People of Today

Debrett's

HM THE QUEEN
Photograph by HRH Prince Andrew
(Camera Press, London)

People of Today

Editor
Patricia Ellis

Co-editor
Juliet Hime

Senior Editor
David Williamson

Published by

DEBRETT'S PEERAGE LIMITED

73/77 Britannia Road · PO BOX 357 · London · SW6 2JY

ISBN 1 870520 04 1

Debrett's People of Today 1991
Published by Debrett's Peerage Limited
73/77 Britannia Road · PO Box 357 · London · SW6 2JY

Printed in England

Data and computer typesetting prepared by Morton Computer Services Limited, Scarborough, Yorks.

Printed and bound by BPCC Wheatons Ltd, Marsh Barton, Exeter

THE CIGARETTE
Davidoff
Davidoff
Davidoff
USING THE RAREST OF DEEP ORANGE VIRGINIA TOBACCOS FOR THE ULTIMATE IN DAVIDOFF TASTE.
MIDDLE TAR As defined by H.M. Government
STOPPING SMOKING REDUCES THE RISK OF SERIOUS DISEASES
Health Departments' Chief Medical Officers

CONTENTS

FOREWORD BY SIR PEREGRINE WORSTHORNE

Traditionally it is a grandee who introduces *Debrett's People of Today,* and I feel it to be symbolic that this year a humble knight of 1990 vintage should have been invited to do the honours. For Debrett's has certainly broadened the circles from which its distinguished people are drawn and can now claim to reflect and celebrate the arrival of Mr Major's classless society.

Debrett's People of Today is to Britain's meritocracy what the Almanach de Gotha was to the European *ancien régime* — a reliable guide to the stock exchange of reputation. Those who compile it have a good idea of the current social values and their judgement can seldom be faulted. Only time will tell whether they have invested in the right people and I shall look forward to further editions with interest.

Meanwhile, it is a reference book on which I shall rely for information that is both accurate and relevant.

Well done, Debrett's.

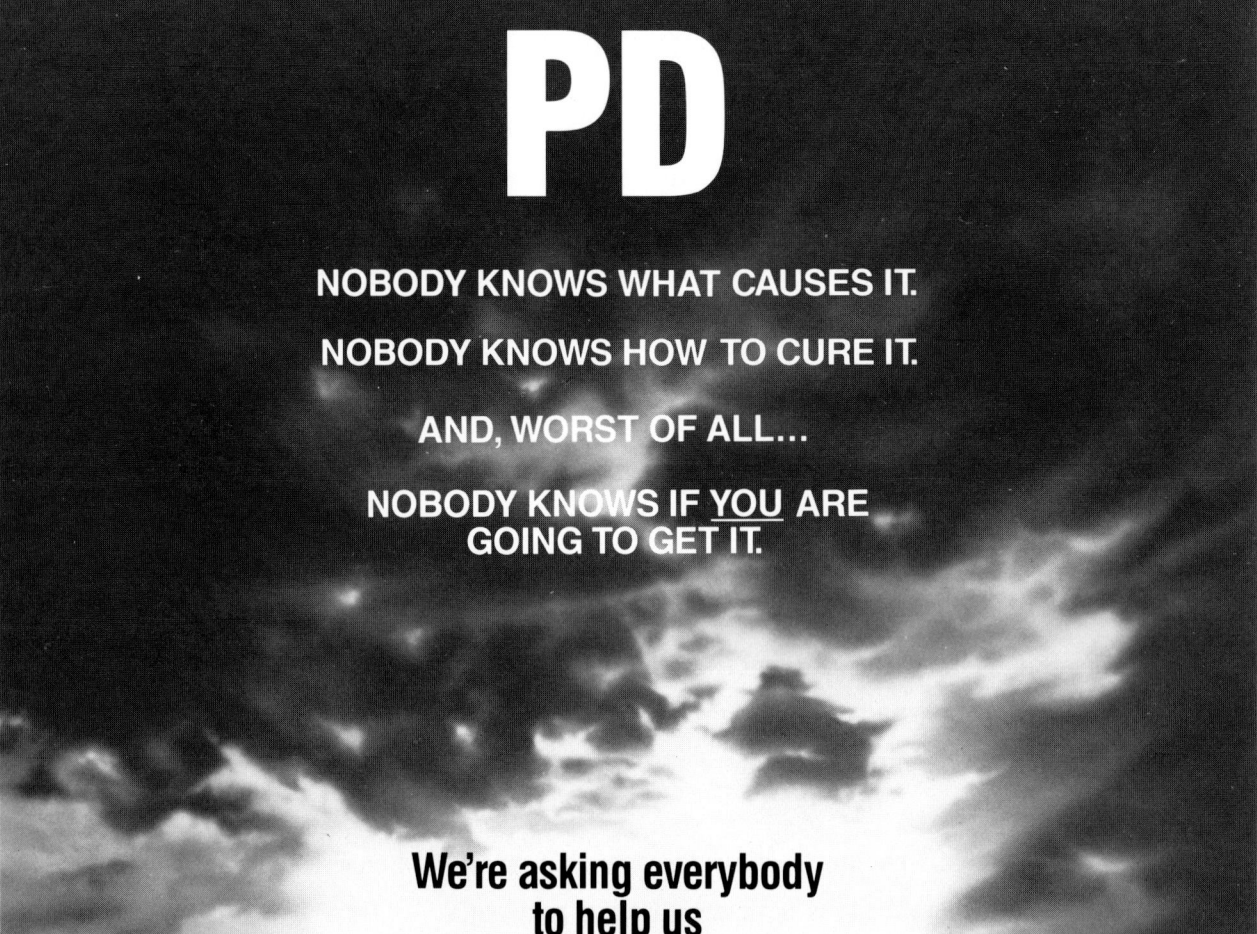

INTRODUCTION

It gives me great pleasure to introduce the fourth edition of *Debrett's People of Today.*

This volume yields not only the result of one year's hard work but also an accumulation of four years' fact finding and checking, deletion and addition, rendering it a most comprehensive and accurate work of reference, now containing over 40,000 biographies relevant to British society.

We at Debrett's are feeling justifiably pleased with ourselves for, not only have we increased the number of entrants in the publication by 5,000, 14 per cent of these being women, but we have also included some interesting new features.

However, before I highlight our new features, I should like to point out that none of our achievements would have been possible without the help and guidance of our distinguished panel of consultant editors, whose names are listed on page 63.

Within the biographical section, we have included a selection of photographs of those entrants whom Debrett's and their experts have chosen as their Personalities of Today.

In the introductory section we have two further new features, 'Parties of the Year' and 'Debrett's Dicta', in addition to the traditional elements. Articles this year have been written by Dame Barbara Cartland and Sara Parkin who give us their somewhat differing views on the role of women in the nineties, and Roger Trafford and David Jewell who air the merits of independent schooling. Hilary Rubinstein casts his expert eye over the current state of British hotels and David Williamson writes on the revival of the Baronetage.

I should like to thank all the staff at Debrett's for their co-operation and assistance in compiling this edition and in particular Taff Hamilton, Juliet Hime, Charles Kidd, Jon Parker, Shelley Roberts, John Verling, Julie West and David Williamson.

Grateful thanks must also go to our parent company, Sterling Publishing Group PLC, for their continued support, and to Michael Preston, Deputy Chairman, who masterminded the project from beginning to end and who inspired us all with his unflagging energy and commitment.

PATRICIA ELLIS

Agros, the group of companies in Poland consisting of:
— Agros Holding S.A. /joint stock company/
— Agros Co. Ltd.
— Trans Agros Co. Ltd.
— Agros Market Co. Ltd.
offers you following services and commodities:

AGROS

Agros Co. Ltd
00-950 Warszawa
8, Chalubińskiego Str.
tel. 301718
tlx. 814391
fax. 300791,2

Agros Co. Ltd deals with export and import of foodstuffs and agricultural products in more than 100 countries all over the world. The company started its trade activity in 1966 and now in its 25th anniversary is reaching a turnover up to 500 million US dollars and over 150 million rubels.
Among the main products Agros exports one can find — alcoholic beverages with the famous Wodka Wyborowa on top, beer, fruit and vegetable preserves, confectionery, forest fruits, tobacco, food concentrates and many others.
Imports consist of coffee, tea, cocoa beans, citrus fruits, bananas, spices, wines, tobacco and tobacco products. Some machinery equipment and production lines for food processing industry, coldstores and other plants are imported by Agros as well. Very large commercial network consisted of several joint stock and limited trading companies such as Agropol Hamburg, Agropol Tokyo, Agropol Antwerp, Agropoland Mexico, Anglo-Dal London and over 60 sole agents, exclusive importers, representatives and so on assures excellent service of Agros turnover.
Welcome to cooperation.

Agros Holding S.A.
Warsaw, 2, Stawki Str.
tel. 6358428, 6359367
tlx. 813654
fax. 6357618

Agros Holding S.A. proposes to all partners its services in the following lines of business:
— creating of pro-export investments
— equipment and machinery leasing services
— registration of new trade marks and brand names in Poland and abroad/EEC included/
— computer model feasibility studies by UNIDO exports for the purpose of new investments
— computer model feasibility studies by UNIDO exports for the purpose of new investments
— supplies imports for food and agricultural industry
— general assistance and advice, legal and organizational, in the area of new investments.

Trans-Agros Co. Ltd.
03-462 Warsaw
61, Swierczewskiego Str.
tel. 185314, 185967
tlx. 817043
fax. 185207

Trans-Agros Co. Ltd — international transport and forwarding offers its specialised transportation means such as:
— refrigerated semitrailers
— tilt and container semitrailers
— road tankers
— tank containers
With Trans-Agros there are no problems when transport perishable cargo to and from Poland.

Agros Market Co. Ltd
00-526 Warsaw
24/26, Krucza Str.
tel. 296883
tlx. 814391
fax. 300791,2

Agros Market Co. Ltd dealing with wholesale trade of foodstuff, offers in permanent saling to wholesale and retail customers a large assortment of foodstuffs of home origin and from abroad. The list is following: coffee, tea, cocoa powder, citrus fruits, and citrus fruit preserves, spices, confectionery, edible fats, alcohol beverages and others. Each order can be effected in a short time.
Welcome to our storehouses!

Debrett's

Dicta for 1991

To commemorate the 1991 edition of People of Today, Debrett's have asked the members of their editorial panel to put forward their suggestions for a "wish-list" for 1991. What follows is a collation of their thoughts, ranging from the pious to the peripheral, from matters of some social moment to purely personal hobby-horses.

One caveat: not every thought on any particular subject comes from the relevant specialist on the panel. Our members have felt free to air themselves on each other's patch, and not the least of our objectives in producing this selection has been to generate speculation as to the provenance of each of the dicta.

Dicta for 1991

Debrett's panel wishes:

THAT *British society would at last stop revelling in its failures and apologising for its successes.*

THAT *the Department of Transport would impose minimum speed limits on motorways, thus depriving the British motorist of his last remaining excuse for not getting back to the inside lane after overtaking.*

THAT *theatre bars would wake up to the fact that their main objective is not necessarily the formation of a queue.*

THAT *television commentators would understand that the presence in a British-won track event of a foreign athlete who once ran in the same race as Kip Keino does not automatically turn that British success into a world-class performance.*

THAT *critics would forego the use of Artspeak in favour of a language which is comprehensible to the intelligent body of lay British society.*

THAT *all British restaurateurs and their staff could take an educational tour of expensive French eating establishments in order that they might learn, once and for all, how not to treat their guests.*

THAT *city journalists would take slightly less obvious pleasure in gloating over the demise of those businessmen whose previous success they uncritically admired, whose hospitality they willingly accepted, and whose activities provided them with the opportunity to ply their own lucrative trade.*

THAT *television interviewers would realise that an interview does not depend for its success on a disdainful presumption that the interviewee is either a liar or a fool.*

THAT *the few remaining unspoilt town centres in Britain might be spared both from development and from illumination with linear yellow paint.*

THAT *opera-and concert-goers would accept that ovinity is not a prerequisite of their attendance, and that they should accordingly feel free not to applaud a bad performance.*

THAT *critics of modern architecture might realise that bad architecture is bad because it is bad, not because it is modern.*

THAT *theatre audiences might learn that they are not obliged to cough, sneeze, whisper or snore simply because there are actors present.*

THAT *football referees might consistently treat a professional foul as a threat to the victim's livelihood rather than as a tiresome technical offence.*

THAT *the length of a hem may be guided by the visual attractiveness of what it covers rather than by the pronouncements of an unaccountable clique.*

THAT *policitians would acknowledge that there is no fair means of taxing people on a local basis, merely differing and variably disadvantageous degrees of unfairness.*

THAT *restaurateurs would appreciate that an unpretentious menu is not an impediment to good cooking.*

THAT *familiarity with Latin and Greek language and culture might no longer be regarded by government educationalists as a bar to a healthy or socially useful existence.*

THAT *men would realise that having a mistress or two wives is even more enjoyable if it escapes the notice of Nigel Dempster.*

THAT *we could all accept that to have tried and failed is better than never to have tried.*

THAT *theatres will finally understand about seating audiences from the centre of a row, so that latecomers merely fill up towards the aisles and are not obliged to clamber over others to get to their seats.*

THAT *the management of the BBC would take the trouble to find out what Radio 3's audience actually wants to listen to.*

THAT *someone would tell (a) the Metropolitan Police that yellow boxes on road junctions are not there purely for decoration, and (b) bus-drivers that they do not signify picnic spots.*

THAT *the English cricket team might be granted a sabbatical.*

THAT *the next government, whichever party forms it, provides theatres with a level of funding which recognises that the Treasury gets far more back in tourism and tax from them than it has ever had to hand out.*

THAT *truth and morality might enter the newspaper industry, preferably from the gutter upwards.*

THAT *the sum of the items on a restaurant menu which a guest has ordered might comprise the entirety of his bill rather than a base figure upon which the restaurateur can exercise his arithmetical ingenuity.*

THAT *the level of financial assistance to museums might be based on the realisation that it is cheaper to prevent their physical collapse than to reconstruct them afterwards.*

THAT *the accountancy profession would ignore the interests of its pocket and recognise that there is a fundamental conflict between auditing a company and providing ancillary services to it.*

THAT *the British government would acknowledge that it could benefit from following the lead given by its Irish counterpart and grant an income tax holiday to creative artists.*

THAT *theatres and concert-halls might open not just for three short evening hours but instead all day as wine bars, bookshops, art galleries and even afternoon cinemas, thereby ensuring their real-estate futures in city centres.*

THAT *users of the English language might resist the American tendency to treat nouns as verbs, adjectives as adverbs, and syntax as a form of literary leprosy.*

THE REVIVAL OF THE BARONETAGE

The announcement in December 1990 that a Baronetcy of the United Kingdom was to be conferred upon Mr Denis Thatcher following his wife's resignation as Prime Minister has put an end to several years of speculation as to the possibility of the revival of this hereditary title, the creation of which had lapsed since 1964.

Although the Order of Baronets was first instituted by King James I in 1611, the title of Baronet had formerly been applied to those members of the nobility who had lost the right of individual summons to Parliament as Barons and was used in this sense in a statute of King Richard II (1377-1399). The famous antiquary Sir Robert Cotton (1571-1631) was consulted by King James I as to the royal prerogative of raising money and, having discovered a patent of Edward III conferring the dignity of a Baronet on William de la Pole in exchange for a monetary consideration, suggested the revival of the title to the King. Accordingly, on 22 May 1611 the hereditary Order of Baronets in England was erected by Letters Patent for the express purpose of the settlement of Ireland. The dignity was to be offered to 200 gentlemen of good birth enjoying a clear estate of £1,000 a year, the condition being that each one should pay into the King's Exchequer in three equal instalments a sum equivalent to three years' pay to 30 soldiers at eight pence per day per man, the first instalment to be paid on the delivery of the patent. The Baronetage of Ireland was erected on 30 September 1611, and that of Scotland (or Nova Scotia) on 28 May 1625, for the purpose of establishing the plantation of Nova Scotia. After the Act of Union between England and Scotland in 1707, no further Baronetcies of England or Scotland were created, the designation becoming Baronet of Great Britain. Following the union of Great Britain and Ireland in 1801, all Baronetcies have been styled of the United Kingdom.

Eighteen gentlemen were created Baronets on the day the Order was created, and it is noteworthy that the first of them, conferred on Sir Nicholas Bacon, of Redgrave, Suffolk, is still held by his descendant as the premier Baronetcy of England. The present Baronet, also Sir Nicholas, is the 14th holder of the title, and by a strange anomaly the 15th holder of another Baronetcy created in 1627 in favour of the first Sir Nicholas Bacon's younger son, Butts Bacon, which merged into the original creation in 1758.

It was fitting that Sir Robert Cotton, who had suggested the revival of the Order, should himself have received the honour among the second batch of Baronets to be created on 29 June 1611. He was also extremely flattered by the King calling him 'cousin' because of his descent from the Bruce family and called himself Robert Bruce Cotton. Alas, the Baronetcy became extinct on the death of the 6th Baronet in 1752.

The first Letters Patent decreed that only two hundred Baronets of England were to exist at any one time, but this limitation soon lapsed and today there are well over 1100 names on the Official Roll of Baronets. The precedence enjoyed by Baronets was fixed by several statements. It was originally stated that no other degree or dignity was ever to be created which would be superior or equal to that of Baronet, while the second Letters Patent stated that no person or persons should have place between them and the younger sons of Viscounts and Barons. Today Baronets rank after the sons of Life Peers and Lords of Appeal in Ordinary and before Knights Grand Cross of the Order of the Bath. Baronets' wives are entitled to the prefix of either 'Dame' (followed by first name) or 'Lady' (followed by surname only), but the use of the former style is now restricted to legal and formal documents only.

Several privileges which were attached to the Baronetage from the inception of the Order have now lapsed. The first of these was the right to be styled 'Honourable,' which fell into disuse early in the 19th century and has never been revived in spite of petitions to the Crown. Another was the right of the eldest sons or heirs apparent of Baronets to claim the honour of knighthood on attaining their majorities. King George IV revoked this privilege, but without prejudicing Letters Patent granted before 19 December 1827, and the last person to claim it successfully was Ludlow Cotter, son of Sir James Lawrence Cotter, 4th Baronet, in 1874. Sir Ludlow never succeeded to the baronetcy as he died unmarried before his father in 1882. A few claims have been made since, but all have been refused.

Baronetcies are usually created with remainder to the heirs male of the body of the grantee, but there have been occasional grants of special remainders, notably in the case of North of Southwell (1920), when, failing heirs male of the body, the destination was to the male issue of the daughters of the first Baronet. Baronetcies of Nova Scotia were sometimes created with remainder to heirs male whatsoever and to 'heirs male and of tailzie.' There are four existing Scottish baronetcies with this last remainder, Dalyell of the Binns, Dunbar of Hempriggs, Hope-Dunbar of Baldoon, and Stirling-Maxwell of Pollok. The present holder of the second of these is a Baronetess, Dame Maureen Dunbar of Hempriggs, or Lady Dunbar of Hempriggs, who established her right to the title in the Lyon Court in 1965.

The Baronets of England and Ireland successfully petitioned King Charles I for permission to wear a badge, but the usage seems to have lapsed after the 17th century. The Baronets of Nova Scotia, however, enjoyed the privilege of wearing the badge of Nova Scotia suspended from an orange-tawny ribbon worn around the neck. In 1929 King George V granted permission to all Baronets, other than those of Scotland, to wear round their necks a badge of the arms of Ulster suspended from an orange ribbon with a narrow border of dark blue on both sides.

The Official Roll of Baronets was established by

Royal Warrant on 23 February 1914 and all Baronets are required to prove their succession and be entered on this before they are legally able to use their titles. The Roll is kept at the Home Office by the Registrar of the Baronetage. The Standing Council of the Baronetage was founded in 1898 to maintain the ancient rights and privileges of the Order.

For some peculiar reason, Baronets have long been cast as dire villains in works of fiction and figured widely as such in Victorian melodramas. We have only to think of the execrable Crawleys in Thackeray's 'Vanity Fair' as an example. There probably have been some wicked Baronets and certainly some wildly eccentric ones, but on the whole they have been no worse and no better than any other section of the community.

The honour now conferred on Denis Thatcher, though it carries very few, if any, privileges, is nevertheless a most appropriate acknowledgement of the supportive role played throughout his wife's premiership by this most English of Englishmen.

David Williamson

BLUEPRINT FOR THE '90s

In 1970 they said it was the beginning of the Romantic Era.

The Royal Philharmonic Orchestra asked me what songs of the '20s and '30s they should play, while in America I sold a million copies of every novel I wrote.

Two years later the publishers woke up, and said to their authors:

'Write like Barbara Cartland with pornography!'

This was the beginning of the permissive era which produced Aids.

In England 'Women's Libbers' were fighting even more violently to prove themselves, not the equal of men, but the superior.

What they succeeded in doing was in getting rid of religion.

Since the very beginning of civilisation the guidelines for mankind have always been through religion. From the totem poles and the witchdoctors, up to the gods of ancient Greece and ancient Rome, to Mohammedanism, Buddhism and Christianity.

The only guidelines given to children today are:

'Don't get caught by the police — they are your enemy!'

In this country, all through the ages, the aristocrats were always supposed to be immoral and so were the peasants. The great middle class was strictly moral and never, in any way, discussed or talked about 'sex'. It was they who extended the great British Empire to cover over one quarter of the world's surface, and it was said that 'the man carried the sword and the woman the Bible!'

What 'Women's Lib' achieved was to make the woman throw away the Bible. Where we had morality in the home, the village, the town and over most of England, we now have 'wife swapping' and many other unpleasant sexual pastimes in small towns.

This resulted in the lapsing of daily prayers in State Schools, so if you wanted your child taught about God you had to pay for him to go to Eton or Harrow, or for a girl to go to some expensive girls' school.

No objection was made by the Archbishop of Canterbury nor any Bishop. The majority of people did not even know it had happened.

It was only finally in 1990, with the assistance of a newspaper, that I managed to bring to the attention of every Member of Parliament what was happening. I received one hundred and fifty letters in return saying that they agreed with me that it was horrifying. The majority admitted they had no idea that prayers had been missing for many years.

The House of Commons and the House of Lords agreed just before Christmas that there should be both prayers and Religious Education in State Schools.

But the damage done over those lost years is horrifying.

We now have, at this moment, the worst child abuse of any country in the world.

London railway stations are where children who have run away from home go at night. They are mostly under fifteen years of age, and wait to be accosted by perverts.

'Women's Libbers' have demanded that women should go back down the mines, when it took a century to get them out of them!

They have made it more important for a woman to have a career rather than a happy marriage. The more advanced of 'Women's Libbers' want to do away with marriage altogether, as was written in a much publicised book:

"Marriage has failed and should be abolished altogether. Love has failed and the only real way to obtain 'good sex' is to have a variety of partners."

As it is, in this country four marriages out of five fail — both Protestant and Catholic.

The Divorce Law, known as the 'Adulteress's Charter', is so appalling in that whatever a man's wife does, he has to give her half of everything he possesses. What is more, she can go on applying for more every year by not agreeing to a Decree Nisi; it is only surprising that any man proposes marriage — promiscuity as advocated by 'Women's Lib' is much easier.

Any policeman or judge will tell you that the young trouble-makers and the hooligans who smash up football grounds are all from broken homes. They have been denied love and they hate the world and want to smash it up.

Also the ghastly crimes inflicted on children are usually perpetrated by the stepfather or the live-in lover.

Apart from this, crime is worse than it has ever been in the whole history of the country. Only one criminal in seven gets caught but even so, prisons are overflowing and it has become unsafe for any child or young woman to walk the streets either in a town or in the country.

What we have to do now, is to go back to morality.

The Prime Ministers of practically every country in Europe have said it is necessary, and so have the Americans. It is going to be a long and hard task to undo the terrible harm which has been done by 'Women's Lib' and the Permissive Era.

It is only women, whose job it has been to hold the Bible, who can get us back to anything that is 'normal'. The first step, in my opinion, and I have been fighting for three years for this, is to have 'wages for wives'. This means that the mother will stay at home with her young children for at least five years, loving them and bringing them up in the right way, before they start school.

For this, she should be given the national wage, which at the moment is about £130 pounds a week.

This means she and her husband could afford to pay the mortgage, and all the other vast bills which today confront a young married couple.

'Wages for Wives' was brought in by the Prime Minister of France in 1988 and it has been a great success. Sweden brought it in last year.

If they can show the way, we, who have always prided ourselves in the past on standing up for what was right and just for our people, can do the same.

This is the only way that we can save the children and bring back morality and the guidelines which are the whole basis of a civilised country.

BARBARA CARTLAND

THE ROLE OF WOMEN IN THE '90s

Identifying the great turning points in human history used to require the long-distance lens of time. Few people alive when the Roman Empire declined, or when Britain changed from a mostly agricultural society to a largely industrial one, for example, would have noticed that history was 'being made' around them.

But as the 20th century draws to a close, the sophisticated communication systems which circle the world mean we can witness history *as it happens.* Roman emperors had to wait for news from Britain to arrive by horseback, but television allowed us to watch the fall of the Soviet Empire *live.* Furthermore, the broadcasting media no longer simply record events; they influence them. Several East European countries, for example, found courage from seeing their neighbours' revolutions taking place.

Nowadays, because news travels so fast, ordinary people can not only observe history being made, they can also take part — they can *make* history.

This is important because during the 1980s our newspapers and TV screens also brought us images of vanishing forests, polluted seas and rivers and impoverished soils. Climate experts have confirmed that, unless we cut down on the amount of greenhouse gases we produce (by a lot and quickly), we are likely to get unpredictable and even catastrophic changes in the weather. Even if only a fraction of the evidence is correct then humankind could be entering a period which any surviving historians might call the Second Dark Age. We have to take preventative action.

Like all pollution, carbon dioxide (the main greenhouse gas) is the inevitable result of using energy. So it is clear that to prevent pollution we will have to restructure our economy so it uses as little energy as possible, We will have to move towards what we might call a 'solar age' where we depend mainly on energy from renewable sources.

This is indeed a great turning point in human history. As great as when we wanted more pulling power for our ploughs but instead of adding one more horse to the team we replaced all the horses with a traction engine and set the industrial age in motion.

However this time, if the climate experts are right, we don't have the luxury of several centuries to turn history round. By and large, governments do know this but seem paralysed in the face of the huge, complicated and speedy changes which will have to be made. Which is where women come in. Not only are women certain to bear the biggest brunt of whatever the future brings, be it good or bad, they also, because of their particular skills and insights, have considerable power to influence the direction it takes.

I think what women do in the 1990s could determine whether we sink into another dark age or turn round and set out towards a sustainable 'solar' future.

This is because women have a way of working and organising which is more in tune with the sort of changes society will have to make. Generally speaking, men prefer to take a step by step approach towards the future, while women (again generally speaking) like to plan ahead and use a combination of instinct and the accumulated knowledge of their experience to tell them which steps are going to take them in the right direction. This way of thinking can save a lot of time.

For example, any woman who has wheeled a push-chair around a city *knows* there is a link between giving motor vehicles priority and a lower quality of environmental and human health. In a recent survey in Finland about future energy needs, men demanded more technology while women proposed conservation measures. That this is the cheapest and easiest way to go forward is, of course, confirmed by energy experts.

Although women are the majority sex and do the majority of work inside and outside the home, they do not hold the majority amongst decision makers. The voice of women and their experience is rarely heard in the governments, industries and institutions which have brought us to the brink of ecological collapse and which have the power to determine what happens next.

Despite improvements over recent years the rate of increase in numbers of women in public life remains disappointing. The fact that only 10% of the entrants in this book are women is my witness. Women's salaries still average less than 75% of men's despite equal opportunities legislation. The majority of jobs done by women is still largely in the supporting/service sector of the economy, and despite the much publicised advent of the new, emancipated male, he is still not doing anything like his whack in the home.

How then are women to take up the challenges of the next decade and make their voices and views heard where it matters? One thing is quite clear, there is obviously no future in merely protesting about our status as 'persistent victims of the system' or waiting passively for rights to be handed out. Although we had a woman prime minister for over a decade, still only 6.3% of MPs are women and the parliamentary working patterns are as hostile to family life as ever! This is in sharp contrast to the preference given to women by Gro Brundtland, prime minister of Norway where women hold over 34% of the seats in parliament.

No, the urgency of the situation requires new strategies. If women are going to play the role they can and should play in the 1990s, they must pour rather than dribble into decision making positions and, equally importantly, *be seen to be doing so.*

Successful women must appear on TV screens, in newspapers and magazines as well as in the statistics of Social Trends but they must also help other women to join them, practically as well as by example. If, for example, each of the women in this year's *Debrett's People of Today* were to extend their personal 'matronage' (a female version of patronage?) to another woman aspiring to public life, the number of entrants could quickly be doubled!

Perhaps the time has come, therefore, for the women's press and women's organisations to look hard at why their readership and membership have fallen so drastically over the last twenty years. Are they tapping into that instinct and collective experience which means most women *know* it will take more than a change of soap powder or face cream to save the rainforest and halt global warming? Are they relevant to the growing number of women who *know* there has to be more to life than looking pretty and being hyper-efficient at home and at work? Are they promoting the sort of role models with which women *want* to identify? The soaring membership of environmental groups over the same period would suggest not.

I freely admit I could not have managed without the advice and example of several women. Simple tips like learning to function despite nerves rather than trying to conquer them (keep the butterflies flying in formation!), or being less not more efficient (women are martyrs to their own efficiency: the more they can do the more they get to do!), do not come from the mainstream women's press but they have helped me to organise my life according to my own values rather than the more manly values which dominate the world around me.

In fact, my greatest inspiration has come not from successful business women in Britain but from women in the Third World; women like Wangari Maathai, the first woman Professor in Nairobi University who, in 1977, founded the Green Belt Movement. Kenyan women were taught to grow trees from seeds in nurseries. But when they set them out in bigger plantations in other villages, the women were careful to pass to other women not only the trees but also information about diet, health, family planning, sustainable agriculture and organising. As Wangari put it 'The period for talking and complaining about the status of women was coming to an end and it appeared appropriate for women to talk around development issues and cause positive change in themselves, environment and country.' Now she is working with the United Nations to introduce similar schemes in 12 other African countries.

It is because of their everyday experience that women all over the world *know* global environmental degradation is caused by what we do in our everday lives. Much will depend therefore on whether women in Britain can do as Wangari Maathai and many other Third World women have done — stop talking and complaining and actually start 'causing positive changes'. Instead of observing on our TV screens more and more environmental degradation and the human misery which goes with it, women have a chance and a responsibility to take part in history and try to steer it in a sustainable direction. We have the skills and we have the knowledge. Our role in the 1990s is to find the courage to put them to work.

SARA PARKIN
Speaker for the Green Party

A CENTENARY CELEBRATION

The Incorporated Association of Preparatory Schools (IAPS) celebrates its centenary during the academic year 1991-2. It is the professional association of the Headmasters and Headmistresses of well over 600 independent preparatory schools in Great Britain and abroad. Members come from schools in Europe, North and South America, the Middle and Far East, East and South Africa, Australia and New Zealand. There are boys' schools, girls' schools, co-educational schools: boarding, day, mixed: in cities, towns and the countryside: the smallest has around 50 pupils the largest over 1000: the Heads are just as various!

Yet it all started — in 1892 — over the size of a cricket ball! A dozen Heads met in a waiting room at Marylebone Station to decide the best ball to be used in interschool matches and no doubt also talked about other matters of common interest. Today, members still talk about problems common to all, despite the great variety of schools, and the IAPS co-ordinates all this from its Headquarters in Kensington Church Street. There are termly District meetings, an annual conference and regular bulletins and circulars which inform and guide members. The IAPS has a full time Director of Education who runs courses for both Heads and their staff. Various committees deal with finance, membership, sport, bursars and Governors and aim to make a little easier the increasingly difficult job of running a school.

As far as parents are concerned, the fact that a school is a member of IAPS implies it has reached certain standards. Until 1978, all independent schools could rely on the Department of Education and Science to provide members of Her Majesty's Inspectorate to examine them regularly and recognise them as efficient. Despite protests, this recognition was discontinued although the Inspectorate has the right to visit independent schools and often does so. The IAPS felt that schools should reach certain standards which would ensure that pupils were being properly educated and, together with other independent schools, set up its own system for accreditation. Each team is led by a former HMI and composed of senior Heads from another part of the country. Standards are laid down concerning payment of staff, qualifications of both Head and staff and facilities for pupils; Heads whose schools do not reach those standards are not elected to membership. In that way, IAPS ensures that parents who send their children to an IAPS school can rely on schools which may differ from each other but which provide a good education. The fact that well over 100,000 children are educated at IAPS schools suggests that parents are generally satisfied with those standards.

The Universal Declaration of Human Rights states that "Parents have a prior right to choose the kind of education that shall be given to their children". Parents may well support that view but it doesn't help them when they want to choose a school! All parents want the best for their children and a good education must be one of the greatest benefits they can give. Some parents live in areas where there are perfectly good maintained schools available and there are plenty of these, of course. Others may choose to send their children at 7 or 8 or even earlier to an independent school. It is worth pointing out that only a handful of these are private schools run for profit. Almost all have their own board of Governors to which the Head is responsible and who supervise the finances of the school. Any excess of income over expenditure has to be put back into the school and the Head, like his staff, earns a salary. Heads are usually able to run their schools in the way they feel is best — a freedom which brings great advantages but great responsibilities too. The market force of parents who are able to send their children to the school down the road is a great incentive to Heads to make the correct decisions! This ability to choose leads to one of the most important advantages of independent schools: a partnership with parents.

There are strong reasons for believing that the years between 8 and 13 are the most vital stage of a child's education because they are the formative years when early promise (or otherwise!) is developed and moulded. A good education will lay down firm foundations in the basic skills of reading, writing and numeracy, hopefully begun from the age of 4 or 5. Prep schools offer small classes and individual care and the staff aim to teach the pupils to work hard and to understand and follow moral values which will help them grow into responsible, considerate adults. The pupils themselves are very far from being children of rich or privately-educated parents. The children come from every sort of home and background and half their parents were educated at local authority schools.

So what should parents look for when they choose a prep school? Although most schools have produced a prospectus for some years, they have become more and more ambitious: they are, after all, in competition with each other! Some retain the services of a public relations firm and some offer video prospectuses. These brochures are necessary and provide background information on costs and what is and is not included in the basic fees. Although it is certainly true to say that the staff and pupils in a school are more important than the facilities, there is no doubt that good equipment helps learning. Sports halls and swimming pools are reasonably common but the library is important too — and the way it is used is even more so. Prep schools have flourished throughout the 1980s and this has been reflected in their facilities and increased size. It is possible to judge a school's facilities but more difficult to estimate its academic success. Children are very varied (thank goodness!) and success for one may be failure for another. The child with a good brain may win a Scholarship but is no more successful than the child who plays a Chopin sonata or one who wins a race or writes a simple story perhaps using a word processor. Prep schools aim to develop the whole personality — the practical and physical as well as the academic and imaginative.

Preparatory schools are also more and more able and willing to offer an education within a traditional school to those who have special needs. Children who are especially gifted in work, sport, music or art need opportunities to use their talents and prep schools can usually provide the facilities and teaching required. Equally, those who are slow or backward or have problems such as dyslexia can be helped by careful, individual teaching. Prep school Heads feel that it is important that pupils from all religions and races grow up together in their schools: a greater understanding of each other's beliefs will help them to be more tolerant as they grow up in a world where tolerance and time for others appear to be increasingly rare.

Many prep schools can also offer the advantages of boarding, whether full or weekly. The days when boys and, less often, girls were sent away from home at the beginning of term and were only seen at the end have long gone. The typical boarder today lives in warm, carpeted rooms and often is only 50 or 100 miles from home and sees parents every two or three weeks. Those whose parents live abroad usually have relations reasonably close and contact between home and school is frequent and friendly. For children with busy, hard-working parents, boarding can provide that increasingly rare commodity: time! There is more time to learn and to enjoy life and other people without the worries of travelling to and from school. The increased use of weekly boarding suggests that parents can see the advantages of using a school very fully during the week and yet join together as a family unit at the weekends.

Preparatory School Heads are certainly joined together as part of the IAPS — and no doubt will enjoy together the Centenary Day in July 1992 with a service in St Margaret's Westminster, a concert given by their pupils in the Barbican and a dinner at Guildhall — but the single and most important asset they will want to carry forward into the next 100 years will be their Independence. To be independent means having the ability to make choices over the education we believe should be offered to our children. There is general awareness among Prep School Heads that the National Curriculum is a worthwhile and positive attempt to ensure good educational standards throughout the country. There is probably less agreement over the details! The Conservative policy is to accept that Independent schools *are* independent and may choose to follow the National Curriculum or not: the Opposition have stated that they will make it compulsory for all schools. We hope that this will not happen because it will remove the valuable element of choice. Independent School Heads and their staff have been wading through the mass of paper which refers to the National Curriculum. They have compared what they are already teaching and have seen that the proposals in the curriculum are often restrictive rather than expansive. For example, most prep schools teach one modern language from the age of nine and then offer others as options. Most teach Latin to some or all of their pupils. The National Curriculum only asks for one language from 11, so time has to be found for teaching the languages prep schools believe to be necessary for pupils who will be part of a multi-lingual European Community, often having to work in Europe.

Heads of prep schools will need to be able to show parents that they are not only reaching the standards required by the National Curriculum but exceeding them; otherwise, why should parents pay for something they can obtain for nothing? Therefore, there is general agreement that the Assessment Tests at 7 and 11 (Key Stages 1 and 2) will be used and prep schools have been involved in the preliminary practice. There are considerable doubts over the amount of time required to give these assessments and the subsequent loss of teaching time. There has been even more disquiet over the time required to complete the Records of Achievement and this is one area where Prep School Heads are glad to be independent and therefore able to choose whether to use hours of teaching time in filling up boxes. It is fair to say that many Heads of maintained schools have similar doubts! However, the independent sector does not in any way ignore Government proposals; it is more likely to study them in depth and to be in a position to provide an alternative, against which the Goverment plans can be measured. An education service completely controlled by a Government cannot be good for a country.

The 1990s, therefore, sees over 600 prep schools, educating 100,000 pupils, in good heart, very much aware of the financial and social problems facing them but determined to offer a service which will help their pupils cope with an ever-changing world where consideration for others should not be confused with weakness and where success is both necessary and remarkably varied.

ROGER TRAFFORD
*Headmaster of Clifton College Preparatory School
and current Chairman of the IAPS*

INDEPENDENT SCHOOLS TODAY

'Public schools are the nurseries of all vice and immorality.' Henry Fielding's view as expressed in 'Joseph Andrews' would receive short shrift today. For years independent schools have been under threat: political or economic. At long last, though, political opponents have turned their attention from outright abolition. They now seek to demonstrate our so-called irrelevance, but they will surely fail. Independent schools are part of the national provision of education in this country and are increasingly seen to be so by politicians, educators, and parents, who in successive opinion polls have shown that they would greet the abolition of independent schools with about as much relish as they would the doubling of the excise duty on a bottle of whisky.

One of the major strengths of the independent sector lies in its diversity. There are schools large and small, boarding and day, co-educational and single sex, as well as schools for the less able and for the talented. Schools which maintain the progressive traditions of their founders and schools which are unashamedly selective and academic; Quaker schools, schools with a military tradition, specialist music schools, sumptuously appointed schools and schools on restricted sites in depopulated city centres: in short, a rich variety of schools responding to parents' needs and wishes.

Why are we so valued by parents and politicians, and why is our influence far beyond that justified by our numbers? One of the reasons is our readiness to initiate, to evaluate, and, if appropriate, to embrace curricular experiment and reform. We are known for achieving outstanding examination results in classrooms which are centres of order and good learning. But the Nuffield Science Project, the Schools' Mathematics Project (SMP), Mathematics for Education and Industry (MEI), Nuffield Modern Languages, A-level Business Studies were all pioneered and developed in independent schools. Many of our schools, while exempt from the provisions of the Education Reform Act, are engaged in national curriculum studies and in helping the Secretary of State to deliver a broad, balanced, and relevant curriculum. We have had considerable influence over the Department of Education and Science's policies on education from 16-19. Independent schools have urged the retention of A-levels as a rigorous and challenging academic examination. A-level study is the flagship of British sixth form education and it may well be the reason why so many come from Europe and the Middle and Far East to join our sixth forms. There has been a discreet but determined erosion of the quality of A-levels over the past few years and further moves in this direction must be carefully monitored and vigorously resisted. We in the independent sector have urged the introduction of a diversity of courses and examinations to meet the needs of the diversity of talents of the new 16-19 year old students. We have argued strongly for greater breadth of study for students of all abilities and we hope to be among the first schools to introduce vocational courses into our sixth forms. Some British sixth-formers were described recently as 'feeling inadequate when confronted by a 17-year-old German exchange student who was studying German, English, Chemistry, Music, and History'. I hope that we will achieve a sixth form curriculum which will make such embarrassment a thing of the past, while allowing our young people to take a proper pride in the fact that this country has produced more Nobel Prize winners than any other in Europe.

Independent schools have become almost the sole suppliers of boarding education as, alas, maintained boarding provision shrinks almost daily. For some children, boarding is the most appropriate form of education. Abundant time available, close relationships between teacher and taught, with dedicated staff and the acceptance of disciplined hard work, are bases of a fine tradition. The quality of life, the advantages of being 24 hours in the same community, encourage an awareness beyond that of the family and the neighbourhood. Boarding schools are powerful weapons to combat any form of disadvantage in education. Disadvantage is suffered not only by those whose families are broken by death or desertion, by children with one parent, but also where circumstances in the home, overcrowding, parents working unsocial hours, or obliged to travel frequently, make it difficult for children to work well. Children from backgrounds such as these will suffer, no matter how conscientious the parent. Many mothers, in particular, far from feeling guilty about sending their children to boarding schools, now welcome the chance to pursue careers. For their children, too, the opportunities available, the companionship of their contemporaries and the friendly supervision by adults, may be infinitely preferable to returning to an empty house and a microwave meal. And boarding schools over the years have successfully reconciled pupils of different religions and races, from rich and poor families, from intellectual and unacademic backgrounds, giving them confidence in their identity and purpose. This work is particularly relevant in contemporary society. The fees of a good boarding school are very considerably less than the cost of maintaining a child at a remand centre or children's home.

Political opponents of independent education have stated their intention to remove our charitable status. Most independent schools are well aware of the need to use the fiscal benefits they receive from charitable status charitably and many have been doing so for years. Many of us use our premises for the benefit of the local community. We have fine facilities: sports centres, all-weather pitches, swimming-baths, tennis courts, theatres, assembly halls, chapels, most of which remain empty or unused for one third of the year. Many schools have devised imaginative schemes to bring the local community and the school community closer together by appropriate use of the buildings. Philanthropy and altruism are part of our tradition and it would be unfortunate to forget that. The McNaughton definition of charity in 1893 includes the relief of poverty which, of course, is the universal attribute of charity; but it then adds ' . . . the advancement of education, the advancement of religion, and other purposes beneficial to the community'. If education is a proper charitable activity, then all education is a proper charitable activity. The Labour Party has stated that independent schools will contine to enjoy charitable status only if they can be shown to be in the national interest. Most of us in independent education believe that the very existence and efficient functioning of our schools is by definition in the national interest. We are playing our part in working on the national curriculum and we are playing an increasingly effective role in the training of teachers. The independent schools must have in front of them the question 'What can we do to serve education for the nation as a whole?' If we do not answer the call of those who originally founded us and set us on our way, if we are ourselves not worthy of our calling, then we deserve to lose our charitable status.

We can do this best by service to others. It is a function of schools like ours to instil in young people a sense of service to the community, a desire to repay by service some of the privileges they have been given by their parents by being educated at independent schools. Perhaps the most famous Haileyburian is Clement Attlee and his life was a life of service right from his childhood — through the Haileybury Boys' Club in Stepney, through local politics there, and eventually service in the highest office of the land. His first contact with the Haileybury Boys' Club, as he wrote in his autobiography 'As It Happened' was ' . . . an event which was destined to alter the whole course of my life'. Community service has been a feature of independent schools for many years now. There can hardly be a school which does not have a community service programme linking it with its local community, with local maintained schools, with local authority homes, and all sorts of agencies. Voluntary Service Overseas, Community Service Volunteers, Schools' Partnership Worldwide, and the Rank Foundation Education Scheme are all making an increasing mark in deprived areas of the country and involving many of the boys and girls in independent schools. It is right that this should be so. There is a danger in communities like ours of insularity. We tend to become preoccupied with our own concerns, important though these may be, and insufficiently aware of a wider world. Most independent schools are Christian communities, upholding and professing the Christian faith. One of the most telling and moving lines in the Prayer Book comes in that marvellous collect, the Second Collect for peace at morning prayer ' . . .whose service is perfect freedom'.

High academic standards, dedicated teaching staffs, good discipline, curricular experiment and reform, the quality of life in boarding schools, and service to others, are all characteristics of the independent sector. A healthy, vigorous, and efficient independent sector is in the national interest and I am proud to be part of it.

DAVID JEWELL
Headmaster of Haileybury and Imperial Service College
and former Chairman of HMC

HOTELS: A HOMILY

At the time of writing, British hoteliers have never had it so bad. The eighties had been like seven fat years: there was, it's true, the occasional blip in a long run of prosperity — the Libyan bombing temporarily halted the growth in tourism — but in general the barometer was set fair, encouraging hotel chains to build larger and grander Hiltons and Marryats, and to splash out in their existing establishments with more rooms, filled with more little extras, not to mention larger items such as gyms, tennis courts, swimming pools, saunas, golf courses and the like. At the same time we witnessed with pleasure the arrival on the scene of many individuals, some of whom had made their money in the city and others who were drop-out executives from big hotel corporations, aspiring to create their own country-house hotel nirvanas — and often making a very good job of their new profession of amateur innkeeper.

Then in the latter part of 1990 and continuing through the bleakest of winters, the bottom dropped out of the market. They say that troubles often come in threes, but this time hoteliers were experiencing a sextuple of miseries: high intererest rates, the poll tax, the Uniform Business Rate, worsening recession, followed by two further body blows, the Gulf War and a renewed outburst of Irish terrorism in the capital, resulting in an almost total collapse of tourism and business travel.

I have no doubt — and this isn't just pious sentiment — that confidence will return, that the habits of weekend breaks, suppressed during the Gulf War, will reassert themselves, that business travel will pick up where it left off, that the Americans and the Japanese, not to mention our fellow-countrymen in the European Community, will be back with their dollars, yen and ecus. But of course some things will never be quite the same again.

I fear that 1991 will see a lot of hotel owners, large and small, failing to meet their commitments. The chief victims will be those who, believing that the upward curve of the economy was irreversible, had borrowed too much and been caught short when the market took a nose-dive. Mega-corporations, with their interests diversified, will have found it easier to survive, but sadly many small personally-owned establishments, including some of the nicest places around, will find it impossible to keep going and will sell — if they are lucky. That quintessentially English experience, the traditional country-house hotel, is likely to become an endangered species: there will still be plenty of establishments calling themselves by that name, but they will often be conference-oriented, company-managed places that bear as much resemblance to the real article as Lymeswold to Stilton. Most at risk in this shake-out will be the relatively recent arrivals, who have not had time to build up a loyal clientele.

Crystal-gazing, what trends can we anticipate in the coming decade? As confidence returns to the world economy, we may expect further demands for beds in major cities. Although high-rise flats are now considered environmentally unsound, I fear that jumbo-sized hotels meeting the demands of jumbo aircraft will continue to sprout. I only hope that they may be less offensive to the eye than some of the monstrosities that have been permitted in the past quarter-century.

Earlier retirement will fertilise the leisure industry, and we shall see more resort hotels, complete with golf and tennis courts, riding facilities and the like, that are already so popular in the US. And the heightened interest in fitness will also impose on the trend-conscious hotel a need to meet the demands of the new fitter traveller. One weary American publisher, a regular visitor to London, was telling me that he was having to give up the *Connaught* as he now found a gym and a swimming-pool crucial to meet the psychic pressures of his hectic schedule.

Significant changes are already taking place in what is on offer in hotel restaurants. People are far more diet-conscious in 1991, and are taking a keener interest than ever before in the quality of the produce as well as of the cooking. Hotels are still inclined to woo customers by massive portions, an overload of vegetables, five-, six- or seven-course set menus, dessert chariots piled high with cholesterol-rich goodies and other ways to damage their health. But I'm convinced that these gargantuan feasts are on their way out. Even the traditional full English (or Scottish, Welsh or Irish) breakfast is losing out to the continental version, and those who like to fuel their tank at the breakfast table are less inclined to need a 3-course lunch a few hours later. Lunch is increasingly honoured in the breach, and the pressure, if you are on a full-board tariff, to eat three hearty meals a day, will lead more people to prefer a half-board arrangement. Hotels that still demand full pension terms in the high season may find themselves facing empty beds. Hotels that fail to offer proper vegetarian options in their restaurants will find themselves with empty tables. And smart hotels will be offering much greater variety in the way of snack lunches than hitherto.

One striking development of the eighties was the rapidity with which the pro-smoking lobby were routed by the opposition. First the Underground, then the buses, and now many airlines, too, have pursued a no-smoking policy. Hotels and restaurants have been slow to catch on to the prevailing mood, and many restaurateurs fear the loss of trade if they impose a total ban. But I am sure we shall see many more no smoking signs in restaurants before the end of the decade, though it's possible that smoking in public places will in any case be made a statutory offence. Even hotels that aren't inclined to turn away compulsive smokers will be offering guaranteed smoke-free rooms for those who are repelled by the traces of stale tobacco smells left by former occupants.

I hope — and believe — that British hotels will

improve their dismal performance in the reception they offer families with children. Hotels on the Continent invariably open their doors to children; they do more than that — they positively cherish their child guests. Many hotels in Britain won't accept children at all — and 'children' in this context may mean even 16-year olds. When, a few years back, I first broached this subject in an introduction to *The Good Hotel Guide,* I received a lot of stick — both from within the catering industry and from individuals who were outraged that the p and q of their favourite hotel sanctuary might be disturbed by brawling youngsters. But already, within a few years, I see attitudes changing. Working parents these days want to spend more leisure time with their young offspring than the previous generation, and will give a wide berth to hotels that fail to provide a genuine welcome to their families. And hoteliers, for their part, are appreciating the importance of cultivating the clientele of tomorrow.

Tipping is another hoary old custom which is being eroded. In a campaign to discredit what I felt to be a blot on the catering industry — it is the *only* industry to countenance the practice — I was grateful to Bernard Levin for reminding his readers that 'you never tip your equals.' Nudging for tips, or leaving the bottom line of a credit card open, is already a thing of the past in many parts of the world — or else has been subsumed by a comprehensive figure 'services and taxes included'. In Australia, if you try to press a coin into someone's hand, you are likely to be told politely but firmly that the pourboire is not required. I don't wish to see people's generous impulses being stifled, but I hate the embarrassment that surrounds this business — how much, to whom and when. But tipping is to some extent a generational habit: younger people feel less compulsion to grease the metaphorical palm than their elders. It is on the way out, and will not, I believe, survive the century.

The greatest hazard that British hoteliers face in the coming decade is the competition from the Continent, and especially from the countries bordering the Mediterranean, where the tariffs are so much lower, the weather so much sunnier and the food, at least in France, incomparably better at whatever price range you choose. The force of that competition will presumably increase after 1992. There is no easy solution, but I hope that hotel-keepers will be able to keep the home fires burning by making their prices keener. One innovation that I would like to see the hotel industry adopt is a stand-by arrangement similar to those which have worked successfully with airlines and in the theatre, whereby — at least in slack seasons — rooms that have not been taken may be offered on the night at, say, half-price to those who are prepared to take their chances and not book in advance. Hotels are traditionally shy of discounting, except for weekend breaks, but anything that will help to maintain good hotels in a thriving condition as we approach the third millenium must be welcomed.

HILARY RUBINSTEIN
Founder and Editor
of the Good Hotel Guide

PARTIES OF THE YEAR

This year, Debrett's have asked John Rendall, Social Editor of Hello!, *to choose the social events of the year. We present his selection below, with photographs on the following four pages.*

For Her Majesty Queen Elizabeth The Queen Mother, 1990 must have felt like one continual party. In addition to a formidable programme of official engagements and charity work, Her Majesty celebrated her 90th Birthday with the adoring British public at a parade in Scotland and the Royal Gala at the London Palladium on Thursday 26th July, and with her family at the Birthday Ball given by HM The Queen at Buckingham Palace.

At the London Palladium the Queen Mother sat with the Queen, Princess Margaret and the Duke of Edinburgh in the Royal Box and enjoyed the stars of British theatre headed by Sir John Gielgud who had created a special theatrical treat for the Queen Mother.

The Prince of Wales's itinerary was seriously curtailed due to his polo accident at Cirencester Polo Club where he shattered his right arm which required lengthy surgery and treatment, leaving the Princess of Wales to carry on their crowded commitments to charities and official engagements.

The Princess of Wales consolidated her national and international position as the most photographed royal in the world and the most popular royal after the Queen. Her attendance at the Phil Collins Concert in the Royal Albert Hall was a brief respite from her continued and valuable contribution to charity fund raising, particularly her favourite charity, Birthright.

The Duke and Duchess of York finally moved into their controversial new home near Sunningdale in Berkshire and threw a House-Warming party for their friends. The Prince and Princess of Wales could not attend, but Viscount Linley, Lady Sarah Armstrong Jones, Susannah Constantine escorted by cricketer Imran Khan, Elton John, Billy Connolly and his wife Pamela Stephenson and the Duchess's father Major Ronald Ferguson were among the guests who dined and danced in the marquee erected in front of the new house which had attracted so many comments because of its size, cost and 'Southfork' (as in the television series, Dallas) architectural style.

Due to his naval commitments the Duke of York was unable to attend the wedding of the year when the Marquess of Blandford married Becky Few Brown at St Mary Magdalene's Church at Woodstock beside the gates to the groom's ancestral home, Blenheim Palace. The Duchess of York sat discreetly in the second row.

Best man was Grand Prix promotor Paddy MacNally, and the Reception was held at Blenheim Palace.

At Chatsworth the Duchess of Devonshire threw the Ball of the Year and over the weekend celebrations the great and glamorous celebrated with estate workers whom the Duchess had 'bussed' from the various Devonshire holdings from Scotland to Cornwall. Traditional aristocratic modesty prevailed when the Duchess was surprised to encounter an uninvited Jerry Hall.

The Princess of Wales's ancestral London home, Spencer House, overlooking Green Park in Mayfair was completely refurbished and made available for very special parties; King Constantine of the Hellenes' Birthday Party (the King and his brother-in-law King Juan Carlos of Spain finally left the party as early office workers arrived for work), Princess Margaret's 60th Birthday Party and Princess Ira von Fürstenberg's 50th Birthday Party.

In the Crystal Ballroom at the Mayfair Hotel, polo-playing Peter Scott threw the surprise party of 1990. Glamorous wife Jan thought she was to dine at Annabel's with a few close friends but was persuaded to drop into the Mayfair for cocktails. The first surprise of the evening was the presence of 250 friends in the Ballroom which had been turned into a pastiche of Zermatt, where Peter and Jan had met ten years ago. The second surprise was Roberta Flack live in cabaret. 'Jan has been giving me flack for years but tonight I give her . . . Roberta'.

Charity Balls continued as considerable fund raisers for charity, the Red October Ball (sponsored by *Hello!*) celebrated the end of the cold war and the demolition of the Berlin Wall and in support of various Scottish charities the Princess Royal joined the Earl and Countess of Erroll in the set reels at the Caledonian Ball held at Grosvenor House. Queen Charlotte's Ball raised over £140,000 and helped save Queen Charlotte's Hospital and at the same time recreate the traditional Deb Season which, after initial charges of being anachronistic, has surprised even its supporters with its popularity. Tickets for this year's Queen Charlotte's Ball and the Berkeley Dress Show (traditionally the beginning of the Deb Season) are already at a premium.

German industrialist Mick Flick and his glamorous wife Maja hosted a dinner party in honour of Herr Flick's mother Marjorie at the Princess of Wales's favourite restaurant, San Lorenzo, and among the guests from Germany were Prince Johannes (since unhappily deceased) and Princess Gloria Thurn and Taxis (described as Princess T.N.T. because of her flamboyant lifestyle), Prince and Princess Michael of Kent and Prince Ernst of Hanover (who, had the Salic Law prevailed in England and Queen Victoria not ascended the British throne, would be the present King of England), and Princess Ernst of Hanover.

An ailing Dame Margot Fonteyn returned to England from her home in Panama and was the guest of honour at a ballet gala and benefit where she was re-united with partner Rudolf Nureyev. At an emotional evening, the Princess of Wales, Princess Margaret, Dame Ninette de Valois and devoted balletomanes paid tribute to the great ballerina who sadly died early this year.

A party of a different kind came to an end when the Rt Hon Margaret Thatcher resigned as Prime Minister. The Iron Lady was no more but her supporters were rewarded for their loyalty throughout her career. Mrs Thatcher (she has insisted that she should still be styled 'Mrs Thatcher' despite her husband's baronetcy) attended the investiture party given for her close advisor, Sir Tim Bell, by his wife, Lady Bell. At the Savoy reception Mrs Thatcher, with Sir Denis, was relaxed and chatted happily with members of the Cabinet before they had to dash back to the House to continue Gulf Crisis debates.

The general impression was that Mrs Thatcher was glad that, for her, the party was over.

JOHN RENDALL

PHOTOGRAPH: THE PRESS ASSOCIATION LTD

HM The Queen

PHOTOGRAPH: DOMINIC O'NEILL

The Princess Royal reeling with Lt-Gen Sir Robert Richardson at the Caledonian Ball, Grosvenor House

PHOTOGRAPH: REX FEATURES

The Prince of Wales with Prince William and Prince Harry

PHOTOGRAPH: DESMOND O'NEILL

HM The Queen presenting the Horse and Hound Grand Military Gold Cup to HM Queen Elizabeth The Queen Mother

PHOTOGRAPH: DOMINIC O'NEILL

The Earl and Countess of Erroll at the Caledonian Ball

PHOTOGRAPH: DESMOND O'NEILL

Ruth, Lady Fermoy

PHOTOGRAPH: REX FEATURES

The Marquess of Blandford marries Miss Rebecca Few Brown at the Church of St Mary Magdalene, Woodstock

PHOTOGRAPH: DESMOND O'NEILL

Dame Margot Fonteyn and the Princess of Wales at the gala in Dame Margot's honour at the Royal Opera House, Covent Garden

PHOTOGRAPH: REX FEATURES

Queen Charlotte's Ball at Grosvenor House: the debutantes of 1990 and their famous cake

PHOTOGRAPH: DESMOND O'NEILL

Dame Margot Fonteyn flanked by Mr Michael Somes and Mr Rudolf Nureyev

PHOTOGRAPH: REX FEATURES

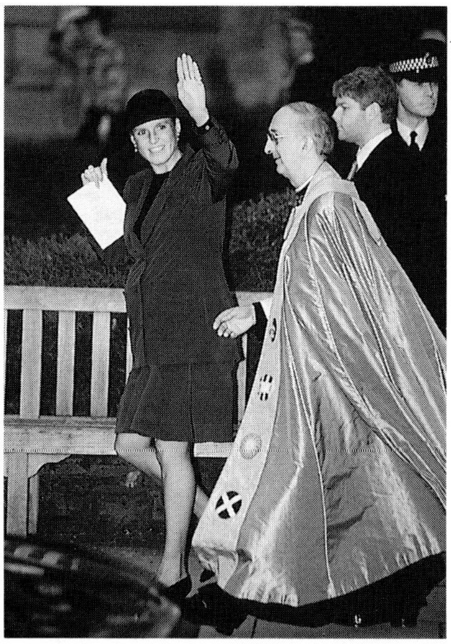

The Duchess of York with the Rt Rev Simon Phipps and Canon John Beckwith at the Blandford-Few Brown wedding

PHOTOGRAPH: DESMOND O'NEILL

Princess Margaret, Countess of Snowdon, with Mr Placido Domingo

PHOTOGRAPH: REX FEATURES

Miss Jade Jagger and Mr Piers Jackson

Mr Bruce Oldfield, Miss Susan George and the Princess of Wales

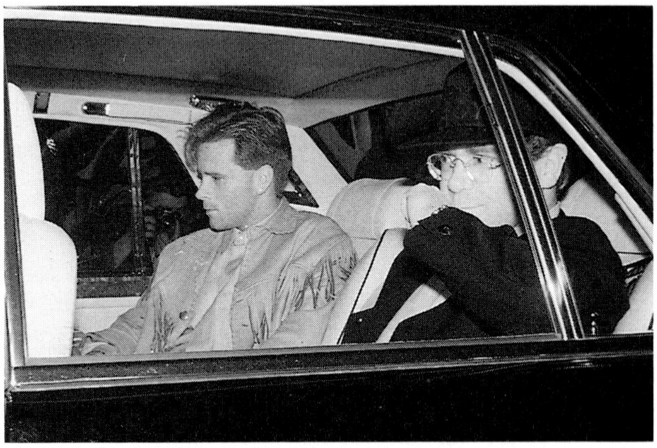

PHOTOGRAPH: REX FEATURES

Mr Elton John arriving at the Duke and Duchess of York's housewarming party at Sunninghill Park, Windsor

PHOTOGRAPH: REX FEATURES

Mr Mick Jagger arriving at the Rolling Stones' end of tour party at the Serpentine Gallery

PHOTOGRAPH: REX FEATURES

Mr and Mrs Michael Caine arriving at the Duke and Duchess of York's housewarming party at Sunninghill Park, Windsor

Viscount Linley with Fleur Rossdale, Organiser of the British Interior Design Exhibition

Princess Ira von Fürstenberg and her son celebrate her 50th birthday party at Spencer House

Lady (Mary) Fairfax at Princess Ira von Fürstenberg's 50th birthday party at Spencer House

PHOTOGRAPH: FERGUS GREER

The former French Ambassador to London, Vicomte de La Barre de Nanteuil with Sir Nicholas and Lady Henderson and Vicomtesse de La Barre de Nanteuil at Pierre Cardin's exhibition at the Victoria and Albert Museum

Sir Denis Thatcher and the Rt Hon Margaret Thatcher at Sir Tim and Lady Bell's investiture party at the Savoy

PHOTOGRAPH: FERGUS GREER

Mr Pierre Cardin and model at his exhibition at the Victoria and Albert Museum

PHOTOGRAPH: RICHARD YOUNG

Prince Johannes and Princess Gloria Thurn and Taxis at Mr Mick Flick's party at San Lorenzo

LONDON CLUBS

American	95 Piccadilly, W1	071-499 2303
Army and Navy	36 Pall Mall, SW1	071-930 9721
Anglo-Belgian	60 Knightsbridge, SW1	071-235 2121
Arts	40 Dover Street, W1	071-499 8581
Athenaeum	107 Pall Mall, SW1	071-930 4843
Beefsteak	9 Irving Street, WC2	071-930 5722
Boodle's	28 St James's Street, SW1	071-930 7166
Brooks's	St James's Street, SW1	071-499 0072
Buck's	18 Clifford Street, W1	071-734 6896
Caledonian	9 Halkin Street, SW1	071-235 5162
Canning	42 Half Moon Street, W1	071-499 5163
Carlton	69 St James's Street, SW1	071-493 1168
Cavalry and Guards'	127 Piccadilly, W1	071-499 1261
City of London	19 Old Broad Street, EC2	071-588 7991
East India, Devonshire, Sports and Public Schools	16 St James's Square, SW1	071-930 1000
Eccentric	9 Ryder Street, SW1	071-930 6133
Farmers	3 Whitehall Court, SW1	071-930 3557
Flyfishers'	24a Old Burlington Street, W1	071-629 6776
Garrick	15 Garrick Street, WC2	071-836 1737
Gresham	15 Abchurch Lane, EC4	071-629 7231
Hurlingham	Ranelagh Gardens, SW6	071-736 8411
Lansdowne	9 Fitzmaurice Place, Berkeley Square, W1	071-629 7200
MCC (Marylebone Cricket Club)	Lord's Cricket Ground, NW8	071-286 3649
National Liberal	1 Whitehall Place, SW1	071-930 9871
Naval and Military	94 Piccadilly, W1	071-499 5163
New Cavendish	44 Great Cumberland Place, W1	071-262 5536
Oriental	Stratford House, Stratford Place, W1	071-629 5126
Portland	42 Half Moon Street, W1	071-499 1523
Pratt's	14 Park Place, SW1	071-493 0397
Queen's	Palliser Road, W14	071-385 3421
Reform	104 Pall Mall, SW1	071-930 9374
Royal Air Force	128 Piccadilly, W1	071-499 3456
Royal Automobile	89-91 Pall Mall, SW1	071-930 2345
Royal Ocean Racing	20 St James's Place, SW1	071-493 2248
Royal Over-Seas League	Over-Seas House, St James's Street, SW1	071-408 0214
Royal Thames Yacht	60 Knightsbridge, SW1	071-235 2121
St Stephen's	34 Queen Anne's Gate, SW1	071-222 1382
Savile	69 Brook Street, W1	071-629 5462
Ski Club of Great Britain	118 Eaton Square, SW1	071-235 4711
Travellers'	106 Pall Mall, W1	071-930 8688
Turf	5 Carlton House Terrace, SW1	071-930 8555
United Oxford & Cambridge University	71 Pall Mall, SW1	071-930 4152
University Women's	2 Audley Square, South Audley Street, W1	071-499 6478
White's	37 St James's Street, SW1	071-493 6671

CLUBS OUTSIDE LONDON

Caledonian	32 Abercromby Place, Edinburgh 3	031 557 2675
Jockey	High Street, Newmarket	0638 663101
Kildare St and University	17 St Stephen's Green, Dublin 2	0001 76 65 23
Ladies Club	29 Queensferry Road, Edinburgh 2	031 225 8002
Leander	Henley-on-Thames	04912 3665
Manchester	50 Spring Gardens, Manchester	061 834 7678
New	86 Princess Street, Edinburgh 2	031 226 4881
Northern Counties	Hood Street, Newcastle-upon-Tyne	0632 326611
Puffin's	c/o Martin's, 70 Rose Street North, Edinburgh	031 225 3106
Royal and Ancient	St Andrews	0334 72112
Royal Irish Automobile	34 Glasgow Street, Dublin 2	001 77 06 68
Royal Scottish Automobile	11 Blythswood Square, Glasgow 2	041 221 3850
Royal Yacht Squadron	Cowes, Isle of Wight	0983 292743
Stephen's Green	9 St Stephen's Green North, Dublin	0001 77 47 44
Ulster	48 High Street, Belfast	0232 230355
Ulster Reform	4 Royal Avenue, Belfast	0232 23411
Western	32 Royal Exchange Square, Glasgow 1	041 221 2016
Yorkshire	17 Museum Street, York	0904 24116

THE ROYAL FAMILY

For full details see *Debrett's Peerage and Baronetage*

HER MAJESTY THE QUEEN, Elizabeth Alexandra Mary; style in the United Kingdom: Elizabeth II, by the Grace of God, of the United Kingdom of Great Britain and Northern Ireland and of Her Other Realms and Territories Queen, Head of the Commonwealth, Defender of the Faith; crowned at Westminster Abbey 2 June 1953; celebrated her Silver Jubilee 1977; er da of His Majesty King George VI (d 6 Feb 1952) and of Lady Elizabeth Angela Marguerite Bowes-Lyon (HM Queen Elizabeth The Queen Mother, *qv)*, da of 14 Earl of Strathmore and Kinghorne; *b* 21 April 1926; *m* 20 Nov 1947, HRH The Prince Philip, Duke of Edinburgh, KG, KT, OM, GBE, PC, *qv*; 3 s, 1 da *(see below); Heir* s, HRH The Prince of Wales, *qv*; Lord High Adm of the United Kingdom; Col-in-Chief: Life Guards, Blues and Royals (Royal Horse Gds and 1 Dragoons), Royal Scots Dragoon Gds (Carabiniers and Greys), 16/5 Queen's Royal Lancers, Royal Tank Regt, RE, Grenadier Gds, Coldstream Gds, Scots Gds, Irish Gds, Welsh Gds, Royal Welch Fus, Queen's Lancashire Regt, Argyll and Sutherland Highlanders (Princess Louise's), Royal Green Jackets, RAOC, Queen's Own Mercian Yeo, Duke of Lancaster's Own Yeo, Corps of Royal Mil Police, Corps of Royal Canadian Engrs, Canadian Forces Mil Engrs Branch, King's Own Calgary Regt, Royal 22e Regt, Govr-Gen's Foot Gds, Canadian Grenadier Gds, Le Regiment de la Chaudière, Royal New Brunswick Regt, 48 Highlanders of Canada, Argyll and Sutherland Highlanders of Canada (Princess Louise's), Royal Canadian Ordnance Corps, Malawi Rifles; Capt-Gen: RA, HAC, Combined Cadet Force, Royal Canadian Artillery, Royal Malta Artillery; Air Cdre-in-Chief: RAuxAF, RAF Regt, Royal Observer Corps, Royal Canadian Air Force Aux; Hon Air Cdre RAF Marham, Cmdt-in-Chief RAF Coll Cranwell, Hon Cmmr Royal Canadian Mounted Police, Master of the Merchant Navy and Fishing Fleets, Head Civil Defence Corps and Nat Hosp Service Reserve; Sovereign of all British Orders of Knighthood, Order of Merit, Royal Order of Victoria and Albert, Order of Crown of India, Order of Companions of Honour, Distinguished Service Order, Imperial Service Order, Order of Canada; Sovereign Head of Order of Hosp of St John of Jerusalem, Order of Australia, The Queen's Service Order of NZ; patron Royal Coll of Physicians Edinburgh and Victoria League for Cwlth Friendship; FRS 1947; Residences: Buckingham Palace, London SW1A 1AA; Windsor Castle, Berkshire; Balmoral Castle, Aberdeenshire; Sandringham House, Norfolk

EDINBURGH, HRH The Duke of; HRH The Prince Philip; KG (1947), KT (1952), OM (1968), GBE (mil 1953), PC (1951, Canada 1957); cr Baron Greenwich, of Greenwich, Co London, Earl of Merioneth, and Duke of Edinburgh (UK 1947); naturalized a British subject and adopted surname of Mountbatten 1947; granted title, style and attribute of Royal Highness 1947; granted style and titular dignity of a Prince of UK 1957; only s of HRH Prince Andrew of Greece and Denmark, GCVO (d 1944), and HRH Princess (Victoria) Alice Elizabeth Julia Marie, RRC (d 1969), da of 1 Marquess of Milford Haven; *b* 10 June 1921; *Educ* Cheam Sch, Salem, Baden, Gordonstoun, RNC Dartmouth; *m* 20 Nov 1947, HM Queen Elizabeth II, *qv*; 3 s, 1 da; 1939-45 War, Mediterranean Fleet (Home Waters) and with British Pacific Fleet in SE Asia and Pacific (despatches, Greek War Cross; 1939-45, Atlantic, Africa, Burma (with Pacific rosette), and Italy Stars; War Medal 1939-45 (with oak leaf) and French Croix de Guerre (with Palm); a personal ADC to HM King George VI 1948; Field Marshal; Capt-Gen RM; Col-in-Chief: Queen's Royal Irish Hussars, Duke of Edinburgh's Royal Regt (Berks and Wilts), Queen's Own Highlanders (Seaforth and Camerons), REME, Intelligence Corps, Army Cadet Force, Royal Canadian Regt, Seaforth Highlanders of Canada, Cameron Highlanders of Ottawa, Queen's Own Cameron Highlanders of Canada, Royal Canadian Army Cadets; Col Grenadier Gds; Hon Col: Edinburgh and Heriot-Watt Univs OTC, Trinidad and Tobago Regt; *Navy:* Adm of the Fleet; Sea Cadet Corps, Royal Canadian Sea Cadets; Marshal of the RAF; Air Cdre-in-Chief: ATC, Royal Canadian Air Cadets; Hon Air Cdre RAF Kinloss; Cmdt-in-Ch and Extra Master Merchant Navy; memb cncl Duchy of Cornwall 1952-, Ranger of Windsor Great Park 1952-, Lord High Steward of Plymouth 1960-; chllr of univs: Salford 1967-71, Wales 1948-, Edinburgh 1952-, Cambridge 1977-; master bench Inner Temple 1954-, elder bro Trinity House 1952, (master 1969-; hon bro Hull 1953-);pres: Amateur Athletic Bd 1952-, Cwlth Games Fedn 1955-, Br Sportsman's Club 1958-, Central Cncl of Physical Recreation 1951-, City & Guilds of London Inst 1951-, ESU of Cwlth 1952-, Guards' Polo Club 1955-, RAS of Cwlth 1958-, Royal Household Cricket Club 1953-, Royal Merchant Navy Sch 1952-, RSA 1952-, World Wild Life Fund British Nat Appeal 1961-; third pres Int Wild Life Fund 1981-; Royal pres Soc of Friends of St George's and Descendants of KGs 1948-; patron and trustee Duke of Edinburgh's Award, chm Duke of Edinburgh's Ctee for Queen's Awards to Industry 1965-; patron UK branch Soc d'Entr'aide of Legion of Honour; Adm and Cdre Royal Yacht Sqdn 1961-68; Adm of Yacht Clubs: House of Lords, Royal Motor, Royal Southern, Bar, Dart, Royal Gibraltar, RNSA, Royal Yacht Club of Victoria (Australia) and of Great Navy State of Nebraska USA; King George VI Coronation Medal 1937, Queen Elizabeth II Coronation Medal 1953; Grand Master and First or Princ Kt of Order of British Empire 1953; FRS 1951

HM QUEEN ELIZABETH THE QUEEN MOTHER; Lady Elizabeth Angela Marguerite, *née* Bowes-Lyon; Lady of the Order of the Garter (1936), Lady of the Order of the Thistle (1937), CI (1931), GCVO (1937), GBE (1927); da of 14 Earl of Strathmore and Kinghorne, KG, KT, GCVO, TD, JP, DL (d 1944) and Nina Cecilia, GCVO (d 1938), da of Rev Charles William Frederick Cavendish-Bentinck (gs of 3 Duke of Portland, who was twice Prime Minister during King George III's reign); *b* 4 Aug 1900: *m* 26 April 1923, HM King George VI (d 6 Feb 1952); 2 da (HM The Queen and HRH The Princess Margaret, *qqv);* Col-in-Chief: 1 Queen's Dragoon Gds, The Queen's Own Hussars, 9/12 Royal Lancers (Prince of Wales's), King's Regt, Royal Anglian Regt, Light Inf, The Black Watch (Royal Highland Regt), RAMC, The Black Watch (Royal Highland Regt) of Canada, The Toronto Scottish Regt, Canadian Forces Medical Services; Hol Col: Royal Yeo, London Scottish (Gordon Highlanders) (TA), Univ of London Contingent OTC; Cmdt-in-Chief: WRNS, WRAC, RAF Central Flying Sch, WRAF, Nursing Corps and Divs St John Ambulance Bde; hon member of Lloyd's; pres British Red Cross Soc 1937-52, since when dep pres; pres Royal Highland and Agric Soc 1963-64; Gold Albert Medal of RSA 1952; Grand Master Royal Victorian Order 1937; pres Univ Coll of Rhodesia and Nyasaland 1957-70, chllr London Univ 1955-81, first chllr Dundee Univ 1967; bencher Middle Temple 1944 (tres 1949); hon fellow London Univ, and of King's Coll London; FRS; appointed Lord Warden and Admiral of the Cinque Ports and Constable of Dover Castle (the first woman to hold this office) 1978; received Royal Victorian Chain 1937; Grand Cross of Legion of Honour; GCStJ; *Residences:* Clarence House, London SW1A 1BA; Royal Lodge, Windsor Great Park, Berks; Birkhall, Ballater, Aberdeenshire; Castle of Mey, Caithness-shire

WALES, HRH The Prince of; HRH The Prince Charles Philip Arthur George; KG (1958, invested and installed 1968), KT (1977), GCB and Great Master of Order of the Bath (1975), AK, QSO, PC 1977; cr Prince of Wales and Earl of Chester 1958 (invested 1969); also Duke of Cornwall and Rothesay, Earl of Carrick and Baron of Renfrew, Lord of the Isles and Great Steward of Scotland; eldest s and h of HM Queen Elizabeth II, *qv*; *b* 14 Nov 1948; *Educ* Cheam Sch, Gordonstoun, Geelong GS Australia, Trinity Coll Cambridge (MA, Polo Half-Blue), Univ Coll of Wales, Aberystwyth; Bar of Gray's Inn 1974 (hon bencher 1975); *m* 29 July 1981, Lady Diana Spencer (*see* Wales, HRH The Princess of); 2s *(see below)*; *Heir,* HRH Prince William of Wales, *qv*; Col-in-Chief: The Royal Regt of Wales (24/41 Foot) 1960-, The Cheshire Regt 1977-, The Gordon Highlanders 1977-, Lord Strathcona's Horse (Royal Canadian) Regt 1977-, The Parachute Regt 1977-, The Royal Regt of Canada 1977-, 2 King Edward VII Own Goorkhas 1977-, The Royal Winnipeg Rifles 1977-; personal ADC to HM 1973-; Col Welsh Guards 1974-; Cdr RN 1976-, Wing Cdr RAF 1976-; Hon Air Cdre RAF Brawdy 1977-; Col-in-Chief Air Reserves Gp of Air Cmd in Canada 1977-, pres: Soc of Friends of St George's and Descendants of KG's 1975-, United World Colls 1978-, The Prince's Trust 1975-; Cdre Royal Thames Yacht Club 1974-, High Steward Royal Borough of Windsor and Maidenhead 1974-; chm: Queen's Silver Jubilee Trust 1978-, The Prince of Wales' Ctee for Wales 1971-; chllr The Univ of Wales 1976-, memb bd Cwlth Devpt Corpn 1979-; patron: The Press Club, Transglobe Expedition, Welsh National Opera, Royal Sch for the Blind, Mary Rose Trust; author of: The Old Man of Lochnagar, A Vision of Britain; Coronation Medal 1953, Queen's Silver Jubilee Medal 1977; *Residences:* Kensington Palace, London W8 4PU; Highgrove House, Doughton, Tetbury, Glos GL8 8TG

WALES, HRH The Princess of; Lady Diana Frances, *née* Spencer; 3 da of 8 Earl Spencer, LVO, DL *(see main text)* and (first wife) Hon Mrs Shand Kydd *(see main text)*; *b* 1 July 1961; *Educ* Riddlesworth Hall, West Heath, Switzerland; *m* 29 July 1981, HRH The Prince of Wales, *qv*; 2 s *(see below)*; former kindergarten teacher

WALES, HRH Prince William of; Prince William Arthur Philip Louis; s and h of HRH The Prince of Wales, *qv*; *b* 21 June 1982

WALES, HRH Prince Henry (Harry) of; Prince Henry Charles Albert David; yr s of HRH The Prince of Wales, *qv*; *b* 15 Sept 1984

YORK, HRH The Duke of; HRH The Prince Andrew Albert Christian Edward; CVO (1979); *cr* Baron Killyleagh, Earl of Inverness, and Duke of York (UK 1986); 2 s of HM The Queen; *b* 19 Feb 1960; *Educ* Gordonstoun, Lakefield Coll Sch Ontario, RNC Dartmouth; Lieut RN, served S Atlantic Campaign 1982 as helicopter pilot HMS *Invincible*; personal ADC to HM The Queen 1984; *m* 23 July 1986, Sarah Margaret Ferguson (*see* York, HRH The Duchess of); 2 da (*see below*) *Residence:* Buckingham Palace, London SW1A 1AA

YORK, HRH The Duchess of; Sarah Margaret, *née* Ferguson; da of Maj Ronald Ivor Ferguson, The Life Guards, and his 1 w, Susan Mary, *née* Wright (now Mrs Hector Barrantes); *b* 15 Oct 1959; *Educ* Hurst Lodge Sunningdale, Queen's Secretarial Coll London; *m* 23 July 1986, HRH The Duke of York, *qv;* 2 da (*see below*)

YORK, HRH Princess Beatrice of; Princess Beatrice Elizabeth Mary; er da of HRH The Duke of York; *b* 8 Aug 1988

YORK, HRH Princess Eugenie of; Princess Eugenie Victoria Helena; yr da of HRH The Duke of York; *b* 23 March 1990

HRH The Prince Edward Antony Richard Louis; CVO (1989); 3 and yst s of HM The Queen; *b* 10 March 1964; *Educ* Gordonstoun, Jesus Coll Cambridge; former house tutor and jr master Wanganui Collegiate Sch NZ; 2 Lieut RM 1983; *Residence:* Buckingham Palace, London SW1A 1AA

HRH THE PRINCESS ROYAL; HRH The Princess Anne Elizabeth Alice Louise; GCVO (1974); declared Princess Royal 13 June 1987; o da of HM The Queen; *b* 15 Aug 1950; *Educ* Benenden; *m* 14 Nov 1973, Capt Mark Anthony Peter Phillips, CVO, ADC (P) (*see main text*); 1 s, 1 da (*see below*); Col-in-Chief: 14/20 King's Hussars, Worcs and Sherwood Foresters Regt (29/45 Foot) and 8 Canadian Hussars (Princess Louise's), Royal Corps of Signals, Canadian Forces Communications and Electronics Branch, Grey and Simcoe Foresters Militia; Ch Cmdt WRNS, Hon Air Cdre RAF Lyneham; pres: Save The Children Fund, British Acad of Film and Television Arts, WRNS Benevolent Trust, Windsor Horse Trials, Royals Sch for Daughters of Offrs of RN and RM (Haslemere); patron: Assoc of WRNS, Communications and Electronics Assoc, Riding for the Disabled Assoc, Jersey Wildlife Trust, R Corps of Signals Assoc, Royal Corps of Signals Instn, Breast Cancer Research Trust, Save the Children Action Group, Army and RA Hunter Trials, Gloucester and N Avon Fedn of Young Farmers' Clubs, Horse of the Year Ball, Benenden Ball; vice-patron British Show Jumping Assoc; Cmdt-in-Ch St John Ambulance and Nursing Cadets; chllr London Univ 1981-; *Residence:* Gatcombe Park, Minchinhampton, Stroud, Glos GL6 9AT

PHILLIPS, Peter Mark Andrew; s of HRH The Princess Royal, *qv*; *b* 15 Nov 1977

PHILLIPS, Zara Anne Elizabeth; da of HRH The Princess Royal, *qv*; *b* 15 May 1981

SNOWDON, HRH The Princess Margaret, Countess of; HRH The Princess Margaret Rose; CI (1947), GCVO (1953), Royal Victorian Chain (1990); yr da of His late Majesty King George VI and Lady Elizabeth Angela Marguerite Bowes-Lyon (HM Queen Elizabeth The Queen Mother, *qv*); *b* 21 Aug 1930; *m* 6 May 1960 (m dis 1978), 1 Earl of Snowdon, GCVO (*see main text*); 1 s, 1 da (*see below*); Col-in-Chief: Royal Highland Fus (Princess Margaret's Own Glasgow and Ayrshire Regt), 15/19 King's Royal Hussars, Princess Louise Fus, Highland Fus of Canada, QARANC; Dep Col-in-Chief Royal Anglian Regt, Hon Air Cdre RAF Coningsby, chllr Univ of Keele; pres: Barnado's Scottish Children's League, Victoria League, Sunshine Homes and Schs for Blind Children (Royal Nat Inst for the Blind), Royal Ballet, NSPCC (and Royal Scottish Soc), Dockland Settlements, Friends of the Elderly and Gentlefolk's Help, Invalid Children's Aid Assoc (also chm cncl), Sadler's Wells Fndn, English Folk Dance and Song Soc, Horder Centres for Arthritics, Girl Guides Assoc, RASE; patron: Princess Margaret Rose Hosp Edinburgh, Royal Coll of Nursing, Nat Cncl of Nurses of UK, London Festival Ballet, Tenovus (Inst of Cancer Research); bencher Lincoln's Inn and tres 1967; Grand Pres of St John Ambulance Assoc and Bde, hon memb and patron of Grand Antiquity Soc of Glasgow; CStJ; *Residence* Kensington Palace, London W8 4PU

LINLEY, Viscount; David Albert Charles Armstrong-Jones; s of HRH The Princess Margaret and s and h of 1 Earl of Snowdon (*see main text*); *b* 3 Nov 1961; *Educ* Bedales, John Makepeace Sch of Woodcraft, Beaminster, Dorset.

ARMSTRONG-JONES, Lady Sarah Frances Elizabeth; da of HRH The Princess Margaret and 1 Earl of Snowdon (*see main text*); *b* 1 May 1964; *Educ* Bedales.

GLOUCESTER, HRH 2 Duke of; HRH Prince Richard Alexander Walter George; GCVO (1974); also Earl of Ulster and Baron Culloden (both UK 1928); 2 but only surv s of HRH the late Prince Henry, 1 Duke of Gloucester (d 1974, 3 s of King George V) and HRH Princess Alice, Duchess of Gloucester, *qv*; *b* 26 Aug 1944; *Educ* Eton, Magdalene Coll Cambridge (MA, Dip Arch); *m* 8 July 1972, Birgitte Eva, GCVO (1989), DStJ (Col-in-Ch Royal Army Educational Corps; pres: London Region WRVS, Royal Alexander and Albert Sch, Cambridge House; patron: Asthma Research Cncl, Bobath Centre), da of Asger Preben Wissing Henriksen, lawyer, of Odense, Denmark, and his 1 w, Vivian, da of late Waldemar Oswald Van Deurs, whose name she assumed; 1 s, 2 da (*see below*); *Heir* s, Earl of Ulster, *qv*; *Career* RIBA, FSA, FRSA; Col-in-Chief: The Gloucestershire Regt 1975-, Royal Pioneer Corps 1977-; Hon Col Royal Monmouthshire RE (Militia) 1977-; pres: Inst of Advanced Motorists 1971-, Cancer Research Campaign 1973-, Nat Assoc of Boys' Clubs 1974-, British Consultants Bureau 1978-, E England Agric Soc 1979-; vice-pres British Leprosy Relief Assoc 1971-; patron: ASH 1974-, Victorian Soc 1976-, Bulldog Manpower Services 1976; ranger of Epping Forest 1975-; Grand Prior Order of St John of Jerusalem 1975-; KStJ; *Residences* Kensington Palace, London W8 4PU; Barnwell Manor, Peterborough, Cambs PE8 5PJ

ULSTER, Earl of ; Alexander Patrick Gregers Richard; s and h of HRH 2 Duke of Gloucester, GCVO, *qv*; *b* 24 Oct 1974

WINDSOR, Lady Davina Elizabeth Alice Benedikte; er da of HRH 2 Duke of Gloucester, GCVO, *qv*; *b* 19 Nov 1977

WINDSOR, Lady Rose Victoria Birgitte Louise; yr da of HRH 2 Duke of Gloucester, GCVO, *qv*; *b* 1 March 1980

GLOUCESTER, HRH Princess Alice, Duchess of; Lady Alice Christabel, *née* Montagu Douglas Scott; GCB (1975), CI (1937), GCVO (1948), GBE (1937); 3 da of 7 Duke of Buccleuch and Queensberry, KT, GCVO, JP (d 1935), and Lady Margaret Alice, *née* Bridgeman (d 1954), 2 da of 4 Earl of Bradford; *b* 25 Dec 1901; *Educ* St James's Sch W Malvern, Paris; *m* 6 Nov 1935, HRH The Prince Henry William Frederick Albert, KG, KT, KP, GCB, GCMG, GCVO, 1 Duke of Gloucester (d 10 June 1974, 3 s of King George V); 1 s (*see above*) and 1 s decd (HRH Prince William, who was killed in an aeroplane accident 28 Aug 1972); Air Chief Marshal WRAF; Col-in-Chief: KOSB, Royal Hussars, RCT; Dep Col-in-Chief Royal Anglian Regt; memb cncl British Red Cross Soc; Dep Cmdt-in-C Nursing Corps and Divs of St John Ambulance Bde 1937-; GCStJ; *Residences* Kensington Palace, London W8 4PU; Barnwell Manor, Peterborough, Cambs PE8 5PJ

KENT, HRH 2 Duke of; Prince Edward George Nicholas Paul Patrick; KG (1985), GCMG (1967), GCVO (1960); also Earl of St Andrews and Baron Downpatrick (both UK 1934); er s of HRH 1 Duke of Kent, KG, KT, GCMG, GCVO, PC (killed on active service 25 Aug 1942, 4 s of King George V), and HRH Princess Marina, CI, GCVO, GBE (d 27 Aug 1968), yst da of HRH late Prince Nicholas of Greece and Denmark; *b* 9 Oct 1935; *Educ* Eton, Switzerland, RMA Sandhurst; *m* 8 June 1961, Katharine Lucy Mary, GCVO (1977) (Controller-Cmdt WRAC and Hon Maj-Gen; Col-in-Chief Army Catering Corps, Hon Col Yorks Volunteers TAVR, chllr Leeds Univ), only da of late Sir William Arthington Worsley, 4 Bt; 2 s, 1 da (*see below*); Maj-Gen (ret) Royal Scots Dragoon Gds; Col-in-Chief: Royal Regt of Fusiliers, Devonshire and Dorset Regt; Col Scots Gds, personal ADC to HM 1966-, GSO II E Cmd 1966-68, company instr RMA Sandhurst 1968-70, cmd C Sqdn Royal Scots Greys 1970-71; Grand Master United Grand Lodge Freemasons of England and Grand Master Order of St Michael and St George; pres: Wellington Coll, Cwlth War Graves Cmmn. Scout Assoc, Technician Educn Cncl; vice-chm British Overseas Trade Bd 1976-; chllr Surrey Univ 1977-; dir British Insulated Callender's Cables 1981-; FRS 1990; *Residences* York House, St James's Palace, London SW1A 1BQ; Anmer Hall, King's Lynn, Norfolk PE31 6RW

ST ANDREWS, Earl of; George Philip Nicholas Windsor; er s, and h of HRH 2 Duke of Kent, KG, GCMG, GCVO, *qv*; *b* 26 June 1962; *Educ* Eton, and Downing Coll Camb; *m* 9 Jan 1988, Sylvana, da of Max Tomaselli; 1 s (Edward Edmund Maximilian George, Lord Downpatrick *b* 2 Dec 1988)

WINDSOR, Lord Nicholas Charles Edward Jonathan; 2 s of HRH 2 Duke of Kent, KG, GCMG, GCVO, *qv*; *b* 25 July 1970

WINDSOR, Lady Helen Marina Lucy; da of HRH 2 Duke of Kent, KG, GCMG, GCVO, *qv*; b 28 April 1964

KENT, HRH Prince Michael of; HRH Prince Michael George Charles Franklin; 2 s of HRH 1 Duke of Kent (killed on active service 1942); *b* 4 July 1942; *Educ* Eton, RMA Sandhurst; *m* 30 June 1978, Baroness Marie Christine Agnes Hedwig Ida, da of late Baron Günther Hubertus von Reibnitz, and formerly wife of Thomas Troubridge, yr bro of Sir Peter Troubridge, 6 Bt; 1 s, 1 da (*see below*); Maj Royal Hussars to 1981; foreign attaché liaison sec MOD 1968-70, UN Force Cyprus 1971, Defence Intelligence Service 1974-76, Army Recruiting Directorate 1976-78, GSO Defence 1974-76, Army Recruiting Directorate 1976-78, GSO Defence Intelligence Staff 1978-81; pres: British Bobsleigh Assoc 1977-, Soc of Genealogists, Inst of Motor Industry 1978-, Royal Patriotic Fund Corpn 1980-, Soldiers', Sailors' and Airmen's Families Assoc 1982-; Cwlth pres Royal Lifesaving Soc; memb: RAC British Motor Sports Cncl, British Olympic Assoc 1977-, HAC; *Residences* Kensington Palace, London W8 4PU; Nether Lypiatt Manor, Stroud, Glos GL6 7LS

WINDSOR, Lord Frederick Michael George David Louis; o s of HRH Prince Michael of Kent, *qv*; *b* 6 April 1979

WINDSOR, Lady Gabriella (Ella) Marina Alexandra Ophelia; o da of HRH Prince Michael of Kent, *qv*; *b* 23 April 1981

HRH Princess Alexandra, the Hon Lady Ogilvy; HRH Princess Alexandra Helen Elizabeth Olga Christabel; GCVO (1960); da of HRH 1 Duke of Kent (killed on active service 1942); *b* 25 Dec 1936; *Educ* Heathfield, Paris; *m* 24 April 1963, Hon Sir Angus Ogilvy, KCVO (*see main text*), 2 s of 12 Earl of Airlie, KT, GCVO, MC; 1 s, 1 da (*see below*); Col-in -Chief: 17/21 Lancers, Queen's Own Rifles of Canada, The King's Own Border Regt, The Canadian Scottish Regt (Princess Mary's); Dep Col-in-Chief LI, Dep Hon Col Royal Yeo TAVR, Air Chief Cmdt Princess Mary's RAF Nursing Service; Hon Cmdt-Gen: Royal Hong Kong Police Force, Royal Hong Kong Aux Police Force; pres: Royal Commonwealth Soc for the Blind, Children's Country Holidays Fund, Queen Alexandra's House Assoc, Star and Garter Home for Disabled Sailors, Soldiers and Airmen, Alexandra Rose Day, British Sch at Rome, Royal Humane Soc; vice-pres British Red Cross Soc; patron Queen Alexandra's Royal Naval Nursing Service; chllr: Lancaster Univ 1964-, Univ of Mauritius 1974-, Hon FRCPS, Hon FRCOG, Hon FFA RCS; *Residences* Thatched House Lodge, Richmond Park, Surrey; 22 Friary Court, St James's Palace, London SW1A 1BQ

OGILVY, James Robert Bruce; o s of HRH Princess Alexandra and Hon Sir Angus Ogilvy, KCVO, *qv*; *b* 29 Feb 1964 *(see main text)*

MOWATT, Mrs Paul; Marina Victoria Alexandra; *née* Ogilvy; o da of HRH Princess Alexandra and Hon Sir Angus Ogilvy, KCVO, *qv*; *b* 31 July 1966; *m* 2 Feb 1990, Paul Julian Mowatt, s of David Mowatt; 1 da (Zenouska *b* 26 May 1990)

For other members of the Royal Family, the Earl of Harewood, KBE, the Hon Gerald Lascelles, the Duke of Fife, Captain Alexander Ramsay of Mar and Lady May Abel Smith, see their entries in the main body of the work.

THE ORDER OF SUCCESSION

The first twenty-five persons in line of succession to the throne

HRH The Prince of Wales
HRH Prince William of Wales
HRH Prince Henry of Wales
HRH The Duke of York
HRH Princess Beatrice of York
HRH Princess Eugenie of York
HRH The Prince Edward
HRH The Princess Royal
Peter Phillips
Zara Phillips
HRH The Princess Margaret, Countess of Snowdon
Viscount Linley
Lady Sarah Armstrong-Jones
HRH The Duke of Gloucester
Earl of Ulster
Lady Davina Windsor
Lady Rose Windsor
HRH The Duke of Kent

(NB Earl of St Andrews would be next in line but for his marriage to a Roman Catholic. His rights are, however, transmitted to his son who follows.)

Lord Downpatrick
Lord Nicholas Windsor
Lady Helen Windsor

(NB HRH Prince Michael of Kent would be next in line but for his marriage to a Roman Catholic. His rights are, however, transmitted to his two children who follow)

Lord Frederick Windsor
Lady Gabriella Windsor
HRH Princess Alexandra, the Hon Lady Ogilvy
James Ogilvy

THE ROYAL HOUSEHOLDS

THE QUEEN'S HOUSEHOLD

Lord Chamberlain, The Earl of Airlie, KT, GCVO, PC
Lord Steward, The Viscount Ridley, TD
Master of the Horse, The Earl of Westmorland, KCVO
Mistress of the Robes, The Duchess of Grafton, GCVO
Lords in Waiting, Lt-Col the Lord Charteris of Amisfield, GCB, GCVO, OBE, QSO, PC (Permanent); The Lord Moore of Wolvercote, GCB, GCVO, QSO (Permanent); The Lord Somerleyton; The Viscount Boyne; The Viscount Long; The Lord Reay; The Earl of Strathmore and Kinghorne; The Lord Cavendish of Furness; The Viscount Astor
Captain, Gentlemen at Arms, The Lord Denham, KBE, PC
Captain, Yeoman of the Guard, The Viscount Davidson
Treasurer of the Household, Alastair Goodlad, MP
Comptroller of the Household, David Lightbown, MP
Vice-Chamberlain of the Household, John Mark Taylor, MP
Ladies of the Bedchamber, The Countess of Airlie, CVO; The Lady Farnham
Extra Ladies of the Bedchamber, The Countess of Cromer, CVO; The Marchioness of Abergavenny, DCVO
Women of the Bedchamber, The Hon Mary Morrison, DCVO; The Lady Susan Hussey, DCVO: Mrs John Dugdale, DCVO; The Lady Elton
Extra Women of the Bedchamber, Mrs John Woodroffe, CVO; The Lady Rose Baring, DCVO; Mrs Michael Wall, DCVO; Lady Abel Smith, DCVO; Mrs Robert de Pass
Equerries, Lt-Col Blair Stewart-Wilson, CVO; W/Cdr David Walker, RAF
Temporary Equerry, Capt the Hon Richard Margesson
Private Secretary, The Rt Hon Sir Robert Fellowes, KCB, KCVO
Deputy Private Secretary, Sir Kenneth Scott, KCVO, CMG
Assistant Private Secretary, Robin Janvrin, LVO
Chief Clerk, Mrs Graham Coulson, MVO
Press Secretary, Charles Anson, LVO
Deputy Press Secretary, John Haslam, LVO
Assistant Press Secretaries, Richard Arbiter; Geoffrey Crawford
Defence Services Secretary, Maj Gen Brian Pennicott
Keeper of the Privy Purse and Treasurer to The Queen, Major Sir Shane Blewitt, KCVO
Deputy Keeper and Deputy Treasurer, John Parsons
Chief Accountant and Paymaster, David Walker, LVO
Personnel Officer, Gordon Franklin, CVO
High Almoner, The Bishop of St Albans (The Rt Rev John Taylor, MA)
Secretary, Royal Almonry, Peter Wright, CVO
Master of the Household, Rear Admiral Sir Paul Greening, KCVO
Deputy Master of the Household, Lt-Col Blair Stewart-Wilson, CVO
Chief Clerk, Michael Jephson, MVO
Comptroller, Lord Chamberlain's Office, Lt-Col Malcolm Ross, OBE
Secretary, LCO, John Titman, CVO
Marshal of the Diplomatic Corps, Lt-Gen Sir John Richards, KCB, KCVO
Vice-Marshal of the Diplomatic Corps, Roger Hervey, CMG
Assistant Marshals of the Diplomatic Corps, Stanley Martin, LVO; Clive Almond, OBE
Secretary, Central Chancery of the Orders of Knighthood, and Assistant Comptroller, LCO, Lt-Col Anthony Mather, OBE
Crown Equerry, Lt-Col Seymour Gilbart-Denham
Superintendent, Royal Mews, Major Albert Smith, MBE
Master of The Queen's Music, Malcolm Williamson, CBE, AO
Poet Laureate, Edward Hughes, OBE
Gentlemen at Arms: Lieutenant, Major Thomas St Aubyn
Clerk of the Cheque and Adjutant, Major Sir Torquhil Matheson of Matheson, Bt
Yeomen of the Guard: Lieutenant, Colonel Alan Pemberton, CVO, MBE
Clerk of the Cheque and Adjutant, Col Greville Tufnell
Clerk of the Closet, The Bishop of Chelmsford (The Rt Rev John Waine, BA)
Deputy Clerk of the Closet, The Rev Canon Anthony Caesar, LVO, MA, MusB, FRCO
Dean of the Chapels Royal, The Bishop of London, PC (The Rt Rev and Rt Hon Graham Leonard)
Sub-Dean of the Chapels Royal, The Rev Canon Anthony Caesar, LVO, MA, MusB, FRCO
Head of the Medical Household and Physician, Dr Anthony Dawson, MD, FRCP
Apothecary to The Queen, Dr Nigel Southward, LVO, MA, MB, BChir, MRCP
Serjeant Surgeon, Barry Jackson, MS, FRCS
Windsor Castle: Constable and Governor, Admiral Sir David Hallifax, KCB, KBE
Superintendent, Major Barrie Eastwood, MBE
Director of the Royal Collection and Surveyor of the Queen's Works of Art, Sir Geoffrey de Bellaigue, KCVO, FSA
Surveyor of The Queen's Pictures, Christopher Lloyd
Librarian, Royal Library, Oliver Everett, LVO
Heralds and Pursuivants, see HER MAJESTY'S OFFICERS OF ARMS

HOUSEHOLD OF QUEEN ELIZABETH THE QUEEN MOTHER

Apothecary to the Household, Dr Nigel Southward, LVO, MA, MB, BChir, MRCP
Clerk Comptroller to the Household, Malcolm Blanch, LVO
Comptroller, Captain Sir Alastair Aird, KCVO
Equerries, Lt-Col Sir Martin Gilliat, GCVO, MBE; Major Sir Ralph Anstruther, Bt, KCVO, MC; Major Raymond Seymour, CVO
Temporary Equerry, Captain Conolly Morris-Adams
Mistress of the Robes, Vacant
Ladies of the Bedchamber, The Dowager Viscountess Hambleden, GCVO; The Lady Grimthorpe, CVO
Women of the Bedchamber, The Dowager Lady Fermoy, DCVO, OBE; Dame Frances Campbell-Preston, DVO; The Lady Elizabeth Basset, DCVO; The Lady Angela Oswald
Lord Chamberlain, The Earl of Dalhousie, KT, GCVO, GBE, MC
Page of Honour, John Carew-Pole
Press Secretary, Major Sir John Griffin, KCVO
Private Secretary, Lt-Col Sir Martin Gilliat, GCVO, MBE
Apothecary to the Household at Royal Lodge, Windsor, Dr John Briscoe, MA, MB, BChir, MRCGP, DObst, RCOG
Treasurer, Major Sir Ralph Anstruther, Bt, KCVO, MC

HOUSEHOLD OF THE PRINCE PHILIP, DUKE OF EDINBURGH

Chief Clerk and Accountant to the Household, Vernon Jewell, MVO
Equerry, Lt Cdr Malcolm Sillars, RN
Temporary Equerries, Capt Michael Hutchings; Capt Alastair Rogers, RN
Private Secretary and Treasurer, Brian McGrath, CVO

HOUSEHOLD OF THE PRINCE AND PRINCESS OF WALES

Apothecary to the Household, Dr Peter Wheeler, MB BS, MRCP, MRCGP
Equerry to The Prince of Wales, Cdr Alastair Watson, RN
Equerry to The Princess of Wales, Sqdn Ldr David Barton, RAF
Temporary Equerry to The Prince of Wales, Capt Davydd Wynne
Ladies in Waiting, Miss Anne Beckwith-Smith, LVO; Viscountess Campden; Mrs Max Pike; Miss Alexandra Loyd; The Hon Mrs Vivian Baring; Mrs James Lonsdale
Private Secretary and Treasurer to The Prince and Princess of Wales, Maj Gen Sir Christopher Airy, KCVO, CBE
Assistant Private Secretaries to The Prince of Wales, Peter Westmacott; Guy Salter
Assistant Private Secretary and Comptroller to The Prince and Princess of Wales, Cdr Richard Aylard, RN
Assistant Private Secretary to The Princess of Wales, Patrick Jephson

HOUSEHOLD OF THE DUKE AND DUCHESS OF YORK

Ladies in Waiting, Mrs John Spooner; Mrs John Floyd
Extra Ladies in Waiting (temporary), Miss Lucy Manners; Mrs Harry Cotterell
Equerry, Capt Alexander Baillie-Hamilton, The Black Watch
Private Secretary and Treasurer, Capt Neil Blair, RN
Comptroller and Assistant Private Secretary, Mrs Jonathan Mathias

HOUSEHOLD OF THE PRINCE EDWARD

Private Secretary and Equerry, Lt-Col Sean O'Dwyer, Irish Guards
Assistant Private Secretary, Mrs Richard Warburton, MVO

HOUSEHOLD OF THE PRINCESS ROYAL

Ladies in Waiting, Mrs Richard Carew Pole, LVO; Mrs Andrew Feilden, LVO; The Hon Mrs Legge-Bourke LVO; Mrs Malcolm Nunneley; Mrs Timothy Holderness-Roddam; Mrs Charles Ritchie; Mrs David Bowes Lyon
Extra Ladies in Waiting, Miss Victoria Legge-Bourke, LVO; Mrs Malcolm Innes, LVO; The Countess of Lichfield
Private Secretary, Lt-Col Peter Gibbs, LVO
Assistant Private Secretary, The Hon Mrs Louloudis

HOUSEHOLD OF THE PRINCESS MARGARET, COUNTESS OF SNOWDON

Apothecary to the Household, Dr Nigel Southward, LVO, MA, MB, BChir, MRCP
Comptroller, Major the Lord Napier and Ettrick, CVO
Equerry, Major the Lord Napier and Ettrick, CVO
Extra Ladies in Waiting, The Lady Elizabeth Cavendish, LVO; Lady Aird, LVO; Mrs Robin Benson, LVO; The Hon Mrs Wills, LVO; Mrs Jane Stevens; The Lady Juliet Townsend, LVO; The Lady Glenconner; The Hon Mrs Whitehead, LVO; The Countess Alexander of Tunis, LVO; Mrs Charles Vyvyan
Personal Secretary, Miss Muriel Murray Brown, CVO
Private Secretary, Major the Lord Napier and Ettrick, CVO

HOUSEHOLD OF PRINCESS ALICE, DUCHESS OF GLOUCESTER

Apothecary to the Household, Dr Nigel Southward, LVO, MA, MB, BChir, MRCP
Clerk Comptroller, Mrs Gordon Franklin
Comptroller, Maj Nicholas Barne
Equerry, Maj Nicholas Barne
Extra Equerry, Lt-Col Sir Simon Bland, KCVO
Ladies in Waiting, Dame Jean Maxwell-Scott, DCVO; Mrs Michael Harvey
Private Secretary, Maj Nicholas Barne

HOUSEHOLD OF THE DUKE AND DUCHESS OF GLOUCESTER

Apothecary to the Household, Dr Nigel Southward, LVO, MA, MB, BChir, MRCP
Clerk Comptroller, Mrs Gordon Franklin
Comptroller, Maj Nicholas Barne
Equerry, Maj Nicholas Barne
Extra Equerry, Lt-Col Sir Simon Bland, KCVO
Ladies in Waiting, Mrs Michael Wigley, CVO; Mrs Euan McCorquodale; Mrs Howard Page; The Lady Camoys (temporary)
Extra Lady in Waiting, Miss Jennifer Thomson
Assistant Private Secretary to the Duchess of Gloucester, Miss Suzanne Marland
Private Secretary, Maj Nicholas Barne

HOUSEHOLD OF THE DUKE AND DUCHESS OF KENT

Apothecary to the Household, Dr Nigel Southward, LVO, MA, MB, BChir, MRCP
Clerk Comptroller, Mrs Antigoni Christodoulou
Temporary Equerry, Capt the Hon Christopher Knollys
Ladies in Waiting, Mrs Fiona Henderson, CVO; Mrs David Napier, LVO
Extra Ladies in Waiting, Mrs Peter Wilmot-Sitwell; Mrs Peter Troughton (temporary); Mrs Julian Tomkins (temporary)
Private Secretary, Cdr Roger Walker, RN

HOUSEHOLD OF PRINCE AND PRINCESS MICHAEL OF KENT

Ladies in Waiting, The Hon Mrs Sanders; Miss Anne Frost; Lady Thompson
Personal Secretary to Prince Michael of Kent, Miss Sally Harvey
Personal Secretary to Princess Michael of Kent, Miss Catherine Fuller

HOUSEHOLD OF PRINCESS ALEXANDRA, THE HON LADY OGILVY

Extra Equerry, Major Peter Clarke, CVO
Lady in Waiting, The Lady Mary Mumford, CVO
Extra Ladies in Waiting, Mrs Peter Afia; The Lady Mary Colman; The Hon Lady Rowley; The Lady Nicholas Gordon Lennox
Private Secretary and Extra Lady in Waiting, Miss Mona Mitchell, CVO

THE QUEEN'S HOUSEHOLD IN SCOTLAND

Hereditary Lord High Constable, The Earl of Erroll
Hereditary Master of the Household, The Duke of Argyll
Hereditary Standard Bearer for Scotland, The Earl of Dundee
Hereditary Bearer of the National Flag of Scotland, The Earl of Lauderdale
Hereditary Keepers:-
Holyrood, The Duke of Hamilton and Brandon
Falkland, Ninian Crichton-Stuart
Stirling, The Earl of Mar and Kellie
Dunstaffnage, The Duke of Argyll
Dunconnel, Sir Fitzroy Maclean, Bt, CBE
Keeper of Dumbarton Castle, Brig A S Pearson, CB, DSO, OBE, MC, TD
Governor of Edinburgh Castle, Lt-Gen Sir John MacMillan, KCB
Dean of the Order of the Thistle, The Very Rev Gilleasbuig Macmillan, MA, BD
Dean of the Chapel Royal, Very Rev Prof R A S Barbour, MC, MA, DD
Physicians in Scotland, Dr Peter Brunt, MD, FRCP; Dr Alexander Muir, MD, FRCPEdin
Surgeons in Scotland, Jetmund Engeset, ChM, FRCS; Ian Macleod, BSc, MD, ChB, FRCS
Apothecary to the Household at Balmoral, Dr Douglas Glass, MB, ChB
Apothecary to the Household at the Palace of Holyrood, Dr John Cormack, MD, FRCGP
Royal Company of Archers:
Capt-Gen and Gold Stick for Scotland, Col the Lord Clydesmuir, KT, CB, MBE, TD
Adjutant, Major the Hon Sir Lachlan Maclean, Bt
Heralds and Pursuivants, see HER MAJESTY'S OFFICERS OF ARMS

HER MAJESTY'S OFFICERS OF ARMS

ENGLAND
College of Arms, Queen Victoria Street, London EC4 4BT

EARL MARSHAL
His Grace the Duke of Norfolk, KG, GCVO, CB, CBE, MC

KINGS OF ARMS
Garter–Sir (Alexander) Colin Cole, KCVO, TD, FSA
Clarenceux–Sir Anthony Richard Wagner, KCB, KCVO, DLitt, FSA
Norroy and Ulster–John Philip Brooke Brooke-Little, CVO, FSA

HERALDS
York (and Registrar)–Conrad Marshall John Fisher Swan, CVO, PhD, FSA
Chester–David Hubert Boothby Chesshyre, LVO, FSA
Windsor–Theobald David Mathew
Lancaster–Peter Llewellyn Gwynn-Jones
Somerset–Thomas Woodcock, FSA
Richmond–Patric Laurence Dickinson

PURSUIVANTS
Portcullis–Peter Brotherton Spurrier
Bluemantle–Terence David McCarthy
Rouge Croix–Henry Edgar Paston-Bedingfeld
Rouge Dragon–Timothy Hugh Stewart Duke

HERALDS EXTRAORDINARY
Norfolk–George Drewry Squibb, LVO, QC, FSA
Wales–Major Francis Jones, CVO, TD, FSA, DL
New Zealand–Phillippe Patrick O'Shea
Surrey (and Earl Marshal's Secretary)–Sir Walter John George Verco, KCVO
Beaumont–Francis Sedley Andrus, LVO
Arundel–Rodney Onslow Dennys, CVO, OBE, FSA
Maltravers–John Martin Robinson, DPhil, FSA

SCOTLAND
Court of the Lord Lyon, HM New Register House, Edinburgh

THE RT HON THE LORD LYON KING OF ARMS
Sir Malcolm Rognvald Innes of Edingight, KCVO, WS, FSA Scot

HERALDS
Albany–John Alexander Spens, RD, WS
Rothesay–Sir Crispin Agnew of Lochnaw, Bt
Ross–Charles John Burnett, FSA Scot

PURSUIVANTS
Kintyre–John Charles Grossmith George, FSA Scot
Unicorn–Alastair Lorne Campbell of Airds, yr, FSA Scot

PURSUIVANTS OF EARLS
(Not forming part of Her Majesty's Household)
Pursuivants to the Earl of Erroll and the Countess of Mar
Slains–Peter Drummond-Murray of Mastrick
(Pursuivant to the Earl of Erroll)
Garioch–David Gordon Allen d'Aldecamb Lumsden of Cushnie
(Pursuivant to the Countess of Mar)

GENERAL TABLE OF PRECEDENCE IN ENGLAND AND WALES

The Queen
The Duke of Edinburgh
The Prince of Wales
The Sovereign's younger sons
The Sovereign's grandsons (according to the seniority of their fathers)
The Sovereign's cousins (according to the seniority of their fathers)
Archbishop of Canterbury
Lord High Chancellor
Archbishop of York
The Prime Minister
Lord High Treasurer (no such office exists at present)
Lord President of the Council
The Speaker of the House of Commons
Lord Privy Seal
Ambassadors and High Commissioners

Above all Peers of their own degree:
Lord Great Chamberlain
Lord High Constable (no such office exists at present)
Earl Marshal
Lord High Admiral (office held by HM The Queen)
Lord Steward of the Household
Lord Chamberlain of the Household

Master of the Horse
Dukes of England
Dukes of Scotland (none created since 1707)
Dukes of Great Britain (1707–1801)
Dukes of Ireland (created before 1801)
Dukes of the United Kingdom (created since 1801)
Eldest sons of Dukes of the Blood Royal (when they are not brothers, grandsons, uncles, or nephews of the reigning sovereign)
Marquesses of England
__________ Scotland (none created after 1707)
__________ Great Britain (1707–1801)
__________ Ireland (created before 1801)
__________ the United Kingdom (created since 1801)
Eldest sons of Dukes
Earls of England (anterior to 1707)
Earls of Scotland (none created after 1707)
Earls of Great Britain (1707–1801)
Earls of Ireland (created before 1801)
Earls of the United Kingdom (created since 1801)
Younger sons of Dukes of the Blood Royal (when they are not brothers, grandsons, uncles or nephews of the reigning sovereign)
Eldest sons of Marquesses
Younger sons of Dukes
Viscounts of England
__________ Scotland (anterior to 1707)
__________ Great Britain (1707–1801)
__________ Ireland (anterior to 1801)
__________ the United Kingdom (created since 1801)
Eldest sons of Earls
Younger sons of Marquesses
Bishop of London
________ Durham
________ Winchester
English Diocesan Bishops (according to date of consecration)
Bishops Suffragan (according to date of consecration)
Secretaries of State (if barons)
Barons of England
Barons of Scotland (none created since 1707)
________ Great Britain (1707–1801)
________ Ireland (anterior to 1801)
________ the United Kingdom (created since 1801)
Lords of Appeal in Ordinary
Commissioners of the Great Seal (those persons who execute the office of Lord High Chancellor when it happens to be vacant)
Treasurer of the Household
Comptroller of the Household
Vice-Chamberlain of the Household
Secretaries of State (when not barons)
Eldest sons of Viscounts
Younger sons of Earls
Eldest sons of Barons
Knights of the Garter
Privy Councillors
Chancellor of the Exchequer
__________ Duchy of Lancaster
Lord Chief Justice
Master of the Rolls
President of the Family Division
The Vice-Chancellor of the Chancery Division
Lord Justices of Appeal, ranking according to date of appointment
Judges of the High Court of Justice, ranking according to date of appointment
Vice-Chancellor of the County Palatine of Lancaster
Younger sons of Viscounts
__________ Barons
Younger sons of Life Peers
Baronets
Knights of the Thistle
Knights Grand Cross of the Bath
Knights Grand Commanders of the Star of India
Knights Grand Cross of St Michael and St George
Knights Grand Commanders of the Order of the Indian Empire
Knights Grand Cross of the Royal Victorian Order
Knights Grand Cross of the Order of the British Empire
Knights Commanders of the Bath
Knights Commanders of the Star of India
Knights Commanders of St Michael and St George
Knights Commanders of the Order of the Indian Empire
Knights Commanders of the Royal Victorian Order
Knights Commanders of the Order of the British Empire
Knights Bachelor
Official Referees of the Supreme Court of Judicature
Circuit Judges
County Court Judges of England and Wales
Masters in Chancery
Master of Court of Protection
Companions of the Bath
Companions of the Star of India
Companions of St Michael and St George
Companions of the Indian Empire
Commanders of the Royal Victorian Order
Commanders of the Order of the British Empire
Companions of the Distinguished Service Order
Lieutenants of the Royal Victorian Order
Officers of the Order of the British Empire
Companions of the Imperial Service Order
Eldest sons of the younger sons of Peers
Eldest sons of Baronets
Eldest sons of Knights of the Garter
Eldest sons of Knights, according to the precedence of their fathers
Members of the Royal Victorian Order
Members of the Order of the British Empire
Younger sons of Baronets
Younger sons of Knights
Esquires
Gentlemen

RELATIVE RANK AND PRECEDENCE IN THE NAVY, ARMY AND AIR FORCE

Navy	Army	Air Force
Admiral of the Fleet	Field Marshal	Marshal of the RAF
Admiral	General	Air Chief Marshal
Vice Admiral	Lieutenant-General	Air Marshal
Rear Admiral	Major-General	Air Vice-Marshal
Commodore	Brigadier	Air Commodore
Captain	Colonel	Group Captain
Commander	Lieutenant-Colonel	Wing Commander
Lieutenant Commander	Major	Squadron Leader
Lieutenant	Captain	Flight Lieutenant
Sub Lieutenant	Lieutenant	Flying Officer
Commissioned Officers from Warrant Rank	Second Lieutenant	Pilot Officer

PRECEDENCE AMONG LADIES.

The daughter of a peer does not lose her own rank should she marry a person not a peer, but if she marries a peer her title and precedence are merged in his, *e.g.*, if the daughter of a duke marries a baron, she takes the rank of a baroness. Maids of Honour* to the Queen Regnant, the Queen Consort, or the Queen Dowager, who are not the daughters of peers, are styled Honourable for life. The widow of a peer, baronet or knight who re-marries does not retain any title or precedence acquired from her previous husband, but may do so only by courtesy. A dowager peeress or the widow of a baronet, while a widow, takes precedence of the wife of the living holder of the title. The divorced wife of a peer or baronet derives no rank or precedence from her former husband but unless she remarries usually retains the title with her christian or forename prefixed (e.g. Mary, Lady Jones). Official rank and precedence is not communicable to the wife, but the wife of a lord mayor has precedence derived from her husband's office.

The Queen
The Queen Mother
The Princess of Wales
The Duchess of York
The Princess Royal
Sister of the Sovereign
Granddaughters of the Sovereign
Wives of the Sovereign's uncles
Wives of the Sovereign's cousins
Cousin of the Sovereign
The Prime Minister
Duchesses of England
———— Scotland
———— Great Britain
———— Ireland
———— the United Kingdom
Wives of the eldest sons of Dukes of the Blood Royal
Marchionesses (in the same order as the Duchesses)
Wives of the eldest sons of Dukes
Daughters of Dukes (while unmarried, or when married to commoners)
Countesses (in the same order as the Duchesses)
Wives of the younger sons of Dukes of the Blood Royal
Wives of the eldest sons of Marquesses
Daughters of Marquesses (while unmarried or when married to commoners)
Wives of the younger sons of Dukes
Viscountesses (in the same order as the Duchesses)
Wives of the elder sons of Earls
Daughters of Earls (while unmarried, or when married to commoners)
Wives of younger sons of Marquesses
Baronesses (in the same order as the Duchesses)
Wives of the eldest sons of Viscounts
Daughters of Viscounts (while unmarried or when married to a commoner)
Wives of the younger sons of Earls
Wives of the eldest sons of Barons
Daughters of Barons (if unmarried, or when married to a commoner)
Maids of Honour
Wives of Knights of the Garter
Privy Councillors (Women)
Wives of the younger sons of Viscounts
Wives of the younger sons of Barons
Daughters of Lords of Appeal
Wives of the sons of Legal Life Peers
Wives of Baronets (according to the dates of creation of titles held by their husbands)
Wives of Knights of the Thistle
Dames Grand Cross of St Michael and St George
Dames Grand Cross of the Royal Victorian Order
Dames Grand Cross of the Order of the British Empire
Wives of Knights Grand Cross of the Bath
Wives of Knights Grand Commanders of the Star of India
Wives of Knights Grand Cross of St Michael and St George
Wives of Knights Grand Commanders of the Indian Empire
Wives of Knights Grand Cross of the Royal Victorian Order
Wives of Knights Grand Cross of the Order of the British Empire
Dames Commanders of the Bath
Dames Commanders of St Michael and St George
Dames Commanders of the Royal Victorian Order
Dames Commanders of the Order of the British Empire
Wives of Knights Commanders of the Bath
Wives of Knights Commanders of the Star of India
Wives of Knights Commanders of St Michael and St George
Wives of Knights Commanders of the Indian Empire
Wives of Knights Commanders of the Royal Victorian Order
Wives of Knights Commanders of the Order of the British Empire
Wives of Knights Bachelor
Commanders of St Michael and St George
Commanders of the Royal Victorian Order
Commanders of the Order of the British Empire
Wives of Commanders and Companions of the Orders of the Bath, the Star of India, St Michael and St George, Indian Empire, Royal Victorian Order, and the British Empire
Wives of Companions of the Distinguished Service Order
Lieutenants of the Royal Victorian Order
Officers of the Order of the British Empire
Wives of Lieutenants of the Royal Victorian Order
Wives of Officers of the Order of the British Empire
Companions of the Imperial Service Order
Wives of Companions of the Imperial Service Order
Wives of the eldest sons of the younger sons of Peers
Daughters of the younger sons of Peers
Wives of the eldest sons of Baronets
Daughters of Baronets
Wives of the eldest sons of Knights of the Garter
Wives of the eldest sons of Knights Bachelor
Daughters of Knights Bachelor
Members of the Royal Victorian Order
Members of the Order of the British Empire
Wives of members of the Royal Victorian Order
Wives of members of the Order of the British Empire
Wives of the younger sons of Baronets
Wives of the younger sons of Knights
Wives of Esquires
Wives of Gentlemen

* No Maids of Honour have been appointed since the reign of King George V and it must be assumed that the dignity has now lapsed and seems unlikely to be revived.

GENERAL TABLE OF PRECEDENCE IN SCOTLAND

GENTLEMEN

The Duke of Edinburgh*
Lord High Commissioner to the General Assembly of the Church of Scotland (during sitting of General Assembly)
Duke of Rothesay (The Prince of Wales)
Sovereign's younger sons
Sovereign's grandsons
Sovereign's Cousins
Lord-Lieutenants of Counties†
Lord Provosts of Cities being *ex-officio* Lord-Lieutenants of Counties of Cities†
Sheriffs Principal†
Lord Chancellor of Great Britain
Moderator of General Assembly of Church of Scotland (during office)
The Prime Minister (if male)
Keeper of the Great Seal of Scotland (the Secretary for Scotland) (if a Peer)
Keeper of the Privy Seal of Scotland (if a Peer)
Hereditary High Constable of Scotland
Hereditary Master of the Household in Scotland
Dukes (as in English Table)
Eldest sons of Dukes of the Blood Royal
Marquesses (as in English Table)
Eldest sons of Dukes
Earls (as in English Table)
Younger sons of Dukes of the Blood Royal
Eldest sons of Marquesses
Younger sons of Dukes
Keeper of the Great Seal (the Secretary for Scotland) (if not a Peer)
Keeper of the Privy Seal (if not a Peer)
Lord Justice-General
Lord Clerk Register
Lord Advocate
Lord Justice-Clerk
Viscounts (as in English Table)
Eldest sons of Earls
Younger sons of Marquesses
Barons or Lords of Parliament (Scotland) (as in English Table)
Eldest sons of Viscounts
Younger sons of Earls
Eldest sons of Barons or Lords of Parliament
Knights of the Garter
Knights of the Thistle
Privy Counsellors
Senators of the College of Justice (Lords of Session), including Chairman of Scottish Land Court
Younger sons of Viscounts
Younger sons of Barons or Lords of Parliament
Baronets
Knights Grand Cross and Knights Grand Commanders of Orders (as in English Table)
Knights Commanders of Orders (as in English Table)
Solicitor-General for Scotland
Lord Lyon King of Arms
Sheriffs Principal (when not within own county)††
Knights Bachelor
Sheriffs
Companions of the Bath
Thence as in English Table

Lord-Lieutenants of Counties and of Counties of Cities during their term of office and with the limits of their jurisdiction have precedence before the Sheriffs Principal having concurrent jurisdiction.

LADIES

The Queen
The Queen Mother
Duchess of Rothesay (The Princess of Wales)
Sovereign's Daughter
Sovereign's Sister
Sovereign's Granddaughters
Wives of Sovereign's Uncles
Wives of Dukes of the Blood Royal
Wives of Princes of the Blood Royal
Sovereign's Cousin
The Prime Minister (if female)
Duchesses (as in English Table)
Wives of the eldest sons of Dukes of the Blood Royal
Marchionesses (as in English Table)
Wives of eldest sons of Dukes
Daughters of Dukes
Wives of younger sons of Dukes of the Blood Royal
Wives of eldest sons of Marquesses
Daughters of Marquesses
Wives of younger sons of Dukes
Countesses (as in English Table)
Viscountesses (as in English Table)
Wives of eldest sons of Earls
Daughters of Earls
Wives of younger sons of Marquesses
Baronesses, or Ladies of Parliament (Scotland) (as in English Table)
Wives of eldest sons of Viscounts
Daughters of Viscounts
Wives of younger sons of Earls
Wives of eldest sons of Barons or Lords of Parliament
Daughters of Barons or Lords of Parliament
Wives of Knights of the Garter
Wives of Knights of the Thistle
Privy Counsellors (women)
Wives of youngers sons of Viscounts
Wives of younger sons of Barons
Wives of Baronets
Dames Grand Cross of Orders (as in English Table)
Wives of Knights Grand Cross and Knights Grand Commanders of Orders (as in English Table)
Dames Commanders of Orders (as in English Tables)
Wives of Knights Commanders of Orders (as in English Tables)
Wives of Knights Bachelor and Wives of Senators of the College of Justice (Lords of Session) including the wife of the Chairman of the Scottish Land Court**
Companions of the Order of the Bath
Thence as in English Table

* By Royal Warrant dated 18 September 1952, it was declared that HRH the Duke of Edinburgh was henceforth to have Precedence next to HM the Queen, thus having place before the Lord High Commissioner.

** Taking precedence among themselves according to the dates of their husbands' creation as Knights or appointment as Senators of the College of Justice, respectively.

† During term of office, and within their respective Counties, Cities, and Sheriffdoms.

†† In Scotland Sheriffs exercise judicial functions.

POSITION OF LETTERS AFTER THE NAME

The abbreviations 'Bt' or 'Bart' (for a Baronet) and 'Esq', if applicable, precede all other letters.

The series of other letters are grouped either by regulations or by custom as follows:

1. Orders and Decorations conferred by the Crown.

2. Appointments in the following order, Privy Counsellor, Aide de Camp to Her Majesty, Honorary Physician to The Queen, Honorary Surgeon to The Queen, Honorary Dental Surgeon to The Queen, Honorary Nursing Sister to The Queen, and Honorary Chaplain to The Queen, viz, PC, ADC, QHP, QHS, QHDS, QHNS and QHC.

3. Queen's Counsel, Justice of the Peace and Deputy Lieutenant, viz. QC, JP and DL.

4. University Degrees.

5. (a) Religious Orders.
   (b) Medical Qualifications.

6. (a) Fellowships of Learned Societies,
   (b) Royal Academicians and Associates,
   (c) Fellowships, Memberships, etc., of Professional Institutions, Associations, etc.,
   (d) Writers to the Signet.

7. Member of Parliament, viz. MP.

8. Membership of one of the Armed Forces, such as RN or RAF.

The following notes are given for guidance.

It is important to keep the group order, even if the individual series of letters in Groups 4, 5 and 6 present difficulties. For further details see the appropriate section.

The nature of the correspondence determines which series of letters should normally be included under Groups 4, 5 and 6. For instance, when writing a professional letter to a doctor of medicine one would normally add more medical qualifications than in a social letter.

On a formal list all the appropriate letters are usually included after each name.

Those who have letters signifying Crown Honours and Awards are usually given only the principal letters in Groups 3, 4 and 5 (e.g. MD, FRCS, FRS).

A peer who is a junior officer in the Armed Forces, is not usually addressed by his Service rank in social correspondence, unless he so wishes, or a letter is forwarded to him at a Service address or club.

1. ORDERS AND DECORATIONS

All the appropriate letters are obligatory in correspondence and lists. The order is laid down for Knights, Dames and others.

They are addressed according to their rank, with the appropriate letters after their name in order of precedence. The use of all these letters is obligatory, e.g John Brown, Esq, CBE, MVO, TD.

The recipient is allowed to use the appropriate letters for the Order from the date of announcement in the 'London Gazette'.

Those promoted within the same Order of Chivalry do not continue to show the letters of the lower class of that Order, e.g. if Brigadier John Smith, OBE, is promoted to CBE he is addressed as Brigadier John Smith, CBE, the OBE being dropped.

Precedence of letters

The full list of honours and awards in order of precedence *of letters* of given below. A baronet has the letters Bt or Bart immediately after the name, and before any letters which signify honours.

It should be noted the VC and GC have precedence of *all* letters signifying Orders (including Knightly grades therein), Decorations and Medals.

The Order of Merit (OM) and Companion of Honour (CH) are important honours which bestow no title on the holder. The letters OM follow GCB, and CH follow GBE.

Some people prefer PC after KG since that is its correct position in order of precedence.

Victoria Cross	VC
George Cross	GC
Knight of the Garter	KG
Knight of the Thistle	KT
Knight/Dame Grand Cross of the Order of the Bath	GCB
Order of Merit	OM
Knight Grand Commander of the Star of India	GCSI
Knight/Dame Grand Cross of the Order of St Michael and St George	GCMG
Knight Grand Commander of the Indian Empire	GCIE
Knight/Dame Grand Cross of the Royal Victorian Order	GCVO
Knight/Dame Grand Cross of the British Empire	GBE
Companion of Honour	CH
Knight Commander of the Bath	KCB
Dame Commander of the Bath	DCB
Knight Commander of the Star of India	KCSI
Knight Commander of St Michael and St George	KCMG
Dame Commander of St Michael and St George	DCMG
Knight Commander of the Indian Empire	KCIE
Knight Commander of the Royal Victorian Order	KCVO
Dame Commander of the Royal Victorian Order	DCVO
Knight Commander of the British Empire	KBE
Dame Commander of the British Empire	DBE
Companion of the Order of the Bath	CB
Companion of the Order of the Star of India	CSI
Companion of the Order of St Michael and St George	CMG
Companion of the Order of the Indian Empire	CIE
Commander of the Royal Victorian Order	CVO
Commander of the Order of the British Empire	CBE
Distinguished Service Order	DSO
Lieutenant of the Royal Victorian Order	LVO
Officer of the Order of the British Empire	OBE
Imperial Service Order	ISO
Member of the Royal Victorian Order	MVO
Member of the Order of the British Empire	MBE
Indian Order of Merit (Military)	IOM
Royal Red Cross	RRC
Distinguished Service Cross	DSC
Military Cross	MC
Distinguished Flying Cross	DFC
Air Force Cross	AFC
Associate, Royal Red Cross	ARRC
Order of British India	OBI
Distinguished Conduct Medal	DCM
Conspicuous Gallantry Medal	CGM
George Medal	GM
Distinguished Conduct Medal of the Royal West African Frontier Force and the King's African Rifles	DCM
Indian Distinguished Service Medal	IDSM
Distinguished Service Medal	DSM
Military Medal	MM
Distinguished Flying Medal	DFM
Air Force Medal	AFM
Medal for Saving Life at Sea	SGM
Indian Order of Merit (Civil)	IOM
Colonial Police Medal for Gallantry	CPM
Queen's Gallantry Medal	QGM
British Empire Medal	BEM
King's Police Medal	KPM
King's Police and Fire Service Medal	KPFSM
Queen's Police Medal	QPM
Queen's Fire Service Medal	QFSM
Colonial Police Medal for Meritorious Service	CPM
Meritorious Service Medal	MSM
Army Emergency Reserve Decoration	ERD
Volunteer Officer's Decoration	VD
Territorial Decoration	TD
Efficiency Decoration	ED
Decoration for Officers of the Royal Naval Reserve	RD
Decoration for Officers of the Royal Naval Volunteer Reserve	VRD
Air Efficiency Award	AE
Canadian Forces Decoration	CD

ORDER OF CANADA

The formation of the Order of Canada was announced in 1967.

The Order, of which the Queen is Sovereign, is divided into the following grades according to its last revised constitution:

CC Companion of the Order of Canada, with precedence after VC and GC before all other letters.
OC Officer of the Order of Canada, with precedence after CC.
CM Member of the Order of Canada, with precedence after OC.

The Cross of Valour, The Star of Courage and The Medal of Bravery have no letters.

ORDER OF AUSTRALIA

The Order of Australia was established in 1975.

The Order, of which The Queen is Sovereign, consists of a General Division and a Military Division and is divided into the following classes:

AK Knight of the Order of Australia, with precedence after the Order of Merit.

AD Dame of Order of Australia, with the same precedence as Knight of the Order of Australia.

AC Companion of the Order of Australia, with precedence after Knight Grand Cross of the Order of the British Empire.

AO Officer of the Order of Australia, with precedence after the Knight Bachelor.

AM Member of the Order of Australia, with precedence after the Distinguished Service Order.

OAM Medal of the Order of Australia, with precedence after the Royal Red Cross (2nd class).

THE QUEEN'S SERVICE ORDER OF NEW ZEALAND

This order was established in 1975. The Order, of which The Queen is Sovereign, is divided into two parts, for Community Service and for Public Services.

There are two divisions:

QSO Companions of The Queen's Service Order, with precedence after Officer of the Order of the British Empire.

QSM The Queen's Service Medal, with precedence after Queen's Gallantry Medal, and before British Empire Medal.

2. PRIVY COUNSELLORS AND APPOINTMENTS TO THE QUEEN

For peers the letters PC are obligatory. For other Privy Counsellors, 'Rt Hon' before the name is sufficient identification. As the other appointments to the Crown (QHP, QHS, etc.) are held for a limited period only, they are not always used by recipients.

3. UNIVERSITY DEGREES

Doctorates in the faculties of Divinity and Medicine (DD, MD) and Masters degrees in the latter (eg MS) are given in all correspondence. Other divinity degrees (eg BD) are sometimes included.

Other degrees in medicine (e.g. MB BS) are sometimes included, especially in professional correspondence, but if one progresses in the same degree only the higher is given.

Doctorates in other faculties are sometimes given, especially if the correspondence concerns the particular profession or subject (e.g. LLD, DSc). Alternatively, except for surgeons, the envelope may be addressed as 'Doctor' before his name, without giving his (or her) degrees.

Other degrees are seldom, and MA and BA never, used in social correspondence, but they are generally included in a formal list.

4. (a) RELIGIOUS ORDERS

Letters for members of religious communities, when used, should be included, e.g. SJ. Some Members of the Order of St. Benedict do not normally use the letters OSB as the prefix of 'Dom' or 'Dame' is held to be a sufficient identification.

(b) MEDICAL QUALIFICATIONS

Fellowships are given in all correspondence (e.g. FRCP, FRCS)

Other qualifications are sometimes given, especially those which are the highest held. They are usually included when writing professionally.

When all letters signifying qualifications are included, as for example in a nominal list, they should appear in the following order. (*Note:* Fellows and Members of each category precede the next category):

Medicine
Surgery (except MRCS)
Obstetrics, Gynaecology and other specialities
Qualifying diplomas (e.g. MRCS, LRCP)
Other diplomas (e.g. DPH, DObst, RCOG)

In practice, a maximum of three series of letters including MD (see Group 3 above) is usually sufficient in ordinary correspondence (e.g. MD, MS, FRCS).

5. (a) FELLOWSHIPS OF LEARNED SOCIETIES

Fellowships fall into two categories:

(a) honorific, i.e. nomination by election,
(b) nomination by subscription.

Normally only honorific fellowships are used in social correspondence (e.g. FRS, FBA). Fellowships by subscription are generally restricted to correspondence concerning the same field of interest, e.g. a writer to a Fellow of the Zoological Society on the subject of zoology will include FZS after the name.

There is no recognized order for placing these letters. Strictly speaking, they should be arranged according to the date of foundation or incorporation of the societies concerned, but some hold that those with a Royal Charter should precede others.

In practice the following is usually adhered to:

(1) Where one society is indisputably of greater importance than another, the letters may be placed in that order; or alternatively the fellowship of the junior society may be omitted.
(2) If such precedence cannot be determined, the letters may be placed in order of conferment. Where this is not known, they may be placed in alphabetical order.
(3) Where a fellow is pre-eminent in a particular subject, his fellowship of a society connected with this interest may either be placed first, or his other fellowships omitted.

The following are some of the principal learned societies, with their dates of incorporation:

Fellow of The Royal Society	FRS	1662
Fellow of The Society of Antiquaries	FSA	1707
Fellow of The Royal Society of Edinburgh	FRSE	1783
Fellow of The Royal Society of Literature	FRSL	1823
Fellow of The British Academy	FBA	1901
Fellow of the Fellowship of Engineering	FEng	1983

Presidents of some societies have special letters to signify their appointment, e.g. The President of the Royal Society has PRS after his name, but these letters are only used within the particular society.

The Royal Society of Literature bestows an award limited to ten recipients, the Companion of Literature. The letters CLit are placed before the Fellowship.

(b) ROYAL ACADEMY OF ARTS, THE ROYAL SCOTTISH ACADEMY, ETC.

It is not suggested that Royal Academicians yield in precedence to fellows of learned societies. In practice the two lists do not coincide.

The President and Past Presidents are indicated as follows:

President of the Royal Academy	PRA
Past President of the Royal Academy	PPRA
President of the Royal Scottish Academy	PRSA
Past President of the Royal Scottish Academy	PPRSA

Royal Academicians and Associates are included as follows:

Royal Academician	RA
Royal Scottish Academician	RSA
Associate of the Royal Academy	ARA
Associate of the Royal Scottish Academy	ARSA

Similarly with other Academies, e.g. President Royal Hibernian Academy (PRHA) and Academicians (RHA).

Honorary Academicians and Associates do not normally use the relevant letters.

(c) FELLOWSHIPS AND MEMBERSHIPS OF PROFESSIONAL INSTITUTIONS, ASSOCIATIONS, ETC.

These letters are usually restricted to correspondence concerning the particular profession.

It is not suggested that professional societies as such yield precedence to learned societies, but in point of fact the two groups do not coincide to any great extent. Most of the senior learned societies which elect fellows are senior in age and importance to the professional. Those whose fellowships are by subscription are generally only used in the particular field of interest. For example, if Mr. John Smith is a Chartered Engineer and a Fellow of the Royal Historical Society, he would normally be described professionally as John Smith, Esq, CEng, FIMechE. When corresponding on historical subjects he is normally described as John Smith, Esq, FRHistS. If both series of letters are placed after his name, it is usual to place first those which concern the particular function or subject.

As there is no recognized order for placing qualifications awarded by different bodies, a recipient usually places these letters on headed paper, business cards, etc. in order of importance to his particular profession.

The Engineering Council

The Engineering Council was granted a Royal Charter in 1981. The object of the Council is to advance the education and training of engineers and technologists, and to promote the science and practice of engineering for the public benefit. The Engineering Council accredits engineering academic courses and training programmes in the UK and registers qualified engineers.

There are 47 Professional Engineering Institutions which are Nominated bodies of The Engineering Council and which work closely with the Council in the qualification and registration areas. Of these 47 Professional Institutions, 17 are chartered. The Engineering Council, through its Board for Engineers' Registration, determines the standards and criteria for the education, training and levels of experience by which Chartered Engineers, Incorporated Engineers and Engineering Technicians may be registered, enabling them to use the designatory letters CEng, IEng, and EngTech respectively. Chartered Engineers must be in membership of a nominated Chartered Engineering Institution, or an institution affiliated body.

The designatory letters CEng, denoting Chartered Engineer, follow immediately after an individual's name and decorations and are followed in turn by the letters F (Fellow) or M (Member) identifying him with the particular institution(s) to which he belongs. Thus J Smith, Esq, OBE, CEng, FICE, MIMechE, is a Chartered Engineer who is a Fellow of the Institution of Civil Engineers and a Member of the Institution of Mechanical Engineers.

The nominated Bodies which are also Chartered Engineering Institutions are: Royal Aeronautical Society, Institution of Civil Engineers, Institution of Chemical Engineers, Institution of Electrical Engineers, Institute of Energy, Institution of Gas Engineers, Institute of Marine Engineers, Institution of Mechanical Engineers, Institute of Metals, Institution of Mining Engineers, Institution of Mining and Metallurgy, Royal Institution of Naval Architects, Institution of Production Engineers, Institution of Structural Engineers, Institute of Measurement and Control, Chartered Institution of Building Services Engineers and the British Computer Society.

Chartered Societies of the Land

Three chartered societies of the land, viz.:

The Royal Institution of Chartered Surveyors
The Chartered Land Agents' Society
The Chartered Auctioneers' and Estate Agents' Institute

united in June 1970 to become the Royal Institution of Chartered Surveyors. Fellows and Professional Associates respectively have the letters FRICS and ARICS.

Incorporated Society of Valuers and Auctioneers

The Incorporated Society of Auctioneers and Landed Property Agents united in April 1968 with The Valuers Institution to form The Incorporated Society of Valuers and Auctioneers, with the letters FSVA and ASVA.

(d) WRITERS TO THE SIGNET

It is customary for the letters WS to follow the name after University degrees and those which signify Fellowship or Membership of a Society or Institution, despite the fact that the WS Society (an ancient Society of Solicitors in Scotland) is frequently considerably older than many Institutions. This is a way of indicating the profession. It is not customary for the letters WS to be used socially.

6. APPOINTMENTS

The letters MP are always shown for a Member of Parliament.

The letters QC are always shown for a Queen's Counsel including a County Court Judge, but not a High Court Judge.

The letters JP for a Justice of the Peace and DL for a Deputy Lieutenant may be included *in that order.* In practice they are often omitted for a peer, or for one with several honours and awards.

Note: There is no official abbreviation for a Lord-Lieutenant, HM Lieutenant or a Vice-Lieutenant.

7. MEMBERSHIP OF ONE OF THE ARMED FORCES

Royal Navy.—The letters 'RN' (or 'Royal Navy', which this Service prefers) are placed after the names of serving officers of and below the rank of Captain. They are also placed after the names of retired Captains, Commanders, and Lieutenant-Commanders where they are prefixed by Naval rank. The letters RNR are likewise used by officers of the Royal Naval Reserve.

Army.—The appropriate letters which signify a Regiment or Corps may be placed after the name for officers on the active list of and below the rank of Lieutenant-Colonel, but are often omitted in social correspondence. These letters are not used for retired officers.

Corps have letter abbreviations (e.g. RE, RAMC, RAOC, RAPC). Most regiments are written in full.

Royal Air Force.—The letters RAF are placed after serving and retired officers, except for Marshals of The Royal Air Force. Officers above the rank of Group Captain do not often use these letters. Similarly with RAFVR.

Royal Marines.—The letters 'RM' (or 'Royal Marines' which some officers prefer) are placed after the names of serving and retired officers of and below the rank of Lieutenant-Colonel. Similarly RMR (Royal Marines Reserve).

FORMS OF ADDRESSING PERSONS OF TITLE

Ecclesiastical and Services prefixes of rank are written before other titles. A High Officer of State or an official holding an important office, should be addressed by his official title when the communication refers to official business.

Eldest Sons of Dukes, Marquesses, and Earls bearing courtesy titles should not be styled "The Rt. Hon." or "The" unless they themselves are Peers or Members of the Privy Council.

Formal conclusions to letters to Peers. The style "I am, my Lord, Your obedient servant" may be used (as applicable), but "Yours faithfully" and "Yours truly" are now more customarily adopted, except for letters to Members of the Royal Family. After the Lambeth Conference 1968 under the guidance of the Archbishop of Canterbury, a simplified form of address for the Clergy of the Church of England was announced.

Commanders, Companions, Officers or Members of any Order and recipients of Decorations and Medals are addressed according to their rank and are entitled to place the recognised initials after their names in the following order:—VC, GC, OM, VA, CI, CH, CB, CSI, CMG, CIE, CVO, CBE, DSO, LVO, (4th class), OBE, QSO, ISO, MVO (5th class), MBE, RRC, DSC, MC, DFC, AFC, ARRC, DCM, CGM, GM, DSM, MM, DFM, AFM, SGM, CPM (for Gallantry), QGM, BEM, KPM, KPFSM, QPM, QFSM, CPM (for Meritorious Service), ERD, TD, ED, RD, VRD, AE, CD.

Succession to hereditary titles. By custom those who have succeeded to peerages and baronetcies are not so addressed until after their predecessor's funeral.

New honours. Knights and Dames of Orders of Chivalry may use their style of "Sir" and "Dame" and the appropriate letters after their names, and Knights Bachelor their style of "Sir" immediately their honours have been announced. Other recipients of honours may also use the appropriate letters. Peers may use their titles after the patent of creation has passed the Great Seal, when their respective Peerage titles will be announced. Full details of forms of address are included in DEBRETT'S CORRECT FORM.

Air Efficiency Award.—The Air Efficiency Award, introduced in 1942 to recognize meritorious Service in the Royal Auxiliary Air Force and the RAFVR, since 1975 officers including retired officers who have received the Award may place AE after their names.

Albert Medal.—In Oct. 1971, The Queen approved the exchange by which holders of the Albert Medal (AM) receive the George Cross. *See* George Cross.

Ambassador (British).—LETTERS.—*Superscription.* (When in the country to which he is accredited only). "His Excellency [preceding all other ranks and titles], HM Ambassador to ______." *Commencement,* "Sir" or socially according to rank. *Conclusion,* "I have the honour to be Sir, Your Excellency's obedient servant." PERSONAL ADDRESS, "Your Excellency."

Ambassador's Wife. She is not entitled to the style "Her Excellency" and is referred to and addressed by name or conversationally as the Ambassadress.

Archbishop.—LETTERS.—*Superscription,* "The Most Rev The Lord Archbishop of ______," *Commencement,* "Dear Archbishop." PERSONAL ADDRESS, "Your Grace" or "Archbishop." On retirement from office he reverts to the style of Bishop.

Archbishop's Wife.—As the wife of an Esquire.

Archdeacon.—LETTERS.—*Superscription,* "The Venerable the Archdeacon of [Ely]." *Commencement,* "Dear Archdeacon." The prefix of the Venerable is not retained after retirement unless the title of Archdeacon Emeritus has been conferred.

Baron.—LETTERS.—*Superscription,* "The Right Hon the Lord ______" or socially "The Lord ______." *Commencement,* "My Lord" or socially "Dear Lord ______." PERSONAL ADDRESS, "My Lord."

Baroness.—LETTERS.—*Superscription,* if a Baroness in her own right "The Right Hon the Baroness ______." or socially "The Baroness ______," or "The Right Hon the Lady ." or "The Lady ______." If the wife of a Baron "The Right Hon the Lady ______," or socially "The Lady ______." *Commencement,* "Madam" or socially "Dear Lady ______." PERSONAL ADDRESS, "Madam." [See also Baron's Widow.]

***If a Baroness in her own right marry a commoner and has issue, the children have the same rank and are addressed as if their father were a Baron.

Baronet.—LETTERS.—*Superscription,* "Sir [Charles] ______ Bt." (The abbreviation "Bart." is also sometimes used). *Commencement,* "Sir." PERSONAL ADDRESS, "Sir" or socially "Dear Sir [Charles]".

Baronet's Widow.—*Same as Baronet's Wife* if present baronet is unmarried. For widows where present incumbent of the title is married ["Dowager"]. As to re-marriage, see "Widows."

Baronet's Wife.—LETTERS.—*Superscription,* if the daughter (i) of a commoner. "Lady ______"; (ii) of a Baron or a Viscount, "The Hon Lady ______"; (iii) of an Earl, a Marquess, or a Duke, "The Lady [Emily] ______." *Commencement,* "Madam.", or socially, "Dear Lady ______." PERSONAL ADDRESS, "Madam."

Baron's Daughter.—LETTERS.—*Superscription,* if married (i) to an esquire, "The Hon Mrs ______"; (ii) to a knight, or a baronet, "The Hon Lady ______"; (iii) to the son of a Baron, or Viscount, or to the younger son of an Earl, "The Hon Mrs ______," or if her husband has a married brother. "The Hon Mrs [William] ______"; (iv) to the younger son of a Marquess or a Duke, "The Lady [Henry] ______." If unmarried, "The Hon [Mary] ______"; (v) to the eldest son of a Duke, Marquess, or Earl by his courtesy title. [*See* also under "Duke's Daughter."] *Commencement,* "Madam." PERSONAL ADDRESS, "Madam," or socially if married to an esquire, "Dear Mrs ______," or according to her husband's rank if a Peer.

Baron's Son.—LETTERS.—*Superscription,* "The Hon [John] ______." *Commencement,* "Sir." PERSONAL ADDRESS, "Sir." or socially "Dear Mr ______." See also "Master of ______.".

Baron's Son's Widow.—*Same as Baron's Son's Wife* so long as she remains a widow. As to re-marriage, see "Widows."

Baron's Son's Wife.—LETTERS.—*Superscription,* "The Hon Mrs [Edward] ______," but if the daughter (i) of a Viscount or Baron "The Hon Mrs ______," (ii) of an Earl, a Marquess, or a Duke, "The Lady [Ellen]." [*See* also under "Duke's Daughter." *Commencement,* "Madam," or socially, if her father an esquire "Dear Mrs ______" or according to her father's rank, if a Peer. PERSONAL ADDRESS, "Madam."

Baron's Widow.—*Same as Baroness* if present Baron is unmarried. For widows where present incumbent of title is married [see "Dowager"]. As to re-marriage, see "Widows."

Bishop (Diocesan).—LETTERS.—*Superscription,* "The Rt Rev the Lord Bishop of ______," *Commencement,* "Dear Bishop."

Bishop (Commonwealth, Church Overseas, Irish, Scottish Episcopal, Suffragan and Welsh).—LETTERS.—*Superscription,* "The Right Rev the Bishop of ______." Exceptions, The Bishop of Meath (Premier Bishop of Ireland), and the Primus of Scotland, who are styled "Most Rev" *Commencement,* "Dear Bishop."

(Bishop retired).—Letters commence "Dear Bishop," and are addressed "The Right Rev [John Smith], DD."

Bishop's Wife.—As wife of Esquire.

Cabinet Ministers.—Are Invariably Privy Counsellors, which see.

Canon.—LETTERS.—*Superscription,* "The Rev Canon [John Smith]." *Commencement,* "Dear Canon, " or "Dear Canon [Smith]." On retirement from office he reverts to the style of other clergy unless he has been appointed a Canon Emeritus.

Chairman of Scottish Land Court, as for Lord of Session.

Circuit Judge.—See "Judge, Circuit."

Clergy.—LETTERS.—*Superscription,* "The Rev John ______." *Commencement,* "Dear Mr (Smith)" or "Dear Father Smith." PERSONAL ADDRESS, "Sir." The Reverend precedes any title: The Rev the Hon It is *incorrect* to write "The Hon and Rev" or "The Rev *Mr.*" Christian name or initals should always be shown.

Consuls [British].—LETTERS.—*Superscription,* "______, Esq, HM ['Consul-General,' 'Consul,' or 'Vice-Consul,' as the case may be] ______," In other respects as an Esquire.

Countess.—LETTERS.—*Superscription,* "The Rt Hon the Countess of ______," or socially "The Countess of ______," In other respects, as Baroness. [See also "Earl's Widow."] *Commencement,* formally "Madam," socially "Dear Lady ______." If a Countess in her own right marries a gentleman of lesser degree than herself, and has issue, the children would have same rank and are addressed as if their father were an Earl.

Dames of Orders of Chivalry prefix "Dame" to their Christian names, adding the initials "GCB," "GCMG," "GCVO," "GBE" "DCB," "DCMG." "DCVO," or "DBE," as the case may be, after the surname. *Commencement,* formally "Madam" or socially "Dear Dame Edith ______" or "Dear Dame Edith." PERSONAL ADDRESS, "Dame Edith."

Dean.—LETTERS.—*Superscription,* "The Very Rev the Dean of ______." *Commencement,* "Dear Dean." PERSONAL ADDRESS, "Sir." The prefix of "The Very Rev" is not retained on retirement.

Degrees.—Those with doctorates of any faculty may be addressed by the appropriate abbreviations after their names, following those of orders, decorations and medals conferred by the Crown. DD should always be included. Masters' and bachelors' degrees are not used in social correspondence. The order of letters signifying doctorates and degrees depends on the individual university which confers them.

Deputy Lieutenant.—The letters DL are usually put after name. They follow JP.

Divorced Ladies. When a lady is divorced she loses any precedence which she gained by marriage. With regard to divorced Peeresses, the College of Arms, acting on an opinion of the Lord Chancellor, has long held that such persons cannot claim the privileges or status of Peeresses which they derived from their husbands. Divorced Peeresses are not summoned to a Coronation as Peeresses. The above remarks apply to ladies who have divorced their husbands as well as to those who have been divorced.

The correct style and description of divorced ladies who have not re-married, nor have taken steps to resume their maiden name with the prefix of Mrs, is as follows:

The former wife of a Peer or courtesy Peer,—Mary, Viscountess ______.

The former wife of a Baronet or Knight,—Mary, Lady ______.

The divorced wife of an "Honourable,"—The Hon Mrs John ______, or alternatively she may prefer to be known as Mrs Mary ______.

The divorced wife of a younger son of a Duke or Marquess,—The Lady John______,

The divorced wife of an untitled gentleman,—Mrs Mary ______ initials.

Dowager Lady is addressed according to her rank. Immediately a peer, or a baronet, marries, the widow of the previous incumbent of the title becomes "The Dowager"; but if there is more than one widow living of previous incumbents of a title, use must be made of the Christian name as a distinction, since the style of Dowager belongs to the senior of the widows for her lifetime. This prefix, however, is very much less used than formerly, use of the Christian name generally being preferred. In such cases ladies are addressed as The Right Hon [Mary], Countess of ______"; or socially as "[Mary], Countess of ______," etc., etc., if a peeress; or, as Ellen, Lady ______," if a Baronet's widow.

Duchess.—LETTERS.—*Superscription,* "Her Grace the Duchess of ______," or socially "The Duchess of ______." *Commencement,* formally "Madam," or socially "Dear Duchess of ______" or "Dear Duchess." PERSONAL ADDRESS, "Your Grace." [See also "Duke's Widow," and for "Duchess of the Blood Royal" *see* "Princess."]

Duke.—LETTERS.—*Superscription,* "His Grace the Duke of ______" or socially "The Duke of______." The very formal style of "The Most Noble" is now rarely used. *Commencement,* "My Lord Duke," "Dear Duke of," or [more usual] "Dear Duke." PERSONAL ADDRESS, "Your Grace." [For "Duke of the Blood Royal" *see* "Prince."]

Duke's Daughter.—LETTERS.—*Superscription,* "The Lady [Henrietta] ." *Commencement,* "Madam," or socially "Dear Lady Henrietta ______" or "Dear Lady Henrietta." PERSONAL ADDRESS, "Madam."

*** If the daughter of a Duke, a Marquess, or an Earl marries a Peer she is addressed according to the rank of her husband. If she marries the eldest son of a Duke, Marquess or Earl she is known by her husband's courtesy title, but if the daughter of a *Duke* or *Marquess* marries the eldest son of an Earl she is sometimes addressed by the courtesy title of her husband, but she may revert to the style of Lady [Mary] Stavordale, i.e. her own title, followed by her husband's courtesy title. His surname must never be used. This form is invariably used by such ladies after divorce.

Duke's Eldest Son, assumes by courtesy a secondary title of his father, and is addressed personally as if he were a Peer without 'The Most Hon' or 'The Rt Hon' *Superscription,* "Marquess of______" (or as title adopted may be).

Duke's Eldest Son's Daughter is by courtesy addressed as if her father were a Peer.

Duke's Eldest Son's Eldest Son assumes by courtesy the third title of his grandfather, and is addressed personally as if he were a peer provided such courtesy title is the title of a Peerage vested in his grandfather. *Superscription,* "Earl of ______" or "Lord______" (or as title adopted may be).

Duke's Eldest Son's Younger Son is by courtesy addressed as if his father were a Peer.

Duke's Eldest Son's Widow, *Same as Duke's Eldest Sons's Wife* so long as she remains a widow. As to re-marriage, *see* "Widows."

Duke's Eldest Son's Wife is known by his courtesy title, and is addressed personally as a peeress without 'The Most Hon' or 'The Rt Hon'.

Duke's Widow, *same as Duchess* if present Duke is unmarried. For widows where present incumbent of title is married [*see* "Dowager"]. As to re-marriage, *see* "Widows."

Duke's Younger Son.—LETTERS.—*Superscription,* "The Lord [Robert] ______." *Commencement,* formally "My Lord," or socially "Dear Lord Robert______," or "Dear Lord Robert." PERSONAL ADDRESS, "My Lord."

Duke's Younger Son's Widow, *same as Duke's Younger Son's Wife.* As to re-marriage, *see* "Widows."

Duke's Younger Son's Wife.—LETTERS.—*Superscription,* "The Lady [Thomas]______." *Commencement,* "Madam," or socially "Dear Lady Thomas ______," or "Dear Lady Thomas."

Earl.—LETTERS.—*Superscription,* "The Right Hon the Earl of ______," or socially "The Earl of ______." In other respects as Baron.

Earl's Daughter, *same as Duke's Daughter.*

Earl's Eldest Son bears by courtesy a lesser (usually the second) title of his father, and is addressed as if he were a Peer but without 'The Rt Hon'. *Superscription,* "Viscount ______."

Earl's Eldest Son's Daughter is by courtesy addressed as if her father were a Peer.

Earls Eldest Son's Son is by courtesy addressed as if his father were a Peer. [If a Scottish Earldom, the eldest may be addressed as "The Master of ______." *See* Master.]

Earl's Eldest Son's Widow, *same as eldest son's Wife* so long as she remains a widow. As to re-marriage, *see* "Widows."

Earl's Eldest Son's Wife is usually known by his courtesy title (for exception see under "Duke's Daughter"), and is addressed personally as if a Peeress but without 'The Rt Hon'.

Earl's Widow, *same as Countess* if present Earl is unmarried. For widows where present incumbent of the title is married [*see* "Dowager"].

Earl's Wife.—*See* "Countess."

Earl's Younger Son, *same as Baron's Son.*

Earl's Younger Son's Widow, *same as Baron's Son's Wife.*

Earl's Younger Son's Wife, *same as Baron's Son's Wife.*

Edward Medal.—In Oct. 1971, The Queen approved the exchange by which holders of the Edward Medal (EM) receive the George Cross. (see George Cross).

Esquire.—LETTERS.—*Superscription,* "[Edward]______, Esq." *Commencement,* "Sir." PERSONAL ADDRESS, "Sir."

Esquire's Widow, *same as Esquire's Wife.* She continues to use her late husband's christian name unless she re-marries, e.g. Mrs John Smith *not* Mrs Mary Smith.

Esquire's Wife.—*Superscription.* "Mrs [Egerton]," or "Mrs [John Egerton]." The former style is applicable if she is the wife of the head of the family, provided that there is no senior widow living, who retains the style for life or until re-marriage.—LETTERS.—*Commencement,* "Madam." PERSONAL ADDRESS, "Madam."

Fire Service Medals.—See Police Medals.

George Cross. The letters GC take precedence after VC, and before all other honours and decorations.

Governor of a Country within the British Commonwealth is styled "His Excellency" [preceding all other ranks and titles] while actually administering a Government and within its boundary (also an officer administering in his absence). If the Governor has not been knighted he is styled "His Excellency Mr John Smith." Esquire should not be used with HE.

Governor-General.—The style of His Excellency precedes all other titles and ranks, and is used while actually administering a Government and within the territory administered.—LETTERS.—*Superscription,* "His Excellency [Sir John] ______, Governor-General of ______" (also an officer administering in his absence). In other respects as for Governor.

Governor-General's Wife.—The style of "Her Excellency" has, since 1924, been confined to the wives of the Govs-Gen of Countries of the Commonwealth within the country administered by her husband.

Governor's Wife.—She is not accorded the style of "Her Excellency."

Grandchildren of Peers.—If the eldest son of a peer predeceases his father and the grandson succeeds to the peerage held by his grandfather, a Royal Warrant is necessary (when such succession has eventuated) to grant to his younger brothers and his sisters, the "rank, title, place, pre-eminence, and precedence" which would have been due to them if their father had survived to inherit the Peerage.

High Commissioner.—*Superscription,* His Excellency [preceding all other ranks, and titles] the High Commissioner for ______." Otherwise as for an Ambassador.

"Honourable" in Commonwealth Countries. The title of "Honourable" is borne *for life* by all Members of the Queen's Privy Council in Canada, Members of the Canadian Senate and Premiers and Lieutenant-Governors of Canadian Provinces, and of the Executive Councils of the Commonwealth of Australia and of the States of Victoria and Tasmania. In Canada the title of "Honourable" is borne *during office* by the following categories of Judges in Canada—Judges of Supreme and Exchequer Courts of Canada the Chief Justices and Judges of the Supreme Courts of Ontario, Nova Scotia, New Brunswick, Alberta and Newfoundland, the Court of Queen's Bench and the Superior Court of Quebec, the Court of Appeal and the Court of Queen's Bench of Manitoba and Saskatchewan, the Court of Appeal and the Supreme Court of British Columbia, the Supreme Court of Judicature of Prince Edward Island, and the Territorial Courts of NW Territories and Yukon Territory. They are eligible to be personally recommended by the Governor-General for Her Majesty's permission to retain the title on retirement. Also in Commonwealth countries all Members of Executive Councils, all Members of Legislative Councils (other than Legislative Councils of Provinces of Canada), and by the Speaker of the Lower House of the Legislatures. It is also used locally by Members of the Executive and Legislative Councils of territories not possessing Responsible Government. The following in Commonwealth Countries are eligible to be recommended to retain the title of "Honourable" on retirement. Executive Councillors who have served for at least three years as Ministers or one year as Prime Minister; Presidents of Senates and Legislative Councils and Speakers of Legislative Assemblies on quitting office after having served three years in their respective offices: Senators and Members of the Legislative Councils on retirement or resignation after a continuous service of not less than ten years.

[*See* also Judges in Commonwealth and Overseas Territories]

Invitations. When sent jointly to married couples at their home address, the envelope should always be addressed to the wife.

Judge of City of London Court, as for Circuit Judge.

Judge in Commonwealth and Overseas Territories.—The title of "The Right Honourable" is borne for life by the Chief Justice of Canada. The title of "Honourable" during tenure of office is borne by Chief Justices and Judges of the High Court of Australia, and the Supreme Courts of New South Wales, Vic, Queensland, S Aust, W Aust, Tasmania, NZ, and the Judges of the Supreme and Exchequer Courts, and the Chief Justices and Judges of certain other Courts in the provinces of Canada; also such Chief Justices and Judges of those Courts as may be specially permitted to bear it after retirement. *Superscription,* "The Hon the Chief Justice," or "The Hon Mr Justice ______." Judges of the Supreme Courts in Commonwealth Countries are styled "The Honourable."

Judge, Circuit.—For the various appointments see Table of General Precedence.—LETTERS. — *Superscription,* "His Honour Judge ______." PERSONAL ADDRESS—"Sir", but when on the Bench, "Your Honour." The prefix of "His Honour," but not "Judge," is retained after retirement from office, but personal address as "Judge" or "Judge Brown" may be continued unofficially in retirement.

Judge of High Court.—LETTERS.—*Superscription,* (official) "The Hon Mr Justice ______." (private) "Sir John ______." *Commencement,* "Sir." PERSONAL ADDRESS, "Sir," but when on the Bench, "My Lord," or, "Your Lordship." *See also* "Lord Chief Justice of England," "Master of the Rolls," "Lord Justice of Appeal," and "Lord of Appeal in Ordinary."

Judges of High Court, Ladies.—LETTERS.—*Superscription,* (official) "The Hon Mrs Justice ______" (private) "Dame Mary Smith ______," *Commencement,* "Madam." PERSONAL ADDRESS, "Madam," but when on the Bench "My Lady" or "Your Ladyship."

Justice of the Peace.—PERSONAL ADDRESS.—When on the Bench, "Your Worship," and in other respects as an Esquire. The letters JP are usually put after name.

Knight Bachelor.—LETTERS.—*Superscription,* "Sir [George] ______." In other respects same as Baronet. The letters KB should *not* be used.

Knight's Wife, *same as Baronet's Wife.* The wife of a clergyman of the Church of England who receives a Knighthood of an Order of Chivalry but consequently not the accolade, retains the style of "Mrs ______."

Knight of an Order of Chivalry, *same as Knight Bachelor,* but adding to the superscription the recognised letters of the Order, such as "GCB," or "KCB". Clergymen of the Church of England and Honorary Knights do not receive the accolade, and consequently are addressed by the letters of the Orders but not the prefix "Sir."

Knight's Widow, *same as Knight's Wife* so long as she remains a widow. As to re-marriage, *see* "Widows."

Lady (untitled). *See* Esquire's wife and widow. Of unmarried daughters, the eldest of the senior generation is styled "Miss [Egerton]." A younger daughter is addressed as "Miss [Helen Egerton]."

Lady Mayoress. *See* "Lord Mayor's Wife."

Lieutenant-Governor.—Isle of Man, Jersey and Guernsey, as for Governor. The style of a Lt-Gov of a Canadian Province is "*The Hon*" (borne for life).

Life Peer.—He is addressed as for an hereditary peer.—*See* "Baron."

Life Peer's Son.—*See* "Baron's son."

Life Peer's Daughter.—*See* "Baron's daughter."

Life Peeress. *See* "Baroness."

Life Peeress in her own right. She is addressed as for an hereditary peeress. *See* "Baroness."

Lord, in Peerage of Scotland.—*See* "Baron."

Lord Advocate.—LETTERS.—*Superscription,* "The Rt Hon the Lord Advocate," or, "The Rt Hon [George] ______." In other respects as an esquire. [The prefix of Rt Hon is not retained after retirement from office, unless a Member of the Privy Council.]

Lord Chancellor.—LETTERS.—*Superscription,* "The Rt Hon the Lord High Chancellor." In other respects as a peer according to his rank.

Lord Chief Justice.—LETTERS.—*Superscription,* "The Lord Chief Justice of England," or "To the Right Hon Lord ______, Lord Chief Justice of England." In other respects as a Judge, except when of noble rank, when he is addressed according to his degree.

Lord High Commissioner to General Assembly of Church of Scotland. —LETTERS.—*Superscription,* "To His Grace the Lord High Commissioner." *Commencement,* "Your Grace." PERSONAL ADDRESS, "Your Grace."

Lord Justice-Clerk.—LETTERS. —*Superscription,* "The Rt Hon the Lord Justice-Clerk" (if a Privy Counsellor), otherwise "The Hon the Lord Justice-Clerk". *Commencement,* "Dear Lord Justice-Clerk." PERSONAL ADDRESS, Addressed for all purposes by their appointments and not by the Judicial Titles with which they take their seats on the bench.

Lord Justice-General.—LETTERS.—*Superscription,* "The Rt Hon the Lord Justice-General". *Commencement,* "Dear Lord Justice-General." PERSONAL ADDRESS, *See* Lord Justice-Clerk.

Lord Justice of Appeal.—LETTERS.—*Superscription,* "The Right Hon Lord Justice," or "To the Right Hon Sir [Robert] ______." In other respects as a Judge of High Court.

Lord Mayor.—LETTERS.— The Lord Mayors of London, York, Belfast, and Cardiff have the privilege of being styled "The Rt Hon"; and permission to use this style has also been granted to the Lord Mayors of Sydney (NSW), Melbourne (Vic), Adelaide (S Aust), Perth (W Aust.), Brisbane (Queensland), and Hobart (Tasmania). *Superscription,* "The Rt Hon the Lord Mayor of ______." or "[Henry ______,] The Rt Hon Lord Mayor of ______," [The prefix of Right Hon is not retained after retirement from office. [*See also* "Lord Provost."]. *Commencement,* "My Lord," or less formally, "Dear Lord Mayor." *Superscription* for other Lord Mayors "The Right Worshipful the Lord Mayor of ______."

Lord Mayor's Wife or Lady Mayoress.—LETTERS.—*Superscription,* "The Lady Mayoress." In other respects as Knight's or Esquire's wife.

Lord of Appeal-in-Ordinary.—*See Baron.*

Lord of Session, Scottish.—LETTERS.— *Superscription,* "The Hon Lord ______." In other respects as a Baron, but children have no courtesy styles. *See* also Lord Justice Clerk and Lord Justice General.

Lord of Session's Wife or Widow.—LETTERS.—*Superscription,* "Lady ______." In other respects as Baron's wife.

Lord Provost.—LETTERS.—*Superscription,* The Lord Provosts of Edinburgh and Glasgow are addressed as "The Rt Hon the Lord Provost," while in office. The prefix may be placed before the name of the holder in the case of the Lord Provost of Edinburgh. In other respects as a Baron. The Lord Provost of Perth, Dundee and Aberdeen are styled "The Lord Provosts of ______."

Lord Provost's Wife. Same as the wife of an Esquire. The style of Lady Provost is incorrect.

Marchioness.—LETTERS.—*Superscription,* "The Most Hon the Marchioness of ______," or socially, "The Marchioness of ______." In other respects as Baroness. [*See also* "Marquess's Widow."]

Marquess.—LETTERS.—*Superscription,* "The Most Hon the Marquess of ______," or less formally, "The Marquess of ______." In other respects as Baron.

Marquess's Daughter, *same as Duke's Daughter.*

Marquess's Eldest Son, *same as Duke's Eldest Son. Superscription,* "Earl of ______" (or as title adopted may be).

Marquess's Eldest Son's Daughter is by courtesy addressed as if her father were a peer.

Marquess's Eldest Son's Eldest Son, *same as Duke's Eldest Son. Superscription,* "Viscount ______" (or as title adopted may be).

Marquess's Eldest Son's Younger Son is by courtesy addressed as if his father were a Peer, viz. "The Hon ______."

Marquess's Eldest Son's Widow, *same as Duke's Eldest Son's Widow.*

Marquess's Eldest Son's Wife is known by his courtesy title, and is addressed personally as a peeress without 'The Rt Hon'.

Marquess's Widow, *same as Marchioness,* if present Marquess is unmarried. For widows where present incumbent of title is married [see "Dowager"]. As to re-marriage see "Widows."

Marquess's Younger Son, *same as Duke's Younger Son.*

Marquess's Younger Son's Widow, *same as Duke's Younger Son's Wife,* As to re-marriage, see "Widows."

Marquess's Younger Son's Wife, *same as Duke's Younger Son's Wife.*

Master.—This title is borne in the *Peerage of Scotland* by the heir apparent or presumptive of a Peer. It is also used *by courtesy* by the eldest son of a Peer by courtesy. In the case of the heir apparent, "Master" is normally used by the eldest son of a Viscount and Lord, as the heirs of the senior grades of the Peerage normally use a courtesy title. He is styled "The Master of ______" (the appropriate title will be found under the Peerage article). If the heir be a woman, she is officially designated "The Mistress of ______" but this title is seldom used. A Master's wife is styled "The Hon Mrs [Donald Campbell"] or according to her husband's rank.

Master of the Rolls.—LETTERS .—*Superscription,* "The Right Hon the Master of the Rolls," or "The Right Hon ______," according to *Commencement,* as "Judge." PERSONAL ADDRESS, "Sir," but when on the Bench, "My Lord," or "Your Lordship."

Mayor (whether man or woman).—LETTERS.—*Superscription,* (if Mayor of a City), "The Right Worshipful the Mayor of ______", (if a Mayor of a Borough or Town Mayor), "The Worshipful the Mayor of ______." *Commencement,* "Sir (or Madam)." In other respects as an Esquire or an Esquire's wife. The form "Dear Mr Mayor" may be used for a man or woman.

Members of the Executive and Legislative Councils.—See Honourable in Commonwealth Countries.

Members of Parliament.—According to rank, but adding the initials "MP" after title or name and honours.

Military Officers.—See "Naval, Military, and Air Force Officers."

Minister of the Crown.—If a Privy Counsellor, see that section, otherwise see Member of Parliament or Grade of Peerage. The social form of "Dear Secretary of State," or "Dear Minister" may be used if the matter concerns the Department.

Moderator of the General Assembly of Church of Scotland. By Order in Council the Moderator has precedence in Scotland and at Court functions immediately after Bishops of the Church of England, and while in office is addressed as "Rt Rev" Former Moderators, "Very Rev."

Naval, Military, and Air Force Officers.—Professional rank should always precede any titles, *e.g.,* "Adm (the Right Hon) the Earl of ______," "Gen the (Right Hon) Lord ______," "Air-Marshal Sir ," but Lieutenants in the Army, Flying Officers and Pilot Officers in the Air Force are addressed by their social and not their professional rank, *e.g.,* "The Hon Benjamin ______, Irish Guards," "George ______, Esq., 11th Hussars," or "William ______, Esq., RAF."

Peers and Peeresses by courtesy.—As commoners they are not addressed as "Rt Hon" or "The" but "Viscount [Brown]" or appropriate title.

Police and Fire Service Medals. The letters KPM, KPFSM, QPM, QFSM and CPM are now placed after the name. If the Colonial Police Medal were awarded for gallantry the letters CPM are placed before BEM, and if for meritorious service after QFSM (see paragraph 4 at beginning of section).

Prebendary.—As for Canon, but substituting the word Prebendary for Canon.

Prime Minister, The.—See Privy Counsellors. The social form of "Dear (Mr.) Prime Minister" may be used if the matter concerns his office.

Prince.—LETTERS.—*Superscription,* (i) the son of a Sovereign "His Royal Highness The Prince [Edward]": (ii) other Princes "His Royal Highness Prince [Michael of Kent]"; (iii) Duke "His Royal Highness The Duke of [Gloucester]." *Commencement,* "Sir," *Conclusion,* "I have the honour to be, Sir. Your Royal Highness's most humble and obedient servant." PERSONAL ADDRESS, "Your Royal Highness," and henceforward as "Sir." [*See also* Royal Family.]

Princess.—LETTERS.—*Superscription,* (i) the daughter of a Sovereign "Her Royal Highness The Princess [Royal]"; (ii) other Princesses "Her Royal Highness Princess [Alexandra], the Hon Lady Ogilvy"; (iii) Duchess "Her Royal Highness The Duchess of [Kent]." *Commencement,* "Madam." *Conclusion,* "I have the honour to be, Madam, Your Royal Highness's most humble and obedient servant." PERSONAL ADDRESS, "Your Royal Highness," and henceforward as "Ma'am." [*See also* Royal Family.]

Privy Counsellors, also spelt PRIVY COUNCILLORS.—LETTERS. — *Superscription,* "The Right Hon ______," but if a peer then as such, followed by the letters "PC," *after* all Orders and Decorations. *Commencement, &c.,* according to the rank of the individual. Privy Counsellors of Northern Ireland, which are no longer created, are entitled to the prefix of Right Hon and are included in this section. Members of the Privy Council of Canada are entitled to the style of "Hon" for life. *Commencement,* as for Esquire or appropriate rank.

Privy Counsellors, Wives of.—They enjoy no special style or precedence as such.

Provost.—As for Dean, but substituting the word Provost for Dean.

Provost (Scotland).—LETTERS.—*Superscription,* "The Provost of ______." *Commencement,* "Dear Provost." PERSONAL ADDRESS, "Provost."

Queen Mother.—LETTERS.—*Superscription,* for formal and state documents, "Her Gracious Majesty Queen Elizabeth The Queen Mother," otherwise "Her Majesty Queen Elizabeth The Queen Mother." *Commencement,* as for the Queen Regnant. *Conclusion,* "I have the honour to remain, Madam, Your Majesty's most humble and obedient servant." PERSONAL ADDRESS, as for the Queen Regnant.

Queen Regnant.—LETTERS.—*Superscription,* for formal and state documents. "The Queen's Most Excellent Majesty." otherwise "Her Majesty The Queen," *Commencement,* "Madam," or "May it please your Majesty." *Conclusion,* "I have the honour to remain Madam, Your Majesty's most humble and obedient servant." PERSONAL ADDRESS, "Your Majesty," and henceforth as "Ma'am."

Queen's Counsel.—LETTERS.—*Superscription,* "______ Esq, QC." In other respects as an Esquire. The letters are used after the name by Circuit Judges, but not by High Court Judges.

Rt Honourable.—This prefix is borne by Privy Counsellors of Great Britain and Northern Ireland, the Governor General of Canada, and Prime Minister and Chief Justice of Canada *for life*; by Earls, Viscounts and Barons: (except peers by courtesy) their wives and widows; and certain Lord Mayors (see Lord Mayors), and Provosts of Edinburgh and Glasgow (see Lord Provosts).

Royal Dukes. —See "Prince."

Royal Family.—On 11 Dec 1917, it was ordained that "The children of any Sovereign of the United Kingdom and the children of the sons of any such Sovereign and the eldest living son of the eldest son of the Prince of Wales, shall have and at all times hold and enjoy the style, title, or attribute of Royal Highness with their titular dignity of Prince or Princess prefixed to their respective Christian names, or with their other titles of honour; and that the grandchildren of the sons of any such Sovereign in the direct male line (save only the eldest living son of the eldest son of the Prince of Wales) shall have the style and title enjoyed by the children of Dukes." [*See* also "Queen Regnant," "Queen Mother." "Prince," and "Princess."]

Rural Deans. No special form of address.

Secretary of State. See "Minister of the Crown" and "Privy Counsellors."

Sheriff.—LETTERS.—*Superscription,* "Sheriff." PERSONAL ADDRESS, Addressed on the bench as "My Lord" or "My Lady" and formally and socially as "Sheriff ______ ."

Sheriff Principal.—LETTERS.—*Superscription,* "Sheriff Principal ____." *Commencement,* "Sheriff Principal." PERSONAL ADDRESS, Addressed on the bench as "My Lord" or "My Lady", and formally and socially as "Sheriff ______ ."

Sovereign, The.—See "Queen Regnant."

Titles just announced.—See paragraph at commencement of this section.

Trinity House, Elder Brethren of are entitled to be called "Captain," with precedence after Naval Captains.

Victoria Cross.—The letters VC take precedence of all other honours and decorations.

Viscount.—LETTERS.—*Superscription,* "The Right Hon the Viscount ______," or socially "The Viscount ______." In other respects as Baron.

Viscountess.—LETTERS.—*Superscription,* "The Right Hon the Viscountess ______." or socially, "The Viscountess." In other respects as Baroness and Baron's widow. [See also "Viscount's Widow"].

Viscount's Son, and his Wife or Widow *same as Baron's.*

Viscount's Daughter, *same as Baron's.*

Viscount's Widow, *same as Viscountess* if present Viscount is unmarried. For widows where present incumbent of title is married [see "Dowager"]. As to re-marriage, see "Widows."

Wales, Prince of. See "Prince" and "Royal Family."

Widows.—A Widow who re-marries *loses* any title or precedence she gained by her previous marriage, and is not recognised as having any claim to bear the title of her deceased husband, *e.g.:* at a coronation or other State ceremonial, the widow of a peer would not be summoned as a peeress if she had subsequently married a commoner; and, if having espoused a peer of lesser degree than her former husband, she would only be recognised by the rank acquired by her last marriage. [*See also* Esquire's Widow.]

CONSULTANT EDITORS

The Panel of Consultant Editors for *Debrett's People of Today* includes the following:

Consultant Editor	**Field**
Mary Rose Beaumont	Visual Arts
Kenneth Fleet	Business & the City
Lynne Franks	Fashion
Paul Gambaccini	Popular Music
Naomi Gornick	Design
Dennis Hackett	Media & Critics
Tony Knox	Public Relations
Desmond Lynam	Sports
Kenneth McLeish	Writers
Sheridan Morley	Stage, Cinema & TV
Michael Preston	Accountancy
Hilary Rubinstein	Hoteliers & Chefs
John Sharkey	Advertising & Marketing
Gillian Widdicombe	Music & Dance

Debrett's

A Readers Guide

The editors would like to point out the following features of a standard entry in *Debrett's People of Today*.

Bracketed forenames indicate name(s) not used by the entrant, the first forename following a bracketed forename is the one commonly used by the entrant.

Well-known colleges and schools are listed without the word college or school.

Children are listed with the names of sons in order of birth first and followed by daughters in order of birth, in accordance with generally accepted genealogical practice.

Careers are set out in chronological order with military service listed first (where applicable), followed by professional career, followed by public career and finally by awards, foreign orders and decorations and fellowships.

Clubs within London are listed omitting the word London; where membership of a club outside London occurs the location of the club follows in brackets.

Style indicates the preferred style to be used in addressing correspondence to an entrant.

A list of abbreviations used in this publication can be found at the back of the book.

DISCLAIMER

A

À COURT ROBINSON, Hon Mrs (Betty Mary); *née* Holmes À Court; da of 4 Baron Heytesbury (d 1949); assumed additional surname à Court 1946; *b* 1902; *m* 1, 1923 (m dis 1946), Cdr Vivian John Robinson, RN; 2 s, 1 da; m 2, 1956, Alfred Esmond Robinson, CBE, MC (d 1975); *Style—* The Hon Mrs À Court Robinson; Combe House, 62 Church Lane, Backwell, Bristol BS19 3JJ (☎ 027 583 2732)

AALDERS, Michael Laurence; s of Prof Laurence Aalders (d 1980), and Kathleen, *née* O'Callaghan; *b* 25 Sept 1944; *Educ* St Ignatius Sch London; *m* 24 Sept 1966, Evelyn Juliet Victoria, da of Pierino Appi (d 1988); 1 s (Dominic Michael b 1972), 1 da (Siobhan Evelyn b 1969); *Career* co fndr Aalders & Marchant Advertising Ltd 1968-82, co fndr and dir The Travel Business Ltd 1978, co fndr and chm The Grayling Co Ltd (PR) 1981, chm Westminster Strategy Ltd, ptnr Badger Antiques; *Recreations* sailing, skiing; *Clubs* Savile; *Style—* Michael Aalders, Esq; 86 Grange Rd, London W5 (☎ 071 579 5072); 4 Bedford Square, London WC1 (☎ 071 255 1100, car 0860 310 369)

AARONOVITCH, David Morris; s of Dr Sam Aaronovitch, of 100 Chetwynd Road, London NW5, and Lavender Geraldine Janet, *née* Walmsley; *b* 8 July 1954; *Educ* William Ellis Sch London, Balliol Coll Oxford, Univ of Manchester (BA); 1 da (Rosa Ann b 5 May 1990); *Career* prodr Weekend World LWT 1984-87 (researcher 1982-84), ed On The Record BBC 1988-90; BBC head of News Westminster 1990-; pres NUS 1980-82; *Recreations* cinema, literature; *Style—* David Aaronovitch, Esq; 29 Countess Rd, London NW5 2XH (☎ 071 485 6515); BBC Westminster, 4 Millbank, London SW1 (☎ 071 973 6010)

AARONS, John Julius Emile; s of Jacob Henry Aarons (d 1945), of Hampstead, and Esther, *née* Cohen (d 1975); *b* 12 Aug 1936; *Educ* Kent Coll Canterbury, St John's Coll Cambridge (BA, MA), Sch of Mil Survey Newbury; *m* 14 Jan 1962, Maureen (Mo) Finley; 1 s (Matthew David Edward b 3 Aug 1969), 3 da (Emma Julia b 25 June 1963, (Sarah) Annabel b 6 Jan 1965, Olivia Rachel b 20 Sept 1967); *Career* surveyor Directorate of Overseas Surveys 1959-63, systems analyst London Boroughs Orgn and Methods Ctee 1963-65, conslt CEIR 1965-67, data processing mangr Wates Ltd 1967-71; The Stock Exchange: systems analyst 1971, dir Inter Market Projects 1987, head Quality of Markets Unit 1990-; parent govr Montpelier Middle Sch 1975-80; *Books* The Useless Land (with Claudio Vita-Finzi); *Recreations* squash, sculling, etymology; *Style—* John Aarons, Esq; 8 Winscombe Crescent, London W5 1AZ (☎ 081 997 7961); The Stock Exchange, Throgmorton St, London EC2N 1HP (☎ 071 588 2355, fax 071 410 6807, telex 88655)

AARONSON, Edward John (Jack); s of Samuel Wolf Aaronson (d 1943), and Sara Jochebed Chaikin (d 1989); *b* 16 Aug 1918; *Educ* C F S London; *m* 7 Sept 1946, Marian, da of Lodwick Davies (d 1984); 2 s (Michael John b 1947, Robin Hugh b 1951); *Career* RA, Palestine to Tunisia 1940-44, India 1945-46, W/S Capt; articled Jackson Pixley & Co 1946-49, fndr gen sec The Anglo Israel C of C London 1950-53, econ advsr (export) GEC 1954-61 (gen mangr overseas operations 1961-63), Celmac Ltd 1964-65, dep chm and pt/t chief exec The Steel Barrel Scammells & Associated Engrs Ltd (later Anthony Carrimore Ltd) 1965-68, industl advsr rising to dir Armitage Industl Hldgs Ltd 1965-68, dir rising to chm George Turton Platt 1966-68, dir E R & F Turner Ltd 1967-68, chm Br Northrop Ltd 1968-73, chm and chief exec (also scheme mangr and Creditors Ctee chm) The G R A Property Tst Ltd 1975-83, non-exec chm Wand F C Bonham and Sons Ltd 1981-88, non-exec dir Camlab Ltd 1982-89, non-exec chm The Reject Shop plc 1985-90; memb: FBI Standing Ctees on overseas credit and overseas investmt from inception 1958-63, Cncl The Export Gp for the Construction Industs 1960-63, Br Greyhound Racing Bd 1975-83, Gen Ctee The Reform Club 1976-79 and 1980-83; chm N G R C Race Course Promoters Assoc 1978-83; FCA 1960, FInstD 1980; *Recreations* family, music, reading, swimming, current affairs; *Clubs* Reform; *Style—* Jack Aaronson, Esq; c/o Equity Recoveries Ltd, Bushey House, Upper Wanborough, nr Swindon, Wilts SN4 0BZ (☎ 0793 790642)

AARONSON, Graham Raphael; QC (1982); s of Jack Aaronson (d 1973), of London, and Dora, *née* Franks; *b* 31 Dec 1944; *Educ* City of London Sch, Trinity Hall Cambridge (MA); *m* 12 Sept 1967, Linda Esther, da of Maj William Smith, of Oxford; 2 s (Oran b 1968, Avi b 1974), 1 da (Orit b 1970); *Career* called to the Bar Middle Temple 1966, md Worldwide Plastics Devpt Ltd 1973-77, fndr Stanford Grange Rehabilitation Centre for Ex-Offenders, advsr on taxation Treasy Israel 1986-, chm Dietary Res Fndn 1989-; *Recreations* photography; *Style—* Graham Aaronson, Esq, QC; Queen Elizabeth Building, Temple, London EC4Y 9BS (☎ 071 936 3131, fax 071 353 1927, telex 8951414)

AARVOLD, His Hon Sir Carl Douglas; OBE (1945), TD (1950), DL (Surrey 1973); s of late Ole Peter Aarvold, of Highnam, W Hartlepool, and late J M Aarvold; *b* 7 June 1907; *Educ* Durham Sch, Emmanuel Coll Cambridge; *m* 1934, Noeline Etrenne, da of Arthur James Hill (d 1935), of Denton Park, Yorks, and gda of Sir James Hill, 1 Bt (d 1936); 3 s; *Career* called to the Bar Inner Temple 1932, in practice N Eastern Circuit, rec of Pontefract 1951-54, judge of the Mayor's and City of London Court 1954-59, common serjeant City of London 1959-64, rec City of London 1964-75; chm: Inner London Probations Ctee 1965-75, City of London QS, Home Sec's Advsy Bd on Restricted Patients 1978-, RAC 1978-81, Statutory Ctee Pharmaceutical Soc of GB 1981-86; pres: Central Cncl of Probation Ctees 1968-75; pres LTA 1962-81; Hon LLD Dalhousie 1962, Hon DLC Durham 1965, hon fell Emmanuel Coll Cambridge; kt 1968; *Style—* His Hon Sir Carl Aarvold, OBE, TD, DL; The Coach House, Crabtree Lane, Westhumble, Dorking, Surrey RH5 6BQ (☎ 0306 882 771)

ABBADO, Claudio; *b* 26 June 1933; *Educ* Conservatorio G Verdi Milan, Hochschule für Musik Vienna; *Career* musical dir: La Scala Milan 1968-86, LSO 1979-86, Euro Community Youth Orchestra 1977-, Gustav Mahler Youth Orchestra 1986-; music dir Vienna State Opera 1986, generalmusikdirektor City of Vienna 1987, princ conductor Berlin Philharmonic 1990-; *Style—* Claudio Abbado, Esq; Staatsoper, A-1010 Vienna, Austria

ABBEY, Henry William; s of John George Abbey (d 1936); *b* 9 April 1925; *Educ* Dulwich; *m* 1950, Kathleen, da of Thomas Adair (d 1978); 5 children; *Career* served RN Aust and Far East as telegraphist; chartered secretary; chm Joint Promotions 1972, dep md William Hill Organisation 1984- (asst md 1980-84); dir: Riley plc 1970-, William Hill Leisure Ltd, Joint Promotions Ltd, Dale Martin Promotions Ltd and various other sporting, leisure and entertainment related cos; memb Lloyds; ACIS; *Recreations* bridge, golf, literature, theatre; *Style—* Henry Abbey, Esq; 11 Heath Drive, Sutton, Surrey (☎ 081 642 2928); William Hill Organization, 19 Valentine Place, London SE1 8QW

ABBOT, Russ; *Career* comedian and actor; turned professional 1965, fndr leader The Black Abbots (cabaret act) 1965-80, solo career launched 1980; early tv guest appearances incl: London Night Out, What's on Next, Who Do You Do, The Comedians, Bruce Forsyth's Big Night; solo tv work: Russ Abbot's Madhouse (ITV) 1981-85, TV specials for ITV, The Russ Abbot Show (BBC) 1986-, Russ Abbot's Christmas Show; tv guest star appearances incl: Des O'Connor Tonight, Live from Her Majesty's, Tarby And Friends, Wogan, The Bob Monkhouse Show, Live from the Palladium; pantomime seasons incl: New Theatre Oxford 1980-81, Davenport Theatre Stockport 1981-82, Alhambra Theatre Bradford 1982-83, Palace Theatre Manchester 1986-87, Hippodrome Theatre Birmingham 1988-89, Mayflower Theatre Southampton 1989-90; star own theatre show: Torquay 1981, Great Yarmouth 1982 and 1987, Blackpool 1983, Southampton 1983-84, Cardiff 1985-86, Bournemouth 1985, Edinburgh 1986, North Pier Blackpool 1986 (biggest ever money-making show of seaside theatre); star of: numerous Madhouse show theatre tours 1982-85 and 1990, Russ Abbot and Friends 1989; West End stage work: Little Me (Prince of Wales Theatre) 1984, One for the Road (Lyric Theatre) 1987; comic creations incl: Cooperman, See You Jimmy-the Scot, Vince Prince, Boggles, Fritz Crackers, Basildon Bond, Wilf, Honest Sid, Barrett Holmes, Val Hooligan, Julio Doubleglazius, Miss Marbles, Dr Profile, Hans Van Rental, Fat Man; chart hits: Atmosphere, All Night Holiday, Lets Go to the Disco (all taken from album I Love a Party); *Awards* five times winner Funniest Man on Television TV Times, Funniest Man on Television in Europe (Euro TV Magazine Assoc) 1983, Best Actor in a TV Commercial (Golden Break Awards) 1990, Top Variety Act (British Comedy Awards) 1990, voted Comedian of the Decade by TV viewers; *Style—* Russ Abbot, Esq; Clifford Elson (Publicity) Ltd, 1 Richmond Mews, off Dean St, London W1V 5AG (☎ 071 437 4822, fax 071 287 6314)

ABBOTT, Diane Julie; MP (Lab) Hackney North and Stoke Newington 1987-; *b* 27 Sept 1953; *Educ* Harrow County Girl's GS, Newnham Coll Cambridge; *Career* admin trainee Home Office, race rels offr NCCL, res Thames TV, reporter TV-am, equality offr ACTT, press and PR offr GLC, princ press offr Lambeth Borough Cncl; memb Westminster City Cncl 1982-86; *Style—* Ms Diane Abbott, MP; House of Commons, London SW1A 0AA

ABBOTT, Reginald James; s of James Joseph Abbott (d 1907), of Norbury, London, and Adeline Mary, *née* Kipling (d 1932); *b* 2 June 1902; *Educ* Univ of London; *m* 16 June 1928, Margaret Ivy (d 1975), da of Ernest Sebire (d 1930), of Newmarket, Melbourne, Aust; 1 s (Geoffrey James Kipling b 20 June 1934); *Career* seconded Admty War Serv MI (IX) 1940-44, Defence Medal; Marconi Int Marine Radio Communications Co: concerned with commercial element radio-TV experiments with Baird 1924-32, Aust 1933, commercial devpt TV 1934-60, res and experiment serv LP records; govt business Europe 1950-60, Royal Fndn of St Katharine 1961; admin sec Nat Playing Fields Assoc London 1962-73, chm Educn and Leisure Ctee Nat Cncl Social Serv 1966-74, vice chm Co Supplying Charities 1963-89, cncl memb and hon advsy offr Local and Co Sports Assocs; Freeman City of London 1931, Liveryman Worshipful Co Drapers 1934; *Recreations* travel; *Style—* Reginald J Abbott, Esq; Chillon, 40 Tongdean Rd, Hove BN3 6QE

ABBOTT, Roderick Evelyn; s of Stuart Evelyn Abbott, OBE, of Cambridge, and Jocelyn, *née* Niemeyer; *b* 16 April 1938; *Educ* Rugby, Merton Coll Oxford (BA); *m* 22 June 1963, Elizabeth McLean, da of Dr Neil McLean; 3 da (Nicola b 1964, Mary b 1966, Melissa b 1972); *Career* Nat Serv RCS 1956-58; Bd of Trade 1962-71; sec SE Econ Planning Cncl 1966-68, FCO 1971-73; EEC Cmmn: DG external rels 1973-, dep head of mission Geneva 1975-79, dir Directorate Gen of External Rels 1982-; *Style—* Roderick Abbott, Esq; EEC Commission, Rue De La Loi 200, 1049 Brussels, Belgium

ABBOTT, Ronald William; CVO (1989), CBE (1979); s of Edgar Abbott (d 1956); *b* 18 Jan 1917; *Educ* St Olaves and St Saviour's GS; *m* 1, 1948, Hilda Mary (d 1972), da of William George Clarke (d 1918); 2 da (Mary Elaine b 1949, Christine Margaret b 1956); m 2, 1973, Barbara Constance, da of Gilbert Hugh Clough (d 1961); *Career* consltg actuary; sr ptnr of Bacon & Woodrow 1972-81; memb Cncl: Inst of Actuaries 1966-74 (treas 1971-73), Indust Soc 1964-84 (life memb 1984), Pensions Mgmnt Inst 1977-81 (vice pres 1978-80); chm Occupational Pensions Bd 1982-87 (dep chm 1973-82); memb Court Worshipful Co of Ironmongers (Master 1986-87); Finlaison medallist Inst of Actuaries 1988; FIA, ASA, FPMI, FRSA; *Recreations* music, theatre; *Clubs* Royal Automobile; *Style—* Ronald W Abbott, Esq, CVO, CBE; 43 Rottingdean Place, Falmer Rd, Rottingdean, E Sussex (☎ 0273 303302); St Olaf House, London Bridge, London SE1 2PE (☎ 071 357 7171)

ABBOTT, Stephen (Steve); s of Wilfred Lockley Abbott, of Bradford, W Yorks, and Lily Templeton, *née* Limbert; *b* 28 July 1954; *Educ* Bradford GS, CCC Cambridge (MA); *m* Karen Lesley Lewis; 1 s (James Alexander b 1989), 1 da (Francesca b 1986); *Career* Price Waterhouse London 1976-79, Hand Made Films London 1979-81, Mayday Management Ltd 1981-, md Prominent Features Ltd 1986-, exec prodr A Fish Called Wanda 1988, prodr American Friends 1990; FCA 1990 (ACA 1979); *Style—* Steve Abbott, Esq; Northcroft Studio, 5 Northcroft Terrace, London W13 9SP (☎ 081 579 2354, fax 081 566 3690); 68A Delancey London NW1 7RY (☎ 071 284 0242, fax 071 284 1004)

ABDELA, His Hon Judge; Jack Samuel Ronald; TD (1948), QC (1966); s of Joseph Abdela (d 1953), of Manchester, and Dorothy Abdela; *b* 9 Oct 1913; *Educ* Manchester GS, Milton Sch Bulawayo, Fitzwilliam Coll Cambridge (MA); *m* 1942, Enid Hope, da of Edgar Dodd Russell (d 1950), of London; 1 s (and 1 s decd); *Career* Nat Serv Lt-Col, served UK, NW Europe WW II; called to the Bar Gray's Inn 1935; judge Central Criminal Ct 1970-86; Liveryman Worshipful Co of Painter Stainers; *Recreations* swimming, tennis, gardening; *Clubs* Savage; *Style—* His Hon Judge Abdela, TD, QC; Tall Trees Cottage, Shipton Under Wychwood, Oxfordshire OX7 6DB (☎ 0993 831520)

ABDELA, Lesley Julia; MBE (1990); da of Frederick Abdela (d 1985), and Henrietta, *née* Hardy (d 1959); Abdela family were shipbuilders in C19 at Manchester Ship Canal (vessels for Amazon rubber trade), and Brimscombe, Stroud, Glos (for river tug boats). From the 1930s, Henrietta and Frederick Abdela built successful catering and frozen food companies; *b* 17 Nov 1945; *Educ* Glendower London, Queen Anne's Caversham, Châtelard Sch Les Avants Switzerland, Queen's Coll Harley St, Hammersmith Coll of Art, London Sch of Printing; *m* 1972 (m dis); 1 s (Nicholas b 1973); *Career* advertising exec Royds London, researcher House of Commons 1976-77, stood for Parl (Lib) in Herts East 1979, fndr all-Party 300 Gp for Women in Politics 1980, US Leader Grant visiting Washington DC, LA, Seattle 1983, studied Third World by residence in the Gambia 1984-86; sr ptnr Eyecatcher Journalism, television and radio bdcaster on politics and travel, feature writer, author, after dinner speaker specialising in Women in the 1990s; FRGS ; *Books* Women with X Appeal (1989); travel books incl: Driving in the USA, Stay Healthy When You Travel (To the Tropics); *Recreations* travel, painting, desert agriculture; *Style—* Ms Lesley Abdela, MBE; Harper's Marsh, King's Saltern, Lymington, Hampshire; La Boursaie, 14140 Tortisambert, France

ABDY, Sir Valentine Robert Duff; 6 Bt (UK 1850), of Albyns, Essex; s of Sir Robert Abdy, 5 Bt (d 1976), and Lady Diana, *née* Bridgeman (d 1967), da of 5 Earl of Bradford; *b* 11 Sept 1937; *Educ* Eton; *m* 1971 (m dis 1982), Mathilde, da of Etienne Coche de la Ferté; 1 s (Robert); *Heir* s, Robert Etienne Eric Abdy b 22 Feb 1978; *Career* set up (with Peter Wilson) Sotheby's first office abroad in Paris and Munich; first rep Smithsonian Inst (Washington DC) in Europe 1983-; *Clubs* Jockey (Paris), The Travellers (Paris); *Style—* Sir Valentine Abdy, Bt; Newton Ferrers, Callington, Cornwall; 13 Villa Molitor, 75016 Paris, France; Clos du Petit Bois, St Martins, Guernsey CI

ABEL, Prof Edward William; s of Sydney John (d 1952), of Kenfighill, and Donna Maria, *née* Grabham (d 1981); *b* 3 Dec 1931; *Educ* Bridgend GS Glamorgan, Univ Coll Cardiff (BSc), Northern Poly London (PhD); *m* 6 Aug 1960, Margaret Rosina, da of Glyndwr Vivian Edwards (d 1974), of Porthcawl; 1 s (Christopher b 23 Oct 1963), 1 da (Julia b 4 April 1967); *Career* Nat Serv 1953-55; res fell Imp Coll 1957-59, lectr and reader Univ of Bristol 1959-71, prof of inorganic chemistry Univ of Exeter 1972; visiting prof: Univ of Br Columbia 1970, Japan 1971, Tech Univ of Braunschweig 1973, Australian Nat Univ Canberra 1990; int sec Int Confs on Organometallic Chemistry 1972-88; Royal Soc of Chemistry: memb Cncl 1978-82 and 1983-89, chm Local Affairs Bd 1983-87, chm Divnl Affairs Bd 1990-, memb Dalton Divnl Cncl 1977-83 and 1987-91, vice pres 1989-91 (pres 1987-89), sec and treas 1977-82; Univ Grants Ctee: memb 1986-89, chm Physical Sci Sub Ctee 1986-89; Cncl for Nat Academic Awards: chm Physical Sci Ctee 1987-91, memb Academic Affairs Ctee 1987-91; nat advsr for chemistry to exec Univ Funding Cncl 1989-, assessor to Res Ctee Poly and Coll Funding Cncl; Royal Soc of Chemistry: Main Gp Chemistry award 1976, Tilden medal and lectr 1981; *Books* Royal Soc Chemistry Specialist Periodical Reports on Organometallic Chemistry Vols 1-20 (jt ed, 1970-), Comprehensive Organometallic Chemistry 9 Vols (exec ed, 1984); *Recreations* gardening, cycling; *Style—* Prof Edward Abel; 1A Rosebarn Avenue, Exeter, Devon EX4 6DY (☎ 0392 70272); Dept of Chemistry, University of Exeter, Exeter, Devon EX4 4QD (☎ 0392 263489, fax 0392 263434 telex 42894 EXUNIV G)

ABEL, Julian David; s of David John Abel, and Heather Diana, *née* Ingram; *b* 10 April 1961; *Educ* St Dunstan's Coll Catford, LSE (BSc); *m* 15 Feb 1986, Donna Christine, da of Christopher Byrne (d 1988); 1 s (Christopher David b 1988); *Career* portfolio mangr CIN Mgmnt Ltd (Br Coal Pension Fund) 1986- (investmt analyst 1984-86); *Recreations* sailing, squash, sub-aqua diving; *Style—* Julian Abel, Esq; CIN Management Ltd, PO Box, 10, Hobart House, Grosvenor Place, London SW1X 7AD (☎ 071 245 6911, fax 071 389 2822, telex 883 770 Ginman G)

ABEL, Kenneth Arthur; CBE (1984), DL (Dorset 1976); s of Arthur Abel, CBE (d 1988), of Yorks, and Francis Ethel, *née* Roome (d 1973); *b* 4 April 1926; *Educ* Durham Sch, Univ of Glasgow, Univ of Durham; *m* 22 Sept 1955, Sarah Matilda, da of Capt Maurice Pugh Poynor, TD (d 1950), of Leics; 3 s (David Arthur b 4 Oct 1957, Paul Anthony b 28 Feb 1958, Godfrey Andrew b 2 July 1960); *Career* RA 1944-48; admitted slr 1952; asst slr: Warwickshire CC 1952-53, Leicestershire CC 1954-59; sr asst slr Northamptonshire CC 1959-63, dep clerk of the peace and of North Riding CC 1963-67, chief exec Dorset CC 1967-, clerk of Itcy Dorset 1967-; memb Assoc of County Chief Execs (past chm); memb Int City Management Assoc; dir: Dorset Enterprise, Dorset Training and Enterprise Cncl; memb Law Soc; *Recreations* golf, skiing, tennis; *Clubs* Sherborne Golf, Dorset Came Down Golf; *Style—* Kenneth Abel, Esq, CBE, DL; Herne's Oak, Bradford Rd, Sherborne, Dorset DT9 6BP (☎ 0935 813200); County Hall, Dorchester, Dorset DT1 1XJ (☎ 0305 204195, fax 0305 204839)

ABEL SMITH, David Francis; s of Sir Alexander Abel Smith, KCVO, TD, JP (d 1980), of Quenington Old Rectory, Cirencester, Glos, and Elizabeth, *née* Morgan (d 1948); *b* 3 Feb 1940; *Educ* Gordonstoun; *m* 18 Nov 1982, Lucy Marie, da of Col Bryce Muir Knox, MC, TD (Lord Lt of Ayr and Arran); *Career* exec dir The Delta Group plc 1974-82 (joined 1961), md Benjamin Priest Group plc 1983-; memb Quenington Parish Cncl 1987-; Freeman City of London, memb Worshipful Co of Fishmongers; *Recreations* foxhunting; *Clubs* Buck's, Pratt's; *Style—* David Abel Smith, Esq; Quenington Old Rectory, Cirencester, Glos GL7 5BN (☎ 028 575 358); Benjamin Priest Gp plc, PO Box 38, Warley, W Mids B64 63W (☎ 0384 66501, fax 0384 64578)

ABEL SMITH, Lady; Henriette Alice; DCVO (1977, CVO 1964), JP (Tunbridge Wells 1955, Glos 1971); o da of Cdr Francis Charles Cadogan, RN (d 1970), and Ruth Evelyn, *née* Howard (d 1962); *b* 6 June 1914; *m* 1, 4 Sept 1939, Sir Anthony Frederick Mark Palmer, 4 Bt (ka 1941); 1 s (Sir Mark Palmer, 5 Bt, *qv*), 1 da; m 2, 17 Feb 1953, Sir Alexander Abel Smith, KCVO, TD, JP (d 1980); 1 s, 1 da; *Career* Lady-in-Waiting to HM The Queen 1949-; *Style—* Lady Abel Smith, DCVO; The Garden House, Quenington, Cirencester, Glos (☎ 028 575 231)

ABEL SMITH, Col Sir Henry; KCMG (1961), KCVO (1950), DSO (1945), DL (Berks 1953); 2 s of Francis Abel Smith, DL (d 1908), of Wilford House, Notts, and Madeline St Maur (d 1951), 4 da of late Rev Henry Seymour, Rector of Holme Pierrepoint; *b* 8 March 1900; *Educ* Eton, RMC Sandhurst; *m* 24 Oct 1931, Lady May, *qv*, o da of Earl of Athlone, KG, GCB, GCMG, GCVO, DSO, PC (d 1957), and HRH Princess Alice, Countess of Athlone, VA, GCVO, GBE (d 1981); 1 s (Richard Abel Smith, *qv*, b 1933), 2 da (Anne b 1932, Elizabeth b 1936); *Career* joined RHG 1919, Capt 1930, Maj 1934, Lt-Col 1944, Col 1946; Hon Cdre RAF; ADC to Earl of Athlone (when govr-gen and CIC S Africa) 1928-31, govr of Queensland 1958-66, administrator Australian Cwlth 1965; KStJ 1958, Kt Order of Orange-Nassau with swords (Netherlands); Hon LLD Queensland Univ; *Recreations* hunting, shooting, fishing, polo; *Clubs* Turf; *Style—* Col Sir Henry Abel Smith, KCMG, KCVO, DSO, DL; Barton Lodge, Winkfield, Windsor, Berks SL4 4RL (☎ 0344 882632)

ABEL SMITH, Lady Mary Elisabeth; *née* Carnegie; da of 10 Earl of Southesk (d 1941); *b* 4 March 1899; *m* 1932, Vice Adm Sir (Edward Michael) Conolly Abel Smith, GCVO, CB (d 1985); 1 s, 1 da; *Style—* The Lady Mary Abel Smith; Ashiestiel, Galashiels, Selkirkshire (089 685 214)

ABEL SMITH, Lady May Helen Emma; *née* Cambridge; o da of 1 Earl of Athlone, KG, GCB, GCMG, GCVO, DSO, PC (d 1957), and HRH Princess Alice, Countess of Athlone, VA, GCVO, GBE (d 1981); ggda of Queen Victoria and last survg gggda of King George III; *b* 23 Jan 1906; *m* 24 Oct 1931, Col Sir Henry Abel Smith, KCMG, KCVO, DSO, DL, *qv*; 1 s, 2 da; *Career* styled HSH Princess May of Teck until 1917; CStJ; *Style—* The Lady May Abel Smith; Barton Lodge, Winkfield, Windsor, Berks SL4 4RL (☎ 0344 882632)

ABEL SMITH, Ralph Mansel; o s of Thomas Abel Smith, JP (d 1983), of Woodhall Park, Watton at Stone, Hertford, and Alma Mary Agatha, *née* de Falbe; *b* 11 Dec 1946; *Educ* Eton; *m* 18 July 1985, Alexandra Clare Ragnhild, da of Maj Ian Stuart Rae Bruce, MC (d 1967), of Highfield, Bells Yew Green, Sussex; 2 s (Thomas Ralph Bruce Abel b 1989, another b 1991); *Career* landowner and farmer; chm: Herts/Middx Branch CLA 1981-86, Herts Co Award Liaison Panel of Duke of Edinburgh's Award Scheme 1976-81; patron of livings of: Watton-at-Stone, Sacombe, Bramfield with Stapleford, Bengeo; High Sheriff Herts 1984-85; memb: E Herts DC 1976-83, Herts CC 1985-89; life govr Haileybury and Imperial Serv Coll 1985; *Recreations* shooting, fishing, music, classical architecture; *Clubs* Buck's, Pratt's, Turf; *Style—* Ralph Abel Smith, Esq; Woodhall Park, Watton-at-Stone, Hertford; Cambusmore Lodge, Dornoch, Sutherland

ABEL SMITH, Col Richard Francis; DL; s of Col Sir Henry Abel Smith, KCMG, KCVO, DSO, DL, *qv*; *b* 11 Oct 1933; *Educ* Eton, Sandhurst, RAC Cirencester; *m* 1960, Marcia, da of Maj-Gen Sir Douglas Kendrew, KCMG, CB, CBE, DSO (d 1989); 1 da (*see* Hon Hubert Beaumont); *Career* RHG (Blues): Escort Cdr and ADC to Govrs of Cyprus 1957-60, Instr RMA Sandhurst 1960-63, ret; co cmmr for Scouts (Notts) 1966-75, cmd Sherwood Rangers Sqdn, Royal Yeo Regt 1967-69 (Hon Col 1979-89); High Sheriff Notts 1978; chm Sports Aid Fndn East Midlands 1979-89; farmer; *Recreations* shooting, fishing, riding; *Clubs* Farmers', Army and Navy; *Style—* Col Richard Abel Smith, DL; Blidworth Dale, Ravenshead, Nottingham NG15 9AL (☎ 0623 792241)

ABEL-SMITH, Lionel; s of Brig-Gen Lionel Abel Abel-Smith, DSO (d 1946), of London, gs of Abel Smith of Woodhall Park, and Frances, da of Gen Sir Harry Calvert, 1 Bt, and Geneviève Lilac Walsh (d 1980); landed gentry (family assumed additional surname of Abel 1922); *b* 1 Sept 1924; *Educ* Haileybury, Merton Coll Oxford (MA); *Career* RNVR 1943-47, Flag Lt to Adm Sir Victor Crutchley, VC (Flag Offr Gibraltar) 1946-47; called to the Bar Lincoln's Inn 1950, in practice Chancery Bar 1950-63; farmer in Sussex 1964; *Recreations* amateur cellist; *Clubs* MCC, Henley; *Style—* Lionel Abel-Smith, Esq; Groves, Peasmarsh, Rye, Sussex (☎ 079 721 338)

ABELL, Sir Anthony Foster; KCMG (1952, CMG 1950); 2 s of George Foster Abell, JP, of Foxcote Manor, Andoversford, Glos (d 1946); bro of Sir George Abell (d 1989); *b* 11 Dec 1906; *Educ* Repton, Magdalen Coll Oxford; *Career* joined Colonial Admin Serv Nigeria 1929, high cmmr Brunei 1950-58, govr and Cdr in Chief Sarawak 1950-59; Gentlemen Usher of the Blue Rod in Order of St Michael and St George 1972-79; *Style—* Sir Anthony Abell, KCMG; Gavel House, Wherwell, Andover, Hants (☎ 026 474 216)

ABELL, (John) David; s of Leonard Abell and Irene Craig, *née* Anderson; *b* 15 Dec 1942; *Educ* Univ of Leeds (BA), LSE (Dip Business Admin); *m* 1, 1967 (m dis 1977), Anne Janette, *née* Priestley; 3 s; m 2, 1981 (m dis), Sandra Dawn, *née* Atkinson; 1 s, 1 da; m 3, Juliana, da of Prof John Lister Illingworth Fennell, of 8 Canterbury Rd, Oxford; *Career* ford Motor Co 1962-65, AEI 1965-67, various appts Br Leyland 1968-72 and 1974-80, First Nat Fin Corpn 1972-73, chm and chief exec Suter plc 1981-; CBIM; *Style—* J David Abell, Esq; The Old Rectory, Branston-by-Belvoir, Grantham, Lincs

ABELL, Prof Peter Malcolm; s of John Raymond Abell (d 1987), and Constance, *née* Moore; *b* 18 Aug 1939; *Educ* Wakefield GS, Univ of Leeds (BSc, PhD); *m* (m dis); 3 s (Paul b 1963, Simon b 1968, Johnathon b 1988); *Career* dir res Industrial Sociology Unit Imp Coll Univ of London 1970-75; prof of sociology: Dept of Sociology Univ of Birmingham 1976-79, Univ of Surrey 1979-; *Books* Model Building in Sociology (1972), Socio-Economic Potential of Producer Co-ops in Developing Countries (1987), The Syntax of Social Life (1988), Support Systems for Co-ops in Developing Countries (1988); *Recreations* walking, music; *Style—* Prof Peter Abell; The Studio, 98 Fellows Road, London NW3; Dept of Sociology, University of Surrey, Guildford, Surrey GU2 5XH (☎ 0483 571281, telex 859331)

ABER, Prof Geoffrey Michael; s of David Aber (d 1988), of Leeds, and Hilda, *née* Madeloff (d 1982); *b* 19 Feb 1928; *Educ* Leeds GS, Univ of Leeds (MB ChB, MD), Univ of Birmingham (PhD); *m* 27 June 1964, Eleanor Maureen, da of Gerald Christopher Harcourt; 1 s (Mark Harrington b 1967), 1 da (Alison Jane b 1965); *Career* Lt and Capt RAMC 1954-56; house physician Brompton Hosp 1957-58, res fell McGill Univ Montreal 1959-60, sr registrar Queen Elizabeth Hosp Birmingham 1960-64, Wellcome sr res fell and hon sr lectr Univ of Birmingham 1964-65, conslt physician N Staffs Hosp Centre 1965-; Univ of Keele: prof and advsr Clinical Res Dept of Postgrad Med 1979-82, prof of renal med 1982-, head Dept of Postgrad Med 1982-89, dean of postgrad med 1989-; MRCP (memb Cncl 1984-87), FRCP 1973; *Recreations* music, sport, motor cars; *Style—* Prof Geoffrey Aber; Greenleaves, Seabridge Lane, Westlands, Newcastle-under-Lyme, Staffs (☎ 0782 613 692); Dept of Postgraduate Medicine, Univ of Keele, Thornburrow Drive, Hartshill, Stoke-on-Trent, Staffs ST5 5BG (☎ 0782 49144 ext 4047, fax 0782 613 847, telex 3 UNKLIB G)

ABERCONWAY, 3 Baron (1911 UK); Sir Charles Melville McLaren; 3 Bt (UK 1902), JP (Denbigh 1946); eld s of 2 Baron Aberconway, CBE (d 1953), and Christabel (d 1974), da of Sir Melville Macnaghten, CB; *b* 16 April 1913; *Educ* Eton, New Coll Oxford (BA); *m* 1, 1941 (m dis 1949), Deirdre, da of John Knewstub; 1 s, 2 da; m 2, 1949, Ann, o da of Mrs Alexander Lindsay Aymer, of New York, and formerly w of Maj Robert Lee Bullard III; 1 s; *Heir* s, Hon (Henry) Charles McLaren, *qv*; *Career* called to the Bar Middle Temple 1937; pres John Brown & Co Ltd 1978-85, (chm 1953-78); chm: Sheepbridge Engineering 1961-79, English China Clays 1963-84 (pres 1984-); dep chm: Sun Alliance & London Insurance Co Ltd until 1985, Westland plc 1979-85; pres RHS 1961-84 (pres emeritus 1984-); cmmr-gen Int Garden Festival of Liverpool 1984; dir Nat Garden Festival Stoke-on-Trent 1986; High Sheriff of Denbighshire 1950; hon fell Inst of Horticulture 1985; *Recreations* gardening, travel; *Style—* The Rt Hon the Lord Aberconway, JP; 25 Egerton Terrace, London SW3 (☎ 071 589 4369); Bodnant, Tal-y-Cafn, N Wales (☎ 0492 650 200)

ABERCORN, 5 Duke of (I 1868); Sir James Hamilton; 15 Bt (I 1660); also Lord Paisley (S 1578), Lord Abercorn (S 1603), Earl of Abercorn and Lord Paisley, Hamilton, Mountcastell, and Kilpatrick (S 1606), Baron of Strabane (I 1617), Baron Mountcastle and Viscount Strabane (I 1701), Viscount Hamilton (GB 1785), Marquess of Abercorn (GB 1790 - title in House of Lords), and Marquess of Hamilton (I 1868); s of 4 Duke of Abercorn (d 1979), and Lady Kathleen Mary, GCVO, *née* Crichton (d 1990), sis of 5 Earl of Erne; *b* 4 July 1934; *Educ* Eton, RAC Cirencester; *m* 1966, Alexandra Anastasia, da of Lt-Col Harold Pedro Phillips (d 1980), of Checkendon Court, nr Reading, also sis of Duchess of Westminster and gda through her m, Georgina, of late Sir Harold Wernher, 3 Bt, GCVO, TD, DL, by his w, late Lady Zia, CBE, *née* Countess Anastasia Mikhailovna (er da of HIH Grand Duke Mikhail Mikhailovitch of Russia, himself gs of Tsar Nicholas I); 2 s (Marquess of Hamilton, Lord Nicholas b 1979), 1 da (Lady Sophie b 1973), *qv*; *Heir* s, Marquess of Hamilton, *qv*; *Career* 2 Lt Grenadier Gds; MP (UU) Fermanagh and S Tyrone 1964-70; dir Local Enterprise Devpt Unit 1971-77; memb Cncl of Europe 1968-70; memb Econ and Social Ctee EEC 1973-78; pres RUKBA 1979-; dir NI Indust Devpt Bd 1982-87, Northern Bank Ltd 1970-, NI Regnl Bd Nationwide Bldg Soc 1971-76; pres The Bldg Socs Assoc 1976-; chm: Templeton Investmt Mgmnt Ltd 1985-, Laganside Devpt Corpn 1989-; High Sheriff Co Tyrone 1970; Ld Lt Co Tyrone; *Recreations* shooting; *Clubs* Brooks's; *Style—* His Grace the Duke of Abercorn, DL; Barons Ct, Omagh, Co Tyrone, N Ireland BT78 4EZ (☎ 066 26 61470); Baronscourt Est Off, Omagh, Co Tyrone (☎ 06626 61683, telex 748111)

ABERCROMBIE, Prof David; s of Lascelles Abercrombie (d 1938), of N Moreton, Didcot, and Catherine, *née* Gatkin (d 1967); *b* 19 Dec 1909; *Educ* Leeds GS, Univ of Leeds, UCL, Sorbonne Paris; *m* 31 Aug 1944, Mary, da of Eugene Marble (d 1973), of Carmel, California; *Career* lectr Inst of English Studies Athens 1938-40, English lectr Cairo Univ 1940-45 and LSE 1945-47 (asst lectr 1934-38); phonetics lectr Univ of Leeds 1947-48, prof Univ of Edinburgh 1964-80 (phonetics lectr 1948-51, sr lectr 1951-57, leader 1957-63), lectr in phonetics and linguistics Univ of Glasgow 1980-81; *Recreations* cricket; *Style—* Prof David Abercrombie; 13 Grosvenor Crescent, Edinburgh EH12 5EL (☎ 031 337 4864)

ABERCROMBIE, (George) Forbes; s of George Francis Abercrombie, VRD, RNVR (d 1978), and Marie, *née* Underhill; *b* 28 March 1935; *Educ* Charterhouse, Gonville and Caius Coll Cambridge, St Bartholomew's Hosp Med Coll (MA, MD); *m* 15 August 1959, Jennifer Elizabeth Dormer, da of Richard Valentine Dormer Kirby (d 1957); 2 s (John Forbes b 1961, Colin Francis b 1963); *Career* conslt urological surgn St Mary's Hosp Portsmouth 1971-; cncl memb Br Assoc of Urological Surgns 1984-87, memb Int Urologica Soc; Liveryman Worshipful Co of Apothecaries 1964 (former memb Livery Ctee); FRCS; *Recreations* golf, salmon fishing, chess; *Style—* Forbes Abercrombie, Esq; Church House, Catherington Lane, Catherington, Hants PO8 0TE (☎ 0705 597 676)

ABERCROMBY, Sir Ian George; 10 Bt (NS 1636), of Birkenbog, Banffshire; s of Robert Ogilvie Abercromby, gs of 5 Bt; suc kinsman 1972; *b* 30 June 1925; *Educ* Lancing, Bloxham Sch Banbury; *m* 1, 1950 (m dis 1957), Joyce Beryl, da of Leonard Griffiths; m 2, 1959, Fanny Mary Udale (Molly), da of Dr Graham Udale-Smith, of Sitio Litre, Puerto de la Cruz, Tenerife; 1 da; m 3, 1976, Diana Marjorie, da of Horace Geoffrey Cockell, and wid of Capt Ian Charles Palliser Galloway; *Heir* none; *Style—* Sir Ian Abercromby, Bt; c/o National Westminster Bank, 224 King's Rd, London SW3

ABERDARE, 4 Baron (UK 1873); Morys George Lyndhurst Bruce; PC (1974), KBE (1984), DL (Dyfed 1985); s of 3 Baron Aberdare, GBE (d 1957); *b* 16 June 1919; *Educ* Winchester, New Coll Oxford; *m* 1946, (Maud Helen) Sarah, da of Sir John Dashwood, 10 Bt, CVO (d 1966); 4 s; *Heir* s, Hon Alastair Bruce; *Career* Welsh Guards 1939-46, min of state DHSS 1970-74, min without portfolio 1974, chm Ctees House of Lords 1976-; chm: Albany Life Assurance 1975-, Metlife (UK) Ltd 1986-; The Football Tst; pres: YMCA of Wales, Tennis and Rackets Assoc, Kidney Research Unit for Wales Fndn; Hon LLD Wales 1985; GCStJ; *Books* The Story of Tennis, Willis Faber Book of Tennis and Rackets; *Recreations* real tennis, rackets; *Clubs* Lansdowne, MCC, All England Lawn Tennis, Queen's; *Style—* The Rt Hon Lord Aberdare, KBE, DL; 32 Elthiron Rd, London SW6 4BW (☎ 01 736 0825)

ABERDEEN, Bishop of (RC) 1977-; Rt Rev Mario Joseph Conti; s of Louis Conti, and Josephine Panicali; *b* 1934; *Educ* St Marie's Convent Sch Springfield Elgin, Blairs Coll Aberdeen, Pontifical Gregorian Univ Rome (STL, PhL); *Career* former jt parish priest St Joachim's Wick and St Anne's Thurso; chm Scottish Catholic Heritage Cmmn, pres Nat Cmmn for Christian Doctrine and Unity; memb: (Roman) Cncl for Promotion of Christian Unity, Bishops' Jt Ctee on Bio Ethical Issues; Hon DD Aberdeen 1989; *Style—* The Rt Rev Mario Conti, Bishop of Aberdeen; Bishop's House, 156 King's Gate, Aberdeen AB2 6BR (☎ 0224 319154)

ABERDEEN AND ORKNEY, Bishop of 1978-; Rt Rev Frederick Charles Darwent; JP; s of Samuel Darwent (d 1957), and Edith Emily, *née* Malcolm (d 1968); *b* 20 April 1927; *Educ* Warbreck Sch Liverpool, Ormskirk GS, Wells Theol Coll; *m* 1, 1949, Edna Lilian (d 1981), da of David Waugh and Lily Elizabeth, *née* McIndoe; 2 da (twins); m 2, 1983, Mrs Roma Evelyn Fraser, elder da of John Michie and Evelyn, *née* Stephen; *Career* served with Royal Inniskilling Fusiliers 1945-48; banker Williams Deacon's (later Williams and Glyn's, now merged with Bank of Scotland) 1943-61; deacon 1963, priest 1964; former rector Strichen, New Pitsligo, Fraserburgh; canon St Andrew's Cathedral Aberdeen 1971, dean Aberdeen and Orkney 1973-78; Hon LTh St Mark's Inst of Theology, Burgess of Guild of the City of Aberdeen 1985; *Recreations* amateur stage (acting and producing), music (especially jazz), calligraphy; *Clubs* The Club of Deir (Aberdeenshire), Rotary International; *Style—* The Rt Rev the Bishop of Aberdeen and Orkney, JP; 107 Osborne Place, Aberdeen AB2 4DD (☎ 0224 646497); Diocesan Office, 16 Crown Terrace, Aberdeen AB1 2HD (☎ 0224 580172)

ABERDEEN AND TEMAIR, 6 Marquess of (UK 1916); Sir Alastair Ninian John Gordon; 14 Bt (NS 1642); also 12 Earl of Aberdeen (S 1682), Lord Haddo, Methlic, Tarves, and Kellie (S 1682), Viscount Formartine (S 1782), Viscount Gordon (UK 1814), and Earl of Haddo (UK 1916); s of 3 Marquess of Aberdeen and Temair, DSO (d 1972), by his 1 w, Cecile, da of George Drummond (ggggs of Andrew Drummond, yr bro of 4 Viscount Strathallan and fndr of Messrs Drummond, the bankers) by Elizabeth (da of Rev Frederick Norman and Lady Adeliza Manners, da of 5 Duke of Rutland); suc er bro 5 Marquess of Aberdeen and Temair 1984; *b* 20 July 1920; *Educ* Harrow; *m* 1950, Anne, *qv*, da of Lt-Col Gerald Barry, MC; 1 s, 2 da; *Heir* s, Earl of Haddo, *qv*; *Career* served WWII Capt Scots Gds; painter; memb Int Assoc of Art Critics, chm Arts Club 1966-76; memb Bach Choir 1939-82; *Recreations* music, people; *Clubs* Arts, MCC, Puffin's; *Style—* The Most Hon the Marquess of Aberdeen and Temair; Quicks Green, Ashamptstead, Berks RG8 8SN (☎ 0491 671331)

ABERDEEN AND TEMAIR, Marchioness of; Anne; da of Lt-Col Gerald Barry, MC (s of William Barry, JP, 4 s of Sir Francis Barry, 1 Bt, by William's w Lady Grace Murray, MBE, da of 7 Earl of Dunmore) who married, 1923, Lady Margaret Pleydell-Bouverie, da of 5 Earl of Radnor; *b* 28 April 1924; *Educ* Godolphin Sch Salisbury, Chapin Sch New York; *m* 1950, 6 Marquess of Aberdeen and Temair, *qv*; 1 s, 2 da; *Career* potter; fell Morgan Library NY; *Recreations* gardening; *Style—* The Most Hon the Marchioness of Aberdeen and Temair; Quicks Green, Ashampstead, Berkshire RG8 8SN

ABERDEEN AND TEMAIR, June, Marchioness of; (Beatrice Mary) June Gordon; CBE (1989, MBE 1971), DL (Aberdeenshire 1971); da of late Arthur Paul Boissier (d 1953); *b* 29 Dec 1913; *Educ* Southlands Sch Harrow, RCM; *m* 29 April 1939, 4 Marquess of Aberdeen and Temair, CBE, TD, KStJ (d 1974); 2 adopted s, 2 adopted da; *Career* musical dir and conductor Haddo House Choral and Operatic Soc 1945-, dir Haddo House Hall Arts Centre; chm: Scottish Children's League 1969, Advsy Cncl Scottish Opera; Hon LLD Aberdeen 1968, DStJ 1977, FRSE 1983, FRCM 1967, GRSM, ARCM; *Style—* The Most Hon June, Marchioness of Aberdeen and Temair, CBE, DL, FRSE; Haddo House, Aberdeen AB41 0ER (☎ 065 15 216)

ABERDOUR, Dr Kenneth Robert; s of Kenneth Aberdour (d 1965), of Chelmsford, and Jennie May Titilah (d 1986); *b* 9 March 1927; *Educ* Trinity GS N London, St Georges Hosp Med Sch, Univ of London (MB); *m* 17 Sept 1960, Jean Rosemary, da of Philip Henry Hardy (d 1977), of Chelmsford; 1 s (Robert b 1964), 1 da (Rosemary b 1961); *Career* conslt radiologist Mid Essex Health Authy 1962; radiologist: The London Clinic, Springfield Med Centre Chelmsford; FRCP, FRCR; *Recreations* gardening, walking; *Style—* Dr Kenneth R Aberdour; The Old Rectory, Wickham Bishops, Witham, Essex CM8 3LA (☎ 0621 891597); Broomfield Hosp, Chelmsford, Essex (☎ 0245 440761)

ABERDOUR, Lord; (John) Stewart Sholto Douglas; s and h of 21 Earl of Morton, *qv*; *b* 17 Jan 1952; *Educ* Dunrobin Castle Sch, Aberdeen Univ; *m* 20 July 1985, Amanda Kirsten, yr da of David John Macfarlane Mitchell, of Castle St, Kirkcudbright; 1 s (Hon John David Sholto, Master of Aberdour b 28 May 1986), 1 da (Hon Katherine Florence b 3 Aug 1989); *Career* ptnr Dalmahoy Farms; *Style—* Lord Aberdour; Haggs Farm, Kirknewton, Midlothian

ABERGAVENNY, 5 Marquess of (UK 1876); John Henry Guy Nevill; KG (1974), OBE (1945), JP (Sussex 1948); also Baron Abergavenny (E 1450 as Baron Bergavenny); 14 Baron, who held the title 1724-45, was the first to be styled Lord Abergavenny), Viscount Nevill, Earl of Abergavenny (both GB 1784), and Earl of Lewes (UK 1876); s of 4 Marquess of Abergavenny (d 1954); *b* 8 Nov 1914; *Educ* Eton, Trinity Coll Cambridge; *m* 1938, Patricia (*see* Abergavenny, Marchioness of); 3 da (and 1 s and 1 da decd); *Heir* nephew, Guy Nevill; *Career* 2 Lt LG 1935, Maj 1942, served NW Europe (despatches), Temp Lt-Col 1945, ret 1946; Hon Col Kent and Co of London Yeo 1948-62, Alderman E Sussex CC 1954-62, tstee Ascot Authy 1952-82, HM Representative at Ascot 1972-82, pres Royal Agric Soc of England 1967 (dep pres 1968 and 1972); former pres: Royal Assoc of Br Dairy Farmers, Assoc of Agric; pres Br Horse Soc 1970-71, memb Nat Hunt Ctee (former Sr Steward), former vice chm Turf Bd; Lord-Lt of E Sussex 1974-89 (Vice-Lt of Sussex 1970-74, DL Sussex 1955), Chllr of Order of the Garter 1977-, pres Cncl of Order of St John, Sussex 1975- (KStJ 1976); former chm: Lloyds Bank Property Co Ltd, Lloyds Bank SE Regional Bd; former dir: Lloyds Bank plc, Lloyds Bank UK Management, Massey-Ferguson Holdings Ltd (ret 1985), Whitbread Investment Co Ltd, Br Equestrian Promotions Ltd, ret; *Clubs* White's; *Style—* The Most Hon the Marquess of Abergavenny, KG, OBE, JP; Eridge Park, Tunbridge Wells, Kent TN3 9JT (☎ 0892 27378); Flat 2, 46 Pont St, London SW1 (☎ 071 581 3967)

ABERGAVENNY, Marchioness of; (Mary) Patricia; DCVO (1981, CVO 1970); da of late Lt-Col John Fenwick Harrison, RHG, and Hon Margery, da of 3 Baron Burnham, DSO; *b* 1915; *m* 1938, 5 Marquess of Abergavenny, *qv*; 3 da (and 1 s and 1 da decd); *Career* Lady of the Bedchamber to HM The Queen 1966- (an Extra Lady of the Bedchamber 1960-66); *Style—* The Most Hon The Marchioness of Abergavenny, DCVO; Eridge Park, Tunbridge Wells, Kent TN3 9JT (☎ 0892 27378); Flat 2, 46 Pont St, London SW1 (☎ 071 581 3967)

ABERNETHY, Barclay Chivas; s of Andrew Abernethy (d 1972), of Aberdeen, and Anne, *née* Hendry (d 1947); *b* 18 Jan 1928; *Educ* Robert Gordon's Coll Aberdeen, Aberdeen Univ and Med Sch (MB ChB); *m* 25 July 1952, Isobel Ellen, da of Charles James Henry Hawke Dennis (d 1978), of Aberdeen; 1 s (Charles Andrew b 1952), 1 da (Sally Anne b 1954, Karen Beverley b 1955); *Career* registrar in gen surgery Middlesex Hosp 1957-60, sr registrar in gen surgery East Fife Area 1960-65, conslt gen surgn Fife Area Hosp Bd 1966-; former pres Kirkcaldy Rotary Club; FRCSEd, FRCS, fell Assoc of Surgns GB and I, fell Assoc of Clinical Anatomists; *Recreations* fishing, curling, gardening; *Clubs* Markinch Curling; *Style—* Barclay C Abernethy, Esq; The Brackens, 10 Abbots Walk, Kirkcaldy, Fife KY2 5NL (☎ 0592 261085); Victoria Hosp, Hayfield Rd, Kirkcaldy, Fife (☎ 0592 261155)

ABERNETHY, (William) Leslie; CBE (1972); s of Robert Abernethy (d 1956), and Margaret, *née* Pickup (d 1935); *b* 10 June 1910; *Educ* Darwen GS; *m* 1937, Irene, da of Walter Holden (d 1968); 1 s (David); *Career* dep co treas Derbyshire CC 1945-48, treas Newcastle upon Tyne Regnl Hosp Bd 1948-50, dep comptroller LCC 1956-64 (asst comptroller 1950-56), treas GLC 1964-72, comptroller of fin servs GLC 1972-73, managing tstee Municipal Mutual Insurance Ltd 1973-1987; dir: Municipal Life Assurance Ltd, Municipal General Insurance Ltd, MLA Unit Trust Management Ltd, OQS Property Management Ltd, OQS Property Development Ltd 1978-87; memb Cncl Chartered Inst of Pub Fin and Accountancy until 1973; FCA; memb IPFA; *Style—* Leslie Abernethy, Esq, CBE; 6 Thornhill Close, Port Erin, Isle of Man

ABIDI, Vilayat Husain; s of Bahadar Husain Abidi (d 1985), of 2a Link St, Defence Housing Soc, Karachi, Pakistan, and Bilquees, *née* Begum; *b* 10 Dec 1934; *Educ* Centenial HS of Christian Coll Lucknow India, Karachi Univ Pakistan (BA); *m* 1, 1960 (m dis 1965), Farhat, da of S F Meerza SQA; 2 s (Ali b 1963, Asad b 1964); m 2, Jawahir, da of Syed Mohammed Siddick (d 1964), of Mecca, Saudi Arabia; *Career* Grindlays Bank 1951-59; (formerly offr mangr & vice pres) sr vice pres United Bank Ltd Pakistan 1960-75, Union Bank Ltd Karachi 1969-71; vice chm and gen mangr United Bank of Lebanon and Pakistan SAL Beirut 1971-75, gen mangr Bank of Credit and Commerce International (BCCI) Lebanon SAL 1977-80, rep for BCCI SA on Bd of Dirs Iran Arab Bank Tehran 1975-79, regnl gen mangr BCCI UK 1980-88, dir BCCI Gibraltar 1980-88; *Clubs* RAC; *Style—* Vilayat Abidi, Esq; Beechcroft, Manor House Drive, Brondesbury Park, London NW6 7DD (☎ 081 459 5939); Consultant, 24 Coniston Court, Kendal St, London W2 2AN (☎ 071 723 4178, 071 724 0832, fax 081 451 0332, car 0860 845115)

ABINGDON, Earl of; *see*: Lindsey and Abingdon, Earl of

ABINGER, 8 Baron (UK 1835); James Richard Scarlett; DL (Essex 1968); s of 7 Baron Abinger, DSO (d 1943); *b* 28 Sept 1914; *Educ* Eton, Magdalene Coll Cambridge; *m* 1957, Isla Carolyn, niece of Sir Henry Rivett-Carnac, 7 Bt, and da of late Vice Adm J W Rivett-Carnac, CB, CBE, DSC; 2 s; *Heir* s, Hon James Scarlett, *qv*; *Career* Hon Lt-Col RA serv France and India, ret 1947; sits as Cons in House of Lords; farmer and co dir; vice pres Byron Soc, former chm Keats-Shelley Meml Soc, memb Exec Ctee CPRE, pres Mid Anglia Centre Nat Tst, former govr ESU; serv Halstead Rural and Braintree Dist Cncls; KStJ; *Recreations* field sports; *Clubs* Carlton, RAC; *Style—* The Rt Hon the Lord Abinger, DL; Clees Hall, Bures, Suffolk (☎ 0787 227227)

ABOYNE, Earl of; Alistair Granville Gordon; s and h of 13 Marquess of Huntly, *qv*; *b* 26 July 1973; *Style—* Earl of Aboyne

ABRAHAM, Sir Edward Penley; CBE (1973); s of Albert Penley Abraham, and Mary, *née* Hearn; *b* 10 June 1913; *Educ* King Edward VI Sch Southampton, Queen's Coll Oxford (MA, DPhil); *m* 1939, Asbjörg Harung, of Bergen, Norway; 1 s; *Career* fell Lincoln Coll Oxford 1948-80 (hon fell 1980-), prof of Chem Pathology Oxford 1964-80; hon fell: Queen's Coll Oxford 1973, Linacre Coll Oxford 1976, Lady Margaret Hall Oxford 1978, Wolfson Coll Oxford 1982, St Peter's Coll Oxford 1983; Chemical Soc Award in Medicinal Chemistry 1975, Royal Soc Mullard medal and prize 1980 (Royal medal 1973), Int Soc of Chemotherapy award 1983; author of med and scientific papers on penicillins, cephalosporins and other substances with biological activity; foreign hon memb American Acad of Arts and Sciences 1983; Hon DSc: Univ of Exeter 1980, Univ of Oxford 1984, Univ of Strathclyde 1989; FRS; kt 1980; *Publications* Biochemistry of Some Peptide and Steroid Antibiotics (1957),

Biosynthesis and Enzymic Hydrolysis of Penicillins and Cephalosporina (1974) ; *Clubs* Athenaeum; *Style—* Sir Edward Abraham, CBE, FRS; Badger's Wood, Bedwells Heath, Boars Hill, Oxford (☎ 0865 735395); Sir William Dunn School of Pathology, Oxford (☎ 0865 275500)

ABRAHAM, Maj-Gen (Sutton) Martin O'Heguerty; CB (1973), MC (1942, and bar 1943); s of Capt Edgar Gaston Furtado Abraham, CB, late ICS (d 1955), and Ruth Eostre, da of Rev Gerald S Davies, master of the Charterhouse, London; *b* 26 Jan 1919; *Educ* Eton, Trinity Coll Cambridge (BA); *m* 1950, Iona Margaret, da of Sir John Stirling, KT, MBE; 2 s, 1 da; *Career* dir of Combat Devpt MOD 1968-71, chief of Jt Servs Liaison Orgn BAOR 1971-73, FO Balanced Force Reductions in Europe 1973-76; sec Bedford Coll Univ of London 1976-82 (govr 1983-85); Col 9/12 Royal Lancers 1978-82; *Style—* Maj-Gen Martin Abraham, CB, MC; c/o Hoare & Co, 37 Fleet St, London EC4 (☎ 071 353 4522)

ABRAHAM, Neville Victor; s of Solomon Abraham (d 1987), and Sarah Raphael; *b* 22 Jan 1937,Calcutta; *Educ* Brighton Coll, Univ of London, LSE (BSc); *Career* sr princ Board of Trade and parly sec Minister of State 1963-71; corporate policy advsr Whitehead Consulting Gp 1971-76; fndr chm and md Amis du Vin Gp and Les Amis du Vin Ltd 1974-86; visiting lectr at leading Business Schs 1974-83; gp exec dir Kennedy Brookes plc 1984-86; dep chm Creative Business Communications plc 1986-; chm and chief exec Lakebird Leisure Ltd 1986-; *Books* Big Business and Government: The New Disorder (1974); *Recreations* music, gardening, walking; *Clubs* RAC; *Style—* Neville Abraham, Esq; 83 Gloucester Terrace, London W2 3HB; 37 Dean St, London W1 (☎ 071 439 2925)

ABRAHAM, Prof Raymond John; s of Judah H Abraham (d 1989), and Elizabeth *née* Harrop; *b* 26 Nov 1933; *Educ* Magnus GS Newark, Univ of Birmingham (BSc, PhD, DSc); *m* 1, 16 Aug 1958 (m dis 1986), June Roslyn; 2 s (David Joseph b 3 Sept 1962, Simon Douglas b 27 Oct 1969), 1 da (Susan Elizabeth b 8 Sept 1959); m 2, 17 Sept 1988, Barbara Ann, da of Henry Broadbent (d 1982); *Career* postdoctoral fell NRC Canada 1957-59, sr fell Nat Physical Lab 1959-61, Univ of Liverpool 1961- (lectr, sr lectr, reader, prof); visiting prof: Carnegie-Mellon 1966-67, Univ of California 1981-89; Ciba-Geigy fell Univ of Trondheim 1979; memb SERC Instrumentation Ctee; memb American Chemical Soc 1981-; *Books* The Analysis of NMR Spectra (1971), Proton and Carbon 13 NMR Spectroscopy (with P Loftus, 1978), Introduction to NMR Spectroscopy (with J Fisher and P Loftus, 1988); *Recreations* squash, gardening, theatre; *Clubs* Birkenhead Constitutional; *Style—* Prof Raymond Abraham; 11 Lawns Ave, Raby Mere, Wirral L63 0NE; The Robert Robinson Labs, The Chemistry Dept, The University of Liverpool, PO Box 147, Liverpool L69 3BX (☎ 051 794 3511, telex 627095 UNILPLG, fax 051 794 3588)

ABRAHAMS, Dr the Noble Anne; *née* Cremona-Barbaro; da of Prof John J Cremona, of Villa Barbaro, Attard, Malta, and Beatrice Cremona-Barbaro, Marchioness of St George; *b* 15 April 1951; *Educ* Convent of the Sacred Heart Malta, Royal Univ of Malta; *m* 24 May 1986, Andrew Leonard Abrahams; 2 da (Hannah b 20 May 1987, Jessica b 18 Jan 1989); *Career* Westminster Hosp 1976, W Middx Hosp 1976, Northwick Park Hosp 1977, The Bethlem Royal and Maudsley Hosp 1977-81, St Thomas's Hosp 1981- 82, lectr in psychiatry Charing Cross Hosp Med Sch 1982-85, conslt psychiatrist Wexham Park Hosp 1985-; MRCS, LRCP, MRCPsych; *Recreations* bridge; *Style—* Dr the Noble Anne Abrahams; c/o Dept of Psychiatry, Wexham Park Hospital, Slough, Berks (☎ 0753 34567)

ABRAHAMS, Maj (Sidney) Anthony George; TD; s of Anthony Claude Walter Abrahams, of Goldsmith Bldg, Temple, London EC4, and Laila, *née* Myking; *b* 30 Oct 1951; *Educ* Bedford Sch; *m* 6 Oct 1979, Kathryn Helen Anne, da of Humphrey John Patrick Chetwynd-Talbot, of South Warnborough, Basingstoke, Hants; 1 s (Thomas b 1985), 2 da (Annika b 1983, Harriett b 1988); *Career* cmmnd 1976, Maj 1984, 4 Bn Royal Green Jackets (V); admitted slr 1978; Wade-Gery and Brackenbury 1980-84, Alexander Farr and Son 1984-88, Wade Gery Farr 1988-, dep registrar Co Ct 1989; Freeman City of London 1985; memb: Worshipful Co of Glazier's 1985, Law Soc; *Recreations* TA, squash, food and drink; *Style—* Maj Anthony Abrahams, TD; Woodfield, Honey Rd, Colmworth, Beds MK44 2LZ (☎ 0230 628996); Wade Gery Farr, 30-32 Bromham Rd, Bedford MK40 2QD (☎ 0234 273 273, fax 0234 3532 110, telex 265871 MONREF G)

ABRAHAMS, Gerald Milton; CBE (1967); s of Isidor Abrahams (d 1943); *b* 20 June 1917; *Educ* Westminster; *m* 1, 1946, Doris, da of late Mark Cole, of Brookline, Mass, USA; 2 da; m 2, 1972, Mrs Marianne Wilson, da of late David Kay, of London; *Career* Maj Br Army WWII, HAC, RHA, served Greece, W Desert and Ceylon; chm and md Aquascutum Gp plc and associated cos 1947-; memb: Br Menswear Guild (chm 1959-61 and 1964-66), Cncl CBI 1965-, Br Nat Export Cncl Ctee for Exports to Canada 1965-70, Consumer Goods Ctee Export Cncl for Europe, Clothing Export Cncl (chm 1966-70, vice pres 1970-), Economic Devpt Ctee for Clothing Indust 1966-69, Clothing Manufacturers' Fedn of GB 1960-82 (chm Exec Cncl 1965-66), North American Advsy Gp BOTB 1978-86 (vice chm 1983-86), Br Clothing Indust Assoc 1982-87; FRSA 1972, CBIM 1979; *Recreations* swimming, golf; *Clubs* Buck's; *Style—* Gerald Abrahams, Esq, CBE; c/o Aquascutum Group plc, 100 Regent St, London W1A 2AQ (☎ 071 734 6090, fax 071 734 0726, telex 264426)

ABRAHAMS, Henry; s of Joseph Henry Abrahams (d 1938), of Leeds, and Florence, *née* Towers (d 1942); *b* 14 Oct 1904; *Educ* Leeds GS, Crawford Coll Berks, Business Sch London; *m* 1, 21 July 1935 (m dis 15 June 1942), Miriam Marion, da of Henry Silbert, of London; m 2, 23 July 1946, Grete, da of Peter Anton Johannes Bork; 2 da (Carol Rosalind (Mrs Le Vay Laurence), Janet Barbara (Mrs Gluckstein)); *Career* industrialist; co fndr A W Securities (mfrs of carpets, plastics, coated fabrics); farmer 1946-59; underwriting memb of Lloyds; ret 1973; supporter of charities and funds through The Henry and Grete Abrahams Charitable Fndn; donations incl: 2 day centres at Israeli hosps, library of med Tel Aviv Univ, paediatric high dependency unit St Mary's Hosp Paddington; created Nurses Endowment Fund; Freeman City of London 1985, memb Worshipful Co of Upholders 1985; Hon PhD Tel Univ 1986; *Recreations* salmon and sea trout fishing, tennis, golf, chess, bridge, travel; *Style—* Henry Abrahams, Esq; 23 Chelwood House, Gloucester Square, London W2 2SY (☎ 071 262 4742)

ABRAHAMS, Ian John; s of Michael Leonard Abrahams (d 1950), and Gertrude Maud, *née* Clavering (d 1983); *b* 23 Nov 1921; *Educ* The Hall Sch Hampstead, Westminster, Pembroke Coll Cambridge (BA, MA); *m* 1, 9 Sept 1947 (m dis 1979), Jill Maude, da of the late Leslie Koppenhagen, of London; 1 s (Michael b 1950), 1 da (Penelope (Mrs Madden) b 1951); m 2, Ruth Daponte, da of the late J Hulme-Smith, of Poonah India; 2 step da (Susan (Mrs Leigh-Wood) b 1948, Sarah b 1957); *Career* WWII 1941-45, Lieut RNVR serv MTB after injury Courtesy Govt USA for RN; chm and chief exec Temple Varnish Co Ltd 1952-53, jt md Ripolin Ltd 1953-55, dir Amalgamated Investment Property Co Ltd 1955-64, chm and chief exec TV Int Ltd 1964-80, Crown Int Prodns Ltd 1969-80, chm TV Applications Ltd 1967-80, Video Communications Ltd 1967-80, dir Crown Cassette Communications Ltd 1967-80, chm Radio Orwell Ltd, chief exec Interservice (Med) Ltd; dir Consumer & Video Hldgs Ltd, chm Monmouth Film Prodn Ltd 1985-88, Chelsea Cable Co Ltd 1984-; vice pres Br Acad of Songwriters, Composers and Authors 1970-, govr: Contemporary Dance Theatre 1971-84, Hall Sch Hampstead; tv and film: Philby A Ruthless Journey 1969, Ivor Novello awards at The Talk of the Town 1972, A Month in the Country 1976, Pictures at an Exhibition with Emerson, Lake and Palmer 1978, Tribute to Her Majesty (with John Mills) 1986, Toga 1990; Capt Cambridge Univ Boxing 1947-48; *Recreations* music, reading, cinema; *Clubs* Hawks Cambridge; *Style—* Ian Abrahams, Esq

ABRAHAMS, Ivor; s of Harry Abrahams (d 1984), of Southport, and Rachel, *née* Kalisky (d 1983); *b* 10 Jan 1935; *Educ* Wigan GS, Southport Sch of Arts and Crafts, St Martins Sch of Art, Camberwell Sch of Art (NDD); *m* 1, Victoria, da of Henry James Taylor; 1 s (Saul Benjamin b 27 March 1966); m 2, Evelyne, da of Andre Horvais; 1 s (Etienne b 17 April 1973); *Career* artist, sculptor, photographer; solo exhibitions incl: Arnolfini Bristol 1971, Mappin Art Gallery Sheffield and Aberdeen Art Gallery 1972, Lijnbaan Centrum Rotterdam 1973, Kölnischer Kunstverien Cologne 1973, Ferens Art Gallery Kingston upon Hull 1979, Portsmouth City Art Gallery 1979, Middlesbrough Art Gallery 1979, Stoke on Trent City Museum 1979, St Enoch's Gallery Glasgow 1980, Warwick Arts Tst London 1982, Bolton Museum and Art Gallery 1984, Yorkshire Sculpture Park Wakefield 1984; gp exhibitions incl: 26 Young Sculptors (Inst of Contemporary Arts London) 1961, Br Art Today (Palazzo Realle Milan) 1976, Silver Jubilee Exhibition (contemporary sculpture, Battersea Park) 1977, New Orleans Museum of Art 1978, Br Art Show 1980, Landscape Prints (Tate Gallery) 1981, Br Sculpture in the 20th Century 1951-80 (Whitechapel Art Gallery) 1982; pub collections incl: Aberdeen Art Gallery and Museum, Arts Cncl of GB, Bibliotheque Nationale Paris, Br Cncl London, Metropolitan Museum New York, Museum of Modern Art New York, Nat Gallery of Australia Canberra, Tate Gallery London, V & A Museum London, Buymans Museum Rotterdam, Denver Museum Colorado, Minneapolis Art Inst, Strasbourg Museum, Walker Art Gallery Liverpool, Wedgwood Museum Stoke on Trent, Wilhem Lembruke Museum Duisburg, Williams Coll Museum of Art Williamstown; book illustrations and photographs, short films and videos; visiting lectr: Birmingham Coll of Art and Crafts 1960-63, Coventry Coll of Art and Crafts 1964-66, Goldsmiths Coll of Art 1968-69, Royal Coll of Art 1980-81, Slade Sch UCL 1982, Winston Churchill fell 1990; ARA 1989; *Recreations* golf, photography, reading, collecting; *Clubs* Chelsea Arts, Colony Room; *Style—* Ivor Abrahams, Esq; The Studio, 112 Shivlard Rd, London W9 (☎ 071 289 6270, 081 969 2505)

ABRAHAMS, Paul Richard; s of Anthony Claud Walter Abrahams, of Brune; and Laila, *née* Myking; *b* 20 April 1962; *Educ* Radley, Downing Coll Cambridge (BA, MA), Darwin Coll Cambridge (PhD, Fencing half blue); *Career* dep defence and aerospace corr Financial Times 1989- (technol corr 1988-89); *Recreations* skiing; *Style—* Paul Abrahams, Esq; Financial Times, 1 Southwark Bridge, London SE1 9HL (☎ 071 873 3650, fax 071 873 3085)

ABRAMOVICH, Solomon; s of Dr Jacob Abramovich (d 1977), and Bronia Maisel (d 1980); *b* 12 Dec 1946; *Educ* Sch of Music, Kaunas Med Sch (MSc, MB BS); *Career* clinical fell Univ of Toronto 1981, chief asst and sr registrar St Bartholomews and Nat Hosp for Nervous Diseases London 1982, conslt ENT Surgn St Mary's Hosp London and Central Middlesex Hosp 1988; hon clinical sr lectr Imperial Coll London 1989; memb: Int Barany Soc, Int Maniere's Soc; FRCS (MRCS), LRCP, MRSM; *Books* Electric Response Audiometry in Clinical Practice (1990); *Recreations* tennis, skiing, playing the violin, music; *Clubs* Savage, Athenaeum; *Style—* Solomon Abramovich, Esq; 24 Downshire Hill, London NW3 (☎ 071 725 1214); 152 Harley St, London W1N 1HH (☎ 071 935 3834, fax 071 224 2574)

ABRAMS, Charles; s of Mozus Mischa Abrams (d 1987), of 5 Turner Close, London NW11, and Evelyn Joyce, *née* Spitzel; *b* 2 Nov 1952; *Educ* St Pauls, Trinity Coll Cambridge (BA); *m* 30 Aug 1987, Georgia Gitelle Devora, da of James Leo Rosengarten of 6 Bishops Ave, London N2 OAN and Naomi Rosengarten, *née* Alexander; 1 da Alexandra Berina Amelia b 29 May 1990); *Career* slr Linklater & Paines 1976-85 (articled 1974), ptnr S J Berwin & Co 1986- (slr 1985-86); various pubns in jls and speaker at seminars on securities and compliance; memb: City Regulatory Panel CBI, Law Soc; *Books* Guide to the Financial Services Act 1986 (jtly, 2 edn 1989); contrib to: CCH Financial Services Reporter, Pension Fund Investment (1987); *Recreations* looking after baby, theatre; *Style—* Charles Abrams, Esq; S J Berwin & Co, 236 Grays Inn Rd, London WC1X 8HB (☎ 071 278 0444, fax 071 833 2860, telex 8814928 WINLAW G)

ABRAMS, (Joseph) David; s of Julius Maurice Abrams (d 1974), of Leeds, and Tilly, *née* Ellis (d 1983); *b* 13 Jan 1928; *Educ* Roundhay Sch Leeds, Univ Coll Oxford (open scholar MA), Middx Hosp Med Sch (DM, DO); *m* 22 Aug 1954, Anita Rosalie, da of Mark Berlyne; 5 da (Susan b 1955, Janet b 1959, Hester b 1963, Wendy b 1966, Rachel b 1973); *Career* Nat Serv RAMC (Command Opthalmologist ME Land Forces) 1953-55; Middx Hosp 1952-53, house surgn Moorfields Eye Hosp 1957-59, conslt opthalmic surgn Central Middx Hosp Gp 1962-72 (sr registrar 1959-61), res assoc Inst of Ophthalmology 1959-69, conslt ophthalmic surgn and teacher Sch of Med Royal Free Hosp 1964-; Instituto Barraquer prize essay 1972; memb BMA, FRSM 1960, FRCS, FCOphth; *Books* Duke-Elder's System of Ophthalmology Vol V (jtly, 1970), Practice of Refraction (1978), Ophthalmology in Medicine (1990); *Recreations* music, ambulistics, paronomasia; *Clubs* Savile; *Style—* David Abrams, Esq; 11 Mercers Place, Brook Green, London W6 7BZ (☎ 071 602 9464); 99 Harley St, London W1N 1DF (☎ 071 935 6362)

ABRAMS, Dr Mark Alexander; s of Abram Abrams (d 1952), of Enfield, Middx, and Anne, *née* Jackson (d 1955); *b* 27 April 1906; *Educ* Latymer Sch, Univ of London (BSc, PhD); *m* 1, 1931 (m dis 1951), Una Strugnell; 1 s (Philip d 1982), 1 da (Evelyn); m 2, 1951, Jean, da of Frederick Bird (d 1974), of Newtown, Connecticut, USA; 1 da (Sarah); *Career* Political Intelligence Dept FO 1941-46; res dir London Press Exchange 1946-70; dir: Res Unit Social Sci Res Cncl 1971-77, Res Unit Age Concern Eng 1977-; *Recreations* listening to music; *Clubs* Civil Service; *Style—* Dr Mark Abrams; 12 Pelham Square, Brighton BN1 4ET (☎ 0273 684573); 60 Pitcairn Rd, Mitcham, Surrey CR4 3LL

ABRAMS, Dr Michael Ellis; s of Sam Philip Abrams, OBE (d 1964), and Ruhamah Emmie, *née* Glieberman (d 1989); *b* 17 Sept 1932; *Educ* King Edward's Sch Birmingham, Univ of Birmingham (MB ChB, BSc); *m* 1962, Rosalind June, da of Nathan Beckman (d 1970); 4 c (Rebecca, Jonathan, Jeremy, Nathan); *Career* dep chief med offr Dept of Health 1985-; FRCP, FFCM; *Recreations* beachcombing; *Style—* Dr Michael Abrams; Department of Health, Richmond House, 79 Whitehall, London SW1A 2NS

ABRAMSKY, Jennifer (Mrs Alasdair Liddell); da of Chimen Abramsky, and Miriam, *née* Nirenstein; *b* 7 Oct 1946; *Educ* Holland Park Sch, UEA (BA); *m* Alasdair D MacDuff Liddell; 1 s, 1 da; *Career* BBC: joined 1969 as progs ops asst, prodr The World At One 1973 (ed 1981), jt prodr special prog on Nixon 1974, ed PM 1978, prodr Radio 4's Budget progs 1979-86, ed Today Prog 1986-87, ed News and Current Affrs Radio 1987-; *Recreations* theatre, music; *Style—* Ms Jennifer Abramsky; BBC, Broadcasting House, Portland Place, London W1A 1AA (☎ 071 580 4468)

ABRAMSON, Sidney; CMG (1979); s of Jacob Abramson (d 1951), of 31 Cadogan St, London, and Rebecca, *née* Cohen (d 1956); *b* 14 Sept 1921; *Educ* Emanuel Sch London, The Queen's Coll Oxford (BA,MA); *m* 1, 15 Dec 1946 (m dis 1958), Lerine, da of Hyman Freedman; 2 s (John b 1947, Richard b 1952); m 2, 1960, Violet Ellen, da of Frederick William Eatley (d 1959); *Career* Interservice Bureau Colombo 1943-46; BOT (later Dept of Trade): 1950-63 and 1965-81 (under sec 1972-81); memb UK Delgn to: OEEC Paris 1957-59, EFTA Geneva 1960, GATT Secretariat Geneva 1963-65; *Recreations* gardening, music; *Style—* Sidney Abramson, Esq, CMG; 26 Arlington, London N12 7JR (☎ 081 445 1264)

ABSE, Dr Dannie; s of Rudolf Abse (d 1964), of Cardiff, and Kate, *née* Shepherd (d 1981); bro of Leo Abse; *b* 22 Sept 1923; *Educ* St Illtyds Coll Cardiff, Univ of Wales Cardiff, King's Coll London, Westminster Hosp London; *m* 4 Aug 1951, Joan, da of John Mercer, of St Helens, Lancs; 1 s (Jesse David b 1958), 2 da (Keren Danielle b 1953, Susanna Ruth b 1957); *Career* RAF 1951-54 Sqdn Ldr i/c Chest Clinic Central Med Estab London; poet, playwright and novelist; sr fell of humanities Princeton Univ 1973-74, pres Poetry Soc 1979-; MRCS, LRCP, FRSL; poetry: After Every Thing Green (1948), Walking Under Water (1952), Tenants of the House (1957), Poems Golders Green (1962), A Small Desperation (1968), Funland and Other poems (1973), Collected Poems (1977), Way Out in the Centre (1981), Ask the Bloody Horse (1986), White Coat, Purple Coat (1989); prose: Ash on a Young Man's Sleeve (1954), Journals from the Ant-Heap (1986); novels: Some Corner of an English Field (1957), O Jones, O Jones (1970); autobiography: A Poet in the Family (1974), A Strong Dose of Myself (1983); plays: House of Cowards (1960), The Dogs of Pavlov (1969), Pythagoras (1976), Gone in January (1978); *Style—* Dr Dannie Abse; c/o The Poetry Society, 21 Earls Court Square, London SW1

ABSE, Leo; *b* 22 April 1917; *Educ* Howard Gardens HS, LSE; *m* 1955, Marjorie Davies; 1 s, 1 da; *Career* WWII serv RAF 1940-45 (arrest for political activities in ME 1944, precipitated Parly debate); slr, sr ptnr in Cardiff law firm; chm Cardiff City Lab Pty 1951-53, memb Cardiff CC 1953-58, Parly candidate (Lab) Cardiff N 1955; MP (Lab): Pontypool 1958-83, Torfaen 1983-87; chm Welsh Parly Pty 1976-87; memb Home Office Advsy Ctees on: the Penal System 1968, Adaption 1972; first chm Select Ctee on Welsh Affairs 1980, memb Select Ctee on Abortion 1975-76, sec Br-Taiwan Parly Gp 1983-87; sponsor or co sponsor of Private Memb's Acts relating to: divorce, homosexuality, family planning, legitimacy, widow's damages, industl injuries, congenital disabilities and relief from forfeiture; sponsor: Children's Bill 1973 (later became Children's Act 1975), Divorce Bill 1983 (later became Matrimonial and Family Proceedings Act) 1985; initiated first Commons debates on: genetic engrg, Windscale, in vitro pregnancies; led Lab anti-devolution campaign Wales 1979; memb Cncl Inst for Study and Treatment of Delinquency 1964-, chm Winnicett Clinic of Psychotherapy 1988-(tstee 1980-), pres Nat Cncl for the Divorced and Separated 1974-, vice pres Br Assoc for Counselling 1985-, chm Parly Friends of WNO 1985-87; memb Ct: Univ of Wales 1981-87, UWIST; Regents' lectr Univ of Calif 1981; *Awards* Best Dressed Man award Clothing Fedn 1962, Order of Brilliant Star (China) 1988; *Books* Private Member: a psychoanalytically orientated study of contemporary politics (1973), In Vitro Fertilisation: past, present and future (contrib 1986), Margaret, daughter of Beatrice: a psychobiography of Margaret Thatcher (1989); *Recreations* italian wines, psychobiography; *Style—* Leo Abse, Esq; Via Poggio di Mezzo, Nugola Vecchia, Livorno, Italy (☎ 586 977022)

ACFIELD, David Laurence; s of Robert Douglas Acfield, of Chelmsford, Essex, and Ena Violet Acfield; *b* 24 July 1947; *Educ* Brentwood Sch, Christs Coll Cambridge (MA); *m* 1973, Helen Mary, da of David Joseph Bradford, of Hutton, Essex; 2 da (Clare b 1977, Rosemary b 1982); *Career* cricketer Essex CCC 1966-87, Olympic fencer (sabre 1968 and 1972), Br Sabre Champion 1969, 1970, 1971 and 1972, BBC TV summarizer (cricket); with Save and Prosper Group Ltd 1987-; *Recreations* birdwatching, wine, films; *Clubs* MCC, Lord Taveners, Essex CCC (ctee memb 1989-), Old Brentwoods, Incogniti; *Style—* David Acfield, Esq; 48 The Furlongs, Ingatestone, Essex CM4 0AH

ACHESON, Prof Sir (Ernest) Donald; KBE (1986); s of Malcolm King Acheson, MC, and Dorothy Josephine, *née* Rennoldson; *b* 17 Sept 1926; *m* Barbara Mary, *née* Castle; 1 s, 5 da; *Career* chief med offr: Dept of Health, DES, Home Office 1984; *Style—* Prof Sir Donald Acheson, KBE; Richmond House, 79 Whitehall, London SW1A 2NS

ACHESON, Frances Russell (Fran); da of Canon Russell Robert Acheson, of Bleddfa, Knighton, Powys, and Richenda Mary, *née* Vale; *b* 4 June 1958; *Educ* Sch of SS Mary & Anne, Abbots Bromley, Univ of York (BA); *Career* ed Herefordshire County Life 1980, sub ed Radio Times 1981-84, sr prodr features arts and educn BBC radio 1984-; jt winner 300 Gp best radio prog Sony nat radio award for best educn and 1990; *Books* Room to Listen Room to Talk (1988), A Taste of Counselling (1989), A Counselling Listener (1989); *Recreations* cooking for greedy friends; *Style—* Ms Fran Acheson; 76 Amelia St, London SE17 3AR (☎ 071 703 6190); BBC Broadcasting House, Portland Place, London W1A 1AA (☎ 071 927 4535, fax 071 323 5060)

ACHESON, Dr (Enid) Joan; da of Ernest Barnett (d 1980), and Eva, *née* Hodgkinson (d 1955); *b* 14 Oct 1926; *Educ* Orme Girls' Sch Newcastle-under-Lyme, Univ of Birmingham (MB ChB, MD, MRCP); *m* Harold William Kennedy (Bill) Acheson, OBE, s of Samuel Acheson (d 1957); 1 s (David b 1955); *Career* Dept Neurology N Staffs Royal Infirmary: res asst 1960-64, clinical res fell Br Heart Fndn 1964-70; clinical res fell Dept of Med Manchester Royal Infirmary 1970-77 (memb Married Womens' Re-Trg Scheme 1977-86), clinical res fell and hon conslt Dept of Med Univ of Manchester Med Sch 1986-89, conslt advsr clinical computing Central Manchester Health Authy; memb Sch Cncl Newcastle-under-Lyme Endowed Schs 1981- (govr 1958-81, vice chm govrs 1959-76, pres of Old Girls' Soc 1963-66, chm govrs 1976-79); memb: BMA 1951, Manchester Med Soc 1971; memb Br Med Informatics Soc 1988; *Books* Strokes - Natural History, Pathology and Surgical Treatment (1975); *Recreations* ornithology, music, embroidery, swimming, fell walking, travel; *Style—* Dr Joan Acheson; Braegarth, Elterwater, Ambleside, Cumbria LA22 9JB (☎ 096 67 355) 6 Appleby Lodge, Wilmslow Rd, Manchester M14 6HZ (☎ 061 224 9469); The Manchester Royal Infirmary, Oxford Rd, Manchester M13 9WL (☎ 061 276 4296)

ACHESON, Hon Patrick Bernard Victor Montagu; s of 5 Earl of Gosford, MC (d 1954), and Caroline Mildred Carter, Countess of Gosford (d 1965); unc and hp of 7 Earl of Gosford; *b* 4 Feb 1915; *Educ* Harrow, Trinity Coll Cambridge (BA), Harvard Univ (MBA); *m* 1946, Judith, da of Frederick B Bate (d 1970), of Waterford, Virginia, USA; 3 s, 2 da; *Career* with International Bank for Reconstruction and Development 1947-65, pres Culligan Water Conditioning Corporation of N Virginia 1966-80; *Recreations* golf, tennis, gardening; *Clubs* Loudoun Golf; *Style—* The Hon Patrick Acheson; Box 71, Waterford, Va 22190, USA (☎ 010 1 703 882 3259)

ACHESON, Prof Roy Malcolm; s of Capt Malcolm King Acheson, MC, MD (d 1962), of Castlecaufield, Co Tyrone, and Dorothy Josephine, *née* Rennoldson (d 1976); *b* 18 Aug 1921; *Educ* Merchiston Castle Sch Edinburgh, Trinity Coll Dublin (BA, MA, ScD), Brasenose Coll Oxford (BA, MA), Radcliffe Infirmary Oxford (BM BCh, DM); *m* 16 March 1950 (m dis 1990), Fiona Marigo, da of Wing-Cdr Vincent O'Brien (d 1950), of Altrincham, Cheshire; 2 s (Malcolm O'Brien b 1950, Vincent Rennoldson b 1960), 1 da (Marigo Fiona b 1963); *Career* enlisted WWII RAC (N Irish Horse) 1942, active serv Algeria and Tunisia, cmmnd RMC Sandhurst 1944, rejoined N Irish Horse, active serv Italy, discharged Lt 1946; prof community med Univ of Cambridge 1976-88 (emeritus prof and fell Churchill Coll 1988-); hon fell Nat Acad of Med in Argentina (elected 1974), govr Action in International Med (AIM); author and ed of several texts and scientific papers; memb: GMC 1978-88, GDC 1983-88, Cambridge Health Authy 1986-88; Hon MA Yale Univ; FRCP, FFOM 1984, FFCM (vice pres 1986-89); *Books* Health, Society and Medicine: An Introduction to Community Medicine (with S Hagard, 1985), Costs and Benefits of the Heart Transplant Programmes at Harefield and Papworth Hospitals (with M Buxton, N Caine, S Gibson and B O'Brien, 1985); *Recreations* choral singing, occasional bird watching, golf; *Clubs* Utd Oxford and Cambridge Univ, Gog Magog Golf; *Style—* Prof Roy Acheson; 8 Kingston St, Cambridge CB1 2NU (☎ 0223 315596); Churchill College, Cambridge CB3 ODS (☎ 0223 336000)

ACKERMAN, Bruce Trevor; s of Gustave Ackerman (d 1966), of Cape Town, South Africa, and Freda, *née* Kahanovitz; *b* 28 Dec 1907; *Educ* Diocesan Coll Cape Town, Cape Town Univ (BA, MBA); *m* 9 Feb 1972, Patricia Anne (d 1989), da of Norman Guy; *Career* dir: German Smaller Co's Investment Trust plc 1985-, Lloyds Merchant Bank Ltd 1985-, First Spanish Investment Tst plc 1988-, Portugal Fund Ltd 1988-; md Lloyds Investment Managers Ltd 1985-; *Recreations* sport, music, classic cars, travel; *Style—* Bruce Ackerman, Esq; Investment Managers Ltd, 48 Chiswell Street, London EC1 (☎ 071 600 4500)

ACKERMAN, Wing Cdr (John) Darral; OBE (1965, MBE 1945); s of Mathew Joliffe (d 1951), of Masterton, NZ, and Phyllis Phoebe, *née* Pearse (d 1962); *b* 6 July 1921; *Educ* Lansdowne Sch Wairarapa, Dannevirke and Levin HS, Victoria Coll Wellington; *m* 22 April 1946, Jean Kathleen, da of Howard Brown (d 1948), of Bramley, Hants; 2 s (Howard b 1947, Neil b 1950); *Career* RNZAF 1940-46, coastal cmd Atlantic 1942-45 (despatches 1943); RAF 1946-74, Bomber Cmd 1948-52; Miny of Supply 1952-58, 1961-64; UK Mission USA 1958-61, Cyprus 1965-68; md Seahorse Sails Ltd 1975-; Half Ton Cup Sailing Championships 1971 and 1973; Queen's Commendation 1958; *Recreations* sailing (racing and cruising); *Clubs* RAF; *Style—* Wing Cdr Darral Ackerman, OBE; 7 Apple Grove, Aldwick Bay, Bognor Regis, W Sussex PO21 4NB (☎ 0243 262311); Seahorse Sails South Ltd, Birdham Pool, Birdham, nr Chichester, W Sussex PO20 7BB (☎ 0243 512195)

ACKERS, Godfrey Lloyd; s of George Lloyd Ackers, OBE (d 1966), and Sylvia Ruth, *née* Tilly (d 1969); *b* 10 Aug 1926; *Educ* King's Sch Canterbury, Trinity Coll Oxford (BA, MA); *m* 4 June 1955, Wendy Bettina, da of William Hunter Lobb, (d 1963); 2 s (Jeremy b 1957, Timothy b 1959), 1 da (Penelope b 1966); *Career* serv RNVR Lt 1944-48; ptnr: Sir M MacDonald & Ptnrs (dir 1976-86), Sir M MacDonald Assocs 1977-85, Sir M MacDonald & Ptnrs (Africa) 1980-86, Associated Consultants & Ptnrs (Khartoum) 1984-87; dir: Sir M MacDonald Ltd 1976-87, Cambridge Educn Cnslts Ltd 1984-87; conslt: Sir M MacDonald & Ptnrs 1986-88, Mott MacDonald Conslt Ltd 1989-; memb: Arbitration Advsy Bd Inst of Civil Engrs 1988-90, Client/Conslts Relationship Ctee Fédération Int des Ingé Conseils 1987-90; CEng, MIWEM, FCIArb; *Recreations* sculling, sailing, Dartmoor; *Style—* Godfrey Ackers, Esq; 26 Kings Orchard, Bridgetown, Totnes, S Devon TQ9 5BX (☎ 0803 866193, fax 0803 867350)

ACKERS, James George; s of James Ackers, and Vera Harriet, *née* Edwards; *b* 20 Oct 1935; *Educ* Oundle, LSE; *m* 1, 1959, Judith Ann Locket; 1 s, 1 da; m 2, 1972, Enid Lydia Silverthorne; *Career* contested (C) Walsall N 1959; former vice chm Bow Group; chm and md Ackers Jarrett Ltd, chm Ackers Jarrett Leasing Ltd; memb Monopolies and Mergers Cmmn 1981-; chm; West Midlands RHA 1982-; Nat Cncl Assoc of Br Chambers of Commerce 1984- (formerly dep chm); former chm West Midlands Chambers of Industry and Commerce; *Style—* James Ackers, Esq; 21A Greycoat Gdns, Greycoat St, London SW1

ACKERY, Prof Duncan Melville; s of William Melville Ackery, of Woodlands, Kirkcudbright, Scotland, and Ruth Frances, *née* Carlisle; *b* 11 Aug 1930; *Educ* Dauntsey's Sch, Univ of Cambridge, Guy's Hosp Med Sch (MA, MB BChir, MSc); *Career* RN 1956-73; currently conslt and hon prof of nuclear med Southampton Univ Hosp; *Style—* Prof Duncan Ackery; The Old Rectory, Eling, Hants SO4 4HF (☎ 0703 864434); Dept of Nuclear Med, Southampton Gen Hosp, Southampton SO9 4XY (☎ 0703 777222 ext 6199)

ACKLAND, Joss (Sidney Edmond Jocelyn); s of Maj Sidney Norman Ackland (d 1981), and Ruth Izod (d 1957); *b* 29 Feb 1928; *Educ* Dame Alice Owens Sch, Central Sch of Speech Training and Dramatic Art; *m* 18 Aug 1951, Rosemary Jean, da of Capt Robert Hunter Kirkcaldy (d 1954); 2 s (Toby b 1966, Paul b 1953, d 1982), 5 da (Melanie b 1952, Antonia b 1956, Penelope b 1958, Samantha b 1962, Kirsty b 1963); *Career* actor; Old Vic Theatre Company 1958-61, artistic dir Mermaid Theatre 1961-63; West End Plays incl: The Hasty Heart, Hotel in Amsterdam, Come As You Are, A Streetcar Named Desire, Collaborators, Captain Brassbounds Conversion; West End Musicals incl: Jorrocks in Jorrocks, Frederik in A Little Night Music, Peron in Evita, Captain Hook and Mr Darling in Peter Pan the musical; played in The Madras House and Jean Seburg at the National Theatre, The Cherry Orchard at Chichester Festival Theatre; national tours: The Dresser and Taming of the Shrew (opening prodns at The Barbican (RSC) 1982), Falstaff in Henry IV parts 1 and 2, Hook and Darling in Peter Pan; recent films incl: The Sicilian 1986, White Mischief 1987, To Kill A Priest 1988, Lethal Weapon II, The Hunt For Red October, To Forget Palermo 1989, Object of Beauty, The Sheltering Desert, The Bridge 1990; recent TV films incl: Shadowlands, First and Last, Clarence Darrow in Never the Sinner 1990, A Murder of Quality 1990; memb: Drug Help Line, Amnesty Int, Covent Garden Community Assoc; *Books* I Must Be in There Somewhere (autobiography 1989); *Recreations* writing, painting, watching movies, bringing up children; *Clubs* Garrick; *Style—* Joss Ackland, Esq; c/o Michael Anderson, ICM Ltd, 388/396 Oxford St, London W1N 9HE (☎ 071 629 8080)

ACKLAND-SNOW, Brian Percy; s of Frank Whittlesey Ackland - Snow (d 1974), and Ivy Jesse Byway; *b* 31 March 1940; *Educ* Harrow Sch of Art; *m* 24 Sept 1960, Carol Avis, da of James Eli Dunsby (d 1963); 1 s (Andrew b 1961), 1 da (Amanda b 1963); *Career* prodn designer and art director; films incl: Death on the Nile, McVicar, Superman III, Room with a View (BAFTA award for production design, Academy award or direction), Maurice, Man in the Brown Suit, Without a Clue, The Secret Garden; memb: BAFTA, AMPAS; *Recreations* historical architecture, archaeology; *Style—* Brian Ackland-Snow, Esq; Quarry Edge, Cookham Dean, Berks (☎ 06284 3387); Camera Masters, Los Angeles (☎ 213 306 0810)

ACKLING, (Walter) Roger; s of Walter Frederick Ackling, of Chillerton, Isle of Wight, and Alice Jean, *née* Lockton; *b* 11 Aug 1947; *Educ* Ealing Art Sch, St Martins Art Sch; *m* 6 Sept 1987, Sylvia, da of Vernon Crowther; *Career* artist; sr lectr Painting Dept Chelsea Sch of Art; over 50 solo exhibitions since 1976 incl: Lisson Gallery London 1976-79, 1981 and 1984, Graeme Murray Edinburgh 1978-79 and 1989, Gillespie/Laage/Salamon Paris 1978, 1981-82, 1984, 1987 and 1991, White Art Tokyo 1985-87, 1989 and 1991, Juda Fine Art London 1987 and 1990; represented by: Hirschland Adler Modern NY, Francoise Lambert Milan, Ann Westin Stockholm; *Recreations* walking, gardening; *Style—* Roger Ackling, Esq; Annely Juda Fine Art, 23 Dering St, London W1R 9AA

ACKNER, Baron (Life Peer UK 1986), of Sutton, Co of W Sussex; Desmond James Conrad Ackner; PC (1980), QC (1961); s of Dr Conrad Ackner, of Yew Tree House, Jordans, Beaconsfield, Bucks, and Rhoda Ackner; *b* 18 Sept 1920; *Educ*

Highgate, Clare Coll Cambridge (hon fell 1983); *m* 1946, Joan Ackner, JP, da of late John Evans, JP, and wid of K B Spence; 1 s, 1 da, 1 adopted (step) da; *Career* served WWII RA and Admiralty Naval Law Branch; barr 1945, QC 1961, rec of Swindon 1962-71, judge High Court Queen's Bench 1971-80, Judge Jersey and Guernsey Courts of Appeal 1967-71, presiding judge W Circuit 1976-79, Lord Justice of Appeal 1980-86; Gen Cncl of the Bar: memb 1957-70, hon treas 1964-66, vice chm 1966-68, chm 1968-70; pres Senate of Inns of Court and Bar 1980-82; chm Law Advsy Ctee Br Cncl 1981-90; dep treas Middle Temple 1983, treas 1984, created Lord of Appeal in Ordinary 1986; *Style*— The Rt Hon Lord Ackner, PC; 7 Rivermill, 151 Grosvenor Rd, London SW1 (☎ 071 821 8068); Browns House, Sutton, Petworth, W Sussex (☎ 079 87 206)

ACKNER, Hon Martin Stewart; o s of Baron Ackner, PC (Life Peer), *qv*; *b* 1951; *Educ* Oundle, Birmingham Univ (BSc); *m* 1983, Janet, da of late C W Williamson; *Style*— The Hon Martin Ackner; Lands Farm, W Anstey, S Molton, Devon

ACKROYD, Christopher Edward; s of Anthony Ackroyd (d 1988), of Rustington, Sussex, and May Patricia Jean, *née* Dixon; *b* 21 Aug 1942; *Educ* Hurstpierpont Coll, Gonville and Caius Coll Cambridge (MA), Middx Hosp Med Sch (MB BChir); *m* 21 Sept 1968, Judith Ann, da of Ernest Albert Talbot, of Taunton, Somerset; 1 s (Oliver Edward b 21 April 1977), 2 da (Emily Kate b 21 Jan 1974, Jessica Louise b 30 Oct 1975); *Career* sr registrar Robert Jones & Agnes Hun Orthopaedic Hosp Oswestry 1973, lectr Dept Orthopaedic Surgery Nuffield Orthopaedic Centre Oxford 1974-76 (reader Dept Orthopaedic Surgery 1976-79), conslt orthopaedic surgn Southmead Gen Hosp and Winford Orthopaedic Hosp 1979-, hon clinical lectr Univ of Bristol 1979-; memb: Bd of Injury 1982-85, Bd of Jl of Bone and Joint Surgery 1983-86; sec Br Orthopaedic Assoc 1987-90 (memb 1973); memb: Br Orthopaedic Res Soc 1976, Girdlestones Soc 1976; FRCS; *Books* The Severely Injured Limb (1983); *Recreations* sailing, gardening, photography, music; *Style*— Christopher Ackroyd, Esq; 2 Clifton Park, Clifton, Bristol BS8 3BS (☎ 0272 730958, fax 0272 730887, car 0836 631989)

ACKROYD, David Edward; s of John Edward Ackroyd (d 1976), and Betty, *née* Mitchell; *b* 9 Aug 1955; *Educ* Chesterfield Sch, Univ of Durham (BSc); *m* 7 July 1984, Sandra Joan; 3 s (Mark Edward b 10 April 1985, Simon William b 24 Sept 1986, Jonathan Paul b 30 July 1988); *Career* actuarial trainee Phoenix Assurance 1976-78; Williams De Broe: joined 1978, head of Gilt Edged Dept 1982, dir 1987-; FIA 1982; *Recreations* squash, golf; *Style*— David Ackroyd, Esq; Danescroft, Manor Way, Knott Park, Oxshott, Surrey KT22 OHU (☎ 0372 843840); Williams De Broe, 6 Broadgate, London EC2M 2RP (☎ 071 588 7511, fax 071 588 1702)

ACKROYD, Jane Victoria Macleod; da of Sir John Robert Whyte Ackroyd, 2 Bt, *qv*, and Jennifer Eileen Macleod, *née* Bishop; *b* 25 Feb 1957; *Educ* Godolphin and Latymer Sch Hammersmith, St Martin's Sch of Art (BA), Royal College of Art (MA); *Career* artist; exhibitions incl: The Albert Exhibition 1983, solo exhibition (Kingsgate Workshops Gallery) 1984, 1985, 1986 and 1987, Anti-thesis (Angela Flowers Gallery) 1986, Anderson O'Day summer exhibition 1987 and 1988, Anderson O'Day Gallery 1988 and 1991, The Royal Academy Summer Exhibition 1988 and 1989; work in public and private collections incl: The Arts Cncl of GB, The Contemporary Arts Soc, The Harlow Arts Tst; dir Kingsgate Workshops; Freeman: Worshipful Co of Carpenters, City of London 1980; *Recreations* walking, music; *Style*— Miss Jane Ackroyd; Kingsgate Workshops, 116 Kingsgate Rd, London NW6 (☎ 071 328 7878); Anderson O'Day Fine Art, 255 Portobello Road, London W11 (☎ 071 221 7592)

ACKROYD, Sir John Robert Whyte; 2 Bt (UK 1956), of Dewsbury, W Riding of Yorks; s of Sir Cuthbert Lowell Ackroyd, 1 Bt, LLD (d 1973), Lord Mayor of London 1955-56; *b* 2 March 1932; *Educ* Bradfield, Worcester Coll Oxford (MA); *m* 1956, Jennifer Eileen McLeod, da of Henry George Stokes Bishop (d 1977), of Stow-on-the-Wold, Glos; 2 s (Timothy b 1958, Andrew b 1961); 2 da (Jane Victoria McLeod b 1957, *qv*, Kate Georgina McBride (Mrs Marion) b 1963); *Heir* s, Timothy Robert Whyte Ackroyd b 7 Oct 1958; *Career* Sword of Hon Mons OCS and cmmnd 2 Lt RA, serv Jordan 1951-52 (ed 'Jordan' 1978, in celebration of Silver Jubilee of HM King Hussein); steward of OUDS 1954; memb Lloyd's, EPAR 1969-75, serv under Maj-Gen L D Grand; dir Martindale Productions Ltd; vice pres Bromley Symph Orch, patron London and Int Sch of Acting; memb Cncl RCM 1980 (hon sec 1986-), hon sec Pilgrims of GB 1965, churchwarden St Mary-Le-Bow Cheapside (Bow Bells), memb Ct City Univ 1989-; Freeman City of London, Liveryman Worshipful Co of Carpenters FRCM 1988, FRSA 1989; *Recreations* music, theatre, travel; *Clubs* Garrick, Oxford Union (life memb); *Style*— Sir John Ackroyd, Bt; Flat 1, 65 Ladbroke Grove, Holland Park, London W11 2PD (☎ 071 727 5465)

ACKROYD, Norman; s of Albert Ackroyd (d 1979), of Leeds, and Clara Briggs (d 1979); *b* 26 March 1938; *Educ* Cockburn HS Leeds, Leeds Coll of Art, RCA; *m* 1, 1963 (m dis 1975), Sylvia, *née* Buckland; 2 da (Felicity b 1964, Justine b 1966); m2, 1978, Penelope, da of Blair Hughes-Stanton; 1 s (Simeon b 1983), 1 da (Poppy b 1981); *Career* artist; recent one-man exhibitions incl: Anderson O'Day Gallery London 1980 and 1988, Associated American Artists Philadelphia 1981 and 1983, Mickelson Gallery Washington DC 1982, Yehudi Menuhin Sch Surrey 1983, Jersey Arts Centre Channel Islands 1984, Dolan/Maxwell Gallery Philadelphia 1985, 1987 and 1989, Dena Clough Gallery Halifax 1986, Nat Museum of Art Santiago Chile 1987, RE London 1988, Compass Gallery Glasgow 1990; pub collections incl: The Br Museum, Tate Gallery, Albertina Museum Vienna, Arts Cncl GB, Boston Museum of Fine Arts, Br Cncl, Chicago Art Inst, Musee D' Art Historie Geneva, Museum of Modern Art NY, National Galleries of Norway, Canada, Scotland and SA, Queensland Art Gallery Aust, Rijksmuseum, V & A; cmmnd murals for: Albany Hotel Glasgow 1974, Albany Hotel Birmingham 1977, Haringey Cncl 1982-83, Lloyds Bank 1990; TV appearances: Artists in Prin (BBC 2) 1981, Paul Sandby (Central) 1987, Prospects of Rivers (Channel 4) 1988; awards: S E States Open exhibition 1969, Bradford International Biennale 1972 and 1982, RE 1984 and 1985, Frechen Triennale Germany 1986; memb RE 1985, ARA 1988; *Recreations* cricket; *Clubs* Chelsea Arts, Arts; *Style*— Norman Ackroyd, Esq

ACKROYD, Peter; s of Graham Ackroyd, and Audrey, *née* Whiteside; *b* 5 Oct 1949; *Educ* Clare Coll Cambridge, Yale Univ; *Career* lit ed Spectator 1971 (managing ed 1977-81); full time writer; Somerset Maugham Prize (1984), the Guardian Fiction Award (1985), Whithead Prize for Best Biography (1984/85); fell RSL; *poetry* London Lickpenny (1973), Country Life (1978), The Diversions of Purley (1987); *biography* Ezra Pound and His World (1980), T S Eliot (1984), Dickens (1990); *novels* The Great Fire of London (1982), The Last Testament of Oscar Wilde (1983), Hawksmoor (1985), Chatterton (1987), First Light (1989); *Style*— Peter Ackroyd, Esq; 43 Doughty St, London WC1N 2LF

ACKROYD, Rev Prof Peter Runham; s of Rev Jabez Robert Ackroyd (d 1978), and Winifred, *née* Brown (d 1971); *b* 15 Sept 1917; *Educ* Harrow, Downing and Trinity Colls Cambridge (MA, PhD), Univ of London (BD, MTh, DD); *m* 1940, Evelyn Alice (d 1990), da of William Young Nutt (d 1926); 2 s (William, Simon), 3 da (Jane, Jenny, Sarah); *Career* clerk in Holy Orders 1957; univ lectr: Leeds 1948-52, Cambridge 1952-61; Samuel Davidson prof of Old Testament studies King's Coll London 1961-82 (emeritus 1982-); visiting prof: Lutheran Sch of Theology Chicago 1967, 1976, Univ of Toronto 1972, Univ of Notre Dame Indiana 1982, Emory Univ Atlanta 1984; special lectures: Selwyn Lectures New Zealand 1970, Haskell Lectures Oberlin Ohio 1984; foreign sec 1987-90; editor: book list Soc for Old Testament Study 1967-73, Palestine Exploration Quarterly 1972-86; pres Soc for Old Testament Study 1972; chm: Cncl Br Sch of Archaeology in Jerusalem 1980-84, Palestine Exploration Fund 1986; *Books Incl:* Exile and Restoration (1968), Israel under Babylon and Persia (1970), I and II Samuel (1971, 1977), I, II Chronicles, Ezra, Nehemiah (1973), Doors of Perception (1978), Studies in the Religious Tradition of the Old Testament (1987); *Recreations* music, reading; *Style*— The Rev Prof Peter R Ackroyd; Lavender Cottage, Middleton, Saxmundham, Suffolk IP17 3NQ (☎ 0728 73458)

ACKROYD, Timothy Robert Whyte; s of Sir John Robert Whyte Ackroyd, 2 Bt, *qv* and Jennifer Eileen McLeod, *née* Bishop; *b* 7 Oct 1958; *Educ* Bradfield, LAMDA; *Career* actor; theatre incl: Agamemnon (nomination Most Promising Newcomer award West End Theatre Critics) 1976, On Approval 1979, Much Ado About Nothing 1980, A Month in the Country 1981, Man and Superman 1982, A Step in the Prisoners 1983, Pygmalion 1984, Another Country 1986, No Sex Please - We're British 1987, Black Coffee 1988, The Reluctante Debutant 1989, Jeffrey Bernard is Unwell 1989-90; films and tv incl: Jack Be Nimble 1979, Martin Luther - Heretic 1983, Creator 1984 (Hollywood), Man and Superman 1985, That Has Such People In It 1987, Pied Piper 1989, Bullseye 1989; dir Martingale Productions 1985-, formed Archview Film Prodns; hon memb Theatre of Comedy 1989; Freeman City of London, Liveryman Worshipful Co of Carpenters 1989; *Recreations* rugby, literature, history, sumo wrestling; *Clubs* MCC; *Style*— Timothy Ackroyd, Esq; Flat 4, 33 Chepstow Rd, London W2 5BP

ACLAND, Sir Antony Arthur; GCMG (1986, KCMG 1982, CMG 1976), KCVO (1976); s of Brig Peter Bevil Edward Acland, OBE, MC, TD, *qv*; *b* 12 March 1930; *Educ* Eton, ChCh Oxford (MA 1956); *m* 1, 6 Nov 1956, (Clare) Anne (d 1984), da of F R Verdon (d 1960), of Liverpool and Sidbury, Devon; 2 s (Simon b 27 March 1958, Nicholas b 6 Feb 1960), 1 da (Lucy b 30 June 1965); m 2, 28 July 1987, Mrs Jennifer Joyce McGougan, da of Col R Dyke, OBE (d 1976), of Bicton, Devon; *Career* HM Dip Serv: joined 1953, ME Centre for Arab Studies 1954, Dubai 1955, Kuwait 1956, FO 1958-62, asst private sec to Sec of State 1959-62, UK Mission to UN 1962-66, head of Chancery UK Mission Geneva 1966-68, head Arabian Dept 1970-72, PPS to Foreign Sec 1972-75; ambass: Luxembourg 1975-77, Spain 1977-79; dep under-sec FCO 1980-82, head HM Dip Serv and perm under-sec FCO 1982-86, ambass Washington USA 1986-91; provost of Eton 1991-; Hon DCL Exeter 1988, Hon LLD College of William and Mary Virginia USA 1991; 1 cl Order of Orange-Nassau Luxembourg, 1 cl Order of Isabel the Catholic Spain; *Recreations* riding, gardening, country pursuits; *Clubs* Brooks's; *Style*— Sir Antony Acland, GCMG, KCVO; c/o Foreign and Commonwealth Office, Downing St, London SW1

ACLAND, Lt-Col Arthur William; OBE (1945), MC (1917), TD (1940); eld s of Col Alfred Dyke Acland, CBE, TD, JP (d 1937), and Hon Beatrice Smith (d 1942), da of Rt Hon W H Smith; *b* 20 Nov 1897; *Educ* Eton, RMC; *m* Dec 1926, Violet Gwendolen (d 1984), da of Rev Canon the Hon Robert Grimston (d 1927); 3 s (David Alfred b 1929, *qv*, Martin Edward b 1932, Charles Robert b 1937); *Career* Grenadier Gds 1916-22, Royal Devon Yeo 1922-40, Cmdg W Somerset Yeo 1940-43, Grenadier Gds 1944-45; WWI France (twice wounded) 1916-18, WWII G1 Welfare France; md W H Smith & Son 1924-64; OStJ; *Recreations* shooting, sailing; *Clubs* Guards, Royal Yacht Squadron; *Style*— Lt-Col Arthur Acland, OBE, MC, TD; Yeomans, 4 Queens Rd, Cowes, Isle of Wight PO31 8BQ (☎ 0983 293345)

ACLAND, David Alfred; s of Lt-Col Arthur William Acland, OBE, MC, TD, *qv*, and Violet Gwendolen, *née* Grimston; *b* 21 Oct 1929; *Educ* Eton, ChCh Oxford (MA); *m* 19 Oct 1960, Serena Elizabeth, da of late Cyril Hugh Kleinwort; 1 s (Harry Alexander b 1963), 1 da (Lucy Henrietta b 1962); *Career* 2 Lt XI Hussars (PAO) 1947-49; chm: Barclays de Zoete Wedd Asset Management Ltd, Barclays de Zoete Wedd Investment Management, Electric & Gen Investment Co plc; vice chm Barclays de Zoete Wedd Property Investment Management; dir: Barclays Fin Servs Ltd, Barclays Bank SA (Switzerland), Kleinwort Overseas Investment Trust plc; vice pres RNLI; *Recreations* sailing, hunting, tennis; *Clubs* Royal Yacht Squadron; *Style*— David Acland, Esq; Seal House, 1 Swan Lane, London EC4R 3UD (☎ 071 623 7777, fax 071 621 9411, telex 9413073)

ACLAND, Lt-Col Sir (Christopher) Guy Dyke; 6 Bt (UK 1890), of St Mary Magdalen, Oxford; MVO (1990); s of Sir Antony Acland, 5 Bt (d 1983), and Margaret, Lady Acland, *qv*; *b* 24 March 1946; *Educ* Allhallows Sch, RMA Sandhurst; *m* 1971, Christine Mary Carden, da of John William Brodie Waring; 2 s (Alexander b 1973, Hugh b 1976); *Heir* s, Alexander John Dyke b 29 May 1973; *Career* Lt-Col RA (former Maj RHA); SO1 Man S (Org) 3 MOD 1990-; *Recreations* sailing, fishing, shooting; *Clubs* Cavalry and Guards, Royal Artillery Yacht, Royal Solent Yacht, Yarmouth Sailing; *Style*— Lt-Col Sir Guy Acland, Bt, MVO

ACLAND, Sir John Dyke; 16 Bt (E 1678, with precedency from 1644), of Columb-John, Devon; eldest s of Sir Richard Thomas Dyke Acland, 15 Bt (d 1990), and Anne Stella, *née* Alford; *b* 13 May 1939; *Educ* Clifton, Magdalene Coll Cambridge (BA, MSc), Univ of West Indies; *m* 9 Sept 1961, Virginia, yr da of Roland Forge, of The Grange, Barnoldby-le-Beck, Lincs; 2 s (Dominic Dyke b 1962, Piers Dyke b 1964), 1 da (Holly Dyke b 1972); *Heir* s, Dominic Dyke Acland b 19 Nov 1990; *Style*— Sir John Acland, Bt; Sprydon, Broadclyst, Devon (☎ 039 282 412)

ACLAND, Maj-Gen Sir John Hugh Bevil; KCB (1980), CBE (1978), DL (Devon 1983); s of Brig Peter Acland, and bro of Sir Antony Acland, GCMG, KCVO, *qv*; *b* 26 Nov 1928; *Educ* Eton; *m* 1953, Myrtle, da of Brig Alastair Crawford (d 1978), of Auchentroig, Stirlingshire; 1 s (Peter b 1954), 1 da (Victoria b 1958); *Career* enlisted Scots Gds 1946 (cmmnd 1948), served with 1 or 2 Bn in Malaya, Cyprus, Egypt, Germany, Kenya, Zanzibar and NI 1949-70, equerry to HRH the Duke of Gloucester 1957-59, Staff Coll 1959, Bde Maj 4 Gds Armd Bde 1964-66, CO 2 Bn Scots Gds 1968-71, Col and BGS MOD 1972-75, Cdr Land Forces Cyprus 1976-78, GOC SW Dist 1978-81, Cdr Commonwealth Monitoring Force S Rhodesia and mil advsr to govr 1979-80, ret 1981; farmer; Hon Col: Univ of Exeter OTC 1980-, Royal Devon Yeo 1983-, Royal Wessex Yeo 1989-; pres Devon RBL 1982-, dir Allied Vintners 1982-, govr Allhallows Sch 1982-; memb: Dartmoor Nat Park Authy 1986, Steering Ctee for Schs Health Educn Unit Univ of Exeter 1987-; chm: Gallant Ordnance 1986-, SW Regnl Working Party on Alcohol 1987-; *Recreations* fly-fishing, arboriculture, destroying vermin; *Clubs* MCC, Blue Seal; *Style*— Maj-Gen Sir John Acland, KCB, CBE, DL; Feniton Court, Honiton, Devon

ACLAND, Lady; Katherine Wilder; da of John Davies Ormond, of Hawkes Bay, NZ; *m* 1935, Sir (Hugh) John Dyke Acland, KBE, JP, sometime MP in NZ (d 1981, himself eld s of Sir Hugh Thomas Dyke Acland, CMG, CBE, who was in his turn gs of Sir Thomas Dyke Acland, 10 Bt, of Columb John); 3 s (John, Mark, Simon), 3 da (Audrey, Evelyn, Sarah); *Style*— Lady Acland; Mount Peel, Peel Forest, South Canterbury, New Zealand

ACLAND, Margaret, Lady; Margaret Joan; da of late Maj Nelson Rooke, HLI, of Badminton; *m* 15 July 1944, as his 2 w, Sir Antony Guy Acland, 5 Bt (d 1983); 1 s (6 Bt, *qv*), 1 da; *Style*— Margaret, Lady Acland

ACLAND, Martin Edward; JP (Herts 1964); s of Lt-Col Arthur Acland, OBE, MC, TD, of Cowes; *b* 31 July 1932; *Educ* Eton; *m* 1956, (Anne) Maureen, *qv*, da of late

Stanley Ryder Runton, of Ilkley, Yorks; 3 s; *Career* formerly 2 Lt 11 Hussars; dir: Mercantile Credit 1970-84, Alexander Hldgs plc 1985-87, Redfearn Nat Glass 1985-88, Cambridge Corporate Consultants Ltd 1985-87; UK dir of Christian Children's Fund; memb: Legal Aid Bd 1988, Herts Family Health Servs Authy 1990; High Sheriff Herts 1978-79; *Recreations* shooting, gun dog training, sailing; *Clubs* Royal Yacht Sqdn, Seaview Yacht; *Style*— Martin Acland, Esq, JP; Standon Green End, Ware, Herts (☎ 0920 438 233)

ACLAND, (Anne) Maureen; *née* Runton; OBE (1988); da of Stanley Ryder Runton (d 1983), of Ilkley, W Yorkshire, and Kathleen Ryder Runton, CBE, *née* Carter (d 1974); *b* 3 Oct 1934; *Educ* privately in England and Paris; *m* 1956, Martin Edward Acland, *qv*, s of Lt-Col Arthur William Acland, MC, OBE; 3 s (Michael Christopher Dyke b 1958, Richard Arthur Dyke b 1962, Peter Edward Dyke b 1964); *Career* FO 1954-56; memb: Cncl St John Herts 1970, London Choral Soc 1970-78 (Cncl 1973-78); co organiser Herts Nat Gardens Scheme 1971-87, tstee and memb Nat Cncl Nat Gardens Scheme 1978-, pres and tstee Herts Nursing Tst 1975-, chm Queen's Nursing Inst 1978-, vice-pres and exec Ctee Dist Nursing Assoc UK 1979, memb Cncl and Grants Ctee Nation's Fund for Nurses 1980, dep co cmmr St John Ambulance Herts 1982-87, cdr St John Ambulance Herts 1987, chm Nat Florence Nightingale Memorial Ctee, memb Cncl Br Holistic Assoc 1987, assoc tstee Florence Nightingale Museum Tst 1988; FRSM 1990 (memb Open Section 1985-), LRAM, FRSA, MRSH; Cdr of the Venerable Order of St John, Chapter Gen OStJ London 1987-; *Recreations* country life, music, gardening, the arts (creative, performing and spectator), tennis, designing and making things; *Clubs* Seaview Yacht, RSM; *Style*— Mrs Maureen Acland, OBE; Standon Green End, Ware, Hertfordshire SG11 1BN (☎ 0920 438 527)

ACLAND, Brig Peter Bevil Edward; OBE (1945), MC (1941), TD (1948), JP (Devon 1962), DL (1948); s of Col Alfred Dyke Acland, CBE, TD, JP (d 1937), and Hon Beatrice Smith (d 1942), da of Rt Hon W H Smith; *b* 9 July 1902; *Educ* Eton, ChCh Oxford (MA); *m* 1927, Bridget Susan, da of late Canon Herbert Barnett; 2 s (Sir Antony Acland, GCMG, KCVO, and Maj-Gen Sir John Acland, KCB, CBE, *qqv*); *Career* Sudan Political Serv 1924-40; served: WWII Abyssinia, N Africa, Aegean (wounded, despatches); Brig 1945, cmd Devon Yeo 1947-51, Hon Col 1952-68; farmer 1946-80; chm Devon Agric Exec Ctee 1948-58, memb Nat Parks Commn 1953-60, T and AF Assoc Devon 1960-67; High Sheriff 1961, vice lt of Devon 1962-78; *Style*— Brig Peter Acland, OBE, MC, TD, JP, DL; Little Court, Feniton, Honiton, Devon (☎ 0404 850202)

ACLAND-HOOD, (Alexander) William; *see*: Fuller-Acland-Hood

ACLOQUE, Hon Mrs (Camilla Anne Bronwen); *née* Scott-Ellis; da of 9 Baron Howard de Walden and 5 Baron Seaford, and his 1 w, Countess Irene Harrach (d 1975); *b* 1 April 1947; *Educ* Convent of the Sacred Heart Woldingham Surrey; *m* 1971, Guy, s of John Acloque (d 1971), of Reigate, Surrey; 1 s, 2 da (twin); *Career* co-heiress to Barony of Howard de Walden; *Style*— The Hon Mrs Acloque; Alderley Grange, Wotton-under-Edge, Glos (☎ 0453 842161)

ACRES, Dr Douglas Ian; CBE, DL; s of Syndey Herbert Acres, MBE, (d 1952), of Benfleet, Essex, and Hilda Emily (d 1979), *née* Chatton; *b* 21 Nov 1924; *Educ* Westcliff HS, Borland's Victoria, London Hosp Med Coll; *m* 17 Sept 1949, Joan Marjorie, da of Charles William Bloxham (d 1966), of Benfleet, Essex; 3 da (Mary b 1952, Jane b 1955, Elizabeth b 1957); *Career* RAF med branch 1951-53 (Acting Sqdn Ldr, vice pres Med Bd, Air Crew Selection Centre, Hornchurch); house surgeon and casualty registrar King George Hosp Ilford 1949-51, GP 1953-84; Md Remploy Ltd 1962-, med correspondent SE Essex Evening Echo 1967-, med advsr Congregation Fedn 1985-; author of articles and chapters on medico-legal matters 1968-; memb: Benfleet UDC 1960-65 (chm Pub Health Ctee), ctee on Mentally Abnormal Offenders 1972-75, Lord Chancellor's Essex Advsy Ctee 1973-84, Int Dept Ctee on Alcoholism 1975-78, Parole Bd 1984-87; chm: Governing Body King John Sch Thundersley 1971-89, Rochford Bench 1974-84 (memb 1958-), Essex Cncl on Alcoholism 1981-86, Cncl Magistrates' Assoc 1984-87; pres Essex Branch Nat Assoc Probation Offrs 1983-89; lay pastor Battlesbridge Free Church and Woodham Ferrers Congregatio Church 1984-; AOC's commendation and vote of thanks E coast flood disaster 1953; Freeman City of London, Liveryman Society of Apothecaries 1968; MRCS, LRCP 1949, MRCGP 1968, DMJ (clin) 1968, OStJ; *Clubs* RSM; *Style*— Dr Douglas Acres, CBE, DL; Thundersley Lodge, Runnymede Chase, Thundersley, Benfleet, Essex SS7 3DB (☎ 0268 793241)

ACTON, Dowager Baroness; Daphne; *née* Strutt; o da of 4 Baron Rayleigh, JP, DL, FRS (d 1947), and his 1 w, Lady Mary Hilda Clements (d 1919), 2 da of 4 Earl of Leitrim; *b* 5 Nov 1911; *m* 25 Nov 1931, 3 Baron Acton, CMG, MBE, TD (d 1989); 5 s, 6 da (1 decd); *Style*— The Rt Hon the Dowager Lady Acton; Marcham Priory, nr Abingdon, Oxon OX13 6NT (☎ 0865 391260)

ACTON, Sir Harold Mario Mitchell; CBE (1965); s of Arthur Mario Acton, and Hortense, *née* Mitchell; *b* 5 July 1904; *Educ* Eton, ChCh Oxford (BA); *Career* served WWII RAF, seconded to SHAEF (Paris) 1944; lectured in English literature Peking National Univ and Normal Coll; author; vice chm Br Inst of Florence; Grand Offr of the Italian Republic; Hon DLitt (New York); FRSL; kt 1974; *Recreations* baiting Philistines; *Clubs* Savile; *Style*— Sir Harold Acton, CBE; Villa La Pietra, Florence, Italy (☎ 496 156)

ACTON, 4 Baron Acton (UK 1869); Sir Richard Gerald Lyon-Dalberg-Acton; 11 Bt (E 1644); also a Patrician of Naples; patron of one living (but being a Roman Catholic cannot present); eldest s of 3 Baron Acton, CMG, MBE, TD (d 1989), and Hon Daphne, *qv*, *née* Strutt, da of 4 Baron Rayleigh; *b* 30 July 1941; *Educ* St George's Coll Salisbury Rhodesia, Trinity Coll Oxford; *m* 1, 28 Aug 1965, Hilary Juliet Sarah (d 1973), 2 da of Dr Osmond Laurence Charles Cookson, of Perth, WA; 1 s (Hon John Charles Ferdinand Harold); m 2, 1974 (m dis 1987), Judith Garfield, da of the Hon Garfield Todd, of Hokonu Ranch, P O Dadaya, Rhodesia (formerly PM of S Rhodesia); m 3, 19 March 1988, Patricia, o da of late M Morey Nassif, of 115 34th Street, South East, Cedar Rapids, Iowa 53403, USA; *Heir* s, Hon John Charles Ferdinand Harold Lyon-Dalberg-Acton b 19 Aug 1966; *Career* barr Inner Temple 1976; dir Coutts & Co 1971-74; sr law offr Zimbabwe Miny of Justice Legal and Parly Affairs 1981-85; writer on American history for academic journals; *Style*— The Rt Hon the Lord Acton; Marcham Priory, nr Abingdon, Oxon; 100 Red Oak Lane SE, Cedar Rapids, Iowa 52403, USA

ACTON-STOW, Derek; OBE (1979); s of Ivor Acton-Stow (d 1972), of E Dean, E Sussex, and Ada Beatrice, *née* Smith; *b* 20 Sept 1929; *Educ* Epsom GS, Kingston College of Art; *m* 1955 (m dis 1959), Julia Weightman; m 2, 25 May 1959, Gwyneth, da of David John Pugh (d 1965), of London; 3 da (Anna b 1959, Katherine b 1962, Harriet b 1968); *Career* architect; Powell and Moya 1953-62; sr ptnr: Derek Stow & Ptnrs 1962-, Harris Stow Ptnrship 1987-; awards incl: Civic Tst 1970, 1973, 1978 and 1986, Concrete Soc 1973, Euro Prize for Architecture 1974, RIBA 1978, Structural Steel 1978 and 1980; memb Cncl Cities of London and Westminster Soc Architects, assoc Soc Artist Architects; Freeman City of London 1984, liveryman Worshipful Co of Chartered Architects 1989; FRIBA 1951, FFB; *Recreations* visual arts, music, literature; *Clubs* Arts; *Style*— Derek Acton-Stow, Esq, OBE; 57 Sutherland St, Pimlico, London SW1V 4JY (☎ 071 834 2599); 14 Old Queen St, Westminster, London SW1H 9HS (☎ 071 222 9237, fax 071 222 8773)

ADAM; *see*: Forbes-Adam

ADAM, Beverley Ann; da of Clement Alfred Adam, and Nora Margaret, *née* Willis; *b* 11 Feb 1953; *Educ* King George V Sch Hong Kong, Univ of Warwick (LLB); *m* 16 April 1977, Graham Robert Starling, s of Arthur Ewart Starling, MBE; 2 s (Gareth b 20 April 1982, Sean b 12 Dec 1985), 1 da (Natasha 12 Nov 1990); *Career* slr and ptnr Linklaters & Paines; memb Worshipful Co of City of London Slrs; memb: Law Soc, UKELA, Ctee Users Ctee of Mayors and City of London Ct, LSLA; *Style*— Miss Beverley Adam; Linklaters & Paines, Barrington House, 59-67 Gresham St, London EC2V 7JA (☎ 071 606 7080, fax 071 606 5113, telex 884349)

ADAM, (David Stuart) Gordon; s of James Adam RCNC (d 1973), and Florence Victoria, *née* Kilpatrick (d 1970); *b* 21 Dec 1927; *Educ* Upper Canada Coll, Queen's Univ Belfast (LLB), Trinity Hall Cambridge (MA, LLM), Harvard Business Sch (AMP); *m* 4 Sept 1965, Rosanne, da of William Watson (d 1979), of Ardlamont; 2 s (James b 1966, Alastair b 1972), 1 da (Alexandra b 1968); *Career* WO 1952-53; called to the Bar Gray's Inn 1951; Barclays Bank: joined 1954, gen mangr 1968, dir Barclays Bank UK 1977-87, dep chm Barclays Trust Company Ltd 1977-82; chm International Trust Group 1983-89; chm Wycombe Abbey Sch 1981-91; *Clubs* Boodle's, Kandahar; *Style*— Gordon Adam, Esq; Mulberry Hill, Wendover, Bucks HP22 6NQ; Quinta dos Ciprestes, Sta Barbara de Nexe, Portugal; 54 Lombard St, London EC3P 3AH

ADAM, Dr Gordon Johnston; MEP (Lab) Northumbria 1979-; s of John Craig Adam (d 1969), of Carlisle, and Deborah Armstrong, *née* Johnston (d 1978); *b* 28 March 1934; *Educ* Carlisle GS, Univ of Leeds (BSc, PhD); *m* 22 Dec 1973, Sarah Jane, da of John Lockhart Seely (d 1990), of Stak Northumberland; 1 s ((John) Duncan b 11 May 1979); *Career* mining engr NCB 1959-79; dep ldr North Tyneside Met Borough Cncl 1975-80; memb Northern Econ Planning Cncl 1974-79; vice chm Euro Parliament's Energy Res and Technol Ctee 1984-; MInstME 1953; *Style*— Dr Gordon Adam, MEP; East House Farm, Killingworth Village, Newcastle upon Tyne NE12 0BQ (☎ 091 216 0154); office: 10 Coach Rd, Wallsend, Tyne and Wear NE28 6JA (☎ 091 263 5838)

ADAM, Nigel David; s of Maj David Lionel Adam, TD, of The Grange, Ruckinge, Ashford, Kent, and Marjorie Diana, *née* Sharpe; *b* 7 April 1946; *Educ* The King's Sch Canterbury, Univ of St Andrews (MA); *m* 29 Aug 1987, Katherine, da of Edward Neil McMillan, of 41 Grapevine Rd, Wenham, Massachusetts, USA; *Career* corr Reuters Europe 1971-78, US ed Euromoney New York 1981-83, dep ed Euromoney London 1983-85, ed Business Magazine 1985-86, managing ed Cornhill Pubns Ltd 1987-89; contrib to jls incl: International Herald Tribune, Financial Times, The European; *Recreations* tennis, squash, cricket, backgammon; *Clubs* RAC; *Style*— Nigel Adam, Esq; Tudor Lodge, Compton Bassett, Calne, Wiltshire SN11 8RA (☎ 0249 816796)

ADAM, Robert Marshall; s of Dr Robert Adam (d 1987) of Claremont, 2 Crescent Rd, Enfield, and Dr Grace Jane Adam, *née* Marshall (d 1991); *b* 12 June 1926; *Educ* Bedales, Christ's Coll Cambridge, Bart's; *m* 17 Oct 1956, Valerie Patricia, da of Sqdn Ldr Roy Travers (d 1965); 4 s (Robert Travers b 10 April 1959, James Thomas Simon b 6 March 1961, William David Roy b 24 June 1966, Matthew Neil Peter b 29 June 1967); *Career* Sub Lt RNVR 1943-47; conslt obstetrician and gynaecologist W Somerset Clinical Area 1965-; memb Hosp Recognition Ctee RCOG 1983-89; memb: BMA, SW Obsetricians and Gynaecologists Soc, N England Obstetricians and Gynaecologists Soc; *Recreations* gardening, reading, travel; *Clubs* Naval; *Style*— Robert Adam, Esq; Sherford House, Sherford, Taunton, Somerset TA1 3RB (☎ 0823 284598); Somerset Nuffield Hospital, Staplegrove, Taunton, Somerset

ADAMS; *see*: Small-Adams

ADAMS, Dr Aileen Kirkpatrick; CBE (1988); da of Dr Joseph Adams, MC (d 1985), of Sheffield, and Agnes, *née* Munro (d 1983); *b* 5 Sept 1923; *Educ* Farringtons Sch Chislehurst Kent, Univ of Sheffield (MB ChB); *Career* clinical fell Massachusetts Gen Hosp Boston USA 1955-57, first asst Nuffield Dept of Anaesthetics Oxford 1957-59, conslt anaesthetist Addenbrooke's Hosp Cambridge 1960-84, sr lectr Lagos Univ Med Sch Nigeria 1963-64, assoc lectr Univ of Cambridge 1977-84, dean Faculty of Anaesthetists RCSEng 1985-88; examiner: Final MB Clinical Pharmacology Univ of Cambridge 1977-80, Final FFARCS 1979-82; dining memb Trinity Hall Cambridge, Univ of Cambridge mass 1977; hon memb Assoc of Anaesthetists of GB and Ireland 1989 (hon sec 1970 vice pres 1976-78), memb Ed Bd Anaesthesia 1972-85; pres: Soc of Anaesthetists of SW Region 1981, East Anglian Assoc of Anaesthetists 1983-85, History of Anaesthesia Soc; memb Cncl RCS 1982-84 and 1985-88; Hon FFA SA 1987, RSM (pres Anaesthetics Section 1985-86), FRCS 1988, FFARCS 1954; *Recreations* choral singing, hill walking, skiing, history; *Style*— Dr Aileen Adams, CBE; 90 High St, Great Abington, Cambridge CB1 6AE (☎ 0223 891523)

ADAMS, Air Vice-Marshal Alexander Annan; CB (1957), DFC (1944); s of Capt Norman Anderson Adams, of Durham; *b* 14 Nov 1908; *Educ* Beechmont Sevenoaks, Switzerland, Austria; *m* 1933, Eileen Mary, da of William Charles O'Neill, of Dublin; 1 s, (and 1 da decd); *Career* cmmnd RAF 1930, Pilot 54 Fighter Sqdn RAF 1931-33, Flying Instr 1933-35, Asst Air Attaché Berlin 1937-39, Intelligence Missions 1940-42, cmd 49 Lancaster Sqdn 1943-44, RAF Station Binbrook 1948-50; NATO Standing Gp Washington 1951-53, Air Attaché Bonn 1955, MOD 1956, COS FEAF 1957-59; Hawker Siddeley Aviation 1961-66; dir Mental Health Fndn 1970-77; *Books* Passing Experiences (1980); *Recreations* Painting; *Clubs* RAF; *Style*— Air Vice-Marshal Alexander Adams, CB, DFC; 31 Saffrons Court, Compton Palace Rd, Eastbourne, East Sussex BN21 1DX

ADAMS, Alfred William David; s of Alfred Adams (d 1928), and Louisa, *née* West (d 1945); *b* 2 April 1905; *Educ* St Lukes Sch, Kingston Tech Coll; *m* 1, 4 Aug 1934 (m dis 1977), Barbara Edith, da of Harold George Ely (d 1960); 1 s (Graham David b 1935), 1 da (Sylvia Lorraine Barbara b 1944); m 2, 1978, Jaqueline Andre Tudor-Pole; *Career* WWII Upper Thames Patrol HG 1940-41, entertainments offr 51 E Surrey Regt 1941-43; unit controller Miny of Tport 1943-51; md: Adams Bros Ltd 1926-52, Adams & Adams Ltd 1936-, George Bristow Ltd 1942-52, Adams Randall Ltd 1970-82; dir Adfin Ltd 1963-; memb Union Fraterneile Franco - Britannique (Br Section) 1951- (pres 1975-); memb New Malden Rotary Club 1954, fndr memb Mitre Club with Sir John Boyd-Carpenter Lord Marchwood 1956; Liveryman Worshipful Co of Clockmakers 1976; MIMI 1936, FIMM 1962, FGEM 1988; *Recreations* veteran Rolls Royces, veteran car rallies; *Clubs* Rolls Royce Euthusiasts, ex Monte Carlo Rally Br Competitors; *Style*— Alfred Adams, Esq; Mon Desir, Coney Six, East Wittering, Chichester, W Sussex PO20 8DL (☎ 0243 671 234); Adams House, Dickerage Lane, New Malden, Surrey KT3 3SF (☎ 081 949 1121)

ADAMS, Prof Anthony Peter; s of Sqdn Ldr Henry William John Adams (d 1986), and Winifred Louise, *née* Brazenor (d 1989); *b* 17 Oct 1936; *Educ* Epsom Coll, Univ of London (MB BS, PhD); *m* 1, 30 Sept 1961 (m dis 1972), Martha Jill Vearncombe, da of Herbert William Davis (d 1985), of Yeovil, Somerset; 2 s (Christopher b 1963, Paul b 1965); m 2, 12 May 1973, Veronica Rosemary, da of Raymond Ashley John, of Maidenhead, Berks; 1 s (Adrian b 1979), 1 da (Jenny b 1975); *Career* conslt anaesthetist and clinical lectr Nuffield Dept of Anaesthetics Oxford 1969-79, prof of anaesthetics Univ of London at United Med and Dental Schs of Guy's and St Thomas's Hosps 1979-, hon conslt anaesthetist Guy's Hosp 1979-; examiner: FFARCS 1974-86, RCVS 1986-, Univ of the W Indies 1986-88, Univ of Wales 1988-, Univ of Singapore

1988, Chinese Univ Hong Kong 1990-; regnl advsr in anaesthetics SE Thames 1980-88, consIt SE Asia WHO 1982; memb: Exec Ctee Anaesthetic Res Soc 1983 (chm 1990-), Safety Ctee Assoc Anaesthetist GB and Ireland 1987-, Cncl Coll of Anaesthetists 1989-; sr Euro Acad of Anaesthesiology 1985- (academician 1981-); visiting professorships incl: Univ of Texas 1983, John Hopkins Hosp Baltimore 1983, Univ of Yale 1984, Univ of Zimbabwe 1985, Univ of W Ontario 1985; memb: Shabbington Parish Cncl 1977-79, Bd of Govrs Sutton HS for Girls 1988-; FFARCS; *Books* Principles and Practice of Blood - Gas Analysis (jtly, 2 edn 1982), Intensive Care (jtly, 1984), Emergency Anaesthesia (jtly, 1986), Recent Advances in Anaesthesia (jtly, 3 edn 1990); *Recreations* cinema, croquet, tennis, badger watching; *Clubs* Royal Soc of Med; *Style*— Prof Anthony Adams; Dept Anaesthetics, Guy's Hospital, London SE1 9RT (☎ 071 955 4047)

ADAMS, Barbara Georgina; *née* Bishop; da of Charles Bishop (d 1980), and Ellaline, *née* Cowdrey (d 1972); *b* 19 Feb 1945; *Educ* Godolphin & Latymer GS, Univ of London (Dip Archaeology), Univ of London (Cert Geology); *m* 27 Sept 1967, Robert Frederick Adams, s of Frederick Adams (ka 1943); *Career* sci asst Entomology and Sub-Dept of Anthropology Br Museum of Nat History 1962-65, curator Petrie Museum of Egyptian Archaeology 1984- (asst 1965-75, asst curator 1975-84); memb: London Fedn of Museums and Art Galleries, London Museum Consultative Ctee, EES, IAE, Palaeopathology Assoc; active memb Lib Pty, candidate for GLC 1982; *Books* Ancient Hierakonpolis (1974), The Koptos Lions (1984), The Fort Cemetery at Hierakonpolis (1987), Predynastic Egypt (1988), ed Shire Egyptology series; *Recreations* geology, film, countryside, museums and galleries; *Style*— Mrs Barbara Adams; Petrie Museum of Egyptian Archaeology, University Coll London, Gower St, London WC1E 6BT (☎ 071 387 7050, ext 2882)

ADAMS, Bernard Charles; s of Charles Willoughby Adams (d 1963), of Ryde, IOW, and Emily Alice, *née* Ambrose (d 1950); *b* 29 Oct 1915; *Educ* King James I Sch IOW; *m* 1, 1942, Marjorie Barrett (d 1986), da of William Henry Frederick Weller (d 1918), of Barnoldswick, Yorks; 3 da (Jane, Gillian d 1983, Catherine d 1973); m 2, 1989, Betty Isabel Tucker, *née* Fei; *Career* TA 1938-39, Nat Serv WWII 57 Wessex Heavy Anti-Aircraft Regt RA, Battle of Britain def of Portsmouth and Southampton, 107 HAA Regt (Mobile) RA in UK, France (Normandy), Belgium, Holland, Germany, Capt RA (despatches); architect; sr architect Derbyshire CC 1951-54, asst co architect Kent CC 1954-59, dep co architect Herts CC 1959-60, co architect Somerset CC 1960-80, vice pres RIBA 1970-72 (memb Cncl 1963-69 and 1970-76); chm: SW Regnl Cncl RIBA 1972-74, Structure of the Profession Study RIBA 1976-79; pres: Co Architects' Soc 1973-74 (vice pres 1971-73), Soc of Chief Architects of Local Authorities (SCALA) 1975-76 (vice pres 1974-75, hon memb 1983-); memb: Nat Consultative Cncl for the Bldg and Civil Engrg Industs 1974-80, Bd of Architectural Studies Univ of Bristol 1964-74; architect advsr to Assoc of CC's 1971-80, fndr chm Architects' Ctee Consortium for Method Bldg 1961-68, fndr memb Taunton Theatre Tst 1972 (memb Tst Ctee 1972-, chm 1986-89); RIBA Architecture Award 1970, Commendation 1974, Heritage Year Award (Euro Architectural Heritage Year) 1975, Civic Tst Awards 1962-68, 1971 and Commendation 1965; ARIBA, FRIBA, FRSA; *Books* contrib to jl of the RIBA and other professional jls; *Recreations* arts, theatre, languages; *Style*— Bernard Adams, Esq; Meadowside, Wild Oak Lane, Trull, Taunton, Somerset TA3 7JT (☎ 0823 272 485)

ADAMS, Dr Bernard George; s of Arthur Adams (d 1975), and Sarah, *née* Morris (d 1971); *b* 9 Aug 1931; *Educ* Univ of London, London Hosp (MSc, MB BS, DPM Acad); *m* 21 Sept 1958, Caryle Ann, da of Robert Julius Steen (d 1968); 2 s (Peter Neil b 1963, James Robert b 1968), 1 da (Madeleine Clare b 1965); *Career* sr registrar: Bethlem Royal and Maudsley Hosps 1965-67, Royal Hammersmith Postgraduate Hosp 1965-67; consIt and hon sr lectr UCH London 1968; conrib to literature on psychopharmacology and liaison psychiatry; FRCP 1973, FRCPsych 1974, FRSM; *Recreations* music, theatre; *Style*— Dr Bernard Adams; 35 Cholmeley Park, Highgate, London N6 5EL; Coutancie, Nanteuil Auriac de Bourzac, France; 7 Wimpole St, London W1 (☎ 071 580 1584)

ADAMS, Bernard Ross Rainsford; s of Charles Bernard Adams, and Marie Edwina, *née* Rainsford; *b* 1 Sept 1939; *Educ* Portora Royal Sch Enniskillen, Trinity Coll Dublin; *m* 21 Sept 1958, Caryle Ann, da of Robert Julius Steen (d 1968); 2 s (Peter Neil b 1963, James Robert b 1968), 1 da (Madeline Clare b 1965); *Career* sr registrar: Bethlem Royal and Mandsley Hosps 1965-67, Royal Hammersmith Postgraduate Hosp 1965-67; Univ Coll Hosp London: consIt 1968 hon sr lectr 1968; conrib to literature on psychopharmacology and liaison psychiatry; FRCP 1973, FRCPsych 1974, FRSM; *Recreations* music, theatre; *Style*— Bernard Adams, Esq; 99 Palewell Park, East Sheen, London SW14 8JJ BBC TV, Villiers House, The Broadway, London W5 2PA (☎ 01 991 8044)

ADAMS, Lady Celia Anne; *née* Fortescue; da (by 1 m) of 7 Earl Fortescue, *qv*; *b* 30 Dec 1957; *m* 10 Dec 1988, David A S Adams, yst s of Dr M S Adams, of Seaview, Isle of Wight; 1 da (b 30 Sept 1990); *Style*— The Lady Celia Adams

ADAMS, David Howard; s of Capt Bernard Adams, RA (d 1982), of Newcastle, and Eve, *née* Glass (d 1987); *b* 15 Nov 1943; *Educ* Manchester GS; *m* 22 June 1969, Zoe, da of Victor Joseph Dwek (d 1989), of Manchester; 2 da (Gisele b 1970, Zanine b 1975); *Career* dir Henry Cooke Lumsden plc 1975, chief exec Henry Cooke Group plc 1988; past chm: Manchester Stock Exchange, Inst for Fiscal Studies NW; memb Worshipful Co of CA's 1978; past memb MENSA, FCA 1967, FRSA 1988; *Recreations* acting, reading, trying to get fit; *Style*— David H Adams, Esq; 1 King St, Manchester M60 3AH (☎ 061 834 2332, fax as phone, telex 667783, car 0836 600714)

ADAMS, Prof David Keith; s of Sidney Adams (d 1976), of Bredon, Worcestershire, and Dagmar Ruth Cawnpore, *née* Judge (d 1985); *b* 11 Aug 1931; *Educ* Abbey House and William Ferrer's GS Tewkesbury, Univ of Rennes, Clare Coll Cambridge (BA, MA), Yale Univ (AM), Oriel and Nuffield Coll Oxford (MA, DPhil); *m* 23 March 1961 (m dis 1981), Virginia Mary Hope, da of Walton White (d 1976), of Edinburgh, Scotland; 3 s (Giles b 4 March 1963, Roderick b 25 Nov 1965, Thomas b 9 June 1967); *Career* Henry fellowship Yale 1954-55, tutor in modern history Univ of Oxford 1955-59, visiting lectr in American studies Univ of Manchester 1959-60, lectr in American studies UCNS 1961 (asst lectr in history 1957-60), ACLS fellowship George Washington Univ 1965-66; Univ of Keele: sr lectr in American studies 1965-72, dir David Bruce Centre for American Studies 1969-, head Dept of American Studies 1965-, prof 1972-; visiting sr scholar Clare Coll Cambridge 1970, visiting prof Univ of Tulsa 1981, visiting scholar Western Carolina Univ 1987; chm: Br-American Assocs London, Canada-UK Colloquia; memb Advsy Ctee Roosevelt Study Centre Middelburg The Netherlands; memb BAAS, OAH, SHAFR; *Books* America in the Twentieth Century (1967), An Atlas of North American Affairs (1969 and 1979), Franklin D Roosevelt and the New Deal (1979), British Documents on Foreign Affairs: North America 1919-1939 (ed 25 vols, 1986-), American Literary Landscapes: The Fiction and the Fact (ed, 1988) Studies in US Politics (ed, 1989); *Recreations* books, gardening; *Style*— Prof David Adams; 17 Springpool, Keele, Newcastle-under-Lyme, Staffs ST5 5BN (☎ 0782 627392); David Bruce Centre for American Studies, University of Keele, Keele, Staffs ST5 5BG (☎ 0782 621111, fax 0782 613847, telex 36113 UNKLI)

ADAMS, Douglas Noel; s of Christopher Douglas Adams (d 1985), and Janet, *née* Donovan (now Mrs Thrift); *b* 11 March 1952; *Educ* Brentwood Sch, St John's Coll Cambridge (BA, MA); *Career* radio and TV writer 1974-78, BBC producer 1978, BBC TV script ed 1978-80, novelist 1979-; Publications: The Hitch Hiker's Guide to The Galaxy (1979), The Restaurant at the End of the Universe (1980), Life, The Universe and Everything (1982), So Long, and Thanks for All the Fish (1984), The Meaning of Liff (with John Lloyd, 1984), The Original Hitch Hiker Radio Scripts (1985), Dirk Gently's Holistic Detective Agency (1987), The Long Dark Tea-Time of the Soul (1988), Last Chance to See (with Mark Cawardine, 1990), The Deeper Meaning of Liff (1990); *Recreations* buying equipment for recreations I think I might like to take up one day; *Clubs* Groucho; *Style*— Douglas Adams, Esq; c/o Ed Victor Ltd, 162 Wardour St, London W1V 3AT (☎ 071 734 4795, fax 071 494 3400)

ADAMS, Douglas William; s of William Adams, of 14 Muirfield, Perth, and Elizabeth, *née* Black; *b* 17 May 1953; *Educ* Perth Acad, Univ of Glasgow (MA, univ golf champion), Univ of Strathclyde (MBA); *m* 28 June 1975, Jacqueline Mary, da of Alfred John Ferguson; 1 s (Euan b 6 Sept 1980), 1 da (Keren Mhairi b 10 Dec 1982); *Career* sr economic asst Scottish Office Edinburgh 1975-78, admin Euro Cmmn Brussels 1978-82; economist: Scottish Devpt Agency Glasgow 1982-86, Scottish Provident Edinburgh 1968-88; mktg dir Templeton Investment Management Ltd Edinburgh 1988-; *Recreations* golf, running; *Clubs* Dunbar Golf, Luffness Golf, Islay Golf; *Style*— Douglas Adams, Esq; Templeton Investment Management Ltd, Templeton House, Atholl Crescent, Edinburgh EH3 8HA (☎ 031 228 3932, 031 228 4506)

ADAMS, Hon Mrs (Eileen Esther); *née* Handcock; da of late 7 Baron Castlemaine; *b* 14 Nov 1931; *m* 1959, Fl-Lt Terence Frank Adams, RAF (ret), son of late Joseph Adams, of Wolverhampton; 2 s (Patrick b 1960, Niall b 1968), 1 da (Siobhan b 1962); *Clubs* RAF; *Style*— The Hon Mrs Adams

ADAMS, Hon Lady ((Mary) Elizabeth); *née* Lawrence; da of 3 Baron Trevethin and (1) Oaksey, DSO, TD, PC (d 1971), and Marjorie, *née* Robinson; *b* 20 Nov 1922; *m* 1954, Sir Philip George Doyne Adams, KCMG, *qv*; 2 s, 2 da; *Style*— The Hon Lady Adams; 78 Sussex Square, London W2

ADAMS, Lady; Esther Marie Ottilie; *née* Overdyck; *m* 1980, as his 2 w, Sir Maurice Edward Adams, KBE (d 1982), sometime Civil Engineer in Chief to The Admiralty; *Style*— Lady Adams; 32 Cavendish Ave, Ealing, London W13 (☎ 01 998 2376)

ADAMS, Gerard (Gerry); MP (Sinn Fein) Belfast West 1983-; s of Gerard Adams; *b* 6 Oct 1948; *Educ* St Mary's GS Belfast; *m* 1971, Colette McArdle; 1 s; *Career* fndr memb Northern Ireland Civil Rights Assoc; interned by British Govt 1971, released for talks with Govt 1972, re-interned 1973; sentenced to 18 months imprisonment for attempted escape; released 1977; charged with IRA membership 1978, but charges unproven and released after seven months; elected to Northern Ireland Assembly 1982; pres Sinn Fein 1983- (vice pres 1978-83); *Books* Peace In Ireland, Politics of Irish Freedom, Falls Memories, Pathway to Peace, Cage 11; *Style*— Gerry Adams, Esq, MP; 51-53 Bothar na bhFal, Beal Feirste BT12 4PD, Northern Ireland; House of Commons, London SW1A OAA

ADAMS, Haldane George; s of George Edward Adams (d 1952), of Paignton, Devon, and Gwendoline Ivy, *née* Hill (d 1988); *b* 12 March 1932; *Educ* King Edward VI Sch Devon; *m* 13 June 1953, Doreen Margaret, da of Maj F A Monaghan, of Emsworth, Hants; 1 s (Stephen b 1953); *Career* cmmnd Lt Light Inf Somerset 1950-53; gen mangr Office Supplies IBM S Africa 1969-75, mktg dir Kores Nordic Ltd 1975-, md Keymax International Ltd 1988-; chm: Govrs Nazeing Park Sch Essex, Thaxted Branch Cons Assoc; vice chm Charity for Physically Handicapped Thaxted Essex; MInstD 1977; *Recreations* sailing, golf; *Style*— Haldane Adams, Esq; Drive House, Watling Lane, Thaxted, Essex (☎ 0371 830 854); Keymax International Ltd, West Rd, Templefields, Harlow, Essex CM20 2AL (☎ 0279 454455, fax 0279 445550, telex 81456)

ADAMS, Prof (James) Hume; s of John Boyd Adams (d 1979), of Paisley, and Elizabeth Scott, *née* Neill (d 1975); *b* 31 Dec 1929; *Educ* Paisley GS, Univ of Glasgow (MB ChB, MD), Univ of London (PhD, DSc); *m* 9 Sept 1954, Eileen Rachel, da of James Lawson (d 1967), of Glasgow; 3 s (Nigel b 21 Jan 1956, Peter b 8 June 1958, Robin b 5 Feb 1961); *Career* Nat Serv RAMC 1955-57; specialist in pathology RAMC 1955-57, MRC res fell London 1957-59, prof of neuropathology Univ of Glasgow 1971- (lectr, sr lectr, read 1959-71); pres Br Neuropathological Soc 1981-83 (sec 1968-76), pres Int Soc of Neuropathology 1990- (sec gen 1978-86); FRCPath 1973 (MRCPath 1963), FRCP Glas 1977 (MRCP Glas 1973), FRSE 1988; *Books* Brain Biopsy (1982), Atlas of Post-Mortem Techniques in Neuropathology (1982), An Introduction to Neuropathology (1988); *Recreations* golf, bridge; *Style*— Prof Hume Adams; 31 Burnhead Rd, Newlands, Glasgow G43 2SU (☎ 041 637 1481); Institute of Neurological Sciences, Southern General Hospital, Glasgow GS1 4TF (☎ 041 445 2466)

ADAMS, Jennifer; *née* Crisp; da of Arthur Roy Thomas Crisp, and Joyce Muriel, *née* Davey; *b* 1 Feb 1948; *Educ* City of London Sch IPRA Staff Coll; *m* 21 Sept 1968, Terence William Adams; *Career* supt Central Royal Parks 1983-; FILAM, Dip PRA, FI Hort; *Clubs* Soroptimists' International; *Style*— Mrs Jennifer Adams; Central Royal Parks, The Storeyard, Hyde Park, London W2 2UH

ADAMS, John Crawford; OBE (1977); s of Dr Archibald Crawford Adams (d 1943), of W Hallam, Derbyshire, and Ethel, *née* Parkin (d 1943); *b* 25 Sept 1913; *Educ* Oakham Sch, Univ of London; *m* 1, 10 Oct 1940, Joan (d 1981), da of W Spencer Elphinstone, MBE (d 1969); m 2, 23 Feb 1990, Marguerite, da of Norman H Cross (d 1968); *Career* MO RAF 1939-45; consIt orthopaedic surgn St Vincent's Orthopaedic Hosp Eastcote Pinn 1948-68; prodn ed jl Bone and Joint Surgery 1954-84, hon consIt orthopaedic surgn St Mary's Hosp London 1980- (consIt 1948-80); FRSM 1950; *Books* Outline of Orthopaedics (1956, 11 edn, 1990), Outline of Fractures (1957, 9 edn 1987), Ischio-Femoral Arthrodesis (1966), Arthritis and Back Pain (1972), Standard Orthopaedic Operations (1976, 3 edn 1985), Shakespeare's Physic, Lore and Love (1989); *Recreations* silversmithing, jazz; *Style*— John Crawford Adams, Esq, OBE; 126 Harley St, London W1 (☎ 071 935 2030)

ADAMS, John Douglas Richard; s of Gordon Arthur Richard Adams (d in enemy hands 1944), and Marjorie Ethel, *née* Ongley (d 1983); *b* 19 March 1940; *Educ* Watford GS, Univ of Durham (LLB); *m* 12 April 1966, Anne Easton, da of Robert Easton Todd (d 1967); 2 da (Katharine b 1975, Caroline b 1978); *Career* called to the Bar Lincoln's Inn 1968; lectr in law: Univ of Newcastle upon Tyne 1963-71, UCL 1971-78; also practised at the Revenue Bar until 1978; special cmmnr of Income Tax 1978-82, current office Registrar of Civil Appeals 1982-; hon lectr St Edmund Hall Oxford 1975-; *Books* International Taxation of Multinational Enterprises (with J Whalley, 1977), Supreme Court Practice (ed, 1990), Atkin's Court Forms (1984), Chitty & Jacob's Queen's Bench Forms (ed, 1987); *Recreations* music, walking, dining; *Style*— J D R Adams, Esq; Royal Courts of Justice, Strand, London WC2A 2LL (☎ 071 936 6017)

ADAMS, Rear Adm John Harold; CB (1967), LVO (1957); s of H V Adams (d 1938), of Alnmouth, Northumberland; *b* 19 Dec 1918; *Educ* Glenalmond; *m* 1, 1943 (m dis 1961), Mary, da of Arthur Parker, of London; 1 s (decd); m 2, 1961, Ione, MVO, JP, da of late Col James Alister Eadie, DSO, TD; 2 s, 2 da; *Career* joined RN 1936, served WWII (despatches), Lt 1941, Lt Cdr 1949, Cdr 1951, Capt 1957, Rear Adm 1966, ACNS (policy) 1966-68, ret; dir Paper Indust Trg Bd and Employers' Fedn of Papermakers 1968-74, DG Br Paper and Bd Indust Fedn 1974-83; md DUO (UK) Ltd (Interview Guidance) 1983-; FIPM; *Recreations* photography, fishing; *Clubs* Army and Navy; *Style*— Rear Adm John Adams, CB, LVO; The Oxdrove House, Burghclere, Newbury, Berks (☎ 063 527 385)

ADAMS, Prof John Norman; s of Vincent Smith Adams, of Lintz Green Cottage, Lintz Green, Tyne & Wear, and Elsie, *née* Davison (d 1964); *b* 24 Dec 1939; *Educ* Newcastle upon Tyne Royal GS, Univ of Durham; *Career* slr in private practice 1965-71, lectr in law Univ of Sheffield 1971-79, called to the Bar Inner Temple 1984, prof of commercial law Univ of Kent 1987- (sr lectr in law 1979-87); visiting prof: Univ of Maryland 1974-75, Nat Law Centre Washington DC 1981, Notre Dame Law Sch Concannon Inst 1986-87, Université Paris X 1989-91; sec Br Literary Artistic Copyright Assoc; *Books* A Bibliography of Eighteenth Century Legal Literature (1982), Franchising (3 edn, 1990), Merchandising Intellectual Property (1987), Understanding Contract Law (1987), Commercial Hiring and Leasing (1989); *Recreations* music, walking; *Clubs* Savage, Lansdowne; *Style*— Prof John Adams; 26 Priory Terrace, London NW6 4DH (☎ 071 328 8676); 5 Wavecrest, Whitstable, Kent CT5 IEH (☎ 0227 274956); Keynes Coll, Univ of Kent, Canterbury CT2 7NP (☎ 0227 764000, fax 0227 274956); 1 Essex Court, Temple, London EC4 9AR (☎ 071 936 3030, fax 071 583 1606)

ADAMS, John Trevor; s of Flt Lt Claude Walter Adams (d 1985) of Wembley, Middx, and Ann Fletcher Gordon, *née* Taylor; *b* 2 April 1936; *Educ* UCS; *m* 6 July 1963, Elizabeth Mary, da of Montague William Lacey (d 1981), of Lytham, Lancs; 1 s (David John b 1968), 1 da (Caroline Mary b 1965); *Career* Nat Serv RASC 1954-56; articled to Temple Gothard 1957-63, audit sr Shipley Blackburn Sutton & Co 1963-68, tax sr Arthur Andersen 1966-68, tax sr and tax ptnr Josolyne Miles and Cassleton Elliot 1968-71, ptnr Clark Whitehill 1972-; FCA 1964; *Recreations* rugby, cricket, badminton, music, fine art; *Style*— John Adams, Esq; 4 Grove Rd, Northwood, Middx HA6 2AP (☎ 09274 24933); 25 New St Square, London EC4 (☎ 071 353 1577, fax 071 583 1720, telex 887422)

ADAMS, Dr Judith Elizabeth; da of Percy Charles Lockyer, of Hale, Cheshire, and Barbara, *née* Bailey; *b* 16 May 1945; *Educ* Roedean, UCH London (MB BS, MRCP); *m* 16 Sept 1972, Prof Peter Harold Adams, s of late Alfred Adams, of Penarth, Wales; 2 s (Charles Edward b 25 Dec 1978, James Lindsay b 26 Jan 1983); *Career* sr lectr in diagnostic radiology Univ of Manchester 1979- (lectr 1976-79), hon conslt radiologist Royal Infirmary Manchester 1978-; author of scientific pubns on: quantitative computed tomography for bone mass measurement, imaging in metabolic bone disorders and endocrine diseases, effective use of radiological resources; chm Examining Bd pt 1 FRCR 1984-89 (examiner 1980-84); memb: Editorial Bd British Journal of Radiology 1984-89, Editorial Bd Skeletal Radiology 1987-, Int Skeletal Soc 1987-; hon sec Br Assoc Clinical Anatomists 1990-; FRCR 1975, FRCP 1988; *Recreations* embroidery, flower arranging, sewing, swimming; *Style*— Dr Judith Adams; Fairholm, Hawley Lane, Hale Barns, Altrincham, Cheshire WA15 0DR; Dept of Diagnostic Radiology, The Medical School, University of Manchester, Oxford Rd, Manchester M13 9PT (☎ 061 275 5117, fax 061 275 5594)

ADAMS, Maj Kenneth Galt; CVO (1979), CBE (1989); s of William Adams, OBE (d 1949), of the Limes, Ranskill, Retford, Notts, and Christina Elisabeth, *née* Hall (d 1948); *b* 6 Jan 1920; *Educ* Doncaster GS, Staff Coll Camberley (psc), Lambeth (MA); *m* 23 Dec 1988, Sally, da of late Col John Middleton, of Fleet, Hants, and widow of Douglas Long; *Career* RASC 1940-59: cmmnd Cairo 1941, WWII served ME and N Africa, DADST WO 1946-48, CO Cdr Kenya 1949-51, DAA & QMG Aldershot 1952, Staff Coll Camberley 1953, DA & QMG HQ Northern Cmd 1954-56, sr instr RASC 1956-59; dir and conslt COS 1962-85, dir Proprietors of Hays Wharf Ltd 1966-70 (joined 1960); Comino fell St George's House Windsor Castle 1976-79 (dir of studies 1969-76), Comino fell RSA 1979-89; vice chm Archbishops' Cncl on Evangelism 1965-77, chm Industl Christian Fellowship 1977-86, chm Southwark Cathedral Cncl 1967-70, patron Nat Soc for Christian Standards in Soc 1985-, indust fell Comino Fndn 1987-; FMS 1970, CBIM 1975, FRSA 1979, FCIT 1980; *Recreations* reading 19th century novels, walking the dog; *Clubs* Army and Navy; *Style*— Maj Kenneth Adams, CVO, CBE; St George's Lodge, 8 Datchet Rd, Windsor, Berks SL4 1QE (☎ 0753 869 708)

ADAMS, Hon Mrs (Marjorie Heather); *née* Davies; JP (1963); yr da of 1 Baron Darwen (d 1950), and Kathleen, *née* Brown (d 1964); *b* 27 Oct 1923; *Educ* Queen Mary's Sch Lytham, Ayton Sch, The Mount Sch York, Rachel McMillan Training Coll; *m* 9 Aug 1944, Frederick Joseph Adams, CBE, son of late Joseph Stephen Adams; 1 s (Christopher Stephen b 1946); *Recreations* painting; *Style*— The Hon Mrs Adams, JP; 2 Beaumont Close, Belper, Derbyshire DE5 OED; 4 Redwood Close, Boverton, Llantwit Major, S Glamorgan CF6 9UT

ADAMS, Surgn Rear Adm Maurice Henry; CB (1965); s of Henry Adams, of Belfast, and Dorothea, *née* Whitehouse; *b* 16 July 1908; *Educ* Queen's Univ Belfast (MB BCh, DOMS); *m* 1938, Kathleen Mary, da of William J Hardy, of Belfast; 1 s (Brian), 2 da (Moya, Patricia); *Career* RN Med Serv 1932-66; *Style*— Surgn Rear Adm Maurice Adams, CB; Canberra, Rock, Wadebridge, Cornwall PL27 6LF

ADAMS, Michael Robert; s of Walter Adams (d 1978), of London, and Dorothy May, *née* Masters (d 1980); *b* 23 Sept 1923; *m* 15 June 1946, Margaret Steven, da of Douglas Carruth Stevenson (d 1977), of Wimbledon; 2 s (Robert Douglas b 7 May 1948, Ian Colin b 10 Oct 1954); *Career* WWII Flt Lt, pilot RAF 1939-47; Lloyd's insur broker 1947-82, dep chm Sedgewicks Ltd 1979-82; chm Lloyd's Insur Brokers Ctee 1975-76, vice pres Insur Inst of London 1975-85; Freeman City of London, fndr memb Worshipful Co of Insurers; ACII; *Recreations* farming, travel; *Style*— Michael Adams, Esq; Crocknorth Farm, East Horsley, Surrey KT24 5TG (☎ 048 653325)

ADAMS, (Adrian) Neil; s of Alfred Cyril Adams, of 144 Dovehouse Drive, Wellesbourne, nr Warwick, and Jean, *née* Wrighley; *b* 27 Sept 1958; *m* 27 Aug 1984, Alison Louise, da of Alan Charles Walker; 1 s (Ashley Neil James); *Career* 8 times Br Open Judo Champion, European Title holder 1979, 1980, 1983, 1984 and 1985, 2 Olympic Silver medals, World Champion 1981; *Books* A Life in Judo (1985), Olympic Judo (Tachiwaza) Standing, Olympic Judo (Newaza) Groundwork, The Neil Adams Guide to Better Judo 1987-88; *Style*— Neil Adams, Esq; The Neil Adams Club, Kenpas Highway, Coventry, Warwicks, (☎ 0203 418282)

ADAMS, Prof Norman Edward Albert; s of Albert Henry Adams, and Elizabeth Winifred Rose, *née* Humphreys; *b* 9 Feb 1927; *Educ* Harrow Art Sch, RCA (ARCA); *m* 1947, Anna Theresa, da of George Baseden Butt (d 1963), of London; 2 s (Jacob b 7 March 1956, Benjamin b 28 Jan 1958); *Career* artist, painter; head Dept of Painting Manchester Poly 1962, prof of fine art Univ of Newcastle upon Tyne 1981, keeper and prof of painting Royal Acad of Arts London 1986-; works incl: murals St Anselm's Church Kennington London 1970, Stations of the Cross Our Lady of Lourdes Milton Keynes 1975, decor for ballet Covent Garden and Sadler's Wells; paintings in many pub collections incl Tate Gallery; Hon MA Newcastle; RWS 1988, ARA 1967, RA 1972; *Recreations* all the arts; *Clubs* Arts; *Style*— Prof Norman Adams; Butts, Horton-in-Ribblesdale, Settle, N Yorks BD24 0HD (☎ 072 96 284); Royal Academy of Arts, Piccadilly, London W1 (☎ 071 439 7438)

ADAMS, Peter Gordon; TD; s of Dr George Stirk Adams, OBE, TD, of Virginia Water, and Marjorie, *née* Gordon (d 1988); *b* 11 Dec 1946; *Educ* Wellington; *m* 2 June 1979, Alice Elizabeth, da of Frank Cromie (d 1983); 2 s (Charles b 22 July 1982, Henry b 30 Jan 1984); *Career* admitted slr 1971; head of legal affrs Associated Gas Supplies Ltd; memb Ctee City of Westminster Law Soc, memb Law Soc; Freeman City of London; *Recreations* skiing; *Clubs* HAC, Cavalry and Guards'; *Style*— Peter Adams, Esq, TD; 59 Markham St, London SW3 3NR (☎ 071 376 5331, fax 071 376 5627)

ADAMS, Sir Philip George Doyne; KCMG (1969, CMG 1959); s of Dr George Basil Doyne Adams (d 1957), and Arline Maud, *née* Dodgson (d 1986); *b* 17 Dec 1915; *Educ* Lancing, ChCh Oxford (MA); *m* 1954, Hon (Mary) Elizabeth Lawrence 2 s (Geoffrey b 1957, Justin b 1961), 2 da (Lucy b 1955, Harriet b 1959); *Career* HM Consular and Dip Serv 1939-75; ambass to Jordan 1966-70, dep sec Cabinet Office 1971-72, ambass to Egypt 1973-75; dir Ditchley Fndn 1977-82; *Clubs* Brooks's; *Style*— Sir Philip Adams, KCMG; 78 Sussex Square, London W2 (☎ 071 262 1547); The Malt House, Ditchley, Enstone, Oxon (☎ 0608 677679)

ADAMS, Richard Borlase; CBE (1982); s of James Elwin Cokayne Adams (d 1961), and Susan Mercer, *née* Porter (d 1985); *b* 9 Sept 1921; *Educ* Winchester, Trinity Coll Oxford; *m* 1951, Susan Elizabeth, da of Col Ronald Streeter Lambert, MC (d 1976); 2 s (Christopher, Jeremy), 1 da (Jill); *Career* served WWII with Rifle Bde ME and Italy; chm: Islay Kerr & Co Ltd Singapore 1963-66; British India Steam Navigation Co Ltd 1970-84 (dir 1966, md 1969); P & O: dir 1970-, dep md 1974, md 1979-84, chief exec 1981-84; dir Clerical Medical and General Life Assurance Soc 1975-88; chm Kent Assoc for the Disabled 1986-; *Recreations* gardening, tennis, golf; *Clubs* Oriental; *Style*— Richard Adams, Esq, CBE; Beacon House, Bethersden, Ashford, Kent TN26 3AE (☎ 023 382 247)

ADAMS, Richard George; s of Evelyn George Beadon Adams, and Lilian Rosa, *née* Button; *b* 9 May 1920; *Educ* Bradfield, Worcester Coll Oxford (MA); *m* 1949, (Barbara) Elizabeth Acland; 2 da (Juliet, Rosamond); *Career* Army Serv 1940-46; entered Civil Serv 1948, ret 1974; author; writer in residence: Univ of Florida 1975, Hollins Coll Virginia; pres RSPCA 1980-82; FRSL, FRSA; *Books* Watership Down (1972, filmed 1978), Shardik (1974), The Plague Dogs (1977, filmed 1982), The Iron Wolf (short stories, 1980), The Girl in a Swing (1980, filmed 1988), Voyage Through The Antarctic (travel book, 1982), Maia (1984), The Bureaucats (1985), Nature Diary (1985); contrib to and ed: Occasional Poets anthology (1986), The Legend of Te Tuna (narrative poem, 1986); Traveller (1988), The Day Gone By (autobiography, 1990); *Style*— Richard Adams, Esq; 26 Church St, Whitchurch, Hants, RG28 7AR

ADAMS, Richard Hugh MacGregor; MBE (1989); s of Ronald Shaw Adams (d 1974), of Gosforth, Newcastle Upon Tyne, and Elizabeth Frances Mary Carew-Hunt, *née* Hunter; *b* 7 Nov 1945; *Educ* Harrow; *m* 1, 19 April 1969 (m dis 1980), Sally Hazel; 1 da (Lucy b 1973); m 2, 25 Sept 1985, Susan Jane, da of George Gray, of Richmond, N Yorks; 1 s (Jack b 1988), 1 da (Rosie b 1985); *Career* md Shaws Biscuits Ltd 1970, chm and md Northumbrian Fine Foods plc 1986-; chm: Sunwheel Foods Ltd 1987, Danish Natural Foods 1987, Country Fitness Foods Ltd 1990; *Recreations* sport, tennis, squash, jogging; *Clubs* Northumberland Lawn Tennis and Squash Rackets; *Style*— Richard Adams, Esq, MBE; Halton Grange, Wall, Hexham, Northumberland (☎ 0434 681293); Northumbrian Fine Foods plc, Dukesway, Team Valley, Gateshead, Tyne and Wear NE11 OQP (☎ 091 482 2611, fax 491 0826, telex 53346)

ADAMS, Prof Robert David; s of William Peter Adams (d 1973), and Marion, *née* Lawton; *b* 13 April 1940; *Educ* Hanley HS, Imp Coll Univ of London (BSc, ACGI, DSc), St John's Coll Cambridge (PhD); *m* 28 Sept 1963, Susan, da of John Felix Waite, GM' of Aston, Market Drayton; 1 s (Joss b 26 Sept 1970), 1 da (Rosie b 11 April 1968); *Career* lectr reader and prof Univ of Bristol Dept of Mechanical Engrg 1967-; chm Western Branch of Cncl of Inst of Mechanical Engrs; memb: Exec Ctee Br Composites Soc, Cncl Plastics and Rubber Inst; FIMechE, FInstP, FPRI; *Books* Structural Adhesive Joints in Engineering (with William C Wake, 1984), over 150 papers in scientific and tech jls; *Recreations* rowing, gardening, wine; *Clubs* Rotary Club of Clifton; *Style*— Prof Robert Adams; 17 Cotham Lawn Road, Bristol BS6 6DU (☎ 0272 247977; Department of Mechanical Engineering, University of Bristol, University Walk, Bristol BS8 1TR (☎ 0272 303030, telex 445938, fax 0272 251154

ADAMS, His Hon Judge (John) Roderick Seton; s of George G Adams (d 1980), of Edinburgh, and M Winifred, *née* Wilson; *b* 29 Feb 1936; *Educ* Whitgift Sch, Trinity Coll Cambridge (MA); *m* 19 April 1965, (Pamela) Bridget, da of Rev David Edmund Rice, MC (d 1978), of Hexham; 3 s (Robert b 5 Jan 1966, James b 14 Aug 1967, John b 9 Oct 1973); *Career* 2 Lt Seaforth Highlanders 1955-56, Capt Parachute Regt 1960-65; called to the Bar Inner Temple 1962, in practice 1968-90, rec Crown Ct 1980-90, circuit judge 1990-; *Recreations* music, fishing; *Style*— His Hon Judge Roderick Adams; 6 Pump Court, Temple, London EC4 (☎ 071 583 6013, fax 071 353 0464); Melness House, Sutherland (☎ 084 756 255)

ADAMS, Terence; s of William Henry Adams (d 1978), and Elsie, *née* Pickering (d 1986); *b* 4 June 1941; *Educ* Stratton GS Biggleswade Beds; *m* 1962, Vera Frances, da of Russell Meachen; 2 s (Christopher Mark b 16 Sept 1965, Paul Stephen b 29 March 1969); *Career* various insurance companies and brokers 1958-71, asst gen mangr (devpt) Cheltenham & Gloucester Building Society 1971-83, chief exec & dir Skipton Building Society 1983-; ACII; *Recreations* golf, music, theatre, travel; *Clubs* Ilkley Golf; *Style*— Terence Adams, Esq; Southwood, 51 Curley Hill, Ilkley, West Yorkshire LS29 0AY (☎ 0943 601155); Skipton Building Society, 59 High St, Skipton, North Yorkshire BD23 1DN (☎ 0756 700500, fax 0756 700257)

ADAMS, William Horace; s of David Horace Adams (d 1965), and Patience, *née* Dixon (d 1963); *b* 15 Aug 1925; *Educ* Stamford Sch, Oakham Sch; *m* 1947, Joan, da of James Pugh (d 1960); 2 s, 2 da; *Career* chartered surveyor; chm: RICS Continental Euro Branch 1981, Waterglade International Holdings plc 1987-; pres: Br Chapter Int Real Est Fndn (FIABCI) 1982-83, Arbitration and Conciliation Cncl FIABCI 1982-90; dir Property Intelligence Ltd 1984-; conslt: Security Pacific National Bank 1984-90, Privatbanken (now Unibank) 1985-, Bankers' Trust Co 1990-, and others; Freeman City of London, Liveryman Worshipful Co of Gardeners; *Recreations* golf; *Clubs* RAC; *Style*— William H Adams, Esq; Westering, 17 Coombe Rd, Otford, Sevenoaks, Kent TN14 5RG (☎ 09592 2565); 15 Les Mesnils du Golf, Evian le Bains, Haute Savoie, France; Waterglade International Holdings plc, Waterglade House, 5/7 Ireland Yard, London EC4V 5DQ (☎ 071 248 8301)

ADAMS, His Excellency Sir William James; KCMG (1991, CMG 1976); s of late William Adams, and late Norah, *née* Walker; *b* 30 April 1932; *Educ* Wolverhampton GS, Shrewsbury Sch, Queen's Coll Oxford; *m* 1961, Donatella, da of late Andrea Pais-Tarsilia; 2 s, 1 da; *Career* Nat Serv, RA 1950-51 ME Land Forces; FO 1954-: MECAS 1955, third sec Bahrain 1956, asst political agent Trucial States 1957, London 1958, second sec 1959, Manila 1960, first sec and private sec to Min of State FO 1963, first sec (info) Paris 1965-69, FCO 1969, counsellor 1971, head of Euro Integration Dept (2) FCO 1971-72, seconded to Econ Cmmn for Africa Addis Ababa 1972-73, cnsllr (developing countries) UK Perm Rep to EC 1973-77, head of Chancery and econ cnsllr Rome 1977-80, asst under sec of state FCO 1980-84; ambassador:

Tunisia 1984-87, Egypt 1987-; Order of the Star of Honour (hon) Ethiopia 1965, Order of the Two Niles (hon) Sudan 1965; *Clubs* Reform; *Style—* His Excellency Sir William Adams, KCMG; c/o Foreign and Commonwealth Office, London SW1A 2AL

ADAMS, William Ralph McClymont; s of Rev Alexander McClymont Adams, and Margaret Swanson, *née* Thomson; *b* 6 March 1915; *Educ* Dollar Acad, Hillhead HS Glasgow, Perth Acad, Heriot-Watt Univ, Edinburgh Coll of Art, architectural training Perth and Edinburgh; *m* Joan Graham, *née* Barry; 1 s, 2 da; *Career* Civil Serv 1939-80; sr conservation offr for Scot 1953-80; specialist in conservation of: carved stone, decorated plaster, painted ornaments; heraldic blazons; vice pres Heraldry Soc of Scotland 1988- (sec 1983-87, fell 1989); FSA (Scot); offr Most Venerable Order of St John of Jerusalem 1982, hon guildsman Ancient Royal Archers Guild of St Sebastian of Knokke Belgium 1984; *Recreations* horticulture, photography, heraldry, history, historic buildings and gardens; *Style—* William Adams, Esq; Limegrove, High St, Gifford, Haddington, E Lothian EH41 4QU (☎ 062 081 617)

ADAMSON, Sir (William Owen) Campbell; o s of late John Adamson, of Kinross; *b* 26 June 1922; *Educ* Rugby, Corpus Christi Coll Cambridge; *m* 1, 1945 (m dis 1984), Gilvray, da of Dr William Allan, of Baildon, Yorks; 2 s, 2 da; m 2, 1984, Mrs J (Mimi) Lloyd-Chandler; *Career* with Richard Thomas & Baldwins and Steel Co of Wales 1947-69; former memb: BBC Advsy Ctee, NEDC, SSRC, Design Cncl, Industl Soc Cncl; formerly vice chm Nat Savings Ctee for England and Wales; dir gen CBI 1969-76; chm: Abbey National Building Society 1978-, Revertex Chemicals 1978-81, Renold Ltd 1982-86 (dir 1976-, dep chm 1981-82); dir: Imperial Group 1976-86, Yule Catto to 1982, Lazard Brothers 1976-87, Doulton & Co 1977-83, Tarmac plc 1980-90; vice pres Inst Manpower Studies 1982-; govr Rugby Sch; kt 1976; *Books* various tech pubns; *Recreations* walking, music; *Clubs* Naval and Military; *Style—* Sir Campbell Adamson; Abbey House, Baker St, London NW1 (☎ 071 486 5555)

ADAMSON, Dr Donald; JP (City of London 1983); s of Donald Adamson (d 1982), and Hannah Mary, *née* Booth; *b* 30 March 1939; *Educ* Manchester GS, Magdalen Coll Oxford, Univ of Paris (MA, MLitt, DPhil); *m* 24 Sept 1966, Helen Freda, da of Frederick Percival Griffiths (d 1970), of Mossley Hill, Liverpool; 2 s (Richard Henry Egerton b 17 Jan 1970, John Daniel b 21 April 1971); *Career* author and historian; visiting fell Wolfson Coll Cambridge; judge Museum of the Year Awards 1979-83, memb Exec Ctee Nat Heritage 1980; memb Cambridge Soc (Kent Branch); Liveryman: Worshipful Co of Haberdashers 1976, Worshipful Co of Curriers 1991; FSA 1979, FRSL 1983, FIL 1989; Lord of the Manor of Dodmore; OStJ 1984, Chevalier Ordre des Palmes Académiques France 1986; *Books* The Genesis of Le Cousin Pons (1966), Dusty Heritage (1971), The House of Nell Gwyn (jtly, 1974), A Rescue Policy for Museums (1980), Balzac Illusions Perdues (1981), Les Romantiques français devant la Peinture espagnole (1985), two translations of Balzac novels; *Recreations* paintings, T S Eliot, gastronomy, water sports; *Clubs* Beefsteak, City Livery; *Style—* Dr Donald Adamson, JP, FSA; Dodmore House, The Street, Meopham, Kent DA13 OAJ; Topple Cottage, Polperro, Cornwall PL13 2RS (car 0836 659418)

ADAMSON, Douglas Thompson; s of W Adamson (d 1933), of London, and Alice Ada, *née* Torrance (d 1980); *Educ* Highgate Sch, Eastbourne Coll, Loughborough Univ; *m* 19 Dec 1959, Jean Valerie, da of Gerald Langford, of Ardenrun, Surrey; 1 s (Stuart Douglas b 16 Sept 1964), 1 da (Sandra Jean b 1 Jan 1962); *Career* 78 Sqdn Aug 1943; bomber cmd, transport cmd, fighter cmd; OC RAF Sharjah 1954-55, OC no 98(F) Sqdn 1956-57, tactics and ops Central Fighter Estab 1957-61, Fighter Command flight safety offr 1961-63; commenced farming 1963, chm RGTA 1975, county chm Camgridgeshire NFU 1984; dir: Cambridge Robotics Ltd, BQM, Search (UK) Ltd; Freeman City of London 1985, Freeman Worshipful Co of Farmers; FInstD, MBIM 1978, memb Lloyds Underwriting 1979; *Recreations* reading, travelling; *Clubs* Royal Air Force; *Style—* Douglas Adamson, Esq; Oak Gates, 6 Woodlands Road, Great Shelford, Cambridge CB2 5LW (☎ 0223 843548); Search (UK) Ltd, St John's Innovation Centre, Cowley Road, Cambridge CB4 4WS (☎ 0223 421116, telex 817739, fax 0223 421114)

ADAMSON, Hamish Christopher; s of John Adamson (d 1985), of Perth, Scotland, and Denise, *née* Colman-Sadd; *b* 17 Sept 1935; *Educ* Stonyhurst, Lincoln Coll Oxford (MA); *Career* admitted slr 1961; The Law Soc: asst sec 1966-81, sec Law Reform and Int Rels 1981-87, dir Int Div 1987-; sec UK Delgn Cncl of Bars and Law Soc's of Euro Community 1981-, exec sec Cwlth Lawyers Assoc 1983-; memb Law Soc; *Books* The Solicitors Act 1974 (1975); *Recreations* plants, books, travel; *Style—* Hamish Adamson, Esq; 133 Hartington Rd, London SW8 2EY (☎ 071 720 4406); The Law Society, 113 Chancery Lane, London WC2A 1PL (☎ 071 320 5759, fax 071 831 0057, telex 261 203)

ADAMSON, Iain Beaton; s of late Alexander Adamson, MBE, journalist and playwright, and late Matilda Beaton Adamson; descendant of noted braggart who fought on both sides in American Civil War, whose son wrote first book on teaching swimming; *b* 22 Aug 1928; *Educ* Glasgow Acad, Euro Travel Scholarship, Univ of Paris (Political Sci Dip); *m* 17 Feb 1962 (m dis 1990), Zita Mary, da of late Vincent Russell James; 1 s (Rory Beaton b 1966), 2 da (Kirstie b 1962, Zita b 1964); *Career* served Seaforth Highlanders, Malay Regt and Gurkha Rifles in Malaya (1948); author and foreign corr; journalist with: Glasgow Herald Orgn, Scottish Daily Express (Glasgow), Daily Mirror London, Santa Monica Outlook USA; foreign corr: France, Germany, Spain, USA; md Iain Adamson & Partners, PR in London, Bristol, Italy; The London Art Coll leisure study coll gp; former TV spokesman for Consumer Cncl; contributor to many jls and newspapers in UK, USA, Canada, Aust, NZ; *Books* author of various biographies including The Old Fox, A Man of Quality, The Great Detective, The Promised Messiah, A Man of God (Military Histories), The Forgotten Men (instruction), Profitable Art; *Recreations* travel, eating; *Style—* Iain Adamson, Esq; Maggs House, Bristol BS8 1QX (☎ 0272 266531, fax 0272 211594)

ADAMSON, Norman Joseph; CB (1981), QC (Scot 1979); s of Joseph Adamson, of Glasgow, and Lily, *née* Thorrat; *b* 29 Sept 1930; *Educ* Hillhead HS, Univ of Glasgow (MA, LLB); *m* 1961, Patricia Mary, er da of Walter Scott Murray Guthrie, of Edinburgh; 4 da; *Career* advocate (Scot) 1957, called to the Bar Gray's Inn 1959; Parly draftsman and legal sec Lord Advocate's Dept London 1965-, legal sec to Lord Advocate and first Parly draftsman for Scot 1979-89, asst counsel to Lord Chm of Ctees House of Lords 1989; elder of Church of Scotland; *Style—* Norman Adamson, Esq, CB, QC; Whiteways, White Lane, Guildford, Surrey (☎ 0483 65301); House of Lords, Westminster, London SW1 (☎ 071 219 3103)

ADAMSON, Paul Malcolm; s of Ivan Adamson (d 1967), and Marjorie, *née* Doughty (d 1974); *b* 21 June 1932; *Educ* Epsom Coll; *m* 15 Feb 1958, Olive, da of Albert Edward Studd; 1 s (Toby Seth Alexander b 1963), 1 da (Isobel b 1960); *Career* Nat Serv RAF 1950-52, Actg Corpl (unpaid) Far East Air Force Malaya 1951-52; Chartered Bank of India Australia and China (London), Bank of Br W Africa (Ghana), md Hopwood Craft Ltd, Bank of the North (Kano Nigeria), United Bank for Africa (Lagos Nigeria), Browning Arms Co (Montreal), US Steel (London), chm XFLO Heat Exchangers Ltd 1976-85; bursar Outward Bound Tst Eskdale Cumbria 1969-; hon memb 3 Bn and 5 Bn Offrs Mess Ghana Regt (5 Bn disbanded following mutiny in Congo 1961), hon memb Dagomba Tribe of N Territories Ghana 1960; AIBDip (lapsed); *Books* many articles in various sporting pubns; *Recreations* shootin', cookin', fishin', travellin', drinkin', snipin' at BNFL; *Clubs* MLAGB; *Style—* Paul Adamson, Esq; Randle How, Eskdale Green, Cumbria (☎ 09403 336); Outward Bound Eskdale, Eskdale Green, Holmrook, Cumbria CA19 1TE (☎ 09403 293, fax 09403 393)

ADAMSON, Stephen James Lister; s of James Lister Adamson (d 1985), and Helen Galloway Begg Adamson (d 1980); *b* 10 July 1942; *Educ* John Lyon Sch, Harrow; *m* 20 May 1972, Elizabeth Margaret, da of John Leslie Tunley (d 1965), of Heswall, Cheshire; 3 s (Neil b 15 Feb 1974, Stuart b 25 Jan 1977, Ross b 19 March 1981); *Career* CA 1966; ptnr: Arthur Young 1978, Ernst & Young 1989; pres Insolvency Practitioners Assoc 1989-90 (memb 1978-); chm Virginia Water Prep Sch; memb Faringdon Ward Club 1988; FIPA 1978; *Recreations* fishing, golf, theatre; *Clubs* IOD; *Style—* Stephen Adamson, Esq; Englewood, Ridgemead Rd, Englefield Green, Surrey; Arthur Young, Rolls House, 7 Rolls Buildings, Fetter Lane, London, EC4A 1NH (☎ 071 831 7130, fax 071 405 2147, telex 888604-262973

ADAMSON, Lt-Col William John Campbell; TD, JP (1951), DL (Angus 1971); s of Capt W Adamson (ka 1915; gn through his m, Norah, da of Rt Hon James Campbell, PC, MP, of Rt Hon Sir Henry Campbell-Bannerman, Liberal PM 1905-08), of Careston Castle, Brechin; *b* 13 March 1914; *Educ* Eton, Trinity Coll Oxford (MA), psc; *m* 1947, Margaret Josephine, da of James Helme (d 1972); 2 s, 3 da; *Career* served WW II, Lt Col Black Watch RHR (wounded); memb Royal Co of Archers (Queen's Body Guard for Scotland); md Careston Estates; memb Angus CC for 24 years, Hon Sheriff Angus; FRICS; *Recreations* farming, foreign travel, shooting; *Style—* Lt-Col William Adamson, TD, JP, DL; Careston Castle, Brechin, Angus (☎ 035 63 242); Nathro Lodge, Lethnot

ADBURGHAM, (Marjorie Vere) Alison; da of Dr Arthur Norman Haig, MD (d 1938), of Yeovil, Somerset, and Agnes Isobel, *née* Stephenson (d 1958); *b* 28 Jan 1912; *Educ* Roedean; *m* 22 Aug 1936, Myles Ambrose Adburgham; 2 s (Thurstan Haig b 1938, Roland Faulkner b 1945), 2 da (Carolyn Ashton b 1941, Jocelyn Alison b 1943); *Career* staff feature writer and fashion ed The Guardian 1954-73; *Books* A Punch History of Manners and Modes (1961), Shops and Shopping 1900-14 (1964, 2 edn 1981), View of Fashion (1966), Women in Print - Writing Women & Women's Magazines from the Restoration to Victoria (1972), Liberty's - A Biography of a Shop (1975), Shopping in Style - London from the Restoration to Edwardian Elegance (1979), Silver Fork Society - Fashionable Life and Literature 1814 to 1840 (1983), A Radical Aristocrat - Sir William Molesworth of Pencarrow (1990); *Clubs* Univ Women's; *Style—* Mrs Alison Adburgham; Tredore Cottage, Little Petherick, Wadebridge, Cornwall PL27 7QT (☎ 0841 540 362)

ADCOCK, Andrew John; s of Reay Stanley Adcock, of Underbarrow, Westmoreland, and Elizabeth, *née* Salter; *b* 10 Sept 1953; *Educ* Kendal GS, Magdalene Coll Cambridge (MA); *m* 17 Sept 1977, Maya (Jessie Maria), da of Maj (Charles) Peter S Ligertwood, of Bagborough, Somerset; 2 s (Oliver William b 1981, Tobias Henry b 1985), 1 da (Annabel Cecilia b 1983); *Career* with Hoare Govett Ltd (stockbrokers) 1975-87, Prolific Gp plc 1987-, memb Stock Exchange; *Recreations* tennis, shooting; *Style—* Andrew Adcock, Esq; 19 Crieff Road, London SW18 (☎ 071 874 8792); 87 222 Bishopsgate, London EC2M 4JS (☎ 071 247 6544)

ADCOCK, Robert Wadsworth; DL (1978); s of Sir Robert Adcock, CBE, DL (d 1990), of Torquay, and Mary Hannah, *née* Wadsworth, of Handforth Hall, Cheshire; *b* 29 Dec 1932; *Educ* Rugby; *m* 26 Oct 1957, Valerie Colston, da of Col Stanley Robins, MBE (Indian Army, d 1974), of Hereford; 1 s (Robert Charles b 1961), 1 da (Olivia Charlotte b 1961); *Career* asst slr Lancs CC 1955-56, asst slr Manchester CC 1956-59, sr slr Berks CC 1959-63, asst clerk (later dep clerk) Northumberland CC 1963-70, dep chief exec Essex CC 1970-76, chief exec Essex CC 1976-, clerk of Essex Lieutenancy 1976-; Assoc of County Cncls: advsr Police Ctee 1976-83, advsr Policy Ctee 1983-, memb Officers Advisory Gp 1983- (chm 1987-); hon sec Assoc of County Chief Execs 1983-90, chm Officers Advice Panel SE Region Planning Conf 1984-88; *Recreations* gardening, ornithology; *Style—* Robert Adcock, Esq, DL; The Christmas Cottage, Great Sampford, Saffron Walden, Essex (☎ 079 986 363); Essex County Council, County Hall, Chelmsford, Essex (☎ 0245 492211 ext 20011, fax 0245 352710, telex 995910)

ADDERLEY, Hon James Nigel Arden; er s and h of 7 Baron Norton, OBE; *b* 2 June 1947; *Educ* Downside; *m* 1971, Jacqueline Julie, da of Guy W Willett, of Alderney; 1 s (Edward James Arden b 1982), 1 da (Olivia Fleur Elizabeth b 1979); *Career* FCA 1970; *Recreations* flying, skiing, music; *Style—* The Hon James Adderley; 1 Picaterre, Alderney, CI

ADDERLEY, Gp Capt Hon Michael Charles; OBE (1960), AFC (and Bar); s of 6 Baron Norton (d 1961); *b* 8 April 1917; *Educ* Radley, Sidney Sussex Coll Cambridge; *m* 1953, Margrethe Ann (d 1986); 3 s, 1 da; *Career* Group Capt RAF (ret); served WWII 1939-45, Malaya 1949-51 (King's Commendation), Korea 1951-52 (American DFC, Bronze Star and Air Medal), Woomera 1957-59, Air Attaché British Embassy Prague 1963-65; *Style—* Gp Capt the Hon Michael Adderley, OBE, AFC; 23 Welham Rd, Norton, Malton, Yorks YO17 9DS

ADDERLEY, Maj Hon Nigel John; s of 7 Baron Norton, OBE; *b* 30 March 1950; *Educ* Downside, RMA Sandhurst; *m* 19 Jan 1991, Teresa M A, da of Maj John Mills, of Vyse House, Winkfield, Berks; *Career* Capt Life Gds; *Style—* Maj the Hon Nigel Adderley

ADDINGTON, Alexandra, Baroness; Alexandra Patricia; yr da of late Norman Ford Millar; *m* 1961 (m dis 1974), 5 Baron Addington (d 1982); 2 s, 2 da; *Style—* The Rt Hon Alexandra, Lady Addington; 9-11 Chalk Hill Rd, Norwich NR1 1SL

ADDINGTON, 6 Baron (UK 1887); Dominic Bryce Hubbard; s of 5 Baron Addington (d 1982), and Alexandra, Baroness Addington, *qv*; *b* 24 Aug 1963; *Educ* Hewett Sch, Norwich City Coll, Univ of Aberdeen; *Heir* bro, Hon Michael Hubbard, *qv*; *Recreations* rugby football; *Clubs* National Liberal; *Style—* The Rt Hon the Lord Addington; 9/11 Chalk Hill Rd, Norwich NR1 1SL

ADDINGTON, Hon Gurth Louis Francis; s of late 6 Viscount Sidmouth; *b* 26 Feb 1920; *Educ* Downside, BNC Oxford (MA); *m* 1950, Patience Gillian, da of late Col L E Travers, RE; 3 s, 6 da (inc 2 sets twins); *Career* served as Flying Offr RAF (aircrew) 1939-45 in Italy and M East; *Style—* The Hon Gurth Addington; 11 Edwin St, Fairlight, NSW 2094, Australia

ADDINGTON, Hon Hiley William Dever; s of late 6 Viscount Sidmouth; *b* 31 Oct 1917; *m* 1942, Brenda Swanney, da of late Robert Charles Wallace, CMG, sometime princ of Queen's Univ Kingston, Canada; 2 s, 1 da; *Career* Lt Cdr RN (ret); sometime chief engr Imp Oil Ltd and conslt Exxon Corporation; *Style—* The Hon Hiley Addington; 1688 Mills St, Sarnia, Ontario, Canada

ADDINGTON, Hon Jeremy Francis; s and h of 7 Viscount Sidmouth; *b* 29 July 1947; *Educ* Ampleforth; *m* 1, 1970, Grete, *née* Henningsen, of Randers, Denmark; 1 s (Steffan b 1966), 1 da (Laura Grete b 1975); m 2, 1986, Una, eldest da of James Coogan, of 54 Compton Bassett, Calne, Wilts; 1 s (John b 29 Nov 1990), 1 da (Anna Frances b 1988); *Style—* The Hon Jeremy Addington; 54 Compton Bassett, Calne, Wiltshire

ADDINGTON, Lt-Col Hon Leslie Richard Bagnall; DFC (1951); 5 s of 6 Viscount Sidmouth; *b* 20 Sept 1923; *Educ* Downside; *m* 1955, Anne, da of Capt Trevor Hume (d 1968), and Sybil, sis of late Sir Maurice Lacy, 2 Bt; 2 s (William b 1956, Richard b 1958), 2 da (Sarah b 1961, Alice b 1964); *Career* served RA 1941-71 Far East, ret as Lt-Col; CO Essex Yeo 1965-66 and 100 (Yeomanry) FD Regt 1967-68; *Clubs* Army and Navy; *Style—* Lt-Col The Hon Leslie Addington, DFC; Polebridge, Sutton Veny, Warminster, Wilts BA12 7AL (☎ 0985 40202)

ADDINGTON, Hon Thomas Raymond Casamajor; MC; s of late 6 Viscount Sidmouth; *b* 7 Jan 1919; *Educ* Downside; *m* 1947, Veronique (d 1970), da of Emile Wirtz, of Antwerp, Belgium; 3 s, 4 da; *Career* Maj (ret) RHA, WWII Commandos 1939-45; *Style—* The Hon Thomas Addington, MC; Highway Farm, nr Calne, Wilts

ADDIS, Dr Bruce John; s of John Henry Addis (d 1942), and Muriel Florence, *née* Cattell; *b* 11 Oct 1942; *Educ* King Edward's Five Ways Sch Birmingham, St Bartholomew's Hosp Med Coll (MB BS); *m* 6 Aug 1966, Rosemary, da of Charles Eltham Kidner, of 9 Wallfield Rd, Bovey Tracey, Devon; 1 s (Mark b 1970), 1 da (Chania b 1968); *Career* Surgn Cdr RN 1968-84, consIt pathologist Royal Naval Hosp Haslar 1978-83; consIt histopathologist: Brompton Hosp, Salisbury Gen Infirmary 1987-; sr lectr Nat Heart and Lung Inst 1984-87, ed Jl of Pathology; memb Cncl Int Acad of Pathology 1988-; FRCPath 1989; *Books* Lung Tumours (ed, 1988), Textbook of Uncommon Cancer (contrib, 1988); *Recreations* music, painting; *Style—* Dr Bruce Addis; Gayton House, Old Dairy Yard, Lower Woodford, Salisbury, Wilts SP4 6NQ (☎ 0722 73590); Dept of Pathology, Salisbury General Infirmary, Fisherton St, Salisbury SP2 7SX (☎ 0722 336212)

ADDIS, Prof Thomas Richard; s of Judge Thomas Addis (d 1952), and Nina, *née* Wallis (d 1967); *b* 31 Aug 1941; *Educ* Univ Coll Sch Hampstead, Univ of Aston (BSc), Brunel Univ (PhD); *m* 14 Sept 1968, Pamela Rose, da of Eric Hubert Housden, of 3 Mayfield Rd, Girton, Cambridge; 1 s (David Thomas b 13 Feb 1981), 1 da (Elizabeth Anne b 12 Sept 1976); *Career* sr tech offr Res and Advanced Devpt Centre ICL Stevenage 1969-81, lectr Dept of Computer Sci Brunel Univ 1981-86, prof of computer sci Univ of Reading 1986-; memb Int Ctee Knowledge Acquisition for Knowledge Based Systems, vice chm BCS Specialist Gp on Expert Systems, memb Ctee IEE C4(Artificial Intelligence) Professional Gp; MInstP 1973, FBCS 1982, FIEE 1990 (MIEE 1983), CEng 1984, CPhys 1985; *Books* Designing Knowledge-Based Systems (1985); *Recreations* riding, sailing, squash; *Clubs* Royal Corinthian Yacht; *Style—* Prof Thomas Addis; Department of Computer Science, University of Reading, PO Box 220, White Knights, Reading RG6 2AX (☎ 0734 318600, fax 0734 751994)

ADDISON, Lt-Col Archibald Randall George; MBE (1971); s of George Anthony Walter Addison (d 1947), and Sheila Mary, *née* Davidson (d 1985); paternal gf was Maj-Gen George Henry Addison, CB, CMG, DSO; maternal g uncle was Dr Randall Thomas Davidson, Archbishop of Canterbury 1903-28; *b* 3 Oct 1933; *Educ* Wellington Coll, RMA Sandhurst; *m* 11 May 1974, Susan Primrose, da of Prof Reginald Victor Jones, CB, CBE, FRS, of 8 Queens Terrace, Aberdeen, and former w of Dr John Thomas Parente, of New York; 1 step s (John Addison formerly Parente b 1965), 1 step da (Gigina Addison formerly Parente b 1964); *Career* cmmnd The Royal Scots 1954; served: Suez Canal Zone, Cyprus, Port Said, Berlin 1954-58; seconded Trucial Oman Scouts 1960-64; served with RS Radfan Aden 1964-65; Staff Coll 1966; HQ 52 Lowland Div 1967-68; served with: Royal Scots, BAOR, N Ireland 1968-71; seconded Abu Dhabi 1971-73; Staff Appt Belize 1975-77 and 1982-83; cmd TA Bn Edinburgh 1979-82, ret 1987; re-employed by MOD in Retired Offr appt; *Recreations* gardening, reading; *Clubs* Northern (Aberdeen); *Style—* Lt-Col Archibald Addison, MBE; The Veldt, Monikie, Angus

ADDISON, Edward Norman; OBE (1987); *b* 28 May 1918; *Educ* Real Gymnasium Vienna; *m* 1 May 1945, Patricia, *née* Saint; 2 da (Vivien b 1946, Jacqueline b 1949); *Career* WWII Army 1940-46; fndr and chm The Addison Tool Co Ltd 1956-, currently dir B Elliott plc; pres MTTA 1990-91 (and 1985-86), chm COMMET 1986-87, pres Comité Européen de Liaison des Importateurs de Machines-Outils 1977-80; FRSA 1988; *Recreations* racehorse owner; *Style—* Edward Addison, Esq, OBE; The Addison Tool Co Ltd, Elliott House, Victoria Road, London NW10 6NY (☎ 081 965 6600, fax 081 993 8767, telex 934211 ADSON G)

ADDISON, Hon Jacqueline Faith; da of 2 Viscount Addison (d 1976), and Brigit Helen Christine, *née* Williams (d 1980); *b* 2 March 1944; *Educ* Chichester HS for Girls, King's Coll London (BA), Univ of Strathclyde (Dip Librarianship); *m* 1966 (m dis 1985), Jeremy Warren Payne, s of Cecil Warren Payne (d 1973), of Old Bursledon, Hants; 3 da (Katy Josephine b 1972, Christina Meriel b 1975, Anna Isabella b 1978); *Career* info specialist; *Style—* The Hon Jacqueline Addison; 16a Bright's Crescent, Edinburgh EH9 2DB (☎ 031 667 6528)

ADDISON, Joseph; CBE (1967); s of Francis Lacy Addison (d 1914); *b* 30 May 1912; *Educ* Eton, Trinity Coll Cambridge; *m* 1938, Wendy Blyth, JP, da of Cecil (Bill) Payn (d 1959), of Durban; 1 s (Michael), 1 da (Jill (Mrs Whiteley)); *Career* WWII Maj Queen's Royal Regt; admitted slr 1936; Linklaters & Paines 1933-46, legal advsr to Anglo-Iranian Oil Co Ltd 1946-54, gen mangr Iranian Oil Participants Ltd 1955-71, chm London Policy Gp of Int Oil Indust 1971; Order of TAJ Iran 1971; *Style—* Joseph Addison, Esq, CBE; The Weir House, Alresford, Hants (☎ 0962 732 320)

ADDISON, 3 Viscount (UK 1945); Michael Addison; s of 1 Viscount Addison, KG, PC, MD, FRCS, sometime MP Shoreditch and Swindon (d 1951); suc er bro, 2 Viscount Addison, 1976; *b* 12 April 1914; *Educ* Hele's Sch Exeter, Balliol Coll Oxford (BA, MA); *m* 1936, Kathleen, da of late Rt Rev and Rt Hon William Wand, KCVO, DD, formerly 110 Bishop of London; 1 s, 2 da; *Heir* s, Hon William Addison; *Career* served RAFVR 1941-45; Civil Service 1935-65, poly lectr 1966-76; memb: RIPA, Assoc of Teachers of Mgmnt; *Style—* The Rt Hon the Viscount Addison; Old Stables, Maplehurst, Horsham, W Sussex (☎ 0403 891298)

ADDISON, Terry Robert; s of Keith Roy Addison (d 1982), and Dorothy Phyllis, *née* Hind (d 1969); *b* 27 Dec 1932; *Educ* Hinckley GS Leics, Leicester Coll of Art, RCA London (Royal scholar, Des RCA); *m* 4 Oct 1958, Anne Jennifer (d 1982), da of Percival White (d 1947); 2 s (Scott b 1961, Ben b 1961), 1 da (Elizabeth b 1970); *Career* Nat Serv 1 RHA, BAOR; interior design consIt; ptnr YRM Architects 1960-78; own practice: Addison Assocs 1978-, Addison Design Pte Ltd Singapore 1983-, AM Assocs 1982-; architectural practice: Addison Sutphin Boston Mass 1982-, Addison Larson Chicago Illinois 1987-; dir: Devpt & Investmt Co, Adsul Ltd 1986-; Fell Soc of Artists and Designers; *Recreations* piano, squash; *Clubs* IOD; *Style—* Terry R Addison, Esq; 23 Emerald St, London WC1N 3QL(☎ 071 831 2800, fax 071 831 0274, telex ADMARC 89669 1TLXIRG, car 0836 209 715)

ADDISON, Hon William Matthew Wand; s and h of 3 Viscount Addison; *b* 13 June 1945; *Educ* King's Sch Bruton, Essex Inst of Agric; *m* 1970, Joanna Mary, da of John Dickinson, of Blyborough Grange, Lincs; 1 s, 2 da; *Style—* The Hon William Addison; Kingerby Hall, Market Rasen, Lincs (☎ 067 382 255)

ADDISON, Sir William Wilkinson; JP (1949), DL (Essex 1973); s of Joseph Addison, of Bashall Eaves; *b* 4 April 1905; *m* 1929, Phoebe, da of Robert Dean, of Rimington, W Yorks; *Career* verderer Epping Forest 1957-; chm Cncl Magistrates Assoc 1970-76; FSA, FRHistS; kt 1974; *Books* Local Styles of the English Parish Church (1982), Farmhouses in the English Landscape (1986), etc; *Style—* Sir William Addison, JP, DL, FSA; Ravensmere, Epping, Essex (☎ 0378 73439)

ADEANE, Baroness; Helen; *née* Chetwynd-Stapylton; da of late Richard Chetwynd-Stapylton; *b* 16 Jan 1916; *m* 1939, Baron Adeane, GCB, GCVO, PC, FSA (Life Peer) (d 1984); 1 s (Hon (George) Edward, CVO, b 1939), 1 da (d 1952); *Style—* The Rt Hon the Lady Adeane; 22 Chelsea Square, London SW3 6LF

ADENEY, (Howard) Martin; s of Rev Arthur Webster Adeney, and Edith Marjorie, *née* Blagden (d 1987); *b* 7 Sept 1942; *Educ* Monkton Combe Sch, Queens' Coll Cambridge (BA); *m* 18 Dec 1971, Ann Valerie, *née* Corcoran; 2 s (William Edward b 3 Sept 1973, Thomas Henry b 7 June 1976), 1 step s (Samuel John Stanton Moore b 29 April 1963); *Career* reporter Guardian 1965-77 (labour corr 1972-77), feature writer Colombo Pubn Bureau 1968-69, industl corr Sunday Telegraph 1977-78, industl ed BBC TV 1982-89 (labour corr 1978-82); head int media rels ICI plc 1989-; memb Westminster City Cncl 1971-74; *Books* The Miners Strike: Loss Without Limit (with John Lloyd, 1986), The Motormakers: The Turbulent History of Britain's Car Industry (1988); *Recreations* walking, garden labouring; *Style—* Martin Adeney, Esq; ICI plc, 9 Millbank, London SW1P 3JF

ADGEY, Dr (Agnes Anne) Jennifer; da of Robert Henry Adgey (d 1973), of Garden Lodge, Newtownards, Co Down, and Sarah Jane, *née* Menown (d 1990); *b* 2 Oct 1941; *Educ* Regent House Sch Newtownards Co Down, Queen's Univ Belfast (MB, MD); *Career* res fell cardiology Presbyterian Med Centre San Francisco 1967-68, consIt cardiologist Royal Victoria Hosp Belfast 1971- (jr house offr 1964-65, sr house offr and registrar 1965-67, sr registrar cardiology 1968-71); memb: Br Cardiac Soc 1973, Assoc Physicians of GB and Ireland 1980, NY Acad of Sci 1983, Resuscitation Cncl UK 1987; fell American Coll Cardiology 1975, examiner RCP London, expert Advsy Panel on Cardiovascular Diseases WHO, examiner RCP Ireland 1988; MRCP 1967, FRCP 1978; *Books* The Acute Coronary Attack (with J F Pantridge, J S Geddes, S W Webb, 1975), Developments in Cardiovascular Medicine (1982), Acute Phase of Ischemic Heart Disease and Myocardial Infarction (ed), numerous papers on cardiology; *Recreations* piano and classical music; *Style—* Dr Jennifer Adgey; 20 Myrtlefield Park, Belfast BT9 6NE (☎ 0232 661693); Regional Medical Cardiology Centre, Royal Victoria Hosp, Belfast BT12 6BA NI (☎ 0232 240503 ext 3223)

ADIE, Jack Jesson; CMG (1962); s of Percy James Adie (d 1948), and Marion, *née* Sharp (d 1957); *b* 1 May 1913; *Educ* Shrewsbury Sch, Magdalen Coll Oxford (BA); *m* 1940, Patricia (d 1978), da of William McLoughlin; 1 s (Peter), 2 da (Susan, Jane); *Career* entered Colonial Admin Serv 1938; served in Zanzibar 1938-48: (on Military Serv 1940-42 in Kenya Regt Occupied Territory Admin, private sec to the Sultan, private sec to the Br Res, sr asst sec; seconded to Colonial Office 1949-51, asst sec Kenya 1951; sec for: Educn and Lab Kenya 1952, Educn Lab and Lands 1954; actg min 1955-56, chief sec Barbados 1957; perm sec for: Forest Devpt, Game and Fisheries Kenya April-Dec 1958, Agric Animal Husbandry and Water Resources; chm: African Land Devpt Bd 1958-59, Central Housing Bd 1959-60, Housing Common Servs Probation and Approved Schs 1960-61, Lab and Housing 1961-62; perm sec for Lab 1962-63; ret 1964; contrib East Africa Annual; temp princ min of overseas devpt 1964-69; Order of Brilliant Star of Zanzibar (4th class) 1947, Coronation Medal 1953; *Recreations* opera; *Style—* J J Adie, Esq, CMG; 3 Braemar, Kersfield Road, Putney, London SW15 3HG (☎ 081 789 8301)

ADIE, Rt Rev Michael Edgar; *see*: Guildford, Bishop of

ADKINS, Frederick Healey (Fred); s of Fred Adkins (d 1945), of Lexington, Kentucky, USA, and Ottilie Maureen, *née* Healey (d 1985); *b* 25 July 1938; *Educ* Nelspruit HS S Africa, Univ of S Africa (memb rugby first team), Dip Inst Mktg S Africa; *m* (Lorraine) Dalmae, da of Henry van Zyl; 3 da (Samantha b 15 Aug 1970, Jessica Dalmae b 14 Nov 1984, Rosalind Healey b 13 Oct 1989); *Career* country mangr Zyma SA 1967-72, nat sales mangr Smith Kline SA 1972-78, mktg dir Bristol-Myers SA 1978-80, int mktg and mgmnt trg consIt Intercontinental Medical Statistics (Europe, N America, S E Asia, Far East) 1981-88, dir Ogilvy and Mather PR 1984-, currently consIt to O & M PR and the pharmaceutical indust, special advsr to UCL; MBIM; *Books* Pharmaceutical Management Manual (1990); *Recreations* study (currently enrolled to Univ of Keele MBA prog); *Style—* Fred Adkins, Esq; 113 Western Avenue, East Acton, London W3 7EB (☎ 081 740 8347); Ogilvy & Mather Public Relations, 33 St John St, London EC1M 4AA (☎ 071 253 5757, fax 081 743 8396)

ADKINS, Roy Ewart; s of Samuel William Ewart Adkins (d 1980), and Elsie, *née* Spooner; *b* 21 June 1931; *Educ* Handsworth GS; *m* 14 May 1960, Barbara May, da of Horace Benjamin Loach; 2 s (John Ewart b 3 Jan 1963, Timothy Benjamin b 3 Feb 1966), 1 da (Louise Elizabeth b 26 May 1961); *Career* Nat Serv 1953-54; ptnr Ault & Co 1966-71 (qualified chartered accountant 1963), ptnr Thornton Baker 1971- (following merger); Grant Thornton (formerly Thornton Baker): ptnr 1971-, chm Insolvency Panel 1973-87, memb and former chm Policy Bd 1978-83, non-exec chm Thornton Baker Associates Limited (Mgmnt ConsIts) 1976-80, chm Ptnrs Nat Annual Conf 1988-90, chm Nat Equity Ptnrs Meetings 1986-91; Insolvency Practitioners Assoc: memb 1971-, memb Law Reform Ctee 1972-78, chm Tech Ctee 1982-84 (memb 1978-84), memb Ethics Ctee 1986-88, chm Regnl Meetings Ctee 1985-88, pres Cncl 1984-85 (memb 1980-86); Soc of Practioners of Insolvency 1990-: fndr memb, memb Cncl, chm Ethics Ctee; memb: Insolvency Practitioners Ctee ICAEW 1986-89, Ethics Ctee ICAEW 1986-88; chm Insolvency Practioners Jt Liaison Ctee 1984-89; memb: Insolvency Serv Steering Bd DTI 1989-, Inst of Credit Mgmnt 1980-; FCA (ACA 1963); *Recreations* theatre, golf; *Style—* Roy Adkins, Esq; Grant Thornton, Enterprise House, 115 Edmund St, Birmingham B3 2HJ (☎ 021 212 4000, fax 021 212 4014)

ADLAM, Lance Edward Stott; s of Edward Douglas Stott Adlam, of Cotleigh, nr Honiton, Devon, and Margaret Elsie, *née* May-Arrindell; *b* 3 April 1944; *Educ* Acton Central Sch, The Elms Secdy Sch Acton, Chiswick Poly, Thames Poly (formerly Hammersmith Coll of Art & Building), Poly of Central London; *m* 1 July 1967, Angela Marie, da of Vivian Egerton Saunders; 2 s (Mark Edward Vivian b 1970, Paul Andrew John b 1972); *Career* architect; Fitzroy Robinson & Partners 1960-71, Bucks Co Architects Dept 1971-78, section ldr Architects Dept Ind Coope Ltd 1978-80, sr architect Fitzroy Robinson Partnership 1980-83, assoc T P Bennett Partnership (formerly T P Bennett & Son) 1983-89 (ptnr 1989-); memb ARCUK 1974, RIBA 1974; *Recreations* badminton, tennis, railway modelling, railway history, philately, genealogy, music, reading; *Clubs* Thame Badminton (chm 1988-), Thame Jr Badminton (coach), Great Western Soc, Romney Hythe & Dymchurch Railway Assoc; *Style—* Lance Adlam, Esq; T P Bennett Partnership, Architects & Planning Consultants, 262 High Holborn, London WC1V 7DU (☎ 071 405 9277, fax 071 405 3568)

ADLAM, (Avis) Marjorie; OBE (1981); da of Richard Michael Charles Collins, of Suffolk, and Milly Elizabeth Rolfe (d 1958); *b* 17 Jan 1913; *Educ* Thetford GS for Girls, Univ of Southampton (BA); *m* 8 April 1939, Bernard Stephen Adlam (d 1976), s of Walter Adlam (d 1962); 3 s (Simon b 1941, Nicholas, *qv*, b 1945 Martin b 1946); *Career* teacher 1939; JP 1952-83, former Bench chm Magistrates Assoc, country rep on Cncl of Probation and After Care (branch chm 1953-85); Hunts, Mid Anglia and Cambs Police Authy 1954-83; memb Bd of Visitors Gaynes Hall Borstal 1973-85; Liveryman Worshipful Co of Spectacle Makers 1986; *Recreations* gardening, lacemaking, needlework; *Style—* Mrs Marjorie Adlam, OBE; The Walnuts, Hail Weston, nr St Neots, Huntingdon, Cambs (☎ 0480 72209)

ADLAM, Nicholas Rolfe; s of Bernard Stephen Adlam (d 1976), of The Walnuts, Hail Weston, St Neots, Cambs, and Avis Marjorie, *née* Collins, OBE, *qv*; *b* 1 Oct 1945; *Educ* Kimbolton Sch; *m* 10 April 1971, Heather Miranda, da of George May (d 1974), of Thatch Cottage, Wyboston, Beds; *Career* chm: Gordon Watts & Co Ltd 1981-89, B S Adlam & Co Ltd 1977; md: Cavingston Properties Ltd 1974-, Cavingston Ltd, Wincomblee Estates Ltd 1985-; non-exec dir Omnibus Workspace Ltd 1977-; jt md: Fennstone Investments Ltd 1990-, Fennstone Properties Ltd 1990-; dir Green Storage Ltd 1990-; Freeman City of London 1967, Liveryman Worshipful Co of Spectacle Makers 1971 (Freeman 1966), memb Guild of Freeman of City of London 1969; *Recreations* horse-racing, travelling, reading balance sheets, cutting grass; *Clubs* E India, RAC; *Style—* Nicholas R Adlam, Esq; c/o East India Club, 16 St James's Square, London SW1Y 4LH (☎ 071 930 1000, fax 071 321 0217, telex 938 041)

ADLARD, David Boyd; s of Clifford Boyd Adlard (d 1985), of Norwich, and Elsie Lawrence, *née* Fielder (d 1990); *b* 13 June 1944; *Educ* Gresham's, Univ of Sussex (BSc), Middlesex Poly (Dip Mgmnt Studies), Kilburn Poly; *m* Aug 1984, Mary Ellen, da of Edward Patrick Healy, of 108 Newton Avenue, North Worcester, Mass; 1 da (Lucy Elizabeth b Nov 1987); *Career* work study engr then prodn mangr Alcan Industries Ltd 1966-73, prodn mangr Cape Universal Building Products 1973-74; chef: various hotels and restaurants France 1975-77 (incl L'Hotel Des Voyageurs Franche Comté), Connaught Hotel Mayfair 1978-81; chef tournant Le Talbooth Restaurant Dedham Colchester Essex 1981-82, pastry chef and asst to Maître D'Hotel Castle Restaurant Leicester Mass USA 1982, restaurant mangr The Terrace Restaurant Dedham Vale Hotel Dedham Colchester Essex 1982, opened Adlard's Restaurant Wymondham Norfolk 1983 (moved restaurant to 79 Upper St Gile's St Norwich 1989) *Awards* (for Adlard's restaurant) Michelin one rosette 1987-89, AA Rosette, Egon Ronay rosette, Good Food Guide 4/5 rating 1990-91 and Exceptional Wine Cellar ranking 1990, Decanter Badoit Restaurant of The Month 1990; memb Académie Culinaire De France (filiale Grande Bretagne) 1988-; *Recreations* wine, computing, reading cookery books, searching for wild mushrooms and dining out; *Style—* David Adlard, Esq; 79a Upper St Giles Street, Norwich, Norfolk NR2 1AB (☎ 0603 611108); Adlards Restaurant, 79 Upper St Giles St, Norwich, Norfolk NR2 1AB (☎ 0603 633522)

ADLER, David Harold; *b* 14 Oct 1941; *Educ* Felsted; *Career* articled clerk Edward Moore & Sons 1961-66, qualified chartered accountant 1966, Roth Manby & Co 1966-68, ptnr KPMG Peat Marwick Mitchell 1972- (joined 1968); pres E Anglian Soc of CAs 1987, chm E Anglian Dist Training Bd 1990-; FCA (ACA 1966); *Recreations* sailing, squash, skiing, bridge; *Style—* David Adler, Esq; KPMG Peat Marwick McLintock, Holland Court, The Close, Norwich, Norfolk NR4 6PY (☎ 0603 620481)

ADLER, George Fritz Werner; OBE (1982); s of Fritz Jacob Sigismund Adler (d 1949), of Cardiff, and Hildegard Julie Lippmann (d 1982); *b* 12 Jan 1926; *Educ* Co GS Penarth, Univ of London (BSc), Univ of Cardiff (Jt Dip in Mechanical Engrg), Imperial Coll London (DIC); *m* 11 June 1949, June Moonaheim Margaret, da of William Charles Nash; 3 da (Helen Margaret Suzanne b 26 April 1951, Fiona Ruth b 22 April 1955, Caroline Francesca Mathilde b 15 Dec 1965); *Career* mangr Water Turbine Valve & Hydraulic Products Divs English Electric Co 1966-71 (graduate apprentice 1945-47, chief devpt engr Rugby 1956-58), mangr Mechanical Products Div Marconi 1962-66 (chief mechanical engr 1958-62), dir of res British Hydromechanics Research Association 1971-86, sec Assoc of Independent Res and Technol Orgns 1986-89; contrib to Kempe's Engineers Yearbook 1956-; fell Univ of Wales Coll of Cardiff; Freeman City of London 1984, Liveryman Worshipful Co of Engrs 1984; memb: Governing Body Imperial Coll 1985-, Engrg Cncl 1986-89; chm Br Nat Ctee for Int Engrg Affairs 1986-89, vice pres Euro Fedn of Nat Engrg Assocs 1987-89, FIMechE (pres 1983-84), FICE 1980, FEng 1981 (treas and memb Cncl 1988-); Eur Ing; *Recreations* crafts, gardening, music, golf; *Clubs* Carlton; *Style—* Eur Ing George Adler, OBE; The Haining, Orchard Close, Longburton, Sherborne, Dorset DT9 5PP (☎ 096321 641)

ADLER, John James; JP (Chelmsford 1987); s of Cdr Alan Adler, RNVR (d 1966); *b* 16 Sept 1935; *Educ* Felsted; *m* 1962, Hilary Anne, da of Reginald Drew, of Essex; 2 s (Michael b 1962, Harry b 1970), 2 da (Fiona b 1964, Julia b 1967); *Career* chm: Cadogan Investments 1970- (md 1966), Tobacco Trade Benevolent Assoc 1977-82; A Oppenheimer & Co 1979-, Medical Academic Unit Broomsfield Hosp, Eastern Cos Rugby Referees, Bd of Visitors HM Prison Chelmsford 1985-87 (now ordinary memb); Master Worshipful Co of Tobacco Makers and Tobacoo Blenders City of London 1982; *Recreations* squash, sailing (Albacore 'Phee Anna'), rugby refereeing; *Clubs* City Livery, Thorpe Bay Yacht; *Style—* John Adler, Esq, JP; c/o A Oppenheimer & Co, 20 Vanguard Way, Shoeburyness, Southend-on-Sea, Essex (☎ 0702 297 785, fax 0702 294 225, telex 99 453)

ADLER, Lawrence Cecil (Larry); s of Louis Adler, and Sadie Hack; *b* 10 Feb 1914; *Educ* Baltimore City Coll; *m* 1, 1938 (m dis 1961), Eileen Walser; 1 s, 2 da; m 2, 1969 (m dis 1977), Sally Cline; 1 da; *Career* mouth organist, journalist and critic; winner Maryland Harmonica Championship 1927, first British stage appearance in CB Cochran's Streamline revue 1934, debut as soloist with Symphony Orchestra Sydney Aust 1939; jt recital tours with dancer Paul Draper US 1941-49; soloist with NY Philharmonic and other maj orchs in US, Eng, Japan and Europe; war tours: for Allied Troops 1943, 1944 and 1945, Germany 1947 and 1949, Korea 1951, Israel 1967 (Six Day War) and 1973 (Yom Kippur War); contrib articles and book reviews: Sunday Times, New Statesman, Spectator, New Society, Observer, Punch; restaurant critic: Harpers and Queen, London Portrait, Boardroom, Chamber Life; columnist: What's On in London, Jazz Express, Jewish Gazette; film scores composed: Genevieve, King and Country, High Wind in Jamaica, The Great Chase; Hon Dip Peabody Conservatory of Music Baltimore, Duke Ellington fell Yale Univ 1988; *Books* Jokes and How to Tell Them (1963), It Ain't Necessarily So (autobiography 1985); *Recreations* tennis, journalism, conversation; *Clubs* Groucho, Paddington Tennis; *Style—* Larry Adler, Esq; c/o MBA Literary Agents Ltd, 45 Fitzroy Street, London W1P 5HR (☎ 071 387 2076)

ADLER, Prof Michael William; s of late Gerhard Adler, and Hella, *née* Hildergard; *b* 12 June 1939; *Educ* Middlesex Hosp Med Sch (MB BS, MD); *m* 1 (m dis 1978), Susan Jean Burnett; m 2, 23 June 1979, Karen Hope Dunnell, da of Richard Henry Williamson (d 1984); 2 da (Zoe b 1980, Emma b 1982); *Career* house offr and registrar in med (Middx Hosp, Central Middx Hosp, Whittington Hosp) 1965-69, lectr St Thomas' Hosp Med Sch 1970-75, sr lectr Middx Hosp Med Sch 1975-79, prof of genito urinary med Middx Hosp Med Sch 1979-; MRC memb: Res Advsy Gp on epidemiological studies of sexually transmitted dieases 1975-80, Working Pty to coordinate lab studies on the gonococcus 1979-83, Working Pty on AIDS 1981-87 (Sub Ctee therapeutic studies 1985-87), Ctee epidemiological studies on AIDS 1985, Ctee on clinical studies of prototype vaccines against AIDS 1987; Jt Ctee of Higher Med Trg: memb Advsy Ctee on genito urinary med 1981-86, sec 1982-83, chm 1984-86; memb EC Working Gp on AIDS 1985-, chm RCP Ctee on Genito Urinary Med 1987- (memb 1981-), advsr Parly All Pty Ctee on AIDS 1987-, tstee Nat AIDS Tst 1987- (chm Grants and Gen Purposes Ctee), dir AIDS Policy Unit 1988-89, memb Cncl Med Soc for Study of Venereal Diseases; DHSS: memb Expert Advsy Gp AIDS 1984-, memb Gp on health care workers 1987, chief sci advsr Res Liaison Gp (Child Health) 1985; memb: Exec Ctee Int Union against Venereal Diseases 1986-, BMA AIDS Working Pty 1986-; advsr in venereology WHO 1983-; fndr ed AIDS (monthly jl) 1986-; FFCM, FRCP, MRCP; *Books* ABC of Sexually Transmitted Diseases (1984), ABC of AIDS (1987), Diseases in the Homosexual Male (ed, 1988); *Recreations* yoga, jogging; *Style—* Prof Michael Adler; Academic Dept of Genito Urinary Medicine, James Pringle House, The Middlesex Hospital, London W1N 8AA (☎ 071 380 9146)

ADLEY, James Anthony; s of John Gordon Adley, and Valerie Elizabeth Rose, *née* Goodman; *b* 7 June 1956; *Educ* Uppingham; *m* 29 March 1981, Ruth Beverley, da of Sidney Middleburgh; 1 s (Joshua b 1989), 1 da (Natasha b 1985); *Career* dir: Charles Sydney Assur Cnslts Ltd, Charles Sydney (Gen Cnslts) Ltd; memb FIMBRA, Chartered Insur Inst; contributor on assur matters to leading specialist magazines; *Recreations* writing, music; *Style—* James A Adley, Esq; c/o Charles Sydney Assurance Consits Ltd, Boundary House, Turner Rd, Edgware, Middx (☎ 081 951 0336)

ADLEY, Robert James; MP (C) Christchurch 1983-; s of Harry Adley, of Hove, Sussex, and Marie Adley; *b* 2 March 1935; *Educ* Uppingham; *m* 1961, Jane Elizabeth, da of Wilfrid Pople (d 1966), of Burnham, Somerset; 2 s (Simon b 1964, Rupert b 1967); *Career* MP (C): Bristol NE 1970-74, Christchurch and Lymington 1974-83; chm: All-Party Parly Tourism Gp, Br-Hungarian Parly Gp, Br-Chinese Parly Gp; dir and mktg conslt Cwlth Holiday Inns of Canada Ltd; memb Nat Cncl for Br Hotels Restaurants and Caterers Assoc, fndr and first chm Brunel Soc, tstee Brunel Engrg Centre Tst, patron SS GB Project, ctee memb Nat Railway Museum York; chm: British-Syrian Parly Gp, Br-ASEAN Parly Gp, Br-Jordanian Parly Gp; vice chm Conservative Transport Ctee; *Books* British Steam in Camera Colour (1979), In Search of Steam (1981), The Call of Steam (1982), To China for Steam (1983), All Change Hong Kong (1984), In Praise of Steam (1985), Wheels (1987), Covering My Tracks (1988), Tunnel Vision (1988), Out of Steam (1990); *Style—* Robert Adley, Esq, MP; c/o House of Commons, London SW1A 0AA

ADLINGTON, Jonathan Peter Nathaniel; s of Sidney Roy Adlington, JP (d 1982), of Mylor, Cornwall, and Patricia, *née* Moxon; *b* 26 April 1949; *Educ* Downside, Univ of Liverpool (LLB); *m* 2 June 1973, Caroline Patricia Lilian Marie, da of Brian BW Bromley, of Crowborough, E Sussex; 1 s (Edward b 25 Dec 1983), 2 da (Emily b 3 May 1975, Tamsin b 19 Sept 1976); *Career* admitted slr 1973; ptnr Trowers and Hamlins 1976- (articled clerk 1971-73); memb Law Soc; *Recreations* sailing; *Clubs* RAC; *Style—* Jonathan Adlington, Esq; Trowers & Hamlins, 6 New Square, Lincoln's Inn, London WC2A 3RP (☎ 071 831 6292, telex 21422, fax 071 831 8700)

ADMANI, Dr (Abdul) Karim; OBE (1987), JP (1974); s of Haji Razzak Admani (d 1954), of Palitana, India, and Hajiani Rahima Admani; *b* 19 Sept 1934; *Educ* Gujrat Univ (BSc), Karachi Univ (MB BS), Univ of London; *m* Seema, da of Charles Robson (d 1947), of South Shields; 1 s (Nadim b 1969), 1 da (Nilofer b 1971); *Career* aonslt physician with special interest in strokes and the elderly; teacher Health Authority 1970-, clinical lectr Sheffield Medical Sch 1972-; dir: Ranmoor Grange Nursing Home Ltd 1975-80, Overseas Doctors Assoc in the UK Ltd 1976- (chm 1981-87, pres 1987-), Sunningdale Yorks Ltd 1983-; county pres BRCS (S Yorks) 1982-; memb: Exec Ctee for Racial Equality in Sheffield 1972- (chm 1978-), Exec Ctee BMA Sheffield 1974-, Gen Medical Cncl in UK 1979-, Central Ctee of Consultant and Specialists in UK 1979-, Exec Ctee Age Concern Sheffield 1982-, Sheffield Health Authy; memb Editorial Bd: Pakistan Medical Bulletin 1974-, Medi-Scene 1981-, ODA News Review 1985-; chm ODTS of ODA 1982-; pres: Muslim Cncl of Sheffield Rotherham and Dists 1978-, Union of Pakistani Orgns in UK and Europe 1979-; magistrate City of Sheffield 1974-; DTM&H (Eng), MRCP, FRCP, FRCPG, FRCPE, FRCM, FRIPHH; *Publications* Guidance for Overseas Doctors in National Health Service in UK (ed, 1982 and 1991); *Recreations* tennis, table tennis, snooker, chess; *Clubs* Abbeydale Rotary, Liberal, Medico-Chirurgical Soc; *Style—* Dr Karim Admani, OBE, JP; 1 Derriman Glen, Silverdale Rd, Sheffield S11 9LQ (☎ 0742 360465); Northern General Hospital, Barnsley Rd, Sheffield (☎ 0742 434343)

ADOLPH, Dr (Moir) Patrick Nelham; s of William Edgar Leonard Adolph (d 1959), of London, and Bridget, *née* Honan (d 1981); *b* 8 March 1931; *Educ* Clongowes Wood Coll, Co Kildare Eire, University Coll Dublin, Nat Univ of Ireland (MB BCh, BAO), Royal Coll of Physicians and Surgeons (Dr Aviation Med), Univ of London (MSc); *m* 17 June 1961, Yvette Mary, da of Donald Hayes; 3 s (William Patrick, Richard Vincent, Christopher Justin); *Career* Unit MO and SMO RAF 1962, RAF Inst of Aviation Med 1971, occupational med advsr to Princ MO HQ RAF Support Cmd, Offr i/c Envirnomental Health Team RAF Halton, Staff MO advsr to Dir of Health and Res 1978, specialist in aviation and occupational med to Royal Saudi Air Force, MO in res Civil Service 1988; Freeman City of London 1960, Liveryman Worshipful Co of Gold and Silver Wyre Drawers 1960; MFOM; *Recreations* bridge, golf, snow skiing; *Style—* Dr Patrick Adolph; Hope Cottage, 12 Hope Lane, Upper Hale, Farnham, Surrey GU9 0HYP (☎ 0252 721 463)

ADRIAN, 2 Baron (UK 1955); Richard Hume Adrian; s of 1 Baron Adrian, OM (d 1977), and Hester, *née* Pinsent, DBE, BEM (d 1966); *b* 16 Oct 1927; *Educ* Westminster, Trinity Coll Cambridge (MA, MB BChir, MD); *m* 1967, Lucy, da of Alban Caroe, of Campden Hill Sq, London W8; *Heir* none; *Career* Nat Serv Capt RAMC 1952-54; Univ of Cambridge: prof cell physiology 1978-, master Pembroke Coll 1981-, vice chllr 1985-87; tstee Br Museum, memb American Philosophical Soc; FRS, FRCP; *Style—* Prof the Rt Hon the Lord Adrian, FRS; The Master's Lodge, Pembroke College, Cambridge (☎ 0223 65862); Umgeni, Cley, Holt, Norfolk (☎ 0263 740597)

ADRIAN (aka WARNE), John Adrian Marie Edward; s of Col John Edward Marie William Warne, REME (d 1971), and Agnes Amelia Diana, *née* Mills; *b* 29 Jan 1938; *Educ* Dulwich Coll London, Salesian Coll Burwash Sussex; *Career* served RAF Cyprus 1955-58; singer and dancer 1959-72; performed at: London Palladium, Moulin Paris, Rouge Paris and Carre Theatre Amsterdam; theatre mangr 1972-86: Nat Youth Theatre, Stoll Moss Theatres London, St Georges Shakespeare Theatre, Garrick Theatre London, Royal Cultural Theatre Amman Jordan, Theatre Royal Windsor; admin and sec Grand Order of Water Rats 1986-; memb: Br Actors Equity, Soc for Theatre Res; *Recreations* theatre research, fencing, swimming and cycling; *Clubs* East India & Public Schools, Green Room; *Style—* John Adrian, Esq; 16 Gloucester Court, Swan St, London SE1 1DQ; Grand Order of Water Rats, 328 Gray's Inn Rd, London WC1X 8BZ (☎ 071 278 3248, fax 071 278 1765)

ADRIEN; *see*: Latour-Adrien

ADVANI, Dr Vik; s of Khema Advani (d 1977), of London, and Gomi Advani (d 1986); *b* 14 June 1950; *Educ* St Xavier's HS Bombay, Hendon Co Sch, Welsh Nat Sch of Med, Univ of Wales (BDS); *Career* cosmetic dentist, portrait painter, sculptor; lectr Children's Dept The London Hosp 1974-75, res into the influence of art in the treatment of handicapped children Univ of Bergen Norway 1976; exhibitions incl: The Arko Gallery Hampstead, Leighton House; one man shows incl: The Power of Portraits London 1987, Watercolours and Pastels London 1988, Say It With Flowers 1989; artistic cmmns incl: Somerset Maugham (portrait bronze), Indira Gandhi (portrait bronze), large murals for Br and Indian charities 1987, portrait of Prince Charles on a polo pony (The Pimm's Book of Polo) 1989; work in pub and private collections:

Holland, Italy, Switzerland, Norway, Germany, USA, Britain, India; lectures incl: Art as Therapy for The Howard League of Penal Reform, Art and Hypnotherapy for Br Soc of Hypnotherapy 1989; set up art workshops in various hosps and with contemporary Br artists on the theatre of art for handicapped children; fundraiser for St John Ambulance London Prince of Wales' Dist, radio and TV appearances, pubns in magazines and jls on holistic and cosmetic dentistry, original christmas greeting cards for children's charities; nat sculpture competition prize for work from Cradle to Grave; *Recreations* painting to music, pursuing serendipity; *Clubs* Travellers, Chelsea Arts; *Style*— Dr Vik Advani; 2 Dukes Lane, off Kensington Church Street, London W8 4JL (☎ 071 937 0772, fax 071 937 0772)

AEBERHARD, John Peter; s of Armin Aeberhard (d 1988), of Switzerland, and Winifred Florence, *née* Ryland; *b* 6 March 1937; *Educ* Bromley Co GS, CCC Oxford (MA); *m* 1964, Penelope Jane, da of Eric John Rankin, MC; 3 s (Matthew John b 25 May 1966, Daniel Edwin b 28 Oct 1969, Peter Joseph b 24 Sept 1971); *Career* press offr: Michelin Tyre Co Ltd 1962-66, English Electric Computers 1966-69; Honeywell: PRO N Europe 1969-75, dir Public Relations UK Ops 1975-78, dir Public Relations and Advertising Honeywell Information Systems Inc Boston Mass 1978-80; md Aeberhard & Partners Ltd 1981-; PRCA (Company membership 1989-); *Recreations* running, walking, jazz; *Style*— John Aeberhard, Esq; Millstones, Egypt Lane, Farnham Common, Buckinghamshire SL2 3LF (☎ 0753 6427390); A Plus Group Ltd, Tithe Barn, Tithe Court, Langley, Berks SL3 8AS (☎ 0753, 586655, fax 0753 586223)

AFFORD, (John) Andrew; s of Jill Afford; *b* 12 May 1964; *Educ* Spalding GS, Stamford Coll of Further Educn; *m* 1 Oct 1988, Lynn, da of (Thomas) James McConnell; *Career* professional cricketer; former amateur Bourne CC, Nottinghamshire CCC 1984-; England A: tour to Kenya and Zimbabwe 1990, 2 Test matches, 2 one-day Ints; honours with Nottinghamshire CCC: County Championship 1987, Benson & Hedges Cup 1989; Gold award winner Benson & Hedges Cup semi-final v Kent 1989; *Recreations* golf, tennis, reading about the Beatles; *Style*— Andrew Afford, Esq; c/o Notts CCC, Trent Bridge, West Bridgford, Nottingham NG2 6AG (☎ 0602 821525)

AFSHAR, Farhad; s of Aziz Afshar Yazdi, and Btoul, *née* Ameli; *b* 4 Dec 1941; *Educ* Lord Wandsworth Coll Hants, London Hosp Med Coll Univ of London (BSc, MB BS, MD); *m* 1, 23 Aug 1968 (m dis 1983), Lucille Anne, da of William E Goodfellow (d 1985); 3 s (Iain b 1970, Daniel b 1973, Brett b 1974), 1 da (Nina b 1977); *Career* fell in neurosurgery Ohio State Univ USA 1974-75, conslt neurosurgeon and sr lectr in neurosurgery London Hosp 1975-85, sr registrar in neurosurgery London and St Bartholomew's Hosp 1977-77, conslt neurosurgeon St Bartholomews Hosp 1985-; numerous chapters and scientific papers on neurosurgery, examiner in surgery Univ of London; FRSM, MRCS, LRCP, FRCS; memb: Soc of Br Neurosurgeons, Congress of American Neurosurgeons, Euro and World Sterotaxic Surgns, World Pituitary Surgns; *Books* Stereotaxic Atlas of Human Brain Stem and Cerebellar Nuclei (1978); *Recreations* photography, natural history, walking; *Style*— Farhad Afshar, Esq; 109 Harley St, London W1 (☎ 071 935 7505); Dept of Neurosurgery, St Bartholomews Hosp, London EC1 (☎ 071 601 8888)

AGA KHAN (IV), HH The; Prince Karim; s of late Prince Aly Khan, and Hon Joan, *née* Yarde-Buller (now Viscountess Camrose), da of 3 Baron Churston, MVO, OBE; gs of HH Rt Hon the Aga Khan (III), GCSI, GCIE, GCVO (d 1957); *b* 13 Dec 1936; *Educ* Le Rosey, Harvard; *m* 1969, Sarah Frances (Sally), o da of Lt-Col A E Croker Poole, and former w of Lord James Crichton-Stuart, s of 5 Marquess of Bute; 2 s (Prince Rahim b 1971, Prince Hussain b 1974), 1 da (Princess Zahra b 1970); *Career* Spiritual Leader and Imam of Ismaili Muslims, granted title HH by HM The Queen 1957, and HRH by late Shah of Iran 1959; *Style*— His Highness the Aga Khan; Aiglemont, 60270 Gouvieux, France

AGAMI, Dr George; s of Dr Alexander Agami (d 1959), and Rose, *née* Goraeb (d 1978); *b* 21 Aug 1928; *Educ* Abbassieh Med Sch Ain Shans Univ Cairo (MB BCh); *m* 14 Nov 1973 (m dis 1989), Marlene, da of Frank Townend (d 1979); 1 s (Daniel Alexander b 10 Jan 1977), 1 da (Rebecca Louise b 16 July 1975); *Career* house offr 1957-58, gen surgery trg 1958-60, private psychiatrist 1960-70, assoc specialist psychiatry 1970-; memb Leics Med Soc; *Style*— Dr George Agami; Woodlands Day Hospital, Carlton Hayes Hospital, Narborough, Leics (☎ 0760 863265)

AGAR, Hon Mark Sidney Andrew; s of 5 Earl of Normanton (d 1967), and Lady Fiona (d 1985), da of 4 Marquess Camden; *b* 2 Sept 1948; *Educ* Gordonstoun; *m* 1, 1973 (m dis 1979), Rosemary, da of Maj Philip Marnham; m 2, 8 Feb 1985, Arabella Clare, da of John Gilbert Gilbey (d 1982), and formerly w of Thomas Charles Blackwell; 2 s (Max John Andrew b 6 April 1986, Charles Christopher Edward b 29 July 1989); *Career* Lt Blues and Royals; farmer and landowner (1200 acres); *Style*— The Hon Mark Agar; Inholmes, Woodlands St Mary, Newbury, Berks

AGBIM, Osita Godfrey; s of Felix Agbim (d 1956) and Amodo Agbim (d 1981); *b* 26 June 1932; *Educ* CKC Coll Nigeria, Univ Coll Dublin; *m* 20 Aug 1960, Beatrice, da of James Okafor (d 1977); 4 s (Raymond b 1961, Stephen b 1963, Anthony b 1966, Paul b 1970), 1 da (Claire b 1977); *Career* conslt surgn; conslt to the Nigeria High Commission London; *Recreations* meditation, jogging; *Style*— Osita Agbim, Esq; 17 Grosvenor Gardens, London NW11 (☎ 081 458 1995); 92 Harley Street, London W1 (☎ 071 486 3499)

AGGETT, Ms Valerie (Mrs John Grenier); da of James William Cocksey (d 1986); *b* 15 Dec 1950; *Educ* Bury GS, Univ of Durham (BA), Coll of Law Guildford; *m* 1 (m dis), Mr Aggett; m 2, 1981, John Allan Grenier, s of Rev George Arthur Grenier (d 1973); 1 step s, 1 step da; *Career* slr; princ and md The HLT Group Ltd 1976- (Queen's Award for Export 1982); *Recreations* motor cruising, tennis, interior design, fashion; *Clubs* RAC, Reform, Queens; *Style*— Ms Valerie Aggett; The HLT Group Ltd, 200 Greyhound Rd, London W14 9RY (☎ 071 385 3377); Plovers, Ruck Lane, Horsmonden, Kent

AGGISS, Liz; da of James Henry Aggiss, of Terling, Essex, and Marie Elizabeth, *née* Chamberlain (d 1975); *b* 28 May 1953; *Educ* Hornchurch GS, Madeley Coll, Nikolais/Louis Dance Theatre NY; *Career* choreographer, performer and artistic dir (in collaboration with Billy Cowie); memb The Wild Wigglers (formed 1982, touring worldwide); work with Divas Dance Co (formed 1985) incl: Torei en Veran Veta Arnold! 1986-87, Eleven Executions 1988, Dorothy and Klaus 1989-91, Die Orchidee im Plastik Karton 1989-91, Drool and Drivel They Care 1990-91, La Petite Soupe 1990-91, French Songs 1991; solo performances incl: Grotesque Dancer 1986-89, Dead Steps/Die Totenschritte 1988-89, Stations of the Angry 1989, Tell Tale Heart 1989, Banda Banda 1989; awards: Colorado Coll scholarship to study with Hanya Holm 1980, Brighton Festival Special award 1989, Brighton Festival Zap award for Dance 1989, Brighton Festival BBC Radio award 1990, Alliance and Leicester award 1990, Time Out/Dance Umbrella award 1990; contrib dance entries Fontana Dictionary of Modern Thought (1988); *Recreations* music, cinema; *Style*— Ms Liz Aggiss; 10/11 Pavilion Parade, Brighton BN2 IRA (☎ 0273 604141)

AGIS, Gaby; *b* 1960; *Career* independent choreographer 1983-; choreographer in residence Riverside Studios 1984-86, launched own co 1985; progs incl: Close Streams (1983), Crossing Under Upwards (1983), Surfacing (1984), Borders (1984), Shouting Out Loud (1984), Between Public Places (1985), Undine and the Still (1985), This Is, What, Where (1985), In Anticipation of Surrender (1986), Fow Fold (1986), Lying On the Warm Concrete (1986), Trail (1986), Kin (1987), Freefall (1988), Don't Trash My Altar/Don't Alter My Trash (1988), MLads (London Symphony Orchestra, 1989), Hess Is Dead (Royal Shakespeare Co, 1989), Dark Hours And Finer Moments (1989), Pale Shelter (1990); performance art venues incl: Whitechapel Art Gallery, Riverside Studios Gallery, The Museum of Modern Art Oxford and Cornerhouse Gallery Manchester; tv and film appearances incl: Hail the New Puritan 1985, Imaginary Women 1986, Freefall 1988; awards incl Distinguished Visitors award of US Govt 1986; *Style*— Ms Gaby Agis

AGIUS, Marcus Ambrose Paul; s of Lt-Col Alfred Victor Louis Benedict Agius, MC, TD (d 1969), and Ena Eleanora, *née* Hueffer; *b* 22 July 1946; *Educ* St George's Coll Weybridge, Trinity Hall Cambridge (MA), Harvard Business Sch (MBA); *m* 1971, Kate Juliette, da of Maj Edmund Leopold de Rothschild, TD, of Hants; 2 da (Marie-Louise Eleanor b 1977, Lara Sophie Elizabeth b 1980); *Career* Lazard Bros & Co Ltd: dir 1981-85, md 1985-90, vice chm 1990-; non exec dir Exbury Gardens Ltd; *Recreations* gardening, tennis, shooting, skiing; *Clubs* White's; *Style*— Marcus A P Agius, Esq; Lazard Bros & Co Ltd, 21 Moorfields, London EC2P 2HT (☎ 071 588 2721, telex 886438, fax 071 638 1051)

AGLIONBY, His Hon Judge Francis John; s of Francis Basil Aglionby, and Marjorie Wycliffe Aglionby; *b* 17 May 1932; *Educ* Charterhouse, CCC Oxford; *m* 1967, Susan Victoria Mary, *née* Vaughan; 1 s, 1 da; *Career* called to the Bar Inner Temple 1956; rec Crown Court 1975-80, bencher Inner Temple 1976; chllr: Birmingham Diocese 1971-, Portsmouth Diocese 1978-; circuit judge (SE) 1980-; *Clubs* Brooks's; *Style*— His Hon Judge Aglionby; The Croft, Houghton, Carlisle, Cumbria CA3 OLD

AGNEW, Hon Mrs (Agneta Joanna Middleton); *née* Campbell; yr da (by 1 m) of Baron Campbell of Eskan (Life Peer), *qv*; *b* 18 Oct 1944; *m* 21 Oct 1966 (m dis 1985), Jonathan Geoffrey William Agnew, er s of late Sir Geoffrey William Gerald Agnew; 1 s (and 1 s decd), 2 da; *Style*— The Hon Mrs Agnew; Flat 1, 30 Pond Place, London SW3 6QP

AGNEW, Sir (John) Anthony Stuart; 4 Bt (UK 1895), of Great Stanhope St, St George, Hanover Square, Co London; s of Maj Sir John Stuart Agnew, 3 Bt (d 1957); *b* 25 July 1914; *Heir* bro, Maj (George) Keith Agnew, *qv*; *Style*— Sir Anthony Agnew, Bt; c/o Blackthorpe Farm, Rougham, Bury St Edmunds, Suffolk

AGNEW, (Alexander James) Blair; s of James Percival Agnew, DL, and Jessie Blair, *née* Anderson (d 1978), of Racecourse Rd, Ayr; *b* 6 Oct 1935; *Educ* Rugby; *m* 1958, Gillian Margaret, da of Maj W D Gray-Newton, of Little Court, Warboys, Cambs, 2 s (Blair, Angus), 1 da (Caroline); *Career* regular offr Royal Scots Fus then Royal Highland Fus 1954-65 (Capt); stockbroker, chm Penney Easton & Co, memb of Cncl of Stock Exchange 1979-85; CBIM; *Recreations* gardening, walking; *Clubs* Army and Navy, Western (Glasgow); *Style*— Blair Agnew, Esq; Drumbarr, Ayr KA6 6BN (☎ 0292 41312); Penney Easton & Co, PO Box 112, 24 George Square, Glasgow G2 1EB (☎ 041 248 2911; telex 777967, code 390)

AGNEW, Hon Mrs (Clare Rosalind); *née* Dixon; da of 2 Baron Glentoran, KBE, and Lady Diana Mary Wellesley, eld da of 3 Earl Cowley (d 1919); *b* 15 Nov 1937; *m* 1965 (m dis 1980), as his 2 w, Rudolph Ion Joseph Agnew; 1 s, 1 da; *Style*— The Hon Mrs Agnew; 35 St Peter's Square, London W6 9NW

AGNEW, Sir (William) Godfrey; KCVO (1965, CVO 1953), CB (1975); s of Lennox Edelsten Agnew (d 1968), of Tunbridge Wells, and Elsie Blyth, *née* Nott (d 1972); *b* 11 Oct 1913; *Educ* Tonbridge; *m* 1, 1939, Ruth Mary (d 1962), da of late Capt Charles Joseph Henry O'Hara Moore, CVO, MC, and late Lady Dorothie, da of 9 Earl of Denbigh and Desmond, GCVO, and Hon Cecilia Clifford, da of 8 Baron Clifford of Chudleigh; 3 s, 3 da (*see* Richard J H Pollen, the Hon Jonathan Davies); m 2, 1965, Nancy Veronica, wid of Adm Sir St John Tyrwhitt, 2 Bt, KCB, DSO, DSC; 2 step s, 1 step da; *Career* served WW II Surrey and Sussex Yeo and RA attaining rank of Maj; admitted slr 1935; joined Pub Tstee Office 1936, dep sec Cabinet Office 1972-74; Privy Cncl: sr clerk 1945-51, dep clerk 1951-53, clerk 1953-54; chm: Sembal Tst 1966-73, Lady Clare Ltd 1970-87 (dir 1948-87); vice-chm Sun Life Assurance Society 1983-84 (dir 1974-84); dir: Seaway Shipping Agencies Ltd 1971-80, Seaway Holdings Ltd 1971-80, Artagen Properties 1976-80, Sun Life Properties 1980-84; memb Bd Hon Tutors Cncl Legal Educn Univ of WI 1973-; conslt: Cncl Engrg Instns 1974-79, Univ Coll Cardiff and Univ of Wales Inst of Sciences and Technol 1982-84; Hon FIMechE, Hon FIMunE, Hon FCIBS, Hon FICE; *Clubs* Army and Navy, Swinley Forest Golf, Rye Golf; *Style*— Sir Godfrey Agnew, KCVO, CB; Pinehurst, Friary Rd, South Ascot, Berks SL5 9HD

AGNEW, Ian Hervey; s of Peter Graeme Agnew, of The Old House, Manaccan, nr Helston, Cornwall, and Mary Diana, *née* Hervey; *b* 19 Aug 1941; *Educ* Stowe, London Sch of Printing & Graphic Arts (Admin Dipl); *m* 4 April 1964, Amanda Barbara, da of Maj A W Read (ka 1944), Inns of Ct Regt, of Water Hall Farm, Ifield Wood, Crawley, Sussex; 2 s (Mark b 1966, Jonathan b 1968); *Career* Lt Inns of Ct and City Yeomanry Regt TA 1962-68; Bradbury Agnew and Co (publishers of Punch): printer 1961-72, dir of subsid cos 1968-72; md Flarepath Printers Ltd 1972-75, proprietor of Edgebury Press (printers) 1978-; dir Iris Fund for Prevention of Blindness London 1987-; *Recreations* shooting, skiing, motor racing (hill climbing classic f3 car); *Style*— Ian Agnew, Esq; Oak Lodge, Ifield Wood, Crawley, Sussex RH11 0LE (☎ 0293 522255); Edgebury Press, 104A Green St, Eastbourne, Sussex (☎ 0323 20810)

AGNEW, Jonathan Geoffrey William; s of late Sir Geoffrey Agnew, and late Hon Doreen, da of 1 Baron Jessel, CB, CMG; *b* 30 July 1941; *Educ* Eton, Trinity Coll Cambridge (MA); *m* 1966 (m dis 1986), Hon Agneta Joanna Middleton, *qv*, da of Baron Campbell of Eskan; 1 s, 2 da; m 2, 1990, Marie-Claire; *Career* fin conslt Morgan Stanley & Co Inc 1983-86 (md 1973-82); chm: Kleinwort Benson Securities Ltd 1987-, Kleinwort Benson Ltd 1989-; chief exec Kleinwort Benson Group plc; dir: Thos Agnew and Sons Ltd, Int Financial Markets Trading Ltd; *Clubs* White's, Automobile (Paris); *Style*— Jonathan Agnew, Esq; 51E Eaton Sq, London SW1W 9BE (☎ 071 235 7589)

AGNEW, Jonathan Herbert; s of David Quentin Hope Agnew (d 1976), and Janet May Dilkes, *née* Malden (d 1981); *b* 7 Nov 1933; *Educ* Clifton; *m* 17 May 1958, (Mary) Mollie Kathleen (d 1982), da of Brig Stannus Grant Fraser, MC (d 1980); 2 s (George b 26 Feb 1962, Michael 22 Oct 1965), 1 da (Susan b 11 May 1963); *Career* RNR Subs; deck offr MN 1952-69, cargo mangr OCL 1970-80, dir Macgregor Ports and Harbours 1980-81, self employed cargo res conslt 1981-; press offr local MS Soc; co-organiser Blackwater Folk Club; *Books* Container Stowage, A Practical Approach (co-author, 1972), Thomas Stowage (co-author 1983); *Recreations* sailing, music (bagpipes); *Clubs* Army and Navy; *Style*— Jonathan Agnew, Esq; 3 Birtwhistle St, Gatehouse of Fleet, Scotland; 11 Ulting Lane, Langford, Maldon, Essex (☎ 0621 55447, fax 0621 56819, telex 995548 LEDA G)

AGNEW, Hon Mrs (Joyce Violet); *née* Godber; er da of 1 and last Baron Godber (d 1976); *b* 23 June 1917; *m* 27 Jan 1937, Andrew Agnew, s of late Sir Andrew Agnew, of Glenlee Park, New Galloway, Kirkcudbright; 3 da; *Style*— The Hon Mrs Agnew; Sweethaws Farm, Crowborough, Sussex TN6 3SS (☎ 0892 655045); Garheugh, Port William, Wigtownshire (☎ 058 15 235)

AGNEW, Julian; *b* 1943; *Educ* Eton, Trinity Coll Cambridge (scholar and sr scholar,

BA); *Career* md Agnew's 1987- (joined 1965, dir 1968); pres BADA 1979-81, chm Soc of London Art Dealers 1986-90, treas Friends of the Courtauld Inst, chm Evelyn Hosp Cambridge; FRSA; *Recreations* grand opera, music, books, tennis, golf; *Style—* Julian Agnew, Esq; Thos Agnew & Sons Ltd, 43 Old Bond St, London W1X 4BA (☎ 071 629 6176, fax 071 629 4359)

AGNEW, Maj (George) Keith; TD; s of Maj Sir John Stuart Agnew, 3 Bt (d 1957); hp of bro, Sir (John) Anthony Stuart Agnew, 4 Bt; *b* 25 Nov 1918; *Educ* Rugby, Trinity Coll Cambridge; *m* 10 July 1948, Baroness Anne Merete Louise, yr da of Baron Johann Schaffalitzky de Muckadell, of Rodkilde, Fyn, Denmark; 2 s (John Keith b 19 Dec 1950, George Anthony b 18 Aug 1953); *Career* Maj Suffolk Yeo (Res); landowner, farmer, forester; JP Suffolk 1949-88; *Style—* Maj Keith Agnew, TD; Blackthorpe Farm, Rougham, Bury St Edmunds, Suffolk

AGNEW, Stephen William; s of Maj Sir John Agnew, 3 Bt, TD, JP, DL (d 1957), and Kathleen, *née* White (d 1971); bro of Sir Anthony Agnew, 4 Bt, *qv*; *b* 31 July 1921; *Educ* Rugby, Trinity Coll Cambridge; *m* 1, 28 June 1947 (m dis 1966), Elizabeth, da of James Brooks Close, of Grey Walls, Aldeburgh, Suffolk; 6 s (Stuart b 30 Aug 1949, Bolton b 21 Oct 1950, Jim b 12 April 1953, Stephen b 5 Dec 1954, Theodore b 17 Jan 1961, St John b 25 Feb 1964), 1 da (Margaret (Mrs Gurney) b 12 Jan 1952); m 2, 1967, Adene Leona Cookson, yst da of Vincent J Brady, DSC (d 1959), of Manly, NSW; *Career* serv WWII 7 Queen's Own Hussars, Lt, Middle E and Italy 1942-46, wounded Sept 1944, invalided out Feb 1946; md Farming Cos in Norfolk 1963-, local dir Sun Alliance and London Insur Gp 1964-85, chm Rogate Farms Pty Ltd NSW 1983-87, dir Aust Regnl Offs Pty Ltd Sydney 1988-; chm: Cawston Coll 1964-71, Norfolk and Norwich Marriage Guidance Cncl 1978-85; memb High Steward Ctee Norwich Cathedral 1962-80, gen cmmr Income Tax 1964-; *Recreations* hunting, shooting, music; *Clubs* Cavalry and Guards, Union (Sydney), Norfolk (Norwich); *Style—* Stephen Agnew, Esq; Oulton Hall, Norwich, Norfolk (☎ 026 387 237)

AGNEW OF LOCHNAW, Sir Crispin Hamlyn; 11 Bt (NS 1629), of Lochnaw, Wigtownshire; Chief of the Name of Agnew; s of Sir Fulque Melville Gerald Noel Agnew of Lochnaw, 10 Bt (d 1975), and Swanzie, da of Maj Esme Nourse Erskine, CMG, MC (descended from the Earls of Buchan), late Consular Serv; *b* 13 May 1944; *Educ* Uppingham, RMA Sandhurst; *m* 27 Aug 1980, Susan Rachel Strang, da of Jock Strang Steel, of Logie (2 s of Sir Samuel Strang Steel of Philiphaugh, 1 Bt, TD, DL, Cornwallis, 2 da of 1 Baron Cornwallis) and Lesley (da of Lt-Col Sir John Graham of Larbert, 3 Bt, VC, OBE, and Rachel, 5 da of Col Sir Alexander Sprot of Stravithie, 1 Bt, CMG); 3 da (Isabel Sevilla Wilhelmina b 1984, Emma Rachel Elizabeth b 1986, Roseanna Celia Nancy b 1989); *Heir* cous, Dr Andrew David Quentin Agnew b 31 Dec 1929; *Career* Maj RHF (ret 1981); advocate 1982; Slains Pursuivant of Arms to the Lord High Constable of Scotland (Th of Erroll) 1978-81, Unicorn Pursuivant of Arms 1981-86, Rothesay Herald of Arms 1986-; ldr of expeditions to: Greenland 1968, Patagonia 1972, Api Himal 1980; memb of expeditions to: Greenland 1966, Antarctica 1970, Nuptse Himal 1975, Everest 1976; *Books* co-author (with Heather Baillie) The Licensing (Scotland) Act 1976 (1989); *Recreations* mountaineering, yachting (yacht 'Pippa's Song'), heraldry, genealogy; *Clubs* Army and Navy; *Style—* Sir Crispin Agnew of Lochnaw, Bt; 6 Palmerston Rd, Edinburgh EH9 1TN (☎ 031 667 4970)

AGNEW-SOMERVILLE, Hon Lady (Margaret April Irene); *née* Drummond of Megginch; 3 and yst da of 15 Baron Strange (d 1982), to which Barony she was co-heiress with her sisters; *b* 3 April 1939; *m* 1963, Sir Quentin Charles Somerville Agnew-Somerville, 2 Bt, *qv*; *Books* A Regency Lady's Fairy Bower (1986); *Style—* The Hon Lady Agnew-Somerville; Mount Auldyn House, Jurby Rd, Ramsey, Isle of Man (☎ 0624 813724)

AGNEW-SOMERVILLE, Sir Quentin Charles Somerville; 2 Bt (UK 1957), of Clendry, Co Wigtown; s of Sir Peter Agnew, 1 Bt (d 1990), and his 1 w, Enid Frances (d 1982), da of Henry Boan, of Perth, W Australia; assumed by Royal Licence 1950 additional surname of Somerville after that of Agnew, and the arms of Somerville quarterly with those of Agnew, on succeeding to the Somerville estate of his maternal unc by m, 2 and last Baron Athlumney, who d 1929, leaving a widow, Margery, da of Henry Boan and sis of Enid, Sir Quentin's mother; *b* 8 March 1929; *Educ* RNC Dartmouth; *m* 1963, Hon Margaret April Irene Drummond, *qv*, da of 15 Baron Strange (d 1982); 1 s, 2 da (Amelia Rachel b 1966, Geraldine Margar b 1967); *Heir* s, James Lockett Charles Agnew-Somerville b 1970; *Career* Sub Lt RN to 1950, when invalided from serv; co dir; *Clubs* Brooks's, Kildare Street and University; *Style—* Sir Quentin Agnew-Somerville, Bt; Mount Auldyn House, Jurby Rd, Ramsey, Isle of Man (☎ 0624 813724)

AGUTTER, Jennifer (Jenny); da of Derek Brodie Agutter, OBE, of London, and Catherine, *née* Lynam; *b* 20 Dec 1952; *Educ* Elmhurst Ballet Sch Camberley Surrey; *m* 4 Aug 1990, Johan Carl Sebastian Tham; *Career* actress; film debut East of Sudan 1964; films incl: Ballerina 1964, Gates of Paradise 1967, Star 1968, Walkabout 1969, The Railway Children 1970, Logan's Run 1975, The Eagle Has Landed 1976, The Man in the Iron Mask 1976, Equus 1976, The Survivor 1980, An American Werewolf in London 1981, Secret Places 1983, Dark Tower 1987, King of the Wind 1989, Child's Play II 1989, The Dark Man 1990; stage performances incl: School for Scandal 1972, Rooted 1973, Arms and the Man 1973, The Tempest (NT) 1974, Spring Awakening (NT) 1974, RSC 1982-83 (Fontanelle in Lear, Regan in King Lear, Alice Arden in Arden of Faversham, Grace in the Body), Breaking the Silence (RSC) 1985, The Unified Field LA 1987, Breaking the Code 1987 (Neil Simon Theatre, NY) 1987, television incl: Long After Summer 1967, The Wild Duck 1971, The Snow Goose 1971, A War of Children 1972, Army 1980, Love's Labours Lost 1984, Silus Marner 1985, Murder She Wrote 1986, The Equaliser 1988, Not a Penny More, Not a Penny Less 1989; awards: Royal Variety Club Most Promising Artist 1971, Emmy (best supporting actress) for The Snow Goose 1971, BAFTA (best supporting actress) for Equus 1976; *Books* Snap (1984); *Style—* Miss Jenny Agutter; Namara Cowan Ltd, 45 Poland Street, London W1V 3DF (☎ 071 434 3871, fax 071 439 6489)

AGUTTER, Richard Devenish; s of Anthony Tom Devenish Agutter (d 1960), and Joan Hildegarde Sabina, *née* Machen (now Mrs Fleming); *b* 17 Sept 1941; *Educ* Marlborough; *m* 29 June 1968, Lesley Anne, da of Kenneth Alfred Ballard, MC, of Giles Barn Cottage, Horsted Keynes, Sussex; 3 s (Rupert William Devenish b 3 Nov 1972, Tom Alexander Devenish b 16 July 1975, Giles Edward Devenish b 6 April 1979); *Career* CA 1964, articled WT Walton & Sons 1960; KPMG Peat Marwick McLintock (formerly Peat Marwick Mitchell): joined 1964, ptnr 1977, currently chm KPMG Int Mergers and Acquisitions Network; Liveryman: Worshipful Co of Goldsmiths, Worshipful Co of Chartered Accountants; FCA (ACA 1964); *Recreations* sailing, gardening; *Clubs* City Livery; *Style—* Richard Agutter, Esq; Great Frenches Park, Snow Hill, Crawley Down, West Sussex RH10 3EE (☎ 0342 716 816); Flat 3, President's Quay House, 72 St Katharines Way, London E1 (☎ 071 702 9113); KPMG Peat Marwick McLintock, 8 Salisbury Square, Blackfriars, London EC4Y 8BB (☎ 071 236 8000, fax 071 832 8252, car 0860 718531)

AH-CHUEN, Sir Moi Lin Jean (Etienne); s of Jean George Ah-Chuen and Li Choi; *b* 22 Feb 1911; *Educ* St Jean Baptiste de La Salle, Chinese HS Mauritius; *m* 1929, Jeanne Hau Man Mui; 5 s, 6 da; *Career* MLA Mauritius 1948-76, Mauritius Govt delgn to UN 1974 and 1976, Cwlth Parly Assoc Mauritius 1948-, Min Local Govt Mauritius 1969-76; chm Chue Wing & Co 1977-; vice-chm Mauritius Union Assur Co 1948-; pres Chinese Cultural Centre 1968-; kt 1980; *Style—* Sir Jean Ah-Chuen; 5 Reverend Lebrun St, Rose Hill, Mauritius (☎ 4-3804)

AHEARNE, Stephen James; s of James Joseph Ahearne (d 1972), and Phyllis Eva, *née* Grigsby; *b* 7 Sept 1939; *Educ* St Ignatius Coll London; *m* 24 April 1965, Janet Elizabeth, da of Jack Ronald Edwards; 2 s (Jeremy b 1966, Thomas b 1968); *Career* CA; md BP Denmark 1978-81; dir: BP Chemicals Int 1981-86, BP Exploration, BP Coal, BP Int 1986-, gp controller BP plc 1986-; *Recreations* tennis, gardening; *Style—* Stephen J Ahearne, Esq; British Petroleum plc, Britannic House, Moor Lane, London EC2 (☎ 071 920 7320)

AHERN, Most Rev John James; *see*: Cloyne, Bishop (RC) of

AHLAS, Lars Peter Richard; *b* 22 Sept 1948; *Educ* Hogre Allmana Lávoverket a Kungsholmen Stockholm, London Sch of Foreign Trade (Dip Shipping & Marine Insur); *m* 1973, Sian Fiona, *née* Holford-Walker; 2 da; *Career* Lt Cdr Royal Swedish Navy 1969-71, Res 1971-; marine insur broker; W K Webster 1971-73, gen mangr Liberian Insur Agency 1973-74, broker Bland Payne 1974-78; dir: Jardine Glanvill Marine 1978-86, Gibbs Insur Hldgs Ltd 1986-; md Marine Div Gibbs Hartley Cooper Ltd 1986-; memb IBRC; *Recreations* shooting, squash, riding; *Clubs* Lansdowne; *Style—* Lars Ahlas, Esq

AHMED, Dr Haroon; s of Mohammad Nizam Ahmed (d 1980), and Bilquis Jehan, *née* Abbasi (d 1988); *b* 2 March 1936; *Educ* St Patrick's Sch Karachi, Imperial Coll London (BSc), Kings Coll Cambridge (PhD); *m* 4 July 1969, Evelyn Anne Travers, da of Alec Thorpe Goodrich; 2 da (Ayesha Fehmina b 12 March 1970, Rehana Sara b 17 Aug 1972); *Career* SEC and Hirst Research Centre 1958-59; Univ of Cambridge: res studentship Kings Coll 1959-62, Turner and Newall res fell 1962-63, univ demonstrator Dept of Engrg 1963-66, fell of Corpus Christi Coll 1967, lectr in engrg 1966-84, reader in microelectronics Cavendish Laboratory 1984-; FEng 1990, FIEE, MInstP; *Books* Introduction to Physical Electronics (with A H Beck, 1968), Electronics for Engineers (with P J Spreadbury, 1973); *Recreations* golf, tennis, skiing; *Style—* Dr Haroon Ahmed; Microelectronics Research Centre, Cavendish Laboratory, Madingley Rd, Cambridge CB3 OHE (☎ 0223 337557, fax 0223 337706)

AHMED, Dr Khurshid; s of Dr Ozair Ahmed (d 1985), of Wakefield, W Yorks, and Mrs R Ahmed; *b* 12 Aug 1963; *Educ* The Queen Elizabeth GS Wakefield, Univ of London (MH, MS); *Career* house offr The Middx Hosp 1987, sr house offr Bart's 1989, sr house offr UCH 1989, rotational sr house offr Charing Cross and Ealing Hosps; memb BMA; *Recreations* travel, photography, cricket; *Clubs* Nat Lib; *Style—* Dr Khurshid Ahmed; 91 Crayford Rd, London N1 (☎ 071 607 5721)

AHRENDS, Peter; s of Steffen Bruno Ahrends, and Margarete Maria Sophie Ahrends; *b* 30 April 1933; *Educ* Architectural Assoc Sch of Architecture (AADipl); *m* 1954, Elizabeth Robertson; 2 da; *Career* architect: Steffen Ahrends & Ptnrs Johannesburg 1957-58, Dennys Lasdun & Ptnrs and Julian Keable & Ptnrs 1959-60; fndr ptnr and dir Ahrends Burton & Koralek 1961, prof of architecture Bartlett Sch of Architecture and Planning UCL 1986-89; princ works incl: Berkeley Library Trinity Coll Dublin 1972, Arts Faculty Bldg 1979, res bldg Keble Coll Oxford 1976, Templeton Coll Oxford 1969-88, Nebenzahl House Jerusalem 1972, warehouse and showroom for Habitat Wallingford, factory for Cummins Engs Shotts, J Sainsbury Supermarket Canterbury 1984, retail HQ WH Smith Swindon 1985, John Lewis Dept Store Kingston 1990, St Marys Hosp Newport IOW 1990, Heritage Centre Dover, stations for extensions Docklands Railway, Br Embassy Moscow; *Clubs* AA; *Style—* Peter Ahrends; 7 Chalcot Rd, London NW1 8LH (fax 071 722 5445)

AHRENS, Christine; da of Jacob Ahrens, and Gesa, *née* Bey; *b* 12 Dec 1961; *Educ* Sumanistisches Gymnasium Hamburg, Cordwainers Coll (Dip SIAD); *Career* shoe designer; designed for films: A View to a Kill, Absolute Beginners; first winter collection 1985, exhibited New York, Milan, Paris 1987-88; made shoes for such designers as: Ally Cappelino, Jasper Conran, David Fielden, Joe-Casely-Hayford; exhibited with London Designer Collections 1988; *Style—* Ms Christine Ahrens; 11 Old Compton Street, London W1 5PH (☎ 071 287 1752)

AICHROTH, Paul Michael; s of Gerald Paul Aichroth, of Vancouver, Canada, and Elsie, *née* Webb; *b* 30 April 1936; *Educ* Alleyn's Sch, King's Coll London, Westminster Med Sch (MB BS, MS); *m* 17 June 1961, Angela, da of Frederick George Joslin, of Bournemouth, Dorset; 1 s (Mark Jonathan Paul); *Career* conslt orthopaedic surgn 1971-: Westminster Hosp, Westminster Children's Hosp, Queen Mary's Hosp Roehampton, Humana Wellington Hosp; author of various papers and thesis on knee disorders; memb Br Orthopaedic Assoc, memb RSM, vice pres SICOT, Hunterian prof RCS 1973; memb BMA 1963, FRCS 1965; *Books* Insall Knee Surgery (contrib, 1974), Harris's Orthopaedics (contrib, 1975), Operative Surgery (contrib, 1990); *Recreations* boats, countryside, Mozart, claret; *Clubs* Athenaeum; *Style—* Paul Aichroth, Esq; Flat 7, 43 Wimpole St, London W1M 7AF (☎ Rooms - 071 935 2349, Res - 071 935 7034); Hydon Wood, Feathercombe Lane, Hambledon, Surrey GU8 4DP (☎ 0483 860 377); Westminster Hospital, London SW1; Wellington Hospital, London NW8

AIKEN, Joan Delano; da of Conrad Potter Aiken, and Jessie McDonald Aiken; *b* 4 Sept 1924; *Educ* privately, Wychwood Sch Oxford; *m* 1, 7 July 1945, Ronald George Brown (d 1955), s of Albert Brown (d 1953); 1 s (John b 1949), 1 da (Elizabeth b 1951); m 2, 2 Sept 1976, Julius Goldstein; *Career* Aorked BBC 1942-43, librarian UN Information Ctee 1943-49, sub ed and features ed Argosy magazine 1955-60, copywriter J Walter Thompson London; author of stories and plays; Guardian award for Children's Literature 1969, Mystery Writers of America Edgar Allan Poe award 1972, Lewis Carroll Shelf award 1962; children's books; adult pubns; memb: Soc of Authors, Writers Guild, Mystery Writers of America; *Books* children's books: All You've Ever Wanted (1953), The Kingdom and the Cave (1960), Black Hearts in Battersea (1964), The Whispering Mountain Cape (1968), Armitage, Armitage, Fly Away Home (1970), Smoke From Cromwell's Time (1970), The Kingdom Under the Sea (1971), A Harp of Fishbones (1972), Winterthing (play, 1972), The Mooncusser's Daughter (1933), The Escaped Black Mamba (1973), Tales of Arabel's Raven (1974), Tale of a One-Way Street (1978), The Skin Spinners (poems, 1976), A Bundle of Nerves (1976), The Faithless Lollybird (1977), Mice and Mendelson (1978), Street (1979), Mortimer's Portrait on Glass (1982), Bridle the Wind Cape (1983), Mortimer's Cross (1983), Up the Chimney Down (stories, 1984), The Last Slice of Rainbow (stories, 1985), Dido and Pa Cape (1986), The Teeth of the Gale Cape (1988), The Erl King's Daughter (1988), Voices Hippo (1988); adult pubns: The Silence of Herondale (1964), The Fortune Hunters (1965), Hate Begins at Home (1967), The Embroidered Sunset (1970), Died on a Rainy Sunday (1972), Castle Barebane (1976), The Smile of the Stranger (1978), The Weeping Ash (1980), A Whisper in the Night (1982), The Way to Write for Children (1982), Foul Matter (1983), Mansfield Revisited (1985), Voices (1988), Blackground (1989), Jane Fairfax (1990), A Fit of Shivers (1990), The Haunting of Lamb House (1991); *Recreations* walking, gardening, listening to music, looking at art, travel; *Style—* Ms Joan Aiken; c/o A M Heath and Co Ltd, 79 St Martins Lane, London WC2N 4AA

AIKEN, Air Chief Marshal Sir John Alexander Carlisle; KCB (1973, CB 1967); s of Thomas Leonard and Margaret Aiken; *b* 22 Dec 1921; *Educ* Birkenhead Sch; *m*

1948, Pamela Jane, da of late H F W Bartlett, of Brook Lodge, Stock, Essex; 1 s, 1 da; *Career* joined RAF 1941, C-in-C NEAF 1973-76; air memb for Personnel 1976-78, dir-gen Intelligence MOD 1978-81; pres: RAF Assoc 1984-85 and 1987-88, cncl Chatham House 1984-90; *Recreations* skiing, walking; *Clubs* RAF; *Style*— Air Chief Marshal Sir John Aiken, KCB; 128 Piccadilly, London W1V 0PY

AIKENS, Richard John Pearson; QC (1986); s of Maj Basil Aikens (d 1983), and Jean Eleonor, *née* Pearson; *b* 28 Aug 1948; *Educ* Norwich Sch, St John's Coll Cambridge (MA); *m* 3 March 1979, Penelope Anne Hartley, da of Hartley Baker (d 1961); 2 s (Christopher b 1979, Nicholas b 1981), 2 step da (Jessica b 1964, Anna b 1966); *Career* called to the Bar 1973, in practice 1974-, jr counsel to the crown common law 1981-86; memb Supreme Court Rules Ctee 1984-88; govr Sedbergh Sch 1988-; *Books* contributing Bullen and Leake on Pleadings and Practice (13 edn, ed); *Recreations* music, the country; *Clubs* Leander; *Style*— Richard Aikens, Esq, QC; Brick Court Chambers, 15-19 Devereux Court, London WC2R 3JJ (☎ 071 583 0777)

AIKIN, Olga Lindholm (Mrs J M Driver); *née* Daly; da of Sidney Richard Daly, of Buckley, Clwyd, and Lilian May, *née* Lindholm (d 1966); *b* 10 Sept 1934; *Educ* Ilford Co HS for Girls, LSE (LLB), King's Coll London, London Business Sch; *m* 1, 1959 (m dis 1979), Ronald Sidney Aikin; 1 da (Gillian); m 2, 1982, John Michael Driver; 1 step da (Katie); *Career* called to the Bar Gray's Inn 1956; lectr: King's Coll London 1956-59, LSE 1959-70, London Business Sch 1971-; dir gen Law Div Lion Int 1985-90, ptnr Aikin Driver Partnership 1988-; memb Cncl ACAS 1982-; *Recreations* collecting cookery books and glass; *Style*— Mrs Olga Aikin; 22 St Lukes Rd, London W11 1DP (☎ 071 727 9791)

AILESBURY, Jean, Marchioness of; Jean Frances Margaret; *née* Wilson; da of John Addison Wilson, of Bodicote, Banbury, Oxon; *m* 1, Sqdn Ldr Richard Williamson, MBE, RAFVR (decd); m 2, 20 Feb 1950, as his 3 w, 7 Marquess of Ailesbury (d 1974); 1 s (Lord Charles Brudenell-Bruce, *qv*); *Style*— The Most Hon Jean, Marchioness of Ailesbury; Bel au Vent, St Lawrence, Jersey, CI

AILESBURY, 8 Marquess of (UK 1821); Sir Michael Sydney Cedric Brudenell-Bruce; 14 Bt (E 1611); also Baron Brudenell (E 1628), Earl of Cardigan (E 1661), Baron Bruce (GB 1746), Earl of Ailesbury (GB 1776), and Earl Bruce and Viscount Savernake (both UK 1821); 30 Hereditary Warden of Savernake Forest; s of 7 Marquess of Ailesbury (d 1974); *b* 31 March 1926; *Educ* Eton; *m* 1, 1952 (m dis 1961), Edwina, da of late Lt-Col Sir Edward Wills, 4 Bt; 1 s, 2 da; m 2, 1963 (m dis 1974), Juliet, da of late Hilary Kingsford; 2 da; m 3, 1974, Caroline, da of late Cdr Owen Wethered, JP, DL, RN; *Heir* s, Earl of Cardigan; *Career* late Lt RHG (reserve); memb London Stock Exchange 1954-; *Style*— The Most Hon the Marquess of Ailesbury; Stable Block, Tottenham House, Marlborough, Wilts

AILSA, 7 Marquess of (UK 1831); Archibald David Kennedy; OBE (1968), DL (Ayrshire); also Lord Kennedy (S 1452), Earl of Cassillis (S 1509), and Baron Ailsa (UK 1806); s of Capt 6 Marquess of Ailsa (d 1957); *b* 3 Dec 1925; *Educ* Pangbourne Nautical Coll; *m* 1954, Mary, da of late John Burn, of Amble, Northumberland; 2 s, 1 da; *Heir* s, Earl of Cassillis; *Career* formerly Lt Scots Gds, Lt-Col Royal Scots Fusiliers (TA), Hon Col Ayrshire Bn ACF 1980-90; patron IOM Rly Soc 1978-, chm Scottish Assoc of Boys Clubs 1978-82; *Clubs* New (Edinburgh), Carlton; *Style*— The Most Hon the Marquess of Ailsa, OBE, DL; Cassillis, Maybole, Ayrshire KA19 7JN

AINGER, David William Dawson; TD (1969); s of Rev John Dawson Ainger (d 1987, Lt Cdr RN), of Weston Super Mare, and Frieda Emily, *née* Brand; *b* 10 March 1935; *Educ* Marlborough, Univ of Oxford (MA), Cornell Univ; *m* 25 July 1964, Elizabeth Ann, da of Albert William Lewis, of 19a Granard Rd, London SW12; 3 s (William b 1969, Luke b 1972, Ruairidh b 1980), 2 da (Katharine b 1966, Siobhan b 1976); *Career* Nat Serv 2 Lt RE 1953-55, AER and TAVR RE and RCT 1955-69; called to the Bar Lincoln's Inn 1961; visiting lectr in law Univ of Southampton 1961-71; *Style*— David Ainger, Esq, TD; 4 Northampton Park, London N1 2PJ (☎ 071 226 1401); 8 Stone Buildings, Lincoln's Inn, London WC2A 3TA (☎ 071 242 5002, fax 071 831 9188, telex 268072)

AINLEY, Sir (Alfred) John; MC (1940); only s of late Rev Alfred Ainley, of Cockermouth, Cumberland; *b* 10 May 1906; *Educ* St Bees Sch, CCC Oxford; *m* 1935, Mona Sybil (d 1981), da of Sidney Wood, of Bromborough, Cheshire; 1 s, 2 da; *Career* barr 1928, chief justice Kenya 1963-68, chm Industl Tbnls 1972-76; kt 1957; *Style*— Sir John Ainley, MC; Horrock Wood, Watermillock, Penrith, Cumbria (☎ Watermillock 268)

AINSCOUGH, Gerry Christopher; s of Gerald Solomon Ainscough, of Wigan, and Anne Maureen, *née* O'Neill; *b* 7 Aug 1964; *Educ* St Thomas More HS Wigan, Leyland Motors Tech Coll, Lancashire Poly; *m* 12 May 1990, Karen Anne, da of William Jones; *Career* Rugby Union centre and fly-half Orrell RUFC; with: Orrell RUFC 1983- (over 300 appearances); rep: Lancashire 1985- (25 appearances, man of the match Co Championship final 1988), North of Eng 1989-, Eng Juniors (tour SA 1987), Eng B (tour Spain 1989, 3 caps); apprentice Leyland Vehicles 1980-84, student mech engr Leyland Trucks 1984-87, mech engr Ingersoll-Rand 1987-88; mech engr Taylor Woodrow 1988-90, professional offr Univ of Wollongong 1990-, project engr Taylor Woodrow 1990-; *Style*— Gerry Ainscough, Esq; 1 Elkstone Close, Winstanley, Wigan WN3 6LQ (☎ 0942 225316); c/o Orrell RUFC, Edge Hall Rd, Orrell, Wigan WN5 8TL (☎ 0695 623193)

AINSLEY, David Edwin; s of Edwin Ainsley, of Bebington, Wirral, Merseyside, and Gertrude Mary, *née* Fletcher (d 1978); *b* 13 Sept 1944; *Educ* Portsmouth GS, Sch of Architecture Univ of Liverpool (BArch); *m* 1, 28 Feb 1970 (m dis 1984), Pauline Elisabeth, da of Aubrey Highton; 2 s (Sam b 21 Sept 1975, Christian b 24 May 1978); m 2, Beatrix Hinchliffe Parry, da of William Ellis, of Tettenhall; 2 step s (Nathan b 22 Dec 1971, Benjamin b 7 Feb 1976); *Career* ptnr in architects and landscape architects firm Ainsley Gommon Wood; winner of several Nat and Int Design Awards incl: Royal Town Planning Inst Commendation, Housing Centre Tst Award, Liverpool Int Garden Festival Best Home Garden, twice winner of RIBA Community Enterprise Scheme Award, Civic Tst Commendation, Welsh Nat Eisteddfod Architecture Prize; fndr memb and former chm Oxton Soc; memb RIBA 1972, FFAS 1986; *Recreations* music; *Style*— David Ainsley, Esq; 24 Village Rd, Oxton, Birkenhead (☎ 051 652 4064); Tynyllwyn, Llanrhaeadr YM, Shropshire SY10 0DA; Ainsley Gommon Wood Architects and Landscape Architects, 1 Price St, Hamilton Square, Birkenhead, Merseyside L41 6JN (☎ 051 647 5511, fax 051 666 2195)

AINSLIE, David Galbraith; s of Patrick David Lafone Ainslie, of Aynhoe Pk, Aynho, nr Banbury, Oxon, and Agnes Ursula, *née* Galbraith; *b* 13 Oct 1947; *Educ* Wellington Coll, Pembroke Coll Cambridge (MA); *Career* admitted slr 1973; joined Dawson & Co 1972, ptnr Lovell White & King 1981-83 (joined 1976), Towry Law & Co Ltd (ind fin advsrs) 1983; dir: Towry Law Tstee Co Ltd 1984, Towry Law Advsy Servs Ltd 1985, Towry Law & Co Ltd 1987; memb: UK Falkland Islands Ctee 1973-, Exec Ctee Falkland Islands Assoc 1977-; tstee UK Falkland Islands Tst 1981-; memb Law Soc 1971-; Freeman City of London, Liveryman Worshipful Co of Haberdashers 1971; *Books* Practical Tax Planning with Precedents (contrib, 1987); *Recreations* fishing, shooting, flying; *Style*— David Ainslie, Esq; The Old Bakehouse, Hampstead Norreys, nr Newbury, Berks RG16 0TE (☎ 0635 201 355); Towry Law Group, Towry Law House, 57 High St, Windsor, Berks SL4 1LX (☎ 0753 868 244, fax 0753 859 719)

AINSLIE, John Bernard (Jack); OBE (1983); s of Capt Charles Bernard Ainslie, MC (d 1937), of Lissadian, S Ascot, Berks, and Eileen, *née* Hollway (d 1962); *b* 2 Aug 1921; *Educ* Harrow, Trinity Coll Oxford; *m* 21 April 1951, Shelagh Lillian, da of Thomas Lawrence Forbes (d 1976), of Chilbolton Cottage, Chilbolton, Stockbridge, Hants; 1 s (Andrew b 1952), 3 da (Sarah b 1952, Serena b 1957, Teresa b 1959); *Career* WWII 1941-46, cmmnd to Royal Berks Regt 1942 serving in the UK and NW Europe till 1945, Capt 2 Royal Lincolns served NW Europe, Egypt and Palestine 1945-46; farmed in partnership at Mildenhall Marlborough 1951-, md Gale and Ainslie Ltd, dir Progressive Pig Prodrs Ltd; formerly: chm Ridgeway Grain, vice chm Gp Cereal Servs; memb: Exec Ctee Community Cncl for Wilts (former chm), Mildenhall Parish Cncl (former chm), Parly candidate (Lib) Devizes 1974 and 1979; Euro Lib candidate: Upper Thames 1979, Wilts 1984; memb Wilts CC 1964- (chm Educn Ctee 1973-77, ldr Lib Gp 1964-85, chm 1985-89), ldr Lib Democrat Gp 1989-, vice pres ACRE; memb: ACC Exec 1985-89, Burnham Ctee 1985-87; FRAgS; *Recreations* music, drama, gardening; *Clubs* Farmers; *Style*— Jack Ainslie, Esq; Pennings, Mildenhall, Marlborough, Wilts SN8 2LT (☎ 0672 513477); Church Farm, Mildenhall, Marlborough, Wilts SN8 2LU (☎ 0672 512385)

AINSLIE, Michael Lewis; s of George L Ainslie, of 100 Netherland Lane, Baysmont, Box 21, Kingsport, Tennessee 37660, and Jean Clare, *née* Waddell; *b* 12 May 1943; *Educ* Vanderbilt Univ (BA), Harvard Business Sch where he was a J Spencer Lover Fellow (MBA); *m* 1, 11 Dec 1971, Lucy Scardino; 1 s (Michael Loren b 28 June 1974); m 2, 13 Dec 1986, Suzanne H Braga; *Career* assoc McKinsey & Co, NYC 1968-71; pres Palmas de Mar, PR 1971-75; sr vice-pres COO N-Ren Corp Cincinnati, 1975-80; pres National Tst for Historic Preservation, Washington DC 1980-84; pres CEO Southeby's Hldgs, Inc 1984-; *Recreations* tennis, golf; *Clubs* Metropolitain, Washington DC, River (NYC), Buck's, Queen's; *Style*— Mr Michael L Ainslie; 150 East 73rd Street, New York 10021, NY; Sotheby's Holdings Inc, 1334 York Avenue, New York 10021, NY

AINSWORTH, Anita, Lady; Anita Margaret Ann; da of Harold Arthur Lett, of Co Wexford; *m* 1946, as his 2 w, Sir John Ainsworth, 3 Bt (d 1981); *Style*— Anita, Lady Ainsworth; 6 Aubury Park Shankill, Co Dublin, Eire

AINSWORTH, Anthony Thomas Hugh; s and h of Sir David Ainsworth, 4 Bt; *b* 30 March 1962; *Educ* Harrow; *Career* Lt Royal Hussars (PWO) 1982-85; *Style*— Anthony Ainsworth, Esq; 10 Paultons House, Paultons Square, London SW3 5DU

AINSWORTH, Sir (Thomas) David; 4 Bt (UK 1916), of Ardanaiseig, Co Argyll; s of Sir Thomas Ainsworth, 2 Bt, by his 2 w, Marie, da of Compton Domvile; suc half-bro, Sir John Ainsworth, 3 Bt, 1981; *b* 22 Aug 1926; *Educ* Eton; *m* 6 May 1957, Sarah Mary, da of Lt-Col Hugh Carr Walford, 17/21 Lancers (ka 1941); 2 s (Anthony, Charles David b 24 Aug 1966), 2 da (Serena Mary (Mrs Peratinos) b 13 March 1958, Tessa Jane (Mrs Fortescue) b 6 Aug 1959); *Heir* s, Anthony Thomas Hugh Ainsworth; *Recreations* shooting, fishing; *Style*— Sir David Ainsworth, Bt; 80 Elm Park Gdns, London SW10; Ashley Hse, Wootton, nr Woodstock, Oxon (☎ 0993 811650)

AINSWORTH, John David; s of George Irving Ainsworth (d 1989), of Bournemouth, and Moyra Rosetta Ainsworth; *b* 27 July 1943; *Educ* Emanuel Sch London, Univ of Southampton (LLB); *m* 4 June 1966, Sally Georgina (d 1990), da of George Goater, of Christchurch, Dorset; 2 s (Nicholas Robert b 13 Jan 1969, Jeremy John b 18 July 1971); *Career* admitted slr 1968; asst slr: White Brooks & Gilman Winchester 1968-71 (articled clerk 1966-68), Harry Ellis & Co Bournemouth 1971-72; ptnr Lester & Russell Bournemouth 1975-88 (asst slr 1972-75), ptnr and head of litigation Lester & Aldridge Bournemouth 1988-, pt/t dep High Ct and Co Ct registrar 1988-; former sec Bournemouth RFC, former chm Dorset Schs Badminton Assoc, vice chm No 3 Area Ctee Legal Aid Bd; memb Law Soc 1968-; *Recreations* golf, tennis, swimming; *Clubs* Lanz Sports, West Hants Lawn Tennis, Queens Park, Mansion House; *Style*— John Ainsworth, Esq; 23 Meyrick Park Cres, Bournemouth, Dorset BH3 7AG (☎ 0202 553839); Lester & Aldridge, Russell House, Oxford Road, Bournemouth Dorset BH1 1BE (☎ 0202 786161, fax 0202 786150)

AINSWORTH, Mavis; da of Reginald Frederick Davenport (d 1967), of Totley, Sheffield, and Wilhelmina, *née* Mynette; *b* 6 Sept 1931; *Educ* Univ of London (BA, PGCE), Univ of Illinois (MA); *m* 8 Aug 1953, Stanley Ainsworth, step s of late Andrew Rutherford Ainsworth, of Heaton Chapel, Stockport; 2 s (Jonathan Grieve b 1960, Quentin Paul b 1961); *Career* head English Dept: Totley Thornbridge Coll of Educn Sheffield 1969-76, Sheffield City Poly 1976-87; dean Faculty of Cultural Studies (with polywide responsibility for initial and inservice teacher trg) 1987-89, dir Sch of Cultural Studies 1989-; *Recreations* theatre, travel, visiting London; *Style*— Mrs Mavis Ainsworth; 139 Dore Rd, Dore, Sheffield S17 3NF; Director of School of Cultural Studies, Sheffield City Poly, Psalter Lane, Sheffield S11 8UZ (☎ 0742 532601, fax 0742 532603, telex 54680 SHPOLY6)

AINSWORTH, Robert David; *b* 10 Dec 1949; *Educ* Dudley GS, Univ of Leeds (BA); *m* 31 July 1971, Alison Elizabeth; 1 da (Rachel b 1976), 1 s (Colin b 1978); *Career* company dir and gp fin dir: The Phoenix Timber Gp plc 1986-, Palma Gp plc 1982-86; FCA; *Recreations* golf, squash; *Style*— Robert D Ainsworth, Esq; Turner House, Station Rd, Elsenham, Bishops Stortford, Herts CM22 6LA; The Phoenix Timber Group plc, Arisdale Avenue, South Ockendon, Essex RM15 5TR (☎ 0708 851801, fax 0708 851850)

AINSWORTH, William Robert; s of William Murray Ainsworth (d 1964), of Stockton-on-Tees, Co Durham, and Emma Laura Mary, *née* Easley (d 1981); *b* 24 June 1935; *Educ* Holy Trinity Sch Stockton-on-Tees, Stockton GS, Sch of Architecture Univ of Durham (BArch); *m* 7 Nov 1959, Sylvia Vivian, da of Norman Brown, of Buenos Aires, Argentina, S America; 3 da (Graciela Glenn b 1960, Anita Susan b 1964, Lucia Emma b 1977); *Career* chartered architect, designer and urban planner, fndr ptnr Ainsworth Spark Assocs 1963- (completed over 2500 projects throughout UK and Europe for local, nat and int companies); working tours of: S America, USA, and Europe; visiting studio tutor Sch of Architecture Newcastle upon Tyne 1961-63; external examiner: Sch of Architecture, Coll of Arts and Technol Newcastle; RIBA: chm Northern Region 1972-73, fndr chm Nat Ctee for Environmental Educn 1977, dir Bd of Servs Ltd London, memb and vice pres Nat Cncl 1980-82; vice pres and hon librarian Br Architectural Library 1987-; bd govr Coll of Arts and Technol 1984-86, initiator of World Day of Architecture in UK 1989; chm: Sculpture Tst Northern Arts (fndr) 1981-, Northumberland and Durham Lord's Taverners; FRIBA 1967, MCSD 1977, IOB 1980, FRSA 1985; *Recreations* cricket, golf, gardening, reading, painting (water colours); *Clubs* Arts (London), Northumberland Golf; *Style*— William Ainsworth, Esq; 1 Edgewood, Darras Hall, Ponteland, Newcastle upon Tyne; Summerhill House (Ainsworth Spark Associates), 9 Summerhill Terrace, Newcastle upon Tyne NE4 6EB (☎ 091 232 3434, fax 091 261 0628, telex 537533)

AIRD, Capt Sir Alastair Sturgis; KCVO 1984 (CVO 1977, LVO 1969); s of Col Malcolm Aird (d 1965); *b* 14 Jan 1931; *Educ* Eton, RMA Sandhurst; *m* 1963, Fiona Violet, LVO (1980), da of Lt-Col Ririd Myddelton (d 1988); 2 da (Caroline (Mrs Allfrey) b 1964, Henrietta b 1966); *Career* cmmnd 9 Queen's Royal Lancers 1951, Adjutant 1956-59, ret 1964; equerry to HM Queen Elizabeth The Queen Mother 1960-63, asst private sec 1964-74, comptroller to HM Queen Elizabeth The Queen Mother 1974-; *Recreations* shooting, fishing, tennis; *Style*— Capt Sir Alastair Aird,

KCVO; 31B St James's Palace, London SW1 (☎ 071 839 6700)

AIRD, Catherine; *see*: McIntosh, Kinn Hamilton

AIRD, Sir (George) John; 4 Bt (UK 1901), of Hyde Park Terrace, Paddington, Co London; s of Col Sir John Renton Aird, 3 Bt, MVO, MC, JP, DL (d 1973), sometime Extra Equerry to King George VI and to HM The Queen, of Forest Lodge, Windsor Great Park, and Lady Priscilla, *née* Heathcote-Drummond-Willoughby, yr da of 2 Earl of Ancaster; *b* 30 Jan 1940; *Educ* Eton, ChCh Oxford (MA), Harvard (MBA); *m* 31 Aug 1968, Margaret Elizabeth, yr da of Sir John Harling Muir, 3 Bt, TD, DL; 1 s, 2 da (Rebecca b 1970, Belinda Elizabeth b 1972); *Heir* s, James John Aird b 12 June 1978; *Career* page of honour to HM 1955-57; engineer Sir Alexander Gibb & Partners 1961-65, mangr John Laing & Co 1967-69, chm and md Sir John Aird & Co 1969-; MICE 1965; *Recreations* skiing, farming; *Clubs* White's; *Style*— Sir John Aird, Bt; Grange Farm, Evenlode, Moreton-in-Marsh, Glos GL56 0NT (☎ 0608 50607)

AIRD, Lady Priscilla; *née* Heathcote-Drummond-Willoughby; yr da of 2 Earl of Ancaster, GCVO, TD, JP, DL (d 1951); co-heiress to Barony of niece, Baroness Willoughby de Eresby, *qv*; *b* 29 Oct 1909; *m* 1939, Col Sir John Renton Aird, 3 Bt, MVO, MC, Gren Gds (d 1973); 1 s, 3 da; *Style*— The Lady Priscilla Aird; Wingrove House, Chipping Campden, Glos

AIREDALE, 4 Baron (UK 1907); Sir Oliver James Vandeleur Kitson; 4 Bt (UK 1886); s of 3 Baron Airedale, DSO, MC (d 1958); *b* 22 April 1915; *Educ* Eton, Trinity Coll Cambridge; *Career* sits as Lib Peer; Maj The Green Howards; barr Inner Temple 1941; dep chm Ctees House of Lords 1961-, dep speaker 1962-; *Clubs* Royal Cwlth Soc; *Style*— The Rt Hon Lord Airedale; Ufford Hall, Stamford, Lincs PE9 3BH

AIREY, Lady; Bridget Georgina; da of Col Hon Thomas Eustace Vesey (d 1946, bro of 5 Viscount de Vesci), and Lady Cecily, Browne(d 1976), da of 5 Earl of Kenmare and a Lady-in-Waiting to HRH Duchess of Gloucester 1947-51, Woman of the Bedchamber to HM Queen Mary 1951-53; *b* 6 Feb 1915; *m* 1947, as his 2 w, Lt-Gen Sir Terence Airey, KCMG, CB, CBE (d 1983, Cdr Br Forces Hong Kong 1952-54); *Style*— Lady Airey; The White Cottage, Bungay Rd, Hempnall, Norwich, Norfolk NR15 2NG (☎ 050 842 214)

AIREY, Clifford; s of Maj William Airey (d 1986), of Preston, Lancashire, and Ellen, *née* Hogg (d 1974); *b* 16 Jan 1939; *Educ* Br Army Schs Overseas, Univ of Liverpool, Univ of Manchester; *m* 1, 23 Jan 1960 (m dis 1980), Maureen, *née* Fowler; 1 s (Shawn James b 1965), 2 da (Dawn Elizabeth b 1960, Rachel Louise b 1967); m 2, 1982, Gina Margarita, *née* Kingdon, 2 s (Sebastian Jon b 1983, Clifford Lloyd b 1985), 1 da (Dominique Ellen 1984); *Career* res ptnr Jubb & Partners consulting engrs 1964-73, sr ptnr Airey and Coles consulting engrs 1973-; sr lectr Plymouth Poly 1967-70; past chm Inst of Structural Engrs, memb Plymouth Philatelic Soc; CEng, FIStructE, MConsE, FFB; *Recreations* fly-fishing, sailing, shooting, stamp and coin collecting; *Style*— Clifford Airey, Esq; 8 Whiteford Rd, Mannamead, Plymouth (☎ 0752 266 456); Kirkby Lodge, Portland Square Lane North, Plymouth, Devon (☎ 0752 229 119/0752 227 983, fax 0752 222 115)

AIREY, Wendy Helen; da of Edward Docherty (d 1976), of Woodfield, Lasswade, Scotland, and Elizabeth Craig, *née* Ross; *b* 26 Jan 1963; *Educ* St Margaret's Sch for Girls, Royal Scottish Acad of Music & Drama, Univ of Glasgow (MSc); *m* 7 May 1988, Timothy Charles Airey, s of Frank L Airey, of Craigmount Ave North, Barnton, Edinburgh; *Career* freelance singer; princ Turin Opera House 1984, singer and pres RAI 1984-85, French Art Song Concerts in Paris Milan and Atlanta 1985, advent concert soloist St Peter's Rome 1987; has given many charity concerts in Scotland especially for Marie Curie Cancer Fndn; *Recreations* riding, polo, swimming; *Clubs* Carlton; *Style*— Mrs W H Airey; 16B Fettes Row, Edinburgh EH3 6RH (☎ 031 556 3272)

AIREY OF ABINGDON, Baroness (Life Peer UK 1979); Diana Josceline Barbara Neave Airey; da of Thomas Giffard, MBE, JP, of Chillington, Staffs (descended from Osbern de Bolebec, Sire de Longueville, *temp* Richard 'Sans Peur' Duke of Normandy, who d 960 and whose sister-in-law, Aveline, Osbern married), and Angela, eld da and co-heir of Sir William Trollope, 10 Bt; *b* 7 July 1919; *m* 1942, Airey Neave, DSO, OBE, MC, TD, MP (assassinated 1979; gggs of Sir Thomas Neave, 2 Bt); 2 s, 1 da; *Career* with Foreign Off and Polish Miny of Info London WWII, thereafter supported husb politically; memb North Atlantic Assembly; tstee: Dorneywood Tst, Imperial War Museum 1985-91, Stansted Park Fndn; Freeman City of London; FRSA; *Recreations* reading, opera, theatre; *Style*— The Rt Hon Baroness Airey of Abingdon; House of Lords, London SW1A 0AA

AIRLIE, 13 Earl of (S 1639); Sir David George Coke Patrick Ogilvy; KT (1985), GCVO (1984), PC (1984), DL (Angus 1964), Lord Lt of Tayside Region - Dist of Angus (1989), JP (1989); also Lord Ogilvy of Airlie (S 1491) and Lord Ogilvy of Alyth and Lintrathen (S 1639); s of 12 Earl of Airlie, KT, GCVO, MC (d 1968), and Lady Alexandra Coke (d 1984), da of 3 Earl of Leicester; *b* 17 May 1926; *Educ* Eton; *m* 1952, Virginia Fortune, CVO (1982; vice-pres Women of the Year, tstee Tate Gallery and Nat Gallery, Lady in Waiting to HM The Queen 1976-), da of John Barry Ryan, of Newport, RI, USA; 3 s (David (Lord Ogilvy), Bruce b 1959, Patrick b 1971), 3 da (Doune b 1953, Jane b 1955, Elizabeth b 1965); *Heir* s, Lord Ogilvy; *Career* Lt Scots Gds 1944; Capt ADC to High Cmmr and C-in-C Australia 1947-48, Malaya 1948-49, resigned cmmn 1950; chief cmmr for Scotland Scout Assoc 1960-61 (treas 1962-86, hon pres 1988); Ensign Royal Co of Archers (Queen's Body Guard for Scotland) 1975-; chm: Schroder's 1977-84, Ashdown Investment Tst, Westpool Investment Tst to 1982 (also resigned directorships), Gen Accident Fire & Life Assur Corpn 1987-; dir: J Henry Schroder Wagg & Co 1961-84 (chm 1973-77), Scottish & Newcastle Breweries 1969-83, Royal Bank of Scotland plc 1983-; Lord Chamberlain of the Queen's Household 1984-; Chllr Royal Victorian Order 1984-; govr Nuffield Hosps 1984-89; CStJ 1981; *Clubs* White's; *Style*— The Rt Hon the Earl of Airlie, KT, GCVO, PC, JP; Cortachy Castle, Kirriemuir, Angus (☎ 05754 231); 5 Swan Walk London SW3 4JJ (☎ 071 352 0296); Lord Chamberlain's Office, Buckingham Palace, London SW1

AIRS, Graham John; s of George William Laurence Airs, of Northampton, and Marjorie, *née* Lewis (d 1967); *b* 8 Aug 1953; *Educ* Newport GS Essex, Emmanuel Coll Cambridge (BA, MA, LLB); *m* 4 April 1981, Stephanie Annette, da of William Henry Marshall; *Career* admitted slr 1978, ptnr Airs Dickinson 1980-84, Slaughter and May 1976-80 (asst slr 1984-87, ptnr 1987-); memb Law Soc, AInstT; *Books* Tolley's Tax Planning (contrib); *Style*— Graham Airs, Esq; 35 Basinghall St, London EC2V 5DB (☎ 071 600 1200, fax 071 726 0038, 071 600 0289, 883486,telex 888926)

AITCHISON, Sir Charles Walter de Lancey; 4 Bt (UK 1938), of Lemmington, Co Northumberland; s of Sir Stephen Charles de Lancey Aitchison, 3 Bt (d 1958); *b* 27 May 1951; *Educ* Gordonstoun; *m* 1984, Susan, yr da of late Edward Ellis, of Hest Bank, Lancs; 1 s (Rory), 1 da (Tessa Charlotte b 1982); *Heir* s, Rory Edward de Lancey b 7 March 1986; *Career* late Lt 15/19 KRH; dir: De Lancey Lands Ltd, Walter Wilson Ltd; ARICS 1989; *Recreations* fishing; *Style*— Sir Charles Aitchison, Bt; White House, Casterton, Carnforth, Lancs LA6 2LF

AITCHISON, Craigie Ronald John; yr s of Rt Hon Lord Aitchison, PC, KC, LLD (Scottish Lord of Session, Lord Justice-Clerk and Lord Advocate Scotland under Ramsay MacDonald; noted for never losing a case involving an indictment on a capital charge when defending); yr bro of Raymund Craigie Aitchison, the writer; *b* 13 Jan 1926; *Educ* Edinburgh Univ, Middle Temple London, Slade Sch of Fine Art; *Career* painter; various one-man shows: Beaux Arts Gallery London (1959, 1960, 1964), Marlborough Fine Arts (London) Ltd (1968), Compass Gallery Glasgow (1970), Basil jacobs gallery London (1971), Rutland Gallery London (1975), Scottish Arts Cncl (1975), M Knoedler & Co Ltd London (1977), Kettles Yard Gallery Cambridge (1979), Arts Cncl Retrospective Exhibition Serpentine Gallery London (1981), David Grob Fine Art London (1981), Artis Monte Carlo Monaco (1985), Albemarle Gallery London (1987, 1989); has participated in many mixed exhibitions; works in: Aberdeen Art Gallery and Museum, Arts Cncl of GB, Glasgow Art Gallery and Museum, Grundy Art Gallery Blackpool, Newcastle Region Art Gallery NSW Australia, Perth City Art Gallery and Museum, Rugby Borough Cncl Collection, Scottish Arts Cncl Edinburgh, Scottish Nat Gallery of Modern Art Edinburgh, Tate Gallery, Walker Art Gallery Liverpool; British Cncl Italian Govt Scholarship 1955, *Awards* Arts Cncl Purchase Award 1965, Edwin Austin Abbey Premier Scholarship 1970, Prize Winner John Moores Liverpool Exhibition 1974, Lorne Scholarship 1974-75, Arts Cncl Bursary 1976, First Johnson Wax Prize RA 1984, Korn Ferry Int Award RA 1989; RA 1988 (ARA 1978); *Style*— Craigie Aitchison, Esq; Montecastelli San Gusme, Siena, Italy; 32 St Mary's Gdns, London SE11 (☎ 071 582 3708)

AITCHISON, (Stephen) Edward; s of Sir Stephen Charles de Lancey Aitchison, 3 Bt (d 1958); *b* 27 March 1954; *Educ* Fettes; *m* 1978, Mrs Harriet M Thomson, yr da of late Dr Henry Miller; 1 s (Stephen Henry b 1981), 1 da (Amanda b 1983); *Career* dir: Walter Willson Ltd, De Lancey Lands Ltd, NISA Ltd; *Style*— Edward Aitchison, Esq; Cuilfail, Apperley Road, Stockfield, Northumberland

AITCHISON, Thomas Milne; MBE (1977); s of William and Jean Aitchison (d 1989), of Viewforth, School Rd, Longridge, W Lothian; *b* 28 May 1930; *Educ* Bathgate Acad, Univ of Edinburgh (BL 1953); *m* 18 Aug 1962, Flora Jane Stewart, da of Robert Paris (d 1965); 3 s (David William Millar b 1964, Iain Robert Paris b 1965, Andrew Thomas Macmillan b 1971); *Career* apprenticeship with MacPherson & Mackay WS Edinburgh 1950-53 (asst 1953-54); legal asst: Motherwell and Wishaw Town Cncl 1954-55, W Lothian CC 1955-61; first legal asst Lanark CC 1962-67, sr depute co clerk Ross & Cromarty CC 1967-75, chief exec Ross & Cromarty DC 1974-78, ptnr P H Young & Co Slrs 1979-83, owner Aitchison & Co SSC Whitburn 1984-90; co treas W Lothian Boy Scouts Assoc 1958-68 (county sec 1960-62); FSA (Scot); *Recreations* yachting, photography, skiing; *Style*— Thomas M Aitchison, Esq, MBE; 12 Merlin Park, Dollar, Clackmannanshire (☎ 025 94 3156)

AITKEN, Alexander William; s of Alexander John Aitken (d 1979), and Freda, *née* Trueman, of Rownhams, nr Southampton; *b* 9 May 1958; *Educ* RAF Changi GS Singapore, Leamington Coll for Boys, The Mountbatten Sch Romsey Hants (played rugby and basketball to County Level); *m* 9 May 1977, Caroline, da of Herbert Douglas Abbott; 2 s (Justin Richard b 1 April 1970, Alexander Joseph b 28 June 1983); *Career* deck hand Scot fishing trawler 1975, waiter Whitbread Wessex Potters Heron Motel Ampfield 1976, asst head waiter The Slipway Restaurant Lymington 1976, head writer Grosvenor Hotel Stockbridge 1976, catering mangr Silhouette Casino 1976-77, restaurant mangr Le Chanteclere Restaurant Cadham Hants 1977-82, The Elizabethan Restaurant Winchester 1982-83, opened Le Poussin Restaurant 1983; *awards* one rosette AA Restaurant Guide, one star Egon Ronay Guide, ed Michelin Guide, 4/5 Good Food Guide, Hampshire Restaurant of the Year 1987, Clover award Ackerman Guide, Out of Town Restaurant of the Year The Times 1990-91; memb: Master Chefs of GB 1986, Br Culinary Inst 1989; *Recreations* sailing, horse riding, scuba diving, mushroom hunting; *Style*— Alexander Aitken, Esq; 57-59 Brookley Road, Brockenhurst, Hampshire SO42 7RB (☎ 0590 23063); Le Poussin Restaurant, 57-59 Brookley Rd, Brockenhurst, Hampshire S042 7RB (☎ 0590 23063, fax 0590 22912, car 0836 561059)

AITKEN, (Peter) Bruce; s of Dr Douglas Crawford Aitken (d 1970), of Carlisle, Cumbria, and Louise Macdonald, *née* Taylor (d 1985); *b* 10 Oct 1941; *Educ* Sedbergh, Univ of Durham, Univ of Newcastle upon Tyne (DipArch); *m* 7 Sept 1974, Ann, da of Frank Edgar Gregory, JP, of Cockermouth, Cumbria; 2 s (Christopher b 1976, Callum b 1979), 1 da (Tamsin b 1981); *Career* ptnr Wilson Mason and Ptnrs Architects 1976-; memb RIBA; *Recreations* golf, sailing; *Clubs* RAC; *Style*— Bruce Aitken, Esq; 26 Ashcombe Ave, Southborough, Surbiton, Surrey KT6 6QA; Wilson Mason and Partners, 3 Chandos St, Cavendish Sq, London W1M 0JU (☎ 071 637 1501, fax 071 631 0525)

AITKEN, Hon Mrs ((Joan) Elizabeth); *née* Rees-Williams; da of 1 Baron Ogmore, TD, PC (d 1976); *b* 1 May 1936; *Educ* Croham Hurst Sch, Mont Olivet Lausanne; *m* 1, 1957 (m dis 1969), Richard St John Harris, actor; 3 s; m 2, 1971 (m dis 1975), Rex Carey Harrison, actor; m 3, 1980, Peter Michael Aitken, gs of 1 Lord Beaverbrook; *Style*— The Hon Mrs Aitken; 14 Lowndes Sq, Kensington, London SW1

AITKEN, Jonathan William Patrick; MP (C) South Thanet 1983-; s of Sir William Aitken, KBE, MP (d 1964), and Hon Lady Aitken, MBE, JP, *qv*; is gn of 1 Baron Beaverbrook and gs of 1 Baron Rugby; bro of Maria Aitken, *qv*, the actress; *b* 30 Aug 1942; *Educ* Eton, ChCh Oxford; *m* 1979, Lolicia Olivera (economist), da of O A Azucki, of Zürich; 1 s (William b 7 Sept 1982), twin da (Victoria, Alexandra b 14 June 1980); *Career* private sec to Selwyn Lloyd 1964-66, foreign corr Evening Standard 1966-71, md Slater Walker (ME) 1973-75, MP (C) Thanet E 1974-1983, fndr and chm Aitken Hume Int 1979-, temp chief exec TV-AM March-April 1983; *Books* A Short Walk on the Campus (1966), The Young Meteors (1967), Land of Fortune: A Study of the New Australia (1971), Officially Secret (1971); *Clubs* Beefsteak, Turf, Pratt's; *Style*— Jonathan Aitken, Esq, MP; 8 Lord North St, London SW1

AITKEN, Maria Penelope Katharine; da of Sir William Aitken, KBE, MP Bury St Edmunds 1950-64 (d 1964, s of Joseph Aitken, 2 s of Rev William Aitken and eld bro of 1 Baron Beaverbrook; Sir William's yr sis Margaret Annie was a Canadian MP in the early 1970s), and Hon Lady Aitken, *qv*, sis of Jonathan Aitken, MP, *qv*; *b* 12 Sept 1945; *Educ* privately, Riddlesworth Hall Norfolk, Sherborne Girls' Sch, St Anne's Coll Oxford; *m* 1, 1968 (m dis), Mark Durden-Smith, yst s of A J Durden-Smith, FRCS, of Kensington; m 2, 1972 (m dis 1980), Nigel Davenport, the actor, *qv*; 1 s (Jack); *Career* actress in (amongst others); Bedroom Farce (NT), Blithe Spirit (NT), Travesties (RSC), The Happiest Days of Your Life (RSC 1984), Waste (RSC 1985); role of: Amanda in 1979/80 London prodn of Noel Coward's Private Lives, Gilda in Coward's Design for Living 1982-83, Sister Mary Ignatius (Ambassadors Theatre 1983), Florence Lancaster in Coward's The Vortex 1989; film work in A Fish Called Wanda 1988; dir: Happy Family by Giles Cooper (Duke of York's Theatre, London 1983), Private Lives by Noel Coward at Oxford Playhouse 1984, After the Ball by William Douglas Home at The Old Vic 1985, The Rivals by Sheridan at the Court Theatre Chicago USA 1985; own chat show (Private Lives) on BBC2; own prodn co Dramatis Personae produced: Happy Family 1983, Sister Mary Ignatius 1983, Acting (series) for BBC2 1988-90; part-time journalist, 1985 documentary (made going up the Amazon) for the BBC; *Books* A Girdle Round the Earth (1986, paperback 1988); *Style*— Miss Maria Aitken; c/o Leading Artists, 60 St James's St, London SW1 (☎ 071 491 4400)

AITKEN, Matthew James; s of John Aitken (d 1965), and Joan, *née* Stockdale-Edge; *b*

25 Aug 1956; *Educ* Leigh Boys' GS, Manchester Poly; *m* Katherine, *née* Williams; 1 da (Isabelle Keeble b 8 March 1990); *Career* professional freelance musician and musicial dir 1980-, audio engr and record prodr 1982-, in prodn team Stock Aitken Waterman 1984-; artists incl: Princess, Hazell Dean, Dead or Alive, Bananarama, Mel and Kim, Sinitta, Rick Astley, Kylie Minogue, Brother Beyond, Jason Donovan, Donna Summer, Sonia, Big Fun, Cliff Richard; charity records incl: Let it Be (Ferry Aid), Help (Comic Relief), Let's All Chant (Help a London Child), Ferry Cross the Mersey (Mersey Aid), Do They Know It's Christmas? (Ethiopia Famine Appeal), You've Got A Friend (Childline); numerous Silver, Gold and Platinum discs; Music Week top producers 1987, 1988 and 1989, Ivor Novello Awards songwriters of the year 1987, 1988 and 1989, wrote most performed works of 1987, 1988 and 1989, BPI best Br prodrs 1988, wrote most performed foreign works of 1989; *Recreations* motor racing, gourmet, computers; *Style—* Matthew Aitken, Esq; 4/7 The Vineyard, Sanctuary St, London SE1 1QL (☎ 071 403 0007, fax 071 403 8202)

AITKEN, Hon Lady (Penelope); *née* Maffey; MBE (1955), JP, WRVS Long Service Medal; da of 1 Baron Rugby, GCMG, KCB, KCVO, CSI, CIE (d 1969); *b* 2 Dec 1910; *m* 1939, Sir William Aitken, KBE, MP (d 1964), s of Joseph Aitken, bro to first Lord Beaverbrook; 1 s (Jonathan Aitken, MP, *qv*), 1 da (Maria Aitken, actress, *qv*); *Career* Justice of the Peace; *Style—* The Hon Lady Aitken, MBE, JP; 2 North Court, Gt Peter Street, London SW1

AITKEN, Robert Nicholas Reid; s of Bruce Ramsey Tweedie Aitken, of Wilmington, Kent, and Anne Constance, *née* Rolfe; *b* 25 Dec 1955; *Educ* Tonbridge; *m* 14 Sept 1985, Katherine Ann, da of William Edward Hampson, of Stamford, Lincs; 1 da (Elizabeth Grace Catherine b 25 Oct 1988); *Career* articled clerk then mangr Touche Ross and Co 1976-83, CA 1980, mangr then ptnr Henderson Crosthwaite and Co 1983-86; dir: Guinness Mahon and Co Ltd (banking subsid Guinness Mahon Hldgs plc) 1986-, Henderson Crosthwaite Ltd (subsid of Guinness Peat Gp) 1987-88; IOD 1979, ACA 1980, memb Int Stock Exchange UK and Ireland 1986; *Recreations* rugby, golf, tropical fish; *Clubs* Blackheath (Rugby) Football, Chislehurst Golf; *Style—* Robert Aitken, Esq; 104 Coleraine Rd, Blackheath, London SE3 7NZ (☎ 081 858 3477); Guinness Mahon and Co Ltd, 32 St Mary at Hill, London EC3P 3AJ (☎ 071 623 9333, fax 071 929 3398, telex 884035 GUIMAN G)

AITKEN, Ronald William; s of Brig William Henry Hutton Aitken (d 1978), of Woking, Surrey, and Mary Dorothea, *née* Davidson (d 1982); *b* 20 Sept 1933; *Educ* Wellesley House, Cheltenham; *m* 3 Nov 1962, Frances Barbara, da of Edward John Wharton Farmer (d 1980), of 36 Buckingham Gate, London SW1; 6 da (Fiona b 1963, Sarah b 1964, Lucinda b 1968, Alexandra b 1970, Penelope b 1975, Georgiana b 1980); *Career* chm: Health Screening Foundation, Ronnie Aitken & Assocs, Courtney Pope (Holdings) plc; dir: Ford Sellar Morris Properties plc, Kells Minerals Ltd, Charles Letts (Holdings) Ltd, N Brown Group plc, Wankel International SA; FCA; *Recreations* golf, tennis, backgammon; *Clubs* Brooks's, NZ Golf; *Style—* Ronald Aitken, Esq; 212 Ashley Gdns, London SW1 (☎ 071 834 3110); 36 Ebury St, London SW1N 0LU (☎ 071 730 9277, fax 071 259 9930)

AITKEN, Timothy Maxwell; er s of Hon Peter Rudyard Aitken (d 1947, yr s of 1 Baron Beaverbrook), by his 2 wife, Marie Patricia, da of Michael Joseph Maguire, of Melbourne, Australia; *b* 28 Oct 1944; *Educ* Repton, Sorbonne, McGill Univ Canada; *m* 1, 10 May 1966, Annette, da of Claus Hansen, of Denmark; m 2, Julie Ruth, da of Charles Filstead; 2 s (Theodore b 1976, Charles b 1979); *Career* chief exec Aitken Hume Int plc; chm: TV-AM Ltd, National Securities & Research Corp Inc; *Clubs* Royal Thames Yacht; *Style—* Timothy Aitken, Esq; c/o Tv - AM, Hawlpy Cres, London NW1 8EF

AITKEN, Lady; Ursula; da of Dr Herbert Wales; *m* 1937, Sir Peter (Arthur Percival Hay) Aitken (d 1984), s of late Canon R Aitken; 1 s, 1 da; *Style—* Lady Aitken; The Lodge, Alde House Drive, Aldeburgh, Suffolk IP15 5EE

AITKEN, Lady; Violet; *née* de Trafford; da of Sir Humphrey Edmund de Trafford, 4 Bt, MC (d 1971), and Hon Cynthia Cadogan who was 3 da of Viscount Chelsea (d 1908); *b* 1926; *m* 1951, as his 3 w, Sir Max Aitken, 2 Bt, DSO, DFC (d 1985; 2 Baron Beaverbrook who disclaimed peerage for life 1964); 1 s (3 Baron Beaverbrook, *qv*), 1 da; *Career* chcllr Univ of New Brunswick Canada 1981-; *Recreations* racing, powerboat racing, hot air ballooning; *Style—* Lady Aitken; Mickleham Downs House, Dorking, Surrey RH5 6DP

AITMAN, David Charles; s of Gabriel Aitman, and Irene Bertha, *née* Polack; *b* 11 April 1956; *Educ* Clifton, Univ of Sheffield (BA); *m* 26 March 1983, Marianne Lucille, da of Edward Atherton; 1 s (Marcus), 2 da (Lauren, Polly); *Career* admitted slr 1982; ptnr Denton Hall Burgin & Warrens, dir Bertelsmann UK Ltd; memb Law Soc, LRAM; *Recreations* squash, wind surfing, music (performing and concert going); *Style—* David Aitman, Esq; Denton Hall Burgin & Warrens, 5 Chancery Lane, Clifford's Inn, London EC4A 1BU

AITON, Keith Martyn Hamilton; s of Alexander Hamilton Aiton, and Margaret Helen Elizabeth, *née* Martyn; *b* 14 Sept 1958; *Educ* Nottingham HS, Sidney Sussex Coll Cambridge; *Career* croquet player 1980-; played for Cambridge in Varsity Match 1980, 1981 and 1982 (capt); team player Nottingham Croquet Club 1983- (joined 1981); played Scotland Home Internationals 1983-85 and 1987-90 (capt 1990); championships incl: British Men's (winner 1987 and 1989), British Open (second 1983, third 1988), President's Cup (third 1984 and 1986), Chairman's Salver (winner 1983); coach: of GB Under 21 Squad 1988-, of winning GB Team for matches v Aust and NZ 1990; qualified as slr 1989, tax specialist Price Waterhouse Nottingham 1990-; *Recreations* chess, golf, Greek mathematics; *Style—* Keith Aiton, Esq; c/o The Croquet Association, Hurlingham Club, Ranelagh Gardens, London SW6 3PR

AKABUSI, Kriss Kezie Uche-Chukwu Duru; s of Daniel Kambi Duru Akabusi, and Clara, *née* Adams; *b* 28 Nov 1958; *Educ* Edmonton Co Comp; *m* 2 April 1982, Monika, da of Heinrich Bernard Udhöfer; 2 da (Ashanti b 19 June 1984, Shakira b 20 Oct 1987); *Career* Army: jr signalman 1975, signalman 1976 (data telegraphist), Lance Corpl (AIPT) 1978, Corpl (AITP) 1980, Sgt SI APTC 1981, Staff Sgt SSI APTC 1985, WOII (QMSI) APTC 1988; athlete: Bronze medallist 4 x 400m relay World Championship 1983, Olympic Silver medallist 4 x 400m relay 1984, UK champion 400m 1984, capt Eng Athletics Team vs USA 1985, Euro and Cwlth 4 x 400m Gold medallist and record holder 1986, finalist 400m hurdles and Silver medallist 4 x 400m relay World Championship 1987, UK 400m hurdles champion 1987, Olympic finalist 400m hurdles 1988, AAA champion 400m 1988, champion Euro and Cwlth 400m hurdles 1990, Gold medallist Euro Championship 4 x 400m 1990, Br record holder 400m hurdles 1990; involved with: Cwlth Games Appeal 1985-86, Olympic Games Appeal 1986-88; *Clubs* Team Solent Athletics; *Style—* Kriss Akabusi, Esq

AKEHURST, Gen Sir John Bryan; KCB (1984), CBE (1976); s of Geoffrey Akehurt, and Doris Akehurst; *b* 12 Feb 1930; *Educ* Cranbrook Sch, RMA Sandhurst; *m* 1955, Shirley Ann, er da of Maj W G Webb, MBE; 1 s, 1 da (both decd); *Career* formerly with Northamptonshire Regt and Malay Regt, cmd 2 Royal Anglian Regt 1968-70, DS IDC 1970-72, Cdr Dhofar Bde Sultan of Oman's Armed Forces 1974-76, dep mil sec (A) MOD 1976-79, GOC Armd Div BAOR 1979-82, Cmdt Staff Coll Camberley 1982-83 (instr 1966-68 and 1972-74), cmd UK Field Army and inspr gen TA 1984-87, Dep Supreme Allied Cdr Europe 1987-90, Col The Royal Anglian Regt 1986-91, chm Cncl TAVRA 1990-; govr Harrow Sch 1982-; Order of Oman (Third Class Mil) 1976; *Books* We Won a War (1982); *Recreations* golf, fly fishing; *Clubs* Army and Navy; *Style—* Gen Sir John Akehurst, KCB, CBE; c/o Midland Bank, Minehead, Somerset TA24 5LH

AKEL, Dr Frederick; s of Maj Joseph B Akel (d 1950), of Wellington, NZ, and Natalie, *née* Alexander; *b* 26 March 1920; *Educ* Wellington Coll NZ, Univ of Otago (BDS); *m* 8 June 1961, Eve, da of Capt Richard Lovett (d 1939), of Camberley, Surrey; 1 s (Julian Lovett b 1962), 1 da (Michele Jane b 1963); *Career* RAMC and RNZADC 1946-48 (ret as Maj); oral surgn; supporter: Cities of London and Westminster C Assoc, Duke of Edinburgh Award Scheme; memb Lloyds; Freeman of the City of London 1981, memb Worshipful Soc of Apothecaries; hon surgn St Dunstan's; FRSM; assoc: Br Assoc of Plastic Surgns, Br Assoc of Oral Surgns; FDSRCS (Edinburgh), FDSR, FDSRACS (Australia); *Recreations* golf, tennis, swimming, sailing, skiing; *Clubs* MCC, Hurlingham, Queen's Tennis, Berkshire Golf, Royal Mid Surrey Golf, Monte Carlo County, RAC, British Ski, Guards Polo, Cawdray Polo; *Style—* DR Frederick Akel; 94 Harley St, London W1N 1AF (☎ 071 235 7347)

AKENHEAD, Robert; QC (1989); s of Lt-Col Edmund Akenhead, TD (d 1990), and Angela Miriam, *née* Cullen; *b* 15 Sept 1949; *Educ* Rugby, Univ of Exeter (LLB); *m* 9 Dec 1972, Elizabeth Anne, da of Maj Frederick Hume Jackson, CMG, OBE, of Tonbridge, Kent; 1 s (Edmund b 1983), 3 da (Eleanor b 1978, Isobel b 1980, Rosalind b 1985); *Career* called to the Bar Gray's Inn 1972; *Books* Site Investigation and the Law (with J Cottington, 1984); *Recreations* cricket, skiing, theatre; *Style—* Robert Akenhead, Esq, QC; 1 Atkin Building, Gray's Inn, London WC1R 5BQ (☎ 071 404 0102, fax 071 405 7456, fax 298623 HUDSON)

AKERS, Colin Arthur; s of Lt Arthur William Akers, JP, RNVR (d 1985), of the Bryn, Yewlands, Hoddesdon, Herts, and Nora Edith, *née* Archer (d 1983); *b* 29 Sept 1931; *Educ* Canford, University Coll Oxford; *m* 8 April 1978, Jean, da of Albert Mills (d 1983), of Carisbrooke, Beech Rd, Hartford, Cheshire; *Career* Nat Serv 1950-52, Gunner tech asst RA Korean War 1951-52; md: EJ Woollard Ltd (horticultural suppliers) 1968-81 (joined 1953), Selfridges Ltd (Wine & Spirits Dept) 1984-; dir Cheshunt Building Soc 1975-; former chm Cheshunt & Waltham Cross C of C, vice pres Herts LTA, hon life memb Broxbourne Sports Club (formerly chm), memb Herts CCC, 105 Caps Herts Co Hockey XI (capt 1958-61); *Recreations* hockey, wine-tasting, classical music; *Clubs* Les Compagnons du Beaujolais, Wine and Spirit Trade; *Style—* Colin Akers, Esq; The Fernery, 110 Bengeo St, Bengeo, Hertford, Herts SG14 3EX (☎ 0992 587300); Selfridges Ltd, 400 Oxford St, London W1 (☎ 071 629 1234)

AKERS-JONES, Sir David; KBE (1985), CMG (1978); s of Walter George Jones, and late Dorothy, *née* Akers; *b* 14 April 1927; *Educ* Worthing HS, Brasenose Coll Oxford (MA); *m* 8 Sept 1951, Jane Ackers-Jones MBE, da of Capt Sir Frank Todd Spickernell, KBE, CB, CVO, DSO (d 1959), and Amice Ivy Delves Broughton (d 1974); 1 s (decd), 1 da; *Career* with Br India Steam Navigation Co 1945-49, Malayan Civil Serv 1954-57; Hong Kong Civil Serv: sec for New Territories 1973-81, sec for City and New Territories admin 1981-83, sec for dist admin 1983-85, chief sec 1985-86, actg govr 1986-87, advr to Govr 1987; chm: Hong Kong Housing Authy, Nat Mutual Insur Hong Kong, Global Asset Mgmnt Hong Kong; WWF Hong Kong and Hong Kong Artists Guild; dir: Sime Darby Hong Kong, Shandwick Hong Kong, Hysan Development Co Ltd; pres Outward Bound Tst, hon pres Hong Kong Mountaineering Union; hon vice pres: Hong Kong Girl Guide Assoc, Scout Assoc of Hong Kong; vice patron Hong Kong Football Assoc; Hon: DCL Univ of Kent 1987, LLD Chinese Univ of Hong Kong 1988; *Recreations* painting, gardening, walking, music; *Clubs* Athenaeum, Royal Over-Seas League, Hong Kong, Kowloon; *Style—* Sir David Akers-Jones, KBE, CMG; Dragon View, Tsing Lung Tau, NT, Hong Kong (☎ 4919319)

AKHTAR, Prof Muhammad; s of Muhammad Azeem Chaudhry; *b* 23 Feb 1933; *Educ* Punjab Univ Pakistan, (MSc), Imp Coll London (PhD, DIC); *m* 3 Aug 1963, Monika E, *née* Schurmann; 2 s (Marcus, Daniel); *Career* res scientist Res Inst for Med and Chemistry Cambridge USA 1959-63, prof and head of biochemistry Univ of Southampton 1987- (lectr 1963-, reader then sr lectr); chm Sch of Biochemical and Physiological Sciences 1983-87, chm Inst of Biomolecular Sciences Univ of Southampton 1989-, author of articles in learned jls; founding fell Third World Acad of Sci 1984; FRS (memb Cncl 1983-85); memb: Royal Soc of Chemistry, American Chem Soc; Biochemical Soc award of Sitara-I-Imtiaz by Govt of Pakistan 1981; *Style—* Prof Muhammad Akhtar, FRS; Dept of Biochemistry, The University, Bassett Crescent East, Southampton SO9 3TU (☎ 0703 595000 ext 4338)

AKISTER, (Roy) Edward; s of Aaron Akister (d 1975), of Lindale, Furness, Lancs, and Jennie, *née* Shaw (d 1974); *b* 22 Oct 1933; *Educ* The Friends' Sch Lancaster, Pinewood Students Unit Berks, Owens Coll Univ of Manchester; *m* 26 Aug 1961, June, da of Robert Curwen (d 1974), of Lancaster, Lancs; 1 s (Simeon James b 15 March 1964), 2 da (Louise b 7 Feb 1962, Victoria b 26 Aug 1972); *Career* mangr Marchwiel Plant and Engrg (aviation) 1970-79, site mangr McAlpine Southern (civil engrg) 1979-85, sr ptnr Easthope Trading Co (design and devpt) 1985-; former ed of 244 magazine; chm: Shropshire and Dist Br Inst of Mgmnt 1978-79, Shropshire Lib Party 1981-84; memb Nat Lib Party Cncl; MBIM, MIIM; *Recreations* bee-keeping, painting, shooting, Guild of One Name Studies, golf; *Clubs* Horsfall Museum (Manchester); *Style—* Edward Akister, Esq; Akehurst Ladywood, Bridge Bank, Iron-Bridge, Shropshire; Easthope Trading Company, Bridge Road, Iron-Bridge, Shropshire (☎ 0952 884132)

AL AZMEH, Prof Aziz; s of Ahmad Malak Azmeh, of Damascus, Syria, and Salma Naboulsi; *b* 23 July 1947; *Educ* Brummana HS Lebanon, Tübingen (MA), Univ of Oxford (DPhil); *m* 31 Aug 1979, Dr Kasturi Sen, da of Keshab Chandra Sen; 1 s (Omar b 27 Dec 1986); *Career* prof of Islamic studies Univ of Exeter 1985-, author of numerous articles on Islam; radio and TV broadcaster on Islamic and Arabic affrs and conslt to various bodies; chm UK section Arab Human Rights Orgn 1987; memb: Arab Club of GB, Br Soc Middle Eastern Studies, Medieval Soc of America, Nat Conf of Univ Profs, Arab Philosophical Assoc, Arab writers' Union; Lesh Beirut; *Books* Ibn Khaldun in Modern Scholarship (1981), Ibn Khaldun (1982), Historical Writing and Historical Knowledge (Arabic, 1983), Arabic Thought and Islamic Societies (1986), The Politics and History of Heritage (Arabic, 1987), Arabs and Barbarians (Arabic, 1990); *Style—* Prof Aziz Al Azmeh; University of Exeter, Department of Arabic & Islamic Studies, Exeter EX4 4JZ (☎ 0392 264028, fax 0392 263108, tlx 42894 EXUNIV G)

ALANBROOKE, 3 Viscount (UK 1946); Alan Victor Harold Brooke; s of 1 Viscount Alanbrooke, KG, GCB, OM, GCVO, DSO (d 1963), and his 2 w, Benita Blanche (d 1968), da of Sir Harold Pelly, 4 Bt, JP, and wid of Sir Thomas Lees, 2 Bt; suc half-bro, 2 Viscount, 1972; *b* 24 Nov 1932; *Educ* Harrow, Bristol Univ (BEd); *Heir* None; *Career* serv Army 1952-72, Germany, Korea, Malaya, UK, Capt RA ret; qualified teacher 1975; lectr for MOD Princess Marina Coll Arborfield 1978-; hon pres Salisbury and Dist Branch The 1940 Dunkirk Veterans 1970; patron 1977-87 and hon pres 1987- The UK Veterans of King Leopold III; *Recreations* private flying, radio control model aircraft, fencing, walking round the edge of Cornwall, restoring property ravaged by tenants; *Style—* The Rt Hon the Viscount Alanbrooke; Ferney Close, Hartley Wintney, Hants RG27 8JG

ALBEMARLE, Countess of; Dame Diana Cicely; DBE (1956); da of Maj John

Grove; *b* 6 Aug 1909; *Educ* Sherborne Sch for Girls; *m* 1931, as his 2 w, 9 Earl of Albemarle, MC (d 1979); 1 da (Lady Anne-Louise Hamilton-Dalrymple, *qv*); *Career* chm: Devpt Cmmn 1948-74, Drama Bd 1964-78, Carnegie UK Tst 1977-82; chm Departmental Ctee on Youth Serv 1958-60; chm Nat Youth Employment Cncl 1962-68; vice chm Br Cncl 1959-74; tstee: Carnegie UK Tst, The Observer until 1977, Glyndebourne Arts Tst 1968-80; *Style*— The Rt Hon the Countess of Albemarle, DBE; Seymours, Melton, Woodbridge, Suffolk (☎ 039 43 2151)

ALBEMARLE, 10 Earl of (E 1696); Rufus Arnold Alexis Keppel; also Baron Ashford and Viscount Bury (both E 1696); s of Viscount Bury (d 1968, eld s of 9 E of Albemarle, MC) and his 2 w, Marina, da of late Lt Cdr Count Serge Orloff-Davidoff, RNVR, and late Hon Elisabeth, *née* Scott-Ellis, 2 da of 8 Baron Howard de Walden; *b* 16 July 1965; *Heir* cousin Crispian Walter John Keppel; *Style*— The Rt Hon the Earl of Albemarle; Piazza di Bellosguardo 10, Florence 50124, Italy; 20A Pembroke Sq, London W8 6PA

ALBERY, Ian Bronson; s of Sir Donald Arthur Rolleston Albery (d 1988), and Ruby Gilchrist, *née* Macgilchrist (d 1956); Ian Albery is the fifth generation in the theatre and both f (Sir Donald Albery) and gf (Sir Bronson Albery) as well as step ggf (Sir Charles Wyndham) were all knighted for servs to the theatre; *b* 21 Sept 1936; *Educ* Stowe, Lycée de Briançon France; *m* 1, 1966 (m dis 1985), Barbara Yuling, *née* Lee; 2 s (Wyndham b 1968, Bronson b 1971); 1 da (Caitlin b 1985), by Jenny Beavan; *Career* Soc of W End Theatre: exec 1965-, pres 1977-79, vice pres 1979-82; tstee Theatres Tst 1977-, memb Drama and Dance Panel Br Cncl 1978-88, dep chm London Festival Ballet Ltd 1984-90, dir Ticketmaster Ltd 1985-, chm and md Donmar Ltd 1986-; prodr or co-prodr of over 50 West End prodns; prodr and md Theatre of Comedy Co Ltd 1987-90, Wyndham Ltd 1987-; *Clubs* Garrick; *Style*— Ian B Albery, Esq; Raspit Hill, Coach Rd, Ivy Hatch, Kent TN15 0PE; Donmar Ltd, Donmar House, 54 Cavell St, Whitechapel, London E1 2HP (☎ 071 790 9937, fax 071 790 6634, fax 264892)

ALBROW, Desmond; er s of Frederick and Agnes Albrow; *b* 22 Jan 1925; *Educ* St Bede's GS Bradford, Keble Coll Oxford; *m* 1950, Aileen Mary Jennings; 1 s, 3 da; *Career* asst ed Sunday Telegraph 1976-87; *Style*— Desmond Albrow, Esq; Totyngton Cottage, 18 Victoria Rd, Teddington, Middx (☎ 081 977 4220)

ALBU, Sir George; 3 Bt (UK 1912), of Grosvenor Place, City of Westminster, and Richmond, Province of Natal, Repub of S Africa; s of Sir George Werner Albu, 2 Bt (d 1963); *b* 5 June 1944; *Educ* Michael House S Africa, Cedara Agric Coll; *m* 23 April 1969, Joan Valerie, da of late Malcolm Millar, of Weybridge, Surrey; 2 da (Camilla Jane b 22 Aug 1972, Victoria Mary b 14 Jan 1976); *Heir* none; *Career* Rifleman Commandos SADF 1963; gen investor; *Recreations* horse racing (flat), motor racing; *Clubs* Victoria (SA), Richmond Country (SA), Pietermaritzburg Natal; *Style*— Sir George Albu, Bt; Glen Hamish, PO Box 62, Richmond 3780, Natal, S Africa

ALBUM, Edward Jonathan Corcos; s of Harry Album (d 1988), of London N3, and Matilda, *née* Corcos; *b* 8 Sept 1936; *Educ* Emanuel Sch, ChCh Oxford (MA); *m* 14 July 1970, Elizabeth Ann, da of Lancelot Ezra, of Belsize Rd, London NW6; 1 s (Richard b 1974), 1 da (Victoria b 1977); *Career* Capt Res TA 1962-70; slr; dir: Leopold Lazarus Ltd, The London Metal & Ore Co Ltd, LMO Investments Ltd, Hartons Estates Ltd, Hartons Gp plc, Int House Assoc Ltd, chm Sanderling Ltd; *Recreations* military history, ornithology, railway preservation; *Clubs* Sir Walter Scott (Edinburgh), Naval and Military, AC Owners; *Style*— Edward Album, Esq; Sanderling House, High St, Cley, Norfolk (☎ 0263 740810); 47 Lyndale Ave, London NW2 2QB (☎ 071 431 2942)

ALBUTT, Dr Kenneth John; s of Leonard John Samuel Albutt, and Doris Rose, *née* Knight; *b* 8 March 1939; *Educ* Handsworth Tech Sch Birmingham, Univ of Aston Birmingham (BSc), Univ of Birmingham (PhD); *m* 14 Sept 1963, Jane Andrée, da of Frederick Blick, of 33 Margaret Grove, Harborne, Birmingham; 1 s (Andrew Scott b 6 June 1968), 1 da (Nicola Jayne b 4 Dec 1966); *Career* sr res metallurgist BSA Gp Res Centre 1962-64, chief metallurgist BSA Motor Cycles Ltd 1967-69; md: Altrincham Labs Ltd (now Amtac Labs Ltd) 1976-82 (gen mangr 1969-71, dir 1971-76), PI Castings Ltd 1982- (tech dir 1974-77), Aical Ltd 1981-; chief exec: PI Castings Gp 1982-85, ATR Gp 1985-; vice pres Br Measurement and Testing Assoc, UK rep Eurolab Gen Assembly, pres Union Int des Labs Independants; memb: Cncl Assoc of Consltg Scis, Advsy Ctee NAMAS; former pres Br Invesmt Casting Trade Assoc; former chm Holmes Chapel Round Table; CEng, FIM 1975, FRSA 1990; *Recreations* shooting, sailing, gardening; *Clubs* 41, Rotary; *Style*— Dr Kenneth Albutt; A T R Group Ltd, Davenport Lane, Broadheath, Altrincham, Cheshire (☎ 061 928 5811, fax 061 927 7023)

ALCHIN, Hon Mrs (Juliet Alers); da of 2 Baron Hankey, KCMG, KCVO; *b* 15 Oct 1931; *m* 1957, Peter John Wrensted Alchin, only s of His Hon Judge Gordon Alchin, AFC (d 1947), of Duffields, Medmenham, Bucks; 1 s (Gordon David b 1961), 2 da (Vanessa Frances b 1962, Chloe Sylvia b 1965); *Career* tech offr for visually handicapped Kent Social Servs 1979-; *Recreations* music, painting, sailing, walking; *Style*— The Hon Mrs Alchin; Parkstone, Clenches Farm Rd, Sevenoaks, Kent (☎ 0732 457 188)

ALCHIN, Peter John Wrensted; s of His Hon Judge Gordon Alchin (d 1947), of Medmenham, nr Marlow, Bucks, and Sylvia, *née* Wrensted (d 1939); *b* 25 July 1928; *Educ* Tonbridge, Hertford Coll Oxford (MA); *m* 23 Feb 1957, Hon Juliet, da of 2 Baron Hankey, KCMG, KCVO; 1 s (Gordon b 1961), 2 da (Vanessa b 1962, Chloe b 1965); *Career* Nat Serv cmmnd 2 Lt York and Lancaster Regt 1947-49; called to the Bar Middle Temple 1951, practised SE Circuit until 1960, legal advsr and co sec in indust (incl 3 years with Turner and Newall Ltd) 1960-70; admitted slr 1970; slr Supreme Court, former ptnr Stephenson Harwood (ret); chm Footpaths Ctee Sevenoaks Soc; Freeman Worshipful Co of Skinners 1947-; *Recreations* painting, music, walking, sailing; *Clubs* Little Ship; *Style*— Peter Alchin, Esq; Parkstone, Clenches Farm Rd, Sevenoaks, Kent TN13 2LU (☎ 0732 45 7188)

ALCOCK, Jonathan Guest; s of Capt Ivor William Guest Alcock, of 80 Biddulph Way, Ledbury, Herefordshire, and Ada Violet, *née* Pike (d 1959); *b* 10 Aug 1955; *Educ* Elliotts Green GS, Harrow Coll of Art; *m* 5 Aug 1978, Nicole Elaine, da of Raimund Frederick Herincx, of Larkbarrow, E Compton, Somerset; 1 s (Sam b 1990); *Career* creative dir Grange Advertising 1981-; *Recreations* tennis; *Style*— Jonathan Alcock, Esq; Grange Advertising Ltd, 113 High St, Berkhamstead, Hertfordshire HP4 2DJ (☎ 04428 74321, fax 0442 874102)

ALCOCK, Prof Leslie; s of Philip John Alcock, and Mary Ethel, *née* Bagley; *b* 24 April 1925; *Educ* Manchester GS, Brasenose Coll Oxford (BA, MA); *m* 29 July 1950, Elizabeth Annie, da of Robert Blair; 1 s (John b 1960), 1 da (Penelope b 1957); *Career* WWII Gurkha Rifles 1943-47; supt of exploration and excavation Dept of Archaeology Govt of Pakistan 1950-52, curator Leeds City Museums 1952-53; prof of archaeology: Univ Coll Cardiff (also lectr and reader) 1953-73, Univ of Glasgow 1973-90; pres: Cambrian Archaeological Assoc 1982, Soc of Antiquaries of Scotland 1984-87; tstee: Nat Museum of Antiquities of Scotland 1973-85, Ancient Monuments Bd Scotland 1974-90; cmmr RC Ancient Monuments: Scotland 1977-, Wales 1986-90; FSA 1957, FRHistS 1969; *Books* Dinas Powys (1963), Arthur's Britain (1971), By South Cadbury is that Camelot (1972), Economy Society and Warfare (1987); *Recreations* music, landscape; *Style*— Prof Leslie Alcock; 29 Hamilton Drive, Glasgow G12 (☎ 041 339 7123)

ALCOCK, Peter John Osborne; s of John Frederick Alcock, OBE, MA (d 1982), of Knaresborough, and Gwendoline Osborne, *née* Sampson; *b* 25 Sept 1936; *Educ* Oundle, McGill Univ (BEng); *m* 2 June 1962, Yvonne, da of Eric Dawson (d 1985); 2 s (John b 1968, Nicholas b 1972), 1 da (Amanda b 1965); *Career* dir: Hunslet 1965-, Greenbat Engineering Ltd 1980-88, Andrew Barclay & Sons Ltd 1982-88, The Leeds TEC Ltd 1990-; chm: Hunslet Engine Co Ltd 1985-, Railway Indust Assoc 1988-90, Poly Enterprises (Leeds) Ltd 1989-; govr Leeds Poly 1988-; *Recreations* skiing, travel; *Style*— Peter Alcock, Esq; Poly Enterprises (Leeds) Ltd, Calverley St, Leeds LS1 3HE (☎ 0532 832600, fax 0532 425733, telex 9312132637)

ALDCROFT, Prof Derek Howard; s of Leslie Howard Aldcroft, and Freda, *née* Wallen; *b* 25 Oct 1936; *Educ* Univ of Manchester (BA, PhD); *Career* lectr in economic history Univ of Leicester and Univ of Glasgow 1960-71; prof of economic history: Univ of Sidney 1973-76, Univ of Leicester 1976- (reader 1971-73); memb Economic History Soc; *Books* incl: From Versailles to Wall Street (1977), The European Economy 1920-80 (1980), Full Employment: The Elusive Coal (1984), The British Economy 1920-51 (1986); *Recreations* tennis, swimming, the stock exchange and gardening; *Style*— Prof Derek Aldcroft; Department of Economic History, The University of Leicester, Leicester LE1 7RH (☎ 0533 522589, fax 0533 522200)

ALDENHAM (AND HUNSDON OF HUNSDON), Mary, Lady; Mary Elizabeth; *née* Tyser; o da of late Walter Parkyns Tyser, of Gordonbush, Brora, Sutherland; *m* 16 July 1947, 5 Baron Aldenham and 3 Baron Hunsdon of Hunsdon (d 1986); 3 s (6 Lord Aldenham, *qv*, Hon George Henry Paul, Hon William Humphrey Durant d 1972), 1 da (Hon Antonia Mary); *Style*— The Rt Hon Mary, Lady Aldenham; Rathgar, The Avenue, Sherborne, Dorset (☎ 0935 817149)

ALDENHAM (AND HUNSDON OF HUNSDON), 6 (and 4) Baron (UK 1896 and 1923 respectively); Vicary Tyser Gibbs; s of 5 Baron Aldenham and 3 Baron Hunsdon of Hunsdon (d 1986); *b* 9 June 1948; *Educ* Eton, Oriel Coll Oxford; *m* 16 May 1980, Josephine Nicola, er da of John Richmond Fell, of Lower Bourne, Farnham, Surrey; 1 s (Hon Humphrey William Fell b 31 Jan 1989), 1 da (Hon Jessica Juliet Mary b 1984); *Heir* s, Hon Humphrey William Fell Gibbs b 31 Jan 1989; *Style*— The Rt Hon Lord Aldenham; Aldenham Wood Lodge, Elstree, Herts WD6 3AA

ALDER, Elisabeth Mary; *née* Artus; da of Rev Hugh Neville More Artus (d 1978), and Phyllis, *née* Row; *b* 1 Nov 1942; *Educ* St Albert's Convent Hinckley, Nuneaton HS for Girls; *m* 1, 18 June 1966 (m dis), David Michael North, s of Douglas Edward North (d 1986), of Penn, Bucks; 1 s (Richard James b 1972), 1 da (Sarah Anne b 1968); m 2, 5 April 1980, Christopher John Alder, s of Rev William Alder, of Silchester, Berks; *Career* WRNS 1960-67 (cmmnd 1963), WRNR 1980-, First Offr 1984, sr WRNR Offr and Ops Trg Offr Southwick RNR, ret list 1989; currently trg offr W Sussex Family Health Services Authy; *Recreations* sailing, music (church), bellringing (campanology); *Clubs* Thorney Island Sailing, Emsworth Slipper Sailing, Ladies' Naval Luncheon; *Style*— Mrs Christopher Alder; 56 Ellesmere Orchard, Westbourne, Emsworth, Hampshire (☎ 0243 375311)

ALDER, Michael; s of Thomas Alder (d 1945), and Winifred Miller (d 1987); *b* 3 Nov 1928; *Educ* Ranelagh Sch Bracknell, Rutherford Coll Newcastle; *m* 1955, Freda, da of John Hall (d 1956); 2 da (Ann, Alison); *Career* with Newcastle Evening Chronicle 1947-59; BBC NE: chief news asst and area news ed Newcastle 1959-69; head of regnl TV devpt BBC 1969-77, controller English Regnl TV BBC 1977-86; chm Appeals Ctee RELATE (marriage guidance) 1990-; *Recreations* gardening, photography, walking, country pursuits; *Style*— Michael Alder, Esq; Red Roofs, Bates Lane, Tanworth in Arden, Warwicks B94 5AR

ALDER, Samuel George (Sam); s of George Parker Alder (d 1981), of Douglas, IOM, and Brenda Margaret, *née* Moore (d 1980); *b* 28 Jan 1944; *Educ* King William Coll IOM, Grey Coll Univ of Durham (BA); *m* 3 Sept 1983, Helen Mary, da of Dr Algernon Ivor Boyd, OBE, of St Johns, Antigua; 1 da (Alison Margaret b 16 Feb 1989); *Career* Whinney Murray & Co (CAs) 1966-71, fin dir EG Mgmnt Ltd 1971-77, md EG Music Ltd 1977-88; mangr: Roxy Music 1972-83, King Crimson 1972-85; chm: EG Music Gp Ltd 1980-, The Villiers Hotel Ltd 1981-, Yeoman Security Gp plc 1986-; sr ptnr Alder Dodsworth & Co (CAs) 1985-, md Old Chelsea Gp plc 1986-, ptnr Athol & Co Ltd 1989-; dir Douglas Gas Light Company; hon treas: Music Therapy Charity Fund Raising Ctee 1975-81, Duke of Edinburgh's Award Int Project 1987, Duke of Edinburgh's Award Special Projects Gp 1988-, Museum of Garden History Appeal Ctee 1989-; tstee: Bishop Barrow's Charity 1985-, LSO Tst 1988-91; sec and treas Nordoff-Robins Music Therapy Centre 1981-, memb Appeals Ctee Royal Acad of Music Fndn 1989-; govr King William's Coll IOM; ACA 1971, FCA 1977; *Recreations* music, farming, history; *Clubs* RAC; *Style*— S G Alder, Esq; The Grange, Onchan, Isle of Man; Old Chelsea Group plc, 63A Kings Rd, London SW3 4NT (☎ 071 730 2162, fax 071 730 1330)

ALDERDICE, Dr John Thomas; s of Rev David Alderdice, of Wellington Manse, 21 Old Galgorm Rd, Ballymena, NI, and (Annie Margaret) Helena, *née* Shields; *b* 28 March 1955; *Educ* Ballymena Acad, Queen's Univ Belfast (MB BCh, BAO); *m* 30 July 1977, Dr Joan Margaret Hill, da of James Hill, of 8 Glenagherty Dr, Ballymena, NI; 2 s (Stephen b 1980, Peter b 1983), 1 da (Anna b 1988); hon lectr in psychotherapy Queen's Univ Belfast 1990-; *Career* conslt psychotherapist E Health and Social Servs Bd 1988; Alliance Pty of NI: memb Exec Ctee 1984, vice-chm 1987, leader 1987-; Westminster Parly candidate June 1987, Euro Parly candidate June 1989; memb Belfast Cncl (Victoria Area) 1989-; exec memb Fedn of Euro Liberal Democrat and Reform Parties; MRCPsych 1983; *Recreations* reading, music; *Clubs* National Liberal; *Style*— Dr John Alderdice; 55 Knock Rd, Belfast BT5 6LB (☎ 0232 793097); Alliance Party Headquarters, 88 University St, Belfast BT7 1HE (☎ 0232 324274, fax 0232 796689)

ALDERMAN, John; s of Edward George Alderman (d 1978), and Eunice, *née* Childs (d 1987); *b* 24 Feb 1936; *Educ* Rotherham GS, Battersea Coll of Tech (Dip Tech in Hotel Mgmnt); *m* 1965, Jean Gwendolen, da of John Raymond Blake; 1 s (Maxwell John b 8 April 1966), 2 da (Jennifer Jean b 29 Nov 1967, Alison Jane b 10 Sept 1969); *Career* hotel mgmnt Jamaica 1961-64, gen mangr 1964-71 (Hertford Hotel, Gifford Hotel, Both Worlds), area mangr CCH 1971-73, md Lithgow Hotels 1973-83, conslt Hall & Woodhouse 1983-88, proprietor Streamside Restaurant and Hotel 1988-; chm Master Innholders 1980-81, nat pres HCIMA 1984-85; Freeman City of London 1978; FHCIMA 1976, Master Innholder 1978, FTS 1980; *Recreations* golf, crossword puzzles; *Clubs* Broadstone Golf; *Style*— John Alderman, Esq; Streamside Hotel & Restaurant, 29 Preston Rd, Weymouth, Dorset DT3 6PX (☎ 0305 833121)

ALDERSON, (John) Antony; s of Henry William Alderson (d 1960) of Sutton Coldfield, Warwick, and Fanny, *née* Woolley (d 1969); *b* 11 July 1924; *Educ* King Edward's Sch Birmingham, Univ of Birmingham (LLB); *m* 19 June 1948, Patricia Joyce, da of Lt Cdr William Leslie Jennings RNVR (d 1980); 1 s (Richard b 1951), 2 da (Ann (Dr Newmark) b 1953, Susan (Mrs Ratcliffe) b 1956); *Career* Sub Lt RNVR 1943-46; slr, former jt sr ptnr Edge and Ellison, chm Wesleyan Assur Soc, dir Aston Villa FC plc; memb Birmingham Law Soc (past pres 1975); *Recreations* gardening, walking; *Clubs* The Birmingham; *Style*— J Antony Alderson, Esq; 9 Hartopp Rd, Sutton Coldfield, W Midlands, (☎ 021 308 0517); Rutland Hse, 148 Edmund St,

Birmingham B3 2JR (☎ 021 200 2001, fax 021 200 1991, fax 336370 EDGECO G)

ALDERSON, Derek; s of Frederick Alan Alderson, of Birtley, Co Durham, and Mary Annie, *née* Brown; *b* 18 Jan 1953; *Educ* Chester-le-Street GS, Univ of Newcastle upon Tyne (MB BS, MD); *m* 19 Oct 1975, Lyn Margaret, da of Anthony Smith, of Pelton, Co Durham; 1 s (Kevin b 1979), 1 da (Helen b 1981); *Career* house offr Royal Victoria Infirmary Newcastle upon Tyne 1976-77, surgical registrar Newcastle AHA 1979-81, Wellcome surgical training fell 1981-83, sr registrar in surgery Northern RHA 1983-88, res fell Washington Univ St Louis USA 1985-86, conslt sr lectr in surgery Univ of Bristol 1988-; memb: Surgical Res Soc, Assoc of Surgns of GS and I, Br Assoc of Surgical Oncology; memb Ctee Pancreatic Soc of GS and I; FRCS 1980; *Recreations* jogging; *Style*— Derek Alderson, Esq; Bristol Royal Infirmary, University Department of Surgery, Marlborough St, Bristol BS2 4HW (☎ 272696)

ALDERSON, Geoffrey Peter; s of Bernard peter Alderson, of 26 Garscube Terrace, Edinburgh EH12, and Janet Kemp, *née* Brown; *b* 26 Oct 1941; *Educ* Edinburgh Acad, Uppingham, Clare Coll Cambridge (BA); *m* 22 April 1966, Patricia Anne (Tish), da of Angus Marsh Scott; 3 s (Andrew b 1967, Timothy b 1969, Anthony b 1971), 2 da (Victoria b 1972, Claire b 1972); *Career* chm Food Serv Equipment Ltd 1983, chm and md Scobie McIntosh Ltd 1984; dir: Revent Int Ltd 1988-, Edinburgh Chamber of Commerce 1988-; chm Catering Equipment Distributors Assoc 1976-78; *Recreations* golf, shooting; *Clubs* Muirfield, New (Edinburgh); *Style*— Geoffrey Alderson, Esq; Scobie & McIntosh Ltd, Bankhead Ave, Sighthill, Edinburgh EH11 4BY (☎ 031 458 5500, telex 727452, fax 031 458 5412)

ALDERSON, John Cottingham; CBE (1981), QPM (1974); s of late Ernest Cottingham Alderson, and Elsie Lavinia Rose; *b* 28 May 1922; *Educ* Barnsley; *m* 1948, Irene Macmillan Stirling; 1 s; *Career* served WWII Warrant Offr Army Physical Training Corps N Africa and Italy; called to the Bar Middle Temple; Police Coll 1954, inspr 1955, dep chief constable Dorset 1964-66, dep asst cmmr (training) 1968, Cmdt Police Coll 1970, asst cmmr (Personnel and Trg Div) 1973, chief constable Devon and Cornwall 1973-83; advsr Centre for Police Studies Univ of Strathclyde 1983-89, conslt on human rights to to Cncl of Europe 1981-, dir of Human Rights Strasbourg; Hon LLD Exeter 1979, Hon DLitt Bradford 1981; *Books* Policing Freedom (1979), Law and Disorder (1984), Human Rights and Police (1984); *Clubs* Royal Overseas League; *Style*— John Alderson, Esq, CBE, QPM; Centre for Police Studies, University of Exeter, Brookfield Annexe, New North Rd, Exeter EX4 4JY

ALDERSON, Maggie Hanne; da of Douglas Arthur Alderson (d 1984), and Margaret Dura, *née* Mackay; *b* 31 July 1959; *Educ* Alleyne's Sch Staffs, Univ of St Andrews (MA); *Career* features ed Look Now, sr writer Woman's World, features ed Honey, commissioning ed You magazine, met features ed Evening Standard, assoc ed ES magazine; memb Br Soc Magazine Eds; *Clubs* Groucho; *Style*— Miss Maggie Alderson; Northcliffe Ho, 2 Derry St, London W8 5EE (☎ 071 938 6000)

ALDERSON, (Arthur) Stanley; s of James Richard Alderson, CBE (d 1970), of Sussex, and Daisy, *née* Cawley (d 1965); *b* 27 April 1927; *Educ* Rutlish Sch Merton, BSc; *m* 4 April 1950, Pauline Olive, da of Clarence Henry Willott (d 1962), of Cornwall; 2 s (Andrew b 1958, Guy b 1960 d 1967); *Career* offr Cadet Royal Fusiliers invalided out after catching polio in India 1945-47; writer and author; *Books* Britain in the Sixties - Housing (1972), Yea or Nay? Referenda in the United Kingdom (1975); *Recreations* literature, theatre, music, walking; *Style*— Stanley Alderson, Esq; St Anthony's Cottage, West Downs, Delabole, Cornwall PL33 9DJ (☎ 0840 213301)

ALDINGTON, 1 Baron (UK 1962) Toby Austin Richard William Low; KCMG (1957), CBE (1945, MBE 1944), DSO (1941), TD and Clasp (1950), PC (1954), DL (Kent 1973); 1 Baron (UK 1962); s of Col Stuart Low, DSO (d on active serv 1942; s of Sir Austin Low, CIE, JP, and Hon Gwen Atkin, da of Baron Atkin, PC (Life Peer, d 1944); *b* 25 May 1914; *Educ* Winchester, New Coll Oxford (BA, MA); *m* 10 April 1947, (Felicité Anne) Araminta, er da of Sir Harold Alfred MacMichael, GCMG, DSO (d 1969), and former w of Capt Paul Humphrey Armytage Bowman; 1 s (Charles b 1948), 2 da (Jane b 1949, Ann b 1956); *Heir* s, Hon Charles Low; *Career* served WWII KRRC 1939-45, Brig BGS5 Corps 1944-45; barr Middle Temple 1939; MP (C) Blackpool N 1945-62, Parly sec MOS 1951-54, min of state BOT 1954-57, dep chm Cons Pty Orgn 1959-63; chm: House of Lords' Select Ctee on Overseas Trade 1984-85, Sub Ctee A House of Lords' Euro Communities Ctee 1989-, Ctee of Mgmnt Inst of Neurology 1961-78, Grindlays Bank 1964-76, Port of London Authy 1971-77, BBC Gen Advsy Cncl 1971-79, Sun Alliance & London Insurance 1971-85, National Nuclear Corporation 1973-80, Westland plc 1978-85, Leeds Castle Fndn 1984-; dep chm GEC 1968-84 (chm 1963-68); dir: Lloyds Bank 1967-85, Citicorp (USA) 1969-83; pres Cons Assoc Ashford Div, tstee Brain Res Tst 1973-, warden Winchester Coll 1979-87, hon fell New Coll Oxford 1976; *Recreations* gardening, golf; *Clubs* Carlton, Beefsteak, Royal St George's Golf, Rye Golf, Royal and Ancient Golf; *Style*— The Rt Hon the Lord Aldington, KCMG, CBE, DSO, TD, PC, DL; Knoll Farm, Aldington, Ashford, Kent TN25 7BY (☎ 0233 720292); Leeds Castle, Maidstone, Kent ME17 1PL (☎ 0622 765400, fax 0622 35616)

ALDISS, Brian Wilson; s of Stanley Aldiss, and May, *née* Wilson; *b* 18 Aug 1925; *Educ* Framlingham Coll, West Buckland Sch; *m* 1, 1949 (m dis 1965); 1 s (Clive b 1955), 1 da (Wendy b 1959); m 2, 11 Dec 1965, Margaret Christie, da of John Manson; 1 s (Tim b 1967), 1 da (Charlotte b 1969); *Career* RCS 1943-47; serv: India, Assam, Burma, Sumatra, Singapore, Hong Kong; bookseller Oxford 1948-56, lit ed Oxford Mail 1957-69; author & critic; prolific lectr and contrib to newspapers and jls; chm Mgmnt Ctee Soc of Authors 1975-78, memb Arts Cncl (Lit Panel) 1978-80, pres World SF 1982-84 (fndr memb), vice pres Soc for Anglo-Chinese Understanding, FRSL 1990; *Books* novels incl: The Brightfount Diaries (1955), Non-Stop (1958), Greybeard (1964), Barefoot in the Head (1969), The Hand-Reared-Boy (1970), Soldier Erect (1971), Frankenstein Unbound (1973), The Malacia Tapestry (1976), A Rude Awakening (1978), Life in the West (1980), The Helliconia Trilogy (1982-85), Forgotten Life (1988); Short Stories Collections incl: Space, Time and Nathaniel (1957), The Canopy of Time (1959), The Saliva Tree (1966), Intangibles Inc (1969), The Moment of Eclipse (1970), Last Orders (1977), Seasons in Flight (1984); non-fiction incl: Cities and Stones (travel) (1966), The Shape of Further Things (1970), Billion Year Spree (1973), Trillion Year Spree (update, 1986), Bury My Heart at W H Smiths (1990); *Recreations* amateur theatricals; *Style*— Brian Aldiss, Esq; Woodlands, Foxcombe Rd, Boars Hill, Oxford OX1 5DL (☎ 0865 735 744)

ALDISS, Thomas Edward; s of Noel Alfred Aldiss, of Caversham, Reading, Berkshire, and Ina Florence, *née* Wyllie (d 1947); *b* 8 Aug 1943; *Educ* Henley GS, Reading Coll of Tech, Univ of Bath; *m* 26 July 1969, Barbara Helen, da of Malcolm Frederick Mitchell, of Lancing, W Sussex; 1 s (David b 1974), 1 da (Suzanne b 1972); *Career* chartered accountant in private practice, princ Aldiss and Co; Freeman City of London; FCA 1972; *Recreations* travel, family, house and garden, wine and food and veteran cycles; *Clubs* Worthing Steyne Rotary; *Style*— Thomas Aldiss, Esq; 19 Broadwater Street East, Broadwater, Worthing, W Sussex (☎ 0903 205 819, fax 0903 214771); Beechcroft, Offington Ave, Worthing, W Sussex

ALDOUS, Bernard Russell; s of Bertie William Aldous, of Haughley, Stowmarket, Suffolk, and Evelyn Rose, *née* Dorling; *b* 5 July 1944; *Educ* Stowmarket County GS; *m* 3 Aug 1968, Patricia Ann, da of Alfred Charles William Greengrass, of Stowmarket; 2 s (Timothy James b 12 Feb 1974, David William b 3 Oct 1981), 2 da (Claire Louise b 16 April 1971, Anna Victoria b 14 May 1978); *Career* qualified mangr Whiting & Partners (chartered accountants) 1967-73 (articled clerk 1962-67), audit mangr Coopers & Lybrand Bristol 1974-76, regnl int mgmnt auditor for SW England and Wales Vestric Ltd (subsid of Glaxo) 1976-78, in practice Bristol 1978-80; ptnr Andrew Moore & Co 1984- (qualified mangr 1980-84); memb for E Anglia Gen Practitioner Bd ICAEW 1989-, pres Ipswich & Colchester Soc of CAs, memb Ctee E Anglian Soc CAs (currently also courses chm and enterprise liaison offr); FCA 1979 (ACA 1968); *Recreations* photography, ornithology, fly fishing, caravanning; *Clubs* Sudbury Institute; *Style*— Bernard Aldous, Esq; 29 Lambert Drive, Acton, Sudbury, Suffolk CO10 6EB (☎ 0787 71507); Andrew Moore & Co, 2 King St, Sudbury, Suffolk CO10 6EB (☎ 0787 881788, fax 0787 880283)

ALDOUS, Charles; QC (1985); s of Guy Travers Aldous (d 1981), of Suffolk, and Elizabeth Angela, *née* Paul; *b* 3 June 1943; *Educ* Harrow, Univ Coll London (LLB); *m* 17 May 1969, Hermione Sara, da of Montague George de Courcy-Ireland (d 1987), of Abington Pigotts Hall, Royston, Herts; 1 s (Alastair b 1979), 3 da (Hermione b 1971 (d 1972), Charlotte b 1973, Antonia b 1975); *Career* barr; called to the Bar (Inner Temple) 1967; *Style*— Charles Aldous, Esq, QC; 7 Stone Buildings, Lincolns Inn, London WC2 (☎ 071 405 3886)

ALDOUS, Hugh Graham Cazalet; s of Maj Hugh Francis Travers Aldous (d 1979), and Emily, *née* Watkinson; *b* 1 June 1944; *Educ* Cheam Sch, Scarborough HS, Univ of Leeds (BCom); *m* 25 Aug 1967, Christabel, da of Alan Marshall (d 1974); *Career* accountant; Robson Rhodes: ptnr 1976, head corp fin consultancy 1983-85, dep managing ptnr 1985-87, managing ptnr 1987-; seconded to Dept of Tport 1976-79; dir: Freightliner Ltd 1979-84, Sealink UK Ltd 1981-84; memb Br Waterways Bd 1983-86, DTI inspr into affairs of House of Fraser Holdings plc 1987-88; FCA 1979 (ACA 1970); *Recreations* walking, tennis, music; *Clubs* RAC; *Style*— Hugh Aldous, Esq; Robson Rhodes, 186 City Road, London EC1V 2NU (☎ 071 251 1644, fax 071 250 0801, telex 885734)

ALDOUS, Lucette (Mrs Alan Alder); da of Charles Fellows Aldous (d 1983), of Sydney, Aust, and Marie, *née* Rutherford; *b* 26 Sept 1938; *Educ* Dux Randwick HS for Girls; *m* 17 June 1972, Alan Richard Alder, s of Richard Alder; 1 da (Floeur Lucette b 2 July 1977); *Career* ballet dancer; prima ballerina Ballet Rambert London England 1957-62; ballerina: London Festival Ballet 1962-66, Royal Ballet Covent Garden 1966-71; prima ballerina Australian Ballet 1972-76, currently guest teacher Australian Ballet, Royal New Zealand Ballet and W Australian Ballet Co; memb: Dance Panel for Performing Arts Bd of Australian Cncl 1986-88, Advsy Cncl Care Australia, Exec Ctee WA Ballet Co; hon memb Imperial Soc of Teachers of Dancing; *Style*— Ms Lucette Aldous; c/o Dance Department, Western Australian Academy of Performing Arts, 2 Bradford St, Mount Lawley, Perth, WA 6050, Aust (☎ 370 6442, fax 370 2910)

ALDOUS, Sir William; s of Guy Travers Aldous, QC (d 1981), and Elizabeth Angela, *née* Paul; *b* 17 March 1936; *Educ* Harrow, Trinity Coll Cambridge (MA); *m* 1960, Gillian Frances, da of John Gordon Henson, CBE; 1 s, 2 da; *Career* called to the Bar Inner Temple 1960, memb jr counsel DTI 1972-76; QC 1976; chm Performing Right Tbnl 1987-88; Justice of the High Ct of Justice (chancery div) 1988-; kt 1988; *Recreations* horses; *Style*— Sir William Aldous; Royal Cts of Justice, Strand, London

ALDRICH, Michael John; s of Charles Albert Aldrich (d 1978), and Kathleen Alice Aldrich (d 1986); *b* 22 Aug 1941; *Educ* Clapham Coll, Univ of Hull (BA); *m* 1962, Sandra Kay, *née* Hutchings; 2 s, 2 da; *Career* md: Rediffusion Computers Ltd 1980-84, Rediffusion Business Electronics Ltd 1983-84, ROCC Corpn 1984-; chm ROCC Computers Ltd 1984-; advsr to HM Govt for info technol 1981-86; pres Inst of Info Scientists 1984-85; chm: Brighton Poly Cncl 1987-89, Brighton Poly Bd 1988-, Videotex Industry Assoc 1986-88, Tavistock Inst Cncl 1989-; *Publications* Videotex - Key to the Wired City (1982), Cable Systems (co-author, 1982), Making a Business of Info (co-author, 1983), Learning to Live with It (co-author, 1985), UK Videotex Market (1986); *Recreations* gardening, reading, riding; *Clubs* Gravetye; *Style*— Michael Aldrich, Esq; ROCC Computers Ltd, Kelvin Way, Crawley, Sussex RH10 2LY (☎ 0293 531211, telex 877369)

ALDRIDGE, (Harold Edward) James; s of William Thomas Aldridge, and Edith, *née* Quayle; *b* 10 July 1918; *Educ* Swan Hill HS Aust, Bradshaw Coll, The War; *m* 16 Oct 1942, Dina, *née* Shenoudah; 2 s (William Daoud, Thomas Hilal); *Career* reporter: Herald and Sun Melbourne 1937-38, Daily Sketch and Sunday Dispatch London 1939; Euro and ME war corr Aust Newspaper Serv and N American Newspaper Alliance 1939- 44, Teheran corr Time and Life 1944; recipient: Rys meml Prize 1945, World Peace Cncl Gold Medal, Int Orgn of Journalists Prize 1967, Lenin Meml Peace Prize 1972, Aust Children's Book Cncl Book of Year Award 1985; *Books* novels incl: Signed With their Honours (1942), Of Many Men (1946), Heroes of the Empty View (1954), I Wish He Would Not Die (1958), The Thinker (1961), The Statesmen's Game (1966), A Sporting Proposition (1973), Mockery In Arms (1974), The Untouchable Juli (1976), Goodbye Un-America (1979); short stories: Gold and Sand (1960); plays: The 49th State (produced 1947), One Last Glimpse (produced 1981); children's books: The Flying 19 (1966), The Marvellous Mongolian (1974), The Broken Saddle (1983); TV scripts for Robin Hood; *Recreations* trout and salmon fishing; *Style*— James Aldridge, Esq; c/o Curtis Brown, 162-168 Regent St, London W1R 5TB

ALDRIDGE, (Michael) John; s of John Edward Aldridge, of Rugby, and Marjorie, *née* Taft; *b* 1 Dec 1942; *Educ* Beckett Sch Nottingham, Brimingham Med Sch (BSC, MB ChB); *m* 4 April 1970, Eva Robin, da of James Nicholson, Harare, Zimbabwe; 4 s (James Hugh b 1971, Gregory b 1972, Stephen b 1974, Nicholas b 1978); *Career* RAMC Lt Col 202 Midland Gen Hosp (cmmnd Capt 1973); house offr Queen Elizabeth Hosp Birmingham 1968-69, then trained in gen and orthopaedic surgery, conslt orthopaedic surgn Coventry and Warwickshire Hosp Coventry 1977-; numerous articles for Nat Coaching Fndn; orthopaedic advsr to Br Amateur Gymnastics Assoc 1981-, memb med cmmn of Int Gymnastics Fedn 1989; memb BMS, fell Br Orthopaedic Assoc; *Books* Stress Injuries to Adolescent Gymnasts' Wrists (1988); *Style*— John Aldridge, Esq; South Lodge, 29 Westfield Rd, Rugby, Warwickshire CV22 6AS (☎ 0788 76583); Coventry and Warwickshire Hospital, Stoney Stanton Rd, Coventry (☎ 0203 224055); 15 Palmerston Rd, Coventry (☎ 0203 678472)

ALDRIDGE, Simon Anthony; s of Maj Anthony Harvey Aldridge, TD, of The Gable, Elstead, Surrey, and Betty Angela, *née* Harbord; *b* 12 April 1942; *Educ* Marlborough, Grenoble Univ France; *m* 23 Feb 1968, Jennifer Roberta Anne, da of Maj Denzil Robert Noble Clarke (d 1986), of Puffins, South Drive, Wokingham; 1 da (Victoria Helmore Elizabeth b 1 May 1969); *Career* md Savory Milln 1986- (ptnr 1969-86), co-chm SBC Stockbrocking 1988-89, dir Baring Securities 1989, chm Northgate Pacific Fund Jersey 1982; dir: French Prestige Fund Paris 1985, Croissance Imobilier Paris 1987; dep chm Croissance Britannia Paris 1987; Chevalier de L'ordre Nat du Merite 1989; *Recreations* golf, shooting, tennis; *Clubs* Cercle de L'Union Interalliée (Paris), City of London; *Style*— Simon Aldridge, Esq; 31 Cadogan St, London SW3 (☎ 071 589 3895); Baring Securities, (☎ 071 329 0329, telex 884287 SBCO G, fax 071 329 8700)

ALDRIDGE, Trevor Martin; s of Dr Sidney Aldridge (d 1972), and Isabel Rebecca, *née* Seelig (d 1960); *b* 22 Dec 1933; *Educ* Frensham Heights Sch, Sorbonne, St John's Coll Cambridge (MA); *m* 1966, Joanna Van Dedem, da of Cyril Van Dedem Edwards, of Isle of Man; 1 s (Neil b 1969), 1 da (Deborah b 1968); *Career* slr (adm 1960); ptnr Bower Cotton & Bower 1962-84; chm of govrs Frensham Heights Sch 1976-; law cmmr 1984-; gen ed Property Law Bulletin 1980-84; *Books* Rent Control and Leasehold Enfranchisement, Letting Business Premises, Leasehold Law, Practical Conveyancing Precedents, Practical Lease Precedents, and others; *Clubs* United Oxford and Cambridge; *Style*— Trevor M Aldridge, Esq; Conquest House, 37/38 John Street, Theobald's Road, London WC1N 2BQ

ALEKSANDER, Prof Igor; s of Branimir Aleksander (d 1972), and Maja, *née* Unger; *b* 26 Jan 1937; *Educ* Marist Bros Coll Johannesburg SA, Univ of Witwatersrand (BSc), Univ of London (PhD); *m* 23 March 1963 (m dis 1977), Myra Jeanette, *née* Kurland; *Career* section head Standard Tel & Cable Co 1958-61, reader Univ of Kent 1968-74; prof and head: Electrical Engrg Dept Brunel Univ 1974-84, Kobler Unit Mgmnt IT Imperial Coll 1984-88; head Electrical Engrg Dept Imperial Coll 1988-; FRSA 1983, FIEE 1988, CEng; *Books* Introduction To Logic Circuit Theory (1971), Microcircuit Learning Computers (1971), Automata Theory: An Engineering Approach (with FK Hanna 1978), The Human Machine (1978), Reinventing Man (with Piers Burnett 1984), Designing Intelligent Systems (1985), Decision And Intelligence (with Forraney and Ghalab 1986), Thinking Machines (with Piers Burnett 1987), An Introduction to Neural Computing (with H Morton 1989); *Style*— Prof Igor Aleksander; Dept of Electrical Engrg, Imperial Coll of Sci and Technol, 180 Queen's Gate, London SW7 2BZ

ALEN-BUCKLEY, Hon Mrs (Giancarla); *née* Forte; 4 da of Baron Forte (Life Peer); *b* 1959; *m* 1981, Michael Ulic Anthony Alen-Buckley; 1 s (Luke Charles Ulic Locke b 6 March 1987), 1 da (Portia b 24 Jan 1991); *Style*— The Hon Mrs Alen-Buckley; 4 Lansdowne Road, Holland Park, London W11

ALESBURY, Alun; s of George Alesbury, of Weybridge, Surrey, and Eveline, *née* Richards; *b* 14 May 1949; *Educ* Tiffin Sch, Cambridge and Seville Univs; *m* 26 June 1976, Julia Rosemary, 6 da of Herbert Archibald Graham Butt (d 1971), of Sibford Gower, Oxon; 1 s (Rupert b 1980), 2 da (Lucy b 1982, Katie Charlotte Julia b 1990) ; *Career* called to the Bar Inner Temple 1974, legal corr The Architect 1976-80, memb Panel of Jr Treasy Counsel (Lands Tbnl) 1978-; fndr memb Local Govt and Planning Bar Assoc 1986 (hon sec 1986-88); pubns incl: Highways (part) Halsburys Laws of England (4 edn), articles on planning law; *Recreations* walking, travel, old buildings, learning Latin languages; *Style*— Alun Alesbury, Esq; Echo Pit House, 26 Fort Rd, Guildford, Surrey (☎ 0483 573 557); 2 Mitre Ct Buildings, The Temple, London EC4 (☎ 071 583 1380)

ALEXANDER; *see*: Hagart-Alexander

ALEXANDER, Hon Mrs (Ada Kate); *née* Bellew; yr da of Richard Bellew (4 s of 2 Baron Bellew and bro of 3 and 4 Barons), and Ada Kate, *née* Gilbey (2 da of Henry Gilbey, who was er bro of Sir Walter Gilbey, 1 Bt); sis of 5 Baron Bellew and was accordingly raised to rank, style and precedence of a Baron's da 1935; *b* 5 March 1893; *m* 1, 1917 (m dis 1936), Charles Domvile (d 1936); 1 s (Maj Denys Barry Herbert Domvile); m 2, 1937, Lt-Col Herbrand Charles Alexander, DSO (d 1965, 2 s of 4 Earl of Caledon); *Style*— The Hon Mrs Alexander; Jenkinstown House, Portarlington, Co Offaly, Ireland (☎ 0502 23459)

ALEXANDER, Prof Albert Geoffrey; s of William Francis Alexander (d 1969), of Kingston upon Hull, and Muriel Katherine, *née* Boreham (d 1989); *b* 22 Sept 1932; *Educ* Bridlington Sch, UCH Dental Sch Univ of London (BDS, MDS, LDSRCS, FDSRCS); *m* 2 June 1956, (Dorothy) Constance, da of Harry Johnson (d 1980), of Orpington; 1 da (Susan Elizabeth b 1959); *Career* Nat Serv Capt RADC 1956-58; dental house surgn UCH 1955-56, lectr in conservative dentistry UCH Med Sch 1960-62, sr lectr conservation and periodontics UCL Dental Sch, prof of conservative dentistry Univ of London 1972 (reader 1969), appointed to chair of conservative dentistry UCL Sch of Med 1976, dean UCL Sch of Dentistry 1977-(vice dean 1974-77); fell: UCL 1986, Int Coll of Dentists; memb: Gen Dental Cncl, Senate Univ of London, Cncl at UCL; memb: BDA, Br Soc for Dental Res, Br Soc for Restorative Dentistry, Federation Dentaire Internationale; *Books* The Prevention of Periodontal Disease (1971), Self Assessment Manual No 3 - Clinical Dentistry (1978), A Companion to Dental Studies (volumes 2 and 3, 1988); *Recreations* photography; *Style*— Prof Albert Alexander

ALEXANDER, Sir Alex(ander Sandor); *b* 21 Nov 1916,Berehovo, Czechoslovakia; *Educ* Charles Univ Prague; *m* 1946, Margaret Irma (Maria), *née* Vogel; 2 s, 2 da; *Career* chm J Lyons & Co 1979-; dep chm Allied-Lyons plc 1982- (dir 1979-); dir Ross Gp Ltd 1954-69 (md and chief exec 1967-69, chm 1969), Imperial Gp 1969-79 (chm Imperial Foods 1969-79, dep chm Br Utd Trawlers 1969-81), Ransomes Sims & Jefferies 1974-83, Bain Dawes plc 1984-86; Inchcape Insur Hldgs 1978-86, Alfred McAlpine plc 1978-, Tate & Lyle 1978-, Unigate Ltd 1978-, London Wall Hldgs plc 1986-, Nat West Bank (SE Region Bd) 1973-84; chm: Theatre Royal (Norwich) Tst 1969-84, Appeals Ctee BRC (Norfolk Branch) 1958-74, chm Royal Opera House Tst 1987-; tstee: Glyndebourne Arts Tst 1975- (vice-chm 1978-), Charities Aid Fndn 1979-86; govr The Royal Ballet,F pres: Br Food Export Cncl 1973-76, Processors & Growers Research Orgn 1978-83; memb: Eastern Gas Bd 1963-72, ct Univ of E Anglia; high sheriff Norfolk 1974; FBIM, FRSA; kt 1974; *Recreations* tennis, shooting, painting, opera, ballet; *Style*— Sir Alex Alexander; Westwick Hall, Westwick, Norwich (☎ 069 269 664); Allied-Lyons plc, Allied House, 156 St John St, London EC1P 1AR (☎ 071 253 9911)

ALEXANDER, Andrew Clive; s of Ronald Fergus Alexander (d 1972), and Doreen, *née* Davies (d 1956); *b* 12 May 1935; *Educ* Lancing; *Career* leader writer Yorkshire Post 1960-65, Parly sketch-writer Daily Telegraph 1966-72, city ed Daily Mail 1984- (Parly sketch-writer and political columnist 1972-84); dir Associated Newspapers; Parly candidate (C) Colne Valley 1963 and 1964; *Books* The Making of the Prime Minister (with Alan Watkins, 1970); *Recreations* landscape gardening, music, weight training; *Clubs* Reform; *Style*— Andrew Alexander, Esq; Pine Hill, Crowhurst, E Sussex TN3 39AA; Daily Mail, Temple House, Temple Avenue, London EC4Y OJA (☎ 071 938 6000)

ALEXANDER, Andrew Robin (Alex); s of Alan Geoffrey Alexander, of 1 Kenneth Ave, Erin, Nr Toronto, Ontario, Canada, and Eileen Joan, *née* Daly; *b* 17 April 1949; *Educ* Colchester Royal GS; *m* 22 June 1970, Jane Walden, da of Howard Alfred Armstrong (d 1984), of 46 West Ave, Clacton-on-Sea, Essex; 2 da (Eve b 1974, Alexandra b 1979); *Career* ptnr Jameson Alexander Law & Co Clacton-on-Sea Essex 1973-; parent govr Colbayns HS, hon memb St John's Ambulance, memb Essex Co Small Bore Rifle Team 1975-, hon treas Clacton-Valence Town Twinning Assoc; FCA 1979; *Recreations* rifleman; *Clubs* The Clacton, The Fellows Soc; *Style*— Alex Alexander, Esq; 26 Arnold Rd, Clacton-on-Sea, Essex CO15 1DE (☎ 0255 429442); Mayfield Chambers, 93 Station Road, Clacton-on-Sea, Essex CO15 1TN (☎ 0255 220044, fax 0255 220999)

ALEXANDER, Anthony Ernest; s of Henry Gustav Alexander (d 1986), and Alice, *née* Polackova; *b* 7 Oct 1945; *Educ* St Paul's, Downing Coll Cambridge (MA); *m* 6 July 1969, Ilana, da of Maurice Raphael Setton, of Jerusalem, Israel; 1 s (Daniel b 17 Sept 1974), 1 da (Sharon b 10 May 1973); *Career* ptnr: Herbert Oppenheimer, Nathan & Vandyk 1973-88 (sr ptnr 1988), Denton Hall Burgin & Warrens 1988-; Freeman Worshipful Co of Slrs 1988; memb: Law Soc 1971, The Pilgrims; *Books* England-Legal Aspects of Alien Acquisition of Real Property (contrib); *Recreations* music and classical studies; *Style*— Anthony Alexander, Esq; Colebrook, Merlewood Drive, Chislehurst, Kent BR7 5LQ (☎ 081 467 1669, fax 081 295 1151); Denton Hall Burgin & Warrens, Five Chancery Lane, Clifford's Inn, London EC4A 1GU (☎ 071 242 1212, fax 071 404 0087, car 0860 375 698, telex 263567/262738 BURGIN G)

ALEXANDER, Anthony George Laurence; s of G W Alexander, of Beaconsfield; *b* 4 April 1938; *Educ* St Edward's Sch Oxford; *m* Frances, *née* Burdett; 1 s, 2 da; *Career* dir Hanson plc; FCA; *Recreations* tennis, golf; *Style*— Anthony Alexander, Esq; Crafnant, Gregories Farm Lane, Beaconsfield, Bucks

ALEXANDER, Anthony Victor; CBE (1987); s of Aaron Alexander (d 1945); *b* 17 Sept 1928; *Educ* Dragon Sch Oxford, Harrow, St John's Coll Cambridge (BA, LLB); *m* 1958, Hélène Esther, da of late Victor Adda; 1 da (Susannah); *Career* insur broker; md Sedgwick Collins (non marine div) 1968-73, chm Sedgwick Forbes UK and dir Sedgwick Forbes Hldgs 1973-78, dir Securicor Gp and Securicor Servs 1977-, dep chm Sedgwick Forbes Ltd 1978-79, dir Sedgwick Gp 1980-; chm: Sedgwick Gp Special Servs 1980-83, Sedgwick Gp Underwriting Servs 1982-85, Br Insur Brokers Assoc (BIBA) 1982-87 (dep chm to 1982); dir ARV Aviation Ltd 1985-88; memb: Mktg of Investmts Bd Organising Ctee 1985-85, Securities and Investmts Bd 1985-88; FCIB, FINE; *Recreations* home and garden, sailing, fishing, antique collecting, woodlands; *Style*— Anthony Alexander, Esq, CBE; 1 St Germans Place, Blackheath, London SE3 (☎ 081 858 5509); c/o Sedgwick Group plc, Sedgwick House, 33 Aldgate High St, London EC3N 1AJ (☎ 071 377 3456)

ALEXANDER, Hon Brian James; s of 1 Earl Alexander of Tunis, KG, GCB, OM, GCMG, CSI, DSO, MC, PC (d 1969 - 3 s of 4 Earl of Caledon); hp of bro, 2 Earl; *b* 31 July 1939; *Educ* Harrow; *Career* Lt Irish Gds (Res); *Clubs* White's; *Style*— The Hon Brian Alexander; 11 The Little Boltons, London SW10 9LJ

ALEXANDER, Hon (Thomas) Bruce; only s of Baron Alexander of Potterhill (Life Peer), *qv*; *b* 31 Dec 1951; *Educ* Oundle, Clare Coll Cambridge (MA); *m* 2, 1984, Susan Joyce Allard; 1 s (Thomas b 1985), 2 step da; *Career* chartered patent agent, European patent attorney, ptnr Boult Wade and Tennant; *Recreations* golf, running; *Clubs* Woking Golf; *Style*— The Hon Bruce Alexander; 49 Northchurch Rd, London N1 4EE (☎ 071 254 1409); Suffolk House, Lidgate, Suffolk; office: 27 Furnival St, London EC4A 1PQ (☎ 071 404 5921, telex 267 271)

ALEXANDER, Byron John; s of Capt Dimitrius Alexander (d 1975), of Athens, and June Doreen, *née* Eddy; *b* 18 May 1942; *Educ* Monkton House Sch; *m* 4 June 1969, Eileen May, da of Eric Leslie Page, of Eastcote, Middx; 2 s (Marc Byron b 4 Oct 1972, James Philip b 25 Dec 1976), 1 da (Nicola Jane b 10 March 1970); *Career* md: Alexander Advertising International Ltd 1969-, Illustra Graphics Ltd 1984-, Illustra Print Ltd 1987-; pres Barker and Associates Florida USA; memb HM Coastguard (Auxiliary Afloat Section) 1973-; memb Guild of Masters, Mates and Engineers; MIPR 1973, MBIM 1975; *Books* Buying a Boat (1972); *Recreations* motor yachting, computers; *Clubs* Royal Corinthian Yacht, Royal Temple Yacht, Oxford Ditch Cricket, Purley Motor Cruiser (hon memb); *Style*— Byron Alexander, Esq; Alexander Advertising International, Alexander House, Wallingford, Oxon, OX10 0XF (☎ 0491 34966, fax 0491 33475, car 0860 877766)

ALEXANDER, Sir Charles Gundry; 2 Bt (UK 1945), of Sundridge Park, Co Kent; s of Sir Frank Alexander, 1 Bt, JP (d 1959), and Elsa, da of Sir Charles Collett, 1 Bt; *b* 5 May 1923; *Educ* Bishop's Stortford Coll, St John's Coll Cambridge (BA, MA); *m* 1, 1944, Mary Neale, o da of late Stanley R Richardson, of Maple Lawn, Lyndhurst, Hants; 1 s, 1 da; m 2, 1979, Eileen Ann, da of Gordon Stewart, of Inveresk, Finchampstead; *Heir* s, Richard Alexander, *qv*; *Career* served WWII Lt RN N Atlantic and Far East; chm Alexander Shipping Co; govr Care Ltd; Master Worshipful Co of Merchant Taylors' 1981-82, Prime Warden Worshipful Co of Shipwrights' 1983-84; *Clubs* RAC; *Style*— Sir Charles Alexander, Bt; Hollytree Farmhouse, North Cadbury, Yeovil, Somerset BA22 7DD (☎ 0963 40159)

ALEXANDER, Sir Darnley Arthur Raymond; CBE (1963); s of late Pamphile Joseph Alexander, MBE, and late Lucy Alexander; *b* 28 Jan 1920,Castries, St Lucia; *Educ* St Mary's Coll St Lucia, UCL; *m* 1943, Mildred Margaret, *née* King (d 1980); 1 s, 1 da; *Career* barr Middle Temple 1942, Chief Justice Nigeria 1975-79; chm Nigerian Law Reform Cmmn 1979-88; CFR 1979; Grand Cdr of the Order of the Niger 1983; kt 1974; *Style*— Sir Darnley Alexander, CBE; Supreme Ct of Nigeria, Lagos, Nigeria

ALEXANDER, Maj-Gen David Crichton; CB (1976); s of James Alexander (d 1978), and Margaret, *née* Craig; *b* 28 Nov 1926; *Educ* Edinburgh Acad, Staff Coll Camberley, RCDS; *m* 1957, Diana Joyce (Jane), da of Sydney Fisher, CVO (d 1980); 1 s, 2 da, 1 step s; *Career* served RM 1944-57, equerry and acting treas to Duke of Edinburgh 1957-60, staff of CDS 1966-69, Col GS to CGRM 1970-73, ADC to HM The Queen 1973-75, MGRM Trg 1975-77; dir-gen ESU 1977-79, cmdt Scottish Police Coll 1979-87; memb Tport Users Consultative Ctee for Scot 1989-, pres SSAFA Fife 1990-, govr Corps of Commissionaires; Freeman City of London, Liveryman Worshipful Co of Painter-Stainers; *Recreations* gardening, fishing, golf; *Clubs* Army and Navy; *Style*— Maj-Gen David Alexander, CB

ALEXANDER, Sir Douglas; 3 Bt (UK 1921), of Edgehill, Stamford, Connecticut, USA; s of Lt-Cdr Archibald Gillespie Alexander, US Coast Guard (d 1978), and Margery Isabel, *née* Griffith; n of Sir Douglas Hamilton Alexander, 2 Bt (d 1983); *b* 9 Sept 1936; *Educ* Rice Univ Houston Texas (MA 1961), Univ of N Carolina (PhD 1967); *m* 1958, Marylon, da of Leonidas Collins Scatterday, of Worthington, Ohio, USA; 2 s (Douglas Gillespie *qv*, Andrew Llewellyn b 14 Jan 1967); *Heir* s, Douglas Gillespie Alexander b 24 July 1962; *Career* pres Edgehill Investment Co; *Style*— Sir Douglas Alexander II, Bt; 145 Main Street, Wickford, Rhode Island 02852, USA

ALEXANDER, Douglas Gillespie; s and h of Sir Douglas Alexander II, 3 Bt; *b* 24 July 1962; *Educ* Reed Coll Portland Oregon (BA); *Style*— Douglas G Alexander, Esq

ALEXANDER, Elsie Winifred May; da of late George Albert Barker, and late Lilian May, *née* Tomlin; *b* 13 Feb 1912; *Educ* Ware GS; *m* 1, 1936 (m dis 1946); 1 da; m 2, 1953, Herbert John Alexander (decd); *Career* dir Alexander - H J Alexander Ltd 1953; started painting and studied art Montelair State Coll USA 1958; work exhibited Christie's and art galleries; sec Wine Trade Art Soc; Freeman: City of London, Worshipful Co of Painter-Stainers; *Recreations* painting in oils, gardening, reading; *Style*— Mrs Elsie Alexander; 20 Parkside Drive, Middx HA8 8JX (☎ 071 958 4440)

ALEXANDER, Ian Douglas Gavin; QC (1989); s of Dr Archibald Douglas Park Alexander (d 1968), of Lancing Sussex, and Dilys, *née* Edwards; *b* 10 April 1941; *Educ* Tonbridge, UCL (LLB); *m* 13 Dec 1969, Rosemary Kirkbridge, da of Kenneth Richards; 1 s (Justin b 6 June 1978), 1 da (Victoria b 26 Jan 1980); *Career* called to the Bar Lincoln's Inn 1964, rec Midland and Oxford circuit 1982-; *Recreations* field sports, sailing, gardening; *Clubs* Naval and Military; *Style*— Ian Alexander, Esq, QC; 13 King's Bench Walk, Temple, London EC4Y 4EN (☎ 071 353 7204, fax 01 583 0252); King's Bench Chambers, Wheatsheaf Yard, High St, Oxford OX1 4EE (☎ 0865 791653, fax 0865 791659)

ALEXANDER, Lady (Elizabeth) Jane; *née* Alexander; da of 6 Earl of Caledon (d

1980), and his 2 w, Baroness Anne-Luise (d 1963), da of late Baron Nicolai de Graevenitz; resumed the name of Alexander by Deed Poll; *b* 1962; *m* 1990, Richard F A Dobbs, s of Sir Richard Dobbs, of Castle Dobbs, Carrickfergus; *Style*— The Lady Jane Dobbs; The Farm, Castle Dobbs, Carrickfergus, Co Antrim, NI

ALEXANDER, John Bernard Alexei; s of B G Alexander, of Gt Haseley, Oxford, and T Alexander, *née* Benckendorf; *b* 23 Aug 1941; *Educ* Westminster, Balliol Coll Oxford; *m* 1 July 1969, Jacquelyn, da of John Bray, of Sydney, Aust; 2 s (Nicolas b 1971, Christopher b 1974); m 2, 14 April 1981, Judy, da of Maj Patrick Chilton, of West Ashling, Sussex; 1 da (Tania b 1982); *Career* merchant banker; dir Hill Samuel & Co Ltd 1973, md LCF Edmond de Rothschild Securities 1984-; *Recreations* skiing, tennis, gardening; *Clubs* Brooks's; *Style*— John B A Alexander, Esq; Old Rectory, Gt Haseley, Oxford; 84 Fenchurch St, London EC3M 4BY (☎ 071 481 0591)

ALEXANDER, Dr John Innis; s of William Bahudur Alexander (d 1984), of Surbiton, Surrey, and Winifred Edith, *née* Cottle; *b* 17 April 1942; *Educ* Kings Coll Sch Wimbledon, Univ Coll and Med Sch London (MB BS, LRCP); *m* 22 April 1978, Susan Diane, da of Philip Lionel Taylor, of Newport, Gwent; 1 s (Christopher b 1982), 1 da (Phyllida b 1980); *Career* sr house offr in anaesthesia Norfolk and Norwich Hosp 1967-68, registrar in anaesthesia Royal Free Hosp London 1968-69, res fell in anaesthesia Scottish Home and Health Dept 1970-72, conslt in anaesthesia and pain relief United Bristol Hosps 1974- (sr registrar in anaesthesia 1969-74); memb: Ed Bd Frontiers of Pain, Steering Gp on Analgesia 1989-; MRCS, FFARCS 1969; memb: Anaesthetic Res Soc 1970, Int Assoc for the Study of Pain 1975; *Books* Postoperative Pain Control (1987); *Recreations* woodwork, swimming; *Style*— Dr John Alexander; Sir Humphry Davy Department of Anaesthesia, Bristol Royal Infirmary, Bristol BS2 8HW (☎ 0272 282163)

ALEXANDER, Kenneth Alston; s of Brig-Gen Sir William Alexander, KBE, CB, CMG, DSO, MP (d 1954), and his 1 wife Beatrice Evelyn, *née* Ritchie (d 1928); *b* 21 Nov 1928; *Educ* Winchester, Trinity Coll Cambridge (BA); *m* 1957, Linda Mary, da of Edward Lefevre, of Cochin and Gargrave, Yorks; 1 s, 3 da; *Career* Royal Tank Regt; chem merchant and manufacturer; chm and chief exec Tennants Consolidated Ltd 1972- (previously holding various directorships within the Tennant Group); *Recreations* shooting, music; *Clubs* RAC; *Style*— Kenneth Alexander, Esq; 69 Grosvenor St, London W1 (☎ 071 493 5451)

ALEXANDER, Prof Sir Kenneth John Wilson; only s of late William Wilson Alexander; *b* 14 March 1922; *Educ* George Heriot's Sch Edinburgh, Dundee Sch of Econs; *m* 1949, Angela-May, da of late Capt G H Lane, RN; 1 s, 4 da; *Career* prof of econs Univ of Strathclyde 1963-80 (on leave 1976-80), dean of Scottish Business Sch 1973-75, princ and vice chllr Univ of Stirling 1981-86; chllr Univ of Aberdeen 1987-; dir: Scottish Television plc, Stakis plc, The Scottish Daily Record and Sunday Mail (1986) Ltd; chm: Highlands and Islands Devpt Bd 1976-81, Michael Kelly Assocs Ltd, Aberdeen Univ Press Ltd, Scottish Industl and Trade Exhibitions Ltd; dep chm Scot Cncl Devpt and Indust; Hon: LLD CNAA 1976, DUniv Stirling 1977, LLD Univ of Aberdeen, LLD Univ of Dundee 1985, DUniv Open Univ 1985, LLD Univ of Strathclyde 1986, DLitt Univ of Aberdeen 1987; CBIM, FRSE, FEIS, FRIAS; kt 1978; *Recreations* sea fishing; *Clubs* Caledonian, Scottish Arts; *Style*— Prof Sir Kenneth Alexander, FRSE; 9 West Shore, Pittenweem, Fife KY10 2NV

ALEXANDER, (William) Leslie; s of William Alexander, and Ann Mary, *née* Craigie; *b* 29 April 1949; *Educ* The Gordon Sch Huntly Aberdeenshire, Univ of Aberdeen; *m* 31 March 1984, Dr Claire Marianne Françoise Dicks-Mireaux, da of Leslie Dicks-Mireaux, of 16 Manor House, Marylebone Rd, London; 1 s (James b 1984), 2 da (Helen b 1985, Sarah b 1987); *Career* sr registrar Moorfields Eye Hosp 1981-84, conslt opthalmic surgn NE Thames RHA 1984-; memb BMA, FRSM, FRCS, FCOpth; *Recreations* reading; *Style*— Leslie Alexander, Esq; 10 Drake Rd, Westcliffe on Sea, Essex SS0 8LP (☎ 0702 334249); Southend Hosp, Prittlewell Chase, Westcliffe on Sea, Essex SS0 0RY (☎ 0702 348911)

ALEXANDER, Leslie William MacBryde; s of Thomas MacKelvie Alexander (d 1964), of Craigie, Moorcroft Rd, Liverpool, and Jane Muir, *née* MacBryde (d 1962); *b* 8 Aug 1917; *Educ* Liverpool Coll, Univ of Liverpool (BArch); *m* 25 March 1950, Margaret, da of Walter Haydn Ellwood (d 1958), of 33 Park View, Cheadle Heath, Cheshire; 1 da (Jane Margaret b 1956); *Career* Capt RE 1940-46 serv in India; architect-arbitrator: visiting lectr on arbitration contract admin and professional practice Univs of Liverpool and York; JP (Liverpool 1971-81); memb: Cncl RIBA 1956-58, Jt Contracts Tbnl 1959-64, Architects Registration Cncl UK 1963-64, Cncl CIArb 1966-80, pres Inst of Arbitrators 1973-74; pres Liverpool Architectural Soc 1956-58, life govr Liverpool Coll 1962-; memb RIBA 1939, FRIBA 1960, FRICS 1960, FCIArb 1964; *Books* The Architect as Arbitrator (2 edn 1978), Handbook of Arbitration Practice (contrib); *Clubs* Royal Over-Seas League; *Style*— Leslie Alexander, Esq; Monreith, 47 Menlove Avenue, Liverpool L18 2EH (☎ 051 722 2491)

ALEXANDER, Sir (John) Lindsay; s of Ernest Daniel Alexander, MC (d 1975), and Florence Mary, *née* Mainsmith; *b* 12 Sept 1920; *Educ* Alleyn's Sch, BNC Oxford (MA); *m* 1944, Maud Lilian, 2 da of Oliver Ernest Collard; 2 s, 1 da; *Career* chm: Ocean Transport & Trading 1971-80, Overseas Container Holdings 1976-82, Lloyds Bank International 1980-85; dep chm Lloyds Bank 1980-88 (dir 1970-91); dir: BP 1975-, Jebsens Drilling 1980-86, Hawker Siddeley 1981-, Lloyds 1988-, Abbey Life 1988-91, Britoil 1988-90; chm Ctee of Euro Shipowners' Assoc 1972-73; pres Chamber of Shipping 1974-75; hon fell BNC Oxford 1977; Cdr Royal Order of St Olav (Norway) 1980; FCIT, CBIM; kt 1975; *Recreations* gardening, music, photography; *Clubs* Brooks's; *Style*— Sir Lindsay Alexander; Lloyds Bank plc, 71 Lombard St, London EC3P 3BS (☎ 071 626 1500)

ALEXANDER, Prof (Robert) McNeill; s of Robert Priestley Alexander (d 1973), of Lisburn, Co Antrim, and Janet, *née* McNeill; *b* 7 July 1934; *Educ* Tonbridge Sch, Trinity Hall Cambridge (MA, PhD); *m* 29 July 1961, Ann Elizabeth, da of Gordon Francis Coulton (d 1947), of Pentney, Norfolk; 1 s (Gordon b 1964), 1 da (Jane b 1962); *Career* sr lectr Univ Coll of N Wales 1968-69 (lectr 1961-68, asst lectr 1958-61); prof of zoology Univ of Leeds 1969-; DSc (Wales) 1969; FRS, FIBiol; *Books* Functional Design in Fishes (1967), Animal Mechanics (1968), Size and Shape (1971), The Chordates (1975), The Invertebrates (1979), Optima for Animals (1982), Elastic Mechanisms in Animal Movement (1988), Dynamics of Dinosaurs and other Extinct Giants (1989), and other books and papers; *Recreations* local history, history of natural history; *Style*— Prof McNeill Alexander; 14 Moor Park Mount, Leeds LS6 4BU (☎ 0532 759218); Department of Pure and Applied Biology, University of Leeds, Leeds LS2 9JT (☎ 0532 332911, fax 0532 332882, telex 556473 UNILDS G)

ALEXANDER, Michael Charles; s of late Rear Adm Charles Otway Alexander, and Antonia, *née* Geermans; *b* 20 Nov 1920; *Educ* Stowe, RMC Sandhurst; *m* 1963 (m dis), Sarah, da of Lt-Col Frederick Wignall; 1 da; *Career* WWII DCLI; 5 (Ski) Bn Scots Gds, 8 Commando (Layforce), HQ 13 Corps GSO3, SBS (POW Colditz 1942-44), 2 SAS regt; WO (civil affrs) Intergovernmental Ctee on refugees 1946, editorial dir Common Ground Ltd 1946-50; located Firuzkoh Central Afghanistan 1952, Himalayan Hovercraft Expedition 1972, Yucatan Straits Hovercraft Expedition 1975, Upper Ganges Hovercraft Expedition 1980, dir Adastra Productions Ltd 1980-; fndr Woburn Safari Serv 1977, Chelsea Wharf Restaurant 1983; co-publisher Wildlife Magazine; FZS, FRGS, fell Royal Soc for Asian Affrs; *Books* The Privileged Nightmare (with Giles Romilly, republished as Hostages at Colditz), Offbeat in Asia, The Reluctant Legionnaire, The True Blue, Mrs Fraser on the Fatal Shore, Discovering the New World, Omai: Noble Savage, Queen Victoria's Maharajah, Delhi-Agra: A Traveller's Companion; *Style*— Michael Alexander, Esq; 48 Eaton Place, London SW1 (☎ 071 235 2724); Skelbo House, Dornoch, Sutherland (☎ 04083 3180)

ALEXANDER, Prof Michael Joseph; s of Joseph Brian Alexander, OBE, JP (d 1984), and Winefred, *née* Gaul (d 1985); *b* 21 May 1941; *Educ* Downside, Trinity Coll Oxford (BA, MA); *m* 1 Sept 1973, Eileen Mary (d 1986), da of Anthony Hamilton McCall; 1 s (Patrick b 1980), 2 da (Lucy b 1977, Flora b 1982); m 2, 11 July 1987, Mary Cecilia Sheahan; *Career* ed William Collins 1963, fell Princeton Graduate Sch 1965, lectr Univ of Calif 1966, ed André Deutsch 1967, reader Univ of Stirling 1985 (lectr 1969), Berry Prof of Eng Lit 1985-; translations incl: The Earliest English Poems (1966), Beowulf (1973); other publications: The Poetic Achievement of Ezra Pound (1977), Twelve Poems (1977), MacMillan Anthology of English Literature (jt ed, 1989); *Style*— Prof Michael Alexander; 62 Hepburn Gardens, St Andrews KY16 9DG; Dept of English, The University, St Andrews KY16 9AL

ALEXANDER, Sir Michael O'Donel Bjarne; KCMG (1988, CMG 1982); s of late Col Hugh O'Donel Alexander, CMG, CBE, and Enid Constance Crichton Neate; *b* 19 June 1936; *Educ* Foyle Coll Londonderry, St Paul's, King's Coll Cambridge, Yale and Berkeley Univs USA (Harkness fell); *m* 1960, Traute Krohn; 2 s, 1 da; *Career* served RN 1955-57; joined FO 1962, asst private sec to Sir Alec Douglas-Home then James Callaghan as successive Foreign Secs 1972-74, cnsllr (Conference on Security and Co-operation in Europe) and subsequently head chancery UK Mission to the UN Geneva 1974-77, head POD FCO 1978-79 (dep head 1977-78), private sec (Overseas Affairs) to PM 1979-81, UK ambass to Vienna 1982-86, UK permanent rep on N Atlantic Cncl Brussels 1986-; *Style*— Sir Michael Alexander, KCMG; c/o Foreign and Commonwealth Office, King Charles St, London SW1; UK Delegation, OTAN/NATO, 1110 Brussels, Belgium

ALEXANDER, Sir Norman Stanley; CBE (1959); s of Charles Monrath Alexander (d 1941), of NZ, and Flora Elizabeth, *née* Reid (d 1944); *b* 25 Oct 1906; *Educ* Hamilton HS NZ, Univ Coll Auckland (MSc), Trinity Coll Cambridge (PhD); *m* 1, 1935, Frances Elizabeth Somerville, da of Kenneth Caldwell (d 1950); 1 s, 2 da; m 2, 1959, Constance Lilian Helen (d 1990), da of Henry Geary (d 1950); *Career* prof of physics: Univ of Malaya 1936-52, Univ Coll Ibadan Nigeria 1952-59; vice chllr Ahmadu Bello Univ of Nigeria 1961-66; advsr on Higher Educn Miny Overseas Dvpt; hon memb Order of the Niger (Nigeria) 1966; kt 1966; *Recreations* gardening; *Style*— Sir Norman Alexander, CBE; Burrowland, Crediton, Devon (☎ 03632 3200)

ALEXANDER, Maj Gen Paul Donald; CB (1989), MBE (1968); s of Donald Alexander, of Dudley, Worcs, and Alice Louisa, *née* Dunn (d 1988); *b* 30 Nov 1934; *Educ* Dudley GS, RMA Sandhurst, Staff Coll Camberley, Nat Def Coll, RCDS; *m* 15 Nov 1958, Christine Winifred Marjorie, da of Fred Coakley, of Dudley, Worcs (d 1966); 3 s (Stephen Nigel b 1959, Richard Neil b 1961, James Robert b 1966); *Career* 2 Lt 1955, Capt 1964, served Hong Kong, seconded KAR in E Africa, army staff duties MOD 1966-67, Sqdn Cdr in UK 1968-69 (NI 1969), DAAG Adj Gens Dept MOD 1970-71, Asst Dir of Def Policy (Col) Central Staff MOD 1977-79, Cmd 1 Div HQ and Signal Regt 1974-76, Cmd Corps RS 1 Br Corps 1979-81, Dep Mil Sec MOD 1982-85, Signal Offr in Chief (Army) 1985-89, Policy Dir MOD 1989-, Hon Col 36 Signal Regt 1991-; Col Cmdt RS 1989-, Admiral RSYC 1989-; memb Herts Ctee E Anglia TAVR Assoc 1989-, chm Royal Signals Assoc 1990-; *Recreations* gardening; *Clubs* Army and Navy; *Style*— Maj-Gen Paul Alexander, CB, MBE; c/o Army and Navy Club, St Jame's Square, London SW1; Ministry of Defence, Metropole Building, Northumberland Ave, London WC2 5BL (☎ 071 218 0596)

ALEXANDER, Richard; s and h of Sir Charles G Alexander, 2 Bt, and his 1 w, Mary, da of Stanley Richardson; *b* 1 Sept 1947; *Educ* Bishop's Stortford Coll; *m* 1971, Lesley Jane, da of Frederick William Jordan, of Orpington; 2 s (Edward Samuel b 1974, James Gundry b 1977); *Career* pub rels offr and ed house magazine Furness Withy Group; Freeman City of London, Liveryman Worshipful Co of Merchant Taylors'; MIPR; *Style*— Richard Alexander, Esq; Wealden Hall, Pilgrims Way, Detling, nr Maidstone, Kent ME14 3JY; Furness Withy Group, Furness House, 53 Brighton Rd, Redhill, Surrey RH1 6YL

ALEXANDER, Richard Thain; MP (C) Newark 1979-; s of Richard Rennie Alexander, of Cockerham, Lancaster, and Gladys Alexander; *b* 29 June 1934; *Educ* Dewsbury GS, UCL, Inst of Advanced Legal Studies London; *m* 1, 1966 (m dis 1984), Valerie Ann, da of Harold Winn (d 1959); 1 s (Nicholas), 1 da (Emma); m 2, 1987, Patricia Diane Hanson; *Career* slr; cmmr for Oaths; former chm Doncaster Nat Insur Appeal Tbnl; sr ptnr Jones Alexander & Co Retford 1964-85, conslt Jones Alexander & Co Retford 1985-90; *Recreations* tennis, riding; *Clubs* Newark Cons, Carlton, Retford Cons; *Style*— Richard Alexander, Esq, MP; 409 Howard Hse, Dolphin Sq, London SW1

ALEXANDER, Rear Adm Robert Love; CB (1964), DSO (1943), DSC (1944); s of Capt Robert Love Alexander, DSO, RD, RNR, of Edinburgh; *b* 29 April 1913; *Educ* Merchiston, RNC Dartmouth; *m* 1936, Margaret Elizabeth, only da of late George Conrad Spring; 1 s, 4 da; *Career* Vice Naval Dep to Supreme Allied Cdr Europe 1962-65; *Style*— Rear Adm Robert Alexander, CB, DSO, DSC; Tythe Barn, South Harting, Hants

ALEXANDER, Roger Michael; s of Hyman Isador Alexander, of London, and Anna, *née* Blumberg; *b* 29 June 1942; *Educ* Dulwich, Law Soc Coll of Law; *m* 26 June 1966, Monica Anne, da of Freddie Freedman; 2 da (Jessica Louise b 6 June 1969, Lucy Katherine b 27 Feb 1971); *Career* admittd slr 1965; Lewis Silkin: ptnr 1965, lead ptnr 1989, head of Mktg Servs Law Gp 1990; hon slr London Marriage Guidance Cncl 1988 (memb Exec Cncl), memb Law Soc 1965; *Recreations* books, photography, gardening, travel; *Style*— Roger Alexander, Esq; Lewis Silkin, 1 Butler Place, Buckingham Gate, London SW1H OPT (☎ 071 222 8191, fax 071 222 4633)

ALEXANDER, William (Bill); s of William Paterson, of Cragside, Coach Rd, Warton, Lancs, and Rosemary, *née* McCormack; *b* 23 Feb 1948; *Educ* St Lawrence Coll Ramsgate, Univ of Keele (BA); *m* 1 June 1979, Juliet Linda, da of Michael Hedley Harmer, of Perrot Wood, Graffham, Petworth, W Sussex; 2 da (Jessie b 1974, Lola b 1979); *Career* assoc dir RSC 1978-91; prodns incl: Volpone 1983, Richard III 1984, The Merry Wives of Windsor 1985, A Midsummer Night's Dream 1986, Twelfth Night, The Merchant of Venice, Cymbeline 1987, Duchess of Malfi 1989, The Taming of the Shrew 1990; *Style*— Bill Alexander, Esq; Rose Cottage, Tunley, Nr Cirencester, Glos; Barbican Theatre, London (☎ 071 628 3351)

ALEXANDER, Dr William David; s of Rev Hugh Crighton Alexander, of Oakington, Cambridge, and Monica, *née* Hill; *b* 9 June 1945; *Educ* Clifton, St Thomas's Hosp Med Sch London (MB BS), MRCP; *m* 12 June 1968, Dr Dorothy Hanson Crawford, da of Sir Theo Crawford, of Langton Green, Tunbridge Wells, Kent; 2 s (Danny b 1970, Theo b 1973); *Career* conslt physician and dir Diabetes Unit Queen Mary's Hosp Sidcup and Bexley Health Authy 1978-; author of various reports and papers on diabetes related topics; chm: Queen Mary's Hosp Med Staff and Exec Ctees 1983-85, SE Thames Diabetes Physicians Gp 1984-88; govr Chislehurst and Sidcup GS 1984-86, hon sec Med Advsy Ctee and med advsr Br Diabetic Assoc 1984-89, conslt memb Dist Mgmnt Bd 1988-; FRCP 1989, FRSPB; memb: BMA, BDA, EASD; *Recreations* taxidermy, Bexley borough choir, beekeeping; *Clubs* Chislehurst Golf; *Style—* Dr William Alexander; Yeomans Hall, 27 Halfway St, Sidcup, Kent DA15 8LQ (☎ 081 302 2678); Diabetes Unit, Queen Mary's Hospital, Sidcup, Kent (☎ 081 302 2678)

ALEXANDER OF POTTERHILL, Baron (Life Peer UK 1974), of Paisley, Co Renfrew; Sir Sir William Picken Alexander; s of Thomas Alexander, of Paisley; *b* 13 Dec 1905; *Educ* Paisley GS, Univ of Glasgow; *m* 1949, Joan Mary, da of Robert Baxter Williamson, of Sheffield; 1 s (Hon (Thomas) Bruce b 1951); *Career* sits as Independent peer in House of Lords; gen sec Assoc Educn Ctees England and Wales 1944-; kt 1960; *Style—* The Rt Hon Lord Alexander of Potterhill; 3 Moor Park Gdns, Pembroke Rd, Moor Park, Northwood, Middx (☎ 092 74 21003)

ALEXANDER OF TUNIS, Countess; Hon Davina Mary; *née* Woodhouse; LVO (1991); da of 4 Baron Terrington; *b* 12 April 1955; *m* 1981, as his 2 w, 2 Earl Alexander of Tunis; 2 da (b 1982 and 1984); *Career* lady in waiting to HRH The Princess Margaret, Countess of Snowdon 1975-79; extra lady in waiting 1979-; *Style—* The Rt Hon the Countess Alexander of Tunis, LVO; 59 Wandsworth Common West Side, London SW18 2ED

ALEXANDER OF TUNIS, 2 Earl (UK 1952); Shane William Desmond Alexander; also Viscount Alexander of Tunis (UK 1946) and Baron Rideau (UK 1952); s of Field Marshal 1 Earl Alexander of Tunis, KG, GCB, OM, GCMG, CSI, DSO, MC, PC (3 s of 4 Earl of Caledon), and Lady Margaret Bingham, GBE, JP (d 1977), da of 5 Earl of Lucan (gs of the Crimean War commander); *b* 30 June 1935; *Educ* Harrow, Ashbury Coll Ottawa; *m* 1, 1971 (m dis 1976), Hilary, da of John van Geest, of Lincs; m 2, 1981, Hon Davina Woodhouse, Extra Lady-in-Waiting to HRH The Princess Margaret, da of 4 Baron Terrington; 2 da (Lady Rose Margaret b 23 April 1982, Lady Lucy Caroline b 20 Sept 1984); *Heir* bro, Hon Brian Alexander, *qv*; *Career* pres Br-American Assocs 1988-; sits as Cons peer in Hse of Lords; patron Br-Tunisian Soc; Lt Irish Gds (res); Lord in Waiting to HM The Queen 1974; dir Int Hosps Gp; Liveryman Worshipful Co of Mercers; *Clubs* MCC; *Style—* The Rt Hon Earl Alexander of Tunis; 59 Wandsworth Common West Side, London SW18 2ED

ALEXANDER OF WEEDON, Baron (Life Peer UK 1988); Robert Scott Alexander; QC (1973); s of late Samuel James Alexander, and Hannah May Alexander; *b* 5 Sept 1936; *Educ* Brighton Coll, King's Coll Cambridge (BA, MA); *m* 1, 1963 (m dis 1973), Frances Rosemary Heveningham Pughe; 2 s, 1 da; m 2, 1978 (m dis), Elizabeth, da of Col C R W Norman; 1 s (decd); m 3, 1985, Marie Sugrue; *Career* barr Middle Temple 1961, bencher 1979; pres King's Coll Assoc 1980- 81; chm of the Bar Cncl 1985-86 (vice-chm 1984-85); a judge of the Cts of Appeal of Jersey and Guernsey 1985-88; govr Wycombe Abbey Sch 1986-; tstee Nat Gallery 1986-; chm Panel on Take-overs and Mergers 1987-; chm Nat Westminster Bank plc 1989-; memb Cncl of Univ of Buckingham 1989-; govr LSE 1989-; chm of Justices 1990-; pres Parkinson's Disease Soc 1990-; *Style—* The Lord Alexander of Weedon, QC; c/o National Westminster Bank plc, 41 Lothbury, London EC2P 2BP

ALEXANDER-SINCLAIR OF FRESWICK, Maj-Gen David Boyd; CB (1980); s of Cdr Mervyn Boyd Alexander-Sinclair of Freswick, RN (d 1979), and Avril Nora, *née* Fergusson-Buchanan (d 1980); *b* 2 May 1927; *Educ* Eton; *m* 1958, Ann Ruth, da of late Lt-Col Graeme Daglish; 2 s, 1 da; *Career* cmdg 3 Bn Royal Green Jackets 1967-69, Cdr 6 Armd Bde 1971-73, GOC 1 Div 1975-77, Chief of Staff UKLF 1978-79, Cmndt Staff Coll 1980-82, ret; *Style—* Maj-Gen David Alexander-Sinclair of Freswick, CB

ALFORD, Prof Bernard William Ernest; s of Ernest Edward Alford (d 1970), of Uffculme, Devon, and Winifred Daisy Alford (d 1966); *b* 17 Oct 1937; *Educ* Tiverton GS, LSE (BSc, PhD); *m* 18 Aug 1962, Valerie Sandra, da of Albert Thomas North (d 1963), of Cullompton, Devon; 2 s (Jonathan Edward b 1970, Dominic James Henry b 1973), 1 da (Naomi Elizabeth b 1968); *Career* asst lectr in econ history LSE 1961-62; Univ of Bristol: lectr then reader in econ and social history 1962-82, prof of econ and social history 1982-, chm Sch of History; numerous contribs to books and learned jls; treas Economic History Soc 1988- (memb Cncl 1979, chm Pubns Ctee 1983-88); memb: Lord Chllrs Advsy Ctee on The Public Records 1988-, Advsy Cncl Inst of Contemporary Br History 1989-, Res Grants Bd Economic and Social Res Cncl 1989-; *Books* A History of the Carpenters Company (with T C Barker, 1968), Depression and Recovery? British Economic Growth, 1918-1939 (1972), W D and H O Wills and the Development of the UK Tobacco Industry, 1783-1965 (1973), British Economic Performance, 1945-1975 (1988), Economic Planning in Britain 1943-1951 (with R Lowe and N Rollings, 1991); *Recreations* family life; *Style—* Prof Bernard Alford; The Bank House, High St, Marshfield, Chippenham, Wilts SN14 8LT (☎ 0225 891660); School of History, University of Bristol, 13-15 Woodland Rd, Bristol BS8 1TB (☎ 0272 303399, fax 0272 732657, telex 445938 BSUNIV G)

ALFORD, Lady; Eileen; *née* Riddell; *m* 1967, as his 2 w, Sir Robert Edmund Alford, KBE, CMG (d 1979), sometime govr and c-in-c St Helena; *Style—* Lady Alford; The Barn, Staple Cross, Sussex

ALFORD, George Francis Onslow; s of Cdr Ian Francis Onslow Alford, RN (ret), of Magnolia House, St Mary Abbots Terrace, London, and Jacqueline Louise, *née* Herbert; *b* 10 Oct 1948; *Educ* Winchester, UCL (BSc); *m* 12 Jan 1974, Adronie Elizabeth, da of late Douglas Crisp Gall, of Chantersell, Nutley, Sussex; *Career* Kleinwort Benson Group 1970-: rep Tokyo Office 1976-80, mangr Middle East Dept 1980-83, gp personnel dir 1987-; md Fendrake Ltd 1982-87; dir London Human Resource Gp 1990; memb: Langbourne Wards Club, United World Club; memb Cncl Br Export Houses Assoc 1984-87; Freeman City of London, Liveryman Worshipful Co of Basketmakers; FIPM; *Recreations* sailing, skiing, riding; *Clubs* Royal Solent Yacht, City Livery; *Style—* George Alford, Esq; Claudian House, 58 Oxberry Ave, London SW6 5SS (☎ 071 736 2298); Kleinwort Benson Group, 20 Fenchurch St, London EC3P 3DB (☎ 071 623 8000, telex 888531)

ALFORD, Mark George; s of Brian George Alford, of Exeter, and Gêne Anne, *née* Heal; *b* 18 Feb 1958; *Educ* Shebbear Coll, London Coll of Furniture (MCSD, LDAD, LCFcert); *m* 7 June 1985, Elizabeth, da of Capt George Peter Adam (d 1962), of York; 2 s (Jamie George b 1 Jan 1987, Tomas David b 12 Nov 1989); *Career* designer; Fitch & Co plc 1983-86, David Davies Assocs; *Recreations* classic cars, skiing; *Clubs* Austin Healey; *Style—* Mark Alford, Esq; 17 Ferndene Rd, Herne Hill, London SE24 0AQ (☎ 071 737 0875); David Davies Associates, 12 Goslett Yard, London WC2H 0EE (☎ 071 437 9070, fax 071 734 0291)

ALFRED, (Arnold) Montague; s of Reuben Alfred, and Bessie, *née* Arbesfield; *b* 21 March 1925; *Educ* Central Fndn Boys' Sch, Imperial Coll London, LSE; *m* 1947, Sheila Jacqueline Gold; 3 s; *Career* dir CELON Div of Courtaulds 1964-69 (head Economics Dept 1953-69); chm BPC Publishing Ltd 1971-81 (dir BPC 1969), chm Caxton Publishing Hldgs 1971-81; chief exec PSA 1982-; 2 perm sec Dept Environment 1982-84; dep chm Ling Kee (UK) 1985-; *Books* Business Economics, Discounted Cash Flow; *Recreations* active in Jewish community affairs; *Style—* Montague Alfred, Esq

ALFREDS, Michael Guy Alexander (Mike); s of John Mark Alfreds (d 1978), and Hylda, *née* Metz; *b* 5 June 1934; *Educ* Bradfield, American Theatre Wing NY, Carnegie-Mellon Inst Pittsburgh Pa USA (BFA); *Career* director; dir of prodns Summer Stock Kennebunkport Maine 1958-59; artistic dir: Theatre West Tucson Arizona 1960, Cincinnati Playhouse-in-the-Park 1961-62; freelance dir: UK repertory theatres and touring opera cos 1963-70, Israeli theatre and tv 1970-75; artistic dir: Khan Theatre Jerusalem 1972-75, Shared Experience 1975-87 (fndr); assoc dir NT 1985 and 1987-88, freelance dir UK and abroad 1983-, currently artistic dir Cambridge Theatre Co; prodns at Shared Experience incl: Arabian Nights Trilogy 1975-77, Bleak House 1977-78, Science Fictions 1978-79, Cymbeline 1979-80, The Merchant of Venice 1981, The Seagull 1981, La Ronde 1982, A Handful of Dust 1982, The Comedy Without A Title 1983, Successful Strategies 1983, False Confidences 1983, Marriage 1984, Too True To Be Good 1986; other prodns incl: Suitcase Packers (Cameri Theatre Tel Aviv 1983, Le Theatre des Nations 1984, Edinburgh Festival 1985), 1001 Nights (Theater der Stadt Heidelberg) 1984, The Cherry Orchard (NT) 1985, The Wandering Jew (NT) 1987, Countrymania (NT) 1987, Blood Wedding (Tarragon Theatre Toronto and Banff Centre) 1988, A Streetcar Named Desire (Tianjin People's Art Theatre China) 1988, Ghosts (Beersheba Municipal Theatre Israel) 1989, The Miser (Oxford Stage Co) 1990, Trouble in Paradise (Talking Pictures) 1990, The Seagull (Oxford Stage Co) 1991; *Awards* (for The Seagull) Best Revival- BTA Drama awards 1982, (for The Cherry Orchard) Best Director-BTA Drama and Plays and Players awards 1986, (for Mandragola (Haifa Theatre) 1971 and Suitcase Packers (Cameri Theatre) 1984) Israel Kinoor David award for Best Director and Best Production; teacher of acting and drama various locations incl: LAMDA, London Opera Centre, Univ of Tel Aviv, Arts Cncl Wellington NZ; author of several articles in professional jls and co-adaptor of Eugene Sue's The Wandering Jew (1987); memb: Arts Cncl Drama Panel 1981-85, Arts Cncl Drama Projects Sub Ctee 1982-85, Mgmnt Ctee The Actor's Centre 1988, Working Pty of Gulbenkian Fndn Enquiry Into Dir Trg (report: A Better Direction) 1987-89; dir: Bd of Almeida Theatre 1982-89, Bd of Shared Experience 1975-, Bd David Glass New Mime Ensemble 1990-; *Style—* Mike Alfreds, Esq; Cambridge Theatre Company, 8 Market Passage, Cambridge CB2 3PF (☎ 0223 357134, fax 0223 467335)

ALI, Dr (Mohammad) Shaukat; s of Shahamat Ali (d 1973), and Hashena Begum; *b* 1 June 1939; *Educ* Kasba High English Sch, Dhaka Govt Coll, Univ Med Coll Dhaka (MB BS), Univ of Liverpool (DTM & H); *m* 30 Sept 1962, Hasina, da of Yakub Ali Bhuiyan, of Chittagong, Bangladesh; 2 s (Sanwar b 1965, Shahrar b 1969), 2 da (Sherlia b 1967, Shabrina b 1977); *Career* registrar in gen med Professorial Unit Chittagong Med Coll Hosp 1964-65, sr registrar in geriatric and gen med KCH 1971-74, conslt physician in geriatric and gen med Greenwich Dist Hosp 1974-; author of various articles; actively involved with: BMA, Overseas Doctors Assoc UK, Bangladesh Med Assoc UK (past pres); currently chm Dist Div of Med; memb BMA 1966, MRCP (Lord) 1973, FRCPI 1984 (MRCPI 1971), FRCP (Glas) 1984, FRCPE 1984; *Books* British Medical Journal (contrib, 1978); *Recreations* photography, gardening, cooking and entertaining; *Clubs* West Kent Medico-Chirurgical Soc; *Style—* Dr Shaukat Ali; Greenwich District Hospital, Vanbrugh Hill, London SE10 9HE (☎ 081 858 8141)

ALISON, Fiona; da of Harry Widdup (d 1976), of Weymouth, Dorset, and Nell Roberts (d 1968); *b* 7 March 1939; *Educ* Weymouth GS, Weymouth Coll, Univ of London (CertEd); *m* 30 June 1962, Peter Alison, s of Youssof Alison; 1 s (Julian Piers b 16 June 1969), 1 da (Elizabeth Charlotte b 10 Jan 1973); *Career* int child photographer 1980-; works incl: children's portraiture 1980-84, children's fashion and advertising photography GB 1984-87, photographic assignments and lectures worldwide 1988- (BIPP nat conf speaker 1990, Enfield Arts Cncl photographic convention speaker 1990, Les Journées Mondiales de L'Image Congres Corsica speaker 1990), exhibition of work at Glaziers' Hall London 1983, numerous appearances on radio and tv, first woman judge BP Chemicals World Photographic Competition 1990, tutor Fuji Film UK Sch of Photography Cyprus and GB 1991; *Awards* Kodak Nat Portrait award winner (first woman to win) 1980, 3M Nat Portfolio award winner (first woman to win) 1983, BIPP Peter Grugeon award (first woman to win) 1988; FBIPP 1988 (LBIPP 1981, ABIPP 1982), FRSA 1982; *Recreations* reading, theatre, scrabble; *Clubs* London Portrait Gp; *Style—* Mrs Fiona Alison; Squirrels, Greystoke, Berkhamsted, Herts HP4 3JJ (☎ 0442 873439); Fiona Alison Studio, 10 Greystoke, Berkhamsted, Herts HP4 3JJ (☎ 0442 873439)

ALISON, Rt Hon Michael James Hugh; PC (1981), MP (C) Selby 1983-; s of J S I Alison, of London and Sydney, Australia; *b* 27 June 1926; *Educ* Eton, Wadham Coll Oxford, Ridley Hall Cambridge; *m* 1958, Sylvia Mary, da of Anthony Haigh, CMG; 2 s, 1 da; *Career* served Lt Coldstream Gds 1944-48; clerk Lazard Bros (merchant bankers) 1951-53, res offr London Municipal Soc 1954-58, memb Kensington Cncl 1956-59, CRD 1958-64, MP (C) Barkston Ash 1964-83, jt Parly under sec DHSS 1970-74; min of state: NI Office 1979-81, Dept of Employment 1981-83; PPS to the Prime Minister 1983-87; second church estates cmmr 1987; *Style—* The Rt Hon Michael Alison, MP; House of Commons, London SW1A 0AA (☎ 071 219 3000)

ALLAIRE, Paul Arthur; s of Arthur E Allaire (d 1960), of Worcester, Mass, USA, and Mrs G P Murphy; *b* 21 July 1938; *Educ* Worcester Polytechnic Inst (BS), Carnegie Mellon Univ (MS); *m* 1963, Kathleen, da of Thomas Buckley (d 1959), of New York; 1 s (Brian b 1964), 1 da (Christiana b 1967); *Career* vice-pres Xerox Corpn 1983-, md Rank Xerox 1980-83; bd memb American Chamber of Commerce 1980-; *Recreations* riding, tennis; *Style—* Paul Allaire, Esq; 727 Smith Ridge Road, New Canaan, Conn 06840, USA

ALLAM, Roger William; s of The Rev William Sydney Allam (d 1977), of St James Vicarage, Muswell Hill, London, and Kathleen, *née* Service; *b* 26 Oct 1953; *Educ* Christ's Hosp Horsham Sussex, Univ of Manchester (BA); *Career* fndr memb Monstrous Regiment Theatre Co; repertory work in Manchester, Birmingham and Glasgow, parts incl: Angelo in Measure for Measure, title role in Macbeth, Macheath in Threepenny Opera, Dr Rock in The Doctor and The Devils; joined RSC 1981 (assoc artist 1990), parts incl: Richmore in Twin Rivals, Conrad in Our Friends in The North, Theseus and Oberon in A Midsummer Night's Dream, Mercutio in Romeo and Juliet, Victor in Today, Ford in The Party, The Officer in The Dream Play, Javert in Les Miserables, Adrian in The Archbishop's Ceiling, Clarence in Richard III, Pimm in Heresies, Brutus in Julius Caesar, Sir Toby Belch in Twelfth Night, Duke Vincentio in Measure for Measure, Benedick in Much Ado About Nothing, Trigorin in The Seagull, Oberon in The Fairy Queen (Aix-en-Provence Festival 1989); tv incl Who Bombed Birmingham? and Ending Up; films incl Wilt; many radio plays; contribs on Mercutio and Duke Vincentio in Players of Shakespeare II and III; *Recreations* playing and listening to music, cooking, drinking red wine; *Clubs* Ronnie Scots; *Style—* Roger Allam, Esq; Meg Poole, c/o The Richard Stone Partnership, 25 Whitehall, London SW1A 2BS (☎ 071 839 6421, fax 839 5002)

ALLAN; *see*: Havelock-Allan

ALLAN, Geoffrey Robert John; s of Dr Robert Leitch Allan (d 1976), and Elsie Kathleen, *née* Stewart; *b* 25 March 1941; *Educ* Strathallan Sch Forgandenny Perthshire, Univ of Glasgow (BDS, Rugby blue), Univ of London (MSc); *m* 1, 1969; 2 s (Christopher Geoffrey b 4 Nov 1973, Nicholas Cochrane Robert b 4 Jan 1975), 1 da (Kimberley b 12 Nov 1977); m 2, Dec 1984, Rosalind Mary, da of David Smith; 1 step s (Gavin David b 10 April 1973), 1 step da (Suzanne Mary b 27 Feb 1975); *Career* trainee rising to shift supt Clyde Paper Co 1960-64; house offr, sr house offr, registrar and sr registrar Glasgow Dental Hosp Canniesburn and Stobhill 1969-77, Eastman Dental Hosp London 1975, conslt in restorative dentistry Guy's Hosp 1977-79, joined Glynn Setchell (now call Glynn, Setchell and Allan) 1979; examiner RCPS Glas 1985-; FDS 1973; memb: BDA, Int Coll of Dentists; *Books* BDA Booklet on Treatment of the Cleft Palate Patient; *Recreations* family, golf, tennis, squash, skiing; *Clubs* Wilderness Golf; *Style—* Geoffrey Allan, Esq; Glynn, Setchell & Allan, 35 Devonshire Place, London W1N 1PE (☎ 071 935 3342)

ALLAN, George Alexander; s of William Allan (d 1976), of 13 Comely Bank Street, Edinburgh, and Janet Peters, *née* Watt (d 1976); *b* 3 Feb 1936; *Educ* Daniel Stewart's Coll Edinburgh, Univ of Edinburgh (MA); *m* 1 Sept 1962, Anne Violet, da of Vibert Ambrose George Veevers, of Kelso; 2 s (Victor Julian Douglas b 1964, Timothy Edward Douglas b 1966); *Career* Edinburgh Univ Air Sqdn 1953-56, CCF RAFVR 1958-66; classics master Glasgow Acad 1958-60; Daniel Stewart's Coll Edinburgh: classics master 1960-63, head of classics 1963-73, housemaster 1966-73; Robert Gordon's Coll Aberdeen: dep headmaster 1973-77, headmaster 1978-; schoolmaster fell commoner Corpus Christi Coll Cambridge 1972-; played rugby for Edinburgh XV 1960-62, Scottish trial 1963; Scottish Div HMC: sec 1980-87, rep on Nat Ctee 1982-83, chm 1988-89; memb Ctee Scottish Cncl of Ind Schs 1988; govr Welbeck Coll 1980-89, burgess of guild City of Aberdeen 1981-; memb HMC 1978; *Recreations* golf, gardening, music, travel; *Clubs* East India and Public Schools, Royal Northern and Univ (Aberdeen); *Style—* George Allan, Esq; 24 Woodend Rd, Aberdeen AB2 6YH (☎ 0224 321733); Robert Gordon's Coll, Schoolhill, Aberdeen AB9 1FR (☎ 0224 646346)

ALLAN, Ian; s of George A T Allan, OBE (d 1952), of Horsham, and Mary Louise, *née* Barnes (d 1963); *b* 29 June 1922; *Educ* St Paul's; *m* 11 Oct 1947, Mollie Eileen, da of Edwin Franklin (d 1942); 2 s (David Ian b 1954, (Edwin) Paul b 1957); *Career* chm Ian Allan Gp (publishers, printers and travel agents) 1962-; govr Christ's Hosp 1944- (almoner 1980-89), treas Bridewell Royal Hosp, chm of govrs King Edward's Sch Witley, memb Dart Valley Light Railway plc (chm 1976-86), vice pres Tport Tst; *Books* many books on railways and associated subjects; *Recreations* swimming, miniature railways, touring, travel; *Style—* Ian Allan, Esq; Terminal House, Shepperton, Middlesex TW17 8AS (☎ 0932 228950, fax 0932 232366, fax 929806 IALLANG)

ALLAN, James Nicholas; CMG (1989), CBE (1976); s of late Morris Edward Allan, and Joan Bach; *b* 22 May 1932; *Educ* Gresham's, LSE; *m* 1961, Helena Susara Crouse; 1 s, 1 da; *Career* ambass Mozambique 1986-89; Directing Staff RCDS 1989-; *Style—* James Allan, Esq, CMG, CBE; c/o Foreign and Commonwealth Office, King Charles St, London SW1A 2AH

ALLAN, John; s of Richard Ferguson Allan, of 12 Celosia Court, Hutchinson Rd, Umbilo, Durban, SA, and Margaret Miller Reid Mason, *née* Ferguson; *b* 25 Nov 1963; *Educ* Glenwood HS Natal SA; *Career* Rugby Union hooker Edinburgh Academicals RFC and Scotland (2 caps); clubs: Glenwood Old Boys RFC 1982-85 (capt U20) and 1988-90 (capt), Northern Transvaal Defence 1986-87, Edinburgh Academicals 1989-; rep: Natal Province U20 1982-83, S African Defence Force XV 1986-87, Natal Province XV 1988-90 (28 caps), S African Select XV 1988-90, Scotland B 1989; Scotland: debut v NZ Dunedin 1990; played Softball Natal Province 1982-85; *Recreations* reading, relaxing in front of TV; *Style—* John Allan, Esq; 120 Rose Street (South Lane), Edinburgh, Scotland EH2 4BB (☎ 031 226 3660, 031 453 6400)

ALLAN, Sheriff John Douglas; s of Robert Taylor Allan, of Edinburgh, and Christina Helen Blythe Allan (d 1970); *b* 2 Oct 1941; *Educ* George Watson's Coll Edinburgh, Univ of Edinburgh (LLB, Dip Mgmnt Studies); *m* 1966, Helen Elizabeth Jean, da of William Aiton (d 1959); 1 s (Graeme b 1967), 1 da (Anne b 1970); *Career* slr and Notary Public; slr 1963-67, dep procurator fiscal 1967-71, sr legal asst Crown Office 1971-76, asst procurator fiscal Glasgow 1976-77, sr asst procurator fiscal Glasgow 1978-79, asst slr Crown Office 1979-83, regnl procurator fiscal for Lothians & Borders 1983-88; Sheriff of S Strathclyde, Dumfries and Galloway at Lanark 1988-; FBIM; *Recreations* youth work, church work, walking; *Style—* Sheriff J Douglas Allan; Minard, 80 Greenbank Crescent, Edinburgh EH10 5SW (☎ 031 447 2593); Sheriff Court, Hope St, Lanark ML11 7NQ (☎ 0555 61531)

ALLAN, Richard Bellerby; *b* 2 Aug 1940; *Educ* Marlborough, Merton Coll Oxford (BA); *m* 17 Sept 1966, Diana Rosemary Cotton, QC; 2 s (Jonathan Bellerby b 28 June 1972, Jeremy Richard b 7 Aug 1974), 1 da (Joanna Frances b 10 March 1977); *Career* KPMG Peat Marwick McLintock: articled clerk 1962-65, qualified sr 1965-69, mangr 1969-77, ptnr 1977-; *Style—* Richard Allan, Esq; KPMG Peat Marwick McLintock, 1 Puddle Dock, Blackfriars, London EC4V 3PD (☎ 071 236 8000)

ALLAN, Robert William; s of William Bennett Allan (d 1986), of NY, USA, and Mona Theresa, *née* Bradley; *b* 4 May 1945; *Educ* Xaverian Coll Brighton; *m* 15 July 1979, Elizabeth, da of John Jackson, of Newcastle; 2 da (Charlotte b 1979, Kirsty b 1982); *Career* admitted slr 1967; ptnr: Roney & Co 1971-73, Simons Muirhead & Allan 1973-86, Denton Hall Burgin & Warrens 1986-; memb Law Soc; *Recreations* skiing, clay pigeon shooting, horse riding; *Clubs* Groucho's; *Style—* Robert W Allan, Esq; 5 Chancery Lane, Clifford's Inn, London EC4A 1BU (☎ 071 242 1212, fax 071 404 0087)

ALLAN, Stephen David; s of Gerry Allan, of London, and Sonja, *née* Geiringer; *b* 26 June 1963; *Educ* City of London Sch; *Career* mangr Fotofast 1981, trainee media exec Yershon Media 1981; The Media Business: media exec 1982, assoc dir 1986, Bd dir holding co 1987, equity shareholder 1988, first dir of new business 1989-; MIPA 1988; *Recreations* golf, shooting, travel; *Clubs* Coombe Hill Golf, John Carpenter, Highbury Rifle; *Style—* Stephen Allan, Esq; The Media Business Group, Media House, 16 Morwell St, London WC1B 3EY (☎ 071 637 7299, fax 071 636 4145)

ALLAN, William Roderick Buchanan; s of James Buchanan Allan, and Mildred Pattenden; *b* 11 Sept 1945; *Educ* Stowe, Trinity Coll Cambridge (MA); *m* 1973, Gillian Gail Colgan; 2 s (Alexander, Robert); *Career* ed *The Connoisseur* 1976-80 (joined staff 1972); arts consultant United Technologies Corporation; latest involvement: Franz Xaver Winterhalter and the Courts of Europe, National Portrait Gallery London, Petit Palais Paris; *Recreations* military history, cooking; *Clubs* Chelsea Arts; *Style—* William Allan, Esq; 54 South Western Rd, St Margaret's, Twickenham, Middx (☎ 081 891 0974)

ALLAN OF KILMAHEW, Baroness; Maureen; da of late Harold Stuart-Clark, of Singapore; *m* 1947, Baron Allan of Kilmahew, DSO, OBE (Life Peer) (d 1979); *Style—* The Rt Hon the Lady Allan of Kilmahew

ALLANBRIDGE, Hon Lord; William Ian Stewart; s of John Stewart, FRIBA (d 1954), and Mrs Maysie Shepherd Service or Stewart (d 1968), of Drimfearn, Bridge of Allan; *b* 8 Nov 1925; *Educ* Loretto, Edinburgh Univ, Glasgow Univ (MA, LLB); *m* 1955, Naomi Joan, da of Sir James Boyd Douglas, CBE (d 1964), of Barstibly, Castle Douglas; 1 s (John), 1 da (Angela); *Career* served WWII Sub-Lt RNVR, escort gp Western Approaches; advocate 1951, advocate depute 1959-64, memb Criminal Injuries Compensation Bd 1969-70, home advocate depute 1970-72, slr gen for Scotland 1972-74, sen of Coll of Justice in Scotland (Scottish Lord of Session) 1977-; QC (Scot) 1965, Sheriff Principal of Dumfries and Galloway 1974; *Recreations* hill walking; *Clubs* New (Edinburgh), RNVR (Glasgow); *Style—* The Hon Lord Allanbridge; 60 Northumberland St, Edinburgh EH3 6JE (☎ 031 556 2823)

ALLANSON-WINN, Hon Owain Gwynedd; 5 and yst s of 5 Baron Headley (d 1935), and his 1 w, Teresa St Josephine, *née* Johnson (d 1919); bro and h of 7 Baron Headley; *b* 15 Feb 1906; *Educ* Bedford Sch; *m* 29 Oct 1938, Ruth, 2 da of late Cecil Orpin, of Strand House, Youghal, Co Cork, and formerly wife of Harry Stuart Pearson; *Style—* The Hon Owain Allanson-Winn; 8 Genevafontein, PO Box 4340, George East, 6539, S Africa

ALLANSON-WINN, Hon Susan Ethel; da of 7 Baron Headley; *b* 26 May 1936; *Style—* The Hon Susan Allanson-Winn

ALLARDICE, His Hon Judge; William Arthur Llewellyn Allardice; DL (Staffs 1980); s of late W C Allardice, MD, FRCSEd, JP, and late Constance Winifred Allardice; *b* 18 Dec 1924; *Educ* Stonyhurst, Univ Coll Oxford (MA); *m* 1956, Jennifer, Ann, da of late G H Jackson; 1 s, 1 da; *Career* called to the Barr Lincoln's Inn 1950; circuit judge (Midland and Oxford) 1972-; *Style—* His Hon Judge Allardice, DL; c/o Courts Administrator, Stafford (☎ 0785 55219)

ALLARDYCE, Hugh Winyett; s of Alexander Allardyce (d 1987), of Tunbridge Wells, Kent, and Phyllis Vandella, *née* de Kantzow; *b* 8 May 1951; *Educ* Bedford Sch, Univ of Leeds; *Career* called to the Bar Middle Temple 1972; *Style—* Hugh Allardyce, Esq; 1 Middle Temple Lane, Temple, London EC4 (☎ 071 583 0659, fax 071 353 0652)

ALLASON, Lt-Col James Harry; OBE (1953); s of late Brig-Gen Walter Allason, DSO (d 1960), and Katharine Hamilton, *née* Poland; *b* 6 Sept 1912; *Educ* Haileybury, RMA Woolwich; *m* 1946 (m dis 1974), Nuala Elveen, da of late John A McArevey, of Foxrock, Co Dublin; 2 s; *Career* cmmnd RA 1932, transfd 3 Carabiniers 1937, served WWII, ret 1953; MP (C) Hemel Hempstead 1959-74, PPS to Sec of State for War 1960-64; *Clubs* White's, Royal Yacht Sqdn; *Style—* Lt-Col James Allason, OBE; 82 Ebury Mews, London SW1 (☎ 071 730 1576)

ALLASON, Julian Edward Thomas; s of Lt-Col James Harry Allason, OBE, FRSA, *qv*; *b* 14 May 1948; *Educ* Downside; *m* 1976, Jessica Marland, da of Richard Thomas Wingert, of Westport, Connecticut, USA; 2 s (James b 1980, Benjamin b 1984), 1 da (Chloe b 1982); *Career* dir: Markham & Markham Ltd 1971-89, Apricot Computers plc 1979-86, Sharp Technol Fund plc 1984-, Megasat Satellite Communications Ltd 1986-89, Elgie Stewart Smith plc 1987-89; md The Blackthorn Gp 1989-; author; publisher Microcomputer Printout Magazine 1979-83; columnist: The Observer 1981-83, Daily Telegraph 1983-86; JP (Inner London) 1973-78; memb Information Technol NEDC Ctee 1984-86; FRSA 1984; Sov Mil Order of Malta; kt 1985, vice chllr 1986-89, Cdr of Merit 1989; kt Constantinian Order of St George 1986 (chllr British delgn 1987-89); *Books* The Pet Companion (1981), English Legal Heritage (co-ed 1979); *Recreations* photography, litigation, fullbore pistol shooting; *Clubs* White's, Jet; *Style—* Julian Allason, Esq; PO Box 41, Wallingford, Oxon OX10 6TD (☎ 0491 641 044)

ALLASON, Rupert William Simon; MP (C) Torbay 1987-; s of Lt-Col James Allason, OBE, of London, and Nuala, *née* McArevey; *b* 8 Nov 1951; *Educ* Downside, Univ Hall Buckland, Univ of Lille, Univ of Grenoble; *m* 1979, Nicole Jane, da of M L Van Moppes (d 1963), of Bermuda; 1 s (Thomas b 1980), 1 da (Alexandra b 1987); *Career* author; euro ed Intelligence Quarterly; *Books* SPY! (with Richard Deacon, 1980), MI5 (1981), A Matter of Trust (1982), MI6 (1983), The Branch (1983), Unreliable Witness (1984), GARBO (with Juan Pujol, 1985), GCHQ (1986), Molehunt (1987), The Friends (1988), Games of Intelligence (1989), The Blue List (1989), Cuban Bluff (1990); *Recreations* skiing, sailing; *Clubs* White's, Special Forces, RYS; *Style—* Rupert Allason, Esq; 310 Fulham Rd, London SW10 (☎ 071 352 1110); House of Commons, London SW1A 0AA (☎ 071 219 4142)

ALLAUN, Frank J; s of Harry Allaun, and Hannah Allaun; *b* 27 Feb 1913; *Educ* Manchester GS; *m* 1, 1941, Lilian (d 1986), da of J Ball, of Manchester; 1 s, 1 da; m 2, 1989, Millicent, *née* Bobker; *Career* MP (Lab) E Salford 1955-83; pres Labour Action for Peace 1963-; chm: Labour Party 1979, Labour Press and Publicity Ctee to 1982, Labour NEC (memb 1967-83); memb Labour Home Policy Ctee to 1982, life memb Nat Union of Journalists; ed Labour's Northern Voice 1953-67; *Style—* Frank Allaun, Esq

ALLAWAY, Percy Albert; CBE (1973); s of Albert Edward Allaway, and Frances Beatrice, *née* Rogers; *b* 22 Aug 1915; *Educ* Southall Tech Coll; *m* 1959, Margaret Lilian Petyt; *Career* EMI: joined 1930, dir 1965-81, dir SE Laboratories 1967-81, chm Electronics 1968-81; EMI subsids: dir Nuclear Enterprises Ltd 1961-81, chm EMIMEC 1968-81 (chm EMI Varian 1969-81); conslt Thorn EMI 1981-82 (memb Exec Mgmnt Bd 1980-81); chm CEI 1980-81; pres Electronic Engrg Assoc 1970; Freeman City of London, Liveryman Worshipful Co of Scientific Instrument Makers; Hon DTech Brunel Univ 1973; FRSA, FEng 1980, FIProdE, FIEE, pres IERE 1976, FIQA; *Style—* Percy Allaway, Esq, CBE; Kroller, 54 Howards Wood Drive, Gerrards Cross, Bucks SL9 7HW (☎ 0753 885028)

ALLCOCK, Anthony (Tony); MBE; s of Ernest Stacey Allcock, and Joan Winifred Allcock (d 1986); *b* 11 June 1955; *Educ* Norwich City Coll; *m* 17 April 1989, Jocelyn Anne (Jossie), da of Antony Frenkel, of Cirencester; 2 step da (Emma Jane b 11 March 1972, Kate Louise b 7 March 1975); *Career* world champion bowls: outdoor champion 1980, 1984, 1988, indoor singles champion 1986, 1987, indoor pairs champion with David Bryant, CBE, 1986, 1987, 1989 1990; chm Glos Special Olympics, patron English Nat Assoc of Visually Handicapped Bowlers; *Books* Improve your Bowls (1988), Step by Step Guide to Bowls (1988), End to End-a year in bowls (1989); *Recreations* countryside, opera, horses, antiques; *Clubs* Cheltenham Bowling, Cotswold and Bentham Country; *Style—* Tony Allcock, Esq, MBE; Cherington, Gloucestershire GL8 8SN (☎ 0285 84 252)

ALLCOCK, John Paul Major; s of John Gladding Major Allcock, CB (d 1986), and Eileen Winifred Arnold, *née* Baiss; *b* 8 July 1941; *Educ* St Edwards Sch Oxford, Kings Coll Univ of London (BSc), Faculté Polytechnique de Mons Belgium (Maitrise en Science Appliquee); *m* 7 Nov 1981, Caroline Anne, da of Arthur Frederick Lyle Rocke, of Olney, Maryland, USA; 1 s (Oliver John Llewelyn b 27 April 1983), 2 da (Arabella Louise b 1 March 1985, Lucinda Anne b 20 Feb 1990); *Career* chartered patent agent 1968, admitted slr 1977, ptnr Bristows Cooke & Carpmael specialising in intellectual property 1981-; memb Law Soc; fell Chartered Inst of Patent Agents 1968, MIEE 1971, C Eng 1971; *Recreations* sailing and walking; *Style—* John Allcock, Esq; 10 Lincoln's Inn Fields, London WC2A 3BP (☎ 071 242 0462, fax 071 242 1232, tlx 27487)

ALLCROFT; *see:* Magnus-Allcroft

ALLDAY, Coningsby; CBE (1971); s of late Esca Allday, and Margaret Allday, of Birmingham; *b* 21 Nov 1920; *Educ* Solihull Sch, Univ of London (BSc); *m* 1945, Iris Helena, da of Frank Spencer Adams, of Birmingham; 1 s, 1 da; *Career* UK Atomic Energy Authority 1959-71 (chief chemist, tech dir, commercial dir, dep md), memb UKAEA 1976-85, md BNFL 1971-86 (chief exec 1975-86, chm 1983-86), chm Allday Nuclear Conslts Ltd 1986-, non-exec dir National Westminster Bank Northern Region 1985-, chm Mintech NW 1986-90; CEng, FIChemE, Hon DSc Univ of Salford; Chevalier de la Legion d'Honneur; *Recreations* gardening, music; *Style—* Coningsby Allday, Esq, CBE; Bredon, 54 Goughs Lane, Knutsford, Cheshire

ALLDIS, Air Cdre Cecil Anderson; CBE (1962), DFC (1941), AFC (1953); 2 s of

John Henry Alldis (d 1943), of Birkenhead, Cheshire, and Margaret Wright Alldis (d 1953); *b* 28 Sept 1918; *Educ* Birkenhead Inst, Emmanuel Coll Cambridge (MA); *m* 1942, Jeanette Claire, da of Albert Edward Collingwood Tarrant (d 1924), of Johannesburg, SA; *Career* served WWII (despatches), Pilot RAF, Asst Air Attaché Moscow 1947-49, Air Attaché Bonn 1963-66, ret 1966; entered Home Civil Serv 1966, MOD 1966-69, seconded to HM Dip Serv 1969, cnsllr (def supply) Bonn 1969-80, ret 1980; sec gen The Air League 1982-90, ret 1990; *Recreations* golf, fishing; *Clubs* Naval & Military; *Style—* Air Cdre Cecil Alldis, CBE, DFC, AFC; Tudor Cottage, Oxshott Way, Cobham, Surrey (☎ 0932 66092)

ALLDIS, Christopher John; s of Flt Lt John Henry Alldis, RAF (d 1981), and Isabel Marjorie, *née* Carter; *b* 16 May 1947; *Educ* Birkenhead Sch, Emmanuel Coll Cambridge (MA, LLB); *m* 14 Sept 1985, Marcia Elizabeth, *née* Kidman; 2 da (Amy Elizabeth b 1987, Rebecca Isabel Amelia b 1989); *Career* called to the Bar Gray's Inn 1970, practising Northern Circuit; *Recreations* gliding, light aviation, skiing, fishing; *Clubs* Naval & Military; *Style—* Christopher Alldis, Esq; Romsdal, 3 Prenton Lane, Birkenhead, Merseyside (☎ 051 608 1828); Peel House, Harrington St, Liverpool (☎ 051 236 4321, fax 051 236 3332)

ALLDIS, John; s of William Alldis, and Nell, *née* Bennet; *b* 10 Aug 1929; *Educ* Felsted, Univ of Cambridge (MA); *m* 23 July 1960, Ursula, da of William Mason; 2 s (Dominic b 1962, Robert b 1964); *Career* Nat Serv Essex Regt 1947-49; formed John Alldis Choir 1962, choral prof Guildford Sch of Music and Drama 1964-77, fndr and conductor London Symphony Chorus 1966-69, conductor London Philharmonic Choir 1969-82, jt chief conductor Radio Denmark 1971-77, Artistic Dir Groupe Vocal de France 1979-83; fell Westminster Choir Coll Princeton USA; ARCO 1956, FGSM 1976, Chev des Arts et des Lettres 1984; *Style—* John Alldis, Esq; 3 Wool Rd, Wimbledon, London SW20 0HN (☎ 081 946 4168)

ALLEN, Prof Adrian; s of Philip John Frances Allen (d 1979), of Bognor Regis, and Mary Isobel, *née* Parry (d 1985); *b* 27 Jan 1938; *Educ* Ch Ch Oxford (MA, DPhil); *m* 22 July 1960, Pauline Elizabeth; 1 s (Adam b 1969), 3 da (Susan b 1961, Deborah b 1965, Katherine b 1967); *Career* Univ of Newcastle upon Tyne: lectr 1967, reader 1976, prof of physiological biochemistry 1980-; *Recreations* ornithology, hill walking; *Style—* Prof Adrian Allen; Department of Physiological Sciences, Medical Sch, Framlington Place, Newcastle upon Tyne NE2 4HH (☎ 091 222 6991, 091 26176151)

ALLEN, Anthony John Rowlatt; s of Stanley Rowlatt Allen, MBE, of 3 Mill Hill, Shoreham By Sea, W Sussex, and Peggy Marion, *née* King; *b* 23 Dec 1943; *Educ* Brighton Coll, Selwyn Coll Cambridge (MA); *m* 15 Oct 1971, Torill, da of Ludwig Berg-Nilsen, of Sarpsborg, Norway; 1 s (Henrik b 9 April 1981), 3 da (Kim b 23 April 1973, Emma b 1 June 1974, Rachel b 7 April 1977); *Career* admitted slr 1971, ptnr Donne Mileham & Haddock 1975-; memb Lewes Town Lab Pty; memb: Law Soc, UK Environmental Law Assoc, Slrs' Family Law Assoc, LMRTPI 1974; *Recreations* walking, sailing; *Style—* Anthony Allen, Esq; 33 Houndean Rise, Lewes, E Sussex BN7 1EQ (☎ 0273 475 014); Donne Mileham & Haddock, Albion House, Lewes, E Sussex (☎ 0273 480 205, fax 0273 480 507)

ALLEN, His Hon Judge; Hon Anthony Kenway; OBE (1946); s of Charles Valentine Allen (d 1956), of Ashtead, Surrey, and Edith Kenway Allen (d 1974); *b* 31 Oct 1917; *Educ* St George's Coll Weybridge, St John's Coll Cambridge (BA), Univ of Freiburg, Univ of Grenoble; *m* 1975, Maureen Margot Murtough, da of Dr Peter Moran (d 1914); *Career* serv WWII RAF, Intelligence Wing Cdr; called to the Bar Inner Temple 1947, circuit judge 1978-; *Recreations* tennis, music, walking, gardening; *Style—* His Hon Judge Allen, OBE; 73 Downswood, Epsom Downs, Surrey (☎ 073 73 50017)

ALLEN, Arnold Millman; CBE (1977); s of Wilfrid Millman and Edith Muriel Allen; *b* 30 Dec 1924; *Educ* Hackney Downs Secdy Sch, Peterhouse Cambridge; *m* 1947, Beatrice Mary Whitaker; 3 s, 1 da; *Career* served Treasy 1945-55, memb Br Waterways Bd 1965-68; UKAEA: memb for fin and admin 1976-81, dep chm 1981-84, chief exec 1982-84, chm 1984-86; *Style—* Arnold Allen, Esq, CBE; Duntish Cottage, Duntish, Dorchester, Dorset (☎ 030 05 258); United Kingdon Atomic Energy Authority, 11 Charles II St, London SW1Y 4QP (☎ 071 930 5454)

ALLEN, Carol; da of William Joseph Allen (d 1949), of Greenford, Middx, and Winifred Rose, *née* Bicknell (d 1973); *Educ* Notting Hill and Ealing HS, Central School of Speech and Drama (Univ of London Dip in Drama, Teaching Dip); *m* 15 June 1973 (m dis 1978), James Dyer, s of Sidney Dyer; *Career* prodn asst BBC TV, prodr COI, freelance broadcaster, LBC 1980-87 (prog presenter, newsreader full time cinema specialist) freelance writer and broadcaster 1987-; freelance work incl: res theatre critic London Talkback Radio's breakfast prog and LBC Newstalk's Michael Parkinson Prog, guest critic BSkyB Movie Show, interviewer and reviewer BBC Radio 2, feature writer for Cosmopolitan and other magazines, film reviews The People newspaper; shortlisted and specially commended in tv section Radio Times Drama awards; memb: Prodr's Assoc, London Screenwriter's Workshop, Critic's Circle, NUJ; *Recreations* the company of friends, books, films, theatre, television; *Style—* Miss Carol Allen; Jacqué Evans Management Ltd, 11A St John's Wood High St, London NW8 7NG (☎ 071 722 4700)

ALLEN, (Michael) Christopher Kinkead; s of Col Robert Langley Kinkead Allen, OBE (d 1976), and Phyllis Mary, *née* Serjeant; *b* 7 Jan 1940; *Educ* Haileybury, Jesus Coll Oxford (MA); *m* 10 April 1976, Jennifer Anne, da of Sir John Rogers Ellis, MBE, of Little Monkhams, Monkhams Lane, Woodford Green, Essex; 1 s (Robert b 1978), 1 da (Kate b 1980); *Career* ptnr: Penningtons slrs 1966-90, Mishcon de Reya slrs 1990; govr St Andrews Sch Woking; *Recreations* squash, tennis, sailing, gardening; *Clubs* Lansdowne; *Style—* Christopher Allen, Esq; Nowhurst Farmhouse, Nowhurst Lane, Broadbridge Heath, N Horsham, W Sussex RH12 3PJ (☎ 0403 69512)

ALLEN, Dr Christopher Michael Colquhoun; s of Christopher Oswald Colquhoun Allen, of Kingsbridge, S Devon, and Barbara Louise, *née* Archer; *b* 1 Dec 1948; *Educ* Eastbourne Coll, Christ's Coll Cambridge (MA, MD, MRCP), Guy's Hosp Med Sch; *m* 28 July 1973, Susan Valerie, da of Alan Douglas Belcher (d 1971), of Sheffield; 1 s (Samuel b 1982), 2 da (Kate b 1978, Joanna b Dec 1979); *Career* sr house offr: renal medicine St Thomas' Hosp 1976-77, Nat Hosp for Nervous Diseases 1977; hon sr registrar Dept of Neurology Guy's Hosp 1979-82 (house offr Med Professorial Unit 1973-74, med registrar 1977-79), neurology registrar Middx Hosp 1982-84, sr registrar in neurology Charing Cross Hosp 1984-86, conslt neurologist Addenbrooke's Hosp Cambridge 1986-; tutor RCP Cambridge Health Dist; FRSM; *Books* The Management of Acute Stroke (1988); *Recreations* listening to Mozart, writing book reviews, teasing professors; *Style—* Dr Christopher Allen; 232 Hills Rd, Cambridge CB2 2QE (☎ 0223 247694) Dept of Neurology, Addenbrooke's Hosp, Cambridge CB2 2QQ (☎ 0223 216759)

ALLEN, Colin Mervyn Gordon; CBE (1978); s of Cecil Gordon Allen (d 1980), of 1 Roundmoor Close, Saltford, Bristol, and Gwendoline Louise Allen, *née* Hutchinson (d 1974); *b* 17 April 1929; *Educ* King Edwards' Sch Bath, Open Univ (BA), Univ of London (MA); *m* 1953, Patricia Mary, da of William Thomas Seddon (d 1943); 2 s (Timothy, Mark), 1 da (Claire); *Career* gen mangr Covent Garden Market Authy 1967-89; pres: Assoc of Wholesale Markets within Int Union of Local Authys 1972-78, Inst of Purchasing and Supply 1982-83; *Style—* Colin Allen, Esq, CBE; 10 Whitecroft Way, Beckenham, Kent BR3 3AG

ALLEN, Rear Adm David; CBE (1985); s of Augustin Victor Allen (d 1974), of Glasgow, and Gladys May, *née* Bradbury (d 1953); *b* 14 June 1933; *Educ* Hutcheson's GS Glasgow, Britannia RNC Dartmouth; *m* 9 June 1962, Margaret Gwendolin, da of Alexander Milross Todd (d 1986), of Shrewsbury; 2 s (Richard b 1963, Stephen b 1966); *Career* RN 1949, Cdr 1970, HMS Fife 1970-72, sec to Naval Sec 1973-75, Fleet Supply Offr 1975-77, Capt 1978, sec to the Controller of the Navy 1978-81, staff and flag offr Naval Air 1981-82, sec to the First Sea Lord 1982-85, cmd HMS Cochrane 1985-87, Rear Adm 1987; *Recreations* family and friends, shooting, fishing, gardening, DIY, reading; *Clubs* Farmers', Landsdowne; *Style—* Rear Adm David Allen, CBE; Defence Services Secretary, Ministry of Defence, Main Building, Whitehall, London SW1A 2HB

ALLEN , (Francis John) David; s of Stanley Roy Allen (d 1942), of Harrow, and Eve Maude, *née* Poulton; *b* 9 Jan 1939; *Educ* Harrow Weald GS, Balliol Coll Oxford (BA); *m* 12 August 1965, Gillian Lilias, da of Jack Johnstone, of West Kirby, Wirral; 1 s (Hugo Richard b 12 Oct 1972), 1 da (Charlotte Luise b 2 Jan 1976); *Career* sr prodr BBC TV, ed BBC Computer Literacy Project 1981-86, prodr and ed Microlive Series BBC TV; winner NY Film Festival 1981, Judges award Royal TV Soc 1982, Times Technol prog of the Year 1985-86, Sony Innovation award 1989 and 1990; *Books* Early Years at School, Measurement in Education, That's the Way the Money Goes, The Computer Book (ed); *Recreations* windsurfing, singing, London Philharmonic Choir; *Style—* David Allen, Esq; 19 Priory Rd, Kew, Richmond, Surrey TW9 3DQ (☎ 081 948 1982); BBC Television Training, BBC Elstree Centre, Borehamwood, Herts (☎ 081 953 6100)

ALLEN, David Robyn; s of Allen Richard David, of The Reach, Smugglers Lane, Bosham, Chichester, W Sussex, and Allen Anne, *née* Douthwaite; *b* 24 Jan 1955; *Educ* Wellington, Charing Cross Hosp Med Sch (MB BS, MS); *m* 30 July 1977, (Anne) Judith, da of William Hutcheson (d 1983); 1 s (Robin William b 14 Sept 1983), 1 da (Kate Victoria b 26 Jan 1985); *Career* house surgn St Richards Hosp Chichester, sr house offr Kingston Hosp 1980; registar: Basingstoke Dist Hosp 1981, Royal Sussex Co Hosp Brighton 1983, St Thomas' Hosp 1984; lectr St Thomas' Hosp 1985; sr registrar: Royal Adelaide Hosp Australia 1987, Southampton and Bath 1989; FRCS 1982; *Style—* David Allen, Esq; 12 Queens Rd, Mortlake, London SW14 8PJ (☎ 081 876 2276); Dept Surgery, St Thomas' Hospital, London SE1 7EH, (☎ 071 928 9292)

ALLEN, Donald George; CMG (1981); s of Sydney George Allen (d 1971), and Doris Elsie, *née* Abercrombie (d 1969); *b* 26 June 1930; *Educ* Southall GS; *m* 1955, Sheila Isobel, da of Wilfred Bebbington (d 1976); 3 s (Stephen, David, Mark); *Career* HM Forces 1949-51; FO 1951-54, The Hague 1954-57, second sec (Commercial) La Paz 1957-60, FO 1961-65, first sec 1962, asst priv sec to Lord Privy Seal 1961-63 and to Min without Portfolio 1963-64, first sec head of Chancery, consul Panama 1966-69, FCO 1969-72, cnsllr on secondment to NI Office Belfast 1972-74, cnsllr and head Chancery UK Perm Delgn to OECD Paris 1974-78, inspr 1978-80, dir Office of Parly Cmmr 1980-82, dep Parly cmmr for admin (ombudsman) 1982-90; memb Broadcasting Complaints Cmmn 1990-; *Recreations* squash, golf, tennis; *Clubs* RAC, Princes Squash; *Style—* Donald Allen, Esq, CMG; 99 Parkland Grove, Ashford, Middx TW15 2JF (☎ 0784 255617)

ALLEN, Fergus Hamilton; CB (1969); s of Charles Winckworth Allen (d 1971), of Dublin, and Marjorie Helen, *née* Budge (d 1986); *b* 3 Sept 1921; *Educ* Newtown Sch Waterford, Trinity Coll Dublin (MA, MAI, ScD); *m* 1947, Margaret Joan, da of Prof Michael J Gorman (d 1982), of Dublin; 2 da (Mary Elizabeth); *Career* dir Hydraulics Res Station 1958-65, chief scientific offr Cabinet Office 1965-69, first civil serv cmmr Civil Serv Dept 1974-81, sr conslt Boyden Int 1982-86; *Recreations* reading, writing, painting; *Clubs* Athenaeum; *Style—* Fergus Allen, Esq, CB; Dundrum, Wantage Rd, Streatley, Berks RG8 9LB (☎ 0491 873 234)

ALLEN, Hon Mrs (Fiona Mary); da of 17 Lord Lovat, DSO, MC, TD; *b* 6 July 1941; *m* 1982, Robin Richard Allen; *Style—* The Hon Mrs Allen; Via Trecento 88, 50025 Montespertoli, (FI), Italy

ALLEN, Hon Mrs (Francesca Nicola); *née* Sternberg; *née* Sternberg; da of Baron Plurenden (Life Peer; d 1978), and Baroness Plurenden, *qv*; *b* 1962; *m* 7 Oct 1989, Douglas G Allen, eldest s of B G Allen, of Scott City, Kansas, USA; *Style—* The Hon Mrs Allen; Plurenden Manor, High Halden, Kent

ALLEN, Hon Judge Francis Andrew; His Hon Judge; s of Andrew Eric Allen and Joan Elizabeth Allen; *b* 7 Dec 1933; *Educ* Solihull Sch, Merton Coll Oxford (MA); *m* 1961, Marjorie Pearce; 1 s, 3 da; *Career* barr 1958; circuit judge 1979-; *Style—* His Hon Judge Allen; 116 Oxford Road, Moseley, Birmingham B13 9SQ (☎ 021 449 1270)

ALLEN, Gary James; s of Alfred Allen, of Sutton Coldfield, W Midlands, and Alice Jane, *née* Herworth; *b* 30 Sept 1944; *Educ* King Edward VI GS Birmingham, Univ of Liverpool (BCom); *m* 10 Sept 1966, Judith Anne, da of William Nattrass (d 1961); 3 s (Andrew b 1969, Anthony b 1971, James b 1979); *Career* md IMI Range Ltd 1973-77; IMI plc: 1978-, asst md 1985-86, md 1986-; chm: IMI Components Ltd 1981-85, Eley Ltd 1981-85, Optilon Ltd 1979-84; non-exec dir: NV Bekaert SA Belgium 1987-, Marley plc 1989-, Birmingham Euro Airways 1989-; memb Cncl: CBI 1986 (W Midlands Regnl Cncl 1983-89), Birmingham Chamber of Indust and Commerce 1983 (vice pres 1989-), Univ of Birmingham 1985-90 (hon life memb Ct 1984), W Midlands Region The Lord's Taverners 1985- (chm 1987-); FCMA 1985, CBIM 1986, FRSA 1988; *Recreations* sport, reading; *Style—* Gary Allen, Esq; IMI plc, PO Box 216, Birmingham B6 7BA (☎ 021 356 4848, telex 336771 IMI KYN G)

ALLEN, Prof Sir Geoffrey; s of John James Allen and Marjorie Allen, of Wingerworth, Derbyshire; *b* 29 Oct 1928; *Educ* Clay Cross Tupton Hall GS, Leeds Univ (BSc, PhD); *m* 1973, Valerie Frances, da of Arthur Duckworth (d 1979); 1 da (Naomi); *Career* scientist; prof of chem physics Manchester Univ 1965-75, prof of chem technol Imperial Coll 1976-81, chm Sci Res Cncl 1977-81 (memb 1976), visiting fell Robinson Coll Cambridge 1980-, head res engrg Unilever 1981-; Hon MSc Manchester; FPRI, FRS 1976, FInstP; kt 1979; *Recreations* walking, talking, eating; *Style—* Professor Sir Geoffrey Allen

ALLEN, mp Graham William; MP (C) Nottingham N 1987-; s of William Allen, and Edna, *née* Holt; *b* 11 Jan 1953; *Educ* Robert Shaw Primary, Forest Fields GS; *Career* local govt sr offr, Nat co-ordinator TU Political Fund Campaign, TU Offr GMB; *Recreations* cricket, walking; *Clubs* Strelley Social, Dunkirk Cricket, Beechdale Community Assoc; *Style—* Graham W Allen, Esq, MP; House of Commons SW1A 0AA (☎ 071 219 4347)

ALLEN, Prof Harry Cranbrook; MC (1944); s of Christopher Albert Allen (d 1960), of London, and Margaret Enid, *née* Hebb (d 1965); *b* 23 March 1917; *Educ* Bedford Sch, Pembroke Coll Oxford (MA), Harvard (Cwlth Fund Fellowship); *m* 23 Aug 1947, Mary Kathleen, da of Frank Andrews (d 1951), of Oxford; 1 s (Franklin), 2 da (Julia, Georgiana); *Career* WWII Sandhurst (OCTU) 1939, The Hertfordshire Regt 1940-44, The Dorset Regt 1944-45, cmdt 43 Divn Educnl Coll 1945, Maj; history fell Lincoln Coll Oxford 1946-55, prof of American history Univ Coll London 1955-71, fndr dir Inst of US Studies Univ of London 1966-71, prof American studies Univ of E Anglia 1971-80; fndr ctee memb Br Assoc for American Studies 1955- (chm 1974-77); ctee memb: Euro Assoc for American Studies 1972-80 (pres 1976-80), Dartmouth RN Review Ctee

1958, RN Educn Advsy Ctee 1960-66, Academic Planning bd Univ of Essex 1962; FRHistS 1955-80; *Books* Great Britain and the United States (1955), British Essays in American History (ed 1957), Bush and Backwoods (1959), The Anglo-American Relationship Since 1783 (1960), The Anglo-American Predicament (1960), The United States of America (1964), Contrast and Connection (ed 1976); *Clubs* Athenaeum; *Style*— Prof H C Allen, MC; 1 Shepard Way, Chipping Norton, Oxfordshire OX7 5BE (☎ 0608 644381)

ALLEN, Prof Howard Godfrey; s of Thomas Charles Allen (d 1971), and Elsie, *née* Fell (d 1979); *b* 17 Oct 1931; *Educ* Haverfordwest GS, Univ of Liverpool (BEng, PhD); *m* 27 July 1957, Margaret, da of late William Edward Bourner, of Middlesbrough; 1 s (Martin b 1963), 1 da (Elizabeth b 1961); *Career* stressman AV Roe Manchester 1955-57, engr Sir William Halcrow and Ptnrs London 1958-60; Univ of Southampton: lectr Dept Civil Engrg 1960, sr lectr 1967, reader 1971, prof of structural engrg 1984-; FIStructE, MICE; *Books* Analysis and Design of Structural Sandwich Panels (1969), Background to Buckling (with P Bulson, 1980); *Recreations* walking, cycling, dinghy-sailing, folk dancing, reading; *Style*— Prof Howard Allen; Department of Civil Engineering, Southampton University, Southampton SO9 5NH (☎ 0703 592870, fax 0703 593017, telex 0703 47661)

ALLEN, Ingrid Victoria (Mrs Alan Barnes); DL (1989); da of Rev Dr Robert Allen (d 1968), of Millifant, Osborne Park, Belfast, and Doris Victoria, *née* Shaw; *b* 30 July 1932; *Educ* Ashleigh House Belfast, Cheltenham Ladies Coll, Queen's Univ Belfast (MB Bch, BAO Hons); *m* 30 may 1972, Alan Watson Barnes, s of Sidney W Barnes, of Old Tiles, Martin Cross, nr Fordingbridge, Salisbury; *Career* house offr Royal Victoria Hosp Belfast 1957-58; Queen's Univ Belfast: Musgrave res fell 1958-59, tutor in pathology 1959-61, Calvert res fell in multiple sclerosis 1961-64; sr registrar Pathology Dept Royal Victoria Hosp 1964-65; Queen's Univ Belfast and Royal Victoria Hosp: sr lectr and conslt in neuropathology 1966-78, reader and conslt in neuropathology 1978-79, prof of neuropathology and conslt and head NI Regnl Neuropathology Serv 1979-; memb: MRC, Multiple Sclerosis Soc, Univ Funding Cncl, BR Malaysian Soc; FRCPath 1975, FRCPI 1985, FRCPGlas 1989 (MRCPGlas 1985); *Books* Demyelinating Diseases in Greenfield's Neuropathology (contrib 4 edn, 1984), Pathology of Demyelinating Disease in McAlpines Multiple Sclerosis (2 edn, 1980); *Recreations* sailing, tennis, reading, Irish history, fashion, architecture; *Clubs* Royal Soc of Med, Royal Ulster Yacht; *Style*— Prof Ingrid Allen, DL; Regional Neuropathology Laboratory, Institute of Pathology, Queen's University of Belfast, Grosvenor Rd, Belfast BT12 6BA (☎ 0232 240503 ext 2019, fax 0232 438024, car 0836 361920)

ALLEN, Janet Rosemary; da of John Algernon Allen (d 1972), of Leicester, and Edna Mary, *née* Orton; *b* 11 April 1936; *Educ* Cheltenham Ladies' Coll, Univ Coll Leicester (BA), Hughes Hall Cambridge (CertEd); *Career* Howell's Sch Denbigh: schoolmistress 1959-75, head of History Dept 1961-75, head of Sixth Form 1965-75, housemistress 1968-75; headmistress Benenden Sch 1976-85; memb: Boarding Schs Assoc Ctee 1980-83, GSA Educnl Sub-C tee 1983-85; vice pres Women's Careers Fndn 1982-, sch govr St Catherine's Bramley Sch; *Recreations* music, drama, walking, swimming; *Clubs* Royal Overseas League; *Style*— Miss Janet Allen; 1 The Broadway, Alfriston, E Sussex BN26 5XL (☎ 0323 870619)

ALLEN, Prof John Anthony; s of George Leonard John Allen (d 1968), and Dorothy Mary, *née* Willoughby (d 1964); *b* 27 May 1926; *Educ* High Pavement Sch Nottingham, Univ of London (BSc, PhD, DSc); *m* 1, 1952 (m dis 1983), Marion Ferguson, da of John Crow (d 1960); 1 s (Hamish John Allen b 1955), 1 da (Elspeth Ferguson Allen b 1959); m 2, 1983, Margaret Porteous, da of James Aitken, of Motherwell; 1 adopted step s (Andrew Alexander Murdoch b 1972); *Career* Sherwood Foresters 1945-46, RAMC 1946-48; asst lectr Univ of Glasgow 1951-54, John Murray student Royal Soc 1952-54, lectr, sr lectr and reader in zoology and marine biology Univ of Newcastle upon Tyne 1954-76, prof of marine biology Univ of London 1976-91, dir Univ Marine Biology Station 1976-91; visiting prof: Univ of Washington 1968/70/71, Univ of W Indies 1976; post doctoral fell and guest investigator Woods Hole Oceanographic Inst 1965-; author numerous pubns and articles on deep sea organisms and shellfish, etc; memb: Natural Environment Res Cncl 1977-83 (chm Univ Affrs Ctee 1975-83), Nature Conservancy Cncl 1982-90 (chm Advsy Ctee on Sci 1984-90), Cncl Marine Biol Assoc UK 1981-83 and 1989-; pres Malacological Soc of London 1982-84; FRSE 1968, FIBiol 1969; *Recreations* travel, admiring gardens, pub lunching, squash; *Style*— Prof John Allen; Drialstone, Isle of Cumbrae, Scotland KA28 0EP (☎ 0475 530 260); Univ Marine & Biological Station, Millport, Isle of Cumbrae, Scotland KA28 0EG (☎ 0475 530 581)

ALLEN, John Derek; CBE (1987); s of William Henry Allen (d 1956), of Cardiff, and Lalla Dorothy, *née* Bowen (d 1987); *b* 6 Nov 1928; *Educ* Cardiff HS, Cardiff Coll of Tech (HND in Bldg); *m* 14 July 1951, Thelma Jean, da of John Henry Hooper (d 1971), of Cardiff; 1 s (Nicholas John b 1961); *Career* civil engr then chm and md John Morgan Group of Cardiff 1947-79, dep chm Land Authy for Wales 1976-, dep chm then chm Cwmbran Devpt Corp 1979-1988, chm Housing for Wales 1988-; treas Nat Fedn of Bldg Trade Employers 1980-83 (pres 1979); Freeman City of London 1980; FCIOB 1980, FBIM 1980, FRSA 1988; *Recreations* fly fishing and golf; *Clubs* Cardiff and County; *Style*— John Allen, Esq, CBE; 6 Egremont Rd, Penylan, Cardiff CF2 5LN (☎ 0222 499 461); Housing for Wales, 25-30 Lambourne Crescent, Llanishen, Cardiff CF4 5ZJ (☎ 0222 747 723)

ALLEN, Hon John Douglas; er s of Baron Croham, GBE (Life Peer), *qv*; *b* 1945; *Educ* BSc, MPhil; *m* 1969, Sheila, o da of Dr A J Ward, of Hemingford Grey, Cambs; 2 s, 1 da; *Style*— The Hon John Allen; 3 Victoria Ave, Sanderstead, Surrey

ALLEN, Very Rev John Edward; s of Rev Canon Ronald Edward Taylor Allen, MC (d 1984), and Isabel Edith, *née* Otter-Barry; *b* 9 June 1932; *Educ* Rugby, Univ Coll Oxford (MA), Fitzwilliam Coll Cambridge (MA), Westcott House Cambridge; *m* 1957, Eleanor, *née* Prynne; 1 s (Christopher), 3 da (Rebecca, Madeleine, Isabel); *Career* chaplain Univ of Bristol 1971-79, vicar Chippenham 1979-82, provost Wakefield West Yorks 1982-; *Recreations* walking, fishing, people; *Style*— The Very Rev John Allen; 1 Cathedral Close, Margaret St, Wakefield, W Yorks WF1 2DQ (☎ 0924 372402)

ALLEN, Maj-Gen John Geoffrey Robyn; CB (1976); s of R A Allen, of Leatherhead, Surrey, and Mrs R A Allen, *née* Youngman; *b* 19 Aug 1923; *Educ* Haileybury; *m* 1959, Ann Monica, da of Kenneth Morford, CBE; 1 s (Christopher b 1962), 1 da (Julia b 1965); *Career* cmmnd KRRC 1942, transfd RTR 1947, dir gen Fighting Vehicles and Engr Equipment MOD 1973-74, dir RAC 1974-76, Sr Army Directing Staff RCDS 1976-78, ret 1979; Col Cmdt RTR 1976-80 (Rep 1978-80); lay observer attached to Lord Chllr's Dept 1979-85; memb: Lord Chllr's Advsy Ctee on Legal Aid 1979-85, Booth Ctee on Matrimonial Procedure 1982-85; Hon Col Royal Yeo (TA) and Hon Col HQ (Westminster Dragons) Sqnd 1982-87; *Recreations* dinghy sailing, gardening; *Clubs* Army and Navy, Bosham Sailing; *Style*— Maj-Gen John Allen, CB; Meadowleys, Charlton, Chichester, West Sussex PO18 0HU (☎ 024363 638)

ALLEN, Prof John Piers; OBE (1979); s of Percy Allen, and Marjorie Isabel Agnes Nash; ggm on the paternal side was Fanny Stirling (1815-1895) whose life has been well documented by historians of the 19 Century theatre; *b* 30 March 1912; *Educ* Aldenham, St John's Coll Cambridge; *m* 1, 1937 (m dis 1944), Modwena Sedgwick; 2 s (Jemmy, Toby); m 2, 1945, Anne Preston (d 1968); 2 s (Simon, Benjamin), 2 da (Charlotte, Harriet); m 3, 1981, Margaret Wootton; *Career* various engagements in profession of theatre 1931-; memb Old Vic Co 1933-34 and 1934-35, drama organizer Left Book Club Theatre Guild 1937, staff of London Theatre Studio 1938; dir Handel's Belshazzar Scala Theatre 1938, Pageant of Music of the People Albert Hall 1939; admin and prodr Glyndebourne Children's Theatre 1945-51, close assoc with UNESCO over children's theatre and educnl drama 1950-60, visit to Aust as UNESCO specialist 1959 and 1961, script-writer and prodr BBC Sch Bdcasting Dept 1951-61, HM inspr of schs with nat responsibility for drama 1961-72, princ Central Sch of Speech and Drama 1972-78, visiting prof of drama Westfield Coll 1979-82; chm: Cncl for Dance Educn and Training 1980-, Conference of Drama Sch, Nat Cncl for Drama Trg various times during 1960s and 70s; vice chm Br Theatre Assoc, lectr City Univ, memb dance and drama panels of CNAA; *Books* Producing Plays for Children (1950), Going to the Theatre (1951), Great Moments in the Theatre (ed 1953), Masters of British Drama (1957), Masters of European Drama (1962), An Elizabethan Actor (1966), Three Medieval Plays (1953), Education Survey No2 - Drama (1968), Drama in Schools: theory and practice (1979), Theatre in Europe (a study of the European Theatre cmmnd by Cncl of Europe, 1981), A History of the Theatre in Europe (1983); *Style*— John Allen, Esq, OBE; The Old Orchard, Lastingham, York YO6 6TQ (☎ 075 15 334)

ALLEN, Judy Christina; da of John Turner Allen (d 1945), and Janet Marion, *née* Beall, of South London; *b* 8 July 1941; *Educ* Privately; *Career* formerly worked in publishing; author; adult fiction: December Flower (1982, televised 1985), Bag and Baggage (1988); junior fiction incl: Something Rare and Special (1985), Travelling Hopefully (1987), Awaiting Developments (1988, winner Children's Section Whitbread prize 1988, winner Friends of the Earth Earthworm Award 1989); author of four radio plays and various guide books and non-fiction for children and adults; winner: Christopher Award (US) for TV version of December Flower, four London Tourist Bd Awards for various London Guidebooks; memb Soc of Authors 1987; *Style*— Miss Judy Allen; c/o Laurence Fitch, Film Rights Ltd, 483 Southbank House, Black Prince Road, Albert Embankment, London SE1 7SJ (Dramatic Agent, ☎ 071 735 8171); c/o Pat White, Rogers Coleridge and White, 20 Powis Mews, London W11 1JN (☎ 071 221 3717)

ALLEN, Keith Howell Charles; s of Edward Allen, and Mary Elizabeth, *née* John; *b* 2 Sept 1953; *Educ* Sir Anthony Browns Brentwood Essex, Brune Park Comp Gosport Hants; *m* 21 July 1984, Alison Mary, da of Peter Benjamin Owen, of Portsmouth; 1 s (Alfie b 11 Sept 1986), 2 da (Sarah b 12 Dec 1979, Lily Rose b 2 May 1985); *Career* actor and writer; performances: Comrades, A Very British Coup, Walter, Scandal, Chicago Joe and The Showgirl, The Yob, The Bullshitters, Gino; writer: The Nightwatchman, Stuck on You Anita, The Yob, Jackson Pace - The Great Years, The Bullshitters, Whatever You Want; *Clubs* The Colony (Zanzibar), Legends; *Style*— Keith Allen, Esq

ALLEN, Kenneth Albert; CBE; s of Albert Allen, and Dorothy Allen; *b* 8 Dec 1927; *m* 22 March 1952, Doreen; 2 s (Keith b 5 July 1953, Lewis b 6 April 1955), 1 da (Kaye b 27 Jan 1962); *Career* Nat Serv RN 1946-48; apprentice compositor Rankin Brothers Ltd Bristol, apprentice compositor monotype operator 1948-50; HMSO: tech clerk 1950-58, tech offr 1959-65, higher tech offr 1965-68, sr exec offr 1968-69, sr works mangr 1970-72, gen mangr 1972-73, dir Tech Servs Div 1973-75, asst sec and dir Prodn Div, dir Middle Band and dir gen printing 1983, grade 4 dir gen printing and publishing 1983-87; non-exec dir The Monotype Corporation plc 1988-; tech conslt BFPMS 1988-, assoc conslt BPIF 1988-; Inst of Printing: chm Nat Tech Ctee 1982-84, vice chm Cncl 1983-87, vice pres 1988-; memb: Printing and Info Tech Divnl Ctee Printing Industs Res Assoc 1982-87, Printing Industs Econ Devpt Ctee 1983-87, Mgmnt Devpt Steering Ctee Br Printing Industs Fedn 1983-85, London Coll Printing Advsy Ctee 1984-87, Statute Law Secretariat 1985-87, Advsy Panel UK Nat Retraining Centre at Pira 1986-87, Statute Law Ctee 1986-87, Pira/BFPMS Chief Execs Gp 1986-87, Tech Advsy Panel HMSO 1989-; chm: Mgmnt Quality Assurance Ctee Printing EDC 1986-87, Printing Industs Quality Assur Cncl 1987-; life memb: Nat State Printers' Assoc (USA) 1987-, Int Govt Printers' Assoc 1987-; tstee Printing Equipment Educnl Tst 1987-; FBIM, FIOP, FIIM; *Recreations* theatre, people; *Clubs* Royal Cwlth Soc; *Style*— Kenneth Allen, Esq, CBE; Earlswood, 5 Yare Valley Drive, Cringleford, Norwich NR4 7SD (☎ 0603 503144, fax 0603 250695); The Monotype Corporation plc, Honeycrock Lane, Salfords, Redhill, Surrey RH1 5JP

ALLEN, Sir (William) Kenneth Gwynne; DL (Beds 1978); er s of Harold Gwynne Allen, JP (d 1960), of Bedford, and Hilda Margaret, *née* Langley (d 1969); bro of (Harold) Norman Gwynne Allen, *qv*; *b* 23 May 1907; *Educ* Westminster, Neuchâtel Univ of Switzerland; *m* 1931, Eleanor Mary (d 1990), o da of late Henry Eeles, of Newcastle-upon-Tyne; 1 s (Charles), 1 da (Caroline); *Career* chm: W H Allen Sons & Co 1955-70 (dir 1937-70, md 1946-70), Amalgamated Power Energy 1968-70; dir: Whessoe Ltd 1954-65, Electrolux 1970-78; chm: Br Internal Combustion Engine Mfrs Assoc 1955-57, BEAMA 1959-61; pres: Br Engrs Assoc 1957-59, Engrg Employers' Fedn 1962-64; Freeman City of London, Liveryman Worshipful Co of Shipwrights; High Sheriff Beds 1958-59; FIMarE, MRINA; kt 1961; *Style*— Sir Kenneth Allen, DL; Manor Close, Aspley Guise, Milton Keynes, Beds MK17 8HZ (☎ 0908 583161)

ALLEN, Leonard; s of Joseph Allen (d 1956), of 50 Fenton Rd, Southbourne, Bournemouth, and Henrietta Emily, *née* Fowle; *b* 30 Nov 1930; *m* 1, 1955 (m dis 1969), Diana, *née* Love; m 2, 27 April 1970, Theodora Jane, da of John Russell (d 1984), of 27 Derby Rd, Caversham, Reading; 1 da (Henrietta Sophie b 1972); *Career* Nat Serv RTR 1949-50; Cons Central Office: agent Reading 1959-64, political educn offr Eastern Area 1964-67 (dep area agent 1967-74), dep dir and head Local Govt dept Cons Central Office 1974-77; dir Fedn of Recruitment and Employment Servs 1977-, sec gen Int Confedn of Temp Work businesses 1990-, vice chm Southern Region UNs Assoc 1955-57, chm Recruitment Soc 1982-84, memb governing body SPCK 1977-80, vice chm Bow Gp 1959-64, memb DOE Advsy Ctee on Womans Employment; govr Battle Abbey Sch; Freeman: City of London 1978, Worshipful Co of Woolmen; *Recreations* conversation, music, reading, art galleries, dining (formally and informally); *Clubs* Athenaeum, Arts, City Livery, London Press, IOD; *Style*— Leonard Allen, Esq; 8 Carmel Ct, Highfield, Marlow, Bucks (☎ 06284 72325); 36-38 Mortimer St, London W1N 7RB (☎ 071 323 4300, car 0836 740 874)

ALLEN, Hon Lionel Paul; s of Baron Allen of Fallowfield, CBE (Life Peer; d 1985); *b* 1943; *m* 1981, Irene Lynwen, *née* Morris; *Style*— The Hon Lionel Allen; Raeburn Farm, Penton, Carlisle, Cumbria CA6 5RX

ALLEN, Louis; s of Louis Levy (d 1922), of Redcar and Middlesbrough, Yorks, and Anne, *née* Allen (d 1959); *b* 22 Dec 1922; *Educ* St Mary Coll Middlesbrough, Univ of Manchester (BA, MA), Univ of Paris; *m* 4 June 1950, Margaret Allen (d 1979), da of George Wilson (d 1941), of Sedgley Park, Prestwich; 4 s (Timothy, John Felix, Mark, Toby), 2 da (Louise b 1952, d 1967, Brigid); *Career* RA followed by Intelligence Corps to Capt 1942-46; serv: India, Burma, SE Asia as Japanese-speaking intelligence offr, despatches 1945, attached UK Mission to Leclerc Saigon 1946; Kemsley res fell Univ Manchester 1947, reader in French Univ of Durham 1983 (lectr 1948, sr lectr 1959); hon fell East Asia Centre Northumbrian Univs 1990-; radio and TV broadcaster: BBC Kaleidoscope, co chm Transatlantic Quiz, co chm Round Br Quiz, etc; memb Gen

Advsy Cncl BBC 1969-75, chm North East Regnl Advsy Cncl 1969-75, memb Cncl Univ of Durham 1962-67; memb: Br Assoc for Japanese Studies (pres 1980), Euro Assoc for Japanese Studies (memb Cncl 1988, hon life memb); life memb: Burma Star Assoc, Indian Army assoc; *Books* Japan. The Years of Triumph (1971), Sittang. The Last Battle (1983), John Henry Newman and the abbé Jager (1976), The End of the War in Asia (1976), Singapore 1941-1942, Burma. The Longest War (1984); *Recreations* military history; *Style*— Louis Allen, Esq; Dun Cow Cottage, North Bailey, Durham DH1 3ES (☎ 091 384 2096); University of Durham, Old Shire Hall, Elvet, Durham City (☎ 091 374 2000, fax 091 374 3740)

ALLEN, Mary; *b* 22 Aug 1951; *Educ* Sch of St Helen and St Katherine, New Hall Cambridge (BA); *Career* actress BBC West End and repertory 1973-76, agent London Management 1977-78, arts sponsorship mangr Mobil Oil Company Ltd 1978-81, asst dir Assoc for Business Sponsorship of The Arts 1982-83, training conslt 1986-, arts mgmnt conslt 1983-90, dir Watermans Arts Centre 1990-; Arts Cncl 1986-90: memb Art Panel, memb Ethnic Minority Arts Ctee, advsr to Percent for Art Steering Gp, chm Public Art Devpt Tst 1983-, memb Bd Cheek by Jowl 1989-, memb Devpt Bd Lambert Dance 1990-; lectr in arts mgmnt for: Br Cncl, City Univ, Leics Poly; *Books* Sponsoring The Arts: New Business Strategies for the 1990s; *Style*— Ms Mary Allen; Waterman's Arts Centre, 40 High St, Brentford, Middlesex TW8 0DS (☎ 081 847 5651)

ALLEN, Dr (Walter) Michael Critten; s of Walter Allen (d 1978), of Southport, and Contance, *née* Critten (d 1982); *b* 12 April 1928; *Educ* Manchester GS, Univ of Manchester, Manchester Med Sch (MB ChB, DMRD); *m* 14 Dec 1955, Dorothy Elizabeth, da of Herbert Norris Crowther (d 1980); 1 s (Patrick Allen b 16 Sept 1961), 1 da (Penelope (Mrs Minto) b 16 Oct 1958); *Career* RAMC Capt 1953-55, Maj TA AER 1955-83, conslt in radiology RARO; conslt radiologist NHS 1955-82, conslt surgn Jockey Club 1981- (hon conslt surgn 1977-81); chm PSM/18 Ctee of BSI (Riding Headwear and Body Protectors Ctee), tstee Stable Lads Welfare Tst; *Recreations* golf; *Clubs* R & A, Royal St George's Golf, Turf, Royal Lytham Golf; *Style*— Dr Michael Allen; 18 Dorin Court, Warlingham, Surrey CR3 9JT (☎ 0883 622055); Jockey Club, 42 Portman Square, London W1H 0EN (☎ 071 486 4921, fax 071 935 8703, telex 21393)

ALLEN, Michael John; s of Edward Thomas Allen, of Bedford, and Dorothy May, *née* Leigh; *b* 11 July 1941; *Educ* Bedford Sch, St Catharine's Coll Cambridge (MA); *m* 22 Oct 1977, Marjolein Christina, da of De Heer Hendrik Casper Wytzes, of Bloemendaal, Netherlands; 2 da (Elizabeth b 1981, Caroline b 1983); *Career* dir of extra mural studies Univ of Cambridge 1980-90, bursar Churchill Coll Cambridge 1990- (fell 1985-), chm of Govrs Comberton Villae Coll; *Recreations* natural history, gardening, squash; *Clubs* Royal Soc of Arts; *Style*— Michael Allen, Esq; Churchill College, Cambridge CB3 0DS (☎ 0223 336112)

ALLEN, Brig Norman Charles; CBE (1990, OBE 1980); s of Leslie Herbert Allen (d 1981), of Hayling Island, and Doris Kathleen, *née* Jones; *Educ* Rutlish Sch, Staff Coll (psc), Nat Defence Coll (ndc); *m* 7 Jan 1961, Lois Allen, da of Robert Keeling (d 1961), of Wimbledon; 2 s (Duncan b 1962, Gordon b 1964), 1 da (Bridget b 1966); *Career* cmmnd Royal Military Police 1957; regimental and staff appts: Britain, Far East, Germany, NI, Berlin, Intelligence Staff SHAPE; Brigadier, Provost Marshal (Army) 1986, ADC to HM the Queen (Col in Chief) 1988; memb: Nat Trust, RNLB, Action Aid, Consumer's Assoc, Wandsworth Deanery Synod; *Recreations* hillwalking, natural history, water colouring, reading, DIY; *Style*— Brig Norman Allen, CBE; Midland Bank, 172 Upper Richmond Rd, London SW15 2SH

ALLEN, Sir Peter Christopher; s of Sir Ernest King Allen, CBE (d 1937), and Florence Mary, *née* Gellathy; *b* 8 Sept 1905; *Educ* Harrow, Trinity Coll Oxford (BSc, MA); *m* 1, 1931, Violet Sylvester (d 1951), da of Sir Ernest Wingate-Saul; 2 da; m 2, 1952, Consuelo Maria Linares Rivas; *Career* chm ICI 1968-71 (joined 1928), pres Canadian Industry Ltd 1959-62, chm ICI of Canada 1959-68; dir: Bank of Montreal 1968-75, BICC 1971-81; chm Br Nat Export Cncl 1970-72, advsy dir New Perspective Fund of Los Angeles 1973-85; govr Harrow Sch; FBIM, FInstD; kt 1967; *Recreations* writing, golf, transport history; *Clubs* Carlton, Royal & Ancient (St Andrews), Augusta Nat; *Style*— Sir Peter Allen; Telham Hill House, nr Battle, E Sussex (☎ 042 46 3150)

ALLEN, Peter Dobson; CBE (1988), DL (1989); s of Frederick Allen (d 1957), of Dewsbury, and Ethel, *née* Dobson; *b* 4 Jan 1931; *Educ* Wheelwright GS Dewsbury, Univ of Birmingham (BSc); *m* 15 Sept 1956, Janet, da of Cyril Thurman (d 1983), of Dewsbury; 3 s (Timothy b 1958, Christopher b 1959, Nicholas b 1963); *Career* Lt RA 1957; BSC 1972-: dir Port Talbot Works 1972-76, md Welsh Div 1976-80, md ops Strip Products Gp 1980-; dir: Benzole Producers Ltd 1982-89, Benzene Mktg Co Ltd 1982-89, ASW Hldgs plc 1987-89, md Br Steel Strip Products 1989-90; High Sheriff Mid Glamorgan 1987-88; memb: Bd West Glamorgan Health Authy 1989-, Cncl and Jt Planning and Resources Ctee Univ of Wales 1989-; CEng, FIM; *Recreations* rugby football, cricket, the turf, music; *Style*— Peter D Allen, Esq, CBE, DL; Furzebrook, Merthyr Mawr Road, Bridgend, Mid Glam CF31 3NS (☎ 0656 655803)

ALLEN, Peter John; s of William George Allen (d 1974), and Florence Rose, *née* Betambeau; *b* 3 July 1949; *Educ* Wellington; *m* 23 June 1973, Jennifer, da of Cyril Robert Groves, of East Sussex; *Career* Kenneth Anderson and Co 1967-68, Centre File 1968-69, Rowe Swann and Co 1969-75, Sheppards and Chase Discretionary Fund Mgmnt 1975-77; Kleinwort Benson Investmt Mgmnt 1977-: asst dir 1985-87, dir 1987-; memb: Inst of Dirs, Int Stock Exchange; MBIM; *Recreations* riding, ballet, circus; *Clubs* RAF; *Style*— Peter Allen, Esq; Hestia, Woodland Way, Kingswood, Surrey KT20 6PA; 1 Churchill Villas, Churchill Rd, The Bourne, Brimscombe, Glos GL5 2UB; Kleinwort Benson Investmt Mgmnt Ltd, 10 Fenchurch St, London EC3M 3LB (☎ 071 623 8000, telex 9413545)

ALLEN, Peter William; s of Alfred William Allen (d 1987), of Sittingbourne, Kent, and Myra Nora, *née* Rogers (d 1982); *b* 22 July 1938; *Educ* Borden GS, Sidney Sussex Coll Cambridge (MA); *m* 1965, Patricia Mary, da of Joseph Frederick Dunk, of Sheffield; 3 da (Samantha, Joanna, Annabel); *Career* RAF 1957-59; joined Coopers & Lybrand 1963: qualified CA 1966, ptnr 1973, chm Int Personnel Ctee 1975-78, ptnr i/c London Off 1983, managing ptnr 1984-90, memb UK Mgmnt Ctee 1984-90, memb Int Exec Ctee 1988-90, dep chm Coopers & Lybrand Deloitte 1990- (memb Bd 1990-), chm Mgmnt Consulting Servs UK and Europe 1990-; Liveryman Worshipful Co of Glaziers and Painters of Glass; FICA 1969; *Recreations* golf; *Clubs* Reform; *Style*— Peter W Allen, Esq; John O'Gaddesden's House, Little Gaddesden, Berkhamsted, Herts HP4 1PF (☎ 044284 2710); Coopers & Lybrand Deloitte, Plumtree Ct, London EC4A 4HT (☎ 071 583 5000, fax 071 822 4652)

ALLEN, Hon Richard Anthony; yr s of Baron Croham, GCB (Life Peer), *qv*; *b* 1950; *Educ* Whitgift Sch Croydon, Southampton Univ (BSc); *m* 1, 1980 (m dis 1986), Karen, o da of F Hughes, of Whetstone, London; m 2, 1988, Gillian Patricia, o da of R Harraway, of Huddersfield; *Career* official Bank of England 1971-, seconded to Bank for Int Settlements Basle 1980-82; *Recreations* music, squash racquets, shooting; *Style*— The Hon Richard Allen; 11 Worcester Close, Shirley, Surrey

ALLEN, Richard Ian Gordon; s of Reginald Arthur Hill Allen, and Edith Alice, *née* Manger; *b* 13 Dec 1944; *Educ* Edinburgh Acad, Univ of Edinburgh (MA), Univ of York (BPhil); *m* 20 May 1988, Lynn Conroy; *Career* conslt UN Econ Cmmn for Euro 1970, res offr NIESR 1971-75, econ advsr Dept of Energy 1975-78, econ advsr HM Treasy 1978-81, sr econ advsr, later asst sec HM Treasy 1981-85, cnsllr econ Br Embassy Washington 1985-87, press sec to Chllr of the Exchequer 1987-88, under sec Int Fin HM Treasy 1988-90; dir European Investment Bank 1988-90, under sec Local Govt Fin HM Treasy 1990-; *Recreations* arts, golf; *Clubs* Royal Wimbledon Golf; *Style*— Richard Allen, Esq; 29 Cleveland Square, London W2 6DD (☎ 071 724 3893); HM Treasury, Parliament St, London SW1 (☎ 071 270 4748)

ALLEN, Richard Paul (Dick); s of Geoffrey B Allen, of Miltoncombe, Yelverton, Devon, and Frances Joan Allen; *b* 21 March 1944; *Educ* Ardingly; *m* July 1965 (m dis), Sally, da of late William Crockett, of East Horsley, Surrey; 1 s (David Giles b 22 Oct 1971), 1 da (Diane Elizabeth b 2 Feb 1969); *Career* Sussex Regt (cadets) 1957-61 (Capt 1960); Br Aerospace Weybridge 1961-62, film ed BBC 1973-; important works incl: Tribal Eye (with Sir David Attenborough), BC, The Bible Lands (with Magnus Magnusson); drama films (BBC) incl: Contact (dir Alan Clarke), Hôtel du Lac (dir Giles Foster, Br Acad Award for Editing 1987), The Most Dangerous Man in the World (dir Gavin Millar), Virtuoso (the story of John Ogden, dir Tony Smith), Portrait of a Marriage (Nigel Nicolson's account of Vita Sackville-West, dir Stephen Whittaker), Deadline (with John Hurt, dir Richard Stroud); other dramas incl: Shackleton (dir Martin Friend), Good as Gold (dir John Glennister), Inappropriate Behaviour (dir Paul Seed), Harry's Kingdom (dir Robert Young), David Copperfield, The Day of the Triffids, When the Boat comes in, Target, Shoestring, Badger Girl (dir photography A Dunn, dir S Paton); *Recreations* yachting, vintage cars, flying opera, wine, books; *Clubs* BBC, RAC; *Style*— Dick Allen, Esq; Gainsborough House, Kew, Surrey TW9 2EA; BBC Television Film Studios, Ealing Green, London W5 (☎ 081 567 6655 ext 807)

ALLEN, Richard Robert Edward; s of Robert Edward Allen (d 1976), of 10 College Precinct, Worcester, and Agnes Mary, *née* Clarke (d 1950); *b* 8 Feb 1933; *Educ* Coll House Sch Worcester, Worcester Sch of Art, Bath Acad of Art, Dept of Educn Univ of Bristol; *m* 13 April 1961, Evelyn Beatrice, da of Phillip Raymond Laurens; 2 da (Rebecca Emily Laurens b 16 June 1966, Alice Mary b 27 Oct 1971); *Career* artist and exhibition/art conslt; lectr in art in colls of art and univ art depts throughout UK, participation in numerous exhibitions, contrib public and private art collections, organiser numerious art photography and other exhibitions in UK, Germany and Belgium; currently dir: Festival France Jersey, Exart Ltd, Exhibition Art and Design Conslts; memb: working party for trg exhibition organisers Arts Cncl, Art Info Registry London, Industl Sponsors Ctee London, Barreau Art Fndn Jersey, Arts Advsy Panel Jersey Heritage Tst; Br Forces Korea Medal 1950-53, UN Serv Medal; FCSD, FRSA; *Recreations* fishing, travelling; *Style*— Richard Allen, Esq; Three Oaks House, Rue Milbrae, La Grande Route de St Laurent, Jersey, CI (☎ 0534 62667); The Studio, Three Oaks House, Rue Milbrae, La Grande Route de St Laurent, Jersey, CI (☎ 0534 73792)

ALLEN, Robert Geoffrey Bruère (Robin); s of Rev Canon Ronald Edward Taylor Allen (d 1984), of Ludlow, and Isabel Edith, *née* Otter-Barry; *b* 13 Feb 1951; *Educ* Rugby, Univ Coll Oxford (BA, PPE); *m* 3 Sept 1977, (Elizabeth) Gay, da of Dr Anthony James Moon, of Rickmansworth; 2 s (Christopher Francis (Kit) b 19 Feb 1983, Luke Anthony b 10 June 1986); *Career* co-organiser Free Representation Unit 1973; called to the Bar Middle Temple 1974; in practise 1976-, employment law advsr to Legal Action Gp 1978-80, legal advsr to local Gout Gp Inst of PR 1988-; contrib: Employment Law Manual (1988), Civil Liberty (1989); sec Lambeth Central Constituency Lab Party 1977; chm: London Youth Advsy Centre 1984-, Bd of Govrs Eleanor Palmer Sch 1988-; *Books* How to Prepare a Case for an Industrial Tribunal (1987); *Recreations* family life, fishing, fighting oppression; *Style*— Robin Allen, Esq; Cloisters, 1 Pump Court, Temple, London EC4Y 7AA (☎ 071 583 0303, fax 071 583 2254)

ALLEN, Dr Thomas Boaz; CBE (1989); s of Thomas Boaz Allen (d 1987), of Seaham, Co Durham, and Florence, *née* Hemmings; *b* 10 Sept 1944; *Educ* Robert Richardson GS Ryhope Co Durham, RCM London (ARCM); *m* 1, 30 March 1968 (m dis 1986), Margaret, da of George Holley (d 1980), of Seaham, Co Durham; 1 s (Stephen Boaz b 31 Jan 1970); m 2, 12 March 1988, Jeannie Gordon Lascelles, da of Norman Gordon Farquharson, of Southbroom, Natal, SA; *Career* singer; princ baritone: Welsh Nat Opera 1969-72, Royal Opera House Covent Garden 1972-77; guest appearances: Metropolitan Opera NY (debut) 1981, Bayerische Staatsoper München 1985, Wiener Staatsoper, Paris Opera, La Scala Milan (opened 1987/88 season as Don Giovanni), ENO, San Francisco Opera, Glyndebourne, Aldeburgh, Salzburg Festivals; memb The Arts for the Earth, bd memb London Int Opera Festival; Hon MA Newcastle 1984, Hon DMus Durham 1988, Hon RAM 1988; FRCM 1988; *Recreations* golf, drawing, ornithology; *Clubs* Effingham Golf; *Style*— Dr Thomas Allen, CBE; c/o John Coast, Manfield House, 376/9 Strand, London WC2 0LR (☎ 071 379 0022)

ALLEN, Timothy Peter Graystoke; s of Maj Desmond Graystoke Allen, MBE, TD (d 1968), and Kathleen Mable, *née* Gray; *b* 15 Sept 1953; *Educ* Cheltenham; *m* 22 July 1978, Sally Christine, da of Capt Charles Jeffrey Clarke Pettifer; 2 da (Victoria Claire Allen b 26 Oct 1980, Jessica Elizabeth Allen b 13 Nov 1986); *Career* trainee CA Messrs Porter Gee & Co, qualified 1977, formed T Allen & Co 1983, amalgamated with C B Heslop 1984 (ptnr 1984-); fndr memb Thatcham Round Table, memb and offr Round Table 25 (Thames Valley), memb Thatcham PCC; ACA 1977, FCA 1983; *Recreations* golf; *Clubs* W Berks Golf; *Style*— Timothy Allen, Esq; C B Heslop & Co, 1 High St, Thatcham, Berks (☎ 0635 68202, fax 0635 71703)

ALLEN, Prof Walter; s of Charles Henry Allen (d 1950), and Annie Maria Allen (d 1950); *b* 23 Feb 1911; *Educ* King Edward's GS Aston Birmingham, Univ of Birmingham; *m* 8 April 1944, Peggy Yorke, da of Guy Lionel Joy; 2 s (John b 1947, Robert b 1951), 2 da (Charlotte b 1949, Harriet b 1959); *Career* features ed Cater's News Agency Birmingham 1935-37, literary ed New Statesman 1960-61; visiting prof of English: Coe Coll Iowa USA 1955-56, Vasser Coll NY 1963-64, Univ of Kansas 1967; prof of English New Univ of Ulster 1967-73, Berg prof of English NY Univ 1970-71, visiting prof Dalhousie Univ Canada 1973-74, prof of English Virginia Poly Inst 1975-76; FRSL; *Books* Innocence is Drowned (1938), Blind Man's Ditch (1939), Dead Man Over All (1950), All in a Lifetime (1959), Get Out Early (1986), Accasting Profiles (1989); literary criticism: Arnold Bennett (1948), The English Novel (1954), Tradition and Dream (1964), The Short Story in English (1981); memoirs: As I Walked Down New Grub Street (1981); *Style*— Prof Walter Allen; 4B Alwyne Rd, London N1 2HH (☎ 071 226 7085)

ALLEN, Dr William Alexander; CBE (1980); s of Frank Allen (d 1965), of Winnipeg, Canada, and Sarah Estelle, *née* Harper (d 1915); *b* 29 June 1914; *Educ* Univ of Manitoba (BArch); *m* 10 Sept 1938, Beatrice Mary Theresa (Tessa), da of Clarence Henry Pearson (d 1930), of Cheriton Fitzpaine, Devon; 2 s (Christopher b 1942, Nicholas b 1944), 1 da (Deborah b 1948); *Career* chief architect Building Research Establishment 1953-61 (joined 1938), princ Architectural Assoc Sch of Architecture 1961-66, jt fndr ptnr Bickerdike Allen Ptnrs 1962-89; memb Cncl RIBA 1954-72 and 1982-89; pres: Inst of Acoustics 1975-76, Ecclesiastic Architects & Surveyors Assoc 1980-81; former vice chm Govrs Sir Frederic Osborn Sch; Hon LLD Univ of Manitoba 1977; FRIBA 1937; fndr memb: Acoustics Soc (later Inst) 1946, hon assoc memb NZ

Inst Arch 1965, memb Ecclesiastic Architects & Surveyors 1975, hon fell American Inst of Architects 1983; Ordem do Merito Portugal 1970; *publications incl:* Sound Transmission in Buildings (with R Fitzmaurice, 1940), Professionalism and Architecture (paper in Encyclopedia of Architecture, 1989), other papers on bldg tech sci and arch; *Recreations* walking, gardening, drawing, writing; *Clubs* Athenaeum; *Style*— Dr William Allen, CBE; 4 Ashley Close, Welwyn Garden City, Herts AL8 7LH (☎ 0707 324178); Bickerdike Allen Ptnrs, 121 Salusbury Rd, London NW6 6RG (☎ 071 625 4411, fax 071 625 0250, telex 263889)

ALLEN, Maj-Gen William Maurice; CB (1983); s of William James Allen, and Elizabeth Jane Henrietta Allen; *b* 29 May 1931; *m* 1956, Patricia Mary Fletcher; 1 da (decd); *Career* joined Army 1949, Dir-Gen Tport and Movements (Army) 1981-83, ret; dir of trg and educn Burroughs Machines Ltd 1983-85; dir European Management Information 1988-, conslt Mondial 1989-, dir Fortis Aviation Group 1990-; *Recreations* rough shooting, economics, gardening, ocean cruising, squash, keeping fit; *Clubs* Overseas, Bristol Channel Yacht; *Style*— Maj-Gen William Allen, CB; c/o Williams & Glyn's Bank Ltd, Holts Farnborough Branch, Lawrie House, 31-37 Victoria Rd, Farnborough, Hants

ALLEN-JONES, Charles Martin; s of Air Vice- Marshall John Ernest Allen-Jones, CBE, of Dunmow, Essex, and Margaret Ena, *née* Rix (d 1974); *b* 7 Aug 1939; *Educ* Clifton Coll Bristol; *m* 25 June 1966, Caroline, da of Keith Beale, OBE (d 1979), of Woodchurch, Kent; 1 s (Christof b 1968), 2 da (Nicola b 1970, Anna b 1972); *Career* articled to Clerk of the Justices Uxbridge Magistrates Ct 1958-60, articled to Vizard Oldham Crowder and Cash 1960-63, slr Supreme Ct 1963, memb City Taxation Ctee 1973-75, head of Corp Dept Linklaters and Paines 1985- (joined 1964, ptnr 1968-, Hong Kong Office 1976-81), memb Hong Kong Banking Advsy Ctee 1978-80; *Recreations* gardening, tennis, travel, reading; *Style*— Charles Allen-Jones, Esq; Barrington House, 59-67 Gresham St, London EC2V 7JA (☎ 071 606 7080, fax 071 606 5113, telex 884349)

ALLEN OF ABBEYDALE, Baron (Life Peer UK 1976); Philip; GCB (1970, KCB 1964, CB 1954); yr s of Arthur Allen (d 1962), of Sheffield, and Louie, *née* Tipper; *b* 8 July 1912; *Educ* King Edward VII Sch Sheffield, Queens' Coll Cambridge (MA); *m* 1938, Marjorie Brenda, da of Thomas John Colton Coe (d 1944); *Career* sits as Independent in House of Lords; second sec Treasy 1963-66, Parly under sec of state Home Office 1966-72; memb Security Cmmn 1973-, chm Gaming Bd for GB 1977-85; memb Tbnl of Inquiry into Crown Agents 1978-82; hon fell Queens' Coll Cambridge; *Style*— The Rt Hon the Lord Allen of Abbeydale, GCB; Holly Lodge, Englefield Green, Surrey TW20 0JP (☎ 0784 432291)

ALLENBY, Hon Mrs (Claude) Bill; Barbara Marion; da of late John Hall, of Felpham, Sussex; *b* 12 June 1917; *m* 1951, as his 2 w, the Hon Claude William Hynman Allenby (d 1975), Lt-Col 11 Hussars (R of O), elected to Cavalry Club Ctee, TV commentator, dir and prodr 1948-75, Guild of TV Prodrs and Dirs Merit Award for prodn of current events 1961; bro of 2 Viscount Allenby; *Career* serv WWII 4 MT WAAF; *Style*— The Hon Mrs C W H Allenby; 29 Hovedene, Cromwell Rd, Hove, Sussex

ALLENBY, 3 Viscount (UK 1919); Michael Jaffray Hynman Allenby; s of 2 Viscount Allenby (d 1984, s of Capt Frederick Allenby, CBE, JP, RN; n of 1 Viscount Allenby, GCB, GCMG, GCVO, and his 1 w (Gertrude) Mary Lethbridge, *née* Champneys (d 1988); *b* 20 April 1931; *Educ* Eton; *m* 29 July 1965, Sara Margaret, o da of Lt-Col Peter Milner Wiggin; 1 s; *Heir* s, Hon Henry Jaffray Hynman Allenby, b 29 July 1968; *Career* Lt-Col Royal Hussars; CO Royal Yeo 1974-77; *Clubs* Cavalry and Guards'; *Style*— The Rt Hon the Viscount Allenby of Meggido; The House of Lords, Westminster, London SW1

ALLENBY, Rt Rev (David Howard) Nicholas; s of William Allenby (d 1944), of London, and Irene Lambert, *née* Spratly (d 1962); *b* 28 Jan 1909; *Educ* House of Sacred Mission, Kelham Theol Coll (MA Lambeth); *Career* deacon 1934, curate St Jude W Derby Liverpool 1934-36, priest 1935, tutor Kelham Theological Coll and public preacher Diocese of Southwell 1936-44, rector Averham with Kelham 1944-57, proctor in convocation Southwell 1950-57, ed Diocesan News and Southwell Review 1950-55, hon canon Southwell 1953-57, personal chaplain to Bishop of Southwell 1954-57, canon emeritus 1957-62, rural dean Newark 1955-57, prov of Soc of Sacred Mission in Aust 1957-62, bishop of Kuching (Sarawak Malaysia) 1962-68, asst bishop Dio of Worcester 1968-; *Books* Pray with the Church (jtly, 1937); *Recreations* reading, painting; *Clubs* Cwlth House; *Style*— The Rt Rev Nicholas Allenby; 16 Woodbine Rd, Barbourne, Worcester WR1 3JB (☎ 0905 27980)

ALLENDALE, Viscountess; Hon Sarah Field; da of 1 Baron Ismay (d 1965); *b* 16 May 1928; *m* 1948, 3 Viscount Allendale; *Style*— The Rt Hon the Viscountess Allendale; Bywell Hall, Stocksfield-on-Tyne, Northumberland; Allenheads Hall, Allenheads, Northumberland

ALLENDALE, 3 Viscount (UK 1911); Wentworth Hubert Charles Beaumont; DL (Northumberland 1961); also Baron Allendale (UK 1906); s of 2 Viscount Allendale, KG, CB, CBE, MC (d 1956), and Violet (d 1979), da of Sir Charles Seely, 2 Bt; *b* 12 Sept 1922; *Educ* Eton; *m* 1948, Hon Sarah Ismay, da of Gen 1 Baron Ismay, KG, GCB, CH, DSO, PC; 3 s; *Heir* s, Hon Wentworth Beaumont; *Career* served WWII Fl-Lt RAFVR (POW); ADC to Viceroy of India 1946-47; Hon Air Cdre 3508 Northumberland; pres Northumberland & Durham Assoc Bldg Socs; OStJ; steward Jockey Club 1963-65; *Style*— The Rt Hon the Viscount Allendale, DL; Allenheads Hall, Allenheads, Hexham, Northumberland (☎ Allenheads 205); Bywell Hall, Stocksfield-on-Tyne, Northumberland

ALLERTON, 3 Baron (UK 1902); George William Lawies Jackson; s of 2 Baron (d 1925); *b* 23 July 1903; *Educ* Eton, RMC; *m* 1, 1926 (m dis 1934), Joyce (d 1953), da of John Hatfeild, of Thorp Arch Hall, Yorks; 1 s; m 2, 1934 (m dis 1947), Hope (d 1987), da of Allan Havelock-Allan, sis of Sir Anthony Allan, 4 Bt, the film producer; m 3, 1947, Anne (d 1989), da of James Montagu; 1 da (decd); *Career* Sqdn Ldr AAF (ret); late Lt Coldstream Gds; *Recreations* golf, shooting; *Clubs* Turf, Pratt's, White's; *Style*— The Rt Hon Lord Allerton; Loddington House, Leics

ALLERTON, Air Vice-Marshal Richard Christopher; CB (1988); er s of Air Cdre Ord Denny Allerton, CB, CBE (d 1977), and Kathleen Mary, *née* Tucker; *b* 7 Dec 1935; *Educ* Stone House Broadstairs, Stowe; *m* 14 March 1964, Marie Isobel Campbell, er da of Capt Sir Roderick Edward François McQuhae Mackenzie (11 Bt, cr 1703), CBE, DSC, RN (d 1986); 2 s (James Roderick Ord b 1967, Christopher Edward Ord b 1970); *Career* Mil Serv RAF, cmmnd 1954; served 1955-78: RAF Hullavington, Oakington, Feltwell, Kinloss, HQ Coastal Cmd, RAF MB SAFI (Malta), HQ Maintenance Cmd, No 3 Sch TT Hereford, RAF Central Flying Sch Little Rissington, RAF Coll Cranwell, student RAF Staff Coll Bracknell, staff HQ RAF Germany, chief instructor S&S WG RAF Coll Cranwell, student Nat Def Coll Latimer, MOD Harrogate; dep dir RAF supply policy MOD 1978-80, station cdr RAF Stafford 1980-82, ADC to HM The Queen 1980-82, student RCDS 1983, air cdre supply and movements HQ Strike Cmd 1983-86, dir gen of supply RAF 1987-90, ret; *Recreations* shooting, fishing, cricket (pres RAF Cricket Assoc 1987-89); *Clubs* RAF; *Style*— Air Vice-Marshal Richard Allerton, CB; c/o Lloyds Bank, 13 Broad St, Launceston, Cornwall PL15 8AG

ALLERY, Stephen Julian; s of George David Allery, of The Close, Salisbury Cathedral, Salisbury, and Phyllis Joyce, *née* Gibson; *b* 7 July 1948; *Educ* City of London Freeman's Sch, Surrey Poly (HND); *m* 1, 1966 (m dis), Susan Eileen, *née* Burnand; 2 s (Dorian Burnand b 1967, Tristan Brett b 1974), 1 da (Tamsin Rachel b 1976); m 2, 1984, Linda Marie, *née* Daniels; 1 s (Daniel Lawrence b 1985); *Career* trainee surveyor and contracts mangr R Manell and Sons 1966-68; contracts mangr and surveyor: J Jarvis and Sons Ltd 1968-71, Clearbrook Property Holdings 1971-74; contracts mangr then area mangr R Durtnell and Sons Ltd 1974-77; Michael Aukett Associates: project mangr 1977-82, ptnr Clover International (project mgmnt co of Michael Aukett Associates) 1982-87, project and construction mgmnt dir Aukett Limited (subsid of Aukett Associates plc) 1987-; MCIM 1970; *Recreations* squash; *Clubs* Wellington Coll Sports, Metropolitan; *Style*— Stephen Allery, Esq; Aukett Limited, 13 Chelsea Embankment, London SW3 4LA (☎ 071 352 0142, fax 071 351 9245, car 0836 374271)

ALLETZHAUSER, Albert Joseph; s of Albert Joseph Alletzhauser, of Madison, Connecticut, and Sydney Louise, *née* Best; *b* 5 Jan 1960; *Educ* Colgate Univ (BA); *m* 8 Aug 1988, Anne, da of Louis Wellington Cabot; *Career* head Int Dept Chintung Investmt Hong Kong 1984-85, sr exec James Capel & Co Tokyo 1986-88; currently princ: Bloomsbury Publishing, Clark Prodn, City Limits Magazine; pres Tiedemann Securities 1989-, chm The Emerging Markets Co 1990-; FRGS; *Books* The House of Nomura (1990); *Style*— Albert Alletzhauser, Esq; 52 Arundel Gardens, London W11 2LB

ALLEYNE, Rev Sir John Olpherts Campbell; 5 Bt (GB 1769), of Four Hills, Barbados; s of Capt Sir John Alleyne, 4 Bt, DSO, DSC, RN (d 1983), and Alice Violet Emily, *née* Campbell (d 1984); *b* 18 Jan 1928; *Educ* Eton, Jesus Coll Cambridge (BA, MA); *m* 28 Sept 1968, Honor Emily Margaret, da of late William Albert Irwin, of Linkview Park, Upper Malone, Belfast; 1 s, 1 da (Clare Emma Gila b 1969); *Heir* s, Richard Meynell Alleyne b 23 June 1972; *Career* deacon 1955, priest 1956; rector of St Matthews Winchester; *Recreations* sailing, mountain walking, astronomy; *Style*— The Rev Sir John Alleyne, Bt; The Rectory, Cheriton Rd, Winchester, Hants (☎ 0962 54849)

ALLFREY, Hon Mrs (Jocelyne); *née* FitzRoy; yr da of Cdr the Hon John Maurice FitzRoy Newdegate, RN (d 1976), and sis of 3 Viscount Daventry, *qv*; raised to the rank of a Viscount's da 1988; *b* 13 July 1929; *m* 1, 26 July 1952 (annulled 1953), Richard John Barton, o s of Col John Seddon Barton, OBE, MC, TD, DL, of Glan-y-Wern Hall, Denbigh; m 2, 18 May 1957 (m dis 1980), Maj Henry John Allfrey, RA (ret), er s of Maj Henry Sydney Allfrey, JP, DL, of Bishop's Acre, Upton Bishop, Ross- on-Wye, Herefordshire; 2 s, 1 da; *Style*— The Hon Mrs Allfrey

ALLFREY, Maj (Henry) John; OBE (1990); s of Maj Henry Sydney Allfrey, JP, DL (d 1975), of The Grange, How Caple, Hereford, and Vera, *née* Hazlehurst (d 1965); *b* 30 Dec 1924; *Educ* Winchester; *m* 1, 18 May 1957 (m dis 1980), Jocelyne, da of Cdr The Hon Maurice FitzRoy-Newdegate (d 1976), of Arbury Hall, Nuneaton, Warwicks; 2 s (David, Charles), 1 da (Lucia); m 2, 18 Oct 1980, Sonia Elisabeth, da of Col Juan Beresford Hobbs (d 1978), of Easthorpe Hall, Kelvedon, Colchester, Essex; *Career* cmmnd RHA 1944, WWII 1945-46 India Malaya and Java, Staff Capt SE Asia Land Forces HQ 1946-48; regtl serv: airborne RHA, Jr Ldrs Regt and Berks Yeo 1948-59, staff coll 1956, GSO II HQ 4 Infantry Div 1957-59, GSO II Brig Author MOD 1959-61; dir: Harp Lager (Southern) 1965-70, Courage (Central) 1967-69, Cou.age (Eastern) 1969-70, Courage (Brewing) 1973-80; md Courage (Central) 1971-79; dir Research into Ageing (registered charity) 1980-89, vice chm and chm Wokingham Cons Assoc 1966-72, govr Elstree Sch 1975-88, fndr and patron Berks Retirement Assoc 1976-89; memb Exec Cncl: Assoc of Med Res Charities, Br Soc for Res into Ageing; FInstD, MInstMktg, memb Inst Fund Raising Mangrs; *Books* from 1959-61: The Nuclear Land Battle, Keeping The Peace, Training For War; *Recreations* fishing, shooting, gardening; *Clubs* Boodle's; *Style*— Maj John Allfrey, OBE; The Dower House, Castle Hedingham, nr Halstead, Essex CO9 3DG (☎ 0787 61108); 25B Wilton Row, London SW1X 7NS

ALLGOOD, Joseph William Edwin; s of Joseph Philip Allgood (d 1938), and Blanche, *née* Strutt (d 1966); *b* 6 Jan 1922; *Educ* Spring Grove GS; *m* 24 Sept 1949, Ann Elizabeth, da of Richard Halsey (d 1955), of Richmond, Surrey; 1 da (Suzanne b 1964), 1 step s (Geoffrey b 1945); *Career* WWII RA 1943-47; served in: N Africa, Italy, Greece, Trieste, Germany (despatches); jeweller; joined Cartier 1938, md Cartier Ltd 1986- (vice chm UK 1983-86); first holder Royal Warrant for HM Queen Elizabeth the Queen Mother (former holder for HM The Queen) on behalf of Cartier for last 12 years; chm Bond St Assoc 1981-83; FGA; *Recreations* golf; *Clubs* Royal OverSeas League, Royal IOD; *Style*— Joseph W E Allgood, Esq; Cartier Ltd, 175-176 New Bond Street, London W1Y 0QA (☎ 071 493 6962)

ALLHUSEN, Hon Mrs (Claudia Violet); *née* Betterton; da of 1 Baron Rushcliffe, GBE, PC (d 1949) by his 1 w; *b* 11 Oct 1917; *m* 1937, Maj Derek Allhusen, CVO, DL, *qv*, s of Lt-Col Frederick Allhusen, CMG, DSO (d 1957); 1 s (Timothy Frederick m 1965 Annabel Morris) and 1 s decd, 1 da (Rosemary Claudia m 1973 Maj Jeremy Groves, 17/21 Lancers); *Recreations* riding; *Clubs* Army and Navy, Cavalry and Guards'; *Style*— The Hon Mrs Allhusen; The Manor House, Claxton, Norwich (☎ 050843 228)

ALLHUSEN, Maj Derek Swithin; CVO (1984), DL (Norfolk 1969); s of Lt-Col Fredrick Allhusen, CMG, DSO (d 1957), of Fulmer House, Fulmer, Bucks, and Enid, *née* Swithinbank (d 1948); *b* 9 Jan 1914; *Educ* Eton, Chillon Coll Switzerland, Trinity Coll Cambridge (MA); *m* 28 April 1937, Hon Claudia Violet, da of 1 and last Baron Rushcliffe, GBE, PC (d 1949); 1 s (Timothy b 1942), 1 da (Mrs Rosemary Groves b 1944) and 1 s decd (Michael d 1960); *Career* served WWII 9 Queen's Royal Lancers France 1940 (wounded), N Africa and Italy (wounded); farmer; high sheriff Norfolk 1958, Standard Bearer Hon Corps of Gentlemen-at-Arms 1981-84 (one of HM's Body Guards of Hon Corps of Gentlemen at Arms 1963-84; chm Riding for the Disabled Norwich and Dist Gp 1968- (vice pres Eastern Region); pres: Royal Norfolk Agric Assoc 1974, National Pony Soc 1982, British Horse Soc 1986-; Freeman City of London, Hon Freeman Worshipful Co of Farriers 1969, Yeoman Worshipful Co of Saddlers; represented Great Britain: Winter Pentathlon Olympic Games 1948, equestrian team Mexico Olympics 1968 (individual Silver, team Gold), Br Olympic Equestrian Team Munich 1972, Equestrianism European Championships Three-Day Event 1957, 1959, 1965, 1967, 1969; Silver Star Medal (USA); *Recreations* riding, shooting, skiing; *Clubs* Cavalry and Guards', Army and Navy; *Style*— Maj Derek Allhusen, CVO, DL; Manor House, Claxton, Norwich, Norfolk (☎ 050843 228)

ALLHUSEN, Lt-Col Richard Christian; s of Lt-Col F H Allhusen, CMG, DSO (d 1957), of Bucks, and Enid, *née* Swithinbank (d 1948); *b* 16 March 1910; *Educ* Eton, Trinity Coll Cambridge; *m* 25 June 1950, Evelyn Jane, da of Lt-Col Sir Richard Chenevix Trench, CIE, OBE (d 1954); 2 s (Christian Henry b 1956, Richard Frederick b 1960), 2 da (Elizabeth Mary b 1952, Rosalind Jane b 1954); *Career* served WWII, adj Lovat Scouts, gen staff offr 2 Scottish Cmd Staff Coll Camberley, Lt-Col Cmdg 21 Army Gp; landowner, farmer; *Recreations* skiing, shooting, arboriculture; *Clubs* Buck's, Army & Navy, MCC; *Style*— Lt-Col Richard C Allhusen; Bradenham Hall, Thetford, Norfolk IP25 7QP (☎ 036 287 279)

ALLINGTON, Edward Thomas; s of Ralph Allington, of Troutbeck Bridge, Cumbria, and Evelyn Hewartson (d 1988); *b* 24 June 1951; *Educ* Lancaster Sch of Art, Central Sch of Art (DipAD), RCA (Herbert Read meml prize); *m* 1974 (sep 1981), Susan Jean Bradley (d 1984); partner 1983, Julia Wood; 1 da (Thalia Evelyn Allington-Wood b 1988); *Career* sculptor; solo exhibitions incl: 1B Kensington Church Walk London 1977, Spacex Gallery Exeter 1981, Exe Gallery Exeter 1982, Spectro Gallery Newcastle upon Tyne 1983, ICA London 1983-84, Lisson Gallery London 1984, Midland Gp Arts Centre Nottingham 1984, Gallery Schmela Dusseldorf 1984, Riverside Studios London 1985, Lisson Gallery London 1985, Northern Centre for Contemporary Art Sunderland 1985-86, Abbot Hall Art Gallery Kendal 1986, Diane Brown Gallery NY 1986, Galerie 565 Aalst Belgium 1986, Galerie Adrien Maeght Paris 1986, Galerie Montenay-Delsol Paris 1986, Marlene Eleini Gallery London 1987, Diane Brown Gallery NY 1987, FUJI TV Gallery Tokyo 1988, Gallery Face Tokyo 1988, Lisson Gallery London 1989, Galerie Faust Geneva 1989; gp exhibitions incl: Summer Show (Serpentine Gallery London) 1976, Objects and Sculpture (Arnolfini Gallery Bristol) 1981, London/NY 1982 (Lisson Gallery London) 1982, Teme Celeste (Museo Civico D'Arte Contemporanea Gibellina Sicily) 1983, Beelden/sculpture 1983 (Rotterdam Arts Cncl) 1983, The Sculpture Show (Hayward and Serpentine Galleries London) 1983, Metaphor and/or Symbol (Nat Museum of Modern Art Tokyo and Nat Museum of Osaka) 1984-85, Space Invaders (Mackenzie Art Gallery Regina and tour Canada) 1985, Time after Time (Diane Brown Gallery NY) 1986, Britain in Vienna 1986, British Art (Kunstlerhaus Vienna) 1986, 3eme Ateliers Internationaux (FRAC Pays de la Loire) 1986, Prospect 86 (Kunstverein Frankfurt) 1986, Vessel (Serpentine Gallery London) 1987, Inside/Outside (Museum van Hedendaagse Kunst Antwerp) 1987, Die Grosse Oper (Bonner Kunstverein Bonn and tour) 1987-88, Britannia 30 Ans de Sculpture (Musée des Beaux Arts Brussels) 1988, British Now Sculpture et Autre Dessins (Musée D'Art Contemporain de Montreal) 1988-89, 2000 Jahre Die Geganwart der Vergangenheit (Bonner Kunstverein Bonn) 1989; most important works incl: His Favourite Was David Smith But She Preferred Dame Barbara Hepworth 1975, Ideal Standard Forms 1980, The Fruit of Oblivion 1982, We Are Time 1985, Building With Missing Columns 1986, Seated in Darkness 1987, Victory Boxed 1987, Light Temple (PAS Heizcraftwerk Saarbrucken) 1989, Inverted Architrave 1990, set for prodn of Apollon La Nuit 1990; *awards* prizewinner John Moore's 16 Liverpool Exhibition 1989, Gregory fell in Sculpture Univ of Leeds; *Style*— Edward Allington, Esq; Lisson Gallery, 67 Lisson St, London NW1 5DA (☎ 071 724 2739, fax 071 724 7124)

ALLINSON, Brian; s of George Raymond Allinson (d 1952), and Ivy Anne, *née* Hardie; *b* 2 Nov 1927; *m* 29 Sept 1956, Mary, da of Stanley Williams (d 1958); 1 s (Derek), 2 da (Claire, Joanne); *Career* RAF physical fitness offr 1945-49; recreation offr City of Cambridge 1963-84, exec sec Br World Games Assoc 1985, dep gen sec Br Olympic Assoc 1985-88, gen sec Cwlth Games Cncl for England 1988-, organisation and mgmnt of Br and English representative sports teams in int events since 1970 incl Olympic, Cwlth and World Games and student games; life fell Inst of Recreation Mgmnt 1954; *Recreations* golf; *Style*— Brian Allinson, Esq; 1 Wandsworth Plain, London SW18 1EH (☎ 081 871 2677, fax 081 871 9104, telex 932 312 BOA G)

ALLINSON, Sir (Walter) Leonard; KCVO (1979, MVO 1961), CMG (1976); s of Walter Allinson (d 1965), and Alice Frances, *née* Cassidy; *b* 1 May 1926; *Educ* Friern Barnet GS, Merton Coll Oxford (MA), RCDS; *m* 1951, Margaret Patricia, *née* Watts; 3 da (incl twins); *Career* dep high cmmr Kenya 1972-73, RCDS 1974, dep high cmmr and min New Delhi 1975-78, high cmmr Lusaka 1978-80, asst under sec (Africa) FCO 1980-82, Br high cmmr Kenya 1982-86 (ret); vice pres Royal African Soc 1982-, memb Cncl Br Inst for E Africa 1988-, hon vice chm Kenya Soc 1990-; *Recreations* reading, collecting driftwood, rough gardening; *Clubs* Oriental; *Style*— Sir Leonard Allinson, KCVO, CMG; c/o National Westminster Bank, 6 Tothill St, London SW1H 9ND

ALLIOTT, George Beckles; s of Hon Sir John Downes Alliott (*qv*), and Patsy Jennifer, *née* Beckles-Willson; *b* 10 Dec 1958; *Educ* Charterhouse, Univ of Warwick (LLB); *m* 4 Feb 1989, Catherine Margaret, da of Anthony Coles; 1 s (b 5 Jan 1991); *Career* Lt Coldstream Gds 1982-85; called to the Bar Inner Temple 1981, practising barrister 1985-; *Recreations* hunting, shooting, apiculture; *Style*— George Alliott, Esq; 2 Harcourt Bldgs, Temple, London EC4 (☎ 071 583 9020, fax 071 583 2686, telex 8956 788)

ALLIOTT, Hon Mr Justice; Hon Sir John Downes Alliott; s of Alexander Clifford Alliott (d 1967), and Ena Kathleen, *née* Downes (now Ellson); *b* 9 Jan 1932; *Educ* Charterhouse, Peterhouse Cambridge (scholar, BA); *m* 1957, Patsy Jennifer, da of late Gordon Beckles-Willson; 2 s (George b 1958, Julian b 1968), 1 da (Katharine b 1967); *Career* cmmnd Coldstream Gds 1950-51; called to the Bar Inner Temple 1955, dep chm E Sussex QS 1970-71, rec of Crown Ct 1972-86, QC 1973, bencher Inner Temple 1980, ldr South Eastern Circuit 1983-86, judge of the High Ct of Justice Queen's Bench Division 1986, presiding judge South Eastern Circuit 1989-; memb Home Office Advsy Bd on Restricted Patients 1983-86; *Recreations* rural pursuits, France, Italy, mil history; *Style*— The Hon Mr Justice Alliott; Royal Courts of Justice, Strand, London WC1

ALLISON, (Samuel) Austin; s of Dr Samuel Allison, of Stedham, W Sussex, and Helen Burns Brighton, *née* Wilson; *b* 30 June 1947; *Educ* Liverpool Coll, Wadham Coll Oxford (BA, BCL); *m* 5 June 1971, June, da of late Henry Edward Brassington, of Crofton, Kent; 2 s (Giles b 1973, Jonathan b 1975); *Career* called to the Bar Middle Temple 1969; private practice at the Bar 1970-87, gp compliance offr Standard Chartered Bank 1987-; memb: Ctee of London and Scottish Bankers (Legal Ctee, Investmt Regulation Ctee), Panel of Arbitrators The Securities Assocs, Commercial Ct Ctee, Bar Assoc of Commerce Fin and Indust Ctee; *Recreations* The Turf; *Style*— Austin Allison, Esq; 47 Elmfield Ave, Teddington, Middx TW11 8BX; 1 Aldermanbury Square, London EC2V 75D (☎ 071 280 7165)

ALLISON, Prof David John; s of Denis Allison (d 1982), of Leeds, and Eileen, *née* O'Connell (d 1986); *b* 21 March 1941; *Educ* Prince Rupert Sch Germany, Wimbledon Coll, KCH London (BSc, MB BS, MD, DMRD, MRCS, MRCP, FFR, FRCR); *m* 16 April 1966, Deirdre Mary, da of Patrick Flynn (d 1975), of New Malden, Surrey; 1 s (Richard b 1970), 2 da (Catherine b 1967, Helen b 1969); *Career* conslt and sr lectr Royal Post Grad Med Sch Univ of London 1975-83, dir of radiology Hammersmith Hosp and Royal Post Grad Med School Univ of London 1983-, author of several publications on cardiovascular and interventional radiology and physiology; memb Fleischner Soc 1979-; memb Cncl: Br Inst Radiology 1985-88, RCR 1987-; Cardiovascular and Interventional Soc of Europe: memb Exec Ctee 1986-, pres 1990-; memb: RCR 1973, Br Inst Radiology 1973, BSG 1978, CIRSE 1980; *Books* Diagnostic Radiology: An Anglo-American Textbook of Imaging Volumes 1, 2 and 3 (with R G Grainger, 1985, 2 edn 1991); *Recreations* gardening, food and wine (at others' expense); *Style*— Prof David Allison; Department of Diagnostic Radiology, Royal Postgraduate Medical School, Hammersmith Hospital, Du Cane Rd, London W12 0HS (☎ 071 740 3123, fax 071 743 5409)

ALLISON, Air Vice-Marshal Dennis; CB (1987); s of George Richardson Allison (d 1951), and Joan Anne Sarah, *née* Little (d 1949); *b* 15 Oct 1932; *Educ* RAF Halton, RAF Coll Cranwell; *m* 16 June 1964, Rachel Anne, da of Air Vice-Marshal John Gerald Franks, CB, CBE, of Schull, Co Cork, Ireland; 1 s (Peter b 1970), 4 da (Jennifer b 1965, Susan b 1965, Rosemary b 1967, Rachel b 1970); *Career* No 87 Sqdn RAF 1955-58, flying instr and Coll Adj Cranwell 1959-61, Sqdn Ldr 1961, OC RAF Sharjah 1961-62, OC Standards Sqdn RAF Strubby 1962-64, Indian Def Servs Staff Coll 1964-65; Wing Cdr 1965, staff HQ 224 Gp Singapore 1965-68, MOD Central Staffs 1968-70; OC Flying Wing RAF Bruggen 1970-72, Nat Def Coll 1972-73, MOD Central Staffs 1973-74, Gp Capt 1974, OC RAF Coningsby 1974-76, Canadian Nat Def Coll 1976-77, MOD Central Staffs 1977-79, Air Cdre 1979, cmdt Central Flying Sch 1979-83, dir flying trg MOD 1983-85, Air Vice-Marshal 1985, dir of Mgmnt and Support of Intelligence 1985-86; chief exec N Western RHA 1990- (regnl gen manger 1978-90); govr Salford Coll of Technol; memb: NHS Trg Authy, Standing Ctee on Post-Grad Educn; Queen's Commendation for Valuable Servs in the Air 1959; *Recreations* golf, bridge, keeping geese; *Clubs* RAF; *Style*— Air Vice-Marshal Dennis Allison, CB; The Old Forge, Castle Bytham, Grantham, Lincs NG33 4RV (☎ 078 081 372); Gateway House, Piccadilly South, Manchester M60 7LP (☎ 061 237 6324)

ALLISON, John; CBE (1975), JP (1966), DL (1975); s of Thomas William Allison (d 1974), and Margaret, *née* Grey (d 1978); *b* 4 Oct 1919; *Educ* Glanmor Secdy Sch, Swansea Tech Coll; *m* 12 April 1948, Elvira Gwendoline, da of William Evan Lewis (d 1945); 1 s (Richard Thomas William b 12 Aug 1956), 2 da (Susan Margaret b 12 May 1949, Jillian b 15 May 1955); *Career* dir: Picton Music Ltd 1969-, Swansea Sound 1974-, Municipal and Mutual Insur Ltd 1982-, Swansea Cork Ferry Co Ltd; memb Swansea Co Borough Cncl 1957-73, ldr City Authy 1967-73, dep Mayor 1966-67 and 1972-73; memb W Glamorgan Co Cncl 1973- (chm 1975-76, ldr 1979-), Assoc of Co Cncls 1973- (chm 1986-88); chm S Wales Police Authy 1987-89; Parly candidate (Lab) Barry 1970; *Recreations* gardening, fishing, golf; *Clubs* The Royal OverSeas League, Morriston Golf; *Style*— John Allison, Esq, CBE, JP, DL; 155 Vicarage Rd, Morriston, Swansea SA6 6DT (☎ 0792 71331)

ALLISON, Ronald William Paul; CVO (1978); s of Percy Allison, and Dorothy, *née* Doyle; *b* 26 Jan 1932; *Educ* Weymouth GS, Taunton's Sch Southampton; *m* 1956, Maureen Angela Macdonald; 2 da; *Career* reporter and corr BBC 1957-73, press sec to HM The Queen 1973-78, md Ronald Allison & Assocs 1978-80; Thames TV: presenter 1978-, controller of sport and outside bdcasts 1980-85, dir corp affrs 1986-89; conslt freelance writer and broadcaster 1989-; chm TV Barter International 1990-; *Books* Look Back in Wonder (1968), The Queen (1973), Charles, Prince of our Time (1978), Britain in the Seventies (1980); *Clubs* RAC; *Style*— Ronald Allison, Esq, CVO; c/o Thames TV, 306 Euston Rd, London NW1 3BB

ALLISON, Shaun Michael; s of Lt Cdr Jorgen Leslie William Michael Allison, (d 1983) of White Cottage, Beenham, Berks; and Honoria Brenda, *née* Magill; *b* 12 Jan 1944; *Educ* Rugby Sch; *m* 14 Sept 1968, Lucy Howard Douglas, da of Lt-Col Charles Robert Douglas Gray, of Chilcombe, Greywell, Basingstoke, Hants; 2 s (Michael Douglas b 1971, Charles Howard b 1977), 1 da (Sophie Louise b 1976); *Career* stockbroker 1967; ptnr Hoare Govett Ltd 1978-85, dir Hoare Govett Securities Ltd 1986-; *Recreations* skiing, shooting, sailing; *Clubs* City of London; *Style*— Shaun M Allison, Esq; Three Oaks, Bramshill, Basingstoke, Hants (☎ 0734 326 270); Hoare Govett Ltd, 4 Broadgate, London EC2 (☎ 071 601 0101)

ALLISON, Dr Simon Philip; s of late Prof Philip Rowland Allison, of Oxford, and Kathleen Allison; *b* 24 Jan 1938; *Educ* Winchester, Trinity Coll Cambridge, Univ of Birmingham (BA, MB ChB, MD); *m* 31 May 1969, Ann Muriel, da of John Percival Bridgens, of Little Aston, Birmingham; 2 da (Elizabeth b 1970, Charlotte b 1973); *Career* house physician: Hammersmith Hosp 1964, Brompton Hosp 1964; registrar Queen Elizabeth Hosp Birmingham 1967; MRC res fell: Univ of Birmingham 1967, Univ of Bristol 1967; Wellcome res fell 1969, conslt physician Gen and Univ Hosps Nottingham 1972; ed in chief Clinical Nutrition jl of Euro Soc Parenteral and Enteral Nutrition; MRCP 1964, FRCP 1976; *Style*— Dr Simon Allison; Long Meadow, Manor Lane, Whatton, Nottingham NG13 9EX (☎ 0949 50835); 11 Regent St, Nottingham (☎ 0602 475475); University Hospital, Nottingham (☎ 0602 709100)

ALLISON, Dr Wade William Magill; s of Lt Cdr (Jorgen Lesley William) Michael Allison, RN (d 1983), and Honoria Brenda, *née* Magill; *b* 23 April 1941; *Educ* Rugby, Trinity Coll Cambridge (MA), ChCh Oxford (MA, DPhil); *m* 1, 9 Sept 1967 (m dis 1988), Sarah Jane, *née* Pallin; 1 s (Thomas b 1977), 3 da (Emma b and d 1968, Harriet b 1972, Rachel b 1974); m 2, 6 Dec 1988, Marilyn Frances (Kate), *née* Easterbrook; *Career* Univ of Oxford: res offr Nuclear Physics Laboratory 1970-75, lectr ChCh Coll 1973-75 (res lectr 1966-71), univ lectr 1976-, sr tutor Keble Coll 1985-89 (tutorial fell 1976-); author of numerous papers and articles on elementary particle physics and experimental methods; fell Royal Cmmn for the Exhibition of 1851 1966-68; *Recreations* sailing, motoring; *Style*— Dr Wade Allison; Southfields, Ludgershall, Aylesbury, Bucks HP18 9PB (☎ 0844 237 602); Keble Coll, Oxford; Nuclear Physics Laboratory, Oxford (☎ 0865 272 734, fax 0865 273 418)

ALLISS, Peter; s of Percy Alliss (d 1975), of Sheffield, Yorkshire, and Dorothy, *née* Rust (d 1973); *b* 28 Feb 1931; *Educ* Queen Elizabeth GS Wimborne Dorset, Crosby House Sch Winton Bournemouth; *m* 1, 1953 (m dis 1968), Joan; 1 s (Gary b 1954), 1 da (Carol b 1960); m 2, 1969 Jaqueline Anne, da of Col Geoffrey Bridgeman Grey, CB, CBE, TD, DL, of Birmingham; 2 s (Simon b 1975, Henry b 1983), 1 da (Sara b 1972); *Career* Nat Serv RAF 1949-51; became professional golfer 1946; played: 8 Ryder Cup matches, 10 Canada Cup (now World Cup) matches; winner: 21 maj events incl open championships of Spain, Portugal, Italy, Brazil; second career as commentator and broadcaster following retirement; former pres: Br Greenkeepers Assoc 1977-86, Ladies Professional Golfers Assoc 1980-86; twice capt PGA 1962-87, pres Nat Assoc of Public Golf Courses; *Books* Bedside Golf (1980), More Bedside Golf (1984), Even More Bedside Golf (1986), Winning Golf (1986), Peter Alliss' Best 100 Golfers, Peter Alliss' Golf to Remember, Lashing the Course, Peter Alliss' Most Memorable Golf, The Duke (novel); *Recreations* conversation (with wine!); *Clubs* Lansdowne, Ritz, Crockfords; *Style*— Peter Alliss, Esq; Alliss Clark Golf Designs, 14 Woodby Drive, Sunningdale, Berkshire SL5 9RD (☎ 0344 872044, fax 0344 872851)

ALLMAN, Bryan; s of Leslie Allman (d 1976), and Ann, *née* Perkin (d 1978); *b* 12 Sept 1929; *Educ* Roundhay Sch Leeds; *m* 14 Sept 1957, Audrey, da of Arther Pollitt (d 1936); 1 s (Christopher John b 7 Aug 1961); *Career* Nat Serv HM RM 1947-49; clerk Burton Gp 1945-51, semi sr audit clerk Blackburn Robson Coates & Co CA 1952-55, chief accountant Darley Mills Gp Ltd 1955-62, fin dir Yorks Hut Co Ltd 1963-64, gp accountant Arthur Johnson (Paper) Ltd 1965-71, chief exec Gower Hldgs plc 1972-; FCCA; *Recreations* golf, walking; *Clubs* Scarcroft (Leeds); *Style*— Bryan Allman, Esq; Grey Gables, Ash Hill La, Shadwell, Leeds (☎ 0532 737 137); Gower Hldgs plc, Holmfield Industrial Estate, Halifax , HX2 9TN (☎ 0422 246 201, fax 0422 249 932, telex 517396)

ALLOTT, Air Cdre Molly Greenwood; CB (1975); da of late Gerald William Allott; *b* 28 Dec 1918; *Educ* Sheffield HS for Girls; *Career* joined WAAF 1941, serv WWII Fighter and Coastal Cmmds, supply branch 1944; appts: Egypt 1945-47, Singapore 1948-50; staff of: AOC in C RAF Germany 1960-63, AOC Fighter Cmmd 1963-66, Trg Cmmd 1971-73; dir WRAF 1973-76, ADC To HM The Queen 1973-76; nat chm Girls Venture Corps 1977-83; cncl memb: Union Jack Club 1976, Main Grants Ctee and Educn Ctee RAF Benevolent Fund 1976-84; FBIM; *Recreations* foreign travel, decorative and fine arts; *Clubs* RAF, Royal Lymington Yacht; *Style—* Air Cdre Molly Allott, CB; 15 Camden Hurst, Milford-on-Sea, Lymington, Hants SO41 0WL

ALLPORT, Denis Ivor; s of late A Allport, and E M, *née* Mashman; *b* 20 Nov 1922; *Educ* Highgate Sch; *m* 1949, Diana, *née* Marler; 2 s, 1 da; *Career* served WWII Indian Army; Metal Box plc: dir 1973, md 1977-79, chief exec 1977-85, dep chm 1979, chm 1979-85; memb Nat Enterprise Bd 1980-83; dir: Beecham Gp 1981-88, Marley plc 1986-; chm Castle Underwriting Agents Ltd 1989-; govr Highgate Sch 1981-, memb Neill Cmmn of Enquiry into Lloyds 1986; CBIM, FRSA; *Style—* Denis Allport, Esq; The Barn, Highmoor, Henley on Thames, Oxon RG9 5DH (☎ 0491 641285)

ALLRED, Prof Henry; s of William Allred (d 1970), of Leigh, Lancashire, and Beatrice Ellen Cooke (d 1960); *b* 4 July 1929; *Educ* Leigh GS Lancashire, Univ of Manchester (DDS, MDS, BDS, LDS); *m* 9 June 1954, Brenda, da of Willam Hoyle (d 1985); 1 da (Josephine Elizabeth b 1960); *Career* house surgn Manchester Dental Hosp 1954, dental practice Walkden Manchester 1954-56, lectr Univ of Manchester 1956-60, conslt in cons dentistry London Hosp 1966-, dean of dental studies London Hosp Med Coll Univ of London 1979-85 (sr lectr in cons dentistry 1961-66, reader 1966-69, prof 1969-); pres Assoc for Dental Educn in Europe; memb: UGC, WHO; Freeman City of London, Liveryman Worshipful Society of Apothecaries; memb: BDA, BSDR, BSRD; FRSM 1961-; *Books* Assessment of the Quality of Dental Care (1977), Public Health in Europe No 7–The Training and Use of Dental Auxiliary Personnel (1977); *Recreations* reading, travel, music; *Clubs* Royal Society of Medicine; *Style—* Prof Henry Allred; 36 Portland Square, London E1 9QR (☎ 071 264 0643); 2 Magistrates Court, Church Lane, Ledbury, Herefordshire; The London Hospital Medical College, Turner St, London E1 2AD (☎ 071 377 7403)

ALLSEBROOK, Peter Winder; CBE (1987), DL (1986); s of Wilton Allsebrook, JP (d 1950), of Skegby Hall, Notts, and Charlotte, *née* Cole (d 1960); *b* 4 Nov 1917; *Educ* Fettes, Caen Univ France, BNC Oxford; *m* 10 Jan 1948, Elizabeth, da of Ulrich Rissik; 3 s (Antony b 1948, Christopher b 1950 (d 1981), Simon b 1962), 2 da (Charlotte b 1953, Katharine b 1957); *Career* enlisted RN 1939, transferred Army, captured Western Desert, POW escaped (despatches), demobbed Lt-Col; TNT Gp: chm TNT (UK) Ltd, dir TNT Ltd, chm TNT Express (UK) Ltd, dir numerous subsids; chm: Truckline Ferries Poole Ltd, Dorset Enterprise Agency Ltd; dir: A H Moody & Son Ltd, Collins Motor Corpn Ltd; md Seeatic Marine Ltd; chm: TEC (Dorset), Princes Tst (Dorset), Baycable Ltd, Dorset Enterprise Agency; cmmr Poole Harbour, dir and former pres The Dorset C of C and Indust, vice pres Red Cross Soc (Dorset Branch), memb Television SW Indust Advs Bd; govr: Clayesmore Sch, Poole GS, Parkstone GS, chm numerous charities; High Sheriff Dorset 1990; FRSA 1967, CBIM, FCIT; Médaille d'Honneur, Queen's award for Industry; *Recreations* sailing; *Clubs* Carlton, Oriental, Achilles, RNSA, Yacht Club de France, Royal Motor Yacht; *Style—* Peter Allsebrook, Esq, CBE, DL; Milton Mill, West Milton, Bridport, Dorset (☎ 030 885391); West Milton, Bridport, Dorset (☎ 030 885432/453, telex 418370 TNT UK G, fax 030 885 280

ALLSOP, Peter Henry Bruce; CBE (1984); s of late Herbert Henry Allsop, and Elsie Hilpern, *née* Whitaker; *b* 22 Aug 1924; *Educ* Haileybury, Caius Coll Cambridge (MA); *m* 1950, Patricia Elizabeth Kingwell Bown; 2 s, 1 da; *Career* called to the Bar Lincoln's Inn 1948, Bencher 1989; chm Sweet & Maxwell 1974-80 (ed 1950-59, dir 1960-64, md 1965-73); md Associated Book Publishers 1968-76, (chm 1976-87, dir 1963, asst mangr 1965-67, chief exec to 1982); memb Cncl Publishers' Assoc (treas 1973-75 and 1979-81, pres 1975-77 pres 1977-78), chm Teleordering Ltd 1978-; dir J Whitaker & Son Ltd 1987-, publishing conslt PUMA 1983-, tstee Yale UP 1981- (vice chm 1984-); chm: Book Trade Ben Soc 1986-, King's Coll Taunton 1986-; dir Woodard Schs (Western Divn) Ltd 1985-; FRSA, FBIM; *Style—* Peter Allsop, Esq; Manor Farm, Charlton Mackrell, Somerton, Somerset

ALLSOP, Prof Richard Edward; s of Edward James Allsop, of Mackworth, Derby, and Grace Ada, *née* Tacey (d 1984); *b* 2 May 1940; *Educ* Bemrose Sch Derby, Queens' Coll Cambridge (MA), UCL (PhD); *m* 23 June 1990, Frances Elizabeth, da of Henry James Killick (d 1978); *Career* sci offr Rd Res Laboratory 1964-66, res fell UCL 1967-69, lectr in tport studies UCL 1970-72, dir Tport Ops Res Gp Univ of Newcastle 1973-76, prof of tport studies UCL 1976-, visitor to Traffic Gp Tport and Rd Res Laboratory 1987-; memb: Rd Traffic Law Review 1985-88, War on Want, Chiltern Soc; convener Rd Environment Working Pty, memb Parly Advsy Cncl for Tport Safety; FCIT 1981, FIHT 1983, C Eng, FICE 1990; *Recreations* photography, theatre, walking; *Style—* Prof Richard Allsop; Transport Studies Group, University College London, Gower St, London WC1E 6BT (☎ 071 387 7050, fax 071 383 5580, telex 296273 UCLENG G)

ALLSOPP, (Harold) Bruce; s of Henry Allsopp (d 1953), of Worthing, Sussex, and Elizabeth May, *née* Robertson (d 1956); *b* 4 July 1912; *Educ* Manchester GS, Univ of Liverpool Sch of Architecture (BArch); *m* 29 Dec 1936, (Florence) Cyrilla, da of John Victor Hearn Woodroffe (d 1938), of Dorking, Surrey; 2 s (Roger Henry b 1941, Christopher John (twin) b 1941); *Career* served WWII RE N Africa and Italy Capt RE; author, artist, historian; chm: Oriel Press Ltd 1962-87, Ind Publishers Guild 1971-72; dir Routledge & Kegan Paul Books 1974-86, fndr memb and chm Soc of Architectural Historians of Great Britain 1959-65, reader in history of architecture Univ of Newcastle 1973-77; occasional TV presenter; Master Art Workers Guild 1970; ARIBA 1935, FRIBA 1955, AMTPI (now MRTPI) 1936, FSA 1968; *Books* incl: Decoration and Furniture (Vol 1 1952, Vol 2 1953), A General History of Architecture (1955), The Future of the Arts (1959), A History of Renaissance Architecture (1959), Architecture (1964), A History of Classical Architecture (1965), Civilization, the Next Stage (1969), Modern Architecture of Northern England (1970), Romanesque Architecture (1971), Ecological Morality (1972), Towards a Humane Architecture (1974), Return of the Pagan (1974), Cecilia (1975), Inigo Jones and the Lords A'Leaping (1975), A Modern Theory of Architecture (1977), Appeal to the Gods (1980), The Country Life Companion to British and European Architecture (1985), Social Responsibility and the Responsible Society (1985), Guide de l'Architecture (1985), Larousse Guide to European Architecture (1985); Architecture of France (with Ursula Clark, 1963), Architecture of Italy (1964), Architecture of England (1964), Historic Architecture of Northumberland (1969), Historic Architecture of Northumberland and Newcastle (1977), English Architecture (1979), The Great Tradition of Western Architecture (1966); articles in Encyclopedia Americana and Encyclopaedia Britannica; *Recreations* music, gardening; *Clubs* Athenaeum; *Style—* Bruce Allsopp, Esq, FSA; Woodburn, 3 Batt House Rd, Stocksfield, Northumberland NE43 7QZ (☎ 0661 842323)

ALLSOPP, Hon Charles Henry; s and h of 5 Baron Hindlip, *qv*; *b* 5 Aug 1940; *Educ* Eton; *m* 18 April 1968, Fiona Victoria Jean Atherley, da of late Hon William Johnston McGowan, 2 s of 1 Baron McGowan; 1 s, 3 da; *Career* late Lt Coldstream Gds; chm Christies UK, dir Christles plc; *Recreations* painting, shooting; *Clubs* White's, Pratt's; *Style—* The Hon Charles Allsopp; The Cedar House, Inkpen, Berks; 9 Cottesmore Gardens, London W8

ALLSOPP, Michael Edward Ranulph; s of Samuel Ranulph Allsopp, CBE (d 1975), of Stansted, Essex, and Hon Norah Hyacinthe, *née* Littleton; *b* 9 Oct 1930; *Educ* Eton; *m* 1953, Patricia Ann, da of Geoffrey H Berners (d 1972), of Faringdon, Oxon; 4 da (Frances Jane Berners (Mrs David Woodd) b 1956, Carolyn Ann Berners b 1957, Davina Hyacinth Berners (m 1987, Sir Nicholas Powell, 4 Bt, *qv*) b 1960, Jessica Elizabeth Berners (twin) (Mrs Edward Leigh Pemberton) b 1960); *Career* Subaltern 7 QOH, Capt Royal Wilts Yeo (TA); chm: Allen Harvey & Ross Ltd 1968-79, London Discount Market Assoc 1974-76, Allied Dunbar & Co Ltd 1979-86, Granville Tst, Granville & Co Ltd, Baronsmead Venture Capital, Strata Investmts, Cater Allen, St David's Investmt Tst plc, Berners Allsopp Estate Mgmnt Co; *Recreations* foxhunting (Master of Old Berks Hounds 1960-81); *Clubs* White's, Pratt's, Cavalry & Guards; *Style—* Michael Allsopp, Esq; Little Coxwell Grove, Faringdon, Oxon SN7 7LW (☎ 0367 240 580, office 0367 240 138, car 0836)

ALLUM, Geoffrey Michael; s of Donald James Allum, and Brenda Mary, *née* Morgan; *b* 12 Oct 1957; *Educ* Hampton Sch, Univ of Aston (BSc), Manchester Business Sch (Dip Business Admin); *m* 31 May 1986, Amanda Jane, da of John Grierson Fleming; *Career* investmt analyst Fielding, Newson-Smith & Co 1982-86, dir Co Nat West Wood Mac 1986-; *Recreations* golf, skiing, reading; *Style—* Geoffrey Allum, Esq; County Natwest, 135 Bishopsgate, London EC2M 3XT (☎ 071 375 8638, fax 071 375 6480, fax 916041)

ALLUM, William Herbert; s of Herbert Edward Allum (d 1987), of Oxford, and Gladys Marion, *née* Bolton; *b* 9 Feb 1953; *Educ* St Edward's Sch Oxford, Univ of Birmingham (BSc, MB ChB, MD); *m* 23 April 1983, (Pamela) Anne, da of Joseph Anthony Collier, of Stratford-upon-Avon; 3 s (Charles b 1985, Henry b 1987, James b 1990); *Career* house offr posts 1977-78, demonstrator in anatomy Univ of Southampton 1978-79, sr house offr in surgery Reading Hosps 1979-80; registrar in surgery: Central Birmingham 1980-82, Hereford Hosps 1982-83; lectr in surgery Univ of Birmingham 1985-88 (hon res fell 1983-85), sr lectr Univ of Leicester and hon conslt surgn Leicester Hosps 1988-; ctee memb Br Stomach Cancer Gp; memb: Surgical Res Soc, Br Assoc of Surgical Oncology; FRCS 1982; *Books* Cancer of the Stomach - Clinical Cancer Monographs 1989 (co-author); *Recreations* golf, cricket; *Clubs* Marylebone Cricket; *Style—* William Allum, Esq; Broadhaven, 9 Link Rd, Stoneygate, Leicester LE2 3RA (☎ 0533 706618); Dept of Surgery, Clinical Sciences Building, Leicester Royal Infirmary, Leicester (☎ 0533 523144)

ALLWARD, Lt-Col (Denis Raymond) Stewart; owner and restorer of Castle Stalker in Argyllshire. The Castle, which derives its name from the Gaelic 'Eilean na Stalcaire' (Island of the Deer Hunter), was last used as a residence, by Campbell of Airds, in the early eighteenth century and became a garrison for Hanoverian soldiers during the last Jacobite Rising; s of Frank Leonard Allward and Daisy Ellen Allward; *b* 18 Nov 1915; *Educ* Friends Sch Saffron Walden, Univ of London (LLB); *m* 1946, Marion, da of John Dunlop; 2 s, 2 da; *Career* HAC 1933-39, served 1939-45, Europe, Gordon Highlanders, London Scottish 1946-1980; slr; *Clubs* HAC, London Scottish; *Style—* Lt-Col Stewart Allward; Allward & Son, 65 Westhall Road, Warlingham, Surrey CR3 9YE (☎ 0883 622768); Castle Stalker, Loch Laich, Appin, Argyllshire (☎ 063 173 234)

ALLWELL-BROWN, Senibo; s of Max Allwell-Brown, MBE (d 1980), and Emily, *née* Hart; *b* 10 March 1935; *Educ* Okrika GS, Univ of Wales (BA); *m* 12 Oct 1963, Hellen Marguerita, da of Ivon Somersall; 1 s (Pubo Duane Dagogo), 4 da (Tumini Helen, Atonye Margeret, Awoibim, Suodienye); *Career* dir: Port Harcourt Flour Mills Ltd 1973-75, African Continental Bank Ltd 1973-75, Pan African Bank Ltd 1975-77, Int Bank for W Africa Ltd 1977-79, Union Bank of Nigeria Ltd 1979-83; memb: Rivers State End Arts and Culture 1977-79, Bd Nigerian Coal Corpn 1975-77, Ctee Banking Experts 1979-80, Cncl Rivers State Univ of Sci and Technol 1984-86, Finima Relocation Ctee 1978-; vice-pres Nigerian Stock Exchange 1987-(memb Cncl 1976-87); chm Bd of Dirs Integrated Data Services Ltd 1988-; FICA 1976; *Recreations* motor boating, reading, golfing; *Style—* Senibo Allwell-Brown, Esq; 47 Obagi Rd GRA Phase one, Port Harcourt, Rivers State, Nigeria (☎ 084 332772); Allwell Brown & Co, Chartered Accountants, 73 Ikwerre Rd, P O Box 242, Port Harcourt, Rivers State, Nigeria (☎ 084 332726, telex 61127 HORINIG)

ALLWOOD, Surgn Capt Michael John; VRD (1964, clasp 1974); s of Edgar Henry Allwood (d 1941), of London, and Florence, *née* Nicholson (d 1979); *b* 31 July 1925; *Educ* St Olave's King's Coll Hosp London (MD, PhD, AKC); *m* 15 July 1950, Rosemary Marguerite, da of James William Stokoe Harrison (d 1977); 3 s (Andrew b 1955, James b d 1962, Christopher b 1963), 3 da (Rosamond b 1952, Camilla b 1959, Cressida b 1966); *Career* RNVR: surgn Lieut 1949, surgn Lt Cdr 1957; RNR: surgn Cdr 1964, hon surgn Capt 1983; res fell Nat Inst Med Res 1951-53, fell Mayo Clinic 1959-60, lectr St Thomas Hosp Med Sch 1954-63, UK Space Gp IAM Farnborough 1963-67, conslt W Midlands RHA 1967-90; pres: CIOMR (NATO) 1980-82 (UK rep 1974-82), Sea Cadet Assoc (Midland Area), RNA (Leamington Spa); *Recreations* walking, travel, naval and military history; *Clubs* Naval; *Style—* Surgn Capt Michael Allwood, VRD; Ridge Barn, Ufton Fields, Ufton, Leamington Spa, Warwicks CV33 9PE (☎ 0926 613844)

ALMENT, Sir (Edward) Anthony John; s of Edward Alment, and Alice Alment; *b* 3 Feb 1922; *Educ* Marlborough, St Bart's Hosp; *m* 1946, Elizabeth Innes Bacon; *Career* conslt obstetrician and gynaecologist Northampton 1960-85; prev: St Bart's Hosp, Norfolk and Norwich Hosp, Queen Charlotte's and Chelsea Hosp for Women, London Hosps; author of various articles on med and wine subjects; former memb Oxford Regnl Hosp Bd and chm Med Advsy Ctee; memb: Oxford RHA 1973-75, UK Central Cncl for Nursing Midwifery and Health Visiting 1980-83; Hon DSc Leicester 1982; MRCS, LRCP, FRCOG (MRCOG 1951, memb Cncl RCOG 1961-67, hon sec 1968-73, pres 1978-81; FRCPI 1979, FRCPE 1981, FRCGP 1982; FRACOG 1985; kt 1980; *Books* Competence to Practice (jtly, 1976); *Recreations* engineering, fishing, wine; *Style—* Sir Anthony Alment; Winston House, Boughton, Northampton NN2 8RR

ALMOND, (Thomas) Clive; OBE (1989); s of Thomas Almond (d 1976), and Eveline, *née* Moss (d 1986); *b* 30 Nov 1939; *Educ* Bristol GS; *m* 4 Sept 1965, Auriol Gala Elizabeth Annette, da of Dr H C Hendry; *Career* joined Dip Serv 1967: FO 1967-68 and 1975-78, High Cmmn Accra 1968-71, Paris Embassy 1971-75, Brussels Embassy 1978-80, Jakarta Embassy 1980-83, HM ambass Brazzaville Embassy 1987-88 (chargé d'affaires 1983-87), asst marshal of the Dip Corps FO 1988-; *Recreations* travel, golf; *Style—* Clive Almond, Esq, OBE; c/o FCO, King Charles St, London SW1A 2AH (☎ 071 210 6402)

ALMOND, David William; s of George Sydney Almond, of Lymington, Hants, and Madge Lilian, *née* Skegg; *b* 24 Oct 1945; *Educ* Purley GS Surrey; *m* 6 June 1970, Elizabeth (Liz), da of Percy Thomas Bisby (d 1978), of Aldwick, Sussex; 2 da (Amanda Jane b 25 Feb 1974, Juliette b 10 March 1977); *Career* CA; articles City of London 1962-67, ptnr Alliotts (formerly Evans Peirson) 1969-; chm: Alliott Peirson Associates 1974-86, Alliott Peirson International 1979-89 (sec 1989-); dir Accounting Firms Associates Inc 1982-; chm: Croydon Soc CA 1979-80 (sec 1975-79), Storrington Rural Pres Soc; treas Pulborough and W Chiltington Scout and Guide Gp; Freeman City of London 1976, memb Ct of Assts Worshipful Co Coachmakers and Coach Harness Makers 1977, Liveryman Worshipful Co of CA's 1980; FCA 1967, ATII 1967, FBIM 1978; *Recreations* sailing, gardening; *Clubs* East India; *Style—* David Almond, Esq; Fryern Place, Storrington, West Sussex RH20 4HG (☎ 0903 743030); Alliotts, 96 High Street, Guildford, Surrey GU1 3DL (☎ 0483 33119, fax 0483 37339)

ALMOND, Prof Jeffrey William; s of Stanley Peter Almond, of Lyndale, Sutton under Whitestone Cliffe, N Yorks, and Joyce Mary, *née* Fountain; *b* 28 June 1951; *Educ* Thirsk Grammar and Mod Sch, Univ of Leeds (BSc), Univ of Cambridge (PhD); *m* 6 Aug 1976, Karen Elizabeth, da of Joseph Batley, of 10 Northolme Circle, Hessle, Humberside; 2 s (Maximilian b 13 Sept 1979, Adam b 8 Nov 1989), 1 da (Gemma b 16 Oct 1981); *Career* scientist Sandoz Forschungsinstitut Vienna 1977-79, lectr Univ of Leicester 1979-85, res fell Lister Inst of Preventative Med 1985, prof of microbiology Univ of Reading 1985-; virus gp convener Soc for Gen Microbiology; *Style*— Prof Jeffrey Almond; Dept of Microbiology, University of Reading, London Rd, Reading RG1 5AQ Berks (☎ 0734 318901)

ALMOND, Martin John; s of Stanley Wilton Almond, and Helen Prescott, *née* Baron (d 1979); *b* 8 May 1946; *Educ* Brooksby Coll of Agric; *m* 12 Dec 1970, Elizabeth Enid; 2 da (Jennifer b 1977, Susan b 1979); *Career* CA; ptnr: H.R Davison & Co 1978-, Robert Parkinson & Co 1981-, Abbey Nursing Homes 1986-; dir Comparative Business Information Ltd 1983-; FCA 1973; *Recreations* walking, gardening, history, reading, family; *Clubs* Royal Over-Seas; *Style*— Martin Almond, Esq; Kingswood House, Buckfastleigh, Devon TQ11 0BL; 100 Queen St, Newton Abbot, Devon TQ12 2E9 (☎ 0626 52 433)

ALPORT, Baron (Life Peer UK 1961), of Colchester, Co Essex; Cuthbert James McCall Alport; TD (1949), PC (1960), DL (Essex 1974); s of Prof Arthur Cecil Alport, MD, (d 1958), of Cairo, and Janet, *née* McCall; *b* 22 March 1912; *Educ* Haileybury, Pembroke Coll Cambridge (BA, MA); *m* 26 Oct 1945, Rachel Cecilia (d 1983), da of Lt-Col Ralph Charles Bingham, CVO, DSO (s of Maj-Gen Sir Cecil Bingham GCVO, KCMG, 2 s of 4 Earl of Lucan, KP, JP); 1 s (Hon Arthur Edward b 22 May 1954), 2 da (Hon Cecilia Alexandra Rose (Hon Mrs Lang) b 3 Sept 1946, Hon Lavender Lilias Carole (Hon Mrs Taylor) b 13 Dec 1950); *Career* served WWII Lt-Col (GSO 1 E Africa 1944-45); barr; MP (C) Colchester 1950-61, Min of State CRO 1959-61, high cmmr Fedn of Rhodesia and Nyassaland 1961-63; sits as ind Cons in Lords, dep speaker House of Lords 1971-, advsr to Home Sec 1974-83; high steward Colchester 1967-; *Clubs* Pratt's, Farmers; *Style*— The Rt Hon the Lord Alport, TD, PC, DL; The Cross House, Layer de la Haye, Colchester, Essex (☎ 0206 634 217)

ALPORT, Hon (Arthur) Edward Bingham; only s of Baron Alport, TD, PC (Life Peer), *qv*; *b* 22 May 1954; *Educ* Haileybury, Exeter Univ (BSc); *m* 1979, Anne Vivian, er da of Patrick Alexander Grove-White, of Crown Piece, Wormingford, Colchester; 2 s (Robert Michael Bingham b 1983, James Richard McCall b 1989), 1 da (Catherine Rachel b 1985); *Career* deputy Lloyd's underwriter 1986; divnl dir Willis Faber & Dumas 1990; Ellis Carson Award 1988; ACII 1979; *Books* Notes Towards a Definition of Moral Hazard (1988); *Recreations* music, writing; *Style*— The Hon Edward Alport; Huckleberry, Church Street, Boxted, Colchester, Essex CO4 5SX

ALSTEAD, Brig (Francis) Allan Littlejohns; CBE (1984); s of Prof Stanley Alstead, CBE, of Glenholme, Glen Rd, Dunblane, Pershire, and Nora, *née* Sowden (d 1980); *b* 19 June 1935; *Educ* Glasgow Acad, RMA Sandhurst, Univ Coll Wales Aberystwyth (MPhil); *m* 4 April 1964, Joy Veronica, da of George Alexander Edwards, of Ghyllbrow, Moorhouse Rd, Carlisle, Cumbria; 2 s (Robert b 24 Dec 1965, Jonathan b 13 Nov 1968); *Career* cmmnd KOSB 1955, RN Staff Coll 1966, Jt Servs Staff Coll 1971, cmd 1 Bn KOSB 1974-76 (despatches 1976), MA to QMG 1976-79, ACOS Log Plans BAOR 1981-84, cmd 51 Highland Bde 1984-87; NATO res fell and reinforcement co-ordinator 1987-90; chief exec Scottish Sports Cncl 1990-, memb Royal Co of Archers (Queen's Bodyguard in Scotland), Dep Hon Col Edinburgh and Heriot-Watt Univs OTC 1990; FBIM 1984, FIPM 1986, FCIT 1989, FInstAM 1990; *Recreations* skiing, running, classical music; *Clubs* RSAC; *Style*— Brig Allan Alstead, CBE; Scottish Sports Council, Caledonia House, Southgyle, Edinburgh EH12 9DQ (☎ 031 317 7200)

ALSTEAD, Prof Stanley; CBE (1960); s of Robert Alstead, OBE, JP (d 1946), and (Sarah) Ann, *née* Deakin, JP (d 1960); *b* 6 June 1905; *Educ* Wigan GS, Univ of Liverpool (MB ChB, MD), Univ of Glasgow; *m* 1, 27 July 1932, Nora (d 1980), da of Matthew William Sowden (d 1961), of Cambria, Whitchurch, Shropshire; 1 s (Allan b 1935); m 2, 15 Sept 1982 (Jessie) Janet McAlpine, da of Louis Pope (d 1924), of Bethshean, Cleland, Lanarkshire; *Career* emergency cmmn RAMC 1942-46, Maj med specialist Casualty Clearing Station UK, N Africa, Italy (despatches), Lt-Col offr i/c med div Gen Hosp Italy and Egypt; Hon Lt-Col RAMC 1946; jr clinical appts Midlands 1929-32, Pollok lectr in pharmacology Univ of Glasgow 1932, physician Highlands and Islands Scotland 1947-48, regius prof of materia medica Univ of Glasgow 1948-70, sr physician Stobhill Gen Hosp Glasgow 1948-70; hon prof and physician Kenyatta Nat Hosp Univ of E Africa 1965-66; memb: Bd of Mgmnt Glasgow Northern Hosps 1948-52, Br Pharmacopoeia Cmmn 1953-57, Standing Ctee on Classification of Proprietary Preparations; jt pres Soc of Friends of Dunblane Cathedral; pres RFPSGlas (now RCPSGlas) 1956-58, Hon FRCPS 1979, FRSEd, FRCPLond, FRCPEd, FRCPS; *Books* jt ed 3 textbooks on pharmacology and therapeutics (1936-70); *Recreations* classical music, English literature; *Clubs* Coll (Glasgow), RSAC; *Style*— Prof Stanley Alstead, CBE; Glenholme, Glen Rd, Dunblane, Perthshire FK15 0DJ (☎ 0786 822 466)

ALSTON, James Douglas; CBE (1967), JP (1960), DL (Norfolk 1981); s of James Alston (d 1958), of Uphall, Norfolk; *b* 6 May 1913; *Educ* Thetford GS, Midland Agric Coll; *m* 1943, Gale Violet May, da of Edward Tyrrell Lewis (d 1934), of Manitoba, Canada; 2 s, 2 da; *Career* served WW II RAF; farmer, chm Eastern Counties Farmers Ltd 1954-68 (pres 1973-83); memb Agric Res Cncl 1957-67, vice chm Royal Norfolk Agric Assoc 1963-83 (pres 1981), chm Plant Breeding Inst Cambridge 1971-83, vice chm Norfolk Agric Station 1973-84, pres Br Friesian Cattle Soc 1983; tstee TSB of Eastern England 1960-80 (vice chm 1979-80); memb Norfolk CC 1969-73; memb Ct and Cncl UEA; *Recreations* shooting; *Clubs* Farmers, Norfolk; *Style*— James D Alston, Esq, CBE, JP, DL; South Lopham Hall, Diss, Norfolk IP22 2LW (☎ 037 977 286)

ALSTON, John Alistair; CBE; s of David Alston (d 1989), of Lavenham, Suffolk, and Bathia Mary Davidson (d 1987); *b* 24 May 1937; *Educ* Orwell Park, Sherborne, RAC Cirencester; *Career* farmer; elected Norfolk CC 1973 (ldr 1981-87 and 1989-, chm 1988), chm Broads Bill Steering Ctee, memb Cncl UEA; *Recreations* shooting, gardening; *Style*— J A Alston, Esq, CBE; Besthorpe Hall, Norfolk NR17 2LJ (☎ (0953) 452138)

ALSTON, (Arthur) Rex; s of Rt Rev Arthur Fawsett Alston (d 1954) suffragan bishop of Middleton, Lancs, of St Leonards-on-Sea, Sussex, and Mary Isabel Tebbutt (d 1957); *b* 2 July 1901; *Educ* Trent Coll, Clare Coll Cambridge (MA, athletics blue); *m* 1, 1932, Elspeth (d 1985), da of Sir Stewart Stockman (d 1926); 1 s (Graham), 1 da (Gay); m 2, 1986, Joan Manthorp Wilson; *Career* BBC commentator on: test cricket 1946-64, rugby union football (incl internationals), athletics (incl 5 Olympic Games), tennis (incl Wimbledon Championships); cricket and rugby corr The Daily and Sunday Telegraph 1966-88; capt: Bedfordshire CC 1928-30, E Midlands and Bedford RUFC; player Rosslyn Park RUFC; *Clubs* East India, MCC; *Style*— Rex Alston, Esq; Garlands, Ewhurst, Cranleigh, Surrey

ALSTON, Richard John William; s of Gordon Walter Alston, and Margaret Isabel, *née* Whitworth; *b* 30 Oct 1948; *Educ* Eton, Croydon Coll of Art; *Career* res choreographer Ballet Rambert 1980-86, artistic dir Rambert Dance Co 1986-; *Style*— Richard Alston, Esq; Rambert Dance Co, 94 Chiswick High Rd, London W4 (☎ 081 995 4246)

ALSTON, Robert John; CMG (1987); s of Arthur William Alston, and Rita Alston; *b* 10 Feb 1938; *Educ* Ardingly Coll, New Coll Oxford (BA); *m* 1969, Patricia Claire, of Essex; 1 s (Jeremy b 1972), 1 da (Nadine b 1970); *Career* Dip Serv: third sec Kabul 1963, Eastern Dept FO 1986, head Computer Study Team FCO 1969, first sec (Econ) Paris 1971, first sec and head of Chancery Tehran 1974, Energy Sci and Space Dept FCO 1977, head Jt Nuclear Unit FCO 1978, political cnsllr UK Delgn to NATO 1981, head Def Dept FCO 1984, ambass Oman 1986-; *Recreations* gardening, travel, music; *Style*— Robert J Alston, Esq, CMG; c/o Foreign and Commonwealth Office, King Charles St, London SW1A 2AH

ALSTON, Robin Carfrae; s of Wilfred Louis Alston, and Margaret Louise, *née* Mackenzie (d 1975); *b* 29 Jan 1933; *Educ* Queen's Royal Coll Trinidad, Lodge Sch Barbados, Rugby, Univ of Br Columbia (BA), Univ of Oxford (MA), Univ of Toronto (MA), Univ of London (PhD); *m* 1957, Joanna Dorothy, da of Harry Ormiston; 2 s (Brent d 1987, Mark), 1 da (Jane); *Career* bibliographer; teaching fell Univ Coll Toronto 1956-58, lectr Univ of New Brunswick 1958-60, lectr in Eng lit Univ of Leeds 1964-76, David Murray lectr Univ of Glasgow 1983; fndr chm and md Scolar Press 1965-73, fndr and md Janus Press 1973-80, conslt bibliographer to Br Library 1977-, ed-in-chief Eighteenth Century Short Title Catalogue 1978-90, ed dir The Ninteenth Century 1985-, prof of library studies Univ of London 1990-, dir School of Library, Archive and Info Studies UCL 1990-; pres Bibliographical Soc 1988-90 (vice pres 1975-88, memb Cncl 1968-74, Pubns Ctee 1970-, ed Occasional Papers 1984-); memb Advsy Ctee Modern Language Assoc of America for the Wing Project 1978-; external examiner Inst of Bibliography Univ of Leeds 1983-, Cecil Oldman lectr Univ of Leeds 1988-89, hon res fell UCL 1987-; FSA 1988; *Publications* Anglo-Saxon Composition for Beginners (1959), Materials for a History of the English Language (2 vols, 1960), An Introduction to Old English (1961, 1962), A Concise Introduction to Old English (1966), Alexander Gil's Logonomia Anglica 1619 (ed with B Danielsson, 1979), Cataloguing Rules for the Eighteenth Century Short Title Catalogue (1977), Bibliography, Machine Readable Cataloguing and the ESTC (with M J Jannetta, 1978), Eighteenth Century Subscription Lists (with F J G Robinson and C Wadham, 1983), The Eighteenth Century Short Title Catalogue: the Br Library Collection (ed, 1983), The Nineteenth Century Subject Scope & Principles of Selection (1986), The Nineteenth Century - Cataloguing Rules (1986), Bibliography of the English Language 1500-1800 (22 vols, 1-12 published to date), The British Library: Past Present Future (1989); *Style*— Robin Alston, Esq, FSA; 16 Medburn St, London; The British Library, Great Russell St, London WC1B 3DG (☎ 071 323 7609)

ALSTON-ROBERTS-WEST, Lt-Col George Arthur; CVO (1988), DL (Warwickshire 1988); yr s of Maj William Reginald James Alston-Roberts-West (ka 1940; the Major's gf James added Alston to his patronymic of Roberts-West 1918. James's ggf, another James, added the name Roberts to his patronymic of West 1808. This second James had as mother one Sarah, da of Christopher Wren, of Wroxall Abbey, Staffs, and a descendant of Sir Christopher Wren the architect), and Constance Isolde, er da of Lord Arthur Grosvenor, JP, DL, 2 s of 1 Duke of Westminster; *b* 23 Nov 1937; *Educ* Eton, RMA Sandhurst; *m* 20 May 1970, Hazel Elizabeth Margaret, yst da of Lt-Col Sir Thomas Russell Albert Mason Cook, JP (ggs of Thomas Cook, fndr of the eponymous tourist agency); extra lady-in-waiting to HRH The Princess of Wales 1981-; *Career* served Gren Gds 1957-80; comptroller Lord Chamberlain's Office 1987-90 (asst comptroller 1981-87), extra equerry to HM The Queen 1982-; *Style*— Lt-Col George Alston-Roberts-West, CVO, DL; Atherstone Hill Farmhouse, Atherstone-on-Stour, Stratford-on-Avon, Warwickshire

ALT, Anthony; *b* 23 March 1946; *Educ* Westminster City Sch, Univ of Hull; *m* Catherine Lurie; 1 s (Nicholas), 1 da (Alexandra); *Career* md N M Rothschild & Sons Ltd; *Recreations* sports, reading, music and family; *Clubs* MCC, Hurlingham, Wentworth; *Style*— Anthony Alt, Esq; N M Rothschild & Sons Limited, New Court, St Swithin's Lane, London EC4P 4DU (☎ 071 280 5000)

ALTAMONT, Earl of; Jeremy Ulick Browne; s and h of 10 Marquess of Sligo; *b* 4 June 1939; *Educ* St Columba's Coll Eire, RAC Cirencester; *m* 1961, Jennifer June, da of Maj Derek Cooper, of Dunlewey, Co Donegal, and Mrs C Heber Percy; 5 da; *Style*— Earl of Altamont; Westport House, Co Mayo, Republic of Ireland

ALTHAM, Hon Mrs (Elizabeth Oona); *née* McNair; da of 1 Baron McNair, CBE, QC, LLD (d 1975); *b* 7 Feb 1913; *m* 1939, Gp Capt John Barrett Altham, CBE; 2 s, 2 da; *Style*— The Hon Mrs Altham; Ivy Cottage, Little Shelford, Cambridge

ALTHAM, Gp Capt John Barrett; CBE (1955); s of Capt Edward Altham, CB, RN (d 1951), and his 1 wife Fiorella Cecil, *née* Willis; gs of Lt-Gen Sir Edward Altham, KCB, KCIE, CMG; *b* 17 March 1909; *Educ* Eton, Trinity Coll Cambridge (MA); *m* 17 June 1939, Hon Elizabeth Oona, eldest da of 1 Baron McNair, CBE (d 1975); 2 s, 2 da; *Career* RAF 1932-62; pilot No 9 (B) Sqdn, CFS course, flying instr Digby, specialist Signals 1937, served WWII Wittering (Fighter Cmd), Empire Air Trg Australia, cmd 80 Signals Wing NW Europe (despatches), chief tech offr CSE Watton, RAF Seletar (Singapore) 1948, Signals staff appointments No 90 Gp, Flying Trg Cmd, Tech Trg Cmd, cmd Communications Gp Allied Air Forces Fontainbleau 1959-62; *Recreations* sailing, golf, landscape gardening; *Clubs* Aldeburgh Yacht, Pitt (Cambridge), Gog Magog Golf; *Style*— Gp Capt John Altham, CBE; Ivy Cottage, Little Shelford, Cambridge (☎ 0223 842182)

ALTHAM, Richard James Livingstone; s of Harry Surtees Altham, CBE, DSO, MC (d 1965), and Alison, *née* Livingstone Learmonth (d 1979); *b* 19 Jan 1924; *Educ* Marlborough, Trinity Coll Oxford (MA); *m* 28 Sept 1957, (Rowena) Jeanne, da of Sir Francis Spencer Portal, 5 Bt (d 1984); 3 s (David b 1959, Robert b 1960, Alastair b 1963); *Career* pilot RAFVR 1941-46, Flt Lt; ICI Ltd 1949-62, jt md Borax Hldgs 1968-82; dir: RTZ plc 1968-87, Boustead plc 1987; memb Cncl: Radley Coll, United World Coll of Atlantic, Ranfurly Library; chm: Fairbridge Drake Soc, Hertfordshire Cheshire Home; *Recreations* reading, gardening, cricket; *Clubs* MCC, RAF; *Style*— Richard J L Altham, Esq; Crunnells Green House, Preston, Hitchin, Hertfordshire (☎ 0462 432163)

ALTHAUS, Sir Nigel Frederick; s of Frederick Rudolph Althaus, CBE (d 1975), and Margaret Frances, *née* Twist (d 1990); *b* 28 Sept 1929; *m* 1958, Anne, da of P G Cardew; 3 s, 1 da; *Career* memb Stock Exchange 1955-89; sr ptnr: Pember & Boyle (stockbrokers) 1975-82, Mullens & Co (stockbrokers to the Government and the Bank of England) 1982-86; sr Govt broker (formally known as sr broker to the National Debt Commissioners) 1982-89; kt 1989; *Style*— Sir Nigel Althaus; c/o Bank of England, Threadneedle St, London EC2R 8AH

ALTHORP, Viscount; Charles Edward Maurice Spencer; s (by 1 m) and h of 8 Earl Spencer, MVO, JP, DL, *qv*; bro of HRH The Princess of Wales (*see* Royal Family); *b* 20 May 1964; *Educ* Maidwell Hall, Eton, Magdalen Coll Oxford; *m* 16 Sept 1989, (Catherine) Victoria, da of John Lockwood, of Barnes, London; 1 da (Kitty Eleanor b 28 Dec 1990); *Career* page of hon to HM The Queen 1977-79; TV correspondent NBC News 1987-; *Clubs* Brooks's; *Style*— Viscount Althorp

ALTMAN, Lionel Phillips; CBE (1979); s of Arnold Altman (d 1955), and Catherine, *née* Phillips (d 1982); *b* 21 Sept 1922; *m* 1; 1 s; m 2, 1977, Jan Mary Borrodell; 2 da; *Career* served HM Forces 1942-46; dir: Carmo Hldgs Ltd 1947-63, Sears Hldgs Motor Gp 1963-72, C & W Hldgs Ltd 1974-77; chm and chief exec Pre-Divisional Investmts

Ltd 1972-; dir: H P Information 1985-, Equity & General plc Gp of Companies 1978- (this gp includes: Equity & General Finance Ltd, Equity & General Finance Estates Ltd, Equity & General Finance (Investmts) Ltd, Equity & General Finance (Rentals) Ltd, Equity & General Finance (Leasing) Ltd, Lease Exchange Ltd, Bluebell Garages (Middlesborough) Ltd, Mountvale Ltd, Western General Trading Ltd, Reid & Lee Ltd, Technology Transfer Assocs Ltd, United Technologists Est, Murie Mines (Pvt) Ltd); pres Motor Agents Assoc 1975-77 (Nat Cncl 1965-); vice-pres and Cncl Inst of Motor Industry 1970-78; chm Industry Taxation Panel; memb: Cncl CBI 1977-, CBI Industl Policy Ctee 1979-, Dun & Bradstreet Industry Panel 1982-; Liveryman Worshipful Co of Coachmakers and Coach Harness Makers; Freeman: City of London, City of Glasgow; *Style*— Lionel Altman, Esq, CBE; The Cottage, Amersham Way, Little Chalfont, Bucks HP6 6SF; 66 Grosvenor St, Mayfair, London W1X 9DB (☎ 071 493 3371)

ALTON, David Patrick; MP (Lib) Liverpool, Mossley Hill 1983-; s of Frederick Alton, and Bridget, *née* Mulroe; *b* 15 March 1951; *Educ* Campion Sch, Christ's Coll of Educn Liverpool; *m* 23 July 1988, Lizzie, *née* Bell; 1 s (Padraig b 1990), 1 da (Marianne b 1989); *Career* city cncllr Liverpool 1972-80 (dep ldr Cncl 1978-79, housing chm 1978-79), nat pres Nat League of Young Liberals 1979, MP (Lib) Liverpool Edge Hill March 1979-83, chm Lib Pty Standing Ctee (policy) 1980-81; Lib chief whip 1985-87; Liberal and Alliance spokesman on NI 1986-87; life vice pres and tstee Crisis at Christmas, Party Sponsor The Jubilee Campaign, pres Liverpool Old People's Hostels Assoc; memb Inst of Journalists; *Books* What Kind of Country (1987), Whose Choice Anyway (1988); *Style*— David Alton, Esq, MP; 25 North Mossley Hill Road, Liverpool L18 (☎ 051 724 6106)

ALTON, Euan Beresford Seaton; MBE (1945), MC (1943); s of William Lester St John Alton (d 1954), of Putney, London, and Ellen Sharpey, *née* Seaton (d 1963); *b* 22 April 1919; *Educ* St Paul's, Magdalen Coll Oxford (MA); *m* 22 Aug 1953, Diana Margaret, da of Dr Colin Ede, MD (d 1967); 1 s (Robert b 1958), 1 da (Sally b 1960); *Career* RA 1939-45; served: Egypt, N Africa, Sicily, Italy; Maj 1945; Colonial Serv HM Overseas Civil Serv 1946-58, Gold Coast Ghana, dist cmmr admin offr class I 1957; Miny of Health Dept of Health & Social Security: joined 1958, asst sec 1961, under sec 1968-76; capt Oxford Univ Rifle Club Half Blue 1946; hon local rep Cruising Assoc 1988- (chm 1984-88); *Recreations* sailing; *Clubs* Stour Sailing, Cruising Assoc; *Style*— Euan Alton, Esq, MBE, MC; Spindlehurst, School Lane, Brantham, nr Manningtree, Essex CO11 1QE (☎ 0206 393419)

ALTRINCHAM, Barony of; *see*: Grigg, John Edward Poynder

ALTY, Prof James Lenton; s of William Graham Alty (d 1959), of Haslingden, Lancs, and Annie Alty (d 1989); *b* 21 Aug 1939; *Educ* King Edward VII Sch Lytham, Univ of Liverpool (BSc, PhD); *m* 16 Jan 1965, Mary Eleanor, da of Thomas Roberts (d 1986), of Llanerchymedd, Anglesey; 2 s (Gareth b 1965, Graham James b 1971), 2 da (Carys Ann b 1967, Sîan Cathryn b 1968); *Career* account exec IBM (UK) Ltd 1971-72 (sr systems engr 1968-71), dir Computer Laboratory Univ of Liverpool 1972-82 (Oliver Lodge res fell 1962-64, Leverhulme res fell 1966-68), exec dir Turing Inst 1984-90, BT prof of computer sci Univ of Strathclyde 1989-90 (prof computer sci 1982-89, dir Scot HCI Centre 1984-90), prof of computer sci Univ of Loughborough 1990-; over forty pubns in academic jls and conf proceedings; memb: Computer Bd for Univs and Res Cncls 1975-81, Cncl Br Computer Soc 1981-84 (fell 1982); *Books* Computing Skills and the User Interface (with M J Coombs, 1982), Human Computer Interaction (with G R S Weir, 1990), Expert Systems: Concepts and Examples (with M J Coombs, 1984); *Recreations* skiing, musical composition; *Clubs* Nat Lib; *Style*— Prof James Alty; 168 Station Rd, Cropston, Leicestershire; Loughborough Univ of Technology, Loughborough, Leicestershire LE11 3TU (☎ 0509 222648, fax 0509 610815)

ALUN-JONES, Sir (John) Derek; s of Thomas Alun-Jones (d 1951), and Madge Beatrice, *née* Edwards (d 1968); *b* 6 June 1933; *Educ* Lancing, St Edmund Hall Oxford; *m* 1960, Gillian, da of Ian Palmer; 2 s (Jeremy b 1961, Nicholas b 1968), 3 da (Carella b 1963, Sophie b 1968, Emma b 1968); *Career* dir: Burmah Oil Trading Co 1974-70, Royal Insur 1981-, Reed Int 1984-90, GKN 1986-88; chm Spectrum Energy and Information Technology Ltd 1990, chm and md Ferranti 1975-90; kt 1987; *Recreations* shooting, fishing, riding; *Style*— Sir Derek Alun-Jones; The Willows, Effingham Common, Surrey KT24 5JE (☎ 0372 58158)

ALVAREZ, Alfred; s of Bertie Alvarez (d 1965), of London, and Katie, *née* Levy (d 1982); *b* 5 Aug 1929; *Educ* Oundle, CCC Oxford (BA, MA); *m* 1, 1956 (m dis 1961), Ursula Barr; 1 s (Adam); m 2, 1966, Anne, da of Jack Gilmore Adams, of Toronto, Canada; 1 s (Luke b 1968), 1 da (Kate b 1971); *Career* poet and author; *Books* The Shaping Spirit (1958), The School of Donne (1961), The New Poetry (ed and introduction, 1962), Under Pressure (1965), Beyond All This Fiddle (1968), Lost (poems, 1968), Penguin Modern Poets No18 (1970), Apparition (poems, 1971), The Savage God (1971), Beckett (1973), Hers (1974), Hunt (1978), Autumn to Autumn and Selected Poems (1978), Life After Marriage (1982), The Biggest Game in Town (1983), Offshore (1986), Feeding the Rat (1988), Day of Atonement (1991); *Recreations* rock climbing, poker, music; *Clubs* Climbers', Alpine; *Style*— A Alvarez, Esq; c/o Aitken & Stone, 29 Fernshaw Rd, London SW10 OTG

ALVES, Colin; OBE (1990); s of Donald Alexander Alves, of Somerset (d 1979), and Marjorie Alice, *née* Marsh (d 1968); *b* 19 April 1930; *Educ* Christ's Hosp, Univ of Oxford (MA); *m* 3 Jan 1953, Peggy, da of Capt Ernest Henry Kember (d 1941); 2 s (William b 1956, Thomas b 1963), 1 da (Rachel b 1954); *Career* lectr King Alfred's Coll Winchester 1959-68, head of Dept Brighton Coll of Educn 1968-74, dir Religious Educn Centre St Gabriel's Coll 1974-77; sec Church Colls of Higher Educn 1977-84, gen sec Gen Synod Bd of Educn and Nat Soc 1984-90; memb: Durham Cmmn on Religious Educn 1967-70, Advsy Ctee on the Supply and Educn of Teachers (ACSET) 1980-85, Nat Advsy Body on Public Sector Higher Educn (NAB) 1983-88, Voluntary Sector Consultative Cncl 1984-88; chm Schs Cncl Religious Educn Ctee 1971-77, sec Assoc of Voluntary Colls 1978-84; Hon MLitt 1989; *publications* Religion and The Secondary School (1968), The Christian in Education (1972), The Question of Jesus (1987); *Recreations* music, walking, gardens; *Clubs* Royal Cwlth Soc; *Style*— Colin Alves, Esq, OBE; 9 Park Rd, Haywards Heath, W Sussex (☎ 0444 454496)

ALVEY, John; CB (1980); s of George Clarence Vincent Alvey (d 1929), and Hilda Eveline, *née* Pellat (d 1955); *b* 19 June 1925; *Educ* Reeds Sch, Univ of London (BSc); *m* 1955, Celia Edmed, da of Dr Cecil Brittain Marson (d 1932); 3 s (David, Peter, Stephen); *Career* chief scientist RAF 1977-80; sr dir of technol Br Telecom 1980-83 (engr-in-chief 1983-86); chm SIRA Ltd 1987-; Hon DSc City Univ, hon fell Queen Mary and Westfield Coll London; FIEE, FEng; *Recreations* skiing, walking, reading, travel; *Style*— John Alvey, Esq, CB

ALVINGHAM, 2 Baron (UK 1929); Robert Guy Eardley; CBE (1977, OBE 1972); s of 1 Baron Alvingham (d 1955), and Dorothea Gertrude Yerburgh (d 1927); *b* 16 Dec 1926; *Educ* Eton; *m* 1952, Beryl Elliot, da of William D Williams, of Hindhead; 1 s (Robert), 1 da (Susannah); *Heir* s, Capt Hon Robert Yerburgh; *Career* formerly Coldstream Gds (joined 1945, cmmnd 1946), serv Palestine, Tripoli, FARELF, S America; Head Staff CDS 1972-74, RCDS 1975, dep dir Army Staff Duties 1975-78, Maj-Gen 1978, dir Army Quartering MOD 1978-81; *Style*— Maj-Gen The Rt Hon Lord Alvingham, CBE; c/o House of Lords, Westminster, London SW1

AMAN, Anthony John; s of John Godfrey Aman (d 1950), of Isle of Wight, and Ursula Mary Simmons (d 1982); *b* 31 March 1932; *Educ* Charterhouse, Pembroke Coll Oxford (MA); *Career* serv RA 1954-56; articled clerk Whinney Smith and Whinney 1954-60, Forestal Land Timber & Railways 1960-64, Mgmnt Selection 1964-66, Nat West Bankgroup 1966-78; dir: County Bank 1969-78, Falcon Resources plc 1981-89; Grovewood Securities 1978-80, dir Falcon Resources plc 1981-89; Freeman City of London, Liveryman Worshipful Co of Makers of Playing Cards; *Clubs* Beefsteak, Carlton, Royal Solent Yacht, Berks Golf, Royal Cinque Ports Golf; *Style*— Anthony Aman, Esq; 133 The Colonnades, Porchester Square, London W2 6AP

AMANN, Prof Ronald; s of George James Amann, of Jesmond Park West, Newcastle upon Tyne, and Elizabeth Clementson, *née* Towell (d 1983); *b* 21 Aug 1943; *Educ* Heaton GS Newcastle upon Tyne, Univ of Birmingham (MSocSci, PhD); *m* 28 Aug 1965, Susan Frances, da of Leslie Peters, of S Porcupine, Ontario, Canada; 2 s (Edmund b 1968, Timothy Frances b 1970), 1 da (Jessica Louise b 1974); *Career* conslt OECD 1965-68; Univ of Birmingham: sr lectr (formerly asst lectr and lectr) 1968-83, dir Centre for Russian and E Euro Studies 1983-89, prof of Soviet politics 1985-, dean Faculty of Commerce and Social Sci 1989-; memb Cncl Sch of Slavonic and E Euro Studies Univ of London, specialist advsr and witness Foreign Affrs Ctee and Ctee on Sci and Technol House of Commons; *Books* Science Policy in the USSR (with Berry and Davies, 1968), The Technological Level of Soviet Industry (with Cooper and Davies), Industrial Innovation in the Soviet Union (with Cooper, 1982), Technical Progress and Soviet Economic Development (with Cooper); *Recreations* walking, modern jazz, cricket; *Style*— Prof Ronald Amann; 4 Naunton Close, Selly Oak, Brimingham B29 4DX (☎ 021 475 7346); Faculty of Commerce and Social Science, The University of Birmingham, Edgbaston, Birmingham 15 (☎ 021 414 6608)

AMBLER, Eric; OBE (1981); s of Alfred Percy Ambler (d 1929), and Amy Madeleine Ambler; *b* 28 June 1909; *Educ* Colfe's GS, Univ of London; *m* 1, 1939, Louise Crombie; m 2, 1958, Joan Harrison; *Career* served WWII Lt-Col Europe, Bronze Star (USA) 1945; novelist and screenwriter; screenplays incl: The Way Ahead (1944), The October Man (1947), The Passionate Friends (1948), Highly Dangerous (1950), The Magic Box (1951), Gigolo and Gigolette in Encore (1952), The Card (1952), Rough Shoot (1953), The Cruel Sea (1953), Lease of Life (1954), The Purple Plain (1954), Yangste Incident (1957), A Night to Remember (1958), Wreck of the Mary Deare (1959), Love Hate Love (1970); *Books* incl: The Dark Frontier (1936), Uncommon Danger (1937), Epitaph for a Spy (1938), Cause for Alarm (1938), The Mask of Dimitrios (1939), Journey into Fear (1940), Judgement on Deltchev (1951), The Schirmer Inheritance (1953), The Night-Comers (1956), Passage of Arms (1959), The Light of Day (1962), The Ability to Kill (essays, 1963), To Catch a Spy (ed and intro, 1964), A Kind of Anger (Edgar Allen Poe award, 1964), Dirty Story (1967), The Intercom Conspiracy (1969), The Levanter (1972, Golden Dagger award, 1973), Dr Frigo (1974, MWA Grand Master award 1975), Send No More Roses (1977), The Care of Time (1981), Here Lies (autobiog, 1985, Dagger award, 1986); *Clubs* Garrick, Savile; *Style*— Eric Ambler, Esq, OBE; c/o Campbell Thomson & McLaughin Ltd, 31 Newington Green, London N16 9PV

AMBRASEYS, Prof Nicholas; s of Neocles Amvrasis, of Athens, and Cleopatra, *née* Yambani (d 1986); *b* 19 Jan 1929; *Educ* Nat Tech Univ of Athens, Imperial Coll London (DIC), Univ of London (PhD, DSc); *m* 25 Aug 1955, Xeni, da of Alexander Stavrou; *Career* lectr Imperial Coll London 1958-61; prof: Univ of Illinois 1962-63, Nat Tech Univ of Athens 1963-64; reader Univ of London 1964-74, prof Imperial Coll London 1974-; FRGS, FGS, FICE, FEng; *Recreations* historical geography, archaeology; *Style*— Prof Nicholas Ambraseys; 19 Bede House, Manor Fields, London SW15 3LT (☎ 081 788 4219); Dept Civil Engrg, Imperial Coll of Sci & Technol, London SW7 2AZ (☎ 071 589 5111, telex 261503)

AMBROSE, Hon Mrs (Angela Francesca Hayward); *née* Blanch; da of Baron Blanch, *qv*; *b* 1950; *m* 1974, Timothy Ambrose; 2 da (Bethany b 1978, Emily b 1981); *Style*— The Hon Mrs Ambrose; 7 Plewlands Ave, Edinburgh

AMBROSE, Prof (Edmund) Jack; s of Hary Edmund Ambrose (d 1940), of Cambridgeshire, and Kate, *née* Stanley (d 1926); *b* 2 March 1914; *Educ* Perse Sch Cambridge, Emmanuel Coll Cambridge (BA, MA), Univ of London (DSc); *m* 31 July 1943, Andrée, da of Alphonse Huck, of Seine, France; 1 s (Edmund David b 1945), 1 da (Philippa Jane b 1948); *Career* WWII secret res Admty 1940-45; res offr (protein structure) Courtauld Basic Res Inst Maidenhead 1945-53 res on cell surfaces in normal and cancer cells Chester Beatty Res I 1953-73, prof and head of Dept of Cell Biology Univ of London 1966-75 (emeritus 1976-); chm Sci Advsy Ctee and advsr in cancer to Govt of India Tata Meml Ho Res Inst Bombay 1965-73, advsr Regnl Cancer Centre Kerala India 1978-, co fndr and advsr Fndn for Med Res (leprosy) Bombay 1975-; res Zoology Section Br Assoc for Advancement of Sci 1968-73, fndr and convener Br Soc of Cell Biology, emeritus memb Int Soc of Biological Differentiation, pres Cell Tissue and Organ Culture Gp; diocesan reader Chichester Diocese 1981-; Queen Elizabeth of Hungary Medal Ordre de St Jean de Malte Paris 1981 (for leprosy work in India); *Books* Cell Electrophoresis (1962), The Cancer Cell in Vitro (jtly, 1968), Biology of Cancer (ed 1968, 2 edn 1975), Cell Biology (jtly, 1970, 2 edn 1975), Nature and Origin of the Biological World (1981), The Mirror of Creation (1990); *Recreations* sailing, pastel sketching; *Clubs* Royal Bombay Yacht; *Style*— Prof Jack Ambrose; The Mill House, Westfield, nr Hastings, E Sussex TN35 4SU (☎ 0424 753933)

AMBROSE, Marie Kosloff; da of Lewis Kosloff (d 1932), of London, and Vera, *née* Wolfson (d 1962); *b* 22 Nov 1916; *Educ* N London Collegiate Sch Middx, Univ Coll Hosp London Univ (LDS, DOrth), Royal Dental Hosp London, Eastman Dept Univ of Rome; *m* 3 Sept 1940, Elwyn Ambrose (d 1971), s of Thomas Ambrose (d 1943), of Shrewsbury; 1 da (Anna (Mrs Whyte) b 1944, d 1985); *Career* dental surgn community gen practice and hosp clinical assistantships 1941-74, specialist orthodontist community serv and teaching Kings Coll 1974-79; memb local dental ctee 1951-63; BDA: pres Met Branch 1977-78, chm Br Cncl 1978-80, memb Rep Bd 1980-88; Women In Dentistry: fndr memb, memb Exec Ctee, archivist, speaker; speaker and memb Exec Ctee 300 Group (for training women for Parl), chaired symposium on politics of health with Extra Mural Dept Univ of London; candidate (Lab) Hampstead local elections 1983; memb Bd Govrs FDR Sch for Physically Handicapped Children; music critic: Musical Opinion (monthly), Hampstead and Highgate Express 1977-; memb: Fawcett Soc, NUJ, Woman Returners Network; life memb: BDA 1986, Women In Dentistry 1988; *Recreations* sailing, music, theatre, travel; *Style*— Ms Marie Ambrose; 32 Belsize Park, London NW3 4DX (☎ 071 794 1255)

AMBROSE, (Neil) Simon; s of Neil Trevor Ambrose (d 1952), and Margaret, *née* Donaldson; *b* 17 May 1950; *Educ* Campbell Coll Belfast, Kings Coll Hosp Med Sch (MB BS, MS); *m* 11 Sept 1976, (Elizabeth) Jane, da of William John Arthur Cowley; 2 s (Benjamin Neil b 1981, Jeremy William b 1983), 1 da (Felicity Jane b 1986); *Career* lectr in surgery Univ of Birmingham 1983-88, conslt surgn and sr clinical lectr Univ of Leeds 1988-, surgical tutor Leeds Eastern Health Authy 1989-, chm Leeds Eastern Dist Audit Ctee; sec Assoc Surgns in Trg 1985-87; FRCS 1979; *Recreations* travel, reading, swimming, golf, gardening, DIY; *Style*— Simon Ambrose, Esq; Rigton Gates, Scarsdale Lane, Bardsey, Leeds LS17 9BH (☎ 0937 74463); St James's Univ Hosp, Beckett St, Leeds LS9 7TF (☎ 0532 433144)

AMERY, Lady Catherine; *née* Macmillan; da of 1 Earl of Stockton (d 1986); *b* 1926; *m* 1950, Rt Hon Julian Amery, *qv*; 1 s, 3 da; *Style*— The Lady Catherine Amery; 112 Eaton Sq, London SW1 (☎ 071 235 1543/7409); Forest Farm House, Chelwood Gate, Sussex

AMERY, Rt Hon Julian; PC (1960), MP (C) Brighton Pavilion 1969-; s of Rt Hon Leopold Stennett Amery, CH, PC (d 1955), and Florence, *née* Greenwood, sister of 1 Viscount Greenwood; *b* 27 March 1919; *Educ* Eton, Balliol Coll Oxford; *m* 1950, Lady Catherine, *qv*, da of 1 Earl of Stockton; 1 s (Leopold b 1956), 3 da (Caroline b 1951, Theresa b 1954, Elizabeth b 1956); *Career* MP (C) Preston N 1950-66; Parly under sec of state and fin sec WO 1957-58, Parly under sec of state Colonial Office 1958-60, sec of state for Air 1960-62; min: Aviation 1962-64, Public Bldg and Works 1970, for Housing and Construction DOE 1970-72; min of state FCO 1972-74; *Clubs* White's, Beefsteak, Carlton, Buck's; *Style*— The Rt Hon Julian Amery, MP; 112 Eaton Square, London SW1 (☎ 071 235 1543/7409); Forest Farm House, Chelwood Gate, Sussex

AMES, Dr Anthony Cyril; s of Cyril Frederick Ames, and Amy Edith, *née* Casey; *b* 7 April 1934; *Educ* Mercers Sch, St Marys Hosp Med Sch Univ of London (BSc, MB BS); *m* 20 May 1961, Gillian Rosemary Tyson, da of Lt-Col J P Walters (d 1952); 1 s (Anthony b 1968), 2 da (Sally b 1963, Samantha b 1965); *Career* conslt chemical pathologist 1969, postgraduate clinical tutor 1971; author of numerous papers on biochemistry and clinical pathology; memb: Nat Quality Assur Advsy Panel for Chemical Pathology 1987-90, Royal Coll of Pathologists Standing Advsy Ctee for Chemical Pathology 1988-90; hon treas Assoc Clinical Pathologists 1990; memb: Welsh Lawn Tennis Coaches Assoc, Assoc of Clinic Pathologists; LRCP, MRCS, FRCPath; *Recreations* marathon running, mountaineering, fly fishing, tennis; *Clubs* Old Mercers, Neath Harriers Athletic; *Style*— Dr Anthony Ames; Tyn-Y-Cwm, Rhos, Pontardawe, W Glamorgan SA8 3EY (☎ 0792 862513); Neath General Hospital Neath, W Glamorgan SA11 2LQ (☎ 0639 641161)

AMES, Gerald George Singleton; s of George Singleton Ames (d 1956), and Florence Christian, *née* Hart (d 1982); *b* 15 April 1927; *Educ* Wade Deacon GS, Manchester Sch of Architecture, (DipArch); *m* 4 Feb 1950, Margaret, da of Frederick Atherton (d 1983), of Hillcrest, Cheshire; 2 s (Stephen b 1956, Mark b 1960); *Career* dir John Finlan Ltd 1956-70; md and deputy chm Finlan Group plc 1970-85; dir Finlan Group plc (company concerned in property design and development, export of building services and components, materials handling and merchanting) 1985-87; *Recreations* sailing, music; *Clubs* Liverpool Artists; *Style*— Gerald Ames, Esq; Glan-Yr-Afon Hall, Llanferres, Mold, Clwyd; Sefton House, Exchange Street East, Liverpool L2 3RD (☎ 051 227 1553, fax 051 236 1046)

AMES, Ruth Winifreda (Mrs Ameresekere); da of Ronald Jackson Cyril Munasinha, of Colombo, Sri Lanka, and Mary Winifreda, *née* Dalpadado; *b* 24 June 1938; *Educ* Ave Maria Convent Negombo Sri Lanka, Good Shepherd Convent Colombo Sri Lanka, City of London Coll, Coll for Distributive Trades London (Dip Advertising); *m* 6 Jan 1960, Ranjit William Ebenezer Ameresekere, s of John William Ebenezer Ameresekere (d 1967); 1 s (Edward Ames); *Career* advertising exec Garland Compton Ltd (now Saatchi and Saatchi) 1964-, i/c new business and accounts Lloyds Advertising 1974-75; md: Ames Advertising 1975-89, RA Advertising Ltd 1989-; ptnr Ames Personnel 1987- (proprietor 1975-87); MCAM; *Recreations* badminton, reading, music; *Clubs* IOD; *Style*— Mrs Ruth Ames; Benting Mead, Lonesome Lane, Reigate, Surrey RH2 7QT; Ames Hse, Kings Cross Lane, South Nutfield, Surrey RH1 5NG (☎ 0737 822122, fax 0737 822133)

AMESS, David Anthony Andrew; MP (C) Basildon 1983-; s of James Henry Valentine Amess (d 1986), and Maud Ethel, *née* Martin; *b* 26 March 1952; *Educ* St Bonaventures GS, Bournemouth Coll of Technol (BFC); *m* 1983, Julia Margaret Monica, da of Graham Harry Arnold, of 7 Ockham Hall, Kingsley, Hants; 1 s (David b 1984), 3 da (Katherine b 1985, Sarah Elizabeth b 1988, Alexandra Charlotte Clementine b 1990); *Career* teacher St John Baptist Jr Mixed Sch Bethnal Green 1970-71, trainee underwriter Leslie & Godwin Agency 1974-76, sr conslt Accountancy Personnel 1976-80, ptnr Accountancy Aims Employment Agency 1981-87, chm Accountancy Solutions 1987; joined Cons Pty 1968, Parly candidate (C) Forest Gate 1974 and 1978, GLC candidate Newham NW 1977, Parly candidate (C) Newham NW 1979; Redbridge Cncl: elected 1981, vice chm Housing Ctee 1981-85, vice chm until 1985; PPS at DHSS 1987 to: Edwina Currie, Michael Portillo, Lord Skelmersdale; currently PPS to Michael Portillo at DOE (previously Min at Dept of Transport 1988); *Recreations* reading, writing, sport, theatre, gardening, popular music; *Clubs* Carlton, Kingswood Squash; *Style*— David Amess, Esq, MP; House of Commons, London SW1A 0AA (☎ 071 219 6387)

AMEY, Julian Nigel Robert; s of Robert Amey, of Fieldways, Barton Seagrave, Kettering, Northants, and Diana, *née* Coles; *b* 19 June 1949; *Educ* Wellingborough Sch, Magdalene Coll Cambridge (MA); *m* 16 Dec 1972, Ann Victoria, da of Thomas Frank Brenchley, CMG, of 19 Ennismore Gdns, London SW1; 3 da (Joanna b 9 Sept 1981, Frances b 12 Oct 1984, Charlotte b 7 Jan 1990); *Career* dir of int sales and marketing Longman Group Ltd 1985-89, exec dir BBC English Speaking Union World Service 1989-; tstee Int House; *Books* Spanish Business Dictionary (1979), Portuguese Business Dictionary (1981); *Recreations* cricket, travel; *Clubs* Hawks', Travellers'; *Style*— Julian Amey, Esq; BBC World Service, Bush House, Strand, London (☎ 071 257 2866, fax 071 430 1985, fax 265781 BBC HQG)

AMEY, Nicholas John; s of John William Thomas Amey, MBE, AFC, JP (d 1990), and Margory Anne, *née* Willis (d 1986); *b* 15 March 1947; *Educ* Wellington; *m* 26 July 1984, Wendy Marion Cecile, da of Gerald Edward Atkinson (d 1964); 1 s (Robert b 1985), 1 step da (Joanna Elizabeth Markey-Amey 1970); *Career* dir Moffatt & Co Ltd insur brokers 1974 (chm and md 1989), md Life Assur brokers 1976; memb Lloyds 1987; md Stronghold Trust Ltd; memb Cons Assoc; Freeman City of London 1978, memb Worshipful Co of Gold and Silver Wyre Drawers; ACII 1976; *Recreations* driving historic sports-racing cars, skiing; *Clubs* Ferrari Owners, Historic Sports Car; *Style*— Nicholas Amey, Esq; The Manor House, Old Knebworth, Herts SG3 6QD (☎ 0438 812 713); Percy House, 796 High Rd, London N17 0DJ (☎ 081 808 3020, fax 081 801 4249)

AMHERST, 5 Earl (UK 1826); Jeffrey John Archer Amherst; MC (1918); also Baron Amherst (GB 1788) and Viscount Holmesdale (UK 1826); s of 4 Earl Amherst (d 1927, gs of 1 Earl, ambass to China 1816 and govr-gen of Bengal 1822-28, whose first w gave her name to the ornamental bird known as Amherst's pheasant), and Hon Eleanor St Aubyn, da of 1 Baron St Levan; *b* 13 Dec 1896; *Educ* Eton, Sandhurst; *Heir* none; *Career* served WW I and II, Maj Coldstream Gds (ret) and Hon Wing Cdr RAF; journalist New York Morning World; former air advsr BR and memb stafff BEA; commercial air pilot; *Books* Wandering Far Abroad (autobiography); *Clubs* Travellers', Cavalry and Guards, Pratt's, Garrick; *Style*— The Rt Hon the Earl Amherst, MC; c/o Royal Bank of Scotland, Drummonds Branch, 49 Charing Cross, London SW1

AMHERST OF HACKNEY, 4 Baron (UK 1892); (William) Hugh Amherst Cecil; s of 3 Baron Amherst, of Hackney, CBE (d 1980), and Margaret, Baroness Amherst, of Hackney, *qv*; *b* 28 Dec 1940; *Educ* Eton; *m* 1965, Elisabeth, da of Hugh Humphery Merriman, DSO, MC, TD, DL (d 1983); 1 s (Hon (Hugh) William Amherst), 1 da (Hon Aurelia Margaret Amherst b 1966); *Heir* s, Hon (Hugh) William Amherst Cecil b 17 July 1968; *Career* dir E A Gibson Shipbrokers Ltd; *Recreations* sailing (yacht "Hal"); *Clubs* Royal Yacht Sqdn, Royal Ocean Racing; *Style*— The Rt Hon the Lord Amherst of Hackney

AMHERST OF HACKNEY, Margaret, Baroness; Margaret Eirene Clifton; da of Brig-Gen Howard Brown, sometime MP Newbury, JP, DL (gs of Sir William Brown, 1 Bt, sometime MP S Lancs, JP, DL); *b* 23 Feb 1921; *m* 1939, 3 Baron Amherst of Hackney, CBE (d 1980); 2 s (4 Baron and Hon Anthony Cecil), 1 da (Hon Mrs Reid); *Style*— The Rt Hon Margaret, Lady Amherst of Hackney; 138 Cranmer Court, London SW3

AMIEL, Jon; s of Barry Conrad Amiel (d 1978), of London, and Anita, *née* Barron; *b* 20 May 1948; *Educ* William Ellis Sch London, Univ of Cambridge (MA); *m* Quinny, da of Leslie Sacks; 2 s (Leo Barry, Jack Barry); *Career* admin Oxford & Cambridge Shakespeare Co 1970-73, literary mangr then assoc dir Hampstead Theatre Club 1973-76, asst then assoc dir Royal Shakespeare Co 1976-78, story ed BBC TV 1978-79; directed numerous prodns for BBC Play for Today 1980-85 incl: Preview, Lunch, A Sudden Wrench, Busted, Gates of Gold, Nobody's Property; directed: series Tandoori Nights Channel 4 1985, film Silent Twins 1986, The Singing Detective 1986, feature film Queen of Hearts 1988, Aunt Julia & The Scriptwriter (US title Tune In Tomorrow) 1990; winner: numerous awards for The Singing Detective, several festival awards for Queen of Hearts and Tune In Tomorrow; *Style*— Jon Amiel, Esq; Angel Films, c/o Newman Harris & Co, 18 Harcourt House, 19 Cavendish Square, London W1 (☎ 081 348 9602)

AMIES, Colin MacDonald; s of Maj George Amies (d 1977), of Drumdevan House, Inverness, and Elizabeth Mary Phillips, *née* MacDonald; *b* 14 May 1940; *Educ* Oundle, Christ's Coll Cambridge (MA); *m* 18 Sept 1965, Catherine Anne (Kate), da of Roland Haddon Lovett (d 1985), of Chatton, Alnwick, Northumberland; 4 s (James b 1968, Simon b 1969, William b 1974, Alexander b 1980); *Career* md Exacta Circuits Ltd 1970-77, mangr mfrg ops STC plc 1977-79, corp fin dir Midland Bank plc 1981-85 (electronics indust advsr 1980-81), dir Anamartic Ltd 1987-, md Advert Ltd 1989- (dir 1985); memb: Scot Regnl Cncl CBI 1971-74, Teaching Co Mgmnt Ctee SERC 1987-90; MICE, CEng; *Recreations* skiing, gardening, tennis; *Clubs* Lansdowne; *Style*— Colin Amies, Esq; Advert Ltd, 25 Buckingham Gate, London SW1E 6LD (☎ 071 630 9811, fax 071 828 9958, car 0896 telex 296923)

AMIES, Sir (Edwin) Hardy; KCVO (1989, CVO 1977); s of late Herbert William Amies; *b* 17 July 1909; *Career* dressmaker by appt to HM The Queen; dir Hardy Amies Ltd 1946-; design conslt to numerous clothing companies worldwide; FRSA; *Style*— Sir Hardy Amies, KCVO; 29 Cornwall Gardens, London SW7; Hardy Amies Ltd, 14 Savile Row, London W1 (☎ 071 734 2436)

AMIES, Timothy John (Tim); s of Maj George Amies (d 1976), of Drumdevan Inverness, and Elizabeth Mary Phillips, *née* MacDonald; *b* 1 July 1938; *Educ* Oundle; *m* 6 Nov 1969, Clare Rosemary, da of John Robert Payne Crawfurd, of Surrey; 3 s (Tom b 1971, Edward b 1973, Harry b 1979), 2 da (Sarah b 1974, Alice b 1985); *Career* 2 Lt Queen's Own Cameron Highlanders 1956-58; CA Casselton Elliott and Co 1959-64, merchant banker Morgan Grenfell and Co 1964-68, stockbroker and ptnr Laurie Milbank and Co 1968-86; Chase Manhattan Bank London 1986-89, dir Chase Investment Bank Ltd 1987-; memb London Stock Exchange; FCA, FSIA; *Recreations* children, reading, walking, golf, gardening; *Clubs* City of London, Inst of Directors, Woburn Country; *Style*— Tim Amies, Esq; The Old Farm, Great Brickhill, Buckinghamshire (☎ 052 526 243); Ballachar, Loch Ruthven, Inverness (☎ 08083 258); Chase Investmt Bank Ltd, Woolgate House, Coleman Street, London EC2 (☎ 071 726 5000, private line 071 726 5327, fax 071 726 7156)

AMIS, Sir Kingsley William; CBE (1981); s of William Robert Amis and Rosa Amis; *b* 16 April 1922; *Educ* City of London Sch, St John's Oxford; *m* 1, 1948, Hilary Ann, da of Leonard Sidney Bardwell; 2 s, 1 da; m 2, 1965 (m dis 1983), Elizabeth Jane Howard, *qv*; *Career* author; *novels:* Lucky Jim (1954, filmed 1957), That Uncertain Feeling (1955, filmed as Only Two Can Play 1962, televised 1986), Take a Girl Like You (1960), One Fat Englishman (1963), The Egyptologists (with Robert Conquest, 1965), The Anti-Death League (1966), Colonel Sun (as Robert Markham, 1968), I Want it Now (1968), The Green Man (1969), Girl, 20 (1971), The Riverside Villas Murder (1973), Ending Up (1974), Jake's Thing (1978), Russian Hide-and-Seek (1980), Stanley and The Women (1984), The Old Devils (winner of the Booker prize 1986, adapted for stage 1989), The Crime of the Century (1987), Difficulties with Girls (1988), The Folks that Live on The Hill (1990); *short stories:* My Enemy's Enemy (1962), Collected Short Stories (1980, enlarged edn 1987); *verse:* A Frame of Mind (1953), A Case of Samples (1956), A Look Round the Estate (1967), Collected Poems 1944-1979 (1979); *belles-lettres:* New Maps of Hell (1960), The James Bond Dossier (1965), The Book of Bond, or Every Man His Own 007 (as William Atanner, 1966), What Became of Jane Austen (1970); *non-fiction:* On Drink (1972), Rudyard Kipling and his World (1975), The Alteration (1976), Every Day Drinking (1983), How's Your Glass? (1984), Great British Songbook (with J Cochrane, 1986); *ed:* G K Chesterton Selected Stories (1972), Tennyson (1972), Harold's Years (1977), The New Oxford book of Light Verse (1978), The Faber Popular Reciter (1978), The Golden Age of Science Fiction (1981), The Amis Anthology (1988), The Crime of the Century (1989); kt 1991; *Recreations* music, thrillers, television; *Style*— Sir Kingsley Amis, CBE; c/o Jonathan Clowes, Iron Bridge House, Bridge Approach, London NW1 8BD

AMIS, Richard Henry Allen; CBE (1983); s of Maj Ivan Roll Amis (d 1970), of the Georgian House, Ripley, Surrey, and Sylvia Emily, *née* Booth (d 1968); *b* 4 May 1932; *Educ* Eton; *Career* Capt (TA) 1955; chm Alfred Booth & Co plc 1974-86, dir Michelin Tyre Co 1982-, chm CBI Health & Safety Ctee 1978-83; JP 1984-87; cncllr Guildford Borough Cncl 1972-83; *Recreations* gardening, walking, historical reading; *Clubs* Carlton; *Style*— Richard Amis, Esq, CBE; The Georgian House, Ripley, Woking, Surrey GU23 6AF (☎ 0483 224353)

AMLOT, Roy Douglas; s of Air Cdre Douglas Lloyd Amlot, CBE, DFC, AFC (d 1979), of Casa Jacaranda, Praia da Luz, Algarve, Portugal, and Ruby Luise, *née* Lawrence; *b* 22 Sept 1942; *Educ* Dulwich; *m* 26 July 1969, Susan Margaret, da of Sir Henry McLorinan McDowell, KBE, of Dulwich; 2 s (Thomas b 1971, Richard b 1978); *Career* called to the Bar Lincoln's Inn 1963, bencher 1987, second prosecuting counsel to Inland Revenue (Central Criminal Ct and London Crown Ct) 1974, first prosecuting counsel to the Crown (Inner London Ct) 1975, jr prosecuting counsel to the Crown (Central Criminal Ct) 1977, sr prosecuting counsel to the Crown (Central Criminal Ct) 1981, first sr prosecuting counsel to the Crown 1987; *Publications* Phipson on Evidence (ed 11 edn); *Recreations* skiing, windsurfing, music, squash; *Clubs* St James's; *Style*— Roy Amlot, Esq, QC; 6 King's Bench Walk, Temple, London EC4

AMORY; *see*: Heathcoat-Amory

AMOS, Alan Thomas; MP (C) Hexham 1987-; s of Cllr William Edmond Amos, of Harpenden, Hertfordshire, and Cynthia Florence Kathleen, *née* Hurford; *b* 10 Nov 1952; *Educ* St Albans Sch, St John's Coll Oxford (MA); *Career* Dame Alice Owen's Sch Herts 1976-84: dir of studies, head of Economics & Politics Dept, head of sixth form; head of Agric & Environment Section Conservative Res Dept 1984-86, asst princ Coll of Further Educn 1986-87; pres Oxford Univ Assoc 1974-75; London Borough of Enfield: cncllr 1978-90, dep ldr cncl, chm Educn Ctee; chm: London

Borough Assoc Educn Ctee 1986-87, Backbench Forestry Ctee 1987; sec: Backbench Tport Ctee 1988, Backbench Educn Ctee 1988; memb: CPA, Inter Parly Union, Br American Parly Gp, Agric Select Ctee 1989, ASA, SPUC; chm All Pty Parly ASH Gp 1990-; *Recreations* badminton, travel, USA politics, bibliophilia; *Clubs* Member English-Speaking Union; *Style—* Alan T Amos, Esq, MP; House of Commons, London SW1A 0AA (☎ 071 219 6251, 0434 603777)

AMOS, Francis John Clarke; CBE (1973); s of Frank Amos (d 1970), and Alice Mary, *née* Clarke (d 1974); *b* 10 Sept 1924; *Educ* Dulwich, Univ of London (BSc), London Poly (Dip Arch), Sch of Planning London (Dip Planning); *m* Geraldine Mercy Amos, MBE, JP, da of Capt Egbert Spear Sutton (d 1977); 1 s (Gideon), 2 da (Zephyr, Felicity); *Career* RIASC, Capt 1942-47; Liverpool City planning offr 1966-73, chief exec Birmingham City 1973-77, sr fell Univ of Birmingham 1977-, special prof of planning and mgmnt Univ of Nottingham 1980-; conslt UN Centre of Human Settlements 1974-, tstee Community Project Fndn 1977-88, tstee dir Action Resource Centre 1976-87; conslt: Venezuela 1978, Tanzania 1978-80, India 1979-, Turkey 1979-80, Kenya 1981-, Pakistan 1981-, Zimbabwe 1981-, Bangladesh 1983, Hong Kong 1983, Ghana 1985, Iraq 1985-, Uganda 1987-, Zambia 1987, Lesotho 1987, Trinidad and Tobago 1988, Ethiopia 1988-89, Br Virgin Islands 1989, Indonesia 1989, Laos 1990, Malta 1990; memb various govt sponsored bodies; memb: Community Work and Area Research Centres Gp 1970-86, Int Soc of City and Regnl Planners 1973-, Exec Ctee Public Serv Announcements 1978-86, Nat Exec Ctee and Cncl Nat Assoc of CAB 1982-86, St George's House Windsor 1981-, Jt Land Requirements Ctee 1982-; hon sec Royal Town Planning Inst 1979- (pres 1971-72); lectr: Workers' Educnl Assoc, Univ Extension Serv, USA, India, Utrecht, Belgrade, Barcelona; int seminars organized by: UN, Orgn for Econ Co-op and Devpt, Int Fedn of Housing and Planning, Int Soc of City and Regnl Planners; visiting prof Tech Coll Univ of Munich 1981; FRSA; *Books* Education for Planning and Urban Governance (1973), City Centre Redevelopment (1973), Planning and the Future (1977), Low Income Housing in the Developing World (1984), and various articles, conference papers and government papers; *Recreations* voluntary social work; *Style—* Francis Amos, Esq, CBE; Grindstones, 20 Westfield Rd, Edgbaston, Birmingham B15 3QG; Coach House, Ashton Gifford, Codford St Peter, Warminster, Wilts; School of Public Policy, Univ of Birmingham, PO Box 363, Birmingham B15 2TT (☎ 021 414 5004, telex Birmingham 338938 SPAPHY G)

AMOS, Roy; s of Leonard Alfred Amos, of Birmingham; *b* 8 Sept 1934; *Educ* King Edward's Sch Aston Birmingham, Birmingham Coll of Commerce; *m* 1956, Marjorie Ann, da of Arnold Hall, of Birmingham; *Career* chm and md Lightning International Ltd 1969-74, exec gp dir IMI plc 1974-; chm Manders Holdings plc; FCMA; *Recreations* tennis, golf; *Clubs* Four Oaks, Sutton Coldfield Golf; *Style—* Roy Amos, Esq; The Lodge, Roman Rd, Little Aston Park, Sutton Coldfield, W Midlands B74 3AA (☎ 021 353 5373)

AMPHLETT, Philip Nicholas; s of Colin Bernard Amphlett, of Farm Field, Wootton Village, Oxford, and Hilda, *née* Price (d 1972); *b* 20 Oct 1948; *Educ* Winchester, Balliol Coll Oxford (BA); *m* 4 Aug 1969, Marjolein Erantha, da of Jan Cornelius de Vries (d 1952), of Eindhoven, Holland; 1 s (Jan b 17 Aug 1972), 2 da (Jessica b 9 Jan 1970, Catherine b 14 Nov 1974); *Career* trainee mangr W H Brandts Sons and Co Ltd 1971-73, dir Henry Ansbacher and Co Ltd 1981-85 (joined 1973), sr vice pres Bank Julius Baer and Co Ltd 1985-; *Recreations* sailing, swimming, tennis; *Style—* Philip Amphlett, Esq; Howletts, Gt Hallingbury, Bishops Stortford, Herts (☎ 0279 54563); Ballaminers Cottage, Little Petherick, nr Wadebridge, N Cornwall; Bank Julius Baer and Co Ltd, Bevis Marks House, Bevis Marks, London EC3A 7NE (☎ 071 623 4211, fax 071 283 6146, telex 887272)

AMPTHILL, 4 Baron (UK 1881); Geoffrey Denis Erskine Russell; CBE (1986); s of 3 Baron Ampthill, CBE, by his 1 w, Christabel, da of Lt-Col John Hart, by his w, Blanche, 4 da of Capt David Erskine (2 s of Sir David Erskine, 1 Bt); suc 1973 and petitioned HM The Queen for a Writ of Summons as Baron Ampthill on death of 3 Baron, the House of Lords Ctee on Privileges deciding in his favour 1976; *b* 15 Oct 1921; *Educ* Stowe; *m* 1, 1946 (m dis 1971), Susan Mary Sheila, da of Hon Charles Winn (2 s of 2 Baron St Oswald, JP, DL) by his 1 w, Hon Olive Paget (da of 1 and last Baron Queenborough, GBE, JP) 2 s (and 1 s decd), 1 da; m 2 1972, (m dis 1987), Elisabeth Anne-Marie, da of late Claude Mallon, of Paris, and of Mme Chavane; *Heir* s, Hon David Russell; *Career* WWII Capt Irish Gds; gen mangr Fortnum & Mason 1947-51, chm New Providence Hotel Co Ltd 1952-58, Theatre Producing Cos 1958-71; (md Theatre Owning Cos 1958-69); dir: Dualvest 1980-87, United Newspapers 1981-, Express Newspapers plc 1985- (dep chm 1989-); dep chm of Ctees House of Lords 1981-, dep speaker 1983-, chm Select Ctee on Channel Tunnel Bill 1987; *Style—* The Rt Hon the Lord Ampthill, CBE; 51 Sutherland St, London SW1 4JX

AMWELL, 3 Baron (UK 1947), of Islington, Co London; Keith Norman Montague; s of 2 Baron Amwell (d 1990), and Kathleen Elizabeth, *née* Fountain; *b* 1 April 1943; *Educ* Ealing GS, Nottingham Univ (BSc), CEng, MICE, MIHT, FGS; *m* 1970, Mary, o da of Frank Palfreyman, of Potters Bar, Herts; 2 s (Hon Ian b 1973, Hon Christopher b 1977); *Heir* s, Hon Ian Montague b 1973; *Style—* The Rt Hon Lord Amwell

AMYES, Julian Charles Becket; s of Charles Becket Amyes (d 1943), and Louise, *née* Wilson (d 1926); *b* 9 Aug 1917; *Educ* Perse Sch Cambridge, Univ of Cambridge (BA); *m* 19 April 1948, Katherine Anne, da of Dr William Smith Allan; 1 s (Sebastian Giles Becket b 6 May 1949), 1 da (Isabelle Alexandra Becket b 13 June 1950); *Career* served Army 1940-46; memb Stratford Meml Theatre Co 1947-49, toured Italy with the Old Vic Co 1950, asst dir Chesterfield Civic Theatre 1950, dir and prodr BBC 1951-56; theatre dir Doctor's Dillema (Saville) 1956; film dir: A Hill in Korea (British Lion) 1956, Miracle in Soho (Rank Org) 1957; memb Bd Granada TV 1964-78 (joined 1958, head of Play Dept 1961-63), freelance dir 1978; memb Director's Guild; *Recreations* swimming, reading, travel; *Style—* Julian Amyes, Esq; 4 Palliser Court, Palliser Rd, London W14 9ED (☎ 071 385 7799)

ANAND, Valerie May Florence; da of John McCormick Stubington (d 1967), of Mitcham, and Florence Louise, *née* Sayers; *b* 1937; *Educ* Mitcham Co Sch for Girls; *m* 26 March 1970, Dalip Singh Anand, s of Sunder Singh Anand; *Career* novelist; typist Sudanese Embassy 1956, shorthand typist then sec Oldhams Press 1956-59, sec then editorial asst Quarry Managers' Journal 1959-60, asst PR offr Institute of Launderers, editorial asst Accountancy 1963-66, journalist Index to Office Equipment & Supplies 1966-69, PR offr E J Poole Associates 1969-71, asst ed then ed house magazine of Heals 1971-75, ed Matthew Hall News 1975-88, full time novelist 1988-; novels: Gildenford 1978, The Norman Prentender 1979, The Disputed Crown 1981, To A Native Shore 1984, King of the Wood 1988, Crown of Roses 1989, The Proud Villeins 1990; memb: Br Assoc of Industl Eds 1976-88, Authors Soc 1989-; *Recreations* walking, reading, conversation and argument, good food and wine, used to ride horses; *Style—* Mrs Valerie Anand; c/o Mr David Grossman, David Grossman Literary Agency, 110-114 Clerkenwell Rd, London EC1M 5SA (☎ 071 251 5046)

ANASTASI, George; s of Michael Anastasi, and Paraskevou, *née* Mattheou; *b* 20 Oct 1941; *Educ* The Quintin Sch London, Goldsmiths Coll London; *m* 19 Dec 1964, Maureen Gillian Gloria, da of Alfred Charles Adams (d 1959); 1 s (Robert Matthew b 23 Nov 1979); *Career* asst vice pres Deltec Trading Co Ltd London 1969-73; mangr: First Boston Corp London 1973-74, Williams & Glyn's Bank Ltd London 1974-78; dir Donaldson Lufkin & Jenrette London 1978-80, exec mangr Arab International Finance Ltd London 1980-83, dir Svenska International plc London 1983-; *Style—* George Anastasi, Esq; 7 Clarendon Way, Chislehurst, Kent (☎ 0689 820112); Svenska House, 3-5 Newgate St, London EC1A 7DA (☎ 071 329 4467, fax 071 329 0036/7, telex 89471)

ANCASTER, Earl of; *see*: Willoughby de Eresby, Baroness

ANCRAM, Earl of; Michael Andrew Foster Jude Kerr; s and h of 12 Marquess of Lothian; *b* 7 July 1945; *Educ* Ampleforth, ChCh Oxford (MA), Edinburgh Univ (LLB); *m* 1975, Lady Jane Fitzalan-Howard, da of 16 Duke of Norfolk, KG, GCVO, GBE, TD, PC (d 1975), and Lavinia, Duchess of Norfolk; 2 da (Lady Clare b 1979, Lady Mary b 1981); *Heir* bro, Lord Ralph Kerr; *Career* advocate (Scot) 1970; MP (C) Berwickshire and E Lothian Feb-Sept 1974, Edinburgh S 1979-87; chm Cons Party in Scotland 1980-83 (vice chm 1975-80), memb Select Ctee on Energy 1979-83, Parly under-sec Scottish Office (Home Affairs and Environment) 1983-87; chm Northern Corporate Communications Ltd 1989-, memb Bd Scottish Homes 1988-90; govr Napier Poly of Edinburgh 1989-90, pres Environmental Medicine Fndn 1988-, chm Waverley Housing Tst 1988-90; *Recreations* photography, folksinging; *Clubs* New (Edinburgh); *Style—* Earl of Ancram; 6 St John's House, 30 Smith Square, London, SW1P 3HF; Monteviot, Jedburgh, Scotland TD8 6UQ

ANDERSON, (William) Ainslie; s of William Anderson, OBE, of 19 Queen's Rd, Aberdeen, and Barbara *née* Gibson; *b* 24 Sept 1925; *Educ* Gordonstoun, Univ of Aberdeen (MB ChB); *m* 29 Sept 1956, late Eileen, da of John Davies, of Dublin; 2 s (William b 1958, James b 1960), 1 da (Susan b 1959); *Career* Garden res fell 1950-52, registrar and sr registrar Aberdeen 1952-61, res fell Univ of Colorado Denver 1959-60, conslt gen surgn Derby 1961-; memb: BMA, RSM, Assoc of Surgns; FRCS, FRCSE; *Recreations* shooting, argument (not at the same time); *Clubs* Country (Derby), Dining (Derby); *Style—* Ainslie Anderson, Esq; Derbyshire Royal Infirmary, London Rd, Derby, Derbyshire (☎ 0332 47141)

ANDERSON, Alastair William; TD (1966); s of Cecil Brown Anderson, of 5 Dorchester Court, Glasgow (d 1965), and Janet Davidson, *née* Bell (d 1966); *b* 9 Aug 1931; *Educ* The High Sch of Glasgow, Univ of Glasgow (BSc); *m* 6 Sept 1957, Jennifer Mary, da of Maj Charles W Markham (d 1942), of Clarkston, Glasgow; 1 s (Keith Charles b 30 July 1962); *Career* Nat Serv cmmnd 2 Lt RE 1954, served Britcom Engr Regt Br Cwlth Forces Korea 1954-56, TA 1956-67, Maj RE; Crouch and Hogg Consultant Engineers: joined 1956, assoc 1966-, ptnr 1971, sr ptnr 1981-90; chm Crouch Hogg Waterman Consulting Engineers 1990-; memb Incorporation of Masons Glasgow 1950; CEng, MConsE, FICE, FIHT, FRSA; *Recreations* golf, gardening, reading, walking; *Clubs* Royal Scottish Automobile; *Style—* Alastair Anderson, Esq, TD; Storrs, 7 Greenbank Ave, Whitecraigs, Giffnock, Glasgow G46 6SG (☎ 041 639 2343); Crouch Hogg Waterman Consulting Civil and Structural Engineers, The Octagon, 35 Baird St, Glasgow G4 0EE (☎ 041 552 2000, fax 041 552 2525, telex 779860)

ANDERSON, Albert Alfred James; OBE (1980); s of Frank Alfred Anderson (d 1963), of Oare, Faversham, Kent, and Alice Morley, *née* Cock (d 1978); *b* 15 April 1909; *m* 26 Dec 1931, Alice Rhoda, da of Hermanus Bertram Rupert Alphonso de Leur (ka 1915), of Strood, Kent; 2 s (John Malcolm b 1939 d 1961, Roger Frank b 1942), 1 da (Margaret (Mrs MacInnes) b 1933); *Career* Cdr V Co 13 Bn, Royal W Kent HG, Maj 1941-46; chm and fndr The Kent Art Printers Ltd, chm World Sporting Publications Ltd (published Athletics Weekly 1946-86); cncllr Rochester City Cncl 1936-58 (alderman 1952); chm: Kent Mayors' Assoc 1975-76, 1980-81 and 1988-89 (fndr memb), Kent Rating Valuation Panel 1971-81 (memb 1957-81), Rochester and Chatham Cons Assoc 1973-76, Tstees Baynards Charity 1980-; pres: Medway Mentally Handicapped Soc 1963-, Rochester and Chatham Parly Constituency 1976-83, Medway Parly Constituency 1983-, Medway C of C 1964-68; hon life pres Medway & Gillingham C of C; govr Sir Joseph Williamson Maths Sch Rochester; Home Office ind memb Canterbury Prison Parole Review Ctee 1973-82, chm Ladies Cookham Wood Borstal Prison Parole Review Ctee 1977-83; Rochester Cathedral: steward, friend, hon fin; Mayor of Rochester, Constable of the Castle, Adm of the River Medway, JP 1951-53; Freeman: City of London 1953, City of Rochester Minnesota USA 1952; Liveryman Worshipful Co of Stationers and Newspaper Makers 1953; *Recreations* golf, voluntary charitable and public work; *Clubs* City Livery, St Stephens, Castle (Rochester); *Style—* Albert Anderson, Esq, OBE; Satis Court, Esplanade, Rochester, Kent ME1 1QE (☎ 0634 842933); Kent Art Printers Ltd, Caxton House, Hopewell Drive, Chatham, City of Rochester-upon-Medway, Kent ME5 7NP (☎ 0634 844644, fax 0634 42114)

ANDERSON, (Pamela) Ann; *née* Bates; da of Kenneth Lindley Bates, of Grantham, and Winifred Ethel, *née* Little (d 1987); *b* 9 Feb 1941; *Educ* Kesteven & Grantham Girl's Sch, Neville's Cross Coll Durham, Univ of Nottingham (BEd, Advanced Diploma in Educn); *m* 30 July 1966, Colin Peter Odell, s of John William Anderson (d 1968), of Grantham; 1 s (Marcus b 1977), 1 da (Caroline b 1979); *Career* head Geography Dept St Hugh's Sch Grantham 1964-73, second dep head William Robertson Comp Sch 1973-80, headmistress and fndr owner of Heathlands Prep Sch 1981-; *Recreations* portrait and porcelain painting, dress design; *Clubs* UK Fedn of Business and Professional Women; *Style—* Mrs Ann Anderson; Endahna House, Somerby Hill, Grantham, Lincs (☎ 0476 62050); Heathlands Preparatory School, Gorse Lane, Grantham (☎ 0476 64444)

ANDERSON, Anthony John; QC (1982); s of A Fraser Anderson (d 1982), and Margaret Gray, *née* Spence (d 1986); *b* 12 Sept 1938; *Educ* Harrow, Magdalen Coll Oxford (MA); *m* 1970, Fenja Ragnhild, da of Havard Gunn, OBE; *Career* 2 Lt Gordon Highlanders 1957-59; called to the Bar Inner Temple 1964; *Recreations* golf; *Clubs* Garrick; *Style—* Anthony Anderson, Esq, QC; 33 Abinger Rd, Bedford Pk, London W4 (☎ 081 994 2857); 2 Mitre Ct Bldgs, Temple, London EC4 (☎ 071 583 1380)

ANDERSON, Dr Arthur John Ritchie (Iain); CBE (1984); s of Dr John Anderson (d 1966), of Pontrhydygroes, and Dorothy Mary Anderson (d 1966); *b* 19 July 1933; *Educ* Bromsgrove Sch, Downing Coll Cambridge (MA, MB BChir), St Mary's Hosp Med Sch; *m* 1959, Janet Edith, *née* Norrish; 2 s (John b 1963, Alan b 1971), 1 da (Margaret b 1965); *Career* gen med and hosp practitioner; memb Regnl Planning Cncl for SE 1977-79; memb NW Thames Regnl Health Authy 1978-85; vice chm Herts CC 1985-87 (ldr 1977-83); chm Crouchfield Tst 1989-, chm Herts Police Authy 1983-86, chief whip and former pres Herts Branch BMA 1989-; MRCGP, MRCS, LRCP, DCH, DRCOG, FRSM; *Clubs* Herts 100 (chm); *Style—* Dr Iain Anderson, CBE; Leaside, Rucklers Lane, King's Langley, Herts WD4 9NQ (☎ 0923 262884); office: The Nap, King's Langley, Herts (☎ 0923 263214)

ANDERSON, (Richard James) Colin; s of Richard Henry Anderson (d 1979), and Roseina, *née* Blaney; *b* 11 May 1954; *Educ* Regent House GS, Univ of Ulster; *m* 18 May 1978, Hilary Ann, da of Wilson Somerville Smyth; 1 s (Kyle), 1 da (Kelly); *Career* trainee Thomson Newspapers Orgn, fndr md and princ shareholder Anderson Advertising Ltd; memb NI Tourist Bd (Govt appt); former cncl memb: NI C of C and Indust, NI Branch Inst of Mktg; rugby rep for: Ulster, Ards Rugby Club, CIYMS

Rugby Club; Duke of Edinburgh's Gold Award (ctee memb NI); MInstM, memb IOD; *Recreations* yachting, skiing, golf, rugby; *Clubs* Ulster Reform, Royal Ulster Yacht; *Style—* Colin Anderson, Esq; Anderson House, Holywood Rd, Belfast BT4 2GU (☎ 0232 760901, fax 0232 761678)

ANDERSON, Rear Adm (Charles) Courtney; CB (1971); s of Lt-Col Charles Anderson (d 1919), Australian Light Horse, and Constance Powell-Anderson, OBE, JP; *b* 8 Nov 1916; *Educ* RNC Dartmouth; *m* 1940, Pamela Ruth, da of Lt-Col William Miles, RM (d 1947); 3 s; *Career* RN 1930, serv WWII, naval attaché Bonn 1962-64, dir Naval Recruiting 1965-68, ADC to HM The Queen 1968, flag offr Admty Interview Bd 1969-71, ed The Board Bulletin 1971-78; *Recreations* gardening, Sea Cadets; *Style—* Rear Adm Courtney Anderson, CB; Bybrook Cottage, Bustlers Hill, Sherston, Malmesbury, Wilts SN16 0ND (☎ 0666 840323)

ANDERSON, David Colville; VRD (1947, clasp 1958), QC (Scot 1957); s of John Lindsay Anderson, of Pittormie, Fife (d 1943), and Etta Colville (d 1949); *b* 8 Sept 1916; *Educ* Trinity Coll Glenalmond (Ashburton Shield winner 1933), Pembroke Coll Oxford (BA), Univ of Edinburgh (Thow scholar, LLB, Maclagan prize in forensic med); *m* 1948, Juliet, yr da of Hon Lord Hill Watson, MC, of Barlanark, Edinburgh (d 1957); 2 s (Laurence and Gavin), 1 da (Lorraine); *Career* WWII Lt RNVR N Sea destroyers and in Norway (despatches); Admty Egerton Prize for 1943 in Naval Gunnery; advocate 1946, lectr in Scots law 1948-60; standing jr counsel War Office 1955-57; Parly candidiate (C): Coatbridge 1955, East Dunbartonshire 1959; MP (C) Dumfries Dec 1963-Sept 1964, slr-gen Scotland 1960-64; chief reporter for public inquiries SO 1972-74, under-sec Civil Serv 1972-74; cmmr Northern Lighthouses 1960-64 (vice chm 1964); Hon Sheriff Lothians 1965-74; chm Industl Appeal Tbnls (Scot) 1970-72; King Haakon VII Freedom Medal (Norway) 1945; subject of the play *The Case of David Anderson, QC* by John Hale (Manchester 1980, Edinburgh 1980, Lyric Hammersmith 1981); *Clubs* New (Edinburgh), Scottish Ornithologists (fndr memb 1936); *Style—* David Anderson, Esq, VRD, QC; Barlanark, 8 Arboretum Rd, Edinburgh EH3 5PD, Scotland (☎ 031 552 3003)

ANDERSON, David Mathieson; s of Rev John Anderson, TD (d 1969), of Glasgow, and Dorothy Mary Elizabeth, *née* Cromb; *b* 22 July 1930; *Educ* Glasgow Acad; *m* 3 April 1961, Alma, da of Allan Fleetham (d 1943); 1 s (John Allan b 11 Sept 1971), 1 da (Gillian Grace b 20 Aug 1964); *Career* Nat Serv PO RAF 1953-55; fin dir Assoc Tees-Side Stores 1962-67, Bank of Scotland 1967-69, non-exec dir Fleming Enterprise Investmt Tst plc 1982, commerical dir Austin Reed Gp 1989- (fin dir 1974-89); memb and treas: Br Clothing Indust Assoc, Br Knitting and Clothing Export Cncl; memb Thirsk Rotary Club; Renter Warden and Liveryman Worshipful Co of Glovers 1978; FCA; *Recreations* gardening, walking; *Clubs* RAC; *Style—* David M Anderson, Esq; The Old Vicarage, Skipton Bridge, Thirsk, N Yorkshire Y07 4SB (☎ 0845 567251); Austin Reed Group plc, P O Box 2, Thirsk, N Yorkshire YO7 1PF (☎ 0845 523611, fax 0845 525536)

ANDERSON, David Munro; s of Alexander Anderson, of St Clements, Jersey, CI, and Jessica Hope, *née* Vincent-Innes; *b* 15 Dec 1937; *Educ* Strathallan Sch, Perth Scotland; *m* 3 April 1965, Veronica Jane, da of Reginald Eric Stevens; 2 s (Angus b 1 Oct 1967, Duncan b 10 Nov 1968), 1 da (Lucy b 29 Sept 1973); *Career* cmmnd The Black Watch 1956-59; The London Scottish 1963-68; dir: Anderson Man Ltd, Anderson Man Investmt Serv Ltd (Hong Kong), Bishopsgate Commodity Serv Ltd, ARMAC Mangrs Ltd (Bermuda), E D and F Man Fin Mkts Ltd, Commodities and Equities Tst Mangrs Ltd (IOM), Mint Ltd (Bermuda), E D and F Man Ltd, Mint Guaranteed (Aust) Ltd; chm Assoc for Futures Investmts; churchwarden Holy Innocents Lamarsh, memb Lamarsh PCC; *Recreations* shooting, skiing, gundog training, the arts; *Clubs* Caledonian; *Style—* David Anderson, Esq; The Old Rectory, Lamarsh, Bures, Suffolk; E D and F Man International, Sugar Quay, Lower Thames Street, London EC3R 6DU (☎ 01 626 8788, fax 01 621 0149)

ANDERSON, David St Kevin; s of Frederic St Kevin Anderson (d 1982), of Worthing, W Sussex, and Eileen Celia, *née* Warwick; *b* 4 Oct 1927; *Educ* Clayesmore; *m* 27 June 1959, Mary Isabella, da of William Garnett Ivory (d 1972), of East Grinstead; 1 s (Nigel St Kevin b 1960), 1 da (Rosanagh Jane b 1962); *Career* RM 1945-46, Lt Royal Fus 1946-48, serv 1 Bn BAOR; with Calico Printers' Association Ltd Manchester 1948-50, WA Beardsell & Co Ltd Madras India 1950-56, Dexion Ltd 1956-70, Gravity Randall Ltd Horsham 1970-75, W C Youngman Ltd 1975-84, Gravity Randall Ltd 1984-87, dir Frank Odell Ltd Teddington 1987-88; conslt NR Associates 1989-; chm Cowden Parish Cncl; churchwarden St Mary Magdalene Cowden; pres Old Clayesmorian Soc; Liveryman Worshipful Co of Vintners; *Recreations* gardening, photography, walking, foreign travel; *Style—* David Anderson, Esq; Medway House, Cowden, Kent TN8 7JQ (☎ 0342 850578)

ANDERSON, Denis Richard; s of Maj Thomas Richard Anderson, of Greenisland, Co Antrim, and Florence, *née* Johnston; *b* 8 Feb 1933; *Educ* Grosvenor HS Belfast, Coll of Art Belfast, Univ of Sheffield (Dip Arch); *m* 24 July 1959 (m dis 1972), Jennifer Mary, da of Alan Basset Ward (d 1978), of Gorse Hill, Baslow, Derbyshire; 1 s (Michael James b 29 Dec 1964), 2 da (Clare Sharon b 15 Nov 1961, Louise Jane b 8 June 1963); *Career* architect in private practice Dublin 1964, in jt practice Diamond Redfern Anderson 1966- (Diamond Partnership in UK 1987-90); private practice Dublin 1991-; Castlepark Village Co Cork: RIAI Commendation 1974, Irish Concrete Soc award 1975, Concours Cembureau Commendation 1975, Euro Architectural Heritage Year medal 1975; Martello Mews Dublin: Europa Nostra Dip Merit 1979, RIAI Triennial medal 1983; Dervock Village Co Antrim RIBA Commendation 1979, Massereene Hosp Co Antrim RICS/Times Conservation Commendation 1980, Morehampton Mews Dublin RIAI Highly Commended 1989, Oak Apple Green Dublin RIAI Triennial medal 1989, West Quay Village and Marina Yeading Middx Regnl award 1990; memb RIBA 1962, fell RIAI 1980; *Recreations* skiing, swimming, cars, birdwatching, painting, cricket; *Clubs* Kildare St and Univ (Dublin), East India, Devonshire, MCC, United Artists (Dublin); *Style—* Denis Anderson, Esq

ANDERSON, Donald; MP (Lab) Swansea E 1974-; s of David Robert Anderson (d 1954), of Swansea, and Eva, *née* Mathias; *b* 17 June 1939; *Educ* Swansea GS, Univ Coll Swansea (BA); *m* 28 Sept 1963, Dorothy Mary, da of Rev Frank L Trotman (d 1969), of Bolivia; 3 s (Robert b 24 Dec 1964, Hugh b 17 Nov 1967, Geraint b 20 Sept 1972); *Career* called to the Bar Inner Temple 1969; memb of FCO 1960-64 (HM Embassy Budapest); lectr in politics Univ Coll Swansea 1964-66; MP (Lab) Monmouth 1966-70; pps: Min of Defence 1969-70, Attorney Gen 1974-79; chm Select Ctee Welsh Affairs 1981-83, oppn spokesman Foreign Affairs 1983-; chm: Welsh Lab Gp 1977-78, Br Zimbabwe Gp, Parly Christian Fellowship 1990-; vice chm: Br French Parly Gp, Br Norwegian Gp, CPA 1987-88; vice chm and treas IPU 1986-90, treas 1990-, sec Br German Parly Gp, chm Nat Prayer Breakfast 1989; cncllr Royal Borough of Kensington and Chelsea 1971-75; Methodist local preacher; hon fell Univ Coll Swansea; Cdr's Cross Order of Fed Repub of Germany for contrib to Br German Relations 1986; *Style—* Donald Anderson, Esq, MP; c/o House of Commons, London SW1A 0AA (☎ 071 219 3425/6562)

ANDERSON, Lady; Doris Norah; er da of Lt-Col John Henry Wybergh (d 1964), of Ewshott, Hants, and Norah Selina, *née* Perceval-Maxwell; *b* 5 Aug 1916; *m* 23 Dec 1942, Lt-Gen Sir Richard Neville Anderson, KCB, CBE, DSO (d 1979), s of Lt-Col Sir Neville Anderson, CBE (d 1963); 2 s; *Recreations* horse breeding, whippet breeding and coursing, judging show ponies and dogs; *Style—* Lady Doris Anderson; Tarrant Keynston House, Blandford, Dorset (☎ 0258 452138)

ANDERSON, Douglas Kinloch; OBE (1983); s of William James Kinloch Anderson, of 12 Abbotsford Court, Edinburgh, and Margaret, *née* Gowenlock Harper; *b* 19 Feb 1939; *Educ* George Watsons Coll Edinburgh, Univ of St Andrews (MA), Univ of Edinburgh; *m* 16 June 1962, Deirdre Anne Kinloch, da of Leonard Walter Loryman (d 1985); 2 s (Peter Douglas b 1968, John William b 1972), 1 da (Claire Deirdre b 1964); *Career* Kinloch Anderson Ltd: dir 1962-72, md 1972-, chm 1980- (Quee's Award for Export Achievement 1979); dir: Edinburgh Capital Ltd, Chamber Devpts Ltd, Edinburgh Mktg Ltd, Lothian & Edinburgh Enterprise Ltd, Edinburgh Vision, Scottish Eastern Investment Trust plc; pres: Edinburgh Assoc of Royal Tradesmen 1986-88, Edinburgh C of C 1988-90; former pres Edinburgh Branch Royal Warrant Holders Assoc; memb: Scottish Tourist Bd 1986-, Edinburgh Festival Cncl 1988-, Scottish Ctee IOD; former memb: Br Airways Consumer Cncl, various ctees Scottish Cncl Devpt Indust, hon memb St Andrews Soc Washington DC 1985; Edinburgh Merchant Company: asst 1976-79, treas 1988-90, Master 1990; *Recreations* fishing, golf, skiing, travel, reading; *Clubs* New (Edinburgh), Bruntsfield Golfing Soc, Caledonian; *Style—* Douglas Kinloch Anderson, Esq, OBE; Dalveen, 7 Barnton Park, Edinburgh EH4 6JF (☎ 031 336 3214); Kinloch Anderson Ltd, Commercial Street/Dock Street, Leith, Edinburgh EH6 6EY (☎ 031 55 1355, fax 031 555 1392)

ANDERSON, Hon Mrs (Emily Mary); da of 3 Viscount Astor (d 1966), and his 2 w, Philippa, da of Lt-Col Henry Hunloke (o s of Maj Sir Philip Hunloke, GCVO) and Lady Anne Cavendish, MBE, JP, 5 da of 9 Duke of Devonshire, KG, GCMG, GCVO, PC, JP, DL; *b* 9 June 1956; *Educ* Francis Holland Sch; *m* 1, 1984, Alan McL Gregory, er s of Donald Gregory, of San Francisco, California, USA; m 2, 7 April 1988, as his 2 w, James Ian Anderson, o s of Capt John Murray Anderson, MC, and Lady Gillian Mary, *née* Drummond, da of 18 Earl of Perth; *Career* photographer; *Style—* The Hon Mrs Emily Anderson; 14 Shalcomb St, London SW10 0HY (☎ 071 351 6554)

ANDERSON, Eric George; s of Charles G Anderson (d 1983), of Alyth, Perthshire, and Margery Drysdale, *née* Taylor; *b* 7 June 1940; *Educ* Dundee HS, Univ of St Andrews (MB ChB), Univ of Salford (MSc); *m* 26 March 1966, Elizabeth Clare (Liz), da of Donald George Cracknell, of The Station, Duror in Appin, Argyll; 1 s (Colin b 1967), 2 da (Fiona b 1969, Heather b 1973); *Career* sr registrar Robert Jones and Agnes Hunt Orthopaedic Hosp Oswestry and Birmingham Accident Hosp 1973-78, conslt orthopaedic surgn Western Infirmary and Gartnavel Gen Hosp Glasgow 1978, hon clinical lectr Univ of Glasgow 1978, clinical assoc Univ of Strathclyde 1979; hon med advsr Scot Amateur Swimming Assoc, hon treas Br Orthopaedic Foot Surgery Soc; memb: Cncl of Collège Internationale de Médécine et Chirurgie du Pied, Jt Advsy Panel Orthotic and Prosthetic Trg and Educn Cncl of England and Wales; memb Editorial Bd: Injury, The Foot; FRCS 1971, FRSM 1973, memb Int Soc Prosthetics and Orthotics 1976, fell Br Orthopaedic Assoc 1978, memb Br Orthopaedic Foot Surgery Soc 1981; FRCS (Edinburgh 1971, Glasgow 1981); *Books* contrib: Common Foot Disorders (1989), The Foot and its Disorders (1991); *Recreations* philately, modelling buses and tramways, music; *Style—* Eric Anderson, Esq; 102 Prestonfield, Milngavie, Glasgow G62 7PZ (☎ 041 956 3594); Department of Orthopaedic Surgery, Western Infirmary, Glasgow G11 6NT (☎ 041 339 8822 Ext 4563); Glasgow Nuffield Hospital, Beaconsfield Rd, Glasgow G12 0PJ (☎ 041 334 9441)

ANDERSON, (William) Eric Kinloch; s of William James Kinloch Anderson, of Edinburgh; *b* 27 May 1936; *Educ* George Watson's Coll, Univ of St Andrews (MA), Balliol Coll Oxford (BLitt); *m* 1960, Anne Elizabeth (Poppy), da of William Mattock Mason (d 1988), of Yorks; 1 s (David b 1961), 1 da (Catherine b 1963); *Career* asst master: Fettes 1960-64 and 1966-70, Gordonstoun 1964-66; headmaster: Abingdon Sch 1970-75, Shrewsbury 1975-80, Eton 1980-; hon fell Balliol Coll Oxford 1989; Hon DLitt St Andrews 1981; FRSE 1985; *Books* Journal of Sir Walter Scott (ed, 1972), Percy Letters, Vol IX (ed, 1989); *Recreations* golf, fishing; *Style—* Eric Anderson, Esq, FRSE; The Cloisters, Eton College, Windsor, Berks

ANDERSON, Prof Sir (William) Ferguson; OBE (1961); s of Capt James Kirkwood Anderson, 7 Scottish Rifles (ka Gaza 1917), and late Sarah Barr Anderson; *b* 8 April 1914; *Educ* Merchiston, Glasgow Acad, Univ of Glasgow (MB ChB, MD); *m* 1940, Margaret Gebbie; 1 s, 2 da; *Career* physician in geriatric med Stobhill Gen Hosp and advsr in diseases of old age and chronic sickness; W Region Hosp Bd Scotland 1952-74, David Cargill prof of geriatric med Univ of Glasgow 1965-79; hon pres Crossroads (Scot) Care Attendant Scheme, hon chm Euro Clinical Section Int Assoc Gerontology; awarded Brookdale Prize from The Gerontological Soc of America 1984; FRCPG, FRCPE, FRCP, FRCP (C), FRCPI, FACP; kt 1974, KStJ 1974; *Books* Practical Management of the Elderly (jtly, 1989); *Recreations* golf; *Clubs* Royal Scottish Automobile; *Style—* Prof Sir Ferguson Anderson, OBE; Rodel, Moor Rd, Strathblane, Glasgow G63 9EX (☎ 0360 70862)

ANDERSON, Lady Flavia Joan Lucy; *née* Giffard; da of 2 Earl of Halsbury, KC (d 1943), and Esmé Stewart Wallace; *b* 20 Sept 1910; *Educ* Queen's Gate Sch; *m* 1933, James Alasdair Anderson (d 1982), of Tullichewan; 1 s (Douglas Hardinge, portraitist and wild-life artist; m 1, 1962, Mary Jenkins; m 2, 1974, Veronica Markes), 1 da (Margaret Minette Rohais, m, 1961, Sir Ilay Campbell, 7 Bt, *qv*) *see* Halsbury, Earl of; *Career* author of six books; Medaille de Vermeil de la Reconaissance Française 1946; *Style—* The Lady Flavia Anderson; 13 Carlton Terrace, Edinburgh EH7 5DD

ANDERSON, Lady Gillian Mary; *née* Drummond; yst da of 16 Earl of Perth, GCMG, CB, PC (d 1951); *b* 17 Feb 1920; *m* 1946, Capt John Murray Anderson, MC and bar (late Seaforth Highlanders, d 1991); 1 s, 3 da; *Style—* The Lady Gillian Anderson; Wilderwick House, E Grinstead, W Sussex (☎ 034 287 242)

ANDERSON, Gordon Alexander; s of Cecil Brown Anderson (d 1965), of Glasgow, and Janet Davidson, *née* Bell (d 1966); *b* 9 Aug 1931; *Educ* The High Sch of Glasgow; *m* 12 March 1958, Eirené Cochrane Howie, da of Richmond Douglas (d 1980), of Troon; 2 s (David b 1958, Colin b 1961), 1 da (Carolyn b 1967); *Career* Nat Serv RN (Sub Lt RNVR) 1955-57; CA 1955; Moores Carson & Watson Glasgow (name changed to McClelland Moores (1958), Arthur Young McClelland Moores (1968), Arthur Young (1985), Ernst & Young (1989)): trainee 1949-55, sr asst 1957-58, ptnr 1958-90, memb Exec Ctee 1972-84, office managing ptnr Glasgow 1976-79, chm 1987-89, dep sr ptnr 1989-90; memb Cncl on Tribunals and its Scottish Ctee 1990-; chm Bitmac Ltd 1990- (dir 1985-), dir Douglas Firebrick Co Ltd 1960-70; dir HS of Glasgow Ltd 1975-81 and 1990-, pres Glasgow HS Club 1978-79, memb Scot Milk Mktg Bd 1979-85; Inst of Chartered Accountants of Scot: memb Cncl 1980-84, vice pres 1984-86, pres 1986-87; FCMA (1984); *Recreations* golf, gardening, opera; *Clubs* Caledonian, Western (Glasgow), Glasgow Golf, Buchanan Castle Golf; *Style—* Gordon A Anderson, Esq; Ardwell, 41 Manse Road, Bearsden, Glasgow G61 3PN (☎ 041 942 2803)

ANDERSON, Hamish; s of Dr James Anderson, of Plymouth, and Joan, *née* Caughey; *b* 12 July 1948; *Educ* Clifton Coll, Kingston Poly (LLB), UCL (LLM); *m* 19 Aug 1972, Linda Stuart, da of Dr Norman Rutherford Carlson; 1 s (James b 1975), 1 da (Bryony b 1977); *Career* admitted slr 1973; pt/t lectr law and res asst Kingston Poly 1969-71, licensed insolvency practitioner 1987-, currently head Insolvency Dept Bond Pearce (joined 1971, ptnr 1977-); memb: Jt Working Pty Insolvency Law Bar and Law Soc

1984-, Insolvency Panel Law Soc 1986-; vice pres Insolvency Lawyers' Assoc 1989-, memb Insolvency Practitioners Assoc; memb: Law Soc, Plymouth Law Soc, Insolvency Lawyers' Assoc, Soc of Practioners of Insolvency Justice, Editional Bd of Insolvency Law & Practice; *Books* Administrators: Part II of the Insolvency Act 1986; *Recreations* shooting, cycling, photography; *Style*— Hamish Anderson, Esq; Maristow Cottage, Maristow, Roborough, Devon PL6 7BZ (☎ 0752 780186); Bond Pearce, 1 The Crescent, Plymouth PL1 3AE (☎ 0752 266633, fax 0752 225350, telex 45404, car 0836 504480)

ANDERSON, Rev Hector David; LVO (1949); s of Rev David Anderson, LLD (d 1922, Clerk in Holy Orders), of Leinster Square, Dublin, and Edith Pope (d 1940); *b* 16 Aug 1906; *Educ* The Abbey Tipperary, Trinity Coll Dublin (MA, BD); *m* 1931, Muriel Louise, da of Edwin Cecil Peters (d 1954), of The Ridgeway, Purleybury Avenue, Purley, Surrey; 1 s (Christopher); *Career* ordained priest Canterbury Cathedral 1931; rector of: Sandringham 1942-55, Swanage, Dorset 1960-69; domestic chaplain to: HM King George VI 1942-52, HM The Queen 1952-55; chaplain to HM The Queen 1955-76; ret; *Style*— The Rev H D Anderson, LVO; Adare, The Hyde, Langton Matravers, Dorset (☎ 423206)

ANDERSON, Prof John Allan Dalrymple; TD (1967), DL (Richmond); s of Lt-Col John Allan Anderson, RAMC (d 1942), and Mary Winifred, *née* Lawson (d 1973); *b* 16 June 1926; *Educ* Loretto, Univ of Oxford (BA, MA), Univ of Edinburgh (MB ChB, MD), Univ of London (DPH); *m* 3 April 1965, Mairead Mary, da of Dr P D Maclaren (d 1967), of Edinburgh; 3 da (Sheena b 1966, Mary b 1968, Anne b 1972); *Career* Nat Serv Capt RAMC 1950-52, Maj RMO 7/9 Royal Scots (TA) 1953-63, Maj 51 Highland Vols OC G Co 1967-70, Lt-Col CO 221 Field Ambulance RAMC (TA), Col London Dist TA 1981-83, Regtl and Dep Hon Col 51 Highland Vols 1983-89, hon civilian consIt to Army (public health med); lectr Dept of Gen Practice Univ of Edinburgh 1954-59, physician and res fell Industrial Survey Unit Dept of Rheumatology Univ of Edinburgh 1960-63, sr lectr preventive med London Sch of Hygiene and Tropical Med 1963-, dir Dept of Community Med Guys Hosp Med Sch (subsequently merged with St Thomas's to form Utd Med and Dental Schs) 1969-90, hon consIt Guys Hosp 1969-90, med dir Occupational Health Serv Lewisham and N Southwark Health Dist 1984-90, academic registrar Faculty of Community Med 1983-89, prof and chm Dept of Public Health and Occupational Med Univ of UAE 1990-; hon physician Royal Scottish Corp, emeritus prof Univ of London 1990; Freeman City of London, Liveryman Worshipful Soc of Apothecaries; FRCP 1987, FFCM 1974, FRCGP 1985, FFOM 1990; *Books* A New Look at Community Medicine (1966), Self-Medication (1970), Bibliography of Back Pain (1978), Epidemiological, Sociological and Enviromental Aspects of Rheumatic Diseases (1987); *Recreations* hill-climbing, golf, bridge; *Clubs* New Edinburgh; *Style*— Prof John Anderson, TD, DL; 24 Lytton Grove, Putney, London SW15 2HB (☎ 081 788 9420); Faculty of Medicine and Health Science, Univ of Utd Arab Emirates, Al Ain, UAE (☎ 010 971 3634717)

ANDERSON, Capt John Charles Lindsay (Jack); VRD (1944 and clasp); s of John Lindsay Anderson (d 1943), of Pittormie, Dairsie, Fife, and Margaret (Etta), *née* Colville (d 1949); *b* 8 Sept 1908; *Educ* Trinity Coll Glenalmond, Pembroke Coll Oxford (MA), Univ of Edinburgh (LLB); *m* 17 Oct 1936, Elsie Margaret (d 1990), da of Capt Andrew Currie Begg (ka 1916), of Kirkcaldy, Fife; 1 s (John b 1938), 2 da (Elizabeth b 1937, d 1979, Sonia b 1944); *Career* Sub Lt E Scot div RNVR 1930, Lt 1934, mobilised 1939, HMS Dunedin (northern patrol) 1939-40, HMS Excellent HA/LA Gunnery Course 1940, gunnery offr HMS Alynbank (convoys) 1940-42, staff HMS Excellent and HMS Queen Charlotte 1943, Lt Cdr 1944, HMS Cochrane (coastal convoys) 1944-45, demobbed 1946, memb Ctee Reconstituting Naval Reserves, Capt RNR 1954 (Cdr 1949), cmd HMS Unicorn Tay Div RNVR (RNR) 1954-59, RNR ADC to The Queen 1959-60; admitted slr 1931; currently consIt J L Anderson (Cupar, Kinross, Glenrothes, Cowdenbeath); arable and fruit farmer; dir: Cupar Corn Exchange Co Ltd, Fife Housing Co Ltd; former chm: The Fife Redstone Quarry Co Ltd, Brackmont Quarry Ltd; memb St Andrews Town Cncl 1938-51 (hon treas 1945-51), Parly candidate (C) W Stirlingshire 1945; hon sheriff 1986-: Tayside Central Fife; fndr and govr The Unicorn Preservation Soc 1968-, pres Royal Caledonian Curling Club 1978-79, chm Kirkcaldy Ice Rink 1978-88; currently: hon pres St Andrews Branch Royal Br Legion Scotland (chm 1968-72), dir Gen Cncl Business Ctee Univ of Edinburgh (memb 1982-88), hon vice-pres Cncl Glenalmond Coll; OStJ 1984; memb Law Soc Scotland 1931 (memb Cncl 1983-86); *Recreations* curling, golf, tennis; *Clubs* Royal and Ancient Golf (St Andrews), New Golf (St Andrews); *Style*— Capt Jack Anderson, VRD; 22 Hepburn Gardens, St Andrews, Fife; Messrs J L Anderson, Solicitors and Estate Agents, 35 Bonnygate, Cupar, Fife (☎ 0334 52331)

ANDERSON, Maj-Gen Sir John Evelyn; KBE (1971, CBE 1963); s of Lt-Col John Gibson Anderson, of Christchurch, NZ, and Margaret, *née* Scott; *b* 28 June 1916; *Educ* King's Sch Rochester, RMA Woolwich; *m* 1944, Jean Isobel, 2 da of Charles Tait, of Tarves, Aberdeenshire; 1 s, 1 da; *Career* cmmnd Royal Signals 1936, Lt-Col 1956, Col 1960, Brig 1964, Maj-Gen 1967, Signal Offr in Chief (Army) MOD 1967-69, ACDS (Signals) 1969-72; Hon Col: 71 (Yeo) Signal Regt TAVR 1969-76, Women's Tport Corps (FANY) 1970-76; dir-gen NATO Integrated Communication System Mgmnt Agency 1977-81, consIt electronics and communications 1981-, exec dir AFCEA Europe Gp 1981-88, dir Space & Maritime Applications Inc 1988-; *Recreations* fishing, gardening; *Clubs* Army & Navy, Flyfishers; *Style*— Maj-Gen Sir John Anderson, KBE; The Beeches, Amport, nr Andover, Hants

ANDERSON, John Heugh; s of Samuel Caldwell Anderson (d 1974), and Jemima Fraser, *née* Cameron (d 1980); *Educ* Queens Park Sr Secdy Sch Glasgow, Jordanhill Coll of Educn, Univ of Strathclyde, Open Univ; *m* 19 Nov 1988, Dorothy Margaret, da of James Holton Beresford; *Career* Nat Serv 1953-55; athletics coach and leisure consultant; teacher Glasgow 1955-64, nat coach AAA 1964-65, Scot nat coach 1965-70, dir of physical recreation Heriot-Watt 1970-74, chief leisure and recreation offr Nuneaton and Bedworth Borough Cncl 1974-84, dir of leisure and recreation London Borough of Southwark 1984-89 (Leisure consIt 1989-); GB team coach track and field for all major championships 1981-90 incl: Olympic Games 1984 and 1988, Cwlth Games 1982 and 1986, World Championships 1983 and 1987, Euro Championships 1982, 1986, 1990, Euro Cup 1981, 1985 1989; over 100 GB athletes coached incl: David Moorcroft, David Bedford, David Jenkins, Linsey MacDonald, Liz McColgan, Judy Simpson, Eugene Gilkes, Lynne Mcintyre; only person to have coached athletes to GB standard in every event, first person to pass all sr AAA coaching awards in all events 1964, first Scotsman to pass full FA Badge 1961, fndr original Passport to Leisure Scheme Nuneaton and Bedworth; sporting achievements: Scot Schs football 1950, footballer Scot Amateur League, finalist LTA W of Scot Doubles Shield; Churchill fell 1971; Olympic coach of the year 1988; *Recreations* coaching the disabled in athletics, reading, walking the dog in the country, jogging, cycling, tennis, golf, computer use; *Style*— John H Anderson, Esq; Port Allen Cottage, Errol, Perthshire PH2 7TH (☎ 08212 855)

ANDERSON, John Stewart; TD (and Bar); s of Percy Stewart Anderson (d 1960), and Mabel France, *née* Jones (d 1962); *b* 3 Aug 1935; *Educ* Shrewsbury, Univ of Manchester (BA), Univ of Salford (MSc); *m* 28 Sept 1963, Alice Beatrice, da of Arthur Shelmerdine, of Holmes Chapel, Cheshire; 1 s (Guy Stewart b 1964); *Career* 2 Lt RE, Lt Suez Reserve 1956, Maj RE TA and RCT 1956-76; architect and planner private and public offices 1962-74, dir Planning and Architecture Lincoln City Cncl 1974-85, consIt architect and town planner practice both nat and int specialising in urban design and conservation 1985-; memb Cncl RTPI (pres 1984), sr vice pres Euro Cncl of Town Planners 1988-90; Freeman: City of London 1988, Worshipful Co of Watermen and Lightermen 1989; ARIBA, FRTPI, FRSA; *Style*— John Anderson, Esq, TD; The Old Stables, Harston, Grantham (☎ 0476 870 424, fax 0476 870 816)

ANDERSON, Mrs Ande; Josephine Clare; *see*: Barstow, Josephine Clare

ANDERSON, Dame Judith Frances Margaret; DBE (1960); da of James Anderson, and Jessie Saltmarsh; *b* 10 Feb 1898; *Educ* Norwood HS S Australia; *m* 1, 1937 (m dis 1939) Prof B H Lehman; m 2, 1946 (m dis 1950), Luther Greene; *Career* stage and screen actress; *Films include* Rebecca (as Mrs Danvers), Spectre of the Rose, Cat on a Hot Tin Roof, A Man Called Horse, Star Trek III (1984); *Stage appearances include* Mourning Becomes Electra (1931), Macbeth (opposite Laurence Olivier, Old Vic 1937), Medea (1947-49, New York and on tour); The Oresteia (1966), Hamlet (1970); *Style*— Dame Judith Anderson, DBE; 808 San Ysidro Lane, Santa Barbara, Calif 93103, USA

ANDERSON, Julian Anthony; s of Sir Kenneth Anderson, of London, and Helen Veronica, *née* Grose (d 1986); *b* 12 June 1938; *Educ* King Alfred Sch, Wadham Coll Oxford (MA); *m* 1983, Penelope Ann, da of Arthur Stanley Slocombe (d 1969); *Career* entered civil serv as asst princ, MAFF 1961, asst private sec to Min 1964-66, princ 1966; seconded FCO as memb UK EEC Accession Negotiation Team 1970-73, asst sec 1973; seconded to FCO as Min (Food and Agric), UK perm rep to EEC 1982-85, under sec Lands and Environmental Affrs 1985-90, resigned Civil Service 1990, presently dir gen Country Landowners Assoc; *Recreations* music, sport, travel, photography, gardening, DIY; *Clubs* United Oxford & Cambridge Univ, Civil Service; *Style*— Julian A Anderson, Esq; Country Landowner Association, 18 Belgrave Square, London SW1X 8PQ

ANDERSON, Keith David; s of Dr Redvers Edward Anderson (d 1947), of Luton, Bedfordshire, and Norah Mary Agnes, *née* Payne (d 1972); *b* 3 June 1939; *Educ* Alton Castle Sch Alton Staffordshire, St Bernardines Coll Buckingham; *m* 1, 27 July 1963 (m dis 1974), Sarah Jane, *née* Beddow; 1 s (Timothy Stuart b 26 Sept 1967), 1 da (Jane Ann b 24 May 1964); m 2, 21 March 1975, Susan Lesley, da of Gordon Rodney Kent, of Princes Risborough, Buckinghamshire; 1 s (Stuart David b 20 July 1978); *Career* Nat Serv 1959-61: Corpl RAPC attached to RNF in 1 Gurkha Inf Bde; local govt offr Aylesbury 1954-64; BBC TV: mangr Alexandra Palace 1965-69, organiser Arts Dept 1970-74, prog planning mangr 1974-78, head prog planning resources 1978-82, gen mangr prog planning 1982-89, controller planning and prog servs 1989-; memb: RTS, BFI; *Recreations* golf, squash; *Clubs* Ellesborough Golf, Western Turville Golf, Holmer Green Squash, Wendover Squash, The Cricketers (London), The Rugby (London); *Style*— Keith Anderson, Esq; BBC TV Centre, Wood Lane, Shepherds Buch, London W12 7RJ (☎ 081 576 1136, 081 743 8000, ext 2936, car 0860 383 639)

ANDERSON, Sir Kenneth; KBE (1962, CBE 1946), CB (1955); s of Walter Anderson (d 1953), of Exmouth, Devon, and Susannah, *née* Chirgwin; *b* 5 June 1906; *Educ* Swindon Secdy Sch, Wadham Coll Oxford (MA); *m* 1932, Helen Veronica (d 1986), da of John Gilbert Grose (d 1965), of Bickington, Devon; 1 s (Julian), 1 da (Shirley); *Career* India Office 1928-47, Mil Govt Germany 1947-48, HM Treasy 1949-52, dep dir-gen and comptroller and accountant-gen GPO 1952-66; Offr Order of Orange-Nassau 1947; *Recreations* music, art; *Clubs* United Oxford and Cambridge Univs; *Style*— Sir Kenneth Anderson, KBE, CB; 7 Milton Close, London N2 0QH (☎ 081 455 8701)

ANDERSON, Leslie William; s of Robert Anderson (d 1966), of Edinburgh, and Janetta Urquart, *née* Wishart; *b* 3 Aug 1940; *Educ* Daniel Stewart's College Edinburgh; *m* 8 Jan 1964, Alexandra Angus, da of Bruce Rennie, of Alexandria, Dunbartonshire; 2 da (Emma b 23 Nov 1972, Sacha b 9 May 1975); *Career* news reporter scot Daily Mail Glasgow 1963-66; scot Daily Express: news reporter 1966-67, dep ind corr 1967-70, ind corr 1970-78; BBC Scot: ind corr 1979-84, parliamentary corr 1984-89, home affairs corr 1989; *Recreations* watching rugby; *Clubs* Caledonian, London; *Style*— Leslie Anderson, Esq; BBC Scotland, Broadcasting House, Queen Margaret Drive, Glasgow (☎ 041 3302 793, fax 041 334 0614)

ANDERSON, Lindsay Gordon; s of late Maj-Gen A V Anderson, and late Estelle Bell Sleigh; *b* 17 April 1923; *Educ* Cheltenham Coll, Wadham Coll Oxford (MA); *Career* Lt KRRC; film and theatre director; assoc artistic dir Royal Court Theatre 1969-75; film documentaries incl: Thursday's Children (Hollywood Academy Award 1953), Every Day Except Christmas (Venice Grand Prix 1957), Raz, Dwa, Trzy (The Singing Lesson) (1967), If you were there.... (1985); feature films incl: This Sporting Life (1963), If....(1968, Grand Prix Cannes 1969), O Lucky Man! (1973), In Celebration (1975), Britannia Hospital (1982), The Whales of August (1987); theatre prods incl: The Long and The Short and The Tall, Serjeant Musgrave's Dance, Billy Liar, In Celebration, The Contractor, Home, The Changing Room, The Farm, Life Class, The Sea Gull, The Bed Before Yesterday, Early Days, Hamlet, The Cherry Orchard, The Playboy of the Western World, In Celebration (New York), Hamlet (Washington DC), Holiday, The March on Russia (Nat Theatre, 1989); for TV: The Old Crowd (Alan Bennett), Free Cinema (film Essay, 1986), Glory! Glory! (Home Box Office, 1988); *Books* Making a Film (1952), About John Ford (1980); *Style*— Lindsay Anderson, Esq; 9 Stirling Mansions, Canfield Gdns, London NW6 3JT

ANDERSON, Mary Margaret; *Educ* Forres Acad, Univ of Edinburgh (MB ChB); *Career* jr posts Scotland and England (incl Hammersmith and St Mary's Hosps), sr registrar St Mary's Hosp London until 1967, consIt obstetrician and gynaecologist Lewisham Hosp London 1967-; chm: Div of Obstetrics and Gynaecology Lewisham Hosp, SE Thames Specialist Sub Ctee (Obstetrics and Gynaecology), Hosp Recognition Ctee RCOG; memb: Scientific Ctee Nat Birthday Tst, Cncl Med Def Union; jr vice pres RCOG 1989-, consIt advsr to the CMO 1990-; FRCOG 1974 (MRCOG 1962); *Books* Anatomy and Physiology of Obstetrics (1979), Handbook of Obstetrics and Gynaecology for House Officers (1981), The Menopause (1983), Pregnancy After Thirty (1984), The A-Z of Gynaecology (1986), Infertility (1987); *Style*— Miss Mary Anderson; 96 Harley St, London W1N 1AF (☎ 071 487 4146)

ANDERSON, Brig Hon Dame Mary McKenzie; *see*: Pihl, Brig Hon Dame M M

ANDERSON, Michael Arthur; JP (Chester 1979); s of Alexander William Anderson (d 1971), and Winifred Ann, *née* Pusill (d 1978); matriculation of Arms granted in 1980 by Lord Lyon, King of Arms, based on Arms granted in 1780 but in use prior to 1665; *b* 23 March 1928; *Educ* LSE (BSc); *m* 1954, Anne, da of Joseph Beynon (d 1965); 2 s (Michael, Richard), 2 da (Sarah, Deborah); *Career* fin dir Caribbean Printers Ltd Trinidad 1960-61, sr fin appts Ford Motor Co and Ford of Europe 1962-67, fin dir Manchester Guardian and Evening News Ltd 1968-69, gp fin dir Tillotson & Son Ltd 1970-71, sr fin appts BL 1972-75, fin dir Mersey Docks & Harbour Co 1975-84; dir: Liverpool Grain Storage & Transit Co Ltd 1979-89, Anderson & Co (CA's) 1984-; business cnsllr to Govt Small Firms Serv 1985-, dir Small Firms Business Advisors Ltd 1989; FCA, FCMA, FIBC; *Books* Anderson Families (1984); *Recreations* genealogy, walking, opera, classical music; *Style*— Michael Anderson, Esq, JP; Kintrave, Wood Lane, Burton, Cheshire, S Wirral L64 5TB (051 336 4349)

ANDERSON, Prof Michael John; s of Ronald Arthur Anderson (d 1981), of Llantwit Major, and Dorothy Alma Anderson; *b* 4 June 1937; *Educ* Taunton Sch, Univ of Bristol (BA); *m* 29 Dec 1973, Alessandra Pierangela Lucia, da of dott Girolamo di Gregorio (d 1983), of Bisceglie, Italy; 2 da (Silvia b 1977, Marina b 1980); *Career* The Welch Regt 1956-58; mangr New Theatre Cardiff 1963-64, lectr in drama Univ of Bristol 1964-78; prof of drama: Univ Coll of North Wales Bangor 1978-90 (chm Standing Ctee of Univ Drama Depts 1979-82), Univ of Kent 1990-; memb Welsh Arts Cncl 1985-90 (chm Drama Ctee), joint sec gen Int Fndn for Theatre Res 1989-; FRSA; *Books* Classical Drama and its Influence (ed, 1965), Anger and Detachment: A Study of Osborne (1976); *Recreations* travel, films; *Clubs* Royal Commonwealth Soc, Circolo Unione Bisceglie (Italy); *Style—* Prof Michael Anderson; 28 Nunnery Fields, Canterbury (☎ 0227 464578); Darwin College, The University, Canterbury (☎ 0227 764000)

ANDERSON, Nigel James Moffatt; MC (1940), DL (1974 Wilts); s of Col John Hubback Anderson, CMG, CBE, MD, of Woodend, Victoria, Aust and Ruthin, Clwyd, N Wales (d 1951), and Ruby Clare, *née* Moffatt (d 1937); *b* 9 March 1920; *Educ* Marlborough, Trinity Coll Oxford (MA); *m* 1 Jan 1942, Phyllis Daphne, da of George McKim Siggins, of Portrush, Co Antrim (d 1963); *Career* cmmnd TA, Lt Royal Welch Fusiliers NW Europe invalided out 1943; forester; Wiltshire CC 1955-85 (chm 1979-84); pres Wiltshire CLA, chm Wilts Scout Cncl, pres Wilts Youth Concert Orchestra; High Sheriff of Wiltshire 1990-91; *Recreations* fishing, gardening; *Clubs* Leander; *Style—* Nigel Anderson, Esq, MC, DL; Hamptworth Lodge, Landford, Salisbury, Wiltshire SP5 2EA (☎ 0794 390215)

ANDERSON, Prof Sir (James) Norman Dalrymple; OBE (mil 1945, MBE mil 1943), QC (1974); s of William Dalrymple Anderson (d 1946); *b* 29 Sept 1908; *Educ* St Lawrence Coll Ramsgate, Trinity Coll Cambridge (sr scholar, MA, LLB, LLD); *m* 1933, Patricia Hope, da of A Stock Givan; 1 s and 2 da (decd); *Career* served WWII in Army as Arab Liaison Offr Libyan Arab Force 1940, Civil Affrs GHQ MEF 1941-46, ret as chief sec (Col); barr; Univ of London: prof of oriental laws 1954-75, dir Inst Advanced Legal Studies 1959-76, dean Faculty of Law 1965-69; pres Soc of Public Teachers of Law 1968-69, chm House of Laity Gen Synod C of E 1970-79; Hon DD Univ of St Andrews 1974; FBA 1970; Libyan Order of Independence 1959; kt 1975; *Recreations* reading, writing (has published 19 books); *Clubs* Athenaeum; *Style—* Prof Sir Norman Anderson, OBE, QC; 9 Larchfield, Gough Way, Cambridge (☎ 0223 358778)

ANDERSON, Prof Olive Ruth; da of Donald Henry Frere Gee (d 1964), and Ruth Winifred, *née* Clackson (d 1950); *b* 27 March 1926; *Educ* King Edward VI GS Louth, St Hugh's Coll Oxford (BA, BLitt, MA); *m* 10 July 1954, Matthew Smith, s of Matthew Smith Anderson (d 1960), of Perth; 2 da (Rachel b 1955, Harriet b 1957); *Career* Dept of History Westfield Coll London: asst lectr 1949-56, lectr 1958-69, reader 1969-86, prof and head of dept 1986-; prof and dep head of dept Queen Mary and Westfield Coll 1989-; Royal Hist Soc: assoc 1953, fell 1968, cnclr 1986-; memb Academic Cncl Univ of London 1989- (Exec Ctee 1990-); *Books* A Liberal State at War (1967), Suicide in Victorian and Edwardian England (1987); *Style—* Prof Olive Anderson; 45 Cholmeley Crescent, Highgate, London N6 5EX (☎ 081 340 0272); Queen Mary and Westfield Coll, Hampstead, London NW3 7ST (☎ 071 435 7141, fax 014 794 2173)

ANDERSON, Hon Mrs (Paulette Anne); *née* Sainsbury; only da of Baron Sainsbury by his 2 w; *b* 2 March 1946; *m* 1970, James Anderson; *Style—* The Hon Mrs Anderson; J Sainsbury plc, Stamford House, Stamford St, London SE1 9LL

ANDERSON, Robert Charles (Bob); s of Harry Charles Anderson (d 1980), and Hazel Irene, *née* Grant; *b* 7 Nov 1947; *Educ* Headlands GS; *m* 26 Sept 1970, Florence Mary, da of Cyril Roy Benstead (d 1976); 1 s (David b 1977), 1 da (Jennie b 1975); *Career* darts player: Gold Cup Winner 1983 and 1986, British Open Champion 1987, World Matchplay Champion 1987, World Masters Winner 1986, 1987 and 1987, World Champion 1988, Pacific Masters Winner 1987, 1988 and 1989; *Recreations* golf, snooker, bowls; *Clubs* Marlborough Golf; *Style—* Bob Anderson, Esq; Limestone Cowboy Promotions Ltd, 38F Gainsborough Ave, Wootton Bassett, Swindon, Wilts SN4 8LA (☎ 0793 848428)

ANDERSON, Dr Robert David; s of Robert David Anderson (d 1956), of 54 Hornton St, London W8, and Gladys, *née* Clayton (d 1973); *b* 20 Aug 1927; *Educ* Harrow, Gonville and Caius Coll Cambridge (MA); *Career* dir music Gordonstoun Sch 1958-62, extra mural lectr Egyptology Univ of London 1966-77, assoc ed The Musical Times 1967-85, conductor Bart's Hosp Choral Soc 1965-90, visiting fell in music City Univ 1983-, admin dir Egypt Exploration Soc's dig at Qasr Ibrim 1976-79 (hon sec 1971-82); music critic for The Times, radio and TV for BBC, co-ordinating ed Elgar Complete Edn 1984-; Freeman: City of London 1977, Worshipful Co of Musicians 1977; Hon DMus City Univ 1985; FSA 1983; *Books* Catalogue of Egyptian Antiquities in the British Museum III, Musical Instruments (1976), Wagner (1980), Egypt in 1800 (jt ed, 1988), Elgar in Manuscript (1990); *Recreations* modulating from music to Egyptology; *Style—* Dr Robert Anderson, FSA; 54 Hornton St, London W8 4NT (☎ 071 937 5146)

ANDERSON, Dr Robert Geoffrey William; er s of Herbert Patrick Anderson, and Kathleen Diana, *née* Burns; *b* 2 May 1944; *Educ* Oxford (BSc, MA, DPhil); *m* 1973, Margaret Elizabeth Callis, da of John Austin Lea; 2 s (William b 1979, Edward b 1984); *Career* keeper of Chem Sci Museum 1980-84; dir: Royal Scottish Museum 1984-85, Nat Museums of Scotland 1985-; *Clubs* Athenaeum; *Style—* Dr Robert Anderson; 11 Dryden Place, Edinburgh (☎ 031 667 8211); Royal Museum of Scotland, Chambers St, Edinburgh (☎ 031 225 7534)

ANDERSON, Prof Robert Henry; s of Henry Anderson (d 1981), and Doris Amy, *née* Callear (d 1977); *b* 4 April 1942; *Educ* Wellington, Univ of Manchester (BSc, MB ChB, MD); *m* 9 July 1966, Christine, da of Keith Ibbotson, of Grantham, Lincs; 1 s (John b 1972), 1 da (Elizabeth b 1970); *Career* travelling fell MRC Univ of Amsterdam 1973, sr res fell Br Heart Fndn Brompton Hosp 1974, Joseph Levy reader in paediatric cardiac morphology Cardiothoracic Inst 1977 (prof 1979), visiting prof Univ of Pittsburgh 1984-91, hon prof Univ of North Carolina 1984-91, visiting prof Univ of Liverpool 1988-91; Excerpta Medica Travel Award 1977, Br Heart Fndn Prize for Cardiovasular Res 1984; FRCPath 1979; *Publications* 350 articles, 225 chapters in books; 23 books incl: Cardiac Anatomy (1978), Cardiac Pathology (1983), Surgical Anatomy of the Heart (1985), Paediatric Cardiology (2 volumes, 1987); *Recreations* music, golf, wine; *Clubs* Roehampton; *Style—* Prof Robert Anderson; 60 Earlsfield Rd, Wandsworth, London SW18 3DN (☎ 081 870 4368); Department of Paediatrics, National Heart & Lung Institute, Dovehouse St, London SW3 6LY (☎ 071 351 8019, fax 071 352 0032)

ANDERSON, Robert O; *Career* dep chm Observer Newspaper Gp 1983- (chm to 1983); chm Atlantic Richfield 1983-; *Style—* Robert Anderson, Esq; Observer Ltd, 8 St Andrews Hill, London EC4V 5JA

ANDERSON, Brig (James) Roy; CBE (1971, OBE 1964); s of George Anderson (d 1964), of Kirn, Argyllshire, and Elizabeth Cecily, *née* Findlater (d 1965); *b* 9 Dec 1919; *Educ* graduate Army Staff Coll; *m* 1, 1948 (m dis 1978), Mollie Agatha, *née* Drake-Brockman; 1 s (Hamish b 1952), 1 da (Sheena b 1954); m 2, 1978, Patricia Mary Philomena Ramsay, da of Dr J J Morrin (d 1952), of 1 Walton Place, London SW3; *Career* Royal Sussex Regt 1939-71; CO (Lt-Col) 3 Bn KAR 1962-64, Asst Mil Sec MOD 1965-66, Regtl Col The Queen's Regt 1966, COS (Brig) Kenyan Armed Forces 1966-70, Divnl Brig The Queen's Divn 1970-71; sales dir Brooke Marine (Warship Div) 1972-84, chm E Anglian Rod Co (wholesale game fishing tackle co) 1984-88, non-exec dir Braunston Canal Marina 1989-; chm Shadingfield Beccles PCC 1983-88; MBIM 1969; *Recreations* game fishing, swimming, gardening; *Clubs* United Service, Naval & Military; *Style—* Brig Roy Anderson, CBE; Cherwell Cottage, Aston-Le-Walls, Northants NN11 6UF (☎ 029 586 737)

ANDERSON, Prof Roy Malcolm; s of James Anderson, and Elizabeth, *née* Watson-Weatherburn; *b* 12 April 1947; *Educ* Duncombe Sch, Richard Hale Sch, Imperial Coll Univ of London (BSc, PhD, DIC); *m* 1, 16 Aug 1974 (m dis 1989), Mary Joan, da of Peter Mitchell; 2, 21 July 1990, Claire, da of Rev Peter Baron; *Career* IBM res fell Oxford Univ 1971-73, head of dept Imperial Coll London 1984- (lectr 1973-1980, reader 1980-82, prof 1982-); author of over 200 scientific jls and books; awarded: Huxley Meml Medal 1982, Zoological Scientific Medal 1982, CA Wright Meml Medal 1986, David Starr Jordan Prize 1986, Chalmers Medal 1988, Weldon Prize 1989; memb: Natural Environment Res Cncl 1988-, Cncl Zoological Soc 1988-, Advsy Cncl On Science and Technol 1989-, Cncl Royal Soc; FRS 1986, FIBiol, FRSS, ARCS; *Books* Population Dynamics of Infectious Diseases (1982), Infectious Diseases of Humans: Dynamics and Control (jtly 1990); *Recreations* croquet, hill walking, music, squash, natural history; *Clubs* Athaeneum; *Style—* Prof Roy Anderson; Biology Dept, Imperial College, University of London, London SW7 2BB (☎ 071 589 5111, fax 071 225 1234)

ANDERSON, Sarah Pia; da of Stewart Angus Anderson, and Eldina Pia Anderson; *b* 19 July 1952; *Educ* The Cedars Sch, Univ of Swansea (BA); *Career* theatre and TV dir; trained as a director at the Crucible Theatre Sheffield (prodns incl Hello and Goodbye, What The Butler Saw, Ashes, The Caucasian Chalk Circle); prodns for the Bush Theatre incl: Blisters, Gin Trap, First Blush Last Resort, The Estuary, These Men, The Nest; prodns for RSC incl: Indigo, Old Year's Eve, Across Oka, Mary and Lizzie; other prodns incl: Rosmersholm (NT, La Mama Theatre NY), Carthagians (Abbey Theatre, Hampstead Theatre), Mary Stuart (Shakespeare Theatre Washington DC), The Winters Tale (Univ of Santa Cruz Shakespeare Festival); TV work incl: Blisters, Stepping Out, Shaping Up, Pity in History, A Silly Little Habit, A Woman Calling (Samuel Beckett award), Summers Awakening, The Raving Beauties Make It Work, In My Experience, This Is History Gran, The Bill (4 episodes); memb Dirs Guild of GB; *Recreations* photography, tennis, swimming; *Style—* Ms Sarah Anderson

ANDERSON, Prof Thomas; s of Frederick Anderson, and May, *née* Barrett (d 1987); *b* 24 July 1947; *Educ* Blaydon GS, Univ of Newcastle upon Tyne (BSc, PhD); *m* 3 Aug 1968, Patricia, da of Robert Ormston; 1 s (Iain b 1972), 1 da (Claire b 1975); *Career* prof of computing science Univ of Newcastle upon Tyne, dir Centre for Software Reliability; MIEEE, FBCS; *Books* Fault Tolerance: Principles and Practice (with P A Lee, 2 edn 1990); ed: Computing Systems Reliability: An Advanced Course (with B Randell, 1979), Resilient Computing Systems (1985); software: Requirements, Specification and Testing (1985), Dependability of Resilient Computers (1989), Safe and Secure Computing Systems (1989); contrib to: Resilient Computing Systems (1985), Software Reliability: Achievement & Assessment (ed B Littlewood, 1987); contrib jtly to: Computing Systems Reliability (with P A Lee and S K Shrivastava, 1979), The Evolution of Fault-Tolerant Computing (with A Avizienis and J C Laprie, 1987), Software Diversity in Computerized Control Systems (ed U Voges, 1988); *Recreations* fellwalking, singing; *Style—* Thomas Anderson, Esq; Centre for Software Reliability, Computing Laboratory, University of Newcastle upon Tyne, Newcastle upon Tyne NE1 7RU (☎ 091 232 4016, fax 091 222 8232, telex 53654 UNINEW G)

ANDERSON, Timothy Donald (Tim); s of Donald Simpson Anderson (d 1976), and Barbara Lucille, *née* Carr (d 1956); *b* 16 Oct 1925; *Educ* Malvern Coll, Clare Coll Cambridge, St Thomas's Hosp (MA, MB BChir); *m* 24 Nov 1956, (Frances) Elizabeth, da of Rev Charles Edward Garrad (d 1958); 1 s (Nick b 9 April 1960), 3 da (Katharine b 26 Jan 1958, Penny b 9 April 1960, Emily b 17 June 1965); *Career* RAMC 1952-54, Capt, temp Maj, MO troopships; res obstetric and gynaecological offr Queen Charlottes Hosp and Samaritan Hosp London 1960-61, registrar in obstetrics and gynaecology St Barts Hosp 1962-64, sr registrar in obstetrics and gynaecology Charing Cross Hosp 1964-66, conslt obstetrician and gynaecologist Windsor and E Berks Dist 1967-89; Athletics blue, English native pole vault record 1949, Gold medal pole vault Br Empire Games 1950, pole vault Olympic Games 1952; chm Oxford Regnl Obstetric and Gynaecological Ctee 1987-89; FRCS, FRCOG, FRSM; *Recreations* skiing, mountain walking, tennis, bicycling, painting; *Clubs* Ski of GB, Hawks, Achilles; *Style—* Tim Anderson, Esq; Eastbank River Rd, Taplow, Maidenhead, Berkshire SL6 OBG (☎ 0628 23139); Western Cottage, Bachelors Acre, Windsor, Berks SL4 1EU (☎ 0753 868450)

ANDERTON, Sir (Cyril) James; CBE (1982), QPM, DL (Greater Manchester); s of Late James Anderton, and Lucy, *née* Occleshaw; *b* 24 May 1932; *Educ* Wigan GS, Univ of Manchester; *m* 1955, Joan; 1 da; *Career* Royal Mil Police 1950-53, Constable rising to Chief Inspr Manchester City Police Force 1953-67, Chief Supt Cheshire Constabulary 1967-68, Asst Chief Constable Leicester & Rutland Constabulary 1968-72, asst to HM Chief Inspr of Constabulary for England and Wales Home Office London 1972-75, Dep Chief Constable Leicestershire Constabulary 1975, Chief Constable Gtr Manchester Police 1976- (Dep Chief Constable 1975-76); pres ACPO 1986-87; Cdr St John Ambulance Gtr Manchester 1989-, co dir 1976-89; pres Manchester Branch BIM, patron NW Co Schs Amateur Boxing Assoc, hon nat vice pres The Boy's Brigade, hon vice pres No 318 Sale Squadron ATC; vice pres: Manchester YMCA, Adelphi Lads' Club Salford, Sharp St Ragged Sch Manchester, Manchester Sch Football Assoc, Gtr Manchester E Scout Cncl, Gtr Manchester Fedn Boys Clubs; NSPCC: pres Junior League of Manchester, memb Exec Ctee Manchester Salford and Dist Branch; patron: NW Eye Res Tst, N Manchester Hosp Broadcasting Serv, NW Campaign for Kidney Donors, Gtr Manchester Ctee Int Spinal Res Tst, Henshaws Soc for the Blind; vice pres Wigan Hospice, pres Bolton Mini Le Mans Annual Charity Race, chm tstees Gtr Manchester Police Community Charity; RSPCA: pres Manchester and District, patron Wigan and Dist; pres: British Coll of Accordionists, Police Athletic Assoc Boxing Section; vice pres Manchester & Dist Branch of the Royal Life Saving Soc, tstee Manchester Olympic Bid Ctee; patron: Sale Branch RNLI, Stockport Canal Tst, Hindley Community Assoc Wigan; memb: Royal Sch of Church Music, Nat Geographic Soc, St Andrews Soc of Manchester, Manchester Literary and Philosophical Soc, The Nat Tst, RSPB, The Cwlth Tst, Wigan Little Theatre, RLSS; hon memb RNCM 1984, Cross Pro Ecclesia et Pontifice 1982, Chevalier de la Confrerie des Chevaliers du Tastevin 1985, hon fell British Coll of Accordionists 1976, Freeman City of London, CBIM, KStJ; kt 1990; *Recreations* home, family; *Style—* Sir James Anderton, CBE, QPM, DL; Greater Manchester Police Force, Police Headquarters, Chester House, Boyer St, Manchester M16 0RE

ANDERTON, John Woolven; OBE (1978), VRD (1958); s of Edward Cooke Anderton (d 1947), of Southport, Lancs, and Anne Nell Amelia, *née* Woolven (d 1965); *b* 8 Aug 1923; *Educ* Terra Nova Sch Birkdale, Worksop Coll; *m* 1, 1951 (m dis 1964), Patricia Thompson-Smith; 2 adopted s (Nigel b 1954, Mark b 1958), 1 adopted da (Sally b 1955); m 2, 1966 (m dis 1974), Pamela Jane Astley-Cooper; m 3, 5 June 1975,

Constance Mary, da of Dr Oswald Richardson (d 1966), of Milford-on-Sea, Hants; *Career* entered RN 1941, serv Fleet Air Arm, cmmnd 1943 serv Atlantic and Russian convoys, Combined Ops Med and Normandy landing, Arctic and Far E, cmd Maj landing craft MTB and SDB, attached Mersey Div RNVR (later RNR) 1946-61, ret Lt Cdr; md E C Anderton Ltd 1947-52, dir 15 real estate cos on Merseyside 1952-64; sometime chm: Merseyside Boy's Club, Exchange Club Liverpool; sometime Parish cncllr Cheshire; hon sec and later dir Br Assoc for Shooting and Conservation (formerly WAGBI) 1957-88 (vice pres 1988-), founded Standing Conf on Countryside Sports 1977; memb: Nature Conservancy Wildfowl Conservation Ctee 1957-73 (chm 1967-69), Home Sec's Advsy Ctee for Protection of Birds 1961-77 (became DOE Ctee 1977-82, then Nature Conservancy Cncl Ctee 1982-84), Medway Panel of Inquiry into Shooting and Angling 1976-79, Int Waterfowl Res Bureau Game Conservation Int 1973-82 (chm Int Advsy Ctee 1981-82); former memb Cncl: Game Conservancy (hon life memb 1988), sometime memb Cncl Soc Wildlife Art for the Nations; fndr memb: UK Fedn of Hunting Assocs of the EEC 1977-87 (sometime vice chm), Cncl for Country Sports; fndr memb and vice chm Long Room Ctee (subsequently Br Shooting Sports Cncl), chm Migratory Birds Project 1981-82, patron Grizedale Soc 1989-, memb Br Pavilion Ctee; sometime memb BFSS: Shooting Ctee, Fox and Pheasant Ctee; sometime memb MAIN, chm and pres Euro Waterfowl Habitat Fund 1990-; delegate World Hunting Exhibition Budapest 1971; UK delegate Ramsar Convention Iran 1971; UK govt delegate Int Conf on Conservation of Wetlands and Waterfowl Heiligenhaven W Germany 1974; Beaufort award 1988; contrib numerous articles to countryside, sporting and shooting press; *Recreations* all countryside activities, landscape gardening, conservation, shooting, sailing, travel, photography, art, dogs, bridge, reading and people; *Clubs* Naval and Military; *Style*— John Anderton, Esq, OBE, VRD; Motte Cottage, Bridge-of-Dee, by Castle Douglas, Kirkcudbrightshire DG7 2AE

ANDERTON, Kenneth John; s of Leslie George Anderton (d 1968), of 10 Windsor Terrace, Penarth, S Glam, and Nina Mary, *née* Harwood; *b* 22 July 1940; *Educ* Penarth GS, Welsh Nat Sch of Med Cardiff; *m* 1, 6 June 1962 (m dis), Elizabeth Sarah, da of Gwillym Jones, of 32 Greenfields Ave, Dinas Powis, Cardiff, S Glam; 1 s (Nicholas Simon b 31 Aug 1974), 2 da (Helen Claire b 19 Feb 1970, Susan Jane b 28 Sept 1972); m 2, 21 Feb 1978, Norah; *Career* house offr: Llandough Hosp Cardiff 1963-64, St Woolos Hosp Newport 1964, Glossop Terrace Hosp Cardiff 1965; sr house offr, then registrar Royal Victoria Hosp Newcastle upon Tyne 1965-68, registrar Ashington Hosp Northumbria 1968-72, lectr Univ Dept Jessop Hosp for Women Sheffield 1972-76, conslt obstetrician and gynaecologist Rotherham Dist Gen Hosp 1976-; author of papers in relevant med jls; chm: Rotherham Branch Relate 1985-86, Rotherham Div BMA 1986-87; FRCOG 1982; *Books* Hormone Replacement Therapy of the Menopause (1976), Psychosexual Problems in Gynaecology (1978); *Style*— Kenneth Anderton, Esq; The Mews, Morthen, Rotherham, South Yorks S66 9JL; Dept of Obstetrics and Gynaecology, Rotherham District General Hospital, Moorgate Rd, Rotherham, South Yorks S60 2AU (☎ 0709 820000)

ANDOVER, Viscount; Alexander Charles Michael Winston Robsahm Howard; s and h of 21 Earl of Suffolk and Berkshire; *b* 17 Sept 1974; *Style*— Viscount Andover

ANDRAE, Michael Anton; s of Emile Anton Andrae (d 1974), of London, and Minnie Jenette Isobel, *née* Nisbett (d 1984); *b* 20 Sept 1932; *Educ* Hornsey County GS, Enfield Tech Coll; *m* 12 March 1955, Laura, da of Alfred George Smith; 2 da (Vivienne Jane b 11 June 1960, Gillian Louise b 16 Oct 1963); *Career* Nat Serv RAF 1951-53; laboratory technician Tottenham Gas Co 1949-50, mgmnt apprentice British Oxygen 1950-51, sales rep A Ling & Co 1953-56, PA to md Medico-Therapeutics Ltd 1956-58, PA to md rising to sales mangr then sales and mktg dir Heinke Ltd 1959-65, dir Heinke-Irelleborg Ltd 1959-65, mktg dir Gemma Group 1965-75, dir Mecco Marine Ltd (UK mktg and distribution co for Pirelli Milan inflatable craft) 1965-75, md and chief exec Hunt Instrumentation Ltd 1972-77; dir: Midar Systems Ltd 1975-87, Bond Instrumentation Gibraltar Ltd 1975-87, Bond Instrumentation (Singapore) PTE Ltd 1975-87 (and alternating chm); commercial dir and co sec Bond Instrumentation and Process Control Ltd 1975-87, full time mktg and business conslt and non-exec dir 1987-; *Awards* President's award Chartered Inst of Mktg 1988; Freeman City of London 1989, Liveryman Worshipful Co of Marketors 1989; CIM: memb 1964, nat treas 1987-88, nat chm 1989-90, Hon FCIM 1990; fell Mktg Inst of Singapore 1988, fell IOD 1985, FRSA 1990; *Recreations* fine art, shooting, fishing; *Style*— Michael Andrae, Esq; Andrae Ryder Associates, Business & Marketing Consultants, Carpenders, Eastwell Towers, Kennington, Ashford, Kent TN25 4PQ (☎ 0233 626868, fax 0233 638528)

ANDREAE-JONES, William Pearce; QC (1984); s of Willie Andreae-Jones (d 1975), and Minnie Charlotte, *née* Andreae (d 1990); *b* 21 July 1942; *Educ* Canford, CCC Cambridge (BA MA); *m* 1978, Anne-Marie, da of Michael Cox; 1 s (William b 1979); *Career* called to the Bar Inner Temple 1965; rec Crown Court 1982-; *Style*— William Andreae-Jones, Esq, QC; 6 Kings Bench Walk, Temple, London EC4 (☎ 071 353 9901)

ANDRESKI, Prof Stanislav Leonard; s of Teofil Andrzejewski (d 1967), and Zofia, *née* Karaszewicz-Tokarzewska (d 1939); *b* 8 May 1919; *Educ* Secdy Sch in Poznan, Univ of Poznan, LSE (BSc, MSc, PhD); *m* 1974, Ruth, da of Maurice Ash (d 1976); 2 s (Adam, Lucas), 2 da (Wanda, Sophia); *Career* Mil Serv Polish Army 1937-47, cmmnd 1944; lectr in sociology Rhodes USA 1947-53, sr res fell in anthropology Univ of Manchester 1954-56; lectr in: econs Acton Tech Coll London 1956-57, mgmnt studies Brunel Coll of Technol London 1957-60; prof of sociology Sch of Social Sciences Santiago Chile 1960-61, sr res fell Nigerian Inst of Social and Econ Res Ibadan Nigeria 1962-64, prof and head of Dept of Sociology Univ of Reading 1964-84 (prof emeritus 1984-), hon prof Polish Univ London 1978-; visiting prof: Dept of Sociology and Anthropology City Coll, City Univ of NY, Dept of Sociology Simon Fraser Univ Canada; memb IPI; *Books* Elements of Comparative Sociology (1964), The African Predicament: a Study in Pathology of Modernisation (1968), The Uses of Comparative Sociology (1969, Spanish ed 1972), Parasitism and Subversion: The Case of Latin America (1970, Spanish ed 1968), Military Organization and Society (1970), Social Sciences as Sorcery (1972; ed: Spanish 1973, German 1974, French 1975, Italian 1977, Japanese 1981), The Prospects of a Revolution in the USA (1973), Max Weber's Insights and Errors (1984, Polish ed 1991), Syphilis, Puritanism and Witch hunts: Historical Explanations in the Light of Medicine and Psychoanalysis with a Forecast about Aids (1989); *Recreations* sailing (yacht Metamorfoza); *Clubs* Cruising Assoc, Berkshire Riding; *Style*— Prof Stanislav Andreski; Farriers, Village Green, Upper Basildon, Reading, Berks RG8 8LS (☎ 0491 671318)

ANDREW, Edward Duxbury; s of Roger Duxbury Andrew (d 1978), of Bury, Lancs, and Winifred Marjorie, *née* Hill; *b* 17 Sept 1936; *Educ* Arnold Sch, Univ of Leeds (BSc); *m* 11 Nov 1959, Patricia, da of Douglas Gaskell (d 1979), of Briercliffe, Nelson, Lancs; 2 s (Mark b 1961, Simon b 1963), 1 da (Kathryn b 1966); *Career* chm: Gaskell plc 1971- (and subsids), Lancashire East Euro Industrialists 1984-; chm and md Andrew Industries Ltd 1969- (and subsids); memb Worshipful Co of Feltmakers of London; *Recreations* yachting, golf, fell walking, swimming, shooting; *Clubs* Royal Yachting Association, Pleasington Golf, RAC, Livery; *Style*— Edward D Andrew, Esq; Greystones, Dinckley, Blackburn, Lancs BB6 8AN (☎ 0254 240098); Andrew Industries Ltd, Walshaw Rd, Bury, Lancs BL8 1NG (☎ 061 7611411, fax 061 763 1156, telex 669809)

ANDREW, Elizabeth Honora; *née* Thomas; da of Dilwyn Thomas, of Pontypridd, S Wales, and Morfydd, *née* Horton (d 1979); *b* 6 March 1946; *Educ* Pontypridd Girls' GS, Univ of London (LLB); *m* 21 July 1967, Kenneth Andrew, s of Arthur James Andrew, of Benfleet, Essex; 2 s (Darius Pleydell b 1974, Giles Sheridan b 1976); *Career* trainee retail and personnel mgmnt Marks & Spencer 1963-65, res asst Welsh Hosp Bd 1965-66, fashion buyer 1966-68, mangr wholesale and retail fashion trade 1968-70; called to the Bar Middle Temple 1974, pt/t legal advsr N London Law Centre 1975-78, tenancy 1981-(specialising commercial law, employment law and gen common law); former parish cncllr Three Rivers Parish Cncl; memb: Bar Assoc for Commerce Fin and Indust, Soc of Eng and American Lawyers, Admin Law Bar Assoc; *Recreations* writing, travel, antiques; *Style*— Mrs Elizabeth Andrew; 15 Old Square, Lincoln's Inn, London WC2 (☎ 071 831 0801, fax 071 405 1387, telex 291543)

ANDREW, Hon Mrs (Gwyneth Margaret); *née* Bruce; yr da of 3 Baron Aberdare, GBE (d 1957); *b* 3 July 1928; *m* 1952, Robert McCheyne Andrew; 1 s, 1 da (1 da decd); *Style*— The Hon Mrs Andrew; Hams Barton, Chudleigh, Newton Abbot, Devon TQ13 0DL (☎ 0626 853133)

ANDREW, Keith Vincent; s of Samuel Albert Andrew (d 1982), and Gladys Andrew (d 1956); *b* 15 Dec 1929; *Educ* Oldham Tech HS (HNC), Manchester Coll of Technol (Grad IMechE); *m* 4 Sept 1954, Joyce; 1 s (Neale John b 17 July 1958), 1 da (Clare Elizabeth b 7 Feb 1956); *Career* Nat Serv REME 1951-53; chief exec Nat Cricket Assoc 1986- (dir coaching 1979-); played for England: v Aust 1954, v W Indies 1963; *Books* Skills of Cricket (1984), Coaching Cricket (1986), The Handbook of Cricket (1989); *Recreations* golf, art (sculpture), history of cricket; *Clubs* MCC; *Style*— Keith Andrew, Esq; National Cricket Association, Lord's Cricket Ground, London NW8 8QZ (☎ 071 289 6098)

ANDREW, Kenneth; s of Arthur James Andrew, of Benfleet, Essex, and Emily Sarah, *née* Elderkin; *b* 21 Dec 1944; *Educ* Enfield Coll of Technol (ONC), Imperial Coll London (MSc, DIC), Univ of Wales (BEng), Int Mgmnt Centre (DPhil); *m* 21 July 1967, Elizabeth Honora, da of Dilwyn Thomas, of Pontypridd, S Wales; 2 s (Darius Pleydell b 16 Nov 1974, Giles Sheridan b 11 May 1976); *Career* apprentice draughtsman 1961-64; NatWest Bank plc 1969-84: various posts including head of operational res, branch mgmnt City and West End London, head of mktg; gp mktg dir Good Relations Group plc 1984-85, dir consumer mktg Europe The Chase Manhattan Bank NA 1985-87, gp dir strategy and mktg National & Provincial Building Society 1987-90, independent business conslt 1990-, industl prof of Fin Servs Mgmnt IMC; Hon MPhil IMCB 1984; MBIM, AIB, MBBA, MInstScB; *Books* The Bank Marketing Handbook (1986), The Financial Public Relations Handbook (1990); *Recreations* swimming, reading, writing, travel; *Style*— Kenneth Andrew, Esq; 3 Cassiobury Park Ave, Watford, Herts WD1 7LA (☎ 0923 220 956, fax 0923 240556)

ANDREW, Prof Malcolm Ross; s of John Malcolm Young Andrew, of Latchley, nr Gunnislake, Cornwall, and Mary Lilian, *née* Faulkner; *b* 27 Jan 1945; *Educ* The Perse Sch Cambridge, St Catharine's Coll Cambridge (BA, MA), Simon Fraser Univ BC Canada (MA), Univ of York (DPhil); *m* 17 Aug 1968, Lena Margareta, da of Gustaf Bernström, of Göteborg, Sweden; 1 s (Christopher b 1980), 1 da (Elizabeth b 1982); *Career* asst English master Haileybury Coll 1973-74, lectr then sr lectr Sch of English and American Studies Univ of Anglia 1974-85, dir Sch of English The Queen's Univ Belfast 1986- (prof of English 1985-); memb Steering Ctee Cncl for Univ English; *Books* On the Properties of Things, Book VII (1975), Poems of the Pearl Manuscript (with R Waldron, 1978), The Gawain-Poet: An Annotated Bibliography (1979), Two Early Renaissance Bird Poems (1984); *Recreations* literature, art, architecture, music; *Style*— Prof Malcolm Andrew; 39 Cranmore Gardens, Belfast BT9 6JL (☎ 0232 667869); School of English, The Queen's University of Belfast, Belfast BT7 1NN, Northern Ireland (☎ 0232 245133 ext 3317)

ANDREW, Nicholas Anthony Samuel; s of Samuel Ogden Lees Andrew (d 1966), of Winchester, and Rosalind Molly Carlyon, *née* Evans (d 1984); *b* 20 Dec 1946; *Educ* Winchester, Queens Coll Cambridge (MA); *m* 28 Nov 1981, Jeryl Christine, da of Col John George Harrison, OBE, TD, DL, *qv*, of Devon; 1 da (Venetia); *Career* CA; ptnr: Robson Rhodes 1986-90, Rawlinson & Hunter 1990-; md Robson Rhodes Financial Services Ltd 1986-90; FIMBRA membership ctee 1986-90; FCA, FCCA; *Books* Yuppies and their Money (1987), Robson Rhodes Personal Financial Planning Manual (jtly,2 and 6 edns), How to Make Yourself Wealthy in the 1990's; *Recreations* golf, music, travel; *Clubs* MCC, RAC; *Style*— Nicholas A S Andrew, Esq; Rawlinson & Hunter, One Hanover Square, London W1A 4SR (☎ 071 493 4040, fax 071 499 7464, telex 928560)

ANDREW, (John) Patrick Ramsay; s of John Ramsay Andrew, of St Saviours, Guernsey, and Betty, *née* Arnold (now Mrs Reginald MacLeod); *b* 25 June 1937; *Educ* Canford; *m* 11 Sept 1976, Philippa Rachel (d 1988), da of Cdr Felix Johnstone (d 1964) (see Peerage and Baronetage, B Derwent); 2 da (Edwina Elizabeth b 1981, Emily Katharine b 1983); *Career* chm Strategy Resources Group, fndr Connaught Gallery; int conslt and co dir; *papers* Utilisation of Appropriate Technology in Education, Healthcare and Rural Development in Asia and Africa; *Recreations* international affairs (memb RIIA), building restoration, offshore sailing, fishing, sculpture; *Clubs* Naval and Military; *Style*— Patrick Ramsay Andrew, Esq; Hill House, Dummer, Hampshire RG25 2AD

ANDREW, Richard Arnold; s of John Ramsay Andrew, of St Saviours, Guernsey, and Beatrice Marjorie Kathleen Betty, *née* Arnol; *b* 4 July 1944; *Educ* Cheltenham; *m* 1, 19 Sept 1965 (m dis 1972), Gillian Kathleen, da of Prof Frank Elliott, of Philadelphia; 2 s (James Richard Elliot b 20 July 1966, Edward Alexander b 7 May 1968); m 2, 27 April 1978, Lady Serena Mary Bridgeman, da of The Rt Hon the Earl of Bradford; *Career* Gallaher Ltd 1964-66, Kleinwort Benson Ltd 1966-72, md Service Holdings Ltd 1972-74, Scandinavian Bank Group plc 1974- (gp dir 1981-); chm: Private Capital Group 1986-, Mortgage Trust Ltd 1989-, Radius Estate Agencies Ltd 1988-; dir Brewin Dolphin & Co Ltd; FInstD; *Recreations* golf, tennis, skiing, shooting, fishing; *Clubs* Brook's, Royal Mid Surrey Golf, Royal Western Yacht; *Style*— Richard Andrew, Esq; 64 Elm Park Rd, London SW3 6AU (☎ 071 351 5131); 51 Lincoln's Inn Fields, London WC2 (☎ 071 831 8772)

ANDREW, Sir Robert John; KCB (1986, CB 1979); s of Robert Young Andrew (d 1980), of Walton-on-the-Hill, Surrey; *b* 25 Oct 1928; *Educ* King's Coll Sch Wimbledon, Merton Coll Oxford (MA); *m* 1963, Elizabeth, da of Walter de Courcy Bayley (d 1951), of Barbados; 2 s (Christopher b 1967, John b 1968); *Career* serv Intelligence Corps 1947-49; joined Civil Serv 1952, serv in MOD, Dip Serv and Civil Serv Dept, dep under sec of state Home Office 1976-83, perm under sec of state NI Office 1984-88; dir Esmée Fairbairn Charitable Tst 1989-; conservator of Wimbledon and Putney Commons 1973-, chm King's Coll Sch Wimbledon 1990- (govr 1976-), memb Cncl Royal Holloway and Bedford New Coll 1989-; *Recreations* carpentry, walking; *Clubs* Utd Oxford and Cambridge Univ; *Style*— Sir Robert Andrew, KCB

ANDREWS, Anthony; *b* 1948; *Educ* Royal Masonic Sch; *Career* actor; tv incl: Brideshead Revisited, Danger UXB, Upstairs Downstairs, Much Ado About Nothing,

Romeo and Juliet, The Fortunes of Nigel, The Beast with Two Backs; film incl: Les Adolescents, Ivanhoe, The Scarlet Pimpernel, Under the Volcano, The Holycroft Covenant, Second Victory, The Light Horseman, Innocent Heroes, Hannah's War; theatre incl: 40 Years On (Apollo Theatre), London Assurance, French Without Tears, The Country Wife, Much Ado About Nothing, One of Us (Greenwich Theatre) 1986, Coming Into Land (NT) 1986; *Style—* Anthony Andrews, Esq; Ginette Chambers, 5th Floor, The Chambers, Lots Road, Chelsea Harbour SW10 0XF (☎ 071 376 7676, fax 071 352 7356)

ANDREWS, Christopher Henry; s of Henry Thomas Gordon, of Beltinge, Kent, and Lorna Beatrix Alexandra, *née* Notton; *b* 24 Jan 1940; *Educ* Chislehurst and Sidcup GS; *m* 27 June 1964, Moira Kathlyn Frances, da of John Alfred Dunn (d 1978), of Truro, Cornwall; 2 da (Carey b 1968, Laura b 1970); *Career* dir Ladbroke Gp PLC 1986- (sec 1974-); FCIS; *Recreations* walking, reading, family; *Style—* Christopher Andrews, Esq; Ladbroke Gp PLC, Chancel House, Neasden Lane, London NW10 2XE (☎ 081 459 8031, fax 081 459 6744, telex 22274)

ANDREWS, Dr Christopher John Horner; s of Capt William Henry Horner Andrews (d 1978), and Jean Romer, *née* Young; *b* 31 Dec 1946; *Educ* High Wycombe Royal GS, St George's Coll Jamaica, Univ of London (MB BS, PhD); *m* 21 Oct 1972, Victoria Catherine, da of Charles Samuel Weston (d 1987); 2 s (Jeremy Charles Horner b 1977, William Jonathan Horner b 1979); *Career* MO Br Antarctic Survey 1972-76, sr house offr in anaesthetics The London Hosp 1976-77, registrar Royal Devon and Exeter Hosp 1977-80, sr registrar Bristol Royal Infirmary 1980-84, conslt Plymouth Health Authy 1984-; hon sec local Hosp Med Staff Ctee; memb: BMA 1972, Assoc of Anaesthetists 1977; FFARCS 1980; *Recreations* fell walking; *Style—* Dr Christopher Andrews; 21 Seymour Park, Mannamead, Plymouth PL3 5BQ (☎ 0752 664830); Derriford Hospital, Dept of Anaesthetics, Derriford Rd, Plymouth PL6 8DH (☎ 0752 792691)

ANDREWS, Rev Clive Francis; s of Francis Edward Andrews (d 1966), of New Malden, Surrey, and Iris Emily Amelia, *née* Barton; *b* 14 Feb 1950; *Educ* King's Coll Sch Wimbledon, King's Coll London (BD, AKC), St Augustine's Coll Canterbury; *m* 20 Feb 1982, Diana Ruth, da of Harry John Scrivener (d 1982), of Burstow, Surrey; 2 da (Siobhan b 1983, Caroline b 1986); *Career* curate Clapham Parish Church 1973-75, curate i/c St Nicholas Kidbrooke 1975-78, diocesan youth advsr Southwark 1979-84, vicar St Augustine's Honor Oak 1984-89, team rector Honor Oak Park Team Ministry 1989, permission to officiate diocese of Salisbury 1989-; project consIt Harris City Technol Coll 1989-90, admin dir City Technol Coll Tst 1990-; memb: Surrey Cncl for Voluntary Youth Orgns 1979-84, London Youth Ctee 1981-83, London S Ctee The Prince's Tst 1984-89 (vice chm 1986-89); chm: Lewisham Youth Ctee 1982-84, Bacon's Sch Bermondsey 1985- (govr 1981-); dir The English Dance Consort 1986-; *Books* A Handbook of Parish Youth Work (1984); *Recreations* building restoration, keyboard playing, walking; *Style—* The Rev Clive Andrews; Cross River Cottage, Donhead St Andrew, Shaftesbury, Dorset SP7 9EQ

ANDREWS, David Roger Griffith; CBE (1980); s of C H R Andrews, and G M Andrews; *b* 27 March 1933; *Educ* Abingdon Sch, Pembroke Coll Oxford (MA); *m* 1963, (Dorothy) Ann, da of B A Campbell, CBE (d 1962); 2 s, 1 da; *Career* exec vice chm BL 1977-81; chief exec Land Rover-Leyland Gp 1982-86 (chm 1981-86); dir: Gwion Ltd, Glaxo Trustees Ltd, Clarges Pharmaceutical Trustees Ltd, Fndn for Sci and Technol; FCMA, CBIM; *Recreations* sailing, photography; *Style—* David Andrews, Esq, CBE; Gainford, Mill Lane, Gerrards Cross, Bucks

ANDREWS, (William) Denys Cathcart; CBE (1980); s of Eugene Andrews (d 1947), of Girvan, and Agnes, *née* Armstrong (d 1964); *b* 3 June 1931; *Educ* Girvan HS, Worksop Coll Notts, Univ of Edinburgh (BL); *m* 11 Nov 1955, May, da of Thomas O'Beirne (d 1985), of Ayr; 2 s (Patrick b 1962, Martin b 1964), 2 da (Caroline (Mrs Harris) b 1960, Alison (Mrs Cosslett) b 1967); *Career* slr; ptnr Shepherd & Wedderburn 1962-; pres Law Soc of Scotland 1978-79 (cncl memb 1972-81, vice pres 1977-78), pt/t memb Lands Tbnl for Scotland 1980-; memb Soc of Writers to HM Signet (fiscal 1987-); *Recreations* gardening; *Clubs* New (Edinburgh); *Style—* Denys Andrews, Esq, CBE; 16 Charlotte Square, Edinburgh EH2 4YS (☎ 031 225 8585, telex 727251, fax 031 225 1110)

ANDREWS, Sir Derek Henry; KCB (1991, CB 1984), CBE (1970); s of late Henry Andrews, and late Emma Jane Andrews; *b* 17 Feb 1933; *Educ* LSE (BA); *m* 1956, Catharine May, *née* Childe (d 1982); 2 s, 1 da; *Career* MAFF: asst princ 1957, asst private sec to Min of Agric, Fisheries & Food 1960-61, princ 1961, asst sec 1968; private sec to PM 1966-70 (under sec 1973, dep sec 1981-87, perm sec 1987); Harvard Univ USA 1970-71; *Style—* Sir Derek Andrews, KCB, CBE; c/o Ministry of Agriculture, Fisheries & Food, 3-8 Whitehall Place, London SW1

ANDREWS, Prof Edgar Harold; s of Richard Thomas Andrews (d 1968); *b* 16 Dec 1932; *Educ* Dartford GS, Univ of London (BSc, PhD, DSc); *m* 1961, Thelma Doris, da of Selby John Walker, of Watford; 1 s (Martyn b 1964), 1 da (Rachel b 1962); *Career* dean Faculty of Engrg QMC (now Queen Mary and Westfield Coll) 1971-74 (prof of materials 1968-); dir: QMC Industrial Research Ltd 1970-88, Denbyware Ltd 1971-81, Materials Technol Consultants Ltd 1974-, Evangelical Press 1975-, Fire and Materials Ltd 1985-88; recipient A A Griffith Silver Medal 1977; FIP, FIM, CEng, CPhys; *Books* Fracture in Polymers (1968), From Nothing to Nature (1978), God, Science and Evolution (1980), The Promise of the Spirit (1982), Christ and the Cosmos (1986); *Recreations* writing, music, church work; *Style—* Prof Edgar Andrews; Redcroft, 87 Harmer Green Lane, Welwyn, Herts (☎ 043 879 376); Queen Mary and Westfield College, Mile End Rd, London E1 4NS (☎ 071 975 5152)

ANDREWS, Ernest Somers; s of Charles Andrews (d 1961), of Manchester, and Dorothy, *née* Tonks (d 1989); *b* 10 June 1928; *Educ* Chorlton GS Manchester, Wigan Mining Coll, Salford Tech Coll, UMIST; *m* 22 Sept 1973, Norma, da of William Wilkinson (d 1974), of Manchester; 3 da (Elizabeth Sarah b 1974, Alexandra Dorothy b 1976, Victoria Mary Jane b 1983); *Career* WWII REME 1946-49; princ Charles Andrews & Sons Consltg Engrs 1956-, dir Northern Res & Devpt Co Ltd 1973-; former pres: Manchester Assoc of Engrs, Rotary Club of Manchester South; former chm Manchester Branch Inst Plant Engrs, memb UMIST Assoc Bd (also NW Section); CEng, FIMechE, FIPlantE, FFB, MConsE; *Recreations* military history, industrial archaeology, gardening; *Style—* Ernest Andrews, Esq; 65 South Drive, Chorltonville, Chorlton-cum-Hardy, Manchester M21 2DZ (☎ 061 881 1265); Charles Andrews & Sons, Charter Buildings, Ashton Lane, Sale, Manchester M33 IWT (☎ 061 973 6782, fax 061 962 0617)

ANDREWS, Dr Gilbert; s of Gnanamuthu Andrews (d 1980), of Madras, India, and Singaram Andrews (d 1947); *b* 14 July 1943; *Educ* Univ of Madras (MB BS); *m* 12 Sept 1970, Saroja, da of Mr Kuppusamy (d 1970); 1 s (Vasanth b 16 Dec 1971), 1 da (Poornima b 23 Oct 1974); *Career* Nat Cadet Corps student wing under offr India; conslt psychiatrist SW Surrey Health Authy, examiner RCPsych, clinical tutor Univ of London; med dir: Lynbrook Clinic Knaphill, Milverton Surbiton (chm), Graceton Surbiton (chm); pres Indian Christian Orgn UK, vice pres MIND Woking; MRCPsych, FRSM; *Books* Therapy Options in Psychiatry, Medical Hypnosis (1977); *Recreations* photography, travel; *Style—* Dr Gilbert Andrews; Lynbrook Clinic, Chobham Rd, Knaphill, Woking, Surrey (☎ 04867 89211, fax 0483 797053, car 0860 206511)

ANDREWS, Prof John Albert; JP (1975-); s of Arthur George Andrews (d 1980), of Newport, Gwent, and Hilda May Andrews (d 1989); *b* 29 Jan 1935; *Educ* Newport HS, Wadham Coll Oxford (MA, BCL); *m* 2 April 1960, Elizabeth Ann Mary, da of Frederick Edward Wilkes (d 1939), of King's Heath, Birmingham; 2 da (Carolyn Elizabeth b 1963, Susan Rebecca b 1966); *Career* called to the Bar Gray's Inn 1960, asst lectr Univ of Manchester 1957-58, lectr Univ of Birmingham 1958-67, vice princ Univ of Wales Aberystwyth 1985-88 (head of Dept of Law 1970-, prof of law 1967-); visiting prof Univs of: Thessaloniki 1974, Cracow 1978, Maryland 1983; ed Legal Studies 1981-; chm: Cncl of Validating Univs 1987-90, Police Promotions Examinations Bd 1987-; pres SPTL 1988-89, memb Police Trg Cncl 1987-, chm Wales Advsy Body for Local Authy Higher Educn Standing Working Gp 1990-, tstee Hamlyn Tst 1969-; *Books* Welsh Studies in Public Law (ed, 1970), Human Rights in Criminal Procedure (ed, 1982), The Welsh Language in the Courts (jtly, 1984), The International Protection of Human Rights (jtly, 1987), Criminal Evidence (jtly, 1987); *Recreations* walking, theatre, food; *Clubs* Brynamlwg; *Style—* Prof John Andrews, JP; Maeshendre, Aberystwyth, Dyfed (☎ 0970 623921); Dept of Law, University College of Wales, Aberystwyth, Dyfed (☎ 0970 622710, fax 0970 611446, telex 35181 ABYUCWG)

ANDREWS, Hon Katharine Ann; da of 1 and last Baron Douglas, of Kirtleside; *b* 26 July 1957; *m* 1984, Geoffrey Andrews; *Career* SRN, HV (Cert), NDN (Cert), SCM; *Style—* The Hon Mrs Andrews

ANDREWS, Mark Björnsen; s of Harry Field Andrews, of Reading, and Ruth Margaret, *née* Legge; *b* 12 July 1952; *Educ* Reading GS, Hertford Coll Oxford (BA); *Career* admitted slr 1976; ptnr Wilde Sapte 1979; memb Law Soc 1974-; *Recreations* playing French horn, singing, outdoor sports and activities, ornithology; *Style—* Mark Andrews, Esq; Wilde Sapte, Queensbridge House, 60 Upper Thames St, London EC4V 3BD (☎ 071 236 3050, fax 071 236 9624, telex 887793)

ANDREWS, (J) Michael G; s of Air Vice-Marshal Jo Andrews, CB, DSO, MC (d 1989), and Bertha Winifred, *née* Bisdee; *b* 6 Nov 1926; *Educ* Shrewsbury, Magdalen Coll Oxford (MA), Harvard Business Sch (MBA); *m* Oct 1988, Sylvia, da of Dr Charles Rothschild (d 1988); 2 da (Carolyn b 1955, Victoria b 1959); *Career* dir: Hill Samuel & Co 1963-68, Samuel Montagu & Co 1968-72; chief exec Brandts 1972-75; non-exec dir incl: Bankside Underwriting Agencies Ltd, McLeod Russell Holdings plc, Credit Lyonnais Capital Mkts, Laing & Cruickshank Investment Management; former non-exec dir: Royal Worcester, Teachers (Distillers); external memb Cncl Lloyds of London 1985-87, memb Advsy Cncl AMBA, former memb Chemical Indust EDC; FCA; *Recreations* fishing; *Clubs* Leander; *Style—* Michael Andrews, Esq; 1 Surrey St, London WC2R 2PS (☎ 071 240 3995, fax 071 831 1133)

ANDREWS, Lady Patricia Ann; *née* Le Poer Trench; da of late 6 Earl of Clancarty; *b* 20 Jan 1928; *m* 1, 1946, Eugene Nicodemus de Szpiganowicz (d 1965), s of late Baron Klemens de Szpiganowicz, of Dobrynic, Poland; m 2, 1977, Alan Sidney Andrews (d 1980); *Style—* The Lady Patricia Andrews; Flat 2, Sunray House, Moory Meadow, Combe Martin, Devon

ANDREWS, Raymond Denzil Anthony; MBE (1953); s of Michael Joseph Andrews (d 1975), of Wolsey Rd, Moor Park, Herts, and Phyllis Marie, *née* Crowley (d 1972); *b* 5 June 1925; *Educ* Highgate Sch, Christ's Coll Cambridge, Univ of London, Univ of Michigan; *m* 28 Sept 1958, (Anne) Gillian Whitlaw, da of David Small (d 1933); 1 s (Michael James b 1964), 1 da (Emily Justine b 1968); *Career* Lt RM 1946, Maj RMR 1968; sr ptnr Andrews Downie & Ptnrs Architects; pres Architectural Assoc 1977-78, Royal Mint Square Housing Competition (first prize); RIBA (vice pres 1984); Order of Al Rafidan of Iraq 1956; *Recreations* sailing (sloop Blaize); *Clubs* Bosham Sailing; *Style—* Raymond Andrews, Esq, MBE; 34 Clarendon Rd, Holland Park, London W11 3AD (☎ 071 727 4129); Andrews Downie & Partners, 6 Addison Ave, London W11 4QR (☎ 071 602 7701, fax 071 602 8480)

ANDREWS, Raymond William John (Ray); s of William Edwin Andrews, of 5 Eastwood Rd, Dudley, W Midlands, an Nell, *née* Walters; *b* 17 June 1944; *Educ* Dudley GS; *m* 24 Dec 1970, Mary Josephine, da of Leonard Edmund Ayres (d 1985); 1 s (Richard Steven b 1971), 1 da (Catherine Elizabeth b 1974); *Career* chm and md Midland Thermal Equipment Ltd 1982-, md Midtherm Engrg 1984-; *Recreations* flying (ratings held PPL and IMC), motor sport; *Style—* Ray Andrews, Esq; Midland Thermal Equipment Ltd, New Rd, Netherton, Dudley, W Mids DY2 8SY (☎ 0384 458800, fax 0384 258572)

ANDREWS, Richard Edward; s of William Reginald Andrews (d 1983), and Agnes Ruby Whiffen; *b* 15 Aug 1936; *Educ* Cambridge HS, St Catharine's Coll Cambridge (MA); *m* 18 Aug 1981, Stephanie Elizabeth, da of Percy Craig, of Motueka, NZ; 1 s, 1 da; *Career* Flt Offr RAF Fighter Cmd 1955-57; sr conslt PA 1965-72, personnel mangr BLMC 1972-74, personnel dir Franklin Mint USA 1974-78, business mangr Cassells 1979, gp personnel dir Dixons Group plc 1980-, dir Dixons Bradford CTC Trust 1988-; FIPM; *Clubs* Savile; *Style—* Richard Andrews, Esq; 29 Farm St, London W1X 7RD (☎ 071 499 3494)

ANDREWS, Stuart Morrison; s of William Hannaford Andrews (d 1975), and Eileen Elizabeth, *née* Morrison (d 1987); *b* 23 June 1932; *Educ* Newton Abbot GS, St Dunstan's Coll, Sidney Sussex Coll Cambridge (MA); *m* 1962, Marie Elizabeth, da of Jacobus Petrus van Wyk, of SA; 2 s (Jeremy b 1963, Christopher b 1966); *Career* headmaster: Norwich Sch 1967-75, Clifton 1975-90; ed Conference 1971-82; dep chm Assisted Places Ctee, nat rep HMC Ctees 1986-87; *Books* Eighteenth Century Europe (1965), Enlightened Despotism (1967), Methodism and Society (1970); *Recreations* walking, writing; *Clubs* East India Sports, Devonshire and Public Schs; *Style—* Stuart Andrews, Esq; 34 St Thomas St, Wells, Somerset BA5 2UX (☎ 0749 670249)

ANDREWS, Dr Vivienne Elizabeth; da of Harry Andrews (d 1985), of London, and Elizabeth Margaret, *née* Byatt; *b* 19 Oct 1951; *Educ* St George's Hosp Med Sch (MB BS, MRCPath); *m* 2 Sept 1978, Dilwyn Allen Morgan, s of George Thomas Morgan, of Sittingbourne; 1 s (Malcolm Edward b 2 March 1989); *Career* conslt haematologist Dartford and Gravesham DHA 1984-; memb: Save the Children Fund, Amnesty Int; memb Br Soc Haematology; *Recreations* flying; *Clubs* Civlair Flying; *Style—* Dr Vivienne Andrews

ANDRUS, (Francis) Sedley; LVO (1982); s of late Brig-Gen Thomas Alchin Andrus, CMG, JP (d 1959), and Alice Loveday, *née* Parr (d 1984); b on first anniversary of d of gf Adm Alfred Arthur Chase Parr, FRGS, sometime a naval ADC to Queen Victoria; *b* 26 Feb 1915; *Educ* Wellington, St Peter's Coll Oxford (MA); *Career* Bluemantle Pursuivant of Arms 1970-72, Lancaster Herald of Arms 1972-82, Beaumont Herald of Arms Extraordinary 1982-; landowner; *Style—* Sedley Andrus, Esq, LVO; College of Arms, Queen Victoria St, London EC4V 4BT (☎ 071 248 2762); 8 Oakwood Rise, Longfield, Kent DA3 7PA (☎ 047 47 5424)

ANDRY, Dr Peter Edward; s of Dr Harold John Andry (d 1963), and Frances Elizabeth *née* Scheerbarth; *b* 10 March 1927; *Educ* Melbourne C of E GS, Melbourne Univ (DMus, ARCM); *m* 1, 11 April 1956 (m dis 1964), Rosemary Jane, da of Lt Hilary Macklin, OBE (d 1965), of 14 Bedford Square; 2 s (Miles, Christopher); m 2, Christine Ann, *née* Sunderland; 1 da (Jennifer); *Career* prodr and freelance musician Aust Bdcasting Cmmn 1949-52, conductor Br Cncl Bursary 1953, prodr Decca Record Co 1954-56; EMI Music: asst mangr HMV 1954-56, asst mangr Int Artists Dept

1962-69, pres Int Classical Div 1972-1989; many recordings with: Inter Alia, Britten, Beecham, Karajan, Klemperer, Menuhin, Callas, De Los Angeles, Dieskau, Richter, Pollini, Rostropovich, Perlman; sr vice pres classical repetoire Warner Classics International 1989; chm and vice pres Barnet Soc MENCAP, chm Music Ctee and memb Cncl RSA, treas Royal Philharmonic Soc, tstee and sec Aust Musical Fndn in London, chm of govrs Music Therapy Charity, hon memb RCM, memb Royal Soc of Musicians of GB; Freeman City of London 1988, Liveryman Worshipful Co of Musicians 1989; Hon DMus City Univ 1990; *Recreations* reading, photography, tennis, running, gardening; *Clubs* Garrick; *Style—* Dr Peter Andry; 82 Corringham Rd, London NW11 7EB (☎ 081 455 8787)

ANFIELD, Elizabeth Margaret; da of Michael Walter Fitton Brown (d 1975), of Mill Hill, London, and Beatrice Elizabeth (Lena), *née* Moore; *b* 20 March 1949; *Educ* North London Collegiate Sch, Univ of Kent at Canterbury (BSc); *m* 19 July 1969 (m dis 1989), Alan Anfield, s of Maj Frederic Ernest Anfield, of Nethy Bridge, Inverness-shire; *Career* CA; memb Exec Ctee: Reading and Central Berks C of C 1985-88 (chm business section 1985), Newbury and W Berks C of C 1985- (chm small business section 1986), Inst of Taxation Thames Valley Branch 1980- (treas 1984-88, sec 1988), md Thames Valley Residential Props plc 1988-; treas Newbury Dist Churches Housing Tst 1984-, sec Newbury Twin Town Assoc 1986-88 (chm 1988-89); FCA, ATII; *Recreations* skiing, theatre, foreign travel; *Style—* Mrs Elizabeth Anfield

ANG, Dr Swee Chai; da of P L Ang, of Singapore, and L H Ang, *née* Lee; *b* 26 Oct 1948; *Educ* Raffles GS, Univ of Singapore (MB BS, MSc); *m* 29 Jan 1977, Francis Khoo, s of Anthony T E Khoo (d 1972), of Singapore; *Career* orthopaedic surgn HS of Beirut 1976-, surgn UN Gaza Strip 1988-89, conslt surgn WHO Gaza and W Bank 1989; fndr memb Br Charity Med Aid for Palestinians; memb BMA, assoc BOA, FRCS; *Books* From Beirut to Jerusalem (1989); *Recreations* music, poetry; *Style—* Dr Swee Ang; Medical Aid for Palestinians, 29 Enford St, London W1H 1DG (☎ 071 723 7760, fax 071 706 1078)

ANGEL, Anthony Lionel; s of William Angel, of 6A Holly Park Gdns, London N3, and Frances Beatrice, *née* Berman; *b* 3 Dec 1952; *Educ* Haberdashers' Aske's, Queens' Coll Cambridge (MA); *m* 2 Nov 1975, Ruth Frances Barbara, da of Ivan Frank Hartog, of 11A Greenheys Close, Northwood, Middx; 2 s (Benjamin b 3 Dec 1978, Jonathan b 18 Sept 1982); *Career* admitted slr 1978; ptnr Linklaters & Paines 1984- (joined 1978); memb: Worshipful Co of Slrs; memb Law Soc; *Recreations* tennis, swimming; *Style—* Anthony Angel, Esq; Linklaters & Paines, Barrington House, 59-67 Gresham St, London EC2V 7JA (☎ 071 606 7080, fax 071 606 5113, telex 884349/888167)

ANGEL, Donald; CBE; *Educ* LSE (BSc Econ); *m* ; 1 s, 1 da; *Career* chm: Birds Eye Wall's Ltd 1981-88, Lipton Ltd 1972-74, Wall's Meat Co Ltd 1974-78, Birds Eye Foods Ltd 1979-81; dir: Trebor Ltd 1987-89, Associated Fresh Foods Ltd 1988-90, Travellers Fare Ltd 1989-; pres UK Assoc of Frozen Food Producers 1984-86; memb Cncl Food and Drinks Fedn 1986-; govr Francis Holland Schs 1975-, memb Cncl GPDST 1988-; *Recreations* opera, antique furniture, gardening; *Style—* Donald Angel, Esq, CBE; 41 Canonbury Square, London N1 2AL

ANGEL, Gerald Bernard Nathaniel Aylmer; s of Bernard Francis Angel (d 1963), and Ethel Angel (d 1988); *b* 4 Nov 1937; *Educ* St Mary's Sch Nairobi Kenya; *m* 1968, Lesley Susan, da of Rev Preb Cyril Kenneth Alfred Kemp (d 1987); 4 s (Matthew b 1971, Thomas b 1975, Benedict b and d 1978, Christopher b 1979), 1 da (Katharine b 1969); *Career* served Kenya Regt 1956-57; called to the Bar Inner Temple 1959, advocate Kenya 1960-62, practiced at Bar 1962-80, registrar Family Div High Ct 1980-91; memb: Judicial Studies Bd 1989-90, Civil and Family Sub Ctee Judicial Studies Bd 1985-90; dist judge 1990, sr dist judge of the Family Div 1991-; memb: Supreme Court Procedure Ctee 1990, Matrimonial Causes Rule Ctee 1991-; ed Industrial Tribunal Reports 1966-78, advsy ed and contributor Atkin's Court Forms (1988); *Style—* Gerald Angel, Esq; 9 Lancaster Avenue, London SE27 9EL; Principal Registry of the Family Division, Somerset House, Strand, London WC2

ANGEL, Dr Heather; da of Stanley Paul Le Rougel, and Hazel Marie, *née* Sherwood; *b* 21 July 1941; *Educ* 14 schs in England and NZ, Univ of Bristol (BSc, MSc); *m* 3 Oct 1964, Martin Vivian Angel, s of Thomas Huber Angel; 1 s (Giles Philip b 25 May 1977); *Career* marine biologist, professional wildlife photographer author and lectr; solo exhibitions: Kodak Exhibition The Natural History of Britain and Ireland (Science Museum) 1981, Nature in Focus (Nat Hist Museum) 1987, The Art of Wildlife Photography (Nature in Art, Gloucester) 1989; television appearances (demonstrating photographic techniques): Me and My Camera 1981, Me and My Camara II 1983, Gardeners' World 1983, Nature 1984, Nocon on Photography 1988; RPS Hood medal 1975, Medaille de Salverte (Société Française de Photographie) 1984; Hon DSc Univ of Bath 1986; Hon FRPS 1986 (FRPS 1972), FBIPP 1972; *Books* Nature Photography: Its Art and Techniques (1972), Photographing Nature (5 vols, 1975), Life in The Oceans (1977), The Book of Nature Photography (1983), Camera in the Garden (1984), The Book of Close-up Photography (1986), A View from a Window (1988), Nature in Focus (1988), Landscape Photography (1989); *Recreations* travelling to remote parts of the world to photograph wilderness areas and unusual aspects of animal behaviour; *Style—* Dr Heather Angel; Highways, 6 Vicarage Hill, Farnham, Surrey GU9 8HJ (☎ 0252 716700, fax 0252 727464)

ANGEL, John Charles; s of James Lee Angel, of 7 Lynceley Grange, Epping, Essex, and Joan Angel; *b* 6 Sept 1939; *Educ* Bancroft's Sch Woodford, London Hosp Med Coll (MB BS, FRCS); *m* 7 Nov 1970, Jacquelyn Carol (Jackie), da of Jack Davies, of 32 Canford Dr, Allerton, Bradford, W Yorks; 1 s (Nicholas b 15 Sept 1973), 1 da (Catherine b 4 March 1972); *Career* conslt orthopaedic surgn Royal Nat Orthopaedic Hosp 1976-; contrib papers and chapters on amputation surgery and slipped upper femoral epiphysis; *Recreations* golf, music; *Style—* John Angel, Esq; Royal Nat Orthopaedic Hosp, Brockley Hill, Stanmore, Middx (☎ 081 954 2300)

ANGEL, Richard Reeve; s of Edward Reeve Angel (d 1988), of Cranford, Northants, and Hope Aldrich Cleaveland Angel (d 1981); *b* 4 Aug 1928; *Educ* Oundle, Univ of Edinburgh; *m* 1951, Margaret Vivien, da of William Warren (d 1956), of Taunton, Somerset; 2 da; *Career* dir: Reeve Angel International 1959-74, Whatman Reeve Angel plc 1974-90, Whatman plc 1990-; pres Br Laboratory Ware Assoc 1970-72; *Recreations* reading, golf; *Style—* Richard Angel, Esq; Spring Walk, Nevill Court, Tunbridge Wells, Kent (☎ 0892 20592); Whatman plc, Springfield Mill, Maidstone, Kent ME14 2LE (☎ 0622 692022)

ANGELL, Prof Ian Oakley; s of Roy Oakley Angell, of Bargoed, Mid Glamorgan, and Eluned (d 1972); *b* 8 June 1947; *Educ* Lewis Sch Pengam Mid Glamorgan, Univ of Wales (BSc), Univ of London (PhD); *m* 30 July 1971, Florence Mary, da of John Graham Davies, of Bargoed, Mid Glamorgan; *Career* lectr Royal Holloway Coll Univ of London 1971-84, sr lectr UCL 1984-86, prof of info systems LSE 1986-; ed MacMillan Info Systems Series; fndr memb Euro Orgn for East-West Cooperation, memb Steering Ctee of UNESCO, memb Regnl Office for Sci and Tech for Europe (Venice), conslt strategic information systems and int and organisational information tech policies; *Books* incl: A Practical Introduction To Computer Graphics (1981), High Resolution Computer Graphics using C (1990), Management Information Systems (1991); *Recreations* opera, ballet, cats, computing; *Style—* Prof Ian Angell; London Sch of Econs and Political Sci, Dept of Info Systems, Houghton St, London WC2A 2AE (☎ 071 405 7686, fax 071 242 0392, telex 24655 BLPES G)

ANGELL-JAMES, John; CBE (1967); s of late Dr John Angell-James, of Bristol, and Emily Cormell, *née* Ashwin; *b* 23 Aug 1901; *Educ* Bristol GS, Univ of London (MB BS), Univ of Bristol (MB ChB); *m* 1930, Evelyn Miriam, da of Francis Over Everard (d 1951), of Devon; 1 s, 2 da; *Career* served WWII Lt-Col RAMC; otolaryngologist; head Dept of Otolargngology Univ of Bristol 1956-66; hon consltg surgn Utd Bristol Hosps 1966-; pres: Br Assoc of Otolaryngologists 1966, Otological Res Soc 1977-; farmer 1950-; FRCP, FRCS, Hon FRCS Edin; *Recreations* shooting, sailing, gardening; *Style—* John Angell-James, Esq, CBE

ANGERS, Brian Mason; s of Ernest Angers (d 1953), and Eunice Mason; *b* 18 Nov 1936; *Educ* Lancaster Royal GS, Oxford Univ (certificate in Mgmnt Studies); *Career* fin dir Cunard Steam-ship Co plc; Nat Serv Sgt RAFC Singapore; dir: Cunard Line Ltd, Cunard Ellerman Ltd, Ritz Hotel (London) Ltd; FCA; *Recreations* tennis, golf; *Clubs* Wentworth; *Style—* Brian M Angers, Esq; Ku-Ring-Gai, Broomfield Park, Sunningdale, Ascot, Berkshire SL5 0JT (☎ 0344 20296); 1 Berkeley St, London W1A 1BY (☎ 071 499 9020)

ANGERSON, Michael John; s of Alfred Angerson (d 1948), of Bristol, and Hilda May, *née* Nichols (d 1988); *b* 28 Jan 1936; *Educ* Sibfold Sch, Univ of Bath (DMS); *m* 28 March 1964, Jean Margaret, da of Edward Charles Dyer, of Langport (d 1976); 2 s (Richard John b 18 Aug 1965, John David b 5 March 1969), 1 da (Claire Ellen b 21 Jan 1967); *Career* chm and md Trylon Group 1974-, dir Landsman's Co Ownership Ltd Huntingdon 1979-; dir: Northampton Common Ownership Devpt Assoc, Industrial Common Ownership Ltd, Industrial Common Ownership Finance Ltd, Industrial Common Ownership Fund plc; *Recreations* furniture restoration, watercolour painting; *Style—* Michael Angerson, Esq; Trylon Ltd, Thrift St, Wollaston, Northants NN9 7QS (☎ 0933 664275, fax 0933 664960, telex 312305 HONDEL G)

ANGGAÅRD, Hon Mrs (Adele Bevyl Alers); da of 2 Baron Hankey, KCMG, KCVO; *b* 31 July 1933; *m* 1964 (m dis 1987), Dr Erik Emil Anggaård; 1 s (Jon), 2 da (Eola, Irene); *Career* int stage designer; *Recreations* tennis, skiing; *Style—* The Hon Mrs Anggaård; Linnegatan 96, 11523 Stockholm, Sweden

ANGLES, James Walker; s of Andrew Angles (d 1961), of Perth, and Barbara Louden, *née* Walker; *b* 27 Dec 1935; *Educ* Perth Acad; *m* 30 Nov 1963, Katherine Gillian, da of Tom Bickerstaff, of Ipswich; 3 da (Alison b 1965, Helen b 1967, Lorna b 1969); *Career* md Britvic Soft Drinks Ltd; *Style—* James W Angles, Esq; Bloomfield Road, Chelmsford, Essex (☎ 0245 261871)

ANGLESEY, 7 Marquess of (UK 1815); Sir George Charles Henry Victor Paget; 10 Bt (I 1730); also Lord Paget of Beaudesert (E 1552) and Earl of Uxbridge (GB 1784); s of 6 Marquess of Anglesey (d 1947), and Lady Marjorie Manners, da of 8 Duke of Rutland; *b* 8 Oct 1922; *Educ* Eton; *m* 16 Oct 1948, Elizabeth Shirley Vaughan, DBE, da of Charles Langbridge Morgan, the writer (*see* Anglesey, Marchioness of); 2 s, 3 da; *Heir* s, Earl of Uxbridge; *Career* Maj RHG 1946; JP 1959-68 and 1983-89; Vice-Lieut of Anglesey 1960-83; dir Wales Nationwide Bldg Soc 1973-89, pres Anglesey Cons Assoc 1949-83, chm Historic Bldgs Cncl for Wales 1977-, tstee National Portrait Gallery 1979-90; memb: National Heritage Memorial Fund 1980-, Royal Cmmn on Historical Manuscripts 1984-; DL Anglesey 1960, Lord-Lieut for Gwynedd 1983-89; FSA, FRHistS, FRSL, Hon FRIBA, Hon DLitt; *Books* The Capel Letters (1955), One-Leg (1961), Sergeant Pearman's Memoirs (1968), Little Hodge (1971), A History of the British Cavalry 1816-1919, Vol I (1973), Vol II (1975), Vol III (1982), Vol IV (1986); *Recreations* music, gardening; *Style—* The Most Hon the Marquess of Anglesey, FSA; Plâs Newydd, Llanfairpwll, Anglesey, Gwynedd (☎ 0248 714330); 5 Walpole St, London SW3 (☎ 071 730 4140)

ANGLESEY, Marchioness of; (Elizabeth) Shirley Vaughan Paget; DBE (1982, CBE 1977); da of late Charles Morgan (novelist), and Hilda Vaughan (novelist); *b* 4 Dec 1924; *Educ* Francis Holland Sch, St James' Sch W Malvern, Kent Place Sch USA; *m* 1948, 7 Marquess of Anglesey; 2 s, 3 da; *Career* chm Nat Fedn of Women's Insts 1966-69, vice chm Govt Working Pty on Methods of Sewage Disposal 1969-70, dep chm Prince of Wales Ctee 1970-80, chm Welsh Arts Cncl 1975-81, memb IBA 1976-81, chm Br Cncl Drama and Dance Advsy Ctee 1981-, chm Broadcasting Complaints Cmmn 1987-, vice chm Museums and Galleries Cmmn 1981-, tstee Pilgrims Tst 1982-; hon fell Bangor UCNW 1990; Hon LLD Univ of Wales 1977; *Style—* The Most Hon the Marchioness of Anglesey, DBE; Plâs Newydd, Llanfairpwll, Gwynedd (☎ 0248 714330)

ANGUS, (William) Jestyn; s of Col Edmund Graham Angus, CBE, MC, TD, DL (d 1983), of Corbridge, Northumberland, and Bridget Ellen Isobel, *née* Spencer (d 1973); *b* 12 Dec 1930; *Educ* Gordonstoun, Harvard Business Sch; *m* 18 Sept 1965, Eleanor Gillian (Mimie), da of Cdr George Frederick Attwood (d 1979); 1 s (Henry b 1966), 1 da (Sarah b 1968); *Career* 2 Lt RA 1949-50, Lt RA (TA) 1950-56; export mangr and market res mangr George Angus & Co Ltd Newcastle upon Tyne and London 1952-59, dir Fire Armour Ltd 1959-65, gp personnel mangr Matthew Hall & Co Ltd 1965-70 (sales mangr 1971-72); sr conslt MSL Mgmnt Selection 1973-82; dir: (Scot) Knight Wendling Ltd 1982-, Glasgow C of C 1975-, The Merchants House of Glasgow; vice pres Dumbarton Scot Cons Assoc; FIPM 1985, MIMC 1986; *Recreations* skiing, tennis, hillwalking, horticulture; *Clubs* Western (Glasgow), Northern Counties (Newcastle upon Tyne); *Style—* Jestyn Angus, Esq; Braeriach, Helensburgh, Dunbartonshire G84 9AH (☎ 0436 72393); Knight Wendling Ltd, 95 Bothwell St, Glasgow G2 7JZ (☎ 041 221 8676, fax 041 204 3913)

ANGUS, Rev (James Alexander) Keith; LVO (1990), TD; s of Rev Walter Chalmers Smith Angus (d 1956), and Isabella Margaret Stephen (d 1979); *b* 16 April 1929; *Educ* HS of Dundee, Univ of St Andrews (MA); *m* 1956, Alison Jane, da of Donald Cargill Daly (d 1951), of Kirkcubrightshire; 1 s (Hugh), 1 da (Alison); *Career* Nat Serv Army TA, RA Capt, TA Royal Chaplains Dept; min: Hoddam Parish Church 1956-67, Gourock Old Parish Church 1967-79, Braemar and Crathie Parish Churches 1979-; domestic chaplain to HM The Queen 1979-; *Recreations* fishing, hillwalking, golf; *Clubs* New (Edinburgh); *Style—* The Rev Keith Angus, LVO, TD; The Manse of Crathie, Crathie, nr Ballater, Aberdeenshire AB3 5UL (☎ 03397 42208)

ANGUS, Sir Michael Richardson; s of William Richardson Angus, and Doris Margaret Breach; *b* 5 May 1930; *Educ* Marling Sch Stroud Glos, Univ of Bristol (BSc); *m* Eileen Isabel May; 2 s, 1 da; *Career* chm Unilever PLC, vice chm Unilever NV; non-exec dir: Whitbread & Co plc, Thorn EMI plc, British Airways PLC; tstee: Leverhulme Tst, Conference Bd (NY);Holland Trade award 1990; Hon DSc Univ of Bristol 1990; CBIM; kt 1990; *Recreations* countryside, wine, puzzles; *Clubs* Athenaum, Univ (NY), Knickerbocker (NY); *Style—* Sir Michael Angus; c/o Unilever PLC, Unilever House, Blackfriars, London EC4P 4BQ (☎ 01 822 5252)

ANGUS, Robin John; s of Ian Gordon Angus, of Forres, Moray, Scotland, and Morag Ann (Sally), *née* Macdonald; *b* 15 Sept 1952; *Educ* Forres Acad, Univ of St Andrews (MA), Peterhouse Cambridge; *m* 20 Aug 1977, Lorna Christine, da of James Smith Campbell (d 1986), of Drumlemble, Argyll, Scotland; *Career* investment mangr Baillie Gifford & Co 1977-81, investment tst analyst Wood Mackenzie & Co 1981-85, dir Personal Assets Tst plc 1984-, asst dir Wood Mackenzie & Co Ltd 1985-88; dir: Hill Samuel Securities Ltd 1985-88, County NatWest Securities Ltd (incorporating Wood Mackenzie & Co Ltd) 1988-; Gen Synod Scottish Episcopal Church: memb, memb faith and order bd, convenor orgn review ctee: memb working pty on fin and ethics Centre for Theology and Public Issues Univ of Edinburgh, auditor and fin advsr Diocese of Moray Ross and Caithness Scottish Episcopal Church, dir Scottish Episcopal Church Clergy Widows and Orphans Fund, tstee and ctee memb Scottish Centre for Economic and Social Res; memb Advsy Cncl Inst of Investmt Mgmnt; *Books* Independence: The Option for Growth (1989), Dictionary of Scottish Church History and Theology (contrib 1990), Independence and the Business Spirit (1991); *Recreations* church work, politics (Scottish Nationalist), history, music, reading, writing verse; *Clubs* New (Edinburgh), Scottish Arts (Edinburgh), Royal Scottish Automobile (Glasgow), McSkate's (St Andrews); *Style*— Robin Angus, Esq; County NatWest Securities Ltd Incorporating Wood Mackenzie & Co Ltd, Kintore House, 74-77 Queen St, Edinburgh, Scotland EH2 4NS (☎ 031 225 8525, fax 031 243 4434/3, telex 72555)

ANGUS, Col William Turnbull Calderhead; s of William Angus (d 1954), of Glasgow, and Elizabeth Galloway, *née* Calderhead (d 1952); *b* 20 July 1923; *Educ* Govan HS, Univ of Glasgow, RMCS; *m* 5 April 1947, Nola Leonie, da of William Alexander Campbell-Gillies (d 1965), of Nairobi; 2 s (Bruce b 1948, Roderigh b 1959), 2 da (Carolyn b 1950, Fiona b 1955); *Career* cmmnd Royal Regt of Artillery 1944, cmd King's African Rifles also Maj GSO2 HQ E Africa 1945-47, tech staff course RMCS 1949-51, Maj TSO2 Inspectorate of Armaments 1951-54, BAOR & Cyprus 1954-57, GSO2 G Tech HQ BAOR 1957-60, TSO2 Ordnance Bd 1960-63, TSO2 Trials Estab Guided Weapons RA 1963-65, post-grad Guided Weapons Course RMCS 1965-66, Lt-Col TSO1 Royal Armament R & D Estab 1966-69, Col asst dir Guided Weapons Trials MOD Procurement Exec 1970-73, memb Ordnance Bd 1973-74, ret 1974; Scottish mangr Blakes Holidays; pres Campbeltown Rotary Club 1985-86; Hon Sheriff in Sheriffdom of N Strathclyde 1986; CEng 1970, MRAeS 1970, FIQA 1972, FBIM 1980; *Recreations* wood-turning, manufacture of spinning wheels; *Style*— Col William T C Angus; Kilchrist Castle, Campbeltown, Argyll PA28 6PH (☎ 0586 53210)

ANKARCRONA, Jan Gustaf Theodor Stensson; s of Sten Stensson Ankarcrona, RVO (d 1981), of Stockholm, Sweden, and Ebba, *née* Countess Mörner; *b* 18 April 1940; *Educ* Östra Real Stockholm, Stockholm Sch of Econ (MBA), Univ of California Berkeley (MBA); *m* 1, 16 June 1968 (m dis 1978), E Margaretha Antonie, da of Erik von Eckermann, of Ripsa, Sweden; 2 s (Johan b 1969, Edward b 1972); m 2, 6 March 1981, Sandra, da of E B Coxe, of New York, USA; 2 da (Aurore b 1983, Ariane b 1988); *Career* Royal Swedish Navy 1958-61, Lt-Cdr Royal Swedish Navy Reserve 1974; Stockholms Enskilda Bank Stockholm 1964-65, Gränges AB Stockholm 1966-69, American Express Securities SA Paris 1969-70, dep md Nordic Bank Ltd London 1971-83, md and chief exec Fennoscandia Bank Ltd London 1983-; OStJ Sweden; *Recreations* shooting, sailing, tennis, music, history; *Clubs* Brooks's, Hurlingham, Nya Sällskapet Stockholm; *Style*— Jan Ankarcrona, Esq; 29 Argyll Rd, London W8 7DA (☎ 071 937 9438); The Old Deanery, Dean's Ct, London EC4V 5AA (☎ 071 236 4060, fax 071 248 4712, telex 892458 FENSCA G)

ANKER, Raymond Thomas; s of Sidney Gerald Anker (d 1983), of Enfield, and Winifred Edith, *née* Singleton; *b* 25 June 1938; *Educ* Enfield Central GS, Enfield Tech Coll; *m* 1 (m dis 1980); 2 s (Danny b 1961, Andrew b 1965); m 2, 17 April 1980, Candy, da of Christopher Manning, of Sandfield Park, West Derby, Liverpool; 2 da (Francine b 1983, Genevive b 1988); *Career* chm and md Ford Halcyon Ltd 1973-; memb: Enfield Cons Assoc, S Cambs Cons Assoc, Broxbourne Business Gp; BSI 1988; *Recreations* politics, reading, wine tasting, squash; *Clubs* Portcullis; *Style*— Raymond Anker, Esq; Ford Halcyon Ltd, New Ford Rd, Waltham Cross, Herts EN8 7PG (☎ 0992 764700, telex 91432, fax 0992 88384, car 0860 336132)

ANNALY, 6 Baron (UK 1863); Luke Richard White; o s of 5 Baron Annaly (d 1990), and his 1 w, Lady Marye Isabel Pepys (d 1958), da of 7 Earl of Cottenham; *b* 29 June 1954; *Educ* Eton, RMA Sandhurst, RAC Cirencester; *m* 1983, Caroline Nina, yr da of Col Robert Hugh Garnett, MBE, of Hope Bowdler Court, nr Church Stretton, Shropshire; 1 s (Hon Luke Henry b 1990), 2 da (Hon Lavinia Marye b 1987, Hon Iona Elizabeth b 1989); *Heir* s, Hon Luke Henry White b 20 Sept 1990; *Career* Lt Royal Hussars 1974-78, RAC Reserve 1978-86; *Style*— The Rt Hon Lord Annaly; Heath Farm, Fritwell, nr Bicester, Oxfordshire OX6 9QS (☎ 0869 345253)

ANNAN, Dr (William) George Taylor; s of James Benjamin Annan (d 1954), and Sarah Araba, *née* Eyeson (d 1983); *b* 22 Feb 1931; *Educ* Adisadel Coll Ghana, UCH Ibadan Nigeria (MB BS London); *m* 29 July 1967, Patricia Ann, da of Samuel Alfred Capenhurst; 3 da (Francesca b 1968, Rebecca b 1970, Georgina b 1973); *Career* sr house offr: gen med City Gen Hosp Stoke on Trent 1963, geriatric med Gen Hosp Northampton 1965-66, chest med Devonshire Road and Victoria Hosp Blackpool 1966-68; registrar: chest med Monsall Hosp Manchester 1968-69, gen med Victoria Hosp Blackpool 1969-73; sr registrar: geriatric med Crumpsall Hosp Manchester 1973-74, gen med Manchester Royal Infirmary 1974; conslt physician geriatric med Blackpool Wyre and Fylde Health Authy 1974-; memb BMA, FRCP 1988 (memb 1972); *Recreations* bridge, gardening, table tennis; *Clubs* Poulton Le Fylde Bridge; *Style*— Dr George Annan; Victoria Hospital, Whinney Heys Rd, Blackpool FY3 8NR (☎ 0253 300000 ext 4862)

ANNAN, John Christopher; s of Alexander Annan, and Christina, *née* Herbertson; *b* 4 Sept 1926; *Educ* Gordonstoun; *m* 1952, Margaret, da of Albert Marlow (d 1943); 1 s, 1 da; *Career* chm A & J C Annan Ltd; underwriting memb Lloyd's; *Recreations* golf, shooting, fishing, sailing; *Clubs* Lloyd's Yacht; *Style*— John Annan, Esq; Lower Snowdon Cottage, Burnhill Green, Staffordshire WV6 7HT (☎ 074 65 224); A & J C Annan Ltd, 53 Waterloo Rd, Wolverhampton, W Midlands WV1 4QJ (☎ 0902 22399)

ANNAN, Baron (Life Peer UK 1965), of Royal Burgh of Annan, Co Dumfries; Noel Gilroy Annan; OBE (1946); s of James Gilroy Annan (d 1965), and Fannie Mildred, *née* Quinn (d 1970); *b* 25 Dec 1916; *Educ* Stowe, King's Coll Cambridge (BA, MA); *m* 30 June 1950, Gabriele, da of Louis Ferdinand Ullstein, of Berlin; 2 da (Hon (Amanda) Lucy (Hon Mrs de Grey) b 13 June 1952, Hon Juliet Louise (Hon Mrs Le Fanu) b 7 Jan 1955); *Career* provost: King's Cambridge 1956-66, UCL 1966-78; vice chllr London Univ 1978-81 (Prof Sir Randolph Quirk succeeded); chm Ctee on Future of Broadcasting 1974-77; tstee: Nat Gallery 1978-85, Br Museum 1963-78; FRHistS; *Clubs* Brooks's; *Style*— The Rt Hon the Lord Annan, OBE; 16 St John's Wood Rd, London NW8 (☎ 071 289 2555)

ANNAND, Richard Wallace; VC (1940), DL (Co Durham 1956); s of Lt Cdr Wallace Moir Annand (k Gallipoli 1915), and Dora Elizabeth Chapman; *b* 5 Nov 1914; *Educ* Pocklington E Yorks; *m* 1940, Shirley Osborne, JP; *Career* cmmnd RNVR 1933, transfd Durham LI 1938, Capt RARO 1948; personnel offr Finchale Abbey Trg Centre for the Disabled 1948-79; *Style*— Richard Annand, Esq, VC, DL; Springwell House, Whitesmocks, Durham

ANNANDALE AND HARTFELL, Dowager Countess of; Margaret Jane; *née* Hunter-Arundell; da of Herbert William Francis Hunter-Arundell, of Barjarg, Auldgirth, Dumfrieshire (who assumed the surname of Hunter-Arundell in lieu of Wadd 1913, on suc to Barjarg estate; s of T H Wadd, of St Leonards-on-Sea, by his w, Mary, da of William A Woodcock, by his w, Marianne, 2 da of William Francis Hunter-Arundell, of Barjarg); *b* 18 Nov 1910; *m* 1940, as his 2 w, Maj Percy Wentworth Hope Johnstone, TD, JP, Lanarkshire Yeomanry RA (TA), *de jure* 10 Earl of Annandale and Hartfell (d 1983); 1 s, 1 da; *Style*— The Rt Hon the Dowager Countess of Annandale and Hartfell; Blackburn House, Johnstonebridge, Lockerbie, Dumfrieshire

ANNANDALE AND HARTFELL, 11 Earl of (S, by Charter, 1662); Patrick Andrew Wentworth Hope Johnstone of Annandale and of that Ilk; DL (Dumfrieshire 1987); also Lord of Johnstone (S 1662), Hereditary Steward of Stewartry of Annandale, Hereditary Keeper of Castle of Lochmaben, and Chief of Clan Johnstone; s of Maj Percy Wentworth Hope Johnstone, TD, JP, RA (TA), *de jure* 10 Earl (d 1983), by his 2 w, Margaret Jane Hunter-Arundell (*qv* Dowager Countess of Annandale and Hartfell); claim to Earldom (which had been dormant since 1792) admitted by Ctee for Privileges of House of Lords, and a writ issued summoning him to Parl in the Upper House 1986; *b* 19 April 1941; *Educ* Stowe, RAC Cirencester; *m* 1969, Susan, o da of Col Walter John Macdonald Ross, CB, OBE, TD, JP, Lord Lt of the Stewartry, of Netherhall, Castle Douglas, Kirkcudbrightshire; 1 s (Hon David Patrick Wentworth, Hope Johnstone, Lord Johnstone and Master of Annandale & Hartfell b 13 Oct 1971); 1 da (Lady Julia Clare b 1974); *Heir* s, Lord Johnstone; *Career* underwriting memb Lloyds 1976-; memb: Solway River Purification Bd 1970-86, Scottish Valuation Advsy Cncl to Sec of State for Scotland 1984-86, Annan Fishery Bd 1983-, Standing Cncl of Scottish Chiefs, various ctees, Dumfries CC 1970-75, Dumfries & Galloway Regnl Cncl 1974-86, chm Royal Jubilee and Prince's Tst for Dumfries and Galloway 1984-88, Royal Scottish Forestry Soc 1981-84; dir: Bowerings Members Agency 1985-88, Murray Lawrence Members Agency 1988-; *Recreations* golf; *Clubs* Puffin's (Edinburgh), Brooks's; *Style*— The Rt Hon the Earl of Annandale and Hartfell, DL; c/o House of Lords, London SW1

ANNESLEY, Lady Frances Elizabeth; yst da of 10 Earl Annesley; *b* 27 July 1957; *Style*— The Lady Frances Annesley; 35 Spring Rise, Egham, Surrey

ANNESLEY, Hon Francis William Dighton; s and h of 15 Viscount Valentia; *b* 29 Dec 1959; *Style*— The Hon Francis Annesley

ANNESLEY, Hon Michael Robert; yst s of 9 Earl Annesley (d 1979); *b* 4 Dec 1933; *Educ* Strode's GS Egham; *m* 1956, Audrey Mary, o da of Ernest Goodwright, of Dartford, Kent; 2 s (Michael Stephen b 1957, Robert Francis b 1962), 1 da (Sheila Marie b 1961); *Career* Warrant Offr RAF; flt simulator engr; dir S and D Leisure Ltd 1984; assoc memb Soc of Licensed Aircraft Engrs and Technols; *Style*— The Hon Michael Annesley; 16 Coltash Road, Furnace Green, Crawley, West Sussex RH10 6JY

ANNESLEY, Nora, Countess; Nora; da of Walter Harrison, of Sapperton, Glos; *b* 5 Nov 1900; *Educ* Sapperton C of E Sch; *m* 1922, 9 Earl Annesley (d 1979); 3 s; *Career* teacher; *Recreations* gardening, knitting, embroidery; *Style*— The Rt Hon Nora, Countess Annesley; 67 Vegal Crescent, Englefield Green, Surrey (☎ 0784 32162)

ANNESLEY, 10 Earl (I 1789); Patrick; also Baron Annesley (I 1758) and Viscount Glerawly (I 1766); s of 9 Earl Annesley (d 1979); *b* 12 Aug 1924; *Educ* Strode's GS Egham; *m* 1947, Catherine, da of John Forrest Burgess; 4 da; *Heir* bro, Hon Philip Annesley, *qv*; *Career* formerly in RN; *Style*— The Rt Hon The Earl Annesley; 35 Spring Rise, Egham, Surrey

ANNESLEY, Hon Philip Harrison; s of 9 Earl Annesley (d 1979), and hp of bro, 10 Earl, *qv*; *b* 29 March 1927; *Educ* Strode's GS Egham; *m* 1951, Florence Eileen, da of late John Arthur Johnston, of Gillingham, Kent; *Career* late REME; *Style*— The Hon Philip Annesley; 48 Shackleton Rd, Tilgate, Crawley, Sussex

ANNETT, Prof John; s of Frederick Annett, and Irene Laura Annett; *b* 7 July 1930; *Educ* Sir Joseph Williamson's Mathematical Sch Rochester, St Peter's Coll Oxford (MA, DPhil); *m* 9 April 1955, Marian Elsie, da of Harold Drabble; 1 s (James Frederick b 1961), 1 da (Lucy Elizabeth b 1958); *Career* Nat Serv RN 1948-50; asst psychologist Burden Mental Res Dept Univ of Bristol 1953-55, res worker Inst of Experimental Psychology Oxford 1955-60, sr res worker Univ of Sheffield 1960-63, lectr Univ of Aberdeen 1963-65, reader Univ of Hull 1968-72 (sr lectr 1965-68); prof of psychology: Open Univ 1972-74, Univ of Warwick 1974-; FBPsS 1980, FErgs 1985, CPsychol 1987; *Books* Feedback and Human Behaviour (1969), Introduction to Psychology (1974); *Recreations* music, watercolouring, gardening; *Style*— Prof John Annett; Department of Psychology, University of Warwick, Coventry CV4 7AL (☎ 0203 523165)

ANNING, Cmmr Raymon Harry; CBE (1982), QPM (1975); *b* 22 July 1930; *m* 1949, Beryl Joan; 1 s (Nicholas b 17 April 1959), 1 da (Julie b 22 July 1955); *Career* E Surrey Regt and Royal Military Police 1948-50; Met Police 1952- 79, HM Inspr of Constabulary for England and Wales 1979-83, cmmr of Police Royal Hong Kong Police Force 1985 - (dep cmmr 1983-85); CBIM 1980; *Style*— Cmmr Raymon Anning, CBE, QPM

ANNIS, Philip Geoffrey Walter; s of Walter Annis, of Bleak House, Windermere, Cumbria, and Lilian Alice, *née* Norris; *b* 7 Feb 1936; *Educ* Sale Co GS Sale Cheshire, Kelsick GS Ambleside Westmorland, Univ of Manchester (BA); *m* 15 June 1967, Olive Winifred, da of Edward Walter Scarlett, OBE, of Ilford, Essex; 1 s (Edward Philip b 30 April 1970); *Career* Nat Serv 2 Lt RA 1957-59, actg Flt Lt RAFVR (T) 1960-62, TA 1961-67, RA (TA); inspr Grade 3 Bd of Inland Revenue 1959-62; Nat Maritime Museum: joined 1962, co-ordinator of museum servs 1971-79, dep dir 1979-86; mangr of regtl history project RA Inst 1986-; FSA 1973, FRHistS 1975; Cdr of the Order of the Lion of Finland 1987; *Books* Naval Swords (1970), Swords for Sea Service (with Cdr W E May, 1970); *Recreations* gardening, walking, reading; *Style*— Philip Annis, Esq, FSA; Royal Artillery Institution, Old Royal Military Academy, Woolwich, London SE18 4DN (☎ 081 854 2242, ext 5613)

ANSARI, Dr Joseph Mohammad Ayub; s of Hakim Mohammad Yusuf Ansari (d 1971), and Hasina Khatoan, *née* Kidwai (d 1971); *b* 25 June 1938; *Educ* Shia Degree Coll Lucknow India (BSc), King Edward VII Med Coll Lahore Pakistan (MB BS); *m* 26 May 1972, Ruth, da of William Haughton Hill (d 1975), of Merseyside; 1 s (Arif b 20 Oct 1974), 1 da (Sarah b 16 Jan 1977); *Career* Dept of Psychiatry Univ of Liverpool: lectr 1971-75, sr lectr 1975-76, clinical lectr 1976-; conslt in psychological med 1976, med dir Regnl Alcohol Univ of Liverpool 1976-, surpervisor for Sr Registrar Training in Psychiatry Merseyside 1986-89; sec and treas NW Div RCPsych, treas Liverpool Psychiatric Soc (former pres); memb: Nat Cncl of Alcohol 1980-, World Psychiatric Assoc 1985-, BMA 1988-; DPM 1970, MPsyMed 1975, FRCPsych 1985; *Books Publications* several contribs on psycho-sexual problems and mental illness in leading medical jls; *Recreations* photography, painting and reading; *Style*— Dr Joseph Ansari; 31 Rodney St, Liverpool L1 9EH (☎ 051 709 8522)

ANSCOMBE, Bernard; s of James Anscomb (d 1981), of Ashmansworth, Newbury, Berkshire, and Edith Minnie, *née* Shephard (d 1984); *b* 25 April 1944; *Educ* St Benedicts Sch; *m* 19 Jan 1985, Catherine Judith, da of Michael Goode; *Career* admitted slr 1970; currently sr ptnr Anscombe Hollingsworth; *Recreations* real tennis; *Clubs* Queen's; *Style*— Bernard Anscombe, Esq; 1 Napier Place, London W14 8LG (☎ 071 602 6339); 19 Pitt St, London W8 4NX (☎ 071 937 4876, fax 071 938 1400)

ANSDELL, Peter Murray Agnew; s of Thomas Agnew Ansdell (d 1966), and Beatrice Frances Clara, *née* St John (d 1957); *b* 8 Aug 1929; *Educ* Winchester, Univ of Lausanne; *m* 25 Oct 1958, Susan Theodora, da of Lt-Col Guy Alexander Ingram Dury, MC (d 1976), of Sussex; 1 s (Paul b 1965), 2 da (Alexandra b 1960, Belinda b 1963); *Career* 2 Lt Coldstream Gds Malaya 1947-49; Eburite Packing 1950-57, Bowater Paper Corp 1957-61, personnel exec William Collins publishers 1966-70 (export mangr 1961, md Heart of England Cottages 1970-); *Recreations* travel, music, tennis, reading, gardening, antiques; *Clubs* Tidapa; *Style*— Peter M A Ansdell, Esq; Iveson House, Ampney St Peter, Cirencester, Gloucestershire GL7 5SH (☎ 0285 851217)

ANSELL, Mark John; s of John Frederick Ansell, of Birmingham, and Irene Francis, *née* Spiers (d 1982); *b* 2 Jan 1952; *Educ* Waverley GS Birmingham; *m* 2 March 1974, Sheila Mary, da of Victor William Marston, of Sutton Coldfield; *Career* CA 1973; ptnr Joslyne Layton Bennett & Co Birmingham 1977 (later merging with Binder Hamlyn), managing ptnr BDO Binder Hamlyn 1988; former chm: City of Birmingham Round Table, Birmingham Rotary Club; ACA 1973, FCA 1977, BMA 1987; *Recreations* golf, football (watching Aston Villa FC); *Clubs* City of Birmingham Round Table, Birmingham Rotary, Walmley Golf; *Style*— Mark Ansell, Esq; BDO Binder Hamlyn, The Rotunda, 150 New St, Birmingham B2 4PD (☎ 021 643 5544, fax 021 643 4665, telex 336015 BINDERG, car 0831 567081)

ANSELL, Col Sir Michael Picton; CBE (1951), DSO (1944), DL (Devon 1966); s of late Lt-Col George Kirkpatrick Ansell, and K Cross; *b* 26 March 1905; *Educ* Wellington, RMC Sandhurst; *m* 1, 1936, Victoria Jacintha Fleetwood (d 1969), da of Sir John Michael Fleetwood Fuller, 1 Bt, KCMG; 2 s, 1 da; m 2, 1970, Eileen, (d 1971), da of late Col E A Stanton, of Brownshill Court, Stroud, Glos, and widow of Maj-Gen Roger Evans, CB, MC; *Career* gazetted 5 Royal Inniskilling Dragoon Gds 1924, served WWII (wounded, POW, discharged disabled 1944), Col 1957-62; chm Br Show Jumping Assoc 1945-64 and 1970-71 (pres 1964-66); hon dir: Horse of the Year Show 1949-75, Royal Int Horse Show 1950-75, Br Horse Soc 1952-73; pres Br Equestrian Fedn 1972-76; Bureau of Fédn Equestre Int 1955-70; pres St Dunstan's 1977-86 (memb 1958-86); High Sheriff Devon 1967; Freeman: Worshipful Co Farriers 1962, Worshipful Co Loriners 1962; Yeoman Worshipful Co Saddlers 1963; Chevalier Order of Leopold (Belgium) 1932, Cdr's Cross Order of Merit (FDR) 1975, Olympic Order Silver 1977; kt 1968; *Books* Riding High, Soldier On, Leopard, The Story of my Horse; *Recreations* polo and show jumping (international 1931-39); *Style*— Col Sir Michael Ansell, CBE, DSO, DL; Pillhead House, Bideford, N Devon EX39 4NF (☎ 0237 472574)

ANSELL, Maj-Gen Nicholas George Picton; OBE (1980); s of Col Sir Mike Ansell, CBE, DSO, DL, of Pillhead, Bideford, Devon, and Victoria Jacintha Fleetwood, *née* Fuller (d 1969); *b* 17 Aug 1937; *Educ* Wellington, Magdalene Coll Cambridge (MA); *m* 17 June 1961, Vivien, da of Col Anthony Donnithorne Taylor, DSO, MC (d 1986), of N Aston, Oxon; 2 s (Mark b 1963, Julian b 1964), 1 da (Clare b 1968); *Career* cmmnd 5 Royal Inniskilling Dragoon Guards 1956 (served BAOR, Libya, Cyprus), Staff Coll Camberley 1970, Bde Maj RAC HQ 1 (BR) Corps 1971-72, instr Staff Coll Camberley 1976-77, CO 5 Royal Inniskilling Dragoon Guards 1977-80, Col GS Staff Coll Camberley 1980-81, OC 20 Armd Bde 1982-83, RCDS 1984, dep chief of staff HQ BAOR 1985-86, dir RAC 1987-89; SDS (Army) RCDS 1990-; govr Hawtreys Sch; *Recreations* country pursuits, riding, fishing, birdwatching; *Clubs* Cavalry and Guards; *Style*— Maj-Gen Nicholas Ansell, OBE; c/o Lloyds Bank plc, Bideford, N Devon

ANSON, Cdr (Norman) Alastair Bourne; OBE (1983); s of Sir (George) Wilfrid Anson, MBE, MC (d 1974), of West Hay, Wrington, Bristol, and Dinah Maud Lilian, *née* Bourne; *b* 14 Oct 1929; *Educ* Winchester; *m* 23 Feb 1952 (m dis 1965), Collette Lavinia, da of Lt-Col Richard Eldred Hindson (d 1964), of Hill Brow, Liss, Hants; 1 s (Richard b 11 Nov 1952), 1 da (Crispin b 5 Sept 1955); m 2, 27 Nov 1968, Lavinia Maude, da of Rear Adm Ion Tower, DSC (d 1917); *Career* RN Coll Dartmouth 1947, Midshipman HMS Triumph and HMS Newcastle Med 1948-49, Sub Lt 1949-51, Lt HMS Bermuda SA 1951-52, HMS Chequers and HMS Chivalrous Med 1952-54, HMS Drake Plymouth 1954-56, CO HMS Carhampton Med 1956-58, Lt Cdr 2 i/c HMS Loch Lomond Persian Gulf 1959-61, naval rep RMA Sandhurst 1961-63, CO HMS Keppel Arctic Fishery Sqdn 1963-65, CO HMS Londonderry Far E 1965-66, asst sec Chiefs of Staff Ctee 1967-69, 2 i/c HMS Fearless 1969-71, Cabinet Office 1972-75, NATO HQ Naples 1975-78, trg dir Sea Cadet Corps 1979-82, ret 1982; memb Panel Lord Chllr's Ind Inquiry Insprs responsible for inquiries on maj trunk road and motorway schemes; sidesman St Martin-in-the-Fields; Freeman City of London 1982, Liveryman Worshipful Co of Tin Plate Workers 1982; FIL 1959, FRGS 1983; *Recreations* music (organist), tennis, skiing, photography; *Clubs* City Livery, The Queen's, Hurlingham; *Style*— Cdr Alastair Anson, OBE; 38 Catherine Place, London SW1E 6HL (☎ 071 834 5991)

ANSON, Colin Shane; s of Anthony John Anson (d 1981), of Highdown, Horam, Sussex, and Rosalind Désirée, *née* Arbuthnot (d 1985); *b* 29 July 1931; *Educ* Dragon Sch, Stowe, Slade Sch of Fine Art (Dip Fine Art); *Career* Art Dept Arts Cncl of GB 1956-66, Picture Dept Christie's 1967-70, Artemis Gp 1971-; dir: David Carritt Ltd (art dealers) 1981- (res asst 1971-81), Artemis Fine Arts Ltd 1981-; *Clubs* Brooks's; *Style*— Colin Anson, Esq; 18 Ripplevale Grove, London N1 1HU (☎ 071 607 2995); David Carritt Ltd, 15 Duke St, St James's, London SW1Y 6DB (☎ 071 930 8733)

ANSON, Vice Adm Sir Edward Rosebery; KCB (1984); s of Ross Rosebery Anson (d 1959), and Ethel Jane, *née* Green; *b* 11 May 1929; *Educ* Prince of Wales Sch Nairobi, RNC Dartmouth; *m* 1960, Rosemary Anne, *née* Radcliffe; 1 s (Jonathan b 1965), 1 da (Mea); *Career* serv Naval Air Sqdns 1952-64, graduated Empire Test Pilots Sch 1957; cmd: HMS Eskimo 1964-66, HMS Juno and Capt 4 Frigate Sqdn 1974-76 (Capt 1971), HMS Ark Royal 1976-78 (last CO of the last traditional Br aircraft carrier); Flag Offr Naval Air Cmd 1979-82, Rear Adm 1980, Vice Adm 1982, COS to C-in-C Fleet 1982-84; Naval Weapons Div Br Aerospace 1984-86, pres and chief exec offr Br Aerospace Inc Washington DC USA 1986-89, sr naval advsr Br Aerospace plc 1989-; FRACS 1982; *Recreations* golf, photography, walking; *Style*— Vice Adm Sir Edward Anson, KCB; c/o Lloyds Bank, 9 High St, Yeovil, Somerset BA20 1RN

ANSON, Lady Elizabeth; *see*: Shakerley, Lady Elizabeth Georgiana

ANSON, James William; CBE (1969); s of Lt-Col George Frank Wemyss Anson, OBE (d 1942); *b* 9 Jan 1915; *Educ* Fettes, Gonville and Caius Coll Cambridge (BA); *m* 1940, Barbara Mary, da of late Gordon Peace, OBE; 1 s, 1 da; *Career* served WWII as Maj 2 Royal Sikhs in Iraq, Persia, Syria, Palestine, Egypt, Western Desert, Italy and Greece, GHQ MEF Cairo, Quetta Staff Coll 1943; chm and md Mackinnon Mackenzie & Co (agents for P&O Steam Navigation Co in India) 1964-69 (joined 1937), tstee Port of Bombay 1965-69, pres Bombay C of C and Indust 1967-68, dep pres Associated Cs of C of India 1967-68, gen mangr Overseas Containers Ltd 1970-77; hon sec Br Italian Soc 1977; Cavaliere of the Order Al Merito della Republica Italiana 1982; *Recreations* golf, gardening, formerly cricket and rugby football; *Clubs* MCC, Royal St George's (Sandwich), Hawks (Cambridge); *Style*— James Anson, Esq, CBE; Courtlands, Pilgrim's Way, Wrotham, Kent TN15 7NN (☎ 0732 822400)

ANSON, Sir John; KCB (1990, CB 1980); s of Sir Edward Anson, 6 Bt (d 1951), and Frances, da of Hugh Pollock (gs of Sir George Pollock, 1 Bt, GCB, GCSI); bro of Rear Adm Sir Peter Anson, 7 Bt, *qv*; *b* 3 Aug 1930; *Educ* Winchester, Magdalene Coll Cambridge (MA); *m* 1957, Myrica, da of Dr Harold Fergie-Woods (d 1961); 2 s, 2 da; *Career* HM Treas 1954-68, fin cnsllr Br Embassy Paris 1968-70, Cabinet Office 1971-74, under-sec HM Treas 1974-77, dep sec HM Treas 1977-87, econ min Br Embassy Washington and UK exec dir IMF and World Bank 1980-83, second perm sec HM Treas 1987-90; *Style*— Sir John Anson, KCB; 18 Church Rd, Barnes, London SW13 9HN (☎ 081 748 6557)

ANSON, Rear Adm Sir Peter; 7 Bt (1831), of Birch Hall, Lancashire; CB (1974); s of Sir Edward Reynell Anson, 6 Bt (d 1951), and Alison, da of Hugh Pollock (gs of Sir George Pollock, 1 Bt, GCB, GCSI); bro of John Anson, CB, *qv*; *b* 31 July 1924; *Educ* RNC Dartmouth; *m* 16 April 1955, Elizabeth Audrey, da of Rear Adm Sir (Charles) Philip Clarke, KBE, CB, DSO (d 1966); 2 s, 2 da; *Heir* s, Philip Anson, *qv*; *Career* RN: Cdr Naval Forces, Gulf 1970-71 (Cdre), asst chief of Def Staff (Signals) 1972-74 (Rear Adm), ret 1975; div mangr satellites Marconi Space and Def Systems Ltd 1977- (asst mktg dir 1975), md Marconi Space Systems Ltd 1984-85 (chm 1985-); CEng, FIEE; *Recreations* shooting, sailing, gardening, golf; *Style*— Rear Adm Sir Peter Anson, Bt, CB; Rosefield, 81 Boundstone Rd, Rowledge, Farnham, Surrey GU10 4AT (☎ 025 125 2724); Marconi Space Systems Ltd; Anchorage Road, Portsmouth, Hants PO3 5PU (☎ 0705 674126)

ANSON, Philip Roland; s and h of Rear Adm Sir Peter Anson, 7 Bt, CB, *qv*; *b* 4 Oct 1957; *Educ* Charterhouse, Chelsea Coll London (BPharm); *Career* pharmacist; Boots 1979-84, Waremoss Chemists Ltd 1984-; MRPharmS 1980, MIPharmM 1980; *Style*— Philip Anson, Esq; 34 Martello Rd, Eastbourne, East Sussex BN22 7SS (☎ 0323 411906); Guy's Pharmacy, 26 Eastbourne Rd, Pevensey Bay, East Sussex BN24 6ET (☎ 0323 761321)

ANSON, Viscount; Thomas William Robert Hugh Anson; s and h of 5 Earl of Lichfield; *b* 19 July 1978; *Style*— Viscount Anson

ANSTEE, Margaret Joan; da of Edward Curtis Anstee (d 1971), and Anne Adaliza, *née* Mills (d 1972); *b* 25 June 1926; *Educ* Chelmsford Co HS for Girls, Newnham Coll Cambridge (MA), Univ of London (BSc); *Career* lectr in spanish Queen's Univ Belfast 1947-48, 3 sec FO 1948-52, admin offr UN Tech Assistance Bd Manila Philippines 1952-54, spanish supervisor Univ of Cambridge 1955-56; UN Tech Assistance Bd: offr i/c Bogota Colombia 1956-57, resident rep Uruguay 1957-59, dir Special Fund progs and UN Info Centre La Paz Bolivia 1960-65, resident rep UNDP Ethopia 1965-67, liaison offr with UN Econ Cmmn for Africa 1965-67, sr econ advsr PM's UK 1967-68, sr asst to cmmr i/c of Study of Capacity of UN Devpt System 1968-69; resident rep UNDP: Morocco 1969-72, Chile and liaison offr with UN Econ Cmmn for Latin America 1972-74; dep to UN Under Sec Gen i/c of UN relief operation to Bangladesh and dep coordinator of UN emergency assistance to Zambia 1973; UNDP NY: dep asst admin and dep regnl dir for Latin America 1974-76, dir Admins Unit for Special Assignments 1976, asst dep admin 1976, asst admin and dir Bureau for Prog Policy and Evaluation 1977-78, asst Sec Gen UN Dept of Tech Cooperation for Devpt 1978-87, special rep of Sec Gen for coordination of int assistance following Mexico earthquake 1985-87, chm advsy gp on review of UN World Food Cncl 1985-86, special coordinator of UN Sec Gen to ensure implementation of Gen Assembly resolution on fin and admin reform of the UN 1986-87; special rep of UN Sec Gen for Bolivia 1982, rep UN Sec Gen at Conf for the Adoption of a Convention Against Illicit Traffic in Narcotic Drugs and Psychotropic Substances 1988, Sec Gen Eighth UN Congress on the Prevention of Crime and the Treatment of Offenders Havana 1990, special rep of the UN Sec-Gen for Peru 1990-, Sec-Gen's co-ordinator for addressing the effects of the Chernobyl disaster 1991-, dir gen UN office Vienna, under sec gen UN, head of centre for Social Devpt and Humanitarian Affrs, co-ordinator of all UN drug control related activities 1987-; *Books* The Administration of International Development Aid (USA 1969), Gate of the Sun: a prospect of Bolivia (ed with R K A Gardiner and C Patterson,1970, USA 1971), Africa and the World (1970); *Style*— Miss Margaret J Anstee; United Nations Office at Vienna, PO Box 500, Room E-1436, A-1400 Vienna, Austria (☎ 21131/5001, 5002, fax 237204/232156, telex 135612 Unations Vienna)

ANSTEY, Caroline Daphne Kathleen; da of Edgar Harold Macfarlane Anstey, OBE, and Marjorie Daphne, *née* Lilly; *b* 7 Nov 1955; *Educ* Henrietta Barnett Sch, Univ of Leeds (BA), Univ of California Berkeley, LSE (PhD); *m* 28 March 1981 (m dis 1989), Simon Herbert Johnson; *Career* res fell Nuffield Coll Oxford 1982-84, political asst to Rt Hon James Callaghan MP (now Lord Callaghan of Cardiff) 1984-86, ed Analysis (BBC Radio Four) 1988- (prodr 1986-88); articles in hist jls on Anglo-American rels; secretariat memb Interaction Cncl; *Recreations* films; *Style*— Miss Caroline Anstey; Broadcasting House, Portland Plc, London W1A 1AA (☎ 071 927 4812, fax 071 580 5780)

ANSTEY, Edgar; s of Percy Lewis Anstey (d 1920), of Bombay, India, and Dr Vera Anstey, *née* Powell (d 1976); *b* 5 March 1917; *Educ* Winchester, Kings Coll Cambridge (MA), UCL (PhD); *m* 3 June 1939, Zoë Lilian, da of John Thomson Robertson (d 1922), of Rangoon; 1 s (David John b 1947); *Career* 2 Lt Dorset Regt 1940-41, Maj directorate for selection of personnel WO 1941-45; asst princ Dominions Office 1938-39, private sec to Duke of Devonshire 1939-40, Home Office 1951-58, sr princ psychologist MOD 1958-64, chief psychologist Civil Serv Cmmn 1964-69 (princ 1945-51), dep chief sci offr and head Res Div Civil Serv Dept 1969-77; cncllr Esher DC 1972-74; pres: N Cornwall Lib Assoc 1984-88 (chm 1982-84), N Cornwall SLD Assoc 1988-90; FBPsS 1949; *Books* Interviewing For The Selection of Staff (with Dr E O Mercer, 1956), Staff Reporting And Staff Development (1961), Committees - How They Work And How to Work Them (1962), Psychological Tests (1966), The Techniques of Interviewing (1968), Staff Appraisal and Development (with Dr CA Fletcher and Dr J Walker, 1976), An Introduction to Selection Interviewing (1978); *Recreations* fell walking, surfing, golf, bridge; *Clubs* Royal Cwlth Soc; *Style*— Dr Edgar Anstey; Sandrock, 3 Higher Tristram, Polzeath, Wadebridge, Cornwall PL27 6TF (☎ 020 886 3324)

ANSTICE, Michael John Christian; MC (1952), TD; s of Vice Adm Sir Edmund Walter Anstice (d 1979), of Inverdunning House, Dunning, Perth, and Leslie Doudney, *née* Ritchie; *b* 5 Oct 1929; *Educ* Wellington, RMA Sandhurst; *m* 11 July 1959, Carolyn May, da of Gerald Richard Powlett Wilson (d 1986), of Cliffe Hall, Piercebridge, Co Durham; 3 s (William b 1960, Mark b 1967, Richard b 1969), 1 da (Penelope b 1962); *Career* Capt 5 Royal Inniskilling Dragoon Gds 1956, Lt Col Cmd Highland Yeomanry 1968, Col Cmdt Angus/Dundee ACF 1968-75, served Germany, Korea, Egypt; ptnr Milldens Partnership Letham Angus (formerly with Jute Industry Ltd Dundee), chm Jute Importers Assoc Dundee 1976-78; *Recreations* shooting, fishing, woodwork; *Clubs* New (Edinburgh); *Style*— Michael J C Anstice, Esq, MC, TD; Melgam House, Lintrathen, Kirriemuir, Angus DD8 5JH (☎ 057 56 269)

ANSTRUTHER, Ian Fife Campbell; s of Douglas Tollemache Anstruther (d 1956, gs of Sir Robert Anstruther, 5 Bt), and his 1 w Enid (d 1964), 2 da of Lord George Granville Campbell; *b* 11 May 1922; *Educ* Eton, New Coll Oxford; *m* 1, 1951 (m dis 1963), (Geraldine) Honor, elder da of late Capt Gerald Stuart Blake, MC; 1 da; m 2, 1963, Susan Margaret Walker, da of Henry St John Paten; 2 s, 3 da; *Career* Capt Royal Corps of Signals, former attache Br Embassy Washington; author; memb Royal Co of Archers (Queen's Body Guard for Scotland); FSA; *Books* I Presume, The Knight and the Umbrella, The Scandal of the Andover Workhouse, Oscar Browning; *Clubs* Brooks's; *Style*— Ian Anstruther, Esq, FSA; Estate Office, Barlavington, Petworth, Sussex GU28 0LG (☎ 079 87 260)

ANSTRUTHER OF THAT ILK, Sir Ralph Hugo; 7 Bt (NS 1694) and 12 Bt (NS 1700), KCVO (1976, CVO 1967), MC (1943), DL (Fife 1960, Caithness 1965); s of late Capt Robert Anstruther, MC, and Marguerite, da of Hugo de Burgh, 3 s of

Thomas de Burgh, of Oldtown, Co Kildare; suc gf Sir Ralph Anstruther, 6 Bt, JP, Lord-Lt of Fife, 1934 and cous Sir Windham Carmichael-Anstruther 11 Bt 1980; *b* 13 June 1921; *Educ* Eton, Magdalene Coll Cambridge (BA); *Heir* cous, Ian Anstruther, *qv*; *Career* Maj (ret) Coldstream Gds; equerry to HM Queen Elizabeth The Queen Mother 1959- (treas 1961-, a private sec 1959-64); memb Royal Co of Archers (Queen's Body Gd for Scotland); hereditary carver to HM The Queen; *Style—* Sir Ralph Anstruther, Bt, KCVO, MC, DL; Balcaskie, Pittenweem, Fife (☎ 0333 311202); Watten Mains, Caithness (☎ 095 582 228)

ANSTRUTHER-GOUGH-CALTHORPE, Sir Euan Hamilton; 3 Bt (UK 1929), of Elvetham Hall, Elvetham, Co Southampton; s of Niall Hamilton Anstruther-Gough-Calthorpe (d 1970), and Martha (who m 2, 1975, Charles Nicholson), da of Stuart Warren Don; suc gf, Brig Sir Richard Anstruther-Gough-Calthorpe, 2 Bt, CBE (d 1985); *b* 22 June 1966; *Educ* Harrow, Royal Agric Coll Cirencester; *Style—* Sir Euan Anstruther-Gough-Calthorpe, Bt; Turner's Green Farm, Elvetham, Hartley Wintney, Hants RG27 8BE

ANTEBI, Raymond Nathan; s of Moise Antebi (d 1970), and Miriam, *née* Farhi; *b* 4 March 1930; *Educ* Lycee Francais Alexandria Egypt, Univ of Bologna (MD), Apothecaries Hall Dublin (LAH), Univ of London (DPM); *m* 1956, Anna, da of Philip Van Der Welde; 2 s (Daniel Leo b 2 April 1957, David Joel b 25 Feb 1960), 2 da (Laura Jane b 7 April 1963, Helen Clare b 10 Nov 1966); *Career* rotating internship United Hosp NY State USA 1954-55, sr house offr Gen Hosp Durham Co 1955-56, registrar Wordsley Hosp Stourbridge 1956-57, pre-registration medicine Darlington Meml Hosp Co Durham 1957-58, pre-registration obstetrics and gynaecology Greenbank Maternity Hosp Co Durham 1958, GP asst Newcastle upon Tyne 1958-59, jr hosp med offr (psychiatry) Moorhaven Hosp S Devon 1959-62, sr registrar and clinical tutor North Regnl Bd Univ of Aberdeen 1962-64; conslt psychiatrist: All Saints Hosp Birmingham, Duke St Hosp and Glasgow Royal Infirmary 1966-80; acting head of Dept of Psychiatry Duke St Hosp 1980-87, physician superintendant and clinical services mangr Eastern Psychiatric Services Glasgow 1987-, clinical teacher Univ of Glasgow; memb RCPSGlas 1979; former psychiatric advsr Student Health Serv Univ of Strathclyde; hon memb Scottish Branch Med and Dental Hypnotic Soc 1982; FRCPS, FRCP, FRCPsych; *publications:* Seven Principles to Overcome Resistance in Hypno-Analysis, Effect of Serum of Schizophrenics on Evoked Cortical Potentials in the Rat, The Need for Elementary Knowledge of Psychology in Dentistry, State Benefits as a Cause of Unwillingness to Work, Accident Neurosis - Entity or Non-Entity, Sexual Dysfunction, Value of Forensic Psychiatry in a Court of Law, Homicide On-lookers, Medical Role of Drug Abuse, Psychological Characteristics of Offenders and Violent Offenders in the West of Scotland; *Style—* Raymond Antebi, Esq; Greater Glasgow Health Board, Gartloch Hospital, Gartloch, Glasgow G69 8EJ (☎ 041 771 0771, fax 041 771 8396)

ANTHONY; *see*: Bank-Anthony

ANTHONY, Barbara (pen name Antonia Barber); da of Derek Wilson, and (Edith Jessie) Julie, *née* Jeal; *Educ* Rye GS, UCL (BA); *m* 1956, Kenneth Charles Anthony (k 1981), s of the late Charles Arthur Anthony ; 2 s (Jonathan Charles b 1968, Nicholas James b 1972), 1 da (Gemma Thi-Phi-Yen b 1974); *Career* writer of children's books 1966-; author of: The Ghosts (1969, filmed as The Amazing Mr Blunden 1971), The Ring in the Rough Stuff (1983), The Enchanter's Daughter (1987), The Mousehole Cat (1990); supporter of: Friends of the Earth, Greenpeace, Ammesty International, Ramblers ASP, Woodland Tst, Nat Tst; *Recreations* walking, sailing, reading, theatre, TV; *Style—* Mrs Barbara Anthony; Hornes Place Oast, Appledore, Ashford, Kent TN26 2BS; c/o Gina Pollinger, 222 Old Brompton Rd, London SW5 0BZ (☎ 071 373 4711, fax 071 373 3775)

ANTHONY, David Gwilym; s of Ernest Anthony (d 1990), and Megan Euron, *née* Davies; *b* 10 Feb 1947; *Educ* Hull GS, St Catherine's Coll Oxford (MA); *m* 8 Oct 1974, (Ellen) Brigid, da of Air Vice-Marshal W J Crisham (d 1987); 1 s (Peter b 1979), 1 da (Jane b 1980); *Career* Barton Mayhew (now Ernst & Young) 1969-73, Dymo Business Systems Ltd 1973-75, Slater Walker Fin Ltd 1975-77, Forward Tst (Ireland) Ltd 1977-82, dir and gen mangr Hitachi Credit (UK) plc 1982-; FCA 1973; *Recreations* walking, table tennis; *Style—* David G Anthony, Esq; Retreat, Church Lane, Stoke Poges, Bucks, SL2 4NZ (☎ 0753 30895); Hitachi Credit (UK) PLC, Hitachi Credit House, Stables Courtyard, Church Rd, Hayes, Middx, UB3 2UH (☎ 081 561 8486, fax 081 561 1206)

ANTHONY, Dr Donald William James (Don); s of George Anthony, of Sidcup, Kent, and Annie Eva Starkey (d 1962); *b* 6 Nov 1928; *Educ* Loughborough Univ of Sci and Technol (Dip Phys Ed), Univ of London (Dip Health Ed), Univ of Leicester (MEd, PhD); *m* 6 June 1958, Jadwiga, da of Wladeslaw Rzeszowski (d 1942); 1 s (Anthony Marek Louis b 14 July 1964); *Career* asst lectr in physical educn Univ of Manchester 1954-56, lectr Loughborough Univ of Technol 1956-59, princ lectr Avery Hill Coll 1959-85; author of several books, journalist, broadcaster; holder of English hammer throwing record and AAA champion 1953, memb Br Olympic Hammer Throwing Team 1956; memb Br Olympic Ctee (chm BOA Educn Ctee), fndr and pres English Volleyball Assoc, advsr IOC Olympic Solidarity, sports admin, conslt to govt and commercial cos; memb: Sports Writers Assoc, Devpt Studies Assoc, World Future Soc, NATFHE; *Books* Know the Game Volleyball (1948), Keeping Fit for All Ages (1962), Success in Volleyball (1962), The PE Teacher's A-Z (1970), How to Keep Fit (1972), A Strategy for British Sport (1980), Field Athletics (1982), Olympic English (1986), Britain and the Olympic Games (1986); *Recreations* tennis, reading, walking; *Style—* Dr Don Anthony

ANTHONY, Evelyn Bridgett Patricia; da of Lt Cdr Henry Christian Stephens, RNVR (d 1953), of Cholderton, Wilts, and Elizabeth, *née* Sharkey (d 1968), of Lower Leeson St, Dublin; ggf Henry Stephens invented writing ink, F H C Stephens invented Dome anti-aircraft trainer 1939-45; *b* 3 July 1928; *Educ* Convent of Sacred Heart Roehampton; *m* 1955, Michael Ward-Thomas, s of Richard Ward-Thomas (d 1954), of Hunsdonbury, Hunsdon, Herts; 4 s (Anthony, Ewan, Christian, Luke), 2 da (Susan, Katharine); *Career* author; has produced 31 novels which have been translated into 19 languages and have sold over 14 million copies; *Books Incl:* The Occupying Power (won Yorkshire Post fiction prize 1973), The Tamarind Seed (made into a major film); *Recreations* nat hunt racing, music, gardening, salerooms; *Style—* Miss Evelyn Anthony; Horham Hall, Thaxted, Essex

ANTHONY, Prof Peter Paul; s of Dr Miklos Anthony (d 1989), and Maria, *née* Sedon (d 1966); *b* 22 June 1933; *Educ* Gymnasia of Eger and Jaszapati, Univ of Budapest Hungary, St Bartholomews Hosp Med Coll Univ of London; *m* 27 May 1961, Mary, da of Norman Capstick (d 1983); 1 s (Stephen), 1 da (Nicola); *Career* sr lectr in pathology and consIt: Univ of East Africa 1969-71, Middx Hosp Med Sch Univ of London 1971-77; sr lectr then reader then prof of clinical histopathology and conslt of Exeter and Royal Devon and Exeter Hosps 1977-; author of over 100 articles reviews and chapters; memb Cncl: Int Acad of Pathology 1988-91 (also 1978-81), Assoc of Clinical Pathologists 1988-91 (also 1981-84), RCPath 1989- (also 1983-87); memb ctees: WHO, BMA, SWRHA; FRCPath 1982 (MRCPath 1968); *Books* Recent Advances in Histopathology vols 10-15 (jtly, 1978-1990), Pathology of the Liver (jt ed, 1 edn 1978, 2 edn 1987); *Recreations* sailing, walking, photography; *Clubs* Starcross Yacht, Exe Yacht; *Style—* Prof Peter Anthony; 2 St Leonards Place, Exeter EX2 4LZ; Royal Devon & Exeter Hospitals, Area Department of Pathology, Church Lane, Exeter (☎ 0392 402943); Postgraduate Medical School, University of Exeter, Barrack Rd, Exeter (☎ 0392 403006)

ANTHONY, Ronald Desmond; s of William Arthur Anthony (d 1987), and Olive Francis, *née* Buck (d 1986); *b* 21 Nov 1925; *Educ* Sidcup and Chistlehurst GS, Imperial Coll of Sci and Technol (BSc, ACGI); *m* Betty Margaret, da of Walter Frederick Newton Croft (d 1971); 4 da (Frances b 1951, Jennifer b 1953, Rebecca b 1957, Sarah b 1958); *Career* served RCS 1943-48; Vickers Armstrongs (Supermarine) 1950-57, Nuclear Power Plant Co 1957-60, inspr of nuclear installations 1960-85, HSE 1974-85, head Safety Policy Div 1977-80 (bd memb 1977-85), chief inspr of nuclear installations 1980-85, engrg conslt 1985-; pres BNES 1987-89, FIMechE, FINucE, MRAeS; *Recreations* golf; *Style—* Ronald Anthony, Esq; 3 Mereside, Orpington, Kent BR6 8ET

ANTHONY, Vivian Stanley; s of Capt Arthur Stanley Anthony (d 1983), of Llandaff, Cardiff, and Ceinwen, *née* Thomas (d 1965); *b* 5 May 1938; *Educ* Cardiff HS, Univ of London, LSE (BSc), Fitzwilliam Coll Cambridge (DipEd); *m* 1969, Rosamund Anne, da of Col Frank McDermot Byrn, of Co Wicklow, Eire; 1 s (Thomas b 1971), 1 da (Jennifer b 1970); *Career* asst master Leeds GS 1960-64, asst master and housemaster Tonbridge 1964-69, lectr in educn Univ of Leeds 1969-71, dep headmaster The King's Sch Macclesfield 1971-76, headmaster Colfe's Sch 1976-90; sec HMC 1990-, chm Econs Assoc 1974-77; external examiner: Univ of Manchester PGCE 1972-75, Univ of Birmingham Cert of Educn at Dudley Coll 1975-78, Univ of Lancaster 1977-79; chief examiner in A and S level economics for Oxford and Cambridge Bd 1975- (examiner 1970-75); memb: Ctee of Chief Examiners to examine common core in A level economics 1980-81, HMC Academic Policy Ctee 1985- (chm 1989-90), Prof Devpt Ctee 1983-88, Teacher Shortage Working Pty 1987-88, CBI/Schools Panel; area 1 chm SHA 1988-89 (memb Educn Ctee 1989-); SHA rep on London Univ Examination Bd 1984-87, SEAC 1980-88, scrutineer Oxford and Welsh Bds; sch master fellowship Merton Coll Oxford; *Books* incl: Monopoly (1968), Overseas Trade (4 edn, 1981), Banks and Markets, Objective Test in A Level Economics (1973), Tour of American Independent Schools (1984), History of Cricket at Colfe's; articles incl: The Economics Association and the Training of Teachers (Economics 1972), The Report of the Working Party on Economics and Economic History (Economics 1973), Report on Records of Achievement (HMC 1989); *Recreations* music (choral singing), rugby football, squash, tennis; *Clubs* E India, Old Colfeians; *Style—* Vivian Anthony, Esq; Headmasters' Conference, 130 Regent Rd, Leicester LE1 7PG

ANTICO, Sir Tristan; AC (1983); s of Terribile Giovanni Antico (d 1965), and Erminia Bertin (d 1979); *b* 25 March 1923; *Educ* Sydney HS; *m* 1950, Dorothy Brigid, da of William Shields; 3 s (William, Damien, Stephen), 4 da (Virginia, Helen, Elizabeth, Veronica); *Career* chm and md Pioneer Concrete Servs Ltd, dir Qantas Airways Ltd 1979-; past chm St Vincent's Hosp Bd; past tstee Art Gallery of New South Wales; Commendatore dell'Ordine della Stella Solidarieta Italiana 1967; kt 1973; *Recreations* horseracing and breeding, swimming, cruising, tennis; *Clubs* Royal Sydney Yacht Squadron, Manly Golf, Tattersall's Australian Jockey, Sydney Turf, American National, Balmoral Beach; *Style—* Sir Tristan Antico, AC; 161 Raglan St, Mosman, NSW 2088, Australia (☎ 969 4070); 11th Floor, 55 Macquarie Street, Sydney 2000 (telex AA21445, fax 251 1595)

ANTON, David; s of James Martin Anton (d 1966), and Sarah Anton (d 1968); *b* 1 April 1936; *Educ* Harrow Co GS; *m* Cynthia Maureen; 1 s (Richard Phillip b 1964), 1 da (Sara Jane b 1969); *Career* CA; articled clerk J & J Sawyer & Co 1952-57, sr chartered accountant Deloitte & Co 1958-66; ptnr: Harmood Banner & Co 1969-70 (mangr 1966-69), Coopers & Lybrand Deloitte (formerly Deloitte Haskins & Sells) 1974- (sr investigations ptnr handling wide variety of fin investigations, expert witness and arbitrator); FCA 1958, memb Br Acad of Experts 1989; *Recreations* sailing, skiing, bridge; *Clubs* Gresham; *Style—* David Anton, Esq; Coopers & Lybrand Deloitte, Plumtree Court, London EC4A 4HT (☎ 071 822 8503, fax 071 822 8500)

ANTONELLI, Count Pietro Hector Paolo Maria; Commendatore Ordine al Merito della Republica Italiana (1983); s of Count Giacomo Antonelli (d 1963; Cavalry Gen, Italian Army), and Countess Luisa Antonelli, *née* Piva (d 1954); of the same family as Cardinal Giacomo Antonelli, sec of State to Pope Pius IX, and of Count Pietro Antonelli, African explorer and diplomat; *b* 14 March 1924; *Educ* Univ of Rome (Degree in Philosophy); *m* (m dis 1976), Countess Maria Benedetta Bossi Pucci; 3 da (Sibilla b 27 April 1947, Santa b 12 Nov 1950, Serena b 18 Jan 1953); *Career* mangr and subsequently dir Hambros Bank Ltd 1972, official Banca Commerciale 1948-62; md: Caboto Spa 1962-72, Banca Provinciale di Depositi e Sconti 1971; *Recreations* yachting; *Clubs* Circolo della Caccia (Rome); *Style—* Count Pietro Antonelli; 12 Eaton Place, London SW1 (☎ 071 235 5923); Hambros Bank Ltd, 41 Tower Hill, London EC3N 4HA (☎ 071 480 5000, fax 071 488 9994, telex 883851)

ANTRIM, 9 Earl of (I 1785); Alexander Randal Mark McDonnell; also Viscount Dunluce, by which title he continues to be known; s of 8 Earl of Antrim, KBE (d 1977), and Angela Christina, da of Col St Mark Sykes; *b* 3 Feb 1935; *Educ* Downside, ChCh Oxford, Ruskin Sch of Art; *m* 1, 1963 (m dis 1974), Sarah Elizabeth Anne, 2 da of Sir John Bernard Vyvyan Harmsworth; 1 s, 2 da (Lady Flora Mary b 1963, Lady Alice Angela Jane b 1964); m 2, 1977, Elizabeth, da of Michael Moses Sacher; 1 da (Lady Rachel Frances b 1978); *Heir* s, Hon Randal Alexander St John McDonnell b 2 July 1967; *Career* keeper of Conservation Tate Gallery 1975-; chm Rathlin Island Tst 1990; memb: Exec Ctee City and Guilds of London Art Sch, Court of Royal Co of Art; dir: Ulster TV, Northern Salmon Co; FRSA; *Style—* Viscount Dunluce; Glenarm Castle, Glenarm, Co Antrim, Northern Ireland

ANTROBUS, Edward Philip; s and h of Sir Philip Coutts Antrobus, 7 Bt, and Dorothy Margaret Mary, *née* Davis (d 1973); *b* 28 Sept 1938; *Educ* Witwatersrand Univ (BSc), Magdalene Coll Cambridge (MA); *m* 7 Oct 1966, Janet Sarah Elizabeth, da of Philip Walter Sceales, of Johannesburg; 1 s (Francis b 1972), 2 da (Barbara b 1968, Sarah b 1970); *Career* mangr Marley Johannesburg, landowner; *Recreations* golf, tennis; *Clubs* Johannesburg Country, Royal Johannesburg Golf; *Style—* Edward Antrobus, Esq; 70 Harry Street, Robertsham, Johannesburg, S Africa (☎ 011 680 3560)

ANTROBUS, Sir Philip Coutts; 7 Bt (UK 1815), of Antrobus, Cheshire; s of Geoffrey Edward Antrobus (gn of Sir Edmund Antrobus, 2 Bt, and gn through his m, Mary, *née* Shakerley, of Sir Charles Shakerley, 1 Bt); suc cous, Sir Philip Antrobus, 6 Bt, MC, 1968; *b* 10 April 1908; *m* 1, 28 Aug 1937, Dorothy Margaret Mary (d 1973), da of late Rev William George Davis, of Grahamstown, SA; 2 s, 1 da; m 2, 1975, Doris Primrose (d 1986), da of late Harry George Watts, and widow of Thomas Ralph Dawkins; *Heir* s, Edward Antrobus; *Career* served WWII (POW); Lord of the Manor of Amesbury; *Recreations* golf; *Clubs* Old Andrean; *Style—* Sir Philip Antrobus, Bt; West Amesbury House, Amesbury, Wilts SP4 7BH (☎ 0980 623860)

ANWAR, Tariq Rafiq; s of Rafiq Anwar (d 1976), of Chiswick, and Edith Fordham, *née* Reich; *b* 21 Sept 1945; *Educ* Walpole GS, Sir John Cass Coll London; *m* 29 Sept 1966, Shirley Natalie, da of John Richard Hills, of Hainault, Essex; 1 s (Dominic b 1967), 1 da (Gabrielle b 1970); *Career* asst film ed; films incl: Mackenna's Gold, Cromwell, Loot; film ed with BBC; best editor BAFTA Awards: Caught on a Train,

Oppenheimer; BAFTA Nominations: Monocled Mutineer, Fortunes of War, Summer's Lease; ACE Nomination for Tender is the Night; memb ACTT; *Recreations* music, tennis, bricklaying; *Style—* Tariq Anwar, Esq; c/o PTA Bugle House, Noel St W1 (☎ 071 439 2282)

ANWYL-DAVIES, His Hon Judge; Marcus John Anwyl-Davies; QC (1967); s of Thomas Anwyl-Davies, MD (d 1971), and Kathleen Beryl, *née* Oakshott; *b* 11 July 1923; *Educ* Harrow, ChCh Oxford (MA); *m* 1, 1954 (m dis 1974), Eva Hilda Elisabeth, *née* Paulson; 1 s, 1 da; m 2, 1983, Myrna Dashoff; *Career* served WWII Capt RA (despatches), Hong Kong and Singapore RA; called to the Bar Inner Temple 1949, legal assessor GMC and GDC 1969-71, circuit judge 1972-, liaison judge Hertford Magistrates 1972-82; vice pres Herts Magistrates Assoc 1975, pres Cncl of HM Circuit Judges 1989; *Recreations* farming, photography; *Clubs* Reform; *Style—* His Hon Judge Anwyl-Davies, QC; c/o Reform Club, 104 Pall Mall, London SW1Y 5EW

AP ROBERT, His Hon Judge; Hywel Wyn Jones; s of Rev Robert John Jones (d 1973), and Mrs Jones, *née* Evans (d 1986); *b* 19 Nov 1923; *Educ* Cardiff HS, CCC Oxford (MA); *m* 1956, Elizabeth, da of J Gareth Davies, of Penarth; 2 da; *Career* WWII FO and Intelligence Corps; called to the Bar Middle Temple 1950, contested Cardiganshire (Plaid Cymru) 1970, chm Industl Tbnls 1970-72, rec of the Crown Ct 1972-75, stipendiary magistrate Cardiff (now S Glamorgan) 1972-75, circuit judge 1975-; hon memb of the Gorsedd of Bards 1972; co ct judge in Mid and W Glamorgan 1985-; *Recreations* Welsh and classical literature, modern languages; *Clubs* Cardiff & County; *Style—* His Hon Judge ap Robert; Law Courts, Cardiff

APPLEBY, His Hon Judge Brian John; QC (1971); s of Ernest Joel Appleby; *b* 25 Feb 1930; *Educ* Uppingham, St John's Coll Cambridge; *m* 1958, Rosa Helena, *née* Flitterman; 1 s, 1 da; *Career* called to the Bar Middle Temple 1953, rec of Crown Ct 1972-88, judge of the Crown Ct 1988-; dep chm Notts QS 1970-71, bencher Middle Temple 1980; dist referee Notts Wages Conciliation Bd NCB 1980-88; memb Notts City Cncl 1955-58 and 1960-63; *Style—* His Hon Judge Brian Appleby, QC; The Poplars, Edwalton Village, Edwalton, Notts (☎ 0602 223814)

APPLEBY, Douglas Edward Surtees; s of late Robert Appleby, and Muriel, *née* Surtees; *b* 17 May 1929; *Educ* Durham Johnston Sch, Nottingham Univ; *m* 1952, June Marrison; 1 s, 1 da; *Career* Corn Products Co (USA) 1958-63, fin dir Wilkinson Sword Co 1963-68; The Boots Co: fin dir 1968-72, md 1973-81, ret; memb Cncl Inst of CA 1971-75 and CBI 1977-81; farmer; FCA; *Style—* Douglas Appleby, Esq; Craigend of Aldbar, West Drums, Brechin, Angus, Scotland

APPLEBY, (Lesley) Elizabeth; QC (1979); (Mrs Michael Collins); o da of Arthur Leslie Appleby, and Dorothy Evelyn, *née* Edwards; *b* 12 Aug 1942; *Educ* Dominican Convent Brewood Staffs, Wolverhampton Girls' HS, Univ of Manchester (LLB); *m* 6 Jan 1978, Michael Kenneth Collins, OBE; 1 s (Andrew b 23 Jan 1980), 1 da (Emma b 13 Feb 1984); *Career* called to the Bar Gray's Inn 1965, ad eundem Lincoln's Inn 1975; in practice Chancery Bar 1966-; memb of Senate of Inns of Court and Bar 1977-80 and 1981-82; bencher Lincoln's Inn 1986, rec Crown Ct; *Recreations* gardening, swimming, golf; *Style—* Miss Elizabeth Appleby, QC; 32 Pembroke Rd, London W8 (☎ 071 602 4141); The Glebe House, Chiddingfold, Surrey; 4/5 Gray's Inn Square, Gray's Inn, London WC1R 5AY (☎ 071 404 5252, fax 071 242 7803)

APPLEBY, George; s of William Appleby (d 1942),of Felling, Gateshead, and Constance, *née* Forrest (d 1979); *b* 2 June 1919; *Educ* private schs, Sch of Mil Engrg and RADAR, Univ of Newcastle upon Tyne; *m* 19 Aug 1955, Doreen, da of James Kidd Reed (d 1969), of Jesmond, Newcastle upon Tyne; 2 s (Stephen Mark b 1956, Jonathan Paul b 1963), 1 da (Carole Anne b 1958); *Career* WWII 1939-46 RE, served 50 Div France (Dunkirk), 8 Army India; clerk G Raillard 1933-34, accountant Bolton & Wawn (now Thornton Baker) 1934-39, sr asst Peat Marwick Mitchell 1946-50, fin exec Armstrong Whitworth Thor Stewart Warner (USA and Italy) 1951-67, conslt advsr 1968-71, fin exec Blyth Harbour Cmmn 1971-78, advsr and instr Seaport Corpn Port Sudan (World Bank and Kuwaiti aid project) 1978-80, port cost accounting expert UN (USA and Turkey) 1980-81, professional accountant Port of London in team at Saudi Arabia (Yanbu project), conslt advsr special devpt area 1982-; FCA, ATII, ABCS; *Recreations* singing, experiments, occasional golf, badminton, bathing; *Style—* George Appleby Esq; 67 Millview Dr, Tynemouth, Tyne and Wear NE30 2QD (☎ 091 2577 516)

APPLEBY, Malcolm Arthur; s of James William Appleby (d 1976), of West Wickham, Kent, and Marjory, *née* Stokes; *b* 6 Jan 1946; *Educ* Hawesdown Co Secdy Mod Sch for Boys, Beckenham Sch of Art, Ravensbourn Coll of Art and Design, Central Sch of Art and Design, Sir John Cass Sch of Art, Royal Coll of Art; *Career* started career as engraver 1968, currently designer for silver and specialist gun engraver (developed gold fusing on to steel and created new silver engraving techniques); work incl: engraving orb on Prince of Wales Coronet, King George VI Diamond Stakes trophy 1978, 500th anniversary silver cup for London Assay Office, V & A seal, condiment set destined for 10 Downing St, major silver cmmn (cup and cover) for Royal Museum of Scotland 1990; work in collections: Aberdeen Art Gallery Nat Museum of Scotland, Royal Armouries, V & A, Crafts BR Museum, Contemporary Arts Soc, Goldsmiths Co, Br Cncl crafts exhibition to Japan, Sotheby's contemporary arts exhibition to Japan, Chicago New Art Forms Exhibition (with the Scottish Gallery); memb Crathes Drumoak and Durris Community Cncl (chm 1981), Br Art Medal Soc; Freeman Worshipful Co of Goldsmiths London 1976; *Recreations* work, standing in the garden, cups of tea with friends and neighbours, less stilton cheese, still darning my very old but colourful pullover; *Style—* Malcolm Appleby, Esq; Crathes Station, Banchory, Kincardineshire AB31 3JN (☎ 033 044 642)

APPLEBY, Martin Thomas Morgan; s of Harold Thompson Appleby (d 1984), and Margaret, *née* Morgan (d 1973); *b* 14 May 1933; *Educ* Downside; *m* 25 April 1959, Angela Mary, da of Dr N E Delaney (d 1967); 2 s (Benedict Mark b 14 July 1960, Thomas Philip Sebastian b 26 Oct 1970), 2 da (Lucy Christina Mary b 5 March 1962), Marica Josephine b 19 June 1963); *Career* Nat Serv 2 Lt RA 1951-53, TA 1953-56; chm Appleby and Son Ltd 1983-84 (md 1966-83), dir Appleby Wesward Gp plc 1984-; chm Van Neste Fndn 1983- (tstee 1966-); *Recreations* sailing, walking, travelling, reading; *Clubs* Royal Western Yacht (Plymouth), Clifton (Bristol); *Style—* Martin Appleby, Esq; Summerleas, Yealm Road, Newton Ferrers, Plymouth Devon; Appleby Westward Group Plc, Callington Rd, Saltash, Cornwall PL12 6LT (☎ 0752 843171, telex 45106, fax 0752 848865)

APPLETON, Lt-Col George Fortnam; OBE (1946), TD (1947), JP (1954), DL (Lancs 1971); s of James Arthur Appleton, JP (d 1961), of Ainsdale, Lancs and Wetwood, Staffs, and Ethel Maude, *née* Fortnam; *b* 23 July 1913; *Educ* Warwick Sch; *m* 1940, Patricia Margaret (d 1990), da of Henry J L Dunlop, memb 1907- Shackleton Antarctic Expedition (d 1931), of Lancs; 1 s (John), 1 da (Jayne); *Career* 2 Lt 5 (Rifle) Bn The King's Regt 1933, Staff Capt 165 Inf Bde 1938, served WWII, Staff Coll 1940, Gen Staff A & Q Branch appts HQ II Corps and HQ Eastern Cmd, Beach Co Cmd D Day Invasion 1944 (despatches twice), DAQMG HQ 12 Corps, 2 Army and Port of Antwerp, AA & QMG HQ 20 L of C Sub Area BAOR; ret co dir and farmer; cmdt Special Constabulary 1950-54, Co Borough cncllr 1949-61, chm: Southport and N Sefton PSD's 1971-83, Southport Juvenile Court Panel 1954; former chm N Lancs and Merseyside Branches Magistrates' Assoc; Co Borough Cncllr 1949-61; High Sheriff Merseyside 1977-78, hon co dir W Lancs BRCS 1964-74, pres Merseyside Co BRCS 1974-79; former fndr chm Merseycare Charitable Tst, former Lancs pres Forces Help Soc and Lord Roberts Workshops; patron: Southport and W Lancs Branch Normandy Veterans Assoc, Southport and Dist Youth Band, Southport and Dist Branch Burma Star Assoc, Dunkirk Veterans Assoc; govr School for Hearing Impaired Children Birkdale; OStJ 1974; *Style—* Lt-Col George Appleton, OBE, TD, JP, DL; Shore House, Shore Rd, Ainsdale, Southport, Lancs PR8 2PU (☎ 0704 78211)

APPLETON, Robert Michael Laurence; s of Laurence Charles Appleton (d 1973), of Wallington, Surrey, and Margaret Mary, *née* Yates (d 1960); *b* 2 April 1931; *Educ* John Fisher Sch Purley; *m* 23 April 1955, Mary Burdett, da of Reginald William Woodford, CBE (d 1980); 1 s (Dominic Robert Gerard), 2 da (Claire Marguerite, Lucy Mary); *Career* Nat Serv RAF 1949-51; Burke Covington & Nash (CA's) 1946-48, Barclays Bank Ltd 1948-49; Vanpoulles Ltd (church furnishers): joined 1951, dir 1969, chm and md 1972-; chm and md Insignia Ltd 1981-, chm and dir Lodge Lane Property Ltd 1986-; dir: Slabbinck NV Belgium 1988-, Gill Vanpoulles Ltd Dublin; treas League of Friends W Park Hosp 1962-72 (memb 1957-90); memb: Purley Tennis Club 1947-55, Downswood Tennis Club 1956-76, Cheam Sports Tennis Club 1979-82, Limpsfield Tennis Club 1982-, St Vincent De Paul Soc 1956-76; FInstD 1969; *Recreations* lawn tennis, golf, bridge; *Style—* Robert Appleton, Esq; 1 Old Westhall Close, Warlingham, Surrey CR3 (☎ 0883 625646); Insignia Ltd, 1-6 Chalice Close, Lavender Vale, Wallington, Surrey SM6 9QS (☎ 081 669 3122, fax 081 669 7192)

APPLEYARD, Bryan Edward; s of Cyril John Snowdon Appleyard (d 1965), and Freda Bendelsen (d 1971); *b* 24 Aug 1951; *Educ* Bolton Sch, King's Coll Cambridge; *m* Christena Marie- Thérèse; 1 da (Charlotte Mary Freda b 26 June 1982); *Career* journalist; S London News Group 1972-75, United Newspapers City Office 1975-76, fin news ed and dep arts ed The Times 1981-84 (journalist 1976-); freelance journalist and author 1985-; contrib to: The Times, Sunday Times, Vogue, Spectator, London Review of Books; tv critic The Tablet, The Bryan Appleyard Interview in The Independent 1990-, weekly columnist The Sunday Times (Bryan Appleyard's Forum); *Awards* Gen Feature Writer of the Year Br Press awards 1986; *Books* The Culture Club (1984), Richard Rogers: A Biography (1986), The Pleasures of Peace (1989); *Recreations* writing; *Clubs* Groucho's, The Academy; *Style—* Bryan Appleyard, Esq

APPLEYARD, (John) Grahame; s of Reuben Appleyard, of Kirkwall, Orkney, and Hazel May, *née* Walker; *b* 26 April 1941; *Educ* Queen Elizabeth's GS Blackburn Lancs, Univ of Sheffield; *m* 29 Aug 1964, Mary Margaret, da of Dr Edward Patrick Moloney (d 1972); 1 s (Christopher b 1967), 2 da (Pamela b 1965, Judith b 1969); *Career* chartered biologist 1980, currently i/c Clinical Chemistry Laboratory St Helens and Knowsley Health Authy; chm govrs St Lukes Primary Sch; AIMLT 1963, SRMLT 1964, FIMLS 1970, MIBiol 1976, MIScT 1979; *Books* Cystathioninuria and B6 Deficiency (1970); *Recreations* reading, writing; *Style—* Grahame Appleyard, Esq; Judante, 58 Westhaven Crescent, Aughton, Ormskirk, Lancs L39 5BW (☎ 0695 422627); Whiston Hospital, Biochemistry Laboratory, Prescot, Merseyside L35 5DR (☎ 051 430 1832)

APPLEYARD, Leonard Vincent; CMG; s of Thomas William Appleyard, of Cawood, W Yorks (d 1979), and Beatrix, *née* Golton (d 1982); *b* 2 Sept 1938; *Educ* Read Sch Drax W Yorks, Queen's Coll Cambridge (MA); *m* 3 May 1964, Elizabeth Margaret, da of John Lees West, Grasmere, Cumbria; 2 da (Caroline b 1965, Rebecca b 1967); *Career* FO 1962, third sec Hong Kong 1964, second sec Peking 1966, second (later first) sec FO 1969; first sec: Delhi 1971, Moscow 1975, HM Treasy 1978; fin cnsllr Paris 1979-82, head of Econ Rels Dept FCO 1982-84, princ private sec 1984-86, ambass to Hungary 1986-89, dep sec Cabinet Office 1989-; *Recreations* music, reading, tennis; *Clubs* Brooks's; *Style—* Leonard Appleyard, Esq, CMG; c/o Foreign and Commonwealth Office, King Charles St, London SW1

APPLEYARD-LIST, Hon Mrs (Caroline Elizabeth); *née* Arbuthnot; yr da of Baroness Wharton, 10 holder of the title (d 1974), and David Arbuthnot; *b* 28 Aug 1935; *m* 1970, Capt Jonathan Cecil Appleyard-List, CBE, RN; 1 da (Zoë b 1973); *Recreations* riding, painting; *Clubs* Soc of Equestrian Artists; *Style—* The Hon Mrs Appleyard-List; Birches, Stanford Common, Pirbright, Surrey

APSLEY, Lord; Allen Christopher Bertram Bathurst; s and h of 8 Earl Bathurst; *b* 11 March 1961; *m* 31 May 1986, Hilary Jane, da of John F George, of Weston Lodge, Albury Surrey; 1 s (Benjamin George Henry b 6 March 1990); *Style—* Lord Apsley

AQUILECCHIA, Prof Giovanni; s of Gen Vincenzo Aquilecchia (d 1959), and Maria Letizia, *née* Filibeck; *b* 28 Nov 1923; *Educ* Lycee T Tasso Rome, Univ of Rome, Univ of Paris, Univ of London; *m* 7 May 1951 (m dis 1973), Costantina Maria, da of Adolfo Bacchetta (d 1940); 2 s (Adolfo b 1952, Vincent b 1956), 1 da (Maria Letizia b 1960); *Career* libero docente di Italiano Univ of Rome 1958-, reader in Italian UCL 1959-61 (lectr 1955-59); prof of Italian: Univ of Manchester 1961-70, Univ of London 1970-; visiting prof: Univ of Melbourne 1983, Univ of Naples 1990; chm Manchester Dante Soc 1961-70, memb Byron Soc 1979-; Hon MA Univ of Manchester 1965, hon res fell UCL 1964-; memb: AUT 1953-, Soc Italian Studies 1954-, Soc Renaissance Studies 1981-; fell Arcadia Accademia Letterazia Italiana 1961-; *Books* Collected Essays on Italian Language and Literature (1971), numerous academic pubns in Italian; *Recreations* walking, swimming; *Style—* Prof Giovanni Aquilecchia; 49 Hanover Gate Mansions, Park Rd, London NW1 (☎ 071 723 8337); Dept of Italian, University College, Gower St, London WC1E 6BT (☎ 071 387 7050 ext 3023)

ARBEID, Murray; s of Jack Arbeid (d 1968), of London, and Ida, *née* Davis (d 1972); *b* 30 May 1935; *Educ* Quintin Sch London; *Career* design asst to Michael Sherard 1952-54, opened own couture business 1955, started Ready-To-Wear Div 1960, opened Sloane St boutique 1982, artistic dir and first collection for Hartnell Bruton St 1988; fndr memb: Fashion Indust Action Gp 1981, Br Fashion Cncl 1985; *Style—* Murray Arbeid, Esq; 202 Ebury St, London SW1W 8UN (☎ 071 259 9292)

ARBIB, Martyn; s of Richard Arbib (d 1975), and Denise Margot, *née* Kelsey; *b* 27 June 1939; *Educ* Felsted; *m* 2 Aug 1969, Anne Hermione (Sally), da of Hugh Parton (d 1973); 2 s (James b 1971, Benjamin b 1980), 2 da (Annabel b 1970, Melanie b 1973); *Career* chm and fndr Perpetual plc 1974-, non-exec dir Kelsey Industries plc 1975-; memb ICAEW 1961; *Recreations* golf, tennis; *Clubs* Huntercombe Golf; *Style—* Martyn Arbib, Esq; 48 Hart St, Henley-on-Thames, Oxon RG9 2AZ (☎ 0491 576868)

ARBON, Paul; DFC; s of Paul Arbon (d 1929), of London, and Elizabeth, *née* Ashe (d 1977); *Educ* Taft Sch, Fountain Valley Sch; *m* 18 May 1946, Joan, da of James Ward Alker (d 1931), of NY City; 4 da (Carol b 1948, Joyce b 1950, Robin b 1952, April b 1958); *Career* WWII Maj US Air Force 1941-45 (served 8 and 20 Air Force); banker; chm of bd Roosevelt & Sons; *Recreations* hunting, fishing; *Clubs* Union Club (Seawanhaka Corinthian Yacht), Soc of the Cincinnati; *Style—* Paul Arbon, Esq, DFC; 46 Limerston St, London SW10 0HH (☎ 071 351 9558); St Jean, Cap Ferrat, France

ARBUTHNOT, Rev Andrew Robert Coghill; s of Capt Robert Wemyss Muir Arbuthnot, MC (d 1962, ggs of Sir William Arbuthnot, 1 Bt, of Edinburgh), and Mary, *née* Coghill; *b* 14 Jan 1926; *Educ* Eton; *m* 1952, Mrs Audrey Dutton-Barker, o da of Denys Billinghurst Johnson, MC, of Midhurst, West Sussex; 1 s (Charles b 1956), 1 da (Caroline b 1954); *Career* WWII Capt Scots Gds (wounded); contested (C) Houghton-le-Spring 1959, chm and chief exec Arbuthnot Latham Hldgs 1974-81, dir

Sun Alliance 1970-; ordained: deacon 1974, priest 1975; missioner London Healing Mission 1983-; *Books* Love that Heals (jtly with his wife), Christian Prayer and Healing; *Recreations* painting, walking; *Style—* The Rev Andrew Arbuthnot; Monksfield House, Tilford, Farnham, Surrey GU10 2AL (☎ 025 18 2233); London Healing Mission, 20 Dawson Place, London W2 4TJ (☎ 071 229 3641)

ARBUTHNOT, David William Patrick; s of Sir Hugh Fitzgerald Arbuthnot, 7 Bt (d 1983), and his 1 w, Elizabeth Kathleen (d 1972); hp of bro, Sir Keith Arbuthnot, 8 Bt; *b* 7 March 1953; *Educ* Wellington; *m* 12 March 1988, Diane, o da of John Yeomans, of Hill House, Baughurst, Hants; 2 da (Phoebe Elizabeth b 18 Nov 1988, Rosanna Mary b 28 Nov 1989); *Career* racehorse trainer; *Recreations* rugby, shooting; *Clubs* Turf; *Style—* David Arbuthnot, Esq; Yew Tree Stables, Compton, nr Newbury, Berks RG16 0QT (☎ 0635 22 427)

ARBUTHNOT, James Norwich; MP (C) Wanstead and Woodford 1987-; yr s of Sir John Sinclair-Wemyss Arbuthnot, 1 Bt, MBE, TD, *qv*, and (Margaret) Jean, *née* Duff; *b* 4 Aug 1952; *Educ* Eton, Trinity Coll Cambridge (MA); *m* 6 Sept 1984, Emma Louise, da of (John) Michael Broadbent, of Avon; 1 s (Alexander Broadbent b 1986), 1 da (Katherine Rose Joste b 1989); *Career* called to the Bar Inner Temple 1975; practising barr 1977-; cncllr RBK&F 1978-87; contested (C) Cynon Valley 1983, 1984; pres Cynon Valley Cons Assoc 1983-; *Recreations* skiing, guitar, theatre; *Style—* James N Arbuthnot, Esq, MP; House of Commons SW1A 0AA (☎ 071 219 4541)

ARBUTHNOT, Sir John Sinclair-Wemyss; 1 Bt (UK 1964), of Kittybrewster, Aberdeen; MBE (1944), TD (1951); s of Maj Kenneth Wyndham Arbuthnot, the Seaforth Highlanders (ka Second Battle of Ypres 1915; ggs of George Arbuthnot, JP, first of Elderslie, himself a yr bro of Sir William Arbuthnot, 1 Bt, of Edinburgh); *b* 11 Feb 1912; *Educ* Eton, Trinity Coll Cambridge (MA); *m* 3 July 1943, (Margaret) Jean, yr da of (Alexander) Gordon Duff (d 1978); 2 s (William Reierson, James Norwich), 3 da (Elizabeth Mary b 27 May 1947, Louise Victoria (Mrs Lancaster) b 26 Oct 1954, Alison Jane b 9 April 1957); *Heir* s, William Reierson Arbuthnot; *Career* dir and chm of tea cos 1934-75; MP (C) Dover 1950-64; PPS to: Min of Pensions 1952-55, Min of Health 1956-57; chm of ctees and temp chm of House of Commons 1958-64; jt hon sec Assoc of Br C of C 1953-59, vice pres Tstee Savings Banks Assoc 1962-75, chm Folkestone and Dist Water Co 1971-87; memb Church Assembly and Gen Synod of C of E 1955-75, second church estates cmmr 1962-64, church cmmr for E 1962-77, tstee Lambeth Palace Library 1964-77; memb KASG; *Recreations* gardening; *Clubs* Carlton; *Style—* Sir John Arbuthnot, Bt, MBE, TD; Poulton Manor, Ash, Canterbury, Kent CT3 2HW (☎ 0304 812516)

ARBUTHNOT, Julia, Lady; Julia Grace; *née* Peake; da of late Col Fredrick Gerard Peake Pasha, CMG, CBE (d 1970), and Elspeth Maclean, *née* Ritchie (d 1967); f campaigned with Lawrence of Arabia after serv in India and Sudan expedition; fndr and cdr of the Arab Legion Jordan; *b* 6 June 1941; *Educ* Oxonford Castle and Minto; *m* 1977, as his 2 w, Sir Hugh Fitzgerald Arbuthnot, 7 Bt (d 1983); *Career* farmer, landowner; *Recreations* hunting, racing, sailing, skiing; *Clubs* Royal Northumberland Yacht; *Style—* Julia, Lady Arbuthnot; Ferme St Jean, Les Bas Adrechs, Callian, Var, France

ARBUTHNOT, Sir Keith Robert Charles; 8 Bt (UK 1823), of Edinburgh; s of Sir Hugh Arbuthnot, 7 Bt (d 1983), by his 1 w, Elizabeth Kathleen (d 1972), da of Sqdn Ldr George Algernon Williams; *b* 23 Sept 1951; *Educ* Wellington, Univ of Edinburgh; *m* 22 May 1982, Anne, yr da of Brig Peter Moore, of Hastings Hill House, Churchill, Oxon; 2 s (Robert Hugh Peter, Patrick William Martin b 13 July 1987), 1 da (Alice Elizabeth Mary b 22 March 1990); *Heir* s, Robert Hugh Peter Arbuthnot, b 2 March 1986; *Style—* Sir Keith Arbuthnot, Bt; Whitebridge, Peebles, Peebles-shire

ARBUTHNOT, William Reierson; s and h of Sir John Arbuthnot, 1 Bt, MBE, TD; *b* 2 Sept 1950; *Educ* Eton; *Career* employed Arbuthnot Latham Hldgs Ltd 1970-76, Joynson-Hicks & Co (slrs) 1978-81; memb Lloyd's; Liveryman Worshipful Co of Grocers; *Recreations* genealogy, computer programming; *Style—* William Arbuthnot, Esq; 14 Ashburn Gdns, London SW7 4DG (☎ 071 370 4907)

ARBUTHNOTT, Col the Hon (William) David; MBE (1964); 2 s of 15 Viscount of Arbuthnott, CB, CBE, DSO, MC; *b* 5 Nov 1927; *Educ* Fettes, RMA Sandhurst; *m* 1955, Sonja Mary, er da of late Col Charles Thomson, CBE, DSO, TD, DL, of Carnoustie; 1 s (Charles b 1956), 2 da (Georgina b 1964, Elizabeth b 1967); *Career* Col (ret) The Black Watch, served Korea 1952-53, Kenya 1953-55, N Ireland 1974 (despatches); Regimental Sec The Black Watch; *Style—* Col the Hon David Arbuthnott, MBE; Old Manse of Strathbraan, Dunkeld, Perthshire PH8 0DY (☎ 035 03 205)

ARBUTHNOTT, Hugh James; CMG (1984); 2 s of Cdr James Gordon Arbuthnott (ggs of 8 Viscount of Arbuthnott); *b* 27 Dec 1936; *Educ* Ampleforth, New Coll Oxford; *m* 1964, Vanessa Rose, o da of Edward Dyer, of Tunbridge Wells; 3 s (Dominic b 1965, Justin b 1967, d 1989, Giles b 1970); *Career* 2 Lt Black Watch; joined FO (subsequently FCO) 1960, third sec Tehran 1961-64, FO 1964-68 (private sec to min of State 1966-68), first sec Chancery Tehran 1971-74, head of Euro Integration Dept (External) FCO 1974-77, cnsllr (Agric and Econ) Paris 1978-80, head of Chancery Paris 1980-83, under sec Int Div ODA 1983-85, ambass to Romania 1986-89, ambass to Portugal 1989-; *Style—* Hugh Arbuthnott, Esq, CMG; c/o Foreign and Commonwealth Office, London SW1A 2AH

ARBUTHNOTT, Hon Hugh Sinclair; 3 and yst s of 15 Viscount of Arbuthnott, CB, CBE, DSO, MC (d 1966), and Ursula, *née* Collingwood (d 1989); *b* 14 Nov 1929; *Educ* Fettes, Gonville and Caius Coll Cambridge (MA), Edinburgh Univ (LLB); *m* 21 Sept 1963, Anne Rosamond, o da of late Charles Bentley Terdre, of Appledore, Cherry Walk, High Salvington, Worthing, Sussex; 1 s (Hugh James Hamilton b 1967), 1 da (Katherine Anne b 1970); *Career* 2 Lt The Black Watch; with Shell Int Petroleum Co 1953-83; FCIS; *Style—* The Hon Hugh Arbuthnott; 7 Birch Close, Boundstone Road, Farnham, Surrey GU10 4TJ; Cairnhill, Forfar, Angus DD8 3TQ

ARBUTHNOTT, Maj James Francis; s of Hugh Forbes Arbuthnott (d 1982, s of late Donald Stuart Arbuthnott, CE, s of 8 Viscount of Arbuthnott), and Janet, da of late Vice Adm Herbert Marshall, of Gayton Hall, Ross, Herefords; *b* 27 April 1940; *Educ* Downside, RMA Sandhurst; *m* 1974, Hon Louisa, *qv*; 2 s, 2 da; *Career* Maj Black Watch; Kt of Honour and Devotion Sov Mil Order of Malta; *Style—* Maj James Arbuthnott; Stone House Cottage, Stone, Kidderminster, Worcs (☎ 0562 69902)

ARBUTHNOTT, 16 Viscount of (S 1641); John Campbell Arbuthnott; CBE (1986), DSC (1945); also Lord Inverbervie (S 1641); s of 15 Viscount of Arbuthnott (d 1966), and Ursula, *née* Collingwood (d 1989); Lord Arbuthnott is the thirty third Laird of Arbuthnott and the twenty seventh in descent from Hugh de Swinton, who acquired the estate of Aberbothenoth, of which he is recorded as having been styled *thanus* and *dominus*, towards the end of the twelfth century, and who was gggggggggggs of Edulf Edulfing, 1 Lord of Bamburgh (d 912); *b* 26 Oct 1924; *Educ* Fettes, Gonville and Caius Cambridge; *m* 1949, Mary Elizabeth Darley, er da of Cdr Christopher Oxley, DSC, RN (himself 2 s of Adm Charles Oxley, JP, and whose yst sis m 14 Viscount of Arbuthnott); 1 s, 1 da (*see* Hon Mrs Smith); *Heir* s, Master of Arbuthnott, *qv*; *Career* served WWII Fleet Air Arm Far E & Pacific; chm: Aberdeen & N Marts 1986- (dir 1973-), Scottish Widows and Life Assoc 1978- (chm 1984-87); dir: Clydesdale Bank 1985-, Scottish N Investmt Tst 1979-85; Lord-Lt Grampian Region (Kincardineshire) 1977-; Britoil plc 1988-90, BP Scot Advsy Bd 1990-; pres: Br Assoc for Shooting and Conservation (formerly WAGBI) 1973-, RZS Scotland 1976-, Royal Scottish Geographical Soc 1982-87; dep chm Nature Conservancy Cncl 1980-85 (chm Scottish Advsy Ctee); memb Royal Cmmn Historic Manuscripts 1987-; Lord High Cmmr to Gen Assembly of Church of Scotland 1986 and 1987; Prior of the Order of St John of Jerusalem in Scotland 1983-; FRSE, FRSA, FRICS; KStJ 1982; *Style—* The Rt Hon the Viscount of Arbuthnott, CBE, DSC, FRSE; Arbuthnott House, by Laurencekirk, Kincardineshire AB3 1PA (☎ home 0561 61226; office 056 12 417)

ARBUTHNOTT, Master of; Hon John Keith Oxley; s and h of 16 Viscount of Arbuthnott, CBE, DSC, *qv*; *b* 18 July 1950; *Educ* Fettes, N Scotland Coll of Agric Aberdeen (Higher Nat Dip, Dip in Farm Business, Organisation and Management); *m* 1974, Jill Mary, eld da of Capt Colin Farquharson, of Whitehouse, Alford, Aberdeenshire; 1 s (Christopher Keith b 20 July 1977), 2 da (Clare Anne b 1974, Rachel Sarah b 1979); *Style—* The Master of Arbuthnott; Kilternan, Arbuthnott, Laurencekirk, Kincardineshire AB30 1NA

ARBUTHNOTT, Prof John Peebles; s of James Anderson Arbuthnott (d 1961), and Jean, *née* Kelly (d 1982); *b* 8 April 1939; *Educ* Hyndland Sr Secdy Sch, Univ of Glasgow (BSc, PhD), Trinity Coll Dublin (MA, ScD); *m* 2 July 1962, Elinor Rutherford, da of John Smillie (d 1986); 1 s (Andrew b 10 Feb 1969), 2 da (Anne b 6 March 1966, Alison b 11 Nov 1974); *Career* res fell Royal Soc 1968-72, sr lectr Dept of Bacteriology Univ of Glasgow 1972-75 (asst lectr 1960-63, lectr 1963-67), bursar Trinity Coll Dublin 1983-86 (prof of microbiology 1976-88), prof of microbiology Univ of Nottingham 1988-, princ elect and vice chllr elect Univ of Strathclyde 1991; author of many papers on microbial pathogenicity; elder of Church of Scotland; memb Cncl Soc of Gen Microbiology 1981-86 (sr ed 1980-84, treas 1987-), meetings sec Fedn of Euro Microbiology Socs 1986-90 (sec 1983-); memb: Microbiological Safety of Food Ctee 1989-90, AFRC Animal Res Bd 1989-, Public Health Laboratory Service, Ctee CAMR 1989-, Soc of Gen Microbiology, Pathological Soc; MIRA 1985, FIBiol 1988, FRSA 1989; *Books* Isoelectric Focussing (jtly, 1974), Determinants of Microbial Pathogenicity (ed, 1983); *Recreations* watching football, Scottish country dancing; *Style—* Prof John Arbuthnott; 43 Cogley Lane, Bingham, Nottingham NG13 8DE (☎ 0949 37723); Department of Microbiology, Queens Medical Centre, University of Nottingham (☎ 0602 709162, fax 0602 422190)

ARBUTHNOTT, Hon Mrs (Louisa Nina); *née* Hughes-Young; 3 da of 1 Baron St Helens, MC, and sis of 2 Baron; *b* 31 Aug 1949; *m* 1974, Maj James F Arbuthnott, *qv*; 2 s (John Patrick b 1977, Albert Michael b 1988), 2 da (Elizabeth b 1980, Florence b 1981); *Style—* The Hon Mrs Arbuthnott; Stone House Cottage, Stone, Kidderminster, Worcs (☎ 0562 69902)

ARBUTHNOTT, Robert; s of Archibald Arbuthnott, MBE, ED (d 1977), and Barbara Joan, *née* Worters (d 1988); *b* 28 Sept 1936; *Educ* Sedbergh, Emmanuel Coll Cambridge (BA, MA); *m* 19 May 1962, (Sophie) Robina, da of Robin Alan Axford; 1 s (Robert Keith b 1968), 2 da (Alison b 1963, Catherine b 1965); *Career* Nat Serv 1955-57, 2 Lt The Black Watch (RHR); Br Cncl 1960-: Karachi 1960, Lahore 1962, London 1964, rep Nepal 1967, rep Malaysia 1973, dir Educational Contracts Dept 1976, controller Personnel Div 1978, rep Germany 1981; RCDS 1986, minister (cultural affairs) New Delhi 1988-; *Recreations* making music, sport, historic places; *Clubs* United Oxford and Cambridge University, Liphook Golf; *Style—* Robert Arbuthnott, Esq; c/o The British Council, 10 Spring Gardens, London SW1A 2BN (☎ 071 930 8466)

ARCHDALE, Sir Edward Folmer; 3 Bt (UK 1928), of Riversdale, Co Fermanagh; DSC (1943); s of Vice Adm Sir Edward Archdale, 2 Bt, CBE (d 1955), and Gerda, da of Frederik Sievers, of Copenhagen; *b* 8 Sept 1921; *Educ* Copthorne Sch, RNC Dartmouth; *m* 24 July 1954 (m dis 1978), Elizabeth Ann Stewart, da of Maj-Gen Wilfrid Boyd Fellowes Lukis, CBE, RM (d 1969); 1 s (Nicholas Edward), 2 da (Annabel Frances b 1956, Lucinda Grace b 1958); *Heir* s, Nicholas Edward Archdale b 2 Dec 1965; *Career* Capt RN (ret), serv WWII (despatches); def conslt, political economist; elected (UUP) Ards Borough Cncl 1989; *Recreations* civilisation; *Style—* Sir Edward Archdale, Bt, DSC; 19 Dermott Rd, Comber, Co Down, NI BT23 5LG (☎ 0247 873195)

ARCHDEACON, Antony; s of Maurice Ignatius Archdeacon (d 1973), of Ruislip, Middx, and Nora Margery May, *née* Ball; *b* 25 Jan 1925; *Educ* Oxford House Sch, Buckingham Univ (LLB); *m* 3 Dec 1956 (m dis 1964), Elizabeth, da of Samuel Percy Ball, of The Cottage, Great Horwood, Bucks; 1 s (Timothy b 1957); *Career* admitted slr 1950, dir Skim Milk Supplies Ltd 1967-, Business Mortgages Tst plc 1969-86, chm Forum of St Albans plc 1985-; pres: Rotary Club Buckingham 1968, Northampton Anglo-German Club 1988-; town clerk Buckingham 1951-71; Freeman: City of London 1972, Worshipful Co of Feltmakers 1972; *Recreations* walking, languages; *Clubs* St Stephen's Constitutional, City Livery; *Style—* Antony Archdeacon, Esq; Trolly Hall, Buckingham MK18 1PT (☎ 0280 812 126, fax 0280 822 105, car 0860 355 748, telex 837204)

ARCHER, Prof Brian Harrison; s of Arthur Cecil Arthur (d 1977), and Elizabeth, *née* Summerscales; *b* 31 July 1934; *Educ* Liverpool Coll, Fitzwilliam House Cambridge (MA), Univ of London (BSc), Univ of Wales (PhD); *Career* cmmnd Kings Regt Liverpool 1955, Maj TAVR 1955-65; schoolmaster Monmouth 1956-69; Inst of Economic Res Univ Coll of N Wales 1969-77: sr res offr, lectr, sr lectr, dir; pro-vice chllr Univ of Surrey 1987- (prof and head of Dept of Mgmnt Studies 1978-); conslt to: Cwlth Secretariat, UNDF, World Bank, WTO; numerous pubns in jls; ind memb devpt and mktg ctees Br Tourist Authy 1984-; FHCIMA , FTS; *Books* The Impact of Domestic Tourism (1973), Demand Forecasting in Tourism (1976), Tourism Multipliers: The State of the Art (1977); *Recreations* travel, watching cricket and rugby; *Style—* Prof Brian Archer; 3 The Cedars, Milford, Godalming, Surrey GU8 5DH; Dept of Management Studies, University of Surrey, Stag Hill, Guildford, Surrey GU2 5XH (☎ 0483 571281, fax 0483 300803, telex 859331)

ARCHER, Bryan Russell; s of Donald Charles Archer (d 1990), and Lillian May, *née* Smith; *b* 18 April 1928; *Educ* Watford GS, Architectural Assoc Sch of Architecture (DipArch); *m* 31 March 1955, Nancy Sheila, da of Stanley James Dean, of Welwyn Garden City, Herts; 2 s (Richard b 1959, Andrew b 1960), 1 da (Susan b 1963); *Career* registered architect 1956; fndr ptnr Archer Boxer Partners 1963, dir Archer Boxer Group Ltd 1978; pres Hatfield C of C 1969-71, dir Herts C of C 1972-80; govr Sherrardswood Sch 1974-85, dist govr Rotary Int 1985-86; memb Worshipful Co of Constructors 1978; FRIBA 1968, FFB 1970; *Recreations* boating; *Clubs* IOD; *Style—* Bryan Archer, Esq; Pennyfathers, Pennyfathers Lane, Harmer Green, Welwyn, Herts (☎ 043 871 4627); Archer Boxer Partners Ltd, ABP House, Salisbury Square, Hatfield, Herts (☎ 0707 269001, fax 0707 275343)

ARCHER, Sir Clyde Vernon Harcourt; *b* 12 Nov 1904; *Educ* Harrison Coll Barbados, Univ of Cambridge; *Career* barrister Gray's Inn; judge Petty Debt Court (Bridgetown Barbados) 1938, legal draughtsman Trinidad and Tobago 1944, slr gen Trinidad and Tobago 1953, puisne judge 1954, chief justice Windward and Leeward Islands 1958, fed justice WI 1958-62, judge Ct of Appeal Bahamas 1971-75; kt 1962; *Publications* Revised Edition of the Laws of Barbados (jointly, 1944); *Style—* Sir Clyde Archer; 40 Graeme Hall Terrace, Christchurch, Barbados

ARCHER, Colin Robert Hill; s of Robin Hamlyn Hill Archer, of Richmond, and Cherrie Mary, *née* Gourlay; *b* 13 Aug 1949; *Educ* Stowe, Univ of Essex (BA); *m* 27 March 1976, (Mary) Jane, da of John Rutherford Blaikie; 1 s (Charles b 18 Aug 1983), 1 da (Sarah b 11 March 1981); *Career* articled clerk then asst mangr Thomson McLintock 1971-77, mangr corp fin Kleinwort Benson 1977-85, divnl dir corp fin BHS plc 1985-86, gp fin controller Storehouse plc 1988-89 (gp co sec 1986-88), gp fin dir Higgs and Hill plc 1989-; FCA; *Recreations* tennis, golf, skiing, reading; *Clubs* Hurlingham, Berkshire Golf; *Style—* Colin Archer, Esq; Higgs and Hill plc, Crown House, Kingston Rd, New Malden, Surrey KT3 3ST (☎ 081 942 8921)

ARCHER, Dr Gordon James; s of Sqdn Ldr Percival John Archer, of 53 Birch Ave, Cleveleys, Lancs, and Doris Elizabeth Archer; *b* 21 Aug 1942; *Educ* Kirkham GS, Univ of Manchester (MB ChB); *m* 21 Sept 1968, Barbara, da of Alwyn Johns, of Greenhedges, 32 Pontardulais Rd, Penllergaer, W Glamorgan; 1 s (Gareth b 9 Oct 1974), 1 da (Joanne b 3 Sept 1976); *Career* med registrar Cardiff Royal Infirmary 1969-71, thoracic med registrar London Chest Hosp 1971-73, sr med registrar Leeds Gen Infirmary 1973-74, conslt physician with special interest chest diseases Stockport AHA 1974-, clinical teacher Univ of Manchester 1983-; memb: Regnl Med Ctee Br Thoracic Soc, NW Regnl Assoc Physicians; chm: Stockport Med Advsy Ctee, Stockport Asthma Care Fund; memb Macclesfield Castle Rotary Club; MRCP 1969, FRCP 1990; *Books* numerous pubns in jls incl: Treatment of Pneumothorax by Simple Aspiration (1983), Results of Pneumothorax Aspiration (1985); *Recreations* golf; *Clubs* Hazel Grove Golf; *Style—* Dr Gordon Archer; Springfield, 14 Moss Lane, Bollington, Macclesfield, Cheshire SK10 5HJ (☎ 0625 572864); Ryley Mount Consulting Rooms, 432 Buxton Rd, Gt Moor, Stockport, Cheshire SK2 (☎ 061 483 9333)

ARCHER, Jasper Rodney; s of Lt-Col Rodney Archer, MC (d 1974); *b* 14 Aug 1941; *Educ* Cheltenham, RMA Sandhurst; *m* 10 Feb 1967, Victoria, da of Eric Leigh (d 1981); 1 s (Nicholas b 1971), 1 da (Sophie b 1973); *Career* 4/7 Royal Dragon Gds 1962-70 (Capt 1965); Charles Barker City 1974-87 (vice chm 1986), vice chm Grandfield Rork Collins 1987-; *Recreations* skiing; *Clubs* Cavalry and Guards; *Style—* Jasper Archer, Esq; 15 Lamont Rd, London SW10; Prestige House, 14-18 Holborn, London EC1 (☎ 071 242 2002)

ARCHER, Jeffrey Howard; s of William Archer, and Lola, *née* Cook; *b* 15 April 1940; *Educ* Wellington Sch Somerset, BNC Oxford (Athletics blues 1963-65, Gymnastics blue 1965, Oxford 100 yds record 1966); *m* 1966, Mary Weeden; 2 s; *Career* politician; memb GLC Havering 1966-70, MP (C) Louth 1969-74; dep chm Cons Pty 1985-86; author; pres: Somerset AAA, Somerset Wyverns; FRSA; *Books* Not a Penny More Not a Penny Less (1975), Shall We Tell The President? (1977), Kane and Abel (1979), A Quiver Full of Arrows (1980), The Prodigal Daughter (1982), First Among Equals (1984), A Matter of Honour (1986), Beyond Reasonable Doubt (1987, play), A Twist in The Tale (1989), Exclusive (1989, play), As the Crow Flies (1991); *Recreations* theatre, cinema, watching Somerset play cricket; *Clubs* MCC, Louth Working Mens; *Style—* Jeffrey Archer, Esq; Alembic House, 93 Albert Embankment, London SE1 (☎ 071 735 0077)

ARCHER, Gen Sir (Arthur) John; KCB (1976), OBE (1964, MBE 1960); s of Alfred Arthur Archer, of Fakenham, Norfolk, and Mildred Archer; *b* 12 Feb 1924; *Educ* King's Sch Peterborough, St Catharine's Coll Cambridge; *m* 1950, (Cynthia) Marie, da of Col Alexander Allan, DSO, MC (d 1967), of Swallowcliffe, Wilts; 2 s; *Career* entered Army 1943, Lt Gen Bde of Gurkhas 1977-78, C-in-C UKLF 1978-79; Col Devonshire & Dorset Regt 1977-79; chief exec Royal Hong Kong Jockey Club 1980-; dir The Hong Kong & Shanghai Banking Corpn; CBIM; *Recreations* light aviation, gliding; *Clubs* Army and Navy, Hong Kong, Royal Hong Kong Jockey, Royal Motor Yacht; *Style—* Gen Sir John Archer, KCB, OBE; c/o Lloyds Bank, Blue Boar Row, Salisbury, Wilts

ARCHER, John Francis Ashweek; QC (1975); s of late George Eric Archer, and Frances, *née* Ashweek; *b* 9 July 1925; *Educ* Winchester, New Coll Oxford (BA); *m* 1960, Doris Mary, *née* Hennessey (d 1988); *Career* served WWII; called to the Bar Inner Temple 1950, rec Crown Court 1974-; memb Criminal Injuries Compensation Bd 1987-; *Style—* John Archer, Esq, QC; 7 Kings Bench Walk, London EC4; 2 Crown Office Row, Temple, London EC4 (☎ 071 353 9337)

ARCHER, John Norman; s of Clifford Banks Archer (d 1973), and Grace, *née* King (d 1984); *b* 27 Feb 1921; *Educ* Wandsworth Sch; *m* 1, 1952, Gladys Joy (d 1985), da of Oliver John Barnes (d 1953), of Kent; m 2, 1986, Anne Lesley Margaret, da of Maj Nicholas Edward Padwick (d 1980), of Berks; step children; *Career* Nat Serv RA Maj 1939-46, Burma 1945; entered Civil Service Bd of Educn 1937: asst princ 1947, princ 1949, Miny of Educn 1960, asst sec Architects and Bldgs Branch Miny of Educn 1962; tech assistance assignments educn: Nigeria, Yugoslavia, Tunisia 1961-63; asst sec Treasy O & M Div 1964, asst sec Mgmnt Servs Devpt Div 1968; under sec: Mgmnt Servs, Civil Serv Dept 1970, Marine Div Dept of Trade 1972-79; md The Int Tanker Owners Pollution Fedn 1979-86; competed Wimbledon Lawn Tennis Championships 1947; Liveryman Worshipful Co of Shipwrights; *Recreations* lawn tennis, bridge, watching cricket; *Clubs* All England Lawn Tennis and Croquet, Kent Cricket, Lawn Tennis of GB, Hurlingham, MCC; *Style—* John N Archer, Esq; 17 Sovereign House, Draxmont, Wimbledon Hill Rd, London SW19 (☎ 081 946 6429)

ARCHER, Prof John Stuart; s of Stuart Leonard Gordon Archer, of Hounslow, Middx, and Joan, *née* Watkinson; *b* 15 June 1943; *Educ* GS for Boys Chiswick, City Univ of London (BSc), Imperial Coll London (PhD, DIC); *m* 30 Sept 1967, Lesley, da of Leslie Arthur Oaksford, of Yeovil, Somerset; 1 s (Adam John b 21 Feb 1975), 1 da (Louise b 19 Jan 1973); *Career* student trainee Imperial Chemical Industs 1961-64, res reservoir engr ESSO Resources Canada 1969-73, petroleum reservoir engr British Gas Corp 1973-74, mangr reservoir studies D&S Petroleum Consits 1974-77, conslt ERC (Energy Resource Consits) 1977-84 (fndr and dir reservoir section 1977-80); Imperial Coll London 1980-: prof of petroleum engrg (former reader), head Dept of Mineral Resources Engrg, dean Royal Sch of Mines; ptnr AWW Petroleum Consits 1984-; memb Soc of Petroleum Engrg 1973, CEng 1974, FInstPet 1977, FInstE; *Books* Petroleum Engineering - Principles and Practice (1986); *Recreations* golf, skiing, walking, gardening, theatre; *Style—* Prof John Archer; Kinghorn Lane, Maidenhead, Berks SL6 7QG; Department of Mineral Resources Engineering, Royal School of Mines, Imperial College of Science Technology and Medicine, Prince Consort Rd, London SW7 2BD (☎ 071 589 5111, fax 071 589 6806, telex 929484)

ARCHER, Prof Margaret Scotford; da of Ronald Archer (d 1964), and Elise, *née* Scotford; *b* 20 Jan 1943; *Educ* Sheffield HS for Girls, LSE (BSc, PhD), Ecole Pratique des' Hautes Etudes Paris; *m* 1 May 1973, (Gilbert) Andrew Jones, s of Kingsley Boardman (d 1975) ; 2 s (Kingsley b 1975, Marcus b 1979); *Career* lectr Univ of Reading 1966-73, prof Univ of Warwick 1979- (reader 1973-79); memb Br Sociological Assoc, pres Int Sociological Assoc; *Books* Social Conflict and Educational Change in England and France 1789-1848 (with M Vaughan, 1971), Contemporary Europe, Class, Status and Power (ed with S Giner, 1971), Students, University and Society (ed, 1972), Contemporary Europe, Social Structures and Cultural Patterns (ed with S Giner, 1978), Social Origins of Educational Systems (1979), The Sociology of Educational Expansion (ed, 1982), Culture and Agency (1988); *Recreations* equestrian; *Style—* Prof Margaret Archer; Monks Court, Deddington, Oxford, Oxon OX5 4TE (☎ 0869 38480); Department of Sociology, University of Warwick, Coventry, Warwickshire CV4 7AL (☎ 0203 523499, fax 0869 37146)

ARCHER, Dr Mary Doreen; da of Harold Norman Weeden (d 1971), and Doreen, *née* Cox; *b* 22 Dec 1944; *Educ* Cheltenham, St Anne's Coll Oxford (BA, MA), Imp Coll London (PhD); *m* 11 July 1966, Jeffrey Howard Archer, s of William Archer (d 1955); 2 s (Harold b 1972, James Howard b 1974); *Career* jr res fell St Hilda's Coll Oxford 1968-72, temp lectr in chemistry Somerville Coll Oxford 1971-72, res fell Royal Inst of Great Britain 1972-76, fell and lectr Newnham Coll Cambridge and lectr in chemistry Trinity Coll Cambridge 1976-86, bye-fell Newnham Coll Cambridge 1987-; non-exec dir: Anglia Television Group 1987-, Mid Anglia Radio plc 1988-, Cambridge and Newmarket FM Radio Ltd 1988-; dir Fitzwilliam Museum Tst 1984-, chm Nat Energy Fndn 1989-, memb Cncl Lloyds 1988-, tstee Science Museum 1990-; FRSC, FRSA; *Recreations* singing, theatre, cats, squash; *Style—* Dr Mary Archer; The Old Vicarage, Grantchester, Cambridge CB3 9ND (☎ 0223 840213, fax 0223 842882); Alembic House, 93 Albert Embankment, London SE1 7TX (☎ 071 735 0077)

ARCHER, Neill John; s of Peter Archer, of 1 Sanvey Lane, Leicester, and Margaret Anne, *née* Munns; *b* 31 Aug 1961; *Educ* Wyggeston Boys' GS Leicester, UEA Norwich, Brevard Music Centre North Carolina USA; *m* 30 Aug 1986, Marilyn, da of late Oscar Dale; 1 da (Sally Anne b 9 Jan 1990); *Career* opera singer, performances incl: Tamino in The Magic Flute (Kent Opera) 1987, Don Quixotte in Don Quixotte in Sierra Morena by Conti (Buxton Festival) 1987, Messiah (QEH) 1988, Don Ottawio in Don Giovanni (Welsh Nat Opera) 1988, Edoardo IV in Riccardo III by Testi (Teatro Regio Torino) 1988, Ubaldo in Armide by Haydn (Buxton Festival) 1988, Carmina Burana by Orff (Edinburgh Festival and BBC TV) 1988, Ferrando in Cosi Fan Tutte (Opera Factory and QEH) 1988, young man and naked youth in Moses and Aaron by Schonberg (BBC SO and BBC Radio 3) 1988, Ferrando in Cosi Fan Tutte (Scottish Opera) 1988, Clem in The Little Sweep by Britten (Thames TV) 1989, Arias in St Matthew Passion (Stavanger Symphony Orchestra) 1989, Andres in Wozzeck (Teatro Regio Parma) 1989, Paradies und Peri by Schumann (Paris Opera) 1989, Clem and Alfred in The Little Sweep (Aldeburgh Festival) 1989, Ferrando in Cosi (Channel 4 TV) 1989, Almaviva in Barbiere di Siviglia (Norske Oper Oslo and Opera North) 1989, Messiah (Welsh Nat Opera and St Davids Hall) 1989, Almaviva and Cassio in Othello (Welsh Nat Opera) 1990, Tamino in Magic Flute (ENO) 1990, Jacqmino in Fidelio (Royal Opera House and BBC Radio) 1990, Pylades in Iphegenia aug Taurus by Gluck (Basel Opera House) 1991; *Recreations* Guardian crossword, golf, pinball; *Clubs* Leicestershire CC; *Style—* Neill Archer, Esq; Athole Still International Management, 113 Church Road, Crystal Palace, London SE19 2PR (☎ 081 653 9595, 081 771 5271, fax 081 771 8172)

ARCHER, (Audrey Barbara) Nikki; *née* Greenall; da of Frank Greenall (d 1951), and late Margaret Ellen, *née* Holiday; *b* 13 Nov 1921; *Educ* Univ of Bristol (BA, CertEd), Guildhall Sch of Music and Drama, London Univ (DipEd); *m* 1, 13 Sept 1947 (m dis 1963), Cecil Watts Paul-Jones, s of Dr Walter Paul-Jones; 1 s (Richard b 3 Sept 1953), 1 da (Miranda (Mrs Scholefield) b 22 Feb 1951); m 2, 8 Oct 1964, Maj John Stafford Archer; *Career* teaching appts 1943-46, asst sec to Assoc of Teachers in Colls and Depts of Educn and Trg Colls Clearing House 1946-49, teaching appts 1949-59, head King Alfred Sch 1960-83 (dep head 1959-60), schoolmistress fell commoner Churchill Coll Cambridge Univ 1972, educnl conslt 1983-; JP Barnet Herts Bench 1971-84; ctee memb: Barnet Branch Nat Marriage Guidance Cncl 1980-82, Secdy Heads Assoc; *Clubs* Bath & County, Army & Navy; *Style—* Mrs Nikki Archer; 15 Manor Rd, Alcombe, Minehead, Somerset TA24 6EH (☎ 0643 6785)

ARCHER, Rt Hon Peter Kingsley; PC (1977), QC (1971), MP (Lab) Warley W 1974-; s of Cyril Kinglsey Archer, MM (d 1974), and May, *née* Baker (d 1976); *b* 20 Nov 1926; *Educ* Wednesbury Boys' HS, UCL (LLB (external), BA), LSE (LLM); *m* 7 Aug 1954, Margaret Irene, da of Sidney Smith (d 1936), of London, Ontario, Canada; 1 s (John Kingsley b 1962); *Career* called to the Bar Gray's Inn 1952, bencher 1974, recorder SE Circuit 1982-; MP (Lab) Rowley Regis and Tipton 1966-74, slr gen 1974-79; oppn frontbench spokesman: Legal Affrs 1981-82, Trade 1982-83; shadow sec NI 1983-87; fell UCL 1978; *Books* The Queen's Courts (1956), Social Welfare and the Citizen (ed, 1957), Communism and the Law (1963), Freedom at Stake (with Lord Reay, 1966), Human Rights (1969), Purpose in Socialism (jtly, 1973), The Role of the Law Officers (1978), More Law Reform Now (co-ed, 1984); *Recreations* music, writing, talking; *Style—* The Rt Hon Peter Archer, QC, MP; House of Commons, London SW1A 0AA (☎ 071 219 4029); 7 Old School Court, Wraysbury, Staines, Middx (☎ 0784 483136)

ARCHER, Peter Monahan; s of Thomas Wilson Archer, and Dorothy Maud, *née* Monahan; *b* 14 March 1942; *Educ* Univ Coll Sch, Coll of Estate Mgmnt; *m* 17 Sept 1966, Gina Susan Constance; 1 da (Francesca b 1972); *Career* dir Lazard Bros & Co Ltd 1986-90, princ The Yarmouth Group (UK) LP 1990-; FRICS 1966; *Style—* Peter Archer, Esq; 6-8 Old Bouce Street, London W1X 3TA

ARCHER, Ronald Walter; s of Norman Ernest Archer, CMG, OBE (d 1970), and Hon Ruth Evelyn, *née* Pease (d 1983), da of 1 Baron Daryngton, PC; *b* 12 Dec 1929; *Educ* Winchester, Magdalene Coll Cambridge (MA); *m* 14 Nov 1959, Catherine Mary, da of Marcus RC Overton (d 1940); 3 s (James b 1960, Michael b 1962, Edward b 1964), 1 da (Mary b 1966); *Career* joined Unilever Ltd (now plc) as economist 1953, fin dir and vice chm Hindustan Lever (Unilever subsidiary in India) 1966-70, commercial dir Unilever plc & NV 1978, personnel dir Unilever plc & NV 1983, plural chief exec of Unilever 1989-; Halifax Bldg Soc: dir 1983, dep chm 1987; *Style—* Ronald Archer, Esq; Unilever plc, Blackfriars, London EC4 (☎ 071 822 6668)

ARCHER, Hon Mrs (Sonia Gina Ogilvie); *née* Birdwood; only da of 2 Baron Birdwood, MVO (d 1962), by his 1 w; *m* 21 July 1956, Geoffrey Thynne Valentine Archer, yst s of Maj Gerald Valentine Archer (d 1958), of High Salvington, Sussex; 1 s (David b 1959), 1 da (Sarah-Jane b 1957); *Career* mangr Hong Kong Arts Festival Soc Ltd 1972-75, various mgmnt positions Hong Kong Arts Centre 1975, exhibition conslt ISCM-ACL (Int Soc for Contemporary Music/Asian Composers League) Conf 1988, dir Archer Gp of Cos Hong Kong; artist; exhibits in Hong Kong; *Recreations* music, choral singing; *Clubs* English Chamber Orch Soc, Hong Kong Arts Centre (life memb), BACSA (Br Assoc of Cemeteries in S Asia); *Style—* The Hon Mrs Archer; 18A Pine Crest, 65 Repulse Bay, Hong Kong (☎ 8121988)

ARCHER, William Frederick (Jock); s of Richard Henry Archer (d 1912), and Alice, *née* Aylett (d 1962); *b* 30 Aug 1906; *Educ* Windsor GS; *m* 30 Aug 1930, Dulcie Mary, da of Frederick Bates (d 1938); 2 s (Dudley Ian b 1933, Paul Richard Hedley b 1938), 1 da (Mary Sherrard (Mrs Gummer) b 1943); *Career* dir Br Celanese Ltd 1962-75 (sec 1955-62); Freeman City of London, Liveryman Worshipful Co of Scriveners; FCIS (pres 1967); *Books* In Retrospect (autobiography); *Recreations* golf; *Style—* Jock Archer, Esq; Heronswood, Rockshaw Rd, Merstham, Surrey (☎ 073 74 3167)

ARCHIBALD, Barony of (UK 1949); *see*: Archibald, George Christopher

ARCHIBALD, Baroness; Catherine Edith Mary; da of Rt Hon Andrew Bonar Law, MP, PM, and Annie Pitcairn, *née* Robley; sister of 1 Baron Coleraine; *m* 1, 1926 (m dis 1941), Kent Colwell; 1 s, 1 da; m 2, 1961, as his 2 w, 1 Baron Archibald (d 1975); *Style—* The Rt Hon the Lady Archibald; 29 Hampstead Hill Gdns, London NW3 2PG (☎ 071 435 8453)

ARCHIBALD, Edward Hunter Holmes (Teddy); s of Walter Archibald (d 1977), of Belfast, and Mary Clare, *née* Ross; *b* 24 Jan 1927; *Educ* Stubbington House, Stowe, Trinity Coll Cambridge (BA, MA); *Career* Springfield Dyeing and Finishing Works Belfast 1948-52, curator of oil paintings Nat Maritime Museum 1952-84, conslt on marine paintings Christie's and Sotheby's; memb: Greenwich Soc, Soc of Nautical Res; FRSA; *Books* The Wooden Fighting Ship in the Royal Navy AD 897-1860 (1968), The Metal Fighting Ship in the Royal Navy 1860-1970 (1972), The Fighting Ship in the Royal Navy AD 897-1984 (1984), Dictionary of Sea Painters (1981, 2 edn 1989); *Recreations* entertaining, looking after my animals, yacht racing, skiing, Cresta run, bobsleighing, collecting glass, pictures, books, armour; *Style—* Teddy Archibald, Esq; 10 Park Vista, Greenwich London SE10, (☎ 081 858 1849)

ARCHIBALD, Prof George Christopher; s of 1 Baron Archibald, CBE (d 1975), and Dorothy Holroyd Edwards (d 1960); disclaimed peerage for life 1975; *b* 30 Dec 1926; *Educ* Phillips Exeter Acad USA, King's Coll Cambridge (MA), LSE (BSc); *m* 1, 1951 (m dis 1965), Liliana Barou (*see* Archibald, Liliana); m 2, 1971, Daphne May Vincent; *Career* served Army 1945-48; prof of econs Univ of BC 1970-; former lectr in econs Univ of Otago NZ and LSE, former prof of econs Univ of Essex; fell Econometric Soc 1976, FRSC; *Books* Theory of the Firm (ed 1971), Introduction to a Mathematical Treatment of Economics (1973); *Style—* Prof G C Archibald; c/o Department of Economics, University of British Columbia, Vancouver, British Coloumbia, Canada

ARCHIBALD, Liliana; da of late Noah Barou; *b* 25 May 1928; *Educ* Kingsley Sch, Geneva Univ; *m* 1951 (m dis 1965), George Christopher Archibald, *qv*; *Career* dir: Adam Bros Contingency Ltd 1970-85, Fenchurch Gp Int Ltd 1985-87, Holman Wade Insur Brokers Ltd 1989-; head of Credit Insur and Export Credit Div EEC 1973-77, EEC advsr Lloyds 1978-85, conslt Belmont Euro Community Law Office Brussels 1985-, dir Holman Wade Ltd 1989-, conslt Coopers Lybrand 1989-; memb Lloyds 1973-; *Style—* Mrs Liliana Archibald; 21 Langland Gdns, London NW3 6QE

ARCHIBALD, Prof (Andrew) Ronald; *b* 12 May 1934; *Educ* Univ of Edinburgh (BSc, PhD); *m* Angela Carr; 3 da (Sarah b 1968, Rachel b 1970, Charlotte b 1972); *Career* prof of microbiological chem and head of Dept of Microbiology Univ of Newcastle upon Tyne 1989-, special res in bacterial cell walls; author of various pubns in scientific lit; *Style—* Professor Ronald Archibald; 19 Linden Rd, Gosforth, Newcastle upon Tyne (☎ 091 2857920); Department of Microbiology, University of Newcastle upon Tyne, The Medical School, Framlington Place, Newcastle upon Tyne NE2 4HH (☎ 091 222 7704, fax 091 222 7736, 53654 UNINEWG)

ARCHIBALD, Wilfred William; s of Cyril Nadalie Archibald (d 1966), of London, and Ethele, *née* Polonski; *b* 13 July 1922; *Educ* Victoria Coll Alexandria Egypt; *m* 28 June 1947, Jean Pauline Scott, da of Alexander William Gibson (d 1961), of Ferring, W Sussex; 1 s (Duncan Archibald b 1948), 2 da (Juliet (Mrs Billingham) b 1949, Christine (Mrs Brewster) b 1959); *Career* WWII Navigator RAF 1940-44; inspr for ME Guardian Royal Exchange Assurance Co 1947-56 (mangr Singapore, Malaysia, Thailand, Borneo 1957-67); seconded to Union Insurance Society of Canton: md 1968-69, overseas mangr GRE Gp Head Office London 1970-77, asst gen mangr (overseas) 1977-86, ret 1986; pres Bd of Govrs Alexandria Schs Tst; govr: City of London Freeman's Sch Ashstead, Mitchell City of London Charity and Educnl Fndn, Lady Eleanor Holles Sch (Cripplegate Schs Fndn); memb: St Michaels Cornhill PCC, Ct of Common Cncl City of London (representing Cornhill) 1986-, Cripplegate Ward Club, Lime St Ward Club, Utd Ward Club, Broadstreet Ward Club; Freeman City of London 1980, Liveryman Worshipful Co of Insurers 1980; *Recreations* farming; *Style—* Wilfred Archibald, Esq; Deakes Manor, Deakes Lane, Cuckfield, West Sussex RH17 5JA (☎ 0444 454151); 184, Andrewes Hse, Barbican, London EC2

ARCULUS, Sir Ronald; KCMG (1979, CMG 1968), KCVO (1980); s of Cecil Arculus, MC (d 1968), and Ethel L Arculus (d 1982); *b* 11 Feb 1923; *Educ* Solihull Sch, Exeter Coll Oxford (MA); *m* 1953, Sheila Mary, da of Arthur Faux (d 1982); 1 s (Gerald), 1 da (Juliet); *Career* WWII, Capt 4 Queen's Own Hussars; entered HM Dip Serv 1947, min (Econ) Paris 1973-77, ambass and perm ldr UK Delgn UN Law of the Sea Conf 1977-79, ambass to Italy 1979-83, ret; dir Glaxo Hldgs 1983-; conslt: Trusthouse Forte 1983-86, London and Continental Bankers 1984-88; govr Br Inst of Florence 1984-; dir King's Med Res Tst 1984-88, special advsr to Min of Tport on Channel Tunnel Trains 1987-88; Freeman City of London 1981; Grand Cross Italian Order of Merit 1980; *Recreations* travel, opera, ballet, fine arts; *Clubs* Army and Navy, Hurlingham; *Style—* Sir Ronald Arculus, KCMG, KCVO; 20 Kensington Court Gdns, London W8 5QF

ARDEE, Lord; John Anthony Brabazon; s and h of 14 Earl of Meath; *b* 11 May 1941; *Educ* Harrow; *m* 1973, Xenia Goudime; 1 s, 2 da (Hon Corinna Lettice b 9 Nov 1974, Hon Serena Alexandra b 23 Feb 1979); *Heir* s, Hon Anthony Jaques Brabazon b 30 Jan 1977; *Career* page of hon to HM The Queen 1956-57, Gren Gds 1960-63; *Style—* Lord Ardee; Ballinacor, Rathdrum, Co Wicklow, Ireland (☎ 0404 46186)

ARDEN, Rt Rev Donald Seymour; CBE (1981); s of Stanley Arden, FLS (d 1942), of Sitiawan (Lower Perak) and Worthing, and Winifred, *née* Morland (d 1968); family a collateral branch of Arden of Harden Hall, Stockport who descend from Eustace de Arden, of Watford, Northants; *b* 12 April 1916; *Educ* St Peter's Coll Adelaide S Aust, Univ of Leeds (BA), Coll of Resurrection Mirfield; *m* 1962, Jane Grace, da of Gerald Riddle (d 1967), of East Ogwell, Devon; 2 s (Bazil, Christopher); *Career* ordained: deacon 1939, priest 1940; curate: St Catherine's Hatcham 1939-40, Nettleden with Potten End 1941-43; asst priest Pretoria African Mission 1944-51; dir Usuthu Swaziland 1951-61 (canon of Zululand and Swaziland); bishop of: Nyasaland 1961, Malawi 1964-71, Southern Malawi 1971-81; archbishop of Central Africa 1971-80, priest i/c St Margaret Uxbridge 1981-86, asst bishop Willesden 1981-, vol asst priest St Alban's N Harrow 1986-; *Books* Youth's Job in the Parish (1938), Out of Africa Something New (1976); *Recreations* photography; *Style—* The Rt Rev Donald Arden, CBE; 6 Frobisher Close, Pinner, Middx HA5 1NN (☎ 081 866 6009)

ARDEN, John; s of C A Arden, and A E Layland; *b* 26 Oct 1930; *Educ* Sedbergh, King's Coll Cambridge, Edinburgh Coll of Art; *m* 1957, Margaretta Ruth D'Arcy; 4 s (and 1 decd); *Career* playwright; works include: Sergeant Musgrave's Dance (1959), The Non-Stop Connolly Show (in collaboration with M D'Arcy), To Present The Pretence (Essays on Theatre, 1978), Silence Among The Weapons (Novel, 1982); *Style—* John Arden, Esq; c/o Margaret Ramsay Ltd, 14A Goodwin's Court, London WC2 (☎ 071 240 0691)

ARDEN, Yves Ralph; s of Charles Henry Arden, MBE (d 1955), of 59 Avenue Hoche, Paris 8, and Annette Lucie, *née* Collignon (d 1982); *b* 15 Dec 1921; *Educ* Ste Croix de Neuilly Paris, Sorbonne; *m* 23 June 1945, Moira Rosemary, da of James Rouse (d 1942), of Sheffield; 1 s (Philip b 1953), 1 da (Denise b 1946); *Career* served WWII 1941-47: W Africa, Italy, Austria; Maj TA 1950-61; dir: Tap & Die Corp Ltd London 1966-69, Tadco Sales Ltd London 1967-69; mktg conslt Yves R Arden & Assocs; conslt ed Special Dictionary Projects References Div Routledge London 1990-; hon conslt: Tunisia in Sheffield 1958-65, Dominican Repub in Sheffield 1959-65; memb Cncl London C of C 1964-71 (chm French Section); *Books* Military Medals and Decorations - A Price Guide for Collectors (1976), Supplement to Kettridge's Dictionary of Technical Terms and Phrases (French/English and English/French, 1980); *Recreations* writing, travel, numismatics; *Style—* Yves Arden, Esq; Hallam Grange, Hallam Grange Rise, Fulwood, Sheffield S10 4BE (☎ 0742 305827)

ARDILES, Osvaldo; s of Arturo Ardiles, of Cordoba, Argentina, and Blanca, *née* Vignoli; *b* 3 Aug 1952; *Educ* Montserrat Sch, Univ of Cordoba and Buenos Aires; *m* 29 Dec 1973, Silvia Navarro; 2 s (Pablo b 1 Feb 1975, Federico b 23 Sept 1978); *Career* professional football manager; player: apprentice Instituto Cordoba 1964 (first team debut 1970), Huracan Buenos Aires 1975-78, Tottenham Hotspur 1978-88, on loan Paris St Germain France 1982, Queens Park Rangers 1988-89, Fort Lauderdale USA 1989, 42 full caps Argentina (debut 1975); mangr Swindon Town 1989-; honours in Argentina: Cordoba League Championship 1972, runners-up Argentinian League 1976, World Cup winners 1978; honours with Tottenham hotspur: FA Cup 1981 and 1982 (runners up 1987), runners up Littlewood Cup 1982, UEFA Cup 1984; promotion to Div 1 Swindon Town 1990 (later cancelled); film actor Escape to Victory 1981; *Recreations* golf, chess, cinema, theatre, reading; *Style—* Osvaldo Ardiles, Esq; Manager, Swindon Town FC, County Ground, Swindon, Wiltshire SN2 2ED (☎ 0793 430430)

ARDRON, Peter Stuart; s of Wilfred Ardron, MBE (d 1982), of 16 Carrmyers, Hare Law, Annfield Plain, Co Durham, and Lucy Muriel, *née* Hawkins; *b* 11 June 1927; *Educ* Stanley GS Stanley Co Durham, INSEAD Fontainebleau, Oxford Centre for Mgmnt Studies; *m* 1956, Marion McWilliams, da of William Ross (d 1972), of Dunoon; 1 s (David), 2 da (Carol, Lesley); *Career* vice chm Barclays Int Ltd 1986-; dir and sr gen mangr: Barclays Bank plc 1985, Barclays Bank Int Ltd 1983-84; gen mangr Barclays Bank Int Ltd 1977-83; dir: Banque de la Société Financière Européenne Paris 1980-, Société Financière Européenne Luxembourg 1980-, Euro-Latinamerican Bank Ltd London 1983-, Barclays Int Hldgs 1985-, Barclays plc 1985-, Barclays Int Ltd 1985-, Int Bank plc 1987-; vice-chm: AK International Ltd 1987-, BAII Ltd 1987; chm Anglo-Romanian Ltd 1987; FIB; *Recreations* cricket, tennis, gardening; *Clubs* Overseas Bankers', MCC; *Style—* P S Ardron, Esq; Oriel Cottage, Rookery Close, Fetcham, Leatherhead, Surrey (☎ 0372 372958); Barclays International Ltd, 54 Lombard St, London EC3P 3AH (☎ 071 283 8989, telex 887591)

ARDWICK, Baron (Life Peer 1970 UK); John Cowburn Beavan; s of late Silas Beavan, and Alderman Emily Beavan, JP; *b* 19 April 1910; *Educ* Manchester GS; *m* 1934, Gladys, *née* Jones; 1 da; *Career* London editor Manchester Guardian 1946, editor Daily Herald 1960-62; MEP (Lab) 1975-79; sits as Labour Peer; *Style—* The Rt Hon The Lord Ardwick; 10 Chester Close, London SW13 (☎ 081 789 3490)

ARENSON, Archy; *b* 5 July 1926; *Educ* Enfield Tech Coll; *m* 1949, Vicky; *Career* non exec dir and conslt Arenson Gp plc 1989-; AMIMechE, AMIEE; *Style—* Archy Arenson, Esq; c/o Arenson Group plc, Lincoln Hse, Colney St, St Albans, Herts AL2 2DX (☎ 0923 85 7200, telex 922171)

ARGENT, Denis John; s of Robert Argent (d 1983), and Ellen, *née* Newman; *b* 28 Aug 1943; *Educ* Cardinal Vaughan Sch; *m* 30 July 1966, Marie Rose, da of John Barnard (d 1980); 3 s (Nicholas b 1968, Phillip b 1970, Christopher b 1973), 1 da (Marianne b 1981); *Career* mgmnt conslt Coopers & Lybrand 1972-79, chief accountant Cancer Res Fund 1979-87, fin dir Royal Pharmaceutical Soc of GB 1987-; FCCA; *Recreations* rugby, squash, golf; *Clubs* MCC, East India, Challoner; *Style—* Denis Argent, Esq; 112 Waxwell Lane, Pinner, Middx (☎ 071 866 1526); 1 Lambeth High St, London SE1 7JN (☎ 071 735 9141)

ARGENT, Douglas; *Career* BBC floor mangr then prodn mangr then dir and prodr; tv series incl: Till Death Us Do Part, Taxi, Feydeau Farces, Liver Birds, Steptoe and Son, Fawlty Towers (BAFTA award 1979), Crimewriters; freelance 1980; tv series incl: Cuckoo Waltz, The Schoolmistress, Astronauts, That Beryl Marsden, Union Castle, The Lady is a Tramp, It takes a Worried Man, Lonelyhearts Kids, Flying Lady, Never the Twain, Anybody for Murder, Edge of Fear; dir corporate video ideas for: Shell Chemicals (UK) Ltd, Lloyds Bank Ltd, Mobil Oil, British Airways, Crown Paints, Guardian Royal Exchange, Trustee Savings Bank; memb: Dirs' Guild of GB, BAFTA (memb Cncl 1978-82, 1984-86, 1990-91); *Style—* Douglas Argent, Esq; 55 Kenton Ave, Sunbury on Thames, Middlesex TW16 5AS (☎ 0932 785892); Michael Ladkin Personal Management (☎ 071 402 6644)

ARGENT, Eric William; s of Eric George Argent, and Florence Mary Argent; *b* 5 Sept 1923; *Educ* Chiswick GS; *m* 1949, Pauline Grant; 2 da; *Career* served WWII; former dir and gen mangr Hastings & Thanet Building Society; dir: Anglia Building Society 1978-87, Nationwide Anglia Building Society 1987-88; FCA, FCBSI; *Style—* Eric Argent, Esq; Fairmount, 104 Longcliffe Road, Grantham, Lincs (☎ 0476 591433)

ARGENT, (Bernard) Godfrey; s of Godfrey Stanley Albert Argent (d 1972), and Helena, *née* Smith; *b* 6 Feb 1937; *Educ* Bexhill GS for Boys Sussex; *m* 1, 11 Nov 1956, Janet Rosemary, *née* Boniface (d 1970); 3 da (Lisa b 1957, Gina b 1958, Susan b 1960); m 2 (m dis 1973), Anne Yvonne, *née* Coxon; m 3, 25 April 1975, Sally Dorothy, *née* McAlpine; 1 da (Jenna b 1980); *Career* Household Cavalry (The Life Gds) 1954-63; freelance photographer 1963, chm Godfrey Argent Ltd 1964-; owner mangr: Walter Bird Photographic Studios (London) 1968, Baron Studios (London) 1974; one man shows incl: Nat Portrait Gallery (London) 1971, Los Angeles 1978 Camera Club (London) 1988; photographer Royal Family 1964-; official photographer: Nat Portrait Gallery (London) 1967-70, Royal Soc of Great Britain 1967-; chm Aux-Air gp of cos 1988; *Books* The Royal Mews (1965), The Household Brigade (1966), The Queens Guards (1966), The Queen Rides (1966), Horses in the Sun (1966), Charles 21st Prince of Wales (1969), World of Horses (1969), Royalty on Horseback (1974); *Clubs* Inanda (SA), Wellington; *Style—* Godfrey Argent, Esq; 49 Campden Hill Rd, Kensington, London W8 7DY (☎ 071 937 4246); 12 Holland St, London W8 4LT (☎ 071 937 4008/0441, fax 071 376 1098, car 0863 621 657)

ARGENT, Malcolm; CBE (1985); s of Leonard James Argent (d 1989), and Winifred Hilda Argent (d 1980); *b* 14 Aug 1935; *Educ* Palmer's Sch Grays Essex; *m* 1, 4 March 1961, Mary Patricia Addis, da of Geoffrey Vivian Stimson (d 1989); m 2, 5 Dec 1986, Thelma Hazel, da of Leonard Eddleston, of Eastry, Kent; 1 s, 1 da; *Career* GPO London Telecom Region: exec offr 1953-62, higher exec offr 1962-66, princ PO HQ 1966-70, private sec to md Telecom 1970-74, personnel controller External Telecom Exec 1974-75; dir: Chm's Office PO Central HQ 1975-77, Eastern Telecom Region 1977; sec: The PO 1978-81, BT Corp 1981-, BT plc 1984-; gp dir and sec BT plc 1989, dir McCaw Cellular Communications Inc 1989-; tstee: BT Staff Superannuation Fund 1981-, BT New Pension Scheme 1986-89; Freeman City of London 1987; FBIM 1980; *Recreations* tennis; *Style—* Malcolm Argent, Esq, CBE; 4 Huskards, Fryerning, Ingatestone, Essex CM4 0HR; British Telecom Centre, 81 Newgate St, London EC1A 7AJ (☎ 071 356 5330, telex 883051, fax 071 356 5520, phone 0860 371776)

ARGENTI, (Ambrose) John Alexander; s of Nicholas A Argenti (d 1961), of London, and Elfrida Mary, *née* Ionides (d 1988); *b* 10 Feb 1926; *Educ* Charterhouse, Trinity Coll Oxford (MA); *m* 29 Dec 1948, Mildred Elfrida, da of Alan George Marshal (d 1973), of Taunton; 1 s (Matthew b 1953), 1 da (Hilary b 1949); *Career* aircraftman (pilot under trg) RAF 1944-45; mgmnt positions Fisons Fertilizers Ltd 1954-68, chm Argenti Systems Ltd 1980; fndr and first treas: Strategic Planning Soc London, Civic Tst Widnes; MBIM 1966; *Books* Corporate Planning - a practical guide (1968), Management Techniques (1970, Matra prize best mgmnt book 1970), A Management System for The Seventies (1971), Systematic Corporate Planning (1974), Corporate Collapse (1976), Practical Corporate Planning (1980 and 1989); *Style—* John Argenti,

Esq; Pettistree Lodge, Woodbridge, Suffolk IP13 0HX; Argenti Systems Ltd, 12 Lower Brook St, Ipswich IP4 1AT (☎ 0728 746466)

ARGUE, (Arnold) Noel; s of William Henry Argue (d 1936), of Sligo, and Bertha Madeline, *née* McMunn (d 1948); *b* 13 Dec 1922; *Educ* St Columba's Coll Rathfarnham, Trinity Coll Dublin (BA, MSc), Univ of Cambridge (MA); *m* 9 Sept 1954, Margaret Mary, da of Robert Anson Francis (d 1917), of Ipswich; 1 s (Christopher); *Career* Nat Serv RAF: AC2 wireless operator and mechanic 1941, LAC 1944; sr observer The Observatories Univ of Cambridge 1960 (jr observer 1953-60); chm: Int Astromonical Union Working Gp on Extragalactic Radio/Optical Reference Frame 1979, Euro Space Agency Hipparcos Input Catalogue Consortium Working Gp for Radio/ Optical Reference Frame 1982; author of approximately 60 papers in astronomical jls; FRAS 1957; *Recreations* music, reading, especially history and biography; *Clubs* Univ of Cambridge Sr Combination Room; *Style—* Noel Argue, Esq; 21 Pierce Lane, Fulbourn, Cambridge (☎ 0223 880279); Univ of Cambridge, The Observatories, Madingley Rd, Cambridge (☎ 0223 337530/48, fax 0223 337523, telex 817297 ASTRON G)

ARGYLE, His Hon Michael Victor; MC (1945), QC (1961); s of Harold Victor Argyle (d 1965), of Highways, Repton, Derby, and Elsie Marion, *née* Richards; *b* 31 Aug 1915; *Educ* Westminster, Trinity Coll Cambridge (MA); *m* 1951, Ann Norah, da of late C A Newton, of Derby; 3 da; *Career* served WWII 7 QOH, Maj; called to the Bar Lincoln's Inn 1938; rec: Northampton 1962-65, Birmingham 1965-70; dep chm Holland Quarter Sessions 1965-71, lay judge Ct of Arches Canterbury 1968-, circuit judge 1970-88 (formerly additional judge of the Central Criminal Ct); pres: Nat Campaign for Restoration of Capital Punishment 1988-, Midland Counties Canine Soc 1988-; Master Worshipful Co of Playing Cards Makers 1984-85 (Jr Warden 1982-83, Sr Warden 1983-84); treas Lincoln's Inn 1984-85; *Books* Phipson on Evidence (10th edition); *Recreations* chess, boxing; *Clubs* Cavalry and Guards', Carlton, Kennel; *Style—* His Hon Michael Argyle, MC, QC; The Red House, Fiskerton, nr Southwell, Notts NG25 0UL

ARGYLL, 12 Duke of (S 1701 and UK 1892); Sir Ian Campbell; 14 Bt (NS 1627), DL (Argyll and Bute 1987); also Lord Campbell (S 1445), Earl of Argyll (S 1457), Lord Lorne (S 1470), Marquess of Kintyre and Lorne, Earl of Campbell and Cowal, Viscount Lochow and Glenilla, and Lord Inveraray, Mull, Morvern and Tiry (all S 1701), Baron Sundridge (GB 1766), Baron Hamilton (GB 1776), hereditary master of HM's Household in Scotland, keeper of the Great Seal of Scotland, keeper of Dunoon, Carrick, Dunstaffnage and Tarbert Castles, Admiral of the Western Isles, hereditary sheriff of Argyll; s of 11 Duke of Argyll (d 1973), by his 2 w Louise, da of Henry Clews; *b* 28 Aug 1937; *Educ* Le Rosey, Trinity Coll Glenalmond, McGill Univ of Canada; *m* 1964, Iona, da of Capt Sir Ivar Iain Colquhoun of Luss, 8 Bt; 1 s, 1 da (Lady Louise Iona b 26 Oct 1972); *Heir* s, Marquess of Lorne; *Career* late Capt Argyll & Sutherland Highlanders; memb Royal Co of Archers (Queen's Body Guard for Scotland); KStJ 1975; *Clubs* White's, New (Edinburgh); *Style—* His Grace the Duke of Argyll, DL; Inveraray Castle, Inveraray, Argyll PA32 8XF (☎ 0499 2275)

ARGYLL, Margaret, Duchess of; (Ethel) Margaret; da of George Hay Whigham (d 1960, fndr and chm of Br and Canadian and American Celanese Corps), and Helen Mann (d 1955), da of Douglas Mann Hannay (Scottish cotton magnate); George Whigham's gf, Robert Whigham, m Jane, da of Sir Robert Dundas, 1 Bt, of cadet branch of Dundas family who became Viscounts Melville; George was bro of: Gen Sir Robert Whigham (Dep CIGS), James (editor Town and Country American magazine), Charles (dir Morgan Grenfell), Gilbert (md Burmah Oil), Walter (dir Bank of England and md London and NE Rlwy); *b* 1 Dec 1912; *Educ* Miss Hewitt's Classes New York, Miss Wolff's London, Heathfield Ascot, Mlle Ozanne Paris; *m* 1, 1933 (m dis 1947), Charles Sweeny; 1 s (Brian), 1 da (Frances: *see* Rutland, 10 Duke of); m 2, 1951 (m dis 1963), as his 3 w, 11 Duke of Argyll (d 1973); *Career* pres Bleakholt Animal Sanctuary Lancs 1968-; helped organise campaign to save Argyll & Sutherland Highlanders 1968; contributor Tatler social diary 1979-81; *Books* Forget Not (autobiography, 1975); *Recreations* animal and child welfare, photography, travel, writing; *Style—* Margaret, Duchess of Argyll

ARIE, Thomas Harry David; s of Dr O M Arie (d 1983), of Reading, and Hedy, *née* Glaser; *b* 9 Aug 1933; *Educ* Reading Sch, Balliol Coll Oxford (MA, BM BCh); *m* 5 July 1963, Dr Eleanor Arie, da of Sir Robert Aitken, of Birmingham; 1 s (Samuel b 1974), 2 da (Laura b 1968, Sophie b 1971); *Career* sr lectr in social med London Hosp 1967-77, conslt psychiatrist Goodmayes Hosp 1969-77; fndn prof of health care of the elderly Univ of Nottingham 1977-, hon conslt psychiatrist Nottingham Health authy 1977-; Fotheringham lectr Univ of Toronto 1979, visting prof NZ Geriatrics Soc 1980, Dozor visiting prof Univ of the Negev 1988, Frölich visiting prof RSM Fndn Univ of California Los Angeles 1991; memb: Central Cncl for Educn and Trg in Social Work 1975-81, Standing Med Advsy Ctee DHSS 1980-84, Ctee on Review Medicines, Res Advsy Ctee Centre for Policy on Ageing, Res Ctee Nat Inst Social Work 1983-90; chm Geriatric Psychiatry Section World Psychiatric Assoc 1989-; Royal Coll of Psychologists: memb Cncl and Ct of Electors, chm Specialist Section on Old Age 1981-86 (vice pres 1983-85); FRCPsych, FRCP, FFCM; *Books* Health Care of the Elderly (ed, 1981), Recent Advances in Psychogeriatrics (ed, 1985); *Style—* Prof T H D Arie; Dept of Health Care of the Elderly, Medical Sch, Queen's Medical Centre, Nottingham NG7 2UH (☎ 0602 709408, 0602 780608, fax 0602 423618, telex 37346 UNINOT G)

ARIF, Saleem; s of Dr S A Quadri, and Sayeed Unisa Quadri; *b* 28 May 1949; *Educ* Birmingham Coll of Art, RCA (MA); *Career* artist; solo exhibitions: Spectro Arts Workshop Newcastle upon Tyne 1982, Bury Metro Arts Assoc Gallery Bury 1982, Midland Gp Nottingham 1983, Kent Univ Gallery Canterbury 1984, Art Heritage Gallery New Delhi 1984, Cymnoza Art Gallery Bombay 1985, Sarla Arts Centre Madras 1985, Br Cncl Div Gallery Calcutta 1985, Ipswich Museum 1986, Winchester Art Gallery 1987, Axiom Gallery Cheltenham 1987, Plymouth Arts Centre 1988, Anderson O'Day Gallery London 1988; gp exhibitions incl: Young Contemporaries (Royal Acad) 1970, First and Third International Biennale Durham 1973 and 1977, Midland View Touring Exhibition 1980, Serpentine Gallery Summer Show London 1981, Hayward Annual London and Edinburgh 1982, Barbican Concourse Gallery London 1982, IAA '73 (Morley Gallery London) 1983, Int Print Biennale Kanagawa Japan 1983, Edward Total Gallery London 1985, Whitechapel (Open/Whitechapel Gallery London) 1986, 1987 and 1989, From Two Worlds (Whitechapel Gallery London and Fruitmarket Gallery Edinburgh) 1986, On a Plate (Serpentine Gallery London) 1990, Graven Images (Harris Museum Preston) 1988, Eight Contemporary British Artists (Galerie Sapet Valance France) 1988, Ways of Seeing (Mestyn Art Gallery Wales Touring, Art Fair Olympia London) 1989, The Other Story (Hayward Gallery London and tours Wolverhampton Art Gallery and Cornerhouse Manchester) 1989-90, Broadgate Art Week London 1990, The Third World and Beyond (Art Int Confrontation of Contemporary Galleria Civica D'Arte Contemporanea Marsala Sicily) 1990; most important works: Itinerary (1972), Dante's Inferno (1980-81, set of forty), Birds of Aspirations (1989), Enchantments of Sky and Earth (1990); Awards: prize winner Young Sculptor of the Year Sunday Telegraph Competition 1971, Arts Cncl of GB 1981, Italian Govt Bursary Florence 1982; artist in residence: Childeric Sch 1983, Ipswich Museum 1986, Elstow Croft Centre Bedford 1987; Br Cncl award 1984, Villers David Fndn travel award to Turkey and Spain 1989; memb: Tstees of Camden Art Centre 1989, Eastern Arts Advsy Arts Panel 1989; *Recreations* collecting Indian contemporary folk art, photography, travelling; *Style—* Saleem Arif, Esq; Space Studios, Britania Works, Dace Road, London E3 (☎ 081 985 4225)

ARIS, John Bernard Benedict; TD (1967); s of John Woodbridge Aris (d 1977), of Sedlescombe, Sussex, and Joyce Mary, *née* Williams (d 1986); *b* 6 June 1934; *Educ* Eton, Magdalen Coll Oxford (BA, MA); *Career* Nat Serv 2 Lt RA Korea, Hong Kong 1952-54, Territorial Serv RA RHA serv in 44 Para Bde, ret Maj 1954-72; LEO Comps Ltd 1958-63, English Electric Comps Ltd 1963-69, ICL 1969-75 (directeur technique Europe de l'Ouest 1972-75), Imperial Group plc 1975-85 (mangr Gp Mgmnt Serv 1982-85), chief exec Nat Comp Centre Ltd 1985-90 (non-exec dir 1981-85), dir IMPACT Programme 1990-; chm FOCUS Private Sector Users' Ctee 1984-85, Alvey User Panel 1985-88; Freeman City of London 1988, fndr Freeman Worshipful Co of Info Technols 1987; FBCS, FInstD, FRSA; *Recreations* travel, music, art, scuba diving, gastronomy; *Style—* John Aris, Esq, TD; NCC Ltd, Oxford Rd, Manchester M1 7ED (☎ 061 228 6333, fax 061 228 2579, telex 66896

ARKELL, Maj James Rixon; TD; s of Peter Arkell, and Anne, *née* Falcon; *b* 28 May 1951; *Educ* Milton Abbey; *m* 7 Sept 1974, Carolyn Jane, da of Charles Ralph Woosnam; 3 s (George b 9 Dec 1978, John b 17 Apr 1983, Alexander b 15 Aug 1985), 1 da (Emma 6 Feb 1976); *Career* cmmnd Royal Wiltshire (Yeo) TA 1976 (joined 1974), Sqdn-Ldr 1983, 2 i/c (V) 1989; md J Arkell & Sons Swindon Wilts, dir Edmont Joinery Ltd Swindon Wilts; *Recreations* shooting, fishing; *Clubs* Special Forces; *Style—* Maj James Arkell, TD; Sterts House, Hannington-Wick, Highworth, Wilts (☎ 0285 810393); Arkells Brewery Ltd, Kingsdown Brewery, Swindon, Wilts (☎ 0793 823 026)

ARKELL, John Heward; CBE (1961), TD; s of Rev H H Arkell, Vicar of Chipping Norton, Oxon, and Gertrude Mary, *née* Heward; *b* 20 May 1909; *Educ* Radley, ChCh Oxford (MA); *m* 1, 1940, Helen Birgit, da of H E Emil Huitfeldt, sometime Norwegian ambass to Denmark; 2 s, 1 da; m 2, 1956 (m dis), Meta, da of Otto Bäche Grundtvig, of Trondheim, Norway; 1 s; *Career* served WWII KRRC 1939, TA; sec Sir Max Michaelis Investment Trust 1931-37, asst sec Cncl for Protection of Rural Eng 1937-39 (vice pres 1984), personnel mangr J Lyons & Co 1945-49; with BBC 1949-70 (controller staff 1949-58, dir staff 1958-60, dir 1960-70), chm Air Tport and Travel Indust Trg Bd 1970-80; dir: The Boots Co 1970-79, The Coates Group of Cos 1970-76, UK Provident Inst 1971-80; sr assoc Leo Kramer International Ltd 1980-86; lay memb Nat Indust Rels Ct 1972-74, memb Cncl Nat Tst 1971-84 (chm Advsy Ctee on Communications 1983), visiting fell Henley Mgmnt Coll 1971-; memb: Cncl CBI 1973-75, Final Selection Bd Civil Serv Cmmn 1978-82; vice pres BIM 1974- (chm Cncl 1972-74, dir BIM Fndn 1976-81), govr Radley Coll 1965-70; gen hon sec and fndr ChCh Oxford Utd Clubs SE London 1932 (later chm, currently jt pres 1986-); composer of light music; CBIM, FRSA, FIPM; *Recreations* music, walking, swimming; *Clubs* Savile, Leander, Lansdowne; *Style—* John Arkell, Esq, CBE, TD; Pinnocks, Fawley, nr Henley-on-Thames, Oxon RG9 6JH (☎ 0491 573017); Glen Cottage, Ringstead Bay, nr Dorchester, Dorset DT2 8NG (☎ 0305 852686)

ARKELL, Julian; s of William Joscelyn Arkell (d 1958), and Ruby Lilian, *née* Percival (d 1983); *b* 22 Oct 1934; *Educ* Bryanston, King's Coll Cambridge (MA); *m* 1, 5 Sept 1964 (m dis 1976); 2 da (Claire b 25 Aug 1966, Katie b 8 July 1968); m 2, 29 April 1983, Elaine; *Career* Shell-Mex and BP Ltd 1956-62, ptnr Robert Matthew Johnson-Marshall & Partners 1972-86 (partnership sec 1962-72), co sec RMJM Ltd 1986-91; conslt: British Invisibles 1985-, RMJM Group 1987-; memb: Fees Ctee RIBA 1974-, Lotis Ctee BI 1981-, Export Fin Panel LCCI 1983-; chm Euro Community Servs Gp Working Pty Brussels; MBIM 1987, MBOU 1962; *Style—* Julian Arkell, Esq; 37 Campden Hill Road, London W8 7DX

ARKELL, Peter; s of Sir Noel Arkell, DL (d 1981), and Olive Arscott, *née* Quick (d 1988); *b* 24 Jan 1923; *m* 12 Aug 1949, Anne, da of Michael Falcon (d 1976), of Burlingham House, Norwich, Norfolk; 1 s (James b 1951), 3 da (Jane b 1950, Alison b 1952, Rosalind b 1954); *Career* Mil Serv RAFVR 1941-45, Flt Lt 26 Sqdn Mustangs 161 Sqdn (Special Duty) Lysander, Tempsford 357 Sqdn (Special Duty) Lysanders BURMA; chm Arkell's Brewery Ltd; *Recreations* riding, fishing, shooting, gardening; *Clubs* Special Forces, RAF, Leander; *Style—* Peter Arkell, Esq; Whelford Mill, Fairford, Gloucestershire; Arkell's Brewery Ltd, Kingsdown, Swindon SN2 6RU

ARKWRIGHT, (Anthony) Mark; s of Maj Anthony Richard Frank Arkwright, and Diana Evelyn Mary, *née* Garle; *b* 15 July 1954; *Educ* Eton, Leeds Sch of Business and Accountancy, RMA Sandhurst; *Career* 9/12 Royal Lancers (PWO) 1975-79 (Capt 1976), Queens Own Yeo 1980-; dir Wise Speke Ltd Stockbrokers 1986; *Recreations* fishing, cresta; *Clubs* Cavalry, Northern Counties; *Style—* Mark Arkwright, Esq; Wise Speke Ltd, Provincial Hse, Albion St, Leeds LS1 6HX (☎ 0532 459341)

ARKWRIGHT, Thomas James; s of Thomas Joseph Arkwright (d 1963), of Holmlea, Wigan Lane, Wigan, Lancs, and Mary Edna, *née* Ashurst; *b* 22 March 1932; *Educ* Mount St Mary's Coll Sheffield, Univ of Liverpool (LLB); *m* 27 Aug 1958, (Margaret) Muriel, da of Wilfred Hague (d 1973), of Trafalgar Rd, Wigan, Lancs; 1 s (Paul b 1962), 5 da (Louise b 1960, Julie b 1963, Clare b 1966, Lucy b 1968, Helen b 1971); *Career* slr; articled to Sir John B McKaig Liverpool 1950-55, currently sr ptnr Cyril Morris Arkwright Bolton, Notary Public; pres: Bolton Catholic Musical and Choral Soc 1968-, Bolton C of C and Indust 1971-73, Bolton Law Soc 1972, Bolton West Cons Assoc 1973-76 and 1989- (sec 1961-66, chm 1966-71, hon life vice pres); dep pres Bolton Coronary Care 1970-, dep treas NW Cons Pty 1972-73, chm NW C of C and Indust 1973, treas and mangr N W Catholic History Soc 1987-90 (hon life memb 1990); memb: Law Soc 1955, Notaries Soc 1960; *Recreations* historical studies, genealogy, walking, gardening; *Clubs* Bolton; *Style—* Thomas Arkwright, Esq; Ivy Cottage, Limbrick, Chorley, Lancs PR6 9EE (☎ 025 72 68646); Churchgate House, 30 Churchgate, Bolton, Lancs BL1 1HS (☎ 0204 35261, fax 0204 363354)

ARLOTT, (Leslie Thomas) John; OBE (1970); s of late William John Arlott, and Nellie Jenvey, *née* Clarke; *b* 25 Feb 1914; *Educ* Queen Mary's Sch Basingstoke; *m* 1, Dawn Rees; 1 s (and 1 s decd); m 2, Valerie France (d 1976); 1 s (and 1 da decd); m 3, 1977, Patricia Hoare; *Career* broadcaster (BBC cricket commentator for 36 years), author, wine writer, topographer, clerk in mental hosp, detective, BBC producer; Parly candidate (Lib) Epping 1955 and 1959; pres Cricketers' Assoc 1968-; Hon MA Southampton Univ 1973, Hon DUniv Open Univ 1981; *Style—* John Arlott, Esq, OBE; c/o The Guardian, 119 Farringdon Rd, London EC1

ARMAGH, Archbishop of (RC), and Primate of All Ireland 1990-; Most Rev Cahal Brendan Daly; s of Charles Daly (d 1939), of Loughguile, Co Antrim, and Susan Daly (d 1974); *b* 1 Oct 1917; *Educ* St Malachy's Coll Belfast, Queen's Univ Belfast (MA), St Patrick's Coll Maynooth (DD), Institut Catholique Paris (LPh); *Career* ordained 1941, classics master St Malachy's Coll Belfast 1945-46, reader in scholastic philosophy Queen's Univ Belfast 1963-67 (lectr 1946-63); consecrated bishop 1967; bishop: Ardagh and Clonmacnois 1967-82, Down and Connor 1982-90; *Books* Morals, Law and Life (1962), Natural Law Morality Today (1965), Violence in Ireland and Christian Conscience (1973), Peace, the Work of Justice (1979); *Recreations* reading, writing; *Style—* The Most Rev Cahal Daly, Archbishop of Armagh; Ara Coeli, Armagh,

N Ireland

ARMAGH, Archbishop of (C of E) 1986-; Most Rev Robert Henry Alexander Eames; s of William Edward Eames, and Mary Eleanor Thompson, *née* Alexander; *b* 27 April 1937; *Educ* Belfast Royal Acad, Methodist Coll Belfast, Queen's Univ Belfast, Trinity Coll Dublin (LLB, LLD, PhD); *m* 1966, (Ann) Christine, da of Capt W M Adrian Reynolds Daly (d 1943); 2 s (Niall b 1967, Michael b 1969); *Career* curate of Bangor Down Dio 1963-66; incumbent of: Gilnahirk Down 1966-74, Dundela Down 1974-75; bishop of Derry and Raphoe 1975-80, bishop of Down and Dromore 1980-86, archbishop of Armagh and primate of all Ireland 1986, chm Archbishop of Canterbury's Int Cmmn on Communion and Women in the Episcopate 1988; *Recreations* sailing, reading; *Clubs* Strangford Yacht, Ringhaddy Yacht, Kildare St and Univ Club (Dublin); *Style—* Most Rev the Archbishop of Armagh, Primate of All Ireland; The See House, Cathedral Close, Armagh BT61 7EE (☎ 0861 522851)

ARMAND SMITH, Dr Nicholas Godfrey; s of Rev Lt Cdr Francis Armand Smith (ret), and Monica Ella Mary, *née* Harden (d 1975); *b* 16 Feb 1943; *Educ* Bryanston, St Mary's Hosp Med Sch Univ of London (MB BS); *m* 13 Sept 1973, Margaret Winifred, da of Francis John Hebbert, ERD, of 488 High Rd, Woodford Green, Essex; 1 s (Henry b 1977), 2 da (Josephine b 1979, Celia b 1985); *Career* conslt epidemiologist WHO 1974-75, specialist in community med Lothian Health Bd 1977-82, dir of public health and dist med offr Salisbury Health Authy 1982-; Wessex regnl advsr in public health med; fell Faculty Public Health Med; *Recreations* cycling, old cars; *Style—* Dr Nicholas Armand Smith; Dept of Public Health, Salisbury Health Authority, Odstock Hosp, Salisbury, Wilts (☎ 0722 336262)

ARMATRADING, Joan Anita Barbara; da of Amos Ezekiel Armatrading, and Beryl Madge, *née* Benjamin; *b* 9 Dec 1950; *Educ* Secdy Sch Birmingham; *Career* first album Whatever's For Us 1972 (with Pam Nestor), stage debut Fairfield Hall Croydon 1972, first non jazz act downstairs at Ronnie Scotts 1973, first major hit Love and Affection 1976, first solo album Joan Armatrading 1976; discs: 3 Silver, 28 Gold, 6 Platinum; concerts: Blackbush with Bob Dylan (before 100,000 plus audience) 1978, Prince's Tst 1982 and 1986, Amnesty Int (Giant Stadium) 1986, Amnesty Int (Secret Policemans' Ball) 1987, Nelson Mandela's 70th Birthday 1988, First King's Tst Swaziland 1989 and 1990; nominated: Grammy Best Female Vocal 1980 and 1983, Best Female Vocal UK 1976 and 1983; key to Sydney 1983, guest of honour St Kitt's Independence Celebration 1983; *Recreations* owner of stud farm, reading British comics, owner of 2 vintage cars; *Style—* Miss Joan Armatrading; c/o Mike Noble, Running Dog Management, 27 Queensdale Place, London W11 4SQ (☎ 071 602 6249, fax 071 602 8755)

ARMES, Timothy Joseph Patrick; s of Harry Armes (d 1986), and Teresa, *née* O'Mahony; *b* 1 Oct 1953; *Educ* St Richard of Chichester Sch, Westminster Tech Coll (ONL), The City Univ; *m* 14 July 1989, Susan McKenzie, da of John Self, of Oxted, Surrey; 1 da (Olivia Charlotte McKenzie b 31 March 1990); *Career* advertising exec; J Walter Thompson 1976-76 (trainee buyer rising to media buyer), media gp head MWK & P 1978-83, media gp dir Young & Rubicam 1983-89, The Media Shop 1990-; memb Educn Ctee The Media Circle; *Recreations* cricket, horse racing, wine, collecting antiques, being a father, opera, theatre, cinema, restaurants, travel; *Clubs* RAC, Middlesex CC; *Style—* Timothy Armes, Esq; The Media Shop, 15 Adeline Place, London WC1B 3AJ (☎ 071 636 6561, fax 071 323 3216)

ARMFIELD, Diana Maxwell; da of (Joseph) Harold Armfield (d 1981), of Ty Newydd, Parc, Bala, Gwynedd, and Gertrude Mary, *née* Uttley (d 1984); *b* 11 June 1920; *Educ* Bedales, Slade Sch, Central Sch of Arts & Crafts; *m* 12 Feb 1949, (Andrew Harold) Bernard Dunstan, s of Albert Ernest Dunstan (d 1960), of Cambridge; 3 s (Andrew Joseph b 1950, David James b 1952, Robert Maxwell b 1955); *Career* cultural activities organiser Miny of Supply 1942-46; tutor Textile Dept Central Sch Art 1949-50, visiting tutor various art schs 1959-, reg exhibitor Royal Acad 1966-; exhibitor: Festival of Br 1951, Tonic for the Nation V&A; artist in residence Perth W Aust 1985; NEAC Centenary Southerbys 1986; one man show Browse & Darby London 1990 (1979, 1981, 1984, 1987); perm collections: cmmns Reuters 1986-87, Contemporary Art Soc Wales 1987, Nat Tst 1988-89, HRH Prince of Wales 1989, Farningdon Tst V&A (textiles), Yale Centre Br Art, Govt Picture Collection, Br Museum Royal Watercolour Soc, Royal W England Acad; memb: Cncl of the Protection of Rural Wales FOE; MCSD 1951, memb NEAC 1970, RWA 1975, RWS 1980, ARA 1989; *Books* Painting In Oils (1982); *Recreations* musical appreciation, singing, gardening; *Clubs* Arts (Dovevst); *Style—* Miss Diana Armfield; 10 High Park Rd, Kew, Richmond, Surrey TW9 4BH (☎ 081 876 6633); Llwynhir, Parc, Bala, Gwynedd

ARMIGER, Paul Gower; OBE; s of Wing Cdr Brian Armiger, of Edinburgh, and Peggy Joyce, *née* Oldfield; *b* 25 Aug 1942; *Educ* Karachi GS India, Cranbrook Sydney Aust, Haileybury and Imp Windsor, Bloxham Sch Banbury Oxon; *m* 28 June 1964, Patricia Gillian, da of Sqdn Ldr Charles Clinch; 2 s (Andrew Gower b 9 April 1968, Steven Paul b 21 Feb 1971); *Career* photographer; staff photographer Montgomery Advertiser and Alabama Journal USA 1960-61, freelance photographer Washington DC (work for: Time, Life, Newsweek, Washington Post, Nat Geographic) 1961-64, freelance photographer The Daily Telegraph London 1965, staff photographer The Daily Telegraph 1967- (covered NI 1969-74, Darien Gap Expedition 1971-); hon memb Naval Air Cmd Sub Aqua Club, fndr memb Br Soc of Underwater Photographers 1969, memb Underwater Archaeological Expeditions Assoc Hollandia Colossus 1967-72; *Awards* second class diver BSAC 1970, holder commercial diver's licence (Part IV Diver at work) 1980; *Recreations* scuba diving, photography, golf, model shipwright (18th century ship models); *Clubs* Press Club (Washington and London), Royal Over Seas League; *Style—* Paul Armiger, Esq; The Daily Telegraph, 181 Marsh Wall, London E14 (☎ 071 538 6399, 0836 256671)

ARMIT, Hon Mrs (Serena Helen Christian); *née* Inskip; da of 2 Viscount Caldecote, DSC; *b* 12 June 1943; *m* 1965, John Andrew Brodie Armit, s of late Maj Cecil Brodie Armit, RAMC; 1 s, 1 da; *Style—* The Hon Mrs Armit; 98 St Paul's Rd, London N1

ARMITAGE, Alexander James (Alex); s of Richard Noel Marshall Armitage (d 1986), of Stebbing Park, Essex, and Lady Caroline Tyrrell, *née* Hay; *b* 17 May 1958; *Educ* Eton; *m* 4 Nov 1987, Carolyn Margery, da of Peter Allen, of Portermouth; 2 da (Sophie Claire b 25 Dec 1987, Daisy Elizabeth Collette b 28 Oct 1990); *Career* dir Farworlds Ltd 1985, chm Noel Gay Artists Ltd 1987 (dir 1980), md Noel Gay Orgn 1987 (dir 1984), dir Billy Marsh Assocs 1988; prodr: Me and My Girl (West End 1987, Broadway 1987), High Society 1987, The Rink 1988; memb Soc West End Theatre 1987; *Recreations* snow skiing, photography, wine and food; *Clubs* Groucho, Lords' Taveners; *Style—* Alex Armitage, Esq; 81 Lonsdale Rd, London SW13 (☎ 081 748 9722); Le Moulin Clos de Clauzel, Donnat, Bagnols-Sur-Ceze, France; The Noel Gay Orgn, 24 Denmark St, London WC2H 8NS (☎ 071 836 3941, fax 379 7027, telex 21760)

ARMITAGE, Edward Phillip (Phil); s of Leslie Armitage, of Barnsley, and Alice Emily, *née* Dufton; *b* 20 Jan 1947; *Educ* Barnsley Holte GS, Univ of Sussex (BSc, MSc, MA); *m* 24 Aug 1974, Elizabeth, da of Joseph Blackburn Sweeney; 1 s (Richard John b 27 Dec 1978), 1 da (Jennifer Elizabeth b 16 Oct 1980); *Career* sr lectr in statistics Coventry Poly 1968-78, res fell and lectr in student assessment Open Univ 1978-85, dir educn and training ICAEW 1990- (examinations offr 1985-90); *Recreations* squash, fell walking; *Style—* Phil Armitage, Esq; Institute of Chartered Accountants, Chartered Accountants Hall, Moorgate Place, London EC2P 2BJ (☎ 071 628 7060, fax 071 920 0547)

ARMITAGE, Maj-Gen Geoffrey Thomas Alexander; CBE (1968, MBE 1945); s of Lt-Col Harold Godfrey Parry Armitage (d 1958), of King's Co, Ireland, and Mary Madeline, *née* Drought (d 1933); *b* 5 July 1917; *Educ* Haileybury, RMA Woolwich; *m* 22 Oct 1949, Monica Wall, da of Frank Wall Poat (d 1972), of Guernsey; 1 s, 1 step da; *Career* cmmnd RA 1937, served WWII (despatches), transferred to Royal Dragoons (1 Dragoons) 1951, cmd 1956-59, instr (GSO1) IDC 1959-60, Col Gen Staff WO 1960-62, Cmdt RAC Centre 1962-65, COS HQ1 BR Corps 1966-68, dir Royal Armd Corps 1968-70, GOC Northumbrian Dist 1970-72, ret 1973; dir CLA Game Fair 1973-80; hon sec Countryside Fndn 1985-; *Recreations* some field sports, writing; *Clubs* Army and Navy, Kennel; *Style—* Maj-Gen Geoffrey Armitage, CBE; Clyffe, Tincleton, nr Dorchester, Dorset DT2 8QR (☎ 0305 848227)

ARMITAGE, Jeremy John; s of Maj Edward John Armitage, of London, and Marthe Ada, *née* Cleyndert; *b* 10 June 1954; *Educ* St Paul's, Edinburgh Coll of Art (BArch, Dip Arch); *m* 4 Jan 1978, Rowena Kathleen, da of Alexander Johnston, JP (d 1988); 2 s (John Joseph b 1981, James William b 1987), 1 da (Hannah Mary b 1979); *Career* architectural asst Western Isles Cncl 1979-80; Campbell and Arnott: joined 1980, opened new Glasgow office and became assoc 1985, ptnr 1987, dir 1989; memb Glasgow Jr C of C; MRIBA 1980, ARIAS 1985, MInstD 1990; *Recreations* sailing, hill walking, curling; *Clubs* The Glasgow Art; *Style—* Jeremy Armitage, Esq; 7 Kirklee Road, Glasgow G12 ORH (☎ 041 334 8522); Campbell & Arbuthnott Ltd, 135 Buchanan Street, Glasgow G1 2JA (☎ 041 221 8011)

ARMITAGE, John Patrick; s of Rev Cyril Moxon Armitage, MVO (d 1966), of St Bride's Rectory, Fleet St, London, and Eva, *née* Brinsmead; *b* 17 March 1935; *Educ* Marlborough; *m* 1, 28 Aug 1965 (m dis 1973), Marah Helen, *née* Douglas; 1 s (Edward b 8 Dec 1967); m 2, 14 Oct 1984, Nicola Caroline, da of Larry Gaines, of Crosstrees, Saltwood, Kent; *Career* Nat Serv cmmnd 2 Lt E Yorks Regt UK, Malaya, Germany 1954-56; sales exec Noel Gay Music Co Ltd 1956-59, dir Ogilvy & Mather Ltd 1971-85 (account exec 1959-71); chm: Primary Contact Ltd 1985-, Ogilvy & Mather Focus Ltd 1988-; memb Mark Soc; *Recreations* golf; *Clubs* Littlestone Rye, Royal & Ancient; *Style—* John Armitage, Esq; Ludwell House, Charing, Kent (☎ 023 371 2469)

ARMITAGE, Prof John Vernon; s of Horace Armitage, and Evelyn, *née* Hauton; through his mother, Prof Armitage is 2 cous of Baron Richardson of Duntisbourne, *qv*; *b* 21 May 1932; *Educ* Rothwell GS, UCL (BSc, PhD), Cuddesdon Coll Oxford; *m* 1963, Sarah Catherine Clay; 2 s; *Career* mathematician; asst master Shrewsbury Sch 1958-59, lectr Durham Univ 1959-67, sr lectr King's Coll London 1967-70, prof Nottingham Univ 1970-75, princ Coll of St Hild and St Bede Durham 1975-; *Books* A Companion to Advanced Mathematics (with H B Griffiths); *Recreations* railways, cricket and most games; *Clubs* Athenaeum; *Style—* Prof John Armitage; The Principal's House, Pelaw Leazes Lane, Durham DH1 1TB (☎ 091 374 3050)

ARMITAGE, Joshua Charles; s of Joshua Armitage (d 1944), of Hoylake, and Kate Louise, *née* Cooke (d 1953); *b* 26 Sept 1913; *Educ* private & public, Liverpool Sch of Art; *m* 27 May 1939, late Catherine Mary, *née* Buckle; 2 da (Judith Penelope b 19 Aug 1944, Lesley Elizabeth b 3 July 1946); *Career* WWII Leading Seaman RNVR 1940-45; freelance artist working under nom de plume Ionicus, assoc with Punch for over forty years, illustrator of over 350 books for leading publishers, twelve watercolours for United Oxford and Cambridge Univ Club in London, closely assoc with PG Wodehouse through Penguin Books, a watercolourist responsible for many pictures with golfing themes; fund raising for many charities; *Recreations* golf, gardening, music; *Clubs* Royal Liverpool Golf; *Style—* Joshua Armitage, Esq; 34 Avondale Rd, Hoylake, Wirral, Cheshire (☎ 051 632 1298)

ARMITAGE, Kenneth; CBE (1969); *b* 18 July 1916; *Career* WWII Army 1939-46; sculptor; solo exhibitions: Gimpel Fils London 1952 (1957, 1980), Bertha Schaefer NY 1956, Paul Rosenberg NY 1958-1962, Br Cncl exhibitions Venice Biennale, then touring museums Paris, Cologne, Brussels, Zürich, Rotterdam, Whitechapel Art Gallery 1959, Br Cncl world touring exhibition 1959-76, Kestner Gesselschaft Hanover and Japan 1960-61, Marlborough Gallery London 1962 and 1965, Art Cncl exhibition touring 10 Eng cities 1972-73, Fuji TV Gallery Tokyo 1978 then Galerie Humanite Nagoya and Gallery Kasahara 1978, Sala Mendoza Caracas Venezuela 1982, Artcurial Paris (retrospective) 1985; gp exhibitions incl: The New Decade (Museum of Modern Art NY) 1955, Guggenheim Int Exhibition NY 1967, Br Sculpture of 20 Century (Whitechapel Gallery) 1982, Br Art of 20 Century (Royal Acad) 1987, then Staatsgalerie Stuttgart; work in private and pub collections worldwide; RCA: hon fell 1965, Hon Dr 1969; *Style—* Kenneth Armitage, Esq, CBE; 22A Avonmore Rd, London W14 8RR

ARMITAGE, Air Chief Marshal Sir Michael John; KCB (1983), CBE (1975); *b* 25 Aug 1930; *Educ* Newport GS, Halton; RAF Coll Cranwell; *m* 1, 1955 (m dis 1969); 3 s; m 2, 1970, Gretl Renate Steinig; *Career* Halton apprentice RAF Coll Cranwell 1947-50; cmmnd 1953, various flying staff and academic appts, OC 17 Sqdn 1967-69, OC RAF Luqa Malta 1972-74, RAF Dir of Forward Policy 1976-78, Dep Cdr RAF Germany 1978-80, Sr RAF Dir Staff RCDS 1980-82, Dir of Service Intelligence 1982-83, Dep Chief Def Staff (Intelligence) 1983, Chief of Def Intelligence MOD 1984-85, air memb for Supply and Orgn, Air Force Bd 1985-87; Cmdt RCDS Studies 1988-89; *Books* Air Power in the Nuclear Age (jtly 2 edn 1985), Unmanned Aircraft (1988), articles in professional journals, lectures on Air Power, Int Affrs and Mil History; *Recreations* field shooting, military history, lecturing; *Clubs* RAF; *Style—* Air Chief Marshal Sir Michael Armitage, KCB, CBE; c/o Lloyds Bank, 6 Pall Mall, London SW1

ARMITAGE, Peter Lockhart; s of Dennis Lockhart Armitage, of Rushton Temple Lane, East Meon, Hants, and Dorothy Margaret, *née* Lamb; *b* 13 Jan 1949; *Educ* Malvern, Univ of Manchester (BA); *m* 7 Aug 1976, Fiona Christine Lilli, da of John Kingsley Hill, of Hen Ysgol, Llanfaethly, Holyhead, Anglesey; 2 s (Michael b 1980, Jonathan b 1985), 1 da (Melanie b 1982); *Career* CA co sec and dir: OCS Gp Ltd 1987, Smarts Gp Ltd 1981, Collie Carpets Ltd 1980, West Leigh Gp Ltd 1989; jt md Smarts Gp Ltd 1985-87 (all cos owned by OCS Gp); jt md J Mason & Son Leek Ltd 1977-78; *Recreations* tennis, sailing, gardening; *Style—* Peter Armitage, Esq; Longmead, Highfields, E Horsley, Leatherhead, Surrey KT24 5AA; OCS Gp Ltd, 79 Limpsfield Road, Sanderstead, Surrey CR2 9LB (☎ 081 651 3211, fax 081 651 4832)

ARMITAGE, (Stephen) Robert; s of Sir Stephen Cecil Armitage, CBE (d 1962), of Nottinghamshire, and Irene, *née* Bowen Smith (d 1984); *b* 19 Jan 1924; *Educ* Harrow; *m* 1, 1951, Jane Elizabeth, da of Dennis Charles Mackie (d 1954); 1 s (Stephen David b 1952), 2 da (Fiona Jane b 1956, Emma Louise b 1958); m 2, 1972, Diana Mary Alethea, da of Patrick Joseph Henry (d 1944); 1 da (Carlotte Diana b 1976); *Career* serv Welsh Gds 1942-47, home and abroad, ret as Capt; joined Armitage Bros plc 1945 as dir (chm 1962-); *Recreations* shooting, fishing, sailing, skiing; *Style—* Robert Armitage, Esq; Hawksworth Manor, Hawksworth, Nottinghamshire NG13 9DB (☎ 0949 50243); Armitage Bros plc, Armitage Hse, Colwick, Nottingham NG4 2BA (☎ 0602 614984, telex 377921, fax 0602 617496)

ARMITAGE, Roger Stuart; s of Eric Armitage (d 1970), and Elsie, *née* Hollingworth;

b 17 April 1943; *Educ* Elland GS; *m* 3 Sept 1966, Wendy, da of Frank Lockwood; 1 s (Martin James b 26 Dec 1970); *Career* CA 1965; Revell Ward (formerly Hirst & Elmslie): articled clerk 1959-64, ptnr 1969, sr ptnr 1990-; ACA 1965, ATII 1965, former pres Huddersfield CAs Students Soc; *Recreations* golf, walking, theatre; *Clubs* Woodsome Hall Golf, Huddersfield Borough Colne Valley Soc (treas); *Style*— Roger Armitage, Esq; Messrs Revell Ward, Chartered Accountants, Norwich Union House, High St, Huddersfield HD1 2LN (☎ 0484 538351, fax 0484 513522)

ARMITAGE, (Henry) St John Basil; CBE (1978, OBE 1968); s of (Henry) John Armitage (d 1978), of Co Tipperary and Lincoln, and Amelia Eleanor, *née* Hall (d 1967); *b* 5 May 1924; *Educ* Lincoln Christ's Hosp, Trinity Coll Cambridge; *m* 1956, Jennifer Gerda, da of Prof Walter Horace Bruford; 1 s (Richard), 1 da (Elizabeth); *Career* served Army 1943-45, Arab Legion 1946, Br Mil Mission to Saudi Arabia 1946-49, mil advsr to Saudi Arabian MOD 1946-51, Desert Locust Control Kenya and Aden Protectorates 1952, mil serv of Sultan of Muscat and Oman 1952-59; resident mangr Gen Geophysical Co (Houston) Libya 1959-60, oil conslt Astor Assocs Libya 1960-61, business conslt ME 1962, joined HM Dip Serv 1962; 1 sec (commercial): Baghdad 1963-67, Beirut 1967-68, Jedda 1968-74; chargé d'affaires Jedda 1968 (also 1969 and 1973); HM cnsllr and consul gen Dubai 1974-78, chargé d'affaires 1975 and 1977, ret 1978; conslt ME affrs; dir: SCF Hldgs London, Socofi Geneva 1979-89; hon sec All Party British Saudi Arabian Parly Gp; *Recreations* cricket, reading, travel; *Clubs* Travellers'; *Style*— St John Armitage, Esq, CBE; The Old Vicarage, East Horrington, Wells, Somerset

ARMSTRONG; *see*: Burnett Armstrong

ARMSTRONG, Andrew Charles; s of Terence George Armstrong, of Elsenham, nr Bishop's Stortford, Herts, and Marion, *née* Rigg; *b* 15 March 1959; *Educ* Newport GS Essex; *m* 4 July 1981, Jacqueline Mary, da of Anthony Rokeby Roberts, of Sheering, nr Bishop's Stortford, Herts; 2 s (Robert Charles b 1985, David Alexander b 1989); *Career* dir Robert Fleming & Co Ltd 1986-; *Recreations* golf; *Style*— A C Armstrong, Esq; Robert Fleming & Co Ltd, 25 Copthall Ave, London EC2R 7DR (☎ 071 638 5858, fax 071 256 5036)

ARMSTRONG, Sir Andrew Clarence Francis; 6 Bt (UK 1841), of Gallen Priory, King's Co; CMG (1959); er s of Edmund Clarence Richard Armstrong, FSA (d 1923), Bluemantle Pursuivant of Arms, and Mary Frances, *née* Cruise, 2 da of Sir Francis Cruise (d 1953); suc his cousin Sir Andrew St Clare Armstrong, 5 Bt (d 1987); *b* 1 May 1907; *Educ* St Edmund's Coll Old Hall Ware, Christ's Coll Cambridge; *m* 1, 8 Jan 1930, Phyllis Marguerite (d 18 Jan 1930), da of Lt-Col Roland Henry Waithman, DSO; m 2, 17 June 1932, Laurel May (d 1988), er da of late Alfred Wellington Stuart, of New Zealand; 1 s (1 s decd); *Heir* s, Lt-Col Christopher John Edmund Stuart Armstrong, MBE, *qv*; *Career* Colonial Admin Serv: W Pacific 1929, Nigeria 1941, perm sec Fed Miny of Mines and Power Nigeria; ret 1961; *Style*— Sir Andrew Armstrong, Bt, CMG; 15 Ravenscroft Rd, Henley-on-Thames, Oxfordshire (☎ 0491 577635)

ARMSTRONG, Lt-Col Christopher John Edmund Stuart; MBE (1979); s and h of Sir Andrew Clarence Francis Armstrong, 6 Bt, CMG, *qv*; *b* 15 Jan 1940; *Educ* Ampleforth, RMA; *m* 1972, Georgina Elizabeth Carey, 2 da of Lt-Col W G Lewis, of Hayling Island; 3 s (Charles Andrew b 1973, James Hugo b 1974, Sam Edward b 1986), 1 da (Victoria Jane b 1980); *Career* Lt-Col RCT; *Style*— Lt-Col Christopher Armstrong, MBE; c/o National Westminster Bank, Marlow, Bucks

ARMSTRONG, Colin Robert; s of Arthur Armstrong (d 1957), and Sylvia Ann, *née* Williamson (d 1945); *b* 4 July 1934; *Educ* Haileybury; *m* 10 Oct 1959, Stella Margaret, da of Harold Bracht (d 1985), of Bogota, Colombia; 1 s (Arthur Guthrie b 9 April 1962), 1 da (Annabel Clare b 16 Sept 1966); *Career* Nat Serv 1952-54: cmmnd Middx Regt 1953, seconded to KAR (active serv E Africa and Malaya); 7 Middx Regt TA 1955-57; dir Tracey & Co (subsidiary of Bank of London and S America) 1963-71, mangr head office Bank of London and S America 1971-74, regnl mangr Lloyds Bank Int 1974-77, gen mangr Banco Anglo Colombiano 1977-81, dir and chief exec (Latin America & Caribbean) Inchcape Overseas Ltd 1981-86, exec dir Inchcape plc 1986-; chm Latin American Trade Advsy Gp 1984-86; memb: exec ctee Canning House 1986, Lloyds 1983-; *Recreations* fly fishing, cricket, ornithology; *Clubs* MCC, East India; *Style*— Colin Armstrong, Esq; The Old House, The Folly, Lightwater, Surrey (☎ 0276 73 258); Inchcape plc, St James House, 23 King Street, London SW1Y 6QY (☎ 071 321 0110, fax 071 321 0604, telex 885 395)

ARMSTRONG, Prof David Gilford; s of Arthur Armstrong (d 1930), of Whitley Bay, Tyne and Wear, and Beatrice Mary, *née* Walton (d 1972); *b* 9 July 1926; *Educ* Whitley Bay GS, Univ of Durham (BSc, MSc, PhD), Univ of Newcastle (DSc); *m* 31 Aug 1963, Susan, da of James Edward Hannah (d 1971), of Ayr, Scotland; 1 s (Neil b 1965), 1 da (Helen b 1967); *Career* lectr in agricultural chemistry Univ of Durham 1951-54 (demonstrator 1946-51), study year Univ of Illinois USA 1952-53, staff appt Nutrition Dept Hannah Res Inst Ayr 1954-62, prof of agriculture biochemistry and nutrition Univ of Newcastle 1968- (reader and head of dept 1963-68), visiting prof Univ of New England Aust 1971; memb Governing Body: Hill Farming Res Orgn 1970-85, Grassland Res Inst 1974-85, Macauley Land Use Res Inst 1985-; memb: Ind Merit Review Ctee 1985-89, Meat and Livestock Res Ctee 1986-, AFRC Animals Ctee 1987-, Inst of Animal Health 1988-, Scientific Ctee on Animal Nutrition EEC; pres Nutrition Soc, pres Northumberland Branch Holstein-Friesian Club 1989, hon res assoc Inst of Grassland and Animal Produce 1987, hon res fell Hannah Res Inst 1989; Hon DSc Univ of Louvain la Neuve 1988; FRSE, FRIC, FIBiol; Ordre du Merite Agricole France 1981; *Recreations* fishing, shooting, golf; *Style*— Prof David Armstrong; Woodcote, 44 North Rd, Ponteland, Northumberland NE20 9UR (☎ 0661 22316); University of Newcastle, Dept of Agricultural Biochemistry and Nutrition, Newcastle upon Tyne NE1 7RU (☎ 091 222 6000, ext 6907, fax 091 222 1182, telex 53654)

ARMSTRONG, Prof David Millar; s of James Armstrong, of Workington, Cumbria, and Jean Alexandra, *née* Millar; *b* 25 May 1941; *Educ* Workington GS, Univ of Oxford (BA, BSc), Australian Nat Univ (PhD); *m* 12 Aug 1964, Lucinda Russell, da of George Graham Kennedy (d 1955); 1 s (James Graham b 1966), 1 da (Katherine Anne b 1965); *Career* prof of physiology Univ of Bristol 1984- (lectr 1968-78, reader 1978-84); memb Neurosciences and Mental Health Bd of MRC; memb: Marine Biological Assoc 1965, Physiological Soc 1968; *Recreations* walking, reading, social and medical historical research; *Clubs* Bristol Scientific; *Style*— Prof David Armstrong; Department of Physiology, School of Medical Sciences, University of Bristol, University Walk, Bristol BS8 1TD (☎ 0272 303471, fax 0272 303497 attn D M Armstrong)

ARMSTRONG, Rt Hon Ernest; PC (1979); s of late John Armstrong, of Crook, Co Durham, and late Elizabeth, *née* Walker; *b* 12 Jan 1915; *Educ* Wolsingham GS, City of Leeds Teacher Training Coll; *m* 1941, Hannah, da of Thomas Lamb, of Sunderland; 1 s (John), 1 da (Hilary, *qv*); *Career* Flying Offr RAF 1942-46 (ME); schoolmaster 1937-52, headmaster 1952-64, chm Sunderland Education Ctee 1960-65; MP (Lab) NW Durham 1964-87, asst Govt whip 1967-69, lord cmmr HM Treasury 1969-70, oppn whip 1970-73, parly under sec DES 1974-75, DOE 1975-79, dep chm Ways and Means Ctee and first dep chm of House of Commons 1981-; dep chm Municipal Mutual Insurance Ltd; vice pres Methodist Conference 1974-75; *Recreations* walking; *Style*— The Rt Hon Ernest Armstrong; Penny Well, Witton-le-Wear, Bishop Auckland, Co Durham (☎ 038 888 397)

ARMSTRONG, Fiona Kathryne; da of Robert Armstrong, of Lancs, and Pauline, *née* Moreland; *b* 28 Nov 1956; *Educ* W R Tuson Coll Preston, Univ of London (BA); *m* 12 Sept 1987, Rodney Thomas Potts, s of Thomas Potts, of Canonbie, Dumfrieshire; *Career* reporter Radio 210 Reading 1980-82, regnl journalist BBC TV Manchester 1982-85, reporter Border TV Cumbria 1985-87, newscaster ITN 1987-; *Recreations* fishing, cooking; *Clubs* Reform; *Style*— Ms Fiona Armstrong; ITN, 200 Gray's Inn Road, London WC1 (☎ 071 833 3000)

ARMSTRONG, Col Geoffrey Russell; DSO (1945), MC (1942), TD (1950); s of William Robinson Armstrong (d 1955), of Banstead, Surrey, and Beatrice, *née* Russell (d 1965); *b* 16 June 1910; *Educ* Sutton Valence; *m* 16 Nov 1945, Elizabeth Peace, da of George William Cole-Hamilton (d 1946), of Hertfordshire; 1 s (Johny b 1946), 1 da (Ruth Margaret b 1949); *Career* joined HAC 1930, cmmnd 1935, Capt 1939, 8 Army Western Desert 1941-42, Maj 1942, Iraq and India 1943, Lt-Col 1944, Burma 1943-45 (despatches), Col 1953; publisher 1953-58; chm and md Mfrg Gp 1958-68; antiquarian bookseller 1968-85; memb Rural Preservation; served in TA Assocs; *Books* The Sparks Fly Upward, various contribs to mil histories; *Recreations* shooting, fishing, deerstalking; *Clubs* Army and Navy, Honourable Artillery Co; *Style*— Col Geoffrey Armstrong,DSO, MC, TD; Axmas Cottage, Rusper, West Sussex

ARMSTRONG, Dr Ian David; s of David Armstrong (d 1986), and Mary, *née* Wardle; *b* 7 April 1943; *Educ* Peebles HS, Heriot-Watt Univ Edinburgh (BSc, PhD); *m* 17 Sept 1965, (Eileen) Carol, da of Flt Lt William Milne; 2 da (Kim b 26 Nov 1967, Sharon b 16 June 1969); *Career* lectr Heriot-Watt Univ 1967-69; Roughton & Ptnrs: sr engr 1969-75, ptnr 1975-85, md 1985; FICE 1972, FIStruct 1972, M Cons E 1984; *Recreations* horticulture, vinery, equine residue culture; *Clubs* Southampton YC; *Style*— Dr Ian Armstrong; Droxford, Hants; Fulham, London; Grenada, Spain; Roughton & Partners, 321 Millbrook Rd West, Southampton SO1 0HW (☎ 0703 705 533, fax 0703 701 060, telex 477 416 RAPCON G)

ARMSTRONG, Prof Isobel Mair; da of Richard Aneurin Jones (d 1953), and Marjorie, *née* Jackson; *b* 25 March 1937; *Educ* Friends Sch Saffron Walden Essex, Univ of Leicester (BA, PhD); *m* 9 Aug 1961, (John) Michael Armstrong, s of Rev Charles Armstrong (d 1947); 2 s (Thomas b 5 Oct 1968, Stephen b 24 April 1975), 1 da (Ursula b 16 Aug 1971); *Career* post doctoral fell in English Westfield Coll London 1962-63, asst lectr then lectr in English UCL 1963-70, lectr then sr lectr in English Univ of Leicester 1970-79, prof of English Univ of Southampton 1979-89; visiting prof: dept of English Princeton Univ, Breadloaf Sch of English MA prog Middlebury Coll Vermont; prof of English Birkbeck Coll London 1989-; fndr ctee memb Ctee for Univ English, co ed Women: A cultural Review 1988; *Books* incl: Every Man Will Shout (with R Mansfield, 1964), The Major Victorian Poets: Reconsiderations (1969), A Sudden Line (1976), Language as Living Form in Nineteenth Century Poetry (1982), Jane Austen: Mansfield Park (1988): contrib incl: Victorian Poetry (1968), Critical Essays on George Eliot (1970), Augustan Worlds (1978), The Oxford Literary Review (1981), Women Reading Women's Writing (1987), Dickens and Other Victorians (1988); reviews incl: Women's Review (1986), Times Literary Supplement (1986); *Recreations* travel, drawing, writing; *Style*— Prof Isobel Armstrong; 15 Furzedown Rd, Highfield, Southampton SO2 1PN; Department of English, Birkbeck College, Malet St, London WC1E 7HX (☎ 071 631 6324)

ARMSTRONG, James Hodgson; s of John James Armstrong (d 1958), of Carlisle, Cumbria, and Margaret Eleanor, *née* Hodgson (d 1959); *b* 11 May 1926; *Educ* Carlisle GS, Univ of Glasgow (BSc); *m* 18 March 1950, Marjorie, da of Victor Allen Cartner (d 1960); 1 s (Hugh b 1954), 1 da (Jane b 1951); *Career* engr; Duff and Geddes consulting engrs Edinburgh 1946-49, Rendel Palmer and Tritton 1948-54 (Scotland, Tyneside, London), specialist geotechnical engr Soil Mechanics Ltd London 1954-60, Harris and Sutherland conslts 1960-63, design of Cwlth Inst; ptnr Building Design Partnership London 1966-89 (joined 1963); visiting prof: Cooper Union Coll NY, Kingston Poly, Queen's Univ Belfast, Univ of Leeds; past pres IStructE, chm tstees Euro Christian Industl Movement, memb Exec Ctee Higher Educn Fndn, chm Design Cncl Undergraduate Engrg Design Awards Panel, govr St James's Schools Kensington, dir Task Undertakings, memb several professional/educnl ctees; FEng 1990 FICE 1951, FIStructE 1951, MACE, MASCE, FGS, FID, FFB, FRSA, FCollP; *Recreations* philosophy, reading, walking, photography; *Clubs* Reform; *Style*— James Armstrong, Esq; 32 Langford Green, London SE5 8BX (☎ 071 733 6808)

ARMSTRONG, Norman Albert; s of Norman Albert Armstrong (d 1943), of Manchester, and Catherine Ellen, *née* McPhillips (d 1988); *b* 13 Dec 1931; *Educ* St Clare's & St Bede's Coll Manchester; *m* 14 Sept 1966, Maureen Monica, da of Martin Joseph McCarthy (d 1988); 2 s (Norman Michael b 21 Aug 1968, John Patrick b 13 Sept 1974), 1 da (Catrina Marie b 13 Aug 1967); *Career* Nat Serv: Sgt RAF Suez campaign, Singapore, Malaya; articled clerk Styler Fray & Whittingham; ptnr: Harry L Price & Co 1960-86 (joined 1958), Hand & Co Birmingham 1964-86, Ernst & Whinny (following merger) 1986-89, Ernst & Young (following merger); Insolvency Practitioners Assoc: fndr memb 1961, memb Cncl 1964-72 and 1978-85, pres 1970-71, chm Ethics Ctee; fndr INSOL, organised first Int Conf Boston Mass 1982; FCA (ACA 1958), fell Insolvency Practitioners Assoc 1961; *Recreations* travel, sailing; *Clubs* Royal Gibraltar Yacht, Royal Scottish Motor Yacht; *Style*— Norman A Armstrong, Esq; New Gap Farm, Birch, Heywood, Lancaster OL10 2QD (☎ 0706 69164); Ernst & Young, Lowry House, 17 Marble St, Manchester M2 3AW (☎ 061 953 9000, fax 061 834 7117, car 0860 414423)

ARMSTRONG, Dr (Nigel) Paul Ireland; s of (Erwin) Paul Armstrong, of Singapore, and Daphne Diana Brewster, *née* Ireland; *b* 24 Oct 1952; *Educ* Caterham Sch, Univ of Manchester (MB ChB, MD); *m* 4 Sept 1976, Josephine Anne, da of David Dickson, of Altrincham, Cheshire; 1 s (William b 1986), 1 da (Katherine b 1984); *Career* registrar UCH 1981-83, sr registrar London Hosp 1983-87, conslt Central Middx Hosp 1987, hon sr lectr St Mary's Hosp Med Sch 1987-; former chm Victor Bonney Soc; MRCOG 1982; *Recreations* swimming, running, gardening; *Clubs* David Lloyd Sports; *Style*— Dr Paul Armstrong; Portland Hospital, 209 Great Portland St, London W1N 6AH (☎ 071 580 4400)

ARMSTRONG, Robert Walter; s of Frederick Lakin Armstrong (d 1981) of Newmarket, and Maureen, *née* Greenwood (d 1979); *b* 15 Jan 1944; *Educ* Kings Mead, Seaford, Uppingham; *m* 1, 5 Nov 1968 (m dis), Elizabeth, da of Marcus Marsh; m 2, 21 April 1979, Mary Anne (decd), da of Hon David Innes-Kerr; m 3, 18 Nov 1989, Jane Robinson, da of John Roberts; *Career* racehorse trainer; best horses trained: Moorestyle, Never So Bold, Shady Heights, Mujtahid, Be My Native; big races won: Prix du Moulin (Longchamp), July Cup (twice, Newmarket), Prix de la Forêt (twice, Longchamp), Coronation Cup (Epsom), Prix de l'Abbaye (Longchamp), Premio Roma (Rome), Vernons Sprint (Haydock), Lockinge (Newbury), Ribbesdale (Royal Ascot), Great Voltigeur Stakes (York), Gimcrack (York), July Stakes (Goodwood), International Stakes (York), Jersey Stakes (Royal Ascot), Diadem Stakes (Ascot), St Simon Stakes (Newbury), Yorkshire Cup (York), Prix Maurice de Gheest (Deanville); *Recreations* tennis, travel, music, arts, flying, motor racing; *Style*— Robert Armstrong, Esq; St Gatien, Newmarket, Suffolk CB8 8HJ (☎ 0638 663333)

ARMSTRONG, Sir Thomas Henry Wait; s of Amos E Armstrong, BMus, of

Peterborough, Northants; *b* 15 June 1898; *Educ* Choir Sch Chapel Royal, King's Sch Peterborough, Keble Coll Oxford, RCM; *m* 1926, Hester (d 1982), da of Rev William Henry Draper (d 1933); 1 s (*see* Baron Armstrong, of Ilminster), 1 da; *Career* serv WWI; organist Exeter Cathedral 1928-33, organist of Christ Church Oxford 1933-55, univ lectr in Music 1937-54, princ RAM 1955-69; student Christ Church Oxford 1939-55, student emeritus 1955, hon student 1981-; FRCM; kt 1958; *Clubs* Garrick; *Style—* Sir Thomas Armstrong; 1 East St, Olney, Bucks MK46 4AP (☎ 0234 711 364)

ARMSTRONG, William O'Malley; s of Brig Alfred Elliott Armstrong, OBE, MC (d 1956), and Marie Josephine Armstrong; *b* 9 Nov 1938; *Educ* Downside, Merton Coll Cambridge (MA); *m* 23 May 1965, Clare Theresa, da of Bernard Collins, CBE (d 1989), of Foxella Matfield Tonbridge Kent; 2 s (Rowland Constantine O'Malley b 1966, Floriam Claud de Bourneviale b 1971); *Career* Knowledge 1963-65, Purnell's History of the Twentieth Century 1966- 68; md Sidgwick & Jackson 1971; sec Barnsbury Action Gp; *Recreations* squash; *Clubs* Garrick, Sobell Sports; *Style—* William Armstrong, Esq; 16 Lonsdale Square, London N1 1EN; Sidgwick & Jackson Ltd, 1 Tavistock Chambers, Bloomsbury Way, London WC1 (☎ 01 242 6081, telex 8952953 SIDJAK G, fax 01 831 0874)

ARMSTRONG-JONES, Lady Sarah; *see:* HRH Princess Margaret, Countess of Snowdon in *Royal Family Section*

ARMSTRONG OF ILMINSTER, Baron (Life Peer UK 1988), of Ashill, Co Somerset; Sir Robert Temple Armstrong; GCB (1983, KCB 1978, CB 1974), CVO (1975); s of Sir Thomas (Henry Wait) Armstrong, *qv*, and Hester Muriel, *née* Draper (d 1982); *b* 30 March 1927; *Educ* Eton, Ch Ch Oxford; *m* 1953 (m dis 1985), Serena Mary Benedicta, er da of Sir Roger James Ferguson Chance, 3 Bt, MC; 2 da (Hon Jane Orlanda b 1954, Hon Teresa Brigid b 1957); m 2, 1985, (Mary) Patricia, o da of Charles Cyril Carlow (d 1957); *Career* asst sec: Cabinet Office 1964-66, Treasury 1967-68; under sec Treasury 1968-70, pps to PM 1970-75, dep under-sec Home Office 1975-77, permanent under sec 1977-79, sec of the Cabinet 1979-87, head Home Civil Service 1981-87; chm Bd of Tstees V & A 1988-, memb Bd of Dirs Royal Opera House Covent Garden 1988- (sec 1968-87); Liveryman Salters' Co 1983; fellow of Eton 1979; hon student Ch Ch Oxford 1985, Rhodes tstee 1975, hon fellow Royal Acad of Music 1985; hon bencher Inner Temple 1986; *Recreations* music; *Clubs* Athenaeum, Brooks's; *Style—* The Rt Hon the Lord Armstrong of Ilminster, GCB, CVO; House of Lords, Westminster, London SW1

ARMYTAGE, Capt David George; CBE (1981); s of Rear Adm Reginald William Armytage, GC, CBE (d 1984), and Sylvia Beatrice, *née* Staveley; cous and hp of Sir Martin Armytage, 9 Bt; *b* 4 Sept 1929; *m* 3 April 1954, Countess Antonia Cosima, er da of Count Cosimo Diodono de Bosdari, and his w Enid, o da of Lt-Col Sir Peter Carlaw Walker, 2 Bt; 2 s (Hugh b 1955, Charles b 1962), 1 da (Davina b 1956); *Career* Capt RN; cmdg HMS Minerva 1968-70, Def Policy Staff 1970-72, Naval Asst to 1 Sea Lord 1972-74, cmd 7 Frigate Sqdn 1976-77, dep dir Naval Warfare 1977-79, Cdre cmdg Standing Naval Force Atlantic 1980-81, sec gen BDA 1981-91, ADC 1981; *Recreations* sailing, shooting; *Clubs* Oriental; *Style—* Capt David Armytage, CBE, RN; Sharcott Manor, Pewsey, Wilts

ARMYTAGE, Lady; (Maria) Margarete; da of Paul Hugo Tenhaeff, of Bruenen, Niederhein; *m* 1949, as his 2 w, Capt Sir John Lionel Armytage, 8 Bt (d 1983); 1 da; *Style—* Margarete, Lady Armytage; The Priory Garden, Kirklees Park, Brighouse, W Yorkshire

ARMYTAGE, Sir (John) Martin; 9 Bt (GB 1738), of Kirklees, Yorkshire; s of Capt Sir John Lionel Armytage, 8 Bt (d 1983), and Evelyn Mary Jessamine, *née* Fox; *b* 26 Feb 1933; *Educ* Eton; *Heir* cousin, Capt David George Armytage, CBE, RN, *qv*; *Style—* Sir Martin Armytage, Bt; Halewell, Withington, Cheltenham, Glos

ARNANDER, Christopher James Folke; s of Per Erik Arnander (d 1933), and Cynthia Anne, *née* Lindsay; *b* 22 Dec 1932; *Educ* Harrow, Oriel Coll Oxford (MA); *m* 7 April 1961, Pamela Primrose, da of David McKenna, CBE; 3 s (Conrad b 1963, Michael b 1964, Magnus b 1970), 1 da (Katharine b 1967); *Career* lectr Univ of Minnesota (USA) 1956-57, Hill Samuel Merchant Bankers 1958-65, Williams & Glyn's Bank 1965-73 (dir 1970), financial exec in Kuwait 1973-79, chief advsr Riyad Bank Saudi Arabia 1979-85, dir Barclays de Zoete Wedd 1985-; memb: Glyndebourne Arts Tst 1964-73 (cncl 1973-), cncllr RCM 1987-, treas Nat Assoc for Care & Resettlement of Offenders 1967-73; *Recreations* music, sports, reading, travel; *Style—* Christopher Arnander, Esq; Barclays de Zoete Wedd, Ebbgate House, 2 Swan Lane, London, EC4R 3TS, (☎ 01 623 2323 fax 8951518)

ARNELL, Richard Anthony Sayer; s of Richard Sayer Arnell (d 1952), and Hélène Marie Ray Scherf (d 1942); *b* 15 Sept 1917; *Educ* Hall Sch, Univ Coll Sch, RCM; *m* 1981, Audrey Millar Paul; 3 da (Jessie, Claudine, Jennifer); *Career* composer, conductor, film maker; princ lectr Trinity Coll of Music 1981- (teacher of composition 1949-81), music conslt BBC N American Serv 1943-46, lectr Roy Ballet Sch 1958-59, ed The Composer 1961-64; chm: Composers' Guild of GB 1965, 1974-75, Jt Ctee Songwriters' and Composers' Guilds 1977-, Young Musicians' Symphony Orch Soc 1973-75; visiting lectr (Fullbright Exchange) Bowdoin Coll Maine 1967-68, visiting prof Hofstra Univ NY 1968-70, music dir and bd memb London Int Film Sch 1975- (chm Film Sch Tst 1981-), music dir Ram Filming Ltd 1980-, dir Organic Sounds Ltd 1982-, Composer of the Year 1966 (Music Teachers Assoc award); compositions include: 5 symphonies, 2 concertos for violin, concerto for harpsichord, concerto for piano, 5 string quartets, 2 quintets, piano trio, piano work, songs, cantatas, organ work, music for string orchestra, wind ensembles, brass ensembles, song cycles, electronic music; opera: Love in Transit, Moonflowers; ballet scores: Punch and the Child for Ballet Soc NY 1947, Harlequin in April for Arts Cncl 1951, The Great Detective for Sadler's Wells Theatre Ballet 1953, The Angels for Royal Ballet 1957, Giselle (Adam) reorchestrated for Ballet Rambert 1965; film scores: The Land 1941, The Third Secret 1963, The Visit 1964, The Man Outside 1966, Topsail Schooner 1966, Bequest for a Village 1969, Second Best 1972, Stained Glass 1973, Wires over the Border 1974, Black Panther 1977, Antagonist 1980, Dilemma 1981; other works: Symphonic Portrait Lord Byron for Sir Thomas Beecham 1953, Landscapes and Figures for Sir Thomas Beecham 1956, Petrified Princess puppet operetta for BBC 1959, Robert Flaherty Impression for Radio Eireann 1960, Musica Pacifica for Edward Benjamin 1963, Festival Flourish for Salvation Army 1965, 2nd piano concerto for RPO 1967, Overture Food of Love for Portland Symphony Orch 1968, My Lady Green Sleeves for Hofstra Univ 1968, Nocturne Prague 1968, I Think of All Soft Limbs for Canadian Broadcasting Corpn 1971, Astronaut One 1973, Life Boat Voluntary for RNLI 1974, Call for LPO 1982, Ode to Beecham for RPO 1986; hon fellow Trinity Coll of Music London (FTCL); *Clubs* Savage; *Style—* Richard Arnell, Esq; 149 Shenley Rd, Borehamwood, Herts WD6 1AH (☎ 01 953 7572); London Int Film Sch, 24 Shelton St, London WC2 (☎ 01 240 0168)

ARNEY, David Barrie; s of Frank Douglas Arney, CBE (d 1983), of Bristol, and Mildred Winifred, *née* Dallin (d 1982); *b* 21 Oct 1933; *Educ* Bristol GS; *m* 25 Aug 1956, Patricia Esme, da of James Edwin Webb (d 1977), of Bristol; 2 da (Louise b 1961, Alison b 1966); *Career* dir: Warwickshire Oil Storage Ltd 1982-89, Bristol Oil Storage Ltd 1988-89, Texaco (UK) Ltd 1984-89; mangr gp ops Texaco Ltd 1987-89, ret; *Recreations* shooting, fishing, golf; *Style—* David B Arney, Esq; 6 Oldbury Grove, Knotty Green, Beaconsfield, Bucks HP9 2AJ (☎ 04946 6847); Texaco Ltd, 195 Knightsbridge, London SW1X 7QJ (telex : 8956681)

ARNISON, Val (Mrs Arthur Brittenden); da of Thomas Arnison, of Wargrave, Berks, and Vera, *née* Christian; *b* 30 Aug 1940; *Educ* Lowther Coll Abergele N Wales; *m* 24 Oct 1975, (Charles) Arthur Brittenden, s of Tom Edwin Brittenden (d 1926); *Career* press and PR offr ICI Ltd 1970-79, asst vice pres and dir PR AMI Health Care Ltd 1982-87, assoc dir Countrywide Communications 1988-; pres Assoc of Women in PR 1978-79 (memb 1975-), memb Foreign Press Assoc 1982-, exec chm Women of the Year Luncheon 1987-89 (memb); MIPR; *Recreations* gardening, reading, music, needlepoint; *Clubs* New Cavendish, RSM; *Style—* Miss Val Arnison; Countrywide Communications, Countrywide Hse, West Bar, Banbury, Oxfordshire (☎ 0295 272 288, fax 0295 270 659)

ARNOLD, Adrian Dawson Bernard; s of Adrian Joseph Arnold (d 1963), and Susan, *née* Dawson Miller; *b* 4 Aug 1947; *Educ* Winchester, Univ Coll Oxford (MA); *Career* Lancing Coll head of classics 1986- (former sr tutor 1982-); chm Sussex Classics Assoc; Liveryman Worshipful Co of Skinners (1983); *Style—* Adrian Arnold, Esq; The Common Room, Lancing Coll, Sussex

ARNOLD, Lt Cdr David John; s of Frank Thomas Arnold, of Rowfold Farm House, Slinfold, Sussex, and Mary Cecily Arnold; *b* 4 June 1939; *Educ* Collyers Sch Horsham, Thames Nautical Trg Coll, HMS Worcester, Univ of London, Univ of Sussex (MA); *m* 17 March 1967, Andrea Damita, da of Carl Georgeff, OBE, of 16 Strathern Kings Park Ave, Crawley, Perth, 6009 W Aust; 2 s (William David Carl b 20 Jan 1970, Henry Michael George b 20 Nov 1977), 1 da (Dianne Katharine Damita b 29 Nov 1972); *Career* Sub Lt RNR 1961, served on minesweepers and submarines, Lt RNR 1964, extra master mariner 1965, navigator nuclear submarine HMS Valiant 1968-69, Lt Cdr RNR 1969, ret 1971; fin dir then chm All Precision Industries 1971-85, chief exec Br Americas Cup Challenges plc 1985-88, md Blue Strip Corp Ltd 1985-, chief exec Yeoman Marine Ltd 1988-; 7 times memb Br Admirals Cup team; once memb: Br Southern Cross team, Br Americas Cup team; co cnllr W Sussex CC 1973-85, memb Southern Water Bd 1980-89, chief race offr Royal Thames YC 1987-; MBIM 1967, FInstD 1984, MInst Navigation 1988; *Books* Tides and Currents (1984); *Recreations* ocean racing, sailing, flying; *Clubs* Royal Thames Yacht, Royal Ocean Racing; *Style—* Lt Cdr David Arnold; Westbrook Hall, Broadbridge Heath, Horsham, W Sussex RH12 3PT (☎ 0403 790168); Yeoman Marine Ltd, Lynchborough Rd, Passfield, Hants GU30 7RN (☎ 0428 77 585, fax 0428 77 405, telex 858593, car 0860 732903)

ARNOLD, David Philip James; s of Philip Arthur Arnold (d 1988), and Christine May, *née* Rowe; *b* 13 Aug 1955; *Educ* Merchant Taylors, Univ of Exeter; *m* 19 Aug 1978, Carol Alice, da of Arthur George Edward Williams (d 1973); 1 da (Kirsten b 7 Feb 1986); *Career* CA; ptnr Ernst & Young 1988; Freeman City of London 1976, Liveryman Worshipful Co of Fishmongers 1982; ICAEW 1979; *Recreations* hockey, squash; *Clubs* City Livery; *Style—* David Arnold, Esq; Ernst & Young, Becket House, 1 Lambeth Palace Rd, London SE1 7EU (☎ 01 928 2000, fax 01 928 1345, telex 885234)

ARNOLD, Brig Giles Geoffrey; CBE; s of Arthur Cecil Arnold, of London, and Ena Genevieve, *née* Jeffree; *b* 10 Jan 1938; *Educ* Westminster, RMA Sandhurst; *Career* cmd 7 Regt RHA 1979-81, mil asst to Cdr Northern Army Gp 1981-84, CRA 2 Inf Div 1984-86, dep cdr Br Forces Hong Kong 1988-90; memb RCDS 1987; ADC 1990; *Recreations* skiing, sailing, shooting; *Clubs* Naval and Military, Royal Artillery Yacht; *Style—* Brig Giles Arnold, CBE; Commandant, Royal School of Artillery, Wiltshire SP4 8QT

ARNOLD, Jacques Arnold; MP (C) Gravesham 1987-; s of Samuel Arnold (d 1985), and Eugenie, *née* Patentine; *b* 27 Aug 1947; *Educ* sch in Brazil, LSE; *m* 22 May 1976, Patricia Anne, da of Dennis Maunder, of Windsor, Berks; 1 s (David Samuel b 1984), 2 da (Hazel Jane b 1979, Philippa Rachel b 1981); *Career* asst gp rep Midland Bank Brazil 1976-78, regnl dir Thomas Cook Gp 1978-84, asst trade fin dir Midland Bank 1984-85, dir American Express Europe Ltd 1985-87; currently: memb Educn, Sci and Arts Select Ctee, sec Cons Backbench Foreign and Cwlth Affrs Ctee, sec Br Latin American Parly Gp, tstee the Environment Fedn; ccncllr Oundle 1981-85; *Style—* Jacques A Arnold, Esq, MP; Fairlawn, 243 London Rd, West Malling, Kent ME19 5AD (☎ 0732 848573); House of Commons, London SW1A 0AA (☎ 071 219 4150)

ARNOLD, James Ronald Matthew; s of Capt Ronald M Arnold (d 1981), of Abington, Northampton, and K Sheila, *née* Chamberlain; *b* 15 Jan 1938; *Educ* Eaglehurst Sch Northampton, Northampton GS; *Career* slr 1960; articled clerk to Mr (now Lord) Boardman, fndr memb Agric Law Assoc, memb Conseil de Direction Comité Europeen de Droit Rural, head Agric Dept Shoosmiths & Harrison, lectr on agric taxation and tenancy law; Notary Public 1971; memb Law Soc 1960; *Recreations* travel, gardening; *Clubs* Northampton and County; *Style—* James Arnold, Esq; Park House, Towcester Northamptons; Shoesmiths & Harrison, 205 Watling St West, Towcester, Northamptons (☎ 0327 50266, fax 0327 53567)

ARNOLD, Prof John André; s of Capt André Eugene Arnold (d 1974), and May, *née* Vickers (d 1977); *b* 30 April 1944; *Educ* Haberdashers' Aske's, LSE (MSc); *m* 11 Jan 1975, Lynne Mary, da of Frederic Reaney Burgess, of Prestbury Cheshire; 2 da (Kate Lynne b 1976, Mandy Louise b 1978); *Career* teaching fell Mgmnt Studies LSE 1967-69; lectr in accounting: Univ of Kent 1969-71, Univ of Manchester 1971-75; prof of accounting Univ of Manchester 1977-86 (sr lectr 1975-77); visiting prof Univ of Washington USA 1981-82; Peat Marwick McLintock prof of accounting Univ of Manchester 1986- (dean Faculty of Econ and Social Studies 1987-89, pro-vice chllr 1990-); dir of res ICAEW 1987-; vice pres Manchester Soc CAs 1989-90 (dep pres 1990-91); Hon MA (Econ) Univ of Manchester; FCA 1967; *Books* Pricing and Output Decisions (1973), Topics in Management Accounting (1980), Accounting for Management Decisions (1983, 2nd edn 1990), Management Accounting Research and Practice (1983), Financial Accounting (1985), Management Accounting: British Case Studies (1987), Managment Accounting: Expanding the Horizons (1987) Financial Reporting: The Way Forward (1990); *Recreations* squash, opera; *Clubs* Marple Cricket & Squash; *Style—* Prof John Arnold; Department of Accounting & Finance, University of Manchester, Manchester, M13 9PL (☎ 061 275 4010, fax 061 275 4023)

ARNOLD, John Irwin Ernest; s of Dr John Irwin Arnold (d 1973), of Southport, and Christina, *née* Henderson; *b* 12 March 1919; *Educ* Manchester GS, Huddersfield Coll, Lincoln's Inn; *m* 13 March 1988, Edith Philippine Hildegard, da of Doctor Franz Hanser (d 1950), of Graz Austria; *Career* RCS WWII 1939-46 served: France and Belgium 1940, Middle East 1940-43, Egypt, Greece, Crete, N Africa, Sicily, Italy, Europe 1944-45; called to the Bar Lincolns Inn 1949; pt/t chm Industl Tbnls 1966-, dep circuit judge 1972-84, asst Parly boundary cmmr 1978-82, pt/t adjudicator immigration appeals 1980-; *Recreations* music, art, architecture, travel, photography; *Style—* John Arnold, Esq; Arley House, Thornhill Rd, Edgerton, Huddersfield HD3 3DD (☎ 0484 424812); 42 Bank St, Sheffield S1 1EE (☎ 0742 751223)

ARNOLD, Rt Hon Mr Justice; Rt Hon Sir John Lewis; PC (1979); s of Alfred Lewis Arnold (d 1917), of London, and E K Arnold; *b* 6 May 1915; *Educ* Wellington; *m* 1, 1940 (m dis 1963), Alice Margaret Dorothea, da of George Cookson (d 1949), of Thursley, Surrey; 1 s, 1 da; m 2, 1963, Florence Elizabeth, da of H M Hague, of Montreal; 1 s, 2 da; *Career* served WW II (despatches); barr Middle Temple 1937,

QC 1958, chm Bar Cncl 1970-72, High Court judge (Family Div) 1972-, pres Family Div 1979-, treas of Middle Temple for 1982; Hon DLitt Reading 1982; kt 1972; *Style*— The Rt Hon Mr Justice Arnold; 6 Pump Court, London EC4 (☎ 01 583 0573); Royal Courts of Justice, London WC2 (☎ 01 936 6189)

ARNOLD, The Very Rev John Robert; s of John Stanley Arnold (d 1977), of Rowan Cottage, Laleham, Middx, and Ivy, *née* Ireland (d 1981); *b* 1 Nov 1933; *Educ* Christ's Hosp, Sidney Sussex Coll Cambridge (MA), Westcott House; *m* 29 Sept 1963, Livia Anneliese, da of Capt Ernst Konrad Franke (d 1944), of Eisleben, Sachsen-Anhalt, Germany; 1 s (Matthew b 1965), 2 da (Frances b 1964, Miriam b 1972); *Career* Nat Serv Intelligence 1952-54, 2 Lt Civil Serv Cmmn Serv Interpreter Cert 1954; ordained: deacon 1960, priest 1961; curate Holy Trinity Millhouses Sheffield 1960-63, Sir Henry Stephenson fell Univ of Sheffield 1962-63, chaplain and lectr Univ of Southampton 1963-72, sec Bd for Mission and Unity 1972-78; dean of: Rochester 1978-89, Durham 1989-; pres and vice chm Conf of Euro Churches 1986-, dir First Conference Estate plc 1978-; chm of Govrs Durham Bow and Chorister Schs 1989-, memb Cncl Univ of Durham 1989-; Order of St Vladimir (Russian Orthodox Church) 1974; *Books* The Eucharistic Liturgy of Taizé (trans, 1962), Strategist for the Spirit (contrib, 1985), Rochester Cathedral (1987); *Recreations* music, literature; *Style*— The Very Rev John Arnold; The Deanery, Durham DH1 3EQ (☎ 091 384 7500)

ARNOLD, Rt Rev Keith Appleby; *b* 1 Oct 1926; *Educ* Winchester, Trinity Coll Cambridge (MA); *m* 9 May 1955, (Deborah) Noreen, da of Thomas Glenwright, of Haltwhistle; 1 s (Jonathan b 1960), 1 da (Judith b 1956); *Career* Coldstream Gds 1945-48, Lt 1946, Actg Capt 1947; curate: Haltwhistle Northumberland 1952-55, St John's Church Edinburgh 1955-61 (rector 1962-69); vicar Kirkby Lonsdale 1969-73, rector and rural dean Hemel Hempstead 1973-80; bishop suffragan of Warwick 1980-90; pres S Warwicks Marriage Guidance Cncl, vice pres Abbeyfield Soc, chm English Villages Housing Assoc; *Recreations* skiing, gardening; *Clubs* Royal Commonwealth; *Style*— The Rt Rev Keith Arnold; White Lodge, Dunstan, nr Alnwick, Northumberland NE66 3TB (☎ 0665 76485

ARNOLD, Malcolm; s of Colin William Arnold (d 1987), of Northwich, Cheshire, and Jane, *née* Powell; *b* 4 April 1940; *Educ* Verdin GS Winsford Cheshire, Loughborough Univ; *m* Madelyn, *née* Morrissey; 1 s (Andrew b 20 Jan 1966), 1 da (Helen b 26 Sept 1964); *Career* athletics coach; dir of coaching Uganda 1968-72, nat athetics coach BAAB 1974-; coach to Olympic teams: Uganda 1968 and 1972, GB and NI 1980, 1984, 1988; coach to: John Akii-Bua (Olympic 400m hurdles champion 1972, world record holder 1972-76), Colin Jackson (Olympic 110m hurdles Silver medal 1988, Cwlth and Euro champion 1990), Kay Morley (Cwlth 110m hurdles champion 1990), numerous Br int athletes *Publications* author of six athletics books; *Recreations* rally driver of enthusiasm but no distinction; *Style*— Malcolm Arnold, Esq; 56 Rolls Avenue, Penpedairheol, Hengoed, Mid Glamorgan CF8 8HQ (☎ 0443 832186, fax 0443 822291)

ARNOLD, Dr Malcolm; CBE (1970); s of William and Annie Arnold, of Northampton; *b* 21 Oct 1921; *Educ* RCM; *m* 1, 1942, Sheila, da of Herbert Nicholson; 1 s, 1 da; m 2, 1963, Isobel Katherine, da of David Inglis Wood Gray; 1 s; *Career* composer; princ trumpet London Philharmonic Orchestra 1942-44 and 1946-48; Ivor Novello for music for Inn of Sixth Happiness 1952, awarded Oscar for music for film Bridge on the River Kwai 1957, bard of Cornish Gorsedd 1969, All Music Composer of the Year 1987; hon Freedom of the Borough of Northampton 1989; Hon DMus: Exeter 1969, Durham 1982, Leicester 1984; Hon RAM; Ivor Novello Award for Outstanding Services to British Music 1986; Hon D Arts and Humane Letters Miami Univ Ohio 1990; FRCM 1983; *Style*— Dr Malcolm Arnold, CBE; 26 Springfields, Attleborough, Norfolk NR17 2PA

ARNOLD, Michael; s of Dr Alan George Arnold (d 1990), and Kathleen, *née* McGuirk (d 1947); *b* 16 Sept 1947; *Educ* Royal Wolverhampton Sch Univ of Reading (BSc); *m* 8 April 1972, Pauline Ann, da of Berwyn Elvet Pritchard; 2 s (David Paul b 4 July 1975, Stuart Michael b 12 May 1978); *Career* actuarial trainee Prudential Assurance Co Ltd 1969-71; Hymans Robertson & Co: joined as actuarial trainee 1971, ptnr 1974, jt sr ptnr; memb Cncl Inst of Actuaries; memb Worshipful Co of Actuaries 1985; FIA 1973; *Recreations* golf, travel; *Clubs* City Livery, Kingswood Golf, Epsom Golf, RAC; *Style*— Michael Arnold, Esq; Hymans Robertson & Co 190 Fleet St, London EC4A 2AH (☎ 071 831 9561, fax 071 831 6800)

ARNOLD, Michael John; s of Thomas Henry Arnold, and Cecily May Arnold; *b* 1 April 1935; *m* 21 Jan 1989, Jane, *née* Benson; *Career* Nat Serv Lt RA 1958-59; Hilton Sharpe & Clark 1951-57, qualified CA 1957, chm AY Management Consultants 1973-83, nat dir Corporate Recovery and Insolvency 1975-89, sole practitioner 1989-, conslt to Electra Kingsway Limited on corp restructuring and recoveries 1990-; hon treas Youth Clubs UK, memb Cncl Racehorse Owners Assoc; FCA, FIMC, FIPA; *Recreations* horse racing, hunting, country; *Clubs* Turf; *Style*— Michael Arnold, Esq; 42 Addison Avenue, London W11 4QP (☎ 071 603 3557, 071 404 8937, fax 071 404 8076)

ARNOLD, (James) Olav; s of Edmund Arnold (d 1954), of Leeds, and (Gjertrude) Marie Mathilde Ravn, *née* Bredal; *b* 18 Oct 1928; *Educ* Stowe, Clare Coll Cambridge (MA); *m* 1, 10 July 1956, Jacqueline Anne Nina (d 1977), da of Harry Wingate (d 1982), of London; 1 s (Christopher b 1960), 2 da (Karen b 1958, Rachel b 1962); m 2, 1 April 1978, Elizabeth Lenwood, da of Prof Roger Wilson, of Yealand Conyers, Carnforth, Lancashire; *Career* Rifle Bde, 2 Lt Green Howards 1947-49; dep md and dep chm E J Arnold & Son Ltd Education Publishers and Suppliers 1952-84, pres Leeds & Holbeck Bldg Soc 1983-85 (dir 1978), chm Leeds Western Dist Health Authy 1986-88; pres: Br Printing Inds Fedn 1977-78, Leeds C of C and Indust 1982-86; govr Leeds Poly 1978-87; chm: Leeds Civic Tst 1983-, Scarcroft Borough Cncl 1974-84; *Recreations* golf, tennis, fishing, painting, music, gardening; *Clubs* Lansdowne, Leeds; *Style*— Olav Arnold, Esq; Manor Close, Thorner Lane, Scarcroft, Leeds LS14 3AL (☎ 0532 892 314)

ARNOLD, (Clifford) Roy; s of Sydney Howard Arnold, and Edna May, *née* Davis; *b* 15 Nov 1932; *m* 22 June 1957, Doreen Margaret, da of William James Davies (d 1976), of Birmingham; 2 s (Stephen b 1962, James b 1964), 2 da (Sally b 1961, Alison b 1970); *Career* Bombadier RA 1957-1958; chief accountant Fulton (TI) Ltd 1970-74, dir Fletcher Homes 1979-, company sec Fletcher Estates 1979-; memb: Exec Ctee Shifnal Town FC, Shifnal (C) Assoc, Shifnal Town Cncl (chm fin ctee 1987-88); FCA; *Recreations* skiing (Alpine), walking, squash; *Clubs* Shifnal Squash, Midlands Ski; *Style*— Roy Arnold, Esq; 18 Vicarage Drive, Shifnal, Shropshire TF11 9AF (☎ 0952 460 635); 95 Mount Pleasant Rd, Shrewsbury SY1 3EL (☎ 0743 236 622)

ARNOLD, Sheila May; da of John Millar Arnold (d 1949), and Mabel, *née* Walker (d 1951); *b* 24 May 1930; *Educ* Royal Coll of Surgns of Ireland (LPCP, LPCS); *m* 4 April 1955, Thomas Matthew Maguire, s of Philip Francis Maguire (d 1932); 2 da (Ailsa Catherine b 1965, Kim Caroline b 1970); *Career* house surgn and physician Richmond Hosp Dublin 1954-55; sr house surgn: Kent and Sussex Hosp 1956, Derbys Royal Infirmary 1957, Newcastle Royal Infirmary 1959; personal physician and surgn to Pres Kwame Nkruma Ghana Med Serv investigating deafness in village children 1959-62, St Mary Abotts Hosp London 1963, sr registrar Guy's and Lewisham Hosps 1970-73, sr conslt ENT surgn Frimley Park Hosp Surrey 1973-; memb: Regnl Med Advsy ctee, Br Soc of Otolaryngologists; LRCP, LRCS 1954, DLO 1961, FRCS 1973, MRSM; *Books* The Vulnerability of the Chorda Tympani Nerve & Middle Ear Disease (paper, 1973); *Recreations* badminton, skiing, swimming, foreign travel, squash; *Style*— Miss Sheila Arnold; Robin Hill, 18 Murdoch Rd, Wokingham, Berks RG11 2DE (☎ 0734 787027); Frimley Park Hosp, Portsmouth Rd, Frimley, Surrey GU16 5UJ (☎ 0276 692777)

ARNOLD, Simon Rory; s of Rory Watkin Williams Arnold (d 1950), and Rosemary Arnold (d 1948); *b* 10 Sept 1933; *Educ* Diocesan Coll S Africa; *m* 1960, Janet Linda, da of Peter J May (d 1980); 1 s (Guy Rory b 1964), 1 da (Clare Louise b 1963); *Career* Lt Duke of Wellington's Regt 1957-59; various directorships with Minet Holdings 1952-84 (dep chm and gp md 1982); chm and chief exec: Bain Dawes plc 1986- (chief exec 1984-), Bain Clarkson Ltd 1987; dir Inchcape plc 1988-; memb Cncl of Lloyds 1991; *Recreations* tennis, golf, walking; *Clubs* Royal Ashdown Golf; *Style*— Simon R Arnold, Esq; Meadows, Ditchling Common, Ditchling, Hassocks, W Sussex (☎ 079 18 4246); 15 Minories, London EC3N 1NJ (☎ 071 481 3232, fax 480 6137, telex 8813411)

ARNOLD, Sue; da of Morny McHarg, and Marjorie James; *Educ* Elmhurst Ballet Sch Camberley, Trinity Coll Dublin (MA); *m* twice; 6 c; *Career* journalist: Lancashire Evening Telegraph Blackburn 1967-68, Evening Standard 1968-69, Tehran Jl 1969-70, The Observer 1970-; *Awards* commended Magazine Writer Br Press awards 1982, Magazine Writer of the Year 1983; *Books* Little Princes (1981), Curiouser & Curiouser (1984); *Recreations* Housewifery; *Clubs* Chelsea Arts; *Style*— Ms Sue Arnold; The Observer, Chelsea Bridge House, Queenstown Rd, Battersea, London (☎ 071 627 0700)

ARNOLD, Sir Thomas Richard; MP (C) Hazel Grove 1974-; s of Thomas Charles Arnold (d 1969), of London, and Helen, *née* Breen; *b* 25 Jan 1947; *Educ* Bedales, Le Rosey, Pembroke Coll Oxford (MA); *m* 4 July 1984, Elizabeth Jane, da of Henry Nevile, of Aubourn Hall, Lincoln, and wid of Robin Smithers; 1 da (Emily b 29 Dec 1986); *Career* theatre prod and publisher; contested (C) Manchester Cheetham 1970, Hazel Grove Feb 1974; pps to: Sec of State for NI 1979-81, Lord Privy Seal/FCO 1981-82; vice-chm Cons Pty 1983-; Freeman City of London, Liveryman of Worshipful Co of Bakers; kt 1990; *Clubs* Carlton, RAC; *Style*— Sir Thomas Arnold, MP; House of Commons, London SW1A 0AA (☎ 071 219 4096)

ARNOLD-BAKER, Prof Charles; OBE (1966); s of Baron Albrecht von Blumenthal, and Alice Wilhelmine, *née* Hainsworth; *b* 25 June 1918; *Educ* Winchester, Magdalen Coll Oxford; *m* 1943, Edith, *née* Woods; 1 s, 1 da; *Career* serv WWII Army Inf and War Off 1940-46; called to the Bar 1948; sec Nat Assoc of Local Cncls 1953-78, memb Royal Cmmn on Common Lands 1955-58; dep chm: Eastern Traffic Cmmrs 1978-90, E Midlands Traffic Cmmrs 1981-86; conslt lectr City Univ 1978-83 (visiting prof 1983-); author and occasional broadcaster; King Haakon VII Freedom medal (Norway) 1946; *Books* The Local Government Act (1972), The Local Government, Planning and Land Act (1980), Local Council Administration (6 ed 1989), The Five Thousand: The Living Constitution (1986); *Recreations* travel; *Clubs* Oxford Union; *Style*— Prof Charles Arnold-Baker, OBE; Top Floor, 2 Paper Buildings, Inner Temple, London EC4 (☎ 071 353 3490)

ARNOLD-BROWN, Adam Sebastian; s of Lt-Col Robert Arnold Brown, MC (d 1945), of Wrotham, Kent, and Mildred Kerry, *née* Brown (d 1966); *b* 6 April 1919; *Educ* Gordonstoun, Trinity Coll Cambridge (BA, MA); *m* 23 July 1949, Jane Leonora, da of Prof Eric Reginald Vincent, CBE (d 1978); 3 da (Siena Laura Joy (Mrs Gold) b 1950, Sheila May (Mrs Churchill) b 1954, Catherine Anne (Mrs Patterson) b 1956); *Career* Nat Serv Seaforth Highlanders 1939-40, Lt and Capt RSF 1940-46; first warden Outward Bound Mountain Sch Eskdale 1949-53, asst master Canford Sch Wimborne Dorset 1953-55; headmaster: Hyderabad Sch Hy Deccan India 1955-58, Kings Choir Sch Cambridge 1958-59, Hazeldene Sch Salcombe Devon 1961-65; asst master Dartington Hall Totnes Devon 1960-61; picture framer and dealer A-B Gallery Salcombe Devon 1965-; memb Ctee S Hams Amenity Soc 1966-68; memb RGS 1949; *Books* Unfolding Character - The Impact of Gordonstoun (1961); *Recreations* formerly tennis, skiing, currently wind-surfing, swimming; *Clubs* RAC; *Style*— Adam Arnold-Brown, Esq; Spindrift, Sandhills Rd, Salcombe, Devon TQ8 8JP (☎ 0548 54 2728); A-B Gallery, 67 Fore St, Salcombe, Devon TQ8 8BU (☎ 0548 54 2764)

ARNOLD-FORSTER, Hon Mrs (Valentine Harriet Isobel Dione); *née* Mitchison; da of Baron Mitchison, CBE, QC (Life Peer; d 1970), and Naomi Mitchison, the authoress; *Educ* Somerville Coll Oxford (BA); *m* 1955, Mark Arnold-Forster (b 16 April 1920, o s of William Edward Arnold-Forster; he is 15 in descent from Robert Maskelynge who was presented, as a freeholder of the manor of Lydiard Milisent, at a court of Henry VI held 5 April 1457); 3 s, 2 da; *Style*— The Hon Mrs Arnold-Forster; 50 Clarendon Rd, London W11

ARNOTT, Sir Alexander John Maxwell; 6 Bt (UK) 1896, of Woodlands, St Anne, Shandon, Co Cork; s of Sir John Arnott, 5 Bt (d 1981); *b* 18 Sept 1975; *Heir* bro, Andrew John Eric Arnott b 20 June 1978; *Style*— Sir Alexander Arnott, Bt; 11 Palmerston Road, Dublin

ARNOTT, Lady; Ann Margaret; da of Terence Alphonsus Farrelly, of Kilcar, Co Cavan; *b* 21 Dec 1942; *Educ* Bridlington High Sch, Cheltenham Ladies Coll, Somerville Coll, Oxford; *m* 1974, Sir John Arnott, 5 Bt (d 1981); 2 s; *Clubs* Univ Womens'; *Style*— Lady Arnott; 11 Palmerston Road, Dublin

ARNOTT, Eric John; s of Capt Sir Robert Arnott, 4 Bt (d 1967), of Ounavarra, Lucan, Co Dublin, Ireland, and Cynthia Anita Amelia, *née* James (d 1948); *b* 12 June 1929; *Educ* Harrow, Trinity Coll Dublin (BA, MB BCh, BAO), Univ of London (DO); *m* 19 Nov 1960, Veronica Mary, da of Capt Arvid Langué Querfeld von der Seedeck (d 1986), of Hazel Bank, Sandy Lane, Hartley, Wintney, Hants; 2 s (Stephen John b 1962, Robert Lauriston John b 1971), 1 da (Tatiana Amelia b 1963); *Career* house offr Adelaide Hosp Dublin 1954-55, registrar Royal Victoria Eye and Ear Hosp Dublin 1956-57, resident offr (later sr resident offr) Moorfields Eye Hosp London 1959-61, sr registrar UCH 1962-65; conslt ophthalmologist: Royal Eye Hosp 1966-72, Charing Cross Hosp and Charing Cross Gp of Hosps 1967-; hon conslt opthalmologist Royal Masonic Hosp 1970-, reader Univ of London 1972-; pres and fndr Euro Soc for Phaco and Laser Surgery, former examiner Br Orthoptic Cncl; pioneer of phacoemulsification in Europe 1968-75, designer intraocular lens implants 1976-; FRCS 1963; FCOphth 1988; *Books* Emergency Surgery (jtly, 1977), Cataract Extraction and Lens Implantation (jtly, 1983), Phacoemulsification (contrib, 1988); *Recreations* swimming, golf; *Clubs* Kildare St (Dublin), Garrick; *Style*— Eric Arnott, Esq; Trottsford Farm, Headley, nr Bordon, Hampshire GU35 8TF (☎ 042 047 2136); 11 Milford House, 7 Queen Anne St, London W1M 9FD (☎ 071 580 1074, fax 071 255 1524)

ARNOTT, (William) Geoffrey; s of Bertie Arnott (d 1975), of Bury Lancs, and Edith May *née* Smith (d 1982); *b* 17 Sept 1930; *Educ* Bury GS, Pembroke Coll Cambridge (MA, PhD); *m* 20 Aug 1955, Vera, da of Wilfrid Hodson (d 1934), of Greenmount, nr Bury, Lancashire; 3 da (Rosemary, Alisonk, Hilary); *Career* asst master Bristol GS 1952, asst lectr in Greek Bedford Coll Univ of London 1955-59, asst dir of examinations Civil Serv Cmmn 1959-60, asst lectr in classics Univ of Hull 1960-61; lectr in classics: Univ of Durham 1961-63, Univ of Newcastle upon Tyne 1963-66; sr lectr in classics Univ of Newcastle upon Tyne 1966-67, prof of Greek Univ of Leeds

1968-; memb Inst for Advanced Studies Priceton USA 1973, visiting foreign scholar Univ of British Columbia Vancouver 1982; visiting prof: Univ of Wellington NZ 1982, Univ of Alexandria Egypt 1983, Univ of Queensland 1987; visiting fell Gonville and Caius Coll Cambridge 1987-88; memb Classical Jls Bd 1970-, govr St Peter's Sch York 1971-83, lectr for NADFAS 1979-, memb Ed Bd of Texts and Commentaries Univs of London and Urbino 1980 -, pres Leeds Birdwatchers Club 1981-84; fell Italian Soc for Study of Classical Antiquity 1981; *Books* Menander's Dyskolos (translated, 1960), Menander Plautus Terence (1975), Menander vol I (1979); *Recreations* birdwatching, 19th century bird-painting, crosswords, photography; *Style—* Prof Geoffrey Arnott; 35 Arncliffe Road, Leeds LS16 9JT, (☎ 0532 333539, fax 0532 336017, telex 556473 UNILDS G)

ARNOTT, Ian Emslie; s of Henry Arnott (d 1967), of Galashiels, and Margaret Hume Paton Emslie (d 1961); *b* 7 May 1929; *Educ* Galashiels Acad, Edinburgh Coll of Art (DA (Edin), Dip TP (Edin)); *m* 17 Sept 1955, Mildred Stella; 1 da (Gillian Elisabeth b 1958); *Career* Flying Offr RAF 1955-57; architect; chm Campbell & Arnott 1963-; awards: gold medal for architecture Royal Scot Acad, Civic Tst (5), Edinburgh Architectural Assoc (2); recent projects: Scot Fin Centre Castle Terrace Edinburgh, Maybury Business Technol Park Edinburgh, AEU HQ London; ARSA, RIBA, ARIAS; *Recreations* walking, travel, music, reading, photography; *Clubs* New (Edinburgh); *Style—* Ian Arnott, Esq; The Rink, Gifford, East Lothian (☎ 062 081 278); Campbell & Arnott, Albany Lane, Edinburgh EH1 3QP (☎ 031 557 1725, fax 031 556 1199)

ARNOTT, John Michael Stewart; s of George Arnott (d 1970), of Kirriemuir, and Winifred Douglas, *née* Livingstone; *b* 12 June 1933; *Educ* King Edward's Sch Birmingham, Peterhouse Coll Cambridge (BA); *m* 2 Jan 1965, (Hazel) Lynne, da of Rev W E Gladstone-Millar, MC (d 1982), of Arbroath; 1 s (Martin b 1967), 1 da (Hilary b 1970); *Career* Flying Offr RAF 1952-54; BBC: Studio mangr 1960, announcer 1961-67, producer 1967-85, ed and mangr Edinburgh 1985-90; vice-chm Countryside Cmmn Scotland 1986- (memb 1982-); chm: Isle of May Bird Observatory 1980-85, Fair Isle Bird Observatory Tst 1983-84; pres Scottish Ornithologists' Club 1984-87, memb Ctee for Scot Nature Conservancy Cncl 1986-; *Recreations* ornithology, hill walking, arctic travel; *Style—* John Arnott, Esq; East Redford House, Redford Rd, Edinburgh EH13 0AS (☎ 031 441 3567)

ARNOTT, Sir (William) Melville; TD (Clasps 1944); s of Rev Henry Arnott (d 1952), of Edinburgh, and Jeanette Main Arnott; *b* 14 Jan 1909; *Educ* George Watson's Coll, Univ of Edinburgh (MB ChB, BSc, MD); *m* 1938, Dorothy Eleanor, er da of George Frederick Seymour Hill, of Edinburgh; 1 s; *Career* serv WWII (siege of Tobruk, despatches 1945); William Withering prof of med Univ of Birmingham 1946-71, prof of cardiology Univ of Birmingham 1971-74 (emeritus 1974-); pres Br Lung Fndn 1984-87, memb Br Heart Fndn; Hon Lt-Col RAMC; Hon MD Birmingham; Hon DSc: Edinburgh 1975, Chinese Univ of Hong Kong 1983; Hon LLD: Rhodesia 1976, Dundee 1976; FRCP, FRCPE, FRCP(C), FRCPath, FACP, FRSE; kt 1971; *Clubs* Naval and Military, London; *Style—* Sir Melville Arnott, TD, FRSE; 40 Carpenter Rd, Edgbaston, Birmingham B15 2JJ (☎ 021 440 2195)

ARNOTT, Prof Struther; s of Charles McCann, and Christina Struthers; *b* 25 Sept 1934; *Educ* Hamilton Acad, Univ of Glasgow (BSc, PhD); *m* 11 June 1970, Greta Maureen, da of James Reginald Edwards, of Dudley; 1 s (Euan b 1973); *Career* res sci MRC Biophysic Units King's Coll London 1960-70 (physics demonstrator 1960-67, dir postgrad studies in biophysics 1967-70); Purdue Univ Indiana USA 1970-86: prof of biology 1970-, head of bio scis 1980-86, vice-pres for res and dean of Graduate Sch 1980-86; Nuffield res fell Green Coll Univ of Oxford 1985-86 sr (visiting fell Jesus Coll 1980-81); princ and vice-chllr St Andrews Univ 1986-; Guggenheim Memorial fell 1985; govr: Sedbergh Sch, Glenalmond Coll Perthshire; FRS, FRSE, FRSC, FIBiol; *Recreations* birdwatching, botanizing; *Clubs* Athenaeum, Caledonian, Royal and Ancient (St Andrews); *Style—* Prof Struther Arnott; 9 The Scores, St Andrews KY16 9AR (☎ 0334 72492); Univ of St Andrews, College Gate, St Andrews KY16 9AJ (☎ 0334 76161, fax 0334 73145)

ARONSON, Sheriff Hazel Josephine; da of Moses Aron Aronson, of Glasgow, and Julia Tobias; *b* 12 Jan 1946; *Educ* Glasgow HS for Girls, Univ of Glasgow (LLB); *m* 17 Dec 1967, John Allan, s of Rev Dr Isaac Kenneth Cosgrove, DL, JP (d 1973); 1 s (Nicholas Joseph b 1972), 1 da (Jillian Abigail b 1970); *Career* advocate The Scottish Bar 1968-79; Sheriff of Lothian and Borders at Edinburgh 1983- (formerly Sheriff of Glasgow and Strathkelvin 1979-83); memb Parole Bd for Scotland 1988-; *Recreations* walking, langlauf, opera; *Style—* Sheriff Hazel J Aronson; 14 Gordon Terrace, Edinburgh EH16 5OR (☎ 031 667 8955); The Sheriff Ct, Lawnmarket, Edinburgh (☎ 031 226 7181)

ARONSTAM, Dr Anthony; s of Alfred Aronstam (d 1975), and Golda, *née* Kagan; *b* 27 May 1934; *Educ* S African Coll Sch, Univ of Cape Town (MB ChB), Univ of Southampton (DM); *m* 28 Feb 1967, Gillian Lesley, da of Leslie Ludlow Hawdon; 2 s (Jeremy b 1968, Benjamin b 1972), 1 da (Suzanne b 1969); *Career* lectr St Georges Hosp Med Sch 1969-70, conslt haematologist Basingstoke 1970-, res fell Univ of Western Ontario 1976-77; memb: Paediatric Advsy Gp World Fedn of Haemophilia, Wessex Regn AIDS Expert Advsy Ctee, N Hampshire Drug Abuse Liason Ctee; chm N Hampshire AIDS Working Pty; FRCPath 1981 (MRCPath 1969); *Books* Haemophilic Bleeding (1985), contrib: Br Journal of Haematology (1976), Journal of Clinical Pathology (1978), British Medical Journal (1979), Lancet (1981), Journal of Paediatrics (1982), Clinical and Laboratory Haematology (1983), Journal of Bone and Joint Surgery (1985 and 1987), Thrombosis Research (1985), Novvelle Revue Francais d'Hematologie (1986), Med Laboratory Science (1988); *Recreations* thinking, sun bathing; *Style—* Dr Anthony Aronstam; Basingstoke District Hospital, Basingstoke, Hants (☎ 0256 473202, fax 0420 84472)

ARRAN, 9 Earl of (I 1762); Sir Arthur Desmond Colquhoun Gore; 11 Bt (I 1662); also Viscount Sudley, Baron Saunders (both I 1758), and Baron Sudley (UK 1884); s of 8 Earl of Arran (d 1983), and Fiona, Countess of Arran, *qv*; *b* 14 July 1938; *Educ* Eton, Balliol Coll Oxford; *m* 1974, Eleanor, er da of Bernard van Cutsem and Lady Margaret Fortescue, *qv*, da of 5 Earl Fortescue; 2 da (Lady Laura Melissa b 1975, Lady Lucy Katherine b 1976); *Heir* kinsman, Paul Annesley Gore, CMG, CVO, JP, *qv*; *Career* Nat Serv cmmnd Gren Gds; asst mangr Daily Mail 1972-73, md Clark Nelson 1973-74, asst gen mangr Daily and Sunday Express 1974; dir Waterstone & Co Ltd 1984-87; a lord-in-waiting (Government whip) 1987, Parly under-sec of state for Armed Forces 1989-; co-chm Children's Country Holidays Fund; *Recreations* tennis, golf, gardening; *Clubs* Turf, Beefsteak, Pratt's; *Style—* The Rt Hon the Earl of Arran

ARRAN, Fiona, Countess of; Fiona Bryde; da of Sir Ian Colquhoun, 7 Bt, KT, DSO, and Geraldine, da of Francis Tennant (2 s of Sir Charles Tennant, 1 Bt; bro of 1 Baron Glenconner); *m* 1937, 8 Earl of Arran (d 1983), journalist and broadcaster; 1 s (9 Earl of Arran, *qv*) and 1 s decd; *Career* first person to average 100 mph in offshore boat (Lake Windermere 1980), awarded Segrave Trophy for outstanding courage on water, land or in the air 1981, holder of first World Electric Boat Record (50.8 mph); Offshore world records: 1972 class 1 (Windermere), 1980 class 2 (Windermere); *Style—* The Rt Hon Fiona, Countess of Arran; Pimlico House, Hemel Hempstead, Herts

ARRINDELL, HE Sir Clement Athelston; GCMG (1984), GCVO (1985), QC (1984); s of George Ernest Arrindell, and Hilda Iona Arrindell (d 1975); *b* 16 April 1931; *Educ* Bradley Private Sch, Basseterre Boy's Elementary, St Kitts-Nevis GS; *m* 1967, Evelyn Eugenia, da of Michael Cornelius O'Loughlin (d 1934), of Basseterre, St Kitts, and his w Dulcie (d 1972); *Career* treas clerk Treas Dept St Kitts 1951-54; barr Lincoln's Inn 1958, practising 1958-66, dist magistrate 1966-72, chief magistrate 1972-78, Puisne judge W Indies Assoc States Supreme Ct 1978-81; govr St Kitts-Nevis 1981-83, govr-gen St Kitts-Nevis 1983-; kt 1982; *Recreations* gardening, piano playing, classical music; *Style—* HE Sir Clement Arrindell, GCMG, GCVO, QC; Government House, St Kitts, West Indies (☎ 2315, 2260)

ARROWSMITH, Anthony; s of Arthur Arrowsmith and Winifred *née* McDonough; *b* 11 May 1945; *Educ* St Chad's Coll Wolverhampton (DipCAM); *m* 4 May 1968, Yvonne Mary da of George Brannon; 1 s (Aidan b 1970), 2 da (Alexa b 1973, Sian b 1982); *Career* dir and chief exec Barkers Birmingham (Charles Barker Black and Gross Ltd) 1976; chm: Barkers Scotland (Charles Barker Scotland Ltd) 1986, Barkers Manchester 1986; dir BNB Resources plc 1987, chief exec Barkers Regional Communications Ltd 1989; MIPA; *Style—* Anthony Arrowsmith, Esq; The Hollies, Histons Hill, Codsall, West Midlands WV8 2ER (☎ 09074 3987, office ☎ 021 236 9501)

ARROWSMITH, Sir Edwin Porter; KCMG (1959, CMG 1950); s of Edwin Arrowsmith (d 1924), of Cheltenham, and Kathleen Eggleston, *née* Porter (d 1971); *b* 23 May 1909; *Educ* Cheltenham, Trinity Coll Oxford (MA); *m* 1936, Clondagh, da of Dr William G Connor (d 1931), of Cheltenham; 2 da; *Career* Colonial Serv: joined 1932, various dist posts in Bechuanaland Protectorate 1932-38, cmmr Turks and Caicos Islands BWI 1940-46, admin Dominica BWI 1946-52, res cmmr Basutoland 1952-56, govr and C-in-C Falkland Islands 1957-64, high cmmr Br Antarctic Territory 1962-64; memb St Dunstan's 1965-; vice-pres: Freshwater Biological Assoc 1983- (memb 1977-83), Royal Cwlth Soc for the Blind 1985- (chm 1970-85); *Recreations* flyfishing; *Clubs* Flyfishers', Hurlingham, Royal Cwlth Soc; *Style—* Sir Edwin Arrowsmith, KCMG; 25 Rivermead Court, London SW6 3RU (☎ 071 736 4757)

ARROWSMITH, John Anthony (Tony); s of Robert Edmund Arrowsmith (d 1983), of North Shields, and Kathleen Mitchel, *née* Cooper (d 1964); *b* 16 Jan 1940; *Educ* Tynemouth GS; *m* 1962, Rosamond Catherine Cecilia (Ros), da of Patrick Eardley (d 1953), of Stoke on Trent; 3 s (Anthony Edmund, John Patrick, Ian Dominic), 1 da (Jacqueline Rose); *Career* md: Ellis Maintenance & Sons Ltd 1976-86, Ellis Manpower Ltd 1976- 86, Tylin CAE Ltd 1979-86; md and chief exec Ellis Mechanical Servs ltd 1987-88, dir Corrall Montenay Ltd 1988, md Ellis Tylin Ltd 1988 (chief exec 1986-88); chm Exec Assoc of GB 1986-87 (dir 1985-88), memb Nat Sporting Club; MIPM, MIOD, MCIOB; *Recreations* golf; *Style—* Tony Arrowsmith, Esq; 86 Sand Lane, Cheam, Surrey SM2 7EP (☎ 081 642 3460); Ellis Tylin Ltd, Tolworth Tower, Ewell Rd, Surbiton, Surrey (☎ 071 390 8911, fax 071 399 8914)

ARROWSMITH, Pat; da of George Ernest Arrowsmith (d 1976), and Margaret Vera, *née* Kingham (d 1976); *b* 2 March 1930; *Educ* Cheltenham Ladies' Coll, Newnham Coll Cambridge (BA), Univ of Ohio, Univ of Liverpool; lesbian ptnr, Wendy Butlin 1962-76; m 11 Aug 1979 (m dis), Donald Gardener; *Career* pacifist and socialist; many short term jobs incl: community organizer Chicago 1952-53, cinema usher 1953-54, social caseworker family Service Unit Liverpool 1954, childcare offr 1955 and 1964, nursing asst Deva Psychiatric Hosp 1956-57, reporter Peace News 1965, gardener Camden BC 1966-68, researcher Soc of Friends Race Relations Ctee 1969-71, case worker NCCL 1971, also worked in farms, cafes, factories and offices; asst ed Amnesty International (joined 1971); organizer: Direct Action Ctee Against Nuclear War, Ctee of 100, CND 1958-68; Parly candidate: (Radical Alliance) Fulham 1966, (Stop the SE Asia War Ctee) Hammersmith 1970, (Independent Socialist) Cardiff SE 1979, gaoled 11 times as political prisoner 1958-85, twice adopted as Prisoner of Conscience by Amnesty International; awarded Holloway Prison Green Arm band 1964; memb: TGWU, CND; *Books* Jericho (1965), Somewhere Like This (1970), To Asia in Peace (1972), Breakout (1975), On the Brink (1981), The Prisoner (1982), Thin Ice (1984), Nine Lives (1990); *Recreations* painting, writing, poetry, swimming; *Style—* Ms Pat Arrowsmith; 132c Middle Lane, London N8 7JP (☎ 081 340 2661); Amnestry International, 1 Easton St, London WC1 (☎ 071 413 5500)

ARROWSMITH, Dr Paul; s of Percy Harold Arrowsmith, and Mary, *née* Travis; *b* 4 Aug 1934; *Educ* Bablake Sch Coventry, Univ of Liverpool (MB CHB); *m* 1, 1 March 1958 (m dis 1985), Janet Frances, da of William Trevor Owen (d 1970); 1 s (Richard), 2 da (Lesley (Mrs Bannister), Wendy (Mrs Pepper)); m 2, 15 April 1985, Patricia Mary Campbell, da of Henry Roberts Wilkinson (d 1964); *Career* sr house offr Walton Hosp Liverpool 1958-60 (house surgn and physician 1957-58), princ GP Hull 1961-80 (asst 1960-61), med offr HM Prison Hull 1980-81 (pt/t 1960-80), sr med offr HM Prison Leeds 1981-85, area princ med offr North East and Yorkshire Prison Service 1985; memb: RSPB, Yorks Naturalist Tst, Hull Med Soc 1970-80 (pres 1979); MBHI; *Recreations* ornithology, horology, walking; *Style—* Dr Paul Arrowsmith; Directorate of Prison Medical Services, Cleland House, Page St, London SW1P 4LN (☎ 071 217 6238)

ARTHUR, Alan David; s of David Edward John Arthur, of 3 Newport Rd, Bedwas, Gwent, and Elizabeth Ann, *née* Howell; *b* 3 July 1949; *Educ* Bedwellty GS, Univ Coll of Wales Aberystwyth (BSc); *Career* CA; joined Deloitte Haskins & Sells direct from Univ and worked in S Wales, W Yorks and Zambia; ptnr in their int practice 1983-84; fdnr and first md Bradford Enterprise Agency 1984-86; ptnr Booth & Co CA's 1986-89, dir corp fin Ernst & Young; FCA 1974, FCIArb 1987; *Recreations* work; *Clubs* Bradford; *Style—* Alan Arthur, Esq; 76 Hallowes Park Rd, Cullingworth BD13 5AR (☎ 0535 273074); Ernst & Young, Clifton House, Clifton Villas, Bradford BD8 (☎ 0274 497153, telex CHACOM G 30C0)

ARTHUR, David Sloan Coullie; s of Rev J W Arthur, OBE (d 1952), of Kikuyu, Kenya, and Evelyn Margaret, *née* Coullie; *b* 23 Feb 1930; *Educ* Univ of Edinburgh (MA, DipEd), Loretto; *m* 5 June 1954, (Alice) Mary, da of R G Frost, of Edinburgh; 3 da (Gillian Margaret b 16 Aug 1959, Seonaid Mary b 29 July 1962, Catriona Caroline b 20 Oct 1967); *Career* 2 Lt RCS 1953, Capt TA RCS 1956; rector Green Faulds High Sch Cumbernauld 1970-76, princ Lomond Sch Helensburgh 1977-86; dir: Dumbarton Dist Trg Assoc 1987-88, Scottish Region Cystic Fibrosis Res Tst 1988; chm: The Samaritans 1972-76 (chm Scottish Regn 1962-66), Dunbarton COMACT Gp 1990-; memb Helensburgh Rotary Club; *Books* Someone To Turn To (1975); *Recreations* tennis, golf, photography, gardening; *Clubs* Royal Over-Seas League; *Style—* David Arthur, Esq; Inverallan, 26 West Argyle St, Helensburgh G84 8DB (☎ 0436 76494, 0436 76791)

ARTHUR, Gavyn Farr; s of Maj the Hon (George) Leonard Arthur, of Bath and London SW3, and (Gladys) Raina Arthur; *b* 13 Sept 1951; *Educ* Harrow, Ch Ch Oxford (MA); *Career* called to the Bar 1975; memb W Circuit Ctee 1988-; chm Res Ctee on Child Care Proceedings 1987, memb Soc Conservative Lawyers; treas Coningsby Club 1987, govr St Bride's Inst Fndn 1989, memb Ct Common Cncl Ward of Farringdon Without 1988; Freeman City of London 1979, memb Worshipful Co of Gardeners; *Recreations* travel, writing, British India, the South Tyrol question; *Clubs* Carlton, Coningsby; *Style—* Gavyn Arthur, Esq; 2 Harcourt Buildings, Temple, London EC4 (☎ 071 353 6961, fax 071 353 6968)

ARTHUR, Prof Geoffrey Herbert; s of William Gwyn Arthur (d 1945), of Cefn Llech,

Llangibby, Gwent, and Ethel Jessie Parry (d 1967); *b* 6 March 1916; *Educ* Abersychan Secdy Sch, Liverpool Univ (BVSc, MVSc), London Univ (FRCVS); *m* 22 Feb 1948, Lorna Isabel, da of Isaac Alec Simpson (d 1969), of Ranworth, Heswall, Ches; 4 s (Richard b 1950, Hugh b 1954, Charles b 1960, James b 1963), 1 da (Angela (Mrs Sheard) b 1948); *Career* lectr in vet med Liverpool Univ 1945-49, prof of vet obstetrics London Univ 1964-73, head of Dept of Surgery RVC 1972-73, prof of vet surgery Univ of Bristol 1974-79, clinical vet prof King Faisal Saudi Arabia 1980-83, regnl postgrad vet dean RCVS 1985; memb Cncl: RCVS, Soc for the Protection of Animals in N Africa; former pres: Br Cattle Vet Assoc, Soc for the Study of Animal Breeding; former memb Cncl: Br Vet Assoc; *Books* Veterinary Reproduction and Obstetrics (6 edn 1989); *Recreations* observing natural phenomena and experimenting, North African travel; *Style—* Prof Geoffrey Arthur; Fallodene, Stone Allerton, Axbridge, Somerset, BS26 2NH (☎ 0934 712 077)

ARTHUR, Lt-Col John Reginald; OBE (1985); s of Col Lionel Francis Arthur, DSO, OBE (d 1952), of Yockley House, Camberley, Surrey, and Muriel Irene, *née* Tilley; *b* 25 June 1935; *Educ* Winchester; *m* 21 Dec 1965, Princess Valerie Isolde Mary de Mahe, da of Prince John Bryant Digby de Mahe, MBE; 2 s (Malcolm Ian Charles b 5 Sept 1969, John Benjamin George b 25 Nov 1971), 1 da (Anneliese Mary b 8 March 1967); *Career* RMA Sandhurst 1954-55, cmmnd Scots Gds 1955, Staff Coll Camberley 1966, Lt-Col 1976, directing staff Nigerian Staff Coll 1976-78, foreign liaison staff MOD 1978-81, project offr Br Army Equipment Exhibition 82 1981-82, PS 12 (Army) MOD 1982-84, ret 1984; co sec Laurence Prust & Co Ltd 1986-90 (joined 1984), co sec Credit Commercial de France (UK) Ltd 1990-; *Recreations* golf, gardening, music; *Clubs* Cavalry and Guards, MCC, Izingari, Free Foresters, Berkshire Golf, Royal St Georges Golf, Hon Co of Edinburgh Golfers; *Style—* Lt-Col John Arthur, OBE; 27 Finsbury Square, London EC2A 1LP (☎ 071 628 1111)

ARTHUR, His Hon Judge; John Rhys Arthur; DFC (1944); s of John Morgan Arthur, JP (d 1973), and Eleanor Arthur; *b* 29 April 1923; *Educ* Mill Hill Sch, Christ's Coll Cambridge (MA); *m* 1951, Joan Tremearne, da of Richard Pickering (d 1961); 2 s, 1 da; *Career* served WW II, Fl-Lt RAF; called to the Bar Inner Temple 1949; asst recorder Blackburn 1970, dep chm Lancs County QS 1970-71, recorder 1972-75, circuit judge 1975-; JP (Lancs) 1970; *Clubs* MCC, Old Millhillians, Athenaeum (Liverpool); *Style—* His Hon Judge Arthur, DFC; Orovales, Caldy, Wirral, Merseyside L48 1LP (☎ 051 625 8624)

ARTHUR, Lady; Margaret; da of late Thomas Arnold Woodcock, OBE, of Ashby de la Zouch; *b* 21 Dec 1924; *Educ* Cheltenham Ladies' Coll, Somerville Coll Oxford; *m* 1946, Sir Geoffrey George Arthur, KCMG (dep under-sec of state FCO 1973-75, master of Pembroke Coll Oxford 1975-84, d 1984); *Clubs* Univ Women's; *Style—* Lady Arthur; 26 Cunliffe Close, Oxford OX2 7BL

ARTHUR, Hon Matthew Richard; 2 s of 3 Baron Glenarthur, OBE, DL, *qv*; *b* 6 March 1948; *Educ* Eton; *m* 1974, Veronica, yr da of Michael Hall, of Kilternan, Co Dublin; 1 s (Matthew Frederick Michael b 1981), 1 da (Jessica Mary b 1979); *Career* Motimoney chiropractor; *Style—* The Hon Matthew Arthur; Bingfield East Quarter, Hallington, Newcastle upon Tyne NE19 2LH (☎ 0434 672219)

ARTHUR, Lt-Gen Sir (John) Norman Stewart; KCB (1985), DL (Stewartry of Kirkcudbright); s of Col Evelyn Stewart Arthur (d 1963), of Montgomerie, Mauchline, Ayrshire, and Elizabeth Burnett-Stuart (d 1976); *b* 6 March 1931; *Educ* Eton, RMA Sandhurst; *m* 1960, Theresa Mary, da of Francis Archibald Hopkinson, of Dundas Farm, Elmsted, Kent; 1 s (Simon b 1967), 1 da (Camilla b 1962), 1 s decd; *Career* cmmnd Royal Scots Greys 1951; CO Royal Scots Dragoon Gds 1972-74 (despatches 1974), 7 Armd Bde 1976-77, GOC 3 Armd Division 1980-82, Dir Personal Servs (Army) MOD 1983-85, Col Cmdt Mil Provost Staff Corps 1983-88, GOC Scot Govr Edinburgh Castle 1985-88, Col The Royal Scots Dragoon Gds (Carabiniers and Greys) 1985-, Col 205 (Scot) Gen Hosp RAMC (v) 1988-; offr Royal Co of Archers (Queen's Body Guard for Scot), memb Br Olympic Team (equestrian three-day event) 1960; vice-pres Riding for the Disabled Edinburgh and Borders 1988-, chm Army Benevolent Fund Scot 1988-, pres Scottish Conservation Projects Tst 1989-; memb: Ctee AA 1990-, Bd of Dirs Edinburgh Mil Tattoo Co 1988-; *Recreations* country pursuits, reading, field sports; *Clubs* Cavalry and Guards', Caledonian Hunt; *Style—* Lt-Gen Sir Norman Arthur, KCB, DL; (☎ 055 663 227)

ARTHUR, Robin Anthony; s of Ronald Arthur, of Folkestone, Kent, and Flore Alzire, *née* Parmentier; *b* 15 Aug 1947; *Educ* Cambridge GS, Univ of London (External); *m* Oct 1968 (m dis 1989), Elizabeth Mary; 1 s (Richard b 1980), 1 da (Lucy b 1982); *Career* called to the Bar Gray's Inn 1976; md: Parmentier-Arthur Holdings plc 1975-, Cambridge Estates Ltd 1982-; *Recreations* rugby, walking, the arts; *Style—* Robin A Arthur, Esq; The Manor House, The Green, Hilton, Huntingdon, Cambridgeshire; 7 The Waits, St Ives, Huntingdon, Cambs (☎ 0480 65522)

ARTHUR, Roland William; s of William Arthur (d 1976), and Olive, *née* Hayward; *b* 21 Dec 1938; *Educ* Monmouth Sch, St Catharines Coll Cambridge (MA); *m* 1 May 1965, Margot Frances, da of Ernest William Anstey (d 1988); 1 s (Robin b 1968), 2 da (Justine b 1967, Sarah b 1962); *Career* admitted slr 1964; St David's Investmt Tst plc: sec 1986, dir 1988; memb Law Soc; *Recreations* squash, golf; *Style—* Roland Arthur, Esq; Llandevaud Court, Llandevaud, Newport, Gwent; Queens Chambers, 2 North St, Newport, Gwent (☎ 0633 244233, fax 0633 246453)

ARTHUR, Sandra, Lady; Sandra Colleen Arthur; da of William Boaz, of Whangarei, New Zealand; *m* 1983, as his 2 w, Hon Sir Basil Arthur, 5 Bt (d 1985, MP (Lab) Timaru, New Zealand 1962-85); *Style—* Sandra, Lady Arthur; Grene Gables, No 3 Rd, Seadown, Timaru, New Zealand

ARTHUR, (James) Stanley; CMG (1977); s of Laurence Arthur (d 1970), and Catherine Jane, *née* Charleson, of Lerwick, Shetland Islands; *b* 3 Feb 1923; *Educ* Trinity Acad Edinburgh, Univ of Liverpool (BSc); *m* 1950, Marion *née* North; 2 s (Stephen, Charles), 2 da (Judith, Shelley); *Career* Scottish Educ Dept 1946-47, Dept of Educ and Sci 1947-66 (princ private sec to Min 1960-62), FO 1966-; resident Br high cmmr: Suva Fiji 1974-78, Bridgetown Barbados 1978-82, St Lucia and St Vincent 1979-82, Grenada 1980-82, Antigua and Barbuda 1981-82; Br govt rep to WI Assoc States 1978-1982, ret 1983; memb: Ct Univ of Liverpool, Central Cncl Royal Cwlth Soc; *Recreations* music, golf; *Clubs* Royal Cwlth Soc; *Style—* Stanley Arthur, Esq, CMG; Moreton House, Longborough, Moreton-in-Marsh, Glos GL56 0QQ (☎ 0451 30774)

ARTHUR, Sir Stephen John; 6 Bt (UK 1841), of Upper Canada; s of Hon Sir Basil Arthur, 5 Bt, MP (d 1985); *b* 1 July 1953; *Educ* Timaru Boys' HS; *m* 1978 (m dis), Carolyn Margaret, da of Burnie Lawrence Diamond, of Cairns, Qld, Australia; 1 s , 2 da (Amanda b 1975, Melanie b 1976); *Heir* s, Benjamin Nathan Arthur b 27 March 1979; *Style—* Sir Stephen Arthur, Bt; Seadown, No 3 Rd, Timaru, New Zealand

ARTHUR, Terence Arthur; s of William Gordon Arthur (d 1971), of West Hartlepool, and Dorothy, *née* Baker; *b* 5 Sept 1940; *Educ* West Hartlepool GS, Univ of Manchester (BSc), Univ of Cambridge (Dip Statistics); *m* 1, 15 May 1965 (m dis 1983), Valerie Ann Marie, da of Stephen Daniels, of Suffolk; 1 s (Richard b 1970), 2 da (Louise b 1966, Frances b 1968); m 2, 25 Nov 1983, Mary Clare, *née* Austick; *Career* asst sec Equity & Law Life Assur Soc 1967 (joined 1963), ptnr Duncan C Fraser & Co Actuaries 1969-76 (joined 1967), T G Arthur Hargrave Actuaries 1976- (fndr 1976) (merged with Bacon and Woodrow 1989); memb: Cncl Inst Actuaries 1977 (treas 1985-86), Co Actuaries; int Capt rugby football 1966; Freeman City of London; FIA 1966, FIS 1975, fell Inst Pensions Mgmnt 1977; *Books* 95 per cent is Crap -A Plain Man's Guide to British Politics (1975); *Clubs* Birmingham Area Sports Internationalists, Wig and Pen; *Style—* Terence Arthur, Esq

ARTHURS, Prof Arnold Magowan; s of James Arthurs (d 1969), of Islandmagee Antrim, and Mary, *née* Scott; *b* 2 Sept 1934; *Educ* Royal Belfast Academical Instn, Queen's Univ Belfast (BSc), Jesus Coll Oxford (MA, DSc); *m* 6 July 1963, Elspeth Marie, da of Arthur John Lonsdale (d 1977), of Hornsea, E Yorks; 3 s (William b 1965, Henry b 1967, Jack b 1971); *Career* praelector mathematics and fell Queen's Coll Oxford 1962; Univ of York: reader 1964, prof mathematics 1976-; memb York Blood Donor Ctee 1983-; FIMA 1970; *Books* Probability Theory (1965), Complementary Variational Principles (1970), Calculus of Variations (1975); *Recreations* music; *Style—* Prof Arnold Arthurs; Department of Mathematics, University of York, Heslington, York YO1 5DD (☎ 0904 433071)

ARTHURTON, Hon Mrs (Phillipa Susan); *née* Mills; yr da of 2 Viscount Mills (d 1988); *b* 25 Feb 1950; *m* 1970, Russell Scott Arthurton; *Style—* The Hon Mrs Arthurton; 96 Pannal Ash Rd, Harrogate, N Yorks

ARTUS, Ronald Edward; CBE (1991); s of Ernest Edward Artus (d 1980), and Doris Isobel Goddard; *b* 8 Oct 1931; *Educ* Sir Thomas Rich's Sch Gloucester, Magdalen Coll Oxford (MA); *m* 1, 1956 (m dis 1987), Brenda Margaret, *née* Touche; 3 s (Colin, Alan, Philip), 1 da (Lucy); m 2, Dr Joan Mullaney; *Career* Prudential 1954-90 (head of econ intelligence 1958-71, sr asst mangr 1973-75, jt sec and chief investmt mangr 1975-82, gp chief investmnt mangr Prudential Corp 1982-90 (exec dir 1984-90)); non-exec dir: Prudential Corp plc 1990-, GEC 1990-, Electro-components plc 1990-, The Slr's Indemnity Fund Ltd 1990-, The Securities Assoc Ltd 1990-, Imperial Cancer Res Technology Ltd 1988-, Celltech Ltd 1980-91; hon fell Soc of Investment Analysts; memb: Accounting Standards Ctee 1982-86, City Capital Markets Ctee 1982-90, Cncl for Inst for Fiscal Studies 1988-, CBI City Indust Task Force; *Recreations* music, art especially Br Sch; *Clubs* MCC; *Style—* Ronald Artus, Esq, CBE; 1 Stephen St, London W1P 2AP (☎ 071 548 3901)

ARULAMPALAM, Thankarajah; s of Richard Kunaratnam Arulampalam (d 1969), of Jaffna, Sri-Lanka, and Anna Annammah, *née* Amerasingham; *b* 28 Dec 1933; *Educ* Jaffna Central Coll Jaffna, St Thomas Coll Mt Lavinia Sri Lanka, Univ of Ceylon Sri Lanka (MB BS); *m* 18 Dec 1967, (Jannette) Lokeswarie, da of Dr John Rasiah Wilson, MBE (d 1984); 1 s (Thanjakumar Hermon Arichandran b 20 Dec 1968), 1 da (Lohini Hemangini b 3 June 1973); *Career* sr house offr in opthalmology St Pauls Eye Hosp Liverpool 1968-69, registrar in ophthalmology Hallamshire Hosp Sheffield 1970-72, sr registrar in ophthalmology Guys Hosp and St Georges Hosp London 1973-77, conslt ophthalmologist Central Notts Health Authy Kings Mill Hosp Notts 1978-; memb GMC and Med Def Union; DO, FRCS, FCOphth; *Recreations* cricket, soccer, hockey, athletics; *Style—* Thankarajah Arulampalam, Esq; 22 Black Scotch Lane, Berry Hill, Mansfield, Nottinghamshire NG18 4JX (☎ 0623 25500); Department of Ophthalmology, Kingsmill Hospital, Mansfield Rd, Sutton in Ashfield, Nottinghamshire (☎ 0623 22515 ext 3366)

ARUNDEL AND BRIGHTON, Bishop (RC) of 1977-; Rt Rev Cormac Murphy-O'Connor; s of Dr George Patrick Murphy-O'Connor (d 1960), of Reading, Berks, and Ellen Theresa, *née* Cuddigan (d 1971); *b* 24 Aug 1932; *Educ* Prior Park Coll Bath, The Ven English Coll Rome, Gregorian Univ Rome (PhL, STL); *Career* ordained to RC Priesthood 1956; parish priest Portswood Southampton 1970-71, rector Venerable Eng Coll Rome 1971-77; first chm Bishops' Ctee for Europe 1979-82, RC co chm of Anglo-Roman Catholic Int Cmmn (ARCIC-II) 1983-; chm TVS Religious Advsrs Panel 1985-; *Recreations* walking, music (pianist), reading; *Style—* The Rt Rev the Bishop of Arundel; St Joseph's Hall, Storrington, Pulborough, W Sussex RH20 4HE (☎ 0903 742172)

ARUNDEL AND SURREY, Earl of; Edward William Fitzalan-Howard; s and h of 17 Duke of Norfolk, KG, CB, CBE, MC, DL; *b* 2 Dec 1956; *Educ* Ampleforth, Lincoln Coll Oxford; *m* 27 June 1987, Georgina Susan, yr da of John Temple Gore; 1 s (Henry Miles, Lord Maltravers b 3 Dec 1987), 1 da (Lady Rachel Rose b 10 June 1989); *Heir* s, Lord Maltravers; *Career* chm: Sigas Ltd; *Recreations* motor racing, skiing, shooting; *Style—* Earl of Arundel and Surrey; Arundel Castle, Arundel, Sussex (☎ 0903 882173); 25 Brynmaer Rd, London SW11 (☎ 071 622 2972); Scar House, Arkengarthdale, Reeth, N Yorks (☎ 0748 84726)

ARUNDELL, Hon Richard John Tennant; s and h of 10 Baron Talbot of Malahide, *qv*; *b* 28 March 1957; *Educ* Stonyhurst, RAC Cirencester; *m* 1984, Jane Catherine, da of Timothy Heathcote Unwin, MFH; 3 da (Isabel Mary b 1986, Emily Rose b 1988, Frances Laura b 1990); *Career* cmmnd Royal Wessex Yeo (TA) 1979; farmer; *Style—* The Hon Richard Arundell; Park Gate Farm, Donhead, Shaftesbury, Dorset (☎ 074 788 423)

ARWYN, Hon Arwyn Hugh Davies; only s of Baron Arwyn (Life Peer, d 1978), and his 2 w, Beatrix Emily Bassett, *née* Organ; *b* 9 April 1949; *Educ* King Edward VI Sch Bath, Truro Sch, Univ of Wales, Sheffield Univ; *m* 1977, Mary Elizabeth Gibson; *Career* Barr Gray's Inn 1972; int lawyer, co dir; *Recreations* sailing, golf; *Clubs* Reform, Roy Fowey Yacht, House of Lords Yacht; *Style—* The Hon Arwyn H D Arwyn; Ewart, Ashley Rd, Bathford, Avon

ARWYN, Baroness; Beatrix Emily Bassett; da of Capt Francis Henry Organ, of St Austell, Cornwall; *m* 6 June 1946, as his 2 w, Baron Arwyn (Life Peer, d 1978); 1 s (Hon Arwyn Hugh Davies. *qv*), 2 step da (Hon Mary Gwynne (Hon Mrs Webb) b 18 Aug 1932, Hon Elisabeth Jocelyn (Hon Mrs Macnab) b 5 July 1938); *Style—* The Rt Hon the Lady Arwyn of Glais; Ormonde, Lostwithiel, Cornwall

ASBURY, Capt John; CBE (1977); s of John Edwards Asbury (d 1979), of Bristol, and Hilda Mary, *née* Brotherston (d 1989); *b* 22 March 1921; *Educ* Bristol GS; *m* 9 Aug 1948, Iona Margaret Amelia, da of Lt W G C Stokes, DSC, RN (d 1975); 3 da (Judith b 1951, Sarah b 1954, Jessica b 1960); *Career* RN: AB 1940, cmmnd Pay/Sub Lt RNVR 1941, staff of Vice Adm Cmdg N Atlantic 1941-42, staff Naval Cmdr Expeditionary Force (Algiers) 1942-44, MID 1943, HMS Erebus at Normandy 1944-45, mine clearance Home Waters and Far E with 11th m/s Flotilla 1945-46; cmmnd Perm List RN 1947, Capt 1966, Cdre Sec to Int Mil Staff of NATO 1973-75; bursar Marlborough Coll 1976-85, govr Wellington Coll Berks 1985-, chm Utd Servs RFC 1968-73; *Recreations* gardening, fishing, boating; *Style—* Capt John Asbury, CBE; Beechcroft, Cross Lane, Marlborough, Wilts SN8 1LA (☎ 0672 54271)

ASCOTT, Robert Henry Charles; s of James Robert Ascott, of London, and Joan Daisy, *née* Le Feuvre; *b* 7 March 1943; *Educ* St Paul's, Trinity Coll Cambridge (MA), Admin Staff Coll Henley; *Career* pres EMI-Capitol de Mexico SA de CV 1975-79, md Emidata 1979-82, gp sr exec Interned 1982-84; bursar Univ of Reading 1984; *Recreations* coaching rowing, choral conducting, singing, organ playing, foreign languages; *Clubs* Leander; *Style—* Robert H C Ascott, Esq; 114 High St, Burbage, Marlborough, Wilts; Univ of Reading, Whiteknights, Reading, Berks

ASFA WOSSEN HAILE SELLASSIE, HIH Meredazmatch; GCMG (Hon 1965), GCVO (Hon 1930), GBE (Hon 1932); Crown Prince of Ethiopia 1930-; eldest s and h of HIM the late Emperor Haile Sellassie of Ethiopia, KG (d 1975), and HIM the late

Empress Menen (d 1962); *b* 27 July 1916; *Educ* privately, Liverpool Univ; *m* 1, 9 May 1932 (m dis 1944), Walatta Israel, da of HH Prince Ras Seyum Mangasha, and widow of Dejazmatch Gabre Sellassie; 1 da (decd); m 2, 8 April 1945, Medfariach Worq, da of Maj-Gen Abebe Damtew; 1 s, 3 da; *Heir* s, HIH Prince Zara Yaqob, b 15 Aug 1953; *Career* fought in Italo-Ethiopian War 1935-36; Grand Cross: Légion d'Honneur (France), Order of Leopold (Belgium), Order of the Netherlands, Order of Rising Sun (Japan), Order of White Elephant (Siam); *Style—* HIH Asfa Wossen Haile Sellassie, GCMG, GCVO, GBE; 82 Portland Place, London W1

ASFOURY, Dr Zakara Mohamed; s of Prof Mohamed El Asfoury (d 1983), of Port Said, Egypt; *b* 5 Aug 1921; *Educ* Port Said Secdy Sch, Cairo Univ, Liverpool Univ, London Univ (BSc, MSc, PhD, MB BCh, MRCS, LRCP), assoc res MD (Univ of Cambridge); *m* 1983, Prof Fadia Hassan, da of late Mohammed Katamesh; *Career* medical practitioner 1947-; res fell, hon demonstator, registrar, sr registrar, conslt physician working at various hosps incl: St Thomas, The London, The N Middx, St Mary's, The High-Land, Red Hill, Liverpool, Cairo; med specialisations incl: gen, rheumatic, tropical and geriatric med; res work incl: first organ transplant RCS 1950, the collagenase enzyme and anticollegenese in man and animals, breaking of kidney stones by VHF currents; memb: The Renal Assoc, The Anatomical Soc, Geriatric Soc, Hunterian Soc; FRSM; *Publications* numerous articles in learned jls, Pregnancy Nephropathy (contrib, 1971), Sympathectomy and the Innervation of the Kidney (1971); *Style—* Dr Z Asfoury; 27 Devonshire Place, London W1N 1PD (☎ 071 486 4342)

ASH, Charles John; s of Leonard John Ash (d 1965), of Cirencester, Glos, and Mary Elizabeth, *née* Watson; *b* 26 Nov 1945; *Educ* Cirencester GS, Hatfield Poly (BSc); *m* 1976, Pamela Monica, da of late Cecil Jenkins; 1 da (Emily Clare b 1978); *Career* Hawker Siddley Dynamics: jr design engr 1964, design engr 1966, sr design engr 1968-72; design engr Broomwade 1967, project leader Instron 1978-82, mangr mechanical engrg Moggridge Associates 1982-; Br Design award for cordless telephone 1990; memb Euro Engrs, MIMechE; *Style—* Charles Ash, Esq; Moggridge Associates, 7-8 Jeffrey's Place, Jeffrey's St, London NW1 9PP (☎ 071 485 1170, fax 071 482 3970)

ASH, Douglas Terence; s of Sydney Alexander Ash, and Doreen Victoria, *née* Gornall; *b* 19 Dec 1947; *Educ* Wallington GS, Univ of Nottingham (BA), Harvard Business Sch (MBA); *m* 19 Aug 1972, Rhona Helen, da of Harold James Bennett (d 1978), former vice-pres Rotary Int; 1 s (Laurence b 1981), 3 da (Belinda 1975, Isobel b 1976, Amelia b 1981); *Career* chief exec MSAS Cargo International, dir various MSAS subsid throughout the World; *Recreations* rugby football; *Style—* Douglas Ash, Esq; Cherry Croft, Kingwood Common, Henley on Thames, Oxon R69 5NA (☎ 04917 234); MSAS Cargo International Cory House, Bracknell, Berks RG12 1AW (☎ 0344 52222)

ASH, Prof Sir Eric Albert; CBE (1982); s of Walter J Ash (d 1970), and Dorothea Cecily, *née* Schwarz (d 1974); *b* 31 Jan 1928; *Educ* Univ Coll Sch, Imperial Coll of Science & Technol (BSc, DIC, PhD, DSc); *m* 30 May 1954, Clare Mosher, *née* Babb; 5 da (Gillian Carol (Mrs Gillian Barr) b 1958, Carolyn Dian b 1960, Lucy Amanda b 1962, Emily Jane b 1966, Jennifer Dian (twin) b 1966); *Career* res fell Stanford Univ California 1952-54, res engr Standard Telecom Labs 1954-63, Pender prof and head of Dept of Electronic and Electrical Engrg UCL 1980-85 (previously sr lectr, reader, prof), rector Imperial Coll of Sci Technol and Medicine 1985-; bd memb Br Telecom 1987-; tstee: Sci Museum 1988-, Wolfson Fndn 1988-; memb Academia Europaea 1989-; Hon degrees: Leicester Univ 1988, Edinburgh Univ 1988, INPG Grenoble 1987, Aston Univ 1987, Poly Univ NY 1988; FEng 1978, FRS 1977; memb: IOD, ABRC; kt 1990; *Recreations* reading, music, swimming, skiing; *Style—* Prof Sir Eric Ash, CBE, FRS; 170 Queen's Gate, London SW7 5HF; Imperial Coll, London SW7 2AZ (☎ 071 589 5111 ext 3000, fax 071 584 7596)

ASH, Peter Edward; s of Albert Edward Ash (d 1945), and Mary Ellen, *née* Hadley; *b* 26 Dec 1924; *Educ* Henry Thornton Sch; *m* 16 Sept 1950, Audrey Edna, da of Bernard Joseph Betts (d 1957); 1 s (Nicholas b 1954), 1 da (Judith b 1952); *Career* Sub Lt (A) RNVR 1943-46; admitted slr 1949; sr ptnr Wright Webb Syrett 1982-90; legal advsr Music Publishers Assoc 1962-90; *Recreations* reading, gardening, crosswords, watching cricket; *Style—* Peter Ash, Esq; 38 Sutton Lane, Banstead, Surrey (☎ 0737 358105); 10 Soho Square, London W1 (☎ 071 439 3111, fax 071 434 1520, telex 22276)

ASH, Rear Adm Walter William Hector; CB (1962); s of Hector Sidney Ash (d 1953), of Portsmouth, Hants, and Mabel Jessy Ash; *b* 2 May 1906; *Educ* City and Guilds Engrg Coll Kensington, RNC Greenwich (Whitworth scholar, John Samuel Scholar, CEng, FIEE) 1927); *m* 1932, Louisa Adelaide, da of late William Salt, of Jarrow-upon-Tyne; 3 da; *Career* chartered electrical engr; electrical engr Admty 1937-39 (asst 1932-37), fleet electrical engr Staff C-in-C Med 1939-40; supt electrical engr: Admty 1940-45, HM Dockyard Hong Kong 1945-48; Cdr HMS Montclare RN 1950-51, Capt Admty RN 1951-54, electrical engr and mangr HM Dockyard Devonport 1954-58, chm IEE S W Sub-Centre 1957-58, Rear Adm 1960, ship design directorate Admty 1959-63; ADC to HM The Queen 1958-60; *Recreations* music (piano and organ); *Style—* Rear Adm Walter Ash, CB; 4 Vavasour Hse, North Embankment, Dartmouth, Devon TQ6 9PW (☎ 0803 834630)

ASHBEE, Dr Paul; *b* 23 June 1918; *Educ* Maidstone Sch, Univ of Leicester (MA, DLitt), Univ of London (Dip Archaeology); *m* 4 Sept 1952, Richmal Crompton Lamburn, da of Thomas Frederick Rhodes Disher (d 1963), of Dulwich; 1 s (Edward b 1953), 1 da (Catherine b 1956); *Career* WWII Royal W Kent and REME 1939-46, control cmmn for Germany Aachen and Dusseldorf HQs 1946-49; carried out for Miny of Works (now English Heritage) 1949-76, co dir Br Museum excavations at Sutton Hoo 1964-71, archaeologist UEA 1968-83; author of numerous papers, articles and reviews for numerous archaeological jls; memb: Royal Archaeological Inst, Wilts Archaeological Soc, Cornwall Archaeological Soc (pres 1976-80, vice pres 1980-84), Kent Archaeological Soc, Prehistoric Soc (Cncl and meetings sec 1960-74); sec Sub Ctee Br Assoc for Archaeological Field Experiments, former sec Neolithic and Bronze Age Ctee Br Archaeology Cncl, Royal Cmmr on Historical Monuments of England 1975-85, memb Area Archaeological Advsy Ctee for Norfolk and Suffolk 1975-79, chm Scole Ctee for E Anglian Archaeology 1979-84; FSA 1958, FRSAIre 1987; *Books* The Bronze Age Round Barrow in Britain (1960), The Earthern Long Barrow in Britain (1970, 2 edn 1984), Ancient Scilly (1974), The Ancient British (1978), Sutton Hoo (contrib, 1976); *Recreations* bibliophilia, historical architecture, E Anglia, dog ownership; *Style—* Dr Paul Ashbee, FSA; The Old Rectory, Chedgrave, Norwich NR14 6ND (☎ 0508 20595)

ASHBOURNE, 4 Baron (UK 1885); (Edward) Barry Greynville Gibson; s of Vice Adm 3 Baron Ashbourne, CB, DSO, JP, of Liphook, Hants (d 1983), and Reta, Baroness Ashbourne, *qv*; *b* 28 Jan 1933; *Educ* Rugby; *m* 25 March 1967, Yvonne Georgina, da of Mrs Flora Ham; 3 s (Hon Charles b 1967, Hon Rodney b 1970, Hon Patrick b 1977); *Heir* s, Hon Edward Charles d'Olier Gibson b 31 Dec 1967; *Career* RN 1951-72: Lt-Cdr, cmd HMS Crofton 1963-64; RN Staff Coll 1965; stockbroker 1972-79; investmt mktg 1979-88; pres Petersfield Branch E Hampshire Cons Assoc; vice pres: Hampshire Autistic Soc, (Europe) Hope Now Int Ministries; chm Joshua Christian Tst; *Recreations* golf, sailing, creative gardening; *Style—* The Rt Hon the Lord Ashbourne; 107 Sussex Rd, Petersfield, Hants GU31 4LB (☎ 0730 64636)

ASHBOURNE, Reta, Baroness; Reta Frances Manning; er da of Ernest Manning Hazeland, of Hong Kong; *b* 2 March 1903; *m* 1929, Vice Adm 3 Baron Ashbourne, CB, DSO (d 1983); 1 s (4 Baron, *qv*), 1 da; *Style—* The Rt Hon Reta, Lady Ashbourne; 56 Chiltley Way, Midhurst Rd, Liphook, Hants

ASHBROOK, 10 Viscount (I 1751); Desmond Llowarch Edward Flower; KCVO (1977), MBE (1945), DL (Cheshire 1949); also Baron Castle Durrow (I 1733); s of 9 Viscount Ashbrook, DL (d 1936), and Gladys, da of Gen Sir George Higginson, GCB, GCVO; *b* 9 July 1905; *Educ* Eton, Balliol Coll Oxford; *m* 8 Nov 1934, Elizabeth, sis of Lady Newton (w of 4 Baron Newton) and da of Capt John Egerton-Warburton (whose f, Piers, was gn of Sir John and Sir Philip Egerton, 8 and 9 Bts, and whose m was Hon Antoinette Saumarez, da of 3 Baron de Saumarez; Piers was ggn of Sir Peter Warburton, 5 and last of the Warburton Baronetcy), by his w Hon Lettice Legh, JP, eld da of 2 Baron Newton); 2 s, 1 da; *Heir* s, Hon Michael Flower; *Career* Maj RA WWII; JP Cheshire 1946-67, Vice Lieut 1961-67; memb Cncl Duchy of Lancaster 1957-77; former chartered accountant; chm Country Gentlemen's Assoc 1955-62; *Style—* The Rt Hon the Viscount Ashbrook, KCVO, MBE, DL

ASHBROOK, Kate Jessie; da of John Benjamin Ashbrook, of Denham Village, Bucks, and Margaret, *née* Balfour; *b* 1 Feb 1955; *Educ* High March Sch, Benenden Sch, Univ of Exeter (BSc); *Career* sec Dartmoor Preservation Assoc 1981-84, gen sec Open Spaces Soc 1984-; memb: Exec Ctee Cncl for Nat Parks, Gen Cncl for Protection of Rural England, Nat Exec Ctee Rambler's Assoc (footpath sec Bucks and W Middx area); sec Countryside Link Gp; *Books* Severnside A Guide to Family Walks (The Southern Quantocks, 1977), The Walks of SE England (contrib A Walk round Denham, 1975), Common Place No More, Common Land in the 1980s (1983), Make for the Hills (1983), Our Common Right (1987); *Recreations* walking, campaigning for access to countryside, music; *Style—* Miss Kate Ashbrook; Telfer's Cottage, Turville, Henley-on-Thames RG9 6QL (☎ 0491 63396); Open Spaces Society, 25A Bell St, Henley-on-Thames RG9 2BA (☎ 0491 573 535)

ASHBROOKE, (Philip) Biden Derwent; s of Philip Ashbrooke (d 1941), of Doveray Place, Porlock, Somerset, and Gladys Derwent, *née* Moger (d 1948); *b* 23 Aug 1925; *Educ* Westminster, St John's Coll Cambridge (MA); *m* 23 Oct 1954, Veronica Philippa, da of Eudo Philip Joseph Stourton (d 1975; ggs of 19 Baron Stourton), of La Grande Maison, St John, Jersey, CI; 1 s (Auberon b 1956, Maj 14/20 Kings Hussars), 1 da (Sophia b 1959, Viscountess Stormont, see Earl of Mansfield and Mansfield); *Career* joined Army 1943, Capt 8 Kings Royal Irish Hussars 1946-47, Capt City of London Yeo (Rough Riders) 1950-56, ADC to H E The Govr of Kenya 1946-47; called to the Bar Gray's Inn 1950; *Clubs* Boodle's; *Style—* Biden Ashbrooke, Esq; La Grande Maison, St John, Jersey, CI

ASHBURNHAM, Capt Sir Denny Reginald; 12 Bt (E 1661), of Broomham, Sussex; s of Sir Fleetwood Ashburnham, 11 Bt (d 1953); co-heir to Barony of Grandison (abeyant since 1328); *b* 24 March 1916; *m* 22 June 1946, Mary Frances, da of Maj Robert Pascoe Mair, of Wick, Udimore, Sussex; 1 s (decd), 2 da; *Heir* gs, James Fleetwood Ashburnham b 17 Dec 1979 (s of John Anchitel Fleetwood Ashburnham (b 1951 d 1981) by his w Corinne, da of D W J O'Brien, of Chelwood Farm, Nutley, E Sussex); *Career* Capt S Staffs Regt; *Style—* Capt Sir Denny Ashburnham, Bt; Little Broomham, Guestling, Hastings, E Sussex

ASHBURTON, 6 Baron (UK 1835); Alexander Francis St Vincent Baring; KG (1969), KCVO (1961), JP (Hants 1951), DL (1973); s of 5 Baron Ashburton (d 1938), by 1 w Hon Mabel Hood (da of 4 Viscount Hood); *b* 7 April 1898; *Educ* Eton, Sandhurst; *m* 17 Nov 1924, Hon Doris Mary Thérèse Harcourt (d 1981), da of 1 Viscount Harcourt; 2 s; *Heir* s, Hon Sir John Baring, KCVO *qv*; *Career* Lt Scots Greys 1917-23, AAF 1939, Gp Capt 1944, ret; CC Hants 1945, CA 1955; md Baring Bros 1928-62 (dir to 1968), former dir Pressed Steel Co and Alliance Assurance; tstee: King George's Jubilee Tst 1949-68, Chantrey Bequest 1963-86; chm: Hants & IOW Police Authy 1967-71, Hampshire Police Authy 1967-71; pres E Wessex TA 1968-70, govr King Edward VII Hosp Fund for London 1971-75 (former treas), receiver-gen to Duchy of Cornwall 1961-74, Vice-Lt Hants and IOW 1951-60, Lord Lt and Custos Rotulorum 1960-73, High Steward of Winchester 1967-78; KStJ 1960; *Style—* The Rt Hon Lord Ashburton, KG, KCVO, JP, DL; Itchen Stoke House, Alresford, Hants SO24 0QU (☎ 096 273 732479)

ASHBY, Anne Mary; da of George Griffiths (d 1942), and Mary Griffiths (d 1965); *b* 2 May 1938; *Educ* Priory Sch Shrewsbury; *m* 26 May 1956, John Ashby; 2 s (Mark b 1961, Edward b 1968), 1 da (Louise b 1971); *Career* SRN Royal Postgrad Hosp 1961, state registered midwife Hammersmith Hosp; co fndr and dir Womens Aid Ltd 1971-83, chm Westminster Womens Aid 1987-, fieldworker Emergency Housing Serv Family Housing Assoc; named a Woman of the Year 1987; *Recreations* reading, swimming, walking; *Clubs* Women of the Year Assoc; *Style—* Mrs Anne Ashby; 12 Reynolds Place, Queens Rd, Richmond, Surrey TW10 6JZ (☎ 081 940 3683)

ASHBY, Brian Sterry; s of Roland Sterry Ashby (d 1978), of Manor House, Moulton, Northants, and Marion Elizabeth, *née* Phillips (d 1976); *b* 28 Aug 1930; *Educ* Bloxham Sch, Trinity Coll Cambridge (MA), Westminster Med Sch (MB MChir); *m* 1, 5 Dec 1953 (m dis 1960), Avis Jean, da of Daniel Howell Harding Thomas (d 1948); 1 s (Phillip Sterry b 31 Jan 1955); m 2, 14 Aug 1961, Gillian Mary Elizabeth, da of William Victor Dawson (d 1946), of Canterbury, Kent; *Career* surgical registrar St James Hosp Balham 1961-63, sr surgical registrar Westminster Hosp 1964-69, res fell Univ of California San Francisco 1966-67, conslt surgn Southend Gen Hosp 1970-, Cutlers Surgical award Worshipful Co of Cutlers 1983, Hunterian prof RCS 1984; memb: Br Soc of Gastroenterology, Assoc of Surgns of GB, RSM; FRCS; *Books* Renal Preservation (1969), contrib to books on surgery of gallstones, choledochoscopy; *Recreations* gardening, driving, collecting Victorian and contemporary water colours, travel; *Style—* Brian Ashby, Esq; Gore House, Ballards Gore, Rochford, Essex SS4 2DA (☎ 0702 258307); Old Keigwin, Mousehole, Penzance, Cornwall TR19 6RR (☎ 0736 731688); Department of Surgery, Southend General Hospital, Southend, Essex SS0 0RY (☎ 0702 348911); Wellesley Hospital, Eastern Ave, Southend, Essex SS2 4XH (☎ 0702 462944)

ASHBY, David Glynn; MP (C) North-West Leicestershire 1983-; s of Robert M Ashby and Isobel A Davidson; *b* 14 May 1940; *Educ* Royal GS High Wycombe, Bristol Univ (LLB); *m* 1965, Silvana Morena; 1 da; *Career* called to the Bar Gray's Inn 1963; in practice on SE Circuit; memb Hammersmith Borough Cncl 1968-71; memb: GLC for W Woolwich 1977-81, ILEA 1977-81; *Recreations* gardening, skiing, music; *Clubs* Hurlingham; *Style—* David Ashby, Esq, MP; 29 Church Street, Appleby Magna, Leics; 132 West Hill, London SW15 2UE

ASHBY, Eric; s of Albert Ashby (d 1932), of Southsea, and (Dorothy) May, *née* Stoner (d 1975); *b* 19 Jan 1918; *Educ* St Jude's Church Sch Southsea Hants; *m* 25 Sept 1975, Eileen, da of Hubert Charles Batchelor (d 1982), of Salisbury, Wilts; *Career* pioneer in filming shy Br animals, started wildlife photography 1930; TV progs incl: The Unknown Forest (1961), The Silent Watcher (1961), A Hare's Life (1963), A Forest Diary (1963), Ponies of the New Forest (1964), Badgers (1966), The Best Of Eric Ashby (1967), At Home With Foxes (1968), The Living Forest (1970), Cranborne

Chase (1973), The Private Life of the Fox (1975), The Year of the Deer (1977), At Home With Badgers (1978), Roadside View (1980), Eye on the Forest (1984), Through Two Cameras (1989), Badger Cottage (1989); memb: New Forest Badger Gp, New Forest Assoc, Hants and IOW Naturalists Tst, CPRE; vice pres Conservative Anti-Hunt Cncl; *Books* The Secret Life of the New Forest (1989); *Recreations* conservation of the precarious New Forest wildlife, caring for rescued foxes; *Style*— Eric Ashby, Esq; Badger Cottage, Linwood, Ringwood, Hampshire BH24 3QT

ASHBY, Baron (Life Peer UK 1973), of Brandon, Suffolk; Eric Ashby; s of Herbert Charles Ashby (d 1933), of Shortlands, Kent, and Helena Chater; *b* 24 Aug 1904; *Educ* City of London Sch, Imperial Coll of Science London (DSc); *m* 1931, Elizabeth Helen Margaret, da of Francis Farries (d 1953), of Castle Douglas, Kirkcudbrightshire, Scotland; 2 s (Hon Michael Farries b 1935, Hon Peter b 1937); *Career* prof of Botany Sydney Univ Aust 1938-46; chm: Aust Nat Research Cncl 1940-42, Professorial Bd Sydney Univ 1942-44; tstee Aust Museum 1942-46, cnsllr and chargé d'affaires Aust Legation Moscow USSR 1945-46, Harrison prof of botany and dir of Botanical Labs Univ of Manchester 1946-50; memb: Advsy Cncl on Scientific Policy 1950-53, Advsy Cncl on Scientific and Industl Research 1954-60; chm Scientific Grants Ctee DSIR 1955-56, vice-chllr Queen's Univ Belfast 1950-59, master Clare Coll Cambridge 1959-75 (fell 1958, life fell 1975-), vice-chm Assoc of Univs of Br Cwlth 1959-61, vice-chllr Cambridge Univ 1967-69, chllr Queen's Univ Belfast 1970-83; sits as memb of SDP in House of Lords; Hon LLD, Hon ScD, Hon DSc, Hon DLitt, Hon DPhil, Hon DCL, Hon DHL; OStJ 1956, Order of Andrés Bello Venezuela 1971(1 Class); hon fell Imp Coll of Science, hon foreign memb American Acad of Arts and Sciences; FRS, Hon FRSE, Hon FRIC; *Books* author of books on biology, environmental politics, and higher education; *Recreations* music; *Style*— The Rt Hon the Lord Ashby, FRS; 22 Eltisley Ave, Cambridge (☎ 0223 356216); Norman Cottage, Brandon, Suffolk

ASHBY, Prof the Hon Michael Farries; er s of Baron Ashby, FRS (Life Peer), *qv*; *b* 20 Nov 1935; *Educ* Campbell Coll Belfast, Queens' Coll Cambridge (MA, PhD); *m* 1962, Maureen, da of James Stewart, of White House, Montgomery, Powys; 2 s, 1 da; *Career* asst prof Harvard Univ 1965-69, prof of Metallurgy Harvard Univ 1969-73, prof of Engineering Materials Cambridge Univ 1973-, ed Acta Metallurgica 1974-; Hon MA Harvard; FRS; *Books* Engineering Materials (parts 1 and 2), Deformation-Mechanism Maps, The Structure and Properties of Cellular Solids; *Recreations* music, design; *Style*— Prof the Hon Michael Ashby, FRS; 51 Maids Causeway, Cambridge CB5 8DE

ASHBY, Dr the Hon Peter; yr s of Baron Ashby, FRS (Life Peer), *qv*; *b* 1937; *Educ* Campbell Coll Belfast, Queen's Univ Belfast (MB BCh, MD); *m* 1967, Moya, da of Surgn Rear Adm Maurice Henry Adams, CB, of Canberra Rock, Cornwall; *Career* prof at Univ of Toronto; *Style*— Dr the Hon Peter Ashby; 42 Bennington Heights Drive, Toronto, Ontario M4G 1A6, Canada

ASHCOMBE, 4 Baron (UK 1892); Henry Edward Cubitt; s of 3 Baron Ashcombe (d 1962) by his 1 w, Sonia, da of Lt-Col Hon George Keppel, MVO, (3 s of 7 Earl of Albemarle); *b* 31 March 1924; *Educ* Eton; *m* 1, 12 Sept 1955 (m dis 1968), Ghislaine, da of Cornelius Dresselhuys, of Long Island and formerly w of late Maj Denis Alexander (afterwards 6 Earl of Caledon); m 2, 1973 (m dis 1979), Hon Virginia Carrington, yr da of 6 Baron Carrington; m 3, 1979, Elizabeth, da of Dr Henry Chipps, of Lexington, Kentucky, and widow of Mark Dent-Brocklehurst, of Sudeley Castle, Glos; *Heir* kinsman, Mark Cubitt, *qv*; *Career* served WW II RAF; consul-gen for Monaco in London 1961-68, chm Cubitt Estates Ltd; *Clubs* White's; *Style*— The Rt Hon the Lord Ashcombe; Sudeley Castle, Winchcombe, Cheltenham, Glos GL54 5JD; Flat 6, 53 Drayton Gardens, London SW10 9RX

ASHCOMBE, Virginia, Baroness; Hon Virginia; *née* Carington; da of 6 Baron Carrington; *b* 23 June 1946; *m* 1973 (m dis 1979), 4 Baron Ashcombe; *Style*— Virginia, Lady Ashcombe; 5 Rutland Gate Mews, London SW7 (☎ 071 584 3678); The Manor House, Bledlow, nr Aylesbury, Bucks (☎ 084 44 3499)

ASHCROFT, George Denman; s of Frederick Ashcroft (d 1941), of Manchester, and Ethel Louise Gertrude, *née* Morgan-Sudlow; *b* 22 Oct 1909; *Educ* Manchester HS of Commerce, Univ of Manchester; *m* 24 June 1944, (Clarice) Dorothy, da of William Alexander Park; 2 da (Jane b 1948, Judith b 1952); *Career* H G 1940-45; civil serv London; accountant 1927-38, industl fin 1938-42 and 1946-50, accountancy branch MOD 1942-46; md Percy Bros Ltd 1950-, dir Int Printers Ltd (IPC Gp) 1960-65, chm Hotspur Press Gp of Co's 1965-; memb Cncl Br Fedn of Printing Industs (memb Fin Ctee and Lab Ctee) 1955-81, pres Lancs & Ches Alliance of Master Printers 1958-60, lay chm Manchester Diocesan Synod (C of E) 1970, chm Diocesan Bd of Fin 1976-; pres: Lancs and Ches Printers Pension Corpn 1965-66, Manchester Soc of CAs; former tbnl memb Miny of Nat Insur, govr St Elphins Sch for Girls Derbys; FCA; *Recreations* golf, walking in Derbyshire hills; *Clubs* Manchester, Naval & Military, Withington Golf; *Style*— George D Ashcroft, Esq; Brantwood, Ballbrook Ave, Didsbury, Manchester M20 0AB; Hotspur House, Whitworth St, W Manchester M1 5QB (☎ 061 236 0374)

ASHCROFT, Kenneth; s of James Martland Ashcroft (d 1969), of Preston, and Mary Winifred, *née* Walker; *b* 22 March 1935; *Educ* Preston GS; *m* 1957, Patricia Maria, da of Henry Hothersall (d 1946), of Preston; 2 da (Jill b 1961, Jayne b 1963); *Career* CA and chartered mgmnt accountant; formerly with Philips Holland and Ford of Europe; dir: Ideal Standard 1970-73, Comet 1973-75, Hepworth-Next 1975-82, Dixons Ltd 1983-85, Amstrad plc 1985-; *Recreations* music, gardening; *Style*— Kenneth Ashcroft, Esq; Fendley Corner, Sauncey Wood, Harpenden, Herts AL5 5DW (☎ 05827 5549); Amstrad plc, Brentwood House, Kings Rd, Brentwood, Essex (☎ 0277 228 888)

ASHCROFT, Dame Peggy - Edith Margaret Emily; DBE (1956, CBE 1951); da of William Worsley Ashcroft and Violet Maud Bernheim; *b* 22 Dec 1907; *Educ* Woodford Sch Croydon and Central Sch of Speech Training and Dramatic Art; *m* 1, 1929 (m dis), Rupert (later Sir Rupert) Hart-Davis; m 2, 1934, Theodore Komisarjevsky; m 3, 1940 (m dis 1966), Jeremy Nicholas Hutchinson, QC (later Lord Hutchinson of Lullington); 1 s, 1 da; *Career* actress; dir Royal Shakespeare Co 1968-; Best Actress Award 1981 Monte Carlo TV Festival; *Style*— Dame Peggy Ashcroft, DBE

ASHCROFT, Philip Giles; s of Edmund Samuel Ashcroft (d 1957), of Newcastle upon Tyne, and Constance Ruth, *née* Giles (d 1960); *b* 15 Nov 1926; *Educ* Newcastle Royal GS, Univ of Durham (LLB); *m* 1, 27 April 1968 (m dis 1983), Kathleen Margaret, *née* Senior; 1 s (Richard b 1969); m 2, 14 Sept 1985, Valerie May, da of Edgar Thomas George Smith (d 1966), of London; *Career* Royal Signals 1944-48; admitted slr 1951; Treasy Slrs Dept 1955-67, asst legal advsr Land Cmmn 1967-71, asst treasy slr 1971-73, under sec legal DTI 1973, legal advsr Dept of Energy 1974-80, dep slr PO 1980-81, slr BT 1981-87, conslt Bldg Socs Cmmn 1988-; memb Law Soc 1951; *Recreations* walking, music; *Style*— Philip Ashcroft, Esq; 24A Rudds Lane, Haddenham, Aylesbury, Bucks HP17 8JP (☎ 0844 291921)

ASHCROFT, Dr Thomas; s of Maj William Gilmour Ashcroft (d 1944), of Urquhart, Morayshire, and Margaret, *née* Anderson (d 1979); *b* 12 July 1933; *Educ* Aberlour HS, Univ of Aberdeen (MB ChB, MD); *m* 15 Sept 1962, Margaret Louise, da of Thomas James (d 1947), of Swansea, Glamorgan; 1 s (Peter b 1970), 3 da (Sarah b 1963, Catherine b 1966, Frances b 1969); *Career* Lt then Capt RAMC 1958-60; house surgn and physician Aberdeen Royal Infirmary 1957-58, sr house offr MRC 1960-61, lectr in pathology Univ of Newcastle upon Tyne 1966-73 (demonstrator in pathology 1961-66), conslt in pathology Leighton Hosp Crewe 1973-79, conslt pathologist Freeman Hosp Newcastle 1979-; FRCPath; *Recreations* hill walking, photography; *Style*— Dr Thomas Ashcroft; 10 Mitchell Ave, Jesmond, Newcastle Upon Tyne NE2 3LA (☎ 091 281 2745); Pathology Dept, Freeman Hospital, Newcastle Upon Tyne NE7 7DN (☎ 091 284 3111 ext 26536)

ASHDOWN, David William; s of William Curtis Thomas, and Jean Vida Ashdown; *b* 11 Dec 1950; *Educ* Wandsworth Comp; *m* 12 Aug 1978, Carol, da of Andrew Allan Smith (d 1963); 2 s (Michael b 1974, Peter b 1979); *Career* photographer: Keystone Press 1968-78, Daily Star 1978-86; chief sports photographer The Independent 1986-; Ilford Press Photographer of the Year 1974, runner-up Br Press Picture Awards 1979, Ilford Sports Picture of the Year 1985, Nikon Press Sports Photographer of the Year 1987, Adidas Euro Sports Picture of the Year 1987, Sports Photographer of the Year 1987; FRPS; *Recreations* golf, old motorbikes; *Style*— David Ashdown, Esq; The Independent, 40 City Rd, London EC1 (☎ 071 253 1222, fax 071 608 1552, car 0836 361 655, telex 9419611)

ASHDOWN, Rt Hon Jeremy John Durham (Paddy); PC (1989), MP (Lib) Yeovil 1983-; s of John W R D Ashdown, and Lois A Ashdown; *b* 27 Feb 1941; *Educ* Bedford Sch, Language Sch Hong Kong; *m* 1961, Jane Courtenay; 1 s (Simon), 1 da (Kate); *Career* RM 1959-72; served: Borneo, Persian Gulf, Belfast; cmd Special Boat Section (SBS) in the Far East; sometime chinese interpreter, joined FCO 1972, first sec to Br Mission to UN Geneva 1974-76; Parly candidate (Lib) 1979, former Lib spokesman Trade and Indust, Educn spokesman 1987, leader Social and Lib Democrats 1988, currently spokesman on NI; *Style*— The Rt Hon Paddy Ashdown, MP; House of Commons, London SW1A 0AA

ASHDOWN, Baroness; Lillian Nell; *née* King; CBE (1971); da of Ralph King (d 1966), of Rhodesia (now Zimbabwe) and London, and Mabel Kathleen King (d 1969); *b* 19 May 1915; *Educ* St Margaret's Harrow, Paris, King's Coll London; *m* 1937, Arnold Silverstone, kt 1964, cr Baron Ashdown (Life Peer) 1974 and d 1977; *Career* served WWII with Mechanised Tport Corps; Westminster City cncllr 1955-65; memb Nat Union Cons Pty 1963-79, vice chm NWAC 1967, chm SE Area Cons Pty 1971-75 (previously chm of women), serv Cons Pty Policy Ctee 1973-79; fndr memb Women's Nat Cancer Campaign 1964- (vice chm 1967-70); govr St George's Hosp 1971-75, pres E Sussex DGAA 1974-78, chm Friends of Moorfield Hosp 1979 and govr Moorfields Special Health Authy; conservator Ashdown Forest 1973-78; pres Westminster SSAFA 1988- (hon sec 1982-88); *Recreations* politics, reading; *Clubs* Carlton; *Style*— The Rt Hon the Lady Ashdown, CBE; c/o Barclays Bank, 8 West Halkin St, London SW1X 8JE

ASHE, Sir Derick Rosslyn; KCMG (1978, CMG 1966); s of Frederick Charles Allen Angelo Patrick Donnelly Ashe (d 1930), and Rosalind, *née* Mitchell; *b* 20 Jan 1919; *Educ* Bradfield, Trinity Coll Oxford (MA); *m* 1957, Mrs Rissa Guinness, da of late Capt Hon Trevor Tempest Parker, DSC, RN (s of Baron Parker of Waddington of the first creation); 1 s (Dominick), 1 da (Victoria); *Career* served WWII Capt (despatches); entered HM Dip Serv 1947; cnsllr: Addis Ababa 1962-64, Havana 1964-66; head Security Dept FO 1966-69, min Br Embassy Toyko 1969-71; HM ambass: Romania 1972-75, Argentina 1975-77; ambass and perm del: First UN Special Session on Disarmament NY 1977-78, Disarmament Conf Geneva 1977-79; ret 1979; Knight of the Order of Orange Nassau with Swords (Netherlands) 1945; *Recreations* gardening, fine arts; *Clubs* Travellers', Beefsteak, White's; *Style*— Sir Derick Ashe, KCMG; Dalton House, Hurstbourne Tarrant, Andover, Hants (☎ 026 476276)

ASHER, Alistair Hugh; s of Robert Alexander Asher, of Nairn, and Jane, *née* Fraser; *b* 30 Dec 1955; *Educ* Norwich Sch, Southampton Univ (LLB), Amsterdam Univ (Dip Euro Law); *m* 25 May 1985, Patricia Margaret, da of Derrick Robinson (d 1979), of Lincoln and Maidenhead; 1 s (Alexander b 9 July 1990), 1 da (Jenny b 29 Sept 1987); *Career* admitted slr 1981; ptnr Allen & Overy 1987-(joined 1979); memb Law Soc; *Recreations* cycling, swimming, squash; *Style*— Alistair Asher, Esq; 9 Cheapside, London EC2V 6AD (☎ 071 248 9898, fax 071 236 2192, telex 8812801)

ASHER, Jane; da of Richard Alan John Asher (d 1969), and Margaret, *née* Eliot; *b* 5 April 1946; *m* Gerald Anthony Scarfe, s of Reginald Thomas Scarfe (d 1972); 2 s (Alexander b 1981, Rory b 1983), 1 da (Katie b 1974); *Career* professional actress; stage appearances incl: Housemaster 1957, Will You Walk A Little Faster (Muriel Webster) Duke of York's Theatre 1960, Peter Pan (Wendy) Scala Theatre 1961, Pygmalion (Eliza Doolittle) Watford, Romeo and Juliet (Juliet) and Measure for Measure (Julietta) City Centre NY 1967, The Philanthopist (Celia) Mayfair Theatre and on Broadway 1970, Old Flames (Sally) Bristol Old Vic 1974, Treats (Ann) Royal Court and Mayfair Theatres 1975, Strawberry Fields (Charlotte) and To Those Born Later National Theatre 1976, Whose Life Is It Anyway? (Dr Scott) Mermaid and Savoy Theatres, Peter Pan (Peter) 1979, Before The Party Queens Theatre 1981 (prodr and performer), Blithe Spirit (Ruth) Vaudeville Theatre 1986, Hence forward.... (Robert and Wife) Vaudeville Theatre 1989, The School for Scandal (Lady Sneerwell) National Theatre 1990; Bristol Old Vic 1965-72: Cleo, Great Expectations, The Happiest Days of Your Life, Sixty Thousand Nights, Romeo and Juliet, Measure For Measure; films incl: Mandy, Greengage Summer, Alfie, Deep End, Henry VIII and His Six Wives, Runners, Dream Child, Paris By Night; TV appearances incl: The Mill on The Floss, The Recruiting Officer, Hedda Gabler, Brideshead Revisited, Love is Old Love is New, Voyage Round My Father, East Lynne, Bright Smiler, The Mistress, Wish Me Luck; BBC radio drama progs incl Crown house; contrib: TV and radio current affrs progs, newspaper and magazine articles; reg columns Daily Telegraph and The Independent; memb Advsy Ctee Childrens Programming TV AM, involved with Dept of Tports' promotion of use of child car restraints; tstee: WWF, Geffrye Museum Ford Martin Fund for Children with Cancer, Child Accident Prevention Tst; memb BAFTA, assoc RADA, govr Molecule Theatre, patron num charities; FRSA; *Books* Jane Asher's Party Cakes (1982), Jane Asher's Quick Party Cakes (1983), Jane Asher's Fancy Dress (1983), Silent Nights for You and Your Baby (1984), Easy Entertaining (1987), Moppy Is Happy (with G Scarfe, 1987), Moppy Is Angry (with G Scarfe, 1987), Keep Your Baby Safe (1988), Jane Asher's Childrens Parties (1988), Calendar of Cakes (1989), Eats for Treats (1990); *Recreations* skiing, reading, music; *Style*— Jane Asher

ASHER, Prof Ronald E; s of Ernest Asher, and Doris, *née* Hurst; *b* 23 July 1926; *Educ* King Edward VI GS Retford Notts, UCL (BA, PhD); *m* 1960, Chin; 2 s (David b 1966, Michael b 1968); *Career* asst Dept of French UCL 1951-53, lectr in linguistics and Tamil SOAS Univ of London 1953-65; Dept of linguistics Univ of Edinburgh: sr lectr 1965-70, reader 1970-77, prof of linguistics 1977-, dean of Faculty of Arts 1986-89, memb of Univ Ct 1989-, vice-princ 1991-; visiting prof: of Tamil Univ of Chicago 1961-62, of linguistics Univ of Illinois 1967, of Tamil and Malayalam Michigan State Univ 1968, of linguistics Univ of Minnesota 1969, Collége de France Paris 1970; FRAS 1964; fell of the Kerala Sahitya Akademi (Kerala Academy of Letters) India 1983, Gold medal of the Akademi for distinguished servs to Malayalam language and lit; *Books* A Tamil Prose Reader (1971), Aspects de la littérature en prose dans le sud de l'Inde (1972), Some Landmarks in the History of Tamil Prose (1973), Scavenger's Son (translation from Malayalam, 1975), Me Grandad 'ad an Elephant (translation from Malayalam, 1980), Towards a History of Phonetics (ed with E J A Henderson, 1981), Tamil (1982), Malayala bhasha-sahitya pathanangal (Malayalam: Studies on Malayalam Language and Literature) (1989), Francus and Samothes: Legendary Monarchs and Nationalism in Renaissance France (1991); *Style*— Prof R E Asher; University of Edinburgh, Department of Linguistics, 15 Buccleuch Place, Edinburgh EH8 9LN (☎ 031 650 3484, fax 031 668 3094, telex 727442 UNIVED G)

ASHFIELD, Gerald William; s of Maj Percy Ashfield (d 1964), of Seaford, Sussex, and Isabella von Herwarth (d 1976); *b* 7 Dec 1910; *Educ* Wellington; *m* 1, 5 March 1935, Lilian (d 1973), da of Maj H Grayson (d 1935) of London; 2 s (Michael b 1938, Philip b 1940); m 2, 28 Sept 1974, Gladys, da of William Miller (d 1965), of London; *Career* Maj Indian Army; memb Stock Exchange 1946-; chm and dir: Practical Investment Co plc, London & St Lawrence Investment Co plc; vice pres Toc H; Lord of the Manor Gt Ashfield Suffolk; *Recreations* golf, walking; *Clubs* Piltdown Golf; *Style*— Gerald Ashfield, Esq; Wilmshurst-Fletching, Nr Uckfield, East Sussex (☎ 082 571 2523); Teather and Greenwood, Salisbury House, London Wall, London EC2M 5TH

ASHFORD, Lady (Winifred) Anne Grizel; *née* Cochrane; only da of Hon Douglas Robert Hesketh Roger Cochrane (d 1942) and sis of 14 Earl of Dundonald; raised to the rank of an Earl's da 1960; *b* 1 Oct 1923; *m* 1967, Alfred Ashford, o s of late Alfred Ashford, of Bromley, Kent; 1 s (Alexis b 1969); *Style*— The Lady Anne Ashford

ASHFORD, Prof Norman Joseph; s of Robert Edward Ashford (d 1979), of London, and Gladys Kathleen, *née* Norman (d 1975); *b* 21 Aug 1935; *Educ* Gunnersbury Sch, UCL (BSc), Georgia Inst of Technol (MSCE, PhD); *m* 13 June 1957, Joan Allison, da of Maurice Hornsby (d 1959), of Sutton in Ashfield; 1 s (Robert Simon b 12 Sept 1962), 1 da (Elizabeth b 18 Nov 1966); *Career* Royal Canadian Engr (Militia) 2 Lt 1961-63, Lt 1963-66; conslt engr Canada 1957-63, asst and assoc prof Florida State Univ 1967-72, prof of tport planning Loughborough Univ of Technol 1972-; author of numerous articles in jnls; dir Aviation Trg Assoc; FICE 1971, FCIT 1972, MASCE 1967; *Books* Transportation Engineering (1972), Airport Engineering (1979), Airport Operations (1984); *Recreations* photography; *Clubs* Royal Cwlth Soc; *Style*— Prof Norman Ashford; 15 The Drive, Woodhouse Eaves, Leicestershire LE12 8RE (☎ 0509 890260); Department of Transport Technology, Loughborough University of Technology, Loughborough, Leicestershire LE11 3TU (☎ 0509 223400, fax 0501 267613, ☎ 34319)

ASHFORD, Peter Desmond; s of Walter George Ashford (d 1985), and Beatrice Narcissa, *née* Davis (d 1985); *b* 31 July 1934; *Educ* Rutlish Sch, Univ of London; *m* 19 Dec 1969, Jennifer Anne, da of Robert James Patrick; 2 da (Elizabeth Anne b 13 July 1971, Catherine Anne b 16 Oct 1974); *Career* Lever Honeyman & Co Chartered Accountants 1951-63 (articled clerk, accountant); Annan & Dexter & Co: joined 1963, seconded to Deloitte Plender Griffiths Annan & Co Ndola Zambia 1965-66, ptnr 1968-71; ptnr: Dearden Lord Annan Morrish 1971-73, Dearden & Co (name change) 1973-76, Dearden Farrow (following merger) 1976-87, Binder Hamlyn (following merger) 1987-89, BDO Binder Hamlyn (name change) 1989-; FCA (ACA 1961); *Recreations* travel, photography; *Clubs* City of London; *Style*— Peter Ashford, Esq; BDO Binder Hamlyn, 20 Old Bailey, London EC4M 7BH (☎ 071 489 9000, fax 071 489 6060, car 0831 460 595)

ASHFORD, Ronald; s of Russell Sutcliffe Ashford (d 1960), of Hilltop, Powntley Copse, Alton, Hants, and Dorothy, *née* Shorland (d 1963); *b* 24 Aug 1932; *Educ* St Edwards Sch Oxford, De Havilland Aeronautical Tech Sch; *m* 18 June 1955, Francoise Louisa Gabrielle, da of Camille Genestal Du Chaumeil (d 1978), of Le Havre, France; 2 s (Mark b 1959, Peter b 1961); *Career* PO RAF 1956-58; flt test engr De Havilland Aircraft Co 1953-56, flt test engr and sr aerodynamicist De Havilland Aircraft Co and Hawker Siddeley Aviation 1958-68, design surveyor Air Registration Bd 1968-72; CAA: design surveyor 1972-82, head Flt Dept 1982-83, dir gen airworthiness 1983-87, head of operational safety 1987-88, gp dir of safety 1988-, bd memb 1988-; memb Exec Bd Euro Jt Aviation Authys; Freeman Guild of Air Pilots and Air Navigators 1990; CEng 1970, FRAeS 1983, FIMechE 1986; *Recreations* walking, gardening, light aircraft flying; *Style*— Ronald Ashford, Esq; Chartcote, Goodley Stock Rd, Crockham Hill, Edenbridge, Kent TN8 6TA (☎ 0732 866252); Aviation House, Gatwick Airport, West Sussex RH6 0YR (☎ 0293 573078, telex 878753, fax 0293 573997)

ASHKENAZY, Vladimir; s of David Ashkenazy, of Moscow, USSR, and Evstolia Plotnova (d 1979); *b* 6 July 1937; *Educ* Moscow Central Sch of Music Moscow Conservatory (second prize Chopin int piano comp 1955, first prize Brussels int piano comp 1956, first prize Tchaikovsky int piano comp 1962); *m* 25 Feb 1961, Thorunn Sofia, da of Johan Tryggvason, of London; 2 s (Vladimir Stefan b 1961, Dimitri Thor b 1969), 3 da (Nadia Liza b 1963, Sonia Edda b 1974, Alexandra Inga b 1979); *Career* concert pianist and conductor; studied under Lev Oborin class Moscow Conservatory 1955, debut with London Symphony Orch solo recital 1962, Royal Philharmonic Orch London 1987-, Radio Symphony Orch Berlin; Hon RAM 1972, Order of Falcon Iceland 1988; *Books* Beyond Frontiers (with Jasper Parrott, 1985); *Style*— Vladimir Ashkenazy, Esq

ASHLEY, Lord; Anthony Nils Christian Ashley-Cooper; s and h of 10 Earl of Shaftesbury; *b* 24 June 1977; *Style*— Lord Ashley

ASHLEY, Sir Bernard Albert; s of Albert Ashley, of Rhayader, Powys, Wales, and Hilda Maud, *née* Woodward; *b* 11 Aug 1926; *Educ* Whitgift Middle Sch, Univ of Wales (DSc Econ); *m* 1949, Laura (d 1985), da of Stanley Mountney (d 1960); 2 s (David, Nicholas), 2 da (Jane, Emma); m 2, 1990, Regine Genevieve Charlotte Chislaine, da of Pierre Burnell (d 1967); *Career* cmmnd Lt Royal Fus 1944-46, seconded 1 Gurkha Rifles 1944-45; chm Laura Ashley Hldgs plc; memb Army Sailing Assoc; FSIA; kt 1987; *Recreations* sailing (yacht 'Quaeso'), swimming, walking; *Clubs* Royal Thames Yacht, Lyford Cay (Nassau); *Style*— Sir Bernard Ashley; 43 Rue Ducale, Brussels, 1000

ASHLEY, Bernard John; s of Alfred Walter Ashley (d 1967), and Vera, *née* Powell (d 1978); *b* 2 April 1935; *Educ* Sir Joseph Williamson's Mathematical Sch Rochester, Trent Park Coll of Educn Herts, Cambridge Inst of Educn (Advanced DipEd); *m* 1957, Iris Frances, da of Harold Edward Holbrook; 3 s (Christopher b 1 Jan 1961, David b 1 June 1963, Jonathan b 17 April 1965); *Career* teacher in Kent until 1965; head teacher: Hertford Heath CP Sch 1965-71, Hartley Jr Sch Newham 1971-77, Charlton Manor Jr Sch London 1977-; writer; novels: The Trouble with Donovan Croft (The Other award 1985, 1974), Terry on the Fence (1975), All My Men (1977), A Kind of Wild Justice (1979), Break in the Sun (1981), Dodgem (1983), High Pavement Blues (1984), Janey (1985), Running Scared (1986), Bad Blood (1988); BBC TV serials: Break In the Sun (1981), Running Scared (1986), The Country Boy (1989), Dodgem (1991); The Secret of Theodore Brown (stage play, Unicorn Theatre London) 1990; memb: Writers' Guild of GB, NAHT; *Recreations* travel, watching football at Tottenham, theatre, concerts; *Style*— Bernard Ashley, Esq; 128 Heathwood Gardens, London SE7 8ER (☎ 081 854 5785); Charlton Manor Junior School, London SE7 7BE (☎ 081 856 6117)

ASHLEY, Cedric; CBE (1984); s of Ronald Bednall Ashley (d 1980), and Gladys Vera, *née* Fincher; *b* 11 Nov 1936; *Educ* King Edward's Sch Birmingham, Univ of Birmingham (BSc, PhD); *m* 1, 1960, Pamela Jane (decd), da of William Turner; 1 s (Paul); m 2, 1965 (m dis 1989), (Marjorie) Vivien, da of Arnold Joseph Gooch (d 1960); 1 s (William b 1971), 1 da (Juliet b 1967); *Career* lectr Univ of Birmingham 1965-73, int tech dir Bostrom Div UOP Ltd 1973-77, dir Motor Indust Res Assoc 1977-87, md Lotus Eng Ltd 1987-88, chm Cedric Ashley and Assocs 1988-, chief exec Br Internal Combustion Engine Res Inst 1989; FIMechE (chm Automobile Div 1990-91), FRSA; *Recreations* walking, motoring; *Clubs* RAC, Anglo Belgian; *Style*— Cedric Ashley, Esq, CBE; 4 The Terrace, Bray, Berkshire SR6 2AR

ASHLEY, Rt Hon Jack; CH (1975), PC (1979), MP (Lab) Stoke-on-Trent 1966-; s of John Ashley (d 1927), and Isabella, *née* Bridge; *b* 6 Dec 1922; *Educ* Ruskin Coll Oxford, Gonville and Caius Coll Cambridge; *m* 1951, Pauline Kay Crispin; 3 da; *Career* former labourer, shop steward convenor Chem Workers' Union, BBC prodr; pps to Sec of State: Econ Affrs 1966-67, DHSS 1974-76; *Style*— The Rt Hon Jack Ashley, CH, MP; House of Commons, London SW1A 0AA

ASHLEY, Maurice Percy; CBE (1978); s of Sir Percy Walter Llewellyn Ashley, KBE, CB (d 1945), and Doris, *née* Hayman (d 1941); *b* 4 Sept 1907; *Educ* St Paul's, New Coll Oxford; *m* 1935, Phyllis Mary Griffiths; 1 s, 1 da; *Career* historian and author; research asst to Sir Winston Churchill 1929-33; journalist with The Guardian and The Times 1933-39, ed Britain Today 1939-40; dep ed The Listener 1946-58 (ed 1958-67); res fell Loughborough Univ of Technol 1968-70; *Books Incl:* Oliver Cromwell (1937), Marlborough (1939), John Wildman: Plotter and Postman (1947), England in the Seventeenth Century (1952, rev 1978), Cromwell's Generals (1954), The Greatness of Oliver Cromwell (1957, rev 1967), Oliver Cromwell and the Puritan Revolution (1958), The Stuarts in Love (1963), Life in Stuart England (1964), Churchill as Historian (1968), A Golden Century 1598-1715 (1969), Charles II: The Man and The Statesman (1971), Oliver Cromwell and His World (1972), The Life and Times of King John (1982), The Life and Times of King William I (1973), The Age of Absolutism 1648-1775 (1974), A Concise History of the English Civil War (1975), Rupert of the Rhine (1976), General Monck (1977), James II (1978), The House of Stuart (1980); *Style*— Maurice Ashley, Esq, CBE; 34 Wood Lane, Ruislip, Middx (☎ 0895 35993)

ASHLEY, Nick Bernard; s of Sir Bernard Albert Ashley, and Laura Ashley, *née* Mountney (d 1985); *b* 15 Jan 1957; *Educ* Caersws Sch Powys Wales, Holland Park Comprehensive Kensington London, St Martins Sch of Art London, Academie Julien Paris, Central Sch of Art and Design London; *m* 7 July 1984, Arabella Jane Campbell, da of Patrick McNair-Wilson, MP; *Career* design dir Laura Ashley Ltd 1980-; *Recreations* motorcycle racing; *Clubs* Hafren Dirt Bike; *Style*— Nick Ashley, Esq; 27 Bagley's Lane, London SW6 2AR

ASHLEY-BROWN, Michael Ashley; s of Lt Col Arthur Basil Brown, TD (d 1987), of Farnham, Surrey, and Myra Anne, *née* Walsh (d 1964); *b* 28 June 1948; *Educ* Cranleigh, Millbrook Sch New York, Coll of Law; *m* 3 June 1972, Rita Julia; 1 s (Miles b 1973), 1 da (Tabitha b 1975); *Career* admitted slr Supreme Ct 1973-; dir: Brown Bros & Taylor Ltd 1985-, Kensington Corpn Ltd 1987-; cncllr York City Cncl 1977-80, co cncllr N Yorks 1977-81; regnl spokesman Br Atlantic Ctee 1982-86, memb Hunter Improvement Soc; Cons candidate Leeds Central 1983; memb Ct and Cncl of York Univ 1978-82, govr Archbishop Holgate GS 1977-82; Freeman City of York; *Recreations* show hunters, skiing, long distance running; *Clubs* Oriental, Yorkshire; *Style*— Michael A Ashley-Brown, Esq; Kepwick Hall, Thirsk, North Yorks (☎ 0845 537286); 106 Micklegate, York YO1 1JX (☎ 0904 55834, fax 0904 30321, car telephone 0836 594908 or 0836 612167)

ASHLEY MILLER, Lt Cdr Peter; s of Cyril Ashley Miller, of Seafield, Overstrand, Norfolk (d 1963), and Marjorie, *née* George (d 1974); *b* 26 Dec 1925; *Educ* RNC Dartmouth; *m* 11 Feb 1956, Catherine Jill, da of Maj John MacNaughton, MC, of Upavon, Wilts (d 1959); 1 s (Mark b 1962), 2 da (Bridget b 1957, Catherine b 1959); *Career* RN 1939-59 in Home, Med and Far East Fleets and Admty; dir: Ionian Bank Ltd 1973-77, Arbuthnot Latham Bank Ltd 1978-; chm: Norland Nursery Trg Coll 1983-, Burlingham House Home for Mentally Handicapped 1984-; FCA; *Recreations* skiing, sailing, shooting; *Clubs* Travellers, Ski (GB), Overseas Bankers, Norfolk Punt; *Style*— Lt Cdr Peter Ashley Miller; Reedham Old Hall, Norwich, Norfolk NR13 3TZ

ASHLEY-MILLER, Dr Michael; s of Cyril Ashley-Miller (d 1963), and Marjorie, *née* George (d 1974); *b* 1 Dec 1930; *Educ* Charterhouse, Hertford Coll Oxford (BA, BM BCh, MA), KCH, London Sch of Hygiene (DPH); *m* 31 May 1958, Yvonne Marcell, da of Cyril Marcell Townend; 3 da (Amanda b 1959, Tessa b 1961, Penny b 1964); *Career* house surgn and physician KCH 1956, SMO Dulwich Hosp 1957; Nat Serv Flt Lt RAF: MO Oakington 1958-60, SMO Colerne 1960; SMO IOW CC 1961-64, MO and SMO MRC HQ 1964-74, SPMO SHHD 1983-86; sec Nuffield Prov Hosp Tst 1986-; FRCP, FRCPEd, FFPHM, FRSM; *Books* Screening for Risk of Coronary Heart Disease (jtly, 1986); *Recreations* walking, reading, visiting cathedrals; *Clubs* RSM; *Style*— Dr Michael Ashley-Miller; 3 Prince Albert Rd, London NW1 (☎ 071 485 6632)

ASHLEY-SMITH, Dr Jonathan; s of Ewart Trist Ashley-Smith (d 1972), of Sutton Valence, Kent, and Marian Tanfield, *née* Smith; *b* 25 Aug 1946; *Educ* Sutton Valence, Univ of Bristol (PhD), Univ of Cambridge; *m* 19 Aug 1967, Diane Louise; 1 s (Joseph Daniel b 1975), 1 da (Zoë Elizabeth b 1985); *Career* V & A: scientific offr 1973-77, keeper Conservation Dept; memb: Crafts Cncl, Cncl for Care of Churches; chm UK Inst for Conservation 1983-84; FIIC 1985, FRCS, CChem 1987, FMA 1988; *Books* Science for Conservators vols 1 - 3 (scientific ed, 1984); *Recreations* legal combinations of driving fast, getting drunk, and heavy rock music; *Clubs* Anglesea; *Style*— Dr Jonathan Ashley-Smith; Conservation Department, Victoria and Albert Museum, London SW7 2RL (☎ 071 938 8568, fax 071 938 8477)

ASHMALL, Harry A; *b* 22 Feb 1939; *Educ* Kilsyth Acad, Univ of Glasgow (MA, MLitt), Jordanhill Coll of Educn; *m* , 2 da; *Career* asst The High Sch of Glasgow 1961-66 (princ teacher of history 1968-71); rector: Forfar Acad 1971-79, Morrison's Acad 1979-; lectr, religious presenter; series incl: In Opposite Corners, The Church and ..., The Apostles' Creed, Sunday Worship; individual presentations incl: Crossfire, Does God Exist After 1984?, Thought for the Day, A Personal View, Voyager, Sixth Sense; chm Scottish Educnl Research Assoc 1980-83, chm Educnl Broadcasting Cncl for Scotland; memb: UNICEF Exec Ctee (UK), UNICEF Mgmnt Ctee, Bd of Mgmnt Scottish Cncl for Research in Educn, Educn Ctee of the SSTA; FBIM, MMIM; *Books* The High School of Glasgow: a history (1976); also various pamphlets and articles; *Recreations* reading, writing, keep fit; *Clubs* New (Edinburgh), East India; *Style*— Harry Ashmall, Esq; Fernbank, Ferntower Rd, Crieff PH7 3DH (☎ 0764 2844)

ASHMOLE, Michael Achille; s of Harold J Ashmole (d 1979); *b* 10 Feb 1939; *Educ* Bemrose GS Derby; *m* 1961, Jean, da of Samuel Higginbottom (d 1943); 2 s (Christopher b 1964, Alexander b 1968), 2 da (Susan b 1962, Brigid b 1966); *Career* RAF 1958-60; chm: Fountain Renewable Resources Ltd, Fountain Timber Products Ltd, Once A Tree Ltd; dir Highland Venison Ltd; chm Scottish Aero Club, exec dir Int Union of Socs of Foresters; FIFor (memb Cncl 1973-78); *Recreations* field sports, flying (sea plane pilot), philately; *Clubs* Catenian Assoc; *Style*— Michael Ashmole, Esq; 111 Burghmuir Rd, Perth, Scotland (☎ 0738 27622)

ASHMORE, Adm of the Fleet Sir Edward Beckwith; GCB (1974, KCB 1971, CB 1966), DSC (1942); s of Vice Adm Leslie Haliburton Ashmore, CB, DSO (d 1974), and late Tamara Vasilievna, *née* Schutt, and bro of Vice Adm William Beckwith Ashmore, *qv*; *b* 11 Dec 1919; *Educ* RNC Dartmouth; *m* 1942, Elizabeth, da of late Rear Adm Sir

Lionel Sturdee, 2 Bt, CBE; 1 s, 1 da (and 1 da decd); *Career* joined RN 1938, asst naval attaché Moscow 1946-47, Capt 1955, Rear Adm 1965, Vice Adm 1968, Vice-Chief Naval Staff 1969-71, Adm 1970, C-in-C Western Fleet 1971, C-in-C Fleet 1971-74, First and Princ Naval ADC to HM The Queen 1974-77, Chief Naval Staff and First Sea Lord 1974-77, Chief Def Staff 1977; govr Sutton's Hosp 1976-; *Clubs* Naval and Military; *Style*— Adm of the Fleet Sir Edward Ashmore, GCB, DSC; c/o Naval Secretary, Ministry of Defence, Whitehall, London SW1

ASHMORE, Vice Adm Sir Peter William Beckwith; KCB (1972, CB 1968), KCVO (1980, MVO (4 Class) 1948), DSC (1942); s of late Vice Adm Leslie Haliburton Ashmore, CB, DSO (d 1974), and late Tamara Vasilievna *née* Schutt, of Petrograd; yr bro of Adm of the Fleet Sir Edward Ashmore, *qv*; *b* 4 Feb 1921; *Educ* Yardley Court, RNC Dartmouth; *m* 1952, Patricia Moray, da of late Adm Sir Henry Tritton Buller, GCVO, CB (d 1960), and Lady Hermione, *née* Stuart, da of 17 Earl of Moray (d 1989); 1 s, 3 da; *Career* midshipman RN 1939, served WWII (despatches), Lt 1941, Equerry to HM The King 1946-1948 (Extra Equerry to HM The Queen 1952), Cdr 1951, Capt 1957, Rear Adm 1966, Chief Staff to C-in-C Western Fleet and NATO C-in-C E Atlantic 1967-69, Vice Adm 1969, Chief Allied Staff NATO Naval HQ S Europe 1970-72; Master of HM's Household 1973-86, ret; *Recreations* golf, tennis, fishing; *Style*— Vice Adm Sir Peter Ashmore, KCB, KCVO, DSC

ASHTON, Andrew Keith Maxwell; s of Sqdn Ldr Hugh Alan Ashton, DFC (d 1989), and Joan Maxwell, *née* Mann; *b* 18 Sept 1950; *Educ* Framlingham Coll, Wells Cathedral Sch, Trent Poly, Univ of London (LLB); *m* 20 April 1985, Dr Patricia Mary White, da of Norman Ernest White (d 1987); 1 s (Richard), 1 da (Catherine); *Career* admitted slr 1974; ptnr Thomas Mallam 1976-; memb: Wallingford Rowing Club, Warborough and Shillingford Soc; memb Law Soc; *Recreations* bringing up children, bar mgmnt, taming the garden; *Clubs* Law Soc; *Style*— Andrew Ashton, Esq; 47 New Rd, Shillingford, Oxon OX9 8EE (☎ 086 732 8424); 126 High St, Oxford OX1 4DG (☎ 0865 244661, fax 0865 721263)

ASHTON, George Arthur; s of Lewis Arthur Ashton (d 1952), and Mary Annie Ashton (d 1964); *b* 27 Nov 1921; *Educ* Llanidloes GS, Birmingham Central Tech Coll; *m* 1, 1948, Joan Rutter (decd); 1 s (Stephen); m 2, 1978, Pauline Jennifer, da of Albert Margett; *Career* HM Forces (wartime) Maj Far East; engrg and mgmnt conslt, ret; chm Seamless Tubes Ltd 1984-86, dep chm Wintech WDA 1984-87; dir: TI Group plc 1969-84, Arthur Lee & Sons plc 1981-; tech dir and business area chm TI Group plc 1978-84; vice pres Advanced Mfrg Technol Res Inst (AMTRI) 1986-; pres BISPA 1973-74; *Recreations* walking, cycling, gardening; *Clubs* Naval and Military; *Style*— George Ashton, Esq; Barn Cottage, Longford, Derby DE6 3DT (☎ 0335 330 561)

ASHTON, Gordon Rayment; s of Gilbert Austin Ashton (d 1985), of Barrow-in-Furness, and Mabel Grace, *née* Rayment; *b* 31 March 1944; *Educ* Ashville Coll, Univ of Manchester (LLB); *m* 20 March 1971, Marion, da of Joseph Turner (d 1972), of Windermere; 1 s (Paul b 1975), 2 da (Deborah b 1973, Clare b 1980); *Career* admitted slr 1967, pt/t chm Social Security Appeal Tbnl 1983-, dep registrar High Ct of Justice 1985-; pres: Grange Rotary Club 1977-78, Furness and Dist Law Soc 1984-86; memb Law Soc 1967; *Recreations* old cars, DIY, computers; *Style*— Gordon Ashton, Esq; Honeypotts, Grange-over-Sands, Cumbria LA11 7EN (☎ 05395 33124); Gedye & Sons, Grange-over-Sands, Cumbria LA11 6DR (☎ 05395 32313, fax 05395 32474)

ASHTON, Hon (Thomas) Henry; s and h of 3 Baron Ashton of Hyde; *b* 18 July 1958; *Educ* Eton, Trinity Coll Oxford; *m* 31 October 1987, Emma Louise, da of Colin Allinson, of Bath; *Career* short service volunteer cmmn with Royal Hussars (PWO), Lt Royal Wessex Yeomanry; reinsurance broker C T Bowring Ltd; *Clubs* Boodle's; *Style*— The Hon Henry Ashton; 4 Poplar Grove, London W6 7RE

ASHTON, Hubert Gaitskell; DL (Essex 1983); s of Sir Hubert Ashton, KBE, MC(d 1979) of Brentwood, and Dorothy Margaret, *née* Gaitskell (d 1983); *b* 27 Jan 1930; *Educ* Winchester, Trinity Coll Cambridge (MA); *m* 1956, Anna-Brita, da of Gustav Bertil Rylander, of Sweden (d 1976); 3 s (Hubert, Peter, Charles), 1 da (Katherine); *Career* 2 Lt Irish Gds 1948-50; Peat Marwick Mitchell 1953-61, J Henry Schroder Wagg & Co (merchant bankers) 1961-85; dir: The Housing Corp 1979-85, Brixton Estate 1983-85, Hanson plc 1985-89, BAA plc 1986-, Lynton plc 1989-, Wheway plc 1989-; chm Close Brothers Gp plc 1989-, Wheway plc 1989-; High Sheriff Essex 1983-84; pres: Essex Co Football Assoc 1984-, Essex Friends of YMCA 1985-; chm Govrs Brentwood Sch 1989; Master Worshipful of Skinners 1986-87; FCA; *Recreations* shooting, eating, drinking, swimming; *Clubs* MCC, City of London; *Style*— H G Ashton, Esq, DL; Wealdside, S Weald, Brentwood, Essex (☎ 0277 73406); 32 Garrick House, Carrington St, London W1 (☎ 071 499 3989); 36 Great St Helen's, London EC3A 6AP (☎ 071 283 2241)

ASHTON, Joseph William (Joe); MP (Lab) Bassetlaw 1968-; s of Arthur and Nellie Ashton, of Sheffield; *b* 9 Oct 1933; *Educ* High Storrs GS, Rotherham Tech Coll; *m* 1957, Margaret Patricia, da of George Lee, of Andover St, Sheffield; 1 da; *Career* journalist; columnist: Daily Star 1979-88, Sunday People 1988-89; PPS to Sec of State for Energy 1975-76, asst govt whip 1976-77, front bench spokesman on energy 1979-81; appeared on What the Papers Say, Granada TV award Columnist of the Year 1984; dir Sheffield Wednesday FC 1990-; *Books* Grassroots (Novel), A Majority of One (Play); *Style*— Joe Ashton, Esq, MP; 16 Ranmoor Park Rd, Sheffield (☎ 0742 301763)

ASHTON, Kenneth Bruce (Ken); s of Harry Anstice Ashton (d 1926), and Olive May, *née* Hawkins; *b* 9 Nov 1925; *Educ* Latymer Upper Sch, Univ of Glasgow; *m* 1955, Anne, *née* Sidebotham; 4 s (Paul, Mark, John, Richard); *Career* Nat Serv RA WWII, Egypt, Italy, Austria, Palestine 1942-47; former sub ed Daily Express and Daily Mail; gen sec NUJ 1977-85 (pres 1975); memb: TUC Printing Indust Ctee 1975-85, TUC Media Working Gp 1977-85, Printing and Publishing Indust Trg Bd 1977-83, Communications Advsy Ctee UK Nat Cmmn for UNESCO 1981-85, Br Ctee Journalists in Europe 1981-86; pres Int Fedn of Journalists 1982-86; *Style*— Ken Ashton, Esq; High Blean, Raydaleside, Askrigg, Leyburn, N Yorks DL8 3DJ

ASHTON, Laraine Gordon; da of Don Ashton, of Amersham, Buckinghamshire, and Helen, *née* Horsfall; *b* 22 March 1946; *Educ* Farmhouse Sch Wendover Bucks; *m* ; 1 s (Claud McCullin Ashton); *Career* model late 1960's and early 1970's; started agency for Mark H MacCormack and his orgn 1975; *Style*— Miss Laraine Ashton; Laraine Ashton-IMG, 18 Marylebone Mews, London W1 (☎ 071 486 8011, fax 071 487 3116)

ASHTON, Rt Rev Leonard James; CB (1970); s of late Henry Ashton, of Chesham, Bucks, and late Sarah, *née* Ing; *b* 27 June 1915; *Educ* Tyndale Hall Trinity Coll Bristol; *Career* ordained 1942, chaplain RAF 1945-74; serv: Far E (incl Br Cwlth Occupation Forces in Japan) 1945-48, Middle E 1954-55 and 1960-61; RAF Coll Cranwell 1956-60, res chaplain St Clement Danes 1965-69, chaplain-in-chief and archdeacon RAF (rank of Air Vice-Marshal) 1969-73; canon and preb of Lincoln Cathedral 1969-73 (canon emeritus 1973-), asst bishop in Jerusalem 1974-76, episcopal canon St George's Cathedral Jerusalem 1976-, bishop in Cyprus and the Gulf 1976-83, hon asst bishop of Oxford 1983, commissary for bishops in Jerusalem and Iran 1983-, episcopal canon St Paul's Cath Cyprus 1989-; hon chaplain to HM The Queen 1967-73; ChStJ 1976; *Recreations* photography, gardening; *Clubs* RAF; *Style*— The Rt Rev Leonard Ashton, CB; 60 Lowndes Ave, Chesham, Bucks (☎ 0494 782952)

ASHTON, Prof Norman Henry; CBE (1976); 2 s of late Henry James Ashton, of Herts, and late Margaret Ann, *née* Tuck; *b* 11 Sept 1913; *Educ* West Kensington Sch, Kings Coll London and Westminster Hosp Med Sch, Univ of London; *Career* Lt-Col RAMC, asst dir of pathology and offr i/c Central Pathological Laboratory M East 1946; dir of pathology Kent and Canterbury Hosp 1941, blood transfusion offr East Kent 1941; Inst of Ophthalmology Univ of London: dir Dept of Pathology 1948-78, reader in pathology 1953, prof of pathology 1957-78, emeritus prof 1978-; FRS 1971; KStJ 1971; *Recreations* painting, gardening; *Clubs* Athenaeum, Garrick; *Style*— Prof Norman Ashton, CBE, FRS; 4 Blomfield Rd, Little Venice, London W9 1AH; Institute of Ophthalmology, Judd St, London WC1H 9QS (☎ 071 387 9621)

ASHTON, Prof Robert; s of Joseph Ashton (d 1979), of Chester, and Edith Frances, *née* Davies (d 1954); *b* 21 July 1924; *Educ* Magdalen Coll Sch Oxford, Univ Coll Southampton, LSE (BA, PhD); *m* 30 Aug 1946, Margaret Alice, da of T W Sedgwick (d 1948), of Dover; 2 da (Rosalind Helen b 1954, Celia Elizabeth b 1961); *Career* WWII served RAF 1943-46; sr lectr in econ hist Univ of Nottingham 1961-63 Casst lectr 1952-54, lectr 1954-61), visiting assoc prof in history Univ of Calif 1962-63, emeritus UEA 1989- (prof Eng hist 1963-89. dean Sch of Eng studies 1964-67, Leverhulm emeritus fell 1989-90), visiting fell All Souls Coll Oxford 1973-74 and 1987; FRHitS 1961; *Books* The Crown and The Money Market 1603-42 (1960), James I By His Contemporaries (1969), The English Civil War 1603-49 (1978), The City and the Court 1603-43 (1979), Reformation and Revolution 1558-1660 (1984); *Recreations* wine, food, old buildings; *Style*— Prof Robert Ashton; The Manor House, Brundall, Norwich NR13 5JY (☎ 0603 713368)

ASHTON, Ruth Mary (Mrs E F Henshel); da of Leigh Perry Ashton, and Marion Lucy, *née* Tryon; *b* 27 March 1939; *Educ* Kenya HS for Girls, Clarendon Sch (lately Abergele), High Coombe Midwife Teachers' Trg Coll (RN 1965, RM 1967, MTD 1970); *m* 7 April 1984, E Fred Henshel; *Career* London Hosp staff midwife and midwifery sister Queen Mother's Hosp Glasgow 1967-69, nursing offr and midwifery tutor King's Coll Hosp London 1971-75, Royal Coll of Midwives 1975-79 (tutor, professional offr); offr sister OStJ; memb Royal Coll of Midwives; *Books* Your First Baby (ed and author, 1980); *Recreations* gardening, sailing, travel; *Clubs* Queenborough Yacht; *Style*— Miss Ruth Ashton; Royal College of Midwives, 15 Mansfield St, London W1M 0BE (☎ 071 580 6523, 071 637 8823, fax 071 436 3951)

ASHTON, William Michael Allingham; MBE (1978); s of Eric Sandiford Ashton (d 1983), of Lytham, St Annes, and Zilla Dorothea, *née* Miles (d 1944); *b* 6 Dec 1936; *Educ* Rossall Sch, St Peter's Coll Oxford (BA, DipEd); *m* 22 Oct 1966, Kay Carol, da of John Stallard Watkins, of New Quay, Dyfed; 2 s (Grant b 1967, Miles b 1968), 1 da (Helen b 1983); *Career* Nat Serv RAF 1955-57; fndr and musical dir Nat Youth Jazz Orchestra 1965-: numerous appearances before royalty incl Royal Variety Performance 1978, toured many countries on behalf of Br Cncl (USA, USSR, Aust, Turkey); memb: Musicians' Union, Br Assoc Jazz Musicians; *Recreations* reading, song writing; *Style*— William Ashton, Esq, MBE; 11 Victor Rd, Harrow, Middx HA2 6PT (☎ 081 863 2717)

ASHTON-BOSTOCK, David Ashton; s of Cdr John Bostock, DSC, RN; additional surname and arms assumed by Royal Licence 1953, at the wish of his great-uncle Samuel Ashton-Yates; *b* 17 Feb 1933; *Educ* Wellington, Maidstone Coll of Art, Byam Shaw Art Sch; *m* 1965 (m dis 1983), Victoria Rosamond, da of Capt Richard White, DSO, RN; 1 s (decd), 1 da; *Career* interior designer; vice pres Alexandra Rose Day, chm Ridley Art Soc, memb Cncl Interior Decorators' and Designers' Assoc; memb Lloyd's; *Recreations* painting, gardening, genealogy; *Style*— David Ashton-Bostock, Esq; Danes Bottom Place, Wormshill, Sittingbourne, Kent (☎ 062 784 476); 28 Sutherland St, London SW1 (☎ 071 834 1696); Ashton-Bostock Interior Decorations, 21 Charlwood St, London SW1 (☎ 071 828 3656)

ASHTON-JONES, Christopher James; *b* 18 March 1948; *Educ* Nailsea GS; *m* 1972, Carmen Mary, *née* Don-Fox; 1 s (George John b 1978), 2 da (Joanna Mary b 1973, Amelia Jane b 1975); *Career* trainee N M Rothschild and Sons 1966-69, institutional sales Hoare Govett 1969-71, investmt analyst and mangr Eastminster Group 1971-73, fin PR exec Leo Burnett 1973-76, exec Dewe Rogerson 1976-79 (sr exec 1979-83), fin PR mangr The BOC Group 1983-85, investor relations dir Dewe Rogerson 1985-88, dir Brunswick Public Relations Ltd 1988-; chm City and Fin Gp Inst of Public Relations 1983-84; MIPR 1978; *Books* This Public Relations Consultancy Business (contrib, 1984); *Recreations* motorboating, gardening, classic cars; *Clubs* City of London, Chichester Yacht; *Style*— Christopher Ashton-Jones, Esq; Brunswick Public Relations Ltd, 15 Lincoln's Inn Fields, London WC2A 3ED (☎ 071 404 5959, fax 071 831 2823)

ASHTON OF HYDE, Marjorie, Baroness; Marjorie Nell; *née* Brooks; JP; da of Hon Marshall Brooks (2 s of 1 Baron Crawshaw), and Florence Brooks; *b* 1901; *Educ* Privately; *m* 1925, 2 Baron Ashton of Hyde, JP, DL (d 1983); 1 s (3 Baron, *qv*), 2 da decd; *Clubs* Parrot; *Style*— The Rt Hon Marjorie, Lady Ashton of Hyde, JP; The Martins, Broadwell, Moreton-in-Marsh, Glos (☎ 0451 30105)

ASHTON OF HYDE, 3 Baron (UK 1911); Thomas John Ashton; TD, JP (Oxon); s of 2 Baron Ashton of Hyde, JP, DL (d 1983), and Marjorie, Baroness Ashton of Hyde, *qv*; *b* 19 Nov 1926; *Educ* Eton, New Coll Oxford; *m* 18 May 1957, Pauline Trewlove, er da of Lt-Col Robert Henry Langton Brackenbury, OBE, of Yerdley House, Long Compton, Shipston on Stour; 2 s, 2 da; *Heir* s, Hon Thomas Henry Ashton b 18 July 1958; *Career* formerly Lt 11 Hussars, Maj Royal Glos Hussars (TA); dir Barclays Bank plc and subsidiary cos 1969-87; *Clubs* Boodle's; *Style*— The Rt Hon the Lord Ashton of Hyde, TD, JP; Fir Farm, Upper Slaughter, Bourton on the Water, Glos (☎ 0451 30652)

ASHTOWN, Sir Nigel Clive Cosby Trench; KCMG (1976, CMG 1966); s of Clive Newcome Trench (d 1964, s of Hon Cosby Godolphin Trench, 2 s of 2 Baron Ashtown), and Kathleen, da of Maj Ivar MacIvor, CIE, hp of kinsman, 6 Baron Ashtown; *b* 27 Oct 1916; *Educ* Eton, CCC Cambridge; *m* 1 Dec 1939, Marcelle Catherine, da of Johan Jacob Clotterbooke Patyn van Kloetinge, of Zeist, Holland; 1 s; *Career* serv KRRC WWII (UK and NW Europe, despatches); Foreign Serv 1946, Cabinet Office 1967, ambass to Korea 1969-71, memb Civil Serv Selection Bd 1971-73, ambass to Portugal 1974-76, memb Police Fire and Prison Serv Selection Bds 1977-86; Order of Dip Serv Merit (Rep of Korea) 1984; *Recreations* golf, photography, looking at other people's gardens; *Clubs* Naval and Military, MCC; *Style*— Sir Nigel Trench, KCMG; 4 Kensington Court Gardens, Kensington Court Place, London W8 5QE

ASHURST, Dr Peter Jeffrey; s of Frederick Ashurst (ka 1941), and Evelyn, *née* Hargreaves; *b* 10 Sept 1934; *Educ* Manchester GS, Manchester Royal Infirmary Univ of Manchester (MB ChB, MD); *m* 1, 1961 (m dis 1982); 1 s (Tim b 1965), 1 da (Jane b 1963); m 2, 11 June 1983, Bonnie Jean, da of Valores Waterman, of San José, Calif; *Career* former conslt dermatologist Aberdeen Teaching Hosps, conslt dermatologist Wolverhampton Dudley and Stourbridge gps of hosps; author of numerous dermatological pubns 1960-70; memb Br Assoc Dermatologists; FRCPE 1985 (MRCPE 1967); *Books* A Manual of Clinical Dermatology (1969); *Recreations* snooker; *Clubs* Stoubridge Inst; *Style*— Dr Peter Ashurst; 8 Summerfield Rd, Wolverhampton WU4 2PP ☎ 0902 24036

ASHWORTH, Dr Bryan; s of Robert Bailey Rothwell Ashworth (d 1959), of Nottingham, and Jessie Isobel, *née* Carley (d 1969); *b* 5 May 1929; *Educ* Laxton Sch Oundle, Univ of St Andrews (MB ChB, MD); *Career* Nat Serv Capt RAMC RWAFF N

Nigeria 1953-55; Wellcome-Swedish travelling res fell Karolinska Hosp Stockholm 1965-66, lectr in neurology Univ of Manchester and hon conslt physician Manchester Royal Infirmary 1966-70, sr lectr in med neurology 1971-, conslt neurologist Northern Gen Hosp Edinburgh then Royal Infirmary and Western Gen Hosps 1971-, dir (non-exec) Robert Bailey & Son plc Stockport 1978-, conslt neurologist Civil Serv Scotland 1988-; hon librarian RCPE 1982-, chm Scottish Assoc Neurological Sciences 1989; FRCP, FRCPE, memb RSM; *Books* Clinical Neuro-ophthalmology (2 edn, 1981), Management of Neurological Disorders (2 edn jtly, 1985), The Bramwells of Edinburgh (1986); *Recreations* writing, walking; *Clubs* Edinburgh Univ Staff; *Style—* Dr Bryan Ashworth; 13/5 Eildon Terrace, Edinburgh EH3 5NL (☎ 031 556 0547); Department of Clinical Neurosciences, Western General Hospital, Edinburgh EH4 2XU (☎ 031 332 2525 ext 4876, fax 031 332 5150)

ASHWORTH, Prof Graham William; CBE (1980); s of Frederick William Ashworth (d 1978), and Ivy Alice, *née* Courtiour (d 1982); *b* 14 July 1935; *Educ* Devonport HS, Univ of Liverpool (BArch); *m* 2 April 1960, Gwyneth Mai, da of John Morgan Jones (d 1959); 3 da (Clare, Alyson, Kate); *Career* architect and planner: London CC 1959-62, Graeme Shankland Assoc 1962-64; architect Civic Tst 1964-65, dir Northwest Civic Tst 1965-73, prof of urban environmental studies 1973-87, res prof urban environmental studies 1987-, dir-gen Tidy Br Gp, chm Ravenhead Renaissance Ltd 1988-; memb Baptist Union Cncl 1975-; assoc pastor Carey Baptist Church Preston 1977-86; dir: Merseyside Devpt Corpn 1981-, Norweb 1985-88; RIBA 1962, FRSA 1968, FRTPI 1969, FBIM 1986; *Books* An Encyclopaedia of Planning (1973); *Clubs* Nat Lib, Athenaeum; *Style—* Prof Graham Ashworth, CBE; Manor Court Farm, Preston New Road, Samlesbury, Preston, Lancs PR5 0UP (☎ 025481 2011); Tidy Britain Gp, The Pier, Wigan WN3 4EX (☎ 0942 824 620)

ASHWORTH, Sir Herbert; s of Joseph Hartley Ashworth (d 1954), of Burnley, Lancs; *b* 30 Jan 1910; *Educ* Burnley GS, Univ of London (BSc, LLB); *m* 1936, Barbara Helen Mary, da of Douglas D Henderson (d 1932), of London; 2 s, 1 da; *Career* chm: Housing Corporation 1968-73, Nationwide Building Society 1970-82; dir The Builder Ltd 1975-80; chm: Surrey and W Sussex Agric Wages Ctee 1974-88, Nationwide Housing Tst 1983-87; kt 1972; *Style—* Sir Herbert Ashworth; 8 Tracery, Park Rd, Banstead, Surrey (☎ 0737 352608)

ASHWORTH, Brig John Blackwood; CBE (1962), DSO (1944); s of Lt-Col Hugh Stirling Ashworth, Royal Sussex Regt (ka 1917), and E M Ashworth; *b* 7 Dec 1910; *Educ* Wellington, RMC Sandhurst; *m* 1944, Eileen Patricia, da of late Maj Herbert Llewellyn Gifford, OBE, Royal Ulster Rifles, and Lady Gooch; 1 da; *Career* cmmnd 1930, served WWII (wounded, despatches twice), Cdr Jt Sch Chemical Warfare 1954, Cdr 133 Inf Bde (TA) 1957, dir Mil Trg WO 1962-65, ADC to HM The Queen 1961-65, Col The Royal Sussex Regt 1963-66, Dep Col Queen's Regt (Royal Sussex) 1967-68; DL Sussex 1972-83; OStJ 1950, Grand Offr Order of House of Orange 1967; *Style—* Brig John Ashworth, CBE, DSO; 16 Castlegate, New Brook St, Ilkley, W Yorks LS29 8DF (☎ 0943 602404)

ASHWORTH, Prof John Michael; s of Jack Ashworth (d 1975), and Mary Constance, *née* Ousman (d 1971); *b* 27 Nov 1938; *Educ* W Buckland Sch, Exeter Coll Oxford (BA, BSc, MA), Univ of Leicester (PhD), Univ of Oxford (DSc); *m* 1, 13 July 1963, Ann (d 1985), da of Peter Knight (d 1977); 1 s (Matthew b 24 Sept 1971), 3 da (Harriet b 23 Oct 1964, Sophia b 2 Dec 1968, Emily b 3 Aug 1970); m 2, 23 July 1988, Auriol Hazel Dawn, da of Capt E B K Stevens, DSO (d 1971); *Career* prof Univ of Essex 1974-79, secondment to central policy review staff 1976-79, under sec Cabinet Office 1979-81, chief scientist CPRS 1979-81; chm: Salford 90 Univ Business Servs Ltd and Business Enterprises Ltd 1981-90, Bd Nat Computer Centre Ltd 1983-; vice chllr Univ of Salford 1981-90, dir LSE 1990-; memb: Library and Info Servs Cncl 1980-84, Bd Granada TV 1986-89, BR (London Mainland) Bd 1987-, Bd Granada Gp 1990-, Manchester Literary and Philosophical Soc, Electronic Indust EDC (NEDO); chm: Bd Salford ITEC 1982-90, Nat Accreditation Cncl for Cert Bodies 1984-88, Info Tech Econ Devpt Cncl; tstee Granada Fndn, pres Res and Devpt Soc, Business in the Community 1988; Colworth medal Biochemical Soc 1972; FIBiol 1973, 1984; *Books* The Slime Moulds (with J Dee, 1970) Cell Differentiation (1972); *Recreations* fell walking, windsurfing; *Style—* Prof John Ashworth; 34 Hawthorn Lane, Wilmslow, Cheshire SK9 6DG (☎ 0625 530559); Univ of Salford, Salford M5 4WT (☎ 061 745 5000, fax 061 745 5040, telex 668680 SULIB)

ASHWORTH, Leonard; CBE (1981); s of James Walter Ashworth (d 1973); *b* 12 Jan 1921; *Educ* Stretford Tech Coll; *m* 1947, Edna, da of Arthur Bromfield (d 1956); 2 children; *Career* Warrant Offr RE SEAC; chief exec Davy McKee Int Ltd; main bd dir Davy Corpn, consulting exec Davy Corpn 1983; memb Process Plant EDC NEDO 1979; chm Br Metallurgical Plant Constructors' Assoc Sept 1981; pres Process Plant Assoc from Aug 1982; chm Mech & Elec Construction Indust Trg Bd 1982; memb EITB 1982; *Recreations* boating; *Clubs* Oriental, Poole Yacht; *Style—* Leonard Ashworth, Esq, CBE; 1 Burnage Court, Canford Cliffs, Poole, Dorset (☎ 0202 700853); Davy Corporation Ltd, 15 Portland Place, London W1A 4DD (☎ 071 637 2821)

ASHWORTH, Piers; QC (1973); s of Tom and Mollie Ashworth; *b* 27 May 1931; *Educ* Christ's Hosp, Pembroke Coll Cambridge; *m* 1, 1959 (m dis 1978), Iolene Jennifer, da of W G Foxley; 3 s, 1 da; m 2, 1980, Elizabeth, da of A J S Aston; *Career* called to the Bar Middle Temple 1956, bencher 1984, rec Crown Ct 1974-, in practice Midland and Oxford Circuit, chm of the Bar Mutual Insurance Fund Ltd; *Style—* Piers Ashworth, Esq, QC; 2 Harcourt Bldgs, Temple, London EC4 YDB (☎ 071 583 9020)

ASKE, Rev Sir Conan; 2 Bt (UK 1922), of Aughton, East Riding of Yorkshire; s of Sir Robert William Aske, 1 Bt, TD, QC, JP (d 1954), by his 2 w Edith; *b* 22 April 1912; *Educ* Rugby, Balliol Coll Oxford (MA); *m* 1, 13 Dec 1948, Vera (d 1960), yst da of late George Rowbotham, of Iffley, Oxford, and former w of Roland Faulkner; m 2, 23 Aug 1965, Rebecca, yr da of Hugh Fraser Grant (d 1967), of Wick, Caithness; *Heir* bro, Robert Aske, *qv*; *Career* serv WWII Dunkirk 1940, Maj E Yorks Regt, ME 1941-51, Sudan Def Force; schoolmaster Hillstone Malvern 1952-69; asst curate: Hagley 1970-72, St John's Worcester 1972-80; chaplain to Mayor of Worcester 1979-80; hon padre 1940 Dunkirk Veterans' Assoc Worcs Branch; *Style—* The Rev Sir Conan Aske, Bt; 167 Malvern Rd, Worcester WR2 4NN (☎ 0905 422817)

ASKE, Robert Edward; 2 s of Sir Robert Aske, 1 Bt, TD, QC, JP, LLD, sometime MP Newcastle E; hp to bro, Rev Sir Conan Aske, 2 Bt, *qv*; *b* 21 March 1915; *m* 1940, Joan Bingham, o da of Capt Bingham Ackerley, of White Lodge, Cobham; 1 s; *Style—* Robert Aske, Esq; 45 Holland Rd, London W14

ASKEW, Barry Reginald William; s of Reginald Ewart Askew (d 1969), and Jane Elisabeth Askew (d 1979); *b* 13 Dec 1936; *Educ* Lady Manners GS Bakewell; *m* 1, 1958 (m dis 1978), June, da of Vernon Roberts; 1 s, 1 da; m 2, 1980, Deborah, da of Harold Parker; *Career* journalist, broadcaster and public relations conslt; trainee reporter upwards Derbyshire Times 1952-57, reporter and sub-ed Sheffield Telegraph 1957-59, reporter, feature writer and broadcaster Raymonds News Agency Derby 1959-61, ed Matlock Mercury 1961-63, indust correspondent, then asst ed, then dep ed Sheffield Telegraph (later Morning Telegraph) 1964-68, assoc ed The Star Sheffield 1968; ed: Lancashire Evening Post 1968-81 (dir 1978-81), News of the World 1981; presenter and anchor man: ITV 1970-81, BBC Radio 4 1971-72, BBC 1 1972, BBC 2 1972-76; memb Davies Ctee to reform hosp complaints procedures in UK 1971-73; campaigning journalist of 1971 IPC Nat Press Awards, journalist of 1977 Br Press Awards, crime reporter of 1977 Witness Box Awards; *Recreations* rugby union, chess, golf, reading; *Clubs* Preston Grasshoppers RFC, Appleby Golf; *Style—* Barry Askew, Esq; School House, Orton, nr Penrith, Cumbria (☎ 05874 434)

ASKEW, Sir Bryan; s of John Pinkney Askew (d 1940), and Matilda Brown; *b* 18 Aug 1930; *Educ* Wellfield GS Wingate Co Durham, Fitzwilliam Coll Cambridge (MA); *m* 10 Aug 1955, Millicent Rose, da of Thomas Henry Holder (d 1966); 2 da (Penelope Jane b 1957, Melissa Clare b 1966); *Career* ICI Ltd 1952-59, Consett Iron Co Ltd (later part of Br Steel Corp) 1959-71, own consultancy 1971-74; Samuel Smith Old Brewery Tadcaster: joined 1974, personnel dir 1982-; Parly candidate gen election (C): Penistone 1964 and 1966, York 1970; chm Yorks RHA 1983; memb: Duke of Edinburgh's Third Cwlth Study Conf Australia 1968, Ct and Cncl Univ of Leeds, Working Gp on Young People and Alcohol, Home Office Standing Conf on Crime Prevention 1987-; FRSA 1986, FRSM 1988; kt 1989; *Style—* Sir Bryan Askew; The Old Brewery, Tadcaster, N Yorks LS24 9SB (☎ 0937 832225, fax 0937 834673)

ASKEW, Henry John; s of Maj John Marjoribanks Eskdale Askew, CBE, *qv*, of Ladykirk, Berwick-upon-Tweed, and Lady Susan Alice, *née* Egerton, *qv*; *b* 5 April 1940; *Educ* Eton; *m* 27 Jan 1978, Rosemary Eileen, da of Dr Charles Edmunds Darby Taylor, of Alnwick House, Little Shelford, Cambridge; 2 s (Jack b 1984, George b 1986); *Career* cmmnd Grenadier Guards 1959-62; dir then md Gerrar & Nat Hldgs plc (formerly Gerrard & Nat Ltd) 1967-; *Recreations* reading, music, opera, ballet; *Clubs* Pratt's; *Style—* Henry Askew, Esq; The Factor's House, Ladykirk, Berwick-upon-Tweed (☎ 0289 309); 77 Chester Row, London SW1W 8JL (☎ 071 730 6151); Gerrard & National Holdings plc, 33 Lombard St, 2nd Floor, London EC3V 9BQ (☎ 071 623 9981, fax 071 623 6173, car 883589)

ASKEW, Ian Voase; MC (1945), DL (E Sussex 1975); s of Sidney Bruce Askew (d 1955), of Buxshalls, Lindfield, Sussex; *b* 9 May 1921; *Educ* Charterhouse, Christ's Coll Cambridge; *Career* serv WWII Italy Capt KRRC; jt master of foxhounds Southdown 1956-66; High Sheriff of Sussex 1969; *Clubs* Army and Navy; *Style—* Ian Askew, Esq, MC, DL; Wellingham Folly, Lewes, E Sussex (☎ 0273 812357)

ASKEW, John Marjoribanks; CBE (1974), JP (Berwicks); s of William Haggerston Askew, JP, of Ladykirk, Berwicks, and Castle Hills, Berwick-upon-Tweed (d 1942), by his w Katherine (herself da of Hon John Gordon, sometime MP for Elgin & Nairn and for Brighton, who was in his turn eld s of Baron Gordon, PC, Lord Advocate for Scotland, a Lord of Appeal in Ordinary and a Life Peer); *b* 22 Sept 1908; *Educ* Eton, Magdalene Coll Cambridge; *m* 1, 1933 (m dis 1966), Lady Susan Alice Egerton, 4 da of 4 Earl of Ellesmere, MVO; 1 s (Henry John), 1 da (*see* Baron Faringdon); m 2, 1976, Priscilla Anne, da of Algernon Ross Farrow (d 1973); *Career* Lt 2 Bn Grenadier Gds 1932, Capt 1940, Maj 1943, served WW II France & Germany; Vice-Lt for Berwickshire 1955-65 (DL 1946-55); Brigadier Royal Co of Archers (Queen's Bodyguard for Scotland); convener: Berwicks CC 1961, Borders Regnl Cncl 1974-82; *Clubs* New (Edinburgh), Boodle's, Pratt's; *Style—* John Askew, Esq, CBE, JP; Ladykirk, Berwicks (☎ 0289 82229); Castle Hills, Berwick-upon-Tweed

ASKEW, Rev Canon Reginald James Albert; s of Paul Askew (d 1953, pioneer of Br Broadcasting), and Amy, *née* Wainwright (d 1976); *b* 16 May 1928; *Educ* Harrow, CCC Cambridge (BA, MA); *m* 1953, Kate, yr da of Rev Henry Townsend Wigley (d 1970, gen sec Free Church Federal Cncl); 1 s (Paul), 2 da (Catherine, Rachel); *Career* curate Highgate 1957-61, lectr and vice princ Wells Theological Coll 1961-69, vicar of Christ Church Lancaster Gate London 1969-73, canon of Salisbury and prebendary of Grantham Borealis 1975; chm The Southern Dioceses' Ministerial Training Scheme 1973-87, princ Salisbury and Wells Theological Coll 1973-1987, dean King's Coll London 1988-90; proctor: Univ of London, Gen Synod of the C of E; memb The Corrymeela Community; *Books* The Tree of Noah (1971); *Recreations* music, gardening, making lino-cuts, cricket; *Style—* The Rev Canon Reginald Askew; Carters Cottage, North Wootton, Somerset BA4 4AF; King's College, Strand, London WC2R 2LS (☎ 071 873 0208)

ASKEW, Lady Susan Alice; *née* Egerton; da of late 4 Earl of Ellesmere, MVO, and Lady Violet, *née* Lambton, da of 4 Earl of Durham; sis of 6 Duke of Sutherland; *b* 1913; *m* 1933 (m dis 1966), Maj John Marjoribanks Askew, Grenadier Gds; 1 s, 1 da (m 3 Baron Faringdon, *qv*); *Style—* The Lady Susan Askew; Stone House, Sprouston, Kelso, Roxburghshire (☎ 0573 24338)

ASKEY WOOD, (John) Humphrey; s of Lt-Col Edward Askey Wood, Leics Regt, and Irene Jeanne, *née* Parry; *b* 26 Nov 1932; *Educ* Winchester, CCC Cambridge (MA); *m* 1981, Katherine Ruth Stewart, da of Capt Horace Alan Peverley (d 1952), Canadian Grenadiar Gds, of Wildwood, St Andrews East, Quebec Canada; 1 s (Jason b 1966), 1 step s (Alexander b 1965), 1 step da (Kate b 1968); *Career* md Consolidated Gold Fields plc 1979-; chm: ARC Ltd 1979-86, De Havilland Aircraft Co Ltd 1956, Hawker Siddeley Aviation Ltd 1964; dir and gen mangr Manchester 1969-75; md Industl and Marine Div Rolls-Royce Ltd 1976-79; memb Cncl CBI 1983, vice-pres Nat Cncl of Bldg Products 1985; *Recreations* fly fishing, sailing, painting; *Style—* Humphrey Askey Wood, Esq; Consolidated Gold Fields Plc, 31 Charles II St, St James's Sq, London SW1Y 4AG (☎ 071 930 6200, telex 883071 Giovan G, fax 071 930 9677)

ASLET, Clive William; s of Kenneth Charles Aslet, and Monica, *née* Humphreys; *b* 15 Feb 1955; *Educ* King's Coll Sch Wimbledon, Peterhouse Cambridge (MA); *m* 27 Sept 1980, Naomi Selma, da of Prof Sir Martin Roth; *Career* Country Life: architectural writer 1977-84, architectural ed 1984-88, dep ed 1989-; founding hon sec The Thirties Soc 1979-87; *Books* The Last Country Houses (with Alan Powers, 1982), The National Trust Book of the English House (1985), Quinlan Terry, The Revival of Architecture (1986), The American Country House (1990); *Recreations* living in London, opera, writing; *Clubs* Garrick, Academy; *Style—* Clive Aslet, Esq; c/o Country Life, King's Reach Tower, Stamford St, London SE1 9LS (☎ 071 261 6969, fax 071 261 5139)

ASPDEN, Hon Mrs (Judith Anne); *née* Nicholls; da of Baron Harmar-Nicholls, JP (Life Peer and 1 Bt); *b* 1941; *m* 1973, Alan Aspden; *Style—* The Hon Mrs Aspden

ASPEL, Michael Terence; s of Edward Aspel, and Violet Aspel; *b* 12 Jan 1933; *Educ* Emanuel Sch; *m* 1, 1957 (m dis), Dian; 2 s (Gregory (decd), Richard); m 2, 1962 (m dis), Ann; 1 s (Edward), 1 da (Jane (twin)); m 3, 1977, Elizabeth Power; 2 s (Patrick, Daniel); *Career* serv Nat Serv KRRC; writer and broadcaster; radio actor 1954-57, BBC TV news reader 1957-68, freelance 1968, Capital Radio disc jockey 1974-84; recently: Thames TV Give Us A Clue, This Is Your Life, LWT Aspel & Company, LWT Child's Play, ITV Telethon 1988; memb: Lord's Taverners, RYA; pres Stackpole Tst, vice pres Baby Life Support Systems, hon vice pres Assoc for Spina Bifida and Hydrocephalus; ordinary fell Zoological Soc of London; *Books* Polly wants a Zebra, Hang on!; *Style—* Michael Aspel, Esq; c/o Bagenal Harvey Organisation, 141-143 Drury Lane, London WC2B 5TB (☎ 071 379 4625)

ASPELL, Col Gerald Laycock; TD (1948), DL (Leicestershire 1952); s of Samuel Frederick Aspell (d 1949), of Queniborough Grange, Leics, and Agnes Maude, *née* Laycock (d 1962); *b* 10 April 1915; *Educ* Uppingham; *m* 1939, Mary Leeson, da of Rev Ion Carroll, of Edmondsham, Dorset; 1 s (Timothy), 2 da (Caroline, Penelope); *Career* Col TA 1933-1984 UK and Burma; CA 1938; ptnr Coopers & Lybrand 1952-78, chm Leicester Bldg Soc 1978-85 (dir 1964-85); chm Uppingham Sch 1977-87 (tstee

1964-87); Vice Lord Lt Leicestershire 1984-90; *Recreations* tennis; *Clubs* Leicestershire; *Style—* Col Gerald Aspell, TD, DL; Laburnum House, Great Dalby, Melton Mowbray, Leics LE14 2HA (☎ 0664 63604)

ASPIN, Peter; s of Thomas Aspin (d 1955); *b* 3 Jan 1933; *Educ* Quarry Bank Sch Liverpool, King's Coll Cambridge (MA); *m* Maureen; 2 children; *Career* professional engr; chm (former md) Allbook & Hashfield Ltd (formerly Giltspur Precision Industries Ltd); *Recreations* shooting; *Style—* Peter Aspin, Esq; Scylla House, Whatton-in-the-Vale, Notts; Allbook & Hashfield Ltd, 153 Huntingdon St, Nottingham (☎ 0602 582721)

ASPIN, William George; s of George Francis Aspin, of The Elms, Willow Ave, Constable Lee, Rawtenstall, Rossendale, Lancs, and Margaret, *née* Joyce; *b* 16 Aug 1954; *Educ* Cardinal Langley GS; *Career* CA; formed W G Aspin & Co 1980, ptnr Dymond Ashworth & Co, Accountants; chm and dir Spiralfair Properties Ltd 1987-; memb Rossendale Round Table; FICA (1983); *Recreations* golf, jogging, reading; *Clubs* Rossendale Golf; *Style—* William George Aspin, Esq; The Elms, Willow Ave, Constable Lee, Rawtenstall, Rossendale, Lancs (☎ 0706 216 442); Dymond Ashworth & Co, Accountants, 19 Ormerod Rd, Burnley, Lancs (☎ 0282 37215)

ASPINALL, Prof David; s of William Aspinall (d 1966), of Blackpool, and Hilda, *née* Whittle (d 1975); *b* 11 Aug 1933; *Educ* King Edward VII Lytham, Univ of Manchester (MSc, PhD); *m* 29 March 1958, Ina Paterson, da of William Kennedy Sillars, of Lytham St Annes; 2 s (Robert b 1962, Edward b 1965), 1 da (Mary b 1960); *Career* visiting assoc prof Univ of Illinois 1966, sr lectr of computer sci Univ of Manchester 1967 (lectr in electrical engrg 1960, lectr in computer sci 1964), prof of electrical engrg Univ Coll Swansea 1970, IEE Silvanus P Thompson lectr 1978-79, prof of computation UMIST 1979- (vice princ 1984-86); chm: IEE PGE2, IFIP TC10; memb Computing Sci Ctee SERC; FBCS 1968, FIEE 1977, CEng 1977; *Books* Introduction To Microprocessors (with E L Dagles, 1976), The Microprocessor & Its Application (1978), Introduction to Microcomputers (with E L Dagles, 1982); *Recreations* gardening, fell walking, golf; *Clubs* Bramall Golf; *Style—* Prof David Aspinall; 16A Darley Ave, West Didsbury, Manchester M20 8XF (☎ 061 445 6622); Dept of Computation, UMIST, PO Box 88, Manchester M60 1QD (☎ 061 200 3300, fax 061 228 7040, telex 666 094)

ASPINALL, John Victor; s of late Col Robert Aspinall, and Mary Grace, *née* Horn, later Lady Osborne (d 1987); *b* 11 June 1926; *Educ* Rugby (asked to leave), Jesus Coll Oxford (sent down); *m* 1, 1956 (m dis 1966), Jane Gordon Hastings; 1 s 1 da; m 2, 1966 (m dis 1972), Belinda Musker; m 3, 1972, Lady Sarah Marguerite Curzon; 1 s; *Career* WWII, Royal Marine 1943-45; fndr: Howletts Zoo Park 1958, Clermont Club 1962, Port Lympne Zoo Park 1973, Aspinall's Club 1978, Aspinall Curzon Club 1984; *Books* Best of Friends (1976); *Style—* John Aspinall, Esq; Howletts, Canterbury, Kent; Port Lympne, Lympne, Kent; 1 Lyall St, London SW1; Noordhoek Manor, Cape Town 7985, SA; 64 Sloane St, London SW1 (☎ 071 235 2768, fax 071 235 4701)

ASPINALL, Hon Mrs (Judith Mary); 4 and yst da of Baron Mackenzie-Stuart (Life Peer); *b* 14 May 1964; *m* 29 July 1989, Nicholas David Aspinall, er s of late Dr Dennis L Aspinall and Mrs M J A Thompson, of Earswick, York; *Style—* The Hon Mrs Aspinall; 30 Edbrooke Road, Maida Vale, London W9

ASPINALL, Martin Mark Charles; s of Charles Nicholas Bernard Aspinall, of family home, Standen Hall, Clitheroe, and Margaret Mary, *née* Worsley-Worswick; *b* 28 April 1951; *Educ* Redrice, RAC Cirencester; *Career* land agent, surveyor, with Miny of Agric and in private practice, chm and md Cotswold Sheepskins & Woollens Ltd 1985; dir Glenisla Property Co Ltd 1987; ARICS; *Recreations* shooting, fishing; *Style—* Martin Aspinall, Esq; c/o Barclays Bank, 128 High St, Cheltenham, Glos; Cotswold Sheepskins & Woollens Ltd, 2A Queens Circus, Montpellier, Cheltenham, Glos (☎ 0242 222377)

ASPINALL, (Harry) Michael; s of Leonard Aspinall (d 1969), of Tunbridge Wells, and Eva, *née* Whitworth; *b* 22 Nov 1926; *Educ* Sutton Valence Sch; *m* 12 Jan 1952, (Joan) Avril Aspinall, da of Maj Lancelot Kaye Machattie Powell, MC (d 1936), of Adelaide, Aust; 1 s (Mark Christopher Leonard b 1957), 1 da (Rebecca Carol (Mrs Bayley) b 1953); *Career* slr; admitted 1948, notary public 1958, sr ptnr Thomson Snell and Passmore 1986-; memb and chm Abbeyfield Tunbridge Wells Soc Ltd; memb: Law Soc 1948, Notaries' Soc 1958; *Recreations* travel, reading, wide interest in art and craft subjects; *Clubs* Royal Ocean Racing, MCC, Ski Club of GB; *Style—* Michael Aspinall, Esq

ASPINALL, Lady Sarah Marguerite; *née* Curzon; da of 5 Earl Howe, CBE, VD, PC (d 1964); *b* 25 Jan 1945; *m* 1, 1966, Piers Raymond Courage (d 1970); 2 s (Jason b 1967, Amos b 1969); m 2, 1972, John Victor Aspinall, s of late Col Robert Aspinall; 1 s (Bassa Wulfhere b 1972); *Style—* The Lady Sarah Aspinall; 1 Lyall St, London SW1

ASPINALL, Wilfred; s of Charles Aspinall (d 1972), and Elizabeth, *née* Cadmen (d 1984); *b* 14 Sept 1942; *Educ* Poynton Secdy Modern Sch, Stockport Coll for Further Educn; *m* 1973, Judith Mary, da of Leonard James Pimlott (d 1979); 1 da (Isabel b 1980); *Career* asst gen sec Nat Westminster Staff Assoc 1969-75, gen sec Confedn of Bank Staff Assoc 1975-79, memb Banking Staff Cncl 1970-77; treas and conslt Managerial Professional and Staff Liaison Gp 1978-79; exec dir Fedn of Managerial Professional and General Assocs (MPG) 1979-, vice pres Confédération Européen des Cadres 1979-; memb: Hammersmith Special Health Authy 1982-90, North Herts Health Authy 1982-6, North West Thames RHA 1986-88; memb Econ and Social Consultative Assembly Brussels 1986-; *Clubs* The Lighthouse, European; *Style—* Wilfred Aspinall, Esq; The Croft, 19 Shillington Rd, Pirton, Hitchin, Herts (☎ 0462 712 316); Tavistock House, Tavistock Sq, London WC1 (☎ 071 383 6194); Brussels Bureau, Bte 49, Rue de la Montagne 34, Brussels 1000, Belgium (☎ 010 32 2 511 2720)

ASPINWALL, Jack Heywood; MP (C) Wansdyke 1983-; *b* 1933; *Educ* Prescot GS Lancs, Marconi Coll Chelmsford; *m* Brenda Jean Aspinwall; *Career* RAF 1949-56, Parly candidate: (Lib) Kingswood Feb and Oct 1974, (C) Kingswood 1979-1983; co dir; *Books* Kindly Sit Down, Tell me Another, Hit me Again, After dinner Stories; *Style—* Jack Aspinwall, Esq, MP; House of Commons, London SW1A 0AA

ASPREY, Algernon; s of George Kenneth Asprey (d 1946), and Charlotte Esta Asprey; *b* 2 June 1912; *Educ* Charterhouse, Sch of Art; *m* 1939, Beatrice, da of Francis Bryant (d 1960); 1 s, 1 da (and 1 da decd); *Career* Capt Scots Gds 1940-46; artist and designer; Asprey Bond St 1933-71 (later md); chm: Purchase Tax Ctee (post war years to its disbandment), Guards' Club 1960-65, Algernon Asprey Ltd 1971-80; pres Bond St Assoc 1968-81 (chm 1965-68); memb Ctee Friends of Royal Acad; Prime Warden Worshipful Co of Goldsmiths 1977-78; *Recreations* painting, sailing, golf; *Clubs* Cavalry and Guards' (hon memb); *Style—* Algernon Asprey, Esq; Magnolia Cottage, Shamley Green, Surrey GU5 0SX (☎ 0483 27 1502)

ASQUITH, Lady (Mary) Annunziata; da of 2 Earl of Oxford and Asquith, KCMG; *b* 28 July 1948; *Educ* Mayfield Sussex, Somerville Coll Oxford; *Career* formerly with Daily Telegraph Magazine; writer, art dealer; *Books* Marie Antoninette (1974); *Style—* The Lady Annunziata Asquith; c/o The Manor House, Mells, Frome, Somerset

ASQUITH, Hon Mrs Paul; Caroline Anne; *née* Pole; yr da of Sir John Gawen Carew Pole, 12 Bt, DSO, TD, *qv*; *b* 11 Jan 1933; *m* 16 July 1963, as his 2 w, Hon Paul Asquith (d 1984), yr s of Baron Asquith of Bishopstone (Life Peer, d 1954); 1 s, 1 da; *Style—* The Hon Mrs Paul Asquith; 41 Quarrendon St, London SW6 (☎ 071 731 3955)

ASQUITH, Hon Dominic Anthony Gerard; s of 2 Earl of Oxford and Asquith, KCMG; *b* 7 Feb 1957; *m* 12 May 1988, Louise E, only da of John E Cotton, of Wollaton, Nottingham; *Style—* The Hon Dominic Asquith; c/o The Manor House, Mells, Frome

ASQUITH, Lady Helen Frances; OBE (1965); da of late Raymond Asquith (ka 1916, Battle of the Somme, s of 1 Earl of Oxford and Asquith); sis of 2 Earl; *b* 1908; *Educ* St Paul's Girls' Sch, Somerville Coll Oxford (BA); *Career* teaching classics in secondary schools, HM inspector of schools; *Style—* The Lady Helen Asquith, OBE; Tynts Hill, Mells, Frome, Somerset

ASQUITH, Hon Luke; er s of Baron Asquith of Bishopstone, PC (Life Peer, d 1954); *b* 18 Nov 1919; *Educ* Winchester; *m* 2 July 1954, (Ethel) Meriel, da of Maurice Cann Evans, of Arrow Lawn, Eardisland, Herefordshire; 2 da; *Career* served 1939-45 War in N Africa, Italy as GOC (3) Liaison Offr 8 Army Tai HQ; *Style—* The Hon Luke Asquith; The Paddock, Broad St, Alresford, Hants SO24 9AN; 31 Trossachs Rd, East Dulwich, London SE22 8PY (☎ 081 693 2239)

ASQUITH, Viscount; Raymond Benedict Bartholomew Michael Asquith; s and h of 2 Earl of Oxford and Asquith, KCMG; *b* 24 Aug 1952; *Educ* Ampleforth, Balliol Oxford; *m* 1978, Clare, da of Francis Pollen (d 1987), and Thérèse, da of His Hon Sir Joseph Sheridan, and gda of late Arthur Pollen (gn of Sir Richard Pollen, 3 Bt) by his w Hon Daphne Baring, da of 3 Baron Revelstoke; 1 s (Mark), 3 da (Magdalen, Frances, Celia); *Heir* s Hon Mark Julian Asquith b 13 May 1979; *Style—* Viscount Asquith; Little Claveys, Mells, Frome, Somerset

ASSCHER, (Adolf) William; s of William Benjamin Asscher (d 1982), and Roosje, *née* van der Molen; *b* 20 March 1931; *Educ* Maerlant Lyceum The Hague Netherlands, London Hosp Med Coll (BSc, MB BS, MD); *m* 1, 1960, Corrie, *née* van Welt (d 1961); m 2, 3 Nov 1962, Jennifer, da of Wynne Lloyd, CB (d 1973), of Cardiff; 2 da (Jane b 1963, Sophie b 1965); *Career* Nat Serv 1949-51 cmmnd Lt RE; jr med appts London Hosp 1957-64; WNSM Cardiff: conslt physician and sr lectr in med 1964-70, reader in med 1970-76, prof of med 1976-80; prof and head Dept of Renal Med Univ of Wales Coll of Med 1980-87; St George's Hosp Med Sch London Univ 1988-: hon conslt physician, dean, prof of medicine; RCP: regnl advsr 1973-77, cnclr 1977-80; chm Ctee on Review of Medicines DHSS 1984-87, memb Welsh Arts Cncl 1985-88, chm Ctee on Safety of Medicines Dept of Health 1987-; memb SW Thames RHA 1988-90, non-exec dir Wandsworth DHA; Liveryman Worshipful Soc of Apothecaries 1960; MRCP 1959, FRCP 1970; memb: Renal Assoc 1962 (sec 1972-77, pres 1986-89), Assoc of Physicians 1970, Med Res Soc 1957 (memb Cncl 1966-6); *Books* The Challenge of Urinary Tract Infections (1981), Nephrology Illustrated (1982), Nephro-Urology (1983), Clinical Atlas of the Kidney (1990); *Recreations* visual arts, golf; *Clubs* Reform, Radyr Golf, Radyr Lawn Tennis (chm 1972-78); *Style—* Prof William Asscher; Dean's Office, St George's Hospital Medical School, Cranmer Terrace, Tooting, London SW17 ORE (☎ 081 672 3122, fax 081 672 6940)

ASSERSON, Ronald Henry; s of David Asserson (d 1937), of London, and Charlotte Shire (d 1983); *b* 4 Jan 1923; *Educ* St Paul's, Univ of London BSc; *m* 1954, Denise Alice, da of Hugo Falk (d 1964), of London; 2 s (Trevor Richard b 1956, Stephen Charles b 1959), 1 da (Janine Karen b 1955); *Career* chm Boosey and Hawkes plc 1985-; dir: Delta Gp plc 1972-85, BRE Ltd 1980-82, Benjamin Priest Gp plc 1985-, Yale and Valor plc 1981-; *Recreations* music, literature; *Clubs* Royal Automobile, City Livery; *Style—* Ronald H Asserson, Esq; 50 Wildwood Road, London NW11 6UP (☎ 081 458 1881); N Chailey Sussex; Boosey and Hawkes plc, Deansbrook Road, Edgeware, Middx HA8 9BB

ASSHETON, Hon Nicholas; Lord of the Manor and Liberty of Slaidburn, Grindleton and Bradford; s of 1 Baron Clitheroe, KCVO, PC (d 1984), and Sylvia, Lady Clitheroe (d 1991), da of 6 Baron Hotham; *b* 23 May 1934; *Educ* Eton, Ch Ch Oxford (MA); *m* 29 Feb 1960, Jacqueline Jill, da of Marshal of the RAF Sir Arthur Harris, 1 Bt, GCB, OBE, AFC (d 1984), of Goring-on-Thames, by his 2 w; 1 s (Thomas b 1963), 2 da (Caroline b 1961, Mary Thérèse b 1967); *Career* formerly 2 Lt Life Gds, Lt Inns of Court Regt; memb Stock Exchange (and Cncl 1969); dir: Coutts & Co, NM UK Ltd; Liveryman Worshipful Co of Vintners; *Clubs* Pratt's, White's; *Style—* The Hon Nicholas Assheton; 15 Hammersmith Terrace, London W6 9TS; Coutts & Co, 440 Strand, London WC1R 0QS (☎ 071 753 1000)

ASSHETON, Hon Ralph Christopher; Lord of the Manors of Downham and Cuerdale; s and h of 2 Baron Clitheroe, *qv*; *b* 19 March 1962; *Educ* Eton; *Style—* The Hon Ralph Assheton

ASTAIRE, Edgar; s of Max Astaire; *b* 23 Jan 1930; *Educ* Harrow; *m* 1958 (m dis 1975); 3 s (Mark b 1959, Simon b 1961, Peter b 1963); *Career* stockbroker; chm Cl-Astaire & Co Ltd 1960-90; Master Worshipful Co of Pattenmakers 1982; *Clubs* MCC, Queen's; *Style—* Edgar Astaire, Esq; 11 Lowndes Close, Lowndes Place, London SW1X 8BZ (☎ 071 235 5757); Cold Comfort Farm, Wendover, Bucks (☎ 0296 623172); Société Générale Strauss Turnbull Securities Ltd, Exchange House, Primrose Street, Broadgate, London EC2A 2DD (☎ 071 638 5699)

ASTBURY, Michael Henry Richardson; s of John Astbury, OBE (d 1968), and Joyce Elsie, *née* Richardson (d 1978); *b* 3 May 1929; *Educ* Edinburgh Acad, Perse Sch Cambridge, St Catharine's Coll Cambridge (MA); *m* 31 March 1959, Margaret, da of Leslie Arthur Hammond (d 1981); 2 s (Peter John Hammond b 5 June 1960, Jonathan Robert Hammond b 27 June 1962); *Career* Nat Serv RAEC 1947-49 (Greece, Egypt); called to the Bar Middle Temple 1953; asst sec Manchester Ship Canal Co 1954-57, sec Employers Fedn of Ceylon 1961-63 (dep sec 1957-61), prosecuting slr DTI 1963-67, dep sec Gen Cncl of the Senate of the Inns of Court and the Bar 1967-77, sec Inc Soc of Valuers and Auctioneers 1977-89; chm Kent Family Health Servs Authy Med Servs Ctee (and dep chm Jt Servs Ctee), chm South Bromley Hospiscare 1990-; sec Kentish Cobnuts Assoc; memb: Panel of Reference Secs MMC, St Peters PCC Ightham Kent; Freeman: City of London, Worshipful Co of Glovers; MCIArb; *Books* Halsburys' Laws of England (contrib, 4 edn), Butterworths Encyclopaedia of Forms and Precedents (advsy ed, 5 edn); *Recreations* sailing, gardening, reading; *Clubs* MCC; *Style—* Michael Astbury, Esq; The Coach House, Oldbury, Ightham, nr Sevenoaks, Kent (☎ 0732 884163)

ASTELL HOHLER, Thomas Sidney; MC (1944); s of Col Arthur Preston Hohler, DSO (d 1919), of Long Crendon Manor, Bucks, and Laline, *née* Astell (later Mrs Stanley Barry); granted the name and arms of Astell Hohler on inheriting the Woodbury and Great Houghton Estate from his maternal uncle Richard Astell 1978; *b* 30 Nov 1919; *Educ* Eton; *m* 1952, (Julie) Jacqueline, da of late Marquis de Jouffroy d'Abbans, of Chateau d'Abbans, Doubs, France; 1 da (Isabelle Jacqueline Laline, m 24 Earl of Erroll, *qv*); *Career* Maj Grenadier Gds, served in WWII in France, N Africa and Italy; ptnr King & Shaxson plc 1946- (chm 1965-84); chm London Discount Market Assoc 1972; Liveryman Worshipful Co of Grocers 1956; *Recreations* shooting, farming; *Clubs* Brooks's, City of London; *Style—* Thomas Astell Hohler, Esq, MC; Wolverton Park, Basingstoke, Hants RG26 5RU (☎ 0635 298200)

ASTILL, His Hon Judge Michael John; s of late Cyril Norman Astill, of Thurnby, Leics, and Winifred, *née* Tuckley; *b* 31 Jan 1938; *Educ* Blackfriars Sch Laxton Northants; *m* 1 June 1968, Jean Elizabeth, da of late Dr John Chisholm Hamilton

Mackenzie; 3 s (Matthew b 28 Dec 1972, James (twin) b 28 Dec 1972, Mark b 11 Nov 1975), 1 da (Katherine b 11 July 1971); *Career* circuit judge Midland and Oxford Circuit 1984; *Recreations* reading, music, gardening, sport; *Style—* His Honour Judge Michael Astill

ASTIN, Prof Alan Edgar; OBE (1989); s of Harold William Astin (d 1974), of Surbiton, Surrey, and Winifred Clara, *née* Phillips (d 1978); *b* 14 June 1930; *Educ* Kingston GS, Kingston upon Thames, Worcester Coll Oxford (MA); *m* 19 March 1955, June Doris, da of Frank Eric Benjamin Bowring (d 1982); 2 s (Anthony b 1958, Neil b 1960); *Career* Nat Serv 1948-50, 2 Lt RASC 1949-50; pro vice chllr Queens Univ Belfast 1974-79 (asst lectr and lectr 1954-67, prof of ancient history 1967-), visiting prof Yale Univ 1966; writer of numerous academic articles; memb Inst for Advanced Study Princeton NJ 1964-65 (1975 and 1983-84); chm Working Party NI 1977-79, chm Arts Cncl of NI 1986- (memb Bd 1980-86), govr Royal Belfast Academical Inst 1977-; MRIA 1973, vice pres Roman Soc 1979-; *Books* The Lex Annalis Before Sulla (1958), Scipio Aemilianus (1967), Cato the Censor (1978), The Cambridge Ancient History (Vols VII-, VII-2, VIII, ed and (contrib 2 edn 1984, 2 edn 1989); *Recreations* music, opera, dance, drama; *Style—* Prof Alan Astin, OBE; Dept of Ancient History, The Queens Univ, Belfast BT7 1NN (☎ 0232 245133)

ASTLEY, David John; s of Robert Joseph Astley (d 1987), of Liverpool, and Joan Margaret Astley (d 1988); *b* 15 April 1953; *Educ* Alsop Comp Sch Liverpool; *m* Denise Michelle, da of Ewart George Mayne; 1 s (Robert George b 19 April 1990), 1 da (Emma Louise b 2 June 1988); *Career* higher clerical offr Chesterfields Hosps 1974-75, asst admin The General Hosp Nottingham 1975-77; dep admin: Wythenshawe Hosp Manchester 1977-79, Withington Hosp Manchester 1979-83; unit admin Walsgrave Hosp Coventry 1983-86; gen mangr: Addenbrookes Hosp Cambridge 1986-90, Norwich Acute Hosps 1991-; memb Inst of Health Serv Mgmnt; *Recreations* swimming, family life, model railways; *Style—* David Astley, Esq; General Manager, Acute Hospitals, Norfolk and Norwich Hospital, Norwich, Norfolk

ASTLEY, Hon Delaval Thomas Harold; s and h of 22 Baron Hastings; *b* 25 April 1960; *Educ* Radley & Durham; *m* 26 July 1987, Veronica, er da of Richard Smart, of Chester; *Style—* The Hon Delaval Astley

ASTLEY, Sir Francis Jacob Dugdale; 6 Bt (UK 1821), of Everleigh, Wilts; s of late Rev Anthony Aylmer Astley, 6 s of 2 Bt; suc kinsman, Capt Sir Francis Henry Rivers Astley-Corbett, 5 Bt, 1943; *b* 26 Oct 1908; *Educ* Marlborough, Trinity Coll Oxford; *m* 1934, Brita Margareta Josefina, da of Karl Nyström, of Stockholm; 1 da; *Career* sr lectr Univ Coll Ghana 1948-62, head of Classics Dept Atlantic Coll St Donat's Castle 1962-69; *Style—* Sir Francis Astley, Bt; 16 Doulton Mews, Lymington Road, London NW6 1XY (☎ 071 435 9945)

ASTLEY, Neil Philip; s of Philip Thomas Astley, of Adelaide, Aust, and Margaret Ivy Astley (d 1976); *b* 12 May 1953; *Educ* Price's Sch Fareham Hants, Univ of Newcastle upon Tyne (BA); *m* 1, 4 Sept 1976 (m dis 1983), Julie Marie Callan; m 2, 8 Oct 1988, Katharine Keens-Soper, da of Henry John Stuffins, of Harrogate; 2 step da (Octavia Claire b 26 Dec 1964, Alice Mary b 22 March 1966); *Career* md and ed Bloodaxe Books Ltd (fndr 1978); awards: Eric Gregory award 1982, Poetry Book Soc Recommendation 1988, Dorothy Tutin award for Servs to Poetry 1989; *Books* Ten North-East Poets (ed, 1980), The Speechless Act (1984), Bossy Parrot (ed, 1987), Darwin Survivor (ed, 1988), Dear Next Prime Minister (ed, 1990); Poetry with an Edge (1988); *Recreations* work; *Style—* Neil Astley, Esq; Bloodaxe Books Ltd, PO Box 1SN, Newcastle upon Tyne NE99 1SN (☎ 091 232 5988)

ASTLEY-COOPER, Alexander Paston; s and h of Sir Patrick Graham Astley-Cooper, 6 Bt; *b* 1 Feb 1943; *Educ* Kelly Coll Tavistock; *m* 1974, Minnie Margeret, da of Charles Harrison (d 1959); *Career* sales office mangr Carton Industry; *Recreations* cricket, badminton, rugby union, theatre, travel; *Style—* Alexander Astley-Cooper, Esq; Gadebridge, 18A Station Rd, Rayleigh, Essex SS6 7HL (☎ 0268 777506)

ASTLEY-COOPER, Sir Patrick Graham; 6 Bt (UK 1821) of Gadebridge, Herts; s of late Col Clifton Graham Astley Cooper, DSO, RA (gs of 2 Bt); suc kinsman Sir Henry Lovick Cooper, 5 Bt (d 1959); *b* 4 Aug 1918; *Educ* Marlborough; *m* 7 April 1942, Audrey Ann Jervoise, yr da of late Major Douglas Philip Jervoise Collas, Military Knight of Windsor; 1 s, 2 da; *Heir* s, Alexander Paston Astley-Cooper; *Career* former sr asst land cmmr MAFF, dir Crendon Concrete Ltd Long Crendon 1973-; *Style—* Sir Patrick Astley-Cooper, Bt; Monkton Cottage, Monks Risborough, Aylesbury, Bucks HP17 9JF (☎ 084 44 4210)

ASTON, Archdeacon of; *see*: Cooper, Ven John Leslie

ASTON, Lady; Eileen Fitzgerald; da of John Bell McNair; *m* 1949, Sir Christopher (Kit) Aston, KCVO (d 1982), sometime chm Powell Duffryn; 1 s (James), 2 da (Joanna, Harriet); *Style—* Lady Aston; 32 Bowerdean St, London SW6 3TW (☎ 071 736 5133)

ASTON, Cdre John Anthony; RN; s of Ernest Gustav Aston (d 1972), and Haley Muriel, *née* Grutchfield (d 1988); *b* 8 June 1939; *Educ* Whitgift Sch, Britannia RNC Dartmouth, Univ of London (BSc); *m* 19 Dec 1970, Elizabeth Constance Mark, da of Rear Adm William Penrose Mark-Wardlaw DSO (d 1952); 2 da (Katie b 1972, Susie b 1975); *Career* Cdr 1973, naval asst to Dir Gen of Weapons (Navy) 1974-76, Admty Surface Weapons Establishment 1976-78, HMS Sheffield 1978-79, staff of C-in-C Fleet 1979-82, exec offr HMS Mercury 1982, Capt 1982, naval attaché Brazil 1983-86, staff of Cdr Br Forces Falklands 1986, Directorate of Naval Plans 1987-89, Cdre 1990, vice pres of Ordnance Bd 1990-; memb: Anglo Brazilian Soc, RNSA; *Recreations* skiing, dinghy sailing, Scottish dancing; *Clubs* The Goat, Thorney Island Sailing; *Style—* Cdre John Aston, RN; 43 Christchurch Rd, St Cross, Winchester, Hants (☎ 0962 862919)

ASTON, Peter George; s of Dr George William Aston (d 1980), and Dr Elizabeth Oliver, *née* Smith (d 1979); *b* 5 Oct 1938; *Educ* Tettenhall Coll, Birmingham Sch of Music (GBSM), Univ of York (DPhil); *m* 13 Aug 1960, Elaine Veronica, da of Harold Neale (d 1942); 1 s (David b 1963); *Career* sr lectr in music Univ of York 1972-74 (lectr 1964-72), dean Sch of Fine Arts and Music UEA 1981-84 (prof and head of music 1974-); music dir: Tudor Consort 1959-65, Eng Baroque Ensemble 1967-70; conductor Aldeburgh Festival Singers 1975-88, gen ed UEA Recordings 1979-, jt artistic dir Norwich Festival of Contemporary Church Music 1981-; published compositions incl: chamber music, church music, opera, choral and orch works; ed complete works of George Jeffreys and music by various Baroque composers; numerous recordings and contribs to int jls; hon patron: Gt Yarmouth Musical Soc, Lowestoft Choral Soc; chm: Eastern Arts Assoc Music Panel 1975-81; Norfolk Assoc for the Advancement of Music 1990-; chorus master Norfolk & Norwich Triennial Festival 1982-85, hon pres Trianon Music Gp 1984-; FTCL, FCI, ARCM, FRSA 1980; *Books* The Music of York Minster (1972), Sound and Silence (jtly 1970, German edn 1972, Italian edn 1980, Japanese edn 1981); *Recreations* bridge, chess, cricket; *Clubs* Athenaeum, Norfolk; *Style—* Prof Peter Aston; Univ of E Anglia, Music Centre, Sch of Fine Arts and Music, Norwich NR4 7TJ (☎ 0603 56161, fax 0603 58553, telex 975197)

ASTON, Col Stanley Collin; OBE (1973), TD and Clasps, DL (Cambs 1960); s of Alfred Ernest Aston (d 1961), of Lincoln; *b* 4 Sept 1915; *Educ* City Sch Lincoln, St Catharine's Coll Cambridge (BA, MA, PhD); *m* 1940, Rosalind Molly, da of Rev Frank Fairfax (d 1964), of Bebington, Cheshire; 1 s, 2 da; *Career* served WWII Suffolk Regt, RM Div, Int Corps; Cambridgeshire Regt and Royal Anglian Regt TA 1946-80, dep hon Col TA Royal Anglian Regt 1972-80, chm Cambs ACF 1947-77 and TA 1967-77; Bye-fellow Magdalene Coll Cambridge 1938-43; St Catharine's Coll Cambridge: fell 1943, dean 1946-57, tutor 1957-59, bursar 1961-79, pres 1980; univ lectr Cambridge 1946-82, visiting prof Ohio State Univ 1955-56 and 1961-62; Doct de l'Univ de Clermont; pres Modern Humanities Research Assoc 1970 (sec 1945-50, chm 1950-68), sec gen Int Fedn for Modern Languages and Literatures 1954-78 (pres 1984-87), pres International Cncl for Philosophy and Humanistic Scis UNESCO 1979-84 (memb 1952-75, vice pres 1975-79); *Books* Peirol, Troubadour of Auvergne (1953), author of numerous articles on medieval romance literatures; editor of journals and bibliographies; *Recreations* sports, music, philately; *Clubs* National Liberal; *Style—* Col Stanley Aston, OBE, TD, DL; c/o St Catharine's College, Cambridge (☎ 0223 338300); 4 Manor Walk, Fulbourn, Cambridge CB1 5BN (☎ 0223 881323)

ASTOR, Bronwen Alun; yst da of His Hon Judge Sir (John) Alun Pugh (d 1971), and Kathleen Mary, *née* Goodyear (d 1970); *b* 6 June 1930; *Educ* Dr William's Sch Dolgellau, Central Sch of Speech and Drama (Dip); *m* 1960, as his 3 w, 3 Viscount Astor (d 1966); 2 da; *Career* teacher, TV announcer, model girl, psychotherapist, runs a Christian retreat house; *Recreations* fishing, tennis, windsurfing; *Style—* Bronwen, Viscountess Astor; Tuesley Manor, Tuesley, Godalming, Surrey GU7 1UD (☎ 0483 417281)

ASTOR, Hon (Francis) David Langhorne; s of 2 Viscount Astor (d 1952), and Nancy, Viscountess Astor, CH, MP (d 1964); *b* 5 March 1912; *Educ* Eton, Balliol Oxford; *m* 1, 1945, Melanie Hauser; 1 da; m 2, 1952, Bridget Aphra Wreford; 2 s, 3 da; *Career* served WW II; The Observer: foreign ed 1946-48, ed 1948-75, dir 1976-81; *Style—* The Hon David Astor; 9 Cavendish Ave, St John's Wood, London NW8 (☎ 071 286 0223); Manor House, Sutton Courtenay, Oxon

ASTOR, David Waldorf; s of Hon Michael Langhorne Astor (MP for Surrey East 1945-51, d 1980, 3 s of 2 Viscount Astor), and his 1 w, Barbara Mary (d 1980), da of Capt Ronald McNeill; n of Hon Sir John Astor, *qv*; *b* 9 Aug 1943; *Educ* Eton, Univ of Harvard; *m* 19 Sept 1968, Clare Pamela, er da of Cdr Michael Beauchamp St John, DSC, RN; 2 s (Henry b 17 April 1969, Tom b 24 July 1972), 2 da (Joanna b 23 June 1970, Rose b 9 June 1979); *Career* short service cmmn in Royal Scots Greys 1962-65; farmer 1973-; dir Jupiter Tarbutt Merlin 1985-, chm Classic FM 1989-; chm Cncl for the Protection of Rural England 1983-; Parly candidate (SDP) Plymouth Drake 1987; FRSA 1988; *Recreations* books, sport; *Clubs* Brooks's, MCC; *Style—* David Astor, Esq; CPRE, 4 Hobart Place, London SW1 (☎ 071 976 6433); Bruern Grange, Milton-under-Wychwood, Oxford OX7 6HA (☎ 0993 830413)

ASTOR, Hon Hugh Waldorf; JP (Berks 1953); s of 1 Baron Astor of Hever (d 1971), and Violet Mary Elliot, da of Earl of Minto; *b* 20 Nov 1920; *Educ* Eton, New Coll Oxford; *m* 1950, Emily Lucy, da of Sir Alexander Kinloch, 12 Bt; 2 s (Robert, James), 3 da (Virginia, Rachel, Jean); *Career* WWII Lt Col Intelligence Corps; dep chm The Times 1959-67; dir: Hambros plc 1960-, Winterbottom Trust 1961-86, Phoenix Assurance 1962-85; memb Cncl of Trusthouse Forte 1962 (chm 1971), exec vice chm Olympia Ltd 1971-73; chm: Times Trust 1967-82, Peabody Donation Fund 1981- (dep chm 1979), Mgmnt Ctee King Edward's Hosp Fund for London 1983-88 (dep chm 1981); High Sherrif Berks 1963; *Recreations* shooting, sailing (motor yacht: Nautacuintli), flying; *Clubs* Brooks's, Buck's, Pratt's, Royal Yacht Sqdn, Royal Ocean Racing; *Style—* The Hon Hugh Astor, JP; Folly Farm, Sulhamstead, Berks RG7 4DF (☎ 0734 302326)

ASTOR, Hon Sir John Jacob; MBE (1945), DL (Cambs 1962); s of 2 Viscount Astor; u of David W Astor, *qv*; *b* 29 Aug 1918; *Educ* Eton, New Coll Oxford; *m* 1, 1944 (m dis 1972), Ana Inez, da of Señor Dr Don Miguel Carcano, (Hon) KCMG, (Hon) KBE, sometime Argentine Ambass to UK; 1 s (Michael Ramon Langhorne m 1979 Daphne Warburg), 1 da (Stella); m 2, 1976 (m dis 1985), Susan, da of Maj Michael Eveleigh; m 3, 16 March 1988, Mrs Marcia de Savary; *Career* served WWII as Maj (French Croix de Guerre and Legion d'Honneur 1945); former JP Cambs; MP (C) Plymouth Sutton 1951-59, PPS to Fin Sec Treasy 1951-52; chm: Governing Body of Nat Inst of Agric Engrg 1963-68, Agric Res Cncl 1968-78, NEDC for Agric Indust 1978-83; steward Jockey Club 1968-71 and 1983-85, memb Horserace Betting Levy Bd 1976-80; kt 1978; *Clubs* White's; *Style—* The Hon Sir John Astor, MBE, DL; The Dower Hse, Hatley Pk, Hatley St George, Sandy, Beds (☎ 0767 50266)

ASTOR, Hon Mrs Michael; Judith Caroline Traill; da of Paul Innes; *m* 1970, as his 3 w, Hon Michael Langhorne Astor (d 1980), 3 s of 2 Viscount Astor; 1 s (Joshua b 1966), 1 da (Polly b 1971); *Style—* The Hon Mrs Michael Astor; Red Brick House, Bruern, Churchill, Oxon

ASTOR, Hon Philip Douglas Paul; yr s of 2 Baron Astor of Hever (d 1984); *b* 4 April 1959; *Educ* Eton (King's Scholar), ChCh Oxford (MA); *Career* called to the Bar 1989; *Style—* The Hon Philip Astor; Flat 3, 6 Embankment Gardens, London SW3 4LJ (☎ 071 351 0018); Tillypronie, Tarland, Aboyne, Aberdeenshire AB3 4XX (☎ 033 98 81238)

ASTOR, Philippa, Viscountess; Philippa Victoria; JP; da of Lt-Col Henry Philip Hunloke, TD (d 1978), and Lady Anne Cavendish, MBE (d 1981), 5 da of 9 Duke of Devonshire, KG, GCMG, GCVO, PC; *b* 10 Dec 1930; *Educ* RADA; *m* 26 April 1955 (m dis 1960), as his 2 w, 3 Viscount Astor (d 1966); 1 da (Hon Emily Mary (Hon Mrs Anderson) b 1956); *Career* stage mangr in various repertory cos and west end prodns prior to marriage; sch governor, charity tstee; *Style—* Philippa, Viscountess Astor, JP; 2 St Albans Grove, London W8 5PN (☎ 071 937 3964)

ASTOR, 4 Viscount (UK 1917); William Waldorf Astor; also Baron Astor (UK 1916); only child of 3 Viscount Astor (d 1966), by his 1 w, Hon Sarah, *née* Norton, da of 6 Baron Grantley; the recurrent forename Waldorf commemorates a village near Heidelberg from which John Jacob Astor (ggf of 1 Viscount) emigrated to the New World in the end of the eighteenth century and later bought lands in the area now covered by New York; *b* 27 Dec 1951; *Educ* Eton; *m* 1976, Annabel Lucy Veronica, da of Timothy Jones (himself s of Sir Roderick Jones, KBE, sometime chm of Reuters, and his w, better known as the writer Enid Bagnold). Annabel's mother was Pandora, *née* Clifford (niece of 11 and 12 Barons Clifford of Chudleigh and sis of Lady Norwich - *see* 2 Viscount Norwich); 2 s (Hon William Waldorf, Hon James Jacob b 18 Jan 1979), 1 da (Hon Flora Katherine b 7 June 1976); *Heir* s, Hon William Waldorf Astor b 18 Jan 1979; *Career* co dir; a Lord in Waiting to HM 1990-; *Recreations* fishing, shooting; *Clubs* White's, Turf; *Style—* The Rt Hon The Viscount Astor; Ginge Manor, Wantage, Oxon (☎ 0235 833228)

ASTOR OF HEVER, Irene, Lady; Lady Irene Violet Freesia Janet Augusta; da of Field Marshal 1 Earl Haig, KT, GCB, DM, GCVO, KCIE (d 1928); *b* 7 Oct 1919; *m* 4 Oct 1945, 2 Baron Astor of Hever (d 1984); 2 s, 3 da; *Career* hon life memb BRCS (holder of Queen's Badge of Honour, chm and pres Kent Branch 1976-82), patron Kent Co Royal Br Legion Women's Section, pres Kent Agric Soc 1981 and 1982, vice pres RNIB, vice patron Nat Asthma Campaign; CStJ; *Style—* The Rt Hon Irene, Lady Astor of Hever; Holly Tree House, French St, Westerham, Kent TN16 1PW (☎ 0959 62141); 11 Lyall St, Eaton Sq, London SW1X 8DH (☎ 071 235 4755)

ASTOR OF HEVER, The Rt Hon the Lord John Jacob Astor; 3 Baron (UK 1956); s of 2 Baron Astor of Hever by his w, Lady Irene Haig, da of 1 Earl Haig, KT, GCB,

OM, GCVO, KCIE; *b* 16 June 1946; *Educ* Eton; *m* 1, 1970 (m dis 1990), Fiona Diana Lennox, da of Capt Roger Harvey, JP, DL, Scots Gds, and Diana (da of Sir Harry Mainwaring, 5 and last Bt, by his w Generis, eld da of Sir Richard Williams-Bulkeley, 12 Bt, KCB, VD, JP, and Lady Magdalen Yorke, da of 5 Earl of Hardwicke); 3 da (Hon Camilla Fiona b 1974, Hon Tania Jentie b 1978, Hon Violet Magdalene b 1980); m 2, 5 May 1990, Hon Elizabeth Constance, da of 2 Viscount Mackintosh of Halifax , OBE, BEM (d 1980), 1 s (Hon Charles Gavin John b 10 Nov 1990); *Heir* s, Hon Charles Gavin John Astor b 10 Nov 1990; *Career* formerly Lt LG served Malaysia, Hong Kong, NI; md: Terres Blanches Services Sarl 1975-77, Valberg Plaza Sarl 1977-82, Honon et Cie 1982-; pres: Astor Enterprises Inc 1983-, Astor France Sarl 1990-; chm Cncl of St John Kent; *Clubs* White's, Cavalry and Guards'; *Style—* The Rt Hon the Lord Astor of Hever; Frenchstreet House, Frenchstreet, Westerham, Kent TN16 1PW (☎ 0959 62783)

ASTWOOD, Hon Mr Justice; Hon Sir James Rufus Astwood; JP; s of late James Rufus Astwood, and Mabel Winifred Astwood; *b* 4 Oct 1923; *Educ* Berkeley Inst Bermuda, Univ of Toronto; *m* 1952, Gloria Preston Norton; 1 s, 2 da; *Career* called to the Bar Gray's Inn 1956; started practice at Jamaican Bar 1956, dep clerk of cts Jamaica 1957-58, stipendiary magistrate and judge Grand Ct Cayman Islands 1958-59, clerk of cts Jamaica 1958-63, res magistrate Jamaica 1963-74, puisne judge Jamaica 1971-73, sr magistrate Bermuda 1974-76, SG Bermuda 1976-77, acting AG Bermuda 1976 and 1977, temp acting dep govr Bermuda during 1977, chief justice Bermuda 1977-; Hon MA Gray's Inn 1985; kt 1982; *Style—* The Hon Sir James Astwood, CJ, Bermuda; Clifton, 8 Middle Rd, Devonshire DV03 Bermuda (☎ 010 1 80292 0263); Chief Justice's Chambers, Supreme Court, Hamilton HM12, Bermuda (☎ 010 180929 21350)

ASTWOOD, Lt-Col Sir Jeffrey Carlton; CBE (1966), OBE (mil 1946), ED (1942); s of late Jeffrey Burgess Astwood, of Neston, Bermuda, and Lilian Maude, *née* Searles; *b* 5 Oct 1907; *Educ* Saltus GS Bermuda; *m* 1928, Hilda Elizabeth Kay, da of Henry George Longhurst Onions, of Aberfeldy, Somerset, Bermuda; 1 s, 1 da; *Career* joined local TF 1924, cmmnd 2 Lt 1926, Capt 1928, Maj 1930, Lt-Col CO Local Forces 1943, organised amalgamation of 2 local forces to form Bermuda Regt 1957; House of Assembly Bermuda: memb 1948-72, memb Exec Cncl and dep speaker 1957-68, speaker 1968-72; min: Agric, Immigration and Lab, Health; pres: Atlantic Investmt and Devpt Ltd, Aberfeldy Nurseries Ltd, J B Astwood & Son Ltd, Astwood Cycles Ltd; chm Vestry St James Church Parish 1950-60; kt 1972; *Recreations* horticulture, theatre; *Clubs* Royal Bermudan Yacht, Directors, RHS Vincent Sq; *Style—* Lt-Col Sir Jeffrey Astwood, CBE, OBE, ED; Greenfield, Somerset, Bermuda (☎ 234 1729, 234 2765)

ATCHERLEY, Sir Harold Winter; s of L W Atcherley, and Maude Lester, *née* Nash; *b* 30 Aug 1918; *Educ* Gresham's, Univ of Heidelberg, Univ of Geneva; *m* 1, 1946 (m dis), Anita Helen, *née* Leslie; 1 s, 2 da; m 2, 25 June 1990, Mrs Elke Jessett, er da of late Dr Carl Langbehn and Mrs Irmgard Langbehn, of Long Melford, Suffolk; *Career* served WWII 18 Inf Div Singapore (POW); Royal Dutch Shell Group 1937-39 and 1946-70 (personnel coordinator), 1 recruitment advsr to MOD 1970-71, chm Armed Forces Pay Review Body 1971-82, memb Top Salaries Review Body 1971-87; memb: Halsbury Ctee of Enquiry into Pay and Conditions of Serv of Nurses and Midwives 1974, Ctee of Inquiry into Remuneration of Membs of Local Authorities 1977; dir British Home Stores Ltd 1973-87, chm Tyzack & Ptnrs 1979-85; memb Mgmnt Ctee Toynbee Hall 1979-90; chm: Toynbee Hall 1985-90, Police Negotiating Bd 1983-85 (dep chm 1982-83), Aldeburgh Fndn 1989-; vice chm Suffolk Tst for Nature Conservation 1987-90; *Style—* Sir Harold Atcherley; Conduit House, The Green, Long Melford, Suffolk (☎ 0787 310 897)

ATHA, Bernard Peter; OBE (1991); s of Horace Michael Atha, of Leeds (d 1984), and Mary, *née* Quinlan (d 1951); *b* 27 Aug 1928; *Educ* Leeds Modern GS, Univ of Leeds (LLB), RAF Sch of Educn (Dip Ed); *Career* Nat Serv FO RAF 1950-52; called to the Bar Gray's Inn 1950; actor and variety artist; films and TV incl: Kes, Coronation St; princ lectr business studies Huddersfield Tech Coll 1973-; elected Leeds City Cncl 1957; contested (Lab): Penrith and Border 1959, Pudsey 1964; vice-chm Sports Cncl 1976-80, memb Arts Cncl 1979-82; chm: Nat Watersports Centre 1978-84, Educn Social Servs and Watch Ctees; current chm: Leisure Servs Ctee, Leeds Co-op Soc, Grand Theatre, City of Varieties, Red Ladder Theatre Co, Yorkshire Dance Centre, Leeds Playhouse, UK Sports Assoc for People with Mental Handicap, Br Paralympic Assoc; memb: Sports Aid Fndn, Sports Aid Tst; former vice chm Leeds West Health Authy; FHSA, FRSA; *Recreations* the arts, sport, politics; *Style—* Bernard Atha, Esq, OBE; 25 Moseley Wood Croft, Leeds LS16 7JJ (☎ 0532 6672 485, 0532 463 000)

ATHANASOU, Dr Nicholas Anthony; s of Anthony James Athanasou (d 1964), and Angela, *née* Pappas (d 1974); *b* 26 April 1953; *Educ* Sydney Boy's High Sch, Univ of Sydney (MB BS), Univ of London (PhD); *m* 27 April 1985, Linda Joan, da of Anthony Hulls, of Chislehurst; *Career* clinical tutor in pathology Univ of Oxford 1983-88; MRCP 1981, MRCPath 1986; *Recreations* cricket, reading; *Style—* Dr Nicholas Athanasou; Nuffield Dept of Pathology, University of Oxford, Level 1, John Radcliffe Hospital, Oxford OX3 9DU (☎ 0865 817250)

ATHERTON, David; s of Robert Atherton, and Lavinia, *née* Burton; *b* 3 Jan 1944; *Educ* Univ of Cambridge (MA); *m* 5 Sept 1970, Ann Gianetta, da of Cdr J F Drake (d 1978), of Ware, Herts; 1 s (John b 14 May 1979), 2 da (Elizabeth b 13 Feb 1974, Susan b 10 June 1977); *Career* conductor, fndr and musical dir London Sinfonietta 1967-73; Royal Opera House: repetiteur 1967-68, res conductor 1968-79; Royal Liverpool Philharmonic Orch: princ conductor and artistic advsr 1980-83, princ guest conductor 1983-86; musical dir and princ conductor San Diego Symphony Orch 1980-87, chief guest conductor BBC Symphony Orch 1985-89, musical dir and princ conductor Hong Kong Philharmonic Orch 1989-; artistic dir and conductor: London Stravinsky Festival 1979-82, Ravel/Varese Festival 1983-84; musical dir and princ conductor Californian Mainly Mozart Festival 1989-; youngest conductor: Henry Wood Promenade Concerts Royal Albert Hall, Royal Opera Hse 1968; Royal Festival Hall debut 1969; performances abroad incl: Europe, M East, F East, Australasia, N America; awards incl: Composers Guild of GB Conductor of the Year 1971, Edison Award 1973, Grand Prix du Disque 1977, Koussevitzky Award 1981, Int Record Critics Award 1982, Prix Caecilia 1982; adapted and arranged Pandora by Robert Gerhard for Royal Ballet 1975; fell Royal Soc of Musicians 1976; *Books* The Complete Instrumental and Chamber Music of Arnold Schoenberg and Roberto Gerhard (ed 1973), Pandora and Don Quixote Suites by Roberto Gerhard (ed 1973), The Musical Companion (contrib 1978), The New Grove Dictionary (1981); *Recreations* travel, squash, theatre; *Style—* David Atherton, Esq; c/o Harold Holt Ltd, 31 Sinclair Rd, London W14 0NS (☎ 071 603 4600, fax 071 603 0019, telex 22339 HUNTER G)

ATHERTON, Dr David John; Dr Desmond Joseph Atherton, of 32 The Firs, Coventry, and Hildegard, *née* Rowe, MBE; *b* 24 April 1949; *Educ* Ampleforth, Pembroke Coll Cambridge (MA, MB BChir); *m* 11 Sept 1971, (Hazel) Anne, da of Dr Rex Malcolm Chaplin Dawson, of Kirn House, Langham, Norfolk; 2 s (James b 1976, Joseph b 1984); *Career* conslt paediatric dermatology 1982-: Hosp for Sick Children Gt Ormond St, St John's Hosp for Diseases of the Skin; sr lectr paediatric dermatology Inst Child Health 1986-; chm Br Soc Paediatric Dermatology; FRCD, MRSH; *Books* Your Child with Eczema (1984); *Recreations* tennis, gardening; *Style—* Dr David Atherton; 20 Harold Rd, London SE19 3DL; Hospital for Sick Children, Great Ormond St, London WC1N 3JH (☎ 071 405 9200, fax 071 829 8643)

ATHERTON, Howard William; s of William Atherton (d 1989), of Sudbury, Suffolk, and Rose Charlotte Atherton (d 1984); *b* 12 Aug 1947; *Educ* Sudbury GS, London Film Sch (BSc); *m* 12 Aug 1972, Janet Ruth Simpson, da of Ronald William, of Lavenham, Suffolk; 1 s (Oliver Luke b 1979), 2 da (Rebecca Louise b 1977, Charlotte Letitia Rose b 1985); *Career* dir of photography; films incl: Helen, Runners, Keep Off the Grass, Fatal Attraction 1986, The Boost 1987, Mermaids 1989; memb Br Soc of Cinematography; *Style—* Howard Atherton, Esq

ATHERTON, Kevin; s of William Edward Atherton, of Douglas, Isle of Man, and Elizabeth, *née* Clague; *b* 25 Nov 1950; *Educ* Douglas HS for Boys IOM, IOM Coll of Art, Fine Art Dept Leeds Poly (BA); *m* 1977, Victoria, da of Francis Sidney Thomas Robinson; *Career* sculptor, artist, lectr in art; pt/t teacher 1978-86: Slade Sch of Fine Art, RCA, Norwich Sch of Art, Winchester Sch of Art, Maidstone Coll of Art, Chelsea Sch of Art, Fine Art Dept Middx Poly, Fine Art Dept South Glamorgan Inst of Higher Educn Cardiff; artist in res London Borough of Richmond upon Thames 1989, Picker lectr in public art Fine Art Dept Kingston Poly 1989, Stanley Picker lectr in Video Performance and pub art Kingston Poly 1990, actg sr lectr in alternative media Fine Art Dept Chelsea Sch of Art 1990-; external examiner: Birmingham Poly 1988-, Bradford and Ilkley Community Coll 1988-, Dartington Coll of Arts Devon 1986-, Limerick Sch of Art and Design 1990-; public collections: Sheffield City Poly, Merseyside CC, Graves Art Gallery Sheffield; cmmns incl: A Body of Work (Tower Hamlets) 1982, Upon Reflection (Islington) 1985, Platforms Piece (BR, Brixton) 1986, Cathedral (Forest of Dean, Glos) 1986, Iron Horses (BR) 1986-87, The Architect (Harlow New Town) 1990, Conversation Piece (Leicester CC) 1990, Art Within Reach (Hampshire Sculpture Tst) 1990, To The Top (New Civic Offices Twickenham) 1990; many exhibitions Eng & Europe; awards incl: Yorkshire Arts Assoc award for Film Work 1973, N Arts Assoc Visual Art award 1974, Arts Cncl of GB Visual Arts awards 1975, 1976 and 1977, ABSA award for Best Cmmn in Any Media 1986; judge Arts Cncl Br Gas Awards 1990-91, specialist advsr CNAA 1985-; *Recreations* the turf; *Style—* Kevin Atherton, Esq; 2 Independent Place, Shacklewell Lane, London E8 2EZ (☎ 071 254 3607)

ATHERTON, Brig Maurice Alan; CBE (1981), JP (Kent 1982), DL (Kent 1984); s of Rev Harold Atherton (d 1975), of Sheffield, and Beatrice, *née* Shaw (d 1958); *b* 9 Oct 1926; *Educ* St John's Sch Leatherhead, Staff Coll Camberley; *m* 28 Aug 1954, Guendolene Mary (Wendi), da of Col James Bryan Upton, MBE, TD, JP, DL (d 1976), of Hotham, York; 1 s (James Patrick b 7 Sept 1966), 1 da (Christine Wendy b 6 March 1965); *Career* cmmnd E Yorks regt 1946 (serv in Egypt, Sudan, Malaysia, Austria, Germany, UK), MA to CBF Hong Kong 1959-62, coll chief instr RMA Sandhurst 1964-67, CO 1 Green Howards 1967-69, GSO 1 NI 1969-70, def advsr Ghana 1971-73; cdr Dover Shorncliffe Garrison 1976-81; Dep Constable Dover Castle 1976-81; magistrate dover Bench 1982-; High Sheriff of Kent 1983-84; county pres: Royal Br Legion 1982-, Men of the Trees 1985-; chm: Kent Ctee Army Benevolent Fund 1984-, Diocesan Property Ctee; *Recreations* shooting, gardening, skiing; *Clubs* Army and Navy, Lansdowne; *Style—* Brig M A Atherton, CBE, JP, DL; Digges Place, Barham, Canterbury, Kent CT4 6PJ (☎ 0227 831420)

ATHERTON, Michael Andrew (Mike); s of Alan Atherton, and Wendy, *née* Fletcher; *b* 23 March 1968; *Educ* The Manchester GS, Downing Coll Cambridge (Cricket blue and capt); *Career* cricketer; former English School's rep, two tours and capt Young England; first class debut Cambridge Univ v Essex April 1987, Lancashire CCC debut v Warwickshire July 1987; int career: England debut v Australia Aug 1989, first full England tour Australia/NZ 1990/91, 13 Test Match appearances to date, 7 One Day Internationals, 3 Test Match centuries, highest score 151 v NZ June 1990; Professional Cricketers Assoc Young Cricketer of Year 1990, Cricket Writers Young Cricketer of Year 1990; *Recreations* reading, golf, squash, rugby, football; *Style—* Mike Atherton, Esq

ATHERTON, Peter; s of Joseph Ignatius Atherton (d 1984), of Wrightington, and Winifred, *née* Marsh; *b* 8 Nov 1952; *Educ* Mount St Mary's Coll Derby, Univ of Birmingham (LLB), Coll of Law; *m* 17 Oct 1981, Jennifer Marie, da of Charles Birch, of Ontario Canada; 1 s (Timothy Peter b 4 Sept 1985), 1 da (Hilary Anne b 4 Jan 1984); *Career* called to the Bar Grays Inn 1975; jr Northern circuit 1978-79; chm Young Barrs Ctee Senate of Inns of Ct and Bar Cncl for England and Wales 1982-83; memb Bar Cncl; *Recreations* tennis, golf, theatre; *Style—* Peter Atherton, Esq; Deans Court Chambers, Crown Square, Manchester (☎ 061 834 4097)

ATHILL, Lady Elizabeth (Liza); *née* Campbell; 2 da of 6 Earl Cawdor; *b* 24 Sept 1959; *m* 4 June 1990, Willie Athill, 3 s of Maj Andrew Athill, of Morston, Norfolk; 1 da (Storm b 10 Dec 1990); *Style—* The Lady Elizabeth Athill

ATHOLL, 10 Duke of (S 1703); George Iain Murray; also Lord Murray of Tullibardine (S 1604), Earl of Tullibardine (S 1606), Earl of Atholl (S 1629), Marquess of Atholl (S 1676), Marquess of Tullibardine (S 1703), Earl of Strathtay and Strathardle (S 1703), Viscount of Balwhidder, Glenalmond and Glenlyon (S 1703), and Lord Murray, Balvenie, and Gask (S 1703); s of Lt-Col George Murray, OBE, RA (ka 1945, s of Sir Evelyn Murray, KCB, himself gggs of Rt Rev Lord George Murray, DD, sometime Bishop of St David's and 2 s of 3 Duke of Atholl, KT), by his w, Hon Angela Pearson (later Hon Mrs Campbell-Preston, d 1981), da of 2 Viscount Cowdray; suc kinsman, 9 Duke of Atholl, 1957; *b* 19 June 1931; *Educ* Eton, Ch Ch Oxford; *Heir* kinsman, John Murray b 1929; *Career* proprietor of the Atholl Highlanders (sole legal private army in UK) Representative Peer for Scotland 1958-63; chm: Westminster Press 1974- (dir 1963-), RNLI 1979-89; dir Pearson Longman 1975-83, vice-pres Nat Tst for Scotland 1977-, memb Red Deer Cmmn 1969-83, pres Int Sheepdog Soc 1982-83 and 1987-88; Capt House of Lords Bridge Team in matches against the Commons 1979-; *Recreations* golf, bridge, shooting, stalking; *Clubs* Turf, White's, New (Edinburgh); *Style—* His Grace The Duke of Atholl; Blair Castle, Blair Atholl, Perthshire (☎ 079 681 212); 31 Marlborough Hill, London NW8 (☎ 071 586 2291); Westminster Press, 8-16 Great New St, London EC4P 4ER (☎ 071 353 1030)

ATIYAH, Sir Michael Francis; s of Edward Selim Atiyah (d 1964), and Jean, *née* Levens (d 1964); *b* 22 May 1929; *Educ* Victoria Coll Egypt, Manchester GS, Univ of Cambridge (MA, PhD); *m* 1955, Lily Jane Myles, da of John Cameron Brown (d 1970); 3 children; *Career* fell Trinity Coll Cambridge 1954-58, Savilian prof of geometry Univ of Oxford 1963-69, prof of mathematics Inst for Advanced Study Princeton USA 1969-72, Royal Soc res prof Mathematical Inst Univ of Oxford 1973-90, pres Royal Soc 1990-, Master Trinity Coll Cambridge 1990-, dir Isaac Newton Inst for Mathematical Scis Cambridge 1990-; Hon ScD Univ of Cambridge; FRS; kt 1983; *Recreations* gardening; *Style—* Sir Michael Atiyah; The Master's Lodge, Trinity College, Cambridge CB2 1TQ (☎ 0223 338412)

ATIYAH, Prof Patrick Selim; s of Edward Selim Atiyah (d 1964), and D Jean C Atiyah, *née* Levens (d 1964); bro of Sir Michael Atiyah, *qv*; *b* 5 March 1931; *Educ* Woking County GS for Boys, Magdalen Coll Oxford (BA, BCL, MA, DCL); *m* 1951, Christine Ann, da of Reginald William Best (d 1978); 4 s (Julian, Andrew, Simon, Jeremy); *Career* asst lectr LSE 1954-55, lectr Univ of Khartoum 1955-59, crown counsel Ghana 1959-61, legal asst Bd of Trade 1961-64, fell New Coll Oxford 1964-70, prof of law ANU (Aust) 1970-73, prof Univ of Warwick 1973-77, prof of English law Oxford 1977-88, ret 1988; *Style*— Prof Patrick Atiyah; 9 Sheepway Court, Iffley, Oxford OX4 4JL (☎ 0865 717637)

ATKIN, Alec Field; CBE (1978); s of Alec and Grace Atkin; *b* 26 April 1925; *Educ* Riley HS, Hull Tech Coll, Hull Univ (BSc, Dip Aero); *m* 1, 1948 (m dis 1982), Nora Helen Darby; 2 s (and 1 s adopted), 1 da; m 2, 1982, Wendy Atkin; *Career* asst md BAC (Military Aircraft Div) 1976-77; md (Military) Aircraft Gp Br Aerospace 1978-81, chm Warton Kingston-Brough and Manchester Div 1978-81, md (Marketing) Aircraft Gp Br Aerospace 1981-82; aviation conslt 1982-; FEng, FIMechE, FRAeS, FRSA; *Style*— Alec Atkin, Esq, CBE; Les Fougères d'Icart, Icart Rd, St Martin, Guernsey, Channel Islands

ATKIN, Peter Richard (Pete); s of Cyril William Atkin, of Cambridge, and Elsie Rose Cowell (d 1980); *b* 22 Aug 1945; *Educ* Perse Sch Cambridge, St John's Coll Cambridge (BA); *m* 24 Nov 1973, Mary Louise, da of Lewis Lynch Lowance, of Manassas, Virginia, USA; *Career* songwriter (with Clive James) and recording artist: 6 albums 1970-75 (collection reissued 1991); scriptwriter, critic; woodwork corr Vole magazine 1976-77, furniture maker, chief prodr BBC Radio Light Entertainment 1986- (producer 1981-, script ed 1983-), head of network radio BBC S and W Bristol 1989-; *Recreations* words, music, wood; *Clubs* Meccano, Eddie Grundy Fan; *Style*— Pete Atkin, Esq; 19 Archfield Rd, Bristol BS6 6BG (☎ 0272 421582); BBC Broadcasting House, Whiteladies Rd, Bristol BS8 2LR (☎ 0272 742112, fax 0272 730793, telex 265781 BSA)

ATKIN, R J; s of Oscar Ridgeway, of 6 Gray's Court, Barrow-on-Soar, Leics, and Agatha Victoria, *née* Hull; *b* 3 Feb 1938; *Educ* Loughborough Coll of Art, Cert Royal Acad Schs; *m* 23 July 1960, Ann, da of Capt Arthur Charles Fawssett, DSO, RN (d 1961); 2 s (Francis Charles Edward b 1961, Richard Bernard b 1963); *Career* artist; exhibited at Royal Soc of Br Artists 1959, Southampton Museum and Art Gallery 1959, RA summer exhibition 1960, 1970, 1975, Royal Watercolour Soc Galleries Bond Street 1961, mixed exhibition Roland Browse and Delbanco Cork Street London and SA 1961 and 1964, Paintings and Sculpture from some Oxford Jr Common Rooms Leics Museum and Art Gallery 1962; one-man show: Plymouth City Museum and Art Gallery 1976, Burton Art Gallery Bideford N Devon 1980, Chenil Art Gallery Kings Road London 1982; paintings in private collections in: GB, Aust, USA, Canada, Germany, Zurich, Lucerne; paintings in public collections incl: Dartington Tst Devon, Devon CC Schs Museum Serv, Lincoln Coll Oxford, Wimbledon Tennis Museum, Plymouth City Museum and Art Gallery; shortlisted for a Gulbenkian Printmakers award 1984; *Recreations* walking; *Style*— R J Atkin, Esq; Workshop 7, West Putford, Devon EX22 7XE (☎ 0409 241435)

ATKIN, Roger Dean; s of (Arthur) James Atkin, of Herne Bay, Kent, and Acie, *née* Dean; *b* 2 April 1939; *Educ* Herne Bay Sch; *m* 21 May 1969, Wendy Anne, da of Sqdn Ldr Thomas Alexander Stewart, DFC, AFC; 2 s (Stewart Dean b 15 April 1971, Alister Graham b 22 August 1973); *Career* signals RAF served UK and W Germany 1959-61; underwriting memb Lloyd's 1980, fndr Atkin Raggett Ltd (Lloyd's broker), dir Edgar Hamilton (Marine) Ltd, chm Atkinsure Ltd; memb Herne Bay UDC 1967-69, chm SE Area Young Cons 1969-70; Freeman City of London 1969; Liveryman: Worshipful Co of Cooks 1972, Worshipful Co of Insurers 1986; MIEx 1975; *Clubs* Royal Over-Seas League, City Livery, Kent and Canterbury; *Style*— Roger D Atkin, Esq; Herne Brow, Pigeon Lane, Herne, Herne Bay, Kent CT6 7ES (☎ 0227 374 423); Edgar Hamilton Group, Lloyd's of London, London EC3

ATKINS, Anthony George; s of Walter George Atkins (d 1975), and Emily Irene, *née* Aldridge; *b* 10 Oct 1939; *Educ* Canton HS Cardiff, Univ Coll Cardiff (BSc), Trinity Coll Cambridge (PhD, ScD), Exeter Coll Oxford (MA); *m* 4 March 1971, Margaret Ann, da of Lt-Col Richard Risely Proud, CVO, OBE (d 1976); 2 s (Philip George b 1973, Richard James b 1976), 1 da (Margaret Ruth b 1980); *Career* US Steel Corpn 1965-67, BSC fell Univ of Oxford 1967-70, assoc prof in mechanical engrg Univ of Michigan 1970-75, res mangr Delta Metal 1975-81, prof of mechanical engrg Univ of Reading 1981-; memb CPRE; FIM 1986, FIMechE 1987, CEng, FRSA 1985, ACIArb 1984; *Books* Strength and Fracture of Engineering Solids (jtly, 1984), A History of GWR Goods Wagons (jtly, 2 edn, 1986), Manufacturing Engineering (jtly, 1987), Elastic and Plastic Fracture (jtly, 2 edn, 1988); *Recreations* music, skiing, woodwork; *Style*— Prof Anthony Atkins; White House, Heads Lane, Inkpen Common, Newbury, Berks RG15 0QS (☎ 048 84 253); School of Engineering and Information Sciences, Box 225, University of Reading, Whiteknights, Reading, Berks, RG6 2AY (☎ 0734 318562, telex 847813, fax 0734 313835)

ATKINS, Brian Lathom; s of Phillip Lathom Atkins (d 1967), and Margaret Mary, *née* Lewis (d 1977); *b* 8 Aug 1947; *Educ* John Bright GS Llandudno, UCNW Bangor (BSc); *m* 1; 1 s (Christopher James b 18 Oct 1973), 1 da (Jane Anne b 2 Feb 1970); m 2, 28 June 1986, Jacqueline Anne, da of Charles Moses Crowe; *Career* nat admin trainee 1969-71, dep hosp sec Sefton Gen Hosp 1971-74, unit admin East Glamorgan Gen Hosp 1974-76, dist gen admin Milton Keynes 1976-80, dist gen admin then dep dist admin West Birmingham Health Authy 1980-87, unit gen mangr Queen Alexandra Hosp Portsmouth and South Hants Health Authy 1987-90, hosp mangr BUPA Gatwick Park Hosp Surrey 1990-; assoc memb Inst of Health Servs Mgmnt 1972-; *Recreations* keeping fit, being at home, music, dining out; *Clubs* Goodwood Golf and Country; *Style*— Brian L Atkins, Esq; BUPA Gatwick Park Hospital, Povey Cross Rd, Horley, Surrey RH6 0BB (☎ 0293 785511, fax 0293 774883)

ATKINS, Eileen June; da of late Arthur Thomas Atkins, and Annie Ellen, *née* Elkins (d 1984); *b* 16 June 1934; *Educ* Latymer GS, Guildhall Sch of Music and Drama (AGSM); *m* 1 (m dis 1965), Julian Glover; m 2, Feb 1978, William B Shepherd; *Career* actress; plays incl: Twelfth Night, Richard III, The Tempest (Old Vic) 1962, The Killing of Sister George (Bristol Old Vic transfd Duke of York, Best Actress Standard award) 1963, The Cocktail Party (Wyndham's transfd Haymarket) 1968, Vivat! Vivat! Regina! (Piccadilly) 1970, Suzanne Andler (Aldwych) 1973, As You Like It (Stratford) 1973, St Joan (Old Vic) 1977, Passion Play (Aldwych) 1981, Medea (Young Vic) 1986, Winter's Tale, Cymbeline, Mountain Language (NT) 1988, A Room of One's Own (Hampstead) 1989, Exclusive (Strand) 1989; films incl: Equus 1974, The Dresser 1984; TV incl: The Duchess of Malfi, Sons and Lovers, Smiley's People, The Burston Rebellion, Breaking Up, The Vision (BAFTA award); hon memb GSM; *Style*— Miss Eileen Atkins; c/o Duncan Heath, Paramount House, 162/170 Wardour St, London W1V 3AT (☎ 071 439 1471)

ATKINS, Frances Elizabeth (Mrs Gerald Atkins); da of Thomas Colyer Venning, MBE, of Windrush, Denton Rd, Ben-Rhydding, Ilkley, Yorks, and Hilary Susan, *née* Harris; *b* 8 Sept 1950; *m* 1, 1973 (m dis 1984), George Alfred Carman, QC; m 2, 1984, Gerald Atkins; *Career* restaurateur; Atkins Restaurant: Great Missenden 1984-86, The Old Plow Inn Speen 1986-88, Farleyer House Aberfeldy 1988-; *Recreations* work, art appreciation, collecting furniture; *Style*— Mrs Gerald Atkins; Farleyer House, Aberfeldy, Perthshire PH15 2JE (☎ 0887 20332); Southstream Ltd, 31 Dashwood Ave, High Wycombe, Berks HP12 3DZ (☎ 0887 20332, fax 0887 29430)

ATKINS, Lady; Gladwys Gwendolen; da of Frank Harding Jones (d 1954), of Harlow, Essex; *m* 1933, Prof Sir Hedley John Barnard Atkins, KBE (surgn, former pres RCS and RSM; d 1983), s of late Col Sir John Atkins, KCMG, KCVO; 2 s (David Hedley, Dr Christopher J Atkins); *Style*— Lady Atkins; 223 Somerset House, 540 Dallas Rd, Victoria BC V8V 1B2, Canada

ATKINS, Dr Peter William; s of William Henry Atkins (d 1988), and Ellen Louise, *née* Edwards (d 1978); *b* 10 Aug 1940; *Educ* Dr Challoner's Amersham, Univ of Leicester (BSc, PhD), Univ of Oxford (MA), UCLA; *m* 20 Aug 1964 (m dis 1983), Judith Ann Kearton; 1 da (Juliet b 1970); *Career* Univ of Oxford: Harkness fell 1964-65, univ lectr physical chemistry 1965-, fell and tutor Lincoln Coll 1965-; visiting prof: China, France, Israel, Japan; Dreyfus lectr California 1980, Firth visiting prof Univ of Sheffield 1984; Meldola medal 1969; *Books* The Structure of Inorganic Radicals (1967), Quanta: A Handbook of Concepts (1974), The Creation (1981), Principles of Physical Chemistry (1982), Solutions Manual for MQM (1983), Molecular Quantum Mechanics (2 edn 1983), The Second Law (1984), Molecules (1987), Chemistry: Principles and Applications (1988), General Chemistry (1989), Inorganic Chemistry (1990), Physical Chemistry (4 edn 1990), Solutions Manual for Physical Chemistry (4 edn 1990); *Recreations* art; *Style*— Dr P W Atkins; Lincoln Coll, Oxford OX1 3DR (☎ 0865 279 797, fax 0865 279 802)

ATKINS, Robert James; MP (C) South Ribble 1983-; s of late Reginald Alfred Atkins, of Gt Missenden, and Winifred Margaret Atkins; *b* 5 Feb 1946; *Educ* Highgate; *m* 1969, Dulcie Mary, da of Frederick Moon Chaplin, of Bexley; 1 s (James b 1979), 1 da (Victoria b 1976); *Career* MP (C) Preston N 1979-1983, former jt sec Cons Parly Def and vice chm Aviation Ctees, nat pres Cons Trade Unionists 1984-87; PPS to: Norman Lamont as Min of State for Indust 1982-84, Lord Young of Graffham as Min Without Portfolio and Sec of State for Employment 1984-87; parly under-sec of State DTI 1987-89, min for roads and traffic Dept of Tport 1989-90, parly under-sec of State Dept of the Environment and min for Sport 1990-; *Recreations* cricket, Holmesiena, ecclesiology, wine; *Style*— Robert Atkins, Esq, MP; House of Commons, London SW1 (☎ 071 219 5080)

ATKINSON, Sir Alec (John Alexander); KCB (1978, CB 1976), DFC (1943); yr s of Rev Robert F Atkinson (d 1943), and Harriet Harrold, *née* Lowdon; *b* 9 June 1919; *Educ* Kingswood Sch Bath, The Queen's Coll Oxford (MA); *m* 1945, Marguerite Louise, da of George Pearson (d 1974); 1 da (Charlotte); *Career* served WWII Flt Lt; entered Civil Serv 1946, dep sec DHSS 1973-76, 2 perm sec DHSS 1977-79; memb: panel of chairmen Civil Serv Selection Bd 1979-88, Occupational Pensions Bd 1981-88; *Recreations* walking, reading, theatre; *Clubs* United Oxford and Cambridge; *Style*— Sir Alec Atkinson, KCB, DFC; Bleak House, The Drive, Belmont, Sutton, Surrey SM2 7DH (☎ 081 642 6479)

ATKINSON, Prof Anthony Barnes (Tony); s of Norman Joseph Atkinson (d 1988), and Esther Muriel, *née* Stonehouse; *b* 4 Sept 1944; *Educ* Cranbrook, Churchill Coll Cambridge (MA); *m* 11 Dec 1965, Judith Mary, da of Alexander Mandeville, of Swansea; 2 s (Richard b 1972, Charles b 1976), 1 da (Sarah b 1974); *Career* fell St John's Coll Cambridge 1967-71, prof of econs Univ of Essex 1971-76, prof Univ of London 1976- (Thomas Tooke prof of econ sci and statistics 1987-), ed Journal of Public Economics 1971-; UAP Sci Prize 1986; pres: Econometric Soc 1988, Euro Econ Assoc 1989, Int Econ Assoc 1989; memb: Royal Cmmn on Distribution of Income and Wealth 1978-79, Retail Prices Advsy Ctee 1984-; vice pres Br Acad 1988-90; Freeman City of London 1983, memb Worshipful Co of Barbers (Liveryman 1985); Hon Dr Rer Pol Univ of Frankfurt 1987, Hon Dr Sci Econ Univ of Lausanne 1988, Hon Dr Univ of Liège 1989; FBA 1984; hon memb American Econ Assoc 1985; *Books* Poverty in Britain (1969), Unequal Shares (1972), Economics of Inequality (1975), Distribution of Personal Wealth in Britain (1978), Lectures on Public Economics (1980), Social Justice and Public Policy (1982), Parents and Children (1983), Unemployment Benefits and Unemployment Duration (1986), Poverty and Social Security (1989); *Recreations* sailing; *Style*— Prof Tony Atkinson; 33 Hurst Green, Brightlingsea, Colchester, Essex CO7 0HA; London Sch of Economics, Houghton St, Aldwych, London WC2A 2AE (☎ 071 955 7481, fax 071 242 2357)

ATKINSON, Prof Anthony Curtis; s of Harold Atkinson (d 1944), of Sidcup, Kent, and Iris Madge Atkinson (d 1990); *b* 22 June 1937; *Educ* Christs Hosp, Univ of Cambridge (MA), Imperial Coll London (PhD); *m* 13 June 1972, Ruth Mary, da of Robert Mantle Rattenbury (d 1970), of Cambridge; 2 da (Alison b 1972, Rachel b 1975); *Career* Shell Chemical Co 1960-64, American Cyanamid NJ USA 1965-67, prof of statistics Imperial Coll 1983-89 (lectr 1969-78, reader 1978-83), prof of statistics LSE 1989-; MISI, FSS; *Books* A Celebration of Statistics (with S Fienberg, 1985), Plots, Transformations, and Regression (1985); *Recreations* music; *Style*— Prof Anthony Atkinson; 2 Eton Villas, London NW3 4SX (☎ 071 722 7021); Department of Statistical and Mathematical Sciences, London School of Economics, Houghton Street, London WC2A 2AE (☎ 071 955 7622, fax 071 242 0392)

ATKINSON, Colin Ronald Michael; s of R E Atkinson; *b* 23 July 1931; *Educ* Durham Univ and others; *m* 1957, Shirley Angus; 2 s, 1 da; *Career* headmaster Millfield 1971- (acting headmaster 1969-70); dir HTV Ltd; chm Edington Sch; pres Somerset County Cricket Club (former capt and chm); memb Cricket Cncl Test and County Cricket Bd; *Style*— Colin Atkinson, Esq; Millfield School, Street, Somerset (☎ 0458 42291, home 0458 33712)

ATKINSON, Daniel Elston; s of Frank Atkinson, of 15 Heene Terrace, Worthing, Sussex, and Elsteen Ann, *née* Curnow (d 1986); *b* 19 March 1961; *Educ* Christ's Hosp; *m* 1989, Catharine Louise, *née* Eccles; *Career* journalist; editorial trainee Thomson Organisation 1980; staff reporter Reading Evening Post 1982-85 (jr reporter 1980-82), ed Executive Magazine 1983-85, dep econ and fin ed The Press Assoc 1985-90, publisher The Extremist Magazine 1987-89; feature contrib BBC Radio Four 1989; staff journalist The Guardian 1989- (covering city fraud, the food industry, gem stones, smuggling and piracy); William Hardcastle Award Young Journalist of the Year 1978, Financial Journalist of the Year 1989, Virgin-Atlantic Travel Writing Award 1989; memb NUJ 1980-; *Recreations* freelance journalism (to pay the mortgage); *Clubs* Ronnie Scott's; *Style*— Daniel Atkinson, Esq; 316 Ben Jonson House, Barbican, London EC2 (☎ 071 588 2855); The Guardian, 119 Farringdon Road, London EC1 (☎ 071 833 4926, fax 071 833 4456)

ATKINSON, David Anthony; MP (C) Bournemouth E 1977-; s of late Arthur Joseph Atkinson, and Joan Margaret, *née* Zink, of Southbourne, Bournemouth; *b* 24 March 1940; *Educ* St George's Coll Weybridge, Coll of Automobile and Aeronautical Engrg Chelsea; *m* 1968, Susan Nicola, da of Dr Roy Pilsworth, of Benfleet, Essex; 1 s (Anthony b 1977), 1 da (Katherine b 1973); *Career* dir Chalkwell Motor Co Westcliff on Sea 1963-72, md David Graham Ltd 1972-78; PPS to Rt Hon Paul Channon as: Min for Civil Service 1979-81, Min for Arts 1981-83, Min for Trade 1983-86, Sec of State for Trade & Indust 1986-87; UK rep on Cncl of Europe and Western European Union 1979-; UK pres: Christian Solidarity Int, Int Soc for Human Rights; *Recreations* mountaineering, rock-climbing, art, architecture, travel; *Style*— David Atkinson, Esq, MP; House of Commons, London SW1A 0AA

ATKINSON, Air Marshal Sir David William; KBE (1982); s of late David William Atkinson, and Margaret Atkinson; *b* 29 Sept 1924; *Educ* Univ of Edinburgh (MB ChB, DPH, DIH); *m* 1948, Mary Sowerby; 1 s; *Career* joined RAF 1949, dir Health and Res 1974-78, princ med offr RAF Strike Cmd 1978-81, dir gen Med Servs 1981-84; dir gen

The Chest Heart and Stroke Assoc 1985-; Freeman City of London, Liveryman Worshipful Soc of Apothecaries; QHP 1978-84; FFCM, MFOM, FFOM, FRCPE; *Style*— Air Marshal Sir David Atkinson, KBE; CHSA House, Whitecross St, London EC1Y 8JJ

ATKINSON, Sir Frederick John (Fred); KCB (1979, CB 1971); s of George Edward Atkinson, and Elizabeth Sabina Cooper; *b* 7 Dec 1919; *Educ* Dulwich, Jesus Coll Oxford; *m* 1947, Margaret Grace, da of Sidney Jeffrey Gibson; 2 da; *Career* HM Treasy 1955-62 and 1963-69, chief econ advsr Dept of Trade and Indust 1970-73, asst sec gen OECD Paris 1973-75, dep sec and chief econ advsr Dept of Energy 1975-77, chief econ advsr to Treasy 1977-79, head Govt Economic Serv 1977-79; hon fell Jesus Coll Oxford; *Books* Oil and the British Economy (with S Hall, 1983); *Style*— Sir Fred Atkinson, KCB; 26 Lee Terrace, Blackheath, London SE3 (☎ 081 852 1040); Tickner Cottage, Aldington, Kent (☎ 0233 720514)

ATKINSON, Dr Harry Hindmarsh; s of Harry Temple Atkinson (late Cmmr of Patents NZ, d 1961), and Constance Hindmarsh, *née* Shields (d 1973); gf, Sir Harry Atkinson (Prime Min of NZ five times between 1873 and 1890, d 1892); *b* 5 Aug 1929; *Educ* Nelson Coll Nelson NZ, Canterbury Univ Coll NZ (BSc, MSc), Cornell Univ, Corpus Christi Coll & Cavendish Lab Cambridge (PhD); *m* 25 March 1958, Anne Judith, da of Thomas Kenneth Barrett (d 1964); 2 s ((Harry) David b 1960, (John) Benedict b 1966), 1 da (Katherine Hindmarsh b 1959); *Career* asst lectr physics Canterbury Univ Coll NZ 1952-53, res asst Cornell Univ USA 1954-55, sr res fell AERE Harwell UK 1958-61, head Gen Physics Gp Rutherford Lab UK 1961-69, staff chief sci advsr to UK Govt Cabinet Office UK 1969-72; UK Sci Res Cncl: head Astronomy Space & Radio Div 1972-78, under sec dir of astronomy space & nuclear physics 1979-83; under sec dir of sci UK Sci & Engrg Res Cncl (incl responsibility for int affrs) 1983-88, under sec (special responsibilities) 1988-; assesor Univ Grants Ctee 1986-89, UK memb EISCAT Cncl 1976-86, chm of Cncl Euro Space Agency 1984-87 (vice chm 1981-84); UK memb of Anglo-Aust Telescope Bd 1979-88, chm Anglo-Dutch Astron Ctee 1981-88, UK delegate Summit Gp on High Energy Physics 1982-; chm and memb steering ctee of Inst Laue Langevin (ILL) Grenoble France 1984-88; UK delegate to Cncl Synchrotron Radiation Facility 1986-88, memb NI Ctee Univ Funding Cncl 1989-, coordinator UK Aust NZ Science Collaboration 1989-, pt/t chief scientist Loss Prevention Cncl 1990-; FRAS; *Recreations* cars, travelling, walking; *Clubs* Athenaeum; *Style*— Dr Harry Atkinson; Science & Engineering Research Council, Polaris House, North Star Avenue, Swindon SN2 1ET (☎ 0793 411000, fax 0793 411099)

ATKINSON, Prof the Rev Canon James; s of Nicholas Ridley Atkinson (d 1942), and Margaret Patience Bradford, *née* Hindhaugh (d 1970); *b* 27 April 1914; *Educ* Tynemouth HS, Univ of Durham (MA, MLitt), Univ of Muenster (DTh); *m* 1 Aug 1939, Laura Jean, da of George Nutley (d 1967); 1 s (Nicholas b 1949), 1 da (Mary b 1945); *Career* curate Newcastle upon Tyne 1937-41, precentor of Sheffield Cathedral 1941-44, vicar St James and Christopher Sheffield 1944-51, res fell Univ of Sheffield 1951-54, canon theologian Leicester Cathedral 1954-56, reader in theology Univ of Hull 1956-66, visiting prof Chicago 1966-67, prof of biblical studies Univ of Sheffield 1967-79, univ memb of Gen Synod 1975-80, fndr and hon dir Centre for Reformation Studies Univ of Sheffield 1979-, examining chaplain to several dioceses; memb: Prep Ctee on Anglican/Roman Catholic Relations, several ctees on Lutheran/Anglican relations, L'Academie Internationale des Sciences Religieuses Brussels; pres Soc for the Study of Theology; *Books* Luther's Early Theological Works (1962), Rome and Reformation (1966), Luther's Works, Vol 44 (1967), Luther and the Birth of Protestantism (1968, 1982), Luther: Prophet to the Church Catholic (1983), The Darkness of Faith (1987); *Recreations* music, gardening; *Style*— Prof the Rev Canon James Atkinson; Leach House, Hathersage, Via Sheffield S30 1BA (☎ 0433 50570)

ATKINSON, Jane Elizabeth; da of William Gledhill (d 1969), and Ethel, *née* Stopps (d 1978); *b* 20 July 1947; *Educ* Kesteven and Seaford HS for Girls; *m* 1, 1967 (m dis 1973), David Hayward; 1 s (Anthony b 1967); m 2, 1975, George Ronald Atkinson; 1 s (Nicholas b 1980), 1 da (Caroline b 1983); *Career* sec until 1975, asst account exec Planned Public Relations International 1975, account exec Welbeck PR 1976, sr client conslt Bell Capper PR 1978, bd dir Eurocom PR 1980, jt md Granard Communications (Eurocom PR merged with Granard Communications 1982) 1988, dep chm The Rowland Company (result of Granard merger with Kingsway PR) 1990; pres Assoc of Women in Public Relations; MIPR; *Recreations* horse riding, cooking, reading, walking; *Style*— Mrs Jane Atkinson; 77 Sutton Court Rd, London W4 3EG (☎ 081 994 7082); The Rowland Company, 67-69 Whitfield St, London W1P 5RL (☎ 071 436 4060, fax 071 255 2131, mobile phone 0836 751089)

ATKINSON, Prof John; s of John Jennings Atkinson (d 1974), and Cecil Prescilla, *née* Sully; *b* 10 March 1942; *Educ* Norwich Sch, Imperial Coll London; *m* 17 July 1978, Josephine, da of John Thomas Kirby, of Brentford, Middx; 2 s (Robert b 1978, Nicholas b 1981); *Career* engr; Coffey & Ptnrs Brisbane 1967-69, Imperial Coll London 1969-73, Univ of Cambridge 1973-76, Univ Coll Cardiff 1976-80, City Univ 1980-; CEng, FICE, FGS; *Books* The Mechanics of Soils (1978), Foundations and Slopes (1981); *Recreations* sailing, surfing, the countryside; *Clubs* Norfolk Broads Yacht, Norfolk Punt; *Style*— Prof John Atkinson; Geotechnical Engineering Research Centre, The City University, Northampton Square, London EC1V 0HB (☎ 071 253 4399)

ATKINSON, Kenneth Neil; s of William Atkinson (d 1972), and Alice, *née* Reid (d 1990); *b* 4 April 1931; *Educ* Kingussie HS; *Career* dep chief conciliation offr Dept of Employment 1968-72, dir youth trg MSC Trg Agency 1983-89 (dir indust trg bd relations 1975-78, dir Scot 1979-82), dir Assoc of Br Travel Agents Nat Trg Bd 1989-; currently chm Prince's Tst Community Venture; ARCM 1961, FIPM 1986; *Recreations* tennis, choral singing, conducting; *Clubs* Royal Scottish Automobile; *Style*— Kenneth N Atkinson, Esq; 57 St Andrews Wharf, 12 Shad Thames, London SE1 2YN

ATKINSON, Prof Michael; s of Herbert Atkinson (d 1975), of Rawdon, Yorks, and Janet, *née* Palliser (d 1962); *b* 27 July 1925; *Educ* Aireborough GS, UCL and UCH (MB BS, MD); *m* 28 March 1951, Iris Margaret Lempriere, da of Rev Herbert Bowman (d 1930), of Leeds; 4 da (Gillian b 1953, Catherine b 1955, Margaret (twin) b 1955, Alison b 1962); *Career* Nuffield travelling fellowship in med 1954-56; conslt physician: Worcester Royal Infirmary 1962, Gen Hosp Nottingham 1973, Univ Hosp Nottingham 1979; special prof in gastroenterology Univ of Nottingham 1984 (ret); pres: Br Soc of Digestive Endoscopy 1977-79, Midland Gastroenterological Soc 1977-79; vice pres (endoscopy) Br Soc of Gastroenterology 1977; FRCP 1966; *Recreations* fellwalking, ornithology; *Clubs* RSM; *Style*— Prof Michael Atkinson; Far Well, Mill Side, Witherslack LA11 6SG

ATKINSON, Michael William; CMG (1985), MBE (1970); *b* 11 April 1932; *Educ* Purley Co GS, Queen's Coll Oxford (BA); *m* 5 March 1963, Veronica Bobrovsky; 2 s (Nicholas b 1963, Paul b 1972), 1 da (Carina b 1967); *Career* HM Dip Serv: HM Embassy Vientiane 1957-59, FO News Dept 1959-60, HM Embassy Buenos Aires 1960-66, seconded to Govt of Br Honduras 1969-71, HM Embassy Madrid 1971-75, NATO Def Coll Rome 1976, HM Embassy Budapest 1977-80, HM Embassy Peking 1980-83, head Consular Dept FCO 1983-85, HM ambass Quito 1985-89, HM ambass Bucharest 1989-; *Style*— Michael Atkinson, Esq, CMG, MBE; c/o FCO (Bucharest), King Charles St, London SW1A 2AH

ATKINSON, Peter Graham; s of William Graham Atkinson (d 1984), of York, and Margaret, *née* Turnbull; *b* 12 Jan 1952; *Educ* Nunthorpe GS York; *m* 14 Sept 1977, Jane Maria, da of Eric Kaiser, of York; 1 s (Christopher Paul b 1984), 1 da (Helen Elizabeth b 1981); *Career* with Barron and Barron 1970-75, Ernst and Whinney (W Africa) 1975-78, chief accountant Claxton and Garland 1978-82, fin dir Yorks Post Newspapers Ltd 1982-; treas: local sch parents assoc, Leeds Chamber of Trade; FCA 1975; *Recreations* family, reading, gardening, swimming; *Style*— Peter Atkinson, Esq; 22 Usher Park Rd, Usher Lane, Haxby, York YO3 8RY (☎ 0904 762854); PO Box 168, Wellington St, Leeds LS1 1RF (☎ 0532 432701, fax 0532 443430, telex 55425)

ATKINSON, Sir Robert; DSC (1941, 2 Bars 1943 and 1944), RD (1947); s of Nicholas Atkinson (d 1944), and Margaret, *née* Bradford; *b* 7 March 1916; *Educ* Univ of London (BSc), McGill Univ Canada; *m* 1, 1941, Joyce, *née* Forster (d 1972); 1 s (Robert), 1 da (Gillian); m 2, 1977, Margaret Hazel Walker; *Career* served WWII 1939-45 (despatches 1943); md: Wm Doxford 1957-61, Tube Investmts (Eng) 1961-67, Unicorn Industs 1967-72; chm: Aurora Hldgs Sheffield 1972-84, Br Shipbuilders 1980-84, Lyons Hldgs Ltd; non-exec dir Stag Furniture Hldgs 1971-; CEng, FEng, FIMechE, FIMarE; kt 1982; *Recreations* salmon fishing, walking; *Clubs* Royal Thames Yacht; *Style*— Sir Robert Atkinson, DSC, RD; Southwood Hse, Itchen Abbas, Winchester, Hants SO21 1AT (☎ 096 278 610)

ATKINSON, Dr Ronald James; s of Robert William Atkinson (d 1974), and Ellen, *née* Whiteside; *b* 8 Sept 1945; *Educ* Bangor GS, Queens Univ Belfast (MD); *m* 25 Oct 1974, (Sarah) Pamela, da of Robert Samuel Gawley (d 1990); 2 da (Claire b 1977, Sarah b 1981); *Career* fell Cancer Res Campaign 1976-78, sr lectr Queens Univ Belfast 1980-, conslt Belfast City Hosp 1980-; numerous contribs in jls; memb: Cncl NI Hospice Ltd, Cncl Irish Assoc for Cancer Res; FRCS, FRCOG; *Recreations* wind surfing, gardening; *Style*— Dr Ronald J Atkinson; 29A Carnreagh, Hillsborough, Co Down, N Ireland BT26 6LJ; Oncology Dept, Whitla Medical Building, 97 Lisburn Rd, Belfast BT9 7BL (☎ 0232 329241 ext 2229)

ATKINSON, Rowan Sebastian; s of Eric Atkinson (d 1984), and Ella May Atkinson; *b* 6 Jan 1955; *Educ* Durham Cathedral Choristers' Sch, St Bee's Cumbria, Univ of Newcastle (BSc), Queen's Coll Oxford (MSc); *Career* actor and writer; for BBC TV 1979-89: Not The Nine O'Clock News, The Black Adder, Blackadder II, Blackadder the Third, Blackadder Goes Forth; theatre performances in London's West End incl: One Man Show 1981 (Soc of West End Theatre Award for Comedy Performance of the Year), The Nerd 1984, One Man Show 1986, Chekhov's The Sneeze 1988; one man show tours to Aust, Canada, USA, and Far East; BBC TV Personality of the Year 1980 and 1989, Br Acad Award 1980; *Recreations* motor cars, motor sport; *Style*— Rowan Atkinson, Esq; c/o PBJ Management, 47 Dean St, London W1V 5HL (☎ 071 434 4278)

ATKINSON, Terry; s of Reginald Atkinson (d 1951), of Thurnscoe, Rotherham, Yorkshire, and Lily, *née* Hampshire; *b* 16 July 1939; *Educ* Wath-upon-Dearne GS South Yorkshire, Barnsley Sch of Art, The Slade Sch of Fine Art Univ of London; *m* ; 2 c; *Career* artist; exhibitions incl: Approaches to Realism 1990, Blue Coats Gallery Liverpool 1990, Oldham Art Gallery 1990, The New Art (Hayward Gallery) 1972, Documenta 5 Kassel W Germany 1972, Contemporanea Paris 1973, Projekt '74 Cologne 1974; cmmnd sculpture with Sue Atkinson for the exhibiton A New Necessity by the Gateshead Garden Festival 1990; author of numerous articles and essays; *Style*— Terry Atkinson, Esq; 12 Milverton Crescent, Leamington Spa, Warwickshire CV32 5NG (☎ 0926 311894); Gimpel Fils Ltd, 30 Davies St, London WC1 1LG (☎ 071 493 2488)

ATKINSON, Prof Thomas; s of Thomas Bell Atkinson (d 1968), of Sacriston, Durham, and Elizabeth Dawson (d 1967); descendant of J J Atkinson, the pioneer of the science of mine ventilation; *b* 23 Jan 1924; *Educ* Sacriston Sch, Royal Sch of Mines London (PhD, DIC, DSc); *m* 1948, Dorothy, da of Harold Price (d 1967), of Tyne and Wear; 1 da (Dorothy b 1951); *Career* RN 1942-46, W/O N Atlantic & SEAC; prof and head of dept of mining engrg Univ of Nottingham 1977-88 (emeritus prof 1988-); chm Consolidated Coalfields Ltd, dir West Seals Ltd; FEng; *Recreations* oil painting; *Clubs* Chaps, Snobs; *Style*— Prof Thomas Atkinson; 27 Kirk Lane, Ruddington, Notts NG11 6NN (☎ 0602 842400); Univ of Notts, Dept of Mining Engrg, Notts NG7 2RD (☎ 0602 506101, telex 37346)

ATKINSON, William Silver; s of Arthur George Atkinson (d 1971), and Kathleen Evelyn May, *née* Fitzgerald (d 1986); *b* 14 Sept 1937; *m* 1963 (m dis 1974), Mary, da of Mark Breadmore, of Bracknell, Berks; *Career* CA; dir: Continental Oil Co Ltd 1979-82, Conoco (UK) Ltd 1982-, Conoco Ltd 1982-, The Arts Club (London) Ltd 1984-, Du Pont Treasury Ltd 1990-; writer and speaker on taxation; sec UK Oil Indust Taxation Ctee 1976-85, hon treas The Arts Club 1985-88 (tstee 1987-); FCA, FTII; *Recreations* opera, walking, wine; *Clubs* Arts, Oriental; *Style*— William Atkinson, Esq; 1 Eton College Rd, London NW3 2BS; Conoco (UK) Ltd, 105 Wigmore St, London W1H 0EL (☎ 071 408 6000)

ATLAY, Robert David; s of Robert Henry Atlay, of 2 Cricket Path, Freshfield, nr Southport, Lancs, and Sarah, *née* Griffiths; *b* 26 June 1936; *Educ* Wirral GS, Univ of Liverpool (MB ChB); *m* 11 Feb 1967, Jean, da of William Alfred Stephen Cole, of 29 Cecil Rd, Prenton, Wirral, Merseyside; 2 da (Josephine b 8 May 1969, Victoria b 3 April 1973); *Career* conslt obstetrician and gynaecologist: Mill Road Maternity Hosp 1970, Royal Liverpool Hosp 1978; clinical lectr in obstetrics and gynaecology and memb Faculty of Med of Liverpool, chm Div Obstetrics and Gynaecology Unit 3 City of Liverpool; examiner: RCOG, Royal Aust Coll Obstetrics and Gynaecology, Univ of Liverpool, Univ of Cambridge, Univ of Manchester, Univ of Birmingham, Univ of Glasgow, Univ of London, Univ of The W Indies; hosp visitor Royal Women's Hosp Brisbane Aust 1981, papers in specialist jls, contrib clinics in obstetrics and gynaecology 1989-; pres Union Professionelle Internationale Obstetrics and Gynaecology; Sec of State appointee memb: Maternity Servs Advsy Ctee, Nat Transplant Panel, English Nat Bd Nursing Midwifery and Health Visiting; hon sec RCOG 1980-87 (memb Cncl 1973-), past pres Waterloo Rugby Union FC; FRCOG; *Recreations* rugby union football, golf, skiing, traditional jazz; *Clubs* Waterloo Football, Formby Golf, Liverpool Artists, Gynaecological Travellers; *Style*— Robert Atlay, Esq; 27 Merrilocks Rd, Blundellsands, Merseyside (☎ 051 924 1160); 35 Rodney St, Liverpool, Merseyside L1 9EN (☎ 051 708 9528); Mill Road Maternity Hospital, Liverpool 6 (☎ 051 260 8787)

ATTA, Hatem Riad; s of Riad Gorgi Atta, of Egypt, and Jozephine Matta, *née* Abrahim (d 1989); *b* 12 Aug 1951; *Educ* Private Mission Sch Egypt, DO London (MB BCh); *m* 26 June 1982, Janet Ann, da of Samuel John Saunders (d 1988); *Career* sr registrar in ophthalmology West Midlands RHA 1983-88, fell in ophthalmic ultrasonography Miami Sch of Med 1986-87, conslt ophthalmic surgn Royal Infirmary 1988-; hon sr lectr Univ of Aberdeen 1988; FRCSEd 1980, FCOPH 1988, memb Oxford Congress; *Books* Techniques and Application of Diagnostic Ultrasound (1990); *Recreations* racquets, sports, golf, scuba diving; *Clubs* Aberdeen Petroleum, British Subaqua; *Style*— Hatem Atta, Esq; Eye Department, Aberdeen Royal Infirmary, Foresterhill, Aberdeen (☎ 0224 681 818)

ATTALLAH, Naim Ibrahim; s of late Ibrahim Attallah, and Genevieve, *née* Geadah; *b* 1 May 1931; *m* 1957, Maria, da of Joseph Nykolyn; 1 s (Ramsay b 1965); *Career* book publisher: Quartet Books, Robin Clark, The Women's Press; magazine proprieter: Literary Review, The Wire; film prodr: The Slipper and the Rose (co-prodr with David Frost 1974), Brimstone and Treacle (exec prodr 1982); theatrical prodr: Happy End (co-presenter Lyric Theatre 1975), The Beastly Beatitudes of Balthazar B (presenter and prodr Duke of York Theatre 1982); fin dir and jt md Asprey of Bond Street, md Mappin & Webb, exec dir Garrard; parfumier (launched Parfums Namara 1985 with Avant L'Amour and Aprés L'Amour, Naïdor in 1986, L'Amour de Namara and Avant by Namara for Men, 1990); *Books* Women (1987), Singular Encounters (1990); *Clubs* Arts, The Acad; *Style—* Naim Attallah, Esq; Namara House, 45-46 Poland Street, London W1V 4AU (☎ 071 439 6750, fax 01 287 4767, telex 919034 NA)

ATTENBOROUGH, Sir David Frederick; CBE (1974); s of late Frederick Levi Attenborough; bro of Sir Richard Attenborough, *qv*; *b* 8 May 1926; *Educ* Wyggeston GS for Boys Leicester, Clare Coll Cambridge (hon fell 1980); *m* 1950, Jane Elizabeth Ebsworth Oriel; 1 s, 1 da; *Career* traveller, broadcaster and writer; joined BBC 1952, controller BBC-2 TV 1965-68, dir of Programmes TV and memb Bd of Management 1969-72; writer and presenter BBC series: Tribal Eye 1976, Life on Earth 1979, The Trials of Life 1990; tstee: World Wildlife Fund Int 1979-, Br Museum 1980-; Hon DLitt: Leicester, City, London, Birmingham; Hon LLD: Bristol, Glasgow; Hon DSc: Liverpool, Heriot-Watt, Sussex, Bath, Ulster, Durham; Hon DUniv Open Univ; FRS; kt 1985; *Publications incl*: Zoo Quest to Guiana (1956), Quest in Paradise (1960), Quest under Capricorn (1963), The Tribal Eye (1976), Life on Earth (1979), The Trials of Life (1990); *Recreations* tribal art, natural history; *Style—* Sir David Attenborough, CBE, FRS; 5 Park Rd, Richmond, Surrey

ATTENBOROUGH, Michael Francis; s of Ralph John Attenborough, CBE, MBE, of Chislehurst, Kent, and Edith Barbara Attenborough (d 1988); *b* 21 Oct 1939; *Educ* Rugby, Trinity Coll Oxford (MA); *m* 7 March 1970, Carol Finlay, da of Dr George Alexander Sharp, of Bishop's Stortford; 1 s (Thomas b 1972), 1 da (Sophie b 1975); *Career* Hodder & Stoughton Ltd: joined 1962, publishing dir 1972-; memb Worshipful Co of Haberdashers 1962; *Recreations* golf; *Clubs* Garrick, Royal St George's Golf, Royal and Ancient Golf of St Andrews, Band of Brothers; *Style—* Michael Attenborough, Esq; 17 Parkgate, London SE3 9XF (☎ 081 318 1914); 47 Bedford Square, London WC1B 3DP (☎ 071 636 9851, fax 071 631 5248, telex 885887)

ATTENBOROUGH, Michael John; s of Richard Samuel Attenborough, and Sheila Beryl Grant, *née* Sim; *b* 13 Feb 1950; *Educ* Westminster, Univ of Sussex (BA, pres Univ Drama Soc); *m* Karen Esther, da of Sydney Victor Lewis (d 1990); 1 s (Thomas Frederick Richard b 13 Oct 1986); *Career* asst dir Gardner Centre Theatre 1972; assoc dir: Mercury Theatre Colchester 1972-74, Leeds Playhouse 1974-79, Young Vic Theatre 1979-80; artistic dir: Palace Theatre Watford 1980-84, Hampstead Theatre 1984-89, Turnstyle Group 1989-90; exec prodr and dir RSC 1990-; freelance work as dir incl prodns for: Open Space Theatre, Red Ladder, Newcastle Playhouse, Citadel Theatre Edmonton, Abbey Theatre Dublin, Royal Court Theatre London and Nat Theatre; dir of over 70 plays to date; former memb Drama Panel: Arts Cncl, Greater London Arts; former memb: Bd Bubble Theatre, Cncl Directors' Guild; dir Susan Smith Blackburn Prize; memb: Cncl RADA, Exec Ctee Arts charitable Tst; nominations: London Theatre Critics award (Best Dir) 1985, Olivier award (Outstanding Achievement as Dir of Hampstead Theatre) 1986; winner Time Out Theatre award for Observe The Sons of Ulster Marching Toward The Somme 1986; *Recreations* being with my family, football, music, theatre; *Style—* Michael Attenborough, Esq; Royal Shakespeare Company, Barbican, London EC2Y 8BQ (☎ 071 628 3351, fax 071 374 0818)

ATTENBOROUGH, Neil Richard; RD 1980 (Bar 1989); s of John William Attenborough, and Eileen, *née* Ward; *b* 4 May 1940; *m* 1, 10 Sept 1968 (m dis 1980), Josephine; 2 s (Paul Alexander b 1971, Tristan Alistair b 1973); m 2, 10 June 1982, Jennifer Mary; 1 s (Thomas William b 1983); *Career* RN 1964-68, Lt Cdr 1968-69; CO: HMS St David, HMS Upton, HMS Waveney; conslt oral and maxillo-facial surgn SW Surrey and NE Hants Dist Authys; inventor and prodr Attenborough Sea Drogue; London Sailing Project Co, memb RNSA; memb: BDA, RSM; FDS RCS (Eng), FDS RCS (Edinburgh); *Recreations* sailing, squash, cricket; *Style—* Neil Attenborough, Esq; Fallowfield, Puttenham, Guildford, Surrey GU3 1AH, (☎ 0483 810216); Mount Alvernia, Harvey Rd, Guildford, Surrey (☎ 0483 38066)

ATTENBOROUGH, Peter John; s of John Frederick Attenborough (d 1967), and Eileen Mabel, *née* Reavell; *b* 4 April 1938; *Educ* Christ's Hosp, Peterhouse Cambridge; *m* 1967, Alexandra Deidre, da of Alexander Henderson Campbell (d 1982), of Derby; 1 s (James b 1969), 1 da (Charlotte b 1971); *Career* asst master Uppingham Sch 1960-75 (head of Classics Dept and housemaster), housemaster Starehe Boys Centre Nairobi 1966-67; headmaster: Sedbergh Sch 1975-81, Charterhouse 1982-; chm: Ind Schs Central Subject Panel for Classics 1976-80, Ind Sch Cmmn Entrance Ctee 1983-88, Schs Arabic Project 1986-87; memb: Ind Schs Curriculum Ctee 1980-83, HMC Academic Policy Ctee 1982-83, HMC Ctee 1986-87 and 1989-90; Liveryman Worshipful Co of Skinners; *Clubs* East India; *Style—* Peter Attenborough, Esq; The Headmaster's House, Charterhouse, Surrey (☎ 0483 426796); Charterhouse Sch (☎ 0483 426794)

ATTENBOROUGH, Philip John; s of (Ralph) John Attenborough, CBE, *qv*; *b* 3 June 1936; *Educ* Rugby, Trinity Coll Oxford; *m* 1963, Rosemary, da of Dr William Brian Littler, CB; 1 s, 1 da; *Career* publisher; chm: Hodder & Stoughton Ltd (joined 1957), Hodder & Stoughton Hldgs 1975-, Lancet Ltd 1977-, dir Book Toheus Ltd 1985-; memb Cncl Publishers Assoc 1976- (pres 1983-85); chm: Book Devpt Cncl 1977-79, Br Cncl Publishers Advsy Ctee 1989-; *Style—* Philip Attenborough, Esq; Coldhanger, Seal Chart, Sevenoaks, Kent TN15 0EJ (☎ 0732 61516); Hodder & Stoughton, Mill Rd, Dunton Green, Sevenoaks, Kent TN13 2YA (☎ 0732 450111)

ATTENBOROUGH, Sir Richard Samuel; CBE (1967); s of Frederick Levi Attenborough (d 1973), and Mary, *née* Clegg (d 1961); bro of Sir David Attenborough, *qv*; *b* 29 Aug 1923; *Educ* Wyggeston GS for Boys Leicester, RADA (Leverhulme scholar); *m* 22 January 1945, Sheila Beryl Grant, *née* Sim, JP (actress), da of Stuart Grant Sim (d 1975), of Hove, Sussex; 1 s (Michael b 13 February 1950), 2 da (Jane (Mrs Holland) b 30 September 1955, Charlotte b 29 June 1959); *Career* joined RAF 1943, flt sgt airgunner/cameraman, seconded RAF film unit 1944, demobilised 1946; actor, film prodr and dir; stage appearances incl: Richard Miller in Ah Wilderness (Intimate Theatre Palmers Green) 1941 (stage debut), Brighton Rock (Garrick) 1943, The Mousetrap (Ambassadors) 1952-54, The Rape of the Belt (Piccadilly) 1957-58; film appearances incl: In Which We Serve (screen debut) 1942, Brighton Rock 1948, The Guinea Pig 1948, Morning Departure 1950, Private's Progress 1956, Dunkirk 1958, I'm All Right Jack 1959, The Angry Silence (also co-prodr) 1960, The League of Gentlemen 1960, The Dock Brief, The Great Escape 1963, Seance On A Wet Afternoon (prodr, Best Actor San Sebastian Film Fest and Br Film Acad) 1964, Guns At Batasi (Best Actor Br Film Acad) 1964, The Flight Of The Phoenix 1966, The Sand Pebbles (Hollywood Golden Globe) 1967, Dr Dolittle (Hollywood Golden Globe) 1967, 10 Rillington Place 1971, The Chess Players 1978; prodr: Whistle Down The Wind 1961, The L-Shaped Room 1962; prodr and dir: Oh! What A Lovely War (16 Int Awards incl Hollywood Golden Globe and BAFTA UN Award) 1969 ; dir: Young Winston (Hollywood Golden Globe) 1972, A Bridge Too Far (Evening News Best Drama Award) 1977, Magic 1978, A Chorus Line 1985; prodr and dir: Gandhi (8 Oscars, 5 BAFTA Awards, 5 Hollywood Golden Globes, Dirs' Guild of America Award for Outstanding Directional Achievement) 1980-81, Cry Freedom (Berlinale Kamera and BFI Tech Achievement Award) 1987; formed: Beaver Films (with Bryan Forbes) 1959, Allied Film Makers 1960; dir Chelsea FC 1969-82; memb: Cncl Br Actors' Equity Assoc 1949-73, Cinematograph Films Cncl 1967-73, Arts Cncl of GB 1970-73; chm: BAFTA 1969-70 (vice pres 1971-), RADA 1970 (memb Cncl 1963-), Capital Radio 1972-, Duke of York's Theatre 1979-, BFI 1981-, Goldcrest Films & TV 1982-87, Ch 4 TV 1987- (dep chm 1980-86), Br Screen Advsy Cncl 1987-, Euro Script Fund 1988-; govr Nat Film Sch 1970-81, dir Young Vic 1974-84, tstee Tate Gallery (Tate Fndn 1986-) 1976-82; pres: Brighton Festival 1984-, Br Film Year 1984-86; Goodwill Ambassador for UNICEF 1987-, pro-chllr Univ of Sussex 1970-; pres: Muscular Dystrophy Gp of GB 1971- (vice pres 1962-71), The Gandhi Fndn 1983-, Arts For Health 1989-; chm: The Actor's Charitable Tst 1956-88, Combined Theatrical Appeals Cncl 1964-88, UK Tstees Waterford-Kamhlaba Sch Swaziland 1976- (govr 1987-), Ctee of Inquiry into the Arts and Disabled People 1983-85; tstee Help A London Child 1975-, govr Motability 1977-, patron Kingsley Hall Community Centre 1982-; Freeman City of Leicester 1990; Evening Standard Film Award for 40 Years Serv to Br Cinema 1983, Order of Merit Euro Film Awards 1988; Hon DLitt: Leicester 1970, Kent 1981, Sussex 1987; Hon DCL Newcastle 1974, Hon LLD Dickinson Penn 1983; fell BAFTA 1983; Martin Luther King Jr Peace Prize 1983, Padma Bhushan India 1983, Commandeur Ordre des Arts et des Lettres France 1985, Ordre de la Legion D'Honneur France 1988; kt 1976; *Books* In Search of Gandhi (1982), Richard Attenborough's Chorus Line (with Diana Carter, 1986), Cry Freedom A Pictorial Record (1987); *Recreations* collecting paintings and sculpture, music, football; *Clubs* Garrick, Beefsteak, Green Room; *Style—* Sir Richard Attenborough, CBE

ATTER, John Perkins; *b* 27 July 1938; *Educ* Worksop Coll; *m* ; 2 da (1 decd); *Career* Lieut Robin Hood Foresters TA; articled clerk Mellors Basdon & Mellors Nottingham 1956-61, audit clerk Peat Marwick Mitchell London 1962-63; fin dir and co sec: J Clerke & Co (Arnold) Ltd 1963-64, Venus Packaging Ltd Ilkeston 1964-70; Shield Packaging Ltd Washington Tyne & Wear: fndr, co sec 1970-75, fin dir 1970-85, commercial dir 1977-79, md 1979-85; sr business advsr English Estates North 1985-86, business support mangr English Estates 1988- (business devpt offr 1986-88); chm Industl & Commercial Membs Ctee A ICAEW (memb 1985-88), fndr memb Bd of Chartered Accountants in Business 1990- (chm Membs Communication Gp 1990-), chm Dina Atter/Shield Cancer Res Fund 1982-; FCA (ACA 1962); *Recreations* rugby, charity work, wood carving, gardening; *Style—* John Atter, Esq; 4 Lumley Thicks, Chester-Le-Street, Co Durham DH3 4HF (☎ 091 385 7189); English Estates, Methven House, Kingsway, Team Valley, Gateshead, Tyne & Wear NE11 0LN (☎ 091 487 4711, fax 091 491 0248)

ATTERBURY, J Michael David; s of Jack Eric Atterbury (d 1977), of Teignmouth, and Joanne Atterbury; *b* 14 June 1935; *Educ* Whitgift Sch; *m* 1959, Margaret Rose, da of William Thomas Evans (d 1971); 1 s, 2 da; *Career* banker; gp sec Barclays Bank plc 1983-; chm Co Secs Panel ICSA; FCIS, FCIB; *Recreations* music, chess, photography, natural history; *Style—* J Michael Atterbury, Esq; New Lodge, Woodham Rise, Horsell, Woking, Surrey GU21 4EE (☎ 04837 62418); Barclays Bank PLC, 54 Lombard St, London EC3P 3AH (☎ 071 626 1567; telex 884970)

ATTERTON, Dr David Valentine; CBE (1981); s of Maj Frank Arthur Shepherd Atterton, MBE (d 1950), and Ella Constance, *née* Collins (d 1940); *b* 13 Feb 1927; *Educ* King's Sch Rochester Kent, Bishop Wordsworth's Sch Salisbury, Peterhouse Cambridge (MA, PhD); *m* 1948, Sheila Ann, da of John McMahon (d 1960); 2 s (Charles, Edward), 1 da (Victoria); *Career* chm Foseco Minsep 1979-87, dep chm Assoc Engrg 1979-86; dir: Investors in Industrial Group plc (formerly Finance for Industry IMI Ltd 1976-89, Barclays Bank plc 1982-, Marks & Spencer plc 1987-, The Rank Organisation plc 1987-, Bank of England 1984-, British Coal 1986-; memb Bd of Govrs Utd World Coll of the Atlantic 1968-85 (chm 1973-79), chm NEDO Iron and Steel Sector Working Pty 1977-82; memb Advsy Cncl for Applied Res and Devpt 1982-85; FEng, FRSA; *Recreations* cartography, notaphilia, Japanese language; *Style—* Dr David Atterton, CBE; The Doctors House, Tanworth in Arden, Solihull, W Midlands B94 5AW; 14 Chesterfield House, South Audley St, London W1Y 5TB (☎ 071 499 8191); Marks & Spencer plc, Michael House, 57 Baker St, London W1A 1DN (☎ 071 935 4422)

ATTEWELL, Prof Peter Brian; s of Ernest Attewell (d 1966), of Ilkeston, Derbys, and Ida Caroline, *née* Bexon (d 1961); *b* 20 Oct 1931; *Educ* Univ of Birmingham (BSc), Univ of Sheffield (PhD, DEng); *m* 21 Dec 1957, Doreen Mary, da of Flt Lt Granville Atack (d 1969), of Heysham, Lancs; 2 da (Jane Elizabeth b 12 Sept 1961, Linda Christine (twin) b 12 Sept 1961); *Career* mgmnt and civil engrg contractors NCB 1956-59 (1950-53), res asst and res fell Univ of Sheffield 1959-65, reader and prof Univ of Durham 1965-; moderator examinations bd Engrg Cncl; FICE; *Books* Principles of Engineering Geology (1976), Soil Movements induced by Tunnelling and their Effects on Pipelines and Structures (1986); *Recreations* swimming; *Style—* Prof Peter Attewell; University of Durham, South Rd, Durham DH1 3LE (☎ 091 374 3922, fax 091 374 2550)

ATTLEE, Air Vice-Marshal Donald Laurence; CB (1977), LVO (1964); s of Maj Laurence Gillespie Attlee (d 1968; bro of 1 Earl Attlee, PM of GB 1945-51), of Groombridge, Sussex, and Letitia, *née* Rotton (d 1973); *b* 2 Sept 1922; *Educ* Haileybury; *m* 2 Feb 1952, Jane Hamilton, da of Capt Robert Murray Hamilton Young, RFC (d 1975), of Tichborne Grange, Hants; 1 s (Charles b 1955), 2 da (Carolyn b 1957, Jenny b 1963); *Career* joined RAF 1942, CO The Queen's Flight 1960-63, CO RAF Brize Norton 1968-70, MOD 1970-75, Air Vice-Marshal 1975, AOA Trg Cmd Brampton 1975-77 (ret 1977); fruit farmer 1977; dir Mid Devon Enterprise Agency, chm mid Devon DC 1989-91 (vice chm 1987-89); *Recreations* genealogy; *Clubs* RAF; *Style—* Air Vice-Marshal Donald Attlee, CB, LVO; Jerwoods, Culmstock, Cullompton, Devon (☎ 0823 680317)

ATTLEE, 2 Earl (UK 1955); Martin Richard Attlee; also Viscount Prestwood (UK 1955); s of 1 Earl Attlee, KG, OM, CH, PC, PM (Lab) 1945-51 (d 1967), and Violet (yst da of Henry Millar and 2 cous of 1 Baron Inchyra); *b* 10 Aug 1927; *Educ* Millfield, Southampton Univ; *m* 1, 1955 (m dis 1988), Anne Barbara, eldest da of late James Henderson, CBE, of Bath; 1 s, 1 da; m 2, 1988, Margaret (Gretta) Deane, o da of late Geoffrey Gouriet, CBE, of Paper House, Hampton Court, Middx; *Heir* s, Viscount Prestwood; *Career* serv Merchant Navy 1945-50; MIPR 1964; asst PRO BR (S Regn) 1970-76, fndr memb of the SDP; memb: All Party Disablement Gp, House of Lords Defence Study Gp; spokesman on Transport and Maritime Affairs for the SDP; dep whip SDP 1988-89, chief whip SDP 1989-; patron of ASPIRE, tstee Countrywide Workshops; dir: WVB Advertising Ltd, Thames Help Tst 1985, Countrywide Workshops Charitable Tst Ltd 1985 , Keith Wilden Public Relations Ltd, Conquest Ltd; contested (SDP) Hampshire European Constituency 1988; *Books* Bluff Your Way in PR (1968); *Recreations* DIY, writing, inventing; *Clubs* Pathfinders; *Style—* The Rt Hon Earl Attlee; 1 Cadet Way, Church Crookham, Fleet, Hants GU13 0UG (☎ 0252 628007)

ATTLEE, Hon Mrs (Rosemary); 2 da of late 1 Baron Elton; *b* 22 Jan 1925; *m* 1, 1946

(m dis 1955), William Yates, er s of William Yates, of Appleby, Westmorland; 1 s (decd), 2 da; m 2, 1955, David Charles Attlee, s of Wilfrid Henry Waller Attlee, MD (d 1962); 1 s, 1 da; *Style—* The Hon Mrs Attlee; Great Woodland Farm, Lyminge, Folkestone, Kent

ATTRIDGE, Elizabeth Ann Johnston; da of Rev John Worthington Johnston (d 1952), and Mary Isobel Giraud, *née* McFadden (d 1957); *b* 26 Jan 1934; *Educ* Richmond Lodge Sch Belfast, Univ of St Andrew (MA); *m* 1 Sept 1956, John Attridge, s of William Christopher Attridge (d 1958), of Worthing; 1 s (John Worthington b 1959); *Career* civil servant; Miny of Educn NI 1955-56; MAFF 1956-: asst princ Land Div, princ Plant Health, asst sec marketing & potatoes and animal health, Tropical Products (chm Int Coffee Orgn), undersec EC Gp 1983-85, Emergencies Food Quality Pesticide Safety Gp until 1989, Animal Health Gp 1989-; *Clubs* Royal Over-Seas League; *Style—* Mrs John Attridge; Ministry of Agriculture Fisheries & Food, Whitehall Place, London SW1

ATTRILL, Kenneth William; s of William James Attrill (d 1980), of Southgate, and Lilian Florence, *née* Dugan (d 1983); *b* 22 June 1917; *Educ* Dame Owen's Sch Islington, Regent St Poly; *m* 22 Dec 1961, da of Lord Gilbert Pope, of 46 Camlet Way, Hadley Wood, Herts; 1 s (Robin b 1968); *Career* Capt Middx Regt 1940-46, attached Princess Louise Kensington Regt Iceland 1942-43 winter warfare instr attached US Forces, rejoined Regt for D-Day landings 1944; ptnr Healey Baker 1952-77 (conslt 1977-87), dir Town Centre Securities plc 1981-; *Recreations* cricket, hockey, golf, sailing, skiing; *Clubs* Carlton, MCC, Royal Burnham Yacht, Hadley Wood Golf, Middx Regt Offrs; *Style—* Kenneth Attrill, Esq; Greyfriars, 393 Cockfosters Rd, Hadley Wood, Herts EN4 0JS (☎ 081 440 2474); Healey Baker, 29 St George St, London W1 (☎ 071 629 9292, fax 071 629 3375, telex 21800 HEABAK G)

ATTWOOD, Frank Albert; s of Eric George Attwood, of Broadstairs, Kent, and Dorothy May, *née* Gifford; *b* 19 Jan 1943; *Educ* Simon Langton GS Canterbury, Leighton Park Sch Reading, Univ of Hull (BSc); *m* 10 July 1985, Pamela Ann Paget, da of Samuel Kennedy Pickavor Hunter, of Broadstone, Dorset; 1 da (Rebecca b 1980); *Career* articled Sir Lawrence Robson 1965-68, CA 1968, chartered sec 1969, ptnr Robson Rhodes 1974-, chief exec offr DRM 1990-; memb: Auditing Practices Ctee 1980-86, ICAEW Insur Sub Ctee; chm APC Lloyd's Working Pty, jt auditor ICEAW; hon treas Schoolmistresses and Governesses Benevolent Inst; Freeman City of London 1989, Liveryman Worshipful Co of Scriveners 1989; FCA, ACIS; *Books* De Paula's Auditing (jtly 1976, 1982, 1986), Auditing Standards From Discussion Drafts to Practice (jtly 1978); *Recreations* rambling, gardening, travel, modern novels, weight training, watching cricket; *Style—* Frank Attwood, Esq; New Malden, Surrey; Robson Rhodes, 186 City Rd, London EC1 (☎ 071 251 1644, 071 251 0256, fax 071 250 0801, car 701 668, telex 885 734); DRM, 1133 Ave of Americas, New York 10036 (☎ 212 382 0493, fax 212 302 4259, telex 42869)

ATTWOOD, Thomas Jaymril; s of Cdr George Frederick Attwood (d 1969), and Avril Sandys, *née* Cargill (d 1963), of NZ, who was ggda of Capt William Cargill (b 1784) who founded Otago province in NZ; *b* 30 March 1931; *Educ* Haileybury, Sandhurst, Harvard and INSEAD (at Fontainebleau) Business Schs; *m* 1963, Lynette, da of late C Lewis; 1 s (Alistair b 1964), 1 da (Caroline b 1966); *Career* chm Cargill Attwood & Thomas (Mgmnt Consultancy Gp) 1965-, pt/t chm POUNC 1982-83; pres Int Conslts Fndn 1978-81, former GLC borough cncllr, memb Exec Ctee Br Mgmnt Trg Export Cncl 1978-85; memb Ct Worshipful Co of Marketors 1985-; FCIM, FIMC, FBIM, FInstD; *Recreations* cricket, travel, music; *Clubs* City Livery, MCC, Lord's Taverners; *Style—* Thomas Attwood, Esq; 8 Teddington Park, Teddington, Middx TW11 8DA (☎ 081 977 8091, fax 081 943 1393)

ATWELL, John David; s of Percival John Cyril Atwell, MBE, of Little Gaynes, Sch Lane, Hamble, nr Southampton, and Doris May, *née* Gardiner; *b* 17 May 1929; *Educ* Peter Symonds Sch Winchester, Univ of Leeds (MB ChB), FRCS (Eng) 1959; *m* 30 April 1960, (Penelope) Susan, da of Lt-Col Roland Douglas Nightingale, MC (d 1962), of Gloucestershire; 2 s (Christopher John b 1961, Michael James b 1965), 1 da (Caroline Susan b 1962); *Career* Nat Serv 2 Lt Royal Corps Signals 1947-49; lectr in paediatric surgery Gt Ormond St Hosp 1963-66, conslt neonatal surgn to St Thomas' Hosp and conslt paediatric surgn to the Westminster Hosp London 1966-69, conslt paediatric surgn to Wessex RHA 1969-, civilian conslt in paediatric surgery to RN 1986-; chm Ct of Examiners RCS 1989 (memb 1983-89), pres Br Assoc Paediatric Surgns 1989-90; external examiner: Univ of London, Univ of Glasgow, RCS Ireland; FRSM, invited cncl memb RCS; *Books* contrib: Current Surgical Practice (1981), Operative Surgery (1983), Management of Vesicoureteric Reflux (1984), Pathology in Surgical Practice (1985), Operative Surgery and Management (1987), Surgery for Anaesthetists (1988); *Recreations* sailing, Old English glass; *Clubs* Royal Southern Yacht, Army and Navy; *Style—* John Atwell, Esq; The Dolphin, High St, Old Bursledon, nr Southampton, Hants SO3 8DJ (☎ 042 121 3336); The Southampton Gen Hosp, The Wessex Regnl Centre for Paediatric Surgery, Tremona Rd, Southampton (☎ 0703 777222 ext 3046)

ATYEO, Donald Leslie; s of Lt Leslie George Gibson Atyeo, and Marjorie Spence, *née* Constable; *b* 10 Feb 1950; *Educ* Geelong Coll Univ of Melbourne; *m* Susan Mabel, da of Harold Archibald Ready; *Career* ed dir Time Out magazine 1989-90 (ed 1981-89), ed 20/20 magazine 1989-90, chief exec Palace Power Station 1990-; *Books* Muhammad Ali The Holy Warrior (1977), Blood & Guts A History of Violence in Sport (1979); *Clubs* Groucho; *Style—* Donald Atyeo, Esq; Palace Music Station, 7 Poland St, London W1 (☎ 071 287 2875)

AUBER, Thomas Fredrick; s of Eric Auber, of Ilford, and Margaret, *née* Wolf (d 1984); *b* 11 Aug 1989; *Educ* Bancroft's Sch Woodford Green Essex, Univ of Oxford (MA); *m* 1965, Jennifer Jane, da of John Berry (d 1942); 2 s (Daniel b 1968, Toby b 1971); *Career* admitted slr 1965; ptnr Gouldens 1971-; past pres Old Bancroftians Assoc; memb Law Soc 1965-; *Recreations* sailing, skiing; *Style—* Thomas Auber, Esq; 40 Cholmeley Crescent, London N6 5HA (☎ 081 340 5712); 22 Tudor St, London EC4Y 0JJ (☎ 071 583 7777, fax 071 583 3051, telex 21520)

AUBREY-FLETCHER, Lt-Col Edward Henry Lancelot; DL (Northants 1983); 4 s of Maj Sir Henry Lancelot Aubrey-Fletcher, 6 Bt, CVO, DSO, Lord-Lt for Bucks; *b* 6 May 1930; *Educ* Eton, New Coll Oxford; *m* 1, 1953, Bridget (d 1977), da of Brig Sir Henry Floyd, 5 Bt, CB, CBE, Lord-Lt for Bucks, and Hon Kathleen, da of 1 Baron Gretton, CBE, VD, TD, PC; 2 s, 1 da; *m* 2, 1981, Baroness Braye, *qv*, da of 7 Baron Braye, DL(d 1985); *Career* serv with Gren Gds until 1980, ret; *Style—* Lt-Col Edward Aubrey-Fletcher, DL; Stanford Hall, Lutterworth, Leics LE17 6DH (☎ 0788 860250)

AUBREY-FLETCHER, Henry Egerton; s and h of Sir John Aubrey-Fletcher, 7 Bt; *b* 27 Nov 1945; *Educ* Eton; *m* 1976, (Sara) Roberta, da of Maj Robert Buchanan, of Evanton, Ross-shire; 3 s (John Robert b 1977, Thomas Egerton b 1980, Harry Buchanan b 1982); *Career* co dir; *Style—* Henry Aubrey-Fletcher, Esq; Town Hill Farm, Chilton, Aylesbury, Bucks (☎ 0844 208196)

AUBREY-FLETCHER, Sir John Henry Lancelot; 7 Bt (GB 1782), of Clea Hall, Cumberland, JP (Bucks); e s of Maj Sir Henry Lancelot Aubrey-Fletcher, 6 Bt, CVO, DSO (d 1969), and his 1 wife Mary Augusta, *née* Chilton (d 1963); *b* 22 Aug 1912; *Educ* Eton, New Coll Oxford (BA); *m* 25 April 1939, Diana Fynvola, o da of late Lt-Col Arthur George Edward Egerton, Coldstream Gds; 1 s (and 1 da decd); *Heir* s, Henry Egerton Aubrey-Fletcher; *Career* Gren Gds 1939-45, Lt Col, left as Hon Maj; called to the Bar 1937; dep chm Quarter Sessions 1959-71, met magistrate 1959-71, recorder Crown Ct 1972-74, High Sheriff of Bucks 1961; *Style—* Sir John Aubrey-Fletcher, Bt, JP; The Gate House, Chilton, Aylesbury, Bucks (☎ 0844 208 347)

AUBURY, Philip Norman; s of Norman Frederick Charles Aubury, of Cheltenham, and Hilary Winifred, *née* Brockman; *b* 9 Aug 1947; *Educ* Saltley GS, Pershore Coll of Hort (NDH); *m* 2 Jan 1967, Elisabeth Ann, da of Clyde Thomas Riley, JP; 1 s (Matthew Philip b 16 Aug 1973), 2 da (Sally-Ann Elisabeth b 15 Feb 1968, Lucy Dawn b 1 Dec 1969); *Career* mangr Roseacre Gdn Centre 1968-74; City of Birmingham: lectr Hort Trg Sch 1974-79, parks mangr Recreation Dept 1979-87; dir Birmingham Botanical Gdns and Glasshouses 1987-; treas Arrow Canoe Club, lectr and judge local hort socs; *Recreations* garden design and construction, conservation; *Style—* Philip Aubury, Esq; Hill Cottage, Scarfield Hill, Alvechurch, Birmingham B48 7SF (☎ 021 445 3895); Birmingham Botanical Gdns and Glasshouses, Westbourne Rd, Edgbaston, Birmingham B15 3TR (☎ 021 454 1860)

AUCKLAND, 9 Baron (I 1789 & GB 1793); Ian George Eden; s of 8 Baron Auckland, MC (d 1957), and Evelyn, 3 da of Col Arthur Hay-Drummond, of Cromlix (nephew of 12 Earl of Kinnoull), the latter's mother Arabella being maternal gda of the 1 Duke of Cleveland. The Duke's paternal gm Grace was gda of Barbara, cr Duchess of Cleveland, by whom Lord Auckland is ninth in descent from Charles II; *b* 23 June 1926; *Educ* Blundell's; *m* 1954, Dorothy Eden, JP (Surrey), da of Henry Joseph Manser, of Eastbourne; 1 s, 2 da; *Heir* s, Hon Robert Eden; *Career* served Royal Signals 1945-48 & London Yeo Sharpshooters TA 1948-53; insur conslt; non-exec dir C J Sims & Co; Lloyd's underwriter 1956-64; vice-pres Royal Soc for Prevention of Accidents; takes Conservative Whip in House of Lords; Order of White Rose of Finland Knight First-Class 1984; *Clubs* City Livery, World Traders; *Style—* The Rt Hon the Lord Auckland; Tudor Rose House, 30 Links Rd, Ashtead, Surrey (☎ 03722 74393)

AUCOTT, John Adrian James; s of Arthur Aucott (d 1955), of Kingsbury, Staffs, and Beryl Joan, *née* Simmonds (d 1984); *b* 20 Jan 1946; *Educ* Coleshill GS; *m* 16 Sept 1969, Angela, da of Alan Baillie, of Rock, Cornwall; 2 da (Katherine Joanne (Kate) b 16 July 1971, Lucy Elizabeth (Lucie) b 6 March 1973); *Career* slr; articled clerk Birmingham, elected sr ptnr Edge & Ellison 1990; chm: Young Slrs Gp 1979-80 (memb 1975-80), Remuneration & Practical Devpt Ctee; memb: Indemnity Insurance Ctee 1982-87 (Treasurer's Ctee 1985-87, Fin Ctee 1987-88), Indemnity Casework Ctee 1987-88, Jt Ctee on the Future of the Legal Profession 1986-88, Gazette Ctee 1985-87, Gazette Advsy Bd 1987-89; dep vice pres Birmingham Law Soc 1990-91 (memb 1969-, memb Cncl 1978-); dir: Slrs Indemnity Fund Ltd 1987-, Slrs Fin and Property Servs Ltd 1988-, Law Soc Services Ltd; non cncl memb Professional and Pub Relns Ctee 1975-78 (former memb), dep registrar High Ct and Co Ct 1983-87; memb Cncl Law Soc 1984- (memb 1969-), memb Birmingham Law Soc 1969-; *Books* contrib to various law pubns and to The Law of Meetings (1987); *Recreations* country sports, wine and gastronomy, family and friends; *Clubs* Midlands Sporting, Belfry Sporting, Wig and Pen; *Style—* John Aucott, Esq; Edge & Ellison Solicitors, Rutland House, 148 Edmund St, Birmingham B3 2JR (☎ 021 200 2001, fax 021 200 1991, car 0831 324094)

AUDAER, Wing Cdr Clifford Harold; s of Harold Audaer (d 1973), of York, and Frances Mary, *née* Whittaker (d 1978); *b* 3 Feb 1928; *Educ* St Michael's Coll, Univ of Leeds (BA, DipEd); *m* 11 Aug 1951, Janet Monro, da of Charles William Hoggard (d 1962); 1 s (Philip Neil b 1959), 1 da (Helen Jane b 1962); *Career* RAF 1950-78: appts incl ADC COS HQ AFCENT Fontainebleau 1956-59 and Chief Linguistic Servs HQ AF S E Naples 1966-69; sec Inst Orthopaedics Univ of London 1978-, chm ARISE the Scoliosis Res Tst; FAA 1978, FBIM 1978; *Recreations* golf, music, theatre; *Clubs* MCC, RAF; *Style—* Wing Cdr Clifford Audaer; Inst of Orthopaedics, Royal Nat Orthopaedic Hosp, Brockley Hill, Stanmore, Middx (☎ 081 954 2300 ext 494)

AUDI, Pierre; *b* 9 Nov 1957; *Educ* Exeter Coll Oxford (BA); *Career* musical and theatrical dir; fndr the Almeida Theatre Islington 1979 (mangr Contemporary Music Festival until 1989), dir numerous operas and plays by living composers and playwrights incl David Rudkin, Botho Straus, Bernard-Marie Kotès, Wolfgang Rihm, Claude Vivier, Michael Finnissy and John Casken; appointed artistic dir De Nederlandse Opera Amsterdam 1988: dir Br premiere Verdi's Jerusalem (Opera North Leeds) and Monteverdi's Il Ritorno di Ulisse in Patria 1990, dir Schöenberg's Die Glückliche Hand and Morton Feldman's Neither 1991; winner Lesley Boosey award for outstanding contribution to Br musical life; *Style—* Pierre Audi, Esq

AUDLAND, Sir Christopher John; KCMG (1987, CMG 1973); s of Brig Edward Gordon Audland, CB, CBE, MC (d 1976), and Violet Mary, *née* Shepherd-Cross (d 1981); *b* 7 July 1926; *Educ* Winchester; *m* 1955, Maura Daphne, da of Gp Capt John Sullivan, CBE (d 1953); 2 s (Rupert b 1960, William b 1966), 1 da (Claire b 1963); *Career* served Br Army 1944-48 RA Temp Capt; entered Diplomatic Serv 1948; serv in FO: Bonn, Strasbourg, Washington, Brussels; memb UK delegation to the negotiations with memb states of the EEC 1961-63, head of Chancery Buenos Aires 1963-67, ldr UK delgn to UN Ctee on the Seabed and Ocean Floor at Rio de Janeiro 1968, head Sci and Technol Dept FO 1968-70, cnsllr and head of Chancery Bonn 1970-73, also dep ldr of the UK delgn to the Four Power negotiations on Berlin; dep sec-gen Cmmn of the Euro Communities 1973-81, dir-gen for Energy CEC 1981-86, ret 1986; hon fell Faculty of Law & visiting lectr on Euro insts Edinburgh Univ 1986-; pro chancellor Univ of Lancaster 1990-; memb: Euro Strategy Bd of ICL 1988-, Lake District Special Planning Bd 1989-, NW Reg Ctee Nat Tst 1987-; vice pres: Europa Nostra 1989-, Int Castles Inst 1990-; *Recreations* gliding, skiing, walking; *Clubs* United Oxford and Cambridge; *Style—* Sir Christopher Audland, KCMG; The Old House, Ackenthwaite, Milnthorpe, Cumbria LA7 7DH (☎ 05395 62202 or 04482 2202, fax 05395 64041)

AUDLEY, Sir (George) Bernard; s of Charles Bernard Audley (d 1928), of Ivy House, Stockton Brook, Stoke-on-Trent, and Millicent Claudia, *née* Collier (d 1989); *b* 24 April 1924; *Educ* Wolstanton GS, Corpus Christi Coll Oxford (MA); *m* 17 June 1950, Barbara, da of Richard Arthur Heath (d 1964); 2 s (Maxwell Charles b 1954, Robert James b 1956), 1 da (Sally Anne b 1959); *Career* served WWII Kings Dragoon Gds 1943-46; asst gen mangr Hulton Press Ltd 1949-57, md TAM Ltd 1957-61, fndr and chm AGB Research 1962-89; chm: Pergamon AGB 1989-90, Caverswall Holdings 1990-; Netherhall House 1962; memb: Indust and Commerce Advsy Ctee William & Mary Tercentenary Tst 1985-89, Arts Access 1986, St Brides Appeal for Restoration & Devpt 1987-; vice pres Periodical Publishers Assoc 1989- (pres 1985-89), visiting prof Business & Mgmnt Middlesex Poly 1989-; Liveryman Worshipful Co of Gold and Silver Wyre Drawers 1975, Freeman City of London 1978; FSS 1960, FMRS 1986, FRSA 1986; kt 1985; *Recreations* golf, reading, travel; *Clubs* Cavalry & Guards, MCC, Rye Golf, Hadley Wood Golf; *Style—* Sir Bernard Audley; Cloister Court, 22-26 Farringdon Lane, London EC1R 3AU (☎ 071 253 3135, fax 071 608 0646, car 0836 500 706)

AUDLEY, 25 Baron (E 1312-13); Richard Michael Thomas Souter; s of Sir Charles Alexander Souter, KCIE, CSI, and Charlotte Dorothy Jesson (sis of Thomas Tuchet-Jesson, f of 23 Baron and the 23 Baron's sis who as Baroness Audley was 24

holder of that title; Charlotte and Thomas were children of Charlotte, da of John Thicknesse-Tuchet, bro of 21 Baron Audley, by her husb Thomas Jesson); suc cous 1973; *b* 31 May 1914; *Educ* Uppingham; *m* 1941, Pauline, da of Dallas Louis Eskell; 3 da; *Heir* all 3 da as coheiresses presumptive: Hon Mrs Carey Mackinnon, Hon Mrs Michael Carrington, Hon Amanda Souter, *qqv*; *Career* WWII Capt RA; fell Chartered Inst of Loss Adjusters; dir Graham Miller & Co (ret 1982); *Recreations* shooting, gardening; *Style—* The Rt Hon The Lord Audley; Friendly Green, Cowden, nr Edenbridge, Kent (☎ 034 286 850682)

AUERBACH, Col Ernest; s of Dr Frank L Auerbach (d 1964), of USA, and Gertrude, *née* Rindskopf; *b* 22 Dec 1936; *Educ* George Washington Univ (BA, JD), US Army General Staff Coll; *m* 1990, Jeanette, da of John Taylor; 1 s (Hans Kevin b 1961); *Career* US Army active serv 1962-70, res 1970-85; serv through rank of Col in Euro Theatre Germany, S Vietnam and the Pentagon; div counsel Xerox Corp 1970-75, mangr attorney NL Industs 1975-77, vice pres and assoc gen counsel CIGNA Corp 1977-83, pres Int Life & Gp Ops CIGNA Corp 1984-89, chm Crusader Life Insur plc 1986-89 (md 1984-86), pres and chief operating offr NY Life Worldwide Hldg Inc 1989-90 ; dir Windsor Life Assur Gp plc 1989-90; ptnr The Schrempf Group plc 1990-; author of published legal business and def articles in: Wall Street Journal, The Officer, American Bar Association Journal, Neue Juristische Wochenschrift, Versicherungsrecht; memb Computer Systems Tech Advsy Ctee US Dept of Commerce 1974, 1976; memb American Cncl on Germany 1979-; Legion of Merit with Oak Leaf Cluster, Bronze Star Medal, Meritorious Service Medal, Army Commendation Medal; *Books* Joining the Inner Circle (1990), The Wall Street Journal on Managing (contrib 1990); *Recreations* writing, running; *Clubs* National Arts (NY), Univ (NY), Inst of Dirs (London); *Style—* Col Ernest Auerbach; 127 E 30th Street, 16D, NY, NY 10016 (☎ 010 1 212 6867400)

AUERBACH, Frank Helmuth; s of Max Auerbach (d 1942), of Berlin, and Charlotte Norah, *née* Borchardt (d 1942); *b* 29 April 1931; *Educ* Bunce Ct Sch Kent, Borough Poly Sch of Art, St Martin's Sch of Art, RCA; *m* 10 March 1958, Julia, da of James Wolstenholme (d 1981); 1 s (Jake b 1958); *Career* artist (painter); pub collections incl: Tate Gallery, Arts Cncl, Br Cncl, Museum of Mod Art NY, Metropolitan Museum NY, Nat Gallery of Australia; exhibited: many one man exhibitions, Arts Cncl Retrospective, Hayward Gallery London 1978, Venice Biennale (Golden Lion), Kunstverein Hamburg 1986, Museum Folkwang Essen, Centro de Arte Reina Sofia Madrid 1987, Riyksmuseum van Gogh Amsterdam 1989; ARCA 1955; *Style—* Frank Auerbach, Esq; c/o Marlborough Fine Art (London) Ltd, 6 Albemarle St, London W1X 4BY

AUGER, George Albert; s of Thomas Albert Auger (d 1977), and Lilian Daisy, *née* McDermott (d 1991); *b* 21 Feb 1938; *Educ* Finchley Co GS; *m* 8 Sept 1962, Pauline June; 2 da (Jacqueline Susan (Mrs Bull) b 1965, Deborah Anne b 1969); *Career* Nat Serv RAF 1957-59; sr insolvency ptnr Stoy Hayward 1978-; memb Cncl Chartered Assoc Certified Accountants 1980-86, pres Insolvency Practioners Assoc 1981-82; chm govrs Channing Sch London; FCCA 1962, MIPA 1967; *Books* Hooper's Voluntary Liquidation (1978); *Recreations* cricket, tennis, opera, porcelain; *Style—* George Auger, Esq; Stoy Hayward, 8 Baker St, London W1M 1DA (☎ 071 486 5888, fax 071 487 3686, telex 367716 H)

AUGHTERSON, William Herbert; s of William Vincent Aughterson, of Melbourne, Aust, and Mary Diana, *née* Wembridge; *b* 21 Dec 1937; *Educ* Xavier Coll Melbourne, Univ of Melbourne, Univ of Essex (MA); *m* 11 June 1960, Patricia Mary, da of Alfred Rowton Giblett; 4 s (Peter b 1963, James b 1965, Paul b 1967, Anthony b 1973), 1 da (Kathleen b 1961); *Career* barr and slr: Supreme Ct of Victoria 1964-, High Ct of Aust 1964-; slr Supreme Ct of England and Wales 1978-; chm Frating Parish Cncl 1977-78, clerk Stanway Parish Cncl 1979-81; memb: Law Inst Victoria 1964, Law Soc 1978, Cwlth Lawyers Assoc 1980, Int Bar Assoc 1990; *Books* The Diseases of Bees (1956); *Recreations* golf, watching cricket; *Clubs* North Countrymans (Colchester), Surrey Co Cricket; *Style—* William Aughterson, Esq; 53 Victoria Rd, Colchester, Essex (☎ 0206 56 2701, fax 0206 769 031)

AUGUST, Dr Paul Jeffrey; s of Capt Arthur August (d 1986), of Hillside, Eddisbury Hill, Delamere, Northwich, Cheshire, and Ella, *née* Davies; *b* 30 Sept 1944; *Educ* Stowe, St Thomas Hosp Med Sch (MB BS); *m* 28 Nov 1966, Lynne Elizabeth, da of Colin Bird, of Trentham, Stoke-on-Trent; 1 s (Piers William b 1978), 4 da (Andrea Elizabeth Mills August b 1968, Sarah Louise Mills b 1971, Susannah Jane b 1976, Poppy Charlotte Rose b 1989); *Career* sr registrar St Thomas Hosp London 1972-75, assoc lectr Univ of Manchester Med Sch 1975, conslt dermatologist Salford and Mersey RHAs 1975-; memb Med Appeal Tbnl 1986, former cncl memb RSM dermatology section; memb Br Med Laser Assoc; FRCP 1987; *Books* Topical Therapeutics (1986); *Recreations* conservatory & garden, golf; *Style—* Dr Paul August; Keepers Cottage, Petty Pool, Whitegate, Northwich, Cheshire (☎ 0606 883178); 23 St John St, Manchester M3 4DT (☎ 061 834 0363)

AUKIN, David; s of Charles Aukin (d 1981), and Regina, *née* Unger; *b* 12 Feb 1942; *Educ* St Paul's, St Edmund Hall Oxford (BA); *m* 20 June 1979, Nancy Jane, da of Herman Meckler, of London and New York; 2 s (Daniel b 1970, Jethro b 1976); *Career* slr 1976-79; dir: Hampstead Theatre 1978-83, Leicester Haymarket Theatre 1983-86; exec dir Royal Nat Theatre 1986-90; head of drama Channel 4 TV 1990-; *Clubs* Garrick, RAC; *Style—* David Aukin, Esq; 27 Manor House Court, Warrington Gardens, London W9 2PZ; National Theatre, South Bank, London (☎ 071 928 2033, fax 071 620 1197); Channel 4 Television, 66 Charlotte St, London W1 (☎ 071 631 4444)

AULD, Margaret Gibson; da of Alexander John Sutton Auld (d 1988), of Cardiff, and Eleanor Margaret, *née* Ingram (d 1980); *b* 11 July 1932; *Educ* Cardiff HS for Girls, Univ of Edinburgh (Cert Nursing Admin, MPhil); *Career* departmental sister Cardiff Maternity Hosp 1957-59 and 1961-66, ward sister Queen Mary Hosp Dunedin NZ 1960, matron Simpson Meml Maternity Pavilion Edinburgh 1968-73 (asst matron 1967), actg chief regnl nursing offr SE Region Scot 1973, chief area nursing offr Borders Health Bd 1973-77, chief nursing offr Scot Home and Health Dept 1977-88; memb: Ctee on Nursing 1970-72, Gen Nursing Cncl Scot 1973-76, Central Midwives Bd Scot 1972-76, Scot Bd BIM 1983-90, Human Fertilization and Embryo Authy 1990-, Scot Ctee of Gen Cncl Cancer Relief Macmillan Fund, Scot Ctee for Action on Smoking and Health; conslt WHO; Hon DSc Queen Margaret Coll Edinburgh 1987 (govr 1989); vice-pres Royal Coll of Midwives 1988, FRCN 1980, CBIM 1981; *Books* How Many Nurses? (1977); *Recreations* reading, music, entertaining; *Style—* Miss Margaret Auld; Staddlestones, Neidpath Rd, Peebles, Scotland EH45 8NN (☎ 0721 29594)

AULD, Hon Mr Justice; Hon Sir Robin Ernest; s of late Ernest Auld; *b* 19 July 1937; *Educ* Brooklands Coll, King's Coll London (LLB, PhD, FKC); *m* 1963, Catherine Elenaor Mary, elder da of late David Henry Pritchard; 1 s, 1 da; *Career* called to the Bar Gray's Inn 1959, QC 1975, rec of Crown Ct 1977-87, bencher 1984 (New York State Bar 1984), legal assessor to Gen Med and Dental Cncls 1982-87, chm Home Office Ctee of Inquiry into Sunday Trading 1983-84, judge High Ct of Justice Queen's Bench Div 1987, presiding judge Western Circuit 1991-; memb Judicial Studies Bd 1989-91 (chm Criminal Ctee 1989-91); Master Worshipful Co of Woolmen 1984-85; kt 1988; *Clubs* Athenaeum; *Style—* The Hon Mr Justice Auld; Royal Courts of Justice, Strand, London WC2A 2LL

AUSTEN, David Lee; s of David Robert Austen, of the Hat and Feathers Pub, Cambridge, and Joan Ellen, *née* Waters; *b* 11 April 1960; *Educ* Maidstone Coll of Art, RCA; partner, Mary Doyle; 1 s (Sam Joseph David b 21 Sept 1986), 1 da (Mia India b 19 Aug 1982); *Career* artist; solo exhibitions: Anthony Reynolds Gallery London 1986, 1988 and 1991, Serpentine Gallery 1987, Arnolfini Bristol 1988, Castle Museum and Art Gallery Nottingham 1989, Currus Los Angeles 1989 and 1991, Frith Street Gallery London 1990, Stephen Solovy Chicago 1991; gp exhibitions incl: Between Ideality & Politics (Gimpel Fils London/NY) 1986, Works on Paper (Anthony Reynolds Gallery London) 1986, On a Plate (Farnham Coll of Art and Serpentine Gallery) 1987, Object and Image: Aspects of British Art in the 1980s (City Museum and Art Gallery Stoke-on-Trent) 1988, Poiesis (Graeme Murray Gallery Edinburgh) 1990; *Style—* David Austen, Esq; 60 Barnes Avenue, Barnes, London SW13 9AJ (☎ 081 741 1182); c/o Anthony Reynolds, Anthony Reynolds Gallery, 37 Cowper St, London EC2A 4AP (☎ 071 253 5575)

AUSTEN, Derek; s of Alan Ewart Walter Austen, OBE (d 1978), of Sunbury on Thames, and Doreen Gladys Nowell, *née* Parr; *b* 7 Aug 1945; *Educ* St Paul's, St John's Coll Cambridge (MA); *Career* CA; Coopers & Lybrand 1968-72, Int Rectifier GB Ltd 1972-75, various positions with Reed Int incl chief accountant, Walker Crosweller Ltd 1975-80; dir: Prudential Portfolio Mangrs Ltd, Prudential Fin Servs Ltd; FCA 1975; *Recreations* squash, sailing, opera; *Clubs* Little Ship, Colets; *Style—* Derek Austen, Esq; 41 Strand on the Green, London W4 3PB; Prudential Financial Services Ltd, 1 Stephen Street, London W1P 2AP (☎ 071 548 3149, fax 01 548 3412)

AUSTEN, Mark Edward; s of Capt George Ernest Austen (d 1987), of Ashtead, Surrey, and Eileen Gladys, *née* Thirkettle; *b* 25 Aug 1949; *Educ* City of London Freemen's Sch; *m* 28 May 1977, Priscilla, da of Reginald Cyril Hart (d 1986), of Chiddingfold, Surrey; 1 s (Timothy b 1980), 1 da (Rachel b 1982); *Career* corp accounts trainee Reecl Int 1967-72, asst fin controller Henry Ansbacher 1972-75, conslt Price Waterhouse 1975-82, ptnr in charge fin servs consltg UK and Euro Price Waterhouse Mgmnt Conslts 1985- (ptnr 1982-85); Freeman City of London; FCMA 1976; *Recreations* music, squash, food; *Clubs* Carlton; *Style—* Mark Austen, Esq; 18 Imber Park Rd, Esher, Surrey KT10 8JB (☎ 081 398 3144); Price Waterhouse Management Consultants, No 1 London Bridge, London SE1 9QL (☎ 071 378 7200, fax 071 403 5265, telex 931709)

AUSTEN-SMITH, Air Marshal Sir Roy David; KBE (1979, CB 1975), DFC (1953); s of D Austen Smith, of Kingsdown, Kent; *b* 28 June 1924; *Educ* Hurstpierpoint; *m* 1951, Patricia Ann, *née* Alderson; 2 s; *Career* RAF; served WWII, Cdr Br Forces Cyprus, AOC Air HQ Cyprus and Admin Sovereign Base Areas Cyprus 1976-78; head Br Def Staff Washington and Def Attaché 1978-81, ret; Gentleman Usher to HM the Queen 1982-; *Style—* Air Marshal Sir Roy Austen-Smith; c/o Nat West Bank, Swanley, Kent

AUSTICK, David; s of Bertie Lister Austick (d 1938), and Hilda, *née* Spink (d 1968); *b* 8 March 1920; *Educ* City of Leeds Sch; *m* 1944, Florence Elizabeth Lomath; *Career* master bookseller Austicks Bookshops, memb Leeds City Cncl 1969-77, MP (Lib) Ripon 1973-74, memb W Yorks CC 1974-79; contested (Lib): Ripon 1974, Cheadle 1979, Leeds Euro Parl 1979; exec chm Electoral Reform Soc Ltd 1984-86 (treas and co sec 1987-), fin sec Electoral Reform (Ballet Serv) Ltd 1989-90; *Recreations* antiquarian books, illustrated books, limited editions, sailing (yacht 'Frontispiece'), nat 12 foot class; *Clubs* Nat Liberal, Fellowship of Reconciliation; *Style—* David Austick, Esq; 16 Oxford St, Harrogate HG1 1SN (☎ 0423 503747, fax 0423 524650); Clarence Place, Burley-in-Wharfedale (☎ 0943 863305); 21 Blenheim Terrace, LS2 9HJ (☎ 0523 432446, fax 0532 425641)

AUSTIN, Brian; s of Harold Austin, and Florence, *née* Elliot; *b* 25 Dec 1929; *Educ* Kettering GS, Leicester Poly Sch of Architecture (Dip Arch); *m* 8 Oct 1955, Gwendoline, da of John Johnson (d 1979); 3 s (Jonathan b 1959, Nigel b 1961, Matthew b 1964); *Career* Nat Serv RE 2nd Lt 1953-55; chartered architect, sr ptnr Featherstone Austin Woodward architects Northampton; ARIBA; *Recreations* campanology, golf; *Clubs* Northampton Town & County; *Style—* Brian Austin, Esq; 24 Gipsy Lane, Kettering (☎ 0536 514910); 30A Billing Rd, Northampton (☎ 0604 34216)

AUSTIN, Dr Colin François Lloyd; s of Prof Lloyd James Austin, of Cambridge, and Jeanne Françoise *née* Guérin; *b* 26 July 1941; *Educ* Lycée Lakanal Paris, Manchester GS, Jesus Coll Cambridge (MA), Ch Ch Oxford (DPhil), Freie Univ W Berlin; *m* 28 June 1967, Mishtu, da of Sreepada Mojumder (d 1963), of Calcutta; 1 s (Topun b 1 Aug 1971), 1 da (Teesta b 21 Oct 1968); *Career* Univ of Cambridge: dir of studies in classics and fell Trinity Hall 1965-, asst lectr 1969-72, lectr 1973-88, reader 1988-; treas: Cambridge Philological Soc 1971-, Jt Ctee Greek and Roman Socs 1983-; FBA 1983; *Books* Nova Fragmenta Euripidea (1968), Menandri Aspis et Samia (1969-70), Comicorum Graecorum Fragmenta in Papyris Reperta (1973), Poetae Comici Graeci 5 vols (1983-); *Recreations* cycling, philately, wine tasting; *Style—* Dr Colin Austin; 7 Park Terrace, Cambridge CB1 1JH (☎ 0223 62732); Trinity Hall, Cambridge CB2 1TJ (☎ 0223 332520)

AUSTIN, Ven George Bernard; s of Oswald Hulton Austin (d 1975), of Bury, Lancs, and Evelyn, *née* Twigg (d 1955); *b* 16 June 1931; *Educ* Bury HS, St David's Coll Lampeter (BA), Chichester Theol Coll; *m* 21 July 1962, Roberta (Bobbie) Anise, da of George Edward Thompson (d 1988), of Luton, Beds; 1 s (Jeremy Paul b 1969); *Career* ordained: deacon 1955, priest 1956; asst chaplain Univ of London 1960; vicar: St Mary's Eaton Bray 1964-70, St Peter's Bushey Heath 1970-88; archdeacon of York 1988-; proctor in convocation 1970-, church cmmr 1978-; *Books* Life of Our Lord (1960), When Will Ye Be Wise? (contrib, 1983), Building In Love (contrib, 1990); *Recreations* cooking, theatre, photography; *Clubs* Athenaeum; *Style—* The Ven the Archdeacon of York; 7 Lang Rd, Bishopthorpe, York, YO2 1QJ (☎ 0904 709 541)

AUSTIN, James Lucien Ashurst; s of Lloyd James Austin, of 2 Park Lodge, Park Terrace, and Jeanne, *née* Guérin; *b* 4 June 1940; *Educ* Lycée Lakanal Paris, Manchester GS, Jesus Coll Cambridge (MA), Courtauld Inst of Art London (post grad degree); *m* 30 July 1969, Pauline Jeannette, da of Paul Aten; 2 s (Thomas b 18 Oct 1974, Benjamin b 7 June 1977), 1 da (Lucie b 27 May 1980); *Career* photographer; Courtauld Inst: asst Photographic Dept 1962-63, photographer to the Conway Library 1973-85; freelance photographer 1965-73 and 1985-; major cmmns incl: Emile Male: Religious Art in France (3 volumes published), The Buildings of England by Nicholas Pevsner (over 15 volumes published), photography of Sainsbury Collection Univ of E Anglia, photographer to artist Ben Nicholson (4 exhibition catalogues published), inventory photography for Nat Trust and English Heritage, catalogue photography for Tate Gallery; photographs of facsimile edns of: Lambeth Palace Apocalypse, Bank of Eng Royal Charter commission and Subscriptions Book, Turner water colours for book on Turner at Petworth; FBIPP 1977 (assoc 1970), memb Assoc of Hist and Fine Art Photographers (1986); *Style—* James Austin, Esq; 24 George Street, Cambridge CB4 1AJ (☎ 0223 65776); Fine Art Photography, 24 George St, Cambridge CB4 1AJ (☎ 0223 359763)

AUSTIN, John; TD; s of John Austin (d 1972), of Chesterfield; *b* 13 April 1927; *Educ*

St George's Sch Harpenden, Univ of Glasgow; *m* 1959, Shirley Frances Bonner, da of Maj G Proctor (d 1979), of Tullydoey, Co Tyrone; 1 s (James b 1960), 1 da (Frances b 1964); *Career* former Capt RASC; former dir and chief exec: J Mann & Son Ltd, Claas (UK) Ltd; former dir: Howard Machinery plc, Ransomes & Rapier Ltd; current chm: Eastern Electricity Consumers Ctee, Ipswich Port Authy; CEng, MIProdE; *Recreations* walking, gardening; *Clubs* RAC; *Style—* John Austin, Esq, TD; The White Cottage, Woodbridge, Suffolk IP12 4BT (☎ 0394 383044)

AUSTIN, Sir Michael Trescawen; 5 Bt (UK 1894), of Red Hill, Castleford, West Riding of York; s of Sir William Austin, 4 Bt (d 1989), and his 1 w, Dorothy Mary, *née* Bidwell (d 1957); *b* 27 Aug 1927; *Educ* Downside; *m* 1951, Bridget Dorothea Patricia, da of late Francis Farrell, of Miltown, Clonmellon, Co Meath; 3 da (Mary b 1951, Jane b 1954, Susan b 1956); *Heir* bro, Anthony Leonard Austin; *Career* served WWII with RNVR; sometime Master of Braes of Derwent; *Style—* Sir Michael Austin, Bt; Idestone Barton, Dunchideock, Exeter, Devon EX2 9UE (☎ 0392 832282)

AUSTIN, Vice Adm Sir Peter Murray; KCB (1976); s of Vice Adm Sir Francis Murray Austin, KBE, CB (d 1953), and Marjorie Jane, *née* Barker (d 1968); *b* 16 April 1921; *Educ* RNC Dartmouth; *m* 1959, Josephine Rhoda Ann Shutte-Smith; 3 s, 1 da; *Career* Naval Cadet 1935, serv WWII at sea, qualified as pilot FAA 1946, Capt 1961, Rear Adm 1971, Flag Offr Naval Air Cmd 1973-76, Vice Adm 1974, ret 1976; ops dir Mersey Docks and Harbour Co 1976-80, dir Avanova Int 1980-89, chm Special Trg Servs 1984-89, md Mastiff Electronic Systems 1990-; CBIM; *Recreations* skiing, sailing, golf; *Clubs* Army and Navy, Royal Yacht Sqdn; *Style—* Vice Adm Sir Peter Austin, KCB

AUSTIN, Richard Russell; s of Prof Colin Russell Austin, of Queensland, Australia, and Patricia Constance, *née* Jack; *b* 25 Aug 1943; *Educ* Cambridgeshire HS, Cambridge Coll of Arts and Technol, RCM; *m* 1, Oct 1969 (m dis 1984), Virginia Anne; 3 da (Emma Rachel b 1969, Kathryn Charlotte b 1970, Elizabeth Jane b 1972); m 2, 31 Aug 1985, Hazel Louise; 1 da (Shami Naomi b 1990); *Career* mangr Table Music Agency 1970-74, admin Aklowa African Dance Co 1979-80, tstee and fndr Jenako Arts Center 1981-88, fndr mangr Orchestre Jazira 1980-85, dir New Era Music Ltd 1988-, fndr and chm New Age Music Assoc 1990-; wrote music for Mandy The Actors Cat released on LP 1976; *Recreations* travel, reading, writing, swimming, photography; *Clubs* RAC; *Style—* Richard Austin, Esq; 64b Colvestone Crescent, London E8 2LJ (☎ 071 249 0034)

AUSTIN, Roger; s of Arthur William Austin (d 1984), and Dorothy Mary Joan, *née* Garrett; *b* 18 April 1947; *Educ* Leamington Coll, Lanchester Coll of Technology (BA); *Career* admitted slr 1973; chm Bishops Itchington Parish Cncl, memb governing body Bishops Itchington Combined Sch; memb Law Soc 1973; *Recreations* cricket, soccer & NH racing; *Clubs* Member of Worcs Warks and Leics CCC, Cheltenham Steeplechase; *Style—* Roger Austin, Esq; 19 Starbold Road, Bishops Itchington, Leamington Spa, Warwickshire CV33 0TQ; 25 Meer St, Stratford-upon-Avon, Warwickshire CV37 6QB (☎ 0789 414444)

AUSTIN, Air Vice-Marshal Roger Mark; AFC (1973); s of Mark Austin (d 1982), and Sylvia Joan, *née* Reed; *b* 9 March 1940; *Educ* King's Alfred GS Wantage; *m* 1, 1963 (m dis 1981), Carolyn de Recourt, *née* Martyn; 2 s (Stuart b 1965, Patrick b 1971), 1 da (Rachel b 1964); m2, 26 July 1986, Glenys Amy Beckley, da of Hugh Glyn Roberts, of Holyhead; 2 step da (Sarah b 1969, Emma b 1972); *Career* RAF: cmmnd 1957, Flying Instr 1960; flying appt: 20 Sqdn 1964, 54 Sqdn 1966, cmd 54 Sqdn 1969, 4 Sqdn 1970; Staff Coll Camberley 1973, cmd 233 OCU 1974, PSO to AOC in C Strike Cmd 1977, cmd RAF Chivenor, ADC to Queen 1980, Staff HQ Strike Cmd 1982, DOR 2 MOD 1984, RCDS 1986, AOIC Central Tactics and Trials Orgn 1987, Dir Gen Aircraft 1 MOD (Procurement Exec) 1987, AOC and Cmdt RAF Coll Cranwell 1989-; *Recreations* walking, transport systems; *Clubs* RAF; *Style—* Air Vice Marshal Roger Austin, AFC; RAF College, Cranwell, Lincs NG34 8HB

AUSTIN, Trevor Herbert; s of Percy Austin (d 1949), of Stockport, Cheshire, and Gladys, *née* Kingdon (d 1968); *b* 21 Feb 1933; *Educ* Stockport GS; *m* 31 Dec 1955, Joan Margaret, da of William Hunt (d 1982), of Stockport, Cheshire; 2 s (Sean, Nicholas), 1 da (Karen); *Career* princ nursing offr Peel Hosp Galashiels 1971-74; Borders Health Bd: gp princ nursing offr 1974-76, area nursing offr 1976-85, chief area nursing offr 1985-; memb: Children's Panel Scot Borders Region 1972-82, Children's Panel Advsy Ctee Borders Regnl Cncl 1984-; memb Royal College of Nursing; *Recreations* member of Roxburgh singers, organist Bowden Kirk Roxburghshire; *Style—* Trevor Austin, Esq; 97 Murrayfield Cottages, Buccleuch Rd, Selkirk, Scotland TD7 5AT (☎ 0750 21579); Borders Health Board, Huntlyburn, Melrose, Roxburghshire, Scotland TD6 9BP (☎ 089682 2662)

AUSTIN, Vivienne; da of Harold Austin, of Lancashire, and Constance Alice, *née* Rose; *b* 10 April 1959; *Educ* Bolton Coll of Art and Design (Dip in Fashion Design, Higher Dip in Fashion Design), St Martins Sch of Art and Design (postgrad); *m* Lawrence Peregrine Blow; *Career* fashion designer and patterncutter: sold menswear collection 1979, designer and prodr stage clothes and jewelry 1982-83; various work for retail firms incl: Miss Selfridge, Wallis, Topshop, C&A, Principles, Richards, Chelsea Girl, Mirror Mirror (Ireland), Demob, Collets, Marks & Spencer, Bennetton, Warehouse (1984-87); magazine work: Over 21 Mizz, International Textiles; produced T-Shirts against animal cruelty for EIA (1988-89); lectures: RCA 1988-, ACL 1989 (in CADCAM); exhibitions incl: winter 89 collection for Int Inst for Cotton, winter 89 Rubber Collection, Satellite Cafe, Docklands fashion show, Infermoda RIBA, Fabrex, BBC Clothes Show, Finesse Designer of the Year Fashion Show, Reactivart Fashion Show; opened Fusion (Retail) Trocadero Piccadilly Circus 1990; memb: EIA, Reactivart, SIAD; *Recreations* weight training, aerobics, exhibitions; *Style—* Mrs Vivienne Austin; 170 Brick Lane, London E1 6RU (☎ 071 247 1599); Cosmic Boom, Afflecks Palace, Church St, Manchester

AUSTIN, William Thomas Frederick; s of Percy Thomas Austin (d 1968), of Stratford upon Avon, and Winifred, *née* Farr (d 1954); *b* 1 Feb 1920; *Educ* Wolverhampton GS, King Edward VI HS Birmingham, Univ of Birmingham (BSc), Cornell Univ; *m* 1, 9 April 1955, Agnes Scott, da of John Mitchell, of Biggar, Lanarkshire; 2 da (Carol Ann b 24 Aug 1957, Morag Elspeth b 21 May 1961); m 2, 12 Sept 1964, Muriel Eileen, da of John Redgrove Taylor (d 1968), of London Colney, Herts; *Career* WW II serv: offr cadet RE 1940-41, 2 Lt (later Lt) 5 FD Co RE 1941-44; Maj (later Lt-Col) Engr and Ry Staff Corps TAVR (now Engr and Tport Corps) 1981; site engr Sir Robert McAlpine & Sons 1940, asst engr R Travers Morgan & Ptnrs 1944-45; Freeman Fox and Ptnrs 1945- (ptnr 1966-85, conslt 1985-): work incl Auckland Harbour Bridge, Forth Road Bridge, M2 and M5 motorways; work in USA on various long span bridges and turnpikes 1950-51; pres: Concrete Soc 1978-79, Inst of Highways and Tport 1984-85; memb Bldg Div Cncl and various ctees BSI 1977-86; Univ of Birmingham: pres Guild of Graduates (London branch) 1983-86, memb Ct 1975-85; memb Glyndebourne Festival Soc 1977-; Freeman City of London, Liveryman Worshipful Co of Paviors 1979; CEng, FICE 1946, FIStructE 1945, FIHT 1959, MASCE 1950; *Recreations* travel, photography, art, opera, literature; *Clubs* RAC; *Style—* William Austin, Esq; 3 Kingfisher Drive, Ham, Richmond, Surrey TW10 7UF (☎ 081 940 7957)

AUSTIN-COOPER, Richard Arthur; o s of late Capt Adolphus Richard Cooper, of Ditton Kent, and Doris Rosina, *née* Wallen; see Burke's Irish Family Records under Cooper (co Tipperary); assumed additional surname of Austin by Deed Poll 1963; *b* 21 Feb 1932; *Educ* Wellingborough GS, Tottenham GS; *m* 1, 28 March 1953 (m dis 1963), Sylvia Anne Shirley Berringer; m 2, 28 Sept 1963 (m dis 1974), Valerie Georgina, da of Henry Drage, of Tottenham, London; 1 s (Matthew b 1969), 1 da (Samantha b 1967); m 3, 19 June 1986, Rosemary Swaisland, *née* Gillespie; *Career* served RA Intelligence Corps 1950-52, 21 SAS Regt, Hon Artillery Co 1952-80, cmmnd 2 Lt TAVR 1968; dep head Stocks & Shares Dept Banque de Paris et des Pays Bas 1969-74; mangr Banking Div Brook St Bureau of Mayfair Ltd 1974-77; chief custodian and London registrar of Canadian Imp Bank of Commerce 1975-78; personnel offr Deutsche Bank AG London Branch 1978-85, sr mangr and head of personnel Deutsche Bank Capital Markets Ltd 1985-90 (ret); fndr Fell Inst of Heraldic and Genealogical Studies, memb Bd of Mgmnt: Barbican YMCA, City of London Central Markets Coal Corn and Rates, Leadenhall Market, Billingsgate Market; memb: Music Mgmnt Ctees 1978-81, Ct of Common Cncl for Cripplegate Ward 1978-81, City of London TAVR Assoc, Mgmnt Ctee Barbican Sch of Music and Drama and mature student (tenor), Irish Peers Assoc; govr: City of London Sch for Girls 1979-80, City of London Freemen's Sch 1980-81, Lansbury Adult Educn Inst 1979-82; life govr Sheriffs' and Recorders' Fund at the Old Bailey 1979-; represented the City of London Corpn on the Gtr London Arts Cncl 1979-80, Freedom of the City of London 1964, final tstee City of London Imp Vols 1980-81; prizes for athletics (including Barclays Bank Cross-Country Championships), operatic singing (tenor), painting; FCIB, FRSA, FHG, FRSAIre, MBIM, FSA (Scot); *Books* Butterhill and Beyond (1991); *Recreations* genealogical research, tenor concerts, gardening, sketching; *Clubs* Special Forces, SAS Old Comrades, Intelligence Corps Old Comrades, Wellingborough GS Old Boys; *Style—* Richard Austin-Cooper, Esq; Butterhill House, 49 Old North Road, Wansford, Cambs PE8 6LB

AUSTWICK, Prof Kenneth; JP (1970); s of Harry Austwick (d 1984), of Morecambe, Lancs, and Beatrice, *née* Lee (d 1954); *b* 26 May 1927; *Educ* Morecambe GS, Univ of Sheffield (BSc, MSc, PhD); *m* 18 Aug 1956, Gillian, da of Frank Griffin (d 1983), of Bromsgrove, Worcs; 1 s (Malcolm b 1959), 1 da (Dawn b 1960); *Career* schoolmaster 1950-59, lectr (later sr lectr) Univ of Sheffield 1959-65, reader Univ of Reading 1965-66, prof Univ of Bath 1966- (pro-vice chllr 1972-75); advsr HO; conslt: OECD, UTA, Br Rail; govr Bath Coll; FSS 1962, FSA 1970; *Books* Teaching Machines (1962), Aspects of Educational Technology Vol Six (1972), Trigonometry (1967), Maths at Work (1985), Mathematics Connection (1985); *Recreations* gardening, wine-making; *Clubs* Royal Cwlth; *Style—* Prof Kenneth Austwick, JP, FSA; Brook Hse, Combe Hay, Bath, Avon (☎ 0225 832541); School of Education, Univ of Bath, Bath, Avon (☎ 0225 826352, fax 0225 62508, telex 826113)

AUTY, Capt Richard Ian; s of Keith Ian Auty, of Nyali, Huntersfield Close, Reigate, Surrey, and Marjorie, *née* Gwinnell; *b* 9 April 1946; *Educ* Trinity Sch of John Whitgift, RAF Coll Cranwell, Coll of Air Trg Hamble; *m* 4 June 1971 (m dis 1984), Carole Marie Brenda Hazel, da of Albert Bacuez (d 1951); 1 s (Charles b 1974), 1 da (Natalie b 1976); *Career* joined BEA 1967, overseas div 1976, sr capt BA; memb: BALPA, RHS; *Recreations* reading, water sports, tennis, golf, theatre; *Clubs* Naval; *Style—* Capt R I Auty; 24 Beechcrest View, Hook, Hampshire

AVEBURY, 4 Baron (UK 1900); Sir Eric Reginald Lubbock; 7 Bt (UK 1806); s of Hon Maurice Fox Pitt Lubbock (yst s of 1 Baron Avebury) and Hon Mary Stanley (eldest da of 5 Baron Stanley of Alderley and sis of the actress Pamela Stanley); suc cousin, 3 Baron 1971; *b* 29 Sept 1928; *Educ* Upper Canada Coll, Balliol Oxford; *m* 1, 1953 (m dis 1983), Kina Maria, da of Count Joseph O'Kelly de Gallagh (a yr s of the family whose head is a Count of the Holy Roman Empire by Imperial Letters Patent of 1767); 2 s (Hon Lyulph Ambrose Jonathan, Hon Maurice Patrick Guy, *qv*), 1 da (Hon Mrs Binney, *qv*); m 2, 1985, Lindsay Jean, da of Gordon Neil Stewart, and of late Pamela Hansford Johnson (Lady Snow), writer; 1 s (Hon John William Stewart b 8 Aug 1985); *Heir* s, Hon Lyulph Ambrose Jonathan Lubbock, *qv*; *Career* 2 Lt Welsh Gds 1949-51; engr with Rolls Royce 1951-56; mgmnt conslt Charterhouse Gp 1960; sits as Liberal in House of Lords; MP (Lib) Orpington 1962-70, Lib chief whip 1963-70; conslt Morgan-Grampian 1970-; dir: C L Projects, 2020 Technology; pres: Fluoridation Soc 1972-85, Conservation Soc 1973-82; chm Parly Human Rights Gp 1976-; memb: Cncl Institute Race Relations 1972-74, Royal Cmmn on Standards of Conduct in Public Life 1974-76; MIMechE, MBCS; *Style—* The Rt Hon the Lord Avebury; 26 Flodden Rd, London SE5 9LH

AVERY, (Marshall) Angus; s of Maj Norman Bates Avery, MC (d 1957), of Redhill, Surrey, and Grace Avery; bro of Gillian Elise Avery, *qv*; *b* 6 May 1933; *Educ* Loretto, Sandhurst; *m* 1975, Penelope Maxwell, da of Alan Berners-Price; 2 s (Archie, Alexander); *Career* Capt Gordon Highlanders 1953-62; md Irish Vintners 1968-70, commercial mangr John Harvey & Sons (España) Ltd 1972-73, dir Waverley Vintners 1974-84, mangr Woodhouse Wines 1987-; *Recreations* sailing, skiing, shooting, squash; *Clubs* Naval & Military; *Style—* Angus Avery, Esq; Iwerne Hill Farmhouse, Iwerne Minster, Blandford Forum, Dorset DT11 8LE (☎ 0747 811867); Hall and Woodhouse Ltd, Blandford Forum, Dorset DT11 9LS

AVERY, Dr Charles Henry Francis; FSA; s of Richard Francis Avery, of Richmond, Surrey, and Dorothea Cecilia, *née* Wharton; *b* 26 Dec 1940; *Educ* KCS Wimbledon, St John's Coll Cambridge (MA, PhD), Courtauld Inst of Art London (Academic Dip); *m* 11 June 1966, (Kathleen) Mary, da of Charles Gwynne Jones, d (d 1969); 3 da (Charlotte Frances b 24 Feb 1970, Susanna Mary (triplet), Victoria Jane (triplet); *Career* dep keeper of sculpture V&A 1965-79, dir Sculpture Dept Christie's 1979-90, currently ind fine art conslt; FSA 1985; Cavaliere Dell'ordine Al Merito della Repubblica Italiana 1979, medal of Ministry of Culture Poland; *Books* Florentine Renaissance Sculpture (1970), Studies in European Sculpture (1981, 1987), Giambologna the Complete Sculpture (1987); *Recreations* writing, reading, tennis; *Clubs* Beckenham Tennis; *Style—* Dr Charles Avery, FSA; Holly Tree House, 20 Southend Road, Beckenham, Kent BR3 1SD

AVERY, Gillian Elise (Mrs A O J Cockshut); da of Maj Norman Bates Avery, MC (d 1957), of Redhill, Surrey, and Grace Avery; sister of (Marshall) Angus Avery, *qv*; *b* 30 Sept 1926; *Educ* Dunottar Sch Reigate; *m* 1952, Anthony Oliver John Cockshut, s of Dr Rowland William Cockshut (d 1977), of Hendon; 1 da; *Career* writer of novels, children's books and non-fiction, A Likely Lad (Guardian Award 1972); chm Children's Books History Soc 1987-90; *Style—* Miss Gillian Avery; 32 Charlbury Rd, Oxford (☎ (0865) 56291)

AVERY, Graham; s of Walter Avery, of Shifnal, Shropshire, and Kathleen, *née* Hawkins; *b* 17 Feb 1945; *Educ* Shrewsbury Coll (HNC); *m* 25 July 1970, Susan Elizabeth, da of Walter Sidney Townes, of Westerfield, nr Ipswich, Suffolk; 1 s (Mark Nigel b 15 Dec 1965), 1 da (Michelle Louise b 28 July 1971); *Career* chm WB Industs plc, proprietor and chm Breckland Gp Hldgs 1964-, chm S Wales Devpt Inc plc 1987-; fndr memb and hon patron Appeal Theatre Gp Ipswich; qualified pilot; *Recreations* tennis, flying, skiing, theatre; *Clubs* IOD; *Style—* Graham Avery, Esq; 19 Charles St, Mayfair, London W1 (☎ 071 499 0056, fax 071 408 1998); Anglia House, 43 Woodbridge Rd East, Ipswich IP4 5QN (☎ 0473 715 751, fax 0473 719 500)

AVERY, Graham John Lloyd; s of The Rev Edward Avery (d 1979), and Alice, *née*

Lloyd; *b* 29 Oct 1943; *Educ* Kingswood Sch Bath, Balliol Coll Oxford (MA), Harvard Univ; *m* 1967, Susan; 2 s (Matthew b 1974, John b 1976); *Career* Miny of Agric Fisheries & Food: entered 1965, princ responsible for negotiations for entry to EC 1969-72, princ private sec to Fred Peart then John Silkin 1976; EC Brussels 1976-; memb cabinets of: Christopher Soames (vice pres external rels) 1973-76, Roy Jenkins (pres) 1977-80, Finn Gundelach (cmmr for agric) 1981, Poul Dalsager (cmmr for agric) 1981, Frans Andriesen (cmmr for agric) 1985-86; served in Directorate Gen for Agric 1981-84 and 1987-90, dir Directorate Gen for External Rels 1990-; Freeman City of Indianapolis, fell Centre for Int Affairs Harvard *Publications* author of articles in various learned jnls; *Style*— Graham Avery, Esq; Commission of The EC, 1049 Brussels, Belgium (☎ 235 4907)

AVERY, Mark Nigel; s of Graham Avery, and Susan Elizabeth, *née* Townes; *b* 15 Dec 1965; *Educ* St Joseph's Coll Ipswich, Northgate HS Ipswich; *Career* croquet player; competitive debut 1979, first Nat Championships 1982, represented England and GB 1986-; achievements incl: Northern champion 1982, Nat champion 1987, Western champion 1989, runner up World Championships London 1989, played in USA 1987-90, memb GB team winning World Team Championships NZ 1990; records: quickest championship match (61 mins v Reid Fleming) World Championships 1989, youngest player to achieve a triple-peel in tournament play aged 14; also winner various football trophies; employment: Ipswich Borough Cncl 1983-88, family building and property co 1988-; *Recreations* all aspects of sport, football, snooker, tennis, keeping fit; *Style*— Mark Avery, Esq; Thurleston Lodge, Henley Road, Ipswich, Suffolk IP1 6TD (☎ 0473 215453)

AVERY JONES, John Francis; CBE (1987); s of Sir Francis Avery Jones, CBE, of Nutbourne, W Sussex, and Dorothea Bessie, *née* Pfirter (d 1983); *b* 5 April 1940; *Educ* Rugby, Trinity Coll Cambridge (MA, LLM); *Career* admitted slr 1966, ptnr Bircham & Co 1970-85, sr ptnr Speechly Bircham 1985-, jt ed Br Tax Review 1974-, memb Ed Bd Simon's Taxes 1977-, visiting prof LSE 1986-; pres Inst Taxation 1980-82; memb: Keith Ctee 1980-84, Cncl Inst of Fiscal Studies 1988-; chm Br Branch Int Fiscal Assoc 1989-, memb Bd Govrs Voluntary Hosp of St Bartholomew; Master Worshipful Co of Barbers 1985-86; memb Law Soc (Cncl 1986-90); *Books* Encyclopedia of VAT (1972), Tax Havens and Measures Against Tax Avoidance and Evasion in the EEC (1974); *Recreations* music particularly opera; *Clubs* Athenaeum; *Style*— John Avery Jones, Esq. CBE; 7 Cleveland Gardens, London W2 6HA (☎ 071 258 1960); Bouverie House, 154 Fleet St, London EC4A 2HX (☎ 071 353 3290 , fax 071 353 4825, telex 22655)

AVON, Countess of; Clarissa; only da of late Maj John Strange Spencer-Churchill, DSO (himself bro of Rt Hon Sir Winston Churchill, KG, OM, CH, TD, PC); *see also* Churchill, John GS; *b* 28 June 1920; *m* 1952, as his 2 w, 1 Earl of Avon, KG, MC, PC (d 1977); *Style*— The Rt Hon the Countess of Avon; 32 Bryanston Square, London W1

AVONSIDE, Rt Hon Lord; Ian Hamilton Shearer; PC (1962); s of Andrew Shearer, OBE, JP, of Dunfermline, and Jessie Macdonald; *b* 6 Nov 1914; *Educ* Dunfermline HS, Glasgow Univ (MA), Edinburgh Univ (LLB); *m* 1, 1942; 1 s, 1 da; m 2, 1954, Janet Sutherland Murray (*see Avonside, Lady*); *Career* served WWII, Maj RA; advocate 1938, QC (Scotland) 1952, sheriff Renfrew and Argyll 1960-62, Lord Advocate 1962-64, Scottish Lord of Session (Senator of the Coll of Justice in Scotland) 1964-84; memb Scottish Univs Ctee of the Privy Cncl 1971-; pres Stair Soc 1975-86; *Clubs* New (Edinburgh); *Style*— The Rt Hon Lord Avonside; The Mill House, Samuelston, E Lothian (☎ 062 082 2396)

AVONSIDE, Lady; Janet Sutherland Shearer; OBE (1956); da of William Murray (d 1932), of Paisley, and Janet Harley Watson; *b* 31 May 1917; *Educ* St Columba's Sch Kilmacolm, Erlenhaus Baden Baden, Univ of Edinburgh; *m* 1953, as his 2 w, Rt Hon Lord Avonside, *qv*; *Career* Parly candidate (C): Glasgow Maryhill 1950, Dundee E 1951, Leith 1955; lectr Dept of Educnl Studies Univ of Edinburgh 1957-69; Scottish govr BBC 1971-76; *Style*— Lady Avonside, OBE; The Mill Ho, Samuelston, E Lothian (☎ 062 082 2396)

AWDRY, Daniel Edmund; TD, DL (Wilts 1979); s of late Col Edmund Portman Awdry, MC, TD, DL, of Coters, Chippenham, Wilts, and Evelyn Daphne Alexandra, JP, *née* French; *b* 10 Sept 1924; *Educ* Winchester, Sandhurst; *m* 1950, Elizabeth, da of Mrs Joan Cattley, of London; 3 da; *Career* served WWII; admitted slr 1950; MP (C) Chippenham 1962-79; pps to: Min of State BOT 1963-64, Slr Gen 1973-74; dir: BET Omnibus Servs 1966-80, Sheepbridge Engrg 1968-79, Rediffusion 1973-79, Colonial Mutual Life Assur Soc 1974-89; *Style*— Daniel Awdry, Esq, TD, DL; Old Manor, Beanacre, nr Melksham, Wilts (☎ 0225 2315)

AWDRY, Henry Godwin; s of Charles Selwyn Awdry, DSO (ka 1918), and Constance Lilias, *née* Bateson (d 1946); *b* 14 Feb 1911; *Educ* Winchester, New Coll Oxford (BA); *m* 5 May 1947, Philippa Joyce, da of Sqdn Ldr Clifford Evans Holman (d 1954); 2 s (Godwin Antony b 1948, Robert Henry b 1951); *Career* 2 Lt Royal Wilts Yeo TA 1934, ret as Maj 1947; admitted slr 1936; ptnr Awdry Bailey & Douglas (ret 1990); govr Dauntsy Sch Fndn 1972-82 (clerk to govrs 1952-72), cncllr Calne and Chippenham RDC 1948-53; memb Law Soc; *Style*— Henry Awdry, Esq; Bottle Farm, Bottlesford, Pewsey, Wilts (☎ 067 2851374) 33 St John St, Devizes, Wilts (☎ 0380 722311)

AWFORD, Ian Charles; s of Joseph Arthur Awford, of Lamorna, Uplyme Rd, Lyme Regis, Dorset, and Eva Rhoda, *née* McPherson; *b* 15 April 1941; *Educ* Wellingborough Sch, Univ of Sheffield (LLB); *m* 1, 24 July 1965 (m dis 1983), Claire Sylvia, da of Ralph Linklater, of 38 Danson Rd, Bexleyheath Kent; 3 s (James b 16 Nov 1967, Giles b 13 Jan 1969, Guy b 27 Sept 1970); m 2, 2 Sept 1989, Leonora Maureen, da of the late Robert James Wilson, of Sydney NSW Aust; *Career* admitted slr 1967; ptnr with Barlow, Lyde & Gilbert 1973-, admitted slr Hong Kong 1988; memb: Int Inst of Space Law of the Int Aeronautics Fedn, Br Space Soc, Int Soc of Air Safety Investigators, Shipping and Aviation Sub Ctee of the City of London Law Soc, Air Law Gp of the Royal Aeronautical Soc, Int American Bar Assoc; chm: Outer Space Ctee of the Int Bar Assoc 1985-90, Aerospace Law Ctee of the Asia Pacific Lawyers Assoc 1987-90, Aerospace Law Ctee of the Inter Pacific Bar Assoc 1990-, Inter Pacific Aerospace Law Assoc 1990-, Conf Ctee Asia Pacific Insurance Conf 1991-; FRAeS 1987; *Books* Developments in Aviation Products Liability (1985), author of various pubns on outer space and aviation legal issues; *Recreations* golf, swimming, art, music, theatre; *Style*— Ian Awford, Esq; 6 Keepier Wharf, 12 Narrow Street, Limehouse, London E14 8DH (☎ 071 790 1694); Barlow Lyde & Gilbert, Beaufort House, 15 St Botolph St, London EC3A 7NJ (☎ 071 247 2277, fax 071 782 8505, telex 913281)

AXFORD, Col Arthur; OBE (1964, MBE 1958), TD (1964), DL (1977); s of Wilfred Axford (d 1981), and Annis, *née* Kershaw (d 1978); *b* 10 Aug 1921; *Educ* Ashton-under-Lyne GS; *m* 20 Nov 1941, Flora Isobel, da of Henry Hampson (d 1962); 2 s (Barry b 1943, Tony b 1948), 1 da (Lynn (Mrs Hayles) b 1954); *Career* RAOC 1939-42, 2 Lt to Capt The Manchester Regt 1942-50, Royal Ulster Rifles 1950-52, Lt-Col Manchester Regt TA 1952-64, dep CO 127 Inf Bde TA 1964-70, Brig 1967, Cmdt East Lancs ACF 1970; ADC to HM The Queen 1965-70; pres Gtr Manchester Spastics Soc; vice pres: Gtr Manchester SSAFA, Inst of Quality Assur; High Sheriff Gtr Manchester 1987; FIPA 1952; *Recreations* golf; *Clubs* Ashton-under-Lyne Golf, Oldham Golf, English Golf Union; *Style*— Col Arthur Axford, OBE, TD, DL; 1 Gorsey Lane, Ashton-under-Lyne, Lancs OL6 9AU (☎ 061 330 4972)

AXFORD, Dr David Norman; s of Norman Axford (d 1961), and Joy Alicia (d 1970); *b* 14 June 1934; *Educ* Merchant Taylors, Plymouth Coll, St Johns Coll Cambridge (BA, MA, PhD), Univ of Southampton (MSc); *m* 1, 26 March 1962 (m dis 1979), Elizabeth Anne Moynihan, da of Ralph J Stiles (d 1973); 1 s (John b 1968), 2 da (Katy b 1964, Sophie b 1966); m 2, 8 May 1980, Diana Rosemary Joan, da of Leslie George Bufton (d 1970); 3 step s (Simon b 1959, Timothy b 1961, Jeremy b 1963), 1 step da (Nicola b 1968); *Career* Nat Serv RAF 1958-60, PO 1958, Flying Offr 1959; Meteorological Office: forecasting and res 1960-68, meteorological res flight and radiosondes 1968-76, asst dir operational instrumentation 1976-80, asst dir telecommunications 1980-82, dep dir observational servs (grade 5) 1982-84, dir of servs and dep to DG of Meteorological Office (under sec grade 3) 1984-89; pres N Atlantic Observing Stations bd 1983-86, chm Ctee of Operational Systems Evaluation 1986-89, vice pres RMS 1989- (memb Cncl and hon gen sec 1983-88) dep sec gen World Meteorological Orgn 1989-; L G Groves Memorial Prize for Meteorology 1970; CEng 1975, FIEE 1982; *Recreations* swimming, reading, good food and wine, garden, music; *Style*— Dr David Axford; En Chenaud, 1183 Bursias, Vaud, Switzerland (☎ 021 824 1009)

AXFORD, Graham David; s of Frederick Axford (d 1982), of Ringwood, Hants, and Hilda Ethel, *née* Sleath (d 1987); *b* 20 June 1925; *Educ* Saltley GS Birmingham, Wyggeston Sch for Boys Leicester; *m* 14 July 1951, Audrey Diane, da of Leonard Bennett; 2 da (Deborah Susan (Mrs Millington) b 24 Jan 1959, Jakki Tracey b 24 April 1961); *Career* Evan H Axford Ltd (family business) 1971-; sports administrator; Cncl Badminton Assoc of England: memb 1976-, dep chm 1983-84, chm 1984-, vice pres 1987-; memb: Warwicks Co Badminton Assoc 1955-, Cncl Int Badminton Fedn 1987-89, W Midland Cncl for Sport and Recreation 1969- (vice chm 1990-); fndr memb Fedn of Sport and Recreational Orgns W Midlands 1965- (chm 1987-); chm: Birmingham Sports Advsy Cncl 1985-, Br Badminton Olympic Ctee 1990-; former club cricket and badminton player; *Recreations* enthusiastic high-handicap golfer, sport generally; *Style*— Graham Axford, Esq; 200 Dog Kennel Lane, Shirley, Solihull, West Midlands B90 4JG (☎ 021 744 3670)

AXTON, Henry Stuart (Harry); s of Wilfrid George Axton, and Mary Louise Laver; *b* 6 May 1923; *Educ* Rock Ferry, Sandhurst; *m* 1947, Constance Mary, da of Lycurgus Godefroy; 1 da; *Career* served WWII N Africa and N W Europe, Royal Tank Regt and Fife and Forfar Yeomanry (wounded 3 times); chm: Brixton Estate plc 1983- (md 1964-83, dep chm 1971-83), Invstmt Cos in Australia and Switzerland, Nuffield Hosp 1976-, St George's Hosp Med Sch 1977-, Chichester Festivities 1989-; dep chm Audit Cmmn 1987-91, dir Cathedral Works Orgn (Chichester) Ltd 1985-, pres Br Property Fedn 1984-86, memb The Archbishop's Cncl Fund 1990; FCA; *Recreations* music, sailing (yacht Alpha IV); *Clubs* Royal Thames Yacht, Royal Ocean Racing; *Style*— Harry Axton, Esq; Hook Place, Aldingbourne, nr Chichester (☎ 0243 542 291); Brixton Estate plc, 22-24 Ely Place, London EC1N 6TQ (☎ 071 242 6898)

AXWORTHY, Geoffrey John; s of William Henry Axworthy (d 1980), and Gladys Elizabeth, *née* Kingcombe (d 1953); *b* 10 Aug 1923; *Educ* Sutton HS Plymouth, Exeter Coll Oxford (MA); *m* 1, 21 Aug 1951, Irene (d 1975); 2 s (Timothy John b 1958, Nigel Peter b 1961), 1 da (Carole Alison b 1954); m 2, Caroline Ann, da of Dr Theodore Griffiths, of Risca, Gwent; 1 s (Christopher Henry b 1986), 1 da (Eliza Jane b 1984); *Career* WWII RAFVR 1942-47; tutor Oxford Delegacy for Extra Mural Studies 1950-51; lectr Coll Arts and Sci Baghdad 1951-56; dir of drama Univ Coll Ibadan Nigeria 1960-67 (lectr 1956-60, fndr dir Univ Sch of Drama and Travelling Theatre), Central Sch Speech and Drama London 1967-70, dir drama Univ Coll Cardiff 1970-88, artistic dir Univ Sherman Theatre 1970-88, dir Sherman Theatre Ltd 1988-; *Recreations* travel; *Style*— Geoffrey Axworthy, Esq; 22 The Walk, West Grove, Cardiff CF2 3AF (☎ 0222 490 696)

AYCKBOURN, Alan; CBE (1987); s of Horace Ayckbourn, and Irene Maude, *née* Worley; *b* 12 April 1939; *Educ* Haileybury; *m* 1959, Christine Helen, *née* Roland; 2 s (Steven, Philip); *Career* playwright, theatre director; artistic dir Stephen Joseph Theatre in the Round Scarborough; *plays incl*: Relatively Speaking (1965), How the Other Half Loves (1969), Time and Time Again (1971), Absurd Person Singular (1972), The Norman Conquests (1973), Absent Friends (1974), Bedroom Farce (1975), Just Between Ourselves (1976), Taking Steps (1979), Seasons Greetings (1980), Way Upstream (1981), Intimate Exchanges (1982), A Chorus of Disapproval (1984), Woman in Mind (1985), A Small Family Business (1987), Henceforward (1987), Man of The Moment (1988), Mr A's Amazing Maze Plays (1988), The Revengers' Comedies (1989), Invisible Friends (1989), Body Language (1990), This Is Where We Came In (1990), Callisto 5 (1990); *Clubs* Garrick; *Style*— Alan Ayckbourn, Esq, CBE; c/o Margaret Ramsay Ltd, 14a Goodwin's Court, St Martin's Lane, London WC2N 4LL (☎ 071 240 0691)

AYKROYD, Sir Cecil William; 2 Bt (UK 1929), of Birstwith Hall, Harrogate, Co York; s of Sir Frederic Alfred Aykroyd, 1 Bt (d 1949), and Lily May (d 1964), da of Sir James Roberts, 1 Bt (d 1935); *b* 23 April 1905; *Educ* Charterhouse, Jesus Coll Cambridge (BA); *Heir* nephew, James Alexander Frederic Aykroyd, *qv*; *Career* dir National Provincial Bank 1958-69; *Style*— Sir Cecil Aykroyd, Bt; Birstwith Hall, nr Harrogate, N Yorks (☎ 0423 770250)

AYKROYD, David Peter; s of Lt-Col George Hammond Aykroyd (d 1972), of The Priory, Nun Monkton, York, and Margaret Roberts Aykroyd (d 1981); *b* 6 June 1937; *Educ* Eton; *m* 30 Oct 1958, (Lydia) Huldine, da of Richard Piggott Beamish, of Castle Lyons, Co Cork, Ireland; 1 s (Nicholas William b 1962, d 1989), 3 da (Amanda Huldine b 1960, Emily Sorrell b 1970, Matilda Rose b 1978); *Career* Nat Serv 2 Lt Coldstream Gds; *Recreations* racing, shooting; *Style*— David Aykroyd, Esq; The Priory, Nun Monkton, York YO5 8ES (☎ 0423 330 334, office 0423 330 131, fax 0423 331 124, car 0836 612 199, telex 57445 YEW G); 6 William Mews, London SW1

AYKROYD, James Alexander Frederic; s of Bertram Aykroyd (d 1983), and his 1 w Margot, *née* Brown; nephew and hp of Sir Cecil William Aykroyd, 2 Bt; *b* 6 Sept 1943; *Educ* Eton, Univ of Aix en Provence, Univ of Madrid; *m* 1973, Jennifer, da of late Frederick William Marshall, MB, BS, DA (Eng), of 3 Penylan Avenue, Porthcawl, Glam; 2 da (Gemma Jane b 1976, Victoria Louise b 1977); *Style*— James Aykroyd, Esq; 5 Highbury Terrace, London N5 1UP

AYKROYD, Michael David; s of late George Hammond Aykroyd, TD, s of Sir William Henry Aykroyd, 1 Bt; hp of cous, Sir William Aykroyd, 3 Bt, MC; *b* 14 June 1928; *m* 1952, Oenone Gillian Diana, da of Donald George Cowling, MBE, of Leeds; 1 s, 3 da; *Style*— Michael Aykroyd, Esq; The Homestead, Killinghall, Harrogate, Yorks

AYKROYD, Lady Sylvia; *née* Walker; da of late Francis Walker, of Huddersfield; *m* 1, Lt-Col Foster Newton Thorne; m 2, 1919, Sir Alfred Hammond Aykroyd, 2 Bt (d 1965); 1 s (and 1 da decd); *Style*— Lady Aykroyd; Marley House, Winfrith Newburgh, Dorchester, Devon

AYKROYD, Sir William Miles; 3 Bt (UK 1920), of Lightcliffe, W Riding, Co of York, MC (1944); s of Sir Alfred Hammond Aykroyd, 2 Bt (d 1965); *b* 24 Aug 1923; *Career* Lt 5 Royal Inniskilling Dragoon Gds 1943-47; dir Hardy Amies 1950-69; *Style*— Sir William Aykroyd, Bt, MC; Buckland Newton Place, Dorchester, Dorset (☎ 030 05 259)

AYLEN, Rear Adm Ian Gerald; CB (1962), OBE (1946), DSC (1942); s of Paymaster Cmdr Alfred Ernest Aylen, RN (d 1946), of Northam, N Devon, and S C M Aylen; *b* 12 Oct 1910; *Educ* Blundells, RNEC Keyham, RNC Greenwich; *m* 1937, Alice Brough, da of Brough Maltby (d 1952), of Westward Hse, N Devon; 1 s, 2 da; *Career* HMS Galatea 1939-41, HMS Kelvin 1942-43, 30 Assault Unit 1944-45, CO RN Engrg Coll 1958-60, Rear Adm 1960, Adm Supt HM Dockyard Rosyth 1960-63; dep sec IMechE 1963-65, asst sec Cncl of Engrg Insts 1965-70, ret 1971; *Style*— Rear Adm Ian Aylen, CB, OBE, DSC; Tracey Mill Barn, Honiton, Devon EX14 8SL

AYLEN, Leo William; s of The Rt Rev Bishop Charles Aylen (d 1972), and Elisabeth *née* Hills (d 1975); *Educ* New Coll Oxford (MA), Univ of Bristol (PhD); *m* Annette Elizabeth, da of Jack Scott Battams (d 1982); *Career* 1riter, actor, director; poetry incl: I, Odyseus (1971), Sunflower (1976), Return to Zululand (1980), Red Alert: this is god warning (1981), Jumping-Shoes (1983); for children: The Apples of Youth (opera 1980), Rhymoceros (poems 1989); contrib to anthologies incl: The Sun Dancing, What Makes Your Toenails Twinkle, Toughie Toffee, High Spirits, Cat's Eyes, Tiger's Eyes, Open the Door; other pubns incl: Greek Tragedy and the Modern World (1964), Greece for Everyone (1976), The Greek Theatre (1985); writer/director films for TV incl: 1065 and All that, Dynamo: a life of Michael Faraday, Who'll Buy a Bubble, Celluloid Love, Steel be my Sister, Six Bites of the Cherry (series); The Drinking Party (nominated for BAFTA award), The Death of Socrates, Soul of a Nation (documentary); radio plays and features incl: The Birds, An Unconquered God, Le Far West; theatre works incl: Down the Arches (lyrics), No Trams to Lime Street (adaption of Alun Owen's play), Antigone (dir of own trans); subject of 3 CBS programmes devoted to his work as poet/ actor; formerly: Hooker Distinguished visiting prof McMaster Univ Ontario, poet in residence Farleigh Dickinson Univ New Jersey; awarded C Day Lewis Fellowship; memb: Poetry Soc of America, Poetry Soc of GB, Writer's Guild of GB, Writer's Guild of America, ACTT, Br Actors' Equity, BAFTA, Int PEN; *Recreations* church organ playing, distance running, mountains; *Clubs* BAFTA; *Style*— Leo Aylen, Esq; 13 St Saviour's Road, London SW2 5HP (☎ 081 674 5949)

AYLESFORD, 11 Earl of (GB 1714); Charles Ian Finch-Knightley; JP (Warwicks 1948); also Baron Guernsey (GB 1702); s of 10 Earl of Aylesford (d 1958); *b* 2 Nov 1918; *Educ* Oundle; *m* 1946, Margaret Rosemary (d 1989), da of Maj Austin Tyer, MVO, TD; 1 s, 2 da; *Heir* s, Lord Guernsey; *Career* served WWII Capt Black Watch; Vice-Lt Warwicks 1964-74, Lord-Lt W Midlands 1974-; former regnl dir Lloyds Bank Birmingham & W Midlands Bd (resigned 1989); memb Water Space Amenity Cmmn 1973-; patron Warwicks Boy Scouts Assoc 1974-; pres: Warwicks CC 1980-, TAVRA 1982; Hon LLD Birmingham 1989; KStJ 1974; *Recreations* shooting, fishing, archery, nature conservation, preservation of wildlife; *Clubs* Fly Fishers; *Style*— The Rt Hon the Earl of Aylesford, JP; Packington Old Hall, Coventry, W Midlands CV7 7HG (☎ 0676 23273, office 0676 22585)

AYLESTONE, Baron (Life Peer UK 1967); Herbert William Bowden; CH (1975), CBE (1953), PC (1962); s of Herbert Henwood Bowden, of Cardiff, and Henrietta, *née* Gould; *b* 20 Jan 1905; *m* 1928, Louisa Grace, da of William Brown, of Cardiff; 1 da; *Career* WWII RAF; MP (Lab): Leicester S 1945-50, SW Div of Leics 1950-67; chief oppn whip 1955-64, lord pres of the cncl ldr of the House of Commons 1964-66, Sec of State for Cwlth Affairs 1966-67, SDP ldr in House of Lords 1981-82, dep speaker Hse of Lords 1983-; chm IBA 1967-75; Gold Medal of Royal TV Soc 1975; *Style*— The Rt Hon the Lord Aylestone, CH, CBE, PC; House of Lords, London SW1

AYLIFFE, Prof Graham Arthur John; s of Arthur Ayliffe (d 1930), of Hambrook, Glos and Winifred Lily, *née* Hart (d 1984); *b* 2 March 1926; *Educ* Queen Elizabeth Hosp Sch Bristol, Univ of Bristol (BSc, MB ChB, MD); *m* 14 Sept 1963, Janet Esther, da of Edwin Alfred Lloyd (d 1977), of Clophill, Beds; 1 s (Richard b 1966), 1 da (Margaret b 1968); *Career* memb scientific staff MRC Industl Injuries and Burns Unit 1964-81, pres Infection Control Nurses Assoc 1976-79, chm Hosp Infection Soc 1979-84, hon dir Hosp Infection Res Laboratory Birmingham 1980- (hon conslt 1964-81), prof of med microbiology Univ of Birmingham 1981-, dir WHO Collaborating Centre In Hosp Infection 1981-, WHO conslt in bacterial diseases, member EEC Ctee On Intensive Care Infection 1986-, chm DHSS Microbiology Advsy Ctee 1986-89; pres: Sterile Servs Mgmt Inst 1988-, Hosp Infection Soc 1988-; chm Int Fedn Infection Control 1990-; FRCPath; *Books* Principles and Practice of Disinfection, Preservation and Sterilisation (co-ed 1981), Drug Resistance in Antimicrobial Therapy (jtly, 1975), Control of Hospital Infection, A Practical Handbook (co-ed, 1981), Hospital Acquired Infection, Principles and Practice (jtly, 1990), Chemical Disinfection in Hospital (jtly, 1984); *Recreations* fencing, fly fishing; *Style*— Prof Graham Ayliffe; 50 Halesowen Rd, Halesowen, West Midlands B62 9BA (☎ 021 422 4233); Hospital Infection Research Laboratory, Dudley Rd Hospital, Birmingham B18 7QH (☎ 021 554 3801 ext 4822, fax 021 551 5562)

AYLING, Air Vice-Marshal Richard Cecil; CB (1965), CBE (1961, OBE 1948); s of Albert Cecil Ayling, LDS (d 1939), of Norwood, London; *b* 7 June 1916; *Educ* Dulwich; *m* 1, 1941, Patricia Doreen (d 1966), da of Karl Wright, of Norbury, Surrey; 1 s, 1 da; m 2, 1971, Virginia, 2 da of Col Frank Davis, of Northwood, Middx; 2 da; *Career* served RNZAF 1940-43, Bomber Cmd RAF 1943-45, Staff Coll 1945, Air Miny (dep dir Policy Air Staff) 1951-54, Station Cdr Bomber Cmd 1954-58, ACDS MOD 1958-59, dir of Orgn Air Miny 1960-61, SASO Flying Trg Cmd 1962-65, MOD 1965-66, AOA RAF Air Support Cmd 1966-69, ret; adjudicator Immigration Appeals 1970-1988; *Recreations* skiing, gardening, sailing; *Clubs* Royal Lymington Yacht; *Style*— Air Vice-Marshal Richard Ayling, CB, CBE; Buckler's Spring, Buckler's Hard, Beaulieu, Brockenhurst, Hants SO42 7XA (☎ 0590 616 204)

AYLMER, Dr Gerald Edward; s of late Capt E A Aylmer, RN, and Mrs G P Aylmer, *née* Evans; *b* 30 April 1926; *Educ* Winchester, Balliol Coll Oxford (MA, DPhil); *m* 1955, Ursula Nixon; 1 s, 1 da; *Career* historian; prof of history and head of dept Univ of York 1963-78, master St Peter's Coll Oxford 1978-91; pres Royal Hist Soc 1984-88 (hon vice pres 1988-); chm: Royal Cmmn on Hist Manuscripts, Editorial Bd History of Parl Tst; FBA; *Style*— Dr Gerald Aylmer; Canal House, St Peter's College, Oxford OX1 2DL (☎ 0865 278 862/278 856/240 554)

AYLMER, Hon (Anthony) Julian; only s, and h of 13 Baron Aylmer; *b* 10 Dec 1951; *Educ* Westminster, Trinity Hall Cambridge; *m* 5 May 1990, Belinda Rosemary, o da of Maj Peter Parker (gs of 6 Earl of Macclesfield), of The Hays, Ramsden, Oxford; *Career* solicitor 1976-; *Style*— The Hon Julian Aylmer; 16 Edgarley Terrace, London SW6 6QF

AYLMER, 13 Baron (I 1718); Sir Michael Anthony Aylmer; 16 Bt (I 1662); s of Christopher Aylmer (d 1955), and his 1 w, Marjorie Marianne Ellison, *née* Barber; suc 2 cous, 12 Baron Aylmer, 1982; *b* 27 March 1923; *Educ* privately, Trinity Hall Cambridge (MA, LLM); *m* 1950, Contessa Maddalena Sofia Maria Gabriella Cecilia Stefania Francesca, da of Count Arbeno Maria Attems di Santa Croce (d 1968), of Aiello del Friuli, and Sofie, eldest da of Prince Maximilian Karl Friedrich zu Löwenstein-Wertheim-Freudenberg; 1 s, 1 da; *Heir* s, Hon Julian Aylmer; *Career* slr 1948; Legal Dept Equity & Law Life Assurance Society 1951-1983; *Recreations* reading, music; *Style*— The Rt Hon The Lord Aylmer; 42 Brampton Grove, London NW4 4AQ (☎ 081 202 8300)

AYLMER, Sir Richard John; 16 Bt (I 1622), of Donadea, Co Kildare; s and h of Sir Fenton Aylmer, 15 Bt (d 1987); *b* 23 April 1937; *m* 16 June 1962, Lise, da of Paul Emile Demers, of Montreal, Canada; 1 s (Fenton Paul), 1 da (Geneviève b 16 March 1963); *Heir* s, Fenton Paul Aylmer b 31 Oct 1965; *Style*— Sir Richard Aylmer, Bt; 3573 Lorne Ave, Montreal, Quebec H2X 2A4, Canada

AYLOTT, David Howard Frederick; s of David Henry Aylott (d 1969), and Anita Maria Celeste, *née* Marchetti (d 1985); *b* 28 May 1914; *Educ* privately; *m* 17 April 1948, Zena Margarita; 1 s (Stuart b 15 Sept 1944), 1 da (Susan b 17 Oct 1949); *Career* RAF 1940-46 (fndr memb of a light entertainment unit producing shows for the serv personnel); various trainee positions in film business 1930-35, make up artist various film studios incl Korda 1935-40, joined MGM Studios Elstree 1946, co fndr (with bro Eric) Eylure Ltd 1947, freelance make-up artist INT Films 1949-60, left film indust to run Eylure Ltd full-time in 1960 (developed internationally successful cosmetic concept which won Queen's Award for Indust in first year), chm Eylure Ltd 1960-; FInstD 1964, FCIM 1989; *Recreations* flying light aircraft, motor cruisers; *Clubs* Oriental; *Style*— David Aylott, Esq; Old Hundred Barn, Tormarton, Avon GL9 1JA (☎ 0454 21211)

AYLOTT, Eric Victor; s of David Henry Aylott (d 1969), of 89 Harmer Green Lane, Welwyn, Herts, and Anita Maria Celeste, *née* Marchetti (d 1968); *b* 20 Oct 1917; *Educ* privately; *m* 30 May 1953, Kathleen, da of Edgar Obbott (d 1953), of Palmers Green; 2 da (Elizabeth, Geraldine); *Career* RAF 1940-46 served ME and Greece 1940-44; film ind make-up artist 1937-59, vice chm Eylure Ltd 1959-; TV appearances with bro David UK NZ and Aust incl: Film Stars of Yesterday, The Movie Greats; MInstD 1964, MInstM 1966; *Books* The Eylure Way of Make-Up (jtly, 1980); *Recreations* football, horse riding, flying (PPL), motor yachting; *Clubs* Oriental, St Pierre Country; *Style*— Eric Aylott, Esq; The Homestead, Raffin Green, Datchworth, Knebworth, Herts (☎ 0438 812297)

AYLOTT, Robert Alexander William; s of Rueben David Aylott (d 1978), of Hampshire, and Colleen Joy, *née* Horne; *b* 21 Dec 1948; *Educ* Charterhouse, Harrison Road Hampshire; *m* 24 Oct 1970, Heather Jean, da of Philip Foot; 1 s (James Alexander Robert b 17 Dec 1973), 1 da (Michelle Heather b 28 Oct 1976); *Career* photo-journalist; darkroom asst: Sport & General Photo Agency Fleet Street 1964-65, Fox Photos London 1966-67; press photographer: Keystone Press Agency Fleet Street 1967-69, Daily Sketch 1969-70, Daily Mail 1970-75; photographer National Enquirer USA 1975-78; proprietor Front Page Press (Newspaper and Publishers) Hampshire 1978-87, photographer Express Newspapers 1987-; winner various awards incl: News Photographer of the Year 1968, Nikon Picture of the Year 1972, World Press Photos Portrait Section 1977; work exhibited at: World Press Photgraphers of the Year 1969, ICA Gallery 1972, first Press Exhibition (Photographers' Gallery London) 1972, contrib various books incl: Photography Year Books 1973-89, Eye Witness and Headline Photography (by Harold Evans), Chronicles of the 20th Century, Slip-Up; fell Inst Inc Photographers 1973, FRPS 1973; *Publications* Cry for Tomorrow (novel, 1973); Local History Publications: Fareham Two Views (1981), Unofficial Guide to Fareham (1982), Isle of Wight Two Views (1982), Gosport Two Views (1982), The Story of Porchester Castle (1983); *Recreations* painting, writing, travel, gardening, art collecting, photographic history; *Clubs* Press; *Style*— Robert Aylott, Esq; Earls Charity, Titchfield, Hampshire PO14 4PD (☎ 0329 42301); Express Newspapers, Ludgate House, Blackfriars Rd, London SE1 (☎ 071 928 8000, car 0831 237030)

AYLWIN, John Morris; s of Waltar Edgar (d 1978), of Worcs, and Rosamund, *née* Byng-Morris; *b* 23 July 1942; *Educ* Uppingham, Emmanuel Coll Cambridge (MA), Guildford Coll of Law; *m* 4 July 1970, Angela, da of Conningsby Deryck Phillips; 2 s (Michael Deryck Morris b 22 April 1972, Christopher John b 16 May 1974); *Career* Richards Butler Solicitors: articled clerk 1965-67, asst slr 1967-72, ptnr 1972-, exec ptnr 1984-; Freeman City of London Slrs Co 1988; memb: Law Soc 1965, City of London Law Soc 1988; *Recreations* tennis, golf, rugby, gardening, theatre; *Clubs* Richmond FC, Dorking RFC; *Style*— J M Aylwin, Esq; Richards Butler, Beaufort House, 15 St Botolph St, London EC3A 7EE (☎ 071 245 6555, fax 071 247 5091)

AYLWIN, Capt (Charles) Kenneth Seymour; s of Claude Aylwin (d 1962), and Evelyn, *née* Brocklebank (d 1971); *b* 5 Nov 1911; *Educ* RNC Dartmouth, RNC Greenwich; *m* 15 July 1939, Islay, da of Maj Ernest Holland (d 1947); 3 s (David b 1940, Nicholas b 1944, Andrew b 1947); *Career* Midshipman 1929-31, Mediterranean and S America 1931, cmmnd Sub Lt, 1931-37 Home Fleet, East Indies, Gibraltar, HMS Excellent 1938, HMS Royal Sovereign 1939, HMS Codrington 1939-40, HMS Euryalus 1940-43, Mediterranean, HMS Valkyrie 1943-44, Staff Flag Offr Western Germany 1944-45, HMS Howe 1946-47, Cdr 1947, Intelligence Div Admty 1948-49, RAF Staff Coll Bracknell 1949, Admty Air and Tactical Divs 1950-51, HMS Liverpool 1952, CO HMS Loch Tralaig 1952, CO HMS Tenacious 1953, RN Air Station Brawdy 1954-55, Capt 1955, Naval Equipment Div Admty 1956, ret 1958; BAT Co Ltd 1958-73: personnel advsr BAT cos ME and Med, ret 1973; memb Wimbledon Borough Cncl 1960-63, hon steward Wimbledon Lawn Tennis Championships 1979-87; memb George Cross Island Assoc 1988; *Recreations* golf, bridge, gardening; *Clubs* Royal Wimbledon Golf, RNC of 1765-85; *Style*— Capt Kenneth Aylwin, RN; 12 Barham Rd, Wimbledon, London SW20 OET (☎ 081 946 6805)

AYRE, John Victor; s of Gp Capt John MacDonald Ayre, CBE (d 1980), and Mary Annie, *née* Hibberd; *b* 11 May 1942; *Educ* King Edward VII Sch Kings Lynn; *m* 18 June 1966, Jean Eva, da of Sqdn Ldr Arthur Frederick Plant, DFF; 1 s (Christopher John William b 12 Dec 1970), 1 da (Caroline Jean b 17 Jan 1968); *Career* CA; articled clerk Allen Baldry Holman & Best London 1959-64, Finnie Ross Welch & Co (now Finnie & Co) 1965-72, Buckley Hall Devin & Co Hull 1972-73; ptnr: Whinney Murray & Co (following merger with Buckley Hall Devin & Co) 1973-89, Ernst & Young (following merger with Whinney Murray & Co) 1989-; pres Humberside & Dist Soc of CA's; FCA 1965; *Clubs* Hull Golf; *Style*— John Ayre, Esq; 4 The Paddock, Swanland, East Yorkshire HU14 3QW; Ernst & Young, Lowgate House, Lowgate, Hull HU1 1JJ

AYRES, Andrew Charles; s of Harry Ayres, of Chinthurst Park, Shalford, Surrey, and Dorothy, *née* Boxall; *b* 13 Dec 1944; *Educ* Reed's Sch Cobham; *m* 28 Sept 1968, Philippa Jill, da of Dr Martin Bristow; 3 s (Christian Andrew Martin b 31 March 1973, Alexander Charles Harry b 25 Sept 1977, Douglas William Robert (twin) b 25 Sept 1977); *Career* articled clerk: Candler Stannard & Co 1962-67, Blake Cassels and Graydon Toronto Canada 1967-68; slr Norton Rose Botterell & Roche 1968-71, ptnr Norton Rose Slrs 1971-; hon legal advsr Surrey Archaeological Soc, hon sec Mr Goschen's Hound's Point to Point; Freeman City of London, Liveryman Worshipful Co Slrs; memb: Law Soc, Baltic Exchange; *Recreations* hunting, steeplechasing, golf, vintage cars; *Clubs* City Univ, W Surrey Golf; *Style*— Andrew Ayres, Esq; Oakhill, Enton Green, Godalming, Surrey; Kempson House, Camomile St, London EC3 (☎ 071 283 2434, fax 071 588 1181, telex 883652)

AYRES, Gillian; OBE (1986); da of Stephen Ayres (d 1969), of Barnes, London, and Florence Olive, *née* Beresford Brown (d 1968); *b* 3 Feb 1930; *Educ* St Paul's Girls' Sch, Camberwell Sch of Art; *m* (m dis); 2 s (James, Sam); *Career* artist; Corham 1959-65, St Martin's 1966-78; head BA Painting Dept Winchester Sch of Art 1978-81; one-woman exhibitions 1956-: Knoedler Gallery London 1966-88, retrospective

Serpentine Gallery 1983, Knoedler Gallery NY 1985, Fischer Fine Art 1990; works in public collections: Tate Gallery, Museum of Modern Art NY; ARA; *Style*— Miss Gillian Ayres, OBE; Tall Trees, Gooseham, nr Bude, Cornwall

AYRES, Dr Jonathan Geoffrey; s of Geoffrey Walter Ayres, and Brenda Ruby, *née* Turpin; *b* 14 Feb 1950; *Educ* Woodhouse GS Finchley, Guys Hosp (BSc, MB BS, MD); *m* 26 July 1980, Susan Marian Ayres, da of Gerald St George Wheeley; 1 s (Peter Michael b 23 June 1987), 1 da (Katherine Louise b 25 Aug 1982); *Career* Guys Hosp: house offr 1974-75, sr house offr 1976-78, res registrar 1979-81, registrar 1978-79 and 1981-82; sr house offr Brompton Hosp 1977-78, sr registrar E Birmingham Hosp 1982-84, conslt physician in respiratory and gen med E Birmingham Hosp and Solihull Hosp, hon sr lectr Univ of Birmingham 1984-; author of numerous scientific pubns; memb: Cncl Br Thoracic Soc (memb PR Ctee, sec Epidemiology Section), Midland Thoracic Soc and W Midlands Physicians Assoc, American Thoracic Soc 1986, Int Epidemiology Assoc 1986; *Recreations* sketching in pencil and watercolors; *Style*— Dr Jonathan Ayres; Dept of Respiratory Medicine, East Birmingham Hosp, Birmingham B9 5ST (☎ 021 766 6611 ext 4475)

AYRES, Pam (Mrs Dudley Russell); da of Stanley William Ayres, (d 1981), Stanford-in-the-Vale, Oxon, and Phyllis Evelyn, *née* Loder; *b* 14 March 1947; *Educ* Faringdon Secdy Modern Sch; *m* 1982, Dudley Russell, s of late Joe Russell; 2 s (William Stanley b 12 Dec 1982, James Joseph b 20 July 1984); *Career* writer and entertainer 1974-; *Style*— Ms Pam Ayres; Dudley Russell, Layston Productions, The Spendlove Centre, Charlbury, Oxon OX7 3PQ (☎ 0608 811311, fax 0608 810116)

AYRES, Rosalind Mary (Mrs Martin Jarvis); da of Sam Johnson (d 1986), of Westbury, Wilts, and Daisy, *née* Hydon (d 1987); *b* 7 Dec 1946; *Educ* George Dixon GS for Girls Birmingham, Loughborough Coll of Educn (Dip Educn); *m* 23 Nov 1974, Martin John Jarvis, s of Denys Jarvis, of Sanderstead, Surrey; *Career* actress; TV: The Mill, The House of Bernarda Alba, Juliet Bravo, The Bounder, Father's Day, Hindle Wakes; Radio: A Room With A View, The Circle, Alphabetical Order; Theatre: Hamlet, The Three Sisters, Uncle Vanya, The Perfect Party (Greenwich Theatre), Dracula (Shaftesubry Theatre), I Claudius (Queens's Theatre), A Dolls House (Thorndike Theatre), Exchange (Vandeville Theatre); Films: The Lovers, Tales from Beyond the Grave, Mr Smith, Cry Wolf, That'll be the Day, Stardust, The Slipper and the Rose; memb: RSC, Stars Organisation for Spastics; *Recreations* interior design, illustration; *Style*— Ms Rosalind Ayres; c/o Michael Whitehall Ltd, 125 Gloucester Rd, London SW7 4TE (☎ 071 244 8466)

AYRTON, Norman Walter; *b* 25 Sept 1924; *Career* WWII serv with RNVR; trained Old Vic Sch 1947-48, memb Old Vic Co 1949 and 1951, memb Staff Old Vic Sch 1949-51, princ LAMDA 1966-72 (asst princ 1954-66), guest dir Aust Cncl for the Arts 1973-74, Australian Opera 1976, 1981 and 1983, memb Faculty of Juillard Sch NY 1974-85, Vancouver Opera 1976-83, dir of opera RAM 1986-90, dean Br American Drama Acad 1986-; Hon RAM 1989; *Recreations* music, travel, gardens; *Style*— Norman Ayrton, Esq; 40A Birchington Rd, W Hampstead, London NW6 4LJ (☎ 071 328 6056); The British American Drama Academy, Cecil Sharpe House, 2 Regents Park Rd, London NW1 4NS (☎ 071 267 4428)

AYTON, Sylvia; da of Donald Ayton, of 49 Brockham Drive, Ilford, Essex, and Florence Mabel, *née* Sabine; *b* 27 Nov 1937; *Educ* Walthamstow Sch of Art (NDD), RCA Fashion Sch (Des RCA); *Career* freelance designer 1959-64; work incl: BEA Air Hostess Uniform autumn ranges for NY USA, collaboration with Doris Langley Moore at Costume Museum Bath, ptnr with Zandra Rhodes (opened Fulham Rd boutique backed by Vanessa Redgrave 1964), outerwear designer Wallis Fashion Gp 1969; lectr Fashion design: Kingston Poly, Ravenstone Coll, Middlesex Poly, Newcastle Poly 1961-; external assessor Fashion and Textile course (BA Hons) 1976-, memb jury RSA Bursary Comp 1982; memb CNAA 1979, FRSA 1987; *Style*— Ms Sylvia Ayton; 28 Eburne Road, London N7 6AU (☎ 071 263 6806); Wallis Fashion Gp Ltd, Garrick Int Centre Garrick Road, Hendon, London NW9 6AQ (☎ 081 202 8252, telex 924895)

AZIZ, Khalid; s of Ahmad Aziz (d 1978), of London, and Sheila Frances, *née* Light; *b* 9 Aug 1953; *Educ* Westminster City Sch, Aitcheson Coll Lahore; *m* 27 March 1974 (m dis), Barbara Elizabeth, da of Harry Etchells, of Sherburn-in-Elmet, Yorks; 2 da (Nadira b 1977, Fleur b 1981); *Career* broadcaster, journalist and dir; prodr presenter: BBC Radio and TV 1970-81, TV South 1981-; presenter: On Course (C4) 1988-89, The Small Business Prog (BBC2/C4) 1990, Starnet Business Programme 1990; TV Journalist of the Year 1987-88; chm Independent Mobility Project, tstee Winchester Med Tst; author: 9 books principally on indian cooking; chm Royal Jubilee and Prince's Tst (Hants), S Counties Bd Prince's Youth Business Tst; vice pres Pestalozzi Int Children's Village; memb Cncl VSO; *Books* The Barclays Guide to Small Business Computing (1990); *Recreations* aviation, fishing, shooting, computers; *Style*— Khalid Aziz, Esq; West Stratton, Winchester, Hants (☎ 0962 89 673)

AZIZ, Suhail Ibne; s of Azizur Rahnan (d 1971), of Bangladesh, and Lutfunnessa Khatoon; *b* 3 Oct 1937; *Educ* RNC Dartmouth, London Univ (MSc Econ); *m* 1960, Elizabeth Ann, da of Alfred Pyne, of Dartmouth; 2 da (Lisa, Rebecca); *Career* served Pakistan Navy 1954-61; personnel mangr Lever Bros Pakistan Ltd 1963-66, served as RAF offr in Br CS 1966-70, indust rels offr London 1970-73, labour rels exec Ford Motor Co UK 1973-74, personnel offr Pedigree Petfoods 1974-78, dir of gen servs divs Cmmn for Racial Equality 1978-81, pa Int Mgmnt Consits 1981-83; head econ and employment div and dep dir London Borough of Lewisham 1984-89, mgmnt conslt Fullemploy Consultancy 1989-, exec memb Nottingham Community Relations Cncl 1975-78; memb: Race Rels Bd Conciliation Ctee 1971-74, Gulbenkian Fndn 1976-82, Home Sec's Standing Advsy Cncl 1977-78, Dept of Employment Min's Employment Advsy Gp 1977-78, Advsy Ctee BBC 1977-82, Employers Panel Industl Tribunals 1978-, Cncl Inst of Mgmnt Consits, Bd of Tstees Brixton Neighbourhood Community Assoc 1979-82; chm Third World Specialist Gp Inst of Mgmnt Consits 1984-, fndr chm E London Bangladeshi Enterprise Agency 1985, advsr Minority Business Devpt Unit City of London Poly 1986; CRE Bursary to USA to study minority econ devpt initiatives 1986, led preparation of Bangladeshi community response to House of Commons Select Ctee report "Bangladeshi in Britain" and assisted organisations in the preparation of implementation plans 1986-, memb QMC London Univ Res Advsy Ctee 1988-; FBIM, MIMC; *Recreations* travel, reading political economy; *Clubs* Sudan (Khartoum), RAF; *Style*— Suhail Aziz, Esq; 126 St Julian's Farm Rd, West Norwood, London SE27 0RR

B

BAART, Leonard William; s of Lein Wilhelmus Baart (d 1973), of S Africa, and Florence Emily, *née* Gilchrist (d 1967); *b* 5 April 1927; *Educ* Kimberley Boys HS, Witwatersrand Univ (BArch); *m* 21 March 1953, Diana Ingrid, da of Richard John Southwell Crowe (d 1980), of Avon; 1 s (John b 1960), 3 da (Veronica b 1954, Fiona b 1956, Angela b 1958); *Career* chartered architect in private practice, cmmnd Architect to English Heritage 1986-89, conslt Architect to English Heritage for Re-Survey of Listed Buildings 1984-87; FRIA, FCIArb, Fellow Worshipful Co of Arbitrators (1985), Freeman City of London (1984); *Recreations* painting (water-colour), golf, squash, tennis, choir singing; *Clubs* Salop (Shrewsbury), Royal Cwlth London, Bulawayo Zimbabwe; *Style—* Leonard W Baart, Esq; Cobden House, Hanwood, nr Shrewsbury (☎ 0743 860322); Bowdler's House, Town Walls, Shrewsbury (☎ 0743 61261/2)

BABBAR, (Rajindar) Paul; s of Arjan Das (d 1933), and Harbhajan Arora; *b* 1930,Amritsar, India; *Educ* MA (Psychology), MA (Economics), LLB; *m* 4 Nov 1956, Kamini, da of Gurdit Singh (d 1983); 1 s (Hemant b 1958), 3 da (Jyotsna b 1961, Monica b 1972, Renuka (twin) b 1972); *Career* practising as Paul Babbar & Co, CAs; vice-chm Hillingdon Community Relations Cncl 1978-81; treas Ruislip Residents Assoc 1979-82; exec memb: Hillingdon Community Relations Cncl 1976-78 and 1982-, Ealing Community Relations Cncl 1984-86; fndr memb (sometime sec and treas) Hillingdon-Amritsar Town Twinning Assoc 1981-89, exec memb Hillingdon Town Twinning Assoc 1978-83, treas Southall Chamber of Commerce 1983-85 (exec memb 1985-); memb Ealing Community Police Liaison Ctee, tstee Southall Info Technol Centre, govr Southall Coll, lay visitor (Ealing, Acton, Southall); FICA; *Recreations* travelling, reading, music, community work; *Clubs* Ruislip-Northwood Rotary; *Style—* Paul Babbar, Esq; The Manor House, The Green, Southall, Middlesex UB2 4BJ (☎ 081 843 1180)

BABBS, Frederick William; s of Fred Albert Babbs, and Agnes, *née* Nickell; *b* 25 July 1929; *Educ* Watford Tech Coll (ONC, HNC), De Haviland Aeronautical Tech Coll; *m* Shirley Ann, da of Reginald George Gilbert; 1 s (David John b 1956), 2 da (Elizabeth Ann b 1960, Joanne Michell b 1969); *Career* student apprentice De Haviland Aircraft, graduate engr Lucas Rotax, chief engr Cox of Watford (chief prodn engr); TI Cox Ltd: tech dir, md, chm; dir Dunlop Cox; memb: Nottingham Bd The Princes Youth Business Tst, The Inst of Br Carriage & Automobile Mfrs; chm Radcliffe on Trent Parish Church Cncl; CEng, FBIM; *Recreations* squash, golf; *Clubs* The Park, Radcliff on Trent Golf; *Style—* Frederick Babbs, Esq; TI Cox Ltd, Glaisdale Parkway, Nottingham NG8 4GP (☎ 0602 287821, telex 37478, fax 0602 899688)

BABER, Hon Mr Justice; Hon Ernest George; CBE (1987); s of late Walter Avertte Baber, and Kate Marion, *née* Pratt; *b* 18 July 1924; *Educ* Brentwood, Emmanuel Cambridge; *m* 1960, Dr Flora Marion, da of late Dr Raymond Bisset Smith; 1 s, 2 da; *Career* served WW II RN; barr Lincoln's Inn 1951, district judge Hong Kong 1967-73, judge of Supreme Court Hong Kong 1973-; *Style—* The Hon Mr Justice Baber, CBE; Supreme Court, Hong Kong

BABINGTON, His Hon Judge; Anthony Patrick; s of Oscar John Gilmore Babington (d 1930), of Monkstown, Co Cork; *b* 4 April 1920; *Educ* Reading Sch; *Career* serv WWII Maj; barr 1948; metropolitan stipendiary magistrate 1964-72, circuit judge 1972-87; Croix de Guerre with Gold Star France 1944; *Books* No Memorial (1954), The Power To Silence (1968), A House In Bow Street (1969), The English Bastille (1971), The Rule of Law In Britain (1978), For The Sake of Example (1983), Military Intervention in Britain (1990); *Clubs* Garrick, Special Forces; *Style—* His Hon Judge Babington; 3 Gledhow Gardens, Kensington, London SW5 0BL (☎ 071 373 4014); Thydon Cottage, Chilham, nr Canterbury, Kent CT4 8BX (☎ 0227 730 300)

BABINGTON, His Hon Judge Robert John; DSC (1942), QC (1965); s of Maj David Louis James Babington (d 1973), and Alice Marie, *née* McClintock (d 1978); *b* 9 April 1920; *Educ* St Columbas Coll Dublin, Trinity Coll Dublin (BA); *m* 2 Jan 1954, (Elizabeth) Bryanna Marguertie, da of Dr Ernest Henry Alton, MC (d 1952); 2 s (Philip b 30 Oct 1954, David b 2 Feb 1961), 1 da (Jane b 22 Sept 1956); *Career* Fleet Air Arm 1940-45; called to the Bar Inns of Court NI 1947, county court judge Fermanagh and Tyrone 1978-; MP N Down Stormont 1968-72; *Recreations* golf; *Clubs* Tyrone County, Special Forces; *Style—* His Hon Judge Babington, DSC, QC; Royal Courts of Justice, Chichester St, Belfast (☎ 0232 235111)

BABOULÈNE (né PHILIE), Bernard Léon; s of Fernand Louis Philie (né Baboulène) (d 1975), and Matilda Philie, *née* Evans (d 1964); noted French painting family; identity changed to Philie 1914, changed back to Baboulene 1957; *b* 1 Sept 1922; *Educ* Ardingly, Magdalen Coll Oxford (BA, MA); *m* 1, 16 June 1952, Doreen Ethel, da of Martin Rabey, of La Mielle du Parcq, Jersey, Channel Is (d 1974); 3 da (Margaret Elizabeth b 1953, Barbara Jean b 1955, Kathryn Hazel b 1963), 1 s (David Louis b 1960); m 2, 5 Oct 1977, Audrey Anne Frances, da of Albert George Conrad Tapster, of London (d 1980); Coronation medals 1937 and 1953, Burma Star 1946, 1939-45, Star 1946; *Career* RAF, 217 Sqdn (Far East), Flt Lt (air navigator) 1941-46; Admty Med Dr General's Dept 1939-41; mgmnt appt in aircraft indust and computers ICT now ICL 1950-64; mgmnt conslt 1964-, formerly exec search conslt (ret 1990); professional tenor taking broadcast recordings and various solo engagements; currently takes exclusive musical tours of Westminster Abbey 10 times a yr; FID MIMC 1972, FIMC 1985; *Recreations* music (singing); *Clubs* Royal Over-seas League, IOD; *Style—* Bernard L Bahouléne, Esq; 10 Richmond Ave, London SW20 8LA (☎ 081 542 8878)

BACCHUS, James; s of Cecil Bacchus, of Billericay; *b* 11 July 1941; *Educ* St Clement Danes London; *m* 1964, Marion, da of Thomas Victor Stratton (d 1970); 3 children; *Career* accountant, fin dir Jessups Hldgs and subsids 1973-; *Recreations* golf; *Clubs* Anglo-American Sporting; *Style—* James Bacchus, Esq; 147 Western Rd, Billericay, Essex

BACH, John Theodore; s of late Dr Francis Bach, and Matine, *née* Thompson; *b* 18 Feb 1936; *Educ* Rugby, New Coll Oxford (MA); *m* 15 April 1967, Hilary Rose, da of late Gp-Capt T E H Birley, OBE; 1 s (Alexander b 1969), 2 da (Emily b 1968, Susannah b 1973); *Career* slr; ptnr Stephenson Harwood 1966-; govr Moorfields Eye Hosp; *Clubs* City Univ; *Style—* John Bach, Esq; 1 St Paul's Churchyard, London EC4M 8SH (☎ 071 329 4422, fax 071 606 0822)

BACHE, Andrew Philip Foley; s of (Robert) Philip Sydney Bache, OBE (d 1984), and late Jessie, *née* Pearman-Smith; *b* 29 Dec 1939; *Educ* Shrewsbury, Emmanuel Coll Cambridge (MA); *m* 20 July 1963, Shăn, da of Rev L V Headley, OBE, of E Tisted, Hants; 2 s (Richard b 1964, Alexander b 1966), 1 da (Samantha b 1974); *Career* HM Dip Serv 1963-; FCO 1963-64, 1968-71, 1974-78, third sec Nicosia, second sec Sofia, first sec Lagos, first sec Vienna (Commercial); cnsllr: Tokyo 1981-85, Ankara 1985-87; head of Personnel Servs Dept FCO 1988; *Recreations* sport, fine arts, travel, ornithology; *Clubs* Jesters, MCC, RCS; *Style—* Andrew Bache, Esq

BACHMANN, Lawrence Paul; s of Jacob G Bachmann (d 1950), of Los Angeles, Ca, and Beatrice, *née* Lashins; *b* 12 Dec 1911; *Educ* Univ of Southern California (BA), Univ of Oxford (MA); *m* 1 (m dis 1966), Jean, *née* Campbell; m 2, 8 May 1967, Bettina, da of Alfred Hart (d 1936), of Rochester, NY; *Career* USAAF: main overseas corr Air Force official jl 1942-45, serv S Pacific 1943, Europe 1944, Europe and Pacific 1944-45, Lt-Col USAFR; asst to head: RKO Studios Hollywood 1933-35, MGM Studios Culver City Ca 1936-42, co-author many Dr Kildare films and others 1936-42, screen writer and novelist 1945-48, in Berlin for US War Dept OMGUS 1948-50, in Berlin for US State Dept 1950-52, novel writing 1952-56, chm and md Paramount Br Prodns London 1956-58, head MGM Br Studios 1959-66, prodr MGM film Whose Life is it Anyway 1982; fell Green Coll Oxford 1983- (memb Vice Chllrs Appeals & Income Generating Ctee); Domus fell St Catherine's Coll Oxford 1990, memb Writers Guild of America 1935; FRSM 1986; *Books* Death in the Dolls House (1943), The Kiss of Death (1946), The Phoenix (1955), The Valley of the Kings (1956), The Lorelei (1957), The Bitter Lake (1969), The Legend of Joseph Nokato (1971), The Ultimate Act (1972); *Recreations* lawn tennis; *Clubs* All Eng Lawn Tennis & Croquet, Garrick, RAF, Beverly Hills Tennis; *Style—* Lawrence Bachmann, Esq; The Manor House, Great Haseley, Oxford OX9 7JY (☎ 0844 279317)

BACK, Patrick; QC (1970); s of late Ivor Back, and Barbara, *née* Nash; *b* 23 Aug 1917; *Educ* Marlborough, Trinity Hall Cambridge; *Career* barr 1940, dep chm Devon QS 1968, ldr Western circuit 1984-; *Style—* Patrick Back, Esq, QC; Flat 3, Marquess House, 74 Marquess Rd, London N1 (☎ 071 226 0991)

BACK, Dr Paul Adrian Auchmuty; s of Arthur William Back, QC (d 1960), of Grahamstown, S Africa, and Mary Helen Margaret, *née* Carter; *b* 30 May 1930; *Educ* St Andrew's Coll Grahamstown S Africa, Rhodes Univ S Africa (BSc), Univ of Cape Town (BSc), Trinity Coll Oxford (Rhodes scholar, PhD, Desborough medal for servs to rowing, Hack Trophy for flying Univ Air Squadron); *m* 1965, Jacqueline Sarah, da of Walter Hide; 3 s (Jonathan Paul b 1966, Rupert James b 1968, Nicholas Hugo b 1976); *Career* Sir Alexander Gibb & Ptnrs: joined 1955, assoc 1967-, ptnr 1970-89, co dir and chief tech dir 1989-; worked on Kariba Hydro-Electric Power Station and Dam 1955-60, worked on several hydro-electric projects incl Samanalawewa and Victoria Dam and Hydro-Electric Projects in Sri Lanka and Kariba North Hydro-Electric Power Station Zambia 1970-, advsr to World Bank on Tarbela Dam 1976-, memb Bd of Advsrs Nat Irrigation Admin of the Philippines Magat Dam 1977-, chm Advsy Panel Shaqikou Hydro-Electric Project China 1984-; chm Panel of Enquiry Kantalai Tank failure Sri Lanka 1986, chm Lesotha Highlands Conslts Review Panel for the Katse Dam 1987-, project dir for design and supervision of construction Cardiff Bay Barrage Wales 1989-; memb Cncl ICE 1989 (FICE 1981, MICE 1961), memb Assoc of Consulting Engrs 1971; ptnr-in-charge Construction News award of the Year for the Victoria Dam Project Sri Lanka (1985); *Books* Seismic Design Study of a Double Curvative Arch Dam (jt author, 1969), P K Le Roux Dam - Spillway Design and Energy Dissipators (jt author, 1973), Hydro-Electric Power Generation and Pumped Storage Schemes Utilising the Sea (1978), Aseismic Design of Arch Dams (jt author, 1980), The Influence of Geology on the Design of Victoria Dam Sri Lanka (jt author, 1982), Automatic Flood Routing at Victoria Dam Sri Lanka; *Recreations* sailing, skiing; *Clubs* RAF London; *Style—* Dr Paul Back; Parsonage Farm, How Lane, White Waltham, Berks SL6 3JP (☎ 0734 343973); Sir Alexander Gibb & Partners, Early House, London Rd, Reading, Berks RG6 1BL (☎ 0734 61061, fax 0734 64088)

BACKHOUSE, David John; s of Joseph Helme Backhouse (d 1989), and Jessie, *née* Chivers, of Devizes, Wilts; *b* 5 May 1941; *Educ* Lord Weymouth Sch Warminster, W of England Coll of Art; *m* 19 July 1975, Sarah Patricia, da of Philip Gerald Barber, CBE (d 1988); 1 s (Theodore b 1980), 2 da (Katharine b 1977, Rosalind b 1984); *Career* sculptor in bronze; many public sculptures in UK; recent cmmns incl: Dolphin Family in London Docklands 1988, Flying Figurehead for Swansea (Winner of Sainsburys' Open Sculpture Competition) 1989, Dance of the Centaurs for Whiteleys of Bayswater 1991; portrait heads and bronzes in collections worldwide; one man exhibitions in: London, NY, Washington; RWA, FRBS, FRSA 1989; *Recreations* landscape gardening, walking, cycling; *Style—* David Backhouse, Esq; Old Post Office, Lullington, Frome, Somerset BA11 2PW (☎ 0373 830319); La Chapelle Pommier, 24340 Mareuil, Dordogne, France; Studio, Old Baptist Chapel, Lower Westwood, Bradford on Avon, Wilts (☎ 02216 6606)

BACKHOUSE, David Miles; s of Jonathan Backhouse, *qv*, and Alice Joan (d 1984), *née* Woodroffe; *b* 30 Jan 1939; *Educ* Eton; *m* 1969, Sophia Ann, da of Col Clarence Henry Southgate Townsend (d 1953); 2 children; *Career* banker; dir: TSB GP plc, Witan Investmt Co plc, Bassett Tst Ltd; govr Royal Agric Coll Cirencester; *Clubs* Boodles, Vanderbilt; *Style—* David Backhouse, Esq; South Farm, Fairford, Glos GL7 3PN (☎ 0285 712225)

BACKHOUSE, Oliver Richard; s of late Maj Sir John Backhouse, 3 Bt, MC; hp of bro, Sir Jonathan Backhouse, 4 Bt; *b* 18 July 1941; *Educ* Ampleforth, RMA Sandhurst; *m* 1970, Gillian Irene, da of L W Lincoln, of Northwood, Middx; 1 adopted s, 1 adopted da; *Career* memb The Stock Exchange; FCA; *Style—* Oliver Backhouse, Esq; 50 Moor Lane, Rickmansworth, Herts WD3 1LG

BACKHOUSE, William; s of Jonathan Backhouse, of Essex, and Alice Joan, *née* Woodroffe (d 1984); *b* 29 May 1942; *Educ* Eton; *m* 1971, Deborah Jane, da of Hon David Edward Hely-Hutchinson (d 1984), of Wilts; 1 s (Timothy b 1981), 2 da (Harriet b 1975, Tessa b 1977); *Career* chm Baring Houston & Saunders Ltd 1984-, chief operating offr Baring Asset Management Ltd 1985-; md: Baring Bros and Co Ltd 1984-85, Baring Fund Managers Ltd 1985-90; FCA; *Recreations* travel, photography, shooting; *Style—* William Backhouse, Esq; Layer Marney Wick, Colchester, Essex CO5 9UT (☎ 0206 330267)

BACKLEY, Steven James; s of John Backley, and Pauline, *née* Hogg; *b* 12 Feb 1969;

Educ Bexley and Erith Tech HS, Loughborough Univ of Technol; *Career* javelin thrower; holder of world jr record in 1989, finished third in overall athletics Grand Prix to Said Aouita and Roger Kingdom 1989, UK record holder 85.90m set in Barcelona 1989, England rep Cwlth Games Auckland NZ 1990, world record holder 90-98m Crystal Palace 1990; *Recreations* athletics; *Clubs* Cambridge Harriers (Bexley); *Style—* Steven Backley, Esq; 22 Beechway, Bexley, Kent D45 3DG (☎ 081 303 4405)

BACON, Baroness (Life Peeress UK 1970); Alice Martha Bacon; CBE (1953), PC (1966), DL (W Yorks 1974); da of Benjamin Bacon, CC (d 1958), of Normanton, Yorkshire; *Educ* Normanton Girls' HS, Stockwell T C, London & London U (external); *Career* schoolmistress; MP (Lab): NE Leeds (1945-55), SE Leeds (1955-70); Min of State: Home Office 1964-67, DES 1967-70; memb Nat Exec Lab Pty 1941-70 (chm of Labour Pty 1950-51); Hon LLD Leeds Univ 1972; (chm of Lab Pty conference 1951); *Style—* The Rt Hon Lady Bacon, CBE, PC, DL; 53 Snydale Rd, Normanton, W Yorks WF6 1NY (☎ 0924 893229)

BACON, Anthony Gordon (Tony); TD (1973); s of Frederick Gordon Bacon, of Ingatestone, Essex, and Dorothy Winifred, *née* Ramsay; *b* 12 May 1938; *Educ* Highgate Sch, Hertford Coll Oxford (BA, MA); *m* 18 Aug 1962, Margaret Jocelyn, da of George Ronald Percival Ross, of Blackmore End, Herts; 3 s (Richard b 1965, Michael b 1967, Timothy b 1970); *Career* Nat Serv RA UK and Hong Kong 1956-58; TA Essex Yeo RHA 1959-74: EY Signal Sqdn, 71 Signal Regt (V); banker Barclays Bank Gp 1961-: UK, Australia, Cote d'Ivoire, Hong Kong, currently corp mangr; churchwarden Kimpton Parish Church; ACIB 1966, FCIS 1985; *Recreations* real tennis, golf, music, country pursuits; *Clubs* Australian, Naval & Military (Melbourne Australia), Overseas Bankers; *Style—* Tony Bacon, Esq, TD; 11 Blackmore Way, Wheathampstead, Herts AL4 8LJ (☎ 0438 832 757); Barclays Bank plc, 9 Gracechurch Street, London EC3V OBB (☎ 071 623 2266)

BACON, Francis; *b* 1909,Dublin; *Career* artist, represented in major museums throughout the world; *Style—* Francis Bacon, Esq; c/o Marlborough Fine Art, 6 Albemarle St, London W1X 4BY

BACON, Francis Thomas; OBE (1967); s of Thomas Walter Bacon (d 1950), of Ramsden Hall, Billericay, Essex, and Edith Mary, *née* Leslie-Melville (d 1950); descendant of Sir Nicholas Bacon, Lord Keeper of the Great Seal *temp* Elizabeth I, and f of Sir Francis Bacon who was also Lord Keeper; *b* 21 Dec 1904; *Educ* Eton, Trinity Coll Cambridge (MA); *m* 1934, Barbara Winifred, da of Godfrey Keppel Papillon (d 1942); 1 s (and 1 s decd), 1 da; *Career* with C A Parsons & Co Ltd Newcastle upon Tyne 1925-40, experimental work on fuel cells King's Coll London 1940-41, temp experiment offr HM Anti-Submarine Experimental Estab 1941-46, experimental work on hydrogen-oxygen fuel cells Cambridge Univ 1946-; conslt on fuel cells: NRDC 1956-62, Energy Conversion Ltd 1962-71, Fuel Cells Ltd 1971-72, Johnson-Matthey 1984-; S G Brown Award and Medal (Royal Soc) 1965, Br Silver Medal (RAeS) 1969, Melchett Medal (Inst of Fuel) 1972, Churchill Gold Medal (Soc of Engrs) 1972, Bruno Breyer Meml Lecture and Medal (Royal Aust Chemical Inst) 1976; Hon DSc Newcastle upon Tyne 1980; FRS, FEng, CEng, MIMechE, Hon FSE; *Publications* Fuel Cells (contrib 1960), Fuel Cells (contrib 1963); many papers on fuel cells; *Recreations* walking in the hills, gardening; *Clubs* Athenaeum; *Style—* Francis Bacon, Esq, OBE, FRS; Trees, 34 High St, Little Shelford, Cambridge CB2 5ES (☎ 0223 843 116)

BACON, Jennifer Helen (Jenny); da of Dr Lionel James Bacon, of Whiteleaf, Crawley, Winchester, Hants, and Joyce, *née* Chapman; *b* 16 April 1945; *Educ* Bedales Sch Petersfield, New Hall Cambridge (BA); *Career* Miny of Lab: entered as asst princ 1967, private sec to Min of State 1971-72, princ Health and Safety at Work Act 1972-74, industl rels legislation 1974-76, princ private sec to Sec of State 1977-78, asst sec Head of Skillcentres in Manpower Servs Cmmn 1978-80, year off travelling in Latin America 1980-81, head Machinery of Govt Div 1981-82, dir of Adult Trg Manpower Servs Cmmn 1982-86; head Schs Branch 3 Nat Curriculum and Assessment Dept of Educn and Sci 1986-89, princ fin offr Dept of Employment 1989-91, dir of strategy and resources Dept of Employment 1991-; visiting fell Nuffield Oxford 1989-; *Recreations* travel, walking, classical music and opera; *Style—* Miss Jenny Bacon; Department of Employment, Caxton House, Tothill St, London SW1 (☎ 071 273 5762, fax 071 273 5030)

BACON, John Maxwell; s of John Anthony Bacon (d 1985), of Beckenham, Kent, and Irene, *née* Roberts; *b* 6 Jan 1949; *Educ* Hawesdown County Secdy Modern Sch Kent; *m* 3 July 1976, Rita, da of Patrick Dempsey; *Career* advtg exec; jr copywriter Young & Rubicam 1969-71, copywriter Collett Dickinson Pearce 1971-73, sr copywriter BMP 1973-78, gp head and creative dir Saatchi & Saatchi 1978-88, exec creative dir Ogilvy & Mather 1988-; winner various advtg awards incl: 3 D&ADA Silver, 3 Gold and 5 Silver Campaign Press awards, 3 Cannes Silver Lions, 5 Clios; memb D&ADA; *Recreations* shooting, fencing, collecting vintage wristwatches, wine; *Style—* John Bacon, Esq; Ogilvy & Mather Ltd, Brettenham House, Lancaster Place, London WC2E 7EZ (☎ 071 836 2466, fax 071 836 5938)

BACON, Maj Keith Ashley; TD (1962); s of Alan Wood Bacon (d 1980), and Margaret, *née* Sherwen; *b* 13 April 1928; *Educ* St Bees Cumbria, Solihull Warwicks; *m* 11 Feb 1954, Elizabeth Margaret, da of John Gibson Nicholson; 1 s (Nicholas b 28 Feb 1955), 3 da (Amanda (Mrs Peet) b 23 Aug 1957, Sarah b 7 May 1961, Joanna (Mrs Hughes) b 12 Nov 1965); *Career* admitted slr 1967, sr ptnr Paisleys; chm DSS Appeal Tbnl, clerk to various charitable tsts; memb Law Soc 1967; *Style—* Maj Keith Bacon, TD; Dearham Mill, Maryport, Cumbria (☎ 0900 812 040); El Pinar 9, Moraira, Spain; Paisleys, 31 Jane St, Workington, Cumbria (☎ 0900 602 235)

BACON, Kenneth Frank; s of Frank Bacon (d 1985), of Brighton, and Ethel Grace, *née* Bishop; *b* 15 Feb 1934; *Educ* Varndean GS, Brighton Tech Coll; *m* 7 July 1956, Cynthia Mary, da of Harry George Green (d 1976); 2 da (Helena b 1963, Blanche b 1967); *Career* md: Magnetic Components Ltd 1972-76, Southern Instrument Hldgs 1976-78; gp chief exec Fairey Hldgs Ltd 1978-81, md Mel Equipment Ltd 1981-83, div md Plessey Communications Div 1983-85, md STC Telecomunications Ltd 1985-87, chm STC-ICL Defence Systems 1987, exec dir Focon Int Ltd; Freeman City of London, Liveryman Worshipful Co of Glass Sellers; CEng, FIEE, CBIM; *Recreations* reading, history; *Clubs* RAC; *Style—* Kenneth Bacon, Esq; Ffowlers Bucke, South Harting, Petersfield GU31 5QB (☎ 0730 825 592); Focon International Limited, Mead House, Bentley, nr Farnham, Surrey (☎ 0420 23935, fax 0420 23937)

BACON, Sir Nicholas Hickman Ponsonby; 14 and 15 Bt (E 1611 and 1627), of Redgrave, Suffolk, and of Mildenhall, Suffolk, respectively; Premier Baronet of England; s of Sir Edmund Bacon, 13 and 14 Bt, KG, KBE, TD, JP, by his w Priscilla, da of Col Sir Charles Ponsonby, 1 Bt, TD, and Hon Winifred Gibbs (da of 1 Baron Hunsdon); Sir Nicholas is 12 in descent from Rt Hon Sir Nicholas Bacon, Lord Keeper of the Great Seal under Elizabeth I 1558-78 (in which latter year he d), His eld s was cr a Bt 1611 and this eld son's 3 s cr a Bt in 1627, Lord Keeper Bacon's 5 s by a second m (but yr s by this w, Anne, da of Sir Anthony Cooke, sometime tutor to Edward VI) was Lord High Chllr & was cr Baron Verulam 1618 and Viscount St Albans 1621 both ext 1626; *b* 17 May 1953; *Educ* Eton, Univ of Dundee; *m* 1981, Susan Henrietta, da of Raymond Dinnis, of Delaware Farm, Edenbridge; 3 s (Henry Hickman b 1984, Edmund b 1986, Nathaniel b 1989); *Heir* s, Henry Hickman Bacon b 23 April 1984; *Career* called to the Bar Gray's Inn 1978; page of honour to HM The Queen 1966-69; *Style—* Sir Nicholas Bacon, Bt; Raveningham Hall, Norwich (☎ 050 846 206)

BACON, Philip Pierre Marie; s of Jean Laurent Bacon, of Paris, France, and Ginette Marie Fournier, *née* Rouquet; *b* 4 Aug 1947; *Educ* Wellington, Lycee Francais London, Univ of Kent; *m* 28 Aug 1973 (m dis 1987), Miriam Anne, da of John J Juviler; 2 s (Jonathan b 10 Jan 1980, Sebastian b 30 May 1983); *Career* press offr London Tourist Bd 1970-72, prodr BBC radio 1972-74, network ed Ind Radio News 1979-80, asst ed LBC radio 1983-89 (prodr 1974-79, ed AM prog 1980-83), ed LBC Crown FM 1989-90; freelance presenter 1990-; chm Radio Acad 1985-89, cncl memb Radio Acad; *Books* The Greater Glory (translator and adapter, 1987); *Recreations* music; *Style—* Philip Bacon, Esq; c/o Arlington Enterprises, 1 Charlotte St, London W1 (☎ 071 580 0702)

BACON, Priscilla, Lady; Priscilla Dora; *née* Ponsonby; DL (Norfolk); eld da of Sir Charles Edward Ponsonby, 1 Bt, TD, DL (d 1976), sometime MP for Sevenoaks (gs of 1 Baron De Mauley), and Hon Winifred Gibbs, JP, eld da of 1 Baron Hunsdon; *b* 3 June 1913; *m* 15 Jan 1936, Sir Edmund Castell Bacon, 13 and 14 Bt, KG, KBE, TD, JP (Lord Lieut of Norfolk 1949-78, d 1982); 1 s (Nicholas Hickman Ponsonby, 14 and 15 Bt), 4 da (Mrs John Bruce, Mrs Stephen Gibbs, Mrs Ronald Hoare, Mrs Paul Nicholson); *Career* Queen Elizabeth II Coronation Medal; *Books* contributed article on Raveningham Hall gardens to New Englishwoman Gardener (1987); *Style—* Priscilla, Lady Bacon, DL; Orchards Raveningham, Norfolk NR14 6NS

BACON, Sir Sidney Charles; CB (1971); s of Charles Bacon; *b* 11 Feb 1919; *Educ* Woolwich Poly, Univ of London (BSc Eng); *Career* md Royal Ordnance Factories and dep chm bd 1972-79, ret; memb Cncl City and Guilds of London Inst 1983-91; FEng 1979, FIMechE, FIProd E; Hon FCGI; kt 1977; *Style—* Sir Sidney Bacon, CB; 228 Erith Rd, Bexley Heath, Kent DA7 6HP

BACON, Timothy Roger; s of Christopher Henry Bacon (d 1956), and Diana Sybil, *née* Richmond Brown; *b* 4 Dec 1947; *Educ* Eton, Univ of Bristol (BSc); *m* 14 Sept 1985, Marylyn Rowan Ogilvie, da of William Arthur Grant; 2 da (Rosalind Sarah b 12 Jan 1987, Laura Charlotte b 11 July 1988); *Career* Brown Shipley & Co Ltd: in trg 1970, Treasy Commercial Loans and Foreign Exchange Depts 1970-79, Corporate Fin Dept 1979-, dir 1988; memb Inst of Bankers; *Recreations* opera, theatre, travel; *Clubs* City University, Pratts; *Style—* Timothy Bacon, Esq; 67 Britannia Rd, London SW6 2JR (☎ 071 731 0408); Brown, Shipley & Co Limited, Founders Court, Lothbury, London EC2R 7HE (☎ 071 606 9833, fax 071 796 4875)

BADAWI, Zeinab Mohammed-Khair; da of Mohammed-Khair El Badawi, of Southgate, London N14, and Asia Mohammed, *née* Malik; *b* 3 Oct 1959; *Educ* Hornsey Sch for Girls, St Hilda's College Oxford (BA), Univ of London (MA); *Career* presenter and journalist in current affrs and documentaries Yorkshire TV 1982-86, current affrs reporter BBC TV 1987-88, newscaster and journalist ITN 1988-; memb NUJ; *Recreations* languages, piano, cinema, music, reading; *Style—* Miss Zeinab Badawi; ITN Independent Television News, 48 Wells St, London W1P 4DE (☎ 081 883 3000, telex 298935)

BADCOCK, Maj-Gen John Michael Watson; CB (1976), MBE (1969), DL (Kent 1980); s of late R D Badcock, MC, JP; *b* 10 Nov 1922; *Educ* Sherborne, Worcester Coll Oxford; *m* 1948, Gillian Pauline, *née* Attfield; 1 s, 2 da; *Career* enlisted in ranks (Army) 1941, cmmnd RCS 1942; served 1945-47: UK, BAOR, Ceylon; serv 1947-68: UK, Persian Gulf, BAOR, Cyprus; cdr 2 Inf Bde and dep constable Dover Castle 1968-71, dep mil sec 1971-72, manning dir (Army) 1972-74, def advsr and head Br Def Liaison Staff Canberra 1974-77, ret; Col Cmdt RCS 1974-80 and 1982-90, master of signals 1982-90, Hon Col 31 (London) Signal Regt (Vol) 1978-83, chm SE TA & VRA 1979-85; *Recreations* rugby, football, cricket, hockey; *Clubs* Army and Navy; *Style—* Maj-Gen John Badcock, CB, MBE, DL; c/o RHQ Royal Signals, 56 Regency St, London SW1P 4AD

BADCOCK, Julian Knighton; MBE (1984); s of Paul Badcock (d 1975), of Cobham, Surrey, and Torfrida Gertrude, *née* Oldfield (d 1981); *b* 24 March 1919; *Educ* St Paul's, King's Coll London (BA, BSc); *m* 2 Sept 1944, Sophie, da of Capt Sergius Peter Skidmore (d 1973), of Athens, Greece; 1 s (Ashley b 1948), 2 da (Jane (Mrs Robb) b 1951, Alice (Mrs Chandler) b 1955); *Career* aniv of London Air Sqdn and RAF Volunteer Res 1938-39 (cmmnd 1939); WWII: navigator and air gunner 44 and 83 Bomber Sqdns 1940-41, navigation instr (memb Aircrew Classification Bd) 1942-43, Empire Air Trg Scheme SA (and liaison offr to Greek Air Force) 1944-45, released Flt Lt 1946 (AE 1947); called to the Bar Lincolns Inn 1949; Br Employers Confedn 1947-50, asst sec and legal advsr to Limestone Fedn and Federated Quarry Owners GB 1950-61, gen mangr and sec to London Port Employers Assoc and assoc Lighterage Tea and Tug Orgns (nat and int) 1961-84, exec dir Trade Association Management Services Ltd, ret 1984; Cobham ward cncllr Esher UDC 1949-67, govr of local schs, chm Esher UDC and ex officio JP for Co of Surrey 1963-64, memb London Dock Labour Bd 1965-68; Freeman: City of London 1977, Worshipful Co of Watermen 1978 (ct memb 1984); *Recreations* voluntary work, historical research; *Clubs* RAF; *Style—* Julian Badcock, Esq, MBE; Abington Orchard, Leigh Place, Cobham, Surrey KT11 2HL (☎ 0932 862969)

BADDELEY, Sir John Wolsey Beresford; 4 Bt (UK 1922), of Lakefield, Parish of St Mary Stoke Newington, Co London; s of Sir John Beresford Baddeley, 3 Bt (d 1979); *b* 27 Jan 1938; *Educ* Bradfield; *m* 1962, Sara Rosalind, da of late Colin Crofts, of Scarborough; 3 da (Sara Alexandra b 1964, Anna Victoria b 1965, Emma Elisabeth b 1972); *Heir* kinsman, Mark Baddeley; *Career* Champagne Bollinger (Mentzendorff & Co Ltd); *Recreations* squash, inland waterways; *Style—* Sir John Baddeley, Bt; Springwood, Sandgate Lane, Storrington, Sussex (☎ 09066 3054)

BADDELEY, Mark David; s of late Mark Baddeley (d 1930), gs of Sir John Baddeley, 1 Bt, and hp of kinsman Sir John Wolsey Baddeley, 4 Bt; *b* 12 May 1921; *Educ* Cliftonville Coll; *Style—* Mark Baddeley, Esq; 22 Woodberry, George V Ave, Margate, Kent

BADDELEY, Nancy, Lady; Nancy Winifred; da of late Thomas Wolsey, of Smallburgh Hall Norfolk; *m* 1929, Sir John Baddeley, 3 Bt (d 1979); 1 s, 2 da; *Style—* Nancy, Lady Baddeley; Bury House, Bury, Pulborough, W Sussex

BADDELEY, Brig Robert John; s of Lt-Col Robert John Halkett Baddeley, MC (d 1954), and Hilda Maitland Dougall, *née* Wardle; *b* 2 July 1934; *Educ* Wellington, RMA Sandhurst; *m* Susan Marian, da of Edwin Colin Neale Edwards, of Eton Coll, Windsor; 2 da (Charlotte b 1965, Emma b 1968); *Career* cmmnd 4/7 Royal Dragoon Gds, ADC Chief of Defence Staff Ghana UN Congo 1960, HQ Malta and Libya 1966, CO 4/7 Royal Dragoon Gds, directing staff Staff Coll Camberley 1976, Def Attaché Tehran 1978, dep dir Army Recruiting 1980, Cdr Br Military Advsy Team Bangladesh 1983, dir of Army Trg 1987, ADC to HM the Queen 1988, Col 4/7 Royal Dragoon Gds 1988; Wilts cncllr 1989; Freeman City of London, Liveryman Worshipful Co of Coachmakers and Coach Harness Makers; *Clubs* Cavalry and Guards, FRGS; *Style—* Brig R J Baddeley; Hazeldon House, Tisbury, Wilts (☎ 0747 870867)

BADDELEY, Stephen John; s of William Baddeley, and Barbara Isobel; *b* 28 March 1961; *Educ* Chelsea Coll Univ of London (BSc); *m* 16 June 1984, Deirdre Ilene *née* Sharman; *Career* badminton player; Eng Nat singles winner: 1981, 1985, 1987; Eng

Nat mens doubles winner: 1985, 1987, 1989; Commonwealth Games: Gold medal team event 1982, 1986, 1990, Gold medal mens singles 1986; winner mens singles: Indian Open 1985, Scottish Open 1986, all-Eng semi-finals 1987; represented Euro against Asia 1983, 1984 and 1986; 143 caps for Eng; hon memb Badminton Writers Assoc, memb and chair Eng Badminton Players Assoc 1989-90, chm World Badminton Players Fedn 1989-90, ret as player 1990, dir coaching and devpt Scottish Badminton Union 1990-; *Books* Badminton In Action (1988); *Recreations* golf; *Style—* Stephen Baddeley, Esq

BADDELEY, Very Rev William Pye; s of William Herman Clinton Baddeley (d 1918), and Louise, *née* Bourdin (d 1920); *b* 20 March 1914; *Educ* privately, Univ of Durham, Cuddesdon Coll Oxford; *m* 1947, Mary Frances Shirley, da of Col Ernest Robert Caldwell Wyatt, CBE, DSO; 1 da (Frances b 1955); *Career* vicar St Pancras 1949-58, dean of Brisbane 1958-67 (diocesan chaplain 1962-67), rector St James's Piccadilly 1967-80, chaplain Royal Academy of Arts 1968-80, area dean of Westminster 1974-80, visiting chaplain Westminster Abbey 1980-, area dean of Westminster 1974-80; commissary to: Primate of Australia 1967-, Bishop of Wangaratta 1970, Archbishop of Papua New Guinea 1972, Bishop of Newcastle NSW 1976; dean emeritus of Brisbane 1980-; dir Elizabethan Theatre Tst 1963-67; pres: Queensland Ballet Co 1962-67, Qld Univ Dramatic Soc 1961-67; life govr Thomas Coram Fndn, chm Malcolm Sargent Cancer Fund for Children 1968-; govr: Burlington Sch 1967-80, Archbishop Tenison's Sch 1967-80; frequent bdcaster on TV and radio in Australia 1958-67; chaplain OStJ 1971; *Recreations* theatre, photography, music; *Clubs* Carlton, Arts, East India; *Style—* The Very Rev William Baddeley; Cumberland House, Woodbridge, Suffolk IP12 4AH (☎ 03943 4104)

BADDILEY, Prof Sir James; s of late James Baddiley and Ivy Logan Cato; *b* 15 May 1918; *Educ* Manchester GS, Univ of Manchester (PhD, DSc), Univ of Cambridge (ScD); *m* 1944, Hazel, yr da of Wesley Wilfrid Townsend; 1 s; *Career* ICI fell Univ of Cambridge 1945-49, swedish MRC fell Wenner-Grens Inst for Cell Biology Stockholm 1947-49, memb of staff Dept of Biochemistry Lister Inst of Preventive Med London 1949-54, Rockefeller Fellowship Harvard Med Sch 1954, prof organic chemistry King's Coll Univ of Durham 1954-77, Karl Folkers visiting prof of biochem Univ of Illinois 1962; Univ of Newcastle upon Tyne: joined 1963, head Sch of Chemistry 1968-78, prof of chemical microbiology Chemical Res Laboratory 1977-83 (dir 1975-83), SERC sr fell Dept of Biochemistry Univ of Cambridge 1981-83, fell Pembroke Coll Cambridge 1981-85 (emeritus fell); memb Cncl: Royal Soc 1977-79, SERC 1979-81; hon memb American Soc of Biochemistry and Molecular Biology; Meldola medal Royal Inst of Chemistry 1947, Corday-Morgan medal Chem Soc 1952 (Tilden lectr 1959, Pedler lectr 1980); Hon DSc Heriot-Watt Univ; Hon DSc Univ of Bath; FRS (Leeuwenhoek lectr 1967, Davy medal 1974); *Style—* Prof Sir James Baddiley, FRS; Hill Top Cottage, Hildersham, Cambridge CB1 6DA (☎ 0223 893055); Dept of Biochemistry, Univ of Cambridge, Tennis Court Rd, Cambridge CB2 1QW (☎ 0223 333600)

BADEL, Sarah; da of Alan Badel (d 1982), of Chichester, West Sussex, and Yvonne, *née* Owen (d 1990); *b* 30 March 1943; *Educ* Poles Convent Sch Herts, Royal Acad of Dramatic Art; *Career* actress; theatrical performances incl: Ellie Dunn in Heartbreak House, Raina in Arms and the Man, Solveig in Peer Gynt, Varya in The Cherry Orchard, The Right Honourable Gentleman, Vivie Warren in Mrs Warren's Profession (NT), (created role of) Rachel in The Black Prince (Aldwych Theatre) 1989; TV credits incl: Flora Poste in Cold Comfort Farm, Katharine in The Taming of the Shrew, Goneril in King Lear, Lizzy Eustace in The Pallisers, Alice in Dear Brutus, Oliver in Dangerous Corner, Joy/Hilary in Small World, Babs in The Irish RM, The Baroness Weber in A Perfect Spy; films incl: The Shooting Party, Not Without My Daughter; radio credits incl: Anna Karenina, Becky Sharp in Vanity Fair, Sister Jeanne in The Devils, Caesar and Cleopatra, Vinnie in Mourning Becomes Electra; winner Best Actress award for Josie in A Moon for the Misbegotten 1978; *Recreations* cooking, bridge; *Clubs* Lansdowne; *Style—* Ms Sarah Badel; c/o Terry Plunkett Green, 4 Ovington Gardens, London SW3 1LS (☎ 071 584 0688)

BADEN, (Edwin) John; s of Percy Baden (d 1972), of Parkstone, Dorset, and Jacoba Geertruij, *née* de Blank; *b* 18 Aug 1928; *Educ* Winchester, CCC Cambridge (BA, MA); *m* 6 Sept 1952, Christine Irene, da of Edward Miall Grose (d 1973), of Farm View, Laughton, Sussex; 2 s (Peter b 1954, David b 1959), 3 da (Ann b 1956, Susan b 1958, Zoë b 1962); *Career* RA and RHA 1947-48, cmmnd 2 Lt, serv Eng Palestine and Tripolitania; audit clerk Deloitte Haskins & Sells London 1951-54, sec and dir H Parrot & Co Ltd London 1955-61, fin advsr C & A Modes Ltd London 1961-63, dir Samuel Montagu & Co Ltd London 1963-78, chm Midland Montagu Industrial Finance 1975-78, md and chief exec Italian International Bank plc 1978-89, md and chief exec Girobank plc 1989-, dir Alliance & Leicester Building Soc 1990-, chm N American Property Unit Trust London, memb Mgmnt Ctee Pan Euro Property Unit Trust London; tstee Int Centre for Res in Accounting Univ of Lancaster; MICAS 1954 (memb Cncl), memb Inst of Taxation 1954; Cavaliere Ufficiale (Order of Merit of the Italian Republic) 1986; *Recreations* sailing, reading; *Style—* John Baden, Esq; The Old Manor House, Chilworth, Surrey GU4 8NE (☎ 0483 61203, fax 0483 577485); Girobank plc, 10 Milk St, London EC2V 8JH (☎ 071 600 6020)

BADEN HELLARD, Ronald; s of Ernest Baden Hellard (d 1975), of Longfield Kent, and Alice May, *née* Banks (d 1980); *b* 30 Jan 1927; *Educ* Liskeard GS, The Poly Sch of Architecture (DipArch), Loughborough Tech Coll (now Loughborough Univ of Technol); *m* 16 Dec 1950, Kay Peggy, *née* Fiddes; 2 da (Sally b 1953, Diana Jacqueline b 1956); *Career* WWII Duke of Cornwalls LI 1945-48, Capt GHQ MELF 1947-48; fndr ptnr: Polycon Gp 1952-, Polycon Building Industrial Consultants 1955-; chm Polycon AIMS Ltd 1984-, chief exec TQM/Polycon 1988-; architect of various industl and commerical bldgs incl Oxford Air Trg Sch at Kidlington; first chm Mgmnt Ctee RIBA 1956-64, developed a number of mgmnt techniques which are now standard mgmnt practice in construction indust; pres S London Soc of Architects 1967-69; BIM: chm SE London Branch 1969-72, chm SE Region 1972-76, memb Nat Cncl 1971-77; cncl memb CIArb 1970-84 (actg sec 1973); Freeman City of London 1981, Liveryman Worshipful Co of Arbitrators 1981; FCIArb 1952, FRIBA 1955, FBIM 1966; *Books* Management in Architectural Practice (1964), Metric Change a Management Action Plan (1971), Training for Change - A Company Action Plan (1972), Construction Quality Coordinators Guide (1987), Managing Construction Conflict (1988); *Recreations* tennis, travel; *Style—* Ronald Baden Hellard, Esq; 97 Vanbrugh Park, Blackheath, London SE3 (☎ 081 853 2006); Polycon Group, 70 Greenwich High Rd, London SE10 (☎ 081 691 7425)

BADEN-POWELL, Carine, Baroness; Carine; da of late Clement Hamilton Crause Boardman, of Johannesburg; *m* 1936, 2 Baron Baden-Powell (d 1962); 2 s, 1 da; *Style—* The Rt Hon Carine, Lady Baden-Powell

BADEN-POWELL, Hon (David) Michael; s of 2 Baron Baden-Powell (d 1962); hp of bro, 3 Baron Baden-Powell; *b* 11 Dec 1940; *Educ* Pierrepont House; *m* 1966, Joan, da of Horace Berryman, of Melbourne; 3 s; *Career* insurance consultant, agent with Australian Mutual Provident Soc 1972-; Freeman City of London, memb Worshipful Co of Mercers; *Style—* The Hon Michael Baden-Powell; 18 Kalang Rd, Camberwell, Vic 3124, Australia (☎ 29 5009)

BADEN-POWELL, Baroness; Patience Hélène Mary; CBE (1986); da of Maj Douglas Batty (d 1982), of Zimbabwe; *b* 27 Oct 1936; *Educ* St Peter's Diocesan Sch Bulawayo; *m* 1963, 3 Baron Baden-Powell, *qv*; *Career* chief cmmr Girl Guides Assoc 1980-85 (int cmmr 1980-85); pres: Cwlth Youth Exchange Cncl 1982-85, National Playbus Assoc; patron: Surrey Antiques Fair, Woodlarks Campsite Tst for the Disabled; dir Laurentian Financial Gp plc, Britannia Cable System Surrey Ltd; *Style—* The Rt Hon the Lady Baden-Powell, CBE; Grove Heath Farm, Ripley, Woking, Surrey GU23 6ES (☎ 0483 224262)

BADEN-POWELL, 3 Baron (UK 1929); Sir Robert Crause Baden-Powell; 3 Bt (UK 1922); s of 2 Baron Baden-Powell (d 1962); *b* 15 Oct 1936; *Educ* Bryanston; *m* 1963, Patience (*see* Baden-Powell, Baroness); *Heir* bro, Hon David Baden-Powell; *Career* RN 1955-57; chief scouts cmmr Scout Assoc 1963-82 (vice pres 1982-), World Scout Fndn 1978-88, dir Boulton Building Soc 1972-88; chm: Quarter Horse Racing UK 1985-88, Br Quarter Horse Assoc 1989-90; *Recreations* Breeding Racing Quarter Horses; *Style—* The Rt Hon the Lord Baden-Powell; Grove Heath Farm, Ripley, Woking, Surrey GU23 6ES (☎ 0483 224262)

BADENI, Count Jan; s of Count Stefan Badeni (d 1961), of Castle of Koropiec, Poland, and Mary, *née* Jablonowska; gs of Count Stanislaus Badeni Head of the State of Galicia; *b* 15 Jan 1921; *Educ* Private; *m* 7 July 1956, June, da of Maj Noel Wilson, JP, of Norton Manor, Malmesbury, Wilts; 1 s (Michael Stefan, *qv*), 1 da (Mary b 1960); *Heir* s Count Michael Badeni; *Career* WWII Sqdn Ldr RAF, served East & Coastal Cmd, also in Malayan Emergency, Cmd Helicopter Sqdns in Malaya & UK on search and rescue duties (lifted 67 casualties) 1955-58; Queen's Commendation for Valuable Serv in the Air 1962; High Sheriff of Wiltshire 1978-79; kt of Honour and Devotion (Polish Assoc) SMO Malta 1971, elected pres Polish Assoc SMD Malta 1990; *Style—* The Count Badeni; Norton Manor, Malmesbury, Wilts SN16 0FN

BADENI, Count Michael Stefan; o s of Count Badeni *qv*, of Norton Manor, Malmesbury, Wilts, and Isita June, *née* Wilson; *b* 31 May 1958; *Educ* Ampleforth, LSE (BSc); *m* 2 Aug 1986, Sarah Peta, da of Peter Briggs, of Hutton Rudby, Cleveland; 1 s (Alexander), 1 da (Amelia); *Career* dir: Henderson Crosthwaite Ltd (joined 1981), Drug and Alcohol Foundation (DAF); memb London Stock Exchange; *Recreations* squash, travelling; *Style—* Count Michael Badeni; Henderson Crosthwaite Ltd, 32 St Mary at Hill, London EC3P 3AJ (☎ 071 283 8577, fax 071 623 1997, telex 884035, 0860 391 231)

BADENOCH, (Ian) James Forster; QC (1989); s of Sir John Badenoch, Kt, DM, FRCP, FRCP (Ed); *b* 24 July 1945; *Educ* Dragon Sch Oxford, Rugby, Magdalen Coll Oxford (MA); *m* Marie-Thérèse Victoria, da of Martin Hammond Cabourn Smith; 2 s (William James Cabourn b 30 Jan 1982, Rory Martin Cabourn b 3 Nov 1984), 1 da (Isabel Grace b 1 Jan 1980); *Career* barr; called to the Bar Lincoln's Inn 1968, memb Inner Temple, rec 1987-; *Books* contrib Medical Negligence (Butterworths 1990); *Recreations* family, tennis, travel; *Style—* James Badenoch, Esq, QC; 1 Crown Office Row, Temple, London EC4Y 7HH (☎ 071 353 1801, fax 071 583 1700)

BADENOCH, Sir John; s of William Minty Badenoch, and Ann Dyer, *née* Coutts; *b* 8 March 1920; *Educ* Rugby, Oriel Coll Oxford (MA); *m* Anne Newnham, da of Prof Lancelot Forster; 2 s, 2 da; *Career* former res asst Dept of Clinical Medicine Oxford, former dir Clinical Studies Univ of Oxford; former conslt physician Oxfordshire Dist Health Authy, univ lectr in med Univ of Oxford; fell Merton Coll; former sr censor and sr vice pres Royal Coll of Physicians; Liveryman Soc of Apothecaries; dir Overseas Liaison Office Royal Coll of Physicians; kt 1984; DM, FRCP, FRCPE; *Recreations* walking, travel, natural history; *Clubs* New (Edinburgh); *Style—* Sir John Badenoch; 21 Hartley Court, 84 Woodstock Rd, Oxford OX2 7PF

BADERMAN, Dr Howard; JP (London, 1981); s of Maxwell Baderman (d 1988), and Esther, *née* Collier (d 1990); *b* 12 Nov 1934; *Educ* Ealing Co GS London, UCL (BSc), UCH Med Sch (MB BS); *m* 4 Sept 1970, Susan, da of Wallace Patten (d 1945); 2 s (Rupert b 1974, James b 1977), 1 da (Sophie b 1972); *Career* conslt physician accident and emergency med UCH London 1970, hon sr clinical lectr Dept of Med Univ of London 1971-, sec and chm Specialist Advsy Ctee Accident and Emergency Med RCPS 19 conslt memb Bloomsbury DHA 1985-89, examiner RCS(Ed) 1982-, conslt advsr accident and emergency med to CMO Dept of Health 1989-, advsr accident and emergency servs WHO; coordinator accident servs: UK Egypt Health Agreement 1983-, UK USSR Health Agreement 1986-; memb: Bd Visitors HM Prisons Wandsworth and Holloway 1982-89, Working Pty Child Sex Abuse Standing Med Advsy Ctee 1987-88, mission on Turkish-Bulgarian migration WHO 1989, Ind Ctee supervision Telephone Info Servs 1986-, Standing Ctee Br Paediatric Assoc on Child Abuse, Parly Action Ctee on Tport Safety; sec Working Pty Prison Med Servs 1988-89; Wilfred Trotter medal surgery 1957, Fellowes Gold medal and Sir William Gower prize medal 1958, Sir Ernest Finch visiting prof sch med Univ of Sheffield 1981; Freeman City Corpus Christi Texas USA 1963; memb CSA, fell UCL 1988, sci fell ZSL; MRCS(Eng) 1959, FRCP(London) 1974 (LRCP 1959, MRCP 1967); *Books* Admission of Patients to Hospital (1973), Management of Medical Emergencies (ed, 1978); *Recreations* European history, fell walking; *Style—* Dr Howard Baderman, JP; 21 Churchill Rd, London NW5 1AN (☎ 071 267 4281); Banty Ghyll, Howgill, Cumbria LA10 5JD; Accident Dept, UCH, London WC1E 4AU (☎ 071 387 9300, telex 071 380 9816)

BADHAM, Douglas George; CBE (1975), JP (Glam 1962); s of late David Badham, JP; *b* 1 Dec 1914; *Educ* Leys Sch Cambridge; *m* 1939, Doreen Spencer Phillips; 2 da; *Career* exec dir Powell Duffryn Group 1938-69; chm: Hamell (West) 1968-, Econ Forestry Gp 1981-88 (dir 1978-88), T T Pascoe 1983-89, Minton Treharne and Davies 1960-84, Worldwide Travel (Wales) until 1985; dir: Align-rite Ltd 1985-88, T H Couch 1985-88, Pascoe Hldgs 1983-88, World Trade Centre Wales Ltd 1985-; chm Powell Duffryn Wagon Co 1965-86; High Sheriff Mid Glamorgan 1976, HM Lt for Mid Glamorgan 1982-85, HM Lord Lt for Mid Glamorgan 1985-89 (DL 1975-82); memb: Welsh Cncl 1971-80, Br Gas Corp 1974-84 (pt/t), BR (Western) Bd 1977-82; chm: Devpt Corp for Wales 1971-80 (memb 1965-83), Nat Health Serv Staff Cmmn 1972-75; dep chm Welsh Devpt Agency 1980-84 (memb 1978-84); memb Wales and The Marches Telecommunications Bd 1973-80; *Style—* Douglas Badham, Esq, CBE, JP; Swyn-y-Coed, Watford Road, Caerphilly, Mid Glam (☎ 0222 882094)

BADHAM, John; s of John William Badham, of Rotherham, Yorks (d 1978), and Wilhemina Frances, *née* Radcliffe (d 1969); *b* 9 Dec 1934; *Educ* Mexborough GS, Sheffield Univ 1953-58 (Dip Arch, ARIBA, Dip TP); *m* 11 Sept 1958, Penelope, da of Francis Henry Stokes, of Potters Bar, Herts; 2 da (Francesca b 1964, Imogen b 1964); *Career* architect; ptnr: The Fitzroy Robinson Partnership 1972-, Edwards Stepan Assocs 1964-72, Sir John Burnet Tait & Ptnrs 1961-64, T P Bennett & Son 1959-61; Freeman Worshipful Co of Chartered Architects 1988; *Recreations* music, piano playing, skiing; *Clubs* Ski (GB); *Style—* John Badham, Esq; 23 Onslow Gardens, London N10 3JT (☎ 081 883 2500); The Fitzroy Robinson Partnership, 77 Portland Place, London W1 (☎ 071 636 8033)

BADHAM, Leonard; s of John Randall Badham, and Emily Louise Badham; *b* 10 June 1923; *Educ* Wandsworth GS; *m* 1944, Joyce Rose Lowrie; 2 da; *Career* md J Lyons & Co 1977, dir Allied-Lyons plc 1978, ret; *Style—* Leonard Badham, Esq; 26 Vicarage Drive, E Sheen, London SW14 8RX

BADNELL, Gordon John; s of Philip John Badnell, and Olive Thurza, *née* Pragnell; *b*

18 Aug 1936; *Educ* Sir William Borlase Sch, Marlow Sch of Architecture, Northern Polytechnic London; *m* 1, 9 Sept 1962 (m dis); 1 s (Piers Apsley John b 1964), 2 da (Imogen Ruth Christina b 1967, Olivia Grace Rebecca b 1973); m 2, 30 Sept 1977, Gillian Elizabeth, da of Kenneth Sydney Rawlins (d 1986), of Treyarnon Bay Cornwall; *Career* 2 Lt Royal Engrs, Troop Cdr Fortress Sqdn Malta 1959-61; chartered architect, princ ptnr Elaine Denby and Gordon Badnell chartered architects 1986- (ptnr 1973-), chm Lahnsohn Arbor Ltd 1982-, dir Tanist Ltd 1985-; *Recreations* art, music, Rotary Club; *Style—* Gordon Badnell, Esq; The Old Bakery, School Lane, Lane End, High Wycombe, Bucks (☎ 0494 882279); 65 High St, Marlow Bucks (☎ 06284 72715)

BADRAWY, Dr Galal Akasha; s of Akasha Badrawy (d 1985), of Cairo, and Sanya Ahmed; *b* 4 June 1946; *m* 1974, Sylvia Anne, da of Edward Hatcher; 1 s (Adam b 1977), 1 da (Sarah b 1980); *Career* house surgn Mansoura Univ Hosp Egypt 1970-71, house physician Dar El Saha Hosp Beirut Lebanon 1971; sr house offr: Accident Emergency & Orthopaedics Princess Margaret Hosp Swindon 1972, Geriatric Med Stratton St Margaret's Hosp Swindon 1972-73, Orthopaedic Surgery Co Hosp York 1973-74; registrar: Naburn & Bootham Park Hosps York 1974-78 (sr house offr 1974), Child and Adolescent Psychiatry Southfield & Fairfield Units York 1978-79, York & Community Psychiatry St Andrew Day Hosp 1979-80; conslt psychiatrist and head Psychiatry Dept Abdulla Fouad Hosp Dammam Saudi Arabia, clinical asst Maudsley & The Bethlem Royal Hosp/Inst of Psychiatry 1982, registrar in psychiatry Horsham and Crawley Gen Hosp 1982-83; locum conslt psychiatrist: Yorkshire RHA (with duties at St Mary's Hosp, Scarborough and Clifton Hosp, Scarborough Dist Hosp) 1983, Trent RHA (with duties at Rauceby Hosp Lincolnshire, Boston Gen Hosp, Skegness Gen Hosp) 1982-85, Ashford Gen Hosp Middx 1985-86; locum conslt: St Thomas' Hosp (based at Tooting, duties at Bec Hosp and Day Hosp Putney) 1986-87, Psychiatric Unit Basingstoke Hosp 1987, Abraham Cowley Unit St Peter's Hosp Chertsey 1987-88; locum conslt psychiatrist Woxham Park Hosp Slough 1988-90; in private practice Harley St 1983- and currently med dir Lister Hosp Chelsea, conslt psychiatrist Charter Nightingale Hosp Lisson Grove 1989- (med dir Arab Unit 1987-89); hon memb American Psychiatric Assoc; memb: RCP, BMA; FRSM; *Publications* Interviews by Harpers and Queen, several Arabic newspapers and by BBC Arabic stations; *Recreations* golf; *Clubs* Wentworth, Les Ambassadeurs; *Style—* Dr Galal Badrawy; High Hedges, 31 London Rd, Camberley, Surrey GU15 3UQ (☎ 0276 22219); 121 Harley St, London W1N 1DH (☎ 071 935 6875, fax 071 224 0651)

BAELZ, Very Rev Peter Richard; s of Eberhard Baelz (d 1986), and Dora, *née* Focke (d 1970); *b* 27 July 1923; *Educ* Dulwich Coll, Christ's Coll Cambridge (MA), Westcott House Cambridge (BD), Univ of Oxford (DD); *m* 15 July 1950, Anne Thelma, da of Edward Cleall-Harding (d 1942); 3 s (Simon b 1951, Nicholas b 1955, Timothy b 1956); *Career* curate: Bournville Birmingham 1947-50, Sherborne Dorset 1950-52; asst chaplain Ripon Hall Oxford 1952-53, rector Wishaw Birmingham 1953-56, vicar Bournville Birmingham 1956-60, dean Jesus Coll Cambridge 1960-72, regius prof of moral and pastoral theology and canon of Christ Church Oxford 1972-79, dean of Durham 1980-88, dean emeritus; OStJ; *Books* Prayer and Providence (1966), The Forgotten Dream (1974); *Recreations* cycling; *Style—* The Very Rev Peter Baelz; 36 Brynteg, Llandrindod Wells, Powys LD1 5NB (☎ 0597 825404)

BAER, Derek Alfred Howard; s of Alfred Max Baer (d 1987), and Olga Maud, *née* Howard (d 1985); *b* 5 Nov 1921; *Educ* Eton, Magdalene Coll Cambridge; *m* 25 June 1948, Elizabeth Sheila, da of Rupert Williams-Ellis, of Glasfryn, nr Pwllheli, Gwynedd; 1 s (Richard b 1949), 3 da (Caroline b 1950, Charlotte b 1953, Susanna b 1962); *Career* WWII: Leics Yeo 1942-45, SO ALFSEA 1945-46; princ Miny of Civil Aviation and Tport 1947-54; with John Govett & Co 1954-79, chm Foreign and Colonial Investment Trust plc 1979-85; dir various public cos incl: The Colonial Mutual Life Assurance Society Ltd (London Bd), Portmeirion Potteries plc, Unilever Pensions Investments Ltd; *Recreations* gardening; *Style—* Derek Baer, Esq; Freshford Hall, Freshford, Bath BA3 6EJ (☎ 0225 722 522, fax 0225 777 388); Foreign and Colonial Management Ltd, Exchange House, Primrose St, London EC2A 2NY (☎ 071 628 8000, fax 071 628 8188)

BAER, Jack Mervyn Frank; yr s of late Frank Baer, and Alix Baer; *b* 29 Aug 1924; *Educ* Bryanston, Slade Sch of Fine Art, UCL; *m* 1, 1952 (m dis 1969), Jean (d 1973), only child of late L F St Clair; 1 da; m 2, 1970, Diana Downes Baillieu, da of Aubrey Clare Robinson; 2 step da; *Career* dir Hazlitt Gallery 1948-, md Hazlitt Gooden & Fox 1973-; chm Soc of London Art Dealers 1977-80; *Clubs* Brooks's, Buck's, Beefsteak; *Style—* Jack Baer, Esq; 9 Phillimore Terrace, W8 (☎ 071 937 6899)

BAERLEIN, Richard Edgar; s of Edgar Baerlein (d 1973), and Dorothy, *née* Dixon (d 1973); *b* 15 Sept 1915; *Educ* Eton, Sidney Sussex Coll Cambridge; *m* 6 April 1950, Lillian Laurette, *née* De Tankerville-Chamberlain; *Career* served WWII (despatches 1942); racing journalist: Sporting Chronicle 1937-39, Evening Standard 1947-57, The Observer 1963-, The Guardian 1968-, The Country Life 1985-, Sporting Life Weekender 1985-; Racing Journalist of the Year 1973, winner of The Sporting Life Napstable 1973, winner of The Sporting Chronicle Napstable 1973; *Style—* Richard Baerlein, Esq; Shergar, 2nd Avenue, Summerley, Felpham, West Sussex (☎ 0243 584995); The Observer, Cheslea Bridge House, Queenstown Rd, London SE1

BAGGALEY, Alan; s of Joseph Baggaley (d 1984), and Alice, *née* Weeden; *b* 24 Sept 1929; *Educ* Univ of Sheffield (BA); *m* 15 Aug 1953, Patricia Mary, da of Frederick Fields (d 1988); 1 s (Kristan Paul), 1 da (Lisa Anne); *Career* RE; architect Shepherd Fowler Architects, sr ptnr Hadfield Cawkwell Davidson & Ptnrs architects engrs and planners 1989 (architect 1953-59, assoc ptnr 1959-63, ptnr 1963-89); memb: IOD, Yorkshire and Humberside Devpt Assoc, Chamber of Commerce, Chamber of Trade; FRIBA; *Recreations* local artist, golf; *Clubs* Sheffield Encouragement of Art, IOD, Artists in Architecture, Abbeydale Golf; *Style—* Alan Baggaley, Esq; Claywood Lodge, 76 Queen Victoria Rd, Totley, Sheffield S17 4HU (☎ 0742 620168); Hadfield Cawkwell Davidson & Partners, Architects Engineers & Planners, 17 Broomgrove Rd, Sheffield S10 2LZ (☎ 0742 668181, fax 0742 666246)

BAGGALEY, David Anthony; s of Geoffrey (d 1944), and Joan, *née* Shackleton (d 1969); *b* 9 Jan 1943; *Educ* Merchant Taylors', Portsmouth Poly (Dip Business Admin); *m* 1965, Betty; 1 s (Jason b 1969), 1 da (Sasha b 1970); *Career* dir fin and investment Girobank plc 1979-85, fin dir Abbey Life Group plc 1985-88, dep md Lloyds Bowmaker Fin Ltd 1989-; FCMA, FCT; *Recreations* sailing, mountaineering; *Clubs* Parkstone Yacht, Fell and Rock Climbing, The Lanz; *Style—* David Baggaley, Esq; Broadwater, 37 Alyth Rd, Talbot Woods, Bournemouth, Dorset BH3 7DG; Lloyds Bowmaker Finance Ltd, Holland House, Oxford Road, Bournemouth BH8 8EZ (☎ 0202 299777)

BAGGE, (Alfred) James Stephen; 2 s of Sir John Alfred Picton Bagge, 6 Bt, ED, DL (d 1990); *b* 7 Dec 1952; *Educ* Eton; *m* 10 Oct 1981, Victoria I, er da of Michael A Lyndon Skeggs, of Oakhall, Cornhill-on-Tweed, Northumberland; 1 da (Edwina Rose b 1985); *Career* Capt Blues and Royals, ADC to Govr S Australia 1975-77; barr 1979, memb Hon Soc of Lincoln's Inn; *Style—* James Bagge, Esq; 28 Luttrell Ave, London SW15; Norton Rose, Kempson House, Camomile St, London EC3 7AN

BAGGE, Sir (John) Jeremy Picton; 7 Bt (UK 1867), of Stradsett Hall, Norfolk; s of Sir John Alfred Picton Bagge, 6 Bt, ED, DL (d 1990), and Elizabeth Helena, *née* Davies; *b* 21 June 1945; *Educ* Eton; *m* 1979, Sarah Margaret Phipps, da of late Maj James Shelley Phipps Armstrong, Agent-Gen for Ontario; 2 s (Alfred James John b 1 July 1980, Albert Daniel Bracewell b 1 April 1985), 1 da (Alexandra Mary Pleasance b 26 Dec 1982); *Heir* s, Alfred James John Bagge b 1 July 1980; *Career* farmer; fin advsr HRH The Crown Prince of Ethiopia 1969-70; chm: West Norfolk Enterprise Agency 1985-, Norfolk RDC; dir: West Norfolk Grain 1983-90, King's Lynn Conservancy Bd 1983-87, Fermoy Centre Fndn 1985-89; cncllr King's Lynn and West Norfolk Borough Cncl 1981, chm Devpt and Estates 1983-; memb: Norfolk Ctee CLA 1986-, Norfolk RCC, Haberdashers' Co; Freeman City of London; FCA; *Recreations* shooting, stalking, hunting, fishing, water skiing; *Clubs* Boodles; *Style—* Sir Jeremy Bagge, Bt; Stradsett Hall, Stradsett, King's Lynn, Norfolk PE33 9HA (☎ 036 64 562); Stradsett Estate Office, Stradsett, King's Lynn PE33 9HA (☎ 036 64 642, fax 036 647846)

BAGGE, Richard Anthony; s of Gordon Roy Bagge (d 1980), and Barbara Joan, *née* Sympson; *b* 5 Aug 1949; *Educ* Broad Green GS, Croydon Tech Coll, London Poly; *m* 15 June 1974, Shirley Anne, da of Reginald Ephraim White; 2 s (Jonathan Richard, Jeremy Edward); *Career* Barclays Bank 1966-70, fund mangr Northcote & Co 1970-75, dir MIM Britannia 1975-; FInstD, FInstSMM; *Recreations* sailing, classic cars, gardening, antiques, music, theatre; *Style—* Richard Bagge, Esq; Bridgeham Lodge, Broadbridge Lane, Smallfield, Surrey; MIM Britannia Unit Trust Managers Ltd, 11 Devonshire Sq, London EC2M 4YR (☎ 071 626 3434)

BAGGE, Thomas Philip (Tom); 3 s of Sir John Alfred Picton Bagge, 6 Bt, ED (d 1990); *b* 4 May 1955; *Educ* Eton, RMAS and RAC Cirencester; *Career* Capt Blues and Royals, ADC to Gen Cmdg 4 Armed Div 1977-78; land agent; ARICS; *Style—* Tom Bagge, Esq; Hall Farm, Irnham, Grantham, Lincolnshire NG33 4JD

BAGIER, Gordon Alexander Thomas; DL (Tyne & Wear 1988); s of Alexander Thomas Bagier, of Glasgow; *b* 1924,July; *Educ* Pendower Secdy Tech Sch Newcastle; *m* 1949, Violet, da of John R Sinclair, of Edinburgh; 2 s, 2 da; *Career* MP (Lab) Sunderland S 1964-1987, pps to Home Sec 1968-69; memb Select Ctee Tport 1980- (chm 1985-87); *Recreations* golf; *Clubs* Westerhope Golf (Newcastle upon Tyne); *Style—* Gordon Bagier, Esq, DL; Rahana, Whickham Highway, Dunston, Gateshead, Co Durham

BAGNALL, John Keith; s of Alfred Studley Bagnall, of Otley, West Yorks, and Margaret, *née* Kirkham (d 1983); *b* 30 Dec 1941; *Educ* Oundle; *m* 10 Oct 1964, Valerie, da of Leslie Moxon (d 1985); 1 s (Stephen b 1968), 1 da (Caroline b 1966); *Career* Alfred Bagnall & Sons Ltd: dir 1962, gp md 1972-; treas Keighley and Dist Trg Assoc 1966-70; memb Standing Ctee: Safety Health and Welfare 1976-79, Fin 1976-, Econ and Public Affrs Gp 1983-; pres: Nat Fedn Painting and Decorating Contractors 1979-80, Fedn of Bldg Specialist Contractors 1983-84; vice pres Bldg Employers Confedn 1986- (memb Nat Cncl 1978-85); FCA 1965, FBIM 1972; *Recreations* tennis, chess; *Style—* John Bagnall, Esq; Dale Lodge, Gilstead Lane, Bingley, West Yorkshire BD16 3LN (☎ 0274 563 867); Alfred Bagnall & Sons Ltd, 6 Manor Lane, Shipley, West Yorks BD18 3RD (☎ 0274 587 227, fax 0274 531 260)

BAGNALL, Kenneth Reginald; QC (1973), QC Hongkong (1983); s of Reginald Bagnall, and Elizabeth Bagnall; *b* 26 Nov 1927; *Educ* King Edward VI Sch Birmingham, Univ of Birmingham (LLB, Ardley Scholar); *m* 1, 1955, Margaret Edith Wall; 1 s, 1 da; m 2, 1963, Rosemary Hearn; 1 s, 1 da; *Career* called to the Bar 1950, dep judge Crown Court 1975-79; chm Hurstwood Timber Co 1972-79; memb Crafts Cncl 1982-84, jt fndr (with HM Govt) of the Bagnall Gallery (operated by the Crafts Cncl 1982-); co fndr: Anglo American Real Property Inst 1980- (chm 1980-82), The New Law Publishing Co Ltd; chm: Editorial Bd New Property Coles Ltd, Brookfield House Estates plc 1989, The New Law Publishing Co Ltd 1991; co fndr The Residential Recovery Company Ltd 1990; Freeman City of London 1972, Liveryman Barber Surgeon Co 1972; *Books* Guide to Business Tenancies (1956), Development Land Tax (1978), Judicial Review (1985); *Style—* Kenneth Bagnall, Esq, QC

BAGNALL, Field Marshal Sir Nigel Thomas; GCB (1985, KCB 1980), CVO (1978), MC (1950, and Bar 1953); s of Lt-Col Harry Stephen Bagnall, and Marjory May Bagnall; *b* 10 Feb 1927; *Educ* Wellington, Balliol Coll Oxford; *m* 1959, Anna Caroline Church; 2 da (Emma, Sarah); *Career* joined Army 1945, cmmnd Green Howards 1946, 6 Airborne Div Palestine 1946-48, Malaya 1949-52, GSO1 (Intelligence) Borneo 1966-67, Cmd 4/7 Royal Dragoon Gds BAOR and NI 1967-69, Cmd RAC BAOR 1970-72, def fell Balliol Coll Oxford 1972-73, sec COS Ctee MOD 1973-75, GOC 4 Div BAOR 1975-77, ACDS (Policy) MOD 1978-80, Cmd 1 (Br) Corps BAOR 1980-83, C-in-C BAOR and Cmd N Army Gp BAOR 1983-85, Chief Gen Staff 1985-88, Col Cmdt RAC 1985-88, Col Cmdt Army Physical Trg Corps 1981-88, ADC Gen to HM The Queen 1985-88; hon fell Balliol Coll Oxford 1986; *Recreations* reading, writing, walking, gardening; *Clubs* Cavalry and Guards; *Style—* Field Marshal Sir Nigel Bagnall, GCB, CVO, MC; c/o Royal Bank of Scotland, Kirkland House, 22 Whitehall, London SW1

BAGNALL SMITH, Corinne Andree Reppin; da of Jameson Reppin Bates, 315 Benfleet Rd, S Benfleet, Essex SS7 1PW, and Andree Josephine Amand Eugenie, *née* Eyskens; *b* 18 March 1961; *Educ* Queenswood Sch; *m* 3 June 1989, Richard Bagnall Smith, s of John Anthony Bagnall Smith, of The Old Kennels, Garsington, Oxon; *Career* trainee asst buyer Harrods 1979-84, conslt Ligne Roset (UK) Ltd 1984-86, sales mangr Van Cleef and Arpels 1987, sales dir Elizabeth Gage 1987-89, dir Chalmet (UK) Ltd 1989-; *Recreations* skiing, swimming, music; *Clubs* Holmes Place, Stocks; *Style—* Mrs Corinne Bagnall Smith; Chaumet (UK) Ltd, 178 New Bond Street, London W1Y 9PD (☎ 071 493 5403, fax 071 408 0620)

BAGNELL, Capt (William) David Armstrong; s of Capt Robert Armstrong Bagnell (Croix de Guerre 1918) (d 1959), of Longdown Chase, Hindhead, Surrey, and Phyllis Evelyn (d 1969), da of Capt George William Taylor, and Lady Elizabeth Emma Geraldine, o da of 4 Earl of Wilton; *b* 21 Aug 1926; *Educ* Eton; *m* 16 May 1962, Caroline Mary, o da of Edward Richard Whittington-Moë (d 1965); 1 s (William Edward Henry b 1966), 1 da (Sophia Mary b 1963); *Career* Capt RHG (Blues), served in WWII Capt Allied Liaison HQ, Belgian Army 1947-48, ret 1955; unsuccessfully contested Hammersmith N Constituency (C) Oct 1959; Hants CC 1964-67, chm E Hants (Petersfield) Cons and Unionist Assoc 1968-73, dep chm Cons Cwlth and Overseas Cncl 1976-83; at talks with World Bank and US Govt Agencies on insurance against political risk 1961; chm DB Investmt Co; underwriting memb of Lloyd's; memb Central Exec Ctee NSPCC 1973-; Chev Order of the Dannebrog (Denmark) 1951; *Recreations* shooting; *Clubs* White's, Buck's; *Style—* Capt David Bagnell; East Worldham House, Alton, Hampshire GU34 3AS (☎ 0420 83143)

BAGOT, 9 Baron (GB 1780); Sir Heneage Charles Bagot; 14 Bt (E 1627); s of late Charles Frederick Heneage Bagot, ggs of 1 Baron; suc half-bro 1979; *b* 11 June 1914; *Educ* Harrow; *m* 1939, Muriel Patricia, da of late Maxwell James Moore Boyle; 1 s, 1 da; *Heir* s, Hon Shaun Bagot; *Career* late Maj Indian Army; *Style—* The Rt Hon The Lord Bagot; 16 Barclay Road, London SW6; Tyn-y-Mynydd, nr Llithfaen, Gwynedd, N Wales

BAGOT, Hon (Charles Hugh) Shaun; s and h of 9 Baron Bagot, *qv*; *b* 23 Feb 1944; *Educ* Abbotsholme; *m* 16 July 1986, Mrs Sally A Stone, da of D G Blunden, of Farnham, Surrey; *Style—* The Hon Shaun Bagot; 16 Barclay Road, London SW6

BAGSHAWE, Prof Kenneth Dawson; CBE (1990); s of Capt Harry Bagshawe (d 1959), of Cliff House, Beesands, Devon, and Gladys, *née* Dawson (d 1983); *b* 17 Aug 1925; *Educ* Harrow County Sch, LSE, St Mary's Hosp Med Sch; *m* 1, 12 Dec 1946

(m dis 1976), Alice, da of Thomas Kelly (d 1924); 1 s (James b 26 April 1959), 1 da (Janita b 2 Mar 1956); m 2, 29 Jan 1977, Sylvia Dorothy Lawler, da of Capt Fred Corben, MC (d 1969); *Career* Sub Lt RNVR 1943-46; jr med appts St Mary's Hosp London 1952-60, res fell John Hopkins Hosp Baltimore USA 1955-56, conslt physician Charing Cross Hosp 1963-75 (sr lectr in med 1961-63), prof of med oncology Charing Cross Hosp Med Sch 1975, 300 papers on various aspects of cancer incl reverse role chemotherapy and generating cytotoxic agents at cancer sites; chm Sci Ctee Cancer Res Campaign 1983-88, chm Exec Ctee and dep chm of Bd various MRC and DHSS Ctees; Hon DSc; FRCOG 1979, FRCR 1984, FRCP 1969, FRS 1989; *Books* Choriocarcinoma (1969), Medical Oncology (1975); *Recreations* walking, photography, invention; *Clubs* Atheneum; *Style—* Prof Kenneth Bagshawe, CBE, FRS; 115 George St, London W1H 5TA (☎ 071 262 6033)

BAGULEY, Maurice Grant; s of Capt William Albert Baguley (d 1947), of Hounslow, Middx, and Phyllis Amy, *née* Laverne (d 1987); *b* 2 May 1926; *Educ* Spring Grove GS, Acton Tech Coll, Brighton Poly, City Univ (MSc); *m* 1, 20 Nov 1948, Ivy Ethel (d 1983), da of Reginald Arthur Coomber (d 1952), of Ashford, Middx; 1 da (Claire Susan b 1953); m 2, 19 Nov 1983, Julie Elizabeth, *née* Barker, wid of Alec John Shickle; *Career* structural draughtsman The Square Grip Co Ltd 1945-46, jr engr J H Coombs & Ptnrs 1946-47, design engr Peter Lind & Co Ltd 1947-48, sr design engr Woodall Duckham 1948-53, ptnr Malcolm Glover and Partners 1953-62, fndr Maurice Baguley and Partners 1962, ret 1973; structural, civil engrg bldg control conslt: City of Westminster, Royal Borough of Kensington and Chelsea, London Borough of Hammersmith and Fulham, London Borough of Hackney, Wandsworth Corp, Tandridge DC; IStructE Awards: Wallace premium 1950, Husband prize 1953, Andrews prize 1953; FICE 1973, FIStructE 1953, MAmerSCE 1974, MConsE 1960; *Recreations* sailing, cruising, pianoforte; *Clubs* Naval, Newhaven Yacht; *Style—* Maurice Baguley, Esq; The Barn, Ivy Mill Lane, Godstone, Surrey RH9 8NF (☎ 0883 724500)

BAHCHELI, Tylan; s of Salih Bahcheli (d 1986), and Zehra, *née* Mustafa (d 1989); *b* 20 Aug 1943; *Educ* The English Sch Nicosia Cyprus, Westminster; *m* 18 March 1965, Marylin Ann, da of Eric Dudley Jenkins, of Downend, Bristol; 1 s (Simon George b 24 Dec 1966), 1 da (Tezel Jane b 19 Sept 1965); *Career* mktg exec T Bath and Co Ltd 1964-70; chm: Dudley Jenkins Assocs Ltd 1984-88 (proprietor 1971-84), Dudley Jenkins Gp plc 1988-; *Recreations* gardening, shooting, reading; *Clubs* Wig and Pen; *Style—* Tylan Bahcheli, Esq; 9 Rostrevor Rd, London SW6 (☎ 071 731 2358); Telford House, Coaley, Nr Dursley, Glos (☎ 0453 860230); Dudley Jenkins Group plc, Axe & Bottle Court, 70 Newcomen St, London SE1 (☎ 071 407 4753, fax 071 407 6294, telex 263496 LISTS G, car 0860 245 881)

BAHRANI, Prof Aladdin Saleem; s of Saleem Bahrani (d 1986), and Bahija, *née* Shamma; *b* 10 March 1930; *Educ* Baghdad Coll Iraq, Queen's Univ Belfast (BSc, MSc, PhD); *m* 1952, Margaret, *née* Sawrey; 1 s (David b 1964), 1 da (Linda b 1955); *Career* apprentice: Ruston and Hornsby Lincoln 1955-56, Metropolitan Vickers Manchester 1956-57; chief marine and mechanical engr Iraq Ports Admins Basrah 1959-63, sr pipeline engr Iraq Petroleum Company Kirkuk 1967-69, chief engr Iraq National Oil Company 1969-70; Queen's Univ of Belfast: lectr 1970-72, sr lectr 1972-77, reader 1977-83, prof of manufacturing engrg 1983-; MIM 1967, FWeldI 1976, FIMechE 1980, FIProdE 1984, FEng 1989; *Recreations* gardening, listening to music, country walking; *Style—* Prof Aladdin Bahrani; 30 Circular Road, Belfast, Northern Ireland BT4 2GA (☎ 0232 768112); Dept of Mechanical and Manufacturing Engineering, Queen's University of Belfast, Belfast BT9 5AH (☎ 0232 245133, fax 0232 661729)

BAIER, Frederick John Watt; s of Francis Clair Wolfgang Baier, of Birkenhead, and Violet, *née* Wood; *b* 15 April 1949; *Educ* Bootham Sch York, Hull GS Kingston upon Hull, Canterbury Coll of Art, Birmingham Coll of Art (Dip AD Furniture), RCA (MA); *m* 1988, Lucy Elizabeth Strachan, the Sculptor, da of David Rankin Strachan (d 1979); 2 da (Billie Anna b 26 Jan 1989, Rebecca b 4 Feb 1990); *Career* furniture designer; in partnership with Barry Joseph Leister and Keith Clarke in Empire Workshops (architectural reclamation, interior schemes and prototype furniture) 1977-79; teaching: Brighton Poly 1979-82, Wendell Castle Sch USA 1986-88, pt/t at RCA and Wilshire Studio 1989-; consultancy work incl: Design Cncl, Crafts Cncl, A B K Architects, Terry Farrell, *qv*, David Davies; exhibitions incl: Furniture Designer Craftsman (RCA) 1977, New Faces (Br Crafts Centre London) 1978, furniture into Sculpture (Ikon Gallery Birmingham) 1979, The Maker's Eye (Crafts Cncl London) 1982, The Furniture Fellow (solo, Northern Arts touring) 1983, Going for Baroque (Midland Gp Nottingham) 1985, British Design (CO1/Kunstlerhaus Vienna) 1986, Keeping up with the Jones (Art and Architecture Gallery USA) 1987, 2D/3D, Art and Craft Made and Designed for the Twentieth Century (Laing Art Gallery Newcastle upon Tyne and Northern Centre for Contemporary Art Sunderland) 1987, Three Ways of Seeing (Crafts Cncl London and touring) 1990; collections and cmmns incl: V & A Museum, Birmingham Museum and Art Gallery, Southern, Arts, Crafts Cncl Gallery, Shipley Art Gallery, Templeton Coll Oxford; awards: Royal Soc of Arts Bursary 1971, Major award Craft Advsy Ctee 1976, Minor award Midlands Arts 1978, Br Crafts award Telegraph Sunday Magazine 1978, Northern Arts Fellowship 1982-83; *Style—* Frederick Baier, Esq; 45 High St, Dewsey, Wiltshire SN9 5AF (☎ 0672 62974, fax 0672 63043)

BAILES, Alyson; da of John-Lloyd Bailes, and Barbara, *née* Martin; *b* 6 April 1949; *Educ* The Belverdere Sch GPDST Liverpool, Somerville Coll Oxford (MA); *Career* entered FCO 1969-; Br Embassy Budapest 1970-74, UK delgn to NATO 1974-76, MOD and FCO 1976-80, Br Embassy Bonn 1981-84, FCO 1984-87, cnsllr Br Embassy Peking 1987-89 dep head of mission Br Embassy Oslo 1990; *Recreations* travel, music, nature; *Style—* Miss Alyson Bailes; c/o Foreign & Commonwealth Office, King Charles St, London SW1A 2AH (☎ 071 270 3000)

BAILEY, (Thomas) Alan; s of Thomas Dobson Bailey, of Ryde, IOW (d 1983), and Violet Vera, *née* Walker (d 1983); *b* 28 Oct 1928; *Educ* Maidstone; *m* 7 Aug 1950, Mary, da of Maj Percy Baldock, IA (d 1973); 1 s (Kimball b 1957); *Career* Nat Serv 1946-49, TA 1949-64 (Capt Intelligence Corps); various local govt appts (incl asst clerk Brentwood DC) 1950-62, under sec RICS 1962-69, chief exec World of Property Housing Trust (now Sanctuary Spiral Hou Group) 1969-79, chm Focus Group of Cos 1969-79, md Andrews Group of Cos 1979-84, chm and md ABS Group of Cos 1979-; chm: Placemakers Luncheon Club 1971-, non-exec dir Asset Corporation Ltd 1989-; former tstee Voluntary and Christian Serv and Phyllis Tst (consequen as dir Help The Aged, Action Aid, and other Charities), dir Int Shakespeare Globe Centre 1981-, tstee Cyril Wood Meml Tst 1980-; visiting lectr Coll of Estate Mgmnt Univ of Reading; MCAM, MIPR, MCIM; *Books* How To Be A Property Developer (1988); *Recreations* drawing, painting, writing; *Clubs* Special Forces, Wig & Pen; *Style—* Alan Bailey, Esq; The Bridge House, Sible Hedingham, Essex; 7 Bradbrook House, Studio Place, London, SW1 (☎ 071 235 3397); 14 Kinnerton Place South, Kinnerton St, London, SW1X 8EH (☎ 071 245 6262, fax 071 235 3916)

BAILEY, Dr Alison George Selborne (Joe); s of George Frederick Selborne Bailey, (d 1969), of Claytons, Bourne End, Bucks, and Mabel Yardley, *née* Guard, (d 1950); *b* 19 July 1915; *Educ* Radley, Gonville & Caius Coll Cambridge (MA), St Bartholomew's Hosp; *m* 15 May 1947, Christine Margeurite, da of Edward Joseph Law Delfosse, of Astons Rd, Moor Park; 2 s (George Henry Selborne b 1953, William Edward Selborne b 1955), 2 da (Alison (Mrs Wilson) b 1949, Margaret (Mrs Jenkins) b 1950); *Career* house surgn: Bart's 1942-43, Addenbrookes Hosp 1942; gen practice Bourne End 1943-86; consulting manipulative surgn 1947-; sr med offr Windsor Racecourse; memb: Bucks LMC 1946-86, Bucks FPC 1950-86, Windsor Med Soc 1943- (pres 1959-60), cncl memb RCS 1983-88 Wooburn PC 1946-69 (chm 1949-61); chm Bd of Govrs Wooburn Infants Primary and Secdy Schs 1946-74, pres Radleian Soc 1986-; pres Radley Mariners 1990-, chm Cains Club 1971-; coach: many coll boats Oxford and Cambridge, Univ of Oxford Boat Race crew 1954 and 1964, Univ of Cambridge for visit to Japan 1954, Brazil 1956; Freeman City of London, Liveryman Soc of Apothecaries 1943; LMSSA 1942, FRGCP 1981, FRCS 1988; *Recreations* riding, rowing; *Clubs* Hawks, Leander; *Style—* Dr Joe Bailey; Clayfield House, Wooburn, High Wycombe, Bucks HP10 0HR (☎ 06285 23203)

BAILEY, Prof Anita Irene; da of Cecil John Bailey, and Irene Maud Mahala, *née* Wakeham; *b* 7 March 1926; *Educ* Jeppe HS for Girls, Univ of Witwatersrand (BSc, MSc), Univ of Cambridge (MA, PhD); *Career* Newnham Coll Cambridge: res fell 1955-58, fell and lectr in physics 1958-64; Smithson res fell The Royal Soc 1958-1964, res scientist MRC Biophysics Res Unit King's Coll London 1964-1970, sr res scientist Fraunhofer Institut für Grenzflächen U Bioverfahrenstechnik Stuttgart W Germany 1970-1976, currently Kodak prof of interface sci Imp Coll London; memb: Soc of Chem Ind 1976-, R Soc Chem 1976-, Royal Inst 1987-; 1851 exhibitioner 1955-58; *Recreations* music, swimming, gardening; *Clubs* Univ Women's; *Style—* Prof Anita Bailey; Hook Heath House, Hook Heath Rd, Hook Heath, Woking, Surrey GU22 0DP (☎ 0483 765598); Department of Chemical Engineering & Chemical Technology, Imperial College of Science, Technology & Medicine, London SW7 2AZ (☎ 071 589 5111, telex 92G 484, fax 071 584 7596)

BAILEY, (Keith Cyril) Austin; s of J Austin Bailey (d 1944), of Swansea; *b* 8 July 1919; *Educ* Wycliffe Coll; *m* 1948, Joan, da of Capt John Thomas (d 1979), of Southampton; 1 s (Clive); *Career* served WWII Capt RACS (POW Singapore 1942; pres S Wales Far East POW Assoc); fomer chm Bailey Carpets, Bailey Carpets Int, Redlands Flooring Distributors (Bristol); former dep chm Tstee Savings Bank for Wales and Border Counties; High Sheriff W Glam 1979-80, chm Friends of the Welsh Cncl of Churches 1983-85, vice chm Swansea and Brecon Diocescan Bd of Fin, vice pres Wales Cncl for the Disabled; memb: Cncl Swansea Univ Coll, Nat Cncl Wholesale Floorcovering Distributors Assoc 1955-87, Rep Body and Governing Body of Church of Wales, IOD Cncl for Wales, Court of Univ of Wales; *Recreations* walking, countryside; *Clubs* City and County (Swansea); *Style—* K C Austin Bailey, Esq; 20 Woodridge Court, Langland Bay, Swansea SA3 4TH (☎ 0792 66836)

BAILEY, Sir Brian Harry; OBE (1976), JP (Somerset 1964), DL (Somerset 1988); s of Harry Bailey, and Lilian, *née* Pulfer; *b* 25 March 1923; *Educ* Lowestoft GS; *m* 1948, Nina Olive Sylvia Saunders; 2 da; *Career* WWII RAF; orgn offr SW District NALGO 1951-82, SW regnl sec TUC 1968-81; memb: Somerset CC 1966-84, SW Econ Planning Cncl 1969-79, MRC 1978-86, Business Educn Cncl 1980-84; chm SW RHA 1975-82, dir Western Orchestral Soc Ltd 1982-; chm: Health Educn Cncl 1983-87, TV South West 1980-; memb NHS Mgmnt Inquiry Team 1983-85; vice chm BBC Radio Br Advsy Cncl 1971-78; memb BBC West Regnl Advsy Cncl 1973-78; memb Advsy Ctee Severn DOE 1978-81; tstee Euro Community Chamber Orch 1987-, regnl pres MENCAP 1984-90; kt 1983; *Style—* Sir Brian Bailey, OBE, JP, DL; 32 Stonegallows, Taunton, Somerset (☎ 0823 461265)

BAILEY, Christopher Bruce (Chris); s of Robert Malcolm Bailey, and Pamela Marion Bailey; *b* 29 April 1968; *Educ* Taverham HS, Norwich City Coll; *Career* tennis player; Br U12 champion 1980, Norfolk number 1: u12, u14, u16, u18; Norfolk sr number 1: 1980, 1982, 1984, 1986; East Regn number 1: u12, u16, u18; East Regn sr number 1: 1980, 1984, 1986; memb and player Br Davis Cup Team: 1987, 1988, 1989; winner Central African Satellite, quarter finalist Stella Artois Championships Queens Club London, semi finalist Livingstone NJ Grand Prix USA; *Style—* Chris Bailey, Esq; 108 Fakenham Rd, Taverham, Norwich, Norfolk NR8 6QD (☎ 0603 867730; car 0860 557907)

BAILEY, Hon Christopher Russell; TD; only s & h of 4 Baron Glanusk; *b* 18 March 1942; *Educ* Eton, Clare Coll Cambridge (BA); *m* 1974, Frances Elizabeth, da of Air Chief Marshal Sir Douglas Charles Lowe, GCB, DFC, AFC, *qv*; 1 s, 1 da; *Career* gen mangr Lumenition 1986-; *Style—* The Hon Christopher Bailey; 51 Chertsey Rd, Chobham, Surrey (☎ 0276 85 6380)

BAILEY, Lady Daphne Magdalene; *née* Cadogan; da of 7 Earl Cadogan by his 1 w Primrose; *b* 23 Oct 1939; *m* 1961, David Malcolm Graham Bailey (b 24 Feb 1934), s of late Ronald Graham Bailey; 2 s, 1 da; *Style—* The Lady Daphne Bailey; The Manor House, Dry Sandford, Abingdon, Oxford

BAILEY, David Royston; s of William Bailey and Agnes, *née* Green; *b* 2 Jan 1938; *m* 1, 1960, Rosemary Bramble; m 2, 1967, Catherine Deneuve, the film actress; m 3, 1975 (m dis 1985), Marie Helvin, *qv*; m 4, 1986, Catherine Dyer; 1 s, 1 da; *Career* photographer; dir of commercials 1966-, dir and prodr of TV documentaries 1968- (titles include Beaton, Warh Visconti); memb Arts Cncl 1983-; retrospectives of his work at: Nat Portrait Gallery 1971, V & A Museum 1983, Int Centre of Photography NY 1984, Royal Acad (gp exhibition) 1989; FRPS, FSIAD, FRSA; *Books* Box of Pinups (1964), Goodbye Baby and Amen (1969), Warhol (1974), Beady Minces (1974), Papua New Guinea (1975), Mixed Moments (1976), Trouble and Strife (1980), NW1 (1982), Black and White Memories (1983), Nudes 1981-84 (1984), Imagine (1985); *Recreations* photography, aviculture, travel; *Style—* David Bailey, Esq

BAILEY, Sir Derrick Thomas Louis; 3 Bt (UK 1919), of Cradock, Province of Cape of Good Hope, Union of South Africa, DFC; s of late Sir Abe Bailey, 1 Bt, KCMG; suc half-bro, Sir John Milner Bailey, 2 Bt (d 1946); *b* 15 Aug 1918; *Educ* Winchester, Ch Ch Oxford; *m* 1, 1946, Katharine Nancy, da of Robert Stormonth Darling, of Kelso, Scotland; 4 s, 1 da; m 2, 1980, Mrs Jean Roscoe; *Heir* s, John Richard Bailey; *Career* Capt S African Air Force, formerly 2 Lt S African Irish; farmer; *Style—* Sir Derrick Bailey, Bt, DFC; Bluestones, Alderney, CI

BAILEY, Diane Jane; MBE (1988); da of William Howard Robb (d 1988), and Doris Elizabeth Robb; *b* 31 Aug 1943; *Educ* Bilston Girls HS; *m* 1, 13 Jan 1962, Alastair Frearson (d 1968), s of Raymond Frearson, of 278 Drummond Rd, Skegness, Lincolnshire; 1 s (Karl b 1964), 1 da (Caroline b 1963); m 2, John Michael Bailey; 1 da (Abigail b 1975); *Career* golf player; Br girl int 1957 to 1961, S Girls Open stroke play champion 1959 and 1961, Staffordshire champion 1961, Br girl champ, finalist Br Ladies Championship 1961, Br int 1961 and 1962, 1968 and 72, Eng int 1961 and 1971, Midland champion 1966, Lincolnshire champ 1966 and 1967, World Cup Team 1968, AVIA Foursomes Championship 1972, capt Cwlth Team 1983, Br capt Vagliano Team 1983 and 1985, capt Curtis Cup Team 1984, 1986 and 1988 (memb 1962 and 1972); currently interior designer; *Recreations* motor cruising, fishing; *Clubs* Royal Motor Yacht, Sussex Motor Yacht, Enville Golf, Reigate Heath Golf, Walton Heath Golf; *Style—* Mrs Diane Bailey, MBE; Plan Magazines Ltd, 45 Station Rd, Redhill, Surrey RH1 1QH (☎ 0737 768261, fax 0737 771662)

BAILEY, Air Vice-Marshal Dudley Graham (Bill); CB (1979), CBE (1970); *b* 12 Sept 1924; *m* 15 May 1948, Dorothy Barbara; 2 da (Deborah b 1956, Caroline b

1957); *Career* served RAF 1943-80; trained as pilot in Canada 1943-45, intelligence duties in Middle East 1946-48, Berlin Airlift No 47 Sqdn 1949, Adjutant 50 Sqdn and Fl Cdr 61 Sqdn (Lincolns) 1950-52, exchange duties with USAF 1952-54 (B36 Aircraft), Flt Cdr 58 Sqdn and OC 82 Sqdn (Canberras) 1955-56, Dept of Operational Requirements, Air Miny 1957-58, Army Staff Coll Camberley 1959, OC 57 (Victors) Sqdn 1960-62, Wing Cdr Ops HQ Middle East Aden 1963-65, Staff of Chief of Def Staff 1965-66, dep dir Air Plans MOD 1966-68, OC RAF Wildenrath 1968-70, sr personnel staff offr HQ Strike Cmd 1970-71, RCDS 1972, dir of personnel (RAF) 1973-74, Sr Air Staff Offr RAF Germany 1974-75, Dep Cdr RAF Germany 1975-76, DG of Personal Serv (RAF) MOD 1976-80, dep md and co sec The Servs Sound and Vision Corp; *Clubs* RAF; *Style—* Air Vice-Marshal Bill Bailey, CB, CBE; Services Sound and Vision Corp, Gerrards Cross SL9 8TN (☎ 024 07 4461, ext 226)

BAILEY, Geoffrey Thomas; s of Thomas Henry Bailey (d 1947), of Preston, Lancs, and Mary Malvina, *née* Harrison (d 1950); *b* 29 June 1912; *Educ* Rossall Sch, Royal Agric Coll, RMC Sandhurst; *m* 30 Sept 1939, Elsie Margaret, da of Harry Ramsden Major Cripps (d 1935), of Shotley, Suffolk; 1 s (William b 1943), 1 da (Janet b 1944); *Career* served WWII 1940-46 RTR: Asst Adj D and M Wing Bovington Camp, Staff Capt 30 Corps HQ Hanover; chartered surveyor, land agent and valuer Holland (Lincs) CC 1948-74, ret; churchwarden: St Mary's Church Frampton, St Michael's Church Frampton W; MRAC, FRICS; *Recreations* rugby, tennis, golf; *Clubs* Fylde, Norwich, Bath Rugby, Woodhall Spa, Boston Golf; *Style—* Geoffrey Bailey, Esq; Hall Lane Cottage, Frampton by Boston, Lincs PE20 1AB (☎ 0205 722259)

BAILEY, George Henry Selborne; s of Dr Alison George Selborne Bailey, of Clayfield House, Wooburn, High Wycombe, Bucks, and Christine, *née* Delfosse (d 1982); *b* 13 Aug 1953; *Educ* Radley, Downing Coll Cambridge (BA); *m* 8 Nov 1986, Allison Gail, da of John Scott Paterson, of Middle Grange, Harpenden; 1 s (Henry George Selborne b 15 Jan 1989); *Career* dir Sotheby's 1979-; ARICS 1978; *Clubs* Leander; *Style—* George Bailey, Esq; Sotheby's 34 New Bond St, London W1 (☎ 071 493 8080)

BAILEY, Glenda Adrianne; da of John Ernest Bailey, and Constance, *née* Groome; *b* 16 Nov 1958; *Educ* Noel Baker Sch Derby, Kingston Poly (BA); *Career* fashion forecasting Design Direction 1983-84, prodr dummy magazine for IPC 1985; ed: Honey magazine 1986, Folio magazine 1987, Br Marie-Claire 1988; winner of Women's Magazine Ed of The Year award 1989 (Br Soc of Magazine Eds); *Style—* Miss Glenda Bailey; 2 Hatfields, London, SE1 9PG (☎ 071 261 5240, fax 071 261 5277, telex 915748 MAGDIVG)

BAILEY, Harry; s of Joseph Henry Lewis Bailey (d 1955), of Yorks, and Lily Groves (d 1953); *b* 28 March 1928; *Educ* Thorne GS, Rotherham Coll of Technol; *m* 1961, Sheila Margaret, da of Stanley Dance (d 1987), of Berks; 3 s (Lewis, David, Howard); *Career* RAF 1946-48, fitter 2 Engines; tech asst Pilkington Bros Ltd 1944-46 (devpt engr 1948-52), mech engr Burmah Oil Co Ltd 1952-60, construction supt Gulf Oil (GB) Ltd 1961-68, dir and gen mangr Motherwell Bridge Nigeria Ltd 1969-71, sales mangr (later sales dir and chief exec Singapore) Matthew Hall plc 1971-85; dir: Matthew Hall Engrg Sdn Bhd Kuala Lumpur 1981-85, Matthew Hall Engrg SE Asia PTE Ltd 1980-85, Matthew Hall Int Devpt Ltd London 1977-85, Shaw and Hatton (Malaysia) Sdn Bhd Kuala Lumpur 1987-, Dovre Hatton As Stavanger Norway 1988-90; md Shaw and Hatton International Ltd 1985-; vice pres Shaw and Hatton US Ltd NY 1987-; MIMechE 1964; *Recreations* swimming, theatre, music; *Clubs* Les Ambassadeurs (London), Tanglin (Singapore), British (Singapore); *Style—* Harry Bailey, Esq; 19 Cookes Lane, Cheam Village, Sutton, Surrey SM3 8QG (☎ 081 644 6262); Shaw and Hatton International Ltd, Ashridge Manor, Forest Road, Wokingham, Berks RG11 5SL (☎ 0734 774177, fax 0734 771210)

BAILEY, Ian Campbell; s of James Rowland Bailey (d 1979), and Hilda Maud, *née* Campbell (d 1958); *b* 5 Oct 1929; *Educ* St Andrew's Coll Dublin, Trinity Coll Dublin (BA, MB BCh, BAO, LM); *m* 18 June 1955, Ruth Kathleen, *née* Johnson; 2 s (Christopher b 1957, Michael b 1961), 1 da (Caroline b 1966); *Career* conslt neurological surgn and sr lectr Univ of E Africa Uganda, sr conslt neurological surgn Royal Victoria Hosp Belfast; memb Cncl Soc of Br Neurological Surgns; FRCS, FRCSI; *Recreations* athletics, tennis, sailing; *Style—* Ian Bailey, Esq; The Blackstone House, Magheragall, Lisburn, Northern Ireland (☎ 0846 621 333); The Royal Victoria Hosptial, Belfast (☎ 0232 240503)

BAILEY, Jack Arthur; s of Horace Arthur and Elsie Winifred Bailey; *b* 22 June 1930; *Educ* Christ's Hosp, Univ of Oxford; *m* 1957, Julianne Mary Squier; 1 s, 2 da; *Career* rugby football corr Sunday Telegraph 1962-74; sec MCC 1974-, sec Int Cricket Conf 1974-; *Style—* Jack Bailey, Esq; 20 Elm Tree Rd, London NW8 (☎ 071 228 6246)

BAILEY, John Richard; s (by 1 m) and h of Sir Derrick Bailey, 3 Bt, DFC; *b* 11 June 1947; *Educ* Winchester, Christ's Coll Cambridge, Univ of Cape Town; *m* 1977, Philippa Jane, da of John Sherwin Mervyn Pearson Gregory, of Monnington-on-Wye, Herefords; 2 s, 1 da; *Style—* John Bailey, Esq

BAILEY, Venerable Jonathan Sansbury; s of Walter Eric Bailey, of Port Erin, IOM, and Audrey Sansbury, *née* Keenan; *b* 24 Feb 1940; *Educ* Quarry Bank HS Liverpool, Trinity Coll Cambridge (MA); *m* 1965, Susan Mary, da of Maurice James Bennett-Jones (d 1980); 3 s (Mark, Colin, Howard); *Career* curate: Sutton Lancs 1965-68, Warrington 1968-71; warden Marrick Priory 1971-76, vicar Wetherby Yorks 1976-82, archdeacon Southend 1982-; *Style—* The Ven the Archdeacon of Southend; 136 Broomfield Rd, Chelmsford, Essex CM1 1RN (☎ 0245 258257, fax 0245 250845)

BAILEY, Kim Charles; s of K Bailey, of Brackley Grange, Brackley, Northants, and Bridgett Anne, *née* Courage (d 1987); *b* 25 May 1953; *Educ* Radley; *m* 31 Oct 1983, Tracey Louise, da of Julian Sutton; *Career* racehorse trainer 1979-; major races won: Seagram Ground National (Mr Frisk), Whitbread Gold Cup (Mr Frisk), SGB Chase (Man O Magic), Bolinger Chase (Man O Magic), Golden Spurs Chase (Man O Magic), H & T Walker Chase (Man O Magic), Scottish Champion Hurdle (Positive), BIC Razor Hurdle (Carnival Air), Anthony Mildway & Peter Cazalet Meml Handicap Chase (twice, Mr Frisk and Shifting Gold), Crown Paints Hurdle (Positive); *Recreations* shooting, cricket, tennis; *Style—* Kim Bailey, Esq; The Old Manor, Upper Lambourn, Newbury, Berkshire (☎ 0488 71483, fax 0488 72978)

BAILEY, (Christian) Martin; s of Dr Leslie Bailey, of Harpenden, Hertfordshire, and Marie Elisabeth, *née* Phillips; *b* 4 Aug 1949; *Educ* Aldwickbury Sch Harpenden Hertfordshire, St Albans Sch Hertfordshire, The Royal Free Hosp Sch of Med (BSc, MB BS, FRCS); *m* 24 April 1971, Jane Nicola Rotha; da of John Stewart Barnfield; 1 s (Simon John Martin b 7 Aug 1975), 1 da (Laura Jane Susanna b 7 June 1978); *Career* past appts: The Royal Free Hosp London (house surgn, house physician, sr house offr), sr house offr (in otolaryngology Royal Nat Throat Nose & Ear Hosp London, in gen surgery The Royal Northern Hosp London), registrar then sr registrar in otolaryngology Royal Nat Throat Nose & Ear Hosp, sr registrar in otolargngology Sussex Throat & Ear Hosp Brighton; TWJ Fndn clinical & research fell in otology & neuro-otology Univ of Michigan USA; present appts: conslt otolaryngologist The Hosp for Sick Children Great Ormond St London and The Royal Nat Throat Nose & Ear Hosp London 1982-, hon conslt otolaryngologist St Luke's Hosp for the Clergy London 1984-; hon sr lectr: Inst of Laryngology & Otology London 1982-, Inst of Child Health 1985-; memb: BMA 1973, Br Assoc of Otolaryngologists 1982; FRSM 1976; *Books* Ear Nose & Throat Nursing (jtly, 1986) Scott-Brown's Otolaryngology (contrib, 1987), author of papers on various aspects of Paediatric Otolaryngology; *Recreations* fell walking, sailing (when time permits!), cars; *Style—* Martin Bailey, Esq; 7 Heathgate, Hampstead Garden Suburb, London NW11 7AR (☎ 081 455 8628); 55 Harley St, London W1N 1DD (☎ 071 580 2426, fax 071 436 1645)

BAILEY, Capt (Oswald) Nigel; OBE (1953); s of Lt-Col Frederick George Glyn Bailey (d 1952), and Lady Janet Lyle Bailey, *née* Mackay (d 1972); *b* 19 June 1913; *Educ* RNCs Dartmouth and Greenwich; *Career* joined RN as cadet 1927, specialised in naval aviation, served as COS to C-in-C Channel 1961-62, rank of Cdre, ret as Capt 1963; *Recreations* fishing, shooting; *Clubs* Army and Navy, IOD; *Style—* Capt Nigel Bailey, OBE, RN; Lake House, Lake, Salisbury, Wilts SP4 7BP (☎ 0980 622138, 0980 622752)

BAILEY, Dr Norman Stanley; s of Stanley Bailey (d 1986), and Agnes, *née* Gale; *b* 23 March 1933; *Educ* East Barnet GS Herts, Rhodes Univ SA (BMus), Vienna State Acad (Dip in Opera, Lieder, Oratorio); *m* 1, 21 Dec 1957 (m dis 1983), Doreen, da of late Leonard Simpson, of Kenya; 2 s (Brian Emeric b 1960, Richard Alan b 1967), 1 da (Catherine Noorah (Mrs Osbourne) b 1961); m 2, 25 July 1985, Kristine, da of Roman Anthony Ciesinski, of USA; *Career* prof of music RCM; regular engagements at world major opera houses and festivals incl: La Scala Milan, Royal Opera House Covent Garden, Bayreuth Wagner Festival, Vienna State Opera, Met Opera NY, Paris Opera, Edinburgh Festival, Hamburg State Opera, English Nat Opera; BBC TV performances: Falstaff, La Traviata, The Flying Dutchman, Macbeth; memb Baha'I world community; Hon DMUS Rhodes Univ S Africa 1986, Hon MRAM 1981; *Recreations* chess, notaphily, golf, microcomputing; *Style—* Dr Norman Bailey; 84 Warham Rd, S Croydon, Surrey CR2 6LB (☎ 081 688 9742); c/o Music International, 13 Ardilaun Rd, Highbury, London N5 2QR (☎ 071 359 5183)

BAILEY, Patricia Lucy; da of Capt Robert Bailey (d 1986), of Blackpool, and Patricia Isobel, *née* Percival; *b* 24 Sept 1940; *Educ* Arnold HS for Girls, Univ of Sheffield (LLB), Univ of Manchester (Adv Dip); *Career* called to the Bar Middle Temple 1969; memb Br Fedn Univ Women Vegetarian Soc; former memb Community Health Cncl; *Recreations* church, languages, playing musical instruments, singing, computers, vegetarian cooking, gardening; *Style—* Miss Patricia Bailey; Hollins Chambers, 64a Bridge St, Manchester (☎ 061 835 3451, fax 061 835 2955)

BAILEY, Paul; s of Arthur Oswald Bailey (d 1948), and Helen Maud, *née* Burgess (d 1984); *b* 16 Feb 1937; *Educ* Sir Walter St John's Sch London, Central Sch of Speech and Drama London; *Career* author; actor 1956-64, writer in residence Univ of Newcastle and Univ of Durham 1972-73, visiting lectr Eng lit North Dakota State Univ 1976-79; winner: Somerset Maugham award 1968, E M Forster award 1973, George Orwell Memorial prize 1977; *Books* At The Jerusalem (1967), Trespasses (1970), A Distant Likeness (1973), Peter Smart's Confessions (1977), Old Soldiers (1980), An English Madam (1982), Gabriel's Lament (1986), An Immaculate Mistake (1990); *Style—* Paul Bailey, Esq; 79 Davisville Road, London W12 9SH (☎ 081 749 2279)

BAILEY, Sir Richard John; CBE (1977); s of Philip Bailey, and Doris Margaret, *née* Freebody; *b* 8 July 1923; *Educ* Newcastle and Shrewsbury; *m* Marcia Rachel Cureton Webb; 1 s, 3 da; *Career* served RN 1942-46, Lt (Destroyers); joined Doulton Fine China 1946- (tech dir 1955-, md 1963-); chm: Royal Doulton 1980- (md 1972-), Royal Crown Derby; dir Central TV; chm Business Initiative; dir West Midlands Industrial Development Assoc; memb Cncl Keele Univ; chm School Cncl Newcastle-Under-Lyme Sch; pres Stoke-on-Trent Repertory Theatre; chm Br Ceramic Manufacturers Federation 1973-47; pres Br Ceramic Soc 1980-81; FICeram, FRSA; kt 1984-; *Recreations* golfing, walking, gardening; *Style—* Sir Richard Bailey, CBE; Roy Doulton Ltd, Minton House, London Rd, Stoke-on-Trent ST4 7QD (☎ 0782 49171, telex MINTON G 36502)

BAILEY, Prof Richard Nigel; s of William Bailey, of Spilsby, Lincs, and Hilda Bailey (d 1959); *b* 21 May 1936; *Educ* Spilsby GS, Univ of Durham (MA, PhD); *m* 3 Sept 1960, Mary Isabel, da of Norman Carmichael (d 1984), of Morpeth, Northumberland; 1 s (Nigel), 1 da (Alison); *Career* lectr in English UCNW 1960-66; Univ of Newcastle: lectr in English 1966-74, sr lectr 1974-80, prof Anglo Saxon civilisation 1980-, dean Faculty of Arts 1985-88, pro vice chllr 1988-; FSA 1975; *Books* Viking-Age Sculpture (1980), Corpus of Anglo-Saxon Sculpture: Cumbria (1988), Dowsing and Church Archaeology (1988); *Recreations* visiting churches and country houses; *Style—* Prof Richard Bailey, FSA; 22 Ridgely Drive, Ponteland, Newcastle upon Tyne NE20 9BL (☎ 0661 23128); University of Newcastle, Newcastle upon Tyne NE1 7RU (☎ 091 222 6000)

BAILEY, Robert John; s of John Bailey (d 1989), and Marie, *née* Boon; *b* 28 Oct 1963; *Educ* Biddulph HS Stoke-on-Trent; *m* 11 April 1987, Rachel; *Career* debut Northants CCC 1982, played for Eng under 15 and Young Eng under 19, full Eng debut 1988; played 4 test matches all v W Indies and 4 one day Internationals; *Style—* Robert Bailey, Esq; Northamptonshire CCC, Wantage RD, Northampton (☎ 0604 32917)

BAILEY, Robin; s of George Henry Bailey (d 1925), of Hucknall, Nottingham, and Thirza Ann Mettam (d 1979); *b* 5 Oct 1919; *Educ* Henry Mellish Sch Nottingham; *m* 6 Sept 1941, Patricia Mary, da of William Oliver Weekes; 3 s (Nicholas, Simon, Justin); *Career* WWII 1940-44 Lt RASC; actor; London appearances incl: Othello 1947, The Rivals 1948, Love in Albania 1949, The Cocktail Party 1950, Pygmalion 1951, A Severed Head 1964, Quartermaine's Terms 1981, Camelot 1982, Beethoven's Tenth 1983, Look Look 1990; NT 1978-88: Volpone, The Country Wife, The Cherry Orchard, Macbeth, For Services Rendered, When We Are Married, Rough Crossing, Mrs Warren's Profession, Six Characters in Search of an Author, Fathers and Sons; TV incl: Bleak House, Potter, Rumpole of the Bailey, I Didn't Know You Cared, Tales From A Long Room; *Clubs* Garrick, MCC; *Style—* Robin Bailey, Esq; 130 Merton Rd, London SW18 5SP (☎ 081 874 8571)

BAILEY, Ronald William; CMG (1961); s of William S Bailey (d 1956), of Southampton; *b* 14 June 1917; *Educ* King Edward VI Sch Southampton, Trinity Hall Cambridge; *m* 1946, Joan Hassall, da of Albert E Gray, JP (d 1959), of Stoke-on-Trent; 1 s, 1 da; *Career* Foreign Serv 1939-75; HM ambass: Bolivia 1967-71, Morocco 1971-75; hon vice pres Soc for the Protection of Animals in N Africa, hon life pres Br-Moroccan Soc; *Books* Records of Oman 1867-1947 (8 vols 1988); *Recreations* gardening; *Clubs* Oriental; *Style—* Ronald Bailey, Esq, CMG; Redwood, Tennyson's Lane, Haslemere, Surrey GU27 3AF (☎ 0428 642800)

BAILEY, Dr (Theodore Robert) Simon; s of Herbert Wheatcroft Bailey (d 1989), of Shepshed, Leics, and Norah Violet, *née* Roberts; *b* 20 Dec 1943; *Educ* King Edward VII GS Coalville Leics, UCL (BSc), UCH Med Sch (MB BS); *m* 26 July 1975, Elizabeth Frances, da of John Harper, OBE, of Oakfield, Salwick, Preston, Lancs; 2 s (Jonathan b 1978, Timothy b 1981); *Career* gp 1973-, sr MO Newmarket Races, clinical teacher Faculty Med Univ of Cambridge, organiser W Suffolk GP Trg Scheme, chm Cambridge Med Answering Serv; *Recreations* music, classic cars; *Style—* Dr Simon Bailey; Lincoln Lodge, Newmarket, Suffolk CB8 7AB (☎ 0638 663 792); Orchard Surgery, Newmarket, Suffolk CB8 8NU (☎ 0638 663 322)

BAILEY, Sir Stanley Ernest; CBE (1980), QPM (1975), DL (1986); s of John William Bailey (d 1962), of London, and Florence Mary, *née* Hibberd (d 1945); *b* 30 Sept

1926; *Educ* Lyulph Stanley Sch Camden Town London; *m* 27 March 1954, Marguerita Dorothea (Rita), da of George Whitbread (d 1963), of London; *Career* Met Police to supt 1947-66, asst chief constable Staffs Police 1966-70, dir Police Res Home Office 1970-72, dep chief constable Staffs 1973-75, chief constable Northumbria Police 1975-, police cdr designate No 2 Home Def Region; memb Assoc of Chief Police Offrs (ACPO) England Wales and N Ireland (vice pres 1984-85, pres 1985-86); chm Ctee first Int Police Exhibition and Conf (IPEC) London 1987, dir and vice chm Crime Concern 1988-, dir Northumbria Coalition Against Crime; police advsr Assoc of Metropolitan Authorities and memb Chernobyl Task Force Ctee 1987-; chm: ACPO Standing Ctee on Intruder Alarms, ACPO Sub Ctee on Crime Prevention, BSI Tech Ctee on Intruder Alarms; vice pres Police Mutual Assur Soc 1986-, active memb Int Assoc of Police Chiefs (memb Exec Ctee 1986), chm Advsy Ctee on Int Policy IACP 1985-89 (dir European World Regnl Office, observer on Private Security Ctee and memb Membership Ctee IAPC); graduate of Nat Exec Inst FBI Acad Washington; ACPO rep at INTERPOL 1986-88; memb Cncl Int Professional Security Assoc, observer Eighth UN Conf on Crime Prevention Havana Cuba 1990, chm First Conf Sr Police at UN Conf 1990; memb Editorial Bd Professional Security; ABIS Ken Bolton award for outstanding contribution to security and crime prevention 1990; lectr on crime prevention and security: USA, Pacific, Far East and Europe; Freeman City of London 1988; CBIM 1987, OStJ 1981; kt 1986; *Books* articles in various police journals on specialist subjects incl management and research; *Recreations* gardening, travel; *Style—* Sir Stanley Bailey, CBE, QPM, DL; Northumbria Police HQ, Ponteland, Newcastle upon Tyne NE20 0BL (☎ 0661 72555)

BAILEY, Stella, Lady; Stella Mary; *née* Chiappini; da of late Charles Chiappini, of 2 Stephen Street, Cape Town, S Africa; *m* 1945, as his 2 wife, Sir John Milner Bailey, 2 Bt (d 1946); *Style—* Stella, Lady Bailey; 123 Kloof Nek Road, Cape Town, South Africa

BAILEY, Sydney Dawson; s of Frank Burgess Bailey, and Elsie May, *née* Farbstein; *b* 1 Sept 1916; *Educ* Univ of Oxford DCL; *m* 26 April 1945, (Jennie Elena) Brenda; 1 s (Martin Dawson b 26 Oct 1947), 1 da (Marion Elizabeth b 27 April 1949); *Career* WWII, Friends Ambulance Unit in Burma and China 1940-46; factory worker 1932-35, bank teller 1936, insurance clerk 1937-40, ed Nat News Letter 1946-48, dir Hansard Soc for Parly Govt and ed Parly Affrs 1948-54, Quaker rep UN 1954-58, visiting scholar Carnegie Endowment for Int Peace 1958-60, numerous articles in learned jls; Rufus Jones Award for contrib to world peace World Acad of Art and Sci 1984; memb: Br Cncl of Churches div of int affrs (former chm), Soc of Friends (Quakers); vice-pres Cncl on Christian Approaches to Defence and Disarmament; memb: RIIA, American Soc of Int Law; *Books* Ceylon (1952), Naissance De Nouvelles Democraties (1953), Parliamentary Government in Southern Asia (1953), Voting in the Security Council (1969), Prohibitions and Restraints in War (1972), Procedure of the UN Security Council (1975), British Parliamentary Democracy (1978), Secretariat of The United Nations (1978), General Assembly of The United Nations (1978), How Wars End (1982), Making of Resolution 242 (1985), War and Conscience in the Nuclear Age (1987), The United Nations: A Short political guide (1989), Four Arab-Israeli Wars and the Peace Process (1990); *Recreations* music, photography, people; *Style—* Sydney D Bailey, Esq; 19 Deansway, London N2 0NG

BAILEY, Terence Michael; s of Thomas Sturman Bailey, and Margaret Hilda, *née* Wright; *b* 20 Oct 1946; *Educ* Kettering GS, Lanchester Poly Coventry (BA); *m* 1, 21 Oct 1972 (m dis), Penelope Ann, da of Geoffrey Lever Butler; 1 s (Tobin b 1976); m 2, 20 July 1985, Susan Jane, da of Frederick Peter Runacres; 3 s (Tim b 1986, Christopher b 1987, David b 1990); *Career* slr to Corby Devpt Corp 1972-73; ptnr Toller Hales & Collcutt Northamptonshire 1973-; *Recreations* skiing, gardening, keep-fit, reading and music; *Clubs* Northants Law Soc, Kettering Golf, RHS; *Style—* Terence M Bailey, Esq; Yew Tree Farm House, Little Oakley, Corby, Northants (☎ 0536 742233); 53-57 High St, Corby, Northants (☎ 0536 67341, fax 0536 400058, telex 341861)

BAILEY, Trevor John; s of Fred Bailey, of Fareham, and Vera Audrey Mary, *née* Turner; *b* 17 April 1947; *Educ* Leeds Poly, Trent Poly, Eastleigh Tech Coll; *m* 7 Aug 1968, Margaret Anne, da of Norman Frederick Smith (d 1983), of Nottingham; 2 s (Nigel b 1974, Simon b 1975); *Career* dir Br Canoe Union 1987- (formerly employed in local govt and water industry); chm of govrs: Hind Leys Community Coll, Castle Donington Community Coll; ACIS 1968, MBIM 1975, DMS; *Recreations* canoeing, walking; *Style—* Trevor Bailey, Esq; British Canoe Union, Adbolton Lane, West Bridgford, Nottingham (☎ 0602 821100, fax 0602 821797)

BAILHACHE, Philip Martin; QC (1989); s of Sqdn Ldr Lester Vivian Bailhache, RAF, and Nanette Ross, *née* Ferguson; *b* 28 Feb 1946; *Educ* Charterhouse, Pembroke Coll Oxford (MA); *m* 1, 1967 (m dis 1982); 2 s (Robert b 1968, John b 1974), 2 da (Rebecca b 1969, Catherine b 1972); m 2, 2 June 1984, Linda, da of Martin Geoffrey Le Vavasseur dit Durell; 1 s (Edward b 1990), 1 da (Alice b 1988); *Career* called to the Bar Middle Temple 1968, called to the Jersey Bar 1969, advocate Jersey 1969-74 (dep for Grouville 1972-74), slr gen Jersey 1975-86, attorney gen Jersey 1986-; chm Jersey Arts Cncl 1987-89; *Recreations* music, the arts, gardening, wine; *Clubs* Reform, United (Jersey); *Style—* Philip Bailhache, Esq, QC; L'Anquetinerie, Grouville, Jersey, Channel Islands (☎ 0534 52533); Attorney-General's Chambers, Royal Court House, St Helier, Jersey (☎ 0534 70011, fax 0534 35330)

BAILIE, Rt Hon Robin John; PC (NI 1971); *b* 6 March 1937; *Educ* Queen's Univ Belfast; *m* 1961, Margaret Frances, da of Charles Boggs; 1 s, 3 da; *Career* slr Supreme Ct of Judicature NI 1961-, MP (NI) Newtownabbey 1969-72, Min of Commerce NI 1971-72; *Style—* The Rt Hon Robin Bailie; 5 Thurloe Close, London SW7 (☎ 071 581 4898); Timbers Parkwall Lane, Lower Basildon, Berks

BAILLIE, Hon Alexander James; yr s of 3rd Baron Burton (by his 1 w); *b* 1 July 1963; *Educ* Eton, Univ of Oxford (scholar); *Clubs* Landowne, BASC; *Style—* The Hon Alexander Baillie

BAILLIE, Andrew Bruce; s of Edward Oswald Baillie (d 1974), and Molly Eva Lavers (Renée), *née* Andrews (d 1985); *b* 17 May 1948; *Educ* King's Coll Sch Wimbledon, Université De Besancon, Univ of Kent (BA); *m* 11 Sept 1976, Mary Lou Meech (d 1988), da of Stanley Harold Palmer (d 1988), of Portsmouth, Hants; 1 s (Oliver b 1984), 2 da (Emma b 1979, Victoria b 1981); *Career* called to the Bar Inner Temple 1970, rec 1989; *Recreations* golf; *Clubs* Caledonian; *Style—* Andrew Baillie, Esq; 2 Dr Johnson's Bldgs, Temple, London EC4 (☎ 071 353 5371)

BAILLIE, Hon Evan Michael Ronald; s and h of 3 Baron Burton by his 1 w Elizabeth; *b* 19 March 1949; *Educ* Harrow; *m* 1970 (m dis), Lucinda, da of Robin Law, of Haverhill; 2 s, 1 da; *Clubs* Brooks's; *Style—* The Hon Evan Baillie; Glencoe, Forbes, NSW 287, Australia

BAILLIE, Sir Gawaine George Hope; 7 Bt (UK 1823); s of Sir Adrian Baillie, 6 Bt (d 1947), and Hon Olive, *née* Paget, da of 1 and last Baron Queenborough, GBE, JP (gs of 1 Marq of Anglesey); *b* 8 March 1934; *Educ* Eton, Univ of Cambridge; *m* 1966, Lucile Margot Gardner, da of Hon Sen Louis P Beaubien, of Ottawa, Canada; 1 s, 1 da; *Heir* s, Adrian Louis Baillie b 26 March 1973; *Career* co dir; *Recreations* golf, tennis, skiing; *Clubs* St George's Golf, Berkshire Golf; *Style—* Sir Gawaine Baillie, Bt; Freechase, Warninglid, Sussex RH17 5SZ (☎ 044 485 296)

BAILLIE, Iain Cameron; s of David Brown Baillie (d 1976), and Agnes Wiseman, *née* Thomson; *b* 14 July 1931; *Educ* Glasgow HS, Univ of Glasgow (BSc), Fordham Law Sch NY (JD); *m* 1959, Joan Mary Christine, da of Dr Allan F Miller (d 1967), of Rickmansworth, Herts; 1 s; *Career* int lawyer; sr Euro ptnr Ladas & Parry (of NY, Chicago, Los Angeles, London, and Munich); admitted NY Bar and Fed Cts incl Supreme Ct (USA); chartered patent agent and registered UK trade mark agent, Euro pate author of numerous articles on business law; memb Inst of Int Practitioners, fell Inst of Trade Marks; *Books* A Practical Management of Intellectual Property (1986), Licensing A Practical Guide for the Businessman (1987); *Recreations* law, walking, model making; *Clubs* Caledonian; *Style—* Iain Baillie, Esq; 20 Chester St, London SW1X 7BL (☎ 071 235 1975); Ladas and Parry, 52 High Holborn, London WC1V 6RR (☎ 071 242 5566, fax 071 405 1908, telex 264255)

BAILLIE, Prof John; s of Arthur Baillie (d 1979), of Glasgow, and Agnes (d 1981); *b* 7 Oct 1944; *Educ* Whitehill Sr Secdy Sch; *m* 3 June 1973, Annette, da of James Alexander; 1 s (Kenneth b 22 Feb 1979), 1 da (Nicola b 13 Oct 1975); *Career* CA; ptnr KPMG Peat Marwick McLintock (formerly Thomson McLintock) 1978; author of various tech and professional papers to professional jls; memb various ctees of ICA 1978-; Johnstone Smith Chair of Accountancy Univ of Glasgow 1983-88, visiting prof of accountancy Heriot-Watt Univ 1988; Hon MA Univ of Glasgow 1983; MICAS 1967; *Books* Systems of Profit Measurement (1985), Consolidated Accounts and The Seventh Directive (1985); *Recreations* keeping fit, reading, golf, music, hill walking; *Clubs* Western (Glasgow), RSAC; *Style—* Prof John Baillie; The Glen, Glencairn Rd, Kilmacolm, Renfrewshire, PA13 4PJ (☎ 050587 3254); 38 Albemarle St, London W1; 1 Puddle Dock, London EC4V 3PD (☎ 071 236 8000)

BAILLIE, Maj Hon Peter Charles; JP (Hants 1968); s of Brig Hon Evan Baillie, MC, TD (d 1941), of Ballindarroch, Scaniport, Inverness; bro of 3 Baron Burton; raised to the rank of a Baron's son 1964; *b* 26 June 1927; *Educ* Eton; *m* 15 Nov 1955, Jennifer Priscilla, yr da of Harold Newgass, GC (d 1984), of Winterbourne, Dorset; 4 da; *Career* served with Life Gds 1945-60, ret as Maj; *Recreations* deer, shooting; *Style—* Maj The Hon Peter Baillie, JP; Wootton Hall, New Milton, Hants (☎ 0425 613722)

BAILLIE, Robin Alexander MacDonald; *b* 20 Aug 1933; *Educ* Larkhall Acad Scotland; *m* 7 Feb 1959, Dr Elizabeth Susan Baillie; 1 s (Jonathan Michael b 20 Oct 1962), 1 da (Caroline Elizabeth b 2 March 1971); *Career* Nat Serv Sub Lt RNVR 1952-54; divnl dir Grindlays Bank plc 1973 (bank offr in Kenya, Uganda and India 1955-66), chief exec Exporters Refinance Corporation Ltd 1972 (joined 1966), md Wallace Brothers Group 1976-77 (joined 1973); Standard Chartered Group: md Standard Chartered Merchant Bank 1977-85, md MAIBL PLC 1983, exec dir 1983-87; non-exec dir: Boustead PLC, Burson-Marsteller Financial Ltd, Capital & Counties plc, London & Strathclyde Trust plc, Standard Chartered PLC, Transatlantic Holdings PLC; chm: Burson-Marsteller Limited, PaineWebber International Bank Limited; FIBScot, FRSA, FInstD; *Recreations* the opera, victorian watercolours, Indian art; *Style—* Robin Baillie, Esq; Burson-Marsteller Ltd, 24-28 Bloomsbury Way, London WC1A 2PX

BAILLIEU, Christopher Latham; MBE (1977); s of Hon Edward Latham Baillieu, and Betty Anne Jardine, *née* Taylor; *b* 12 Dec 1949; *Educ* Radley, Jesus Coll Cambridge (Rowing blue); *m* 8 Sept 1984, Jane Elizabeth, da of Robert Price Bowie; 2 s (Charles Latham b 31 May 1985, Edward Latham b 22 July 1990), 1 da (Olivia Clare b 3 Oct 1987); *Career* oarsman; rowed for: Radley Coll 1967-68 (competed Jr Int 1967), Univ of Cambridge 1970-73, Leander Club 1973-84, GB 1973-83; bronze medallist double sculls Euro Championships 1973; World Championships: bronze medallist double sculls 1974 and 1975, Gold medallist 1977, Silver medallist 1978, fourth place 1979), fourth place single sculls 1981 (sixth place 1982); Silver medallist double sculls Olympic Games 1976 (fourth place double sculls 1980); longest standing record at Henley Royal Regatta for double sculls set in 1973 (6.59, held with Mike Hart); called to the Bar Lincoln's Inn (Walter Wrigglesworth scholarship 1975), co dir, tv rowing commentator; Sir Winston Churchill travelling fellowship 1976, steward Henley Royal Regatta 1984; *Recreations* old buildings, most art, modern history; *Style—* Christopher Baillieu, Esq, MBE; Leander Club, Henley-on-Thames, Oxon

BAILLIEU, Hon David Clive Latham; yr s of 2 Baron Baillieu (d 1973); *b* 2 Nov 1952; *Educ* Radley, Cranfield Sch of Management (MBA); *Career* slr 1979; *Recreations* hill-walking, opera and classical music, swimming, tennis; *Clubs* Lansdowne; *Style—* The Hon David Baillieu; 3a Redcliffe Rd, London SW10 9NR (☎ 071 352 1198)

BAILLIEU, Hon Edward Latham; 3 s of 1 Baron Baillieu, KBE, CMG (d 1967); *b* 17 Oct 1919; *Educ* Winchester, BNC Oxford (MA); *m* 1942, Betty Anne Jardine, da of Henry Taylor; 2 s, 1 da; *Career* served WWII Capt RHA (invalided out); ret stockbroker, ptnr Hoare Govett; chm: NM (UK) Ltd until 1990, RTZ 1967-77, ANZ Bank 1967-80; chm Royal Humane Soc 1977-90; former dep grand master of Utd Grand Lodge (Freemasons) 1982; *Recreations* shooting, golf; *Clubs* Boodle's, Leander, Melbourne, Swinley Forest Golf, MCC; *Style—* The Hon Edward Baillieu; Tangle Copse, West Drive, Sunningdale, Berks (☎ 0344 842301)

BAILLIEU, 3 Baron (UK 1953); James William Latham Baillieu; er s of 2 Baron Baillieu (d 1973), and his 1 w, Anne Bayliss, *née* Page; *b* 16 Nov 1950; *Educ* Radley, Monash Univ Melbourne (BEc); *m* 1, 1974 (m dis 1985), Cornelia, da of late William Ladd; 1 s; m 2, 1985, Clare, da of Peter Stephenson; *Heir* s, Hon Robert Latham Baillieu, b 2 Feb 1979; *Career* 2 Lt Coldstream Gds 1970-73; Banque Nationale de Paris 1978-80; assoc dir Rothschild Australia Limited 1980-88, gen mangr Capital Markets Manufacturers Hanover Australia Ltd 1988-89, assoc dir Standard Chartered Ltd 1990-; *Clubs* Boodle's, Australia (Melbourne); *Style—* The Rt Hon the Lord Baillieu; c/o Mutual Tst Pty Ltd, 360 Collins St, Melbourne, Victoria 3000, Australia

BAILLIEU, Maj the Hon Robert Latham; MBE (1945), TD; 2 s of 1 Baron Baillieu, KBE, CMG (d 1967); *b* 18 July 1917; *Educ* Winchester, Magdalen Coll Oxford (MA); *m* 1949, Delphine Mary, yr da of the late Edgar Hastings Dowler; 2 s, 2 da; *Career* Maj Middx Yeo WWII (despatches); slr 1954; vice chm Banque Belge Ltd and md Dawnay Day Ltd; md: Henry Ansbacher & Co Ltd, Fraser Ansbacher Ltd; dir: C H Goldrei, Foucard & Son Ltd, View Forth Investmt Tst Ltd; ret; *Recreations* golf; *Clubs* Sloane; *Style—* Maj the Hon Robert Baillieu, MBE, TD; Abingdon Court, Abingdon Villas, London W8

BAILWARD, Hon Mrs ((Diana) Penelope Florence); *née* Sclater-Booth; eldest da of 3 Baron Basing (d 1969), and Mary Alice Erle, *née* Benson (d 1970); *b* 29 Jan 1925; *Educ* Downham Bishops Stortford; *m* 1946, James Tennant Bailward, s of Cdr Maurice William Bailward, RN (ret) (d 1958), of Penny's Hill Lodge, Ferndown, Dorset; 1 s (Christopher John b 1949), 1 da (Clare Penelope b 1947); *Career* served WW II Lance Corpl FANY; *Recreations* music (principally singing); *Style—* The Hon Mrs Bailward; Causeway House, Radipole, Weymouth, Dorset DT4 9RX (☎ 0305 783916)

BAILY, John Leslie; s of Leslie Baily (d 1976), and Margaret Baily, *née* Jesper; *b* 1 Aug 1933; *Educ* Ackworth Sch, Northern Poly, Univ of Leeds (Dip Arch, PhD); *m* 21 Nov 1959, Maureen May, da of Capt William Jenkins (d 1967); 2 s (Paul b 1963, Christopher b 1964); *Career* architect and historian; princ John Baily & Assocs, md In House Property Mgmnt Ltd, architect and clerk of works to Dean and Chapter Lincoln Cathedral; FFAS, ARIBA; FRSA; *Recreations* travel; *Clubs* Yorkshire; *Style—* John

Baily, Esq; 4 Minster Yard, Lincoln; Midland Bank, Parliament St, York; Almsford House, Beckfield Lane, York YO2 5PA (☎ 0904 783079)

BAILY, Lady Sarah Dorothea; *née* Boyle; el da of Rear Adm 9 Earl of Glasgow, CB, DSC; *b* 3 June 1941; *m* 1962, John Edward Baily, elder s of late Brig Michael Henry Hamilton Baily, DSO; 2 s, 2 da; *Style—* The Lady Sarah Baily; 27 Park Walk, London SW10

BAIN, Angus Hugh Uniacke; s of Dr George Alexander Bain (d 1981), of Sheffield, and Sheila Beatrice, *née* Uniacke (d 1988); *b* 31 July 1940; *Educ* Uppingham; *m* 1, 24 March 1965 (m dis 1972); m 2, 3 May 1973, Jane Verel, da of Wing Cdr Coleman, AFC, of Malta; 1 s (Hugo Alastair Uniacke b 28 April 1974); *Career* memb Stock Exchange 1962, dir How Gerrard Vivian Gray 1989-; *Recreations* golf, tennis, racing, cricket, football; *Clubs* City of London, Royal Wimbledon Golf; *Style—* Angus Bain, Esq; 27 Titchwell Rd, London SW18 (☎ 081 874 9461); Burne House, 88 High Holburn, London WC1V 7EB (☎ 071 831 8883, fax 071 831 9883, telex 883 850)

BAIN, Prof George Sayers; s of George Alexander Bain, of 181 Leighton Ave, Winnipeg, Canada, and Margaret Ioleen, *née* Bamford (d 1988); *b* 24 Feb 1939; *Educ* Winnipeg State Sch System, Univ of Manitoba (BA, MA), Univ of Oxford (DPhil); *m* 1, 24 Aug 1962 (m dis 1987), Carol Lynne Ogden, da of Herbert Fyffe White (d 1986); 1 s (David Thomas b 1969), 1 da (Katharine Anne b 1967); m 2, 28 Dec 1988, (Frances) Gwynneth Rigby, *née* Vickers; *Career* Royal Canadian Navy Reserve, Midshipman 1957-60, Sub Lt 1960, Lt 1963, ret 1963; Industl Rels Res Unit of SSRC Univ of Warwick: dep dir 1970-74, acting dir 1974, dir 1975-81; Univ of Warwick: titular prof 1974-79, Pressed Steel Fisher prof of industl rels 1979-89, chm Sch of Industl and Business Studies 1983-89; princ London Business Sch 1989-; memb res staff Royal Cmmn on Trade Unions and Employers Assoc (The D Cmmn) 1966-67, conslt to Nat Bd for Prices and Incomes 1967-69; memb: Mechanical Engrg Econ Devpt Ctee NEDO 1974-76, Ctee of Inquiry on Industl Democracy 1975-76, Cncl ESRC 1986-, Nat Forum for Mgmnt Educn and Devpt 1988-90; chm Cncl of Univ Mgmnt Schs 1987-90, frequent arbitrator/mediator for ACAS; *Books* Trade Union Growth and Recognition (1967), The Growth of White-Collar Unionism (1970), The Reform of Collective Bargaining at Plant and Company Levels (co-author 1971), Social Stratification and Trade Unionism (1973), Union Growth and the Business Cycle (1976), A Bibliography of British Industrial Relations (1979 and 1985), Profiles of Union Growth (1980), Industrial Relations in Britain (ed 1983); *Clubs* Reform; *Style—* Professor George Bain; London Business School, Sussex Place, Regent's Park, London NW1 4SA (☎ 071 262 5050, fax 071 724 7875)

BAIN, Iain Stuart; s of James Bain, MC (d 1971), of Kirkcudbright, and Frances Mary Hamilton, *née* Shaw (d 1984); *b* 16 Feb 1934; *Educ* Fettes, St Edmund Hall Univ of Oxford; *m* 14 June 1958, Susan, da of Kenneth Herbert Forbes (d 1981), of Englefield Green; 2 da (Kirsty b 1961, Catriona b 1964); *Career* Nat Serv Cmmnd 2 Lt 1 Bn Seaforth Highlanders 1953-55; Scottish Champion Hammer Thrower 1956-57 and 1959, Scotland and GB Rep 1959; prodn mangr The Bodley Head 1966-72, publisher The Tate Gallery 1972-; chm Printing Hist Soc 1984-89, tstee Thomas Bewick Birthplace Tst 1985-90; Liveryman Worshipful Co of Stationers and Newspaper Makers 1990; FSA 1988; *Books* A Memoir of Thomas Bewick (1975, 1979), Thomas Bewick: Vignettes (1979), The Watercolours & Drawings of Thomas Bewick & His Workshop Apprenti (1981), The Workshop of Thomas Bewick: a pictorial survey (1989); *Recreations* printing and publishing history, printing and typography at the hand-press, folk music and pipe music of Scotland and Northumberland; *Clubs* Athenaeum, Double Crown; *Style—* Iain Bain, Esq; New Cottage, Newnham, Baldock, Hertfordshire SG7 5JX; The Tate Gallery, Millbank, London SW1P 4RG

BAIN, Neville Clifford; s of Charles Alexander Bain, of St Kilda, Dunedin, NZ, and, Gertrude Mae, *née* Howe (d 1986); *b* 14 July 1940; *Educ* Kings HS Dunedin NZ, Otago Univ Dunedin NZ (MCom); *m* 18 Sept 1987, Anne Patricia; from previous m, 1 s (Peter John b 1965), 1 da (Susan Mary nb 1963), 1 step da (Kristina Knights b 1979); *Career* gp fin dir and dep chief exec Cadbury Schweppes plc; dir: Cadbury Schweppes Overseas Ltd, Cadbury Schweppes Australia, Cadbury Schweppes S A, Cadbury India Ltd, Amalgamated Beverages GB, Reading Scientific Servs Ltd, Itnet Ltd; non-exec dir London Int Gp plc; gp chief exec Coats Viyella plc 1990-; CMA, FCA, ACIS, FBIM, FRSA; *Recreations* music, sport, photography; *Style—* Neville C Bain, Esq; Inglewood House, 21 Ince Rd, Burwood Park, Walton on Thames, Surrey KT12 5BJ; Coats Viyella plc, 28 Savile Row, London W1X 2DD (☎ 071 734 4030, car 0860 860135)

BAIN, Prof William Herbert; s of J H Bain (d 1981), and MSS, *née* Sadler; *b* 20 Nov 1927; *Educ* Glasgow HS, Univ of Glasgow (MB ChB), Univ of Chicago (MD), FRCS (Glasgow and Edinburgh); *m* 19 Sept 1959, (Maud) Helen, da of James Craigie (d 1985); 2 s (Douglas, Donald), 1 da (Susan); *Career* lectr in experimental surgery Univ of Glasgow 1958 (Hall fell 1953), Andrews fell Univ of Chicago 1961, sr lectr in surgery 1962, reader in cardiac surgery 1975, titular prof in cardiac surgery 1981; ret 1990; memb Br Standards Inst, pres Scot Thoracic Soc 1987, pres Soc of Cardio-thoracic Surgns of GB 1989; Freedom City of Glasgow 1945; fell American Coll of Chest Physicians 1961; *Books* Cardiovascular Surgery (1967), Handbook of Intensive Care (1981); *Recreations* golf, sailing, fishing; *Style—* Prof William Bain; Dept of Cardiac Surgery, Western Infirmary, Glasgow G11 6NT (☎ 041 339 8822)

BAIN SMITH, Lady Corisande; da of 8 Earl of Tankerville (d 1971), of Chillingham, Northumberland and Violet, Countess of Tankerville, JP, *née* Pallin; *b* 10 April 1938; *Educ* St James West Malvern, Oxford Univ; *m* 1963, Lt Cdr Timothy Bain Smith, CPA, RN, s of Lt-Col George Stewart Bain Smith, GC (d 1972); 2 s (James b 1964, Charles b 1966); *Style—* Lady Corisande Bain Smith; Wickens Manor, Charing, Kent

BAINBRIDGE, Beryl; da of Richard Bainbridge, and Winifred Baines; *b* 21 Nov 1934; *Educ* Merchant Taylors' Sch Liverpool, Arts Educnl Schs Tring; *m* 1954 (m dis), Austin Davies; 1 s, 2 da; *Career* actress, writer; columnist for The Evening Standard 1987-; *Plays*: Tiptoe Through the Tulips (1976), The Warriors Return (1977), Its a Lovely Day Tomorrow (1977), Journal of Bridget Hitler (1981), Somewhere More Central (TV 1981), Evensong (TV 1986); *Books*: A Weekend with Claud (1967, revised edn 1981), Another Part of the Wood (1968, revised edn 1979), Harriet Said.... (1972), The Dressmaker (1973), The Bottle Factory Outing (1974, Guardian Fiction Award), Sweet William (1975, film 1980), A Quiet Life (1976), Injury Time (1977, Whitbread Award), Young Adolf (1978), Winter Garden (1980), English Journey (1984, TV series), Watson's Apology (1984), Mum and Mr Armitage (1985), Forever England (1986, TV series 1986), Filthy Lucre (1986), An Awfully Big Adventure (1989); Hon Litt D Liverpool; FRSL; *Books* The Bottle Factory Outing (1974, Guardian Fiction Award), Injury Time (1977, Whitbread Award); *Style—* Miss Beryl Bainbridge; 42 Albert St, London NW1 (☎ 071 387 3113)

BAINBRIDGE, Cyril; s of Arthur Herman Bainbridge (d 1966), and Edith, *née* Whitaker (d 1988); *b* 15 Nov 1928; *Educ* Negus Coll Bradford; *m* 20 Jan 1953, Barbara Hannah, da of Sydney Crook; 1 s (Christopher b 1958), 2 da (Susan b 1954, Amanda b 1958); *Career* Nat Serv Army 1947-49; author and journalist; reporter: provincial newspapers 1944-54, Press Association 1954-63; The Times: joined 1963, dep news ed 1967-69, regnl news ed 1969-77, managing news ed 1977-82, asst managing ed 1982-86, ed data mangr 1986-88; pres Inst of Journalists 1978-79 (vice-pres 1977-78, fell 1986); memb: Press Cncl 1980-90, Nat Cncl for Trg Journalists 1983-87; *Books* The Brontes and Their Country (1978, revised edn 1990), Brass Triumphant (1980), North Yorkshire and North Humberside (1984, revised edn 1989), One Hundred Years of Journalism (ed 1984), Pavilions on the Sea (1986); *Recreations* reading, walking; *Style—* Cyril Bainbridge, Esq; 98 Mayfield Ave, London NI2 (☎ 081 445 4178)

BAINBRIDGE, John Philip; s of Philip James Bainbridge, of Mottingham, London, and Joan Winifred, *née* Walker; *b* 28 Aug 1946; *Educ* Chislehurst and Sidcup GS; *m* 2 May 1970, Marilynne Ailsa, da of Stanley Joseph Kesler (d 1985), of Cranleigh, Surrey; 2 s (Daniel b 1979, James b 1981); *Career* dir Schroder Unit Tsts Ltd 1988- (joined Schroder Gp 1973); FCA; *Recreations* home, family, gardening, cricket; *Style—* John Bainbridge, Esq; Baltic House, The Common, Cranleigh, Surrey GU6 8SL (☎ 0483 275949); Schroder Unit Trusts Ltd, 36 Old Jewry, London EC2R 8BS (☎ 071 382 6000, fax 071 382 6737, tlx 885029)

BAINBRIDGE, Philip; s of Leonard George Bainbridge, of 16 Derek Drive, Sneyd Green, Stoke-on-Trent, and Lilian Rose, *née* Wilkinson; *b* 16 April 1958; *Educ* Hanley HS Stoke-on-Trent, 6 Form Coll Borough Road Coll of Educn; *m* 22 Sept 1979, Barbara, da of John Edwards, of 50 East Court, North Wembley, Middlesex; 1 s (Neil b 11 Jan 1984), 1 da (Laura b 15 Jan 1985); *Career* cricketer; Gloucestershire CCC: debut 1977, capped 1981, vice capt 1985-88, benefit year 1989, ret 1990; appearances: first class 255, One Day 233; memb: England Schoolboys U19's 1976 (U15's 1972), Nat Assoc of Young Cricketers U19's; played: young England v Australia 1977, MCC v New Zealand 1990, English Counties Tour Zimbabwe 1985; supply teacher 1979-84, mktg mangr Gloucester CCC 1985-88, ptnr in own business Rhodes Leisure 1989-; U23 Batsman of the Year 1981, Wisden Cricketer of the Year 1985; *Recreations* all sports, travel, photography; *Style—* Philip Bainbridge, Esq; c/o Rhodes Leisure, 414 Speedwell Rd, Kingswood, Bristol, BS15 1ES (☎ 0272 618337, fax 0272 353277)

BAINES; *see*: Grenfell-Baines

BAINES, Alan Leonard; s of Leonard Baines (d 1989), of Newark, and Edna, *née* Hackston (d 1985); *b* 7 May 1948; *Educ* Chadderton GS Lancashire; *m* 1982, Carole, da of Colin Johnson; *Career* articled clerk Joseph Crossley & Sons Manchester; accountant Price Waterhouse 1970-74, ptnr Stoy Hayward 1976- (joined 1975, specialist advsr on problems of corporate strategies and family owned businesses); FCA, FBIM, FInstD; *Recreations* the Br coast and countryside, music, theatre; *Style—* Alan Baines, Esq; Stoy Hayward, Foxhall Lodge, Gregory Boulevard, Nottingham NG7 6LH (☎ 0602 626578, fax 0602 691043)

BAINES, Garron John; s of Roy Hubert Baines, of Tadgells, Housham Tye, Harlow, Essex, and Jillian Ann, *née* Wheeley; *b* 25 Aug 1952; *Educ* Oundle; *m* 6 July 1974, Irene Joyce, da of Richard Rennie Williams, of 19 Broadstone Ave, Port Glasgow, Renfrewshire, Scotland; 2 da (Laura Lockhart b 1 Nov 1978, Fiona Suzanne b 8 June 1982); *Career* former newspaper journalist E Midland Allied Press, writer Ind TV News 1977, dep ed Channel Four News 1989 (news ed 1982); *Recreations* talking, walking, television; *Style—* Garron Baines, Esq; Weffells, Purton End, Debden, Saffron Walden, Essex CB11 3JT (☎ 0799 41079); ITN, 48 Wells St, London W1 (☎ 071 637 2424, fax 071 255 2125)

BAINES, Dr Geoffrey Fielden; s of Lt-Col Frank Baines, MC, TD (d 1969), of 14 Southport Rd, Chorley, Lancs, and Constance Muriel, *née* Fielden (d 1981); *b* 8 Aug 1931; *Educ* Rossall Sch, Univ of St Andrews (MB ChB); *m* 11 April 1984, Janet Mary, da of Maj Ronald Revell (d 1957), of 135 Stoneclough Rd, Radcliffe, Manchester; 3 s (Richard b 1958, Paul b 1960, Geoffrey 1984), 3 da (Helen b 1963, Madeleine b 1985, Catherine b 1987); *Career* Nat Serv med offr RAMC Blandford Camp 1957-59; conslt physician in cardiology Kettering Gen Hosp 1970-, dist clinical tutor 1973-81, chm Med Sub Ctee Oxford RHA 1979-81, dep regnl advsr ORHA 1988-; memb Br Cardiac Soc 1989; memb RSM 1970, FRCPEd 1977, FRCP 1978; *Style—* Dr Geoffrey Baines; The Cottage, Main St, Great Addington, Kettering, Northamptonshire (☎ 0536 78223); Cardiology Department, Kettering General Hospital, Kettering, Northants NN16 8UZ (☎ 0536 410666, fax 0536 411482)

BAINS, Lawrence Arthur; CBE (1983), DL (Gtr London 1978); s of late Arthur Bains, and Mabel, *née* Payn; *b* 11 May 1920; *Educ* Stationers' Co's Sch; *m* 1954, Margaret, da of Sir William J Grimshaw (d 1958); 2 s, 1 da; *Career* chm: GLC 1977-78, Haringey Health Authy 1981-; dir: Bains Bros Ltd, Crowland Leasing Ltd; memb Lloyd's; *Clubs* City Livery; *Style—* Lawrence Bains, Esq, CBE, DL; Crowland Lodge, 100 Galley Lane, Arkley, Barnet, EN5 4AL (☎ 081 440 3499)

BAINS, Malcolm Arnold; JP (Norfolk Island), DL (Kent 1976); s of Herbert Bains, of Newcastle upon Tyne; *b* 12 Sept 1921; *Educ* Hymers Coll, Univ of Durham (LLB); *m* 1, 1942 (m dis 1961), Winifred Agnes Davies; 3 s; m 2, 1968, Margaret Hunter; *Career* slr; clerk of Kent CC and clerk to Lieutenancy of Kent 1970-74; fell ANU and advsr to NSW Govt Australia 1977-78; chm Local Govt Review Bd of Victoria 1978-79; head Norfolk Island Public Serv 1979-82; JP (Norfolk Island); FRSA; *Books* The 'Bains' Report on Local Authority Mgmnt 1973; *Style—* Malcolm Bains Esq, JP, DL; Somers Cottage, Lamer Street, Meopham, Kent; PO Box 244, Norfolk Island, via Australia 2899

BAINTON, Lady Annabel Elizabeth Hélène; *née* Sutherland; da of Countess of Sutherland in her own right (who adopted the surname of Sutherland according to Scots law 1963) and her husb Charles Janson, DL; *b* 16 May 1952; *m* 29 Oct 1982, John Vernon Bainton, s of late John Richard Bainton, of Point Piper, Sydney, Australia; 2 s (Edward b 1983, Nicholas b 1988), 1 da (Alice b 1985); *Style—* The Lady Annabel Bainton; 9 Eaton Sq, London SW1

BAINTON, Richard Leslie; s of Richard Bainton (d 1970); *b* 4 March 1923; *Educ* Christ Church Cathedral GS; *m* 1954, Ruth; 1 s, 3 da; *Career* md Portland Gp of Cos 1977- (exec dir 1969-); *Recreations* golf, youth and church work; *Clubs* Badgemore Golf; *Style—* Richard Bainton Esq; Apnagar, 139 Wilderness Rd, Earley, Berks (☎ 0734 873156, office 0734 866 777)

BAIRD, Sir David Charles; 5 Bt (UK 1809), of Newbyth, Haddingtonshire; s of William Arthur Baird, JP, DL (himself 2 s of Sir David Baird, 3 Bt, JP, DL, by his w Hon Ellen Stuart, 2 da & coheir of 12 Lord Blantyre). The present Bt's mother was Lady Hersey Conyngham, 3 da of 4 Marquess Conyngham; suc unc, Sir David Baird, 4 Bt, MVO, JP, DL, 1941. Sir David's ggg uncle, the Rt Hon Sir David Baird, 1 Bt, KCB, PC, was a distinguished soldier & himself gn of Sir James Baird, 2 Bt, of Saughton; *b* 6 July 1912; *Educ* Eton, Univ of Cambridge; *Heir* nephew, Charles Stuart Baird b 1939; *Style—* Sir David Baird, Bt; 52 Old High St, Kirkcudbright DG6 4JX

BAIRD, Prof David Tennant; s of Sir Dugald Baird (d 1986), and Mathilda Deans, *née* Tennent, CBE (d 1983); *b* 13 March 1935; *Educ* Aberdeen GS, Univ of Aberdeen, Trinity Coll Cambridge (BA), Univ of Edinburgh (MB ChB, DSc); *m* 29 Jan 1964, Frances Diana, da of Francis Lichtveld, of Amsterdam, Holland; 2 s (Dugald Francis b 1967, Gavin Tennent b 1969); *Career* conslt gynaecologist Royal Infirmary Edinburgh 1970-, prof obsterics and gynaecology Univ of Edinburgh 1977-85 (sr lectr and conslt gynaecologist 1970-72), clinical res prof reproductive endocrinology MRC 1985- (dep dir Unit of Reproductive Biology 1972-77); memb MRC 1989-; FRCP Ed 1971, FRCOG 1972, FRSE; *Books* Mechanism of Menstruation (1983); *Recreations* ski-mountaineering, golf; *Style—* Prof David Baird, FRSE; Dept of Obstetrics And

Gynaecology, Univ of Edinburgh, 37 Chalmers St, Edinburgh (☎ 031 229 2575)

BAIRD, James Andrew Gardiner; s and h of Sir James Baird, 10 Bt, MC, of The Old Vicarage, Arreton, Isle of Wight and Mabel Annie Gill; *b* 2 May 1946; *Educ* Eton; *m* 1984 (m dis), Jean Margaret, da of Brig Sir Ian Liddell Jardine, 4 Bt, OBE, MC (d 1982), of Coombe Place, Meonstoke, Southampton; *Recreations* shooting, fishing, photography; *Clubs* Boodles; *Style—* James Baird Esq; 68 Lessar Avenue, Clapham Common, London SW4 9HQ (☎ 071 673 2035)

BAIRD, James Hewson; s of James Baird, MBE, of Carlisle, and Ann Sarah, *née* Hewson (d 1988); *b* 28 March 1944; *Educ* Austin Friars, Creighton Sch Carlisle, Univ of Newcastle (BSc); *m* 7 March 1969, Clare Rosalind, da of Frederick Sidney Langstaff, of Colchester; 3 da (Emma Jane b 6 April 1973, Deirdre Helen b 13 Feb 1975, Katherine Sally b 26 July 1978); *Career* hydrologist and agriculturalist Essex River Authy 1968-74, princ engr Anglian Water Authy 1974-75, policy offr Nat Water Cncl 1975-80; dir: admin ICE 1982-85 (asst 1980-82), Assoc Municipal Engrs 1985-86, external affrs FCEC 1986-87; chief exec BVA 1987-; MIWES 1970-87; *Clubs* London Rugby; *Style—* James Baird, Esq; British Veterinary Association, 7 Mansfield St, London (☎ 071 636 6541, fax 071 436 2970)

BAIRD, Lt-Gen Sir James Parlane; KBE (1973); s of Rev David Baird, of Lochgoilhead, Argyllshire, and Sara Kathleen Black; *b* 12 May 1915; *Educ* Bathgate Acad, Edinburgh Univ (MD); *m* 1948, Anne Patricia, da of David Patrick Anderson, of Houghton, Arundel, Sussex; 1 s, 1 da; *Career* cmmnd RAMC 1939, Cmdt and Dir of Studies Royal Army Med Coll 1971-73, Dir-Gen AMS 1973-77; med advsr Nat Advice Centre for Postgrad Educn 1977-84; QHP 1969; awarded Hilal-i-Quaid-i-Azam (Pakistan); FRCP; FRCPE; *Style—* Lt-Gen Sir James Baird, KBE; c/o Royal Bank of Scotland, Kirkland House, Whitehall, London SW1

BAIRD, Sir James Richard Gardiner; 10 Bt (NS 1695), MC; s of late Capt William Frank Gardiner Baird, 2 s of 8 Bt; suc unc, Maj Sir James Hozier Gardiner Baird, 9 Bt, MC, 1966; *b* 12 July 1913; *Educ* Eton, Univ Coll Oxford; *m* 1941, Mabel Ann Tempest, da of Algernon Gill; 2 s, 1 da; *Heir* s, James Andrew Gardiner Baird; *Career* formerly Capt Kent Yeo; hon treas The Ada Cole Meml Stables Ltd; *Style—* Sir James Baird, Bt, MC; Church Farm House, Guist, Norfolk NR20 5AJ (☎ 036284 808)

BAIRD, Dr John Alexander; s of John Wilson Baird (d 1963), of Edinburgh, and Agnes Fairrie, *née* Newlands (d 1990); *b* 28 Aug 1947; *Educ* Daniel Steward Coll, Univ of Edinburgh (BSc, MB ChB, MD); *m* 6 Oct 1972, Ann, da of Robert Easson (d 1988), of Edinburgh; 3 s (Colin b 1974, Douglas b 1977, Andrew b 1979); *Career* physician supt State Hosp Carstairs 1985- (conslt forensic psychiatrist 1981-85); chm Standing Ctee On Difficult Prisoners 1988- (memb 1985-); MRC Psych 1978; *Recreations* hill walking, wine; *Clubs* Medico Legal Soc; *Style—* Dr John Baird; State Hospital, Carstairn Junction, Lanark ML11 8RP (☎ 0555 840 293)

BAIRD, Roger Neale; s of John Allan Baird, of Edinburgh, and Margaret Edith, *née* Shand; *b* 24 Dec 1941; *Educ* Daniel Stewarts Coll Edinburgh , Univ of Edinburgh (BSc, MB ChB, ChM); *m* 12 Oct 1968, Affra Mary, da of Douglas Varcoe-Cocks (d 1964); 1 s (Richard b 1972), 1 da (Susan b 1970); *Career* sr house offr and registrar Royal Infirmary Edinburgh 1969-73 (house surgn 1966-67), res scholar in clinical surgery 1967-69, lectr and sr lectr Univ of Bristol 1973-81, Fulbright scholar Harvard Med Sch Mass 1975-76, conslt surgn Royal Infirmary Bristol 1981-; FRCS, FRCSEd; *Books* Diagnosis and Monitoring in Arterial Surgery (1980), Human Disease for Dental Students (1981); *Recreations* golf, skiing, travel; *Clubs* Army and Navy; *Style—* Roger Baird, Esq; 23 Old Sneed Park, Stoke Bishop, Bristol BS9 1RG (☎ 0272 685523); Consultant Surgeon, Royal Infirmary, Bristol BS2 8HW (☎ 0272 282737, fax 0272 252736)

BAIRD, (John) Stewart; s of John Baird (d 1971), and Louisa Jane Wright, *née* Stewart; *b* 8 June 1943; *Educ* Allan Glens Sch Glasgow, Univ of Glasgow; *m* 22 March 1985, Lorna Jane, da of Andrew Bayne, of 7 James Place, Stanley, Perthshire; 1 s (Andrew b 14 Aug 1977), 3 da (Karen b 12 May 1969, Emma b 12 Nov 1972, Amanda b 1 Jan 1977); *Career* Pannell Kerr Forster: apprentice Glasgow 1962-67, audit sr Liberia 1967-68, ptnr Gambia 1968-72, ptnr Sierra Leone 1972-85, ptnr London 1985-87, managing ptnr London 1987-; memb IOD, Freeman City of London 1987, Liveryman Worshipful Co of Loriners 1987; memb: Inst CAs of Scotland 1967-, Inst of CAs of Ghana 1977-, Insolvency Practioners Assoc; Royal Order of the Polar Star (Sweden, 1985); *Recreations* golf, reading; *Clubs* Caledonian, Walton Health Golf, Kingswood Golf; *Style—* Stewart Baird, Esq; Glenshee, 10 Warren Lodge Drive, Kingswood, Surrey, KT20 6QN (☎ 0737 832010); Pannell Kerr Forster, 78 Hatton Garden, London EC1N 8JA (☎ 071 831 7393, fax 071 405 6736, car 0836 210893, telex 295298)

BAIRD, Dr (Thomas) Terence; CB (1977); s of Ven Thomas Baird, Archdeacon of Derry (d 1967), of Strabane, Co Tyrone, and Hildegarde, *née* , Nolan (d 1919); *b* 31 May 1916; *Educ* Haileybury, Queen's Univ Belfast (MB BCh, BAO, DPH, FFPHM); *m* 1, 1940, Joan, da of Dr Douglas Edward Crosbie, MC (d 1952), of Londonderry; 2 da (Eileen, Sheelagh); m 2, 1982, Mary Wilson, da of Henry Claudius Powell (d 1966), of Manchester; *Career* RN 1940-46, Surgn Lt RNVR; served: N Atlantic, Indian Ocean, SW Pacific Ocean; med practitioner; dep co med offr Berks CC 1950-54, SMO Welsh Bd of Health 1956-62, chief surgn for Wales St John Ambulance Bde 1958-62, CMO Dept of Health and Social Servs NI 1972-78; QHP 1976; landowner (30 acres); memb GMC 1976-80, chm: NI Med Manpower Advsy Ctee, NI Advsy Ctee on Infant Mortality and Handicap; MRCPEd, FRCPI, FFCM, FFCMI; CStJ 1955; *Recreations* fishing, forestry; *Clubs* Carlton; *Style—* Dr Terence Baird, CB; 2 Kensington Rd, Belfast BT5 6NF (☎ 798020); Port-a-Chapel, Greencastle, Co Donegal (☎ 077 21038)

BAIRD, Vice Adm Sir Thomas Henry Eustace; KCB (1980), DL (Ayr and Arran 1982); s of Geoffrey Henry, and Helen Jane Baird; *b* 17 May 1924; *Educ* RNC Dartmouth; *m* 1953, Angela Florence Ann Paul, of Symington, Ayrshire; 1 s, 1 da; *Career* joined RN 1941, COS to C-in-C Naval Home Cmd 1976-77, Rear Adm 1976, dir gen Naval Personal Servs 1978-79, Vice Adm 1979, Flag Offr Scotland and NI, Cdr N Sub Area E Atlantic and N Sub Area Channel 1979-82, ret 1982; chm Erskine Hosp Exec Ctee 1986; *Recreations* shooting, fishing, golf, DIY; *Clubs* Army & Navy, Prestwick Golf; *Style—* Vice Adm Sir Thomas Baird, KCB, DL

BAIRD-SMITH, Robin Jameson; s of John Helenus Baird-Smith (d 1977), and Jean Marjorie Guthrie, *née* Priestman, OBE; *b* 21 July 1946; *Educ* Winchester, Trinity Coll Cambridge (BA); *m* 17 Jan 1976, Sarah Mary-Ann, da of Charles Stevens Hedley, MC (d 1976); 2 s (Max b 1978, Archie b 1979), 1 da (Leonora b 1981); *Career* publisher Darton Longman and Todd Ltd 1968-78; ed dir: Collins Publishers 1978-84, Constable Publishers 1985-; opera critic Mail on Sunday Newspaper 1989-; former chm Guild of Catholic Writers; *Books* Living Water (1985), Winter's Tales (1986/87/88/89/90), God of the Impossible (1986); *Recreations* music, travel, gardening; *Clubs* Travellers, Beefsteak; *Style—* Robin Baird-Smith, Esq; Constable and Company Ltd, 3 The Lanchesters, 162 Fulham Palace Rd, London W6 9ER (☎ 081 741 3663, fax 081 748 7562)

BAIRSTO, Air Marshal Sir Peter Edward; KBE (1981, CBE 1973), CB (1980), AFC (1957); s of late Arthur Bairsto, and Beatrice, *née* Lewis; *b* 3 Aug 1926; *Educ* Rhyl GS; *m* 1947, Kathleen, *née* Clarbour; 2 s, 1 da; *Career* RN 1944-46, RAF 1946-84, ret Air Marshal; mil aviation advsr Ferranti Scottish Group (now GEC Ferranti Defence Systems) 1984-, vice chm (Air) Highland TAVRA 1984-90, HM cmmr Queen Victoria Sch Dunblane 1984-; memb: Scottish Sports Cncl 1985-90, Cncl RAF Benevolent Fund 1985-, Scottish Air Cadet Cncl 1988-, St Andrews Links Tst 1989-; Hon Cd RE Field Sqdns Northern Gp ADR(V), CBIM; *Recreations* gardening, shooting, fishing, golf; *Clubs* RAF, New (Edinburgh), New Golf St Andrews, Royal and Ancient Golf St Andrews; *Style—* Air Marshal Sir Peter Bairsto, KBE, CB, AFC; Lucklaw House, Logie, by Cupar, Fife (☎ 0334 870546)

BAIRSTOW, Maria Elizabeth Jane; *née* Frank; da of Sir Robert John Frank (d 1987), of Ruscombe End, Waltham St, Lawrence, Berks, and Angela Elizabeth, *née* Cayley; *b* 26 Jan 1952; *Educ* Hampden House Sch Great Missenden Bucks; *m* 13 Sept 1975, Vivian Murray Bairstow, s of Alan Murray Bairstow, of 34 Manor Way, Egham, Surrey; 1 s (George b 1987), 1 da (Katharine b 1982); *Career* slr Fordyce Bairstow Egham Surrey; involved with local C of C and Church, govr Manorcroft Sch Egham; memb Law Soc 1981; *Recreations* family, dramatic society, squash; *Clubs* Wentworth Golf; *Style—* Mrs Maria Bairstow; Englewick, Englefield Green, Surrey TW20 0NX (☎ 0784 436645); Milton House, 27 Station Rd, Egham, Surrey TW20 9LD (☎ 0784 436121, 0784 432277 and 0784 431115, fax 0784 439 659)

BAKER *see also*: Arnold-Baker, Sherston-Baker

BAKER, Anthony Castelli; LVO (1980), MBE (1975); s of Alfred Guy Baker (d 1956), Wing Cdr RAFVR, and Luciana Maria Lorenzo Baker, *née* Castelli Spinola; *b* 27 Dec 1921; *Educ* Merchant Taylors'; *Career* munitions worker 1940-41, RAFVR 1941-46, served UK, ME and Italy, Flt Lt; HM Diplomatic Serv 1946-81; served Rome and Paris 1946-50; third sec: Prague 1951, Hamburg 1953, Milan 1954; third later second sec: Athens 1959, Beirut 1963, first sec: Cairo 1965, Naples 1968, Turin 1970; first sec commercial: Calcutta 1972, Port of Spain 1976; consul: Montreal 1975, Genoa 1979-81; ret 1981; Order of Merit (Italy) 1980; *Recreations* travelling, watching cricket, jazz music; *Clubs* MCC, RAF, Gloucestershire CCC; *Style—* Anthony Baker, Esq, LVO, MBE; Box 91, 17100 La Bisbal, Girona, Spain (☎ 72 490438); c/o 2/44 Elsworthy Road, London NW3 3BU

BAKER, Anthony Frank (Tony); s of Frank Cyril Baker, of Southampton, and Gwendoline Maggie, *née* Bushell; *b* 29 March 1940; *Educ* Taunton's Sch Southampton; *m* 19 Sept 1964, Sally, *née* Slinn, step da of Dudley Fitzroy Harding; 2 s (Paul Michael b 4 April 1968, Jonathan Alan b 30 April 1971); *Career* cricket administrator; chief exec Hampshire CCC 1986- (hon treas 1978-86), former chm Southern Cricket League; tax offr Inland Revenue 1958-60, trainee CA 1961-66, mangr chartered accountants Winchester 1966-68, ptnr Brooking Knowles and Lawrence 1968-86; ACA 1966; former cricket player: Old Tauntonians CC, Southampton Touring CC, Club Cricket Conference, Hampshire CCC second eleven; represented Southampton and Southern Area basketball; *Recreations* playing golf, watching football and cricket, travel, collecting cigarette cards; *Style—* Tony Baker, Esq; Hampshire CCC, Northlands Rd, Southampton, Hants SO9 2TY (☎ 0703 333788, fax 0703 330121)

BAKER, Anthony James Morton; s of Harris James Morton Baker (d 1960), of N Barningham, Norfolk, and Cicely Margaret, *née* Howgate (d 1986); *b* 30 Jan 1932; *Educ* Gresham's, Emmanuel Coll Cambridge (MA, LLM); *m* 19 July 1958, Vivienne Marguerite, da of Alexander Barclay Loggie, MBE (d 1967); 1 s (Malcolm b 1961), 1 da (Katherine (Mrs McGoldrick) b 1963); *Career* Nat Serv 2 Lt RA 1951-52; TA: Lt RA 1952-54, Lt Norfolk Yeo 1954-55, Lt RA 1955-58, Capt RA 1958-60; admitted slr 1958; ptnr: Walters and Hart 1960-72, Walters Vandercom and Hart 1972-78, Walters Fladgate 1978-87; sr ptnr: Walters Fladgate 1988, Fladgate Fielder 1988-; chm: CT Baker Ltd, Larner Brothers Ltd pres: Old Greshamian Club 1985-87, Bucks Co Hockey Assoc 1981-84; memb Cncl Hockey Assoc 1980-87; memb Law Soc; *Recreations* mens hockey, golf, reading; *Clubs* Beaconsfield Golf, Sheringham Golf, Royal Norwich Golf; *Style—* Anthony Baker, Esq; 15 Cosway St, London NW1 5NR (☎ 071 723 9601); The Old Farm, West Runton, Cromer, Norfolk NR27 9QJ; Heron Place, 3 George St, London W1H 6AD (☎ 071 486 9231, fax 071 935 7358, telex 28578)

BAKER, Brian James; s of Trevor George Baker, of Uppingham, Leicestershire, and Joan Eunice, *née* Duffin; *b* 19 Nov 1964; *Educ* Uppingham Community Coll, Rutland Sixth Form Coll; *Career* chef de cuisine Hambleton Hall Hotel 1982-; two stages with the Roux Brothers London educnl tour San Francisco and Flordia 1990; awards: Michelin Star 1986, Badoit Restaurant of the Year 1987; contrib articles to: The Independent (My Favourite Place To Eat), Vogue, House & Garden; *Recreations* sailing, tennis, swimming, horseriding, collecting old cookery books; *Style—* Brian Baker, Esq; 3 Thistleton Road, Market Overton, Rutland, Leicestershire (☎ 0572 838225); Hart Hambleton plc, t/a Hambleton Hall Hotel, Hambleton, Nr Oakham, Rutland, Leicestershire LE15 8TH (☎ 0572 756991, fax 0572 724721)

BAKER, Caroline Christian; da of Maj Hugh Armitage Baker, MC (d 1972), of Risence, Argentina, and Nettie Christian, *née* Cook; *b* 8 Jan 1943; *Educ* Northlands Buenos Aires; 1 da (Elodene Baker Murphy b 1984); *Career* asst to Shirley Conran at the Observer 1966-68, fashion ed Nova Magazine 1968-76, freelance fashion contributor Vogue Magazine 1976, fashion ed Cosmopolitan 1980-83, fashion ed Sunday Times 1987-90, fashion designer Mirabella 1990; *Recreations* swimming, tennis, painting, writing; *Style—* Ms Caroline Baker; 111 Aylmer Rd, London; Murdoch Magazines, Kings House, London W1

BAKER, Christopher James; s of James Alfred Baker, and Alice Marjorie Baker, *née* Yeomans; *b* 5 Nov 1951; *Educ* Dulwich, Christ's Coll Cambridge (MA); *m* 27 March 1978, Anne Elizabeth Sylvia, da of Francis George James Morris, of 172 Oxbridge Lane, Stockton-on-Tees; 2 s (James b 1981, Francis, b 1985), 2 da (Amy b 1983, Hannah b 1988); *Career* principal HM Treasy 1973-80; banker Morgan Grenfell & Co Ltd 1981-83, dir Hill Samuel Bank Ltd 1987-89 (joined 1983), corp fin ptnr Coopers & Lybrand Deloitte 1990-; *Recreations* walking, motoring, photography; *Style—* Christopher J Baker, Esq; Woodlands, 18 Carrwood Road, Wilmslow, Cheshire SK9 5DL (☎ 0625 529663); office: Abacus Court, 6 Minshull Street, Manchester M1 3ED (☎ 061 247 4081)

BAKER, Christopher Paul; s of Roland Midelton Baker (d 1949), and Hilda May, *née* Paul (d 1968), of Clifton; *b* 31 Oct 1925; *Educ* Marlborough; *m* 1956, Jane, da of Maj-Gen Sir Charles Dunphie, CB, CBE, DSO, of Wincanton, *qv*; 2 s, 1 da; *Career* Army 1944, served Egypt and Palestine 1945-77 (Capt); insur broker (Lloyd's), ret; former dir Glanvill Enthoven & Co Ltd and subsidiary cos; dep chm Mid Southern Water Co, memb Cncl of the Water Co (Pension Fund) Tstee Co; *Recreations* gardening, steam trains, preservation of the Book of Common Prayer; *Style—* Christopher Baker, Esq; Broad Oak House, Odiham, Hants RG25 1AH (☎ 0256 702482)

BAKER, Christopher William (Chris); s of Christopher Charles Robert Baker, of Dartford, Kent, and Annie Sarah Elizabeth, *née* Palmer; *b* 19 April 1934; *Educ* Collyers GS Horsham, Prince of Wales Nairobi Kenya; *m* 1, 31 March 1962, Marie Estelle (d 1966), da of Reginald Nutkins; 2 s (Christpher Graham b 12 January 1965, Terence Geoffrey b July 1966); m 2, 7 June 1969, Julia Ann, da of Joseph Barton; 1 s (Trevor Ian Robert b 26 June 1972); *Career* clerk Coopers & Lybrand London 1957-64 (Dar Es Salaam 1951-57), chief accountant and co sec Amalgamated Oxides (1939) Ltd 1965-66, Barnaby Engineering (1950) Ltd, ptnr Hacker Young 1977- (joined 1972);

permanant govr and tstee Canterbury Oast; FCA; *Recreations* table tennis, orienteering, road running, walking, the countryside; *Clubs* YCMA; *Style—* Chris Baker, Esq; 87 Avenue Road, Erith, Kent DA8 3AT (☎ 0322 341722); Hacker Young, St Alphage House, 2 Fore St, London EC2Y 5DH (☎ 071 588 3611, fax 071 638 2159)

BAKER, Colin Charles; s of Charles Ernest Baker (d 1971), and Lily Catherine Baker; *b* 8 June 1943; *Educ* St Bedes Coll Manchester, Coll of Law, LAMDA; *m* 1, 1976 (m dis 1979), Liza Goddard; m 2, 20 Sept 1982, Marion Elizabeth, da of Kenneth Wyatt; 1 s (Jack b and d 1983), 3 da (Lucy b 1985, Belinda b 1988, Lalage b 1990); *Career* actor; major roles incl: Prince Anatol War in and Peace (BBC TV) 1971, Paul Merroney in The Brothers (BBC TV) 1973-76, The Doctor in Dr Who (BBC TV) 1983-86; memb and vice-pres Wildlife Hosp Tst; memb: Cncl of Mgmnt and Appeals Ctee Fndn for the Study of Infant Deaths, Equity 1969, Equity Cncl 1990; *Style—* Colin Baker, Esq; c/o Barry Burnett Organisation, Suite 42/43 Grafton House, 2-3 Golden Square, London W1 (☎ 071 437 7048)

BAKER, David Leon; s of Jack Charles Baker, of Baker St, London, and Joan, *née* Grannard; *b* 14 May 1950; *Educ* St Marylebone GS London, Caton & Wallis Coll London; *m* 23 June 1974, Helen Amanda (Monday), da of Gerald Stone, of 36 York Terrace West, Regents Park, London NW1; *Career* Edward Erdman (Surveyors): asst negotiator, assoc ptnr 1975, ptnr and dir 1978, sr office ptnr 1987 (network mangr for N USA and Europe 1987), dir corp business 1989-; dep res Brokerage Ctee Int Real Estate Fedn, memb Steering Ctee Office Agents Soc; Freeman City of London 1990; MFB, FFB, mmeb Land Inst, fell Property Conolts Soc; *Recreations* rugby, cricket, athletics, tennis, local government, architectural and historic London, the tehatre; *Style—* David Baker, Esq; Edward Erdman Surveyors, 9-13 Grosvenor Street, London W1X OAD (☎ 071 629 8191, fax 071 409 3124, telex 28169, car 0836 656527)

BAKER, Donald Raglan; s of Alfred James Baker (d 1941), of London, and Lilian Kate, *née* Walker (d 1974); *b* 20 June 1922; *Educ* Merchant Taylors'; *m* 11 March 1950, Margaret Elizabeth (Peggie); 2 s (Timothy b 1953, Jeremy b 1958), 1 da (Claire b 1962); *Career* camps sec The Crusaders' Union 1947-57, bursar and sec London Bible Coll 1957-70, dir and gen mangr Phillips Fine Art Auctioneers 1972-87, dir Study Centre for the History of Fine and Decorative Arts 1985-; memb: Nat Tst, Bible Soc, NSPCC, Tear Fund, Samaritans, RSC, Stratford upon Avon Soc; memb Soc of Scribes and Illuminators; Freeman: City of London 1947, Worshipful Co of Merchant Taylors 1947; *Recreations* calligraphy, walking, desk work; *Clubs* Halls Croft (Stratford-upon-Avon); *Style—* Donald Baker, Esq; 3 Narrow Lane, Stratford-upon-Avon, Warwickshire CV37 6DP (☎ 0789 295019)

BAKER, Rev (Walter) Donald; s of Archibald Baker (d 1946), of Birkenhead, and Edith Alice, *née* Barber (d 1942); *b* 29 July 1906; *Educ* St Aidan's Coll; *m* 31 Aug 1934, Dorothea Frances, da of Harper Marrs (d 1944); 1 s (Ronald Duncan b 7 Sept 1935); *Career* officiating chaplain: RAF Hockering 1948, RAF Coltishall 1952, RAF Digby 1956; hon chaplain ATC 1965; organist and choirmaster: West Church Ballymena 1928, Portrush Parish Church 1932, Lanark Parish Church 1935; rector: Elsing with Bylangh 1947, Lamas with Scottow and Little Hautbois 1950; vicar St Paul with St Stephen Old Ford London 1958, rector Hanwell London 1964, vicar St Stephen Upper Holloway 1969, conductor Wenfield Singers 1965, princ Victoria Coll of Music 1988; pres Lincoln Diocesan Guild of Bellringers 1956; cncllr Mitford and Launditch RDC; life govr Royal Hosp and Home for Incurables Putney; Freeman City of London 1961, Liveryman Worshipful Co of Musicians 1968 (Almoner 1988); DLitt; FRSA, LTCL, MRST; *Books* Organ and Choral Aspects and Prospects (contrib 1958); *Clubs* City Livery; *Style—* The Rev Donald Baker; 8 Bishop St, London N1 (☎ 071 359 3498); St James Garlickythe, Garlick Hill, London EC4 (☎ 071 236 1719)

BAKER, His Honour Judge Geoffrey; QC (1970); er s of Sidney Baker (d 1963), of Bradford, and Cecilia Baker; *b* 5 April 1925; *Educ* Bradford GS, Univ of Leeds; *m* 1948, Sheila, da of M Hill, of Leeds; 2 s, 1 da; *Career* called to the Bar 1947; rec: Pontefract 1967-71, Sunderland 1971-72, Crown Ct 1972-78; circuit judge 1978-; pres Leeds Law Graduates Assoc, chm Univ of Leeds Convocation 1987; *Style—* His Honour Judge Geoffrey Baker, QC; c/o Courts Administrator, Bank House, Park Place, Leeds LS1 5QS

BAKER, Prof Geoffrey Howard; s of Albert Baker (d 1976), of 4 Senior Ave, Marton, Blackpool, and Dorothy, *née* Howard; *b* 27 Dec 1931; *Educ* Arnold Sch Blackpool, Sch of Architecture Univ of Manchester (Dip Arch), Univ of Newcastle upon Tyne (PhD); *m* 1, 11 Jan 1966 (m dis 1988), Margaret Anne, *née* Gilmour; 1 s (Kieran Roderick Michael b 14 April 1968); m 2, Carolynn, da of Carl E Gillum, of Chanute, Kansas, USA; *Career* architect; Grenfell Baines and Hargreaves Preston 1957-59, SW Cooke and Ptnrs Birmingham 1959-60, Norman and Dawbarn London 1960-62; lectr: Plymouth Sch of Architecture 1962-64, Univ of Newcastle upon Tyne Sch of Architecture 1964-76; visiting lectr and critic: Plymouth Poly, Univ of Sheffield; visiting prof: Queen's Univ Belfast 1981, Univ of Arkansas (and programme dir); external examiner Huddersfield Poly 1976-85, reader Sch of Architecture and Interior Design Brighton Poly 1976-87 Open Univ: co-organiser course A305, external examiner course A305, writer and presenter six TV programmes, dir summer sch Univ of Sussex 1975; currently prof architecture Tulane Univ New Orleans USA; assoc RIBA 1959; *Books* Le Corbusier: An Analysis of Form (1984, 2 edn 1989), Le Corbusier: Early Works by Charles-Edouard Jeanneret-Gris (1987), Design Strategies in Architecture: An Approach to the Analysis of Form (1989); *Recreations* swimming, travel, soccer, opera; *Style—* Prof Geoffrey Baker; School of Architecture, Tulane University, New Orleans, Louisana 70118 USA (☎ 504 891 3451)

BAKER, George William; CBE (1977, OBE 1971), VRD (1952 and clasp 1979); s of George William Baker (d 1956), and Lilian Turnbull, *née* Best (d 1976), of Priors Haven, Babbacombe, Devon; *b* 7 July 1917; *Educ* Chigwell Sch, Hertford Coll Oxford; *m* 1942, Audrey Martha Elizabeth, da of Robert Day Barnes (d 1965); 2 da (Susan, Pamela m 5 Baron Coleridge, *qv*); *Career* Lt Cdr RNVR, London Div RNVR 1937-62; war serv RN 1939-45: N Atlantic, Norway, Med, S Atlantic, Indian Ocean, Persian Gulf, India, Ceylon, Singapore, Malaya, Java seas, American seaboard, Combined Ops 1942-45; colonial admin serv Tanganyika 1946-62: asst colonial attaché Washington 1957, def sec Tanganyika 1959, head of Tanganyika Govt Info Dept 1959-62; first sec and dir Br Info Servs Br High Commission Freetown 1962-65, served FCO 1965-69, first sec and head of chancery Br Embassy Kinshasa 1969-72, dep Br govt rep St Vincent and Grenada 1972-74, Br high cmmr to Papua New Guinea 1974-77; vice pres Royal African Soc 1970-; chm: Heathfield Ctee Sussex Housing Assoc for the Aged 1979-84, Waldron Branch Wealden Cons Assoc 1983-84, E Sussex Ctee VSO, Exeter Flotilla 1987-90; E Devon Luncheon Club; ctee memb Devon Branch Oxford Soc; memb Sidmouth Dramatic Soc, ed The Clockmakers' Times 1987-, conslt Operation Raleigh; Freeman: City of London 1980-, Worshipful Co of Clockmakers 1981 (Liveryman 1984, Steward 1987), memb Guild of Freemen; *Recreations* photography, cabinet making, fishing, sailing, cricket, flying, rugby union; *Clubs* MCC, SES, Exeter Flotilla, City of London, Queen Hithe Ward; *Style—* George Baker Esq, CBE, VRD; Crosswinds, Coreway, Sidford, Sidmouth, Devon EX10 9SD (☎ 039 55 78845)

BAKER, Gordon Meldrum; s of Ralph Gordon Walter John Baker, of Burnham-on-Sea, Somerset, and Kathleen Margaret Henrietta Dawe, *née* Meldrum; *b* 4 July 1941; *Educ* St Andrew's Sch Bridgwater, Univ of Bradford (MSc); *m* 8 April 1978, Sheila Mary, da of Edward Megson (d 1977); *Career* Lord Chllr's dept 1959-66; Dip Serv 1966: Cwlth Office 1966-68, FCO (formerly FO) 1968-69, Br High Commision Lagos 1969-72, first sec W Africa Dept FCO 1973-75, res clerk FCO 1974-75 (and 1976-78), sabbatical at Bradford Univ 1975-76, FCO 1976-78 (Sci and Technol (later Maritime, Aviation and Environment) Depts), first sec head of Chancery and HM Consul Brasilia 1978-81, asst head Mexico and Central America Dept FCO 1982-84, cnsllr FCO 1984, seconded to British Aerospace plc 1984-86, cnsllr head of Chancery and HM Consul-Gen Santiago 1986-90, Royal Coll of Defence Studies 1990; *Recreations* reading, walking, watching birds, amateur dramatics; *Style—* G M Baker, Esq; c/o FCO, King Charles St, London SW1A 2AH

BAKER, Guy Christopher Scott; s of George Henry Baker (d 1980), of Rothley, Leics, and Phyllis Harriett Scott (d 1985); *b* 18 March 1945; *Educ* Loughborough GS; *m* 3 Nov 1979, Caroline Anne, da of Thomas Matthew Lockton; 1 da (Josephine Elizabeth b 10 Dec 1981); *Career* articled clerk A C Palmer & Co 1962, CA 1968, ptnr Ernst & Young 1989- (ptnr with previous merged firms 1974-); memb: Insolvency Practitioners Assoc, Soc of Practitioners of Insolvency 1990; *Recreations* golf; *Clubs* Rothley Park Golf, Charnwood Forest Golf, The Farmers; *Style—* Guy Baker, Esq; 13 Westfield Lane, Rothley, Leicester LE7 7LH (☎ 0533 303004); Ernst & Young, Provincial House, 37 New Walk, Leicester LE1 6TU (☎ 0533 549818, fax 0533 551357)

BAKER, Dr (John) Harry Edmund; s of late Joseph Elmer Grieff Baker, and Mary Irene Elizabeth, *née* Bolton; *b* 8 Jan 1949; *Educ* Epsom Coll, The Middx Hosp Med Sch Univ of London (BSc, MB BS, MRCP); *Career* Maj RAMC TA, specialist pool HQ AMS, Br Army Trauma Life Support Team, chief med advsr ACFA/CCFA, lately DADMS (TA) HQ W Mid Dist; lectr Univ of Nottingham Med Sch 1976-77, registrar Nat Hosp for Nervous Diseases 1977-80, sr registrar Nat Spinal Injuries Centre Stoke Mandeville 1980-83, Midland Spinal Injury Centre Oswestry 1983-85, conslt in spinal injuries and rehabilitation med S Glamorgan Health and Welsh Health Common Servs Authy 1985-, conslt advsr in rehabilitation Dept of Social Security Nat Pensions Office, pubns in med jls on immediate care & emergency handling of spinal co injury, mgmnt of spinal injuries at accident sites, accident and disaster med; asst surgn in chief St John Ambulance Bde, chm Professional Panel St John Aero Med Servs, vice chm Wales and memb Exec Bd (UK) Br Assoc of Socs of Immediate C memb Med Bd of St John Ambulance (Priory for Wales), med advsr Nat Rescue Trg Cncl; memb Cncl: Int Soc of Aeromedical Servs, Int Med Soc of Paraplegia, World Assoc of Emergency and Disaster Med; conslt advsr to Conjoint Ctee of the Voluntary Aid Socs; advsr and lectr in mgmnt of spinal cord injury to: Fire Servs, NHS Trg Authy, Ambulance Serv, Med Equestrian Assoc, Various Equestrian bodies, RAC, MSA, various other motor sports orgns, Mountain Rescue Team, RLSS; CStJ 1988; Fell NY Acad Sci (USA) 1988; *Books* Management of Mass Casualties (contrib 1980); *Style—* Dr Harry Baker; 56 Bridge St, Llandaff, Cardiff CF5 2EN (☎ 0222 578 091); 5 Bridge Rd, Llandaff, Cardiff CF5 2PT (☎ 0222 569 900); Rookwood Hospital, Fairwater Rd, Llandaff, Cardiff CF5 2YN (☎ 0222 566 281, 0222 555 677, car 0860 346 fax 0222 555 156, answering serv 0426 910 256)

BAKER, Dr Harvey; s of Isaac Baker (d 1971), and Rose, *née* Rifkin (d 1982); *b* 19 Aug 1930; *Educ* Univ of Leeds (MB, ChB, MD); *m* 6 June 1960, Adrienne Dawn, da of Leonard Lever, of London; 1 s (Laurence b 1961), 2 da (Caroline b 1962, Marion b 1967); *Career* Capt RAMC served KAR Kenya 1955-57; conslt physician The London Hosp 1968-; pres St Johns Hosp Dermatological Soc 1973, conslt dermatologist 1968-, pres Br Assoc Dermatologists 1990-91; FRCP (London); *Books* Concise Text Book of Dermatology (1979), Clinical Dermatology (1989); *Recreations* music, literature; *Style—* Dr Harvey Baker; 16 Sheldon Ave, Highgate, London N6 4JT (☎ 081 340 5970); 152 Harley St, London W1 (☎ 071 935 8868, fax 071 224 2574)

BAKER, Maj-Gen Ian Helstrip; CBE (1977, MBE 1965); s of Henry Hubert Baker, and Mary Clare, *née* Coles; *b* 26 Nov 1927; *Educ* St Peter's Sch York, St Edmund Hall Oxford; *m* 1956, Susan Anne, da of Maj Henry Osmond Lock, of York House, Dorchester, Dorset; 2 s, 1 s decd, 1 da; *Career* cmmnd RA 1948, transfered to RTR 1955, Staff Coll 1959, DAAG HQ17 Gurkha Div Malaya 1960-62, OC Parachute Sqdn RAC 1963-65, Instr Staff Coll and Brevet Lt-Col 1965, GSO1 Chiefs of Staff Ctee MOD 1966-67, CO 1 RTR 1967-69, 1970, Col RTR 1970-71, Brig 1972, Cdr 7 Armd Bde 1972-74, RCDS 1974, BGS HQ UKLF 1975-77, Maj Gen 1978, Asst Chief of Gen Staff MOD 1978-80, GOC NE Dist 1980-82, Col Cmdt RTR 1981-86, sec UCL 1982-; fell St Catharine's Coll Cambridge 1977; *Recreations* skiing, sailing, outdoor pursuits; *Style—* Maj-Gen Ian Baker, CBE; University College London (☎ 071 380 7000); c/o Barclays Bank, Dorchester, Dorset

BAKER, Sir (Allan) Ivor; CBE (1944), JP (Cambridgeshire 1954), DL (Cambridgeshire 1973); s of late Allan Richard Baker (d 1942), of Easton-on-the-Hill, Stamford, Lincs; *b* 2 June 1908; *Educ* Bootham York, King's Coll Cambridge, Harvard; *m* 1935, Josephine, da of late A M Harley, KC, of Brantford, Ontario, Canada; 3 s, 1 da; *Career* chm Baker Perkins Holdings 1944-75; kt 1972; *Style—* Sir Ivor Baker, CBE, JP, DL; 214 Thorpe Rd, Peterborough PE3 6LW (☎ 0733 262437)

BAKER, Dame Janet Abbott; DBE (1976, CBE 1970); da of Robert Abbott Baker and May, *née* Pollard; *b* 21 Aug 1933; *Educ* The Coll for Girls York; *m* 1957, James Keith Shelley; *Career* singer; memb Munster Tst; Hon DMus: Oxford, Cambridge, London, Birmingham, Hull, Lancaster, Leeds, Leicester, York; hon fell St Anne's Coll Oxford; Hon DLitt Bradford, Hon LLD Aberdeen; holder of Hamburg Shakespeare Prize and Copenhagen Sonning Prize, Gold medal Royal Philharmonic Soc 1990; FRSA; *Books* Full Circle (autobiog 1982); *Style—* Dame Janet Baker, DBE; c/o Ibbs & Tillett Ltd, 18b Pindock Mews, London W9 2PY

BAKER, Jennifer Myrle; da of Colin Hamilton Macfie (d 1981), and Beatrice Mary, *née* Hogg (d 1975); *b* 22 Aug 1949; *Educ* Whyteleafe Co GS for Girls, Mackie Acad Stonehaven, Inverness Royal Acad, Univ of Edinburgh (BSc); *m* 4 Jan 1980, Martin John, s of (William) Stanley Baker, KBE (d 1976); 3 s (Liam b 1982, Alexander b 1986, Shaun b 1989); *Career* asst gen mangr Hard Rock Cafe 1972-75; dir: Rock Biz Pix 1976-80, Martin Baker Enterprises Ltd 1984-, Hemisphere Prodns Ltd 1988-; freelance writer 1980- (several episodes for Storybook Int Hemisphere Prodns HTV Ltd); *Recreations* gardening, walking, reading; *Style—* Mrs Martin Baker; 61 Deacon Rd, Kingston, Surrey KT2 6LS; Hemisphere Prodns Ltd, 105 Mount St, London W1Y 5HE (☎ 071 493 5041, fax 071 499 3024)

BAKER, His Honour Judge John Arnold Baker; DL (Surrey 1986); s of late William Sydney Baker, MC, and Hilda Dora, *née* Swiss; *b* 5 Nov 1925, Calcutta; *Educ* Plymouth Coll, Wellington, Wadham Coll Oxford (MA, BCL); *m* 1954, (Edith Muriel) Joy, *née* Heward; 2 da; *Career* admitted slr 1951, barr 1960, circuit judge 1973; contested (Lib): Richmond 1959 and 1964, Dorking 1970; chm Lib Party Exec 1969-70, pres Medico-Legal Soc 1986-88; *Recreations* music, boating; *Style—* His Honour Judge Baker, DL; c/o The Crown Court, Canbury Park Rd, Kingston upon Thames, Surrey (☎ 081 549 5241)

BAKER, Rt Rev John Austin; *see*: Salisbury, Bishop of

BAKER, John Bellyse; s of Bellyse Baker (d 1947), of Highfields, Audlem, and Lilian, *née* Crosland (d 1971); *b* 29 Nov 1915; *Educ* Pownall Sch; *m* 4 Oct 1952, Josephine

May, da of Maj Joseph Henry Hendersen (d 1958), of Rosemeath, Wilmslow; 1 s (John b 1956), 1 da (Charity b 1960); *Career* joined family business Parr Baker & Co Ltd Manchester cotton mfrs 1934 (dir 1944, chm 1947-); chm N Staffs Hunt Supporters Club; *Publications* Highfields Audlem (1982); *Recreations* ornithology, painting, fox hunting; *Style—* John Baker, Esq; Highfields, Audlem, nr Market Drayton, Cheshire (☎ 0630 3825)

BAKER, His Honour Judge John Burkett; QC (1975); s of Philip and Grace Baker, of Finchley; *b* 17 Sept 1931; *Educ* Finchley Catholic GS, Univ Coll Exeter; *m* Margaret Mary Smeaton, of East Ham; 3 s (1 decd), 7 da; *Career* called to the Bar 1957, circuit judge 1978-; *Style—* His Hon Judge J Burkett Baker; 43 The Ridgeway, Enfield, Middx

BAKER, (Cecil) John; s of Frederick William Baker (d 1944), and Mildred Beatrice, *née* Palmer (d 1965); *b* 2 Sept 1915; *Educ* Whitgift, LSE (LLB, BSc); *m* 1, 1942 (m dis 1965), Kathleen Cecilia Henning; 1 s (John Howard); m 2, 1971, Joan Beatrice, da of Henry Thomas Barnes (d 1950), of Farnborough, Kent; 1 da (Amanda Claire b 7 Nov 1971); *Career* sec Insur Inst of London 1945-49, investmt mangr London Assurance 1950-64, investmt conslt Hambros Bank Ltd 1964-74; chm: Pension Fund Property Unit Trust 1966-87, Charities Property Unit Trust 1967-87, Victory Insurance Holdings Ltd 1979-85, British American Property Unit Trust 1982-87, United Real Property Unit Trust plc 1983-86, Alliance & Leicester Building Society (formerly Alliance Building Society) 1981-, Hunting Gate Group 1980-90; dir: Abbey Life Group plc 1985-88, Alliance Building Society 1970; FIA 1948, ACII 1937; *Recreations* golf; *Clubs* Savile; *Style—* John Baker, Esq; 3 Tennyson Court, 12 Dorset Square, London NW1 6QB (☎ 071 724 9716); 49 Park Lane London W1Y 4EQ (☎ 071 629 6661, fax 071 408 1399)

BAKER, John Derek; s of Bertie Baker (d 1972), of Walsall, and Edith Annie Doris Baker, *née* Sheldon; *b* 8 May 1932; *Educ* Queen Marys GS Walsall; *m* 1955, Mary Elizabeth, da of John Herbert Hancox (d 1970); 1 s (Richard b 1959), 2 da (Elizabeth b 1957, Catherine b 1966); *Career* CA, sr ptnr Baker & Co; fndr chm Walsall Gp Chartered Accountants 1978; dir: West Bromwich Building Soc 1984-, Arbor Accounting Servs Ltd, Arbor Estates Ltd, Walsall Unionist Hldgs Ltd, Unionist Buildings Ltd, WBBS (SRS) Ltd, Walsall Chamber of Commerce and Industry, Walsall Chamber of Commerce Engrg Trg Centre Ltd, Arbor Fin Servs Ltd; appointed magistrate Walsall Bench 1971 (chm Walsall Bench 1987); chm Walsall Parish Church Restoration Appeal Ctee 1978-; memb of Worshipful Co of Chartered Accountants in England & Wales 1980; Freeman City of London; FCA; *Recreations* gardening & bridge; *Style—* John D Baker, Esq; 16 Broadway, North Walsall, West Midlands WS1 2AN (☎ 21661)

BAKER, Prof John Hamilton; s of Kenneth Lee Vincent Baker, QPM, of Hintlesham, Suffolk, and Marjorie, *née* Bagshaw; *b* 10 April 1944; *Educ* King Edward VI GS Chelmsford, Univ Coll London (LLB, PhD), Univ of Cambridge (MA, LLD); *m* 20 April 1968, Veronica Margaret, da of Rev William Stephen Lloyd, TD (d 1971), Vicar of Southsea and Berse Drelincourt, Denbighshire; 2 da (Alys b 1973, Anstice b 1978); *Career* called to the Bar Inner Temple 1966 (hon bencher 1988); lectr in law Univ Coll London 1967-71 (asst lectr 1965-67, fell 1990, fell St Catharine's Coll Cambridge 1971-, lectr in legal history Inns of Ct Sch of Law 1973-78; Univ of Cambridge: librarian Squire Law Library 1971-73, lectr 1973-83, jr proctor 1980-81, reader 1983-88, prof of Eng legal history 1988-; visiting prof: Euro Univ Inst Florence 1979, Harvard Law Sch 1982, Yale Law Sch 1987, NY Univ Law Sch 1988-; jt literary dir Selden Soc 1981-; FRHistS 1980, FBA 1984; *Books* Introduction to English Legal History (1971, 3 ed, 1990), English Legal Manuscripts (1975, 1978), The Reports of Sir John Spelman (1977-78), Manual of Law French (1979, 2 ed, 1990), The Order of Serjeants at Law (1984), English Legal Manuscripts in the USA (1985, 1990), The Legal Profession and the Common Law (1986), Sources of English Legal History: Private Law to 1750 (with S F C Mi 1986), The Notebook of Sir John Port (1986), Readings and Moots in the Inns of Court, Part II: Moots (with S E Thorne, 1990); *Style—* Prof J H Baker; 75 Hurst Park Ave, Cambridge CB4 2AB (☎ 0223 62251); St Catharine's Coll, Cambridge CB2 1RL (☎ 0223 338317, fax 0223 338340)

BAKER, (Norman) Keith; s of Norman Baker (d 1985), of Bedford, and Lilian Hopper, *née* Robson; *b* 25 April 1945; *Educ* Doncaster GS, Bedford Modern Sch; *m* 1973, Elizabeth Rhoda, da of John Avery Stonehouse; 2 da (Amelia Elizabeth b 1978, Alice Harriet Clarissa b 1981); *Career* Coopers & Lybrand: Bedford 1964-70, supervisor London 1970-72, mangr 1972, expert witness 1973, audit gp mangr Hong Kong 1973-75, sr mangr Audit & Investigations Bedford 1976-87; Neville Russell Chartered Accountants: joined 1987, ptnr 1988-, tech ptnr for Luton Bedford and Milton Keynes regns, staff ptnr Milton Keynes in charge of Total Duality Mgmnt Prog and Litigation Support servs; FCA 1975 (ACA 1970); *Recreations* golf, crosswords, furniture renovation, squash; *Clubs* Howsbury Golf; *Style—* Keith Baker, Esq; 113 Kimbolton Road, Bedford MK41 9DP (☎ 0234 352484); Neville Russell Chartered Accountants, Sovereign Court, 202 Upper Fifth St, Silbury Boulevard, Central Milton Keynes MK9 2JB (☎ 0908 664466, fax 0908 690567, car 0831 388272)

BAKER, Rt Hon Kenneth Wilfred; PC (1984), MP (C) Mole Valley 1983-; s of late Wilfred M Baker, OBE, of Twickenham, Middx, and Mrs Baker, *née* Harries; *b* 3 Nov 1934; *Educ* St Paul's, Magdalen Coll Oxford; *m* 1963, Mary Elizabeth, *qv*, da of William Gray Muir, of Edinburgh; 1 s, 2 da; *Career* industl conslt; MP (C): Acton 1968-70, St Marylebone 1970-1983; PPS to ldr of oppn 1974-75, min of state Indust (special responsibility info technol) 1981-84, min for Local Govt 1984-85, sec of DOE 1985-86, sec of state for Educn and Sci 1986-89, chm of the Cons Party and chllr of the Duchy of Lancaster 1989-, Home Sec 1990-; memb Exec 1922 Ctee 1975-81, chm Hansard Soc 1978-81; *Books* I Have No Gun But I Can Spit (1980), London Lines (1982), The Faber Book of English History in Verse (1988), Unauthorised Versions: Poems and Their Parodies (1990); *Style—* The Rt Hon Kenneth Baker, MP; House of Commons, London SW1A 0AA

BAKER, Mark Alexander Wyndham; s of Lt Cdr Alexander Arthur Wyndham Baker (d 1969), and Renée Gavrelle Stenson, *née* Macnaghten; *b* 19 June 1940; *Educ* Prince Edward Sch Salisbury Rhodesia, Univ Coll Of Rhodesia and Nyasaland (BA), Christ Church Oxford (BA, MA); *m* 30 July 1964, Meriel, da of Capt Edward Hugh Frederick Chetwynd-Talbot, MBE, of Milton Lilbourne, Pewsey, Wilts; 1 s (Alexander b 1968), 1 da (Miranda b 1970); *Career* UKAEA 1964-89: various admin appts 1964-76, sec AERE Harwell 1976-78 (gen sec 1978-81), dir of personnel and admin Northern Div 1981-84, authy personnel offr 1984-86, authy sec 1986-89; exec dir corp affairs and personnel Nuclear Electric plc 1989-; *Recreations* squash, bridge, walking, gardening, words; *Clubs* United Oxford and Cambridge Univ, Antrobus Dining (Cheshire); *Style—* Mark Baker, Esq; Nuclear Electric plc, Barnett Way, Barwood, Gloucester GL4 7RS (☎ 0452 654251)

BAKER, Mary Elizabeth; da of William Gray Muir, WS (d 1959), of Edinburgh, and Betty, *née* Montgomery (d 1976); *b* 5 Feb 1937; *Educ* St Mary's Wantage, Univ of St Andrews; *m* 1963, Kenneth Baker, MP, *qv*; 1 s, 2 da; *Career* teacher 1959-67, dir Thames TV 1975-, govr Bedford Coll 1980-85, chm London Tourist Bd 1980-83; dir: Avon Cosmetics Ltd 1981-, Barclays Bank UK Ltd 1983-88, Barclays Bank plc 1988-; Prudential Corp plc 1988-, memb Womens' National Cmmn 1973-8; chm: Holiday Care Serv 1986-, Thames/LWT Telethon Tst 1987-89; fell Tourism Soc; govr Westminster Sch 1982-88, tstee Ind Bdcasting Telethon Tst 1989-, chm Tourist Bd Working Party (Tourism for All) 1988/89, vice pres Opportunities for People with Disabilities 1990-, pres Women in Mgmnt 1990-; Freeman City of London; *Books* Days of Decision-Women (part author, 1987); *Style—* Mrs Mary Baker; c/o The Secretary, Johnson Smirke Building, 4 Royal Mint Court, London EC3N 4HJ

BAKER, Michael Findlay; s of Rt Hon Sir George Baker PC (d 1984), of Rickmansworth Herts and Portpatrick Wigtownshire, and Jessie Raphael, *née* Findlay; *b* 26 May 1943; *Educ* Haileybury and ISC, BNC Oxford (BA); *m* 1973, Sarah Hartley Overton; 2 da (Helen Mary Hartley b 1976, Hannah Elizabeth Findlay b 1979); *Career* called to the Bar 1965; sec Nat Reference Tribunal for the Coolmining Indust 1973-; *Recreations* mountaineering, cross country running; *Clubs* Alpine, Climbers'; *Style—* Michael Baker, Esq, QC; Oakford, Standon, Ware SG11 1LT (☎ 0920 822144); Fountain Court, Temple, London EC4Y 9DH (☎ 071 583 3335)

BAKER, Michael Glendrew; s of Wing Cdr A Stanley Baker, of Abbey Cottage, Turvey, Bedfordshire, and Audrey, *née* Laing; *b* 3 July 1947; *Educ* Bedford Mod Sch,Univ of Leicester, Manchester Business Sch (DipBA, PhD); *m* 1970 (m dis 1983); 2 s (Alexander b 1974, Thomas b 1978), 1 da (Lucinda b 1976); *Career* dir Kleinwort Benson Ltd 1985-(exec asst mangr, mangr asst dir 1972-85); *Recreations* family, skiing, sailing; *Style—* Michael Baker, Esq; Kleinwort Benson Ltd, 20 Fenchurch St, London EC3P 3DB (☎ 071 956 5940)

BAKER, Prof Michael John; TD (1971); s of John Overend Baker (d 1960), of York, and Constance Dorothy, *née* Smith (d 1979); *b* 5 Nov 1935; *Educ* Worksop Coll, Gosforth & Harvey GS, Univ of Durham (BA), Univ of London (BSc), Harvard (Cert ITP, DBA); *m* 1959, Sheila, da of Miles Bell (d 1964), of Carlisle; 1 s (John), 2 da (Fiona, Anne); *Career* served in TA 1953-55, 2 Lt RA 1956-57, Lt 624 LAA Regt RA (TA) 1958-61, Capt City of London RF 1961-64, Capt PWO 1965-67; salesman Richard Thomas & Baldwins (Sales) Ltd 1958-64, lectr Hull & Medway COT's 1964-68, FME fell 1968-71, res assoc Harvard Business Sch 1969-71, prof Strathclyde Univ 1971-, dean Strathclyde Business Sch 1978-84 (dep princ 1984-); md: Baker Gordon (Business Res) Ltd 1973-90, Westburn Publishers Ltd 1982-, Stoddard Sekers Int plc 1983-, Scottish Tport Gp 1987-; chm: Scottish Mktg Projects Ltd 1986-, Inst of Mktg 1987, SGBS Ltd 1990-; Secretary of State for Scotland's nominee Scottish Hosps Endowment Res Tst 1984-, memb Chief Scientist's Ctee SHHD 1985-; SCOTBEC 1973-85 (chm 1983-85); memb UGC Business & Mgmnt Ctee 1985-89; FCIM, FCAM, FRSA, FScotVec; *Books* Marketing New Industrial Products (1975), Innovation: Technology, Policy & Diffusion (1979), Marketing: Theory & Practice (2 edn, 1983), Market Development (1983), Marketing Management and Strategy (1985), Marketing: An Introductory Text (4 edn, 1985), Organisational Buying Behaviour (1986), The Marketing Book, The Role of Design in International Competitiveness (1989), Marketing and Competitive Success (1989); *Recreations* travel, gardening, DIY, sailing (Lurline III and Ornsay); *Clubs* Royal Overseas League; *Style—* Prof Michael Baker, TD; Westburn, Helensburgh, Scotland (☎ 0436 74686); Univ of Strathclyde, Glasgow G4 0RQ (☎ 041 5524400)

BAKER, His Hon Judge Michael John David; s of Ernest Bowden Baker (d 1979), and Dulcie, *née* Davies; *b* 17 April 1934; *Educ* Trinity Sch of John Whitgift, Univ of Bristol (LLB); *m* 4 April 1958, Edna Harriet, da of John Herbert Lane (d 1950); 1 s (Matthew b 1963), 1 da (Amanda b 1961); *Career* Flying Offr RAF 1957-60; admitted slr 1957, ptnr Glanvilles 1962-88, coroner S Hamps 1973-88, rec Crown Ct 1980-88, circuit judge 1988; *Recreations* walking, swimming, tennis, theatre, photography; *Clubs* The Law Soc, RAF; *Style—* His Hon Judge Michael Baker; c/o 131 London Rd, Waterlooville, Hampshire (☎ 0705 251414)

BAKER, Michael Verdun; s of Albert Ernest Thomas Baker, of Rochford Way, Frinton-on-Sea, Essex, and Eva Louisa Florence, *née* Phillips; *b* 30 July 1942; *Educ* Caterham Sch; *m* 21 Sept 1963, Rita Ann, da of Walter James Marks, of 7 Kirkland Ave, Clayhall, Ilford, Essex; 2 da (Carolyn b 1967, Louise b 1970); *Career* insur official Alliance Assurance Co Ltd 1959-63, O & M systems analyst Plessey Co 1963-66, sr conslt Coopers & Lybrand 1967-72; The Stock Exchange: talisman project dir 1972-78, settlement dir 1978-82, admin dir 1982-84, divnl dir settlement servs 1984-87, exec dir mkts 1987-90, chief exec Assoc of Private Client Investmt Mangrs and Stockbrokers 1990-; author of various booklets and brochures on O & M, clerical work mgmnt and Stock Exchange settlement; memb: ISE APCIMS Exec Ctee, UK Equity Settlement Review Ctee; chm Securities Indust Liaison Ctee; *Recreations* running, photography, travel, squash, record collecting; *Clubs* Bigbury GC; *Style—* Michael Baker, Esq; Association of Private CLient Investment Managers and Stockbrokers, 20 Dysart St, London EC2A 2BX (☎ 071 334 8993)

BAKER, Nicholas Brian; MP (C) N Dorset 1979-; *b* 23 Nov 1938; *Educ* Clifton, Exeter Coll Oxford; *m* 1970, (Penelope) Carol, da of Maj Edward Nassau Nicolai d'Abo, KOYLI (RARO); 1 s, 1 da; *Career* PPS to: Min State Armed Forces 1981 and Procurement 1983, Michael Heseltine Sec of State for Def 1984-86, Lord Young of Graffham Sec of State for Trade and Indust 1987-88; govt whip 1989-; ptnr Frere Cholmeley Slrs 1973-; *Clubs* Blandford Constitutional, Wimborne Cons; *Style—* Nicholas Baker, Esq, MP; House of Commons, London SW1A 0AA

BAKER, (William) Nigel Whiston; s of Francis Cecil Whiston Baker (d 1952), and Gladys, *née* Davies; *b* 4 Jan 1934; *Educ* St Edwards Sch Oxford, Univ of London Middx Hosp Med Sch (MB, MS); *m* 29 Nov 1962, Daphne Cicely Kempe, da of John Kempe Clarke (d 1977); 2 da (Helen b 1964, Charlotte b 1966); *Career* Capt RAMC 1960-62; res fell St Marks Hosp 1967-69 (former resident surgical offr), sr registrar Westminster Gp Hosps 1970-77, conslt gen surgn Ashford Hosp 1977-; memb RSM, Br Soc of Gastroenterology; *Style—* Nigel Baker, Esq; 77 Elers Rd, Ealing, London W13 9QB (☎ 081 567 8817); Ashford Hospital, Ashford, Middx TW15 3AA (☎ 0784 251188, fax 0784 255696)

BAKER, Paul Kenneth Hay; s of George Kenneth Baker (d 1976), of Beckenham, and Margaret Elizabeth Hay, *née* Greenaway; *b* 20 Feb 1948; *Educ* Eastbourne Coll; *Career* mangr Deloitte Haskins & Sells CAs 1967-78, dir accounting servs RAC 1978-83, fin dir Deinhard & Co Ltd Wine Shippers 1983-, gp fin controller W J Marston Holdings Ltd 1989-90, fin mangr The King's Sch Canterbury 1990-; memb: Croydon Dist Soc of CAs, Ctee London Philharmonic Soc; chm and former treas Crystal Palace FC Vice Presidents' Club; FCA 1979 (ACA 1972), FBIM 1980; *Clubs* Croydon Dining (former pres and sec), Kent CCC, Croydon Cons, Croham Hurst GC, RAC; *Style—* Paul Baker, Esq

BAKER, His Hon Judge Paul Vivian; QC (1972); s of Vivian Cyril Baker (d 1976), and Maud Lydia, *née* Jiggins (d 1979); *b* 27 March 1923; *Educ* City of London Sch, Univ Coll Oxford (BA, BCL, MA); *m* 2 Jan 1957, Stella Paterson, da of William Eadie (d 1942); 1 s (Ian David b 1958), 1 da (Alison Joyce b 1960); *Career* Flt Lt RAF 1941-46; called to the Bar Lincoln's Inn 1950, practised at Chancery Bar 1951-83, bencher Lincoln's Inn 1979, circuit judge 1983-; ed Law Quarterly Review 1971-87 (asst ed 1960-70); Freeman City of London 1946; *Books* Snell's Principles of Equity (jt ed 24-29 edn, 1954-90); *Recreations* music, walking, reading; *Clubs* Athenaeum, Arts; *Style—* His Hon Judge Paul Baker, QC; 9 Old Square, Lincoln's Inn, London WC2A 3SR (☎ 071 2422633)

BAKER, His Hon Judge; Peter Maxwell; QC (1974); s of Harold Baker (d 1971), and Rose Baker; *b* 26 March 1930; *Educ* King Edward VII Sch Sheffield, Exeter Coll Oxford; *m* 1954, Jacqueline Mary, da of William Marshall, of Sheffield; 3 da; *Career* barr 1956, Crown Court recorder 1972-83, circuit judge 1983-; *Recreations* owner yacht: 'Susajo II' (seamaster 30 TSDY); *Style*— His Hon Judge Baker, QC; 28 Snaithing Lane, Sheffield, S10 3LG; 2 Harcourt Buildings, Temple, London EC4Y 9DB (☎ 071 353 1394)

BAKER, Peter Portway; AFC (1957); s of Wing Cdr Alfred Guy Baker (d 1955), of Beaconsfield, Bucks, and Luciana Maria Lorenza, *née* Castelli; *b* 2 Sept 1925; *Educ* Merchant Taylors', St John's Coll Oxford; *Career* RAF: U/T Aircrew 1944, GD Offr (Pilot Offr) 1945, memb 201, 209 and 230 Sqdns as pilot 1946-49, Central Flying Sch 1949, flying instr (Flt Lt) 1949-52, Empire Test Pilots Sch 1953, test pilot A and AEE Boscombe Down 1954-56, tutor (Sqdn-Ldr) Empire Test Pilots Sch 1957-59, voluntarily resigned 1959, test pilot Handley Page Ltd 1959 (test flying Dart Herald and Victor aircraft); BAC Weybridge 1962: joined 1962, test pilot for VC10 BAC 1-11 and Concorde aircraft, asst chief test pilot Concorde 1969, dep chief test pilot BAe Filton Div 1980 (ret 1982); CAA Airworthiness Div 1982 (chief test pilot 1986-87, ret 1987), self employed aviation conslt and freelance commercial pilot 1987-; Queens commendation for Valuable Serv in the Air, RP Alston Meml Medal 1978; Liveryman Worshipful Co Air Pilots and Air Navigators 1971 (Freeman 1961-); memb: Royal Aeronautical Soc 1964, Soc of Experimental Test Pilots 1965; *Recreations* walking, reading, aviation; *Clubs* RAF, MCC; *Style*— Peter Baker, Esq, AFC; Flat 2, 44 Elsworthy Rd, London NW3 3BU (☎ 071 722 4759)

BAKER, Richard Douglas James; OBE (1976), RD (1978); s of Albert Baker and Jane Isobel Baker; *b* 15 June 1925; *Educ* Kilburn GS, Peterhouse Cambridge; *m* 1961, Margaret Celia Martin; 2 s; *Career* served WWII RN; broadcaster and author; BBC TV newsreader 1954-82, TV Newscaster of the Year (Radio Industs Club) 1972, 1974 and 1979; presenter: Omnibus (BBC 1) 1983, Start the Week (Radio 4) 1970-87, Baker's Dozen (Radio 4) 1971-88, Melodies For You (Radio 2) 1988-, Richard Baker Compares Notes (Radi 4) 1989-; Hon LLD: Strathclyde 1979, Aberdeen 1982; Hon FRCM, Hon FLCM; *Style*— Richard Baker, Esq, OBE, RD; Hadley Lodge, 12 Watford Rd, Radlett, Herts (☎ 081 379 4625)

BAKER, Richard William Shelmerdine; s of Lt-Col Charles Bradbeer Baker (d 1979), and Vera Margaret, *née* Shelmerdine; *b* 17 Jan 1933; *Educ* Buxton Coll; *m* 1 (m dis 1975), Teresa Mary Elizabeth, *née* Smith; 1 s (David b 22 Feb 1960), 1 da (Lisa b 31 July 1962); m 2, 30 May 1975, Vanda, da of Percy William Macey (d 1989); *Career* Nat Serv 1951-53, cmmnd 2 Lt, transfd AER 1953, Lt 1954, Actg Capt 1960; mgmnt post Marks and Spencer 1954-60, sales dir and gp md Barbour Index Ltd 1972-79; sr vice pres and gen mangr Sun Life Assurance Co of Canada (rep 1960-72, memb Sr Advsy Cncl for Int Ops), md Sun Life of Canada (UK) Ltd; chm: Sun Life of Canada Unit Managers Ltd, Sun Life of Canada Home Loans Ltd; dir Life Assurance and Unit Trust Regulatory Orgn; pres GB Wheelchair Basketball Assoc; MIOD; *Recreations* horseracing, golf, tennis, cricket, collecting antiques; *Clubs* Canada, East India, MCC; *Style*— Richard Baker, Esq; Wissenden House Oast, Bethersden, Kent TN26 3EL (☎ 023 382 352); Fisher House, Hillside Park, Sunningdale, Berks SL5 9RP (☎ 0990 22664); Sun Life of Canada, Basing View, Basingstoke, Hants RG21 2DZ (☎ 0256 841414, fax 0256 460067, car 0831 414 385, telex 858654)

BAKER, Prof Robert George; s of Reginald Henry Baker (d 1981), of Dinton, Wilts, and Ellen Louise (d 1984); *b* 6 Dec 1930; *Educ* Bishop Wordsworth's Sch Salisbury, Fitzwilliam House Cambridge (MA, PhD); *m* 30 July 1955, Anne, da of Norman Watts Ramsden (d 1965), of Boughton Northants; 1 s (Stephen John b 1957, d 1975), 2 da (Caroline Jane b 1958, Katharine Elizabeth b 1962); *Career* head metallurgical res Welding Inst 1959, asst res mangr British Steel 1970, supt Materials Applications Div Nat Physical Laboratory 1973, dir res Glacier Metal Co 1977, conslt materials engr 1982-, industl fell Wolfson Coll Oxford 1983-85, assoc prof Brunel Univ 1984-; FIM 1969, FWeldI 1968, CEng 1978; *Books* The Microstructure of Metals (with Prof J Nutting, 1965); *Recreations* painting, walking, reading, photography; *Style*— Prof Robert Baker; PO Box 105, Slough, SL2 3YZ (☎ 02814 2818, fax 081 977 0227)

BAKER, Robert James; s of John Edward Baker (d 1990), and Margaret Elsie Mary, *née* Palmer; *b* 9 Dec 1947; *Educ* Univ of East Anglia (BA); *m* 15 June 1973, Beverley Joan, da of Paul Archdale Langford (d 1976); 2 da (Hannah Alice b 1979, Amy Margaret b 1981); *Career* dir Hobsons Publishing plc; *Recreations* art, antique collecting, racing; *Clubs* Reform; *Style*— Robert Baker, Esq; Porters Farm, Over, Cambridge (☎ 0954 30761); Hobsons Publishing plc, Bateman St, Cambridge (☎ 0223 35455)

BAKER, Robin Richard; s of Walter Richard Baker (d 1975), and Victoria Rebecca, *née* Martin (d 1988); *b* 31 Dec 1942; *Educ* RCA (maj travelling scholar, Fulbright scholar, MA), Univ of California, Thames Poly; *m* 1, 1966 (m dis 1970), Teresa Osborne-Saul; m 2, 1971 (m dis 1975), Tamar Avital; m 3, 1981 (m dis 1988), Angela Mary Piers Dumas; *Career* designer; designer with: Joseph Ezcherick Associates San Francisco 1964-65, Russell Hodgeson & Leigh (architects) 1965-66; fndr own design practice (maj exhibitions cmmns from Arts Cncl of GB, Br Airports Authy and Nat Tst) 1966-79, princ lectr (with resp for computor studies) Chelsea Sch of Art 1982-83, computor advsr Art & Design Inspectorate ILEA 1984-86, specialist advsr in computing Ctee for Arts & Design CNAA 1985-88, visitor in computing Art & Design Inspectorate and Poly of Hong Kong 1985, dir of computing RCA 1987; design computing conslt to: Conran Fndn's Museum of Design 1987-, Comshare Ltd 1987-88, Arthur Young 1988-89, Burtons Ltd 1988-89, Design Cncl 1990-, Marks & Spencer 1990-; author of numerous articles in design technology jls; *Style*— Robin Baker, Esq; Director of Computing, Royal College of Art, Kensington Gore, London SW7 2EU (☎ 071 584 5020, fax 071 225 1487)

BAKER, Roy Horace Ward; s of Horace John Baker (d 1964), of London, and Florence Amelia, *née* Ward (d 1971); *b* 19 Dec 1916; *Educ* Lycée Corneille Rouen, City of London Sch; *m* 1, 1940 (m dis 1944), Muriel Constance, da of Late Evelyn Edward Bradford; m 2, 1948 (m dis 1987), Joan Sylvia Davies, da of Alfred William Robert Dixon; 1 s (Nicholas Roy b 18 Aug 1950); *Career* army serv 1940-46 (cmmnd Bedfordshire and Hertfordshire regt 1941, army Kinematograph serv 1943); prodn runner to Asst Dir Gainsborough Studios Islington 1934-40; dir of more than 30 feature films incl: The October Man (1946), Morning Departure (1949), Don't Bother to Knock (in Hollywood, 1952-53), Night Without Sleep (in Hollywood), Inferno (in Hollywood), Tiger in the Smoke (1956), The One That Got Away (1957), A Night to Remember (1958), The Singer Not the Song (1960), Two Left Feet (1962), Quatermass and the Pit (1967), The Anniversary (1967), Asylum (1972); dir of more than 100 TV Series incl: The Avengers, Danger UXB, Minder, Irish RM, Flame Trees of Thika; NY Critics Circle (for A Night to Remember) for direction: Golden Globe, Christopher; Paris Convention du Cinema Fantastique grand prix for Asylum 1972; *Recreations* books, music, joinery, turnery; *Clubs* Athenaeum; *Style*— Roy Baker, Esq; 2 St Albans Grove, London W8 5PN (☎ 071 937 3964)

BAKER, Hon Mr Justice (Thomas) Scott Gillespie; s of Rt Hon Sir George Gillespie Baker, OBE (d 1984), and Jessie McCall, *née* Findlay (d 1983); *b* 10 Dec 1937; *Educ* Haileybury, Brasenose Coll Oxford; *m* 1973, Margaret Joy Strange; 2 s, 1 da; *Career* called to the Bar 1961, rec Crown Ct 1976-88, QC 1978, memb Chorleywood UDC 1965-68, memb Warnock Ctee 1982-84, bencher Middle Temple 1985, justice of the High Ct Family Div 1988-, presiding judge Wales and Chester Circuit 1991; *Recreations* golf, fishing; *Clubs* MCC; *Style*— The Hon Mr Justice Scott Baker; Royal Courts of Justice, Strand, London WC2

BAKER, Stephen; OBE (1987); s of late Arthur Baker, and late Nancy Baker; *b* 27 March 1926; *Educ* Epsom Coll, Clare Coll Cambridge; *m* 1950, Margaret Julia Wright; 1 s, 2 da; *Career* md Br Electricity Int 1978-, dir Davy Ashmore 1963, chm and chief exec Davy Utd Engineering, Ashmore Benson Pease Ltd and Loewy Robertson Engineering 1968, md Kearney & Trecker Ltd 1970; former chief indust advsr Dept of Trade; FIMechE; *Style*— Stephen Baker, Esq, OBE; 75 Slayleigh Lane, Sheffield S10 3RG

BAKER, Susan Mary; da of Lt Leo Kingsley Baker, DFC, RFC (d 1986), and Eileen Frida, *née* Brooks (d 1982); *b* 22 July 1930; *Educ* Stroud HS, Francis Holland Sch, RCM; *m* 12 July 1958, William Bealby-Wright, s of George Edward Wright (d 1931) (stage name George Bealby); 1 s (Edmund b 1962), 1 da (Sarah b 1960); *Career* violinist mangr Barrow Poets 1960-; princ performances incl: UK festivals 1960s and 1970s, 4 tours in America 1969-71; one woman show Violins Fiddles and Follies 1976-, princ performances incl: Edinburgh Int Festival, Brighton, Belfast; solo album Fiddles and Follies; promoter of classical concerts in Somerset; memb Musicians Union; ARCM; *Recreations* cooking, swimming; *Style*— Miss Susan Baker; 70 Parliament Hill, Hampstead, London NW3 2TJ (☎ 071 435 7817)

BAKER, Prof Terry George; s of George William John (d 1987), of Lymington, Hants, and Eugenia, *née* Bristow; *b* 27 May 1936; *Educ* Coventry Tech Secdy Sch, UCNW Bangor (BSc), Univ of Birmingham (PhD), Univ of Edinburgh (DSc); *m* 23 Aug 1958, Pauline, da of Alfred Archer (d 1969), of Coventry; 3 s (Paul Stephen b 6 Jan 1960, Noel Terence b 4 Dec 1962, Martin Christopher b 20 June 1966); *Career* science master Woodlands Boys Sch Coventry 1959-61; Univ of Birmingham: res student 1961-64, MRC res fell 1964-67, lectr in anatomy 1967-68; sr lectr in obstetrics and gynaecology Univ of Edinburgh 1975-79 (lectr 1968-75), pro vice chllr Univ of Bradford 1986-89 (prof of biomedical sciences 1980-); author of numerous pubns in learned jls; memb Bradford Health Authy 1982-86, memb Sub-Ctee on Educn Inst of Med Laboratory Sci 1985-88, govr Huddersfield Poly 1986-89; MRCPath, FIBiol, FIMLS, FRSE; *Books* incl: Radiation Biology of the Foetal and Juvenile Mammal (contrib, 1969), Human Reproduction: Conception and Contraception (contrib, 1973), Ovarian Follicular Development and Function (contrib, 1978), Functional Morphology of the Human Ovary (contrib, 1981), Comparative Primate Biology (contrib, 1986), Visual Problems in Childhood (contrib, 1990); *Recreations* music, wood carving, photography; *Style*— Prof Terry Baker, FRSE; Hollybrook, 30 Queen's Rd, Ilkley, W Yorkshire LS29 9QT (☎ 0943 602510); Department of Biomedical Sciences, University of Bradford, Richmond Rd, Bradford BD7 1DP (☎ 0274 733466 ext 215, fax 0274 309742, telex 51309 UNIBFD

BAKER, Wei Mei; *b* 2 May 1949; *Educ* Malaysian Schs; *m* 1975, Stephen Andrew Baker; *Career* fin dir Leopold Joseph & Sons Ltd 1985-91, non-exec dir RLJ Finance Ltd 1986-91, chm International Banking Information systems User Group 1988-91; *Clubs* Whitstable Yacht; *Style*— Mrs Mei Baker; Hobbits Oast, Goodnestone, Faversham, Kent (☎ 0795 532 555); 31-45 Gresham St, London EC2V 7EA (☎ 071 588 2323, fax 071 726 0105, telex 886454-5)

BAKER-BATES, Merrick Stuart; s of Eric Tom Baker-Bates (d 1986), and Norah Stuart, *née* Kirkham (d 1981); *b* 22 July 1939; *Educ* Shrewsbury, Hertford Coll Oxford (MA), Coll of Europe Bruges; *m* 6 April 1963, Chrystal Jacqueline, da of John Hugh Mackenzie Goodacre, of Court Farm House, Frowlesworth Rd, Ullesthorpe, Leics; 1 s (Jonathan b 1966), 1 da (Harriet b 1969); *Career* journalist Brussels 1962-63; HM Dip Serv 1963, third sec (later second sec) Tokyo 1963-68, FCO 1968-73; first sec: (info) Washington 1973-76, (commercial) Tokyo 1976-82 (later cnsllr); dir Cornes & Co Ltd and rep dir Gestetner (Japan) Ltd Tokyo 1982-85; rejoined Dip Serv 1985, dep high cmmr and cnsllr (commercial and economic) Kuala Lumpur 1986, head South America Dept FCO 1989-90, head S Atlantic and Antarctic Dept and cmmr Br Antarctic Territory 1990-; *Recreations* photography, golf, things Japanese; *Clubs* Brooks's, Tokyo; *Style*— Merrick Baker-Bates, Esq; c/o Foreign & Commonwealth Office, London SW1A 2AH

BAKER-CARR, Air Marshal Sir John Darcy; KBE (1962, CBE 1951), CB (1957), AFC (1944); s of Brig-Gen Christopher Teesdale Baker-Carr, CMG, DSO (d 1949), and Sarah de Witt, *née* Quinan; *b* 13 Jan 1906; *Educ* Harrow, Phillips Acad USA, MIT; *m* 30 June 1934, Margery Alexandra Grant, da of Maj-Gen Alister Grant Dallas, CB, CMG (d 1931); *Career* joined RAF 1929, No 32 Fighter Sqdn UK 1930-31, flying boats RAF Calshot and Iraq 1931-34, special armament course 1934-35, Western Area Andover 1935-37, No 3 Bomber Gp Mildenhall 1937-38, R & D air testing of aircraft 1938-45, Br Air Cmmn Washington 1945-46, Central Fighter Estab 1947-48, dir Dept of Personnel 1948-49, dir of armament R & D Miny of Supply 1949-51, Imperial Def Coll 1951-52, Cmdt RAF St Athan 1953-56, HQ Fighter Cmd 1956-59, AOC No 41 Gp Andover 1959-61, Air Marshal controller Engrg and Equipment 1962-64; ret 1964; *Style*— Air Marshal Sir John Baker-Carr, KBE, CB, AFC; Thatchwell Cottage, King's Somborne, Hants

BAKER CRESSWELL, Charles Addison Fitzherbert; OBE (1973), TD (1965), DL (N'mberland 1983); s of Capt A J Baker Cresswell, DSO, RN, of Budle Hall, Bamburgh, N'mberland, and Mrs A J Baker Cresswell; *b* 20 March 1935; *Educ* Winchester, RAC; *m* 28 July 1964, Barbara, da of Ralph Henry Scrope (d 1981), of South Thorpe, Barnard Castle, Co Durham; 3 s (John Addison b 18 May 1965, Edward Joe b 28 Feb 1967, Ralph Robert b 10 May 1969); *Career* Nat Serv 2 Lt 1 Bn The Rifle Bde (despatches); TA: Lt (later Maj) 7 Bn The Royal N'mberland Fus 1955-70, Lt-Col raised and cmd The Northumbrian Volunteers 1970-73, Col dep cdr NE Dist 1973-75; farmer; Parly candidate (Cons) Berwick-on-Tweed 1975 and 1979; *Recreations* environmental studies; *Clubs* Farmers, London Business Sch Alumnae; *Style*— Charles Baker Cresswell, Esq, OBE, TD, DL; Bamburgh Hall, Bamburgh, Northumberland NE69 7AB, (☎ 06684 230)

BAKER WILBRAHAM, Randle; s & h of Sir Richard Baker Wilbraham, 8 Bt; *b* 28 May 1963; *Educ* Harrow; *Career* London Fire Bde 1983-89; Fine Art Course V & A Museum 1989-90; *Style*— Randle Baker Wilbraham Esq; Rode Hall, Scholar Green, Cheshire ST7 3QP (☎ 0270 873237)

BAKER WILBRAHAM, Sir Richard; 8 Bt (GB 1776); s of Sir Randle John Baker Wilbraham, 7 Bt, JP, DL (d 1980); *b* 5 Feb 1934; *Educ* Harrow; *m* 2 March 1962, Anne Christine Peto, da of late Charles Peto Bennett, OBE, of Jersey; 1 s, 3 da; *Heir* s, Randle Baker Wilbraham, *qv*; *Career* late Lt Welsh Gds; dir: J Henry Schroder Wagg & Co 1969-89, Westpool Investment Tst plc 1974-, Brixton Estate plc 1985-, Charles Barker plc 1986-89, Really Useful Gp plc 1985-90, Severn Trent plc 1989-, Bibby Line Gp Ltd 1989- (dep chm), Majedie Investments plc 1989-, Grosvenor Estate Hldgs 1989- (dep chm); tstee Grosvenor Estate 1981-; govr: Harrow Sch 1982, Nuffield Hosps 1990-; *Clubs* Brooks's, Pratts; *Style*— Sir Richard Baker Wilbraham, Bt; Rode Hall, Scholar Green, Cheshire ST7 3QP (☎ 0270 873237)

BAKEWELL, Joan Dawson; da of John Rowlands and Rose, *née* Bland; *b* 16 April

1933; *Educ* Stockport HS for Girls, Newnham Coll Cambridge; *m* 1, 1955 (m dis 1972), Michael Bakewell, 1 s, 1 da; m 2, 1975, Jack Emery (theatre prodr); *Career* broadcaster and writer; arts corr BBC TV 1981-87, presenter Heart of the Matter 1988-; columnist Sunday Times; pres Soc of Arts Publicists; *Books* The New Priesthood (with Nicholas Gardham), A Fine & Private Place (with John Drummond), The Complete Traveller; *Style*— Ms Joan Bakewell; BBC Television, Television Centre, Wood Lane, London W12

BAKKER, Paul-Jan; s of Hubertus Antonius Bakker, of The Hague, Netherlands, and Wilhelmina Hendrika Bakker-Goos; *b* 19 Aug 1957; *Educ* Hugo De Groot Scholengemeenschap The Hague; *Career* professional cricketer; Quick CC The Hague 1965-85, Greenpoint CC SA winters 1981-86; Hampshire CCC 1984-; non-contract player 1984, professional 1985, debut 1986, awarded county cap 1989; MCC tour Pa USA 1990 and Namibia 1991; Holland: played in first int under 19 tournament, 51 full appearances, tour England and UAE; first Dutchman to play first class county cricket; J & B cricketer of the month 3 times, cricketer of the year Hants press 1989; military serv Holland (private pilots cert), ski holiday organiser Switzerland during off seasons; *Recreations* golf, skiing, newspapers, good food, meeting people, generally enjoying life; *Style*— Paul-Jan Bakker, Esq; Hampshire CCC, County Cricket Ground, Northlands Road, Southampton SO9 2TY (☎ 0703 333788)

BALAGUER-MORRIS, José; s of Vicente Balaguer Martin (d 1975), of Barcelona, Spain, and Emma Morris Irrisarry; *b* 6 Oct 1933; *Educ* Jesuit Sch Barcelona, Barcelona Univ Med Sch, King's Coll Dental Sch London (BDS, Sr Conservation prize), Karolinska Institutet Stockholm (Leg Tand); *m* 8 Sept 1962, Ann-Britt, da of late Vidar Sahlin; 1 da (Anna Cristina b 28 May 1967); *Career* dental technician Barcelona and London, house surgeon King's Coll London 1970, lectr Karolinska Institutet Tandlakare Hogskolan Stockholm 1970-71, private dental surgeon and pt/t clinical lectr KCH and UCH Dental Schs 1971-72, clinical lectr UCH 1971-72, sr clinical lectr UCH Dental Sch 1975-82 (pt/t clinical lectr 1972-75); in private practice London and Oxford 1972-; UK corr Revista Europea de Estomatologia, advsr in Spanish language to FDI Lexicon; memb: BDA 1970, Swedish Dental Assoc 1971, Euro Prosthodontic Assoc (fndr) 1979, Int Coll of Dentists 1985, Int Prosthodontic Assoc 1986, Br Soc of Endodontics (memb Cncl 1987), Br Soc of Periodontology, Br Soc of Cons Dentistry, Int Dental Fedn (FDI); memb Delta Sigma Delta fraternity; *Recreations* tennis, mountain walking, collecting wine, Latin and Punic wars, historical literature, travel to historical places; *Clubs* Bisham Abbey Tennis; *Style*— Jose Balaguer-Morris, Esq; 90 Harley St, London W1N 1AF (☎ 071 935 2240, fax 071 224 4158); 4 Moreton Rd, Oxford OX2 7AX (☎ 0865 57808)

BALCHIN, Robert George Alexander; s of Leonard George Balchin (d 1968), and Elizabeth, *née* Skelton; the Balchin family settled in Surrey c1190, Sir Roger de Balchen owning lands in both Normandy and Surrey, Adm Sir John Balchin (1669-1744) was Governor of Greenwich RN Hosp; *b* 31 July 1942; *Educ* Bec Sch, Univ of London, Univ of Hull (MEd, Adv Dip Ed); *m* 1970, Jennifer, da of Bernard Kevin Kinlay (d 1975), of Cape Town; 2 s (Alexander b 1975, Thomas (twin) b 1975); *Career* asst master Chinthurst Sch 1964-68, head English Dept Ewell Sch 1968-69, dir Hill Sch Westerham 1980- (headmaster 1972-80); dir gen St John Ambulance 1984-90, chm Campaign for a Gen Teaching Cncl 1981-; memb: Surrey CC 1981-85, Centre for Policy Studies 1982-; treas E Surrey Cons Assoc 1982-85, dep area treas Cons Pty 1983-86, vice chm Cons Pty SE England 1986-90, Cons treas for SE England 1990-, conslt dir Cons Central Office 1988-; chm: Grant-Maintained School Trust 1989, Pardoe-Blacker Publishing Ltd 1989; Hon DPhil Northland Open Univ Canada 1985, Freeman and Liveryman Worshipful Co of Goldsmiths 1987; Hon FCP 1987, Hon FHS 1987; Commander's Cross (Pro Merito Melitensi SMOM) 1987; KStJ 1984; *Books* Emergency Aid in Schools (1984), New Money (1985), Choosing a State School (jtly, 1989); *Recreations* restoration of elderly house; *Clubs* Athenaeum, Carlton, St Stephen's Constitutional; *Style*— Robert Balchin, Esq; New Place, Lingfield, Surrey RH7 6EF (☎ 0342 834543); 7 Ashley Ct, Westminster, SW1P 1EN; 239-245 Vauxhall Bridge Road, London SW1 (☎ 071 828 9855)

BALCHIN, Prof William George Victor; s of Victor Balchin (d 1944), of Aldershot, Hants, and Ellen Winifred Gertrude, *née* Chapple (d 1988); *b* 20 June 1916; *Educ* Aldershot HS, St Catharine's Coll Cambridge (BA, MA), Kings Coll London (PhD); *m* 10 Dec 1939, Lily, da of Henry Gordon Kettlewood (d 1965), of Otley, Yorks; 1 s (Peter Malcolm b 6 Sept 1940), 2 da (Anne Catharine b 10 Oct 1948, Joan Margaret b 10 May 1942 d 1985); *Career* WWII hydrographic offr Hydrographic Dept Admiralty 1939-45; jr demonstrator in geography Univ of Cambridge 1937-39 (geomorphologist Cambridge Spitsbergen Expedition 1938), lectr Univ of Bristol Regnl Ctee on Educn and WEA tutor 1939-45, lectr King's Coll London 1945-54 (geomorphologist on US Sonora-Mohave Desert Expedition 1952), prof of geography and head dept Univ Coll Swansea 1954-78 (dean of Science 1959-61, vice-princ 1964-66 and 1970-73), emeritus prof 1978-, Leverhulme emeritus fell 1982; RGS: Open Essay prize 1936-37, Gill Memorial award 1954, memb Cncl 1962-65 and 1975-88, chm Educn Ctee 1975-88, vice pres 1978-82, chm Ordnance Survey Ctee 1983-; Geographical Assoc: conference organiser 1950-54, memb Cncl 1950-81, tstee 1954-77, pres 1971, hon memb 1980; BAAS: pres (Section E Geography) 1972, treas 2 Land Utilisation Survey of Britain 1961-, chm Land Decade Educnl Cncl 1978-83; memb: Meteorological Ctee MOD 1963-69, Br Nat Ctee for Geography 1964-70, 1976-78 and Cartography 1961-71, Nature Conservancy Ctee for Wales 1959-68, Hydrology Ctee ICE 1962-76, Court of Govrs Nat Mus Wales 1966-74, Univ Coll Swansea 1980-, St Davids Coll Lampeter 1968-80, Univ of Bradford Disaster Prevention Unit 1989-; vice pres Glamorgan Co Naturalist Tst 1961-80; hon FKC 1984; FRGS 1937, FKMetS 1945, FRCSoc 1978; *Books* Geography and Man (3 vols, ed 1947), Climatic and Weather Exercises (with A W Richards 1949), Practical and Experimental Geography (with A W Richards 1952), Cornwall Making of the English Landscape (1954), Geography for the Intending Student (ed 1970), Swansea and Its Region (ed, 1971), Living History of Britain (ed, 1981), Concern for Geography (1981), The Cornish Landscape (1983); *Recreations* travel, writing; *Clubs* Royal Cwlth Soc, Geographical; *Style*— Prof William Balchin; 10 Low Wood Rise, Ben Rhydding, Ilkley, W Yorks LS29 8AZ (☎ 0943 600 768)

BALCOMBE, Rt Hon Lord Justice; Rt Hon Sir (Alfred) John; PC (1985), QC (1969); er s of Edwin Kesteven Balcombe (d 1986), of London, and Jane Phyllis, *née* Abrahams (d 1982); *b* 29 Sept 1925; *Educ* Winchester, New Coll Oxford (BA, MA); *m* 24 May 1950, Jacqueline Rosemary, yr da of Julian Cowan (d 1957), of Harrow, Middx: 2 s (Peter b 1955, David b 1958), 1 da (Jennifer (Mrs Suthers) b 1952); *Career* called to the Bar Lincoln's Inn 1950; bencher 1977; high court judge (Family Div) 1977, Lord Justice of Appeal 1985-; Liveryman Worshipful Co of Tin Plate Workers (Master 1971); kt 1977; *Books* Exempt Private Companies (1953); *Clubs* Garrick; *Style*— The Rt Hon Lord Justice Balcombe; Royal Courts of Justice, Strand, London WC2A 2LL

BALCON, Jonathan Michael Henry; TD (1965); s of Sir Michael Balcon (d 1977), film prodr, and Aileen Freda, *née* Leatherman; *b* 7 Dec 1931; *Educ* Eton, Gonville and Caius Coll Cambridge; *m* 1 Oct 1955, Hon Sarah Patricia Mills, *qv*, da of 5 Baron Hillingdon (d 1982); 3 da (Deborah b 1956, Sarah-Clair b 1957, Henrietta b 1960); *Career* TA 1951-67, City of London Yeo (Rough Riders) 1951-62 (cmmnd 1956), Inns of Court and City Yeo 1962-67 (Maj 1966 cmdg B Sqdn); underwriting agent at Lloyds, dir C I de Rougemont & Co Ltd, chm Michael Balcon Productions Ltd; Kent Special Constabulary 1967- (Cmdt C Div); pres Sevenoaks Combined Div St John Ambulance, memb Kent Ctee SE TAVRA (chm Recruiting Kent 1983-87); Queen's Jubilee medal, Special Constabulary Long Service medal and bar; *Recreations* shooting; *Clubs* City of London; *Style*— Jonathan Balcon, Esq, TD; The Grey House, Seal, Sevenoaks, Kent (☎ 0732 61592/61819); C I de Rougemont & Co Ltd, 71-74 Mark Lane, London EC3 (☎ 071 481 9277)

BALCON, Raphael; *b* 26 Aug 1936; *Educ* King's Coll Med Sch (MB BS, LRCP, MRCP, MD); *Career* resident house physician King's Coll Hosp London 1960, resident house surgn Dulwich Hosp London 1961, resident house physician London Chest Hosp 1961, sr house physician St Stephens Hosp London 1962-63, US pub health fell Dept of Med Wayne State Univ Coll of Med Detroit USA 1963-64, locum med registrar St Thomas and St Stephens Hosps 1964, fell and hon registrar King's Coll Hosp London 1965, med registrar King's Coll Hosp London 1966, sr registrar Nat Heart Hosp London 1967-70 (registrar 1966-67); currently: conslt cardiologist, clinical co-ordinator, memb Mgmnt Gp Royal Brompton and Nat Heart and Lung Hosp Victoria Park, hon sr lectr Nat Heart and Lung Inst; dean Cardiothoracic Inst 1976-80, memb DHSS Pacemaker Advsy Ctee 1979-84, hon treas Br Cardiac Soc 1981-86; memb: Cardiology Ctee RCP 1983-86, Fin Ctee RCP 1986-, Cncl Br Coronary Intervention Soc 1990-, Ethical and Legal Ctee Br Cardiac Soc 1990-; memb Br Cardiac Soc 1969-, FACC 1970, FRCP 1977, fndr fell Euro Soc of Cardiology 1986-; author numerous pubns in learned jls; *Style*— Raphael Balcon, Esq; 68 Gloucester Crescent, London NW1 7EG

BALCON, Hon Mrs (Sarah Patricia); *née* Mills; da of 5 Baron Hillingdon, MC, TD; *b* 1933; *Educ* Westonbirt; *m* 1955, Jonathan Michael Henry Balcon, TD, o s of late Sir Michael Balcon; 3 da (Deborah b 1956, Sarah Clair b 1957, Henrietta b 1960); *Career* tstee Harrison Zoological Museum, vice pres Kent Girl Guide Assoc; *Recreations* travelling, paleontology, fine arts; *Style*— The Hon Mrs Balcon; The Grey House, Seal, Sevenoaks, Kent (☎ 0732 61592)

BALDERSTONE, Sir James Schofield; s of James Schofield Balderstone (d 1953), and Mary Essendon, *née* Taylor (d 1960); *b* 2 May 1921; *Educ* Scotch Coll Melbourne; *m* 1946, Mary Henrietta, da of William James Tyree; 2 s (James, Richard), 2 da (Susan, Elizabeth); *Career* gen mangr (Aust) Thomas Borthwick & Sons 1953-67; chm: Australian Meat Exporters Federal Cl 1963-64, Squatting Investment Company Ltd 1966-73, Commonwealth Government Working Group on Agricultural Policy Issues and Options for the 1980's 1981-82, Stanbroke Pastoral Company 1982- (md 1964-81), Broken Hill Proprietary Company Ltd 1984-89 (dir 1971-, chm 1984-), Vic Br Bd AMP Soc 1984-90 (dir 1962-); dir: Commerical Bank of Australia 1979-81, Westpac Banking Corporation 1981-84, NW Shelf Development Party Ltd, Woodside Petroleum Ltd 1976-83; princ: Bd AMP Soc 1979-, ICI Aust Ltd 1981-84 (chm 1990-), Chase AMP Bank 1985- (chm 1990-); pres Inst of Public Affairs 1981-84; memb: rep Meat Exporters on Australian Meat Bd 1964-67, Export Devpt Cncl 1968-71; kt 1983 *see Debrett's Handbook of Australia and New Zealand for further details*; *Recreations* farming, reading, watching sport; *Clubs* Australian, Melbourne, Union (Sydney), MCC, Queensland; *Style*— Sir James Balderstone; 115 Mont Albert Rd, Canterbury, Vic 3126, Australia (☎ 836 3137); Level 32, 600 Bourke St, Melbourne, Australia 3000 (☎ 03 609 3644, fax 03 602 4019)

BALDING, Ian Anthony; s of Gerald Matthews Balding (d 1956), of Weyhill, nr Andover, Hants, and Eleanor, *née* Hoagland (d 1987); *b* 7 Nov 1938; *Educ* Marlborough, Millfield, Christ's Coll Cambridge (Rugby blue); *m* 25 Aug 1969, Emma Alice Mary, da of late Peter Hastings-Bass; 1 s (Andrew Matthews b 29 Dec 1972), 1 da (Clare Victoria b 29 Jan 1971); *Career* racehorse trainer 1964-; notable horses trained incl: Glint of Gold, Mrs Penny, Mill Reef, Forest Flower; trained for: HM Queen Elizabeth The Queen Mother (won Imperial Cup with Insular), HM The Queen 1964-, Paul Mellon KBE 1964-; maj races won in UK: Derby, King George VI & Queen Elizabeth Stakes, Eclipse Stakes, Dewhurst Stakes 4 times, Imperial Cup (nat hunt), 1000 Guineas (Ireland), Nat Stakes twice (Ireland); races won abroad: Italian Derby, St Leger twice, 2000 Guineas, Prix de L'Arc de Triomphe, Prix Ganay, Prix de Diane, Prix Vermaille, Prix de L'Abbaye de Long Champ, Grosser Preis von Baden twice, Preis von Europa 3 times; second leading flat trainer in first full year 1965, leading trainer 1971, leading int trainer 3 times; amateur nat hunt jockey winning over 70 races 1954-64 (incl Nat Hunt Chase Cheltenham), winning jockey various hunter chase and point to point races 1964- (winner two point to points on Experimenting 1990); rugby: Bath 1956-66, Dorset & Wiltshire 1956-66, Cambridge Univ 1959-62, various appearances Southern Cos, currently Newbury Faded Blues; boxing Cambridge Univ, cricket Crusaders; *Recreations* jt master Berks & Bucks Drag Hunt, skiing, squash, tennis, golf, cricket; *Style*— Ian Balding, Esq; Park House, Kingsclere, Newbury, Berks RG15 8PZ (☎ 0635 298274/298210, fax 0635 298305)

BALDOCK, Brian Ford; s of Ernest John Baldock, of 12 Ferry Road, Teddington, Middx, and Florence, *née* Ford (d 1983); *b* 10 June 1934; *Educ* Clapham Coll London; *m* 1 (m dis 1966), Mary Lillian, *née* Bartolo; 2 s (Simon b 1958, Nicholas b 1961); m 2, 30 Nov 1968, Carole Anthea, da of F R Mason (d 1978); 1 s (Alexander b 1970); *Career* Lt Royal W Kent Regt 1952-53, Corps of Royal Mil Police 1953-55; mgmnt trainee Procter & Gamble Ltd 1956-61, assoc dir Ted Bates Inc 1961-63, mktg mangr Rank Organisation 1963-66, dir Smith & Nephew 1966-75, vice pres Revlon Inc (Europe, ME and Africa) 1975-78, md Imperial Leisure & Retail 1978-86, gp md Guinness plc; cncl memb Lord's Taverners; Freeman: Worshipful Co of Brewers 1988, City of London 1988; FInstM 1976, fell Mktg Soc 1988, FRSA 1987; *Recreations* theatre, music, travel; *Clubs* Lord's Taverners; *Style*— Brian Baldock, Esq; The White House, Donnington, Newbury, Berkshire (☎ 0635 41200); Guinness plc, 39 Portman Sq, London W1 (☎ 081 965 7700, fax 081 961 8727, telex 23822)

BALDREY, Frank William; s of William Baldrey (d 1960), of London; *b* 7 Jan 1921; *Educ* City of London Sch, King's Coll London (BSc); *m* 1, 1946, Nancy (d 1969), da of William Mullins (d 1945), of Co Mayo; 2 s, 2 da; m 2, 1974, Patricia, da of Francis Clements (d 1974), of Droitwich; *Career* md Stanley Bridges Ltd until 1967, chm Garringtons Ltd to 1976, chief exec IP & SD BOC Ltd to 1984; dir: Technicare International NOWSCO UK Gp, S Wales Forgemaster; CEng, FICE, FIMechE, FIEE; *Recreations* sports administration, horse racing; *Style*— Frank Baldrey, Esq; Deancroft, Cookham Dean, Berks (☎ 0628 486699)

BALDRY, Antony Brian; MP (C) Banbury 1983-; known as Tony; eldest s of Peter Edward Baldry, and Oina, *née* Paterson; *b* 10 July 1950; *Educ* Leighton Park, Univ of Sussex (BA, LLB), Lincoln's Inn; *m* 1979, Catherine Elizabeth, 2 da of Capt James Weir, RN (ret), of Chagford, Devon; 1 s, 1 da; *Career* barr and publisher; PA to Mrs Thatcher in Oct 1974 election, in ldr of oppn's office Mar-Oct 1975, awarded Robert Schumann Silver medal (for contributions to Euro politics) 1978, memb Carlton Club Political Ctee, contested (C) Thurrock 1979, memb Parly Select Ctee on Employment 1983-85, PPS to Lynda Chalker 1985-87, PPS to John Wakeham 1987-, Parly under sec Dept of Energy 1990-; dir Newpoint Gp 1974-; *Recreations* walking, beagling; *Clubs* Carlton; *Style*— Antony Baldry Esq, MP; Ho of Commons, London SW1

BALDWIN, Hon Mrs (Alison Mary); *née* Sandilands; da of 14 Lord Torphichen; *b* 18 July 1944; *m* 1966, David Maurice Baldwin, s of Maurice Balwin, of 43 Laxey Rd,

Rotton Pk, Birmingham 16; 2 da; *Style—* The Hon Mrs Baldwin; 30 Rochford Ave, Shenfield, Essex

BALDWIN, Barry Anthony; s of Joseph Patrick Baldwin (d 1977), and Nina, *née* Brazier; *b* 7 Jan 1935; *Educ* King's Coll Sch Wimbledon; *m* 1, 1958 (dis 1973); m 2, 1976, Liz, da of John McKeown; 3 s (Christopher Richard b 15 July 1959, Mark Jonathan b 31 Aug 1961, Paul Stephen b 27 March 1964); *Career* articled clerk Russell and Mason 1953-58; Price Waterhouse 1958-: mangr 1963-69, ptnr Bristol 1969-75, ptnr i/c Ind Business Gp London 1975-83, seconded to CRD 1980-82, ptnr i/c Windsor office 1983-85, nat dir Ind Business Servs 1983-88, dir Ind Business Servs Europe 1988-, chm Emerging Business World Executive 1991-; chm Union of Ind Cos 1986-87, vice pres Small Business Bureau, hon special advsr to Small Firms Min, econ advsr to the Union of Ind Cos, rapporteurs expert Econ and Social Ctee of EC 1983, 1985 and 1986, memb Cncl Small Business Res Tst; memb: Lambeth Lewisham and Southwark Area Health Authy 1980-82, Lewisham and N Southwark Dist Health Authy 1982-83; co-opted special tstee Guy's Hosp, hon dir Theatre Royal Windsor; FCA (ACA 1958); *Books* Management Training for Owners of SME's (with Sue Palmer, 1983), A UK Loan Guarantee Scheme (with Bill Poeton, 1981); *Recreations* golf, theatre, rugby football; *Style—* Barry Baldwin, Esq; Price Waterhouse, Southwark Towers, 32 London Bridge St, London SE1 9SY (☎ 071 939 3000, fax 071 378 0647)

BALDWIN, Christopher William Kennard; s of Peter Godfrey Kennard Baldwin (d 1979), of Lindsay Hill, Antigua, W Indies, and Joan Lillian, *née* Burgess-Driver; *b* 26 Dec 1945; *Educ* Skinners Sch; *m* 5 March 1984, Emma Margaret, da of Lt-Col Humphrey Crossman, JP, DL, of Cheswick House, Berwick upon Tweed, Northumberland, and Lady Rose Crossman, o da of Field Marshal 1 Earl Alexander of Tunis, KG, GCB, OM, GCMG, CSI, DSO, MC, PC (d 1969); 1 s (John Lindsay Alexander b 23 Jan 1989); *Career* landowner Bedgebury Estate Kent; capt Br Bobsleigh Team, Br Bobsleigh Champion (Cervinia 1974, St Moritz 1976); chm Kent Co Ctee Game Conservancy Tst 1987-; *Recreations* shooting, skiing, fishing; *Style—* Christopher Baldwin, Esq; Twyssenden Manor, Bedgebury, Goudhurst, Kent

BALDWIN, David Arthur; CBE; s of Isaac Arthur Baldwin (d 1983), of Twickenham, and Edith Mary, *née* Collins; *b* 1 Sept 1936; *Educ* Twickenham Tech Coll, Wimbledon Tech Coll; *m* 1961, (Jacqueline) Anne, da of Frederick Edward Westcott (d 1947), of Twickenham; 1 s (Richard David b 1975), 1 da (Sarah b 1967); *Career* radio engr EMI Ltd 1954-63, sales engr Solartron Ltd 1963-65, sales engr and mangr Hewlett Packard Ltd 1965-73, euro mktg mangr Hewlett Packard SA 1973-78, chm Hewlett Packard Ltd 1988- (md 1978-88); memb: Electronics Indust Sector Gp NEDO, ITSA and Butcher IT Skills Shortage Ctee, Cncl Econ and Fin Planning Ctee CBI, Ct of Brunel Univ, Ct of Cranfield Inst of Technol, Cncl for Indust and Higher Educn, PITCOM, Berks Assoc of Boys Clubs; vice chm Thames Action Res Gp for Educn and Trg; Freeman City of London, memb Guild of Info Technologists; FIEE, MIERE, MInstD, MInstM; *Recreations* golf, skiing, photography, painting; *Clubs* RAC; *Style—* David Baldwin, Esq, CBE; Hewlett Packard Ltd, Cain Road, Bracknell, Berks RG12 1HN (☎ 0344 360000, fax 0344 362224)

BALDWIN, Jan; da of Joseph John Baldwin, of 67 The Leys, Chipping Norton, Oxon, and Catherine Agnes, *née* Freeman; *b* 12 Dec 1946; *Educ* Chipping Norton GS, Bicester GS, Royal Coll of Art (MA); *m* 10 Dec 1988, Prof Henry Philip Wynn, s of Arthur Wynn; 2 step s (Hamish Wynn, Robin Wynn); *Career* therapy radiographer NY 1967-74, asst to photographer Tessa Traeger 1974-79, freelance photographer 1981-; memb AFAEP; *Recreations* film, theatre, travelling; *Style—* Ms Jan Baldwin; 11 Gibraltar Walk, London E2 7LH (☎ 071 729 2664)

BALDWIN, Prof John Evan; s of Evan Baldwin (d 1976), and Mary, *née* Wild (d 1983); *b* 6 Dec 1931; *Educ* Merchant Taylors' Crosby, Queens' Coll Cambridge (Clerk Maxwell scholar BA, MA, PhD); *m* 20 Sept 1969, Joyce, da of Alexander Thomas Cox (d 1979); *Career* Univ of Cambridge: res fell later fell Queens' Coll Cambridge 1956-74 and 1989-, demonstrator in physics 1957-62, asst dir of res 1962-81, reader 1981-89, dir Mullard Radioastronomy Observatory 1987-, prof of radioastronomy 1989-; memb SERC Ctees and Bds 1971-; FRAS 1957-, memb Int Astronomical Union 1961-; *Recreations* mountain walking, gardening; *Style—* Prof John Baldwin; Cavendish Laboratory, Madingley Rd, Cambridge CB3 0HE (☎ 0223 337299, fax 0223 63263, telex 81292)

BALDWIN, Maj-Gen Peter Alan Charles; s of Alec Baldwin, and Anne, *née* Dance; *b* 19 Feb 1927; *Educ* King Edward VI GS Chelmsford; *m* 1, 1953, Judith Elizabeth Mace; m 2, 1982, Gail J Roberts; *Career* enlisted 1942, served WWII, Korean War, Borneo Ops (despatches 1967), ACOS Jt Exercises Div AFCENT 1976-77, CSO HQ BAOR 1977-79; dir Radio IBA 1987-90 (dep dir 1979-87), chief exec Radio Authy 1991-; *Recreations* cricket, theatre, golf; *Clubs* Army and Navy, MCC; *Style—* Maj-Gen Peter Baldwin; c/o Lloyds Bank Ltd, 7 Pall Mall, London SW1Y 5NA

BALDWIN, Sir Peter Robert; KCB (1977, CB 1973); s of Charles Baldwin (d 1962) and Katie Isobel, *née* Field (d 1957); *b* 10 Nov 1922; *Educ* City of London Sch, CCC Oxford; *m* 1951, Margaret Helen Moar; 2 s; *Career* served FO 1942-45, Gen Register Office 1948-54, Treasy 1954-62, Cabinet Off 1962-64; Treasy 1964-76: under-sec 1968-72, dep sec 1972-76; 2 perm sec DOE 1976, perm sec Dept of Tport 1976-82 (when ret); chm: S E Thames RHA 1983-, RSA 1985-87, PHAB 1982-87, Civil Serv Sports Cncl 1978-82; vice chm Automobile Assoc Ctee 1990-; memb: Public Fin Fndn 1984-, Charities Aid Fndn 1990; vice pres: RSA 1987-, RNID 1983-90; *Style—* Sir Peter Baldwin, KCB; 123 Alderney St, London SW1V 4HE (☎ 071 821 7157)

BALDWIN, Prof Robert William; s of William Baldwin, and Doris, *née* Mellor; *b* 12 March 1927; *Educ* Univ of Birmingham (BSc, PhD); *m* 19 July 1952, Lilian; 1 s (Robert Neil b 1957); *Career* dir Cancer Res Campaign Laboratories 1960-, prof of tumour biology Univ of Nottingham 1971-; memb Cancer Res Campaign; FRCPath 1973, fell Royal Inst Biology 1979; *Books* Monoclonal Antibodies for Cancer Detection and Therapy (1985), Immunology of Malignant Diseases (1987); *Recreations* gardening; *Style—* Prof Robert Baldwin; Cancer Research Campaign Laboratories, University of Nottingham, Nottingham NG7 2RD (☎ 0602 484848, fax 0602 586630)

BALDWIN, Roger James Maxwell; s of George Maxwell Baldwin (d 1984), of Brixham, Devon, and Norah Joan, *née* Smith; *b* 2 Aug 1939; *Educ* Orange Hill CG Mill Hill (Dip Arch Hons); *m* 7 Oct 1967 (m dis 1988) Heather, da of Andrew Douglas Kyd (d 1979); 2 s (Mark b 1973, Jonathan b 1980), 1 da (Lara b 1976); *Career* racing driver 1964-, chartered architect; ptnr Baldwin Beaton Everton Isbell 1970, Baldwin Everton Ptnrship 1976-; Freeman: City of London 1975, Worshipful Co of Constructors 1975; RIBA; *Recreations* work, drawing, reading, antiques, driving, tennis, karate; *Style—* Roger Baldwin, Esq; Keatings, Nuthurst, Horsham, West Sussex RH13 6RG; Baldwin Everton Partnership, Coach House Yard, London NW3 1QD (☎ 071 435 0153, fax 071 431 2982)

BALDWIN OF BEWDLEY, 4 Earl (UK 1937); Edward Alfred Alexander Baldwin; also Viscount Corvedale (UK 1937); s of 3 Earl (d 1976, 2 s of 1 Earl, otherwise Stanley Baldwin, thrice PM and 1 cous of Rudyard Kipling); *b* 3 Jan 1938; *Educ* Eton, Trinity Coll Cambridge (MA); *m* 1970, Sarah MacMurray, da of Evan James, of Upwood Park, Abingdon, Oxon (and sis of Countess of Selborne); 3 s (Viscount Corvedale, Hon James Conrad b 1976, Hon Mark Thomas Maitland b 1980); *Heir* s, Viscount Corvedale, *qv*; *Style—* The Rt Hon The Earl Baldwin of Bewdley; Manor Farm House, Godstow Rd, Upper Wolvercote, Oxon OX2 8AJ (☎ 0865 52683)

BALES, Kenneth Frederick; CBE (1990); s of Frederick Charles Bales (d 1981), of Ilford, Essex, and Deborah Alice (d 1983); *b* 2 March 1931; *Educ* Buckhurst Hill GS, LSE (BSc), Univ of Manchester (DSA); *m* 16 Aug 1958, (Margaret) Hazel, da of John Austin (d 1946), of Dumfries, Scotland; 2 s (Stewart Mark b 22 Oct 1959, Craig Austin b 2 Sept 1961), 1 da (Shona Kay b 9 April 1963); *Career* hosp sec Southport Hosp Mgmnt Ctee 1958-62, regnl staff offr Birmingham Regnl Hosp Bd 1965-68 (regnl trg offr 1962-65), sec W Birmingham Hosp Mgmnt Ctee 1968-73; W Midlands Regnl Health Authy: regnl admin 1973-84, regnl gen mangr 1984-90, regnl md 1990-; assoc Inst of Health Serv Mgmnt; *Recreations* swimming, sports viewing and painting; *Style—* Kenneth Bales, Esq, CBE; West Midlands Regional Health Authority, Arthur Thomson House, 146 Hagley Rd, Birmingham B16 9PA (☎ 021 456 1444, fax 021 454 4406, telex 339973)

BALFE, Richard Andrew; MEP (Lab) London S Inner 1979-; s of Dr Richard Joseph Balfe (d 1985), of Yorks, and Dorothy Lillias, *née* De Cann (d 1970); *b* 14 May 1944; *Educ* Brook Secdy Modern Sch Sheffield, LSE (BSc); *m* 1, 1976 (m dis 1984), Vivienne Patricia, *née* Job; 1 s (Richard Geoffrey Clement b 10 April 1980); m 2, 22 March 1986, Susan Jane, da of John Honeyford, of Cambridge; 1 da (Alexandra Mary Jane b 9 March 1988); *Career* 1 Bn London Irish Rifles TA 1961-67; FO 1965-67, res offr Finer Ctee on One Parent Families 1970-72, political sec Royal Arsenal Co-op 1973-79, dir CWS Ltd 1979-80; memb GLC 1973-77; patron Med Aid for Palestine, chm Ethiopia Soc; *Books* Housing in London (1977), Human Rights in Turkey (1985); *Recreations* reading, walking; *Clubs* Reform, Lewisham Labour; *Style—* Richard Balfe, Esq, MEP; 132 Powis St, London SE18 6NL (☎ 081 855 2128, fax 081 316 1936); 97-113 rue Belliard, 1040 Bruxelles, Belgium (☎ 010 322 284 5406, fax 010 322 284 9406)

BALFOUR; *see*: FitzGeorge-Balfour

BALFOUR, Charles George Yule; s of Eustace Arthur Goschen Balfour, and Dorothy Melicent Anne, *née* Yule; *b* 23 April 1951; *Educ* Eton; *m* 1, 18 Sept 1978 (m dis 1985), Audrey Margaret, da of HP Hoare (d 1983), of Stourhead, Wilts; m 2, 1987, Svea Maria, da of Ernst-Friedrich Reichsgraf von Goess, of Carinthia, Austria; 1 s (George Eustace Charles b 8 Dec 1990); *Career* Hoare Govett 1971-73, Hill Samuel 1973-76, Dillon Read 1976-79, exec dir Banque Paribas London 1979-; memb Queen's Body Guard for Scotland (The Royal Co of Archers); *Recreations* shooting, fishing; *Clubs* Turf, White's, City of London, Puffins; *Style—* Charles Balfour, Esq; 15 Oakley St, London SW3 (☎ 071 352 2764); 68 Lombard St, London EC3V 9EH (☎ 071 929 4545, fax 071 726 6761, telex 945881)

BALFOUR, Christopher Roxburgh; s of Archibald Roxburgh Balfour (d 1958), and Lilian, *née* Cooper (d 1989); strong links with S America 1850-1960 via Balfour Williamson & Co; *b* 24 Aug 1941; *Educ* Ampleforth, Queen's Coll Oxford (BA); *Career* merchant banker Hambros Bank Ltd 1968-87 (appointed dir 1984); *Recreations* horses, tennis, shooting, bridge, skiing; *Clubs* Pratts; *Style—* Christopher R Balfour, Esq; 35 Kelso Place, London W8 (☎ 071 937 7178); Hambros Bank Ltd, 41 Tower Hill, London EC3N 4HA (☎ 071 480 5000)

BALFOUR, Cdr Colin James; DL (Hants 1973-); s of Maj Melville Balfour, MC (d 1962), of Wintershill Hall, Durley, Hants, and Margaret (Daisy) Mary, *née* Lascelles (d 1972); *b* 12 June 1924; *Educ* Eton; *m* 27 Aug 1949, Prudence Elisabeth, JP, da of Adm Sir Ragnar Colvin, KBE, CB (d 1954), of Curdridge House, Curdridge, Hants; 1 s (James b 1951), 1 da (Belinda (Mrs Hextall) b 1953); *Career* RN 1942, serv HMS Nelson Med 1943, D Day and N Russian Convoys 1944-45, HMS Cossack Korean War 1950-52, RN Staff Coll 1955, 1 Lt HM Yacht Britannia 1956-57, Cdr 1957, Cmd HMS Finisterre 1960-62, res 1965; CLA: chm Hants Branch 1980-81 (pres 1987), chm Legal and Parly Sub Ctee and memb Nat Exec Ctee 1982-87; pres Hants Fedn of Young Farmers Clubs 1982; liason offr Hampshire Duke of Edinburgh's Award Scheme 1966-76, memb Hampshire Local Valuation Panel 1971-81 (chm 1977-), govr and vice chm Lankhills Special Sch Winchester 1975-80, chm of govrs Durley C of E Primary Sch 1980-; High Sheriff of Hampshire 1972; Freeman City of London, Liveryman Worshipful Co of Farmers 1983; *Recreations* shooting, small woodland mgmnt; *Clubs* Brook's, Pratts; *Style—* Cdr Colin Balfour, DL, RN; Wintershill Hall, Durley, Hants SO3 2AL; Flat 4, Cygnet House, 188 Kings Rd, London SW3

BALFOUR, Eustace Arthur Goschen; s of late Lt-Col Francis Cecil Campbell Balfour, CIE, CVO, CBE, MC and gn of 1 E of Balfour, KG, OM, PC (d 1930), and Hon Phyllis Evelyn Goschen (d 1976), da of 2 Viscount Goschen; h to Earldom of Balfour; *b* 26 May 1921; *Educ* Eton; *m* 1, 1946 (m dis 1971), Anne, da of late Maj Victor Yule; 2 s (Roderick, Charles) (*see* Lady Tessa Balfour); m 2, 1971, Mrs Paula Susan Cuene-Grandidier, da of late John Maurice Davis, MBE; *Career* served WWII, Capt Scots Guards, 1939-46, N Africa, Italy and Greece; wounded Anzio beach head; *Clubs* Naval and Military; *Style—* Eustace Balfour, Esq

BALFOUR, Hon Francis Henry; TD; s of 1 Baron Riverdale, GBE, (d 1957); *b* 25 Aug 1905; *Educ* Oundle; *m* 1, 1932, Muriel Anne (d 1970), da of late Rear Adm Ralph Berry; 2 s, 2 da; m 2, 1971, Daphne Cecelia Keefe, da of A C Moss, of Rochfort, Bathampton, Bath; *Career* Vice-Consul for Denmark 1946-50; kt of Order of Dannebrog (Denmark); *Style—* The Hon Francis Balfour, TD; Holcombe Cottage, Holcombe Lane, Bathampton, Bath BA2 6UN (☎ 0225 60811)

BALFOUR, 4 Earl of (UK 1922); Gerald Arthur James Balfour; JP (E Lothian 1970); also Viscount Traprain (UK 1922); s of 3 Earl (d 1968, nephew of 1 Earl, otherwise Arthur Balfour, PM (C) 1902-05) and Jean Lily (d 1981), da of late Rev John James Cooke-Yarborough (fourth in descent from George, 2 s of Sir George Cooke, 3 Bt); *b* 23 Dec 1925; *Educ* Eton, HMS Conway; *m* 14 Dec 1956, Mrs Natasha Georgina Lousada, da of late Capt George Anton, of Archangel, Russia; *Heir* kinsman, Eustace Balfour; *Career* master mariner; cncllr E Lothian till 1974; served in Merchant Navy WWII; *Clubs* Association of International Cape Horners, English Speaking Union; *Style—* The Rt Hon the Earl of Balfour, JP; Whittingehame Tower, Haddington, E Lothian (☎ 036 85 208)

BALFOUR, Hugh Crawford; s of John Selby Balfour (d 1987), of West Wittering, and Elizabeth Barbara, *née* Crawford; *b* 21 Sept 1936; *Educ* Felsted, Univ of Sussex (Dip Civil and Struct Engrg); *m* 3 Sept 1966, Ethne Gillian, da of Maurice James Bennett-Jones (d 1980), of Grange Hollies, Grange Lane, Gatacre, Liverpool; 2 s (Robert David b 4 May 1972, Martin Hugh b 25 May 1976), 2 da (Sarah Elizabeth b 13 March 1968, Catherine Hilary b 24 Oct 1969); *Career* engr specialising in water supply, involved with sewage treatment pollution prevention: UK, Mali, Senegal; ptnr Balfours Consltg Engrs 1966-88, regnl dir Mott MacDonald 1988-; chm Friends City of Sheffield Youth Orch; FICE, Fell Soc French Engrs & Consltg Engrs; *Recreations* veteran cars; *Clubs* RAC; *Style—* Hugh Balfour, Esq; Ranmoor, 8 Sherbrook Rise, Wilmslow, Cheshire, SK9 2AX; (☎ 0625 537136)

BALFOUR, Rear Adm (George) Ian Mackintosh; CB (1962), DSC (1943); s of Tom Stevenson Balfour (d 1912), and Ina Mary, *née* Tabuteau (d 1953); *b* 14 Jan 1912; *Educ* RNC Dartmouth; *m* 8 Aug 1939, (Gertrude) Pamela Carlyle, da of late Major Hugh Carlyle Forrester, DL, of Tullibody House, Cambus; 2 s (David b 1944, ka HMS Sheffield Falklands 1983, Patrick b 1950), 1 da (Jane b 1953); *Career* HMS Emperor of India 1929-30, HMS Cornwall and HMS Kent (China) 1930-32, Sub Lt's courses 1932-

33, HMS Viceroy 1933-34, HMS Carlisle (SA), and on loan as ADC to Govr Gen, Flag Lt to C in C 1935-37, HMS Caledonia 1937-39, Lt HMS Kelvin 1939-42 (despatches 1941); i/c: HMS Foxhound 1942, HMS Decoy 1942-43, HMS Tuscan 1943, HMS Scourge 1943-45, HMS Solebay 1945-46, HMS Onslow 1946; jt planning staff Cabinet Offices 1946-48, American jt staff course 1948, exec offr HMS Triumph 1948-50, jt servs staff course 1950, asst dir of Plans Admty 1951, Capt of Plans Washington 1952-54, i/c HMS Osprey 1954-56, i/c and Capt D2 HMS Daring 1956-58, dir of offrs appointments Admty 1958-60, sr directing staff (Navy) IDC 1960-63, ret 1963; chief appeals offr and dep sec Cancer Res Campaign 1963-78 (memb Cncl 1978-86), vice pres RN Sch Haslemere (former govr); *Recreations* fishing; *Style—* Rear Adm Ian Balfour, CB, DSC; Westover, Farnham Lane, Haslemere, Surrey GU27 1HD (☎ 0428 643876)

BALFOUR, Dr (Elizabeth) Jean; CBE (1981), JP (Fife 1963); da of late Maj-Gen Sir James Syme Drew, KBE, CB, DSO, MC (d 1955), and late Victoria Maxwell of Munches; *b* 4 Nov 1927; *Educ* Univ of Edinburgh (BSc); *m* 1950, John Charles Balfour, *qv*; 3 s; *Career* dir A J Bowen & Co, ptnr Balbirnie Home Farms; dir: Chieftain Industries 1983-85, Scot Dairy Trade Fedn 1983-86; pres Royal Scot Forestry Soc 1969-71, chm Countryside Cmmn Scot 1972-83; vice pres: Scot Youth Hostel Assoc, Scot Coll of Agric 1982 (govr 1958-89); dir Scot Agric Colls 1987-89; memb: Fife CC 1958-70, Nature Conservancy Cncl 1973-80, Scot Economic Cncl 1978-83, Court Univ of St Andrew's 1983-87; dep chm Seafish Indust 1987-90; hon fell Zoological Soc of Scotland; fell Inst of Biology; Hon DSc Univ of St Andrews 1977; FRSE, FICF; *Clubs* Farmers; *Style—* Dr Jean Balfour, CBE, JP, FRSE; Kirkforthar House, Markinch, Glenrothes, Fife (☎ 0592 752233); Scourie, by Lairg, Sutherland; Balavoulin, Glenfincastle, Pitlochry, Tayside

BALFOUR, John Charles; OBE (1978), MC (1943), JP (Fife 1957), DL (Fife 1958); s of late Brig Edward Balfour, CVO, DSO, OBE, MC, and Lady Ruth, CBE, *née* Balfour (d 1967), da of 2 Earl of Balfour (d 1945), and Lady Elizabeth Bulwer-Lytton, da of 1 Earl of Lytton; *b* 28 July 1919; *Educ* Eton, Trinity Coll Cambridge; *m* 1950, Jean, *née* Drew, *qv*; 3 s; *Career* memb Royal Co of Archers (Queen's Bodyguard for Scotland) 1949-; chm Fife Area Health Bd 1983 (memb 1981-87), tstee Nat AIDS Tst 1987-; vice Lord Lt Fife 1988; *Style—* John Balfour, Esq, OBE, MC, JP, DL; Kirkforthar House, Markinch, Glenrothes, Fife KY7 6LS (☎ 0592 752233)

BALFOUR, John Manning; s of James Richard Balfour, and Eunice Barbara, *née* Manning; *b* 2 Oct 1952; *Educ* Fettes Coll Edinburgh, Worcester Coll Oxford (MA); *Career* slr Frere Cholmeley 1979- (ptnr 1986-); *Books* Air Law (contrib ed, 1988); *Recreations* swimming, reading; *Clubs* Lansdowne; *Style—* John Balfour, Esq; 52 Ingestre Court, Ingestre Place, London W1R 3LU (☎ 071 437 2420); Frere Cholmeley, 28 Lincoln's Inn Fields, London WC2A 3HH (☎ 071 405 7878, fax 071 405 9056, telex 27623)

BALFOUR, Lady; (Catharine) Marjorie; da of Sir Charles Rugge-Price, 7 Bt (d 1953); *b* 5 Jan 1904; *m* 1930, Lt-Gen Sir Philip Maxwell Balfour, KBE, CB, MC (d 1977); *Style—* Lady Balfour; Bridles, Donhead St Mary, Shaftesbury, Dorset

BALFOUR, Hon Mark Robin; s and h of 2 Baron Riverdale; *b* 16 July 1927; *Educ* Aysgarth Sch Yorks, Trinity Coll Sch Port Hope Canada; *m* 1959, Susan Ann, da of Robert Percival Phillips, of Sheffield; 1 s (Anthony Robert b 1960), 2 da (Nancy Ann b 1963, Kate Frances b 1967); *Career* chm: Sheffield Rolling Mills Ltd 1969-75, Balfour Darwins Ltd 1971-75, Light Trades House Ltd, Finglands Servs Ltd (property co); proprietor Multilog Logging Tools; non-exec dir: W M Ridgway & Sons 1964-72 (also dep chm), BSC Special Steels Bd 1970-73, Newton Chambers 1972; pres Nat Fedn of Engineer's Tool Mfrs 1974-76; memb: Exec Ctee BISPA 1967-75, Economic Devpt Cncl for Machine Tools 1975-78, Aust Br Trade Assoc Cncl, Aust & NZ Trade Advsy Ctee (BOTB) 1975-86; High Sheriff South Yorkshire 1986-87; memb: Sheffield C of C Sheffield (pres 1979), ctee SSAFA; chm Cncl of Mgmnt Ashdell Schools Tst; memb: Worshipful Co of Blacksmiths, Co of Cutlers in Hallamshire (Master 1969-70); Freeman City of London; guardian Sheffield Assay Office; vice counsul for Finland in Sheffield 1962-; *Clubs* Sheffield; *Style—* The Hon Mark Balfour; Fairways, Saltergate Lane, Bamford, nr Sheffield, Derbys S30 2BE (☎ 0433 51314)

BALFOUR, Michael John; JP; s of Duncan Balfour (d 1952), of Englefield Green, Surrey, and Jeanne Germaine, *née* Picot (d 1974); *b* 17 Oct 1925; *Educ* Eton, Christ Church Oxford (MA); *m* 15 Sep 1951, Mary Campbell, da of Maj-Gen Sir William Ronald Campbell Penney, KBE, CB, DSO, MC (d 1964), of Stanford Dingley, Berks; 3 s (James b 1952 d 1974, William b 1955, Andrew b 1963), 1 da (Emma b 1953); *Career* WWII RAF 1944-47; Bank of England: joined 1950, sr advsr euro affrs 1973, chief advsr 1976, asst dir overseas affrs 1980-83, alternate dir Bank for Int Settlements 1972-85; chm: Balgonie Estates 1975- (dir 1955-), IMI Capital Markets (UK) Ltd 1987-, IMI Securities Ltd 1988-; dep chm IMI Bank (Int) 1987-; *Recreations* fishing, boating, music; *Style—* M J Balfour, Esq, JP; Harrietfield, Kelso, Roxburghshire TD5 7SY (☎ 0573 24825); 17 Shrewsbury Mews, London W2 5PN; IMI Capital Markets (UK) Ltd, Walbrook House, 23-29 Walbrook, London EC4N 8BB (☎ 071 283 6264, fax 071 283 2279, telex 941 9091 IMI CAP)

BALFOUR, Nancy; OBE (1965); da of Alexander Balfour, and Ruth Macfarland Balfour; *b* 1911; *Educ* Wycombe Abbey, Lady Margaret Hall Oxford; *Career* asst ed The Economist 1948-72, chm Contemporary Art Soc 1976-82, vice chm Crafts Cncl 1983-5; chm: Art Servs Grants 1983-89, Arts Research Ltd 1990-; *Style—* Miss Nancy Balfour, OBE; 36E Eaton Square, London SW1 (☎ 071 235 7874)

BALFOUR, Neil Roxburgh; s of Archibald Roxburgh Balfour, and Lilian Helen, *née* Cooper (d 1989); *b* 12 Aug 1944; *Educ* Ampleforth, Univ Coll Oxford (BA); *m* 1, 23 Sept 1969 (m dis 1978), HRH Princess Elizabeth of Yugoslavia; 1 s (Nicholas b 6 June 1970); m 2, 4 Nov 1978, Serena Mary Churchill, da of Edwin F Russell; 1 s (Alastair b 20 Aug 1981), 1 da (Lily b 29 Nov 1979), 2 step da (Morgan b 19 June 1973, Lucinda b 14 Aug 1975); *Career* called to the Bar Middle Temple 1968; Baring Bros 1968-74, Euro Banking Co 1974-83 (dir 1980-83), chm York Trust Group plc 1983-; MEP Yorks N 1979-84; *Books* Official Biography of Prince Paul of Yugoslavia (1980); *Recreations* bridge, golf, tennis, fishing and shooting; *Clubs* Turf, White's, Royal St George's; *Style—* Neil Balfour, Esq; 55 Warwick Sq, London SW1V 2AJ (☎ 071 834 6974); Dawyck Hse, Stobo, nr Peebles, Tweeddale, Scotland EH45 9JU; Babcock Prebon plc, 155 Bishopsgate, London EC2N 3DA (☎ 071 522 2222); York Trust Ltd, 4 City Rd, London EC1Y 2AA (☎ 071 374 2344)

BALFOUR, (George) Patrick; s of David Mathers Balfour, CBE, of Little Garnstone Manor, Seal, Sevenoaks, Kent, and Mary Elisabeth, *née* Beddall (d 1988), gs of George Balfour, MP; *b* 17 Sept 1941; *Educ* Shrewsbury Sch, Pembroke Coll Cambridge (MA); *m* 18 March 1978, Lesley Ann, da of John Denis Johnston, of Glenfuir, Fidra Rd, N Berwick, Scotland; 3 s (James David Johnston b 1980, Matthew Alexander Patrick b 1982, Hugo Charles Beddall b 1989); *Career* slr, ptnr Slaughter and May 1973; dir Slrs Benevolent Assoc; memb Law Soc; *Recreations* theatre, opera, golf, country pursuits; *Style—* Patrick Balfour, Esq; 70 Lansdowne Rd, London W11 (☎ 071 221 7814); 35 Basinghall St, London EC2V 5DB (☎ 071 600 1200, fax 071 726 0038, telex 883486)

BALFOUR, Peter Edward Gerald; CBE (1984); s of Brig Edward William Sturgis Balfour, CVO, DSO, OBE, MC (d 1955), and Lady Ruth, CBE (d 1967), *née* Balfour, da of 2 Earl of Balfour (d 1945), and Lady Elizabeth Bulwer-Lytton, da of 1 Earl of Lytton; *b* 9 July 1921; *Educ* Eton; *m* 1, 1948 (m dis 1967), Lady Grizelda, *née* Ogilvy, da of 7 (12 but for attainder) Earl of Airlie, KT, GCVO, MC (d 1968); 2 s, 1 da; m 2, 1968, Diana Wainman; 1 s, 1 da; *Career* served Scots Guards 1940-54; chm and chief exec Scottish and Newcastle Breweries 1970-83; chm: Selective Assets Tst 1978- (dir 1962-), Charterhouse plc 1985-90, First Charlotte Assets Tst; dir: Royal Bank of Scotland 1971-91, Br Assets Tst plc; pres Scottish Cncl (Devpt and Indust) 1986- (chm Exec Ctee 1978-85); *Style—* Peter Balfour, Esq, CBE; Scadlaw House, Humbie, E Lothian (☎ 087 533 252)

BALFOUR, Richard Creighton; MBE (1945); s of Donald Creighton Balfour and Muriel, *née* Fonçeca; *b* 3 Feb 1916; *Educ* St Edward's Sch Oxford; *m* 1943, Adela Rosemary, *née* Welch; 2 s; *Career* chief accountant Bank of England 1970-75; pres: Royal Nat Rose Soc 1973-74, World Fedn of Rose Socs 1983-85; int rose judge, Dean Hole medallist 1974, Gold medallist World Fedn of Rose Socs 1985, Aust Rose Award 1989; Liveryman and Upper Warden Worshipful Co of Gardeners, Freeman City of London; *Books* photographs in many books incl Classic Roses by Peter Beales; *Style—* Richard Balfour, Esq, MBE; Albion House, Little Waltham, Chelmsford, Essex CM3 3LA (☎ 0245 360410)

BALFOUR, Robert Peter; s of Peter Balfour (d 1988), of Southport, and Evelyn, *née* Murgatroyd; *b* 5 Nov 1942; *Educ* Liverpool Inst, Univ of Liverpool (MB ChB, DTM&H); *m* 11 Sept 1965, Jean Margaret, da of Frederick Faram (d 1980), of Stockport; 2 s (David b 21 Oct 1974, Jonathan b 16 July 1976), 1 da (Sharon b 27 Oct 1970); *Career* jr hosp appts Liverpool 1966-68, med offr Vom Christian Hosp Nigeria 1969-72, jr hosp appts Chester, Liverpool, Bangor and Cardiff 1972-80, conslt obstetrician and gynaecologist 1980-; chm Fedn of Doctors Who Respect Human Life; FRCOG; *Style—* Robert Balfour, Esq; Heddfan, Marine Walk, Ogmore-by-Sea, Bridgend, Mid Glamorgan (☎ 0656 880034); Princess of Wales Hospital, Bridgend, Mid Glamorgan (☎ 0656 662166)

BALFOUR, Robert Roxburgh; s of Alexander Norman Balfour, and Elizabeth Eugenie, *née* Cowell; *b* 29 June 1947; *Educ* Tabley House, Grenoble Univ (Dip), Madrid Univ (Dip); *m* 31 Jan 1973, (Camilla) Rose, da of Michael George Thomas Webster, of The Vale, Woodside, Windsor Forest, Berks; 1 s (Rupert Alastair b 23 April 1976), 2 da (Camilla Louise b 11 May 1979, Lara Selina b 1 June 1983); *Career* md Bell Lawrie White Financial Services Ltd 1984, dir Bell Lawrie White Ltd 1987; memb: Red Deer Cmmn 1984-, Firearms Consultative Ctee 1989-90; IBRC 1980; *Recreations* shooting, photography; *Style—* Robert Balfour, Esq; Wester Dawyck, Stobo, Peebleshire EH45 9JU (☎ 072 16226); Bell Lawrie White Ltd, 7 Drumsheugh Gardens, Edinburgh EH3 7QH (☎ 031 225 2566, fax 031 225 3134, telex 72260)

BALFOUR, Roderick Francis Arthur; s of Eustace Arthur Goschen Balfour, and Anne, *née* Yule; *b* 9 Dec 1948; *Educ* Eton, London Business Sch (sr exec program); *m* 14 July 1971, Lady Tessa Balfour, da of 17 Duke of Norfolk; 4 da (Willa b 1973, Kinvara b 1975, Maria b 1977, Candida b 1984); *Career* ptnr Grieveson Grant and Co Stockbrokers 1972-81, investmt dir Jessel Toynbee and Co 1981-83, int and UK investmt dir Union Discount Co of London plc 1983-90, dir Rothschild Trust Corporation 1990-; Freeman City of London 1977, Liveryman Worshipful Co of Clothworkers 1986; *Recreations* tennis, skiing, water skiing; *Clubs* White's, City of London, Hurlingham; *Style—* Roderick Balfour, Esq; Burpham Lodge, Arundel, West Sussex BN18 9RR; NM Rothschild & Sons Ltd, New Court, St Swithin's Lane, London EC4P 4DU (☎ 071 280 5000, fax 071 929 5239)

BALFOUR, Lady Tessa Mary Isobel; *née* Fitzalan Howard; da of 17 Duke of Norfolk, CB, CBE, MC, DL, *qv*; *b* 30 Sept 1950; *m* 1971, Roderick Francis Arthur Balfour, s of Eustace Arthur Goschen Balfour, *qv*; 4 da (Willa Anne b 1973, Kinvara Clare b 1975, Maria Alice Jubilee b 1977, Candida Rose b 1984); *Style—* Lady Tessa Balfour

BALFOUR, William Harold St Clair; s of Francis Edmund Balfour (d 1974), of Edinburgh, and Isobel MacIntosh Shaw, *née* Ingram (d 1980), originally of Balgonie, Fife, then of Westray, Orkney; *b* 29 Aug 1934; *Educ* Hillfield Sch Ontario Canada, Edinburgh Acad, Univ of Edinburgh; *m* 1, 10 June 1961 (m dis 1983), (Janette) Patricia, da of late Donald Mowbray Waite, of Penn House Farm, Penn, Bucks; 1 s (Michael St Clair b 1966), 2 da (Sonia Jane b 1962, Jillian Clare b 1964); m 2, 1989, Mrs (Alice) Ingsay Macfarlane; 2 step da (Catherine b 1974, Emma b 1972); *Career* TA 1953-60; slr; ptnr Balfour & Manson 1962-; clerk to Admission of Notaries Public in Scotland 1973-; pt/t tutor Univ of Edinburgh 1981-86, assessor Scottish Arts Cncl 1988-, memb Scottish Home and Health Dept Prison Visiting Ctee 1965-70; chm: Basic Space Dance Theatre 1980-86, Friends of Talbot Rice Art Centre, Central Edinburgh New Town Assoc, Garvald Tst; memb Ctee: Scottish Assoc of Counselling, Wellspring; sec Scottish Photography Gallery Fruit Market Gallery Edinburgh, tstee Edinburgh Rudolf Steiner Sch; memb: Law Soc of Scotland 1960-, Inst of Dirs 1980-, City of Edinburgh Business Club 1962-, Int Bar Assoc 1988-; *Recreations* sailing, walking, bird watching, travel; *Clubs* New (Edinburgh), Royal Forth Yacht; *Style—* William Balfour, Esq; 58 Frederick St, Edinburgh EH2 ILS (☎ 031 225 8291, fax 031 225 5687); 11 Nelson St, Edinburgh EH3 6lF (☎ 031 556 7298)

BALFOUR-LYNN, Dr Lionel Peter; *b* 4 May 1928; *Educ* Hurstpierpoint Coll, Christ's Coll Cambridge, Guy's Hosp London (MA, MD, BChir, MRCS, LRCP, DCH); *m* 1952, June Anne; 1 da (Alison b 1955), 2 s (Simon b 1957, John b 1961); *Career* Flt Lt RAF 1954-56; paediatric registrar Hillingdon Hosp 1956-58; American Hosp Ruislip: sr paediatric specialist 1958-68, conslt paediatrician 1968-70; hon lectr in paediatrics: Brompton Hosp 1970-74, Royal Postgraduate Sch Hammersmith Hosp 1974-; med offr Westfield Coll Univ of London 1958-; chm Br Fellowship of the Israel Med Assoc 1985-; memb Hampstead Med Soc 1958-, FRSM; *Recreations* golf, tennis, cricket, skiing; *Clubs* RSM; *Style—* Dr Lionel Balfour-Lynn

BALFOUR OF BURLEIGH, Lady; Jennifer Ellis; da of E S Manasseh (d 1962), of London, and Phyllis Annette, *née* Barnard (d 1971); *b* 27 Oct 1930; *Educ* St Paul's Girls' Sch, Lady Margaret Hall Oxford; *m* 1, 12 Dec 1951 (m dis 1968), John Edward Jocelyn Brittain-Catlin (d 1987), s of Sir George Edward Gordon Catlin (d 1979), and his 1 w, Vera Brittain; 3 s (Daniel b 1953, Timothy b 1961, William b 1966); m 2, 30 Oct 1971, 8 Lord Balfour of Burleigh, *qv*; 2 da (Hon Victoria b 1973, Hon Ishbel b 1976); *Career* public relations executive: Butter Information Cncl 1953-55, Patrick Dolan & Assoc 1955-56; sr public relations executive Erwin Wasey Ruthrauff & Ryan 1956-61; conslt PR advsr to a number of maj clients including Acrlan, Hoover, Vono, Carnation Milk, Littlewoods Stores, Scottish Crafts Centre 1961-71; dir: Jamaica Street Ltd property developers 1980-; mangr London & Scottish Property Services 1985-; dir: Scottish Opera 1990-, ECAT Ltd (Edinburgh Contemporary Arts Tst) 1989-; memb bd Link Housing Assoc 1974- (chm Central Region Ctee); chm Ochil View Housing Assoc 1988-; special arts advsr to bd Centresound Community Radio for Central Scotland 1990-; memb: Citizens Advice Bureau Alloa 1988-; exec ctee Clackmannan Social & Liberal Democrats since inception, author of paper on housing policies for Scotland and writer of numerous booklets, pamphlets, newspaper and magazine articles; FRSA 1990; *Recreations* music, theatre; *Clubs* New (Edinburgh); *Style—* The Rt Hon the Lady Balfour of Burleigh; Brucefield, Clackmannan, Scotland FK10 3QF (☎ 0259 30228)

BALFOUR OF BURLEIGH, 8 (*de facto* and 12 but for the Attainder) Lord (S 1607);

Robert Bruce; er s of 7 Lord Balfour of Burleigh (11 but for the Attainder, d 1967); *b* 6 Jan 1927; *Educ* Westminster; *m* 30 Oct 1971, Jennifer Ellis, da of E S Manasseh (d 1962), and former w of John Edward Jocelyn Brittain-Catlin; 2 da (Hon Victoria b 7 May 1973, Hon Ishbel b 28 Sept 1976); *Heir* (hp) da, Hon Victoria Bruce b 7 May 1973; *Career* foreman and supt English Electric Co Ltd Stafford & Liverpool 1952-57; gen mangr: Eng Electric Co India Ltd 1957-64, Eng Electric Netherton Works 1964-66, D Napier & Son Ltd 1966-68; dir: Bank of Scotland 1968-91, Wm Lawson Distillers Ltd. 1984- (dep govr 1977-91), Tarmac plc 1981-90, Scottish Investment Trust plc 1971-; Forestry Cmmr 1971-74; chm: Scottish Arts Cncl 1971-80, Edinburgh Book Festival 1982-87, National Book League Scotland 1981-86, Cablevision (Scotland) plc 1983-, The Turing Institute 1983-, Viking Oil Ltd 1971-80, Fedn of Scottish Bank Employers 1977-86, Assoc of Business Sponsors of the Arts Scot 1990-; treas: Royal Soc of Edinburgh 1989-, Royal Scottish Corpn 1967-; Chllr Univ of Stirling 1988-; CEng, FIEE, Hon FRIAS, FRSE; *Style—* The Rt Hon the Lord Balfour of Burleigh, FRSE; Brucefield, Clackmannan FK10 3QF (☎ 0259 30228); 13 Dean Terrace, Edinburgh EH4 1ND (☎ 031 343 6568)

BALFOUR OF INCHRYE, 2 Baron (UK 1945); Ian Balfour; s of 1 Baron Balfour of Inchrye, MC, PC (d 1988), and his 1 w Diana Blanche (d 1982), da of Sir Robert Grenville Harvey, 2 Bt; *b* 21 Dec 1924; *Educ* Eton, Magdalen Coll Oxford; *m* 28 Nov 1953, Josephine Maria Jane, o da of Morogh Wyndham Percy Bernard; 1 da (Roxane, *see* Hon Mrs Laird Craig); *Heir* none; *Career* author and composer; *Books* Famous Diamonds (1987); *Recreations* reading, walking, watching cricket and association football; *Style—* The Hon Ian Balfour; 10 Limerston Street, London SW10 0HH

BALFOUR OF INCHRYE, Mary, Baroness; Mary Ainslie; yr da of Baron Albert Peter Anthony Profumo, KC (d 1940), and Martha Thom, *née* Walker; sis of John Profumo, *qv*; *b* 7 May 1911; *m* 2 Jan 1947, as his 2 w, 1 Baron Balfour of Inchrye, PC, MC (d 1988); 1 da (Mary Ann, *see* Hon Mrs Sutherland Janson); *Style—* The Rt Hon Mary, Lady Balfour of Inchrye; End House, St Mary Abbots Place, London W8 6LS

BALFOUR PAUL, Major Lyon; TD; s of Lt-Col John William Balfour Paul, DSO, DL (d 1957) (sometime Marchmont Herald and s of Sir James Balfour Paul, KCVO, Lord Lyon King of Arms (d 1931)), and Muriel Cassels, *née* Monteith (d 1964); *b* 21 April 1914; *Educ* Sedbergh, Edinburgh Coll of Art (Architect); *m* 28 May 1954, Carola Mary Eve, da of Lt Col A H Marlowe, QC, MP; 1 s (Hugh b 1955), 4 da (Fiona b 1956, Veronica b 1957, Philippa b 1959, Mary b 1964); *Career* joined Lovat Scouts (TA) 1935, Major WWII served Faroe Islands, Italy; architect; ptnr winemaking firm Inverness, farmer on Isle of Mull; memb Queens Bodyguard for Scotland; ARIBA; *Recreations* fishing, shooting, skiing, piping; *Clubs* New (Edinburgh); *Style—* Major Lyon Balfour Paul, TD; Eskadale Cottage, Kiltarlity, Invernesshire (☎ 0463 550); Moniack Castle, Kirkhill, Inverness (☎ 046 383 283)

BALGONIE, Lord; David Alexander Leslie Melville; s and h of 14 Earl of Leven and (13 of) Melville, DL; *b* 26 Jan 1954; *Educ* Eton; *m* 1981, Julia Clare, yr da of Col I R Critchley, of Lindores, Muthill, Perths; 1 s (Hon Alexander b 1984), 1 da (Hon Louisa Clare b 1987); *Heir* s Hon Alexander Leslie Melville; *Career* Lt Queen's Own Highlanders RARO 1979-81, relinquished commission 1981, reappointed to RARO July 1981; dir: Wood Conversion Ltd Slough 1984-, Treske Shop Ltd London 1988-; *Style—* Lord Balgonie; The Old Farmhouse, West Street, Burghclere, Newbury, Berks RG15 9LB (0635 27241)

BALKWILL, Richard Stephen; s of Michael Y Basanta Balkwill (d 1985), of Semley, Shaftesbury, Dorset, and Bridget Home de Selincourt (d 1970); *b* 12 June 1946; *Educ* Charterhouse, ChCh Oxford (MA); *m* 5 July 1975, Elisabeth Ruth, da of Air Marshal Sir Thomas Warne-Browne, KBE, CB, DSC (d 1963), of Chilbolton, Stockbridge, Hants; 1 da (Emily Victoria b 14 April 1976); *Career* Ginn & Co 1968-72, primary schs ed Thos Nelson & Sons 1972-77, dir operations and servs Macmillan Education 1989 (sr primary ed 1977-78, dir primary sch publishing 1979-83, dir schs publishing 1983-84, publishing dir 1984-88); md Heinemann Childrens Reference 1990-; chm of govrs of primary sch; *Books* Livelihoods (4 book series, 1977); *Recreations* music, choral singing, writing, canal cruising, steam railways; *Clubs* Savile; *Style—* Richard Balkwill, Esq; Pitts, Great Milton, Oxford OX9 7NF (☎ 0844 279506); Heinemann Children's Reference, Halley Ct, Jordan Hill, Oxford OX2 8EJ (☎ 0865 311366)

BALL, Alan Hugh; s of late Sir (George) Joseph Ball, KBE (d 1961), and his wife, Mary Caroline, *née* Penhorwood (d 1957); *b* 8 June 1924; *Educ* Eton; *m* 1948, Eleanor Katharine Turner; 2 s, 1 da; *Career* dir Lonrho Ltd and associated cos (chm and jt md 1961-72); *Style—* Alan Ball Esq; The Old Mill, Ramsbury, Wilts (☎ 0672 266)

BALL, Air Marshal Sir Alfred Henry Wynne; KCB (1976, CB 1967), DSO (1943), DFC (1942); s of Capt J A E Ball, MC (d 1957), and Josephine Hilda Wynne, *née* Rowland-Thomas, of Rostrevor, Co Down and BNR India; *b* 18 Jan 1921, Rawalpindi, Br India; *Educ* Campbell Coll Belfast, RAF Coll Cranwell, RAF Staff Coll, JSSC, IDC; *m* 1942, Nan, da of late A G McDonald, of Tipperary; 3 s, 1 da; *Career* served WWII RAF Lysander Spitfire and Mosquito Sqdn (despatches twice), Air Medal (USA) 1943, asst COS SHAPE 1968-71, dir gen of RAF Orgn 1971-75; UK mil rep CENTO Ankara 1975-77, Dep C-in-C RAF Strike Cmd 1977-78, ret 1979; mil advsr ICL 1979-83; vice chm: (Air) TAVRA Cncl 1979-84, Hon Air Cdre RAuxAF 1984-; Hon FBCS 1984; *Recreations* golf, bridge; *Clubs* RAF, Phyllis Court, Huntercombe; *Style—* Air Marshal Sir Alfred Ball, KCB, DSO, DFC, FBCS

BALL, Anthony George (Tony); MBE (1986); s of Harry Clifford Ball, of Bridgwater, Somerset, and Mary Irene Ball; *b* 14 Nov 1934; *Educ* Bridgwater GS, Bromsgrove Coll of Further Educn; *m* 27 July 1957, Ruth, da of Ivor Parry Davies (d 1976), of Mountain Ash, S Wales; 2 s (Kevin, Michael), 1 da (Katherine); *Career* indentured engrg apprentice Austin Motor Co 1951, responsible for launch of Mini 1959, sales mangr Austin Motor Co 1962-66, sales and marketing exec BMC 1966-67, chm Barlow Rand UK Motor Gp 1967-78 (md Barlow Rand Ford S Africa 1971-73 and Barlow Rand Euro Ops 1973-78), md Br Leyland Overseas Trading Ops 1978-82; dir: BL Cars, BL International, Rover Triumph, Austin Morris, Jaguar Cars, Jaguar Rover Triumph Inc (USA) and BL overseas subsidiaries; chm Nuffield Press 1978-80, chm and md BL Europe and Overseas 1979-82, chief BL Cars World Sales 1979-82 (responsible for BL's Buy British campaign and launch of Austin Metro 1980); chief exec Henlys plc 1982-83; chm: Tony Ball Assocs plc (marketing, product launch and sales promotion agency), Tony Ball Conslts; dep chm Lumley Insurance; dir: Customer Concern Ltd, Jetmaster UK, Jetmaster Int Ltd; Freeman City of London 1980; Liveryman: Worshipful Co of Coach Makers and Coach Harness Makers 1980, Worshipful Co of Carmen 1983; FCIM 1981 (for launch of Metro and servs to Br motor indust); hon memb City & Guilds of London (for educational and vocational servs 1982), 1984 Prince Philip Medal for Mktg Achievement and Servs to Br Motor Indust; mktg advsr to Sec of State for Energy 1983-87; responsible for UK dealer launch of Vauxhall Astra for Gen Motors 1984; launches for: Mercedes-Benz, Fiat, Bedford, GM Europe; mktg advsr to sec of State for Wales 1987-; marketing exec, broadcaster, writer, lectr and after-dinner speaker; FIMI, ACIArb; *Books* A Study of the Marketing of the Welsh Craft Industry (1988); *Recreations* military history, theatre, after-dinner speaking, sharing humour; *Clubs* Oriental; *Style—* Tony Ball, Esq, MBE; Blythe House, Bidford-on-Avon, Warwicks B50 4BY (☎ 0789 778015); 249 Grove End Gardens, Grove End Rd, St John's Wood, London NW8 (☎ 071 286 0899); Tony Ball Associates plc, 174/178 North Gower St, London NW1 2NB (☎ 071 380 0953)

BALL, Arthur Beresford; OBE (1971); s of Charles Henry Ball (d 1943), and Lilian Houlden, *née* Hinde (d 1945); *b* 15 Aug 1923; *Educ* Bede Collegiate Boys' Sch, UEA (BA, MA); *m* 1961, June Stella, da of Edward John Luckett (d 1977); 1 s (Jonathan), 2 da (Abigail, Johanna); *Career* HM Dip Serv 1949-80: Bahrain, Tripoli, MECAS, Ramullah, Damascus, Kuwait, New Orleans, Saọ Paulo, Lisbon, Jedda, Ankara; Br Consul-Gen Perth WA 1978-80; ret 1980; *Recreations* ice skating, historical studies; *Style—* Arthur Ball, Esq, OBE; 15 Eccles Road, Holt, Norfolk NR25 6HT

BALL, Brian James; s of Gordon Ball (d 1981), of Ossett, Yorkshire, and Edna, *née* Stonehouse (d 1974); *b* 28 June 1930; *Educ* Woodhouse Grove Apperley Bridge Bradford, Leeds Hotel Sch (Dip); *m* 3 Sept 1955, (Anne) Barbara, da of William Gibson; 1 s (Richard James Gibson b 1 July 1960), 1 da (Alison Jane Gray b 18 Feb 1958); *Career* trainee Hotel des Trois Couronnes Vevey Switzerland 1953-54, restaurant mangr Lewis's Leeds 1954-56, gen mangr Gambit Restaurant Leeds 1956-59; British Petroleum Co: catering admin mangr 1959-67, HQ catering mangr 1967-69, gp catering advsr (responsible for catering and accommodation for BP GP Worldwide) 1969-83; proprietor and chm Calcot Ventures Ltd of Calcot Manor Country House Hotel and Restaurant 1983-; pres and chm Cncl HCIMA 1976/77, fndr chm Chiltern Cheshire Home Gerrards Cross; Catey awards Newcomer of the Year; Freeman City of London 1980, Master Innholder 1989; FHCIMA 1971; *Recreations* golf, theatre, music, reading; *Clubs* Sloane, 190; *Style—* Brian Ball, Esq; Calcot Manor, nr Tetbury, Gloucestershire GL8 8YJ (☎ 0666 890391, fax 0666 890394)

BALL, Sir Charles Irwin; 4 Bt (UK 1911), of Merrion Sq, City of Dublin, and Killybegs, Co Donegal; s of Sir Nigel Gresley Ball, 3 Bt (d 1978), and Florine Isabel, *née* Irwin; *b* 12 Jan 1924; *Educ* Sherborne; *m* 2 Sept 1950 (m dis 1983), Alison Mary, o da of Lt-Col Percy Holman Bentley, MBE, MC, of Farnham, Surrey; 1 s, 1 da (Diana Margaret b 1955); *Heir* s, Richard Bentley Ball, *qv*; *Career* served WWII and to 1947 in RA (Capt 1946); chartered accountant Peat Marwick Mitchell 1950-54; former dir: Kleinwort Benson (vice-chm 1974-76), memb Br Tport Docks Bd 1971-82, dep chm Associated British Ports Holdings 1982-; dir: Sun Alliance & London Insurance 1971-83, Tunnel Hldgs 1976-82, Rockware Gp 1978-84, Peachey Property Corp 1978-88 (chm 1981-88); chm: Barclays Merchant Bank 1976-77 (dir Barclays Bank 1976-77), Telephone Rentals 1981-89 (vice-chm 1978-81, dir 1971-89); chm Silkolene Lubricants 1989-; Master Worshipful Co of Clockmakers 1985; FCA 1960; *Style—* Sir Charles Ball, Bt; Appletree Cottage, Heath Lane, Ewshot, Farnham, Surrey (☎ 0252 850208)

BALL, Christopher Charles; s of Reginald Charles Ball, of Essex, and Amelia Ellen, *née* Garner; *b* 25 Dec 1945; *Educ* Harold Hill GS; *m* 17 July 1971, Frances Jean, da of Philip Elliott, of Barry Island, Wales; 1 s (Ian b 1987); *Career* dir: Capel-Cure Myers 1986, Linton Nominees Ltd 1986, Richardson Glover and Case Nominees Ltd 1986, Key Fund Managers Ltd 1990, National Investment Group 1990; memb Stock Exchange; *Recreations* golf, reading, shooting; *Style—* Christopher Ball, Esq; 147 Western Rd, Leigh-on-Sea, Essex (☎ 0702 711032); The Registry, Royal Mint Court, London EC3N 4EY (☎ 071 488 4000, fax 071 481 3798, telex 9419251)

BALL, Sir Christopher John Elinger; er s of late Laurence Elinger Ball, OBE, and Christine Florence Mary, *née* Howe; *b* 22 April 1935; *Educ* St George's Sch Harpenden, Merton Coll Oxford (MA); *m* 1958, Wendy Ruth, da of Cecil Frederick Colyer; 3 s (David, Peter, Richard), 3 da (Helen, Diana, Yasmin); *Career* 2 Lt Para Regt 1955-56; lectr English language Merton Coll Oxford 1960-61, lectr in comparative linguistics SOAS Univ of London 1961-64; Lincoln Coll Oxford: fell and tutor of English language 1964-79, sr tutor for admission 1971-72, bursar 1972-79, hon fell 1981; Keble Coll Oxford: warden 1980-88, hon fell 1989; hon fell Merton Coll Oxford 1987; chm Bd of Nat Advsy Body for Public Sector Higher Educn in England 1982-88, sec Linguistics Assoc of GB 1964-67, pres Oxford Assoc of Univ Teachers 1968-71, publications sec Philological Soc 1969-75, chm Oxford Univ English Bd 1977-79, founding fell Kellog Forum for Continuing Educn Univ of Oxford 1988-89, chm Educn-Indust (Indust Matters) RSA 1988-90, RSA fell in continuing Educn 1989-, Jt Standing Ctee for Linguistics 1979-82, memb Conf of Colls Fees Ctee 1979-85; memb: Gen Bd of the Faculties 1979-82, Hebdomadal Cncl 1985-89, CNAA 1982-88 (chm English Studies Bd 1973-80, Linguistics Bd 1977-82), BTEC 1984-90, IT Skills Shortages Ctee (Butcher Ctee) 1984-85, CBI IT Skills Agency 1985-88, CBI Trg Task Force 1988-89, CBI Educn and Trg Affrs Ctee 1989-; Cncl and Exec Templeton Coll Oxford 1981-; govr St George's Sch Harpenden 1985-89, Centre for Medieval and Renaissance Studies Oxford 1987-90, chm Brathay Hall Tst 1990-, Manchester Poly 1989- (hon fell 1988), hon fell Poly of Central London 1990, chm High Educn Info Servs Tst 1987-90, visiting prof in higher educn Leeds Poly 1989-, educnl consIt to Price Waterhouse 1989-; jt founding ed (with late Angus Cameron) Toronto Dictionary of Old English 1970, memb Editorial Bd Oxford Review of Education 1984-; Hon DLitt CNAA; FRSA 1987; kt 1988; *Books* Fitness for Purpose (1985); *Clubs* Utd Oxford and Cambridge Univ; *Style—* Sir Christopher Ball; 45 Richmond Rd, Oxford OX1 2JJ (☎ 0865 310800)

BALL, David Martin James; s of Rev Thomas William Ball, of Perth, W Aust, and Anne, *née* Rice; *b* 29 Sept 1943; *Educ* Annadale GS, Lisburn Tech Coll, Belfast Coll of Arts and Tech (Dip Civil Eng); *m* 1, 1969 (m dis 1985); 3 da (Heidi b 5 Oct 1974, Joanna b 14 Aug 1977, Victoria b 20 Nov 1980); m 2, 31 May 1986, Jacqueline Bernadette Margaret Mary, da of Maj Fredrick Jocelyn Clarke, of little Bylands, Cavendish Rd, St George's Hill, Weybridge, Surrey; *Career* civil engr Middle Level Cmmrs March Cambridge 1965-66, gen mangr A L Curtis (ONX) Ltd Chatteris Cambridge 1966-70, chm and md David Ball Group Cambridge 1970-; chm: Cambridge Energy Management Group 1982, Cambridge Philharmonic Soc 1986, CN-FM Radio Ltd (local commercial radio) 1988; govr Anglia Higher Educn Coll, memb Cncl Midland Examining Group, vice chm and co fndr Cambridge Enterprise Agency; vice chm: Cambridge Work Relations Gp, Parochial Church Cncl; memb: Cncl Soc for Application of Res, memb Ely Synod; tstee Pye Fndn; FBIM 1981, fell Inst Refractory Engrs 1981, FRSA 1985; *Recreations* gardening, tennis, walking; *Style—* David Ball, Esq; Freckenham House, Freckenham, Suffolk IP28 8HX (☎ 0638 720975); David Ball Group plc, Huntingdon Rd, Bar Hill, Cambridge CB3 8HN (☎ 0954 780687, fax 0954 782912, tlx 817213 BALL CO G, car 0836 738826)

BALL, Denis William; MBE (1971); s of William Charles Thomas Ball, of 17 Warburton Close, Park Lane, Eastbourne, Sussex, and Dora Adelaide, *née* Smith; *b* 20 Oct 1928; *Educ* Tonbridge, BNC Oxford (MA); *m* 5 Aug 1972, Marja Tellervo (d 1987), da of Osmo Lumijarvi, of Sontula 42, Toijala, Finland; 2 s (Christian b 1975, Robin b 1976), 1 da (Sasha b 1981); *Career* served RN 1947-49, RNR 1953-85 (Lt Cdr 1958-); housemaster The King's Sch Canterbury 1954-72 (asst master 1953-72), headmaster Kelly Coll Tavistock 1972-85; dir: Western Bloodstock Ltd 1986-, James Wilkes plc 1987, Perkins Foods plc 1987-, Redbridge Properties Ltd 1990-; conslt Throgmorton, Investment Management Ltd 1987-88; Squash Rackets for Oxford Univ and Kent Real Tennis for Jesters and HMC 1972-85, HMA 1972-85; tstee Tavistock Sch 1972-85, vice chm of Govrs St Michael's Sch Tawstock 1974-; memb: Ickham PCC 1986- (treas 1990-), Johnson Club 1987-; *Recreations* Elizabethan history, cryptography, literary and mathematical puzzles, cricket, real tennis, golf; *Clubs* East India, Devonshire, Sports and Public Schools, MCC; *Style—* Denis Ball, Esq, MBE;

Ickham Hall, Ickham, nr Canterbury, Kent

BALL, (Wilfred) Dennis; s of Frederick Thomas Ball (d 1989), and Ethel, *née* Cope (d 1973); *b* 27 Sept 1922; *Educ* Queen Elizabeth's GS Tamworth, Wednesbury Commercial Coll, Br Tutorial Inst; *m* 1, 19 Oct 1946 (m dis 1974), Jean Mildred, da of late Albert Bates; 1 s (David John Wilfred Lumley b 9 Dec 1952), 1 da (Elaine Patricia (Mrs Bates) b 29 Nov 1947); m 2, 10 Aug 1974, Marian Ball, JP, da of William Merrifield (d 1985), 2 da (Anne Margaret b 1 May 1977, Helen Patricia b 10 July 1979); *Career* Corpl RAF 1942-46 (despatches); accountant Brockhouse Trading Facilities Ltd 1952-57, co sec and accountant subsids of FMC Ltd 1957-65, orgn and methods offr (later chief exec) J Brockhouse & Co Ltd 1965- dir Brockhouse Ltd (parent co) 1968-; Brockhouse Gp: asst md 1968-84, fin dir 1970-84, conslt 1984-; hon auditor: St John Ambulance W Midland Co, Canon St Baptist Church Handsworth; memb: Local Branch Assoc of Corporate Treas, Birmingham and Midlands Soc of Fin, W Midlands Regnl Bd BIM; patron Sandwell Dist Spastics Soc; FAIA 1982, FCT 1979, CBIM 1982; *Recreations* gardening, reading, travel; *Style—* Dennis Ball, Esq; 54 Hinstock Rd, Handsworth Wood, Birmingham B20 2EU (☎ 021 554 5957)

BALL, Florine, Lady Florine Isabel; da of late Col Herbert Edwardes Irwin; *m* 1922, Sir Nigel Gresley Ball, 3 Bt (d 1978); *Style—* Florine, Lady Ball; Greenbanks Nursing Home, 29 London Rd, Liphook, Hampshire

BALL, Geoffrey Arthur; s of Henry Arthur Ball, of Bristol, and Phyllis Edna, *née* Webber; *b* 4 Aug 1943; *Educ* Cotham GS Bristol; *m* 1968, Mary Elizabeth, da of late S George Richards, of Bristol; 3 s (Nicholas b 1971, Nathan b 1972, Thomas b 1975), 1 da (Esther b 1977); *Career* chm and chief exec CALA plc; dir: The Scottish Mortgage & Tst plc, Stenhouse Western Ltd, The Standard Life Assur Co; memb: Scottish Arts Cncl, ISCO (Scotland); asst to the Master's Ct of The Co of Merchants of the City of Edinburgh; Clydesdale Bank Young Business Personality of the Year 1983; FCA; *Recreations* golf, music; *Clubs* New (Edinburgh), MCC; *Style—* Geoffrey Ball, Esq; 34 Colinton Rd, Edinburgh EH10 5DG (☎ 031 337 1528); CALA plc, 42 Colinton Rd, Edinburgh EH10 5BT (☎ 031 346 0194, fax 031 346 4190, car 0836 700565)

BALL, Prof Sir (Robert) James; s of Arnold James Hector Ball; *b* 15 July 1933; *Educ* St Marylebone GS, Queen's Coll Oxford (BA, MA), Univ of Pennsylvania (PhD); *m* 1, 1954 (m dis 1970), Patricia Mary Hart Davies; 1 s (Charles), 3 da (Stephanie, Deborah, Joanne) and 1 da decd; m 2, 1970, Mrs Lindsay Jackson, *née* Wonnacott; 1 step s (Nigel); *Career* Flying Offr Navigator RAF 1952-54; res offr Oxford Univ Inst of Statistics 1957-58, IBM fell Univ of Pennsylvania 1958-60, lectr (subsequently sr lectr) Univ of Manchester 1960-65, prof of economics London Business Sch 1965- (govr 1968-84, dep princ 1971-72, princ 1972-84); dir: Ogilvy & Mather Ltd 1969-71, Economic Models Ltd 1971-72, Barclays Bank Trust Co 1973-86, Tube Investments 1974-84; memb Ctee To Review Nat Savings (Page Ctee) 1971-73, chm Legal & General Group plc 1980-, econ advsr Touche Ross & Co 1984-; dir: IBM UK Ltd 1979-, London & Scottish Marine Oil (LASMO) 1988-, Royal Bank of Canada 1990-; tstee: Foulkes Fndn 1984-, Civic Tst 1986-, Economist Newspaper 1987-; memb British-North American Ctee 1985-; Marshall Aid Commemoration cmmr 1987-; fell Econometric Soc 1973, CBIM 1974, FIAM 1985; Freeman City of London 1987; Hon DSc Aston Univ 1987, Hon DSocSci Manchester 1988; kt 1984; *Books* An Econometric Model of the United Kingdom (1961), Inflation and the Theory of Money (1964); ed: Inflation (1969), The International Linkage of National Economic Models (1973); Money and Employment (1982), Toward European Economic Recovery in the 1980's (with M Albert, 1984), numerous articles in professional jls; *Recreations* gardening, chess; *Clubs* RAC; *Style—* Prof Sir James Ball; London Business School, Sussex Place, Regent's Park, London NW1 4SA (☎ 071 262 5050, fax 071 724 7875, telex 27461)

BALL, Dr John Macleod; *b* 19 May 1948; *Educ* Mill Hill Sch, St John's Coll Cambridge (open exhibitioner, BSE), Univ of Sussex (DPhil); *Career* Dept of Mathematics Heriot-Watt Univ 1972-74, SRC postdoctoral res fellowship Brown Univ USA 1972-74; Heriot-Watt Univ: lectr in mathematics 1974-78, reader in mathematics 1978-82, prof of applied analysis 1982-; visiting prof Dept of Mathematics UCLA 1979-80, sr fell SERC 1980-85, visiting prof Laboratoire d'Analyse Numérique Université Pierre et Marie Curie Paris 1987-88, Ordway visiting prof Univ of Minnesota 1990; exec ed Proceedings A RSE; memb Editorial Bds of: Analyse Nonlineaire (Instut Henri Poincaré), Archive for Rational Mechanics and Analysis, Journal of Elasticity, Physica D, Dynamics and Differential Equations, Proceedings A Royal Soc of London; author of numerous pubns; Whittaker prize Edinburgh Mathematical Soc 1981, jr Whitbread prize Royal Soc of London 1982, Keith prize RSE 1990; chm Steering Ctee Int Centre for Mathematical Scis Edinburgh, memb: Scientific Advsy Bd Issac Newton Inst Cambridge, Royal Soc Sectional Ctee 1, Scientific Ctee 1 Euro Congress of Mathematics; FRS 1989, FRS; *Style—* Dr John Ball, FRS, FRSE

BALL, Jonathan Macartney; s of Christopher Edward Ball (d 1978), and Dorothy Ethel, *née* Macartney; *b* 4 June 1947; *Educ* Truro Sch, The Arch Assoc (AA Dipl); *m* 29 June 1974, Victoria Mary Ogilvie, da of Dr Anthony Michael Ogilvie Blood, of Irstead House, Stratton, Bude, Cornwall; 2 da (Jemima Veryan b 1976, Morwenna Victoria b 1979); *Career* chartered architect, princ The Jonathan Ball Practice 1974-; Concrete Soc award (mention) 1981 and 1986, RIBA award (commendation) 1983, CPRE/CLA Henley award 1981; occasional lectr, conference speaker, contrib to architectural periodicals, assessor for RIBA architecture awards; memb Architectural Advsy Bd Plymouth Poly; RIBA: memb Cncl 1981-, chm Parly Liaison Ctee 1981-87, vice pres 1983-85, hon sec 1988-; RNLI sr Helmsman-Bude Lifeboat, chm Bude Surf Life Saving Club, Service award-Surf Life Saving Assoc GB; memb Worshipful Co of Chartered Architects 1986, Freeman City of London 1987; ACIArb 1978, FRSA 1985; *Recreations* enjoying Cornwall; *Clubs* Athenaeum; *Style—* Jonathan Ball, Esq; Tregarthens, Diddies Rd, Stratton, Bude, Cornwall EX23 9DW (☎ 0288 352198); The Jonathan Ball Practice, Chartered Architects, 5 Belle Vue, Bude, Cornwall EX23 8JJ (☎ 0288 355557, fax 0288 355826)

BALL, Kevin Anthony; s of Cyril Boyce Ball, of Hastings, East Sussex, and Patricia, *née* Harris; *b* 12 Nov 1964; *Educ* Hastings GS; partner, Sharon Lesley, da of Jack Butchers; 1 s (Luke Kevin b 30 Sept 1987); *Career* professional footballer; apprentice Coventry City 1981-82 (no appearances); Portsmouth 1982-90: debut v Shrewsbury Town 1984, 111 appearances, 4 goals; Sunderland 1990-: debut v Tottenham Hotspur 1990, over 25 appearances, 3 goals; only player to capt Sussex under 19 team whilst still in fifth form; promotion to Div 1 Portsmouth 1987; *Recreations* reading autobiographies, listening to music; *Style—* Kevin Ball, Esq; Sunderland FC, Roker Park, Grantham Rd, Roker, Sunderland, Tyne & Wear SR6 9SW (☎ 091 514 0332)

BALL, Rt Rev Michael Thomas; *see*: Truro, Bishop of

BALL, Rev Canon Peter William; s of Leonard Wevell Ball (d 1976), of St Albans, and Dorothy Mary, *née* Burrows; *b* 17 Jan 1930; *Educ* Aldenham Sch, Worcester Coll Oxford (MA), Cuddesdon Coll; *m* 11 Sept 1956, Angela Jane, *née* Dunlop; 1 s (Michael b 1961), 2 da (Lucy b 1957, Katharine b 1959); *Career* 2 Lt RA 1948; curate All Saints Poplar 1955-61, vicar The Ascension Wembley 1961-68, rector St Nicholas Shepperton 1968-84, area dean Spelthorne 1972-84, prebendary St Paul's Cathedral 1976-84, canon residentiary and chllr St Paul's Cathedral 1984-, chapter treas 1985-, dir Post Ordination Trg and Continuing Ministerial Educn Kensington Area 1984-87; chaplain: Associated Rediffusion TV 1961-68, Thames Television 1970-; fndr and chm Catechumenate Network 1984-, dir Samaritans Brent and NW Surrey 1965-75; Freeman of the City of London 1986; *Books* Journey into Faith (1984), Adult Believing (1988); *Style—* The Rev Canon Peter Ball; 1 Amen Ct, London EC4M 7BU (☎ 071 248 1817)

BALL, Richard Bentley; s and h of Sir Charles Irwin Ball, 4 Bt; *b* 29 Jan 1953; *Educ* Dragon Sch Oxford, Sherborne, Leicester Univ; *Career* chartered accountant with: Peat Marwick Mitchell 1975-82, Int Computers Ltd 1982-; ACA; *Recreations* tennis, hockey, squash; *Clubs* Roehampton, Hampstead Westminster Hockey; *Style—* Richard Ball, Esq; 11 Rotherwood Rd, London SW15 1LA (☎ 081 785 9887)

BALL, Tony; *see*: Ball, Anthony George

BALL, Trevor Mackenzie; s of William Albert Jardine Ball (d 1965), and Margaret, *née* Bushell; *b* 15 May 1931; *m* 28 Aug 1958, Norah Julia, da of Edward John Fitz-Henny; 2 da (Sarah Katherine MacKenzie b 5 Jan 1964, Clare Louise Mackenzie (Mrs Kirtley) b 17 July 1965); *Career* articled clerk Fryer Sutton Morris Chartered Accountants 1954-59, fndr own practice Trevor M Ball & Co 1965, ptnr Stoy Hayward (following merger) 1989-; hon treas: The Norfolk Soc Co Branch CPRE 1986-, Age Concern Norfolk 1988-, Norfolk Drug and Alcohol Abuse Soc 1990-; Norfolk Hist Bldgs Tst 1990-; fin dir Norwich Puppet Theatre 1987-; memb: Norwich Cathedral, Norfolk Gdns Tst, Nat Tst; fndr memb King Harold Dining Club 1966; fell RSPB, FCA (ACA 1960); *Style—* Trevor M Ball, Esq; 50 The Close, Norwich, Norfolk NR1 4EG (☎ 0603 764264, fax 0603 764412)

BALLANTINE, Dr Brian Neil; *b* 27 Jan 1936; *Educ* Queen Elizabeth Sch, Univ of London (BSc), St Bart's London (MB BS); *m* 18 Dec 1982, Annette; *Career* occupational physician; chm to UK Offshore Ops Assoc Med Advsy Ctee; MFOM 1988 (RCP), DIH 1985 (London Univ); *Style—* Dr Brian Ballantine; Red Lion House, The Lee, Gt Missenden, Bucks HP16 9NH (☎ 024 020 339); British Gas plc, 59 Bryanston St, London W1A 2AZ (☎ 071 723 7030)

BALLANTINE, Dr Robert Ian Waverley; s of Richard Waverley Head Ballantine, CBE (d 1965), and Olive Norma, *née* Law (d 1973); *b* 15 May 1922; *Educ* Wellington, Univ of London St Bart's Hosp (DA); *m* 13 April 1946, Jill Muriel, da of Col Cyril Helm, DSO, OBE, MC (d 1972); 2 s (Alistair b 1948, Giles (twin) b 1948), 1 da (Alison b 1952); *Career* resident anaesthetist Addenbrookes Hosp Cambridge 1947, chief asst anaesthetist Hillingdon and Harefield Hosps 1947-52, asst prof of anaesthesia Johnson Willis Hosp Richmond Virginia USA 1956, sr anaesthetist St Bart's 1978-86 (house surgn 1946, res anaesthetist 1947, conslt anaesthetist 1952-86), teacher in anaesthetics Univ of London; memb: BMA 1946-, Assoc of Anaesthetists 1946-; MRCS, LRCP, FFARCS; The Most Distinguished Order of Paduka Seri Laila Jasa (SLJ) of Brunei; *Books* General Anaesthesia For Neurosurgery (1960); *Recreations* golf, gardening, jazz music, reading; *Style—* Dr Robert Ballantine

BALLANTINE, Capt Ronald George; LVO (1952); s of William Henry Ballantine (d 1961), of Dublin, and Catherine Dalgairns, *née* Roberts (d 1982); *b* 2 Aug 1913; *Educ* Plymouth Coll, Plymouth Sch of Art; *m* 4 April 1942, Cherrie Julian Maybeth, da of George Whitby (d 1966), of Yeovil and Colombo; 2 s (Nicholas Whitby b 1942, Alistair Nigel Stuart b 1946), 1 da (Clare Catherine b 1954); *Career* Capt Imperial Airways 1937, chief pilot Hong Kong Airways 1947-49, flight mangr BOAC 1957-59, dir flight ops Malaysia Singapore Airline 1969-71; Newbury CAB 1972-83; King's Commendation for valuable serv in the air 1943; Freeman City of London, Liveryman Worshipful Co Air Pilots and Air Navigators; *Recreations* tennis, gardening, travelling; *Clubs* Naval & Military; *Style—* Capt Ronald Ballantine, LVO; Hitchens, Woolton Hill, Newbury, Berkshire RG15 9TX (☎ 0635 253 565)

BALLARD, Maj Anthony William; s of Maj John Francis Ballard, of Over Worton Heath Farm, Oxon, and Jean Carolina, *née* Rawle; *b* 27 May 1957; *Educ* Eton, RMA Sandhurst; *m* 25 Oct 1986, Petronella Johanna Antonia Maria, da of Sjoerd Wiegersma, of Amsterdam; 1 da (Charlotte Antonia Carolina b 25 Oct 1989); *Career* Sandhurst 1976, cmmnd 1 Bn Welsh Gds 1977, Gds Depot 1979, 1 Bn Welsh Gds 1980 (Falklands 1982), SO3 G2/G3 HQ Logistic Support Gp 1987, SO3 G3 (Log/Trg) HQ UK Mobile Force 1988, Maj 1 Bn Welsh Gds 1989-; hon sec Combined Servs Polo Club 1990-; *Recreations* polo, hunting; *Clubs* Cavalry and Guards, Mounted Infantry, Guards Polo; *Style—* Maj A W Ballard; Over Worton Heath Farm, Oxon OX5 4EH (☎ 060 883 237)

BALLARD, Beatrice Rosalind; da of James Graham Ballard, of Shepperton, Middx, and Mary, *née* Matthews (d 1964); *b* 29 May 1959; *Educ* St David's Sch Ashford Middx, UEA (BA), City Univ of London (Journalism Dip); *Career* reporter New Statesman 1981, writer and researcher Radio Times 1981-82, asst prodr and dir John Craven's Newsround BBC TV 1983-85; prodr: special progs LWT 1986-88, Saturday Night Clive and Clive James Postcard Documentaries BBC TV 1988-; memb: ACTT, NUJ; *Recreations* film, music, travel, working, squash; *Style—* Ms Beatrice Ballard; 43 Bollo Lane, Chiswick, London W4 5LS; BBC Television, Kensington House, Richmond Way, London W14 0AX (☎ 081 895 6611, fax 081 895 6975, telex 265781)

BALLARD, (Richard) Graham John; s of Alfred John Ballard (d 1979), of Worcs, and Ada Mary (d 1981); *b* 17 Jan 1927; *Educ* Prince Henry's GS Evesham, Wadham Coll Oxford (MA), Cambridge Univ (MA); *m* 10 July 1954, Domini Gabrielle, da of Dr Alfred Johannes Wright (d 1942), of Bucks; 2 s (Sebastian John b 1961, Toby Graham Dominic b 1963); *Career* chm and md Liebigs Rhodesia Ltd 1973-78, md Brooke Bond Kenya 1978-83, dir Tea Board of Kenya 1978-83, chm British Business Assoc Kenya 1982-83; bursar and fell Christs' Coll Cambridge 1983-; chm: Cambridge Univ Lodging House Syndicate 1986-, Cambridge Univ Stewards Ctee 1986-; memb Overseas Ctee Save The Children Fund 1984-, sr tres Cambridge Univ Opera Soc 1985-, tstee Wesley House Cambridge 1986; *Recreations* opera, chamber music, reading, French culture; *Style—* Graham Ballard, Esq; 23 Bentley Rd, Cambridge CB2 2AW (☎ 0223 323547); Christ's College, Cambridge CB2 3BU (☎ 0223 334949)

BALLARD, Kenneth Alfred; MC (1944); s of Charles John Ballard, of Cromer Lodge, Glengall Rd, Woodford Green, Essex (d 1930), and Elizabeth Anne Ballard (d 1950); *b* 17 Sept 1915; *m* 30 March 1940, Ann, da of Frederick Joseph Anthony, of Warley Road, Woodford Green, Essex, and Peaches Close, Cheam, Surrey; 3 da (Lesley Ann b 1947, Gillian Elizabeth b 1949, Patricia Katherine b 1951); *Career* RA 1940-, cmmnd 1941, served W Desert, Italy (MC), France, Germany, Holland; dir: Murray Pipework Ltd 1964-78, Patent Lightning Crusher Ltd 1965-85; chm: K A Ballard Ltd, Ballard Fired Heaters Ltd, Medium Trading Co Ltd, Prematechnik (UK) Ltd, Baynard Engrg Co Ltd; elected memb Ct of Common Cncl Corp of London, chm City of London Police 1973-77; Sheriff of London 1978-79; chm New Victoria Hosp Kingston 1965-73, tstee Castle Baynard Educnl Tst; govr: Christ's Hosp, Bridewell Hosp, City of London Freemen's Sch; *Recreations* music, photography; *Style—* Kenneth Ballard, Esq, MC; Giles Barn Cottage, Church Lane, Horsted Keynes, Danehill, Sussex (☎ 0825 790 795)

BALLARD, Peter; s of William Stanley Ballard (d 1979), and Bronwen Rowena (d 1965); *b* 24 Feb 1942; *Educ* John Lyon Sch Harrow, Univ of London; *m* 16 Sept 1972, Anne de Riemer, da of Dr Lawrence Claude de Riemer (Toby) Epps (d 1986); 2 da

(Bronwen Rowena b 1975, Sarah Rhiannon b 1975); *Career* asst prodr BBC TV 1969-78; BBC Enterprises: sales exec 1978-80, mktg mangr 1980-82, head of educn and trg sales 1982-87, head of TV sales 1987-89, dep dir broadcasting services 1989-; MCIM, memb Royal TV Soc; *Recreations* cinema, theatre, photography, music; *Style*— Peter Ballard, Esq; BBC Enterprises Ltd, Woodlands, 80 Wood Lane, London W12 0TT (☎ 081 576 2000, tlx 934678, fax 081 749 0538)

BALLARD, Richard Michael; s of Michael Agar Ballard, and Junella, *née* Ashton (d 1960); *b* 3 Aug 1953; *Educ* St Edmund's Coll Ware, Queens' Coll Cambridge (MA); *m* 28 Feb 1981, Penelope Ann, da of Dilwyn John Davies, DFC (d 1988), of Glamorgan; 2 s (Hayden b 1984, Thomas b 1985), 1 da (Sophie b 1987); *Career* admitted slr 1978; ptnr Freshfields 1984-; memb Law Soc; *Recreations* sport, wine, country pursuits; *Style*— Richard Ballard, Esq; Nether Hall, Pakenham, Suffolk; Whitefriars, 65 Fleet St, London (☎ 071 936 4000, fax 071 248 3487, telex 889292)

BALLARD, (Geoffrey) William; s of Geoffrey Horace Ballard, CBE, JP, DL (d 1990), of Orchard House, Abberley, Worcestershire, and Dorothy Sheila (d 1979); *b* 30 May 1954; *Educ* Malvern, Univ of Bristol (BSc); *m* 12 April 1980, Louisa Alden, da of David Chavasse Alden Quinney, of Reins Farm, Sambourne, Redditch, Worcestershire; 3 s (George b 1984, William b 1987, Jeffrey b 1988), 1 da (Celia b 1986); *Career* CA, fndr Ballards 1985-; scholar FCEC, fndr memb Tolzey Debating Soc; FCA 1989; *Recreations* farming, sailing; *Style*— G W Ballard, Esq; Stud Farm, Abberley, Worcs WR6 6AU (☎ 0299 896617); Morgan House, 1 Tagarell Road, Droitwich, Worcs WR9 8DS (☎ 0905 794504, 0831 241967, fax 0905 779956)

BALLENTYNE, Donald Francis; CMG (1985); s of Henry Quiney Ballentyne (d 1971), of London, and Frances Rose, *née* McLaren (d 1985); *b* 5 May 1929; *Educ* Haberdashers' Aske's; *m* 10 June 1950, Elizabeth, da of Leslie Alfred Heywood, of Benson, Oxon; 1 s (Christopher John b 1950), 1 da (Sarah Leslie (Mrs Michael Pringle) b 1957); *Career* served HM Forces 1948-50; joined HM Foreign Serv 1948; jr attaché Berne and Ankara; consul: Munich 1957-59, Stanleyville 1961-62, Cape Town 1962-65; first sec and dep head of mission Luxembourg 1965-69, Havana 1969-72; cnsllr (commercial): The Hague 1974-78, Bonn 1978-82; dep head of mission East Berlin 1982-84, consul gen Los Angeles 1984-89; *Recreations* sailing, riding, tennis, music; *Clubs* St James's; *Style*— Donald Ballentyne, Esq, CMG

BALLIN, Robert Andrew; s of Harold Ballin (d 1976), of E Dean, E Sussex, and Mollie Ballin, *née* Dunn (d 1989); *b* 8 July 1943; *Educ* Highgate Sch, City of London Coll; *m* 27 Nov 1975, Serena Mary Ann, da of Richard Goode, OBE, (d 1966), of Chelsea, London SW3; 1 s (Edward b 1980), 2 da (Annabel b 1981, Chloe b 1985); *Career* Shell-Mex and BP Ltd 1962-67, SH Benson Ltd 1967-69, Gallagher-Smail/Doyle Bernbeck 1969-73, FCB Ltd 1973-74, int account dir and dep to md Impact-FCB Belgium 1975-77, dep chm FCB Advertising Ltd 1988 (dir 1977); *Recreations* music, theatre, sport; *Clubs* Naval and Military, RAC, MCC, Annabel's; *Style*— Robert Ballin, Esq; The Old Vicarage, Froxfield, Marlborough, Wilts (☎ 0488 682736); FCB Advertising Ltd, 82 Baker St, London W1 (☎ 071 935 4426, telex 263526)

BALLINGALL, Patrick Chandler Gordon; MBE; s of Col David Charles Gordon Ballingall, MC, RAMC (d 1973), of E Sussex, and Rosa Beatrice, *née* Chandler (d 1974); *b* 5 Dec 1926; *Educ* Loretto, Univ of Edinburgh, Emmanuel Coll Cambridge (MA); *m* 10 May 1951, Mary Hamilton (May), da of Robert Brown Mackie, OBE (d 1978), of E Sussex; 1 s (James b 11 May 1958), 1 da (Anne (Hon Mrs Lever) b 12 Oct 1954); *Career* Lt RA, serv in Greece Palestine and Egypt; admitted slr 1953; ptnr Barwell Blakiston & Ballingall 1959-89, conslt 1990-; chm: Lewes Cons Assoc 1978-81, E Sussex Cons Euro Constituency Cncl 1984-90; memb Law Soc (pres Sussex Law Soc 1974-75); *Style*— Patrick Ballingall, Esq, MBE; 4 Chyngton Gardens, Seaford, East Sussex BN25 3RP (☎ 0323 893866); Barwell, Blakiston & Ballingall, 10 Sutton Park Rd, Seaford, East Sussex BN25 1RB (☎ 0323 899331, fax 0323 890108)

BALLS, Alastair Gordon; s of Rev Ernest George Balls, of Stevenson, Ayrshire, Scotland, and Elspeth Russell, *née* McMillan; *b* 18 March 1944; *Educ* Hamilton Acad Lanarkshire, Univ of St Andrews (MA), Univ of Manchester (MA); *m* 26 Nov 1977, Beryl May, da of John Nichol, of Harlow, Essex; 1 s (Thomas b 1979), 1 da (Helen b 1982); *Career* asst sec Treasy Govt of Tanzania 1966-68, economist Dept of Tport UK Govt 1969-73, sec Cairncross Ctee on Channel Tunnel 1974-75, sr econ advsr HM Treasy 1976-79, under sec DOE 1983-87, chief exec Tyne & Wear Urban Devpt Corpn 1987-; CBIM 1988; *Recreations* fishing, camping; *Clubs* Wylam Angling; *Style*— Alastair Balls, Esq; Scotswood House, Newcastle Business Park, Newcastle upon Tyne NE4 7YL (☎ 091 226 1234, fax 091 226 1388)

BALLS, (Henry) Derek; s of Maj Henry Burgess Balls, TD (d 1960), and Gladys Jane, *née* Harris (d 1948); *b* 31 July 1923; *Educ* City of London Sch; *m* 24 July 1950, Sheila Muriel, da of Harold Chiesman (d 1985), of Beckenham, Kent; 1 s (Richard b 12 May 1953), 3 da (Christine b 11 March 1952, Catharine b 25 May 1959, Rosemary b 28 Sept 1961); *Career* Army 1941-46, Capt 7 Light Cavalry (Indian Army), served India, Burma, Japan; memb Common Cncl City of London 1970-, dep Cripplegate Ward 1977; chm: Bd of London Sch 1983-86, City of London Health Ctee 1977-80, Epping Forest and Open Spaces Ctee 1990-; Liveryman Worshipful Co of Innholders (Master 1977-78); JP Essex 1975-86; FHCIMA 1980; *Recreations* skiing, shooting, sailing, fishing; *Clubs* City Livery, Royal Burnham Yacht; *Style*— Derek Balls, Esq; Greengates, Albion Hill, Loughton, Essex; Balls Bros Ltd, 311 Cambridge Heath Rd, London E2 9LQ (☎ 071 739 6466, fax 071 729 0258)

BALLS, Geoffrey Robert; s of Victor Leslie Balls, of 18 Harrow Rd, Carshalton, Surrey, and Ellen, *née* MacNaboe; *b* 28 Sept 1989; *Educ* Trent Poly (BA), Garnett Coll (CertEd), Univ of Warwick (MSc);; *m* 31 Aug, Eileen Mary, da of Patrick O'Regan, of Laheme Cross, Baltimore, Co Cork, Eire; 1 s (Matthew), 3 da (Jessica, Stephanie, Catherine); *Career* Plessey Radar Ltd 1979-82, Cray Research (UK) Ltd 1982-87, head of Info Systems Channel Four TV Ltd 1987-; memb RTS; *Style*— Geoffrey Balls, Esq; Channel Four Television Ltd, 60 Charlotte St, London, W1P 2AX (☎ 071 927 8646, fax 071 637 1495, telex 892355)

BALMER, Sir Joseph Reginald; JP; s of Joseph Balmer, of Birmingham; *b* 22 Sept 1899; *Educ* King Edward's GS Birmingham; *m* 1927, Dora, da of A Johnson; *Career* nat chm Guild of Insur Officials 1943-47; kt 1965; *Style*— Sir Joseph Balmer, JP; 26 Stechford Lane, Ward End, Birmingham (☎ 021 783 3198)

BALMFORTH, Ven Anthony James; s of Rev Joseph Henry Balmforth (d 1943), and Daisy Florence, *née* Mawby (d 1973); *b* 3 Sept 1926; *Educ* Sebright Sch Wolverley Worcs, BNC Oxford (MA), Lincoln Theol Coll; *m* 16 April 1952, Eileen Julia, da of James Raymond Evans (d 1939); 1 s (Timothy b 19 Feb 1954), 2 da (Theresa b 7 Aug 1958, Anne b 5 Dec 1964); *Career* served Army 1944-48; ordained 1952, curate Mansfield 1952-55; vicar: Skegby Notts 1955-61, St John's Kidderminster 1961-65; rector Kings Norton Birmingham 1965-79 (rural dean 1973-79), canon of Birmingham Diocese 1976-79, archdeacon of Bristol and canon Bristol Cathedral 1979-90 (now ret); memb Gen Synod of C of E 1982-90; *Recreations* gardening; *Style*— The Ven A J Balmforth; Slipper Cottage, Stag Hill, Yorkley, Gloucestershire GL15 4TB (☎ 0594 364019)

BALNIEL, Lord; Anthony Robert Lindsay; s and h of 29 Earl of Crawford and (12 of) Balcarres, PC, *qv*; *b* 24 Nov 1958; *Educ* Eton, Univ of Edinburgh; *m* 12 Aug 1989, Nicola yst da of Antony Bicket, of Derwas, Dolwen, N Wales; *Career* dir J O Hambro Investment Management Ltd; *Clubs* New (Edinburgh); *Style*— Lord Balniel; Balcarres, Colinsburgh, Fife

BALOCH, Dr Nusrat; da of Abdullah Channah (d 1989), of Hyderabad, Sind, Pakistan, and Zeenat Channah; *b* 20 Aug 1944; *Educ* St Mary's Sch Hyderabad Pakistan, Liaquet Med Coll Hyderabad Pakistan, Univ of Sind (MB BS), Univ of London (DObstRCOG, DPM), MRCPsych, FRCPsych; *m* 14 Nov 1966, Dr Khadim Hussain Baloch, s of Ali Mohammed Baloch (d 1971) of Karachi, Pakistan; *Career* house offr med gynaecology and obstetrics Gen Hosp Ashton under Lyne 1967-68, sr house offr gynaecology and obstetrics Forest Gate Hosp London 1968, conslt psychiatrist Severalls Hosp Colchester 1974- (registrar psychiatry 1968-71, sr registrar psychiatry 1971-74); memb: Sindhi Doctors Assoc UK, Overseas Doctors Assoc UK, Pakistan Med Soc UK, Hosp Conslts Assoc UK; *Recreations* theatre, music, cinema, travel; *Style*— Dr Nusrat Baloch; Little Court, London Rd East, Dedham, Colchester, Essex CO7 6BW (☎ 0206 323006); Severalls Hospital, Colchester, Essex CO4 5HG (☎ 0206 852271 ext 2795)

BALOGH, Baroness; Catherine; da of Arthur Cole (d 1968, Fell of King's Coll Cambridge); *Educ* Univ of Cambridge, W London Hosp (MRCS, LRCP); *m* 1, Dr Storr; 3 da; m 2, 1970, as his 2 w, Baron Balogh (d 1985; Life Peer UK 1968), of Hampstead; *Career* psychiatrist; writer; *Books* Growing Up (1975), The World of Freud (contrib 1972) Discipline in Schools (contrib 1973), over 30 books for children; *Style*— The Rt Hon the Lady Balogh; Flat 5, 12 Frognal Gardens, London NW3

BALOGH, Hon Christopher Thomas; yr s of Baron Balogh (d 1985), and his 1 wife, Penelope Noel Mary Ingram, *née* Tower (d 1975); *b* 16 Nov 1948; *Educ* Westminster, King's Coll Cambridge; *Style*— The Hon Christoper Balogh; 30 Daleham Gardens, London NW3

BALOGH, Hon Stephen Bernard; er s of Baron Balogh (d 1985), and his 1 wife, Penelope Noel Mary Ingram, *née* Tower (d 1975); *b* 18 Jan 1946; *Educ* Westminster, Balliol Coll Oxford; *Style*— The Hon Stephen Balogh; Loweswater Hall, Cockesmouth, Cumbria

BALOGUN, Anthony; s of Janet Balogun; *b* 26 Dec 1959; *Educ* Compton Coll, Univ of Nevada Reno (BSc); *Career* basketball player; selected GB Olympic Basketball Team 1984 and 1988, co-capt England Basketball Team 1989 (first cap 1983), runner-up Carlsberg Basketball League for MVP 1989; *Style*— Anthony Balogun, Esq; Thames Valley Basketball Club, Jubilee Terrace Beehive Rd, Amen Corner, Bracknell, Berks RG12 47P (☎ 0344 424827)

BALSTON, His Honour Judge Antony Francis; s of Cdr Edward Francis Balston, DSO, RN, of Oast Ho, Crowhurst, Battle, E Sussex, and Diana Beatrice Louise, *née* Ferrers; *b* 18 Jan 1939; *Educ* Downside, Christ's Coll Cambridge (MA); *m* 1966, Anne Marie Judith, da of Gerald Ball (d 1971); 2 s (James b 1967, Andrew b 1969), 1 da (Alexandra b 1972); *Career* RN 1957-59; ptnr Herington Willings & Penry Davey Slrs 1966-85; recorder 1980, hon recorder of Hastings 1984; circuit judge 1985; *Recreations* gardening; *Style*— His Honour Judge Antony Balston; Elmside, Northam, Rye, E Sussex (☎ 079 7252270)

BALY, Dr Monica Eileen; da of Albert Frank Baly (d 1953), of Shirley, Surrey, and Annie Elizabeth, *née* Marlow (d 1961); *b* 24 May 1914; *Educ* St Hilda's Sch for Girls London, Open Univ (BA), Univ of London (PhD); *Career* WWII: Sister Princess Mary RAF Nursing Serv 1942-46, ME and Italian campaigns (despatches 1944); chief nursing offr Displaced Persons Div Germany (Br Zone) FO 1949-51, regnl nursing offr W Area Royal Coll of Nursing 1951-74, lectr and examiner in nursing Univ of London; official historian Nightingale Fund Cncl, fndr Royal Coll of Nursing History of Nursing Soc, vice chm Arthritis Res Cncl Bath, lectr history of nursing England and N America; FRCN 1986, centenary fell Queen's Inst Nursing; ed History of Nursing Jl; *Books* History of the Queen's Nursing Institute (1987), Nursing and Social Change (2 edn, 1980), Professional Responsibility (2 edn, 1984), District Nursing (2 edn, 1987), Florence Nightingale and the Nursing Legacy; *Recreations* music particularly opera, theatre; *Style*— Dr Monica Baly; 19 Royal Cres, Bath BA1 2LT (☎ 0225 424 736)

BALY, Patrick Thomas; s of Albert Frank Baly (d 1956), and Annie Elizabeth, *née* Marlow (d 1967); *b* 22 Feb 1921; *Educ* Whitgift Middle Sch Croydon; *m* 5 Nov 1949, Margaret Elizabeth, da of Percival Allen Butland (d 1965); 1 s (Nigel b 1957), 1 da (Gillian b 1962); *Career* RAF 1941-46; ptnr: Hatfield Dixon Roberts Wright & Co 1956-84, Rowley Pemberton Roberts & Co 1967- (sr ptnr 1976-80), Pannell Kerr Forster (vice chm Nat Exec 1980-82); official liquidator De Lorean Motor Cars Ltd 1982-; memb Bd of Mgmnt Royal Masonic Hosp 1985- (hon tres and tstee 1987-), memb Worshipful Co of Gold and Silver Wyre Drawers; FCA 1951; *Recreations* cricket, tennis, fly-fishing; *Clubs* MCC, Flyfishers'; *Style*— Patrick Baly, Esq

BAMBER, David James; s of Ernest Bamber, of Walkden, Salford, and Hilda, *née* Wolfendale; *b* 19 Sept 1954; *Educ* Walkden Co Secdy Modern Sch, Farnworth GS, Univ of Bristol, RADA; *m* July 1982, Julia Swift (the actress), da of David Swift; *Career* actor; theatre: Joseph and His Amazing Technicolour Dreamcoat (Palace Theatre Westcliff) 1979, Outskirts (RSC Warehouse) 1981, Oresteia (NT) 1981, Masterclass (Leicester Haymarket, Old Vic, Wyndhams) 1983-84, Kissing God (Hampstead) 1984, Amadeus 1986; NT: Charlie (The Strangeness of Others) 1988, John Littlewit (Bartholomew Fair) 1988, Horatio (Hamlet) 1989, Streaky Bacon (Racing Demon) 1990-91, Mole (Wind in the Willows) 1990-91; tv: Call Me Mister (BBC) 1986, Cockles (BBC) 1983; film: Privates on Parade 1982, High Hopes 1988; RADA William Peel prize, Carol Brahams Musical Comedy prize, Bancroft Gold medal; *Recreations* listening to music, playing the piano, trying to keep fit usually at a gym, being married to Julia; *Style*— David Bamber, Esq; c/o Michael Ladkin Personal Management (☎ 071 402 6644)

BAMBERG, Harold Rolf; CBE (1968); s of Ernest Bamberg; *b* 17 Nov 1923; *Educ* Fleet Sch and William Ellis Sch Hampstead; *m* 1957, June Winifred, da of John Clarke; 1 s, 2 da (and 1 s, 1 da of a former m); *Career* chm Bamberg Group Ltd, Eagle Aircraft Services Ltd; *Style*— Harold Bamberg Esq, CBE; Harewood Park, Sunninghill, Berks

BAMBOROUGH, John Bernard; s of John George Bamborough (d 1931), and Elsie Louise, *née* Brogden; *b* 3 Jan 1921; *Educ* Haberdashers' Aske's, Hampstead Sch, New Coll Oxford; *m* 1947, Anne, da of Olav Indrehus (d 1984), of Indrehus, Norway; 1 s (Paul), 1 da (Karin Cecilia); *Career* RN 1941-46, Lt Instr Europe; fell and tutor Wadham Coll Oxford 1947-62 (lectr in English 1951-62), princ Linacre Coll Oxford 1962-88, pro vice chllr Univ of Oxford 1966-88; *Style*— John Bamborough, Esq; 18 Winchester Rd, Oxford (☎ 0865 59886); Linacre Coll, St Cross Rd, Oxford (☎ 0865 271650)

BAMBRIDGE, Anthony Martin; s of Sidney Ernest, and Millicent Rose, *née* Reekie (d 1990); *b* 27 Aug 1935; *Educ* Buckhurst Hill County HS, LSE; *m* 1960, Judith Pauline, *née* Swingland; 2 s (Daniel b 1967, Jacob b 1969), 1 da (Emma b 1965); *Career* reporter The Economist 1960-64, business and news ed The Observer 1964-76, PR dir Unilever 1976-77, The Sunday Times 1977- (business ed, managing ed news, managing ed features, currently exec ed); *Books* Ambush (with Robin Morgan and James Adams, 1989); *Style*— Anthony Bambridge, Esq; The Sunday Times, 1 Pennington St, London E1 (☎ 071 782 5000)

BAMFORD, Alan George; CBE (1985), JP (1977); s of James Ross Bamford (d 1976), of Liverpool, and Margaret Emily, *née* Ramsay; *b* 12 July 1930; *Educ* Prescot GS, Borough Road Coll (Cert Ed), Univ of Liverpool (Dip Ed, MEd), Univ of Cambridge (MA); *m* 7 Aug 1954, Joan Margaret, da of Arthur William Vint (d 1985), of Hastings; 4 s (Stephen Mark b 1955, Timothy David b 1959, Simon John b 1960, Peter Andrew b 1967); *Career* Corpl RAF 1948-50; teacher then dep headmaster Lancs Primary Schs 1952-62, lectr in educn Univ of Liverpool 1962-63, sr lectr Chester Coll 1963-66, princ lectr and head of dept St Katharine's Coll Liverpool 1966-71; princ: Westhill Coll Birmingham 1971-85, Homerton Coll Cambridge 1985-; memb: Advsy Ctee on Religious Broadcasts BBC Radio Birmingham 1972-8 Cncl Br and Foreign Sch Soc 1972-85; chm Birmingham Assoc of Youth Clubs 1972-85; memb: Br Cncl of Churches Standing Ctee on Theological Educn 1979-82, Cncl of Mgmnt Central Register and Clearing House 1982-, Exec Ctee Assoc of Voluntary Colls 1979-86; Birmingham Cmmn 1977-85; govr London Bible Coll 1981-89; memb: Cncl Nat Youth Bureau 1974-80, Exec Ctee Standing Conf on Studies in Educn 1978-87 (sec 1982-84), Educn Ctee Free Church Fed Cncl 1978-1990, Ctee Standing Conf on Principals of Colls and Insts of Higher Educn Cambridge Health Authy (and tstee) 1987-90, Voluntary Sector Consultative Cncl 1987-88, Standing Ctee on Educn and Trg of Teachers (vice chm 1988, chm 1989) Hon MA Univ of Birmingham 1981; FRSA 1975; *Recreations* travel, photography; *Clubs* Royal Cwlth Soc, United Oxford and Cambridge; *Style—* Alan Bamford, Esq, CBE, JP; Principal's House, Homerton College, Cambridge CB2 2PH (☎ 0223 411 141)

BAMFORD, Anthony Paul; DL (Staffs 1989); s of Joseph Cyril Bamford, *qv*; *b* 23 Oct 1945; *Educ* Ampleforth, Grenoble Univ; *m* 1974, Carole Gray Whitt; 2 s, 1 da; *Career* joined JCB on shop floor 1962, chm and md J C Bamford Excavators Ltd 1976-, non-exec dir Tarmac plc 1987; Young Exporter of the Year 1972, Young Businessman of the Year 1979; pres: Burton on Trent Cons Assoc 1987-, Staffs Agric Soc 1987-88; memb: Design Cncl, Presidents Ctee CBI; Individual Leadership award PA Consulting Group 1990; High Sheriff Staffs 1985-86; Hon MEng Univ of Birmingham 1987, Hon Dr Univ of Keele 1988, Chevalier de l'Ordre National du Merite 1989; *Clubs* BRDC, Pratts; *Style—* Anthony Bamford, Esq, DL; J C Bamford Excavators, Rocester, Uttoxeter, Staffs (☎ 0889 590312)

BAMFORD, Colin; s of Firth Bamford (d 1986), of Blackburn, Lancs, and Edna, *née* Cockshutt; *b* 28 Aug 1950; *Educ* Queen Elizabeth's GS Blackburn, Trinity Hall Cambridge (scholar, MA); *m* 31 Jan 1975, Nirmala Rajah Bamford, da of Hon Mr Justice AP Rajah, of Singapore; 2 s (Rowan Firth Rajah b 13 March 1980, Daniel Chelva Rajah b 26 July 1986), 1 da (Roxanne Vijaya Rajah b 6 May 1990); *Career* Herbert Oppenheimer Nathan and Vandyk: articled clerk 1972-74, asst slr 1974-77, ptnr 1977-88; ptnr Richards Butler 1988-; *Style—* Colin Bamford, Esq; Richards Butler, Beaufort House, 15 St Botolph St, London EC3 7EE (☎ 071 247 6555, fax 071 247 5091)

BAMFORD, David John; s of Samuel John Bamford, of Wellingborough, Northants, and Joan Sullivan, *née* Greenwood; *b* 28 June 1955; *Educ* Wellingborough GS, Univ of Aberdeen (MA); *m* 19 July 1979, Meyni Maria, da of Corneluus Timmer, of Oosterend, Texel, Netherlands; 1 s (Thomas Rosh b 1981); *Career* BBC: political researcher Monitoring Serv 1980-83, journalist World Serv News 1983-86, Ankara corr 1986-87, N Africa corr 1988-89; contrib 1986-89: The Guardian, Middle East Int, Middle East Economic Digest; *Style—* David Bamford, Esq; 1 The Crofts, Little Paxton, Huntingdon, Cambs (☎ 0480 212581); BBC World Service News, PO Box 76, Bush House, Strand, London (☎ 071 257 2684)

BAMFORD, Brig (Percy) Geoffrey; CBE (1959, OBE 1951), DSO (1944); s of Lt-Col Percy Bamford, OBE, TD, JP (d 1951), of Cottage Field, Ightham, Kent; *b* 23 May 1907; *Educ* Cranleigh Sch, RMA Sandhurst; *m* 1930, Betty Fallding (d 1981), da of Lt-Col Henry Joseph Crossley, CIE, RAMC (d 1939); 1 s (and 1 da decd); *Career* Brig, Cdr 150 Inf Bde 1954-56, Col The Lancs Fusiliers 1955-64; *Recreations* hunting; *Clubs* Army and Navy; *Style—* Brig Geoffrey Bamford, CBE, DSO; Brook End Cottage, Kitebrook, Moreton-in-Marsh GL56 0TA (☎ 0608 74 257)

BAMFORD, John William; OBE (1991); s of William Harry Bamford (d 1961), of Thrapston, and Harriet Ethel, *née* Fogell (d 1969); *b* 27 Aug 1918; *Educ* Kimbolton, Open Univ (BA); *m* 11 Oct 1941, Denise Mary, da of Hubert Morris; 3 da (Penelope b 1950, Ann b 1957, Sarah b 1959); *Career* WWII 1940-46; local govt offr 1935-78, city treas Westminster 1974-78, pub fin conslt; memb Chapter Gen, chm London Cncl; St John Ambulance: dep pres, cdr, dir London Dist; Freeman City of London 1978, Liveryman Worshipful Co of Gardeners 1983; memb: IPFA 1949, FRVA 1964; KStJ 1985 (OStJ); *Recreations* reading, crosswords, watching cricket, gardening; *Clubs* MCC; *Style—* John Bamford, Esq, OBE; 21 West Way, Pinner, Middx HA5 3NX (☎ 081 866 4869)

BAMFORD, Joseph Cyril; CBE (1969); Cyril Joseph Bamford (d 1953), of the Parks, Uttoxeter, Staffs; *b* 21 June 1916; *Educ* St John's Alton Staffs, Stonyhurst; *m* 1941, Marjorie, da of William Griffin, of Uttoxeter, Staffs; 2 s (Anthony Paul, *qv*, Mark Joseph); *Career* chm and md J C Bamford Excavators 1945-76; Hon DTech (Loughborough) 1983; *Style—* Joseph Bamford, Esq, CBE; PO Box 229, Rue du Maupas 49, Ch-1000 Lausanne 9, Switzerland

BAMFORD, Richard Brian; DL (1987); s of Dr James Brian Bamford, DL (d 1979), and Eileen Mary, *née* Leeming (d 1990); *b* 24 April 1938; *Educ* Wellington, Selwyn Coll Cambridge (MA); *m* 8 April 1978, Elizabeth Ann, da of Lt-Col H W Faure Walker; 1 s (John b 1981), 1 da (Peggy b 1979); *Career* Nat Serv 2 Lt 1 Bn XX Lancashire Fusiliers Cyprus; slr; Slrs Disciplinary Tribunal 1984-; Mayor of Ely 1988-89; *Recreations* shooting, golf; *Clubs* Royal Worlington (Capt 1986/87), Royal West Norfolk; *Style—* Richard Bamford, Esq, DL; Vineyard Lodge, Market Place, Ely, Cambs CB7 4NP (☎ 0353 662203)

BAMJI, Dr Andrew Nariman; s of Dr Nariman Sorabji Bamji (d 1978), of Highgate, London N6, and Dr Joan Elizabeth Bamji, *née* Jermyn; *b* 14 Aug 1950; *Educ* Highgate Sch, The Middlesex Hosp Med Sch Univ of London (MB BS); *m* 10 June 1978, Elizabeth Mary, da of Raymond William Millard, of Wembdon, Bridgwater, Somerset; 1 s (Nicholas b 1985), 1 da (Alexandra b 1981); *Career* conslt in rheumatology and rehabilitation: SE Thames RHA Brook Gen Hosp 1983-89, Queen Mary's Hosp Sidcup 1983- (dir Elmstead Younger Disabled Unit 1985-, clinical tutor and dir of med educn 1990-), Chelsfield Park Hosp Kent 1987-, chm Jt Care Planning Gp for the Younger Disabled Bealy Health Authy 1990-; memb BMA, FRCP 1989; *Books* Atlas of Clinical Rheumatology (jt ed, 1986); *Recreations* antiques, gardening, pianola; *Style—* Dr Andrew Bamji; Greylands, 58 Goddington Lane, Orpington, Kent BR6 9DS; Queen Mary's Hospital, Frognal Ave, Sidcup, Kent DA14 6LT (☎ 081 302 2678, fax 081 308 0457); Chelsfield Park Hospital, Bucks Cross Road, Chelsfield, Kent BR6 7AG (☎ 0689 877855)

BAMPFYLDE, Hon David Cecil Warwick; s of 6 Baron Poltimore (d 1978), and Margret Mary (d 1981), da of 4 Marquis de la Pasture (cr France 1768); *b* 3 March 1924; *Educ* Eton; *m* 1950, Jean Margaret, da of Lt-Col Patrick Kinloch Campbell; 3 s; *Style—* The Hon David Bampfylde; Coombe Lea, Malmesbury, Wilts

BAMPTON, Deborah Ellen; da of Albert Richard Bampton, of 68 Castlefields, Istead Rise, Meopham, Kent, and Ann Ceila, *née* Johnson; *b* 7 Oct 1961; *Career* capt England Women's Football Team, former player mangr Millwall Lionesses; *Style—* Miss Deborah Bampton; 1, The Spires, Wilmington, Kent

BANATVALA, Prof Jangu Edal; s of Dr Edal Banatvala (d 1981), and Ratti, *née* Shroff; *b* 7 Jan 1934; *Educ* Forest Sch London, Gonville & Caius Coll Cambridge (MA), London Hosp Med Coll (MD, DCH, DPH, Sir Lionel Whitby medal); *m* 15 Aug 1959, Roshan, da of Jamshed Mugaseth (d 1950); 3 s (Nicholas b 1961, Jonathan b 1963, Christopher b 1967), 1 da (Emma-Jane b 1968); *Career* res fell Univ of Cambridge 1961-64, post doctoral fell Yale Sch of Med 1964-65; St Thomas' Hosp Med Sch (later Utd Med and Dental Sch): sr lectr 1965-71, reader in clinical virology 1971-75, prof 1975-; vice pres: RCPath 1987-90 (registrar 1985-87), Cncl Med Def Union 1987-; pres Euro Assoc against Virus Disease 1983-85; chm: Sub Ctee on Measles Mumps and Rubella (CDVIP) Med Res Cncl 1985-, Dept of Health Advsy Gp on Hepatitis 1990-;memb Jt Ctee on Vaccination and Immunisation 1986-; examiner in pathology for MB Univs of: London, Cambridge, W Indies, Riyadh; examiner in virology RCPath; elected memb Univ of London Senate 1987; Freeman City of London 1987, Liveryman Worshipful Soc of Apothecaries; memb: Soc Gen Microbiology 1970-, BMA 1970-, Royal Soc of Tropical Med and Hygiene 1983-; MRCP, FRCPath; *Books* Current Problems in Clinical Virology (1971), Principles and Practice of Clinical Virology (jtly, 1987, 2 edn 1990); *Recreations* watching sports in which one no longer performs (rowing, cricket), playing tennis, exercising retrievers (infrequently), music; *Clubs* Athenaeum, Leander, MCC; *Style—* Prof Jangu Banatvala; Little Acre, Church End, Henham, nr Bishop's Stortford, Herts CM22 6AN; Department of Virology, United Medical and Dental School of St Guy's and St Thomas' Hospitals, St Thomas' Campus, Lambeth Palace Rd, London SE1 7EH (☎ 071 928 9292 ext 2405, fax 071 633 0775)

BANBURY, Martin John; s of Raymond Francis Banbury, of Fareham, and Molly Louise Banbury; *b* 30 March 1957; *Educ* Chelsea Coll London (BSc); *m* Sarah, da of Peter Andrew Campbell, 2 da (Amber Sarah Edna b 1 Dec 1986, Emma Lucy b 24 June 1988); *Career* mktg exec; Mktg Dept of Procter & Gamble 1979-82, Cussons 1982-84, Britvic 1984-85; jt chm Communicator One plc 1985-; memb: Inst of Sales Promotion, Sales Promotion Conslts Assoc; FIOD; *Recreations* flying, sailing; *Style—* Martin Banbury, Esq; 31 Whiteadder Way, London E14 9UR (☎ 071 987 4554); Communicator One plc, 15/17 St Cross St, London EC1N 8UN (☎ 071 831 3622, fax 071 242 1061)

BANBURY, (Nigel Graham Cedric) Peregrine; s of Ralph Cecil Banbury (d 1951), of Ebury St, London, and Florence Leslie St Clair Keith; *b* 23 May 1948; *Educ* Gordonstoun; *m* 1, 17 Nov 1973, Rosemary Henrietta Dorothy, da of Capt Anthony Henry Heber Villiers, of The Old Priory, Woodchester, Glos; m 2, 28 Sept 1978, Susan Margaret, da of Lt-Col Joseph Patrick Feeny, of Estoril, Portugal (d 1970); 2 s (Alexander b 1981, Ralph b 1987); *Career* Coutts & Co 1967-70, stockbroker 1971-81, Robert Fleming 1981-86, dir EBC Amro Asset Management Ltd 1986-87, head Investmt Dept Coutts & Co 1987-; Freeman City of London; *Recreations* shooting, skiing, gardening, golf; *Style—* Peregrine Banbury, Esq; Coutts & Co, 440 Strand, London WC2R 0QS (☎ 071 753 1000)

BANBURY OF SOUTHAM, 3 Baron (UK 1924); Sir Charles William Banbury; 3 Bt (UK 1902); s of 2 Baron Banbury, DL (d 1981), and Hilda, *née* Carr (m dis 1958; she m 2, Maj R Gardner, MC); *b* 29 July 1953; *m* 1984 (m dis 1986), Lucinda Trehearne; *Style—* The Rt Hon The Lord Banbury of Southam; The Mill, Fossebridge, nr Cheltenham, Glos

BANCE, Prof Alan Frederick; s of Frederick Bance, and Agnes Mary, *née* Wilson; *b* 7 March 1939; *Educ* Grocers Co Sch, UCL (BA), Univ of Cambridge (PhD); *m* 30 Aug 1964, Sandra, da of John Davis, of Hove, W Sussex; 2 da (Georgia b 1972, Miriam b 1976); *Career* lectr Univ of Strathclyde 1965-67, sr lectr Univ of St Andrews 1981 (lectr 1967-81); prof: Univ of Keele 1981-84, Univ of Southampton 1984-; memb Ctee Modern Humanities Res Assoc 1980-, ed Germanic Section Modern Language Review; *Books* The German Novel 1945-60 (1980), Theodor Fontane: The Major Novels (1982), Weimar Germany: Writers and Politics (ed, 1982), Ödön von Horváth 50 Years On (ed with I Huish, 1988); *Recreations* walking, gardening, researching, foreign travel; *Style—* Prof Alan Bance; German Dept, University of Southampton, Highfield, Southampton SO9 5NH (☎ 0703 592210, fax 0703 593939, tlx 47661)

BANCEWICZ, John; s of Dr Anthony Bancewicz, of Airdrie, Lanarkshire, and Helen, *née* Ulinskas (d 1950); *b* 26 March 1945; *Educ* St Aloysius Coll Glasgow, Univ of Glasgow (BSc, MB ChB), Univ of Manchester (ChM); *m* 5 Jan 1972, Margaret Kathleen, da of Dr Charles Douglas Anderson, MC; 1 s (Peter b 1973), 1 da (Ruth b 1976); *Career* res fell Harvard Med Sch 1974-75, lectr in surgery Univ of Glasgow 1976-79, reader in surgery and conslt surgn Univ of Manchester 1988- (sr lectr 1979-88); FRCS (Glasgow) 1973; *Recreations* sailing, hill walking; *Style—* John Bancewicz, Esq; 10 Syddal Rd, Bramhall, Cheshire SK7 1AD (☎ 061 439 2508); University of Manchester, Dept of Surgery, Hope Hospital, Salford M6 8HD (☎ 061 789 7373, fax 061 787 7432)

BANCROFT, Hon Adam David Powell; yr s of Baron Bancroft, GCB (Life Peer); *b* 1955; *Educ* King's Coll Sch Wimbledon, LSE (BSc); *m* 1985, Amanda C, da of late A J McCance, of London SW19; *Career* wine supplier; *Style—* The Hon Adam Bancroft; 51 Rossiter Rd, London SW12 (☎ 081 675 1832)

BANCROFT, Brig Donald Royle Jackson; OBE (1961); s of Maj Peter Henson Bancroft (d 1969), and Florence Adolphine, *née* Jackson (d 1962); *b* 18 July 1916; *Educ* RMA Sandhurst; *m* 1 (m dis), Phyllis Catherine, *née* Angas (d 1977); m 2, 8 May 1948, Elizabeth Ann Rosetta, da of Maj Lawrence Lee Bazeley Angas, MC (d 1972), of S Aust, London and New York; 1 s (Richard Lee b 23 Nov 1950), 1 da (Catherine Clare Elizabeth b 3 March 1949); *Career* cmmnd KSLI 1936; WWII: France and Burma (despatches), Korea (despatches), E Africa (despatches); cmd KSLI 1953-56, cmd 149 Inf Bde 1962-65, def attaché and cdr Cwlth Mission Korea 1966-68, ret 1968; farmer 1968-, breeder of Sussex Cattle and Blonde d'Acquitaine; pres Kilndown Br Legion, vice pres Bewl Fly-Fishers; *Recreations* shooting, fishing; *Clubs* Naval and Military; *Style—* Brig Donald Bancroft, OBE; Chicks Farm, Kilndown, Cranbrook, Kent (☎ 0892 890 396); Flat 19, 34 Sloane Court West, London SW3 (☎ 071 730 1058)

BANCROFT, Baron (Life Peer UK 1981); Ian Powell Bancroft; GCB (1979, KCB 1975, CB 1971); s of Alfred Ernest Bancroft (d 1954), and L Bancroft; *b* 23 Dec 1922; *Educ* Coatham Sch, Balliol Coll Oxford (hon fell); *m* 1950, Jean Hilda Patricia, da of David Richard Swaine; 2 s, 1 da; *Career* WWII served Rifle Bde; joined Treasy 1947, Cabinet Office 1957-59, PPS to Chllr of Exchequer 1964-66, under sec Treasy 1966-68, under sec CSD 1968-70, dep sec to Dir Gen Orgn & Estabmnts (DOE) 1970-72, cmmr of Customs & Excise and dep chm Bd 1972-73, second perm sec CSD 1973-75, perm sec Enviroment 1975-77, head Home Civil Serv and perm sec CSD 1978-81; dir: Bass 1982-, The Rugby Gp 1982-, (ANZ) Grindlays Bank 1983-, Sun Life Assur 1983-, Bass Leisure Ltd 1984-, ANZ McClaughand Merchant Bank 1987-; visiting fell Nuffield Coll Oxford 1973-81, chm Tstees Mansfield Coll Oxford 1981-, memb Mgmnt Bd Royal Hosp and Home Putney 1982- (chm 1984-88), vice-pres Bldg Socs Assoc 1983-, govr Cranleigh Sch 1983-, memb Advsy Cncl on Pub Records 1983-88, pres Bldg Centre Tst 1987-; *Style—* The Rt Hon the Lord Bancroft, GCB; House of Lords, London SW1

BANCROFT, Hon Simon Powell; er s of Baron Bancroft, GCB (Life Peer); *b* 3 Sept 1953; *Educ* KCS Wimbledon, LSE (BSc); *m* 1985, Vicki Lynn, da of Glenn Rosenqvist, of Dallas, Texas; 1 s (Nicholas b 19 Jan 1990), 1 da (Megan b (twin) 19 Jan 1990); *Career* asst vice pres Swett & Crawford (wholesale insurance brokers) Dallas USA; *Recreations* squash, racquetball; *Style*— The Hon Simon Bancroft; 2001 Bryan Tower, Suite 3970, Dallas, Texas 75229, USA (☎ 214 742 8131)

BAND, David; s of David Band (d 1988), of Ledaig, Argyll; *b* 14 Dec 1942; *Educ* Edinburgh Acad, Rugby, St Edmund Hall Oxford (MA); *m* 1 June 1973, Olivia Rose, da of Benjamin Brind; 1 s (David Robert Benjamin b 2 March 1978), 1 da (Isabelle Olivia Eve b 4 May 1981); *Career* various positions JP Morgan/Morgan Guaranty Trust Co 1964-81, exec vice pres Morgan Guaranty Trust Co 1987-88 (sr vice pres New York 1981-86), md Morgan Guaranty Ltd London 1986-87, dep chm The Securities Assoc 1986-88, chm JP Morgan Securities London 1987-88, dir Barclays plc/Barclays Bank plc 1988-, chief exec Barclays de Zoete Wedd Holdings Ltd 1988-; *Recreations* golf, tennis; *Clubs* Hon Co of Edinburgh Golfers; *Style*— David Band, Esq; Barclays de Zoete Wedd Holdings Ltd, Ebbgate House, 2 Swan Lane, London EC4R 3TS (☎ 071 623 2323, fax 071 956 4612, telex 8812124 BZW G)

BAND, His Hon Judge; Robert Murray Niven Band; MC (1944), QC (1974); s of Robert Niven, and Agnes Jane Band; *b* 23 Nov 1919; *Educ* Trinity Coll Glenalmond, Hertford Coll Oxford; *m* 1948, Nancy Margery Redhead; 2 da; *Career* barr 1947; circuit judge 1978-; *Style*— His Hon Judge Band, MC, QC

BAND, Thomas Mollison (Tom); s of late Robert Boyce Band, and Elizabeth, *née* Mollison; *b* 28 March 1934; *Educ* Perth Acad; *m* 9 May 1959, Jean McKenzie, da of Robert Brien, JP; 1 s (Ewan b 1960), 2 da (Susan b 1962, Margaret b 1966); *Career* Nat Serv RAF 1952-54; joined CS 1954, princ BOT 1966-73, dir Location of Indust DOI Scotland 1973-76, asst sec SO 1976-84, dir Historic Buildings & Monuments 1984-87, chief exec Scottish Tourist Bd 1987-; dir: Taste of Scotland Ltd 1989, Forth Bridge Centenary Trust Ltd 1989-, Edinburgh C of C 1989-, Edinburgh Marketing Co Ltd 1989-; FSA Scot 1984, FIT 1988; *Recreations* skiing, gardening, beating; *Style*— Tom Band, Esq; Heathfield, Pitcairngreen, Perth (☎ 073 883 403); Scottish Tourist Board, 23 Ravelston Terr, Edinburgh (☎ 031 332 0350)

BANDEY, Derek Charles; s of Percy William Bandey (d 1942), of Bedford, and Beatrice Ellen, *née* Lawrence (d 1965); *b* 9 Nov 1924; *Educ* Bedford Modern Sch; *m* 2 Aug 1949, Mary, da of John Henderson Hutcheson (d 1954); 2 da (Pamela Ann b 15 March 1944, d 1971, Jill Mary b 18 Feb 1951); *Career* MN: cadet 1941-45, 3 Offr 1945-47, 2 Offr 1947-49, 1 Offr 1949-51, Master Mariner (foreign going) 1951; William M Mercer Fraser Ltd (formerly Met Pensions Assoc Ltd) 1951-: office mangr 1956-59, area mangr 1959-65, dir 1965-71, dep md 1971-75, md 1975-82 (ret), conslt 1982-; pres: Pensions Mgmnt Inst 1976-78, Soc of Pension Conslts 1978-82; chm Occupational Pension Schemes Jt Working Gp 1980-81, memb Cncl Nat Assoc of Pension Funds (chm Educn Ctee and Parly Ctee) 1981-88 (previously 1970-77); FPMI; *Recreations* sailing, voluntary work; *Style*— Derek Bandey, Esq; 4 Hunters Way, Chichester, W Sussex, PO19 4RB (☎ 0243 527 831)

BANDON, Countess of; Lois; da of Francis Russell, of Victoria, Australia; *m* 1, Sqdn-Ldr Frederick Arthur White, RAF; m 2, 1946, as his 2 w, Air Chief Marshal 5 Earl of Bandon, GBE, CB, CVO, DSO (d 1979, when the title became extinct); *Style*— The Rt Hon the Countess of Bandon

BANERJEE, Dr Arup Kumar; JP; s of Ansumali Banerjee (d 1984), and Maya, *née* Chatterjee; *b* 28 Nov 1935; *Educ* Univ of Calcutta Med Coll (MB BS); *m* 23 March 1959, Dr Aleya Banerjee, da of late Nakuleswar Banerjee; 3 s (Arpan b 14 Feb 1960, Anjan b 12 Sept 1962, Avijit b 2 Dec 1969); *Career* various jr hosp appts in India and UK 1958-67, sr registrar in med Southend Gen Hosp 1967-68, lectr in med Univ of Malaya Med Sch Kuala Lumpur 1968-71, sr registrar in elderly med Portsmouth and Southampton Univ Hosps 1971-73, conslt physician in elderly med Bolton Gen Hosp 1973-, hon lectr in geriatric med Univ of Manchester 1975-; conslt to Nat Health Advsy Serv; various pubns on med topics; memb: Nat Cncl and Exec Br Geriatrics Soc, Central Conslts and Specialists Ctee BMA, Geriatric Ctee RCP London; non-exec memb NWRHA, memb Panel of Experts for Nat Registered Homes Tbnl, chm Bolton Med Exec Ctee; memb: Br Geriatrics Soc, BMA, FRCP Glasgow 1979 (MRCP Glasgow 1965), FRCPE 1980 (MRCPE 1967), FRCP 1982 (MRCP 1967); *Books* Haematological Aspects of Systematic Disease (contrib 1976), The Principles and Practice of Geriatric Medicine (1985, 1990); *Recreations* travel, music, literature; *Style*— Dr Arup Banerjee, JP; 2 Pilling Field, Egerton, Bolton BL7 9UG (☎ 0204 55482); Department of Medicine for the Elderly, Bolton General Hospital, Minerva Rd, Farnworth, Bolton BL4 0JR (☎ 0204 390685/6, 0204 22444)

BANERJEE, Baladeb; s of B C Banerjee (d 1973), of Calcutta, India, and Gouri, *née* Ganguly; *b* 22 Aug 1938; *Educ* Univ of Calcutta (BSc, MA, LLB); *m* 1, 1966 (m dis 1977), Ella; 1 s (Robin b 1974), 1 da (Ranju b 1968); m 2, 27 June 1984, Baruna; *Career* barr of the Middle Temple 1970; chm Social Security Appeals Tbnl; vice chm Bengali Inst, memb Panel of Arbitrators; FCIArb 1977-; *Recreations* social work, cricket; *Style*— Baladeb Banerjee, Esq; 64a Melrose Ave, London NW2 (☎ 081 452 3697); 1 Stone Buildings, Lincoln's Inn, London WC2 (☎ 071 405 6879)

BANERJI, Sara Ann; da of Sir Basil Mostyn, and Anita Mostyn; *b* 6 June 1932; *Educ* various schs and convents GB and S Rhodesia; *m* Ranjit Banerji; 3 c (Bijoya b 13 Dec 1957, Sabita b 26 Jan 1960, Juthika b 18 Nov 1963); *Career* writer; books: Cobwebwalking, The Wedding of Jayanthi Mandel, The Teaplanter's Daughter, Shining Agnes, Absolute Hush; memb PEN Int; *Recreations* painting, gardening, cooking, interior decor, company (especially of husband, daughters, sons-in-law and grandchildren); *Style*— Mrs Sara Banerji; 7 London Place, Oxford OX4 1BD; Gina Murray Pollinger, 222 Old Brompton Rd, London

BANG, Christian Francis Lanyon; s of Christian Lucien Bang, of White House, Old Bosham, nr Chichester, W Sussex, and Agnes Elizabeth Lanyon, *née* Penno; *b* 12 Aug 1948; *Educ* Forres and Crookham Court; *Career* HAC 1967-75; CA Blease Lloyd & Co 1967-72, Thomson McLintock & Co 1973-76, Robson Rhodes 1977-78, Norton Warburg Ltd 1979-80, sr ptnr Christian Bang and Co 1981-; dir several cos incl Bow Gp 1975-84; FCA; *Recreations* riding, sailing; *Clubs* Itchenor Sailing; *Style*— Christian Bang, Esq; 44 Cathcart Rd, London SW10 9JQ; Francis House, Francis St, London SW1P 1DE (☎ 081 834 6262)

BANGOR, 7 Viscount (I 1781); Edward Henry Harold Ward; also Baron Bangor (I 1770); s of 6 Viscount Bangor, PC, OBE; *b* 5 Nov 1905; *Educ* Harrow, RMA Woolwich; *m* 1, 1933 (m dis 1937), Elizabeth, da of Thomas Balfour, JP, of Wrockwardine Hall, Wellington, Salop; m 2, 1937, May Kathleen (d 1969), da of W Middleton, of Shanghai; m 3, 1947 (m dis 1951), Leila Mary (d 1959), da of David Rimington Heaton, DSO; 1 s; m 4, 1951, Mrs Marjorie Alice Simpson, da of late Peter Banks; 1 s (Hon Edward Ward), 1 da (Hon Mrs (Sarah) Baker - the actress Lalla Ward); *Heir* s, Hon William Ward; *Career* broadcaster and journalist, sometime Reuter's correspondent in China and Far East; BBC news observer: Finland 1939-40, Libya 1941, Germany 1945, worldwide 1947-65; *Clubs* Savile, Garrick; *Style*— The Rt Hon The Viscount Bangor; 59 Cadogan Square, London SW1 (☎ 071 235 3202)

BANGOR, Bishop of 1983-; Rt Rev John Cledan Mears; s of Joseph Mears (d 1972), of Aberystwyth, and Anna Lloyd Mears (d 1968); *b* 8 Sept 1922; *Educ* Ardwyn GS Aberystwyth, Univ Coll of Wales Aberystwyth (BA, MA), Wycliffe Hall Oxford; *m* 1949, Enid Margaret, da of James Tudor Williams (d 1952), of Glamorgan; 1 s (Wyn b 1950), 1 da (Eleri b 1955); *Career* curate: Mostyn 1947-49, Rhosllannerchrugog 1949-55; vicar of Cwm 1955-58, lectr (chaplain) St Michael's Coll Llandaff, subwarden UC of Wales Cardiff 1967-73 (lectr 1959-67), vicar of Gabalfa 1973-82, clerical sec Governing Body 1977-82, hon canon of Llandaff Cathedral 1981; author of articles on: Eucharistic Sacrifice, Prayers For the Dead, Comparative Religion, Marriage and Divorce; *Recreations* hill walking, long distance paths; *Style*— The Rt Rev the Bishop of Bangor; Ty'r Esqob, Bangor, Gwynedd LL57 2SS (☎ 0248 362895)

BANHAM, Belinda Joan; CBE (1977), JP; da of Col Charles Henry Unwin (d 1939), of Chelsea, and Winifred Woodman, *née* Wilson (d 1922); *Educ* privately, West Bank Sch, Univ of London (BSc); *m* 1939, Terence Middlecott Banham, s of Rev Vivian Greaves Banham, MC (d 1973); 2 s (John, Simon), 2 da (Susan, Joanna); *Career* chm: Cornwall & Isles of Scilly Health Authy 1967-77, Kensington Chelsea & Westminster FPC 1979-85, Paddington & N Kensington Health Authy 1981-86; non-exec dir and vice-chm Lambeth Southwark and Lewisham Family Health Authy 1990-; memb: SW Regnl Hosp Bd 1965-74, MRC 1979-87; vice chm Disabled Living Fndn 1983-90; memb Lambeth Southwark & Lewisham FPC 1987-90; conslt Health Servs Div Business Sciences Ltd; *Style*— Mrs Terence Banham, CBE, JP; Ponsmaen, St Feock, Truro, Cornwall TR3 6QG (☎ 0872 862275); 81 Vandon Court, Petty France, London SW1

BANHAM, John Michael Middlecott; s of Terence Middlecott Banham, and Belinda Joan Banham, CBE, JP, *née* Broadbent; *b* 22 Aug 1940; *Educ* Charterhouse, Queens' Coll Cambridge (MA); *m* 30 Oct 1965, Frances Barbara Molyneux, da of Cdr R M Favell, DSC, RN, of St Buryan, Cornwall; 1 s (Mark Richard Middlecott b 1968), 2 da (Serena Frances Tamsin b 1970, Morwenna Bridget Favell b 1972); *Career* temp asst princ Dip Serv 1962-64, mktg exec J Walter Thompson 1964-65, mktg dir Mktg Div Reed International 1965-69; McKinsey & Co Inc 1969-83: assoc 1969-75, princ 1975-80, dir 1980-83; first controller Audit Cmmn for Local Authorities 1983-87, dir gen CBI 1987-; Hon LLD Bath, Hon DSc Loughborough Univ of Technol; *Books* numerous reports on mgmnt, health and local authy servs; *Recreations* gardening, cliff walking, sailing, ground clearing; *Clubs* Travellers, Oriental; *Style*— John Banham, Esq; Centre Point, 103 Oxford St, London WC1A (☎ 071 379 7400)

BANISTER, (Halcyone) Judith; da of Charles John Banister (d 1953), of Torquay, and May, *née* Fowler (d 1972); *b* 8 May 1925; *Educ* Richmond Co Sch for Girls, King's Coll London (BA); *Career* asst ed Watchmaker, Jeweller and Silversmith 1948-60, PRO Smiths' Clocks & Watches Ltd 1961-63, hon ed Proceedings of the Silver Soc 1961-87, pt/t curator silver and jewellery museum of James Walker Ltd 1964-84, ed The Goldsmiths' Review 1985-87; ed Right Ahead Putney Cons Assoc 1948-60; PRO to various membs of antique, silver and jewellery trades 1963-; Freeman City of London 1977, Liveryman Worshipful Co of Goldsmiths 1984; hon memb Silver Soc 1961-, FGA 1959; *Books* Old English Silver (1965), English Silver (1965), Gli Argenti Inglese (1966, in English 1969), Late Georgian and Regency Silver (1971), Mid-Georgian Silver (1972), Collecting Antique Silver (1972), Country Life Pocket Book of Silver (1982); *Style*— Miss Judith Banister; 20 Marlborough Gdns, Lovelace Rd, Surbiton, Surrey KT6 6NF (☎ 091 399 1707)

BANISTER, (Stephen) Michael Alvin; s of Dr Harry Banister (d 1963), of Grantchester, Cambridge, and Idwen, *née* Thomas (d 1980); *b* 7 Oct 1918; *Educ* Eton, King's Coll Cambridge (MA); *m* 1944, Rachel Joan, da of Claude Vivian Rawlence (d 1967), of Weybridge, Surrey; 4 s (Peter, Christopher and David (twins), Huw); *Career* Maj HG 1944; FO 1939-45; Min of Civil Aviation 1946, private sec to 6 successive Mins of Tport & Civil Aviation 1950-56, asst sec Miny of Tport and Bd of Trade 1956-70, UK Shipping Delg UNCTAD 1964, under sec DOE and Dept of Tport 1970-78, UK dep in Euro Conf of Mins of Tport 1976-78; dir Taylor & Francis Ltd 1978-, fndr ed Transport Reviews 1981-; memb Nat Insur Appeals Tribunal 1978-85, sec Br and Foreign Sch Soc 1978-; *Recreations* country, walking, singing, formerly cricket (played Univ of Cambridge vs Aust 1938); *Style*— Michael Banister, Esq; Bramshaw, Lower Farm Rd, Effingham, Surrey (☎ 0372 452778); BFSS, Richard Mayo Hall, Eden St, Kingston on Thames (☎ 081 546 2379); T & F, 4 John St, London (☎ 071 405 2237)

BANISTER, (John) Michael; s of Frederick Banister (d 1963); *b* 30 Nov 1924; *Educ* St Peter's Sch York, BNC Oxford (MA); *m* 1960, Thelma, da of William Smart, of Solihull; 1 s, 1 da; *Career* chm Toon & Heath 1972-84 (md 1961-72), dir Royds Toon & Heath Ltd 1984-85, ret 1986; FIPA; *Recreations* philately, bridge, genealogy; *Clubs* Rotary; *Style*— Michael Banister, Esq; 102 Ladbrook Rd, Solihull, W Mids B91 3RW (☎ 021 705 3332)

BANKES, James Leslie Kennerley; *b* 10 March 1935; *Educ* King Edward VII Sch Kings Lynn, St Mary's Hosp Med Sch Univ of London (MB BS); *m* 1962, Josephine Anne, *née* Kingswell; 2 s (Angus Geoffrey Kingswell b 17 Feb 1964, Marcus James Kennerley b 27 Jan 1967); *Career* various appts as sr house offr, registrar and sr registrar (St Mary's Hosp, Western Ophthalmic Hosp, Moorfields Eye Hosp), conslt ophthalmic surgn St Mary's Hosp 1969-; hon conslt ophthalmic surgn Royal Hosp Chelsea and St Luke's Hosp for the Clergy, subdean St Mary's Hosp Med Sch Univ of London, former sec Ophthalmological Soc of the UK; Master Worshipful Co of Spectacle Makers 1991; memb BMA, FRCS, FCOphth; *Style*— James Bankes, Esq; 64 Kingsley Way, Hampstead Garden Suburb, London N2 0EW (☎ 081 455 9044); 107 Harley Street, London W1N 1DG (☎ 071 580 3614, fax 071 935 5187)

BANKES, Hon Mrs (Juliet Anne); *née* Williamson; da of 3 Baron Forres (d 1978), and Gillian Ann Maclean, *née* Grant (who *m* 2, 1968, Miles Herman de Zoete, who d 1987); *b* 29 Aug 1949; *m* 1972, Nigel John Eldon Bankes; 1 s, 2 da; *Style*— The Hon Mrs Bankes

BANKHEAD, Jack William; s of Franck James Bankhead, and Rita, *née* Jones; *b* 29 Dec 1942; *Educ* Wandsworth Comp; *m* 30 Sept 1967, Ann Christina, da of Frank Trotter; 2 s (William John b 17 May 1972, Barney Jack b 28 May 1975), 1 da (Corina Ann b 13 Jan 1979); *Career* advertising photographer; art studio mangr 1972, estab own studio 1979; notable campaigns incl series for John Player Special; *Recreations* tennis, skiing, swimming; *Style*— Jack Bankhead, Esq; 31B Harbour Yard, Chelsea Harbour, SW10

BANKS, Brian; s of Albert Edward Banks (d 1981), of London, and Evylyn Lilian, *née* Bilyard (d 1981); *b* 2 July 1938; *Educ* Henry Thornton GS; *m* 6 Oct 1962, Barbara Eileen, da of Edward Townsend (d 1973), of London; 2 s (Andrew Nicholas b 1964, Alexander James b 1973), 1 da (Joanne b 1967); *Career* res analyst L Messel & Co 1964-66, investmt mangr Nat Provident Inst 1966-68, md Britannia Arrow Hldgs 1975-78 (investmt dir 1968-78), dir Dunbar Gp and md Dunbar Fund Mangrs 1978-83, chm Guildhall Investmt Mgmnt 1983-86, md Asset Tst plc 1986-89; Freeman City of London; memb Worshipful Co of Carmen; *Recreations* golf; *Clubs* RAC, MCC, City Livery; *Style*— Brian Banks, Esq; Johnson Fry Asset Managers plc, Dorland House, 20 Regent St, London SW1Y 4PZ (☎ 071 839 5688, fax 071 839 4348, telex 9419723, AssetM, car 0836 234949)

BANKS, Hon Mrs (Caroline Veronica); *née* Hamilton-Russell; da of 10 Viscount Boyne, JP, DL; *b* 15 Feb 1957; *m* 1975, David George Fothergill Banks, FRICS; 1 s,

1 da; *Style*— The Hon Mrs Banks; Upper Norton, Bromyard, Herefordshire; Banks and Silvers (Chartered Surveyor), 66 Foregate St, Worcester (☎ 0905 23456)

BANKS, Colin; s of William James Banks (d 1985), and Ida Jenny, *née* Hood (d 1976); *b* 16 Jan 1932; *Educ* Rochester Sch of Art; *m* 1961, Caroline Grigson; 1 s, 1 da (decd); *Career* fndr ptnr Banks & Miles (graphic designers) 1958-; design conslt: Zoological Soc 1962-82, Br Cncl 1968-83, E Midlands Arts Assoc 1974-77; art ed Which? 1964-; design advsr: Natural Environment Res Cncl, London Tport, BT, Property Servs Agency, IMechE, SERC, Fndn Roi Bandonin, MOH MacDonald Consltg Engrs, Portsmouth Poly, UN Univ Tokyo and Helsinki; mangr Blackheath Sch of Art 1981-90;IBA Heinrich Mann medal 1971, Gold medal Brno Biennale 1986, Green Award for redesign of phonebook RSA 1989, Silver medal Leipzig Book Fair 1989, Best German Printed Book Frankfurt 1989, BBC Environmental prize 1990; treas Mala Project for Childrens Educn and Welfare India, memb Association Typographiare Internationale; FRSA, FCSD, FSTD; *Books* Social Communication; *Recreations* Indian life and society; *Clubs* Arts, Dirs NY, Wynkyn de Worde (past chm), Double Crown (pres); *Style*— Colin Banks, Esq; Banks & Miles, 1 Tranquil Vale, Blackheath, London SE3 0BU (☎ 081 318 1131)

BANKS, Dr David Charles; s of Charles William John Banks (d 1961), of Brighton, and Jenny Frances Kathleen, *née* Puttick (d 1981); *b* 11 Dec 1938; *Educ* Varndean GS Brighton, The London Hosp Univ of London (MB BS, MD); *m* 3 Aug 1963, Judith Elizabeth, da of Horace Kingsley Evershed; 2 s (Peter b 1964, Philip b 1971), 2 da (Elizabeth b 1966, Gill b 1969); *Career* house offr London Hosp and sr house offr assoc hosps 1962-67, med registrar KCH 1967-69, MRC res fell Med Unit Univ of Nottingham 1969-72, Anglo American res fell Br Heart Fndn at American Heart Assoc 1972-73, assoc in med Harvard Univ 1972; City Hosp Nottingham: conslt physician and pt/t sr lectr in therapeutics 1973-82, conslt physician 1982-, unit gen mangr 1984-86; dist gen mangr Nottingham Health Authy 1986-; memb: Exec Ctee Univ Hosp Assoc, Ethical Ctee SmithKline Beecham Pharmaceuticals, Liver Club 1975, European Cardiac Soc, Cardiac Soc 1979, Assoc of Physicians 1982; FRCP 1979 (MRCP 1966); *Books* ABC of Medical Treatment (1979); *Recreations* walking, golf, photography; *Style*— Dr David Banks; The Mill House, Caythorpe, Nottingham NG14 7ED (☎ 0602 663092); City Hospital, Hucknall Rd, Nottingham NG5 1PB (☎ 0602 691169)

BANKS, Baron (Life Peer UK 1974); Desmond Anderson Harvie Banks; CBE (1972); s of James Banks, OBE; *b* 23 Oct 1918; *Educ* UCS Hampstead; *m* 1948, Barbara, da of Richard Taylor Wells; 2 s; *Career* served WWII M East & Italy KRRC & RA as Maj (Chief PRO Allied Mil Govt Trieste 1946); sits as Liberal Peer in Lords; life assur broker, dir Tweddle French & Co (Life & Pensions) Ltd 1973-; chm Lib Pty Exec 1961-63 & 1969-70; pres: Lib Pty 1968-69, Nat Liberal Club; memb For Affrs & Soc Securities Panel 1961-, Lib Spokesman soc servs 1977-, Dep Lib Whip Ho Lds 1977-, pres Lib Euro Action Gp 1971-; Parly Candidate (Lib): Harrow E 1950, St Ives 1955, SW Herts 1959; vice chm Euro Atlantic Gp 1979-, Br Cncl Euro Movement 1979-; elder of the Utd Reformed Church; *Style*— The Rt Hon Lord Banks CBE; 58 The Ridgeway, Kenton, Middx (☎ 081 907 7369)

BANKS, Frank David; s of Samuel and Elizabeth Banks; *b* 11 April 1933; *Educ* Liverpool Collegiate Sch, Carnegie Mellon Univ; *m* 1, 1955, Catherine Jacob; 1 s, 2 da; m 2, 1967, Sonia Gay Coleman; 1 da; *Career* chm H Berkeley (Hldgs) Ltd, dir Constructors John Brown Ltd 1974-; FCA; *Style*— Frank Banks Esq; Town House, Ightham, Sevenoaks, Kent TN15 9HH

BANKS, Geoffrey Alan; s of William Hartley Banks, of Rothwell, Leeds, and Elsie, *née* Banks; *b* 7 Aug 1936; *Educ* Rothwell GS, Leeds Poly (HNC); *m* 17 Sept 1960, Enid, da of Sgt Rowland Robinson (d 1980), of Leeds; 2 da (Alison Caroline, Sarah Jane); *Career* dir Matthew Hall International Development 1981-88, dir Matthew Hall Mining and Materials 1983-88, md Qualter Hall and Co Ltd 1984- (sales dir 1977-82, dep md 1982-84), dir Telfos Holdings plc 1990-, md Hunslet GMT Ltd 1990-, chm EXCIL Electronics Ltd 1990-; chm Round Table Rothwell 1974, pres Rotary Club Rothwell 1983; memb Cncl: Yorks EEF, ABMEC; CEng 1986, Fell Inst Mining Engineers 1987, memb Inst Mech Engrs 1989; *Recreations* cricket, squash, caravaning, garden; *Style*— Geoffrey Banks, Esq; Qualter Hall & Co Ltd, PO Box 8, Johnson St, Barnsley (☎ 0226 205761, telex 54697, fax 0226 286269, car 0836 639126)

BANKS, James Alastair Crawford; s of Maj Alastair Arthur Banks, MC, of Thursley, Surrey, and Ann Paton, *née* Crichton; *b* 11 March 1947; *Educ* Dover Coll, Greenwich HS USA, Grenoble Univ France; *m* 15 May 1976, Sally Christable, da of Richard Geoffrey Hugh Coles, of Sandleheath, Fordingbridge, Hants; 2 s (Alastair b 1979, Stuart b 1981); *Career* works mangr H Taylor (Drums) Ltd 1972-78, dir and gen mangr Victor Blagden Ltd 1978-88, gp business devpt exec Blagden Industs plc 1988-; chm E London Area Ctee CBI 1987 (memb London Regnl Cncl 1987), pres Barking & Dagenham COC 1987-89, chm Barking & Dagenham Trg Initiative Ltd 1987-89, govr Meadgate Primary Sch Gt Baddow 1988; *Recreations* sailing, squash, bridge, skiing, badminton, theatre; *Style*— James Banks, Esq; Brickwalls, High St, Great Baddow, Essex, CM2 7HQ (☎ 0245 72053); Blagden Industries plc, Tonman Hse, 63-77 Victoria St, St Albans, Herts AL1 3LR (☎ 0727 40907, fax 0727 47460)

BANKS, John; s of John Banks (d 1982), of Rainhill, Lancs, and Jane, *née* Dewhurst (d 1987); *b* 2 Dec 1920; *Educ* Univ of Liverpool (BEng, MEng); *m* 18 Aug 1943, Nancy Olive, da of William James Yates (d 1947), of St Helens, Lancs; 2 s (John Rodney b 30 Oct 1944, Roger Howard b 20 July 1947); *Career* exec chm BICC Res & Engrg Ltd 1975-84, exec dir BICC plc, bd memb St James Venture Capital Fund Ltd 1985-89; visiting prof Univ of Liverpool; Freeman City of London, Liveryman Worshipful Co of Engineers; FEng 1983, FIEE (pres 1982-83); *Recreations* golf, music, bridge; *Clubs* Seaford Golf; *Style*— John Banks, Esq; Flat B1, Marine Gate, Marine Drive, Brighton BN2 5TQ (☎ 0273 690756)

BANKS, (Ernest) John; s of Ernest Frederick Banks, and Marian Blanche, *née* Nuttall; *b* 2 July 1945; 1 da (Charlotte Frederique Marianne b 5 May 1983); *Career* gp chm and chief exec offr Young and Rubicam Gp Advertising Agency; memb: The Prince's Youth Business Trust, The Prince's Trust, Business in the Community; MInstM, memb Market Res Soc GB, FIPA; *Clubs* Bucks, Carlton, RAC; *Style*— John Banks, Esq; Young & Rubicam Ltd, Greater London House, Hampstead Rd, London NW1 7QP (☎ 071 380 6555, fax 071 380 6570, telex 25 197)

BANKS, (William) Lawrence; s of Richard Alford Banks, CBE, of Herefords, and Lilian Jean, *née* Walker (d 1973); *b* 7 June 1938; *Educ* Rugby, ChCh Oxford (MA); *m* 1963, Elizabeth Christina, da of Capt Leslie Swain Saunders, DSO, RN, (d 1988), of Northants; 2 s (Richard b 1965, Edward b 1967); *Career* merchant banker; dep chm Robert Fleming & Co Ltd; hon treas and chm Cncl Royal Postgrad Med Sch Hammersmith, hon treas RHS; tstee: Chevening Estate, Chelsea Physic Garden, Hereford Mappa Mundi Tst; *Recreations* gardening, fishing, shooting, theatre; *Clubs* MCC, Pratts; *Style*— Lawrence Banks, Esq; 13 Abercorn Place, London NW8 9EA (☎ 071 624 5740); Robert Fleming & Co Ltd, 25 Copthall Ave, London EC2R 7DR (☎ 071 638 5858)

BANKS, Lynne Reid; da of Dr James Reid-Banks (d 1953), and Muriel Alexandra Marsh (d 1982, actress stage name Muriel Alexander); *b* 31 July 1929; *Educ* various schs in Canada, Italia Conti Stage Sch, RADA; *m* Chaim Stephenson; 3 s (Adiel b 1965, Gillon b 1967, Omri b 1968); *Career* actress 1949-54, reporter ITN 1955-62, teacher of English in Israel 1963-71; full time writer and lectr 1971-; visiting teacher Tanzania Int Sch 1988; author of numerous plays for stage, tv and radio; *Books* The L-Shaped Room (1960), An End to Running (1962), Children at the Gate (1968), The Backward Shadow (1970), Two is Lonely (1974), Defy the Wilderness (1981), The Warning Bell (1984), Casualties (1987); biographical novels: Dark Quartet, The Story of the Brontes (1976), Path to the Silent Country (sequel, 1977); books for young adults: One More River (1973), Sarah and After (1975), My Darling Villain (1977), The Writing on the Wall (1981), Melusine, a Mystery (1988); childrens' books: The Adventures of King Midas (1977), The Farthest-Away Mountain (1977), I, Houdini (1978), The Indian in the Cupboard (1980), Maura's Angel (1984), The Fairy Rebel (1985), Return of the Indian (1986), Secret of the Indian (1989); history: Letters to My Israeli Sons (1979), Torn Country, An Oral History of Israel's War of Independence (1982); *Recreations* theatre, gardening, talking; *Style*— Ms Lynne Reid Banks; c/o Sheila Watson, Watson Little Ltd, 12 Egbert St, London NW1 8LJ (☎ 071 722 9514)

BANKS, Sir Maurice Alfred Lister; s of Alfred Banks, FRCS, and Elizabeth, *née* Davey; *b* 11 Aug 1901; *Educ* Westminster, Univ of Manchester (BSc); *m* 1933, Ruth, da of Perry D Hall, of Philadelphia; 1 s, 2 da; *Career* joined Anglo Persian Oil Co 1924; Br Petroleum: md 1960, dep chm 1965, ret 1967; chm Bd of Trade Dept Ctee to enquire into Patent Law and Procedure 1967-70; chm Laird Gp 1970-75; FRIC, MIChemE; kt 1971; *Style*— Sir Maurice Banks; Beech Copice, Kingswood, Surrey (☎ 0737 2270)

BANKS, Norman Dinsdale; s of William Dinsdale Banks, MBE (d 1963), and Rose Mary, *née* Sculpher (d 1983); *b* 18 May 1929; *Educ* St Dunstan's Coll Catford London, Univ of London (LLB); *m* 3 Jan 1970, Gwendoline Georgina, da of Flt Lt George Frederick Stubbings (d 1974); *Career* called to the Bar Lincoln's Inn 1952; conslt ed Rating and Valuation Reporter 1978-; chm W Lewisham Cons Assoc 1966-68, memb LLC (Cons) 1961-65, Lewisham Borough Cncl 1959-71 (ldr Cncl 1968-71); *Recreations* gardening, walking, one bull terrier; *Style*— Norman Banks, Esq; 1 Essex Court, Temple, London EC4Y 9AR (☎ 071 936 3030, fax 071 583 1606)

BANKS, Philip Francis; *b* 27 Aug 1933; *Educ* Univ of London (BSc); *m* 1957, Judith Monica; 1 da (Jessica); *Career* Nat Serv Lt Army; md A T Kearney Ltd 1978-85, chm Mgmnt Conslts Assoc 1983, head Int AT Kearney Inc 1986-; *Recreations* politics; *Clubs* Lansdowne; *Style*— Philip Banks, Esq; Ferndale, Pool Hayes Lane, Willenhall, Staffs (☎ 0902 65834); Kearneys, Lon Ednyfed, Criccieth, Gwynedd (☎ 076 671 2926)

BANKS, Robert George; MP (C) Harrogate 1974-; s of late George Walmsley Banks, MBE, and Olive Beryl, *née* Tyler; *b* 18 Jan 1937; *Educ* Haileybury; *m* 1967, Diana Margaret Payne Crawfurd; 4 s, 1 da; *Career* Lt Cdr RNR; memb Paddington Borough Cncl 1959-65, jt fndr dir Antocks Lairn Ltd 1963-67; jt sec Cons Parly Def Ctee 1976-79, memb Cncl of Europe and W Euro Union 1977-81, chm Anglo-Sudan Gp 1983- (sec 1978-83), vice chm All-Pty Tourism Gp 1979- (sec 1974-79); PPS to: Min of State FO 1979-82, Min of State for Overseas Devpt FO 1981-82; memb Select Ctee on Foreign Affrs 1982-83; memb: N Atlantic Assembly 1981-, Acts Alcohol Educn & Res Cncl 1982-88; *Books* Britain's Home Defence Gamble (jtly, 1979); New jobs from Pleasure 1985; *Recreations* travel, contemporary art, architecture; *Style*— Robert Banks, Esq, MP; House of Commons, London SW1

BANKS, Robert James; s of Maj Kenneth Banks (d 1986), of Yalding, Kent, and Nona Banks; *b* 26 Feb 1951; *Educ* Dover Coll, Univ of Wales (BSc); *Career* called to the Bar Inner Temple 1978; co fndr Yalding and Nettlestead Protection Soc; *Recreations* antiques, country pursuits; *Style*— Robert J Banks, Esq; 12 South Square, Grays Inn, London, WC1 (☎ 071 242 1052)

BANKS, Roderick Charles l'Anson; s of Charles l'Anson Banks, of Kingston upon Thames, and Suzanne Mary Gwendoline, *née* Hall; *b* 5 Dec 1951; *Educ* Westminster, UCL (LLB); *m* 11 Aug 1979, Susan Elizabeth Lavington, da of His Hon Judge Albert William Clark, *qv*, of Worthing, Sussex; 2 s (Oliver b 1982, Frederick b 1986); *Career* called to the Bar Lincoln's Inn 1974, legal author; fndr memb Centre for Dispute Resolution; memb Country Landowners Assoc; *Books* co-ed: Lindley on Partnership (14 edn 1979, 15 edn 1984), Lindley & Banks on Partnership (16 edn 1990), Encyclopaedia of Professional Partnerships (1987); *Recreations* reluctant gardener, TV/video addict; *Style*— R C l'Anson Banks, Esq; 3 Stone Buildings, Lincolns Inn, London WC2A 3XL (☎ 071 242 4937, fax 071 405 3896) REF TW)

BANKS, Hon Mrs (Rowena Phyllis); *née* Joynson-Hicks; 2 da of 4 Viscount Brentford, *qv*; *b* 23 Oct 1967; *m* 16 Dec 1989, Simon J Banks, yr s of M J Banks, of Bishop's Stortford, Herts; *Style*— The Hon Mrs Banks; c/o The Rt Hon the Viscount Brentford, Newick Park, East Sussex BN8 4SB

BANKS, Tony; MP (Lab) Newham North West 1983-; *b* 1943,April; *Educ* Archbishop Tenison's GS Kennington, Univ of York, LSE; *Career* sponsored by TGWU, contested (Lab): East Grinstead 1970, Newcastle North Oct 1974, Watford 1979; sometime political advsr to Dame Judith Hart, head of res AUEW 1968-75; asst gen sec Assoc of Bdcasting and Allied Staffs 1976-83; memb: Co-operative Pty, GLC 1970-77 and 1981-86, Cncl of Europe and Western Euro Union Select Ctee on Procedure; chm: GLC Gen Purposes Ctee 1975-77, Arts Ctee 1981-83, London Gp Lab MPs 1987-; last chm GLC 1985-86, London Whip 1988-; former memb Bd: NT, ENO, London Festival Ballet, London Orchestral Concert Bd, Treasy Select Ctee; *Style*— Tony Banks, Esq, MP; House of Commons, London SW1

BANNEN, Ian; s of John James Bannen (d 1958), of Coatbridge, Scotland, and Agnes Clare, *née* Galloway (d 1976); *b* 29 June 1928; *Educ* St Aloysius Jesuit Sch Glasgow, Grace Dieu Prep Sch Leics, Ratcliffe Coll Leics; *m* 16 Nov 1978, Marilyn, da of John Salisbury (d 1984), of Wrexham; *Career* Nat Serv RE; actor; RSC 1951-54, first West End appearance as Marco in A View from the Bridge Comedy 1956-57, title role in Sergeant Musgrave's Dance (Royal Court) 1958, Jamie in Long Day's Journey into Night (Globe) 1958-59, Julian in Toys in the Attic (Piccadilly) 1960; RSC 1961-62: title role in Hamlet, Orlando (to Vanessa Redgrave's Rosalind) in As You Like It, Mercutio in Romeo and Juliet, Iago to Sir John Gielgud's Othello; Yvonne Arnaud Theatre: Dick Dudgeon in The Devils Disciple 1965, The Brass Hat 1972; Hickey in The Iceman Cometh (Royal Lyceum Edinburgh 1974, London Arts and Wintergarten Theatres 1958), Judge Brack to Janet Suzmann's Hedda Gabler (Duke of York's and Edinburgh Festival 1977, Hugh in Translations (Hampstead Theatre and NT, winner Critics' award Actor of the Year) 1981-82, Tyrone in Moon for the Misbegotten (Riverside, Mermaid, American Repertory Harvard and Broadway) 1983-84; recent films and TV incl: Hope and Glory (Best Supporting Actor nomination BAFTA), Flight of the Phoenix (Oscar nomination), Gandhi, Gorky Park, Eye of the Needle, Defence of the Realm, Tinker Tailor Soldier Spy, George's Island, Ghost Dad, The Big Man, Uncle Vanya, The Common Pursuit, Murder in Eden; vice pres Catholic Stage Guild; memb: St Vincent de Paul Soc, American Acad (AMPAS) 1966-, BAFTA; *Recreations* walking, swimming, reading, photography; *Style*— Ian Bannen, Esq; c/o London Management, 235-241 Regent St, London W1 (☎ 071 493 1610)

BANNER; *see*: Harmood-Banner

BANNER, Christopher Victor; s of Samuel Victor Banner (d 1981), of Whinhurst,

Birkenhead, and Nora Dorothy, *née* Stott (d 1968); *b* 4 March 1936; *Educ* Stowe; *m* 1 (m dis 1974), Elizabeth Anne, da of Col R C Blair; 2 da (Juliette Christine b 11 Oct 1964, Fiona Jane b 23 June 1966); m 2, 12 May 1977, Alison Hilary, da of Stanley Gardner; 1 da (Charlotte Sarah b 29 March 1979); *Career* Nat Serv 1 Lt 21 Field Regt RA, TA Capt 359 Medium Regt RA; laboratory technician Shell Mex BP 1956-57, plant asst J Bibby and Sons 1957-58; Samuel Banner Ltd: sales rep, dir of mktg, md; *Recreations* golf, tennis; *Clubs* Racquetts (Liverpool), Artists (Liverpool); *Style*— Christopher Banner, Esq; Samuel Banner and Co Ltd, 59 Sandhills Lane, Liverpool L5 9XL (☎ 051 922 7871, fax 051 922 0407, telex 627025)

BANNER, (David) Ian; s of John David Banner, of Uddingston, Glasgow (d 1989), and Georgina Stewart, *née* Johnston; *b* 14 April 1936; *Educ* Uddingston GS, Univ of Glasgow (BL); *m* 18 June 1975, Mary Elizabeth, da of John Rourke, of Greenock (d 1974); 2 da (Peta b 1978, Clare b 1981); *Career* cmmnd RAF during Nat Serv, flying offr; slr, sr ptnr Neill Clerk of Greenock and Glasgow; chm Sir Gabriel Wood's Mariners' Home Greenock 1982-, chm Greenock Dist Scout Cncl 1989-; *Recreations* tennis, curling, bridge, scouting; *Style*— D Ian Banner, Esq; 33 The Esplanade, Greenock (☎ 0475 20621); 3 Ardgowan Sq, Greenock (☎ 0475 24522, fax 0475 84339)

BANNERMAN, Barbara, Lady; Barbara Charlotte; yr da of Lt-Col Alexander Cameron, OBE, IMS (d 1932), of Southwold, Suffolk; *m* 27 July 1932, Lt-Col Sir Donald Arthur Gordon Bannerman, 13 Bt (d 1989); 2 s (Sir Alexander Patrick, 14 Bt, Sir David Gordon, 15 Bt), 2 da (Ruth Mary Charlotte (Mrs Massey) b 1937, Janet Elizabeth Naomi (Mrs Jackson) b (twin) 1937); *Style*— Barbara, Lady Bannerman; Upwood, 8 Shepley Road, Barnt Green, Worcs

BANNERMAN, Celia Elizabeth; da of Hugh Bannerman, and Hilda, *née* Diamond; *b* 3 June 1944; *Educ* Drama Centre London; *m* Edward Klein; *Career* director and actress; staff dir NT 1978-80 (Lies In Plastic Smiles, Making Love, The Passion, Lark Rise, Strife, Fruits of Enlightenment), assoc dir Bristol Old Vic 1982-83 (Quartermaine's Terms, Translations, The White Devil, Good Fun, Enemy of The People, The Price), assoc dir Theatre Royal Stratford (Sleeping Beauty, Magni, The Proposal); directed: Hank Wangford Band (Edinburgh Festival), La Ronde (Bristol Old Vic), Jack And The Beanstalk (Shaw Theatre London); worked on setting up and prodn of Little Dorrit with Derek Jacobi for Sands Films 1985-86; dir: Beached (Croydon Warehouse) 1987, Bet Noir (Young Vic Studio) 1987, Sinners and Saints (Croydon Warehouse) 1988; assoc prodr The Fool 1989-90, Brookside (Mersey TV) 1990; actress, theatre incl: Dolly in you Never Can Tell (Haymarket London), Lucy in The Rivals (Haymarket), Miranda in The Tempest (Glasgow Citizens), Cecily in The Importance of Being Earnest (Haymarket), Cynthia in The Double Dealer (Royal Ct), Come As You Are (New Theatre London), Viola in Twelfth Night (Regents Park), Katherine in Perkin Warbeck (Other Place RSC), Lady Anne in Richard III (Other Place RSC), Mrs Galy Gay in Man is Man (Other Place RSC); TV incl: Elizabeth Bennett in Pride and Prejudice, Cecily in The Importance of Being Earnest, Lady Diana Newbury in Upstairs Downstairs; film appearances incl: Rachel in The Tamarind Seed, title role in Biddy 1983, Milliner in Little Dorrit 1987; memb Dirs' Guild of GB; *Style*— Ms Celia Bannerman; Harriet Cruickshank, 97 Old South Lambeth Rd, London SW 1XU (☎ 071 735 2933)

BANNERMAN, (James Charles) Christopher; s of Prof Lloyd Charles Bannerman, of Ontario, Canada, and Ethel Leah, *née* Dakin; *b* 23 Feb 1949; *Educ* Univ of Kent at Canterbury (BA); *m* 2 Sept 1988, Sara Elizabeth, da of Thomas Haig; *Career* dancer Nat Ballet of Canada 1968-72, dancer and choreographer London Contemporary Dance Theatre 1975-; choreographed: Treading, The Singing, Sandsteps, Shadows in the Sun, Unfolding Field, Ascending the Climbing Frame, Coils of Silence; head of Sch of Dance Middx Poly; *Recreations* gardening, travel, wilderness canoe trips in Canada; *Style*— Christopher Bannerman, Esq; 136 Dukes Ave, Muswell Hill, London N10 2QB (☎ 081 883 1314); c/o LCDT, 16 Flaxman Terrace, London WC1 (☎ 071 387 0324)

BANNERMAN, Sir David Gordon; 15 Bt (NS 1682), of Elsick, Kincardineshire; OBE (1976); yr s of Sir Donald Arthur Gordon Bannerman, 13 Bt (d 16 Aug 1989), and Barbara Charlotte, *née* Cameron; suc bro Sir Alexander Patrick Bannerman, 14 Bt (d 21 Nov 1989); *b* 18 Aug 1935; *Educ* Gordonstoun, New Coll Oxford (MA); *m* 25 June 1960, Mary Prudence, er da of Rev Philip Frank Ardagh-Walter, Vicar of Woolton Hill, Hants; 4 da (Clare Naomi b 1961, Margot Charlotte b 1962, Arabella b 1965, Clodagh Isobel Rose b 1975); *Heir* kinsman, Mordaunt Francis Bannerman b 22 Dec 1907; *Career* 2 Lt Queen's Own Cameron Highlanders 1954-56, HOMCS (Tanganyka) 1960-63, MOD 1963-; *Style*— Sir David Bannerman, Bt; Upwood, 8 Shepley Rd, Barnt Green, Worcester; Royal Bank of Scotland, Holt's Whitehall Branch, Kirkland House, Whitehall, London SW1

BANNERMAN, (George) Gordon; s of George Bannerman (d 1961), of Glasgow; *b* 25 Feb 1932; *Educ* Glasgow HS, Glasgow Acad, Sidney Sussex Coll Cambridge (MA); *m* 1959, Ann, da of James Gemmell (d 1977), of Milngavie; 1 s, 1 da; *Career* actuary; dir and actuary C T Bowring & Layborn Ltd 1972, dir and chief actuary Fenchurch Fin Servs Ltd 1987; ACII, AIA, ASA, FPMI, FFA; *Style*— Gordon Bannerman, Esq; 37 Westbury Rd, London N12 7PB (☎ 081 445 1795)

BANNERMAN, Joan, Lady; Joan Mary; da of late John Henry Wilcox, of Tadcaster, Yorks; *m* 1977, Sir Alexander Patrick Bannerman, 14 Bt (d 1989); *Style*— Joan, Lady Bannerman; 73 New Causeway, Reigate, Surrey

BANNINGTON, Adrian John (Barney); s of Donald Bertram Bannington, of Tollesbury, Essex, and Sylvia Ada, *née* Mann; *b* 4 April 1956; *Educ* Lucton Boys Secdy Sch Loughton, W Hatch Tech High Chigwell, NE London Poly; *m* 19 Sept 1981, Elizabeth Jennifer Jane, da of Capt Peter Richardson, JP, of Loughton, Essex; 1 da (Amy Louise b 16 April 1985); *Career* Saffery Champness (formerly Saffery Sons & Co) 1975-1988: articled 1979, qualified CA 1980, mangr 1985-88; fin dir: Planning Res & Systems plc 1988-90, Telehouse International Corporation of Europe Ltd 1990-; memb ICAEW; *Recreations* sailing, golf, chess; *Style*— Barney Bannington, Esq; 9 Chapel Rd, Epping, Essex (☎ 0378 72625); Telehouse International Corporation of Europe Ltd, Coriander Ave, London E14 (☎ 071 512 0550)

BANNISTER, Brian; s of Norman Bannister, and Sarah Ann, *née* Jolly; *b* 31 Dec 1933; *Educ* King Edward VII Sch Lytham St Annes, Birmingham Sch of Architecture (Dip Arch); *m* 1, 5 April 1961 (m dis 1973), Pauline Mary, da of Jack Miller (d 1987), of Preston, Lancs; 1 s (Dominic b 3 Feb 1964, d 1981), 1 da (Karen b 23 July 1962); m 2, 25 May 1973, Avril, da of James Wigley Allen (d 1987); 1 s (Richard b 8 July 1975), 1 da (Katie 10 Feb 1979); *Career* Nat Serv 1958-59; architect Lancs CC 1956-58 and 1969; John H D Madin and Ptnrs: sr architect 1959-64, assoc 1964-68; assoc i/c Watkins Grey Woodgate International (Birmingham Office) 1968; ptnr: Burman Goodhall and Ptnrs 1970-72, Brian Bannister and Assocs 1972-85, Brian Bannister Partnership 1985-; dir Co-ordinated Project Management Ltd 1971-, dir and co sec BMW Properties Ltd 1986-; sub ed Architecture West Midlands 1970-75, memb Ctee Birmingham Architectural Assoc 1972-84 (vice pres 1980-82, pres 1982-84); ARIBA 1958, FBIM 1980; *Recreations* golf, squash, sailing; *Clubs* Edgbaston Golf, Edgbaston Priory; *Style*— Brian Bannister, Esq; 180 Lordswood Rd, Harborne, Birmingham B17 8QH (☎ 021 426 3671); Brian Bannister Partnership, Belmont House, 40 Vicarage Rd, Edgbaston, Birmingham B15 3EZ (☎ 021 454 7373, fax 021 454 7109); BMW Properties Ltd, Belmont House, 40 Vicarage Rd, Edgbaston, Birmingham B15 3ES (☎ 021 454 4764); Co-ordinated Project Mgmnt Ltd, Belmont House, 40 Vicarage Rd, Edgbaston, Birmingham B15 3ES (☎ 021 454 1516)

BANNISTER, (Richard) Matthew; s of Richard Neville Bannister, of Sheffield, and Olga Margaret, *née* Bennett; *b* 16 March 1957; *Educ* King Edward VII Sch Sheffield, Univ of Nottingham (LLB); *m* 1, 23 June 1984, Amanda Gerrard, da of Dr (Alexander) Percy Walker, of Bentfield, Prestwick, Ayrshire; 1 da (Jessica b 3 Dec 1984); m 2, 14 Jan 1989, Shelagh Margaret, *née* MacLeod; 1 s (Joseph b 1 May 1990); *Career* BBC presenter and reporter: Radio Nottingham 1978-81, Radio One Newsbeat 1983-85; head of news Capital Radio 1987-88 (presenter reporter and prodr 1981-83, asst head of news 1985-87), managing ed Greater London Radio 1988-91, chief asst to BBC's Dir of Corporate Affrs 1991-; memb: Radio Acad, Nat Tst; *Recreations* opera, theatre, rock music, collecting P G Wodehouse first editions; *Style*— Matthew Bannister, Esq; BBC, Broadcasting House, London W1 (☎ 071 580 4468)

BANNISTER, (Arthur) Neil; s of Arthur Bannister (d 1974), of Lytham, Lancashire, and Ida, *née* Powner; *b* 27 Aug 1936; *Educ* The Grammer Sch Manchester, Blackpool Catering Coll; *Career* Nat Serv personal cook GOC-C London dist 1955-57, stagiaire La Tour d'Argent Paris 1957-59, various asst mgmnt posts George Hotel Edinburgh 1960-68, co-proprietor Tullich Lodge 1968-; travelling scholarship HCI, Master Innholder 1981; Freeman City of London 1981; FCMA 1976 (MHCIMA 1955); *Clubs* Travellers'; *Style*— Neil Bannister, Esq; Tullich Lodge, Ballater, Aberdeenshire, Scotland AB3 5SB (☎ 03397 55406, fax 03397 55397)

BANNISTER, Sir Roger Gilbert; CBE (1955); s of late Ralph Bannister and Alice Bannister, of Harrow; *b* 23 March 1929; *Educ* Univ Coll Sch, Exeter and Merton Coll Oxford (MA, MSc), Harvard Univ; *m* 1955, Moyra, da of Per Jacobsson (chm IMF), of Sweden; 2 s, 2 da; *Career* first man to run the four minute mile 1954; hon conslt neurologist: Nat Hosp Nervous Diseases London, St Mary's Hosp London, Oxford Regnl and Dist Health Authy; master Pembroke Coll Oxford 1985-; hon fell: Merton Coll Oxford, UMIST 1974, Exeter Coll Oxford 1979; Hon LLD Liverpool 1972, Hon DLitt Sheffield 1978; Doctorate: Jyvaskyla Univ Finland 1983, Univ of Bath 1984, Univ of Rochester NY USA 1985, Univ of Pavia Italy 1986, Williams Coll USA 1987; FRCP; kt 1975; *Style*— Sir Roger Bannister, CBE; The Master's Lodgings, Pembroke College, Oxford OX1 1DW (☎ 0865 276 444)

BANNOCK, Graham Bertram; s of Eric Burton Bannock (d 1977), and Winifred, *née* Sargent (d 1972); *b* 10 July 1932; *Educ* Crewkerne Sch, LSE (Bsc); *m* 26 Feb 1971, Françoise Marcelle, *née* Vranck; 1 s (Laurent Graham b 1972); *Career* Sgt RASC 1950-52; market analyst Ford Motor Co 1955-56; asst mangr: market res Richard Thomas & Baldwins Ltd 1957-58, Rover Co 1958-60; sr admin OECD Paris 1960-62; chief of econ and market res Rover Co 1962-67; mangr Advanced Progs Ford of Europe Inc 1968-69, dir Res Ctee of Inquiry on Small Firms 1970-71; md: Econ Advsy Gp Ltd 1971-81, Economist Intelligence Unit Ltd 1981-84; chm Graham Bannock & Ptnrs Ltd 1985-, exec dir Central Banking Publications Ltd 1990-; *Books* Business Economics and Statistics (with A J Merrett, 1962), The Juggernauts (1971), The Penguin Dictionary of Economics (with R E Baxter and Evan Davis, 1972), How to Survive the Slump (1975), Smaller Business in Britain and Germany (1976), The Economics of Small Firms (1981), Going Public (1987), The Economist International Dictionary of Finance (1989), Governments and Small Business (with Sir Alan Peacock, 1989), Taxation in the European Community (1990); *Recreations* badminton, gymnastics, karate, the arts; *Clubs* Royal Automobile, London World Traders; *Style*— Graham Bannock, Esq; Graham Bannock & Partners Ltd, 53 Clarewood Court, Crawford St, London W1H 5DF (☎ 071 723 1845)

BAŃSKI, Norman Alexander Fyfe Ritchie; s of Richard Carol Stanislaw Bański, Lt 9 Polish Lancers, of Kincardineshire (d 1970), and Marion Alexandra Watt Fyfe (now Mrs George A Ritchie); *b* 3 Aug 1955; *Educ* Laurencekirk Secdy Sch, Mackie Acad Stonehaven, Univ of Aberdeen (LLB); *Career* slr and NP; ptnr W J C Reed & Sons, registrar births deaths and marriages, cemetery clerk, census offr (S Kincardine) 1981 and 1991; sec and dir: Milltown Community (maladjusted children), Grampian Gliding Club Ltd; tstee various local charitable tsts, dir Howe O'The Mearns Developments Ltd; hon vice pres: Laurencekirk and Dist Angling Assoc, PM Lodge St Laurence 136; past princ: Chapter Haran 8, Office Bearer Provincial Grand Lodge Kincardineshire; memb: Grand Lodge of Scotland, Law Soc of Scotland, Scottish Law Agents Soc, Assoc of Registrars for Scotland, WWF, Esk Dist Fishery Bd, Laurencekirk Business Assoc; *Recreations* golf, angling, clay pigeon shooting, sailing, philately, rugby, gliding; *Clubs* Laurencekirk and Dist Angling Assoc, Caledonian Golf, Montrose, MacKie Acad, F P Rugby, Lodge St Laurence 136, Chapter Haran 8; *Style*— Norman Bański, Esq; W J C Reed & Sons, Royal Banks Buildings, Laurencekirk

BANSZKY VON AMBROZ, Baroness Caroline Janet; da of Harold Arthur Armstrong White (d 1982), of East Molesey, Surrey, and Janet Bell Symington, *née* Clark; *b* 24 July 1953; *Educ* Wycombe Abbey Sch, Univ of Exeter (BA); *m* 31 March 1984, Baron Nicholas Laszlo Banszky von Ambroz of Hungary, qv, s of Baron Dr Laszlo Banszky von Ambroz; 2 da (Genevra b 15 April 1985, Antonella b 1 Aug 1987); *Career* articled clerk rising to audit asst mangr KPMG Peat Marwick McLintock; N M Rothschild & Sons Ltd: Corp Fin Div 1981-84, Admin Div 1984-, chief fin offr 1988, exec dir 1989-; Liveryman Worshipful Co of Farriers 1978-; FCA 1991 (ACA 1978); *Recreations* children, riding, skiing; *Clubs* Roehampton; *Style*— Baroness Nicholas Banszky von Ambroz; N M Rothschild & Sons Ltd, New Court, St Swithins Lane, London EC4P 4DU (☎ 071 280 5000, fax 081 929 1643)

BANSZKY VON AMBROZ, Baron (Hungary) Nicholas Laszlo; s of Baron Dr Laszlo Banszky von Ambroz (d 1965), of London, and Veronica, *née* Racz (now Lady Wyatt of Weeford); *b* 18 July 1952; *Educ* Westminster, Worcester Coll Oxford (MA); *m* 31 March 1984, Caroline Janet, *qv*, da of Harold Arthur Armstrong While, of East Molesey, Surrey; 2 da (Genevra b 15 April 1985, Antonella b 1 Aug 1987); *Career* merchant banker; N M Rothschild & Sons Ltd 1974-84, Charterhouse J Rothschild Gp 1984-86, Smith New Court plc 1986- (head corp fin, dir 1988); *Recreations* riding, skiing, cooking; *Clubs* Roehampton; *Style*— Baron Nicholas Banszky von Ambroz; Smith New Court plc, Smith New Court House, P O Box 293, 20 Farringdon Road, London EC1M 3NH (☎ 071 772 1000, fax 071 772 2919, telex 9413941 SNCA G)

BANTON, Prof Michael Parker; JP (Bristol) 1966; s of Francis Clive Banton (d 1985), of Maids Morton, Buckingham, and Kathleen Blanche, *née* Parkes (d 1945); *b* 8 Sept 1926; *Educ* King Edwards Sch Birmingham, LSE Univ of London (BSc), Univ of Edinburgh (PhD, DSc); *m* 23 July 1952,(Rut) Marianne, da of Lars Robert Jacobson (d 1954), of Lulea, Sweden; 2 s (Sven Christopher b 1953, Nicholas b 1956), 2 da (Ragnhild b 1955, Dagmar b 1959); *Career* Sub-Lt RNVR 1946-47; lectr in social anthropology Univ of Edinburgh 1955-62 (reader 1962-65), prof of sociology Univ of Bristol 1965- (pro vice chllr 1985-88), memb Royal Cmmn on: Criminal Procedure 1978-81, Civil Disorders in Bermuda 1978; memb UN Ctee for Elimination of Racial Discrimination 1986-; pres Royal Anthropological Inst 1987-89; *Books* The Coloured Quarter (1955), West African City (1957), White and Coloured (1959), The Policeman in the Community (1964), Roles (1965), Race Relations (1967), Racial Minorities (1972), Police-Community Relations (1973), The Idea of Race (1977), Racial and Ethnic Competition (1983), Promoting Racial Harmony (1985), Investigating Robbery

(1985), Racial Theories (1987), Racial Consciousness (1988); *Style*— Prof Michael Banton, JP; The Court House, Llanvair Discoed, Gwent NP6 6LX (☎ 0633 400 208); University Dept of Sociology, 12 Woodland Rd, Bristol BS8 1UQ (☎ 0272 30 30 30, ext 3141)

BANVILLE, John; *Educ* Christian Brothers' Schs, St Peter's Coll Wexford; *m* Janet Dunham; 2 s (Colm, Douglas); *Career* journalist 1969-; currently lit ed The Irish Times; novelist; *Books*: Long Larkin (short stories, 1970), Nightspawn (1971), Birchwood, Doctor Copernicus, Kepler, The Newton Letter, Mefisto, The Book of Evidence (shortlisted Booker prize 1989); *Awards* incl: Allied Irish Banks Fiction prize, American-Irish Fndn award, James Tait Black Meml prize, Guardian prize for fiction, Guinness Peat Aviation award; *Style*— John Banville, Esq; Secker & Warburg Ltd, Michelin House, 81 Fulham Rd, London SW3 6RB

BÁNYÁSZ, His Excellency Dr Rezso; *b* 9 Jan 1931; *Educ* Budapest Univ; *m* 1951, Irén Horváth; 2 s; *Career* Hungarian ambass to UK 1981-84; state sec and chm Information Office of Hungarian Govt 1984-; *Style*— HE Dr Rezso Bányász; Information Office, 1-3 Kossuth Square, Budapest, Hungary

BAR, Geoffrey; s of Frank Gordon Henry Bar (d 1979); *b* 19 March 1929; *Educ* Aldenham; *m* 1954, Jeannie Campbell Penton, da of Arthur Wellington Blackwood (d 1964); 3 s; *Career* asst md Dickinson Robinson Group, divnl chief exec DRG Packaging; chief exec: Milk Mktg Bd 1981-85, Dairy Crest Ltd 1985-; FCA; *Recreations* tennis, sailing, music, squash, skiing; *Clubs* Royal Lymington Yacht, Milford Country; *Style*— Geoffrey Bar, Esq; 6 Leicester House, Ditton Close, Thames Ditton, Surrey (☎ 081 398 4101); Dairy Crest House, Portsmouth Road, Surbiton, Surrey KT6 5QL (☎ 081 398 4155, telex 8956671)

BARBARY, Lady Pamela Joan; *née* Nugent; o da of 12 Earl of Westmeath (d 1971), and Doris, *née* Imlach (d 1968); *b* 31 Jan 1921; *m* 23 Sept 1950, Lt-Col Peter John Barbary, OBE, GM, TD, DL (d 1969), eldest s of late Brig John Ewart Trounce Barbary, CBE, TD, ADC, DL, of Trevarth House, Gwennap, Cornwall; 1 s, 1 da; *Career* sometime Section Officer WAAF; *Style*— The Lady Pamela Barbary; Briar Rose Cottage, 17 Landeryon Gdns, Penzance, Cornwall TR18 4JN

BARBER, Albert James; *b* 14 June 1943; *Educ* Canterbury Coll of Art; *Career* joined George Rainbird Publishing Studio, writer and dir of Playschool 1975 and Play Away, deviser, prodr and dir of Think of a Number 1978 (BAFTA Award, ABU Prize), deviser and prodr of Think Again 1981 (BAFTA nomination, Emmy nomination, Prix Jennes Award, ABU Prize), prodr Windmill 1987 (BAFTA nomination), prodr Grange Hill 1989 (dir 1988, BAFTA nomination); memb Royal Inst of GB; *Recreations* sub aqua, graphic design, photography; *Clubs* BSAC; *Style*— Albert Barber, Esq; BBC TV Centre, London W12 7JR

BARBER, Anthony Julian; s of Frank Douglas Barber, of Wandsworth, London, and Elizabeth Joan, *née* Nolan; *b* 28 March 1960; *Educ* Dulwich, St John's Coll Oxford (scholar, BA); *m* 6 Oct 1990, Pauline Anne, *née* Tunnicliffe; *Career* corr Reuters News Agency: joined 1981, US 1982-83, Austria 1983-84, Poland 1984-85, USSR 1985-87, US 1987-88, Yugoslavia 1989-90; foreign specialist writer Independent on Sunday 1990-; *Recreations* chess, assembling archives on the Spanish Inquisition; *Style*— Anthony Barber, Esq; The Independent on Sunday, Newspaper Publishing plc, 40 City Rd, London EC1Y 2DH (☎ 071 415 1331, fax 071 415 1366)

BARBER, Baron (Life Peer UK 1974), of Wentbridge, W Yorks; Anthony Perrinott Lysberg Barber; TD, PC (1963); s of late John Barber, CBE, of Doncaster, and Musse, *née* Lysberg; *b* 4 July 1920; *Educ* Retford GS, Oriel Coll Oxford (MA, LLB); *m* 1, 1950, Jean Patricia (d 1983), da of Milton Asquith, of Wentbridge; 2 da (Hon Louise Patricia Lysberg b 1951, Hon Josephine Julia Asquith (Hon Mrs Bradby) b 1952); m 2, 8 Sept 1989, Mrs Rosemary Youens, da of Canon Youens of Brodsworth; *Career* called to the Bar 1948; MP (C): Doncaster 1951-64, Altrincham and Sale 1965-74; Chllr of Exchequer 1970-74; chm Cons Pty Orgn 1967-70; chm Standard Chartered Bank 1974-87; memb: Franks Ctee on The Falklands 1982, Cwlth Eminent Persons Gp on SA 1985-86; *Style*— The Rt Hon The Lord Barber, TD, PC; House of Lords, London SW1

BARBER, Antonia; *see*: Anthony, Barbara

BARBER, Colin Thomas; s of Frank Barber, OBE, of Folkestone, Kent, and Lilian Barber, MBE; *b* 8 Feb 1948; *Educ* Haileybury, Kingston Coll of Advanced Technol, Univ of London (BSc Econ); *m* 9 June 1973, Diana Elizabeth, da of Peter Parkyn (d 1987), of SA; *Career* CA 1972; dir: Scac UK Ltd, Socomar Ltd, F Barber Properties Ltd; memb Bidborough Gardening Assoc, Bidborough Amateur Dramatic Soc, Tonbridge Oast Theatre; FCA 1979; *Recreations* gardening, spectating amateur dramatics, tennis, bridge, watching rugby union and American football; *Clubs* Old Haileyburian RFC, Bidborough Tennis, Leigh Tennis, The Club, The Danish, CGA, IOD; *Style*— Colin T Barber, Esq; Bidborough Close, Frank's Hollow Rd, Bidborough, Kent TN3 0UD; c/o Scac UK Ltd, 9 Fairway, Green Lane, Hounslow, Middlesex TW4 6BU

BARBER, Prof David John; s of George William Barber (d 1981), and Amelia Sarah, *née* Harris (d 1973); *b* 14 Feb 1935; *Educ* Wanstead HS London, Univ of Bristol (BSc, PhD); *m* 1, 26 July 1958 (m dis 1974), Vivien Joan, da of Leslie George Hayward (d 1969); 2 s (Douglas b 1961, Peter b 1961, d 1979), 2 da (Rosalind b 1964, Alison b 1966); m 2, 17 Oct 1975, Jill Elizabeth Edith, da of Frank Joseph Sanderson, of Great Holland, Essex; 1 s (Alastair b 1978); *Career* investigator Alcan Int 1959-62, gp leader Nat Bureau of Standards USA 1963-65 (scientist 1962-63); visiting scholar: Univ of California 1970-71, 1980 and 1989, Pennsylvania State Univ 1979-80; pro vice chllr Univ of Essex 1981-85 (lectr 1965-74, sr lectr 1974-7 1979-), visiting scholar State Univ of NY 1989; vice pres Mineralogical Soc (GB) 1987-88 (memb cncl 1985-88); memb: Inst of Physics, Mineralogical Soc GB, Mineralogical Soc USA, Royal Microscopical Soc; *Books* Introduction to the Properties of Condensed Matter (with R Loudon, 1989), Deformation Processes in Minerals, Ceramics and Rocks (ed with P G Meredith, 1990); *Recreations* sailing, gardening, carpentry; *Clubs* Royal Harwich Yacht; *Style*— Prof David Barber; Physics Department, University of Essex, Wivenhoe Park, Colchester, Essex CO4 3SQ (☎ 0206 873388, fax 0206 873598, telex 98440 UNILIB

BARBER, David Stewart; s of Jack Barber (d 1961), of Manchester, and Margaret, *née* Hall (d 1960); *b* 21 Sept 1931; *Educ* Rossendale GS; *m* 25 Jan 1965, Hazel Valerie, da of Francis Smith (d 1968), of Whitstable, Kent; 1 s (Nicholas b 1968), 1 da (Suzanna b 1971); *Career* 2 Lt Lancs Fus 1950-52; trainee and subsequently mangr Imperial Tobacco Co (John Player & Sons 1952-57, PA mgmnt consits (various appts) 1958-69, divnl chief exec Bovis Ltd 1969-71, chm and chief exec Halma plc 1972-; *Recreations* tennis, golf; *Style*— David Barber, Esq; Halma plc, Misbourne Court, Rectory Way, Amersham, Bucks HP7 0DE (☎ 0494 721111, fax 0494 728032)

BARBER, (Thomas) David; s and h of Sir William Barber, 2 Bt, TD; *b* 18 Nov 1937; *Educ* Eton, Trinity Coll Cambridge (MA); *m* 1, 1972 (m dis 1975), Amanda Mary, da of Frank Rabone, and wid of Maj Michael Healing, Gren Guards; 1 s (Thomas b 14 March 1973); m 2, 1978, Jeannine Mary, former w of John Richard Boyle (gs of Col Lionel Boyle, CMG, MVO, himself ggs of 7 Earl of Cork and Orrery), by whom she had 3 s, and da of Capt Timothy John Gurney by his w Bridget, half sister of Sir Christopher de Bathe, 6 and last Bt; 1 s (W Samuel T b 23 Sept 1982), 1 da (Sarah b 19 June 1981); *Career* 2 Lt RA 1957-58; *Style*— David Barber, Esq; Windrush House, Inkpen, nr Newbury, Berks RG15 0QY (☎ 048 84 419)

BARBER, Sir Derek Coates; s of Thomas Smith-Barber (d 1967), of The Thatched House, nr Stradbroke, Suffolk, and Elsie Agnes, *née* Coates (d 1967); descendant of John Coates whose three sons due to a disagreement swore not to bear his name 1870, instead they adopted Coates Cotts and Coutts; *b* 17 June 1918; *Educ* RAC Cirencester; *m* 1 (m dis 1981); m 2, 1983, Rosemary Jennifer Brougham, da of Lt Cdr Randolph Brougham Pearson, RN (ka 1946); *Career* farmer and land conslt; fndr memb Farming & Wildlife Advsy Gp 1969-, environment conslt Humberts Chartered Surveyors 1972-, ed chm BBC's Central Agric Advsy Ctee 1974-80, conslt Humberts Landplan 1974-89, chm Countryside Cmmn 1981-91, chm Booker plc Countryside Advsy Bd 1990-; pres: Glos Naturalist's Soc 1982-, pres RSPB 1990- (chm 1976-81, vice pres 1982-90), patron Lancs Heritage Tst 1990, bd memb Centre for Econ and Environmental Devpt 1983-, tstee Farming and Wildlife Tst 1984-, memb Advsy Ctee Centre for Agric Strategy 1985-88, dep chm The Groundwork Fndn 1985-91, vice pres Ornithology Soc of ME 1987-; memb Cncl: Rare Breeds Survival Tst 1987-, Br Tst for Ornithology 1987-89; awards: John Haygarth Gold medal in Agric 1939, Bledisloe Gold medal for Distinguished Servs to UK Agric 1969, Queens Silver Jubilee medal 1977, RSPB Gold medal for Servs to Wildlife Conservation 1983, Massey-Ferguson Agric award 1989; Hon FRAgS 1986, Hon DSc Univ of Bradford 1986; kt 1984; *Books* Farming for Profits (with Keith Dexter 1961), Farming in Britain Today (with Frances and J G S Donaldson 1969), Farming and Wildlife: a Study in Compromise (1971), A History of Hamberts (1980); *Recreations* birds, farming; *Clubs* Farmers; *Style*— Sir Derek Barber; Chough House, Gotherington, Glos GL52 4QU (☎ 0242 673908)

BARBER, Donald Christopher (Chris); s of Donald Barber, CBE (d 1957), of West Byfleet, Surrey, and Henrietta Evelyn Barber, JP, *née* Dunne; *b* 17 April 1930; *Educ* King Alfred Sch, St Paul's, Guildhall Sch of Music; 2 previous m; 1 da (Caroline Mary b 1980); m 3, 6 June 1984, Renate Martha Barber-Hilbich, da of Arno Hilbich (d 1986), of Germany; 1 s (Christopher Julian b 1985); *Career* jazz musician; plays: trombone, trumpet, baritone horn, contra bass; formed amateur band then played in cooperative band with Ken Colyer 1949-54; fndr and ldr Chris Barber's Jazz Blues Band 1954-: over 120 LPs, extensive tours to USA, Japan, Aust, ME and E and W Europe, playing approx 250 engagements each year; hon citizen New Orleans LA USA; *Recreations* motor racing and snooker; *Style*— Chris Barber, Esq; Cromwell Management, The Coach House, 9A The Broadway, St Ives, Huntingdon, Cambridgeshire PE17 4BX (☎ 0480 65695, fax 0480 495382)

BARBER, Edmund Patrick Harty; s of Maj Leslie Bernard Michael Barber (d 1983), of Marley House, Marley Commom, Haselmere, and Ellen, *née* Harty; *b* 25 Aug 1946; *Educ* Glenstal Abbey Sch Co Limerick, Univ Coll Dublin; *m* 20 Dec 1969, Elizabeth Marguerite, da of Eric Fowler Sherriff, of Tewin, Welwyn, Herts; 1 s (Samuel), 2 da (Catherine, Lucy); *Career* CA 1973- (specialising in int tax work and acquisition and disposal); dir: Rigidized Metals Ltd, Courtyard Leisure plc; Freeman City of London, memb Worshipful Co of Chartered Accountants; FCA 1973; *Recreations* squash, golf; *Clubs* Naval and Military, Leander; *Style*— Edmund Barber, Esq; 1 Harmer Green Lane, Digswell, Welwyn, Herts (☎ 043 871 6088); Flat 2, 25 Maiden Lane, Covent Garden, London WC2E 7NA (☎ 071 379 0422); 17-18 Henrietta St, Covent Garden, London WC2E 8QX (☎ 071 379 7711, fax 071 240 2618, telex 266489)

BARBER, Hon Sir (Edward Hamilton) Esler; s of late Rev John Andrew Barber, and Maggie Rorke; *b* 26 July 1905; *Educ* Hamilton Coll Vict, Scots Coll Sydney, Scotch Coll Melbourne, Melbourne Univ; *m* 1954, Constance, da of Capt C W Palmer; 1 s, 1 da; *Career* barr 1929, puisne judge Victoria Supreme Court Aust 1965-77, QC (Victoria) 1955; kt 1976; *Style*— Hon Sir Esler Barber; 1 St George's Court, Toorak, Vict 3142, Australia (☎ 24 5104)

BARBER, Frank; s of Sidney Barber, and Florence, *née* Seath; *b* 5 July 1923; *Educ* W Norwood Central Sch; *m* Dec 1945, Gertrude Kathleen, *née* Carson; 2 s (John b 1951, Alan b 1947 decd), 1 da (Ann b 1948); *Career* WWII Flt Lt RAFVR 1942-46; Lloyd's 1939-, underwriter Frank Barber & Others 1962-81; ptnr: Morgan Fentiman & Barber 1968-, GS Christensen and Partners 1986-; memb: Ctee of Lloyds (1977-80, 1981-85 and 1987), Cncl of Lloyds (1983-85 and 1987); chm Lloyd's Underwriters Non Marine Assoc 1972; dep chm: Br Insurers Euro Ctee 1983, dep chm Lloyd's 1983-84; *Recreations* music, walking, sailing; *Clubs* Royal Dart Yacht, Lloyd's Yacht; *Style*— Frank Barber, Esq; Godden House, Godden Green, Sevenoaks, Kent, TN15 0HP (☎ 0732 61170); Morgan Fentiman & Barber, Lloyd's, London (☎ 071 327 3744, fax 071 623 8233)

BARBER, Glynis Sharon; da of Frederick Werndly Barry van der Riet, of Durban, SA, and Heather Maureen, *née* Robb (d 1973); *Educ* Mountview Theatre Sch; *Career* actress; TV: Blake's 7 1981, Jane 1982, Dempsey and Makepeace (Harriet Makepeace) 1984-86, Visitors 1986; Films: The Wicked Lady 1982, Jekyll and Hyde - The Edge of Sanity 1988, Tangier, Terror, The Hound of the Baskervilles; *Recreations* tennis, yoga, reading; *Style*— Miss Glynis Barber; c/o James Sharkey, 15 Golden Square, London W11 (☎ 071 434 3801)

BARBER, Graham Lister; s of William Lister Barber, JP (d 1976), of Wimbledon, and Marjorie Gertrude, *née* Grose (d 1978); *b* 20 Aug 1930; *Educ* Uppingham; *m* 15 Sept 1956, Carol Valentine, da of Douglas Colinson Brown, of Wimbledon; 2 s (Miles b 1958, Mark b 1960), 1 da (Emma Rose b 1963); *Career* Nat Serv Lt RASC 1949-51; chm and md F H Barber & Co Ltd Fulham 1976- (md 1965, dir 1956); chm: Assoc Dept Stores 1965, Drapers Chambers of Trade 1986-88; first chm Assoc Ind Stores 1976-78, vice chm Sunday Special Campaign 1988-, dir Retail Consortium Cncl 1986; chm Winnowing Club 1966-67, pres Twenty Club 1975-76; memb Glovers Co; *Recreations* golf, bridge; *Clubs* Royal Wimbledon Golf; *Style*— Graham Barber, Esq; Flat 2, 36 Lingfield Rd, Wimbledon, London SW19 7DN (☎ 081 946 4654); F H Barber & Co Ltd, 427-429 North End Rd, Fulham, London SW6 (☎ 071 385 6666)

BARBER, Prof (James Hill) Hamish; s of Richard Barber (d 1988), and Isobel McInnes, *née* Hill (d 1974); *b* 28 May 1933; *Educ* The Edinburgh Acad, Univ of Edinburgh (MB ChB, MD); *m* 20 Sept 1958, Patricia May, *née* Burton (d 1981); 1 s (Colin McInnes b 26 Jan 1964), 3 da (Susan Janet b 29 June 1959, Penelope Jane b 6 Jan 1961, Nicola Lynne b 2 Aug 1963); *Career* Sqdn Ldr Med Branch RAF 1958-63; GP: Callander 1964-66, Livingston 1966-72; Norie Miller prof of gen practice Univ of Glasgow 1974- (sr lectr gen practice 1972-74); hon conslt physician: Glasgow Royal Infirmary 1974-, Western Infirmary 1974-; past memb Chief Scientist Ctee SHHD; memb: BMA, AUTGP, RCGP; FRCGP, FRCP, DRCOG; Bronze medal Univ of Helsinki 1983; *Books* General Practice Medicine (1975), Towards Team Care (1981), General Practice Medicine (2 edn, 1984); *Recreations* sailing, model boat building, photography; *Clubs* SMC, Clyde Cruising, Royal Highland Yacht; *Style*— Prof Hamish Barber; Ledaig, 74 Drumlin Drive, Milngavie, Glasgow G62 6NQ (☎ 041 956 5920); Dept of Gen Practice, Woodside Health Centre, Barr St, Glasgow G20 (☎ 041 332 8118)

BARBER, Dr James Peden; s of John Barber (d 1973), and Carrie Barber (d 1967); *b* 6 Nov 1931; *Educ* Liverpool Inst HS, Pembroke Coll Cambridge, Queen's Coll Oxford (MA, PhD); *m* 3 Sept 1955, (Margaret) June Barber, da of Henry James McCormac, of Beetham, Cumbria; 3 s (Michael James b 1958, Andrew John b 1959, Mark Henry b

1965), 1 da (Anne Elizabeth b 1965); *Career* Nat Serv PO RAF 1950-52; dist offr 1956-61, HM CS Overseas Uganda 1956-63, asst sec to PM and clerk to cabinet 1961-63; lectr Univ of NSW Aust 1963-65, lectr in govt Univ of Exeter 1965-69 (seconded to Univ Coll Rhodesia 1965-67), prof of political sci Open Univ 1969-80, master Hatfield Coll Univ of Durham 1980-, pro vice chllr and sub warden Univ of Durham 1987-; pres Soc of Fells 1985-88; advsr to House of Commons Select Ctee on Foreign Affrs 1990; memb RIIA 1968; Uganda Independence Medal; *Books* Rhodesia: The Road to Rebellion (1967), Imperial Frontier (1968), South Africa's Foreign Policy (1973), European Community: Vision and Reality (1974), The Nature of Foreign Policy (1975), Who Makes British Foreign Policy? (1977), The West and South Africa (1982), The Uneasy Relationship: Britain and South Africa (1983), South Africa: The Search for Status and Security (1990); *Recreations* hockey, walking, choral singing; *Clubs* Royal Cwlth Soc; *Style—* Dr James Barber; Kingsgate House, Bow Lane, Durham City DH1 3ER (☎ 091 384 8651); Hatfield College, University of Durham, North Bailey, Durham City DH1 3RQ (☎ 091 374 3160, fax 091 374 3740, telex 537351 DURLIB G)

BARBER, John Norman Romney; s of George Ernest Barber, and Gladys Eleanor Barber; *b* 22 April 1919; *Educ* Westcliff HS; *m* 1941, Babette, da of Louis Chalu (d 1975); 1 s; *Career* dir: Ford Motor Co Ltd 1955-65, AEI 1966-67; dep chm BL Motor Corp 1973-75 (dir 1968-75); chm: Aberhurst Ltd 1976-89, A C Edwards Engineering 1977-81; dir: Acrow plc 1977-84, Good Relations Group plc 1979-84, Amalgamated Metal Corp 1980-81, Spear and Jackson International plc 1980-85; dep chm: John E Wiltshier Gp plc 1980-88, Cox and Kings 1980-81; chm: C and K Consulting Gp 1981-88, UK Investments 1985-; dir Economists Advsy Gp 1981-, chm Advsy Ctee on Investmt Grants to BOC 1967-68; memb: Royal Cmmn on Med Educn 1965-68, Advsy Cncl for Energy Conservation 1974-75; vice pres Soc of Motor Mfrs and Trades 1974-76; CBIM; *Style—* John Barber, Esq; Balcary, Earleswood, Cobham, Surrey KT11 2BZ; 38 Spring St, London W2 1JA (☎ 071 224 9100)

BARBER, Lynn (Mrs David Cardiff); da of Richard Barber, of Ebbesborne Wake, Wilts, and Beryl Barber; *b* 22 May 1944; *Educ* The Lady Eleanor Holles Sch for Girls, St Anne's Coll Oxford (BA); *m* 1 Sept 1971, David Maurice Cloudesley Cardiff, s of Maj Maurice Cardiff, CBE, of Little Haseley, Oxford; 2 da (Rose b 1975, Theodora b 1978); *Career* asst ed Penthouse magazine 1967-72, staff writer Sunday Express Magazine 1984-89, feature writer Independent on Sunday 1990-, winner of Br Press Awards Magazine Writer of the Year 1986 and 1987; *Books* How to Improve Your Man in Bed (1973), The Single Woman's Sex Book (1975), The Heyday of Natural History (1980); *Recreations* gossip; *Style—* Ms Lynn Barber; The Independent on Sunday, 40 City Rd, London EC1Y 2DB (☎ 071 253 1222)

BARBER, Nicholas Charles Faithorn; s of Bertram Harold Barber (d 1982), and Nancy Lorraine, *née* Belsham (d 1984); *b* 7 Sept 1940; *Educ* Ludgrove Sch, Shrewsbury, Wadham Coll Oxford (MA), Univ of Columbia NY (MBA); *m* 8 Jan 1966, Sheena Macrae, da of Donald Graham (d 1984); 2 s (James Henry b 1969, George Belsham b 1974), 1 da (Fenella Macrae b 1972); *Career* Ocean Group plc: joined 1964, dir 1980-, gp chief exec 1987-; dir: Costain Group plc 1990, Royal Insurance Holdings plc 1991-; tstee nat museums and galleries Merseyside 1986-, vice pres Liverpool Sch of Tropical Med; memb: Advsy Ctee Tate Gallery Liverpool, govr Shrewsbury Sch; CBIM; *Recreations* mountain walking, destructive gardening; *Clubs* Oxford and Cambridge, MCC; *Style—* Nicholas Barber, Esq; Ocean Group plc, 47 Russell Sq, London WC1B 4JP (☎ 071 636 6844, fax 071 636 0289, telex 291689)

BARBER, Paul Jason; s of Victor William Barber, of Peterborough, Cambs, and Phyllis May, *née* Lamb; *b* 21 May 1955; *Educ* The King's Sch Peterborough; *m* 30 Aug 1980, Jennifer, da of John Douglas Redford, of Peterborough, Cambs; 2 s (Michael James b 1 Oct 1984, Stephen Daniel b 23 April 1987); *Career* hockey player; Bronze medal: Euro Cup 1979, Olympic Games 1984; Silver medal: World Cup 1986, Euro Cup 1987; Gold medal Olympic Games 1988; Hockey Player of the Year 1983; memb Chartered Inst of Bldg; *Recreations* travel, golf, most sports generally; *Style—* Paul Barber, Esq; 48 Glendale Ave, Wash Common, Newbury, Berks; c/o G Percy Thentham Ltd, Theale, Reading, Berks

BARBER, Philip Petley; s of Ernest Walter Barber (d 1953), of Moseley, Birmingham, and Stratford upon Avon, and Hilda, *née* McMichael (d 1933); *b* 22 Sept 1917; *Educ* Sebright Sch Wolverley; *m* 18 December 1947, Magdalene Emma (d 1990); 1 s (John Petley b 1953); *Career* TA (Royal Warwicks) RE 1939, cmmnd RA 1941, served BAOR (wounded Rhine crossing 1944), staff Capt 50 AA Brigade 1945-46; articled to Clement Geoffrey Keys (Clement Keys & Co Chartered Accountants Birmingham) 1936, ptnr Clement Keys & Co (Birmingham) 1951 (ret as sr ptnr 1983); appointed approved auditor (Industrial Provident Soc Act) 1954, conslt 1983-89, tstee Hallfield Prep Sch Edgbaston 1979; FCA 1947; *Recreations* golf; *Clubs* Edgbaston Golf; *Style—* Philip Barber, Esq; Sardon Cottage, 24 Woodfield, Belbroughton, Worcs DY9 9SW (☎ 0562 730982)

BARBER, Stephen David; s of Dr Frederick Barber, and Edith Renate Wolfenstein (d 1987); *b* 15 March 1952; *Educ* Univ Coll Sch, LSE (BSc); *m* 1 April 1978, Suzanne Jane, da of Graham Hugh Presland (d 1986); 1 s (Andrew Charles b 1985), 1 da (Claire Louise b 1982); *Career* ptnr Price Waterhouse 1985- (joined 1976); FCA; *Recreations* family, skiing, running, films; *Style—* Steve Barber, Esq; Southwark Towers, 32 London Bridge St, London SE1 9SY (☎ 071 939 3000, fax 071 378 0647, telex 884 657)

BARBER, Stephen Douglas; s of Frank Douglas Barber, journalist and author, of London, and Joan Elizabeth, *née* Nolan; *b* 18 Jan 1955; *Educ* Dulwich, St John's Coll Oxford (MA); *m* 9 April 1983, Kimiko, of Kobe; *Career* Samuel Montagu & Co Ltd 1977-, dir MIM Limited 1985-90, md MIM Tokyo KK 1987-90, pres MIM Investment Trust Management Co Ltd 1990-; memb: Liszt Soc (UK), Guild of Rahere, Asiatic Soc of Japan; *Recreations* book reading and collecting, fresh air, drawing; *Style—* Stephen Barber, Esq; 3-20-2 Ebisu, Shibuya-Ku, Tokyo, Japan (☎ 03 5566 1122); INVESCO MIM plc, 11 Devonshire Square, London EC2M 4YR (☎ 071 626 3434)

BARBIERI, Margaret Elizabeth; da of Ettore Barbieri, and Lea Barbieri; *b* 2 March 1947; *Educ* Durban, Royal Ballet Sr Sch; *m* 1982, Iain Webb; 1 s (Jason Alexander b July 1987); *Career* sr princ Sadler's Wells Royal Ballet 1974-90, guest artist with Birmingham Royal Ballet, freelance teacher and coach 1990-; *Style—* Miss Margaret Barbieri; Chiswick, London W4

BARBOR, Dr Peter Ronald Hubback; JP (City of Nottingham 1980); s of Dr Ronald Charles Blair Barbor (d 1989), and Yvonne, *née* Hubback; *b* 7 May 1936; *Educ* Haileybury, Clare Coll Cambridge (BA, MB), St Thomas's Hosp; *m* 4 Sept 1965, Patricia, da of Dr N J P Hewlings, DSO, of Banbury; 2 s (Edward Patrick b 1966, Sam Ronald b 1968), 1 da (Amelia Frances b 1971); *Career* physician; worked in WI 1967, Vietnam 1970, Libya 1985; conslt paediatrician Univ Hosp Nottingham 1973-; memb of NSPCC Central Exec and chm Professional Advsy Ctee; chm Br Paediatric Assoc Standing Ctee on Child Abuse; FRCP; *Books* Essential Paediatrics (contrib), Hospital Paediatrics, Understanding Child Abuse (1987), Parents' Guide to Childhood Cancer (ed); *Recreations* reading, squash, tennis, skiing; *Style—* Dr Peter R H Barbor, JP; The Old Vicarage, Ab Kettleby, Melton Mowbray LE14 3JA (☎ 0664 822912); University Hospital, Nottingham (☎ 0602 421421)

BARBOUR, Alec Walter; CBE (1989); s of George Freeland Barbour (d 1948), of Fincastle House, Pitlochry Perthshire, and Hon Helen Victoria, *née* Hepburne-Scott (d 1982); *b* 15 Jan 1925; *Educ* Rugby, Univ of Edinburgh (BSc); *m* 6 Sept 1950, Hazel Thomson, da of William Byers Brown, of Peebles (d 1960); 3 s (John b 1951, Alastair b 1953, Walter b 1956), 2 da (Jean b 1958, Kirstie (twin) b 1958); *Career* agric advsr E Scot Coll of Agric 1948-52; ptnr Renton Finhayson Land Agents and Surveyors Aberfeldy Perthshire 1960-75 (conslt 1975-79), factor Duke of Atholl Estates Perthshire 1975-89; pres Bd of Govrs E Scot Coll of Agric 1982-90, vice chm Scot Agric Colls 1985-90; memb Cncl NFU Scot 1960-70 (memb and chm Local Ctees 1954-91); FRICS 1960; *Style—* Alec Barbour, Esq, CBE; Mains of Bonskeid, Pitlochry, Perthshire PH16 5RN (☎ 0796 3234)

BARBOUR, Anthony George; adopted s of George Richard Barbour (d 1989), of Bolesworth Castle, Tattenhall, Chester, and s of Eva Elizabeth, *née* Houry (d 1983); *b* 19 Oct 1938; *Educ* Stowe and New Coll Oxford; *m* 12 Nov 1976, Diana Caroline, da of David Blackwell, of South View Cottage, Combe, Oxford; 2 da (Nina Caroline b 1980, Cleo Diana b 1986); *Career* dir: Bolesworth Estate Co Ltd 1960-, Paramount plc 1989-; chm Cheshire CLA 1986-87, Parly candidate (Cons) Crewe 1964 and 1966; High Sheriff of Cheshire 1987-88; memb Agric Land Tbnl 1976-89; *Recreations* art collector, shooting, tennis; *Clubs* Brooks's; *Style—* Anthony Barbour, Esq; Bolesworth Castle, Tattenhall, Chester GH3 9HQ (☎ 082 925 369)

BARBOUR, (John) Roy; s of Alexander Ewan Barbour (d 1964), of Lanarkshire, and Mary Hart, *née* Cornwall (d 1970); *b* 25 Nov 1929; *Educ* Uddingston GS, Royal Tech Coll Glasgow (now Univ of Strathclyde); *m* 4 July 1953, Jean Livingstone Trotter, da of Flt Lt Alexander Thompson (d 1981), of Ashgill, Lanarkshire; 1 s (Ewan b 1961), 1 da (Jane b 1957); *Career* Nat Serv 1953-55, cmmnd 2 Lt 1954, cmmnd Lt TA 1957, Maj 1964 (cmd 128 Corps FD PK SQM RE, 105 Plant SQM RE), posted R of O 1970; Cooper MacDonald & Ptnrs: sr civil engr 1962-67 and 1967-68, assoc ptnr 1968-70, ptnr 1970-; Lanarkshire Co Youth Half Mile champion 1947; Freeman City of London, memb Worshipful Co of Constructors; MConsE, FICE, FIHT, FFB, FIArb; *Recreations* overseas travel, walking, gardening; *Clubs* RAC; *Style—* Roy Barbour, Esq; Anavryta, 3 Grove Rd, Camberley, Surrey GU15 2DN (☎ 0276 22590); Cooper McDonald Plc Consulting Engrs, Loxford House, East St, Epsom, Surrey KT17 1HG (☎ 0372 728511, fax 0372 742129, telex 24667 IMPEMP-G, car 0836 779136)

BARBOUR OF BONSKEID, Very Rev Prof Robert Alexander Stewart (Robin); MC (1945); s of Dr George Freeland Barbour of Bonskeid and Fincastle, Pitlochry (d 1946); s of Rev Robert Barbour, and his w Charlotte, 2 da of Sir Robert Fowler, 1 Bt (Btcy cr 1885, extinct 1902), and Hon Helen Victoria, *née* Hepburne-Scott (d 1982), eldest da of 9 Lord Polwarth, CBE, DL; *b* 11 May 1921; *Educ* Rugby, Balliol Coll Oxford (MA), St Mary's Coll St Andrews (BD), Yale Univ (STM); *m* 18 March 1950, Margaret Isobel, da of Lt-Col Harold Pigot (d 1982), of Beccles; 3 s (Freeland b 1951, David b 1954, Andrew b 1959), 1 da (Alison b 1956); *Career* late Maj Scot Horse; lectr then sr lectr in New Testament language, literature and theology Univ of Edinburgh 1955-71, prof of New Testament exegesis Univ of Aberdeen 1971-85; dean Chapel Royal Scot 1981-91, Chaplain in Ordinary to HM The Queen in Scot 1976-91, prelate Priory of Scot of Order of St John 1977-; master Christ's Coll Aberdeen 1977-82; chm govrs Rannoch Sch 1971-77, chm Scot Churches' Cncl 1982-86; Hon DD St Andrews 1979; *Books* The Scottish Horse 1939-45 (1950), Traditio-Historical Criticism of the Gospels (1972), What is the Church for? (1973); *Recreations* music, rural pursuits; *Clubs* New (Edinburgh); *Style—* The Very Rev Prof Robert Barbour of Bonskeid, MC; Fincastle, Pitlochry, Perthshire PH16 5RJ (☎ 0796 3209)

BARBY, Hon Mrs (Rosemary Gail); *née* Pritchard; er da of Baron Pritchard (Life Peer); *b* 1946; *m* 1, 1967 (m dis 1977), Ernest Raymond Anthony Travis, *qv*; m 2, 1979, Ian Barby; 1 s, 1 da; *Style—* The Hon Mrs Barby

BARCCANI-DUNSTON, Marcus Armand Chrystos Frans; s of Capt James Frans Barccani-Dunston (d 1945), and Mildred Evelyn, *née* Sydney (d 1984); *b* 18 Oct 1944; *Educ* Univ of Calif Berkeley (BA, MA), Citie Universite de Paris, California Coll (Cert in Teaching), Church Univ Modesto (PhD); *m* 10 June 1989, Anna Marce, da of Capt Dr Demetrius Karsant, of San Fransisco; *Career* teacher and counsellor Alameda Co Juvenile Hall Calif Jan-July 1965, counsellor Stiles Hall YMCA Alameda Calif July-Dec 1965, cultural co-ordinator JL Magnes Meml Museum Berkeley Calif 1968-69, market res analyst MARC Research San Bruno Calif 1971-72, owner and mangr Le Domaine Estate Vineyards Lac Marc de la Belle Quebec Canada 1974-; pres: Lasting Impressions San Bafael Calif 1978-80, Mil-Jim Inc San Rafael 1978- (vice pres, sales mangr, buyer 1973-78), SM-JM Inc Lahaina Maui & San Rafael California 1982-; regent and first conslt to Pres Univ of Calif Berkeley 1983-, sole proprieter Autographia San Rafael; memb: Psychoanalytic Inst of San Francisco, World Affairs Cncl San Francisco, Smithsonian Inst Washington DC, English-Speaking Union (vice pres Sri Lanka), Order of Charles V (Spain), Order of Belgae-Hispanica; Duque de Barcani-Duaston (Spain), Fuedal Baron of Tonbridge, Lord of Dunston Manor; *Books* Real Magic (with Issaz PF Bonewits, 1971); *Recreations* shooting, stalking; *Style—* Marcus Barccani-Dunstan, Esq; 450 Taraval Street, Flat 202, San Francisco, California, USA; 15 Unthank Rd, Norwich NR2 2PA (☎ 0603 612769, fax 0603 762251)

BARCHARD, John Harley; s of William Stanley Barchard (d 1981), of Silvergates, Tranby Park, Hessle, Humberside, and Gladys Evelyn, *née* Bright (d 1956); *b* 22 Aug 1927; *Educ* Hymers Coll, Pocklington Sch; *m* 7 June 1975, Marguerite Claire, da of Oscar Ernest Warburton, of 10 Westella Way, Kirkella, Hull, Humberside; *Career* md: Barchards Ltd (family business founded 1873), Barchards Hldgs Ltd, Barchards (Timber) Ltd; *Recreations* shooting; *Style—* John Barchard, Esq; The Mount, N Ferriby, Humberside (☎ 0482 631628); Barchards Ltd, Gibson Lane, Melton, N Ferriby, Humberside (☎ 0482 633388, telex 592528, car 0860 818838, fax 0482 633751)

BARCLAY, Capt Charles Geoffrey Edward; s of Maj Maurice Edward Barclay (d 1962), of Brent, Pelham Hall, Buntingford, Herts, and Margaret Eleanor, *née* Pryor; *b* 13 Aug 1919; *Educ* Eton, Magdalene Coll Cambridge (MA); *m* 1, 14 June 1947, Laura May (d 1972), da of late Lt-Col Thomas Slings MC, of Danceys, Clavering, Saffron Walden, Essex; 3 s (Thomas Patrick Edward b 16 Jan 1951, Robert Charles William b 26 Dec 1957, Maurice James b 19 Aug 1959), 1 da (Diana Margaret (Mrs Pyper) b 10 March 1949); m 2, 10 May 1985, Kathleen Ann, da of late Sir Edward Foster, of Newton, Bridgnorth, Shropshire; *Career* served N Somerset Yeo 1939-46, Palestine, Syria, Western Desert, Sicily, Italy, France, Belgium, Holland and Germany (despatches, wounded twice); farmer; memb Cncl Royal Agric Soc of England 1959-, chm Hatfield Forest Nat Tst Mgmnt Ctee 1964; master of fox hounds Puckeridge 1947-; High Sheriff Herts 1990; Freeman: City of London, Worshipful Co of Farriers; memb: NFU, Country Landowners Assoc; *Recreations* all fields sports, travel, British countryside; *Clubs* Cavalry & Guards, Farmers; *Style—* Capt Charles Barclay; Brent Pelham Hall, Buntingford, Herts (☎ 0279 777 220); Estate Office, Brent Pelham, Buntingford, Herts (☎ 027 9777 223)

BARCLAY, Christopher Francis Robert; CMG (1967); s of Capt Robert Barclay (d 1941), of Toddington, Beds, and Annie Douglas Dowdeswell, *née* Davidson (d 1958); *b* 8 June 1919; *Educ* Summer Fields, Eton, Magdalen Coll Oxford (MA); *m* 1, 29 Sept

1950 (m dis 1962), Clare Justice, da of Sir John Monro Troutbeck, GBE, KCMG (d 1970), of Horsham; 2 s (Christopher b 1951, John b 1954), 1 da (Jane b 1955); m 2, 14 June 1962, Diana Elizabeth, da of Cdr (John) Michael Goodman (ka 1940); 1 s (Charles b 1963), 1 da (Henrietta b 1966); *Career* Army Offr Cadet 1939; RB: 2 Lt 1940, Capt 1942, Maj 1943; served ME (Egypt, Palestine, Iraq), demobbed 1946; Dip Serv: FO 1946, Br Embassy Cairo 1947, FO 1950, Br Embassy Bonn 1953, FO 1956, Br Embassy Beirut 1959, FO 1960, cnsllr and head Info Res Dept 1962, head Personnel Dept (trg and gen) FCO 1967, asst sec Civil Serv Dept 1969, DOE 1973, sec Govt Hospitality 1976-80; memb Cncl City Univ 1976-84, chm Jt Nat Horse Educn and Trg Cncl 1988-90; Freeman City of London 1942, Master Worshipful Co of Saddlers 1983-84 (Liveryman 1942); FRSA 1984; Cdr of the Order of the Infante DOM Henrique Portugal 1979; *Recreations* fishing, gardening; *Clubs* Army and Navy; *Style—* Christopher Barclay, Esq, CMG; Croft Edge, Hollyhock Lane, Painswick, Glos GL6 6XH (☎ 0452 812 332)

BARCLAY, Sir Colville Herbert Sanford; 14 Bt (NS 1668); s of late Rt Hon Sir Colville Adrian de Rune Barclay, KCMG, 3 s of 11 Bt; suc unc, Sir Robert Cecil de Belzim Barclay, 13 Bt, 1930; *b* 7 May 1913; *Educ* Eton, Trinity Coll Oxford; *m* 1949, Rosamond Grant Renton, da of late Dr W Armstrong Elliott, of Chandler's Ford, Hants; 3 s; *Heir* s, Robert Colraine Barclay; *Career* 3 sec Dip Serv 1938-41; WWII Lt Cdr RNVR; *Books* Crete, Checklist of Vascular Plants; *Clubs* Naval; *Style—* Sir Colville Barclay, Bt; Pitshill, Petworth, W Sussex (☎ 079 85 341)

BARCLAY, David William; s of Theodore Barclay, of Desnage Lodge, Bury St Edmunds; *b* 29 Nov 1942; *Educ* Harrow, Trinity Coll Cambridge; *m* 1967, Celia, da of Maj Hugh Cairns, MC, of St Boswell's, Roxburghshire; 1 s, 1 da; *Career* local dir Barclays Bank: Pall Mall 1973-79, Ipswich 1979-85, London Northern 1985-87; regnl dir E Anglia Reg Barclays Bank 1988-; *Recreations* shooting, fishing; *Clubs* Boodle's, Pratt's; *Style—* David Barclay, Esq; Desnage Lodge, Higham, Bury St Edmunds, Suffolk (☎ 0638 750254)

BARCLAY, Hugh Maben; s of William Barclay (d 1972), and Mary Frances, *née* Laird (d 1983); *b* 20 Feb 1927; *Educ* Fettes, Gonville and Caius Coll Cambridge (MA); *m* 8 Sept 1956, Margaret Hilda Hope, da of George Gilbert Hope Johnston (d 1973), of Beith, Ayrshire and latterly of Sevenoaks, Kent; 2 c (Alison b 1957, David b 1961); *Career* RA Egypt 1948-50; Dept of the Clerk of the House of Commons: joined 1950, sr clerk 1955, dep princ clerk 1967, clerk of Standing Ctees 1976, clerk of Private Bills 1982, clerk of Pub Bills 1988-; *Style—* Hugh Barclay, Esq; 37 Stockwell Green, London SW9 9HZ (☎ 071 274 7375); House of Commons, London SW1 0AA (☎ 071 219 3255)

BARCLAY, James Christopher; s of Theodore David Barclay (d 1981), and Anne Millard, *née* Bennett; *b* 7 July 1945; *Educ* Harrow; *m* 1975, Rolleen Anne, da of Lt-Col Walter Arthur Hastings Forbes, (d 1987); 2 children; *Career* bill broker; chm and jt md Cater Allen Ltd (bankers) 1981-, chm Cater Allen Holdings plc 1985-; *Recreations* fishing, shooting; *Clubs* Pratt's; *Style—* James Barclay, Esq; Cater Allen Holdings plc, 20 Birchin Lane, London EC3V 9DJ (☎ 071 623 2070; telex 888553/4)

BARCLAY, Joseph Gurney; s of Sir Roderick Edward Barclay, GCVO, KCMG, *qv*; *b* 17 Jan 1946; *Educ* Harrow, St Edmund Hall Oxford; *m* 1978, Joanna, da of late Brig Anthony Douglas Brindley, CBE; 1 s, 2 da; *Career* local dir Barclays Bank Birmingham 1978-85, res dir (then dep chm) Barclays Bank SA Paris 1986-; *Recreations* shooting, travel; *Clubs* Cercle de L'Union Interalliée (Paris), Brooks'; *Style—* Joseph Barclay, Esq; c/o Barclays Bank, 54 Lombard St, London EC3

BARCLAY, Brig Neil; DL (Shropshire 1986); s of Eric Lionel Barclay (d 1974), of Chelmsford, Essex, and Muriel Clare, *née* Copeland (d 1975); *b* 18 April 1917; *Educ* Private; *m* 27 Sept 1941, Mary Emma (Mollie), da of David Scott-Shurmer (d 1964), of Bicknacre, Essex; 1 s (John Allardice b 7 Aug 1944), 3 da (Jane Allardice b 13 Jan 1947, Mary Allardice b 23 Sept 1954, Emma Allardice b 4 Nov 1957); *Career* RHA TA 1933-38, RA 1939-51; served: Gibraltar, Malta, Cyprus, Egypt, Palestine, at sea with the RN, W Africa, NW Europe (Airborne Forces), India; transferred RAOC 1951; served: Libya, Persia, Egypt, Germany, E Africa, S Arabia and Persian Gulf; Lt-Col 1958, Col 1964, Brig 1968; writer and journalist 1933-39; sr planning inspr then sr princ DOE 1972-89; Cdr St John Ambulance Shropshire; memb: Co Ctee SSAFA, jt TA/Cadet Ctee; vice chm ABF Shropshire; pres: ACF League Branch, RA Assoc Branch; FASMC 1962, FBIM 1968, FCIArb 1973; KStJ 1987; *Recreations* talking, gardening; *Clubs* Army & Navy, Muthaiga (Nairobi); *Style—* Brig Neil Barclay, DL; Strinebrook House, The Hincks, Lilleshall, Newport, Shropshire (☎ 0952 604204)

BARCLAY, Norman Veitch Lothian; s of James Barclay, JP (d 1963), and Florence, *née* Lothian (d 1976); *Educ* Trinity Coll Glenalmond, St John's Coll Cambridge (MA); *m* 1, 20 Jan 1954, Joan, da of George Ogg; 3 s (James b 1955, Rupert b 1957, Jeremy b 1958); m 2, 20 Sept 1969, Thérèse Ann, da of Lt Cdr O M De Las Casas, LVO, OBE, RN; 2 s (Maxwell b 1970, Alexander b 1974); *Career* dir (former chief exec) Aberdeen Combworks Ltd (now MacFarlane Gp plc); GB bobsleigh champion 1958-60, Gold medallist 4 man bob Cwlth Winter Games 1958, GB luge champion 1960-63, memb luge team 1964-68, winner of many class 1 and 2 powerboat races, first boat round Britain 1969, first Trans-Irish waterskier, first winter Trans-Alpine balloon crossing 1972; *Recreations* all winter sports, speedsports, golf, diving, ballooning; *Clubs* Turf, Lyford Cay, RSAC, St Moritz Sporting, St M Tobogganing (Cresta), UKOBA Dracula etc; *Style—* Norman Barclay, Esq; Eyreton House, Quarterbridge, Douglas, Isle of Man

BARCLAY, Peter Maurice; CBE (1984); s of George Ronald Barclay, OBE (d 1975), and Josephine Stephanie, *née* Lambert (d 1968); *b* 6 March 1926; *Educ* Bryanston, Magdalene Coll Cambridge (MA); *m* 1953, Elizabeth Mary, da of Herbert H S Wright, of Wellington Coll; 1 s (Simon), 2 da (Alison, Nicola); *Career* RNVR 1944-46 Sub Lt; admitted slr 1952; sr ptnr Beachcroft & Co 1964-74, ptnr Beachcrofts 1974-88; govr Bryanston Sch 1972-88, tstee Joseph Rowntree Meml Tst 1974-; chm: Ctee of Role and Tasks of Social Workers 1981-82, St Pancras Housing Assoc 1983, Social Security Advsy Ctee 1985-; pres Nat Inst for Social Work 1988 (chm 1973-85), cncl memb Policy Studies Inst 1989-; *Recreations* gardening, walking, painting; *Style—* Peter Barclay, Esq, CBE; Ferry Hill, E Portlemouth, nr Kingsbridge, S Devon (☎ 054 884 3443); Flat 4, 43 Ladbroke Grove, London W11 3AR

BARCLAY, Richard Fenton; s of Rev Gilbert Arthur Barclay (d 1972), of Holly Cottage, Lamer Lane, Wheathampstead, Herts, and Dorothy Catherine Topsy, *née* Studd (d 1980); *b* 3 Dec 1926; *Educ* Greshams Sch, Trinity Coll Cambridge (MA); *m* 27 April 1957 (sep), Alison Mary, da of Stanley Richard Cummings, of East Culme, Cullompton, Devon; 3 s (Charles b 1962, Angus b 1964, Michael b 1967), 1 da (Juliet b 1959); *Career* WWII Sub Lt RNVR 1944-46; from clerk to sr local dir Barclays Bank plc 1948-86; dep chm Nat Provident Inst 1987- (dir 1967), dir Portsmouth Building Society 1987-; memb: Ctee of Mgmnt RNLI, Ct of the Mary Rose; tstee Hampshire and the Islands Historic Churches Tst, memb Fundraising Ctee Univ of Southampton; Freeman City of London; FCIB, FIOD; *Recreations* history, travel; *Clubs* Army & Navy; *Style—* Richard Barclay, Esq; Solent House, 28 Cliff Road, Hill Head, Fareham, Hants PO14 3JT (☎ 0329 662 128)

BARCLAY, Robert Colraine; s and h of Sir Colville Herbert Sanford Barclay, 14 Bt, *qv*; *b* 12 Feb 1950; *m* 1980, Lucilia Saboia, da of Carlos Saboia de Albuquerque, of Ipanema, Rio de Janeiro; 1 s, 1 da; *Career* CA; *Style—* Robert Barclay, Esq; Pitshill, Petworth, W Sussex GU28 9AZ

BARCLAY, Sir Roderick Edward; GCVO (1966, KCVO 1957, CVO 1953), KCMG (1955, CMG 1948); s of late J Gurney Barclay, and Gillian, *née* Birkbeck; *b* 22 Feb 1909; *Educ* Harrow, Trinity Coll Cambridge; *m* 1934, Jean, da of late Sir Hugh Gladstone, of Capenoch, Dumfries; 1 s, 3 da; *Career* Dip Serv 1932-69: PPS to Sec of State for Foreign Affrs 1949-51, ambass Denmark 1956-60, dep under sec of state 1960-63, ambass Belgium 1963-69; dir: Slough Estates 1969-84, Barclays Bank International 1971-77, Banque de Bruxelles 1971-77; chm Barclays Bank SA (France) 1970-74 (dir 1969-79); *Books* Ernest Bevin and the Foreign Office 1932-69 (1975); *Style—* Sir Roderick Barclay, GCVO, KCMG; Great White End, Latimer, Bucks (☎ 0494 76 2050)

BARCLAY, Stephen Robert; s of James Barclay, and Edna, *née* Brown; *b* 8 Nov 1961; *Educ* Ardrossan Acad, Glasgow Sch of Art (BA); partner Ilka Johannsen; 1 da (Gwen Johannsen b 17 April 1990); *Career* artist 1985-; with Paton Gallery London 1985-88, joined Raab Gallery London 1988; solo exhibitions incl: Paton Gallery London 1987, Raab Gallerie Berlin 1989, Raab Gallery London 1989; gp exhibitions incl: Royal Glasgow Inst of Fine Arts Annual Exhibition 1984, Christmas Show (Compass Gallery Glasgow) 1984-85, Smith Biennial (Third Eye Centre Glasgow) 1985, Ayr Midland Gp Nottingham 1985, Contemporary Art on the Theme of Gardens (Stoke-on-Trent City Museum and Art Gallery) 1985, New Art New World (Jack Barclay's Ltd London) 1985, Autumn Show (Paton Gallery London) 1986 and 1987, British Art in Malaysia 1987, New British Painting - Object and Image Aspects of British Art in the 1980's (touring USA) 1988, Metropolis (Raab Gallery London) 1988, Opening Exhibition (Raab Gallery Millbank London) 1989, Turning the Century: The New Scottish Painting (Raab Gallery Millbank London) 1990, Gallerie Gian Ferrari Milan 1980, Three Generations of Scottish Painters (Beaux Arts Gallery Bath) 1990; work in pub collections incl: Aust Nat Gallery, Contemporary Arts Soc London, Cleveland Gallery, Tyne and Wear Museum Newcastle, Metropolitan Museum of Modern Art NY; *Awards* Hospitalfield Summer Scholarship 1983, Adam Bruce Thomson award 1984; *Recreations* gliding, sailing; *Clubs* Angus Gliding; *Style—* Stephen Barclay, Esq; The Guynd, Carmyllie, Arbroath, Angus, Scotland DD11 2QR (☎ 0241 6296)

BARCLAY, Timothy Humphrey; s of Rev Humphrey Gordon Barclay, CVO, MC (d 1955), of Thurgarton Lodge, Norwich, and Evermar Beatrice, *née* Bond Cabbell (d 1975); *b* 18 June 1923; *Educ* Stowe; *m* 23 June 1947, June, da of Thomas Ramsden (d 1960), of Middleton Tower, King's Lynn; 1 s (Thomas Julian b 12 June 1950); *Career* RN 1941-46; Rootes Group 1946-50, farmer and agent 1950-, rep Bonhams Auctioneers E Anglia 1965-85, dealer fine arts 1960-; High Sheriff of Norfolk 1983-84; master and huntsman: W Norfolk Foxhounds 1958-68 (sec 1953-58), Sennow Park Harries 1970-75; pres N W Norfolk Cons Assoc 1984, steward and dir Falzenham Race Course 1955; Liveryman Worshipful Co of Farriers 1976, hon life memb BHS; *Recreations* hunting, fishing, shooting, coursing; *Clubs* MCC, Norfolk, Allsorts; *Style—* Timothy Barclay, Esq; Middleton Tower, King's Lynn, Norfolk PE32 1EE (☎ 0553 840 203)

BARCLAY-BROWN, Kenneth; s of Maj Robert Barclay-Brown, OBE, and Margaret Nancy, *née* Frizelle; *b* 3 Aug 1929; *Educ* Britannia RNC Dartmouth, RNC Greenwich; *m* 12 Sept 1959, Susan, da of Richard (Dick) Gillard; 2 s (Simon b 4 Feb 1962, James b 7 Jan 1967), 1 da (Kerry b 6 July 1960); *Career* cmmnd Sub Lt RN 1949, seconded Royal Aust Navy 1950-53, qualified TAS course 1956, staff BRNC Dartmouth 1959-60, CO HMS Brocklesby 1961-63, Cdr 1964, naval offr i/c Takoradi Ghana 1964-66, SO dir of naval equipment (DNE) 1966-68, ret 1969; Grieveson Grant & Co (now Kleinwort Benson): joined 1969, ptnr 1977, dir Kleinwort Grieveson Investment Management 1986-88; dir CCL Financial Group 1989; memb Stock Exchange 1974, AMSIA; *Recreations* golf, fishing, sailing, windsurfing, squash, tennis, photography, skiing; *Clubs* Hankley Common Golf, Rye Golf, SCGB; *Style—* Kenneth Barclay-Brown, Esq; Isington Close, Isington, nr Alton, Hants GU34 4PR (☎ 0420 22041)

BARCLAY-TIMMIS, Dr Kenneth Frank John; TD; s of Brig William Frank De-Chaunce Timmis, and Elizabeth Sara, *née* Archer; descendent of Capt Gabriel Archer who landed (1607) in N America and named Cape Cod and was a fndr of Jamestown; *b* 18 Oct 1939; *Educ* UCS, UCL (BSc), Canada (PhD), Univ of Aston (MSc); *m* 1, 1962, Marie Barclay; 2 s (Paul b 1965, Jonathan b 1966), 1 da (Sarah b 1963), m 2, 1981, Janet Christine, da of Capt Joseph Philip Howe; 1 da (Victoria b 1982); *Career* Inns of Ct Regt 1976-, Maj RGJ (TAVR); chm: European Development Group Ltd 1986-, DPK Ltd, Hospital Computer System (UK) Ltd, Computer International Hospital Equipment Ltd, International Supplies Ltd 1975-; cncllr Ivinghoe Div Bucks; *Recreations* golf; *Clubs* Army and Navy, RAC, Buckingham Golf; *Style—* Dr Kenneth Barclay-Timmis, TD; Springhill House, Hethe, Oxfordshire (☎ 0869 278350)

BARCLAY-WHITE, Dr Barclay Egon Oram; s of Carl Jack Barclay-White (d 1981), of Weybridge, Surrey, and Phyllis Blauche, *née* Showler; *b* 27 June 1927; *Educ* King's Coll Sch Wimbledon, Univ of London, California USA (DDS); *m* 1, 1952 (m dis 1979), Sheila Meredith Bailey; 2 s (Adam Meredith Barclay b 1966, Jason Meredith Barclay b 1969), 2 da (Belinda Meredith Barclay b 1951, Amanda Meredith Barclay b 1953); m 2, 16 Sept 1979, Cathy Mary Bernadette, da of John Gregson (d 1975), of Weybridge and Shepperton; 1 s (Barclay John Gregson b 1987), 1 da (Genevieve Gregson b 1983); *Career* dentist in Weybridge until 1978, dir Dominfast Investments Ltd 1973-, fndr and non-exec dir Capital Radio plc; memb RCS, LDS; *Recreations* worrying (so I'm told); *Clubs* Naval & Military; *Style—* Dr Barclay Barclay-White; Warren Cottage, Camp End Rd, Weybridge, Surrey KT13 0NR (☎ 0932 850547, fax 0932 850547, car 0831 421650)

BARD, Dr Basil Joseph Asher; CBE (1968); s of late Abram Isaac Bard, of Finchley, and Anita Bard; *b* 20 Aug 1914; *Educ* Owen's Sch, RCS (Imperial Coll); *m* 1942, Ena Dora, da of late B Birk, of Newcastle upon Tyne and London; 3 s; *Career* called to the Bar Gray's Inn 1938; 1939-49: Coal Cmmn, Miny of Supply, Miny of Aircraft Prodn Fedn of Br Indust; National Resource Development Corp 1950 (md 1970-74); chm: New Product Management (NPM) Group 1977-83, Birmingham Mint Ltd 1977-82, Transcan Video Ltd 1978-82, Xtec 1983-86; dir: First National Financial Corporation 1974-76, The Technology and Innovations Exchange (TIE) 1982-83, Interflex Structural Coatings Ltd 1984-89, Scanning Technology Ltd 1984; chm Promicro Ltd 1986-; Hon Life memb: Licensing Execs Soc 1989-, Fndn for Sci and Technol 1990-; pres: Anglo-Jewish Assoc 1977-83, Jewish Memorial Cncl 1982-89; *Clubs* Athenaeum; *Style—* Dr Basil Bard, CBE; 23 Mourne House, Maresfield Gardens, London NW3 5SL (☎ 071 435 5340; business 071 328 8138)

BARDA, Robin John Blackmore; s of Gaston Barda (d 1978), of Lausanne, Switzerland, and Cecilia Marjorie, *née* Blackmore; *b* 19 Oct 1947; *Educ* Bryanston, Magdalen Coll Oxford (BA); *m* 6 Sept 1980, Louisa Anne Maxwell, da of Lawrence Thorne Stevenson (d 1985); 3 da (Tabitha b 1983, Arabella b 1986, Persephone b 1988); *Career* freelance singer and musician 1970-75, called to the Bar Gray's Inn 1975; *Recreations* singing, music, squash; *Clubs* United Oxford and Cambridge; *Style—* Robin Barda, Esq; 4 Paper Buildings, Temple, London EC4Y 7EX (☎ 071 583 0816, fax 071 353 4979)

BARDER, Brian Leon; s of Harry Barder, and Vivien Barder; *b* 20 June 1934; *Educ*

Sherborne, St Catharine's Coll Cambridge (BA); *m* 1958, Jane Maureen; 1 s, 2 da; *Career* 2 Lt 7 RTR 1952-54; Colonial Office 1957, private sec to Perm Under Sec 1960-61, HM Dip Serv 1965, first sec UK mission to UN 1964-68, FCO 1968-70, first sec and press attaché Moscow 1971-73, cnsllr and head of Chancery Br High Cmmn Canberra 1973-77, Canadian Nat Def Coll Kingston Ontario 1977-78, head Central and Southern (later Southern) African Dept FCO 1978-82; ambass to: Ethiopia 1982-86, Poland 1986-88; high cmmr: to Nigeria and ambass (non resident) to Benin 1988-91, designate to Australia 1991-; Hon Cdr of the Order of the Niger (Nigeria) 1989; *Clubs* Utd Oxford & Cambridge Univ, Cwlth Tst; *Style—* Brian Barder, Esq; c/o Foreign & Cwlth Office, London SW1A 2AH

BARDHAN, Dr (Pokalath) Gouri; da of Maj-Gen Pokalath Ram Kumar, of Bangalore, India, and Rohini, *née* Ezhuthachan; *b* 6 March 1943; *Educ* Univ of Madras (MB BS, DCH); *m* 15 Dec 1972, Karnadev Bardhan, s of Maj-Gen Pramathanath Bardhan (d 1966); 1 s (Satyajeet b 11 Nov 1977), 1 da (Suchitra Kaveri b 30 Sept 1980); *Career* conslt haematologist Doncaster Royal Infirmary 1984-; former memb Doncaster DHA; MRCP, FRCPath; *Recreations* reading, music, crafts; *Style—* Dr Gouri Bardhan; Haematology Department, Doncaster Royal Infirmary, Armthorpe Rd, Doncaster DN2 5LT (☎ 0302 366666)

BARDHAN, Dr Karna Dev; s of Maj-Gen Pramatha Nath Bardhan (d 1966), of Pune, India, and Anima, *née* Chaudhuri; *b* 16 Aug 1940; *Educ* Christian Med Coll of Vellore Univ of Madras (MB BS), Univ of Oxford (Rhodes scholar, DPhil); *m* 15 Dec 1972, Dr Gouri Bardhan, da of Maj-Gen P Ram Kumar, of Bangalore, India; 1 s (Satyajeet b 11 Nov 1977), 1 da (Suchitra Kaveri b 30 Sept 1980); *Career* house physician Oxford and Hammersmith Hosp London 1968-69, registrar Royal Hosp Sheffield 1969-70, conslt physician Dist Gen Hosp Rotherham 1973-, hon lectr in gastroenterology Sheffield Univ 1973- (lectr in med 1970-72); memb: Br Soc of Gastroenterology, Assoc of Physicians of GB and Ireland; *Books* Perspectives in Duodenal Ulcer (1980), Topics in Peptic Ulcer Disease (ed, 1987); *Recreations* photography; *Style—* Dr Karna Bardhan; 26 Melrose Grove, Rotherham S60 3NA (☎ 0709 372288); District General Hospital, Moorgate Road, Rotherham S60 2UD (☎ 0709 820000, fax 0709 820007)

BARDSLEY, Andrew Tromlow; JP (Essex 1975); s of Andrew Bardsley (d 1950), of Ashton-under-Lyne, Lancs, and Gladys Ada, *née* Tromlow; *b* 7 Dec 1927; *Educ* Ashton-under-Lyne GS, Manchester Regnl Coll of Art, UMIST; *m* 27 Nov 1954, (June) Patricia, da of Patrick Ford (d 1968), of Ashton-under-Lyne; 1 s (Dr Philip Andrew b 6 April 1958), 1 da (Catherine Patricia b 17 March 1962); *Career* served RN communications branch 1946-49; borough engr and surveyor Worksop Borough Cncl 1963-69; dir Tech Servs: Corby New Town 1969-71, Luton Co Borough Cncl 1971-73; gen mangr Harlow Devpt Corp 1973-80, princ Westgate Devpt Consultancy 1981-; gen cmmr of Taxes for England and Wales 1987-; CEng, FICE; *Recreations* golf, tennis, music appreciation, most spectator sports; *Clubs* Ferndown Golf (Dorset); *Style—* Andrew Bardsley, Esq, JP; 25 Charlotte Close, Talbot Village, Poole, Dorset (☎ 0202 537954); 19 Copper Court, Sawbridgeworth, Herts CM21 9ER (☎ 0279 723 210)

BAREAU, Paul Louis Jean; OBE (1971); s of Louis Bareau (d 1925), and Elisa van Caneghem (d 1909); *b* 27 April 1901; *Educ* Athénée Antwerp, Dulwich, LSE (BCom); *m* 15 Sept 1934, Katharine Dorothy, da of Basil Gibson, ICS (d 1950); 2 s (Michael b 1936, Peter b 1942), 2 da (Juliet b 1935, Suzanne b 1939); *Career* econ journalist and conslt: Statist 1926-29, Financial News 1929-33, News Chronicle 1933-44; UK Treasy (Washington) 1944-47, News Chronicle 1947-58 (City ed 1953-58), ed The Statist 1961-67, lectr on Comparative Banking LSE 1947-51; econ advsr: Publishing Corp, Mirror Group Newspaper 1968-, Barclays Bank Group 1967-80; dir: M & G Investment Management 1973-, Halifax Building Society (London Bd) 1974-76, UK Provident Inst 1959-73, dir Broadstone Investment Trust 1973-81; hon fell LSE; *Recreations* music; *Clubs* Reform, Political Economy; *Style—* Paul Bareau, Esq, OBE; Glebe Lodge, Crondall, Farnham, Surrey (☎ 0252 850294); Mirror Group, City Office, Holborn Circus EC1P 1DQ (☎ 071 822 3885)

BAREFOOT, Peter Thomas; s of Herbert John Leslie Barefoot, GC (d 1958), and Amy Gladys, *née* Goddard; *b* 20 Jan 1924; *Educ* Ipswich Sch, Architectural Assoc Sch of Architecture (AA Dip); *m* 3 July 1948, Patience Heaslop, da of John Francis Cunningham, OBE (d 1932), of London W1; 1 s (Guy b 1957), 3 da (Ann b 1949, Julia b 1951, Sara b 1953); *Career* WWII RN 1943-46 (hostilities only), Petty Offr Med Combined Ops; chartered architect in private practice 1954-, chartered designer 1976-; architect: Stevenage Devpt Corp 1949-50, County Hall LCC 1951-54; work incl: Suffolk Hosp Buildings (Bronze Medal RIBA), Elizabeth Court sheltered housing for old people at Aldeburgh (Miny of Housing and Civic Tst Awards) 1962-63, Club House for Royal Harwich Yacht Club 1966-68, WVRS Housing Assoc (DOE Award) 1969-70, Peter Runge House conf centre in Westminster for Industl Soc (The Times/RICS Conservation Award) 1970-71, 273 dwellings Central Lancs New Town 1975-76, sheltered housing and hostel Brixton for Church Housing Assoc 1980-83, laboratory for prof of surgery St Bart's Hosp London 1986; drawings and models have been exhibited at: Royal Acad Summer Exhibition, RIBA, the AA, Le Grand Palais Paris; *Recreations* sailing, travel; *Clubs* Royal Harwich Yacht, Waldringfield Sailing; *Style—* Peter Barefoot; 1 Gaston Street, East Bergholt, Colchester CO7 6SD (☎ 0206 298 422)

BARENBOIM, Daniel; s of Enrique Barenboim, and Aida, *née* Schuster; *b* 15 Nov 1942, Buenos Aires; *Educ* Santa Cecilia Acad Rome, coached by Edwin Fischer, Nadia Boulanger and Igor Markevitch; *m* 1, 1967, Jacqueline du Pré, OBE, violoncellist (d 1987), da of Derek du Pré (d 1990) , by his w Iris Maud, *née* Greep (d 1985); m 2, Nov 1988, Elena Bashkirova; *Career* pianist and conductor; musical dir Orchestre de Paris 1975-89, Chicago Symphony Orch 1991-; Israel Philharmonic Orch (debut) 1953, Royal Philharmonic Orch 1956, Berlin Philharmonic Orch 1963, NY Philharmonic 1964; reg tours to Aust, N and S America, Far East; regular appearances at Bayreuth, Edinburgh, Lucerne Prague and Salzburg Festivals; Beethoven medal 1958, Paderewski medal 1963; *Style—* Daniel Barenboim, Esq; c/o Daniel Barenboim Secretariat, 5 Place de la Fusterie, 1204 Geneve, Switzerland

BARFETT, Ven Thomas; s of Rev Thomas Clarence Fairchild Barfett (d 1968), and Mary Deborah, *née* Hancock (d 1961); *b* 2 Oct 1916; *Educ* St John's Leatherhead, Keble Coll Oxford (BA, MA); *m* 1945, Edna, da of Robert Toy (d 1924); 1 s (Paul), 1 da (Susan); *Career* asst curate: Christ Church Gosport 1939-43, St Francis Gladstone Park NW10 1944-47, St Andrew Undershaft London 1947-49; asst sec London Diocesan Cncl for Youth 1944-49, vicar St Paul Penzance Dio of Truro 1949-55, rector Falmouth Dio of Truro 1955-77, sec Truro Diocesan Conf 1952-67, proctor in Convocation 1958-77, memb Gen Synod C of E 1977-82 (memb Central Bd of Fin C of E 1969-77), church cmmr 1975-82, memb Pension Bd C of E 1973-85 (chm Investmts Fin Ctee 1985), archdeacon of Hereford and residentiary canon of Hereford Cathedral 1977-82 (canon treas of Cathedral), chaplain to HM The Queen 1975-86, archdeacon emeritus 1982; chm Cornwall Family History Soc 1985-88; Freeman City of London 1973, Freeman Liveryman Worshipful Co of Scriveners' 1976; asst chaplain OStJ 1963 (sub chaplain 1971); Jubilee medal 1977; *Books* Trebarfoote - A Cornish Family (1975), Hatchments in Britain (ed Cornish section, 1988); *Recreations* genealogy, heraldry; *Clubs* Oxford and Cambridge; *Style—* The Ven Thomas Barfett; Treberveth, 57 Falmouth Rd, Truro, Cornwall TR1 2HL (☎ 0872 73726)

BARFIELD, Brian Michael; s of Isom Bennett Barfield, and Georgina Margaret, *née* Aiken (d 1983); *b* 21 Jan 1945; *Educ* Friends Sch Lisburn, Trinity Coll Dublin (BA); *Career* sr prodr of arts progs BBC NI 1972-77, (announcer and presenter 1968-72), dep ed Kaleidoscope Radio 4 1979-85 (sr prodr of talks and documentaries 1977-79), head of planning and business mgmnt Radio 3 1988- (planning ed 1985-); *Recreations* walking and visiting country graveyards; *Style—* Brian Barfield, Esq; BBC, 16 Langham St, London W1A 1AA (☎ 071 927 4617, fax 071 637 3009, telex 265781)

BARFORD, Clive Julian Stanley; s of Maj Edward James Barford, MC (d 1979), late Royal Horse Guards (Special Reserve), and Hon Grace Lowrey Stanley (later Hon Mrs Buckmaster), da of 1 and last Baron Ashfield; *b* 11 May 1933; *Educ* Eton; *m* 1961, Helen Gay Woodroffe, da of Hon Mr Justice (Sir Peter Harry Batson Woodroffe) Foster, MBE, TD; 1 s (James Edward Clive b 1972), 3 da (Emma Jane b 1962, Amanda Helen b 1964, Charlotte Gay b 1967); *Career* chm and md Aldworth Investments Ltd and Abex Ltd, memb Lloyd's; *Recreations* shooting, golf, gardening; *Clubs* Buck's; *Style—* Clive Barford, Esq; Pibworth House, Aldworth, Berks (☎ 0635 578495)

BARFORD, Sir Leonard; s of William Barford, of Harley House, Sutton Road, Seaford, Sussex, and Ada Barford; *b* 1 Aug 1908; *Educ* Dame Alice Owen's Sch, St Catharine's Coll Cambridge; *m* 1939, Betty Edna, da of Thomas Crichton, of Plymouth; 2 s; *Career* dep chm Horserace Totalisator Bd 1974-77, chief inspector Taxes Bd of Inland Revenue 1964-73; kt 1967; *Style—* Sir Leonard Barford; Harley House, 79 Sutton Rd, Seaford, E Sussex (☎ 893364)

BARFORD, Hon Mrs (Marian Woodruff); *née* Stanley; da of 1 and last Baron Ashfield (d 1948), and Grace Lowrey, *née* Woodruff (d 1962); *b* 1906; *m* 1, 1927 (m dis 1934), James Hart Rutland, s of Archibald Hart Rutland; 1 s; m 2, 1934 (m dis 1940), James Henry Royds, eldest s of Col Albert Henry Royds, OBE; 1 da; m 3, 1940 (m dis 1954), Ralph Arthur Hubbard, eldest s of Capt Gerald Hubbard; 2 da; m 4, 1964 (m dis 1971), Edward James Barford, MC (d 1979), s of James Golby Barford, JP, of Gayhurst, Peterborough; *Style—* The Hon Mrs Barford; Dormy House, Ridgemount Rd, Sunningdale, Berks

BARGE, Ronald Mansfield; DSC (1942), VRD (1950), DL (Dunbartonshire 1972); s of Lt-Col Kenneth Barge, DSO, MC, DL, JP, IA (d 1971), and Debonair Eva Ruth, *née* Mansfield (d 1959); *b* 10 Nov 1920; *Educ* Trinity Coll Glenalmond, Glasgow Art Sch, Univ of Munich, Univ of Durham, RCA; *m* 1950, Elizabeth Ann, da of Col John Robertson Lamberton, DSO, MC (d 1974), of Helensburgh; 3 s (Nigel, Alastair, Henry), 3 da (Rosanna, Veronica, Lisa); *Career* salmon farmer; chm: Otter Ferry Salmon Ltd, Onshore Aquaculture; dir: Bitmac Tport Ltd, Bitmac Ltd; *Recreations* art, gardening, fishing; *Clubs* Royal Northern & Clyde Yacht, Mudhook Yacht; *Style—* Ronald Barge, Esq, DSC, VRD, DL; Whistlers' Hill, Rhu, Dunbartonshire (☎ 0436 820285); Evanachan, Otterferry, Argyll (☎ 070 082284)

BARHAM, David George Wilfrid; JP (Kent 1961), DL (Kent 1976); s of Harold Arthur Barham (d 1978), of Rolvenden, Kent, and Edith Dulcie Brown, *née* Taylor (d 1988); *b* 6 Oct 1926; *Educ* Malvern, RAC Cirencester (Dip Estate Mgmnt); *m* 28 Oct 1955, Catherine Margaret, da of Col Rixon Bucknall, MBE (d 1975), of Rotherfield, Sussex; 3 s (William b 1958, Edward b 1962, Robert b 1965), 1 da (Jennifer b 1957); *Career* Lt RHG 1944-48; farmer, land agent in private practice; general cmmr taxation 1960-; former chm Kent Branch CLA, memb Kent CC for Tenterden 1959-69; chm: Kent TAVRA Assoc 1975-81, Kent Ctee COSIRA (now Rural Devpt Cmmn) 1982-89; High Sheriff of Kent 1974-75; FRICS; *Recreations* gardening, country pursuits; *Clubs* Army and Navy, RAC; *Style—* D G W Barham, Esq, JP, DL

BARHAM, (Geoffrey) Simon; s of Denis Patrick Barham (d 1978), of Cavendish, Suffolk, and Pleasance, *née* Brooke; *b* 23 Dec 1945; *Educ* Malvern, Christ's Coll Cambridge (BA, MA); *m* 18 Sept 1976, Sarah, da of Rev Godfrey Seebold; 1 s (Thomas b 1980), 1 da (Lucy b 1979); *Career* called to the Bar Lincoln's Inn 1968; rec 1987; *Clubs* Norfolk; *Style—* Simon Barham, Esq; Wensum Chambers, Wensum Street, Norwich, Norfolk (☎ 0603 617 351)

BARING, Hon James Cecil; s of 4 Baron Revelstoke, *qv*; *b* 16 Aug 1938; *Educ* Eton; *m* 1, 1968, Aneta Laline Dennis, da of late Erskine Arthur Hamilton Fisher, of Mickleham, Surrey; 2 s; m 2, 1983, Sarah, da of William Edward Stubbs, MBE; 1 da; *Style—* The Hon James Baring

BARING, Hon John; s and h of 4 Baron Revelstoke, *qv*; *b* 2 Dec 1934; *Educ* Eton; *Style—* The Hon John Baring

BARING, Sir John Francis; 3 Bt (UK 1911), of Nubia House, Northwood, Isle of Wight; s of Capt Raymond Alexander Baring (d 1967), and Margaret Fleetwood, JP, DL, *née* Campbell-Preston; suc unc Sir Charles Christian Baring, 2 Bt (d 1990); *b* 21 May 1947; *Educ* Eton, RAC Cirencester, LSE; *m* 1971, Elizabeth Anne, yr da of late Robert D H Pillitz, of Superi 1552, Buenos Aires, Argentina; 2 s (Julian Alexander David b 1975, James Francis b 1984), 1 da (Andrea Hermione b 1977); *Heir* s, Julian Alexander David Baring b 1975; *Career* with: Citibank NA 1971-72, Chemical Bank 1972-84, Kidder Peabody & Co Inc 1984-89, GPA Group Ltd 1989; *Clubs* Union (NY); *Style—* Sir John Baring, Bt; 17 East 96th Street, New York, NY 10128, USA; June Road, North Salem, NY 10560, USA

BARING, Hon Sir John Francis Harcourt; KCVO (1990, CVO 1980); s and h of 6 Baron Ashburton, *qv*; *b* 2 Nov 1928; *Educ* Eton (fellow 1982), Trinity Coll Oxford (MA); *m* 1, 1955 (m dis 1984), Hon Susan Mary Renwick, da of 1 Baron Renwick, KBE; 2 s, 2 da; m 2, 27 Oct 1987, Mrs Sarah Crewe, da of John Spencer Churchill, and Mrs Angela Culme Seymour; *Career* chm: Baring Bros & Co 1974-89 (md 1955-74), Barings plc 1985-89 (dir 1985-), Stratton Investment Tst plc 1986-;dir: Br Petroleum Co plc 1982-, Bank of England 1983-, Jaguar plc 1989-, Outwich Investment Tst 1965-86, Royal Insurance Co 1964-82 (dep chm 1975-82), Dunlop Holdings 1981-84; memb President's Ctee of CBI 1976-79; chm: Ctee on Fin for Industry (NEDC) 1980-86, Accepting Houses Ctee 1977-81; receiver-gen Duchy of Cornwall 1974-90, Lord Warden of the Stannaries and keeper of the Privy Seal of the Duke of Cornwall 1990-; Rhodes Tstee 1970- (chm 1987-); tstee Nat Gallery 1981-87; hon fell Hertford Coll Oxford 1976, hon fell Trin Coll Oxford 1989; kt 1983; *Style—* The Hon Sir John Baring, KCVO; Lake House, Northington, Alresford, Hants SO24 9TG (☎ 0962 734293); Baring Brothers & Co, 8 Bishopsgate, London EC2N 4AE (☎ 071 280 1000)

BARING, Louise Olivia; da of Aubrey George Adeane Baring (d 1987), and Marina, *née* Bessel; *b* 28 July 1957; *Educ* Queen's Gate Sch; *Career* journalist; letters arts and home affrs writer Britain section The Economist 1983-89, commissioning ed You magazine The Mail on Sunday 1989-90, asst features ed The Independent on Sunday 1990-; *Style—* Ms Louise Baring; Flat 7, 39-40 Queens Gate, London SW7 5HR (☎ 071 581 8641); The Independent On Sunday, 40 City Rd, London EC1Y 2DH (☎ 071 253 1222)

BARING, Lady Rose Gwendolen Louisa; *née* McDonnell; DCVO (1972, CVO 1964); er da of 7 Earl of Antrim (d 1932), and Margaret Isabel (d 1974), da of Rt Hon John Gilbert Talbot; *b* 23 May 1909; *m* 22 April 1933, Francis Anthony Baring (ka 1940), s of Hon Hugo Baring (s of 1 Baron Revelstoke, OBE), and Lady Evelyn, *née* Ashley-Cooper, da of 8 Earl of Shaftesbury; 2 s, 1 da; *Career* woman of the bedchamber to HM The Queen 1953-73, extra woman of the bedchamber 1973-; *Style—* Lady Rose Baring, DCVO; 43 Pembroke Square, London W8

BARING, Hon Mrs (Sarah Katherine Elinor); *née* Norton; o da of 6 Baron Grantley (d 1954); *b* 20 Jan 1920; *Educ* private; *m* 1, 14 June 1945 (m dis 1953), 3 Viscount Astor (d 1966); 1 s; m 2, 17 April 1953 (m dis 1965), Thomas Michael Baring, eldest s of Maj Edward Baring, of Heronry House, Beckley, Sussex; 1 s; *Style*— The Hon Mrs Baring; 23 Scarsdale Villas, London W8

BARING, Hon Mrs (Susan Mary); *née* Renwick; OBE (1984), JP (Hants 1965); prefers style of Hon Mrs to that of Hon Lady; da of 1 Baron Renwick, KBE (d 1973); *b* 5 June 1930; *m* 1955 (m dis 1984), Hon Sir John Francis Harcourt Baring, *qv*; 2 s, 2 da; *Career* chm Hampshire Probation Ctee 1978-82; vice chm Central Cncl of Probation Ctees 1979-82; memb Parole Bd for England and Wales 1971- 74 and 1979-83; pres Hampshire Assoc of Youth Clubs 1977-79; devpt offr Richmond Fellowship 1984-86; prospective Parly Alliance candidate for Reading East 1987; memb Cncl King's Coll London 1979-; vice chm Delegacy King's Coll Med Sch 1989-; chm: Br Inst of Human Rights 1989-, Nat Birthday Tst 1989-, Tstees NW London Housing Assoc; *Recreations* walking, reading, music, family; *Style*— The Hon Mrs Baring, OBE, JP; 13 Alexander St, London W2 5NY

BARING, Lt-Col Thomas Michael; TD; s of late Maj ET Baring, and Virginia Ryan Baring (d 1988); *b* 24 Oct 1927; *Educ* Brooks Sch Andover Mass USA, Ch Ch Oxford; *m* 1, March 1953 (m dis 1965), The Hon Sarah Katherine Elinor Norton, da of Richard, 6 Baron Grantley; m 2, 11 June 1966, Gillian Ann Rosemary, da of Col Arthur Rupert Woolley DSO, OBE; 1 da (Constance Nina b 12 July 1970); *Career* short serv cmmn 10 Royal Hussars, Col and Cmd Leicestershire and Derbyshire Yeo 1966 until TA disbanded 1968; md Baring Industries, fine art conslt Baring Fine Art; fndr and pres of Stourhead Polo Club; *Recreations* polo; *Clubs* Army and Navy; *Style*— Lt-Col Thomas Baring, TD

BARING, Hon Vivian John Rowland; 2 s of 3 Earl of Cromer, KG, GCMG, MBE, PC, *qv*; *b* 12 June 1950; *m* 1974, his 2 cous, Lavinia Gweneth (extra lady-in-waiting to HRH The Princess of Wales), er da of Sir Mark Baring, KCVO (d 1988); 2 s (Rowley b 1977 (page of honour to HM The Queen 1989-), Thomas b 1979), 1 da (Camilla b 1985); *Career* dir: Gen Tours Ltd, Instone West Ltd, Courier Printing & Publishing Co Ltd, Essex Chronicle Series Ltd, Gloucestershire Newspapers Ltd, The Cheltenham Newspaper Co Ltd, The Print Works (Gloucester) Ltd; dep pres Kent County St John Ambulance; memb Cncl of St John: Kent 1978-88 (chm 1985-87), Glos 1988- (chm 1989-); *Clubs* White's; *Style*— The Hon Vivian Baring; The Stone House, Lower Swell, Stow on the Wold, Glos GL54 1LQ (☎ 0451 30622)

BARKER, Hon Adam Campbell; s of Baroness Trumpington of Sandwich (Jean, *née* Campbell-Harris) (Life Baroness), *qv*, and William Alan Barker, of Sandwich, Kent (d 1988); *b* 31 Aug 1955; *Educ* The Kings Sch Canterbury, Queens' Coll Cambridge (MA); *m* 1985, Elizabeth Mary, da of Eric Marsden, OBE; 1 s (Christopher Adam b 1989), 1 da (Virginia Giverny b 1987); *Career* lawyer; assoc Webster & Sheffield NY 1980-90, counsel Sedgwick Detert Moran & Arnold 1990-; barr 12 King's Bench Walk London 1978-80; *Recreations* golf, tennis, horse racing, bridge; *Clubs* Oxford and Cambridge, Royal St George's (Sandwich), Hurlingham, Pilgrims; *Style*— The Hon Adam Barker; Rose Cottage, 54 King St, Sandwich, Kent CT13 9BL (☎ 0304 617256); 169 East 90th Street 9, NY, NY 10128, USA (☎ 010 212 369 0723); 41st Floor, 59 Maiden Lane, NY, NY 10038, USA (☎ 010 212 422 0202)

BARKER, Prof (Sidney) Alan; s of Philip Henry Barker (d 1962), of 36 Elmbridge Rd, Perry Barr, Birmingham, and Gladys, *née* Allen; *b* 13 April 1926; *Educ* Handsworth GS, Univ of Birmingham (BSc, PhD, DSc); *m* 8 March 1952, Miriam Ruth, da of Harry May (d 1968), of 15 Marion Rd, Smethwick, Warley, W Mid; 1 s (Richard Charles Stuart b 15 Sept 1968), 2 da (Jane Alison (Mrs Shirley) b 11 Aug 1957, (Helen) Elizabeth (Mrs Farra) b 19 May 1961); *Career* Mackinnon student of Royal Soc 1951-53, lectr Univ of Birmingham 1954-55, Rockerfeller res fell Univ of California and Rutgers Univ 1955-56; Univ of Birmingham: lectr 1956-62, sr lectr 1962, reader 1965, prof 1969-; cwlth res fell Queens Univ Canada 1967, author of numerous papers and patents; memb Derbyshire Archaeological Soc: FRSC 1967; *Books* Polysaccharides of Microorganisms (1960), Carbohydrates of Living Tissues (1962); *Recreations* genealogy; *Clubs* Staff House, Senior Common Room, Univ of Birmingham; *Style*— Prof Alan Barker; 1 Abdon Ave, Selly Oak, Birmingham B29 4NT (☎ 021 475 5209); Chemistry Dept, Univ of Birmingham, PO Box 363, Edgbaston, Birmingham B15 2TT (☎ 021 414 4457, fax 021 414 4403); Barker Consultancy Services and Barker Technical Services, 1 Abdon Ave, Selly Oak, Birmingham B29 4NT

BARKER, Sir Alwyn Bowman; CMG (1962); s of late Alfred James Barker, of Mt Barker, S Australia; *b* 5 Aug 1900; *Educ* St Peter's Coll Adelaide, Geelong GS, Adelaide Univ (BE, BSc); *m* 1926, Isabel Barron, da of Sir Edward Lucas (d 1950); 1 s (Donald, decd), 1 da (Shirley); *Career* gen mangr Chrysler Aust Ltd 1940-52; chm: Kelvinator Aust Ltd 1967-80 (md 1951-67), Adelaide Electrolysis Ctee 1935-78, Industl Devpt Advsy Cncl 1968-70; chm of bd Municipal Tramways Tst 1953-68, dep chm Aust Mineral Fndn 1969-83; pres: Australian Inst of Mgmnt SA Div 1952-54 (fedn pres 1952-53 and 1959-61), Instn of Prodn Engrs (Aust Cncl) 1970-72; memb: Faculty of Engrg Univ of Adelaide 1937-66 (lectr in industl engrg 1929-54), Mfrg Industs Advsy Cncl 1958-72, R & D Advsy Ctee 1967-72; John Storey Meml Medal 1965, Jack Finlay Nat Award 1965; *see Debrett's Handbook of Australia and New Zealand for further details*; grazier (6000 acres); Hon FAIM, CEng, FIAM, FIEAust; kt 1969; *Publications* Three Presidential Addresses (1954), William Queale Memorial Lecture (1965); *Clubs* Adelaide; *Style*— Sir Alwyn Barker, CMG; 51 Hackney Rd, Hackney, 5069, South Australia (☎ 010 618 362 2838)

BARKER, Hon Mrs (Angela Margaret); o da of 10 Baron Dufferin and Clandeboye, *qv*; *Educ* Sydney Univ (BSc), Mitchel Coll Charles Sturt Univ (Dip Ed); *m* 1965, Clifton Elliott Barker, BSc; 1 s (Stephen Michael b 1969), 3 da (Zoë Frances b 1971, Lucinda Alice b 1975, Karina Emily b 1980); *Career* teacher Sci Dept Abbotsleigh Wahroouga; *Style*— The Hon Mrs Barker; 141 Campbell Drive, Wahroonga, NSW 2076, Australia

BARKER, Anthony; QC (1985); s of Robert Herbert Barker, of Barlaston, Stoke-on-Trent, Staffs, and Ellen Doreen, *née* Maskery; *b* 10 Jan 1944; *Educ* Newcastle-under-Lyme HS, Clare Coll Cambridge (BA); *m* 12 Feb 1983, Valerie Ann, da of Dr William Chatterley Baird, of Caterham, Surrey; 2 da (Sarah Louise b 1971, Vanessa Ann b 1973), 1 step s (Scott William Kenneth Ellis b 1975); *Career* called to the Bar 1966; rec of the Crown Ct 1985; *Style*— Anthony Barker, Esq, QC; Hilderstone House, Hilderstone, Nr Stone, Staffs (☎ 088 924 331); 5 Fountain Ct, Steelhouse Lane, Birmingham 4 (☎ 021 236 5771)

BARKER, Anthony Arnold; s of Kenneth Walter Barker, of Toys Hill, Westerham, Kent, and Dorothy Vere, *née* Arnold (d 1981); *b* 28 June 1934; *Educ* Gordonstoun; *m* 1, Patricia Anne Butler (d 1972); m 2, 1974, Valerie Jean, da of Cdr Henry James Norman William Taylor, RN (ret) (d 1981); 3 s (Timothy, James, Matthew), 2 da (Caroline, Lucy); *Career* Nat Serv RA 1952-54; sales mangr: 1940 Gp of Cos 1957-59, Marlowe Cleaners 1959-60; founding dir Harlequin Cleaners Ltd 1960-72 (md 1967-72), dir Harlequin Engineering 1964-68, md Commodore Cleaners Ltd 1967-72, sales and marketing conslt Tony Steven Assoc 1962-67, conslt Clissold Stevens Administration Services 1962-75; chm and md: Anthony A Barker Ltd 1972-, Anthony A Barker (The Argyle Laundry) Ltd 1973-, Anthony A Barker (The Dry Cleaner) Ltd 1973-; non-exec dir Laundry Wise Ltd 1990-; memb Nat Cncl Assoc Br Launderers and Cleaners 1985-87; Freeman City of London, Liveryman Worshipful Co of Launderers 1984; FIOD; *Recreations* reading, collecting, antiques, washing other peoples linen; *Clubs* Naval and Military, RMYC; *Style*— Anthony Barker, Esq; The Old Rectory, Durweston, Blandford Forum, Dorset

BARKER, (Brian) Ashley; OBE (1975); s of George Henry Barker (d 1980), of Aley Green, Beds, and Evelyn Dorothy, *née* Chandler; *b* 26 May 1927; *Educ* Luton GS, AA London (Dip Arch); *m* 1, 27 Feb 1960 (m dis 1973), Eirian Whittington, *née* Jenkins; 2 s (James b 1961, David b 1964), 2 da (Rhiannon b 1963, Charlotte b 1967); m 2, 29 May 1973, (Sheila) Ann Margaret, da of Lt-Col George Broadhurst (d 1954), of Cheltenham; *Career* architect and conslt on historic bldgs; surveyor of historic bldgs GLC (head of div) 1970-86, head of London div Historic Bldgs and Monuments Cmmn for England 1986-88; currently conslt in private practice; chm Assoc for Studies in the Conservation of Historic Bldgs 1970-89; memb: London Diocesan Advsy Ctee for the Care of Churches 1978-, Faculty Jurisdiction Cmmn 1980-84, Cathedrals Advsy Cmmn for England 1986, Canterbury Cathedral Fabric Ctee 1987-, St Paul's Cathedral Fabric Ctee 1990-; tstee Civic Tst 1989-; Freeman City of London 1972, memb Worshipful Co of Chartered Architects 1985 (jr warden 1990; FSA 1966, FRIBA 1967 (assoc 1949); *Recreations* music, visual arts; *Clubs* Athenaeum; *Style*— Ashley Barker, Esq, OBE, FSA; 39 Kensington Park Gardens, London W11 2QT (☎ 071 727 9148, fax 071 792 9672)

BARKER, Audrey Lilian; da of Harry Barker (d 1963), and Elsie Annie Dutton (d 1976); *b* 13 April 1918; *Educ* secdy schs in Kent and Surrey; *Career* writer; memb Exec Ctee Eng Centre Int PEN 1981-85; memb Panel of Judges for: Katherine Mansfield Prize 1984, Macmillan Silver Pen Award for Fiction 1986, Short Stories 1989, Arts Cncl Writers' Bursaries 1989; *Awards* Atlantic Award in Lit 1946, Somerset Maugham Award 1947, Cheltenham Festival of Lit Award 1963, Arts Cncl Award 1970, SE Arts Creative Book Award 1981, Macmillan Silver Pen Award 1987,Soc of Authors Travelling Scholarship 1988; FRSL; *Books* Innocents (1947), Apology for a Hero (1950), Novelette (1951), The Joy Ride (1963), Lost Upon the Roundabouts (1964), A Case Examined (1965), The Middling (1967), John Brown's Body (1969), Femina Real (1971), A Source of Embarrassment (1974), A Heavy Feather (1979), Life Stories (1981), Relative Successes (1984), No Word of Love (1985), The Gooseboy (1987), The Woman Who Talked to Herself (1989), Any Excuse for a Party (1991); *Style*— Ms A L Barker; 103 Harrow Rd, Carshalton, Surrey SM5 3QF

BARKER, Barry; MBE (1960); s of Francis Walter Barker (d 1974),and Amy Barker, *née* Rumsey; *b* 28 Dec 1929; *Educ* Ipswich Sch, Trinity Coll Oxford (MA); *m* 1954, Vira, da of Jehangir Dubash, of Bombay, India; 2 s (Christopher, David); *Career* sec: Bombay C of C and Indust 1956-62, The Metal Box Co of India Ltd 1962-67; dir Shipbuilding Indust Bds 1967-71, conslt DOI 1972, sec Pye Holdings Ltd 1972-76; memb: Nat Cncl for Vocational Qualificationns, Nat Forum for Mgmnt Educn and Devpt; chm Consultative Cncl of Professional Mgmnt Organisations; sec and chief exec ICSA (formerly Chartered Inst of Secs) 1976-89; memb: Nat Cncl for Vocational Qualifications, Business and Technician Educn Cncl, Nat Forum for Mgmnt Educn and Devpt, Bd of Mgmnt RSA Examinations, Bd of Mgmnt The Young Vic; chm Consultative Cncl of Professional Mgmnt Orgns; *Recreations* theatre, arts; *Clubs* Oriental; *Style*— Barry Barker, Esq, MBE; 82 Darwin Court, Gloucester Ave, London NW1 7BQ

BARKER, Barry William; s of William John Walter Barker, of Witham, Essex, and Doris Catherine Margaret, *née* Bruton (d 1986); *b* 11 Aug 1946; *Educ* George Green's GS, Camberwell Sch of Art (DipAd); *m* 1, 1968 (m dis) Beatrice Joyce Cooper; m 2, Claire Francesca (formerly Mrs Griffiths), da of Derek Omaney Raby Noble; 1 s (William Paul b 20 March 1989), 2 step c (Annie Griffiths b 6 Dec 1977, Graham Griffiths b 15 March 1979); *Career* pt/t lectr various art schs 1967-73, dir of exhibitions ICA 1973-76; dir: Barry Barker Gallery 1976-79, John Hansard Gallery 1980-87, Arnolfini Gallery 1987-90; asst dir of regnl exhibitions South Bank Centre 1990-; curator of numerous exhibitions of contemporary art incl: Pier & Ocean (Hayward Gallery) 1979, L'Different (John Hansard Gallery) 1986, Falls The Shadow (Hayward) 1986, Decor: By Marcel Broothaers (ICA) 1976; numerous contribs to jls and catalogues of contemporary art; *Recreations* family, learning to play golf; *Style*— Barry Barker, Esq; Exhibitions Dept, South Bank Centre, Belvedere Rd, London SE1 8XZ (☎ 071 921 0862)

BARKER, Bridget Caroline; da of Michael John Barker, of 14 Bollinwood Chase, Wilmslow Park, Wilmslow, Cheshire, and Brenda, *née* Sawdon (d 1987); *b* 7 March 1958; *Educ* Haberdashers' Monmouth Sch for Girls, Univ of Southampton (LLB); *Career* admitted slr 1983; Macfarlanes 1983- (ptnr 1988-); Skadden Arps Slate Meagher & Flom NY 1986-87; memb: Law Soc, Int Bar Soc, Assoc of Women Slrs, City of London Slrs Co; *Recreations* tennis, travel; *Style*— Ms Bridget Barker; 10 Norwich Street, London EC4A 1BD (☎ 071 831 9222, fax 071 831 9607)

BARKER, Charles Richard; s of Brian Barker (d 1982), of Halifax , and Sybil Mabel, *née* Busfield; *b* 24 March 1951; *Educ* Hipperholme GS Halifax , Imperial Coll of Sci and Technol Univ of London (BSc); *Career* CA, trained Spicer and Pegler, Robson Rhodes, dir and sec Low Moor Properties Ltd 1974, sole practitioner 1979-; FCA; *Style*— Charles Barker, Esq; Hill Top House, Main Street, Burley-in-Wharfedale, Ilkley, West Yorkshire (☎ 0943 862 912)

BARKER, Christopher Shelley; DL (S Yorks, 1984); s of Ernest Anthony Barker, CBE (d 1979), of Lindrick, nr Worksop, and Barbara Mary, *née* Bishop; *b* 13 Nov 1932; *Educ* Rugby, New College Oxford (BA); *m* 11 June 1960, Jennifer Mary, da of Harold Sydney Biggs (d 1981), of Hornsea; 3 da (Caroline, Victoria, Belinda); *Career* Nat Serv RE 1950-52 (cmmnd 1951), TA RE 1952-62; admitted slr 1959; ptnr: H Shelley Barker & Son 1960-68, Neals & Shelley Barkers 1969-77, Broomheads 1978-87 (sr ptnr from 1981); sr ptnr Dibb Lupton Broomhead 1988-; directorships incl: Dengel & Barker (Holdings) Ltd and subsids (chm 1983-), Circuitt & Hinchcliffe Ltd and subsids, Rittal Holdings Ltd and subsids; tstee Sheffield Town Tst 1984-, Talbot Tsts 1962-; gen cmmr of taxes 1967-72, memb Cncl Univ of Sheffield 1964- (treas 1971-79, pro chllr 1979-87, chm 1981-87); Freeman Co of Culters in Hallamshire, Hon LLD Univ of Sheffield 1988; memb Law Soc; *Recreations* golf; *Clubs* R & AGC, Lindrick Golf, Hunstanton Golf, Royal Worlington & Newmarket Golf; *Style*— Christopher Barker, Esq, DL; Lion Cottage, Firbeck, nr Worksop, Notts S81 8JT (☎ 0709 817 011); The Old School House, Brancaster, West Norfolk PE31 8AP (☎ 0485 210 689; Dibb Lupton Broomhead, Fountain Precinct, Balm Green, Sheffield S1 1RZ (☎ 0742 760 351, fax 0742 700 568, car tel 0837 273 094, telex 547566)

BARKER, Rt Rev Clifford Conder Barker; TD (1971); s of Rev Sidney Barker (d 1979), and Kathleen Alice, *née* Conder (d 1973); *b* 22 April 1926; *Educ* Middlesbrough HS, Oriel Coll Oxford (BA, MA), St Chad's Coll Durham (Dip Theol); *m* 1, 14 Aug 1952, Marie (d 1982), da of Richard Edwards (d 1958); 1 s (Richard b 1960), 2 da (Helena b 1954, Catherine b 1962); m 2, 23 July 1983, Audrey Vera Gregson, da of Charles Ernest Fisher (d 1961); 2 step s (Timothy b 1954, Simon b 1955), 1 step da (Louise b 1959); *Career* Green Howards 1944-48 (cmmnd 1946), Chaplain TA 1958-74; ordained: deacon 1952, priest 1953; curate: All Saints Scarborough 1952-55, Redcar

1955-57; vicar: Sculcoates Hull 1957-63, Rudby in Cleveland with Middleton 1963-70, St Olave York 1970-76; rural dean: Stokesley 1965-70, City of York 1971-76; canon and prebendary York Minster 1973-76, consecrated bishop 1976, bishop of Whitby 1976-83, bishop of Selby 1983-91; *Recreations* most sports, gardening, music, travel, crosswords, natural history; *Clubs* Yorkshire; *Style—* The Rt Rev C C Barker, TD; 15 Oak Tree Close, Strensall, York YO3 5TE (☎ 0904 490406)

BARKER, Clive; s of Leonard Barker, of Liverpool, and Joan Ruby Revill; *b* 5 Nov 1952; *Educ* Quarry Bank GS Liverpool, Univ of Liverpool (BA); *Career* playwright and film dir; plays: Dog, History of the Devil, Frankenstein in Love, Colossus, Subtle Bodies, Paradise Street, Crazyface, Secret Life of Cartoons; films: Hellraiser, Nightbreed; *Books* Books of Blood Vols I-VI (1984), Vols 4,5,6 (1985), The Damnation Game (1986), Weaveworld (1987), Cabal (1989), The Great and Secret Show (1989); *Style—* Clive Barker, Esq

BARKER, Clive; s of Samuel Lawrence Barker (d 1987), of Middlesbrough, Yorkshire, and Lily, *née* Dawson (d 1970); *b* 29 June 1931; *Educ* Acklam Hall GS Middlesbrough, Bristol Old Vic Theatre Sch, Univ of Birmingham (BA); *m* 1, 21 March 1964, Josephine, *née* Benson (decd); 2 s (John Jesse b 30 Dec 1960, Brendan Samuel b 5 March 1965); m 2, 15 Aug 1983, Susan Edna, da of Raymond George Bassnett; 1 s (Luke Alexander Bassnett b 31 July 1989), 2 da (Vanessa Jane Bassnett b 11 Aug 1977, Rosanna Bassnett Barker b 7 Feb 1985), 1 step da (Lucy Mercedes Bassnett-McGuire b 30 Sept 1972); *Career* freelance actor, dir, writer and other theatrical employment 1955-66; festivals organiser Centre 42 1961-63, lectr in theatre practice Dept of Drama and Theatre Arts Univ of Birmingham, assoc dir Northcott Theatre Exeter 1974-75, lectr Jt Sch of Theatre Studies Univ of Warwick 1975-; memb Theatre Workshop Co 1955-; performing first productions incl: The Hostage 1958, Fings Ain't Wot They Used T'be, The Good Soldier Schweik 1956, The Merry Roosters Pantomime 1963, Twang!!! 1965, Oh What A Lovely War 1964; worked repertory theatres: Carlisle 1956, Canterbury and Exeter 1960-63, Royal Ct Theatre 1960; dir first Br productions incl: The Lion in Love 1960, Enter Solly Gold 1962, The Dice 1963, The Police 1963, Vassa Zhelessnova 1972; work abroad: acting coach Bühne der Stadt Köln 1974, dir Dr Faustus (Deutsches Nat Theatre Weimar) 1983, assoc dir Teatro Libre de Bogota 1985, dir Oroonoko (Teatro Colon Bogota) 1986; teaching posts incl: dir of courses Nat Youth Theatre 1964-70, Br Cncl Exchange fell Humboldt Univ of Berlin 1981, Landsdown visitor Univ of Victoria BC Canada 1986; memb Bd of Dirs: Centre 42 1961-71, 7:84 Theatre Co 1980-, Albatross Arts Project and Geese Theatre 1987- (chm 1989-), Int Workshop Festival 1990-; memb: Int Symposium on the Trg of Theatre Dirs Warsaw 1980, Int Sch of Theatre Anthropology Bologna 1990-; pres Br Pirandello Soc 1983-88, assoc dir Almost Free Theatre 1974-82, chm of the Tstees Inst of Drama Therapy 1989-, tstee Interaction 1967-; assoc ed Theatre Quarterly 1978-81; jt ed: New Theatre Quarterly 1984-, (with Susan Bassnett) New World Theatre Series 1989-; various radio documentaries; author plays for TV, theatre and radio; *Books* Theatre Games, A New Approach to Theatre Training (1977), Brecht: The Days of the Commune (translation with Arno Reinfrank, 1978), Woche Für Woche (1971); *Recreations* cricket; *Style—* Clive Barker, Esq; Woodstock House, The Square, Wolvey, Hinckley, Leics LE10 3LJ; Joint Sch of Theatre Studies, University of Warwick, Coventry CV4 7AL (☎ 0203 523351)

BARKER, Sir Colin; *b* 20 Oct 1926; *m* 15 Sept 1951, Beryl; 3 s (Keith, Roger, Paul), 1 da (Heather); *Career* chm: British Technology Group 1983-, British Investment Trust plc 1985-, CIN Management Limited 1985-, MCD Group Limited 1990-, Globe Investment Trust plc 1990-; dir National Coal Board 1984-, Edinburgh Fund Managers plc 1988-, Torotrack (Holdings) Limited 1989-, Malvern UK Index Trust plc 1990-, currently non-exec dir Reed International plc; FRSA; kt; *Style—* Sir Colin Barker; British Technology Group, 101 Newington Causeway, London SE1 6BU

BARKER, David; QC (1976); s of Frederick Barker (d 1987), of The Old Cottage, Woodhouse, Leics, and Amy Evelyn, *née* Lundie; *b* 13 April 1932; *Educ* Sir John Deane's GS, Univ Coll London (LLM), Univ of Michigan (USA); *m* 1957, Diana Mary Vinson, da of Alan Duckworth (d 1981), of Hill House, Rochdale, Lancs; 1 s (Jonathan), 3 da (Jane, Rachel, Caroline); *Career* RAF Flt Lt 1956-58; rec of the Crown Court 1974, bencher Inner Temple 1985, memb Criminal Injuries Compensation Bd 1990-; *Style—* David Barker, Esq, QC; Nanhill, Woodhouse, Eaves, Leics (☎ 0509 890 224); 7 King's Bench Walk, EC4; Francis Taylor Bldg, Temple, London EC4 (☎ 071 353 7768)

BARKER, David; s of Samuel Barker, of 162 Rochdale Rd, Royton, Oldham, Lancs, and Alice, *née* Bailey; *b* 31 March 1943; *Educ* N Chadderton Sch, Royal Coll Advanced Technol Salford; *m* 2 s (Simon David b 23 Sept 1965, Timothy Jason b 5 Nov 1968); *Career* md Styles & Wood Ltd 1966-, chm Meridian Holdings Group 1981-; memb Bd of Dirs: Wembley Stadium 1984, Young Presidents Organisation Inc 1986-; exec chm Crown Store Equipment Inc USA 1987; JP Oldham Bench 1976-86; chm Oldham Round Table 1976-77, nat cncllr Round Table Br and Ireland 1979-82, chm Pennine Chapter 1985-86 and int sr vice pres Euro Middle E & Africa Young Presidents Organisation Inc 1989-91; memb IOD, FInstD; *Recreations* skiing, walking, flying; *Clubs* St James's (Manchester); *Style—* David Barker, Esq; 2 Evenholme, Green Walk, Bowdon, Cheshire WA14 2SL (☎ 061 954 7030, fax 061 954 0498); Meridian Holdings Ltd, St James House, 8th Floor, Pedleton Way, Salford, Manchester M6 5JA (☎ 061 854 7030, fax 061 954 0498)

BARKER, David Edward; s of Edward Reginald Barker, of Radlett, Herts, and Frances Barker, *née* Solly; *b* 28 May 1946; *Educ* Bushey Sch, Watford Art Coll; *m* 9 Oct 1971, Jennifer Ann, da of Ernest Farnham (d 1960), of Morden, Surrey; 1 s (Leo Farnham b 1979), 1 da (Cassia Eve b 1978); *Career* art dir Leo Burnet London 1966-68, creative gp head J Walter Thompson London New York 1970-75 (art dir 1968-70); creative dir: Rupert Chetwynd 1975-79, Benton & Bowles London 1979-80, Geers and Gross 1980-84; fndr and creative dir Humphreys Bull & Barker 1984-86, fndr and exec creative dir KHBB 1986-90, dir The Reject Shop plc 1990, fndr chm and creative dir Barker & Ralston 1991-; *Recreations* motor racing, photography, music; *Clubs* BARC, BRSCC; *Style—* David Barker, Esq; 2 Physic Place, 70 Royal Hospital Road, London SW3 4HP (☎ 071 351 3535, fax 071 352 3237)

BARKER, Prof David Faubert; s of Faubert Barker (d 1980), and Doreen Maude, *née* Hitchcock (d 1955); *b* 18 Feb 1922; *Educ* Bryanston, Magdalen Coll Oxford (BA, DPhil, MA, DSc); *m* 1, 16 June 1945 (m dis 1977), Kathleen Mary Frances, da of William Pocock (d 1951); 3 s (Ian b 1947, Jolyon b 1952, Guy b 1954), 2 da (Susan b 1948, Jillian b 1955); m 2, 29 Jan 1978, Patricia Margaret, *née* Drake; 1 s (John b 1970), 1 da (Annabel b 1974); *Career* demonstrator Dept of Zoology Univ of Oxford 1947-50, dean Faculty of Sci Univ of Hong Kong 1959-60 (prof of zoology 1950-), prof of zoology Univ of Durham 1962-87, Sir Derman Christopherson fell Univ of Durham Res Fndn 1985-86 (emeritus prof 1987-); emeritus fell Leverhulme Tst 1989-91; memb Physiological Soc, sr memb Anatomical Soc; *Recreations* gardening; *Style—* Prof David Barker; Dept of Biological Sciences, Univ of Durham, South Rd, Durham DH1 3LE (☎ 091 374 3341)

BARKER, Dennis Malcolm; s of George Walter Barker (d 1970), of Oulton Broad, and Gertrude Edith, *née* Seeley (d 1979); *b* 21 June 1929; *Educ* Royal GS High Wycombe, Lowestoft GS; *m* Sarah Katherine, *née* Alwyn; *Career* journalist and author; Suffolk Chronicle and Mercury 1947-48, E Anglian Daily Times 1948-58, Express and Star Wolverhampton (property ed, theatre and radio critic, columnist) 1958-63, Guardian (Midlands corr, then in London, feature writer, general columnist, media corr, People profile columnist) 1963-; occasional broadcaster BBC Radio Stop The Week Programme 1974-76; chm: Suffolk branch NUJ 1958 (sec 1953-58), Home Counties Dist Cncl 1956-57; memb: Writers Guild of GB, Soc of Authors, Broadcasting Press Guild; *Books* non-fiction: The People of the Forces Trilogy (Soldiering On 1981, Ruling The Waves 1986, Guarding The Skies 1989), One Man's Estate (1983), Parian Ware (1985), Fresh Start (1990); novels: Candidate of Promise (1969), The Scandalisers (1974), Winston Three Three Three (1987); *Recreations* painting, sailing, music, cinema; *Style—* Dennis Barker, Esq; 67 Speldhurst Road, London W4 1BY (☎ 081 994 5380); The Guardian, 119 Farringdon Road, London EC1R 3ER (☎ 071 278 2332)

BARKER, Prof Geoffrey Ronald; s of Ronald James Barker (d 1982), and Edith Gertrude, *née* Fisher (d 1985); *b* 4 April 1943; *Educ* Univ of London Guy's Medical Dental Sch (BSc, MB BS, BDS), Univ of Manchester (MSc); *m* 14 Nov 1977, Jane McEwen, da of Daniel Trushell, of Kilbarchan; 2 s (Simon b 26 July 1979, Matthew 24 June 1981); *Career* consIt oral and maxillofacial surgn RAMC (V) 372 MFST, Maj 1985-; med practitioner Channel Islands Alderney and Guernsey 1974-78; Univ of Birmingham Med and Dental Schs 1978-81: hon registrar, hon sr registrar, lectr in oral surgery and oral med; sr lectr and hon consIt in oral and maxillofacial surgery and oral med Manchester Med and Dental Schs 1981-87; Dept of Oral Surgery Medicine and Pathology Univ of Wales Coll of Med Cardiff 1987- (prof, consIt and head of Dept); memb: Dental Ctee Med Def Union, Local Dental Ctees for S Wales; ex surgn St John Ambulance; FRCS 1985, MRCS, LRCP, LDSRCS, FDSRCS 1979; *Recreations* photography, walking, golf; *Clubs* Royal Army Medical; *Style—* Prof Geoffrey Barker; 24 Duncan Close, Old Church Hill, St Mellons, Cardiff CF3 9NP (☎ 0222 797366, 0426 9593261); 87 Green Pastures, Heaton Mersey, Cheshire SK4 3RB (☎ 061 442 5565); Department Oral Surgery Medicine & Pathology, University of Wales College of Medicine, Heath Park, Cardiff CF4 4XY (☎ 0222 742445 ext 2442)

BARKER, George Granville; s of George Barker (d 1961), and Marion Frances, *née* Taaffe (d 1955); *b* 26 Feb 1913; *Educ* Marlborough Rd Sch London; *m* 1963, Elspeth Roberta Cameron, da of Robert Langlands, of Kelso, Scotland; 3 s, 2 da; *Career* writer; prof of Eng lit Imperial Tohoku Univ Japan 1939-40, visiting prof NY State Univ, Arts fellowship Univ of York; author of various collected poems, essays and two plays; *Style—* George Barker, Esq; Bintry House, Itteringham, Aylsham, Norfolk (☎ 0263 87240); c/o Faber & Faber Ltd, 3 Queen's Square, London WC1

BARKER, Godfrey Raymond; s of Harold Lindsey Barker (d 1973), and Alys, *née* Singleton (d 1988); *b* 14 April 1945; *Educ* Dulwich, Cambridge, Oxford and Cornell Univs (MA, DPhil); *m* 17 Feb 1974, Ann, da of Frederick Botsford Callender, of Pasadena, California; 1 s (Frederick George Lindsey b 28 Oct 1983); *Career* Cons Res Dept 1966-67, fell and tutor Cornell Univ 1967-69, editorial trainee ITN 1969-72, 2nd sec UN Dept FO 1972, sr feature writer Now magazine 1979-81; The Daily Telegraph: political reporter 1972-79, parly sketchwriter and leader writer 1981-89, arts ed 1986, arts and political columnist 1989-; *Recreations* campaigning for the National Heritage, opera, lieder, cricket; *Clubs* Beefsteak; *Style—* Godfrey Barker, Esq; 26 Charles St, Berkeley Square, London W1 (☎ 071 499 8516); The Daily Telegraph, 181 Marsh Wall, London E14 (☎ 071 538 5000)

BARKER, Prof Graeme William Walter; s of Reginald Walter Barker (d 1987), and Kathleen, *née* Walton (d 1981); *b* 23 Oct 1946; *Educ* Alleyn's Sch London, St John's Coll Cambridge (Henry Arthur Thomas open scholar, BA, MA, PhD), Br Sch at Rome (Rome scholar in classical studies); *m* 3 Jan 1976 (m dis 1991), Sarah Miranda Buchanan; 1 s (Lewis William b 26 May 1983), 1 da (Rachel Jessica b 14 Feb 1980); *Career* sr lectr in prehistoric archaeology Univ of Sheffield 1981-84 (lectr 1972-81), dir Br Sch at Rome 1984-88, prof of archaeology Univ of Leicester 1988-; chm Soc for Libyan Studies; memb: Editorial Bd CUP and Journal of Mediterranean Archaeology, Leics Archaeological Advsy Ctee, Br Acad State Studentships Ctee; FSA 1979; *Books* Landscape and Society in Prehistoric Central Italy (1981), Archaeology and Italian Society (co-ed with R Hodges), Prehistoric Farming in Europe (1985), Beyond Domestication in Prehistoric Europe (co-ed with C Gamble, 1985), Cyrenaica in Antiquity (co-ed with J Lloyd and J Reynolds, 1985), Roman Landscapes (co-ed with J Lloyd, 1991); *Recreations* walking, swimming, skiing, reading; *Style—* Prof Graeme Barker, FSA; 55 Knighton Drive, Leicester LE2 3HD (☎ 0533 708132); School of Archaeological Studies, University of Leicester, University Rd, Leicester LE1 7RH (☎ 0533 522612, fax 0533 5222000, telex 342750)

BARKER, Graham Harold; TD (1985); s of Harold George Barker (d 1962), of Cambridge, and Dorothy, *née* Speechley (d 1986); *b* 11 Jan 1949; *Educ* Cambridge GS, King's Coll London, St George's Hosp Med Sch London (MB BS, AKC); *m* 23 Sept 1978, Esther Louise, da of John Owen Farrow, of Norwich; 1 s (Douglas Graham b 23 June 1982), 1 da (Louise Elizabeth b 9 Jan 1987); *Career* Surgn 217 (L) Gen Hosp RAMC (V) 1973-, Capt 1974, Maj 1980; lectr Inst of Cancer Res London 1977-79, registrar Queen Charlotte's and Chelsea Hosps London 1980, sr registrar in gynaecology and obstetrics Middx Hosp and UCL 1981-87, currently gynaecologist St George's Hosp London and Portland Hosp for Children London; memb: Br Soc for Colposcopy and Cervical Pathology, Br Gynaecologicial Cancer Soc, Gynaecological Res Soc, Chelsea Clinical Soc; AKC, Astor fell Harvard Univ Hosps 1984; Freeman City of London, Liveryman Worshipful Co of Apothecaries 1980; MRCOG 1978, FRCSEd 1979; *Books* Family Health And Medicine Guide (1979), Your Search For Fertility (1981), Chemotherapy of Gynaecological Malignancies (1983), The New Fertility (1986), Your Smear Test - A Guide To Screening, Colposcopy And The Prevention Of Cervical Cancer (1987), Overcoming Infertility (1990); *Recreations* writing, the organ, trumpet, piano; *Style—* Graham Barker, Esq, TD; 12 Wolsey Close, Kingston Upon Thames, Surrey KT2 7ER (☎ 081 942 2614); 8 Denham Way, Cambersands, Rye, East Sussex; St George's Hosp, Blackshaw Rd, London SW17 (☎ 081 672 1255)

BARKER, John; *Educ* RCM London, Salzburg Mozarteum (Lovro von Matačič); *Career* conductor; has worked with Br Opera Cos incl: Glyndebourne Festival (memb music staff), Sadler's Wells (chorus master, conductor), ENO (head of music, conductor), The Royal Opera (head Music Staff, currently head Music Dept); at Covent Garden has conducted: Le Nozze di Figaro, Don Giovanni, Troilus and Cressida, Peter Grimes, Madame Butterfly, Tosca, Turandot, Lucia di Lammermoor, Il Trovatore, La Boheme; conductor Royal Ballet 1988-89: Sleeping Beauty, Romeo and Juliet; repertoire at Sadler's Wells and ENO incl: Mozart, Rossini, Saint-Saëns, Verdi, Offenbach, Johann Strauss, Humperdinck, Stravinsky, Wagner (incl the Ring Cycle), Williamson's The Violins of St Jaques and Lucky Peter's Journey (world premiere); conducted: Carmen in Seoul, concert with Baltsa and Carreras in Tokyo on 1986 Far East Tour, two concerts with Domingo Royal Opera House 1988; conducted orchs incl: London Philharmonic, Boston Symphony, Radio Eireann Symphony, Bournemouth Symphony, Orquestra Sinfonica Mexico City; *Style—* John Barker, Esq

BARKER, John Alfred; s of Alfred Barker (d 1990), of Holborn, London, and Miriam Alice, *née* Kerley; *b* 2 Dec 1929; *Educ* Neale's Mathematical Sch, City of London Coll;

m 22 Sept 1962, Margaret Coutts, da of Thomas Coutts Smith (d 1948), of 1 Waterside St, Sandford, Stonehouse, Lanark; *Career* Intelligence Corps TA and AVR 1959-69; Stock Exchange 1950-64, Inner London Probation Serv 1965-90, memb Local Review Ctee HM Prison Wandsworth 1986-; memb: Corp of London Common Councilman Cripplegate Without 1981-, Special Health Authy Bethlem Royal and Maudsley Hosps 1983-, Bd of Mgmnt Barbican YMCA 1986- (chm 1990-), City Parochial Fndn Central Governing Body 1989-, Nat Cncl of YMCA's Nat Bd 1989-, London Homes for the Elderly 1989-; upper warden Cripplegate Ward Club; govr: Bridewell Royal Hosp 1982, City of London Sch for Girls 1982, King Edward's Sch Witley Surrey 1989; tstee: Soc for Relief of Homeless Poor 1982, Neales Educnl Fndn 1983, Charity of John Land 1983; Freeman: City of London 1970, Worshipful Co of Basketmakers 1973; FRGS 1979, FZS 1980, FInstD 1984, MBIM 1985; *Recreations* travel, hill and mountain walking, club man; *Clubs* Reform, Guildhall, City Livery; *Style—* John Barker, Esq; 319 Willoughby House, Barbican, London EC2Y 8BL (☎ 071 628 5381)

BARKER, John Francis Holroyd; CB (1984); s of Rev C H Barker, and B A Barker, *née* Bullivant; *b* 3 Feb 1925; *m* 1954, Felicity Ann Martindale; 3 da; *Career* dir of music Abingdon Sch 1950-54, War Office (later MOD) 1954-85, conslt Cabinet Office 1985-; *Style—* J F H Barker, Esq, CB; c/o Coutts & Co, 440 Strand, London WC2R 0QS

BARKER, Air Vice-Marshal John Lindsay; CB (1963), CBE (1946), DFC (1945); s of Dr Abraham Cockroft Barker (d 1971), and Lilian Alice, *née* Woods (d 1969); *b* 12 Nov 1910; *Educ* Trent Coll, BNC Oxford; *m* 1948, Eleanor Margaret Hannah, da of E B Williams, of Co Cork; 1 s; *Career* RAFO 1930, RAF 1933, served WWII, air attaché Rome 1955-58, Cdr Royal Ceylon Air Force 1958-63, ret; called to the Bar Middle Temple 1947; Order of Merit (Italy) 1958; *Recreations* sailing, golf, photography; *Clubs* RAF; *Style—* Air Vice-Marshal John L Barker, CB, CBE, DFC; The Old Cider Press Mill, Court Frogmore, Kingsbridge, South Devon TQ7 2PB (☎ 0548 531746)

BARKER, Rear Adm John Perronet; CB (1985); s of Gilbert Barker (d 1969; gs of Thomas Perronet Barker, constructional engr, who built all the waterless gasholders in Britain in the 1930s), and Dorothy Gwendoline, *née* Moore (d 1972), of Edgbaston, Birmingham; *Educ* Nautical Coll Pangbourne; *m* 1955, (Evelyn) Priscilla Summerson, da of Sir William Christie, KCIE, CSI, MC (d 1983), of Gerrards Cross, Bucks; 2 s (b 1957 and 1959); *Career* joined RN 1948, supply offr HMS Lagos 1957-58, Britannia RN Coll Dartmouth 1958-61, sec to Br Naval Attaché Washington 1961-64, sec to ACNS (Warfare) 1964-67, supply offr HMS Hampshire 1967-68, sec to Controller of the Navy 1972-76, Royal Acoll of Defence Studies 1977, dir Fleet Supply Duties MOD 1978-80, Cdre HMS Centurion 1980-83, Rear Adm 1983, COS to C-in-C Naval Home Cmd 1983-85, ret RN 1986; chm IYRU Youth Sailing Ctee 1986-; memb Cncl: Sea Cadet Assoc 1986-, Shaftesbury Homes and ARETHUSA 1988-, administrator Mission to Seamen 1987-, chm Assoc of RN Offrs 1987-; Liveryman of Worshipful Company of Shipwrights 1983; *Recreations* yacht racing and administration, gardening, DIY; *Clubs* RN Sailing, Midland Sailing, Royal Yacht Sqdn; *Style—* Rear Adm John Barker, CB; c/o Lloyds Bank plc, Colmore Row, Birmingham B3 3AD

BARKER, John Sowerby Gartside; s of Lt-Col Robert Hewitt Barker, JP (d 1961), of Todmorden and Rochdale (MP (Ind) Sowerby 1919-22), and Violet Kathleen, *née* Gartside (d 1982); *b* 27 June 1921; *Educ* King Edward VII Sch Lytham St Annes; *m* 15 Sept 1951, Judith Mary, da of Herbert Wilson Collier, JP, (d 1977), of Gloucester; 2s (Robert, Richard), 2 da (Hazel, Sara); *Career* WWII served 1941-46, Maj RA (despatches 1946); articled F Hunter Gregory & Lord 1938, qualified CA 1949, commercial appt 1948-53, ptnr F Hunter Gregory & Lord (merged with BDO Binder Hamlyn 1974) 19 (conslt 1987-); former pres NW Soc CAs 1983-84, memb Bacup Rotary Club, treas Rochdale Music Soc; MICA; *Recreations* music, pianoforte, rugby, tennis, golf; *Style—* John Barker, Esq; BDO Binder Hamlyn, 7-9 Irwell Terrace, Bacup, Lancs OL13 9AJ, (☎ 0706 873 213, fax 0706 874 211)

BARKER, Jonathan David; s of Thomas William Barker, and Dorothy Joan Barker; *b* 17 July 1949; *Educ* Victoria Boys' Sch Watford, Cassio Coll of Futher Educn Watford, Birkbeck Coll London (BA, Frank Newton prize for English), Poly of N London (Postgrad Dip in Librarianship & Info Sci); *m* 23 July 1983, Deirdre Mary, da of Cornelius Joseph Shanahan; *Career* arboriculturalist Whippendell Woods Watford 1969-70, library asst Kensington Central Reference Library 1970-72, poetry librarian Arts Cncl Poetry Library 1973-88, asst sec Poetry Book Soc Ltd 1973-83, literature offr Literature Dept The Br Cncl 1988-; pubns: Arts Council Poetry Library Short-Title Catalogue (6 edn 1981), Selected Poems of W H Davies (ed, 1985), Poetry Book Society Authology (ed, 1986), The Art of Edward Thomas (ed, 1987), Thirty Years of The Poetry Book Society: 1956-1986 (ed, 1988), Norman Cameron Collected Poems and Selected Translations (jt ed, 1990); contrib critical articles to reference books, adjudicator numerous poetry competitions; ALA 1985; *Recreations* music, gardening, travelling, book collecting; *Clubs* ICA; *Style—* Jonathan Barker, Esq; Literature Dept, The British Council, 10 Spring Gardens, London SW1A 2BN (☎ 071 930 8466, fax 071 839 6347)

BARKER, Kenneth; s of Raymond Charles Barker, of Leics, and Ivy, *née* Blackburn; *b* 15 Aug 1947; *Educ* Gateway Sch Leics; *m* 1, 30 Oct 1970 (m dis 1983), (Elizabeth) Peris, da of Thomas Stephens (d 1985); 1 s (Michael b 1974); m 2, 8 July 1987, Julie, da of Joseph Casling (d 1984); 1 s (Edward b 1984); *Career* CA; F W Clarke & Co (later Touche Ross & Co) 1964-78, Barker Crowfoot 1978-; treas and memb: Leicester CC 1962-82, Old Lancastrians Football Club 1963-85; treas Leics Badminton Assoc 1981-84; FCA 1979; *Recreations* golf, badminton; *Clubs* Glen Gorse Golf, Coalville Badminton; *Style—* Kenneth Barker, Esq; The Old Coach House, Church Lane, Dunton Bassett, Lutterworth, Leics (☎ 0455 202140); Barker Crowfoot, Lonsdale, High St, Lutterworth, Leics (☎ 0455 557322, fax 0455 554144)

BARKER, Capt Nicholas John; CBE (1982); s of Lt Cdr John Frederick Barker, DSC, RN (ka 1940), and Jillian, *née* Paget (d 1943); *b* 19 May 1933; *Educ* Canford, Naval Colls and Staff Coll, Churchill Coll (def fellowship 1983-84), Univ of Cambridge; *m* 1, 10 Aug 1957 (m dis 1989), Elizabeth Venetia, *née* Redman; 2 s (Henry b 1959, Benjamin b 1964), 2 da (Louise (Mrs Townsend) b 1961, Emma (Mrs Payne) b 1962); m 2, 4 March 1989, Jennifer Jane, da of Cdr Richard Douglas Cayley, DSO and two bars, RN (ka 1943); 2 step da (Antonia b 1958, Jessica (Mrs Cushnib) b 1963); *Career* RN; eight seagoing cmds incl: HMS Arrow 1975-77, HMS Endurance (Falklands) 1980-82, Fishery Protection Sqdn 1984-86, HMS Sheffield 1987-88; MOD Naval Sec Dept 1977-79; chm: Sea Safety Centre Ltd North East Marine Services Ltd; dir: Glowsafe Ltd, Marr Tech Servs; ptnr Nicholas Barker Consultancy; nat chm Royal Nat Mission to Deep Sea Fishermen, memb Nat Cncl Br Maritime League; memb: S W Atlantic Gp, Jubilee Tst (patron local Ctee); Younger Bro Trinity House London 1967; Hon Col Royal Marines RMR Tyne 1990; Freeman City of London, Liveryman Worshipful Co of Fishmongers 1986; FBIM 1977, MNI 1979, FRGS 1982; Royal Order of Merit Class IV Norway 1988; *Books* The Falklands, a Common Denominator (1984); novels incl: Red Ice (1987, voted one of best novels NY Times 1987), Rig (1990); *Recreations* shooting, fishing, golf, spectating almost any sport, reading - current affairs; *Clubs* Naval, Northern Counties; *Style—* Capt Nicholas Barker, CBE, RN; Low Farnham Farmhouse, Sharperton, Rothbury, Morpeth, Northumberland NE65 7AQ (☎ 0669 40275); The Sea Safety Centre, Barrack St Entrance, South Dock, Sunderland (☎ 091 514 5037, fax 091 510 8108)

BARKER, Nicolas John; s of Sir Ernest Barker (d 1960), and Olivia Stuart, *née* Horner (d 1976); *b* 6 Dec 1932; *Educ* Westminster, New Coll Oxford (MA); *m* 11 Aug 1962, Joanna Mary Nyda Sophia, da of Col Henry Edward Mariano Cotton, OBE (d 1988); 2 s (Christian b 1964, Cosmo b 1973), 3 da (Emma b 1963, Olivia b 1963, Cecilia b 1969); *Career* Rupert Hart-Davis Ltd 1959, asst keeper Nat Portrait Gallery 1964, Macmillan and Co 1965, OUP 1971, dep keeper Br Library 1976, ed The Book Collector 1965; *Books* The Publications of the Roxburghe Club (1962), The Printer and the Poet (1970), Stanley Morison (1972), The Early Life of James McBey (1977), Bibliotheca Lindesiana (1977), The Oxford University Press and the Spread of Learning (1978), A Sequel to an Enquiry (with J Collins, 1983), Aldus Manutius and the Development of Greek Script and Type (1985), The Butterfly Books (1987), Two East Anglian Picture Books (1988), Treasures of the British Library (compiler, 1989); *Clubs* Garrick, Beefsteak; *Style—* Nicolas John Barker, Esq; 22 Clarendon Rd, London W11 3AB (☎ 071 727 4340); British Library, Great Russell St, London WC1B 3DG (☎ 071 323 7550, telex 21462)

BARKER, Hon Mrs (Olwen Gwynne); *née* Philipps; JP; da of 1 and last Baron Kylsant (d 1937); *b* 1905; *m* 1, 1925 (m dis 1937), 7 Baron Suffield; m 2, 1937, Lt-Col Frank Richard Peter Barker, TD, RA (d 1974), s of late Christopher Barker, of Oakhyrst Grange, Caterham, Surrey; 1 s (Timothy Gwynne, *qv*); *Style—* The Hon Mrs Barker, JP; Lund Court, Nawton, York

BARKER, Dr Pamela Margaret Wentworth; da of Leslie Oliver Barker (d 1974), and Irene, *née* Duckett (d 1968); *b* 5 Nov 1929; *Educ* Ipswich HS Univ of Leeds (BSc, MB ChB, DPM); *Career* conslt psychiatrist Highland Health Bd 1978-, clinical sr lectr in mental health Univ of Aberdeen 1981-; FRSM 1983, MRC PSych; *Recreations* motor vehicle maintenance; *Style—* Dr Pamela Barker; Burnside, Leachkin Rd, Inverness IV3 6NW; Craig Dunain Hospital, Inverness IV3 6JU (☎ 0463 234101)

BARKER, Patricia Margaret (Pat); da of Moira Drake; *b* 8 May 1943; *Educ* Grangefield GS, LSE (BSc); *m* 29 Jan 1978, David Faubert Barker, s of Faubert Barker (d 1980); 1 s (John b 1970), 1 da (Annabel b 1974); *Career* novelist; MGM film Stanley and Iris starring Fonda and de Niro based on Union 1990, Jt Winner Fawcett Prize 1983, elected one of twenty Best of British Young Novelists 1983; memb literature panel Northern Arts; memb: Soc of Authors 1983, PEN 1989; *Books* Union Street (1982), Blow your House Down (1984), The Century's Daughter (1986), The Man Who Wasn't There (1989); *Recreations* swimming, walking, yoga, reading; *Style—* Mrs Patricia Barker; c/o Anne McDermid, Curtis Brown, 162-168 Regent St, London W1R 5TB (☎ 071 872 0331)

BARKER, Paul; s of Donald Barker (d 1981), and Marion, *née* Ashworth (d 1989); *b* 24 Aug 1935; *Educ* Hebden Bridge GS, Calder HS, BNC Oxford (MA); *m* 1960, Sally, da of James Huddleston (d 1965); 3 s (Nicholas b 1961, Tom b 1966, Daniel b 1973), 1 da (Kate b 1963); *Career* Nat Serv cmmnd Intelligence Corps 1953-55; lectr École Normale Supérieure Paris 1958-59; writer and broadcaster; ed staff: The Times 1959-63, Economist 1964-65; ed New Society 1968-86 (staff writer 1964, asst ed 1965-68); social policy ed Sunday Telegraph 1986-88, columnist London Evening Standard 1987-, assoc ed The Independent Magazine 1988-90, social and political coloumnist The Sunday Times 1990-; visiting fell Centre for the Analysis of Social Policy Univ of Bath 1986-; dir: The Fiction Magazine 1982-87, Pennine Heritage 1978-86; *Books* A Sociological Portrait (ed, 1972), One for Sorrow, Two for Joy (ed and contrib, 1972), The Social Sciences Today (ed, 1975), Arts in Society (ed and contrib, 1977), The Other Britain (ed and contrib, 1982), Founders of the Welfare State (ed, 1985); *Recreations* architecture; *Style—* Paul Barker, Esq; 15 Dartmouth Park Ave, London NW5 1JL (☎ 071 485 8861)

BARKER, Peter William; CBE (1988), DL (1990); *Career* chm Fenner PLC (power transmission engrs) 1982-; chm: J H Fenner & Co, Fenner Int; dir: Mastabar Mining Equipment, James Dawson & Son, Neepsend plc, Fenner America, Fenner (India), Fenner (Australia), Fenner (S Africa), Fenner Industl Controls, Fenner SA, Fenner GmbH; vice chm: CBI Yorks, Humberside Regnl Cncl; memb: CBI Nat Cncl, Yorks and Humberside Regnl Industl Devpt Bd; CBIM, FIIM, FInstD, FCIM, FRSA; *Clubs* Hurlingham, Oriental; *Style—* Peter W Barker, Esq, CBE, DL; Fenner PLC, PO Box 3, Welton Hall, Welton, Brough, N Humberside HU15 1PQ (☎ 0482 668111)

BARKER, Richard Philip; s of Philip Watson Barker (d 1971), and Helen May, *née* Latham (d 1957); *b* 17 July 1939; *Educ* Repton, Trinity Coll Cambridge (MA), Univ of Bristol (Cert Ed); *m* 30 July 1966, Imogen Margaret, da of Sir Ronald Montague Joseph Harris, KCVO, CB, of Slyfield Farmhouse, Stoke D'Abernon, Surrey; 2 s (Jolyon b 1967, Thorold b 1971), 1 da (Rosalind b 1969); *Career* asst master: Bedales Sch 1963-65, Marlborough Coll 1967-81; dir A Level Business Studies Project 1966-75, lectr Inst of Educn London 1974-75, headmaster Sevenoaks Sch 1981-; memb various ctees HMC; Understanding Business (series ed, 1975-); *Recreations* fishing, sailing, beekeeping, educational matters; *Clubs* RSA; *Style—* Richard Barker, Esq; Sevenoaks School, Sevenoaks, Kent TN13 1HU (☎ 0732 455133, fax 0732 456143)

BARKER, Ronnie (Ronald William George Barker); OBE (1978); s of Leonard and Edith Barker; *b* 25 Sept 1929; *Educ* Oxford HS; *m* 1957, Joy Tubb; 2 s, 1 da; *Career* actor; winner of eighteen awards for performances, including three Br Acad Awards; *Style—* Ronnie Barker, Esq, OBE; High Tamarisks, Loudwater, Bucks SL4 3BL

BARKER, Simon; s of Roy Barker (d 1982), of Rochdale, Lancashire, and Irene Barker; *b* 4 Nov 1964; *Educ* Pendlebury HS Swinton Manchester, Tuson Coll Preston; *m* 14 June 1987, Teresa Rean, da of Kenneth Knowles; *Career* professional footballer; Blackburn Rovers 1982-88: debut v Swansea City 1983, 221 appearances, 42 goals; Queens Park Rangers 1988-; joined for a fee of £400,000, debut v Manchester Utd 1988, over 100 appearances; 4 England under 21 caps 1985-86; Full Members Cup winners Blackburn Rovers 1987; *Style—* Simon Barker, Esq; Queens Park Rangers, Rangers Stadium, South Africa Road, Shepherds Bush, London W12 7PA (☎ 081 743 0262, fax 081 749 0994)

BARKER, Thomas Christopher; s of Col Rowland Barker, OBE, MC (d 1965), of Brighton, and Kathleen Maude, *née* Welch (d 1956); *b* 28 June 1928; *Educ* Uppingham, New Coll Oxford (MA); *m* 3 Sept 1960, Griselda Helen, da of Robert Cormack (d 1982), of Ayr; 2 s (Christopher b 1964, Robert b 1966), 1 da (Rosanna b 1961); *Career* 2 Lt Worcs Regt 1945; HM Dip Serv: third sec Paris 1953-55, second sec Baghdad 1955-58, first sec Mexico City 1962-67 (also head of Chancery and consul), cnsllr and head of Chancery Caracas 1969-71, under sec Belfast 1975-76; curator Scottish Nat War Meml 1978-88 (sec to tstees 1988-); FSAS 1988; *Style—* Thomas Barker, Esq; Carmurie, South St, Elie, Fife KY9 1DN; Scottish National War Memorial, The Castle, Edinburgh EH1 2YT

BARKER, Thomas Lloyd; s of Edmund Cadwaladyr Barker, of Loughton, Essex, and Patricia Josephine May, *née* Yates (d 1982); *b* 11 Jan 1939; *Educ* Bancroft's Sch, Univ of Birmingham (LLB); *m* 2 Oct 1971, Edwina Ethel, da of Albert Edward Wright, of Chelmondiston, Suffolk; 1 s (Thomas Oliver b 1972), 1 da (Charlotte b 1974); *Career* admitted slr 1967; currently ptnr Vanderpump and Sykes, Notary Public 1977; lay memb and chm Serv Ctees Redbridge and Waltham Forest Family Health Service

Authy, memb Ctee Buckhurst Hill and Loughton Green Belt Preservation Soc; tstee Barts-Oxford Family Study of Childhood Diabetes, special constable HAC; Freeman City of London 1981, Liveryman Worshipful Co Farriers 1981 (asst Ct 1988); memb: Law Soc, Soc Provincial Notaries; *Recreations* horse riding, walking, historical res; *Clubs* HAC; *Style—* Thomas Barker, Esq; Clovelly, 45 Hillcrest Rd, Loughton, Essex (☎ 081 508 1199); Vanderpump and Sykes, Lough Point, Gladbeck Way, Enfield, Middx (☎ 081 366 9696, fax 081 807 5347)

BARKER, Timothy Gwynne; s of Lt-Col (Frank Richard) Peter Barker (d 1974), of Lund Ct, Nawton, York, and Hon Olwen Gwynne, *née* Philipps, *qv*; *b* 8 April 1940; *Educ* Eton, Jesus Coll Cambridge (MA), McGill Univ Montreal; *m* 14 July 1964, Philippa Rachel Mary, da of Brig Mervyn Christopher Thursby-Pelham, OBE, of Ridgeland House, Finchampstead, Berks; 1 s (Christopher b 1970), 1 da (Camilla b 1968); *Career* dept chief exec Kleinworth Benson Group plc 1990- (joined 1988), vice chm Kleinwort Benson Ltd 1989- (dir 1973-); DG Panel on Takeovers and Mergers, Cncl for the Securities Indust 1984-85; *Style—* Timothy Barker, Esq; Kleinwort Benson Ltd, PO Box 560, 20 Fenchurch St, London EC3P 3DB

BARKER, Trevor; s of Samuel Lawrence Barker (d 1987), of Middlesbrough, and Lilian, *née* Dawson (d 1970); *b* 24 March 1935; *Educ* GS; *m* 7 Sept 1957, Joan Elizabeth, da of Frederick Cross (d 1972), of Stockton-on-Tees; 1 s (Roy b 21 Feb 1961), 1 da (Karen (Mrs Dent) b 17 July 1958); *Career* articled to Leonard C Bye FCA Middlesbrough, Price Waterhouse & Co 1957-58, Cooper Bros 1958-62, practised in Leyburn Yorks 1962-70, chm and chief exec Gold Case Travel Ltd 1964-77, dir Ellerman Wilson Lines Ltd 1977-80; chm and chief exec: John Crowther Group plc 1981-88, William Morris Fine Arts plc 1982-88, Alpha Consolidated Holdings Ltd 1988-; dep chm and chief exec Blanchards plc 1988-, chm Micklegate Group plc 1989-; memb Bd of Peterlee and Aycliffe Development Corp 1986-88; Freeman City of London, Liveryman Worshipful Co of Woolmen; FCA 1957, FRSA 1989; *Recreations* racing thoroughbreds, golf, opera, books; *Style—* Trevor Barker, Esq; Windways, 323 Coniscliffe Rd, Darlington, Co Durham, DL3 8AH (☎ 0325 350436); Arnison House, 139 High St, Yarm, Cleveland TS15 9AY (☎ 0642 786250, car 0860 517839)

BARKER, Sir William; KCMG (1967, CMG 1958), OBE (1949); s of Alfred Barker (d 1961), of Leigh, Lancs; *b* 19 July 1909; *Educ* Univ of Liverpool, Univ of Prague; *m* 1939, Margaret, da of Thomas P Beirne, of Leigh, Lancs; 1 s, 1 da; *Career* Br Ambass to Czechoslovakia 1966-68, Bowes prof of Russian Univ of Liverpool 1969-76; *Style—* Sir William Barker, KCMG, OBE; 19 Moors Way, Woodbridge, Suffolk IP12 4HQ (☎ 03943 3673)

BARKES, Neville Rogerson; TD; s of W Barkes, MD, of Northumberland, and Kathleen Herbert Ranken; *b* 11 July 1924; *Educ* Sedbergh, Edinburgh Univ; *m* 1952, Gillian, da of Col J C B Cookson, DSO, DL, of Meldon Park, Morpeth, Northumberland; 2 s (Richard, George), 1 da (Caroline); *Career* Capt 6 RHA 1946-47, Lt-Col 272 (N) Field Regt RA (TA) 1965-67; dir: British Electrical & Manufacturing Co 1953-88, TSB Holdings 1980-82; TSB Group Computer Services 1981-1984; chm: TSB Computer Services 1973-84, TSB NE 1980-83; memb TSB Central Bd 1980-86, dir Central Trustee Savings Bank 1982-86; memb TSB England and Wales 1983-86; Dir: TSB Group plc 1985-89, TSB England and Wales plc 1986-89; *Recreations* shooting, gardening; *Clubs* Northern Counties; *Style—* Neville Barkes, Esq, TD; West Muckleridge, Matfen, Northumberland NE20 0SQ (☎ 0661 886 230)

BARKSHIRE, (Robert Renny St John) John; CBE (1990), TD (1970), JP (Lewes 1980), DL (E Sussex 1986); s of Robert Hugh Barkshire, CBE, *qv*; *b* 31 Aug 1935; *Educ* Bedford Sch; *m* 1, 1960 (m dis 1990), Margaret Elizabeth, da of Leslie Robinson (d 1986), of Great Dunmow, Essex; 2 s (Charles b 1963, William b 1965), 1 da (Sarah b 1969); m 2, 1990, Audrey Witham; *Career* Nat Serv 2 Lt Duke of Wellington's Regt 1953-55, TA HAC 1955-74 (CO 1970-72), (Regt Col 1972-74); banker; Cater Ryder & Co 1955-72 (jt md 1963-72); chm: Mercantile House Holdings plc 1972-87, Alexanders Laing & Cruickshank Holdings Ltd 1984-88; 100 acre farm in E Sussex; non-exec dir: Extel Group 1979-87 (dep chm 1986-87), Household Mortgage Group 1985-, Savills plc 1988-, Sun Life Assurance 1988-; memb Advsy Bd: IMM Div of Chicago Mercantile Exchange 1981-84, Bank Julius Baer & Co Ltd (London) 1988-; dir LIFFE 1982- (chm: FFWP 1980, LIFFE St Ct 1981, LIFFE 1982-85); chm: Ctee on Market in Single Properties 1985-, Int Commodities Clearing Exchange 1986-90; gen cmmr for Income Tax City of London 1981-; memb Regular Forces Employment Assoc Cncl; govr: Eastbourne Coll (dep chm), Roedean 1984-89; chm Bedford Sch 1984-89, cmmr Duke of York's Royal Mil Sch Dover; chm: Chiddingly and Dist Br Legion 1982-87, Reserve Forces Assoc 1983-87, Sussex TA Ctee 1983-85, SE TAVR Assoc 1985-, City of London TAVRA 1989, Hon Col 6/7 Queens Regt, vice chm TA Sport Bd 1983- (memb 1979-) fin advsr Victory Services Club 1981-, dir Offrs' Pensions Society Investment Co 1982-; Freeman City of London, Liveryman Worshipful Co of Farmers; ACIB; *Recreations* sailing, shooting; *Clubs* City of London, Cavalry and Guards, MCC, Royal Fowey Yacht; *Style—* John Barkshire, Esq, CBE, TD, JP, DL; Hazelhurst Farm, Three Leg Cross, Ticehurst, E Sussex TN5 7LF (☎ 0580 200 382)

BARKWORTH, Paul Raymond Braithwaite; JP; s of Frederic Basil Stileman Barkworth, of Eastbourne, E Sussex, and Beryl Nellie, *née* Wright; *b* 26 Jan 1947; *Educ* Monkton Combe Sch; *m* 18 June 1970, Janet Elizabeth, da of Charles Arthur Crees, of Plymouth; *Career* CA; public practice, dir Baptist Insurance Co plc 1985, chm Baptist Housing Assoc 1988, memb of Cncl Baptist Union of GB, parish cncllr; memb: IOD, Bristol Chamber of Commerce and Industry; Freeman City of London; FCA; *Recreations* motor cycling, music, travel, photography; *Clubs* Bristol Commercial Rooms; *Style—* P R B Barkworth, Esq, JP; Tranby House, Norton Lane, Whitchurch, Nr Bristol BS14 0BT (☎ 0272 837101); Bristol Chambers, 6/10 St Nicholas Street, Bristol BS1 1UQ (☎ 0272 294 833, fax 0272 221 493); Oakfield House, Oakfield Grove, Clifton, Bristol BS8 2BN (☎ 0272 23700, fax 0272 732741)

BARKWORTH, Peter Wynn; s of Walter Wynn Barkworth (d 1974), of Bramhall, Cheshire, and Irene May, *née* Brown (d 1972); *b* 14 Jan 1929; *Educ* Stockport Sch, RADA; *Career* actor; theatre: Crown Matrimonial 1972 (BAFTA award Best Actor 1974), Donkey's Years 1976, Can You Hear Me At The Back? 1979, A Coat of Varnish 1982, Siegfried Sassoon 1986, Hidden Laughter 1990; television: Professional Foul (BAFTA Best Actor award 1977), The Power Game, Manhunt, Telford's Change, The Price, Late Starter, The Gospel According to St Matthew; dir: Sisterly Feelings, Night and Day; prodr, dir independent prodn co Astramead Ltd; *Books* About Acting (1980), First Houses (1983), More About Acting (1984); *Recreations* walking, looking at paintings, gardening; *Style—* P Barkworth, Esq; 47 Flask Walk, London NW3 1HH (☎ 071 794 4591); c/o Duncan Heath Associates Ltd, Paramount House, 162 Wardour St, W1V 3AT (☎ 071 439 1471)

BARLEY, Dr Victor Laurence; s of George Alec Barley, of 7 Larkfield Drive, Harrogate, Yorks, and Evelyn Mary Barley (d 1971); *b* 16 June 1941; *Educ* Stamford Sch Lincolnshire, Univ of Cambridge (MA, MB BChir), Univ of Oxford (MA, DPhil); *m* 25 Jan 1969, Janet, da of Dr Stanley Devidson Purcell, of 226A Old Church Rd, Clevedon, Avon; 1 s (Peter b 3 Dec 1969), 3 da (Elizabeth b 6 Jan 1972, Madeline (twin) b 6 Jan 1972, Christine b 16 July 1981); *Career* conslt radiotherapist and oncologist Bristol 1978-, gen mangr Radiotherapy and Oncology Centre Bristol 1988-; memb Br Inst Radiology; FRCSEd, FRCR; *Recreations* music; *Style—* Dr Victor Barley; 11 Barrow Court Mews, Barrow Court Lane, Barrow Gurney, Bristol BS19 3RW (☎ 027546 3006); Bristol Radiotherapy and Oncology Centre, Horfield Rd, Bristol BS2 8ED (☎ 0272 282415)

BARLOW, Sir Christopher Hilaro; 7 Bt (UK 1803), of Fort William, Bengal; s of Sir Richard Barlow, 6 Bt, AFC (d 1946), and Rosamund Sylvia, *née* Anderton; *b* 1 Dec 1929; *Educ* Eton, McGill Univ (BArch); *m* 1952, Jacqueline Claire de Marigny, da of John Edmund Audley (d 1980); 1 s (and 1 s decd), 2 da; *Heir* s, Crispian John Edmund Audley Barlow; *Career* architect; *Clubs* Royal Cwlth Soc, The Crow's Nest; *Style—* Sir Christopher Barlow, Bt; 18 Winter Ave, St John's, Newfoundland A1A 1T3, Canada (☎ 709 726 5913)

BARLOW, Crispian John Edmund Audley; s and h of Sir Christopher Hilaro Barlow, 7 Bt, *qv*; *b* 20 April 1958; *Educ* Marine Electronics, Coll of Fisheries, St John's, Newfoundland; *m* 1981, Anne Waiching Siu; *Career* sr inspector of police Royal Hong Kong Police Force (inspector 1978-); memb Int Assoc of Bomb Technicians and Investigators; assoc Inst of Explosive Engrs; *Recreations* shooting, sailing; *Clubs* OCH, 100 club; *Style—* Crispian Barlow, Esq; c/o Royal Hong Kong Police Headquarters, Arsenal Street, Hong Kong

BARLOW, David John; s of F Ralph Barlow, of Birmingham, and Joan, *née* Barber; *b* 20 Oct 1937; *Educ* Leighton Park Sch, Queen's Coll Oxford, Univ of Leeds (MA, DipEd, DipESL); *m* 1; 3 s (John, Andrew, Simon); m 2, 1981, Sanchia Beatrice, da of Marcel Oppenheimer; 2 s (Luke, Nathan), 1 da (Imogen); *Career* gen sec ITCA 1980-81, sec BBC 1981-83; controller BBC: Public Affrs and Int Relations 1983-85, Public Affrs 1985-87, Regnl Bdcasting 1987-90; seconded to EBU in Geneva as Eureka coordinator 1990, controller Int Relations BBC 1991-; *Clubs* English Speaking Union, BAFTA, Royal TV Soc; *Style—* David Barlow, Esq; 1 St Joseph's Close, Olney, Bucks MK46 5HD; c/o BBC Broadcasting House, London W1A 1AA

BARLOW, Erasmus Darwin; s of Sir Alan Barlow, 2 Bt, GCB, KBE (d 1968); *b* 15 April 1915; *Educ* Marlborough, Trinity Coll Cambridge, UCH Med Sch (MA, MB BChir, FRCPsych); *m* 1938, Brigit, da of Ladbroke Black, of Wendover; 1 s, 2 da; *Career* res fell and conslt psychiatrist St Thomas's Hosp 1951-66, chm Bath Inst of Med Engrg 1976-88; Master Worshipful Co of Scientific Instrument Makers 1976-77; sec Zoological Soc of London 1980-82; chm and dep chm Cambridge Instrument Co 1964-79; *Recreations* home, garden, music, travel; *Clubs* Savile; *Style—* Erasmus Barlow, Esq; Elbrook House, Ashwell, Baldock, Herts SG7 5NE

BARLOW, James Alan; s and h of Sir Thomas Barlow, 3 Bt, DSC, DL, *qv*; *b* 10 July 1956; *Educ* Highgate, Univ of Manchester (BSc); *Career* metallurgist; res engr The Welding Institute Cambridge 1978-82; mangr: Harland & Wolff Belfast 1982-84, Glassdrumman House Annalong 1984-; *Style—* James Barlow, Esq; The Beatings, Glassdrumman Rd, Annalong, Co Down; Glassdrumman House, Annalong, Newry, Co Down BT34 6QN (☎ 039 67 68585)

BARLOW, James Mellodew; s of Capt Cecil Barlow (d 1988), of Oldham, and Florence Patricia, *née* Mellodew; *b* 23 Dec 1943; *Educ* Mill Hill Sch, Univ of Nottingham (LLB); *Career* admitted slr 1967; ptnr Clifford Chance (formerly Coward Chance) 1980-; hon sec Cumberland LTC 1976-82; memb Worshipful Co of Slrs 1980; memb Law Soc 1967, ATII 1968; *Recreations* squash, tennis, skiing, fell walking, bridge; *Clubs* Old Mill Hillians; *Style—* James Barlow, Esq; 11 Edmunds Walk, London N2 0NH (☎ 081 883 6972); Clifford Chance, Royex House, Aldermanbury Square, London EC2V 7LD (☎ 071 600 0808, fax 071 726 8561, telex 8959991)

BARLOW, Sir John Kemp; 3 Bt (UK 1907), of Bradwall Hall, Cheshire; s of Sir John Denman Barlow, 2 Bt (d 1986), and Hon Diana Helen Kemp, yr da of 1 Baron Rochdale; *b* 22 April 1934; *Educ* Winchester, Trinity Coll Cambridge; *m* 1962, Susan, da of Col Sir Andrew Horsbrugh Porter, 3 Bt, DSO; 4 s; *Heir* s, John William Marshall b 12 March 1964; *Career* farmer; chm Majedie Investmts plc; chm Rubber Growers Assoc 1974-75; *Clubs* Brooks's, Jockey (Steward 1988-90), City of London; *Style—* Sir John K Barlow, Bt; Bulkeley Grange, Malpas, Cheshire SY14 8BT

BARLOW, Richard Leonard; s of Leonard Wilfrid Barlow (d 1982), and Shelagh Sutherland (d 1986); *b* 14 March 1948; *Educ* Kendal GS, Moseley Hall GS, LSE (LLB); *Career* called to the Bar Middle Temple 1970, in practice in Manchester 1971-73, Customs and Excise Solicitor's Office (Grade 5) 1973-1988, in practice in Leeds 1988-; *Recreations* piano, horse racing, literature; *Style—* Richard Barlow, Esq; 22 East Parade, Leeds LS1 5BU (☎ 0532 452702, fax 0532 420683)

BARLOW, Roy Oxspring; s of George Barlow, and Clarice Barlow; *b* 13 Feb 1927; *Educ* King Edward VII Sch Sheffield, Queen's Coll Oxford, Univ of Sheffield; *m* 1957, Kathleen Mary Roberts; 2 s, 1 da; *Career* slr, rec Crown Ct 1975; *Style—* Roy Barlow, Esq; The Cottage, Oxton Rakes, Barlow, Sheffield (☎ 0742 890652)

BARLOW, Sir Thomas Erasmus; 3 Bt (UK 1902), DSC (1945), DL (Bucks 1976); s of Sir Alan Barlow, 2 Bt, GCB, KBE (d 1968); *b* 23 Jan 1914; *Educ* Winchester; *m* 1955, Isabel, da of late Thomas Munn Body, of Middlesbrough; 2 s, 2 da; *Heir* s, James Barlow; *Career* RN 1932, Capt, ret 1964; *Recreations* birdwatching, wildlife conservation; *Clubs* Athenaeum, Savile; *Style—* Sir Thomas Barlow, Bt, DSC, DL; 45 Shepherds Hill, Highgate, London N6 5QJ (☎ 081 340 9653)

BARLOW, Sir (George) William; s of Albert Edward Barlow and Annice Barlow; *b* 8 June 1924; *Educ* Manchester GS, Univ of Manchester (BSc); *m* 1948, Elaine Mary Atherton, da of William Adamson; 1 s, 1 da; *Career* chm Ransome Hoffman Pollard 1971-77, PO 1977-80 (organised sep PO and Br Telecom), Design Cncl 1980-86; dir: Thorn EMI plc 1980, Racal Telecom plc 1988; chm: BICC plc 1985-, Ericsson Ltd 1988-, Bain & Co Inc UK 1988-, Engrg Cncl 1988-; pres BEAMA 1986-87; dep pres Assoc of Lancastrians in London 1991; Hon DSc: Cranfield 1979, Bath 1986, Aston 1988; Hon DTech Liverpool Poly 1988; FEng, FIMechE, FIEE, CBIM; kt 1977; *Style—* Sir William Barlow; 4 Parkside, Henley-on-Thames, Oxon RG9 1TX; BICC Devonshire House, Mayfair Place, London W1X 5FH

BARLOW, (John) William Marshall; s and h of Sir John Kemp Barlow, 3 Bt; *b* 12 March 1964; *Style—* William Barlow, Esq; Bulkeley Grange, Malpas, Cheshire

BARLTROP, Prof Donald; s of Albert Edward Barltrop (d 1976), and Mabel, *née* Redding (d 1984); *b* 26 June 1933; *Educ* Southall GS, Univ of London (BSc, MB BS, MD); *m* 1 Aug 1959, Mair Angharad, da of Rev Richard Evan Edwards (d 1971), of Swansea; 2 s (Andrew b 1965, Richard b 1968), 1 da (Elen b 1970); *Career* Capt RAMC 1959-61; Fulbright scholar Harvard Univ 1963-64, Wellcome sr res fell in clinical sci 1968-74, reader in paediatrics: St Mary's Hosp 1975-78, Westminster Hosp 1978-82); prof of child health Westminster Hosps Univ of London 1982-, adjunct prof of community health Tufts Univ Boston Mass 1984-; examiner: RCP, Univs of London, Capetown, Hong Kong, Al-Fateh Tripoli; memb: Lead and Health Ctee DHSS Working Pty (Composition of Infant Foods Ctee), Steering Ctee on Food Policy and Surveillance MAFF; chm Westminster Children Res Tst; medical advsr: Bliss, Buttle Tst; Freeman City of London 1977, Liveryman Worshipful Co of Barbers 1978; FRCP; *Books* Mineral Metabolism in Paediatrics (jtly, 1969), Children in Health and Disease (jtly, 1977); *Recreations* offshore sailing; *Clubs* Naval, RNVR Yacht; *Style—* Prof Donald Barltrop; 7 Grove Rd, Northwood, Middx (☎ 09274 26461); Westminster Childrens Hosp, Vincent Sq, London (☎ 01 746 8622, fax 834 8834, telex 919263 RIVHAG)

BARLTROP, Roger Arnold Rowlandson; CMG (1987), CVO (1982); s of Ernest William Barltrop, CMG, CBE, DSO (d 1957), and Ethel Alice Lucy, *née* Baker (d

1966); the Barltrop family origins lie in Essex, and those of the Bakers in London and (earlier) Yorkshire; *b* 19 Jan 1930; *Educ* Solihull Sch, Leeds GS, Exeter Coll Oxford (MA); *m* 1962, Penelope Pierrepont, da of Denys Neale Dalton (d 1986); 2 s (Paul, Richard), 2 da (Fiona, Mary); *Career* RN 1949-50, RNVR, RNR 1950-64 (Lt-Cdr); HM Dip Serv: served India, Nigeria, Rhodesia, Turkey, Eastern Caribbean and Ethiopia, ambass (formerly high cmmr) to Fiji and concurrently high cmmr to Nauru and Tuvalu 1982-89, ret 1990; *Recreations* sailing, opera, genealogy; *Clubs* Royal Cwlth Soc, Royal Suva Yacht, Fiji; *Style*— R A R Barltrop, Esq, CMG, CVO; c/o Commonwealth Trust, 18 Northumberland Ave, London WC2N 5BJ

BARNABY, Dr (Charles) Frank; s of Charles Hector Barnaby (d 1932), and Lilian, *née* Sainsbury; *b* 27 Sept 1927; *Educ* Andover GS, Univ of London (BSc, MSc, PhD); *m* 19 Dec 1982, Wendy Elizabeth, da of Francis Arthur Field, of Adelaide, Aust; 1 s (Benjamin b 1977), 1 da (Sophie b 1975); *Career* physicist: AWRE Aldermaston 1951-57, UCL 1957-67; exec sec Pugwash Conf on Sci and World Affrs 1967-71, dir Stockholm Int Peace Res Inst 1971-81, guest prof Free Univ of Amsterdam 1981-85, author 1985-; Hon Doctorate Free Univ of Amsterdam; *Books* Man and the Atom (1972), Nuclear Energy (1975), Prospects for Peace (1975), Verification Technologies (1986), Future Warfare (1986), Star Wars (1987), The Automated Battlefield (1987), The Gaia Peace Atlas (1989), The Invisible Bomb (1989); *Recreations* astronomy, bird watching; *Style*— Dr Frank Barnaby; Brandreth, Station Rd, Chilbolton, Stockbridge, Hants SO20 6AW (☎ 0264 860423)

BARNARD, Baroness; Lady Davina Mary; *née* Cecil; da of 6 Marquess of Exeter, KCMG (d 1981), and 1 w, Lady Mary Montagu Douglas Scott, da of 7 Duke of Buccleuch; *b* 1931; *m* 1952, 11 Baron Barnard, *qv*; *Career* DStJ; *Style*— The Rt Hon the Lady Barnard; Selaby Hall, Gainford, Darlington, Co Durham DL2 3HF (☎ 0325 730 206)

BARNARD, Capt Sir George Edward; 2 s of Michael Barnard, and Alice Louise Barnard; *b* 11 Aug 1907; *m* 1940, Barbara Emma (d 1976), da of Percy Vann Hughes; 1 s; *Career* dep master Trinity House 1961-72 (elder brother 1958); treas Int Assoc of Lighthouse Authorities 1961-72, tstee Nat Maritime Museum 1967-74, fell Nautical Inst 1975 (pres 1972-75); FRSA; kt 1968; *Style*— Capt Sir George Barnard; Warden, Station Rd, Much Hadham, Herts (☎ 027 984 3133)

BARNARD, 11 Baron (E 1698); Harry John Neville Vane; TD (1960), JP (Durham 1961); patron of ten livings; s of 10 Baron Barnard, CMG, OBE, MC, TD, JP (d 1964), and Dowager Baroness Barnard, *qv*; *b* 21 Sept 1923; *Educ* Eton, Durham Univ Business Sch (MSc); *m* 8 Oct 1952, Lady Davina Mary Cecil, DStJ, *qv*, da of 6 Marquess of Exeter (d 1981); 1 s, 4 da; *Heir* s, Hon Henry Vane; *Career* Flying Offr RAFVR 1942-46, Northumberland Hussars 1948-66, Lt-Col Cmdg 1964-66, Hon Col 7 Bn LI 1979-89, pres N of England TAVRA 1974-77; landowner, farmer; cncllr Durham 1952-61, memb Durham Co Agric Exec Ctee 1953-72 (chm 1970-72), pres Durham Co Branch CLA 1965-88 ; pres: Durham Co St John Cncl 1971-88, Durham Co Scout Assoc 1972-88, Durham and Cleveland Co Branch Royal Br Legion 1973, Durham Wildlife Tst 1984; memb: Durham Co Branch BRCS 1969-86, Cncl BRCS 1982-85 (vice chm 1987); Lord Lt and Custos Rotulorum Co Durham 1970-88 (Vice Lt 1969-70, DL 1956); KStJ 1971; *Clubs* Brooks's, Durham County, Northern Counties (Newcastle); *Style*— The Rt Hon the Lord Barnard, TD, JP; Raby Castle, P O Box 50, Staindrop, Darlington, Co Durham DL2 3AY (☎ 0833 60751)

BARNARD, Prof John Michael; s of John Claude Southard Barnard (d 1976), and Dora Grace, *née* Epps; *b* 13 Feb 1936; *Educ* King Alfred's GS Wantage Berks, Wadham Coll Oxford (BA, BLitt, MA); *m* (m dis); 1 s (Jason b 1966), 2 da (Josie b 1963, Clio b 1965); *Career* Nat Serv sr radar technician RAF 1954-56; res asst Dept of English Yale Univ USA 1961-64, visiting lectr English Dept Univ of Calif at Santa Barbara USA 1964-65; Sch of English Univ of Leeds: lectr then sr lectr 1965-78, prof 1978-; gen ed Longmans Annotated Poets 1977-, Br Acad Warton lectr 1989; memb Mid Wharfedale Parish Cncl 1974-84; memb Cncl Bibliographical Soc 1990; *Books* Congreve's The Way of the World (ed, 1972), Pope: The Critical Heritage (ed, 1973), John Keats: The Complete Poems (1973, 3 edn 1988), Etherege's The Man of Mode (ed 1979 (reprinted in Five Restoration Comedies, 1984), John Keats (1987), John Keats: Selected Poems (ed, 1988); *Recreations* cricket, travel; *Clubs* Johnson; *Style*— Prof John Barnard; School of English, University of Leeds, Leeds LS2 9JT (☎ 0532 334730, telex 556473 UNILDS G)

BARNARD, Sir Joseph Brian; JP (1973), DL (N Yorks 1988); s of Joseph Ernest Barnard (d 1942), and Elizabeth Loudon Barnard (d 1980); *b* 22 Jan 1928; *Educ* Sedbergh; *m* 21 Jan 1959, Suzanne Hamilton, da of Clifford Bray, of Ilkley, W Yorks; 3 s (Nicholas b 1960, Simon (twin) b 1960, Marcus b 1966); *Career* cmmnd KRRC 1946-48; dir: Joseph Constantine Steamship Line Ltd 1952-66, Teesside Warehousing Co Ltd 1966-, NE Electricity Bd 1987-90; chm: E Harsley Parish Cncl 1973-, Allertonshire Petty Sessional Div 1981-, govrs Ingleby Arncliffe C of E Primary Sch 1981-, NE Electricity Consultative Cncl 1987-90; pres Yorks area Cons Trade Unionists, Yorks Magistrates Ct Ctee 1981-, patron St Oswalds E Harsley, vice chm Nat Union of Cons and Unionist Assocs 1988-, chm Yorks Area Cons 1983-88; kt 1986; *Recreations* walking, shooting, gardening; *Clubs* Carlton; *Style*— Sir Joseph Barnard, JP, DL; Harlsey Hall, Northallerton, N Yorks DL6 2BL (☎ 0609 82 203)

BARNARD, Hon Lance Herbert; AO; s of Hon H Barnard; *b* 1 May 1919; *Educ* Launceston Tech Coll; *m* 1; 1 da; m 2, 1962, Jill, da of Senator H Cant; 1 s, 2 da (and 1 da decd); *Career* state pres Tasmanian Branch Australian Lab Party, Min for Defence 1972-75, dep PM 1972-74, Australian ambass to Sweden, Norway and Finland 1975-78; *Style*— Hon Lance Barnard, AO; 6 Bertland Court, Launceston, Tasmania 7250, Australia

BARNARD, Michael John; s of Cecil William Barnard, and Gladys Irene Mary, *née* Hedges; *b* 4 May 1944; *Educ* Licensed Victuallers Sch Slough; *m* 1, 12 March 1965 (m dis 1979), Jennifer, da of Charles Tyrrill; 1 s (Matthew b 15 Sept 1971); m 2, Charlotte Susan, da of Sir Kenneth Berrill; *Career* journalist: Kent Web Offset Group 1962-66, Westminster Press 1966-67 and 1968-71; managing ed First Features Ltd 1967-68, prodn dir Macmillan Magazines 1971-79, chm and md Macmillan Production Ltd 1979-; dir: Macmillan Publishers Ltd 1982-, Macmillan Ltd 1985-, Macmillan Publishers Group Admin Ltd 1988-; chm: Macmillan Distribution Ltd 1988-, Macmillan Information Systems Ltd 1988-; non-exec dir: Periodical Publishers Association Ltd 1988-, Gill & Macmillan Ltd 1990-; chm Printing Div Printing Industs Res Assoc; MAIE 1988; *Books* Magazine and Journal Production (1986), Introduction to Print Buying (1987), Inside Magazines (1989); *Recreations* swimming, reading; *Style*— Michael Barnard, Esq; Macmillan Ltd, 4 Little Essex St, London WC2R 3LF (☎ 071 836 6633, fax 071 379 4204, telex 262024 MACMIL G)

BARNARD, Surgn Rear Adm (Ernest Edward) Peter; s of Lionel Edward Barnard (d 1965), of Milford on Sea, and Ernestine, *née* Lethbridge (d 1986); *b* 22 Feb 1927; *Educ* schs in UK and S Aust, St John's Coll Oxford (DPhil); *m* 1955, Joan Marion, da of Arthur William Gunn (d 1984), of Grays, Essex; 1 s (Christopher), 1 da (Penelope); *Career* exec dir Med Cncl on Alcoholism; formerly: Surgn Rear Adm (Operational Med Support) 1982-84, dep med dir gen (Naval) 1980-82; publications on underwater medicine and physiology 1962-85; FFCM; *Recreations* gardening, photography; *Clubs* RSM; *Style*— Surgn Rear Adm Peter Barnard; Chesilcote, Chapel Rd, Swanmore, Southampton SO3 2QA (☎ 04893 2373); 1 St Andrews Place, London NW1 4LB (☎ 071 487 4445)

BARNARD, Robert; s of Leslie Barnard (d 1969), and Vera Doris, *née* Nethercoat; *b* 23 Nov 1936; *Educ* Colchester Royal GS, Balliol Coll Oxford, Univ of Bergen Norway (DPhil); *m* 1963, Mary Louise Tabor, da of Geoffrey Tabor, of Armidale, Aust; *Career* lectr in English lit Univ of New England Armidale NSW 1961-66, lectr and sr lectr Univ of Bergen Norway 1966-76, prof of English lit Univ of Tromsoø Norway 1976-83; author; *Books incl* Death of An Old Goat (1974), Unruly Son (1978), Mother's Boys (1981), Sheer Torture (1981), A Corpse in a Guilded Cage (1984), A Short History of English Literature (1984), Out of the Blackout (1985), The Skeleton in the Grass (1987), City of Strangers (1990); memb: Soc of Authors, Crime Writers' Assoc (memb Ctee 1988-91), Brontë Soc; *Recreations* walking, opera, Edwin Drood; *Style*— Robert Barnard, Esq; Hazeldene, Houghley Lane, Leeds LS13 2DT (☎ 0532 638955); agents Peters, Fraser and Dunlop, 503/4 The Chambers, Chelsea Harbour, London SW10 0XF (☎ 071 376 7676)

BARNARD, Stephen Geoffrey; s of Geoffrey Thomas Barnard, of Beech Cottage, Sudbourne, Suffolk, and Diana Pixle, *née* Rivron; *b* 4 May 1950; *Educ* Gresham's Sch, Univ of Southampton (LLB); *m* 4 Oct 1980, Jane Elizabeth Lisa, da of Dr Oliver Vivian Maxim, of the Windhovers, Gretton, Northants; *Career* slr 1974; Herbert Smith: joined 1976, NY 1980-82, ptnr 1983; *Recreations* golf, bridge, walking, birds, skiing; *Style*— Stephen Barnard, Esq; Herbert Smith, Exchange House, Primrose St, London EC2A 2HS (☎ 071 374 8000)

BARNARD, Dowager Baroness; Sylvia Mary; o da of Herbert Straker (d 1929), of Hartforth Grange, Richmond, Yorks, and Gwendolin Georgiana, née Cradock (d 1932); *b* 26 Aug 1898; *m* 14 Oct 1920, 10 Baron Barnard, CMG, OBE, MC (d 1964); 2 s, 1 da; *Career* late Chief Cmdt ATS; *Style*— The Rt Hon the Dowager Lady Barnard; The White House, Gainford, Darlington DL2 3DN (☎ 0325 730 389)

BARNE, Lady Elizabeth Beatrice; *née* Montgomerie; da of 17 Earl of Eglinton and Winton (d 1966), and Ursula Joan, da of Hon Ronald Bannatyne Watson (d 1987); *m* 1976, Maj Christopher Miles Barne; 1 s; *Style*— Lady Elizabeth Barne; Culeaze Farm, Wareham, Dorset

BARNE, Hon Mrs (Janet Elizabeth); *née* Maclean; o da of Baron Maclean, KT, GCVO, KBE, PC (Life Peer and 11 Bt, d 1990), and (Joan) Elizabeth, *née* Mann; *b* 27 Dec 1944; *m* 1974, Maj Nicholas Michael Lancelot Barne, Scots Guards (ret); 2 s (Alasdair Michael Fitzroy b 1979, Hamish Nicholas Charles b 1981); *Style*— The Hon Mrs Barne; Blofield House, Blofield, Norfolk

BARNEBY, John Henry; s of Lt-Col Henry Habington Barneby, TD, DL, of Llanerch-Y-Coed, Dorstone, Herefordshire, and Angela Margaret, *née* Campbell (d 1979); *b* 29 July 1949; *Educ* Radley, ChCh Oxford (MA); *m* 2 Dec 1978, Alison (Sophie), da of Alan David Donger, of Winchester; 1 s (Thomas Henry b 1985), 2 da (Emily Henrietta b 1981, Laura Katherine b 1982); *Career* dir: C Czarnikow Ltd 1984-, Czarnikow Holdings Ltd 1989-; *Style*— John Barneby Esq; Cleveland Farm House, Longcot, Faringdon, Oxfordshire (☎ 0793 783 220), 66 Mark Lane, London EC3 (☎ 071 480 9333, fax 071 480 9500)

BARNEBY, Col Michael Paul; s of Capt Richard Paul Barneby (d 1944), of Longworth, Hereford, and Vera Margery Freedman, *née* Bromilow; *b* 29 March 1939; *Educ* Radley; *m* 13 April 1973, Bridget Mary, da of Col Arthur Gordon Roberts, DSO, of Crickhowell, Powys, S Wales; 3 da (Camilla b 1974, Vanessa b 1976, Georgina b 1980); *Career* cmmnd 1958 15/19 The King's Royal Hussars; served principally in: Germany, NI, Hong Kong where cmd Royal Hong Kong Regt (Vols) 1981-83, ret Army 1988; clerk to Worshipful Co of Salters; *Recreations* hunting, shooting; *Clubs* Cavalry and Guards; *Style*— Col Michael P Barneby; The Old Vicarage, Preston Candover, Hants RG25 2EJ (☎ 025 687 248)

BARNES; *see*: Gorell Barnes

BARNES, Anthony David; s of Cecil James (d 1975), of Hove, and Mary Grace, *née* Pardey; *b* 19 June 1934; *Educ* Brighton Hove and Sussex GS, Univ of Birmingham (BSc, MB ChM); *m* 11 July 1959, Patricia Mary, da of John Frederick Pyatt (d 1977), of Stone; 1 s (Simon David b 1961), 2 da (Sarah Anne Louise b 1963, Joanna Mary b 1966); *Career* Univ of Birmingham: lectr in anatomy 1959-60, Leverhulme res fell 1960-62; United Birmingham Hosp: surgical trainee 1962-69, conslt surgn 1969-; RCS: Arris & Gayle lectr, Hunterian prof, regnl advsr 1984-90; chm UK Transplant 1972-82; FRCS; memb: BMA, Br Transplant Soc, Br Endocrine Surgns Assoc, Assoc of Surgns; *Recreations* fishing, farming; *Style*— Anthony Barnes, Esq; 25 Metchley Park Rd, Edgbaston, Birmingham B15 2PQ (☎ 021 454 2607); Queen Elizabeth Hosp, Queen Elizabeth Medical Centre, Edgbaston, Birmingham B15 2TH (☎ 021 472 1311, car 0860 342648)

BARNES, (Charles) Antony; s of Charles Herbert Barnes (d 1965), of Hampstead, London, and Nellie Gertrude, *née* Croxton (d 1963); *b* 5 July 1925; *Educ* Westminster; *m* 8 Sept 1951, Margaret Helen, da of Frank Cuthbert Jones, of Montgomeryshire; 1 s (David b 1954); *Career* dir: City Merchants Bank Ltd, ACA Ltd, CA Tstees Ltd, FCA Ltd, Manor Fields Est Ltd, Soc of Inc Acct Ltd; ex dir: Samuel Montagu & Co Ltd and subsids 1986, various other cos; memb Cncl ICAEW; *Recreations* theatre, classical music, opera; *Clubs* Hurlingham; *Style*— Antony Barnes, Esq; 3 Selwyn House, Manor Fields, Putney Hill, London SW15 3LR

BARNES, Carol Lesley; da of Lesley Harry Barnes, of London SW16, and Alexandra Barnes; *b* 13 Sept 1944; *Educ* St Martin in the Fields HS, Univ of Sheffield (BA), Univ of Birmingham (Cert Ed); *m* 30 July 1981, Nigel Thomson, s of Hugh Thomson, of Brighton; 1 s (James b 25 May 1982), 1 da (Clare b 14 July 1979); *Career* presenter LBC Radio 1973-74, reporter World at One BBC Radio 4 1974-75, reporter and presenter ITN 1974-90; *Recreations* exercise, flying, skiing; *Style*— Ms Carol Barnes; ITN, Wells St, London W1 (☎ 071 637 2424)

BARNES, Christian William; s of Oswald Edward Barnes, of Gt Houghton, Northants, and Gillian, *née* Ralph; *b* 20 June 1959; *Educ* Uppingham, Univ of Durham (BA); *m* 1987, Melanie Joy, da of Kenneth Royston Eades; 1 s (Elliot James Royston b 6 Feb 1991); *Career* advertisement sales mangr Dominion Press Ltd 1981-82, asst account mangr then account dir Leo Burnett Ltd 1982-87, fndr ptnr and co dir Barnes Vereker Allen Ltd 1987-; *Recreations* music, theatre, travel; *Style*— Christian Barnes, Esq; Barnes Vereker Allen Ltd, 3 Lloyds Wharf, Mill St, London SE1 2BA (☎ 071 231 3100, fax 071 231 6868)

BARNES, Clive Leslie; s of Harry Leslie Barnes (d 1981), of Warwick, and Mabel Caroline, *née* Reed (d 1963); *b* 14 Sept 1940; *Educ* Cheltenham Coll; *m* 1, 27 Nov 1965 (m dis 1987), Miriam Rosalind, da of Francis Vincent Everard, of Bucks; 2 s (Luke b 1968, Thomas b 1969); m 2, 17 Feb 1989, Sally Anne, da of Douglas Arthur Bayes, of Hanmer, Salop; *Career* CA; Midland Counties & Olympic Trialist Hockey; *Recreations* real tennis, lawn tennis, skiing; *Clubs* Farmers; *Style*— Clive L Barnes, Esq; Ettington Hall, Ettington, Stratford-upon-Avon (☎ 0789 740515); 22 Queens Rd, Coventry (☎ 0203 56331)

BARNES, Dr Colin Greenhill; s of Harold Albert Barnes (d 1975), of Pinner, Middx, and Marjorie Mary *née* Pottle; *b* 4 July 1936; *Educ* Mill Hill Sch, The London Hosp Med Coll Univ of London (BSc, MB BS); *m* 22 Sept 1962, Marian Nora, da of William Goss Sampson (d 1984), of Exeter, Devon; 2 s (Graham b 1964, Peter b 1966);

Career conslt physician in rheumatology The Royal London Hosp 1968-, teacher The London Hosp Med Coll Univ of London 1974-, rheumatologist London Independent Hosp 1986-, hon conslt rheumatologist St Lukes Hosp for the Clergy 1987-; chm: Exec Fin Ctee Arthritis and Rheumatism Cncl for Res 1977-, Mgmnt Ctee Kennedy Inst of Rheumatology 1977-; pres Br League Against Rheumatism 1982-85, assoc ed Annals of the Rheumatic Diseases 1982-88, pres Euro League Against Rheumatism 1989- (vice pres 1987-89); FRCP (London) 1978, memb: BMA, British Soc for Rheumatology; hon memb: Swiss Soc of Rheumatology, Aust Rheumatology Assoc; fell RSM; *Books* Behcets Syndrome (jt ed, 1979), Behcets Disease (jt ed, 1986); contrib: Clinical Rheumatology, Copeman's Textbook of Rheumatology, The Foot; *Recreations* gardening, music (classical), opera, skiing, travel; *Clubs* Reform, RSM; *Style*— Dr Colin Barnes; 96 Harley St, London W1N 1AF (☎ 071 486 0967) Dept of Rheumatology, The Royal London Hosp, London E1 1BB (☎ 071 377 7784)

BARNES, Daniel Sennett; CBE (1977); s of John Daniel Barnes; *b* 13 Sept 1924; *Educ* Dulwich, Univ of London (BSc); *m* 1955, Jean A Steadman; 1 s; *Career* md Sperry Gyroscope 1971-82, Electronic Systems and Equipment Div Br Aerospace (formerly Sperry Gyroscope) 1982-86; dir: Sperry Ltd 1971-82, Sperry AG Switzerland 1979-83; pres Electronic Engrg Assoc 1981-82, memb of Bd Bracknell Devpt Cncl 1976-82; chm: Berks and Oxon Area Manpower Bd, Manpower Servs Cmmn 1983-88; CEng, FIEE; *Style*— Daniel Barnes, Esq, CBE

BARNES, (James) David Francis; CBE (1987); s of Eric Cecil Barnes, CMG (d 1987), and Jean Margaret Procter, *née* Dickens; *b* 4 March 1936; *Educ* Shrewsbury, Univ of Liverpool; *m* 1 May 1963, (Wendy) Fiona Mary, da of John Leighton Riddell, of Limetree House, Gawsworth, Macclesfield, Cheshire; 1 s (Jonathan Mark b 8 July 1967), 1 da (Alison Jane b 9 Nov 1964); *Career* Nat Serv 1958-60, cmmnd N Battery (The Eagle Troop) 2 Regt RA; ICI Pharmaceuticals Div: euro mangr 1968, overseas dir 1971, dep chm 1977; chm ICI Paints Div 1983, exec dir ICI plc 1986; non exec dir Thorn EMI plc 1987; Thames Valley Hospice: chm of Capital Appeal 1984-88, vice pres 1987; NEDO: chm Pharmaceuticals Economic Devpt Ctee, chm Biotechnology Working Party 1989; FInstD 1983, CBIM 1987, FRSA 1988; *Recreations* fishing, shooting, gardening; *Style*— David Barnes, Esq, CBE; ICI plc, 9 Millbank, London SW1P 3JF (☎ 071 834 4444, fax 071 834 2042, telex 21324 ICIHQG)

BARNES, David Stewart; s of Herbert Stewart Barnes (d 1978), of Salford Lancs, and Kate Myfanwy, *née* Jones; *b* 6 Sept 1938; *Educ* Salford GS, King's Coll Univ of Durham (soccer first team), Univ of Manchester (Dip Arch, second and third year design prizes, soccer first team full maroon colours, Univ athletic union soccer colours); *m* June 1967, Gwendoline Edith Irene, da of Thomas Foster (d 1986); 1 da (Sarah Kate b 11 May 1972); *Career* asst architect: Cruickshank & Seward Manchester 1964-68, Building Design Partnership Manchester 1968-69; princ ptnr Barnes Heap & Assoc Glossop Derbyshire 1969-74, architect ptnr Building Design Partnership 1979- (project architect 1974-79); *awards* for Chloride Technical Ltd Swinton Manchester: RIBA award 1978, Structural Steel Design award 1979; Civic Trust award for Gtr Manchester County Fire Serv HQ 1981, Class 3 Office of the Year award for Building Design Partnership Office Sheffield 1983; RIBA Northwest Regnl award for Gtr Manchester Museum of Sci and Indust Manchester: 1989, RICS/ Times Conservation commendation 1989; MRIBA 1965-; *Recreations* soccer, golf; *Clubs* Manchester Univ Soccer (past pres), Manchester Univ XXI; *Style*— David Barnes, Esq; Building Design Partnership, Sunlight House, PO Box 85, Quay St, Manchester M60 3JA (☎ 061 834 8441, fax 061 832 4280)

BARNES, Sir Denis Charles; KCB (1967, CB 1964); s of Frederick Charles Barnes (d 1944); *b* 15 Dec 1914; *Educ* Hulme GS Manchester, Merton Coll Oxford; *m* 1938, Patricia, da of Col Charles Murray Abercrombie, CMG, CBE (d 1933), of Prestbury, Cheshire; *Career* entered Home Civil Service 1938, dep sec Miny of Labour 1964-66, perm sec 1966-73, chm Manpower Services Cmmn 1973-75; dir Glynwed Ltd, Gen Accident Fire & Life Assur Corp 1976-85, pres Manpower Soc 1976-, perm sec Dept of Employment 1968-73, FIPM; *Clubs* Savile; *Style*— Sir Denis Barnes, KCB; The Old Inn, 30 The Street, Wittersham, Kent (☎ 079 77 528)

BARNES, Edward Campbell; s of Hubert Turnbull Barnes, and (Annie) Mabel, *née* Latham; *b* 8 Oct 1928; *Educ* Wigan Coll; *m* 1950, Dorothy, *née* Smith; 1 s, 2 da; *Career* head children's progs BBC TV 1978-86; prodr/dir: Treasure Houses 1986, All Our Children 1987-90; BAFTA Specialist Progs Craft award 1969, Silver medal Royal TV Soc 1986, Pye Award for services on childrens' TV 1986; *Books* 25 Blue Peter Books and 8 Blue Peter Special Assignment Books, Blue Peter - The Inside Story (1989); *Recreations* cricket, Bali, opera; *Clubs* BAFTA; *Style*— Edward Barnes, Esq

BARNES, Frederick Brian; s of Frederick George James Barnes (d 1984), of Berks, and Agnes Ethel, *née* Colgate; *b* 1 Sept 1937; *Educ* Slough GS, LSE (BSc); *m* 1962, Susan Felicity, da of James Michael Pattemore (d 1986); 1 s (Christopher James b 1968), 2 da (Katherine Helen b 1965, Victoria Jane b 1970); *Career* flying offr RAF 1958-61; First National Finance Corporation 1970-76, assoc dir Assocs Capital Corporation (chm and md 1976-), Assocs International Management Co, pres 1984; *Recreations* golf, ballet, horse racing; *Clubs* Stoke Poges Golf; *Style*— Brian Barnes, Esq; Assoc House, PO Box 200, Windsor, Berks (☎ 0753 857100)

BARNES, Gerald William; s of George William Barnes (d 1977), and Violet, *née* Stevens (d 1975); *b* 4 Sept 1928; *Educ* Southend HS, Brentwood Sch; *m* 4 Dec 1954, Jean Dorothy, da of James Robert Hills; 1 s (Robin Richard b 1963); *Career* Nat Serv 13/18 Royal Hussars; CA 1956, budget offr International Computers Ltd 1957-59; fin dir: Pembroke Carton and Printing Co Ltd 1959-64, W S Cowell Ltd and Cowells plc 1964-87; corp conslt 1988-, chm Alderman Printing and Bookbinding Co Ltd 1989-; former chm Parish Cncl, Rotarian, involvement in number of local charities and clubs; various past offices held in Br Printing Indust Fedn (pres East Angl Alliance, memb Fin Ctee, Educn Ctee, Eastern Regnl Bd, chm Book Prod Section); FCA 1956; *Recreations* cricket, theatre, travel; *Clubs* Ipswich and Suffolk; *Style*— Gerald Barnes, Esq; Sweynes, 1 Church Crescent, Sproughton, Ipswich, Suffolk IP8 3BJ (☎ 0473 742760)

BARNES, Harold (Harry); MP (Lab) Derbyshire NE 1987-; s of Joseph Barnes, of Easington Colliery, Co Durham, and Betsy, *née* Gray; *b* 22 July 1936; *Educ* Ruskin Coll Oxford, Univ of Hull; *m* 14 Sept 1963, Elizabeth Ann, da of Richard Stephenson (d 1983); 1 s (Stephen b 1968), 1 da (Joanne b 1972); *Career* RAF 1954-56; railway clerk 1952-54 and 1956-62; lectr Univ of Sheffield 1966-87, (dir mature matriculation courses 1984-87); variety of positions NE Derbys Constituency Lab Pty 1970-87; memb Cncl of Nat Admin Cncl of Independent Lab Pubns 1977-80 and 1982-85; memb ctee stage: Local Govt Fin Act 1988, Employment Act 1989, Football Spectator Act 1989, Educn (Student Loans) Act 1990, NI (Emergency Provisions) Bill 1990-; memb Select Stees Euro Legislation 1989-, Members Interests 1990-; vice chm: Lab Back-Bench Ctee on NI 1989-, E Midlands Gp Labour MPs 1990-; chm New Consensus; *Style*— H Barnes, Esq, MP; 16 Gosforth Lane, Dronfield, Sheffield S18 6PR (☎ 0246 412 588); House of Commons, London SW1A 0AA (☎ 071 219 4521)

BARNES, Capt James David Kentish; s of Arthur James Kentish Barnes (d 1976), of Caldecot, Caldy, Wirral, Cheshire, and Hester Beatrice, *née* Cromwell-Jones; *b* 18 April 1930; *Educ* Eton, Sandhurst; *m* 1, 1955 (m dis), Julie Ann; 1 s (Timothy James Kentish b 1961), 1 da (Nicola Jane Kentish b 1963); m 2, 1975, Susan Mary, da of Maj-Gen James Francis Harter DSO, MC, DL (d 1965), of Whalebone House, Langham, Colchester; *Career* Capt 5 Royal Inniskilling Dragoon Gds 1950-57, served Korea, ME, Germany; joined John Waterer Sons & Crisp (md 1967-84), currently md and chm Dobbies of Edinburgh; fell RHS; *Recreations* cricket, golf, gardening, shooting, fishing; *Clubs* MCC, The Honourable Co of Edinburgh Golfers, Cavalry and Guards; *Style*— Capt James Barnes; Biggar Park, Biggar, Lanarks (☎ 0899 29185); Dobbie & Co Ltd, Melville Nurseries, Lasswade, nr Dalkeith, Midlothian

BARNES, James Frederick; CB (1982); s of Wilfred Barnes (d 1984), and Doris Martha, *née* Deighton (d 1985); *b* 8 March 1932; *Educ* Taunton's Sch Southampton, The Queen's Coll Oxford (BA, MA); *m* 1957, Dorothy Jean, da of William Jeffrey Drew (d 1980); 1 s (Richard), 2 da (Amanda, Elizabeth); *Career* chartered engr, dep chief scientific advsr MOD 1987-89; chm of govrs Yateley Manor 1981-88, church warden All Saint's Farringdon 1984-89, lay memb Winchester Diocesan Synod 1985-89, stewardship advsr Dio of Monmouth 1989-; *Recreations* garden, local history; *Style*— James Barnes, Esq, CB; Monmouth Diocesan Offices, 64 Caerau Rd, Newport, Gwent NP9 4HJ

BARNES, Lady; Joan Alice Katherine; *née* Schwabe; da of Prof Randolph Schwabe, Slade Prof at London Univ and memb of Royal Soc Painters in Watercolours; *m* 1941, Sir Harry Jefferson Barnes, CBE (d 1982), sometime dir Glasgow Sch of Art; 2 da (and 1 s decd); *Style*— Lady Barnes; 11 Whittingehame Drive, Glasgow (☎ 041 339 1019)

BARNES, John Alfred; s of John Joseph Barnes (d 1953), of Sunderland, and Margaret Carr, *née* Walker (d 1984); *b* 29 April 1930; *Educ* Bede Boys' GS Sunderland, Univ of Durham (BSc, MA, MEd); *m* 7 Aug 1954, Ivy May, da of Robert Rowntree Walker (d 1981), of Sunderland; 2 da (Shirley May b 30 Oct 1957, Jennifer Anne b 16 June 1960); *Career* Nat Serv RAF 1948-49; teacher Grangefield GS Stockton-on-Tees 1953-57, asst educn offr Barnsley Co Borough 1957-61, dir of educn City of Wakefield 1963-68 (dep dir 1961-63), chief educn offr City of Salford 1968-84; dir-gen City & Guilds of London Inst 1984-; chm: Assoc Colls of Further Educn 1980-81, Northern Examining Assoc 1979-82, Assoc Lancs Sch Examining Bd 1972-84; hon sec Assoc Educn Offrs 1977-84, treas NFER 1979-84, pres Educn Devpt Assoc 1980-85; Freeman City of London 1989; FRSA 1973, FITD 1986; *Recreations* cultural activities, foreign travel; *Clubs* Athenaeum; *Style*— John Barnes, Esq; Two Oaks, 37 Woodfield Park, Amersham, Bucks HP6 5QH (☎ 0494 726120); City & Guilds of London Inst, 76 Portland Place, London W1N 4AA (☎ 071 278 2468, fax 071 436 7630, telex 266586)

BARNES, Sir (Ernest) John Ward; KCMG (1974), MBE (Mil 1946); s of Rt Rev Ernest William Barnes, Bishop of Birmingham (d 1953), and Adelaide, da of Sir Adolphus Ward, Master of Peterhouse Cambridge; *b* 22 June 1917; *Educ* Winchester, Trinity Coll Cambridge (MA); *m* 1948, Cynthia Margaret Ray, JP, da of Sir Herbert Stewart, CIE; 2 s, 3 da; *Career* WWII Lt-Col RA (US Bronze Star 1946); HM Dip Serv 1946-77: ambass to Israel 1969-72, ambass to The Netherlands 1972-77; dir: Alliance Investment Co 1977-87, Whiteaway Laidlaw & Co 1979-88; chm Sussex Rural Community Cncl 1982-87, memb Cncl Univ of Sussex 1981-85 (vice chm 1982-84), chm of govrs Hurstpierpoint Coll 1983-87; *Books* Ahead of his Age (1979); *Clubs* Athenaeum, Beefsteak, Brooks's, MCC; *Style*— Sir John Barnes, KCMG, MBE; Hampton Lodge, Hurstpierpoint, W Sussex BN6 9QN (☎ 0273 833247); 20 Thurloe Place Mews, London SW7 2HL (☎ 071 584 9652)

BARNES, Jonathan; s of Albert Leonard Barnes, and Kathleen Mabel, *née* Scoltock; *b* 26 Dec 1942; *Educ* City of London Sch, Balliol Coll Oxford; *m* Jennifer Mary, da of Ormond Postgate; 2 da (Catherine, Camilla); *Career* Univ of Oxford: fell Oriel Coll 1968-78, fell Balliol Coll 1978-, lectr in philosophy 1968-, prof of ancient philosophy 1989-; visiting appointments at: Univ of Chicago, Inst for Advanced Study Princeton, Univ of Massachusetts Amherst, Univ of Texas Austin, Wissenschaftskolleg Zu Berlin, Univ of Edmonton, Univ of Zurich, Istituto Italiano per gli Studi Filosfici Naples; FBA 1987; *Books* The Ontological Argument (1972), Aristotle's Posterior Analytics (1975), The Presocratic Philosophers (1979), Aristotle (1982), Early Greek Philosophy (1987), The Toils of Scepticism (1990); *Recreations* rowing, tennis, tapestry, crosswords; *Style*— Jonathan Barnes, Esq; Balliol College, Oxford OX1 3BJ (☎ 0865 277754, fax 0865 270708 ATTN BALLIOL)

BARNES, Dame (Alice) Josephine Mary Taylor; DBE (1974); Dame Josephine Warren; da of late Rev Walter W Barnes (d 1959), and Alice Mary, *née* Ibbetson; sis of Francis Walter Ibbetson Barnes, *qv*; *b* 18 Aug 1912; *Educ* Oxford HS, LMH Oxford, Univ Coll Hosp Med Sch; *m* 1942 (m dis 1964), Sir Brian Warren, *qv*; 1 s, 2 da; *Career* consulting obstetrician and gynaecologist Charing Cross Hosp and Elizabeth Garrett Anderson Hosp; pres: Women's Nat Cancer Control Campaign 1974-, BMA 1979-80; memb Cncl Advertising Standards Authy 1980-; FRCP, FRCS, FRCOG; *Books* Lecture Notes on Gynaecology (6 edn 1988), Scientific Foundations of Obstetrics and Gynaecology (ed 3 edn 1986); *Recreations* music, gastronomy, motoring, foreign travel; *Style*— Dame Josephine Barnes, DBE; 8 Aubrey Walk, London W8 7JG (☎ 071 727 9832)

BARNES, Sir Kenneth; KCB (1977, CB 1970); s of Arthur Barnes and Doris Barnes, of Accrington, Lancs; *b* 26 Aug 1922; *Educ* Accrington GS, Balliol Coll Oxford; *m* 1948, Barbara Ainsworth; 1 s, 2 da; *Career* permanent sec Dept of Employment 1976-82; *Style*— Sir Kenneth Barnes, KCB; South Sandhills, Sandy Lane, Betchworth, Surrey, RH3 7AA, (☎ 0737 842445)

BARNES, Dr (Nicholas) Martin Limer; s of Geoffrey Lambe Barnes, of Craven Arms, Shropshire and Birmingham (d 1984), and Emily *née* Dicken (d 1976); *b* 18 Jan 1939; *Educ* King Edwards Sch Birmingham, Imperial Coll London (BSc), Univ of Manchester Inst of Sci and Technol (PhD); *m* 23 Feb 1963, Diana Marion, da of Barrie Campbell (d 1968); 1 s (Matthew b 1966), 1 da (Kate b 1964); *Career* res fell Univ of Manchester 1968-71, ptnr Martin Barnes and Partners 1971-85; ptnr Coopers and Lybrand Deloitte, mgmnt conslt Martin Barnes Project Mgmnt; Churchill Fellowship 1971, FEng, FICE, FCIOB, CBIM, FAPM, (chm 1986-), FInstCES (pres 1978-86), FRSA, MBCS, ACIArb, ACGI; *Books* Measurement in Contract Control (1977), The CESMM2 Handbook (1986), Engineering Management: Financial Control (ed, 1990); *Recreations* railway and canal history, victorian paintings; *Style*— Dr Martin Barnes; 322 Shakespeare Tower, Barbican, London EC2Y 8DR (☎ 071 628 3961); Coopers and Lybrand Deloitte, Hillgate House, 26 Old Bailey, London EC4M 7PL (☎ 071 583 5000, fax 071 236 2367)

BARNES, Michael Cecil John; s of Maj Cecil Horace Reginald Barnes, OBE (d 1969), and Katherine Louise, *née* Kennedy (d 1988); *b* 22 Sept 1932; *Educ* Malvern, CCC Oxford (MA); *m* 21 April 1962, Anne, da of Basil Mason (d 1974), of London; 1 s (Hugh b 1963), 1 da (Katy b 1966); *Career* Nat Serv 2 Lt The Wilts Regt, served Hong Kong 1952-53; MP (Lab) for Brentford and Chiswick 1966-74; chm Electricity Consumers Cncl 1977-83, dir UK Immigrants' Advsy Serv 1984-90; Legal Services Ombudsman 1991-; chm: Hounslow Arts Tst 1974-82, Notting Hill Social Cncl 1976-79, Housing Action Centre N Kensington 1980-87; memb: Nat Consumer Cncl 1975-80, Advertising Standards Authy 1979-85; Burgess City of Bristol 1953; *Recreations* walking, swimming, dogs; *Style*— Michael Barnes, Esq; 45 Ladbroke Grove, London W11 3AR (☎ 071 727 2533); 84 Monkton Deverill, nr Warminster, Wilts BA12 7EX;

Office of the Legal Services Ombudsman, 22 Oxford Court, Manchester M2 3WQ (☎ 061 236 9532)

BARNES, (David) Michael William; QC (1981); s of David Charles Barnes (d 1954), and Florence Maud, *née* Matthews (d 1967); *b* 16 July 1943; *Educ* Monmouth Sch, Wadham Coll Oxford (BA); *m* 10 Sept 1970, Susan Dorothy, da of William Turner; 3 s (Andrew b 1972, Edmund b 1974, Peter b 1979); *Career* barr Middle Temple 1965; hon res fell Lady Margaret Hall Oxford 1979; recorder of Crown Court 1984; ed 15, 16 and 17 edns of Hill & Redmans Law of Landlord and Tenant; *Style—* Michael Barnes, Esq, QC; 2 Paper Bldgs, Temple, London EC4

BARNES, Neil Richard; s of Maj Harold William Barnes (d 1981), of W Wickham, Kent, and Mary Mabel, *née* Butchart (d 1980); *b* 14 Jan 1947; *Educ* Sutton Valence Sch, Univ of Reading (BSc); *m* 18 Sept 1971, Susan Jane, da of Douglas Norman Smith, of Beckenham, Kent; 1 s (Stephen b 24 May 1979), 1 da (Nicola b 20 Nov 1975); *Career* md IDC Property Investmts 1979-91, divnl dir AMEC Properties Ltd 1991-; pres Round Table W Wickham 1990-91 (chm 1986-87); Freeman City of London, Liveryman Worshipful Co of Masons; FRICS 1983; *Recreations* golf, badminton; *Style—* Neil Barnes, Esq; AMEC Properties Ltd, 7 Baker St, London W1M 1AB (☎ 071 935 9384)

BARNES, Peter; s of Frederick Barnes (d 1955), and Martha (d 1981); *b* 10 Jan 1931; *Educ* Stroud GS; *m* 18 Oct 1961, Charlotte Beck; *Career* playwright and dir; plays incl: The Ruling Class (1968), Leonardo's Last Supper and Noonday Demons (1969), Lulu (1970), The Devil is an Ass (1973), The Bewitched (1974), The Frontiers of Farce (1976), Laughter! (1978), Antonio (1979), Red Noses (1985), Sunsets and Glories (1990); radio plays incl: Barnes' People I, II, III (1981-86), More Barnes' People (1989); films incl: Leonardo's Last Supper (1971), The Ruling Class (1972); directed: Lulu (1970), Bartholomew Fair (1977), Frontiers of Farce (1976), Antonio (1979), The Devil Himself (1980), Somersaults (1981), Bartholomew Fair (1987); written and directed for TV: The Spirit of Man (1989), Nobody Here But Us Chickens (1989); awards: Winner of the John Whiting Award (1969), Evening Standard Award (1969), Best Radio Play Award (1981), Olivier Award (1985), Royal TV Soc Drama Award (1989); FRSL 1984; *Style—* Peter Barnes, Esq; 7 Archery Close, Connaught St, London W2; Margaret Ramsay Ltd, 14A Goodwins Ct, St Martins Lane, London WC1 (☎ 071 240 0691)

BARNES, Peter Robert; CB (1981); s of Robert Stanley Barnes, and Marguerite, *née* Dunkels; *b* 1 Feb 1921; *Educ* Eton, Trinity Coll Cambridge; *m* 1955, Pauline Belinda Hannen; 2 s, 1 da; *Career* called to the Bar Inner Temple 1947; Dept Pub Prosecutions: legal asst 1951, sr legal asst 1958, asst slr 1970, asst dir 1974, princ asst dir 1977, dep dir 1977-82; pres Video Appeals Ctee 1985-; *Style—* Peter Barnes, Esq, CB; The Old Vicarage, Church Lane, Witley, Surrey (☎ 0428 684509)

BARNES, Dr Robert Sandford; s of William Edward Barnes (d 1981), of Maghull, Lancs, and Ada Elsie, *née* Sutherst (d 1983); *b* 8 July 1924; *Educ* Ormskirk GS, Univ of Manchester (BSc, MSc, DSc); *m* 16 Aug 1952, Julia Frances Marriott, da of Roger Douglas Marriott Grant (d 1978), of IOW; 1 s (Richard b 1963), 3 da (Philippa b 1956, Alison b 1958, Penelope b 1959); *Career* radar res Admty Res Estab Witley 1944-47; head irradiation branch AERE Harwell 1962-65 (scientist 1948-62), visiting scientist N American Aviation California 1965; head Metallurgy Div Harwell 1966-68, dir BISRA 1969-70 (dep dir 1968), chief scientist Br Steel Corp 1975-78 (dir R & D 1970-75); chm: Ruthner Continuous Crop Ltd 1976-78, Robert S Barnes Consits Ltd 1978-; tech advsr: to the Bd BOC Ltd 1978-79, BOC Int 1979-81; princ Queen Elizabeth Coll, Univ of London 1978-85; Hadfield meml lecture 1972, John Player lecture 1976; memb Cncl Backpain Assoc 1979-, pres Inst of Metalluqists 1982-85; Rosenhain medal 1964; Freeman City of London 1984, Liveryman Worshipful Co of Engrs 1984; FInstP 1961, FIM 1965, FRSA 1976, CEng 1977; *Recreations* cruising (yacht Cassis of St Helier); *Clubs* Athenaeum, Cruising Assoc; *Style—* Dr Robert S Barnes; Pigeon Forge, Daneshill, The Hockering, Woking, Surrey (☎ 0483 761529)

BARNES, Hon Ronald Alexander Henry; yr s of 3 Baron Gorell, CBE, MC (d 1963); hp of 4 Baron; *b* 28 June 1931; *Educ* Harrow, New Coll Oxford; *m* 1957, Gillian Picton, yst da of late Picton Hughes-Jones, of Henstridge, Somerset; 1 s, 1 da; *Career* late Lt Royal Fusiliers, seconded KAR, Capt Royal Northumberland Fusiliers (TA); formerly Public Relations Offr P&O Orient Lines; sr ptnr Stockton & Barnes (estate agents); *Style—* The Hon Ronald Barnes; Fernbank, Mingoose, Mount Hawke, Truro, Cornwall (☎ 0209 890310)

BARNES, Rosemary (Rosie); MP (SDP) Greenwich 1987; da of Alan Allen, of Nottingham, and Kathleen, *née* Brown; *b* 16 May 1946; *Educ* Bilborough GS, Univ of Birmingham (BSoc Sci); *m* 1967, Graham Barnes; 2 s (Dannyt b 1973, Joseph b 1985), 1 da (Daisy b 1975); *Career* mgmnt trainee Unilever (Research Bureau Ltd) 1967-69, mktg exec Yardley 1969-72, primary teacher 1973, freelance researcher 1973-87; *Style—* Mrs Rosemary Barnes, MP; 21 Egerton Drive, Greenwich, London SE10 8JR (☎ 071 692 8452)

BARNES, Timothy Paul; QC (1986); s of the late Arthur Morley Barnes, of The Homestead, Seal, Nr Sevenoaks, Kent, and Valerie Enid Mary, *née* Wilks; *b* 23 April 1944; *Educ* Bradfield, Christs Coll Cambridge (MA); *m* Aug 1969, Patricia Margaret, da of Leslie Ralph Gale (d 1974); 1 s (Christopher b 1973), 3 da (Olivia b 1975, Jessica b 1978, Natasha b 1986); *Career* called to the Bar Gray's Inn 1968; asst rec 1983, rec 1987, memb of Midland and Oxford circuit; *Recreations* hockey, gardening, music; *Clubs* MCC; *Style—* Timothy P Barnes, Esq, QC; The White House, Crooms Hill, London, SE10 8HH (☎ 081 858 1185); 2 Crown Office Row, Temple, London, EC4 (☎ 071 353 1365)

BARNETSON, Hon (William) Denholm; s of Baron Barnetson (Life Peer, d 1981), and Joan Fairley, *née* Davidson; *b* 30 May 1955; *Educ* Cranleigh Sch, Sorbonne Paris; *Career* journalist/foreign corr Utd Press Int Washington DC: Paris 1980-81, NY 1981-83, Washington 1983-85, Hong Kong, New Delhi 1985-88, India, Islamabad, Pakistan 1988-91, Saudi Arabia 1991-; *Style—* The Hon W Denholm Barnetson; c/o Broom, Chillies Lane, Crowborough, E Sussex TN6 3TB; UPI, Eye Street, Washington DC, USA

BARNETSON, Baroness; Joan Fairley; da of William Fairley Davidson (d 1958), and Augustina, *née* Bjarnadottir (d 1969); *b* 22 July 1918; *m* 1940, William Denholm, Baron Barnetson (Life Peer 1975, kt 1972, d 1981); 1 s (Denholm), 3 da (Astraea, Louise, Julia); *Recreations* sculpture, tapestry; *Style—* The Rt Hon the Lady Barnetson; Broom, Chillies Lane, Crowborough, East Sussex TN6 3TB (☎ 0892 655748)

BARNETT, Col Anthony Francis (Tony); OBE (1982); s of Walter Francis Barnett (d 1967), of Hockley, Essex, and May Lillian, *née* White (d 1984); *b* 19 May 1933; *Educ* Brentwood Sch Essex; *m* 31 July 1957, Sheila Rose (d 1980), da of Charles Douglas Tomkinson, of Bradford on Avon, Wilts; 1 s (Martin b 1962), 2 da (Caroline 1960); *Career* cmmnd Army 1952, Staff offr RMA Sandhurst 1962-64, 99 Gurkha Inf Bde Sarawak 1965-66, CO Army Catering Corps Army Apprentice Coll 1977-79, HQ Dir Army Catering Corps 1979-81, Cdr Catering Gp 1983-85, Col and dep dir HQ Dir Army Catering Corps 1985-88; memb Fencing Ctee Asian Games Singapore 1965; FHCIMA 1984, FBIM 1989; *Recreations* writing plays and short stories, cricket, eating out, theatre; *Clubs* Army and Navy; *Style—* Col Tony Barnett, OBE; Little Foxes, 21 Huntsmead, Ashdell Park, Alton, Hampshire (☎ 0420 85287); c/o HQ DACC, St Omer Barracks, Aldershot, Hants

BARNETT, Dr Anthony Howard (Tony); s of Geoffrey Barnett, and Beulah, *née* Statman; *b* 29 May 1951; *Educ* Roundhay GS Leeds, Univ of London Kings Coll Hosp (BSc, MB BS, MD); *m* 11 Nov 1975, Catherine Elizabeth Mary, da of John O'Donnell (d 1977); 3 s (James John, Jonathan Andrew, Robert David), 3 da (Clare Joanne, Sarah Suzanne, Anna Lucy); *Career* sr fell MRC 1979-81, sr registrar in med diabetes and endocrinology Ch Ch NZ and Southampton 1981-83, sr lectr and conslt physician Univ of Birmingham 1983- (reader in med 1989-); memb : Br Diabetic Assoc, Euro Assoc Study of Diabetes; former sec NZ Diabetes Assoc 1981-82; MRCP 1978; *Books* Immunogenetics of Insulin Dependant Diabetes (1987), Hypertension and Diabetes (1990); *Recreations* reading, sport and family; *Style—* Dr Tony Barnett; E Birmingham Hosp, Undergraduate Centre, Birmingham B9 5ST (☎ 021 766 6611 ext 4006, fax 021 773 6736)

BARNETT, Maj Benjamin George; MBE (1946), TD; s of Col George Henry Barnett, CMG, DSO (d 1942), of Glympton Park, Oxon, and Mary Dorothea, *née* Lowbridge-Baker; *b* 5 Dec 1912; *Educ* Malvern; *m* 1943, Delia, JP, da of Maj Sir Algernon Peyton, 7 Bt (d 1962); 2 s, 1 da; *Career* served with Oxfordshire Yeomanry, Maj, ret 1947; ret memb Stock Exchange; High Sheriff Oxfordshire 1969; *Recreations* shooting, fishing; *Style—* Maj Benjamin Barnett, MBE, TD; Woodbine Cottage, Swifts House, nr Bicester, Oxon (☎ 0896 346819)

BARNETT, His Hon Judge Christopher John Anthony; QC (1983); s of Richard Adrian Barnett, of Battle, Sussex, and Phyllis, *née* Cartwright (d 1947); *b* 18 May 1936; *Educ* Repton, Coll of Law London; *m* 31 Oct 1959, Sylvia Marieliese (Marlies), da of George Lyn Ashby Pritt (d 1983); 2 s (Peter b 1962, Marcus b 1970), 1 da (Susannah b 1965); *Career* Nat Serv with Kenya Regt and Kenya Govt, Dist Offr (Kikuyu Gd) 1954-56; Kenya Govt Serv 1956-60; dist offr H Overseas Civil Serv in Kenya 1960-62; called to the Bar Gray's Inn, 1 rec of the Crown Court 1982; circuit judge 1988; chm SE Circuit Area Liaison Ctee 1985-88; memb: Court of Univ of Essex 1983-, Wine Ctee Circuit 1984-88; *Recreations* cricket, tennis, walking; *Clubs* Kenya Kongonis Cricket; *Style—* His Hon Judge Barnett, QC; 4 Paper Buildings, Temple, London EC4Y 7EX (☎ 071 583 7765, fax 071 353 4674)

BARNETT, Correlli Douglas; s of D A Barnett; *b* 28 June 1927; *Educ* Trinity Sch Croydon, Exeter Coll Oxford; *m* 1950, Ruth Murby; 2 da; *Career* writer and historian; keeper of the Churchill Archives Centre and fell Churchill Coll Cambridge 1977-; FRHistS, FRSL; *Style—* Correlli Barnett, Esq; Catbridge House, E Carleton, Norwich

BARNETT, (Ulric) David; s of Peter Cedric Barnett (d 1980), and Sylvia Irina, *née* Kenny; *b* 29 Sept 1942; *Educ* Eton, Magdalen Coll Oxford; *m* 4 Jan 1969, Marie-Jane Hélène, da of Capitaine de Fregate Jean Levasseur (d 1947); 2 s (Rory b 1971, Oliver b 1979), 1 da (Natalie b 1974); *Career* joined Cazenove & Co Stockbrokers 1965 (ptnr since 1972); *Clubs* MCC, City Univ; *Style—* David Barnett, Esq; 12 Tokenhouse Yard, London EC2R 7AN

BARNETT, Air Chief Marshal Sir Denis Hensley Fulton; GCB (1964, KCB 1957, CB 1956), CBE (1945), DFC (1940); yst s of Sir Louis Edward Barnett, CMG, CM (d 1946), and Mabel Violet, *née* Fulton; *b* 11 Feb 1906; *Educ* Christ's Coll NZ, Clare Coll Cambridge (MA); *m* 1939, Pamela, yst da of Sir Allan John Grant (d 1955); 1 s, 2 da; *Career* cmmnd RAF 1929, served WW II Bomber Cmd, AOC-in-C RAF Tport Cmd 1959-62, RAF Near East, Cdr Br Forces Cyprus and Admin Sovereign Base Area 1962-64, ret; memb Weapons R & D AEA 1965-72; *Style—* Air Chief Marshal Sir Denis Barnett, GCB, CBE, DFC; River House, Rushall, Pewsey, Wilts SN9 6EN

BARNETT, Eric Oliver; s of Eric Everard Barnett (d 1989), of Johannesburg, S Africa, and Maud Emily Louise, *née* Oliver (d 1948); *b* 13 Feb 1929; *Educ* St John's Coll Johannesburg, Witwatersrand Coll of Art, Univ of Cape Town, Univ of S Africa, Univ of Natal, UCL; *m* 1, 13 Feb 1950, Louise Francesca (d 1984), da of Nicholas Peter Lindenberg (d 1978), of Durban; m 2, 13 March 1986, Vivienne, da of Samuel Arthur Goodwin, of Northwood, London; *Career* lectr psychology Univ of Natal 1957; Arthur Barnett Fndn: res dir 1963-71, vice chm 1969-71, chm 1971-; chm Rural Ecology & Resources Ctee Southern Africa 1978-; *Recreations* music, painting, history of sci, salmon fishing, shooting; *Style—* Eric Barnett, Esq; Baldarroch House, Murthly, Perthshire (☎ 073 871 309)

BARNETT, Col Gordon; MBE (1976); s of Ernest Barnett (d 1980), of Stoke on Trent, and Eva Hodgkinson (d 1955); *b* 26 May 1936; *Educ* Newcastle under Lyme HS, RMA Sandhurst; *m* 4 June 1960, Carole Phyllis, da of George Brian Townsend (d 1982), of Weybridge, Surrey; 2 s (Simon b 1963, Jonathan b 1965); *Career* Nat Serv N Staffordshire Regt 1955, Offr Cadet RMA Sandhurst 1956-58, cmmnd RCS 1958, cdr signals Qatar Defence Force (Lt-Col) 1979-81, controller UK Army Telecoms (Col) 1982-86, cdr Sultan of Oman's Armed Forces Signals (Col) 1986-89; mktg mangr Racal Communications Ltd 1989-; MISM 1966, MBIM 1978; hon comm Indian Army Signal Corps (rank Maj) 1976; *Recreations* photography, walking; *Style—* Col Gordon Barnett, MBE; Hill Cottage, Thames St, Sonning-on-Thames, Berkshire (☎ 0734 696693); Racal Radio Ltd, 472 Basingstoke Rd, Reading, Berks (☎ 0734 875181)

BARNETT, Baron (Life Peer UK 1983), of Heywood and Royton, in Greater Manchester; Joel Barnett; PC (1975), JP (Lancs 1960); s of Louis Barnett (d 1964), of Manchester, and Ettie Barnett (d 1956); *b* 14 Oct 1923; *Educ* Derby Street Jewish Sch, Manchester Centl HS; *m* 11 Sept 1949, Lilian Stella, da of Abraham Goldstone (d 1965); 1 da (Hon Erica Hazel b 7 Aug 1951); *Career* served WW II, RASC; sr ptnr J C Allen & Co Manchester 1954-74; Parly candidate (Lab) Runcorn 1959, MP (Lab) Lancs Heywood and Royton 1964-83; chm Lab Party Econ and Financial Gp 1967-70; memb: Public Accounts Ctee 1966-71, Public Expenditure Ctee 1971-74, Select Ctee on Tax Credits 1973; chief sec Treasury 1974-79 (oppn spokesman Treasury 1970-74, Cabinet memb 1977-79), chm Commons Select Ctee Public Accounts 1979-83; oppn spokesman (Lords) Treasury 1983-86; memb Hallé Soc of Manchester 1982-; hon visiting fell Strathclyde Univ 1980-, tstee V & A 1983-, vice pres Assoc of Metropolitan Authorities 1983-; vice chm BBC 1986-; chm Hansard Soc for Parly Govt 1984-90; Hon LLD Univ of Strathclyde 1983; govr Birkbeck Coll Univ of London; pres RIPA 1988-; dir various public and private cos; FCCA; *Books* Inside the Treasury (1982); *Recreations* hiking, reading, music, theatre; *Style—* The Rt Hon the Lord Barnett, PC, JP; 7 Hillingdon Rd, Whitefield, Manchester M25 7QQ (☎ 061 766 3634); 92 Millbank Court, 24 John Islip St, London SW1 (☎ 071 927 4620); Vice-Chairman's Office, BBC, Broadcasting House, London W1A 1AA (☎ 071 927 4620, fax 071 637 0705, telex 268781, car 0860 545 981)

BARNETT, Joseph Anthony; CBE (1983); s of Joseph Edward Barnett (d 1962), and Helen Yanocatis (d 1976); *b* 19 Dec 1931; *Educ* St Albans Sch, Pembroke Coll Cambridge (MA); *m* 1960, Carolina Johnson, da of Baldwin Rice (d 1974), of USA; 1 s (Lindsay b 1965), 1 da (Sujata b 1970); *Career* Unilever Ltd 1954-58; Br Cncl 1958; overseas serv: E Pakistan 1958-63, India 1967-71, Ethiopia 1971-75, Brazil 1978-83, rep Japan 1983-; *Style—* Joseph Barnett, Esq, CBE; The Thatch, Stebbing Green, Gt Dummow, Essex (☎ 037 186 352); Br Cncl, 2 Kagura Zaka-1 Chome, Shinjuku-Ku, Tokyo 162, Japan

BARNETT, Hon Mrs (Kathleen Irene Mary); *née* Hennessy; da of 1 Baron Windlesham, OBE (d 1953); *b* 1914; *Educ* private; *m* 1947, Wilfred Ernest Barnett, 3 s of Ernest Barnett, of Chesterfield, Derbyshire; 2 s (Robin George, Nicholas James);

Style— The Hon Mrs W Barnett; Pullington Cottage, Benenden, Cranbrook, Kent (☎ 0580 240435)

BARNETT, Kenneth Thomas; CB (1979); yr s of Frederick Charles Barnett (d 1975), and Ethel, *née* Powell (d 1965); *b* 12 Jan 1921; *Educ* Howard Gdns HS Cardiff; *m* 1943, Emily May, da of Edward Lovering (d 1962); 1 da; *Career* served RAF 1941-46 as radar mechanic (NCO); entered Miny of Tport 1937, exec offr Sea Tport 1946-51, accountant offr and sec to Divnl Sea Tport Offr ME Port Said 1951-54, higher exec and sr exec posts Roads Divs 1954-61, princ Fin Div 1961-65, asst sec then under sec Ports 1965-71; under sec: Cabinet Office (on secondment) 1971-73, Housing Dept of Environment 1973-76; dep sec Housing 1976-80, ret 1980; dir Abbey Data Systems Ltd 1984-; *Style—* Kenneth Barnett, Esq, CB; The Stone House, Frith End, nr Bordon, Hants (☎ 0420 472856)

BARNETT, Kim John; s of Derek Barnett of Stoke-on-Trent, and Doreen, *née* Haywood; *b* 17 July 1960; *Educ* Leek HS; *Career* professional cricketer; Derbyshire CCC: debut 1979, awarded county cap 1982, capt 1983-, 260 appearances; England: 4 Test matches 1988-89 (highest score 80 v Aust Headingley 1989), one day Int v Sri Lanka Oval; 1 unofficial Test v SA, 4 one day Ints v SA; Derbyshire record holder for centuries scored (32) and number of runs in one day cricket; 10 one day man of the match awards; *Recreations* horse-racing, most sports, reading; *Style—* Kim Barnett, Esq; Derbyshire CCC, County Ground, Nottingham Rd, Derby (☎ 0332 383211)

BARNETT, Hon Mrs (Laura Miriam Elizabeth); da of Baron Weidenfeld (Life Peer), by his 1 w; *b* 1953; *Educ* Univ of Oxford (MA); *m* 1976, Christopher Andrew Barnett; 3 s (Benjamin b 1979, Rowan b 1981, Nathaniel b 1984), 1 da (Clara b 1986); *Style—* The Hon Mrs Barnett; Awdry House, Sunnyside, West Lavington, nr Devizes, Wilts SN10 4HU

BARNETT, Michael Gerald; s of Gerald Barnett, of Fordham, Cambs, and Edwina May, *née* Fordham; *b* 24 Jan 1951; *Educ* Soham GS, Imperial Coll London (BSc); *m* 6 Oct 1973, Vivienne Joy, da of Robert Nicholas; 1 s (Philip James b 31 July 1982), 1 da (Stefanie Michelle b 9 April 1976); *Career* Friends Provident: actuarial student 1973, numerous actuarial positions until 1981, actuary 1981, pensions actuary 1985, pensions marketing mangr 1986, gp pensions mangr 1987 asst gen mangr (pensions) 1990; ARCS, FIA 1981; *Recreations* golf, music, theatre; *Clubs* Mannings Heath Golf, The Debtors' (actuarial); *Style—* Michael Barnett, Esq; 39 Irwin Drive, Horsham, West Sussex RH12 1NL (☎ 0403 66823); Friends Provident, Pixham End, Dorking, Surrey RH4 1QA (☎ 0306 740123)

BARNETT, Sir Oliver Charles; CBE (1954, OBE (Mil) 1946), QC (1956); s of Charles Frederick Robert Barnett (TA, ka 1915); *b* 7 Feb 1907; *Educ* Eton; *m* 1945, Joan, da of W H Eve (Capt 13 Hussars, ka 1917), and gda of Rt Hon Sir Harry Eve (d 1940, High Court Judge); *Career* called to the Bar 1928, Judge Advocate Gen of the Forces 1963-68, bencher Middle Temple 1964, dep chm Somerset QS 1967-71; kt 1968; *Clubs* Brooks's, Pratt's; *Style—* Sir Oliver Barnett, CBE, QC; The Almonry, Stogumber, nr Taunton, Somerset (☎ 0984 56291)

BARNETT, Prof Stephen; s of Wolfe Barnett, of Hull, and Sylvia, *née* Sugar; *b* 1 July 1938; *Educ* Univ of Manchester (BSc, MSc, DSc), Univ of Loughborough (PhD); *m* 5 June 1960, Naomi Joan, da of Joseph Vine, of Sussex; 1 s (David Michael b 13 Sept 1969); *Career* dean engrg Univ of Bradford 1988-90 (reader engrg maths and sr lectr 1969-80, prof applied maths 1981-90), prof in applied maths Univ of Essex 1990-; chm Conf of Univ Profs Applied Maths 1988-; FIMA 1968, MIEE 1978, CEng 1978; *Books* Matrices in Control Theory (1971, 2 edn 1984), Introduction to Mathematical Control Theory (1975, 2 edn 1985), Polynomials and Linear Control Systems (1983), Mathematical Formulae (with T M Cronin 1971, 4 edn 1986); Natrixes, methods and applications (1990); *Recreations* hiking, photography, collecting ephemera; *Style—* Prof Stephen Barnett; Dept of Mathematics, Univ of Essex, Colchester CO6 3DZ (☎ 0206 873040)

BARNETT, William Evans; QC (1984); s of Alec Barnett (d 1981), of Penarth, S Glam, and Esmé Georgiana, *née* Leon (d 1989); *b* 10 March 1937; *Educ* Repton, Keble Coll Oxford (BA, MA); *m* 24 July 1976, Lucinda Jane Gilbert, JP, da of Richard William Gilbert (d 1980), of Addington, Surrey; 2 s (Nicholas b 1978, James b 1980); *Career* Nat Serv RCS 1956-58; barr 1962, joined Midland and Oxford Circuit 1963; memb Personal Injuries Litigation Procedure Working Pty 1976-78, rec Crown Ct 1981; memb: Panel of Arbitrators Master Insurers' Bureau 1987, Croydon Medico-Legal Soc; *Recreations* golf, photography, gardening, DIY; *Clubs* Surrey Tennis & County, RAC; *Style—* William Barnett, Esq, QC; Carleon, 6 Castlemaine Avenue, S Croydon, Surrey CR2 7HQ (☎ 081 688 9559); 12 King's Bench Walk, Temple, London EC4Y 7EL (☎ 071 583 0811, fax 071 583 7228)

BARNEWALL, Peter Joseph (Joe); s and h of Sir Reginald Robert Barnewall, 13 Bt, *qv*; *b* 26 Oct 1963; *Educ* St Joseph's Nudgee Coll, Univ of Queensland (BAgrSc (Econ)); *m* 1988, Kathryn Jane, da of Patrick Carroll, of Brisbane, Queensland; *Career* Lt served with Australian Army Reserve, Queensland Univ Regt 1981-86; 2/14 Light Horse (Queensland Mounted Inf) 1987-; agric economist; *Recreations* game shooting, running, photography, tennis; *Clubs* United Service, Tamborine Mountain RSC; *Style—* Joe Barnewall, Esq; 16 Akala St, Camp Hill, Queensland 4152, Australia

BARNEWALL, Sir Reginald Robert; 13 Bt (I 1623); s of Sir Reginald John Barnewall, 12 Bt (d 1961); *b* 1 Oct 1924; *Educ* Xavier Coll Melbourne; *m* 1, 1946, Elsie Muriel (d 1962), da of Thomas Matthews Frederick, of Brisbane, Queensland; 3 da; m 2, 1962, Maureen Ellen, da of William Daly, of S Caulfield, Victoria; 1 s; *Heir* s, Peter Joseph Barnewall b 26 Oct 1963; *Career* wool grower, cattle breeder, orchardist; former dir Island Airways Pty Ltd (Pialba, Qld), operator and owner Coastal-Air Co (Qld) 1971-76, former dir and vice chm J Roy Stevens Pty Ltd; *Style—* Sir Reginald Barnewall, Bt; Innisfree, Westcliff Road, Mount Tamborine, Queensland 4272, Australia

BARNEY, Charlotte Mary Elizabeth; da of Ashley R G Raeburn, of Dulwich, London, and Esther, *née* Johns; *b* 29 June 1954; *Educ* James Allen's Girls' Sch Dulwich, Somerville Coll Oxford (MA); *m* 21 Oct 1989, William David Iain Barney, s of (William) Guy Barney; *Career* analyst/graduate trainee Overseas Dept Bank of England 1975-78, exec Corp Fin Dept Hill Samuel 1980-81 (exec Project Fin Dept 1978-80), journalist Investors' Chronicle 1981-85, account dir Good Relations City 1985-86; dir: Streets Financial Strategy 1987 (asst dir 1986-87), Citigate Communications Ltd 1987-; *Recreations* music, skiing, riding, Dorset countryside; *Style—* Mrs Charlotte Barney; Citigate Communications Limited, 7 Birchin Lane, London EC3V 9BY (☎ 071 623 2737, fax 071 623 9050)

BARNICOAT, Wing Cdr David Ross; s of Frank Ross Barnicoat (d 1977), and Olive Mary, *née* Collins (d 1982); *b* 21 July 1925; *Educ* Cranbrook Sch, Wadham Coll Oxford, RAF Coll Cranwell; *m* 1, 25 March 1944, Audrey Margaret, da of Harold Wilson (d 1981); 1 s (Ian b 1946), 2 da (Jacqueline b 1944, Jennifer b 1950); m 2, 1960, Elizabeth Christine, da of Maurice Cecil Johnes Lloyd (d 1950); 1 s (Oliver b 1963), 1 da (Katherine b 1965); *Career* RAF Offr 1944-75, Wing Cdr Air Attache Cairo; sr ptnr D R Barnicoat Assoc 1975-, chm B&B Serv Conslts Ltd 1977-; FBIM, FInstD; *Recreations* travel, skiing, swimming, boating; *Clubs* RAF; *Style—* Wing Cdr David R Barnicoat; Garden House, Wyke Hall, Gillingham, Dorset SP8 5NS (☎ : 0747 823409; Villa Pasqualino, Porto Cervo, Costa Smeralda, Sardinia

BARNS-GRAHAM, Patrick Allan; TD; s of Allan Barns-Graham (d 1957), of Lymekilns, and Wilhelmina Menzies, *née* Bayne-Meldrum; *b* 19 Feb 1915; *Educ* Sedbergh; *m* 31 Dec 1944, Daphne Blanche Rosemary, da of Lt William Henry Braisty Skaife-d'Ingerthorpe, RNVR; 2 s (Allan b 1948, Peter b 1951), 2 da (Rosemary b 1946, Christina b 1959); *Career* RA (TA): 2 Lt 1938, Capt 1940, Maj 1942, serv M East 1935-45, demobilised as Maj; CA Thomson McLintock & Co Glasgow 1938; Brownlee & Co plc: account sec 1946, sec 1948, dir 1958, md 1968, chm 1973-80; dir: Alliance Alders and assoc cos 1973-80, Diversion Insurance Timber Trade UK Ltd; Lord Dean Guild of City of Glasgow 1977-87, dir Glasgow C of C 1969-77, chm Glasgow Humane Soc 1977-87 (dir 1976-90), preceptor Royal Incorporation of Hutcheson's Hosp 1987-90; MICAS; *Recreations* formerly shooting and fishing; *Style—* Patrick Barns-Graham, Esq, TD; Braehead, Blanefield, Stirlingshire G63 9AP (☎ 0360 70249)

BARNSLEY, Prof (David) Graham; s of David Barnsley (d 1982), and Mabel Grace, *née* Beech; *b* 16 Jan 1936; *Educ* Stand GS Whitefield Manchester, Univ of Manchester (LLB, LLM); *m* 21 May 1960, Blanche, da of George Richard Charles Thompson, of Blackburn, Lancs; 2 da (Helen Ruth b 1962, Gail Elisabeth b 1964); *Career* admitted slr 1960, lectr Univ of Manchester 1960-66, dean Faculty of Law Univ of Leicester 1976-82 (sr lectr 1966-73, pro law 1973-); memb: The Gideons Int, Soc of Pub Teachers of Law, Law Soc; *Books* Conveyancing Law and Practice (3 edn, 1988), Land Options (1978); *Recreations* walking, gardening, philately, lay preaching; *Style—* Prof Graham Barnsley; Faculty of Law, University of Leicester, Univ Rd, Leics LE1 7RH (☎ 0533 522345, telex 347250 LEICUN G)

BARNSLEY, Thomas Edward; OBE (1975); s of Alfred E Barnsley and Ada F Nightingale; *b* 10 Sept 1919; *Educ* Wednesbury Boys' HS; *m* 1947, Margaret Gwyneth Llewellin; 1 s, 1 da; *Career* md Tube Investments 1974-82; dir H P Bulmer Hldgs 1982-87; FCA; *Style—* Thomas Barnsley, Esq, OBE; Old Rectory, Llanelidan, nr Ruthin, Clwyd (☎ 08245 633)

BARNSLEY, Victoria; da of T E Barnsley, OBE, of The Old Rectory, Llanelidan, Ruthin, N Wales, and Margeret Gwyneth, *née* Llewellin; *b* 4 March 1954; *Educ* Loughborough HS for Girls, Beachlawn Oxford, UCL (BA), Univ of York (MA); *Career* fndr and publisher Fourth Estate Publishers 1984 (winner of first Sunday Times best publisher award 1988); *Clubs* Groucho; *Style—* Ms Victoria Barnsley; 9 Kensington Place, London W8 (☎ 071 229 3718); Fourth Estate, Classic House, 289 Westbourne Grove, London W11 (☎ 071 727 8993, fax 071 792 3176)

BARNWELL, Hon Mrs (Elizabeth Mary); *née* Shore; da of 6 Baron Teignmouth (d 1964); *b* 1916; *m* 1942, Maj Charles John Patrick Barnwell, yr s of late Frederick Arthur Lowry Barnwell, of Hinton St George, Somerset; 1 s (and 1 s decd); *Style—* The Hon Mrs Barnwell; Standerwick, Fivehead, Taunton, Somerset TA3 6PT (☎ 0460 281228)

BARON, Alexander; s of Barnet Baron (d 1977), and Fanny, *née* Levinson (d 1974); *b* 4 Dec 1917; *Educ* Hackney Downs Sch; *m* 4 Aug 1960, Delores, da of Sidney Lopez Salzedo (d 1987); 1 s (Nicholas b 1969); *Career* WWII 1940-46 Army serv in Sicily and NW Europe; novelist and scriptwriter; many film scripts, TV plays and classic serials for the BBC incl Vanity Fair (1987); *Books incl* From the City, From the Plough (1948), There's No Home (1950), The Human Kind (1953), Franco is Dying (1977); *Style—* Alexander Baron, Esq; c/o Lemon and Durbridge, 24 Pottery Lane, London W11

BARON, Anthony; s of John Baron, and Doreen, *née* Eastman; *b* 26 Sept 1950; *Educ* LSE (BSc), QMC London (MSc); *m* 13 Nov 1970(m dis 1984), Ruzena Eliska Michaela, da of Dr Ctibor Haluza; 2 da (Andrea b 9 July 1975, Georgina b 4 April 1978); m 2, Jane Edith Mary, da of John Patrick Lynch; *Career* sr info offr Central Office of Info 1973-77, UK economist Hoare Govett 1977-81, chief economist Savory Milln & Co 1981-83, ptnr Laurie Milbank & Co 1983-87, md Chase Investmt Bank 1987-; memb Int Stock Exchange; *Recreations* swimming, squash; *Style—* Anthony Baron, Esq; Prior House, Cleeve Prior, Nr Evesham, Worcs; 5 Westwood Park, London SE25; Chase Investment Bank, Woolgate House, Coleman St London EC2P 2HD (☎ 071 726 3183, fax 071 726 5952, telex 8958831)

BARON, (Henry William) Anthony; s of Alfred Edward Baron (d 1981), of Brackens Pinhoe, Exeter, Devon and Constance Evelyn, *née* Palmer (d 1972); *b* 31 Dec 1917; *Educ* Oundle, Trinity Coll Cambridge (MA, MB MChir), St Bart's Hosp; *m* 2 July 1952, (Margaret) Ann, da of Maj Geoffrey Thomas Floyd, of Birkenhead, Bombay; 1 s (Andy Anthony John Prescot b 4 Jan 1955), 1 da (Elizabeth Ann b 24 April 1957); *Career* RAMC Capt served in Far east 1943-46; res fell St Georges Hosp 1950- 54 (surgical first asst 1947-50); conslt surgn 1950-80: St Margaret's Hosp Epping, Princess Alexandra Hosp Harlow, Ongar War Meml Hosp, Waltham Abbey Memorial Hosp; Freeman City of London 1955, Liveryman Worshipful Soc of Apothecaries 1952; memb BMA 1942, RSM 1947, FRCS 1946; *Recreations* reading, shooting; *Clubs* United Oxford and Cambridge Univ, MCC; *Style—* Anthony Baron, Esq; 3 Lansdowne Place, Hove, E Sussex; 66 Shepherds Hill N 6; 103 Los Pinos, El Rosario, Marbella, Spain (☎ 0273 735 853); 17 Harley St, London W1N 1DA (☎ 071 935 1928)

BARON, Cecil Saul; s of Henry (Harry) Donald Baron (d 1973), of Brondesbury Park, and Henrietta (Hetty) Ethel, *née* Solomons (d 1973); *b* 18 Feb 1925; *Educ* Haberdashers Askes, Univ of Cambridge, LSE (B Com); *m* 31 March 1962, Caroline Ann, da of Stanley Victor Blackman (d 1982); 1 da (Lyn Harriet Ruth b 27 Sept 1963); *Career* WWII Capt RCS served India and Burma; fin offr Chain Store Fin Tst 1955-56, mangr Lloyds and Scot Group subsidiary 1957-59, dir S Essex Motors 1960-64, pa to chm and gp co sec Oxley Industries 1965-78, md Central Motor Institute 1979-, md Small Business Computers, Microcomputer Conslt and conslt Planned Solutions Ltd 1990-; hon auditor Thos Martyn Fdn; FCA 1962; *Recreations* overseas travel, swimming; *Style—* Cecil Baron, Esq; 6 Stradbrook, Bratton, nr Westbury, Wilts

BARON, Prof Denis Neville; s of Dr Edward Baron (d 1964), of London, and Lilian Dolly, *née* Silman (d 1985); *b* 3 Oct 1924; *Educ* Univ Coll Sch London, Middx Hosp Med Sch Univ of London (MB BS, MD, DSc, MA); *m* 6 Dec 1951, Yvonne Else, da of Hugo Stern (d 1963), of Dresden and London; 1 s (Justin b 1963), 3 da (Leonora b 1954, Jessica b 1956, Olivia b 1958); *Career* Flt Lt RAF (med branch) 1946-49; Royal Free Hosp and Sch of Med London: conslt chemical pathologist, reader in chemical pathology 1954-63, prof chemical pathology 1963-88, vice dean 1977-79; Rockefeller fell Univ of Chicago 1960-61; visiting prof various overseas posts; senator Univ of London 1985-88, tutor in medical ethics St Mary's Hosp Med Sch 1989-; ed in chief Clinical Science 1966-68, chm Assoc of Profs of Chemical Pathology 1980-81; memb: Medicines Cmmn 1982-89, Standing Med Advsy Ctee DHSS 1966-74, Med Ctee Chem Def Advsy Bd 1969-76 (conslt 1976-), Camden & Islington AHA 1978-81, Barnet Health Authy 1982-85 and 1989-, Assoc 1990-, govr Henrietta Barnett Sch 1987-; Liveryman Worshipful Soc of Apothecaries 1951; memb BMA 1945, FRSA 1952, FRCPath 1963 (vice pres 1972-75), FRCP 1971; *Books* New Short Textbook of Chemical Pathology (fifth edn jtly 1989), Units, Symbols, and Abbreviations (ed, 4 edn 1988); *Recreations* opera, gardening, sight-seeing; *Clubs* RSM; *Style—* Prof D N Baron; 47 Holne Chase, London N2 0QG (☎ 081 458 2340)

BARON, Frank; *b* 15 May 1947; *Educ* Tulse Hill Sch; *m* 1983, Lorna Margaret, da of Brian Dearnaley; 2 s (Christopher b 1983, Alexander b 1987); *Career* asst photographer Keystone Press Agency 1963-67, photographer Daily Sketch 1967-72, fndr and photographer Sporting Pictures 1972-85, sports photographer The Guardian 1985-; winner Sports Picture of the Year 1974; fndr memb Professional Sports Photographers' Assoc; *Recreations* tennis; *Clubs* Telford Lawn Tennis; *Style—* Frank Baron, Esq; 12 Ederline Avenue, Norbury, London SW16 (☎ 081 679 3056); The Guardian, 119 Farringdon Rd, London EC1 (☎ 071 278 2332)

BARON, Dr (Jeremy) Hugh; s of Dr Edward Baron (d 1964), and Lillian Hannah (Dolly) Baron (d 1984); *b* 25 April 1931; *Educ* Univ Coll Sch Hampstead, Queen's Coll Oxford (MA, DM), Middx Hosp Med Sch London; *m* 8 Sept 1960, Wendy, da of Dr Samuel Barnet Dimson; 1 s (Richard b 1964), 1 da (Susannah b 1968); *Career* Capt RAMC Royal Herbert Hosp Woolwich, BMH Singapore and Malaya, jr specialist med and offr i/c Med Div BMH Kuala Lumpur Malaya 1956-58; house physician, registrar, lectr, sr registrar Middx Hosp and Med Sch London 1954-67, MRC Eli Lilly travelling fell and fell gastroenterology Mount Sinai Hosp NY USA 1961-62, conslt physician Prince of Wales and St Ann's Hosps Tottenham 1968-71, sr lectr and conslt Depts Surgery and Med Royal Postgrad Med Sch and Hammersmith Hosp 1968-, conslt physician St Charles Hosp London 1971-, conslt physician and gastroenterologist St Mary's Hosp and hon clinical sr lectr St Mary's Hosp Med Sch London 1988-; sr hon ed RSM 1984-90, chm Med Writers Gp of The Soc of Authors 1985-87, pres Br Soc of Gastroenterology 1988-89, chm Mgmnt Ctee Br Health Care Arts Centre 1989-; Liveryman Worshipful Soc of Apothecaries 1972; memb: BMA, Med Res Soc, Surgical Res Soc; FRCP, FRCS; *Books* Carbenoxolone Sodium (1970), Clinical Tests of Gastric Secretion (1978), Foregut (1981), Cimetidine in the 80s (1981), Vagotomy in Modern Surgical Practice (1982), St Charles Hospital Works of Art (1984), History of The British Society of Gastroenterology, 1937-1987 (1987); *Recreations* looking; *Style—* Dr J H Baron; Dept of Surgery, Royal Postgrad Med Sch Hammersmith Hosp, Du Cane Rd, London W12 ONN (☎ 081 743 2030 ext 2035, fax 071 740 3179)

BARON, Stuart Robert; s of Robert Baron; *b* 16 Oct 1957; *Career* designer Benchmark 1980-81, designer Michael Peters and Ptnrs 1981-82, creative dir (graphics) David Davies Assoc 1982-; *Style—* Stuart Baron, Esq; David Davies Associates, 12 Goslett Yard, London WC2H 0EE (☎ 071 437 9070, fax 071 734 0291)

BARON, Dr (Ora) Wendy; da of Dr Samuel Barnet Dimson, of London, and Gladys Felicia, *née* Sieve; *b* 20 March 1937; *Educ* St Paul's Girls', Courtauld Inst of Art (postgrad studentship, BA, PhD); *m* 1, 1960, Dr Jeremy Hugh Baron, s of Edward Baron; 1 s (Richard Jon b 1964), 1 da (Susannah Eve b 1968); m 2, 1990, David Joseph Wyatt, s of Frederick Wyatt; *Career* Leverhulme Tst Fund fellowship 1972-74; keeper of Govt art Collection 1978; *Books* Sickert (1973), Miss Ethel Sands and Her Circle (1977), The Camden Town Group (1979); *Style—* Dr Wendy Baron; Government Art Collection, c/o Office of Arts & Libraries, Horse Guards Road, London SW1P 3AL (☎ 071 928 8516, fax 071 928 6172)

BARON COHEN, Gerald; s of Morris Baron Cohen (d 1972), of Cardiff, S Glam, and Miriam, *née* Nicholsby (d 1987); *b* 13 July 1932; *Educ* Univ of Wales (BA); *m* 12 June 1962, Daniella Naomi, da of Hans Israel Weiser, of Telaviv, Israel; 3 s (Jonathon Ammon b 1964, Erran Boaz b 1968, Sacha Noam b 1971); *Career* CA, co dir, ed Mosaic 1960-62, dep ed New Middle East 1967-68; past pres Bnai Brith First Lodge 1979-80 (nat treas 1984) vice chm Hillel Fndn 1970-, past vice chm Union Jewish Students, chm Bamah Forum for Jewish Dialogue; FCA 1954; *Style—* Gerald Baron Cohen, Esq; 70 Wildwood Road, London NW11 6UJ (☎ 081 458 1552); 760 Finchley Rd, London NW11 7TH (☎ 081 455 0994)

BARR, Prof Allan David Stephen; s of Rev Prof Allan Barr (d 1988), of 1 Drylaw Ave, Blackhall, Edinburgh, and Agnes Christina, *née* Dryburgh (d 1978); *b* 11 Sept 1930; *Educ* Daniel Stewart's Coll Edinburgh, Univ of Edinburgh (BSc, PhD); *m* 16 Dec 1954, Eileen Patricia, da of Patrick Redmond (d 1971), of 99 Hadleigh Rd, Frinton-on-Sea; 2 s (David b 28 Jan 1957, Richard b 22 Sept 1960), 1 da (Christina b 7 May 1967); *Career* student apprentice Bristol Aeroplane Co Filton Bristol 1947-49, Fulbright scholar and visiting prof Cornell Univ Ithaca NY USA 1964-65, reader Dept of Mech Engrg Univ of Edinburgh 1965-72 (former asst, lectr, sr lectr 1952-72), prof and head of Dept of Mech Engrg Univ of Dundee 1972-85, Jackson prof of engrg Univ of Aberdeen 1985-; memb Scot Ctee of Univ Funding Cncl; CEng, FIMechE, FRSE; *Recreations* fly fishing, oil painting; *Clubs* Royal Northern and University (Aberdeen); *Style—* Prof Allan D S Barr, FRSE; The Orchard, Auchattie, Banchory, Kincardineshire AB31 3HP (☎ 033 02 5244)

BARR, David; s of Walter Barr (d 1981), latterly of Glasgow, and Betty, *née* Shulman; *b* 15 Oct 1925; *Educ* Haberdasher's Aske's, Brookline HS Boston USA, Univ of Edinburgh, UCL (LLB); *m* 8 June 1960, Ruth, da of David Weitzman, QC, MP (d 1987); 1 s (Andrew b 9 April 1961), 1 da (Frances b 14 March 1964); *Career* RN 1943-47; admitted slr 1953; met stipendiary magistrate 1976; JP Inner London Area 1963-76, dep chm N Westminster PSD 1968-76, chm Inner London Juvenile Panel 1969; mangr Finnant House Sch 1955-81 (chm & tstee 1973-); Freeman City of London 1959; *Recreations* book collecting, bridge; *Clubs* Garrick, MCC; *Style—* David Barr, Esq; Highbury Corner Magistrates Court, London N7 (☎ 071 607 6757)

BARR, Derek Julian; s of Peter Joachim Barr, of 1 Woodspring Rd, London SW19, and Ingrid Gerda, *née* Dannenbaum; *b* 16 Sept 1945; *Educ* St Paul's, Imperial Coll (BSc, ACGI); *m* 19 Dec 1970, Zoe Maxine, da of Wing Cdr Jack Leon Elson-Rees (d 1962); 2 s (James b 1976, Nicholas b 1981), 2 da (Katrina b 1972, Annabelle b 1974); *Career* chemical engr (expert in industl drying and process technol), md Barr & Murphy 1974- (founded firm with father 1962); awarded Queen's Award for Export Achievement 1976; FIChemE 1987; *Recreations* skiing, sailing, tennis, music; *Clubs* IOD, Roehampton; *Style—* Derek Barr, Esq; Wifflescombe, 1 Vineyard Hill Rd, London SW1 7JL (☎ 071 946 1044); B & M House, 48 Bell St, Maidenhead, Berks SL6 1BR (☎ 0628 776177, fax 0628 776118)

BARR, Graham Robert; s of Robert Barr (d 1986), of Roundhay, Leeds, and Barbara Moyra Mary, *née* Keene; *b* 25 Jan 1926; *Educ* Rounday GS, Kitson Coll; *m* 16 March 1985, Diane, da of Raymond Thomas Mastin; 1 da (Emma Victoria b 16 Jan 1975); *Career* investmt mangr Stockbrokers, sales and mktg mangr Wardley Investment Services, conslt to Cresvale Asset Management; dir: Lineham Farm Ltd, Lineham Leasing Ltd; *Recreations* shooting, fishing, gun dogs; *Clubs* Sloane; *Style—* Graham Barr, Esq; Barkwood, Breary Lane East, Bramhope, Leeds (☎ 0831 528977)

BARR, Ian; s of Peter McAlpine Barr (d 1961), of Dalserf, Lanarkshire, and Isobel Baillie (d 1979); *b* 6 April 1927; *Educ* Boroughmuir HS Edinburgh; *m* 1951, Gertrud Karla, da of August Otto Odefey (d 1976), and Anny Petersen (d 1980), of Schleswig-Holstein; 2 da (Karen, Kirsten); m 2, 1988, his cousin Margaret Annie, da of Andrew McAlpine Barr (d 1959); *Career* Post Office: asst postal controller NW region 1955, inspr of postal servs 1957, asst controller planning HQ 1962, Staff Coll Henley on Thames 1965-66, princ 1966, memb CS Selection Bd 1966-71, asst sec 1971-76, regnl dir Eastern Postal Region 1976, dir bldgs mechanisation and planning HQ 1978-81, dir Estates Exec 1981-84, chm Scottish Bd 1984-88; chm Post Office Nat Arts Ctee 1976-87, pres Conference Européenne des Postes et des Télécommunications (Bâtiments) 1982-86; memb: Br Materials Handling Bd 1978-81, bd Girobank Scotland 1984-88, Scottish Cncl CBI 1984-88; chm: Saltire Soc 1986-87, Scottish Ctee Assoc for Business Sponsorship of the Arts 1986-88; dir Scottish Nat Orch 1988-90; tstee: Endocrine Res Tst Western Gen Hosp Edinburgh 1987-, Lamp of Lothian Collegiate Tst 1988-, High Blood Pressure Fndn 1990-; memb: Cncl Edinburgh Festival 1988-89, Scottish Convention Ctee and Signatory to its report 'A Claim of Right for Scotland' 1988; *Recreations* composing serial music, constructing a metaphysical system; *Style—* Ian Barr, Esq; Scott House, Newcastleton, Roxburghshire TD9 0QU

BARR, Prof James; *b* 20 March 1924; *Educ* Daniel Stewart's Coll Edinburgh, Univ of Edinburgh (MA, BD), Univ of Oxford (DD); *Career* served WWII pilot RN Fleet Air Arm; ordained min Church of Scotland 1951, min Church of Scotland Tiberias Israel 1951-53; prof of New Testament Presbyterian Coll Montreal Canada 1953-55; prof of Old Testament lit and theology: Univ of Edinburgh 1955-61, Princeton Theological Seminary 1961-65; prof of Semitic languages and literatures Univ of Manchester 1965-76, Oriel prof of the interpretation of holy scripture Oxford 1976-78, regius prof of Hebrew Oxford 1978-89 (emeritus regius prof 1989-), prof of Hebrew Bible Vanderbilt Univ Nashville Tennessee 1989-; ed: Jl of Semitic Studies 1965-76, Oxford Hebrew Dictionary 1974-80; del OUP 1979-89, Crown appointee Governing Body SOAS London 1980-85; pres: Soc for Old Testament Study 1973, Br Assoc for Jewish Studies 1978; memb Inst for Advanced Study Princeton 1985; visiting prof: Ormond Coll Melbourne Aust 1968 and 1982, Hebrew Univ Jerusalem 1973, Univ of Chicago 1975 and 1981, Univ of Strasbourg 1975-76, Brown Univ Providence RI 1985, Univ of Otago NZ 1986, Univ of SA Pretoria 1986, Vanderbilt Univ 1987, 1988; Burkitt medal for Biblical Studies (Br Acad) 1988; Hon: DD Knox Coll Toronto 1964, MA Univ of Manchester 1969, DD Dubuque Univ Iowa 1974, DD St Andrews 1974, DD Edinburgh 1983, DTheol Univ of SA 1986, doctorate Faculté de Théologie Protestante Paris 1988, DD Victoria Univ Toronto 1988; Guggenheim Res fellowship 1965, hon fell SOAS 1975, corresponding memb Göttingen Acad of Scis 1976, memb Norwegian Acad of Scis and Letters 1977, hon fell Oriel Coll Oxford 1980, hon memb Soc of Biblical Lit (USA) 1983, FBA 1969, FRAS 1969; *Books* The Semantics of Biblical Language (1961), Biblical Words for Time (1962), Old and New in Interpretation (1966), Fundamentalism (1977), Holy Scripture: Canon, Authority, Criticism (1983) Escaping from Fundamentalism (1984), The Variable Spellings of the Hebrew Bible (1989); *Style—* Prof James Barr; 6 Fitzherbert Close, Iffley, Oxford OX4 4EN; 4400 Belmont Park Terrace, No 203, Nashville TN 37215 USA

BARR, Sheriff Kenneth Glen; o s of Rev Gavin Barr, and Catherine McLellan, *née* McGhie; *b* 20 Jan 1941; *Educ* Ardrossan Acad, Royal HS, Univ of Edinburgh; *m* 1970, Susanne Crichton Keir; *Career* Sheriff S Strathclyde Dumfries and Galloway 1976-; *Style—* Sheriff Kenneth Barr; Sheriff Court House, Dumfries

BARR, (John) Malcolm; CBE (1982); s of Robert Barr (d 1964), and Edith, *née* Midgley (d 1968); *b* 23 Dec 1926; *Educ* Shrewsbury, Clare Coll Cambridge (MA, LLM); *m* 27 Aug 1955, Elaine Mary, da of Harold Rhodes (d 1956); 2 da ((Margaret) Clare (Mrs Whitaker) b 1956, Janine Ruth (Mrs Oddy) b 1959); *Career* Sub Lt RNVR 1944-48; Barr & Wallace Arnold Trust plc 1952-: chm and gp md 1962-88, gp exec chm 1988-; non-exec dir: Leeds Permanent Building Society 1970 (pres 1989), Hickson International plc 1971; pres City of Leeds YMCA, chm Fin Ctee Br Show Jumping Assoc, memb Fin Ctee Fedn Equestre Internationale, dir Br Equestrian Promotion Ltd; High Sheriff W Yorks 1978; FRSA; *Recreations* drama, literature, music, show jumping, sailing; *Clubs* Royal Ocean Racing, Climbers'; *Style—* Malcolm Barr, Esq, CBE; Group Executive Chairmam, Barr & Wallace Arnold Trust plc, 3 Killingbeck Drive, York Rd, Leeds LS14 6UF (☎ 0532 499322, fax 0532 491192, car 0836 505150)

BARR, Hon Mrs (Penelope Carol); yst da of Baron Crowther-Hunt (Life Peer d 1987); *b* 1955; *m* 23 July 1988, Andrew A Barr, er s of W G Barr, of Oxford; 1s (William Norman b 8 May 1990); *Style—* The Hon Mrs Barr; 30 Upland Park Road, Oxford

BARR, His Honour Judge; Reginald Alfred Barr; s of Alfred Charles Barr (d 1950); *b* 21 Nov 1920; *Educ* Christ's Hosp, Trinity Coll Oxford; *m* 1946, Elaine, 2 da of James William Charles O'Bala Morris, of Llanstephan, Carmarthenshire; *Career* barr 1954, circuit judge 1970; *Style—* His Hon Judge Barr; 42 Bathurst Mews, Hyde Pk, W2 (☎ 071 262 5731)

BARR, Stuart Alan; DL (W Yorks 1987); s of Robert Barr (d 1960), and Edith, *née* Midgley (d 1963), of Shadwell, Leeds; *b* 18 Nov 1930; *Educ* Shrewsbury; *m* 1 (m dis 1964); 2 s (Nicholas, Robert); m 2, 1969, Karin Johanne, da of Col Donald Blake Smiley, DFC, RCAF (d 1985), of Florida, USA; 2 da (Lucinda b 1971, Camilla b 1976); *Career* Maj Queen's Own Yorks Dragoons (TA), Lt 9 Queen's Royal Lancers; dep chm and md Barr & Wallace Arnold Trust; dir: Wallace Arnold, Trust Motors, Wass Ltd, BCB Motor Factors, Wallace Hotels Ltd, Robert Sibbald Travel Agents, Wayahead Fuel Services, Wilks & Meade; High Sheriff W Yorks 1984; vice pres: Leeds Tradesmen's Inst, Yorks Area Boy Scouts Assoc; pres: Knaresborough Div St John Ambulance, W Yorks Youth Assoc; memb High Steward's Cncl and tstee York Minster; Freeman City of London; *Recreations* racing, shooting; *Clubs* Cavalry and Guards; *Style—* Stuart Barr, Esq, DL; Barr & Wallace Arnold Trust plc, 3 Killingbeck Drive, Leeds LS14 6UF (☎ 0532 499322)

BARRACLOUGH, Air Chief Marshal Sir John; KCB (1970, CB 1969), CBE (1961), DFC (1942), AFC (1941); s of late Horatio Leonard Barraclough, of London, and Marguerite Maude Barraclough; *b* 2 May 1918; *Educ* Cranbrook Sch; *m* 1946, Maureen, da of Dr William John McCormack, of Wicklow, and niece of George, Noble Count Plunkett; 1 da (Moy (Mrs David Scott)); *Career* Air Vice-Marshal 1964; dir Public Relations Air Ministry 1961-64, vice CDS 1970-72, air sec 1972-74; Cmdt RCDS 1974-76, vice chm Commonwealth War Graves Cmmn 1981-; FIPM, MBIM, MIPR; *Style—* Air Chief Marshal Sir John Barraclough, KCB, CBE, DFC, AFC; Crapstone House, Buckland Monachorum, Devon (☎ 082 285 3639); c/o Barclays Bank, 11 Newgate st, EC1

BARRACLOUGH, Lt-Col Michael Charles; OBE (1986); s of Maj Ernest Barraclough (d 1942), of Kenya, and Margery, *née* Goulden (d 1962); *b* 1 July 1923; *Educ* Haileybury; *m* 22 Jan 1949, Anne Marie, da of Capt Henry D'Olier Vigne (d 1982), of Essex; 1 s (Charles Henry Thomas b 1950), 1 da (Jane b 1953); *Career* cmmnd 22 Dragoons 1942-45, 4/7 Royal Dragoon Gds 1945-71, cmd 4/7 RDG 1964-66, Staff Coll 1957, DAAG & QMG HQ RAC 1 Br Corps 1958-60, GSO 2 HQ Land Forces Persian Gulf 1962-64, GSO (OPS) Allied Forces AFCENT 1967-69, GSO Royal Armament R & D Estab 1969-71; gen sec Homoeopathic Tst for Res & Educn & Faculty of Homoeopathy 1972-89; *Recreations* fishing, shooting; *Clubs* Cavalry and Guards'; *Style—* Lt-Col M C Barraclough, OBE; Ivy Cottage, Mill Green, Ingatestone, Essex CM4 0HY (☎ 0277 352769)

BARRACLOUGH, Robert James; s of Charles Brayshaw Barraclough, of Wosehill, Wokingham, Berks, and Winifred Elizabeth Gibson, *née* Moulton; *b* 17 April 1942; *Educ* Bootham Sch York; *m* 8 Sept 1973, Julian Mary, da of Frederick George Fennell (RN); 4 s (Paul Anthony b 9 March 1974, Nicholas Charles b 5 Aug 1975, Timothy Nigel b 31 May 1977, Tristan Toby William b 15 Aug 1978); *Career* Robson Rhodes Chartered Accountants Bradford: articled clerk 1960-65, audit sr 1965-68, audit mangr 1968-71, ptnr 1971-90 (gen client serv ptnr, ptnr in charge of audit practice W Yorks); estab Forensic Accountancy and Litigation Support Unit in N England Haines Watts Bradford 1990-; memb Yorks Numismatic Soc (pres 1975), hon treas Bradford C of C

1988, memb Br Acad of Experts 1989; FCA 1965; *Recreations* badminton, theatre, fell walking, numismatics, scouting; *Clubs* Bradford; *Style—* Robert Barraclough, Esq; Haines Watts, Sterling House, 133 Barkerend Road, Bradford BD3 9AU (☎ 0274 393666, fax 0274 307364)

BARRAN, Sir John Napoleon Ruthven; 4 Bt (UK 1895); s of Sir John Leighton Barran, 3 Bt (d 1974), and Hon Alison (d 1973), da of 9 Lord Ruthven of Freeland, CB, CMG, DSO; n of Sir David Barran, chm of the Midland Bank and former chm Shell; *b* 14 Feb 1934; *Educ* Heatherdown Ascot, Winchester; *m* 1965, Jane Margaret, da of Sir Stanley George Hooker, CBE (d 1984), and his 1 w Hon Margaret Bradbury, da of 1 Baron Bradbury; 1 s, 1 da (Susannah Margaret b 1981); *Heir* s, John Ruthven Barran b 10 Nov 1971; *Career* Lt 5 Royal Inniskillen Dragoon Gds 1952-54; in advertising 1956-63, served Br High Cmmn Ottawa 1964-67; head Viewdata Unit COI 1978-85; head of Info Technol Unit 1985-87; *Recreations* shooting, fishing, gardening, entertaining; *Clubs* RAC; *Style—* Sir John Barran, Bt; 17 St Leonard's Terrace, London SW3 (☎ 071 730 2801); The Hermitage, East Bergholt, Suffolk (☎ 020 028 8236); Middle Rigg Farm, Sawley, Yorkshire (☎ 076 586 207)

BARRASFORD, Tig; s of Capt Thomas George Barrasford (d 1981), of Wokingham, and Florence Cavell, *née* Mayo; *b* 20 July 1947; *Educ* The John Bright GS Llandudno, Llandrillo Tech Coll Colwyn Bay (Nat Dip in Hotel Keeping and Catering); *m* 5 Oct 1968, Sheelagh Mary, da of Owen O'Hagan; 2 s (Simon b 22 Oct 1971, Paul b 18 March 1974), 1 da (Zoë b 25 March 1978); *Career* trainee mangr Grand Metropolitan Hotels 1968-70; Trust House Forte Hotels: asst mangr Both Worlds Gibraltar 1970-71, dep mangr Eastgate Hotel Lincoln 1972, food and beverage mangr Appollonia Beach Hotel Cyprus 1973, gen mangr Parkview Hotel Durban SA 1974-75, gen mangr Excelsior Hotel Glasgow 1975-77, ops control mangr THF UK Hotels 1977-78, area dir Scotland THF UK Hotels 1979-80, ops exec Exclusive Hotels THF 1981, ops dir International Hotels THF 1981-82; proprietor Bryn Cregio Garden Hotel Peganwy 1983-86 (responsible for BTA Commendation, Michelin Guide, Relais Routiers, Ashley Courtenay); Aga Khan Fund for Econ Devpt: chief exec Serema Lodges and Hotels Kenya 1986-90, md Serema Tourism Promotion Sevrs SA 1991-; fndr memb Welsh Rarebits (mktg consortium of high quality, ind Welsh hotels), winner Master Innholders award; Freeman City of London, memb Worshipful Co of Innholders 1985; MHCIMA 1977, FHCIMA 1990; *Recreations* golf, windsurfing, sailing, eating good food and drinking good wine; *Clubs* The North Wales Golf (Llandudno), The Llandudno and County; *Style—* Tig Barrasford, Esq; Secretariat of His Highness The Aga Khan, Aiglemont, Gouvieux, France (☎ 010 334 458 4000, fax 010 334 458 2000)

BARRASS, Christopher Patrick; s of Maj Patrick Rae Barrass, of Chobham, Surrey, and Ann Delory, *née* Bertram; *b* 12 Nov 1953; *Educ* Dauntsey Sch Wiltshire; *Career* chief reporter: Westminster Press Surrey Herald 1976-78, Sutton Seibert Publishing 1980-82; md Sovereign Servs 1979-82, conslt Granard Communications 1982-85, dir Edelman Public Rels 1987-89 (assoc dir 1985-87), chief exec Integrated Marketing and Communications 1989-; memb: Exec Ctee Clandon Soc, Clandon Horticultural Soc, Surrey Downs Gp; *Recreations* classic cars, literature, arts, water and snow skiing; *Style—* Christopher Barrass, Esq; Integrated Marketing and Communications, IMC House, 20A Berkeley St, London W1 (☎ 071 495 3475)

BARRASS, Gordon Stephen; s of James Stephen Barrass (d 1984) and Mary, *née* Quinn (d 1971); *b* 5 Aug 1940; *Educ* Hertford GS, LSE (BSc Econ), SOAS; *m* 1965, Alice Cecile Oberg (d 1984); *Career* HM Dip Serv 1965-: Peking 1970-72, Cultural Exchange Dept FCO 1972-74, UKMIS Geneva 1974-78, memb Planning Staff FCO 1979-82, counsellor 1983; RCDS 1983; seconded to: MOD 1984-86, Cabinet Office 1986- (under sec 1991-); *Recreations* Chinese and western art, classical archaeology, opera, travel, books; *Clubs* Athenaeum; *Style—* Gordon S Barrass, Esq; Foreign and Commonwealth Office, King Charles St, London SW1A 2AH

BARRATT, Eric George; s of Frank Barratt, of Stokenchurch, Bucks; *b* 15 April 1938; *Educ* Oriel Coll Oxford (MA); *Career* sr ptnr MacIntyre Hudson; dir: Cmmn for the Newtowns, Esthwaite Estate Ltd, Ely Place Investmts, Heathfield Sch Ltd, Grangehouse Investmnts Ltd, SC Brannan & Sons Ltd, Avonmore Stud Ltd; treas and fell Oriel Coll; FCA; *Clubs* Athenaeum, Carlton, City of London; *Style—* Eric Barratt, Esq; Stockfield, Stokenchurch, Bucks (☎ 0494 482284); MacIntyre Hudson, 28 Ely Place, London EC1N 6LR (☎ 071 242 0242)

BARRATT, Jeffery Vernon Courtney Lewis; s of Arnold Douglas Courtney Lewis, and Edith Joyce, *née* Terry; *b* 31 Oct 1950; *Educ* Scots Coll Wellington NZ, Univ of Adelaide (LLB), Univ of Sydney (LLB,LLM); *Career* articled clerk Giovanell and Burges 1971-73, slr Stephen Jaques and Stephen 1973-75, trg ptnr Norton Rose 1987- (ptnr 1979-, estab Bahrain Office 1979-82), memb Editorial Bd Butterworths Jl of Int Banking and Fin Law; author of numerous articles on selling Loan Assets and Sterling Commercial Paper in learned jls; memb: London Legal Educn Ctee, Law Soc, IBA, QMC (Summer Sch Faculty); *Recreations* cricket, squash, skiing, tennis, opera; *Clubs* Hampstead Cricket (Capt 1987), RAC, MCC; *Style—* Jeffery Barratt, Esq; Norton Rose, Kempson House, Camomile St, London EC3A 7AN (☎ 071 283 2434, fax 071 588 1181, telex 883652)

BARRATT, Sir Lawrence Arthur (Lawrie); *b* 14 Nov 1927; *m* 1, 1951 (m dis 1984); 2 s; m 2, 1984, Mary Sheila Brierley; *Career* Barratt Developments plc (UK's largest private house bldg co at mid-Dec 1981): fndr 1958, former chm and md, now life pres; FCIS; kt 1982; *Recreations* golf, shooting, sailing; *Style—* Sir Lawrie Barratt; Wingrove House, Ponteland Rd, Newcastle upon Tyne NE5 3DP (☎ 091 2866811)

BARRATT, Michael Fieldhouse; s of Wallace Milner Barratt (d 1980), and Doris, *née* Fieldhouse (d 1934); *b* 3 Jan 1928; *Educ* Rossall and Paisley GS; *m* 1, 1952 (m dis), Joan Francesca Warner; 3 s (Mark, Andrew, Paul), 3 da (Eve, Jane, Rachel); m 2, 1977, Dilys Jane, da of David Morgan (d 1985); 2 s (Oliver, Barnaby), 1 da (Jessica); *Career* entered journalism Kemsley Newspapers 1945, ed Nigerian Citizen 1956, reporter Panorama 1963; presenter: 24 Hours 1965-69, Nationwide 1969-77, Songs of Praise 1977-82, Reporting London 1983-88; radio question master Gardeners' Question Time 1973-79; Hon LLD Univ of Aberdeen; FRHS; *Books* Michael Barratt (1973), Down to Earth Gardening Book (1974), Michael Barratt's Complete Gardening Guide (1977), Golf with Tony Jacklin (1978); *Recreations* cricket, golf, listening; *Clubs* Lord's Taverners, Reform; *Style—* Michael Barratt, Esq; 5/7 Forlease Rd, Maidenhead, Berks SL6 1RP (☎ 0628 770 800)

BARRATT, Oliver William; s of Lt-Col Roger Barratt, MBE, of Cowmire Hall, Kendal, and Diana Norah, *née* While; *b* 7 July 1941; *Educ* Radley, Edinburgh and East of Scotland Coll of Agric (SDA); *Career* sec: The Cockburn Assoc (The Edinburgh Civic Tst) 1971-, The Cockburn Conservation Tst 1978-; vice chm Scottish Assoc for Public Tport; tstee: Scottish Historic Bldgs Tst, Lothian Bldg Preservation Tst; memb Soc of Architectural Historians 1980; *Recreations* the hills, travel, most of the arts; *Style—* Oliver Barratt, Esq; 1 London St, Edinburgh EH3 6LZ (☎ 031 556 5107); The Cockburn Association, Trunk's Close, 55 High St, Edinburgh EH1 1SR (☎ 031 557 8686)

BARRATT, Peter William; s of Robert Leslie Barratt (d 1974), of Jersey, CI, and Winifrid Irene, *née* Kirton; *b* 1 May 1934; *Educ* De La Salle Coll Salford, Prior Park Coll Bath; *m* 1, 22 June 1960 (m dis 1983), Shirley, da of Charles Littler (d 1955), of Swinton, Lancs; 1 s (Nigel b 1962), 2 da (Elizabeth b 1964, Jacqueline b 1966); m 2, 1990, Pamela Rose, da of Jonah Shapiro; *Career* articled clerk EA Radford Edwards Manchester 1952-59, Ashworth Sons Barratt (stockbrokers) 1959-89: ptnr 1961, memb Stock Exchange 1961-, sr ptnr 1968-88, dir FPG Securities Ltd (acquired Ashworth Sons & Barratt 1988) 1988-; memb Broughton Park RFC 1952-72 (IXV), Lancs RFC 1966-70 (Eng trial 1969); memb Catenian Assoc; FCA; *Recreations* squash, theatre, antiques, reading, history; *Clubs* Alderley Edge Squash & Tennis, Broughton Park RFC, Lancs RFC; *Style—* Peter Barratt, Esq; The Corner House, Brook Lane, Alderley Edge, Cheshire SK9 7QQ

BARRATT, Robin Alexander; QC (1989); s of Harold Robert Mathew Barratt (d 1974), of Godalming, and Phylis Lily Barratt (d 1968); *b* 24 April 1945; *Educ* Charterhouse, Worcester Coll Oxford (MA); *m* 1 April 1972, Gillian Anne, da of Peter Ellis; 1 s (Richard), 3 da (Sarah, Caroline, Joanna); *Career* called to the Bar Middle Temple 1970; cncllr London borough of Merton 1978-86; *Recreations* music, fell walking, reading; *Style—* Robin Barratt, Esq, QC; 2 Mitre Court Buildings, Temple, London EC4 (☎ 01 583 1355)

BARRATT, (Francis) Russell; CB (1975); s of Frederick Russell Barratt (d 1957); *b* 16 Nov 1924; *Educ* Durban HS, Clifton, Univ Coll Oxford; *m* 1, 1949 (m dis 1978), Janet Mary, *née* Sherborne; 3 s; m 2, 1979, Josephine Norah Harrison, da of Brig D McCririck (d 1947); *Career* Intelligence Corps 1943-46 (Capt 1946); HM Treasy 1949-82 (dep sec 1973-82), dir Amdahl (UK) 1983-; *Recreations* reading, music, golf; *Clubs* Athenaeum; *Style—* Russell Barratt, Esq, CB; Little Paddocks, Smallhythe Rd, Tenterden, Kent TN30 7LY (☎ 058 06 3734)

BARRATT BROWN, Dr Michael; s of Alfred Barratt Brown, of Ruskin Coll Oxford (d 1947), and Doris Eileen, *née* Cockshott (d 1984); *b* 15 March 1918; *Educ* Dragon Sch Oxford, Bootham Sch York, CCC Oxford (MA); *m* 1, 12 Aug 1940, Frances Mary, da of Edward Mayo Hastings Lloyd (d 1963), of Hemel Hempstead Herts; 2 s (Christopher John b 1945, Richard Rollo b 1947); m 2, 17 July 1948, Eleanor Mary, da of David Jacob Singer, of Penn Bucks (d 1933); 1 s (Daniel b 1949), 1 da (Deborah b 1950); *Career* lectr and writer; sr lectr industl studies Univ of Sheffield 1959-77, princ Northern Coll Barnsley 1977-83; chm: Third World Information Network Ltd, Twin Trading Ltd 1984-; dir Bertrand Russell Peace Fndn, pres Soc of Industl Tutors 1983-, hon fell Sheffield City Poly 1984, Hon Doctorate Open Univ 1985; *Books* most important works: After Imperialism (1963 Spanish, Portuguese and Italian edns), What Economics is About (1970 Italian edn), From Labourism to Socialism (1972), The Economics of Imperialism (1974 Spanish, Portuguese and Italian edns Information at Work (1978), Models in Political Economy (1984 US edn), European Union: Fortress or Democracy (1991) Ed Bds: New Reasoner, Universities and Left Review, New Left Review, Spokesman, Institute for Workers Control, Conference of Socialist Economists, New Socialist; *Recreations* gardening, boating; *Style—* Dr Michael Barratt Brown; Robin Hood Farm, Baslow, Nr Bakewell, Derbyshire (☎ 0246 58 2281); 345 Goswell Rd, London EC1 (☎ 071 837 8222)

BARRAUD, Hon Mrs (Jane); *née* King-Hall; da of Baron King-Hall (Life Peer, d 1966); *b* 1930; *m* 1951, Yves Barraud, s of Dr J Barraud (d 1941), of Lausanne, Switzerland; 3 s; *Style—* The Hon Mrs Barraud; Les Saules, Les Cullayes, Vaud, Switzerland

BARRELL, Alan Walter; s of Leslie Walter Barrell, of Waltham Forest, Essex, and Margaret Louise Emily Barrell; *b* 21 July 1940; *Educ* Willesden GS, Cambridge Coll of Arts and Technol (DipM); *m* 3 March 1963, Pamela Mollie, da of Marcel Herbert Whitley, of Southend, Essex; 2 s (James, Julian), 2 da (Helene, Louise); *Career* gp chief exec Domino Printing Sciences plc 1984-90; chm: Domino AmJet Ltd (UK), Domino AmJet Inc (USA), Domino GmH (Germany), Domino AmJet BV; chm Transatlantic Expansion Ltd Cambridge; govr Thetford GS, tstee Cambs Work Relations Gp, vice chm of govrs Hills Rd 6 Form Coll Cambridge; FCIM, FIOD, FBIM, MRSH; *Style—* Alan Barrell, Esq; 6 Hills Ave, Cambridge CB1 4XA (☎ 0223 249597); Transatlantic Expansion Ltd, Cambridge (☎ 0223 411015)

BARRELL, Anthony Charles; s of William Frederick Barrell (d 1973), and Ruth Eleanor, *née* Painter; *b* 4 June 1933; *Educ* Friars Sch Bangor, Kingston GS, Univ of Birmingham, Imperial Coll London (BSc); *m* 26 Jan 1963, Jean, da of Francis Henry Hawkes, and Clarice Jean Silke, of Budleigh Salterton, Devon; 1s (Andrew Mark b 1966), 1 da (Samantha Ruth b 1968); *Career* chemist Miny of Supply (later War Dept) 1959-64, commissioning engr African Explosives and Chem Industs 1964-65, shift mangr MOD 1965-66; HM Factory Inspectorate 1966-78 (chem inspr, supt specialist inspr), head Major Hazards Assessment Unit 1978-85, dir of technol Health and Safety Exec 1985-90, dir Hazardous Installations Policy 1990, chief exec North Sea Safety Dept of Energy 1990-; CEng 1974, FIChemE 1984, Eur Ing 1988, memb Cncl IChemE 1989-, FEng 1990; *Recreations* offshore sailing, fell walking, reading; *Clubs* West Kirby Sailing; *Style—* Anthony Barrell, Esq; Sanderling, Baskervyle Rd, Gayton, Wirral L60 8NJ (☎ 051 342 8255); Department of Energy, Palace Street, London SW1E 5HE (☎ 071 238 3109, fax 071 834 3712, telex 918777 ENERGY G)

BARRELL, Joan; *Career* magazine publisher; IPC Magazines 1959-71: first female advertisement rep, advertisement mangr Honey magazine 1965 (former fndr), fndr Fashion magazine 1967, only female gp mangr (Honey, Fashion and Petticoat magazines) 1968, merchandise mangr all IPC Women's magazines 1970-71; National Magazine Company 1971-: assoc publisher Vanity Fair magazine 1971 and fndr and assoc publisher Cosmopolitan magazine 1972, fndr and publisher Company magazine 1978, only female dir National Magazine Co 1981-, dir COMAG distributors 1984-, publishing dir Country Living magazine 1986-; pres Women's Advtg Club of Britain 1975-, former chm Advtg Ctee Gtr London Fund for the Blind and BACUP, chm Publicity Club of London 1989-90; greatest female contribution towards advertising 1977-78 Adwoman Awards 1978; memb: Int Advtg Assoc, Euro Union of Women, Marketing Gp of GB, Nat Cncl of Women in GB; MInstD; *Books* The Business of Women's Magazines (jtly, 1 edn 1979, 2 end 1988); *Style—* Ms Joan Barrell

BARRETT; *see*: Scott-Barrett

BARRETT, David Nicholas; s of Kenneth Sidney Barrett, of Killearn, and Jennifer Mary Comber, *née* Pope; *b* 25 July 1963; *Educ* Balfron HS, Univ of Edinburgh, Jordanhill Coll; *m* 25 June 1988, Wendy Margaret, da of E Douglas Burch, of West Wellow Hants; 1 da (Amy Jane b 9 July 1990); *Career* Rugby Union full back West of Scotland RFC; club: Strathendrick RFC 1979-83, West of Scotland RFC 1983- (toured Canada 1983); rep: Glasgow (won Inter-Dist Championships 1990), Scotland B (debut v Ireland 1990, 3 caps); physical educn teacher Glasgow Acad 1988-; *Recreations* rugby, cricket, golf; *Style—* David Barrett, Esq; West of Scotland Rugby Club, Milngavie (☎ 041 956 3116)

BARRETT, Edwin Radford (Ted); s of William Barrett (d 1963), and Florence Adeline, *née* Kohlar; *b* 26 March 1929; *Educ* Itchen Sch Southampton, Burnley GS Lancs, Univ of London (BSc); *m* 26 Sept 1957, Patricia, da of Egbert Shuttleworth; 1 s (Nicholas Radford b 1960), 1 da (Juliet Jane b 1964); *Career* PA to non conformist Chaplain RAF 1951-52; reporter and sub ed Evening Telegraph Blackburn 1952-56, sub ed Press Assoc London 1956-59; Daily Telegraph: joined 1959, seconded to Sports Room 1959, dep sports ed 1962, sports ed 1979-88, sports managing ed 1988-90; sports broadcaster and freelance writer: Sports Report, Overseas Serv BBC 1960-80's; memb Inst of Journalists; *Books* Oxford Companion to Sports and Games (contrib, 1975); *Recreations* golf; *Clubs* Press Golfing Soc, Upminster Golf; *Style—* Ted Barrett, Esq; 12 Oak Ave, Upminster, Essex (☎ 04022 24709)

BARRETT, Frank Michael; s of Ernest Edward Barrett (d 1976), of Dagenham, Essex, and Dorothy Sophia, *née* Bentley Allen (d 1988); *b* 17 July 1944; *Educ* Goresbrook Secdy Modern; *m* 16 March 1968, Elaine Joan, da of John Henry Alfred Humby (d 1974); 2 s (Michael Frank b 24 April 1971, Christian David b 15 May 1973); *Career* Keystone Press Agency: messenger 1959, developing boy in glazing room then darkroom, printer, finally full photographer until 1977 (covered Royal Tours and Montreal Olympic Games); freelance photographer 1978; Daily Star: joined 1978, Royal photographer 1988-90, chief photographer 1990; stories covered incl: official birthday pictures of HRH Prince Charles 1977, Kidney transplant pictures 1980, Argentina during Falklands War 1982, Boy George pop concerts in Japan, Wham pop tour of China, Bob Geldoff in Ethiopia and Live Aid concert at Wembley, Ireland - USA World Championship fights with Barry McGuigan, USSR hero of Chernobyl, drug running in Thailand, Princess Diana, in Australia and Middle East, The Romanian Revolution, murder squads in Brazil 1990, the Gulf Conflict, two election tours with Margaret Thatcher; Best Agency Photographer 1977, British press photographer of the Year 1977, News Photographer of the Year 1980, British Press Photographer of the Year 1990; memb NUJ; *Recreations* supporting Arsenal football club, tennis; *Style—* Frank Barrett, Esq; 1 Green Lane, Chislehurst, Kent BR7 6AG (☎ 081 467 0955); Daily Star-Express Newspapers, Ludgate House, 245 Blackfriars Rd, London EC1 (☎ 071 922 7353, car 0860 327304)

BARRETT, Air Cdre Frederick Onslow Barrington Oliver (Barry); CBE (1968), DFC (1945); s of Edwin Victor George Oliver Barrett (d 1930), of London, and Edith, *née* Haines (d 1971); *b* 21 Dec 1918; *Educ* City of London Sch; *m* 11 June 1976, Penelope Gay Rowland, da of Ralph Rowland Absalom, of Brechfa, Carmarthen, Wales; *Career* RAF 1938-72: operational serv Europe and Africa 1939-45, SASO HQ No 38 Gp 1968-71, dir Flight Safety RAF and Army Air Corps 1972-73, graduate RAF Staff Coll, JSSC, RAF Flying Coll; md: Air Gregory Ltd, Surrey and Kent Flying Sch; Exec Air Birmingham; dir Air Gregory Petroleum Servs 1973-75, gen mangr Aviation Dept GKN 1976-81, conslt GKN 1982-84, aviation conslt and aircraft broker 1982-; dir: Fortis Aviation Group 1990-, Magnum Aviation 1990-; vice pres SSAFA for Warwicks; Freeman City of London 1984, Liveryman Worshipful Co of Air Pilots and Navigators 1984 (asst to Ct 1989); *Recreations* golf, fishing; *Clubs* RAF; *Style—* Air Cdre Barry Barrett, CBE, DFC; Ct Farm House, Lower Fulbrook, Warwick CV35 8AS (☎ 0926 624 379)

BARRETT, Guy Crossland; OBE (1986); s of John Catton Barrett (d 1982), and Marian Braithwaite (d 1980); *b* 17 March 1925; *Educ* Giggleswick Sch, Bradford Tech Coll; *m* 1950, Mavis, da of Nathaniel James Yeadon (d 1968), of Leeds; 2 s (James b 1955, Richard b 1957), 1 da (Elizabeth b 1951); *Career* structural engr; chm Henry Barrett Group plc 1987- (md 1965-87); pres: Royal Pigeon Racing Assoc 1976-79, Bradford C of C 1977-79, Br Constructional Steel Work Assoc 1983-86, La Féderation Colombophile Internationale 1983-87; Euro Convention for Constructional Steelwork 1988-89; CEng, FIStructE; *Recreations* shooting, pigeon racing; *Clubs* Bradford; *Style—* Guy Barrett, Esq, OBE; Fence End, Calverley Lane, Horsforth, Leeds LS18 4ED (☎ 0532 582655); Henry Barrett Group plc, Barrett House, Dudley Hill, Bradford BD4 9HU (☎ 0274 682281)

BARRETT, John; s of Reginald Frank Barrett (d 1973), of Crewkerne, Somerset, and Doris Elsie, *née* Cummings; *b* 7 Jan 1933; *Educ* Crewkerne GS; *m* 29 March 1958, Phyllis Margaret, da of Ernest George Edward Prentice (d 1975), of Croydon, Surrey; 1 s (Andrew John b 1964), 1 da (Helen Margaret b 1967); *Career* RAF 1951-54; CA 1962; Price Waterhouse: joined 1963, sr mangr 1967, ed PW Reporter 1983-, archivist 1983-, ed PW Euro News 1988-; author of various articles on genealogy; chm Merton Historical Soc 1977-79, fndr chm Wimbledon Nat Tst Assoc 1981-84, Sec Albert Reckill Charitable Tst 1969-, chm local PTA 1976-78, sch govr 1977-78; official guide: City of London 1985-, London Borough of Islington 1986-; Freeman City of London, memb Guild of Freemen; FCA; *Recreations* London history, genealogy; *Style—* John Barrett, Esq; 28 Melbury Gardens, London SW20 0DJ (☎ 081 946 3865); Price Waterhouse, Southwark Towers, 32 London Bridge St, London SE1 9SY

BARRETT, John Barbenson; s of George William Barrett, of Jersey, and Vera, *née* Simon; *b* 19 July 1950; *Educ* De La Salle Coll Jersey; *m* 1 June 1974, Joan Madelene, da of Francis John Le Corre; 1 s (Simon), 2 da (Caroline, Louise); *Career* CA; ptnr BDO Binder, sr ptnr Carnaby Barrett; FICA 1975; *Recreations* flying, reading; *Style—* John Barrett, Esq; La Platiere, Le Hocq, St Clement, Jersey; Carnaby Barrett, Seaton House, Seaton Place, St Helier, Jersey (☎ 0534 21565, fax 0534 21987, telex 4912337)

BARRETT, Rev Prof (Charles) Kingsley; s of Rev Fred Barrett (d 1957), and Clara, *née* Seed (d 1941); *b* 4 May 1917; *Educ* Shebbear, Pembroke Coll Cambridge (BA, MA, BD, DD); *m* 1944, Margaret, da of Percy Leathley Heap (d 1952), of Calverley, Yorkshire; 1 s (Martin), 1 da (Penelope); *Career* prof of divinity Univ of Durham 1958-82 (lectr in theology 1945-58), visiting lectureships and professorships in Euro, Aust, NZ and USA; contrib to learned jls and symposia; pres Studiorum Novi Testamenti Societas 1973-74; Burkitt medal for Biblical Study 1966, Forschungspreis of the Von Humboldt-Stiftung 1988; FBA 1961; *Books* incl: The Holy Spirit and The Gospel Tradition (1947), Gospel According to St John (1955, 2 edn 1978), The Gospel of John and Judaism (1975), Essays on Paul (1982), Essays on John (1982), Freedom and Obligation (1985); *Style—* The Rev Prof C K Barrett; 22 Rosemount, Plawsworth Rd, Durham DH1 5GA

BARRETT, Michael Joseph; s of Michael Joseph Barrett, MBE (d 1983), of Acklam, Middlesbrough, Cleveland, and Hilda Patricia, *née* Davey (d 1991); *b* 15 Oct 1943; *Educ* Ratcliffe Coll Leics, Advanced Mgmnt Programme Harvard Business Sch; *m* 7 Sept 1967, Sheila Katherine, da of Arnold Willis Little, of 49 Tunstall Ave, Billingham, Cleveland; 1 s (Peter b 1982), 1 da (Louise b 1973); *Career* underwriter and insurance broker; chief exec offr Alexander Stenhouse Europe Ltd and subsidiaries, dir Bekouw Mendes BV Amsterdam; memb Cncl Soc Gen de Courtage d'Assurances Paris; *Recreations* fishing, shooting; *Clubs* Annabel's; *Style—* Michael Barrett, Esq; Grey Poplars, Danesbury Park, Bengeo, Herts SG14 3HX (☎ 0992 553485); Alexander Stenhouse Europe Ltd, 10 Devonshire Square, London EC2M 4LE (☎ 071 621 9990, telex 920368, fax 071 621 9950)

BARRETT, Roderic Westwood; s of Frederic Cecil (d 1976), and Edith Jante, *née* Harper; *b* 8 Jan 1920; *Educ* St Christopher Letchworth, The Central Sch of Art and Design London; *m* 9 Oct 1943, Lorna Marguerite, da of Josiah Cullum Blackmore (d 1960); 2 s (Jonathan Oliver b 7 Oct 1944, Mark Alexander b 27 Feb 1951), 1 da (Kristin Marguerite b 21 July 1946); *Career* visiting instr in drawing at Central School of Art and Design 1947-68, tutor at Royal Acad Schs 1968-, visiting lectr Philips Exter Acad New Hampshire USA; one man shows: London 9, Cambridge 2, Oxford 2, Castle Museum Norwich, Lamont Gallery New Hampshire USA, Share Gallery Boston USA; works displayed in Univs of: Southampton, Warwick, Keele, Essex; works displayed at: Bath festival, Llubljana, Manchester, Bristol, Royal Acad, Wildersteins, Beaux Arts, London GP, Boston Arts festival, Pittsburg, NY, Princeton; works purchased by: V and A Museum, Lamont Gallery USA, Chelmsford and Essex Museum, Southend and Epping Museum; works in private collections in: France, Italy, Switzerland, Belgium, USA; pres Colchester Art Soc; supporter of: CND, Shelter and Green Peace; *Recreations* playing piano, talking with friends, gardening, tennis, reading; *Style—* Roderic Barrett, Esq; Rooks End, Church Lane, Stanway, Colchester, Essex C03 5LR (☎ 0206 210517)

BARRETT, Rodney James; s of Sidney Wilson Barrett (d 1977), and Dorothy Lucy Barrett (d 1961); *b* 7 April 1947; *Educ* Paston Sch N Walsham Norfolk, Univ of Essex (BA); *m* 23 Sept 1968, Janet Ann, da of Albert Edward Sealey (d 1957); 1 s (Daniel b 1975), 1 da (Anna b 1978); *Career* res asst Univ of Essex 1968-70, res assoc Univ of Manchester 1970-71, fin res dir Hoare Govett 1983-89 (bank analyst 1971), exec dir Goldman Sachs International 1989-; ASIA; *Recreations* entertaining family and friends, following horse-racing from a safe distance; *Style—* Rod Barrett, Esq; Goldman Sachs Int,5 Old Bailey, London ECHM 7AH (☎ 071 489 2537)

BARRETT, (Alan) Roger; s of Lester Barrett (d 1970), of Leeds, and Nancy Cowling, *née* Clark; *b* 2 Dec 1941; *Educ* St Peter's Sch York; *m* 1977, Diana Kathryn, da of Ernest North (d 1985); 1 da (Jane Elizabeth b 1982); *Career* articled clerk Coulson & Co Scarborough 1958-64, qualified chartered accountant 1963, personal asst to ptnr Norman Hurtley & Co Leeds 1964-72, ptnr Spicer & Pegler (later Spicer & Oppenheim, then Touche Ross & Co) 1972-91, ptnr Barrowcliff & Co Leeds 1991-; chm Leeds Branch Inst of Taxation 1981-83, sec Yorks and Midland Regns Glass & Glazing Fedn 1972; ACA 1963, ATII 1964, memb Soc of Assoc Execs 1986; *Recreations* theatre, opera, gardening, walking; *Style—* Roger Barrett, Esq; 2 Oakwood Park, Leeds LS8 2PJ (☎ 0532 403420); Barrowcliff & Co, 46 Park Place, Leeds LS1 2SY (☎ 0532 451652, fax 0532 341478)

BARRETT, Stephen Jeremy; CMG (1982); s of Wilfred Phillips Barrett (d 1978), of Keene Valley, NY, and Dorothy, *née* Sommers (d 1987); *b* 4 Dec 1931; *Educ* Westminster, Ch Ch Oxford (BA, MA); *m* 1958, Alison Mary, da of Col Leonard George Irvine (d 1972); 3 s (Timothy b 1959, Nicholas b 1960, Matthew b 1962); *Career* Dip Serv 1955-, head of Chancery Helsinki Embassy 1965-68, cnsllr and head of Chancery Prague Embassy 1972-74, head of SW Euro Dept FCO 1974, princ private sec to Foreign and Cwlth Sec 1975, head of Sci and Technol Dept FCO 1976-77, fell Centre for Int Affrs Harvard Univ 1977-78, cnsllr Ankara 1978-81, head Br Interests Section Tehran 1981, dir of communications and tech servs FCO 1981-84; ambass: Prague 1985, Warsaw 1988-; *Recreations* climbing small mountains, reading; *Clubs* Travellers, Ausable; *Style—* Stephen Barrett, Esq, CMG; c/o Foreign & Cwlth Office, King Charles St, London SW1

BARRETT, (Nicholas) Vincent John; s of Sidney Gordon Barrett, of East Hyde, Harpenden, Herts, and Francine Constance Alice, *née* Collins; *b* 9 June 1956; *Educ* Haileybury & ISC, Guy's Hosp (BDS), Univ of Texas San Antonio (MS), M D Anderson Cancer Hosp (Cert in Maxillofacial Prosthodontics); *Career* Guy's Hosp: house surgn Dept of Oral Maxillofacial Surgery Feb-July 1980, house offr Dept of Prosthetic Dentistry 1980-81, assoc in gen dental practice Feb-June 1981, dental practice London 1985-; appts also held: Westminster Hosp 1985-90, King's Coll Dental Sch 1986-87, Guy's Hosp Dental Sch 1986-; Newland Pedley travelling scholar 1981, American Dental Soc award 1981; memb: American Coll of Prosthodontics 1983, M D Anderson Cancer Hosp Assocs 1985, American Dental Soc of London 1986 (hon sec 1990-), Int Coll of Prosthodontics 1987, American Dental Soc of Europe 1987, Int Soc for Dental Ceramics 1990; *Books* Colour Atlas of Occlusion and Malocclusion (jtly, 1991); *Recreations* tennis, squash, swimming, theatre, art; *Style—* Vincent Barrett, Esq; 38 Devonshire St, London W1N 1LD (☎ 071 935 8621)

BARRETT-LENNARD, Rev Sir Hugh Dacre; 6 Bt (UK 1801); s of Sir Fiennes Cecil Arthur Barrett-Lennard (d 1963), gggs of 1 Bt; suc kinsman, Sir (Thomas) Richard Fiennes Barrett-Lennard, 5 Bt, OBE, 1977; *b* 27 June 1917; *Educ* Radley, Pontifical Beda Coll Rome; *Heir* cous, Richard Barrett-Lennard; *Career* served WW II Capt Essex Regt (despatches); ordained in Roman Catholic Church 1950; priest London Oratory 1950-; *Recreations* in Scotland; *Style—* The Rev Sir Hugh Barrett-Lennard, Bt; The Oratory, South Kensington, London SW7 (☎ 071 589 4811)

BARRETT-LENNARD, Richard Fynes; s of Roy Barrett-Lennard (d 1979); hp of kinsman, Rev Sir Hugh Barrett-Lennard, 6 Bt; *b* 6 April 1942; *Style—* Richard Barrett-Lennard Esq

BARRETTO, Dr John Harold; s of Harold James Barretto (d 1974) and Winifred Annie Alexander (d 1990); *b* 6 Nov 1941; *Educ* Newells Sch Horsham Surrey, King's Coll Sch Wimbledon, St Bartholomews Hosp Univ of London (MB BS, MRCS, LRCP); *m* 31 July 1964, Jeanette, da of Reginald Owens, of Phoenix, Arizona; 2 s (Mark b 15 July 1965, Dominic b 6 June 1975); *Career* house surgn and house physician Canadian Red Cross Meml Hosp Taplow Bucks 1965; sr house offr: Gynaecology St Bartholomews Hosp 1966, Accident and Neuro-Surgy Radcliffe Infirmary Oxford 1967; in general private practice 1968-; FRSM; *Recreations* shooting, tennis, squash, skiing; *Clubs* Hurlingham; *Style—* Dr John Barretto; 64 Oakwood Court, Addison Rd, London W14 (☎ 071 602 2342); 134 Harley St, London W1 (☎ 071 580 1101)

BARRIE, Dr Dinah; da of Maj Claude Montague Castle, MC (d 1940), of London, and Mary Alice Patricia, *née* Armstrong; *b* 23 May 1936; *Educ* St James's Convent Sch, St Thomas's Hosp Med Sch (MB BS); *m* Aug 1963, Dr Herbert Barrie, *qv*; 1 s (Michael Robert b 1968), 1 da (Caroline Dinah b 1965); *Career* med registrar: Worthing Gen Hosp 1960-61, Edgware Gen Hosp 1961-63; asst lectr then lectr St Thomas' Hosp 1963-67; currently conslt microbiologist: Charing Cross Hosp (sr registrar 1970-72), Parkside Hosp Wimbledon and New Victoria Hosp Kingston; articles on microbiology in med jls; memb: Hosp Infection Soc, Br Soc Antimicrobial Chemotherapy; FRCPath 1984 (MRCPath 1972); *Recreations* reading and gardening; *Style—* Dr Dinah Barrie; 3 Burghley Ave, Coombe Hill, Surrey KT3 4SW (☎ 081 942 2836); Dept of Microbiology, Charing Cross Hosp, Fulham Palace Rd, London W6 8RF (☎ 081 846 7257, fax 081 846 7261)

BARRIE, Dr Herbert; *b* 9 Oct 1927; *Educ* Wallington County GS, UCL and Med Sch London (MB BS, MD); *m* 1963, Dinah Castle; 1 s (Michael), 1 da (Caroline); *Career* hon conslt paediatrician Charing Cross Hosp 1966-, sr physician 1984-86, hon conslt paediatrician Parkside Hosp Wimbledon; examiner Univ of London and RCP; FRCP; *Recreations* tennis, writing; *Style—* Dr Herbert Barrie; 3 Burghley Ave, Coombe Hill, New Malden, Surrey KT3 4SW (☎ 081 942 2836); Parkside Hospital, London SW19 5NX

BARRIE, Jane Elizabeth; da of William Pearson, of Somerset, and Bessie, *née* Knowles; *b* 11 Sept 1946; *Educ* Bishop Fox GS for Girls, Imperial Coll of Sci & Technol (BSc); *m* 12 Dec 1970, Dr William Robert Ian Barrie, s of Dr Robert Barrie, of Somerset; *Career* stockbroker; regnl dir Nat West Stockbrokers 1990-; dir Somerset Trg and Enterprise Cncl, pres Soroptimist Int of GB and I 1990-91, chm of govrs Bishop Fox's Sch Taunton 1984-; chm: Somerset & Avon Constabulary Taunton Deane, West Somerset Div Crime Prevention Panel 1987-; memb Int Stock Exchange 1973-, ARCS; *Recreations* sailing, bridge; *Clubs* Royal Dart Yacht; *Style—* Mrs Jane E Barrie; Hollydene, Kingston St Mary, Taunton, Somerset TA2 8HW (☎ 0823 451388); Nat West Stockbrokers, Bridgwater House, 3-5 Corporation St, Taunton, Somerset TA1 4AJ (☎ 0823 336622, fax 0823 338660)

BARRINGTON, Lady; Constance Doris; da of Ernest James J Elkington, of London;

m 1930, Sir Charles Barrington, 6 Bt (d 1980); 2 da; *Style*— Lady Barrington

BARRINGTON, Douglas John; OBE; s of John Frederick Barrington (d 1964), of Mount Lawley, West Australia, and Ethel Hannah Douglas (d 1981); *b* 9 Oct 1920; *Educ* Modern Sch Perth W Aust; *m* Clare Rachel Mary (d 1989), da of C Cuthbert Brown, of Malaya; 1 da (Prudence Rachel b 1954); *Career* serv WWII Lieut RANVR, Gunnery Offr destroyer flotilla Med (despatches 1945); Lygon Arms Broadway Worcs: mangr 1945, dir 1946, md 1956, owner and chm 1970-86, dir 1986-; fndr and chm Prestige Hotels 1966; dir Savoy Hotel Management plc 1986, Gordon Russell plc (chm 1980-82), Gleneagles Hotels plc 1980-82, Savoy Hotel Management plc 1986-90, Lucknam Park plc, Chester International plc, F Copson plc, Profile Management & Specialist Recruitment Ltd, Ashford International plc, Cassel Hotels & Restaurnats plc, Balmoral International Ltd; memb: Main Bd BTA 1973-74, Exec Ctee, Fin Ctee and Cncl Int Hotel Assoc (chm Fin Ctee 1979-83, pres 1982-84), Cncl World Travel Market 1987-, A A Liaison Ctee Br Hotels Restaurants and Caterers Assoc 1972-(chm Nat Cncl 1980-82, memb Bd of Mgmnt and Hotel Advsy Panel 1972-86); pres: Br Assoc of Hotel Accountants 1984-87, The Hotel and Catering Benevolent Assoc 1990-; *Awards* Queens award (first country inn to receive this honour) 1971 and 1985, Catey award for Tourism 1988, Catey award for Lifetime Achievement 1989; cncllr Wychavon DC 1970-76, former chm Broadway Parish Cncl, memb Broadway Cons Assoc, chm Hotel Sector Br Wildlife Year 1986-87; Master Innholder 1978, Freeman City of London 1980, memb Worshipful Co of Innholders 1985; FHCIMA, ACIS; *Recreations* travel, reading, tennis and golf (rather badly); *Clubs* Army & Navy; *Style*— Douglas Barrington, Esq, OBE

BARRINGTON, Sir Nicholas John; KCMG (1990, CMG 1982), CVO (1975); s of Eric Alan Barrington (d 1974), of Trumpington, Cambridge, and Agnes Mildred, *née* Bill; *b* 23 July 1934; *Educ* Repton, Clare Coll Cambridge (MA); *Career* 2 Lt RA 1952-54; FO (Persian language trg) 1957-58, language student Tehran 1958-59, oriental sec Kabul 1959-61, FO 1961-63; UK Delgn to Euro Communities 1963-65, first sec Pakistan 1965-67; Euro Econ Dept FCO and private sec Perm Under Sec CRO 1967-68, asst private sec FO 1968-72, head of Chancery and cnsllr Japan 1972-75, FO 1975-78, cnsllr Cairo 1978-81, head of Br Interests Section Tehran 1981-83, UK Mission to UN (NYC), econ summit coordinator 1984, asst under sec of state (public depts) 1984-87, ambass later high cmmr to Pakistan 1987-; Order of Sacred Treasure (third class) Japan 1975; FRSA-; fell: Royal Soc of Asian Studies, Egypt Exploration Soc; *Recreations* tennis, drawing, theatre; *Clubs* Athenaeum, Royal Cwlth Soc; *Style*— Sir Nicholas Barrington, KCMG, CVO; c/o Foreign and Commonwealth Office, King Charles St, London SW1; 33 Gilmerton Court, Trumpington, Cambridge

BARRINGTON, Raymond Lewis; s of Walter Lewis Barrington (d 1990), of Redland, Bristol, and Muriel, *née* Adams (d 1980); *b* 25 July 1928; *Educ* St Brendans Coll Bristol; *m* 14 March 1953, Shirley, da of George William Yarwood (d 1981), of Hilperton, Wilts; 1 da (Katharine b 1958); *Career* Nat Serv Glos Regt 1946-48; mgmnt conslt Peat Marwick Mitchell & Co 1957 (consultancy ptnr 1963, ret 1981), chm Fairford Electronics Ltd 1982 (chm and md 1985); hon treas Kingsbridge Cons Club 1982-, town cncllr Kingsbridge 1982-87, dist cncllr South Hams 1983- (chm Housing 1988-); Freeman City of London 1977, Liveryman Worshipful Co of Wheelwrights 1977; FCA 1963, FCMA 1966, Hon FBCS (pres 1973-74); *Recreations* golf, crossword solving; *Clubs* Thurlestone Golf; *Style*— Raymond Barrington, Esq; Lukes Farm, Kingsbridge, Devon (☎ 0548 853933); Fairford Electronics Ltd, Coombe Works, Derby Rd, Kingsbridge, Devon (☎ 0548 857494, fax 0548 853118)

BARRINGTON-CARVER, John; s of John Henry Carver, of Heatherby, Southway, Hillside Rd, Sidmouth, and Grace Elaine, *née* Dowell; *b* 8 Dec 1941; *Educ* Queen Elizabeth Sch Kingston, Britiannia Royal Naval Coll Dartmouth; *m* 2 Jan 1965, Judith Rosemary, da of Douglas Arthur Garrett (d 1981); 1 da (Nicola Wyn Louise b 30 Sept 1965); *Career* RN: joined BRNC Dartmouth as Gen list Cadet 1960, asst Gunnery offr HMS Lowestoft 1962, Navigating offr HMS Wasperton 1964, seconded RN TRG team Kenya ak Cmdg Offr KNS Chui 1966, seconded to RN Trg Team Kenya, ret at own request 1968; metals analyst and commodity and fin futures broker 1968-85 (with Metal Traders Ltd, Metal Traders Far East (Tokyo) Ltd, Fergusson Wild Ltd, Parisbas Warburg Becker, Arab International Securities); dir: Streets Financial Communications 1985, Ogilvy & Mather Public Relations 1988, sr conslt Ogilvy Adams & Rinehart 1990- (internal transfer); memb Fund Raising Ctee Queen Elizabeth Hosp for Sick Children Hackney; *Recreations* shooting, sailing, antique restoration; *Clubs* Special Forces, Hurlingham; *Style*— John Barrington-Carver, Esq; Ogilvy Adams & Rinehart, Chancery House, Chancery Lane, London WC2A 1QU (☎ 071 405 8733, fax 071 831 0339 carver)

BARRINGTON-WARD, Dr Edward James; s of Sir Lancelot Barrington Ward, KCVO, FRCS (d 1953), of St Edmunds, and Catherine (Mamie), *née* Reuter (d 1984); *b* 19 July 1942; *Educ* Eton, Gonville and Caius Coll Cambridge, St Bartholomews Hosp (MA, MBChir); *m* 24 July 1969, Brigid, da of William J Concannon Tuam, of Co Galway; 2 da (Elaine b 1971, Catherine b 1973); *Career* GP Bury St Edmunds 1970-87; med dir: St Nicholas Hospice Bury St Edmunds 1986-87, Highland Hospice Inverness 1987; cncl memb BASC 1935-82, fndr chm research/conservation Ctee BASC, memb Disciplinary Ctee BASC 1977; tstee Youth & The Countryside Educn Tst, vice pres Fenland Wildfowlers Assoc; MRCS, LRCP; *Recreations* shooting, fly fishing; *Style*— Dr Edward J Barrington-Ward; c/o Natwest Bank, 7 Cornhill, Bury St Edmunds; Highland Hospice, Ness House, 1 Bishops Rd, Inverness (☎ 0463 243132)

BARRINGTON-WARD, Frank; s of Frank Ward (d 1940), and Florence Bertha, *née* Thompson (d 1936); *b* 8 April 1928; *Educ* King Edward V1 Sch Aston Birmingham, St Catherine's Coll Oxford (MA); *m* 11 Aug 1951, Heather Beatrice, da of Reginald Walter William Warmington (d 1947); 3 s (Miles b 1956, Simon b 1957 d 1985, Piers b 1963); *Career* Army 1946-48, RAEC HQ Berlin 1947; overseas magistrate Fiji 1971-74, high court dist registrar Birmingham 1974-80, high court dist and co court registrar Oxford 1980-; memb: Rotary Club Oxford, Oxfordshire CC 1958-67; memb Law Soc 1956; *Recreations* rowing, skiing; *Clubs* Frewer Oxford, Leander, Henley Oxon, SCGB; *Style*— Frank Barrington-Ward, Esq; Crown Ct Co Ct, Oxford Combined Ct Centre, St Aldate's, Oxford OX1 1TL (☎ 0865 248448)

BARRINGTON-WARD, Simon; *see*: Coventry, Bishop of

BARRIT, Desmond; s of Samuel Islwyn Brown, and Gwyneth, *née* West (d 1970); *b* 19 Oct 1944; *Educ* Garw GS; *Career* actor; Brogard in Scarlet Pimpernel (Chichester and Her Majesty's); Nat Theatre: Archille Blond in The Magistrate, chauffeur in Jacobowsky, Charlie in 3 Men on a Horse (also at Vaudeville); RSC 1988-89 (Trinculo in Tempest, Gloucester in King Lear, Porter/Ross in Macbeth, Tom Errand in Constant Couple, Banjo in The Man Who Came to Dinner 1990-91, Antipholus in Comedy of Errors; Clinton in The Liar Old Vic); organiser of charity events incl: Samaritans, The Lighthouse, Children in Need, Children North East; Clarence Derwent award for Trinculo; Olivier award for Best Comedy 1988; *Recreations* antiques, cooking, travel; *Style*— Desmond Barrit, Esq; Hope & Lyne, 18 Leonard St, London EC2A 4RH (☎ 071 739 6200)

BARRON, Derek Donald; s of Donald Frederick Barron (d 1967), of Beckenham, Kent, and Hettie Barbara, *née* McGregor; *b* 7 June 1929; *Educ* Beckenham GS, Univ Coll London; *m* 16 June 1963, Rosemary Ingrid, da of Lionel George Brian (d 1984); 2 s (Andrew b 1965, Adam b 1968); *Career* served Intelligence Corps 1947-49; Ford: tractor mangr 1951, Tractor Gp 1961, Ford Italiana 1963-70, mktg assoc US 1970-71, gen sales mangr overseas mkts Ford US 1971-73, md Ford Italy 1973-77, gp dir Southern Euro sales Ford Europe 1977-79, sales and mktg dir Ford Brazil 1979-82, vice pres Ford Motor de Venezuela 1982-85, dir and vice pres ops Ford Brazil 1985-86, chm Ford Motor Credit Co Ltd 1986-; chm and chief exec Ford Motor Co Ltd 1986-; pres SMMT 1990; cncl memb: Prince's Youth Business Tst, Business in the Community; Hon DUniv Essex 1989; CBIM 1987, FIM 1987, FIMI 1987; *Clubs* RAC; *Style*— Derek Barron, Esq; Ford Motor Co Ltd, Warley, Essex (☎ 0277 253000, fax 0277 262066, telex 995311 FORDCO G)

BARRON, Sir Donald James; DL (N Yorks 1971); s of Albert Gibson Barron, of Edinburgh, and Elizabeth, *née* Macdonald; *b* 17 March 1921; *Educ* George Heriot's Sch Edinburgh, Univ of Edinburgh; *m* 1956, Gillian Mary, da of John Saville, of York; 3 s, 2 da; *Career* chartered accountant; chm: Rowntree Mackintosh 1966-81, Midland Bank plc 1982-87 (dir 1972-, vice chm 1981-82), Ctee London & Scottish Bankers 1986-1987 (memb 1985-87); dir Investors in Industry Gp plc 1980-; dep chm: Canada Life Assur Co of GB Ltd 1980-, Canada Life Unit Tst Managers Ltd 1980-; dir: Canada Life Assurance Co Toronto 1980-, Univ Grants Ctee 1972-81, BIM Foundation 1977-80 (memb Cncl BIM 1978-80); memb Bd of Banking Supervision 1987-89, tstee Joseph Rowntree Foundation 1966-73 and 1975- (chm 1981-); memb: Cncl CBI 1966-81 (chm CBI Educn Fndn 1981-84), NEDC 1983-85; kt 1972; *Recreations* golf, tennis, gardening; *Clubs* Athenaeum, Yorkshire (York); *Style*— Sir Donald Barron, DL; Greenfield, Sim Balk Lane, Bishopthorpe, York (☎ 0904 705 675); Joseph Rowntree Foundation, The Homestead, 40 Water End, York YO3 6LP (☎ 0904 629241)

BARRON, Dr (Thomas) Hugh Kenneth; s of Thomas Bertrum Barron (d 1963), of Worthing, and Florence Nightingale Kingston (d 1990); *b* 27 July 1926; *Educ* Epsom Coll, New Coll Oxford (MA, DPhil); *m* 11 July 1956, Gillian Mary, da of Owen Aubrey Sherrard (d 1962), of Lyme Regis; 3 s (Thomas b 1957, William b 1960, James b 1963), 1 da (Ruth b 1969); *Career* petty offr (Radar) UK 1944-47; asst res offr Div of Pure Physics Nat Res Cncl Ottawa 1957-58 (post doctorate fell 1955-57); Univ of Bristol: lectr Sch of Chemistry, reader in theoretical chemistry 1968-77, reader in chem physics 1977, head of Hons Sch of Chem Physics, ret 1988; princ res scientist CSIRO Sydney 1975-76; author of papers and review articles on thermal expansion and other thermodynamic properties of solids; *Style*— Dr Hugh Barron; 3 Carnarvon Rd, Redland, Bristol (☎ 0272 243956); School of Chemistry, Univ of Bristol, Bristol (☎ 0272 303682)

BARRON, Iann Marchant; s of William A Barron (d 1974), and Lilian E Barron (d 1969); *b* 16 June 1936; *Educ* Univ Coll Sch, Christ's Coll Cambridge (MA); *m* 1961 (m dis 1989), Jacqueline Rosemary, da of Arthur W Almond (d 1978); 2 s (Marc b 1965, Simon b 1967), 2 da (Clare b 1963, Sian b 1969); *Career* chief strategic offr Inmos International plc 1984-89 (dir 1978-89); md: Inmos Ltd 1981-88, Computer Technology Ltd 1965-72, Microcomputer Analysis 1973-78; industl prof Univ of Bristol 1985-, visiting prof Westfield Coll Univ of London 1976-78, visiting fell Sci Policy Res Unit Univ of Sussex 1977-1978, visitng fell Queen Mary Coll Univ of London 1976, hon fell Bristol Poly 1986, RW Mitchell medal 1983, J J Thompson Medal IEE 1986, author of tech papers; distinguished fell Br Computer Soc 1986; memb Cncl Univ Coll Sch 1983-; Hon DSc: Bristol Poly 1988, Univ of Hull 1989; *Publications* The Future with Microelectronics (with Ray Curnow 1977), technical papers; *Style*— Iann M Barron, Esq; Barrow Ct, Barrow Gurney, Bristol

BARRON, Kevin John; MP (Lab) Rother Valley 1983-; s of Richard Barron; *b* 26 Oct 1946; *m* 1969; 1 s, 2 da; *Career* coal miner, NUM exec for Maltby colliery, pres Rotherham and District TUC; *Style*— Kevin Barron, Esq, MP; House of Commons, London SW1

BARROS D'SA, Aires Agnelo Barnabé; s of Inaçio Francisco Purificação Saude D'Sa (d 1978), of London, and Maria Eslinda Inez D'Sa, *née* Barros; *b* 9 June 1939; *Educ* Duke of Gloucester Sch, Queen's Univ Belfast (MB BCh, BAO, MD), FRCS Edinburgh, FRCS England, ECFMG Certificate USA; *m* 12 May 1972, Elizabeth Anne, da of Hugh Austin Thompson (d 1984), of Belfast; 4 da (Vivienne, Lisa, Miranda, Angelina); *Career* clinical teacher and vascular surgn; Providence Med Centre Seattle USA 1977-78, conslt Royal Victoria Hosp Belfast 1978, Hunterian Professorship RCS 1979, James IV Surgical Traveller to N America and Australia and SE Asia 1983, Rovsing and Tcherning lectr Denmark 1987, jt lectureship RCS Edinburgh and Acad of Med Singapore 1989, examiner FRCS (Edinburgh) 1984; memb: Exec Cncl GB and I Vascular Surgical Soc 1986, ed Bd Euro Jl of Vascular Surgery 1987; regnl advsr RCS 1988, RCSE rep on NI Cncl for Post Grad Med Educn 1989; prodr of Carotid Endarterectomy Teaching Film (winner merit award Assoc of Surgns); memb: Vascular Advsy Ctee of Vascular Soc 1983, Clinical Res Awards Advsy Ctee DHSS NI 1986, Surgical Training Ctee NI 1989-, Earth Life Assoc, Friends of the Earth, Greenpeace; FRSM, FRCS, FRCSEd; *Books* author and reviewer of numerous pubns on vascular surgery; *Recreations* music, books and painting; *Style*— Aires Barros D'Sa, Esq; Vascular Surgery Unit, Royal Victoria Hospital, Belfast BT12 6BA (☎ 0232 240503 ext 3680, fax 240899, telex 747578 (QUBMED.G))

BARROS D'SA, Alban Avelino John; s of Inaçio Francisco Purificação Saude D'Sa (d 1978), of London, and Maria Eslinda Inez, *née* Barros; *b* 25 Oct 1937; *Educ* Teacher Training Coll Nairobi Kenya, Univ of Bristol (MB ChB), LRCP; *m* 22 July 1972, Gwenda Anne, da of Richard Arthur Davies, of Coventry; 1 s (Ian James b 30 April 1976), 1 da (Sonia Helen b 4 Sept 1974); *Career* house surgn and physician Bristol Royal Infirmary 1967-68, memb staff Faculty of Anatomy Univ of Bristol 1968-69, sr house offr in surgery (renal transplantion, orthopaedic, traumatic and general thoracic surgery) Bristol Hosps 1969-71, registrar surgery and urology Musgrove Park Hosp Taunton 1971-74, Pfizer res fell (also tutor in surgery and hon sr registrar) Royal Postgrad Med Sch and Hammersmith Hosp 1974-75, sr registrar surgery Univ Hosp of Wales Cardiff and Singleton Hosp Swansea, conslt surgn Walsgrave Hosp Coventry and St Cross Hosp Rugby 1979-, clinical dir in surgery St Cross Hosp Rugby 1990-, surgical tutor RCS England 1987-; examiner (FRCS) in gen surgery for RCS Edinburgh 1990-, memb Ct Univ of Bristol 1969-; memb: Midland Vascular Soc, Br Soc of Gastroenterology, Midland Gastroenterology Assoc, Midland Surgical Soc, Rugby and Dist Med Soc; MRCS, FRCSEd, fell Assoc of Surgns GB and Ireland; *Books* Rhoads Textbook of Surgery (contrib, 5 edn, 1977) numerous pubns in med jls on oesophageal, gastric, pancreatic and vascular surgery; *Recreations* travel; *Style*— Alban Barros D'Sa, Esq; 40 Nightingale Lane, Westwood Gardens, Coventry CV5 6AY (☎ 0203 675181); Walsgrave Hospital, Coventry; St Cross Hospital, Rugby; 5 Davenport Rd, Coventry; 56 Regent Street, Rugby (☎ 0203 602020, 0788 572831)

BARROTT, Michael Anthony Cooper; s of Brian Robert James Barrott (d 1963), and Betty Doreen, *née* Berryman; *b* 9 Dec 1954; *Educ* Reading Sch, St John's Coll Oxford (MA); *m* 29 May 1982, Elizabeth Jelisaveta, da of Stojan Stosic of Pimlico, London; *Career* Price Waterhouse 1976-87, gp financial controller The Private Capital Gp 1987-89, fin dir Mortgage Tst Ltd 1988-89, md Private Capital (Financial Servs) Ltd 1989-; FCA (1990, ACA 1979), MBIM 1987; *Recreations* music, skiing, restoring Georgian houses; *Style*— Michael Barrott, Esq; Mortgage Trust Ltd, Park Lodge, London Rd, Dorking, Surrey RH4 1RG (☎ 0306 75544, 0306 75557)

BARROW, Andrew James; s of Gerald Ernest Barrow, MBE, of Corners, 2 The Broadway, Gustard Wood, Wheathampstead, Herts, and Angela Eileen, *née* Frank; *b* 17 May 1954; *Educ* King's Sch Canterbury, Univ of Nottingham (LLB); *m* 16 April 1983, Helen Elizabeth, da of Brian Carter; 2 s (Charles Andrew b 24 May 1984, Frederick Nicholas b 26 May 1986), 1 da (Clementine Elizabeth b 17 March 1988); *Career* slr; Travers Smith Braithwaite: articled clerk 1976-78, asst slr 1978-83, ptnr 1983-; memb City of London Slrs Co; memb: Law Soc, Int Bar Assoc; *Recreations* golf, tennis, family; *Clubs* Burhill, E Sussex Nat (Castledown); *Style—* Andrew Barrow, Esq; 10 Snow Hill, London EC1A 2AL (☎ 071 248 9133, telex 887117, fax 071 236 3728, car 0831 386119)

BARROW, Anthony John Grenfell; s and h of Capt Sir Richard John Uniacke Barrow, 6 Bt; *b* 24 May 1962; *Style—* Anthony Barrow, Esq

BARROW, Brian Morris; s of Geoffrey Barrow (d 1963), of Torquay, and Winifred Horbury Gaston, *née* Morris (d 1967); *b* 16 Jan 1924; *Educ* HMS Worcester, Stanford Univ (BSc); *m* 1, 1948, Jane Vandervort; 1 s (Andrew), 3 da (Pamela, Victoria, Melanie); m 2, 1963, Joan Barnes; m 3, 1975, Kari Elisabeth, da of Per Aasen (d 1985), of Hamar, Norway; 2 s (Nicolai b 1976, Jonathan b 1981); *Career* Naval Offr 1941-46, N and S Atlantic, Indian Ocean, Pacific; petroleum geologist: Peru 1951-54, Colombia 1954-58, Bolivia 1958, Ecuador 1958-60, Nigeria 1960-63, USA 1963-64, UK 1964-68, Argentina 1968-71, Sweden 1971-74, Norway 1974-84; chm UK A J Drilling Ltd 1984-; *Recreations* sailing, fishing, shooting; *Clubs* Royal Norwegian Yacht (Oslo); *Style—* Brian M Barrow, Esq; 4 Primrosebank Ave, Cults, Aberdeen AB1 9PD (☎ 0224 861994); A J Drilling Ltd, Wood Offshore Centre, Greenbank Crescent, Aberdeen AB1 4BG (☎ 0224 248181, fax 0224 248292)

BARROW, Hon Mrs (Hilary Ann); *née* Evans; o da of Baron Evans of Hungershall (Life Peer); *b* 22 July 1931; *m* 1954 (m dis 1963), William John Barrow, s of Hugh P Barrow, of Ockley, Surrey; 2 s (Sebastian b 1955, Ashley b 1958), 1 da (Melanie b 1961); *Style—* The Hon Mrs Barrow; Duck Cottage, Puncknowle, Dorchester, Dorset DT2 9BW

BARROW, Dr Jack; s of Stanley Barrow (d 1963), of Surrey, and Winifred Evelyn, *née* Fox; *b* 14 Dec 1916; *Educ* City of London Sch, St Thomas's Hosp Med Sch (MB BS); *m* 10 March 1942, Mariane Wynne, da of Robert Noel Anderson (d 1966), of Glos; 1 s (Peter b 1947), 1 da (Ann b 1949); *Career* Capt RAMC served ME and Burma 1942-46; conslt in genito-urinary med to Home Office (ret 1990), physician i/c Dept of Genito-Urinary Med St Thomas's Hosp, ret 1981; past pres Med Soc for Study of Veneral Diseases 1980-81; author of works on genito-urinary medicine and contributor to medical textbooks; MRCS, LRCP, FRSM; *Recreations* walking, gardening; *Style—* Dr Jack Barrow; 1 Lauriston Rd, Wimbledon, London SW19 4TJ; Carters Cottage, Sherrington, Warminster, Wilts BA12 0SN; Albert Embankment Consltng Rooms, 199 Westminster Bridge Rd, London (☎ 071 928 5485)

BARROW, Prof John David; s of Walter Henry Barrow (d 1979), of London, and Lois Miriam, *née* Tucker; *b* 29 Nov 1952; *Educ* Ealing GS, Van Mildert Coll Univ of Durham (BSc), Magdalen Coll Oxford (DPhil); *m* 13 Sept 1975, Elizabeth Mary, da of James William East (d 1978), of London; 2 s (David Lloyd b 1978, Roger James b 1981), 1 da (Louise Elizabeth b 1984); *Career* jr res lectr ChCh Oxford 1977-80, Lindemann fell English Speaking Union Cwlth 1977-78, Miller fell Univ of California Berkley 1980-81, Nuffield fell 1986-87, Gifford lectr Univ of Glasgow 1988, Samuel Locker award 1989, Scott Meml lectr Leuvan 1989, prof of astronomy Univ of Sussex 1989- (lectr 1981); external examiner Open Univ, Collingwood Meml lectr Durham 1990, memb ctees SERC; FRAS, memb Int Astronomical Union; *Books* The Left Hand of Creation (1983), The Anthropic Cosmological Principle (1986), L'Homme et le Cosmos (1984), The World Within the World (1988); *Recreations* athletics; *Style—* Prof John Barrow; Astronomy Centre, Univ of Sussex, Falmer, Brighton BN1 9QH (☎ 0273 606755 ext 3100, fax 0273 678097, telex 877159 BHVTXS G)

BARROW, Julian Gurney; s of G Erskine Barrow (d 1979), and Margaret Armine Macinnes (d 1977); bro of Simon Hoare Barrow, *qv*; *b* 28 Aug 1939; *Educ* Harrow; *m* 1971, Serena Catherine Lucy, da of Maj John Harington (d 1983); 2 da; *Career* landscape and portrait painter; pres Cheslea Art Soc; *Recreations* painting, travel; *Style—* Julian Barrow, Esq; 33 Tite St, London SW3 4JP (☎ 071 352 4337)

BARROW, Kate, Lady; (Alison) Kate; da of Capt Russell Grenfell, RN (d 1954), naval historian and naval correspondent for The Times during WWII, and Helen Sidney Lindsay-Young, yst da of Col George Sidney Sheppard, CMG, JP; *b* 24 June 1940; *m* 1961 (m dis 1976), Capt Sir Richard John Uniacke Barrow, 6 Bt; 1 s (Anthony b 1962), 2 da (Nony b 1963, Frances b 1971); *Career* Seccombe Marshall & Campion plc; Freeman City of London 1980; *Style—* Kate, Lady Barrow; 55 Ongar Rd, London SW6 1SH

BARROW, Capt Sir Richard John Uniacke; 6 Bt (UK 1835); s of Maj Sir Wilfrid Barrow, 5 Bt (d 1960); *b* 2 Aug 1933; *Educ* Beaumont; *m* 1961 (m dis 1976), (Alison) Kate, da of late Capt Russell Grenfell, RN; 1 s; 2 da; *Heir* s, Anthony John Grenfell Barrow b 24 May 1962; *Career* served Irish Gds 1952-60; Int Computers and Tabulators Ltd 1973; *Style—* Capt Sir Richard Barrow, Bt

BARROW, Robert; s of Frederick Barrow, of Congleton, and Hannah, *née* Carless; *b* 27 Dec 1949; *Educ* Sandbach Sch, Univ of Warwick, North Staffs Poly (BSc); *m* 14 Oct 1972, Pamela, da of Kenneth Stuart Snelgrove; 1 da (Alethea Mary Fiona b 20 June 1980); *Career* on mgmnt staff Computing Div British Railways Bd 1972-77, conslt ICL Ltd 1977-82, co-fndr and dir of res and devpt JSB Computer Systems Ltd 1982-; winner Design Cncl award for JSB Multiview computer windowing product 1989, nominated for Duke of Edinburgh's special designers prize 1989; MBCS 1976, CEng 1990; *Style—* Robert Barrow, Esq; JSB Computer Systems Ltd, Cheshire House, Castle St, Macclesfield, Cheshire SK11 6AF (☎ 0625 433618, fax 0625 433948, car 0860 736959)

BARROW, Simon Hoare; s of G Erskine Barrow (d 1979), of IOM, and Margaret Armine MacInnes (d 1977); *b* 4 Nov 1937; *Educ* Harrow, Ch Ch Oxford, Hill Sch Pennsylvania ESU Exchange; *m* 1, 1964 (m dis 1977), Caroline Peto Bennett; 1 s (Thomas), 3 da (Sasha, Emmeline, Rebecca); m 2, 1983, Sheena Margaret, da of Maj-Gen Sir John Anderson, KBE; 2 da (Kate, Florence); *Career* 2 Lt Scots Gds 1956-58; dir Charles Barker Group 1978 (now BNB Resources), chief exec Ayer Barker 1978, chief exec Barkers Human Resources 1987; *Recreations* sailing; *Clubs* Brooks's; *Style—* Simon Barrow, Esq; 16 Chelsea Embankment, London SW3 4LA (☎ 071 352 7531); Barkers Human Resources, 30 Farringdon St, EC4 (☎ 071 634 1180)

BARROW, Simon Richard; s of Brig Richard Barrow, CBE (d 1977), of Liphook, Hants, and Jean, *née* McKay; *b* 11 Jan 1936; *Educ* Charterhouse; *m* 17 Aug 1962, Kirsten Ingrid Louise, da of Niels-Christian Stenderup (d 1990); 3 da (Louise Ingrid Jean b 9 Nov 1964, Pernille Margaretha b 10 Oct 1966, Nicola Kirsten b 31 March 1972); *Career* Binder Hamlyn 1954-60, Darling & Co (Sydney Aust) 1961-65, Schroder Wagg & Co Ltd 1965-67, Kleinwort Benson Ltd 1967-84 (dir 1979-84), ptnr Ernst & Whinney 1984-87, dir Henry Ansbacher & Co Ltd 1987-89; former dir First Independent Corporate Finance Ltd; memb Worshipful Co of Skinners 1957; memb ICAEW; *Recreations* golf, tennis, skiing, opera; *Clubs* City of London, Liphook Golf; *Style—* Simon Barrow, Esq; Fiddlers Copse, Rickmans Lane, Plaistow, Nr Billinghurst, West Sussex RH14 0NT

BARROWCLOUGH, Sir Anthony Richard; QC (1974); s of Sidney Barrowclough, of 28 Albion St, W2; *b* 24 June 1924; *Educ* Stowe, New Coll Oxford; *m* 1949, Mary Agnes, yr da of Brig Arthur Francis Gore Pery-Knox-Gore, CB, DSO (d 1954); 1 s (Richard b 1953), 1 da (Claire b 1956); *Career* called to the Bar Inner Temple 1949; rec of the Crown Ct 1972-; parly cmmr for Admin 1985-90, Health Serv cmmr 1985-90; kt 1988; *Style—* Sir Anthony Barrowclough, QC; The Old Vicarage, Winsford, nr Minehead, Somerset

BARRY; *see*: Milner-Barry

BARRY, Anthony James; s of late Edmund Barry, of Douglas, IOM; *b* 31 July 1931; *Educ* Old Swan Inst, Liverpool Coll of Bldg; *m* 1958, Margaret, da of William Foulkes; 1 s, 1 da; *Career* chm Business and Technical Educn Cncl, memb Cncl of Nat Academic Awards, md R Mansell (Westminster); dir Englemere Services Ltd; treas Chartered Inst of Bldg (past pres); *Recreations* swimming, reading, shooting, flying; *Clubs* Sonning Working Men's, RAC, The Livery; *Style—* Anthony Barry, Esq

BARRY, Anthony Morgan (Tony); s of Patrick Ian Barry, of Dulwich, and Catherine Elizabeth, *née* Skone; *b* 1 Oct 1965; *Educ* Alleyns Sch, Hounslow Borough Coll (HND); *Career* advertising exec; sr copywriter Leagas Shafron Davis Chick 1988-, tutor Design and Art Direction Course 1990-; awards: Silver award Creative Circle 1990; Silver award and commendation Campaign Poster Awards 1990; *Recreations* football, draughts, polo, theatre, films; *Clubs* The Fridge, National Films Theatre, ICA, Millwall FC; *Style—* Tony Barry, Esq; 77 St James Drive, Wandsworth, London SW17; Leagas Shafron Davis Chick, 1 Star St, London W2 1QD (☎ 071 724 7020)

BARRY, Prof Brian William; s of William Paul Barry (d 1982), and Jean, *née* Manson (d 1959); *b* 20 April 1939; *Educ* Univ of Manchester (BSc, DSc), Univ of London (PhD); *m* 26 March 1966, Betty Barry, da of John Hugh Boothby, of Portsmouth; 1 s (Simon John b 1967); *Career* community and industl pharmacist 1960-62, asst lectr and lectr Univ of London 1962-67, sr lectr and reader Portsmouth Poly 1967-77, prof Univ of Bradford 1977-; memb Ctee on Safety of Meds; FRSC 1976, fell Royal Pharmaceutical Soc 1982; *Books* Dermatological Formulations: Percutaneous Absorption (1983), author of numerous res papers, books and chapters; *Recreations* swimming, walking, golf; *Clubs* Royal Cwlth; *Style—* Prof Brian Barry; School of Pharmacy, University of Bradford, Bradford BD7 1DP (☎ 0274 733466)

BARRY, Sir (Lawrence) Edward Anthony Tress; 5 Bt (UK 1899), of St Leonard's Hill, Clewer, Berks, and Keiss Castle, Wick, Caithness-shire; Baron de Barry of Portugal, Lord of the Manors of Ockwells and Lillibrooke, Berks; s of Maj Sir Rupert Barry, 4 Bt, MBE (d 1977); *b* 1 Nov 1939; *Educ* Haileybury; *m* 1968 (m dis 1990), Fenella, da of Hilda Hoult, of Knutsford, Cheshire; 1 s, 1 da; *Heir* s, William Rupert Philip Tress Barry b 13 Dec 1973; *Career* former Capt Grenadier Gds; *Style—* Sir Edward Barry, Bt; 3 Sunnyside Cottages, Warehorne Rd, Hamstreet, Kent (☎ 023 373 2454)

BARRY, James Edward; s of James Douglas Barry (d 1971), of Southgate, Glamorgan, and Margaret Agnes, *née* Thornton; *b* 27 May 1938; *Educ* Merchant Taylors' Crosby, Brasenose Coll Oxford (MA); *m* 11 June 1963, (Ann) Pauline; 3 s (Matthew b 28 Sept 1967, David b 23 Jan 1972, William b 23 Dec 1976); *Career* Nat Serv RASC and Intelligence Corps 1957-59; called to the Bar Inner Temple 1963, practiced NE circuit 1963-85, stipendiary magistrate South Yorks 1985-; rec of Crown Ct 1985-; *Recreations* reading, home life; *Style—* James Barry Esq; Law Courts, College Rd, Doncaster, South Yorkshire DN1 3HS

BARRY, Lady Margaret; *née* Pleydell-Bouverie; da of 6 Earl of Radnor, CIE, CBE (d 1930); *b* 26 June 1903; *m* 1923, Lt-Col Gerald Barry, MC (d 1977), late Coldstream Guards, elder s of William James Barry, JP (d 1952), 4 s of Sir Francis Tress Barry, 1 Bt; 1 s, 5 da; *Style—* Lady Margaret Barry

BARRY, Dr Michael; s of Maj Francis Patrick Barry, MC, TD (d 1964), and Margaret Julia, *née* Hunter; *b* 9 March 1934; *Educ* Repton, Pembroke Coll Cambridge, The London Hosp (BA, MB BChir, MD); *m* 4 July 1964, Helen Margaret, da of Capt Hector Lloyd Price, MC (d 1979); 1 s (Timothy b 14 April 1965), 1 da (Susannah b 3 May 1967); *Career* Nat Serv Capt RAMC 1960-63, Maj Ghana Armed Forces 1961-62; The London Hosp 1958-60: house physician, house surgeon registrar in pathology, fell in gastroenterology Cornell Med Centre NY Hosp 1968-69, sr registrar in med the Royal Free Hosp 1969-74 (registrar in med 1963-65, hon lectr in med 1966-68), conslt physician Taunton and Somerset Hosp 1974-; MRCP 1960, FRCP 1979; *Recreations* gardening, photography, ornithology; *Style—* Dr Michael Barry; Woodville, Haines Hill, Taunton, Somerset (☎ 0823 337847); Taunton and Somerset Hosp, Taunton, Somerset (☎ 0823 333444)

BARRY, (John) Michael; s of Thomas Ernest Barry, MBE (d 1942), and Mary Josephine, *née* Furlong (d 1964); *b* 20 April 1924; *Educ* Dulwich Coll, Queen's Coll Oxford (BA, MA, DPhil); *m* 8 Sept 1956, Elaine Mary, da of Ryle Edward Charles Morris (d 1972), of Carmarthen; 2 s (Thomas b 1958, Alexander b 1960), 1 da (Veronica b 1965); *Career* res fell Univ of Chicago 1948-51, lectr in agric sci Univ of Oxford Univ 1951-, fell St John's Coll Oxford 1960-, (estates bursar 1977-87); author of numerous scientific books and pubns; treas Oxford Boat Club 1967- (memb Oxford crew 1946 boat race); *Recreations* hunting; *Clubs* Vincent's, Leander; *Style—* Michael Barry, Esq; Shilton House, Shilton, Oxon OX8 4AG (☎ 0993 842369); St John's Coll, Oxford OX1 3JP (☎ 0865 277300)

BARRY, Rt Rev (Noel) Patrick; 2 s of Dr T St J Barry (d 1962), of Wallasey, Cheshire, and Helen Agnes, *née* Walsh (d 1977); *b* 6 Dec 1917; *Educ* Ampleforth, St Benet's Hall Oxford (MA); *Career* headmaster Ampleforth 1964-79 (housemaster 1954-64); chm: Headmasters' Conf 1975, Conf of Catholic Colls 1973-75; Abbot of Ampleforth 1984-; *Style—* The Rt Rev Patrick Barry, OSB; Ampleforth Abbey, York (☎ 043 93 421)

BARRY, (Donald Angus) Philip; CBE (1980, OBE 1969); s of John Angus Barry (d 1946), and Dorothy Ellen Averill; *b* 16 Sept 1920; *Educ* Fort Augustus Abbey Sch; *m* 1942, Margaret Ethel Balfour, da of David Orr, MD (d 1941); 5 s (Michael, Hugh, Gavin, Nigel, Richard), 1 da (Philippa); *Career* dir: John Barry Ltd 1946-81 (md 1965-81), Swanfield Mill Ltd 1963-; memb: visiting ctees HM Borstal Instns Edinburgh, Dumfries, Polmont 1946-58 (chm 1965-81), SACTO 1953-58, Parole Bd for Scotland 1968-80 (chm 1974-80); chief inspr of prisons for Scotland 1981-85; ret; *Clubs* Univ of Edinburgh Staff; *Style—* Philip Barry, Esq, CBE; c/o Bank of Scotland, 28 Bernard St, Edinburgh EH6 6OD

BARRY, Lady Sarah Sue; *née* Stanhope; da of 11 Earl of Harrington; *b* 12 Dec 1951; *Educ* Lawnside; *m* 1970, Robert John Barry; 3 s (Mark b 1972, Guy, Tristan (twins) b 1975); *Career* involved in bloodstock business with husband; *Recreations* art, gardening; *Style—* Lady Sarah Barry; Mellon Stud, Kildimo, Co Limerick, Eire (☎ 061 393329, fax 061 393541)

BARRY, Sheila, Lady; Sheila Georgina Veronica; da of Maj George Joseph Francis White, MBE, of Longacre, Andover Rd, Winchester; *m* 12 May 1951, as his 2 w, Maj Sir Rupert Barry, 4 Bt, MBE (d 1977); 3 s (Timothy b 1952, Nicholas b 1957, Jonathan b 1960) 2 da (Tara b 1954, Xandra b 1962); *Style—* Sheila, Lady Barry; Brisley Rise, Willesborough Lees, Ashford, Kent

BARSTOW, Josephine Clare (Mrs A Anderson); CBE (1985); da of Harold Barstow, of Sussex, and Clara Edith, *née* Shaw; *b* 27 Sept 1940; *Educ* Univ of

Birmingham (BA), London Opera Centre; *m* 1, 1964 (m dis), Terry Hands; m 2, 1969, Ande Anderson; *Career* opera singer, freelance 1971-; most important roles: Violetta (Traviata), Elisabeth de Valois (Don Carlos), Lady Macbeth (Mtsensk), Amelia (Masked Ball), Leonora (Forza del Destino), Salome, Arabella, The Marschallin (Der Rosenkavalier), Jenufa, Emilia Marty (The Makropoulos Case), Katya Kabanova, Leonore (Fidelio), Sieglinde, Mimi (La Boheme), Tosca, Minnie; Hon DMus Univ of Birmingham; *Recreations* breeding Arabian horses (stud farm in Sussex); *Style*— Miss Josephine Barstow, CBE; c/o John Coast, Manfield House, 376/9 Strand, Covent Garden, London WC2R OLR

BARSTOW, Stan; s of Wilfred Barstow (d 1958), and Elsie, *née* Gosnay; *b* 28 June 1928; *Educ* Ossett GS; *m* 1951, Constance Mary, da of Arnold Kershaw (d 1935); 1 s (Neil), 1 da (Gillian); *Career* novelist, short story-writer, script writer for TV; dramatisations incl: Joby, A Raging Calm, South Riding (RTS Writer's Award 1975), A Kind of Loving, Travellers and A Brother's Tale; has also written for radio and theatre; hon fell Bretton Coll; Hon MA Open Univ; *Publications* A Kind of Loving (1960), The Desperadoes (1961), Ask Me Tomorrow (1962), Joby (1964), The Watchers on the Shore (1966), A Raging Calm (1968), A Season with Eros (1971), The Right True End (1975), A Brother's Tale (1980), The Glad Eye (1984), Just You Wait and See (1986), B- Movie (1987), Give us this Day (1989); *Style*— Stan Barstow, Esq; c/o Lemon, Unna & Durbridge Ltd, 24 Pottery Lane, London W11 4LZ (☎ 071 727 1346)

BART, Lionel; *b* 1 Aug 1930; *Career* songwriter, composer, lyricist; lyrics written incl: Lock Up Your Daughters (1959), Fings Ain't Wot They Used t'Be (and music, 1959), Oliver! (and music and book, 1960), Blitz! (and music and direction, 1962), Maggie May (and music, 1964); film scores incl: Serious Charge, In the Nick, Heart of a Man, Let's Get Married, Light Up the Sky, The Tommy Steele Story, The Duke Wore Jeans, Tommy the Toreador, Sparrers Can't Sing, From Russia with Love, Man in the Middle; writer of many hit songs; awards incl: Ivor Novello Award (1957, 1959, 1960 and 1989), Variety Silver Heart for Show Business, Personality of the Year Broadway USA (1960), Antoinette Perry Award (Tony) for Oliver! (1962), Gold Disc Award for the soundtrack of Oliver! (1969), Ivor Novello Jimmy Kennedy Award (1985), Golden Break Award (1990); *Style*— Lionel Bart, Esq; c/o 8-10 Bulstrode St, London W1M 6AH

BARTELL, Lt-Col Kenneth George William; CBE (1977); s of William Richard Aust Bartell and Daisy Florence, *née* Kendall; *b* 5 Dec 1914; *Educ* Coopers' Co's Sch; *m* 1955, Lucie Adèle George; *Career* pres: Br Chambers of Commerce in France 1974-76 and 1978-79 (hon vice pres), Br Chambers of Commerce in Europe 1977-80; FCIB; *Style*— Lt-Col Kenneth Bartell, CBE; 5 Ave St Honore d'Eylau, Paris 75116, France (☎ 4553 69 48)

BARTHOLOMEW, Hon Mrs (Noreen); da of 3 Viscount Long, TD, DL (1967); *b* 21 Jan 1921; *m* 1947, Capt John Cairns Bartholomew, TD, o son of late John Bartholomew, of Rowde Court, Devizes; 2 s, 1 da; *Style*— The Hon Mrs Bartholomew; Poulshot House, Poulshot, Devizes, Wilts

BARTHROPP, Wing-Cdr Patrick Peter Colum; DFC (1941), AFC (1953); s of Capt Elton Peter Maxwell D'Arley Barthropp, and Winifred Mary, *née* Maxwell (d 1920); *b* 9 Nov 1920; *Educ* Ampleforth; *m* 1, Barbara Pal (m dis); m 2, 29 Aug 1962, Elizabeth Lady Rendlesham, da of Col Robin Cowper Rome, MC, of Monks Hall, Glemsford, Suffolk; *Career* RAF joined 1938, 602 Sqdn 1940 (Battle of Br), 91 Sqdn 1941 (298 operational flights), 122 Sqdn 1942 (POW 1942-45, escaped twice), Empire Test Pilots Sch 1945, Boscombe Down test pilot 1945-49, Fighter Wing Ldr 1950-52, OC admin Hong Kong 1952-54, OC RAF Honiley 1954-56, Wing-Cdr RAF Cottishall 1956-58, ret 1958; fndr Patrick Barthropp Ltd (luxury chauffeur drive private hire Co) 1958, sold Co to Savoy Hotel plc 1986; tstee Douglas Bader Fndn, pres 613 Sqdn Assoc; Freeman City of Hull (1941); ARAeS, Cross of Lorraine, Order of King Haakon VII (Class II); *Books* Paddy (Autobiography Second edn 1987); *Recreations* shooting, fishing; *Clubs* RAF, Aspinalls, Marks, Harry Bar; *Style*— Wing Cdr Patrick Barthropp, DFC, AFC; The Cottage, Berwick St James, Salisbury, (☎ 0722 790476); Camelot Barthropp Ltd, Headfort Place, London SW1X 7DE, (☎ 071 235 0234, telex 8952647 CAMBAR)

BARTLAM, Thomas Hugh; s of Howard Bennett Bartlam (d 1970), and Mary Isobel Bartlam, *née* Lambert; *b* 4 Dec 1947; *Educ* Repton, Selwyn Coll Cambridge (MA); *m* 4 June 1977, Elizabeth Gabriel, da of Andrew David Arthur Balfour, Beech House, Shalford, Surrey; 2 s (Edward b 1979, Henry b 1985), 1 da (Harriet b 1981); *Career* merchant banker; dir: Charterhouse Bank 1984-89, Charterhouse Venture Capital Fund, Charterhouse Buy-Out Fund, Charterhouse Business Expansion Fund, Intermediate Capital Gp 1989-, Fenchurch Insur Gp (non exec) 1989-; *Recreations* opera, gardening; *Clubs* MCC, City of London; *Style*— Thomas H Bartlam, Esq; Blounce House, South Warnborough, nr Basingstoke, Hants (☎ 0256 862 234); 49 Bow Lane, London EC4 (☎ 071 329 0434)

BARTLE, Ronald David; s of Rev George Clement Bartle, of Surrey, and Winifred Marie Bartle; *b* 14 April 1929; *Educ* St John's Sch Leatherhead, Jesus Coll Cambridge (MA); *m* 1981, Hisako, da of Shigeo Yagi (d 1983), of Japan; 1 s (Nicholas b 1967), 1 da (Elizabeth b 1965) (both by former m); *Career* Nat Service 1947-49, RAEC 1948, army athletic colours 1954; called to the Bar Lincoln's Inn, practised in leading criminal chambers 1956-72; dep circuit judge 1974-78; candidate 1958 and 1959; met stipendary magistrate 1972, chm Inner London Juvenile Cts 1973-79; memb: HO Advsy Cncl on Drug Abuse 1987, HO Ctee on Magistrate's Cts Procedure 1989; Freeman City of London 1976; elected Steward of Worshipful Co of Basket Makers 1987; memb Royal Soc of St George; *Books* Introduction to Shipping Law (1958), The Police Officer in Court (1984), Crime and the New Magistrate (1985), The Law and the Lawless (1987); *Recreations* reading, walking, travel, relaxing at home; *Clubs* Lansdowne, Garrick; *Style*— Ronald D Bartle, Esq; c/o Bow St Magistrates Court, London WC2 (☎ 071 434 5270)

BARTLES-SMITH, Ven Douglas Leslie; s of Leslie Charles Bartles-Smith (d 1975), of Salop, and Muriel Rose Bartles-Smith; *b* 3 June 1937; *Educ* Shrewsbury Sch, St Edmund Hall Oxford (MA), Wells Theol Coll; *m* 1967, Patricia Ann, da of James Garlick Coburn (d 1971), of Derbyshire; 2 s (Andrew James b 1969, Peter Nathaniel b 1976), 1 da (Sarah Elizabeth b 1971); *Career* Nat Serv 1956-58, 2 Lt RASC 1957, Lt 1958; curate St Stephens Westminster 1963-68, priest i/c St Michael and All Angels and All Souls 1968-72 (vicar 1972-75), vicar St Lukes Battersea 1975-85 (rural dean 1981-85), archdeacon of Southwark 1985-; *Books* Urban Ghetto (co-author 1976); *Recreations* Shrewsbury Town football, travel, reading; *Style*— The Ven the Archdeacon of Southwark; 1A Dog Kennel Hill, E Dulwich, London SE22 8AA (☎ 071 274 6767)

BARTLETT, Anthony David (Tony); s of Clifford Sydney McDonald Bartlett, of Ash, Surrey, and Sylvia Patricia, *née* Samson; *b* 21 Feb 1951; *Educ* Stamford Sch Lincs; *m* 19 April 1980, Cathy Yoon Pow, da of Hiu Hon Leung, of Malaysia; 1 s (Joshua b 1984), 1 da (Melissa b 1982); *Career* CA; Neville Russell & Co 1971-74, ptnr Coopers & Lybrand 1984- (joined 1975); fell Singapore Inst of Accountants, FICA; *Recreations* swimming, theatre, gardening; *Clubs* RAC, Surrey Tennis and Country; *Style*— Tony Bartlett, Esq; 39 Brambledown Rd, Wallington, Surrey SM6 OTF (☎ 081 647 8164); Coopers & Lybrand, Plumtree Ct, London EC4A 4HT (☎ 071 583 5000, 071 822 4507, fax 071 822 4652, telex 887470)

BARTLETT, (Harold) Charles; s of Charles Henry Bartlett, and Frances Kate; *b* 23 Sept 1921; *Educ* Eastbourne GS, Eastbourne Sch of Art, RCA (ARCA); *m* 1, 1950 (m dis), Elizabeth, *née* Robertson; 1 s (Dr Charles Bartlett b 1956); m 2, 1970, Olwen Elizabeth Jones; *Career* WWII served RCS 1942-45; artist; many one man exhibitions in London, exhibited widely in UK and abroad, work in private and public collections; official purchases incl: V&A, Arts Cncl of GB, Nat Gallery of S Australia, Albertina Collection Vienna; pres Royal Soc of Painters in Watercolours, fell of the Royal Soc of Painters Etchers and Engravers; RWS, RE; *Recreations* music, sailing; *Style*— Charles Bartlett, Esq; St Andrews House, Fingringhoe, Colchester, Essex CO5 7BG (☎ 0206 28 406)

BARTLETT, Hon Mrs (Charlotte Trewlove); *née* Ashton; er da of 3 Baron Ashton of Hyde, TD; *b* 22 Feb 1960; *m* 21 March 1987, Andrew Donald Bartlett, o s of late D W Bartlett; *Style*— The Hon Mrs Bartlett

BARTLETT, Prof Christopher John; s of Sqdn-Ldr Reginald George Bartlett (d 1977), and Winifred Kathleen, *née* Luther (d 1978); *b* 12 Oct 1931; *Educ* Univ Coll Exeter (BA), LSE (PhD); *m* 7 Aug 1958, Shirley Maureen (d 1988), da of Alfred Briggs (d 1958); 3 s (Paul b 1960, d 1962, Roger b 1963, Nigel b 1965); *Career* asst lectr Univ of Edimburgh 1957-59; lectr: Univ of the W Indies Jamaica 1959-62, Queens Coll Dundee 1962-68; prof Univ of Dundee 1978 (reader 1968-78); memb Scottish Examination Bd 1984; FRHistS 1967, FRSE 1989; *Books* Great Britain and Sea Power 1815-53 (1963), Castlereagh (1966), The Long Retreat 1945-70 (1972), The Rise and Fall of the Pax Americana (1974), History of Postwar Britain (1977), The Global Conflict 1880-1970 (1984), British Foreign Policy in the Twentieth Century (1989); *Style*— Prof Christopher Bartlett; History Department, The University, Dundee DD1 4HN (☎ 0382 23181 ext 4511)

BARTLETT, George Robert; QC (1986); s of Cdr Howard Volins Bartlett, RN (d 1988), of Putney, and Angela Margaret, *née* Webster; *b* 22 Oct 1944; *Educ* Tonbridge, Trinity Coll Oxford (MA); *m* 6 May 1972, Dr Clare Virginia, da of Gordon Chalmers Fortin, of Castle Hedingham; 3 s (William b 1973, Frederick b 1979, Charles b 1982); *Career* barr Middle Temple 1966, rec Crown Court 1990; *Recreations* cricket and other games; *Style*— George R Bartlett, Esq, QC; The Court House, East Meon, Petersfield, Hants GU32 1NJ; 2 Mitre Court Buildings, Temple, London, EC4Y 7BX (☎ 071 583 1380, telex 28916)

BARTLETT, James Michael Gilbert; s of Maj Michael George Bartlett, TD, and Elizabeth Marjorie, *née* Grieve; *b* 21 March 1947; *Educ* Bromsgrove; *m* 20 Sept 1975, (Patricia) Anne, da of Ronald Dean Cranfield (d 1976); 1 s ((James) Michael Ronald b 1981), 1 da (Catherine Anne b 1978); *Career* princ Bartlett & Co CAs 1983, sr ptnr Bartlett Hall & Co CAs 1989, dir several private cos; chm Winchcombe Deanery Synod 1980, memb Gloucs Diocesan Synod 1980, dir Gloucs Diocesan Bd of Fin 1982, treas Gloucs Branch Cncl for Preservation of Rural England 1987; Freeman City of London 1979, Liveryman Worshipful Co of Builders Merchants; FCA 1971, FBIM 1988; *Recreations* sailing, riding; *Clubs* Royal Ocean Racing, Royal Northumberland Yacht; *Style*— James Bartlett, Esq; Cleeve House, West Approach Drive, Cheltenham, Gloucestershire (☎ 0242 575000); Bartlett & Co, 80a Eastgate St, Gloucester, GL1 1QN (☎ 0452 501635, fax 0452 304585)

BARTLETT, Sir John Hardington David; 4 Bt (UK 1913), of Hardington-Mandeville, Somerset; s of Sir (Henry) David Hardington Bartlett, 3 Bt, MBE (d 1989), and his 1 w, Kathlene Rosamund, 2 da of Lt-Col W H Stanbury, of Putney; *b* 11 March 1938; *Educ* St Peter's Guildford; *m* 1, May 1966, Susan Elizabeth (d 1970), da of Norman Waldock, of Gt Bookham, Surrey; 1 da (Nicola Jane b 20 April 1969); m 2, 19 June 1971, Elizabeth Joyce, da of George Thomas Raine, of Kingston; 2 s (Andrew Alan b 26 May 1973, Stephen b 5 July 1975); *Heir* s, Andrew Alan Bartlett b 26 May 1973; *Career* co dir, engr; electrical and gen engrg; *Recreations* construction design and model making, fine wines; *Style*— Sir John Bartlett, Bt; Hardington House, Ermyn Way, Leatherhead, Surrey KT22 8TW

BARTLETT, John Vernon; CBE (1976); s of late Vernon F Bartlett and Olga, *née* Testrup; *b* 18 June 1927; *Educ* Stowe, Trinity Coll Cambridge (MA); *m* 1951, Gillian, da of late Philip Hoffmann, of Sturmer Hall, Essex; 4 s; *Career* consulting engr; sr ptnr and jt chm Mott Hay & Anderson; pres Inst of Civil Engrs 1982-83; FEng, FICE, FASCE, FIEAust; *Recreations* sailing; *Clubs* REYC; *Style*— John Bartlett, Esq, CBE; Mott Hay & Anderson, 20/26 Wellesley Rd, Croydon, Surrey CR9 2UL (☎ 081 686 5041)

BARTLETT, Keith; s of Charles Windsor Bartlett (d 1958), and Olive May Bartlett; *b* 10 June 1944; *Educ* Pontllanfraith GS, Welsh Nat Sch of Med (MB BCh); *m* 23 April 1968, Lilian Mary, da of Alan Oakley Davis (d 1988); 1 s (Paul Andrew b 1974), 2 da (Nicola Ann b 1969, Andria Louise b 1970); *Career* conslt radiotherapist: Univ Hosp Saskatoon Saskatchewan 1976-78, Wolverhampton 1978; locum GP Wordsley W Midlands 1978-79, conslt radiotherapist ARI Aberdeen 1979-; winner of Zworykin Prize for paper on Bioengineering (Inst of Electrical Engrs) 1989; memb: Panel of Specialists in Radiotherapy, Scot Breast Trials Steering Ctee Edinburgh; dir Radiotherapy Res Gp Aberdeen; initiated RAWW-Frequency Hyperthermia Scotland 1980, immuno modulation for breast cancer 1990; DMRT 1972, FRCR 1976; *Recreations* music, live recording, car maintenance, target shooting, electronics; *Style*— Keith Bartlett, Esq; Granville, 58 Victoria St, Dyce, Aberdeen AB2 0EL (☎ 0224 722221); Radiotherapy & Oncology Dept, Aberdeen Royal Infirmary (☎ 0224 681818)

BARTLETT, Maj-Gen (John) Leonard; CB (1985); s of Frederick Bartlett (d 1941), of Liverpool, and Eva, *née* Woods (d 1984); *b* 17 Aug 1926; *Educ* Holt GS; *m* 1952, Pauline, da of James Waite (d 1979); 2 s (Nigel, David); *Career* cmmnd RAPC 1946, served Hong Kong, Singapore, BAOR, War Office, Washington, Malta, Libya, HQ MELF 1966-67 (despatches), staff pmr and offr i/c FBPO Berlin 1968-69, GS01 (Sec) NATO Military Agency for Standardisation 1969-71, cmmd pmr Hong Kong 1972-74, Col GS MOD 1974-76, chief pmr ADP and Station Cdr Worthy Down 1976-79, chief pmr BAOR 1980-82, pmr-in-chief and inspr of Army Pay Servs 1983-86, ret; mgmnt conslt; Col Cmdt RAPC 1987; Freeman City of London 1984; MBCS, FBIM; *Recreations* golf; *Clubs* Lansdowne, Royal Winchester Golf, Meon Valley Golf; *Style*— Maj-Gen Leonard Bartlett, CB; Lloyds Bank Ltd, The Sq, Wickham, Hants PO17 5JQ

BARTLEY, (Joseph) Haydn; s of Joseph Henry Bartley (d 1968), of Cardiff, and Gertrude Lucy, *née* Wilde (d 1983); *b* 13 April 1929; *Educ* Whitchurch GS Cardiff; *m* 15 June 1957, Dianne Evine, da of Harry Rupert Marjoram, of Cardiff; 1 s (Richard b 1961), 1 da (Deborah b 1959); *Career* trg instr RAPC Nat Serv 1950-52; CA; sr ptnr Hopkin Bartley Jones & Co (until 1986), admin Merrils Ede slrs Cardiff 1987-; vice chm Welsh Assoc of Youth Clubs 1984-, scout ldr 1947-65, youth ldr 1967-85, deacon local Church 1972-87, chm local Festival Ctee 1988; memb: Soc Incorporated Accountants 1956, FCA 1964; *Clubs* Cardiff Athletic, Glamorgan Wanderers Rugby Football; *Style*— Haydn Bartley, Esq; 12 Rhiwbina Hill, Rhiwbina, Cardiff (☎ 0222 624 781)

BARTMAN, Barry David; s of John Bartman, of London NW8, and Lillian, *née* Mitchell; *b* 3 July 1941; *Educ* City of London Sch, LSE (BSc Econ); *m* 8 Oct 1966,

Ennis, da of Maj Edward Guy Patrick Jessiman (d 1977), of Shoreham-by-Sea, Sussex; 1 s (Nicholas b 1972), 1 da (Carolyn b 1969); *Career* CA and fin advsr; dir: Polyfield Servs Ltd, The Beckenham Gp plc, Capital Wholesale Ltd; FCA; *Recreations* tennis, skiing, astronomy, classical music, antique clocks; *Style—* Barry D Bartman, Esq; Orford, 11 Park Avenue South, Harpenden, Herts AL5 2DZ (☎ 05827 69731); 17 Albemarle St, London W1 (☎ 071 495 3909, fax 071 495 3141)

BARTOLO, David Charles Craig; s of Albert Edward Bartolo, of Malta, and Evelyne Valerie Jean, *née* Callie; *b* 21 July 1949; *Educ* Queen Elizabeth GS Carmarthen, St Mary's Hosp Med Sch Univ of London (MB BS, MS); *m* 20 April 1974, Lesley Anne, da of Raymond Jeremy; 1 s (James b 1985), 2 da (Victoria b 1979, Rebecca b 1980); *Career* sr registrar S Western RHA 1982-86, sr registrar St Mark's Hosp London 1985, hon conslt surgn Bristol Royal Infirmary 1987-90, conslt sr lectr Univ of Bristol 1987-90, conslt surgn Royal Infirmary of Edinburgh Lothian Health Bd 1990; Hunterian prof RCS 1984-85, Moynihan travelling fell Assoc of Surgns of GB and Ireland 1987, jt winner Patey Prize MRS 1988, jt winner New England surgical prize American Soc of Colon and Rectal Surgns 1988; memb Cncl Section of Coloproctology RSM, memb Surgical Res Soc, memb Br Soc of Gastroenterology; FRCS 1976; *Style—* David Bartolo, Esq; Easter Hatton House, Kirknewton, Edinburgh EH27 8EB (☎ 031 333 3797); The Royal Infirmary of Edinburgh, Edinburgh EH2 9YW (☎ 031 229 2477)

BARTOLOME; *see*: de Bartolome

BARTON, Prof (Barbara) Anne; *née* Roesen; da of Oscar Charles Roesen (d 1955), of New York, and Blanche Godfrey Williams (d 1968); *b* 9 May 1933; *Educ* Bryn Mawr Coll Pennsylvania USA (BA), Cambridge Univ (PhD); *m* 1, 1957 (m dis 1968), William Harvey Righter; m 2, Aug 1969, John Bernard Adie Barton, s of the late Sir Harold Montagu Barton, of London; *Career* Cambridge Univ 1962-72 (fell Girton Coll 1962-72), Hildred Carlile prof Bedford Coll Univ of London 1972-74, fell and tutor New Coll Oxford 1974-84; Grace II prof of English Cambridge Univ 1984-; fell Trinity Coll Cambridge 1986-; hon fell New Coll Oxford 1989-; *Books* Shakespeare and the Idea of the Play (1962), Introductions to the Comedies, The Riverside Shakespeare (1974), Ben Jonson, Dramatist (1984), The Names of Comedy (1990); *Recreations* travel, opera, fine arts; *Style—* Prof Anne Barton; Leverington Hall, Wisbech, Cambridgeshire PE13 5DE; Trinity College, Cambridge CB2 1TQ (☎ 0223 338 466)

BARTON, David Garbutt; s of James Richard Barton (d 1983), of York, and Marion Joyce, *née* Garbutt; *b* 29 Jan 1937; *Educ* St Peters Sch York, Emmanuel Coll Cambridge, Univ Coll Hosp Med Sch Univ of London (MA, MB BChir, MRCS, LRCS, DCH, DObst RCOG, FPCert); *m* 2 April 1961, Bernice Ann, da of George Birnie Banton, of Wallasey; 2 s (Sebastian b 1963, Hugo b 1968); *Career* 2 Lt 5 W Yorks Regt (TA) 1958, Lt 1960, resigned 1962; GP Herne Bay Kent 1968-; co surgn St John Ambulance Kent, memb ST John Cncl for Kent, Freeman City of London 1977; Liveryman Worshipful Soc of Apothecaries 1977; FRCS (Ed) 1969, FRCGP 1976; OStJ 1990; *Books* Child Care in General Practice (contrib, 2 edn 1982); *Recreations* theatre, ballet, opera, memb Glyndbourne; *Clubs* BMA London, Kent and Canterbury, Kent CCC; *Style—* Dr David Barton; 64 Western Esplanade, Herne Bay, Kent CT6 8DN; Lower Chitty Farm, Chislet, nr Canterbury, Kent; St Annes Surgery, Herne Bay, Kent (☎ 0227 366 945)

BARTON, Derek; s of Ronald Pascoe Barton (ka 1944), and Hetty Iris Barton; *b* 16 Oct 1934; *Educ* Henry Thornton GS; *m* 24 Aug 1956, Angela Mary, da of Patrick O'Connell, of Oxford; 2 da (Julie Ann b 3 Sept 1957, Deborah b 19 March 1963); *Career* RAF Police 1952-55; advertisement rep TV Times 1957-60, advertisement mangr IPC 1960-67; Farming Press: advertisement mangr 1967-70, advertisement dir 1970-74, jt md 1974-76, chm and md 1976-; *Recreations* travel, golf, DIY; *Style—* Derek Barton, Esq; Pleasant View, Norman Close, Felixstowes, Suffolk IP11 9NQ, (☎ 0394 272 700), Farming Press Ltd, Wharfedale Rd, Ipswich (☎ 0473 241122

BARTON, Eric James; s of James Barton (d 1957), and Robina Edith, *née* Beveridge; *b* 2 Nov 1953; *Educ* Cumbernauld HS, Univ of Glasgow (MA), Univ of Strathclyde (LLB); *m* 13 July 1978, Heather, da of George Kennedy, of Cumbernauld; 3 s (Iain b 1980, Stuart b 1982, Graeme b 1989); *Career* slr; tstee and co sec Cumbernauld and Kilsyth Enterprise Trust Ltd 1985-, sr ptnr Barton & Hendry Slrs; *Recreations* literature, historical reading; *Style—* Eric J Barton, Esq; 60 Grampian Rd, Stirling; Barton & Hendry Slrs, Fleming House, Tryst Rd, Cumbernauld (☎ 0236 735446, fax 0236 735451)

BARTON, Maj-Gen Eric Walter; CB (1983), MBE (1966); s of Reginald John Barton (d 1968), and Dorothy, *née* Bradfield (d 1965); *b* 27 April 1928; *Educ* St Clement Danes Sch, Royal Mil Coll of Sci (BSc), UCL (Dip Photogrammetry); *m* 1, 1963 (m dis 1983), Margaret Ann, *née* Jenkins; 2 s; m 2, 1984, Pamela Clare Frimann, da of late Reginald D Mason, of Winchelsea; *Career* RE 1948, served Middle East 1948-52, E Africa 1957-59, Middle East 1965-67; asst survey dir MOD 1967-70, dep dir Ordnance Survey 1972-74, geographic advsr HQ AFCENT 1974-76, dir surveys and prodn Ordnance Survey 1977-80, Maj-Gen 1980, dir of Mil Survey 1980-84, Col Cmdt RE 1982-87, Hon Col TA 1984-89; dir Caravan Club 1984-; *Recreations* water sports, numismatics; *Clubs* Army and Navy, Geographical; *Style—* Maj-Gen Eric Barton, CB, MBE; c/o Barclays Bank, Winchester SO23 8RG

BARTON, (Alan) John; s of Alan Luke Barton (d 1971), of Copthorne Rd, Rickmansworth, Herts, and Helen, *née* Pullen; *b* 9 Nov 1927; *Educ* Watford GS; *m* 1, 18 July 1953 (m dis 1970), Pamela Elizabeth, da of John Errington Gibbs (d 1961); 1 s (Richard b 4 Jan 1962), 1 da (Anne-Marie b 15 Nov 1963); m 2, 8 April 1982, Angela, da of Leslie Maddock Brew (d 1972), of Mettingham Castle, nr Bungay, Suffolk; *Career* Fleet Air Arm 1945-47; md (formerly gen mangr) Brew Bros Ltd 1972-83, chm and md Pennington Cross Garage Ltd 1983-; vice-pres Kensington and Chelsea C of C 1987- (chm and pres 1979-87); Freeman City of London 1981, Liveryman Worshipful Co of Coachmakers and Harness Makers 1981; FID 1980; *Recreations* sailing, photography; *Clubs* RAC, Royal Lymington Yacht; *Style—* John Barton, Esq; 24 Stanford Rd, London W8 5PZ (☎ 071 937 6855); 33 Milford Rd, Lymington, Hants SO41 8DH (☎ 0590 673 227, car 0836 511 197)

BARTON, John Bernard; s of Bernard Cecil Leslie Barton, and Agnes Jane Gemmell, *née* Thomson (d 1973); *b* 22 Jan 1934; *Educ* Winchester; *m* 1965, Sarah Maud, da of His Hon Judge L K A Block; 1 s (Bernard David Grenfell b 18 Sept 1969), 2 da (Katherine Maud b 19 Feb 1967, Agnes Mary b 27 Jan 1972); *Career* Nat Serv 1952-54; articled clerk Mellors Basden & Mellors Nottingham 1954-59; ptnr Peat Marwick Mitchell & Co (now KPMG Peat Marwick McLintock) 1970- (joined 1959); Liveryman Worshipful Co of Tallow Chandlers; FCA; *Clubs* Army & Navy, City Livery Club; *Style—* John Barton, Esq; Haysden House, Haysden, Tonbridge, Kent TN11 9BE; KPMG Peat Marwick McLintock, 1 Puddle Dock, London EC4V 3PD (☎ 071 236 8000, fax 071 583 1938)

BARTON, John Bernard Adie; CBE (1981); s of Sir Harold Montagu Barton (d 1963), and Joyce, *née* Wale (d 1988); *b* 26 Nov 1928; *Educ* Eton, King's Coll Cambridge (BA, MA); *m* 1968 (Barbara) Anne Righter (Prof Anne Barton, *qv*), da of Oscar Charles Roesen; *Career* drama dir and adaptor; assoc dir RSC 1964-; dir and co-dir of numerous plays incl: Othello 1972, Richard II 1973, Dr Faustus 1974-75, King John 1974-75, Cymbeline 1974-75, Much Ado about Nothing 1976, Winter's Tale 1976, Troilus & Cressida 1976, King Lear 1976, Midsummer Night's Dream 1977, Pillars of the Community 1977, The Way of the World 1977, The Merchant of Venice 1978, Love's Labour Lost 1979, The Greeks 1980, Hamlet 1980, Titus Andronicus 1981, Two Gentlemen of Verona 1981, La Ronde 1982, Life's a Dream 1983, The Devils 1984, Dream Play 1985, The Rover 1986, The Three Sisters 1988, Coriolanus 1989; dir: School for Scandal (Haymarket Theatre 1983), own adaption of The Vikings (Den Nat Scene, Bergen, Norway) 1983, Coriolanus 1989; fell King's Coll Cambridge 1954-60; *Books* The Hollow Crown (1962, 1971), The War of The Roses (1970), The Greeks (1981), La Ronde (1981); *Recreations* travel, chess, work; *Style—* John Barton, Esq, CBE; 14 De Walden Court, 85 New Cavendish St, London W1 (☎ 071 580 6196/071 636 7031)

BARTON, Martin; s of Walter Barton, of 215 Cyncoed Rd, Cardiff, and Sadie, *née* Shipman (d 1990); *b* 7 May 1944; *Educ* Quakers Yard GS nr Cardiff, Co GS Merthyr Tydfil S Wales; *m* 6 May 1969, Jeanette, da of Arran Lermon (d 1988), of Cardiff; 1 s (David b 1970), 1 da (Susannah b 1972); *Career* articled clerk Leyshon & Lewis CAs Merthyr Tydfil 1963-68, ptnr Curitz Berg & Co 1971 (joined 1970), formed own practice Barton Felman & Co 1979 (Barton Felman & Cotsen 1981, Barton Cotsen & Co 1983, Bartons 1990); memb: Cardiff Utd Synagogue, Cardiff Bridge Club; ACA 1968, FCA 1976; *Recreations* bridge, badminton; *Style—* Martin Barton, Esq; 15 Ty Gwyn Crescent, Cyncoed, Cardiff (☎ 0222 481471); Lermon Court, Fairway House, Links Business Park, St Mellons, Cardiff ☎ 0222 777756)

BARTON, Nicholas James; s of Sqdn Ldr Ronald Cecil Nicholson Barton (d 1986), and Mary Carty, *née* Farrell; *b* 28 May 1935; *Educ* Westminster, Cambridge Univ (MA, MB BChir); *m* 13 Aug 1960, Margaret Anne Joyce, da of Sgt Leslie Holman Rowe, DFM (d 1978); 2 s (Neil b 1961, David b 1972), 3 da (Katherine b 1963, Jane b 1963, Clare b 1966); *Career* conslt hand surgn Nottingham Univ Hosp and Harlow Wood Orthopaedic Hosp 1971-, civilian conslt in hand surgery to the RAF 1980-, ed Jl of Hand Surgery 1987-; chm Nomenclature Ctee Int Fedn of Socs for Surgery of the Hand; hon memb: S African Soc for Surgery of the Hand, Brazilian Soc for Surgery of the Hand; corresponding memb American Soc for Surgery of the Hand, pres Br Soc for Surgery of the Hand 1989; FRCS, FBOA; *Books* The Lost Rivers of London (1962), Fractures of the Hand and Wrist (ed, 1988); *Recreations* walking, reading, watching cricket; *Style—* Nicholas Barton, Esq, FRCS; Department of Hand Surgery, Queen's Medical Centre, Nottingham NG7 2UH (☎ 0602 421421 ext 44337)

BARTON, (Malcolm) Peter Speight; s of Michael Hugh Barton, of Brockenhurst, Hants, and Diana Blanche, *née* Taylor; *b* 26 March 1937; *Educ* St Edward's Sch Oxford, Magdalen Coll Oxford (BA); *m* 7 Sept 1963, Julia Margaret, da of Hon James Louis Lindsay, *qv*; 2 s (Henry (Harry) b 1967, Christopher b 1970), 1 da (Fenella b 1965); *Career* Nat Serv 2 Lt Oxford and Bucks LI (later 1 Greenjackets) 1955-56, Capt London Rifle Bde Rangers TA 1960-63; admitted slr 1964; ptnr Travers Smith Braithwaite 1967-86; memb Stock Exchange 1986; md corp fin Lehman Bros International 1986-; memb: Law Soc, Int Bar Assoc, Cncl Br Inst of Int and Corp Law; Cncl Br Inst of Int and Comparative Law; *Recreations* walking, shooting, skiing; *Clubs* City of London, City of Law; *Style—* Peter Barton, Esq; Primrose Hill, Hawkhurst, Kent (☎ 058075 2132); 29 Campden St, London W8 (☎ 071 229 4006); Lehman Brothers International, 1 Broadgate, London EC2M 7HA (☎ 071 260 2931 & 071 601 0011)

BARTON, Sheila Elizabeth; s of George Richard Andrews (d 1979), and Marjorie Anne Andrews; *b* 4 Jan 1929; *Educ* Beverley HS, Hull Tech Coll; *m* 1 Jan 1950, Gerald Douglas Barton, s of Douglas Stanley Barton (d 1957); 3 da (Sally b 1953, Jane b 1955, Lucy b 1958); *Career* co dir and housewife; dir: Humbrol Ltd 1957-76, Saluja Hldgs Ltd 1987-; tstee Charity of William Turner Beverley 1965-; *Recreations* swimming, tennis; *Clubs* Beverley Decorative and Fine Arts Soc; *Style—* Mrs Gerald D Barton; Cherry Burton, Beverley, E Yorks HU17 7RF (☎ 0964 550242)

BARTON, Stephen James; s of Thomas James Barton, of Birkenhead, Merseyside, and Vera Margaret, *née* Francis (d 1983); *b* 4 May 1947; *Educ* Birkenhead Sch, Jesus Coll Cambridge (MA), Coll of Law; *m* 20 Apr 1974, Catherine Monica Lloyd, da of Arthur Frederick Buttery (d 1986); 2 da (Tamsin b 1975, Claire b 1977); *Career* admitted slr 1971; ptnr Herbert Smith Slrs 1978- (asst slr 1971-78, articled 1969); memb: UK Oil Lawyers Gp, Soc for Computers and Law, Insolvency Lawyers' Assoc; Freeman City of London Slrs Co; memb: Law Soc, IBA; *Books* contributing ed Butterworths Co Law Serv 1985-; *Recreations* photography, gardening, walking, river cruising, reading; *Style—* Stephen Barton, Esq; Exchange House, Primrose St, London EC2A 2HS (☎ 071 374 800, fax 071 496 0043, telex 886633)

BARTRAM, Dr Clive Issell; s of Henry George Bartram, of 42 Blenheim Drive, Oxford, and Muriel Barbara, *née* Partridge; *b* 30 June 1943; *Educ* Dragon Sch Oxford, St Edward Sch Oxford, Westminster Hosp Med Sch (MB BS); *m* 29 Oct 1966, Michele Juliette Francois, da of John Anthony Beeston Clark (d 1988), of 11 Northanger Ct, Grove St, Bath; 2 s (Damian b 1970, Guy b 1974); *Career* conslt radiologist St Bart's Hosp 1974; St Mark's Hosp: conslt radiologist 1974, dean of postgraduate studies 1985-88 (subdean 1976), chm Radiology Div 1987; radiologist King Edward VII Hosp 1978; FRCR 1972, FRCP 1985; *Books* Clinical Radiology in Gastroenterolgoy (1981), Radiology in Inflammatory Bowel Disease (1983); *Recreations* walking, theatre, music; *Style—* Dr Clive Bartram; 89 Normandy Ave, Barnet, Herts EN5 2NJ (☎ 081 449 9751); St Mark's Hosp, City Rd, London EC1V 2PS (☎ 081 601 7918)

BARTRUM, Patrick Hugo; s of Stanley Hugo Bartrum (d 1939), of Kent, and Kathleen Joan, *née* Ellis (d 1987); *b* 12 Jan 1926; *Educ* Charterhouse, New Coll Oxford (BA); *m* 1950, Jacqueline Luigia, da of Albert Alfred Jucker (d 1980), of Cheshire; 2 s (Hugo b 1951, Oliver b 1957), 1 da (Giulia b 1954); *Career* served Grenadier Gds (Lt) 1944-47; Sun Alliance Insurance Gp: gen mangr 1976-88, dir 1978-90; dir Nat Supervisory Cncl for Intruder Alarms 1972-80 (chm 1979-80), The Motor Insurance Repair Res Centre 1977-82; memb of HO Standing Ctee for Crime Prevention 1976-80; memb Bd of Govrs Chartered Insur Inst Coll of Insurance 1984-; pres: Insurance Inst of London 1980-81, Chartered Insurance Inst 1985-86; *Recreations* skiing, hill walking, tennis, bridge, opera; *Clubs* RAC; *Style—* Patrick Bartrum, Esq; Prospect House, Whitchurch-on-Thames, Pangbourne, Berkshire (☎ 0734 842158)

BARTTELOT, Col Sir Brian Walter de Stopham; 5 Bt (UK 1875), OBE (1983), DL; s of Lt-Col Sir Walter Barttelot, 4 Bt (d 1944), and Sara, da of late Lt-Col Herbert Ravenscroft, JP, of The Abbey, Storrington, Sussex; *b* 17 July 1941; *Educ* Eton, Sandhurst, Staff Coll Camberley; *m* 1969, Hon Fiona, *née* Weld-Forester, *qv*; 4 da; *Heir* bro, Robin Barttelot; *Career* equerry to HM The Queen 1970-71; mil sec to Maj-Gen Cmdg London Dist and Household Div 1978-80, CO 1 Bn Coldstream Gds 1983-85, gen staff HQ BAOR 1985-86; Regt Lt-Col cmdg Coldstream Gds 1987-, Col Foot Guards 1989-; Liveryman Worshipful Co of Gunmakers 1980; *Clubs* Buck's, Cavalry and Guards', Pratt's, Farmers'; *Style—* Col Sir Brian Barttelot, Bt, OBE, DL; Stopham Park, Pulborough, W Sussex RH20 1EB

BARTTELOT, Hon Lady ((Mary Angela) Fiona); *née* Weld-Forester; da of late 7 Baron Forester and Marie, da of Sir Herbert Perrott, 6 Bt, CH, CB; *b* 26 Feb 1944; *m* 1969, Col Sir Brian Walter de Stopham Barttelot, 5 Bt, *qv*; 4 da; *Career* memb Inst of King Edward VII Hosp Midhurst 1981-; county pres Sussex St John Ambulance Bde

1989-; *Style*— The Hon Lady Barttelot; Stopham Park, Pulborough, W Sussex

BARTTELOT, Robin Ravenscroft; s of Lt-Col Sir Walter Barttelot, 4 Bt (d 1944), and Sara, *née* Ravenscroft; bro and h of Lt-Col Sir Brian Barttelot, 5 Bt; *b* 15 Dec 1943; *Educ* Seaford Coll, Perth Univ W Aust; *m* 1987, Teresa, er da of late Kenneth Greenlees; 1 s (Hugo Ravenscroft b 7 April 1990), 1 da (Emily Rose b 1 May 1988); *Career* stockbroker; *Style*— Robin Barttelot, Esq

BARWELL, David John Frank; s of James Howard Barwell, of Abbey Rd, Harborne, Birmingham, and Helen Mary, *née* Phillips (d 1986); *b* 12 Oct 1938; *Educ* Lancing, Trinity Coll Oxford (MA), Institut des Hautes Etudes Internationales Geneva; *m* 1968, Christine Sarah, da of Joseph Henry Carter, (d 1969), of Manor Farm, Brickhill, Bucks; 1 s (Thomas b 1976); *Career* FCO 1965, Aden 1967, Baghdad 1968, Bahrain 1971, Cairo 1973, FCO 1976, Nicosia 1982, Paris 1985, FCO 1989; *Recreations* Gregorian chant, singing Bach, wandering round the Mediterranean; *Style*— David Barwell, Esq; c/o Foreign & Commonwealth Office, King Charles Street, London SW1; British Embassy, Paris

BARWELL, Hon Mrs (Sheila Margaret Ramsay); *née* McNair; 2 da of 1 Baron McNair, CBE, QC; *b* 19 Feb 1918; *m* 1946, John Harold Barwell (d 1983), s of Reginald Barwell (d 1959), of Swavesey, Cambs; 1 s (Hugh John b 1949), 3 da (Alice Marjorie Sheila b 1947, Lucy Elizabeth b 1951, Claire Bridget b 1953); *Style*— The Hon Mrs Barwell; 33 Fulbrooke Rd, Cambridge CB3 9EE

BARWICK, David John; JP; s of Richard Robert Oliver Barwick, OBE (d 1982), and Phylis Mary, *née* Goodban; *b* 10 Sept 1932; *Educ* St Lawrence Coll Ramsgate; *m* 4 Oct 1958, Gillian Cowell, da of Gerald Cowell Williams (d 1985); 3 s (Richard b 1960, Jonathan b 1961, Jeremy b 1963), 1 da (Susan); *Career* builder; md RJB (Plant) Ltd 1974-90, chm R J Barwick & Sons Ltd 1982-90 (dir 1960-87, md 1975-90); pres Southern Region Bldg Employers Confedn 1984; FBIM, FCIOB; *Recreations* golf, gardening; *Clubs* Royal Cinque Ports Golf (Capt 1991), IOD; *Style*— David J Barwick, Esq, JP; Overglen, St Clare Rd, Walmer, Deal, Kent CT14 7QB (☎ 0304 374897); Coombe Valley Rd, Dover, Kent CT17 0UJ (☎ 0304 203716, fax 0304 240293)

BARWICK, Norman; s of John Barwick (d 1963), of Bristol, and Gertrude, *née* Liddell (d 1927); *b* 12 June 1917; *Educ* Sexey's Sch Bruton Somerset; *m* 21 Sept 1940, Esme Maud Sophia (d 1985), da of Edward Peters (d 1942), of Bristol; 1 s (John b 1946), 1 da (Susan b 1944); *Career* mil serv: RA rising to rank of Maj 1939-46, Adj 181(M) HAA Regt 1943-44; legal advsr for welfare Army & RAF Middle East Forces; admitted slr 1939; Law Soc Divorce Dept Newcastle upon Tyne 1947-57; private practice: Sunderland 1957-66, Havant 1966-89; *Style*— Norman Barwick, Esq; 9 Hudshaw Gardens, Hexham, Northumberland (☎ 0434 607346); Longcrofts, 13 The Pallant, Havant, Hants (☎ 0705 492295)

BARWICK, Stephen Royston; s of Roy Barwick, of Briton Ferry, and Margaret Barwick; *b* 6 Sept 1960; *Educ* Cwrt Sart Comp Sch, Dwr-y-Felin Comp Sch; *m* 12 Dec 1987, Margaret Ann, da of Iowerth John; 1 s (Michael Warren b 25 Sept 1990); *Career* professional cricketer; debut Glamorgan CCC 1981, awarded county cap 1987; represented Welsh Schs under 18; Benson & Hedges Gold award 1984, young bowler of the month 1983; *Recreations* sea fishing, watching football and rugby; *Style*— Stephen Barwick, Esq; Glamorgan CCC, Sophia Gardens, Cardiff CF1 9XR (☎ 0222 343478)

BASING, 5 Baron (UK 1887); Neil Lutley Sclater-Booth; s of 4 Baron Basing (d 1983), and his 1 w Jeanette (d 1957), da of late Neil Bruce MacKelvie, of New York; *b* 16 Jan 1939; *Educ* Eton, Harvard (BA); *m* 1967, Patricia Ann, da of George Bryan Whitfield (d 1967), of New Haven, Conn, USA; 2 s (Hon Stuart, Hon Andrew b 1973); *Heir* s, Hon Stuart Whitfield Sclater-Booth b 18 Dec 1969; *Clubs* Harvard, Meadow Brook; *Style*— The Rt Hon the Lord Basing; 112 East 74 St, NY, NY 10021, USA (☎ 010 1212 535 1945); 60 Broad St, NY, NY, USA (☎ 010 1212 269 0049)

BASINGSTOKE, Bishop Suffragan of, 1977-; Rt Rev Michael Richard John Manktelow; s of Sir (Arthur) Richard Manktelow, KBE, CB (d 1977), of Dorking, and (Edith) Helen Saxby (d 1965); *b* 23 Sept 1927; *Educ* Whitgift Sch Croydon, Christs's Coll Cambridge (BA, MA), Chichester Theol Coll; *m* 1966, Rosamund, da of Alfred Mann, of Penrith; 3 da (Helen b 1967, Elizabeth b 1969, Katharine b 1971); *Career* ordained deacon 1953, priest 1954; curate Boston Lincs 1953-57, chaplain Christ's Coll Cambridge 1957-61, chaplain and sub warden Lincoln Theol Coll 1961-66; vicar: Knaresborough 1966-73, St Wilfrid's Harrogate 1973-77; rural dean Harrogate 1972-77, bishop of Basingstoke 1977-, canon residentiary of Winchester Cathedral 1977-91; pres: Anglican and Eastern Churches Assoc 1980-, Assoc for Promoting Retreats 1982-87; *Books* Forbes Robinson: Disciple of Love (ed, 1961); *Recreations* walking, reading, music; *Clubs* Nat Liberal; *Style*— The Rt Rev the Bishop of Basingstoke; Bishop's Lodge, Skippetts Lane West, Basingstoke, Hants RG21 3HP (☎ 0256 468193)

BASKETT, Dr Peter John Firth; s of Sir Ronald Gilbert Baskett, OBE (d 1972), and Joan Shirley Staples, *née* Firth (d 1982); *b* 26 July 1934; *Educ* Belfast Royal Acad, Campbell Coll Belfast, Queens Coll Cambridge (BA, MB BCh), Queens Univ Belfast (MB BCh, BA); *m* 1 (m dis 1972), Hazel; 1 s (Simon Patrick b 1963), 1 da (Lucy Jane b 1965); m 2 (m dis 1989), Margaret Jean; 1 da (Olivia Catherine Marie b 1978); m 3, 5 April 1989, Christine Mary; *Career* TA RAMC (V) 1982-: Capt 1982-84, Maj 1984-87, Lt-Col 1988-; hon civilian conslt in resuscitation to the Army; conslt anaesthetist Royal Infirmary and Frenchay Hosp Bristol 1966-, sr clinical lectr Univ of Bristol 1966-; author of numerous chapters and articles in books and med jls; hon sec Assoc of Anaesthetists 1978-80, hon sec RSM Anaesthesia 1980-82, fndr memb Resuscitation Cncl UK 1983-, chm Br Assoc for Immediate Care 1984-86, Euro Resuscitation Cncl 1988-, memb Bd Faculty of Anaesthetists 1984-88, vice pres Assoc of Anaesthetists 1985-88, chm Monospecialist ctee Union of Euro Med Specialists 1985-88 (UK rep 1982-), academician Euro Acad of Anaesthesiology 1985-, pres Euro Section World Fedn of Socs of Anaesthesiology 1986-90 (hon sec 1982-86), memb Cncl Coll of Anaesthetists 1988-, chm Euro Resuscitation Cncl 1988-, pres World Assoc Emergency and Disaster Med 1989- (hon sec 1979-89), pres Assoc of Anaesthetists 1990- (pres elect 1989-90); memb Worshipful Soc of Apothecaries 1986; FFARCS 1963; hon memb Aust Soc of Anaesthetists; *Books* Immediate Care (with Dr J Zorab, 1976), Pre Hospital Immediate Care (1981), Medicine for Disasters (with Dr R Weller, 1988), Cardiopulmonary Resuscitation (1989), Resuscitation Handbook (1989); *Clubs* Clifton, RSM; *Style*— Dr Peter Baskett; 14 All Saints Rd, Clifton, Bristol BS8 2JJ (☎ 0272 732732, fax 0272 735629); Department of Anaesthesia, Frenchay Hospital, Bristol BS16 1LE (☎ 0272 701212/702020, fax 0272 574414)

BASRA, Dev; s of Bishan Singh Basra, and Harbans, *née* Kaur; *b* 9 Jan 1942; *Educ* Col Brown Sch Dehra Dun India, Medical Coll Amritsar (MB BS, Best Artist); *m* 1, 1966; 2 c (Sukhdev, Devina); m 2, 25 Nov 1989, Sara Victoria, da of Harold James Hill; *Career* Surgn various NHS hosps 1966-76, private practice aesthetic plastic surgery 1977-, professional sculptor 1986-, studied sculpture under Martine Vaugel New York Acad of Art; Exhibitions: International Contemporary Art Fair (Shore Gallery) 1989, Maclaurin Art Gallery Ayr 1989; vice pres Federation Europeene des Societes Nationales de Chirurgie Esthetique, pres Indian Assoc of Cosmetic Surgns, charter memb Int Soc of Aesthetic Surgery; memb: Int Acad of Cosmetic Surgery, Japanese Assoc of Aesthetic Surgns; former sec Br Assoc of Cosmetic Surgns; FRCS 1976, FRSM; *Books* The Ageing Skin (1986); *Recreations* sculpture, photography, painting, design; *Style*— Dev Basra, Esq; 111 Harley St, London W1N 1DG (☎ 071 486 8055, 071 487 4654)

BASS, Neville M; s of Arthur Bass, of Manchester; *b* 8 June 1938; *Educ* Manchester GS, Univ of Manchester, Turner Dental Sch (LDS, BDS, VU), Eastman Dental Inst (Dip Orth); *m* 6 Jan 1968, Mona; 2 s (Alexander b 1970, Anthony b 1973); *Career* house surgn Manchester Dental Hosp 1960-61, Eastman Dental Hosp London 1961-62, (registrar orthodontic and paedodontic depts 1962-63), gen dental practice 1964-65, conslt orthodontist USAF London 1965-69, private practice 1969-, postgrad teaching staff Royal Dental Hosp London 1972-76; Angle Soc of Europe: memb 1974-, sec 1978-81, memb Scientific Ctee 1988-; certification Br Orthodontic Cert Bd 1984 (memb mgmnt ctee 1985-) memb Tweed Orthodontic Fndn USA; postgrad orthodontic teaching staff London Hosp Med Coll Dental Sch 1989-; FOS, FRCS (Eng); *Recreations* sculpting, jogging, weight training, swimming, skiing, reading, jazz and classical music, wind surfing, sailing; *Style*— Neville M Bass, Esq; 4 Queen Anne St, London W1 (☎ 071 580 8780)

BASSET, Lady Carey Elizabeth; *née* Coke; da of 5 Earl of Leicester; *b* 5 May 1934; *m* 1960, Bryan Ronald Basset, o surviving s of Ronald Lambart Basset (d 1972), and Lady Elizabeth Basset, *qv*; He is the sr rep of the ancient family of Basset of Tehidy, Cornwall, whose ancestor, Thurstan Basset, is said to have come to England with William the Conqueror; 3 s (David b 1961, Michael b 1963, James b 1968 a Page of Honour to HM The Queen); *Style*— The Lady Carey Basset; 10 Stack House, Cundy St, SW1 (☎ 071 730 2785); Quarles, Wells-next-Sea, Norfolk NR23 1RY (☎ 0328 738 105)

BASSET, Lady Elizabeth; *née* Legge; DCVO (1989, CVO); 2 da of 7 Earl of Dartmouth, GCVO (d 1958); *b* 5 March 1908; *Educ* at home; *m* 1931, Ronald Lambart Basset (d 1972, whose mother Rebecca was da of Sir William Salusbury-Trelawny, 10 Bt); 1 s (*see* Lady Carey Basset) and 1 s decd; *Career* extra woman of the bedchamber to HM Queen Elizabeth the Queen Mother 1958-82, full time woman of the bedchamber 1982-; *Recreations* reading, writing (3 anthologies published); *Style*— The Lady Elizabeth Basset, DCVO; 67 Cottesmore Court, Stanford Rd, London W8 (☎ 071 937 1803)

BASSETT, David Thomas (Dave); s of Harold Thomas Bassett, and Joyce Mary, *née* Spicer; *b* 4 Sept 1944; *Educ* Roxeth Manor Secdy Sch; *m* 8 July 1972, Christine, da of Thomas Edward Carpenter; 2 da (Carly Dawn b 12 July 1979, Kimberley Anne b 12 Feb 1982); *Career* professional football manager; amateur player Walton & Hersham 1970-75; Wimbledon: semi-professional player 1975-78, professional player 1978-79 with 36 league appearances in Wimbledon's first season in the Football League, asst mangr and coach 1978-81, mangr 1981-87; mangr: Watford 1987-88, Sheffield Utd 1988-; 10 England amateur caps 1972-75; capt Walton & Hersham Amateur Cup Winners 1973; achievements as mangr: Wimbledon promoted to Div 3 1981, Div 4 Championship 1983 (after relegation 1982), promoted ot Div 2 1984 and Div 1 1986, Sheffield Utd promoted to Div 2 1989 and Div 1 1990; 7 mangr of the month awards, special merit awards for taking Wimbledon into Div 1 from Bells Whiskey and LWT; *Style*— Dave Bassett, Esq; Sheffield United Football Club, Bramall Lane, Sheffield S2 4SU (☎ 0742 738955, fax 0742 723030)

BASSETT, Prof Douglas Anthony; s of Hugh Bassett, and Annie Jane Bassett; *b* 11 Aug 1927; *Educ* Llanelli GS for Boys, Univ Coll of Wales Aberystwyth (BSc, PhD); *m* 1954, Elizabeth Menna, da of Gwylim Roberts; 3 da (Sarah, Sian, Rhian); *Career* lectr Univ of Glasgow 1954-59, keeper of geology Nat Museum of Wales 1959-77 (dir 1977-85); chm: Ctee for Wales Water Resources Bd 1968-73, Advsy Ctee for Wales Nature Conservancy Cncl 1973-85; The Assoc of Teachers of Geology: fndr chm 1967, pres 1969, ed 1969-74; fndr memb and dir Nat Welsh-American Fndn 1980-87, memb Ordnance Survey Review Ctee 1978-80; hon professorial fell Univ of Wales Cardiff Coll 1977-; Officier de l'Ordre des Art et des Lettres 1984, Silver medal Czechoslovak Soc for Int Relations 1985, Aberconway medal Instn of Geologists 1985; *Style*— Dr Douglas Bassett; 4 Romilly Rd, Canton, Cardiff CF5 1FH (☎ 0222 227823); Nat Museum of Wales, Cardiff CF1 3NP (☎ 0222 397951)

BASSETT, John Cecil; s of Cecil John Bassett (d 1990), and Elizabeth Bassett (d 1977); descendant of J T Bassett, sometime mason contractor involved in Royal Albert Hall and Alexandra Palace; *b* 13 Jan 1928; *Educ* Cheshunt GS; *m* 20 Mar 1953, Josephine, da of Ernest Saunders White (d 1964; descendant of Thomas White, of Stonehouse Manor, Gloucester); 2 s (Peter John b 1955, Robert Edward b 1965); *Career* Nat Serv RE 1946-49; chartered surveyor, incorporated rating valuer, arbitrator; erstwhile surveyor of works Egypt 1949; three times examination prizewinner RICS; pres: Rating and Valuation Assoc (now IRRV) 1974, Rating Surveyors Assoc 1982; serving memb and father of Cncl IRRV; memb: cncl London C of C and Indust, Lands Tbnl Consultative Ctee; advsr to many city insts incl: Bank of England, Corporation of Lloyd's, Stock Exchange, Olympia & York; memb IRRV, ACIArb, FRICS, FInstD; *Publications* author of numerous tech articles; Bean and Lockwood's Rating Valuation Practice (co-author 6 and 7 edns); *Recreations* sailing, rugby football; *Clubs* Gresham, Little Ship; *Style*— John C Bassett, Esq; 19 Solent Ave, Lymington, Hants SO41 9SD (☎ 0590 676388); 22 Sandstone, 5 Kent Rd, Kew, Richmond (☎ 081 948 5618); 71 Queen Victoria St, London EC4V 4DE (☎ 071 236 4040)

BASSETT, Trevor; QFSM (1986); s of Richard Bassett (d 1972), of Thaxted, Essex, and Bessie, *née* Whyard (d 1973); *b* 10 Jan 1936; *Educ* Newport GS Essex; *m* 24 June 1967, Rosemary Louise; 1 s (Richard b 1969), 1 da (Emma b 1971); *Career* Nat Serv 1957-59; divnl offr II Essex Fire Brigade 1971-73: pt/t 1954-57, full time 19 leading fireman 1962-63, sub offr 1963-64, station offr 1964-68, asst divnl offr 1968-70, divnl offr III 1970-71; sr divnl offr Somerset Fire Brigade 1975-76 (divnl offr I 1973-75), dep chief fire offr Wilts 1976-83, chief fire offr Dorset 1983-; chief and asst chief Fire Offrs Assoc; fell Inst of Fire Engrs 1986; *Recreations* campanology, woodworking; *Style*— Trevor Bassett, Esq; Hengistbury, Winterbourne Steepleton, Dorchester, Dorset DT2 9LQ; Dorset Fire Brigade HQ, County Hall, Dorchester, Dorset DT1 1XJ (☎ 0305 204871, fax 0305 204974)

BASSNETT, Peter; s of Herbert Bassnett, and Emma, *née* Bacon; *b* 6 Dec 1940; *Educ* Stand GS Manchester; *m* 12 March 1965, Gabrielle Charlotte, *née* Hall; 2 da (Samantha Jane b 1970, Annabelle b 1972); *Career* dir field ops Abbey Life 1982-86 (agency mangr 1971-82), sales dir Aetna Life Insurance Co Ltd 1986-, md Westminster Ltd 1989; memb judging panel Br Quality Assoc; FLIA; *Recreations* sailing; *Clubs* Royal Motor Yacht; *Style*— Peter Bassnett, Esq, QFSM; 21 Branksome Towers, Westminster Rd, Poole, Dorset BH13 6JT

BASTABLE, Arthur Cyprian; OBE (1984); s of Herbert Arthur Bastable (d 1943), and Edith Ellen, *née* Allen (d 1954); *b* 9 May 1923; *Educ* St Georges Sch Harpenden, Univ of Manchester (BSc); *m* 3 April 1946, Joan, da of David Cardwell (d 1990); 1 s (Roger b 1952), 1 da (Susan b 1955); *Career* served WWII RNVR; chartered electrical engr; Fielden Electronics Ltd 1947-50, Ferranti plc 1950-88, sales mangr Vac Physics Dept Scot Gp Ferranti 1957-71, gen mangr Ferranti Dundee 1971-86, dir Ferranti Astron Ltd 1983-86, dir Ferranti Industry/Electronics Ltd 1984-86; memb: Dundee Port Authy, Scot Cncl CBI 1980, Dundee and Tayside C of C (pres 1970-71); CEng,

FIEE, FBIM; *Recreations* sailing, skiing, hill-walking; *Clubs* Danish, Royal Tay Yacht, Scottish Ornithologists; *Style*— Arthur Bastable, Esq, OBE; Hunters Moon, 14 Lorne Street, Monifieth, Dundee DD5 4DU (☎ 0382 532 043)

BASTIN, Prof John Andrew; s of Authur Edward Bastin (d 1930), of London and Emma Lucy Price, *née* Dunk (d 1955), of Essex; *b* 3 Jan 1929; *Educ* Sir George Monoux GS, CCC Oxford (BA), Univ of London (PhD); *m* 1, 1959 (m dis 1982); 1 s (Richard Edward b 28 Feb 1964), 1 da (Claire Damaris b 2 Jan 1962); m 2 1985, Aida Baterina, da of Felicano Delfino (d 1985), of Sala Cabuyao, Laguna, Luzon; *Career* Nat Serv Leading Seaman RN 1948-49; lectr Univ of Nigeria Ibadan 1952-56, res fell Univ of Reading 1956-59; Queen Mary Coll Univ of London 1959-84: lectr, reader in astrophysics, prof, head of dept, now emeritus prof; initiated res gp in Far Infrared Astronomy 1960-75 (discovered solar enhancements at these wavelengths assoc with sunspots, lunar dumbbel formation and seismic propagation, the liquification model and limitations of earths atmosphere for astronomy), princ investigator NASA US Lunar Samples prog (for infrared and ther measurements made with lunar rock) 1969-76, Leverhulme emeritus fell (light scattering applied to landscape) 198 landscape painting currently exhibited in several London and provinc galleries; Hon MA Oxon 1956; FRAS (former memb Cncl); *Recreations* architecture, music, tennis; *Style*— Prof John Bastin; 27 Endwell Road, Brockley London SE4 2NE (☎ 071 635 8501)

BASTYAN, Lady (Victoria Eugénie Helen); *née* Bett; da of William Bett, of St Leonard's-on-Sea, Sussex, and Marguerite, *née* Hay; *b* 24 Jan 1907; *Educ* governess Schs in: Russia, England, Switzerland; *m* 1944, Lt-Gen Sir Edric Montague Bastyan, KCMG, KCVO, KBE, CB (d 1980); 1 s (David Ion Gordon b 1945); *Career* WWII secretarial duties 1939-45 (despatches); DStJ 1969; *Clubs* Special Forces, Queen Adelaide (Adelaide); *Style*— Lady Bastyan; Flat 42, 52 Brougham Place, N Adelaide, 5006, S Australia

BASUALDO, Hon Mrs (Lucy); *née* Pearson; da of 3 Viscount Cowdray; first cous of Duke of Atholl and third cous of Duke of Marlborough, through her paternal gm, Agnes, da of Lord Edward Spencer Churchill, 5 s of 6 Duke of Marlborough; *b* 11 April 1954; *Educ* Daneshill Basingstoke; *m* 1972 (m dis 1978), Capt (Hector) Luis Juan Sosa-Basualdo, s of Lt-Col Hector Sosa-Basualdo, of Inocencio Sosa, Argentina; 1 s (Rupert Peregrine b 1976), 1 da (Charlotte Pearson b 1974); *Career* landowner, farmer; *Recreations* skiing, tennis, polo; *Clubs* Piping Rock (Long Island NY), Wellington (Palm Beach); *Style*— The Hon Mrs Basualdo; 370 Park Avenue, Box 48, New York, NY 10022, USA; Cowdray Park, Midhurst, Sussex; Dunecht, Aberdeenshire

BASUROY, Dr Ratish; s of Ramesh Basuroy (d 1947), of Calcutta, India, and Chinmoyee Basuroy; *b* 27 April 1937; *Educ* Univ of Calcutta (MB BS); *m* 16 Jan 1971, Namita, da of Tarapada Biswas (d 1985); 3 s (Raja b 6 July 1974, Rono b 6 Sept 1976, Robin b 15 May 1981); *Career* IA 21 Bengal Med NCC sr under offr, Capt 93 NCC Co Calcutta India 1963-64; demonstrator in anatomy Calcutta Nat Med Coll 1963-64, surgical registrar various hosps in UK 1965-70, registrar in genito-urinary med St Thomas's Hosp London 1971, sr registrar Bournemouth and Southampton gp of hosps 1971-73, physician in charge Dept of Genito-Urinary Med E Dorset Health Authy conslt in genito-urinary med W Dorset and Southampton Univ gp of hosps clinical tutor of gen practitioners Dorset Health Authy, clinical tutor in genito-urinary med Univ of Southampton 1974; contrib articles to: Br Med Jl, Genito-Urinary Med Jl, Br Jl of Clinical Practice, Br Jl of Sexual Med; reviewer of books for The Br Jl Genito-Urinary Med 1986-; conslt surgn for Br Pregnancy Advsy Serv Bournemouth 1974-90, memb SAC in genito-urinary med of The JCHMT RCP 1982-86, former chm Wessex Genito-Urinary Physicians Sub Ctee to Wessex RHA (memb Ctee 1981), memb and chm SAC Visiting Team RCP 1983-, dep chm Genito-Urinary Med Sub Ctee BMA 1984-89 (memb Cncl 1982-89); memb: CCHMS Ctee of BMA 1985-89, Wessex Regnl Aids Expert Ctee 1986-89, Bournemouth and Poole Med Soc, Conslt and Sr Registrar Appt Ctee WRHA 1973-; memb Cncl Med Soc for the Study of Veneral Diseases 1989-(1982-85); memb: BMA, RCPED 1986; FRCS 1968, FRCPE 1989; *Recreations* photography, philately, numismatics, reading, finance; *Style*— Dr Ratish Basuroy; Dept of Genito-Urinary Medicine, Royal Victoria Hospital, Gloucester Rd, Bournemouth BH7 6JF (☎ 0202 395201 ext 3369, 0202 398548)

BATCHELOR, Andrew Goolden Grant; s of Lt Col Hugh Thomas Nicolas Batchelor (d 1976), and Margaret Irene, *née* Grant; *b* 28 Aug 1951; *Educ* Whitchurch HS, St Mary's Hosp Med Sch Univ of London (BSc, MB BS); *m* 3 Nov 1973, Rosemary Marion, da of William Hugh Gibson, of Melksham, Wilts; 1 s (Thomas b 18 April 1980), 1 da (Elizabeth b 12 Oct 1983); *Career* surgical res King Edward VII Hosp Paget Bermuda 1978-79, sr house offr in gen surgery St Mary's Hosp London 1979-80, registrar in gen surgery Queen Elizabeth II Hosp Welwyn Gdn City 1980-81, sr house offr in plastic surgery Wexham Park Hosp Slough 1981-82, registrar in plastic surgery Nottingham City 1982-84, sr registrar W of Scotland Regnl Plastic Surgery Unit 1984-86, clinical lectr in surgery Univ of Leeds 1986-, conslt plastic surgn: St James Hosp Gen Infirmary Leeds 1986- S York Dist Hosp 1988-; memb: Br Microsurgical Soc 1982, Br Soc of Head and Neck Oncologists 1986, Br Asoc of Plastic Surgns 1986, Br Assoc of Aesthetic Plastic Surgns 1988; FRCS, FRCS (Plastic Surgns); *Books* contrib: Essential Surgical Practice (1988), Tissue Expansion (1989); *Recreations* sailing, shooting; *Style*— Andrew Batchelor, Esq; Dunleary, Off Street Lane, Roundhay, Leeds LS8 1DF, (☎ 0532 664009); Dept of Plastic Surgery, St James's University Hospital, Beckett St, Leeds LS8 1DF, (☎ 0532 433144 ext 5112)

BATCHELOR, Prof Bruce Godfrey; s of Ernest Walter Batchelor (d 1982), of Rugby, Warwickshire, and Ingrid Maud, *née* Wells; *b* 15 May 1943; *Educ* Lawrence Sherrif Sch Rugby, Univ of Southampton (BSc, PhD); *m* 21 Aug 1968, Eleanor Gray, da of Percy William Pawley, of Cardiff; 2 c (Helen b 1969, David b 1972); *Career* engr Plessey Co Ltd 1968-70, lectr Univ of Southampton 1971-80, conslt Br Robotic Systems Ltd 1980-86, prof Univ of Wales Coll of Cardiff 1981-; conslt 3M Co USA 1984-, Vision Dynamics Ltd 1987-; author of 150 tech articles; memb: IEE 1972, SPIE 1983; CENG 1972, FRSA 1984; *Books* Practical Approach Pattern Classification (1975), Pattern Recognition, Ideas In Practice (ed, 1978), Automated Visual Inspection (ed, 1985), Intelligent Image Processing in Prolog (1991); *Recreations* Presbyterian Church, walking, swimming, photography; *Style*— Prof Bruce Batchelor; School of Electrical Electronic & Systems Engineering, University of Wales College of Cardiff, PO Box 904 Cardiff CF1 3YH (☎ 0222 874390, fax 0222 874192, telex 497368)

BATCHELOR, Prof Sir Ivor Ralph Campbell; CBE (1976); s of Ralph C L Batchelor, and Muriel, *née* Shaw; *b* 29 Nov 1916; *Educ* Edinburgh Acad, Univ of Edinburgh; *m* 1941, Honor Wallace Williamson; 1 s, 3 da; *Career* emeritus prof of psychiatry Univ of Dundee (ret 1982); memb: MRC 1972-76, Royal Cmmn on the NHS 1976-79, Scottish Hosp Endowments Res Tst 1984-90; FRSE 1960-, hon fell RCPsych 1984-; kt 1981; *Clubs* Athenaeum, Royal and Ancient Golf; *Style*— Prof Sir Ivor Batchelor, CBE, FRSE

BATCHELOR, Prof (John) Richard; s of Basil William Batchelor, CBE (d 1956), of Pembury, Kent, and Esme Clare, *née* Cornwall; *b* 4 Oct 1931; *Educ* Marlborough, Emmanuel Coll Cambridge, Guy's Hosp Med Sch; *m* 23 Jul 1955, Dr Moira Ann, da of William McLellan (d 1987), of Tadworth, Surrey; 2 s (Andrew b 1957, Simon b 1962), 2 da (Annabel b 1959, Lucinda b 1964); *Career* Nat Serv MO RAMC 1957-59; lectr and sr lectr Dept of Pathology Guy's Hosp Med Sch 1962-67; dir Blond McIndoe Res Centre Queen Victoria Hosp East Grinstead; prof of: transplantation res RCS 1967-79, tissue immunology Royal Postgrad Med Sch 1979-82, immunology Royal Postgrad Med Sch 1982-; memb MRC Grants Ctees and Cell Bd 1972-78; chm: Arthritis & Rheumatism Cncl Grants Ctee 1986-88, Scientific Coordinating Ctee 1988-; pres Int Transplantation Soc 1988-90; memb Court Worshipful Co of Skinners (Master 1984-85); FIBiol; *Recreations* tennis, skiing; *Clubs* Brooks' & Queen's; *Style*— Prof Richard Batchelor; Little Ambrook, Nursery Rd, Walton-on-the-Hill, Tadworth, Surrey KT20 7TU (☎ 0737 812 028); Dept of Immunology, Royal Postgraduate Medical School, Hammersmith Hospital, Du Cane Rd, London W12 0NN (☎ 081 740 3225)

BATCHELOR, Stephen James; s of Frank Ralph Batchelor, of The Spinney Mynthurst, Leigh, Reigate Surrey, and Doreen Majorie Batchelor; *b* 22 June 1961; *Educ* Millfield; *m* 20 May 1989, Jaqueline Sarah Chennery, da of Micheal Simmonds; 1 da (Anna Kate b 20 Jan 91); *Career* hockey player; Silver medallist Champions Trophy, Bronze medallist Los Angeles Olympic Games 1984, Silver medallist World Cup London 1986, Silver medallist European Cup Moscow 1987, Gold Medallist Olympic Games Seoul 1988; *Style*— Stephen Batchelor, Esq; The Spinney, Mynthurst, Leigh, nr Reigate, Surrey (☎ 0293 862 849)

BATE, Anthony; s of Hubert George Cookson Bate (d 1986), and Cecile Marjorie, *née* Canadine (d 1973); *b* 31 Aug 1927; *Educ* King Edward VI Sch Stourbridge Worcs, Central Sch of Speech & Drama; *m* 22 May 1954, Diana Fay, da of Kenneth Alfred Charles Cawes Watson (d 1939), of Seaview, IOW; 2 s (Gavin Watson b 25 Feb 1961, Mark Hewitt b 23 Sept 1963); *Career* Nat Serv RNVR 1945-47; actor; entered professional theatre 1953, first West End appearance Inherit the Wind (St Martin's) 1960, Treasure Island (Mermaid Theatre) 1960, Happy Family (Hampstead Theatre Club) 1966, Much Ado About Nothing and Silence (RSC Aldwych) 1969, Find Your Way Home (Open Space Theatre) 1970, Eden End (tour) 1972, Economic Necessity (Haymarket Leicester) 1973, Getting Away with Murder (Comedy Theatre) 1976, Shadow Box (Cambridge Theatre) 1979, The Old Jest (tour) 1980, A Flea in her Ear (Plymouth Theatre Co) 1980, Little Lies (Wyndhams Theatre) 1983, Master Class (tour) 1984, The Deep Blue Sea (Theatre Royal Haymarket) 1988; first TV appearance 1955; numerous appearances since incl: Philby Burgess and Maclean 1976, The Dutch Train Hijack 1976, The Seagull 1977, An Englishman's Castle 1978, The Trial of Uri Urlov 1978, Tinker Tailor Soldier Spy 1978, Crime and Punishment 1979, T'is A Pity She's A Whore 1979, The Human Crocodile 1980, Smiley's People 1981, A Woman Called Golda 1981, Artists and Models 1983, War and Rememberance 1986, Game Set and Match 1987, Countdown to War 1989; films incl: The Set Up 1961, Stopover Forever 1963, Act of Murder 1964, Davey Jones' Locker 1964, Ghost Story 1973, Bismark 1975, Give My Regards to Broad Street 1982, Exploits at West Poley 1985, Eminent Domaine; memb BAFTA; *Recreations* listening to music; *Style*— Anthony Bate, Esq; c/o Al Parker Ltd, 55 Park Lane, London W1Y 3LB (☎ 071 499 4232)

BATE, Jennifer Lucy; da of Horace Alfred Bate, and Dorothy Marjorie, *née* Hunt; *b* 11 Nov 1944; *Educ* Tollington GS, Univ of Bristol (BA); *Career* asst organist St James Muswell Hill 1955-78, superintendant Shaw Library LSE 1966-69, became a full time professional musician 1969-, specialist in eighteenth century Eng organ music, frequently appears with Dolmetsch Ensemble at Haslemere Festival of Early Music; world authy on works of Olivier Messiaen (composer), soloist at Br première Livre du Saint Sacrement (Olivier Messiaen) Westminster Cathedral, and opened a series on the complete organ works of Messiaen on Radio France in the presence of the composer; designed (with NP Mander Ltd) portable pipe organ and (with Wyvern Organs) a new type of computer organ; has made over 30 recordings incl: From Stanley to Wesley, complete organ works of Franck and Messiaen (of which Livre du Saint Sacrement gained Grand Prix du Disque); collaborator with many British composers having works written for her incl: Blue Rose Variations (by Peter Dickinson), Fenestra (by William Mathias); awards: GLAA Young Musician 1972, Personnalité de l'Année (France) 1990; Silver plaque for services to music: Alassio (Italy), Garbagna (Italy); memb: Royal Soc of Musicians, Royal Philharmonic Soc, Br Music Soc, Incorporated Soc of Musicians; FRCO, LRAM (organ performer), ARCM (organ performer); *Music Published* Introduction and Variations on an Old French Carol, Four Reflections, Hommage to 1685, Toccata on a Theme of Martin Shaw, Grove's Dictionary of Music & Musicians (contrib); *Recreations* gardening, cooking, philately; *Style*— Miss Jennifer Bate; 35 Collingwood Ave, Muswell Hill, London N10 3EH (☎ 081 883 3811, fax 081 444 3695); Bureau de Concerts Maurice Werner, 7 Rue Richepance, 75008 Paris, France (☎ 010 331 40 15 92 80, fax 010 331 42 60 30 49)

BATE, Kenneth James (Ken); s of Maj Ernest James Bate, MBE, of Dudley, West Midlands, and Mary Joyce Adelaine, *née* Morgan (d 1970); *b* 20 June 1943; *Educ* Oldswinford Hosp Sch Stourbridge, Univ of Aston Birmingham (BSc, Dip Arch); *m* 26 Sept 1968, Susan Kay (d 1982), 2 s (Simon b 1972, Matthew b 1975); *Career* princ architect Wolverhampton Borough Cncl 1975-79, regnl architect Tarmac Construction Ltd 1979-84; ptnr: Quest Design Group, Quest Bloomer Tweedale (architects and town planners); memb Ordre des Architects France; memb RIBA 1976; *Recreations* sailing; *Style*— Kenneth J Bate, Esq; Quest Design Group, St Marks Chapel Ash, Wolverhampton, W Midlands WV3 0T2 (☎ 0902 714499, telex 35518 QUESA G)

BATE, Rex; OBE (1980); s of Ferdinand Bate (d 1958), of Solihull, and Kate Emeline, *née* Batchelor (d 1975); *b* 18 June 1911; *Educ* West Bridgford Sch, Univ of Loughborough; *m* 1937, Peggie, da of James Heron Watt (d 1955), of Ealing; 1 s (Richard), 2 da (Penelope, Sara); *Career* RE attached Indian Army 1940-45, served Burma Army and XIV Army in Burma, Lt-Col; chartered electrical and mechanical engr; dir: Brush Electrical Eng Co Ltd 1946-54, Enfield Cables Ltd 1954-58, Renold Ltd 1973-80 (md 1959-73); chm London Assoc for the Blind 1975-90; *Recreations* music, rowing, fishing, bridge; *Clubs* East India and Sports, Leander; *Style*— Rex Bate, Esq, OBE; The Dial House, Chobham, Surrey GU24 8NA (☎ 0276 858176)

BATE, Terence Charles; s of Harry James Bate (d 1975), of Preston, Lancs, and Annie Evelyn, *née* Gore (later Graffy); *b* 3 Oct 1930; *Educ* Hele's Sch Exeter, Univ of Liverpool (BVSc), Lancashire Poly (LLB); *m* 24 Feb 1961, Mary Evelyn, da of Capt Herbert Edgar Newth (d 1964); 2 s (Anthony John b 1961, Christopher David b 1962), 2 da (Carolyn Mary b 1964, Nicola Anne b 1967 d 1969); *Career* vet surgn; ptnr practice 1955-85, former vet advsr Assoc of DC's, vet surgn W Lancs DC 1979-85, asst chief vet offr RSPCA 1987-; former pt/t lectr: Manchester Poly, Lancs Coll of Agric; called to the Bar Lincoln's Inn 1986; memb: Cncl BVA 1978-, Cncl Vet Pub Health Assoc (former pres); Cert Dip AF; MRCVS; *Recreations* cycling, running, walking; *Clubs* Cyclists' Touring; *Style*— Terence C Bate, Esq; Lowden Lodge, Lowden Hill, Chippenham, Wilts SN15 2BT (☎ 0249 651385); RSPCA Headquarters, Causeway, Horsham, West Sussex RH12 1HG (☎ 0403 64181, fax 0403 41048)

BATE-WILLIAMS, John Robert Alexander; yr s of Maj Michael Thomas Jerome Bate-Williams, RA (ret), of Wootra Brook, Bindoon, Western Aust, and Rosemary Suzanne, *née* Bate (d 1979); *b* 25 Sept 1951; *Educ* private tuition, Whitefriars Sch, Stoke-on-Trent Coll of Building and Commerce, Univ of Wales (LLB); *m* 4 Aug 1984, Elizabeth Anne, da of Richard Lippiatt; 1 s (Rory b 1987), 1 da (Rosemary b 1989);

Career called to the Bar Inner Temple 1976; memb Hon Soc of Inner Temple 1976; *Recreations* travel, rowing, tennis; *Clubs* Jokers; *Style—* John Bate-Williams, Esq; 4 Swan Studios, 69 Deodar Rd, London, SW15 2NV (☎ 081 874 5739); Tie Cross Cottage, Murcott, Crudwell, nr Malmesbury, Wilts (☎ 06667 617); 1 Temple Gardens, Temple, London EC4Y 9BB (☎ 071 583 1315, fax 071 353 3969)

BATELY, Prof Janet Margaret; da of Maj Alfred William Bately, TD (d 1985), and Dorothy Maud, *née* Willis (d 1988); *b* 3 April 1932; *Educ* Somerville Coll Oxford (Dip Comparative Philology, MA); *m* 20 Aug 1964, Leslie John, s of John Summers (d 1965), of Bromley, Kent; 1 s (Michael b 23 Aug 1966); *Career* reader in engrg Birkbeck Coll Univ of London 1970-76 (asst lectr 1955-58, lectr 1958-69), head of Dept of English King's Coll London 1980- (prof 1977-); FKC 1986, FBA 1990; memb: cncl EETS 1980-, Advsy Ctee ISAS 1985-, Exec Ctee FONTES 1985-, Project Ctee SASLC 1987; *Books* The Old English Orosius (1980), The Anglo Saxon Chronicle: MSA (1986); *Recreations* music, gardening; *Style—* Prof Janet Bately; 86 Cawdor Cres, London W7 2DD (☎ 081 567 0486); King's College, University of London, Strand, London WC2 R2LS (☎ 071 873 2594)

BATEMAN, Barry Richard James; *b* 21 June 1945; *Educ* Univ of Exeter (BA); *m* Christine; 1 s (James b 1980); *Career* res dir Hoare Govett 1972-75 (investmt analyst 1967-72), mktg dir Datastream 1975-81, sr mktg dir Fidelity Int Mgmnt Ltd 1981-86, md Fidelity Investmt Servs Ltd 1986-; memb Soc of Investmt Analysts; *Recreations* photography, music, E Type Jaguars, writing; *Clubs* Jaguar Drivers; *Style—* Barry Bateman, Esq; High Trees, Pine Coombe, Shirley Hills, Croydon, Surrey CR0 5HS (☎ 081 656 8638); Fidelity Investment Services Ltd, Oakhill House, 130 Tonbridge Rd, Hildenborough, Tonbridge, Kent TN11 9DZ (☎ 0732 361 144, fax 0732 832 792, telex 957 344 FIMLO)

BATEMAN, Dr Christopher John Turner; s of Sir Geoffrey Hirst Bateman, of Thorney, Graffham, W Sussex, and Lady Margaret Bateman; *b* 3 June 1937; *Educ* Marlborough, Univ Coll Oxford (MA, BM Bch), St Thomas's Hosp Med Sch; *m* 1, 1961, Hilary (d 1984), da of James Stirk, of Worcester; 1 s (Alastair b 1963), 2 da (Jennifer b 1964, Caroline b 1966); m 2, 1986, Joan Valerie, da of Dr J Cann, of Southampton; *Career* conslt haematologist: Chichester Health Authy 1973, King Edward VII Hosp Midhurst; vice chm St Wilfrids Hospice Chichester; Freeman City of London 1961, Asst Worshipful Co of Haberdashers; FRCPath 1982; *Recreations* fishing, tennis, golf, shooting; *Style—* Dr Christopher Bateman; Waterleas, West Ashling, Chichester, W Sussex PO18 9LE; St Richards Hospital, Chichester PO19 4SE (☎ 0243 788 122, ext 706)

BATEMAN, Cynthia (Mrs Norman Livesey); da of Harry Bateman (d 1985), of Eccleton, Chorley, Lancs, and Bessie, *née* Gray; *b* 24 April 1940; *Educ* Ormskirk GS; *m* 5 Oct 1963, Norman Livesey; *Career* French translator Leyland motors Ltd 1959-63; Lancashire Evening Post 1960-76 (news reporter, feature writer, travel ed, news ed); sports writer (specialising in professional soccer) The Guardian 1988- (feature writer and sub ed Manchester office 1976-88); awarded: Willie Clissett Prize for Newspaper Practice Nat Cncl for Trg of Journalists 1963, Thomson Travel Award 1969, IPC Press Award commendation 1969; hon memb 12 LI RA; memb RSPCA; *Recreations* travel, walking (English setter), tennis, sailing, racing pigeons; *Clubs* Western Isles Yacht; *Style—* Ms Cynthia Bateman; The Guardian, 119 Farringdon Road, London EC1R 3ER (☎ 071 278 2332)

BATEMAN, Derek; s of Thomas Bateman, of Ellesmere Port, and Millicent, *née* Blackburn; *b* 8 Feb 1949; *Educ* Stanney Secdy Modern Tech Sch; *m* 5 Aug 1978, Jenny, da of Samuel Howarth (d 1986), of Gateshead, Tyne and Wear; 4 step s (Hilton b 1960, Sean b 1965, Wayne b 1967, Craig b 1971), 1 step da (Jaqualine b 1962); *Career* engr Vauxhall Motors 1965-70, machinist and fitter Vauxhall 1970-82; elected: borough cncllr Ellesmere Port and Neston 1974-78, cncllr 1977- (dep ldr Cncl and chm Strategic Planning and Transportation Ctee); chm: Manchester Ship Canal Steering Ctee, Nat Public Tport Forum; vice chm: Assoc of CCs Planning and Tport Ctee and Sub Ctee 1987-88; *Recreations* Lab Pty; *Style—* Derek Bateman, Esq; 168 Cambridge Rd, Ellesmere Port, Cheshire (☎ 051 355 6575); County Hall, Chester (☎ 0244 602 194, fax 0244 603 800)

BATEMAN, Derek Walls; s of David Charteris Graham Bateman, of Selkirk, and Mary Ann, *née* Walls; *b* 10 May 1951; *Educ* Selkirk HS, Edinburgh Coll of Commerce; *m* 11 Nov 1972, Alison, *née* Edgar; 2 da (Eilidh b 24 March 1975, Lucy b 11 Nov 1978); *Career* trainee journalist Scotsman Publications 1968-71; reporter: Edinburgh Evening News 1971-73, Glasgow Herald 1973-86; reporter and presenter BBC TV (Scotland) 1986-88, political ed Scotland on Sunday 1988-; currently contrib: Sky TV, Scottish TV, Radio Clyde, Radio Scotland; currently advsr On The Record BBC TV; finalist Young Journalist of the Year Edinburgh Evening News 1973, runner-up Reporter of the Year Glasgow Herald 1986; memb: Selkirk Merchant Co, NUJ 1968; *Books* Unfriendly Games (with Derek Douglas, 1986); *Recreations* golf, rugby union, reading; *Clubs* Dunbar Golf; *Style—* Derek Bateman, Esq; Ty Mawr, Boggs Farm Steading, Pencaitland, Tranent, East Lothian EH34 5BD (☎ 0875 340 538); Scotsman Publications, 20 North Bridge, Edinburgh EH1 1YT (☎ 031 243 3590, car 0860 796792)

BATEMAN, Sir Geoffrey Hirst; s of Dr William Hirst Bateman, JP (d 1959), of Rochdale, Lancs, and Ethel Jane, *née* Scrimgeour (d 1964); bro of Sir Ralph Melton Bateman, *qv*; *b* 24 Oct 1906; *Educ* Epsom Coll, Univ Coll Oxford; *m* 1931, Margaret, da of Sir Samuel Turner (d 1955); 3 s, 1 da; *Career* surgn St Thomas's 1938-71; memb Cncl Royal Coll of Surgeons 1963-67; kt 1972; *Recreations* golf, fishing; *Style—* Sir Geoffrey Bateman; Thorney, Graffham, Petworth, W Sussex GU28 0QA (☎ 079 86314)

BATEMAN, Col Giles Barthrop; OBE (1982); s of Sqdn Ldr Anthony Edward Barthrop Bateman (d 1970), and Dorothea May Pryce, *née* Aspinall (d 1973); *b* 10 Jan 1939; *Educ* Sutton Valence, Staff Coll, Nat Def Coll; *m* 31 Dec 1966, Susan Jennifer (Sue), da of Robert Ben Chalcraft, of Greenford, Middlesex; 2 s (Noel Christopher Barthrop b 1969, Alexander James Barthrop (Alex) b 1972); *Career* cmmnd Queen's Own Royal W Kent Regt 1958; regtl and staff posts incl: England and Cyprus 1958, Kenya 1961, Br Guiana 1964, Singapore 1965-67, Bahrain 1968, NI 1969 and 1975, Aust 1976-78; Sch of Serv Intelligence 1982-85, MOD Def Intelligence and Gen Staff posts 1985-90; *Recreations* gardening, music, books; *Clubs* Royal Cwlth Soc; *Style—* Col Giles Bateman, OBE; c/o Lloyds Bank, Hawkhurst, Kent; MOD, Main Building, Whitehall Ave, London SW1 (☎ 071 218 6789)

BATEMAN, Dr Nigel Turner; s of Sir Geoffrey Hirst Bateman, *qv* and Lady Margaret, *née* Turner; *b* 3 April 1943; *Educ* Marlborough, Univ Coll Oxford, St Thomas' Hosp (BM BCh, MRCP); *m* 10 Dec 1966, Susannah Christian, da of Cdr A Denis Bulman, of The Old Manse, Midlem, by Selkirk, Scotland; 4 s (Thomas Andrew b 1969, Patrick Edward b 1971, Colin David b 1972, Michael Geoffrey b 1981); *Career* War Memorial scholarship Univ Coll Oxford 1962, assoc prof preventive med Univ of Wisconsin 1978-79, conslt physician St Thomas' Hosp 1980-; Liveryman Worshipful Soc of Apothecaries 1985, Freeman City of London 1985; FRCP 1985; *Books* Respiratory Disorders (with IR Cameron, 1983); *Recreations* tennis, golf, fishing, hill walking; *Style—* Dr Nigel Bateman; St Thomas' Hospital, London SE1 7EH (☎ 071 928 9292)

BATEMAN, Paul Terence; s of Nelson John Bateman (d 1984), and Frances Ellen, *née* Johnston; *b* 28 April 1946; *Educ* Westcliff HS, Univ of Leicester (BSc); *m* 18 Jan 1970, Moira; 2 s (Michael b 1973, Timothy b 1977); *Career* Save and Prosper Gp Ltd 1967-: graduate in secretarial dept 1967-68, asst to gp actuary 1968-73, mktg mangr 1973-75, gp mktg mangr 1975-80, gp mktg and devpt mangr 1980-81, exec dir mktg and devpt 1981-88, chief exec 1988-; exec dir Robert Fleming Holdings Ltd 1988-, dir Lautro Ltd 1988-; chm bd of govrs Westcliff HS for Boys; *Recreations* yachting, squash; *Clubs* Royal Burnham Yacht; *Style—* Paul Bateman, Esq; 25 Plymtree, Thorpe Bay, Essex SS1 3RA (☎ 0702 587152); Save and Prosper Group Ltd, 1 Finsbury Ave, London EC2M 2QY (☎ 071 588 1717, fax 071 247 5006, telex 883838 SAVPRO G)

BATEMAN, Peter Tremellen Campion; s of Capt Geoffrey Campion Bateman, of Ladymead, Flower Walk, Guildford, and Margery Prudence, *née* Tremellen (d 1985); *b* 12 June 1928; *Educ* Clifton, Hertford Coll Oxford (MA); *m* 1 May 1954, Janet Katherine, da of Capt Ernest Hyatt Box (d 1953), of Guildford; 2 s (Nicholas Peter b 1955, Dominic Charles b 1960), 1 da (Anna Katherine b 1958); *Career* Nat Serv RASC 1947-49, 2 Lt 1948; md GC Bateman Ltd (family co of Ophthalmic Opticians) 1975- (dir 1954); chm: Soc of Opticians 1968-70, Optical Info Cncl 1987-88; capt Hertford Coll RUFC 1951, memb Guildford Round Table 1952-64; Freeman City of London, Liveryman Worshipful Co of Spectacle Makers 1971; *Recreations* skiing, swimming, photography, oil painting; *Style—* Peter Bateman, Esq; Holly House, Goose Rye Rd, Worplesdon, Surrey (☎ 0483 232 636); The Hallams, Littleford Lane, Shamley Green, Guildford, Surrey GU5 0RH (☎ 0483 893 933)

BATEMAN, Sir Ralph (Melton); KBE (1975); 3 s of Dr William Hirst Bateman, JP (d 1959), of Rochdale, Lancs, and Ethel Jane, *née* Scrimgeour (d 1964); bro of Sir Geoffrey Hirst Bateman, *qv*; *b* 15 May 1910; *Educ* Epsom Coll, Univ Coll Oxford (MA); *m* 1935, Barbara Yvonne, 2 da of Herbert Percy Litton (d 1939), of Heywood, Lancs; 2 s, 2 da; *Career* chm Stothert and Pitt 1977-85; dep chm: Rea Bros 1979-85 (dir 1977-), Furness Withy 1979-84 (dir 1977-84); former chm Turner and Newall plc; pres Confedn of Br Indust 1974-1976, former dep chm Crosby Woodfield, vice pres and former chm of govrs Ashridge Coll of Mgmnt, former chm of Cncl Buckingham Univ, Adm Waco Fleet Texas Navy USA; hon fell Univ of Manchester Inst of Sci and Technol; Freeman City of Waco Texas USA; Hon DSc: Univ of Salford, Univ of Buckingham; FCIS, CBIM, FRSA, FIOD; *Style—* Sir Ralph Bateman, KBE; 2 Bollin Court, Macclesfield Rd, Wilmslow, Cheshire SK9 2AP

BATEMAN, Richard Harrison; s of Herbert F A Bateman, of Southborough, Kent, and Minnie, *née* Harrison (d 1986); *b* 21 April 1945; *Educ* Hampton Sch; *m* 1 April 1967, Maureen Winifred, da of Michael Devaney; 1 s (Stephen Harrison b 7 April 1968), 1 da (Kate Mary b 12 May 1970); *Career* with Coutts & Co 1963-67, Charles Fulton & Co (Int Money Brokers) 1967-70, Kirkland Whittaker Gp Ltd 1970- (dir 1978-); chm London Subsidiaries: KW (Foreign Exchange) Ltd, KW (Sterling) Ltd, KW (Currency Deposits) Ltd 1986-; England rugby football trials 1966; *Recreations* sports, metaphysical poetry; *Clubs* Richmond RFC; *Style—* Richard Bateman Esq; Kirkland Whittaker Group Ltd, 76-80 Great Eastern Street, London EC2A 3JL (☎ 071 739 0099, fax 071 739 7629, telex 894710)

BATES, Alan Arthur; s of Harold Arthur Bates (d 1976), of Bank House, Bradbourne, Derbyshire, and Florence Mary, *née* Wheatcroft; *b* 17 Feb 1934; *Educ* Herbert Strutt GS Belper Derbys, RADA; *m* 1970, Victoria Valerie, da of Roland Ward (d 1980); 2 s (Tristan b Nov 1970 d 1990, Benedick (twin) b Nov 1970); *Career* RAF 1952-54; actor; Theatre: English Stage Co (Royal Court Theatre London): The Mulberry Bush, Cards of Identity, Look Back in Anger, The Country Wife, In Celebration; West End: Long Day's Journey into Night, The Caretaker, The Four Seasons, Hamlet; Butley (London and NY) (Evening Standard Best Actor Award 1972, Antoinette Perry Best Actor Award 1973), Poor Richard (NY), Richard III and The Merry Wives of Windsor (Stratford, Ontario), Venice Preserved (Bristol, Old Vic), Taming of the Shrew (Stratford-on-Avon) 1973, Life Class 1974, Otherwise Engaged (Queen's) 1975 (Variety Club of GB Best Stage Award 1975), The Seagull (Duke of York's) 1976, Stage Struck (Vaudeville) 1979, A Patriot for Me (Chichester, Haymarket) 1983, Victoria Station and One for the Road (Lyric Studio) 1984, The Dance of Death (Riverside Studios Hammersmith) 1985, Yonadab (NT) 1985, Melon (Haymarket) 1987, Much Ado About Nothing and Ivanov (double bill at Strand Theatre 1989); Films: The Entertainer, Whistle Down the Wind, A Kind of Loving, The Running Man, The Caretaker, Zorba the Greek, Nothing but the Best, Georgie Girl, King of Hearts, Far from the Madding Crowd, The Fixer (Oscar Nomination), Women in Love, The Three Sisters, A Day in the Death of Joe Egg, The Go-Between, Second Best (prodr), Impossible Object, Butley, In Celebration, Royal Flash, An Unmarried Woman, The Shout, The Rose, Nijinsky, Quartett, The Return of the Soldier, The Wicked Lady, Duet for One, Prayer for the Dying, Pack of Lies, We think the World of You, Mr Frost, Dr M, Hamlet 1990, Shuttlecock 1990; Television: Plaintiff and Defendant, Two Sundays, The Collection 1977, The Mayor of Casterbridge 1978, Very Like a Whale, The Trespasser 1980, A Voyage Round My Father, Separate Tables, An Englishman Abroad 1983 (BAFTA Best TV Actor award 1984), Dr Fisher of Geneva 1984, The Dog It Was That Died 1988, 102 Boulevard Haussmann 1990; *Recreations* driving, swimming, riding; *Style—* Alan Bates, Esq; c/o Chatto & Linnit, Prince of Wales Theatre, Coventry St, London W1 (☎ 071 930 6677)

BATES, Allan Frederick; CMG (1958); s of John Frederick Lawes Bates (d 1953), of Plumstead, London, and Ethel Hannah, *née* Potter (d 1958); *b* 15 July 1911; *Educ* Woolwich Central Sch, Univ of London, Open Univ (BA); *m* 1937, Ena Edith, da of John Richard Boxall (d 1944), of Charlton, London; 3 s; *Career* fin sec: Cyprus 1952-60, Mauritius 1960-64; CA 1959-; md Devpt Bank Mauritius 1964-70; IMF fin advsr: Bahamas Govt 1971-74, Lesotho 1971-74; accounts advsr Belize 1982-; *Recreations* painting, carving; *Clubs* Royal Cwlth Soc, IOD; *Style—* Allan Bates, Esq, CMG; 5 Redford Ave, Coulsdon, Surrey (☎ 081 660 7421)

BATES, Christopher; s of Alan Douglas Bates, of Gedling, Nottingham, and Alma, *née* Atkins; *b* 10 Oct 1962; *Educ* Carlton Le Willows Sch Gedling Nottingham; *Career* oarsman; Newark Rowing Club 1973-81, Nottingham Boat Club and Notts County Rowing Assoc 1981-; 38 caps England and GB 1983-; Nat Championships: represented Newark 1980, Silver medal lightweight coxless fours 1982, Gold medal 1983, 1984, 1988 (2), 1990 (2), Silver medal 1985; medals won at int events: 4 Gold Henley Royal Regatta, Gold Tokyo Henley, 2 Gold 2 Silver 1 Bronze unofficial Euro Championships Lucerne, Gold Cwlth Games 1986; also World Championships: Silver 1983, 1986 and 1987, Bronze 1984 and 1990; records: Lightweight four 1986 Cwlth Games, Ladies Plate Henley Royal Regatta 1989, world lightweight eight 1990; employed in family firm; *Recreations* motor boats, classic sports cars; *Style—* Christopher Bates, Esq; 2 St Ervan Rd, Wilford, Nottingham NG11 7BU (☎ 0602 818727); Nottinghamshire County Rowing Association, National Water Sports Centre, Nottingham (☎ 0602 821212)

BATES, Prof Colin Arthur; s of Ralph Mehew Bates (d 1965), and Annie Kathleen, *née* Cooper; *b* 7 May 1935; *Educ* City of Norwich Sch, Univ of Nottingham (BSc, PhD); *m* 29 July 1961, Margaret, da of Edmund Green, of Nottingham; 2 s (Julian Michael b 1967, Richard Daniel b 1971), 1 da (Karen Nicola (Mrs Eden) b 1965);

Career sr res asst Stanford Univ California USA 1961; Univ of Nottingham: demonstrator 1958, research assoc 1959, lectr in physics 1962, sr lectr in physics 1970, reader in theoretical physics 1974, prof 1984, prof and head of dept 1987-; FInstP, CPhys; *Books* various scientific articles; *Recreations* aquarist, sport, garden; *Style*— Prof Colin Bates; 26 Lime Grove Ave, Chilwell, Nottingham NG9 4AR (☎ 0602 255568); Physics Dept, The University, Nottingham, NG7 2RD (☎ 0602 484848 ext 2828, fax 0602 229792, telex 37345 UNINOT G)

BATES, Air Vice-Marshal David Frank; CB (1983); s of S F Bates (d 1977), and N A Bates, *née* Story; *b* 10 April 1928; *Educ* RAF Coll Cranwell; *m* 1954, Margaret Winifred, *née* Biles; 1 s, 1 da; *Career* RAF: Station Cdr Uxbridge 1974-75, dir of Personnel Ground 1975-76, dir Personnel Mgmnt (ADP) 1976-79, air offr admin HQ RAF Support Cmd 1979-82; bursar of Warwick Sch 1983-85; *Recreations* cricket, most sports, gardening, model railways; *Clubs* RAF, MCC; *Style*— Air Vice-Marshal David Bates, CB; c/o Lloyds Bank Ltd, 73 Parade, Leamington Spa, Warwickshire CV32 4BB

BATES, Sir David Robert; s of Walter Vivian Bates (d 1937), of Co Tyrone, and Mary Olive Bates; *b* 18 Nov 1916; *Educ* Royal Belfast Academical Inst, Queen's Univ Belfast, UCL; *m* 1956, Barbara, da of Joseph Bailey, DSO, of Qld; 1 s, 1 da; *Career* Queen's Univ Belfast: prof of theoretical physics 1968-73, res prof 1973-83, emeritus prof 1983-; Smithsonian Regent's fell Harvard-Smithsonian Center for Astrophysic 1983-84; FRS; kt 1978; *Recreations* reading (history, biography); *Style*— Sir David Bates, FRS; 1 Newforge Grange, Belfast BT9 5QB (☎ 0232 665640)

BATES, Sir (John) Dawson; 2 Bt (UK 1937), MC (1943); s of Rt Hon Sir Dawson Bates, 1 Bt, OBE (d 1949), and Muriel (d 1972), da of Sir Charles Cleland, KBE, MVO; *b* 21 Sept 1921; *Educ* Winchester, Balliol Coll Oxford; *m* 30 April 1953, Mary Murray, da of late Lt-Col Joseph Murray Hoult, RA, of Norton Place, Lincoln; 2 s, 1 da; *Heir* s, Richard Dawson Hoult Bates b 12 May 1956; *Career* WWII Maj Rifle Brigade; regnl dir Nat Tst, ret; FRICS; *Style*— Sir Dawson Bates, Bt, MC; Butleigh House, Butleigh, Glastonbury, Somerset

BATES, Edward Robert; s and h of Sir Geoffrey Bates, 5 Bt, MC; *b* 4 July 1946; *Educ* Gordonstoun; *Style*— Edward Bates, Esq; Gyrn Castle, Llanasa, Holywell, Clwyd (☎ 074 585 3500)

BATES, Sir Geoffrey Voltelin; 5 Bt (UK 1880), MC (1942); o s of Maj Cecil Robert Bates, DSO, MC (d 1935), and Hylda Madeleine (d 1960), da of Sir James Heath, 1 Bt; suc (1946) unc, Sir Percy Bates, 4 Bt, GBE; *b* 2 Oct 1921; *Educ* Radley; *m* 1, 12 July 1945, Kitty (d 1956), da of Ernest Kendall-Lane, of Saskatchewan; 2 s; m 2, 31 July 1957, Hon Olivia Gwyneth Zoë FitzRoy (d 1969), da of 2 Visc Daventry; 1 da (and 1 da decd); m 3, 1971, Mrs Juliet Eleanor Hugolyn Whitelocke-Winter, da of late Cdr G Whitelocke, RN, and wid of Edward Winter; *Heir* s, Edward Bates; *Career* High Sheriff Flintshire 1969, Maj (ret) Cheshire Yeomanry; *Recreations* hunting, shooting, fishing; *Style*— Sir Geoffrey Bates, Bt, MC; Gyrn Castle, Llanasa, Holywell, Clwyd (☎ 0745 853500)

BATES, (Michael) Jeremy; s of Samuel Bates, of Solihull, West Midlands, and Marjorie, *née* Bourne; *b* 19 June 1962; *Educ* Strodes GS, Tudor Grange Comp Sch Solihull, Solihull Sixth Form Coll; *Career* tennis player; turned professional 1980; nat champion: under 12 1974, under 18 1979 and 1980, sr 1985, 1988, 1990; county champion various levels 1973-80; represented GB: int events at various levels, Galea Cup, Euro Youth Championships, Coupe Jean Beeker, Kings Cup 1980-84, Euro Cup 1985-90, Davis Cup 1984-90; achievements incl: mixed doubles champion Wimbledon 1987, mens doubles runner-up Aust Open 1988, doubles champion Queens Club 1990, mixed doubles champion Aust Open 1991 (semi-finalist mens doubles); Br number one 1988; various LTA awards incl Sr Player of the Year; *Recreations* golf, guitar, karate; *Style*— Jeremy Bates, Esq; Pier House, Strand on the Green, Chiswick, London (☎ 081 994 1444)

BATES, John Fielding; s of Arnold Fielding Bates, OBE (d 1961), of Sheffield, and Winifred Margaret, *née* Crosland (d 1965); *b* 11 May 1925; *Educ* Trent Coll, Kings Coll Cambridge, Rotherham Tech Coll, City Poly London (BSc); *m* 31 July 1954, Joan, da of John Elliott (d 1976), of Sheffield; 3 s (Martin b 1957, James b 1960, Timothy b 1964); *Career* RAF 1943-47 (PO 1 Offr Air Sea Rescue 1945-46, FO Personnel Offr HQ Med Cairo, AHQ Malta, HQ 90 Gp Medmenham 1946-47), released 1947; asst engr Charles Brand and Son 1952-57, res engr E Middlesex Main Drainage for J D and D M Watson (later Watson Hawksley) 1957-64 (ptnr 1969-85, sr conslt 1985-); FICE 1971, MConsE 1973; *Recreations* sailing, boating; *Style*— John F Bates, Esq; 17 Marlow Mill, Mill Rd, Marlow, Bucks, SL7 1QD (☎ 06284 867108); Watson Hawksley, Terriers House, Amersham Rd, High Wycombe, Bucks HP13 5AS (☎ 0494 26240, fax 0494 22074, telex 83439 WATSON G)

BATES, Maj-Gen Sir (Edward) John Hunter; KBE (1969, OBE 1952), CB (1965), MC (1944); s of Ernest Bates (d 1954), of Bournemouth; *b* 5 Dec 1911; *Educ* Wellington, Corpus Christi Coll Cambridge (MA); *m* 1947, Sheila Ann, da of Maj Herbert Norman (d 1962), of Victoria, BC, Canada; 2 s, 2 da; *Career* dir RA WO 1961-64, Cmdt RMCS 1964-67, Col Cmdt RA 1966-76, dir Royal Def Acad 1967-69, Special Cmmr Duke of York's Royal Mil Sch 1972-; personnel dir Thomson Regnl Newspapers 1969-78, master Worshipful Co of Haberdashers 1978-79; *Recreations* fishing, shooting; *Clubs* Army and Navy, Rye Golf; *Style*— Maj-Gen Sir John Bates, KBE, CB, MC; Chaffenden, Frensham Rd, Rolvenden Layne, Cranbrook, Kent TN17 4NP (☎ 0580 241 536)

BATES, Lilian Marie-Adrienne; *née* Loir; da of Dr Adrien-Charles Loir (d 1941), of Paris, and Helene Catherine, *née* de Montes (d 1946); *b* 7 Nov 1908; *Educ* Cours du Parc Monceau Paris, Faculte de Medecine Paris (MD, DPH); *m* 7 March 1934, Ralph Marshall Bates, OBE, s of William Bates (d 1945), of Saltash, Cornwall; 1 s (Ralph), 2 da (Liliane, Elisabeth); *Career* med asst Miny of Health Paris 1933-34, sr med offr (mental health) Essex CC 1948-60; conslt psychiatrist: NE Essex Health Authy 1960-81, NE Met Regnl Hosp Bd 1952-68; life memb Assoc Francaise pour l'Avancement des Sciences 1930-; MRCPsych 1971, memb BMA 1948; *Books* Notions de Droit Administratif a l'Usage du Medecin Fonctionnaire d'Hygiene (1933); *Recreations* playing the harp, gardening (especially growing vegetables); *Clubs* English Speaking Union; *Style*— Dr Lilian Bates; 66 North Rd, Highgate Village, London N6 4AA (☎ 081 348 1376)

BATES, Malcolm Rowland; s of late Rowland Bates, of Waterlooville, Hants; *b* 23 Sept 1934; *Educ* Portsmouth GS, Univ of Warwick, Harvard Grad Sch of Business Admin; *m* 1960, Lynda, da of Maurice Price, of Bristol; 3 da; *Career* jt md Wm Brandt's & Sons 1972-75; chm: Picker International Inc, A B Dick Inc, GEC Inc, GEC Alsthorm NV, Eurolec NV, GPT Ltd, General Domestic Appliances Ltd, Associated Electrical Industries Ltd, Eng Electric Co Ltd; dep md GEC plc 1985-; *Recreations* classical music, reading, tennis; *Style*— Malcolm Bates, Esq; Mulberry Close, Croft Rd, Goring-on-Thames, Oxon RG8 9ES (☎ 0491 872214)

BATES, Hon Mrs (Margaret Eleanor); *née* Shepherd; o da of 1 Baron Shepherd, PC; *b* 14 Feb 1922; *m* 1949, Theodore Leonard Bates, s of late Theodore Leonard Bates, of 95 North Street, NW8; 1 s (Andrew Michael b 1952), 1 da (Suzanne Katherine Michèle b 1960); *Style*— The Hon Mrs Bates; 3 Victoria Cottages, Lydiate Lane, Lynton, N Devon

BATES, Peter Edward Gascoigne; CBE (1987); s of James Edward Bates (d 1952), and Esme Grace Gascoigne, *née* Roy (d 1960); *b* 6 Aug 1924; *Educ* Kingston GS, SOAS Univ of London, Lincoln Coll Oxford; *m* 15 Dec 1947, Jean Irene Hearn, da of Brig W Campbell Grant, MC, RA (d 1966); 2 s (Jeremy b 3 March 1949, Nigel b 23 Feb 1953), 1 da (Deborah b 13 Feb 1957); *Career* cmmnd Intelligence Corps 1944, serv India, Burma, Malaya, Japan 1944-46, released 1946 with rank of Capt; Malayan Civil Serv 1947-55, Rolls-Royce Ltd 1955-57, Bristol Aircraft Ltd (later British Aircraft Corpn) 1957-64; Plessey Co plc (formerly Ltd): gen mangr Plessey Radar 1967-71 (md Radar Div 1971-76), dep chm Plessey Electronic Systems Ltd 1976-86; dir General Technology Systems Ltd 1986-, chm BDMI Ltd 1986-; memb: Cncl Electronic Engrg Assoc 1973-85 (pres 1976), Cncl SBAC 1978-86 (pres 1983-84), Br Overseas Trade Bd 1984-87; FRSA 1988; *Recreations* golf, theatre, gardening; *Clubs* Army and Navy, Royal Wimbledon Golf; *Style*— Peter Bates, Esq, CBE; 12 Lindisfarne Rd, Wimbledon, London SW20 0NW (☎ 081 946 0345); General Technology Systems, Brunel Science Park, Kingston Lane, Uxbridge UB8 3PQ (☎ 0895 56767, fax 0895 32078, telex 295 607 GENTEL G)

BATES, Peter Francis; s of Lt-Col Charles Donald Bates (d 1979), and Gladys Elizabeth, *née* Wilson; *b* 12 Aug 1934; *Educ* Friends Sch Lisburn NI, Royal GS Lancaster, Gonville and Caius Coll Cambridge (MB, BA, MB BChir), St Mary's Hosp London; *m* 1, Aug 1964 (m dis 1970), Cynthia Joan, da of Leslie Herbert Trace, of Twickenham, Middx; m 2, June 1971 (m dis 1980), Maggie, da of Bernard Wright; *Career* W Middx Hosp 1961-64, surgical registrar Hillingdon Hosp 1965-68; hon tutor: Royal Coll of Surgeons 1974-83, Guy's Hosp 1981; conslt gen surgn Dartford and Gravesham Health Dist 1974-; memb: Hosp Conslt Specialists Assoc, Br Assoc of Surgical Oncology, Euro Soc of Oncology, Br Soc of Gastroenterology, Br Assoc of Surgns of GB and Ireland, Br Computer Assoc, World Medical Assoc; Freeman: Guild of the City of London 1988-, City of London 1983; memb Worshipful Co of Apothecaries 1983 (memb Cncl 1990); FRCSI 1967, FRCS 1969; *Recreations* theatre, skiing, books, collecting pictures, sculpture; *Clubs* Oxford and Cambridge, Arts, Wig and Pen, Rugby, Livery; *Style*— Peter F Bates, Esq; 1 River Court, 82 St George's Square, London SW1V 3QX (☎ 071 821 0768); 144 Harley St, London W1 (☎ 071 935 0023, Voice Bank 0426911205)

BATES, Robert Alexander; s of Richard William Bates, of Haywards Heath, Sussex, and Barbara Joan, *née* Gully (d 1990); *b* 20 Sept 1941; *Educ* Emanuel Sch; *m* 1966, Susan Margaret, da of Geoffrey; 1 s (Richard Alexander b 1970), 1 da (Emma Lucy b 1967); *Career* CA 1965; ptnr Moore Stephens 1971- (articled clerk 1959-64); Freeman of the City of London; *Recreations* reading, golf, gardening; *Style*— Robert Bates, Esq; Moore Stephens, St Paul's House, Warwick Lane, London EC4P 4BN (☎ 071 248 4499)

BATES, Stewart Taverner; QC (1970); s of John Bates (d 1946), of Greenock; *b* 17 Dec 1926; *Educ* St Andrews Univ, CCC Oxford; *m* 1950, Anne Patricia, da of David West, of Pinner; 2 s, 4 da; *Career* barr 1954, memb Bar Cncl 1962-66; recorder 1981-; *Style*— Stewart Bates, Esq, QC; The Grange, Horsington, Templecombe, Somerset (☎ 0963 0521)

BATES, Dr Thelma Dorothy; da of William Cyril Johnson (d 1970), and Dorothy Florence, *née* Proudman (d 1986); *b* 18 Aug 1929; *Educ* Orme Girls Sch Staffs, Univ of Birmingham (MB ChB); *m* 23 July 1960, (Sidney Edward) Mills Bates; 2 s (Richard b 1963, Charles b 1964), 1 da (Anne b 1961); *Career* conslt radiotherapist and oncologist St Thomas' Hosp 1968-, dir SE London Radiotherapy Centre 1986-, conslt oncologist St Christopher's Hospice; vice pres Royal Coll of Radiologists 1988-, memb GMC 1989-; FRACR, FRCR, FRSA 1986, memb RSM; *Recreations* art collector; *Style*— Dr Thelma Bates; Saxonwood, Albany Cl, Blackhills, Esher, Surrey KT10 9JR (☎ 0372 464851); St Thomas' Hosp, Dept of Radiotherapy and Oncology, London SE1 7EH (☎ 071 922 8030)

BATES, William Paul Norman; s of Maj-Gen Sir John Bates, KBE, CB, MC, of Rolvenden, Kent, and Sheila Ann, *née* Norman; *b* 29 Oct 1953; *Educ* Stonyhurst, UCL (BSc, DipArch); *m* 29 Sept 1979, Carolyn Anne Lothian, da of William Patrick Lothian Nicholson (d 1972); 1 s (Robert b 1988), 2 da (Fenella b 1982, Annabel b 1985); *Career* architect RIBA 1980, formed own practice 1984, dir Scorpio Estates Ltd 1986-; Liveryman Worshipful Co of Haberdashers; *Recreations* skiing, golf, family; *Clubs* MCC; *Style*— William Bates, Esq; Martins Farm Oast, Collier St, nr Tonbridge, Kent TN12 9SD (☎ 089 273 602)

BATESON, Alec John; s of Rear Adm Stuart Latham Bateson, CB, CBE, DL (d 1980), of Pine's Nook, Ridlington, nr Uppingham, Rutland, and Marie Elphinstone Fleming, *née* Cullen (d 1985); *b* 23 Jan 1925; *Educ* Rugby, Trinity Coll Oxford (scholar elect); *m* 1, 3 June 1950, (Alice) Barbara (d 1985), da of (Alexander) Comrie Cowan, MC (d 1937), of 5 St Petersburg Place, London W2; 2 s (David Stuart b 1955, Hugh Comrie b 1957), 1 da (Julia Mary (Mrs Robert Langton) b 1951); m 2, 11 Oct 1986, (Isabel) Phillippa, da of Albert Cyril Sharwood (d 1978), widow of Douglas James Roper Austin (d 1979); *Career* The Rifle Bde 1943-1947, HQ 6 Airlanding Bde, 1 Para Bde in Palestine 1945-47, Capt 1946; admitted slr Lincoln's Inn 1950; Trower Still & Keeling 1947-87 (ptnr 1955-), Hamlins Grammer & Hamlins 1970-86 (sr ptnr), Trowers & Hamlins 1987-90 (conslt 1990-); memb: The Lowtonian Soc 1973-90, Slrs Disciplinary Tbnl 1975-, Cncl Queen's Nursing Inst 1986-; pres Holborn Law Soc 1978-79 (ctee memb 1969-82), tstee Herts Nursing Tst 1985-; memb Law Soc 1950-; *Recreations* reading, travel; *Clubs* Law Soc, Inst of Dir; *Style*— Alec J Bateson, Esq; Bradley Springs, Codicote, Nr Hitchin, Herts SG4 8TH; Trowers & Hamlins, 6 New Sq, Lincolns Inn, London, WC2A 3RP (☎ 071 831 6292, fax 071 831 8700)

BATESON, Fergus Dingwall; s of Owen Latham Bateson, KC (d 1947), of Penrose, Kings Rd, Berkhamsted, Herts, and Eileen Mary Havelock, *née* Collins (d 1965); *b* 26 April 1930; *Educ* Westminster, Hertford Coll Oxford (BA); *m* 11 April 1957, Ann Margaret, da of Dr Jared Totten (d 1959), of Lochnell, Northchurch, Berkhamsted, Herts; 3 s (James b 1961, Alexander b 1962, Charles b 1965), 1 da (Lucinda b 1960); *Career* admitted slr 1956; sr ptnr Thomas Cooper and Stibbard 1990- (ptnr 1959, sr ptnr 1986-1990), London corr Europe Magazine 1990-; chm CPC Ctee C Party Eastern Area 1967-70, memb Runciman Advsy Ctee On Historic Wreck Sites 1974-, tstee Nautical Museums Tst 1983-; Liveryman Worshipful Co of Solicitors 1970, Freeman City of London 1970; memb Law Soc; *Books* Digest of Commercial Laws of the World (contrib 1966); *Recreations* amateur theatre, bridge; *Clubs* Mitre; *Style*— Fergus Bateson, Esq; 18 Fishpool St, St Albans, Herts AL3 4RT (☎ 0727 59340); Thomas Cooper & Stibbard, 52 Leadenhall St, London EC3A 2DJ (☎ 071 481 8851, fax 071 480 6097, telex 886334)

BATESON, John Swinburne; s of William Swinburne Bateson (d 1970), and Kathryn Urquart, *née* Lyttle; *b* 11 Jan 1942; *Educ* Appleby GS, Lancaster Royal GS; *m* 30 Jan 1964, Jean Vivien, da of Robert Forsyth (d 1977); 1 s (John William Swinburne b 1972), 2 da (Kathryn Ann b 1967, Janet Mary b 1969); *Career* dir: Fairclough Construction Group plc 1980-82, Batesons Hotels (1958) Ltd; chief exec AMEC plc 1988- (dir 1982-88); *Recreations* gardening, chess, light aviation, golf; *Clubs* Blackpool and Fylde Aero; *Style*— John Bateson, Esq; Clayton Croft, Ribchester Rd, Clayton-le-Dale, Blackburn, Lancashire (☎ 0254 40748); AMEC plc, Sandiway House, Northwich, Cheshire, CW8 2YA (☎ 0606 883885, telex 669708)

BATESON, Lynne; *b* 16 Aug 1952; *Educ* Univ of London (external student, BSc); *Career* gen reporter Pudsey News 1973-77, feature writer Yorkshire Evening Post 1978-81; city writer: Utd Newspapers 1981-84, Thomson Regnl Newspapers 1984-86, personal fin writer Daily Express 1986-87, features ed Money Magazine 1987-88, personal fin ed Sunday Express 1988-; winner: special commendation Bradford & Bingley's Personal Fin Journalist of the Year award 1990; *Recreations* horror and history books, Wagner, Puccini, Debussy and soul, oriental food, hot baths; *Style*— Ms Lynne Bateson; Personal Finance Editor, Sunday Express, Ludgate House, 245 Blackfriars Rd, London SE1 9UX

BATESON, Prof Paul Patrick Gordon; s of Capt Richard Gordon Bateson (d 1956), and Solvi Helene, *née* Berg (d 1987); *b* 31 March 1938; *Educ* Westminster, King's Coll Cambridge (BA, PhD, ScD); *m* 20 July 1963, Dusha, da of Kenneth Matthews, of Halesworth, Suffolk; 2 da (Melissa b 1968, Anna b 1972); *Career* Stanford Univ California 1963-65; Univ of Cambridge: Harkness fell, sr asst res 1965-69, lectr in zoology 1969-78, dir Sub Dept Animal Behaviour 1976-88, reader in animal behaviour 1978-84, prof of ethology 1984-; Provost King's Coll Cambridge 1988- (fell 1984-88); FRS 1983; *Books* Growing Points of Ethology (ed with R A Hinde, 1976), Perspectives in Ethology Vols 1-8 (ed with P Klopper, 1972-89), Mate Choice (ed, 1983), Defended to Death (with G Prins & Others, 1984), Measuring Behaviour (with P Martin, 1986), The Domestic Cat (ed with D Turner, 1988); *Clubs* United Oxford Cambridge; *Style*— Prof Patrick Bateson; Provost's Lodge, Kings College, Cambridge CB2 1ST (☎ 0223 350411)

BATEUP, John Brian; s of John Maynard Bateup (d 1971), of Horsmonden, Kent, and Dorothy Nellie, *née* Rose; *b* 22 Aug 1949; *Educ* The Judd Sch Tonbridge Kent; *m* 5 Jan 1974, Christine Anne, da of Rev William Preston, of Horsmonden, Kent; 3 s (Matthew b 1983, Timothy b 1986, Andrew b 1989), 2 da (Helen b 1975, Anne b 1977); *Career* actuary; md: Reliance Mutual Insurance Society Ltd 1982-, The British Life Office Ltd, Reliance Fire and Accident Insurance Corporation Ltd, Reliance Unit Managers Ltd, Reliance Pension Scheme Trustee Ltd; FIA; *Recreations* sport, especially table-tennis; *Clubs* IOD, Actuarial Dining; *Style*— John B Bateup, Esq; Reliance House, Tunbridge Wells, Kent TN4 8BL (☎ 0892 510033, fax 0892 510676)

BATH, 6 Marquess of (GB 1789); Sir Henry Frederick Thynne; 9 Bt (GB 1641), ED; also Viscount Weymouth and Baron Thynne of Warminster (GB 1682); s of 5 Marquess, KG, CB, PC (d 1946), and Violet, da of Sir Charles Mordaunt, 10 Bt; *b* 26 Jan 1905; *Educ* Harrow, Christ Church Oxford; *m* 1, 1927 (m dis 1953), Hon Daphne, da of 4 Baron Vivian, DSO; 2 s, 1 da; m 2, 1953, Virginia Penelope, da of late Alan Parsons and formerly w of Hon David Francis Tennant; 1 da; *Heir* s, Viscount Weymouth; *Career* formerly Maj Royal Wilts Yeo, memb of Cncl of HRH The Prince of Wales 1933-36, sat as MP for Frome Div of Somerset (C) Oct 1931-Oct 1935; chm Football Pools Panel 1966-87; JP Wilts 1938-80; *Style*— The Most Hon the Marquess of Bath, ED; Job's Mill, Crockerton, Warminster, Wilts (☎ 0985 212279); Longleat, Warminster, Wilts

BATH AND WELLS, Bishop of 1987-; Rt Rev Dr George Leonard Carey; s of George Thomas Carey, and Ruby Catherine, *née* Gurney; *b* 13 Nov 1935; *Educ* Bifrons Secdy Modern Sch, London Coll of Divinity, Kings Coll London (ALCD, BD, MTh, PhD); *m* 25 June 1960, Eileen Harmsworth, da of Douglas Cunningham Hood; 2 s (Mark Jonathan b 28 Feb 1965, Andrew Stephen b 18 Feb 1966), 2 da (Rachel Helen b 30 May 1963, Elizabeth Ruth b 26 Oct 1971); *Career* Nat Serv 1954-56, serv Egypt, Shaibah Iraq; curate St Mary's Islington 1962-66; lectr: Oakhill Theol Coll London 1966-70, St John's Theol Coll Notts 1970-75; vicar St Nicholas' Church Durham 1975-82, princ Trinity Coll Bristol 1982-87; memb cncl Bath Int Art Festival, patron and pres of many organizations; Freeman of the City of Wells 1990; Archbishop designate of Canterbury 1991; *Books* I Believe in Man (1976), God Incarnate (1977), The Church in The Market Place (1982), The Great Acquittal (1983), The Gate of Glory (1985), The Meeting of The Waters (1986); *Recreations* walking, reading, music, family life; *Style*— The Rt Rev the Bishop of Bath and Wells; The Palace, Wells, Somerset BA5 2PD (☎ 0749 72341, fax 0749 79355)

BATHAM, Cyril Ernest Kila Northwood; s of Ernest Northwood Batham (d 1941), and Susan Penelope, *née* Herridge (d 1940); *b* 29 June 1909; *Educ* Bishop Veseys GS Sutton Coldfield Warks; *m* 8 Aug 1931, Alys Gillian, da of Ernest Drinkwater (d 1962), of Ross-on-Wye, Herefordshire; 1 da (Ruth Penelope (Mrs Bell) b 28 Feb 1948); *Career* Yorks Insurance Co Ltd (now General Accident Fire & Life Assurance Corp plc): mangr Bristol Branch 1946-57, mangr Manchester Branch 1957-63, liaison offr Paris 1963-67, head office underwriter 1967-72; insur broker Mann Rutler & Collins (Life & Pensions) Ltd 1972-76, company dir QC Correspondence Circle Ltd 1976-; lectr on Freemasonry; ed Ars Quator Confonatorum 1975-; chm Bristol Old Vic Theatre Club 1955, asst Summer Sch for Teachers of Eng Stratford-upon-Avon 1948-71; Freeman: City of London 1972, Worshipful Co of Gold and Silver Wyre Drawers 1972; OSTJ 1980; ACII 1928; *Recreations* theatre, classical music; *Style*— Cyril Batham, Esq; 17 Romeland, Waltham Abbey, Essex EN9 1QZ (☎ 0992 713 527); QC Correspondence Circle Ltd, 60 Great Queen Street, London WC2A 5BA (☎ 071 405 7340 or 071 831 2493)

BATHO, Antoinette, Lady; Antoinette Marie; da of Baron Paul d'Udekem d'Acoz, of Ghent, Belgium; *m* 28 May 1934, Sir Maurice Benjamin Batho, 2 Bt (d 1990); 3 s (1 decd), 2 da; *Style*— Antoinette, Lady Batho; Carlton Hall, Saxmundham, Suffolk (☎ 0728 2505)

BATHO, Prof Gordon Richard; s of Walter Batho (d 1955), of Ealing, W London, and Harriet Emily, *née* Dymock (d 1988); *b* 27 Feb 1929; *Educ* Ealing GS for Boys, UCL (BA), Inst of Educn London (PGCE), Royal Holloway Coll London (MA); *m* 5 Sept 1959, Hilary, da of Alfred Crowson (d 1963), of Bakewell, Derbyshire; 2 s (Richard b 1965, Paul b 1969); *Career* sr history master Ilfracombe GS 1953-55, sr lectr educn Univ of Sheffield 1966-74 (asst lectr 1956, lectr 1958), emeritus prof of educn Univ of Durham 1988 (prof 1975-88); visiting lectr: McMaster Univ 1963, Univ of BC 1963-64 and 1966, Carleton Univ 1964; vice-pres Hist Assoc, lately chm Standing Conf on Studies in Educn, reviews ed British Journal of Educational Studies 1989-; FRHistS 1956, (Assoc) 1954, chm Durham Thomas Harriot Seminar 1977-; *Books* Household Papers of Henry Percy (1564-1632) Royal Historical Society (1962), Calendar of the Talbot Papers, Historical MSS Commission (1972) Political Issues In Education (1989); *Recreations* gardening, historical visiting; *Style*— Prof Gordon Batho; 3 Archery Rise, Durham DH1 4LA (☎ 091 3868908); School of Education University of Durham, Leazes Rd, Durham (☎ 091 374 3497)

BATHO, (Walter) James Scott; s of Walter Scott Batho (d 1967), of Barton on Sea, and Isabella Laidlaw, *née* Common (d 1970); *b* 13 Nov 1925; *Educ* Epsom Co GS, Univ of Edinburgh (MA); *m* 25 Aug 1951, Barbara, da of Percy Gerald Kingsford (d 1968), of Ashtead; 2 s (Paul b 1954, Mark b 1956), 2 da (Elizabeth (Mrs Earl) b 1959, Julia (Mrs Bridge) b 1963); *Career* Sub Lt RNVR 1943-46; Civil Serv 1950-85; private sec to Perm Under Sec War Office 1956, Miny of Public Bldg and Works 1963-70; DOE: under sec 1979, regnl dir Eastern Regn and chm Regnl Bd 1983; chm London and Quadrant Housing Tst 1989; memb: Guildford Diocesan Synod, Diocesan Bd of Fin; pres Ashtead Choral Soc; *Recreations* singing, reading, gardening; *Clubs* Naval; *Style*— James Batho, Esq; Bushpease, Grays Lane, Ashtead, Surrey KT21 1BU (☎ 0372 273471)

BATHO, Sir Peter Ghislain; 3 Bt (UK 1928); s of Sir Maurice Benjamin Batho, 2 Bt (d 1990), and Antoinette Marie, da of Baron Paul d'Udekem d'Acoz, of Ghent, Belgium; *b* 9 Dec 1939; *Educ* Ampleforth, Writtle Farm Inst; *m* 29 Oct 1966, Lucille Mary, da of late Wilfrid Francis Williamson, of The White House, Saxmundham, Suffolk; 3 s; *Heir* s, Rupert Sebastian Ghislain Batho b 26 Oct 1967; *Style*— Sir Peter Batho, Bt; Park Farm, Saxmundham, Suffolk IP17 1DQ

BATHURST, Lady (Elizabeth) Ann; da of Capt Hon Chandos Graham Temple-Gore-Langton (d 1921), and Ethel Frances, da of the Rev A L Gore; sis of 7 Earl Temple of Stowe; raised to rank of Earl's da 1941; *b* 3 April 1908; *m* 1927, Gp Capt Peter Bathurst, RAF (d 1970), o son of late Lt-Col Hon (Allen) Benjamin Bathurst, 3 s of 6 Earl Bathurst; 2 s; *Style*— The Lady Ann Bathurst; 12A Northanger Court, Grove St, Bath, Avon BA2 6PE

BATHURST, Adm Sir (David) Benjamin; GCB (1991, KCB 1987); s of late Gp Capt Peter Bathurst, and Lady Ann Bathurst, qv; *b* 27 May 1936; *Educ* Eton, Britannia RN Coll Dartmouth; *m* 1959, Sarah, *née* Peto; 1 s, 3 da; *Career* joined RN 1953; qualified: pilot 1960, helicopter instr 1964; Fleet Air Arm appts incl: 2 years exchange with 723 and 725 Sqdns RAN, sr pilot 820 Naval Air Sqdn, CO 819 Naval Air Sqdn, HMS Norfolk 1971, naval staff 1973, CO HMS Ariadne 1975, naval asst to First Sea Lord 1976, Capt 5 Frigate Sqdn HMS Minerva 1978, RCDS 1981, dir Naval Air Warfare 1982, flag offr 2 Flotilla 1983-85, dir gen Naval Manpower and Trg 1985-86, Chief of Fleet Support 1986-89, Cdr in Chief Fleet, Cdr in Chief Eastern Atlantic Area, Allied Cdr in Chief CHANNEL 1989-91, Vice Chief Def Staff 1991- ; Liveryman Guild of Air Pilots and Navigators; *Recreations* gardening, shooting, fishing; *Clubs* Army and Navy, MCC; *Style*— Admiral Sir Benjamin Bathurst, GCB; c/o Coutts and Co, 440 Strand, London WC2

BATHURST, Lady (Joan) Caroline; *née* Petrie; da of James Alexander Petrie (d 1977), of London, and Adrienne Johanna, *née* van den Bergh; *b* 2 Nov 1920; *Educ* Wycombe Abbey Sch, Newnham Coll Cambridge (BA, MA); *m* 8 Aug 1968, Sir Maurice Edward Bathurst, CMG, CBE, QC, *qv*, s of Edward John James Bathurst (d 1978), of East Horsley, Surrey; 1 step s (Adrian Edward b 1948); *Career* Dip Serv 1947-72; FO 1947-48, second sec The Hague 1948-50, FO 1950-54 (first sec 1953), UK High Cmmn and Embassy Bonn 1954-58, FO (later FCO) 1958-71, cnsllr 1969, head Euro Communities Info Unit FCO 1969-71; memb UK delgn to Colombo Plan Consultative Ctee Jogjakarta 1959, advsr Br Gp Inter-Parly Union 1962-68; Offr Order of Leopold (Belgium) 1966; *Recreations* genealogy, gardening, music; *Clubs* Utd Oxford and Cambridge; *Style*— Lady Bathurst; Airlie, The Highlands, East Horsley, Surrey KT24 5BG (☎ 04865 3269)

BATHURST, Hon David Charles Lopes; s of 2 Viscount Bledisloe, QC (d 1979); *b* 15 Dec 1937; *Educ* Eton, Magdalen Oxford; *m* 1967, Mary Cornelia, da of Andrew Kirkwood McCosh, of Coulter Lanarks; 3 da; *Career* 2 Lt 12 Royal Lancers 1956-58; pres Christie Manson & Woods 1978-84 (New York); *Clubs* Boodle's, White's; *Style*— The Hon David Bathurst; South Lodge, E Heath Rd, London NW3 (☎ 071 794 6999)

BATHURST, Hon George Bertram; TD; s of Lt-Col Lord Apsley, DSO, MC, TD, MP (k on active serv 1942); bro of 8 Earl Bathurst, DL; *b* 12 March 1929; *Educ* Eton, Trinity Coll Oxford; *m* 1973, Susan, da of Malcolm Messer, of Manor Farm House, Tarlton, Glos; *Career* late Capt Royal Wilts Yeomanry, late Lt 10 Hussars; *Style*— The Hon George Bathurst, TD; Hullasey House, Tarlton, Cirencester, Glos

BATHURST, 8 Earl (GB 1772); Henry Allen John Bathurst; DL (Glos 1960); also Baron Bathurst (GB 1711) and Baron Apsley (GB 1771); s of Lt-Col Lord Apsley, DSO, MC, TD, MP (k on active serv 1942) and late Lady Apsley, CBE; suc gf (7 Earl) 1943; *b* 1 May 1927; *Educ* Eton, Ch Ch Oxford, Ridley Coll Canada; *m* 1, 1959 (m dis 1976), Judith Mary, da of late Amos Christopher Nelson, of Fosse Corner Cirencester; 2 s, 1 da; m 2, 1978, Gloria, da of Harold Edward Clarry, of Vancouver, and wid of David Rutherston; *Heir* s, Lord Apsley; *Career* Lt 10 Royal Hussars 1946-48, Royal Glos Hussars 1948-59 Capt TA; master VWH Hounds 1950-64, jt master VWH Hounds 1964-66; Lord in Waiting 1957-61; chllr Primrose League 1959-61; jt Parly under sec Home Office 1961-62; govr Royal Agric Coll; pres: Royal Forestry Soc 1976-78, Inst of Sales & Mktg Mgmnt 1981-, Assoc of Prof Foresters 1983-86; memb Cncl CLA & TGO; dir Forestor Ltd; *Clubs* White's, Cavalry; *Style*— The Rt Hon the Earl Bathurst, DL; Manor Farm, Sapperton, nr Cirencester, Glos (☎ 0285 76 407)

BATHURST, Sir Maurice Edward; CMG (1953), CBE (1947), QC (1964); o s of late Edward John James Bathurst, of E Horsley, Surrey, and late Annie Mary Bathurst; *b* 2 Dec 1913; *Educ* Haberdashers' Aske's Hatcham, King's Coll London (LLB, LLD), Columbia Univ New York (LLM), Gonville and Caius Coll Cambridge (PhD); *m* 1, 1941 (m dis 1963), Dorothy Eunice, da of late W S Stevens, of Gravesend, Kent; 1 s; m 2, 1968, Joan Caroline, da of James Alexander Petrie; *Career* slr 1938-56, called to the Bar Gray's Inn and Inner Temple 1957, bencher Gray's Inn 1970; legal advsr Br Info Services 1941-43, legal advsr Br Embassy Washington 1943-46, legal memb UK Delgn to UN 1946-48, dep legal advsr Control Cmmn Germany 1949-51, legal advsr to UK High Cmmn for Germany 1951-55, judge Supreme Court Br Zone 1953-55, legal advsr to Br Embassy Bonn 1955-57, Br judge Arbitral Cmmn Germany 1968-69; memb Panel of Presidents Arbitral Tbnls Int Telecommunications Satelite Orgn 1974-78; memb UK Delgns: UNRRA, WHO, UN Gen Assembly, NATO Status of Forces Conf; memb: Panel of Arbitrators Int Centre for Settlement of Investment Dept 1968-87, UK Ctee UNICEF 1959-84; hon visiting prof of int law King's Coll London 1967-77 (hon fell); judge Arbitral Tbnl and Mixed Cmmn for the Agreement on German External Debts 1977-1988; memb: Gen Cncl of the Bar 1970-71, Senate of Inns of Court 1971-73, Senate of Inns of Court and the Bar 1974-77; pres Br Insur Law Assoc 1971-75; vice pres: Br Inst of Int and Comparative Law, Br Acad of Experts; Master Worshipful Co of Haberdashers 1980-81 (chm Govrs Haberdashers Aske's Hatcham Schs 1972-80); Freeman: City of London, City of Bathurst NB; Hon DCL, Sacred Heart NB; kt 1984; *Style*— Sir Maurice Bathurst, CMG, CBE, QC; Airlie, The Highlands, East Horsley, Leatherhead, Surrey KT24 5BG (☎ 04865 3269)

BATISTE, Spencer Lee; MP (C) Elmet 1983-; s of Samuel Batiste, and Lottie Batiste; *b* 5 June 1945; *Educ* Carmel Coll, Sorbonne, Univ of Cambridge; *m* 1969, Susan Elizabeth, da of late Ronald William Atkin; 1 s, 1 da; *Career* slr; contested (C) Sheffield, Chesterfield and NE Derbyshire Euro election 1979; vice chm Nat Bd Small Business Bureau; memb Cncl Univ of Sheffield; law clerk Sheffield Assay Office; memb Br Hallmarking Cncl; pres Cons Trade Unionists, former memb Energy Select Ctee; former PPS to min of State for: Indust and Info Technol, Def Procurement; PPS to Leon Brittan, vice pres Cmmn of the Euro Community; *Recreations* gardening, reading, photography; *Style*— Spencer Batiste, Esq, MP; House of Commons, London SW1A 0AA (☎ 071 219 6054)

BATLEY, John Geoffrey; OBE (1987); s of John William Batley (d 1971), of Keighley, W Yorks, and Doris, *née* Midgeley (d 1985); *b* 21 May 1930; *Educ* Keighley GS; *m* 1953, Cicely Anne, da of William Bean Pindar, of Bradford; 1 s (John), 1 da (Janet); *Career* BR: trained and qualified as chartered engr NE Region 1947-53, asst divnl engr Leeds 1962, mgmnt servs offr BR HQ London 1965, dep princ Br Tport Staff Coll Woking 1970, divnl mangr Leeds 1976, dep chief sec BRB London 1982, sec BR Bd

1984-87; World Bank/Tanzanian Railway Corp project coordinator Tanzania 1988-90; CEng, MICE, MCIT; *Recreations* walking, golf, gardening; *Clubs* Savile; *Style*— John Batley, Esq, OBE; c/o Savile Club, 69 Brook St, London W1Y 2ER (☎ 071 629 5462)

BATLEY, Lawrence; s of John Arthur Batley (d 1947), of Huddersfield, and Beatrice, *née* Fawley; *b* 15 Feb 1914; *Educ* Hillhouse Central Sch Huddersfield; *m* 5 June 1937, Dorothie Hepworth, da of Wilfred Boothroyd (d 1918), of Huddersfield; 1 da (Rita b 30 March 1940); *Career* Cash and Carry wholesaler; inventor and pioneer of Cash and Carry in GB May 1958; fndr and chm Batleys of Yorkshire; originator and sole sponsor of Lawrence Batley Int Golf tournament 1981; dir Lawrence Batley Art Centre Bretton Hall Wakefield; *Recreations* golf, swimming; *Clubs* Huddersfield Borough; *Style*— Lawrence Batley, Esq; Heaton Park House, Heaton Road, Huddersfield HD1 4HX (☎ 0484 544211); Batleys plc, Leeds Road, Huddersfield HD2 1UN (☎ 04845 44211)

BATSFORD, Sir Brian Caldwell Cook; s of late Arthur Caldwell Cook, of Gerrards Cross, Bucks; assumed mother's maiden name by deed poll 1946; *b* 18 Dec 1910; *Educ* Repton; *m* 1945, Joan (Wendy), da of Norman Cunliffe (d 1964), of Oxford; 2 da; *Career* served WWII Flt Lt RAF; chm B T Batsford (publishers) 1952-74 (pres 1974-76); Parly candidate (Nat Govt) Chelmsford 1945, MP (C) Ealing S 1958-74, asst Govt whip 1962-64, Oppn dep chief whip 1964-67, chm House of Commons Library Ctee 1970-74; Alderman GLC 1967-69, fell Chartered Soc Designs 1971, pres Old Reptonian Soc 1973, govr Repton Sch 1973, vice pres RSA 1975- (chm 1973-75); exhibited: Arts Cncl exhibition, British Landscape Painting 1850-1950 (Hayward Gallery) 1983, one-man exhibition (Parker Gallery) 1987; hon RI 1985, hon memb Soc of Graphic Art 1987; kt 1974; *Books* The Britain of Brian Cook (1987); *Recreations* painting, gardening; *Clubs* Pratt's; *Style*— Sir Brian Batsford; Buckland House, Mill Road, Winchelsea, E Sussex TN36 4HJ (☎ 0797 226131)

BATT, Reginald Joseph Alexander; s of Benjamin and Alice Harriett Batt; *b* 22 July 1920; *m* 1951, Mary Margaret Canning; 1 da; *Career* called to the Bar Inner Temple 1952; recorder SE Circuit 1982-, bencher 1986; *Style*— Reginald Batt, Esq; 6 King's Bench Walk, Temple, London EC4Y 7DR (☎ 071 583 0410)

BATT, William Frederic; MBE (Mil 1945), JP, DL; s of Lt-Col Reginald Cossley Batt, CBE, MVO, of Gresham Hall, Norwich (d 1952), by his 1 w Violet, *née* Knowles (d 1910); *b* 4 April 1904; *Educ* Winchester, Sandhurst; *m* 1928, Hon Elisabeth (d 1988), 1 s, 2 da (and 1 s decd); *Career* Maj Coldstream Gds 1924-29 and 1939-45 (served NW Europe); High Sheriff Norfolk 1963, ret landowner and farmer; memb Gen Synod C of E; *Clubs* Cavalry and Guards; *Style*— William Batt Esq, MBE, JP, DL; Chaucer's Farm, Gresham, Norwich (☎ 026 377 223)

BATTEN, (William) Henry; TD (1963), JP (Dorset 1960-); s of Col Herbert Copeland Cary Batten, DSO (d 1963), of Aldon House, Yeovil, Somerset, and Dorothy Lilian Hyde, *née* Milne (d 1951); *b* 29 Jan 1926; *Educ* Marlborough; *m* 2 Sept 1950, Susan Helen Frances, da of Sir Philip Colfox, 1 Bt, MC, of Symondsbury Manor, Bridport, Dorset; 2 s (David Henry Cary b 3 March 1952, Michael John b 29 Jan 1960), 2 da (Tessa Mary b 22 Oct 1953, Caroline Bridget b 13 July 1955); *Career* cmmnd Lt RM 1944-48, cmmnd 294 Field Regt TA (Queens Own Dorset Yeomanry) 1948-64, ret Maj; admitted slr 1954, sr ptnr Batten & Co (slrs and land agents) 1963-90; chm Wessex Water Bd, clerk Yeovil Gen Cmmrs for Income Tax 1964-, vice pres Royal Bath and West and Southern Counties Soc, vice chm Sherborne RDC; *Recreations* foxhunting, sailing; *Clubs* Royal Cruising; *Style*— Henry Batten, Esq, TD, JP; Church Farm, Ryme Intrinseca, Sherborne, Dorset (☎ 0935 872 482); Church Ho, Yeovil, Somerset (☎ 0835 236 85, fax 0935 706 054, telex 46124)

BATTEN, Sir John Charles; KCVO (1987); s of Raymond Wallis Batten, JP (d 1979), of Worthing, Sussex, and Kathleen Gladys, *née* Charles (d 1982); *b* 11 March 1924; *Educ* Mill Hill Sch, St Bartholomews Med Coll Univ of London (MB BS, MD); *m* 14 Oct 1950, Anne Mary Margaret, da of John Augustus Oriel, CBE, MC; 1 s (Mark b 1957), 3 da (Elizabeth b 1951, Sarah b 1953 d 1955, Clare b 1957); *Career* Surgn Capt RHG 1947-49; jr hosp appts St George's and Brompton Hosps 1946-57; physician: St George's Hosp 1958-79 (now hon physician), Brompton Hosp 1959-87 (now hon physician), King Edward VII Hosp for Offrs 1968-89; physician to HM the Queen 1974-89, head HM Med Household 1981-89; censor 1977 and sr censor 1981 RCP; pres: Med Protection Soc, Br Lung Fndn, Cystic Fibrosis Res Tst; Freeman Worshipful Co of Apothecaries; FRSM; memb: Assoc of Physicians, Br Thoracic Soc; *Recreations* music, sailing, plants; *Style*— Sir John Batten, KCVO; 7 Lion Gate Gardens, Richmond, Surrey TW9 2DF

BATTEN, Mark Wilfrid; s of late Edward Batten, and late Elizabeth, *née* Denne; *Educ* Chelsea Sch of Art; *m* 1933, Elsie May Owston Thorneloe (d 1961); 1 da (Griselda); *Career* sculptor; direct carver in stone; sculptures on Old Bodleian Library and Trinity Coll Oxford and Goldershill Park N London; in USA, Aust, Pakistan; pres Roy Soc of Br Sculptors 1956-61; memb: RBA, RBS, RSA; hon memb Nat Sculpture Soc of USA; *Books* Direct Carving in Stone; *Clubs* Chelsea Arts; *Style*— Mark Batten, Esq; Christian's River Studio, Dallington, Heathfield, Sussex TN21 9NX

BATTEN, Stephen Duval; QC (1989); s of Brig Stephen Alexander Holgate Batten, CBE (d 1957), and Alice Joan, *née* Royden, MBE (d 1990); *b* 2 April 1945; *Educ* Uppingham, Pembroke Coll Oxford (BA); *m* 5 June 1976, Valerie Jean, da of George Ronald Trim (d 1982); 1 s (Henry b 1978), 1 da (Sarah b 1980); *Career* called to the Bar Middle Temple 1968, rec Crown Court 1987; *Recreations* golf, sheep farming; *Style*— Stephen Batten, Esq, QC; 3 Raymond Buildings, Gray's Inn, London WC1R 5BH (☎ 071 831 3833, fax 071 242 4221)

BATTERBURY, His Hon Judge Paul Tracy Shepherd; TD 1972 (and 2 bars 1978 and 1984), DL (Greater London 1986), rep DL (London Borough of Haverling 1989-); s of Hugh Basil John Batterbury (d 1986), of Sidcup, and Inez, *née* Shepherd; *b* 25 Jan 1934; *Educ* St Olaves GS, Univ of Bristol (LLB); *m* 11 April 1962, Sheila Margaret, da of John Arthur Watson, of Eltham; 1 s (Simon b 1963), 1 da (Sarah b 1967); *Career* RAF 1952-55, Maj RA (TA) 1959-85; called to the Bar Inner Temple 1959, dep circuit judge 1975-79, recorder 1979-83, circuit judge 1983-; memb: Sidcup and Chislehurst UDC 1960-62, Greenwich Borough Cncl 1968-71 (chm Housing Ctee 1970-71); fndr tstee St Olave's Prep Sch New Eltham 1969-, fndr chm Gallipoli Meml Lectures 1985, vice pres SE London St John Ambulance 1988-; Liveryman Worshipful Co of Plumbers; *Recreations* walking, caravanning; *Clubs* Civil Service; *Style*— His Hon Judge Batterbury, TD, DL; 5 Paper Buildings, Temple, London EC4 (☎ 071 583 9275)

BATTERSBY, Prof Alan Rushton; s of William Battersby (d 1967), and Hilda, *née* Rushton (d 1972); *b* 4 March 1925; *Educ* Leigh GS, Univ of Manchester (BSc, MSc), Univ of St Andrews (PhD), Univ of Bristol (DSc), Univ of Cambridge (ScD); *m* 18 June 1949, Margaret Ruth, da of Thomas Hart (d 1965); 2 s (Martin b 29 July 1953, Stephen b 24 April 1956); *Career* lectr in chemistry: Univ of St Andrews 1948-53, Univ of Bristol 1954-62; second chair organic chem Univ of Liverpool 1962, elected to chair of organic chemistry Univ of Cambridge 1969 (elected to 1702 chair 1988); non-exec dir Schering Agrochemicals Ltd; Hon: DSc Rockerfeller Univ NY 1977, LLD Univ of St Andrews 1977, DSc Univ of Sheffield 1986, DSc Heriot-Watt Univ 1987; FRS 1966; memb: Deutsche Akademie der Naturforscher Leopolding (Germany) 1967, Soc Royal de Chimie (Belgium) 1987; hon memb American Acad of Arts and Sci (USA) 1988; *Recreations* music, camping, sailing, gardening and fly fishing; *Style*— Prof Alan Battersby, FRS; 20 Barrow Rd, Cambridge CB2 2AS (☎ 0223 63799); University Chemical Laboratory, Lensfield Rd, Cambridge CB2 1EW (☎ 0223 336400, fax 0223 336362)

BATTERSBY, Eric Worsley; OBE (1965, MBE (Mil) 1946); s of Charles Worsley Battersby (d 1952), of Pountney Copse, Alton, Hants, and Susie Agnes Shelly, *née* Kennard-Davies (d 1964); *b* 18 April 1916; *Educ* Marlborough Coll; *m* 13 July 1946, Edna Iris Prudence, da of Col John Norman Gwynne (d 1969), of Toronto; 3 s (Nicholas b 1947, d 1990, Timothy b 1949, Simon b 1953), 1 da (Tessa b 1956, d 1959); *Career* joined Indian Police Burma 1935-40, ADC to Govr of Burma Hon Sir Archibald Cochrane (successor Rt Hon Sir Reginald Dorman-Smith) 1940-42, staff duties Eastern Army India Cmd 1942-44, Maj Force 136 SOE Far East 1944-46, demobbed 1946; civil servant; civil asst WO 1946, Malaya 1946-48, Jamaica 1955-57, seconded to FO 1960-65, MOD 1965-76, ret 1976; chm Warsash and Dist Art Gp; Freeman City of London 1944, Liveryman Worshipful Co of Fishmongers; *Recreations* painting, golf; *Style*— Eric Battersby, Esq, OBE

BATTERSBY, Rita; da of John Baybutt, and Zena May, *née* Cowell; *b* 29 Sept 1942; *Educ* Wigan Mining & Tech Coll; *m* 21 March 1964, Albert Battersby, OBE, s of Albert Battersby, (d 1952); 2 da (Zena b 26 Jan 1965, Debra b 9 March 1967); *Career* fndr VDU Installations Ltd 1977; awards: First award winner Industrial Achievement Award 1981, Runner-up Business Woman of the Year 1986, Inst of Sales and Marketing mgmt award 1988; memb local PCCA 1986; *Recreations* swimming, sailing; *Style*— Mrs Rita Battersby; VDU Installations Ltd, 43 Western Rd, Bracknell, Berks, RG12 1RW (☎ 0344 424000, fax 0344 424063, telex 846545 VDUINS G)

BATTERSBY, Robert Christopher; MBE (1971), MEP (C) Humberside 1979-; s of late Maj Robert Luther Battersby, MM, RFA, late IA, and Dorothea Gladys, *née* Middleton; *b* 14 Dec 1924; *Educ* Edinburgh Univ, Cambridge Univ (BA, MA), Sorbonne, Toulouse Univ; *m* 1, 1949 (m dis), June Scriven; 1 da; m 2, 1955, Marjorie Bispham; 2 s, 1 da; *Career* RA and Intelligence Corps 1942-47, Lt RARO; mangr Dowsett Gp; dir Associated Engineering and Guest-Keen and Nettlefolds Gps; principal administrator European Cmmn 1973-79; dep chief whip (EDG) 1983-86, chief whip 1987-; chm Fisheries Sub Ctee European Parliament 1979-84 (vice-chm 1984-87); vice-chm: EP-China Interparly Delgn 1981-87; EP-USSR Delegation 1987-; *Clubs* Carlton; *Style*— Robert Battersby, Esq, MBE, MEP; West Cross, Rockshaw Road, Merstham, Surrey

BATTIE, David Anthony; s of Donald Charles Battie (d 1988), of Woking, and Peggy Joan Battie; *b* 22 Oct 1942; *Educ* King James 1 Sch; *m* 1 Jan 1972, Sarah, da of Philip James Francis (d 1987), of Merstham Surrey; 2 da (Henrietta Victoria b 17 Aug 1977, Eleanor Har June 1980); *Career* dir Sothebys 1976, BBC TV Antiques Roadshow 1977-; *Books* Price Guide to 19th Century British Pottery (1975), Price Guide to 19th Century British Porcelain (1979), Sothebys Guide to Porcelain (ed, 1990); *Recreations* book binding; *Style*— David Battie, Esq; Sotheby's 34/35 New Bond St, London W1A 2AA (☎ 071 408 5366)

BATTISCOMBE, Christopher Charles Richard; s of Lt-Col Christopher Robert Battiscombe (d 1989), and Karin Sigrid, *née* Timberg (d 1983); *b* 27 April 1940; *Educ* Wellington Coll, New Coll Oxford (BA); *m* 1972, Brigid Melita Theresa, da of Peter Northcote Lunn; 1 s (Max b 1977), 1 da (Antonia b 1975); *Career* MECAS 1963; 2 sec FO (later FCO) 1963, 3 sec Kuwait 1965; asst priv sec to Chllr of Duchy of Lancaster 1969; UK del OECD Paris 1971; 1 sec UK mission to UN New York 1974, FCO 1978, cnsllr Cairo 1981, Paris 1984, cnsllr FCO 1986-90, HM ambass to Algeria 1990-; *Recreations* golf, tennis, skiing; *Clubs* Kandahar; *Style*— Christopher Battiscombe, Esq

BATTISCOMBE, (Esther) Georgina; da of George Harwood, MP (d 1912), and Ellen, *née* Hopkinson (d 1965); *b* 21 Nov 1905; *Educ* St Michael's Oxford, Lady Margaret Hall Oxford (BA); *m* 1 Oct 1932, Lt-Col Christopher Francis Battiscombe, s of Christopher William Battiscombe (d 1917); 1 da (Aurea (Mrs Morshead) b 1935); *Career* biographer; reviews and articles in: The Times, Country Life, Times Literary Supplement, many other periodicals; James Tait Black prize best biography of the year for John Keble; memb: Diocesan Ctee for Care of Churches, Redundant Churches Ctee; county organiser St John Red Cross Hosp Libraries; FRSL; *Books* Charlotte Mary Yonge (1943), Two on Safari (1946), English Picnics (1949), Mrs Gladstone (1956), John Keble (1963), Queen Alexandra (1969), Lord Shaftesbury (1974), Reluctant Pioneer (Elizabeth Wordsworth) (1978), Christina Rossetti (1981), The Spencers of Althorp (1984); *Recreations* looking at churches, bird watching; *Clubs* University Women's; *Style*— Mrs Georgina Battiscombe; 40 Phyllis Court Drive, Henley-on-Thames, Oxon RG9 2HU (☎ 0491 574830)

BATTLE, John; MP (Lab) Leeds W 1987-; s of John Battle, and Audrey, *née* Rathbone (d 1982); *b* 26 April 1951; *Educ* Upholland Coll, Univ of Leeds (BA); *m* 12 April 1977, Mary Geraldine, da of Jerry Meenan; 1 s (Joseph b 1978), 2 da (Anna b 1981, Clare b 1982); *Career* trg for RC priesthood 1969-73, res offr to Derek Enright MEP 1979-83, nat co-ordinator Church Action on Poverty 1983-87; cncllr Leeds 1980-87, chm housing ctee Leeds CC 1983-85; *Style*— John Battle, Esq, MP; 26 Victoria Park Ave, Leeds LS5 3DG

BATTY, Andrew James; s of Francis Leslie Batty (d 1971), and Pamela, *née* Ball; *b* 12 April 1956; *Educ* Roundhay GS, Jacob Kramer Coll Leeds; *Career* copywriter Charles Walls Advertising 1975-79, creative dir Severn Advertising 1979-81, dir MCS Robertson Scott Yorks 1981-82, chm and md Creative Mktg Servs 1982-; chm: Publicity Assoc of Bradford, Yorkshire Advertising and Communications Training; MSIAD 1978, MCAM 1979, MInstM 1981, MBIM 1984, FInstSMM 1987; *Recreations* voluntary activities in advertising training, local history; *Style*— Andrew Batty, Esq; 4 Moor Park Villas, Far Headingley, Leeds LS6 4BZ (☎ 0532 787669); Creative Marketing Services, 153-155 Sunbridge Rd, Bradford, W Yorkshire BD1 2NU (☎ 0274 309311, fax 0274 306595)

BATTY, John Christopher Ralph; s of Ralph Frank Batty, of London, and Georgina, *née* Chambers; *b* 13 Sept 1941; *Educ* Brighton Coll, Manchester Univ (BSc), Cranfield Inst of Tech (MBA), Coll of Law; *m* Sept 1986, Hannah-May Eugenia, da of Eugene Stuart Lyddane, MD (d 1986), of Washington DC, USA; *Career* admitted slr 1968, articled Slaughter and May (asst slr 1968-74), counsel Lloyds Bank Int Ltd 1978-81, ptnr Berwin Leighton 1983-89; dir: Science Business Interface plc 1988-, Beta Sigma Ltd and subsidiaries 1988-; memb: London Mathematical Society 1964, Int Bar Assoc; *Recreations* music, history of mathematics, Dr Samuel Johnson, Samuel Pepys; *Style*— John Batty, Esq; c/o Park House, 16 Finsbury Circus, London EC2M 7DJ (☎ 071 638 3366, fax 071 382 9089)

BATTY, Peter Wright; s of Ernest Faulkner Batty (d 1986), of Surrey, and Gladys Victoria, *née* Wright (d 1979); *b* 18 June 1931; *Educ* Bede GS Sunderland, Queen's Coll Oxford (MA); *m* 1959, Anne Elizabeth, da of Edmund Stringer, of Devon; 2 s (David, Richard), 1 da (Charlotte); *Career* feature writer Financial Times 1954-56, freelance journalist 1956-58, prodr BBC TV 1958-64, memb original Tonight Team (ed 1963-64); other BBC prodns incl: The Quiet Revolution, The Big Freeze, The Katanga Affair, Sons of the Navvy Man; exec prodr and assoc head of Factual Programming ATV 1964-68; prodns include: The Fall and Rise of the House of Krupp (Grand Prix for Documentary Venice Film Festival 1965, Silver Dove Leipzig Film Festival 1965), The Road to Suez, The Suez Affair, Vietnam Fly-in, Battle for the Desert; chief exec

Peter Batty Prodns 1970-; recent programmes directed produced and scripted for BBC TV ITV and Channel 4 incl: The Plutocrats, The Aristocrats, Battle for Cassino, Battle for the Bulge, Birth of the Bomb, Farouk Last of the Pharaohs, Operation Barbarossa, Superspy, Spy Extraordinary, Sunderland's Pride and Passion, A Rothschild and his Red Gold, Search for the Super, The World of Television, Battle for Warsaw, The Story of Wine, The Rise and Rise of Laura Ashley, The Gospel According to St Michael, Battle for Dien Bien Phu, Nuclear Nightmares, A Turn Up In a Million, Il Poverello, Swindle!, The Algerian War, Fonteyn and Nureyev The Perfect Partnership, The Divided Union, A Time for Remembrance, Swastika Over British Soil; contrib to The World at War series; *Books* The House of Krupp (1966), The Divided Union (1987), La Guerre d'Algerie (1989); *Recreations* walking, reading, listening to music; *Clubs* White Elephant; *Style—* Peter Batty, Esq; Claremont Ho, Renfrew Rd, Kingston, Surrey KT2 7NT (☎ 081 942 6304, telex 262433 MONREF G 2685, fax 081 336 1661)

BATTY, Dr Vincent Bernard; s of Henry Joseph Batty, of London, and Ena Violet, *née* Cavenagh; *b* 8 June 1951; *Educ* St Aloysius Coll Highgate, Middx Hosp Med Sch (BSc, MBBS, DMRD, MSc, FRCR); *m* 21 Feb 1987, Dr Wilma, da of Rolf Westensee, of Grahamstown, SA; 1 s (Adam b 1980), 2 da (Louise b 1980, Anke b 1989); *Career* house physician Watford Gen Hosp 1977, house and casualty surgn Middx Hosp 1978, GP Hythe Hants 1979, conslt radiology and nuclear med Southampton Gen Hosp 1984 - (registrar radiology 1979, sr registrar radiology 1982), sr registrar ultrasound and nuclear med Royal Marsden Hosp 1984; *Books* Nuclear Medicine In Oncology (ed, 1986); *Recreations* squash, gardening, music, photography; *Style—* Dr Vincent Batty; Denny Cottage, Denny Lodge, Lyndhurst, Hants SO43 7FZ (☎ 0703 292918); Dept of Nuclear Medicine, Southampton General Hospital, Tremona Rd, Southampton SO9 4XY (☎ 0703 777222)

BATTY, Sir William Bradshaw; TD (1946); s of Rowland Batty, and Nellie Batty; *b* 15 May 1913; *Educ* Hulme GS Manchester; *m* 1946, Jean Ella Brice; 1 s (and 1 s decd), 1 da; *Career* chm Ford Motor Co 1972-75, ret; pres SMMT 1975-76; FBIM; kt 1973; *Recreations* golf, sailing, gardening; *Clubs* Royal Western Yacht; *Style—* Sir William Batty, TD; Glenhaven Cottage, Riverside Rd West, Newton Ferrers, S Devon

BATTY SHAW, Patricia Dorothy Mary; CBE (1982), JP (Norfolk 1968), DL (Norfolk 1989); da of Dr Graham Heckels, of Norwich, and Dorothy Clark (d 1980); *b* 18 Nov 1928; *Educ* Wimbledon HS for Girls, Univ of Southampton; *m* 1954, Dr Anthony Batty Shaw, s of Dr Harold Batty Shaw (d 1936); 1 da; *Career* tax cmmr Wymondham 1975- (chm 1987-), nat chm Nat Fedn of Women's Inst 1977-81, dep chm Norfolk Magistrates Ctee 1985-87; memb: VEA Cncl 1978-85, Devpt Cmmn 1981-90, AG Wages Bd England and Wales 1984-, Eng Advsy Ctee on Telecommunciations 1985-88, Archbishop's Cmmn of Rural Affrs 1988-90; govr Norwich HS for Girls 1981-; tstee: Theatre Royal Norwich 1982-88, Charities Aid Fndn 1983-90; AMIA; *Style—* Mrs Anthony Batty Shaw, CBE, JP, DL; Appleacre, Barford, Norwich NR9 4BD (☎ 0603 545 268)

BATY, Clifford John; s of Herbert Thomas Baty (d 1937), and Ethel Beatrice, *née* Garrod (d 1989); *b* 6 Nov 1934; *Educ* Haberdashers' Aske's, Hampstead Sch, North Western Poly; *m* 19 March 1960, Brenda Anne, da of Edward Laurie Fonceca (d 1955); 1 da (Helen Jane b 1967); *Career* ATV Network Ltd: accountant 1963-74, fin controller 1974-77, fin dir 1977-81; Central Independent Television plc: dir of fin 1982-88, commercial dir 1988-; *Recreations* golf, bridge; *Style—* Clifford Baty, Esq; Central Independent Television plc, Central House, Broad St, Birmingham

BAUDINO, Dr Catherine Anne; da of Jean Rene Baudino, and Anne-Marie, *née* Camus; *b* 26 Oct 1952; *Educ* Lycee Francais De Londres, UCL (BA, PhD); *Career* dir Institutional Investor 1980-87; chief exec: Maxwell Satellite Communications Ltd 1987-89, Baudino Enterprises Ltd 1989-; *Recreations* opera, theatre, wine and food; *Style—* Dr Catherine A Baudino; Baudino Enterprises, 217A Ashley Gardens, Emery Hill St, London SW1P 1PA (☎ 071 828 2449, fax 071 233 6268)

BAUER, Eran Nicodemus; s of Capt Jacob Bauer, RAMC (d 1961), and Gitta, *née* Gaal; *b* 25 Feb 1954; *Educ* King GS Grantham; *Career* Parachute Regt 16 Ind Co (V) 1973-78; dir: Universal Cleaning Services (historic bldgs restoration conslt), Civil Def Supply 1980-, Satrade Ltd (Satra Group), Anglo-Societ Trade/Technology 1988-; co-designer and inventor of mil and police special ops equipment, patented first interlocking riot shield; contrib pubns on police tech; security conslt to Govt depts; memb: RUSI for Def Studies, RAeS; *Recreations* architecture, architectural drawing and rendering, flying, hunting (Blankney hunt), sports sponsorship, writing; *Style—* Eran Bauer, Esq; The Old Rectory, Wellingore, Lincoln LN5 0JF (☎ 09522 810388); Civic Defence Supply, Wellingore, Lincoln LN5 0JF (☎ 0522 810388 3 lines, telex 56472 CIVDEF G, fax 0522 811353)

BAUER, Gerard Miet; s of Dr Jacob Bauer (d 1961), and Gitta, *née* Gaal; *b* 16 Aug 1956; *Educ* Kings GS Grantham, Carmarthen Art Sch Dyfed; *Career* professional artist 1968-; work in oils incl: portraiture, equine, illustrator for RAF and overseas calendars; dir: Civil Defence Supply 1980-, Satrade Ltd (Satra Group) Anglo-Soviet Trading 1988-; co patentee interlinking riot shields and designer of police equipment; memb: Lincolnshire and Humberside Arts, Royal Aeronautical Soc; *Recreations* riding, music, art and architecture, travel; *Style—* Gerard Bauer, Esq; The Old Rectory, Wellingore, Lincoln LN5 0JF; Civil Defence Supply, Wellingore, Lincoln LN5 0JF (☎ 0522 810388, fax 0522 811353, telex 56472)

BAUER, Baron (Life Peer UK 1983), of Market Ward in the City of Cambridge; Prof Peter Thomas Bauer; s of Aladar Bauer (d 1944), of Budapest, Hungary; *b* 6 Nov 1915; *Educ* Scholae Piae Budapest, Gonville and Caius Coll Cambridge (MA); *Career* reader in agric economics Univ of London 1947-48, economics lectr Univ of Cambridge 1948-56, Smuts reader Cwlth Studies Univ of Cambridge 1956-60, prof of economics LSE 1960-83; fell Gonville and Caius Coll Cambridge 1946-60 and 1968-; FBA; *Publications* The Rubber Industry (1948), West African Trade (1954), The Economics of Underdeveloped Countries (with B S Yamey, 1957), Economic Analysis and Policy in Underdeveloped Countries (1958), Indian Economic Policy and Development (1961), Markets, Market Control and Marketing Reform (with B S Yamey, 1968), Dissent on Development (1972), Aspects of Nigerian Development (1974), Equality, the Third World and Economic Delusion (1981), Reality and Rhetoric: Studies in the Economics of Development (1984); *Clubs* Garrick; *Style—* The Rt Hon the Lord Bauer; House of Lords, Westminster, London SW1

BAUER, Willy Benedikt (*né* Gegen-Bauer); s of Willy Gegen-Bauer (d 1990), of Stuttgart, Germany, and Maria, Elizabeth, *née* Schuhbauer (d 1965); *b* 8 Nov 1937; *Educ* GS and HS Biberach Germany, Hotel Sch Heidelburg (Diploma); *Career* hotelier; mgmnt trg Hotel Rad Biberach Germany 1957-60; hotel trg: Lausanne and Geneva Switzerland 1961-62, Grand Hotel Eastbourne 1962-63, Grand Metropolitan Hotel London 1963-65, banqueting mgmnt trg Hilton International London 1965; various mgmnt positions Trust Houses 1965-69; gen mangr Trust House Forte: Red Lion Colchester 1969-71, Cairn Hotel Harrogate 1971-72, St George's Hotel Liverpool 1972-75, Hyde Park Hotel 1975-80; exec dir and gen mangr Grosvenor House Park Lane 1980-81, gen mangr The Savoy London 1982-83, md The Savoy Management Ltd (The Savoy, The Lygon Arms, Wiltons Restaurant) 1983-89, chief exec Wentworth Group 1989; *Awards* European Hotelier of the Year 1985, Hotel of the Year award 1988; Freeman City of London 1987; memb: Master Innholders 1987, Advsy Bd Acad of Culinary Arts 1988, Chaine de Rotisseurs, Reunion des Gastronomes, Savoy Gastronomes; Bd of Friends Univ of Surrey Food & Wine Soc 1986, Bd of Govrs Acad of Culinary Arts plc 1990, RAGB 1990; FHCIMA 1987; *Recreations* music, theatre, sport, gardening, architecture, design, antiques; *Clubs* The Duke's 100-1990, Dulwich & Sydenham Hill Golf, Wentworth Golf, St James's, RAC, One Ninety Queens Gate, Les Ambassadeurs; *Style—* Willy Bauer, Esq; Wentworth Group Holdings, Wentworth Drive, Virginia Water Surrey GU25 4LS (☎ 0344 845216, fax 0344 845415)

BAUGHAN, Julian James; QC (1990); s of Prof E C Baughan, CBE, and Mrs E C Baughan; *b* 8 Feb 1944; *Educ* Eton, Balliol Coll Oxford (scholar, BA); *Career* called to the Bar Inner Temple 1967; prosecuting counsel DTI 1983-90, rec 1985-; *Style—* Julian Baughan, Esq, QC; 13 Kings Bench Walk, Temple, London EC4Y 7EN (☎ 071 353 7204)

BAUGHAN, Michael Christopher; s of Prof Edward Christopher Baughan, CBE; *b* 25 April 1942; *Educ* Westminster; *m* 1975, Moira, da of Percy Levy; 2 s; *Career* md Lazard Brothers, dir Goode Durrant plc; memb Bd of Govrs Westminster Sch; memb Slrs Disciplinary Tbnl; *Style—* Michael Baughan, Esq; 21 Moorfields, London EC2P 2HT

BAUGHEN, Rt Rev Michael Alfred; *see*: Chester, Bishop of

BAUM, (John) David; *b* 23 July 1940; *Educ* Univ of Birmingham (MB ChB, MD), Univ of Glasgow (DCh), Univ of London (MSc); *m* 5 Jan 1967, Angela Rose Goschalk; 4 s (Benjamin b 1970, Joshua b 1971, Jacob b 1974, Samuel Alexander b 1980); *Career* house physician Queen Elizabeth Hosp 1963, house surgn W Middx Hosp 1964, house physician Birmingham Children's Hosp 1964 (RMO 1965), dep RMO Middx Hosp 1966; Hammersmith Hosp: neonatal resident 1967, paediatric registrar 1968, sr registrar paediatrics 1970; Univ of Oxford: lectr 1972, clinical reader in paediatrics 1974-85 (hon conslt paediatrics Oxfordshire Health Authy); Univ of Bristol: prof of child health 1985-, founding dir Inst of Child Health 1988-; visiting prof: Univ of Colorado Med Center 1969, Univ of Porto Alegre Brazile 1976, Med Coll of S Africa 1982, Hadassah Hosp and Med Sch Jerusalem and West Bank Hosps Israel 1985, Palma de Mallorca 1987, Royal Children's Hosp and Monash Med Centre Melbourne Australia 1987, Sophia's Children's Hosp and Univ Hosp Rotterdam Netherlands 1988, Ben Gurion Univ of the Negev Israel 1988-89, Royal Soc of Med NY USA 1989; external examiner med schs in England, Ireland, Sweden, Hong Kong and Addis Ababa, Ethiopia since 1976; memb editorial bds and contrib numerous papers to learned jls; memb numerous nat and int ctees; tstee: CLIC (Cancer and Lenkaemia in Childhood) Tst, ARTHOS (Arts in Hosps Fndn), Bristol Family Conciliation Serv, The Musicspace Tst; Percy J Neate res fell of Worshipful Co of Clothworkers 1968; professorial fell St Catherine's Coll Oxford 1977; FRCP 1977 (MRCP 1966), memb numerous scientific socs, FRSA 1990; BPA Guthrie medal 1976, Prix de la Vulgarisation Medicale 1981; *Books* Clinical Paediatric Physiology (with S Godfrey, 1979), Human Milk Processing, Fractionation and Nutrition of the Low Birth Weight Baby (with A F Williams, 1984), Care of the Child with Diabetes (with A L Kinmonth, 1985), Child Health - The Complete Guide (with S Graham-Jones, 1989), Care of the Child with Life Threatening Disease (with Mother F Dominica and R Woodward, 1990); *Recreations* visual arts, environmental affairs; *Style—* Prof David Baum; 19 Charlotte St, Bristol BS1 5PZ (☎ 0272 260448); Inst of Child Health, Royal Hospital for Sick Children, St Michael's Hill, Bristol BS2 8BJ (☎ 0272 285383)

BAUM, Prof Harold; s of Isidor Baum (d 1980), and Mary, *née* Rosenberg (d 1974); *b* 14 Nov 1930; *Educ* Halesowen GS Worcs, Univ of Birmingham (BSc, PhD); *m* 30 Oct 1962, Patricia Glenda, da of Maj George Magrill, OBE, JP, of Roehampton, London; a direct desc of The Marahil, Jacob Moelln, a great 14 C Rabbi; 1 s (David b 1965), 2 da (Mandy b 1967, Alison b 1969); *Career* King's Coll London: prof of biochemistry 1968, head of Dept of Biochemistry and dean of Faculty of Life Scis 1987-, head of Sch of Life Basic Med and Health scis 1989-; dir Taylor and Francis Gp Ltd; radio and TV broadcaster; chm Professional and Educnl Ctee Biochemical Soc 1981-, chm of govrs S Thames Coll 1983-87, memb Cncl Glynn Research Fndn, tstee Nuffield Chelsea Curriculum Tst; treas Internal Fedn of Scientists for Soviet Refuseniks; FRSC, CChem, FIBiol, CBiol; *Recreations* squash, skiing, songwriting, bridge; *Clubs* Roehampton; *Style—* Prof Harold Baum; Yew Trees, 356 Dover House Rd, London SW15 5BL (☎ 081 789 9352, 081 788 2471); King's College London; Campden Hill Rd, London W8 (☎ 071 333 4646, fax 071 937 5690)

BAUM, Louis Clarence; s of Rudolf Josef Baum (d 1984), and Heather, *née* Shulman; *b* 15 March 1948; *Educ* SA Coll Sch, Univ of Cape Town (BA); *m* 1971 (m dis 1982), Stephanie, *née* Goodman; 1 s (Simon b 1979); *Career* author of childrens' books; journalist: Cape Times 1979-84, The Bookseller 1984-; ed The Bookseller 1980-, dir J Whitaker & Sons; *Books* JuJu and the Pirate (1983), I Want to see the Moon (1984), After Dark (1984), Are We Nearly There? (1986), Joey's Coming Home Today (1989); *Recreations* writing; *Clubs* The Groucho (dir 1984-); *Style—* Louis Baum, Esq; J Whitaker & Sons Ltd, 12 Dyott St, London WC1A 1DF (☎ 071 836 8911, fax 071 836 6381)

BAUM, Prof Michael; s of Isidor Baum (d 1980), and Mary, *née* Rose (1974); *b* 31 May 1937; *Educ* George Dixons GS Birmingham, Univ of Birmingham Medical Sch (MB ChB, ChM); *m* 12 Sept 1965, Judith, da of Reuben Marcus, of Newcastle upon Tyne; 1 s (Richard b 20 Sept 1966), 2 da (Katie b 19 April 1969, Suzanne b 22 March 1973); *Career* lectr in surgery King's Coll London 1969-72, sr lectr in surgery (later reader) Welsh Nat Sch of Medicine 1972-79, prof of surgery King's Coll Sch of Medicine and Dentistry 1980-90, hon dir Cancer Res Campaign Clinical Trials Centre 1980-, prof of surgery Inst of Cancer Res 1990-; memb: UK Coordinating Ctee for Cancer Res (chm Breast Cancer Sub Ctee), Advsy Ctee Dept of Health; chm: Br Breast Gp, Higher Degrees Ctee Univ of London (vice chm Bd of Studies in Surgery); Hon Doctorate of Medicine Univ of Gotenberg 1986; FRCS 1965; *Books* Breast Cancer The Facts (1984, 2 edn 1988); *Recreations* theatre, literature, philosophy, food, wine, skiing; *Clubs* Athenaeum, Royal Soc of Medicine; *Style—* Prof Michael Baum; Department of Academic Surgery, Institute of Cancer Research, Royal Marsden Hospital, Fulham Rd, London SW3 (☎ 071 352 8171, fax 071 351 5410)

BAVIDGE, Elizabeth Mary; JP (1979); da of Walter Robert Ashton (d 1972), and Mary Newton, *née* Donaldson (d 1986); *b* 24 Aug 1945; *Educ* Carlisle & Co HS for Girls, Univ of Newcastle upon Tyne (BA); *m* 1972, Nigel Patrick Bavidge, s of Dr Kenneth George Scott Bavidge (d 1972); 2 c (Gabrielle Mary b 1972, Fintan Nicholas Ashton b 1975); *Career* graduate trainee Shell-Max & BP Ltd 1967-72, pt/t lectr in English language and literature Percival Whitley Coll 1980-87, lectr in flexible learning opportunities Airedale & Wharfedale Coll Leeds 1987-; nat pres Nat Cncl of Women 1990-92 (nat vice pres 1988-90); *Books* Let's Talk to God (1980); *Recreations* playing the piano, making bread, speaking french, eating; *Style—* Mrs Elizabeth Bavidge, JP; The National Council of Women of Great Britain, 36 Danbury St, London N1 8JU (☎ 071 354 2395)

BAVIN, Timothy John; *see*: Portsmouth, Bishop of

BAVISTER, Edward John; CBE (1988); s of Aubrey John Bavister (d 1974), of Herts, and Ethel, *née* Dennis; *b* 19 April 1933; *Educ* Berkhamsted Sch, St John's Coll

Cambridge (MA); *m* 1958, Barbara Jean, da of Harold Foster (d 1973), of Cumbria; 3 da (Heather Jane b 1960, Anne Kirsten b 1962, Gillian Fiona b 1965); *Career* chartered engr; dep md John Brown plc 1987- (dir 1982-); FEng, FIChemE; *Recreations* sailing, walking, opera; *Clubs* Oriental; *Style—* Edward Bavister, Esq, CBE; Marsham Cottage, Marsham Way, Gerrards Cross, Bucks (☎ 0753 882415); John Brown plc, 20 Eastbourne Terrace, London W2 6LE (☎ 071 262 8080, telex 263521)

BAWDEN, Nina Mary (Mrs Austen Kark); *née* Mabey; da of Cdr Charles Mabey (d 1976), and Ellaline Ursula May, *née* Cushing (d 1986); *b* 19 Jan 1925; *Educ* Ilford County HS for Girls, Somerville Coll Oxford (MA); *m* 1 Oct 1946 (m dis 1954), Henry Walton Bawden, s of Victor Bawden; 2 s (Robert Humphrey Felix b 1951, Nicholas Charles b 1948 d 1982); m 2, 5 Aug 1954, Austen Steven Kark, s of Maj Norman Benjamin Kark, of East India Club, St James's Square, London; 1 da (Perdita Emily Helena b 1957); *Career* novelist; *Books* Devil by the Sea (1955), Just Like a Lady (1960), In Honour Bound (1961), Tortoise by Candlelight (1963), Under the Skin (1964), A Little Love, A Little Learning (1965), A Woman of My Age (1967), The Grain of Truth (1969), The Birds on the Trees (1970), Anna Apparent (1972), George Beneath a Paper Moon (1974), Afternoon of a Good Woman (1976), Familiar Passions (1979), Walking Naked (1981), The Ice House (1983), Circles of Deceit (1987), Family Money (1991); *for children* The Secret Passage, On The Run, The White Horse Gang, A Handful of Thieves, Squib, Carrie's War, The Peppermint Pig, The Finding, Keeping Henry, The Outside Child; Prizes: Yorkshire Post Novel of the Year Award (1976), Guardian Award for Children's Fiction (1976), Booker Short List for Circles of Deceit (1987); JP Surrey 1969-76; memb Video Appeals Ctee; FRSL; *Recreations* food, films, theatre, travel, politics, garden croquet; *Clubs* Groucho, Oriental; *Style—* Miss Nina Bawden; 22 Noel Road, London N1 8HA (☎ 071 226 2839); 19 Kapodistriou, Nauplion, Greece

BAXENDALE, Lady Elizabeth Joan; *née* Fortescue; da of 5 Earl Fortescue, KG, PC, CB, OBE, MC, (d 1958); *b* 1 Oct 1926; *m* 1946, Maj William Lloyd (John) Baxendale, JP, DL (d 1982), s of Capt Guy Vernon Baxendale (d 1969), of Framfield Place, Uckfield, Sussex ; 2 s, 1 da; *Style—* Lady Elizabeth Baxendale; Hailwell House, Framfield, Uckfield, E Sussex (☎ 082 580 256)

BAXENDALE, Lily; da of Herbert Baxendale (d 1959), and Rebecca Baxendale (d 1983); *b* 7 Aug 1924; *Educ* Accrington GS, Bedford Coll London (BSc); *Career* md Biorex Laboratories Ltd 1983- (sec and dir 1950-83); Queens Award for Tech Innovation 1972; CChem; *Style—* Miss Lily Baxendale; Biorex Laboratories Ltd, 2 Crossfield Chambers, Gladbeck Way, Enfield, Middx EN2 7HT (☎ 081 366 9301, fax 081 367 4627)

BAXENDALE, Thomas Dawtrey; s of Hugo Lloyd Baxendale, JP (d 1957), of Chidmere House, Chidham, W Sussex, and Eleanor Sibyl Mitford, *née* Oliver (d 1968); *b* 7 April 1937; *Educ* Eton; *Career* 2 Lt Welsh Grds 1957-58; called to the Bar Inner Temple 1962; in practice in Chancery 1963-, barr Lincolns Inn 1967, underwriting memb Lloyds 1970-, memb Syndicate 89 Ctee 1984-89; memb Ct Corpn of Sons of the Clergy 1972-; *Recreations* gardening, art, travel; *Clubs* Cavalry and Guards, Pratt's; *Style—* Thomas Baxendale, Esq; Chidmere House, Chidham, Chichester, Sussex; 24 Old Buildings, Lincoln's Inn, London WC2A 3UJ (☎ 071 404 0946, fax 071 405 1360)

BAXENDELL, Sir Peter Brian; CBE (1972); s of Lesley Wilfred Edward Baxendell (d 1968), and Evelyn Mary, *née* Gaskin; *b* 28 Feb 1925; *Educ* St Francis Xavier's Liverpool, Royal Sch of Mines (ARSM, BSc); *m* 1949, Rosemary, da of Herbert Leo Lacey; 2 s, 2 da; *Career* dir Shell Transport and Trading 1973- (chm 1979-85); chm Ctee of Mds Royal Dutch Shell Gp of Cos 1982-85; dir: Hawker Siddeley Group plc 1984- (chm 1986-), Inchcape PLC 1986-, Sun Life Assurance Co of Canada 1986-; memb Univ Grants Ctee 1983-89; Cdr of the Order of Orange-Nassau 1985; FEng 1978; fell Imperial Coll London 1983; Hon DSc: Heriot-Watt 1982, Queen's Univ of Belfast 1986, Univ of London 1986, Univ of Technology Loughborough 1987; *Recreations* tennis, fishing; *Clubs* Hurlingham; *Style—* Sir Peter Baxendell, CBE; Shell Centre, London SE1 7NA (☎ 071 934 2772)

BAXI, Vibhaker Kishore; s of Kishore Jayantilal Baxi (d 1967), and Indira Kishore Baxi; *b* 25 Dec 1947; *Educ* Brooklands Co Tech Coll Surrey, Univ of Surrey Guildford (BSc), Brunel Univ Uxbridge (PGCE), Manchester Business Sch (MBA); *m* 12 Nov 1978, Hina, da of Indulal Vaikunthrai Vaidya, of India; 1 da (Mamta b 1982); *Career* fin inst account offr Citibank Dubai 1975-76, asst treas Citibank NA Dubai 1976-78; treas: Citibank NA Bahrain 1979-80, Chem Bank Hong Kong 1981-85; head and md Money Mkt & Securities Trading Chem Bank London 1985-89, sr risk mangr (interest rates) Hong Kong & Shanghai Banking Corpn London 1989; *Style—* Vibhaker Baxi, Esq; 22 Sherwood Rd, London NW4 1AD (☎ 081 203 1503); Hong Kong Bank, 99 Bishopsgate, London EC2P 2LA (☎ 071 588 4591, fax 071 256 7637, telex 886340)

BAXTER, Glen; s of Charles Bertie Baxter, of Leeds, and Florence Mary, *née* Wood (d 1988); *b* 4 March 1944; *Educ* Cockburn HS Leeds, Leeds Coll of Art (NDD); *m* Carole Agis; 1 s (Harry b 1978), 1 da (Zoë b 1975); *Career* pt/t lectr Goldsmiths Coll London 1974-87; exhibitions: Gotham Book Mart Gallery NY 1974, 1976 and 1979, Fuller Goldeen San Francisco 1986, ICA London 1981, Museum of Modern Art, Oxford 1981, Nigel Greenwood 1981, 1983, 1987 and 1990, Galleria Del Cavallino Venice 1984, Royal Festival Hall 1984, Holly Solomon Gallery NY 1985 and 1988, Sydney Biennale 1986, Samia Gallery Paris 1987 and 1989, Musée de L'Abbaye Sainte-Croix Les Sables D'Olonne 1987, MUHKA Antwerp 1988, DC Art Sydney Australia 1990; *Books* The Impending Gleam (1981), Atlas (1982), His Life (1983), Jodhpurs in the Quantocks (1987), Charles Malarkey and the Belly Button Machine (with William and Bren Kennedy), Welcome to the Weird World of Glen Baxter (1989), The Billiard Table Murders - A Gladys Babbington Morton Mystery (1990); *Recreations* croquet, marquetry; *Clubs* Chelsea Arts, Groucho, Ale and Quail; *Style—* Glen Baxter, Esq; Aitken & Stone, 29 Fernshaw Rd, London SW10 0TG (☎ 071 351 7561)

BAXTER, Dr (William) Gordon; OBE (1964), DL (Morayshire 1985); s of William Alexander Baxter (d 1973), of Fochabers, Moray, and Ethelreda, *née* Adam (d 1963); *b* 8 Feb 1918; *Educ* Ashville Coll Harrogate, Univ of Aberdeen (BSc); *m* 26 Sept 1952, Euphemia Ellen (Ena), da of Thomas William Robertson (d 1955), of Castlepark, Huntly; 2 s (Andrew b 1958, Michael b 1962), 1 da (Audrey b 1961); *Career* res and devpt mangr ICI Explosives Ltd 1940-45; returned to family business WA Baxter & Sons Ltd: prodn dir 1946, md 1947, chm and md 1973; chm: Baxters of Speyside Ltd, Gordon & Ena Baxter Ltd, Grampian Food Technol Centre Ltd; former dir Grampian Regnl Bd of Bank of Scot; memb: Scot Cncl for Devpt and Indust, Cncl Royal Warrant Holders Assoc, Aberdeen Assoc Royal Warrant Holders, Scot Cons Party's Business Gp, Cncl Food Mfrs Fedn, N American Advsy Gp to the BOTB; Hon LLD Univ of Strathclyde 1987; MIOD 1970, FIGD 1983; *Recreations* fishing; *Clubs* Caledonian; *Style—* Dr Gordon Baxter, OBE, DL; Speybank House, Fochabers, Morayshire IV32 7HH (☎ 0343 821234); W A Baxter & Sons Ltd, Fochabers, Morayshire IV32 7LD (☎ 0343 820393, fax 0343 820286, telex 73327, car 0836 6529348)

BAXTER, Hon Mrs (Helen Margaretta); *née* Maude; da of 7 Viscount Hawarden (d 1958); *b* 23 Aug 1921; *Educ* Bedgebury Park Goudhurst Kent; *m* 10 May 1947, (Walter) Peter Baxter (d 1977), eldest s of Col Donald Baxter, MC (d 1969), of Longburton House, Sherborne, Dorset; 1 s (Charles), 3 da (Joanna, Margaretta, Victoria); *Style—* The Hon Mrs Baxter; Stourbridge House, Milton-on-Stour, Gillingham, Dorset (☎ 0747 823222)

BAXTER, Maj-Gen Ian Stuart; CBE (1982, MBE 1973); s of Charles Henry Baxter (d 1972), of Pendle, nr Nelson, Lancs, and Edith May, *née* Trinder; *b* 20 July 1937; *Educ* Ottershaw Sch; *m* 19 Aug 1961, Meg Lillian, da of Ronald Bullock, of Pensnett, Brierly Hill, Staffs; 3 da (Deborah b 1962, Louise b 1964, Marianna b 1971); *Career* cmmnd RASC 1958, regtl duty in UK, Kenya, India, NI (2 Lt, Capt) 1958-69, Staff Coll Camberley (Maj) 1970, DAA and QMG 8 Inf Bde Londonderry 1971-73, OC 60 Sqdn RCT 1973-74, NDC 1974-75, GSO 1 DS Staff Coll Camberley (Lt-Col) 1975-78, CO 2 Armd Div Tport Regt RCT 1978-80, Col AQ Commando Forces RM and Col Station Cdr Plymouth (incl Falklands campaign) 1980-84, RCDS 1984, Brig dir army recruiting MOD 1985-87, Maj-Gen ACDS (L) MOD 1987-90; Col Cmdt RCT 1989; ret 1990; antique dealer 1990-; *Recreations* antique restoration, gardening; *Style—* Maj-Gen Ian S Baxter, CBE; c/o Barclays Bank, 17-21 High Street, East Grinstead, West Sussex

BAXTER, John Lawson; DL (1988); s of Maj John Lawson Baxter, ERD (d 1983), of Coleraine, NI, and Enid Maud Taggart, *née* Adamson; *b* 25 Nov 1939; *Educ* Oundle, Trinity Coll Dublin (BA BComm), Queens Univ (LLB), Tulane Univ USA (LLM); *m* 28 Dec 1967, Astrid Irene, da of Max Eitcl, of Dungannon, Co Tyrone; 3 s (Warren Max John b 17 Sept 1968, David Robert b 19 Aug 1970, Max Douglas Lawson b 18 July 1973); *Career* admitted slr 1964, memb NI Assembly 1973-75, min of info NI Exec 1974, former memb NI Health Bd; pres Coleraine C of C 1969 and 1989; memb NI Law Soc; *Recreations* golf, fishing; *Clubs* Royal Portrush Golf, Portstewart Golf; *Style—* John Baxter, Esq, DL; c/o Wray & Baxter Slrs, 25 New Row, Coleraine, NI BT52 1AD (☎ 0265 54014, fax 0265 43403)

BAXTER, Keith Stanley; s of Capt Stanley Baxter-Wright (d 1960), of Swansea, and Emily Marian, *née* Howell (d 1972); *b* 29 April 1933; *Educ* Newport HS, Barry GS, RADA (Bronze medal); *Career* actor; stage: Oxford Repertory Co Playhouse Oxford Sept 1956, London debut Ralph in Tea & Sympathy (Comedy Theatre) April 1957, Hippolytus in Phedre (Stephen Joseph's Theatre in the Round) Nov 1957, Jean Pierre in Change of Tune (Strand Theatre) May 1959, Prince Hall in Chimes at Midnight (Opera House Belfast) March 1960, Roger in Time and Yellow Roses (St Martin's Theatre) May 1961, King Henry VIII in A Man for All Seasons (Anta Theatre, NY) Nov 1961, Howard in The Affair (Henry Miller's Theatre, NY) Sept 1962, Gino in Where Angels Fear To Tread (St Martin's) July 1963, Inspector in Torpe's Hotel (Yvonne Arnand, Guildford) Oct 1965, Valentine in You Can Never Tell (Haymarket) Jan 1966, Bob Acres in The Rivals (Haymarket) Oct 1966, Baldo in Avanti (Booth Theatre, NY) Feb 1968, Hooner in The Country Wife (Chichester) 1969, Octavius Caesar in Antony & Cleopatra (Chichester) 1969, Milo in Sleuth (St Martin's Theatre) Feb 1970 and (Music Box Theatre, NY) Nov 1970, Macbeth in Macbeth (Birmingham Repertory Theatre) Oct 1972, Vershinin in Three Sisters (Greenwich) Jan 1973, Benedick in Much Ado About Nothing (Lyceum, Edinburgh) Sept 1973, Rico in Tonight We Improvise (Chichester) 1974, Antony in Antony & Cleopatra and Witwoud in The Way of the World and Vershinin in Three Sisters (Stratford, Ontario) 1976, King in Red Devil Battery Sign (Phoenix Theatre) July 1977, Lord Illingworth in A Woman of No Importance and Dorante in The Inconstant Couple (Chichester) 1978, Patrick in A Meeting By the River (Palace Theatre, NY) March 1979, Bill in Home and Beauty (Kennedy Centre) June 1979, Hamlet in Hamlet (Citadel Theatre, Edmonton, Canada) Sept 1979, Sherlock Holmes in the Penultimate Case of Sherlock Holmes (Hudson Guild, NY) May 1980, Jason Carmichael in Romantic Comedy (Barrymore Theatre, NY) Sept 1980, Frederick in Undiscovered Country and Antony in Antony & Cleopatra and Kean in Kean (Hartford Stage Co) 1981, Gwilym in 56 Duncan Terrace (Citadel Theatre, Edmonton, Canada) Feb 1982, Narrator in Oedipus Rex (Philadelphia Opera) Oct 1982, Antony in Antony & Cleopatra (Young Vic) April 1983, Evelyn and Rupert in Corpse (Apollo) July 1984 and (Helen Hayes Theatre, NY) Dec 1984 and (Footbridge Theatre, Sydney, Aust) July 1986, Carleton in Light Up the Sky (Globe Theatre) July 1987; Dafydd in Barnaby and The Old Boys (Vaudeville Theatre) Dec 1989, Elyot in Private Lives (Aldwych) Sept 1990, Cassini in Julius Caesar (Hartford Stage Co, USA) March 1991; TV: Young May Moon 1958, Man & Superman 1958, Incident at Echo Six 1958, Dead Secret 1959, Sweet Poison 1959, After the Party 1960, Square Dance 1960, Jealousy 1962, Rewards of Silence 1963, For Tea on Sunday 1963, Nobody Kills Santa Claus 1964, I've Got A System 1964, Curtains For Sheila 1965, St Joan 1966, Love Story 1966, Shakespeare 1976; Films: The Barretts of Wimpole St 1956, Peeping Tom 1958, Chimes At Midnight 1967, Love in Mind 1968, Ash Wednesday 1973, Le Regenta 1974, Berlin Blues 1989; Radio: King Arthur in Arthur the King 1990; dir: Red Devil Battery Sign 1977, Time & The Conways 1988; Plays Written: 56 Duncan Terrace (1982), Cavell (1982), Barnaby & The Old Boys (1989); winner: Theatre World award NY 1961, Drama Desk award NY 1972; *Recreations* the sea; *Style—* Keith Baxter, Esq; ICM, 388/396 Oxford St, London W1N 9HE (☎ 071 629 8080)

BAXTER, Margaret Eleanor (Maggie); da of Charles Frank Alexander Baxter, JP, of Shaftesbury, Dorset, and Eleanor Frances Mary, *née* Bloomer; *b* 7 July 1947; *Educ* Godolphin Sch Wiltshire, Open Univ (BA); *m* 1 (m dis); ptnr 2, common law husband, George Sean Baine, s of Roney Baine (d 1988), of Belfast; 1 s (Alex b 13 May 1981), 1 da (Holly b 30 Jan 1985), 2 step s (Jack b 10 Feb 1972, Kieran b 25 May 1974); *Career* project dir Action Res Centre 1972-75, dir Dame Colet House Settlement Stepney 1975-80, vol orgns offr London Borough of Camden 1982-89, advsr Baring Fndn 1989-; tstee: Tst for London, City Parochial Fndn; govr Beckford Sch, chm Hampstead Sch PTA, memb Ctee W Hampstead Community Assoc; *Recreations* family, theatre, cinema, tennis; *Style—* Ms Maggie Baxter; 40 Hillfield Rd, London NW6 1PZ (☎ 071 794 2636)

BAXTER, Prof Murdoch Scott; s of John Sawyers Napier Baxter (d 1977), and Margaret Hastie, *née* Murdoch; *b* 12 March 1944; *Educ* Hutchesons' Boys' GS, Univ of Glasgow (BSc, PhD); *m* 3 Aug 1968, Janice, da of James Henderson (d 1990), of Shawlands, Glasgow; 1 foster s (John b 1969); *Career* visiting res fell (Apollo 11 Lunar Res) State Univ of NY 1969-70, sabbatical res conslt IAEA International Laboratory of Marine Radioactivity Monaco (radioactive waste disposal) 1981-82; Univ of Glasgow: lectr in environmental radiochemistry Dept of Chemistry 1970-85, dir Scottish Univ Res and Reactor Centre 1985-90, prof Univ of Glasgow 1985-, dir IAEA International Laboratory of Marine Radioactivity Monaco 1990-; memb: Challenger Soc, Scottish Marine Biological Assoc, NERC COGER Ctee, various IAEA expert gps, Ed Bd Journal of Radioanalytical and Nuclear Chemistry; fndr and ed Journal of Environmental Radioactivity (Elsevier Applied Sci Pubn); author of more than 120 res papers in scientific lit; CChem, FRSC 1984, FRSE 1989; *Recreations* sports, walking; *Clubs* Queens Park FC; *Style—* Prof Murdoch Baxter; IAEA International Laboratory of Marine Radioactivity, 19 Ave des Castellans, Principality of Monaco MC 98000 (☎ 33 93 50 44 88, telex 47 93 78 ILMR, fax 33 93 25 73 46)

BAXTER, Reginald de St Clair; s of Henry George Charles Baxter (d 1971), of Smitenwood House, Offord Cluny, Huntingdon, Cambridgeshire, and Ethel, *née* Palmer (d 1972); *b* 3 Aug 1918; *Educ* Kimbolton Sch Huntingdon, Cambridge Sch Certificate, Guildhall Sch of Music and Drama; *Career* WWII serv RA 1939-45;

1939-45 star, France & Germany star, Def Medal, End of War Medal; marine broker Sedgwick Collins & Co Ltd 1936-60, chief hull broker Pitman & Dean Ltd 1960-70 (later dir and md), md J H Minet, Baxter & Co Ltd 1970- (new broking house Reginald Baxter & Co (Insurance Brokers) Ltd formed 1977); memb Lloyds's 1963; close friend of Ivor Novello, established his memorial in crypt of St Paul's Cathedral, subsequently close friend of Noel Coward; Freeman City of London 1964, Worshipful Co of Carmen 1965; *Recreations* musical theatres; *Clubs* Reform; *Style—* Reginald Baxter, Esq; Cityside House, 40 Adler Street, London E1 1EE (☎ 071 247 3203, fax 071 377 1995)

BAXTER, Dr Roger George; s of Rev Benjamin George Baxter, and Gweneth Muriel, *née* Causer (d 1989); *b* 21 April 1940; *Educ* Handsworth GS Birmingham, Univ of Sheffield (BSc, PhD); *m* 1967, Dorothy Ann, da of Albert Leslie Cook (d 1949); 1 s (Philip b 1968), 1 da (Fiona b 1972); *Career* lectr Dept of Applied Mathematics Univ of Sheffield 1966-70 (jr res fell 1965-66), under master Winchester Coll 1976-81 (asst mathematics master 1970-81), headmaster Sedbergh Sch 1982-; govr: Bramcote Sch Scarborough, Hurworth House Sch Darlington, Mowden Hall Sch Northumberland, The Cathedral Choir Sch Ripon, Cundall Manor Sch York; memb: HMC Academic Policy Ctee (1985-90), Common Entrance Ctee; FRAS, FRSA; *Books* author of various papers on numerical studies in magnetoplasm diffusion with applications to the F-2 layer of the ionosphere including contrib to Proceedings of the Royal Society; *Recreations* production of opera, opera, music, cooking, wine; *Clubs* E India; *Style—* Dr Roger Baxter; Birksholme, Sedbergh, Cumbria LA10 5HQ (☎ 05396 20491); Sedbergh Sch, Sedbergh, Cumbria LA10 5HG (☎ 05396 20535)

BAXTER-WRIGHT, Keith; *see*: Baxter, Keith

BAYFIELD, Stephen Peter; s of Stanley William Henry Bayfield, of Harlow, and Eileen Lilian, *née* Sears; *b* 21 May 1954; *Educ* Brays Grove Harlow; *m* 20 July 1974, Margaret Anne, da of Edwin Stanley Barrett, of Brockholes, nr Huddersfield; 2 s (Richard b 1981, Mark b 1986), 1 da (Sarah b 1983); *Career* Inland Revenue 1976-78, Frazer Whiting & Co CA 1978-81, princ Robson Rhodes 1985- (joined 1981); memb Inst Taxation 1979; *Recreations* athletics, swimming; *Style—* Stephen Bayfield, Esq; Robson Rhodes, 186 City Rd, London EC1V 2NU (☎ 071 251 1644/ 071 251 0316 (after 6 pm), 0245 468123, fax 071 250 0801, telex 885734)

BAYLEY, Prof Frederick John (Fred); s of Frederick John Bayley (d 1974), of Greenhithe, Kent, and Kate, *née* Dalley (d 1967); *b* 30 July 1928; *Educ* Gravesend GS, King's Coll Newcastle, Univ of Durham (BSc, MSc, PhD, DSc); *m* 1 April 1950, Norma June, da of Robert Ferguson (d 1969), of Whitley Bay, Northumberland; 2 s (Robert b 1952, Keith b 1963), 1 da (Janette (Mrs Clark) b 1956); *Career* scientific offr Nat Gas Turbine Estab Farnborough 1948-51, res engr Pametrada Res Station Wallsend 1951-53; reader (formerly lectr) in mechanical engrg Univ of Durham (later Newcastle) 1955-65 (James Clayton res fell mechanical engrg 1953-55), sr pro vice chllr Univ of Sussex 1988- (prof mechanical engrg 1966-, dean engrg 1979-80, pro vice chllr sci 1980-85); memb: Aeronautical Res Cncl 1965-75, Def Scientific Advsy Ctee 1977-81; FIMechE 1966; *Books* Introduction to Fluid Dynamics (1958), Heat Transfer (with J M Owen and A B Turner, 1972), numerous scientific and tech papers; *Recreations* photography, walking; *Clubs* Athenaeum; *Style—* Prof Fred Bayley; Camberley, Firle Rd, Seaford, E Sussex (☎ 0323 490024); Univ of Sussex, Falmer, Brighton, E Sussex (☎ 0273 606755)

BAYLEY, Gordon Vernon; CBE (1976); s of Capt Vernon Bayley (d 1949), and Gladys Maud, *née* Sharp (d 1985); *b* 25 July 1920; *Educ* Abingdon Sch Oxon; *m* 25 Aug 1945, (Miriam Allenby) Theresa, da of Frederick Walter Ellis (d 1959); 1 s (Mark b 1960), 2 da (Angela b 1946, Susan b 1948); *Career* joined HM Forces 1940, cmmnd RA, Maj 1945; asst actuary Equitable Life Assur Soc 1949, ptnr Duncan C Fraser & Co 1954-57, gen mangr and actuary Nat Provident Inst 1964-85 (asst sec 1957, jt sec 1959); chm: Swiss Reinsurance Co (UK) Ltd 1985-, Life Offices Assoc 1969-70; memb: Occupational Pensions Bd 1973-74, Steering Bd Companies House 1988-91, Ctee to Review Functioning of Fin Institutions 1977-80; chm Bd Govrs Abingdon Sch 1979-83; Freeman Worshipful Co of Insurers 1979; FIA 1946 (pres 1974-76), FSS 1947, FIMA 1976, CBIM 1980; *Recreations* skiing, sailing; *Clubs* Athenaeum, English Speaking Union, Sea View Yacht; *Style—* Gordon Bayley, Esq, CBE; The Old Manor, Witley, Surrey GU8 5QW (☎ 042868 2301); 71-77 Leadenhall St, London EC3A 2PQ (☎ 071 623 3456, fax 071 623 5819, telex 884380 SRUK G)

BAYLEY, Michael Hugh Headington; s of Lt Frederic Hugh Bayley (d 1938), and Elsa Dorothy Bayley (d 1987); *b* 13 Oct 1922; *Educ* Imperial Service Coll Windsor, Sch of Architecture Oxford (Dip Arch); *m* 7 Aug 1948, Pauline Denys, da of Gustav Oppenheimer (d 1945), of Raymead, Maidenhead, Berks; 2 s (Hugh b 1952, Antony b 1964), 2 da (Justine b 1950, Annabel b 1961); *Career* cmmnd Cheshire Regt 1944, Kensington Regt France and Germany 1944-45, OBLI 6 Airborne 1945, 6 Palestine RASC Greece 1946, Lieut; chartered architect in private practice 1959-, asst to Diocesan Architect for Bucks 1956-59; memb: Maidenhead Civic Soc, Maidenhead C of C, Berks Local Hist Assoc; ARIBA; *Recreations* drawing, local history and legends, celtic place names; *Style—* Michael Bayley, Esq; New Britwell, Westmorland Rd, Maidenhead, Berks SL6 4HD (☎ 0628 20576)

BAYLEY, Prof Peter Charles; s of William Charles Abell Bayley (d 1939), and Irene Evelyn Beatrice, *née* Heath (d 1962); *b* 25 Jan 1921; *Educ* The Crypt Sch Gloucester, Univ Coll Oxford (MA); *m* 30 June 1951 (m dis), Patience, da of Sir George Norman Clark; 1 s (Nicholas), 2 da (Rosalind, Clare); *Career* RA 1941-46; master of Collingwood Coll Durham 1972-78, emeritus prof Univ of St Andrews 1985- (Berry prof of English 1978-85), emeritus fell Univ Coll Oxford 1987- (fell 1947-72); *Books* The Faerie Queene (ed, vol 1 1965, vol 2 1966), Edmund Spenser, Prince of Poets (1971), Loves and Deaths (ed, 1972), A Casebook on The Faerie Queene (ed, 1977), On Selected Poems of John Milton (1982), An ABC of Shakespeare (1985); *Style—* Prof Peter Bayley; 63 Oxford St, Woodstock, Oxon OX7 1TJ (☎ 0993 812300)

BAYLEY, Prof Peter James; s of John Henry Bayley, of Portreath, Cornwall, and Margaret, *née* Burness; *b* 20 Nov 1944; *Educ* Redruth GS, Emmanuel Coll Cambridge (MA, PhD), Ecole Normale Superieure Paris; *Career* fell: Emmanuel Coll Cambridge 1969-71, Gonville and Caius Coll Cambridge 1971-; Drapers prof of French Univ of Cambridge 1985- (lectr in French 1978-85); Officier des Palmes Academiques France 1988; *Books* French Pulpit Oratory 1598-1650 (1980), Selected Sermons of the French Baroque (1983); *Recreations* Spain, wine and food, gardening; *Style—* Prof Peter Bayley; Department of French, Sidgwick Ave, Cambridge CB3 9DA (☎ 0223 335009)

BAYLEY, Stephen Paul; s of Donald Sydney Bayley, of Staffs, and Anne, *née* Wood; *b* 13 Oct 1951; *Educ* Quarry Bank Sch Liverpool, Univ of Manchester (BA), Univ of Liverpool (MA); *m* 29 Sept 1981, Flo, da of Richard Ernest Fothergill, of London; 1 s (Bruno b 3 June 1985), 1 da (Coco b 9 March 1987); *Career* history and theory of art lectr: Open Univ 1974-76, Univ of Kent 1976-80; dir: Boilerhouse Project 1981-86, Conran Fndn 1981-, Arts Fndn 1990-; principal Eye-Q Limited 1990-, chief exec The Design Museum 1981-90; memb Design Policy Ctee LRT, govr History of Advertising Tst; FRSA; Chevalier des Arts et Lettres 1989; *Books* In Good Shape (1979), Albert Memorial (1981), Harley Earl (1983), Conran Directory of Design (1985), Sex, Drink and Fast Cars (1986), Commerce and Culture (1989); *Recreations* words, pictures, food, drink, travel, sport; *Clubs* Savile, Chelsea Arts Acad; *Style—* Stephen Bayley, Esq; Eye-Q Limited, 30 Chelsea Wharf, London SW10 0QJ (☎ 071 351 5084, fax 071 351 5128)

BAYLIS, Rear Adm Robert Goodwin (Bob); CB (1984), OBE (1964); s of Harold Goodwin Baylis (d 1963), and Evelyn May, *née* Whitworth (d 1961); *b* 29 Nov 1925; *Educ* Highgate Sch, Univ of Cambridge (MA); *m* 1949, Joyce Rosemary, da of Lawrence Dyer Churchill (d 1952); 2 s (Mark, Nicholas), 1 da (Rachel); *Career* joined RN 1943; Fleet Weapons Engr Offr 1973-75, Capt RN Engrg Coll 1975-78, staff of Vice Chief of Def Staff 1979-80; chief exec R G Baylis & Associates (mgmnt and engrg conslt), conslt GEC Avionics, dir Reliability Consultants Ltd, pres Ordnance Bd 1980-84; chm Nuffield Theatre Tst, assoc memb (emeritus) Aust Ordnance Cncl; memb: Univ of Southampton Devpt Tst, Euro Atlantic Group; *Recreations* windsurfing, theatre, tennis; *Clubs* Landsdowne, Owls; *Style—* Rear Adm Bob Baylis, CB, OBE; Broadwaters, 4 Cliff Rd, Hill Head, Fareham, Hants PO14 3JS (☎ 0329 663392)

BAYLISS, Dr Christopher Richard Butler; s of Sir Richard Bayliss, KCVO, and Margaret Joan, *née* Lawson; *b* 10 Oct 1945; *Educ* Rugby, Clare Coll Cambridge (MA, MB BCh); *m* 20 May 1978, (Felicity) Nicola, da of Ivor Adye (d 1972); 1 s (Timothy Richard b 1985), 2 da (Clare Alexandra b 1982, Lucy Margaret b 1988); *Career* sr registrar X-ray Dept Royal Postgrad Med Sch Hammersmith Hosp London 1976-79, conslt med diagnostic imaging Royal Devon and Exeter Hosp 1979-; memb Central Conslts and Specialists Ctee; FRCR; *Recreations* skiing, golf; *Clubs* East Devon Golf, Budleigh Salterton; *Style—* Dr Christopher Bayliss; St Johns, Exton, Devon EX3 0PL (☎ 0392 875117); Royal Devon & Exeter Hosp, Exeter, Devon (☎ 0392 405153)

BAYLISS, Jeremy David Bagot; s of Edmund Bayliss (d 1990), of Guernsey, and Marjorie Clare Thompson (d 1983); *b* 27 March 1937; *Educ* Harrow, Sidney Sussex Coll Cambridge (MA); *m* 1962, Hon Mrs Mary Selina Bayliss, 3 da of 2 Viscount Bridgeman, KBE, CB, DSO, MC (d 1982); 3 s (Jonathan Andrew Bagot b 2 Jan 1964, Richard Charles b 11 Dec 1965, Patrick Thomas Clive b 6 March 1968); *Career* Nat Serv 2 Lt Coldstream Gds 1956-57; Gerald Eve & Company: joined 1960, ptnr 1967, jt sr ptnr 1988, sr ptnr 1990-; chm Gerald Eve Financial Services Ltd 1989-; memb Gen Cncl RICS 1987-, pres Planning and Devpt Div RICS 1989-90; memb Rating Surveyors Assoc 1976, FRICS 1971 (ARICS 1962); *Recreations* gardening, shooting, reading, tapestry work; *Clubs* Boodles; *Style—* Jeremy Bayliss, Esq; Sheepbridge Court, Swallowfield, nr Reading, Berkshire RG7 1PT (☎ 0734 883218, fax 071 491 1825, car 0836 685693)

BAYLISS, John Leslie; s of Leslie William Bayliss (d 1987), of Birmingham, and Ellen, *née* Rose; *b* 29 Nov 1940; *Educ* Handsworth GS Birmingham, Univ of Leeds (BSc), Univ of Aston; *m* 19 March 1966, Fiona Lennox, da of Frederick Charles Hicks, of Wootton Bassett, Wilts; 3 s (Richard b 1969, Jonathan b 1971, David b 1974); *Career* distribution mangr Lucas Batteries Ltd 1973-78, dir Flockvale Ltd 1982 (divnl mangr 1978-81); chm: Flockvale Distribution Ltd 1982-, Idealcare Ltd 1982-, Sollihull Business and Educn in Ptnrship, Midland Express Parcels Ltd 1986-; memb Solihull Careers Assoc, vice chm of govrs Lyndon Sch Solihull, ctee memb 1 Solihull Scout Gp; author of numerous papers and articles in professional jls; FBIS 1984, FILDM 1984, FBIM 1985, FInstD 1987, FInstAA; *Recreations* badminton, family history, industrial archeaology; *Style—* John Bayliss, Esq; 44 Links Drive, Solihull, W Mids B91 2DL; Flockvale Distribution Ltd, Minworth Industrial Pk, Sutton Coldfield, W Mids B76 8AH (☎ 021 351 6111, fax 021 351 4895, car 0831 522143)

BAYLISS, Hon Mrs (Mary Selina); *née* Bridgeman; da of 2 Viscount Bridgeman, KBE, CB, DSO, MC (d 1982); *b* 14 Jan 1940; *m* 1962, Jeremy David Bagot Bayliss, s of Edmund Bayliss; 3 s; *Career* memb Court of Reading Univ 1982; govr Chiltern Nursery Training Coll; *Recreations* music, gardening; *Style—* The Hon Mrs Bayliss, JP; Sheepbridge Court, Swallowfield, nr Reading, Berks RG1 1PT

BAYLISS, Sir Noel Stanley; CBE (1960); s of Henry Bayliss (d 1948), of NSW, and Nelly Stothers; *b* 19 Dec 1906; *Educ* Melbourne HS, Queens Coll Univ of Melbourne, Lincoln Coll Oxford, Univ of California Berkeley; *m* 1933, Nellie Elise, da of Arthur Banks, of Los Angeles; 2 s; *Career* prof of chemistry Univ of W Australia 1938-71 (emeritus 1972); memb Aust Univs Cmmn 1959-70, memb Hong Kong Univs and Polys Grants Cmmn 1966-73, chm Murdoch Univ Planning Bd 1970-73; kt 1979; *see Debrett's Handbook of Australia and New Zealand for further details*; *Recreations* music, golf; *Clubs* Royal Perth Yacht, Nedlands Golf (WA); *Style—* Sir Noel Bayliss, CBE; 104 Thomas St, Nedlands, W Australia 6009 (☎ 010 619 386 1453)

BAYLISS, Sir Richard Ian Samuel; KCVO (1978); s of late Frederick William Bayliss, of Tettenhall, and late Muryel Anne Bayliss; *b* 2 Jan 1917; *Educ* Rugby, Clare Coll Cambridge, St Thomas' Hosp London (MD); *m* 1, 1941 (m dis 1956), Margaret Joan Lawson; 1 s, 1 da; m 2, 1957, Constance Ellen, da of Wilbur J Frey, of Connecticut; 2 da; m 3, 1979, Marina, wid of Charles Rankin; *Career* conslt physician: Westminster Hosp 1954-81, King Edward VII's Hosp for Offrs 1964-86; med dir Swiss Reinsurance Co 1969-85, physician to HM The Queen 1970-82, head of HM's Med Household 1973-82, dir and vice chm Private Patients Plan plc 1979-89, dir J S Pathology plc 1980-90, hon med advsr Nuffield Hosps 1981-88, asst dir RCP Res Unit London 1982-88; second vice pres RCP 1983-84; hon fell Clare Coll Cambridge, memb Med Advsy Panel ITC, conslt Biotechnology Investments Ltd; FRCP; *Recreations* skiing, photography, music; *Clubs* Garrick; *Style—* Sir Richard Bayliss, KCVO; Flat 7, 61 Onslow Sq, London SW7 3LS (☎ 071 589 3087)

BAYLY, Vice Adm Sir Patrick Uniacke; KBE (1968), CB (1965), DSC (1944) and two bars (1944, 1951); s of Lancelot F S Bayly (d 1951), and Eileen M Bayly, of Nenagh, Co Tipperary; *b* 4 Aug 1914; *Educ* Aravon Bray Co Wicklow, RNC Dartmouth; *m* 1945, Moy Gourlay, da of Robert Gourlay Jardine, of Newtonmearns, Scotland; 2 da (Caroline, Jennifer); *Career* midshipman 1932, combined ops 1941-43, Lt Cdr 1943, HMS Mauritius 1944, Cdr 1948, Korean War 1952-53, Capt 1954, IDC 1957, Capt (D) 6 Destroyer Sqdn 1958, staff SACLANT Norfolk Va 1960, C of S Med 1962, Rear Adm 1963, Flag Offr Sea Trg 1963, Adm pres RNC Greenwich 1965, Vice Adm 1967, C of S COMNAVSOUTH Malta 1967, ret 1970; dir The Maritime Tst 1971-88, chm Falklands Appeal 1983-89; *Style—* Vice Adm Sir Patrick Bayly, KBE, CB, DSC and two bars; Dunning House, Liphook, Hants (☎ 0428 723116)

BAYMAN, Margaret Elizabeth; da of George William Walsh, of 28 South Park, Lytham, Lytham St Annes, Lancs, and Janet Featherstone, *née* Firth; *b* 2 Aug 1943; *Educ* Fylde Lodge HS for Girls Stockport, Arnold HS for Girls Blackpool Lancs; *m* 9 Sept 1967, Paul Aubrey Robert Bayman, s of Capt Aubrey Fredrick James Bayman, of 14 Romney Rd, New Malden, Surrey; 2 s (David b 1973, Matthew b 1974), 2 da (Catherine b 1969, Sarah b 1970); *Career* accountant Retail Suppliers Ltd 1989-; treas: Claygate Scout Gp 1982-89, PTA Claremont Fan Court Sch 1988-; FCA (1968); *Recreations* reading, theatre, history; *Style—* Mrs Margaret Bayman; 45 Oaken Lane, Claygate, Esher, Surrey

BAYNE, Dr Nicholas Peter; CMG (1984); s of Capt Ronald Bayne, RN (d 1978), and Elisabeth Margaret, *née* Ashcroft; *b* 15 Feb 1937; *Educ* Eton, ChCh Oxford (MA, DPhil); *m* 1961, Diana, da of Thomas Wilde, of Bideford, N Devon; 2 s (and 1 decd); *Career* HM Dip Serv; ambass Zaire 1983-85; non resident ambass: Congo 1984-85, Rwanda and Burundi 1984-85; UK perm rep OECD Paris 1985-88, dep under sec of state FCO 1988-; *Style—* Dr Nicholas Bayne, CMG; c/o Foreign and Commonwealth Office, King Charles St, London SW1

BAYNE-JARDINE, Colin Charles; s of Brig Christian West Bayne-Jardine, CBE, DSO, MC (d 1959), and Isobel Anna, *née* Forman; *b* 8 Jan 1932; *Educ* Marlborough, Univ Coll Oxford (MA), Univ of Bristol (MEd); *m* 7 Sept 1957, (Helen) Elizabeth, da of Arthur Douglas Roberts, OBE (d 1979); 4 s (John b 1958, Charles b 1960, Thomas b 1962, Andrew b 1963); *Career* 2 Lt RA BAOR; Capt RA TA; teacher: St Paul's Sch Concord New Hampshire USA 1956-57, Upper Canada Coll Toronto Canada 1957-58, Glasgow Acad 1958-61, Blundell's Sch 1961-65, Henbury Sch Bristol 1966-69, Univ of Bristol 1969-70; headmaster: Culverhay Sch Bath 1970-76, Henbury Sch Bristol 1976-85; sr inspr (secdy) Staffs 1986-88, princ co inspr Hereford and Worcester 1988-; chm of govrs Downs Sch Wraxall, memb Local Review Ctee Bristol Prison, memb Cncl Cheltenham Coll; *Books* Mussolini and Italy (1966), World War Two (1968), World War Two and Its Aftermath (1986); *Style*— Colin Bayne-Jardine, Esq; The Half Timbered Barn, Church Lane, Eldersfield, Glos GL19 4NP; Education Office, Castle St, Worcester WA1 3AG (☎ 0905 763763)

BAYNES, Christopher Rory; s and h of Sir John Baynes, 7 Bt, *qv*; *b* 11 May 1956; *Career* ACA 1982; *Style*— Christopher Baynes, Esq

BAYNES, Sir John Christopher Malcolm; 7 Bt (UK 1801); s of Lt-Col Sir Rory Malcolm Stuart Baynes, 6 Bt (d 1979), and Ethel Audrey, *née* Giles (d 1947); *b* 24 April 1928; *Educ* Sedbergh, RMA Sandhurst, Univ of Edinburgh (MSc); *m* 1955, Shirley Maxwell, da of Robert A Dodds, of Foxbury House, Lesbury, Alnwick, Northumberland (d 1952); 4 s (Christopher, *qv*, b 1956, Timothy b 1957, Simon b 1960, William b 1966); *Heir* s, Christopher Rory, b 11 May 1956; *Career* Ranks and Sandhurst 1946-48; Offr 1948-72; Lt-Col (ret) Cameronians (Scot Rifles) 1948-68, Malaya 1952 (despatches), Aden 1966, cmd 52 (L) vols 1969-72; Queen's Own Highlanders 1968-72; writer; Order of the Sword 1 Class (Sweden) 1965; *Publications* Morale: A Study of Men and Courage (1967 and 1987), The Jacobite Rising of 1715 (1970), The Soldier in Modern Society (1971), Vol IV of The History of The Cameronians (Scot Rifles) (1971), Soldiers of Scotland (1988), The Forgotten Victor: The Life of General Sir Richard O'Connor (1989), A Tale of Two Captains (1990); *Recreations* shooting, fishing, golf, reading; *Clubs* Army and Navy; *Style*— Lt-Col Sir John Baynes, Bt; Talwrn Bach, Llanfyllin, Powys SY22 5LQ (☎ 069 184 576)

BAYNES, Pauline Diana; da of Frederick William Wilberforce Baynes, CIE, and Jessie Harriet Maud Cunningham; *b* 9 Sept 1922; *Educ* Beaufront Sch Camberley, Farnham Sch of Art, Slade Sch of Art; *m* 1961, Fritz Otto Gasch; *Career* designer and book illustrator; *Style*— Miss Pauline Baynes; Rock Barn Cottage, Dockenfield, Farnham, Surrey (☎ 0428 713306)

BAYNHAM, Prof (Alexander) Christopher; s of Alexander Baynham (d 1965), of Stroud, Glos, and Dulcie Rowena, *née* Rees (d 1959); *b* 22 Dec 1935; *Educ* Marling Sch, Univ of Reading (BSc), Univ of Warwick (PhD), RCDS; *m* 5 Aug 1961, Eileen May, da of George Wilson, of Tadcaster, Yorks; 2 s (Andrew b 27 April 1965, Peter b 13 Oct 1966), 1 da (Sharon b 8 March 1968); *Career* Civil Serv 1955-: dir Royal Signals and Radar Estab 1984-86, dir Royal Armament R & D Estab 1986-89, princ Cranfield Inst of Technol Campus; involved in local church activities; *Style*— Prof Christopher Baynham; Cranfield Inst of Technol, Shrivenham, Swindon, Wilts SN6 8LA (☎ 0793 785437)

BAYNTUN-COWARD, Hylton Henry; s of Leslie Lancelot Coward (d 1982), of Combe Royal, Bath, and Constance Louise Muriel, *née* Bayntun; *b* 17 Nov 1932; *Educ* Cheltenham; *m* 1 June 1963, Charlotte Anne Wentworth, da of Sir John Gibbons, 8 Bt (d 1982), of Preston, Dorset; 2 s (Edward b 1966, Jo b 1972), 2 da (Emma b 1964, Polly b 1970); *Career* antiquarian bookseller, md George Bayntun incorporating Robert Riviere 1954-, proprietor George Gregory Gallery 1963-, fndr Museum of Bookbinding 1977, vice pres Antiquarian Booksellers' Assoc (Int) 1990- (hon treas 1977-80 and 1986-90, pres 1980-82); *Recreations* farming, conservation; *Style*— Hylton Bayntun-Coward, Esq; Dunkerton Grange, nr Bath BA2 8BL (☎ 0761 32366); Manvers St, Bath BA1 1JW (☎ 0225 466000)

BAZALGETTE, Rear Adm Derek Willoughby; CB (1976); yr s of Harry L Bazalgette (d 1953); *b* 22 July 1924; *Educ* RNC Dartmouth; *m* 1947, Angela Hilda Vera, da of Sir Henry Hinchliffe (d 1980); 4 da; *Career* RN 1938-76, Admiral Pres Royal Naval Coll Greenwich 1974-76, ADC 1974; princ Netley Waterside House 1977-83 (local govt); HQ cmmr Scout Assoc 1977-87; Independent Inquiry inspr 1983-; memb General Synod 1985, treas Corp of the Sons of the Clergy 1988; *Clubs* Lansdowne; *Style*— Rear Adm Derek Bazalgette, CB; The Glebe House, Newtown, Fareham, Hants (☎ 0329 833138)

BAZLEY, Thomas John Sebastian; s and h of Sir Thomas Bazley, 3 Bt, *qv*; *b* 31 Aug 1948; *Style*— Thomas Bazley, Esq

BAZLEY, Sir Thomas Stafford; 3 Bt (UK 1869); s of late Gardner Sebastian Bazley, o s of 2 Bt; suc gf, Sir Thomas Sebastian Bazley, 2 Bt, 1919; *b* 5 Oct 1907; *Educ* Harrow, Magdalen Coll Oxford; *m* 1945, Carmen, da of J Tulla; 3 s, 2 da; *Heir* s, Thomas John Sebastian Bazley, *qv*, b 31 Aug 1948; *Style*— Sir Thomas Bazley, Bt; Eastleach Downs Farm, Eastleach Turville, Cirencester, Glos GL7 3PX

BEACH, Gen Sir (William Gerald) Hugh; GBE (1980, OBE 1966), KCB (1976), MC (1944); s of Maj-Gen William Henry Beach, CB, CMG, DSO (d 1952), and Constance Maude, *née* Cammell; *b* 20 May 1923; *Educ* Winchester, Peterhouse Cambridge (MA), Univ of Edinburgh (MSc); *m* 1951, Estelle Mary (d 1989), da of Gordon Henry, of Epsom, Surrey; 3 s, 1 da; *Career* served WWII RE, N W Europe and Far East, Lt-Col 1963, Brig 1968, Cdr 12 Inf Bde BAOR 1968-71, dir Army Staff Duties MOD 1971-74, Maj-Gen 1971, Cmdt Staff Coll Camberley 1974-75, dep C-in-C UK Land Forces 1976-77, master-gen of the Ordnance 1977-81, Hon Col Cambridge Univ OTC 1979-89; Vice-Lord-Lt Gtr London 1981-87 (DL 1981); warden St George's House Windsor 1981-86, memb Security Cmmn 1982-, Chief Royal Engr 1982-87, chm Study Gp on Censorship to Protect Mil Info 1983, dir The Cncl for Arms Control 1986-89; chm: Rochester 2000, Winchester Diocesan Cncl for the Care of Churches, Gordon's Sch Fndn, Govrs of Bedales Sch, Governing Body of the Church Army; patron Venturers Search and Rescue, pres Sheffield Branch CPRE, memb Governing Body of SPCK; Hon DCL Univ of Kent; *Recreations* sailing, skiing; *Clubs* Farmers', Royal Lymington Yacht; *Style*— Gen Sir Hugh Beach, GBE, KCB, MC; The Ropeway, Beaulieu, Hants (☎ 0590 612269)

BEACHAM, Stephanie; *b* 28 Feb 1947; *Educ* Convent of the Sacred Heart Whetstone, QEGGS, RADA, Mime School Paris; *m* ; 2 da (Phoebe b 1974, Chloe b 1977); *Career* actress; stage performances incl: Tea Party and the Basement Duchess Theatre 1969, London Cuckolds Royal Court Theatre 1977, Venice Preserved NT 1985, The Rover RSC 1988; TV performances incl: Tenko 1982, Connie 1984, The Colbys and Dynasty (ABC TV USA) 1985-87 and 1988-89, Sister Kate (NBC TV USA) 1989-; film Nightcomers; spokesperson American Speech Language and Hearing Assoc; *Style*— Ms Stephanie Beacham; 1131 Alta Loma, West Hollywood, CA 90069 USA (☎ 213 652 6254)

BEADLE, Geoffrey Richard Munro; s of Richard Frederick William Beadle (d 1964), of Birchington, Kent, and Lily May-Ena, *née* Green (d 1976); *b* 23 March 1929; *Educ* Chatham House GS Ramsgate, Balliol Coll Oxford (BA, MA); *m* 11 Aug 1966, Cosette Helene May, da of Septimus Frederick Oswald Harris, of Lee-on-the-Solent, Hants; 1 da (Philippa Helen b 1969); *Career* Gunner Nat Serv RA 1951, 2 Lt 58 Med Regt RA 1952-53, discharged HAC (TA) 1953-57; admitted slr 1957; asst slr Pearless de Rougemont & Co E Grinstead 1957-58, sr ptnr Boys & Maughan Margate and Canterbury 1989 (joined 1958, ptnr 1961); pres Rotary Club Sandwich 1964-65 (vice pres 1963-64), musical dir Dover Choral Soc 1967-88, churchwarden Kingston nr Canterbury 1974-81; *Recreations* singing, choir training, golf, reading; *Clubs* United Oxford and Cambridge Univ; *Style*— Geoffrey Beadle, Esq; 14 New Dover Rd, Canterbury, Kent CT1 3AP (☎ 0227 459817); Messrs Boys & Maughan, 1 St Margarets St, Canterbury, Kent CT1 2TT (☎ 0227 464481, fax 0227 762311)

BEAKBANE, (Henry) Renault; s of Henry Beakbane, of Stourport-on-Severn (d 1953); *b* 28 April 1923; *Educ* Leighton Park, Univ of Leeds, LSE (BSc); *m* 1951, Joan, da of Henry Epton Hornby, OBE, of Zimbabwe (d 1976); 2 s, 1 da; *Career* Colonial Serv Tanganyika 1946-50, chm Beakbane Ltd; Master Worshipful Co of Glovers 1979; Quaker; CBIM, FRSA; *Recreations* riding (horses Gemini of Lockmeadow, Myricaria); *Clubs* BHS (bridleway offr W Midlands Regn), The Ludlow Hunt; *Style*— Renault Beakbane, Esq; Jacob's Ladder, Low Habberley, Kidderminster, Worcs DY11 5RF

BEAL, Anthony Ridley; s of Harold Beal, and Nesta Beal; *b* 28 Feb 1925; *Educ* Haberdashers' Aske's, Downing Coll Cambridge; *m* 1, 1958, Rosemary Jean Howarth (d 1989); 3 da; m 2, 1990, Carmen Dolores Carter; *Career* chm Heinemann Educnl Books 1979-85, md Heinemann Educnl Books (Int) 1979-85, dir Heinemann Gp of Publishers 1973-85, chm Educational Publishers Cncl 1980-83; memb Cncl of the Publishers Assoc 1982-86; *Books* D H Lawrence, D H Lawrence: Selected Literary Criticism; *Style*— Anthony Beal, Esq; 19 Homefield Rd, Radlett, Herts (☎ 0923 85 4567)

BEALBY, Walter; s of Harry Bealby, of Nottingham, and Heulwen, *née* Morris; *b* 8 Jan 1953; *Educ* Henry Mellish GS Nottingham, Univ of Bristol (BA); *m* 22 Nov 1980, Finnula Leonora Patricia, da of Daniel O'Leary, of Abingdon, Oxon; 1 s (Thomas Henry b 21 Jan 1985), 1 da (Polly Megan b 5 July 1988); *Career* called to the Bar Middle Temple 1976; Blackstone scholarship 1977; *Recreations* loafing; *Clubs* Nat Lib; *Style*— Walter Bealby, Esq; 9 King's Bench Walk, Temple, London EC4 7DX (☎ 071 353 5638, fax 071 353 6166)

BEALE, Prof Hugh Gurney; s of Charles Beale, TD, of Birmingham, and Anne Freeland, *née* Gurney-Dixon (d 1953); *b* 4 May 1948; *Educ* The Leys Sch Cambridge, Exeter Coll Oxford (BA); *m* 18 July 1970, Jane Wilson, da of Nathan Cox (d 1980), of Clarkton, N Carolina; 2 s (Ned b 1977, Thomas b 1979), 1 da (Martha b 1981); *Career* lectr Univ of Connecticut 1969-71, called to the Bar Lincoln's Inn 1971, lectr UCW Aberystwyth 1971-73, reader Univ of Bristol 1986-87 (lectr 1973-86), prof of law Univ of Warwick 1987-; memb Commission for Euro Contract Law 1987-; *Books* Remedies for Breach of Contract (1980), Contract Cases and Materials (with W D Bishop and M P Furmston, 1985); *Recreations* fishing, music, walking; *Style*— Prof Hugh Beale; School of Law, University of Warwick, Coventry CV4 7AL (☎ 0203 523185, fax 0203 524105)

BEALE, (Alfred) James; s of Alfred James Beale (d 1950), of Edinburgh, and Thomasina Wilkie, *née* Robertson (d 1990); *b* 12 July 1935; *Educ* George Heriot's Sch, Univ of Edinburgh (MA); *m* 30 Aug 1958, Kathleen, da of George Edward McHugh; 1 s (David Alistair b 31 Jan 1963), 1 da (Susan Carole b 4 Dec 1960); *Career* Nat Serv 2 Lt 1 Bn Royal Scots 1957-59; brand mangr Procter & Gamble Ltd 1959-64; P A Consulting Gp: mktg 1964-68, mktg supervisor 1968-72, regnl mangr NI 1972-77, dir in charge NE Eng 1978-, chief exec P A Cambridge Economic Consultants 1987-; govr Ulster Coll 1974-77, pres NI Chamber of Commerce and Indust 1977-78, nat chm Chartered Inst of Mktg 1991- (chm NI branch 1975-76, chm NE branch 1983-84), chm Northumbria branch BIM 1983-85, govr Centre for Info on Language Teaching and Res; memb: Product Devpt Ctee Business and Tech Educn Cncl (chm Languages Panel), Prog Advsy Gp Poly and Colls Funding Cncl, Indust Lead Bodies (responsible for languages, accountancy and mktg standards); FCIM, FBIM, FIMC, FInstD; *Books* Irish Salesman Under The Mircoscope (1981); *Recreations* golf; *Style*— James Beale, Esq; Hallbankfield, Newcastle Road, Corbridge, Northumberland NE45 5LN (☎ 0434 632158); P A Consulting Group, A Floor, Milburn House, Dean St, Newcastle upon Tyne NE1 1LE (☎ 091 232 8038, fax 091 232 2557)

BEALE, Nicholas Clive Lansdowne; s of Prof Evelyn Martin Lansdowne Beale, FRS (d 1985), and Violette Elizabeth Anne, *née* Lewis; *b* 22 Feb 1955; *Educ* Winchester, Trinity Coll Cambridge (MA); *m* 16 July 1977, Christine Ann, da of Peter Macpoland, of Bedford; 1 s (Rupert Christopher Lansdowne b 1977), 1 da (Rebecca Merryn Elizabeth b 1980); *Career* md Beale Electronic Systems Ltd 1977-85, exec vice chm Beale Int Technol Ltd 1985-88, conslt McKinsey & Co 1988-89; chm: Beale Hldgs 1988-, Sciteb 1989-; author of various technical articles and speeches at int confs on computer communications; *Recreations* piano, sulkido; *Clubs* IOD; *Style*— Nicholas Beale, Esq; 1 Leighton Mansions, Queens Club Gardens, London W14 9SQ; Whitehall, Wraysbury, Staines, Middx TW19 5NJ

BEALE, Maj-Gen Peter John; QHP (1988); s of Basil Hewett Beale (d 1987), of Romford, Essex, and Eileen Beryl, *née* Heffer; *b* 18 March 1934; *Educ* St Paul's Cathedral Choir Sch, Felsted, Gonville & Caius Coll Cambridge (BA), Westminster Hosp (MB BChir, DTM & H); *m* 22 Aug 1959, Julia Mary, da of John Clifton Winter; 4 s (Simon Russell b 12 Jan 1961, Timothy John b 17 Jan 1962, Andrew Mark (twin) b 17 Jan 1962, Matthew James Robert b 25 Jan 1974), 2 da (Katie Louise b 28 June 1964, Lucy Ann b 10 Dec 1967, d 1971); *Career* RARO 34 LAA Regt RA 1960-63, trainee and specialist physician 1963-71, conslt physician 1971-, cmd med 2 div 1981-83, Col Armd 3 1983-84, cmd med 1 Br Corps 1984-87, cmd med UKLF 1987-90; author of various articles in med jls on mil med matters; pres Army Squash Assoc; memb: BMA, RSM; FRCP, MFCM, MRCS; *Recreations* golf, squash, tennis; music: conducting, singing; *Clubs* Tidworth Golf (pres); *Style*— Maj-Gen Peter Beale; DMSD, MOD, First Avenue House, High Holborn, London WC1V 6HE (☎ 071 430 5418)

BEALE, Trevor Howard; s of Thomas Edward Beale, CBE, JP, of West Lodge Park, Hadley Wood, Herts, and Beatrice May, *née* MacLaughlin (d 1986); *b* 28 Nov 1934; *Educ* Westminster, Trinity Coll Cambridge (MA); *m* 5 May 1962, Susan Jane, da of Philip Reginald Brierley, of Maple Cottage, Chalfont St Peter, Bucks; 3 s (Andrew b 30 Nov 1963, Christopher b 20 Nov 1967, Nicholas b 30 Dec 1969), 1 da (Philippa b 5 Nov 1965); *Career* called to the Bar Gray's Inn 1960; md Beales Ltd 1970; churchwarden St Michael's Highgate 1979-82; Third Warden Worshipful Co of Bakers 1990; FHCIMA 1990; *Recreations* music; *Style*— Trevor Beale, Esq; Bunkers House, Gaddesden Row, nr Hemel Hempstead, Herts; West Lodge Park, Hadley Wood, Herts (☎ 081 440 8311)

BEALES, Prof Derek Edward Dawson; s of Edward Beales (d 1984), and Dorothy Kathleen, *née* Dawson; *b* 12 June 1931; *Educ* Bishop's Stortford Coll, Sidney Sussex Coll Cambridge (BA, MA, PhD, LittD); *m* 14 Aug 1964, Sara Jean (Sally), da of Francis Harris Ledbury (d 1971); 1 s (Richard Derek b 1967), 1 da (Christina Margaret (Kitty) b 1965); *Career* Nat Serv Sgt RA 1949-50; Sidney Sussex Coll Cambridge: res fell 1955-58, fell 1958-, vice master 1973-75, univ asst lectr 1962-65, lectr 1965-80, prof of modern history 1980-, chm Bd of History 1979-81; visiting lectr Harvard Univ 1965; ed Hist Journal 1971-75; memb: Univ Library Syndicate Cambridge 1981-89, Gen Bd of the Faculties 1987-89, Br Acad 1989; author articles in learned jls; FRHistS (memb Cncl 1984-88); *Books* England & Italy 1859-60 (1961),

From Castlereagh to Gladstone (1969) , The Risorgimento and the Unification of Italy (1971), History & Biography (1981), History Society & the Churches (ed with Geoffrey Best, 1985), Joseph II: in the Shadow of Maria Theresa 1741-80 (1987); *Recreations* music, walking, bridge; *Style*— Prof Derek Beales; Sidney Sussex Coll, Cambridge CB2 3HU (tel 0223 338800)

BEALES, Peter Leslie; *b* 22 July 1936; *Educ* Aldborough Secdy Modern, Norwich City Coll; *m* 23 Sept 1961, Joan Elizabeth, *née* Allington; 1 s (Richard b 9 April 1970), 1 da (Amanda b 10 Sept 1968); *Career* Nat Serv RA 1955-57; apprentice Le Grice Roses 1952-55 (also pt/t course at Norfolk Sch of Horticulture), mangr Hillings Nurseries Surrey 1958-62, fndr Peter Beales Roses 1963-; memb Ctee Historic Rose Gp of Royal Nat Rose Soc, chm Attleborough and Dist C of C 1987-89, pres Attleborough Rotary Club 1989-90; memb Inst of Horticulture 1986, hon life memb Bermuda Rose Soc 1986; Lester E Harrell award for significant contrib to heritage roses USA 1987; *Books* Georgian and Regency Roses (1978), Early Victorian Roses (1978), Late Victorian Roses (1980), Edwardian Roses (1980), Classic Roses (1985), Twentieth Century Roses (1988); *Recreations* antiquarian books, photography; *Clubs* Attleborough Rotary; *Style*— Peter Beales, Esq; Peter Beales Roses, London Rd, Attleborough, Norfolk NR17 1AY (☎ 0953 454707, fax 0953 456845)

BEALEY, Prof Frank William; s of Ernest Bealey (d 1951), of Netherton, Dudley, and Nora, *née* Hampton (d 1982); *b* 31 Aug 1922; *Educ* King Edward VI GS Stourbridge, LSE (BSc, DScEcon); *m* 2 July 1960, Sheila, da of James Hurst (d 1955); 1 s (William b 20 Nov 1968), 2 da (Rachel b 14 Sept 1963, Rosalind b 11 March 1967); *Career* Finnish Govt scholar at Univ of Helsinki 1948-49, res asst for Passfield Tst LSE 1950-51, extra-mural lectr Univ of Manchester (Burnley area) 1951-52; asst lectr (also lectr and sr lectr) Univ of Keele 1952-64, prof of politics Univ of Aberdeen 1964-, visiting fell Yale 1980; organiser Parly All-Party Gp Social Sci and Policy 1984-89; FRHistS 1971; Order of the Blyskiwicka (Poland) 1979; *Books* Labour and Politics (with Henry Pelling, 2 edn 1982), Constituency Politics (with J Blondel and W P McCann, 1965), The Social and Political Thought of the British Labour Party (1970), The Post Office Engineering Union (1976), The Politics of Independence (with John Sewel, 1981), Democracy in the Contemporary State (1988); *Recreations* watching football and cricket, swimming, darts; *Clubs* Economicals Assoc Football and Cricket; *Style*— Prof Frank Bealey; The Cottage, Duncanstone, Insch, Aberdeenshire AB5 6YU (☎ 046 43 523); Department of Politics, The University, Aberdeen AB9 2UB (☎ 0224 272716)

BEAMENT, Sir James William Longman; o s of Tom Beament (d 1958), of Crewkerne, Somerset; *b* 17 Nov 1921; *Educ* Crewkerne GS, Queens' Coll Cambridge (MA, ScD), London Sch of Tropical Med (PhD); *m* 1962, (Sara) Juliet, yst da of Prof Sir Ernest Barker (d 1959); 2 s; *Career* princ scientific offr Agric Res Cncl to 1961; fell and tutor Queens' Coll Cambridge 1962-67, reader Univ of Cambridge 1967-69, head of Dept of Applied Biology Univ of Cambridge 1969-89, emeritus prof of agric and life fell Queens' Coll Cambridge 1989-; chm NERC 1978-81; kt 1980; *Recreations* composing music, playing music, DIY; *Clubs* Farmers', Amateur Dramatic (Cambridge); *Style*— Sir James Beament; 19 Sedley Taylor Rd, Cambridge CB2 2PW (☎ 0223 246045)

BEAMISH, Adrian John; CMG (1988); s of Thomas Charles Constantine Bernard Beamish (d 1948), and Josephine Mary, *née* Lee (d 1968); *b* 21 Jan 1939; *Educ* Prior Park Coll Bath, Cambridge Univ (BA); *m* 1965, Caroline, da of Dr John Lipscomb, of Chilham, Kent; 2 da (Catherine b 1966, Antonia b 1968); *Career* HM Dip Serv; third sec Tehran, second sec FO, first sec Paris; dir Br Info Servs New Delhi, dep head Personnel Operations FCO, cnsllr Bonn 1981-85; head Falklands Islands Dept FCO 1985-87, ambass Lima 1987-89, under sec for Americas and Australasia FCO 1989-; *Recreations* books, plants; *Style*— Adrian Beamish, Esq, CMG; c/o Foreign and Commonwealth Office, London SW1

BEAMISH, Michael John; s of Lewis Stanley Beamish (d 1983), and Beatrice Ivy, *née* Beazley; *b* 9 May 1916; *Educ* Keys Coll Sussex (no longer in existence), Worthing Art Coll; *m* 21 Sept 1963 (m dis 1979), Christine Ann, da of Frank Alfred Nichols; *Career* designer John Michael Gp 1969-72, freelance interior design conslt UK and abroad 1972-82, fndr Prizelake Ltd and Prizelake Southern Ltd interior design conslts 1982- (Prizelake USA 1988-); clients incl: Glyndebourne Festival Opera, Br Maritime Museum; memb: Master Builders Fedn, Fedn Master Craftsmen; *Recreations* boating, keep fit and weight training, swimming, art, architecture; *Style*— Michael Beamish, Esq; Bearlands, Dyke Rd Ave, Brighton, Sussex BN1 5NU; Singing Waters, 501 Solar Isle Drive, Fort Lauderdale, Florida USA; P O Box 995, Brighton BN1 5NU (☎ 0273 559 630, fax 0273 564 436)

BEAMONT, Wing Cdr Roland Prosper; CBE (1965, OBE 1953), DSO (1943 and bar 1944), DFC (1941, and bar 1942), DFC (USA 1945), DL (Lancashire 1977); s of Lt-Col E C Beamont, of Summersdale, Chichester (d 1957), and Dorothy Mary, *née* Haynes (d 1950); *b* 10 Aug 1920; *Educ* Eastbourne Coll; *m* 1, 1942, Shirley (d 1945), da of Bernard Adams, of Chelsea; 1 da (Carol); m 2, 1946, Patricia, da of Capt Richard Galpine Raworth, of Harrogate; 1 step s (Richard), 2 da (Patricia, Elizabeth); *Career* RAF Fighter Cmd 1939-46 (despatches 1940); chief test pilot English Electric 1947-60, dep chief test pilot British Aircraft Corp Weybridge 1960-65; dir of flight ops: British Aircraft Corp, British Aerospace Warton 1965-78, Panavia (Tornado prog) 1971-79; Master Pilot and Liveryman Guild of Air Pilots, hon fell Soc of Experimental Test Pilots of USA, memb Battle of Britain Fighter Assoc; FRAeS; *Books* Phoenix into Ashes (1968), Typhoon and Tempest at War (1979), Testing Years (1980), English Electric Canberra (1982), Fighter Test Pilot (1986), English Electric P1 Lightning (1984), My Part of the Sky (1988), Testing Early Jets (1990); *Recreations* fishing, aviation; *Clubs* RAF, Sweatford Flyfishers, Bustard Flying (hon memb); *Style*— Wing Cdr Roland Beamont, CBE, DSO, DFC, DL; Cross Cottage, Pentridge, Salisbury SP5 5QX

BEAN, Basil; CBE (1985); s of Walter Bean (d 1976), of York, and Alice Louise Chambers (d 1978); *b* 2 July 1931; *Educ* Archbishop Holgate Sch York; *m* 1956, Janet Mary, da of Frederick Cecil Rex Brown (d 1961), of West Bromwich; 1 da (Rachel); *Career* chief exec: Nat House Bldg Cncl 1985-, Merseyside Devpt Corporation 1980-85; gen mangr Northampton Devpt Corpn 1977-80; memb: Chartered Inst of Pub Finances and Accountancy, Br Waterways Bd 1985-88; hon fell Incorp Assoc of Architects and Surveyors; *Recreations* travel, walking, bridge; *Clubs* Royal Cwlth, Northampton and Co; *Style*— Basil Bean, Esq, CBE; National House Building Council, Buildmark House, Chilthern Ave, Amersham, Bucks HP6 5AP (☎ 0494 434 477)

BEAN, Christopher Robin; *b* 25 Aug 1934; *Educ* Bungay GS Suffolk; *m* 31 March 1956, Mavis Kathleen; 2 da (Susan b 5 April 1958, Judith Marie b 27 Feb 1960); *Career* dep chm and chief exec Dubilier Int plc; *Recreations* interested in all sporting activities; *Style*— Christopher R Bean, Esq; Dubilier International plc, Dubilier House, Radley Rd, Abingdon, Oxon OX14 3XA (☎ 0235 28271)

BEAN, Hugh Cecil; CBE (1970); s of Cecil Walter Claude Bean, MBE (d 1975), and Gertrude Alice, *née* Chapman (d 1982); *b* 22 Sept 1929; *Educ* Beckenham GS, RCM; *m* 16 April 1963, Mary Dorothy, da of Henry Unwin Harrow (d 1981); 1 da (Fiona b 8 May 1969); *Career* Grenadier Gds 1949-51; prof of violin RCM 1954, ldr Philharmonia Orchestra 1956-67, assoc ldr BBC Symphony Orchestra 1967-69, ldr LSO 1969-71, co ldr Philharmonia Orchestra 1989-; memb Music Gp of London 1951-88; recordings: Elgar Violin Concerto (EMI), Vivaldi's Seasons (Decca), numerous works of chamber music for various cos; memb Royal Philharmonic Soc; FRCM 1968; *Recreations* model aircraft, steam railways, record collecting; *Style*— Hugh Bean, Esq, CBE; 30 Stone Park Ave, Beckenham, Kent BR3 3LX (☎ 081 650 8774)

BEAN, Rev Canon John Victor; s of Albert Victor Bean (d 1961), and Eleanor Ethel Bean (d 1975); *b* 1 Dec 1925; *Educ* Gt Yarmouth GS, Univ of Cambridge (MA), Salisbury Theological Coll; *m* 1955, Nancy Evelyn, da of Capt Thomas Allen Evans, MC (d 1964); 2 s (Simon, Martin), 2 da (Judith d 1961, Rosalind); *Career* war serv RNVR; ordained deacon 1950, priest 1951, various appts in diocese of Portsmouth, vicar St Mary Cowes 1966-91, canon emeritus Portsmouth Cathedral 1991- (hon canon 1970-91), priest i/c All Saints Gurnard 1978-91; chaplain to HM The Queen 1980-; *Recreations* boatwatching, photography, tidying up; *Clubs* Gurnard Sailing, Cowes Rotary, Cowes Golf; *Style*— Rev Canon John Bean; 4 Parkmead Court, Park Road, Ryde, Isle of Wight PO33 2HD (☎ 0983 812516)

BEAN, Margaret; da of Alexander John Bean (d 1958), of 39 Thorburn Rd, Colinton, Edinburgh, and Isobel, *née* Knowles (d 1974); *b* 25 Aug 1942; *Educ* George Watson's Ladies' Coll Edinburgh, Univ of Edinburgh (MA); *Career* HM Dip Serv 1970-72, clerk Royal College of Surgeons Edinburgh 1983; *Recreations* genealogy, study of languages, cinema, horse riding; *Style*— Miss Margaret Bean; Royal College of Surgeons of Edinburgh, Nicolson St, Edinburgh EH8 9DW (☎ 031 556 6206, fax 031 557 6406)

BEANEY, Linda Margaret; da of Kenneth Ashley Beaney, of Gidea Park, Essex, and Kathleen Margaret, *née* Stainforth; *b* 1 Dec 1952; *Educ* Coborn Sch for Girls London; *Career* trainee property sales negotiator Edward Erdman & Co Mayfair London 1969; Hampton & Sons: joined 1976, ptnr 1981, md London 1989-; dir Hornchurch Theatre Trust Ltd 1985-90, jt chief exec Hamptons Residential Developments 1989-; Freeman City of London 1984; memb Land Inst 1988, MInstD 1991; *Recreations* theatre, tennis, skiing; *Style*— Ms Linda Beaney; 25 Thames Quay, Chelsea Harbour, London SW10 0UY; The Red House, Great Warley, Essex CM13 3HX; Hamptons, 6 Arlington Street, St James's, London SW1A 1RB (☎ 071 493 8222)

BEARCROFT, (Joseph) Peter; s of Arthur William Bearcroft (d 1975), of 17 Filey Rd, Scarborough, and Elizabeth Jane, *née* McKinley (d 1982); *b* 15 July 1923; *Educ* St Mary's GS, Hummersknott nr Darlington, Queensland Univ Brisbane Aust, Balliol Coll Oxford (MA); *m* 14 June 1952, Dr Rosalind Irene Bearcroft, da of Albert Victor Chamberlain, MBE (d 1978); 1 s (Philip b 13 March 1964), 2 da (Charlotte b 5 June 1962, Emma b 19 May 1968); *Career* flying cadet Fleet Air Arm 1942, flying trg with US Navy 1943-44, Sub Lt RNVR, flying control offr Fleet Air Army HQ for the Normandy Landings 1944, TAMY I and MONAB 5 Aust SE Asia Cmd 1945, demob Lt RNVR 1946; jr commercial asst ICI Ltd Distribution Centre Billingham, trainee Manchester Assurance Co Ltd 1949, trainee tech asst Howards & Sons (Ilford) Ltd; Horlicks Ltd 1950-63: mgmnt trainee, market res offr, asst to co sec, head of Mktg Div; dir Pristine Products Ltd and Airwick Ltd; BR Bd 1963-83: dir of mktg (HQ) 1963-65, freight mktg and sales mangr, chief freight mangr Western Region (Paddington) HQ, freight mktg advsr (HQ) 1978-83, ret 1983; business cnsllr DTI and Dept of Employment 1983-86, currently private industl mktg conslt and business advsr; underwriting memb Lloyds 1981; fndr chm: Railway Mktg Soc 1971-83, Tport and Distribution Gp Inst of Mktg (memb Nat Cncl); memb Ctee for Terotechnol with DTI 1973-78; fndr memb SDP 1981; memb Catholic Union, prov pres Caterian Assoc 1990; Freeman City of London, Liveryman Worshipful Co of Marketors 1976; fell: CIT, Chartered Inst of Mktg, Inst of Logistics and Physical Distribution Mgmnt; *Recreations* swimming, golf, reading, travelling; *Clubs* MCC, Cricketers; *Style*— Peter Bearcroft, Esq; Barming Place, Maidstone, Kent ME16 9ED (☎ 0622 727844)

BEARCROFT, Dr Rosalind Irene; da of Victor Albert Chamberlain, MBE (d 1978), of Penylan, Cardiff, and Irene Mary Chamberlain, MBE, *née* Price; *b* 16 May 1926; *Educ* Howell's Sch, Univ of Wales (BSc), Somerville Coll Oxford (BA, MA), UCH (MB BS, DPM); *m* 14 June 1952, (Joseph) Peter Bearcroft, s of Arthur William Bearcroft (d 1975), of Scarborough; 1 s (Philip b 1964), 2 da (Charlotte b 1962, Emma b 1968); *Career* held jr hosp Dr appts in London and Wales, sr registrar St Ebba's Hosp Epsom Surrey; conslt psychiatrist: Maidstone Hosp, Kent and Sussex Hosp Tunbridge Wells; conslt in child and family psychiatry Tunbridge Wells; chm: Regnl Speciality Sub Ctee on Child and Adolescent Psychiatry Met Health Authy (SE), Tunbridge Wells Health Dist Div of Psychiatry; rep on: Kent Police Advsy Ctee for Maidstone Health Dist, Kent Child Protection Ctee for RCPsych, Speciality Sub Ctee on Psychiatry Thames RHA; memb: Cncl Catholic Union (memb Issues Ctee), Guild of Catholic Drs, Conslt and Specialists Assoc; vice pres and fndr memb Parenthood; memb BMA, FRCPsych; *Recreations* travelling, swimming, reading, gardening; *Style*— Dr Rosalind Bearcroft; Barming Place, Maidstone, Kent ME16 9ED (☎ 0622 727844/ 0831 231831)

BEARD, Allan Geoffrey; CB (1979); s of Maj Henry Thomas Beard (d 1969), and Florence Mercy, *née* Baker (d 1954); *b* 18 Oct 1919; *Educ* Ormskirk GS; *m* 21 June 1945, Helen Matthews, da of Michael James McDonagh (d 1956); 1 da (Mary Taylor); *Career* Capt RE 1940-46; under-sec DHSS until 1979; hon treas Motability 1985-; *Recreations* gardening; *Clubs* RAC; *Style*— Allan Beard, Esq, CB; 51 Rectory Park, Sanderstead, Surrey CR2 9JR (☎ 081 657 4197)

BEARD, Andrew; s of Richard Geoffrey Beard, of Sheffield, and Constance Lorna, *née* Booth; *b* 17 July 1943; *Educ* Rishworth Sch; *m* 23 Oct 1982, Barbara Anne, da of Ralph Gordon Bristow; 3 s (Matthew Andrew b 11 Feb 1972, Duncan Edward b 9 June 1973, Jonathan Charles b 14 Nov 1983), 1 da (Harriet Emma Kate b 30 March 1988); *Career* articed clerk Knox Burbidge Henderson Sheffield 1960-65, ptnr Pannell Kerr Forster 1972- (following a series of mergers), nat dir of Business Servs Pannell Kerr Forster 1985-89; pres Sheffield and Dist Soc of CAs 1991-; FCA (ACA 1965); *Recreations* DIY, sailing; *Style*— Andrew Beard, Esq; Pannell Kerr Forster, 4 Norfolk Park Rd, Sheffield S2 3QE (☎ 0742 767991, fax 0742 753538)

BEARD, Malcolm Douglas; s of Harold William Poynter Beard (d 1982), and Doris Helena, *née* Cuthbert; *b* 26 April 1930; *Educ* Buckhurst Hill Co HS; *m* 11 Sept 1954, (Edith) Jeanne, da of Charles Edward May; 2 s (Graham Michael b 28 March 1958, David Christopher b 8 April 1960), 1 da (Gillian Margaret b 30 June 1955); *Career* RN 1949-51; Fred Olsen Lines Oslo Norway 1947-49, H Maclaine & Co Ltd London 1951-52, Galbraith Pembroke & Co Ltd 1952-68 (dir 1963-68), proprietor MD Beard & Co Ltd 1968-; memb The Baltic Exchange London; vice chm Old Buckwellian Assoc, capt St John's Badminton Club Buckhurst Hill; Freeman City of London 1978, Liveryman Worshipful Co of Shipwrights 1978; *Recreations* tennis, badminton; *Clubs* City Livery; *Style*— Malcolm D Beard, Esq; 17 Luctons Ave, Buckhurst Hill, Essex (☎ 071 504 7850); Pine Lodge, Grove Ave, West Mersea, Essex(☎ 0206 382034); M D Beard & Co Ltd, 25 Phipp St, London EC2A 4NP (☎ 071 490 3361, fax 071 739 8093

BEARD, (Christopher) Nigel; s of Albert Leonard Beard (d 1958), of Castleford, Yorks, and Irene, *née* Bowes (d 1968); *b* 10 Oct 1936; *Educ* Castleford GS Yorks, UCL (BSc); *m* 1969, Jennifer Anne, da of Thomas Beckerleg Cotton, of 35 Mountside, Guildford, Surrey; 1 s (Daniel b 1971), 1 da (Jessica b 1973); *Career* supt land ops and reinforcement policy studies Def Operational Analysis Estab 1968-73, chief planner strategy GLC 1973-74, dir London Docklands Devpt Orgn 1974-79; sr mangr New Business Devpt ICI Millbank 1979-; Parly candidate (Lab): Woking 1979, Portsmouth North 1983; memb: SW Thames RHA 1978-86, Royal Marsden Cancer Hosp and Inst of Cancer Res 1981-; FRSA; *Recreations* reading, sailing, talking; *Clubs* Athenaeum, Royal Instn; *Style*— Nigel Beard, Esq; Lanquhart, The Ridgway, Pyrford, Woking, Surrey (☎ 0932 348963); ICI plc, 9 Millbank, London SW1P 3JF (☎ 071 834 4444)

BEARD, Prof Richard William; s of Brig William Horace Gladstone Beard (d 1989), and Irene, *née* Foote; *b* 4 May 1931; *Educ* Westminster, Christ's Coll Cambridge (MA, MB BChir), St Bart's Hosp (MD); *m* 1, 28 Aug 1957 (m dis 1979), Jane Elizabeth, *née* Copsey; 2 s (Charles b 3 Sept 1959, Nicholas b 27 March 1962); m 2, 24 Feb 1979, Irene Victoire, da of Comte de Marotte de Montigny (d 1973), of Chateau de Libois, Belgium; 1 s (Thomas b 14 Dec 1979); *Career* obstetrician and gynaecologist RAF Changi Singapore 1957-60; house surgn Chelsea Hosp for Women 1961-62, asst obstetrician Univ Coll Hosp 1963-64; sr lectr and hon conslt: Queen Charlotte's and Chelsea Hosps 1967-68, King's Coll Hosp 1968-72; prof of obstetrics and gynaecology St Marys's Hosp Med Sch 1972-; advsr Social Servs Select Ctee House of Commons 1978-90, civilian conslt advsr in obstetrics and gynaecology RAF 1983-, conslt advsr in obstetrics and gynaecology Chief Med Offr DHSS 1984-; RCOG: chm Scientific and Pathology Ctee 1983-86, chm Birthright Res Ctee 1987-90, memb Cncl 1988-; FRCOG 1972; *Books* Fetal Medicine (1974), Fetal Physiology and Medicine (2 edn, 1983); *Recreations* tennis, sailing, chinese history; *Clubs* Garrick; *Style*— Prof Richard Beard; 64 Elgin Crescent, London, W11 2JJ (☎ 071 221 1930); Department of Obstetrics and Gynaecology, St Mary's Hospital Medical School, Paddington, London W2 1PG (☎ 071 725 1461, fax 071 724 7349)

BEARD, Robert Ian (Rob); s of Reginald Oliver Beard (d 1968), of Rottingdean, Sussex, and May F Beard (d 1970); *b* 14 Sept 1932; *Educ* Epsom County GS Epsom Surrey, Univ of Bristol (BA); *m* 8 Oct 1961, Diane Betty, da of Jack R Sanders, of Cheam, Surrey; 2 s (Duncan Richard, Alex Neil), 1 da (Joanna Louise (Mrs Newman)); *Career* chief exec Spicer and Pegler Assoc 1968-79, ptnr Touche Ross & Co (formerly Spicer and Oppenheim) 1966-; FCA, FIMC, FInstD; *Recreations* swimming, gardening, photography, theatre, reading; *Style*— Rob Beard, Esq; Frenchlands, Ockham Road South, E Horsley, Surrey KT24 6SN; Touche Ross & Co, Friary Court, 65 Crutched Friars, London EC3 (☎ 071 480 7766); Domaine de St Pierre, Plan de la Tour, Var, France

BEARDMORE, Prof John Alec; s of George Edward Beardmore, of Burton on Trent, and Anne Jean, *née* Warrington; *b* 1 May 1930; *Educ* Burton on Trent GS, Birmingham Central Tech Coll, Univ of Sheffield (BSc, PhD); *m* 26 Dec 1956, Anne Patricia, da of Frederick William Wallace (d 1951); 3 s (James b 1960, Hugo b 1963, Charles b 1965), 1 da (Virginia b 1957); *Career* radar operator RAF 1948-49; res demonstrator Univ of Sheffield 1954-56, Cwlth Fund Fell (Harkness) Columbia Univ NY 1956-58, visiting asst prof of plant breeding Cornell Univ 1958, lectr in genetics Univ of Sheffield 1958-61, prof of genetics and dir Genetics Inst Univ of Groningen The Netherlands 1961-66, sr fell Nat Sci Fndn Pennsylvania State Univ 1966, prof of genetics Univ Coll Swansea 1966- (head of dept 1966-87), dean of sci UCS 1974-76 (vice princ 1977-80, dir Inst of Marine Studies 1983-87, head Sch of Bio Sci 1988-); hon sec Inst of Biology 1980-85 (vice pres 1985-87); memb: NERC Aquatic Life Sci Ctee 1982-87 (chm 1984-87), Br Nat Ctee for Biology 1983-87; chm CSTI Bd 1984-85; FIBiol, FRSA, FLS; Univ of Helsinki medal (1980); *Books* Marine Organisms: Genetics Ecology and Evolution (co ed with B Battaglia, 1977); *Recreations* bridge, hill walking; *Clubs* Athenaeum; *Style*— Prof John A Beardmore; 153 Derwen Fawr Road, Swansea SA2 8ED (☎ 0792 206 232); School of Biological Sciences, Univ Coll Swansea, Swansea SA2 8PP (☎ 0792 295 382, fax 0792 295 447, telex 48149 U

BEARDSWORTH, Maj-Gen Simon John; CB (1984); s of Paymaster Capt Stanley Thomas Beardsworth, RN (ka 1941), and late Pearl Sylvia Emma (Biddy), *née* Blake; *b* 18 April 1929; *Educ* St Edmund's Coll, RMA Sandhurst, Royal Mil Coll of Science (BSc); *m* 1954, Barbara Bingham, da of Brig James Bingham Turner, RA (d 1963); 3 s; *Career* cmd 1 Royal Tank Regt 1970-71, Project Mangr 1973-77 (Col), Dir of Projects 1977-80 (Brig), Dep Cmdt Royal Mil Coll of Science 1980-81, Maj-Gen 1981, Vice Master Gen of the Ordnance 1981-84, ret; self employed conslt in defence procurement; *Recreations* game shooting, helping out at horsey events, writing a book, travel, garden; *Clubs* Army & Navy; *Style*— Maj-Gen S J Beardsworth, CB; c/o Lloyds Bank plc, 27 Fox Street, Chard, Somerset TA20 1PS

BEARE, Stuart Newton; s of Newton Beare (d 1985), of Lutterworth, Leicestershire, and Joyce Atkinson (d 1962); *b* 6 Oct 1936; *Educ* Clifton Coll, Clare Coll Cambridge (MA, LLB); *m* 1974, Cheryl, da of John Douglas Wells (d 1983); *Career* asst slr Simmons & Simmons 1964-66 (articled clerk 1961-64); Richards Butler: asst slr 1966-69, ptnr 1969-88, sr ptnr 1988-; memb: Ct of Asst City of London Slrs Co, Law Soc, Baltic Exchange; titular memb Comité Maritime International; *Recreations* gentle mountaineering, skiing and travel; *Clubs* Alpine, City of London, Oriental, MCC; *Style*— Stuart Beare, Esq; Richards Butler, Beaufort House, 15 St Botolph Street, London EC3A 7EE (☎ 071 247 6555, fax 071 247 5091)

BEARMAN, Alan Peter; s of Alexander Bearman (d 1976), of London, and Esther Bearman; *b* 15 Nov 1934; *Educ* Newbury GS, City of London Sch for Boys; *m* 9 Sept 1958, (Adrienne) Cecilia, da of Harry Labozer, of London; 2 s (Robert Simon b 1960, David Laurence b 1968), 2 da (Lisa Caron (Mrs Harrison) b 1962, Juliette Tamara b 1970); *Career* CA; ptnr Warner Bearman 1956-, fin dir Arthur Shaw & Co plc 1986-; FCA 1956, ATII 1965; *Recreations* tennis, cricket, bridge, reading; *Clubs* White Elephant; *Style*— Alan Bearman, Esq; Warner Bearman, 16 Wimpole St, Cavendish Square, London W1M 8BH (☎ 071 580 6341, fax 071 580 6925)

BEARMAN, Garth Russell; s of Russell Legerton Bearman (d 1986), and Barbara Maye Fester, *née* Limb (d 1971); *b* 3 Oct 1946; *Educ* Harrow; *m* 26 Jan 1972, Diana Jane, da of Clair Morrel Waterbury, of Virginia Water, Surrey; 1 s (Christian), 1 da (Katherine); *Career* chief exec Robert Fraser Insurance Brokers Ltd; *Recreations* polo, tennis, squash; *Clubs* Turf, Naval and Military, City, Cowdray Park Polo, Lloyd's Saddle; *Style*— Garth Bearman, Esq; Harcombe House, Ropley, nr Alresford, Hampshire; Robert Fraser Insurance Brokers Ltd, 32/38 Leman Street, London E1 (☎ 01 481 0111, telex 894460, fax 01 481 9377

BEARN, Dr Jennifer Anne; da of Edward Michael Bearn, and Margaret Elizabeth, *née* Tisdall; *b* 1 July 1955; *Educ* Convent of Holy Family Littlehampton Sussex, Bognor Regis Sch Sussex, Guys Hosp Med Sch (BSc, MB BS, MRCP); 1 da (Alice b 10 March 1987); *Career* sr house offr in gen med Whittington Hosp London 1981-83, offr in neurology Nat Hosp For Nervous Diseases Queen Sq 1983-84; registrar in psychiatry Maudsley Hosp 1984-87, lectr Inst of Psychiatry 1987-; MRCPsych 1987, memb BMA; *Recreations* reading victorian novels, squash, swimming, playing trumpet; *Style*— Dr Jennifer Bearn; 46 Mayflower Rd, London SW9 9LA (☎ 071 247 1975); Inst of Psychiatry, De Crespigny Park, London SE5 (☎ 071 703 6333)

BEARPARK, (Peter) Andrew; s of Geoffrey Raymond Bearpark, of Rochdale, and Elizabeth Antonie, *née* Hulsken; *b* 28 March 1953; *Educ* Rochdale GS, Queen Elizabeth Coll, Univ of London (BSc); *m* 10 Sept 1976 (m dis 1989), Teresa Mary, da of Peter John Rombaut, of Leigh on Sea; 2 da (Jennifer b 1980, Caroline b 1982); *Career* asst head SE Asia Devpt Div 1977-80, princ ODA 1981-83 (memb 1973-76), first sec Br High Cmmn Harare Zimbabwe 1983-86, private sec to PM 1986-89, chief exec Punchline 1989; *Recreations* walking; *Style*— Andrew Bearpark, Esq; Punchline, 10-12 Ely Place, London EC1N 6TY (☎ 071 405 1750, fax 071 430 0990, telex 21512)

BEARSTED, 4 Viscount (UK 1925); Sir Peter Montefiore Samuel; 4 Bt (UK 1903), MC (1942), TD (1951); 2 s of 2 Viscount Bearsted, MC (d 1948), and Dorothea (d 1949), da of late E Montefiore Micholls; *b* 9 Dec 1911; *Educ* Eton, New Coll Oxford; *m* 1, 11 Oct 1939 (m dis 1942), Deirdre du Barry; m 2, 20 March 1946, Hon Elizabeth Adelaide (d 1983), da of Baron Cohen, PC (Life Peer, d 1973), and widow of Capt Arthur John Pearce-Serocold, Welsh Gds; 2 s, 1 da; m 3, 2 Feb 1984, Nina Alice Hilary, da of Reginald John Hearn, of London, and widow of Carmichael (Michael) Charles Peter Pocock, CBE; *Heir* s, Nicholas Alan b 22 Jan 1950; *Career* Maj Warwicks Yeomanry; dep chm Hill Samuel Gp 1965-82 (dir 1935-87); pres Mayborn Group plc 1946-; chm: Dylon Int 1958-84, Hill Samuel & Co (Ireland) 1964-84, Samuel Properties 1982-86 (dir 1961-86); dir: Shell Transport and Trading 1938-82, Trades Union Unit Tst Managers 1961-82, Gen Consolidated Investmt Tst 1975-82; Royal Free Hosp: chm Cncl Sch of Med 1973-82 (memb 1948-87), chm Bd of Govrs 1956-68 (govr 1939-68); pres Norwood Child Care 1962-79 (treas and chm 1948-62); *Recreations* golf, shooting; *Clubs* White's; *Style*— The Rt Hon the Viscount Bearsted, MC, TD; Farley Hall, Farley Hill, nr Reading, Berks (☎ 0734 733242); 9 Campden Hill Court, London W8 7HX (☎ 071 937 6204)

BEASANT, Dave; s of Cecil Hugh Beasant, of Willesden, Brent, and May Edith, *née* Timms; *b* 20 March 1959; *Educ* Willesden HS; *m* Sandra Dawn, da of Victor Albert Harris; 2 s (Nicholas David b 23 Oct 1985, Samuel James b 8 April 1988); *Career* professional footballer; 340 league appearances Wimbledon 1980-88, 20 league appearances Newcastle Utd 1988-89 (joined for a fee of £850,000), over 100 appearances Chelsea 1989- (joined for a fee of £725,000); England: 6 B caps, 2 full caps, memb World Cup squad Italy 1990; first goalkeeper to capt FA Cup Final team Wimbledon 1988, first goalkeeper to Dave penalty in FA Cup Final; honours with Wimbledon: Div 4 Championship 1983, FA Cup 1988; honours with Chelsea: Div 2 Championship 1989, Zenith Data Systems Cup 1990; *Books* Tales of the Unexpected: The Dave Beasant Story; *Recreations* golf; *Style*— Dave Beasant, Esq; c/o David Clatworthy, Ultra Management, The Penthouse, 22 The Green, West Drayton, Middlesex UB7 7PQ (☎ 0895 431964, fax 0895 446164)

BEASLEY, Alan Walter; s of Frederick Hancock Beasley (d 1980); *b* 10 Feb 1935; *Educ* King Edward VI GS Nuneaton; *m* 1960, Margaret, da of Frederick Payne; 3 s (Andrew b 1961, Nigel b 1963, Stephen b 1969); *Career* dir: Charrington Industrial Holdings 1974-77 (when taken over by Coalite Group), Coalite Group Bd 1979-90 (ret), Ashton-Vernon Ltd 1990; chief exec Great Central Merchants Ltd 1990- (joined 1986); Midland Region CBI: memb 1981-87 and 1988-90, Nat Cncl memb 1988-90, vice chm 1988-90; dep chm Bolsover Enterprise Agency Ptnrship 1988-; FCA; *Recreations* sport, reading, travel, theatre, home and garden, family, rotary; *Style*— Alan Beasley, Esq; 694 Chatsworth Rd, Brookside, Chesterfield, Derbys S40 3PB (☎ 0246 568785)

BEASLEY, Lady Alexandra Mariota Flora; *née* Egerton; da of 6 Earl of Wilton (d 1927); *b* 9 Nov 1919; *m* 1939 (m dis 1962), Patrick Beasley, s of Henry Herbert Beasley, of Eyrefield House, Curragh, Co Kildare; 1 da; *Style*— Lady Alexandra Beasley; Chimney Cottage, Gressenhall, East Dereham, Norfolk

BEASLEY-MURRAY, Rev Dr Paul; s of Rev Dr George Raymond Beasley-Murray, of Hove, East Sussex, and Ruth, *née* Weston; *b* 14 March 1944; *Educ* Trinity Sch of John Whitgift Croydon, Jesus Coll Cambridge (MA), Univ of Zurich, Univ of Manchester (PhD), N Baptist Coll, Int Baptist Theological Seminary Switzerland; *m* 26 Aug 1967, Mrs Caroline Wynne Beasley-Murray, JP, da of Arthur Maelor Griffiths, of Wrexham, North Wales; 3 s (Jonathan Paul b 6 Aug 1969, Timothy Mark b 19 Nov 1971, Benjamin James b 6 March 1976), 1 da (Susannah Caroline Louise b 21 Sept 1973); *Career* prof of New Testament Nat Univ of Zaire at Kisangani (in assoc with Baptist Missionary Soc) 1970-72, pastor Altrincham Baptist Church Altrincham Cheshire 1973-86, princ Spurgeons Coll London 1986-; memb Cncl Baptist Union of GB, exec memb Mainstream; memb: Gen Ctee Baptist Missionary Soc, Theological and Academic Ctee Baptist World Alliance, Studiorum Novi Testament Societas 1973; *Books* Turning the Tide (with Alan Wilkinson, 1980), Pastors Under Pressure (1989), Dynamic Leadership (1990); *Recreations* walking, music; *Style*— The Rev Dr Paul Beasley-Murray; Spurgeon's College, South Norwood Hill, London SE25 6DJ (☎ 081 653 1235, fax 081 653 1235)

BEASTALL, John Sale; s of Howard Bestall, and Marjorie Betty, *née* Sale, of Milford on Sea, Hants; *b* 2 July 1941; *Educ* St Paul's, Balliol Coll Oxford (BA); *Career* HM Treasy: asst princ 1963-66, asst private sec to Chllr of Exchequer 1966-67, princ 1967-68 and 1971-74, (Civil Serv Dept 1968-71), private sec to Paymaster Gen 1974-75, asst sec 1975-79 and 1981-85 (Civil Serv Dept 1979-81); asst sec DES 1985-87, treasy offr of Accounts 1987-; *Recreations* christian youth work; *Clubs* Utd Oxford and Cambridge; *Style*— John Beastall, Esq; HM Treasury, Parliament St, London SW1

BEATON, Ian Gordon; s of Gordon Beaton, of 4 Spencer Park, London (d 1968), and Elsie Mary, *née* Allen (d 1963); *b* 27 Aug 1924; *Educ* Dulwich Coll; *m* 4 April 1953, Joan Elizabeth, da of Robert Charles Ridgwell, of Southgate, London (d 1974); 1 s (Alastair b 1954), 1 da (Jane b 1959); *Career* RNVR Sub-Lieut (E) gun mounting engineer; dept md The 600 Gp plc; FCA, FCMA; *Recreations* books, glass, gardening, occasional golf; *Style*— Ian G Beaton, Esq; The White Cottage, Bulstrode Way, Gerrards Cross, Bucks (☎ 0753 882897); Hytheend House, Chertsey Lane, Staines, Middx (☎ 0784 61545, telex 23997, fax 0784 63405)

BEATON, Chief Superintendent James Wallace; GC (1974); s of J A Beaton, and B McDonald; *b* 16 Feb 1943; *Educ* Peterhead Acad, Aberdeenshire; *m* 1965, Anne C Ballantyne; 2 da; *Career* chief superintendent Metropolitan Police 1983- (chief inspr 1979-83); *Style*— Chief Superintendent James Beaton, GC; 12 Embry Way, Stanmore, Middx (☎ 081 954 5054)

BEATON, Norman Lugard; s of William Solomon Beaton (d 1982), of Georgetown, Guyana, and Ada Agatha, *née* MacIntosh (d 1962); *b* 31 Oct 1934; *Educ* Queen's Coll Georgetown, Teachers Training Coll (CertEd), Inst of Educn London (DipEd); *m* 1, 16 May 1958, Gloria, da of Sidney Moshette (d 1949), of Georgetown, Guyana; 4 s (Jayme Lugard b 1958, Jeremy Lester b 1962, Norman Lyle b 1964, William Godfrey b 1968), 1 da (Kim Agatha b 1960); m 2 (m dis 1980), Caroline Ann Cliff; m 3, Jean Davenport; *Career* actor; Nat Theatre: National Health Tyger 1971, Cato Street 1971, Measure for Measure 1981, The Caretaker 1981, You Can't Take it With You 1983; Royal Court Theatre: Play Mas 1974, Rum and Coca Cola 1976, Sargent Ola and his Followers 1979; West End: The Tempest 1970, Threepenny Opera 1972, Signs of the Times 1973, Play Mas 1974, Black Mikado 1975-76; Murderous Angels (Dublin) 1971, The Mahabaratha (Paris) 1987; films: Two for Birdie 1971, Pressure 1973, Black Joy 1977, Black Christmas 1977, Eureka 1982, Big George is Dead 1986, Playing Away 1988, Mighty Quinn 1988, When Love Dies 1989; TV: The Fosters 1976-77, Empire Road 1978-79, Dead Head 1985, Desmond 1989-90; Citizens (BBC Radio 4) 1990-; Film Actor of the Year Variety Club of GB 1977, Golden Sunrise Award Afro-Caribbean Post 1979, Br Cwlth Union Award to Indust 1988, Best TV Personality Entertainments Enterprise 1990, Best TV Actor Base Awards (UK) 1990; UK Civil

Rights Lambeth Plaque of Honour 1990, Black Theatre Forum; Accademia Italia Delle Arti e Del Lavoro 1980; Br Actors' Equity 1965, PRS 1990; Images Caraîbes Honour (Deuxiéme Festival de Film Caribéen) 1990; *Books* Beaton But Unbowed (1987); *Recreations* cricket, horse racing; *Clubs* Mortons; *Style—* Norman Beaton, Esq; Frazer-Skemp Management Ltd, 34 Bramerton St, Chelsea, London SW3 5LA (☎ 071 352 3771, fax 071 352 1969)

BEATSON, Jack; s of John James Beatson (d 1961), and Miriam, *née* White; *b* 3 Nov 1948; *Educ* Whittingehame Coll Brighton, Univ of Oxford (BCL, MA); *m* 1973, Charlotte, da of Lt-Col John Aylmer Christie-Miller, CBE, *qv*, of Bourton-on-the-Hill, Glos; 1 s (Samuel J b 1976), 1 da (Hannah A b 1979); *Career* called to the Bar Inner Temple 1972, law lectr Univ of Bristol 1972-73, fell Merton Coll Oxford 1973-, law cmmr England and Wales 1989-, memb Editorial Bd Law Quarterly Review; visiting prof: Osgoode Hall Law Sch Toronto 1979, Univ of Virginia 1980 and 1983; *Books* Administrative Law: Cases and Materials (jtly 1983, 2 edn 1989), Chitty on Contracts (jt ed, 1989); *Recreations* travelling, gardening; *Clubs* Utd Oxford and Cambridge; *Style—* Jack Beatson, Esq; Law Cmmn, Conquest House, 37-38 John St, Theobalds Rd, London WC1N 2BQ (☎ 071 242 0861, fax 071 242 1855)

BEATTIE, Dr Alistair Duncan; s of Alexander Nicoll Beattie (d 1965), of Paisley, and Elizabeth McCrorie, *née* Nisbet (d 1961); *b* 4 April 1942; *Educ* Paisley GS, Univ of Glasgow (MB ChB, MD); *m* 29 Oct 1966, Gillian Margaret, da of Dr James Thomson McCutcheon (d 1964); 3 s (Duncan b 16 Feb 1970, Douglas b 30 April 1975, Neil b 26 Aug 1979), 2 da (Charlotte b 23 May 1968, Deirdre b 25 May 1972); *Career* res fell Scottish Home and Health Dept 1969-73, lectr materia medica Univ of Glasgow 1973-76, res fell MRC Royal Free Hosp 1974-75, conslt physician S Gen Hosp Glasgow 1976-; W Scotland regnl postgrad med advsr; hon sec RCPSGlas, hon treas Med and Dental Def Union of Scotland; MRCP 1973, FRCPG 1983, FRCP 1985; *Books* Emergencies in Medicine (jt ed, 1984), Diagnostic Tests in Gastroenterology (1989); *Recreations* golf, music; *Clubs* Douglas Park Golf; *Style—* Dr Alistair Beattie; 228 Queen Victoria Drive, Glasgow G13 1TN (☎ 041 959 7182); Southern General Hospital, Glasgow G51 4TF (☎ 041 445 2466)

BEATTIE, Charles Noel; s of Michael William Beattie (d 1956), of Sussex, and Edith, *née* Lickfold (d 1964); *b* 4 Nov 1912; *Educ* Lewes GS, Univ of London (LLB); *m* 2 Aug 1972, Wendy, da of John Lawrenson, of Norfolk; 3 da (Elizabeth b 1947, Patricia b 1947, Lucy b 1976); *Career* WWII Capt RASC 1939-45 (despatches); served: Egypt, Libya, Tunisia, Yugoslavia, Italy; called to the Bar Lincoln's Inn 1946; *Style—* Charles N Beattie, Esq; 27 Old Buildings, Lincoln's Inn, London WC2; Leckmelm Estate, Loch Broom, Ullapool, Ross-Shire

BEATTIE, David; CMG (1989); s of George William David Beattie, and Norna Alice, *née* Nicolson; *b* 5 March 1938; *Educ* Merchant Taylors' Sch Crosby, Lincoln Coll Oxford (BA, MA); *m* 1966, Ulla Marita, da of Allan Alha (d 1987), of Helsinki, Finland; 2 da; *Career* Nat Serv RN 1957-59; RNR: Sub Lt 1959-62, Lt 1962-67; Dip Serv 1963-: FO 1963-64, Moscow 1964-66, FO 1966-70, Nicosia 1970-74, FCO 1974-78, dep head (former cnsllr) UK delgn to negotiations on mutual reduction of forces and armaments and associated measures in Central Europe (Vienna) 1978-82, cnsllr (commercial) Moscow 1982-85, head of Energy Sci Space Dept FCO 1985-87, min and dep UK permanent rep to NATO Brussels 1987-; *Recreations* walking, bridge, history of the House of Stuart; *Clubs* Travellers'; *Style—* David Beattie, Esq, CMG; UK Delgn to NATO Brussels; c/o Foreign and Commonwealth Office, King Charles Street, London SW1A 2AH

BEATTIE, Hon Sir David Stuart; GCMG (1980), GCVO (1981) QSO (1985); s of Joseph Nesbitt Beattie; *b* 29 Feb 1924; *m* 1950, Norma, da of John Macdonald; 3 s, 4 da; *Career* barr, slr; QC (1965); judge Supreme (now High Ct) of NZ 1969-80, govr-gen of NZ 1980-85; chm: Royal Cmmn on the Cts 1978-79, Ministerial Ctee on Sci and Technol 1986, NZ Int Festival of the Arts; pres NZ Olympic and Cwlth Games Assoc; patron: NZ Rugby Football Union, NZ Squash Raquets; Hon LLD; *Style—* The Hon Sir David Beattie, GCMG, GCVO, QSO; 18 Golf Rd, Heretaunga, Upper Hutt, New Zealand

BEATTIE, Capt George Kenneth; CBE (1984), RD (1968, bar 1978) DL (Greater London 1982); s of Harold Beattie, JP (d 1956), of Didsbury, Manchester, and Isobel Kerr-Muir, *née* Gallaher; *b* 5 Oct 1931; *Educ* Harrow, Trinity Coll Oxford; *m* 5 Sept 1964, Hon Jane Katherine, *née* Herbert, da of Baron Tangley, KBE (Life Peer, d 1973), of Tangley Way, Blackheath, Guildford, Surrey; 3 da (Sarah b 1965, Joanna b 1966, Alison b 1968); *Career* RNVR 1952, Nat Serv RN 1954-56, cmd patrol craft Cyprus, joined London Div RNVR 1957, Capt RNR 1978, cmd London Div (HMS President) 1979-83; called to the Bar Gray's Inn 1958, practised at Admty Bar as counsel/maritime arbitrator, ADC to HM The Queen 1981-83; memb HM Lieutenancy City of London 1983, vice chm (Navy) Greater London TAVR Assoc 1984-89; panel memb Lloyds Salvage Arbitrators 1983-; tstee RN Museum Portsmouth 1990; Freeman City of London, memb Worshipful Co of Watermen and Lightermen of the River Thames; Liveryman Worshipful Co of Shipwrights; *Recreations* sailing, music; *Clubs* Naval, Royal Cruising, Royal Naval Sailing Assoc; *Style—* Capt George Beattie, CBE, RD, DL, RNR; Big Oak, Churt, Surrey (☎ 0428 713163); Queen Elizabeth Building, Temple, London EC4Y 9BS (☎ 071 353 9153, fax 071 583 0126, telex 26276 INREM G)

BEATTIE, James; OBE (1964), TD, JP (Wolverhampton 1949-), DL (Stafford 1952-); s of Arthur Beattie (d 1957), and Christine Brown; *b* 30 Sept 1914; *Educ* Repton; *m* 22 Sept 1939, Joan, da of Dr Arthur Avent; 1 s (David b 1942), 1 da (Victoria b 1944); *Career* md James Beattie plc 1948-79 (chm 1979-); Mayor of Wolverhampton 1951-52 (memb Borough Cncl 1935-56); chm Wolverhampton Borough Justices 1959-64, cmmnr of Income Tax 1958-84; TA 1932-48, chm Wolverhampton Savings Ctee 1958-66; FRSA 1972; *Recreations* golf, bridge; *Clubs* Royal and Ancient Golf, Staffordshire County Cricket; *Style—* James Beattie, Esq, OBE, TD, JP, DL; Perton Orchard, Pattingham Rd, Perton, Wolverhampton WV6 7HD (☎ 0902 700266)

BEATTIE, Jennifer Jane Belissa; da of Maj Ian Dunbar Beattie (d 1987), of Brighton, Sussex, and Belissa Mary Hunter Graves, *née* Stanley; *b* 20 July 1947; *Educ* Queen Anne's Sch Caversham; *Career* slr; ptnr: Blacket Gill & Langhams 1973-77 (joined 1972), Blacket Gill & Swain 1977-85, Beattie & Co 1985-; vice pres Women's Nat Cancer Control Campaign 1986- (dep chm 1983-86); memb Law Soc 1972; *Recreations* skiing, tennis, reading, dog walking; *Clubs* Naval & Military; *Style—* Miss Jennifer Beattie; 41 Great Percy St, London WC1 (☎ 071 278 5203); St Martins, East Bergholt, Suffolk; 9 Staple Inn, Holborn, London WC1V 7QH (☎ 071 831 1011, fax 071 831 8913)

BEATTIE, Dr John Ogilvie; s of Dr Peter Beattie, of Glasgow, and Isobel, *née* Murray; *b* 4 Aug 1952; *Educ* St Aloysius' Coll Glasgow, Univ of Glasgow (MB ChB, DCH); *m* 19 July 1982, Marie Therese, da of John Scullion, of Glasgow; 3 s (Stephen b 6 Oct 1984, David b 17 March 1986, Christopher b 30 July 1988); *Career* sr registrar Dept of Child Health Univ Hosp Nottingham, currently conslt paediatrician Forth Valley Health Bd (cystic fibrosis clinic Royal Hosp for Sick Children Glasgow); memb: BPA, BMA; FRCP; *Recreations* fishing, sleep; *Style—* Dr John Beattie; 36 Albert Place, King's Park, Stirling FK8 2RG (☎ 0786 79761); Stirling Royal Infirmary, Livilands, Stirling FK8 2AU (☎ 0786 73151); Royal Hospital for Sick Children, York Hill, Glasgow G3 8SJ

BEATTIE, Mary Frances Pamela Aufrere; MBE (1990), JP (1963), DL (Essex 1979); da of Col Henry Haslett Beattie (d 1960), of Heath Lodge, Lexden, Colchester, Essex, and Gwendolin Edith, *née* Morton (d 1958); *b* 15 July 1922; *Educ* St Marys Sch Colchester, Princess Helena Coll Hitchin Herts; *Career* chm: Essex Probation Ctee 1986-, Windyridge Probation Home; chm Bd of Govrs Princess Helena Coll Hitchin Herts 1970; *Recreations* bridge, tennis; *Style—* Miss Mary Beattie, MBE, JP, DL; Heath Lodge, Lexden, Colchester, Essex, (☎ 0206 572493)

BEATTIE, Noel Cunningham; s of Samuel Beattie (d 1984), and Annie Adair, *née* Heslip; *b* 30 Dec 1941; *Educ* Belfast Royal Acad; *m* 7 Sept 1967, (Margaret) Annette, da of Thomas John Malcomson; 1 s (Alistair Samuel Noel b 1970), 1 da (Andrea Margaret b 1972); *Career* co sec Northern Bank Ltd; dir Northern Bank: Fin Servs Ltd, Leasing Ltd, Nominees Ltd, Pension Tst Ltd, Equipment Leasing Ltd, (IOM) Ltd, Commercial Leasing Ltd, Industrial Leasing Ltd; dir Causeway Credit Ltd; *Recreations* photography, hill walking, music; *Style—* Noel Beattie, Esq; Northern Bank Limited, Donegall Square West, Belfast BT1 6JT (☎ 0232 245277, ext 3521)

BEATTY, 3 Earl (UK 1919); David Beatty; also Viscount Borodale and Baron Beatty (UK 1919); s of 2 Earl Beatty, DSC (d 1972); *b* 21 Nov 1946; *Educ* Eton; *m* 1, 23 June 1971 (m dis 1983), Anne, da of A Please, of Wokingham; 2 s (Viscount Borodale, Hon Peter Wystan b 28 May 1975); m 2, 18 June 1984, Anoma Corinne Wijewardene; *Heir* s, Viscount Borodale, *qv*; *Career* photographer and writer; *Style—* The Rt Hon the Earl Beatty; 2 Larkhall Place, Larkhall, Bath, Avon

BEATTY, Col Michael Philip Kenneth; CBE (1990), TD (1971) and Bars (1977, 1987), DL (Staffs 1980); s of Col George Kenneth Beatty, MC, MRCS, LRCP (d 1962), of Upland Grange, Kidderminster; *b* 9 June 1941; *Educ* St Edward's Sch Oxford; *m* 13 Dec 1969, Frances Elizabeth, JP, o da of Richard Nathaniel Twisleton-Wykeham-Fiennes (ggs of 16 Baron Saye and Sele); 4 da (Geraldine, Zazie, Katie, Caroline); *Career* Glynwed International 1965-84; chm and md BGS Ltd; cmmnd Queen's Own Mercian Yeomanry 1978-80, TA Col Western District 1985-90, TA Col UKLF 1990, Hon Col 35 Midland Signal Regt (Vols) 1986-91; ADC to HM The Queen 1987-90; gen cmmr of taxes; *Recreations* restoring ruined old houses, gardening; *Style—* Col Michael Beatty, CBE, TD, DL; Tixall Farmhouse, Tixall, Stafford ST18 0XT

BEATTY, Hon Nicholas Duncan; s of 2 Earl Beatty, DSC (d 1972); *b* 1 April 1961; *Educ* Eton, Exeter Univ (BA); *m* 29 Sept 1990, Laura Mary Catherine, da of Charles Wiliam Lyle Keen, of St Mary's Farm, Beenham, Berks, and Lady (Priscilla) Mary Rose, *née* Curzon, da of 6 Earl Howe, CBE; *Style—* The Hon Nicholas Beatty

BEATY, Robert Thompson (Bob); s of Laurence Beaty, of 12 Castlebay Court, Ayreshire, and Elizabeth (Beattie), *née* Todd; *b* 13 Oct 1943; *Educ* Hamilton Acad, Univ of Glasgow (Hoover scholar, BSc); *m* Anne Veronica, da of George Gray Gillies (d 1990); 2 s (Kenneth Robert b 23 Dec 1968, Steven Gillies b 5 Oct 1971); *Career* trainee then test engr Hoover Cambuslang 1966-68; IBM: quality engr Greenock Plant 1968-69, Uithoorn Devpt Laboratory Holland 1969-71, World Trade HQ White Plains NY 1973-74, second level mgmnt 1974 (mgmnt 1971), functional mangr quality assurance 1976-78, PCB Business Unit 1978-80, various sr mgmnt positions 1980-87, asst plant mangr 1987-89, dir of ops European HQ Paris 1989-; memb Bd of Inverclyde Enterprise Tst 1987, FIEE 1985, FIProdE 1987, FEng 1989; *Recreations* golf, jogging, hillwalking, cycling, car restoration, DIY; *Style—* Bob Beaty, Esq; Glenside, 89 Newton St, Greenock, Renfrewshire PA16 8SG (☎ 0475 22027); 15bis Avenue Clarisse, 92420, Vaucresson, France (☎ 33 1 47 41 33 60); IBM Eurocoordination, Tour Pascal, La Défense 7 Sud, Cedex 40 (☎ 33 1 47 67 76 95)

BEAUCHAMP; *see*: Proctor-Beauchamp

BEAUCHAMP, Linda Marie (Linsey); da of Capt Leroy John Beauchamp, of Oklahoma, and Nancy, *née* Kulper (d 1978); *b* 3 March 1960; *Educ* Arts Educnl Sch, Univ of Oxford (BA); *Career* actress; theatre work incl: Ophelia in Hamlet (tour of ME) 1987, Ophelia in Hamlet and Junie in Brittanicus (Salisbury) 1989, Gloria in You Never Can Tell, (York) 1986, Julia in The Rivals, (Bristol Old Vic) 1986; TV incl: Cathy McGee in Kinsey 1991, Constance in Sophia and Constance 1988, Tender is the Night 1986, Anna in Anna of the Five Towns 1985; *Style—* Ms Linsey Beauchamp; c/o Janet Welch Personal Management, 486 Chiswick High Road, London W4 5IT (☎ 081 994 1697)

BEAUCHAMP, Brig Vernon John; s of Herbert George Beauchamp (d 1952), of Waterlooville, Hants, and Vera Helena, *née* Daly; *b* 19 Sept 1943; *Educ* Portsmouth GS; *m* 27 Nov 1971, Anne Marie, da of Evind Teunis Van Den Born (d 1982), of Renkum, Holland; 2 s (Mark b 9 Dec 1972, Dominic b 16 Oct 1975); *Career* commissioned into Royal Warwickshire Fusiliers 1963, transferred to 2 Gurkha Rifles 1969; serv in Germany, UK, Borneo, HK, Malaysia; Army Staff Coll 1976, Brigade Maj 20 Armoured Brigade 1977-79, Nat Def Coll 1981, Commandant 2 Bn 2 Gurkha Rifles 1981-84, sr staff appts MOD and HQ BAOR 1984-88, commander 48 Gurkha Infantry Brigade 1987-89; *Recreations* golf, running; *Style—* Brig Vernon Beauchamp; Headquarters 48 Gurkha Infantry Brigade, Hong Kong, British Forces Post Office 1 (☎ 0 4837101)

BEAUCLERK, Lady Emma Caroline de Vere; o da of 14 Duke of St Albans; *b* 22 July 1963; *Educ* Roedean, St John's Coll Cambridge, UEA; *Style—* The Lady Emma Beauclerk; Canonteign, Exeter, Devon EX6 7RH

BEAUCLERK, Lord James Charles Fesq de Vere; s of 13 Duke of St Albans, OBE (d 1988); *b* 6 Feb 1949; *Educ* Eton; *Style—* Lord James Beauclerk; Barn House, Midgham, Reading, Berks RG7 5UG

BEAUCLERK, Lord John William Aubrey de Vere; s of 13 Duke of St Albans, OBE (d 1988); *b* 10 Feb 1950; *Educ* Eton; *Career* explorer and freelance journalist 1970-85, relief and devpt worker in Third World; *Style—* Lord John Beauclerk; c/o Oxfam, Africa South, 274 Banbury Road, Oxford OX2 7DZ

BEAUCLERK, Lord Peter Charles de Vere; s of 13 Duke of St Albans, OBE (d 1988); *b* 13 Jan 1948; *Educ* Eton; *m* 1972 (m dis), Beverley June, *née* Bailey, of California; 1 s decd (Robin), 1 da (Angela b 1974); *Career* served RNR 1966-69; property investmt and devpt; *Recreations* skiing, sail boarding; *Style—* Lord Peter Beauclerk; 2726 Shelter Island Drive 332, San Diego, California 92106, USA

BEAUCLERK-DEWAR, Peter de Vere; RD (1980) and bar (1990), JP (Inner London 1983); s of James Dewar, MBE, GM, AE (d 1983), and Hermione de Vere (d 1969), yr da and co-heir of Maj Aubrey Nelthorpe Beauclerk, of Little Grimsby Hall, Lincs (d 1916, heir-in-line to Dukedom of St Albans); recognised by Lord Lyon King of Arms 1965 in additional surname and arms of Beauclerk; *b* 19 Feb 1943; *Educ* Ampleforth; *m* 1967, Sarah Ann Sweet Verge, da of Maj Lionel John Verge Rudder, DCLI, of Bibury, Glos; 1 s (James William Aubrey de Vere b 1970), 3 da (Alexandra Hermione Sarah b 1972, Emma Diana Peta b 1973, Philippa Caroline Frances b 1982); *Career* Lt Cdr RNR; genealogist: Falkland Pursuivant Extraordinary 1975, 1982, 1984, 1986 and 1987; usher: (Silver Stick) Silver Jubilee Thanksgiving Serv 1977, (Liaison) HM Queen Elizabeth The Queen Mother's 80th Birthday Thanks Serv 1980; hon treas: Inst of Heraldic and Genealogical Studies 1979- (Hon FHG), Royal Stuart Soc 1985-; heraldry conslt to Christie's Fine Art Auctioneers 1979-; chm Assoc of Genealogists and Record Agents 1982-83, chief accountant Archdiocese of Westminster 1982-85; dir: Mgmnt

Search International Ltd 1985-87, Five Arrows Ltd 1986-87, Clifton Nurseries (Holdings) Ltd 1986-88, Room Twelve Ltd 1987-88; founded Peter Dewar Associates 1988; govr More House Sch SW1 1986-; memb Queen's Body Guard for Scotland (Royal Co of Archers) 1981-; kt of Hon and Devotion SMO Malta 1971 (Dir of Ceremonies Br Assoc 1989-), kt Sacred Mil Order of Constantine St George 1981; OStJ 1987; Cdr of Merit with Swords "Pro Merito Melitensi" 1989; Liveryman Haberdashers' Co; FBIM, FFA, FInstSMM, FSA Scot, SAT; *Books* The House of Nell Gwyn 1670-1974 (co-author), The House of Dewar 1296-1991, The Family History Record Book, contributor to many pubns; *Clubs* Puffin's, New (Edinburgh); *Style*— Peter Beauclerk-Dewar, Esq, RD, JP; 45 Airedale Ave, Chiswick, London W4 2NW (☎ 081 995 6770, fax 081 747 8459); Holm of Huip, By Stronsay, Orkney Islands

BEAUFORT, Duchess of; Lady Caroline Jane Somerset; *née* Thynne; da (by 1 w) of 6 Marquess of Bath; *b* 28 Aug 1928; *m* 1950, 11 Duke of Beaufort, *qv*; 3 s, 1 da; *Style*— Her Grace the Duchess of Beaufort; Badminton House, Avon; 90 Eaton Terrace, London SW1

BEAUFORT, 11 Duke of (E 1682); David Robert Somerset; also Baron Herbert of Raglan, Chepstow and Gower (E 1506), Earl of Worcester (E 1513), Marquess of Worcester (E 1642) and hereditary keeper of Raglan Castle; s of Henry Somerset, DSO (d 1965; ggs of 8 Duke), and Bettine (d 1978), yr da of Maj Charles Malcolm (bro of Sir James Malcolm, 9 Bt); suc Kinsman, 10 Duke of Beaufort, KG, GCVO, PC, 1984; *b* 23 Feb 1928; *Educ* Eton; *m* 1950, Lady Caroline Thynne, *qv*, da of 6 Marquess of Bath; 3 s, 1 da; *Heir* Marquess of Worcester, *qv*; *Career* late Lt Coldstream Gds; chm Marlborough Fine Art 1977-; *Clubs* White's; *Style*— His Grace the Duke of Beaufort; Badminton House, Glos GL9 1DB

BEAUMAN, Christopher Bentley; s of Wing Cdr Eric Bentley Beauman (d 1989), of Chester Row, London, and Katharine Burgoyne, *née* Jones; *b* 12 Oct 1944; *Educ* Winchester, Trinity Coll Cambridge, Johns Hopkins Sch of Advanced Int Studies and Columbia Univ (Harkness fell); *m* 1, 1966 (m dis 1976), Sally, *née* Kinsey-Miles; m 2, 1976, Nicola, da of Dr Francis Mann, of Manchester Sq, London; 1 s, 1 da, 3 step c; *Career* corp fin exec Hill Samuel 1968-72; dir: Guinness Mahon 1973-76, FMC Ltd 1975-81; advsr to Chm: BSC 1976-81, Central Policy Review Staff 1981-83, Morgan Grenfell Group 1983- (planning dir 1989-); *Recreations* reading, family, London; *Style*— Christopher Beauman, Esq; 35 Christchurch Hill, London NW3 (☎ 071 435 1975)

BEAUMONT, Bryan Kenneth; s of Cyril Beaumont (d 1918); *b* 16 July 1918; *Educ* Firth Park Sch Sheffield; *m* 1940, Kathleen (d 1987), da of Henry Greaves (d 1948); 1 da; *Career* chm Luncheon Vouchers Ltd 1970-82; fin dir: Express Dairy Foods 1975, Express Dairy 1980-83; FCA; *Recreations* listening to music, reading, gardening, golf; *Style*— Bryan Beaumont, Esq; 20 York Avenue, East Sheen, London SW14 7LG

BEAUMONT, Hon Charles Richard; s of 3 Viscount Allendale; *b* 8 March 1954; *Educ* Eton, Royal Agric Coll; *m* 27 Oct 1979, Charlotte Sybil, da of Lt-Col Richard Ian Griffith Taylor, DSO, MC, JP, DL; 2 s (Edward b 1983, Harry b 1987), 1 da (Laura b 1985); *Career* farmer; co dir; *Recreations* skiing, cricket, tennis; *Clubs* Turf, Northern Counties, Borderers Cricket, Cloth Cap; *Style*— The Hon Charles Beaumont; Swallowship House, Hexham, Northumberland NE46 1RJ (☎ 0434 603891)

BEAUMONT, His Hon (Herbert) Christopher Beaumont; MBE (1948); s of Maj Gerald Beaumont, MC (d 1933), of Woolley Moor House, Wakefield, and Gwendolene, *née* Haworth; *b* 3 June 1912; *Educ* Uppingham, Worcester Coll Oxford; *m* 1940, Helen Magaret Gordon, da of William Mitchell Smail, of Edinburgh; 1 s, 2 da; *Career* formerly ICS and FO; barr 1951-72, circuit judge 1972-89; *Recreations* european travel; *Clubs* Brooks's, Yorkshire (York); *Style*— His Hon Christopher Beaumont, MBE; Minskip Lodge, Boroughbridge, N Yorks (☎ 0432 32 2365)

BEAUMONT, Christopher Hubert; s of Hubert Beaumont, MP (d 1948), and Beatrix Beaumont (d 1982); *b* 10 Feb 1926; *Educ* W Monmouth Sch Pontypool, Balliol Coll Oxford (MA); *m* 1, 31 Aug 1959, Catherine (d 1971), da of Eric Clark (d 1982); 2 s (Simon b 1962, Guy b 1964); m 2, 28 June 1972, Sara Patricia, da of Cdr William Magee, RN (d 1976); 1 da (Justine b 1973); *Career* served RN 1944-47 (Sub-Lt, RNVR); called to the Bar Middle Temple 1950, rec Crown Ct 1981-; chm Agric Land Tbnl Eastern Area 1985- (dep chm 1979-85); asst dep Coroner Inner W London 1963-81; *Books* Law Relating to Sheriffs (1968), Town and Country Planning Act 1968 (1969), Town and Country Planning Acts 1971 and 1972 (1972), Land Compensation Act 1973 (with W G Nutley, 1973), Community Land Act 1975 (with W G Nutley, 1976), Planning Appeal Decisions (jt ed with W G Nutley, in series from 1968-); *Style*— Christopher H Beaumont, Esq; Rose Cottage, Lower Eashing, Godalming, Surrey GU7 2QG (☎ 0483 416316); 2 Harcourt Buildings, Temple, London EC4Y 9DB (☎ 071 353 8415)

BEAUMONT, Ernest George; s of George Bunzl (d 1976); *b* 9 Aug 1921; *Educ* Austria, Univ of Manchester, Univ of London; *m* 1947, Eva Marie, da of Walter Dux, of London; 3 c; *Career* interned on the IOM 1940 before being allowed to serve REME; chm Bunzl plc 1981-90 (former md and dep chm); *Recreations* golf, filming, travel, theatre; *Clubs* RAC; *Style*— Ernest Beaumont, Esq; Wych Elm, Fitzgeorge Ave, New Malden, Surrey KT3 4SH (☎ 081 949 6500); Bunzl plc, Friendly House, 21-24 Chiswell St, London EC1 (☎ 071 606 9966)

BEAUMONT, Sir George Howland Francis; 12 Bt (E 1661); s of Sir George Arthur Hamilton Beaumont, 11 Bt (d 1933); *b* 24 Sept 1924; *Educ* Stowe; *m* 1, 1949 (m annulled 1951), Barbara, da of William Singleton; m 2, 1963 (m dis 1985), Henrietta Anne, da of late Dr Arthur Weymouth; 2 da (twins); *Heir* none; *Career* formerly warrant offr Australian Army; Coldstream Gds, Lt 60 Rifles WW II; *Clubs* Lansdowne; *Style*— Sir George Beaumont, Bt; The Corner House, Manor Court, Stretton-on-Fosse, nr Moreton-in-Marsh, Glos GL56 9SB

BEAUMONT, Hon Hubert Wentworth; s of Baron Beaumont of Whitley (Life Peer); *b* 12 April 1956; *Educ* Gordonstoun, S Bank Poly; *m* 1980, Katherine Emma, da of Richard Abel Smith, *qv*; 2 s (George b 1985, Richard b 1989), 1 da (Amelia b 1983); *Career* farmer; *Style*— The Hon Hubert Beaumont; Harristown House, Brannockstown, Kildare, Republic of Ireland

BEAUMONT, Janet Elizabeth; da of Cdr Surg Robert Holden Tincker, RNVR, DSO (d 1982), of Painswick, Gloucestershire, and Kathleen Aldrich *née* Bates; *b* 5 Jan 1937; *Educ* St Mary's and St Anne's Secdy Sch Uttoxeter, Univ of Surrey (MPhil); *m* 19 July 1958, Stephen Francis Beaumont, s of Hugh Beaumont (d 1936), of Ipswich; 2 s (Robert Stephen b 1959, James Hugh b 1961), 1 da (Elizabeth Frances b 1964); *Career* CA 1973; lectr Oxford Poly 1973-82; fin dir OSS Scaffolding Ltd 1983-; FCA; *Style*— Mrs Janet Beaumont; Rye Farm, Culham, Abingdon, OX14 3NN (☎ 0235 20484); Oxford House, Pony Rd, Cowley, Oxford (☎ 0865 748488)

BEAUMONT, John Richard; s of Stanley Beaumont, of Denmead, Hampshire, and Winifred Louise, *née* Williams (d 1984); *b* 22 June 1947; *Educ* Wolverhampton GS, Merton Coll Oxford (BA, MA); *m* 18 Oct 1986, Susan Margaret, da of Ivan Stanley Blowers, of Oulton Broad, Suffolk; 1 da (Anna Jane b 1988), 1 step s (Christopher Jones b 1983); *Career* schoolmaster Buckingham Coll Harrow 1969-71; Shelter Nat Campaign for the Homeless Ltd: regnl organiser W Mids 1971-73, nat projects dir 1973-74; legal offr: Alnwick DC Northumberland 1974, Thurrock Borough Cncl 1974-75; called to the Bar Inner Temple 1976, memb Northern Circuit, pt/t legal advsr Assoc Newspapers plc; former memb: Mgmnt Ctees of Bradford Housing and Renewal Experiment (SHARE), North Islington Housing Rights Project; *Recreations* walking, reading history and victorian literature; *Style*— John Beaumont, Esq; 9 Valley Way, Knutsford, Cheshire (☎ 0565 3419); Queens Chambers, 5 John Dalton St, Manchester (☎ 061 834 6875/4738, fax 061 834 8557); 5 Essex Ct, Temple, London

BEAUMONT, Major Keith John Lancelot; TD (1976); s of Frank Charles Beaumont (d 1987), of Worthing, Sussex, and Dorothy Kate, *née* Turner (d 1971); *b* 7 May 1937; *Educ* Alleyns & Dulwich Colls; *Career* RAVR 1959-63 Flying Offr, Middx Yeomanry (TA) 1963-79; Royal Signals: Lt 1963, Capt 1970, Actg Maj 1976; dir: Dominion Assoc Leasing Ltd, Dominion Corp Fin Ltd; chief exec Dominion Credit & Fin Ltd 1983-, underwriter Lloyds 1989; vice chm Execs Assoc of GB; Freeman City of London 1978; Liveryman: Worshipful Co of Joiners 1973, Worshipful Co of Carmen 1983; FCIM 1973, Worshipful Co of Carmen 1983; FICM; *Recreations* golf, shooting, arts, racehorse owner; *Clubs* Cavalry & Guards, St George's Hill Golf; *Style*— Maj Keith Beaumont, TD; Elbury, Oxshott Way, Cobham, Surrey, KT11 2RO (☎ 0932 65914); Dominion Credit & Finance Ltd, Dominion House, 49 Parkside, Wimbledon SW19 5RB (☎ 081 947 1150)

BEAUMONT, Hon Mark Henry; 2 s of 3 Viscount Allendale; *b* 21 July 1950; *Educ* Eton; *m* 1982, Diana Elizabeth, yst da of Lt-Col J E Benson, of Chesters, Humshaugh, Northumberland; 2 s (George Richard Benson b 19 July 1987, John Wentworth b 28 Nov 1989); *Style*— The Hon Mark Beaumont; Dilston House, Corbridge, Northumberland (☎ 0434 633137)

BEAUMONT, Martin Dudley; s of Patrick Beaumont, JP, DL, of Donadea Lodge, Clwyd, and (Doreen Elizabeth) Lindesay, *née* Howard; *b* 6 Aug 1949; *Educ* Stowe, Magdalene Coll Cambridge (MA); *m* 12 June 1976, Andrea Evelyn, da of John Wilberforce, of The Red House, Corbridge; 3 da (Alice b 11 July 1980, Jessica 22 Dec 1981, Flora b 4 Oct 1989); *Career* ptnr Peat Marwick McLintock (formerly Thomson McLintock) 1983-87 (dir 1980-87), gp fin dir Egmont Publishing Group 1987-90; dir: World Int Publishing Ltd 1987-90, Ward Lock Ltd 1987-89; chief exec Children's Best Sellers 1990, fin controller and sec Norwest Cooperative Society Ltd 1990-; memb Parochial Church Cncl; FCA 1977, MIMC 1981; *Recreations* shooting, fishing, tennis; *Style*— Martin Beaumont, Esq; Beech Cottage, Hand Green, Tarporley, Cheshire CW6 95N (☎ 082973 2994)

BEAUMONT, Mary Rose; da of Charles Edward Wauchope (d 1969), and Elaine Margaret, *née* Armstrong-Jones (d 1965); *b* 6 June 1932; *Educ* Prior's Field Godalming Surrey, Courtauld Inst Univ of London (BA); *m* 1955, Timothy Wentworth Beaumont (Baron Beaumont of Whitley, *qv*), s of Michael Wentworth Beaumont; 2 s (Hubert Wentworth b 1956, Alaric Charles Blackett b 1958, d 1980), 2 da (Atalanta Armstrong b 1961, Ariadne Grace b 1963); *Career* writer and art critic for newspapers and periodicals incl: Financial Times, Sunday Telegraph, Art International, Arts Review, Art and Design; author of numerous catalogue introductions for individual artists, teacher at art schs and polys, lectr at Tate Gallery and National Gallery; exhibition curator: for Br Cncl in E Europe and Far East 1983-87, The Human Touch (Fischer Fine Art) 1986, The Dark Side of The Moon (Benjamin Rhodes Gallery) 1990; Picker Fellowship at Kingston Poly; exec and memb Cncl Contemporary Arts Soc 1980-90; *Recreations* listening to opera and reading novels; *Clubs* Chelsea Arts; *Style*— Ms Mary Rose Beaumont; 70 Marksbury Avenue, Richmond, Surrey TW9 4JF (☎ 081 876 1929)

BEAUMONT, Hon Matthew Henry; 4 s of 2 Viscount Allendale, KG, CB, CBE, MC (d 1956); *b* 10 April 1933; *Educ* Bradfield; *m* 1, 1959 (m dis 1972), Anne Christina Margaret, da of Gerald Hamilton; 1 s, 1 da; m 2, 1973, Belinda Jane Elizabeth, da of late Harold David Cuthbert, of Beaufront Castle, Hexham, Northumberland; *Career* underwriting memb of Lloyd's 1960; *Clubs* Boodle's; *Style*— The Hon Matthew Beaumont

BEAUMONT, (John) Michael; Seigneur of Sark (cr 1565) 1974-; s of late Lionel (Buster) Beaumont, and Enid, *née* Ripley; gs of Dame Sibyl Mary Hathaway, DBE, Dame of Sark, whom he suc on her death; *b* 20 Dec 1927; *Educ* Loughborough Coll; *m* 1956, Diana, *née* La Trobe-Bateman; 2 s; *Heir* s, Christopher Beaumont; *Career* aircraft design engineer to 1975; *Style*— Michael Beaumont, Esq; La Seigneurie, Sark, Channel Islands (☎ 048 183 2017)

BEAUMONT, Hon (Edward) Nicholas Canning; CVO (1986, MVO 1976), DL (Berks 1982); 3 s of 2 Viscount Allendale, KG, CB, CBE, MC (d 1956); *b* 14 Dec 1929; *Educ* Eton; *m* 1953, Jane Caroline Falconer, da of Alexander Lewis Paget Falconer Wallace, JP, of Candacraig, Strathdon, Aberdeen; 2 s (Thomas b 1962, Henry b 1966, a page of hon to HM Queen Elizabeth The Queen Mother 1979-82); *Career* joined Life Gds 1948, Capt 1956, ret 1960; asst to clerk of the course Ascot 1964-69, clerk of the course and sec to the Ascot Authy 1969; OBStJ 1988 (SBStJ 1982), pres Berkshire St John 1988, Vice Lord Lt Berkshire 1989; *Style*— Capt the Hon Nicholas Beaumont, CVO, DL; Secretary's Office, Ascot Racecourse, Ascot, Berks (☎ 0990 22211)

BEAUMONT, Sir Richard Ashton; KCMG (1965, CMG 1955), OBE (1949); s of A R Beaumont (d 1962), of Uppingham, Rutland, and Evelyn Frances, *née* Rendle; *b* 29 Dec 1912; *Educ* Repton, Oriel Coll Oxford; *m* 1, 1942, Alou (d 1985), da of M Camran, of Istanbul; 1 da; m 2, 24 Feb 1989, Mrs Melanie E M Anns, da of H Brummel; *Career* served WWII; joined HM Consular Serv 1936, served Beirut and Damascus; FO: joined 1945, head of Arabian Dept 1959, ambass Morocco 1961-65, ambass Iraq 1965-67, dep under-sec of state 1967-69, ambass Egypt 1969-72; chm: Anglo-Arab Assoc 1979-, Arab-Br C of C 1980; tstee Thomson Fndn 1974-; *Style*— Sir Richard Beaumont, KCMG, OBE; 14 Cadogan Sq, London SW1

BEAUMONT, Hon Richard Blackett; 2 s of 2 Viscount Allendale, KG, CB, CBE, MC (d 1956); *b* 13 Aug 1926; *Educ* Eton; *m* 1971, Lavinia Mary (sometime Governess to HRH The Prince Edward), da of late Lt-Col Arnold Keppel (gggs of Rt Rev Hon Frederick Keppel, sometime Bishop of Exeter and 4 s of 2 Earl of Albemarle); *Career* joined RNVR 1944, Sub Lt 1946; PA to Sir Walter Monckton Hyderabad 1947-48, joined James Purdey and Sons 1949 (dir 1952), ADC to Sir Donald MacGillivray Malaya 1954-55, chm James Purdey and Sons 1971-; Master Gunmakers' Co 1969 and 1985; *Books* Purdey's, The Guns and the Family (1984); *Recreations* shooting, travel; *Clubs* White's, Turf, Beefsteak, Pratt's; *Style*— The Hon Richard Beaumont; Flat 1, 58 South Audley St, London W1 (☎ 071 499 5845)

BEAUMONT, Rupert Roger Seymour; s of Robert Beaumont, of London, and Peggy Mary Stubbs, *née* Bassett (d 1988); *b* 24 Feb 1944; *Educ* Wellington, Univ of Grenoble France; *m* 24 Feb 1968, Susie Diane, da of Noel Sampson James Wishart; 1 s (James b 1971), 1 da (Juliet b 1972); *Career* articled clerk Beaumont & Son 1962-68, admitted slr 1968, with Appleton Rice and Perrin NY USA 1968-69, ptnr Slaughter and May 1974- (joined 1969, Hong Kong office 1976-81); memb Law Soc 1973; *Books* author various articles for learned jls; *Recreations* tennis, fishing, carpentry; *Clubs* Cavalry and Guards; *Style*— Rupert Beaumont, Esq; 35 Basinghall Street, London EC2V 5DB (☎ 071 600 1200, fax 071 726 0038/071 600 0289, telex 883486/888926)

BEAUMONT, Hon Wentworth Peter Ismay; s and h of 3 Viscount Allendale; *b* 13 Nov 1948; *Educ* Harrow; *m* 1975, Theresa Mary Magdalene, da of Frank More O'Ferrall (d 1977); 1 s, 3 da; *Career* farmer; chm of Northumberland Association of

Boys' Clubs; *Recreations* shooting, skiing, horseracing; *Clubs* Jockey, Northern Counties, White's; *Style*— The Hon Wentworth Beaumont; Bywell Castle, Stocksfield-on-Tyne, Northumberland (☎ 0661 842450; office: 0661 843296)

BEAUMONT, William Anderson; CB (1986), OBE (1961), AE (1958); s of William Lionel Beaumont, of Nesbit Hall, Pudsey, W Yorks (d 1956), and Ivy Mima, *née* Anderson (d 1990); *b* 30 Oct 1924; *Educ* Moorlands Sch Leeds, Terrington Hall York, Cranleigh, ChCh Oxford (MA, DipEd); *m* 1, 24 Aug 1946, Kythé, da of Maj Kenneth Gordon Mackenzie, Canadian Army (d 1988); 1 da (Kythé Victoria b 1958); m 2, June 1989, Rosalie Jean Underhill, *née* Kinloch, wid of Judge Michael Underhill, QC; *Career* md: Beaumont and Smith Ltd Pudsey Yorks (textile manufacturers) 1954-66, Henry Mason (Shipley) Ltd (Textile Manufacturers) 1966-76; asst sec Welsh Office Cardiff 1976-82, Speaker's sec House of Commons 1982-86; ret; active in various official and semi-official bodies incl: memb Panel of Chm Civil Serv Selection Bd, vice chm Franco-Br Soc, dir St David's Forum (Fforum Dewi Sant); *Recreations* inland waterways; *Clubs* RAF, Civil Service, United Services (Cardiff); *Style*— William Beaumont, Esq, CB, OBE, AE; 28 Halford Rd, Richmond, Surrey (☎ 081 940 2390)

BEAUMONT, William Blackledge (Bill); OBE (1982); s of Ronald Walton Beaumont, of Croston, Lancs, and Joyce, *née* Blackledge; *b* 9 March 1952; *Educ* Ellesmere Coll; *m* 1977, Hilary Jane, da of Kenneth Seed, of Iken House, Freckleton, Preston, Lancs; 2 s (Daniel b 1982, Samuel b 1985); *Career* co dir J Blackledge and Son Ltd 1981; dir: Red Rose Radio 1981, Chorley and District Bldg Soc 1983; England Rugby capt 1977-82, Br Lions capt SA 1980, Barbarians capt, Lancashire capt, capt England to Grand Slam 1980; BBC sports analyst: Grandstand, Rugby Special; team capt Question of Sport (BBC); *Books* Thanks to Rugby (autobiography, 1982); *Recreations* golf, boating; *Clubs* E India, Royal Lytham Golf, Fydle RUFC; *Style*— Bill Beaumont Esq, OBE

BEAUMONT-DARK, Anthony Michael; MP (C) Birmingham Selly Oak 1979-; s of Leonard Cecil Dark; *b* 11 Oct 1932; *Educ* Birmingham Coll of Arts and Crafts, Univ of Birmingham; *m* 1959, Sheelagh Irene, da of R Cassey; 1 s, 1 da; *Career* investmt analyst and company dir, memb Birmingham Stock Exchange 1958-, conslt Smith Keen Cutler PLC 1958- (ptnr 1959-85); dir: Wigham Poland (Midlands) Ltd 1960-, National Exhibition Centre Ltd 1971-73, J Saville Gordon PLC 1989-, TR High Income Tst 1990-, Cope Allman International Ltd 1972-89; Birmid Qualcast PLC 1983-89, chm Birmingham Executive Airways 1983-86; memb: Central Housing Advsy Ctee DOE 1970-76, Treasy Civil Serv Select Ctee 1979-, Birmingham City Cncl 1956-67, W Midlands County Cncl 1973-87 (chm Fin Ctee 1977-83); contested (c) Birmingham Aston 1959 and 1964; govr: Univ of Aston 1980, Univ of Birmingham 1984; tstee Birmingham Copec Housing Tst 1975; Alderman 1967-74, Hon Alderman 1967-; *Clubs* Carlton; *Style*— Anthony Beaumont-Dark, Esq, MP; House of Commons, SW1

BEAUMONT OF WHITLEY, Baron (Life Peer UK 1967); Timothy Wentworth Beaumont; o s of late Maj Michael Wentworth Beaumont, TD (d 1958, gs of 1 Baron Allendale) by 1 w, Hon Faith Muriel, *née* Pease (d 1935), da of 1 Baron Gainford; *b* 22 Nov 1928; *Educ* Eton, Gordonstoun, ChCh Oxford; *m* 13 June 1955, Mary Rose, yr da of Lt-Col Charles Edward Wauchope, MC; 2 s (1 decd), 2 da; *Career* vicar of Christ Church Kowloon Hong Kong 1957-59 (resigned Holy Orders 1979, resumed 1984); proprietor various periodicals incl Time and Tide and New Christian 1960-70; pres Lib Pty 1969-70 (head of orgn 1965-66), del to Parly Assembly Cncl of Europe and Western Euro Union 1974-77; chm Studio Vista Books 1963-68; dir Green Alliance 1977-79; Lib spokesman House of Lords on educn, arts and the environment 1967-85; vicar of St Luke's and St Philip's (The Barn Church) Kew 1986-; *Books* Where Shall I Place My Cross? (1987); *Style*— The Rev The Rt Hon Lord Beaumont of Whitley; 70 Marksbury Avenue, Richmond, Surrey

BEAUREPAIRE, Dame Beryl Edith; DBE (1981, OBE 1975); da of E L Bedggood; *b* 24 Sept 1923; *Educ* Fintona GS Victoria, Univ of Melbourne; *m* 1946, Ian Francis Beaurepaire, CMG, former Lord Mayor of Melbourne; 2 s; *Career* WAAAF 1942-45; memb Nat Exec YWCA of Australia 1969-77; chm: Victoria Women's Ctee Section Lib Pty 1973-76, Bd of Mgmnt Fintona Girls' Sch 1973-87, Fed Women's Ctee Lib Pty 1974-76; Australian Children's TV Fndn: bd memb 1982-88, vice pres 1986-88; vice pres Victoria Div Lib Pty 1976-86, convenor Nat Women's Advsy Cncl 1978-82; memb: Cncl Aust War Meml 1982- (chm 1985-), Bd of Victoria's 150 Authy 1982-86, memb Bd Bi-centennial Multicultural Fndn 1988-; pres Victorian Assoc of the Most Excellent Order of the Br Empire 1987-90; Queen's Silver Jubilee Medal 1977; *Style*— Dame Beryl Beaurepaire, DBE; 18 Barton Drive, Mount Eliza, Victoria 3930, Australia

BEAVEN, John Lewis; CMG (1986), CVO (1983, MVO 1974); s of Charles Beaven (d 1967), and Margaret Beaven (d 1973); *b* 30 July 1930; *Educ* Newport HS Gwent; *m* 1, 1960 (m dis), Jane Beeson; 1 s, 1 da; m 2, 1975, Jean McComb Campbell; *Career* Flying Offr RAF Res 1948-50; BOT 1947; HM Dip Serv 1956-90; dep consul-gen New York and dir Br Trade Devpt Off NY 1978-82, consul-gen San Francisco 1982-86, ambass Khartoum 1986-90 (ret); US rep to Save the Children Fund 1990-; *Recreations* computing, music, tennis, walking, needlepoint; *Clubs* Brook (New York); *Style*— John Beaven, Esq, CMG, CVO; Scannell Rd, Ghent, NY 12075, USA (☎ 518 392 2152)

BEAVERBROOK, 3 Baron (UK 1917); Sir Maxwell William Humphrey Aitken; 3 Bt (UK 1916); s of Sir Max Aitken, 2 Bt, DSO, DFC (d 1985; suc as 2 Baron Beaverbrook 1964, which he disclaimed for life 1964) by his 3 w, Violet (*see* Lady Aitken); *b* 29 Dec 1951; *Educ* Charterhouse, Pembroke Coll Cambridge; *m* 1974, Susan Angela (Susie), da of Francis More O'Ferrall and Angela (niece of Sir George Mather-Jackson, 5 Bt, and da of Sir Anthony Mather-Jackson 6 Bt, JP, DL, by his w, Evelyn, da of Lt-Col Sir Henry Stephenson, 1 Bt, DSO); 2 s (Maxwell b 1977, Alexander Rory b 1978), 2 da (Charlotte 1982, Sophia b 1985); *Heir* s, Hon Maxwell Francis Aitken, b 17 March 1977; *Career* dir Ventech Ltd 1983-86, chm and pres Ventech Healthcare Inc 1988- (chm 1986); govt whip House of Lords 1986-88; treas: Cons Party 1990- (dep treas 1988-90), Euro Democratic Union 1990-; tstee Beaverbrook Fndn 1974- (chm 1985-); memb Cncl Homeopathic Tst 1989-, chm Nat Assoc of Boys' Clubs; *Clubs* White's, Royal Yacht Squadron; *Style*— The Rt Hon the Lord Beaverbrook; House of Lords, London SW1

BEAVIS, Air Chief Marshal Sir Michael Gordon; KCB (1981), CBE (1977, OBE 1969), AFC (1962); s of Walter Erle Beavis (d 1972), of Haverhill, and Mary Ann, *née* Sarjantson; *b* 13 Aug 1929; *Educ* Kilburn GS; *m* 9 Dec 1949, Joy Marion, da of Arthur Olwen Jones (d 1974); 1 s (Simon Anthony b 1 Jan 1960), 1 da (Lynn Alison Deborah b 16 April 1956); *Career* joined RAF 1947, Air Marshal 1981, AOC-in-C RAF Support Cmd 1981-84, Air Chief Marshal 1984, Dep C-in-C Allied Forces Central Europe 1984-86, ret 1987; dep chm Tubular Exhibition Gp 1989-; Liveryman Guild of Air Pilots and Navigators 1982; CBIM; *Recreations* golf, travel; *Clubs* RAF; *Style*— Air Chief Marshal Sir Michael Beavis, KCB, CBE, AFC; c/o Lloyds Bank plc, 202 High Street, Lincoln LN5 7AP

BEAZER, Brian Cyril; s of Henry George Beazer; *b* 22 Feb 1935; *Educ* Wells Cathedral Sch; *m* Patricia; 1 da (Susan Jill b 28 Jan 1963); *Career* Beazer plc: joined 1958, bldg mangr 1958-68, md 1968-83, chm and chief exec 1983-; *Recreations* walking, reading, history and theology; *Style*— Brian Beazer, Esq; The Weavers House, Castle Combe, Wiltshire; Beazer PLC, Beazer House, Lower Bristol Rd, Bath, Avon BA2 3EY (☎ 0225 428401, telex 449397)

BEAZLEY, Rev Prof John Milner; s of Ernest Victor Beazley (d 1968), of Manchester, and Alice, *née* Milner (d 1968); *b* 8 Nov 1932; *Educ* William Hulmes' GS, Univ of Manchester (MB ChB, MD, FRCOG); *m* 12 July 1958, Barbara Winifred, da of Thomas Geoffrey Child (d 1941); 2 s (Simon b 1960, Andrew b 1964), 2 da (Susan b 1962, Ruth b 1968); *Career* sr lectr in obstetrics and gynaecology Queen Charlotte's Maternity Hospital 1968-72, dean Faculty of Medicine Univ of Liverpool 1988- (prof of obstetrics and gynaecology 1972-); ordained minister C of E Diocese of Chester 1986); Hon FACOG 1989; memb: RCOG, BMA, RSM; Order of the Yugoslav Flag with Gold Star 1982; *Books* Aspects of care in labour (jtly, 1983), Fetal growth retardation: diagnosis and treatment (jt ed, 1989); author of numerous medical and non medical publications; *Recreations* training and judging field trial pointers & setters; *Style*— The Rev Prof John Beazley; Gourley Grange, Gourley's Lane, Grange, West Kirby, Wirral L48 8AS (☎ 051 625 5353); Univ Dept of Obstetrics and Gynaecology/Faculty of Medicine, Royal Liverpool Hospital, Prescott St, Liverpool L7 8XP (☎ 051 709 0141, telex 627095 UNILPL G, fax 051 708 6502)

BEAZLEY, Peter George; MEP (EDG) Beds 1979-; s of late Thomas Alfred Beazley, and Agnes Alice Mary Beazley; *b* 9 June 1922; *Educ* Highgate Sch, St John's Coll Oxford; *m* 1945, Joyce Marion, *née* Sulman; 1 s (Christopher John Pridham b 1952), 2 da (and 1 da decd); *Career* ICI 1947-78: dir ICI Italia 1965-73, dir ICI Fibres and ICI Europa 1969-73, md ICI Europa Fibres Gmbh 1969-73; vice chm and md South African Nylon Spinners and Pan Textiles 1973-77, res fell Royal Inst of Int Affairs 1977-78; *Clubs* Oriental, Royal Institution, Willingdon Golf; *Style*— Peter Beazley, Esq, MEP; Rest Harrow, 14 The Combe, Ratton, Eastbourne, E Sussex (☎ 0323 504460); 4 Bridgewater Court, Little Gaddesden, Herts (☎ 044 284 3548)

BEBB, Maureen Mary; da of Carl Burcham Bebb, of 16 Compton Place Rd, Eastbourne, Sussex, and Mary Ethel, *née* Barnes; *b* 16 Sept 1938; *Educ* St Maur's Convent Weybridge Surrey, Rosslyn House Weybridge Surrey; *Career* BBC Radio: sec 1956, studio mangr 1961, prog planner World Serv 1966, sr then chief prog planner World Serv 1973, chief asst directorate World Serv 1983-; *Recreations* opera, theatre, travel, food, wine, bridge; *Clubs* Ski Club of GB; *Style*— Miss Maureen Bebb; BBC World Service, Bush House, Strand, London WC2 4PH (☎ 071 257 2097, fax 071 240 8926, telex 265781)

BEBBINGTON, Andrew John Price; s of Jack Price Bebbington (d 1987), of Hazel Grove, nr Stockport, Cheshire, and Elizabeth, *née* Riding; *b* 10 March 1952; *Educ* Stockport GS; *m* 8 March 1975, Heather Winifred, da of Benjamin Harold Linton (d 1954); *Career* CA: Neville Russell 1969-75, Dearden Farrow 1977-82, own practice 1982-; FCA 1976; *Recreations* sport, military modelling; *Clubs* Hale Barns Cricket; *Style*— Andrew J P Bebbington, Esq; 13 Rushside Rd, Cheadle Hulme, Cheadle, Cheshire, SK8 6NW (☎ 061 485 7136)

BECCLE, Geoffrey Stephen; s of Louis Francis Beccle (d 1964), and Amelia, *née* Gittleson (d 1936); *b* 6 July 1933; *Educ* Bradfield; *m* 3 June 1961, Angela Rosalind Vere, da of Edward Thomas Marshall (d 1973); 2 s (Simon Edward, Richard Stephen); *Career* Nat Serv flying offr RAF 1956-58; admitted slr 1956, ptnr Geoffrey S Beccle and Co; memb Law Soc; *Recreations* lawn tennis, golf, bridge, horse racing; *Clubs* All England Lawn Tennis and Croquet, MCC, Buck's, RAF, Berkshire Golf; *Style*— Geoffrey Beccle, Esq; 18 Stanhope Gardens, London SW7 5RQ (☎ 071 581 2346, fax 071 259 2635)

BECHER; *see*: Wrixon-Becher

BECHMANN, Hon Mrs (Elizabeth Suzanne); *née* Duke; o da of 2 Baron Merrivale, OBE (d 1951); *b* 27 Aug 1921; *m* 1, 1942 (m dis 1953), Capt Jean Pompei, French Air Force, s of Louis Pompei; 1 s, 1 da; m 2, 1955, Jacques Bechmann, s of René Bechmann; 1 s; *Clubs* Chantilly Golf; *Style*— The Hon Mrs Bechmann; La Charité, 60 500 Vineuil-St Firmin, Chantilly, France (☎ 010 33 4457 0169)

BECK, Rev Brian Edgar; s of Alfred George Beck, of Tooting, London, and Cicely Annie, *née* Roots (d 1987); *b* 27 Sept 1933; *Educ* City of London Sch, Corpus Christi Coll Cambridge, Wesley House Cambridge (MA); *m* 9 Aug 1958, Margaret Elizabeth Christie, da of William Ernest Ludlow (d 1952), of Basingstoke, Hants; 3 da (Eleanor (Mrs Cribb) b 1961, Julia b 1963, Marian b 1966); *Career* asst tutor Handsworth Coll 1957-59, ordained methodist minister 1960, E Suffolk Circuit 1959-62, St Paul's United Theol Coll Limuru Kenya 1962-68, princ Wesley House Cambridge 1980-84 (tutor 1968-80), sec Methodist Conf 1984-; *Books* Reading the New Testament Today (1977), Christian Character in the Gospel of Luke (1989); contrib to: Christian Belief: A Catholic-Methodist Statement (1970), Unity the Next Step? (1972), Suffering & Martyrdom in the New Testament (1981); *Recreations* walking, DIY; *Style*— The Rev Brian E Beck; 76 Beaumont Road, Purley, Surrey CR8 2EG (☎ 081 645 9162); 1 Central Buildings, Westminster, London SW1H 9NH (☎ 071 222 8010, fax 071 930 5355)

BECK, Charles Theodore Heathfield; s of Richard Theodore Beck, and Margaret Beryl, *née* Page; *b* 3 April 1954; *Educ* Winchester, Jesus Coll Cambridge (MA); *Career* Bank of England 1975-79; JM Finn & Co stockbrokers: joined 1979, ptnr 1984, fin ptnr 1988; Freeman City of London 1980, Liveryman Worshipful Co of Broderers 1981; AMSIA 1980; *Recreations* fencing, japanese fencing, archaelogy; *Style*— Charles Beck, Esq; c/o J M Finn & Co, Salisbury House, London Wall, London EC2M 5TA (☎ 071 628 9688, fax 071 628 7314, telex 887281)

BECK, Clive; s of Sir Edgar Charles Beck, CBE, and his 1 wife, Mary Agnes, *née* Sorapure; *b* 12 April 1937; *Educ* Ampleforth; *m* 28 April 1960, Philippa Mary, da of Dr Philip Flood (d 1968), of Wimbledon; 3 s (David b 28 July 1962, Andrew b 22 Sept 1964, Simon b 30 Dec 1965), 3 da (Nicola b 17 Feb 1961, Emma b 19 Dec 1967, Sarah b 16 July 1971); *Career* 2 Lt The Life Guards 1955-57; joined John Mowlem & Co 1957, joined SGB Gp plc 1967 (dir 1968, chm 1985); rejoined John Mowlem & Co plc as dep chm and jt md on acquisition of SGB by Mowlem 1986; Freeman of City of London 1960, Liveryman Worshipful Co of Plaisterers; *Recreations* fishing, shooting, golf; *Clubs* Buck's, Royal Wimbledon Golf, Swinley Forest Golf; *Style*— Clive Beck, Esq; John Mowlem & Co plc, Lion Court, Swan St, Isleworth, Middx (☎ 081 568 9111, fax 081 569 9975, telex 24414)

BECK, Dr Eric Robert; s of Dr Adolf Beck (d 1986), of 24 Cyprus Gdns, London, and Helen, *née* Marhold; *b* 26 Aug 1934; *Educ* St Paul's, UCL (BSc, MB BS); *m* 1, 18 Aug 1956, Patricia Chapman (d 1975); 1 s (Martin b 1963), 1 da (Helen Carol b 1959); m 2, 29 Feb 1980, Pamela Mary, da of Francis Leonard Bretherton (d 1987), of 6 Elgar Drive, Kempsey, Worcs; 1 da (Lucy Claire b 1985); *Career* conslt physician Whittington Hosp London 1969-, hon sr clinical lectr in med UCH and Middx Hosp 1971-, recognised teacher Univ of London 1971-, sec Part 2 Examination Bd MRCP(UK) 1986-; fndr memb and former treas NHS Conslts Assoc, cncl memb Mayer-Lismann Opera Workshop; memb BMA; MRCP 1961, FRCP 1974; *Books* Whittington Postgraduate Medicine (1974), Tutorials in Differential Diagnosis (1974, 1982); *Recreations* opera, squash, hill walking; *Style*— Dr Eric Beck; 59 Glasslyn Rd, London N8 8RJ (☎ 081 340 1564); Whittington Hospital, London N19 5NF (☎ 071 272 3070); Royal College of Physicians, St Andrew's Place, Regents Park, London NW1 4LE (☎ 071 935 1174)

BECK, Prof John Swanson; s of John Beck (d 1976), of Glasgow, and Mary, *née*

Barbour (d 1976); *b* 22 Aug 1928; *Educ* Glasgow Acad, Univ of Glasgow (BSc, MB, MD); *m* 10 June 1960, Marion Tudhope, da of Lt Cdr John Clendinning Paterson, DSO (d 1970), of Glasgow; 1 s (John b 1962), 1 da (Patricia Mary Swanson b 1965); *Career* lectr Univ of Glasgow 1958-63, sr lectr Univ of Aberdeen 1963-71, prof of pathology Univ of Dundee 1971-; MRC: memb Cell Bd 1978-82, chm Breast Tumour Panel 1979-; chm clinical and Biomed Res Ctee Scot Home and Health Dept 1983-; memb: Incorporation of Masons Glasgow 1960, Tayside Heath Bd 1983-, Chief Scientist Ctee Scottish Home & Health Dept 1983-, Cncl RSE 1986-89, Med Advsy Bd LEPRA 1987-, Nat Biol Standards Bd 1988-; bonnetmaker craftsman Incorporated Trades Dundee 1973; FRCPG 1965, FRCPE 1966, FRCPath 1975, FRSE 1984, FIBiol 1987; *Recreations* DIY work; *Clubs* Clyde Canoe, Royal Cwlth Soc; *Style*— Prof John Beck, FRSE; 598 Perth Rd, Dundee, Tayside DD2 1QA (☎ 0382 562298); Pathology Department, Ninewells Hospital and Medical School, Dundee (☎ 0382 60111 ext 3120)

BECK, Lesley Susan Barron; da of Laurence Barron Beck, and Marjorie Stewart, *née* Reid; *b* 10 July 1964; *Educ* Jordanhill Coll Sch, Perth Coll of Further Educn, Motherwell Coll of Further Educn, Université de Savoie, Strathclyde Graduate Business Sch; *Career* slalom skier; Br jr champion 1980 and 1982, Br sr champion 1982 and 1984-87, Le Sauze Grand Prix winner 1984, Bronze medallist N American series 1986; memb: Br World Championship Team 1985-89, Br Olympic Team 1984 and 1988; completed 10 World Slalom Championships 1987, athletes' rep to Br Olympic Ctee 1984-; *Recreations* other sports, rock climbing, grass skiing, cycling, photography, reading non fiction; *Clubs* Scottish Ski, Bearsden Ski; *Style*— Ms Lesley Beck; 2 Crosslet Ave, Dumbarton G82 3NR (☎ 0389 62039); British Ski Federation, 258 Main Street, East Calder, West Lothian EH53 0EE (☎ 0506 884 343)

BECK, Dr Michael Hawley; s of William Hawley Beck, of Crewe, Cheshire, and June Aldersey, *née* Davenport; *b* 20 Oct 1948; *Educ* Sandbach Sch, Univ of Liverpool (MB ChB); *m* 18 March 1978, Gerralynn (Lynn), da of John Harrop (d 1986), of Worsley, Manchester; 2 s (Jamie b 1979, Robin b 1981); *Career* sr house offr: Clatterbidge Hosp Wirral 1972-74, neurosurgery Walton Hosp 1974; registrar in med Trafford Health Authy 1976-77, registrar and sr registrar in dermatology Salford Health Authy 1977-81 (sr house offr gen med 1974-76), conslt dermatologist NW RHA 1981-; dermatological advsr to the Ileostomy Assoc of UK and Ireland 1982, chm NW Regnl Sub-Ctee on Dermatology 1985-88, hon assoc lectr in dermatology Univ of Manchester 1981; ctee memb and meeting sec Br Contact Dermatitis Gp; memb: Euro Contact Dermatitis Soc, Int Contact Dermatitis Computer Gp, American Contact Dermatitis Soc, Dowling Club 1977; author various articles in med jls and books relating to clinical dermatology and contact dermatitis; MRCP 1977, FRSM 1981; memb: NEDS 1981, BAD 1981; *Recreations* geneaology; *Style*— Dr Michael Beck; 23 St John St, Manchester M3 4DT (☎ 061 832 3080)

BECK, Sir (Edgar) Philip; s of Sir Edgar Charles Beck, CBE, of 13 Eaton Place, London, and his 1 wife Mary Agnes, *née* Sorapure; *b* 9 Aug 1934; *Educ* Ampleforth, Jesus Coll Cambridge (MA); *m* 1, 1957 (m dis), Thomasina Joanna Jeal; 2 s (Adam, Thomas); m 2, 7 Feb 1991, Bridget Alexandra, da of Brig Roderick Heathcoat-Amory, MC, and formerly w of Michael R L Cockerell; *Career* chm John Mowlem and Co, dir of various associated cos; chm Federation of Civil Engrg Contractors 1982-83; kt 1988; *Recreations* sailing, flying; *Clubs* Royal Yacht Sqdn, Buck's; *Style*— Sir Philip Beck; Lion Court, Swan St, Isleworth, Middx (☎ 081 568 9111, fax 081 847 4802, telex 24414)

BECK, Baron (Rudolph) Rolf; s of Baron Dr Otto Beck, and Baroness Margaret Beck; *b* 25 March 1914; *Educ* Theresanium Mil Acad, Geneva Univ, Lausanne Univ, Vienna Univ; *m* 1, 1944 (m dis), Elizabeth Lesley Brenchley (decd), da of Capt Fletcher, RN; 1 s (Stephen b 1948); m 2, 1979 (m dis), Countess (Signe) Mariana Sophie, da of Count Carl Göran Axel Mörner af Morlanda, of Sweden, and formerly w of Count von Rosen; m 3, 1990, Susan Cleland, da of Geoffrey Outram; *Career* petrochem engr and researcher, fndr various companies, chm and md Slip and Molyslip Gp of Cos 1939-; fndr memb Scientific Exploration Soc, corporate memb Euro Atlantic Gp, vice pres Small Business Bureau, sustaining memb American C of C; *Clubs* RAC, Royal Scottish Automobile, Royal Harwich Yacht, W Mersey Yacht, Hurlingham, Union Interalliée (Paris), Princeton (New York); *Style*— Baron Rolf Beck; 62 Bishops Mansion, Bishops Park Rd, London, SW6 6DZ (☎ 071 731 3021) Cap Davia, Marine De Davia, Ile Rousse, Corsica (☎ 95 600625); Molyslip Holdings Ltd, Reform Rd, Maidenhead, Berks SL6 8BY (☎ 0628 74991, telex 849850)

BECK-MACKAY, Colin; s of Capt John Mackay, RFC (d 1957), of Sutherland, and Patricia Kat *née* Beck (d 1972); *b* 31 Aug 1947; *Educ* Univ of Loughborough, RMA Sandhurst; *Career* Home Civil Serv 1972, hon sec Br Field Sports Soc 1980, memb Scot Shooting Liaison Ctee 1989; *Recreations* fishing, shooting, military history; *Clubs* Naval; *Style*— Colin Beck-Mackay, Esq; Boreland Cottage, Southwick, Dumfries DG2 8AN

BECKER, Basil George Christie; VRD (1964); s of Leslie Becker (d 1976), of Frinton, and Elizabeth Webster, *née* White (d 1966); *b* 17 May 1928; *Educ* Shrewsbury; *m* 1952, Gillian, da of Henry Paul Dawson (d 1984); 1 s, 1 da; *Career* served RM 1944-47, RMR 1948-65; chm Contract Cleaning and Maintenance Assoc 1972-74; dir: R J Barwick and Son, The Kent Chemical Co Ltd; Master Worshipful Co of Horners 1987, Sr Warden Worshipful Co of Environmental Cleaners 1989; *Recreations* golf, gardening, sailing; *Clubs* City Livery, RAC; *Style*— Basil Becker, Esq, VRD; c/o National Westminster Bank plc, 96 Fenchurch St, London EC3M 4EN

BECKER, (Edward) Lionel; s of Isaac (Jack) Becker (d 1956), and Sadie, *née* Reiss; *b* 5 Jan 1926; *Educ* King George V Sch Southport, Univ of Manchester (BA); *m* 1 (m dis 1978), Dora-Jean (d 1989); 3 da (Karen Beverley (now Mrs Wright) b 1954, Jacqueline (now Mrs Mohar) b 1956, Nicola Shelley b 1969); m 2, 1979, Deborah Ann (d 1988); 1 da (Rachel Jayne b 1979); m 3, 28 Oct 1988, Joyce Carole; *Career* chm: Euro Corporate Services Group 1977-, Apollo Leisure Group 1979-86; dep chm Triumph Apollo Theatre Production Ltd 1982-86; FCA 1950, FTII 1965; *Recreations* golf; *Style*— Lionel Becker, Esq; 19 Calle de Felipe II, Sotogrande, Cadiz, Spain (☎ 010 34 56 792356); European Corporate Services Group, 37 Lime Wall Rd, Gibraltar (☎ 010 350 76513, fax 010 350 79523)

BECKERMAN, Dr Wilfred; s of Morris Beckerman (d 1968), of London, and Matilda, *née* Pavilotsky (d 1963); *b* 19 May 1925; *Educ* Ealing GS, Trinity Coll Cambridge (MA, PhD); *m* 22 June 1952, Nicole Geneviève Ritter (d 1979); 1 s (Stephen b 19 March 1955), 2 da (Deborah b 5 Sept 1961, Sophia b 10 Dec 1962); *Career* WWII serv RN 1943-46 (Sub Lt RNVR 1944-46); econ advsr to Pres BOT 1967-69, prof of political econs Univ of London and head Dept Political Econ UCL 1969-75, fell Balliol Coll Oxford 1965-69 and 1975-, reader in econs Univ of Oxford 1977-, Elie Halevy prof Int Nat d'Etudes Politiques Paris 1976-77, pres Section F (Econs) Br Assoc for Advancement of Sci 1978; memb: Royal Cmmn on Environmental Pollution 1970-73, Cncl Royal Econ Soc 1990-; govr and memb Exec Ctee Nat Inst Econ and Social Res 1972-; *Books* The British Economy in 1975 (with assocs, 1965), International Comparisons of Real Incomes (1966), An Introduction to National Income Analysis (1968, trans Japanese Portuguese Spanish), The Labour Government's Economic Record 1964-70 (ed, 1972), In Defence of Economic Growth (1974, trans Swedish Dutch Japanese), Measures of Leisure Equality and Welfare (1978), Poverty and the Impact of Income Maintenance Programmes (1979), Slow Growth in Britain: Cause and Consequences (ed, 1979), Poverty and Social Security in Britain since 1961 (1982), Wage Rigidity and Unemployment (ed, 1986); *Recreations* swimming, skiing, tennis; *Clubs* Reform; *Style*— Dr Wilfred Beckerman; Balliol College, Oxford OX1 3BJ (☎ 0865 277713, fax 0865 277803)

BECKET, Michael Ivan; *b* 11 Sept 1938; *Educ* Wynyard Sch Ascot, Sloane Sch Chelsea, Open Univ; *Career* Nat Serv 1957-59; lathe operator Elliot Bros (London) Ltd 1956-57, exhibition organiser Shell International Petroleum 1959-61, journalist Electrical & Radio Trading 1961, market res Young & Rubicam 1962; civil serv 1962-68 (Bd of Trade, Nat Bd for Prices and Incomes, Nat Econ Devpmnt Office); Daily Telegraph 1968-; *Books* Computer by the Tail (1972), Economic Alphabet (1976), Bluff Your Way in Finance (1990); *Style*— Michael Becket, Esq; 9 Kensington Park Gardens, London W11 (☎ 071 727 6941); Daily Telegraph, 4 Fore St, London EC2Y 5DT (☎ 071 538 5000)

BECKETT, Allan Harry; MBE; s of George William Harry Beckett, MM (d 1949), of Belvedere, Kent, and Emma Louise, *née* Stokes (d 1983); *b* 4 March 1914; *Educ* East Ham Secdy Sch, London Univ (BSc); *m* 25 June 1949, Ida Gwladys, da of Kenbryd Morris James, DCM (d 1983), of Keston, Kent; 2 s (Michael b 1950, Timothy b 1953), 1 da (Sian b 1957); *Career* engrg asst: A J Bridle 1934-35, HM Office of Works 1935-37; bridge designer Br Steelwork Assoc 1937-38, asst site engr Woolwich Arsenal Chief Architects Dept 1938-39; RE 1940, 142 OCTU 1940, cmmnd 2 Lt 1941, Capt 1942, Staff Maj 1942, tech advsr in field 21 Army RE 1944, seconded to BAOR 1945; sr engr Sir Bruce White, Wolfe Barry and Ptnrs Conslting Engrs 1946 (ptnr 1957-, sr ptnr 1983-); FICE, MIConsE; *Books* numerous tech papers on engrg; *Recreations* sailing; *Clubs* St Stephens and Erith Yacht; *Style*— Allan Beckett, Esq, MBE; Thistledown, Wood Way, Farnborough Park, Kent; 83 Abbey St, Faversham, Kent (☎ 06898 52193); 270 Vauxhall Bridge Road, Westminster, London SW1V 1BB (☎ 071 233 6423, fax 071 834 7265)

BECKETT, Bruce Probart; s of Capt James Donald Lancaster Beckett (d 1969), and Florence Theresa, *née* Probart (d 1983); *b* 7 June 1924; *Educ* Rondebosch Boys HS Cape Town, Cape Town Univ (BArch), UCL (DipTP); *m* 9 May 1957, Jean, da of William Low McDonald (d 1949); 2 s (John, Malcolm), 3 da (Elizabeth, Janet, Margaret); *Career* sea cadet RNVR SA Div 1938-42 (later cadet petty offr RNVR), WWII SANF seconded RN 1942, midshipman 1943, Sub Lt 1944; active serv: S Atlantic, W Africa, Med, Western Approaches; Lt Indian Ocean 1946, Antartic Expdn SANR 1948, escort to HM King George VI and Royal Family Visit to South Africa 1948 in HMS Nigeria, Lt Cdr 1950, resigned cmmn 1960; architect: Lightfoot Twentyman-Jones & Kent 1951-59, Arthur Kenyon & Ptnrs 1960-61; civil serv 1961-84: sr architect WO 1961-64, supt architect DGRD and MPBW 1964-67, chief architect and under sec Scottish Office 1967-84; ptnr Hutchison Locke & Monk 1984-86; in private practice as chartered architect, town and country planner and building conslt, hon sec Cape Town Architectural Assoc, sr vice pres Edinburgh Architectural Assoc, cncllr Royal Incorporation of Architects (Scotland), vice pres RIBA; cncllr ARCUK 1968-; MISA, FRIBA, FRIAS, FRTPI, FCIOB; *Recreations* gardening, drawing, water colour painting, DIY; *Clubs* New (Edinburgh), Arts, Western Province Sports (Cape Town); *Style*— Bruce Beckett, Esq; Summerfield, Vines Cross Rd, Horam, nr Heathfield, E Sussex TN21 OHE (☎ 04353 2042)

BECKETT, Maj-Gen Denis Arthur; CB (1971), DSO (1944), OBE (1960); s of Archibald Edward Beckett (d 1976), of Radlett, Herts, and Margery Mildred, *née* Robinson (d 1954); *b* 19 May 1917; *Educ* Forest Sch Essex, Chard Sch Somerset; *m* 1, 1946, Elizabeth, da of Col Guy Edwards, DSO, MC (d 1962), of Rockcliff House, Upper Slaughter, Glos; 1 s (Nigel); m 2, 1978, Nancy Ann, da of Charles Bradford Hitt (d 1957), of Gross Pointe, Michigan, USA; *Career* Maj-Gen (late Parachute Regt), COS Far East Land Forces 1966-68, dir Personal Servs (Army) 1968-71; *Clubs* Army and Navy, Lansdowne; *Style*— Maj-Gen Denis Beckett, CB, DSO, OBE; 12 Wellington House, Eton Rd, London NW3 4SY

BECKETT, Hon Edward John; s and h of 4 Baron Grimthorpe, OBE; *b* 20 Nov 1954; *Educ* Hawtreys, Harrow; *Style*— The Hon Edward Beckett

BECKETT, Maj-Gen Edwin Horace Alexander; CB (1988), MBE (1974); s of William Alexander Beckett (d 1986), of Sheffield, and Doris, *née* Whitham (d 1989); *b* 16 May 1937; *Educ* Henry Fanshawe Sch, RMA Sandhurst; *m* 1963, Micaela Elizabeth Benedicta, yr da of Col Sir Edward Malet (d 1990); 3 s (Simon b 1965, Alexander b 1979, Thomas b 1980), 1 da (Diana b 1964); *Career* cmmnd West Yorks Regt 1957; regtl serv: Aden (despatches 1968), Gibraltar, Germany, NI; DAA and QMG 11 Armd Bde 1972-74, CO 1 PWO 1976-78 (despatches 1977), GSO1 (DS) Staff Coll 1979, Cmdt Jr Div Staff Coll 1980, Cdr UKMF and 6 Field Force 1981, Cdr UKMF 1 Inf Bde and Tidworth Garrison 1982; dir: Concepts MOD 1983-84, Army Plans and Progs MOD 1984-85; chief of staff HQ BAOR 1985-88, head of Br Def Staff and def attaché Washington DC; *Recreations* fishing, golf; *Clubs* Naval and Military; *Style*— Maj-Gen Edwin Beckett, CB, MBE

BECKETT, Frank Blair; s of Frank Beckett (d 1967), and Janet Catherine, *née* Blair (d 1981); *b* 30 Oct 1941; *Educ* Glasgow Acad, Univ of Glasgow; *m* 7 Sept 1972, Sandra Margaret, da of Percy John Green (d 1966); 1 s (Graham Frank b 20 Dec 1974), 2 da (Julie Margaret b 7 Dec 1976, Sally Jane b 5 Jan 1979); *Career* accountant; Kerr Macleod & MacFarlane: joined as apprentice 1960, mangr 1968, ptnr 1974 (merged with Deloitte Haskins & Sells 1974), staff and student recruitment and tech ptnr until 1985, ptnr i/c of audit practice Leeds office 1985, ptnr i/c of Audit and Investigations Dept 1990 (merged with Coopers & Lybrand 1990); lectr to students and membs of Scot Inst of CAs 1969-73, memb Rep Ctee Deloitte Haskins & Sells 1987-90; govr: Glasgow Acad 1983-89, Forest Sch Knaresborough 1988- (dep chm 1990-); MICAS, ACA; *Clubs* Glasgow Academical, Golf House, Harrogate Golf; *Style*— Frank Beckett, Esq; Alverthorpe, 29 Wheatlands Rd East, Harrogate, North Yorkshire HG2 8QS (☎ 0423 502525); Coopers & Lybrand Deloitte, Albion Court, 5 Albion Place, Leeds LS1 6JP (☎ 0532 431343, 0532 424009)

BECKETT, John Michael; yr s of Horace Norman Beckett, MBE, and Clarice Lillian, *née* Allsop; bro of Sir Terence Norman Beckett, *qv*; *b* 22 June 1929; *Educ* Wolverhampton GS, Magdalen Coll Oxford; *m* 1955, Joan Mary, o da of Percy Rogerson; 5 da; *Career* barrister; former chief exec Br Sugar; chm Woolworth Hldgs; *Style*— John Beckett, Esq; Belton House, Rutland, Leics (☎ 057 286 682)

BECKETT, Margaret Mary; MP (Lab) Derby S 1983-; da of Cyril Jackson, and Winifred Jackson; *b* Jan 1943; *Educ* Notre Dame HS, Manchester Coll of Sci and Technol; *m* 1979, Lionel A Beckett; *Career* sometime metallurgist sponsored by TGWU as Miss Margaret Jackson, MP (Lab) Lincoln Oct 1974-79 (contested same Feb 1974), asst govt whip 1975-76, princ res Granada TV 1979-83; front bench responsibility for social security 1984-89, shadow chief sec to The Treasy 1989-; memb: Lab Pty NEC 1980-81, 1985-86, 1988-89, Tribune Gp, Fabian Soc, CND; *Style*— Mrs Lionel Beckett, MP; House of Commons, London SW1

BECKETT, Sir Martyn Gervase; 2 Bt (UK 1921), MC (1945); s of Hon Sir William Gervase Beckett, 1 Bt (d 1937), bro of 2 Baron Grimthorpe, and Lady Marjorie (d 1964), da of 5 Earl of Warwick and wid of 2 Earl of Feversham; *b* 6 Nov 1918; *Educ* Eton, Trinity Coll Cambridge (BA); *m* 1941, Hon Priscilla Léonie Helen Brett, da of 3

Viscount Esher, GBE (d 1964); 2 s, 1 da; *Heir* s, Richard Gervase Beckett; *Career* Capt Welsh Gds 1944-45; architect; tstee: Wallace Collection 1972- (chm 1976-), Br Museum 1978-88; chm Yorkshire Regnl Ctee Nat Tst 1980-85; memb Cncl of Mgmnt Chatsworth House Tst 1981-; tstee: CPRE Tst 1983-90, Doyly Carte Charitable Tst 1985-; memb Cncl RSPB 1985-87; ARIBA 1952, FRSA 1982; *Recreations* painting, piano; *Clubs* Brooks's, MCC; *Style—* Sir Martyn Beckett, Bt, MC; 3 St Alban's Grove, London W8 (☎ 071 937 7834); Kirkdale Farm, Nawton, Yorks (☎ 0751 31301)

BECKETT, Hon Oliver Ralph; 2 s of 2 Baron Grimthorpe (d 1963); *b* 21 Aug 1918; *Educ* Eton, Trinity Coll Cambridge; *m* 6 April 1944, Hélène Agnes, da of Constantine Fessas, and formerly w of Richard Tasker Evans; 2 da; *Career* author and lecturer; FRSA; *Books* J F Herring and Sons, Horses and Movement; *Style—* The Hon Oliver Beckett; 55 Carlisle Ave, St Albans, Herts AL3 5LX (☎ 0727 62389)

BECKETT, Hon Lady (Priscilla Léonie Helen); *née* Brett; da of 3 Viscount Esher, GBE (d 1963); *b* 31 May 1921; *m* 1941, Sir Martyn Beckett, 2 Bt, MC, *qv*; 2 s, 1 da; *Style—* The Hon Lady Beckett; 3 St Alban's Grove, London W8 (☎ 071 937 7834)

BECKETT, Hon Ralph Daniel; s of 4 Baron Grimthorpe, OBE; *b* 11 April 1957; *m* 22 Jan 1987, Susanna W, er da of Colin Townsend-Rose; *Style—* The Hon Ralph Beckett

BECKETT, Richard Gervase; QC; s and h of Sir Martyn Beckett, 2 Bt, MC, *qv*; *b* 27 March 1944; *Educ* Eton; *m* 1976, Elizabeth Ann, da of Maj (Charles) Hugo Waterhouse; 1 s (Walter Gervase b 16 Jan 1987), 3 da; *Career* called to the Bar Middle Temple 1965, QC 1988; *Recreations* walking; *Clubs* Pratts, Portland; *Style—* Richard Beckett, Esq, QC; 33 Groveway, London SW9 (☎ 071 735 3350)

BECKETT, Sir Terence Norman; KBE (1987, CBE 1974); s of Horace Norman Beckett, MBE, and Clarice Lillian, *née* Allsop; bro of John Michael Beckett, *qv*; *b* 13 Dec 1923; *Educ* engrg cadet 1943-45, LSE (BSc); *m* 1950, Sylvia Gladys Asprey; 1 da (Alison b 1960); *Career* served WWII Capt REME (UK, India, Malaysia); RARO 1949-62; Ford Motor Co Ltd: co trainee 1950, mangr product planning staff 1955-63 (responsible for Cortina, Transit Van and D series truck), exec dir 1966, md and chief exec 1974-80, chm 1976-80; dir ICI 1976-80; DG CBI 1980-87 (memb Cncl 1976-80); pt/t memb CEGB 1987- (dep chm 1990); conslt Milk Mktg Bd and Dairy Trade Fedn, pres IVCA 1987-; memb: Top Salaries Review Body 1987-, Engrg Industs Cncl 1975-80, BIM Cncl 1976-80 (Gold medal 1980), Cncl Automotive Div IMechE 1979-80, NEDC 1980-87; chm Governing Body London Business Sch 1979-86 (hon fell 1987-); memb Court Cranfield Inst of Technol 1977-82; govr Nat Inst Econ and Soc Res 1978-; govr and memb Court LSE 1978-; memb Ct and Cncl Univ of Essex 1986- (chm Cncl and pro-chllr 1989-); memb Cncl BTO 1986-; vice pres Conf on Schs Science and Technol 1979-80; govr Chigwell Sch 1986-; hon memb REME Instn 1990; Hon DSc: Cranfield 1977, Heriot-Watt 1981; Hon DSc (Econ) London 1982; Hambro Businessman of the Year 1978, hon fell Sidney Sussex Coll Cambridge 1981-, Stamp lectr Univ of London 1982, Pfizer lectr Univ of Kent 1983; FEng, FIMechE, CBIM, FIMI (vice pres 1974-80); *Recreations* ornithology, music; *Clubs* Athenaeum; *Style—* Sir Terence Beckett, KBE; c/o Barclays Bank plc, 74 High St, Ingatestone, Essex CM4 9BW

BECKETT, William Alan; s of William Alexander Beckett (d 1986), of Sheffield, and Doris, *née* Whitham; *b* 5 Jan 1946; *Educ* High Storrs GS; *m* 30 Sept 1965, Linda, da of George Frederick Sanders, of Walsall; 1 s (Marcus b 1966), 3 da (Sarah b 1967, d 1985, Rachel b 1971, Clare b 1971); *Career* md: William Beckett & Co (Plastics) Ltd 1972-, Roder Beckett Fine Art Ltd 1975-83, Polyplas Ltd 1987-; co-chm SCI SAFE; *Recreations* cricket, tennis, occasional skier, potential golfer; *Style—* William Beckett, Esq; 274 Ecclesall Rd South, Sheffield S11 9PS (☎ 0742 351405); William Beckett & Co (Plastics) Ltd, Unit 5, Tinsley Industrial Park, Shepcote Way, Sheffield S9 1TH (☎ 0742 434399, fax 0742 560196, telex 547241)

BECKETT, Hon William Ernest; yst s of 3 Baron Grimthorpe (d 1963); *b* 30 June 1945; *Educ* Eton; *m* 15 June 1968, Virginia Helen Clark, o da of Michael Clark Hutchison, sometime MP for Edinburgh; 1 s, 1 da; *Career* Lt 9/12 Royal Lancers (POW) 1964-68; conslt electronic publishing; *Recreations* sailing, shooting, skiing, windsurfing, hunting, tennis; *Style—* The Hon William Beckett; The Estate House, Serlby, nr Bawtry, S Yorks (☎ 0777 818282)

BECKINGHAM, Dr David Clive; s of Capt Clive Walter Beckingham (d 1954), of Inverness-shire, and Alice, *née* Hatcher; *b* 8 Aug 1928; *Educ* St Andrews Sch Eastbourne, Harrow, New Coll Oxford (MA, BM BCh); *m* 12 Aug 1972, Mary Chaldecot, da of Thomas Preston Everett, of Gwent; 1 da (Sarah Jane b 1975); *Career* Royal Navy 1956-75: PMO HMS Albion, SMO and conslt gynaecologist RN Hosp Gibraltar, PMO HMS Hermes, ret Surgeon Cdr; conslt physician Cardiff Royal Infirmary and Royal Gwent Hosp Newport 1976-; past chm Gwent Div BMA; memb: Welsh Cncl BMS, Welsh Ctee for Hosp Medical Services, (past) Welsh Medical Ctee, Gwent Medical Ctee (chm 1980-82), Gwent District Health Authy Mgmnt Team 1979-; chm S Gwent Medical Exec Ctee; MRCOG; *Recreations* sailing, swimming, cooking, military history, Spain; *Clubs* Army and Navy, Pall Mall, United Services (Cardiff); *Style—* Dr David C Beckingham; The Gables, Llandevaud, Gwent NP6 2AF (☎ 0633 400921); Dept GU Medicine, Royal Gwent Hospital, Newport (☎ 0633 52244)

BECKMAN, Hon Mrs (Angela Clare); o da of Baron Mais, GBE, ERD, TD, JP, DL (Life Peer); *b* 4 Nov 1946; *Educ* St Margaret's Bushey, House of Citizenship; *m* 1976, Robert Beckman, of Washington DC; *Style—* The Hon Mrs Beckman; 11100 River Rd, Potomac, Maryland 20854, USA

BECKMAN, Michael; QC; s of Nathan Beckman, and Esther, *née* Sonabend; *b* 6 April 1932; *Educ* King's Coll London (LLB); *m* 1, 1966 (m dis), Sheryl Robin, *née* Kyle; 2 da (Amanda, Natasha); m 2, 1990, Jennifer Johnson, *née* Redmond; *Career* Nat Serv; called to the Bar Lincoln's Inn 1954; head of Chambers; *Recreations* tennis, food, wine, cinema, theatre, travel, people, animals; *Style—* Michael Beckman, Esq, QC; Bullards, Widford, Herts SG12 8RQ; St Germaine de Talloires, 74290 Veyrier du Lac, France; 19 Old Buildings, Lincoln's Inn, London WC2 3UR (☎ 071 831 6381); 3 East Pallants, Chichester (☎ 0243 784538)

BECKWITH, Lady Antonia Pamela Mary; *née* Crichton; da of 5 Earl of Erne (d 1940), and Lady Davidema, da of 2 Earl of Lytton; *b* 18 April 1934; *Educ* privately; *m* 1, 1953, Timothy William Wardell, Sub-Lt (ret) RN, gs of Sir Kenneth Crossley, 2 Bt; 3 s, 2 da; m 2, 1981, Charles William Beckwith; *Recreations* hunting, fishing; *Clubs* Meath Hunt; *Style—* The Lady Antonia Beckwith; Highfield, Dunsany, Co Meath, Eire

BECKWITH, Rev Canon John Douglas; o s of William Albert Beckwith (d 1977), of Leeds, and Gladys Rubery, *née* Barley (d 1989); *b* 6 July 1933; *Educ* Leeds Modern, King's Coll London (AKC); *Career* Nat Serv War Office 1951-53; ordained: deacon 1958, priest 1965; sr tutor Ijebu-Igbo GS and lectr Molusi Coll W Nigeria 1960-62, tutor Eltham Coll 1964-69, chaplain Gothenburg 1969-70, chaplain to Bishop of Edmonton 1970-77 (hon chaplain 1977-84), dir of ordinands 1970-77, vicar St Anne Highgate 1977-88, canon Gibraltar Cathedral and commissary Diocese in Europe 1984-, priest i/c Bladon-cum-Woodstock 1988-; memb Br Factory Gothenburg 1969, tstee Highgate Cemetery 1979-87, chm Church Needlework News 1979-; Freeman City of London 1979, Liveryman Worshipful Co of Broderers 1979; Order of Thyateira and GB (First Class) 1974; *Recreations* graphic and applied arts, writing, pilgrimages; *Clubs* City Livery, Nikaean; *Style—* The Rev Canon John Beckwith; Woodstock Rectory, Oxford OX7 1UQ (☎ 0993 811415)

BECKWITH, Peter Michael; s of Col Harold Andrew Beckwith (d 1966), of Hong Kong, and Agnes Camilla McMichael, *née* Duncan (d 1980); *b* 20 Jan 1945; *Educ* Harrow, Emmanuel Coll Cambridge (MA); *m* 19 Oct 1968, Paula, da of late Robin Stuart Bateman, of Cliftonville, Kent; 2 da (Tamara Jane b 1970, Clare Tamsin b 1972); *Career* slr Supreme Court of Judicature 1970-, dep chm London and Edinburgh Tst plc 1983-; *Recreations* association football, tennis, skiing, opera, gardening, dogs; *Clubs* Riverside Racquets, OHAFC, Downhill Only, Covent Garden Friends; *Style—* Peter Beckwith, Esq; 243 Knightsbridge, London SW7

BECTIVE, Earl of; Thomas Michael Ronald Christopher Taylour; s and h of 6 Marquess of Headfort; *b* 10 Feb 1959; *Educ* Harrow, Royal Agric Coll Cirencester; *m* 17 Oct 1987, Susan Jane, da of Charles Anthony Vandervell (d 1987), of Burnham, Bucks; 1 s (Hon Thomas Rupert Charles Christopher b 18 June 1989); *Heir* s, Hon Thomas Rupert Charles Christopher; *Career* Estate Agency, John D Wood and Co; *Style—* Earl of Bective; Cusby Farm, Bride, Ramsey, Isle of Man

BEDDALL, Hugh Richard Muir; s of Herbert Muir Beddall (d 1952), and Jennie, *née* Fowler (d 1973); *b* 20 May 1922; *Educ* Stowe, Ecole de Commerce Neuchatel Switzerland; *m* 22 June 1946, Monique Henriette, da of Herman Haefliger (d 1953), of Neuchatel, Switzerland; 3 s (Richard Grant Muir b 1949, Keith Ian Muir b 1954, Alastair Clive Hugh b 1962), 1 da (Angela Claire Muir b 1951); *Career* 2 Lt RM 1941, Lt 1941, Capt 1944, troop cdr A Troop 45 RM Commando and 1 Commando Bde HQ; chm: Muir Beddall and Co Ltd 1962-, C T Bowring & Co Ltd 1963-83; memb Lloyd's 1943-; *Recreations* shooting, racing; *Clubs* Buck's, E India, Pilgrims'; *Style—* Hugh Muir Beddall, Esq; 53 Cadogan Square, London SW1X OHY (☎ 071 235 9461)

BEDDARD, Dominic Anthony Hamilton; s of Terence Elliot Beddard (d 1966), and Ursula Mary Howard, *née* Gurney Richards, BEM (d 1985); *b* 14 May 1937; *Educ* Cheam Sch, Eton; *m* 17 Sept 1966, Susan Claire, da of Leslie Leo Stevens, of E Sussex; 1 s (Matthew b 1968), 2 da (Emma b 1969, Henrietta b 1971); *Career* KRRC (60 Rifles) 1955-56, cmmnd 1955, served Libya and Cyprus, TA (Queen Victorias Rifles, Queens Royal Rifles, 4 Bn Royal Green Jackets) 1958-69, Capt 1961, Major 1964; NSU (GB) Ltd 1957-62, ptnr Wilson Smithett and Co 1968 (joined 1962); church warden St Thomas á Becket Brightling 1979-84, sec Brightling Village Tst 1985, chm Tea Brokers Assoc of London 1986 and 1988; *Recreations* golf, gardening; *Clubs* Lansdowne, Royal Green Jackets London; *Style—* Dominic Beddard, Esq; Wyland Wood, Robertsbridge, E Sussex; Wilson Smithett & Co, Sir John Lyon House, Upper Thames St, London EC4V 3LS (☎ 071 236 0611, fax 071 236 4976, telex 888627)

BEDDARD, Lt-Col Jonathan Patrick Owen; MBE (1981); s of Terence Elliot Beddard (d 1966), and Ursula Mary Howard, *née* , Gurney-Richards, BEM (d 1985); *b* 17 March 1944; *Educ* Cheam Sch, Eton; *m* 4 Dec 1979, Felicity Victoria, da of Lt-Col Granville Reginald Arthur Brooking, of Sussex; 1 s (Henry Terence b 1981), 1 da (Genevieve Daisy b 1984); *Career* served Far East, Ops in Borneo 1963-64, Instructor Jungle Warfare Sch 1967-69, Loan Service Fiji 1972-74, Staff Coll Camberley 1977, Ops N Ireland 1969, 1971, 1981, BAOR 1970-72 and 1982-85, CO 2 Bn Royal Green Jackets 1983-85, MOD 1985-87; dir London Portfolio Services Ltd; Freeman City of London, Liveryman Worshipful Co of Skinners; *Recreations* fencing, subaqua, diving; *Clubs* Epee, British Sub Aqua (instructor), Landsdowne; *Style—* Lt-Col Jonathan Beddard, MBE; Barnfield House, Hawkhurst, Kent TN18 4PX (☎ 05805 2388); C Hare and Co, 37 Fleet St, London EC4; London Portfolio Services, 52 Grosvenor Gardens, London W1A 0AU

BEDDARD, His Hon Judge Nicholas Elliot; s of Terence Elliot Beddard (d 1966), of Kensington, London, and Ursula Mary Hamilton Howard, *née* Gurney-Richards, BEM (d 1985); *b* 26 April 1934; *Educ* Cheam Sch, Eton; *m* 25 Apr 1964, Gillian Elisabeth Vaughan, da of Llewelyn Vaughan Bevan (d 1987), of Cambridge; 2 s (James b 1966, Benedict b 1968), 1 da (Emily b 1974); *Career* Royal Sussex Regt 1952-54, cmmnd 1953, TA 1955-64; mgmnt trainee United Africa Co 1955-58, asst pub policy exec RAC 1958-68, called to the Bar Inner Temple 1967, practiced SE Circuit 1968-86, rec Crown Ct 1986, circuit judge 1986; memb Cncl HM Circuit Judges 1986; fndr memb Barnsbury Singers; Freeman City of London, Liveryman Worshipful Co of Skinners 1957; *Recreations* choral singing, squash, golf; *Clubs* Lansdowne, Orford Sailing; *Style—* His Hon Judge Beddard; Farrar's Building, Temple, London EC4Y 7BD (☎ 071 583 9241)

BEDDINGTON, (Julian) Roy; s of Reginald Beddington, CBE (d 1961), of Old Basing, and Sybil Elizabeth, *née* Henriques (d 1939); *b* 16 June 1910; *Educ* Rugby, CCC Oxford, Slade Sch of Art, Florence Sch of Art; *m* 1 (m dis), Anna, *née* Griffith; 2 da (Phillipa (Mrs Foulkes), Rosa (Dr Denniston)); m 2, 1961, Diana Mary, da of W Dobson, of Marnhull, Dorset; 1 da (Sarah Anne); *Career* RA Lt Intelligence Offr 38 AA Bde, invalided out; London Electrical Engrs; fisheries office MAFF; artist, illustrator, author and poet; rep GB Olympic Games (Art) London, cmmnd to paint Winston Churchill in Silver Jubilee Procession; seven one man exhibitions incl: Bond Street, Grafton Gallery, Ackermann, Walker's Gallery; other exhibitions incl: Whitechapel Art Gallery, NEAC; fishing corr Country Life; vice pres Salmon & Trout Assoc; chm Fisheries' Ctee Hampshire River Bd; FRSA; *Books* The Adventures of Thomas Trout (1939), To be a Fisherman (1955), The Pigeon and the Boy (1957), Pindar, a Dog to Remember (1979), A Countryman's Verse (1981); illustrator: The Happy Fisherman, River to River, Alexander and Angling, Riverside Reflections, Beyond the Caspian, Two in a Valley; *Recreations* fishing, gardening; *Clubs* Arts; *Style—* Roy Beddington, Esq; Home Farm, Chute Cadley, nr Andover, Hants (☎ 026 470 282)

BEDDOES, Air Vice-Marshal John Geoffrey Genior; CB (1980); s of Algernon Geoffrey Beddoes (d 1967), and Lucy Isobel, *née* Collier (d 1935); *b* 21 May 1925; *Educ* Wirral GS; *m* 1947, Betty Morris, *née* Kendrick; 3 s; *Career* pilot trg in Rhodesia and Egypt 1943-45, served 114 Sqdn Italy and Aden 1945-46, No 30 Sqdn Abingdon and Berlin Airlift 1947-49, flying instr RAF Coll Cranwell and Central Flying Sch 1950-55, Flt Cdr No 57 Sqdn Canberra 1955, Air Miny 1956-57, Flying Coll 1958, Flt Cdr No 57 Sqdn 1959-61, sc Bracknell 1962, OC 139 (Jamaica) Sqdn 1963-65, Wing Cdr Ops HQ No 3 Gp 1965-67, directing Staff Coll of Air Warfare 1968-69, OC RAF Laarbruch 1969-71, MOD dep dir Operational Requirements 1971-73, HQ 2 ATAF Asst COS Offensive Operations 1974-75, MOD Dir Operational Requirements 1975-78, DG aircraft (2) MOD Procurement Exec 1978-81, ret; chm St Gregory's Tst Norwich, memb Norfolk CC (Watton Div 1989); FRAeS; *Recreations* gardening, DIY, golf; *Clubs* RAF; *Style—* Air Vice-Marshal John Beddoes, CB; White Stables, Stow Bedon, Norfolk (☎ 095 383 524)

BEDDOW, Cecil Miles (Bill); s of late Leslie Towne Beddow, of Southwold; *b* 18 Sept 1920; *Educ* King's Sch Bruton Somerset; *m* 1947, Modwena Keyna, da of late Thomas Austin Rafferty, of Paris, France; 2 s (1 decd), 1 da; *Career* Jardine Matheson and Co Hong Kong 1949-53; Carreras/Rothmans Ltd to 1960, dir Aspro-Nicholas to 1969; fin dir F W Woolworth and Co 1969-73; advsr Morgan Grenfell 1973-86; chm and chief exec London and Midland Industls plc, chm Aspro-Nicholas (Tstees) Ltd; dir: Yule Catto and Co plc, Amersham International plc, McPhersons (UK) Ltd, Harold Holt Ltd, Oriflame Int SA, Gordon and Gotch Hldgs plc; fell and memb Cncl of Royal

Soc of Arts Manufacturers and Commerce; FCA; *Recreations* swimming, skiing; *Clubs* Carlton, Garrick; *Style*— Bill Beddow, Esq; Flat 7, Seven Princes Gate, London SW7 (☎ 071 584 8391; work: 071 723 5123); Robbers Wood, Lymore, Lymington, Hants

BEDDOW, (Frank) Howard; s of late Frank Harold Beddow, and late Ethel, *née* Urmsom; *b* 8 May 1927; *Educ* Birkenhead Sch, Univ of Liverpool (MB ChB, MChOrth); *m* 31 July 1964, Ann Lilian, da of late Albert Edward Collins; *Career* RAMC, Lt 1951, Capt 1952-53; conslt orthopaedic surgn: Whiston and Rainhill Hosp 1962-72, Royal Liverpool Hosp (formerly Liverpool Royal Infirmary), Sefton Gen Hosp, Sir Alfred Jones Meml Hosp 1972-; univ appts: memb Med Appeal Tbnl 1969-, pt/t clinical lectr in orthopaedic surgery, examiner for MB ChB and MChOrth 1972-, memb of Bd of Orthopaedic Studies 1972-, chm Regnl Sub-Ctee in Orthopaedic Surgery 1986-88, memb Regnl Med Ctee 1986-88, chm Postgrad Advsy Panel in Orthopaedic Surgery 1989-; memb Cncl Br Orthopaedic Assoc 1984-86 (fell 1963-), vice pres Liverpool Med Inst 1985-86 (cncl memb 1976-87, memb 1954-); RCS: regnl advsr in orthopaedic surgery 1986-, rep on Physiotherapy Bd 1988-; memb Hoylake Civic Soc; FRCSE 1956, FRCS 1988; *Books* The Surgical Management of Rheumatoid Arthiritis (1988); *Recreations* gardening, canal boating, photography; *Clubs* Nantwich & Border Counties Yacht; *Style*— Howard Beddow, Esq; 72 Rodney St, Liverpool L1 9AF (☎ 051 709 2177)

BEDELIAN, Haro Moushegh; OBE (1986); s of Moushegh Haroutune Bedelian (d 1974), and Annig, *née* Nigogosian; *b* 6 March 1943; *Educ* English Sch Nicosia Cyprus, St Catharine's Coll Cambridge (MA); *m* 1970, Yvonne Mildred, da of Stephen Gregory Arratoon, of London; 1 s (Stephen b 1973), 2 da (Lisa b 1975, Claire b 1978); *Career* md Balfour Beatty Ltd 1989- (dir 1988-); memb Cncl Inst of Civil Engrs 1987-90, FEng 1989-; *Recreations* squash; *Clubs* RAC; *Style*— Haro M Bedelian, Esq, OBE; Bryn Stoke, 30 Downs Way, Tadworth, Surrey (☎ 073 781 3261); Balfour Beatty, 7 Mayday Rd, Thornton Heath, Surrey CR4 7XA (☎ 081 684 6922)

BEDELL, Geraldine Claire; da of Albert John Bedell (d 1982), and Iris Myrtle Wright; *b* 22 Aug 1956; *Educ* Wanstead HS, Lady Margaret Hall Oxford (MA); *m* 1981, Jon Norton, s of John Norton; 1 da (Henrietta b 20 July 1983), 1 s (Freddie b 31 June 1987); *Career* journalist Surrey and South London Newspapers 1979-80, account mangr Leo Burnett Ltd 1980-81, journalist Gulf Daily News 1982-86; freelance writer specialising in social affairs 1987-; contrib to: The Independent, The Times, The Independent On Sunday, The Guardian, Sunday Times, Harpers and Queen; TV reporter: Special Inquiry, The Family (LWT, 1991); *Recreations* gossiping with my sister, being lectured on politics by my husband, squabbling with my children; *Clubs* City Women's Network, The Smithfield Group; *Style*— Ms Geraldine Bedell; 71 Cleveland Road, London N1 3ES (☎ 071 359 4153); Studio Five, Panther House, 38 Mount Pleasant, London WC1X 0AP (☎ 071 278 7953, fax 071 837 5505)

BEDELL-PEARCE, Keith Leonard; s of Leonard Bedell-Pearce, of Purley, Surrey, and Irene, *née* Bedell; *b* 11 March 1946; *Educ* Trinity Sch of John Whitgift, Univ of Exeter(LLB), Univ of Warwick, Graduate Business Sch (MSc); *m* 2 Oct 1971, Gaynor Mary, da of Frederick Charles Pembarthy Trevelyan, of Exeter, Devon; 1 s (Jack b 1980), 2 da (Olivia b 1976, Harriet b 1988); *Career* systems analyst: Plessey 1969-70, Wiggins Teape 1970-72; Prudential 1972-: computer projects mangr 1972-75, legal dept 1975, slr 1978, gen mangr Field Operations 1986 (additional responsibility for mktg 1987), dir 1988-; chief exec and dir Prudential Financial Services Ltd 1991-; dir: Prudential Portfolio Mangr Ltd 1985, Prudential Unit Tst Mangrs Ltd 1986, various Prudential subsid cos, Staple Nominees Ltd 1991-; memb: Law Soc, Mktg Soc; *Books* Checklists for Data Processing Contracts (1978), Computers & Information Technology (1979, 2 edn 1982); *Recreations* shooting, squash, tennis; *Style*— Keith Bedell-Pearce Esq; 142 Holborn Bars, London EC1N 2NH (☎ 071 405 9222, fax 071 831 1625, car 0860 368 751, 0836 286 830, telex 266431)

BEDFORD, Alan Frederick; s of Frederick Thomas Bedford (d 1967), of London, and Muriel Evelyn, *née* Sampson; *b* 14 May 1947; *Educ* Strand GS, Westminster Med Sch (MB BS, MChOrth), FRCS; *m* 11 Dec 1971, Janine Wendy, da of Kenneth Charles Smithson, of Thurston, Suffolk; 2 s (Mark b 1981, Nicholas b 1985), 1 da (Anna b 1984 d 1984); *Career* conslt in traumatic and orthopaedic surgery to E Anglian RHA 1982-; memb: Br Orthopaedic Assoc, BMA; *Recreations* wine, photography, horticulture; *Clubs* Nibblers; *Style*— Alan Bedford, Esq; Hydene Cottage, Hawkedon, Bury St Edmunds, Suffolk IP29 4DR (☎ 0284 89483); West Suffolk Hospital, Hardwick Lane, Bury St Edmunds, Suffolk (☎ 0284 763131); St Edmunds Hospital, St Mary's Square, Bury St Edmunds (☎ 0284 701371)

BEDFORD, Alfred William (Bill); OBE, AFC; s of Lewis Alfred Bedford (d 1926), of Delamore House, Boyer St, Loughborough, Leics, and Edith, *née* Lawrence; *b* 18 Nov 1920; *Educ* Loughborough Coll; *m* 30 Nov 1941, Mary, da of Frederick Bryer Averill (d 1975); 1 s (Peter b 28 May 1946), 1 da (Janet b 1 Nov 1948, d 1976); *Career* joined RAF 1940, fighter pilot 1941-45 (flying Hurricanes, Thunderbolts and Mustangs in the Far East and Europe), graduate Air Fighting Trg Unit 1944, qualified flying instr 1945, graduate Empire Flying Sch 1947, graduate Empire Test Pilots' Sch 1949 (later tutor), res test pilot Experimental Flying Dept Royal Aircraft Estab Farnborough (also detached to Nat Gas Turbine Estab on Jet Engine Res), resigned RAF 1951; experimental test pilot Hawker Aircraft Ltd 1951-67 on fighter aircraft (chief test pilot 1956), made first flights and involved with the devpt of the Harrier V/STOL aircraft; Hawker Siddeley Aviation/Br Aerospace: int mktg mangr, regnl exec SE Asia (latterly dedicated to Indonesia); aviation conslt 1986-; first chm and fndr memb Test Pilots' Gp Royal Aeronautical Soc; pres: Godalming and Farncombe Branch RAF Assoc, Godalming Sqdn ATC; held aircraft and glider records, frequent lectr and writer on aircraft-related topics; FRAeS, memb Soc of Experimental Test Pilots; awarded First Class Wings of the Indonesian Air Force; *Recreations* walking, swimming, squash, tennis, nature; *Clubs* RAF, Esher Squash, British Aerospace Squash; *Style*— A W Bedford, Esq, OBE, AFC; The Chequers, West End Lane, Esher, Surrey KT10 8LF (☎ 0372 462285)

BEDFORD, Anthony Peter; s of Philip Derek Bedford, MP (d 1962), and Jean Rachel, *née* Whyman; *b* 30 Sept 1951; *Educ* Kings Sch Canterbury, St Catherine's Coll Oxford (MA), Univ of London (MPhil); *m* 14 March 1974, Anita Susan, da of Charles Hamilton-Matthews, of Cornwall; 1 s (Tobias b 1974), 1 da (Anouska b 1977); *Career* conslt clinical psychologist; head of Psychology Dept St Andrews Hosp Northampton 1974-84; dir: Psychiatric and Psychological Conslt Servs Ltd 1981-, psychological servs AMI Psychiatric Div 1984-87, Centre for Occupational Res 1984-, The Rehabilitation Gp 1989-; *Recreations* riding; *Style*— Anthony P Bedford, Esq; The Old Rectory, East Martin, Nr Fordingbridge, Hants; 14 Devonshire Place, London W1 (☎ 071 935 0640)

BEDFORD, Bishop of 1981-; Rt Rev David John Farmbrough; 2 s of late Charles Septimus Farmbrough, and Ida Mabel Farmbrough; *b* 4 May 1929; *Educ* Bedford, Lincoln Coll Oxford; *m* 1955, Angela Priscilla, da of Walter Adam Hill; 1 s, 3 da; *Career* ordained: deacon 1953, priest 1954, priest i/c St John's Hatfield 1957-63, vicar of Bishop's Stortford 1963-74, archdeacon of St Albans 1974-81; *Recreations* sailing, gardening; *Style*— The Rt Rev The Bishop of Bedford; 168 Kimbolton Rd, Bedford MK41 8DN (☎ 0234 357551)

BEDFORD, David Vickerman; s of Leslie Herbert Bedford, CBE (d 1989), and Lesley Florence Keitle (d 1987); *b* 4 Aug 1937; *Educ* Lancing, RAM; *m* 1, 4 Sept 1958 (m dis 1968), Maureen, *née* Parsonage; 2 da (Tamara b 1960, Chloe b 1962); m 2, 27 Sept 1970 (m dis 1986), Susan, da of Gorgon Pilgrim; 2 da (Sarah b 1969, Emily b 1971); *Career* composer of over 100 published musical pieces to date, assoc visiting composer Gordonstoun Sch 1984, youth music dir Eng Sinfonia 1986; pres Br Music Info Centre 1988; chm Assoc of Professional Composers 1991; *Recreations* cricket, squash, film; *Style*— David Bedford, Esq; 39 Shakespeare Rd, London NW7 4BA (☎ 081 959 3165)

BEDFORD, (Charlotte) Gaby; *née* Martin-Langley; da of Charles Harold Martin-Langley (d 1977), and Ruby, *née* Middleton Rowe; *b* 14 June 1943; *Educ* St Monicas Sch for Girls, Falmouth County HS for Girls; *m* 1, 1965 (m dis 1966), Raymond Argent; m 2, 18 May 1974, Piers Errol James Bedford, s of Errol Bedford, of 23 Farmer St, London W8; 2 s (James Simon b 12 May 1966, Timothy Piers James b 15 Sept 1975); *Career* film prodr Eyeline Films Ltd 1970-74, dir and prod Piers Bedford Productions Ltd 1974-; fndr and dir: Component Editing Ltd 1984-89, Component TV Productions Ltd 1987- (client work incl: IBA, Memorex Computers, Telstar Records, Royco Varia Investment); area collection organiser Greenpeace, memb Cons Pty; *Recreations* skiing, gardening; *Style*— Mrs Piers Bedford; 5 Woodstock Rd, Bedford Park, London W4 1DS (☎ 081 747 0069); Saltings, Park Rd, Aldeburgh, Suffolk; The Component Gp, 1 Newman Passage, London W1P 3PF (☎ 071 631 4400, fax 081 995 0137)

BEDFORD, 13 Duke of (E 1694); John Robert Russell; also Baron Russell (E 1539), Earl of Bedford (E 1550), Baron Russell of Thornhaugh (E 1603), Marquess of Tavistock (E 1694), Baron Howland (E 1695); s of 12 Duke (d 1953); *b* 24 May 1917; *m* 1, 1939, Mrs Clare Gwendolen Hollway, da of late John Bridgman; 2 s; m 2, 1947 (m dis 1960), Hon Lydia Yarde-Buller, da of 3 Baron Churston, MVO, OBE (d 1930), and late Duchess of Leinster, and wid of Capt Ian Archibald de Hoghton Lyle, Black Watch; 1 s; m 3, 1960, Mme Nicole Milinaire, da of Paul Schneider, of Paris; *Heir* s, Marquess of Tavistock; *Career* Coldstream Gds WW II (invalided out); *Style*— His Grace The Duke of Bedford; Les Ligures, 2 Rue Honoré Labande, MC98000 Monaco

BEDFORD, Lydia, Duchess of; Hon Lydia; *née* Yarde-Buller; 3 da of 3 Baron Churston, MVO, OBE (d 1930); *b* 17 Oct 1917; *m* 1, 1938, Capt Ian Archibald de Hoghton Lyle, Black Watch (d 1942); 1 s (Sir Gavin Lyle, 3 Bt, *qv*), 1 da; m 2, 1947 (m dis 1960) 13 Duke of Bedford, *qv*; *Style*— Lydia, Duchess of Bedford; Ribsden Cottage, Chertsey Road, Windlesham, Surrey

BEDFORD, Peter Wyatt; s of David Edwin Wyatt Bedford (d 1979), of Hampshire, and Ruth Lakin, *née* Jackson; *b* 9 March 1935; *Educ* Spyway Sch Langton Matravers Dorset, Marlborough; *m* 1959, Valerie Clare, da of John Walton Collins, of IOW; 4 s (Rupert b 1960, Julian b 1962, Mark b 1963, Hugo b 1970); *Career* dir Fenchurch Insurance Holdings Ltd, chm Fenchurch Insur Brokers Ltd; chm Royal Human Soc; *Recreations* golf, shooting, horseracing; *Clubs* MCC, Sunningdale, Swinley Forest; *Style*— Peter Bedford, Esq; Elderfield House, Herriard, Basingstoke, Hampshire (☎ 025 683 339); 89 High Road, South Woodford, London E18 2RH (☎ 081 505 3333)

BEDFORD, Hon Mrs (Sarah); *née* Lyttelton; twin da of 10 Visc Cobham, KG, GCMG, GCVO, TD, PC (d 1977); *b* 10 June 1954; *Educ* The Abbey Sch Malvern Wells; *m* 1976, C Nicholas Bedford; 2 da; *Style*— The Hon Mrs Bedford; Armsworth Hill Cottage, Old Alresford, Hants

BEDFORD, Sybille; OBE (1982); da of Maximilian von Schoenebeck (d 1923), and Elizabeth, *née* Bernard (d 1937); *b* 16 March 1911; *Educ* privately educated Italy France and England; *Career* author and literary journalist; *Books* A Visit to Don Otavio The Sudden View (1953), A Legacy (1956), The Best We Can Do: The Trial of Doctor Bodkin Adams (1958), The Faces of Justice (1960), A Favourite of the Gods (1962), A Compass Error (1968), Aldous Huxley: A Biography (Vol I 1973, Vol II 1974), Jigsaw (1989), As It Was (1990); FRSL 1964, memb Soc of Authors, vice pres Eng Centre PEN 1981; *Recreations* reading, wine, cookery; *Clubs* Reform; *Style*— Mrs Sybille Bedford, OBE

BEDFORD RUSSELL, Maj Anthony; s of Harold George Bedford Russell (d 1958), of London, and Lilian May, *née* Longmore-Mavius; *b* 20 April 1930; *Educ* Eton, RMA Sandhurst; *m* 26 April 1955, Jane March, da of Lt John Hughes, RNVR (ka 1943), of London; 3 s (Mark b 1957, James b 1959, Christopher b 1962); *Career* Regular Army 1948-83, Coldstream Gds UK, Cyprus, Egypt, Br Guyana, BAOR, Malay Regt 1958-61; Asst Mil Attaché Saigon 1966-68, Intelligence Corps 1968: SHAPE, Australia; Maj; apptd entomologist (butterflies) to Indonesian phase of Op DRAKE 1980; lectr, entomologist, furniture restorer; FRES, FRGS; *Recreations* philately, bridge, tennis, lapidary, natural history, photography, fly-fishing, language, travelling; *Style*— Maj Anthony Bedford Russell; The Post House, Porton, Salisbury, Wilts SP4 0LF (☎ 0980 610796)

BEDINGFELD, Sir Edmund George Felix Paston-; 9 Bt (E 1660); co-heir to Barony of Grandison (abeyant since *temp* Edward III); s of Sir Henry Edward (Paston-)Bedingfeld, 8 Bt (d 1941), and Sybil, *née* Lyne-Stephens (d 1985 aged 101); *b* 2 June 1915; *Educ* Oratory Sch, New Coll Oxford; *m* 1, 1942 (m dis 1953), Joan Lynette (d 1965), da of Edgar G Rees, of Llwyneithin, Llanelly; 1 s, 1 da; m 2, 1957, Agnes Danos (d 1974), da of late Miklos Gluck, of Budapest, Hungary; m 3, 1975, Peggy Hannaford-Hill, of Fort Victoria, Rhodesia (now Zimbabwe); *Heir* s, Henry Edgar (Paston-)Bedingfeld, *qv*; *Career* Maj Welsh Gds; md Handley Walker (Europe) Ltd 1969-80; Freeman City of London 1988, Liveryman Worshipful Co of Bowyers; *Recreations* ornithology, heraldry, fly fishing; *Clubs* Naval and Military; *Style*— Sir Edmund Bedingfeld, Bt; 153 Southgate St, Bury St Edmunds, Suffolk (☎ 0284 4764); Oxburgh Hall, Kings Lynn, Norfolk

BEDINGFELD, Henry Edgar Paston-; s and h of Maj Sir Edmund George Felix (Paston-)Bedingfeld, 9 Bt, *qv*, and his 1 w, Joan Lynette, *née* Rees (d 1965); *b* 7 Dec 1943; *Educ* Ampleforth; *m* 7 Sept 1968, Mary Kathleen, da of Brig Robert Denis Ambrose, CIE, OBE, MC (d 1974); 2 s (Richard Edmund Ambrose b 8 Feb 1975, Thomas Henry b 6 Sept 1976), 2 da (Katherine Mary b 4 Oct 1969, Charlotte Alexandra b 6 May 1971); *Career* chartered surveyor 1968; fndr chm Norfolk Heraldry Soc 1975-80, vice pres 1980-; Rouge Croix Pursuivant of Arms 1983-; sec Standing Cncl of the Baronetage 1984-88; memb Cncl: Norfolk & Norwich Genealogical Soc, Norfolk Record Soc, The Heraldry Soc; vice pres Cambridge Univ Heraldic and Genealogical Soc; Freeman City of London 1985, Liveryman Worshipful Cos of Scriveners and Bowyers; Kt of Sov Mil Order of Malta 1975; *Books* Oxburgh Hall - The First 500 years (1982); *Recreations* redecorating; *Clubs* Norfolk (Norwich); *Style*— Henry Bedingfeld, Esq; Oxburgh Hall, King's Lynn, Norfolk PE33 9PS (☎ 036 621 269); The College of Arms, Queen Victoria St, London EC4V 4BT (☎ 071 236 6420, fax 071 248 4707)

BEDSER, Alec Victor; CBE (1982, OBE 1964); s of Arthur Bedser (d 1978), and Florence Beatrice, *née* Badcock (d 1989); *b* 4 July 1918; *Career* WWII RAF 1939-46, served in France with BEF 1939-40, evacuated S of Dunkirk 1940, Fl Sgt served N Africa, Sicily, Greece, Italy, Austria 1942-46; cricket player: Surrey professional staff 1946-60 (memb of Surrey winning team when championship won 7 consecutive years 1952-59), played for England in First Test after war at Lords v India 1946, record Test debut taking 22 wickets in first two Test matches, played 51 Test Matches for

England, 21 times for England against Aust; memb England cricket team to: Aust and NZ 1946-47, SA 1948-49, Aust and NZ 1950-51, Aust and NZ 1954-55; asst mangr Aust and NZ 1962-63; mangr England team: to Aust and NZ 1974-75, to Aust and India 1979-80; journalist and tv commentator England Tour of Aust 1958-59; memb: England Test Team Selection Panel 1962-85 (chm 1969-82); Surrey CCC: memb Ctee 1961-, vice pres, pres 1987-88); memb MCC Cricket Ctee; *Recreations* golf, gardening, cricket, charities; *Clubs* MCC, Surrey CCC, E India and Sports, W Hill Golf; *Style—* Alec Bedser, Esq, CBE; c/o Initial Contract Services Ltd, Lincoln House, 33-34 Hoxton Square, London N16 NN (☎ 071 739 3566)

BEEBEE, Meyrick Frederick Legge; JP (Radnorshire 1966), DL (1962); s of Meyrick John Legge Beebee (d 1956), of Womastron, Radnorshire; *b* 16 July 1910; *Educ* RNC Dartmouth; *m* 1, 1935 (m dis 1960), Jean Mary Joy, da of Cdr K Walker, RNVR; 1 s, 2 da; m 2, 1962, Angela Inez Green, da of Santos Diego (d 1924); 2 s, 3 da; *Career* served RN 1924-49; memb Foreign Office 1949-58; md Woodcemair Ltd 1959-72; vice chm Welsh Conservatives 1975-80; memb: Powys Magistrates' Ctee and Probation After-Care Ctee 1974-80, Dyfed-Powys Police Authority; *Clubs* Army and Navy; *Style—* Meyrick Beebee, Esq, JP, DL; 26 Lower Sloane St, London SW3

BEECH, (Thomas) Hugh; s of Capt John Beech, RE (ka 1918), of Kuala Lumpur, and Anna Nellie, *née* Scott; *b* 21 June 1917; *Educ* Sir Roger Manwood's Sch, Gonville and Caius Coll Cambridge (BA, MA); *m* 7 Sept 1940 (Ethel) Nancy, da of Arthur Horace Papworth (d 1955), of 77 The Avenue, Muswell Hill; 1 s (John Greatrex b 24 Oct 1947); *Career* actuarial conslt 1956, asst actuary Leslie & Godwin 1961, co actuary and statistician Int Computers and Tabulators (dir of pension tst fund) 1962, co dir (later dir) Antony Gibbs Pensions 1964, dir Martin Paterson Assocs 1972, sole proprietor Micro Consul (software consulting agency) 1982; vice pres Bedhampton CC; Freeman City of London 1979, memb Worshipful Co of Actuaries 1979; AIA 1956, FIA 1958, FSS 1961, FPMI 1976; *Recreations* pianist, dance band leader, steam train enthusiast; *Clubs* Chelsea Arts, Argonauts, Coda; *Style—* Hugh Beech, Esq; Downing Cottage, 11 Havant Rd, Bedhampton, Hants (☎ 0705 475149)

BEECH, Sydney John; s of Sydney Beech, of Stoke-on-Trent, Staffs, and Ruth, *née* Baskeyfield; *b* 6 Feb 1945; *Educ* Hanley HS, Univ of Sheffield (BA); *m* 6 Sept 1969, Jean Ann, da of Bertram Gibson, of Gillow Heath, Biddulph, Staffs; *Career* graduate trainee Peat Marwick Mitchell & Co 1966-69, lectr in accounting taxation and quantitative techniques 1969-72, PA to ptnr Lyon Griffiths and Co 1972-74 (ptnr 1974-86, sr ptnr 1986-); memb of Clark Whitehill Assocs (memb Exec Ctee); FCA, ATII; *Recreations* golf, weightlifting, music; *Clubs* Hill Valley Golf and Country, Dabbers Golf Soc; *Style—* S J Beech, Esq; 8 Woodland Ave, Nantwich, Cheshire (☎ 0270 629 586); Lyon Griffiths & Co, 63-67 Welsh Row, Nantwich, Cheshire (☎ 0270 624 445, fax 0270 623 916)

BEECHAM, Alan; *b* 12 June 1935; *Educ* Boston GS, Open Univ (BA); *m* (m dis); 2 s (Jonathan b 1967, Christopher b 1969); *Career* Nat Serv Royal Lincolnshire Regt Malaya 1955-57; journalist 1951-62; newspapers: Lincs Standard Series, Southern Times, Southern Journal, Surrey Comet, News Chronicle, Daily Express; external news serv BBC 1961-62; radio news and current affrs BBC 1962-89: chief sub ed 1967-69, duty ed 1969-70, sr duty ed 1970-78, asst ed radio news 1978-87, news output ed 1987-89; for radio: general election, euro election, referenda, budget, local and by-election news progs, Falklands War coverage, Royal Weddings 1964-89; created modern BBC internal news agency and news serv between London and local radio, currently media conslt and freelance journalist; FRSA (Silver medal, advanced English); *Recreations* media, theatre, cinema, writing; *Style—* Alan Beecham, Esq; 7 Thalia Close, Greenwich, London SE10 (☎ 081 858 7887)

BEECHAM, Jeremy Hugh; s of Laurence Beecham (d 1975), of Newcastle upon Tyne, and Florence, *née* Fishkin (d 1986); *b* 17 Nov 1944; *Educ* Royal GS Newcastle upon Tyne, Univ Coll Oxford (MA); *m* 7 Jul 1968, Brenda Elizabeth, da of Dr Sidney Woolf; 1 s (Richard b 1973), 1 da (Sara b 1972); *Career* admitted slr 1968; ptnr Allan Henderson Beecham & Peacock 1968-; memb: Local & Regnl Govt Sub Ctee Lab Pty NEC 1971-83, President's Ctee Business in the Community 1988-, Cncl Neighbourhood Energy Assoc 1987-89, Theatre Royal Tst 1985-; dir N Devpt Co Ltd 1986; cncllr Newcastle upon Tyne 1967- (chm: Social Serv Ctee 1973-77, Policy and Resources Ctee 1977-, Fin Ctee 1979-85; leader 1977-); vice chm AMA 1986- (dep chm 1984-86), cmmr English Heritage 1983-87; Parly candidate (Lab) Tynemouth 1970; vice chm Northern Regnl Cncls Assoc 1985-; hon fell Newcastle upon Tyne Poly 1989; *Recreations* reading (esp novels and history), music; *Clubs* Manors Social (Newcastle upon Tyne); *Style—* Jeremy Beecham, Esq; 39 The Drive, Gosforth, Newcastle upon Tyne (☎ 0912 851 888); 7 Collingwood St, Newcastle upon Tyne (☎ 0912 325 048); Civic Centre, Newcastle upon Tyne (☎ 0912 610 352)

BEECHAM, Shirley, Lady; Shirley Jean; da of Albert George Hudson; *m* 1959, as his 3 w, Sir Thomas Beecham, 2 Bt, CH (d 1961) internationally renowned conductor, composer, author and wit; *Career* dir and tstee Sir Thomas Beecham Tst Ltd, formerly admin RPO; *Style—* Shirley, Lady Beecham; The West Wing, Denton House, Denton, Harleston, Norfolk IP20 OAA (☎ 098 686 780)

BEECHEY, Prof (Ronald) Brian; s of Albert Ernest Beechey, of Heckmondwike, Yorks, and Edna Beechey; *b* 24 April 1931; *Educ* Whitcliffe Mount GS, Cleckheaton, Univ of Leeds (BSc, PhD); *Career* Scientific Staff MRC 1956-58, lectr Univ of Southampton 1958-63, princ scientist Shell Res Ltd 1963-83, prof and head Dept of Biochemistry UCW Aberystwyth, author of articles in scientific jls; memb AFRC (memb Animals Res Ctee), treas Biochemical Soc; FRSC 1970; *Clubs* Lensbury; *Style—* Prof Brian Beechey; Kolbe, The Cliff, Borth, Dyfed SY24 5NN (☎ 0970 871395); Department of Biochemistry, University College of Wales, Aberystwyth, Dyfed SY23 3DD (☎ 0970 622291, fax 0970 622307, telex 35181 ABYUCW G)

BEECHING, Baroness; Ella Margaret Beeching; da of William John Tiley, of Maidstone, Kent; *m* 1938, Baron Beeching (d 1985, Life Peer UK 1965); *Style—* The Rt Hon the Lady Beeching; Barnlands, 97 High Street, Lindfield, W Sussex RH16 2HN

BEEDHAM, Brian James; CBE (1989); s of James Victor Beedham (d 1973), of Nottingham, and Nina Florence Grace, *née* Zambra (d 1964); *b* 12 Jan 1928; *Educ* Leeds GS, Queen's Coll Oxford (MA); *m* 1960, (Ruth) Barbara, da of Werner Zollikofer (d 1975), of Zurich; *Career* Capt RA 1950-52; journalist; foreign ed The Economist 1964-89 (assoc ed 1989-); *Recreations* music, walking; *Clubs* Travellers; *Style—* Brian Beedham, Esq, CBE; 9 Hillside, London SW19 (☎ 081 946 4454); The Economist, 25 St James's St, London SW1 (☎ 081 839 7000)

BEEDHAM, Trevor; s of Herbert Victor Beedham (d 1955), of Nottingham, and Olive Mildred, *née* Spikings; *b* 30 July 1942; *Educ* High Pavement GS Nottingham, Univ of London (BDS, MB BS); *m* 21 May 1966, Anne, da of Maj James Darnbrough-Cameron (d 1977), of Bardon Hall, Bardon, Leics; 2 s (Robin b 28 July 1971, Martyn b 29 June 1973), 1 da (Erica b 11 April 1969); *Career* sr registrar The London Hosp 1979; conslt obstetrician and gynaecologist Tower Hamlets Health Authy (The London Hosp) 1981-; examiner: Univ of London 1982-, Soc of Apothecaries, The Examining Bd in England 1984-88; Freeman City of London 1984, Liveryman Worshipful Co of Apothecaries 1988; FRSM, MIBiol 1979, FRCOG 1989 (memb 1977); *Books* Treatment and Prognosis in Obstetrics and Gynaecology (with J G Grudzinskas, 1988), The Examination of Women (in Hutchison's Clinical Methods, 1989); *Recreations* swimming, skiing; *Clubs* City Livery; *Style—* Trevor Beedham, Esq; 127 Harley St, London W1 1DJ (☎ 071 935 8157)

BEEKE, Peter James; s of Leonard James Beeke (d 1966), of London, and Violet Ruth Beeke (d 1985); *b* 2 May 1942; *Educ* Erith GS, UCL; *m* 14 Aug 1970 (m dis 1987), Gillian Mary, da of John Patterson Irvine, of London; 1 s (James b 1977), 1 da (Eleanor b 1975); *Career* programmer W H Smith & Son 1962, chief programmer Br Euro Airways 1964, mgmnt conslt Peat Marwick Mitchell 1967, gen mangr Woolwich Bldg Soc 1984 (formerly data processing mangr and asst gen mangr), gen mangr Pearl Assurance; MBCS 1970, FCBSI 1987; *Recreations* rugby football, golf, music, personal counselling; *Style—* Peter Beeke, Esq; Pearl Assurance plc, Thorpewood, Peterborough PE3 6SA (☎ 0733 292301, fax 0733 558172)

BEELEY, Sir Harold; KCMG (1961, CMG 1953), CBE (1946); s of Frank Arthur Beeley (d 1966), of Southport, Lancs, and Ada, *née* Marsh; *b* 15 Feb 1909; *Educ* Highgate Sch, Queen's Coll Oxford; *m* 1, 1933 (m dis 1953), Millicent Mary, da of late W G Chinn, of Newton Abbot, Devon; 2 da; m 2, 1958, Patricia Karen, da of William Cecil Shields, OBE, and widow of Capt R N B Brett-Smith; 1 da, 1 step s, 2 step da; *Career* lectr: Queen's Coll Oxford 1935-38, UC Leicester 1938-39; entered Foreign Serv 1946, ambass Saudi Arabia 1955, asst under sec FO 1956-58, dep UK rep to UN 1958-61, ambass UAR 1961-64 and 1967-69, UK rep Disarmament Conf Geneva 1964-67, lectr QMC 1969-75; pres Egypt Exploration Soc 1969-88; chm: World of Islam Festival Tst 1973-, Egyptian-Br C of C 1981-; memb RIIA 1939-45; *Style—* Sir Harold Beeley, KCMG, CBE; 38 Slaidburn St, London SW10 (☎ 071 351 0997)

BEER, Andrew Michael Salisbury; s of Adolphus Sharman Beer (d 1983), of Thame, Oxford, and Elsie Margaret Emily, *née* Williams; *b* 26 Aug 1939; *Educ* Shrewsbury; *m* Elizabeth Julia, *née* Dawes; 2 c; *Career* ptnr Wilde Sapte 1969- (joined 1968); memb: City of London Slrs Co, Law Soc; *Recreations* rugby; *Clubs* Law Soc RFC; *Style—* Andrew Beer, Esq; Wilde Sapte, Queensbridge House, 60 Upper Thames St, London EC4V 3BD (☎ 071 236 3050, fax 071 236 9624)

BEER, Fritz Bedrich Frederick; OBE (1979); s of Capt Berthold Beer (d 1942), and Jeanette, *née* Glasner (d 1941); *b* 25 Aug 1911; *Educ* Realgymnasium Brno, Charles Univ Prague, Univ of Dijon, LSE; *m* 30 July 1940, Ursula Rosemary, da of Dr Franz Davidson (d 1942); 1 da (Maria Pauline (Mrs Lacheze) b 11 Feb 1943); *Career* 5 Cavalry Regt Czechoslovak Army 1936-38, Czechoslovak Armoured Bde with Br Forces 1940-45; journalist and writer: dep ed Peoples Illustrated Weekly Prague 1934, scriptwriter and political commentator BBC German Serv 1945-72, radio and tv feature writer for West German Stations 1948-79, London corr German Newspapers 1956-79; Literary Peace Prize Moscow 1934, Franz Brunner Journalism Prize Essen 1968; pres Foreign Press Assoc 1978-80, PEN Centre of German Speaking Authors Abroad 1988-; Czechoslovak Military Medal 1944; *Books* Shots at Dawn (1931), Black Coffres (1934), The House on the Bridge (1949), Intervention in CSSR (1968), The Future Does Not Yet Work (1969); *Recreations* reading, music, gardening, DIY; *Style—* Fritz Beer, Esq, OBE; Hill House, 31b Arterberry Rd, London SW20 8AG (☎ 081 946 0178)

BEER, Ian David Stafford; JP (Middlesex 1981-); s of William John Beer (d 1976), of Surrey, and Doris Ethel, *née* Rose; *b* 28 April 1931; *Educ* St Catharine's Coll Cambridge (MA, PGCE); *m* 1960, Angela Felce, 2 da of Lt-Col Eric Spencer Gravely Howard, MC, RA (d 1977); 2 s (Martin b 1962, Philip b 1965), 1 da (Caroline b 1967); *Career* 1 Bn Royal Fusiliers Berlin 1949-51; bursar Offershaw Sch 1955, housemaster Marlborough Coll 1957-61 (asst master 1955-57); headmaster: Ellesmere Coll Shropshire 1961-69, Lancing Coll Sussex 1969-81, Harrow Sch 1981-; chm: HMC 1980, Physical Educn Working Gp on the Nat Curriculum, Advsy Ctee ISJC 1988-; govr Whitgift Fndn, memb Exec Ctee RFU 1985-; JP: Shropshire 1962-69, West Sussex 1969-81; tstee: Welfare Tst, RMC; *Recreations* rugby football, gardening, natural history; *Clubs* Hawks (Cambridge), East India and Sports; *Style—* Ian D S Beer, Esq, JP; Peel House, Football Lane, Harrow on the Hill, Middlesex HA1 3EA (☎ 081 869 1200); Harrow School, Harrow on the Hill, Middlesex HA1 3HW (☎ 081 869 1200)

BEER, James Edmund; s of Edmund Huxtable Beer (d 1965), and Gwendoline Kate Beer; *b* 17 March 1931; *Educ* Torquay Boys GS; *m* 1953, Barbara Mollie, da of Francis Tunley (d 1960); 2 s, 1 da; *Career* dir of fin Leeds CC until 1978, fin advsr AMA until 1978; rate support grant negotiator until 1978; dir: Short Loan and Mortgage Co 1978-87, Shortloan (Leasing) Co 1978-87, London and University Financial Futures Ltd 1983-87; fin advsr London and Cambridge Investments Ltd 1987-88; public sector conslt: Citicorps Insurance Brokers Ltd, The Co-operative Bank, London Ctee YHDA; Liveryman Worshipful Co of Basketmakers 1981-; *Recreations* walking, theatre, swimming; *Clubs* City Livery, Gresham; *Style—* James Beer, Esq; 48 High Ash Ave, Alwoodley, Leeds LS17 8RG (☎ 0532 683907)

BEER, Prof John Bernard; s of late John Bateman Beer, and late Eva, *née* Chilton; *b* 31 March 1926; *Educ* Watford GS, St John's Coll Cambridge (MA, PhD); *m* 7 July 1962, Gillian Patricia Kempster, *née* Thomas; 3 s (Daniel, Rufus, Zachary); *Career* RAF 1946-48; lectr Univ of Manchester 1958-64; Univ of Cambridge: res fell St John's Coll 1955-58, fell Peterhouse 1964-, univ lectr 1964-78, reader 1978-87, prof of English lit 1987-; *Books* Coleridge the Visionary (1959), The Achievement of E M Forster (1962), Coleridge's Poems (ed, 1963), Milton Lost and Regained (1964), Blake's Humanism (1968), Blake's Visionary Universe (1969), Coleridge's Variety: Bicentenary Studies (ed, 1974), Coleridge's Poetic Intelligence (1977), Wordsworth and the Human Heart (1978), Wordsworth in Time (1979), E M Forster: A Human Exploration (ed with G K Das, 1979), A Passage to India: Essays in Interpretation (ed, 1985); *Recreations* walking in town and country; *Style—* Prof John Beer; Peterhouse, Cambridge CB2 1RD (☎ 0223 338254, fax 0223 337578)

BEER, Lionel Edwin; s of Edwin John Beer (d 1986), of Paignton, Devon, and Phoebe, *née* Hill; *b* 5 Feb 1940; *Educ* S Devon Tech Coll Torquay; *Career* antique dealer; contrib various books on the paranormal and UFO's, regular appearances on radio and tv; publisher Spacelink Magazine 1967-71, organiser of first UFO study course to be held at an academic inst in London Morley Coll 1979, coordinator land London Int UFO Congresses 1979 and 1981, vice pres Br UFO Res Assoc (fndr memb 1962); life memb: Assoc of Railway Preservation Socs, Assoc for the Scientific Study of Anomalous Phenomena, Br Unidentified Flying Object Res Assoc, English Heritage, The Nat Tst; *Books* The Moving Statue of Ballinspittle and Related Phenomena (1986); *Recreations* travel; *Style—* Lionel Beer, Esq; 115 Hollybush Lane, Hampton, Middlesex TW12 2QY (☎ 081 979 3148)

BEER, Prof (Anthony) Stafford; *b* 25 Sept 1926; *Educ* Whitgift Sch, UCL, Univ of Manchester (MBA); *Career* WWII Gunner RA cmmnd Royal Fus, Co Cdr 9 Gurkha Rifles 1945, Staff Capt Intelligence Punjab, army psychologist 1947, Capt Royal Engrs; prodn controller Samuel Fox 1949-56, head of operational res and cybernetics United Steel 1956-61, fndr and md SIGMA (Science in General Management) Ltd 1961-66 (dir parent co Metra International), devpt dir International Publishing Corporation 1966-70; freelance conslt: Ernst & Whinney 1970-87, Govt of Chile 1971-73, pres offices of Mexico, Venezuela and Uruguay; fndr and dir Metapraxis Ltd 1984-87; academic career: visiting prof of cybernetics Univ of Manchester 1969-, prof of gen systems

Open Univ 1970-71, adjunct prof of social systems scis Wharton Sch Univ of Pa 1981-87 (adjunct prof of statistics and operations res 1972-81); visiting prof: Concordia Univ Montreal 1992, Univ of British Columbia 1982, Business Sch Univ of Durham 1990-; distinguished cybernetican in res McCluhan Prog Univ of Toronto 1984, res prof of managerial cybernetics Univ Coll Swansea 1990-, adjunct prof of educn Univ of Toronto 1990-; Silver medal Royal Swedish Acad for Engrg Scis 1958, Lanchester prize Operations Res Soc of America 1966, Resolution of the United States House of Representatives for wise and objective counsel 1970, McCulloch plaque American Soc of Cybernetics 1970, life membership plaque Austrian Soc for Cybernetics 1984, Freeman City of London 1970, Hon LLD Concordia Univ Montreal 1988, hon fell St David's Univ of Wales 1989, hon prof of organisational transformation Sch of Info Sci and Technol Liverpool Poly 1990; fell RSS (regnl chm and memb Industl Relations Ctee 1953-59), FREconS; memb: Operational Res (memb Cncl 1958-62 and 1969-72, pres 1970-71), Operations Res Soc of America, Societe Francaişe de la Recherche Operationelle, Royal Inst of Philosophy, Soc for Gen Systems Res (govr and pres 1971-72), Teilhard Centre for the Future of Man 1975; pres World Orgn of Systems and Cybernetics, govr Int Cncl for Computer Communication; hon fell Int Inst Social Intervention; FWA; *Books*Cybernetics and Management (1959), Management Science (1968), Brain of the Firm (1 edn 1972, 2 edn 1981), Designing Freedom (1974), Platform for Change (1975), Transit (poems, 1977), The Heart of the Enterprize (1979), Diagnosing the System for Organisations (1985), Pebbles to Computers: The Thread (1986); *Recreations* staying put; *Clubs* Athenaeum; *Style*— Prof Stafford Beer; 34 Palmerston Square, Toronto, Ontario, Canada M6G 2S7 (☎ 0101 416 535 0396)

BEERLING, John William (Johnny); s of Raymond Starr Beerling, and May Elizabeth Julia, *née* Holden; *b* 12 April 1937; *Educ* Sir Roger Manwood's GS Sandwich Kent; *m* 1959, Carol Ann, *née* Reynolds; 1 s (David John b 1965), 1 da (Julie Margaret b 1963); *Career* Nat Serv wireless fitter RAF 1955-57; BBC: joined 1957, studio mangr 1958, prodr 1962, head Radio 1 Programmes 1983, controller Radio 1 1985-; *Publications* Emperor Rosko's DJ Handbook (1976); *Recreations* photography, skiing, angling; *Style*— Johnny Beerling, Esq; Egton House, Langham St, London W1A 1AA (☎ 071 927 4561, fax 071 323 4726)

BEESLEY, Mark Christopher; s of George Carter Beesley, and Agnes Winifred Ross; *b* 22 Sept 1945; *Educ* St Joseph's Acad London; *m* 1968, Margaret Clare, da of Sean Byrne, of Ireland; 3 s (Stephen b 1972, Christopher b 1974, David b 1978), 1 da (Clare b 1982); *Career* CA; accountant at Royal London Mutual Insur Soc Ltd 1974-; dir: Royal London Unit Tst Managers Ltd 1980-, Triton Fund Managers Ltd 1986-, Atrium Mgmnt Ltd 1982-, Royal London Asset Mgmnt Ltd, RLAM (Nominees) Ltd, Neptune Fund Mangrs Ltd, Royal London Homebuy Ltd; FCA; *Style*— Mark Beesley, Esq; Rodings, 65 Mill Road, Great Totham, Maldon, Essex CM9 8DH (☎ 0621 891946); Royal London House, Middleborough, Colchester, Essex CO1 1RA (☎ 0206 761761)

BEESON, Andrew Nigel Wendover; s of Capt Nigel Wendover Beeson (d 1944), and Ann Margaret, *née* Sutherland; *b* 30 March 1944; *Educ* Eton; *m* 1, 1971 (m dis 1983), Susan Roberta Caroline, da of Guy Standish Gerard (d 1981); 1 s (James Gerard b 26 March 1976), 1 da (Susanna Caroline b 27 June 1973); m 2, 12 July 1986, Carrie Joy, da of Norman Joseph Martin, of Majorca; 1 da (Alexandra Robina Martin b 4 Sept 1989); *Career* stockbroker; ptnr Capel-Cure-Carden 1972-85; dir: ANZ Merchant Bank 1985-87, ANZ McCaughan 1987-89; chief exec Beeson Gregory Ltd 1989-; *Recreations* real tennis, rackets, shooting, collecting; *Clubs* White's, Pratt's, MCC, Swinley; *Style*— Andrew N W Beeson, Esq; 21 Warwick Square, London SW1V 2AB (☎ 071 834 2903); Beeson Gregory Ltd, The Registry, Royal Mint Court, London EC3N 4EY (☎ 071 488 4040, fax 071 481 3762, car 0836 202374)

BEESON, Bryan Douglas; s of Walter Beeson (d 1976), and Muriel, *née* Posthill; *b* 26 July 1960; *Educ* Heathfield Sr High, Coll of Arts & Technol, Consett Tech Coll; *Career* squash player; turned professional 1985; honours incl: Northern champion under 16 to under 19, Northumbria jr champion under 16 to under 19, winner Yorks League (Harrogate), winner Northumbria League (Gateshead), winner Nat League (Lambs and Cannons); first int cap Home Ints 1985; total 58 caps incl: Home Ints 6 times (Gold medals), Euro Championships 6 times (Gold medals), World Championships England (Bronze medal) and Singapore (Bronze medal); mechanical technician in plant engrg; *Recreations* golf, windsurfing, reading; *Style*— Bryan Beeson, Esq; c/o Squash Rackets Assoc, Westpoint, 33-34 Warple Way, London W3 ORG

BEESON, Headley Thomas; s of Thomas Benjamin Beeson (d 1942), of Headley Park, Headley, nr Epsom, Surrey, and Elizabeth, *née* Brezovits; *b* 20 Aug 1942; *Educ* Clark's GS Surbiton; *m* 7 Sept 1968, Lesley Ann, da of Roland Conrad Wontner, of Heathlands, Woodside Rd, Cobham, Surrey; 1 s (Miles b 1973), 1 da (Caroline b 1975); *Career* Fenn & Crosthwaite (stockbrokers) 1962-67, investmt mgmnt and mktg Barclays Bank Group 1967-81, dir N M Schroder Unit Trust Managers Ltd 1981-88, Schroder Investment Management Ltd 1988-; AMSIA 1972; *Recreations* rowing, motor sports; *Style*— Headley Beeson, Esq; Courtlands, 14 The Ridings, Cobham, Surrey KT11 2PU (☎ 0372 843 230); Schroder Investment Management Ltd, 36 Old Jewry, London EC2R 8BS (☎ 071 382 6000 or 071 382 6498, fax 071 382 6965, tlx 885029)

BEESON, Very Rev Trevor Randall; s of Arthur William Beeson (d 1979), and Matilda Beeson (d 1980); *b* 2 March 1926; *Educ* King's Coll London, St Boniface Coll Warminster (MA); *m* 1950, Josephine Grace, da of Ernest Joseph Cope (d 1974); 2 da (Jean, Catherine); *Career* dean of Winchester 1987-; FKC; *Books* The Church of England in Crisis (1973), Discretion and Valour (1974), A Vision of Hope (1984); *Recreations* gardening, cricket; *Style*— The Very Rev the Dean of Winchester; The Deanery, Winchester SO23 9LS; Grove House, Church St, St Clements, Sandwich, Kent

BEETHAM, Lady (Eileen Joy); da of Arthur Leslie Parkinson (d 1968), of Polegate, and Adeline, *née* Wood; *b* 19 March 1910; *Educ* Godolphin Salisbury; *m* 1933, Sir Edward Beetham, KCMG, CVO, OBE (d 1979), s of Dr Fredrick Beetham (d 1943); 1 da; *Career* worked for the Navy in Freetown, W Africa 1941-45; *Clubs* Phyllis Court, Anglo-Belgian; *Style*— Lady Beetham; 26 Adam Court, Henley-on-Thames, Oxon RG9 2BJ (☎ 0491 574865)

BEETHAM, Marshal of the RAF Sir Michael James; GCB (1978, KCB 1976), CBE (1967), DFC (1944), AFC (1960), DL (Norfolk 1989); s of Maj George C Beetham, MC (d 1953), of Broadstairs, Kent; *b* 17 May 1923; *Educ* St Marylebone GS; *m* 1956, Patricia Elizabeth, da of Henry Lane, of Christchurch, NZ; 1 s, 1 da; *Career* joined RAF 1941, Bomber Cmd 1943-46 (flying 30 combat missions in Lancaster bombers of 50 Sqdn), psa 1952, idc 1967, Dir Ops (RAF) MOD 1968-70, Cmdt RAF Staff Coll 1970-72, ACOS (plans and policy) SHAPE 1972-75, Dep C-in-C Strike Cmd 1975-76, C-in-C RAF Germany and Cdr 2 Allied Tactical Air Force 1976-77, Chief of the Air Staff 1977-82, Air ADC to HM the Queen 1977-82, Marshal of the RAF 1982; dir: Brixton Estate plc 1983-, GEC Avionics Ltd 1984- (chm 1986-90); chm Tstees RAF Museum 1983-90, govr Cheltenham College 1983-; Hon Air Cdr RAuxAF 1983-; FRSA, FRAeS; *Clubs* RAF; *Style*— Marshal of the RAF Sir Michael Beetham, GCB, CBE, DFC, AFC, DL; c/o RAF Club, Piccadilly, London W1

BEETHAM, Roger Campbell; LVO (1976); s of Henry Campbell Beetham (d 1986), of Burnley, Lancashire, and Mary, *née* Baldwin (d 1978); *b* 22 Nov 1937; *Educ* Peter Symonds Sch Winchester, BNC Oxford (MA); *m* 1, 1965 (m dis 1986), Judith, *née* Rees; m 2, 19 Dec 1986, Christine Marguerite, da of Adrien Malerme, of Callas, S France; *Career* HM Dip Serv 1960-: UK Delgn to Disarmament Conf Geneva 1962-65, Washington 1965-68, FCO 1969-72, Helsinki 1972-76, EC Cmmn 1977-81, cnsllr (econ & commercial) New Delhi 1981-85, head Maritime Aviation & Environment Dept FCO 1985-90, ambass Senegal (also non-resident Cape Verde, Guinea, Guinea-Bissan and Mali) 1990-; Order of the White Rose of Finland 1976; *Recreations* travel, cooking, wine; *Clubs* Travellers'; *Style*— Roger Beetham, Esq, LVO; FCO, King Charles St, London SW1A 2AH

BEETON, David Christopher; s of Ernest Walter Beeton, and Ethel Louise, *née* Lemon; *b* 25 Aug 1939; *Educ* Ipswich Sch, King's Coll London (LLB); *m* 6 July 1968, Elizabeth Brenda; 2 s (Thomas b 1970, Samuel b 1972); *Career* admitted slr 1966; chief exec Bath City Cncl 1973-85, sec The Nat Tst 1985-89, chief exec Historic Royal Palaces 1989; *Recreations* swimming, historic buildings, cooking; *Style*— David Beeton, Esq; 5 Moreton Terrace Mews South, London SW1V 2NU; Hampton Court Palace, East Molesey, Surrey KT8 9AU (☎ 081 977 7222, fax 081 977 9714)

BEEVERS, Dr (David) Gareth; s of Rev Charles Edward Beevers, CBE (d 1973), sometime Rector of The Lophams, Norfolk, and Mabel, *née* Charlton (d 1991); *b* 4 June 1942; *Educ* Dulwich, The London Hosp Med Coll (MB BS, MD); *m* 30 Sept 1967, Michèle, da of Peter Barnett, of Royston, Herts; 1 s (Robert Charles Josiah b 15 Feb 1976), 2 da (Hellen Elizabeth Michèle b 7 June 1969, Rachel Victoria b 30 Nov 1972); *Career* clinical scientist MRC Blood Pressure Unit Western Infirmary Glasgow 1972-77, reader in med Univ of Birmingham 1977-, hon conslt physician Dudley Rd Hosp Birmingham 1977-; ed Jl of Human Hypertension, sec Br Hypertension Soc; FRCP 1981; memb: BMA, Assoc of Physicians GB and Ireland; *Books* Hypertension in Practice (with G A MacGregor, 1987); *Recreations* collecting; *Style*— Dr Gareth Beevers; Dept of Medicine, Dudley Road Hosp, Birmingham B18 7QH (☎ 021 554 3801)

BEEVOR, Antony Romer; s of Miles Beevor, of Welwyn; *b* 18 May 1940; *Educ* Winchester, New Coll Oxford; *m* 1970, Cecilia, da of John Hopton (d 1969); 1 s, 1 da; *Career* slr Ashwort Morris Crisp 1962-72, Hambros Bank 1974- (exec dir 1982-, on secondment dir gen Panel on Takeovers and Mergers 1987-89); *Style*— Antony Beevor, Esq; 20 Radipole Rd, London SW6 (☎ 071 731 8015)

BEEVOR, Carola, Lady; Carola; da of His Hon Judge Jesse Basil Herbert, MC, QC (d 1971), and Hon Isabella Russell, *née* Rea, *qv*; *b* 17 July 1930; *Educ* St Paul's Girls' Sch, St Hugh's Coll Oxford (MA); *m* 1966 (m dis 1975), as his 2 w, Sir Thomas Agnew Beevor, 7 Bt; *Career* economist US Embassy London 1958-67; *Books* Debrett's Register of Yachts (ed, 1983); *Recreations* sailing (owner of 'Isla'), dog showing, beagling; *Clubs* Pin Mill Sailing; *Style*— Carola, Lady Beevor; Lark Cottage, Pin Mill, Ipswich, Suffolk (☎ 047 384 579)

BEEVOR, Sir Thomas Agnew; 7 Bt (GB 1784); s of Cdr Sir Thomas Beevor, 6 Bt (d 1943), and Edith Margaret, *née* Agnew (d 1985, having m 2, 1944, Rear Adm Robert Alexander Currie, CB, DSC); *b* 6 Jan 1929; *Educ* Eton, Magdalene Coll Cambridge; *m* 1, 1957 (m dis 1965), Barbara Clare, yst da of Capt Robert Lionel Brooke Cunliffe, CBE, RN (ret); 1 s, 2 da; m 2, 1966 (m dis 1975), Carola, da of His Hon Judge Jesse Basil Herbert, MC, QC; m 3, 1976, Mrs Sally Elisabeth Bouwens, da of Edward Madoc, of White Hall, Thetford; *Heir* s, Thomas Beevor; *Style*— Sir Thomas Beevor, Bt; Hargham Hall, Norwich

BEEVOR, Thomas Hugh Cunliffe; s and h of Sir Thomas Beevor, 7 Bt; *b* 1 Oct 1962; *Style*— Thomas Beevor Esq; Hargham Hall, Norwich

BEGG, Alastair Currie; s of Henry Currie Begg (d 1983), of Edinburgh, and Rosemary Anne, *née* Kemp; *b* 6 Feb 1954; *Educ* King's Sch Canterbury, Sidney Sussex Coll Cambridge (MA); *m* 12 June 1982, Patricia Barbara Wigham, da of Sir George Wigham Richardson, Bt (d 1981), of Benenden, Kent; 1 s (Andrew b 1985), 1 da (Camilla b 1984); *Career* admin trainee Home Civil Serv 1976-78, Bank of America International Ltd 1978-81, dir Kleinwort Benson Investment Management Ltd 1987 (joined 1981-); memb Int Stock Exchange; *Style*— Alastair Begg, Esq; Monks Manor, Fir Toll Lane, Mayfield, E Sussex TN20 6NE (☎ 0435 872429); 10 Fenchurch St, London EC3M 3LB (☎ 071 956 5005, fax 071 623 5519, telex 9413545

BEGG, Alexander Hugh; s of Norman Fraser Buchanan Begg (d 1952), and Olive Jane, *née* Wood (d 1982); *b* 23 Jan 1931; *Educ* St Paul's, Nautical Coll Pangbourne, RNC Dartmouth; *m* 18 April 1958, Robin, da of Horace Victor Gundry, of Sydney, Australia; 3 da (Nicola b 1959, Alexandra b 1960, Louisa b 1962); *Career* Lieut RN (ret 1958); served in HM Submarines in Mediterranean and Far East; md Thomson Television Int Ltd 1961-63, chief exec Overseas Operations Thomson Orgn 1963-65, md Thomson Yellow Pages Ltd 1965-71, chm and md London Editions Ltd 1971-78, md Siemssen Hunter Ltd 1979-84, deputy chm and chief exec Seymour Int Press Distributors Ltd 1984-89; dir: K James and Son Ltd, London Office Facilities Ltd; *Recreations* golf; *Clubs* Carlton, Royal Wimbledon Golf, Rye Golf; *Style*— A H Begg, Esq; 29 Holmead Rd, London SW6 2JD (☎ 071 731 8346, car ☎ 0836 224042)

BEGG, Prof David Knox Houston; s of Robert William Begg, of Glasgow, and Sheena Margaret, *née* Boyd; *b* 25 June 1950; *Educ* Kelvinside Acad Glasgow, Univ of Cambridge, Univ of Oxford (MPhil), Massachusetts Inst of Technol (PhD); *Career* Lloyds fell in econs Worcester Coll Oxford 1977-86, visiting prof Princeton Univ 1979, res dir Centre Econ Forecasting London Business Sch 1981-83, res fell Centre Econ Policy Res 1983-, founding managing ed of Economic Policy 1984-, advsr econ policy res Bank of England 1986, prof of econs Birkbeck Coll Univ of London 1987-; memb: Academic Panel HM Treasy 1981-, Res Awards Advsy Ctee Leverhulme Tst 1987-; specialist advsr: Treasy and Civil Serv Ctee House of Commons 1983, House of Lords Euro Communities Ctee 1988-89, Commission of the Euro Cmmn 1989-90, Federal Govt of Czechoslovakia 1990-91; *Books* The Rational Expectations Revolution in Macroeconomics (1982), Economics (with S Fischer and R Dornbusch, 1984, 2 edn 1987), Monitoring European Integration: The Impact of Eastern Europe (1990); *Recreations* travel, eating, gambling; *Style*— Prof David Begg; Dept of Economics, Birkbeck College, 7 Gresse St, London W1P 1PA (☎ 071 631 6414, fax 071 631 6498)

BEGG, Prof Hugh MacKemmie; s of Hugh Alexander Begg (d 1978), of Glasgow, and Margaret Neil, *née* MacKemmie; *b* 25 Oct 1941; *Educ* HS of Glasgow, Univ of St Andrews, Univ of BC; *m* 20 July 1968, Jane Elizabeth, da of Charles Wilfred Harrison, of Salt Spring Island, BC; 2 da (Mary Margaret b 26 April 1970, Susan Morven b 28 Sept 1973); *Career* asst lectr Univ of St Andrews 1966-67, res fell Tayside Study 1967-69, lectr Univ of Dundee 1969-76, asst dir Tayside Regnl Cncl 1976-79, head Sch of Town and Regnl Planning Duncan of Jordanstone Coll and Univ of Dundee 1981- (sr lectr 1979-81), conslt UN devpt project 1986-; memb Exec RTPI Scotland; MCIT 1980, FRSA 1988, FRTPI 1989; *Recreations* hill walking, puppy walking, guide dogs; *Clubs* Monifieth and Dist Rotary; *Style*— Prof Hugh Begg; 4 Esplanade, Broughty Ferry, Dundee DD5 2EL (☎ 0382 79642); School of Town and Regional Planning, Duncan of Jordanstone College of Art/Dundee University, Perth Rd, Dundee DD1 4HT (☎ 0382 23261)

BEGG, John Alexander Sutherland; s of Daniel Begg, of Wick (d 1984); *b* 2 July 1938; *Educ* Wick HS, Aberdeen Univ, Edinburgh Univ; *m* 1978, Lesley, da of Donald

Nichol, of The Wirral; 3 children; *Career* md: Lewis's Ltd (dept store) 1981-; *Style—* John Begg, Esq; Petwood, Heath Lane, Willaston, S Wirral L64 1TR

BEGG, Dr Robert William; CBE (1977); s of David Begg (d 1968), and Elizabeth Young Thomson; *b* 19 Feb 1922; *Educ* Greenock Acad, Univ of Glasgow (MA); *m* 1948, Sheena Margaret, da of Archibald Boyd (d 1958), of Largs; 2 s (David b 1950, Alan b 1954); *Career* CA; tstee Nat Galleries of Scot; memb Ct Univ of Glasgow 1986-90, exec memb Nat Tst for Scot 1986-90, pres Glasgow Inst of Fine Arts 1987-90, memb Museums and Galleries Cmmn 1988-; Hon DUniv of Glasgow 1990; *Recreations* painting; *Clubs* Glasgow Art, New (Edinburgh); *Style—* Robert Begg, Esq, CBE; 3 Colquhoun Dr, Bearsden, Glasgow G61 4NQ (☎ 041 942 2436); Moores Rowland, Allan House, 25 Bothwell St, Glasgow G2 6NL (☎ 041 221 6991, fax 041 221 2685, telex 777036)

BEGG, Admiral of the Fleet Sir Varyl (Cargill); GCB (1965, KCB 1962, CB 1959), DSO (1952), DSC (1941); s of Francis Cargill Begg (d 1952), of Henley-on-Thames, and Muriel Clare Robinson; *b* 1 Oct 1908; *Educ* St Andrews Sch Eastbourne, Malvern; *m* 1943, Rosemary, da of Francis Edward Cowan (d 1961), of Helens Bay, NI; 2 s (Timothy, Peter); *Career* entered RN 1926, Gunnery Offr 1933, Cmdr 1942, Capt 1947, idc 1954, Rear Adm 1957, Vice Adm 1960, Adm 1963, PMN 1966, Chief of Naval Staff and First Sea Lord 1966-68, ret; Govr and C-in-C Gibraltar 1969-73; KStJ 1969; *Style—* Admiral of the Fleet Sir Varyl Begg, GCB, DSO, DSC; Copyhold Cottage, Chilbolton, Stockbridge, Hants (☎ 026 474 320)

BEGGS, Roy; MP (UU) East Antrim 1983-; *b* 20 Feb 1936,Belfast,; *Educ* Ballyclare HS, Stranmillis Training Coll; *m* ; 2 s, 2 da; *Career* teacher Larne HS 1957; memb Larne Borough Cncl 1973-, Mayor of Larne 1978-83; elected NI Assembly for Stormont 1982, chm Economic Devpt Ctee 1982-84; chm NE Educn and Library Bd 1985- (vice chm 1981-85); pres Assoc Educn and Library Bds NI 1984-85; vice pres Gleno Valley Young Farmers Club; memb Ulster Farmers Union; *Style—* Roy Beggs, Esq, MP; House of Commons, London SW1

BEHAN, Prof Peter Oliver; s of Patrick Behan (d 1985), and Mary Ellen, *née* Ryan; *b* 8 July 1935; *Educ* Christian Brothers Schs Athy, Univ of Leeds (MB ChB, MD); *m* 23 Aug 1968, Dr Wilhelmina Behan, da of Dr William Hughes (d 1981); 2 s (Miles b 1973, Edmund b 1977), 1 da (Charlotte b 1969); *Career* demonstrator in pathology Univ of Cambridge, res fell in psychiatry and special res fell neurology Univ of Harvard, special res fell neurology Univ of Oxford, asst prof of neurology Univ of Boston; Univ of Glasgow: lectr, sr lectr, reader, prof of neurology; med patron Scot Motor Neurone Disease Assoc; memb: Neuroimmunology Res Gp World Fedn of Neurology, Rodin Acad for Dyslexia Res; FRCP, FRCPG, FRCPI, FACP, fell American Neurological Assoc, hon fell Norwegian Neurological Assoc; *Books* Clinical Neuroimmunology (with S Curie, 1978), Clinical Neuroimmunology (with W Behan and J Aarli, 1987); *Recreations* salmon fishing, gardening; *Clubs* Savile; *Style—* Prof Peter Behan; 17 South Erskin Pk, Bearsden, Glasgow G61 4NA (☎ 041 942 5113); Department of Neurology, Institute of Neurological Sciences, Southern General Hospital, Glasgow G51 4TF (☎ 041 445 2466 or 041 445 2466 ext 4334)

BEHARRELL, Steven Roderic; s of late Douglas Wells Beharrell, TD, and Pamela, *née* Pearman Smith; *b* 22 Dec 1944; *Educ* Uppingham; *m* 10 June 1967, Julia Elizabeth, da of William Wilson Powell, DL; 2 da (Victoria Jane b 5 Aug 1971, Rebecca Clare b 9 Oct 1973); *Career* admitted slr 1969; ptnr Denton Hall Burgin & Warrens 1973-90, fndr ptnr Beharrell Thompson & Co 1990-; Freeman Worshipful Co of Drapers; memb: Law Soc, Int Bar Assoc; *Style—* Steven Beharrell, Esq; 5 Chancery Lane, London EC4A 1BU (☎ 071 242 1212, fax 071 404 0087, telex 263 567

BEHRENS, James Nicholas Edward; s of Col William Edward Boaz Behrens (d 1989), of Homegarth, Swinton Grange, Malton, N Yorks, and Dulcie Bella, *née* Mocatta; *b* 22 Dec 1956; *Educ* Eton, Trinity Coll Cambridge (scholar, MA); *m* 6 Sept 1986, Sally, da of Michael Templeton Brett, of Harpsden Hill, Harpsden, Henley-on-Thames, Oxfordshire; 1 da (Deborah b 1987); *Career* Astbury scholar Middle Temple 1978, barr 1979-; *Books* Wordperfect for the Legal Professions (1991); *Recreations* music, photography, local church; *Clubs* Lansdowne; *Style—* James Behrens, Esq; 13 Old Square, Lincoln's Inn, London WC2A 3UA (☎ 071 242 6105, fax 071 405 4004, tlx 262205

BEHRENS, John Stephen; JP (1970); s of Edgar Charles Behrens, CBE, JP (d 1975), of Norwood House, Ilkley, Yorks, and Winifred Wrigley, *née* Luckhurst (d 1976); *b* 9 July 1927; *Educ* Rugby; *m* 1964, Kathleen Shirley, da of Richard Alfred Leicester Billson, JP (d 1949); 2 s (Charles, James), 1 da (Philippa); *Career* dir Sir Jacob Behrens and Sons Ltd and subsidiary cos; chm: Francis Willey (British Wools 1935) Ltd and subsidiary cos, John Smith and Sons (Shrewsbury) Ltd, Craig Home for Children, Bradford Tradesmen's Homes; pres Country Wool Merchants Assoc; *Style—* John Behrens, Esq, JP; Park Green, Littlethorpe, Ripon, N Yorks (☎ 0765 872 62); Ravenscliffe Mills, Calverley, Pudsey, W Yorks (☎ 0274 612 541)

BEILL, Air Vice-Marshal Alfred; CB (1986); s of Gp Capt Robert Beill, CBE, DFC (d 1970), and Sophie, *née* Kulczycka; *b* 14 Feb 1931; *Educ* Rossall, RAF Coll Cranwell; *m* 1953, Vyvian Mary, da of Dr Basil Crowhurst-Archer (d 1981); 4 da (Francesca b 1956, Jacqueline b 1957, Anna-Louise b 1961, Miranda b 1962); *Career* cmmnd RAF 1952; serv in: UK, Aden, Singapore, Cyprus; student RAF Staff Coll 1964, joint servs Staff Coll 1968 and on staff 1970-73, ADC to HM The Queen 1974-75, Air Vice Marshal 1984, dir gen of Supply (RAF) 1984-87, ret 1987; appeals sec King Edward VII's Hosp for Offrs, pres RAF Swimming Assoc 1982-87 (life vice pres 1987-); *Clubs* RAF; *Style—* Air Vice-Marshal Alfred Beill, CB; c/o Lloyds Bank plc, Cox's and King's Branch, 7 Pall Mall, London SW1Y 5NA; Appeals Office, King Edward VII's Hospital for Officers, 6 Buckingham Place, London SW1E 6HR (☎ 071 828 4454)

BEISHON, Dr (Ronald) John; s of Arthur Robson Beishon, of Brighton, and Irene, *née* Westerman; *b* 10 Nov 1930; *Educ* Battersea Poly, Birkbeck Coll London (BSc), Univ of Oxford (D Phil); *m* 25 March 1955, Gwenda Jean; 2 s (Marc, Daniel), 2 da (Jessica, Judith); *Career* Nat Serv marine engr RASC 1951-53; tech offr ICI 1954-58, section ldr BICC 1958-61; sr res offr Univ of Oxford 1961-64, lectr Univ of Bristol 1964-68, reader Univ of Sussex 1968-71, prof Open Univ 1971-80; dir: South Bank Poly 1980-85, North London Poly 1985-87, Assoc for Consumer Res; chief exec Consumer's Assoc; memb: Exec Ctee Int Orgn of Consumer Unions (IOCU), Exec Ctee Nat House Builders Assoc; govr Brighton Poly; CEng, FRSA, MIM, MWeldI, AFBPsS; *Recreations* squash; *Clubs* Wig and Pen; *Style—* Dr John Beishon; 421 Ditchling Rd, Brighton BN1 6XB (☎ 0273 552 100); 2 Marylebone Rd, London NW1 4DX (☎ 071 486 5544)

BEIT, Sir Alfred Lane; 2 Bt (UK 1924); s of Sir Otto (John) Beit, KCMG (d 1930); *b* 19 Jan 1903; *Educ* Eton, ChCh Oxford (MA); *m* 20 April 1939, Clementine Mabell Kitty, da of Maj the Hon Clement Bertram Ogilvy Freeman-Mitford, DSO (ka 1915), s of 1 Baron Redesdale; *Heir* none; *Career* Sqdn RAFVR (ret); MP(C) SE Div of St Pancras Oct 1931-June 1945 (Parly candidate May 1929); PPS (unpaid) to Fin Sec to War Off 1935-38, sec of state for Colonies 1944-45; former memb Advsy Ctee of Tanganyika Concessions Ltd; tstee Beit Tst; Hon LLD Nat Univ of Ireland; *Clubs* Brooks's, Carlton, Kildare St and University (Dublin); *Style—* Sir Alfred Beit, Bt; Russborough, Blessington, Co Wicklow, Republic of Ireland

BEITH, Alan James; MP (Lib Dem) Berwick-upon-Tweed 1973; o s of James Beith (d 1962), of Poynton, Cheshire, and Joan Beith; *b* 20 April 1943; *Educ* King's Sch Macclesfield, Balliol and Nuffield Colls Oxford; *m* 1965, Barbara Jean Ward; *Career* lectr Dept of Politics Univ of Newcastle upon Tyne 1966-73; Parly candidate (Lib) Berwick-upon-Tweed 1970, Lib chief whip 1976-85, Lib dep ldr and foreign affrs spokesman 1985-87, Treasy spokesman Lib Democrats 1988-, memb House of Commons Cmmn and Treasy Select Ctee; *Recreations* walking, music; *Clubs* Nat Liberal; *Style—* Alan Beith, Esq, MP; 28 Castle Terrace, Berwick-upon-Tweed, Northumberland

BEKER, Prof Henry Joseph; s of Jozef Beker (d 1960), and Mary, *née* Gewaid; *b* 22 Dec 1951; *Educ* Kilburn GS, Univ of London (BSc), Open Univ (PhD); *m* 30 Oct 1976, Mary Louise, *née* Keilthy; 2 da (Hannah Louise b 1979, Josephine Tamara b 1988); *Career* sr res asst Dept of Statistics Univ Coll Swansea 1976-77, princ mathematician Racal Comsec Ltd 1977-80 (chief mathematician 1980-83), dir of res Racal Research Ltd 1983-85, dir of systems Racal-Chubb Security Systems Ltd 1985-86, md Racal-Guardata Ltd 1986-88, exec chm Zergo Ltd 1988-; visiting prof IT Westfield Coll Univ of London 1983-84, visiting prof of info technol Royal Holloway and Bedford New Coll London 1984; MIS, MIEE, CEng, AFIMA; *Books* Cipher Systems (with Prof F C Piper, 1982), Secure Speech Communications (with Prof F C Piper, 1985); *Recreations* music, reading, travel; *Style—* Prof Henry Beker; Communications House, Winchester Rd, Basingstoke, Hants RG22 4AA (☎ 0256 818800)

BEKHIT, Dr Sawsan Mansour; da of Mansour Bekhit (d 1971), of Cairo, Egypt, and Nelly, *née* Boulos (d 1978); *b* 21 Oct 1929; *Educ* Helwan GS, Univ of Cairo (MB BCh); *m* 22 Aug 1956, Dr Kamal Ghattas, s of Abdel Messih Ghattas; 2 s (Khalid b 24 Feb 1958, Rammy b 6 April 1962); *Career* internship Kasr-el-Aini Hospital 1953-55, res med offr Obstetrics and Gynaecology Kuwait Emiri Hosp 1955-60; res med offr: Bearsted Memorial Hosp Hampton Court 1963-64, Gulson Hosp Coventry 1964-65, St Cross Hosp Rugby 1965-66; hon registrar Bart's 1966-67 (registrar 1967-70), conslt locum Watford Hosp 1970-85, conslt obstetrician Mother's Hosp London 1972-77; conslt gynaecologist: Metropolitan Hosp London 1972-75, Humana Hosp, Clementine Churchill Hosp Harrow; private practice Harley Street 1974-; FRCOG 1982, FRSM 1968, FRCSEd, FRCSI, fell Huntarian Soc, LMSSA, memb BMA 1965; *Style—* Dr Sawsan Bekhit; 57 Harley Street, London W1N 1DD (☎ 071 636 4424)

BELCHAMBER, Peter John; s of John Belchamber (d 1983), of Derbyshire, and Sheila, *née* Warwick; *b* 5 Sept 1943; *Educ* Monkton Combe Sch, Nottingham Peoples Coll, Alexander Hamilton Inst (Dip Business Admin); *m* 2 Sept 1972, Margaret Anne Elizabeth, da of George William Bowes (d 1968), of Hutton Mount, Essex; 1 s (James), 2 da (Emma, Fiona); *Career* journalist Nottingham Evening Post 1962-66, ed Nottingham Observer 1965-67, account mangr Ogilvy and Mather 1967-71, account dir J Walter Thompson 1971-74, dir Charles Barker Lyons 1976-86, md Charles Barker Traverse-Healy 1986-88, dir College Hill Assocs 1988; church reader, fndr memb Exec Ctee Br Assoc of Cancer United Patients 1986-; hon PR advsr: Nat Assoc for Welfare of Children in Hosp, Wishing Well Appeal Gt Ormond St Hosp for Children; memb Open College of the Arts; *Books* East Midlands Airport (1965); *Recreations* opera, ballet, reading, music, cricket; *Clubs* Scribes; *Style—* Peter Belchamber, Esq; Oakwood, High St, Whittlesford, Cambridge (☎ 0223 833 729); 4 College Hill, London EC4 (☎ 071 236 2020)

BELCHAMBERS, Anthony Murray; s of Lyonel Eustace Belchambers (d 1981), of Ashburton, Devon, and Dorothy Joan, *née* Wylie; *b* 14 April 1947; *Educ* Christ Coll Brecon; *m* 14 Jan 1980, Penelope Brabazon, *née* Howard; *Career* called to the Bar Inner Temple, in practice W circuit 1972-75; lawyer: DTI 1975-82, Dir of Public Prosecutions 1982-84, Treasy 1984-86; co sec and gen counsel Assoc of Futures Brokers and Dealers 1986-89, gen counsel Jt Exchanges Ctee 1989-; *Recreations* tennis, riding, bridge; *Clubs* HAC; *Style—* Anthony Belchambers, Esq; Kensington, London W8; Joint Exchange Ctee, 28-29 Threadneedle St, London EC2R 8BA (☎ 071 283 1345)

BELCHER, Anthony Dennis (Tony); s of Dennis Frederick Belcher, of Chertsey, and Kathleen Patricia, *née* Backhouse; *b* 26 Feb 1957; *Educ* Salesian Coll Chertsey, Polytechnic of the South Bank (BSc); *m* 16 May 1981, Andrea Margaret, da of Victor Ernest Whatley; 2 s (Nicholas Anthony b 8 July 1983, Shaun Anthony b 21 Feb 1987); *Career* Mellersh & Harding: trainee surveyor 1975, salaried ptnr 1985, youngest equity ptnr in recent years 1990; FRICS 1981, ACIArb; *Recreations* skiing, badminton, squash, fishing, restoration of French house, golf, travel; *Clubs* English Setter Assoc; *Style—* Tony Belcher, Esq; Mellersh & Harding, 43 St James's Place, London SW1A 1PA (☎ 071 499 0866, fax 071 799 2010, car 0836 600838)

BELCHER, John Leonard; s of Leonard Charles Belcher, and Hannah Joan, *née* Collins; *b* 27 Oct 1949; *Educ* Kesteven Coll, Univ of Nottingham, Univ of London; *Career* educationalist; lectr Open Univ 1974-75, asst prof of sociology American Coll of Switzerland 1975-80, various academic appts in US 1980-83, dir external rels QMWC London 1983, chief of public affrs The United Nations Univ 1990-; memb various ctees concerning educn incl: Ed Bd International Education, ECS Exec Ctee Br Cncl, Exec Bd Euro Assoc for Int Educn, Essex CC Educn Ctee; *Recreations* music, running, skiing, reading, travel; *Style—* John Belcher, Esq; 3 Grange Cottages, Low Rd, Barrowby, Grantham, Lincs NG32 1DL; Queen Mary and Westfield Coll, Univ of London, Mile End Rd, London E1 4NS (☎ 071 975 5071, fax 071 981 5497, telex 893750)

BELDAM, Robert Geoffrey; CBE (1975); s of late Ernest Asplan Beldam; *b* 3 Jan 1914; *Educ* Repton, Corpus Christi Coll Cambridge (MA); *Career* chm and md: Beldam Lascar Seals Ltd, Auto-Klean Filtration Ltd; memb: CBI Cncl 1965-86, CBI Smaller Firms Cncl 1965-79 (chm 1965-74), CBI London Regnl Cncl 1952-80 and 1981-87, SE Econ Planning Cncl 1966-73 (acting chm 1971), Woking UDG 1947-70 (chm 1954-55); Brunel Univ: memb Ct, life memb 1966-, memb Cncl representing CBI 1962-87, memb Fin Ctee and sites bldgs (chm 1982-87); FCA, CEng, FIMarE; *Recreations* travel, gardening, historic buildings, education; *Clubs* MCC, Carlton; *Style—* Robert Beldam, Esq, CBE; Rocombe, Grange Rd, Horsell, Woking Surrey GU21 4DA (☎ 0483 761400)

BELDAM, Rt Hon Lord Justice; Rt Hon Sir (Alexander) Roy Asplin; PC (1989); s of George William Beldam (d 1937), of Brentford and Shiness Lodge, Lairg, and Margaret Frew Shettle, formerly Beldam, *née* Underwood; *b* 29 March 1925; *Educ* Oundle, BNC Oxford; *m* 1953, Elisabeth Bryant, da of Frank James Farr (d 1969), of Hong Kong; 2 s (Rufus, Royston), 1 da (Alexandra); *Career* served WWII Sub-Lt RNVR Air Branch 1943-46; called to the Bar 1950, QC 1969, bencher 1977; rec Crown Court 1972-81, High Court judge (Queen's Bench) 1981-89; presiding judge Wales and Chester circuit 1985; Lord Justice of Appeal 1989-; chm The Law Cmmn 1985-89; kt 1981; *Style—* The Rt Hon Lord Justice Beldam; Royal Courts of Justice, Strand, London WC2 2LL

BELFAST, Earl of; (Arthur) Patrick Chichester; s and h of 7 Marquess of Donegall; *b* 9 May 1952; *Educ* Harrow, RAC Cirencester; *m* 14 Oct 1989, Caroline M, er da of Maj Christopher Philipson, of Elmdon, Saffron Walden, Essex; 1 s (James, Viscount Chichester b 19 Nov 1990); *Heir* s, Viscount Chichester b 19 Nov 1990; *Career* Lt Coldstream Gds, ret 1977; entered Cater Allen (Bill Brokers), resigned

1986; *Recreations* shooting, racing (horses); *Style*— Earl of Belfast

BELGEONNE, Capt Peter Edward; s of Capt Oscar Victor Belgeonne, (Kt Order of Crown of Belgium), of Antwerp (d 1936), and Gabriele, *née* Gysels (d 1974); *b* 7 Dec 1915; *Educ* Antwerp, Louvain Univ; *m* 1, (m dis 1947), Terry Verellen; 2 s (Philip b 1938, Rudy b 1939), 2 da (Vivian b 1940, Nicolette b 1943); m 2, 24 July 1948, Berenice (decd), da of Charles Fletcher Lumb (d 1969); 1 s (Clive b 1958), 1 da (Alexandra b 1959); *Career* OCTU Staff Coll, Int Corps SOE, Capt 1944, served England, Belgium, Germany, France (ret 1946); chm and md English subsidiary of French Gp (Chemicals) 1951-85 (ret); formerly chm Bourbon Products Ltd, PE Belgeonne Ltd; Kt Order of Crown of Belgium 1945, Kt Order of Agric Merit France 1982; *Recreations* painting, reading, riding, travel; *Clubs* Arts London; *Style*— Capt Peter E Belgeonne; Ballycronigan, Kilrane, Co Wexford, Ireland (☎ 01035353 33185)

BELHAVEN, Master of; Hon Frederick Carmichael Arthur Hamilton; s and h of 13 Lord Belhaven and Stenton; *b* 27 Sept 1953; *Educ* Eton; *m* 1981, Elizabeth Anne, da of S V Tredinnick, of Naldretts Court, Wisborough Green, W Sussex; 2 s (William Richard b 30 Dec 1982, James Frederick b 25 Dec 1984); *Style*— The Master of Belhaven

BELHAVEN AND STENTON, Ann, Lady; (Elizabeth) Ann; da of late Col Arthur H Moseley, DSO, of Hastings Rd, Warrawee, NSW; *m* 1952 (m dis 1973), 13 Lord Belhaven and Stenton; 1 s, 1 da; *Style*— Lady Ann Belhaven and Stenton; 15 Duke St, Sydney, NSW, Australia

BELHAVEN AND STENTON, 13 Lord (S 1647); Robert Anthony Carmichael Hamilton; s of 12 Lord Belhaven and Stenton (d 1961); *b* 27 Feb 1927; *Educ* Eton; *m* 1, 1952 (m dis 1973), (Elizabeth) Ann, da of late Col Arthur Moseley, DSO, of NSW; 1 s, 1 da; m 2, 1973 (m dis 1986), Rosemary, da of Sir Herbert Williams, 1 Bt, MP (d 1954), sis of Sir Robin Williams, Bt, *qv*, and formerly w of Sir Ian Mactaggart, 3 Bt; 1 adopted da; m 3, 1986, Malgorzata Maria, da of Tadeusz Pobog Hruzik-Mazurkiewicz, of Krakow, Poland; 1 da (Alexandra Maria b 1987); *Heir* s, Master of Belhaven; *Career* Army 1945-48, cmmnd Cameronians 1947; farmer 1950-72, cook 1972-80; sits as Conservative in House of Lords; *Recreations* writing children's stories, growing vegetables; *Clubs* Army and Navy; *Style*— The Rt Hon the Lord Belhaven and Stenton; 16 Broadwater Down, Tunbridge Wells, Kent

BELL, Alan Scott; s of late Stanley Bell, of Sunderland, and late Iris, *née* Scott; *b* 8 May 1942; *Educ* Ashville Coll, Selwyn Coll Cambridge (MA), Univ of Oxford (MA); *m* 1966, Olivia, da of Prof J E Butt, FBA; 1 s (Nicolas), 1 da (Julia); *Career* asst registrar royal Cmmn on Historical Manuscripts 1963-66, asst keeper Nat Lib of Scotland 1966-81, visiting fell All Souls Coll Oxford 1980, librarian Rhodes House Library Oxford Univ 1981-; FRHistS; *Books* Sydney Smith (1980), Leslie Stephen's Mausoleum Book (ed, 1976), Lord Cockburn (1979); *Clubs* Beefsteak, Brooks's; *Style*— Alan Bell, Esq; Rhodes House Library, South Parks Rd, Oxford OX2 3RG (☎ 0865 270 907)

BELL, Dr Albert Elliot; s of James Albert Bell (d 1980), of Glasgow, and Mary Fletcher, *née* Elliot (d 1979); *b* 26 Nov 1924; *Educ* George Heriot's Sch Edinburgh, Univ of Glasgow (MA, MB ChB); *m* 15 Feb 1965, (Mary) Fiona Jean, da of James Neil McCully (d 1963), of Renton, Dunbartonshire; 3 s (Neil b 1967, Angus b 1968, Keith b 1972); *Career* sgt pilot RAF 1944-47; various positions in industry 1939-51, dep gp med supt Glasgow Royal Infirmary and assoc hosps 1962-63, asst dean faculty of med Glasgow 1963-69, med offr then sr med offr Scottish Home and Health Dept 1970-85, community med specialist Fife Health Bd 1985-87, hon sr lectr Usher Inst Univ of Edinburgh 1987-89; memb: Faculty of Community Med 1980, Faculty of Public Health Med 1989; fndr memb Br Blood Transfusion Soc; *Recreations* golf, walking, reading, music; *Clubs* Royal Dornoch Golf, Gullane Golf, Baberton Golf; *Style*— Dr Albert Bell; 6B Juniper Park Rd, Juniper Green, Midlothian EH14 5DX (☎ 031 453 3692); Department of Community Medicine, Usher Institute, University of Edinburgh, Teviot Place, Edinburgh (☎ 031 667 1011)

BELL, Maj Alexander Fulton; s of Harry Bell, OBE (d 1984), of Viewpark, St Andrews, Fife, and Sophia McDonald, *née* Fulton (d 1991); *b* 20 Jan 1937; *Educ* Shrewsbury, RMA Sandhurst, Dundee Coll of Tech and Commerce; *m* 1, 4 Jan 1969, Sophia Lilian Elizabeth Morgan (d 1971), da of Cdr Donald Hugh Elles, RN, of N Tullich, Inveraray, Argyll; 2 s (Harry b 7 Dec 1969, Thomas b 25 Feb 1971); m 2, 23 April 1984, Alison Mary, da of John Cole Compton, MBE, of Ward of Turin, Forfar, Angus; *Career* cmmnd Argyll and Sutherland Highlanders 1957, Capt HM The Queen's Gd Balmoral 1963, Adj 1 Bn Singapore/Borneo 1964-65, serv Cyprus, BAOR, Malaya, Borneo, Berlin; ADC to GOC 51 Highland Div 1966, ret 1969; Maj 1/51 Highland Vols TAVR 1972-74, Home Serv Force 1982-83; sales exec Assoc Br Maltsters 1969; ABM (parent Dalgety plc): sales mangr 1971, dir of sales 1973-87, dir of mktg Pauls Malt (parent Harrisons and Crossfield plc) 1987-89 dir of sales J P Simpson & Co (Alnwick) Ltd 1989-; chm and pres Inst of Mktg (Tayside branch) 1975-77, memb Advsy Cncl Dundee Coll of Commerce 1976-78, govr Ardvreck Sch Crieff 1982-86; MIBrew 1970, MInstM 1972, MBIM 1975, MCIM 1989; *Recreations* golf, fishing, shooting, skiing, walking; *Clubs* Royal & Ancient (St Andrews), The Hon Co of Edinburgh Golfers, Highland Bde; *Style*— Maj Alexander Bell; Drumclune, By Forfar, Angus DD8 3TS (☎ 0575 72074); Simpsons Malt Ltd, Berwick-Upon-Tweed TD15 2UZ (☎ 0289 330033, fax 0575 73477, car 0860 425136)

BELL, Sheriff Andrew Montgomery; s of James Montgomery Bell (d 1953), of Edinburgh, and Mary, *née* Cavaye (d 1975); *b* 21 Feb 1940; *Educ* The Royal HS, Univ of Edinburgh (BL); *m* 3 May 1969, Ann Margaret, da of William Robinson (d 1956), of Darlington, Durham; 1 s (James b 1972), 1 da (Lucy b 1970); *Career* slr 1961-74; Sheriff of: S Strathclyde, Dumfries and Galloway at Hamilton 1979-84, Glasgow and Strathkelvin at Glasgow 1984-90, Lothian and Borders 1990-; memb Faculty of Advocates 1975; *Style*— Sheriff Andrew Bell; Sheriff's Chambers, Sheriff Court House, Lawnmarket, Edinburgh EH1 2NG (☎ 031 226 7181)

BELL, Andrew Richard; s of Richard Erskine Bell, of Little Bookham, Surrey, and Sandra Hayhurst *née* Smith; *b* 23 July 1960; *Educ* Glyn Sch Epsom, Mansfield Coll Oxford (MA); *Career* asst dir E B Savory, Milln and Co 1981-86, assoc dir Wood MacKenzie and Co 1986-88, dir Kleinwort Benson Securities 1988-; memb: Int Stock Exchange, Soc Investment Analysts; *Recreations* skiing, horse-riding, running, tennis, football; *Clubs* RAC, United Oxford and Cambridge; *Style*— Andrew Bell, Esq; Kleinwort Benson Securities Ltd, 20 Fenchurch St, London, EC3P 3DB (☎ 01 623 8000, fax 01 623 4572, telex 922241

BELL, Ann Forrest (Mrs Robert Lang); da of Dr John Forrest Bell (d 1966), and Marjorie, *née* Byrom (d 1984); *b* 29 April 1940; *Educ* Birkenhead HS (GPDST), RADA; *m* 23 Dec 1971, Robert Lang, s of Robert Lang (d 1962); 1 da (Rebecca Catherine b 1974), 1 s (John Stephen Jervis b 1975); *Career* actress; roles for TV incl: Jane Eyre, For Whom the Bell Tolls, Three Sisters, Uncle Vanya, The Lost Boys, Double First, Tumbledown, Tenko; theatre: Old Vic Seasons, The Philanderer (NT), Veterans, Eclipse (Royal Court Theatre); *Recreations* reading, swimming, walking dogs; *Style*— Ms Ann Bell; c/o Julian Bellrage Associates, 60 St James St, London SW1 (☎ 071 491 4400)

BELL, Anthony Holbrook (Tony); s of late Alan Brewis Bell, of Abergele, Clwyd, and Kathleen Burton, *née* Holbrook, of Waco, Texas, USA; *b* 7 Nov 1930; *Educ* Haberdashers Aske's; *m* 15 Sept 1956, Lorraine Every, da of Leslie Charles Wood (d 1956), of Stanmore, Middx; 1 s (Ian Charles b 1958), 1 da (Susan Nicola (Mrs Auden) b 1960); *Career* Nat Serv cmmnd 2 Lt RA 1949, Lt 1950; chm: A H Bell and Co (Insur Brokers) Ltd 1979-80, A H Bell and Co (Fin Planning) Ltd, Bell Eteson and Co Ltd, Pennine (Derby) Insur Servs 1983-87; dir Derbyshire Bldg Soc; former: pres Insur Inst of Derby, Capt Chevin Golf Club; pres Derby RFC 1987-89; ACII 1961, ACIArb 1971, FBIBA 1974; *Recreations* golf, rugby football; *Clubs* Chevin Golf, Derby RFC; *Style*— Tony Bell, Esq; Hob Hill Cottage, Hazelwood, Derby DE6 4AL (☎ 0332 840747); AH Bell and Co (Insurance Brokers) Ltd, Avenue House, 3 Charnwood St, Derby DE1 2GT (☎ 0332 372111, fax 0332 290786, car 0860 603921)

BELL, Christopher Charles; s of Lendon Bell (d 1986), and Dorothea Anne, *née* Preston (d 1989); *b* 31 Dec 1945; *Educ* Marlborough, Pembroke Coll Cambridge (BA); *m* 1, 1969 (m dis 1976), Caroline Robey, 1 s (Edward b 5 Feb 1975), 1 da (Clarissa b 11 June 1973); m 2, 1977, Dinah, da of Col John Erskine Nicholson; 2 da (Rowena b 3 April 1981, Octavia b 9 Dec 1982); *Career* slr; articled clerk Crossman Block & Keith 1969-71, ptnr Travers Smith Braithwaite 1974- (asst slr 1971); *Style*— Christopher Bell, Esq; Travers Smith Braithewaite, 6 Snow Hill, London EC1A 2AL (☎ 071 2489133)

BELL, Christopher John; TD; s of Alfred Bell (d 1979), and Dorothy Craven, *née* Fletcher; *b* 11 Jan 1929; *Educ* Worksop Coll; *m* 1951, Margaret, da of Thomas Beaumont (d 1938); 1 s (Richard), 1 da (Susan); *Career* chm M M Bell and Sons Ltd (cardboard box mfrs); pres Br Paper Box Assoc 1978-80; pres Packaging Employers Confedn 1980-82, regnl cncl CBI 1979-82; nat treas Br Box and Packaging Assoc and Nat Packaging Confedn; dir Richard Bell Design (Leeds) Ltd; *Recreations* gardening, scouting; *Style*— Christopher Bell, Esq, TD; 529 Fulwood Rd, Sheffield (☎ 0742 305272); M M Bell & Sons Ltd, 102 Arundel St, Sheffield S1 3BA (☎ 0742 24740/29839)

BELL, Christopher Robert; s of Stanley Bell (d 1987), of Carlisle, and Alice May, *née* Sewell (d 1969); *b* 14 Sept 1942; *Educ* Carlisle GS; *m* 9 Sept 1967, Alice Anne, da of Edward Irving Latimer, of Annan, Dumfries & Galloway; 1 da (Anne b 1971); *Career* fin dir Stead McAlpin & Co Ltd 1982- (asst accountant 1966-80, accountant and co sec 1980-); hon treas Carlisle Cathedral Old Choristers Assoc; MICAS 1966; *Recreations* church organist, choral singing, railway enthusiast; *Style*— Christopher Bell, Esq; Carillon, 24 Moorville Drive South, Carlisle CA3 0AW (☎ 0228 28816); Stead McAlpin & Company Limited, Cummersdale Print Works, Carlisle CA2 6BT (☎ 0228 25224, fax 0228 512070, telex 64266 STEADM G)

BELL, Colin Murray; s of Vernon Robert Bell (d 1989), of Lymington, Hants, and Nell, *née* Yates (d 1979); *b* 11 Jan 1927; *Educ* Southgate Co Sch; *m* 9 Dec 1949, Elizabeth Fryns, da of Francois Joseph Fryns (d 1963), of La Calamine, Belgium; 3 s (Godfrey b 1951, Colin b 1952, Michael b 1959), 1 da (Teresa b 1953); *Career* RHA Sgt Europe, ME 1943-48; newspaper dir and building co chm; dir: Bennett Bros (Journal Newspapers) Ltd 1959-65 (md 1962-65), Colchester Chamber of Commerce Ltd 1968 (pres 1983-85), Weekly Newspaper Advertising Bureau 1970-80 (chm 1974-75), Audit Bureau of Circulations 1973-81 (chm 1979-81), Verified Free Distribution Ltd 1982-85 (chm 1983-5), Regional Newspaper Advertising Bureau Ltd 1980-90 (vice-chm 1985-90) Colchester Business Enterprise Agency Ltd 1982- (chm 1983-5); *Recreations* walking, golf; *Clubs* IOD; *Style*— Colin Bell, Esq; Essex County Newspapers, Oriel House, North Hill, Colchester, Essex CO1 1TZ

BELL, David Charles Maurice; s of R M Bell, of London, and M F Bell (d 1973); *b* 30 Sept 1946; *Educ* Worth Sch, Trinity Hall Cambridge (BA), Univ of Pennsylvania (MA); *m* 30 Dec 1972, Primrose Frances, da of E S Moran (d 1973); 2 s (Charles Alexander b 1978, Thomas George b 1981), 1 da (Emma Theodora b 1975); *Career* Oxford Mail and Times 1970-72; Financial Times: int ed 1978-80, asst ed feature 1980-85, managing ed 1985-89, advert dir 1989-; dir Financial Times Group 1991-, chm Islington SDP 1981-86, dir Ambache Chamber Orch 1987-; *Recreations* theatre, cycling, family, Victorian social history; *Style*— David Bell, Esq; 35 Belitha Villas, London N1 1PE (☎ 071 609 4000); Financial Times, No 1 Southwark Bridge, London SE1 9HL

BELL, Dr Donald Atkinson; s of Robert Hamilton Bell (d 1989), and Gladys Mildred, *née* Russell (d 1979); *b* 28 May 1941; *Educ* Royal Belfast Acad Inst, Queens Univ Belfast (BSc), Southampton Univ (PhD); *m* 25 March 1967, Joyce Louisa, da of James Conroy Godber; 2 s (Alistair b 1971, Richard b 1973); *Career* res asst Kings Coll London 1962-66, princ sci offr Nat Phys Lab 1966-77, dep chief sci offr DTI 1978-82, dir Nat Engng Laboratory 1983-90, visiting prof Strathclyde Univ; FIMechE 1987, MIEE 1978; *Style*— Dr Donald Bell; National Engineering Lab, East Kilbride, Glasgow G75 0QU

BELL, Douglas Maurice; CBE (1972); s of Alexander Dunlop Bell of Shanghai, China (d 1938) and Nora Sunderland (d 1966); gn of Dr Joseph Bell of Edinburgh, the original of Sherlock Holmes; *b* 15 April 1914; *Educ* Cathedral School Shanghai, The Edinburgh Academy, St Andrews University (BSc); *m* 7 Nov 1947, Elizabeth Mary, da of Charles William Edelsten, Exmouth (d 1955); 1 s (Benjamin b 1952), 2 da (Janet b 1950, Margaret b 1951); *Career* md: ICI Ltd Billingham Div 1955-57, ICI Ltd Petrochemical Div 1958-61; chm: ICI Europe Ltd 1961-73, Tioxide Ltd and assoc companies 1973-8; dir Bekaert NV (Belgium) 1973-; chm: TWIL Gp (Tinsley Wire Industries Ltd) 1978-; pres Soc of Chem Industry 1976-8; hon fell: BIM, Inst of Chem Engineering; Hon LLD St Andrews Univ; Kt Commander of Order of Civil Merit (Spain) 1971; Commander Order of Leopold II (Belgium) 1973; *Recreations* sports, gardens; *Clubs* Edinburgh Academicals, Wasps Rugby Football, St Andrews Alumis, Waterloo Golf (Brussels), Anglo Belgian, West Sussex Golf; *Style*— Douglas Bell, Esq, CBE; Stocks Cottage, West Chiltington, Sussex RH20 2JW (☎ Chiltington 2284)

BELL, Dr (Geoffrey) Duncan; s of Sqdn Ldr Robert Charles Bell, of 20 Linden Rd, Gosforth, Newcastle upon Tyne, and Phyllis Pearl Hunter Codling; *b* 19 June 1945; *Educ* Royal GS Newcastle upon Tyne, St Bartholomew's Hosp Med Coll, Univ of London (MB BS, MS, MD); *m* 21 June 1969, Joanna Victoria, da of Capt Joseph Henry Patterson (d 1981); 2 s (Jonathan b 8 March 1970, Robert b 13 Oct 1977), 2 da (Anne-Helénè b 30 Oct 1973 d 1975, Karen b 7 May 1980); *Career* lectr in med St Bartholomew's Hosp Med Sch 1973-76, sr lectr in therapeutics Univ of Nottingham 1976-83, conslt gastroenterologist Ipswich Hosp 1983-; memb Assoc of Physicians 1979, chm working party on endoscopic safety and monitoring Br Soc of Gastroenterology, fndr memb Suffolk branch Br Digestive Fndn, Hunterian prof RCS 1990; MRCS 1968, LRCP 1968, MRCP 1970, FRCP 1985; *Recreations* canoeing, boxing, rowing; *Style*— Dr Duncan Bell; Swiss Farm, Falkenham, Ipswich, Suffolk IP10 0QU (☎ 03948 249); Dept of Medicine, The Ipswich Hospital, Ipswich, Suffolk IP4 5DP (☎ 0473 712233)

BELL, Gavin Paterson; s of Gavin Bell, and Annie, *née* Gribbin; *b* 29 July 1947; *Educ* Hutcheson's Boys GS Glasgow; *Career* political reporter; apprentice Scottish Daily Mail and Daily Record 1966-71, Agence France-Presse Paris 1971-73, National Enquirer Florida 1973-75, Reuters (based in London, Beirut and Paris) 1975-86, The Times (based in London, Delhi, Seoul and Johannesburg) 1986-, currently SA corr; carried Olympic torch at Seoul Games Korea 1988; *Recreations* reading, writing, running, retracing travels of Robert Louis Stevenson; *Clubs* Bellahouston Harriers Glasgow; *Style*— Gavin Bell, Esq; The Times, 1 Pennington St, London E1 9XN (☎

Johannesburg 0102711 290780, fax 0102711 234619)

BELL, Sir Gawain Westray; KCMG (1957), CBE (1955, MBE mil 1942); s of William Westray Bell (d 1947); *b* 21 Jan 1909; *Educ* Winchester, Univ of Oxford (BA); *m* 1945, Silvia, da of Maj Adrian Cornwell-Clyne, MBE (d 1969); 3 da; *Career* 2 Lt TA 1929-32, served WWII ME, Kaimakam Col Arab Legion; Sudan Political Serv 1931, seconded to Palestine Govt 1938-41, dist cmmr Sudan Political Serv 1945-49, dep Sudan agent Cairo 1949-51, dep civil sec Sudan Govt 1953-54, perm sec Miny of Interior Sudan 1954-55; HM Political Agent Kuwait 1955-57, govr Northern Nigeria 1957-62; sec gen: Cncl ME Trade 1963-64, S Pacific Cmmn 1967-70; vice-pres: Exec Ctee LEPRA 1984- (chm 1972-84), Anglo-Jordanian Soc 1985-; pt/t chm CS Selection Bds 1972-77; memb Govt Body SOAS Univ of London 1971-81; Order of Independence 3 Class (Jordan) 1944; KStJ 1959 (memb Chapter Gen 1964-89); *Books* Shadows on the Sand (1983), An Imperial Twilight (1989); *Recreations* walking, riding, gardening, swimming; *Clubs* Army and Navy; *Style—* Sir Gawain Bell, KCMG, CBE; 6 Hildesley Court, East Ilsley, Berks RG16 0LA (☎ 063 528 554)

BELL, Hon Mrs (Heather Doreen); *née* Parnell; yst da of 6 Baron Congleton (d 1932), and Hon Edith Mary Palmer Howard, MBE (d 1980), da of Baroness Strathcona and Mount Royal in her own right; *b* 11 Jan 1929; *m* 23 April 1960, (Robert) Peter Mangin Bell, *qv*; 2 s, 1 da; *Style—* The Hon Mrs Bell; Sarsen House, 5 Mead Rd, St Cross, Winchester, Hants (☎ 0962 65320)

BELL, Ian; s of John Robert Bell (d 1967); *b* 29 May 1942; *Educ* Hymers Coll Hull; *m* 1965, Kate, da of George Stead; 3 s (James b 1969, Charles b 1971, Nicholas b 1977); *Career* asst gen mangr Leeds Permanent Bldg Soc 1977-81, gen mangr (Devpt) Provincial Bldg Soc 1981-82, gen mangr (Ops) Nat and Prov Bldg Soc 1983-87, md Town and Country Bldg Soc 1987, local dir Commercial Union Assur Co Ltd; chm Met Assoc of Bldg Socs; Freeman City of London; FCII, FCBSI, MBIM; *Recreations* shooting, skiing, sailing; *Style—* Ian Bell, Esq; 52 Hurlingham Rd, Fulham, London SW6 3RQ; Town and Country Bldg Soc, 12 Devereux Ct, London WC2R 3JJ (☎ 071 353 2438, fax 071 353 2933)

BELL, Rear Adm John Anthony; CB (1977); s of Mathew Bell (d 1948), of Dundee, and Mary Ann Ellen, *née* Goss (d 1979); *b* 25 Nov 1924; *Educ* St Ignatius Coll, Univ Coll of S Wales (BA, BSc, LLB); *m* 1946, (Eileen) Joan, da of Daniel Woodman (d 1934); 3 da; *Career* RM 1943-45, RAN 1948-52, SACLANT USA 1961-64, dir Naval MET 1973-75, Rear Adm 1975, dir Naval Educn 1975-79; called to the Bar Gray's Inn 1970; educn sec BBC 1979-83; vice-pres United Servs Catholic Assoc 1979-; chm Kent Ecumenical Cmmn 1982-; pres Kent Area RN Assoc 1982-; vice pres RN Assoc 1983-; dep chm Police Complaints Bd 1983-; KSG 1983; *Recreations* swimming, travel, France; *Style—* Rear Adm John Bell, CB; The Beild, Conifer Ave, Hartley, Kent DA3 8BX (☎ 047 47 2485)

BELL, Sir John Lowthian; 5 Bt (UK 1885); s of Sir Hugh Francis Bell, 4 Bt (d 1970); *b* 14 June 1960; *Educ* Glenalmond, RAC Cirencester; *m* 22 June 1985, Venetia Mary Frances, 2 da of J A Perry, of Llanstefan, Monkton Heathfield, Taunton, Somerset; 1 s (John Hugh b 1988); *Heir* s, John Hugh Bell b 1988; *Career* farmer; *Recreations* fishing, shooting; *Style—* Sir John Bell, Bt; Arncliffe Hall, Ingleby Cross, Northallerton, N Yorks (☎ 060 982 202)

BELL, John Nicholson; s of John Joseph Bell (d 1973), and Mary Annie, *née* Wills of 2 Fell View, Wigton; *b* 14 Dec 1947; *Educ* Nelson Thomlinson GS Wigton, Univ of Manchester (BA); *m* 10 Aug 1979, Jeanette Wynn, da of Thomas Arthur Jones; 1 s (John Alexander b 9 Feb 1987), 1 da (Emma Jane b 18 Aug 1980); *Career* bowls player; memb: Wigton Throstle Nest Bowling Club 1960-70, Wigton Bowling Club 1970-, England Outdoor Int team (39 caps) 1978-, England Indoor Int team (24 caps) 1983-, 5 man England team World Bowls Championships (Melbourne 1980, Aberdeen 1984, Auckland 1988); minor championship wins: 9 Outdoor Club Singles, 3 Cumbria Indoor Singles, 3 Cumbria Champion of Champions Singles; runner up: Granada Superbowl Singles 1984, EIBA Nat Singles 1984, Hong Kong Int Singles 1983 and 1984, EBA Nat Triples 1985; Bronze medallist EBA Gateway Masters 1985; major titles incl: EBA Triples champion 1976, EBA Singles Champion 1983, Gold medallist (World Fours) 1984, Br Isles Singles champion 1984, Gold medallist (world team) 1980 and 1988; Bronze medallist (World Fours & Triples) 1988; played rugby for Cumbria (full-back) 1972-75; currently asst dir for Mktg promotion and tourism Econ, Devpt & Planning Dept Carlisle City Cncl (joined 1970); Cumbria Sports Personality of Year 1979, pres of Cumbria County Bowling Assoc 1981, winner Vaux Silver Star award 1979, 1980 and 1984; *Recreations* music, humour (after dinner speaking); *Style—* John Bell, Esq; Bangla, Cross Lane, Wigton, Cumbria (☎ 06973 43124)

BELL, John Sydney; s of Percy Bell (d 1970),of Northampton, and Florence Annie, *née* Jones; *b* 5 Oct 1930; *Educ* Northampton GS, St Catharine's Coll Cambridge, (MA); *m* 5 March 1966, Margot Diana, da of Wing Cdr Cedric Alfred Wright, of Worlebury, Weston-Super-Mare; 2 s (Stuart b 1967, Edward b 1971), 1 da (Caroline b 1969); *Career* Nat Serv RAF Pilot Offr 1949-50; admitted slr 1957, ptnr Aplin Stockton Fairfax , Slrs 1968- (sr ptnr 1987-), Notary Public, clerk to Cmmrs of Income Tax; chm N Oxfordshire Cons Assoc 1980-85 (vice pres 1986-), pres Banbury C of C 1986-87; memb Law Soc 1957; *Recreations* horticulture, model engrg; *Style—* John Bell, Esq; The Manor House, Overthorpe, Banbury, Oxon (☎ 0295 710005); Aplin Stockton Fairfax , 36 West Bar, Banbury, Oxon (☎ 0295 251234)

BELL, Joseph; CBE (1953); s of Joseph Bell (d 1941), and Elizabeth, *née* Phillips (d 1926); *b* 15 July 1899; *Educ* Alderman Wood Sch Co Durham; *m* 1926, Edith (d 1980), da of Matthew Adamson (d 1909); 1 s (Joseph Arthur), 1 da (Constance, d 1953); *Career* RNVR 1917-19; Newcastle upon Tyne City Police 1919-33; chief constable Hastings 1933-41; asst chief constable City of Manchester 1941-43 (chief constable 1943-58); ret 1958; *Style—* Joseph Bell, Esq, CBE; Norwood, 246 Windlehurst Rd, Marple, Cheshire SK6 7EN (☎ 01 427 3129)

BELL, Col (Francis Cecil) Leonard; DSO (1945), MC (1943), TD (1949); s of Cecil Walker Bell (d 1947), of Lincolnshire, and Frances Ethel, *née* Heath (d 1967); *b* 25 Sept 1912; *Educ* St Christopher's Eastbourne, Gresham's; *m* 16 Dec 1942, Mary Wynne, da of Lt Col A L B Jacob, DSO (d 1958), of Surrey; 1 s (Simon b 1949), 1 da (Elizabeth b 1943); *Career* Lt Col cmd 6 Bn Lincolnshire Regt 1944-45; (despatches 1940, 1943, & 1945) served Dunkirk, N Africa, Italy, Greece; Hon Col 4/6 Bn Royal Lincolnshire Regt 1962-67; Hon Col Royal Lincolnshire Regt TA 1967; slr 1936, legal advsr Lloyds Bank plc 1965-76, chm Legal Ctee Banking Fedn of EEC 1974-75; *Recreations* fishing, shooting; *Style—* Col Leonard Bell, DSO, MC, TD; Cross Glades, Chiddingfold, Godalming, Surrey (☎ 042 868 3430)

BELL, Lady Lilias Catriona Maighearad; *née* Graham; yst da of 7 Duke of Montrose, *qv*; *b* 16 Feb 1960; *Educ* Univ of St Andrew's (Robert T Jones meml scholarship); *m* 7 July 1990, Jonathan D Bell, s of Michael Bell, of N Z; *Career* mgmnt devpt conslt; *Style—* The Lady Lilias Bell; Montrose Estates, Drymen, by Glasgow

BELL, Martin George Henry; s of Leonard George Bell (d 1968), of Loughton, and Phyllis, *née* Green; *b* 16 Jan 1935; *Educ* Charterhouse; *m* 2 Jan 1965, Shirley, da of William Henry Wrightson (d 1960), of Bournemouth; 2 s (Thomas b 1966, Jeremy b 1969); *Career* admitted slr 1961, sr ptnr Ashurst Morris Crisp (ptnr 1963-); Freeman City of London, memb Worshipful Co of Slrs; memb: Law Soc, Int Bar Assoc; assoc memb American Bar Assoc; *Style—* Martin Bell, Esq; Mulberry, Woodbury Hill, Loughton, Essex IG10 1JB (☎ 081 508 1188); Broadgate House, 7 Eldon Street, London EC2M 7HD (☎ 071 247 7666, fax 071 377 5659, telex 887067 ASHLAW)

BELL, Martin Irvine; MBE (1985); s of George Alfred Bell (d 1975), and Margaret Martin, *née* Young; *b* 9 Dec 1938; *Educ* King's Park Sr Secdy Sch, Univ of Glasgow (BSc); *m* 5 Sept 1962, Joyce Hislop, da of John Shearer (d 1972); 1 s (Adrian b 1971), 1 da (Fiona b 1965); *Career* engrg dir Barr and Stroud Ltd 1984-85 (asst md operations 1985, chief exec 1988-), chm and non-exec dir A and S Engineering Designs 1985-; *Recreations* sailing, skiing, squash, music, reading; *Clubs* Royal Northern and Clyde Yacht, Helensburgh Sailing; *Style—* Martin Bell, Esq, MBE; 7 Lower Sutherland Crescent, Helensburgh, Dunbartonshire G84 9PG (☎ 0436 72606); Barr and Stroud Ltd, Caxton St, Anniesland, Glasgow G13 1HZ (☎ 041 954 9601, telex 778114 BS GLWG, fax 041 954 2380)

BELL, Martin Neil; s of Flt Lt Arthur Rodney Bell, RAF, of Harrogate, and Dorothy Jean, *née* Little; *b* 6 Dec 1964; *Educ* George Watson's Coll Edinburgh, Internatsschule Für Skisportler Stams Austria; *Career* skier; British champion: jr 1978-80, slalom 1981, 1987 and 1989, giant slalom 1980 and 1986, downhill 1981 and 1986; Australia and NZ Cup winner 1981, Australian slalom champion 1981, FIS downhill winner Italy 1985, fifth World Cup downhill Sweden 1986, FIS Super G winner Canada 1986, eigth Olympic downhill Canada 1988 (best Br men's Olympic skier Ski Survey Magazine); ski coach Harrogate Ski Centre, conslt ICI Tactel; Br Ski Fedn Rep British Olympic Ctee; *Books* The British Ski Federation Guide to Better Skiing (contrib, 1986), Let's Go Skiing (1990); *Recreations* tennis, squash, football, volleyball, grass skiing; *Clubs* Kandahar, Harrogate Ski, Scottish Ski, Ski Club of GB, Riverside Racquet Centre; *Style—* Martin Bell, Esq; 32 Wildcroft Manor, London SW15 3TT (☎ 081 785 6589); IMG, The Pier House, Strand-on-the-Green, London W4 3NN (☎ 081 994 1444, fax 071 935 5820)

BELL, Mary, Lady; Mary; JP (Yorks 1972); da of George Howson, MC (d 1936), of Hambledon Bucks; *b* 2 Nov 1923; *Educ* Univ of Edinburgh (MB ChB, DObst, RCOG); *m* 1959, as his 2 w, Sir Hugh Francis Bell, 4 Bt (d 1970); 4 s (*see* Sir John Bell, 5 Bt); *Career* ret doctor; farmer; *Recreations* travel, reading history; *Clubs* Farmers'; *Style—* Mary, Lady Bell, JP; The Hollins, East Rounton, Northallerton, N Yorks DL6 2LG (☎ 060 982 617)

BELL, Michael Jaffray de Hauteville; s of Capt C L de Hauteville Bell, DSC, RD, RNR (d 1972); *b* 7 April 1941; *Educ* Charterhouse; *m* 1965, Christine Mary, *née* Morgan; 1 s, 4 da; *Career* ptnr R Watson and Sons 1967-, actuary to various life assurance cos in UK and overseas; FIA 1964, ASA, FPMI; *Style—* Michael Bell, Esq; R Watson & Sons, Watson House, London Rd, Reigate, Surrey RH2 9PQ

BELL, Michael John Vincent; s of Christopher Richard Vincent, OBE, and Violet Irene Edith Lorna (Jane) Bell, MBE (d 1989), of Ditchling, Sussex; *b* 9 Sept 1941; *Educ* Winchester, Magdalen Coll Oxford; *m* 3 Sept 1983, Mary, da of John William Shippen (d 1957), of Shiremoor, Northumberland; 1 s (John b 1985), 2 da (Julia b 1987, Jane b 1989); *Career* res assoc Inst for Strategic Studies 1964-65, asst princ MOD 1965, asst private sec to Sec of State for Def 1968-69, princ MOD 1969, private sec to Perm Under Sec MOD 1973-75, asst sec MOD 1975, on loan to HM Treasy 1977-79, asst under sec MOD 1982, asst sec gen def planning and policy NATO 1986-88, dep under sec of state (Fin) MOD; *Recreations* motor cycling, mil history; *Style—* Michael Bell, Esq; MOD, London SW1A 2HB (☎ 071 218 6182)

BELL, (William) Michael; s of William Bell, and Hilda, *née* Taylor (d 1984); *b* 16 Sept 1944; *Educ* Berwick upon Tweed GS; *m* 4 Oct 1969, Helen Robina, da of William John Brown (d 1978), of Langleeford, Wooler, Northumberland; 3 da (Alison b 1971, Sarah b 1974, Lesley b 1977); *Career* CA; Thornton Baker & Co 1967-70, G A Wheeler & Co Wisbech 1970 (ptnr 1972-); memb Wisbech Rotary 1982- (hon asst sec 1985-87, hon sec 1987-), clerk to and govr St Peter's Junior Sch Wisbech 1971-, memb St Peter and St Paul PCC 1972-85 (hon treas 1972-85); FCA; *Recreations* golf; *Clubs* Sutton Bridge Golf (capt 1989-90, hon treas 1983-), Thetford Golf; *Style—* Michael Bell, Esq; Apple Acre, Park Lane, Leverington, Wisbech, Cambs PE13 5EH (☎ 0945 870 736); G A Wheeler & Co, 30 Old Market, Wisbech, Cambs PE13 1NE (☎ 0945 582 547)

BELL, Dr Patrick Michael; s of Benjamin Jonathan Bell (d 1982), and Jane, *née* McIllveen; *b* 9 March 1953; *Educ* Friends Sch Lisburn Co Antrim, Queens Univ Belfast (MB BCh, BAO, MD); *m* 28 June 1979, (Dorothy Lavina) Patricia, da of Canon Leslie Walker, of Larch House, Ballylesson, Co Down; 1 s (Jonathan b 1987), 2 da (Jane b 1980, Katie b 1982); *Career* DHSS res fell Royal Victoria Hosp and Belfast City Hosp 1981-82; sr registrar Royal Victoria Hosp 1982-84, Mayo Fndn fell in endocrinology Mayo Clinic USA 1984-85, sr registrar Belfast City Hosp 1985-86, conslt physician Royal Victoria Hosp 1986-; Central Exec Ctee and policy convenor Alliance Pty of NI; MRCP 1979, FRCP (Glas) 1988, MRCPI 1989; *Books* Multiple Choice Questions in Medicine (1981); *Style—* Dr Patrick Bell; 14 Clonevin Park, Lisburn, Co Antrim BT29 3BL (☎ 0846 674703); Wards 9 and 10, Royal Victoria Hospital, Grosvenor Rd, Belfast BT12 6BA (☎ 0232 240503 ext 3423)

BELL, Prof Peter Frank; s of Frank Bell, of Sheffield, and Ruby, *née* Corks; *b* 12 June 1938; *Educ* Univ of Sheffield (MB ChB); *m* 26 Aug 1961, Anne, da of Oliver Jennings (d 1981), of Dewsbury, Yorks; 1 s (Mark b 1967), 2 da (Jane Marie b 1962, Louise b 1963); *Career* registrar in surgery Sheffield Health Bd Sheffield Yorks 1963-65, Sir Henry Wellcome Travelling Fell Wellcome Fndn Denver Coll USA 1968-69 sr lectr in surgery Univ of Glasgow 1969-74 (lectr 1963-68), Fndn prof of surgery Univ of Leics 1974-; author numerous articles in learned jls; memb Leics Orgn for Relief of Suffering, chm Organising Ctee Transplant Games, former pres Surgical Res Soc, former sec Int Transplantation Soc; FRCS 1965, FRCS Glasgow 1969; *Books* Operative Arterial Surgery (1983), Surgical Aspects of Haemodialysts (1985), Vascular Surgery (ed and contrib, 1985), Arterial Surgery of the Lower Limb (1991); *Recreations* painting, gardening, woodwork; *Clubs* Leics; *Style—* Prof Peter Bell; 22 Powys Ave, Oadby, Leicester (☎ 0533 709579); Department of Surgery, Clinical Sciences Building, Leicester Royal Infirmary, Leicester LE2 7LX (☎ 0533 523142)

BELL, Prof Quentin (Claudian Stephen); 2 s of Clive Bell (d 1964), the author and art critic, and Vanessa, *née* Stephen (d 1961), the artist; nephew of Virginia Woolf; *b* 19 Aug 1910; *m* 1952, Anne Olivier Popham; 1 s, 2 da; *Career* painter, potter, author; emeritus prof of history and theory of art Univ of Sussex; DLitt Newcastle 1983; FRSA, FRSL; *Books* Ruskin (1963), Bloomsbury (1968), Virginia Woolf, a biography (1972), A New and Noble School (1982), The Brandon Papers (1985), Bad Art (1989); *Clubs* Reform; *Style—* Prof Quentin Bell; 81 Heighton Street, Firle, Sussex

BELL, Quentin Ross; s of Ross Bell, and Violet Martha, *née* Douglas; *b* 24 June 1944; *Educ* Presentation Coll Reading; *m* Hilary Sian, da of Vernon Jones; 2 da (Verity Ross, Henrietta Ross); *Career* various positions: Reading Standard, Thomson Newspapers, Haymarket Publishing, Safari Holidays, Bell Capper Assoc; presently The Quentin Bell Organization plc 1973-; MIPR, MInstD, memb Chartered Inst of Mktg; *Books* How To Win in PR; *Recreations* collecting art, clocks, watches and parrots, cars, wine, walking; *Clubs* RAC; *Style—* Quentin Bell, Esq; Rydal Mount, Heath Rd, Weybridge, Surrey KT13 8SX (☎ 0932 844945); Watermill Lodge, Eggesford, Chulmleigh, Devon; La Cohérance, Crespin 81350, Valderies, Tarn, France; The Quentin Bell Organization plc, 22 Endell St, Covent Garden, London WC2H 9AD (☎ 071 379 0304, fax 071 379 5483, car 0836

BELL, Sir (George) Raymond; KCMG (1973), CB (1967); eldest s of William Bell (d 1954), of Bradford, and Christabel, *née* Appleton; *b* 13 March 1916; *Educ* Bradford GS, St John's Coll Cambridge; *m* 1944, Joan Elizabeth, o da of William George (d 1951), of London, and Christina Coltham; 2 s, 2 da; *Career* WW II Lt RNVR; entered Civil Serv 1938, sec Fin Office of UK High Cmmr (Canada) 1945-48, dep sec HM Treasy 1966-72 (asst sec 1951, under sec 1960), memb UK delgn to Brussels Conf 1961-62 and 1970-72, vice pres Euro Investmt Bank 1973-78, ret 1978; hon vice pres EIB 1978-; *Style—* Sir Raymond Bell, KCMG, CB; Quartier des Bories, Aouste-sur-Sye, 26400 Crest, Drôme, France (☎ 75 25 26 94)

BELL, (John) Robin Sinclair; s of Ian Cardean Bell, OBE, MC (d 1967), of Edinburgh, and Cecile *née* Rutherford (d 1980); *b* 28 Feb 1933; *Educ* The Edinburgh Acad, Loretto Sch, Worcester Coll, Oxford (BA), Univ of Edinburgh (LLB); *m* 27 Apr 1963, Patricia, da of Edward Upton, of Whitby, N Yorkshire; 4 s (Charles b 1965, d 1969, Patrick b 1967, Peter b 1970, Jonathan b 1972); *Career* Nat Serv cmmnd Royal Scots Berlin 1951-53, Capt TA 1953-63; slr; Coward Chance slrs 1961-62, sr ptnr Tods Murray WS Edinburgh 1987 (ptnr 1963); non-exec dir: Edinburgh Financial Trust plc 1983-87, Upton and Southern Holdings plc; memb Cncl Law Soc Scotland 1975-78; memb Co Law Ctee Law Soc Scotland; *Recreations* salmon fishing, gardening; *Clubs* New (Edinburgh), The Royal Scots (Edinburgh); *Style—* Robin Bell, Esq; 66 Queen St, Edinburgh EH2 4NE (☎ 031 226 4771)

BELL, Rodger; QC (1982); s of John Thornton Bell (d 1974), and Edith, *née* Rodger; *b* 13 Sept 1939; *Educ* Brentwood Sch, BNC Oxford; *m* 27 Sept 1969, (Sylvia) Claire, only surv da of William Eden Tatton Brown, CB, of Berkhamsted, Herts, by his w Aileen Hope Johnston, da of late Joseph Knox Sparrow, MC; 1 s (Benjamin b 1970), 3 da (Natasha b 1972, Lucinda b 1975, Sophie b 1982); called to the Bar Middle Temple 1963; rec of Crown Ct 1980, legal memb Mental Health Review Tbnl 1983, memb Parole Bd 1990; *Recreations* running, rowing; *Clubs* Thames Hare and Hounds, Achilles, Dacre Boat, Thames Rowing; *Style—* Rodger Bell, Esq, QC; 14 Castello Avenue, London SW15 6EA (☎ 081 788 3857); 1 Crown Office Row, Temple, London EC4Y 7HH (☎ 071 353 1801)

BELL, Roger Wallace; s of Frederick Nelson Bell, and Kathleen Joyce, *née* Slater; *b* 23 June 1941; *Educ* Primary Sch Trinidad W Indies, Gosfield's Boy's Sch Essex; *m* 1, Sally Warick (m dis); 2 da (Deborah Jane b 1964, Joanne Louise b 1966); m 2, June 1988, Pamela Annette, *née* Nolan; *Career* articled Edmond D White 1958-67; site accountant Br Oxygen Co Ltd 1967-69, fin controller Hoke Int Ltd 1969-73, co accountant John Brown Earl & Wright Ltd 1973-80, accounting mangr John Brown Engrg Ltd 1980-83, fin controller Earl and Wright Ltd 1983-86; computer consult 1986- (practice suspended since heart transplant in 1988); treas Br Heart Fndn (Reading Branch) 1988-; FCA; *Recreations* computer programming, walking, reading, travel, fund raising; *Style—* Roger Bell, Esq; 25 Purfield Drive, Wargrave, Berkshire, RG10 8AP (☎ 075322 2720)

BELL, (Alexander) Scott; s of William Scott Bell (d 1973), of Falkirk, Scotland, and Catherine Irene, *née* Traill; *b* 4 Dec 1941; *Educ* Daniel Stewart's Coll Edinburgh; *m* 12 Oct 1965, Veronica Jane, da of James Simpson (d 1985), of Edinburgh; 2 s (Scott b 1968, David b 1970), 1 da (Victoria b 1974); *Career* md Standard Life Assur Co 1988- (joined 1958); dir: Bank of Scotland 1988-, The Hammerson Property Investmt and Devpt Corpn plc 1988-, Scottish Fin Enterprise 1989-; FFA 1966, FPMI 1978; *Recreations* golf, travel, reading; *Clubs* New (Edinburgh), Bruntsfield Links Golfing Soc; *Style—* Scott Bell, Esq; Standard Life Assurance Co, 3 George St, Edinburgh EH2 2XZ (☎ 031 245 6011, fax 031 245 6010, telex 72530)

BELL, Hon Mrs (Serena Frances); *née* Fairfax ; da of 13 Lord Fairfax of Cameron (d 1964); *b* 12 Dec 1952; *m* 1976, W Robert G Bell; 1 s (b 1986), 2 da; *Style—* The Hon Mrs Bell

BELL, Sheriff Principal Stewart Edward; QC (1982); s of Charles Edward Bell (d 1947), of 9 Botanic Crescent, Glasgow, and Rosalind, *née* Stewart (d 1964); *b* 4 Aug 1919; *Educ* Kelvinside Acad Glasgow, Trinity Hall Cambridge (BA, MA), Univ of Glasgow (LLB); *m* 1, 1948, Isla Janet Malcolm (d 1983), da of James Spencer (d 1978), of Jersey; 3 da (Adelin, Fiona, Linda); m 2, 1985, Margaret Virginia, da of Andrew St Clair Jameson (d 1978), of Edinburgh; 2 step da (Virginia, Jane); *Career* WWII cmmnd Loyal Regt 1939, serv Singapore, Malaya Lt (POW); advocate 1948-61, sheriff Glasgow 1961-82, sheriff princ of Grampian Highland and Islands 1983-88; *Recreations* highland bagpipe; *Clubs* New (Edinburgh); *Style—* Sheriff Principal Stewart Bell, QC; 14 Napier Rd, Edinburgh EH10 5AY (☎ 031 229 9822)

BELL, Stuart; MP (Lab) Middlesbrough 1983-; s of Ernest and Margaret Rose Bell; *Educ* Hookergate GS Durham; *m* 1, 1960, Margaret, da of Mary Bruce; 1 s, 1 da; m 2, Margaret, da of Mary Allan; 1 s; *Career* barr Gray's Inn; sometime journalist; joined Lab Pty 1964, contested (Lab) Hexham 1979, memb Newcastle City Cncl 1980-83; legal advsr Trade Unions for Lab Victory N Region; PPS to Dep Ldr Lab Pty (Rt Hon Roy Hattersley); memb: Police and Criminal Evidence Bill Ctee, Soc of Labour Lawyers, Fabian Soc, Co-operative Soc, Gen and Municipal Boilermakers and Allied Trade Union; front bench spokesman for the Oppn on NI 1984; fndr memb Br-Irish Parly Body 1990; memb Children's Bill Ctee 1989; *Publications* Paris 69, Days That Used To Be, When Salem Came to the Boro, How to Abolish the Lords (Fabian tract), The Principles of US Customs Valuation (legal pubn), Annotation of the Children Act (legal pubn); *Recreations* short story and novel writing; *Style—* Stuart Bell, Esq, MP; House of Commons, London SW1A 0AA

BELL, Sir Tim John Leigh; s of Arthur Leigh Bell (d 1963), of SA, and Greta Mary, *née* Findlay; *b* 18 Oct 1941; *Educ* Queen Elizabeth GS Barnet Herts; *m* 11 July 1988, Virginia Wallis, da of Dr John Wallis Hornbrook, of Sydney, Aust; 1 da (Daisy Alicia Wallis b 1988); *Career* md Saatchi & Saatchi 1970-75, chm and md Saatchi & Saatchi Compton 1975-85, gp chief exec Lowe Howard-Spink Campbell Ewald 1985-87, special advsr to chm NCB, dep chm Lowe Howard-Spink & Bell 1987-89, chm Lowe Bell Communications 1987-; chm: Pub Affrs Ctee WWF, Fund Raising Ctee Sports Aid Fndn, PR Ctee Gtr London Fund for Blind 1979-86, Cncl Royal Opera House 1982-85, Steering Ctee Per Cent Club; memb Indust Ctee Save The Children, govr BFI 1983-86; FIPA; Kt 1990; *Recreations* golf, politics; *Clubs* Harry's, Marks, RAC; *Style—* Sir Tim Bell; Lowe Bell Communications, 7 Hertford St, London W1Y 7DY (☎ 071 495 4044, fax 071 491 9860)

BELL, William Archibald Ottley Juxon; s of William Archibald Juxon Bell (d 1970), late of Pendell Court, of Bletchingley Surrey, and Mary Isabel Maude, *née* Ottley (d 1969); *b* 7 July 1919; *Educ* Eton, Trinity Coll Oxford (MA); *m* 19 July 1947, Belinda Mary, da of Geoffrey Dawson (d 1944), of Langcliffe Hall, Settle, and late Hon Cecilia, *née* Lawley; 2 s (Robert b 1950, Nicholas b 1952), 3 da (Georgiana (Mrs Heskins) b 1948, Caroline (Mrs Llewellyn) b 1955, Joanna (Mrs Goodwin) b 1958); *Career* WWII Temp Capt Welsh Gds 1940-45; served: N Africa, Italy, Austria; FO: entered 1945, Egyptian dept 1945-46, political private sec to High Cmmr India 1946-47; private sec to exec dirs Br South Africa Company 1947-50, dir King & Shaxson plc (Bill-brokers) 1950- (md 1950-70); memb for Chelsea GLC & ILEA 1970-86; chm: Diocesan Bd of Fin Oxfordshire 1974-75, GLC Historic Bldgs Ctee 1977-81, Heritage of London Tst 1980- (fndr), Oxfordshire Bldgs Tst 1987-; memb: London Advsy Ctee English Heritage 1986-90, Ctee Oxfordshire Historic Churches Tst; High Sheriff Oxfordshire 1978-79; *Recreations* shooting, golf tennis, painting; *Clubs* White's, Pratt's; *Style—* William Bell Esq; 165 Cranmer Ct, London SW3 3HF (☎ 071 589 1033); Cottisford House, nr Brackley, Northamptonshire NN13 5SW (☎ 02804 848247); c/o English Heritage, Chesham House, 30 Warwick St, London W1R 6AB (☎ 01 734 8144)

BELL, William Edwin; CBE (1980); s of Cuthbert Edwin Bell (d 1961), and Winifred Mary, *née* Simpson; *b* 4 Aug 1926; *Educ* Birmingham Univ, Royal Sch of Mines; *m* 1952, Angela Josephine, da of Flt Lt E Vaughan, MC (d 1931); 2 s, 2 da; *Career* exec Royal Dutch/Shell Gp, dir Shell Int 1980-84, non exec dir Costain Gp plc, chm Enterprise Oil plc 1984-; CBIM, FInstPet; *Recreations* golf, sailing (yacht 'Bel Esprit'); *Clubs* Chichester Yacht, Nevill Golf; *Style—* William Bell, Esq, CBE; Fordcombe Manor, nr Tunbridge Wells, Kent

BELL, William Lewis; CMG (1970), MBE (1945); s of Frederick Robinson Bell (d 1957), of Cheltenham, and Kate Harper, *née* Lewis (d 1984); *b* 31 Dec 1919; *Educ* Hymers Coll Hull, Oriel Coll Oxford; *m* 1 Sept 1943, Margaret, da of William Giles (d 1957), of Carmarthen; 1 s (Richard Jeremy Giles), 1 da (Rosalind Margaret (Mrs N S Bowlby)); *Career* Glos Regt 1940-46: Capt and Adj 2 Bn 1942, Maj and DAAG 49 WR Inf Div 1943-46; HM Colonial Admin Serv Uganda: Dist offr 1946-54, asst fin sec 1954, dep sec to Treasy 1956, perm sec to Min of Educn 1958-62; dir Cox & Danks Ltd MI Gp 1963-64, sec Westfield Coll Univ of London 1964-65, founding head Br Devpt Div for Caribbean Miny of Overseas Devpt 1966, UK dir Caribbean Devpt Bank 1970-72, founding dir gen Tech Educn & Trg Orgn Miny of Overseas Devpt 1972-77, info offr Univ of Oxford 1977-84; chm Uganda Nat Parks 1962, pres Uganda Sports Union 1961-62; fell Econ Devpt Inst World Bank 1958; *Recreations* watching cricket, Caribbeana, gardening; *Clubs* MCC, Vincent's; *Style—* William Bell, Esq, CMG, MBE; Hungry Hatch, Fletching, E Sussex, TN22 3SH (☎ 082 572 3415)

BELL DAVIES, Vice Adm Sir Lancelot Richard; KBE (1977); s of Vice Adm Richard Bell Davies, VC, CB, DSO, AFC (d 1966), and Mary Pipon Bell Davies, *née* Montgomery (d 1975); f VC Gallipoli Campaign one of the first RNAS pilots; *b* 18 Feb 1926; *Educ* Boxgrove Sch Guildford, RNC Dartmouth (13 year old entry); *m* 1949, Emmeline Joan, da of Prof G J H Molengraaff (d 1961), of Holland; 1 s (Richard William b 1955), 2 da (Emmeline Anne b 1950, Daphane Alexandra b 1956); *Career* Midshipman HMS Norfolk 1943 Battle of North Cape, joined submarines 1944; cmd: HMS Subtle 1953, HMS Explorer 1955, HMS Leander 1962, HMS Forth 1967; dir naval warfare 1969, Capt HMS Bulwark 1972-73, naval attaché Washington DC 1973-75, supreme allied cdr Atlantic Rep Europe 1975-78, cmdt NATO Def Coll Rome 1978-81; chm Sea Cadet Cncl 1983; CBIM; *Recreations* sailing, gardening; *Clubs* Royal Yacht Sqdn, Naval and Military, RNSA; *Style—* Vice Adm Sir Lancelot Bell Davies, KBE; Holly Hill Lodge, 123 Barnes Lane, Sarisbury Green SO3 6BH (☎ 04895 73131)

BELL-SALTER, David Basil; s of Capt Basil Owen Bell-Salter, RN (d 1976), and May Bowcher, *née* Tustin (d 1985); *b* 22 Jan 1921; *Educ* Imperial Service Coll Windsor; *m* 21 April 1942, Elfia, da of Maj Adolph Kagans (d 1964); 1 da (Maria Cristina b 17 Oct 1961); *Career* RAF 1939-46, Flt Lt Fighter Cmd, fought in France May 1940 and Battle of Britain Aug/Sept 1940; int timber specialist and conslt; Montague L Meyer Ltd 1946-57, Colonial Devpt Corpn 1957-61, gen mangr Br Guiana Timbers Ltd 1959-61, emigrated NY USA; mangr Balfour Williamson Inc and United Africa Co 1961-69; pres: Int Wood Products Inc 1969-81, DBS Inc 1981-88; sole proprietor David Bell-Salter; *Recreations* sailing, clay target shooting; *Clubs* The Lumbermen's (Memphis), St Georges Soc of NY; *Style—* David Bell-Salter, Esq; 379 North Highland St, Memphis, Tennessee 38122, USA; David Bell-Salter, PO Box 22681, Memphis, Tennessee 38122 0681; 6 York Terrace West, Regents' Park, London NW1

BELLAIGUE; *see*: de Bellaigue

BELLAIRS, Prof Angus d'Albini; s of Nigel Bellairs (d 1979) and, Kathleen, *née* Niblett (d 1946); *b* 11 Jan 1918; *Educ* Stowe, Queens' Coll Cambridge (MA), UCH London (DSc); *m* 5 July 1949, Madeline Ruth, da of Trevor Morgan (d 1973), of Bell Croft House, Southowram, Halifax , Yorks; 1 da (Vivien St Joseph b 1959); *Career* WWII RAMC 1942-46, Med Offr 4 Div Engrs, Maj Operational Res Section 14 Army; served: N Africa, ME, Italy, India, Burma, Washington; lectr Univ of Cambridge 1951-53; St Mary's Hosp Med Sch Univ of London: reader in anatomy and embryology 1953-70, prof of vertebrate morphology 1970-82 emeritus prof 1982-; pres First World Congress of Herpetology 1989; MRCS, LRCP; fell: Inst of Biology, Linnean and Zoological Socs; *Books* The World of Reptiles (with R Carrington, 1966), The Life of Reptiles 2 Vols (1969), Reptiles (with J Attridge, fourth edn 1975), The Isle of Sea Lizards (novel), First World Congress of Herpetology (1989); *Recreations* natural history (especially reptiles and cats), antiques, modern novels; *Style—* Prof Angus Bellairs; 7 Champion Grove, London SE5 8BN (☎ 01 274 1834)

BELLAK, John George; *b* 19 Nov 1930; *Educ* Rose Hill Sch Tunbridge Wells, Uppingham, Haute Ecole Commerciale Lausanne Switzerland, Clare Coll Cambridge (MA); *m* Mary Prudence (Pru); 3 s (Max b 1962, Leo b 1966, Benjy b 1968), 1 da (Maria b 1964); *Career* J Whittingham & Sons Ltd 1952-58, A Hoffmann & Co Ltd 1958-68; Doulton & Co Ltd 1968-83: sales dir (fine china), commercial dir Tableware Ltd, mktg dir 1972, dep md, Euro distributive NV Royal Doulton (Belgium) SA, md Royal Doulton Tableware Ltd 1980; chm: Royal Crown Derby Porcelain Co Ltd, Lawleys Ltd; memb: Cncl CBI, Ct Univ of Keele, Cncl of Newcastle-under-Lyme Schs; Parly candidate (Cons): Kingston upon Hull West 1964, Keighley; treas Ripon Div Cons Assoc 1967; chm Severn Trent Water Authy (now Severn Trent plc) 1983; FRSA; *Recreations* politics, shooting, ornithology, wild life, conservation, ancient Chinese artefacts; *Clubs* Carlton; *Style—* John Bellak, Esq; Severn Trent plc, 2297 Coventry Rd, Birmingham, West Midlands B26 3PU (☎ 021 722 4000, fax 021 722 4477, car 0836 507295, telex 339333)

BELLAMY, Alan Nicholas Fothergill; s of Gilbert Bernard Bellamy (d 1965), and Nina, *née* Fothergill; *b* 2 Nov 1939; *Educ* Nottingham HS, Birmingham Univ (BSc); *m* 10 Jan 1970, Dorothy Jane, da of Leslie Stuart Hooley (d 1984); 1 s (Jonathan b 1972, d 1979), 2 da (Vanessa b 1970, Amanda b 1973); *Career* dir Hestair plc; chm: Hestair Intercraft Ltd, Hestair Intercraft Pty Ltd, Hestair Mclaren Ltd; *Style—* Alan N F Bellamy, Esq; 50 Hawthorn Lane, Wilmslow, Cheshire (☎ 0625 532 651); 17 Buckingham Gate, London SW1

BELLAMY, Prof David James; s of Thomas James Bellamy (d 1988), and Winifred May, *née* Green (d 1979); *b* 18 Jan 1933; *Educ* Sutton County GS, Chelsea Coll of Sci and Technol (BSc), Bedford Coll London (PhD); *m* 3 Jan 1959, (Shirley) Rosemary, da of Frederick Herbert Froy, (d 1959); 2 s (Rufus b 8 June 1966, Eoghain b 9 May 1975), 3 da (Henrietta b 14 Feb 1970, Brighid b 7 March 1972, Hannah b 24 June 1978); *Career* Univ of Durham: lectr in botany 1960-68, sr lectr in botany 1968-82, hon prof of adult educn 1982-; special prof of botany Univ of Nottingham 1987-, visiting prof of natural heritage studies Massey Univ NZ 1989; dir: Botanical Enterprises Ltd, David Bellamy Assocs, (fndr) Conservation Fndn NZ, Conservation Fndn London; tv work: Life in Our Sea (BBC) 1970, Bellamy on Botany (BBC) 1973, Bellamy's Britain (BBC) 1975, Bellamy's Europe (BBC) 1977, Botanic Man (ITV) 1979, Up a Gum Tree (BBC) 1980, Backyard Safari (BBC) 1981, The Great Seasons (BBC) 1982, Bellamy's New World (BBC) 1983, You Can't See The Wood (BBC) 1984, Seaside Safari (BBC)

1985, The End of the Rainbow Show (ITV) 1986, Bellamy's Bugle (ITV) 1986, Turning the Tide (ITV) 1986, Bellamy's Birds Eye View (ITV) 1988, Moa's Ark (TVNZ) 1990, Don't Ask Me (ITV), It's Life (ITV), It's More Life (ITV), The Gene Machine (ITV), Swallow (ITV), Bellamy on Top of the World (ITV), Paradise Ploughed (ITV), Bellamy Rides Again (BBC); *Books* Bellamy on Botany (1972), Peatlands (jtly, 1973), Bellamy's Britain (1974), Life Giving Sea (1975), Green Worlds (jtly, 1975), The World of Plants (1975), It's Life (1976), Bellamy's Europe (1976), Botanic Action (1978), Botanic Man (1978), Half of Paradise (1979), Forces of Life (1979), Bellamy's Backyard Safari (1981), The Great Seasons (jtly, 1981) Il Libro Verde (1981), Discovering the Countryside (1982 and 1983), The Mouse Book (jtly, 1983), Bellamy's New World (1983), The Queen's Hidden Garden (jtly, 1984), Bellamy's Ireland (1986), Turning the Tide (jtly, 1986) Bellamy's Changing Countryside (1987) England's Last Wilderness (jtly, 1989) England's Lost Wilderness (jtly, 1990), Wetlands (jtly, 1990), Wilderness Britain (jtly, 1990), How Green are You (jtly, 1991), Tomorrow's Earth (jtly, 1991), Plants Patients and People (jtly, 1991); memb various professional ctees and recipient of many awards; Open Univ, Hon DSc CNAA; FLS, FIBiol, FRGS, fell Inst of Environmental Sci; Order of the Golden Ark (Netherlands) 1988, Commemoration medal (NZ) 1990; *Style—* Prof David Bellamy; Mill House, Bedburn, Bishop Auckland, Co Durham DL13 3NN

BELLAMY, (Kenneth) Rex; s of Sampson Bellamy (d 1958), and Kathleen May, *née* English (d 1988); *b* 15 Sept 1928; *Educ* Woodhouse GS Sheffield; *m* 12 May 1951, Hilda, da of Edwin O'Shea (d 1972); 1 step da (Alannah b 10 April 1940); *Career* Nat Serv RA and RASC 1946-49; sports and feature writer: Sheffield Telegraph 1944-46 and 1949-53, Birmingham Gazette 1953-56, The Times (mainly tennis and squash corr) 1956-89; author and freelance journalist 1989-; memb Inst of Journalists; *Books* Teach Yourself Squash (with Leslie Hamer, 1968), The Tennis Set (1972), Squash, A History (1978, revised edn 1988), The Peak District Companion (1981), Walking the Tops (1984), Game, Set and Deadline (1986), Love Thirty (1990); *Recreations* hill walking, golf; *Clubs* Cowdray Park Golf; *Style—* Rex Bellamy, Esq; 8 Guillards Oak, Midhurst, W Sussex GU29 9JZ (☎ 0730 814230)

BELLAMY, Richard Anthony; s of late Maj Roland Cecil Bellamy, OBE, TD, JP, DL, and Kathleen Alice, *née* Beacock; *b* 21 March 1939; *Educ* Shrewsbury; *m* 1965, Wendy, *née* Hopwood; 2 s, 1 da; *Career* fndr chm Avia Fuels (UK) Ltd; memb Cncl Univ of Hull 1981-87; Liveryman Worshipful Co of Coach and Harness Makers; High Sheriff Humberside 1980-81; FInstPet; *Recreations* shooting; *Clubs* Army and Navy, Rotary; *Style—* Richard A Bellamy, Esq; Parklands, Barnoldby-Le-Beck, Great Grimsby, S Humberside (☎ 0472 823680)

BELLANY, Prof Ian; s of James Bellany (d 1984), of Sheffield and Bristol, and Jemima, *née* Emlay; *b* 21 Feb 1941; *Educ* Preston Lodge, Prestonpans, Firth Park Sheffield, Balliol Coll Oxford, (BA, MA, DPhil); *m* 7 Aug 1965, Wendy Ivey, da of Glyndwr Thomas (d 1978), of Gilwern, Abergavenny; 1 s (Alastair b 1968), 1 da (Alison b 1971); *Career* asst princ FCO 1965-68, res fell Aust Nat Univ Canberra 1968-70; Univ of Lancaster: lectr in politics (sr lectr 1974-79), prof of politics and dir of the Centre for the Study of Arms Control and Int Security 1979-; founding ed Arms Control, memb advsy panel on Disarmament FCO; external examiner: Int Rels LSE 1985-88, Int Studies Univ of Birmingham 1989-; *Books* Australia in the Nuclear Age, Anti-Ballistic Missile Defence in the 1980s (ed), The Verification of Arms Control Agreements (ed), The Nuclear Non Proliferation Treaty (ed), New Conventional Weapons and Western Defence (ed), A Basis for Arms Control; *Recreations* carpentry and computing; *Style—* Prof Ian Bellany; University of Lancaster, Bailrigg, Lancaster, LA1 4YL (☎ 0524 65 201)

BELLANY, John; s of Richard Weatherhead Bellany (d 1985), of Port Seton, E Lothian, Scotland, and Agnes Craig Maltman Bellany; *b* 18 June 1942; *Educ* Cockenzie Sch E Lothian, Preston Lodge Prestonpans, Edinburgh Coll of Art (DA), RCA (MA); *m* 1, 19 Sept 1964 (m dis 1974), Helen Margaret, da of late Harold Percy of Golspie, Sutherland, Scotland; 2 s (Jonathan b 22 Dec 1965, Tristan b 21 Aug 1968), 1 da (Anya b 30 Sept 1970); m 2, 1980, Juliet Gray, *née* Lister (d 1985); m 3, 1986, his first wife Helen Margaret; *Career* lectr in fine art Winchester Sch of Art 1969-73, head Faculty of Painting Croydon Coll of Art 1973-78, visiting lectr in painting RCA 1975-84, lectr in fine art Goldsmiths Coll London 1978-84, artist in residence Victorian Coll of the Arts Melbourne Aust 1983; Maj Arts Cncl Award 1981, jt 1 prize Athena Int Award 1985; maj one man exhibitions: Drian Gallery London 1970, 1971, 1972, 1973 and 1974, Aberdeen City Art Gallery 1975, Acme Gallery London 1977 1980, Scottish Arts Cncl Gallery 1978, 3rd Eye Centre Glasgow 1979, Southampton Art Gallery, Rosa Esman Gallery NY 1982, 1983, 1984, Beaux Arts Gallery Bath 1989 and 1990, Fischer Fine Art London 1986, 1987, 1989 and 1991, Scot Nat Gallery of Modern Art 1986 and 1989, Raab Gallery Berlin 1989; Arts Cncl touring exhibition 1983: Ikon Gallery Birmingham, Walker Art Gallery Liverpool, Graves Art Gallery Sheffield; Arts Cncl touring exhibition 1984: Christine Abrahams Gallery Melbourne, Dusseldorf Gallery Perth Aust, Roslyn Oxley Gallery Sydney Aust; Nat Portrait Gallery 1986, Ruth Siegel Gallery NY 1988 and 1990, Galerie Kirkhaar Amsterdam; retrospective exhibitions: Scot Nat Gallery of Modern Art 1986, Serpentine Gallery London, RCA Gallery 1987, Kusthalle Hamburg 1989, Roslyn Oxley Gallery Aust, Butler Gallery Kilkenny Castle, Hendrix Gallery Dublin, 3rd Eye Centre Glasgow (prints) 1988; public collections: Aberdeen Art Gallery, Arts Cncl of GB, Br Cncl, Br Govt Collection Whitehall, Contemporary Arts Soc, Hatton Art Gallery, Kelvingrove Art Gallery, Leeds Art Gallery, Leicester Art Gallery, Middlesborough Art Gallery, Nat Gallery of Poland Warsaw, Nat Library of Congress Washington USA, Museum of Modern Art NY, Met Museum NY, Nat Portrait Gallery, Nat Gallery of Modern Art Scotland, Gulbenkian Museum Lisbon, J F Kennedy Library Boston USA, V & A, Br Museum, Tate; maj gp exhibitions: British Romantic Painting Madrid, El Greco (Mystery and Illumination) Nat Gallery, Br Cncl touring exhibition Every Picture tells a Story Singapore and Hong Kong, Eros in Albion House of Messaccio Italy, Scottish Art since 1990 Nat Gallery of Scotland and Barbican London, Scotland Creates 1990, The Great British Art Show 1990; fell commoner Trinity Hall Cambridge 1988; Hon RSA 1987, elected ARA 1986; *Clubs* Chelsea Arts, Scottish Arts (Edinburgh); *Style—* John Bellany, Esq; 2 Windmill Drive, Clapham Common, London SW4 9DE; 19 Great Stuart St, Edinburgh, Scotland; c/o Fischer Fine Art, 30 King St, St James's, London SW1 (☎ 071 839 3942)

BELLEW; *see*: Grattan-Bellew

BELLEW, Hon Bryan Edward; s and h of 7 Baron Bellew; *b* 19 March 1943; *Educ* Eton, RMA Sandhurst; *m* 1968, Rosemary Sarah, er da of Maj Reginald Kilner Brasier Hitchcock, of Meers Court, Mayfield, Sussex; 2 s (Patrick Edward b 1969, Anthony Richard Brooke b 1972); *Career* Maj (ret) Irish Gds; *Style—* Maj the Hon Bryan Bellew; Barmeath Castle, Togher, Drogheda, Co Louth, Eire

BELLEW, Hon Christopher James; 2 s of 7 Baron Bellew; *b* 3 April 1954; *Educ* Eton; *m* 1984, Hon Rose Griselda, *née* Eden, yst da of 7 Baron Henley, and former w of Stuart Ballin; *Style—* The Hon Christopher Bellew; 56 Margravine Gardens, London W6 8RJ

BELLEW, Hon Sir George (Rothe); KCB (1961), KCVO (1953, CVO 1950, MVO 1935); s of Hon Richard Bellew, by his w Gwendoline, da of William R J Fitzherbert Herbert-Huddleston, of Clytha; *b* 13 Dec 1899; *Educ* Wellington, ChCh Oxford; *m* 1935, Ursula Kennard, da of Anders Eric Knös Cull; 1 s; *Career* served WW II RAFVR (despatches); registrar Coll of Arms 1935-46; genealogist Order of the Bath 1950-61, OStJ 1951-61; Knight Principal of Imperial Soc of Knights Bachelor 1957-62 (Dep Knight Princ 1962-71); Garter Principal King of Arms 1950-61; Inspector of Regimental Colours 1957-61; Sec of the Order of the Garter 1961-74; FSA; kt 1950; *Style—* Hon Sir George Bellew, KCB, KCVO, FSA; The Grange, Old Park Lane, Farnham, Surrey (☎ 0252 715146)

BELLEW, 7 Baron (I 1848); Sir James Bryan Bellew; 13 Bt (I 1688); s of 6 Baron Bellew, MC; suc f 1981; *b* 5 Jan 1920; *m* 1, 1942, Mary Elizabeth (d 1978), er da of Rev Edward Hill, of West Malling; 2 s, 1 da; m 2, 1978, Gwendoline, da of Charles Redmond Clayton-Daubeny, of Bridgwater, Somerset, and of Bihar, India, and formerly w of Maj P Hall; *Heir* s, Hon Bryan Bellew; *Career* late Capt Irish Gds, served WW II; *Style—* The Rt Hon The Lord Bellew; Barmeath Castle, Togher, Drogheda, Co Louth, Eire (☎ 041 5 12 05)

BELLEW, Hon Patrick Herbert; s of Richard Eustace Bellew (d 1933, 4 s of 2 Baron Bellew) by his 2 w Gwendoline (herself da of William Reginald Joseph Fitzherbert Herbert-Huddleston, JP, DL, of Clytha Park, Monmouthshire, and Sawston Hall, Cambs, by his first w, Charlotte Giffard, one of the Giffards of Chillington; *see* Giffard, Peter); half-bro of 5 Baron Bellew, MBE (d 1975); granted, rank, title and precedence of a Baron's s 1935; *b* 2 April 1905; *Educ* privately, Cambridge Univ; *m* 1, 1936, Hon Catherine Moya de la Poer Beresford (m dis 1946 and who d 1967), da of 5 Baron Decies, DSO, PC (d 1944); 1 s (John); m 2, 1954, Helen Carol, da of late Walter Clinton Louchheim, of New York; *Career* Lt RNVR 1938; *Style—* The Hon Patrick Bellew; Litchfield, Connecticut, USA

BELLEW, Hon Mrs (Rose Griselda); *née* Eden; da of 7 Baron Henley (d 1977); *b* 17 Nov 1957; *m* 1976 (m dis 1979), Stuart Ballin; m 2, 1984, Hon Christopher Bellew, *qv*, yr s of 7 Baron Bellew; *Style—* The Hon Mrs Bellew; 56 Margravine Gardens, London W6

BELLI, Dr Anna-Maria; da of Bartolomeo Antonio Luigi Belli, of 9 Lon Cynfor, Cwmgyn, Swansea, West Glam, and Carmen, *née* Lombardelli; *b* 5 Aug 1957; *Educ* Glanmôr Sch for Girls, Univ of London, Middx Hosp Med Sch (MB BS); *Career* sr registrar in radiology St George's Hosp 1985-87 (registrar 1982-85); sr lectr and hon conslt in radiodiagnosis: Univ of Sheffield 1987-90, Royal Postgraduate Medical School Hammersmith Hospital London 1990-; memb: BMA 1981, BIR 1983, CIRSE 1988, BSIR 1988; FRCR 1985, BMLA 1989; *Books* Pros and Cons in PTA and Auxiliary Methods (contrib 3 edn, 1989); *Style—* Dr Anna-Maria Belli; Dept of Radiology, Royal Postgraduate Medical School, Hammersmith Hospital, London W12 ONN (☎ 081 743 2030)

BELLINGER, Christopher Henry; s of Clifford Bellinger, Cardiff, S Wales, and Margaret Joy, *née* Boddington; *b* 20 Feb 1943; *Educ* Abingdon Sch Berkshire; *m* 24 June 1972, Diana Penelope Margaret, da of Maj Frank Albert Bowater (d 1982), of London; *Career* BBC TV: film dept Wales 1964-70, TV presentation 1971-78, prodr Multi-Coloured Swap Shop, ed Saturday Superstore 1982, ed Going Live! 1986; *Books* Saturday Superstore Book (2 edns), The Going Live! Book (1988); *Recreations* reading, walking, photography; *Style—* Christopher Bellinger, Esq; BBC Television Centre, London W12 7RJ (☎ 081 576 1979, fax 081 740 8835)

BELLINGER, Sir Robert Ian; GBE (1967); s of David Morgan Bellinger, of Cardiganshire, by his w Jane Ballantine Deans; *b* 10 March 1910; *Educ* Church of England Sch; *m* 1962, Christiane Marie Louise, da of Maurice Clement Janssens, of Brussels; 1 s, 1 da; *Career* chm: Kinloch (PM) Ltd 1964-75, Nat Savings Ctee 1970-75 (pres 1972-75), Danish Trade Advsy Bd 1977-82; dir Rank Organisation 1971-83; Lord Mayor of London 1966-67; one of HM Lieutenants City of London 1976-; dir Arsenal FC 1960-, chm Fin Ctee BBC, govr BBC 1968-71; Gentleman Usher of the Purple Rod, Order of the Br Empire 1969-85, KStJ 1966; kt 1964; *Style—* Sir Robert Bellinger, GBE; Penn Wood, Fulmer, Bucks (☎ 0753 662029)

BELLINGHAM, Prof Alastair John; s of Stanley Herbert Bellingham, of Ewell, Surrey, and Sybil Mary, *née* Milne; *b* 27 March 1938; *Educ* Tiffin Boys' Sch Kingston upon Thames, UCH Med Sch London; *m* 24 May 1963, (Valerie) Jill, da of Kenenth Morford (d 1971); 3 s (James b 24 April 1964, Richard b 14 April 1969, Paul b 25 Feb 1973); *Career* Mackenzie-Mackinnon Streatfeild fell RCP 1968-69, res fell Univ of Washington USA 1969-70, sr lectr haematology UCH Med Sch London 1971-74; prof of haematology: Univ of Liverpool 1974-84, Kings Coll London 1984-, former sec Br Soc for Haematology 1984-87, memb Cncl RC Path 1987-90; FRCP 1976, FRCPath 1986 (vice pres 1990-); *Recreations* photography, oenology, viticulture, claret testing; *Style—* Prof Alastair Bellingham; 13 Barnmead Rd, Beckenham, Kent BR3 1JF (☎ 081 778 0730); Dept of Haematological Medicine, Kings College School of Medicine & Dentistry, Bessemer Rd, London SE5 9RS (☎ 071 326 3080)

BELLINGHAM, Anthony Edward Norman; s of Sir Roger Bellingham, 6 Bt (d 1973); bro and hp of Sir Noel Bellingham, 7 Bt; *b* 24 March 1947; *Educ* Rossall; *Style—* Anthony Bellingham, Esq

BELLINGHAM, Henry Campbell; MP (Cons) Norfolk North West 1983-; s of (Arthur) Henry Bellingham (d 1959), and June Marion Cloudesley, *née* Smith; *b* 29 March 1955; *Educ* Eton, Magdalene Coll Cambridge, Cncl of Legal Educn; *Career* called to the Bar Middle Temple 1978; elected MP for North West Norfolk 1983-87, vice chm Cons Backbench Smaller Business Ctee 1987- (jt sec 1983-87), jt memb Environment Select Ctee 1987-, chm Cons Cncl on Eastern Europe 1989-; *Clubs* Whites, Pratts; *Style—* Henry Bellingham, Esq, MP; House of Commons, London SW1

BELLINGHAM, Lynda (Mrs Nunzio Peluso); da of Capt D J Bellingham, and Ruth Bellingham; *b* 31 May 1948; *Educ* Convent GS, Central Sch of Speech and Drama; *m* 22 July 1981, Nunzio Peluso; 2 s (Michael b 1983, Robert Ciro b 1988); *Career* actress; W End appearances: Noises Off, Look No Hans, Double Double; TV appearances incl: Mackenzie, Dr Who, Funny Man, All Creatures Great and Small, Second Thoughts (LWT), star of Oxo adverts; *Style—* Ms Lynda Bellingham; c/o Saraband Associates, 265 Liverpool Rd, London N1 (☎ 071 609 5313)

BELLINGHAM, Sir Noel Peter Roger; 7 Bt (GB 1796); s of Sir Roger Bellingham, 6 Bt (d 1973); *b* 4 Sept 1943; *Educ* Lindisfarne Coll; *m* 1977, Jane, da of Edwin William Taylor, of Sale, Cheshire; *Heir* bro, Anthony Bellingham, *qv*; *Career* accountant; *Style—* Sir Noel Bellingham, Bt; 20 Davenport Park Rd, Davenport, Stockport, Cheshire (☎ 061 483 7168)

BELLIS, John Herbert; s of Thomas Bellis (d 1953), of Wernto, Llanfairfechan, Gwynedd, and Jane Blodwen, *née* Roberts (d 1980); *b* 11 April 1930; *Educ* Friars GS Bangor, Univ of Liverpool (LLB); *m* 4 Mar 1961, Sheila (Helen), da of Alastair McNeil Ford (d 1979), of Rhos on Sea, Clwyd; 2 s (Nicholas, Mark), 1 da (Linda); *Career* Nat Serv 2 Lt The Welch Regt 1953-55; admitted slr 1953; princ John Bellis & Co Penmaenmawr Gwynedd 1958-84; chm Industl Tbnls Manchester 1984-; Parly candidate (L) Conway Carnarvonshire 1959-64; *Recreations* golf, gardening, horse racing, walking; *Style—* John Bellis Esq; Heron Watch, 148 Grovelane, Cheadle Hulme, Cheadle, Cheshire SK8 7NH (☎ 061 439 7582); Alexandra House, Parsonage Gardens, Manchester (☎ 061 833 0581)

BELLIS, Michael John; s of Herbert Henry Bellis (d 1976) of Sherborne, Dorset, and Marjori Dudley, *née* Charlton; *b* 28 April 1937; *Educ* Bancrofts Sch Woodford Green; *Career* Nat Serv RCS 1956-58; admitted slr 1968; cmmr for oaths 1973, sr ptnr Edward Oliver of Bellis 1975-; chm Med Serv Ctee FPC London Boroughs of Redbridge and Waltham Forest 1978-89, former vice pres W Essex Law Soc, former pres Rotary Club Ilford; Freeman City of London, Liveryman Worshipful Co of Bakers; memb Law Soc 1968; *Recreations* collecting rare books, travel in the USA, growing and eating asparagus; *Style—* Michael John Bellis, Esq; Beck Farm Coach House, The Street, Kelling, Holt, Norfolk NR25 7EL (☎ 026 370 435); Edward Oliver & Bellis, City House, 9 Cranbrook Rd, Ilford, Essex (☎ 081 553 1214, fax 081 501 0021)

BELLOS, Prof David Michael; s of Nathaniel Bellos, of London, and Katharine Mabel, *née* Shapiro; *b* 25 June 1945; *Educ* Westcliff HS, Univ of Oxford (BA, MA, DPhil); *m* 1, 31 Dec 1966 (m dis 1985), Ilona, da of Sandor Roth (d 1945); 1 s (Alexander b 1969), 2 da (Amanda b 1971, Olivia b 1974); m 2, 1 July 1989, Susan Esther Currie, da of Prof A C Lendrum; *Career* fell Magdalen Coll Oxford 1969, lectr in French Univ of Edinburgh 1972, prof of French Univ of Southampton 1982, prof and head dept of French Studies Univ of Manchester 1985; Chevalier De l'Ordre Des Palmes Academiques France 1988; *Books* Balzac Criticism in France, 1850-1900 (1976), Georges Perec, Life, A User's Manual (trans, 1987); *Recreations* cycling; *Style—* Prof David Bellos; 2 Kingston Ave, Manchester M20 8SB; Jolibert, 24130 Monfaucon, France; Dept of French Studies, Univ of Manchester, Manchester M13 9PL (☎ 061 275 3212)

BELLOW, Hon Stephen Jeremy; o s of Baron Bellwin, JP (Life Peer); *b* 1953; *Educ* Leeds GS, Leeds Poly; *m* 1974, Marilyn Stern; 1 s (Adam b 1989), 1 da (Milena b 1986); *Style—* The Hon Stephen Bellow; The Oval, 25a Bracken Park, Scarcroft, Leeds LS14 3HZ (☎ 0532 892325)

BELLVILLE, Lady Lucinda Ruth; *née* Wallop; da of Viscount Lymington (d 1984), and sis of 10 Earl of Portsmouth; *b* 9 Feb 1956; *m* 1984, Patrick Anthony Ewen Bellville, s of late Anthony Seymour Bellville, late Lt Grenadiers Guards, of Bembridge, Isle of Wight; 3 s (Blaise b 1985, Oscar b 1986, Archie b 1988); *Style—* The Lady Lucinda Bellville; The White House, Bembridge, Isle of Wight

BELLWIN, Baron (Life Peer UK 1979); Irwin Norman Bellow; JP (Leeds 1969); s of Abraham and Leah Bellow; *b* 7 Feb 1923; *Educ* Leeds GS, Univ of Leeds (LLB); *m* 1948, Doreen Barbara Saperia; 1 s, 2 da; *Career* alderman Leeds CC 1968-, ldr Leeds City Cncl 1975-79; Parly under sec of state DOE 1979-83, min of state for Local Govt 1983-84; bd memb New Towns Cmmn 1985-; non-exec dir: Taylor Woodrow plc 1985-, Sinclair Goldsmith plc 1987-, Mountleigh Bp plc 1987-, Trimoco plc 1987-; *Recreations* golf; *Clubs* Moor Allerton (hon pres); *Style—* The Rt Hon The Lord Bellwin, JP; Woodside Lodge, Ling Lane, Scarcroft, Leeds LS14 3HX (☎ 0532 892908)

BELMONT, Michael Jeremy Kindersley; s of Capt Algernon Spencer Belmont, RA (ka 1944), and Hon Margaret Marion, *née* Kindersley (d 1981), er da of 1 Baron Kindersley, GBE; *b* 26 Feb 1930; *Educ* Eton; *m* 27 May 1953, Virginia Ann, da of Vernon George Tate, MC (d 1955); 2 s (Piers b 1954, Antony b 1956), 1 da (Lisa b 1959); *Career* 10 Royal Hussars (POW) 1948-51; dir: LASMO, Ivory & Sime, Monterey Tst, Frobisher Tst; memb Exec Ctee NSPCC 1961-66 (dep vice chm 1966-69); Freeman City of London, Liveryman Worshipful Co of Fishmongers 1955; *Recreations* shooting, golf, gardening; *Clubs* City of London, Pratt's, Bohemian (San Francisco); *Style—* M J K Belmont, Esq; 52 Warwick Square, London SW1V 2AJ (☎ 071 834 9955); Gaunt Mill, Standlake, Oxon (☎ 0865 300 227); Ivory & Sime plc, 7 Chesham Place, London SW1X 8HN (☎ 071 823 1520, fax 071 823 1473)

BELMORE, 8 Earl (I 1797); John Armar Lowry-Corry; also Baron Belmore (I 1781) and Viscount Belmore (I 1789); s of 7 Earl Belmore, JP, DL (d 1960) and Gloria Anthea Harker; *b* 4 Sept 1951; *Educ* Lancing; *m* 1984, Lady Mary Jane Meade, 2 da of 6 Earl of Clanwilliam (d 1989); 2 s (Viscount Corry b 1985, Hon Montagu G G Lowry-Corry b 1989); *Heir* s, Viscount Corry, *qv*; *Career* farmer; *Recreations* art; *Clubs* Kildare Street Dublin; *Style—* The Rt Hon the Earl of Belmore; The Garden House, Castle Coole, Enniskillen, N Ireland BT74 6JX (☎ 0365 322463)

BELOFF, Hon Jeremy Benjamin; yr s of Baron Beloff (Life Peer), *qv*; *b* 1943; *m* 1973, Carol Macdonald; 2 s (Nicholas b 1975, Jonathan Max b 1986), 1 da (Catherine b 1978); *Style—* The Hon Jeremy Beloff; Glenwood, Templewood Lane, Farnham Common, Bucks SL2 3HW

BELOFF, Baron (Life Peer UK 1981), of Wolvercote, Co Oxfordshire; Sir Max Beloff; er s of Simon Beloff, and Mary Beloff; *b* 2 July 1913; *Educ* St Paul's, CCC Oxford (MA, DLitt); *m* 1938, Helen, da of Samuel Dobrin; 2 s; *Career* sits as Cons in House of Lords; fell CCC Oxford 1937-39, asst lectr Univ of Manchester 1939-46, Nuffield reader in comparative study of instns Oxford Univ 1946-56 (Nuffield fell 1947-57), Gladstone prof of govt and public admin Oxford Univ 1957-74, fell All Souls Coll Oxford 1957-74 (emeritus fell 1980-), princ UC Buckingham 1974-79, supernumerary fell St Antony's Coll Oxford 1975-84; memb Wilton Park Academic Cncl until 1983; Hon LLD: Pittsburgh USA, Manchester; Hon DCL Bishop's Canada; Hon DLitt: Bowdoin USA, Buckingham; Hon DUniv Aix-Marseille III; FBA, FRHistS, FRSA; kt 1980; *Style—* The Rt Hon Lord Beloff; Flat 9, 22 Lewes Crescent, Brighton BN2 1GB (☎ 0273 688622)

BELOFF, Hon Michael Jacob; QC (1981); er s of Baron Beloff (Life Peer), *qv*; *b* 19 April 1942; *Educ* Eton, Univ of Oxford (MA); *m* 1969, Judith Mary Arkinstall; 1 s, 1 da; *Career* called to the Bar Gray's Inn 1967, bencher 1988; former lectr Trinity Coll Oxford; legal corr: New Society, The Observer; rec Crown Court 1985, dep judge of the High Court 1989; *Style—* The Hon Michael Beloff, QC; 58 Park Town, Oxford

BELOFF, Nora (Mrs Clifford Makins); da of Simon Beloff (d 1964), and Marie Katzin Beloff; *b* 24 Jan 1919; *Educ* King Alfred Sch London, Lady Margaret Hall Oxford (BA); *m* 10 March 1977, Clifford George Makins; *Career* Political Intelligence Dept FO (UK and Paris) 1940-46; Reuters News Agency (Paris Office) 1945-46, Paris corr The Economist 1946-50; editorial staff The Observer 1948-77: chief political corr 1964-76, corr (Paris, Washington, Moscow, Brussels, roving); *Books* The General Says No (1963, French translation 1964), Transit of Britain (1973), Freedom Under Foot (1976), No Travel Like Russian (1979, USA edn Inside the Soviet Empire: Myth Reality 1980), Tito's Flawed Legacy (1985, USA 1986, Italian translation 1987, Slovonic translation 1990); *Recreations* walking, conversation; *Clubs* Chatham House, London Library; *Style—* Miss Nora Beloff; 11 Belsize Rd, London NW6 4RX (☎ 071 586 0378)

BELPER, 4 Baron (UK 1856); (Alexander) Ronald George Strutt; s of 3 Baron (d 1956), by 1 w, Hon Dame Eva Bruce, DBE, JP, da of 2 Baron Aberdare; bro of Lavinia, Duchess of Norfolk; *b* 23 April 1912; *Educ* Harrow; *m* 1940 (m dis 1949), Zara Sophie Kathleen Mary, da of Sir Harry Mainwaring, 5 Bt; 1 s; *Heir* s, Hon Richard Strutt; *Career* formerly Maj Coldstream Gds; *Style—* The Rt Hon The Lord Belper; Kingston Hall, Nottingham

BELSHAW, Prof Deryke Gerald Rosten; s of Leonard Gerald Belshaw (d 1987), of Ash Vale, nr Aldershot, Hants, and Phyllis Guiver, *née* Rosten; *b* 9 Sept 1932; *Educ* Hampton GS, Selwyn Coll Cambridge (MA), Hertford Coll Oxford (Dip Agric Econ); *m* 15 Aug 1959, Audrey Gladys, da of John Newell, MBE, VMH (d 1984), of Ringwood, Hants; 1 s (Jeremy b 1960), 2 da (Sarah b 1962, Anna b 1963); *Career* Nat Serv RA seconded to RWAFF Nigeria, gunner 1954, 2 Lt 1955, Lt 1956; res offr Sch of Agric Univ of Cambridge 1958-60, sr lectr then reader in agric economics Makerere Coll Univ of E Africa 1964-70 (lectr 1960-64), prof of rural devpt Sch of Devpt Studies Univ of E Anglia 1985- (sr then reader in agric economics 1970-85, dean 1981-84), FAO food strategy advsr Govt of Ethiopia Overseas Devpt Gp Ltd Univ Anglia 1986-89 (ODA economic advsr Govt of Kenya 1970-72, UNDP and F regnl devpt advsr Govt of Tanzania 1974-77); memb: Ed Bd of Rural Development Abstracts, Bd of Dirs World Vision of Br, tstee Traidcraft Ltd; *Books* Agriculture and Rural Development Programme Review, Kenya (1987), Farm Finance and Agricultural Development (1988), Towards a Food and Nutrition Strategy for Ethiopia (1989); *Recreations* vinous evaluation; *Style—* Prof Deryke Belshaw; School of Development Studies, University of E Anglia, Norwich NR4 7TJ Norfolk (☎ 0603 56161, fax 0603 505262, telex 975 UEA)

BELSHAW, Kenneth John Thomas; s of John Everton Belshaw, and Lilian Elizabeth, *née* Stewart; *b* 14 May 1952; *Educ* Orangefield Sch for Boys Belfast; *m* 24 Nov 1979, Iris Elizabeth, da of Sydney Miller McKeown, of Shanliss, Stewartstown, Co Tynone, N Ireland; 1 s (Stephen John Doran b 1987), 1 da (Maeve Elizabeth b 1983); *Career* recruitment consult; md: Grafton Recruitment Ltd (Ireland's largest employment agency), Grafton Recruitment UK Ltd 1982-; *Recreations* fine wines, reading; *Clubs* Kildare St and Univ (Dublin); Cranmore, 27 Eaton Sq, Dublin 6, Ireland (☎ 0001 900323), Grafton Recruitment, 37-40 Upper Mound St, Dublin 2 (☎ 0001 684388, fax 0001 614897)

BELSKY, Franta; s of Josef Belsky (d 1963), and Martha Grunbaum (d 1973); *b* 6 April 1921; *Educ* Acad of Fine Arts Prague, RCA London; *m* 1944, Margaret, da of Albert Edward Owen, DSO (d 1959); *Career* gunner France 1940, Normandy 1944; sculptor; taught in art schs 1950-55, pres Soc of Portrait Sculptors 1963-68, govr St Martin's Sch of Art 1967-; work in: Nat Portrait Gallery, collections in USA, collections in Europe, numerous CC's, industl shipping and private cos and educn authorities; works incl: Paratroop Meml Prague 1947, statue of Cecil Rhodes Bulawayo 1953, Triga Knightsbridge 1958, Astronomer Herschel Meml Slough 1969, Jamestown Harbour Docklands 1988, Euro Shell Centre fountains; portraits include: Queen Mother 1962, HM The Queen 1981, Prince Andrew 1963 and 1984, Prince Philip 1979, Prince William 1985, statue of Sir Winston Churchill for Churchill Meml and Library in US and bust in Churchill Archives Cambridge 1971, Harry S Truman, Lord Cottesloe, Queen Mother 80 Birthday Crown Coin; Jean Masson Davidson Award for distinction in Portrait Sculpture; FRBS; *Books* illustrations and contributions to various books and journals; *Recreations* skiing, gardening, amateur archaeology; *Style—* Franta Belsky, Esq; 12 Pembroke Studios, London W8 6HX

BELSON, Col Philip Charles Euan; TD (1947); s of Fredrick Charles Belson (d 1952), and Hilda Carlyon, *née* Euan-Smith (d 1954); blessed Thomas Belson - beatified in Rome 1987; 1815 Lt Gen Sir C P Belson commanded the Gloucestershsire Regt at the Battle of Waterloo; *b* 15 Dec 1915; *Educ* Westminster, Staff Coll (psc); *m* 21 Dec 1945, Sheila Agnes, da of Edwin Chappel Keliher (d 1968); 1 s (Euan Charles b 1962), 3 da (Anne Julie b 1947, Adelle Carolyn b 1949, Nicola Mary b 1954); *Career* Col RA 1939-44 and 1946-64, seconded Parachute Regt 1944-45; served BEF France 1939-40, Maj Rhine Crossing 1945, Lt-Col Liaison Offr to US Army 1957-60, Lt-Col (Hon Col) War Office 1962-64 (ret); dir R and M Management Consultants Ltd 1965-80; *Recreations* sailing, skiing; *Clubs* Royal Lymington Yacht, Royal Artillery Yacht; *Style—* Col Philip Belson, TD; Old Bank House, Beaulieu, Hampshire SO42 7YA (☎ 0590 612141)

BELSTEAD, 2 Baron (UK 1938); Sir John Julian Ganzoni; 2 Bt (UK 1929), PC (1983), JP (Ipswich), DL (Suffolk 1979); s of 1 Baron Belstead, JP, DL (d 1958), sometime MP Ipswich and PPS to postmaster-gen 1924; *b* 30 Sept 1932; *Educ* Eton, Christ Church Oxford; *Heir* none; *Career* Parly sec: DES 1970-73, NI 1973-74, Home Office 1979-82; min of state: FCO 1982-83, MAFF 1983-87, Environment Countryside and Water DOE 1987-88; Lord Privy Seal and Ldr of House of Lords 1988-90; paymaster gen and dep to Sec of State Northern Ireland Office 1990-; chm Governing Bodies Assoc 1974-79; Hon Freeman City of London 1990; *Clubs* MCC, All England Lawn Tennis and Croquet (Wimbledon); *Style—* The Rt Hon the Lord Belstead, PC, JP, DL; House of Lords, London SW1A 0PW (☎ 071 219 3000)

BELSTEAD, John Sydney; s of Eric Kenneth, and Kathleen Phyllis, *née* Curling (d 1985); *b* 16 Sept 1945; *Educ* Univ of Leeds (MB ChB); *m* 14 July 1969, Dr Susan Margaret Goord, da of Austin Arthur Goord; 3 da (Philippa b 1972, Stephanie b 1974, Anna b 1976); *Career* surgn Manorom Christian Hosp Thailand 1978-85, conslt Accident and Emergency Ashford Hosp 1985-; memb: Casualty Surgeons Assoc, Christian Med Fellowship; fell British Orthopaedic Assoc, FRCS Ed 1972, FRCS Ed Orth 1981; *Books* Aids to Post Graduate Surgery (1978); *Recreations* church, DIY; *Style—* John Belstead, Esq; A & E Dept, Ashford Hospital, London Rd, Ashford, Middx TW15 3AA (☎ 0784 258712, fax 0784 251188)

BELTON, Anthony John (Tony); s of Stanley Louis Belton, of Oxshott, and Frances Lillian, *née* Mercer; *b* 6 April 1941; *Educ* Tiffin Sch, Magdalen Coll Oxford (MA); *Career* info systems mangr LRB 1986-88 (GLC 1964-86), divnl dir Hoskyns Pub Sector Div 1988-; cncllr London Borough of Wandsworth, chm various voluntary orgns and sch governing bodies; MBCS; *Recreations* politics, sport, films; *Style—* Tony Belton, Esq; 99 Salcott Rd, London SW11 6DF (☎ 071 223 1736); Hoskyns plc, 95 Wandsworth Rd, London SW8 2LX (☎ 081 553 6800)

BELTON, Capt Christopher Patrick Richard; s of John Joseph Belton (d 1962), and Phyllis Mary, *née* Stevens; *b* 15 Dec 1933; *Educ* Oakham Sch, HMS Conway; *m* 1, 30 March 1960 (m dis 1969), Deborah Parker; 1 s (David b 22 Nov 1965), 1 da (Joanna b 14 Feb 1963); m 2, 30 April 1970 (m dis 1987), Elizabeth Claire Leacock; 1 s (Thomas b 6 June 1980), 1 da (Camilla b 30 Oct 1981); m 3, 29 Jan 1988, Yolande Nicola, da of Leonard Charles Wright Robinson (d 1990); *Career* transferred from Royal Mail Lines to RN 1954; Cmd HM Submarines: Truncheon 1966-67, Osiris 1969-70, Churchill 1973; exec offr: HMS Dido 1970-72, HMS Bristol 1980-81; Cmd Royal Bahamas Def Force 1981-83, Queens Harbour Master Plymouth 1983-85, ret 1988; asst sec Civil Serv 1988, dir of Marine Serv (Naval) 1988-; Younger Brother of Trinity House 1973; MRIN 1970; *Recreations* golf, shooting, sailing, reading, theatre; *Clubs* Army and Navy, MCC; *Style—* Capt Christopher Belton, RN; Draycott Farm, Draycott, Yeovil, Somerset BA22 8EE (☎ 0935 840171); Ministry of Defence, Foxhill, Bath BA1 5AB (☎ 0225 883448, fax 0225 883180)

BELTON, Leslie Frederick; DFC (1944); s of Ernest Joseph George Belton (d 1943), of Streetly, Sutton Coldfield, and Gertrude Ann, *née* Allsopp (d 1970); *b* 14 Sept 1912; *Educ* King Edward VI Sch Birmingham, Birmingham Coll of Art and Crafts (ATD); *m* 28 Dec 1939, Helen Grace, da of Charles Rodgers, OBE (d 1946), of Watford; 1 s (John), 1 da (Sally); *Career* RAF U/T pilot RAFVR 1940, cmmnd 1941; flying instr: RAF Coll Cranwell 1941, RAF Brize Norton heavy gliders 1942; Bomber Cmd 1943, 149 E Indian Sqdn 1944, completed tour of ops 1944; pt/t instr Birmingham Coll of Art 1934-37; teacher of arts and craft: the GS Rye Sussex 1937-39, the GS Adwick-le-Street 1939-40; asst Winchester Sch of Art 1946-51, teacher Trg Dept Bournemouth Coll of Art 1951-54, head Swindon Sch of Art 1954; one man annual exhibition of pastels and water colours Bembridge and Henley 1977-82; fndr Basingstoke Art Club 1948 (past pres, vice pres, hon fndr memb, fell of the club), memb Reading Guild of Artists; *Recreations* caravanning, swimming, gardening; *Style—* Leslie Belton, Esq, DFC; 132 Westwood Rd, Tilehurst, Reading, Berks RG3 6LL (☎ 0734 425867)

BELTON, Michael Norman; s of Alfred Belton, of Birmingham, and Emma Elizabeth, *née* Grantham; *b* 25 Jan 1947; *Educ* Hansworth GS Birmingham, Inst of Health Service Management; *m* Joyce, da of Robert Gillies; 2 s (Richard b 31 July 1987, Stephen b 21 March 1989); *Career* dep hosp sec South Birmingham Hosp Mgmnt Ctee 1969-72, asst hosp sec East Birmingham Hosp Mgmnt Ctee 1973-74, dep hosp community administrator Birmingham Dist Health Authy 1975-77 (dep hosp administrator 1974-75); Newcastle Dist Health Authy: sector administrator 1978-82, unit administrator 1982-85, unit gen mangr 1985-87; chief exec North Tees Health Authy 1991- (dist gen mangr 1987-90); AHSM; *Recreations* lecturing, public speaking, music, reading, swimming and cycling; *Clubs* Rotary (Thornaby and Yarm); *Style—* Michael Belton, Esq; North Tees General Hospital, Hardwick, Stockton on Tees, Cleveland TS19 8PE (☎ 0642 672122, fax 0642 602995)

BELTRAMI, Joseph; s of Egidio Beltrami (d 1971), and Isabel, *née* Battison; *b* 15 May 1932; *Educ* St Aloysius Coll Glasgow, Univ of Glasgow (BL); *m* 18 Jan 1958, Brigid, da of Edward Fallon; 3 s (Edwin Joseph b 23 Sept 1962, Adrian Joseph b 8 Nov 1964, Jason Joseph b 23 Sept 1967); *Career* Intelligence Corps 1954-56: attached to Br Mil Delgn to Euro Def Community at Br Embassy Paris, Detachment Cdr Field security SW Dist Taunton; admitted slr 1956, ptnr Beltrami & Co (slr in cases of only two Royal pardons in Scotland this century: Maurice Swanson 1975, Patrick Meehan 1976); instructed in more than 300 murder trials; formerly: pres Bothwell Bowling Club, mangr and coach Bothwell AFC; memb Scottish Law Soc; *Books* The Defender (1980), Glasgow - A Celebration (contrib, 1984), Tales of the Suspected (1988), A Deadly Innocence (1989); *Style—* Joseph Beltrami, Esq; Blenio, Bothwell, Scotland (☎ 0698 852374); 93 West Nile St, Glasgow (☎ 041 221 0981)

BEMROSE, (William) Alan Wright; s of Col William Lloyd Bemrose, OBE, TD, of Umtali, Zimbabwe, and Lucy Mabel Lewis (d 1982); *b* 13 June 1929; *Educ* Repton; *m* 1, 21 July 1952 (m dis 1984), (Elizabeth) Anne, da of John William Rose (d 1955), of Duffield; 1 da (Sarah b 15 July 1959); m 2, 31 Aug 1985, Elizabeth (Nibby), da of Reginald William Melling, of Downderry, Cornwall; *Career* Sherwood Foresters (Notts & Derby), RCS, Selous Scouts Rhodesia; chief exec Br Historic Bldgs Tst 1983-, Historic Bldgs & Monuments Cmmn (HBMC): princ conslt Bldgs At Risk 1, memb Advsy Ctees Bldgs and Areas 1984-; Derbyshire CC: memb 1964, alderman 1967, chm of fin 1967-74, ldr CC 1968-74, vice chm 1977-79; tstee Chatsworth House Tst 1982-, govr Sir John Port's Charity (Repton Sch) 1965-, fndr chm Derbyshire Historic Tst 1974-, memb Historic Bldgs Cncl for England 1979-84; Freeman and Liveryman Worshipful Co of Stationers and Newspaper Makers 1952, memb Ct of Assts 1979-87; FRSA 1985; *Recreations* hunting, equestrian sports; *Style—* Alan Bemrose, Esq; Tinkersley Farm, Great Rowsley, Derbyshire DE4 2NJ (☎ 0831 178015, fax 0629 825385)

BEN-DAVID, Zadok; s of Moshe Ben-David, of Israel, and Hana Ben-David; *b* 1949; *Educ* Bezalel Acad of Art and Design Israel, Univ of Reading, St Martin's Sch of Art; *Career* asst to NH Azaz 1974, Sculpture teacher St Martin's Sch of Art 1977-82, teacher Ravensbourne Coll of Art and Design 1982-85, visiting artist Stoke-on-Trent Museum 1987; sculptor; pub cmmns: Rauncorn Shopping City 1977, Tel-Hai Museum Israel 1983, Harlow Essex 1984, Villa Nova de Cerviera Portugal 1986, Forest of Dean Sculpture Project Gloucs 1988, Tel Aviv Promenade Israel 1989, Keren Karev Jerusalem 1990, ORS Building Tel Aviv 1990; solo exhibitions incl: AIR Gallery London 1980, Woodlands Art Gallery London 1982, 121 Gallery Antwerp 1984, Benjamin Rhodes Gallery London 1985, 1987, 1990, Art and Project Amsterdam 1986, Albert Totah Gallery NY 1987, Newcastle Poly Gallery 1988, Luba Bilu Gallery Melbourne 1989, Collins Gallery Glasgow 1990, Milburn & Arte Gallery Sydney 1991; gp exhibitions incl: Atlantis Gallery London 1983, 80 Years of Sculpture (Israel Museum) Jerusalem 1984, Who's Afraid of Red Yellow & Blue? (Arnolfini Gallery Bristol) 1985, From Two Worlds (Whitechapel Art Gallery) 1986, IV Int Biennale Portugal 1986, Ek'ymose Art Contemporain Bordeaux 1987, Israeli Artists Brooklyn Museum NY 1988, Fresh Paint Israel Museum Jerusalem 1988, Museum of Israeli Art Ramat Gan Israel 1988, Galerie Albrecht Munich (with Joel Fisher and Franz Bernhard) 1989, Gimmel Gallery Jerusalem 1990; various collections in: UK, Europe, Israel, USA, Aust; jointly represented Israel Venice Biennale 1988 (with Moti Mizrachi); *Style—* Zadok Ben-David, Esq; 36 Brecknock Road, London N7 ODD (☎ 071 607 1596); Benjamin Rhodes Gallery, 9 New Burlingham Place, London W1X 1SB (☎ 071 434 1768/9, fax 071 287 8841)

BENARDOUT, Raymond; s of Nissim Benardout, of London SW7, and Betty, *née* McInnes (d 1967); *b* 27 March 1942; *Educ* St Vincent's, John Perryn, The Elms; *m* 10 March 1966, Linda Susan, da of Al Berlin (d 1979); 1 s (Marc Nissim 1 Feb 1967), 1 da (Nicola Bettina b 5 Sept 1968); *Career* estab Raymond Benardout purveyors of antique rugs tapestries and textiles 1961-, dir Benni Ltd, author numerous books and articles; chm Knightsbridge Group, memb Ctee Knightsbridge Assoc; memb: IOD, BADA; *Books* Turkoman Rugs (1974), Turkish Rugs (1975), Tribal Rugs (1976), Nomadic Rugs (1977), Caucasian Rugs (1978), Antique Rugs (1983); *Recreations* golf, travel; *Clubs* RAC; *Style—* Raymond Benardout, Esq; 5 William Street House, William St, Knightsbridge, London SW1X 9HL (☎ 071 235 0504); 4 William Street, Knightsbridge, London SW1X 9HL (☎ 071 235 3360, fax 071 823 1345)

BENCE, John Douglas; *b* 18 June 1932; *Educ* King Edward Sch Birmingham; *m* Jennifer Patricia; 5 children; *Career* vice pres Euro Packaging Operations, Stone Container Corp; dir: Touring Club of GB and I, Inst of Packaging Ltd, The Caravan Club Ltd, Europa Carton AG; chm Cartomills SA; hon treas the Caravan Club; *Recreations* sailing, caravanning; *Clubs* Royal Thames Yacht, Royal Lymington Yacht; *Style—* John Bence, Esq; The Old Vicarage, Cholesbury, nr Tring, Herts (☎ 024 029 695); Stone Container Corp, 195 Knightsbridge, London SW7 1RG (☎ 071 589 6381, fax 071 589 6514)

BENCE, Hon Mrs (Patricia Mary); *née* Dent; da of Baroness Furnivall (d 1968, herself da of 14 Baron Petre and co-heir with Lord Mowbray, Segrave and Stourton to the Baronies of Strange de Blackmere, Talbot, Howard, and others; the Barony of Furnivall, abeyant since the d in 1777 of the 9 Duke of Norfolk who was also 18 Baron Furnivall, was called out in her favour by Letters Patent 1913) and co-heiress to that Barony of Furnivall, abeyant since 1968; *b* 4 April 1935; *Educ* Mayfield Sussex; *m* 1, 1956 (m dis 1963), Capt Thomas Hornsby (d 1967); 1 s (Francis Walton Petre b 1958), 1 da (Clare Mary Petre b 1957); m 2, 1970, Roger Thomas John Bence; 1 s (Richard William Petre b 1976), 1 da (Katharine Rosamond Petre b 1971); *Style—* The Hon Mrs Bence; Trotwood, 11 Gresham Rd, Limpsfield, Oxted, Surrey (☎ 088 33 714 062)

BENCE-TROWER, Nicholas Alexander; s of Capt Peter Alexander Bence-Trower, DL, RN, of West Meon, Hants, and Sheena Margaret, *née* Grant; *b* 21 Feb 1957; *Educ* Winchester; *m* 14 Oct 1989, Nicola Sophie, da of Ralph Stuart Bell; *Career* J Henry Schroder Wagg & Co Ltd 1977-; Freeman City of London 1978, Liveryman Worshipful Co of Drapers 1982; *Recreations* golf, skiing, flying, cinema and theatre; *Style—* Nicholas Bence-Trower, Esq; 47 Sloane Gardens, London SW1W 8ED (☎ 071 730 7277); J Henry Schroder Wagg & Co Ltd, 120 Cheapside, London EC2V 6DS (☎ 071 382 6000, fax 071 382 3950, telex 8850529)

BENCE-TROWER, Capt Peter Alexander; DL (Hants 1985); s of Richard Alexander Bence-Trower, of Medmenham, Bucks, and Violet Elizabeth Mabel, *née* Weatherall; *b* 10 Jan 1925; *Educ* Winchester; *m* 9 June 1951, Sheena Margaret, da of Lewis Russell Harley Grant (d 1945), of Langside, Peebles; 2 s (Nicholas Alexander b 21 Feb 1957, Mark Grant b 16 May 1960), 2 da (Anna Marguerite b 22 Sept 1961, Caroline Jane b 30 April 1965); *Career* Midshipman HMS Glasgow and HMS Malaya 1944, HMS King George V 1945, Sub Lt i/c HMS Tahay, minesweepers Iceland and Butt of Lewis 1945-47, Lt HMS Liverpool 1947, Flag Lt to 1 Sea Lord (Lord Fraser of N Cape) 1950-51, qualified as navigation specialist HMS Actaeon (S Africa and S America) 1952-54, HMS Vanguard 1954, Lt Cdr 1955, HMS Battleaxe 1956, Army Staff Coll Camberley 1957, HMS Newfoundland 1958-60, HMY Britannia 1960, i/c HMS Carron 1961, Cdr i/c HMS Surprise 1962-64, SO ops to C in C Portsmouth 1964-66, i/c HMS Ghurkha 1966, Capt i/c HMS Protector 1967-68, naval attaché HM Embassy Paris 1969-71, RCDS 1971, Capt of the Fleet 1972, ret 1973; dir: The Glenlivet Whisky Co 1958-64, JCS Computer Bureau 1976-80; govr Queen Mary's Coll 1980-87, tstee Wessex Med Tst 1982-88 and 1990-, pres Hants branch Nat Deaf Child Soc; High Sheriff of Hampshire 1983; Freeman City of London 1946, Past Master Worshipful Co of Drapers 1984; *Recreations* fishing, golf, travel; *Clubs* White's, Royal Yacht Sqdn, Army & Navy; *Style—* Capt Peter Bence-Trower, DL, RN; West Meon House, West Meon, Hampshire GU32 1JG; Glendalloch, Glenlivet, Banffshire (☎ 073 086 278)

BENDALL, David Vere; CMG (1966), MBE (1945); s of John Manley Bendall (d 1970); *b* 27 Feb 1920; *Educ* Winchester, King's Coll Cambridge (BA); *m* 1941, Eve Stephanie Merrilees, da of Charles Galpin (d 1928), of Colombo; 1 da; *Career* Grenadier Guards 1941-46; HM Dip Serv 1946-71, asst under sec of state 1969-71; merchant banker 1971-; chm: Morgan Grenfell Int 1982-86, Morgan Grenfell Italy, Banque Morgan Grenfell en Suisse 1978-90, Banca Nazionale de Lavoro Investment Bank plc 1986-; Br Red Cross Soc 1981-85; OStJ 1986; *Recreations* tennis, shooting; *Clubs* Boodle's; *Style—* David Bendall, Esq, CMG, MBE; 3 Eaton Terrace Mews, London SW1 (☎ 071 730 4229); Ashbocking Hall, Ipswich, Suffolk (☎ 0473 890262)

BENDALL, Dr (Michael) John; s of Edward Lewis Bendall (d 1987), of Risca, Gwent, and Edna May, *née* Williams (d 1983); *b* 7 June 1943; *Educ* Pontwaun GS Risca Gwent, Univ of London (BSc, MB BS), Univ of Nottingham (DM); *m* 4 Jan 1969, Patricia, da of Herbert Wyndham Jenkins (d 1980), of Newport, Gwent; 2 s (David b 1975, Thomas b 1977), 2 da (Megan b 1973, Elinor b 1983); *Career* conslt physician in geriatric med Colchester 1974-78, sr lectr and conslt physician in health care of the elderly Nottingham 1978-; memb: Br Geriatrics Soc, BMA; PCC St Luke's Church Nottingham; FRCP 1986; *Recreations* music, theatre, reading, photography, golf; *Style—* Dr John Bendall; Department of Health Care of the Elderly, University of Nottingham Medical School, Queen's Medical Centre, Nottingham NG7 2UH (☎ 0602 421421, fax 0602 423618)

BENDALL, Vivian Walter Hough; MP (C) Ilford North 1978-; s of Cecil Aubrey Bendall (d 1963), and Olive Alvina, *née* Hough (d 1980); *b* 14 Dec 1938; *Educ* Broad Green Coll Croydon; *m* 1969; *Career* surveyor and valuer; Cons backbench ctee positions held: vice chm Employment, sec Foreign and Cwlth Affrs, vice chm Transport; *Recreations* cricket, motor sport; *Clubs* Carlton, Essex CC; *Style—* Vivian Bendall, Esq, MP; 25 Brighton Rd, Croydon, Surrey

BENEDICTUS, David Henry; s of Henry Jules Benedictus (d 1990), of Winter Lodge, Cookham Dean, Berkshire, and Kathleen Constance, *née* Richardo; *b* 16 Sept 1938; *Educ* Eton, Balliol Coll Oxford (BA), State Univ of Iowa; *m* 1971, Yvonne Daphne, da of late Harvey Antrobus; 1 s (Leo b 1977), 1 da (Chloe b 1979); *Career* author, critic, prodr, dir; story ed and dir BBC1 Wednesday Play 1965-66, Thames TV trainee dir 1968, asst dir RSC 1971, antiques corr Evening Standard 1980-82, commissioning ed Channel 4 Drama Series 1984-86, readings ed BBC 1989-, fndr and dir Kingston Books, numerous TV and theatre credits; memb ctee Br Screen Advsy Cncl, chm Censorship Ctee and memb Exec Cncl Writer's Guild; chm 28 Gp Amnesty Int; *Books* author of more than 20 incl: several books on London, The Fourth of June, The Rabbi's Wife, A Twentieth Century Man, Floating Down to Camelot; *Recreations* chess, golf, piano playing, food, bank managers, dogs; *Style—* David Benedictus, Esq; 19 Oxford Rd, Teddington, Middx TW11 0QA (☎ 081 977 4715); Room 6097, BBC Broadcasting House, London W1A 1AA (☎ 071 927 5547)

BENEY, Cedric Ivor; s of Frederick William Beney, CBE, QC (d 1986), and Irene Constance, *née* Ward-Meyer, the concert pianist; *b* 12 July 1917; *Educ* Mill Hill Sch, Univ of Reading; *m* 1, 1968, Mercia Silverthorne (d 1976); m 2, 1977, Suzanne Joselyn Frances Neville; 1 step da (Christine b 1953); *Career* WWII Lance Corpl RASC BEF 1929-41 (invalided out); worked in book publishing 1937-39, farmer 1948-50, estate mangr 1950-68, private proprietor 1968-77; *Recreations* gardening, music, reading, opera; *Style—* Cedric I Beney, Esq; Mandalay, 3 Horns Park, Bishopsteignton, Teignmouth, S Devon TQ14 9RP

BENGER, Patrick; s of Harold Albert Benger (d 1978), of Worcester, and Mildred Nancy, *née* Freeman (d 1988); *b* 29 Sept 1939; *Educ* Farnborough GS, Royal Aircraft Estab Tech Coll; *m* 20 Oct 1966, Frances Ann, *née* Finch; 1 da (Georgina Anne b 1968); *Career* asst experimental offr RAE Farnborough, seconded as tech offr E African Meteorological Dept Tanganyika 1962-64; conslt meteorologist to offshore indust: Middle East 1965-71, N Sea and Europe 1972-; md Seaplace Ltd 1985-; scientific advsr Hampshire Co Emergency Planning Orgn; FRMetS; author of technical papers and articles on meteorological aspects of offshore installation techniques; *Recreations* shooting, antique collecting; *Clubs* Naval; *Style—* Patrick Benger, Esq; c/o National Westminster Bank plc, 39 The Borough, Farnham GU9 7NR

BENHAM, David Hamilton; s of George Frederick Augustus Benham (d 1980), and Pamela Ruth, *née* Kellond; *b* 7 Jan 1942; *Educ* Univ of Southampton; *m* 14 Sept 1968, Ann Pyta, da of Sqdn Ldr L L Thomas, DFC (d 1975); 1 s (Nicholas Hamilton b 18 March 1971), 1 da (Fiona-Jane Teresa b 1 Oct 1973); *Career* admitted slr 1970, ptnr Bischoff and Co Commercial; Freeman City of London 1980, Liveryman City Livery Co 1980; memb Law Soc; *Recreations* squash, photography, collecting antiques, power boating; *Clubs* Lambs, Colets, Royal Southampton Yacht; *Style—* David H Benham, Esq; Bischoff and Co, Epworth House, 25 City Rd, London EC1 (☎ 071 628 4222, fax 071 638 3345, telex 885062)

BENHAM, Keith Peter; s of Peter Gray Benham, and Susan Phoebe, *née* Brown; *b* 10 March 1943; *Educ* Marlborough; *m* 26 Nov 1969, Merilyn Anne, da of Maj Philip Norman Holbrook (d 1990); 3 da (Samantha b 1972, Lucy b 1974, Henrietta b 1978); *Career* slr; ptnr Linklaters & Paines 1973-, (articled clerk 1963, asst slr 1968-73); memb Southern Region Bd of BR 1989-, govr St Mary's Sch Calne 1989-; memb: City of London Law Soc 1963-, The Law Soc 1963-; Freeman City of London 1968, memb Worshipful Co of Slrs (memb Co Law Sub Ctee 1976-85); *Recreations* gardening, sailing, skiing, tennis; *Clubs* City Law, Sea View Yacht; *Style—* Keith Benham, Esq; Linklaters & Paines, Barrington House, 59/67 Gresham St, London EC2V 7JA (☎ 071 606 7080, fax 071 606 5113, telex 884349, 888167)

BENHAM, Peter Carr; MBE (Mil 1945), TD (1946); s of Gerald Carr Benham, MC,

TD (d 1962); *b* 17 June 1918; *Educ* Uppingham; *m* 1940, Eileen Mary, *née* Adams; 1 s; *Career* WWII Maj Field Artillery N Africa and Normandy; slr 1947, coroner for Borough of Colchester 1958-74, chm Colchester Permanent Building Society 1977-80; *Recreations* golf (represented Essex at golf, hockey and squash rackets); *Clubs* Colchester Garrison Officers, Frinton Golf; *Style—* Peter Benham, Esq; MBE, TD; 21 Queens Rd, Colchester, Essex (☎ 0206 572019)

BENINGTON, Prof Prof Ian Crawford; s of George Crawford Benington (d 1980), of Tunbridge Wells, Kent, and Edith, *née* Green; *b* 24 Feb 1938; *Educ* Dalriada Sch Ballymoney Co Antrim, Queen's Univ Belfast (BDS); *m* 10 July 1967, Eileen Agnes, da of Thomas Irwin (d 1988), of 16 Knockbracken Park, Belfast; 1 s (David b 28 May 1974), 1 da (Fiona b 3 April 1973); *Career* serv Army Cadet Force N Irish Horse 1950-58; dental staff Queen's Univ Belfast 1961-62, sr registrar Eastman Dental Hosp and Inst of Dental Surgery London 1965-72, conslt Glasgow Dental Hosp and Sch 1972-78, dir Sch Clinical Dentistry Royal Victoria Hosp Belfast 1989- (sr lectr and conslt 1978-83, prof dental prosthetics and head Dept Restorative Dentistry 1985-90); chm Specialist Advsy Ctee for Higher Trg in Restorative Dentistry RCS, memb Eastern Health and Social Servs Bd in NI; FDSRCS, FFDRCSI; memb: BDA, RSM; *Recreations* music, hill walking; *Clubs* East India; *Style—* Prof Ian Benington; 10 Hampton Park, Belfast BT7 3JC (☎ 0232 692050); Department of Restorative Dentistry, School of Dentistry, Royal Victoria Hospital, Grosvenor Rd, Belfast BT12 6BA (☎ 0232 240503 ext 2107, fax 0232 438861)

BENJAMIN, George; s of William Benjamin, and Susan, *née* Bendon; *b* 31 Jan 1960; *Educ* Westminster, Paris Conservatoire, King's Coll Cambridge (MA, MusB), IRCAM Paris; *Career* composer, conductor, pianist; visiting prof composition RCM 1985-, dir Ensemble Musique Oblique Paris 1989-; princ works incl: Ringed by the Flat Horizon 1980 (performed BBC Proms then over 40 times worldwide), A Mind of Winter for soprano and orch (Aldeburgh Festival) 1981, At First Light (cmmnd by London Sinfonietta) 1982, Three Studies for solo piano 1982-85, Jubilation (written for London Schs Symphony Orch) 1985, Antara, for computerised keyboards and ensemble (cmmnd for 10 anniversary of Pompidou Centre Paris) 1987 (subject of BBC TV documentary), Cascade (written for London Philharmonic Orch) 1989-90, Upon Silence for mezzo-soprano and 5 violins (written for Fretwork) 1990; conductor of orchs in: UK, France, Italy, USA; awards incl: Lili Boulanger award Boston 1985, Koussevitsky Int Record award 1987, Grand Prix du Disque Paris 1987, Gramophone Contemporary Music award 1990; *Style—* George Benjamin, Esq; c/o Faber Music, 3 Queen Square, London WC1N 3AU (☎ 071 278 2654)

BENJAMIN, John Circus; s of Bernard Benjamin, of 12a The Mount, Wembley Park, Middx, and Doris, *née* Mindel; *b* 15 Jan 1955; *Educ* John Lyon Sch Middx; *m* 27 June 1986, Patricia Adele Ruane, da of Sqdn Ldr Michael Joseph Francis Burgess, of 193 Hale Rd, Hale, Cheshire; *Career* Phillips Auctioneers: cataloguer, sr cataloguer, mangr 1976-, dir Jewellery Dept 1986-, dir 1990-; regular lectr on history of jewellery; FGA 1976; *Clubs* Lansdowne; *Style—* John Benjamin, Esq; 101 New Bond Street, London W1Y 0AS (☎ 071 499 1827, fax 071 629 8876, telex 298855 BLEN G)

BENJAMIN, (Isaac) Louis; s of Benjamin Benjamin, and Harriet, *née* Boekbinder; *b* 17 Oct 1922; *Educ* Highbury Co Secdy Sch; *m* 23 May 1954, Vera Doreen, da of Thomas Frederick Ketteman; 2 da (Reica (Mrs Gray) Diane); *Career* served WWII with RAC in India, Burma and Singapore; joined Moss Empires Ltd 1937, 2 asst mangr London Palladium 1945, asst mangr and box office mangr Victoria Palace 1948, gen mangr Winter Gardens Morecmbe; sales controller Pye Records: sales controller 1959, gen mangr 1962, md 1963, chm 1975-80; jt md ATV Corp 1975-80; Stoll Moss Theatres Ltd: md 1980-81, chief exec 1982-85, pres 1985-89; pres British Music Hall Soc; Entertainment Artistes Benevolent Fund: vice pres 1971-82, life govr 1982-; presenter of Royal Variety Performance 1979-85, memb Exec Ctee Variety Club of GB, hon memb Cncl NSPCC; Companion of Grand Order of Water Rats; *Style—* Louis Benjamin Esq; Cranbourn Mansions, Cranbourn Street, London WC2 (☎ 01 437 2274, fax 01 434 1217)

BENJAMIN, Prof Ralph; CB (1980); s of Charles Benjamin (d 1944), and Claire, *née* Stern (d 1944); *b* 17 Nov 1922; *Educ* Ludwig Georg's Gymnasium Darmstadt Germany, Rosenberg Coll St Gallen Switzerland, St Oswald's Coll Ellesmere Salop, Imperial Coll London (BSc, ACGI, PhD, DSc); *m* 1951, Kathleen Ruth, *née* Bull; 2 s (John b 28 June 1956, d 1987, Michael b 30 Dec 1959); *Career* joined RN Scientific Serv 1944, head of res and dep chief scientist Admiralty Surface Weapons Estab: 1960-64, dir Admiralty Underwater Weapons Estab (and dir MOD HQ) 1964-71, dir of sci and technol GCHQ 1971-82, head communications techniques and network Supreme HQ Allied Powers in Europe 1982-87; visiting prof: Imperial Coll London 1988-, UCL 1988-; IEE Marconi Premium 1965, Heinrich Hertz Premium 1980 and 1984, Judo Black Belt, RN Diving Offrs Cert, first ascent North Face Cima di Moro; FIEE 1976, FCGI 1981, FEng 1983 (CEng 1962), FRSA 1984; *Books* Modulation, Resolution and Signal Processing (1966), numerous articles in learned jls; *Recreations* hill-walking, skiing, watersports, work; *Clubs* Athenaeum; *Style—* Prof Ralph Benjamin, CB; 13 Bellhouse Walk, Rockwell Park, Henbury, Bristol BS11 OUE (☎ 0272 821333)

BENJAMIN, Prof Sidney; *b* 6 June 1928; *Educ* Bancroft Sch Essex, Cambridge Univ (MA); *m* 1951, Golda Julia, *née* Blinder; 1 s, 1 da; *Career* served RAF 1946-49; Prudential Assurance Co 1952-59, Ferranti Computers 1959-62, ptnr Bacon & Woodrow 1964- (joined 1962); Inst of Actuaries: memb Cncl 1961-85, chm Res Ctee 1964-87; visiting prof actuarial science The City Univ; memb Cncl RSS 1982-84, chm Dystonia Soc; awarded Inst of Actuaries Gold Medal 1985; FIA, FIS, FBCS, ASA; *Recreations* painting, sketching; *Clubs* Actuaries, Gallio (past chm); *Style—* Prof Sidney Benjamin; Bacon & Woodrow, St Olaf House, London Bridge City, London SE1 2PE (☎ 071 357 7171, fax 071 378 8428/8470, telex 8953206 BWLON G)

BENJAMIN, Prof Thomas Brooke; s of Capt Thomas Joseph Benjamin (d 1964), of Wallasey, Merseyside, and Ethel Mary, *née* Brooke (d 1972); *b* 15 April 1929; *Educ* Wallasey GS, Univ of Liverpool (BEng), Univ of Yale (MEng), Univ of Cambridge (PhD); *m* 1, 1956 (m dis 1974), Helen Gilda-Marie, *née* Ginsburg; 1 s (Peter b 1965), 2 da (Lesley b 1958, Joanna b 1960); *m* 2, 26 Feb 1978, Natalia Marie-Thérèse, *née* Court; 1 da (Victoria b 1982); *Career* reader in hydrodynamics Univ of Cambridge 1967-69 (asst dir res 1956-67), prof of mathematics and dir Fluid Mechanics Res Inst Univ of Essex, first Sedleian prof of natural philosophy Univ of Oxford 1979-, fell Queen Coll Oxford, adjunct prof Pennsylvania State Univ 1988-; visiting appts at Univs in USA: Michigan 1962, Univ of Calif San Diego 1966-67, Chicago 1980, Wisconsin 1980-81, Houston 1985, Univ of Calif Berkeley 1986; memb: Cncl Royal Soc 1979-81 and 1990-, Scholarships Ctee Royal Commission for 1851 Exhibition 1980-; chm Royal Soc Mathematical Educn Ctee 1979-85; chm Nat Conf Univ Professors 1989-; Hon DSc Bath 1989; FIMA 1962, FRS 1966; *Recreations* music, steam railways; *Style—* Prof Brooke Benjamin, FRS; 8 Hernes Rd, Oxford OX2 7PU (☎ 0865 54439); Mathematical Institute, 24/29 St Giles, Oxford OX1 3LB (☎ 0865 273525, fax 0865 273543)

BENJAMIN, Victor Woolf; s of Harry Benjamin, and Dorothy, *née* Cooper; *Educ* Malvern; *m* 3 s (Daniel John, Bruce Adam, Harry), 2 da (Lucy Ann, Ruth Miranda); *Career* leading coder (special) RN 1956-58; admitted slr 1956; ptnr Berwin leighton; dep chm: Lex Service plc, Tesco plc; chm Central Cncl for Jewish Social Serv, dir Blackheath Concert Halls; memb Law Soc; *Recreations* sailing, skiing, opera; *Clubs* City of London, Savile, Royal Thames; *Style—* Victor Benjamin, Esq; Adelaide House, London Bridge, London EC4R 9HA (☎ 071 623 3144, fax 071 623 4416, telex 886420, car 0860 286 896)

BENN, Rt Hon Anthony Neil Wedgwood (Tony); PC (1964), MP (Lab) Chesterfield 1984-; s of 1 Viscount Stansgate, DSO, DFC, PC (d 1960); suc as 2 Viscount 1960, but made it known that he did not wish to claim the Viscountcy; disclaimed his peerage for life 31 July 1963, having unsuccessfully attempted to renounce his right of succession 1955 and 1960; *b* 3 April 1925; *Educ* Westminster, New Coll Oxford; *m* 1949, Caroline Middleton, da of late James Milton De Camp, of Cincinnati, USA; 3 s, 1 da; *Career* WW RAFVR 1943-45, RNVR 1945-46; joined Lab Pty 1943, MP (Lab) Bristol SE 1950-60 and 1963-83; memb Nat Exec Ctee Lab Pty 1959-60 and 1962 (chm 1971-72), candidature for leadership Lab Pty 1976 for dep leadership 1971 and 1981; Postmaster-Gen 1964-66, min of Technol 1966-70 (also temporarily held portfolios Aviation 1967 and Power 1969), oppn spokesman Trade and Indust 1970-74, sec of state for Indust and min for Post and Telecommunications 1974-75, sec of state for Energy 1975-79; pres EEC Council of Energy Mins 1977, chm Campaign Gp 1987-; chm Lab Home Policy Ctee until 1982; memb until 1982: Labour-TUC Liaison Ctee, Women's Ctee, Tribune Gp; *Books* The Privy Cncl as a Second Chamber (1957), The Regeneration of Britain (1964), The New Policies (1970), Speeches (1974), Arguments for Socialism (1979), Arguments for Democracy (1981), Writings on the Wall a radical and socialist anthology 1215-1984 (ed 1984), Fighting Back: speaking out for Socialism in the Eighties (1988); Out of the Wilderness Diaries 1963-67 (1987), Office Without Power Diaries 1968-72, Against the Tide Diaries 1973-76, Conflicts of Interest Diaries 1977-80; *Style—* The Rt Hon Tony Benn, MP; 12 Holland Park, London W11

BENN, Hon David Julian Wedgwood; s of 1 Viscount Stansgate, DSO, DFC, PC (d 1960); bro of Rt Hon Tony Benn; *b* 28 Dec 1928; *Educ* Balliol Coll Oxford; *m* 1959, June Mary, da of late Ernest Charles Barraclough; 1 s, 1 da; *Style—* The Hon David Benn; St Andrew's House, 113 Mycenae Rd (☎ 081 858 0912); Stansgate Cottage, nr Steeple, Southminster, Essex

BENN, (Edward) Glanvill; s of Sir Ernest Benn, Bt, CBE (d 1954), and Gwendolen Dorothy Benn, JP, *née* Andrews; *b* 31 Dec 1905; *Educ* Harrow, Clare Coll Cambridge; *m* 4 Jun 1931, (Beatrice) Catherine Benn, MBE, da of Claude Newbald (d 1943), of Wallington, Surrey; 1 s (James b 1944), 1 da (Elizabeth b 1936); *Career* MOI 1939, 2 Lt E Surrey Regt 1940, Adj 11 Bn E Surrey Regt 1941-42, Staff Coll Camberley 1943, Bde Maj 138 Bde Italy 1944, GSO2 Land Forces Adriatic 1945 (despatches); office boy NY Times 1925; dir: Ernest Benn Ltd publishers 1928-75, Benn Bros Ltd publishers 1928-75 (chm 1945-75), Exchange Telegraph Co Ltd 1961-72 (chm 1969-72); tstee Advertising Benevolent Soc 1951-71 (cncl memb 1937-61, chm Fin Ctee 1950-60), chm Advertising Advsy Ctee ITA 1959-63, hon treas Cwlth Press Union 1967-77 (hon life memb 1975), appeals chm Newspaper Press Fund 1971, pres Periodical Publishers Assoc 1976-77; Liveryman Worshipful Co of Stationers and Newspaper Makers 1935 (Master 1977-78); *Clubs* Reform, Aldeburgh Golf; *Style—* Glanvill Benn, Esq; Crescent Cottage, Aldeburgh, Suffolk IP15 5HW; Benn Bros plc, Sovereign Way, Tonbridge, Kent

BENN, Hilary James Wedgwood; s of Rt Hon Tony Benn, PC (disclaimed Viscountcy of Stansgate for life 1963); *b* 26 Nov 1953; *Educ* Holland Park Sch; *m* Rosalind (d 1979); *Career* Labour memb Ealing Cncl, researcher with ASTMS, chm Acton Labour Party; *Style—* Hilary Benn, Esq; 19 Rothschild Rd, Acton Green, London W4

BENN, Dr John Meriton; CB (1969); s of Ernest Benn (d 1935), of Burnley, and Emily Louise, *née* Hey (d 1957); *b* 16 July 1908; *Educ* Burnley GS, Christ's Coll Cambridge (BA, MA); *m* 1933, Valentine Rosemary, da of William Seward (d 1932), of Hanwell, Middlesex; 2 da (Susan, Diana); *Career* Miny of Educn for NI: inspr of schs 1935-44, princ 1944-51, asst sec 1951-64, perm sec 1964-69; cmmr for complaints for NI 1969-73, Parly cmmr for admin for NI 1972-73; ret; chm: NI Civil Serv Appeals Bd 1974-78, NI Schs Examinations Cncl 1974-81; memb Senate Queen's Univ of Belfast 1973-86 (pro-chllr 1979-86); *Style—* Dr John Benn, CB; 7 Tudor Oaks, Holywood, Co Down BT18 0PA (☎ 02317 2817)

BENN, Sir (James) Jonathan; 4 Bt (UK 1914), of The Old Knoll, Metropolitan Borough of Lewisham; s of Sir John Andrews Benn, 3 Bt (d 1984), and Hon Ursula Lady Benn, da of 1 Baron Hankey, *qv*; *b* 27 July 1933; *Educ* Harrow, Clare Coll Cambridge; *m* 2 July 1960, Jennifer Mary, eldest da of Dr Wilfred Vivian Howells, OBE (d 1987), of The Ferns, Clun, Shropshire; 1 s, 1 da (Juliet b 1966); *Heir* s, Robert Ernest Benn, *qv*; *Career* dir Reedpack Ltd 1988-90, chm and chief exec Reed Paper and Bd (UK) Ltd 1978-90, chm J & J Maybank Ltd 1988-90; pres Br Paper and Bd Industs Fedn 1985-87; *Style—* Sir Jonathan Benn, Bt; Fielden Lodge, Tonbridge Rd, Ightham, nr Sevenoaks, Kent TN15 9AN

BENN, Melissa Anne Wedgwood; da of Rt Hon Tony Benn, PC (disclaimed Viscountcy of Stansgate for life 1963); *b* 20 Feb 1957; *Educ* Holland Park Sch; *Style—* Miss Melissa Benn

BENN, Nigel Gregory; s of Dixon Benn, of Ilford, Essex, and Loretta Benn; *b* 22 Jan 1964; *Educ* Loxford Comp Sch; *m* 22 Jan 1991, Sharon Crowley; 2 s (Dominic, Reece), 1 da (Sade); *Career* served 1 Bn RRF W Germany and N Ireland 1980-85; professional middleweight boxer; began fighting career whilst in the Army; amateur career: memb West Ham ABC Club, London ABA Middleweight champion 1986, Nat ABA Middleweight champion 1986, winner 48 fights (1 defeat); professional boxing debut v Graeme Ahmed 1987; *Major or titles* Cwlth Middleweight Title: won v Abdul Umuru Sanda (Muswell Hill) April 1988, defended v Anthony Logan (Kensington) Oct 1988 (Fight of the Year BBBC 1988, Int Fight of the Year Boxing News 1988), defended v David Noel (Crystal Palace) Dec 1988, defended v Mike Chilambe (Kensington) Feb 1989, lost v Michael Watson (Finsbury Park) May 1989 (Fight of the Year BBBC, Domestic Fight of the Year Boxing News); WBO Middleweight Title: won v Doug de Witt (Atlantic City) April 1990 (Fight of the Month Boxing Illustrated, Fight of the Month Boxing Monthly, Best Middleweight Fighter of the Year Boxing Illustrated, voted third Biggest Upset of 1990 Boxing Weekly, third Best Int Fight of 1990 Boxing Weekly), defended v Iran Barkley (Las Vegas) Aug 1990 (Fight of the Month Boxing Illustrated, Fight of the Month Boxing Monthly, Round of the Year (Round 1) Boxing Weekly), lost v Chris Eubank (NEC Birmingham) Nov 1990 (British Fight of the Year Boxing Weekly, fifth Best Int Fight of 1990 Boxing Weekly, Fight of the Year BBBC, Domestic Fight of the Year Boxing News); professional boxing record: 29 fights, 27 victories (25 by KO, 2 by points), 2 defeats; *Awards* Best Young Boxer (Boxing Writers' Club) 1987, British Fighter of the Year (Boxing Weekly readers) 1990, Best Middleweight Puncher of 1990 (The Ring), fourth Most Destructive Puncher in the World 1990 (KO Magazine); debut single Stand and Fight released 1990; *Recreations* music, keep fit, all sports; *Style—* Nigel Benn, Esq; c/o World Sports Corpn, 212 Tower Bridge Road, London SE1 2UP (☎ 071 378 0009, fax 071 403 1040, telex 010390 G VIN B)

BENN, Capt Sir Patrick Ion Hamilton; 2 Bt (UK 1920); s of late Col Ion Bridges Hamilton Benn, s of 1 Bt; suc gf, Capt Sir Ion Hamilton Benn, 1 Bt, CB, DSO, TD,

RNVR, (d 1961); *b* 26 Feb 1922; *Educ* Rugby; *m* 1959, Edel Jorgine, da of late Col W S Lobach, formerly Royal Norwegian Army; *Heir* none; *Career* Capt Res of Offrs late Duke of Cornwall's Light Infantry, Maj Norfolk ACF; *Style*— Capt Sir Patrick Benn, Bt; Rollesby Hall, nr Gt Yarmouth, Norfolk NR29 5DT

BENN, Robert Ernest (Robin); s and h of Sir Jonathan Benn, 4 Bt, and Jennifer Mary, da of Dr Wilfred Vivian Howells, OBE; *b* 17 Oct 1963; *Educ* Judd Sch, Tonbridge, CCC Cambridge (MA); *m* 1985, Sheila Margaret, 2 da of Dr Alastair Macleod Blain, of Braco Lodge, Elgin, Moray; *Career* CA Touche Ross & Co London 1985-; *Recreations* music, walking, photography; *Style*— Robin Benn, Esq; 6, Rangers Square, Hyde Vale, Greenwich SE10 8HR (☎ 081 691 0120)

BENN, Stephen Michael Wedgwood; s of Rt Hon Tony Benn PC, MP and h to Viscountcy of Stansgate, which was disclaimed by his f for life 1963; *b* 21 Aug 1951; *Educ* Holland Park Sch, Keele Univ; *Career* memb: Inner London Educn Authority, General Purposes Ctee 1986-; *Books* The White House Staff (1984), Politics and International Relations (1979); *Style*— Stephen Benn, Esq

BENN, Timothy John; s of Sir John Andrews Benn, 3 Bt, and Hon Ursula Helen Alers, *née* Hankey; *b* 27 Oct 1936; *Educ* Harrow, Clare Coll Cambridge (MA), Princeton, Harvard Business Sch USA; *m* 1982, Christina Grace Townsend; *Career* served HM Forces 2 Lt Scots Gds 1956-57; Benn Brothers Ltd: memb Bd 1961-82, md 1972-82, dep chm 1976-81; chm Benn Brothers plc 1981-82; Ernest Benn: memb Bd 1967-82, md 1973-82, chm and md 1974-82; chm: Timothy Benn Publishing 1983-, Bouverie Publishing Co 1983-, Buckley Press 1984-, Bouverie Data Services 1986-, Henry Greenwood and Co 1987-, Dalesman Publishing Co 1989-, Stone & Cox 1989-; pres Tonbridge Civic Soc 1982-87; *Books* The (Almost) Compleat Angler (1985); *Recreations* writing, toymaking; *Style*— Timothy Benn, Esq; The Priory, Bordyke, Tonbridge, Kent TN9 1NN

BENN, Hon Lady (Ursula Helen Alers); *née* Hankey; o da of 1 Baron Hankey, GCB, GCMG, GCVO, PC (d 1963); *b* 5 Feb 1909; *Educ* Priors Field Godalming; *m* 1929, Sir John Benn, 3 Bt (d 1984); 2 s (Sir Jonathan Benn, Bt, Timothy John Benn, *qqv*), 3 da; *Career* teacher of The Alexander Technique; *Style*— The Hon Lady Benn; High Field, Pastens Rd, Limpsfield, Oxted, Surrey

BENNARD, Hon Mrs (Edith Ellen); *née* Quibell; JP (Parts of Lindsay Lincs); da of 1 and last Baron Quibell (d 1962); *b* 1904; *m* 1954, Eric Bennard Cuthbert, who took name of Bennard by deed poll 1962, s of G E Cuthbert (d 1960), of Scawby, Lincs; *Career* dir Quibell and Hardy Ltd; pres RSPCA, Scunthorpe; Mayoress of Scunthorpe 1953-54; *Style*— The Hon Mrs Bennard, JP; Sweeting Thorns, Holme Lane, Raventhorpe, Scunthorpe, S Humberside

BENNER, Patrick; CB (1975); s of Henry Grey Benner (d 1971), of Ipswich, and Gwendolen May, *née* Freeman (d 1974); *b* 26 May 1923; *Educ* Ipswich Sch, Univ Coll Oxford (BA); *m* 1952, Joan Christabel, da of John Godfrey Beresford Draper (d 1972); 2 da (Lucy, Mary); *Career* admin civil servant 1949-84; dep sec: Cabinet Office 1972-76, DHSS 1976-84; *Style*— Patrick Benner, Esq, CB; 44 Ormond Crescent, Hampton, Middlesex TW12 2TH (☎ 081 979 1099)

BENNER, Peter Charles (Priddis); s of Charles William Benner (d 1978), of Balcombe, Sussex, and Joyce, *née* Oldroyd (d 1976); *b* 1 June 1937; *Educ* Ardingly Coll Sussex, Downing Coll Cambridge (BA, MA); *m* 16 Jan 1965, Elizabeth Anne, da of Ronald Wilkinson Kenyon, of Horsham, W Sussex; 2 da (Tracy Caroline Alice b 10 Dec 1965, Lucinda Diana Kate b 17 May 1969); *Career* admitted slr 1963; sr ptnr Charles Benner & Son 1976-86, ptnr Houseman Rohan & Benner 1986-; NP 1979; chm Sussex Co Young Cons 1964-65, treas SE Area Young Cons 1965-66, parish cncllr Slaugham W Sussex, chm Mid Sussex Gp of Slrs 1983-84; memb Law Soc 1963; *Recreations* Sussex local history, old cars, dog walking; *Clubs* Utd Oxford and Cambridge Univ; *Style*— Peter Benner, Esq; Pear Trees, Warninglid, Haywards Heath, W Sussex RH17 5TY (☎ 0444 85 251); Aberdeen Ho, Haywards Heath, W Sussex RH16 4NG (☎ 0444 414 081, fax 0444 457 384, telex 877555 LAWYER G)

BENNET, Rev the Hon George Arthur Grey; s of 8 Earl of Tankerville (d 1971), and hp of n, 10 Earl of Tankerville; *b* 12 March 1925; *Educ* Radley, CCC Cambridge, Clifton Theol Coll; *m* 1957, Hazel (Jane) Glyddon, da of late Ernest W G Judson, of Bishopswood, Chard, Somerset; 2 s, 1 da; *Career* sr physics master Clifton Coll; ordained 1969, vicar Shaston Team Ministry 1973-80, rector Redenhall Harleston Wortwell and Needham 1980-90; *Books* Electricity and Modern Physics (1965); with T B Akrill and C J Millar: Physics (1979), Practice in Physics (1979); *Style*— The Rev the Hon George Bennet; 112, Norwich Rd, Wymondham, Norfolk (☎ 0953 601284)

BENNET, George Charters; s of George Charters Bennet (d 1968), and Euphemia, *née* Igoe; *b* 8 Aug 1946; *Educ* Holycross Acad, Univ of Edinburgh Med Sch (BSc, MB ChB); *m* 17 June 1978, (Kathryn) Louise, da of Dr Bernard G Willam Spilbury; 3 s (George b 1979, Simon b 1982, Matthew b 1987); *Career* former appts: London, Oxford, Southampton, Toronto; currently: conslt surgn Royal Hosp for Sick Children Glasgow, hon clinical lectr Univ of Glasgow; FRCS, FBOA; *Books* Paediatric Hip Disorders (1987); *Recreations* hill walking, gardening; *Style*— George Charters, Esq; Tamarack House, Moor Rd, Strathblane, Stirlingshire (☎ 0360 70233); Royal Hosp For Sick Children, Yorkhill, Glasgow G3 8SJ (☎ 041 339 8888)

BENNET, Hon Ian; s of 8 Earl of Tankerville (d 1971), and his 2 w, Violet, *qv*; *b* 16 April 1935; *Educ* Radley, CCC Cambridge (MA Agric); *Career* Lt RNR; farmer and landagent; mangr Chillingham Estates 1961-83; chm Northumbria Region Historic Houses Assoc 1982-85, vice chm Duke's Sch Alnwick (govr 1983-); memb (C) Berwick-upon-Tweed Borough Cncl 1983- (Cons Gp ldr 1987-); memb River Tweed Cmmn 1983-, pres Governing Cncl Chillingham Wild Cattle Assoc 1990- (memb 1967-, vice pres 1988-90); *Recreations* shooting, forestry; *Style*— The Hon Ian Bennet; Estate House, Chillingham, Alnwick, Northumberland NE66 5NW (☎ 066 85 213)

BENNETT, (Frederick Onslow) Alexander Godwyn; TD; s of Alfred Bennett, of Sulhamstead, Berks, and Marjorie Muir Bremner; *b* 21 Dec 1913; *Educ* Winchester, Trinity Coll Cambridge; *m* 18 Nov 1942, Rosemary, er da of Sir Malcolm Perks, 2 Bt; 1 s, 4 da; *Career* served WWII, cmmnd 8 RB (TA) 1939, Lt Col GSOI SHAEF 21 Army Gp (despatches twice), US Bronze Star; joined Whitbread and Co 1935; chm: Whitbread and Co Ltd 1972-77, Whitbread Investment Co Ltd 1977-88; chm Brewers Soc 1970-72; pres Kent CCC 1983; Master Worshipful Co of Brewers 1965; *Clubs* MCC; *Style*— Alexander Bennett, Esq, TD; Grove House, Selling, Faversham, Kent (☎ 0227 752250)

BENNETT, Andrew Francis; MP (Lab) Denton and Reddish 1983-; *b* 9 March 1939; *Educ* Univ of Birmingham; *m* 2 s, 1 da; *Career* teacher, NUT, memb Oldham Borough Cncl 1964-74, contested (Lab) Knutsford 1970, MP (Lab) Stockport North Feb 1974-83; memb Select Ctees: (Jt Standing Ctee) Statutory Instruments, (former Standing Ctee) Violence in the Family, Members' Interests 1979-83, Social Services 1979-; chm PLP Health and Social Services Gp, sec PLP Civil Liberties Gp, oppn front bench spokesman Educn 1983-88; *Style*— Andrew Bennett, Esq, MP; House of Commons, London SW1

BENNETT, Andrew John; s of Leonard Charles Bennett, and Edna Mary, *née* Harding (d 1984); *b* 25 April 1942; *Educ* St Edwards Sch Oxford, Univ Coll N Wales Bangor (BSc), Univ of W Indies Trinidad, Univ of Reading (MSc); *Career* Lt 6/7 Bn Royal Welch Fus TA 1961-66; VSO Kenya 1965-66, agric res offr Govt of St Vincent W Indies 1967-69, maize agromist Govt Republic of Malawi 1971-74, chief res offr (agric) Regnl Miny of Agric Southern Sudan 1976-80; Overseas Devpt Admin FCO London: agric advsr 1980-83, nat resources advsr SE Asia Devpt Div Bangkok 1983-85, head Br Devpt Div in the Pacific Fiji 1985-87, chief nat res advsr 1987-; memb: Cncl RASE, TAA; *Recreations* walking, boating; *Style*— Andrew Bennett, Esq; Overseas Development Administration, Eland House, Stag Place, London SW1E 5DH (☎ 071 273 0513)

BENNETT, Chris John Arthur; s of Stanley Arthur Bennett (d 1973), and Beatrice Rose, *née* Helsdon (d 1990); *b* 22 Aug 1947; *Educ* Ewell Castle Sch; *m* 1, 25 Jan 1975 (m dis 1985), Barbara Lois, da of Michael Burn, of Somerset; 1 s (Benjamin James b July 1980); m 2, 2 April 1988, Jennifer Margaret, da of Herbert Edward Dabnor, of Macclesfield, Cheshire; *Career* sales dir Autochem Instruments Ltd 1978-79, sr ptnr Bennett & Co 1979-81; md: C B Scientific Ltd 1981-, Bennett & Co Ltd 1985-, Biopack Ltd 1989-; *Recreations* sailing; *Style*— Chris Bennett, Esq; Field House, Newton Tony, Salisbury, Wiltshire (☎ 0980 643 21); Bennett & Co, Field House, Newton Tony, Salisbury, Wiltshire SP4 OHF (☎ 0980 64488, fax 0980 64327); Biopack Ltd, Field House, Newton Tony, Salisbury, Wiltshire SP4 0HF (☎ 0980 64488, fax 0980 64327)

BENNETT, Christopher Heal; s of Philip Hugh Pemberthy Bennett, CBE, and Jeanne Reynolds, *née* Heal; *b* 15 March 1945; *Educ* Harrow, Univ of London, Open Univ (BA); *m* 29 May 1971 (m dis), Mary Ruth, da of Ernest Samuel Stock; 1 s (Jeremy b 1977), 1 da (Georgina b 1973); *Career* ptnr Richard Ellis 1985, chm Nat Ctee Industl Agents Soc 1988 (memb 1982, treas 1984, vice-chm 1986); treas North Colchester Constituency Cons Assoc 1983-85; Freeman City of London 1971, Liveryman Worshipful Co of Painter Stainers; FRICS; *Recreations* reading, walking; *Clubs* RAC; *Style*— Christopher Bennett, Esq; Lynwood House, North Entrance, Saxmundham, Suffolk (☎ 0728 3557); Price Waterhouse (Budapest), Alagut Utca 5, 1013 Budapest, Hungary (☎ 361 155 9801)

BENNETT, Clive Frank; s of Oswald Bartram Tom Bennett, of Budleigh Salterton, Devon, and Olive Helena, *née* Archer; *b* 28 Aug 1945; *Educ* The Dragon Sch Oxford, St Lawrence Coll Ramsgate; *m* 22 Feb 1969, Jill, da of Ken Alexander Woodward; 2 s (Patrick Martin b 2 Nov 1971, Graham Neal b 24 Sept 1973), 1 da (Kim Sara b 11 Aug 1975); *Career* auditor Peat Marwick Mitchell London 1968-69 (auditor Johannesburg 1969-71); Grant Thornton Oxford: articled clerk 1963-67, mangr 1972-73, client service ptnr 1973-80, managing ptnr 1980-88, memb Nat Policy Bd 1985-87, int practice ptnr 1987-, regnl managing ptnr Central Region 1989-; Freeman City of Oxford; FCA (ACA 1968); *Recreations* yachting, white water kayaking, squash, skiing, keeping fit, reading, travelling; *Clubs* Clarendon (Oxford), various sports clubs; *Style*— Clive Bennett, Esq; Grant Thornton, 1 Westminster Way, Oxford (☎ 0865 244977, fax 0865 724420)

BENNETT, (George) Colin; s of Rowland Bennett, OBE (d 1973), and Mary, *née* Hutchinson (d 1972); *b* 10 May 1924; *Educ* Rydal Sch, Trinity Hall Cambridge; *m* 1953, Mary Christina Barron, *née* Jones; 2 s (Mark, Michael), 1 da (Georgina); *Career* slr, Notary Public; *Recreations* sport, jazz, photography; *Clubs* MCC; *Style*— Colin Bennett, Esq; Colwyn, Woodlands Lane, Gt Oakley, Corby, Northants (☎ 0536 743475); office: West St, Kettering, Northants (☎ 0536 513195)

BENNETT, David Anthony; s of Albert Henry Bennett, of 498 Warwick Rd, Solihull, West Midlands, and Doris May Ward; *b* 4 Oct 1948; *Educ* Harold Malley GS Solihull, Portsmouth Poly, John Hopkins Univ, Sch of Advance Int Studies (scholar, BSc, Dip Int Affrs); *Career* stagiaire and admin Euro Cmmn 1973-74, Econ Planning Div British Gas 1977-84, dir pub affrs Eurofi plc 1984-87, md Powerhouse Europe 1987-; dir: Powerhouse Europe 1987-, dir Powerhouse Group Ltd 1989-, conslt speaker in EC issues for Euro Cmmn, sec Lab Economics, Fin and Taxation Assoc (LEFTA) 1974-81, Parly candidate (SDP/Alliance) 1983 and 1987, Euro Parly candidate 1984, alternate memb Econ and Social Ctee of Euro Communities 1982-84, expert Econ and Social Ctee 1990-91; *Books* The European Economy in 1975 (1975); *Recreations* tennis, skiing, walking, travel, theatre; *Style*— David Bennett, Esq; 1 The Vat House, 27 Regent's Bridge Gardens, London SW8 1HD (☎ 071 735 0241); Powerhouse Europe Ltd, 26 Westbourne Grove, London W2 5RH (☎ 071 221 3754, fax 071 221 0723)

BENNETT, Dudley Paul; s of Patrick James Bennett, of Bognor Regis, and Mary, *née* Edmondson; *b* 4 Aug 1948; *Educ* Bradfield, Univ of London (LLB); *m* 24 May 1986, Patricia Ann, da of James Kinnear Martin, of Notts; 2 da (Olivia Mary b 4 Feb 1988, Emma Jayne b 5 Oct 89); *Career* called to the Bar Inner Temple 1972; rec Crown Ct 1988-; *Recreations* gardening, travel; *Style*— Dudley Bennett, Esq; 50 High Pavement, Nottingham (☎ 0602 503 503)

BENNETT, Dr (Albert) Edward; s of Albert Edward Bennett (d 1973), and Frances Anne, *née* Owen (d 1971); *b* 11 Sept 1931; *Educ* Univ Coll Sch, The London Hosp Medical Coll (Arnold Thompson prize for Medical and Surgical Diseases of Children); *m* 1 Feb 1957, Jean Louise, da of Lawrence Dickinson (d 1980); 2 s (Mark Edward Hurley b 1957, Neil Edward Francis b 1965); *Career* Surgeon Lt RN 1957-60; medical offr The Wellcome Fndn 1960-64, sr lectr Dept of Clinical Epidemiology and Social Medicine St Thomas's Hosp Medical Sch Univ of London 1964-70, dir Health Servs Evaluation Gp Univ of Oxford 1970-77, prof and head Dept of Clinical Epidemiology and Social Medicine St George's Hosp Medical Sch Univ of London 1974-81; dir: Directorate of Health and Safety Cmmn of the Euro Communities 1981-87, Directorate of Nuclear Safety Industry and Environment and Civil Protection 1987-; FFPHM 1972, FFOM 1984, FRCP; *Books* Questionnaires in Medicine (1975), Recent Advances in Community Medicine (ed, 1978), Communications Between Doctors and Patients (1976); *Recreations* music, cinema, gardening; *Clubs* Athenaeum; *Style*— Dr Edward Bennett; Avenue des Pins 4, Kraainem, Brussels, Belgium B1950 (☎ 02 767 5947); Commission of the European Communities, 200 Rue De La Loi, Brussels, Belguim (☎ 02 2354049, fax 02 236 3041, telex 21877 COMEUB)

BENNETT, Francis Ernest Herman; CBE (1963); s of Sir Ernest Nathaniel Bennett (d 1947), of Cwmllecoediog, Aberangell, Machynlleth, and Marguerite, *née* Kleinwort; bro of Rt Hon Sir Frederic Mackarness Bennett, *qv*; *b* 5 Nov 1916; *Educ* Westminster, New Coll Oxford; *m* 1947, Hon Ruth Gordon, *qv*, da of 1 Baron Catto, CBE (d 1959); 2 s; 1 da (Olivia); *Career* WWII Capt 1939-46; third sec to HM Legation Bucharest 1947-49; sec-gen Lib Int 1951-52; called to the Bar 1953, chm WJ Cox Ltd 1959-74, dep chm Cons GLC 1975-76 (chief whip 1959, alderman and chief whip 1965-79), chm and cmmr Advsy Ctee on Gen Cmmrs of Income Tax 1978-; memb Court Brunel Univ, former govr London Festival Ballet; Hon DUniv Brunel Univ; *Recreations* skiing, shooting, travelling, entomolgy; *Clubs* Reform, Carlton; *Style*— Francis Bennett, Esq, CBE; C Hoare and Co, 37 Fleet St, London EC4

BENNETT, Rt Hon Sir Frederic (Mackarness); DL (Greater London 1990), PC (1985); 2 s of Sir Ernest Nathaniel Bennett (d 1947), of Cwmllecoediog, Aberangell, Machynlleth, and Marguerite, *née* Kleinwort; bro of Francis Ernest Herman Bennett, *qv*; *b* 2 Dec 1918; *Educ* Westminster; *m* 1945, Marion Patricia, da of late Maj Cecil Burnham, OBE, of Manor Farm, Rustington, Sussex; *Career* serv WWII RA; called to the Bar Lincoln's Inn 1946; contested (C) Burslem 1945, MP Reading North (C) 1951-55, Torquay 1955-87; ldr Br Delegation to Cncl of Europe and WEU 1979-87 (vice pres 1979-87); chm and dir of various cos; Lord of the Manor of Mawddwy; Cdr Order of Phoenix (Greece) 1963, Star of Pakistan (Sithari, Pakistan) 1964, Cdr Polonia Restituta (Poland) 1977, Grand Cdr's Cross 1984, Order of Al-Istiqlal (Jordan) 1980, Cdr Isabel la Catolica (Spain) 1982, Hilal-i-Quaid-i-Azam (Pakistan) 1983, cdr Order of Merit (Germany) 1989, Grand Cross Order of Polonia Restituta First Class 1990, Knight Commander The Knightly Order of Vitez (Hungary) 1990; Hon LLD Univ of Istanbul 1984; Freeman City of London 1984; kt 1964; *Books* Reds under the Bed, or the Enemy at the Gate - and Within (1979, 3 edn 1982); *Recreations* shooting, skiing, sailing; *Clubs* Carlton, Beefsteak; *Style—* The Rt Hon Sir Frederic Bennett; Cwmllecoediog, Aberangell, nr Machynlleth, Powys (☎ 065 02 430); Oswego Island, St Davids, Bermuda; 2 Stone Bldgs, Lincoln's Inn, London WC2 (☎ 071 242 3900)

BENNETT, Dr Gerald Charles Joseph; *b* 28 July 1951; *Educ* Welsh Nat Sch of Med Cardiff (MB, BCh); *Career* lectr geriatric med St George's Hosp Tooting 1980-84, currently conslt in geriatric med Royal London Hosp; written numerous articles, chapters in books, and made TV and radio appearances; memb Exec Ctee Age Concern Greater London; MRCP 1980, memb Med Protection Soc; *Books* Alzheimers Disease and Other Causes of Confusion (1989); *Recreations* ballet, travel; *Style—* Dr Gerald Bennett; 46 Gerrard Rd, London N1 8AX (☎ 071 359 9320); The Royal London Hosp, Mile End, Dept of Health Care of the Elderly, Bancroft Rd, London E1 4DG (☎ 071 377 7843/4/5)

BENNETT, Capt Gordon Beresford; s of Ernest Bennett (d 1977), of Abbotts Way, Newcastle, Staffs, and Annie, *née* Beresford (d 1978); *b* 14 May 1922; *Educ* The HS Newcastle-under-Lyme Staffs; *m* 10 Jan 1948, Iris McFarlane (Mac), da of Harold Mayhew (d 1970), of 7 The Chine, Saltburn, Yorks; 2 da (Rosemary Elizabeth (Mrs Smeaton) b 1951), Catherine Rosamund (Mrs McIlroy) b 1954); *Career* S Staff Regt 1941-42, OCTU Lanark and Sandhurst 1942-43, cmmnd 6 Bn Royal Northumberland Fus 1943, 3 Div Reconnaissance Regt Reconnaissance Corps 1943, served in Italy with 44 Recon Regt, 56 Div and GHQ, CMF, demobbed 1946; Donald H Bates and Co Stoke on Trent: ptnr 1953-88, sr ptnr 1981-88, currently conslt; pres: N Staffs Soc of CAs 1971-72, Staffs Salop and Wolverhampton Soc of CAs 1982-83; memb: ICAEW 1952, FCA; *Recreations* walking, photography, gardening; *Clubs* Br Pottery Mfrs Fedn; *Style—* Gordon Bennett, Esq; Glen How, Park Wood Drive, Baldwins Gate, Newcastle, Staffs (☎ 0782 680 711); Donald H Bates & Co, 110 Lichfield St, Hanley, Stoke on Trent ST1 3DS (☎ 0782 262 121, fax 0782 287 246)

BENNETT, (Jeffery) Graeme; *b* 30 May 1942; *Educ* Univ of Queensland (MB BS); *Career* cardiac surgn Nat Heart Hosp, sr lectr Nat Heart and Lung Inst; FRCS, FRCSEd; *Recreations* golf, art; *Clubs* Hurlingham, Royal Wimbledon Golf; *Style—* Graeme Bennett, Esq; National Heart Hospital, Westmoreland St, London W1 (☎ 071 486 4433, fax 071 487 4326)

BENNETT, Guy Patrick de Courcy; s of Patrick John de Courcy Bennett, of Thames Ditton, and Pamela Mary Ray, *née* Kirchner; *b* 27 Oct 1958; *Educ* Wimbledon Coll, Manchester Univ (BSc); *m* 5 Nov 1988, Monica Beatrice, da of Alfred Cecil Francis Brodermann (d 1974); 1 da (Emily b 1990); *Career* investmt analyst Equity & Law Life 1980-83, dir Marketable Securities Div CIN Mgmnt 1984-; *Recreations* tennis, squash; *Style—* Guy Bennett, Esq; 10 Jedburgh St, Clapham Common, London SW11 5QB (☎ 071 350 1200); PO Box 10, Hobart House, Grosvenor Place, London SW1X 7AD (☎ 071 389 7014)

BENNETT, Sir Hubert; s of Arthur Bennett, JP, and Eleanor, *née* Peel; *b* 4 Sept 1909; *Educ* Victoria Univ, Manchester Sch of Architecture; *m* 1938, Louise F C Aldred; 3 da (Louise, Elizabeth, Helen); *Career* architect in private practice; chief architect to LCC and GLC 1956-71, exec dir English Property Corp 1971-79; assessor: Vauxhall Cross Competition, City Poly Hong Kong 1982; conslt architect for guest palace for HM Sultan of Oman 1982, architect to UNESCO Paris 1982; memb RIBA Cncl (1952-55, 1957-62, 1965-66, 1967-69); recipient of various architectural and design awards; FRIBA; kt 1970; *Recreations* golf; *Style—* Sir Hubert Bennett; Broadfields, Ripsley Park, Liphook, Hants GU30 7JH (☎ 0428 724176)

BENNETT, Hugh Peter Derwyn; QC (1988); s of Peter Ward Bennett, OBE, and Priscilla Ann, *née* Troughton; *b* 8 Sept 1943; *Educ* Haileybury, ISC, Churchill Coll Cambridge (MA); *m* 6 Dec 1969, Elizabeth, da of James Whittington Landon, DFC; 1 s (Vivian Hugh James b 16 Nov 1974), 3 da (Ursula Ann b 29 Jan 1971, Henrietta Mary b 1 July 1973, Rosamond Elizabeth b 13 Sept 1976); *Career* called to the Bar 1966, asst rec 1987, rec Crown Ct 1990, memb Supreme Ct Rule Ctee 1988; hon legal advsr Sussex Co Playing Fields Assoc 1988-, pt/t chm Horserace Betting Levy Appeal Tbnl 1989-; govr Lancing Coll 1981-, fell SE Div Woodard Corp 1987-; *Recreations* cricket, tennis, shooting and fishing; *Clubs* MCC; *Style—* Hugh Bennett, Esq, QC; Queen Elizabeth Building, Temple, London EC4Y 9BS (☎ 071 583 7837, fax 071 353 5422)

BENNETT, Ian Howard; s of John Fitzroy Bennett (d 1986), of Woodford Green, Essex, and Marjorie Grace Winifred, *née* Howard (d 1979); *b* 24 July 1943; *Educ* Forest Sch, St Edmund Hall Oxford; *m* 14 April 1973, Jane Victoria, da of Harold Elmy, of Farnham, Surrey; 2 s (Toby b 1975, Alexander b 1981), 1 da (Emily b 1979); *Career* purchasing offr Ford Motor Co 1965-67, sales exec IBM (UK) Ltd 1967-81, regnl sales mangr Amdahl (UK) Ltd 1981-84, md Digital Publishing Systems Ltd 1985-88, sales dir DPS Typecraft Ltd 1988-; *Recreations* skiing, hockey, golf, tennis, squash; *Style—* Ian Bennett, Esq; 17 Parkmore Close, Sunset Ave, Woodford Green, Essex (☎ 081 504 2045); Acorn House, Great Oaks, Basildon, Essex (☎ 0268 523471, fax 0268 281090, car 0836 214020)

BENNETT, James Douglas Scott; s of Andrew Carmichael Bennett, (d 1983), of Edinburgh, and Margaret Catherine, *née* Nelson; *b* 1 March 1942; *Educ* Fettes, Univ of Edinburgh (MA); *m* 14 June 1969, Lorna Elizabeth Margaret, da of John Trevor William Peat (d 1974); 2 s (Hamish b 1974, Fraser b 1977); *Career* dir: Anglo Continental Tst 1972-5, Chloride Alcad Ltd 1978-81, East of Scotland Industrial Investments plc 1984-, John Menzies plc 1981-; CA; memb: Accounts Commission for Local Authy in Scot 1983-, Scot Provident Inst 1989; FBIM, FRSA; *Recreations* golf, reading; *Clubs* New (Edinburgh), Denham Golf, IOD, Luffness New (Murrayfield); *Style—* James Bennett, Esq; John Menzies plc, 108 Princes St, Edinburgh (☎ 031 225 8555)

BENNETT, Jeremy James Balfe; s of Arthur Henry Bennett (d 1968), and Anne Gladys Bennett (d 1976); *b* 20 Jan 1934; *Educ* Repton; *m* 24 April 1965, Shelagh Winifred, da of Robert Jones (d 1968); 3 da (Sarah b 1962, Charlotte b 1967, Jane b 1967); *Career* cmmnd Sherwood Foresters, Cheshire Yeomanry (TA); dir Grants of St James's Ltd 1975; md Grants Wine & Spirit Merchants 1978; chm: London Wine Importers 1981, Wine & Spirit Educn Tst 1988, Acad of Wine Service 1988; corp affrs dir Euro Cellars Ltd 1987; *Recreations* photography, music, reading, walking; *Clubs* Cavalry and Guards'; *Style—* Jeremy Bennett, Esq; The Vine House, Rooks Lane, Broughton, nr Stockbridge, Hants SO20 8AZ (☎ 0794 301219); c/o European Cellars, St James's House, Guildford Business Park, Guildford, Surrey (☎ 0483 64861)

BENNETT, Col John Stanley; OBE (1977); s of Stanley Alfred Bennett (d 1972), of Bexhill-on-Sea, and Ethel Burdiss, *née* Smith (d 1988); *b* 20 Oct 1933; *Educ* Melville Coll Edinburgh, Farnborough GS, Royal Mil Acad Sandhurst; *m* 17 Aug 1960, Pauline Mary, da of Bernard Joseph Edsforth, of Accrington, Lancs; 1 s (Timothy b 1963), 2 da (Jane b 1964, Anne b 1965); *Career* cmmnd RA 1954, CO 5O MSL Regt RA BAOR 1974-77, GSOI MOD Defence Sales Orgn 1977-80, CIG RSA 1982-86, Col GS MOD Directorate of Mgmnt Audit 1986-89; MBIM 1977; *Recreations* country and fell walking, music, reading, gardening; *Clubs* Royal Cwlth Soc; *Style—* Col John Bennett, OBE; St Leonards-on-Sea, E Sussex

BENNETT, Leon Samuel; s of Solomon Bennett, of Caesarea, Israel, and Freda, *née* Canter; *b* 14 June 1935; *Educ* Liverpool Coll, Liverpool Univ (LLB); *m* 6 Feb 1966, Beverley Elaine, da of Solomon (Sid) Levene (d 1980); *Career* slr; chm Fund Raising Ctee Stapely Home and Hosp 1972-89; Freeman of Hale 1986; *Recreations* golf, squash, tennis, snooker, bridge; *Clubs* Racquet (Liverpool), Lee Park Golf (Liverpool); *Style—* Leon S Bennett, Esq; Thimble Cottage, 16 Hale Rd, Hale, Cheshire L24 5RE (☎ 051 425 2184); 46 Castle St, Liverpool L2 7LA (☎ 051 277 1126)

BENNETT, Dowager Lady; Leopoldine; da of Leopold Armata, of Vienna; *m* 1938, as his 2 w, Sir Albert Bennett, 1 Bt (d 1945); *Style—* Dowager Lady Bennett; c/o 46 High Point, Weybridge, Surrey

BENNETT, Lilian Margery; *née* Barnett; da of Maurice Sydney Barnett, of London (d 1981), and Sophia Levy (d 1975); *b* 22 Aug 1922; *Educ* West Ham Secondary Sch; *m* 2 Nov 1952, Ronald, s of Alec Bennett (d 1974), of London; 1 s (Jonathan b 1954); *Career* dir: Thermo-Plastics Ltd 1957-68, Manpower plc 1968-, Girlpower Ltd 1968-, Overdrive plc 1968-; memb The Parole Board & Community Serv Volunteers Employment Panel; FRSA; *Recreations* reading, music, community work; *Style—* Mrs Lilian Bennett; 67 Porchester Terrace, London W2 3TT (☎ 071 262 4001); Manpower plc, 66 Chiltern St, London W1M 1PR (☎ 071 224 6688, fax 071 224 5267)

BENNETT, Linda Margaret; da of Norman James Turner (d 1981), of Swanage, Dorset, and Margaret Doris, *née* Kneller; *b* 28 Aug 1950; *Educ* Sutton HS GPDST, UCW Aberystwyth (BSc); *m* 28 Aug 1982, Thomas John Paterson, s of Thomas Bennett, of Amesbury, Wilts; *Career* regnl mangr Angus Fire Armour 1972-78, dir Rayner Advertising 1978-81; Eros Mailing: client servs dir 1982-87, md 1987-; MInstM, FIOD; *Recreations* water skiing, snow skiing, sailing; *Style—* Mrs Linda Bennett; Eros Mailing, Central Way, Feltham, Middx TW14 0TG (☎ 081 751 6373, fax 081 751 6562, telex 24346)

BENNETT, Martin Malcolm Bertram; s of Bertram Frederick Ernest Bennett (d 1984), of Herne Bay, and Lilli, *née* Giersdorf (d 1985); *b* 31 Jan 1952; *Educ* Simon Langton GS Canterbury, Gonville and Caius Coll Cambridge (MA); *m* 17 Oct 1981, Jacqueline Mary, da of Herbert Percy Gambrell (d 1982), of Whitstable; 2 da (Laura b 1987, Alicia b 1989); *Career* admitted slr 1976, ptnr Nabarro Nathanson 1982-; *Recreations* trying to relax; *Style—* Martin Bennett, Esq; Nabarro Nathanson, 50 Stratton St, London W1X 5FL (☎ 071 493 9933, fax 071 629 7900, telex 881 3144 NABARO G)

BENNETT, (John) Martyn; s of Dr John Garner Bennett, JP, of Crosby, Liverpool, and Dorothy, *née* Batty; *b* 14 Feb 1946; *Educ* Rydal Sch, Liverpool Univ (LLB); *m* 6 Sept 1980, Catherine Elizabeth, da of Cornelius Raphael O'Leary (d 1988); 2 s (Henry b 1985, Edwin b 1987); *Career* lectr in law 1967-68, barr Gray's Inn 1969, Northern Circuit 1969-, dir Bennett Safety Wear Ltd and assoc cos 1984-, memb Area Legal Aid Ctee 1986-; asst rec 1988; various contributions to legal jls; represented N Wales at rugby 1967-69, chm Rydal Bankhall Youth Centre 1980-83, govr local Primary Schools 1986-88; memb Family Law Bar Assoc; *Recreations* watching rugby, fell walking; *Clubs* Liverpool Racquet, Waterloo Football; *Style—* Martyn Bennett, Esq; Stanthorne House, Burton Lane, Duddon, Cheshire CW6 0EP (☎ 082 924 303); Peel House, 5/7 Harrington St, Liverpool, L2 9QA (☎ 051 236 4321); 5 Essex Court, Temple, London EC4Y 9AH

BENNETT, Mrs John; Mary Letitia Somerville; da of Rt Hon Herbert Albert Laurens Fisher, OM, FRS (d 1940), and Lettice, *née* Ilbert; *b* 9 Jan 1913; *Educ* Oxford HS, Somerville Coll Oxford; *m* 1955, John Sloman Bennett, CMG (d 1990), s of late Ralph Bennett; *Career* princ St Hilda's Coll Oxford 1965-80; *Style—* Mrs John Bennett; 25a Alma Place, Oxford

BENNETT, Michael; s of late Frank Carlton Bennett (d 1973); h to Btcy of cousin, Sir Ronald Bennett, Bt, *qv*; *b* 15 Feb 1924; *m* 1952, Janet Hazel Margaret, da of Brig Edward Joseph Todhunter, TD; 1 s, 2 da; *Style—* Michael Bennett, Esq; Flat 70, Albert Hall Mansions, London SW7

BENNETT, Dr Michael Camm; s of Francis Camm Bennett (d 1971), of Bath, Somerset, and Lilian Mabel, *née* Pegler (d 1951); *b* 29 Sept 1929; *Educ* King Edward VI Sch Bath, King's Coll London (BSc, PhD); *m* 9 Jan 1954, Mollie, da of Alan Charles Riches (d 1962), of Beetley, Norfolk; 1 s (Richard b 1957), 2 da (Jane b 1955, Suzanne b 1962); *Career* sr physical chemist Imperial Coll of Tropical Agric Trinidad 1954-59; Tate & Lyle: head of Physical Chemistry Res Dept London 1960-68, dir tech servs 1969-75, dir engrg 1975-85; chm: British Charcoals & Macdonalds, Process Technologies, Farrow Irrigation Smith-Mirrlees 1975-85 (md Int Div 1985-87, dir in Ltd Co 1986-89, gp tech dir 1987-89, ret 1989); chm Int Soc Sugar Cane Technologists 1974-80; pres: Sugar Processing Res Inc USA 1978-82, Br Soc of Sugar Cane Technologists 1981-87, Sugar Indust Technologists Inc USA 1982-83; CChem, FRSC 1976, memb Soc Chem Indust 1968; George & Eleanor Meade Award 1970 USA, SASTA Golden Jubliee Award 1975 South Africa, The Crystal Award 1978 USA; *Recreations* gardening, walking, shooting, sailing; *Style—* Dr Michael Bennett; Arden, Pastens Rd, Limpsfield Chart, Surrey RH8 0RE (☎ 0883 722 171)

BENNETT, Prof Michael David; s of Stanley Roland Bennett, and Marion, *née* Woods; *b* 6 Oct 1943; *Educ* Gravesend Boys GS, Univ Coll Wales Aberystwyth (BSc, PhD); *m* 28 Aug 1971, Anita Lucy, da of Harry Ring, of 51 Milroy Ave, Northfleet, Kent; 1 s (Nathan b 1980), 2 da (Michelle b 1976, Danielle b 1977); *Career* res scientist (cytogeneticist) Plant Breeding Inst Cambridge 1968-87, Venture res fell BP 1986-, keeper of Jodrell Laboratory Royal Botanic Gardens Kew 1987-; FLS 1988; *Recreations* gardening, reading, bible study; *Style—* Prof Michael Bennett; 2 Kew Palace Cottages, Royal Botanic Gardens, Kew, Richmond, Surrey TW9 3AQ (☎ 081 948 9280); Jodrell Laboratory, Royal Botanic Gardens, Kew, Richmond, Surrey TW9 3DS (☎ 081 940 1171, fax 081 948 1197, telex 296694 KEWGAR)

BENNETT, Neil Roger; s of Eric Joseph Bennett, of Tillington, Staffs, and Alice, *née* Savage; *b* 12 May 1956; *Educ* Wolverhampton GS, Trinity Coll Cambridge (MA, DipArch); *Career* architect; projects include: TV AM Headquarters 1981-84, Charing Cross and Embankment Place Devpt 1985-88; project dir: Terry Farrell Ptnrship 1986-89, Burn Bennett Cook 1989-(ptnr); memb MIND; memb RIBA 1980; *Style—* Neil Bennett, Esq; 35 Arlington Avenue, London N1 7BE (☎ 071 354 5602); Pont Evans, Ceinws, Corris, Gwynedd; Burn Bennett Cook, 114 Great Portland St, London W1N 6EP (☎ 071 636 8868, fax 071 323 5205)

BENNETT, Prof (Stanley) Neville; s of late Stanley Bennett, of Preston, Lancs, and Gladys, *née* Welch; *b* 25 July 1937; *Educ* Kirkham GS, Univ of Lancaster (BEd, PhD); *m* 18 March 1961, Susan Gail, da of Peter Umney, of Foyers, Scotland; 1 s (Neil b 1961), 2 da (Louise b 1963, Sara b 1964); *Career* radio offr Mercantile Marine 1956-61, radio engr Br Aerospace 1961-64, prof of educnl res Univ of Lancaster 1978-85 (res offr 1969-72, lectr and sr lectr 1972-78), dir Centre for Res on Teaching and Learning Univ of Exeter 1987- (prof of educn 1985-); memb: Br Educnl Res Assoc, American Educnl Res Assoc, Euro Assoc for Res on Learning and Instruction; *Books*

Teaching Styles and Pupil Progress (1976), Focus on Teaching (1979), Open Plan Schools (1980), The Quality of Pupil Learning Experiences (1984), A Good Start (1989), From Special to Ordinary Schools (1989); *Recreations* gardening, travel, DIY, walking, reading; *Style*— Prof Neville Bennett; School of Education, University of Exeter, St Lukes, Exeter, Devon (☎ 0392 264794)

BENNETT, Nicholas Jerome; MP (Cons) Pembroke 1987-; s of Peter Ramsden Bennett, and Antonia Mary Bennett (d 1984); *b* 7 May 1949; *Educ* Univ of London (BA), Univ of Sussex (MA); *Career* former: teacher, lectr and educn offr; cllr London Borough of Lewisham 1974-82 (ldr of the oppn 1979-81), memb ILEA 1978-81, contested Hackney Central Gen Election 1979; memb Select Ctee on Welsh Affairs PPS to Roger Freeman, MP, Min of S of Tport 1990-, parly under-sec of State for Wales 1990-; *Recreations* swimming, history, transport, browsing in second hand bookshops; *Style*— Nicholas Bennett, MP; c/o House of Commons, London SW1 (☎ 071 219 4415)

BENNETT, Dr Peter Norman; s of Norman Bennett (d 1989), and Elizabeth Jane, *née* Ogston; *b* 25 Nov 1939; *Educ* Nairn Acad, Univ of Aberdeen (MB ChB, MD); *m* 31 Aug 1963, Jennifer Mary, da of Eric Arthur Brocklehurst, of Hull, N Humberside; 2 s (Michael John b 1965, Neil Robert b 1968), 1 da (Sally Ann Elizabeth b 1972); *Career* lectr in med Univ of Aberdeen 1967-71, Wellcome res fell UCH London 1971-73, lectr Royal Postgrad Med Sch 1973-76, conslt physician in clinical pharmacology and dir of Clinical Pharma Unit Royal United Hosp Bath 1976-, assoc dean School of Postgrad Med Univ of Bath 1989 (sr lectr in clinical pharmacology 1976-90, dir Centre for Med Studies 1978, reader in clinical pharmacology); memb Br Pharmacological Soc (treas Clinical Section 1982-87), chm Euro Working Gp on Drugs and Breast Feeding 1983-; *Books* Clinical Pharmacology (with D R Laurence, 1987), Multiple Choice Questions on Clinical Pharmacology (with D R Laurence and F Stokes, 1988), Drugs and Human Lactation (ed, 1988); *Recreations* fishing; *Clubs* Royal Commonwealth; *Style*— Dr Peter Bennett; Denmede, Southstoke Rd, Combe Down, Bath, Avon BA2 5SL (☎ 0225 823255, fax 0225 332886)

BENNETT, His Hon Judge Raymond Clayton Watson; s of Harold Watson (Church Army Capt, d 1941), and Doris Helena, *née* Edwards (later Bennett, d 1988); *b* 20 June 1939; *Educ* Glasgow Acad, Bury GS, Univ of Manchester (LLB); *m* 24 April 1965, Elaine Margaret, da of William Haworth, of Clitheroe; 1 s (John b 1966), 1 da (Jane b 1969); *Career* slr Blackburn 1964-72; called to the Bar Middle Temple 1972; Northern Circuit 1972-, rec of Crown Ct, circuit judge 1989-; memb Hon Soc of Middle Temple; *Recreations* tennis, squash, sailing, cycling; *Style*— His Hon Judge Bennett; c/o The Crown Court, Manchester

BENNETT, Sir Reginald Frederick Brittain; VRD (1944); s of Samuel Robert Bennett (d 1964), and Gertrude, *née* Brittain (d 1946); *b* 22 July 1911; *Educ* Winchester, New Coll Oxford (MA, BM BCh), LMSSA, Inst of Psychiatry London (DPM); *m* 1947, Henrietta, da of Capt Henry Berwick Crane, CBE, RN (d 1987); 1 s (Timothy), 3 da (Antonia, Medina, Belinda); *Career* Surgn Lt Cdr RNVR and Fleet Air Arm Pilot 1939-46; MP (Cons) Gosport and Fareh 1950-79, PPS Iain Macleod 1954-63; chm: Parly and Scientific Ctee 1959-61, Parly Anglo-Italian Ctee 1969-79, Catering Sub Ctee 1970-79; vice pres Parly Franco-British Ctee 1972-79, memb Servs Ctee; wine conslt and co dir; chm Nadder Wine Co Ltd 1985-, dir Italian General Shipping Co Ltd 1977-; chm: Amateur Yacht Research Soc 1972-90, World Sailing Speed Record Cncl (IYRU) 1980-, RYA Speed Sailing Ctee 1980-; Grande Officiale Italian Order of Merit 1977; kt 1979; *Recreations* yacht racing, foreign travel, basking in the sun; *Clubs* White's, Imperial Poona Yacht (cdre); *Style*— Sir Reginald Bennett, VRD; 30 Strand-on-the-Green, London W4 3PH (☎ 081 995 1777)

BENNETT, Richard Rodney; CBE (1977); s of H Rodney and Joan Esther Bennett; *b* 29 March 1936; *Educ* Leighton Park, Royal Acad of Music; *Career* composer; memb Gen Cncl Performing Right Soc 1975-, vice-pres London Coll of Music 1983-; *Style*— Richard Bennett, Esq, CBE; c/o Mrs Keys, London Management, Regent House, 235 Regent St, London W1

BENNETT, Robert; s of late Robert Bennett, and Emily, *née* Clegg; *b* 16 June 1940; *Educ* Rossall; *m* 5 Oct 1963, Alice Mary, da of late George William Ormerod; 1 s (Robin b 1964 d 1966), 2 da (Georgina b 1967, Jill b 1968); *Career* chm Lancs CCC 1987- (cricketer 1962-66); mangr England A Team to Zimbabwe and Kenya 1990; *Style*— Robert Bennett, Esq; Pippin Bank, Braaid Rd, Marown Douglas, Isle of Man

BENNETT, Prof Robert John; s of Thomas Edward Bennett, of Southampton, and Kathleen Elizabeth, *née* Robson; *b* 23 March 1948; *Educ* Taunton's Sch Southampton, St Catharine's Coll Cambridge (BA, MA, PhD); *m* 5 Nov 1971, Elizabeth Anne, da of William Allen, of Eastrington, Humberside; 2 s (Phillip Stewart Edward b 1982, Richard John Charles b 1986); *Career* lectr UCL 1973-78, visiting prof Univ of California Berkeley 1978, lectr Univ of Cambridge 1978-85 (fell tutor and dir of studies Fitzw Coll 1978-85), prof LSE 1985-; memb: Govt and Law Ctee ESRC 1982-87, Cncl Inst of Br Geographers 1985-87 (treas 1990-); chm Election Studies Advsy Ctee ESRC 1987-88, conslt to Commons Employment Ctee 1988-89; FRGS 1982; *Books* incl: Environmental Systems: Philosophy, Analysis and Control (with R J Chorley, 1978), Optimal Control of Spatial Systems (with K C Tan, 1984), Local Business Taxes in Britain and Germany (with G Krebs, 1988); *Recreations* craft work, the family; *Style*— Prof Robert Bennett; London School of Economics, Houghton St, London WC2A 2AE

BENNETT, Robert Michael; s of Frederick William Bennett (d 1980) of Friern Barnet, London, and Doris Annie, *née* Mallandaine (d 1990); *b* 29 Nov 1944; *Educ* Woodhouse GS Finchley, Northampton Coll of Advanced Technol (first and second year Dip Technol), Enfield Tech Coll (HND, IEE part III); *m* 1969 Norma, *née* Baldwin; 1 s (Simon Michael b 1971); *Career* apprenticeship trg Eastern Electricity Bd Wood Green 1963-68; design/contracts engr Christy Electrical Ltd Chelmsford 1969-72, electrical design engr Posford Pavry & Ptnrs London (civil structural & building servs consltg engrs) 1972-73, sr electrical engr James R Briggs & Associates Hampstead (building servs consltg engrs) 1973-76, electrical assoc Donald Smith Seymour & Rooley London 1981-86 (sr electrical engr 1976-81), electrical engrg ptnr Building Design Partnership London 1986-; chm South Bucks Area IEE; CEng 1978, FCIBSE 1985, FIEE 1987, Eur Ing 1988; *Books* Electricity and Buildings (jt author, 1984); *Recreations* golf, skiing, theatre-going; *Clubs* Hazlemere Golf (Bucks), Beaconsfield 41; *Style*— Robert Bennett, Esq; Building Design Partnership, PO Box 4WD, 16 Gresse St, London W1A 4WD (☎ 071 631 4733, 071 437 3223, fax 071 631 0393, 071 734 6851)

BENNETT, Ronald Alistair; CBE (1986), QC (1959); s of Arthur George Bennett, MC (d 1946), of Edinburgh, and Edythe, *née* Sutherland (d 1970); *b* 11 Dec 1922; *Educ* Edinburgh Acad, Edinburgh Univ, Balliol Coll Oxford (MA, LLB); *m* 1950, Margret, da of Sigursteinn Magnusson (d 1985), Consul Gen for Iceland; 3 s (Mark, Sigurdur, Magnus), 3 da (Ingibjorg, Vivien, Fleur); *Career* 79 (Scottish Horse) Medium Regt RA 1943-45, Capt RAOC, India and Japan 1945-46; advocate Scotland 1947; Vans Dunlop Sch in Scots Law and Conveyancing 1948; standing cnsl to Miny of Labour and Nat Serv 1957-59; Sheriff Princ: Roxburgh, Berwick, Selkirk 1971-74, S Strathclyde, Dumfries and Galloway 1981-82, N Strathclyde 1982-83; lectr in mercantile law: Edinburgh Univ 1956-68, Heriot-Watt Univ 1968-75; chm: Medical Appeal Tribunals (Scotland) 1971-, Agric Wages Bd for Scotland 1973-, Local Govt Boundaries Cmmn for Scotland 1974-, Northern Lighthouse Bd 1974, Industl Tribunals (Scotland) 1977-; War Pensions Tribunal 1983-; Arbiter Motor Insurers' Bureau Appeals 1975-; memb Scottish Medical Practices Ctee 1976-88; *Books* Bennett's Company Law (2 edn 1950), Fraser's Rent Acts in Scotland (2 edn 1952), Scottish Current Law and Scots Law Times Sheriff Ct Reports (1948-74, ed), Ct of Session Reports (1976-88, ed); *Recreations* gardening, music, reading; *Clubs* New (Edinburgh); *Style*— Ronald Bennett, Esq, CBE, QC; Laxamyri, 46 Cammo Rd, Edinburgh EH4 8AP (☎ 031 339 6111)

BENNETT, Sir Ronald Wilfrid Murdoch; 3 Bt (UK 1929); o s of Sir Wilfred Bennett, 2 Bt (d 1952), and Marion Agnes, OBE (d 1985), da of James Somervell, of Sorn Castle, Ayrshire; *b* 25 March 1930; *Educ* Wellington Coll, Trin Coll Oxford; *m* 1, 1953, Rose-Marie Audrey Patricia, o d of Maj A L J H Aubépin; 2 da; m 2, 1968, Anne, da of late Leslie George Tooker; m 3, Princess Victoria Komukyeya of Toro (d 1988); *Heir* kinsman, Mark Edward Francis Bennett b 5 April 1960; *Style*— Sir Ronald Bennett, Bt

BENNETT, Roy Grissell; CMG (1971), TD (1946); s of Charles Ernest Marklew Bennett (d 1962), and Lilian, *née* Bluff (d 1972); *b* 21 Nov 1917; *Educ* privately, RMC Sandhurst; *Career* served WWII Maj 17/21 Lancers; 24 Lancers D Day, 2 Lothian Border Horse 2 in Cmd; dir: Vavasseur and Co Penang 1948-52, Maclaine Watson and Co Singapore 1956-72 (chm 1960-72); chm: Singapore Anti Tuberculosis Assoc 1958-62, Singapore Int Chamber of Commerce 1968-70; ctee memb and chm: Rubber Assoc Singapore 1960-72, Singapore Chamber of Commerce Rubber Assoc 1960-72; chm: Pilkington SEA Pte Ltd 1972-89, Fibre Glass Pilkington Malaysia 1972-89, Racehorse Spelling Station (Malaya) 1976-, Beder Int Singapore; fndr chm Utd World College SEA 1970-78 (now memb bd), fndr chm Riding for the Disabled Assoc of Singapore; patron Singapore Polo Club (chm 1968-70), dep chm Singapore Turf 1966-88; IOD; *Recreations* polo (5 handicap 1967-78), racing, swimming, shooting, travelling, gardening, photography, people of all races, building projects; *Clubs* Cavalry and Guards', Tanglin, British (Singapore), Turf, Polo, Polo (Penang), Swimming (Penang), Victoria Racing (Melbourne); *Style*— Roy Bennett, Esq, CMG, TD; Oak Tree House, S Holmwood, Surrey RH5 4NF (☎ 0306 889414); Taman Indera, 22 Jalan Perdana, Johore Bharu, 80300, Malaysia (☎ 010 60 7234 505, fax 607 249006)

BENNETT, Hon Mrs (Ruth Gordon); *née* Catto; yst da of 1 Baron Catto, CBE, PC (d 1959); *b* 1919; *m* 1947, Francis Ernest Herman Bennett, CBE, *qv*; 2 s, 1 da; *Career* serv WWII LACW RAF 11 Gp HQ 1942-45, Pilot Offr 1945-46; *Style*— The Hon Mrs Bennett; C Hoare and Co, 37 Fleet St, London EC4

BENNETT, Stephen Scott; s of Montague Bennett (d 1976), and Rachel, *née* Lopez-Dias, of Sutton; *b* 6 Dec 1946; *Educ* Rutlish Sch Merton; *m* 22 June 1969, Bobbi, da of Leon Hanover; *Career* qualified CA 1968, tax specialist Fuller Jenks Beecroft 1968-70, ptnr Accountancy Tuition Centre 1970-78; Deloitte Haskins & Sells: dir of educn 1978-82, ptnr 1982-, head of Mergers and Acquisitions; chm and chief exec Craton Lodge of Knight Group Plc; ctee memb Merton RFC; FCA 1968, FCCA 1973, AT11 1970; *Recreations* squash, rugby, drama; *Clubs* RAC; *Style*— Stephen Bennett, Esq; Foxcote, 50 West Hill, Sanderstead, Surrey (☎ 081 657 4228); Craton Lodge & Knight Group Plc, Lyric House, 149 Hammersmith Rd, London W14 (☎ 071 602 7272, fax 071 602 1586)

BENNETT, Todd Anthony; s of Anthony Henry Jack Bennett, of Southampton, and Jean Patricia, *née* Marshall; *b* 6 July 1962; *Educ* Romsey Sch, Barton Peveril VI Form; *m* 19 Sept 1987, Vanessa Lorraine, da of Peter Frank Drodge, of Romsey, Hants; *Career* sprinter; Euro Jr Championships 1981 Gold 400m and Silver 4 x 400m, Euro Championships 1982 Silver 4 x 400m, Cwlth Games 1982 Gold 4 x 400m, World Championships 1983 Bronze 4 x 400m, Olympics 1984 Silver 4 x 400m, Euro Indoor 1985 Gold 400m (world record), World Indoor 1985 Silver 400m, Cwlth Games 1986 Silver 200m and Gold 4 x 400m, Euro Indoor 1987 Gold 400m, Euro Championships Gold 4 x 400m, World Championships 1987 Silver 4 x 400, Olympics 1988 fifth 4 x 400m; *Recreations* golf, basketball, gardening; *Style*— Todd Bennett, Esq; Sandmartins, 8 The Street, Binsted, Nr Alton, Hants GU34 4PB (☎ 0420 23235); Hampshire Family Health Services, Friarsgate, Winchester (☎ 0962 853361)

BENNETT, Trevor Tyrer; s of Tom Bennett (d 1950), of Preston, Lancs, and Isabella, *née* Tyrer; *b* 8 July 1932; *Educ* Preston GS; *m* 1, 7 June 1951, (m dis 1983), Barbara Alice, da of Walter Bateman, of Barton; 1 s (Richard b 1964), 2 da (Susan (Mrs Cox) b 1952, Nicola b 1969); m 2, 11 Aug 1984, Judith Anne, da of Anthony Morris, of Wellington; 1 s (Charles b 1986); *Career* admitted slr 1955; sr ptnr Russell & Russell 1984-90 (ptnr 1960-84); dir Nat Assoc Investment Clubs Ltd; former pres: Bolton Jr Chamber of Commerce, Bolton Investment Club; memb Law Soc 1955; *Books* Guide to Buying Property in Portugal, Guide to Buying Property in Spain, Guide to Buying Property in France; *Recreations* cinema, books, travel, spectator sports; *Clubs* 41; *Style*— Trevor Bennett, Esq; White Oaks, Brook Lane, Alderley Edge, Cheshire SK9 7RU; (☎ 0625 583 596); Casa Das Castanhas, Foia, Monchique, Algarve, Portugal; Bennett & Co Solicitors, Bridge House, 2 Heyes Lane, Alderley Edge, Cheshire (☎ 0625 586937, fax 0625 585362, car 0860 622141, telex 9312111071)

BENNETT, Dr William Arthur; s of Thomas Arthur Bennett (d 1964), of Kensington, London, and Alic Maud, *née* Cressey (d 1947); *b* 10 Nov 1930; *Educ* Latymer Upper Sch, Gonville and Caius Coll Cambridge (BA), Univ of London (Academic DipEd), Univ of Cambridge (PhD); *m* 7 Aug 1954, Doreen May, da of Leonard Albert Humphreys (d 1978), of East Barnet, Herts; 1 s (Geoffrey William Michael b 1959), 1 da (Joanne b 1960); *Career* Nat Serv RAF 1949-51; sr lectr modern languages Ealing Tech Coll 1962-65, asst dir of res in applied linguistics Univ of Cambridge 1965-74, reader in French linguistics King's Coll London 1974-; memb: Philological Soc, Linguistics Assoc of GB, Soc for French Studies, Henry Sweet Soc; *Books* Aspects of Language and Language Teaching (1968 and 1969), Applied Linguistics and Language Learning (1974); *Recreations* walking, talking; *Style*— Dr William Bennett; Arncliffe, 20 Haslingfield Rd, Harlton, Cambridge CB3 7ER (☎ 0223 262 586); King's College London, The Strand, London WC2R 2LS (071 836 5454)

BENNEY, (Adrian) Gerald Sallis; s of Ernest Alfred Sallis Benney, and Aileen Mary, *née* Ward; *b* 21 April 1930; *Educ* Brighton GS, Brighton Coll of Art (Nat Dip), Royal Coll of Art (Des RCA); *m* 4 May 1957, Janet, da of Harold Neville Edwards, of Rawlins Farm, Ramsdell, nr Basingstoke, Hants; 3 s (Paul b 1959, Jonathan b 1961, Simon b 1966), 1 da (Genevieve b 1962); *Career* REME 1949-51; designer and maker of domestic and liturgical silver; started workshop in London in 1955, conslt designer to Viners Ltd 1957-59; holder of Royal Warrants to: HM The Queen 1974-, HRH The Duke of Edinburgh 1975-, HM Queen Elizabeth The Queen Mother 1975-, HRH The Prince of Wales 1980-; memb: Govts Craft Advsy Ctee 1972-77, advsy ctee UK Atomic Energy Ceramics Centre 1979-83; metalwork design advsr to Indian Govt 1977-78, chm Govt of India Hallmarking Survey 1981, memb Br Hallmarking Cncl 1983-88, export advsr and conslt designer to Royal Selangor Pewter Co Kuala Lumpur 1986-; commenced Reading Civic Plate 1960; Freeman: City of London 1957, Borough of Reading 1984; Liveryman Worshipful Co of Goldsmiths 1964; Hon MA Univ of Leicester 1963; RDI (Royal Designer to Industry) 1971, FRSA 1971; *Recreations* walking, landscape gardening, painting; *Style*— Gerald Benney, Esq; Beenham House, Beenham, nr Reading, Berks (☎ 0734 744 370)

BENNION, Francis Alan Roscoe; s of Thomas Roscoe Bennion (d 1968), of Hove, Sussex, and Ellen Norah, *née* Robinson (d 1986); *b* 2 Jan 1923; *Educ* John Lyon's Sch Harrow, Univ of St Andrews, Balliol Coll Oxford (MA); *m* 28 July 1951 (m dis 1975), Barbara Elizabeth, da of Harry Arnold Braendle (d 1964), of Little Hadham, Herts; 3 da (Sarah, Carola, Venetia); m 2, 2 Nov 1977, Mary Anne, wid of William Field, da of Patrick Lynch (d 1962), of Limerick; *Career* WWII Flt Lt Pilot RAFVR 1941-46; called to the Bar Middle Temple 1951, in practice 1951-53 and 1985-; lectr and tutor law St Edmund Hall Oxford 1951-53, memb Parly Cncl 1953-65 and 1973-75, sec-gen RICS 1965-68; constitutional advsr: Pakistan 1956, Ghana 1959-61, Jamaica 1969-71; govr Coll Estate Mgmnt 1965-68, co-fndr and first chm Professional Assoc Teachers 1968-72, fndr and first chm World of Property Housing Tst (now Sanctuary Housing Assoc) 1968-72 (vice pres 1986-); fndr: Statute Law Soc 1968 (chm 1978-79), Freedom Under Law 1971, Dicey Tst 1973, Towards One World 1979; co-fndr Areopagitica Educnl Tst 1979; chm Oxford City FC 1988-89; *Books* Constitutional Law of Ghana (1962), Professional Ethics (1969), Tangling With The Law (1970), Consumer Credit Control (1976-), Consumer Credit Act Manual (1978, 3 edn 1986), Statute Law (1980, 3 edn 1990), Statutory Interpretation (1984), Victorian Railway Days (1989); *Recreations* cricket, Victoriana, old railways; *Clubs* MCC; *Style*— Francis Bennion, Esq; 62 Thames St, Oxford OX1 1SU

BENNITT, (Mortimer) Wilmot; s of Rev F W Bennitt (d 1947), of The Rectory, Bletchley, Bucks, and Honoria, *née* Booth (d 1960); *b* 28 Aug 1910; *Educ* Charterhouse, Trinity Coll Oxford (MA); *m* (m dis 1952), Cecilia Bowman; *Career* RAF Motor Boat Crew 1940-43 LAC, intelligence offr FO 1943-44; under sec Miny of Works 1951-63 (1935-51), Land Cmmn 1966-71; hon sec Islington Soc 1961-63 and 1985-, chm Islington Archaeology and History Soc 1988-; *Books* Guide to Canonbury Tower (1962); *Recreations* theatre, local history; *Clubs* United Oxford and Cambridge Univ; *Style*— Wilmot Bennitt, Esq

BENSON, Sir Christopher John; s of late Charles Woodburn Benson and Catherine Clara, *née* Bishton; *b* 20 July 1933; *Educ* Worcester Cathedral Kings Sch, The Incorporated Thames Nautical Training Coll HMS Worcester; *m* 1960, Margaret Josephine, OBE, JP, da of Ernest Jefferies Bundy; 2 s; *Career* Sub Lt RN; dir Arndale Developments Ltd 1965-69; fndr chm: Dolphin Developments, Dolphin Property Ltd 1969-72; asst md The Law Land Co Ltd 1972-74, former dir Sun Alliance and London Insurance Group (West End Bd), dir House of Fraser plc 1982-86, chm MEPC 1988- (dir 1974-, md 1976-88), dir Sun Alliance and London Insurance plc 1988-; chm: Property Advsy Gp to the Dept of the Enviroment 1988-90, Reedpack Ltd 1989-90, The Books Company plc 1990-, The Housing Corporation 1990-; pres Br Property Fedn 1981-83; memb: Investment Ctee BP Pension Fund 1979-84, Cncl Marlborough Coll 1982-90; underwriting memb of Lloyds 1979-; dir Royal Opera House Covent Gdn Ltd 1984-; chm: Civic Tst 1985-90, London Docklands Devpt Corpn 1984-88; Freeman: Worshipful Co of Watermen and Lightermen; Guild of Air Pilots and Air Navigators 1980-; tstee Metropolitan Police Museum, hon fell Wolfson Coll Cambridge, hon bencher Middle Temple 1984-; FRICS; *Recreations* farming, aviation, opera, swimming; *Clubs* Garrick, City Livery, Naval, RAC, MCC; *Style*— Sir Christopher Benson

BENSON, Clifford George; s of George Benson, of 112 Blackshots Lane, Grays, Essex, and Doris Lilian, *née* Jennings; *b* 17 Nov 1946; *Educ* RCM; *m* 1 Sept 1973, Dilys Morgan, da of Robert Davies, of Craig Wen, Bwlch-y-Gwynt Rd, Llysfaen, nr Colwyn Bay, Clwyd; 2 da (Sarah b 22 July 1975, Emily b 8 Aug 1977); *Career* concert pianist; first prize with Levon Chilingirian on violin BBC Beethoven Duo Competition 1969, Royal Festival Hall debut playing Rachmaninov 3 Piano Concerto 1970, first prize with Levon Chilingirian Int Duo Competition Munich 1971, recital with Thea King and Peter Pears Aldeburgh Festival 1975, performed constant Lambert Piano Concerto 1975, world premiere of Richard Rodney Bennet's Three Romantic Pieces for BBC Pebble Mill Howard Ferguson 80th birthday concert 1988; performed solo piano recitals and concertos world-wide incl: Canada, Middle and Far East, USA, Czechoslovakia, Europe; regular broadcaster BBC Radio 3; recordings with: Deutsche Grammophon, CBS, Hyperion, Chandos, CRD; compositions incl: Three Pieces for Piano 1983, Mozart goes to Town (piano duet) 1985, Au Revoir Sylvie 1988; memb ctee Tonbridge Music Club; life memb RCM Student's Union, memb ISM; *Style*— Clifford Benson, Esq

BENSON, David Holford; s of Lt-Col Sir Reginald (Rex) Lindsay Benson, DSO, MVO, MC (d 1968), of Cucumber Farm, Singleton, nr Chichester, Sussex, and Leslie, *née* Foster (d 1981); half-bro (through his mother's former marriage to Condé Nast) of Lady Bonham-Carter (*see* Lord Bonham-Carter); *b* 26 Feb 1938; *Educ* Eton, Univ of Madrid; *m* 1964, Lady Elizabeth Mary, *née* Charteris, da of 12 Earl of Wemyss and (8 of) March, KT, JP; 1 s, 2 da; *Career* merchant banker; dir and vice chm: Kleinwort Benson Group plc, British Gas plc, Wemyss and March Estate Co, Marshall Cavendish, The Rouse Co; tstee Charities Official Investmt Fund; *Recreations* painting; *Clubs* White's, ESU; *Style*— David Benson, Esq; 11 Brunswick Gardens, London W8 (☎ 071 727 4949); Cucumber Farm, Singleton, Sussex (☎ 024 363 222)

BENSON, David Wilbert; s of Wilbert Thomas Benson (d 1956), of South Africa, and Lilian Ethel, *née* Verner (d 1980); *b* 25 July 1929; *Educ* King Edward VII Sch Johannesburg, Univ of Witwatersrand (DNF, BSc); *m* Feb 1968, Vera Evelyn, da of Sydney Coking, formerly Mrs Sugg; 1 step da (Penelope Jennifer Ann Sugg b 1948); *Career* sales engr G H Langler Johannesburg 1949-52; actor in UK incl experience at Old Vic, Manchester Library Theatre, Birmingham Repertory, Westminster Theatre 1952-57; freelance journalist 1957-60, journalist Today Magazine 1961-64, dep ed Motor Magazine 1964-65; Daily Express 1965-; feature writer 1965-, motoring corr 1970-, motoring ed 1980-; motoring ed Sunday Express 1987-; Conoco Motoring Writer of the Year 1984, Conoco Special award 1985, British Press Awards Campaigning Journalist of the Year 1985; memb Guild of Motoring Writers 1961 (chm 1976); *Books* Hunt v Lauda; *Recreations* swimming; *Clubs* BRDC, BARC, Wig and Pen; *Style*— David Benson, Esq; 28 St Georges Square, Narrow Street, London E14 8DL (☎ 071 791 0906); Express Newspapers plc, Ludgate House, 245 Blackfriars Rd, London SE1 9UX (☎ 071 922 7101, 071 928 8000, fax 071 620 1654)

BENSON, Lady Elizabeth Mary; *née* Charteris; o surviving da of 12 Earl of Wemyss, KT, *qv*; *b* 2 July 1941; *m* 17 Oct 1964, David Holford Benson, yr son of late Lt-Col Sir Reginald Lindsay (Rex) Benson, DSO, MVO, MC (d 1968), by his wife, Leslie, formerly wife of late Condé Nast, and da of late Volney Foster, of Illinois, USA; 1s, 2 da; *Style*— Lady Elizabeth Benson; 11 Brunswick Gdns, London W8 (☎ 071 727 4949)

BENSON, Prof Frank Atkinson; OBE (1988), DL (South Yorks 1979); s of late John Benson and late Selina Benson; *b* 21 Nov 1921; *Educ* Ulverston GS, Univ of Liverpool (BEng, MEng), Univ of Sheffield (DEng, PhD); *m* 1950, Kathleen May, *née* Paskell; 2 s; *Career* prof and head of Dept of Electronic and Electrical Engrg Univ of Sheffield 1967-87 (emeritus prof 1987-); FIEE, FIEEE; *Style*— Prof Frank Benson, OBE, DL; 64 Grove Rd, Sheffield S7 2GZ (☎ 0742 363 493); Dept of Electronic and Electrical Engineering, Univ of Sheffield, Mappin St, Sheffield S1 3JD (☎ 0742 768 555)

BENSON, (John) Graham; s of Marshall Benson, of Stanmore, Middx, and Beatrice, *née* Stein; *b* 29 April 1946; *Educ* Central Foundation Boys' GS London; *m* 13 May 1978, Christine Margaret, da of John James Fox, of Verwood, Dorset; 1 da (Fay Cecily b 1 Nov 1983); *Career* stage mangr in theatre 1965-68, TV prodn mangr and assoc prodr Drama Plays Dept BBC 1968-76; prodr: Premiere Films BBC 1976, Fox for Euston films 1979; euro prodn exec The Robert Sigwood Group 1980, freelance independent prodr 1982-86, md Consolidated Productions 1986, controller of drama for TVS and dir Telso Communications 1987-; freelance prodr many films including: Thank You Comrades 1978, A Hole in Babylon (BBC1) 1978, Outside Edge (LWT) 1982, Red Monarch theatrical feature C4) 1982, Meantime (Central/C4) 1983, Charlie (Central) 1983, Honest Decent and True (BBC2) 1984, Coast to Coast (BBC1) 1984; memb Exec Ctee Br Film and TV Prodrs Assoc 1981-90 (now The Prodrs Assoc), chm BAFTA 1985-87 (memb Cncl 1980-); fell Royal Soc of Arts Mfrg and Sci 1987; *Recreations* food, drink, literature, opera, cricket, travel, walking; *Clubs* Savile, Surrey CCC.; *Style*— Graham Benson, Esq; TVS, Television Centre, Northam, Southampton SO9 5HZ (☎ 0703 834126, fax 0703 221598)

BENSON, Baron (Life Peer UK 1980); Henry Alexander Benson; GBE (1971, CBE 1946); s of Alexander Stanley Benson, and Florence Mary, *née* Cooper; *b* 2 Aug 1909; *Educ* Johannesburg; *m* 1939, Anne Virginia, da of Charles Macleod; 2 s, 1 da; *Career* former ptnr Coopers and Lybrand, pres ICAEW 1966; chm Royal Cmmn on Legal Servs 1976-79; tstee Times Tst 1967-81; advsr to Govr of Bank of England 1975-83; hon master of Bench of Inner Temple 1983; sits as Independent in House of Lords; FCA; kt 1964; *Recreations* shooting, sailing; *Clubs* Brooks's, Royal Yacht Sqdn, Jockey; *Style*— The Rt Hon Lord Benson, GBE; 9 Durward House, 31 Kensington Court, London W8 5BH (☎ 071 937 4850)

BENSON, James; s of Henry Herbert Benson and Olive, *née* Hutchinson; *b* 17 July 1925; *Educ* Bromley GS, Emmanuel Coll Cambridge (MA); *m* 1950, Honoria Margaret, da of Patrick Hurley (d 1952), of Dublin; 1 da; *Career* served WW II RNVR, N Atlantic and East Indies; advertising exec: with Kemsley 1948-58, Mather and Crowther Ltd (subsequently Ogilvy and Mather Ltd) 1959-78 (dir 1960, md 1967, chm 1970); with Ogilvy and Mather International (parent co) (dir 1966, vice-chm 1970-); govr Brasilinvest SA 1977-, (memb advsy bd 1984); chm international ctee American Assoc of Advertising Agencies; chm of tstees American Assocs of the Royal Acad 1983-; *Recreations* travelling, fishing, music, reading, writing; *Style*— James Benson Esq; 550 Park Avenue, New York, NY 10021, USA (☎ 212 355 0291); Kelsey Rd, Box 271, Sheffield, Mass 01257, USA

BENSON, Jane Elliott; LVO (1981); da of Frank Elliott Allday, DL, TD (d 1970), and Agnete, *née* Kuhn; *b* 19 Dec 1937; *Educ* St James West Malvern, St Hildas Coll Oxford (MA); *m* 23 July 1964, Robin Stephen, s of Col Sir Rex Benson, DSO, MC, MVO (d 1969); 2 da (Lucinda b 1965, Camilla b 1968); *Career* Royal Household; Lady in waiting to Princess Margaret 1963-; Courtauld Inst of Art: hon sec friends 1972-84, appeal organiser 1983-90, sponsorship conslt 1990-; memb centenary appeal ctee St Hildas Coll 1989-; *Recreations* tennis, gardening, travelling; *Clubs* Queens, Vanderbilt; *Style*— Mrs Jane Benson, LVO; 11 Kensington Gate, London W8 5NA

BENSON, Lady Jane Helen Harbord; *née* Lowther; da of 7 Earl of Lonsdale, *qv*; *b* 13 Nov 1947; *m* 1, 19 Dec 1968 (m dis 1970), Gary Hunter Wooton, of California, USA; m 2, 6 Dec 1978, Robert Charles Benson, eldest son of Lt Cdr Nicholas Robin Benson, RN (eldest son of Guy Holford Benson by his wife, Lady Violet Catherine, widow of Hugo Francis, Lord Elcho, and da of 8 Duke of Rutland); 2 da (Laura Jane b 1980, Sophie Camilla b 1984); *Career* master of Ullswater Fox Hounds; ctee memb: Red Cross, Lifeboat Assoc; *Recreations* scuba diving, gun dogs, tennis, sailing; *Style*— The Lady Jane Benson; Glebe House, Lowther, Penrith, Cumbria (☎ 09312 270)

BENSON, Sir (William) Jeffrey; s of Herbert Benson (d 1950), of Bramley, Leeds, and Lilian Benson, *née* Goodson (d 1950); *b* 15 July 1922; *Educ* West Leeds HS; *m* 8 Sept 1947, Audrey Winifred, da of Ebineezer Parsons (d 1962), of Canterbury; 2 s (Martin Jeffrey b 22 March 1954, Stephen Nigel b 10 Feb 1957); *Career* RAF 1941-46 (despatches); National Westminster Bank plc: joined National Provincial Bank 1939, regnl exec dir 1968-73, gen mangr 1973-75, dep gp chief exec 1975-77, gp chief exec 1978-82, dep chm 1987; chm Export Advsy Cncl 1982-87, chm 600 Group plc 1987-; FCIB, FIOB (pres 1983-85) kt 1987; *Recreations* golf; *Clubs* Clifton Phyllis Court; *Style*— Sir Jeffrey Benson; Auben, 24 Spencer Walk, Rickmansworth, Herts WD3 4EZ (☎ 0927 778 260); Hythe End House, Chertsey Lane, Staines, Middx TW18 3EL (☎ 0784 61 545)

BENSON, John Blair; s of Robert Spence Thom Benson, of Ascot Ct, Glasgow, and Anna Margaret, *née* Blair; *b* 6 Sept 1945; *Educ* Clydebank HS, Strathclyde Univ (BA); *m* 9 Aug 1969, Anne, da of Albert Carter (d 1978); 3 da (Joanne b 28 Sept 1971, Victoria b 2 Dec 1974, Sarah b 8 Oct 1976); *Career* dir gp personnel servs Scottish & Newcastle Breweries 1978-84; gp personnel dir: Nabisco Group Ltd 1984-87, Reed International Manufacturing Group 1987-88; dir personnel and corp servs Reedpack Ltd 1988-90, chm PDB Ltd 1990-; FIPM; *Recreations* golf, hill walking, art literature; *Style*— John Benson, Esq

BENSON, Julian Riou; s of Maj-Gen Edward Riou Benson, CB, CMG, CBE (d 1985), of Well House, Aldermaston, Berkshire, and Isolda Mary Stuart, *née* Shea; *b* 17 May 1933; *Educ* Winchester, New Coll Oxford (BA); *m* 1 Oct 1960, Lilias Jane, da of Lt-Col Gerald Alan Hill-Walker (d 1980), of Maunby Hall, Thirsk, Yorkshire; 2 s (John b 1961, Charles b 1966), 2 da (Camilla b 1963, Fiona b 1970); *Career* Nat Serv 2 Lt 11 Hussars (Prince Albert's Own) 1952-53; bank clerk Barclays Bank 1956-59; Laing & Cruickshank stockbrokers 1959-89: ptnr 1959-71, dir 1971-84, dir corporate fin div 1984-89, ret 1989; chm: Bourne End Properties plc, Video Magic Leisure Gp plc; *Recreations* stalking, skiing, gardening; *Clubs* White's, MCC; *Style*— Julian Benson, Esq; The Old Rectory, Abbotts Ann, Andover, Hampshire SP11 7NR (☎ 0264 710 389)

BENSON, Mark Richard; s of Frank Edward Benson, of Oxted, Surrey, and Judith Ann, *née* Harrison; *b* 6 July 1958; *Educ* Sutton Valence; *m* Sarah Patricia, da of Laurence Waitt; 2 s (Laurence Mark Edward b 16 Oct 1987, Edward Robert b June 1990); *Career* professional cricketer; Kent CCC: debut 1980, awarded county cap 1981, benefit 1991, capt 1991-; 1 Test match England v India Edgbaston 1986; *Recreations* horse racing, swimming; *Style*— Mark Benson, Esq; c/o Kent County Cricket Club, St Lawrence Ground, Canterbury CT1 3NZ (☎ 0227 456886)

BENSON, (Dorothy) Mary; da of Cyril Benson (d 1968), of Pretoria, SA, and Lucy, *née* Stubbs (d 1953); *b* 9 Dec 1919; *Educ* Pretoria Girls' HS; *Career* memb staff Br High Cmm SA 1939-41, Women's Army Aux Serv 1941-45; pa to: DQMG GHQ Middle East, CAO Allied Armies in Italy (Capt), Cmdt Mil Liaison Greece, Cdr Br Section Four-Powered Govt Vienna; sec to David Lean 1947-49, a fndr and sec The Africa Bureau London 1952-56; UN: testified before Ctee on Apartheid 1963, testified before Ctee On Human Rights 1970 (1964, 1966); testified before Congressional Ctee on SA Washington; memb Ctee Nat Campaign for the Abolition of Capital Punishment; *Books* Tshekedi Khama (1960), The African Patriots (1963), South Africa: The Struggle for a Birthright (1985), Nelson Mandela (1986, 1990), At The Still Point (1988), A Far Cry - The Making of A South African (1989); BBC Radio Programmes on Nelson Mandela, Robben Island, Thomas Wolfe and Rainer Maria Rilke; *Recreations* reading, movies, theatre; *Style*— Miss Mary Benson; 34 Langford Court, London NW8

9DN (☎ 071 2867850)

BENSON, Hon Michael D'Arcy; yr s of Baron Benson, GBE (Life Peer), *qv*; *b* 23 May 1943; *Educ* Eton; *m* 1969, Rachel Candia Woods; 1 s (Charles D'Arcy b 1976), 2 da (Catherine Rachel b 1971, Harriet Anne b 1974); *Career* memb Research Dept L Messel & Co (Stockbrokers) 1965-67 (clerk on dealing floor 1963-65); Lazard Brothers & Co Ltd: joined 1967, dir Lazard Securities Ltd 1978 (head Private Client Dept and admin dir 1980), jt md Lazard Securities Ltd 1980, dir Lazard Securities (Jersey) Ltd 1981-82, dir Lazard Bros & Co (Jersey) Ltd 1981-82, dir Lazard Securities (HK) Ltd 1984-85, dir Lazard Bros & Co (Guernsey) Ltd 1984-85; md Scimitar Asset Management Ltd (London) 1985; dir: Standard Chartered Merchant Bank Ltd 1985, Gracechurch Nominees Ltd 1985, Scimitar Global Asset Management Ltd 1986, Scimitar Asset Management Asia Ltd 1986, Scimitar Asset Management (CI) Ltd 1986, Scimitar Worldwide Selection Fund Ltd 1986, Scimitar Asset Management (Singapore) Ltd 1988, Chartered Financial Holdings Ltd 1990; chm Scimitar Unit Trust Managers Ltd 1989; *Style*— The Hon Michael Benson; 34 St John's Ave, London SW15 6AN (☎ 081 788 3828); Scimitar Asset Management Ltd, Dashwood House, 69 Old Broad Street, London EC2M 1QS (☎ 071 588 6868, fax 071 374 2353)

BENSON, Michael Stewart; s of late Seymour Stewart Benson, AFC (Air Cdre RAF ret), of Haughley, Suffolk, and late Eva Margaret, *née* Sully; *b* 23 July 1929; *Educ* Rugby; *m* 20 June 1953, Mary Scott, da of Lt-Col James Kenneth Matheson, MC (d 1956), of Sotik, Kenya; 1 s (Peter b 13 Feb 1956), 1 da (Sarah b 30 April 1958); *Career* Army 1947-49, cmmnd 2 Lt RA 1948; Br-American Tobacco Co Ltd: mgmnt pupil UK 1949, purchasing mangr E Africa 1951, area mktg mangr E Africa 1957, sales mangr Tripoli 1958; Givaudan and Co Ltd (subsid of Hoffmann La-Roche): asst to md 1962, sales dir 1970, md 1977, non-exec chm 1989-; non-exec dir Treatt plc Bury St Edmunds 1989-; chm Br Fragance Assoc 1987-89, memb PCC Parish of All Saints Dane Hill Sussex 1985- (church warden 1982-88); *Recreations* fly fishing, sailing; *Clubs* Caledonian, Lansdowne; *Style*— Michael Benson, Esq; High Pines, Church Lane, Dane Hill, Haywards Heath, Sussex RH17 7EU (☎ 0825 790583); Givaudan & Co Ltd, Whyteleafe, Surrey CR3 0YE (☎ 0883 623377, fax 0883 626414, telex 28558)

BENSON, Peter Charles; s of Robert Benson (d 1970), of The Anchorage, Baildon, Yorks, and Dorothy, *née* Cartman; *b* 16 June 1949; *Educ* Bradford GS, Univ of Birmingham (BSocSc); *Career* called to the Bar Middle Temple 1975; practised on NE Circuit 1975-; junior of NE Circuit 1979-80, asst rec of the Crown Ct 1991-; tstee Henry Scott Fund; treas Bradford Cricket Club; pres Hon Soc of Gentleman Troughers; *Recreations* golf, reading, conversation; *Clubs* Ilkley Golf, Ilkley Bowling; *Style*— Peter Benson, Esq; Bygreen Cottage, Parish Ghyll Drive, Ilkley, Yorkshire (☎ 0943 601245); Fifth Floor, St Paul's House, Park Square, Leeds LS1 2ND (☎ 0532 455866, fax 0532 455807, car 0860 558393)

BENSON, Hon Peter Macleod; er s of Baron Benson, GBE (Life Peer), *qv*; *b* 1940; *Educ* Eton, Univ of Edinburgh (MA); *m* 1, 1970 (m dis 1987), Hermione Jane Boulton; 1 s (Edward Henry b 1975), 2 da (Candida Jane b 1972, Hermione Emily b 1980); m 2, 3 Aug 1989, Señora Maria de los Angeles Martin, da of Don Victoriano Martinez Latasa; *Career* CA; ptnr Coopers & Lybrand; *Recreations* shooting, golf; *Clubs* Brooks's, Hurlingham, MCC, Tandridge Golf; *Style*— The Hon Peter Benson; 22 Larpent Ave, London SW15 (☎ 081 788 3758); Coopers & Lybrand, Plumtree Court, Farrington St, London EC4 (☎ 071 583 5000)

BENSON, Richard Anthony; s of Douglas Arthur Benson (d 1983), and Muriel Alice, *née* Fairfield (d 1984); *b* 20 Feb 1946; *Educ* Wrekin Coll, Inns of Court Sch of Law; *m* 15 Sept 1967, Katherine Anne, da of Tom Anderson Smith, Highfield, Whiteway, Gloucestershire; 1 s (Jake Alexander Fairfield b 22 Feb 1970), 2 da (Amy b 26 April 1972, Chloe Kate b 25 Aug 1981); *Career* called to the Bar Inner Temple 1974, in practice Midland & Oxford Circuit 1975; *Recreations* flying, offshore cruising, drama, after dinner speaking; *Clubs* Northampton & County, British Airways Flying, Bar Yacht; *Style*— Richard Benson, Esq; Clematis Cottage, Rectory Road, Great Haseley, Oxfordshire OX9 7JL (☎ 0844 279 298); 1 Kings Bench Walk, Temple, London EC4Y 7DB (☎ 071 353 8436)

BENSON, Robert Charles; s of late Lt Cdr Nicholas Robin Benson, of Barn Court, Coln St Denni Cheltenham, and Barbara, *née* Kitchiner; *b* 17 Nov 1952; *Educ* Eton, Univ of Southampton (BSc); *m* 6 Dec 1978, Lady Jane, da of 7 Earl of Lonsdale, of Askham Hall, Penrith, Cumbria; 2 da (Laura Jane b 1980, Sophie Camilla b 1984); *Career* land agent and sporting mangr Lowther Estates 1976, dir Lakeland Investment Co 1980; chm: North West Br Field Sports Soc, Lowther Driving Trials and Country Fair; memb Ctee: Timber Growers UK, Country Land Owners Assoc, Br Deer Soc; sch govr; *Recreations* shooting, hunting, tennis; *Clubs* MCC; *Style*— Robert Benson, Esq; Glebe House, Lowther, Penrith, Cumbria (☎ 09312 270); Lakeland Investments, Estate Office, Lowther, Penrith, Cumbria (☎ 09312 577)

BENSON, Robin Stephen; s of Lt-Col Sir Rex Benson, DSO, MVO, MC (d 1968), of 30 Cadogan Place, London SW1, and Leslie, *née* Foster (d 1981); *b* 11 Aug 1934; *Educ* Eton, Balliol Coll Oxford; *m* 23 July 1964, Jane Elliott, LVO, da of Col F E (Bill) Allday, OBE, TD, DL; 2 da (Lucinda b 1965, Camilla b 1968); *Career* Lt 9 Lancers 1952-54; marketing mangr Holt Products Ltd 1965-71, dir Bensonic Ltd 1971-84, chm and md Herbert Johnson Ltd 1984-89, chm S Lock Ltd 1990-; MInstM 1969; *Recreations* shooting, tennis, music, motor racing; *Clubs* Whites, Queens, Vanderbilt Racquet; *Style*— Robin Benson, Esq; 11 Kensington Gate, London W8

BENSON, Roger Scholes; s of Thomas Scholes Benson, of Radcliffe-on-Trent, Nottingham, and Jane, *née* Bridge (d 1955); *b* 20 Oct 1932; *Educ* Roundhay Sch Leeds; *m* 15 Oct 1955, Hilary Margaret, da of late George Morris Brown, of Nottingham; 3 da (Jane b 1957 d 1983, Jo b 1959, Nicky b 1962); *Career* CA 1954; taxation mangr Peat Marwick Mitchell & Co 1954-59, own practice Benson Brooks West Bridgford Nottingham 1959-79, fin dir Speedograph-Richfield 1980-, sales dir British Precision Spring Ltd 1989-; hotelier Burleigh Court Hotel Minchinhampton Glos 1980-; parish cnllr 1967-76, rural dist cnllr 1972-76; Rotarian 1963-81, past pres Rotary Club of W Bridgford; FCA 1959 (memb Ctee 1973-81); *Recreations* golf, cricket, travel; *Clubs* Minchinhampton Golf, Bramcote Cricket (Notts); *Style*— Roger Benson, Esq; Cornerstones, Burleigh, Stroud, Glos (☎ 0453 886409); Burleigh Court Hotel, Stroud, Glos (☎ 0453 883804, fax 0453 886870)

BENSON, Ross; s of Stanley Ross Benson, of St John's Wood, London, and Marbella, Spain, and Mabel, *née* Greaves; b 29 Sept 1948; *b* 29 Sept 1948; *Educ* Sydney GS, Gordonstoun; *m* 1, 1968 (m dis 1974), Beverly Jane, da of K A Rose; 1 s (Dorian Ross b 1974); m 2, 1975 (m dis 1986), Zoé, da of G D Bennett; 1 da (Anouchka b 1975); m 3, 27 Nov 1987, Ingrid, da of Dr Eric Canton Seward; 1 da (Arabella b 1989); *Career* journalist and broadcaster; dep diary ed: Daily Mail 1968-71, Sunday Express 1971-72; Daily Express: joined 1973, foreign news ed 1975-76, specialist writer 1976-78, US W Coast corr 1978-82, chief foreign corr 1982-87, chief feature writer 1987-88, diary ed 1988-; Int Reporter of the Year Br Press Awards 1983; The Ross Benson Programme LBC Newstalk 1990; *Books* The Good, the Bad and the Bubbly (with George Best); *Recreations* skiing, motor racing, fishing; *Style*— Ross Benson, Esq; c/o Daily Express, Blackfriars Rd, London SE1 (☎ 071 922 1148)

BENSON, Stephen; s of A Benson; *b* 7 June 1943; *Educ* Highgate, Magdalen Coll Oxford; *m* 1966, Jacqueline, *née* Russell; 3 da; *Career* dir: Davidson Pearce 1974-89, Dave Rogerson 1989-90; head corp devpt Action Aid (charity) 1990-; *Recreations* music, running; *Style*— Stephen Benson, Esq; 8 Laurier Rd, London NW5 (☎ 071 485 0287, office: 071 281 4101)

BENSON, Maj William Arthur; TD, DL (Northumberland 1953); 2 s of Walter John Benson (d 1923), of Newbrough Hall, Hexham, Northumberland; bro of John Elliott Benson, *qv*; *b* 27 June 1905; *Educ* Eton; *m* 1948, Adela Clare Thomasine (d 1980), 3 da of Maj William Percy Standish (d 1922), of Marwell Hall, Hants, and former w of Cdr John Samuel Hervey Lawrence, RN; *Career* Maj with Northumberland Hussars, served WWII Greece, W Desert, Normandy; memb Cncl Royal Agric Soc of England 1949 (hon show dir 1955-62, dep pres 1963); High Sheriff Northumberland 1951; *Clubs* Cavalry; *Style*— Maj William Benson, TD, DL; Newbrough Hall, Hexham, Northumberland (☎ 0434 74202)

BENTALL, John Anthony Charles (Tony); s of Frank Bentall (d 1975), of Beckenham, Kent, and Freda, *née* Hooper (d 1966); *b* 16 Jan 1929; *Educ* Dulwich, Lincoln Coll Oxford (BA, MA); *m* 23 March 1963, Brenda Kathryn, da of Francis Scaife; 2 c (Andrew Christopher b 17 Feb 1969, Suzanna Kathryn b 20 July 1972); *Career* Nat Serv RA 2 lt 1948-49; articled clerk Woolgar Hennell Scott-Mitchell & Co CAs 1952-57, qualified chartered accountant 1956, tax sr Cooper Bros 1957-59, audit mangr Layton-Bennett Billingham & Co 1961-63 (audit sr 1959-61); ptnr: Viney Price & Goodyear 1963, merged to become Viney Merretts 1970, merged Binder Hamlyn 1980-89; ret 1989; memb Appeal Ctee (Disciplinary Scheme) ICAEW 1980-; Freeman City of London 1978, memb Worshipful Co of Chartered Accountants in England and Wales; FCA 1966 (ACA 1956); *Recreations* charitable matters, golf, theatre going, hill walking, gardening; *Clubs* East India, Vincents Oxford, MCC; *Style*— Tony Bentall, Esq; 24 Stanley Avenue, Beckenham, Kent BR3 2PX (☎ 081 658 0827)

BENTALL, (Leonard Edward) Rowan; DL (Greater London 1977); s of Leonard H Bentall, JP (d 1942), of Oakwood Court, Leatherhead, Surrey; *b* 27 Nov 1911; *Educ* Eastbourne Coll; *m* 1, 1937, Adelia Elizabeth (d 1986), yr da of David Hawes (d 1946), of Holly Hill, Meopham, Kent; 3 s, 2 da; m 2, 1987, Katherine Christina Allan; *Career* served WWII, cmmnd Royal Welch Fusiliers 1941; pres Bentalls plc 1978- (dir 1936-78, md 1963-78, chm 1968-78); pres Steadfast Sea Cadet Corps, govr and vice pres The Horse Rangers Assoc, patron Portsmouth Dist Eight Army Old Comrades Assoc; Freeman City of London; Cavaliere Order Al Merito della Republica Italiana 1971-; *Books* My Store of Memories (1974); *Recreations* ornithology, gardening; *Clubs* RAC, IOD; *Style*— Rowan Bentall, Esq, DL

BENTATA, (Morris) David Albert; s of Robert Victor Bentata (d 1961), of Didsbury, Manchester, and Joyce Ethel, *née* Weinberg; *b* 22 Oct 1913; *Educ* Blundell's, ChCh Oxford (BA, MA); *m* 20 Feb 1964, Alison Jessica, da of Christopher Henley Boyle Gilroy, of Boundstone, nr Farnham, Surrey; 1 s (Robert b 5 Nov 1968), 1 da (Victoria b 10 Feb 1966); *Career* Nat Serv: enlisted N Staffs Regt 1957, OCS Eaton Hall and Mons 1957-58, cmmnd 2 Lt Intelligence Corps 1958, serv BAOR 1958-59, cmmnd Lt Intelligence Corps (TA) 1959, RARO 1963; md M Bentata & Son Ltd 1962-67, fndr int mangr Hill Samuel & Co Ltd 1969-72 (investmt analyst 1968-69), int investmt mangr Charterhouse Japhet Ltd 1972-79, dir Charterhouse Investmt Mgmnt Ltd 1986-88 (int dir 1979-86), md Charterhouse Portfolio Mangrs Ltd 1986-88, chm and fndr Bentata Assocs Ltd 1988-, dir: Pegasus Fin Hldgs Ltd 1989, Gandalf Explorers Int Ltd (fndr) 1989; elected Lloyds underwriter 1976; vice chm and chm Stoke d'Abernon Residents Assoc 1969-77, memb ctee Oxshott Cons Assoc 1969-72; memb The Sherlock Holmes Soc of London; Liveryman Worshipful Co of Feltmakers 1983 (Steward 1989), Freeman City of London 1984; AMSIA 1969, FInstD 1988, FRGS 1988; *Recreations* full-bore rifle shooting, travel; *Clubs* City of London; *Style*— David Bentata, Esq

BENTHALL, Jonathan Charles Mackenzie; s of Sir (Arthur) Paul Benthall, KBE, of Benthall Hall, Broseley, Salop, and Mary Lucy, *née* Pringle (d 1988); *b* 12 Sept 1941; *Educ* Eton, King's Coll Cambridge (MA); *m* 23 Oct 1975, Zamira, da of Sir Yehudi Menuhin OM, KBE, of London; 2 s (Dominic b 1976, William b 1981); *Career* sec ICA 1971-73, dir RAI 1974-, ed Anthropology Today 1985- (RAIN 1974-84); Save the Children Fund: former memb UK Child Care Ctee, memb Assembly 1990-, Overseas Advsy Ctee 1990-; memb Assoc of Social Anthropologists 1983; Chevalier de l'Ordre des Arts et des Lettres France 1973; FRSA; *Books* Science and Technology in Art Today (1972), The Body Electric Patterns of Western Industrial Culture (1976); *Recreations* listening to music, swimming, skiing; *Clubs* Athenaeum; *Style*— Mr Jonathan Benthall; 212 Hammersmith Grove, London W6 7HG; 50 Fitzroy St, London W1P 5HS

BENTHALL, Margaret; da of Sydney Woolhouse-Clarke (d 1968), of Bowerham House, Lancaster, and Emilie, *née* Stanton (d 1964); *b* 17 Aug 1917; *Educ* Ackworth Sch Yorkshire, Univ of Liverpool (Dip Arch); *m* 11 July 1953, John D'Aguilar Lawrence Benthall, s of Maj John Lawrence Benthall, CBE, TD (d 1947), of Holly Bowers, Chistlehurst; *Career* architect; ptnr CWB Architects & Conservation Specialists 1985-; memb SPAB; RIBA; *Recreations* embroidery, gardening; *Style*— Mrs Margaret Benthall; The Coach House, Keytes Lane, Bourton-on-the-Hill, Moreton-in-Marsh GL56 9AG (☎ 0386 700646)

BENTHALL, Maxim Trevor; s of Leslie Norman Benthall, of Northants, and Gwendoline Alice Benthall; *b* 25 March 1947; *Educ* Royal GS High Wycombe, Architectural Assoc Sch of Architecture (AA Dipl); *m* (m dis); 2 da (Karen b 1975, Sarah b 1979); *Career* architect; dir Ian C King Architects Ltd; RIBA; *Recreations* boating, fishing, painting; *Style*— Maxim Benthall, Esq; 21 Earlsfield Rd, London SW18

BENTHALL, Sir (Arthur) Paul; KBE (1950); s of Rev Charles Francis Benthall (d 1936), of Teignmouth, and Annie Theodosia Benthall; *b* 25 Jan 1902; *Educ* Eton, Ch Ch Oxford; *m* 1932, Mary Lucy (d 1988), da of John Archibald Pringle (d 1952), of Horam, Sussex; 4 s (including Jonathan Charles Mackenzie, *qv*); *Career* chm Amalgamated Metal Corpn 1959-73; dir: Chartered Bank 1953-72, Royal Insur Co and assoc cos 1953-73; pres Assoc Chambers of Commerce of India 1950 and 1948; FLS; *Clubs* Oriental, Lansdowne; *Style*— Sir Paul Benthall, KBE; Benthall Hall, Broseley, Salop (☎ 0952 882254)

BENTHAM, Prof Richard Walker; s of Richard Hardy Bentham (d 1980), of Woodbridge, Suffolk, and Ellen Walker, *née* Fisher (d 1983); *b* 26 June 1930; *Educ* Campbell Coll Belfast, Trinity Coll Dublin, (BA, LLB); *m* 16 May 1956, Stella Winifred, da of Henry George Matthews (d 1969), of Hobart, Tasmania; 1 da (Stella); *Career* called to the Bar Middle Temple 1955; lectr in law: Univ of Tasmania Hobart 1955-57, Univ of Sydney NSW 1957-61; visiting scholar UCL 1961-62, BP Legal dept 1961-83 (dep legal adsr 1979-83); Univ of Dundee: prof of petroleum and mineral law, dir Centre for Petroleum and Mineral Law Studies 1983-; pubns in learned journals in the UK and Overseas; govr Heatherton House Sch Amersham 1969-83, bd memb Scot Cncl for Arbitration 1988-, cncl memb ICC Inst of Int Business Law and Practice 1988-, Br nominated memb IEA Dispute Settlement Centre's Panel of Arbitrators 1989-; memb: Int Law Assoc (cncl memb 1980-90), Int Bar Assoc 1978-; FRSA 1986; *Books* State Petroleum Corporations (with W G R Smith, 1987), Precedents in Petroleum Law (with W G R Smith, 1988); *Recreations* cricket, military history; *Clubs* Dundee Univ; *Style*— Prof Richard Bentham; Centre for Petroleum and Mineral Law Studies, The University of Dundee, Park Place, Dundee, Scotland (☎ 0382 23181 ext 4298, fax 0382 201 604)

BENTINCK; *see*: Cavendish-Bentinck

BENTINCK, Lady Anna Cecilia; yr da of 11 Earl of Portland, *qv*; *b* 18 May 1947; *m* 1, 1965 (m dis 1974), Jasper Hamilton Holmes; 2, 1975 (m dis 1977), Nicholas George Spafford Vester; resumed her maiden name; issue (by Arnold George Francis Cragg); 2 s (Gulliver Jack Bentinck Cragg b 1978, George Finn Gareth Bentinck Cragg b 1980), 1 da (Charlotte-Sophie Camden Bentinck Cragg b 1988); *Style—* The Lady Anna Bentinck; 64 Croftdown Road, London NW5 1EN

BENTINCK, Lady (Alexandra Margaret) Anne; da of 7 Duke of Portland, KG (d 1977); *b* 6 Sept 1916; *Career* CStJ; *Style—* The Lady Anne Bentinck; Welbeck Woodhouse, Worksop, Notts

BENTINCK, Lady Sorrel Deirdre; er da of 11 Earl of Portland, *qv*; resumed maiden name 1990; *b* 22 Feb 1942; *m* 1972 (m dis 1988), Sir John Philip Lister Lister-Kaye, 8 Bt; 1 s, 2 da; *Style—* The Lady Sorrel Bentinck; 18 Rankeillor St, Edinburgh EH8 9HZ

BENTINCK (VON SCHOONHETEN), Baron Steven - Carel Johannes; s of Baron Adolph Willem Carel Bentinck von Schoonheten (former Dutch Ambass to London), and Baroness Thyssen-Bornemisza von Kaszony (sister of Baron Heini Thyssen); male heir of the Barons Bentinck, founded by Johan Bentinck (recorded in Heerde 1361-86) from whom the Dukes of Portland also descend; *b* 1 March 1957; *Educ* Sunningdale, The American Sch in Paris, Valley Forge Mil Acad USA, Brunel Sch of Econ UK; *m* Nora, da of Fernand de Picciotto, and formerly w of Prince Adan Czartoryski; *Career* chm: Applied Power Technology Int, Scientia Ltd; *Clubs* Turf; *Style—* Baron Steven Bentinck; 20 The Vale, London SW3

BENTLEY, (Henry) Brian; s of John Clarence Hayes Bentley (d 1972), and Emily Mary, *née* Church; *b* 9 Aug 1933; *Educ* Castleford GS, Open Univ (BA), CNAA (MPhil), Univ of Leeds (MEd); *m* 30 Nov 1957, Sylvia Mary, da of William Drabble (d 1984), of Thrybergh, Rotherham; 1 s (Phillip John Henry b 1971), 2 da (Alison Deborah (Mrs Clark) b 1960, Susan Lesley (Mrs Jackson) b 1965); *Career* Nat Serv RAF served war RAF hosps 1955-57; trained nurse Rotherham Hosp 1951-55, RGN 1954; princ Sch of Radiography Gen Infirmary at Leeds 1968- (radiographer 1957-68); memb: Leeds Univ Gp for Study of Ageing, Univ of Leeds Bone and Mineral Res Gp, Ctee Yorks Branch Soc of Radiographers (chm 1972-74 and 1978-80), Cncl Coll of Radiographers 1974-84 (pres 1981-82); co ordinating sec Leeds Med Gp; external examiner Univ of Dublin, examiner Coll of Radiographers (various bds); examiner: MSc degree in Imaging Technology Univ of Liverpool, BSc (Hons) Radiography South Bank Polytechnic and Guy's Hospital London; dir of education NETRHA Charterhouse Coll of Radiography 1990-; memb Garforth St Mary's PCC; FCR (1966), FRIPHE (1985); *Books* A Textbook of Radiographic Science (editor 1986); contrib many paper to learned jnls; *Recreations* traction engine rally, church choir; *Style—* Brian Bentley, Esq; Fairfield, Aberford Rd, Garforth, Leeds LS25 1PZ (☎ 0532 862 276); The General Infirmary At Leeds (☎ 0532 432 799)

BENTLEY, His Hon Judge David Ronald; QC (1984); s of Edgar Norman Bentley (d 1982), and Hilda, *née* Thirlwall (d 1959); *b* 24 Feb 1942; *Educ* King Edward VII Sch Sheffield, Univ Coll London (LLB, LLM); *m* 1978, Christine Elizabeth, da of Alec Stewart (d 1978); 2 s (Thomas b 1985, David b 1989); *Career* called to the Bar, rec 1985, circuit judge North Eastern Circuit 1988-; *Recreations* legal history, literature, cinema, dogs; *Style—* His Hon Judge David Bentley, QC

BENTLEY, The Ven Frank William Henry; s of Nowell James Bentley (d 1945), and May Sophia Bentley, *née* Gribble; *b* 4 March 1934; *Educ* Yeovil Boys GS, Kings Coll London (AKC); *m* 1, 28 Sept 1957, Murial (d 1958), da of Maj Lionel Stewart Bland (d 1983); 1 s (Michael b 1958); m 2, 29 Oct 1960, Yvonne Mary, da of Bernard Henry Wilson; 2 s (Stephen b 1962, Richard b 1971), 1 da (Frances b 1964); *Career* curate Shepton Mallet 1958-62, rector Kingsdon with Podymore Milton 1962-66; curate in charge: Yeovilton 1962-66, Babcary 1964-66; vicar Wiveliscombe 1966-76, rural dean Tone 1973-76, vicar St John in Bedwardine 1976-84; rural dean Martley and Worcester West 1979-84, hon canon Worcester Cathedral 1981-84, archdeacon Worcester (and residentiary Cathedral canon) 1984-; memb General Synod 1986-; *Recreations* gardening, motoring; *Style—* The Ven Frank Bentley; 7 College Yard, Worcester WR1 2LA (☎ 0905 25046); Diocesan Office, The Old Palace, Deansway, Worcester WR1 2JE (☎ 0905 20537)

BENTLEY, Prof George; s of George Bentley (d 1964), and Doris, *née* Blagden; *b* 19 Jan 1936; *Educ* Rotherham GS, Univ of Sheffield (MB, ChB, ChM); *m* 4 June 1960, Ann Gillian, da of Herbert Hutchings (d 1953); 2 s (Paul b 4 March 1964, Stephen b 2 March 1966), 1 da (Sarah b 2 Dec 1962); *Career* lectr in anatomy Univ of Birmingham 1961-62, surgical registrar Sheffield Royal Infirmary 1963-65, orthopaedic registrar Orthopaedic Hosp Oswestry 1965-67, sr orthopaedic registrar Nuffield Orthopaedic Centre Oxford 1967-69, instr in orthopaedics Univ of Pittsburgh USA 1969-70; Oxford Univ 1970-76: lectr, sr lectr, clinical reader in orthopaedics; prof of orthopaedics: Univ of Liverpool 1976-82, Univ of London 1982-; hon conslt orthopaedic surgeon Royal Nat Ortho Hosp 1982-;FRCS 1968; *Books* Rob and Smith Operative Surgery - Orthopaedics Vols I and II (conslt 1990), Mercer's Orthopaedic Surgery (jt ed 1983); *Recreations* music, tennis, horology; *Style—* Prof George Bentley; 120 Fishpool St, St Albans, Herts AL3 4RX (☎ 0727 51600); University Department of Orthopaedics, Royal National Orthopaedic Hospital, Stanmore, Middlesex HA7 1LP (☎ 081 954 2300 ext 531/532)

BENTLEY, Howard; s of Wilfred Bentley (d 1970), of Southampton, and Wynifred Bentley; *b* 5 Oct 1944; *Educ* Peter Symond's Winchester; *m* 1966, Margaret, da of James Montague; 1 s (Nicolas b 1973), 1 da (Kate b 1976); *Career* mgmnt trainee RHM 1966-68, nat account mangr Green Shield Stamps 1972-75 (account mangr 1968-72); account mangr: Marden Kane 1975-76, IMP 1976-77; account dir MKM Group 1978-79, managing ptnr TCC 1979-84, restaurateur 1985-87; md: Bentley & Co 1987-90, Bentley Clark Consultancy 1990-; *Recreations* food, wine, golf, rugby, listening to Brian Redhead; *Style—* Howard Bentley, Esq; Bentley Clark Consultancy, Commonwealth House, Chalkhill Rd, London W6 8DW (☎ 081 846 8585, fax 081 846 9052, car 0836 502384)

BENTLEY, John Philip; s of Roland Cunard Bentley (d 1917), of Bexley Heath, Kent, and Margaret, *née* Budd (d 1951); *b* 5 Jan 1916; *Educ* Christ's Hosp Horsham, Charing Cross Hosp Univ of London (MB BS); *m* 31 Oct 1945, Daphne Kathleen, da of Col Charles Burridge Rennick, OBE (d 1968), of Bournemouth; 1 s (Christopher b 1940); *Career* WWII Flying Offr RAF 1940; jr surgn: RAF Halton 1940, RAF Hosp Ely 1940-42; Sqdn Ldr CO 1 Mobile Surgical Unit RAF (India) 1943-45, Wing Cdr CO 66 Mobile Field Hosp (India) 1945-46; surgical registrar Charing Cross Hosp 1946-49, Moynihan Fellowship Assoc of Surgns 1947, Cwlth fell Harkness Fndn 1947-48, lectr surgery Columbia Univ NY 1948; conslt surgn: Connaught Hosp London 1948, Harrow Hosp 1949, Wanstead Hosp 1950, Italian Hosp 1959, ret 1982; private conslt practice Harley St 1949-82; Freeman City of London, Liveryman Worshipful Co of Apothecaries; FRSM 1938, memb BMA 1938, FRCS 1942, FACS 1955; *Recreations* music, gardening, sailing; *Clubs* RAC, Hurlingham, West Mersea Yacht; *Style—* John Bentley, Esq; 1 Victoria Esplanade, West Mersea, Colchester, Essex CO5 8AT (☎ 0206 382 452)

BENTLEY, Michael John; s of Leopold John Bentley, (d 1987), and Ann Margaret, *née* MacGillivray (d 1968); *b* 23 Nov 1933; *Educ* Morrisons Acad Crieff Perthshire; *m* 24 June 1961, Sally Jacqueline, da of Stanley Bertram James Hogan, of Bexhill-on-Sea, Sussex; 4 s (Jeremy b 26 March 1963, Rupert b 29 April 1966, Andrew b 4 March 1968, David b 27 Aug 1970); *Career* Lehman Brothers (investmt bankers NY) 1959; S G Warburg & Co Ltd: joined 1962, dir 1968-76; dir Mercury Securities Ltd 1974-76, dir and exec vice pres Korea Merchant Banking Corporation Seoul 1977-79, dir Lazard Bros & Co Ltd 1977-80, jt vice chm J Henry Schroder Wagg & Co Ltd 1980-85, dir Schroders plc 1980-83, (gp md corp fin 1983-85), chm Electra Management Services Ltd 1986-, dep chm and chief exec Electra Investment Trust plc 1986-89 (jt dep chm 1989-); dep chm Electra Kingsway Managers Holdings Ltd 1989-; chm: Fin Ctee London Borough of Islington 1968-71, Islington Nat Savings Ctee 1968-71; FCA 1963 (ACA 1958); *Recreations* music, opera, sailing, gardening; *Clubs* Links (New York); *Style—* Michael Bentley, Esq; Electra Investment Trust plc, 65 Kingsway, London WC2B 6QT (☎ 071 831 6464, fax 071 404 5388, telex 265525 ELECG G)

BENTLEY, Susan Jane; da of Dennis Herbert Bentley, of Caterham, Surrey, and Shirley Constantine, *née* Nineham; *b* 19 July 1955; *Educ* Notre Dame Convent, Univ of Dundee (BSc); *Career* CA; Ernst & Whinney 1977-87, gp acquisitions exec Abaco Investmts plc (now part of Br & Cwlth Hldgs Plc) 1987-89, assoc dir corp devpt Br & Cwlth Hldgs PLC 1989; ACA 1980; *Recreations* skiing, tennis, entertaining, music; *Style—* Ms Susan Bentley; Kings House, 36-37 King St, London EC2V 8BE (☎ 071 600 0840)

BENTLEY, Hon Mrs (Victoria Elizabeth); *née* Mansfield; da of 5 Baron Sandhurst, DFC; *b* 30 Jan 1957; *Educ* Benenden, Bordeaux Univ; *m* 1978, (Charles) James Sharp Bentley, s of Kenneth Bentley, of Balmuir, Angus; 1 s (James b 1982), 1 da (Sophie b 1985); *Recreations* skiing, riding, tennis; *Style—* The Hon Mrs Bentley

BENTLEY, Sir William; KCMG (1985, CMG 1977); s of Lawrence Bentley, and Elsie Jane Bentley; *b* 15 Feb 1927; *Educ* Bury HS, Univ of Manchester, Wadham Coll Oxford, Coll of Europe Bruges; *m* 1950, Karen Ellen, *née* Christensen; *Career* joined FO 1952, head Far Eastern Dept FCO 1974-76, ambass The Philippines 1976-81, high cmmr to Malaysia 1981-83, ambass Norway 1983-87; chm: Coflexip (UK) Ltd, Duco Ltd, Diodex International Ltd, Soc of Pensions Conslts, Roehampton Inst; advsr French Petroleum Inst; bd memb: Kenmore Refrigeration Equipment, Dyno Industs (UK); *Style—* Sir William Bentley, KCMG; 48 Bathgate Rd, London, SW19; Oak Cottage, Great Oak Lane, Crickhowell, Powys

BENTON, Kenneth Carter; CMG (1966); s of William Alfred Benton (d 1944), and Amy Adeline, *née* Kirton; *b* 4 March 1909; *Educ* Wolverhampton GS, London Univ; *m* 1938, Winifred (Peggie), da of Maj Gen Charles Pollock, CB, CBE, DSO (d 1929); 1 s, 2 step s (1 decd); *Career* HM Foreign Serv: Vienna, Riga, Madrid (twice), Rome (twice) Lima, cncllr Rio 1966-68, ret; *Books* eleven thrillers, two historical novels; *Recreations* painting, writing; *Clubs* Detection; *Style—* Kenneth Benton, Esq, CMG; 2 Jubilee Terrace, Chichester, W Sussex PO19 1XL (☎ 0243 787148)

BENTON, Peter Faulkner; s of Shirley Faulkner Benton (d 1985), of India and Haslemere Surrey, and Hilda Dorothy Benton; *b* 6 Oct 1934; *Educ* Oundle, Queens' Coll Cambridge (MA); *m* 1959, Ruth Stansfeld, da of Robert Stanley Cobb, MC, of Nairobi and Kidlington, Oxon; 2 s (Robert, Thomas), 3 da (Sarah, Juliet, Katherine); *Career* co dir and business conslt specialising in information technology; chm Euro Practice Nolan Norton and Co 1984-87; dir: Turing Inst 1985-, Singer and Friedlander Ltd 1983-89, Tandata Hldgs 1983-89; formerly md then dep chm Br Telecom 1978-83; memb: PO Bd 1978-81, gp bd Gallaher Ltd 1973-77; dir gen BIM 1987-, chm Enfield Health Authy 1986-, ind memb Br Library Advsy Cncl, memb Indust Devpt Advsy Bd, gen chm World Bank Confs on Catastrophe; *Publications* Riding the Whirlwind (1990), articles on science, information technology and management; *Recreations* reading, conversation; *Clubs* Athenaeum, United Oxford and Cambridge Univ, The Pilgrims, Highgate Literary and Scientific; *Style—* Peter Benton, Esq; Northgate House, Highgate Hill, London N6 5HD (☎ 081 341 1133)

BENTOVIM, Dr Arnon; s of Zvi Harry Bentovim (d 1989), and Gladys Rachel, *née* Carengold (d 1985); *b* 24 July 1936; *Educ* St Thomas' Hosp London (MB BS, DPM); *m* 1, 2 April 1958 (m dis 1987), Cecily Anne; 1 da (Ayalah b 1970); m 2, 1989, Marianne; *Career* psychoanalyst, family and child psychiatrist; registrar Maudsley Hosp 1962-66, sr registrar and consit child psychiatrist Hosps for Sick Children Gt Ormond St 1966, consIt Tavistock Clinic 1975-, consIt specialist advsr to House of Commons Select Ctee 1978-79; fndr: CIBA Fndn Study Gp, Trg Advsy Gp for the Sexual Abuse of Children, first sexual treatment prog in UK at Hosps for Sick Children 1981-; pubns on: child psychiatry, family therapy, aspects of child abuse; fndr memb: Assoc for Family Therapy, Br Assoc for the Prevention of Child Abuse and Neglect, Inst of Family Therapy; FRCPsych 1966; *Books* Family Therapy, Complimentary Frameworks of Theory and Practice (1984-89), Child Sexual Abuse within the Family: Assessment & Treatment (ed, 1988); *Recreations* music (particularly jazz), theatre, opera, travel; *Style—* Dr Arnon Bentovim; Hospitals for Sick Children, Great Ormond St, London WC1N 3JH (☎ 01 405 9200); Tavistock Clinic, 120 Belsize Lane, London NW3; Institute for Family Therapy, 43 New Cavendish St, London W1

BENYON, Thomas Yates; s of Capt Thomas Yates Benyon (d 1958, s of Capt Thomas Yates Benyon (d 1893) and Hon Christina Philippa Agnes, OBE, da of 11 Baron North, JP), and his 2 wife, Joan Ida Walters (d 1982); *b* 13 Aug 1942; *Educ* Wellington Sch Somerset, RMA Sandhurst; *m* 1968, (Olivia) Jane, da of Humphrey Scott Plummer by his w, Hon Pamela, *née* Balfour, da of 2 Baron Kinross, KC; 2 s, 2 da; *Career* former Lt Scots Gds, served Kenya, Muscat; MP (C) Abingdon 1979-83; chm: Assoc of Lloyd's Membs 1982-86, Homecare Residential Services plc, Milton Keynes Health Authy 1990-; *Recreations* hunting, music; *Clubs* RAC, Pratt's; *Style—* Thomas Benyon, Esq; The Old Rectory, Adstock, Buckingham, Bucks MK18 2HY (☎ 029671 3308); 17 Marshall St, London W1

BENYON, William Richard; DL (1970), MP (Cons) Milton Keynes 1983-; s of Vice Adm Richard Benyon, CB, CBE (d 1968, 2 s of Sir John Shelley, 9 Bt, JP, DL, a distant cous of the Shelley Bts who produced the poet, and Marion, da of Richard Benyon), and Eve, twin da of Rt Rev Lord William Cecil, sometime Bp of Exeter (2 s of 3 Marquess of Salisbury); the Adm changed his name to Benyon by Deed Poll on inheriting the Benyon estates of his cous Sir Henry Benyon, Bt; William Benyon is ggs of the Conservative PM, Lord Salisbury; *b* 17 Jan 1930; *Educ* RNC Dartmouth; *m* 1957, Elizabeth Ann, da of Vice Adm Ronald Hallifax , CB, CBE (d 1943), of The Red House, Shedfield, Hants; 2 s (Richard, Edward); 3 da (Catherine, Mary, Susannah); *Career* RN 1947-56; MP (C) Buckingham 1970-83, PPS to Paul Channon as Min of Housing 1972-74, oppn whip 1974-77, memb exec 1922 Ctee 1982-89; JP Berks 1962-77; *Clubs* Boodle's, Pratt's; *Style—* William Benyon, Esq, DL, MP; Englefield House, Englefield, Reading, Berks (☎ 0734 302 221); House of Commons, London SW1 (☎ 071 219 4047)

BERE, Rennie Montague; CMG (1957); s of Rev Montague Acland Bere (d 1947), and Sarah Lucy Troyte, *née* Griffith (d 1942); *b* 28 Nov 1907; *Educ* Marlborough, Selwyn Coll Cambridge (MA); *m* 13 April 1936, (Anne) Maree, da of Cecil Charles Barber (d 1962), of Ceylon; *Career* HM Overseas Serv 1930-55, provincial cmmr Uganda 1951-55; dir and chief warden Uganda Nat Parks 1955-60, pres Cornwall Tst for Nature Conservation 1967-70; author of books on wildlife in Africa and Cornwall; *Books* The Wild Mammals of Uganda (1962), The Way to the Mountains of the Moon

(1966), The African Elephant (1966), Birds in an African National Park (1969), Antelopes (1970), Crocodile's Eggs for Supper (folk tales, 1973), Wildlife in Cornwall (1970), The Book of Bude and Stratton (with B D Stamp, 1980), The Nature of Cornwall (1982); author of various articles in Alpine and other jls; *Recreations* mountaineering, cricket, walking, watching wildlife; *Clubs* Alpine, Climbers', Royal Cwlth Soc; *Style*— Rennie Bere, Esq, CMG; West Cottage, Bude Haven, Bude, N Cornwall (☎ 0288 352082)

BERENDT, Lady Frances Virginia Susan; *née* Ryder; da of 6 Earl of Harrowby and Helena Blanche Coventry; *b* 20 June 1926; *Educ* St Hugh's Oxford; *m* 1949, Frank Ernest Berendt, s of Siegfried Berendt (d 1947), of London; 1 s (Anthony), 1 da (Susan); *Career* dir and permissions ed Calibre (Cassette Library for the Blind and Handicapped); *Style*— Lady Frances Berendt; 34 The Marlowes, Boundary Road, NW8

BERENDT, Richard Arthur; s of Harold Berendt (d 1971), of Roydon, Essex, and Winifred, *née* Chipperfield; *b* 14 June 1926; *Educ* The Coll Bishops Stortford, Univ of Reading (BSc Agric); *m* 7 June 1952, Jean Marr, da of Lt-Col Arthur Cyril Robert Croom-Johnson (d 1964), of Sloane Square, London; 1 s (Peter b 1956), 1 da (Julia b 1963); *Career* served HAC 1948-59, Capt; gen mangr Shell Chemical Co E Africa and Central Africa 1966-71, dir Berendt Bros Ltd 1972-81; fin advsr 1976-; *Recreations* golf, beekeeping; *Clubs* Farmers; *Style*— Richard A Berendt, Esq; Kelsale Place, Kelsale, Saxmundham, Suffolk IP17 2RD (☎ (0728 602410); Hill Samuel Investment Services Ltd, Mount Pleasant House, Huntingdon Road, Cambridge CB3 0BL (☎ 0223 462233)

BERENS, David John Cecil (Henry); yst s of Herbert Cecil Benyon Berens, MC (d 1981), of Bentworth Hall Alton, Hants, and Moyra Nancy Mellard, niece and adopted da of 1 and Baron Greene, PC, OBE, MC, KC; descendant of Joseph Berens, of Kevington, Kent (b 1775), whose ancestors accompanied William of Orange from Holland in 1688; 6 generations have matric at ChCh Oxford; *b* 7 Oct 1939; *Educ* Eton, ChCh Oxford (MA); *m* 3 Oct 1963, Janet Roxburgh, yst da of Archibald Roxburgh Balfour, MC (d 1958), of Dawyck, Peeblesshire; sister of Christopher and Neil Balfour (*qqv*); 2 s (Archie b 1965, Jasper b 1970), 2 da (Emily b 1967, Henrietta b 1981); *Career* merchant banker; Lazard Bros 1962-72, invest mangr Trafalgar House 1972-82, md London Trust 1982-85; exec dir Tyndall Holdings 1985-89; memb Nat Cncl and chm Housing Mgmnt Ctee Carr Gomm Soc; *Recreations* arts, literature, sport, motor-cycling, shooting; *Clubs* White's, Pilgrims; *Style*— Henry Berens, Esq; 71 Church Rd, Wimbledon Village, SW19 5AL; 9A Gloucester St, Pimlico SW1V 2DB; Yew Tree Cottage, Bentworth, Alton, Hants GU34 5LE

BERESFORD, Lord Charles Richard de la Poer; 2 s of 8 Marquess of Waterford; *b* 18 Jan 1960; *m* 1984, Maria Teresa, da of Gabriel Donoso Phillips, of Santiago, Chile; 1 s (William b 24 June 1990), 1 da (Carolina b 1989); *Style*— The Lord Charles Beresford; Curraghmore, Portlaw, Co Waterford

BERESFORD, Christopher Charles Howard; s of (Richard) Marcus Beresford (d 1968), of Oundle, and Diana Katharine, *née* Howard; *b* 9 July 1946; *Educ* The Dragon Sch, Rugby, Trinity Coll Cambridge (MA); *m* 5 May 1973, (Philippa) Susan, da of Dennis Yates (d 1968); 1 s (Nicholas b 1979), 2 da (Antonia b 1975, Fiona b 1977); *Career* CA; ptnr KPMG Peat Marwick McLintock 1981-; vice chm Br Ski Club for the Disabled; Liveryman Worshipful Co of Grocers; FCA; *Recreations* skiing, tennis, shooting, badminton, bridge; *Clubs* City Livery, Ski Club of GB; *Style*— Christopher Beresford, Esq; KPMG Peat Marwick McLintock, 1 Puddle Dock, Blackfriars, London EC4V 3PD (☎ 071 236 8000, fax 071 832 8888, telex 8811541 PMM LON G)

BERESFORD, Lord James Patrick de la Poer; 3 s of 8 Marquess of Waterford; *b* 10 Dec 1965; *Style*— The Lord James Beresford; Curraghmore, Portlaw, Co Waterford

BERESFORD, Marcus de la Poer; s of Anthony de la Poer Beresford, TD, of Harrow-on-the-Hill, Middx, and Emmala Mary Alwina, *née* Canning; *b* 15 May 1942; *Educ* Harrow, St John's Coll Cambridge (MA); *m* 25 Sept 1965, Jean Helen, da of H T Kitchener, of Shepreth, Cambs; 2 s (Thomas, William); *Career* Smiths Industs 1960-83 (operating gp md 1979-83), dir and gen mangr Lucas Electronics & Systems 1983-85; md: Siemens Plessey Controls Ltd 1985-, Traffic Systems Int Ltd 1988-; dir: SICE SA (Spain), Elsydel SA (France), Dorset C of C and Indust; chm Bd of Govrs Bournemouth Poly; Freeman City of London 1963, Liveryman Worshipful Co of Skinners; FIEE, MIMechE, CEng, FInstD; *Recreations* golf; *Style*— Marcus Beresford, Esq; Siemens Plessey Controls Ltd, Sopers Lane, Poole, Dorset BH17 7ER (☎ 0202 782294, fax 0202 782331, telex 41272)

BERESFORD, Hon Marcus Hugh Tristam de la Poer; only s and heir of 6 Baron Decies (by 2 w); *b* 5 Aug 1948; *Educ* St Columba's Coll, Univ of Dublin (MLitt); *m* 1, 1970 (m dis 1974), Sarah Jane, only da of Col Basil Gunnell; m 2, 1981, Edel Jeanette, da of late Vincent Ambrose Hendron, of Dublin; 1 s (Robert b 1988), 1 da (Louisa b 1984); *Style*— The Hon Marcus Beresford; Straffan Lodge, Straffan, Co Kildare, Ireland

BERESFORD, Meg; da of John Tristram Beresford, CBE (d 1988), and Anne Isobel, *née* Stuart Wortley; *b* 5 Sept 1937; *Educ* Sherborne Sch for Girls, Univ of Warwick (BA); *Career* gen sec CND 1985-; *Recreations* hill walking, gardening, reading; *Style*— Ms Meg Beresford; Campaign For Nuclear Disarmament, 22-24 Underwood ST, London N1 7JG

BERESFORD, Lord Patrick Tristram de la Poer; s of 7 Marquess of Waterford (d 1934); *b* 16 June 1934; *Educ* Eton, RMA Sandhurst; *m* 1964 (m dis 1971), Mrs Julia Carey, da of Col Thomas Cromwell Williamson, DSO (d 1987); 1 s, 1 da; *Career* Capt RHG (ret); bloodstock agent; Chef d'Équipe Br 3 Day Event Team 1985; *Clubs* White's; *Style*— The Lord Patrick Beresford; Fairview Cottage, Wicks Green, Binfield, Berks RG12 5PF (☎ 0344 860976)

BERESFORD, Philip Charles Francis Martin; s of Major W B Beresford MC Cumbers, Liss, Hants (d 1980), and Winifred, *née* Cooper; *b* 25 Oct 1949; *Educ* Rossall Sch Fleetwood Lancs, Univ of Southampton (BSc), Univ of Strathclyde (MSc), Univ of Exeter (PhD); *Career* examinations sec RCOG 1978-79, journalist Engineering Today Magazine 1979-81, city reporter Sunday Telegraph 1982-83, Sunday Times 1983-90 (business reporter, transport corr, industl ed, dep business ed), ed Management Today 1990-; *Books* Sunday Times Book of Rich (1990); *Recreations* running, reading, cinema, trains, wine; *Style*— Dr Philip Beresford; Management Today, 30 Lancaster Gate, London W2 3LP (☎ 071 413 4184, fax 071 413 4138)

BERESFORD, Lady William Rachel Wyborn; *née* Page; yr da of late George Kennett Page, JP, of Upton Lodge, Bursledon, Hants, and Edith Mary, *née* Hill; *b* 5 July 1908; *Educ* Godolphin Sch Wilts; *m* 1945, Maj Lord William Mostyn de la Poer Beresford (d 1973), 2 s of 7 Marquess of Waterford ; 2 da (Meriel, Nicola); *Style*— The Lady William Beresford; The Thatched Cottage, Church Lane, Stradbally, Co Waterford (☎ 24275)

BERESFORD-ASH, John Randal; s of Maj Douglas Beresford-Ash, DSO, DL (d 1976), of Co Londonderry, N Ireland, and Lady Helena Betty Joanna Rous (d 1969); *b* 21 Jan 1938; *Educ* Eton; *m* 27 March 1968, Agnes Marie Colette, da of Comte Jules Marie Guy de Lamberterie, L'Ensouleiada Av de Bénéfiat, Cannes, France; 3 da (Melanie b 1968, Louisa-Jane b 1971, Angelique b 1978); *Career* Londonderry Grand Jury 1959-68, High Sheriff Co Londonderry 1976, farmer; pres Afghan Aid (Ireland) 1986-; *Recreations* golf; *Style*— John R Beresford-Ash, Esq; Ashbrook, Drumahoe, Co Londonderry, N Ireland (☎ (0504) 49223)

BERESFORD JONES, David; s of Capt Sidney Albert Jones, RD, RNR (d 1975), of Bournemouth (former Capt Queen Mary and Queen Elizabeth), and Bertha Mary Moldram, *née* Barnes; *b* 19 Aug 1936; *Educ* King's Sch Bruton; *m* 1, 12 Sept 1959 (m dis 1972), Sheila, *née* Lewis; 2 da (Nicola b 1963, Sarah b 1965); m 2, 19 Aug 1972, Lynda Caroline, da of Kenneth Roy Dolleymore (d 1976); 1 s (Edward b 1976), 1 da (Caroline b 1979); *Career* Pilot Offr RAF 1954-56; dir: Bland Welch (Reinsurance Brokers) Ltd 1971-74, Bland Payne Reinsurance Brokers Ltd 1974-76; chm: Steel Burrill Jones Group plc 1990- (co fndr 1977), Steel Burrill Jones Ltd 1985-; FRSA 1990; *Recreations* cricket, real tennis, golf, hockey, tennis; *Clubs* MCC, HAC, RTC (Hampton Court), Tulse Hill and Honor Oak, Roehampton, IOD; *Style*— David Beresford Jones, Esq; 100 Whitechapel, London E1 1JG (☎ 071 247 8888, fax 071 377 0020, telex 886129)

BERESFORD-PEIRSE, Sir Henry Grant de la Poer; 6 Bt (UK 1814), of Bagnall, Waterford; s of Sir Henry Beresford-Peirse, 5 Bt, CB (d 1972), and Margaret, Lady Beresford-Peirse, *qv*; *b* 7 Feb 1933; *Educ* Eton, Ontario Agric Coll; *m* 1966, Jadranka, da of Ivan Njerš, of Zagreb; 2 s; *Heir* s, Henry Beresford-Peirse; *Career* investment mgmnt; *Recreations* tennis, golf, country homes in Yorkshire and Portugal; *Clubs* Cavalry and Guards; *Style*— Sir Henry Beresford-Peirse, Bt; Bedall Manor, Bedale, N Yorks (☎ 0677 22811); 34 Cadogan Square, London SW1 (☎ 071 589 1134)

BERESFORD-PEIRSE, Henry Njerš de la Poer; s and h of Sir Henry Grant de la Poer Beresford-Peirse, 6 Bt; *b* 25 March 1969; *Educ* Harrow; *Recreations* cricket, golf, tennis; *Style*— Henry Beresford-Peirse, Esq; c/o Bedall Manor, Bedale, N Yorks

BERESFORD-PEIRSE, Margaret, Lady; Margaret; da of Frank Morrison Seafield Grant, of Knockie Whitebridge, Inverness-shire, and Caroline Frances Grant, *née* Philips; *b* 15 Oct 1907; *Educ* Cheltenham Ladies Coll; *m* 1932, Sir Henry Campell de la Poer Beresford-Peirse, 5 Bt, CB (d 1972); 2 s (Sir Henry Grant de la Poer Beresford-Peirse, 6 Bt, John David de la Poer), 1 adopted da (Mary, m Andrew, yr s of Sir John Gilmour, Bt, *qv*, of Montrave Fife Scotland; 2 s (Robert, David)); *Clubs* Lansdowne; *Style*— Margaret, Lady Beresford-Peirse; Bedall Manor, Bedale, N Yorks (☎ 0677 22811); Monte Elvas, S Bras de Alportel, Algarve, Portugal (☎ 089 42843)

BERESFORD-STOOKE, Lady; Creenagh; da of Sir Henry George Richards, KBE, KC (d 1928), sometime Chief Justice of Allahabad, and Frances Maud Lyster, OBE, *née* Smythe; *m* 1931, Sir George Beresford-Stooke, KCMG (d 1983), Gentleman Usher of the Blue Rod 1959-71; 1 s, 1 da; *Career* CStJ; *Style*— Lady Beresford-Stooke; Little Rydon, Hillfarrance, Taunton, Somerset TA4 1AW (☎ 0823 461640)

BERESFORD-WEST, Michael Charles; QC (1975); s of Arthur Charles West and Ida Dagmar West; *b* 3 June 1928; *Educ* St Peters, Portsmouth GS, Brasenose Coll Oxford (MA); *m* 1956 (m dis), Patricia Eileen, *née* Beresford; 2 s, 1 da; m 2, 1986, Sheilagh Elizabeth Davies; *Career* Intelligence Serv Middle East; called to the Bar 1952, Western Circuit 1953-65, South Eastern Circuit 1965, rec of the Crown Court 1975-83; chm Ind Schools Tbnl 1974-80; *Recreations* tennis, music, swimming; *Clubs* Oxford and Cambridge, MCC (1949-79), Hampshire Hogs, Aldeburgh Golf, Aldeburgh Yacht, Bar Yacht; *Style*— Michael Beresford-West, Esq, QC; 1 Grays Inn Square, London WC1R 5AG

BERG, Adrian; s of Charles Berg, and Sarah, *née* Sorby; *b* 12 March 1929; *Educ* Charterhouse, Gonville and Caius Coll Cambridge (MA), Trinity Coll Dublin (H DipEd), St Martin's Sch of Art, Chelsea Sch of Art (NDD), RCA; *Career* Nat Serv 1947-49; artist; selected one-man exhibitions: five at Arthur Tooth & Sons Ltd 1964-75, three at Waddington Galleries 1978-83, Waddington Galleries Montreal and Toronto 1979, Hokin Gallery Inc Chicago 1979, Rochdale Art Gallery 1980, The Picadilly Gallery 1985 and 1988, Serpentine Gallery London 1986, Walker Art Gallery Liverpool 1986; permanent exhibitions: Arts Cncl of GB, Br Cncl, Br Museum, Euro Parl, Govt Picture Collection, Hiroshima City Museum of Contemporary Art, The Tate Gallery, Tokyo Metropolitan Art Museum; *Style*— Adrian Berg, Esq; The Piccadilly Gallery, 16 Cork St, London W1X 1PF (☎ 071 629 2875)

BERGEL, Hon Mrs (Alexandra Mary Swinford); *née* Shackleton; only da of Baron Shackleton, KG, OBE, PC (Life Peer); *b* 15 July 1940; *Educ* Raven's Croft Sch Eastbourne, Trinity Coll Dublin; *m* 1969, Richard Charles Bergel, yr s of Hugh Charles Bergel, of Stamford Brook House, W6; 2 s; *Style*— The Hon Mrs Bergel; Dolphin House, Cricket Hill, Yateley, Hants

BERGENDAHL, (Carl) Anders; s of Carl Johan Bergendahl, of Djursholm, Sweden, and Ingrid Bergendahl (d 1964); *b* 20 March 1952; *Educ* Djursholm's Samskola Sweden, Stockholm Sch of Econs; *m* 18 March 1984, Maria, da of Stephen Heineman (d 1967); 2 s (David b 11 Sept 1985, Alexander b 18 June 1987); *Career* assoc Merrill Lynch 1977-, md Merrill Lynch Capital Markets 1985-; *Recreations* sailing, tennis, squash, skiing; *Clubs* Sallskapet, RAC; *Style*— Anders Bergendahl, Esq; 25 Ropemaker St, Ropemaker Place, London EC2Y 9LY (☎ 071 867 2800, fax 071 867 4455)

BERGER, Vice Adm Sir Peter Egerton Capel; KCB (1979), LVO (1960), DSC (1949); s of Capel Colquhoun Berger (d 1941), and Winifred Violet, *née* Levett-Scrivener (d 1981); *b* 11 Feb 1925; *Educ* Harrow; *m* 1956, June Kathleen, da of Cdr Frederick Arthur Pigou, RN (d 1979); 3 da (Sarah b 1959, Louisa b 1961, Katy b 1964); *Career* joined RN 1943, Normandy and S of France landings in HMS Ajax 1944, Lt 1946, Yangtse Incident in HMS Amethyst 1948, Lt Cmdr 1953, Cdr 1956, Fleet Navigating Offr Home Fleet 1956-58, Navigating Offr HM Yacht Britannia 1958-60, i/c HMS Torquay 1962-64, Capt 1964, i/c HMS Phoebe 1966-68, Cdre, Clyde 1971-73, Rear Adm 1973, Asst Chief of Naval Staff (Policy) 1973-75, COS to C-in-C Fleet 1976-78, Flag Offr Plymouth, Port Adm Devonport, Cdr Centl Sub Area E Atlantic and Cdr Plymouth Sub Area Channel 1979-81; bursar and fell Selwyn Coll Cambridge 1981-91; Hon MA Cambridge 1984; *Recreations* reading history, shooting, fishing; *Style*— Vice Adm Sir Peter Berger, KCB, LVO, DSC; Linton End House, Linton Road, Balsham, Cambs CB1 6HA; Selwyn College, Cambridge CB3 9DQ (☎ 0223 335891)

BERGHAHN, Marion; da of Herbert Koop (d 1978), and Ilse Voigt; *b* 14 Sept 1941; *Educ* Univ of Hamburg, Univ of Paris, Univ of Freiburg (DPhil), Univ of Cambridge (Certificate of Anthropology), Univ of Warwick (PhD); *m* 29 Dec 1969, Volker R Berghahn, s of Dr Alfred Berghahn, of Steinradweg 19, 3011 Barsinghausen, West Germany; 2 s (Sascha b 1973, Melvin b 1978), 1 da (Vivian b 1976); *Career* fndr publishing firm 1983; memb: Ind Publishers Guild 1983, Anthropological Soc 1989; *Books* The Image of Africa In Afro-American Literature (1976), Continental Britons German Jewish Refugees from Nazi Germany (1984); *Recreations* music; *Clubs* Sloane; *Style*— Ms Marion Berghahn; 77 Morrell Ave, Oxford OX4 1JJ

BERGNE, Hon Mrs ((Phyllis) Dorothy); *née* Borwick; yr da of 3 Baron Borwick (d 1961) by his 1 w; *b* 24 Aug 1916; *m* 1963, as his 2 wife, John A'Court Bergne (d 1978), s of Hervey A'Court Bergne (d 1941), of Budleigh Salterton, Devon; *Career* late Flying Offr WAAF; *Style*— The Hon Mrs Bergne; 16 Woodlane, Falmouth, Cornwall (☎ 0326 312430)

BERGSSON, Gudni; s of Bergur Gudnason, of Hadaland 11, Reykjauik, Iceland, and

Hjordis Bodvarsdottie; *b* 21 July 1965; *Educ* Breidagerdi Sch, Rettarholt Sch, Sund Sch, Univ of Iceland; *m* Elin Konradsdottir, da of Konrad David Johannesson (d 1985); *Career* professional footballer; amateur (131 appearances) FC Valur Iceland 1983-88 (Icelandic champions 1985 and 1987, Cup winners 1988); Tottenham Hotspur 1988-; Iceland caps: 1 under 16, 5 under 18, 4 under 21, 35 full 1984-; jr champion Iceland 1979, Young Player of the Year Iceland 1984; Player of the Year: The Morning Paper Iceland 1987, Daily Paper Iceland 1988; handball: 5 under 18 Iceland caps, jr champion Iceland 1977, 1978, 1980, 1981, 1983 and 1986; *Recreations* family and friends, sports, golf, chess, travelling; *Style—* Gudni Bergsson, Esq; Keystone, 60 London Rd, St Albans, Herts AL1 1NG

BERGSTROM, Prof (Albert) Rex; s of Albert Victor Bergstrom (d 1945), of Christchurch, NZ, and Lily, *née* Markland (d 1976); *b* 9 July 1925; *Educ* Christchurch Boys HS NZ, Univ of NZ (MCOM), Univ of Cambridge (PhD); *m* 12 Dec 1960, Christine Mary, da of Basil Egmont Arnold (d 1968), of Auckland, NZ; 1 s (Carl b 1961); *Career* RNZAF 1945-46; reader in economics LSE 1962-64, prof of econometrics Univ of Auckland 1965-70, prof of economics Univ of Essex 1971-; fell Econometric Soc; *Books* The Construction and use of Economic Models (1967), Statistical Inference in Continuous Time Economic models (ed, 1976), Stability and Inflation (jt ed, 1978), Continuous Time Econometric Modelling (1990); *Recreations* music, opera; *Style—* Prof Rex Bergstrom; 46 Regency Lodge, Avenue Rd, St John's Wood, London NW8 5ED (☎ 071 586 6259); 28B Creffield Rd, Colchester, Essex CO3 3HY (☎ 0206 43092); Department of Economics, University of Essex, Wivenhoe Park, Colchester CO4 3SQ (☎ 0206 872725)

BERGVALL, Prof Ulf Erik Gottfrid; s of Capt Harald Bergvall (d 1961), of Strängnäs, Sweden, and Essan, *née* Holm; *b* 1 Dec 1930; *Educ* Strängnäs Hal Sweden, Karolinska Inst Stockholm Sweden (ML, MD); *m* 15 Dec 1951, Margareta, da of Bertil Hälleraåd, of Örebro, Sweden; 2 s (Mats b 1960, Ola b 1969), 4 da (Maria b 1954, Johanna b 1956, Lovisa b 1963, Amanda b 1965); *Career* sr registrar and asst head radiology Serafimerlasarettet Stockholm 1963-67 (Sabbatsbergs Hosp Stockholm 1958-63), asst head radiology Danderyds Hosp Stockholm 1968-70, asst head neuroradiology Karolinska Hosp Stockholm 1970-76 (sr registrar neuroradiology 1967-68), head radiology II Huddinge Univ Hosp Stockholm 1982-83 (conslt neuroradiologist 1976-82), visiting prof and prof neuroradiology CHU de la Timone Marseille France 1984-85, conslt neuroradiologist Royal Hallamshire Hosp Sheffield 1986- (visiting prof and hon conslt 1983-84); assoc ed Acta Radiologica 1971-83; memb Swedish, Scandinavian and Euro Socs of Neuroradiology; memb: Swedish Soc of Med, RSM; *Recreations* gliding, sailing, mountain walking; *Clubs* Timmermansorden (Stockholm, Sweden); *Style—* Prof Ulf Bergvall; X-Ray Department, Royal Hallamshire Hospital, Sheffield S10 2JF (☎ 0742 766222)

BERIOSOVA, Svetlana; da of Nicolas Beriozoff, of Zurich, and Maria Beriosova (d 1942); *b* 24 Sept 1932; *Educ* Vilzak Schollar Sch of Ballet; *m* 1959 (m dis 1974) Mohammed Masud Khan (d 1989); *Career* ballet dancer; joined Grand Ballet de Monte Carlo 1947; danced with: Metropolitan Ballet 1948-49, Sadler's Wells Theatre Ballet 1950-52, Sadler's Wells Ballet (now The Royal Ballet); cr leading roles in: Designs for Strings, Fancrulla delle Rose, Trumpet Concerto, Pastorale, The Shadow, Armida, Prince of the Pagodas, Antigone, Baiser de la Fee, Diversions, Persephone, Images of Love; classical roles incl: Le Lac des Cygnes, The Sleeping Beauty, Giselle, Coppelia, Sylvia, Cinderella, Nutcracker; has danced with Royal Ballet in: USA, France, Italy, Aust, SA, Russia; guest: Belgrade, Granada, Milan (La Scala), Stuttgart, Bombay, Paris, Vienna, NZ, Zurich; film The Soldier's Tale 1966, numerous tv appearances, currently teaches worldwide; *Recreations* the arts; *Style—* Ms Svetlana Beriosova

BERKE, David Maurice; *b* 12 May 1935; *m* 11 Feb 1962, Esther, *née* Ovicher; 1 s (Jonathan b 23 Jan 1967), 1 da (Caroline Shear b 12 May 1963); *Career* articled clerk: C D Bromhead & Co Plymouth, Lubbock Fine London 1951-57; CA and audit mangr: Kemp Chateris London, Gainsley Harrison London; ptnr Berke Fine 1960- (now Neville Russell); FCA 1957, ATII 1962; *Style—* David Berke, Esq; Neville Russell, 246 Bishopsgate, London EC2M 4PB

BERKELEY, Andrew Wilson Atkins; s of Andrew Berkeley, JP (d 1952), of Cookstown, Co Tyrone, NI, and Mabel Berkeley; *b* 15 July 1936; *Educ* Rainey Sch Co Derry, Queen's Univ Belfast (BSc), Harvard Business Sch (AMP); *m* 30 Nov 1968, Carolyn Blyth Hinshaw Ross, of Milngavie, Glasgow, Scotland; 2 da (Kirsten b 16 Nov 1972, Iona b 27 April 1978); *Career* HAC Inf Bn TA 1966-67; called to the Bar Gray's Inn 1965; memb legal dept ICI Ltd 1966-78, dir ICI Petroleum Ltd 1978-81; admitted slr 1980; sec The British National Oil Corporation 1981-84, dir legal corp affrs STC plc 1984-87, gp gen counsel Laporte plc 1987-; vice chm Section for Energy and Nat Resources Law Int Bar Assoc 1979-83; Law Soc: memb Standing Ctee on Revenue Law, chm Ctee on Petroleum Taxation 1980-84; memb Cncl Inst of Industl and Commercial Law and Practice, Int C of C Paris; ACIArb 1986; *Recreations* riding; *Clubs* Athenaeum; *Style—* Andrew Berkeley, Esq; 49 Arden Rd, London N3 3AD (☎ 081 346 4114); Laporte House, Kingsway, Luton, Beds LU4 8EW (☎ 0582 21212)

BERKELEY, David James; s of Aubrey William Grandidier Berkeley, of Reigate, Surrey, and Sheena Elsie, *née* Turner; *b* 7 Aug 1944; *Educ* Rugby; *m* 28 Sept 1968, Gay Veronica, da of Robert Geoffrey William Hudson, MBE, of Naivasha Kenya; 2 da (Georgina b 1972, Louisa b 1975); *Career* chm and md: Brown Shipley (Jersey) Ltd, Brown Shipley Offshore Holdings Ltd; dir Brown Shipley and Co Ltd London; chm: Brown Shipley Stockbroking (CI) Ltd, Brown Shipley Tst Co (CI) Ltd, Brown Shipley Tst Co (IOM) Ltd, Brown Shipley (Isle of Man) Ltd; memb Stock Exchange; FCA; *Recreations* lawn tennis, hockey, English watercolours; *Clubs* Overseas Bankers, Public Schools Old Boys, LTA; *Style—* David J Berkeley, Esq; La Grange, St Mary, Jersey, Channel Islands (☎ 0534 81760); Brown Shipley (Jersey) Ltd, PO Box 583, 1 Waverley Place, St Helier, Jersey, Channel Islands JE4 8XR (☎ 0534 67557)

BERKELEY, Frederic George; s of Dr Augustus Frederic Millard Berkeley (d 1952), of Kennington, and Anna Louisa, *née* Inniss (d 1954); *b* 21 Dec 1919; *Educ* Elstree Sch, Aldenham, Pembroke Coll Cambridge (MA); *m* 1; 1 s, 1 da (1 da decd), 1 step s; m 2, 1988, Helen Kathleen Lucy; 1 step s, 1 step da; *Career* served WWII, Maj Normandy (wounded); slr, ptnr Lewis and Lewis 1951-70, vice chm and chm Legal Aid Area Ctee 1964-70, master Supreme Ct 1971, chief master Supreme Ct Taxing Office 1988-; gen ed Butterworths Costs Serv; *Recreations* reading, gardening, travel, writing; *Style—* Frederic Berkeley, Esq; The Royal Courts of Justice, The Strand, London WC2A 2LL (☎ 071 936 6227); 10 Dover House, Abbey Park, Beckenham, Kent BR3 1QB

BERKELEY, Hugh Rowland Comyns; s of Rowland Frank Brackenbury Berkeley, of Little Heronden, High St, Hawkhurst, Kent, and Margaret, *née* Kelleher; *b* 22 July 1938; *Educ* St George's Coll Weybridge Surrey, Neuchatel Business Sch Neuchatel Switzerland; *m* 30 June 1962, Cherry, da of Lt Cdr Humphrey Cleveland Hookway, DSC; 2 s (Robert b 11 Sept 1964, Neil b 17 May 1966), 1 da (Theresa b 10 March 1969); *Career* aviation broker Stewart Smith Lloyds of London 1959 (CT Bowring 1958), ptnr Berkeley Haulage & Co 1961; md: Berkeley Invicta Ltd 1977, D & H Holdings 1984; FInstD 1980, FBIM 1981, AInstM 1981; *Recreations* rugby, flying, skiing; *Clubs* Tonbridge Rugby; *Style—* Hugh Berkeley, Esq; Ethnam, Ethnam Lane, Sandhurst, Kent TN18 5PS (☎ 0580 850217); 191 Bravington Rd, Maida Vale, London; D & H Holdings Ltd, Maidstone Rd, Matfield, Tonbridge, Kent TN12 7JN (☎ 089272 2202, fax 089272 3507, telex 95539 BERK G, car 0836 553707)

BERKELEY, Humphry John; s of Capt Reginald Cheyne Berkeley, MC (d 1935), sometime Liberal MP, and his 2 w Hildegarde (Mrs Hildegarde Tinne); *b* 21 Feb 1926; *Educ* Malvern, Pembroke Coll Cambridge; *Career* pres Cambridge Union 1948, served at Cons Political Centre 1949-56, chm Coningsby Club 1952-55, DG UK Cncl Euro Movement 1956-57; MP (C) Lancaster 1959-66; joined Labour Pty 1970, fought North Fylde (Lab) Oct 1974, joined SDP 1981, contested (SDP) Homefields Ward of Hounslow for Borough Cncl election May 1982, contested Southend East (SDP Liberal Alliance) 1987, rejoined Labour Pty 1988; dir: Caspair Ltd, Island Devpts, Sharon Allen Leukaemia Tst 1984-; *Books* The Power of the Prime Minister (1968), Crossing the Floor (1972), The Life and Death of Rochester Sneath (1974), The Odyssey of Enoch - A Political Memoir (1976), The Myth that will not Die - The Formation of the National Government (1978), Faces of The Eighties (with Jeffrey Archer, 1987); *Clubs* Savile; *Style—* Humphry Berkeley, Esq; 3 Pages Yard, Church St, Chiswick, London W4 (☎ 081 994 5575)

BERKELEY, (Robert) John Grantley; TD (1967), JP (Glos 1960), DL (Glos 1982, Hereford and Worcester 1983); s of Capt Robert George Wilmot Berkeley (d 1969, himself 13 in descent from Hon Thomas Berkeley (4 s of 1 Baron Berkeley cr 1421, gs of 4 Baron Berkeley cr 1295, and descended in direct male line from Eadnoth the Staller, pre-Conquest Anglo-Saxon nobleman at Court of King Edward the Confessor) by his 2 w Isabel, da and co-heir of Thomas Mowbray, 1 Duke of Norfolk and Hon Myrtle, da of 14 Baron Dormer; *b* 24 July 1931; *Educ* Oratory Sch, Magdalen Coll Oxford; *m* 25 Jan 1967, Georgina Bridget, eld da of Maj Andrew Charles Stirling Home Drummond Moray (d 1971), of Easter Ross, Comrie, Perthshire; 2 s (Robert Charles b 1968, Henry John Mowbray b 1969); *Career* Maj Queen's Own Warwicks Yeo 1963; jt master Berkeley Hunt 1960-84; High Sheriff: Worcs 1967, Glos 1982-83; *Clubs* Cavalry and Guards; *Style—* R J Berkeley, Esq, TD, JP, DL; Berkeley Castle, Glos (☎ 0453 810 202); Spetchley Park, nr Worcester (☎ 090 565 224)

BERKELEY, Baroness (E 1421); Mary Lalle Foley Berkeley; da of Col Frank Wigram Foley, CBE, DSO (d 1949), and Eva Mary Fitz-Hardinge, Baroness Berkeley (d 1964); *b* 9 Oct 1905; *Heir* sister, Hon Mrs Gueterbock; *Style—* The Rt Hon the Lady Berkeley; Pickade Cottage, Gt Kimble, Aylesbury, Bucks (☎ 084 44 3051)

BERKELEY, Michael Fitzharding; s of Sir Lennox Randolph Francis Berkeley, CBE (d 1989), of 8 Warwick Ave, London, and Elizabeth Freda, *née* Bernstein; *b* 29 May 1948; *Educ* Westminster Cathedral Choir Sch, The Oratory, Royal Acad of Music (ARAM), post grad work with Richard Rodney Bennett, *qv*; *m* 19 Nov 1979, Deborah Jane Coltman, da of Guy Coltman Rogers (d 1976), of Stanage Park, Knighton, Powys; 1 da (Jessica Rose b 28 June 1986); *Career* composer and broadcaster; phlebotonist St Bartholomew's Hosp 1969-71, announcer BBC Radio 1974-79, regular broadcaster on music and the arts BBC radio and TV 1974-; music panel advsr Arts Cncl of GB, memb Central Music Advsy Ctee BBC 1986-89; memb Gen Advsy Cncl BBC 1990-; assoc composer Scottish Chamber Orch 1979; pres Presteigne Festival; compositons incl: Meditation (Guiness prize for composition) 1977, Primavera 1979, Uprising 1980, Wessex Graves 1981, Oratorio Or Shall We Die? 1982, Music from Chaucer 1983, Fierce Tears 1984, Pas de Deux 1985, Songs of Awakening Love 1986, Organ Concerto 1987; The Red Macula 1989, Gethsemane Fragment 1990, Entertaining Master Punch 1991; memb: Composer's Guild of GB, APC; *Recreations* contemporary painting, walking, hill farming; *Style—* Michael Berkeley, Esq; 49 Blenheim Crescent, London W11 2EF (☎ 071 229 6945)

BERLIAND, David Michael; s of Jasha Berliand (d 1976), and Phyllis, *née* Doresa; *b* 17 Dec 1935; *Educ* Charterhouse; *m* 1961, Diana Jill, da of Antony Maynard Puckle (d 1989), of Hants; 1 s (Richard b 1962), 2 da (Louise b 1964, Penelope b 1967); *Career* Nat Serv Lt RA Germany 1955; dir: Bain Clarkson Ltd (insurance brokers) 1987-, Inchcape Insurance Holdings Ltd; Freeman Worshipful Co of Insurers; *Recreations* tennis, golf; *Clubs* Boodles, MCC; *Style—* David Berliand, Esq; Bridgefoot Farm, Ripley, Surrey (☎ 0483 224354); 15 Minories, London EC3N 1NJ (☎ 071 481 3232, fax 071 488 2693, telex 8813411)

BERLIN, Sir Isaiah; OM (1971), CBE (1946); s of Mendel and Marie Berlin, of London; *b* 6 June 1909; *Educ* St Paul's CCC Oxford; *m* 1956, Aline, da of Baron Pierre de Gunzbourg, of Paris and formerly w of Dr Hans Halban; *Career* served WWII with Miny of Info and Foreign Office; Chichele prof of social and political theory Oxford Univ 1957-67, visiting prof of humanities City Univ NY 1966-71, pres Wolfson Coll Oxford 1966-75; pres Br Acad 1974-78; fell: New Coll Oxford 1938-50, All Souls Coll Oxford; memb bd of dirs Royal Opera House Covent Garden 1954-65 and 1974-87; tstee Nat Gallery 1975-85; awarded Erasmus Prize 1983 for promoting Euro culture Commandeur de l'Ordre des Arts et des Lettres 1990; recipient of hon doctorates from British, Israeli and American Univs; FBA; kt 1957; *Books* Karl Marx (1939, 1978), First Love by I A Turgenev (translation, 1950), The Age of Enlightenment (1956), Four Essays on Liberty (1969), Vico and Herder (1976), Concepts and Categories (1978), Russian Thinkers (1978), Against the Current (1979), Personal Impressions (1980), The Crooked Timber of Humanity (1990); *Style—* Sir Isaiah Berlin, OM, CBE; All Souls College, Oxford

BERMAN, Caroline Frances Esther; da of Lawrence Sam Berman, CB, *qv*, and Kathleen Doreen, *née* Lewis; *b* 8 May 1958; *Educ* North London Collegiate Sch, Univ of Sussex (BA); *m* 23 Nov 1986, Jonathan David Chattyn Turner, s of Dr Maxwell Herman Turner; 1 s (Jacob), 1 da (Camilla); *Career* ed Mills and Allen Communications 1979-82, viewdata mangr Standby Travel Pubns 1982-83, journalist Computing Magazine 1983-85, media ed Campaign Magazine 1985, freelance journalist 1986-; Times/Hewlett Packard Computer Journalist of the Year (features) 1984; *Recreations* theatre, painting, walking, playing with Jacob and Camilla; *Style—* Ms Caroline Berman

BERMAN, Franklin Delow; CMG (1987); s of Joshua Zelic Berman, of Cape Town, and Gertrude, *née* Levin; *b* 23 Dec 1939; *Educ* Rondebosch Boys HS, Univ of Cape Town (BA, BSc), Wadham and Nuffield Colls Oxford (MA); *m* 24 July 1964, Christine Mary, da of Edward Francis Lawler (d 1978); 2 s (Jonathan b 1966, Stefan b 1968), 3 da (Katharine b 1972, Judith b 1972, Victoria b 1972); *Career* HM Dip Serv 1965, asst legal advsr FCO 1965-71, legal advsr Br Mil Govt Berlin 1971-72, legal advsr Br Embassy Bonn 1972-74, legal cnsllr FCO 1974-82, cnsllr UK Mission UN 1982-85, dep legal advsr FCO 1988-; chm: Dip Serv Assoc 1979-82, Staff Tbnl Int Oil Pollution Compensation Fund 1985-; *Recreations* reading, walking, choral singing, gardening; *Style—* Franklin Berman, Esq, CMG; Foreign and Commonwealth Office, King Charles St, London SW1A 2AH (☎ 071 270 3000)

BERMAN, Lawrence Sam; CB (1975); s of Jack Berman, and Violet Berman (d 1980); *b* 15 May 1928; *Educ* St Clement Danes GS, LSE (BSc, MSc); *m* 1954, Kathleen D Lewis; 1 s (Richard), 1 da (Caroline); *Career* Central Statistical Office 1952-72, dir of statistics DTI 1972-83, statistical advsr Caribbean Tourism R & D Centre Barbados 1984-85; *Recreations* travel, theatre, collecting bow ties; *Style—* Lawrence Berman, Esq, CB; 10 Carlton Close, Edgware, Middx HA8 7PY (☎ 081 958 6938)

BERMAN, Richard Andrew; s of Laurence S Berman, CB, and Kathleen, *née* Lewis; *b* 3 April 1956; *Educ* Haberdashers' Aske's, Churchill Coll Cambridge (BA, MA); *m* 31 Aug 1985, Susan, *née* Charles; *Career* treas Andrea Merzario Spa 1980-83, gp treas

Heron Corporation plc 1984; dir: IFM Term Investments Ltd 1985-90, Pine St Investments Ltd 1987-90; md FVL Corporate Finance Ltd 1987-; dir and head of International Mergers and Aquisitions Credit Lyonnais Securities 1990-; memb ACT; *Recreations* eclectic collecting, walking, reading; *Style—* Richard Berman, Esq; PO Box 1270, London W4 4AX

BERMANT, Chaim Icyk; s of Azriel Bermant (d 1962), of Glasgow, and Feiga, *née* Daets (d 1971); *b* 26 Feb 1929; *Educ* Queens Park Sch Glasgow, Univ of Glasgow (MA, MLitt), LSE (MSc); *m* 16 Dec 1962, Judy, da of Fred Weil, of Jerusalem; 2 s (Azriel b 1968, Daniel b 1972), 2 da (Alisa b 1963, Evie b 1966); *Career* staff writer: Scottish TV 1957-59, Granada TV 1959-61; journalist Jewish Chronicle 1961-66, author; *Style—* Chaim Bermant, Esq; c/o Aitken and Stone, 29 Fernshaw Rd, London SW10 OTG

BERMINGHAM, Gerald Edward; MP (Lab) St Helens South 1983-; s of late Patrick Xavier Bermingham and Eva Terescena Bermingham; *b* 20 Aug 1940; *Educ* Cotton Coll, Wellingborough GS, Univ of Sheffield; *m* 1, 1964 (m dis), Joan; 2 s; m 2, 1978, Judith; *Career* barr formerly slr, memb Sheffield City Cncl 1975-79, contested (Lab) Derbyshire SE 1979; *Style—* Gerald Bermingham, Esq, MP; House of Commons, London SW1

BERNARD, Sir Dallas Edmund; 2 Bt (UK 1954), of Snakemoor, Co Southampton; s of Sir Dallas Gerald Mercer Bernard, 1 Bt (d 1975); *b* 14 Dec 1926; *Educ* Eton, CCC Oxford (MA); *m* 1, 1959 (m dis 1978); 3 da (Juliet Mary b 1961, Alicia Elizabeth b 1964, Sarah Jane b 1968); m 2, 1979, Mrs Monica J Montford, da of late James Edward Hudson; 1 da (Olivia Louise b 1981); *Heir* none; *Career* dir: Morgan Grenfell and Co Ltd 1964-77, Morgan Grenfell Holdings Ltd 1970-79, Italian International Bank plc 1978-89; memb Monopolies and Mergers Cmmn 1973-79; chm: Nat and Foreign Securities Trust Ltd 1981-86, Thames Trust Ltd 1983-86; dir: Dreyfus Intercontinental Investment Fund NY 1970-, Dreyfus Dollar International Fund NY 1982-; memb Cncl Girls Pub Day Sch Tst 1978-; *Clubs* Brooks', Lansdowne; *Style—* Sir Dallas Bernard, Bt; 8 Eaton Place, London SW1X 8AD

BERNARD, Jeffrey Joseph; s of Maj Oliver Bernard, OBE, MC, (d 1939); *b* 27 May 1932; *Educ* Pangbourne; *m* 1978, Susan; 1 da (by previous m); *Career* journalist and columnist; formerly with New Statesman, Sporting Life, Daily Mirror, Pacemaker; feature writer Sunday Times Mag, reviewer Punch, racing columnist Harpers and Queen, columnist Private Eye; writer 'Low Life' column The Spectator for the past 14 years; subject of play by Keith Waterhouse 'Jeffrey Bernard is Unwell'; *Recreations* cooking, music, racing, drinking with friends; *Clubs* Colony Room, Chelsea Arts, Groucho; *Style—* Jeffrey Bernard, Esq

BERNARD, Lady Jennifer Jane; er da of Air Chief Marshal 5 and last Earl of Bandon, GBE, CB, CVO, DSO (d 1979), and his 1 w, (Maybel) Elizabeth (*see* Holcroft, Elizabeth, Lady); *b* 30 April 1935; *Style—* Lady Jennifer Bernard; Padworth House, Reading, Berks

BERNARD, (Francis) William Wigan; s of Brig Ronald Playfair St Vincent Bernard, DSO, MC, IA (d 1943), and Katharine Etheldreda, *née* Wigan (d 1978); *b* 5 June 1924; *Educ* Bedford Sch, BNC Oxford (MA); *m* 7 Feb 1958, Margaret Renee, da of Capt Wilfrid Harry Dowman, RNVR (d 1936), of Weymouth; 1 s (James b 1959), 4 da (Catherine b 1960, Antonia b 1961, Frances (twin) b 1961, Sarah b 1964); *Career* Capt RA 1942-47; ADC to Govr Gen of Fedn of Rhodesia and Nyasaland (Lord Llewellin) 1953-57, Maj Rhodesia and Nyasaland Def Staff 1955-58, dir Central African Bldg Soc; cncllr Salisbury 9 yrs, memb St John Ambulance Bde, Cdr for Jersey 1987 (see also Who's Who of Central Africa 1968); CStJ 1990; *Recreations* ornithology, tennis; *Clubs* Boodles; *Style—* William Bernard, Esq; Herupe House, St John, Jersey, CI (☎ 0534 65358)

BERNAYS, Richard Oliver; s of Robert Hamilton Bernarys, MP (MP for Bristol North 1931-45, ka 1945), and Nancy, *née* Britton (d 1987); *b* 22 Feb 1943; *Educ* Eton, Trinity Coll Oxford (MA); *m* 12 Feb 1972, Karen, da of Russell Henry Forney, of New Castle, PA, USA (d 1979); 3 da (Lucy b 1975, Mary b 1977, Amy b 1979); *Career* vice chm Mercury Asset Mgmnt plc, dir Mercury Fund Managers; *Recreations* golf, fishing; *Clubs* Brooks's, Rye Golf; *Style—* Richard Bernays, Esq; 82 Elgin Crescent, London W11 2JL; 33 King William St, London EC4R 9AS

BERNERS, Baroness (15 in line, E 1455); Vera Ruby Williams; *née* Tyrwhitt; da of Maj the Hon Rupert Tyrwhitt, 5 s of Emma Harriet, Baroness Berners (12 holder of title *de jure* and seventeenth in descent from Edward III); *b* 25 Dec 1901; *Educ* Ladies Coll Eastbourne, St Agnes E Grinstead; *m* 1927, Harold Williams, JP; 2 da; *Heir* (co-heiresses) daughters, Hon Mrs P V Kirkham and Hon Mrs R T Pollock, *qqv*; *Career* nursing Guy's Hosp; *Recreations* gardening; *Style—* The Rt Hon the Lady Berners; Ashwellthorpe, Charlton Lane, Cheltenham, Glos (☎ 0242 519595)

BERNEY, John Verel; JP (Norfolk 1957); s of George Augustus Berney (d 1952), of Morton Hall, Norfolk, and Marjory Scott, *née* Verel (d 1966); *b* 17 Feb 1924; *Educ* Radley, Clare Coll Cambridge (BA); *m* 1, 3 Jan 1950 (m dis 1984), Jill, da of Capt Gilbert Philip Makinson (d 1935), of Sydney, Aust; 1 s (Ralph), 3 da (Philippa (Mrs Moll), Sylvia, Rosalind); m 2, 23 March 1984, Pauline Jenkins, da of Ernest George Emms, of South Cottage, Pulham Market, Norfolk; *Career* WWII served Capt Royal Norfolk and Hants Regts (wounded) 1942-47; landowner, farmer; memb: CLA Norfolk Ctee 1957-, High Sheriff Norfolk 1978; Agric Land Tbnl (also Land Drainage Section); *Recreations* shooting, fishing, beagling, walking, travel; *Clubs* Norfolk (Norwich); *Style—* John Berney, Esq, JP; Hockering House, E Dereham, Norfolk (☎ 0603 880339)

BERNEY, Sir Julian Reedham Stuart; 11 Bt (E 1620), of Parkehall in Redham, Norfolk; s of Lt John Berney (k on active serv Korea 1952) and Hon Jean (who m 2, P Jesson; and 3, M Ritchie), da of 1 Viscount Stuart of Findhorn, CH, MVO, MC, PC; suc gf 1975; *b* 26 Sept 1952; *Educ* Wellington, N E London Poly; *m* 1976, Sheena, da of Ralph Day, of Danbury, Essex; 2 s (William b 1980, Hugo Ralph b 1987), 1 da (Jessica Mary b 1982); *Heir* s, William Reedham John Berney b 29 June 1980; *Career* chartered surveyor, ARICS; *Recreations* sailing, hill walking; *Clubs* Royal Ocean Racing; *Style—* Sir Julian Berney, Bt; Reeds House, 40 London Rd, Maldon, Essex CM9 6HE (☎ 0621 853420)

BERNS, Richard Michael; s of Leonard Berns (d 1978), of Cobham, Surrey, and Elizabeth Grace, *née* Turner; *b* 16 Aug 1947; *Educ* Dulwich; *m* 16 Dec 1972, Roberta, da of Robert Dunlop Fleming (d 1978), of Perth, Scotland; 1 s (Ashley b 1969), 1 da (Antonia b 1974); *Career* slr; jt sr ptnr Piper Smith and Basham; dir: Ansad Properties (Manchester) Ltd 1979-87, District and Central Finance Ltd 1979-87, Grange Park Securities Ltd 1981-87, TNC Properties Ltd 1988-89; life govr Imperial Cancer Res Fund; memb Law Soc; *Recreations* sailing, skiing, tennis; *Style—* Richard M Berns, Esq; Leigh Hill House, Leigh Hill Rd, Cobham, Surrey (☎ 0932 62284); 31 Warwick Square, London SW1 (☎ 071 828 8685, telex 916604 PSBG, fax 071 630 6976, car 0836 227 653)

BERNSEN, Svend Aage; s of Hans Henrik Bernsen (d 1966), and Johanne, *née* Loenborg; *b* 23 April 1934; *Educ* commercial training in Denmark, Germany and the UK; *m* 28 Feb 1959, Vivienne, da of Edwin Brace (d 1973); 2 da (Karen b 1959, Elizabeth b 1966); *Career* Ess-Food Denmark (Danish bacon factories' export assoc): joined 1959-, head clerk 1961, head of Dept 1968, sales dir 1973, md Ess-Food (UK) Ltd 1977, group md 1986-; dir Danish Bacon Company plc; chm: Ess-Food Danepak Ltd, Anglo-Danish Food Transport Ltd, Bacon Distribution Centre Ltd, Ess-Food Fresh Meat Ltd; *Recreations* golf; *Style—* Svend Bernsen, Esq; White Lodge, 24 Astons Rd, Moor Park, Northwood, Middlesex HA6 2LD (☎ 09274 25076); Ess-Food (UK) Group Ltd, Howardsgate, Welwyn Garden City, AL8 6NN (☎ 0707 323421, car ☎ 0836 200421)

BERNSTEIN, Baron Anthony Webber; s of Cyril Philip (d 1952), of Manchester, and Dorothy, *née* Webber (d 1985); *b* 22 Sept 1938; *Educ* Clifton; *m* 16 Aug 1961, (Sara) Frances, da of Lazarus Rayman (d 1948), of Singapore and Manchester; 3 s (Simon Laurence b 20 Aug 1963, Jeremy Paul b 16 Oct 1965, Robin Daniel b 27 Feb 1970); *Career* Cyril Bernstein Ltd (now Bernstein Gp plc): dir 1964-72, md 1972-85, chm 1985-; chm: Honmark Int Ltd, Century Locks Ltd; treas Br Furniture Mfrs Assoc 1984-88, memb Funiture EDC 1985-88, pres NW Furniture Trades Fedn 1983-87 (offr 1966-86, treas 1979-83); *Recreations* football, swimming, water-skiing, tennis; *Style—* Baron Bernstein, Esq; Richmond House, Norman's Place, Altrincham, Cheshire WA14 2AB (☎ 061 941 2404); Bernstein Gp plc, PO Box 33, Middleton, Manchester M24 1AR (☎ 061 653 9191, fax 061 653 5392, telex 668111 OODAIR)

BERNSTEIN, Prof Basil Bernard; s of Percival Bernstein (d 1972), and Julie Bernstein (d 1931); *b* 1 Nov 1924; *Educ* Christ Coll Finchley, LSE; *m* 22 Nov 1955, Marion, da of Samuel Black (d 1955), of Manchester; 2 s (Saul b 17 Nov 1959, Francis b 24 Aug 1965); *Career* RAF 1942-46; teacher City Day Coll 1954-60; Inst of Educn Univ of London: hon res asst 1960-62, reader sociology of educn 1963-67, prof sociology of educn 1967-79, Karl Mannhiem prof in sociology of educn 1979-, sr pro-dir 1983-89, pro dir (res) 1983-89; DLitt Univ of Leicester 1974, FilHDr Univ of Lond 1980, DUniv Open Univ 1983, Phd Univ of Rochester USA 1989; *Books* Poder, Education of Conscience (1988); Class, Codes and Control: vol I (1971), vol II (1973), vol III (1975); Routledgedregon Paul (with W Brandis, 1974), Selection and Control (1974), Macht Kontroll och Pedagogic Lisor Farlay Lund (ed with U Lundgran, 1983); *Style—* Prof Basil Bernstein; 90 Farquhar Rd, Dulwich, London SE19 1LT (☎ 081 670 6411); Institute of Education, University of London, 20 Bedford Way, London WC2 (☎ 071 636 1500)

BERNSTEIN, Dr Robert Michael; s of Dr Fred Julian Bernstein (d 1986), and Dr Emilie Ellen Bernstein, *née* Guthmann; *b* 31 Dec 1947; *Educ* Highgate Sch, King's Coll Cambridge (MA, MD, BChir), UCH Med Sch; *m* 29 Sept 1978, Frances Jane Northcroft, da of Dr Christopher Tibbits Brown, of North Mill, Wareham; 2 s (Jonathan b 1979, Nicholas b 1983), 2 da (Laura b 1981, Alice b 1986); *Career* sr registrar Royal Post Grad Med Sch 1981-85, visiting scientist Cold Spring Harbor Laboratory USA 1983-84, conslt rheumatologist and clinical lectr Univ of Manchester and Manchester Royal Infirmary 1985-; memb: Rheumatology Sub Ctee and columnist RCP, Ed Bd Clinical and Experimental Rheumatology, nat ctee Br SLE Aid Gp, GMC; FRCP 1990 (MRCP 1975); *Recreations* mountains, music; *Style—* Dr Robert Bernstein; 23 Anson Rd, Manchester M14 5BZ (☎ 061 225 1135)

BERNSTEIN, Ronald Harold; DFC (1944), QC (1969); Mark Bernstein, and Fanny, *née* Levinson; *b* 18 Aug 1918; *Educ* Swansea GS, Univ Coll Swansea, Balliol Coll Oxford; *m* 4 Jan 1955, Judy, da of David Levi; 3 s (Mark b 1959, John b 1961, Daniel b 1965), 1 da (Sarah b 1963); *Career* cmd: 654 Air Op Sqdn RAF 1944-45, 661 Air Op Sqdn R AUX AF 1954-55; called to the Bar Middle Temple 1948, rec Crown Court 1975-90, bencher Middle Temple 1975, dep official referee 1982-90; FCIArb 1983 (currently vice pres), Hon ARICS, Hon FSVA; *Books* Handbook of Rent Review (1982), Handbook of Arbitration Practice (1987); *Clubs* Athenaeum; *Style—* Ronald Bernstein, Esq, DFC, QC; Temple Chambers, Falcon Court, 32 Fleet St, London EC4Y 1AA (☎ 071 353 2484, fax 071 353 1261)

BERNSTEIN, Baron (Life Peer UK 1969), of Leigh; Sidney Lewis Bernstein; s of Alexander and Jane Bernstein; bro of late Cecil Bernstein (jt fndr with him of Granada) and unc of Alex Bernstein, chm Granada Gp; *b* 30 Jan 1899; *Educ* LLD; *m* 1954, Sandra, da of Charles Malone, of Toronto; 1 s, 2 da; *Career* fndr Film Soc 1924, memb Middx CC 1925-31, chm Granada Group Ltd 1934-79; pres 1979-: Granada Group plc, Granada TV, Granada Leisure Ltd, Granada TV Rental, Granada Motorway Services; films advsr Miny of Info 1940-45, liaison Br Embassy Washington 1942; chief Film Section: AFHQ N Africa 1942-43, SHAEF 1943-45; lectr in film and int affrs NY Univ and Yale; memb Resources for Learning Consultative Ctee Nuffield Fndn 1965-72, govr Sevenoaks Sch 1964-74; *Clubs* Garrick; *Style—* The Rt Hon the Lord Bernstein; 36 Golden Square, London W1R 4AH (☎ 071 734 8080)

BERRAGAN, Maj-Gen Gerald Brian; CB; s of William James Berragan (d 1982), of 24 Green Dykes Lane, York, and of Marion Beatrice Berragan; *b* 2 May 1933; *Educ* various schs in India and UK; *m* Anne Helen, da of David Boyd Kelly (d 1971), of York; 3 s (Howard Neil b 1959, Nigel Boyd b 1962, Nicholas Jeremy b 1967); *Career* cmmnd REME 1954, Lt attached 7 Hussars, trans RAOC 1956, Capt UK Belgium and Germany, Staff Coll 1966, served Maj York & BAOR, Lt Col 1972; Cmd: RAOC 3 Div 1976-78, AQMC HQ N I 1978-80; Col 1978, HQ DGOS 1978-80, Brig 1980, Cmd COD Chilwell 1980-82, Cmd COD Bicester 1982-83, Dir Supply Ops Army 1983-85, Maj Gen DGOS 1985-88; chief exec Inst of Packaging 1988-; FBIM, FInstPS; *Recreations* sailing, skiing, tennis; *Clubs* Athenaeum, Army and Navy; *Style—* Maj-Gen Gerald Berragan, CB

BERRIDGE, David; s of William Berridge, of Hull, and Phyllis, *née* Langley; *b* 12 Nov 1947; *Educ* Hull GS, Univ of Hull (MA); *m* 19 July 1969, Barbara May, da of James Sutherland, of Willerby, nr Hull; 1 s (Christopher b 1970), 4 da (Lisa b 1971, Emma b 1975, Kathryn b 1978, Amy b 1987); *Career* CA; fndr and princ D Berridge, sr lectr Humberside Coll, dir Hull Collectors Centre 1976-77, accountant Rediffusion Ltd 1972-73, hon treas Anlaby Community Care Assoc, involved in local charity work; FCA, ACIS; *Recreations* reading, jogging, watching rugby league; *Style—* David Berridge, Esq; 31 Westella Way, Kirkeua, Hull HU10 7LN (☎ 0482 650 747)

BERRIDGE, Dr Michael John; s of George Kirton Berridge and Stella Elaine, *née* Hards; *b* 22 Oct 1938; *Educ* Univ Coll of Rhodesia and Nyasaland (BSc), Univ of Cambridge (PhD); *m* 5 March 1965, Susan Graham, *née* Winter; 1 s (Paul b 19 March 1969), 1 da (Rozanne b 4 June 1967); *Career* post doctoral fell Univ of Virginia 1965-66, res assoc Case Western Res Univ 1967 (post doctoral fell 1966-69); Univ of Cambridge: sr scientific offr Unit of Invertebrate Chemistry and Physiology 1969, chief sci offr Unit of Insect Neurophysiology and Pharmacology 1987-; fell Trinity Coll cambridge 1972; awards incl: Feldberg Prize 1984, The King Faisal Int Prize in Sci 1986, Louis Jeantet Prize in Med 1986, William Bate Hardy Prize (Cambridge Philosophical Soc) 1987, Abraham White Scientific Achievement Award (George Washington Univ Sch of Med) 1987, Gairdner Fndn Int Award 1988, Baly Medal (RCP) 1989, Albert Lasker Basic Med Res Award 1989; FRS 1984; *Recreations* golf, gardening; *Style—* Dr Michael Berridge, FRS; 13 Home Close, Histon, Cambridge CB4 4JL (☎ 0223 232416); Dept of Zoology, Downing St, Cambridge CB2 3EJ (☎ 0223 336600 ext 6603, fax 0223 461954)

BERRIDGE, (Donald) Roy; CBE (1980); s of (Alfred) Leonard Berridge (d 1966), of Peterborough, and Pattie Annie Elizabeth, *née* Holloway; *b* 24 March 1922; *Educ* King's Sch Peterborough; *m* 1945, Marie, da of Harold Kinder (d 1958), of Leicester; 1 da; *Career* chm South of Scotland Electricity Bd 1977-82, dir Howden Gp plc 1982-

88; FEng, FIMechE; *Style*— Roy Berridge, Esq, CBE; East Gate, Chapel Square, Deddington, Oxford OX5 4SG (☎ 0869 38400)

BERRIEDALE, Lord; Alexander James Richard Sinclair; s and h of 20 Earl of Caithness, *qv*; *b* 26 March 1981; *Style*— Lord Berriedale

BERRILL, Geoffrey William; s of William George Berrill (d 1969), of Cheam, Surrey, and Ada Alice, *née* Martin; *b* 4 June 1948; *Educ* Uppingham; *m* 10 June 1972, Karen Peta, da of Peter Frank (d 1974), of Tadworth, Surrey; 2 da (Victoria b 6 April 1977, Charlotte b 3 Oct 1979); *Career* dir: Alexander Howden Insur Brokers Ltd 1980-83, Alexander Howden Ltd 1983-85, Halford Shead & Co Ltd 1984-86, Hartley Cooper Assoc Ltd 1986-; Freeman City of London 1969, Liveryman Worshipful Co of Glass Sellers 1969 (apprentice 1962); *Recreations* walking, gardening; *Style*— Geoffrey Berrill, Esq; Rook Hall, Kelvedon, Essex CO5 9DB; Bishops Court, 27-33 Artillery Lane, London E1 7LP (☎ 01 247 5433, fax 01 377 2139, telex 8950791)

BERRILL, Sir Kenneth; GBE (1988), KCB (1971); s of Stanley Berrill, of London; *b* 28 Aug 1920; *Educ* LSE, Trinity Coll Cambridge; *m* 1, 1941 (m dis), Brenda West; 1 s; m 2, 1950 (m dis), June, da of Arthur Phillips, of London; 1 s (Simon, *qv*), 1 da; m 3, 1977, Jane Marris; *Career* served WWII REME; economist; former fell and bursar: St Catharine's Coll Cambridge, King's Coll Cambridge; prof MIT 1962; special advsr Treasy 1967-69, chief econ advsr 1973-74, head CPRS Cabinet Off 1974-80; chm Vickers da Costa 1981-85 (joined 1980); memb of The Stock Exchange London 1981-85; dep chm: Univs Superannuation Scheme 1980-85, General Funds Investmt Tst 1982-85, govt nominee on Review Bd for Govt Contracts 1981-85; nominated memb Cncl of Lloyds 1983-88; chm: Securities & Investmt Bd 1985-88; Robert Horne Gp 1987-; pro-chllr Open Univ (chm governing body) 1983-; *Style*— Sir Kenneth Berrill, GBE, KCB; 207 Queen's Quay, 58 Upper Thames Street, London EC4V 3EH

BERRILL, Simon Philip; s of Sir Kenneth Berrill, GBE, KCB, *qv*, and June Myrtle Berrill; *b* 17 Aug 1953; *Educ* Westminster, Magdalen Coll Oxford (BA, MBA); *m* 6 Feb 1988, Anneke, da of Alan John Waple, OBE (d 1986); 1 s (Daniel Philip b 1988); *Career* called to the Bar Middle Temple 1975; GEC Ltd 1978; dir: Michael Laurie and Ptnrs Inc 1981, Morgan Grenfell Laurie Ltd 1988; chief exec Benlox plc 1988, md J W O'Connor & Co Ltd 1990-; *Style*— Simon Berrill, Esq; 9 Duncan Terrace, London N1 8BZ; Princeton House, 271-273 High Holborn, London WC1V 7EE

BERRIMAN, Sir David; s of late Algernon Edward Berriman, OBE, and late Enid Kathleen, *née* Sutcliffe; *b* 20 May 1928; *Educ* Winchester, New Coll Oxford (MA), Harvard Business Sch (PMD course); *m* 1, 1955 (m dis 1969), Margaret Lloyd, *née* Owen; 2 s; m 2, 1971, Shirley Elizabeth, *née* Wright; *Career* Citibank 1952-56, Ford Motor Co UK 1956-60, AEI Hotpoint 1960-63, United Leasing Corp 1963-; dir: Morgan Grenfell Holdings (formerly Morgan Grenfell) 1963-73, Guinness Mahon 1973-87, Cable and Wireless plc 1975-88, Bahrein Telecom Co 1982-88, Britannia Building Society 1983-, British Screen Finance Ltd 1985-, Videotron Corp Ltd 1989-, Sky Television plc (formerly Satellite Television plc) 1981-89 (chm 1981-85), East European Development Ltd 1990-, Kent Community Housing Tst 1990-; chm: Bunzl Textile Holdings Ltd 1978-88, Alban Communications Ltd 1983-90, NE Thames RHA 1984-90; dep chm Nat Film and TV Sch 1989- (dir 1977-), memb Br Screen Advsy Cncl (formerly Interim Action Ctee on Future of Br Film Indust), former memb Govt Ctee on Harland and Wolff Diversification; chm govrs MacIntyre (for the Mentally Handicapped); govr United Med and Dental Schs of St Thomas' and Guy's Hosps 1982-84; FCIB, CBIM; kt 1990; *Books* XYZ Case; *Recreations* golf, tennis; *Clubs* RAC, Royal St George's Golf; *Style*— Sir David Berriman; Britannia Building Society, Newton House, Leek, Staffs ST13 5RG

BERRINGTON, Prof Hugh Bayard; s of William Majilton Berrington (d 1986), of Ewell, Surrey, and Grace Constance, *née* Smith (d 1931); *b* 12 Dec 1928; *Educ* Ewell Castle Sch Surrey, Nuffield Coll Oxford, Univ of London (BSc); *m* 9 Aug 1965, Catherine Margaret, da of Sqdn Ldr JC Llewellyn Smith, of W Bagborough, Somerset; 1 s (Andrew William b 25 Jan 1967), 3 da (Lucy Margaret b 20 Feb 1969, Sarah Constance b 2 April 1971, Mary Edith b 23 July 1974); *Career* Nat Serv RAF 1947-49; jr clerk Barclay's Bank Ltd 1944-47, Divnl Health Office and Co Educn Dept Surrey CC 1949-53, admin asst Divnl Health Office Wimbledon 1953-54, lectr Univ of Keele 1959-65 (asst lectr 1956-59), prof of politics Univ of Newcastle upon Tyne 1970- (reader 1965-70); memb SDP, vice pres Political Studies Assoc of UK; *Books* Backbench Opinion in the House of Commons 1955-59 (jtly, 1961), Backbench Opinion in the House of Commons 1945-55 (1973), Change in British Politics (ed, 1984); *Recreations* walking; *Style*— Prof Hugh Berrington; Department of Politics, University of Newcastle upon Tyne, Newcastle upon Tyne NE1 7RU (☎ 091 222 6000 ext 7530, fax 091 222 8107)

BERRINGTON, Richard Norman; *b* 25 July 1930; *Educ* Loughborough Endowed Sch; *m* Freda Mary; 1 s (Richard), 1 da (Rachel); *Career* md Manesty Machines Ltd (winner Queen's Award for Export Achievement), cncllr DTI Enterprise Initiative, vice chm Vertec Ltd, dir Medirise Ltd; FCA, FInstD; *Recreations* music, golf, gardening; *Style*— R N Berrington, Esq; Summerdown, Castle Hill, Prestbury, Cheshire SK10 4AS; Vertec Ltd, Leslie Hough Way, Salford Univ Business Park, Salford M6 6AJ

BERRISFORD, Simon Netcott; s of Julian Antony Berrisford of Little Manor, Wroxton, Oxon, and Penelope Nance-Kivell, *née* Netcott; *b* 29 Dec 1963; *Educ* Shiplake Coll; *Career* oarsman; memb Leander Club, competed at Henley 1981-, first cap 1985; Henley Royal Regatta: Ladies Plate 1985, Stewards Cup 1988, Silver Nickel Goblet 1989; competed World Rowing Championships 1985, 1987, 1989 (Silver medal coxless pairs), fourth Olympics Seoul 1988; one of only three male English rowers to compete in two disciplines at World Championships (coxed pairs and coxless pairs Yugoslavia 1989); former salesman: Collingridge flower stall New Covent Garden, Wellington Vintners Crowthorne; stock clerk Cecil Macdonald London; *Recreations* water-skiing, snow-skiing, vintage cars; *Style*— Simon Berrisford, Esq; 25 Westfield Road, Caversham, Reading, Berkshire RG4 8HL (☎ 0734 482427)

BERRY, Hon Adrian Michael; s of Baron Hartwell, MBE, TD (Life Peer); *b* 15 June 1937; *Educ* Eton and Ch Ch Oxford; *m* 1967, Marina Beatrice, da of Cyrus Sulzberger, of Paris; 1 s, 1 da; *Career* sci corr Daily Telegraph 1977-; *publications:* The Next Ten Thousand Years (1974), The Iron Sun (1977), From Apes to Astronauts (1980), High Skies and Yellow Rain (1983), The Super-Intelligent Machine (1983), Ice With Your Evolution (1986), Koyama's Diamond (fiction) (1984), Labyrinth of Lies (fiction) (1986), Harrap's Book of Scientific Anecdotes (1989); *Style*— The Hon Adrian Berry; 11 Cottesmore Gardens, London W8

BERRY, Andrew Piers; s of Donald Michael Berry, of Gibraltar, and Patricia Margaret, *née* Connelan; *b* 11 Aug 1957; *Educ* Rugby, Univ of Reading (LLB); *m* 12 April 1986, Anne Josephine, da of Robert Blagbrough; *Career* admitted slr 1984; ptnr Payne Hicks Beach 1987- (articled clerk 1982-84, asst slr 1984-87); *Style*— Andrew Berry, Esq; Payne Hicks Beach, 10 New Sq, London WC2A 3QG (☎ 071 242 6041 fax 071 405 0434)

BERRY, Anthony Arthur; s of Francis Berry (d 1936), of London, and Amy Marie Freeman (d 1966); family have been wine merchants in Exeter and 3 St James's St London since 1700s; *b* 16 March 1915; *Educ* Charterhouse, Trinity Hall Cambridge (BA); *m* 1953, Sonia Alice, da of Sir Harold Graham-Hodgson, KCVO (d 1960); 1 s (Simon), 1 da (Victoria); *Career* wine merchant, chm Berry Bros and Rudd Ltd 1965-85 (dir 1946-); chm Wine Trade Benevolent Soc 1968, cellarer Saintsbury Club 1978-; Master Worshipful Co of Vintners 1980-81; *Recreations* golf, walking; *Clubs* Boodle's, Royal St George's Golf, Royal Wimbledon Golf, Saintsbury, Bath and County; *Style*— Anthony Berry, Esq; 4 Cavendish Crescent, Bath BA1 2UG (☎ 0225 422669); Windy Peak, St Margaret's Bay, Kent CT15 6DT (☎ 0304 952413)

BERRY, Brig Anthony Edward; OBE (1982); s of Edward Joseph Berry, and Jean, *née* Larkin; *b* 4 Dec 1938; *Educ* RMA Sandhurst; *m* 3 Dec 1966, Sally, da of Lt-Col John Cairnes (ka 1943), of Dublin; 1 s (Nicholas Anthony b 1968), 1 da (Suzanna Claire b 1972); *Career* cmmnd KRRC 1958, Staff Coll 1970, CO 4 Bn Royal Green Jackets 1977-79, def advsr Br High Cmmn Islamabad 1989-; CStJ 1983; *Recreations* fishing; *Clubs* Army and Navy; *Style*— Brig Anthony Berry, OBE; c/o Ministry of Defence, Whitehall, London SW1

BERRY, Hon Mrs (Bride Faith Louisa); *née* Fremantle; 3 da of 3 Baron Cottesloe, CB, VD, TD (d 1956), and Florence, *née* Tapling (d 1956); *b* 1 July 1910; *Educ* PNEU Sch Burgess Hill, Girton Coll Cambridge; *m* 20 Aug 1936, John Berry, CBE, DL, FRSE *qv*; 2 s, 1 da; *Style*— The Hon Mrs Berry; The Garden House, Tayfield, Newport-on-Tay, Fife DD6 8HA (☎ 0382 543118)

BERRY, Dr (Anne) Caroline; da of Charles Rushton Elliott (d 1989), of Jersey, CI, and Evelyn Anne, *née* Le Cornu (d 1986); *b* 1 April 1937; *Educ* Bedgebury Park Sch, The Middlesex Hosp London (MB BS, PhD); *m* 13 June 1958, (Robert James) Sam; 1 s (Andrew b 1963), 2 da (Alison b 1963, Susan b 1965); *Career* conslt clinical geneticist Guys Hosp 1979-; MRCP 1987; *Books* Rites of Life: Christians & Biomedical Decision Making (1987); *Style*— Dr Caroline Berry; SE Thames Regional Genetics Centre Guys Hospital London SE1 9RT (☎ 071 955 4648)

BERRY, Claude de Pomeroy; s of Capt Paul Berry (d 1965), of St Helier, Jersey, CI, and Violet Ellen Patricia, *née* Lysaght; *b* 15 Aug 1938; *Educ* Wellington, RMA Sandhurst, RAC Cirencester; *m* 1, 30 March 1961 (m dis 1983), Caroline Stafford Robinson, da of Capt Christopher Scott-Nicholson (ka 1945), of Whitecroft, Annan, Dumfriesshire; 2 s (Dominic b 18 Dec 1963, John b 7 June 1966); m 2, 5 June 1986, Meg, da of Edward Gerald Hart Jackson (d 1963), of Filg Bucks; *Career* cmmnd 16/5 Lancers 1958-61; farmer Scotland 1962-78, ptnr John Sale and Ptnrs (chartered surveyors) 1975-78, dir Tryon Gallery Ltd 1980- (joined 1978); ARICS 1973; *Books* Collecting Sporting Art (contrib, 1988), The Racehorse in Twentieth Century Art (1989); *Recreations* racing, hunting, ornithology, reading; *Clubs* Boodle's, Twelve; *Style*— Claude Berry, Esq; 61 Iverna Court, Kensington, London W8 6TS (☎ 071 937 1742); Mill Farm, Cadeleigh, Tiverton, Devon EX16 8HJ (☎ 088 45 245); Tryon Gallery Ltd, 23/24 Cork St, London W1X 1HB (☎ 071 734 6961/2256)

BERRY, Prof Francis; s of James Berry (d 1952), of Malay States and Cheltenham, and Jane, *née* Ivens (d 1915); *b* 23 March 1915; *Educ* Hereford Cathedral Sch, Dean Close Sch, Univ of London (BA), Univ of Exeter (MA); *m* 1, 4 Sept 1947, Nancy Melloney (d 1967), da of Cecil Newton Graham (1929); 1 s (Scyld), 1 da (Melloney Poole); m 2, 1969 (m dis 1971), Patricia Tyler, da of John Gordon Thomson; m 3, 9 April 1979, Eileen Marjorie, da of Charles Eric Lear; *Career* 4 Bn Devonshire Regt 1939-46, Malta 1940-43; Univ of Sheffield 1947-70: asst lectr, lectr, sr lectr, reader, prof of English; prof of English Royal Holloway Coll Univ of London 1970-80 (emeritus prof 1980-); visiting appts: Carleton Coll Minnesota 1951-52, Jamaica 1957, India 1966-67; visiting fell Aust Nat Univ Canberra 1979; visiting prof: Malawi 1980-81, Japan 1983, NZ 1988; FRSL 1969; *Books* The Iron Christ (1938), Murdock and Other Poems (1947), The Galloping Centaur (1952), Herbert Read (1953), Poets' Grammar (1958), Poetry and the Physical Voice (1958), Morant Bay (1961), The Shakespeare Inset (1965), Ghosts of Greenland (1967), I Tell of Greenland (1977), From the Red Fort (1984); *Recreations* following first class cricket; *Clubs* Hampshire (Winchester); *Style*— Prof Francis Berry; 4 Eastgate St, Winchester, Hants SO23 8EB (☎ 0962 854439)

BERRY, Frank Alfred John; s of Frank Walter Berry (d 1966), and Elsie Mary, *née* Gibbs; *b* 3 Feb 1930; *Educ* Edmonton Latymer; *m* 17 Sept 1955, Cicely Edith, da of Arthur Ernest Stockhausen (d 1971); 1 s (John b 1961), 2 da (Janet b 1959, Elizabeth b 1965); *Career* dir: Sun Life Assur plc, Sun Life Unit Servs Ltd, Sun Life Direct Mktg Ltd, Sun Life Pensions Mngmnt Ltd, Sun Life Portfolio Counselling Servs Ltd, Sun Life Promotions Ltd, Sun Life Tst Mngmnt Ltd; *Recreations* bowls, philately; *Style*— Frank Berry, Esq; Broadwater, Woodlands Rd, Portishead, Bristol BS20 9HE; Sun Life Assurance Society plc, Sun Life Court, St James Barton, Bristol BS1 3TH

BERRY, Dr Hedley; s of Edward Basil Berry, and Mathilde Josephine Berry (d 1982); *b* 18 Feb 1943; *Educ* Reading Sch, Wadham Coll Oxford (MA, DM); *m* 27 June 1974, Sonia, da of Joseph Tchoudy; 1 s (Michael b 1976); *Career* conslt physician and rheumatologist Kings Coll Hosp 1976-; memb Br Soc of Rheumatology; memb RSM, FRCP; *Books* Rheumatology and Rehabilitation (1985); *Recreations* music, travelling, eating, theatre; *Style*— Dr Hedley Berry, Esq; 21 Dorset Drive, Edgware, Middx HA8 7NT; 96 Harley St, London (☎ 071 486 0967); Kings Coll Hosp, London SE5

BERRY, Ian Andrew; s of W S Berry, and Shirley, *née* Mackay; *b* 10 Jan 1953; *Educ* Univ of Toronto (BA); *m* 30 April 1983, Helen; *Career* trg Canadian Imperial Bank of Commerce 1976-80; Fixed Income Dept: Eliott and Page Fin Conslts 1980-82, Canada Permanent Tst 1982-84; dir Scotia McCleod (formerly McCleod Young & Weir) 1987- (trader 1984-87); *Style*— Ian Berry, Esq; Scotia McCleod, 3 Finsbury Sq, London, EC2 (☎ 071 256 5656)

BERRY, Ian Robert; s of Lt-Col Frank Berry, IA (d 1982), and Mary Margaret Ann, *née* Chater (d 1973); *b* 29 Nov 1933; *Educ* Charterhouse, Open Univ (BA), Univ of Southampton (MSc); *m* 19 Sept 1959, Elizabeth Douglas, da of James Smurthwaite (d 1975); 2 s (Robert James b 1962, Michael John b 1966), 2 da (Elizabeth Jane b 1960, Jennifer Ann b 1965); *Career* Nat Serv; 2 Lt RAPC 1954-56, Army Emergency Reserve, Lt and Paymaster RAPC 1956-60, Capt RE (144 Bomb Disposal Regt) 1961-71; co sec: Sealectro Ltd 1968-69, Savage and Parsons 1970-74; fin dir Savage Industries Ltd 1975-77; sr lectr Portsmouth Poly 1978-; pres Bushey and Oxhey Rotary Club 1977-78, vice pres Int Commn Paritaire (Euro Dip in Business and Mgmnt); FCA 1972 (ACA 1962), FCMA 1971 (ACMA 1966); *Recreations* sailing, photography; *Style*— Ian Berry, Esq; 51 Park Rd, Hayling Island, Hants PO11 0HT (☎ 0705 466693); Portsmouth Poly Business School, Locksway Rd, Milton, Portsmouth, Hants (☎ 0705 844182)

BERRY, Jack; s of Harry Berry (d 1989), and Nancy, *née* Potter (d 1953); *b* 7 Oct 1937; *Educ* Boston Spa Secdy Modern Sch; *m* 30 Oct 1962, Josephine Mary Thames; 2 s (Alan Warwick b 30 May 1963, Martin Stratford b 13 April 1965); *Career* horse-racing trainer; apprentice flat race jockey (no winners) then nat hunt jockey for 16 years (first winner 1954); record for a northern trainer with 127 flat winners in a season 1990; *Books* It's Tougher at the Bottom (1991); *Style*— Jack Berry, Esq; Moss Side Racing Stables, Crimbles Lane, Cockerham, Lancashire (☎ 0524 791179)

BERRY, Jamie Alistair Jagoe; s of Raymond Berry, of Dower House, Stonor, Oxon, and Phyllis, *née* Pegg; *b* 22 Dec 1955; *Educ* Harrow; *m* 15 Dec 1979, Veronica Charlotte Herbert, da of Col F H Scobie; *Career* GT Management plc 1973-81, md Berry Asset Management plc 1981-, dir Berry Starquest plc (investment trust); FIMBRA (memb Cncl 1984-87); *Recreations* sailing, shooting; *Clubs* City of London, Annabel's; *Style*— Jamie Berry, Esq; Gowan House, 71 Gowan Avenue, London SW6;

The Chambers, Chelsea Harbour, London SW10 (☎ 071 376 3476)

BERRY, John; CBE (1968), DL (Fife 1969); s of William Berry, OBE, DL (d 1954), of Tayfield Fife; *b* 5 Aug 1907; *Educ* Eton, Trinity Coll Cambridge (BA, MA), Univ of St Andrews (PhD); *m* 1936, Hon Bride Faith Louisa Fremantle, *qv*, da of 3 Baron Cottesloe, CB, VD, TD (d 1956); 2 s (William, Peter), 1 da (Margaret); *Career* res offr Biological Res Station Univ Coll Southampton 1932-36 (dir 1936-39); chief press censor Scotland 1940-44, biologist and info offr N of Scotland Hydro-Electric Bd 1944-49; dir Nature Conservation in Scotland 1949-67; fndr memb Int Union for Conservation of Natural Resources (first pre its Cmmn on Ecology); environmental conservation and fisheries advsr N Scotland Hydro Bd 1 dir Br Pavillion, EXPO 71, Budapest 1971; advsr S of Scotland Electricity Bd, ind advsr to other authorities 1973-89; memb Court Univ of Dundee and of various Ct Appt Bds and Ctees, notably the Tay Estuary Res Centre (Int); Br official rep Int Symposium on Hydropower and the Environment Guya 1976; invited prof 'Cursurile de Vara Internationale' held in Al I Cuza Un Moldavia 1980; conslt on environmental conservation and freshwater fisheries, specialist on environmental and wildlife conservation and in water projects and their environmental and sociological impacts; Hon LLD Dundee Univ 1970; FRSE 1936; *Studies* Future Power Generation having regard to environmental conservation (financed by New Zealand Conservation Cncl 1970 and 1975), Hydropower and the Environment, the Upper Mazaruni Devpt Project (UK Miny of Overseas Devpt, Nat Sci Res Cncl Guyana, 1976), Nature Reserves and Conservation in Iran (Iranian Miny for the Environment and the Br Cncl, 1975); *Recreations* natural history (especially wild geese and insects), music; *Clubs* New (Edinburgh); *Style—* John Berry, Esq, CBE, DL, FRSE; The Garden House, Tayfield, Newport-on-Tay, Fife DD6 8HA (☎ 0382 543118)

BERRY, Michael Robert William; s of William Berry (d 1976), and Lilian Gretton, *née* Buckley; *b* 8 May 1930; *Educ* Mill Hill Sch; *m* 19 June 1954 (m dis); 2 s (Simon Frederick Michael b 23 Sept 1959, Timothy Robert James b 26 May 1961); *Career* Capt RAPC attached to 1 Bn KOSB 1954-56; CA; accountant Rack Engrg Ltd 1957-58, fin dir Sulzer Bros UK Ltd 1959-72, currently chm and md English Lakes Hotels Ltd; vice chm and ministers nominee Northern Cncl for Sport and Recreation, dir Cumbria Trg and Enterprise Cncl; FCA; *Recreations* walking, dogs, gardening, Cumbrian bibliophile; *Clubs* Old Millhillians; *Style—* Michael Berry, Esq; Pool Garth, Cartmel Fell, Grange-Over-Sands, Cumbria LA11 6NS (☎ 05395 31571); English Lakes Hotels Ltd, Low Wood, Windermere, Cumbria LA23 1LP (☎ 05394 33773, fax 05394 34275, telex 65273)

BERRY, Hon Nicholas William; s of Baron Hartwell, MBE, TD (Life Peer); *b* 3 July 1942; *Educ* Eton, ChCh Oxford; *m* 1977, Evelyn, *née* Prouvost; 2 s (William b 1978, Alexander b 1981); *Style—* The Hon Nicholas Berry; 22 Rutland Gate, London SW7

BERRY, Norman Stevenson McLean; s of James Stevenson Berry, of Glasgow, and Mary Jane, *née* Oliver; *b* 23 Jan 1933; *Educ* Shawlands Acad Glasgow, Univ of Glasgow (BSc), Univ of Strathclyde (BSc); *m* 20 Oct 1965, Sheila Margaret, da of John Allan McMillan, DSO (d 1967), of Glasgow; 2 s (David John b 1969, Andrew James b 1970), 1 da (Ruth Margaret b 1966); *Career* student then asst engr Hugh Fraser & Partners 1952-57, Public Works Dept Eastern Nigeria 1957-61 (exec engr Roads Dept 1957, zone engr for Rural Water Supplies Programme 1958-61), water and sewerage engr Public Works Dept Solomon Is 1967-71; Babtie Shaw & Morton: asst engr water supply 1961-67, projects engr 1967, assoc 1975, ptnr 1977 (responsible for the Kielder Transfer Works incl 30km of hard rock tunnelling); awards: Telford Medal for paper on Kielder Transfer Works ICE 1983, Telford Premium for paper on Kielder Experimental Tunnel Final Results ICE 1984, Inst Medal for paper on Large Diameter Flexible Steel Pipes for the Transfer Works of the Kielder Water Scheme IWES 1986; renovation convener and treas Findlay Meml Church Glasgow; FICE, FIWEM; memb American Soc of Civil Engrs; *Clubs* Royal Scot Automobile; *Style—* Norman Berry, Esq; 2 Fintry Gardens, Bearsden, Glasgow G61 4RJ (☎ 041 942 0637); Babtie Shaw & Morton, 95 Bothwell St, Glasgow G2 7HX (☎ 041 204 2511, fax 041 226 3109, telex 77202)

BERRY, Very Rev Peter Austin; s of Austin James Berry, of Worcs, and Phyllis Evelyn Brettell; *b* 27 April 1935; *Educ* Solihull Sch, Keble Coll Oxford (BA, MA); *Career* Capt Intelligence Corps (TA); bishop's chaplain Coventry Cathedral 1963-70, midlands regnl offr Community Relations Cmmn 1970-73, vice-provost of Coventry 1977-86, canon emeritus Coventry Cathedral 1986- (canon residentiary 1973-86); fell Lanchester Coll Coventry 1985-, provost of Birmingham 1986-; *Recreations* theatre, architecture; *Clubs* St Paul's (Birmingham); *Style—* The Very Rev Peter A Berry; Provost's House, 16 Pebble Mill Road, Birmingham B5 7SA (☎ 021 472 0709); The Round House, Ilmington, Warwickshire (☎ 060 882 518); Birmingham Cathedral, Colmore Row, Birmingham B3 2QB (☎ 021 236 6323)

BERRY, Peter Fremantle; s of John Berry, CBE, DL, of Newport-on-Tay, Fife, and Hon Bride Faith Louisa, *née* Fremantle (*see* Burke's Landed Gentry for Berry, Debrett for Fremantle); *b* 17 May 1944; *Educ* Eton, Lincoln Coll Oxford (MA); *m* 1972, Paola, da of Giovanni Padovani (d 1951); 1 s (Richard b 1979), 2 da (Sara b 1974, Anna b 1977); *Career* mgmnt appts Harrisons & Crosfield plc SE Asia 1967-73, dir Anglo-Indonesian Corp plc 1974-82; dir assocs and subsids notably: Anglo-Asian Investmts Ltd, Ampat Rubber Estate Ltd Sumatra, Central Province Ceylon Tea Hldgs Ltd, Colman & Co (Agric) Ltd, Walker Sons & Co Ltd; Crown Agents For Oversea Govts and Admins: dir Asia and Pacific (res Singapore) 1982-84, dir ME Asia and Pacific 1984, md and Crown Agent 1988; dir: Thomas Tapling & Co Ltd, various subsids and assocs of Crown Agents; memb Bd Resource; *Recreations* travel, wildlife, country pursuits; *Clubs* RAC; *Style—* Peter Berry, Esq; 58 Pyrland Rd, N5 (☎ 071 226 3908); office: St Nicholas House, Sutton, Surrey (☎ 081 643 3311, telex 267103)

BERRY, Richard Gomer; s of Hon Denis Gomer Berry, TD, DL (d 1983), and his 2 w, Pamela, *née* Wellesley (d 1987); n and hp of 2 Viscount Kemsley; *b* 17 April 1951; *Educ* Eton; *m* 9 May 1981, Tana-Marie, er da of Clive William Lester, of Beaufre, Beaulieu, Hants; *Career* dir: Trans Europe Timber Ltd 1990-, C & L Lester (1990) Ltd 1990-; *Recreations* sailing, dendrology; *Clubs* IOD; *Style—* Richard Berry, Esq; Brockenhurst Park, Brockenhurst, Hants SO42 7QP (☎ 0590 22244); P O Box 9, Brockenhurst, Hants SO42 7XW (☎ 0590 612553, fax 0590 612549, telex 47208 BAOBAB G, car 0860 391924)

BERRY, Prof Robert James; s of Albert Edward James Berry (d 1952), of Preston, Lancs, and Nellie, *née* Hodgson (d 1956); *b* 26 Oct 1934; *Educ* Shrewsbury, Gonville and Caius Coll Cambridge (BA, MA), Univ Coll London (PhD, DSc); *m* 13 Jun 1958, Anne Caroline, da of Charles Rushton Elliott; 1 s (Andrew b 11 July 1963), 2 da (Alison (twin) b 11 July 1963, Susan b 26 June 1965); *Career* lectr Royal Free Hosp of Med 1962-78 (later reader, then prof), prof of genetics UCL 1978-; govr Monkton Coombe Sch 1979-; memb: Gen Synod of C of E 1970-90, Cncl NERC 1981-87; pres: Linnean Soc 1982-85, British Ecological Soc 1987-89, Euro Ecological Fedn 1990-; treas Mammal Soc 1981-87, vice pres Zoological Soc of London 1988-90, memb Human Fertilization and Embryology Authy 1990-, tstee Nat Museums and Galleries on Merseyside; FIBiol 1974, FRSE 1981; *Publications* Teach Yourself Genetics (1965, 3 edn 1977), Adam and the Ape (1975), Natural History of Shetland (jtly, 1980), Neo Darwinism (1982), Free to be Different (jtly, 1984), Natural History of Orkney (1985), God and Evolution (1988); ed: Biol of the House Mouse (1981), Evolution in the Galapagos (1984), Encyclopaedia of Animal Evolution (1986), Nature, Natural History and Ecology (1987); Evolution Ecology and Environment Stress (1989); *Recreations* walking, resting; *Style—* Prof Robert Berry, FRSE; Quarfseter, Sackville Close, Sevenoaks, Kent TN13 3QD; Department of Biology, Medawar Building, University College London, Gower St, London WC1E 6BT (☎ 071 380 7170, fax 071 380 7026)

BERRY, Dr Roger Julian; RD (1986); s of Sidney Norton Berry (d 1975), of NY, USA, and Beatrice, *née* Mendelson (d 1989); *b* 6 April 1935; *Educ* Stuyvesant HS NY, New York Univ (BA), Duke Univ Durham N Carolina (BSc, MD), Magdalen Coll Oxford (DPhil, MA); *m* 25 Sept 1960, (Joseline) Valerie Joan Berry, da of John Henley Butler, of Ramsey, Isle of Man; *Career* RNR 1971-; sea serv in HM submarines: Courageous, Swiftsure, Superb, Orpheus; HM Ships: Dido, Scylla; recalled to serv as PMO: HMS Dolphin, HMS Defiance, HMS Neptune, HMS President RNR 1980-83; PMO (Reserves) 1987-88, Surgn Capt Med Trg (Reserves) 1989-90; house offr New Haven Med Centre Yale Univ 1958-59, American Cancer Soc fell and MO Churchill Hosp Oxford 1959-60, sr investigator US Nat Cancer Inst 1960-62, postdoctoral fell Helen Hay Whitney Fndn 1962-65, MRC external staff and head Radiobiology Laboratory Churchill Hosp O 1965-74, clinical lectr in radiobiology Univ of Oxford 1969-76, hon conslt med radiobiologist United Oxford Hosps 1970-76, head of Neutron and Therapeutic Effects Gp, MRC Radiobiology Unit Harwell 1974-76, Sir Brian Windeyer prof of oncology Middx Hosp Med Sch 1976-87, dir health and safety and environmental protection BNF PLC 1987-, QHP 1987-89; Borden award for med res Duke Univ 1958, Roentgen prize Br Inst Radiology 1970, Knox Lectr RCR 1981, Florence Blair-Bell meml lectr Liverpool Med Inst 1982, Stanley Melville meml lectr Coll of Radiographers 1987, Finzi lectr Radiology Section RSM 1989; memb: Nat Radiological Protection Bd 1982-87, Radioactive Waste Management Advsy Ctee DOE 1984-87, Ctee on Med Aspects of Radiation in the Environment Dept of Health 1 Main Cmmn of Int Cmmn on Radiological Protection 1985-89; vice-chm Br Ctee on Radiation Units and Measurements 1984- (memb 197 pres Br Inst Radiology 1986-87 (hon sec 1970-73, vice-pres 1983-86); Freeman City of London 1982, Liveryman Worshipful Soc of Apothecaries 1984 (Yeoman 1981); FRCP 1978 (MRCP 1971), FRCR 1979, hon FACR 1983, MFOM 1988; OStJ 1990; *publications* Manual on Radiation Dosimetry (with NW Holm, 197 contrib chapters to: Oxford Textbook of Med, Florey's Textbook of Pathology; *Recreations* sailing, music; *Clubs* Naval and Military, Royal Naval Sailing Assoc; *Style—* Dr Roger Berry, RD; Well Cottage, Parkgate Rd, Mollington, Chester CH1 6JS (☎ 0244 851367); British Nuclear Fuels PLC, Risley, Warrington, Cheshire WA3 6AS (☎ 0925 835022, fax 0925 817625 tlx 627581)

BERRY, Hon Lady; Sarah Anne; *née* Clifford-Turner; da of Raymond Clifford-Turner, and Zöe *née* Vachell; *b* 9 March 1939; *m* 5 April 1966, as his 2 w, Hon Sir Anthony George Berry (k in the IRA bomb explosion at the Grand Hotel, Brighton, 1984); yst s of 1 Viscount Kemsley (d 1968); 1 s, 1 da; *Style—* The Hon Lady Berry; Fox's Walk, Shurlock Row, Reading, Berks RG10 OPB

BERRY, Lady Seraphina Mary; *née* Erskine; er da of 17 Earl of Buchan, JP; *b* 14 July 1961; *m* 31 March 1990, Steven K Berry, er s of Maj Roy Berry, of Witham, Essex; *Style—* The Lady Seraphina Berry

BERRY, (Roger) Simon; QC (1990); s of Kingsland Jutsum Berry, of Tenerife, and Kathleen Margaret, *née* Parker; *b* 9 Sept 1948; *Educ* St Brendan's Coll Bristol, Univ of Manchester (LLB); *m* 1974, Jennifer Jane, da of Jonas Birtwistle Hall; 3 s (Richard James b 27 Nov 1979, Nicholas Peter b 25 June 1981, William Patrick b 11 Aug 1986); *Career* admitted slr 1973, ptnr Stanley Wasbrough (now Veale Wasbrough) 1975-77; called to the Bar Middle Temple 1977; memb: Middle Temple, Lincoln's Inn, Western Circuit, Chancery Bar Assoc, Ctee Chancery Bar Assoc 1984 and 1985; *Recreations* family, cycling, skiing, keeping fit; *Clubs* Ski Club of GB, Riverside; *Style—* Simon Berry, Esq, QC; 9 Old Square, Ground Floor, Lincoln's Inn, London WC2A 3SR (☎ 071 405 4682, fax 071 831 7107)

BERRY, Stephen Ronald; s of Ronald Lenard Berry, of Canford Cliffs, Poole, Dorset, and Maureen Ann Berry; *b* 23 May 1954; *Educ* Univ of Pennsylvania (BSc), Harvard Business Sch (MBA); *m* 3 April 1976, Bonnie Tatem, da of Philip Williams; 1 da (Elaina Tatem b 26 Oct 1984); *Career* treasy mangr Bankers Tst Co 1979-88, md The Tickle Gp Ltd 1989; dir: Hacking Jack Ltd, Euromania Ltd; *Recreations* skiing, squash, art; *Style—* Stephen Berry, Esq; 88 Englewood Rd, London SW12 9NY (☎ 081 675 8450)

BERRY, William; WS; s of John Berry, CBE, DL, *qv*, of Tayfield; *b* 26 Sept 1939; *Educ* Eton, Univ of St Andrews, Univ of Edinburgh (MA, LLB); *m* 1973, Elizabeth, da of Sir Edward Warner, KCMG, OBE, of Blockley, Glos; 2 s (John b 1976, Robert b 1978); *Career* sr ptnr Murray Beith & Murray WS Edinburgh, dep chm Scottish Life Assurance Co; dir: Scot American Investment Co, Fleming Universal Investment Trust, Dawnfresh Seafoods Ltd, Incheape Family Investments Ltd, various other cos; memb Royal Co of Archers (Queens Bodyguard for Scotland); dep chm Edinburgh Int Festival 1985-89, chm Newtown Concerts Soc Edinburgh, tstee Royal Botanic Garden Edinburgh; *Recreations* music, shooting, forestry; *Clubs* New (Edinburgh); *Style—* William Berry, Esq, WS; 39 Castle St, Edinburgh 2; Tayfield, Newport-on-Tay, Fife

BERRY OTTAWAY, Peter; s of Cecil Berry Ottaway (d 1986), of Sutton St Nicholas, Hereford, and Myfanwy, *née* Thomas; *b* 17 Feb 1942; *Educ* Steyning GS, Univ of London (BSc), Univ Coll of Rhodesia and Nyasaland; *m* 21 Dec 1963, Andrea, da of Richard Sampson, ED, of Illinois, USA; 2 s (Gareth b 10 July 1965 (decd), Charles b 9 Oct 1986), 2 da (Samantha b 20 April 1969, Georgina b 17 Jan 1981); *Career* cmmnd Trg Branch RAFVR 1968- (currently Sqdn Ldr); res scientist Zambian Govt WHO 1963-65; res mgmnt: Unilever Ltd 1965-67, General Foods Ltd 1967-74; int consultancy in food technol, food sci and nutrition 1974-81, dir sci and technol (Europe) Shaklee Corporation California USA 1981, md Berry Ottaway & Assocs Ltd, dir Mercia Testing Laboratories Ltd, consulting scientist 1987-; memb Duke of Edinburgh's Award Ctee Herefordshire (sec 1977-82); CBiol, FRSH 1974, MIBiol 1978, FIFST 1981, MRIPHH; *Books* Food for Sport (1985), Nutrition In Sport (ed with Dr D H Shrimpton, 1986); *Recreations* light aviation, hill walking, art; *Clubs* RAF; *Style—* Peter Berry Ottaway, Esq; The Cedars, St Margaret's Rd, Hereford HR1 1TS (☎ 0432 276 368); Berry Ottaway & Assocs Ltd, Plough Lane, Hereford HR4 0EL (☎ 0432 270 886, fax 0432 270 808, telex 35302)

BERRYMAN, John Dennis; s of William Roberts Berryman, and Dorothy, *née* Morcom; *b* 3 Jan 1927; *Educ* Plymouth Coll, BNC Oxford; *m* 4 April 1955, Barbara, da of Joseph Brooks; 1 s (Peter John b 27 Sept 1959), 1 da (Lesley b 1 Jan 1956); *Career* Nat Serv writer and leading writer RN; called to the Bar Middle Temple 1951, barr W Circuit 1952-54, dep chief clerk Met Magistrates Cts 1954-58, clerk to Nuneaton and Atherstone Justices Warwick 1958-62, clerk to Havering Justices in Outer London and Brentwood Justices in Essex 1962-70, clerk to Croydon Justices 1970-88; *Books* Anthony and Berryman's Magistrates' Court Guide (jt author, 1966), Anthony and Berryman's Legal Guide to Domestic Proceedings (jt author, 1968), Anthony and Berryman's Guide to Licensing Law (jt author, 1967); *Recreations* reading, golf, bridge; *Clubs* Tavistock Golf, Yelverton Golf; *Style—* John Berryman, Esq; 30 Widewell Rd, Roborough, Plymouth PL6 7DW (☎ 0752 791757)

BERRYMAN, Lady; Muriel Alice Ann; *née* Whipp; CBE (1972); da of James Henry

Whipp, of Sydney, NSW; *m* 1925, Lt-Gen Sir Frank Horton Berryman, KCVO, CB, CBE, DSO (d 1981); 1 s, 1 da; *Style—* Lady Berryman, CBE; 17 Wentworth St, Point Piper, Sydney, NSW 2027, Australia

BERTELSEN, Aage; s of Jens Bertelsen (d 1947), of Denmark; *b* 2 Sept 1921; *Educ* engineering sch Denmark; *m* 1958, Dorthe, da of August Hald, of Denmark (d 1960); 1 s, 1 da; *Career* md Celcon Ltd 1956-, chm 1979-; *Recreations* bridge, gardening; *Clubs* Danish, Norwegian; *Style—* Aage Bertelsen Esq; Chalford, Traps Hill, Loughton, Essex (☎ 081 508 1778)

BERTHON, Vice Adm Sir Stephen Ferrier; KCB (1979); s of Rear Adm Charles Pierre Berthon, CBE (d 1965), of Deddington, Oxon, and Ruth, *née* Ferrier; *b* 24 Aug 1922; *Educ* RNC Dartmouth; *m* 1948, Elizabeth, da of Henry Leigh-Bennett; 2 s, 2 da; *Career* served WWII RN, Dep Chief Def Staff (Operational Requirements) 1978-80, ret 1981; *Recreations* riding, hunting, gardening, walking; *Clubs* Army and Navy; *Style—* Vice Adm Sir Stephen Berthon, KCB; Garden House, Stert, Devizes, Wilts (☎ 0380 3713)

BERTHOUD, Anne Dorothy; da of George Esmond Berthoud (d 1943), and Dorette Edmee, *née* Oswald; *b* 5 Sept 1942; *Educ* Lyce'e de Jeunes Filles de Rabat Morocco, Lausanne Univ Switzerland (MA); *Career* gallery owner; publishing editions Rencontre Lausanne 1966-68, Linguistic Dept Mexico Olympic Games 1968, sec to Del in Athens of Int Ctee of the Red Cross (Geneva) 1969-71, head Film Dept of French Inst (London) 1971-76, Douglas Rae Management (lit agency) 1976-78, Hester Van Royen Gallery (Covent Garden) 1978-81, Anne Berthoud Gallery 1981-; *Style—* Ms Anne Berthoud; 4A Stanley Crescent, London W11 2NB (☎ 071 437 1645)

BERTHOUD, Sir Martin Seymour; KCVO (1985), CMG (1985); s of Sir Eric Berthoud, KCMG (d 1989), and Ruth Tilston (d 1988); *b* 20 Aug 1931; *Educ* Rugby, Magdalen Coll Oxford (BA, Capt Oxford Rugby Fives and Half Blue); *m* 10 Dec 1960, Marguerite Joan Richarda, da of Col Desmond Phayre, of Collatons, Bow, Crediton, Devon; 3 s (Colin b 1962, Charlton b 1963, Christopher b 1967), 1 da (Isabella b 1968); *Career* HM Dip Serv: third sec Tehran 1956-58, first sec Manila 1961-64, first sec Pretoria/Cape Town 1968-71, first sec Tehran 1971-74, cnsllr Helsinki 1974-77, head N American Dept FCO 1977-79 (inspectorate 1979-82), cnsllr and consul gen Sydney 1982-85, high cmmr Port of Spain 1985-; memb: Nat Tst, WWF; Cdr Order of the Lion Finland (1976); *Recreations* tennis, squash, golf, bird-watching, photography; *Clubs* Utd Oxford & Cambridge Univs; *Style—* Sir Martin Berthoud, KCVO, CMG; Gillyflower Cottage, Stoke by Nayland, Colchester CO6 4RD (☎ 0206 263 237); British High Commission, Furness House, Independence Sq, Port of Spain, Trinidad & Tobago (☎ 010 1809 625 2861, fax 0101 809 623 0621)

BERTIE, HMEH Prince and Grand Master of the Sovereign Military Hospitaller Order of St John of Jerusalem, of Rhodes and of Malta; Frà Andrew Willoughby Ninian; er s of Lt Cdr the Hon James Willoughby Bertie, RN (d 1966; yst s of 7 Earl of Abingdon), and Lady Jean Crichton-Stuart, *qv*, yr da of 4 Marquess of Bute, KT; *b* 15 May 1929; *Educ* Ampleforth, Ch Ch Oxford (MA), Sch of African and Oriental Studies London Univ; *Career* Lt Scots Guards 1948-50; with City Press 1954-57, Ethicon 1957-59, Worth Sch 1960-83; elected Prince and Grand Master of the Sovereign Military Hospitaller Order of St John of Jerusalem, of Rhodes and of Malta 1988; Pro Hungria medal (SM Order of Malta) 1957, Grand Offr Order of Agatha (San Marino) 1984, Order of the Annunziata (House of Savoy) 1988; collar: of the Constantine Order of St George 1988, of the Order of Merit of the Central African Republic 1988, of the Order of Merit of the Republic (Italy) 1990, of Order of Merit (Chile), of the Southern Cross of Brazil 1990, of the Order of the Liberator San Martin (Argentina) 1990, of Order of Prince Henry the Navigator (Portugal) 1989; Grand Cross of the Legion of Honour (France) 1989; *Recreations* reading, gardening, judo, fencing; *Clubs* Turf, RAC, Caccia (Rome), Scacchi (Rome), Casino (Malta); *Style—* His Most Eminent Highness the Prince and Grand Master of the Sovereign Military Hospitaller Order of St John of Jerusalem, of Rhodes and of Malta; Via Condotti 68, 00187 Rome, Italy (☎ 010 396 679-8851; fax (010 396) 679- 7202; telex , 612622 SMOM)

BERTIE, Lady Jean; Crichton-Stuart; da of 4 Marquess of Bute, KT (d 1947); *b* 28 Oct 1908; *m* 1928, Hon James Willoughby Bertie (d 1966), yst s of 7 Earl of Abingdon; 2 s (Andrew Willoughby Ninian, *qv*, (Charles) Peregrine Albemarle, *qv*); *Career* Dame Grand Cross of Honour and Devotion SMOM; *Style—* Lady Jean Bertie; Casa De Piro, Attard, Malta, GC

BERTIE, Hon Mrs Arthur; Lillian Isabel; da of late Charles Cary-Elwes, KM (ie Knight of Malta), and Edythe Isabel, da of Sir John Roper-Parkington, JP, DL, consul gen for Montenegro, fndr memb of Entente Cordial; *b* 23 June 1902; *Educ* Sacred Heart Convent Roehampton; *m* 1, 1925, Lt Cdr Francis Crackanthorpe, RN (decd), 1 s (David), 1 da (Antonia); m 2, 1949, as his 2 wfe, Maj Hon Arthur Michael Cosmo Bertie, DSO, MC, 2 s of 7 Earl of Abingdon (d 1957); *Style—* The Hon Mrs Arthur Bertie; The Red House, Sudbury, Suffolk CO10 6TD

BERTIE, (Charles) Peregrine Albemarle; s of Lt Cdr the Hon James Willoughby Bertie, RN (d 1966, yst s of 7 Earl of Abingdon), and Lady Jean Crichton-Stuart, *qv*, yr da of 4 Marquess of Bute, Kt; bro of the Prince and Grand Master SMOM, *qv*; *b* 2 Jan 1932; *Educ* Ampleforth; *m* 20 April 1960, Susan Griselda Ann Lyon, da of Maj John Lycett Wills, of Allanbay Park, Binfield, Berks; 1 s (David Montagu Albemarle b 12 Feb 1963), 1 da (Caroline Georgina Rose b 16 March 1965); *Career* Capt Scots Gds 1950-54; memb Stock Exchange; High Sheriff of Berkshire 1986-87; kt of Honour and Devotion SMOM; memb Queen's Bodyguard for Scot (Royal Co of Archers), Liveryman Worshipful Co of Armourers and Brasiers; OStJ; Kt Cdr Order of St Gregory the Great 1983, Cdr of Merit with Swords Order Pro Meriot Melitensi; *Clubs* Turf, White's, Pratt's; *Style—* Peregrine Bertie, Esq; Henry Cook Lumsden plc, Crowne House, 56/58 Southwark Street, London SE1 1UL (☎ 071 962 1010)

BERTLIN, Dennis Percy; s of Percy Walter Bertlin (d 1952); *b* 18 May 1911; *Educ* Manchester GS, Univ of Liverpool (BEng, MEng); *m* 1954, Patricia, da of Dr Ashley Daly (d 1977); 2 s, 3 da; *Career* WWII Lt-Col RE BEF France, 1 Army N Africa, 21 Army Gp; consulting engr; sr ptnr Bertlin and Ptnrs 1960-81 (conslt 1981-), offr Order of Orange Nassau (Netherlands) 1946; FICE, FCIArb; *Recreations* chess, gardening, painting; *Clubs* Savile, Royal Thames Yacht, Royal Cruising, Royal Ocean Racing; *Style—* Dennis Bertlin Esq; Castlefield, Bletchingley, Surrey RH1 4LB (☎ 0883 74 3186)

BERTRAM, Anthony Allan (Tony); s of Gp Capt Ian Anstruther Bertram (d 1962), and Dorothy Cecil, *née* Eliott-Lockhart; gggs of John Bateman, fndr of Melbourne, Australia, and ggggs of Dr Arnaud de Lapeyre, physician to Napoleon; *b* 6 June 1926; *Educ* Stowe, Univ Coll Oxford (MA); *m* 8 Aug 1968, Carin, da of Christian Langöe-Conradsen (d 1984), of Stockholm, Sweden; 1 da (Grizel Louisa Christine b 1972); *Career* subaltern: QVO Corps of Guides India 1946-47, 15/19 KRH Palestine and Sudan 1947-48; gp offr ROC Edinburgh 1958-71; steamer agent Gladstone Lyall, Calcutta (India) and Khulna (E Pakistan now Bangladesh) 1951-52, commodity broker Hale and Son (London) 1954-55, translator Indonesian Legation Stockholm 1955-56; now farming; made first Br guideless traverse Aiguille de Grépon to Aiguille (Alps) 1950, first traverse Äpartjaåkko Gp (Lapland) 1959, first ascents of peaks and ridges and major traverse of Paårte gr Ryggaåsberget (Lapland) 1961, private expedition in Langtanlg Himal (Nepal) with minor first ascen Tibeta Frontier 1962; *Recreations* travel; *Clubs* Alpine, Himalayan; *Style—* Tony Bertram, Esq; Nisbet, Culter, Biggar, Lanarkshire (☎ 0899 20530)

BERTRAM, Dr Brian Colin Ricardo; s of Dr George Colin Lawder Bertram, of Graffham, Sussex, and Dr Cicely Kate Ricardo Bertram; *b* 14 April 1944; *Educ* Perse Sch Cambridge, St John's Coll Cambridge (BA, PhD, TH Huxley Award Certificate of Commendation); *m* 3 May 1975, Katharine Jean, da of Francis Blaise Gillie, CBE (d 1981); 1 s (Nicholas Blaise Ricardo b 1983), 2 da (Joanna Mary Ricardo b 1981, Felicity Kate Ricardo (twin) b 1983); *Career* res fell Serengeti Res Inst Tanzania 1969-73, sr res fell King's Coll Cambridge 1976-79, curator of mammals Zoological Soc of London 1980-87, dir gen The Wildfowl & Wetlands Tst 1987-; FIBiol 1979; *Books* Pride of Lions (1978); *Recreations* family, animals, garden, friends; *Clubs* Zoological; *Style—* Dr Brian Bertram; Fieldhead, Amberley, Stroud, Glos GL5 5AG (☎ 0453 872796); The Wildfowl & Wetlands Trust, Slimbridge, Glos GL2 7BT (☎ 0453 890333, fax 0453 890827)

BERTRAM, John Alexander; s of Maj David Craig Bertram, GM, TD (d 1990), of Kent, and Phyllis Mary Bertram (d 1986); *b* 2 March 1934; *Educ* Forest Sch, Dover Coll, Univ of London (LLB); *m* 4 April 1959 (m dis 1985), Elizabeth Sarah, da of Hugh Gwylym Hughes; 1 s (Mark b 1966), 1 da (Jane b 1963); *Career* RASC 1957-59, 2 Lt 1958; admitted slr 1957; ptnr Thomson Snell & Passmore Solicitors 1964-; pres Tunbridge Wells Tonbridge and Dist Law Soc 1984; memb Law Soc 1957; *Clubs* Army and Navy; *Style—* John Bertram, Esq; The Coach House, Cabbage Stalk Lane, Tunbridge Wells, Kent (☎ 0892 356 99); Thomson Snell & Passmore, Lyons East St, Tonbridge, Kent (☎ 0732 771 411, telex 957263 TSPTON G)

BERTRAM, Dr (Cicely) Kate; da of Harry Ralph Ricardo (d 1974), and Beatrice Bertha, *née* Hale (d 1975); *b* 8 July 1912; *Educ* Hayes Ct, Kent, and Newnham Coll Camb (MA, PhD); *m* 28 Sept 1939, George Colin Lawder Bertram, s of Francis George Lawder Bertram, CBE (d 1938); 4 s (Mark b 1942, Brian b 1944, Roger b 1946, William b 1950); *Career* zoological research in Africa 1935-36, memb Col Off Nutrition Survey in Nyasa Land 1939, adviser on Freshwater Fisheries to Palestine Govt 1940-43, joint research with husband on Sea-Cows (Sirenia) 1962-79; tutor Lucy Cavendish Collegiate Soc Camb 1965-70, (pres 1970-79); JP Cambs and Isle of Ely 1959-79; *Recreations* travel, sylviculture, bell ringing; *Clubs* English Speaking Union; *Style—* Dr Cicely Bertram

BERTRAM, Peter John Andrew; s of Capt George Robert Bertram (d 1936), and Ann Mary, *née* Regan (d 1984); *b* 26 April 1930; *Educ* Henry Mellish Sch Nottingham, Göttingen Univ Germany; *m* 14 Sept 1957, Winifred Rita, da of Wilfred Henry Parr (d 1974); 2 s (Christopher b 1958, Timothy b 1964), 1 da (Nicola b 1961); *Career* CA in own practice P J A Bertram; md Old Market Square Securities Ltd 1984-; dir: Ryland Group Ltd, Longcliffe Golf Co Ltd, Premier Portfolio Group plc, Denham Grange Ltd; tstee The Shand Tst; FCA, FCMA, FCT; *Recreations* golf, bridge, music, literature, travel; *Clubs* RAC, Royal Overseas League, Longcliffe Golf; *Style—* Peter Bertram, Esq; Cedar House, Nanpantan, Loughborough, Leics (☎ 0509 239 253); 89 Thomas More House, Barbican, London EC2 (☎ 071 588 8431)

BERTRAM, Robert David Darney; WS (1969); s of David Noble Stewart Bertram (d 1981), of Edinburgh, and Angela Jean Weston, *née* Devlin; *b* 6 Oct 1941; *Educ* Edinburgh Acad, Oriel Coll Oxford (MA), Edinburgh Univ (LLB); *m* 23 Sept 1967, Patricia John, da of John Laithwaite, formerly of Prescot, Lancashire; 2 s (Andrew b 1972, Nicholas b 1975); *Career* ptnr Dundas and Wilson CS Edinburgh 1969-, non-exec dir The Weir Gp plc 1983; memb: VAT tbnl, Tech Ctee Inst Taxation 1986, Scottish Law Cmmn 1978-86, examiner Law Soc Scotland, memb Scottish review panel on Reform of Law on Security over Moveables 1986; ATII; *Recreations* books; *Clubs* Scottish Arts, Edinburgh Univ Staff; *Style—* R D Bertram, Esq, WS; 4 Arboretum Rd, Edinburgh (☎ 031 225 1234, fax 031 556 5594, telex 72404)

BERTRAM, Dr Roger Charles Ricardo; s of George Colin Lawder Bertram, of Ricardo's Graffham, Petworth, Sussex, and Cicely Kate Ricardo Bertram, JP, *née* Ricardo; *b* 23 Feb 1946; *Educ* Friends Sch Saffron Walden, St John's Coll Cambridge (MA), Inst of Educn of Univ of London, Sch of Clinical Med Univ of Cambridge; *m* 29 June 1968, Julia Ruth, da of Prof Richard Stanley Peters, of Inst of Educn Univ of London; 2 s (Aldous b 18 Sept 1984, Tarquin b 11 Sept 1989), 3 da (Rebecca b 16 June 1971, Esther b 16 May 1974, Beatrice b 9 May 1983); *Career* head Biology Dept Netherhall Sch Cambridge 1974-76, ptnr in gen practice Linton; sec Cambridge Med Soc, memb local Med Ctee; *Recreations* riding, gardening, reading; *Style—* Dr Roger Bertram; Linton House, Linton, Cambridgeshire (☎ 0223 891 368); The Health Centre, Linton, Cambs (☎ 0223 891 456)

BERTRAM, (Charles) William; s of Lt-Col Richard Bertram, of High Barn, Shenington, nr Banbury, and Elizabeth Florence Oriana, *née* Bedwell; *Educ* Sherborne, Architectural Assoc (AADip); *m* 16 Nov 1963, Victoria Harriette, da of Reginald Addington Ingle, of The Little Manor, Loves Hill, Timsbury, nr Bath; 1 s (Robert William b 1970), 2 da (Clare Victoria Harriette b 1965, Josephine Alice b 1967); *Career* fndr architectural practice William Bertram and Fell Bath 1969 (cons architects to Abbotsbury 1972); converted: Royal Crescent Hotel into 5 star hotel, Cliveden into hotel 1986-89; conslt to Eastern Region Duchy of Cornwall 1989, currently involved in building a classical piece in Bath; received: UK Cncl Euro Architectural Heritage Year award 1975, Civic Tst award for conservation of Abbotsbury Village Dorset, Civic Tst award for Dower House Bath 1986, Bath Conservation Area Advsy Ctee Environmental award 1987, award for environmental design St Ann's Place and Environs; tstee Bath Preservation Tst 1966-68, listed in Architects Registration Cncl of UK; memb Br Soc of Architects, MRIBA; *Books* An Appreciation of Abbotsbury (1973); *Recreations* tennis, gardening, sketching, gardens; *Clubs* Bath and County; *Style—* William Bertram, Esq; Woodrising, Loves Hill, Timsbury, nr Bath, Avon (☎ 0761 70718); 5 Gay St, Bath BA1 2PH (☎ 0225 337273)

BESLEY, Crispian George; s of Christopher Besley, of Wimbledon, London, and Pamela Geraldine Margaret Edgeworth, *née* David; *b* 21 Nov 1958; *Educ* Wellington; *m* 10 Sept 1988, Elizabeth Charlotte (Libby), da of Thomas Bridger; *Career* formerly dir Prudential Bache Securities Japan 1987, dir Smith New Court Int 1987-; *Recreations* motor racing and collecting classic cars; *Clubs* City Univ, Landsdowne, Annabel's, The Tasting Club; *Style—* Crispian Besley, Esq; Smith New Court plc, Chetwynd House, 24 St Swithins Lane, London EC4N 8AE (☎ 071 626 1544, fax 071 623 3132, telex 945754)

BESLY, Lt-Col John Richard Seymour; s of Ernest Withers Francis Besly, CMG (d 1964), and Helen Judith Besly (d 1974); *b* 28 Sept 1931; *Educ* Winchester; *m* 21 Jan 1958, Dinah Priscilla (d 1987), da of Brig Adrian Clements Gore, DSO, of Ashford, Kent; 2 s (Adrian Thomas Francis b 1963, Michael John b 1966), 3 da (Emma Belinda b 1958, Lucinda Mary b 1960, Sarah Jane Beatrice b 1964); *Career* military service 1950-78, joined 3 Bn Gren Guards, Adjt (12 Bn) 1955-57, Staff Coll 1963, BLI ST CYR 1962-69, 2 i/c 1 Bn 1970-72, Offr leading 2 Bn 1972-74, AGMG London Dist 1974-77; Location of Offices Bureau 1978-80; development offr King's Coll London 1980-82, dir of fund raising Br Heart Fndn 1989- (regnl dir 1983-89); *Recreations* sailing, shooting, tennis swimming; *Clubs* Aldeburgh Yacht; *Style—* Lt-Col John R S Besly; Marsh Hill, Hazelwood, Aldeburgh, Suffolk IP15 5PI (☎ 0728 452210)

BESSBOROUGH, 10 Earl of (I 1739, UK 1937); Frederick Edward Neuflize Ponsonby; DL (W Sussex 1977); also Baron Bessborough (I 1721), Viscount Duncannon (I 1723), Baron Ponsonby of Sysonby (GB 1749); s of 9 Earl of Bessborough, GCMG, PC (d 1956) and Roberte, JP (GCStJ), da of Baron Neuflize, of Paris; *b* 29 March 1913; *Educ* Eton, Trin Coll Cambridge; *m* 1948, Mary, da of Charles A Munn, of New York and Paris; 1 da; *Heir* (to Irish Earldom and UK Barony only) cous, Arthur Ponsonby; *Career* sits as Cons House of Lords; pres Euro-Atlantic Gp; first sec (formerly second sec) Br Embassy Paris 1944-49, merchant banker Robert Benson, Lonsdale and Co Ltd 1950-56, dir ATV Ltd 1955-63 and other cos; Parly sec for science 1963-64, jt Parly under-sec of state for educn and science 1964, dep chm Metrication Bd 1969-70, min of state Miny of Technol 1970, chm Ctee of Enquiry into Research Assocs 1971-73; MEP 1972-79, vice-pres and dep ldr Cons Gp 1973-77; chm Stansted Park Fndn 1984-; UK memb of Bentinck Prize Jury; pres: Men of the Trees, Chichester Festival Theatre Tst, Br Theatre Assoc; author of plays and other publications; OStJ, FRGS, FRSA; Chevalier of Legion of Honour; Memb American Philosophical Soc; *Clubs* Turf, Garrick, Beefsteak, Roxburghe; *Style—* The Rt Hon Earl of Bessborough DL; Stansted Park, Rowland's Castle, Hants PO9 6DX (☎ 0705 412223); 4 Westminster Gdns, London SW1P 4JA (☎ 071 828 5959)

BESSER, Aubrey Derek; s of Hyman Besser (d 1982), and Leah Geller; *b* 27 Nov 1929; *Educ* Rutlish GS, Hove County GS; *m* 6 May 1962, Susan Elisabeth, da of Leslie Edward Hutchinson (d 1967), of Hove, Sussex; 3 da (Julia b 1964, Sarah b 1967, Abigail b 1970); *Career* md Steel and Oil Import/Export, Metal Enterprises and Co (London) Ltd 1952-87; *Recreations* tennis, bridge, swimming; *Clubs* Tramp, Les Ambassadeurs, Griffin; *Style—* Aubrey Besser, Esq; Metal Enterprises and Co (London) Ltd, 2 Grosvenor Gardens, London SW1W 0DH (☎ 071 730 6134, fax 071 730 0740, telex 916475)

BESSEY, Gordon Scott; CBE (1968); s of late Edward Emerson Bessey, of Gt Yarmouth, and Mabel Bessey; *b* 20 Oct 1910; *Educ* Heath Sch Halifax , St Edmund Hall Oxford (BA, Dip Ed, MA); *m* 1937, Cynthia, da of late William Bird, of Oxford; 1 s, 3 da; *Career* teacher Keighley and Cheltenham 1933-37, admin asst Surrey 1937-39, asst (later dep) educn offr Norfolk 1939-45, dep educn offr Somerset 1945-49; dir of educn: Cumberland 1949-74, Cumbria 1974-75; memb Youth Serv Devpt Cncl 1960-67, chm Working Pty on Pt/t Trg of Youth Leaders 1961-62, pres Assoc of Chief Educn Offrs Soc 1969-70, chm Educnl Advsy Cncl of IBA (formerly ITA) 1970-74, treas Soc of Educn Offrs 1971-74; chm: East Cumbria Community Health Cncl 1974-79, Assoc of Community Health Cncls in England and Wales 1977-79, Voluntary Action Cumbria 1978-84; Hon DCL Newcastle upon Tyne 1970; *Recreations* fishing, golf, fell walking, ornithology; *Clubs* Border & County (Carlisle); *Style—* Gordon Bessey, Esq, CBE; 8 St George's Crescent, Carlisle (☎ 0228 22253)

BEST, (William) Alan; s of William George Best (d 1966), and Mabel, *née* Watters (d 1962); *b* 1 Sept 1944; *Educ* Portadown Coll; *m* 7 Sept 1968, Valerie Anne, da of Samuel Derby; 2 da (Nicola Anne b 16 Sept 1972, Joanne Claire b 10 June 1974); *Career* clerk: Lurgan Rural Dist Cncl 1963-66, Lurgan Borough Cncl 1966-68; sr clerk NI Trg Exec 1968-70; personnel mangr: Ormeau Bakery Ltd 1970-74, Tenneko-Walker (UK) Ltd 1974-75; Eastern Health and Social Servs Bd: dist personnel offr 1975-78, asst chief offr (personnel) 1978-84, gp administrator 1984-90; dir of management and personnel HPSS Management Executive 1990-; MIPM 1972, ASA(NI) 1978; memb Lagan Valley Ex Tablers Club, treas Lagtan Valley AC, pres Perennials RFC; *Style—* Alan Best, Esq; HPSS, Management Executive, Dundonald House, Belfast (☎ 0232 650111)

BEST, Anthony Arthur; s of late Arthur Best, and Dorothy Rose Amelia Best; *b* 11 Oct 1935; *m* 31 March 1962, Mary Anne; 2 s (Mark b 1963, Nigel b 1965), 1 da (Natalie b 1968); *Career* exec dir: Rothschild Intercontinental Bank (London) 1968-74, Amex Bank London (dir subsdiary Bds) 1974-75; gen mangr Pierson, Heldring and Pierson Amsterdam (dir Pierson, Heldring and Pierson London) 1975-78, gen mangr Pierson, Heldring and Pierson; dir Polcreate 1980-; sr exec Amsterdam-Rotterdam Bank NV, Amsterdam 1980-82; md The Royal Trust Co of Canada London; dir: Royal Trust Bank (Jersey) Ltd, Royal Trust Bank (Isle of Man) 1982-86; vice chm Charterhouse (Suisse) SA, Geneva 1987-; md Charterhouse Bank Ltd 1986-; FCIB; *Recreations* gardening; *Clubs* Overseas Bankers, Walbrook Ward, European Atlantic; *Style—* Anthony A Best, Esq; Lodgefield, Newdigate Rd, Beare Green, Dorking, Surrey (☎ 0306 711341); Charterhouse Bank Ltd, 1 Paternoster Row, London EC4M 7DH (☎ 071 248 8000, fax 071 248 6522, telex 884276)

BEST, Hon Mrs Caroline; *née* Kinnaird; da of 13 Lord Kinnaird; *m* 1, 1970 (m dis 1986), Christopher Wigan, s of Algernon Wigan; 1 s, 1 da; *m* 2, 1986, James Douglas Best; 2 s; *Style—* The Hon Mrs Best; 80 Portland Rd, London W11

BEST, Gary Martin; s of Charles William Best, of South Shields, and Doreen, *née* Wright; *b* 6 Oct 1951; *Educ* South Shields Grammar Tech Sch, Exeter Coll Oxford (MA), Oxford Dept of Educn (PGCE); *m* 9 Aug 1975, Frances Elizabeth, da of Edward Albert Rolling, of Redruth; 1 da (Claire Frances b 1981); *Career* asst history teacher King Edward's Sch Bath 1974-80, head of Sixth Form Newcastle under Lyme Sch 1983-87 (head of history 1980-83), headmaster Kingswood Sch 1987-; Methodist local preacher; *Books* Seventeenth-Century Europe (1980), Wesley and Kingswood (1988); *Recreations* painting, music, reading, walking; *Style—* Gary Best, Esq; Summerfield, Coll Rd, Bath BA1 5SD (☎ 0225 317907); Kingswood Sch, Bath BA1 5RG (☎ 0225 311627)

BEST, Dr Geoffrey Francis Andrew; s of Frederick Ebenezer Best (d 1940), and Catherine Sarah Vanderbrook, *née* Bultz; *Educ* St Paul's Sch, Trinity Coll Cambridge (BA, PhD), Univ of Harvard (as Joseph Hodges Choate Fell); *m* 9 Jul 1955, (Gwenllyan) Marigold, da of Reginald Davies, CMG; 2 s (Simon Geoffrey b 1956, Edward Hugh b 1958), 1 da (Rosamund Margaret b 1961); *Career* 2 Lt RAEC 1946-47; asst lectr Univ of Cambridge 1956-61; Univ of Edinburgh: lectr 1961-66, Sir Richard Lodge prof of history 1966-73; Univ of Sussex: prof of history 1974-85, dean Sch of European Studies 1980-82; visitor and res fell LSE 1982-88; sr assoc memb St Antony's Coll Oxford 1988-; visiting fell: All Souls Coll Oxford 1969-70, Woodrow Wilson Center Washington DC 1978-79, Aust Nat Univ 1984; BRCS: chm Principles and Law Ctee 1980-84, hon conslt on Humanitarian Law 1985-91; *Books incl:* Temporal Pillars (1964), Mid-Victorian Britain (1971), Humanity in Warfare (1980), Honour Among Men & Nations (1982), War & Society in Revolutionary Europe (1982), The Permanent Revolution (1988); *Style—* Dr Geoffrey Best; 19 Buckingham St, Oxford OX1 4LH

BEST, Capt George Frederic Matthew; OBE (1985), RN; s of Adm The Hon Sir Matthew Robert Best, KCB, DSO, MVO (d 1940), of Crockway, Maiden Newton, nr Dorchester, Dorset, and Annis Elizabeth, *née* Wood (d 1971); *b* 14 Dec 1908; *Educ* Britannia RNC Dartmouth, RN Staff Coll; *m* 26 July 1940, Rosemary Elizabeth, da of John Chadwick Brooks, OBE (d 1964); 1 s (John b 1948), 1 da (Georgina (Mrs Connaughton) b 1944); *Career* WWII 1939-45 served: Atlantic, W Africa, E Indies, Rangoon (despatches); Mil Staff Ctee UN 1946-48, CO HMS Loch Quoich Persian Gulf 1948-50, exec offr RN Air Station Ford 1950-52, liaison offr Staff of Br Naval C-in-C Med (at HQ Allied Forces S Eur 1952-54, 4 Minesweeping Sqdn 1954-56, dep dir Naval Intelligence Admty 1956-58, Cdr Arabian Seas and Persian Gulf, Naval Cdr S Arabian Cmd 1958-60; cncllr Dorset 1962-85, Avon and Dorset River Authy 1963-73, dep chm Wessex Regnl Water Authy 1973-85, chm Dorset Rural Devpt Area Jt Ctee 1984-89; *Recreations* sailing, shooting, fishing, gardening; *Clubs* Army and Navy; *Style—* Capt George Best, OBE, RN; Wallhayes, Nettlecombe, Bridport, Dorset (☎ 030 885 358)

BEST, His Hon Judge Giles Bernard; s of Hon James William Best, OBE (d 1960), of Hincknowle, Melplash, Bridport, Dorset, and Florence Mary Bernarda, *née* Lees (d 1961); *b* 19 Oct 1925; *Educ* Wellington, Jesus Coll Oxford; *Career* Lt RM 1944-48; called to the Bar Inner Temple 1951, dep chm Dorset QS 1967-72, rec 1972-75, circuit judge 1975-; *Recreations* gardening, fishing; *Style—* His Hon Judge Best

BEST, Henry Nicholas; yst s of Hon James William Best, OBE, VD (d 1960, yst s of 5 Baron Wynford), and Florence Mary Bernarda (d 1961), da of Sir Elliott Lees, 1 Bt, DSO; *b* 3 May 1930; *Educ* Wellington; *m* 30 July 1963, Elisabeth Rose Ursula, da of Hans Joachim Druckenbrodt (d 1977), of Marburg, Germany; 2 s, 1 da; *Career* md until 1990: Anglo Blackwells Ltd (Queen's Award for Export Achievement 1979 and 1985), SKW Metals UK Ltd; gen mangr Molypress 1990; tstee Catalyst Museum of the Chemical Indust Widnes Cheshire; FIOD; *Recreations* hill walking, gardening, reading, local affrs; *Style—* Henry Nicholas Best, Esq; Bank House, Goldford Lane, Bickerton, Malpas, Cheshire SY14 8LL (☎ 0829 782287)

BEST, Hon John Philip Robert; only s and heir, of 8 Baron Wynford, MBE; *b* 23 Nov 1950; *Educ* Radley, Keele Univ (BA), RAC Cirencester; *m* 10 Oct 1981, Fenella Christian Mary, o da of Capt Arthur Danks, MBE, TD, and Hon Serena Mary, da of 4 Baron Gifford; 1 s (Harry Robert Francis b 1987), 1 da (Sophie Hannah Elizabeth b 1985); *Career* ARICS land agency div 1979; *Style—* The Hon John Best; The Manor, Wynford Eagle, Dorchester, Dorset DT2 0ER (☎ 0300 20763)

BEST, John Robert Hall; s of Robert Dudley Best; *b* 11 Feb 1929; *Educ* Leighton Park, Christ's Coll Cambridge; *m* 1961, Avril; 2 s; *Career* chm Best & Lloyd 1975- (md 1970-); tstee William Dudley's Tst; *Clubs* Savile, Thames Hare and Hounds; *Style—* John Best, Esq; 16 Oak Hill Drive, Edgbaston, Birmingham B15 (☎ 021 454 8702); Best & Lloyd Ltd, William St West, Smethwick, Warley, W Midlands B66 2NX (☎ 021 558 1191)

BEST, Keith Howard; OBE (1983); s of Herbert Henry Best (d 1958), of Sheffield, and Margeret, *née* Appleyard (d 1925); *b* 16 Jan 1923; *Educ* High Storrs GS, Univ of Sheffield (BEng); *m* 5 April 1947, Maire Raymonde, da of George Ernest Lissenden (d 1965); 2 s (Jonathan b 1949, Clive b 1952), 1 da (Sarah b 1947); *Career* served WWII 1942-46, parachute sqdns RE France and Germany, Lt 1944, Palestine 1945, Capt; Husband and Co: asst engr Sheffield 1947-54, princ engr Ceylon 1954-57, ptnr London 1957-70; Bullen and Ptnrs: ptnr Croydon 1970-81, ptnr Durham 1981-88, sr ptnr 1988-89, conslt 1989-; memb Cncl Inst Structural Engrs 1968-71, BR sec Societe des Ingenieurs et Scientifiques de France 1976, memb EDC (civil engrg) 1978-84; chm: Maritime Engrg Gp ICE 1981-84, Assoc Consulting Engrs 1987-88, N region Engrg Cncl 1988-90; Freeman City of London, Liveryman Worshipful Company of Engrs 1985; FICE 1958, FIStructE 1957, FEng 1983; *Recreations* sailing; *Clubs* Army and Navy, Royal Engr Yacht; *Style—* Keith Best, Esq, OBE; 7 Chessingham Gardens, York YO2 1XE (☎ 0904 701744); Neville Court, Nevilles Cross, Durham DH1 4ET (☎ 091 384 8594, fax 091 384 6082)

BEST, Keith Lander; TD; s of Peter Edwin Wilson Best (d 1984), of Beeches, Pitt Lane, Hurstpierpoint, West Sussex, and Margaret Louisa, *née* Ambrose; *b* 10 June 1949; *Educ* Brighton Coll, Keble Coll Oxford (BA, MA); *m* 28 July 1990, Elizabeth Margaret Gibson; *Career* Maj 289 Parachute Batty RHA (V) and Commando Forces, serv on HMS Bulwark 1976, naval gunfire liason offr; called to the Bar Inner Temple 1971, barr in Old Steine Brighton 1971-87; borough cncllr Brighton 1976, MP (Cons) Anglesey 1979-87, PPS to Sec of State for Wales 1981-84, direct mail conslt Nat Children's Home 1987, dir Prisoners Abroad 1989; memb UNA Disarmament Ctee, chm The Hollyhead Festival Ltd; Freeman City of London, Liveryman Worshipful Co of Loriners; FRSA; *Books* Write Your Own Will (1978), The Right Way to Prove a Will (1980); *Recreations* walking, skiing, photography, being useful; *Style—* Keith Best, Esq, TD; 15 St Stephen's Terrace, London SW8 1DJ (☎ 071 735 7699); 7 Alderley Terrace, Holyhead, Anglesey, Gwynedd LL65 1NL (☎ 0407 762972); Prisoners Abroad, 82 Rosebery Ave, London EC1R 4RR (☎ 071 833 3467, car 0830 615 665)

BEST, Dr Michael Howard; s of Benjamin Frederick Best (d 1989), of Sidcup, Kent, and Betty Noreen, *née* Crawley (d 1970); *b* 6 Aug 1948; *Educ* Chislehurst and Sidcup GS for Boys, Univ of Newcastle upon Tyne (MB BS); *m* 4 July 1981, Sylvia Renée Martina, da of Hermann Rolf Pabst; *Career* house physician Dryburn Hosp Durham and house surgeon in paediatrics Newcastle Gen Hosp 1973-74, registrar Dept of Psychological Med Royal Victoria Infirmary Newcastle upon Tyne 1974-77, sr registrar Bethlem Royal and Maudsley Hosps London 1977-82; conslt psychiatrist: Frenchay Hosp and Glenside Hosp Bristol 1982-86, Charter Nightingale Hosp London 1987-89; in private practice 1989-; MRCPsych 1977; *Recreations* swimming, fell walking, antiquarian medical books, history of spa medicine; *Style—* Dr Michael H Best; 18 Upper Wimpole St, London W1M 7TB (☎ 071 935 3940); Consulting Room, 18 Upper Wimpole St, London W1M 7TB

BEST, Norman Alexander; CBE (1980); s of Harold Ernest Best (d 1954), and Emily, *née* Webster; *b* 5 May 1924; *Educ* St Gregorys Luton, Eggars GS Alton; *m* 11 Sept 1948, (Valerie) Mary, JP, da of Frank Archibald Appleton (d 1968); 1 s (Nicholas b 1964), 3 da (Julia b 1949, Hilary b 1953, Vivienne b 1954); *Career* WWII Dorset Regt and Queen's Own Royal W Kent Regt, serv with 8 Army N Africa and Italy 1943-47; legal profession 35 years (ret); Southampton City Cncl: cncllr 1967-, leader 1972 and 1976-84, leader Cons Gp 1972-88, memb various ctees (incl Policy and Resources, Economic Devpt); Hampshire CC: cncllr 1973-, vice chm Cons Gp 1973, memb Policy Resources Ctee, chm Public Protection Ctee 1973-, memb Economic Strategy Panel, memb Coastal Conservation Panel; ACC: memb exec 1974-, memb Consumer Service Ctee 1974-90, memb Fire and Emergency Planning Ctee 1974-; Nat Jt Cncl for Local Authy Fire Bdes 1974-, Advsy Ctee on control of pollution of the sea 1974-90; LACOTS (fndr chm 1979); memb: Univ of Southampton Ct and Cncl, Mayflower Theatre Tst; dir: Southampton City Leisure Ltd, Southampton Economic Development Corporation Ltd; Sheriff and Dep Mayor of Southampton 1988-89 (Mayor 1989-90); pres Southampton Test Cons Assoc 1981-, memb Wessex Area Cons Local Govt Advsy Ctee; pres Age Concern Southampton 1987-, vice pres Hants CCC; Freeman City of London; FInstLEx; *Recreations* cricket, photography; *Style—* Norman Best, Esq, CBE; 1 Bassett Ct, Bassett Ave, Bassett, Southampton, Hants SO1 7DR (☎ 0703 769320)

BEST, Hon Patrick George Mathew; yst s of 7 Baron Wynford (d 1943), and Evelyn Mary Aylmer, *née* May (d 1929); *b* 5 Oct 1923; *Educ* Wellington Coll; *m* 29 March 1947, Heather Elizabeth, yr da of Hamilton Alexander Gardner (d 1952), of London and Assam; 4 s (Christopher b 1948, Michael b 1951 d 1952, David b 1953, Philip b 1960), 1 da (Clare b 1945); *Career* Lt RNVR, Channel, Atlantic, Med 1941-46; chm Wiggins Teape Gp 1979-84; dir: BAT Industs 1979-84, BAT US Inc 1980-84; non-exec dir Ranks Hovis Macdougal 1984; Master Worshipful Co of Ironmongers 1985-; FRSA, CBIM; offr Ordre de la Couronne (Belgium) 1982; FRSA; *Recreations* skiing, theatre, the arts, golf; *Clubs* Boodle's; *Style—* The Hon Patrick Best; Monk's Hse,

Durford Wood, Petersfield, Hants (☎ 0730 893176)

BEST, Sir Richard Radford; KCVO 1990, CBE (1989, MBE 1977); s of Charles Ronald Best (d 1960), and Frances Mary, *née* Raymond; *b* 28 July 1933; *Educ* Worthing HS, Univ Coll London (BA); *m* 1, 1957, Elizabeth Vera, *née* Wait (d 1968); m 2, 18 Jan 1969, Mary Kathleen Susan, da of Ernest Harry Wait (d 1977); 1 s (John Radford b 1973), 2 da (Anne Elizabeth Mary b 1961, Clare Caroline Frances b 1964); *Career* Home Office 1957-66; Dip Serv 1966-: second sec (info) Lusaka 1969, first sec (econ) Stockholm 1972, first sec (commercial) New Delhi 1979, actg dep high cmmr Calcutta 1982, asst head Personnel Ops Dept FCO 1983, dep high cmmr Kaduna 1984, ambass Iceland 1989-; BBC 'Brain of Britain' 1966; *Clubs* Royal Overseas League, Nigeria Britain Assoc (life memb); *Style—* Sir Richard R Best, KCVO, CBE; c/o FCO, King Charles St, London SW1 2AH

BEST, Richard Stuart; OBE (1988); s of Walter Stuart Best, JP, DL (d 1984), and Frances Mary, *née* Chignell (d 1967); *b* 22 June 1945; *Educ* Shrewsbury, Univ of Nottingham (BA); *m* 1, 1970 (m dis 1976), Ima Akpan; 1 s (Peter b 1971), 1 da (Lucy b 1974); m 2, 1978, Belinda Janie Tremayne, da of Geoffrey Eustace Stemp, DFC, of Neill's Cottage, Lamberhurst, Kent; 1 s (William b 1984), 1 da (Jessica b 1981); *Career* dir: Br Churches Housing Tst 1970-73, Nat Fedn of Housing Assocs 1973-88, Joseph Rowntree Fndn 1988-; sec Duke of Edinburgh's Inquiry into Br Housing 1984-86, cmmr Rural Devpt Cmmn 1989-, chm RDC Social Advsy Panel 1990-; memb: Social Policy Ctee of C of E Bd for Social Responsibility 1986-, BBC/IBA Central Appeals Advsy Ctee 1988-, Exec Ctee Assoc Charitable Fndns 1989-, Community Advsy Panel IBM UK Ltd 1990-; *Clubs* Travellers; *Style—* Richard Best, Esq, OBE; Joseph Rowntree Foundation, The Homestead, 40 Water End, York YO3 6LP (☎ 0904 629241, 0904 620072)

BEST-SHAW, Sir John Michael Robert; 10 Bt (E 1665), of Eltham, Kent; s of Cdr Sir John Best-Shaw, 9 Bt, RN (d 1984), and Elizabeth Mary Theodora, eld da of late Sir Robert Heywood Hughes, 12 Bt of East Bergholt; *b* 28 Sept 1924; *Educ* Lancing, Hertford Coll Oxford (MA), London Univ (CertEd); *m* 1960, Jane, da of Alexander Guthrie; 2 s (Thomas b 1965, Samuel b 1971), 1 da (Lucy b 1961), and 1 child decd; *Heir* s, Thomas Joshua, *qv*; *Career* late Capt Queen's Own Royal W Kent Regt, served WW II NW Europe; with Fedn Malaya Police 1950-58, church work 1959-71, teaching 1972-82, social work 1982-; *Recreations* gardening, writing; *Clubs* Royal Cwlth Soc; *Style—* Sir John Best-Shaw, Bt; The Stone House, Boxley, Maidstone, Kent ME14 3DJ (☎ 0622 757524)

BEST-SHAW, Thomas Joshua; s and h of Sir John Michael Robert Best-Shaw, 10 Bt, *qv*; *b* 7 March 1965; *Educ* Maidstone GS, Univ of Reading (BSc); *Career* Surveyor; Freeman of the City of London, Liveryman Worshipful Co of Vintners; *Recreations* piano, sketching, golf; *Style—* Thomas Best-Shaw, Esq; The Stone House, Boxley, Maidstone, Kent ME14 3DJ (☎ 0622 757524)

BESTERMAN, Prof Edwin Melville Mack; s of Theodore Besterman (d 1976), of Thorpe Mandeville, and Evelyn, *née* Mack (d 1964); *b* 4 May 1924; *Educ* Stowe, Trinity Coll Cambridge (BA, MA), Guys Hosp (MB), Univ of Cambridge (MD, Raymond Horton Smith prize); *m* 23 Sept 1944 (m dis 1955), Audrey, *née* Heald; m 2, 9 Jul 1955 (m dis 1978), Eleanor, *née* Till; 4 s (Harvey, Tristram, Adam, Gregory) from foregoing marriages; m 3, 7 July 1987, Perri Marjorie, da of Roy Burrowes, of Kingston, Jamaica; *Career* MO Outpatient Dept Guys Hosp 1947, house physician Br Post-graduate Med Sch Hammersmith 1948, registrar rheumatic unit Canadian Red Cross Memorial Hosp 1949-52, lectr Inst of Cardiology and Nat Heart Hosp 1953-55, sr registrar Middlesex Hosp 1956-62; conslt cardiologist: St Marys Hosp, Paddington Green Children's Hosp 1962-85; visiting cardiologist Malta Govt 1966-85, head conslt Royal Post-graduate Med Sch Hammersmith 1981-85; hon conslt cardiologist Univ of W Indies Jamaica 1986-; FRCP, FACC; *Books* Paul Woods Diseases of Heart and Circulation (contrib, 1968), author of numerous articles on cardiological topics in learned journals; *Recreations* photography, breeding German Shepherd dogs, gardening; *Clubs* Liguanea (Jamica); *Style—* Prof Edwin Besterman; Airy View, Stockfarm Road, Golden Spring, St Andrew, Jamaica, W I (☎ (Jamaica) 942 2308); PO Box 340, Stony Hill, Kingston 9, Jamaica; Dept of Medicine, Univ of West Indies, Mona, Kingston 7, Jamaica, W I (☎ (Jamaica) 9271707)

BESWICK, David John; s of David Beswick (d 1991), and Winifred Anne, *née* Davies (d 1985); *b* 30 Nov 1944; *Educ* Longton HS for Boys Stoke-on-Trent, Birmingham Coll of Food and Drink (Nat Dip Hotel Keeping); *m* 1 April 1967, Pauline Ann, da of late Arthur John Bayliss; 2 da (Allison Jane b 7 Aug 1968, Amanda Louise b 8 March 1971); *Career* mgmnt trainee Grosvenor House Park Lane 1963-65, asst mangr Grosvenor House Sheffield 1965-67, gen mangr Gulf Hotel BOAC Bahrain 1967-74, res mangr Sheraton Heathrow Hotel 1974-76, gen mangr Holiday Inns Inc Lagos Tel Aviv and Bermuda 1976-82, dir and gen mangr Broughton Park Hotel Preston 1982-89, gen mangr Dalmahoy Hotel Golf and Country Club 1989-; Master Innholder 1989-, Freeman City of London 1989; FHICMA 1975; *Recreations* golf, gardening, study of wine; *Clubs* Rotary; *Style—* David Beswick, Esq; Dalmahoy Hotel Golf and Country Club, Kirknewton, Midlothian EH27 8EB (☎ 031 333 1845, fax 031 335 3203)

BESWICK, Hon Frank Jesse; s of Baron Beswick, PC (Life Peer), (d 1987); *b* 12 May 1949; *Educ* Latymer Upper Sch; *Style—* The Hon Frank Beswick; 28 Skeena Hill, SW18

BETHEL, David Percival; CBE (1983); s of William George Bethell (d 1982), of Lydney, Glos, and Elsie Evelyn Gladys, *née* Cossins (d 1984); *b* 7 Dec 1923; *Educ* King Edward VI Sch Bath & Crypt GS, West of England Coll of Art, Univ of Bristol (NDD, ATD); *m* 1943, Margaret Elizabeth, da of Alexander John Dent-Wrigglesworth (d 1957); 1 s (Paul), 1 da (Ruth); *Career* designer and educator; lectr Stafford Sch of Art 1951-54, vice princ Coventry Coll of Art 1955-56 (princ 1965-69), dep dir Leics Poly 1969-73 (dir 1973-87); pres Nat Soc for Art Educn 1965-66; memb: Cncl Int Soc for Educn through Art 1970-77, Cncl for Educnl Technol 1974-80, Cncl CNAA 1975-81 (chm Ctee for Art and Design 1975-81), Hong Kong Univ and Poly Grants Ctee 1982-, Nat Advsy Body for Public Sector Higher Educn 1982-87; chm: Design Cncl Educn Ctee 1981-89, Chartered Soc of Designers' Educn Ctee 1987-, Planning Ctee for Academic Awards Hong Kong 1986-87, Hong Kong Provisional Cncl for Academic Award 1987-, chm Hong Kong Cncl for Academic Awards 1989-, East Midlands Regnl Advsy Cncl for Further Educn Academic Bd 1977-81, Ctee of Dirs of Polys 1975-81, Study of Primary Health Care Serv in E Midlands 1987-88, Cwlth of Australia Visiting Fellowship 1979-, Cyril Wood Tst, Jt NAB/UGC/SED Gp for Town & Country Planning 1985-; vice chm Inter-Univ Cncl for Higher Educn Overseas 1981-83; Hon LLD Leics 1979, Hon DLitt Loughborough 1987; ARWA, FSAE, FSTC, FRSA, FCSD; *Recreations* travel, genealogy; *Clubs* Athenaeum; *Style—* David Bethel, Esq, CBE; Stoke Lodge, 48 Holmfield Road, Stoneygate, Leics LE2 1SA (☎ 0533 704921)

BETHEL, Martin; QC (1983); s of Rev Ralph Arnold Bethel (d 1946), and Enid Ambery, *née* Smith; *b* 12 March 1943; *Educ* Kingswood Sch, Fitzwilliam Coll Cambridge (MA, LLM); *m* 14 Sept 1974, Kathryn Jane, da of Isaac Allan Denby, of Riddlesden, Keighley, Yorkshire; 2 s (Thomas b 1980, William b 1981), 1 da (Sarah b 1976); *Career* called to the Bar Inner Temple 1965; recorder Crown Ct 1979-; *Recreations* sailing, skiing; *Style—* Martin Bethel, Esq, QC; Pearl Chambers, 22 East Parade, Leeds LS1 5BU (☎ 0532 452702, fax 0532 420683)

BETHEL, Dr Robert George Hankin; s of Horace Hankin Bethel (d 1961), of London and Eastbourne, and (Eileen Maude) Mollie, *née* Motyer; *b* 7 June 1948; *Educ* Eastbourne GS, Pembroke Coll Cambridge (BA, MA, MB BChir), St Mary's Hosp Med Sch; *Career* med practitioner; house physician Queen Elizabeth II Hosp London 1972, house surgn Nottingham Gen Hosp 1973, SHO Northwick Park Hosp and Clinical Res Centre Harrow 1974, registrar W Middx Univ Hosp 1974-76, gen med practitioner Englefield Green and Old Windsor 1976-; course tutor The Open Univ 1979-80, hosp practitioner in geriatrics 1980-, trainer for GP (Oxford region) 1984-, advsy ed Horizons 1988-; author of various scientific papers in med jls with particular interest in rheumatological and gen practice topics; memb Cncl Section of Gen Practice RSM 1990-; chm The Cambridge Soc (Surrey branch) 1988- (sec 1982-85); wandsman St Paul's Cathedral 1988-, vice chm Old Windsor Day Centre 1989-, memb Soc of Genealogists; Freeman City of London 1977, memb Guild of Freemen City of London 1979, Liveryman Worshipful Co of Apothecaries 1981 (Freeman 1977), memb United Wards' Club of the City of London ; FRSM 1975, MRCGP 1979, FRSH 1989; *Recreations* genealogy, books, gardening; *Clubs* United Oxford & Cambridge Univ; *Style—* Dr Robert Bethel; Newton Court Medical Centre, Burfield Rd, Old Windsor, Berkshire SL4 2QF (☎ 0753 863 642)

BETHELL, Dr Hugh James Newton; s of Brig Richard Brian Wyndham Bethell, DSO (d 1990), of Pilton House Barn, Pilton, nr Shepton Mallet, Somerset, and Jackomina Alice, *née* Barton (d 1979); *b* 31 March 1942; *Educ* Tonbridge, St John's Coll Cambridge (BA), Guys Hosp (MB BChir, DObstRCOG); *m* 1, 1968, Astrid Jill, née Short (d 1979); 2 da (Katharine Emma b 25 Dec 1969, Christina Louise b 12 April 1973); m 2, 1984, Lesley, *née* Harris; *Career* cardiac registrar Charing Cross Hosp 1969-72, dermatology registrar Guys Hosp 1972-74; princ in gen practice 1974-; dir Alton Coronary Rehabilitation Unit 1976-, chm Advsy Ctee on Coronary Rehabilitation to the Coronary Prevention Gp 1987-, dir Cardiac Rehabilitation Unit London Bridge Hosp 1987-, MO Sunday Times Nat Fun Run 1985-, fndr chm Alton Joggers; author of various articles; MRCP 1970, MRCGP 1974; *Recreations* running, cinema; *Style—* Dr Hugh Bethell; Farringdon Hurst, Nr Alton, Hants GU34 3DH (☎ 0420 58 592) The Health Centre, Alton, Hants (☎ 0420 84676)

BETHELL, Hon James David William; s of 5 Baron Westbury, MC; *b* 22 Feb 1952; *Educ* Harrow; *m* 1, 1974, Emma Hermione, da of Malise Nicolson, of Frog Hall, Tilston, Malpas, Cheshire; 2 da; m 2, 21 Nov 1987, Mrs Sally Le Gallais; 1 da (b 31 May 1988); *Career* racehorse trainer; *Recreations* shooting; *Style—* The Hon James Bethell; Downs House, Chilton, Didcot, Oxon OX11 0RR (☎ 0235 834333)

BETHELL, Lady Jane; *née* Pleydell-Bouverie; eldest da of 7 Earl of Radnor, KG, KCVO (d 1968), and his 1 w, Helen Olivia, *née* Adeane; *b* 14 Sept 1923; *Educ* Godolphin Sch Salisbury; *m* 27 Sept 1945, Richard Anthony Bethell, *qv*; 2 s (Hugh, William), 2 da (Camilla, Sarah); *Style—* The Lady Jane Bethell; Rise Park, Hull, Humberside HU11 5BL (☎ 0964 562241)

BETHELL, Prof Leslie Michael; s of Stanley Bethell (d 1969), and Bessie, *née* Stoddart; *b* 12 Feb 1937; *Educ* Cockburn HS Leeds, UCL (BA, PhD); *m* 1961 (m dis 1983); 2 s (Ben b 1966, Daniel b 1967); *Career* lectr in history: Univ of Bristol 1961-66, UCL 1966-74 (reader 1974-86); prof of Latin American history Univ of London 1986-, dir Inst of Latin American Studies Univ of London 1987-; *Books* The Abolition of the Brazilian Slave Trade (1970); ed: The Cambridge History of Latin America: Colonial Latin America (vol I & II 1984), From Independence to c 1870 (vol III 1985), From c 1870 to 1930 (vol IV & V 1986), Mexico, Central America and the Caribbean since 1930 (vol VII 1990), Spanish South America since 1930 (vol VIII 1991); *Style—* Prof Leslie Bethell; 2 Keats Grove, Hampstead, London NW3 2RT (☎ 071 435 5861); Institute of Latin American Studies, 31 Tavistock Square, London WC1H 9HA (☎ 071 387 5671, fax 071 388 5024)

BETHELL, 4 Baron (UK 1922) Nicholas William Bethell; 4 Bt (UK 1911), MEP (EDG) London NW 1979-; s of Hon William Gladstone Bethell (d 1964), 3 s of 1 Baron Bethell; suc cous 1967; *b* 19 July 1938; *Educ* Harrow, Pembroke Coll Cambridge (PhD); *m* 1964 (m dis 1971), Cecilia Mary Lothian (d 1977), da of Prof Alexander Mackie Honeyman (d 1988), of Oldtown, Ardgay, Ross-shire; 2 s (Hon James Nicholas, Hon William Alexander b 18 March 1969); *Heir* s, Hon James Nicholas Bethell b 1 Oct 1967; *Career* takes Cons Whip in House of Lords; chm Freedom of the Skies Campaign (lobby gp against Europe airline fares cartel); sub-editor TLS 1962-64; script editor BBC Radio Drama 1964-67; a govt whip 1970-71, nominated MEP 1975-79; *Books* Gomulka, The War Hitler Won, The Last Secret, Russia Besieged, The Palestine Triangle, The Great Betrayal, (translator) Cancer Ward by Alexander Solzhenitsyn, Elegy to John Donne by Joseph Brodsky; *Recreations* poker, cricket; *Clubs* Pratt's, Garrick, Carlton, MCC; *Style—* The Rt Hon the Lord Bethell, MEP; 73 Sussex Sq, London W2 2SS (☎ 071 402 6877)

BETHELL, Richard Anthony; JP (Humberside 1950); eld s of Lt-Col (William) Adrian Vincent Bethell (d 1941), of Rise Park, Hull, and Watton Abbey, nr Driffield, and Cicely, da of Sir John Richard Geers Cotterell, 4 Bt, by his w, Lady Evelyn Gordon-Lennox, da of 7 Duke of Richmond, KG; *b* 22 March 1922; *Educ* Eton; *m* 27 Sept 1945, Lady Jane, *qv*, da of 7 Earl of Radnor, KG, KCVO (d 1968); 2 s, 2 da; *Career* landowner and farmer; 2 Lt Life Gds 1941, served UK and overseas 1941-45; DL Humberside 1975; Lord-Lieut 1983-, High Sheriff Humberside 1976-77; *Recreations* hunting, shooting, racing, farming; *Style—* Richard Bethell, Esq, JP; Rise Park, Hull, Humberside HU11 5BL (☎ 0964 56 224)

BETHELL, Maj the Hon Richard Nicholas; MBE (1979); s and h of 5 Baron Westbury, MC; *b* 29 May 1950; *Educ* Harrow, RMA Sandhurst; *m* 1975, Caroline, da of Richard Palmer, JP, of Swallowfield, Berks; 1 s, 2 da; *Career* Maj Scots Gds 1982; Officer Brother Order of St John; *Style—* Maj the Hon Richard Bethell, MBE

BETHELL-JONES, Richard James Stephen; s of Geoffrey Bethell-Jones (d 1977), and Nancy Hartland, *née* Martin; *b* 16 Sept 1945; *Educ* St Johns Leatherhead, Univ of Cambridge; *m* 15 Sept 1973, Sarah Landells, da of Lt-Col Felix Hodson; 2 da (Jessica b 1977, Harriet b 1979); *Career* admitted slr 1970, ptnr Wilde Sapte 1975-; memb Worshipful Co of Slrs 1984; *Recreations* tennis; *Style—* Richard Bethell-Jones, Esq; Queensbridge House, 60 Upper Thames St, London EC4V 3BD (☎ 071 236 3050, fax 071 236 9624, telex 887793)

BETHENOD, Gilles Marie Nicolas; s of Maurice Bethenod (d 1980), of Paris, and Solange Salteur De La Serraz; *b* 28 Sept 1948; *Educ* Ecole Des Roches, Paris Univ; *m* 26 Oct 1974, Sylvie Paule Jeanne, da of Yvon Colin (d 1988); 2 s (Alexis b 18 Oct 1975, Nicolas b 20 Jan 1977), 1 da (Marie Astrid b 10 Oct 1979); *Career* Offr French Navy (reserve); Banque Nationale de Paris 1975-86, dep md Yamaichi Int Europe Ltd 1986-; *Recreations* tennis, skiing; *Style—* Gilles Bethenod, Esq; 51 Rue des Missionaires, 7800 Versailles, France; Yamaichi International (Europe) Ltd, Finsbury Ct, 111/117 Finsbury Pavement, London EC2A 1EQ (☎ 071 638 5599, fax 071 588 4602, telex 887414)

BETHUNE, Sir Alexander Maitland Sharp; 10 Bt (NS 1683); s of Sir Alexander Sharp Bethune, 9 Bt, JP (d 1917), by Elisabeth (d 1935), da of Frederick Maitland-Heriot; *b* 28 March 1909; *Educ* Eton, Magdalene Coll Cambridge; *m* 11 Jan 1955, (Ruth) Mary, da of James Hurst Hayes, of Marden House, East Harting, Sussex; 1 da (Lucy b 1959); *Heir* none; *Career* formerly Capt Intelligence Corps; dir Contoura

Photocopying Ltd, Copytec Services Ltd; *Recreations* golf, Scottish history; *Style—* Sir Alexander Sharp Bethune, Bt; 21 Victoria Grove, London W8

BETHUNE, Hon Sir (Walter) Angus; s of Frank Pogson, and Laura Eileen Bethune; *b* 10 Sept 1908; *m* 1936, Alexandra, da of P A Pritchard; 1 s, 1 da; *Career* premier and treas of Tasmania 1969-72; pastoralist; kt 1979; *see Debrett's Handbook of Australia and New Zealand for further details*; *Style—* The Hon Sir Angus Bethune; 553 Churchill Avenue, Sandy Bay, Tasmania 7005

BETT, Michael; CBE (1990); s of Arthur Bett, OBE, and Nina, *née* Daniells; *b* 18 Jan 1935; *Educ* Aldenham, Pembroke Coll Cambridge (MA); *m* 3 Oct 1959, Christine Angela Bett, JP, da of Maj Horace Reid, JP; 1 s (Timothy Mark b 1961), 2 da (Sally Maria b 1963, Lucy Ann b 1965); *Career* dir Industl Rels Engrg Employers Fedn 1970-72; personnel dir: GEC 1972-77, BBC 1977-81; BT personnel dir 1981-85, md LCS div, md BT UK 1985-91, vice chm British Telecom plc 1990-; former memb: Pay Bd, May Ctee of Inquiry into UK Prison Serv, Ctee of Inquiry into Water Dispute 1983, Griffiths Inquiry into NHS Mgmnt, Armed Forces Pay Review Body, Manpower Servs Cmmn, Cncl Cranfield Inst of Technol; memb Cncl: Inst of Manpower Studies, Int Mgmnt Centre Buckingham; vice pres Royal TV Soc, dir Eng Shakespeare Co; chm: Nurses Pay Review Body, Mgmnt Ctee Bromley CABX; DBA (honoris causa IMCB), CBIM, FIPM, FRSA; *Style—* Michael Bett, Esq, CBE; Colets Well, The Green, Otford, Sevenoaks, Kent

BETT, Nigel; s of Philip Bett, of Rochester, Kent, and Molly, *née* Robertson; *b* 2 Sept 1949; *m* 17 Sept 1977, 2 s (Philip b 11 March 1981, George b 30 Dec 1985); *Career* club cricket: The Band of Brothers, The Mote CC, The Blue Mantles, The Oundle Rovers; mktg mangr Kent CCC 1978-87 (joined as head gateman 1977), sec Sussex CCC 1987-; *Recreations* all sports, collecting ties; *Clubs* MCC, Kent CCC; *Style—* Nigel Bett, Esq; Sussex County Cricket Club, County Ground, Eaton Rd, Hove, East Sussex BN3 3AN (☎ 0273 732161, fax 0273 771549)

BETTINSON, John Richard; s of Harold Richard Bettinson, MC (d 1986), of Edgbaston, and Barbara, *née* Keene (d 1984); *b* 27 June 1932; *Educ* Haileybury, Univ of Birmingham (LLB); *m* 1 Nov 1958, (Margaret) Angela, da of Richard Good (d 1955), of Edgbaston; 1 s (Richard b 1961), 1 da (Hayley b 1963); *Career* Lt 3 Carabiniers 1955-57; admitted slr 1955; ptnr Shakespeares Birmingham; chm: Victoria Carpet Hldgs plc, Assay Office Birmingham, Birmingham Repertory Theatre Ltd, Birmingham Research Park Ltd; dep chm Concentric plc, pres W Midland Rent Assessment Panel; dep treas Univ of Birmingham; chm: Age Concern England, Birmingham Area Health Authy 1973-82, Nat Assoc of Health Authys 1976-79; gen cmmr for Income Tax 1970-; Freeman Worshipful Co of Glaziers; memb Law Soc; *Recreations* theatre, bricklaying, reading; *Clubs* Cavalry and Guards'; *Style—* John Bettinson, Esq; Storey House, 4 Pritchatts Rd, Edgbaston, Birmingham B15 2QT (☎ 021 455 7588); 10 Bennetts Hill, Birmingham B2 5RS (☎ 021 632 4199, fax 021 643 2257)

BETTISON, Kenneth Henry David; s of Alfred Hanson Bettison (d 1941), of Manchester, and Emily, *née* Holland (d 1986); *b* 29 July 1925; *Educ* Manchester GS; *m* 7 June 1947, Ona Patricia, da of Alfred Ratcliffe (d 1965), of Preston; 1 s (Paul), 1 da (Fiona); *Career* Capt REME 1946-49; mktg dir Rockwell Graphic Systems 1977-85 (former Goss Printing Press Co Ltd Preston, joined 1949, London mangr 1955, sales mangr 1959, sales dir 1975, ret 1985), chm Graphic Systems Int Ltd 1987-; memb: Cncl of Printing Inst Res Assoc, Cncl of Br Printing Machinery Assoc (vice-chm) 1956-85; gp scout leader Scouts Assoc; CEng, MIMechE 1952, MIOP 1965, FInst SMM 1982; *Recreations* travel, dining out, swimming, egg craft; *Style—* Kenneth Bettison, Esq; Seven Elms, 81A Salisbury Rd, Worcester Park, Surrey KT4 7BZ; Graphic Systems International Ltd, Caxton House, 23 Vicarage Rd, Blackwater, Camberley, Surrey GU17 9AX (☎ 0276 37377, fax 081 330 7146, car 083638 2000, 083638 2003)

BETTISON, Paul David; s of Capt Kenneth Henry David Bettison, of Worcester Park, Surrey, and Ona Patricia, *née* Ratcliffe; *b* 18 April 1953; *Educ* Tiffin Boys Sch Kingston-Upon-Thames; *m* 15 May 1976, Jean Margaret, da of Flt Lt Kenneth Charles Bradshaw, of Ewell, Epsom, Surrey; 2 da (Clare Louise b 1983, Emily Margaret b 1985); *Career* memb mgmnt Rockwell Graphic Systems Ltd 1978-87, md Graphic Systems Int Ltd 1987-; dir: Factistel Ltd 1988-, Tolerans Ingol (UK) Ltd 1990-, Topeta Limited 1990-; FInstSMM 1979; *Recreations* travel, cars, wine; *Style—* Paul Bettison, Esq; Longdown House, Mickle Hill, Little Sandhurst, Camberley, Surrey GU17 8QL; Graphic Systems International Ltd, Caxton House, 23 Vicarage Rd, Blackwater, Camberley, Surrey GU17 9AX (☎ 0276 37337, fax 0276 37319, telex 858902 BARON G, car 0836 287050)

BETTON, David John William; s of John Clifford Betton, of Milverton, Taunton, Somerset, and Evelyn Naomi, *née* Byatt; *b* 30 Dec 1947; *Educ* Dulwich Coll, Emmanuel Coll Cambridge (BA, MA); *m* 6 Jan 1968 (m dis 1975), Christine Judith Patey, da of Very Rev Edward Patey, Dean of Liverpool, Merseyside; m 2, 5 Sept 1980, Nicola Mary Mallen, da of John McGregor Carter (d 1983); 1 s (Jack David McGregor), 3 da (Victoria Christine Naomi, Polly Nicola, Nancy Evelyn Mary); *Career* called to the Bar 1972; sr legal advsr HM Customs and Excise 1976-86, nat dir of VAT Clark Whitehill CAs 1986-; Freeman City of London, Liveryman Worshipful Co of Plumbers; *Recreations* cricket, theatre, walking; *Clubs* MCC, RAC; *Style—* David Betton, Esq; 32 Thaxted Rd, Saffron Walden, Essex CB11 3AA (☎ 0799 27958); 25 New Street Square, London EC4A 3LN (☎ 071 353 1577, fax 071 583 1720, telex 887422)

BETTON, Michael; s of Very Rev John Richard Betton, dean of Bocking (d 1985), and Marjorie Phyillis, *née* Paine; *b* 4 Feb 1962; *Educ* Ipswich Sch, St Edmund Hall Oxford (BA, MA); *m* 29 June 1985, Margaret Claire, da of Reginald Seal, of Langley Mill, Derbyshire; 1 da (Charlotte Hannah b 1988); *Career* mgmnt trainee Suffolk Group Radio 1984-85, station co ordinator Saxon Radio 1985-86; Ocean Sound: prog controller 1986-89, prog dir 1989; prog dir and dep md 1989-90, md 1990, operatio dir Southern Radio 1990; *Recreations* walking, Scottish islands; *Style—* Michael Betton, Esq; Ocean Sound, Whittle Avenue, Segensworth West, Fareham, Hampshire PO15 5PA (☎ 0489 589911, telex 47474 OCEANS G, fax 0 589453)

BETTS, Anthony George (Tony); s of George Betts (d 1974), and Bridget Jane, *née* Shivnen (d 1984); *b* 26 June 1939; *Educ* De La Salle Coll Sheffield, Univ of Birmingham (BSc); *m* 1, 1962 (m dis 1975), Margaret Agnes Johnston; 1 s (John Alexander b 1963), 1 da (Karen Ann b 1964); m 2, 1977, Jane Alison Monica Howard Smith; 1 s (Sean Anthony b 1980), 1 da (Christina Jane b 1982); *Career* articled clerk Foster & Stephens 1960-1963, qualified chartered accountant 1963, ptnr Touche Ross & Co 1967-; FCA 1974 (ACA 1964); *Recreations* golf, squash, skiing; *Clubs* Edgbaston Priory, Edgbaston Golf; *Style—* Tony Betts, Esq; Touche Ross & Co, Newater House, 11 Newhall St, Birmingham B3 3NY (☎ 021 200 2211, fax 021 236 1513)

BETTS, Rt Rev Bishop Stanley Woodley; CBE (1967); s of Hubert Woodley Betts (d 1950), of Cambridge, and Lilian Esther, *née* Cranfield (d 1962); *b* 23 March 1912; *Educ* The Perse Sch Cambridge, Jesus Coll Cambridge (MA); *Career* curate St Paul's Cheltenham 1935-38, chaplain RAF 1938-47, sr chaplain BAFO Germany 1946-47, Cmdt RAF Chaplain's Sch 1947, chaplain Clare Coll Cambridge 1947-49, vicar Holy Trinity Cambridge 1949-56, bishop of Maidstone to HM Forces 1956-66, dean of Rochester 1966-77, chm Bd of the Church Army 1970-80; vice-pres: Lee Abbey, Wadhurst Coll (chm of Cncl 1976-84); *Clubs* The National; *Style—* Rt Rev Stanley Betts, CBE; 2 Kings Houses, Old Pevensey, E Sussex BH24 5JR (☎ 0323 762421)

BETTS, Air Vice-Marshal (Charles) Stephen; CBE (1962); s of Herbert Charles Betts (d 1971), of Nuneaton, Warwicks, and Edith Whiting, *née* French (d 1979); *b* 8 April 1919; *Educ* King Edward VI Sch Nuneaton, Sidney Sussex Coll Cambridge (MA); *m* 1, 1943 (m dis 1964), Pauline Mary (d 1965) da of Lt-Col P Heath, IA; 2 da (Susan, Stephanie); m 2, 1964, Margaret Doreen, da of Col Walter Herbert Young, DSO (d 1941), of Farnham, Surrey; *Career* Engr Offr RAF 1941-74, Asst Cmdt RAF Coll Cranwell 1971, Air Offr cmdg No24 Gp Rudloe Manor 1972-74, head Inspection and Control Div The Armaments Control Agency Western Euro Union Paris 1974-84; ret; *Recreations* travel, music; *Clubs* RAF; *Style—* Air Vice-Marshal Stephen Betts, CBE; Cranford, Weston Rd, Bath BA1 2XX (☎ 0225 310995); Le Moulin de Bourgeade, Bourg du Bost, 24600 Riberac, France (☎ 53 90 96 93)

BETTS, William Reuben; s of William Louis Betts (d 1961), and Doris Pumfrey (d 1977); *b* 27 June 1924; *Educ* St John's Sch Leatherhead Surrey; *m* 24 May 1950, Barbara Nellie, da of James George Wilkin (d 1941); 1 da (Rosemary Frances); *Career* chartered surveyor; sr ptnr Burrows & Day, Chartered Surveyors 1977-85; Kent County Agric Soc: vice chm 1971-84, hon life govr 1984-; chartered memb Weald of Kent Round Table 1957- (fndr memb Lagos, Nigeria 1963), pres Central Assoc Agricultural Valuers (Kent) 1977-79, pres Ashford Cattle Show; FRICS RICS (chm Kent branch 1980); assoc Chartered Auctioneers and Estate Agents Inst 1948-; *Recreations* beekeeping, DIY; *Clubs* Elwick Ashford; *Style—* William R Betts, Esq; Ilex Cottage, Bramble Lane, Wye, Ashford, Kent TN25 5EH (☎ 0233 812693)

BETZ, Charles John Paul; s of Col Francis Betz (d 1949), of California, and Martha Abusdal Flannery (d 1988); *b* 8 Sept 1946; *Educ* American Grad Sch of Int Management (MIM), Univ of Stanford (Cert), California State Univ (BS), Univ of Uppsala Sweden (Cert); *m* 6 Dec 1969, Birgitta, da of Erik Gideon Thorell, of Solleron, Sweden; 2 s (Christian Michael b 1977, Clark Paul Erik b 1982), 2 da (Anika Ingrid b 1975, Martina Mary b 1980); *Career* dir customer serv Transworld Airlines NY 1970-72, regnl vice pres Bank of America London 1979-86 (various appts San Francisco 1973-76, vice pres NY 1976-79), md Carre Orban and Ptnrs 1986-; chm and organizer Champion Polo Benefit, bd memb Ham Polo Club, polo mangr Vale of Aylesbury; *Recreations* polo; *Clubs* Salskopet (Sweden), Ham Polo; *Style—* Charles Betz, Esq; Atkins Farm, Great Missenden, Buckinghamshire (☎ 02406 4054); 2809 Raccoon Trail, Pebble Beach, California, USA (☎ 408 372 2429); Carre, Orban and Partners, 7 Curzon St, London W1 (☎ 071 491 1266, fax 071 491 4609, car 0860 234 554)

BEUTHIN, Allan John Elrick; *née* Burnett; s of Prof R C Beuthin, of Johannesburg, S Africa, and Beryl Ada, *née* Bray; *b* 19 Jan 1944; *Educ* St Stithians Coll, Parktown Boys HS S Africa; *m* 15 April 1968, Sharon Alice, da of Lawrence John Landey; 1 s (Charles Lawrence b 1975), 1 da (Teresa b 1971); *Career* dir Menell Jack Hyman & Co 1962-68, memb Johannesburg Stock Exchange 1969-78, memb The Stock Exchange London 1980-, dir Merrill Lynch Ltd 1985-88; *Recreations* golf, cycling, theatre; *Clubs* Hadley Wood Golf; *Style—* Allan Beuthin, Esq; 26 Beech Hill Ave, Hadley Wood, Herts (☎ 081 440 1304)

BEVAN; *see*: Evans-Bevan

BEVAN, Brian Eyrl; s of Eric Clarence Bevan (d 1978), of Sydney, Aust, and Veida Alice, *née* Leggett (d 1979; *b* 24 June 1924; *Educ* Bondi Public Sch, Randwick Intermediate HS; *m* 20 April 1949, Grace Doreen, da of William Henry Allison, of Grappenhall, Cheshire; 2 da (Jennifer Lorraine, Jeanette Susanne); *Career* WWII, Aust Navy Pacific area 1941-45; signed professional forms for Warrington Rugby League Club 1946; scored world record number of tries (796, incl 100 hat tricks), won numerous int medals and caps, appeared in 2 Wembley finals; *Style—* Brian Bevan, Esq; 21 Dunes Ave, South Shore, Blackpool, Lancashire FY4 1PY (☎ 0253 401342)

BEVAN, Rear Adm Christopher Martin; CB (1978); s of Humphrey Charles Bevan (d 1982), and Mary, *née* Mackenzie; *b* 22 Jan 1923; *Educ* Stowe, Victoria Univ Wellington NZ; *m* 1948, Patricia Constance, da of Rev Arthur William Bedford (d 1950); 1 s, 3 da; *Career* joined RN 1942, ADC to HM The Queen 1976, Flag Offr Medway and Port Adm Chatham 1976-78; under-treas Gray's Inn 1980-89; *Recreations* theatre, music, photography; *Clubs* Boodle's, Hurlingham; *Style—* Rear Adm Christopher Bevan, CB; c/o C Hoare & Co, 37 Fleet St, London EC4P 4DQ

BEVAN, (Andrew) David Gilroy; MP (C) Birmingham, Yardley 1979-; s of Rev Thomas John Bevan (d 1944), and Norah, *née* Gilroy (d 1974); bro of Prof Peter Gilroy Bevan, CBE, *qv*; *b* 10 April 1928; *Educ* King Edward VI Sch Birmingham; *m* 1967, Cynthia Ann Villiers, da of T J Boulstridge; 1 s, 3 da; *Career* served on Birmingham CC and later W Midlands CC 1959-80; princ A Gilroy Bevan Incorporated Valuers and Surveyors; chm: Conservative Backbench Tourism Ctee, Parly Road Passenger Transport Co; vice chm Urban Affairs Ctee; FCIA 1954, MRSH 1957, FIAAS 1962 (past chm W Midlands branch), FSVA 1968 (past chm W Midlands branch), FRVA 1971, FFB 1972; *Recreations* gardening, walking; *Clubs* Carlton; *Style—* David Bevan, Esq, MP; House of Commons, London, SW1A 0AA (☎ 071 219 4539, 021 308 6319)

BEVAN, Hon Mrs (Hilary Evelyn Spicer); *née* Pakington; da of 5 Baron Hampton, OBE; *b* 24 May 1914; *m* 1938, David John Vaughan Bevan, TD, 2 s of late Penry Vaughan Bevan, Fell of Trin Coll, Camb, and bro of Dr Edward Vaughan Bevan, *qv*; 3 s, 2 da; *Style—* The Hon Mrs Bevan; Kingsland, Bledington, Oxford

BEVAN, Dr James Stuart; s of Peter James Stuart Bevan (d 1968), of London, and Phyllis Marjorie, *née* Enthoven (d 1978); *b* 28 Sept 1930; *Educ* Bryanston, Trinity Coll Cambridge (MA, MB BChir); *m* 21 April 1962, Rosemary, da of John Mendus (d 1988), of Pembroke; 1 s (Richard Stuart b 1964), 1 da (Katharine b 1966); *Career* Capt and jr specialist in medicine RAMC, active serv Malaya and Singapore 1958-59; princ GP 1960-, sr med conslt AA, med advsr London Coll of Music and other orgns; chm Fndn of Nursing Studies, sec of Ethics Ctee Humana-Wellington Hosp; memb BMA 1955; MRCGP 1962, DObstRCOG; *Books* Your Family Doctor, Anatomy and Physiology, Pocket Medical and First Aid Guide; *Style—* Dr James Bevan; 9 Hill Rd, London NW8 9QE (☎ 071 286 8340); 6A Palace Gate, London W8 5NF (☎ 071 589 2478)

BEVAN, John Penry Vaughan; s of Llewelyn Vaughan Bevan (d 1987), and Hilda Molly, *née* Yates; *b* 7 Sept 1947; *Educ* Radley, Magdalene Coll Cambridge (BA); *m* 1, 1971 (m dis 1976), Dinah, *née* Nicholson; 2 da (Amelia b 1972, Lucinda b 1975); m 2, 12 May 1978, Veronica, *née* Aliaga-Kelly; 1 s (Henry b 1981), 1 da (Charlotte b 1985); *Career* called to the Bar Middle Temple 1970, sr prosecuting counsel to the Crown at Central Criminal Ct, rec 1987-; *Recreations* sailing, tennis; *Clubs* Leander, Aldeburgh Yacht, Orford Sailing; *Style—* John Bevan, Esq; 2 Harcourt Buildings, Temple, London EC4 (☎ 071 353 2112)

BEVAN, John Stuart; s of Frank Oakland Bevan, of Stour Row, Dorset, and Ruth Mary, *née* Sadler; *b* 19 Nov 1935; *Educ* Eggar's GS, Jesus Coll Oxford (MA), St Bart's Hosp Med Coll (MSc); *m* 30 July 1960, Patricia Vera Beatrice, da of Alfred Charles William Joyce, of Shillingstone, Dorset; 2 s (David b 16 Nov 1961, Robin b 14 Aug 1966), 2 da (Elizabeth b 19 Dec 1962, Sally b 22 March 1965); *Career* Harefield Hosp (Pathology Lab) 1954-56, physicist UKAEA 1960-62, lectr and sr lectr S Bank

Poly (previously Borough Poly) 1962-73, dir of educn ILEA 1979-82 (asst then sr asst educn offr 1973-76, dep offr 1977-79), sec NAB 1982-88, dir Educn Servs LRB 1989-; dep co cmmr Kent and chm Nat Activities Bd Scout Assoc; memb Exec Ctees: ATTI 1968-73 (pres 1972-73), NUT 1970-73, AEO 1977-82 (chm 1981-82); hon fell: S Bank Poly 1988, Westminster Coll Oxford 1990; Hon DUniv Surrey 1990; FInstP 1972; *Books* The Space Environment (jtly, 1969); *Recreations* scouting, mountaineering; *Style—* John Bevan, Esq; 4 Woodland Way, Bidborough, Tunbridge Wells, Kent TN4 0UX (☎ 0892 27461); LRB, Globe House, Temple Place, London WC2 3HP (☎ 071 633 1698)

BEVAN, Jonathan Stuart Vaughan; s of Dr Edward Vaughan Bevan, TD, DL, (d 1988), and Joan Margot, *née* Goddard; *b* 15 June 1940; *Educ* St Faiths Cambridge, Bedford Sch; *m* 17 Sept 1960 (m dis 1986), Victoria Judith Helen, da of Hugh Leycester (d 1952), of Hilton, Hunts; 3 da (Charlotte Victoria b 1961, Francesca b 1963, Tiffany Alice b 1965); *Career* dep export dir and PA to chm Pye of Cambridge 1959-66, joined Grievson Grant and Co 1966-85 (assoc memb 1968, ptnr 1970); dir: Kleinwort Benson Securities 1985-88, Alexander Laing and Cruikshank Securities 1988-90; chm and memb of exec local Cons Orgn 1963-72, memb Cambridge Rowing Soc, dist cmmr Cambridgeshire Pony Club 1981-85, life pres St Moriz Sporting Club 1984-, chm and chief exec SMOMC 1984-; FRGS; memb: London Stock Exchange 1970, Stock Exchange 1987; *Books* Very Large Numbers (1984); *Recreations* tobogganinng, shooting, walking; *Clubs* St Moriz Tobagganning, SMOMC; *Style—* Jonathan Bevan, Esq; 17 Eaton Terrace, London SW1; (☎ 071 730 3344); La Forge Les Houches, Mont Blanc, France; 5 Chasa Cattaneo, Maistra 46 St Moritz, Switzerland

BEVAN, (Edward) Julian; s of Capt Geoffrey Bevan, and Barbara, *née* Locke; *b* 23 Oct 1940; *Educ* Eton; *m* 17 Sept 1966, Bronwen Mary, da of Brig James Windsor Lewis, DSO, MC; 2 s (David, Dickon), 2 da (Anna, Henrietta); *Career* called to the Bar Grays Inn 1962; standing counsel Inland Revenue 1973-77, first sr treasy counsel Central Criminal Court 1989 (jr treasy counsel 1977-84, sr treasy counsel 1984), master of the bench Grays Inn 1989; *Clubs* Whites, Garrick; *Style—* Julian Bevan, Esq; Queen Elizabeth Buildings, Temple, London EC4 (☎ 071 583 5766)

BEVAN, Prof Peter Gilroy; CBE (1983); s of Rev Thomas John Bevan (d 1944), and Norah Gilroy (d 1974); bro of (Andrew) David Gilroy Bevan, MP, *qv*; *b* 13 Dec 1922; *Educ* King Edwards HS Birmingham, Univ of Birmingham Med Sch (MB ChB, ChM), Univ of London; *m* 1949, Patricia Joan (d 1985), da of Maj-Gen Rufus Henry Laurie (d 1960); 1 s (Jonathan), 1 da (Deirdre); m 2, Beryl Margaret, da of Arthur Harold Jordau Perry (d 1944); *Career* RAMC (Capt) BAOR 1947-49; conslt surgn Dudley Rd Hosp Birmingham 1958-87, advsr in gen surgery to the CMO 1975-84, post grad dir Univ of Birmingham Med Sch 1978-87, author of various papers on surgery and surgical trg; memb Cncl RCS 1971-83 (vice pres 1980-81), fndr chm W Midlands Oncology Assoc 1974-79, vice pres Br Assoc of Surgical Oncologists 1975-78, pres Pancreatic Soc of GB 1977, UK rep to EEC on Med Trg Advsy Ctee 1980-85 (on Monospecialist Section of Surgery 1975-84), advsr in gen surgery to the RN 1983-88; pres: Br Inst of Surgical Technols 1983-, Assoc of Surgns of GB and I 1985; dir Overseas Dr's Trg Scheme (RCS) 1987-90, med memb Pensions Appeal Tbnls 1987-89, chm DHSS Steering Gp on Operating Theatres 1989, memb Med Appeals Tbnls 1989-, pres W Midlands Surgical Soc 1986, chm Joint Planning Advsy Ctee 1990-; FRCS 1952, MRCP, LRCP; *Books* Reconstructive Procedures in Surgery (1981); *Recreations* music, painting, inland waterways, golf, photography; *Clubs* Edgbaston Golf; *Style—* Prof Peter Gilroy Bevan, CBE; 10 Russell Rd, Moseley, Birmingham B13 8RD (☎ 021 449 3055)

BEVAN, (John) Peter; s of George Bevan (d 1986), of Liverpool, and Eileen Bevan (d 1975); *b* 29 Oct 1942; *Educ* Liverpool Inst HS; *m* 1966, Susan Jane, da of Sir Harold McDonald Steward; 1 s (Nicholas John b 9 March 1971), 1 da (Amanda Jayne b 8 June 1968); *Career* chartered accountant; articled clerk 1959-64, ptnr 1971, managing ptnr Grant Thornton Liverpool office 1990-; ACA 1964; *Recreations* golf, football; *Clubs* Woolton Golf (former capt), Liverpool Lyceum (pres 1989-90); *Style—* Peter Bevan, Esq; Grant Thornton, 1-3 Stanley St, Liverpool L1 6AD (☎ 051 227 4211, fax 051 227 3429)

BEVAN, Rev Canon Richard Justin William; s of Rev Richard Bevan (vicar of St Harmon Radnorshire, d 1928), and Margaret Mabel, *née* Pugh; *b* 21 April 1922; *Educ* St Edmund's Sch Canterbury, St Augustine's Coll Canterbury, St Chad's Coll, Univ of Durham (BA, LTh), Lichfield Theol Coll; *m* 4 Sept 1949, Sheila Rosemary, da of Thomas Barrow (d 1963), of Fazakerley, Liverpool; 4 s (Roderick, Nicholas, Timothy, Christopher b 1967, d 1968), 1 da (Rosemary); *Career* ordained Lichfield Cathedral: deacon 1945, priest 1946; asst curate Stoke-on-Trent 1945-49, chaplain Aberlour Orphanage Scotland 1949-51, asst master Towneley Tech HS Burnley 1951-60, licence to officiate Diocese of Blackburn 1951; hon asst curate: Church Kirk 1951-56, Whalley 1956-60; rector St Mary-le-Bow Durham 1964-74, vicar United Benefice St Oswald with St Mary-le-Bow Durham 1964-74; chaplain: Univ of Durham 1961-74 (convenor of chaplains 1966-74), Durham Girls' HS 1966-74, St Cuthbert's Soc Univ of Durham 1966-74, St Aidan's Soc Univ of Durham 1960-64, Trevelyan Coll Univ of Durham 1966-72; examining chaplain to Bishop of Carlisle 1970-, govr St Chad's Coll Durham 1969-89, rector Grasmere 1974-82, canon residentiary Carlisle Cathedral 1982-89 (treas and librarian 1 vice dean 1986-89), chaplain to HM The Queen 1986-; first pres and fndr memb Grasmere Village Soc; theol conslt Churchman Publishing Ltd 1986-; Hon ThD Geneva Theol Coll 1972, Hon PhD Columbia Pacific Univ 1980, Hon ThD Univ of Greenwich USA 1990; *Books* Steps to Christian Understanding (ed 1959), The Churches and Christian Unity (ed 1964), Durham Sermons (ed 1964), Unfurl the Flame (poetry, 1980), A Twig of Evidence: Does Belief in God Make Sense? (1986); *Recreations* poetry, reading, musical appreciation, train travel; *Clubs* Victory Services; *Style—* The Rev Canon Richard Bevan; Beck Cottage, Burgh by Sands, Carlisle, Cumbria CA5 6BT; The Cathedral, Carlisle, Cumbria

BEVAN, Brig Timothy David Vaughan (Tim); s of Maj D J V Bevan, TD (1986), and Hon Hilary Evelyn, *née* Pakington; *b* 20 Aug 1939; *Educ* Abberley Hall, Shrewsbury Sch; *m* 1, 1964 (m dis 1988), Jill Sarah Murrell; 1 s (Simon David Vaughan b 16 Sept 1970), 1 da (Charlotte Hilary Vaughan b 19 April 1968); m 2, Penelope Edyth McCloy, da of Douglas Lavers, of Auckland NZ; *Career* CO 2 LI Brig 1979-81, cmd I5 Inf Bde 1987-90; *Recreations* theatre, history, painting; *Clubs* Army and Navy; *Style—* Brig Tim Bevan; Lloyds Bank Ltd, 16 Cheriton High St, Folkestone, Kent CT19 4EU

BEVAN, Sir Timothy Hugh; s of late Hugh Bevan, and Pleasance, *née* Scrutton; *b* 24 May 1927; *Educ* Eton; *m* 1952, Pamela, da of late Norman Smith; 2 s, 2 da; *Career* called to the Bar Middle Temple 1950, joined Barclays Bank 1950, chm 1981-87 (dep chm 1973-81), chm BET plc 1988-; kt 1984; *Style—* Sir Timothy Bevan; c/o BET plc, Stratton House, Piccadilly, London W1X 6AS (☎ 071 629 8886)

BEVAN, Rear Adm Timothy Michael; CB (1986); s of Thomas Richard Bevan (d 1967), and Margaret Richmond Bevan, *née* Turnure (d 1974); *b* 7 April 1931; *Educ* Eton; *m* 1970, Sarah, da of Maj Claude Thorburn Knight, of Sussex; 3 s (Thomas b 1973, Michael b 1975, Richard b 1977); *Career* RN 1949; cmd: HMS Decoy 1966, HMS Caprice 1967-68, HMS Minerva 1971-72, HMS Ariadne 1976-78; HMS Ariadne and Capt of 8 Frigate Sqdn 1980-82, Britannia RNC 1982-84, Asst CDS (Intelligence) 1984-87, ret 1987; *Style—* Rear Adm Timothy Bevan, CB

BEVAN-THOMAS, Philip Morgan; s of William Ewart Thomas (d 1970), of 67 Grand Ave, Worthing, and Doris Winifred, *née* Morgan (d 1966); *b* 2 Dec 1934; *Educ* Cheltenham, St Edmund Hall Oxford (MA); *m* 18 June 1962, Janet Mary, da of Eric Walter Ward (d 1979), of 13 Manor Close, Havant; 2 s (Giles b 1965, Oliver b 1967); *Career* Nat Serv 2 Lt RA 1953-55, Capt TA RHA (Para) 1958-63; slr; ptnr: Francis and Parkes 1964-86, Field Seymour Parkes 1987-; pres Berks, Bucks and Oxford Law Soc 1982-83, dir Slrs Benevolent Assoc, chm Shiplake Parish Council 1985; memb Law Soc 1963-; *Recreations* sailing, golf; *Clubs* Huntercombe Golf, Leander, Sea View Yacht; *Style—* Philip Bevan-Thomas, Esq; The Moorings, Wharfe Lane, Henley-on-Thames, Oxford RG9 2LL (☎ 0491 572143); The Old Coroners Ct, 1 London St, Reading RG1 4QW (☎ 0734 391011, fax 0734 502704)

BEVERIDGE, Brian Francis; s of Maj-Gen Arthur J Beveridge, CB, OBE, MC (d 1959), of Dublin, and Sheila, *née* Macnamara (d 1952); *b* 7 May 1933; *Educ* St Conleth's Coll Dublin, Ampleforth, Univ Coll Dublin (MB BCh); *m* 20 July 1968, Victoria, da of Ronald Barton-Wright, of Northampton; 3 s (Richard b 1969, Dominic b 1972, Edward b 1975); *Career* cmmnd Capt 155 (L) Field Ambulance RAMC (TA) 1963, transferred to RARO III 1969; sr house offr in ophthalmology Professorial Unit Edinburgh Royal Infirmary 1962-64, registrar (ophthalmology) Birkenhead and Northampton Gen Hosps 1964-66, MO Nat Eye Bank (Moorfields and E Grinstead) 1966-70, registrar Corneoplastic Unit E Grinstead 1968-70, sr registrar Birmingham and Wolverhampton Eye Hosps 1970-74, conslt ophthalmic surgn Whipp's Cross Eye Unit 1974-; chm Regnl Advsy Ctee on Ophthalmology NE Thames RHA 1988-, memb Hunterian Soc; Fell Coll of Ophthalmologists 1988, FRSM 1980, FRCSEd 1970; *Recreations* swimming, skiing, travel; *Style—* Brian Beveridge, Esq; 8 The Charter Rd, Woodford Green, Essex IG8 9QU (☎ 081 504 2301); Whipps Cross Eye Unit, Whipps Cross Hospital, London E11 1NR (☎ 081 539 5522 ext 235); Holly House Hospital, High Rd, Buckhurst Hill, Essex 1G9 5HX (☎ 081 505 3311)

BEVERIDGE, George William; s of George Beveridge (d 1978), of Saline, Fife, and Margaret Patricia, *née* McLeod; *b* 23 Feb 1932; *Educ* Dollar Acad, Univ of Edinburgh (MB ChB); *m* 16 March 1962, Janette, da of John Millar, CBE (d 1978), formerly Lord Provost of Edinburgh; 2 s (Iain George b 25 Sept 1966, Alastair John b 13 March 1969), 2 da (Carolyn Janette b 1 May 1963, Susan Patricia b 7 Dec 1964); *Career* Nat Serv RAMC 1957-59, Capt RMO 2 Royal Tank Regt; conslt dermatologist The Royal Infirmary Edinburgh and pt/t hon sr lectr Univ of Edinburgh 1965-; author of articles in jls on acne, drug reactions and skin tumours; pres Scot Dermatological Soc 1982-85, elder Church of Scot; FRCPE 1970 (MRCPE 1961); *Recreations* gardening, golf; *Style—* George Beveridge, Esq; 8 Barnton Park View, Edinburgh EH4 6HJ (☎ 031 336 3680); Dept of Dermatology, The Royal Infirmary, Edinburgh EH3 9YW (☎ 031 229 2477 ext 4128, fax 031 229 8769)

BEVERIDGE, Dr Gordon Smith Grieve; s of Victor Beattie Beveridge (d 1983), and Elizabeth Fairbairn, *née* Grieve (d 1971); *b* 28 Nov 1933; *Educ* Inverness Royal Acad, Univ of Glasgow (BSc), Royal Coll of Sci and Technol Glasgow (ARCST), Univ of Edinburgh (PhD); *m* 1963, Geertruida Hillegonda Johanna, da of Gerrit Hendrik Bruijn (d 1944); 2 s, 1 da; *Career* lectr in chem engrg Univ of Edinburgh 1962-67, sr lectr and reader in chem engrg Heriot-Watt Univ 1967-71, prof of chem engrg Univ of Strathclyde 1971-86, vice chllr Queen's Univ Belfast 1986-; memb: Cncl Soc of Chem Ind 1978-88 (vice pres 1985-88), Engrg Cncl 1981-, Engrg Bd of SERC 1983-86, Chem Econ Devpt Ctee NEDO 1983-87; Harkness fell the Cwlth Fund (NY), resident at Univ of Minnesota 1960-62; dir Cremer & Warner Ltd; CEng, FEng 1984, FIChemE (memb Cncl 1975-, pres 1984-85), FRSE 1974, FRSA 1988, MRIA 1989; *Recreations* Scottish and Dutch history; *Clubs* Caledonian; *Style—* Dr Gordon Beveridge, FRSE; 10 Eglinton Crescent, Edinburgh EH12 5DD; The Vice-Chancellors Lodge, 16 Lennoxvale, Belfast BT9 5BY

BEVERIDGE, John Caldwell; QC (1979); s of Prof William Ian Beardmore Beveridge, of Canberra, and Patricia Dorothy Nina, *née* Thomson; *b* 26 Sept 1937; *Educ* Jesus Coll Cambridge (MA, LLB); *m* 1, 2 Aug 1973 (m dis 1989), Frances Ann Clunes Grant Martineau, da of Dr John Sutherland, of Edinburgh; m 2, 7 July 1989, Lilian Moira Weston, da of John Weston Adamson (d 1977), of Oldstead Hall, N Yorkshire; *Career* barr, rec Crown Ct (Western Circuit) 1975-, bencher Inner Temple 1987; QC NSW Australia 1980; Freeman City of London 1965, Liveryman Worshipful Co of Goldsmiths; *Recreations* hunting, shooting; *Clubs* Brooks's, Beefsteak, Pratt's, Turf; *Style—* John Beveridge, Esq, QC; Batheacton Court, Taunton, Somerset TN4 2AJ (☎ 0984 2461, 0984 24612); 5 St James's Chambers, Ryder St, London SW1 6QA (☎ 071 839 2660); 4 Pump Court, Temple, London EC4 (☎ 071 353 2656, car 0836 250691)

BEVERLEY, Lt-Gen Sir Henry York La Roche; KCB (1991), OBE (1979); s of Vice Adm Sir York Beverley, KBE, CB (d 1982), and Maria Theresa Matilda, *née* Palazio (d 1957); *b* 25 Oct 1935; *Educ* Wellington; *m* 3 Aug 1963, Sally Anne, da of Alistair Maclean (d 1973); 2 da (Lucy Anne b 15 Nov 1965, Sara Elizabeth b 13 March 1968); *Career* ADC to Govr Gen NZ 1961-62, 41 Commando RM 1962-65, exchange offr US Marine Corps 1965-66, Staff Coll Camberley 1968, Jt Servs Staff Coll 1971, staff of SNO W Indies 1971-73, BM HQ 3 Commando Bde RM 1973-75, DS Camberley 1975-77, CO 42 Commando RM 1978-80, Cmdt CTC RM 1980-82, dir RM Personnel MOD 1982-84, Cmd 3 Commando Bde RM 1984-86, Maj-Gen TRSF RM 1986-88, COS DCGRM 1988-90, Cmdt Gen RM 1990-; *Recreations* cricket, golf, cross country skiing; *Clubs* Army and Navy; *Style—* Lt-Gen Sir Henry Beverley, KCB, OBE; c/o Ministry of Defence, Whitehall, London SW1

BEVERTON, Prof Raymond John Heaphy; CBE (1968); s of Edgar John Beverton (d 1968), of London, and Dorothy Sybil Mary, *née* Heaphy; *b* 29 Aug 1922; *Educ* Forest Sch Snaresbrook, Downing Coll Cambridge (BA, MA); *m* June 10 1947, Kathleen Edith, da of Frederick Henry Marner (d 1956), of London; 3 da (Susan Lorinda b 1950, Julia Rosemary b 1953, Valerie Louise b 1955); *Career* operational res 1942-45; fisheries lab MAAF Lowestoft Suffolk: res scientist 1947-65, dep dir 1959-65; sec Natural Environment Res Cncl 1965-80, prof Dept Applied Biology UWIST 1983- 87, prof and head Sch of Pure and Applied Biology Univ of Wales and Coll of Cardiff 1987-; Hon DSc Univ of Wales 1989; FIBiol 1973, FRS 1975; *Books* On The Dynamics of Exploited Fish Populations (with S J Holt, 1957); *Recreations* gardening, music, DIY, golf; *Style—* Prof Raymond Beverton, CBE, FRS; Montana, Old Roman Rd, Langstone, Gwent, South Wales NP6 2JU (☎ 0633 412 392); School of Pure & Applied Biology, University of Wales, PO Box 915, Cardiff CF1 3TL (☎ 0222 874 305, fax 0222 371 921)

BEVES, Brian Montague; s of Montague Hebb Beves (d 1943), of Hove, and Dorothy Hamlyn, *née* Lawrence-Smith (d 1960); *b* 8 Jan 1924; *Educ* Haileybury, King's Coll Cambridge (MA); *m* 28 Sept 1957, Carolyn Langworthy, da of Rear-Adm Cecil Ramsden Langworthy Parry (d 1977), of Coachmans, Wesbourne, Sussex; 2 da (Lucy b 1959, Frances b 1963); *Career* temp admin appt FO 1945-47; special corr The Times on Antartic Expdn 1948; served in Sudan Political Serv 1951-54; broker and underwriter Lloyd's (Sedgwick Collins) 1955-73, ret 1973; chm Hereford Diocesan Bd of Fin 1980-90; memb Gen Synod and Central Bd of Fin C of E 1990-; *Recreations* gardening, music; *Style*— Brian Beves, Esq; Abbey House, Ledbury, Herefords HR8 1BP (☎ 05312762)

BEVINGTON, Christian Veronica; da of Michael Falkner Bevington, of St Neots, Cambs, and Dulcie Marian, *née* Gratton (d 1979); *b* 1 Nov 1939; *Educ* St James's West Malvern; *m* 7 Oct 1961 (m dis 1974), Frederick David Andrew Levitt, OBE, s of late Frederick Charles Levitt; 1 s (Aldhun b 1965), 2 da (Alison b 1963, Evelyn b 1966); *Career* called to the Bar Inner Temple 1961, Lincoln's Inn (ad eundem) 1971; head of Chambers 1981-, asst rec SE Circuit; subscriber Hampstead Soc, subscribing memb Justice; memb: Criminal Bar Assoc, Family Law Bar Assoc; *Recreations* music-organ and harpsichord; *Clubs* Reform; *Style*— Ms Christian Bevington; Cloisters, 1 Pump Court, Temple, London EC4, (☎ 071 583 5123 ext 0018, fax 071 353 3383)

BEVINS, Anthony John; s of Rt Hon John Reginald Bevins, *qv*; *b* 16 Aug 1942; *Educ* Liverpool Collegiate GS, LSE (BSc); *m* 1965, Ruchira Mistuni, da of Kshitis Roy, of Santiniketan, West Bengal, India; 1 s (Robert b 1968), 1 da (Nandini b 1972); *Career* VSO 1964-66; political corr: Liverpool Daily Post 1970-73 (sub ed 1967-70), Sunday Express 1973, The Sun 1973-76, Daily Mail 1976-81, The Times 1981-86; political ed The Independent 1986-; *Style*— Anthony Bevins, Esq; Press Gallery, House of Commons, London SW1

BEVINS, Rt Hon John Reginald; PC (1959); s of John Milton and Grace Eveline Bevins, of Liverpool; bro of Kenneth Milton Bevins, *qv*; *b* 20 Aug 1908; *Educ* Liverpool Collegiate Sch; *m* 1933, Mary Leonora, da of J O Jones, of Liverpool; 3 s (including Anthony John, *qv*); *Career* postmaster-gen 1959-64; parly sec: Miny Housing and Local Govt 1957-59 (pps to Min 1951-53), Miny Works 1953-57; MP (C) Toxteth 1950-64, fought Toxteth West and Edgehill 1945 and 1947; served WW II RASC MEF and Europe; *Style*— The Rt Hon John Bevins; 37 Queen's Dve, Liverpool L18 2DT (☎ 051 722 8484)

BEVINS, Kenneth Milton; CBE (1973), TD (1951); s of John Milton Bevins (d 1928), of Liverpool, and Grace Eveline Bevins, bro of Rt Hon John Reginald Bevins; *b* 2 Nov 1918; *Educ* Liverpool Collegiate Sch; *m* 1, 1940, Joan Harding (d 1969); 2 da; m 2, 1971, Diana, da of the late Godfrey J Sellers, of Keighley; *Career* WWII: 136 Field Regt RA incl with 14 Army Burma 1943-46, Maj RA (TA); Royal Insurance Co: sec 1957, gen mangr 1963, dep chief gen mangr 1966, chief gen mangr 1970-80, dir 1970-89; dir Fire Protection Assoc 1963-77 (chm 1966-68), dir Trade Indemnity Co 1970-80 (chm 1975-80), chm Br Insur Assoc 1971-73, Mutual & Federal Insurance Co Ltd 1971-80, dir British Aerospace PLC 1981-87; memb: Jt Fire Res Orgn Steering Ctee 1966-68, Home Sec's Standing Ctee on Crime Prevention 1967-73, Exec Ctee City Communications Centre 1976-80, Bd British Aerospace 1980-81, Govt Ctee to review Export Credit Guarantee Dept 1983-84; *Recreations* travel, gardening, reading, photography, painting, handiwork; *Clubs* Army and Navy, Oriental; *Style*— Kenneth Bevins, Esq, CBE, TD; Linton, The Drive, Sevenoaks, Kent TN13 3AF (☎ 0732 456909)

BEVIS, Prof Michael John; s of Bernard John Bevis, of Jersey, Channel Islands, and Kathleen Mary Balston; *b* 25 April 1940; *Educ* De La Salle Coll Jersey CI, Univ of London (BSc, PhD); *m* 23 May 1964, Diana, da of Edgar Holloway; 1 s (Andrew John b 12 Jan 1968), 2 da (Katie Ann b 30 April 1965, Sarah Jane b 11 March 1972); *Career* lectr then sr lectr then reader Dept of Metallurgy and Materials Sci Univ of Liverpool 1965-; Brunel Univ: joined 1977-, prof and head Dept of Non-Metallic Materials 1977-84, prof and head Dept of Materials Technol 1984-87, res prof and dir Wolfson Centre 1987-; *awards* A A Griffith medal and prize of Inst of Metals 1988, Swinburne medal and prize of Plastics and Rubber Inst 1990; FInstP 1971, fell Inst Metals 1977, FPRI 1980, FEng 1986; *Style*— Prof Michael Bevis; Wolfson Centre for Materials Processing, Brunel Univ, Uxbridge, Middlesex UB8 3PH (☎ 0895 74000, fax 0895 32806)

BEWES, Michael Keith; *b* 4 March 1936; *Educ* Marlborough, Emmanuel Coll Cambridge (MA); *m* 10 Oct 1964, (Patricia) Anrôs, *née* Neill; 3 s (Jonathan b 1965, Nicholas b 1967, Anthony b 1971), 1 da (Rebecca b 1973); *Career* Nat Serv 2 Lt RA 1954-56; BR 1959-66, mgmnt devpt offr Royal Exchange Assurance 1966-68; Guardian Royal Exchange Assurance plc 1968: personnel mangr, field servs mangr, mangr corp affrs and personnel devpt, asst gen mangr; chm Insurance Indust Training Cncl 1982-88; The Chartered Insurance Inst: treas 1985-87, dep pres 1987-88, pres 1988-89; memb Governing Cncl Business in the Community; govr: Stowe Sch, The Coll of Insurance; tstee Dio of Central Tanganyika, chm of Cncl Scripture Union, chm Stowe Sch Educnl Servs Ltd; FITD 1983, FRSA 1989; *Recreations* fly fishing, heraldic painting, photography, music, Napoleon commemorative medals, sport various - lawn tennis and hockey at county level; *Clubs* RAC, Hawks; *Style*— Michael Bewes, Esq; Clifton House, Church Lane, Lexden, Colchester, Essex CD3 4AE (☎ 0206 42710); Guardian Royal Exchange Assurance plc, 68 King William St, London EC4N 7BU (☎ 071 283 7101, 883232, 071 283 5605)

BEWES, Rev Prebendary Richard Thomas; s of Rev Canon Thomas Francis Cecil Bewes, and Nellie Sylvia Cohu, *née* De Berry; *b* 1 Dec 1934; *Educ* Marlborough, Emmanuel Coll Cambridge (MA), Ridley Hall Theol Coll Cambridge; *m* 18 April 1964, Elisabeth Ingrid, da of Lionel Jaques; 2 s (Timothy b 1966, Stephen b 1971), 1 da (Wendy b 1968); *Career* vicar: St Peter's Harold Wood Essex 1965-74, Emmanuel Northwood Middx 1974-83; rector All Souls Langham Place London 1983-, prebendary St Paul's Cathedral 1988; Freedom of the City of Charlotte N Carolina USA 1984; memb Guild of Br Songwriters 1975; *Books* God in Ward 12 (1973), Advantage Mr Christian (1975), Talking About Prayer (1979), The Pocket Handbook of Christian Truth (1981), John Wesley's England (1981), The Church Reaches Out (1981), The Church Overcomes (1983), On The Way (1984), Quest For Life (1985), Quest For Truth (1985), The Church Marches On (1986), When God Surprises (1986), The Resurrection (1989), A New Beginning (1989); *Recreations* tennis, photography, broadcasting, reading, writing; *Style*— The Rev Prebendary Richard Bewes; 12 Weymouth St, London W1N 3FB (☎ 071 580 6029); All Souls Church 2 All Souls Place, London W1N 3DB (☎ 071 580 6029, fax 071 426 3019)

BEWICKE-COPLEY, Hon Thomas David (Percy); yr s of 6 Baron Cromwell and hp to er bro, 7 Baron; *b* 6 Aug 1964; *Educ* Summerfields Oxford, Eton, Webber-Douglas Acad of Dramatic Art London (Dip); *Career* actor (as Percy Copley), season at Brunton Theatre Scotland Sept-Nov 1985, Augustus Gloop in Charlie and the Chocolate Factory 1985-86, Gala performance for Save The Wells (Royal Opera House) 1986, Giant Gormless and Lagopus Scoticus in "The Old Man of Lochnagar" based on the book by HRH The Prince of Wales 1986-87, Frederick Willow in "Bless The Bride" (Sadlers Wells) 1987; *Recreations* jazz music, ukulele, bagpipes, banjo, collects 78 rpm records; *Style*— The Hon Thomas Bewicke-Copley; Flat 1, 52 Braxted Park, London SW16 3AU (☎ 071 764 4273)

BEWLEY, Dr Beulah Rosemary; da of John B Knox (d 1975), of Coulsdon, Surrey, and Ina, *née* Charles; *b* 2 Sept 1929; *Educ* Trinity Coll Dublin (MB BCh, MA, MD), Univ of London (MSc); *m* 20 April 1955, Dr Thomas Henry Bewley, s of Dr A G Bewley (d 1980), of Dublin; 1 s (Henry John b 1963), 4 da (Susan Jane b 1958, Sarah Elizabeth b 1959, Louisa Mary b 1961, Emma Caroline b 1966); *Career* conslt sr lectr in public health med St George's Hosp Med Sch London; SWTRA reg post grad tutor in public health med; memb: GMC, previous Central Ctee for Educn of Social Workers; former pres Med Women's Fedn; FFCM 1980; *Recreations* music, travel, food; *Clubs* RSM; *Style*— Dr Beulah R Bewley; 11 Garrads Rd, London SW16 1JU (☎ 081 769 1703); Department of Public Health Sciences, St George's Hospital Medical School, London SW17 0RE (☎ 081 672 9944)

BEWLEY, Dr Thomas Henry; CBE (1988); s of Dr Geoffrey Bewley (d 1980), and Victoria Jane, *née* Wilson (d 1953); *b* 8 July 1926; *Educ* Rugby, St Columbus Coll Dublin, Trinity Coll Dublin (BA, MB, MA, MD); *m* 20 April 1955, Beulah, da of John Knox (d 1975); 1 s (Henry b 1963), 4 da (Susan b 1958, Sarah b 1959, Louisa b 1961, Emma b 1966); *Career* conslt psychiatrist 1961-88: St Thomas Hosp, St George's Hosp, Tooting Bec Hosp; hon sr lectr St George's Hosp Med Sch 1988-, WHO expert Advsy Panel on Drug Dependence and Alcohol Problems 1988- pres Royal Coll Psychiatrists 1984-87 (dean 1977-82), physician memb Social Security and Med Appeal Tbnls 1987-, memb Parole Bd 1988; Hon MD Univ of Dublin 1987; FRCPI 1963, FRCPsych 1972, FRCP (London) 1988; *Style*— Dr Thomas Bewley, CBE; 11 Garrads Rd, London SW16 1JU (☎ 081 769 1703)

BEWLEY, Brig William Patrick (Bill); s of James Patrick Francis Bewley (d 1978), and Ellen Keane (d 1975); *b* 25 March 1937; *Educ* St Francis Xaviers Coll, Univ of Liverpool, RMCS (MSc); *m* 19 Aug 1964, Jean Morag, da of Dr C C Connochie (d 1975); 3 s (James b 5 Jan 1967, Linus b 8 Dec 1967, Francis b 11 March 1970), 2 da (Helen b 14 Sept 1965, Rachel b 29 March 1969); *Career* Nat Serv 1960, 1 Guards Bde 1960-62, 51 Bde of Gurkhas 1962-64; computer programmer 1964-68; MOD: 1968-70, 1972-74, 1976-80, 1983-87; HQ Army Air Corps 1970-72, co cdr BAOR 1974-76, RMCS 1980-83, garrison cdr 1987-; memb regnl ctee Nat Computing Centre (chm of Seminar Sub-Ctee); MBCS, FBIM; *Recreations* country pursuits, history, art; *Clubs* Army and Navy, Shrivenham; *Style*— Brig W P Bewley; HQ Bicester Garrison, Bicester, Oxon OX6 0LD (☎ 086 925 3311)

BEWSHER, (John) Gowen; s of Edmund Gordon Bewsher (d 1952), and Decima Mary, *née* Cross (d 1978); *b* 11 Jan 1935; *Educ* Mill Hill; *m* 1, 29 July 1959 (m dis 1977), Moiya Ann, *née* Kelly; 3 s (Guy b 1962, James b 1965, Charles b 1971), 2 da (Elizabeth b 1964, Charlotte b 1971); m 2, 21 July 1979, Angela Margaret, da of Gerald Austin Reed, of Maidenhead, Berks; *Career* Nat Serv RAF 1953-55; chm Group Four Advertising 1986- (md 1976-86); govr Mill Hill Sch 1974-; Freeman City of London 1982, Liveryman Worshipful Co of Needlemakers 1984; FInstD, MInstM; *Books* Nobis - The Story of a Club (1979); *Recreations* cruising, politics, genealogy; *Clubs* United and Cecil, Phyllis Court, Old Millhillians, Int Churchill Soc; *Style*— Gowen Bewsher, Esq; The Bridge House, High Street, Eton, Windsor, Berks (☎ 0753 868000, fax 0753 840952, car 0836 293255)

BEXON, Michael Laurence; MC (1945); s of MacAlister Bexon, CBE (d 1976), of High Wycombe, and Nora Hope, *née* Jenner (d 1976); bro of Roger Bexon, *qv*; *b* 28 June 1923; *Educ* Denstone Coll, St John's Coll Oxford (MA); *m* 1949, Joan Agnes Mary, da of Joseph Austin (d 1938), of Wadhurst; 2 s (Julian, Dominic); *Career* WWII Capt North Irish Horse 1941-46, served Italy and Palestine; Capt Westminster Dragoons TA 1957-62; joined Dunlop Rubber Co Ltd 1948 (Denmark 1950-54, Lebanon 1954-56, India 1960-65); dir: Dunlop Hldgs (formerly Dunlop Rubber) 1967-83, Sumitomo Rubber Industs Ltd 1970-84; mgmnt conslt 1983-; *Style*— Michael Bexon, Esq, MC; 14a Ashley Gardens, London SW1P 1QD (☎ 071 834 7362)

BEXON, Roger; CBE (1985); s of MacAlister Bexon, CBE (d 1976), of High Wycombe, and Nora Hope, *née* Jenner (d 1976); bro of Michael Laurence Bexon, *qv*; *b* 11 April 1926; *Educ* St John's Coll Oxford (MA), Univ of Tulsa Oklahoma (MS); *m* 1951, Lois Loughran Walling; 1 s, 1 da; *Career* geologist and petroleum engr Trinidad Petroleum Devpt Co Ltd 1946-57; Br Petroleum Co: E Africa 1958-59, Libya 1959-60, Trinidad 1961-64, London 1964-66, mangr N Sea Ops 1966-68, gen mangr Libya 1968-70, regnl coordinator ME London 1971-73, gen mangr Exploration and Prodn London 1973-76; md: BP Exploration Co Ltd London 1976-77, BP Co 1981-86 (dep chm 1983-86); chm: Laporte plc 1986-, Goal Petroleum plc 1990-; dir: Standard Oil Co 1982-86 (dir and sr vice pres 1977-80), BP Canada Inc 1983-87, BICC 1985-, Lazard Bros 1986-, JH Fenner (Hldgs) 1986-89, Cameron Iron Works 1987-89, Astec (BSR) 1989-; *Recreations* golf, reading, crosswords; *Style*— Roger Bexon, Esq, CBE; c/o Laporte plc, 3 Bedford Square, London WC1B 3RA (☎ 071 580 0223)

BEXSON, Peter James; s of Thomas William Bexson (d 1984), of E Molesey, Surrey, and Elsie Constance, *née* Cox (d 1986); *b* 2 May 1926; *Educ* Glasgow Acad, Gonville and Caius Coll Cambridge (BA), Coll of Estate Mgmnt Univ of London; *m* 7 Feb 1953, Edna May, da of Harold Glover, of Hartley, Dartford, Kent; 2 s (Robert b 9 July 1956, William b 18 May 1961); *Career* WWII cadet pilot Canada and USA 1944-45, instr PT Branch Germany 1946-47; chief surveyor Greencoat Properties 1956-63; ptnr: Graves Son & Pilcher 1963-86, Stiles Harold Williams 1986-; memb Gen Cncl RICS (chm Conduct Investigation Ctee), pres Int Real Estate Fedn Paris, memb London Rent Assessment Panel DOE, valuation conslt Mid Sussex DC, former pres Soc of London Ragamuffins; Freeman City of London, Liveryman Worshipful Co of Tallow Chandlers, Liveryman Worshipful Co of Painter Stainers; FRICS 1961; *Recreations* walking, travel; *Clubs* RAC, London Scottish FC, RSAC; *Style*— Peter J Bexson, Esq; 1 Paxton Terrace, London SW1V 3DA (☎ 071 834 4565); 18 Hanover Square, London W1R 9DA (☎ 071 499 2323)

BEYFUS, Drusilla Norman (Mrs M Shulman); da of late Norman Beyfus, and late Florence Noël Barker; *Educ* RN Sch, Channing Sch; *m* 1956, Milton Shulman; 1 s (Jason), 2 da (Alexandra, Nicola); *Career* assoc ed Queen Magazine 1958-63, home ed The Observer 1963-64, assoc ed Daily Telegraph colour supplement 1964-70, ed Brides Magazine 1971-79, assoc ed British Vogue Magazine Condé Nast 1979-86, ed Harrods Magazine 1987-88, columnist Daily Mail magazine 1988-89, visiting tutor Central St Martin's Coll of Art 1989-; author and broadcaster; *Books* Lady Behave (co-author), The English Marriage, The Bride's Book, The Art of Giving; *Style*— Miss Drusilla Beyfus; 51G Eaton Square, London SW1 (☎ 071 235 7162)

BEYNON, David William Stephen; s of William Henry Beynon (d 1983), and Eileen Beynon; *b* 14 March 1934; *Educ* King Edward VII Sch Sheffield, Trinity Hall Cambridge (MA); *m* 23 Sept 1961, Joyce Noreen, da of George Trevor Richards, of Wallasey, Ches; 2 s (Stephen b 1965, Daniel b 1971), 1 da (Jane b 1962); *Career* Nat Serv RA 1952-54; ICI: joined 1954, commercial appts ICI Petrochemicals Div 1954-77, head of policy Gps Dept London 1977-79, dep chm Plastics Div 1979-81, gp dir Petrochemicals and Plastics Div 1981-87, dir ICI Chemicals & Polymers Ltd 1987-, dir ICI Resources Ltd 1987-; dir Euro Vinyls Corp 1987-, pres Br Plastics Fedn 1987-88 (memb Cncl 1980-); memb Cncl: Assoc of Euro Plastics Mfrs (APME) 1987-, Assoc of Euro Petrochem Mfrs (APPE) 1986-; memb Ctee Euro Petrochem Assoc (EPCA) 1987-; capt: Gt Ayton CC 1971-76, Welwyn Garden City CC 1980-86; Freeman City of London 1984, Liveryman Worshipful Co of Horners 1983; *Recreations* family, cricket; *Clubs* Forty, MCC; *Style*— David Beynon, Esq; ICI Chemicals and Polymers Ltd, The Heath, Runcorn, Cheshire (☎ 0928 513339, car 0836 628796, telex 629655)

BEYNON, (Ernest) Geoffrey; s of late Frank William George Beynon, and Frances Alice, *née* Pretoria, *née* Kirkpatrick (d 1990); *b* 4 Oct 1926; *Educ* Borden GS Sittingbourne, Univ of Bristol (BSc, CertEd); *m* 2 Aug 1956, Denise Gwendoline, da of late Frederick Charles Rees; 2 s (David Michael b 25 July 1957, Peter b 16 Nov 1961), 1 da (Dina b 16 June 1959); *Career* RA 1947-49; mathematics master

Thornbury GS Glos 1950-56, sr mathematics master and sixth form master St George GS Bristol 1956-64, asst sec Asst Masters Assoc 1964-78, jt gen sec Asst Masters and Mistresses Assoc 1979-87; former chm Teachers' Panel Burnham Primary and Secdy Ctee 1985-87; memb Ct Univ of Bristol, mangr and tstee Muntham House Sch Horsham; memb Ctee: Welwyn Garden City Soc, St Albans dist Hertford Co Assoc of Change-Ringers; Charter Fell The Coll of Preceptor (Hon FCP) 1985; memb RIPA; *Recreations* campanology, canal boating, walking, books; *Style*— Geoffrey Beynon, Esq; 3 Templewood, Welwyn Garden City, Herts AL8 7HT (☎ 0707 321 380)

BEYNON, Prof Sir (William John) Granville; CBE (1959); s of late William Beynon, and Mary Beynon, of Dunvant, Swansea; *b* 24 May 1914; *Educ* Gowerton GS, Univ Coll Swansea; *m* 1942, Megan Medi, da of Arthur Morgan James; 2 s, 1 da; *Career* scientific offr Nat Physical Laboratory 1938-46; lectr Univ Coll Swansea 1946-58; prof and head of Dept of Physics UCW Aberystwyth 1958 memb SRC 1976-81; numerous pubns in scientific jls; FRS; kt 1976; *Style*— Prof Sir Granville Baynon, CBE, FRS; Bryn Eithin, 103 Dunvant Rd, Swansea, Wales (☎ 0792 203585); Caebryn, Caergôg, Aberystwyth, Wales

BEYNON, Prof John David Emrys; s of John Emrys Beynon (d 1973), and Elvira, *née* Williams; *b* 11 March 1939; *Educ* Pontywaun GS Risca Gwent, Univ of Wales (BSc), Univ of Southampton (MSc); *m* 28 March 1964, Hazel Janet, da of Albert Hurley (d 1983); 2 s (Graham b 1968, Nigel b 1968), 1 da (Sarah b 1966); *Career* scientific offr DSIR Radio and Space Res Station Slough 1962-64, reader Dept of Electronics Univ of Southampton (lectr, sr lectr) 1964-77, prof of electronics UWIST Cardiff 1977-79; Univ of Surrey: prof of electrical enrg 1979-90, head Dept of Electronic and Electrical Engrg 1979-83, pro vice chllr 1983-87, sr pro vice chllr 1987-90; princ King's College London 1990-; FIEE 1979 (MIEE 1968), FIERE 1979, FRSA 1982, FEng 1988; *Books* Charge Coupled Devices and Their Applications (1980); *Recreations* music, photography, travel; *Style*— Dr John D E Beynon; Chalkdene, Great Quarry, Guildford, Surrey (☎ 0483 503 458); King's College, Strand, London WC2R 2LS (☎ 071 873 2292 fax : 071 872 0204)

BEYNON, Timothy George (Tim); s of George Beynon (d 1976), of Mumbles, Swansea, and Fona Inanda, *née* Smith; *b* 13 Jan 1939; *Educ* Swansea GS, King's Co Cambridge (MA); *m* 1 March 1979, Sally Jane, da of John Wilson, of Foresters Lodge, Ashridge Park, Little Gaddesden, Berkhamsted, Herts; 2 da (Sorrel b 1974, Polly b 1976); *Career* asst master City of London Sch 1962-63; Merchant Taylors Sch: joined 1963, housemaster 1970-78, sr master 1977-78; headmaster: Denstone Coll 1978-86, The Leys Sch 1986-90; expdns: Petra (overland) 1961, Spain, Hungary, Austria, Romania (ornithological); Denstone Expdn to Inaccessible Island 1982/83, sci advsr on wetland reserves to Glamorgan Co Naturalists Tst; memb: Eng Cncl 1986-89, Oxford and Cambridge Sch Examination Syndicate Appts Ctee; FRGS 1973, HMC 1978; *Recreations* ornithology, fishing, shooting, sport, music, expeditions; *Style*— Tim Beynon; The Croft, College Rd, Denstone, Uttoxeter, Staffs

BHAN, Dr Girdari Lal; s of Arjun Nath Bhan (d 1955), and Laxmi Bhan; *b* 25 Dec 1943; *Educ* Med Coll Srinagar India (MB BS), MRCP (UK); *m* 31 Aug 1968, Supriya, da of Varkie Cherian; 2 da (Archana b 7 Oct 1969, Kanchan b 25 Nov 1975); *Career* sr house offr: med East Birmingham Hosp 1974-75, neurology Midland Centre for Neurosurgery and Neurology 1976; registrar med East Birmingham Hosp 1977-79, sr registrar North West RHA 1980-81, conslt physician Royal Oldham Hosp 1982-; memb: BMA, RSM, Br Geriatrics Soc; *Recreations* classical music, gardening; *Style*— Dr Girdari Bhan; Consultant Physician, Royal Oldham Hospital, Rochdale Road, Oldham, Lancashire OL1 2JH (☎ 061 6278480)

BHANJI, Dr Sadrudin; s of Rahimtulla Harji Bhanji (d 1969), and Anna Lyna Mary, *née* Goodman; *b* 23 Feb 1942; *Educ* Manchester GS, Guy's Hosp Med Sch (MB BS, MD); *m* 29 May 1967, Janice Irene, da of Bruce Ogilvy Brown (d 1987); 1 s (Nicholas b 1977); *Career* various house appts and registrarships Guys Hosp 1965-71, res worker Inst of Psychiatry 1971-73, sr registrar Maudsley Hosp 1973-77, conslt psychiatrist Exeter Health Authy and sr lectr in adult mental illness Univ of Exeter 1977-; memb various local NHS ctees, former examiner Coll of Occupational Therapists and RCPsych; FRCPsych 1985 (MRCPsych 1977); *Books* Medical Aspects of Anorexia Nervosa (1988); *Recreations* antique collecting, boating; *Clubs* Exe Vale Social; *Style*— Dr Sadrudin Bhanji; Wonford House Hospital, Exeter EX2 5AF (☎ 0392 403625)

BHARUCHA, Dr Chitra; da of George Gnanadickam, of Madras, India, and Mangalam, *née* Ramaiya; *b* 6 April 1945; *Educ* Christian Med Coll Vellore India (MB BS); *m* 18 Jan 1967, Hoshang Bharucha, *qv*, s of Kaikusru Bharucha, of Bombay, India; 2 da (Anita b 3 June 1972, Tara b 8 Jan 1974); *Career* currently dep dir NI Blood Transfusion Serv and conslt haematologist Belfast City Hosp; memb: Med Women's Fedn, WHO; MRCPath; *Style*— Dr Chitra Bharucha; 15 Richmond Court, Lisburn, Northern Ireland BT27 4QU (☎ 0846 678347); Northern Ireland Blood Transfusion Service, 89 Durham St, Belfast BT12 4GE (☎ 0232 321414); Belfast City Hospital, Lisburn Rd, Belfast BT9 7AD

BHARUCHA, Dr Hoshang; s of K H Bharucha, and Shirin, *née* Motivala; *b* 18 Nov 1937; *Educ* Christian Medical Coll Vellore India; *m* 18 Jan 1967, Dr Chitra Bharucha, *qv*; 2 da (Anita b 1972, Tara b 1974); *Career* conslt pathologist Royal Victoria Hosp Belfast, sr lectr in pathology Queen's Univ of Belfast 1974-; FRCPath 1974; *Recreations* badminton, tennis; *Style*— Dr Hoshang Bharucha; 15 Richmond Ct, Lisburn, N Ireland BT27 4QU (☎ 0846 678347); 144 Head Rd, Kilkeel, N Ireland; The Queens Univ of Belfast, Dept of Pathology, Grosvenor Rd, Belfast BT12 6BL (☎ 0232 240503 ext 3274)

BHATTACHARYYA, Mukti Nath; s of Manju Gopal Bhattacharyya (d 1981), of Calcutta, and Santilata Mukherjee (d 1936), of Calcutta; *b* 22 Jan 1935; *Educ* Univ of Calcutta (MB BS, Dip Gynaecology and Obstetrics), FRCOG London 1983 (MRCOG 1964); *m* 18 Oct 1969, Brenda Kathleen, da of L Evans Esq, of Wolverhampton; 2 s (Neil b 27 Nov 1972, Robin b 10 Dec 1973); *Career* Int R G Kar Med Coll Calcutta 1959-61; Teaching Hosp Calcutta: res in surgery, med, obstetrics and gynaecology 1959-62; registrar in obstetrics and gynaecology Wisbech Hosp 1963-64, sr house offr obstetrics and gynaecology Huddersfield Hosp 1964, registrar in obstetrics and gynaecology Stockport 1965-67, registrar in diagnostic radiology Manchester 1967-70, conslt in genito-urinary med Royal Infirmary Sheffield 1973-79 (sr registrar in venereology 1971-73), conslt physician Manchester Royal Infirmary 1979-, hon lectr Univ of Manchester 1979-; memb and chm Manchester BMA 1987-90 (sec 1984-87); memb: Genito Urinary Med Advsy Subctee NW Region, Manchester Med Soc, Med Soc for Study of Venereal Diseases, Int Soc for Study of Vulvar Diseases, Int Soc Venereal Diseases and Treponematoses, Int Soc for Res into Sexually Transmitted Diseases, North of Eng Obstetrics and Gynaecological Soc; *Books* pubns incl numerous papers to professional med jls; *Recreations* astronomy, music, sports, travel; *Clubs* Manchester Rotary; *Style*— Mukti Bhattacharyya, Esq; 56 Green Pastures, Heaton Mersey, Stockport SK4 3RA (☎ 061 432 3832); Manchester Royal Infirmary, Oxford Rd, Manchester M13 9WL (☎ 061 276 1234)

BHAURA, Kulbir Singh; s of Harkishan Singh Bhaura, of Southall and Kirpal, *née* Kaur; *b* 15 Oct 1955; *Educ* Julundur India, Featherstone Sch Southall Middx; 1 s (Nicholas Banns b 25 Sept 1981); *Career* sales and promotions mangr Merican Sport; hockey player, 147 int caps for England and GB, Olympic Games 1984 Bronze Medallist, World Cup 1986 Silver Medallist, Olympic Games 1988 Gold Medallist; capt: Indian Gymkhana Hockey Club, Middx Co Hockey team (nat champions 1987-88); *Recreations* hockey, music, badminton, family; *Style*— Kulbir Bhaura, Esq; 64 Alexandra Rd, Kew, Richmond, Surrey (☎ 081 940 5135); Mercian Sports, 151-152 Maybury Rd, Woking, Surrey GU21 5LJ (☎ 0483 757677)

BIBBY, Sir Derek James; 2 Bt (UK 1959), of Tarporley, Co Palatine of Chester; MC (1945), DL (Cheshire 1987); s of Maj Sir (Arthur) Harold Bibby, 1 Bt, DSO, DL (d 1986), and Marjorie Guthrie, *née* Williamson (d 1985); *b* 29 June 1922; *Educ* Rugby, Trinity Coll Oxford (MA); *m* 11 Jan 1961, Christine Maud, da of Rt Rev Frank Jackson Okell, Bishop of Stockport (d 1950); 4 s (Michael James, Geoffrey Frank Harold b 18 Feb 1965, Peter John b 26 March 1969, David Richard b 10 Aug 1970), 1 da (Jennifer Margaret b 3 March 1962); *Heir* s, Michael James Bibby b 2 Aug 1963; *Career* WWII as Capt RA 1942-46 (wounded, MC); ptnr Bibby Bros & Co 1950 (joined 1946); chm: Bibby Bros & Co (Management) Ltd 1978-, Bibby Line Ltd (now Bibby Line Group Ltd) 1969-88, Bibby Line Group Ltd 1989-, Renray Group Ltd 1987- (dir 1986); pres Indefatigable and Nat Sea Training Sch for Boys; chm Birkenhead Boys' Club; MIOD; Chev de l'Ordre du Merite Maritime (France) 1978; *Recreations* gardening, tennis, shooting; *Clubs* Royal Cwlth Soc; *Style*— Sir Derek Bibby, Bt, MC, DL; Willaston Grange, Hadlow Rd, Willaston, S Wirral, Cheshire L64 2UN (☎ 051 327 4913); Bibby Line Group Ltd, 401 Norwich House, Water St, Liverpool L2 8UW (☎ 051 236 0492, fax 051 236 1163, telex 629241

BIBBY, (John) Roland; s of William Henry Bibby (d 1947), of Morpeth, and Margaret Jane, *née* Davison (d 1963); *b* 17 May 1917; *Educ* King Edward VI GS Morpeth, Durham Univ (King's Newcastle) (BA); *m* 12 Aug 1948, Winifred Maude, da of Robert Tweedie (d 1971), of Morpeth; 1 s (John Trevor b 1949), 1 da (Katherine Marie b 1953); *Career* WWII The Border Regt 1940-44, The Royal Warwickshire Regt 1944-46, served India and Burma (Capt and Adj); sec Gateshead Cncl of Social Servs 1947-52, teacher 1952-82, head of history Blyth Ridley HS; local historian, researcher and writer on Northumbrian history, lore, language and conservation 1946-, ed of Northumbriana magazine 1975-, lectr on Northumbrian history 1947-, lectr on language 1955-; Hon MA Univ of Newcastle 1987; pres Northumbrian Pipers' Soc 1980-; fell Northumbrian Language Soc 1986-; *Recreations* Northumbrian history, law, language, conservation; *Style*— Roland Bibby, Esq; Westgate House, Dogger Bank, Morpeth, Northumberland NE61 1RF (☎ 0670 513308)

BIBICA ROSETTI, Princess Raoul; Dorothy; *née* Acton; da of Henry Acton (ggs of Lt-Gen Joseph Acton, bro of Sir John Acton, 6 Bt, by his w, Eleanora Countess Berghe von Trips) and Elly, da of Prince Cleon Rizo Rangabe, of Greece; *b* 20 April 1893; *m* 1921, Prince Raoul Bibica Rosetti (d 1967), sometime Greek ambass to Canada and s of Prince Salvator Bibica Rosetti; 1 da (Princess Lobanov-Rostovsky, *qv*); *Style*— Princess Raoul Bibica Rosetti; Swallowdale, 67 Woodruff Avenue, Hove, Sussex BN3 6PJ

BICÂT, Col André; OBE (1943); s of Joseph Bicat, and Emelia Julia, *née* Bowra; *b* 27 Dec 1909; *m* 24 May 1944, (Marianne) Packly, da of Gen T Tchermoeff; 2 s (Anthony b 11 March 1945, Nicholas b 23 Feb 1949), 1 da (Christina b 9 Jan 1947); *Career* Nat Serv Col 1940-45; artist; painter, sculptor, printmaker, ceramist; works in pub and private collections incl: Br Museum, V & A, galleries and museums in London, Paris, USA, Canada, Aust, India, Hong Kong and Holland; tutor: RCA, City and Guilds of London Art Sch; visiting tutor Univ of Reading; *Style*— André Bicât, OBE; 233 Putney Bridge Rd, London SW15 2PU

BICESTER, 3 Baron (UK 1938); Angus Edward Vivian Smith; s of late Lt-Col the Hon Stephen Edward Vivian Smith, 2 s of 1 Baron by Lady Sybil McDonnell (da of 6 Earl of Antrim); 4 cous once removed to Lord Carrington, the Foreign Sec; suc unc 1968; *b* 20 Feb 1932; *Educ* Eton; *Heir* bro, Hugh Charles Vivian Smith; *Style*— The Rt Hon The Lord Bicester; House of Lords, SW1

BICHAN, Dr Herbert Roy; *b* 5 Nov 1941; *Educ* Univ of Aberdeen (BSc), Univ of Leeds (PhD); *m* Fiona Keay; 1 s (Michael Roy b 8 May 1969), 2 da (Inga Jane b 16 Feb 1967, Susan Elizabeth b 1 Aug 1971); *Career* chm The Robertson Gp plc, former pres Inst of Mining and Metallurgy; Adrian Fell Univ of Leicester 1988; FIMM, MIGeol; *Recreations* golf; *Style*— Dr Roy Bichan; The Robertson Group plc, Ty'n-y-Coed, Llandudno, Gwynedd LL30 1SA (☎ 0492 581811, fax 0492 583416, telex 61216 ROBRES G)

BICK, David Robert; s of Roy Leslie Samuel Bick, and Vera Grace, *née* Collis; *b* 9 April 1957; *Educ* Glyn GS Epsom, Univ of Essex; *m* 21 July 1984, Susan Christine, da of Joseph Esmond Stobbs (d 1979); 2 da (Antonia b 1987, Harriet b 1989); *Career* PA to David Atkinson MP 1979-80; exec: KH Publicity Ltd 1981-81, Shandwick Conslts Ltd 1981-83; account dir Good Relations City Ltd 1984-85 (account mangr 1983-84), dir and jt fndr Lombard Communications plc 1985-; cncllr London Borough of Lambeth 1980-86 (chm Amenity Servs 1982); *Recreations* theatre, reading, cricket, cinema; *Style*— David R Bick, Esq; 12 Groveland Court, Bow Lane, London EC4M 9EH (☎ 071 236 5858, fax 071 236 6128)

BICKERSTAFF, Hon Mrs (Sara Gillian Mary); *née* Bramall; o da of Baron Bramall, GCB, OBE, MC (Life Peer), *qv*; *b* 16 April 1951; *m* 12 June 1987, Dr Edwin R Bickerstaff; *Style*— The Hon Mrs Bickerstaff; St Helens, The Close, Trevone, Padstow, Cornwall

BICKERSTETH, Edward; s of Rev Canon Edward Monier Bickersteth, OBE (d 1976), of Worton, nr Devizes, Wilts, and Katharine, *née* Jelf (d 1936); *b* 27 April 1915; *Educ* Haileybury, ChCh Oxford (MA); *m* Elspeth, da of Dr Hector Charles Cameron (d 1959), of Witley, Surrey; 3 s (Michael b 1948, Anthony b 1951, Peter b 1956); *Career* asst private sec to the High Cmmr in Palestine 1937-38, Sudan Political Serv 1938-55, overseas dir and asst dir personnel Reckitt & Colman plc 1955-75; memb Chm's Panel Civil Serv Selection Bd 1976-87; *Recreations* fishing, walking; *Clubs* Travellers; *Style*— Edward Bickersteth, Esq; 29 The Close, Salisbury, Wilts SP1 2EJ (☎ 0722 322 449)

BICKERSTETH, Rt Rev John Monier; KCVO (1989); yr s of Rev Canon Edward Monier Bickersteth, OBE (d 1976); *b* 6 Sept 1921; *Educ* Rugby, Ch Ch Oxford (MA); *m* 1955, Rosemary, yr da of Edward Cleveland-Stevens (d 1962), of Gaines, Oxted; 3 s, 1 da; *Career* Capt RA 1941-46; ordained 1951; curate Moorfields Bristol 1950-54, curate i/c and min i/c St John Hurst Green Southwark 1954-62, vicar St Stephen Chatham Rochester 1962-70, hon canon Rochester Cath 1968-70; bishop of: Warrington 1970-75, Bath and Wells 1975-87; chaplain and sub prelate Order of St John 1977-, Clerk of the Closet to HM The Queen 1979-89, took seat in House of Lords 1981, memb Cncl Marlborough Coll 1981; Freeman City of London 1978; chm: Bible Reading Fellowship 1978-90, Royal Sch of Church Music 1977-89; *Recreations* country pursuits; *Clubs* Royal Cwlth Soc; *Style*— The Rt Rev John Bickersteth, KCVO; Beckfords, Newtown, Tisbury, Wilts SP3 6NY (☎ 0747 870479)

BICKERTON, Peter W; *b* 4 July 1940; *Educ* Abbotsholme Sch Derbyshire, Univ of Durham (BSc), INSEAD, Univ of Grenoble; *m* 1967, Anne da of John Mitchell, of Cheltenham; *Career* Koch-Light Laboratories Ltd 1962-65, New Prods Devpt Exec Miles Laboratories 1965-68, Fisons plc 1968-75; Sime Darby Gp: gp treas 1975-80, fin dir Western Div 1980-83; Manufacturers Hanover Ltd: assoc dir 1983-84, exec dir 1984-87, md 1987-; *Recreations* classical music; *Style*— Peter Bickerton, Esq;

Manufacturers Hanover Ltd, The Adelphi, 1-11 John Adam St, London WC2N 6HT (☎ 071 932 3537, telex 839 8774)

BICKET, Henry Brussel; JP (Liverpool 1960), DL (Merseyside 1977); s of Alexander Bicket (d 1981), of Oxton, Merseyside, and Amelia, *née* Brussel (d 1967); *b* 1 June 1922; *Educ* Radley, Brasenose Coll Oxford; *m* 21 April 1956, Katharine Morris, da of Clarence Hascy Young (d 1957), of Greenwich, Conn USA; 2 s (Henry Alexander Clarence (Harry) b 1961, Robert Morris b 1963), 2 da (Margreta Elizabeth Simpson b 1957, Jennie Hascy b 1958); *Career* Ordinary Seaman RN 1940-41; RNVR (Midshipman 1941-42, Sub-Lt 1942-43, Lt 1943-50), Lt Cdr RNR 1950; md The Alexandra Towing Co Ltd 1972-83 (chm 1972-88), chm Euro Tug Owners Assoc 1983-84, pres Br Tug Owners Assoc 1986- (chm 1972-74), chm Liverpool Shipowners Assoc 1980-88, regnl advsy dir Barclays Bank plc; chm: Spirit of Merseyside Tst, Fairbridge Drake Soc Merseyside; memb: Liverpool Shipwreck and Humane Soc, Merseyside Assoc for Alcoholism; High Sheriff 1983-84; *Recreations* boating, gardening; *Clubs* Royal Yacht Sqdn, Royal Ocean Racing, Naval and Military, Liverpool Racquet; *Style—* Henry Bicket, Esq, JP, DL; 3 The Orchard, N Sudley Rd, Liverpool L17 6BT; Achahoish Lodge, By Lochgilphead, Argyll; 43 Castle St, Liverpool 2 (☎ 051 227 2151)

BICKFORD, James David Prydeaux; s of William Alfred John Prydeaux Bickford, of Lloyds Bank, Pall Mall, London W1, and Muriel Adelyn, *née* Smythe (d 1973); *b* 28 July 1940; *Educ* Downside; *m* 24 April 1965, Carolyn Jane, da of Maj William Arthur Richard Sumner (d 1943); 3 s (Nicholas b 1966, James b 1967, Peter John b 1972); *Career* slr of the Supreme Ct 1963, in practice with J J Newcombe & Co Devon 1963-69, memb crown counsel and legal advsr to Turks and Caicos Island Govt 1 asst legal advsr then counsellor to the FCO, legal advsr Br Military Govt Berlin 1979-82, currently under sec of state MOD; memb Panel of Legal Experts Int Telecommunications Satellite Orgn, chm Assembly Maritime Satellite Orgn 1985-87; memb Law Soc; *Books* Land Dealings Simplified in the Turks and Caicos Islands (1971); *Recreations* the family, fishing; *Style—* David Bickford, Esq; c/o National Westminster Bank, Torrington, Devon

BICKFORD SMITH, John Roger; CB (1988), TD (1950); er s of late Leonard W Bickford Smith, of Camborne, Cornwall, and Anny Grete, *née* Huth (d 1986); *b* 31 Oct 1915; *Educ* Eton, Hertford Coll Oxford; *m* 1, 1939 (m dis), Cecilia Judge, er da of W W Heath, of Leicester; 2 s; m 2, 1972, Baronin Miranda von Kirchberg-Hohenheim; *Career* called to the Bar Inner Temple 1942, bencher 1984; master of the Supreme Ct Queen's Bench Div 1967-88; sr master and Queen's Remembrancer 1983-88; Master Worshipful Co Bowyers 1986-88; *Clubs* Garrick; *Style—* John Bickford Smith, Esq, CB, TD; 65 Gibson Sq, London N1 ORA

BICKFORD-SMITH, Hon Mrs (Joan Angel Allsebrook); da (by 1 m) of 1 Viscount Simon, GCSI, GCVO, OBE, PC, QC (d 1954); *b* 8 Aug 1901; *m* 1924, Capt John Allan Bickford-Smith, RN (ret) (d 1970); 1 s decd, 2 da; *Style—* The Hon Mrs Bickford-Smith; Brackenlea, Shawford, Winchester, Hants

BICKFORD-SMITH, Peter Michael; s of Michael George Bickford-Smith (d 1975), of Helston Cornwall, and Joyce Mallileu Bickford-Smith, MBE, *née* Coates (d 1984); *b* 23 April 1947; *Educ* Harrow, RAC Cirencester; *m* 1 May 1971, Margaret Mary, da of Lt Cdr David Verney, *qv*, of Truro; 1 s (Michael Rupert David b 27 March 1984), 3 da (Sacha Ann Mary b 21 March 1975, Charlotte Ann Bertha b 22 Feb 1977, Stephanie May b 1 May 1989); *Career* memb Stock Exchange 1974; pres BRCS Cornwall; chm Garden Soc, county chm Game Conservancy Cornwall, pres Royal Cornwall Show 1990; memb Clockmakers Co 1974; *Recreations* shooting, fishing, gardening, sailing; *Clubs* Royal Cornwall Yacht; *Style—* Peter Bickford-Smith, Esq; Trevarno, Helston, Cornwall (☎ 0326 572022)

BICKMORE, Peter Christopher; s of Lt-Col Lawrence Hyde Neild Bickmore, OBE, of 31A High St, Sandwich, Kent, and Anne Windsor Lewis, *née* Drummond (d 1985); *b* 4 April 1943; *Educ* Charterhouse; *m* 22 July 1975, Isabel Margaret, da of Maj-Gen Lord Michael Fitzalan Howard, KCVO, MC, of Fovant House, Fovant, nr Salisbury, Wiltshire; 2 s (Andrew Ralph b 1979, Rupert Nicholas b 1985), 1 da (Fiona Clare b 1981); *Career* Lt short serv cmmn Life Gds 1962-68; md Pegasus Insurance Services Ltd 1979-88; currently: dir Bloodstock Agency plc, md BBA Insurance Services Ltd, dir Robert Fraser (Bloodstock) Ltd (Lloyds Brokers); Freeman City of London 1964, Liveryman Worshipful Co of Skinners 1969; memb Insur Brokers Registration Cncl 1986; *Recreations* tennis, golf, shooting; *Clubs* White's, Turf, Pratt's; *Style—* Peter Bickmore, Esq; 32-38 Leman St, London E1 8EW (☎ 071 702 1213, fax 071 481 2096, telex 894460, car 0860 280795)

BICKNELL, Claud; OBE (1946); s of Raymond Bicknell (d 1927), of Newcastle upon Tyne, and Phillis Ellen, *née* Lovibond (d 1957); *b* 15 June 1910; *Educ* Oundle, Queens' Coll Cambridge (MA); *m* 1, 15 Dec 1934, Esther Irene (d 1958), da of Rev Kenneth Norman Bell (d 1951), of Oxford; 1 s (Mark, *qv*, b 1936), 3 da (Meriel (Mrs Mastroyannopoulou) b 1939 d 1977, Clare (wife of Dr Sir John Richard Shelley, 11 Bt) b 1943, Phillis (Mrs Jones) b 1949); m 2, 7 May 1960, Christine Betty, CBE, da of Walter Edward Reynolds (d 1940), of Dulwich; *Career* WWII Auxiliary Fire Serv Newcastle upon Tyne 1939-41, Nat Fire Serv 1941-45, sr fire staff offr Home Office 1943-45; admitted slr 1934; Stanton Atkinson & Bird Newcastle upon Tyne 1934-70, law cmmr 1970-75, chm of industl tbnls 1975-83; dir Northern Corp Ltd 1939-53, memb Planning Bd Lake Dist Nat Park 1951-70 (chm Devpt Control Ctee 1957-70), memb Lord Jellicoe's Ctee on Water Resources in the NW 1963, pres Newcastle upon Tyne Incorporated Law Soc 1969, chm Newcastle upon Tyne Housing Improvement Tst Ltd 1966-70; *Clubs* Garrick, Alpine; *Style—* Claud Bicknell, Esq, OBE; Aikrigg End Cottage, 115 Burneside Road, Kendal, Cumbria LA9 6DZ

BICKNELL, Eric Arthur; s of Frederick Arthur Bicknell (d 1974), and May, *née* Downes (d 1943); *b* 11 Dec 1919; *Educ* Beaufort House Sch, Hammersmith Sch of Bldg Arts and Crafts; *m* 16 Feb 1941, Patricia Marie, da of Augustus Markland (d 1936); 2 s (Brian b 1946, Stephen b 1950); *Career* served RM 1940-46, Capt; mangr and dir A Stone & Sons Ltd 1946, md H C Wakefield & Sons Ltd 1951, dir and gen mangr Troy Gp of Cos 1954, founded EA Bicknell & Sons Ltd 1955, chm Bicknell Holdings plc; FCIOB 1955, FFB 1975, MJMA 1962; *Recreations* golf, soccer, tennis, racing; *Clubs* Clifton, Univ & Literary, Long Ashton Golf, Bristol Central Tennis; *Style—* Eric Bicknell, Esq; Penthouse A, Marklands, Julian Rd, Sneyd Park, Bristol, Avon BS9 1NP; Bicknell Holdings plc, Merstham Rd, Bristol BS2 9TQ

BICKNELL, John; s of Peter Barrie Bicknell, and Lorna Mary Graham, *née* Farmer; *b* 28 July 1958; *Educ* Sir Winston Churchill Co Secdy Sch Surrey, Offershaw Sch Surrey, NE London Poly (BA), Slade Sch of Fine Art Univ of London (Boise travelling scholar, HDip, Slade Prize); *m* Christina, da of Manthos Dorees; *Career* artist; solo exhibitions: Paintings Drawings and Prints (Carlile Gallery London) 1987, Painting and Prints (Pomeroy Purdy Gallery London) 1990; gp exhibitions incl: Sainsbury Centre for Visual Arts UEA 1980, Stowells Trophy (Royal Acad of Arts) 1983, New Graduate Art (Christies Contemporary Art) 1983, Leicester exhibition for schs and colls (Beaumanor Hall Loughborough) 1984, Athens International Awards (Mall Galleries) 1985, Open Studio exhibition (Wapping) 1985, XXV Joan Miró (Barcelona and touring Spain) 1986, Drawings (Carlile Gallery) 1986, Walker Art Gallery 1987, South Bank Picture Show Royal Festival Hall) 1987, For Sale (Minories Gallery) 1988, Art '89 (Islington Centre) 1989, Summer Exhibition (Pomeroy Purdy Gallery) 1989, New Talent (Schuster Gallery Florida) 1989, Christies New Contempories (RCA Galleries) 1989, Ninth Bath Fair 1989, Painting and Sculpture (Leeds Poly Gallery) 1990, Gallery Artists (Pomeroy Purdy Gallery) 1990, Fifth Br Int Contemporary Art Fair (Olympia) 1990, A View of the New (Br Over-Seas League) 1990; works in collections: Slade Collection, Boise Scholarship Collection, Leicester Collection for Schs and Colls, County National Westminster Bank, Reed International, private collections in England, Europe, Israel and USA; theatre work: asst designer studio ATA (Athens) prodn of White Nights by Fyodor Dostoeusky 1988, designer The Night is Not Dark (Gate Theatre) 1990; awards: Greater London Arts award, 1986, prizewinner John Moores Liverpool Exhibition 1987, second prize South Bank Bd, Henry Moore Printmaking fellowship Leeds Poly 1989-90; *Style—* John Bicknell, Esq; Pomeroy Purdy Gallery, Jacob Street Studios, Mill Street, London SE1 2BA (☎ 071 237 6062)

BICKNELL, Julian; s of Wing Cdr Nigel Bicknell, DSO, DFC (d 1990), and Sarah Greenaway, *née* Leith; *b* 23 Feb 1945; *Educ* Winchester, Kings Coll Cambridge (MA, DipArch); *m* 18 Nov 1967, Treld, da of Arthur K A Pelkey (d 1979), of West Hartford Connecticut USA; 1 s (Titus P b 1971), 1 da (Poppaea E b 1982); *Career* architect; asst (later ptnr) Edward Cullinan 1966-72; tutor and dir of Project Office RCA 1973-80: The Old Gaol, Abingdon (RIBA award 1976), The Garden Hall and Library, Castle Howard (Carpenters award 1984); staff architect Arup Assocs (reconstruction of Bedford Sch) 1981-84; private practice 1984-: Henbury Rotonda, HM Ambassador's Residence Moscow, Upton Viva Nagara Country Club Japan; external examiner Leeds Poly Sch of Architecture 1990, tutor Prince of Wales Summer Sch 1990; FRIBA 1971, FFB 1985, AA 1987, FRSA 1988; *Books* The Design for Need Papers (1979); *Recreations* architecture, music, the countryside; *Style—* Julian Bicknell, Esq; 29 Lancaster Park, Richmond, Surrey (☎ 081 940 3929); The White Cottage, Fontmell Magna, Dorset; office, 78 St Martins Lane, London WC2 (☎ 071 836 5875)

BICKNELL, Mark; s of Claud Bicknell, OBE, *qv*, of Aikrigg End Cottage, Burneside Road, Kendal, Westmoreland, and Esther Irene *née* Bell (d 1958); *b* 21 April 1936; *Educ* Winchester, CCC Cambridge (MA); *m* 1, 28 April 1962, Jennifer Claire, *née* Fairley (d 1977); 2 s (William b 1966, Tristan Samuel (Sam) b 1969), 1 da (Georgia (twin) b 1966); m 2, 19 Aug 1978, Countess Ilona Esterhazy; 1 s (Charles Esterhazy b 1979); *Career* Nat Serv, 2 Lt RTR; engrg appts: UKAEA 1961-62 (apprentice 1959-61), Charrington & Co Ltd 1963-64, J D & D M Watson 1964-66, Morganite Carbon Ltd 1967, Pencol 1967-70; J D & D M Watson 1970-78 (chief mechanical engr 1973, ptnr 1977), ptnr Watson Hawksley 1978-; ACE: memb cncl 1979-82, 1983-86 and 1988-, hon treas 1989-; FIMechE 1975, FICE 1982, MConsE 1978; *Books* author of various tech papers in learned jls; *Clubs* Alpine, Leander; *Style—* Mark Bicknell, Esq; 11 High St, Nettlebed, Henley on Thames, Oxon RG9 5DA (☎ 0491 641 619); Watson Hawksley, Terriers House, Amersham Rd, High Wycombe, Buckinghamshire HP13 5AJ (☎ 0494 26240, fax 0494 22074, telex 83439)

BICKNELL, Stephen Alan; s of Alan Bicknell, of The Birches, West Chiltington, Sussex, and Vivienne, *née* Colwell; *b* 30 Sept 1951; *Educ* Andover; *m* 19 July 1980, Karen Wendy, da of Edward Shotnik; 2 da (Kirstie b 24 Nov 1982, Susannah b 7 Aug 1984), 1 s (Christopher b 4 Sep 1986); *Career* trained in industl photography with Walter Gardner of Worthing 1968-72, freelanced London 1972-76, started own studio business Horsham 1976- (specialised in creative industl photography at Billingshurst 1985); Industrial Ilford award 1987, highly commended Ilford Folio 1988 and 1989; FBIPP 1986; *Style—* Stephen Bicknell, Esq; Ashley House, Swan Corner, Pulborough, W Sussex (☎ 07982 2324); Steve Bicknell Photography, Unit 7 Eagle Industrial Estate, Brookers Rd, Billingshurst, West Sussex RH14 9RZ (☎ 0403 78431, fax 0403 785368, car 0860 610758)

BIDDISS, Prof Michael Denis; s of Daniel Biddiss (d 1984), of Orpington, and Eileen Louisa, *née* Jones (d 1984); *b* 15 April 1942; *Educ* St Joseph's Acad Blackheath, Queens' Coll Cambridge (MA, PhD); *m* 8 April 1967, Ruth Margaret, da of Dr Frederick Fox Cartwright, of Milverton, Somerset; 4 da (Clare b 1969, Kate b 1972, Sarah b 1974, Beth b 1977); *Career* fell and dir of studies in history and social and political sciences Downing Coll Cambridge 1966-73, lectr and reader in history Univ of Leicester 1973-79, prof of history Univ of Reading 1979- (dean of the Faculty of Letters and Social Sci 1982-85); visiting professorships: Univ of Victoria BC Canada 1973, Univ of Cape Town SA 1976 and 1978, Monash Univ Aust 1989; chm History at the Univs Defence Gp 1984-87; memb cncl: Historical Association 1985- (pres 1991-), Royal Historical Soc 1988-; hon fell Faculty of History of Med Worshipful Soc of Apothecaries 1986- (Osler medal 1989); FRHistS 1974; *Books* Father of Racist Ideology (1970), Gobineau: Selected Political Writings (ed, 1970), Disease and History (jtly, 1972), The Age of the Masses: Ideas and Society in Europe since 1870 (1977), Images of Race (ed, 1979), Thatcherism: Personality and Politics (jt ed, 1987); *Recreations* cricket, mountain walking, music and opera; *Style—* Prof Michael Biddiss; Department of History, University of Reading, Whiteknights, Reading RG6 2AA (☎ 0734 318146)

BIDDLE, Donald Frank; s of Kenneth Barrington Biddle, of Poole, Dorset, and Judy Hill, *née* Downie (d 1964); *b* 6 March 1933; *Educ* Uppingham; *m* 3 Oct 1963, Anne Muriel, da of Maj Charles Deane Cowper; 2 s (Justin b 1968, Mark b 1971), 2 da (Georgina b 1973, Anne-Marie (twin) b 1973); *Career* 2 Lt RA Germany 1956-57, HAC 1957-63; Price Waterhouse 1957-62, sr audit ptnr Smith and Williamson 1962-, gen cmmr of Taxation 1970-87 and 1989-; tstee: English Language Servs Int 1963-, Ada Lewis Housing Tst 1967-82 (chm 1978-80), Samuel Lewis Housing Tst 1978-; CA Cons Pty at local and area levels, sec Int Dragon Assoc 1982-89; memb Olympic Yachting Ctee 1964-74; FCA; *Recreations* yachting, skiing, wine; *Clubs* Carlton, Boodle's, Royal Yacht Sqdn; *Style—* Donald F Biddle, Esq; The Old House, Milton-on-Stour, Gillingham, Dorset (☎ 0747 823487); 23 Eaton Place, London SW1 (☎ 071 235 8950); 1 Riding House St, London W1A 3AS (☎ 071 637 5377, telex 25187, fax 071 631 0741)

BIDDLE, Prof Martin; s of Reginald Samuel Biddle (d 1971), and Gwladys Florence, *née* Baker (d 1986); *b* 4 June 1937; *Educ* Merchant Taylors', Pembroke Coll Cambridge (BA, MA), Univ of Oxford (MA); *m* 1, 9 Sept 1961 (m dis 1966), Hannelore Bäcker; 2 da (Joanna b 1962, Barbara b 1965); m 2, 19 Nov 1966, Birthe, da of Landsretssagfoører Axel Th Kjoølbye (d 1972), of Soønderborg, Denmark; 2 da (Signe b 1969, Solvej b 1971); *Career* 2 Lt 4 RTR 1956, Ind Sqdn RTR Berlin 1956-57; asst inspr of ancient monuments Miny of Public Bldg and Works 1961-63, lectr in medieval archaeology Univ of Exeter 1963-67, visiting fell All Souls Coll Oxford 1967-68, dir Winchester Res Unit 1968-, dir Univ Museum and prof of anthropology and history of art Univ of Pennsylvania 1977-81, lectr of the house ChCh Oxford 1983-86, Astor sr res fell in medieval archaeology Hertford Coll Oxford 1989-; author of numerous articles; excavations with: Sir Mortimer Wheeler St Albans and Stanwick 1949 and 1952, Dame Kathleen Kenyon Jericho 1957-58; fieldwork: Nonsuch Palace 1959-60, Winchester 1961-71, St Albans 1978 and 1982-84, Repton 1974-88, Holy Sepulchre Jerusalem 1989-90; archaeological conslt: Canterbury Cathedral, St Albans Abbey and Cathedral Church, Eurotunnel, British Telecom; chm: Rescue The Trust for Br Archaeology 1971-75, Winchester in Europe (Nat Referendum 1975); served Cons Pty Ctees in Winchester 1973-77 (and currently Oxford 1982-); cmmr Royal

Cmmn on the Historical Monuments of England 1984-; hon kt of the Hon Soc of Kts of the Round Table 1971; Freeman: Worshipful Co Merchant Taylor's 1963, City of London 1963; Univ of Pennsylvania: Hon MA 1977, Hon Phi Beta Kappa 1978; FSA 1964, FRHists 1970, FBA 1985; *Books* Future of London's Past (1973), Winchester in the Early Middle Ages (ed 1976), Object and Economy in Medieval Winchester (1990), Approaches to Urban Archaeology (1991), King Arthur's Round Table (1991); *Recreations* travel, especially Hellenic and Middle East, reading; *Clubs* Athenaeum; *Style—* Prof Martin Biddle, FSA; 19 Hamilton Rd, Oxford OX2 7PY (☎ 0865 513 056); Hertford College, Oxford OX1 3BW (☎ 0865 279422)

BIDDLE, Neville Leslie; s of Walter Alan Biddle, of Nannerch Lodge, Nannerch, N Wales, and Beryl Mary, *née* Meadows; *b* 24 April 1951; *Educ* Wrekin, Univ Coll Wales Abertstwyth (BSc); *m* 2 Oct 1976, Sheila Ruth, da of Parimal Kumar Sen (d 1973); 3 da (Caroline b 22 Nov 1980, Josephine 27 July 1982, Rebecca 2 June 1986); *Career* called to the Bar Grays Inn 1974; elected to Northern circuit 1975, currently in practice Liverpool; *Style—* Neville Biddle, Esq; Peel House, Harrington St, Liverpool L2 9QA (☎ 051 236 4321)

BIDDULPH *see also*: Maitland Biddulph

BIDDULPH, Hon Edward Sidney; s of 3 Baron Biddulph (d 1972); *b* 16 Nov 1934; *Educ* Eton; *Career* Lt RHG 1955; ret fruit farmer; *Recreations* racing, shooting, gardening; *Clubs* White's; *Style—* The Hon Edward Biddulph; Ribston Lawn, Much Marcle, Ledbury, Herefordshire HR8 2ND (☎ 053 184 204)

BIDDULPH, Hon Fiona Mary Maitland; da of 4 Baron Biddulph (d 1988); *b* 28 Aug 1961; *Educ* Courtauld Inst of Art (BA); *Career* journalist; *Style—* The Hon Fiona Maitland Biddulph

BIDDULPH, Sir Ian D'Olier; 11 Bt (E 1664); s of Sir Stuart Royden Biddulph, 10 Bt (d 1986), and Muriel Margaret, *née* Harkness; *b* 28 Feb 1940; *Educ* Slade Sch Warwick Queensland; *m* 1967, Margaret Eleanor, o da of late John Gablonski, of Oxley, Brisbane; 1 s, 2 da; *Heir* s, Paul William Biddulph b 30 Oct 1967; *Career* grazier; *Style—* Sir Ian Biddulph, Bt; Fernway Poll Hereford Stud, Mail Service 23, Mount Walker, via Rosewood, Queensland 4340, Australia

BIDDULPH, Baroness; Lady Mary Helena; *née* Maitland; eldest da of Viscount Maitland (ka 1943; s and h of 15 Earl of Lauderdale), and Helena Ruth, *née* Perrott; *b* 23 Oct 1938; *m* 9 April 1958, 4 Baron Biddulph (d 1988); 2 s (5 Baron, Hon William Ian Robert Maitland Biddulph, *qv*), 1 da (Hon Fiona Maitland Biddulph, *qv*); *Style—* The Rt Hon Lady Biddulph; Makerstoun, Kelso, Roxburghshire TD5 7PA

BIDDULPH, 5 Baron (UK 1903); (Anthony) Nicholas Colin Maitland Biddulph; er s of 4 Baron Biddulph (d 1988), and Lady Mary Maitland, da of Viscount Maitland, s of 15 Earl of Lauderdale; *b* 8 April 1959; *Educ* Cheltenham, RAC Cirencester; *Heir* bro, Hon William Ian Robert Maitland Biddulph, *qv*; *Career* interior designer; *Recreations* shooting; *Clubs* Raffles; *Style—* The Rt Hon Lord Biddulph; Makerstoun, Kelso, Roxburghshire TD5 7PA

BIDE, Sir Austin Ernest; o s of Ernest Arthur Bide (d 1918), and Eliza, *née* Young (d 1976); *b* 11 Sept 1915; *Educ* Acton County Sch, Univ of London; *m* 1941, Irene, da of Ernest Auckland Ward (d 1953); 3 da; *Career* Maj 21 Army GP Germany; Dept of Govt chemist until 1940; joined Glaxo Laboratories Ltd (Res Dept) 1940, consecutively head Chem Investigation and Devpt Dept, pa to Dep MD Glaxo Laboratories Ltd, head of patents and trademarks; first factory mangr Montrose 1951, dep sec Glaxo Laboratories Ltd 1954 (sec 1959-65), dir Glaxo Group 1963, dep chm Glaxo Holdings 1971-73 (chm and chief exec 1973-85, hon pres 1985-), non exec dir J Lyons & Co Ltd 1977-78, non-exec chm BL 1982- (non-exec dir 1977-82); chm: QCA Ltd 1985-88, Microtest Research Ltd 1987-90, United Environmental Systems Ltd 1988-; CBI: chm Res and Technol Ctee 1977-87, memb Cncl 1976-88, memb Cos Ctee 1974-80, memb Pres Ctee 1983-87, memb Univs Polys and Indust Ctee 1984, memb Industl Performance Steering Gp 1985-87; chm: Nat Appeal Ctee Salisbury Cathedral 1986-, Nat AIDS Tst 1987-; vice pres Inst of Industl Mangrs; memb: Imperial Soc for Knights Bachelor 1980-, Ct of Br Shippers' Cncl 1984- (chm 1989), Advsy Ctee on Indust to the Vice Chllrs and Princs of the Affrs of the Univ Grants Ctee 1984-, Cncl Inst of Manpower Studies 1985-, body to review the affrs of the Univ Grants Ctee 1985; chm Visiting Ctee Open Univ 1982-89, tstee Br Motor Indust Heritage Tst 1983-86; Hon DSc Queen's Univ Belfast; CBIM: memb Cncl 1976-88, memb Companion's Ctee, chm Fin Ctee and dir BIM Fndn 1977-79; BIM Gold medal (for outstanding achievements in mgmnt of Glaxo Group 1982); FRSC, FIEx, FInstD, Hon FIChemE, Hon FICE 1983; kt 1980; *Recreations* fishing, handicrafts; *Clubs* Hurlingham; *Style—* Sir Austin Bide

BIDE, Margaret Helen; da of Herbert William Bide (d 1957), of Hillcrest, Runfold, Farnham, Surrey, and Helen Maud, *née* Edmunds (d 1984); gggf Richard Bide (1802-70), founded in 1854 Alma Nurseries of Farnham Surrey, ggf Samuel Bide (1842-1915), developed and expanded the business, known this century as S Bide & Sons Ltd, horticulturalists, farmers and hop growers; business remained in the family until closing nursery 1971 and farm 1982; *b* 15 March 1937; *Educ* Farnham Sch of Art (now W Surrey Coll of Art and Design) (Nat Dip in Design), Univ of Leeds (post grad study); *Career* head dept of textiles W Surrey Coll of Art and Design Farnham 1973-85 (lectr 1965-67, sr lectr 1967-73); developing own textile mill in Wales 1987-; *Style—* Miss Margaret Bide; 44 Beavers Rd, Farnham, Surrey GU9 7BD (☎ 0252 722367)

BIDGOOD, John Claude; s of Edward Charles Bidgood (d 1967), of Leeds; *b* 12 May 1914; *Educ* London Choir Sch, Woodhouse Tech Sch; *m* 1945, Sheila Nancy, da of Dr James Walker-Wood (d 1968), of Harrogate; 1 s, 2 da; *Career* MP (C) Bury and Radcliffe 1955-64; chm: Anglo-Dominion Finance Co, A-D Construction, A-D Trading; dir: Bidgood Holdings, Edward Bidgood & Co, Bidgood Larsson Ltd, Wright & Summerhill, R Horsfield & Co; Freeman City of London, Liveryman Worshipful Co of Horners, Alderman Chapeltown Corporation; *Recreations* music, travel; *Clubs* Naval and Military, City Livery, Leeds; *Style—* John Bidgood, Esq; The Old Joinery, Walton, Wetherby, W Yorks (☎ home 0937 844028, work 0532 459068)

BIDWELL, Sir Hugh Charles Philip; GBE (1989); s of Edward Bidwell, and late Elizabeth Bidwell; *b* 1 Nov 1934; *Educ* Stonyhurst; *m* 1962, Jenifer Celia; 2 s, 1 da; *Career* Nat Serv cmmnd E Surrey Regt, seconded to 1 Bn KAR Nyasaland; Viota Foods Ltd 1956-70: dir 1962-67, md 1967, dir Robertson Foods plc (parent Co of Viota Foods plc 1969-70); chm: Pearce Duff Holdings Ltd 1970-85 (acquired by Gill & Duffus Group plc 1984), Gill & Duffus Foods 1984-85, Ellis Son & Vidler Ltd 1986-88; dir: Glendronach Distillery Co Ltd 1989-, Baskin-Robbins Eastern Ltd 1990-; non-exec dir Riggs AP Bank Ltd 1989-; vice chm Allied-Lyons Eastern Ltd 1990- (chief exec and dir 1988-); Lord Mayor of London 1989-90, Sheriff City of London 1986-87, Alderman Billingsgate Ward; pres: Billingsgate Ward Club, Billingsgate Christian Mission & Dispensary, Fishmongers' & Poulterers' Inst; govr Berkhamsted schs; memb: Exec Ctee Food Manufacturers Fedn 1973-76, Cncl London C of C and Indust 1976-85, Food from Britain Cncl (chm Export Bd 1983-86), pres Br Food Export Cncl 1980-87, dep pres Food and Drink Fedn 1985 and 1986; memb: Exec Cncl Br - Soviet C of C 1989-, Cncl Sino - Br Trade Cncl 1989-, Euro Trade Ctee (BOTB) 1989-, Cncl China Br Trade Gp 1990-; dir Br Invisibles; memb Worshipful Co of Grocers (Master 1984-85), Hon Liveryman Worshipful Co of Marketors'; *Recreations* golf, tennis, cricket, fishing; *Clubs* Boodles, City of London, Denham Golf (Capt 1980), Royal St George's, MCC; *Style—* Sir Hugh Bidwell, GBE; 59 Eaton Mews North, London SW1 (☎ 071 235 7762); Waterlane Farm, Bovington, Herts HP3 ONA (☎ 0442 832179)

BIDWELL, Sydney James; MP (Lab) Ealing - Southall 1974-; s of late Herbert Emmett Bidwell, of Southall; *b* 14 Jan 1917; *Educ* Nat Cncl of Lab Colls; *m* 1941, Daphne, da of late Robert Peart, of Southall; 1 s, 1 da; *Career* former: railwayman, memb NUR, offr Southall Trades Cncl; lectr, memb Southall Borough Cncl 1951-55; contested (Lab): Herts E 1959, Herts SW 1964; tutor organiser NCLC TUC London regnl offr up to election 1966, sponsored by TGWU, MP (Lab) Southall 1966-74, chm Tribune Gp 1975-, vice chm PLP Tport Gp 1977, former memb Select Ctee on Race Relations and Immigration, memb Select Ctee on Tport 1979-; *Books* Red White & Black, Turban Victory; *Recreations* artist, soccer enthusiast; *Style—* Sydney Bidwell, Esq, MP; House of Commons, London SW1

BIELCKUS, Colin David; s of Louis Reginald Bielckus, of Thornhill, Southampton, and Lorna Elizabeth Mary Bielckus; *b* 17 June 1956; *Educ* King Edward VI Sch Southampton, Univ of E Anglia (BSc); *m* 11 Oct 1981, Lorraine, da of Reginald Alexander, of Southampton; *Career* CA; audit mangr Alliott Millar Fareham 1985-90, audit ptnr Alliott Millar Fareham 1990-; *Recreations* railways, collecting books, collecting beermats, collecting cacti and other succulent plants; *Style—* Colin Bielckus, Esq; 2 Lilydale Cottages, Portsmouth Rd, Lowford, Southampton SO3 8EQ (☎ 042 121 4681); Alliott Millar, Kintyre House, 70 High St, Fareham, Hants (☎ 0329 822232, fax 822402)

BIENKOWSKI, Jan Stanislaw; s of Zygmunt Witymir Bienkowski (d 1978) Polish Air Force Col, and Halina Wita Bienkowska, *née* Grzybowska; *b* 7 Nov 1948; *Educ* Salesian Coll, Univ of Surrey, AA Sch of Architecture (BSc Eng, AADip); *m* 21 Sept 1974, Zofia Joanna, da of Leszek Josef Rybicki, Maj 15 Lancers (Polish Cavalry); 1 s (Andrzej b 1984), 2 da (Lidia b 1977, Monika b 1978); *Career* chartered architect; asst architect John R Harris (London & ME) 1975-77, architect The Fitzroy Robinson Partnership London 1977-79, founding ptnr Spiromega Partnership (architects & designers) 1980-, jt md Blythe Projects plc 1985-89; dir: Myviad Ltd 1986-89, H and B Projects Ltd 1989-; chm Bienkowski & Co plc 1990-; MCSD, memb RIBA; *Recreations* landscape painting, sailing, squash; *Style—* Jan S Bienkowski, Esq; 86 Ranelagh Rd, London W5 5RP (☎ 081 579 1623); 259 King St, London W6 9LW (☎ 081 748 8525, fax 081 748 5094)

BIFFA, Richard Charles; s of Richard Frank Biffa, and Alice Ethel Amiens, *née* Berryman; *b* 23 Dec 1939; *Educ* Berkhamsted Sch; *m* 19 Feb 1983, Gillian, da of William L Poole-Warren (d 1978); 2 s (Matthew b 1969, Antony b 1972), 1 da (Harriet b 1984); *Career* chm and md Biffa Ltd 1977-85; chm Rechem Int Ltd 1985-; treas Nat Assoc of Waste Disposal Contractors 1985- (vice pres 1975-77); *Recreations* tennis, squash, sailing; *Clubs* Phyllis Court, Henley; *Style—* Richard C Biffa, Esq; Rechem International Ltd, Astor House, Station Road, Bourne End, Bucks SL8 5YP

BIFFEN, Rt Hon (William) John; PC (1979), MP (C) North Shropshire 1983-; s of Victor W Biffen, of Otterhampton, Somerset; *b* 3 Nov 1930; *Educ* Dr Morgan's GS Bridgwater, Jesus Coll Cambridge (BA); *m* 1979, Mrs Sarah Wood, *née* Drew; 1 step s, 1 step da; *Career* with Tube Investments Ltd 1953-60, Economist Intelligence Unit 1960-61; MP (C) Oswestry 1961-83; chief sec to Treasy 1979-81, trade sec 1981-82, lord pres of the Cncl 1982-83, ldr House of Commons 1982-87, Lord Privy Seal 1983-87; dir: Glynwed International 1987-, J Bibby & Sons 1988-, Rockware Group 1988-; *Style—* The Rt Hon John Biffen, MP; c/o House of Commons, London SW1

BIGGAR, (Walter) Andrew; CBE (1979, OBE 1967), MC (1945); s of Walter Biggar (d 1949), of Grange, Castle Douglas, and Margaret, *née* Sproat (d 1965); *b* 6 March 1915; *Educ* Sedbergh, Univ of Edinburgh (BSc); *m* 11 June 1945, Patricia Mary Irving, da of William Elliot (d 1949), of Middletoun, Stow, Midlothian; 1 s (Michael b 1949), 1 da (Susan b 1947); *Career* WWII 1939-46, cmmnd Royal Signals (POW Germany 1940-45); dir Caledonian Investment & Finance Co 1986-89; Rowett Res Inst 1935-54; farmer 1956-89; memb: Agric Res Cncl 1969-79, Scottish Agric Devpt Cncl 1971-81; govr Grassland Res Inst 1961-80; dir and tstee: Scottish Soc for Crop Res 1958-88, Animal Diseases Res Inst 1960-; chm: Animals Bd Jt Consultative Orgn for Res in Age 1973-1980, Moredun Animal Health Tst 1988-; govr St Margaret's Sch Edinburgh 1959-79; hon fell Animal & Grassland Res Inst 1980, FRAgS 1969; *Recreations* photography, rugby football; *Style—* W Andrew Biggar, Esq, CBE, MC; Magdalene Hall, St Boswells, Roxburghshire, Scotland (☎ 0835 23741)

BIGGART, Alastair Ross; s of Thomas Biggart (d 1985), and Mary Gladys Biggart, of 6 St Matthews Drive, Bickley, Bromley, Kent; *b* 13 Aug 1933; *Educ* Canford Sch, Univ of Loughborough (BSc, pres Univ Boat Club); *m* 1 Sept 1962, Mary Margaret Neill, da of James William Roxburgh Murray; 1 s (Iain William Murray b 13 Nov 1969), 3 da (Fiona Margaret b 11 Sept 1963, Kirsty Mary b 16 Dec 1964, Alison Elizabeth b 7 Nov 1967); *Career* Nat Serv pilot RAF 1956-58; asst engr: tunnelling project London Sir Robert McAlpine & Sons Ltd 1958-59, Design Office Balfour Beatty & Co Ltd 1959-61; sub agent: John Howard & Co Ltd 1961-62, Edmund Nuttall Ltd 1963-64 (Clyde Dry Dock Project), Mitchell Brothers Sons & Co Ltd 1964-65 (Victoria Line Underground London); dir: Mitchell Brothers 1965-70 (responsible for tunnel projects), Edmund Nuttall Ltd 1972-80 (contracts mangr 1970-71); md R L Priestley Ltd 1981-82 (part of Nuttall Group); Lilley Construction: tunnel mangr 1983-84, dir with responsibility for tunnelling projects 1984-85, tech dir (Cairo) 1985-87, asst construction dir for all tunnelling and precast work on the Channel Tunnel Transmanche-Link 1987-89 (ops dir 1989-); holder of Br patent for Double Gate Valve for use with slurry machines; FICE 1971, FEng 1990; *Publications* The Bentonite Tunnelling Machine (Proceedings ICE, 1973, awarded Telford Gold medal), The Bentonite Tunnelling Machine at Warrington (jtly, Symposium Tunnelling '76, 1976), Slurry Face Machine Tunnelling (Proceedings RETC, 1979), The Channel Tunnel (Channel Tunnel Conf Paris, 1989); *Recreations* sailing, shooting, running, youth club, building wall, converting old buildings; *Clubs* RAF; *Style—* Alastair Biggart, Esq; St Oswald House, Paddlesworth, Folkestone, Kent CT18 8AD (☎ 0303 893254); Transmanche Link, Beaumont House, Channel Tunnel Site, Old Folkestone Rd, Dover, Kent CT17 9UD (☎ 0304 242990, fax 0304 240809, car 0860 377601)

BIGGART, (Thomas) Norman; CBE (1984), WS; o s of Andrew Stevenson Biggart, JP, and his w Marjorie Scott; *b* 24 Jan 1930; *Educ* Morrisons Acad Crieff, Univ of Glasgow (MA, LLB); *m* 1956, Eileen Jean Anne Gemmell; 1 s, 1 da; *Career* RN 1954-56, Sub Lt RNVR; slr; ptnr Biggart Baillie & Gifford WS Glasgow & Edinburgh 1959-; dir Clydesdale Bank plc 1985-; chm: New Scotland Insur Gp plc 1989 (dir 1986-), Beechwood Glasgow plc 1989-; pres Business Archives Cncl Scot 1977-86; memb: Scot Tertiary Educn Advsy Cncl 1984-87, exec Scot Cncl Devpt and Indust 1984-, Cncl on Tbnls (chm Scot Ctee) 1990-, Scot Records Advsy Cncl 1985-; hon memb American Bar Assoc 1982; OStJ 1968; *Recreations* golf, hill-walking; *Clubs* Royal Scottish Automobile, Western (Glasgow); *Style—* Norman Biggart, Esq, CBE, WS; Gailes, Kilmacolm, Renfrewshire PA13 4LZ (☎ 050 587 2645)

BIGGIN, Alan Keith; s of Herbert Biggin, of Bradford, W Yorks, and Ada, *née* Richardson; *b* 19 Dec 1949; *Educ* Hanson GS, Bradford, W Yorks; *m* 27 May 1978, Angela (Susan), da of Clifford Crompton (d 1966); *Career* CA; trg and (later audit mangr) Deloitte Haskins & Sells, fin controller CH Industrials PLC 1978-79; sr ptnr: A K Biggin & Co 1980-87, Bostocks CAs 1987-90; memb: Cs of C in Bradford Halifax

Kirkless and Wakefield, Borough Club in Huddersfield, Exec Club at Bradford City AFC, Bradford Civic Soc; FCA, MBIM; *Recreations* golf, squash, fishing, shooting; *Clubs* West Bradford Golf; *Style—* Alan Biggin, Esq; The Counting House, Wade House Rd, Shelf, nr Bradford HX3 7PB (☎ 0274 673 642); St Georges House, 7 St Georges Square, Huddersfield HD1 1LA (☎ 0484 530 647); La Plata House, 147 Sunbridge Rd, Bradford BD1 2NA; Empire House, 15 Mulcture Hall Rd, Halifax HX1 1SP (☎ 0422 359412); Oakwell House, 643A Roundhay Rd, Oakwell, Leeds LS8 4BA (☎ 0532 405261)

BIGGINS, Christopher; s of William Biggins, of Salisbury, Wilts, and Pamela Parsons; *b* 16 Dec 1948; *Educ* St Probus Salisbury, Bristol Old Vic Theatre Sch; *Career* actor, dir and personality; govr St Dunstan's Coll Catford, tstee All Hallows by the Tower; Freeman City of London; *Recreations* eating, swimming, enjoying life; *Style—* Christopher Biggins, Esq; IMG, The Pier House, Strand on the Green, Chiswick W4 3NN (☎ 081 994 1444)

BIGGLESTONE, John George; s of John Bigglestone, and Lillian Bigglestone (d 1978); *b* 10 Aug 1934; *Educ* Bablake Sch, Coventry; *m* 22 Dec 1984, Annette Vivian, da of Kenneth Bull, of Devizes; *Career* professional photographer, journalist, broadcaster and lectr 1951-; photographic clients incl many leading indust cos; sr lectr in photography Salisbury Coll of Art 1966-; nat examiner photographic courses City & Guilds of London Inst, memb Photographic Educn Gp, educn corr The Photographer; presenter of seminars to professional photographers; ABIPP, ARPS, memb IOJ; *Recreations* learning; *Style—* John Bigglestone, Esq; The Gables, Potterne Park, Devizes (☎ 0380 72 5709); Salisbury College of Art, Southampton Rd, Salisbury (☎ 0722 23711)

BIGGS, Bryan George; s of George William Biggs, of Barnet, Herts, and Barbara Anne, *née* Bonner; *b* 13 Oct 1952; *Educ* Queen Elizabeth's GS for Boys Barnet, Barnet Coll of Art (fndn course), Liverpool Poly (BA); *m* 12 May 1979, Christine, da of John Edward Landells; 2 s (Michael William b 22 May 1982, Jonathan Richard b 7 July 1988), 1 da (Laura Frances b 1 May 1985); *Career* admin asst Bluecoat Soc of Arts 1975-76, dir Bluecoat Gallery 1976-; organiser of over 175 exhibitions at Bluecoat and other venues in UK and abroad incl: Duncan Grant- Designer 1980, Cover Versions 1981, Derek Boshier-Drawings 1983, Paper Trails 1984, Liverpool/Cologne exchange programme 1987-; author of numerous articles and reviews for art press; catalogue essays incl: Ray Walker Murals (Bluecoat) 1987, New North (Tate Gallery Liverpool) 1990; memb: Performance Art Advsy Panel Arts Cncl of GB 1986-87, Bd Merseyside Moviola 1990-; *Recreations* drawing, record collecting; *Style—* Bryan Biggs, Esq; 5 Elmbank Rd, Mossley Hill, Liverpool L18 1HR (☎ 051 733 8546); Bluecoat Gallery, School Lane, Liverpool L1 3BX (☎ 051 709 5689)

BIGGS, Lewis; s of Ian Biggs, of Culachy, Fort Augustus, Inverness-shire, and Penelope, *née* Torr; *b* 22 April 1952; *Educ* Wellington, New Coll Oxford (BA, scholar), Courtauld Inst Univ of London (MA); *m* 1983, Ann, da of Michael Compton; 1 s (Nicholas b 1989), 1 da (Alison b 1987); *Career* gallery co-ordinator Arnolfini Bristol 1979-84, exhibition offr Fine Art Dept Br Cncl 1984-87, curator of exhibitions Tate Gallery Liverpool 1987-90 (curator 1990-); memb ICOM 1983-; *Style—* Lewis Biggs, Esq; Tate Gallery Liverpool, Albert Dock, Liverpool L3 4BB (☎ 051 709 3223, fax 051 709 3122)

BIGGS, Brig Michael Worthington; CBE (1962, OBE 1944); s of Lt Col Charles William Biggs, OBE (d 1965), of Montpellier Grove, Cheltenham, Glos, and Winifred Jesse Bell, *née* Dickinson (d 1932); *Educ* Cheltenham, RMA Woolwich, Pembroke Coll Cambridge (MA); *m* 1940, Katharine Mary, da of Sir Walter Harragin, CMG, KC (d 1966); 2 da (Patricia, Hilary); *Career* mil serv RE (cmmnd 1931) and King's African Rifles, incl active serv in Palestine, Abyssinia (BM) and Burma (GSO1 & CRE) E Africa Cmd 1960-63, dir of Quartering (Army) 1963-66; gp bldg exec Forte's Holdings 1966-67; mangr Welwyn Garden City and Hatfield Cmmn for the New Towns 1967-78, pres KAR & EAF Offrs Dinner Club 1972, chm Herts Bldg Preservation Tst 1978-86, memb Cncl Town & Country Planning Assoc 1978-84, memb Exec Ctee Herts Soc 1978; Freeman City of London 1985; CEng, MICE; *Recreations* tennis, golf; *Clubs* Army & Navy; *Style—* Brig Michael Biggs, CBE; Strawyards, Kimpton, Hitchin, Herts SG4 8PT (☎ 0438 832498)

BIGGS, Neil William; s of Sir Lionel Biggs (d 1985), of 151 Richmond Park Rd, Bournemouth, and Doris Rose, *née* Davies; *b* 29 March 1939; *Educ* Shrewsbury; *m* 1 Sept 1969, Shirley Evelyn, da of Albert Harfield Simpson (d 1957); *Career* slr; ptnr: Withington Petty & Co (Manchester) 1962-73, Masons (London) 1973-; NP; involved in CAB and numerous artistic socs; memb Law Soc; *Recreations* swimming, theatre, literature; *Clubs* RAC; *Style—* Neil Biggs, Esq; 40 South Hill Park, London NW3 2SJ; 30 Aylesbury St, London EC1R 0ER (☎ 071 490 4000, fax 071 490 2545, telex 8811117)

BIGGS, Norman Linstead; s of Joseph John Biggs (d 1965), and Dorothy Linstead (d 1982); *b* 2 Jan 1941; *Educ* Selwyn Coll Cambridge (BA, MA), Univ of London (DSc); *m* 1, 1968 (m dis 1975), Rita Elizabeth, *née* Kelly; m 2, 20 March 1976, Christine Mary, da of Eric Richard Farmer, of Bromley, Kent; 1 da (Juliet b 1980); *Career* lectr Univ of Southampton 1963-70, reader in pure mathematics Royal Holloway Coll Univ of London 1976-88 (lectr 1970-76), prof of mathematics LSE 1988-; memb Ctee London Mathematical Soc 1985-89 (chm Computer Sci Ctee 1985-89, memb Cncl 1979-85); memb Br Numismatic Soc; *Books* Finite Groups of Automorphisms (1971), Algebraic Graph Theory (1974), Graph Theory 1736-1936 (jtly 1976), Interaction Models (1977), Permutation Groups and Combinatorial Structures (jtly 1979), Discrete Mathematics (2 edn 1989), Introduction to Computing With Pascal (1989); *Recreations* metrology and numismatics; *Style—* Prof Norman Biggs; LSE, Houghton St, London WC2A 2AE (☎ 071 955 7640, fax 071 242 0392, telex 24655 BLPES G)

BIGGS, Sir Norman Parris; s of John Gordon Biggs, and Mary Sharpe Dickson; *b* 23 Dec 1907; *Educ* John Watson's Sch Edinburgh; *m* 1936, Peggy Helena Stammwitz (d 1990); 2 s (Nigel, Alastair), 1 da (Lindsay); *Career* Bank of England 1927-46; dir: Kleinwort, Sons & Co 1946-52, ESSO Petroleum 1952-66 (chm 1968-72), Gillet Bros Discount 1963-71; chm: Williams & Glyn Bank 1972-76, United Int Bank 1970-79; dep chm Privatbanken Ltd 1980-83, dir Banco de Bilbao 1981-87; memb Bullock Ctee Industl Democracy 1976; kt 1977; *Style—* Sir Norman Biggs; Northbrooks, Danworth Lane, Hurstpierpoint, Sussex (☎ 0273 832022)

BIGGS, Prof Peter Martin; CBE (1987); s of (George) Ronald Biggs (d 1985), and Cécile Agnes, *née* Player (d 1981); *b* 13 Aug 1926; *Educ* Bedales Sch, Cambridge Sch Mass USA, RVC (BSc), Univ of Bristol (PhD), Univ of London (DSc); *m* 9 Sept 1950, Alison Janet, da of late Malcolm Christian Molteno; 2 s (Andrew b 20 May 1957, John b 15 Nov 1963), 1 da (Alison (Mrs Stanley) b 28 May 1955); *Career* RAF: univ short course Queens Univ 1944-45, air crew undertraining, remustered Corp, demobbed 1948; lectr in veterinary clinical pathology Univ of Bristol 1955-59 (res 1953-55); Houghton Poultry Res Station: head Leukosis Experimental Unit 1959-7, dep dir 1971-73, dir 1974-86; visiting prof RVC Univ of London 1982-, dir AFRC Inst for Animal Health 1986-88, Andrew D White prof-at-large Cornell Univ USA 1988-, chm Scientific Advsy Ctee Animal Health Tst; memb: Vet Prods Ctee, Meds Cmmn 1973-, Advsy Ctee on Dangerous Pathogens 1988-; Hon DVM Maximillian Univ Munich Germany, Hon DUniv of Liege Belgium, Wolf Fndn Prize in Agric 1989; FRCVS, FRCPath, FIBiol, CBiol, FRS; *Recreations* music, boating, photography; *Clubs* Farmers; *Style—* Prof Peter Biggs, CBE, FRS; Willows, London Rd, St Ives, Huntingdon, Cambs PE17 4ES (☎ 0480 63471)

BIGGS, Prof William Derrick; OBE (1987); s of William Chaplin Biggs (d 1960), and Frances Anne, *née* Rendell (d 1954); *b* 7 July 1923; *Educ* Nether Edge GS Sheffield, Univ of Sheffield (AMet), Univ of London (BSc), Univ of Birmingham (PhD); *m* 28 Sept 1946, Doreen (d 1984), da of Francis Woollen (d 1967), of Sheffield; 1 s (Andrew), 1 da (Jennifer); *Career* metallurgist and res mangr Murex Welding Processes 1947-58, lectr Univ of Cambridge and fell and tutor Christ's Coll Cambridge 1958-73, prof of building technol Univ of Reading 1973-88, conslt engr 1988-; sch govr, govr Farnborough Tech Coll; FInst Structural Engrs, FCIOB, CEng, hon ARICS; *Books* Brittle Fracture of Steel (1960), Mechanical Behaviour of Engineering Materials (1966), Mechanical Design in Organisms (1976); *Recreations* work, reading, listening to music; *Style—* Prof William Biggs; Beaufort House, Spring Lane, Aston Tirrold, Didcot, Oxon

BIGHAM, (Derek) Alastair; s of Capt Robert Alexander Bigham (d 1968), and Dorothy May, *née* Bowyer (d 1963); *b* 7 March 1926; *Educ* Whitgift Sch, Trinity Hall Cambridge, Univ Coll Oxford (MA); *m* 1, 22 Aug 1952 (m dis 1983), June Diana, da of Lt Col John Grenville Fortescue (d 1964), of Stowford Grange, Lewdown, N Devon; 2 da (Diana Susan (Mrs W Grundy) b 1954, Julia Rosemary b 1959); m 2, 3 April 1984, Mary Elizabeth, *née* Gregory; *Career* war serv RM subsequently Lt Seaforth Highlanders 1944-48; barr 1952, legal advsr/pa to Lloyds Brokers, pa to sec RIBA, chartered land agent (estate mgmnt) and chartered surveyor (Planning and Devpt Div) partnership in practice Bath 1959-69, specialised bar practice environmental and real property Middle Temple 1969-82; chm: Rent Assessment Panel 1971-82, Industrial Tribunals (full-time) 1982-, UK Ministerial Delegation at Conf on the Environment Bern 1976, Ctee of Agric Law Assoc (UK) 1978-82; conslt to: Euro Cmmn 1979-, Cmmn Permanente Droit et Technique of Int Union of Advocates 1979-; memb Cmmn on Enviromental Policy Law and Admin of Int Union for Conservation of Nature and Natural Resources (IUCN) 1980-; memb International Council of Environmental Law 1984-, visiting Fell Sheffield Univ 1986; memb Windsor Borough Cncl 1954-58, Som CC 1967-77 (chm Co Planning Ctee 1969-70), short listed for four Party seats (C) prior to 1969; FCIArb 1965, FRICS 1972, MI Env Sc 1974, FRSA 1980; *Books* The Law and Administration Relating to Protection of the Environment (1973), The Impact of Marine Pollution (with others, 1980); *Recreations* natural history, history, visual arts, fly fishing, shooting; *Style—* Alastair Bigham, Esq; 1 Simon Ct, Graham Rd, Ranmoor, Sheffield S10 3GR, South Yorkshire (☎ 0742 307392); Office of the Industrial Tribunals, 14 East Parade, Sheffield S1 2ET (☎ 0742 760348)

BIGHAM, Hon Andrew Charles; yst s of 3 Viscount Mersey and Lady Nairne (12 holder of that title), *qqv*; *b* 26 June 1941; *Educ* Eton, Worcester Coll Oxford; *Career* short serv cmmn Ir Gds 1964-66; asst master (and sr French master) Aysgarth Sch Bedale N Yorks 1968-89; asst master Sunningdale Sch 1989-; *Style—* The Hon Andrew Bigham; Bignor Park, Pulborough, Sussex (☎ 079 87 214)

BIGHAM, Hon David Edward Hugh; s of 3 Viscount Mersey and Lady Nairne; *b* 14 April 1938; *Educ* Eton; *m* 2 Jan 1965, Anthea Rosemary, da of Leo Seymour, of Easterknowe Farm, Stobo, Peebles, Border District; 3 s (Charles Richard Petty b 21 April 1967, Patrick David Hugh b 21 Aug 1969, James Edward Conway b 12 March 1973), 1 da (Lucinda Emma b 5 Nov 1965); *Clubs* Buck's; *Style—* The Hon David Bigham; Hurston Place, Pulborough, West Sussex RH20 2EW (☎ 0903 74 2428)

BIGHAM, Hon Edward John Hallam; s and h of 4 Viscount Mersey; *b* 23 May 1966; *Educ* Eton, Balliol Coll Oxford; *Career* professional musician; *Style—* The Hon Edward Bigham; 1 Rosmead Rd, London W11 2JG

BIGHAM, Hon (Ralph) John; s of 2 Viscount Mersey, PC (d 1956); *b* 3 Aug 1913; *Educ* Eton; *m* 1954, Cicely Ruth (d 1986), yst da of Percy Johnson, of Douglas, IOM; *Career* OStJ; *Style—* The Hon John Bigham

BIGSBY, Prof Christopher William Edgar; s of Maj Edgar Edward Leo Bigsby (d 1968), and Ivy May, *née* Hopkins; *b* 27 June 1941; *Educ* Sutton GS, Univ of Sheffield (BA, MA), Univ of Nottingham (PhD); *m* 9 Oct 1965, Pamela Joan, da of Stephen Joseph Lovelady; 2 s (Gareth Christopher b 1968, Ewan James b 1976), 2 da (Kirsten Rebecca b 1972, Bella Juliet Natasha b 1974); *Career* prof of American Studies UEA; writer and broadcaster; TV with Malcolm Bradbury: The After Dinner Game 1975, Stones 1976; radio: Patterson (with Malcolm Bradbury) 1983, Fictions 1984, Long Day's Journey 1988; *Books* Confrontation and Commitment 1967, Albee 1969, Three Negro Plays (1969), The Black American Writer: 2 vols (1971), Dada and Surrealism (1972), Edward Albee (1975), Superculture (1975), Approaches to Popular Culture (1976), Tom Stoppard (1980), The Second Black Renaissance (1980), Contemporary English Drama (1981), A Critical Introduction to 20th Century American Drama: 3 vols (1982), Joe Orton (1982), The Radical Imagination and the Liberal Tradition (1982), David Mamet (1985), Cultural Change in the United States since World War II (1986), Plays by Susan Glaspell (1987), File on Miller (1987), Arthur Miller and Company (1990); *Recreations* so far undiscovered; *Style—* Prof Christopher Bigsby; 3 Church Farm, Colney, Norwich NR4 7TX, (☎ 0603 56048); School of English and American Studies, University of East Anglia, Norwich NR4 7TJ (☎ 0603 57171)

BILBY, David; s of Walter Bilby (d 1983), and Violet Florence, *née* Trinder; *b* 19 Jan 1943; *Educ* Archbishop Temple Sch; *m* 25 Sept 1965, Ann Kathleen, da of Harold Poulter (d 1983); 2 s (Jonathan b 1971, Andrew b 1980), 1 da (Laura b 1969); *Career* sales/showroom dir Garrard Crown Jewellers 1985-88, formed David Bilby & Ptnrs Ltd 1988, chm and md Bilby & Holloway (Fine Jewels Silver & Objets D'Art) 1988-; FGA 1963; *Style—* David Bilby, Esq; 13A Grafton St, Mayfair, London W1X 3LA (☎ 071 495 4636, fax 071 495 5946)

BILES, Michael James; s of Walter James Biles, of Little Chalfont, Bucks, and Olive Irene, *née* Dawson; *b* 23 June 1946; *Educ* St Nicholas GS Northwood, Univ of Nottingham (BA); *m* 18 Sept 1971, Angela Rosemary, da of Geoffrey Walter Griffin (d 1979), of Newport Pagnell, Bucks; 1 s (Alexander James Walter b 10 June 1981), 1 da (Louise Elizabeth b 21 Feb 1979); *Career* qualified CA 1970, chm Exec Ctee Robson Rhodes 1987- (ptnr 1977); treas Hornsey Housing Trust Ltd 1982-89; FCA 1970; *Recreations* Devon, all sports, surfing, walking, family; *Style—* Michael Biles, Esq; Robson Rhodes, 186 City Rd, London EC1V 2NU (☎ 071 251 1644, fax 071 250 0801)

BILLETER, Alex (Pierre); s of Maurice Billeter, of Switzerland, and Beate, *née* Oesterle (d 1985); *b* 10 April 1944; *Educ* Gymnase Cantonal de Neuchatel, Swiss Inst of Technol (ETH) Zurich Switzerland (Dip Arch); *Career* ptnr: Billeter & Thompson chartered architects, Dupuis and Billeter architects SIA Geneva; pt/t teacher in architecture N London Poly, works in UK, Switzerland and Africa; memb RIBA, SIA; *Recreations* friends, saxophone, music, books, travels (Africa); *Style—* Alex Billeter, Esq; Billeter & Thompson, 39 Marylebone High St, London W1M 3AB (☎ 071 486 7434)

BILLETT, Cncllr John Anthony; s of Ernest Edward Billett (d 1981), of Middlesex, and Angelina Christina Billett, *née* Martinelli; *b* 22 June 1945; *Educ* Ealing County GS, Dartmouth Royal Naval Coll; *m* 3 July 1971, Carole Elizabeth, da of Harold Edward Jarvis; 1 s (Christian b 1976), 1 da (Elizabeth b 1986); *Career* RN pilot 1962-71; insur broker princ 1971-72, American International Group 1972-81 (UK production mangr, dep regnl dir E Africa, dep regnl dir ME, gen mangr Netherlands, dir of Ops Caribbean); vice pres The Continental Corporation (regnl dir Euro, ME) 1981-85, chm Continental Hellas; dir: Continental Life, Continental Pensions; dir and conslt Tillinghast Nelson and Warren Ltd 1985-87; chm and chief exec Barkers Finance Services Ltd; *Recreations* squash, shooting, sailing, golf; *Clubs* Chiltern Squash, Glyfada Golf; *Style—* Cncllr John A Billett; Barkers Farmhouse, Little Chalfont, Buckingham HP7 9JY (☎ 049476 2026); Barkers Financial Services Ltd, 13 Station Approach, Northwood, Middlesex HA6 2XN

BILLINGHAM, Hon Mrs (Brenda Dolores Bowden); da of Baron Aylestone, CBE, PC (Life Peer); *b* 17 Feb 1929; *m* 1951, John Leonard Billingham; 1 s, 1 da; *Style—* The Hon Mrs Billingham; 67 Kingsmead Av, Worcester Park, Surrey

BILLINGTON, Guy; s of Reginald Arthur Billington (d 1960), of 1 Arterberry Rd, London, and Constance May, *née* Riches; *b* 12 Nov 1946; *Educ* King's Coll Sch Wimbledon, St John's Coll Cambridge (MA); *m* 5 July 1966, Christine Ellen, da of Rev Frederick Charles Bonner, of 4 Ham View, Upton upon Severn, Worcs; 2 da (Nicole b 13 Dec 1966, Suzanne b 21 Jan 1971); *Career* articled clerk Lovell White and King 1969-72, ptnr McKenna and Co 1972- (asst slr); memb City of London Slr's Co; memb Law Soc; *Recreations* rugby, music, scuba diving; *Clubs* Rosslyn Park Football, BSAC; *Style—* Guy Billington, Esq; 16 Belvedere Grove, London SW19 7RL (☎ 081 946 4889); McKenna and Co, Mitre House, 160 Aldersgate St, London EC1A 4DD (☎ 071 606 9000, fax 071 606 9100, telex 27251 CDE Box 724)

BILLINGTON, (Edward) John; RD, DL; s of Edward Billington, and Nesta, *née* Boxwell; *b* 21 Dec 1934; *Educ* Uppingham; *m* 5 Dec 1964, Fenella, da of Dr Hamilton-Turner; 2 s (Edward b 1966, Richard b 1970), 1 da (Suzetta b 1968); *Career* RNR 1953-86; commodity broker; chm Edward Billington & Son Ltd; DL, High Sheriff (Mersyside 1990-91); memb NW Bd DTI, dep treas Univ of Liverpool, tstee Nat Museums and Galleries on Merseyside; CBIM; *Style—* John Billington Esq, RD, DL; Cunard Building, Liverpool L3 1EL

BILLINGTON, Lady Rachel Mary; *née* Pakenham; da of 7 Earl of Longford, KG, PC, and sis of Lady Antonia Pinter (*see* Lady Antonia Fraser); *b* 11 May 1942; *Educ* Univ of London; *m* 1967, Kevin Billington (b 12 June 1934, film, theatre and tv dir), s of Richard Billington, of Warrington, Lancs; 2 s, 2 da; *Career* author; *Books* A Women's Age, Occasion of Sin, Theo and Matilda; *Style—* Lady Rachel Billington; 30 Addison Ave, London W11 4QR; The Court House, Poyntington, nr Sherborne, Dorset

BINDER, Alan Naismith; OBE (1974); s of Frederick John Binder (d 1961), of Hampshire, and Kathleen Mary, *née* Darker (d 1967); *b* 4 Aug 1931; *Educ* Bedford Sch, Magdalen Coll Oxford (MA); *m* 1958, Gillian Patricia, da of George Francis Wilson, of Sussex; 1 s (Jonathan b 1962), 2 da (Jennifer b 1958, Stephanie b 1959); *Career* dir Shell International Petroleum Co Ltd 1984, pres Shell International Trading Co 1987; *Recreations* tennis, skiing, reading, music; *Clubs* Carlton, Leander, MCC; *Style—* Alan Binder, Esq, OBE; Old Place, Speldhurst, Kent TN3 0PA (☎ 089 286 3227); Shell Centre, London SE1 7NA (☎ 071 934 5878)

BINDMAN, Geoffrey Lionel; s of Dr Gerald Bindman (d 1974); *b* 3 Jan 1933; *Educ* Royal GS Newcastle-upon-Tyne, Oriel Coll Oxford; *m* 1961, Lynn Janice; 3 children; *Career* slr; Bindman & Partners London NW1; chm Legal Action Gp 1976-78, legal advsr Cmmn for Racial Equality 1977-83, hon visiting prof of law UCL 1990-, cncllr London Borough of Camden 1971-74 (dep ldr 1973-74); *Recreations* book collecting, music, walking; *Clubs* Law Society; *Style—* Geoffrey Bindman Esq; 1 Euston Rd, London NW1 2SA (☎ 071 278 8131)

BING, Hon Mrs (Christian Keith); da of 15 Viscount of Arbuthnott, CB, CBE, DSO, MC (d 1966); *b* 1 Oct 1933; *Educ* Univ of Edinburgh; *m* 1954, Cdr Peter John Bing, OBE, RN, s of William Leslie Bing, of High Hedges, Crowborough, Sussex; 3 s, 1 da; *Style—* The Hon Mrs Bing; The Cottage, Hillside, Montrose, Angus

BING, Peter John; OBE (1974); s of William Leslie Bing, of High Hedges, Crowborough, Sussex; *b* 30 Aug 1925; *Educ* Felsted, RNC Dartmouth, RNEC Plymouth; *m* 1954, Hon Christian Keith, da of 15 Viscount of Arbuthnott, CB, CBE, DSO, MC; 3 s, 1 da; *Career* midshipman HMS Berwick 1945, Lt Cdr 806 Seahawk Sqdn, HMS Centaur 1955, cdr DAEO HMS Hermes 1963-64, Jt Servs Staff Coll 1964, dir RN Air Engrg Sch 1968-71 (ret 1974); mangr first Offshore Trg Centre for the Oil Indust 1975-82, bd sec OPITB Montrose 1983-90, mgmnt conslt 1990-; dir Montrose C of C, memb Cncl Humberside Offshore Trg Assoc Hull 1986-90; CEng, FIMechE, FCIS, FBIM, FInstPet; *Recreations* restoring houses, hockey (Devon & RN), cricket (RN); *Clubs* Army and Navy; *Style—* Peter Bing, Esq, OBE; The Cottage, Hillside, Montrose, Angus (☎ 0674 83 267)

BING, Robert Fill; s of Alec George Bing, of 23 Harcourt Drive, Canterbury, Kent, and Kate Isobel, *née* Theobald; *b* 9 Feb 1945; *Educ* Simon Langton GS, Canterbury, Univ of Sheffield (MB ChB); *m* 11 Oct 1969, Ann, da of Philip Walter Grunsell (d 1987); 2 s (Andrew b 1971, Simon b 1977), 1 da (Emma-Jane b 1974); *Career* res registrar in hypertension United Sheffield Hosps 1972-74 (med training rotation 1969-72), clinical res fell MRC Univ of Sussex 1974-76, currently sr lectr in med Univ of Leicester (lectr 1976-81) and hon conslt physician Leics Health Authy; memb Exec Ctee Br Hypertension Soc, govr Alderman Newtons Sch Leicester, memb Assoc of Physicians of GB and Ireland 1984; FRCP 1984 (memb 1971); *Style—* Robert Bing, Esq; Department of Medicine, University of Leicester, Leicester

BINGHAM, Charlotte; *see*: Brady, Hon Mrs (C M T)

BINGHAM, Lord; George Charles Bingham; s and h of 7 Earl of Lucan; *b* 21 Sept 1967; *Style—* Lord Bingham

BINGHAM, Hon Hugh; s of 6 Earl of Lucan, MC (d 1964); *b* 24 April 1939; *Educ* Charterhouse, Hertford Coll Oxford; *Style—* The Hon Hugh Bingham; 6 Gledhow Gardens, London SW5 (☎ 071 373 4489)

BINGHAM, Dr James Stewart; TD (1982); s of Dr William Bingham, of Blue Hayes, Craigavad, Co Down, N Ireland, and Norah Mary, *née* Beckett; *b* 31 July 1945; *Educ* Campbell Coll Belfast, Queen's Univ Belfast (MB BCh, BAO, DObstRCOG, FRCOG); *m* 21 Sept 1974, Elizabeth Eleanor, da of Charles Arnold Stewart; 1 s (Stewart Mark b 20 Jan 1983); *Career* Univ Offrs Trg Corp 1963-69, 253 (NI) Field Ambulance and 217 (L) Gen Hosp RAMC 1969-83, resigned as Lt Col, currently Maj RARO; house physician and surgn The Royal Victoria Hosp Belfast 1969-70; sr house offr: in obstetrics Royal Maternity Hosp Belfast 1970-71, in gynaecology Belfast City Hosp 1971-72, in gynaecology Musgrove Park Hospital Belfast Feb-July 1972; sr house offr in gen surgy Harare Hosp Salisbury Rhodesia Aug-Dec 1973 (registrar in obstetrics and gynaecology 1972-73); sr registrar in obstetrics and gynaecology: Waveney Hosp Ballymena NI Feb-July 1974, Harare Hosp 1974-75; sr resident in obstetrics & gynaecology Vancouver Gen Hosp Canada Feb-July 1975; The Middlesex Hosp London: sr registrar in genitourinary med 1975-77, conslt 1977-, dir of serv 1983-; hon treas Med Soc for Study of Venereal Disease 1986- (memb Cncl 1979-82 and 1983-86); memb: Bd of Examiners for Dip in Genitourinary Med Soc of Apothecaries of London 1982, Working Party on Med Audit in Genitourinary Med RCP, Genitourinary Sub Ctee CCSC BMA 1986- (rep of Sub Ctee on CCSC 1989); rep RCOG on Specialist Advsy Ctee in Genitourinary Med RCP 1988 (and sec 1990-), rep of Middx and Univ Coll Hosp on Univ Hosp Assoc 1989-90, organiser course on sexually transmitted diseases and HIV infection for GPs Middx Hosp 1988, memb Editorial Bd International Journal of STD and AIDS 1990-; FRCOG 1989; memb: BMA, RSM, Med Soc for the Study of Venereal Disease, Soc for the Study of Sexually Transmitted Diseases in Ireland, Int Union Against the Venereal Disease and Treponematoses, Br Soc for Colposcopy and Cervical Pathology; *Books* Sexually Transmitted Diseases (1984, edn 1990); *Recreations* British military history with particular emphasis on the Anglo-Irish contribution, reading military and political biographies, gardening; *Style—* Dr James Bingham, TD; James Pringle House, The Middlesex Hospital, London W1N 8AA (☎ 071 436 2377, 071 380 9152)

BINGHAM, Hon John Edward; TD; s of 5 Earl of Lucan, GCVO, KBE, CB, TD, PC (d 1949); *b* 29 Feb 1904; *Educ* Eton, Trinity Coll Cambridge (MA); *m* 1942, Dorothea, da of late Rev John Kyrle Chatfield; 3 s (Nicholas Charles b 1943, Peter John b 1945, David Julian b 1951); *Career* late Derbyshire Yeo and 2 SAS Regt; 1939-45 War in N Africa; *Clubs* Pratt's, ESU; *Style—* The Hon John Bingham; Nicholls, Udimore, Rye, East Sussex (☎ 0797 223120)

BINGHAM, John Temple; o s of Rear Adm the Hon Barry Stewart Bingham, VC, OBE (d 1939), and Vera Maud Temple, *née* Patterson; kinsman and hp of 8 Baron Clanmorris, *qv*; *b* 22 Feb 1923; *m* 28 April 1949, Joan Muriel Bown (d 1955); *Style—* John Bingham, Esq; Flat 1, 48 Holland Road, London W14 8BB

BINGHAM, Prof Nicholas Hugh; s of Robert Llewelyn Bingham (d 1972), of Dolgellau, and Blanche Louise, *née* Corbitt; *b* 19 March 1945; *Educ* Tadcaster GS, Trinity Coll Oxford (MA), Churchill Coll Cambridge (PhD); *m* 13 Sept 1980, Cecilie Ann, da of Ralph William Gabriel (d 1973), of Leigh-on-Sea; 1 s (James b 1982), 1 da (Ruth b 1985); *Career* prof of mathematics Royal Holloway and Bedford New Coll Univ of London 1985- (lectr then reader Westfield Coll 1969-84, reader 1984-85); ed book reviews 1981-90; memb London Mathematical Soc, Inst of Mathematical Statistics; RSS; *Books* Regular Variation 1987; *Recreations* chess, running, gardening, swimming; *Style—* Prof Nicholas Bingham; 13 Woodside Grange Rd, London N12 8SJ (☎ 081 445 5779); Mathematics Dept, Royal Holloway and Bedford New College, University of London, Egham Hill, Egham, Surrey TW20 0EX (☎ 0784 443115)

BINGHAM, Stephen Denis; OBE; s of Cdr Francis Bingham, RN (d 1986); *b* 28 June 1934; *Educ* Ampleforth, St Catharine's Coll Cambridge (BA); *m* 1962, Elizabeth, da of Cdr G Paine, RN (d 1980); 3 s (Benedict, Thomas, Patrick), 2 da (Emma, Catherine); *Career* Lt Irish Gds; md Sodastream Ltd 1974-78; gp md Servotomic Ltd 1986-88, memb Bd Peterborough Devpt Corpn, nat dir Plan International UK; *Recreations* sailing, indifferent golf, painting; *Style—* Stephen Bingham, Esq, OBE; Geeston, Ketton, Stamford, Lincs (☎ 0780 720135)

BINGHAM, Rt Hon Lord Justice; Rt Hon Sir Thomas Henry Bingham; PC (1986); s of Dr Thomas Henry Bingham, of Reigate, Surrey, and Catherine, *née* Watterson; *b* 13 Oct 1933; *Educ* Sedbergh, Balliol Coll Oxford; *m* 1963, Elizabeth, o da of Peter Loxley (d 1945); 2 s, 1 da; *Career* called to the Bar 1959, jr counsel Dept of Employment 1968-72, QC 1972, ldr Investigation into Supply of Petroleum and Petroleum Prods to Rhodesia 1977-78, High Ct judge (Queen's Bench Div) 1980-86, Lord Justice of Appeal 1986-; kt 1980; *Style—* The Rt Hon Lord Justice Bingham; Royal Courts of Justice, Strand, London WC2

BINGLEY, Clive Hamilton; s of Alexander Hamilton Bingley (d 1985), and Stella, *née* Hanscomb (d 1981); *b* 2 April 1936; *Educ* Highgate Sch, St Johns Coll Johannesburg, Univ of Oxford (MA); *m* 16 March 1963, Anne Edith, da of Basil Henry Chichester-Constable (d 1968); 3 da (Miranda b 1964, Kate b 1966, Zillah b 1968); *Career* ed New Library World 1970-77; dir numerous publishing cos incl: Book Publishing Development plc, The Athlone Press Ltd, Library Association Publishing Ltd, Lund Humphries Publishers Ltd; hon treas The Nat Book League 1980-84, hon fell The Library Assoc 1986, co fndr The London Book Fair; *Books* Book Publishing Practice (1966), The Business of Book Publishing (1970); *Recreations* switching off; *Clubs* Savile; *Style—* Clive Bingley, Esq; 16 Pembridge Rd, London W11 3HL (☎ 071 229 1825)

BINGLEY, Lt-Col Robert Noel Charles; s of Col Robert Albert Glanville Bingley, DSO, OBE, MVO (d 1977), of Higher Eggbeer, Exeter, Devon, and Sybil Gladys Williamson, *née* Duff; *b* 28 Dec 1936; *Educ* Abberley Hall Malvern Worcs, Charterhouse; *m* 23 Nov 1962, Elizabeth Anne, da of Col Thomas Charles Stanley Haywood, OBE, JP, DL, of Gunthorpe, Oakham, Rutland; 2 s (Piers b 1967, Alexander b 1971), 1 da (Claire b 1963); *Career* Troop Ldr 11 Hussars (PAO) 1957, Staff Capt HQ 17 Div Malaya Dist 1965, Staff Coll Pakistan 1969, GSO 2 MOD 1970, 2 i/c Royal Hussars 1972, NDC 1974, instr Australia Army Staff Coll 1976, CO Royal Yeo 1977; antique dealer 1978-; memb Cancer Relief MacMillan Fund; *Recreations* shooting, fishing, waterskiing; *Clubs* Kingswater Ski; *Style—* Lt-Col Robert Bingley; Wing House, Oakham, Rutland (☎ 057 285 314); Coul Cottage, Scatwell, Marybank by Muir-of-Ord, Ross-shire; Robert Bingley Antiques, Church St, Wing, Oakham, Rutland, LE15 8RS (☎ 057 285 725)

BINKS, William Richard; s of William Henry Binks (d 1961), of London, and Ellen French, *née* Wintle (d 1943); *b* 29 Jan 1922; *Educ* Downshall Secdy Sch, Univ of London (LLB); *m* 21 May 1943, Kathleen Elsie, da of Frederick John Le May (d 1976), of Eastbourne; 1 s (Alan), 1 da (Karen); *Career* Flt Lt RAF 1942-46, Res 1946-52; admitted slr 1965, sr ptnr Binks Stern and Ptnrs 1982- (ptnr 1965-); memb Law Soc; *Recreations* sailing; *Clubs* RAF, Royal Ocean Racing, Royal Burnham Yacht; *Style—* William R Binks, Esq; 91 Manor Road, Chigwell, Essex IG7 5PN (☎ 081 500 8664); Queens House, 55/56 Lincoln's Inn Fields, London WC2A 3LT (☎ 071 404 4321, fax 071 405 5040, car 0836 202 519 295408)

BINNEY, Ivor Ronald; s of Ronald Frederick Binney (d 1979), and Ethel Alice, *née* Dredge (d 1990); *b* 11 Oct 1929; *Educ* Haberdashers' Aske's; *m* 1957, Susan Mary Campbell, da of Capt John Calendar Ritchie (d 1939); 1 s (Hugo), 3 da (Emma, Lucy, Sara); *Career* dir: CT Bowring & Co Ltd 1970-87 (dep chm), Terra Nova Insurance Co Ltd 1970-87, Marsh & McLennan Cos Inc 1980-87, A J Archer & Co Ltd 1987-; chm Syndicate Underwriting Management Ltd (formerly AUA4) 1987-, conslt Insurance and Reinsurance 1987-; Lloyds: ctee memb 1978-81 and 1984-87, cncl memb 1984-87; *Recreations* golf; *Clubs* MCC, Pilgrims; *Style—* Ivor Binney, Esq; Southease Place, Southease, nr Lewes, Sussex

BINNEY, Marcus Hugh Crofton; OBE (1983); s of late Lt Col Francis Crofton Simms, MC, and Sonia (d 1985), da of Rear Adm Sir William Marcus Charles Beresford-Whyte, KCB, CMG (she m 2, 1955, as his 2 wife, Sir George Binney, DSO, who d 1972); *b* 21 Sept 1944; *Educ* Eton, Magdalene Coll Cambridge (BA); *m* 1, 1966 (m dis 1976), Hon Sara Anne Vanneck (d 1979), da of 6 Baron Huntingfield; m 2 , 1981, Anne Carolyn, da of Dr T H Hills of Merstham, Surrey; 2 s (Francis Charles Thomas b 1982, Christopher Crofton b 1985); *Career* writer; ed Country Life 1984-86 (architectural writer 1968-77, architectural ed 1977-84); ed Landscape 1987-; sec UK Ctee Int Cncl on Monuments and Sites 1972-81, dir Railway Heritage Tst 1984-, pres SAVE Britain's Heritage 1984- (chm 1975-84); co-organiser: The Destruction of the Country House (exhibition V & A) 1974, Change and Decay: the Future of our Churches (V & A) 1977; *Books* Change and Decay: the future of our churches (with Peter Burman 1977), Chapels and Churches: who cares? (with Peter Burman 1977), Preservation Pays (with Max Hanna 1978), Railway Architecture (ed jtly 1979), Our

Past Before Us (ed jtly 1981), The Country House: to be or not to be (with Kit Martin, 1982), Preserve and Prosper (with Max Hanna 1983), Sir Robert Taylor (1984), Our Vanishing Heritage (1984); contrib: Satanic Mills (1979), Elysian Gardens (1979), Lost Houses of Scotland (1980), Taking the Plunge (1982), SAVE Gibraltar's Heritage 1982, Vanishing Houses of England (1983), Time Gentlemen Please (1983), Great Railway Stations of Europe (1984); *Style*— Marcus Binney, Esq, OBE; Domaine des Vaux, St Lawrence, Jersey, CI

BINNEY, (Harry Augustus) Roy; CB (1950); s of Harry Augustus Binney (d 1960), of Churston, Devon; *b* 18 May 1907; *Educ* Royal Dockyard Sch Devonport, Univ of London (BSc); *m* 1944, Barbara (d 1975), da of Jeffrey Poole (d 1952), of Harborne, Birmingham; 3 s, 1 da (and 1 da decd); *Career* undersec BOT 1947-50, dir-gen BSI 1950-72 (memb Cncl Int Standards Orgn Geneva 1951-72 (vice pres 1964-69), chm CEN (ctee for Euro Standards) 1963-65, UN advsr on standards Cyprus 1974-77; FKC, FRSA; *Recreations* gardening; *Style*— Roy Binney, Esq, CB; Hambutts Orchard, Edge Rd, Painswick, Glos (☎ 0452 813718)

BINNEY, Hon Mrs (Victoria Sarah Maria); *née* Lubbock; da of 4 Baron Avebury, *qv*, and his 1 w, Kina Maria, *née* O'Kelly de Gallagh; *b* 27 April 1959; *m* 1983, Alan Binney; 2 s (Archie b 1983, Alastair b 1985); *Career* ptnr in EDIT (Editorial Information Technology); dir Recruit Media Ltd; contested (Lib) Hackney Borough Cncl 1982; *Style*— The Hon Mrs Binney; 225 Evering Road, London E5 8AL

BINNIE, Dr Colin David; s of Horace David Binnie, of Leigh-on-Sea, Essex, and Doris Amy, *née* Read (d 1966); *Educ* Felstead, Univ of Cambridge (MD, MA, BCh), Guy's Hosp Med Sch; *m* 31 Oct 1964, (Florence) Margaret, da of George Shields (d 1980); 1 s (Jonathan Nicholas b 1968), 1 da (Caroline b 1965); *Career* physician i/c Dept of Clinical Neurophysiology Bart's and Southend Hosp 1972-76, head of clinical neurophysiology serv Inst Voor Epilepsie Bestrjding Heemstede Netherlands 1976-86, conslt clinical neurophysiologist Bethlem Royal Hosp and Maudsley Hosp 1986-; memb: Cncl EEC Soc, Int League Against Epilepsy, Electroencephalography and Clinical Neurophysiology Educnl Bd, Electrophysiological Tech Assoc; memb: RSM 1965, Assoc Br Clinical Neurophysiologists 1970, Br Assoc for Neurophsychiatry 1988; MRCS, LRCP; *Books* A Manual of Electroencephalographic Technology (1982), Biorhythms and Epilepsy (1986), numerous pubns on Electroencephalography and Epilepsy; *Recreations* opera, computing, languages; *Style*— Dr Colin Binnie; Dept of Clinical Neurophysiology, Maudsley Hosp, Denmark Hill, London SE5 8AZ (☎ 071 703 6333, fax 071 703 0179)

BINNIE, John; *b* 7 June 1935; *Educ* Falkirk HS, Univ of Glasgow (BSc); *m* 6 July 1960, Caroline Kerrison, *née* Muirhead; 2 s (John b 20 Sept 1962, David b 6 Dec 1964), 1 da (Kathryn b 4 Jan 1967); *Career* Esso Petroleum Co Ltd 1958-63, ICI and Nalfloc Ltd 1963-73, Allied Colloids Gp plc 1973-; pres Bradford C of C 1989-, dir 48 Gp (Br Traders with China); *Recreations* golf, gardening, bridge; *Style*— John Binnie, Esq; Allied Colloids Gp plc, P O Box 38, Low Moor, Bradford BD12 0JZ (☎ 0274 671267, fax 0274 606499, telex 51646)

BINNING, Kenneth George Henry; CMG (1976); s of Henry Binning (d 1976), of Wivenhoe, Essex, and Hilda, *née* Powell (d 1987); *b* 5 Jan 1928; *Educ* Bristol GS, Balliol Coll Oxford (MA); *m* 28 Feb 1953, Pamela Dorothy, da of Alfred Edward Pronger (d 1963), of Streatham, London; 3 s (Simon Kenneth b 1955, Julian Charles b 1957, Marcus Adam b 1963), 1 da (Susanna Clare b 1960); *Career* Nat Serv Capt RAEC 1950-52; HM Treasy 1952-59 (private sec to Fin Sec 1956), UK AEA 1959-65, seconded Miny of Technol 1965-67 and 1969, asst dir Progs Analysis Unit 1967-69, DG Concorde Prog (UK) 1973-76, cr Invest in Br Bureau 1976-80, govt dir BSC 1980-82, dir govt rels NEI plc 1983-; *Recreations* music, gardening; *Clubs* Reform; *Style*— Kenneth Binning, Esq, CMG; 12 Kemerton Road, Beckenham, Kent BR3 2NJ (☎ 081 650 0273); NEI plc, Tavistock House East, Woburn Walk, Burton St, London WC1 (☎ 071 387 9393)

BINNING, Lady Nora Kathleen; da of 10 Earl Annesley; *b* 27 March 1950; *m* 1969, John Binning; 2 s, 2 da; *Style*— Lady Nora Binning; 6 Baron's Way, Egham, Surrey

BINNINGTON, Bernard Thomas; s of Richard Binnington, (d 1963), of Jersey, and Florence Mary, *née* Quenault; *b* 23 Nov 1930; *Educ* Victoria Coll Jersey; *m* 28 Sept 1953, Elizabeth Rowley, da of James Davidson (d 1979), of Edinburgh; 1 s (Alan Richard), 1 da (Anne Elizabeth); *Career* exec dir: Chelsea Hotels Ltd 1955-, Pioneer Coaches Ltd 1965-; dir Samuel Montagu & Co (Jersey) Ltd 1979-87, chm Jersey Electricity Co Ltd 1982-88 (dir 1976-82), dir A Degruchy & Co Ltd 1987-; St Helier Jersey Parliament: dep 1969 and 1972, senator 1975, 1982 and 1987; pres: Jersey Hotel and Guest House Assoc 1966-68, States of Jersey Harbours and Airport Ctee 1981-; chm Jersey Tport Authy 1981-; MHCIMA 1974; *Recreations* sailing, music; *Style*— Bernard Binnington, Esq; La Rochelle, St Aubin, Jersey (☎ 0534 43303); Chelsea Hotel, St Helier, Jersey (☎ 0534 30241)

BINNS, Christopher; s of Herbert Chester Binns (d 1988), of Norwich, and Winifred Ann Binns; *b* 28 June 1941; *Educ* Birmingham Coll of Food & Domestic Art; *m* 5 July 1969, Brenda Margaret, da of Leslie Flowers; 2 s (Gregory Haston b 22 Oct 1970, Adam James b 16 Nov 1977), 1 da (Sarah Marie b 13 May 1972); *Career* Strand Hotels Ltd 1960-70: trainee mangr London hotels, devpt of provincial hotels in Birmingham 1963 and Nottingham 1969, latterly asst gen mangr Albany Hotel Nottingham; Property Partnerships (Hotels) Ltd: Mangr Hotel Nelson Norwich 1970-72, gen mangr Hotels Div 1972-75, md 1975-89 (also dir Property Partnership PLC); md Waveney Inns Group Diss Norfolk 1990-; chm: E Anglia Branch BHRCA 1974-75 and 1987-90, E Anglia Branch HCIMA 1974-75, Best Western E Anglia Region 1977-78; fndr chm: Norwich & Dist Hoteliers Assoc 1977-78, Norwich Tourist Assoc 1980-82: memb: Dist MSC 1977-79, Exec Ctee E Anglia Tourist Bd 1978-82; dir Norwich Area Tourism Agency 1982-90, govr Norwich City Coll 1988-91; Freeman City of London 1981; FHCIMA (HCIMA 1960), Master Inn Holder 1980 (vice chm 1989-90), CBIM 1988; *Recreations* wine, badminton, mountain climbing, conservation; *Style*— Christopher Binns, Esq

BINNS, Colin; s of Arthur Thomas Binns, of Charleston House, Blackpool, and Amy Evelyn Binns; *b* 20 April 1942; *Educ* Arnold Sch, Leeds Sch of Architecture (Dip Arch); *m* 25 Feb 1967, Pamela, da of Kenneth Crook, of Dugvesta De Espana, Torremolinos; 2 da (Joanna b 1969, Nina b 1971); *Career* architect and designer; main projects incl: Fort Regent Leisure and Conference Centre Jersey 1970, ICI Petrochemicals HQ Wilton 1976, housing assoc projects 1976-82, indust projects 1982-85, leisure projects 1985-90; RIBA design prize 1966, RIBA award 1976, BDA award 1976, Civic Tst Award 1979; chm: Design and Art Courses Advsy Panel Preston Coll, BDP Art Soc; former memb Ctee Lancs region CPRE; memb RIBA; *Recreations* sculpture, photography, sketching; *Clubs* Fylde Fencing; *Style*— Colin Binns, Esq; Building Design Partnership, Vernon St, Moor Lane, Preston (☎ 0772 59383, fax 0772 201378 telex 677160)

BINNS, David John; CBE (1989); s of Henry Norman Binns, OBE (d 1959), of Grimsby, and Ivy Mary, *née* Baker (d 1981); *b* 12 April 1929; *Educ* Rossall Sch, Univ of Sheffield (LLB); *m* 6 July 1957, Jean Margaret, da of Lt Cdr Frank Newton Evans, DSC (d 1968), of Hoylake; 1 s (Jonathan b 1964), 1 da (Caroline b 1959, d 1962); *Career* admitted slr 1954; Warrington Co Borough: asst slr 1954-55, chief asst slr 1955-58, dep town clerk 1958-69; gen mangr: Warrington Devpt Corp 1969-81, Warrington and Runcorn Devpt Corp 1981-89; memb Warrington Health Authy 1990-; former chm: Warrington Round Table, Stockton Heath Playmakers; *Recreations* gardening, walking, swimming, music; *Clubs* Warrington; *Style*— David Binns, Esq, CBE; 4 Cedarways, Appleton, Warrington, Cheshire WA4 5EW (☎ 0925 62169)

BINNS, Prof Kenneth John; s of Harold Gladstone Binns (d 1972), of 14 Mauldeth Rd, Withington, Manchester, and Helen Cecilia, *née* Moss (d 1975); *b* 4 Aug 1934; *Educ* Xaverian Coll Manchester, Univ of Manchester (BSc), Univ of Southampton (DSc); *m* 5 May 1962, Patricia Ann, da of James Patrick McGrath (d 1979); 2 da (Louise, Jane); *Career* reader Univ of Southampton 1972-83, prof of electrical engrg Univ of Liverpool 1983-; hon ed IEE Proceedings Part B; FIEE, FRSA; *Books* Analysis and Computation of Electric and Magnetic Field Problems (jtly, 1973), Vibration and Audible Noise in A.C. machines (jtly, 1986); *Recreations* gardening, badminton; *Style*— Prof Kenneth Binns; The University of Liverpool, Department of Electrical Engineering and Electronics, PO Box 147, Brownlow Hill, Liverpool L69 3BX (☎ 051 794 4500, fax 051 794 4540, telex 627095)

BINNS, Malcolm; s of Douglas Priestley Binns (d 1988), of Keighley, Yorkshire, and May, *née* Walker; *b* 29 Jan 1936; *Educ* Bradford GS, RCM; *Career* prof RCM 1961-65; concert pianist: London debut 1959, debut Promenade Concerts 1960, regular performances at Proms 1962-, Royal Festival Hall debut 1961, has appeared in London Philharmonic seasons 1962-; soloist with all major Br orchs, over 30 recordings, first complete recording of Beethoven Piano Sonatas on original instruments, played Far E and toured with Scot Nat Orch and Limbourg Orch 1987-88; ARCM; *Recreations* gardening; *Style*— Malcolm Binns, Esq; c/o Ibbs and Tillett, 18B Pindock Mews, London W9 2PY (☎ 071 2867526)

BINSTED, John Wadkin; s of George Percy Binsted, and May Emma, *née* Wadkin; *b* 6 Oct 1923; *Educ* Worthing HS; *m* 17 June 1950, Gloria Patricia, da of Albert Harry Bringes; 2 s (Andrew John Bringes b 8 March 1953, David Christopher b 11 Aug 1954), 2 da (Julia Gloria (Mrs Doig) b 3 Jan 1957, Elizabeth Angela b 20 Oct 1966); *Career* 1 Br Airborne Corps RCS 1943-45, served Arnhem 1944, Lt RCS MELF 1946-47 served Cairo, Alexandria, Ismailia, Capt RCS E Africa 1947-48 served Nairobi; CA; Arthur Stubbs and Spofforth 1948-51, audit mangr Ogden Hibberd Bull and Langton 1951-54, fin dir and sec BSA Motor Cycles Ltd Birmingham 1954-70, gp controller Br Utd Shoe Machinery Gp Leicester 1971-73, dir fin and admin Whittaker Ellis Ltd Staffs 1973-77, accountancy servs MOD 1977-87, ind fin intermediary J W Binsted Fin Servs Co; chm Civilian Ctee 194 ATC Sqdn 1960-, tstee Solihull Sch Parent's Assoc Careers Fund 1975-, dir Solihull Masonic Temple 1978-; former pres Solihull Sch Parents' Assoc 1970; FCA 1954, FIMBRA 1987; *Recreations* golf, tennis; *Clubs* Olton GC, Solihull Cricket and Tennis; *Style*— John Binsted, Esq; Brueton Hse, 34 Brueton Ave, Solihull, W Mids B91 3EN; Southwinds Ct, 26 West Parade, West Worthing, W Sussex (☎ 021 705 2581)

BINT, Dr Adrian John; s of Arthur Herbert Bint, of Birmingham, and Lily, *née* Naylor; *b* 3 April 1948; *Educ* Moseley GS Birmingham, Univ of Birmingham (MB ChB); *m* 12 June 1971, Marilyn Joyce, da of Charles Bourne Wathes, of Kingsbury nr Tamworth, Staffs; 1 s (Alastair Halford b 1974), 1 da (Nicola Sarah b 1975); *Career* conslt microbiologist Royal Victoria Infirmary Newcastle 1979-; meetings sec Br Soc for Antimicrobial Chemotherapy 1980-83; memb: Cncl Assoc of Clinical Pathologists 1983-86, Editorial Bd Jl of Clinical Pathology 1988-; FRCPath 1989 (MRCPath 1977); *Recreations* fell walking, badminton; *Style*— Dr Adrian Bint; The Royal Victoria Infirmary, Newcastle-upon-Tyne NE1 4LP (☎ 091 232 5131)

BINTLEY, David Julian; s of David Bintley, of Honley, Huddersfield, and Glenys, *née* Ellinthorpe; *b* 17 Sept 1957; *Educ* Holme Valley GS, Royal Ballet Upper Sch; *m* 12 Dec 1981, Jennifer Catherine Ursula, da of Bernard Mills, of San Diego, California, USA; 1 s (Michael b 21 March 1985); *Career* Sadlers Wells Royal Ballet 1976-: debut The Outsider 1978, res choreographer and princ dancer 1983-86; res choreographer and princ dancer Royal Ballet 1986-; winner: Evening Standard award for Choros and Consort Lessons 1983, Laurence Olivier award for performance in Petrushka (title-role) 1984, Manchester Evening News award for Still Life at the Penguin Café 1988; other works incl: Galanteries 1986, Allegri Diversi 1987, Hobson's Choice 1989; *Style*— David Bintley, Esq; c/o Royal Opera House, Covent Garden, London WC2 (☎ 071 240 1200)

BION, Dr Julian Fleetwood; s of Dr Wilfred Ruprecht Bion, DSO (d 1979), of Oxford, and Francesca, *née* Purnell; *b* 30 July 1952; *Educ* Harrow, Charing Cross Hosp, Univ of London (MB BS); *m* 15 June 1985, Nitaya, da of Sanit Tangchurat (d 1979), of Bangkok, Thailand; *Career* previous appts in anaesthesia gen med and cardiology, sr anaesthetist Red Cross surgical team Thai-Cambodian border 1983, sr lectr in intensive care Univ of Birmingham 1989-; memb: Intensive Care Soc, Assoc of Anaesthetists, BMA; MRCP 1980, FFARCS 1982, FCAnaes 1988; *Style*— Dr Julian Bion; University of Birmingham, Queen Elizabeth Hospital, Birmingham 15 2TH (☎ 021 472 1311)

BIRCH, Prof Bryan John; s of Arthur Jack Benjamin Birch, and Mary Edith, *née* Buxton; *b* 25 Sept 1931; *Educ* Shrewsbury, Trinity Coll Cambridge (BA, PhD); *m* 1 July 1961, Gina Margaret, da of late Digby Henry Christ; 2 s (Colin b 1962, Michael b 1964), 1 da (Alison b 1968); *Career* fell: Trinity Coll Cambridge 1956-60, Churchill Coll Cambridge 1960-62; sr lectr and reader Univ of Manchester 1962-65, fell and prof of arithmetic BNC 1985- (reader 1966-85); FRS 1972; *Recreations* theoretical gardening, opera, admiring marmots; *Style*— Prof Bryan Birch, FRS; Green Cottage, Boars Hill, Oxford OX1 5DQ (☎ 0865 735367); Math Institute, 24-29 St Giles, Oxford (☎ 0865 273528)

BIRCH, Clive Francis William; s of Raymond William Birch, CBE (d 1980), and (Olive Edith Charlton) Valerie, *née* Fry; *b* 22 Dec 1931; *Educ* Uppingham; *m* 1, 1957 (m dis 1961), Gillian May, *née* Coulson; m 2, 1961 (m dis 1978), Penelope Helen, *née* Harman; 1 s (James b 1962), 1 da (Emma b 1964); m 3, 16 April 1983, Carolyn Rose, da of Thomas Desborough (d 1978); 1 step s (Jamie b 1974), 1 step da (Katie b 1970), 1 adopted s (Richard b 1957), 1 adopted da (Cally b 1959); *Career* Nat Serv radar RAF 1950-52; office jr Stretford Telegraph 1952, reporter Stockport Express 1953, dist reporter Kent and Sussex Courier 1953, chief reporter Herts Newspapers 1954, ed Bucks Examiner 1956, press offr Frigidaire Div General Motors Ltd 1958, product devpt Metro-Cammell Weyman Ltd 1959, gp advertisement mangr Modern Transport Publishing Co Ltd 1965, mangr Electrical Press Ltd 1966; dir: Birch Bros Ltd 1966-, Illustrated Newspapers 1969; ed Illustrated London News 1970, dir Northwood Publications Ltd 1971, md designate Textile Trade Pubns Ltd 1972, publishing dir Mercury House Ltd 1973, fndr chm and md Barracuda Books Ltd 1974-, dir Quotes Ltd 1985-; hon life memb Chiltern Car Club 1956-; voluntary memb: Ind Publishers' Guild 1975-, Royal Soc for Nature Conservation 1981- (Promotion and Educn Ctee 1981-84); vice pres and fndr chm Buckingham and Dist Chamber of Trade Commerce and Indust 1983-, hon life memb Inst of the Royal Corps of Tport 1985-, fndr chm Buckingham Heritage Tst 1985-; cncllr: Radclive-cum-Chackmore PCC 1983-, Radclive-cum-Chackmore Cncl 1987-; govr Royal Latin Sch Buckingham 1989-, former memb Cncl Chesham Round Table; Freeman City of London 1960-; Worshipful Co of Carmen: Freeman and Liveryman 1960-, Ct of Assts 1966-, Master 1984-85, Past Master 1985, Dep Master 1988-89; memb Carmen's Awards Ctee 1969-, fndr chm

Carmen's Charity Ball 1985 (memb Ctee 1988-91); FRSA 1980, FSA 1981; *Books* incl: The Book of Chesham (1974), The Book of Aylesbury (1975), The Book of Amersham (with Leslie Pike, 1976), The Freedom-History and Guilds of the City of London (jtly, 1982), Buckingham in Camera (1987), Chiltern Thames in Camera (1990); *Style—* Clive Birch, FSA; Radclive Hall, Nr Buckingham (☎ 0280 812743); Les Autels St Bazile, Calvados, France; Meadows House, Well St, Buckingham MK18 1EW (☎ 0280 814441)

BIRCH, Gp Capt David Brendon Thomas; OBE (1981); s of William David Birch (d 1988), and Elizabeth, *née* O'Sullivan (d 1985); *b* 9 June 1933; *Educ* Paddington Tech Coll; *m* 24 May 1958, Margaret, da of John George William Coe (d 1988); 2 s (Jason Eugene St John b 1963, Alastair Guy Sinclair b 1969), 1 da (Hilary Lorraine b 1966); *Career* cmmnd Flt Lt: engrg offr 215 Sqdn RAF Changi Singapore 1963-65, armament trials offr A&AEE RAF Boscombe Down 1965-67; Sqdn-Ldr: OC Mechanical Engrg Air Sqdn RAF Abingdon 1967-69, armament project mangr RARDE Fort Halstead 1969-73, OC Armament Engrg Sqdn RAF Honington 1973-75; Wing Cdr: armament staff offr HQ STC RAF High Wycombe 1975-78, OC Engrg Wing RAF Bruggen FRG 1978-81, Aircraft Engrg Authy HQ RAFSC RAF Brampton 1981-83, OC RAF Engrg Fl RAF Stanley Falklands 1983-84; Gp Capt: staff offr engrg HQ18 Gp RAF Northwood 1984-86, memb Ordnance Bd 1986-; CEng 1966, MRAES 1966, FIMechE 1981, FBIM 1986; *Recreations* sailing, golf, philately, caravaning; *Clubs* RAF; *Style—* Gp Capt David Birch, OBE; Room 1704, Ordnance Board, Empress State Building, Lillie Rd, London SW6 1TR (☎ 071 385 1244 ext 3578)

BIRCH, Dennis Arthur; CBE (1977), DL (W Midlands 1979); s of George Howard Birch (d 1960), of Wolverhampton, and Leah, *née* Draycott; *b* 11 Feb 1925; *Educ* Wolverhampton Municipal GS; *m* 1948, Mary Therese, da of Bernard Lyons (d 1964); 1 da (Imelda); *Career* draughtsman and estimator John Thompson Ltd Wolverhampton 1942-64, PR exec George Wimpey and Co Ltd Birmingham 1966-77; mktg mangr: C Bryant and Son Birmingham 1978-83, E Manton Ltd Birmingham 1983-; *Style—* Dennis Birch, Esq, CBE, DL; 3 Tern Close, Wolverhampton Road East, Wolverhampton (☎ 090 73 3837); E Manton Ltd, 100 Saltley Rd, Birmingham (☎ 021 359 5987)

BIRCH, Frank Stanley Heath; s of John Stanley Birch (d 1985), and Phyllis Edna, *née* Heath (d 1981); *b* 8 Feb 1939; *Educ* The Grammar Sch for Boys Weston-super-Mare, Univ Coll Cardiff (BA), Univ of Birmingham; *m* 7 Sept 1963, Diana Jacqueline, da of William Walter Frederick Davies, of Chislehurst, Kent; 1 da (Jocelyn b 1968); *Career* various appts City Treas Dept Cardiff 1962-69, chief auditor Dudley CBC 1969-73, asst chief exec W Midlands CC 1974-76 (asst co treas 1973-74), chief exec Lewisham London Borough Cncl 1976-82, town clerk and chief exec Croydon 1982-; memb Cncl Order St John for Gtr London (Prince of Wales dist) 1986-, vice pres Gtr London St John Ambulance Bde for Gtr London 1988-; OStJ (1988); Freeman City of London 1980; IPFA 1969, MBIM 1969, FRSA 1980; *Recreations* music, travel, the countryside; *Style—* Frank Birch, Esq; Town Clerk's Office, Taberner House, Park Lane, Croydon CR9 3JS (☎ 081 686 4433, fax 081 760 0871)

BIRCH, Henry Langton; MBE (1944), TD, JP (Chester 1955), DL (Cheshire 1966); s of Arthur Lyle Birch (d 1967), of Chester; *b* 7 March 1915; *Educ* Charterhouse, Oriel Coll Oxford; *m* 1948, Helen Margaret (d 1984), da of Capt Harvey Blease (ka 1915); 1 da; *Career* Lt-Col (Hon Col) TA; admitted slr 1939; *Style—* Henry Birch, Esq, MBE, TD, JP, DL; Lion House, Tattenhall, nr Chester (☎ 0829 70347)

BIRCH, James; s of Simon Birch, of London, and Bettine, *née* Coventry; *b* 24 July 1956; *Educ* Milton Abbey Sch, Aix-en-Provence Univ (Dip Histoire D'Art); *Career* Christies 1976-78 (Old Masters Dept and 1950s Rock and Roll Dept), opened own gallery Kings Rd 1983, opened Birch & Conran Gallery Soho 1987, collecting Messerchmidt bubble cars; organised "A Salute to English Surrealism" (Colchester, Hull City Art Gallery, Newcastle) instigated Francis Bacon exhibition in Moscow; Liveryman Worshipful Co of Fishmongers 1980; *Recreations* backgammon; *Clubs* Groucho's, Colony Room, Little House; *Style—* James Birch, Esq; 40 Dean St, Soho, London W1 (☎ 071 434 1246)

BIRCH, John Allan; CMG (1987); s of Dr C Allan Birch (d 1983); *b* 24 May 1935; *Educ* Leighton Park Sch, CCC Cambridge (MA); *m* 5 March 1960, Primula Haselden; 3 s (James b 1962, Alexander b 1963, Henry b 1969), 1 da (Melanie b 1967); *Career* Nat Serv Army 1954-56; joined HM Dip Serv 1959; serv: Paris, Singapore, Bucharest, Geneva, Kabul, Budapest; RCDS 1977; ambass and Br dep perm rep to UN 1986-89, ambass Hungary 1989-; *Recreations* skiing, tennis; *Clubs* Athenaeum; *Style—* John Birch, Esq, CMG; Foreign and Commonwealth Office, London SW1

BIRCH, Dr John Anthony; s of Charles Aylmer Birch (d 1966), of Leek, Staffs, and Mabel, *née* Greenwood (d 1971); *b* 9 July 1929; *Educ* Trent Coll Notts, RCM; *Career* Nat Serv RCS 1949-50; organist and choirmaster St Thomas's Church Regent St 1950-53, accompanist St Michael's Singers 1952-58, organist and choirmaster All Saints Church Margaret St London 1953-58, sub-organist HM Chapels Royal 1957-58, organist and master of the choristers Chichester Cathedral 1958-80, prof RCM 1959-, re-established the Southern Cathedrals Festival with Cathedral Organists of Salisbury and Winchester 1960, musical advsr Chichester Festival Theatre 1962-80, choirmaster Bishop Otter Coll Chichester 1963-69, accompanist Royal Choral Soc 1965-70 (organist 1966-), md CA Birch Ltd Staffs 1966-73 (rep 1950-66), univ organist Univ of Sussex 1967- (visiting lectr in music 1971-83), special cmmr Royal Sch of Church Music, organist and choir dir Temple Church 1982-, organist & Royal Philharmonic Orchestra 1983-, curator-organist Royal Albert Hall 1984-; concert appearances: France, Belgium, Germany, Switzerland, Netherlands, Spain, Portugal, Scandinavia, Far E; recital tours: Canada and US 1966 and 1967, Aust and NZ 1969, SA 1978; examiner Assoc Bd Royal Schs of Music 1958-77, fell Corpn of SS Mary and Nicolas (Woodard Schs) 1973-; govr Hurstpierpoint Coll 1974-, govr St Catherine's Bramley 1981-89; pres RCO 1984-86 (memb Cncl 1964-); hon MA Univ of Sussex 1971, hon DMus Lambeth 1989; ARCM, LRAM, FRCM 1981, FRCO (chm); *Recreations* collecting pictures; *Clubs* Garrick, New (Edinburgh); *Style—* Dr John Birch; 13 King's Bench Walk, Temple, London EC4Y 7EN (☎ 071 353 5115); Fielding House, The Close, Salisbury, Wilts SP1 2EB (☎ 0722 412 458)

BIRCH, John Richard; s of Cedric Ronald Birch, of 36 Gervase Drive, Dudley, W Mids, and Joan Mary, *née* Stafford; *b* 1 April 1945; *Educ* Dudley GS, Birmingham Univ; *m* 17 Aug 1968, Maureen May, da of John Thomas Sanders, of Netherton, W Mids; 1 da (Amanada Jayne b 3 April 1971); *Career* Br Fed Ltd: Tech Sales mangr 1976-81, Electronics dir 1981-84, md 1984-; 1975: C ENG, MIEE, MIERE; *Recreations* golf; *Style—* John Birch, Esq; 9 St Johns Close, Swindon, Dudley, W Mids DY3 4PQ (☎ 0384 279592); British Federation Ltd, Castle Mill Works, Dudley, W Mid, DT1 4DA (☎ 0384 455400 (459400 night), fax 0384 455554, telex 337416)

BIRCH, Mark; s of Arthur Birch (d 1978), and Mary Birch (d 1953); *b* 6 Sept 1949; *Educ* South Chadderton, Lancs; *m* 20 Sept 1969, Joyce Patricia, da Herbert Lynn; 3 c (Samantha b 17 March 1970, Jill b 21 Dec 1974, Nicholas b 15 Dec 1977); *Career* jockey; winner of: Gimcrack Stakes York on Sun and Gold, Ebor Handicap York, November Handicap Doncaster (twice) on Swingit Gunner and Young Benz, Chester Cup (twice) on Sea Pigeon; seven times Champion Northern jockey; *Recreations* fishing, gardening, crosswords; *Style—* Mark Birch, Esq; c/o MH Easterby, Habton Grange, Great Habten, N Yorks

BIRCH, Peter Gibbs; s of William Birch (d 1971), and Gladys, *née* Gibbs (d 1971); *b* 4 Dec 1937; *Educ* Allhallows Sch; *m* 17 March 1962, Gillian Heather, da of Leonard Brace Sale Benge; 3 s (James b 1964, Simon b 1967, Alexander b 1970), 1 da (Sophie b 1972); *Career* Nat Serv 2 Lt Royal West Kent Regiment 1956-58; Nestle UK, Switzerland Singapore Malaysia 1958-65, mktg positions Gillette 1965-68, Gillette Aust (Melbourne) 1969-71; gen mangr: Gillette NZ 1971-73, Gillette SE Asia 1973-75; gp gen mangr Gillette Africa ME and Eastern Europe 1975-81, md Gillette (UK) 1981-84, gp chief exec Abbey National 1984-; dir: Hoskyns Group plc, Argos PLC 1990; chm Cncl of Mortgage Lenders 1991; pres Middx Assoc of Boys Clubs; *Recreations* swimming, wind surfing, cycling, skiing; *Style—* Peter G Birch, Esq; Abbey National plc, Baker St, London NW1 (☎ 071 612 4131)

BIRCH, Robin Arthur; s of Arthur Birch, and Olive Birch; *b* 12 Oct 1939; *Educ* King Henry VIII Sch Coventry, Ch Ch Oxford (MA); *m* 15 Dec 1962, Jane Marion Irvine, da of Vivian Sturdy (d 1965); 2 s (David b 1965, Michael b 1967); *Career* Civil Serv: princ Miny of Health 1966-69 (asst princ 1961-66), seconded Interdepartmental Social Work Gp 1969-70, Home Office 1970-72, asst sec DHSS 1973, princ private sec to Ldr of House of Commons 1980-81, under sec DHSS 1982, seconded NAO as asst auditor gen (undersec) 1984-86, dir regnl orgn DSS 1988-90, dep sec (grade 2) and head Policy Group DSS 1990-; hon sec Friends of Christ Church Cathedral Oxford 1978-; *Recreations* family and friends, books, listening to music; *Clubs* Oxford Union; *Style—* Robin Birch, Esq; DSS, Richmond House, 79 Whitehall, London SW1A 2NS (☎ 071 210 5459)

BIRCH, Roger; CBE (1987), QPM (1980); s of John Edward Lawrence Birch (d 1981), and Ruby Birch; *b* 27 Sept 1930; *Educ* Teignmouth GS, Torquay GS, King's Coll Taunton; *m* Jeanne Margaret, da of Herbert Ernest Head (d 1976); 1 s (Steven); *Career* cadet RNC Dartmouth 1949-50, Pilot Offr RAF Canada 1950-52; joined Devon Police 1954, served in CID and Uniform Branch rising to chief supt 1954-72, asst chief constable Mid Anglia Constabulary 1972, dep chief constable of Kent 1974; chief constable: Warwickshire 1978, Sussex 1983; dir Police Extended Interviews; chm Int Affrs Advsy Ctee ACPO 1988- (vice pres 1986-87, pres 1987-88), vice chm Euro Section Int Assoc of Chiefs of Police 1989-, UK vice pres The Royal Life Saving Soc (chm SE Region); tstee: Police Dependants Tst, Gurney Fund for Police Orphans; memb: Cncl of the Inst of Advanced Motorists, Guild of Experienced Motorists; CBIM; *Recreations* swimming, music; *Clubs* RAF; *Style—* Roger Birch, Esq, CBE, QPM; Sussex Police HQ, Malling House, Lewes, E Sussex (☎ 0273 475432)

BIRCH REYNARDSON, Maj Richard Francis; s of Lt-Col Henry Thomas Birch Reynardson, CMG (d 1972), of Adwell, Oxon, and Diana Helen, *née* Ponsonby (d 1962); *b* 26 Sept 1926; *Educ* Eton; *m* 18 June 1951, Mary, da of Major Sir John Crocker Bulteel, KCVO, DSO, MC (d 1955), of Devon; 1 s (Charles Crocker b 1963), 2 da (Sara b 1952, Marie-Therese b 1960); *Career* cmmnd Grenadier Guards 1945,ADC to C in C Far East Land Forces 1948-49, PA to chm Combined Chiefs of Staff Pentagon 1949-51; ptnr Myers & Co Stockbrokers (now Capel Cure Myers) 1960-73; dir Goddard Kay Rogers and Assocs 1981-89; *Recreations* shooting, fishing; *Clubs* Whites, The Turf, Pratts; *Style—* Maj Richard F Birch Reynardson; The Stables, Brailes House, Brailes Banbury, Oxon; Old London House, 32 St James's Square, London SW1 (☎ 071 930 5100)

BIRCH REYNARDSON, William Robert Ashley; s of Lt-Col Henry Thomas Birch Reynardson, CMG (d 1972), and his 1 w Diana Helen, *née* Ponsonby (d 1962); *b* 7 Dec 1923; *Educ* Eton, Ch Ch Oxford; *m* 30 Nov 1950, (Pamela) Matnika, da of Lt-Gen Sir (Edward) Thomas Humphreys, KCB, CMG, DSO; 1 s (Thomas), 2 da (Juliet (Mrs Stewart-Brown) Clare (Mrs Hopkinson)); *Career* cmmnd 9 QR Lancers 1941, served in N Africa and Italy; called to the Bar Inner Temple 1950; sr ptnr and chm Thomas Miller, ret 1987; dir Graham Miller & Co; hon sec Br Maritime Law Assoc, vice pres Comité Maritime Int; High Sheriff of Oxfordshire 1974-75; past memb Bullingdon RDC; *Recreations* hunting, shooting, painting, gardening; *Clubs* Cavalry and Guards', Pratt's, City of London; *Style—* William Birch Reynardson, Esq; Adwell House, Tetsworth, Oxfordshire OX9 7DQ (☎ 084 428 204); 111 Marsham Court, Marsham Street, London SW1 (☎ 071 630 1191)

BIRCHALL, Adrian Philip; s of Wilfred Birchall (d 1977), and Mona Winifred, *née* Hibbert; *b* 11 Oct 1946; *Educ* Up Holland GS, Univ of Birmingham (BSocSci); *m* 1 (m dis), 6 July 1968, Jacqueline Mullis; m 2, 9 Oct 1981, Elizabeth Anne, da of Harold Lowe (d 1979); 1 s (Andrew Philip Lowe b 24 Oct 1983), 1 da (Jessica Elizabeth Anne b 1 March 1985); *Career* advertising exec; teacher in mathematics Croydon and Wimbledon Secdy Sch, media res mangr and planning gp head Lintas Ltd 1969-73, media gp mangr McCann-Erickson 1973-75, media dir BBDO 1975-79, media dir and dep md Geers Gross 1979-85, vice chm DMB & B 1986-90, chm DMB & B Media Centre 1991-; FIPA 1981; *Recreations* theatre, music, sport; *Style—* Adrian Birchall, Esq; The DMB & B Media Centre, 5 Charles II Street, London SW1

BIRCHALL, Prof (James) Derek; OBE (1990); s of David Birchall (d 1961), and Dora Mary, *née* Leather (d 1976); *b* 7 Oct 1930; *m* 2 June 1956, Pauline Mary (d 1990), da of Benjamin Jones, OBE, KPFSM (d 1966); 2 s (Shaun Nicolas Paul, Timothy Martin); *Career* RCS 1952-54; ICI sr res assoc 1975-, fell Wolfson Coll Oxford 1977-79; assoc prof: Brunel Univ 1985, Univ of Sheffield 1989; visiting prof Massachusetts Inst of Technol 1984-86; memb: various SERC ctees and panels, HM Treas IM Panel 1988-89; FRSC, FRS 1982, FICeram; *Recreations* old books; *Style—* Prof Derek Birchall, OBE, FRS; Braeside, Stable Lane, Mouldsworth, Chester CH3 8AN (☎ 09284 320); Imperial Chemical Industries plc, PO Box 11, The Heath, Runcorn, Cheshire WA7 4QE (☎ 0928 51 3465)

BIRCHALL, Mark Dearman; s of Maj Peter Dearman Birchall, CBE, and Susan Auriol Charrington (d 1972); *b* 26 July 1933; *Educ* Eton, Trinity Coll Oxford; *m* 6 July 1962, Helen Iona, da of Capt Alexander Francis Matheson (d 1976), of Conon Bridge, Ross-shire; 1 s (John b 1970), 2 da (Clare b 1965, Katharine b 1967); *Career* Nat Serv 1951-53; stockbroker 1956-82; ptnr Mullens and Co 1966-82; dir: Careerplan 1973-, Christian Weekly Newspapers Ltd 1979-, Lella plc 1984-90; memb Gen Synod 1980-; *Books* The Gospel Community and its Leadership (with John Tiller, 1987); *Recreations* wild flowers, walking; *Style—* Mark D Birchall, Esq; 3 Melrose Rd, London SW18 1ND

BIRD; *see*: Martin Bird

BIRD, Rev Dr Anthony Peter; s of Rev Prebendary Albert Harry Bird (d 1986), and Noel Whitehouse, *née* Oakley (d 1940); *b* 2 March 1931; *Educ* St John's Sch Leatherhead, St John's Coll Oxford (BA, MA), Birmingham Univ (MB, ChB); *m* 29 Sept 1962 (m dis 1981), Sabine, *née* Boehmig; 2 s (Markus b 1963, Dominic b 1973), 1 da (Stephanie b 1965); *Career* Nat Serv 1949-50, cmmnd RASC; ordained Lichfield Cath: deacon 1957, priest 1958; asst curate St Mary's Stafford 1957-60, chaplain and vice princ Cuddesdon Theol Coll 1960-64; medical practitioner Hosp Appts 1970-71, gen practitioner Birmingham 1972-73; princ Queen's Theol Coll Birmingham 1974-79, recognized lectr Dept of Theol Birmingham Univ 1974-; gen practitioner Balsall Heath Birmingham 1979-; memb Advsy Ctee on Sexual Offences 1976-80, Parole Bd 1978-80; Freedom of Information Campaign Award 1987; *Books* The Search for Health: A Response from the Inner City (1981); *Recreations* swimming, walking, music, reading; *Style—* The Rev Dr Anthony Bird; 93 Bournbrook Rd, Birmingham B29 7BX; Edward

Rd Health Centre, 43 Edward Rd, Birmingham B12 9JB (☎ 021 440 2574)

BIRD, Hon Mrs (Catherine Mary); da of 15 Baron Dormer (d 1975); *b* 2 April 1950; *m* 1973, Christopher J G Bird; *Style—* The Hon Mrs Bird; 45 Addison Ave, London W11

BIRD, David Charles; s of George Henry Bird (d 1985), of Teddington, and Grace Jesse, *née* Parsley; *b* 14 June 1943; *Educ* Stanley Road Secdy Mod, Twickenham Tech Sch, Kingston Coll (ONC); *m* 1 March 1969, Margaret Ann, da of Stanley Bourne, of Rye, Sussex; *Career* angler; Rye & Dist Angling Soc (approx 100 appearances) 1973-; angling admin 1972-, pres Nat Fedn of Anglers (300,000 membs) 1987-; *Recreations* angling; *Style—* David Bird, Esq; 95 Brunswick Road, Ealing, London W5 1AQ (☎ 081 997 6848)

BIRD, (George) Eric; s of Capt George Albert Bird (d 1965), of Kenton, Middx, and Winifred Fanny, *née* Hood (d 1973); *b* 9 Nov 1913; *Educ* Harrow GS , RMC Sandhurst; *m* 11 May 1968, Adrienne Sandra, da of Haydn Alexander King, of Canons Park, Edgware, Middx; 1 s (Alexander Hamilton b 1969); *Career* RTR; dir: Claudius Ash Sons and Co (USA) Inc 1947-52, Amalgamated Dental Co Ltd 1954-77; patent and trademark conslt 1977-; tstee Morse-Boycott Bursary Fund, govr Felpham Community Coll, memb PROBUS, memb Arundel CC, memb Chichester Festival Theatre; Arundel dist cncllr; *Recreations* theatre-going, ecclesiology, reading; *Style—* Eric Bird, Esq; 3 Glynde Cres, Felpham, Bognor Regis, West Sussex PO22 8T (☎ 0243 867171)

BIRD, Brig Garth Raymond Godrey; s of Herbert William Bird Norther (d 1945), of Surrey, and Nora Constance Shaw, *née* Vernon (d 1957); *b* 4 Sept 1909; *Educ* Stonyhurst, RMC Sandhurst; *m* 19 Sept 1942, Elizabeth Mary, da of the late Sir Leonard Vavasour, Bt (Capt RN); 2 s (Christopher b 1946, Anthony b 1952), 1 da (Fiona b 1953), 1 step s (Simon De Walters b 1941); *Career* regular soldier The Sherwood Foresters 1929-62, served N Africa and Italy 1939-45, CO 2 Foresters Anzio 1944, CO 1 Foresters BAOR 1945-48, GSO1 Western Cmd 1949-52, Col (mil attaché) Br Embassy Belgrade 1952-55, Brig 1956, CO Bde 1956-59, CO Home Counties Dist 1959-62; ADC to HM The Queen 1959-62; army interpreterships in French and Italian; exec Br Nat Export Cncl 1962-72; *Recreations* hunting, shooting; *Clubs* Naval and Military; *Style—* Brig Garth R G Bird; Oast House, Gt Broadhurst Broad Oak, Heathfield, E Sussex TN21 8UX; Lloyds, Cox and Kings, 6 Pall Mall, London SW1

BIRD, Harold Dennis (Dickie); MBE (1986); s of James Harold Bird (d 1969), and Ethel Bird, *née* Smith (d 1978); *b* 19 April 1933; *Educ* Raley Sch Barnsley; *Career* Test and World Cup Final cricket umpire; only man to umpire 3 World Cup finals (W Indies v Australia Lord's 1975, W Indies v England Lord's 1979, and W Indies v India Lord's 1983), umpire of World Cup India 1987, umpire Queen's Silver Jubilee Test Match (England v Aust Lords 1977), umpire Centenary Test Match (England v Aust Lords 1980), umpire Bi-centenary Test Match (MCC v Rest of World Lords 1987), only umpire of both men's and women's World Cup Finals (women's World Cup NZ 1982), umpire 122 int cricket matches and 46 test matches and many other cricketing events (incl Gillett, Nat West and Benson and Hedges Cup Finals), qualified MCC advanced Cricket Coach, player Yorkshire and Leicestershire Co Cricket Club; Yorkshire Personality of the Year 1977; *Books* Not Out (1978), That's Out (1985), From The Pavillion End (1988); *Clubs* Lord's Taverners; *Style—* Dickie Bird Esq, MBE; White Rose Cottage, 40 Paddock Rd, Staincross, Barnsley, Yorks S75 6LE (☎ 0226 384491); Test and County Cricket Board, Lords Cricket Ground, London NW8 8QN (☎ 071 286 4405)

BIRD, John Alfred William; MEP Midlands West 1987-; s of John William Bird (d 1978), and Elsie Louisa, *née* Hallett (d 1945); *b* 4 Feb 1926; *Educ* Bushbury Hill Secdy, Wolverhampton and Staffordshire Coll of Technol; *m* 21 Sept 1946, Gwendoline, da of Robert Davies (1971), of New Broughton, Wrexham, North Wales; 2 s (David John b 1 April 1948, Julian Robert b 18 June 1954); *Career* army serv Infantry 1943-47; Wolverhampton Borough PC 1947-49, gear cutter Henry Meadows Ltd 1949-51, personnel HM Hobson Ltd and Lucas Aerospace 1963-82 (turner 1951-63), MEP 1987-; memb: Wolverhampton Borough Cncl 1962-88 (chm Educn Ctee 1972-80, ldr 1973-87), W Midlands CC 1973-81, vice pres AMA (Educn Ctee 1972-80, Cncl 1972-87), AEC 1972-75, EC 1974-75, W Midlands Econ Planning Cncl 1974-79, chm W Midlands Cncls 1986-87; pres Norwest Chartered Inst of Mktg 1990-91; hon fell Sci and Technol Wolverhampton Poly; *Recreations* sport, soccer, brass band music; *Style—* John Bird, Esq, MEP; Old Bank Chambers, Lich Gates, Wolverhampton WV1 1TY (☎ 0902 712366, fax 0902 20276)

BIRD, John Andrew; s and h of Sir Richard Bird, 4 Bt; *b* 19 Jan 1964; *Style—* John Bird Esq

BIRD, Capt Lionel Armitage; LVO (1972); s of George Armitage Bird (d 1976), and Noreen Phyllis, *née* Bailey (d 1967); *b* 6 Oct 1928; *Educ* RNC Dartmouth; *m* 17 Aug 1957, Barbara Jane, da of Scott Henry (d 1963); 1 s (Simon b 1960), 1 da (Amanda b 1961); *Career* HM Yacht Britannia 1970-72, naval attaché Paris 1973-75, CO HMS Fearless 1974-77; lectr: Br Atlantic Ctee, Peace through NATO; life memb and former chm RNFA; *Recreations* fishing, cricket, golf gardening, horse racing; *Clubs* RN Cricket; *Style—* Capt Lionel A Bird, LVO; Manor Farmhouse, Trent, Sherborne, Dorset DT9 4SW (☎ 0935 850 576)

BIRD, Michael David; s of Sqdn Ldr David Bird (d 1970), of Letchworth, Herts, and Monica Lilian, *née* Bradley; *b* 21 July 1942; *Educ* Hitchin Sch, Univ of Manchester; *m* 8 June 1968, Kay Elisabeth, da of Elystan John Wilson, of Oakley, Beds; 1 s (David b 1972), 1 da (Rosemary b 1970); *Career* project mangr Binder Hamlyn Fry & Co 1966-73, gen mangr Fairview Estates plc 1973-74, md Br Debt Servs plc 1974-76, Michael D Bird & Assocs freelance consultancy 1976-78, dir Resource Evaluation Ltd 1979-; hon treas Letchworth Golf Club, past capt Letchworth Tennis Club; underwriting memb Corpn of Lloyds 1977; FCA 1966, FIMC 1971, MICM 1979; *Recreations* golf, duplicate bridge, tennis, racing; *Style—* Michael Bird, Esq; Park Gate, 21 Tothill St, London SW1H 9LL (☎ 071 222 1212, fax 071 233 0735, car 0831 490576)

BIRD, Sir Richard Geoffrey Chapman; 4 Bt (UK 1922); s of Sir Donald Geoffrey Bird, 3 Bt (d 1963); *b* 3 Nov 1935; *Educ* Beaumont; *m* 1, 1957, Gillian Frances (d 1966), da of Bernard Haggett; 2 s, 4 da; m 2, 1968, Helen Patricia, da of Frank Beaumont, of Pontefract; 2 da; *Heir* s, John Andrew Bird b 19 Jan 1964; *Style—* Sir Richard Bird, Bt; 39 Ashleigh Road, Solihull, W Midlands B91 1AF

BIRD, Richard Herries; CB (1983); s of Edgar Clarence Frederick Bird, and Armorel, *née* Dudley-Scott; *b* 8 June 1932; *Educ* Winchester, Clare Coll Cambridge (BA); *m* 1963, (Margaret) Valerie, da of Edward Robson Sanderson; 2 da (Caroline b 1964, Julia b 1966); *Career* joined Civil Service 1955; private sec to perm sec Miny of Tport 1958-60, PPS to Min Tport 1966-67, under-sec Dept of Educn and Science 1975-80, dep sec DES 1980-; *Recreations* music, reading, gardening; *Clubs* Reform; *Style—* Richard Bird, Esq, CB; Department of Education and Science, Elizabeth House, London SE1 7PH (☎ 071 934 9956, telex 23171)

BIRD, Thomas Arthur; DSO (1942), MC (and bar 1941); s of Arthur Wheen Bird (d 1953), of Crockmore, Fawley, Henley-On- Thames, and Eveline Mary, *née* Huggins (d 1950); *b* 11 Aug 1918; *Educ* Winchester, Architectural Assoc Sch of Architecture (Dip AA); *m* 9 March 1946, Alice, da of Prof Jerome Clarke Hunsaker (d 1984), of Louisburg Square, Boston, Mass, USA; 2 s (Antony b 1947, Nicholas b 1948), 1 da (Sarah (Mrs Squires) b 1956); *Career* WWII 2 Bn RB ME (wounded 3 times) 1939-43, ADC to Field Marshal Lord Wavell in India (Maj) 1943, 2 i/c 8 Bn RB in NW Europe (wounded) 1944, ADC to Field Marshal Lord Wilson in Washington (Maj) 1945; fndr ptnr Bird and Tyler Assocs (architects) London and Cambridge 1952-85, practising from home at Turville Heath House Henley-on-Thames 1985-; High Sheriff of Bucks 1989; RIBA 1949; *Recreations* shooting, gardening, tennis, drawing; *Clubs* Boodle's; *Style—* Thomas Bird, Esq, DSO, MC; Turville Heath House, Turville Heath, Henley-on-Thames (☎ 049163 331)

BIRD, Rt Hon Vere Cornwall; PC (1982); *b* 9 Dec 1909; *Educ* St John's Boys' Sch Antigua, Salvation Army Trg Sch Trinidad; *Career* memb Exec Antigua Trades and Labour Union 1939- (pres 1943-67), memb Antigua Legislative Cncl 1945, memb Exec Cncl 1946, ctee chm Exec Cncl 1951-56 in which capacity instituted Peasant Devpt Scheme, whereby land was redistributed and development loans were made possible, min Trade and Prodn 1956, first chief minister Antigua 1960, co-fndr Caribbean Free Trade Assoc 1965, first premier Antigua 1967-71 (when lost seat in Parly), MP (Antigua) 1976, first PM of Antigua and Barbuda 1981-; *Style—* The Rt Hon Vere Bird Sr; Office of the Prime Minister, Antigua and Barbuda, West Indies

BIRD-WILSON, Air Vice-Marshal Harold (Birdy); CBE (1962), DSO (1944), DFC (1940, bar 1943), AFC (1946, bar 1955); s of Harold Bird-Wilson (d 1957), and Victoria Mabel, *née* Cooper (d 1962); *b* 20 Nov 1919; *Educ* Liverpool Coll; *m* 21 March 1942, Audrey, da of Robert James Wallace, MVO, OBE (d 1963); 1 s (Robert Stuart b 30 Nov 1943), 1 da (Caryl b 22 June 1945); *Career* joined RAF 1937, 17 Fighter Sqdn Kenley 1938, WWII served France, Dunkirk and Battle of Britain, Flt Cdr 234 Spitfire Sqdn 1941, (despatches) Sqdn Ldr 152 Sqdn then 66 Sqdn 1942, Wing Ldr 83 Gp 1943, chm and gen Staff Sch Fort Leavenworth USA 1944, Wing Ldr Harrowbeer Spitfire Wing later Bradwell Bay and Mustang Fighter wing at Bentwaters 1944-45, CO first jet conversion unit 1945-46, CO air fighting devpt sqdn Central Fighter Estab 1946-47, Ops Staff HQ MEAF 1948, RAF Staff Col 1949, personal SO to C in C MEAF 1949-50, RAF Flying Coll Manby 1951, OC tactics (later AFDS), Central Fighter Estab 1952-54, staff BJSM Washington USA 1954-57, staff air sec dept Air Miny 1957-59, CO RAF Coltishall 1959-61, staff intelligence Air Miny 1961-63, AOC and Cmdt Central Flying Sch 1963-65, AOC Hong Kong 1965-67, dir of flying R & D Miny of Technol 1967-70, AOC 23 Gp 1970-73, cdr S Maritime Air Region Mount Batten 1973-74, ret 1974; dep chief exec Br Aircraft Corp Riyad Saudi Arabia 1974-76, mil liaison Br Aerospace, ret 1984; Czechoslovak Medal of Merit first class 1945, Dutch DFC 1945; *Clubs* RAF; *Style—* Air Vice-Marshal Harold Bird-Wilson, CBE, DSO, DFC, AFC; Whytecroft, Gong Hill Drive, Lower Bourne, Farnham, Surrey GU10 3HQ

BIRDWOOD, Dowager Lady; Joan Pollock; *née* Graham; da of Christopher Norman Graham, of Ealing; *m* 22 Feb 1954, as his 2 w, 2 Baron Birdwood, MVO (d 1962); *Career* independent patriot candidate Bermondsey By-Election 1983; *Style—* The Rt Hon the Dowager Lady Birdwood; 114 Gunnersbury Ave, London W5

BIRDWOOD, 3 Baron (UK 1938), of Anzac and of Totnes, Devon; Sir Mark William Ogilvie Birdwood; 3 Bt (UK 1919); s of 2 Baron, MVO (d 1962), and (Elizabeth) Vere Drummond, CVO, da of Lt-Col Sir George Drummond Ogilvie, KCIE, CSI; *b* 23 Nov 1938; *Educ* Radley, Trinity Coll Cambridge; *m* 27 April 1963, Judith Helen, er da of Reginald Gordon Seymour Roberts; 1 da (m 1987 Earl of Woolton, *qv*); *Career* former 2 Lt RHG; J Walter Thompson Cambridge Conslts, vice pres Boyden Int, Wrightson Wood (md 1984), chm Martlet Ltd 1986-; dir: Du Pont Pixel Systems Ltd (formerly Benchmark Technol), Comac plc, Scientific Generics Ltd 1989; *Clubs* Brooks's; *Style—* The Rt Hon the Lord Birdwood; Russell House, Broadway, Worcs WR12 79V; 5 Holbein Mews, London SW1W 8NW

BIRDWOOD, Lt-Col Richard Douglas Davis; MC (1942), JP (Devon 1964), DL (1964); s of Lt-Col Gordon Birdwood (d 1945); *b* 5 Jan 1905; *Educ* Clifton, Peterhouse Cambridge (MA); *m* 1930, Phyllis, JP, da of Lt-Col Sir Thomas Bilbe-Robinson, GBE, KCMG, (d 1939); 2 s, 1 da; *Career* High Sheriff Devon 1962, Mayor Bideford 1963; pres: Torrington Farmers' Hunt, Devon County Agric Assoc 1970, Royal N Devon Golf Club 1977, Appledore Branch RNLI; Hon Freeman Borough of Bideford 1972; *Recreations* fishing, golf; *Style—* Lt-Col Richard Birdwood, MC, JP, DL; Horwood House, Horwood, Bideford, Devon (☎ 027 185 231)

BIRDWOOD, Baroness; (Elizabeth) Vere Drummond; CVO (1972, MVO 1958); da of Lt-Col Sir George Drummond Ogilvie, KCIE, CSI (d 1966); *b* 7 Aug 1909; *m* 7 March 1931 (m dis 1954), 2 Baron Birdwood, MVO (d 1962); 1 s, 1 da; *Career* priv sec to govr of Sind 1942-45; administrator King Edward VII's Hosp for Offrs 1950-72, ed Public Record Office 1972-; vice-chm Provident Assoc for Med Care 1977-82 (bd memb 1958-82); memb AHA: Westminster, Kensington, Chelsea 1973-76; memb Chelsea Borough Cncl 1954-60; *Style—* Vere, Lady Birdwood, CVO; 11 Whitelands House, Cheltenham Terrace, London SW3 4QT

BIRK, Baroness (Life Peer UK 1967); Alma Lillian Birk; JP (Highgate 1952); da of late Barnett Wilson, of London, and Alice, *née* Tosh; *Educ* S Hampstead HS, LSE; *m* 1939, Ellis Samuel Birk, *qv*; 1 s, 1 da; *Career* sits as Lab Peer in House of Lords; memb Fabian Soc 1946-; Parly candidate (Lab) Ruislip-Northwood 1950 and Portsmouth West 195 former lectr and visitor Holloway Prison, assoc ed Nova 1965-69, memb London Pregnancy Advsy Service 1968-; a baroness-in-waiting to HM the Queen 1974, under sec of state DOE 1974-79, min of state Privy Cncl Office 1979; govr and tstee Raymond Mander and Joe Mitchenson Theatre Collection, dir New Shakespeare Co 1979-; tstee: Balfour Diamond Jubilee 1982-, Jerusalem Fndn 1982-, Health Promotion Research Tst 1983- (vice chm 1990-), Stress Syndrome Fndn 1983-; vice-pres Family Planning Assoc 1983-; oppn spokesman (Lords) Environment 1983-86, Arts Heritage Broadcasting 1986-; govr Br Film Inst 1980-87; memb Cncl RSA 1983-87; FRSA; *Recreations* theatre, travelling, trying to relax; *Style—* The Rt Hon Baroness Birk, JP; 3 Wells Rise, Regents Park, London NW8 7LH (☎ 071 722 6226)

BIRK, Ellis Samuel; s of Barnett Birk, of London and Newcastle; *b* 30 Oct 1915; *Educ* Clifton, Jesus Coll Cambridge; *m* 1939, Baroness Birk (Life Peer), *qv*; 1 s, 1 da; *Career* slr 1945; chm Central Independent Television Pension Fund Tstees 1985-, dir Jewish Chronicle 1957-; *Clubs* Garrick, Royal Automobile; *Style—* Ellis Birk, Esq; 3 Wells Rise, Regents Park, London NW8 7LH (☎ 071 722 6216)

BIRKBECK, Capt Henry; DL; eldest s of Maj Henry Anthony Birkbeck, MC, JP, DL (d 1956), of Westacre High House; bro of William Birkbeck, *qv*; *b* 15 Nov 1915; *Educ* Eton, Magdalene Coll Cambridge; *m* 1939, Nadine Mary, da of Maj Francis Wilfred Gore-Langton (d 1931), of Tingewick, Buckingham; 1 s, 4 da; *Career* Capt Grenadier Gds; landowner and farmer; *Recreations* ornithology, shooting, fishing, ARICS; *Clubs* Cavalry and Guards'; *Style—* Capt Henry Birkbeck, DL; Westacre High House, Castleacre, King's Lynn, Norfolk PE32 2BW (☎ 0760 755203)

BIRKBECK, John Oliver Charles; yr s of Lt-Col Oliver Birkbeck (d 1952), of Little Massingham House, Kings Lynn, Norfolk, and Lady (Mary) Joan Wilhelmina Cator, *née* Fitzclarence; *b* 22 June 1936; *Educ* Gordonstoun, RAC Cirencester; *m* 2 May 1964, Hermione Anne, o da of Maj D'Arcy Dawes (d 1967), of Leacon Hall, Warehorne, Ashford, Kent; 1 s (Oliver Benjamin b 1973), 2 da (Lucy Claire b 1966, Rosanna Mary b 1974); *Career* chm: Breckland Dist Cncl 1987-88 (memb 1969-), Norfolk County Cncl 1989 (chm Planning Ctee, memb 1970-), Norfolk Historic

Buildings Tst 1987-, Norfolk Windmills Tst 1988-; vice chm Norfolk Churches Tst 1990-, church warden Litcham All Saints 1980-; *Recreations* shooting, gardening; *Clubs* White's, Norfolk; *Style*— John Birkbeck, Esq; Litcham Hall, Kings Lynn, Norfolk PE32 2QQ (☎ 0328 701 389)

BIRKBECK, Mark Nigel Thomas; s of Capt Maurice Birkbeck (d 1972), and Billie, *née* Hoyland; *b* 2 July 1948; *Educ* Eshton Hall Yorks; *m* Linda Mary, da of William Hird, of Fern Croft, Casterton, Kirkby Lonsdale; 2 s (Patrick Mark b 14 Dec 1972, Tom Mackenzie b 19 March 1985), 2 da (Alexandra Robin b 18 June 1976, Georgina Amy b 27 Jan 1983); *Career* chm Mark Birkbeck & Co (Westmorland Woollens, estab 1971), Jumpers Ltd (retail div), Sheepskin Warehouse Shops Ltd (retail div); *Recreations* fishing, shooting, rugby; *Style*— Mark Birkbeck, Esq; Low Gale, Cowan Bridge, Carnforth, Lancs; Strathtulcham, Advie, Nr Grantown on Spey, Morayshire (☎ 0468 71542); Bridge Mill, Cowan Bridge, Carnforth, Lancs (☎ 0468 71071, fax 0468 72058, car 0836 523967, telex 65109 MB CO G)

BIRKBECK, Hon Mrs (Mary); *née* Crossley; JP (1966, Huntingdon and Peterborough); o da of 2 Baron Somerleyton, MC (d 1959), and Bridget, MBE, JP, *née* Hoare; *b* 3 Feb 1926; *m* 7 July 1950, Maj William Birkbeck, DL, Coldstream Guards (ret), yst s of late Maj Henry Anthony Birkbeck, MC, JP, DL, of Westacre, Norfolk; 1 s, 3 da; *Style*— The Hon Mrs Birkbeck, JP; Bainton House, Stamford, Lincs, (☎ 740227)

BIRKBECK, Mary Joan; da of Col Oliver Birkbeck (d 1953), of Lt Massingham House, King's Lynn, Norfolk and Wilhelmina Joan Mary, *née* Fitzclarence; *b* 13 Sept 1931; *Educ* Hatherop Castle; *Career* Nat Coursing Club Trainer, second woman to train Waterloo Cup Winner 'Modest NewDown' 1973; *Recreations* horse racing, hunting, coursing; *Clubs* National Coursing; *Style*— Miss Mary Birkbeck; Mill House, Harpley, King's Lynn, Norfolk PE31 6TT (☎ 048 524 204)

BIRKBECK, William; DL (Huntingdon and Peterborough 1965, subsequently Cambs); yst s of Maj Henry Anthony Birkbeck, MC, JP, DL (d 1956), of Westacre High House, Norfolk, and Sybil, *née* Harley (d 1948); bro of Capt Henry Birkbeck, *qv*; *b* 13 April 1922; *Educ* Eton; *m* 7 July 1950, Hon Mary Crossley, JP, *qv*, o da of 2 Baron Somerleyton, MC; 1 s, 3 da; *Career* Coldstream Gds 1941-57, Maj; banker: dir Barclays Bank 1970-86, Bank of Scotland 1971-85; *Recreations* country sports; *Clubs* Army and Navy; *Style*— Maj William Birkbeck, DL; Bainton House, Stamford, Lincs (☎ 740227)

BIRKENHEAD, Lord Bishop of, 1974-; Rt Rev Ronald Brown; s of Fred Brown (d 1977), and Ellen, *née* Billington (d 1969); *b* 7 Aug 1926; *Educ* Kirkham GS, St John's Coll, Univ of Durham (BA DipTheol); *m* 14 July 1951, Joyce (d 1987), da of William Hymers (d 1955); 1 s (Laurence Frederick Mark b 1953), 1 da (Janet Elizabeth b 1956); *Career* vicar: Whittle-le-Woods Lancs 1956-61, St Thomas' Halliwell Bolton 1961-70; rector and rural dean Ashton-under-Lyne Lancs 1970-74, bishop Birkenhead 1974; *Recreations* DIY activities, antiques; *Style*— The Rt Rev the Lord Bishop of Birkenhead; Trafford House, Victoria Crescent, Queen's Park, Chester CH4 7AX (☎ 0244 675895)

BIRKENHEAD, Countess of; Hon Sheila; *née* Berry; DL (Northants 1979); da of 1 Visc Camrose; *b* 3 May 1913; *m* 1935, 2 Earl of Birkenhead, TD (d 1985, extinct); 1 da; (1 s dec'd); *Career* authoress; lady-in-waiting to HRH Princess Marina, Duchess of Kent 1949-53; chm Northants Branch CPRE 1975-89, vice-pres RSL 1975-, chm Keats-Shelley Assoc 1977-89; *Recreations* reading, gardening, watching tennis; *Style*— The Rt Hon the Countess of Birkenhead, DL; 24 Wilton St, SW1 (☎ 071 235 4111); Charlton, Banbury, Oxon (☎ 0295 811224)

BIRKETT, Brig (John) Brian; OBE (1958); s of John Guy Giberne Birkett (d 1967), of Cambrian House, Burgess Hill, Sussex; *b* 2 Oct 1916; *Educ* Marlborough, RMA Woolwich; *m* 1941, Emily Margaret, da of John Higginson; 2 s (1 decd), 1 da; *Career* served WWII, France, Belgium and Germany, Lt-Col 1958, Brig 1966, Brig gen staff MOD 1966-69; dir Trade Assoc 1969-83; Master Worshipful Co of Ironmongers 1974; *Recreations* active outdoor occupations; *Clubs* Army and Navy, Boodle's, Harlequin FC, MCC; *Style*— Brig Brian Birkett, OBE; West Tillingham House, Upper Hartfield, Sussex

BIRKETT, 2 Baron (UK 1958); Michael Birkett; s of 1 Baron Birkett (d 1962); *b* 22 Oct 1929; *Educ* Stowe, Trinity Coll Cambridge; *m* 1 (m dis), 10 Oct 1960, Mrs Junia Crawford (d 1973), da of Harold Elliott; m 2, 1978, Gloria, da of Thomas Taylor, of Queen's Gate, London; 1 s; *Heir* s, Hon Thomas Birkett b 25 July 1982; *Career* film prodr 1961-; prodns incl: The Caretaker, Marat/Sade, A Midsummer Night's Dream, King Lear; dep dir Nat Theatre 1975-77, conslt to Nat Theatre on films, TV and sponsorship 1977-79, dir Recreation and the Arts GLC 1979-86; pres BRIT Sch for Performing Arts and Technol Croydon 1980; Master Worshipful Co of Curriers' 1975-76; *Recreations* the arts; *Style*— The Rt Hon The Lord Birkett; House of Lords, London SW1

BIRKETT, Michael Phillip; *b* 30 May 1948; *Educ* Leicester Coll of Art, Leeds Polytechnic (BA Hons), Garnett Coll, RCA (MA); *Career* UK team contrib Paris Biennale 1969, asst designer Purcell Miller Tritton 1970-72, studio designer Replicards Ltd 1972-73, designer Purcell Miller Tritton 1973-77, lectr London Coll of Furniture 1978-83, freelance designer Gordon Bowyer & Partners 1980-81, princ lectr and co-ordinator of interior design studies Bournemouth & Poole Coll of Art & Design 1983-85; sr interior designer Space Planning Services Consultancy Group plc 1985-88; assoc ptnr Purcell Miller Tritton & Partners 1988-; BTEC moderator of spatial design BTEC HND 1985-90, external assessor Chelsea Sch of Art 1990-; *Style*— Michael Birkett, Esq; Purcell Miller Tritton & Partners, No 1 Tideway Yard, Mortlake High St, London SW14 8SN (☎ 081 392 1277)

BIRKETT, Peter Philip; s of Philip Walker Birkett (d 1945), of Lincoln, and Kathryn, *née* Tidy; *b* 19 Aug 1944; *Educ* Dauntsey's Sch Devizes Wilts; *m* Christine Sally; 2 da (Alice Emily, Rosamund Kate); *Career* reporter: Kent Messenger Maidstone Kent 1963-68, Daily Sketch 1968-70, Sunday Telegraph 1970-74, Daily Telegraph 1974-79, Daily Mail 1979-84; news ed Daily Telegraph, ed Peterborough Column in Daily Telegraph 1984-89, foreign ed Daily Mail 1989-; *Recreations* fishing, gardening; *Style*— Peter Birkett, Esq; Daily Mail, 2 Derry St, London W8 (☎ 071 938 6000)

BIRKETT, Peter Vidler; QC (1989); s of Neville Lawn Birkett JP, of Kendal, Cumbria, and Marjorie Joy, *née* Vidler; *b* 13 July 1948; *Educ* Sedbergh Sch Yorkshire, Univ of Leicester (LLB); *m* 11 Dec 1976, Jane Elizabeth, da of Robert Hall Fell, MBE (d 1981); 2 s (Nicholas Robert b 20 Dec 1984, Michael Peter Vidler b 12 Dec 1986); *Career* called to the Bar Inner Temple 1972, barr N Circuit 1972-, rec Crown Court 1989; memb Honorable Soc The Inner Temple; *Recreations* golf, skiing, music; *Clubs* Wilmslow Golf; *Style*— Peter Birkett, Esq, QC; 18 St John St, Manchester M3 4EA (☎ 061 834 9843)

BIRKIN, Sir (John) Derek; TD (1965); s of Noah Birkin, and Rebecca, *née* Stranks; *b* 30 Sept 1929; *Educ* Hemsworth GS; *m* 1 April 1952, Sadie, da of Ernest Wade-Smith; 1 s (Michael b 16 April 1957), 1 da (Alison (Mrs Lear) b 16 July 1958); *Career* 2 Lt RA (Nat Serv) 1948-50, Maj TA; md: Velmar Ltd 1966-67, Nairn Williamson Ltd 1967-70, Tunnel Holdings Ltd 1971-75; chm and md Tunnel Holdings Ltd 1975-83, dir The Rio Tinto-Zinc Corpn 1982- (dep chief exec 1983-85, chief exec and dep chm 1985-); dir: Smiths Industs Ltd 1977-84, British Gas Corporation 1982-85, George Wimpey plc 1984-, CRA Ltd (Aust) 1985-, Rio Algom Ltd (Canada) 1985-, British Steel plc (formerly British Steel Corporation) 1986-, The Merchants Trust plc 1986-, Barclays Plc 1990-; memb: Cncl of The Industrial Soc 1985-, Top Salaries Review Bd 1986-89; tstee Royal Opera House Trust 1990-; CBIM 1980, FRSA 1988; kt 1990; *Recreations* opera, rugby, cricket; *Clubs* MCC, Harlequins; *Style*— Derek Birkin, Esq, TD; The RTZ Corporation plc, 6 St James's Sq, London SW1Y 4LD (☎ 071 930 2399, fax 071 930 3249, telex 24639 RTZLDN G)

BIRKIN, Sir John Christian William; 6 Bt (UK 1905), of Ruddington Grange, Notts; o s of Sir Charles Birkin, 5 Bt (d 1985), and Janet Ramsay, *née* Johnson; *b* 1 July 1953; *Educ* Eton; *Heir* Kinsman, James Francis Richard Birkin b 27 Feb 1957; *Career* BBC TV, dir Compound Eye Productions; *Style*— Sir John Birkin, Bt; 23 St Luke's St, London SW3 5RP (☎ 071 351 4810)

BIRKMYRE, Archibald; s and h of Sir Henry Birkmyre, 2 Bt; *b* 12 Feb 1923; *Educ* Radley; *m* 1953, Gillian Mary, o da of late Eric M Downes, OBE; 1 s, 2 da (*see* Hon John Fellowes); *Career* Capt RA Burma 1941-45; memb London Stock Exchange; *Recreations* golf, shooting, fishing; *Clubs* Boodle's; *Style*— Archibald Birkmyre, Esq; The Old Presbytery, Buckland, Faringdon, Oxon, SN7 8QW (☎ 036 787253)

BIRKMYRE, Sir Henry; 2 Bt (UK 1921), of Dalmunzie, Co Perth; s of Sir Archibald Birkmyre, 1 Bt, CBE (d 1935); *b* 24 March 1898; *Educ* Wellington; *m* 1922, Doris Gertrude, da of Col Herbert Austen Smith, CIE (d 1949); 1 s, 1 da; *Heir* s, Archibald Birkmyre; *Career* serv WWI with RFA in France; former co dir; *Recreations* golf; *Clubs* Rye Golf, Cooden Beach Golf; *Style*— Sir Henry Birkmyre, Bt; Tudor Rest, 2 Calverley Park Gardens, Tunbridge Wells, Kent TN1 2DX

BIRKS, Dr Jack; CBE (1975); s of Herbert Horace Birks (d 1950), and Ann Birks; *b* 1 Jan 1920; *Educ* Ecclesfield GS, Univ of Leeds (BSc, PhD); *m* 1948, Vere Elizabeth, da of Barnard Burrell-Davis (d 1960); 2 s, 2 da; *Career* engr; md BP 1978-82 (ret); chm: Charterhouse Petroleum plc 1982-86, NMI Ltd 1982-85, BMT 1985-, Mountain Petroleum 1988-, North American Investment Trust; dir: Wimpey Gp 1982-90, Midland and Scot Resources 1982-, Petrofina (UK) 1986-89, Bellwether Exploration Co 1988-, BP Minerals International 1982-85, London American Energy NV 1982-88, Mountain Petroleum 1985-; memb: SRC 1976-80, Meteorological Ctee 1977-82, Cncl Univ of Surrey 1982-87, Maritime League 1982-86, Royal Inst 1982-85 and 1988-; pres Inst of Petroleum 1984-86; Hon LLD: Univ of Aberdeen 1981, Univ of Surrey 1981; CEng, FEng, FIMM, FInstPet, FIMechE; *Recreations* golf, tennis; *Clubs* Athenaeum, Norfolk; *Style*— Dr Jack Birks, CBE; British Maritime Technology Ltd, Orlando House, Waldegrave Rd, Teddington, Middlesex TW11 8LZ (☎ 081 943 5544); 1a Alwyne Rd, Canonbury, London N1 (☎ 071 226 4905); High Silver, High St, Holt, Norfolk (☎ 0263 712847); High Bank, Laceys Lane, Niton, Isle of Wight (☎ 0983 730282)

BIRKS, His Hon Judge Michael; s of Falconer Moffat Birks, CBE (d 1960) and Monica Katherine Lushington, *née* Mellor (d 1957); *b* 21 May 1920; *Educ* Oundle, Trinity Coll Cambridge (MA); *m* 1947, Ann Ethne, da of Capt Henry Stafford Morgan; 1 da; *Career* ft 22 Dragoons; slr 1946, asst registrar Chancery Div of High Ct 1953, asst county ct registrar 1960; registrar Birkenhead and Chester Gp of County Cts 1961-66, West London County Ct 1966-83, rec 1979, circuit judge S Eastern Circuit 1983-; advsy ed Atkins Ct Forms 1966-; *Books* Gentlemen of the Law (1960), contrib to fourth edn Halsbury's Laws of England; *Recreations* painting, sailing; *Style*— His Hon Judge Michael Birks

BIRKS, Prof Peter Brian Herrenden; s of Dr Peter Herrenden Birks, and (Maud) Mary, *née* Morgan; *b* 3 Oct 1941; *Educ* Trinity Coll Oxford (MA), UCL (LLM); *m* 29 Oct 1984, Jacqueline Susan; *Career* lectr UCL 1967-71, law fell Brasenose Coll Oxford 1971-81, prof of civil law Univ of Edinburgh 1981-88, prof of law Univ of Southampton 1988-89, visiting prof Aust Nat Univ 1989, Regius prof of civil law Univ of Oxford and professorial fell All Souls Coll Oxford 1989-; memb: Lord Chllr's Advsy Ctee on Legal Educn 1989-, SEAC Ctee on social sciences 1989-; hon sec Soc of Public Teachers of Law 1989-; FBA 1989; *Books* The Legal Mind (ed with N MacCormick), The Institutes of Justinian (with G McLeod, 1986), Introduction to the Law of Restitution (1989), New Perspectives in the Roman Law of Property (ed, 1989); *Clubs* Athenaeum; *Style*— Prof Peter Birks; 8 Cobden Crescent, Oxford OX1 4LJ (☎ 0865 727170); All Souls College, Oxford OX1 4AL (☎ 0865 279379, fax 0865 279 229)

BIRLEY, Lady; Elinor Margaret; da of Eustace Corrie Frere, FRIBA (d 1944), and Marion Edith Grant; *b* 15 Oct 1904; *Educ* Dragon, St Leonard's Sch St Andrews Fife, Lady Margaret Hall Oxford (MA); *m* 1930, Sir Robert Birley, KCMG (d 1982, sometime headmaster of Charterhouse and Eton), s of Leonard Birley, CSI, CIE; 1 da (Rachael) (1 da decd); *Recreations* reading, gardening, grandchildren; *Style*— Lady Birley; Lomans, West End, Somerton, Somerset (☎ 0458 72640)

BIRLEY, Marcus Oswald Hornby Lecky (Mark); s of Sir Oswald Birley (d 1952); *Educ* Eton, Univ Coll Oxford; *m* 1954 (m dis 1975), Lady Annabel Vane-Tempest-Stewart, d of 8 Marquess of Londonderry; 2 s, l da; *Clubs* White's, Bath, Travellers' (Paris), Jockey (Paris), The Brook (New York); *Style*— Mark Birley, Esq

BIRLEY, Richard Yvon; s of Stephen Harvey Yvon Birley, of Br Columbia (d 1941), and Erica Pressey (d 1971); *b* 16 Jan 1928; *Educ* RNC Dartmouth; *m* 1, April 1953 (m dis 1958), Constance, da of Richard Rheem, of San Francisco (d 1975); m 2, August 1958, Maureen Ann, da of James McNicol, of Perth, Scot; 4 s (Richard b 1954, Jeremy b 1959, Mark b 1962, Stephen b 1965), 1 da (Nicolette b 1956); *Career* RN Lt Submarines 1944-55; Shell Internat (London, Hague, S Africa, Iran) 1957-66; dir: Wm Brandts and Sons Ltd 1969-72, Edward Bates 1972-75; md KCA Drilling Ltd 1975; chm: Rea Bros Leasing 1976-, TLS Range plc 1988-; *Style*— Richard Birley, Esq; 24 Baltic Street, London EC1Y OTB (☎ 071 251 9111, 1991, fax 071 251 2609)

BIRLEY, Prof Susan Joyce; *Educ* Univ Coll London (BSc), Harvard (Int Teachers Prog scholar), Univ of London (PhD); *Career* lectr: Dunsmore Sch 1964-66, Dept of Econs and Mgmnt Lanchester Poly 1966-68; sr lectr Mgmnt Sch Poly of Central London 1970-72 (lectr 1968-70), sr res fell City Univ 1972-74, visiting lectr INSEAD 1978, sr res fell London Business Sch 1979-82 (lectr 1974-79), prof of strategy and entrepreneurship Coll of Business Univ of Notre Dame 1982-85 (adjunct assoc prof 1978-82); Cranfield Institute of Technology 1985-90 (dir Cranfield Entrepreneurship Res Centre, dir of res, Philip and Pauline Harris prof of entrepreneurship), dir of res and prof of mgmnt The Management School Imperial College of Science Technology and Medicine 1990-; chm Newchurch & Co; govr Harris City Technol Coll 1990; memb: NI Econ Cncl 1988, PCFC 1988- Advsy Panel on Deregulation DTI, E European Links Advsy Bd Br Cncl; Freeman City of London; *Books* The Small Business Casebook (1979), New Enterprises (1982), The British Entrepreneur (jtly, 1990), Building European Ventures (ed, 1990); *Style*— Prof Susan Birley; Imperial College of Science Technology and Medicine, The Management School, Prince Consort Rd, London SW7 2BP (☎ 071 589 5111)

BIRMINGHAM, Bishop of 1987-; Rt Rev Mark Santer; s of Rev Canon Eric Arthur Robert Santer (d 1979), of The Chaplain's Lodge, St Cross, Winchester, Hants, and Phyllis Clare, *née* Barlow (d 1978); *b* 29 Dec 1936; *Educ* Marlborough, Queens' Coll Cambridge (MA), Westcott House Cambridge; *m* 3 Oct 1964, Henriette Cornelia, da of Willem Antoine Gerard Westrate (d 1987), of Driebergen; 1 s (Diederick b 1969), 2 da (Hendrika b 1966, Miriam b 1967); *Career* ordained: deacon

1963, priest 1964; asst curate Cuddesdon and tutor Cuddesdon Theol Coll Oxford 1963-67, fell and dean Clare Coll Cambridge 1967-72, asst lectr in divinity Univ of Cambridge 1968-72, princ Westcott House Cambridge 1973-81, bishop of Kensington 1981-87; co-chm Anglican-Roman Catholic Int Cmmn 1983-; hon fell Clare Coll Cambridge 1987; memb Cncl Nat Assoc for Care and Resettlement of Offenders 1985-; Freeman City of London 1984; *Books* The Phenomenon of Christian Belief (contrib, 1970), Documents in Early Christian Thought (1975), Their Lord and Ours (contrib, 1982), The Church and State (contrib, 1984), Dropping the Bomb (contrib, 1985); *Style*— The Rt Rev the Bishop of Birmingham; Bishop's Croft, Old Church Rd, Harborne, Birmingham B17 0BG (☎ 021 427 1163, fax 021 426 1322)

BIRMINGHAM, 7 Archbishop of (RC) 1982-; Most Rev Maurice Noël Léon Couve de Murville; s of Noël Couve de Murville, and Marie, da of Sir Louis Souchon; 4 cous once removed of Maurice Couve de Murville, French PM 1968-69; *b* 27 June 1929, in France; *Educ* Downside, Trinity Coll Cambridge (MA), Institut Catholique Paris (STL), Sch of Oriental and African Studies Univ of London (MPhil); *Career* priest 1957, curate St Anselm's Dartford 1957-60, priest i/c St Francis Moulsecoomb 1961-64; Catholic chaplain: Univ of Sussex 1961-77, Univ of Cambridge 1977-82; *Style*— The Most Rev Maurice Couve de Murville; Archbishop's House, St Chad's Queensway, Birmingham B4 6EX (☎ 021 236 5535)

BIRNBERG, Benedict Michael; s of Jonas Birnberg (d 1970), and Naomi Hilda, *née* Bentwich (d 1988); *b* 8 Sept 1930; *Educ* Minehead GS, King's Sch Canterbury, Corpus Christi Coll Univ of Cambridge (BA); *m* 29 April 1968, Triantafyllia (Felitsa), da of Kyriakos Matziorinis (d 1946); 1 da (Ariadne b 1971); *Career* admitted slr 1958; sr ptnr B M Birnberg and Co; chm NCCL 1974; chm Lewisham CAB 1979-84; govr Greenwich Theatre Ltd 1974-78; *Recreations* music, theatre, politics; *Style*— Benedict Birnberg, Esq; 4 Eliot Place, Blackheath, London SE3 (☎ 081 852 1937); 103 Borough High St, London SE1 (☎ 071 403 3166)

BIRNIE, John; s of John Birnie, of Ellon, Aberdeenshire, and Helen, *née* Russell (d 1982); *b* 31 Oct 1935; *Educ* Peterhead Acad; *m* 20 June 1962, Helen Summers, da of Andrew Taylor (d 1965), of Fraserburgh; 2 s (Russell b 1964, Owen b 1972, Linzi b 1967); *Career* Gordon Highlanders, WO 1954-57; cmmnd RAPC (TA) 1957-67, transferred to RARO 1967; scholarship Sparbanken Stockholm 1975; mangr Aberdeen TSB: Stornoway 1975-79, Elgin 1979-86; sr fin advsr Hill Samuel; fndr Scottish Landowners Fedn; treas: Moray and West Banff Cons and Unionist Assoc, Banff and Moray Centre Nat Tst for Scotland; chm Local Mutual Improvement Assoc; former: pres Jr Chamber, pres Speakers Club, sec Rotary Club, memb local community cncl; ACIB 1962; *Recreations* fishing, walking, gardening; *Style*— John Birnie, Esq; Druimchoille, Fochabers, Moray

BIRNIE, Lady (Marguerite) Kathleen; *née* Courtenay; 3 da of Rev 16 Earl of Devon (d 1935), and Marguerite, *née* Silva (d 1950); *b* 15 Feb 1911; *m* 22 Nov 1933, Col Eugene St John Birnie, OBE (d 1976), s of Cyril Montague Birnie (d 1958), of Melbourne, Australia; 2 da (Marguerite Susan b 1934, Angela Patricia Jane b 1936); *Style*— Lady Kathleen Birnie; The Cottage, Longparish, Hants (☎ 026 472 346)

BIRO, Val Balint Stephen; s of Dr Balint Biro (d 1944), of Budapest, Hungary, and Margaret, *née* Gylahazi (d 1982); *b* 6 Oct 1921; *Educ* Cistercian Sch Budapest, Central Sch of Art and Design London; *m* 1, 1945 (m dis), Vivien, da of A H Woolley; 1 da (Melissa b 1951); m 2, 1970, Marie-Louise Ellaway, da of P Christofas; 1 step s (Philip b 1956), 1 step da (Caroline b 1961); *Career* author and illustrator; memb AFS London 1942-45, studio mangr Sylvan Press London 1944-46, prodn mangr C & J Temple London 1946-48, art dir John Lehmann Ltd London 1948-53, freelance illustrator designer; cncllr 1966-70, memb and chm governing bodies Amersham Coll of Art & Design 1974-84; author and illustrator of about 40 children's books incl series of Gumdrop books (about a vintage car); also author of: Hungarian Folktales (1981), The Magic Doctor (1982), The Hobyahs (1985), Tobias and the Dragon (1989), Look-and-Find ABC (1990), Rub-a-Dub-Dub Nursery Ryhmes (1991); illustrator of over 300 books incl: Worlds Without End (Denys Val Baker, 1945), The Prisoner of Zenda (Anthony Hope 1961), Wizard of Oz books (L Frank Baum 1965- 67), The Good Food Guide (1971), The Wind in the Willows (Kenneth Grahame, 1983), The King's Jokes (Margaret Mahy, 1987); contrib weekly illustrations Radio Times 1951-72; named among Top Hundred Authors in list from PLR 1990; FCSD, memb Soc of Authors; *Recreations* vintage car motoring; *Clubs* Vintage Sports Car, Vintage Austin Register; *Style*— Val Biro, Esq

BIRRELL, James Gibson; WS (1979); s of James Adamson Birrell, of 5-6 Fettes Rise, Edinburgh, and Louisa Elizabeth, *née* Silvester; *b* 10 June 1948; *Educ* Loretto, Queen Mary Coll, Univ of London (BA); *m* 15 Aug 1970, Angela Hilary, da of Eric Robert Soame, of Radley Rd, Abingdon, Oxon; 2 s (Gordon b 1976, David b 1978), 1 da (Jane b 1982); *Career* slr 1972; ptnr: Brodies 1976-85, Dickson Minto 1985-; external examiner in Commercial Law Univ of Edinburgh, memb Insolvency Practioners Adjudication Panel (Scot); memb Law Soc: Eng and Wales 1972, Scotland 1975; *Books* contrib Stair Memorial Encylopaedia (1987); *Recreations* music, photography, skiing, squash, golf; *Clubs* Caledonian; *Style*— James Birrell, Esq, WS; 26 Kinnear Rd, Edinburgh, EH3 5PE (☎ 031 552 1077); 11 Walker St, Edinburgh, EH3 7NE (☎ 031 225 4455, fax 031 225 2712); Royal London House, 22/25 Finsbury Square, London EC2A 1DS (☎ 071 628 4455, fax 071 628 0027)

BIRSAY, Lady; Robina Margaret; only da of J G Marwick, FSA (Scot), sometime Provost of Stromness, Orkney; *Educ* Univ of Edinburgh (MB ChB); *m* 1945, Sir Harald Robert Leslie, Hon Lord Birsay, KT, CBE, TD, QC, DL (d 1982), a Lord of Session; 1 s, 1 da; *Career* Capt RAMC (despatches); *Style*— Lady Birsay; Queenafjold, Birsay, Orkney KW17 2LZ (☎ 085 672 286); 5/34 Oswald Rd, Edinburgh EH9 2HR (☎ 031 662 0324)

BIRSE, Peter Malcolm; s of Peter Alexander McCauley Birse, of 7 MacKenzie St, Carnoustie, Scotland, and Margaret Cumming, *née* Craib; *b* 24 Nov 1942; *Educ* Arbroath HS, Univ of St Andrews (BSc); *m* 25 Jan 1969, Helen, da of Paul Stanley Searle, of Bishopston, Bristol; 2 s (James Peter Alexander b 1971, Robert Archibald b 1975), 1 da (Bridget b 1969); *Career* engr John Mowlem Ltd 1963-65, engr and project mangr Gammon Ghana Ltd 1965-67, contract mangr Gammon (UK) Ltd 1967-70, established Birse Gp plc (construction gp) 1970-; chm Peter Birse Charitable Tst; MICE 1971; *Recreations* sailing, skiing, tennis, golf, fishing; *Clubs* Royal Ocean Racing; *Style*— Peter Birse, Esq; Flat 4, Welbeck House, 62 Welbeck St, London W1; High Hall Etton, Beverley, Humberside, HU17 7PE (☎ 0430 810 230); c/o Birse Gp plc, Humber Rd, Barton-On-Humber, Humberside, DN18 5BN (☎ 0652 33222, fax 0652 33360, telex 527442, car 0831 272 572)

BIRT, Alan Beckett; CBE (1979); s of Guy Capper Birt, CVO (d 1972), and Roberta, *née* Ross (d 1976); *b* 24 June 1915; *Educ* Wellington, St Thomas's Hosp Med Sch Univ of London (MB BS); *m* 1, 15 Sept 1939, Joyce Staunton (d 1986), da of Capt Husband, IMS, DSO (d 1916), of India; 1 s (Christopher Alan b 1942), 3 da (Rosemary Alison (Mrs Zakrzewski) b 1946, Alix Mary (Mrs Barbabas) b 1948, Jennifer Anne (Mrs Garner) b 1950); m 2, 4 Oct 1986, Peggy Jean, wid of Mr F Wilkinson (d 1977); *Career* Maj RAMC 1941-45: N Africa, Sicily, Italy 1942-45 (Lt-Col Italy and Greece 1945-46); St Thomas's Hosp London: casualty offr 1937, house surgn 1938, surgical registrar and tutor 1939-41; conslt surgn: Norfolk & Norwich Hosp, Jenny Lind Children's Hosp Norwich 1946-79; examiner in surgery: Univ of Cambridge, Univ of Edinburgh 1975-80; memb and chm Specialist Advsy Ctee for Gen Surgery of the Four Royal Colls of Surgns, past pres and fell The Assoc of Surgns of GB and Ireland, cncl memb The Int Trauma Fndn 1984-, memb Soc of Thoracic Surgns of GB, fell Assoc of Surgns of Poland (elected 1972); Hon ScD Univ of East Anglia 1979; MRCS, LRCP, FRCS; *Books* chapters in British Practice - Surgical Progress (1961), numerous articles in scientific surgical jls; *Recreations* gardening, mountain climbing, sailing; *Style*— Alan Birt, Esq, CBE; 264A Reepham Rd, Hellesdon, Norwich, Norfolk NR6 5SP (☎ 0603 787199)

BIRT, John; s of Leo Vincent Birt, of Richmond, Surrey, and Ida Birt; *b* 10 Dec 1944; *Educ* St Mary's Coll Liverpool, St Catherine's Coll Oxford (MA); *m* 14 Sept 1965, Jane Frances, da of James Harris Lake (d 1982, 2 Lt US Navy), of Chevy Chase, Maryland, USA; 1 s (Jonathan b 1968), 1 da (Eliza b 1971); *Career* prodr Nice Time 1968-69, jt ed World in Action 1969-70, prodr The Frost Programme 1971-72, exec prodr Weekend World 1972-74, head current affrs LWT 1974-77, co prodr The Nixon Interviews 1977, controller of features and current affrs LWT 1977-81, dir of programmes LWT 1982-87, dep dir gen BBC 1987-; memb: Wilton Park Academic Cncl 1980-83, Media Law Gp 1983-, Working Pty on the New Technols Broadcasting Res Unit 1981-83 (memb Exec Ctee 1983-87); FRTS; *Style*— John Birt Esq; BBC, Broadcasting House, London W1A 1AA (☎ 071 580 4468)

BIRTS, Peter William; QC 1990; s of John Claude Birts (d 1969), of Sussex, and Audrey Lavinia, *née* McIntyre; *b* 9 Feb 1946; *Educ* Lancing, St John's Coll Cambridge (MA); *m* 24 April 1971, Penelope Ann, da of Wing Cdr Anthony Eyre, DFC (d 1946); 1 s (William b 1979), 2 da (Melanie b 1972, Charlotte b 1975); *Career* called to the Bar Gray's Inn 1968; recorder S Eastern Circuit 1989; Freeman of City of London 1967, Liveryman Worshipful Co of Carpenters 1967; elected to Bar Cncl 1990; *Books* Trespass: Summary Procedure for Possession of Land (with Alan Willis, 1987), Remedies for Trespass (1990); *Recreations* music, shooting, tennis; *Clubs* Hurlingham; *Style*— Peter Birts, Esq, QC; Farrar's Building, Temple, London EC4Y 7BD (☎ 071 583 9241, fax 071 583 0090)

BIRTWISTLE, Maj-Gen Archibald Cull; CB (1983), CBE (1976, OBE 1971); s of Walter Edwin Birtwistle, and Eila Louise, *née* Cull; *b* 19 Aug 1927; *Educ* St John's Coll Cambridge (MA); *m* 1956, Sylvia Elleray; 2 s, 1 da; *Career* cmmnd RCS 1949, serv Korea (despatches), Dep Cmdt RMCS 1975-79, Chief Signal Offr BAOR 1979-80, Signal Offr-in-C (Army) 1980-83, ret; memb Def Spectrum Review Ctee, Col Cmdt RCS 1983-, Hon Col 34 (Northern) Signal Regt (Volunteers) 1988-90; Master of Signals and Col Cmdt RCS 1990-; CEng, MIEE; *Recreations* gardening; *Style*— Maj-Gen Archibald Birtwistle, CB, CBE; c/o Nat West Bank plc, 97 High St, Northallerton, N Yorks DL7 8PS

BIRTWISTLE, Hon Mrs (Diana); *née* Barnewall; o da of 19 Baron Trimlestown (d 1990), and his 1 w, Muriel, *née* Schneider (d 1937); *b* 13 Oct 1929; *m* 1954, Anthony Gerard Astley Birtwistle, yst s of James Astley Birtwistle, of Hoghton, nr Preston, Lancs, and Wroxton, Banbury, Oxon; 4 da; *Style*— The Hon Mrs Birtwistle; Hatch Hill House, Hindhead, Surrey (☎ 042 873 60 4388)

BIRTWISTLE, Sir Harrison; s of Frederick Birtwistle (d 1985), and Margaret, *née* Harrison (d 1970); *b* 15 July 1934; *Educ* Royal Manchester Coll of Music, RAM London (LRAM); *m* 4 Jan 1958, Sheila Margaret Wilhelmina, da of George Duff (d 1986); 3 s (Adam b 1959, Silas b 1963, Thomas b 1965); *Career* composer; visiting fell Princeton Univ USA 1968; visiting prof of music Swarthmore Coll Pennsylvania USA 1975; visiting Slee Prof State Univ NY at Buffalo USA 1977; Harkness Fell Univ Colorado Boulder USA 1969; associate dir music Nat Theatre London 1976-88; Hon FRMCM and ARMCM Royal Northern Coll of Music 1986; Evening Standard Award for Opera 1986; Grawemeyer Award Univ Louisville Kentucky USA 1986; Hon Fell: RAM, Akademie der Kunst Berlin; chevalier des Arts et des Lettres (France) 1986; kt 1988; *Recreations* fishing, walking; *Style*— Sir Harrison Birtwistle; c/o Allied Artists, 42 Montpelier Square, London SW7 1JZ (☎ 071 589 6243, fax 071 581 5269)

BIRTWISTLE, Sue Elizabeth; da of Frank Edgar Birtwistle (d 1987), of Northwich, Cheshire, and Brenda Mary, *née* Higham; *b* 12 Dec 1945; *m* 14 July 1973, Richard Charles Hastings Eyre, s of Cdr Richard Galfredus Hastings Giles Eyre; 1 da (Lucy b 25 Sept 1974); *Career* theatre dir: Royal Lyceum Theatre in Educn Co 1970-72, Nottingham Playhouse Roundabout Co 1973-78, freelance 1978-80; freelance TV prodr 1980-; films incl: Hotel Du Lac (BAFTA award 1987, ACE award 1988), Scoop, V (Royal TV Soc award), Or Shall We Die, Dutch Girls, Ball-Trap on the Côte Savage; memb Arts Cncl Drama Panel 1975-77; memb ACTT 1979; *Recreations* the countryside, books, theatre, music, croquet; *Style*— Miss Sue Birtwistle; c/o Peter Murphy, Curtis Brown, 162-168 Regent St, London W1 (☎ 01 872 0331)

BISCHOFF, Winfried Franz Wilhelm; s of Paul Helmut Bischoff, of Dunkeld, Johannesburg SA, and Hildegard, *née* Kühne; *b* 10 May 1941; *Educ* schs in Germany, Marist Bros Johannesburg SA, Univ of Witwatersrand Johannesburg (BCom); *m* 1972, Rosemary Elizabeth, da of Hon Leslie John Leathers, *qv*; 2 s (Christopher b 1973, Charles b 1975); *Career* merchant banker; formerly with Chase Manhattan in NY, md Schroders Asia Ltd (formerly Schroders & Chartered Ltd) Hong Kong 1971-82, chm J Henry Schroder Wagg and Co Ltd London 1983-, gp chief exec Schroders plc 1984-; *Recreations* golf, opera, music, the country; *Clubs* Hurlingham, Woking GC, Frilford Heath GC; *Style*— Winfried Bischoff, Esq; 28 Bloomfield Terrace, London SW1W 8PQ; J Henry Schroder Wagg and Co Ltd, 120 Cheapside, London EC2V 6DS (☎ 01 382 6000, telex London 885029)

BISCOE, Michael; s of Guy Biscoe (d 1967), of London, and Sheila Mary, *née* Seymour Chalk; *b* 4 May 1938; *Educ* Westminster, Selwyn Coll Cambridge (MA, Dip Arch); *m* 28 Jan 1967, Kari Jetten, da of Edward Beresford Davies, of Cambridge; 1 s (Guy b 14 May 1970), 1 da (Henrietta b 5 Jan 1968); *Career* Nat Serv 2 Lt 43 LAA Regt RA, serv Cyprus 1956-58; sr ptnr Biscoe & Stanton 1977- (ptnr 1967-); Liveryman: Worshipful Co of Leathersellers 1972, Worshipful Co of Chartered Surveyors 1975; memb RIBA, FRICS; *Recreations* music, golf, rowing, shooting, fishing; *Clubs* Carlton, RAC, Chelsea Arts; *Style*— Michael Biscoe, Esq; Biscoe & Stanton Architects, 1 Snow Hill Court, London EC1A 2EJ (☎ 071 248 5258, fax 071 248 3768, car 0836 210 244)

BISCOE, Prof Timothy John; s of Rev W H Biscoe, TD (d 1969), and M G A Biscoe, *née* Middleton (d 1989); *b* 28 April 1932; *Educ* Latymer Upper Sch, London Hosp Med Coll (BSc, MB BS); *m* 17 Sept 1955, Daphne Miriam, da of W P Gurton; 1 s (Max), 2 da (Sarah, Mandy); *Career* short serv cmmn RAMC 1958-61; Inst of Animal Physiology Babraham Cambridge 1962-, Inst of Advanced Studies Canberra 1965-, Cardiovascular Research Institute San Francisco Med Centre 1968, chm Dept of Physiology Univ of Bristol 1975 (joined 1969, prof 1970), vice provost UCL 1990, Jodrell prof Dept of Physiology UCL 1979- (chm 1979-1988); pubns in scientific jls and books on neurobiology; memb: Cncl Res Def Soc (exec), Exec Ctee Save Br Sci; FRCP; *Recreations* reading, writing; *Clubs* Garrick; *Style*— Prof Timothy Biscoe; Dept of Physiology, University College London, Gower St, London WC1E 6BT (☎ 071 380 7129, fax 071 383 7005)

BISHOP, Alan Henry; CB (1989); s of Robert Dick Bishop (d 1968), and May Douglas, *née* Watson (d 1968); *b* 12 Sept 1929; *Educ* George Heriots Sch Edinburgh,

Univ of Edinburgh (MA); *m* 30 March 1959, Marjorie Anne, da of Joseph Henry Conlan (d 1988); 1 s (Keith b 1961), 1 da (Susan b 1960); *Career* asst princ Dept of Agric 1954-59, private sec to Lord John Hope (Lord Glendevon) and G Leburn (jr mins SO) 1958-59, princ Dept of Agric and Fisheries Scotland 1960-63 and 1967-68, first sec Food and Agric Copenhagen and The Hague 1963-66; asst sec: Scot Devpt Dept 1968-69, Royal Cmmn on the Constitution 1969-73, SO 1973-80; asst under sec of state SO 1980-84; princ estab offr 1984-89, HM Chief Inspr of Prisons for Scotland 1989-; *Recreations* contract bridge, theatre, golf, reading; *Clubs* New (Edinburgh), Murrayfield Golf (Edinburgh), Melville Bridge (Edinburgh); *Style*— Alan Bishop, Esq, CB; Beaumont Court, 19/8 Wester Coates Gardens, Edinburgh EH12 5LT (☎ 031 346 4641); St Andrews House, Edinburgh EH1 3DE (☎ 031 244 2335)

BISHOP, (William) Archie; s of Evelyn Archie Bishop (1979), and Gertrude, *née* Pocock (1988); *b* 21 July 1937; *Educ* Thames Nautical Training Coll, Sir John Cass Coll, Coll of Law; *m* 8 April 1961, Joan Beatrice, da of Charles Edward Skerman (d 1983); 1 s (Mark b 14 Feb 1966), 1 da (Paula b 24 Feb 1963); *Career* deck offr P & O Line 1954-60; Holman Fenwick & Willan: mangr Admiralty Dept 1960-70, ptnr 1970-89, sr ptnr 1989-; Freeman: City of London, Worshipful Co of Watermen and Lightermen, City of London Solicitors Co; memb Law Soc; *Recreations* golf, horse riding, hunting, fishing, painting; *Clubs* IOD; *Style*— Archie Bishop, Esq; Holman, Fenwick & Willan, Marlow House, Lloyds Avenue, London EC3N 3AL (☎ 071 488 2300, fax 071 481 0316)

BISHOP, Christopher David; s of Joseph Charles Bishop, and Zephyr Ethel, *née* Breese; *b* 8 Sept 1938; *Educ* Eastbourne Coll; *m* 22 July 1961, Judith, da of Harry Leonard Wise (d 1986); 3 s (David Charles b 1962, Simon Christopher b 1965, Guy Elliott b 1970), 1 da (Lucinda b 1968); *Career* articled clerk then mangr Baker Sutton and Co 1956-71, co sec GR Merton (Agencies) Ltd 1971-74, princ Christopher Bishop and Co 1974-85, ptnr Ernst and Whinney now Ernst & Young 1985-; FCA; *Recreations* hunting, equestrian sports, golf; *Clubs* City of London; *Style*— Christopher Bishop, Esq; Becket House, 1 Lambeth Palace Rd, London SE1 7EU (☎ 071 928 2000, fax 071 928 1345, telex 885234)

B'SHOP, Dr (Arthur) Clive; s of Charles Henry Bishop (d 1966), of Newcastle, Staffs, and Hilda, *née* Clowes; *b* 9 July 1930; *Educ* Wolstanton Co GS Newcastle Staffs, King's Coll London (BSc, PhD); *m* 8 Sept 1962, Helen, da of Joseph Bennison (d 1983), of Stoke-on-Trent; 1 da ((Elizabeth) Anne b 1965); *Career* Nat Serv Educn Branch RAF 1955-57; geologist HM Geological Survey Edinburgh 1954-58, lectr in geology Queen Mary Coll London 1958-69; Br Natural History Museum: princ sci offr 1969-72, dep keeper 1972-74, keeper of mineralogy 1975-89, dep dir 1982-89; fell King's Coll London 1985; Membre d'Honneur La Societe Jersiaise 1983; memb GA (pres 1978-80), life memb Mineralogical Soc (pres 1978-80); FGS; *Books* An Outline of Crystal Morphology (1967), Hamlyn Guide to Minerals, Rocks and Fossils (with W R Hamilton and A R Woolley, 1974); *Recreations* painting; *Style*— Dr Clive Bishop; 4 Viewfield Rd, Bexley, Kent DA5 3EE (☎ 081 302 9602)

BISHOP, David Broughton Gibson; s of Col A W G Bishop, MC (d 1979); *b* 1 Feb 1933; *Educ* Wellington, Jesus Coll Cambridge; *m* 1974, Judith, *née* Brown; 1 s, 1 da; *Career* slr; sr ptnr Baileys Shaw & Gillett 1979-88 (ptnr 1961); dir Syndicate Administration and other cos; *Recreations* cricket, skiing, shooting, gardening, antiques; *Clubs* Sunningdale Golf, United Oxford and Cambridge; *Style*— David Bishop, Esq; Old Rectory, Easton, nr Winchester, Hants (☎ 096 278 205); Baileys Shaw and Gillett, 17 Queen Square, London WC1N 3RH (☎ 071 837 5455)

BISHOP, David Charles; s of Kenneth Charles Bishop, MBE, of Sedbergh, Cumbria, and Margaret Cecilia Bishop, JP, *née* Birtwistle; *b* 6 April 1947; *Educ* Sedbergh, Gonville and Caius Coll, Cambridge (MA); *m* 6 June 1980, Ann Winifred, da of Leslie Brian Tallon (d 1984), of Blundellsands; 1 s (Michael b 1983), 1 da (Julia b 1984); *Career* admitted slr 1972; ptnr Laces & Co, Notary Public 1984, ptnr Lace Mawer Slrs 1988; memb Law Soc; *Recreations* ornithology; *Style*— David Bishop, Esq; 14 Wrigleys Close, Freshfield, Liverpool L37 7DT (☎ 07048 73819); Lace Mawer, Solicitors, 43 Castle St, Liverpool L2 9SU (☎ 051 236 2002, fax 051 236 2585, telex 627229, car 0831 117927)

BISHOP, (Thomas) David; s of Thomas Challis Bishop (d 1981), of Conifer, Underhill Park Road, Reigate, Surrey, and Mary, *née* Simmons; *b* 22 Aug 1934; *Educ* Charterhouse; *m* 20 Sept 1966, Josephine Anne, da of Lionel Mitchell Robinson, of Rodney, Brockenhurst, Hants; 1 s (Jeremy b 1970), 1 da (Belinda b 1973); *Career* Nat Serv RA 1955-56; slr 1960, ptnr Hunters 1961-, clerk Worhsipful Co of Masons 1986-87; *Recreations* cricket, tennis, skiing, shooting, classical music, travelling; *Clubs* Boodle's, MCC; *Style*— David Bishop, Esq; Spur Point, Marley Heights, Haslemere, Surrey (☎ 0428 3050); 9 New Square, Lincoln's Inn, London WC2A 3QN (☎ 01 242 4931)

BISHOP, Errol Simon Owen; s of Dr Peter Maxwell Farrow Bishop (d 1979), and Winifred Phyllis, *née* Thurston (d 1981); *b* 1 Aug 1938; *Educ* Charterhouse, Univ of Southampton (BSc); *m* ; 1 s (Max b 1970), 2 da (Charlotte b 1966, Katherine b 1970); *Career* dir and gp md Dihurst Holdings Ltd 1976-80, dir and dep chm Systems Designers Int Ltd 1976-81; currently: exec dir Barclays Developement Capital Ltd and related cos, dir Carpet Express Hldgs Ltd, Mecro Gp Ltd, Ashwood Holdings, NE Technol Ltd; CEng, MIMechE, FBIM; *Recreations* motor racing, DIY; *Style*— Errol Bishop, Esq; Parnells, Witherenden Hill, Burwash Common, E Sussex; Barclays Developement Capital Ltd, Pickfords Wharf, Clink St, London SE1 9DG (fax 071 407 3362)

BISHOP, Sir Frederick Arthur; CB (1960), CVO (1957); s of late A J Bishop, of Bristol, and Mary Shaw; *b* 4 Dec 1915; *Educ* Colston's Hosp, Univ of London (LLB); *m* 1940, Elizabeth Finlay, da of Samuel Stevenson, of Belfast; 2 s, 1 da; *Career* Miny of Food 1947, PPS to Min of Food 1949-52, asst sec to Cabinet Office 1952-55, PPS to PM 1956-59; dep sec: Cabinet 1959-61, MAFF 1961-64; perm sec Miny of Land and Natural Resources 1964-65; dir: S Pearson and Sons Ltd 1966-70, Pearson Longman Ltd 1970-77; dir-gen Nat Tst 1971-75; dir: English China Clays, Lloyds Bank Ltd (Devon and Cornwall) 1975-86; kt 1975; *Style*— Sir Frederick Bishop, CB, CVO; Manor Barn, Bramshott, Liphook, Hants

BISHOP, Sir George Sidney; CB (1958), OBE (1947); s of late Joseph Bishop, of Wigan, Lancs; *b* 15 Oct 1913; *Educ* Ashton-in-Makerfield GS, LSE; *m* 1, 1940 (m dis 1961), Marjorie, da of C H Woodruff, of Illingworth; 1 da; m 2, 1961, Una, da of late C F C Padel, of Inkpen, Berks; *Career* joined Civil Serv 1940, under-sec MAFF 1949 (dep sec 1959-61), chm Bookers Int Hldgs Ltd 1964-70, vice chm Int Wheat Cncl 1959, dir Nigerian Sugar Co Ltd 1966-70; Booker McConnell Ltd: vice chm 1970-71, chm 1972-79, dir 1961-, dir Ibec (agribusiness assoc of Booker McConnell) to 1983; chm West India Ctee 1969-71, memb Panel for Civil Serv Manpower Review 1968-70; dir: Barclays Bank Int 1972-, Barclays Bank 1974-, Rank Hovis McDougall 1976-, Int Basic Economy Corpn USA; kt 1975; *Style*— Sir George Bishop CB, OBE; Brenva, Egham's Wood Rd, Beaconsfield, Bucks (☎ 0494 3096)

BISHOP, Jack Stanley; s of Albert Bishop (d 1970), of Cippenham, Slough, Berks, and Rhoda Bishop (d 1970); *b* 2 Sept 1918; *Educ* Cof E; *m* 3 June 1939, Megan Elsie Ada, da of Leonard John Kilby (d 1983), of Stoke Poges, Slough, Berks; 3 s (Jack E b 18 Feb 1941, Derek V b 5 June 1946, Peter D b 4 Sept 1948); *Career* served Army WWII 1939-45, fought in the desert, Sicily, Italy and Germany; chm and dir: Bishops Holdings Ltd, JS Bishop & Co Ltd, Bishop Swimming Pools Ltd, Bishops Civil Engrg Co Ltd, William Wood & Son Ltd, Bishop Sports and Leisure Ltd, Bishops Commercial Admin Ltd, Holiday Habitats Ltd, Shorters Construction Co Ltd, Olympic Golf (Devpts) Ltd, Beechwood Nurseries Ltd, Slough Masonic Hall Ltd, Thames Chilton Chamber of Commerce and Indust, Harmud Properties Ltd; chm and dir Inst of Swimming Pool Engrs, (fell 1980-); past pres: Thames Chiltern Chamber of Commerce and Indust (current cncl memb), Windsor Eton and Dist Royal Warrant Holders Assoc (current cncl memb), Royal S Bucks Agric Assoc, Slough Rotary Club, 4 Nat Trade Assocs; former chm Berkshire Fire Liaison Ctee, former Bucks County Cncllr, former govr Bd of Dirs of Slough Coll of HE, pres League of Friends of the Slough Hosps, Holder of the Royal warrant for HM the Queen and HM the Queen Mother; Freeman City of London 1976, Master of the Worshipful Co of Glovers London 1989-90; FBIM 1975; *Recreations* travel, sport; *Clubs* City Livery, Guards Polo, Slough Rotary; *Style*— Jack Bishop, Esq; Bishops Court, East Burnham Park, Allerds Rd, Farnham Royal, Slough SL2 3TJ (☎ 0753 643505); Bishop House, Bath Rd, Taplow, Nr Maidenhead, Berks SL6 0NY (☎ 0628 604444, fax 0628 665647, telex 849325, car 0860 334773)

BISHOP, James Drew; s of Sir (Frank) Patrick Bishop, MBE, MP (d 1972), and his 1 wife Vera Sophie, *née* Drew (d 1953); *b* 18 June 1929; *Educ* Haileybury, CCC Cambridge; *m* 1959, Brenda, da of George Pearson; 2 s; *Career* The Times: foreign corr 1957-64, foreign news ed 1964-66, asst ed features 1966-70; ed Illustrated London News 1971-1987; dir: Illustrated London News and Sketch Ltd 1971, Int Thomas Publishing Ltd 1980-85; ed in chief Illustrated London News Pubns 1987-; memb Advsy Bd Annual Register 1970-; *Books* A Social History of Edwardian Britain (1977), A Social History of the First World War (1982), The Story of the Times (with Oliver Woods, 1983), Illustrated Counties of England (ed, 1985); *Recreations* reading, walking; *Clubs* Oxford and Cambridge, MCC; *Style*— James Bishop, Esq; 11 Willow Rd, London NW3 (☎ 071 435 4403); 20 Upper Ground, London SE1 9PF (☎ 071 928 2111)

BISHOP, John Andrew; s of Sidney Bishop (d 1978), and Winnie Bishop; *b* 1 Aug 1946; *Educ* London GS; *m* 20 March 1972, Bernadette; 2 s (Sebastian Luke b 11 April 1974, Oliver Sam b 30 Jan 1977); *Career* photographer; worked regularly for: Vogue, Elle (Br, French, Italian), Harpers, Tatler, Marie Curie; also worked for major advertisers including: L'Oreal, Max Factor, Harrods, Next, Austin Reed, Laura Ashley; *Recreations* sports; *Style*— John Bishop, Esq; 126 Shirland Rd, London W9 (☎ 071 286 8136)

BISHOP, John Anthony Fremantle; s of Evan Winfrid Bishop, OBE, of 9 Mead Rd, Pennington, Lymington, Hants, and Mary, *née* Godwin-Smith (d 1983); *b* 17 Feb 1949; *Educ* Warminster Sch, LAMDA; *Career* BBC TV: floor asst 1971, asst floor mangr, then prodn mangr 1974, dir of Light Entertainment 1980, prodr light entertainment 1984, exec prodr 1988, asst head of variety in light entertainment 1988-; *Recreations* theatre and swimming; *Style*— John Bishop, Esq; BBC Television, TV Centre, Wood Lane, London W12 (☎ 081 576 7941, fax 081 743 2457)

BISHOP, Dr John Edward; s of Reginald John Bishop, and Eva, *née* Lucas; *b* 23 Feb 1935; *Educ* Cotham Sch Bristol, St John's Coll Cambridge (MA, MusB), Univ of Reading, Univ of Edinburgh (DMus); *Career* asst dir then sr dir of Music Worksop Coll 1958-72; Birmingham Sch of Music 1972-86: dir of studies, head of sch, head of admissions, then head of organ studies; freelance musician 1986-; former pres: Birmingham, Sheffield and Bristol Organists' Assocs; former govr of City of Birmingham Poly; dir of music Cotham Parish Church Bristol, dir Bristol Highbury Singers, chm Bristol Centre Inc Soc of Musicians; conslt in organ studies Wells Cathedral sch; hon fell Birmingham Sch of Music 1986; FRCO (chm), ADCM ISM (chm Bristol Centre); *Recreations* walking, savouring the countryside, railways; *Style*— Dr John Bishop; 98 High Kingsdown, Bristol BS2 8ER (☎ 0272 423373)

BISHOP, John Maurice; s of Edwin Maurice Bishop, of Paignton, Devon, and Joyce Emily, *née* Edmunds; *b* 6 May 1947; *Educ* Sherborne, Queen Mary Coll Univ of London (LLB); *m* 1, 30 March 1970 (m dis 1985), Maureen, *née* Maloney; 1 s (Edward b 19 Dec 1973), 4 da (Laura b 6 March 1976, Sophie b 10 Nov 1979, Alice b 26 July 1982, Chloe (twin) b 26 July 1982); m 2, 18 April 1986, Virginia, *née* Welsh; 1 step da (Sophie b 22 April 1980); *Career* slr; Masons: articled clerk 1969-71, asst slr 1971, salaried ptnr 1972, equity ptnr 1973, managing ptnr 1987-90, sr ptnr 1991-; offical referee Solicitors' Assoc (chm 1990-); memb Law Soc 1969, MFB 1975, CIArb 1980; *Recreations* golf, horseriding, shooting; *Clubs* Rye Golf; *Style*— John Bishop, Esq; Masons (Solicitors), 30 Aylesbury St, London EC1R 0ER (☎ 071 490 4000, fax 071 490 2545)

BISHOP, John Michael; s of Lt Wilfred Charles John Michael Bishop (d 1988), of Whitstable, Kent, and Margery Bains, *née* Emmerson; *b* 1 March 1947; *Educ* Kent Coll Canterbury, LSE (LLB); *m* 12 Aug 1982, Laurie Marie, da of Lyman Charles Harris (d 1980), of Virginia Beach, Virginia, USA; 2 da (Heather Virginia, Lucy Cecilia); *Career* Kent and Co of London Yeomanry (TA) 1965-67; head barr of chambers at 7 Stone Buildings Lincolns Inn 1986, head of chambers at 31 Watling St Canterbury Kent 1988-; memb Hon Soc Middle Temple Lincoln's Inn; *Recreations* photography, antiquarian books; *Style*— John Bishop, Esq; Greenfields, Pean Hill, Whitstable, Kent

BISHOP, Dame (Margaret) Joyce; DBE (1963, CBE 1953); 2 da of Charles Benjamin Bishop (d 1933), and Amy Stewart Tyndall (d 1965); *b* 28 July 1896; *Educ* Edgbaston HS Birmingham, Lady Margaret Hall Oxford (MA); *Career* English mistress Herfordshire and Essex HS 1918-24; head mistress: Holly Lodge HS Smethwick Staffs 1924-35, Godolphin and Latymer Sch London 1935-63; memb Working Pty set up by Min of Educn to enquire into recruitment of women to teaching profession 1947; pres Assoc of Head Mistresses 1950-52; memb: Secdy Sch Examinations Cncl 1950-62, UGC 1961-63, Cncl for Professions Supplementary to Med 1961-70, TV Res Ctee 1963-69; chm Jt Ctee of Four Secdy Assocs 1956-58; FKC 1973; *Recreations* listening to cassettes, theatre; *Style*— Dame Joyce Bishop, DBE; 22 Malbrook Rd, Putney, London SW15 6UF (☎ 081 788 5862)

BISHOP, Kevin John; s of Lindsay Bishop, and Mary Inez, *née* King; *b* 6 June 1949; *Educ* South Bromley Coll, Plymouth Poly Coll of Art (BA); *Career* TV dir: Wogan 1984-86, Kenny Everett TV Show 1986-87, Paul Daniels Magic Show 1987, French and Saunders 1987-88, Victoria Wood 1989, HM Queen Mother's 90th Birthday Gala; TV prodr: Michael Barrymore's Saturday Night Out 1988-89, The Laughter Show 1989, Rory Bremner 1990-91, Rita Rudner 1991, The Childrens' Royal Variety Performance 1991; *Style*— Kevin Bishop, Esq; BBC TV, Wood Lane, London W12 (☎ 081 743 8000)

BISHOP, Martin Egerton; s of Louis Egerton Bishop (d 1973), of Worthing, Sussex; *b* 8 June 1929; *Educ* St Edwards Sch Oxford, Univ of St Andrews; *m* 22 April 1961, Ann, da of Keith Ernest Thurley (d 1980), of Padstow, Cornwall; 2 da (Samantha b 1966, Georgina b 1968); *Career* RA 1947-49; London Stock Exchange 1959-, Greig Middleton and Co 1988-; memb The Bows Gp, vice chm Bristol Stock Exchange; memb Int Stock Exchange; *Recreations* photography, music; *Style*— M E Bishop, Esq; The Thatched Cottage, Mawgan-in-Meneage, Helston, Cornwall (☎ 032 622 306);

Greig, Middleton & Co, Court House, Tailors Court, Broad St, Bristol BS1 2EX (☎ 0272 264013, car 0836 311773)

BISHOP, Michael David; CBE (1986); s of Clive Leonard Bishop (d 1980), and Lilian, *née* Frost (d 1989); *b* 10 Feb 1942; *Educ* Mill Hill; *Career* chm: Airlines of Britain Hldgs plc, Manx Airlines 1982-, Loganair 1983-, London City Airways 1986-; chm and md Br Midland Airways (joined 1964), dir Airtours plc 1987-; memb: E Midlands Elec Bd 1980-83, E Midlands Bd Central Ind TV plc 1981-; chm D'Oyly Carte Opera Tst; *Recreations* music; *Clubs* St James's (Manchester), Union (Sydney); *Style—* Michael Bishop, Esq, CBE; Donington Hall, Castle Donington, nr Derby (☎ 0332 810 741, telex 37172)

BISHOP, Stanley Victor; MC (1944); s of George Stanley Bishop (d 1963), of SA, and Elsie Gordon, *née* Milne (d 1967); *b* 11 May 1916; *Educ* Leeds Sch; *m* 30 Apr 1946, Dorothy Primrose, da of Ralph Herbert Dodds, MC (d 1951), of Berwick-upon-Tweed; 2 s (John Stuart b 3 April 1947, Richard Anthony b 31 Mar 1949), 1 da (Victoria Jane b 23 Jan 1957); *Career* Cerpl 1 London Scottish 1937-40, cmmnd W Yorks Regt 1940, 2 Lt 2 W Yorks Regt 1941-42 (ME), Capt ME Training Centre 1942-43, 2 W Yorks 1943-44 (ME, Burma, Maj 1944), W Yorks ITC 1944-45; chief cost accountant A E Reed & Co Ltd 1945-51; comptroller: Petters Ltd 1951-56, Costains 1956-59, Massey Ferguson Tractors 1959-60 (plans coordinator UK 1960-61, worldwide 1961-63); fin dir Perkins Ltd 1963-65 (gen mangr Madrid 1965-66), chief exec British Printing Corpn 1966-71, dir Massey Ferguson Europe 1973-78, mgmnt conslt/non exec dir with various co's 1971-73 and 1978-; memb Cncl BIM 1967-70; FCA, FICA 1937, FBIM (Cncl 1967-70), FInstD; *Books* Business Planning and Control (1966); *Recreations* swimming, gardening; *Style—* Mr Stanley Bishop, Esq, MC; Halidon, Rogers Lane, Ettington, Stratford-upon-Avon

BISHOP, Thomas Frederick (Tim); s of Frederick Stanley Bishop (d 1970), and Edith Gertrude, *née* Pore (d 1968); *b* 4 April 1937; *Educ* St Olaves and St Saviors GS London, Timaru Boys HS New Zealand, Canterbury Coll, Univ of New Zealand; *m* 13 march 1959, Jennifer Clare, da of Darcley Francis Hocking (d 1963); 1 s (Tristram b 1961), 1 da (Charlotte b 1959); *Career* nat dir Arthur Young McClelland Moores and Co 1977-82 (ptnr 1975), chm Spicer and Pegler Assoc 1987 (md 1983-87), Spicer and Oppenheim Conslts 1987 (chm of UK Consltng Operations 1988); *Recreations* tstee Rye art gallery; *Style—* Tim Bishop, Esq; Spicer and Oppenheim, 13 Bruton St, London (☎ 071 480 7766)

BISHOP, Instr Rear Adm Sir William Alfred; KBE (1955, OBE 1941), CB (1950); s of Alfred Bishop (d 1954), of Purley, Surrey; *b* 29 May 1899; *Educ* Whitgift Sch, CCC Cambridge (MA); *m* 1929, Stella Margaret Bishop, MBE (d 1985), da of Robert Warner Macfarlane, of Hobart, Tasmania (d 1985); *Career* RN 1922, Dir of Naval Educn Serv 1948-56, Naval ADC to HM The King 1950, Instr Rear Adm 1951, ret; *Style—* Instr Rear Adm Sir William Bishop, KBE, CB; Windmill Court, St Minver, Wadebridge, Cornwall PL27 6SB (☎ 0208 862890)

BISHOP-KOVACEVICH, Stephen; s of Nicholas Kovacevich, and Loretta, *née* Zuban; *b* 17 Oct 1940; *Educ* Berkeley HS California; *Career* concert pianist; studied with Dame Myra Hess, worldwide concert tours, Kimber Award California 1959, Hertz Scholar 1959-61, Mozart Prize London 1962, Edison Award for Bartok Piano Concerto no 2; conductor: co-princ Orch St Johns, guest Aust Chamber Orch; int chair piano studies RAM; *Books* Schubert Anthology; *Recreations* films, table tennis, tennis, chess, indian food; *Style—* Stephen Bishop-Kovacevich, Esq; c/o Terry Harrison Artists Management, 9A Penzance Pl, London W11 4PE (☎ 01 221 7741, telex 25872 TERRYH G, fax 01 221 2610)

BISHOPP, Colin Philip; s of Clement Walter Bishopp, of Lymm, Cheshire, and Alison Moray, *née* Stewart (JP); *b* 10 Oct 1947; *Educ* Manchester GS, St Catharine's Coll Cambridge (BA, MA); *m* 1, (m dis), Margaret, da of William Norman Bullock; 1 s (Daniel Toby Nicholas b 15 July 1979), 1 da (Corinna Jayne b 4 April 1973); m 2, Anne-Marie Jeanne, da of René Émile Jean Baissac; 1 s (Maxime Andrew Colin b 9 Feb 1990); *Career* articled clerk Sole Sawbridge & Co London and A W Mawer & Co Manchester; admitted slr 1971; ptnr A W Mawer & Co (became Lace Mawer 1988) 1973-; chm VAT Tribunals 1990-; memb Law Soc 1980; *Recreations* golf, computers; *Style—* Colin Bishopp, Esq; Ladycroft, Congleton Rd, Alderley Edge, Cheshire SK9 7AA (☎ 0625 586463); Lace Mawer, 42 King Street West, Manchester M3 2NU (☎ 061 236 2002, fax 061 832 7956, car 0860 894940)

BISSELL, Frances Mary; da of Robert Maloney, and Mary, *née* Kelly; *b* 19 Aug 1946; *Educ* Goyt Bank HS Cheshire, Cape Town HS, Allerton HS Leeds, Univ of Leeds (BA); *m* 12 Dec 1970, Thomas Emery Bissell, s of Thomas Wilson Bissell (d 1975), of Pittsburgh, USA; 1 step da (b 1958); *Career* VSO Nigeria 1965-66, asst Ecole Normale 1968-69, The British Cncl 1970- (leave of absence 1987-), freelance writer, author, broadcaster and conslt on cookery and food 1983-, The Times Cook 1987-; fndr memb Guild of Food Writers 1985; *Books* A Cooks Calendar (1985), The Pleasures of Cookery (1986), Ten Dinner Parties for Two (1988), The Sainsbury's Book of Food (1989), Oriental Flavours (1990); *Recreations* writing and cooking; *Style—* Mrs Thomas Bissell; c/o The Times, Saturday Review, 1 Pennington St, London E1 9XN (☎ 071 782 5187, fax 071 782 5841, telex 262 141)

BISSILL, Hon Mrs (Charmiane Elizabeth Violet Cecilia); *née* Wilson; da of 3 Baron Nunburnholme; *b* 4 Aug 1930; *m* 19 Jan 1957, William Rippon Bissill (d 1983), er s of William Norman Bissill (d 1936), of Cranmer House, Aslockton; 1 s (and 1 s decd), 1 da; *Style—* The Hon Mrs Bissill; Cranmer House, Aslockton, Notts (☎ 0949 50226)

BISSILL, Mrs Eileen; *née* Grey; da of Sir John Foley Grey, 8 Bt (d 1938), and Jean Jessie Mary, *née* De Sales la Terriere; *b* 1 Feb 1922; *Educ* privately; *m* 1, 5 Feb 1942 (m dis 1946), 11 Earl of Harrington; 1 s, 2 da (1 decd); m 2, 23 Jan 1947, John Philip Bissill, s of William Norman Bissill; 1 da (Alexandra Diana b 15 Feb 1950); *Recreations* fishing, shooting, gardening; *Style—* Mrs Eileen Bissill; Enville Hall, Stourbridge, Worcs

BISSILL, Raymond Norman; s of Herbert Cyril Bissill (d 1973), of Chestfield, Whitstable, Kent, and Evelyn Violet, *née* Sydney; *b* 14 Oct 1938; *Educ* Chatham GS for Boys, Medway Coll of Technol (Dip in Bldg); *m* 7 Feb 1975, Sally Ann, da of Maj Roy Albert Smith, MBE (ret), of Whitstable, Kent; 2 s (Adam b 1976, James b 1977), 1 da (Abigail b 1974); *Career* chm and md: Abbey Grove Securities Ltd, R Bailey and Co Ltd, Errill Securities Ltd, Bailey Builders Ltd; pres The Canterbury and Dist Bldg Employees Confedn 1979-81, chm The E Kent Jt Consultative Ctee of Bldg 1987-88; FInstD, FCIOB; *Recreations* squash, skiing, windsurfing; *Clubs* Kent and Canterbury, Whitstable Yacht; *Style—* Raymond N Bissill, Esq; Penraevon, Chestfield Rd, Chestfield, Whitstable, Kent; R Bailey and Co Ltd, Malvern House, Broad St, Canterbury, Kent (☎ 0227 768445, fax 0227 450569)

BLACH, Rudolf Karl (Rolf); s of Paul Samuel Blach (d 1940), and Hedwig Jeanette Blach (d 1968); *b* 21 Jan 1930; *Educ* Berkhamsted Sch, Trinity Coll Cambridge, St Thomas's Hosp London (MA, MB BChir, MD); *m* 26 March 1960, Lynette Cecilia (Lyn), da of Jaffray Andrew Conynghame Sceales; 2 s (Thomas b 1962, Richard b 1968), 1 da (Catherine b 1964); *Career* Lt RAMC 1956 (Capt 1957); conslt ophthalmic surgn St Mary's Hosp Paddington 1963-70, hon conslt ophthalmologist Royal Postgrad Med Sch Hammersmith 1967-74, conslt ophthalmologist St Dunstans 1967, conslt surgn Moorfields Eye Hosp 1969-, Dean Inst of Ophthalmology Univ of London 1985-; Freeman City of London 1967, Liveryman Worshipful Soc of Apothecaries; FRCS, FCOphth, FRSM; *Style—* Rolf Blach, Esq; 88A College Rd, Dulwich, London SE21 7NA (☎ 01 693 1917); Lister House, 11/12 Wimpole St, London W1M 7AB (☎ 01 636 3407)

BLACK, Alan William; s of William Black, of 7 Oddicombe Croft, Styvechale, Coventry, and Agnes Whyte Buchanan, *née* Wilson; *b* 21 Feb 1952; *Educ* King Henry VIII Sch, Kings Coll London (LLB); *Career* slr; ptnr Linklaters and Paines 1983-; Freeman Worshipful Co of Slrs 1983; memb Law Soc; *Recreations* tennis, opera and early music, Far East, searching for Schrodinger's cat; *Clubs* The Second Eleven, The Inner Theatre, Pacific; *Style—* Alan Black, Esq; House 11, 29 Mount Kellett Rd, The Peak, Hong Kong; Linklaters & Paines, Barrington House, 59-67 Gresham St, London EC2; 14th Floor, Alexandra House, Central, Hong Kong

BLACK, Alastair Kenneth Lamond; CBE (1989), DL (Gtr London 1978); s of late Kenneth Black, and Althea Joan, *née* Hanks (d 1984); *b* 14 Dec 1929; *Educ* Sherborne, Law Soc Sch of Law; *m* 1955, Elizabeth Jane, da of Sir Henry Darlington, KCB, CMG, TD (d 1959); 1 s (Rupert), 2 da (Sarah, Susan); *Career* admitted slr 1953; Nat Serv Lt Intelligence Corps 1953-55; ptnr Messrs Burchell and Ruston 1953-; Dep Sheriff Co of London then Gtr London 1953-74, Under Sheriff Gtr London 1974-; clerk to the Gen Cmmrs of Income Tax for the Divs of Holborn, Finsbury, St Paul's, Covent Garden 1966-, clerk to the Bowyers Co 1985-; memb House of Laity Gen Synod 1982-, lay reader 1983-; pres Under Sheriffs Assoc 1987- (vice pres 1985-87), memb cncl Shrievalty Assoc, 1985-; *Books* contrib to: Halsbury's Laws of England (4 edn vol 25 1978, vol 42 1983), Atkins Court Forms (3 edn vol 19 1972, revised edn 1985, vol 22 1986, vol 36 1977), Execution of a Judgment, Oyez Practice Notes (6 edn 1979, 7 edn 1986); *Recreations* horse racing, gardening, travel; *Style—* Alastair Black, Esq, CBE, DL; South Lodge, Guildford Road, Effingham, Surrey, 2 Serjeants' Inn, Fleet Street, London EC4Y 1LL (☎ 071 353 5385)

BLACK, Col Anthony Edward Norman; OBE (1981); s of Arthur Norman Black (d 1973), of Hove, Sussex, and Phyllis Margaret, *née* Ranicar (d 1989); *b* 20 Jan 1938; *Educ* Brighton Coll, RMA Sandhurst, Army Staff Coll Camberley; *m* 1 October 1963, Susan Frances, da of Maj John Watt Copeland (d 1965), of Ilkley, W Yorks; 2 s (Simon b 12 July 1965, Michael b 13 March 1968); *Career* cmmnd RE 1957, served Kenya, Aden, Germany, Cyprus, army staff course Camberley 1970, GSOI Ghana Armed Forces Staff Coll 1976-78, CO 36 Engr Regt 1978-80, Col GS MGO Secretariat 1980-82, cmd Engrs Falkland Is 1983, Cmdt Army Apprentices Coll Chepstow 1983-86, ret 1987; currently chief exec cmmr The Scout Assoc; FBIM 1983; *Recreations* dinghy sailing, walking, gardening, bird-watching; *Clubs* Cwlth Tst; *Style—* Col Anthony Black, OBE; The Scout Association, Baden-Powell House, Queen's Gate, London SW7 5JS (☎ 071 584 7030, fax 071 581 9953)

BLACK, Barrington; s of Louis L Black, and Millicent, *née* Brash; *b* 16 Aug 1932; *Educ* Roundhay Sch, Univ of Leeds (LLB); *m* 19 June 1962, Diana Heller, JP, da of Simon Heller; 2 s (Matthew b 1965, Jonathan b 1968), 2 da (Harriette b 1963, Anna b 1971); *Career* admitted slr 1956, asst rec Inner London Crown Court, chm Inner London Juvenille Court 1986-; Metropolitan Stipendiary magistrate 1984; memb: Inner London Probation Ctee, Br Acad Forensic Sci 1976-; former pres Univ of Leeds Union, memb Court and Cncl Univ of Leeds, vice pres NUS; *Recreations* music, opera, ski-bobbing; *Style—* Barrington Black, Esq; Marylebone Magistrates Court, London (☎ 071 706 1261)

BLACK, Colin Hyndmarsh; s of Robert Black, and Daisy Louise, *née* Morris; *b* 4 Feb 1930; *Educ* Ayr Acad, Fettes, Univ of St Andrews (MA), Univ of Edinburgh (LLB); *m* 1955, Christine Fleurette, *née* Browne; 1 s, 1 da; *Career* ptnr i/c investmt mgmnt Brander and Cruickshank Aberdeen 1957-71, dep chm Globe Investment Trust 1983-90 (joined 1971); chm: Scottish Widows' Fund and Life Assurance Society 1987-, Association of Investment Trust Companies 1987-89; non-exec dir: Temple Bar Investment Trust 1963-, Clyde Petroleum 1976-, Electra Investment Trust 1975-, Kleinwort Benson Group plc 1988-, Scottish Power 1990-; chm Kleinwort Benson Investment Management Ltd 1988-; *Recreations* golf, gardening, reading, walking labradors; *Clubs* New (Edinburgh); *Style—* Colin Black, Esq; Kleinwort Benson Investment Management Ltd, P.O. Box 191, 10 Fenchurch St, London EC3M 3LB (☎ 071 956 6600, fax 071 929 0296, telex 9413545)

BLACK, Conrad Moffat; OC (1990); *b* 25 Aug 1944; *Educ* Carleton Univ (BA), Laval Univ (LLL), McGill Univ (MA); *m* 1978, Joanna Catherine Louise; 2 s, 1 da; *Career* chm: Daily Telegraph plc 1979- (dir 1985-), Hollinger Inc (and chief exec) 1985-, Argus Corporation Ltd 1979- (chief exec 1985-), The Ravelston Corporation Ltd (and chief exec offr) 1979-; dep chm American Publishing Company 1987-, vice chm Norcen Energy Resources Ltd 1986-; dir: Canadian Imperial Bank of Commerce 1977- (memb Exec Ctee 1987-), Confederation Life Insurance Co 1977-, Eaton's of Canada Ltd 1976-, Algoma Central Railway 1984-, Brascan Ltd 1986-, Hees International Bancorp Inc 1986-, Tridel Enterprises Inc 1986-, Canadian Marconi Company 1988-, The Financial Post Company Ltd 1988- The Clarke Inst of Psychiatry Fndn 1989- (tstee 1983), Henry Birks and Sons Ltd 1990-,The Spectator (1828) Ltd 1990-, Uniemdia (1988) Inc 1990- (chm 1988-90); memb: Chm's Cncl of the American Soc, The Int Inst for Strategic Studies, The Trilateral Cmmn, Steering Ctee and Adsvy Gp, Advsy Bd St Mary's Hosp West Palm Beach Florida; patron The Malcolm Muggeridge Fndn; Hon LLD: Carelton Univ 1989, St Francis Xavier 1979, McMaster Univ 1979; Hon LittD Univ of Windsor 1979; Order of Canada 1990; *Books* Duplessis (1977); *Clubs* Everglades (Palm Beach), Toronto, Toronto Golf, York, University, Mount Royal (Montreal); *Style—* Conrad Black, Esq, OC; c/o 10 Toronto St, Toronto, Ont M5C 2B7, Canada (☎ 416 363 8721); The Daily Telegraph plc, Peterborough Court at South Quay, 181 March Wall, London E14 9SR

BLACK, Sir Cyril Wilson; JP (London 1942), DL (Surrey 1957, Gtr London 1966); s of Robert Wilson Black, JP (d 1951), and Annie Louise, *née* North; *b* 8 April 1902; *Educ* King's Coll Sch Wimbledon; *m* 1930, Dorothy Joyce, da of Thomas Birkett (d 1962), of Wigston Hall, Leicester; 1 s, 2 da; *Career* chartered surveyor; MP (C) Wimbledon 1950-70; mayor: Wimbledon 1945-47 (memb borough cncl 1942-65), Merton 1966-67 (memb borough cncl 1965-78); chm Surrey CC 1956-59 (memb 1943-65, vice chm 1953-56); conslt to Knight and Co Estate Agents and Surveyors; chm: Temperance Permanent Building Soc 1939-73, Beaumont Properties 1947-80, M F North Hotels Gp 1948-81, London Shop Property Tst 1951-79; nat treas Girls' Bde 1939-69 (vice pres 1969-), treas Boys' Bde 1962-69 (hon vice pres 1970-), hon treas London Baptist Assoc 1942-76 (pres 1965-66, life memb 1976-); memb: Baptist Union Cncl (vice pres 1969-70, pres 1970-71), Free Church Federal Cncl, Cncl of Christians and Jews; pres: Christian Union for the Estate Profession, UK Alliance, 18F (Wimbledon) Sqdn Air Training Corps, Wimbledon and Merton Dist Scout Cncl 1974-; FRICS, FRSA; kt 1959; *Recreations* teetotaller and anti-drink campaigner, reading, music, public and Christian work; *Style—* Sir Cyril Black, JP, DL; Rosewall, Calonne Rd, London SW19 (☎ 01 946 2588); Windmill Cottage, Sea Way, Middleton-on-Sea, Sussex (☎ 024 369 2288)

BLACK, (William) David Anthony; s of William Milnes Black, of Clwyd, and Dorothy Charlotte, *née* Harrison; *b* 19 June 1938; *Educ* Stonyhurst, Manchester Univ (BSc); *m*

2 April 1964, Charmain Jennifer, da of Sidney Stewart Downing (d 1986); 1 s (William Benjamin David b 1965), 2 da (Nicola Louise b 1967, Jane Ruth b 1979); *Career* chm and md: Harrison and Jones Gp Ltd 1976- (dir 1962-76), Bysingwood Gp Ltd 1973-; *Recreations* shooting, vintage motor racing, steamboating; *Clubs* RAC, Bugatti Owners; *Style—* David Black, Esq; Douglas Bank Farm, Appley Bridge, via Skelmersdale, Lancs (☎ 0257 52844); Harrison and Jones Gp Ltd, Swan Mill, Middleton Junction, Manchester (☎ 061 643 2468)

BLACK, Sir (Robert) David; 3 Bt (UK 1922), of Midgham, Co Berks; s of Sir Robert Andrew Stransham Black, 2 Bt, ED (d 1979); *b* 29 March 1929; *Educ* Eton; *m* 1, 1953 (m dis 1972), Rosemary Diana, da of Sir Rupert John Hardy, 4 Bt; 2 da (Diana Sarah (Mrs Mark Newton) b 1955, Joanna Rosemary b 1966), and 1 da decd; m 2, 1973, (Dorothy) Maureen, da of Maj Charles Robert Eustace Radclyffe, and wid of Alan Roger Douglas Pilkington; *Career* formerly Maj Royal Horse Gds and Maj Berks and Westminster Dragoon Yeo 1964-67; jt MFH Garth and S Berks Hunt 1964-72; vice-chm Berks Eastern Wessex TAVR 1985-; Hon Col 94 (Berks Yeo) Signal Sqdn 1988-; *Clubs* Cavalry and Guards; *Style—* Sir David Black, Bt; Elvendon Priory, Goring, nr Reading, Berks (☎ 0491 872 160); Shurrery Lodge, Shebster, Thurso, Caithness (☎ 084 781 252)

BLACK, Don; s of Morris Blackstone (d 1979), of Hackney, London, and Betsy, *née* Kersh (d 1966); *b* 21 June 1938; *Educ* Cassland Rd Sch Hackney; *m* 7 Dec 1958, Shirley Kitty, da of James Berg; 2 s (Grant Howard b 28 Jan 1961, Clive Darren b 24 Aug 1963); *Career* office jr New Musical Express 1955, music publisher, professional comedian, agent and mangr for Brian Epstein's NEMS co; lyricist; films incl: Born Free, To Sir With Love, Diamonds are Forever, Ben, The Man With The Golden Gun, Thunderball, True Grit; musicals incl: Billy, Aspects of Love, Song and Dance; lyricist for well known composers incl: Andrew Lloyd Webber, John Barry, Henry Mancini, Elmer Bernstein, Charles Aznavour, Quincy Jones, Jule Styne, Charles Strouse; Oscar award (for Born Free 1966), Golden Globe, 4 Ivor Novello awards, 3 Tony Nominations, numerous Platinum, Gold and Silver discs; chm Br Acad of Songwriters Composers and Authors 1986-, frequent broadcaster and chm of the Vivien Ellis prize held at the Guildhall Sch of Music; *Recreations* swimming, snooker; *Clubs* RAC, Groucho, St James's; *Style—* Don Black, Esq; c/o John Cohen, Clintons, Wellington House, 6-9 Upper St Martin's Lane, London WC2H 9DF (☎ 071 379 6080, fax 071 240 9310)

BLACK, Donald Sinclair; s of Frank Charles Briscoe Black (d 1988), of 26 Learmonth Terrace, Edinburgh, and Anne Betty Hirst, *née* Sinclair (d 1989); *b* 4 July 1941; *Educ* Merchiston Castle Sch Edinburgh, Edinburgh Univ (LLB); *m* 30 Sept 1972, (Evelyn) Bronwen Louise, da of William Kennedy, of Sidmouth, Devon; 3 s (Roderick b 1975, Graeme b 1979, Alistair b 1982), 1 da (Tamara b 1973); *Career* CA; articled Deloittes (Edinburgh) 1963-67, Royal Bank of Scotland Investmt Dept 1967-68, Edinburgh Fund Mangrs Fund 1968-70, dir Panmure Gordon & Co Ltd 1975-(joined 1970); memb Lloyd's; MICAS 1966; *Recreations* skiing, tennis; *Style—* Donald Black, Esq; 244 Residence Mondzeu, Verbier, Switzerland; 19 Ennismore Ave, Guildford, Surrey GV1 1SP; Panmure Gordon Co Ltd, 9 Moorfields Highwalk, London EC2 (☎ 071 628 4010, fax 071 920 9305, telex 883832)

BLACK, Dr (Ann) Dora; *b* 2 July 1932; *Educ* Univ of Birmingham (MB ChB), Inst of Psychiatry (DPM); *m* 4 Dec 1955, Jack Black; 2 s (David b 1960, Andrew b 1961), 1 da (Sophie b 1963); *Career* conslt child and adolescent psychiatrist Edgware Gen Hosp 1968-84 Royal Free Hosp 1984-; author of chapters and papers on: bereavement in childhood, family therapy, ethics, educn; assoc ed British Journal Psychiatry; chm Inst of Family Therapy London, memb Cncl Cruse (nat charity for bereavement care); MRCPsych 1971, FRCPsych 1979; *Books* Child Psychiatry and the Law (jtly, 1989); *Recreations* travel, theatre, friends; *Style—* Dr Dora Black; Royal Free Hospital, London NW3 (☎ 071 794 0500)

BLACK, Sir Douglas Andrew Kilgour; s of Rev Walter Kilgour Black (d 1951), and Mary Jane *née* Crichton; *b* 29 May 1913; *Educ* Forfar Acad, Univ of St Andrews; *m* 1948, Mollie, da of Edward Thorn (d 1962); 1 s, 2 da; *Career* served WW II in RAMC as Maj (India); prof of med Univ of Manchester 1959-78, chief scientist DHSS 1973-77; chm Working Pty on: Inequalities in Health 1977-80, Childhood Leukaemia in W Cumbria 1983-84; pres: RCP 1977-83, BMA 1984-85; KStJ 1989; kt 1973; *Books* Invitation to Medicine (1987), Recollections and Reflections (1987); *Recreations* reading, writing; *Clubs* Athenaeum; *Style—* Sir Douglas Black; The Old Forge, Duchess Close, Whitchurch-on-Thames, nr Reading RG8 7EN (☎ 073 57 4693)

BLACK, Geoffrey Howard (Geoff); s of Robert Black, of Liverpool, and Rene Black; *b* 23 Dec 1948; *Educ* Quarry Bank HS Liverpool, private accountancy colls; *m* 26 May 1972, Linda Margaret, da of Joseph Dowsing (d 1959); 2 s (Andrew b 1980, Michael b 1989), 2 da (Rachel b 1976, Susannah b 1978); *Career* princ GH Black and Co 1976-83, chief examiner A' level accountancy Univ of London Exam Bd 1983, head of accountancy Cambridgeshire Coll of Arts and Technol 1984-88, ptnr The Guidelines Ptnrship ed conslts 1986-; Parly candidate Lib Liverpool Garston Constituency gen elections 1974, Parly agent Lib Shrewsbury Constituency gen election 1979; FCA 1971; *Books* Financial Accounting (1986), Accounting Standards (1987), Applied Economics (contrib, 1989); *Recreations* avoiding sporting activities; *Clubs* University Centre, Cambridge; *Style—* Geoff Black, Esq; 18 Pretoria Rd, Cambridge CB4 1HE (☎ 0223 314 668, fax 0223 64619)

BLACK, Air Vice-Marshal George Philip; CB (1987), OBE (1967), AFC (1962, and bar 1971); s of William Black, and Elizabeth Edward, *née* Philip; *b* 10 July 1932; *Educ* Aberdeen Acad, Jt Servs Staff Coll, RCDS; *m* 1954, Ella Ruddiman, da of Edwin Stanley Walker (d 1961); 2 s (Stuart Douglas b 1955, Ian Craig b 1959); *Career* RAF, pilot/gen duties branch, air def; served in Central Euro Theatre incl Med; several appointments in NATO; ADC to HM The Queen 1981-83; CO 111 Sqdn 5 Sqdn RAF Wildenrath; cdr socl; Cmdt ROC; sr def advsr GEC-Marconi; *Recreations* military aviation, philately, model railways; *Clubs* RAF; *Style—* Air Vice-Marshal George Black, CB, OBE, AFC; The Grove, Warren Lane, Stanmore, Middx HA7 4LY (☎ 081 954 4819)

BLACK, Ian Roger Maclean; s of Lewis Worcester Maclean Black (d 1973), of Gillingham, and Norah, *née* Greenwood; *b* 30 July 1949; *Educ* Kings Sch Rochester, Univ of Warwick (BSc), IMCB (MBA); *m* 29 June 1974, Madeleine Alix, da of Howard Richard Clutterbuck, of Combe St Nicholas, Somerset; 2 da (Emma b 1977, Stephanie b 1980); *Career* chief scientist Forth River Purification Bd 1985-89, princ Dames & Moore Int 1989; CChem, MRSC, MBIM; *Recreations* cycling, squash, alpine gardening; *Style—* Ian Black, Esq; Booth House, 15-17 Church St, Twickenham TW1 3NJ (☎ 081 891 6161, fax 081 891 4457, telex 929861)

BLACK, Jack; *b* 9 Jan 1932; *Educ* Towcester GS, Hendon County Sch, UCL (LLB); *m* 4 Dec 1955, (Ann) Dora, da of Sqdn Ldr Philip Braham, MBE, of Barnet, Herts; 2 s (David b 1960, Andrew b 1961), 1 da (Sophie b 1963); *Career* Nat Serv RASC 2Lt, battalion courts martial offr and asst adjutant 1954-56; admitted slr 1954; sr ptnr Heald Nickinson 1984- (ptnr 1956-); memb Cncl: Int Copyright Soc, Common Law Inst of Intellectual Property, The Bentham Club UCL; memb Legal Ctee German Chamber of Indust and Commerce UK; chm: Intellectual Property Cmmn Union Internationale des Avocats, Br Literary and Artistic Copyright Assoc 1985-; former chm of Cncl King Alfred Sch Hampstead; memb Law Soc; fndr memb: Br-German Jurists Assoc 1970, Slrs Euro Gp; FRSA; *Books* An Introduction to EEC Law (contrib, 1972), Halsbury's Laws of England EC vols (contrib 5 edn, 1986); *Recreations* the arts, travel; *Clubs* Reform, Groucho; *Style—* Jack Black, Esq; Heald Nickinson, 48 Bedford Square, London WC1B 3DS (☎ 071 636 8010, fax 071 580 7521, telex 268003 RETAIN G)

BLACK, Sir James Whyte; *b* 14 June 1924; *Educ* Beath HS, Univ of St Andrew's (MB ChB); *Career* prof and head of Dept of Pharmacology Univ Coll London 1973-77; dir of therapeutic research Wellcome Research Laboratories 1978-84; prof of Analytical Pharmacology 1984-; awarded Nobel Prize for Medicine 1988; FRCP, FRS; kt 1981; *Style—* Sir James Black, FRS; Analytical Pharmacology Unit, Rayne Institute, 123 Coldharbour Lane, London SE5 9NU (☎ 071 274 7437)

BLACK, Adm Sir (John) Jeremy; KCB (1987), DSO (1982), MBE (1963); s of Alan Henry Black, and Gwendoline, *née* Westcott; kinsman Capt George Blagdon Westcott k in cmd of HMS Majestic at the battle of the Nile 1798; *b* 17 Nov 1932; *Educ* RNC Dartmouth; *m* 1958, Alison Pamela, da of Col Philip Thomas Barber, MC (d 1965), Baluch Regt; 2 s (Simon b 1967, Julian b 1968), 1 da (Carolyn b 1965); *Career* served in HMS Belfast (Korean War, Malaysian Emergency) 1950, specialized in naval gunnery 1958, CO HMS Fiskerton (Borneo confrontation) 1962, CO HMS Decoy (Far E and Mediterranean) 1968, Naval Staff Appts 1970, 1975 and 1980, RCDS 1979; elected yr bro of Trinity House; CO HMS Invincible (Falklands War) 1982, Flag Offr 1 Flotilla 1983-, Asst Chief Naval Staff 1984-, Dep Chief of Def Staff (Systems) 1986, C in C Naval Home Cmd 1989, Flag ADC to HM The Queen 1989; Cdre RNSA 1989-, memb Cncl RUSI 1987-89, chm Race Ctee Whitbread Round The World Race 1990-; Order of Royal Star of Brunei (1963); *Recreations* history, sailing; *Clubs* Cwlth Trust, RUSI IISS, Royal Yacht Sqdn, RN Sailing Assoc (Cdre 1989-); *Style—* Adm Sir Jeremy Black, KCB, DSO, MBE

BLACK, Lady; Joan Edna; da of George Fairbrother, of Birkenhead, and Gertrude Campbell Shanks; *m* 1955, Sir Misha Black, OBE (d 1977); 2 s, 1 da; *Style—* Lady Black; 78 Primrose Mansions, Prince of Wales Drive, SW11; Thistley Common, Boyton End, Halstead, Essex

BLACK, John Alexander; CBE (1983); s of Arthur Alexander Black (d 1958); *b* 8 July 1923; *Educ* Cheltenham, Univ of Birmingham; *m* 1950, Joan, da of Henry Knight (d 1954); 2 da; *Career* dir: AA Black Ltd 1948-63, Charles Barker Gp Ltd 1976-83, Birmingham Convention and Visitor Bureau Ltd 1982-87, Task Undertakings Ltd 1988-89; gen cmmr for Income Tax 1966-72, chm: Bd of Mgmnt Birmingham Cncl of Social Serv 1964-67 (memb 1960-74), S Birmingham Hosp Mgmnt Ctee 1972-74 (memb 1971-72), Langleys & Hoffman Ltd 1972 (dir 1963-72, vice chm and md 1970-72), Charles Barker Black & Gross Ltd 1976-83, (vice chm 1972-75, dep chm 1975-76), Solihull AHA 1977-82, Charles Barker Scotland Ltd 1980-83, Solihull Health Authy 1982-88, Birmingham Venture 1985-88; pres: Birmingham Jr C of C 1956-57, Birmingham Publicity Assoc 1974-75, Birmingham Chamber of Indust & Commerce 1981-82 (hon treas 1974-78); *Recreations* gardening, woodturning, walking, photography; *Style—* John A Black, Esq, CBE; 2 Old Hay Gardens, Dore, Sheffield S17 3HG (☎ 0742 350182)

BLACK, Kingsley; s of James Edward Black, of Luton, and Laurene Elaine, *née* Griffiths; *b* 22 June 1968; *Educ* Cardinal Newman HS, Luton Sixth Form Coll; *Career* professional footballer; Luton Town 1986-: memb coll then professional, debut v Queens Park Rangers 1987, over 100 appearances; represented England Schs under 18; Northern Ireland: debut v France 1988, 14 full caps; Littlewoods Cup winners Luton Town 1988; *Recreations* antiques, gardening; *Style—* Kingsley Black, Esq; Luton Town FC, 1 Maple Rd, Luton, Bedfordshire (☎ 0582 411622)

BLACK, Lady; Margaret; da of John Milton Saxton (d 1951), of Belfast; *m* 1940, Sir Harold Black (sometime Sec to NI Cabinet and Dep Sec NI Office; d 1981), s of Alexander Black (d 1946), of Belfast; 1 s, 1 da; *Style—* Lady Black; c/o 102 Moneymore Rd, Cookstown, Co Tyrone, N Ireland

BLACK, Michael Donald Gordon; MC (1953); s of Lt Col M G Black, OBE (d 1946), of Edenwood, Cupar, Fife, and Gladys Temple Thomson (d 1972); *b* 7 Sept 1932; *Educ* Sedbergh; *m* 2 May 1958, Priscilla Mary Amy, da of Lt Col John William Cecil Holt (d 1981), of Belmont, Devoran, Truro, Cornwall; 1 s (Michael Jamie Gordon b 1 March 1965), 2 da (Charlotte Mary Temple Gordon b 13 Jan 1960, Marie-Claire Gordon b 18 April 1962); *Career* Nat Serv, Black Watch 1950-52, Maj Black Watch TA 1952-67; tstee of Savings Bank in Kirkcaldy (later Tayside Savings Bank, now TSB Scot) 1958-87, dir TSB Scot, dir Michael Nairn and Co Ltd (now Nairn and Williamson) 1960-79, chm and chief exec Nairnflair Ltd (now Forbo Nairnflair Ltd 1979-; farmer 1972-; memb Lloyds 1979-; *Recreations* shooting, fishing, management of estate; *Clubs* Army and Navy; *Style—* Donald Black, Esq; Edenwood, Cupar, Fife KY15 5NX (☎ 0334 53159); Forbo-Nairnflair Ltd, Woodside Road, Glenrothes, Fife (☎ 0592 758943, fax 0592 753968, telex 728225)

BLACK, Lady Moorea; *née* Hastings; JP; da of 15 Earl of Huntingdon (d 1990), and his 1 w, Cristina, da of Marchese Casati; *b* 4 March 1928; *m* 1, 1957 (m dis 1966), Woodrow Wyatt (later Lord Wyatt of Weeford), *qv*; 1 s (Pericles Plantagenet James Casati b 1963); m 2, 1967, Brinsley Black; 1 s (Octavius Orlando Irvine Casati b 1968); *Career* JP; *Style—* The Lady Moorea Black, JP; 17 Lansdowne Walk, London W11 3AH (☎ 071 727 3528)

BLACK, Peter; JP; s of Peter Blair Black, of 3 Tudor Close, Ealing, London, and Cissie Crawford, *née* Samuel; *b* 22 April 1917; *Educ* Sir Walter St John Battersea, Bearsden Acad, London Sch of Building; *m* 1952, Mary Madeleine, da of Dr Joseph Hilly (d 1930), of Philadelphia, USA; 1 s (Peter b 1957), 3 da (Susan, Ann, Margaret); *Career* memb GLC 1982-87, chm Thames Water Authy 1973-78, pres Pure Rivers Soc 1976-, leader GLC Group to Moscow and Leningrad 1971; sr ptnr P Blair and Ptnrs 1984-; former memb: Thames Conservancy Bd, Met Water Bd, Cncl Nat Fedn of Housing Socs; Freeman City of London; *Recreations* small boats, fishing; *Clubs* Middleton Sports, Sewers Synonymous; *Style—* Peter Black, Esq, JP; The New House, 101A Limmer Lane, Felpham, Bognor Regis, Sussex PO22 7LP (☎ 0243 582054)

BLACK, (Francis) Peter; s of Francis Raymond Black (d 1985), and Rosina Mary, *née* De Burgh; *b* 20 Aug 1932; *Educ* Gunnersbsury GS, Hammersmith Coll of Art; *m* 15 March 1958, Jillian Elsie; 2 da (Susan b 1961, Caroline b 1964); *Career* architect with Norman and Dawbarn for 4 years designing Imperial Coll building; joined Scott Brownrigg and Turner 1961 (ptnr 1970-); bldgs include: Sport City Dubai, three airports in Iraq; pres Chertsey Agric Assoc 1990; Ecclesia et Pontifici (Vatican) 1990; RIBA, FSIAD, FCSD, FRSA, MBIM; *Recreations* runs a small farm at Englefield Green specialising in breeding and showing Dexters, short-legged rare breed of British cattle; *Style—* Peter Black, Esq; Sandylands Home Farm, Wick Road, Englefield Green, Surrey TW20 0HJ (☎ 0784 32782); Scott Brownrigg and Turner, 10-13 King Street, London WC2E 8HZ (☎ 071 240 2961, telex 25897, fax 071 831 1231)

BLACK, Prof Robert; QC (1987); s of James Little Black,of Lockerbie, Scot, and Jeannie Findlay, *née* Lyon; *b* 12 June 1947; *Educ* Lockerbie Acad, Dumfries Acad, Univ of Edinburgh (LLB), McGill Univ Montreal (LLM); *Career* advocate of the Scot Bar 1972, sr legal offr Scot Law Commn 1975-78, in practice Scot Bar 1978-81, prof of Scots Law Univ of Edinburgh 1981- (lectr 1972-75); temp Sheriff 1981-; gen ed The

Laws of Scotland: Stair Meml Encyclopaedia 1988- (dep, then jt gen ed 1981-88); memb: Exec Cncl Scot Nat Dictionary Assoc, Legal Ctee RSSPCC; *Books* An Introduction to Written Pleading (1982), Civil Jurisdiction: The New Rules (1983); *Recreations* beer, wine, tea (not always in that order); *Clubs* Sloane, Scot Arts (Edinburgh); *Style*— Prof Robert Black, QC; 6/4 Glenogle Rd, Edinburgh EH3 5HW (☎ 031 557 3571); Dept of Scots Law, Old Coll, Sth Bridge, Edinburgh EH8 9YL (☎ 031 667 1011, fax 031 662 4902, telex 727442)

BLACK, Robert Anderson; s of Thomas Black (d 1960), of Tarriebank, Arbroath, and Agnes, *née* Leggat; *b* 8 March 1923; *Educ* Giggleswick Sch, Glasgow Univ; *m* 20 Sept 1956, Mary Wallace, da of William Lees Weir (d 1948), of Carnoustie, Angus; 2 s (Tony b 1959, Robert b 1961), 2 da (Kay b 1957, Susan b 1962); *Career* WWII Ferry Serv Admty 1943-46; md Tarriebank Estates 1946-61, chm and md Border Oats Ltd 1979-; pres Br Oatmeal and Barley Millers Assoc 1986-88 (vice pres 1984-86), memb Cereal Ctee Agric Food Res Cncl 1987-88-; fndr memb NSPPA, memb Carnyllie Community Fund, fndr Angus SC; LIBiol, MInstM; *Recreations* golf, fishing, curling; *Clubs* Royal Overseas, CGA, Chirnside Curling; *Style*— Robert Black, Esq; Edington Hill House, Chirnside, Duns, Berwickshire TD11 3LE (☎ 089 081 723); Border Oats Ltd, Edington Mill, Chirnside, Duns, Berwickshire TD11 3LE (☎ 089 081 252, telex 727176)

BLACK, Sir Robert Brown; GCMG (1962, KCMG 1955, CMG 1953), OBE (1949, MBE (Mil) 1948); s of Robert Black (d 1929), of Blair Lodge, Stirlingshire, and Catherine Black; *b* 3 June 1906; *Educ* George Watson's Coll Edinburgh, Univ of Edinburgh (MA); *m* 1937, (Elsie) Anne, da of Allan Stevenson (d 1960), of Edinburgh; 2 da; *Career* Capt Intelligence Corps (Special Ops) Far East, 43 special mil missions; Colonial Admin Serv; govr and C-in-C: Singapore 1955-57, Hong Kong 1958-64; cmmr Cwlth War Graves Cmmn 1964-82; pres Int Social Serv (GB) 1973-82 (chm 1965-73); chm Clerical, Medical and General Life Assur Soc 1975-78; Hon LLD Hong Kong Univ, Chinese Univ of Hong Kong; KStJ 1955; Grand Cross Order of Merit (Peru) 1962; *Recreations* fishing, walking; *Clubs* E India Sports Devonshire and Public Schools; *Style*— Sir Robert Black, GCMG, OBE; Mapletons House, Ashampstead Common, nr Reading, Berks RG8 8QN (☎ 0635 201 254)

BLACK, Dr Robert Monro; s of Thomas Henry Black (d 1944), and Ada, *née* Wright (d 1930); *b* 13 Jan 1925; *Educ* Eltham Coll Kent, Kings Coll London (BSc), Sir John Cass Coll, Univ of London (MSc, PhD); *m* 29 Oct 1957, Beatrice Maud, da of Albert Ernest Higgs (d 1949); *Career* res chemist BICC plc 1945-87: (seconded to AIERE Harwell 1953-55), head Irradiation Dept 1955-61, head Physical Chemistry Dept 1961-68, PA to Dir Res and Engrg 1968-72, special projects and info 1972-87; memb Soc History Alchemy and Early Chemistry; Freeman City of London, Freeman (by servitude) Worshipful Co of Merchant Taylors; FChem Soc 1945, memb Soc Chemical Industries 1945, ARIC 1950; *Books* Electric Cables in Victorian Times (1972), The History of Electric Wires and Cables (1983) author or co-author numerous scientific and tech papers; *Recreations* music, reading, freemasonry; *Style*— Dr Robert Black; 93 Roxborough Ave, Isleworth, Middlesex TW7 5HH (☎ 081 560 8519)

BLACK, Roger Anthony; s of David Harrison Black, and Thelma Royds, *née* Culshaw; *b* 31 March 1966; *Educ* Portsmouth GS; *Career* athlete; represented UK 1985-; honours incl: Gold medal 400m and 4 x 400m Euro Jr Championships 1985, Gold medal 400m and 4 x 400m Cwlth Games 1986, Gold medal 400m and 4 x 400m Euro Championships 1986 and 1990, Silver medal 4 x 400m World Championships 1987; Br 400m record 1986; male athlete of the year Br Athletic Writers' Assoc 1986; *Recreations* guitar, song writing, tennis, arts; *Style*— Roger Black, Esq; AAA, Edgbaston House, 3 Duchess Place, off Hagley Rd, Edgbaston, Birmingham B16 8NM (☎ 021 456 4050)

BLACK, Russell; s of Samuel Joseph Black, of Cardiff, and Muriel, *née* Lustig; *b* 12 Oct 1957; *Educ* Cardiff HS, Salford Univ (BSc); *Career* CA; Gerald Edelman & Co 1979-83, Stoy Hayward 1983-86, tax ptnr Glazers 1987-; ACA 1983, ATII 1987; *Recreations* tennis, golf, soccer, music, flying; *Style*— Russell Black, Esq; Glazers, 843 Finchley Road, London NW11 8NA (☎ 081 458 7427, fax 081 458 8504, telex 268695)

BLACK, Prof Samuel (Sam); MBE (1969); s of Lionel Black (d 1960), of London, and Sophia, *née* Divinsky (d 1968); *b* 6 Jan 1915; *Educ* Owens Sch, Northampton Engrg Coll, Univ of London; *m* 1, 24 June 1939, Muriel Cecilia Emily (d 1982), da of Cornelius George Snudden (d 1924), of Woodford, Essex; 1 s (Christopher), 1 da (Patricia); m 2, 27 Sept 1986, (Lucy) Gwendoline, da of George Bowles (d 1969), of Northampton; *Career* RAMC 1941-46; head of PR: Assoc of Optical Practitioners 1946-55, Br Electrical and Allied Mfrs Assoc 1955-60; PR advsr London C of C 1965-72, PR cnsllr 1961-, memb Miny of Health Ophthalmic Optical Advsy Ctee Optical Whitley Cncl; chm Inst Public Relations, pres Int Public Relations Assoc, sec Finchley Chess Club; visiting prof Coll of St Mark and St John Plymouth 1989; Freeman City of London 1956, Liveryman Worshipful Co of Spectacle Makers 1956; hon prof relations Univ of Stirling 1988; FBIM, FRSA, FBCO, FSMC, MJI; Hon FIPR; *Books* Practical Public Relations (1962), Exhibiting Overseas (1971), Role of Public Relations in Management (1972), Businessman's Guide to The Centrally Planned Economies (1972), Public Relations in the 1980's (1979), Exhibitions and Conferences from A-Z (1989), Introduction to Public Relations (1989); *Recreations* chess, travel; *Clubs* Reform; *Style*— Prof Sam Black, MBE; Keswick House, 3 Greenway, London N20 8EE (☎ 081 445 5256, fax 081 446 9108, telex 262433 ref 3237)

BLACK, Sheila Psyche; OBE (1986); da of Clement Johnston Black, and Mildred Beryl Black; *b* 6 May 1920; *Educ* Dorset, Switzerland and RADA; *m* 1, 1939 (m dis 1951), Geoffrey Davien; 1 da (and 1 s decd); m 2, 1951 (m dis 1973), L A Lee Howard; *Career* woman's ed Financial Times 1959-72, specialist feature writer nat newspaper and magazines, author of several books, dir MAI plc 1976-; memb: Liquor Licensing Law Reform Ctee 1967-70, Price Cmmn 1973-77, Cncl IOD 1975-, Nat Consumer Cncl 1981-, Ctee on Privacy and Related Matters 1989-90; chm Gas Consumers Cncl 1980-89; *Style*— Miss Sheila Black, OBE; 12A Earls Court Gardens, London SW5 0TD (☎ 071 373 3620)

BLACK, Thomas Charteris; s of John Sutherland Charteris Black (d 1967), and Gertrude Margaret, *née* Stout (d 1976); *b* 12 Sept 1914; *Educ* Univ Coll Sch Frognall London, Sch of Pharmacy London; *m* 28 March 1942, (Violet) Lorna, da of Brig-Gen William Denman Croft, CB, DMG, DSO (d 1968), of Mawnan Smith, Cornwall; 1 s (Peter b 1952), 2 da (Jane b 1943, Susan b 1945); *Career* HG 1940-41: Cdr No 1 Platoon, No 3 Co, 1 Co of London Bn, Cdr Buckingham Palace Detachment of Kings Gd 1941; seaman RN Patrol Serv 1941-42; cmmnd Fighter Direction Offr 1942; RNVR: Sub Lt HMS Victorians RNVR 1942-43, Lt HMS Ukussa 1944, Lt HMS Valiant 1944, Lt HMS Boxer 1945, Lt Cdr HMS Glory 1945-46; Menley & James Ltd: factory worker 1930-33, office mangr 1933-39, manufactured Stilboestrol 1938-39, mktg mangr 1939-41 and 1946-49, mktg dir 1949-56; mangr of commercial devpt Pfizers Ltd 1957-59, mktg mangr Miles Ltd 1959-67, vice pres of int ops Miles Inc USA 1969-79 (mktg dir Ames Div 1967-69); sec local Royal Br Legion, treas local Cons branch; Liveryman Worshipful Soc Apothecaries 1951, Freeman City of London 1952; MPharmS 1938, FRSA 1951, FRPharmS 1977; *Recreations* sailing, bowls, walking; *Style*— Thomas Black, Esq; Michaelmas, Convent Close, St Margarets-at-Cliffe, Dover, Kent CT15 6JD (☎ 0304 853142)

BLACK, Virginia; da of (Morice) William Black, of Birmingham, and Mabel Florence, *née* Jones; *b* 1 Oct 1943; *Educ* Kings Norton GS Birmingham, RAM; *m* 1965, Howard Davis, s of Howard Davis; 2 s (Guy b 25 Sept 1969, Oliver b 6 Jan 1972); *Career* solo harpsichordist specialising in the virtuoso repertoire; tours abroad incl: USA, NZ, Aust, France, Germany, Austria, Poland, Sweden; appearances at major early music festivals incl: Göttingen Handel Festival, Herne, York, Carmel Bach Festival; major venues incl: South Bank, Carnegie Hall, NY, Vienna's Konzerthaus; half of duo with Howard Davis (baroque violin); many live broadcasts and TV appearances in UK and abroad; concerts with: Eng Chamber Orch Ancient Acad of Music, professor of harpsicord RAM; recordings incl: Scarlatti Sonatas (1985), Soler Sonatas (1987), J C Bach (1987), Mozart Violin and Keyboard Sonatas (with Howard Davis 1988), Brandenburg 5 with Consort of London (1989), The Essential Harpsichord (1989), J S Bach - Goldberg Variations (1990), The Complete Keyboard Works of Rameau (1991); Gramophone's Critics Choice of the Year for Soler Sonatas; *Recreations* interior design, creative cookery; *Style*— Virginia Black; 123 Sheering Rd, Old Harlow, Essex CM17 0JP (☎ 0279 431337); Melanie Turner Management, 203 Murchison Rd, London SW3 5NB (☎ 071 376 3758)

BLACKABY, Frank Thomas; s of Rev Edgar Percival Blackaby (d 1977), and Muriel Ruth, *née* Hawkins (d 1977); *b* 25 Oct 1921; *Educ* Perse Sch Cambridge, Emmanuel Coll Cambridge (BA); *m* 1, 27 Oct 1961, Elizabeth; 1 s (Mark b 1962); m 2, 31 Dec 1975, Mary Mildred, da of Hon Arthur John Palmer Fuller-Acland-Hood (d 1964), of Somerset; 2 c (Susan Acland-Hood b 1977, John Acland-Hood b 1979); *Career* dep dir Nat Inst of Economic and Social Research 1971-81, dir Stockholm Int Peace Research Inst 1981-86; ed: British Economic Policy 1960-74, Cambridge Univ Press 1978, World Armaments and Disarmament Yearbooks; *Recreations* tennis; *Style*— Frank T Blackaby, Esq; 9 Fentiman Road, London SW8 (☎ 071 735 3193)

BLACKADDER, Elizabeth Violet; OBE (1982); da of Thomas Blackadder (d 1941), of Falkirk, and Violet Isabella, *née* Scott (d 1984); *b* 24 Sept 1931; *Educ* Falkirk HS, Univ of Edinburgh, Edinburgh Coll of Art; *m* 1956, John Houston, s of Alexander Anderson Houston (d 1947); *Career* artist; lectr Sch of Drawing and Painting Edinburgh Coll of Art 1962-86; numerous solo exhibitions since 1960 (Mercury Gallery 1965-), shows regularly at Royal Scottish Acad and Royal Acad, Tapestry designs (woven by Dovecot Studies) in private collections Fleming Holdings Ltd Reckitt Colman; *solo exhibitions incl*: Retrospective (Scottish Arts Cncl & touring) 1981-82, Retrospective (Aberystwyth Arts Centre & touring) 1989; *works in the collectins of*: Scottish Arts Cncl, Scottish Nat Gallery of Modern Art, Scottish Nat Portrait Gallery, Nat Portrait Gallery, Govt Art Collection, Kettle's Yard Univ of Cambridge, Univ of Edinburgh, Hunterian Art Gallery Univ of Glasgow, Univ of St Andrews, Univ of Stirling, Nat Museum of Women in the Arts Washington DC, McNay Art Museum San Antonio Texas, Heriot Watt Univ, Robert Fleming Holdings Ltd; Guthrie award Royal Scottish Acad 1963, Pimms award Royal Acad 1983, Watercolour Fndn Royal Acad 1988; memb: Soc of Scottish Artists, Royal Glasgow Inst of the Fine Arts, Royal Scottish Soc of Painters in Watercolours; hon memb Royal W of Eng Acad, hon fell RIAS; Hon D Litt: Heriot Watt Univ 1989, Univ of Edinburgh 1990; RSA 1972, RA 1976; *Recreations* gardening and golf; *Style*— Ms Elizabeth Blackadder, OBE; 57 Fountainhall Rd, Edinburgh EH9 2LH (☎ 031 667 3687)

BLACKADDER, Dr Eric Sutton; RD (1968, clasp 1978); s of John Williamson Blackadder (d 1946), of Falkirk, and Phoebe Euodia, *née* Sutton (d 1973); *b* 25 Nov 1927; *Educ* Falkirk HS, Edinburgh Univ (MB ChB); *m* 28 July 1955, Jean, da of William Law Gordon (d 1985), of Sunningdale; 2 s (Mark b 1956, John b 1957), 1 da (Averil b 1959); *Career* Nat Serv Surgn Lt RNVR 1953-55; RNR 1958-81: Surgn Lt Cdr 1960, Surgn Cdr 1965, ret 1981; jr hosp appts 1952-58, princ in gen practice 1958-68, fell in med admin Scottish Home and Health Dept 1968-70, med inspr of factories 1970-71, dep dir of med servs Health and Safety Exec 1977-80 (sr employment med advsr 1972-77), chief med offr BBC 1980-84, gp med dir BUPA 1986-; govr BUPA Med Fndn Ltd 1986-, exec govr BUPA 1987-; dir: BUPA Health Insur 1987-, BUPA Int 1987-; hon lectr Dept of Gen Practice Univ of Edinburgh 1963-68, hon clinical lectr in community med Univ of Glasgow 1975-77, guest lectr Dept of Social Med Univ of Edinburgh and Dept of Occupational Med Univ of Dundee 1968-77; cncl memb Rotary Club of London 1987-91, vice pres Int Med Assoc for Radio and TV 1980-84, hon treas Int Assoc Physicians for Overseas Servs 1986-90, chm fin ctee Royal Inst of Public Health and Hygiene 1988- contrib numerous articles to medical and scientific jls; FRCP Glasgow 1983 (MRCP 1980), MRCPE 1985, FRCPE 1988 (MRCPE 1985), FFOM 1984 (MFOM 1978), MRCGP 1961, MFCM 1974, FRSM, fell Royal Inst of Public Health and Hygiene, memb BMA; *Recreations* sailing, golf; *Clubs* R & A, Royal Burgess Golfing Soc of Edinburgh, Royal Naval Sailing Assoc, Royal Yachting Assoc; *Style*— Dr Eric Blackadder, RD; 2 Gloucester Gate Mews, Regents Park London NW1 4AD (☎ 071 486 7758) BUPA, Provident House, Essex St, London WC2R 3AX (☎ 071 353 5212, fax 071 353 0134, telex 883059)

BLACKBURN, Bishop of 1989-; Rt Rev Alan David Chesters; s of Herbert Chesters (d 1982), of Huddersfield, W Yorks, and Catherine Rebecca, *née* Mountfort (d 1984); *b* 26 Aug 1937; *Educ* Elland GS, St Chad's Coll Durham (BA), St Catherine's Coll Oxford (MA), St Stephen's House Oxford; *m* 23 July 1975, Jennie, da of Thomas Davison Garrett (d 1973), of Sunderland, Tyne and Wear; 1 s (David b 1977); *Career* curate St Anne Wandsworth London 1962-66, chaplain Tiffin Sch Kingston upon Thames 1966-72, hon curate St Richard Ham 1967-72, dir of Educn Dio of Durham 1972-85, rector of Brancepeth 1972-85, hon canon Durham Cathedral 1975-55, archdeacon Halifax 1985-89; C of E Gen Synod: memb 1975-, memb Standing Ctee 1985-89, vice chm Bd of Educn 1984-, chm Bd of Educn Schs Ctee 1984-90; church cmmr 1982-89, govr St Chad's Coll Durham 1980-89, memb Advsy Cncl Radio Leeds 1987-89; *Recreations* railways, walking; *Style*— The Rt Rev the Bishop of Blackburn; Bishop's House, Ribchester Road, Blackburn BB1 9EF

BLACKBURN, Capt (David) Anthony James; LVO (1978); s of late Lt J Blackburn, DSC, RN, and late Mrs M J G Pickering-Pick; *b* 18 Jan 1945; *Educ* Taunton Sch, RNC Dartmouth; *m* 1973, Elizabeth Barstow; 3 da; *Career* cmd HMS Kirkliston 1972-73, Equerry-in-Waiting to HRH The Duke of Edinburgh 1976-78, exec offr HMS Antrim 1978-81; Cmd: HMS Birmingham 1983-84, Capt 3 Destroyer Sqdn HMS York 1987-88; Cdre Clyde and Naval Base Cmd Clyde 1990-; *Style*— Capt Anthony Blackburn, LVO, RN

BLACKBURN, Archdeacon of; *see*: Robinson, The Ven (William) David

BLACKBURN, Barrie; s of Harold Blackburn, of Harlow, Essex, and Kathleen May, *née* King (d 1984); *b* 23 June 1948; *Educ* Marling Sch Stroud, Univ of Leeds (BCom); *m* 9 Jan 1971, Julie Maureen, da of Phillip Ronald Baker, of Abingdon, Oxon; 2 s (David Charles b 1971, Luke b 1979), 1 da (Jane b 1984); *Career* articled clerk Touche Ross & Co 1970-75, taxation mangr Davy Corporation plc 1975-84, gp taxation controller The Plessey Co Plc 1984-87, gp dir of taxation TI Group Plc 1987-; FCA, ATII; *Recreations* skiing, reading, watching sport, gardening; *Style*— Barrie Blackburn Esq; Woodbrook, 13 Stony Wood, Harlow, Essex CM18 6AU (☎ 0279 424495); TI Group plc, Foxcombe Court, Abingdon Business Park, Abingdon, Oxon OX14 1DZ (☎ 0235 555570, fax 0235 555818)

BLACKBURN, David Michael; s of Rudolph Isaac Blackburn, of London, and Esther Sybil, *née* Levy; *b* 23 Dec 1937; *Educ* City of London Sch, St John's Coll Cambridge (MA, LLM); *m* 1, 11 Jan 1962 (m dis 1969), Louise Joy, da of Louis Courts, of London; 1 s (James b 1964), 1 da (Deborah b 1963); m 2, 30 April 1970, Janice, da of Louis Brown (d 1987); 2 s (Oliver b 1971, Joshua b 1973); *Career* slr; ptnr Courts & Co 1962-81; dir: Rosehaugh plc 1979-85, Rosehaugh Stanhope Developments plc 1983-, Blackburn Assoc Ltd 1986-; property project conslt 1985-; memb Law Soc 1962; *Style*— David Blackburn, Esq; 6 Rosslyn Mews, London NW3 1NN (☎ 071 431 3467, fax 071 435 0332, car 0836 229)

BLACKBURN, Frank Victor; s of John Martin Blackburn (d 1975), and Mabel Gregg (d 1951); *b* 29 Oct 1931; *Educ* numerous schs; *m* 1, 27 Sept 1952 (m dis 1969), Dorothea, da of Franz Schibitschek; 2 s (Mark b 1954, Fraser b 1957), 1 da (Susan b 1955); m 2, 3 Sept 1969, Gwendoline, da of Cecil Jones; *Career* served RE 1949-54; md Frank V Blackburn (Printers) Ltd 1955-70, freelance wildlife photographer 1970-, chm Nature Photographers Ltd 1980-86; major contrib of natural history photographs to leading pubns worldwide; TV and radio appearances; *Books* Natural History Photography (jtly, 1974); *Recreations* darkroom activities, bird watching, natural history, good music, reading, hill walking, fishing; *Style*— Frank Blackburn, Esq; 15 Dolley's Hill, Normandy, Guildford, Surrey GU3 2AJ (☎ 0483 811569)

BLACKBURN, George Richard (Dick); VRD (1958); s of Robert Blackburn, OBE (d 1955), of Bowcliffe Hall, Boston Spa, E Yorks, and Jessica Tryphena, *née* Thompson; *b* 19 Feb 1917; *Educ* Sherborne, Christ's Coll Cambridge (MA), LAMDA (ALAM); *m* 6 March 1947, Dulcie May (d 1989), da of Frederick Garrod (d 1985), of Leiston, Suffolk; 1 s (Robert Wesley b 27 Aug 1952), 1 da (Susan Patricia b 15 Dec 1947); *Career* QORWK, LRB and KOYLI Regts Army 1940-41, Lt (A) RNVR 1941-46; Pilot Fleet Air Arm served: UK, Trinidad, Canada, Gibraltar, N Africa, Atlantic Convoys, CO Aircraft Ferry Sqdn; Pilot: Flt-Lt RAFVR 1949-52 Lt Cdr RNVR 1952-58, RNR 1958-72, ret 1967; apprentice trainee Rolls Royce 1939, called to the Bar Inner Temple 1948, private practice NE circuit 1951-56 (participated first Legal Aid scheme 1952), dir legal advsr Tiltman Langley Ltd 1952-57, lawyer and legal advsr Shell Mex and BP Ltd 1956-63, self-employed dir (business encompassing farm, garage and airfield) 1963-67, mangr legal dept Hotel and Catering Indust Trg Bd Middx 1967-71, gp legal offr Calor Gp Slough 1971-82, ret 1982 (still involved in private work); memb: Bar Assoc Commerce Fin and Indust, Fleet Air Arm Offr's Assoc; *Recreations* family, church and social work (for elderly), freemasonry, flying, law, theatre, keeping fit, tennis, swimming; *Clubs* RAF, Naval; *Style*— Dick Blackburn, Esq, VRD; 26 Pearl Court, Cornfield Terrace, Eastbourne, E Sussex BN21 4AA (☎ 0323 644050)

BLACKBURN, John Graham; MP (C) Dudley W 1979-; s of Charles Frederick Blackburn (d 1969), and Grace Blackburn; *b* 2 Sept 1934; *Educ* Liverpool Collegiate Sch, Univ of Liverpool; *m* 1958, Marjorie, da of George Thompson (d 1974), of Wigan; 1 s, 2 da; *Career* formerly police offr Liverpool; sales dir Solway Engrg 1965-; memb POUNC 1972-; Freeman Cities of London and Tel Aviv; *Recreations* yachting (yacht 'Tobermory'); *Clubs* Wolverhampton and Bilston Athletic, Traeth Coch Yacht (Anglesey); *Style*— John Blackburn, Esq, MP; 906 Howard House, Dolphin Square Westminster, London

BLACKBURN, Michael John; s of Francis Blackburn (d 1970), and Ann Elizabeth, *née* Thornley (d 1973); *b* 25 Oct 1930; *Educ* Kingston GS; *m* 19 March 1955, Maureen Beatrice, da of Arnold Dale; 1 s (Alastair b 1957), 2 da (Fiona b 1958, Anna b 1966); *Career* managing ptnr Touche Ross International plc 1984-90; chm: Touche Ross 1990 (ptnr 1960-), GEI International plc 1990-; FCA 1953, CBIM 1986; *Recreations* horse racing, gardening; *Clubs* City of London; *Style*— Michael Blackburn, Esq; Touche Ross & Co, Hill House, 1 Little New St, London EC4 3TR (☎ 071 936 3000, fax 071 583 8517, telex 884739)

BLACKBURN, Peter Hugh; s of Hugh Edward Blackburn, of Bladford, Yorkshire (d 1964), and Sarah, *née* Moffatt; *b* 17 Dec 1940; *Educ* Dovai Sch, Univ of Leeds (BA), Univ of Poitiers (Dip French), Harvard Business Sch (AMP); *m* 17 March 1967, Gillian Mary, da of William Francis Popple, of Yorkshire; 3 da (Joanna Clare b 1968, Catherine Elizabeth b 1970, Louise Mary b 1973); *Career* articled clerk RS Dawson & Co Chartered Accountants 1962-66, fin controller John Mackintosh & Sons Ltd Norwich 1967-72 (works accountant Halifax 1966-67); Rowntree Mackintosh: fin dir Overseas Div 1972-75, asst md rising to md 1975-84, gp bd dir 1982-88, chm UK and Eire Regn 1985-88; Nestle SA (following takeover): md Rowntree UK 1968-, dir Int Chocolate & Confectionary Strategy 1989-90, chm and md Nestle UK 1991-; chm Cncl Festival of Languages Young Linguists Competition 1985-89; memb: Cncl Univ of York 1989-, CIHE 1990-; memb Worshipful Co of Merchant Adventurers York 1989; hon fell Inst of Linguists 1989; FCA 1976 (ACA 1966); *Recreations* fell walking, swimming, photography; *Clubs* Yorkshire (York); *Style*— Peter Blackburn, Esq; The Nestle Co Ltd, St Georges House, Croydon CR9 1NR (☎ 081 686 3333)

BLACKBURN, Brig Raymond Forrester; s of Rev William Erskine Blackburn (d 1954), of Aberdeen, and Ella Forrester, *née* Brander (d 1974); *b* 29 Jan 1929; *Educ* Edinburgh Acad, Aberdeen GS, Univ of Aberdeen (MB ChB, DPH); *m* 4 June 1966, Ann Delyse, da of William George Hubbard (d 1977), of Kew Gardens, London; *Career* Nat Serv (Korea, Japan and Malaya) 1953-55; CO: 23 Parachute Field Ambulance 1968-70, Br Mil Hosp Hong Kong 1970-73; chief instr and dep cmdt RAMC Trg Centre 1973-74, Asst DGMAS MOD 1974-77, dep dir Med Servs BAOR 1977-79; med cdr: Horse Gds London 1979-82, HQ NI 1982-85, Hong Kong 1985; asst surgn gen 1986; DRCOG 1957, MFCM 1972, FBIM 1972; *Recreations* photography, wild life, gardening; *Style*— Brig Raymond Blackburn; c/o The Royal Bank of Scotland, Lawrie House, Victoria Rd, Farnborough, Hants

BLACKBURN, Richard John; s of Tom Binks Blackburn (d 1973), and Mabel, *née* Cleal; *b* 22 Feb 1938; *Educ* Eastbourne Coll, Worcester Coll Oxford (MA); *m* 3 Sept 1966, Jennifer Ann Yelland; 1 s (Alistair James b 1 June 1971), 2 da (Joanna Clare b 24 Oct 1968, Sophie Jane b 20 Sept 1974); *Career* Nat Serv cmmnd RASC 1956-58; Touche Ross & Co: articled clerk 1961-64, chartered accountant 1965-, ptnr 1969-, London 1961-81 and 1986-, Glasgow 1981-86, various mgmnt appts 1979-86; memb Cncl: Roedean, Hazelwood Sch Oxted; Freeman City of London 1988; FCA 1975 (ACA 1965); *Recreations* sailing, skiing, Br domestic architecture; *Clubs* City of London, Utd Oxford and Cambrige Univ, Royal Northern and Clyde Yacht; *Style*— Richard Blackburn, Esq; Wexcombe, Warlingham, Surrey CR6 9HQ (☎ 0883 622725); Touche Ross & Co, Hill House, 1 Little New St, London EC4A 3TR (☎ 071 936 3000, fax 071 583 8517)

BLACKBURN, Ronald Henry Albert; s of Sydney James Blackburn (d 1954), of Prestbury, Knock, Belfast, and Ellen Margaret Selina, *née* German (d 1952); *b* 9 Feb 1924; *Educ* Royal Belfast Academical Inst, Univ of London (LLB); *m* 13 Sept 1950, Annabell, da of John Hunter (d 1941), of Whiteabbey, NI; 2 s (Alan b 1952, Paul b 1957); *Career* WWII FO 1943-45; NI Parly reporting staff 1946-52, 2 clerk asst Parly 1952-62 (clerk asst 1962-71, clerk of the Parliaments 1971-73), clerk NI Assembly 1973-79, clerk NI Constitutional Convention 1975-76, memb NI Planning Appeals Cmmn 1980-89 (ret); memb Cwlth Parly Assoc 1952-79 (attended confs in Malaysia, Gibraltar, CI, London and IOM); *Recreations* gardening, golf; *Style*— Ronald Blackburn, Esq; Trelawn, 9 Jordanstown Rd, Newtownabbey, Co Antrim, NI BT37 0QD (☎ 0232 862035)

BLACKBURN, Thomas; s of Thomas Blackburn (d 1987), of Preston; *b* 22 July 1932; *Educ* Oundle; *m* 1955, Diana Christine, da of William Ascough Lillico (d 1983), of Barnet; 1 s, 2 da; *Career* engr dir: C Seward & Co Holdings 1960-, Shard Bridge Co 1980- (chm 1984); jt md C Seward & Co 1967- (chm 1987), chm C Seward (Properties) Ltd 1989-; *Recreations* shooting, fishing; *Style*— Thomas Blackburn, Esq; Hill Top Farm, Thornley with Wheatley, Longridge, Preston, Lancs PR3 2TY (☎ 0772 783353); C Seward and Co Ltd, West View, Ribbleton, Preston, Lancs PR1 5JA (☎ 0772 796424)

BLACKBURN, William Howard; s of Thomas Cather Johnston Blackburn (d 1960), and Elizabeth, *née* Jones (d 1978); *b* 23 Dec 1932; *Educ* Holt Sch, Univ of Liverpool (LLB); *m* 1, 9 April 1960, Marie-Therese (d 1983), da of Gen Andre Dorange (d 1985); m 2, 23 July 1985, Chloe Marya Tickell, da of Sir James Gunn (d 1964); 2 s (Alexander b 1963, James b 1965); *Career* ptnr Theodore Goddard Paris 1957-62; IBM 1962-84: mangr legal dept, co sec, md Euro office SA; memb: Br Cncl Law Advsy Ctee, Inst of Actuaries Appeals Bd, UK Delgn to CCBE, cncl Law Soc; chm Int Ctee Law Soc; *Recreations* golf; *Clubs* RAC, Royal Mid-Surrey Golf; *Style*— William Blackburn, Esq; 18 Alma Square, London NW8 9QA (☎ 071 286 5273, fax 071 266 2627); c/o Theodore Goddard, 150 Aldersgate St, London EC1A 4EJ (☎ 071 606 8865, fax 071 606 4390)

BLACKBURNE, Lady; Bridget Senhouse Constant; *née* Wilson; da of James Mackay Wilson, JP, DL (d 1934), of Currygrane, Co Longford, and Amy Alice Goldie-Taubman (d 1944); *b* 28 Sept 1903; *Educ* privately; *m* 1935, Sir Kenneth William Blackburne, GCMG, GBE, (d 1980); 1 s (Martin d 1985), 1 da (Jean (Mrs Richard Hall)); *Style*— Lady Blackburne; Garvagh, Ballasalla, Isle of Man (☎ 0624 823640)

BLACKER, Dr Carmen Elizabeth; da of Carlos Paton Blacker, and Helen Maude, *née* Pilkington; *b* 13 July 1924; *Educ* Benenden Sch, SOAS Univ of London (BA, PhD), Somerville Coll Oxford (BA), Radcliffe Coll USA, Keio Univ Tokyo 1951-53; *Career* univ lectr in Japanese Univ of Cambridge 1958- (fell Clare Hall 1965-) visiting prof Columbia Univ 1965, Princeton 1979; FBA; pres Folklore Soc 1982-84; Order of the Precious Crown (Japan); *Books* The Japanese Enlightenment: a study of the Writings of Fukuzawa Yukichi (1964), The Catalpa Bow: a study of Shamanistic Practices in Japan (1975); *Recreations* walking, comparative mythology; *Style*— Dr Carmen Blacker; Willow House, Grantchester, Cambridge CB3 9NF (☎ 0223 840196); Faculty of Oriental Studies, Sidgwick Ave, Cambridge (☎ 0223 335172)

BLACKER, Hon Mrs - Hon Caroline Susan Dean; da of Rev Lord Soper, and Marie Gertrude Dean; *b* 11 Aug 1946; *Educ* Queenswood, Univ of Exeter (BA); *m* 1975, Terence Blacker, s of Gen Sir Cecil Hugh Blacker, KCB, OBE, MC, *qv*; 1 s (Alexander b 1977), 1 da (Alice b 1979); *Style*— The Hon Mrs Blacker; 91 Wendell Rd, London W12 (☎ 081 743 8746)

BLACKER, Gen Sir Cecil Hugh; GCB (1975, KCB 1969, CB 1967), OBE (1960), MC (1944); s of Col Norman Valentine Blacker, DSO, MC (d 1958), and Olive Georgina, *née* Hope (d 1978); *b* 4 June 1916; *Educ* Wellington, RMC Sandhurst; *m* 26 Feb 1947, Felicity Mary, da of Maj Ivor Buxton, DSO, TD (d 1969), and wid of Maj John Rew (ka 1943); 2 s; *Career* 2 Lt Royal Inniskilling Dragoon Gds 1936, GOC-in-C Northern Cmd 1969-70, vice CGS 1970-73, Adj-Gen 1973-76, ret 1976; ADC to HM The Queen 1962-64, ADC (Gen) to HM The Queen 1974-76; pres: Br Showjumping Assoc 1976-80, Br Equestrian Fedn 1980-84; chm Racecourse Security Servs Ltd 1980-83; memb Horserace Betting Levy Bd 1980-83; dep sr steward Jockey Club 1984-86; FBIM 1973; *Recreations* painting, hothouse gardening; *Clubs* Jockey; *Style*— Gen Sir Cecil Blacker, GCB, OBE, MC

BLACKER, Hon Mrs; Hon Mary Rose; er da of 2 Baron Rathcavan (o da by his 1 w); *b* 26 Aug 1935; *m* 1960, David Stewart Wellesley Blacker, JP, DL, er twin s of Lt-Col Latham Valentine Stewart Blacker, OBE, of Cold Hayes, Liss, Hants (whose maternal gm was Marie Leszczynska, ggda of last Elector of Posen and gt grand-niece of Stanislas Leszczynski, Count of Lesno and, as Stanislaw I, King of Poland, hence cous to all the descendants of Louis XV of France by his m with Marie Leszczynska, King Stanislaw I's da) by Col Blacker's w Lady Doris Peel, JP, o da of 1 E Peel; 3 s (Barnaby b 1961, William b 1962, Rohan b 1966); *Style*— The Hon Mrs Blacker; Molecomb, Goodwood, Chichester, Sussex

BLACKETT, Captain (John) Beauchamp; s of Maj (Christopher) William (Stewart) Blackett (d 1985), of Arbigland by Dumfries, and Kathleen Charlotte, *née* Williams-Wynn; *b* 6 May 1939; *Educ* Eton; *m* 1, 15 Jan 1964 (m dis 1977), Sarah Jennifer, da of James Withycombe (d 1984), of Bury Farm, Studham, Dunstable; 2 s (James b 1964, Edward b 1969), 1 da (Annabel b 1966); m 2, 1977, Susan Elizabeth, da of Michael Badger, of Chilson, Charlbury, Oxon; 2 da (Flora b 1978, Letitia b 1983); *Career* Coldstream Gds 1957-70; chm: Ashdown (Leadenhall) Ltd 1970-90, Ashdown (Leadenhall) plc 1990-, Beauchamp's Restaurant 1989; Co Pres SSAFA Dumfries; chm: Dumfries Prison Visiting Ctee 1982-85, Congregational Bd Kirkbean Church; Freeman City of London 1989; FInstD 1970; *Recreations* polo, shooting, fishing, gardening; *Clubs* Pratt's, Beauchamp's Tap; *Style*— Capt Beauchamp Blackett; Arbigland, Dumfries DG2 8BQ (☎ 038788 283); Quinta da Escocia, Pincho, Bensafrim, Lagos, Algarve; Ashdown (Leadenhall) Ltd, 23-25 Leadenhall Market, London EC3 (☎ 071 626 1949/0178)

BLACKETT, David John; s of Capt Frederick Herbert Blackett, of Edinburgh, and Mary, *née* Watson (d 1982); *b* 22 Aug 1950; *Educ* Dollar Academy Scotland, Univ of Edinburgh (B Com); *m* 1979, Anita Mary, da of Grareth Evans; 1 s (Matthew Gareth b 9 March 1988), 1 da (Sarah Louise b 12 Dec 1984); *Career* apprentice chartered accountant Graham Smart & Annan 1970-73, merchant banker N m Rothschild & Sons Ltd 1973-, seconded to venture in Malaysia with Bumiputera Merchant Bankers 1975-77, md N M Rothschild & Sons (Singapore) Ltd 1979-86, dir N M Rothschild & Sons Ltd 1983-, md N M Rothschild & Sons (Hong Kong) Ltd 1986-; MICAS 1975; *Recreations* polo, sailing, golf, tennis, photography; *Clubs* Oriental (London), Guards Polo, Royal Hong Kong Yacht, Jurong Golf & Country, Sheko' Golf; *Style*— David Blackett, Esq; N M Rothschild & Sons (Hong Kong) Ltd, 16th Floor, Alexandra House, Central, Hong Kong (☎ 5255 333)

BLACKETT, Francis Hugh; s of Sir Hugh Douglas Blackett, 8 Bt (d 1960); hp to btcy of bro, Sir George Blackett, 10 Bt; *b* 16 Oct 1907; *Educ* Eton; *m* 1, 1950, Elizabeth Eily Barrie (d 1982), da of late Howard Dennison, of Valparaiso, Chile; 2 s, 2 da; m 2, 1985, Catherine Joan, da of late Edward Watson, of Bloxham, Oxon; *Career* Maj The Royals (ret), served WWII; *Style*— Francis Blackett, Esq; Ramshope Lodge, Catcleugh, Otterburn, Newcastle upon Tyne NE19 ITZ

BLACKETT, Sir George William; 10 Bt (E 1673); s of late Sir Hugh Blackett, 8 Bt; suc bro, Sir Charles Douglas Blackett (d 1968); *b* 26 April 1906; *m* 1, 1933, Euphemia Cicely (d 1960), da of late Maj Nicholas Robinson, of Frankton Grange, Shropshire; m 2, 1964, Daphne Laing, da of late Maj Guy Laing Bradley, TD, of Bridge End House, Hexham; *Heir* bro, Maj Francis Hugh Blackett, *qv*; *Career* Shropshire Yeo and CMP WW II; *Style*— Sir George Blackett, Bt; Colwyn, Corbridge-on-Tyne, Northumberland (☎ Corbridge 2252)

BLACKETT, Hon Mrs (Geva Charlotte Caroline); *née* Winn; o da of 5 Baron St Oswald, *qv*; *b* 15 Sept 1955; *m* 12 June 1987, John Simon Blackett, er s of John Harold

Booth Blackett, of Whalton, Northumberland; 2 da (Helena Charlotte Rose b 22 1988, Camilla Harriet Eve b 23 Nov 1989); *Style*— The Hon Mrs Blackett; The Corner House, Markham Lane, Scredington, Sleaford, Lincs NG34 OAW

BLACKETT, Hon Nicolas Maynard; s of Baron Blackett, OM, CH (Life Peer, d 1974); *b* 25 May 1928; *Educ* Univ Coll Sch London and Univ of Bristol; *m* 1951, Patricia Kathleen Tankins, of Bristol; 1 s (Peter b 1962); *Career* research scientist; Inst of Cancer Research London 1954-83, ret; *Style*— The Hon Nicolas Blackett; 18 Farquhar Road, London SW19

BLACKETT-ORD, His Hon Judge (Andrew) James; CVO (1988); 2 s of John Reginald Blackett-Ord, JP (d 1967), of Whitfield Hall, Hexham, Northumberland, and Lena Mary, *née* Blackett-Ord (d 1961); yr bro of John Christopher Blackett-Ord, *qv*; *b* 21 Aug 1921; *Educ* Eton, New Coll Oxford (MA); *m* 9 June 1945, Rosemary, da of Edward William Bovill (d 1966), of Brook House, Moreton, Essex; 4 s (Christopher b and d 13 Feb 1946, Charles b 6 Feb 1948, Mark b 10 May 1950, Benjamin James b 12 Feb 1963), 1 da (Nicola Mary Lena (Mrs George St Leger Granville) b 25 Oct 1961); *Career* Lt Scots Guards, served in UK, N Africa and Italy 1941-46 (prisoner (Anzio) 1944-45); called to the Bar Inner Temple 1947, Lincoln's Inn 1948; county court judge 1971; vice chllr Co Palatine of Lancaster, memb Cncl of Duchy of Lancaster and High Court Judge (Chancery Div) Northern Area 1973-87; chllr Dio of Newcastle-upon-Tyne 1971-; Bencher Lincoln's Inn 1985; *Recreations* rural life, reading, travel; *Clubs* Garrick, Lansdowne; *Style*— His Honour A J Blackett-Ord, CVO; Helbeck Hall, Brough, Kirkby Stephen, Cumbria (☎ 09304 323)

BLACKETT-ORD, John Christopher; JP (1960); elder s of John Reginald Blackett-Ord, JP (d 1967), of Whitfield Hall, Hexham, Northumberland, and Lena Mary, *née* Blackett-Ord (d 1961); bro of Andrew James Blackett-Ord, *qv*; *b* 30 Sept 1918; *Educ* Eton, New Coll Oxford; *m* 1, 1941, Elisabeth Hamilton (d 1977), da of Maj Charles Mitchell, DSO, OBE (d 1958), of Pallinsburn, Cornhill on Tweed; 1 s, 2 da; m 2, 1985, Pamela Margaret, da of Frederic Blagden Malim, of Myddylton House, Saffron Walden (d 1964), and widow of John Humphrey Edmund Craster (d 1983); *Career* Maj served in Scots Guards 1939-45 (Italy 1943-45); FRICS 1949; farmer; *Recreations* shooting, fishing; *Clubs* Lansdowne; *Style*— John Blackett-Ord, Esq, JP; Old Rectory, Whitfield, Hexham, Northumberland (☎ home 0434 345228, office 0434 345273)

BLACKETT-ORD, Mark; s of His Hon Judge Andrew James Blackett-Ord, CVO, *qv*, and Rosemary, *née* Bovill; *b* 10 May 1950; *Educ* Eton, New Coll Oxford; *m* 2 Dec 1981, Carol Theresa Anne, da of Sir David Scott-Fox, KCMG (d 1984); 3 da (Katherine b 1983, Elinor b 1986, Constance b 1988); *Career* called to the Bar Lincoln's Inn 1974; *Books* Hell-Fire Duke (1981), ed Partnership Law in Halsbury's Laws of England (1981); *Recreations* restoration of ancient buildings; *Style*— M Blackett-Ord, Esq; Warcop Hall, Warcop, Appleby, Cumbria; 81 Church St, Stoke Newington, London N16; 2 New Square, Lincoln's Inn, London WC2A 3RU (☎ 071 242 6201, fax 071 831 8102)

BLACKFORD, Sqdn Ldr Peter Fitzgerald; s of Joseph Blackford (d 1959), and Sheila, *née* O'Halligan (d 1952); *b* 22 Nov 1920; *Educ* Tonbridge, RAF Coll Cranwell; *m* 23 July 1943, Sheila, da of Lt-Col Henry Joseph Higgs (d 1936), of Notts; 4 s (Timothy b 1945, Christopher b 1948, Jeremy b 1952, Patrick b 1954); *Career* reg RAF offr 1938-57, wartime ops in UK and Europe, ret as Sqdn Ldr 1957; subsequently worked as personnel mangr in several cos incl Wellcome Foundation 1969-82; *Recreations* gardening; *Style*— Sqdn Ldr Peter F Blackford; Shode House, Dux Lane, Plaxtol, nr Sevenoaks, Kent

BLACKFORD HICKMAN, Rivers; s of late Leslie Blackford Hickman, and late Rose Alice, *née* Begg; *b* 15 July 1936; *Educ* Cheltenham; *m* 1966, Patricia May, da of Richard Alfred Coombs (decd); 1 s (Gavin b 1966), 2 da (Susan b 1958, Amanda b 1962); *Career* Nat Serv Lt Army, serv in Malaya 1954-56; admitted slr 1964; rec of the Crown Ct 1987-; *Recreations* hunting, watching son compete Motor Cross; *Style*— Rivers Blackford Hickman, Esq; The Coach House, Upper End, Birlingham, Pershore, Worcs WR10 3AA; 16 Broad St, Pershore, Worcs; 3 Foregate St, Worcester

BLACKHURST, Christopher Charles (Chris); s of Donald Blackhurst, of Barrow-in-Furness, Cumbria, and Rose Bestwick, *née* Wood; *b* 24 Dec 1959; *Educ* Barrow-in-Furness GS, Trinity Hall Cambridge (MA); *m* 2 Aug 1986, Lynette Dorothy Wood, da of Philip Grice; 1 s (Harry Max Thomas b 20 Sept 1987), 1 da (Daisy Natasha b 25 Dec 1988); *Career* articled clerk Cameron Markby 1982-84, asst ed International Financial Law Review (Euromoney Publications) 1985-86, sr writer Business Magazine 1987-88 (staff writer 1986-87), dep ed Insight The Sunday Times 1990 (business reporter 1989-90), city ed Sunday Express 1990; TSB/PIMS Fin Journalist of the Year 1988; *Recreations* golf, tennis, playing with the children, walking the dog; *Clubs* Clare Hill Golf (Esher); *Style*— Chris Blackhurst; Sunday Express, Ludgate House, 245 Blackfriars Rd, London SE1 9UX (☎ 071 922 7313/7316)

BLACKIE, John Walter Graham; s of Walter Graham Blackie (d 1972); *b* 2 Oct 1946; *Educ* Uppingham, Univ of Cambridge, Harvard Univ, Merton Coll Oxford, Univ of Edinburgh; *m* 1972, Jane; *Career* advocate 1974, lectr in Scots law Univ of Edinburgh 1975 (sr lectr 1988-), visiting lectr Univ of Göttingen 1981-90, dir Blackie & Son Ltd (Publishers) 1970; *Recreations* sailing, playing wind instruments; *Style*— John Blackie, Esq; The Old Coach House, 23a Russell Place, Trinity, Edinburgh EH5 (☎ 031 552 3103)

BLACKISTON, Galton Benjamin; s of B L J Blackiston, of Boat House, Blakeney, Norfolk, and Anne, *née* Skerrett-Rogers; *b* 13 Aug 1962; *Educ* Homewood Sch Tenterden Kent; *m* 12 Dec 1987, Tracy Jane Rowe; 1 s (Sydney); *Career* weekly stall Rye Market 'Galtons Goodies' 1979, trained under John Tovey of Miller Howe 1980-86, head chef Miller Howe 1986- (involved with pub demonstrations for tv and radio and work in USA, SA and Canada); *Recreations* eating out, wine, reading cookery books old and new, golf; *Style*— Galton Blackiston, Esq

BLACKLEDGE, Michael Glyn; s of Edward John Blackledge (d 1981), of Bromley, Kent, and Winifred May, *née* Hemsley; *b* 24 Oct 1954; *Educ* Colfe's GS Lee London, South Bank Poly (Dip Estate Mgmnt), Garnett Coll (Cert Ed); *m* 21 Aug 1976, Janet May, da of Edward Arthur Connell, of Beckenham, Kent; 2 s (Jonathan b 1984, Alexander b 1990); *Career* surveyor Thames Water Authy 1974-78; valuer: City of Westminster 1978-79, London Borough of Croydon 1979-81; sr lectr: Vauxhall Coll of Bldg and Further Educn 1981-88, Thames Poly 1988-89; sr surveyor King & Co 1989-, tutor Coll of Estate Mgmnt 1989-; Freeman City of London, memb Worshipful Co of Feltmakers; ARICS 1978; *Recreations* writing, golf, soccer, wargaming and computing; *Style*— Michael Blackledge, Esq; King & Company, Chartered Surveyors, 7 Stratford Place, London W1N 9AE (☎ 071 493 4933, fax : 071 409 0469, 071 409 7458)

BLACKLEE, Andrew Gimson; s of Frederick Phillips Blacklee, of Rose Cottage, East Haddon, Northants, and Sylvia May, *née* Gimson; *b* 26 Jan 1955; *Educ* Magdalen Coll Sch Northants, Mill Hill Sch London, Leicester Poly (BSc); *m* 1 June 1985, Jillian Mary, da of Dr John Clough, of 923 Finchley Rd, Golders Green, London; *Career* commercial surveyor; Douglas L January & Ptnrs Cambridge 1976-77, Hillier Parker May & Rowden London 1977-79; dir Leslie Furness & Co 1979-; FRICS; *Recreations* skiing, travel, scuba, motor sports, running, swimming; *Style*— Andrew Blacklee, Esq; 27 Leinster Mews, Hyde Park, London W2 3EY (☎ 071 402 7106); Leslie Furness & Company, 6 Princes Street, Hanover Square, London W1 (☎ 071 408 2172)

BLACKLEE, Jillian Mary; da of Dr John Henry Harper Clough, of London NW11, and Margaret Vaughan, *née* Edwards; *b* 30 March 1955; *Educ* Wycombe Abbey Sch High Wycombe Bucks, The Middx Hosp London (Dip Physiotherapy); *m* 1 June 1985, Andrew Gimson Blacklee, s of Frederick Phillips Blacklee, of Northampton, England; *Career* physiotherapist: Northwick Park Hosp 1976-79, Thermalbaeder Bad Ragaz Switzerland 1979-81; sr physiotherapist: Behring Krankenhaus W Berlin 1981-83, St Mary's Hosp London 1983-86, Paddington Community Hosp London 1986-; MCSP 1976; *Recreations* snow skiing, classical flute; *Style*— Mrs Jillian Blacklee; 27 Leinster Mews, Hyde Park, London W2 3EY (☎ 071 402 7106); Paddington Community Hosp, 7A Woodfield Rd, London W9 (☎ 071 286 6669, ext 210)

BLACKLEY, Ian Lorimer; s of John Lorimer Blackley, JP, of Berscar, Closeburn, Thornhill, Dumfriesshire, and Christina Ferrier, *née* Aitken; *b* 14 Dec 1946; *Educ* Sedbergh, St Catharine's Coll Cambridge (MA); *m* 7 Sept 1981, Pamela Ann Helena, da of Maj Marten H G Belt of Abbotsham, N Devon; 1 s (Giles b 3 Nov 1983); *Career* joined HM Diplomatic Serv 1969; served in: MECAS Lebanon 1971, Tripoli 1972, Berlin 1973, Damascus 1974, FCO 1977, Beirut 1980, The Hague 1982; asst head Middle East Dept FCO 1986, cnsllr and dep head of mission Kuwait; *Recreations* fly fishing; *Clubs* Naval and Military; *Style*— Ian Blackley, Esq; c/o FCO, King Charles St, London SW1A 2AH

BLACKLEY, John Lorimer; JP; s of John Blackley (d 1951); *b* 22 Nov 1915; *Educ* Sedbergh; *m* 1940, Christina Ferrier, da of Robert Stepford, of Dumfries; 1 s; *Career* farmer; chm W Cumberland Farmers' Ltd 1976-, EFG (New Lands) Ltd 1976-; *Recreations* angling, shooting, gardening; *Clubs* Farmers'; *Style*— John Blackley, Esq, JP; Berscar, Closeburn, Thornhill, Dumfriesshire (☎ Closeburn 246)

BLACKLEY, Neil Ramsay; s of (Samuel) Ramsay Blackley, OBE, of Hamdon House, New Galloway, Kirkcudbrightshire, and Deirdre, *née* Wilson; *b* 30 Aug 1955; *Educ* Malvern, Imperial Coll London (BSc), London Business Sch (MBA); *m* 8 Nov 1986, Susan Valerie, da of Keith Lawrence Porter, of Plover, 1 Kenwyn Rd, Torquay; *Career* shipping analyst Lindsay Blee (chartering) Ltd 1979-82; investmt analyst: Esso Pension Fund 1982-83, James Capel 1983-; memb Business Graduates Assoc; ACGI 1977, MBIM; pubns incl: The Design Consultancy Marketplace, The Global Advertising Marketplace, The Global Recruitment Services Marketplace, The James Capel Media Book; *Recreations* squash; *Style*— Neil Blackley, Esq; 19 Gordon Rd, Grove Park, London W4 (☎ 081 994 5586); James Capel & Co, James Capel House, 6 Bevis Marks, London EC3 (☎ 071 621 0011)

BLACKMAN, Carol Anne; da of Herbert Owen Francis Smith, and Gladys, *née* Huggins; *b* 11 March 1947; *Educ* Univ of Southampton (BA), Univ of Bradford (MSc); *m* 28 March 1970 (m dis 1981), Robert Stephen Blackman, s of Jack Blackman; *Career* dir industl liason London Management Centre, vice pres industl Marketing Research Assoc 1985- (chm 1981-86, vice chm 1982-84), chm Educn Ctee; memb: Market Research Soc, Chartered Inst of Marketing, Marketing Educn Gp, Assoc for Mgmnt Educn Devpt; *Recreations* sailing, golf; *Style*— Ms Carol Blackman; Polytechnic of Central London, Management Centre, 35 Marylebone Rd, London NW2 5LS (☎ 071 911 5060); Management and Marketing Studies, 33 High St, Westerham, Kent (☎ 0959 61424); B & W Associates, Deni House, 11 The Warren, Chesham, Bucks HP5 2RX (☎ 0494 771325)

BLACKMAN, Dr Lionel Cyril Francis; s of Ernest Albert Cecil Blackman (d 1949), of Grange Hill, Essex, and Amy McBain (d 1979); *b* 12 Sept 1930; *Educ* Wanstead Co High, Univ of London (BSc, PhD, DIC); *m* 15 Oct 1955 (m dis 1983), Susan Hazel, da of Leonard Edward Arthur Peachey (d 1978), of Western Lullingfields; 1 s (Stuart b 1956), 1 da (Suzanne b 1959); *Career* sr res fell Royal Naval Scientific Serv 1955-57, ICI res fell and lectr Imp Coll London 1957-60, asst dir and dir of chem res BR 1960-64, dir and dir gen Br Coal Utilisation Res Assoc 1964-70, dir of res Fibreglass Ltd 1971-78, gen mangr and dir of res British American Tobacco Co Ltd 1978-84; memb: Parliamentary and Scientific Ctee, UN Industl Liason Gp for Sci and Technol, Non Metallic Materials and Chemicals Ctee DTI, bd of Studies univs of London Sheffield and Surrey; FRSC 1960, SFInstE 1965, CEng 1972, CChem 1975; *Books* Modern Aspects of Graphite Technology (1970), Athlectic World Records (1988); *Recreations* garden, music, wine; *Clubs* Athenaeum; *Style*— Dr Lionel Blackman; Griffin House, Knowl Hill, The Hockering Woking GU22 7HL (☎ 0483 766328)

BLACKMORE, (Edward) Anthony; s of Hilary Blackmore (d 1986), of Midhurst, and Florence Olive, *née* Simpson (d 1982); *b* 9 April 1933; *Educ* Winchester, Emmanuel Coll Cambridge (BA); *m* 5 Sept 1959, Caroline Ann, da of Oliver Haworth Jones (d 1978); 2 s (James b 1960, Simon b 1964), 1 da (Emma b 1962); *Career* admitted slr 1957; asst slr Slaughter and May 1957-59, sr ptnr Simpson Curtis 1988 (asst slr 1959-62, ptnr 1962-90); non-exec dir Liberty plc; memb Ctee Leeds Law Soc 1970-90 (pres 1990), visiting prof commercial practice Leeds Poly 1989; Freeman City of London Slrs Co; memb Law Soc; *Recreations* skiing, swimming; *Clubs* The Leeds; *Style*— Anthony Blackmore, Esq; 41 Park Square, Leeds LS1 2NS (☎ 0532 433 433, fax 0532 445 598, car 0860 227 373, telex 44376)

BLACKMORE, Antony John; s of John Wilfrid Blackmore, of The Rectory Cottage, Brandesburton, E Yorks, and Marjorie, *née* Sims; *b* 3 Sept 1949; *Educ* The King's Sch Canterbury, Magdalene Coll Cambridge (MA, Athletics blue), Hull Sch of Architecture (DipArch); *m* 28 Dec 1973, Helena Mary, da of Arthur Reynolds Carter; 3 s (John Robin b 30 Dec 1975, Edward Antony James b 23 July 1979, Timothy Andrew John b 26 Sept 1985), 2 da (Charlotte Sophie d 1977, Charlotte Mary b 6 Feb 1981); *Career* architect; Blackmore Son & Co Hull 1980-, architect Lincoln and York Dioceses 1984-, regnl panel architect Nat Assoc of Almshouses; Civic Tst Awards for Hart Homes Hornsea and Mary Lowther Hosp Ackwor 1989; involved in the restoration of many churches and almshouses, exec cmmr Georgian Soc for E Yorks, memb Hunsley Beacon Beagles, gen cmmr Inland Revenue (Hull); memb: RIBA 1975, EASA 1982; *Recreations* athletics, gardening, heraldry; *Clubs* Arts, Hawks (Cambridge); *Style*— Antony Blackmore, Esq; The Old Rectory, Brandesburton, Driffield, E Yorks (☎ 0964 542 904); Kilmun, Loch Avich, by Taynuilt, Argyll; Blackmore Son & Co, Blaydes House, High St, Hull HU1 1PZ (☎ 0482 26406)

BLACKMORE, Courtenay Thomas Gardner; 2 s of late Rev Canon Alfred T G Blackmore, of Apple Trees, Steeple Ashton, Wilts; *b* 16 Oct 1922; *Educ* Oakham Sch, Keble Coll Oxford (pres Oxford Union Soc); *m* 26 Oct 1957, as her 2 husb, Lady Pamela, *qv*, da of 1 and last Earl of Kilmuir (d 1967); 1 s, 2 da; *Career* formerly with ICI; head of admin Lloyd's 1975-83; memb: Cncl Sail Trg Assoc 1978-, Exec Ctee Industl Soc 1976-84, Churchill Group 1980-90; ptnr Project Client Conslts 1984-; dir: Lloyd's of London Press Ltd 1973-89, Royal Institution; chm Bd of Delegates RIBA Architecture Awards Tst Fund 1989-; Freeman City of London; FIPM, FRSA, Hon FRIBA; *Publications* Professional Studies in British Architectural Practice (contrib 1989), The Client's Tale (1990); *Recreations* gardening, reading, photography, painting; *Clubs* Architecture, Carlton, MCC, 1900; *Style*— Courtenay Blackmore, Esq; 61 Riverview Gdns, Castelnau, London SW13 9Q2

BLACKMORE, Lady Pamela Maxwell; *née* Fyfe; JP (Inner London); da of 1 and last Earl of Kilmuir, GCVO, PC (d 1967); *b* 14 Oct 1928; *Educ* Crofton Grange, LMH Oxford; *m* 1, 24 May 1950, Clive Wigram (d 1956), o s of late Nathan Graham

Wigram; 1 da; m 2, 26 Oct 1957, Courtenay Thomas Gardner Blackmore, *qv*; 1 s, 2 da; *Career* memb Exec Ctee and Appeals Ctee Peckham Settlement 1975-89; chm S Eastern Greenwich and Woolwich Div Inner London Bench 1983-86 (dep chm 1976-83 and 1986-), memb Inner London Probation Ctee 1986-90, memb David Isaac Ctee 1980-, chm Ilderton Project 1989-; Freeman City of London; *Style*— The Lady Pamela Blackmore, JP; 61 Riverview Gardens, Castelnau, London SW13 9QZ (☎ 081 741 1239)

BLACKSHAW, Alan; VRD (1970); s of Frederick William Blackshaw (d 1983), of Blundellsands, Liverpool, and Elsie, *née* MacDougall (d 1978); *b* 7 April 1933; *Educ* Merchant Taylors' Sch Crosby, Wadham Coll Oxford (MA); *m* 1, 1956 (m dis 1983), Jane Elizabeth Turner; 1 da (Sara); m 2, 1984, Dr Elspeth Paterson, da of late Rev Gavin C Martin; 1 s (Alasdair b 1985), 2 da (Elsie b 1987, Ruth b 1990); *Career* RM 1954-56, RMR 1954-74, Capt; business conslt and author; civil servant 1956-79; dir gen Offshore Supplies Office 1977-78 (head of Coal Div 1978-79); pres Br Mountaineering Cncl 1973-76, memb: Scot Cncl for Devpt and Indust 1974-78, Scot Sports Cncl 1990-; conslt dir Strategy International Ltd 1979-; sec (Edinburgh Branch) Oxford SOC 1989-; chm: Br Ski Fedn 1984-86, Nat Mountain Centre Plas y Brenin 1986-, Alpinism Cmmn Union Internationale des Associations d'Alpinisme 1990-; memb Sports Cncl 1990-; Freeman City of London 1966; FRGS, FInstPet; *Books* The Alpine Journal (ed 1968-70), Mountaineering (3 edn, 1975); *Recreations* mountaineering, skiing, canoeing, windsurfing; *Clubs* Alpine, Ski of GB, Royal Scot Automobile; *Style*— Alan Blackshaw, Esq, VRD; 2 Clark Rd, Edinburgh EH5 3BD (☎ 031 531 3153); Les Autannes, Le Tour, Argentiere, France (☎ 50 54 12 20)

BLACKSTONE, Baroness (Life Peeress UK 1987), of Stoke Newington, Greater London; Tessa Ann Vosper Evans; *née* Blackstone; er da of late Geoffrey Vaughan Blackstone, CBE, GM (d 1989), of Bures, Suffolk, and Joanna, *née* Vosper; *b* 27 Sept 1942; *Educ* Ware GS for Girls, London Sch of Economics and Political Science (BSc, PhD); *m* 1963 (m dis), Thomas Charles Evans (d 1985); 1 s (Hon Benedict Evans, *qv*), 1 da (Hon Liesel, *qv*); *Career* assoc lectr in sociology Enfield Coll of Technology 1965-66; asst lectr then lectr in social admin LSE 1966-75; fell Centre for Studies in Social Policy 1972-74; advsr Central Policy Review Staff Cabinet Office 1975-78; prof of educational administration Univ of London Inst of Education 1978-83; dep education offr (Resources) ILEA 1983-86; clerk to the Authority and dir of Education ILEA April-Nov 1986; Rowntree Special res fell Policy Studies Inst 1986-87; master Birkbeck Coll Univ of London 1987-; chm: Fabian Soc 1984-85, General Advisory Cncl BBC 1988-, Institute for Public Policy Res 1988-; memb: Arts Cncl Planning Board 1986-90, Board Royal Opera House 1987-, Management ctee King Edward's Hosp Fund for London; dir Fullemploy Group; *Books* Students in Conflict, LSE in 1967 (1970, co-author), A Fair Start: The Provision of the Pre-School Education (1971); The Academic Labour Market: Economic and Social Aspects of a Profession (1974, and 1982, co-author), Disadvantage and Education (1982, co-author); Testing Children: Standardised Testing in Local Education Authorities and Schools (1983, co-author), Response to Adversity (1983, co-author), Inside the Think Tank: Advising the Cabinet 1971-83 (1988, co author), Prisons and Penal Reform (1990); *Style*— The Rt Hon Barness of Blackstone; 2 Gower St, London WC1 (☎ 071 636 0067); Birkbeck College, Malet St, London WC1 (☎ 071 631 6274)

BLACKTOP, Rev Graham Leonard; s of Leonard Blacktop (d 1981), and Grace Ivy May, *née* Evans (d 1988); *b* 21 July 1933; *Educ* Christ's Coll Finchley; *m* 9 May 1959, Alison Margaret, da of Kenneth Campbell; 3 da (Louise b 1960, Catherine b 1962, Ruth b 1965); *Career* cmmnd Royal Fusiliers City of London Regt and Royal W African Frontier Force 1951-54, TA Middx Regt (Duke of Cambridge's Own) and Herts Regt 1954-61; jr clerk Standard Bank of S Africa 1949-51, md Alexanders Discount plc 1983- (joined 1954); contrib articles to: Euromoney, American Banker, Jnl of the Inst of CAs in Scotland, Jnl of the Cricket Soc; non-stipendary Anglican priest (ordained 1985); Liveryman: Worshipful Co of Painter-Stainers 1969, Worshipful Co of Parish Clerks 1980; *Recreations* watching cricket, travel; *Clubs* MCC, Army & Navy; *Style*— The Rev Graham Blacktop; 52 Shepherd's Way, Rickmansworth, Herts WD3 2NL (☎ 0923 772022); Alexanders Discount plc, Broadwalk House, 5 Appold Street, London EC2A 2DA (☎ 071 588 1234)

BLACKWELL, Sir Basil Davenport; s of late Alfred Blackwell, and late Hilda Kathleen Sophia Bretherick (later Mrs Lloyd); *b* 8 Feb 1922; *Educ* Leeds GS, St John's Coll Cambridge (MA), Univ of London (BSc Eng); *m* 1948, Betty, da of Engr Capt Meggs, RN; 1 da (Susan); *Career* vice chm and chief exec Westland Gp of Cos 1974- (dep chm and chief exec 1984-85); chm: Westland Helicopters Ltd 1976-85, Br Hovercraft Corpn 1979-85, Normalair-Garrett Ltd 1979-85; FEng (1978), Hon DSc Bath (1984), FIMechE, FRAeS (Gold Medal 1982); kt 1983; *Recreations* gardens, gardening; *Clubs* United Oxford and Cambridge; *Style*— Sir Basil Blackwell; High Newland, Newland Garden, Sherborne, Dorset DT9 3AF (☎ (0935) 813516)

BLACKWELL, Colin Roy; s of John Harris (d 1931), of Witheridge, and Marjorie Grace Blackwell (d 1982); *b* 4 Sept 1927; *Educ* West Buckland, Univ of Bristol (BSc); *m* 1979, Susan Elizabeth, da of Brig Cecil Hunt, CBE (d 1985), of Chichester; *Career* cmmnd 83 LAA Regt RA served ME 1946-48; Freeman Fox and Ptnrs Conslt Engrs: joined 1951, site engr Gold Coast (later Ghana) 1955-57, sr engr 1957-68, princ engr 1969-82; dir Freeman Fox Ltd 1983-87, int conslt on telescopes and observatories Acer Freeman Fox 1987-; memb: CIRIA Res Ctee 1976-79, Br Cncl Mission to Saudi Arabia 1985, BSI CSB Ctee 1986-; FICE, FASCE, FRAS, FRSA; *Clubs* Athenaeum; *Style*— Colin Blackwell, Esq; 34 Drayton Gardens, London SW10 9SA (☎ 071 370 1145, fax 071 835 1351); Acer Consultants Ltd, Acer House, Medawar Road, The Surrey Research Park, Guildford, Surrey GU2 5AR (☎ 0483 35000, fax 0483 35051)

BLACKWELL, Dr John Charles; CBE (1988); s of Charles Arthur Blackwell (d 1989), and Louisa Amy, *née* Sellers; *b* 4 Nov 1935; *Educ* Glynn GS Ewell Surrey, Dudley Coll of Educn (CertEd), Univ of Bristol (BA, MEd, PhD); *m* 1, 3 Aug 1961 (m dis 1973), Julia, *née* Rose; 1 s (Mark Frazer Charles b 23 Aug 1963); m 2, 1978, Inger Beatrice Lewin; 1 step s (Patrick Richard b 23 Oct 1967); *Career* Met Police Cadet 1952-53, RAF 1954-56; teacher Dempsey Secdy Sch London 1958-60; British Cncl: asst rep Tanzania 1966-70, educn offr Calcutta India 1971-72, asst educn offr New Delhi India 1973-75, head Schs and Teacher Educn Unit London 1976-78; asst cultural attache Br Embassy Washington DC 1979; British Cncl: dir Educn Contracts Dept London 1980-83, rep Indonesia 1983-89, dir Educn and Sci Div London 1989-; chm Educn and Trg Export Ctee 1989-; memb: Bd Br Accreditation Cncl 1990-, Bd Int Agric Trg Prog 1990-; *Recreations* angling, boating; *Style*— Dr John Blackwell, Esq, CBE; Education and Science Division, British Council, 10 Spring Gardens, London SW1A 2AH (☎ 071 930 8466, fax 071 839 6347, telex 8952201 BRICON G)

BLACKWELL, Nigel Stirling; s of Richard Blackwell, DSC (d 1980), and Marguerite, *née* Holliday; *b* 18 March 1947; *Educ* Winchester, St Edmund Hall Oxford (MA); *m* 22 Sept 1984, Eliza Pumpelly, da of Frank Mauran III, of 109 Benefit St, Providence, Rhode Island; 1 s (Richard Raphael Holliday b 17 June 1989), 1 da (Georgina Stirling b 27 July 1986); *Career* dep chm and chief exec offr Blackwell N America 1979-86, jt md BH Blackwell 1980-83 (dir 1974), chm Blackwell Scientific 1990 (dir 1980-), md The Blackwell Gp 1983-89, chm and md Blackwell Retail Gp 1983-89, chm Basil Blackwell Ltd 1985-, dir Munksgaard Publishers Copenhagen 1987-, chm Blackwell Publishing 1989-, dir Western Provident Assoc 1990-; memb Ranfurly Library Serv, chm Richard Blackwell Scholarship Tst; Freeman Worshipful Co of Stationers and Newspapermakers; *Recreations* country pursuits; *Clubs* Brooks's, Leander (Henley-on-Thames), Dunes (Narragansett RI), Vincents, Itchenor Sailing; *Style*— Nigel Blackwell, Esq; The Blackwell Publishing Group, 50 Broad St, Oxford OX1 3BQ (☎ 0865 791862, fax 0865 791638, telex 83118 BWELOX G)

BLACKWOOD, Brian; s of George Blackwood, of Reigate, Surrey, and Eva Blackwood; *b* 4 Feb 1926; *Educ* Redhill Tech Coll, Inverness HS, Architectural Assoc, Northern Poly, Univ Coll London (Dip TP), Univ of York Inst of Advanced Architectural Studies (Dip Conservation Studies); *m* 1950 (m dis 1974); 1 s, 2 da; *Career* artist, photographer, architect, conservationist, town planner and leading authy on lives and works of architects Smith and Brewer; local govt 1945-70; Tunbridge Wells Borough Cncl 1951-62, Stevenage Devpt Corp 1962-66, head of design Herts Co Planning Dept 1966-70; architectural advsr The Victorian Soc 1974-75; memb: St Albans Diocesan Advsy Ctee 1972-77, City of Cambridge Listed Bldgs Panel 1974-, Cncl Ancient Monuments Soc 1982-, Cases Ctee Herts Conservation Soc 1987-, N Herts Crime Prevention Panel 1977-89; Freeman City of London 1979, Liveryman Worshipful Co of Painter-Stainers 1984; FRSA 1947, ARIBA 1961, FRIBA 1968, AMTPI 1968, FRTPI 1974, FSAScot 1972, ARHistS 1976, FSAI 1976, FRGS 1983, fell Cambridge Philosophical Soc 1986, FLS 1990; *Recreations* archaeology, coffee, lichen, music, writing; *Clubs* Art Workers Guild; *Style*— Brian Blackwood, Esq; Ebony House, Whitney Drive, Stevenage, Herts SG1 4BL (☎ 0438 725111)

BLACKWOOD, Wing-Cdr (George) Douglas Morant; s of James Hugh Blackwood (d 1951), of London, and Sybil Mary, *née* Morant; *b* 11 Oct 1909; *Educ* Eton, Clare Coll Cambridge; *m* 22 Feb 1936, Phyllis Marion, da of Sir John Caulcutt, KCMG, (d 1942); 1 s ((John) Michael Douglas b Dec 1942), 1 da (Maureen Lavinia b March 1940); *Career* cmmnd RAF 1932, sqdn-ldr formed 1 Czech Fighter Sqdn 1940, served Battle of Britain wing-cdr 1941, Czech wing 2nd TAF 1944 (despatches twice), ret 1945; ed Blackwoods' Magazine 1952-72 (gggs of William Blackwood fndr), ret 1976; Czech War Cross 1940, Czech first class 1944; *Recreations* countryside, sports; *Style*— Wing-Cdr Douglas Blackwood; Airhouse, Oxton, Lauder, Berwickshire (☎ 057 85 225)

BLACKWOOD, Hon John Francis; s and h of 10 Baron Dufferin and Clandeboye, *qv*; *b* 18 Oct 1944; *Educ* Barker Coll Hornsby, Univ of NSW (BArch); *m* 1971, (Annette) Kay, da of Harold Greenhill, of Seaforth, Sydney, NSW; 1 s (Francis Senden b 6 Jan 1979), 1 da (Freya Jodie b 1975); *Career* architect in private practice; ARAIA; *Style*— The Hon John Blackwood; 169 Anson Street, Orange, NSW 2800, Australia

BLACKWOOD, Lilian, Lady; Lilian Margaret; da of late Fulton J MacGougan, of Vancouver; *m* 1921, Sir Francis Elliot Temple Blackwood, 6 Bt (d 1979); *Style*— Lilian, Lady Blackwood; c/o Rivesdale Convalescent Hospital, 1090 Rio Lane, Sacramento, California 35822, USA

BLACKWOOD, Hon Peter Maurice; yr s of 10 Baron Dufferin and Clandeboye, *qv*; *Educ* Knox GS Wahroonga, Macquarie Univ (BA); *m* 1979, Kay Lynette, *née* Winkle; 1 da (Alice b 1982)

BLAGG, Nikola Kate; da of Cedric Charles Blagg, of Peterborough, and Enid, *née* Hancock; *b* 27 Sept 1955; *Educ* Stewards Comp Harlow Essex, UCL (BSc); *m* Kevin Michael O'Connell; 1 s (Sam b 25 Oct 1988); *Career* media trainee Albany Advertising International 1979-80, media exec rising to assoc dir managing Int Media Dept D'Arcy MacManus & Masius (now DMB&B) 1980-85, media dir rising to md MJP/Carat International (int media planning and buying) 1985-; memb Int Advtg Assoc 1980-; *Style*— Ms Nikola Blagg; MJP/Carat International, Broadway House, 2-6 Fulham Broadway, London SW6 1AA (☎ 071 381 8010, 071 385 3233)

BLAGG, Dr Thomas Frederick Colston; s of Lt-Col Thomas Colston Blagg (d 1983), of Brunsell Hall, Car-Colston, Notts, and Loys Willis, *née* Cope (d 1989); *b* 10 Aug 1942; *Educ* Oakham, Keble Coll Oxford (BA, MA), Inst of Archaeology Univ of London (PhD); *Career* admitted slr 1967; in practice 1967-70, freelance archaeologist 1970-78, memb educn serv Br Museum 1978; lectr in archaeology Univ of Kent 1978-; FSA 1983; *Books* The Roman Riverside Wall and Monumental Arch in London (jtly, 1980), Papers in Iberian Archaeology (jtly, 1984), Military and Civilian in Roman Britain (jtly, 1984), Excavations at Mal Millien, Malta (jtly, 1990), The Early Roman Empire in the West (jtly, 1990); *Recreations* travel (wine and ruins), shooting, London; *Style*— Dr Thomas Blagg; Rutherford College, The University, Canterbury, Kent CT2 7NX (☎ 0227 764000)

BLAHNIK, Manolo; s of E Blahnik (d 1986), and Manuela, *née* Rodrigo-Acosta; *b* 28 Nov 1943; *Educ* Univ of Geneva, Louvre Art Sch Paris; *Career* designer of shoes and furniture; co proprietor 1973-; winner: Fashion Cncl of America award 1988, Hispanic Inst Washington Autonio Lopez award 1990, Br Fasion Cncl award 1990, Fashion Cncl of America (won for second time) 1991, American Leather New York Award 1991; *Recreations* travel and painting; *Style*— Manolo Blahnik, Esq; 49-51 Old Church St, London SW3 (☎ 071 352 8622, 071 352 3863)

BLAIR, Sir Alastair Campbell; KCVO (1969, CVO 1953), TD (1950), WS (1932), JP (Edinburgh 1954); 2 s of late William Blair, WS, of Edinburgh, and late Emelia Mylne Campbell; *b* 16 Jan 1908; *Educ* Charterhouse, Clare Coll Cambridge (BA), Univ of Edinburgh (LLB); *m* 1933, Catriona Hatchard, o da of late Dr William Basil Orr, of Edinburgh; 4 s (incl Robin Orr Blair and Michael Campbell Blair, *qv*); *Career* former ptnr Dundas & Wilson, CS; sec Royal Co of Archers (Queen's Body Guard for Scotland) 1946-59, Capt 1982-84, purse bearer to The Lord High Cmmr to the Gen Assembly of the Church of Scotland 1961-69; *Style*— Sir Alastair Blair, KCVO, TD, WS, JP; 7 Abbotsford Court, Colinton Rd, Edinburgh EH10 5EH (☎ 031 447 3095)

BLAIR, Dr Alastair William; s of Dr Lyon Blair (d 1941), and Isobel, *née* Breen; *b* 11 Aug 1936; *Educ* Harris Acad, Univ of St Andrews (MB ChB); *m* 16 Oct 1970, Irene Elizabeth Greenhill Blair; 2 s (Oliver b 1972, Roderick b 1975); *Career* house offr and registrar posts Maryfield and Kings Cross Hosps Dundee and Gt Ormond St Hosp London, lectr in child health Univs of Dundee and Aberdeen, Welcome Swedish res fell Sweden, sr registrar paediatrics Southmead Hosp Bristol, conslt paediatrician Fife Hosp, hon sr lectr in child health Univs of St Andrews and Edinburgh; memb: Hosp Conslts and Specialists Assoc, Nat Assoc of Clinical Tutors; sec and treas Scottish Paediatric Soc; *Books* Prenatal Paediatrics: a Handbook for Obstetricians and Paediatrician (1971); *Recreations* sailing, private flying, jazz; *Style*— Dr Alastair Blair; Paediatric Unit, Victoria Hosp, Kirkcaldy, Fife KY2 5AH (☎ 0592 261155, fax 0592 202248)

BLAIR, Angus Ogilvie; s of Douglas Blair, of 56 Abbots View, Haddington, E Lothian, and Agnes, *née* Erskine; *b* 13 May 1965; *Educ* Knox Acad Haddington; *m* 3 March 1988, Janice Margaret da of Charles McGoff; 1 s (Jamie Angus b 19 May 1990); *Career* bowler; winner: Haddington Club Championship 1981 (joined club 1974), East Lothian Junior Singles 1981, East Lothian Under 25 Championship 1985; 12 Caps (indoors) 1987-90, 15 Caps (outdoors) 1984 and 1987-90; Scottish Singles Champion (Queen's Park Glasgow) 1986, Br Isles Singles champion (Llanelli Wales) 1987, Scottish Pairs champion (Queens Park Glasgow) 1988, World Classic Pairs winner (Australia) 1988, British Isles Pairs Champion (Worthing England) 1989; slater and plasterer 1981; *Recreations* snooker, golf; *Style*— Angus Blair, Esq; 6 Seggarsdean

Terrace, Haddington, East Lothian EH41 4RJ (☎ 062 082 2750)

BLAIR, Anthony Charles Lynton; MP (Lab) Sedgefield 1983-; s of Leo Charles Lynton Blair and late Hazel Blair; *b* 6 May 1953; *Educ* Durham Choristers Sch, Fettes, St John's Coll Oxford; *m* 1980, Cherie Booth, 2 s, 1 da; *Career* called to the Bar Lincoln's Inn 1976; *Style—* Anthony Blair, Esq, MP; House of Commons, London SW1A 0AA

BLAIR, Astra; da of Col Douglas George Waugh (d 1949), and Nell, *née* Sanders (d 1984); *b* 2 Sept 1932; *Educ* St Mary's Convent Kent, RAM; *m* 27 March 1954, Raimund Frederick Herincx, s of Florent Herincx (d 1975); 1 s (Gareth James b 10 May 1966), 2 da (Nicole (Mrs Alcock) b 20 Aug 1955, Gemma b 20 July 1964); *Career* professional singer 1955-69; ran Quinville Concert Tst (charity for disabled and handicapped children) jtly with husband 1967-79, ran opera and concerts Music Mgmnt, dir Music and Musicians Artists Mgmnt 1972-, co-fndr Assoc of Artists against AIDS 1987; events presented to raise funds for AIDS: Anglo-French Gala Paris 1987, concert Edinburgh 1989, Royal Gala Drury Lane 1989; co-ordinator of recording of Br opera singers' An Anthology of English Song (all proceeds to AIDS res and Milestone Hospice Edinburgh), involved with Nat AIDS Tst 1988-89, involved with charity gala The Opera House Manchester (funds for women and children in Manchester); memb English Vineyard Assoc, memb Br Assoc of Concert Agents; *Recreations* walking, travelling, theatre, entertaining; *Style—* Ms Astra Blair; Monks Vineyard, Larkbarrow, East Compton, Shepton Mallet, Somerset

BLAIR, Lt-Gen Sir Chandos; KCVO (1972), OBE (1962), MC (1941, and Bar 1944); s of Brig-Gen Arthur Blair, DSO (KOSB, d 1947), and Elizabeth Mary, *née* Hoskyns; *b* 25 Feb 1919; *Educ* Harrow and RMC Sandhurst; *m* 1947, Audrey Mary, da of F Guy Travers; 1 s, 1 da; *Career* 2 Lt Seaforth Highlanders 1939, served WWII 2 and 7 Seaforth Highlanders, Lt-Col 1957, Brig 1964, GOC 2 Div BAOR 1968-70, Maj-Gen 1968, Defence Servs Sec MOD 1970-72, GOC Scotland and govr of Edinburgh Castle 1972-76, Lt-Gen 1972; *Style—* Lt-Gen Sir Chandos Blair, KCVO, OBE, MC; c/o Bank of Scotland, Gullane, East Lothian

BLAIR, Prof Gordon Purves; s of Gordon Blair (d 1984), and Mary Helen, *née* Jones; *b* 29 April 1937; *Educ* Larne GS, The Queen's Univ of Belfast (BSc, PhD, DSc); *m* 23 July 1964, Norma Margaret, da of James Millar (d 1979); 2 da (Rosemary b 15 June 1969, Alison b 2 March 1973); *Career* asst prof New Mexico State Univ 1962-64; The Queen's Univ of Belfast 1989-: lectr mechanical engrg 1964-71, sr lectr 1971-73, reader 1973-76, prof 1976-82, head of dep 1982-89, pro vice chllr 1989-; vice chm automobile div IMechE, FIMechE 1976, FSAE 1979, FEng 1982; *Books* The Basic Design of Two-Stroke Engines (1990); *Recreations* fishing, golf; *Clubs* Cairndhu Golf, Royal Portrush Golf; *Style—* Prof Gordon Blair; 9 Ben Madigan Park South, Newtownabbey, Co Antrim NI BT36 7PX (☎ 0232 773280); Department of Mechanical & Manufacturing Engineering, School of Mechanical and Process Engineering, Ashby Building, The Queen's University of Belfast BT9 5AH (☎ 0232 245133, fax 02 661729)

BLAIR, Lionel; *b* 12 Dec 1936; *m* 21 March 1967, Susan; 2 s (Daniel Mark b 6 Aug 1968, Matthew James b 26 June 1982), 1 da (Lucy Jane b 18 July 1971); *Career* boy actor in Watch on the Rhine (Stratford and the West End); choreography for and appearing with (on ATV): Dave King, Arthur Askey, Roy Castle, Jo Stafford, Harry Secombe, Bob Hope and Sammy Davis Jr; appeared in Royal Variety Performance 1968; TV shows incl: Give Us A Clue, Name That Tune; recent work incl: Jim in Mr Cinders, cameo role in Absolute Beginners, Seasons Greetings (with Marti Caine), starred in There's a Girl in my Soup; memb: Help the Aged (Stage for Age), Grand Order of Water Rats; *Books* Stage Struck (autobiog); *Style—* Lionel Blair, Esq; c/o Peter Charlesworth, 68 Old Brompton Rd, London SW7 3LQ (☎ 01 581 2478)

BLAIR, Louise Caroline Marian; da of Donald A Blair, of Brighton and the Outer Hebrides, and Alexandria, *née* Mackenzie-Macarthur; *b* 10 May 1958; *Educ* Canterbury Coll of Art, Hornsey Sch of Art (BA), Chelsea Sch of Art (MA); *m* 1981 (m dis 1989), Simon Edmonson; *Career* artist; lectr in fine art Univ of Newcastle 1980-81; solo exhibitions: Cockpit Theatre London 1981, Nicola Jacobs Gallery London 1983, 1985, 1986 and 1989; gp exhibitions incl: Young Contemporaries (ICA London) 1977, 1978 and 1980, Stowells Trophy (Royal Acad London) 1977 and 1978, Summer Exhibition Royal Acad London) 1980, Sets for Station House Opera (Waterloo Gallery London) 1982, Passion and Power (Gracie Mansion Gallery NY) 1985, Heads (Nicola Jacobs Gallery London) 1986, Winter '89 (Nicola Jacobs Gallery London) 1989; in pub collection The Contemporary Art Soc; has designed clothes for various commercials; *Recreations* dress design, writing, gardening; *Clubs* Chelsea Arts; *Style—* Miss Louise Blair; Nicola Jacobs Gallery, 9 Cork Street, London W1

BLAIR, Michael Campbell; s of Sir Alastair Campbell Blair, KCVO, TD, WS, *qv*; *b* 26 Aug 1941; *Educ* Cargilfield Sch Edinburgh, Rugby, Clare Coll Cambridge (MA, LLM), Yale Univ USA (MA); *m* 1966, Halldóra Isabel, da of Richard Anthony Conolly Tunnard, DL, of Lincs; 1 s (Alastair Magnus b 1974); *Career* called to the Bar Middle Temple 1965; circuit admin Midland and Oxford Circuit 1982-86, under sec Lord Chllrs Dept 1982-1987 (joined 1966, private sec to Lord Chllr and dep Sgt at Arms House of Lords 1968-71), Cabinet Office Top Mgmnt Prog 1986, dir legal servs The Securities and Investmts Bd 1987-, memb Gen Cncl of the Bar 1989-, chm Bar Assoc for Commerce Fin and Indust 1990-; *Books* Sale of Goods Act 1979 (1980); *Recreations* family life; *Clubs* Athenaeum; *Style—* Michael Blair, Esq; The Securities and Investment Board, Gavrelle House, 3-11 Bunhill Row, London EC1Y 8RA

BLAIR, Nicholas Peter; s of Maj Peter Blair, TD, and Ann De Quincey, *née* Walker; *b* 22 Feb 1949; *Educ* Wood Tutorial Coll; *Career* Collett Dickenson Pearce and Ptnrs Ltd 1967-71, md BSB Dorland Ltd 1989- (vice chm 1971-); Freeman: City of London 1970, Worshipful Co of Dyers 1970; MIPA, MInstM; *Recreations* shooting, horseracing; *Clubs* Buck's; *Style—* Nicholas Blair, Esq; 41 Southwood Park, Highgate, London N6 5SG (☎ 081 348 5730); BSB Dorland Ltd, 121-141 Westbourne Terrace, London W2 6JR (☎ 071 262 5077, fax 071 724 7876, car 0836 311111, telex 27778)

BLAIR, Robin Orr; WS (1965); s of Sir Alastair Campbell Blair, KCVO, *qv*; *b* 1 Jan 1940; *Educ* Rugby, Univ of St Andrews (MA), Univ of Edinburgh (LLB); *m* 20 May 1972, (Elizabeth) Caroline McCallum, da of Ian McCallum Webster (d 1973), of Walberswick, Suffolk; 2 s (Matthew b 1974, Benjamin b 1976), 1 da (Alice b 1980); *Career* ptnr Davidson & Syme WS 1967-74, non-exec dir Tullis Russell & Co Ltd 1978-, chm Top Flight Leisure Gp 1987- (non-exec dir 1977-), managing ptnr Dundas & Wilson CS 1988- (ptnr 1974, managing ptnr 1976-83), chm Scottish Solicitors' Staff Pension Fund 1985- (non-exec dir 1978-); Purse Bearer to the Lord High Cmmr to the Gen Assembly of the Church of Scotland 1988-; sec Assoc of Edinburgh Royal Tradesmen 1966-, memb Queen's Bodyguard for Scotland (Royal Co of Archers) 1970-; memb Law Soc of Scotland 1965; *Recreations* skiing, hill walking; *Clubs* New (Edinburgh), Hon Co of Edinburgh Golfers; *Style—* Robin Blair, Esq, WS; 2 Greenhill Park, Edinburgh EH10 4DW (☎ 031 447 4847); 25 Charlotte Square, Edinburgh EH2 4EZ (☎ 031 225 1234, fax 031 225 5594, telex 72404

BLAIR, Dr (George) Stewart; s of George Blair (d 1980), of 58 Brisbane St, Greenock, and Wilhelmina, *née* Montgomerie; *b* 28 July 1936; *Educ* Greenock Acad, Univ of Glasgow (BDS, DDS), RCPS Glas (FDS, HDD); *m* 8 Aug 1968, Ishbel Campbell, da of David Russel (d 1979), of 31 Queens Crescent, New Stevenston, Motherwell; 2 s (Alistair b 1969, Andrew b 1971); *Career* Nat Serv RADS Capt (former Lt), served in Aden Bahrain, Trucial Oman; gen dental practitioner Greenock 1962-65, registrar Glasgow Dental Hosp 1965-67 (house surgn 1958-60), lectr Univ of Glasgow 1968-73, sr lectr Univ of Newcastle 1973-, hon conslt Newcastle Health Authy 1973-; vice chm Rep Bd BDA; chm: Regnl Dental Ctee Northern RHA, Div of Dentistry Newcastle HA; memb BDA 1958, BAOMS 1966, BSDR 1968, RCPS 1968, EBDSA 1972, IADR 1968, FDI 1987; *Recreations* golf, rugby union football; *Clubs* Ponteland Golf, Greenock Wanderers Rugby Football, Medical Rugby Football; *Style—* Dr Stewart Blair; 45 Cheviot View, Ponteland, Newcastle upon Tyne NE20 9BH (☎ 0661 22367); Newcastle Dental Hospital, Richardson Rd, Newcastle upon Tyne NE2 4AZ (☎ 091 232 5131)

BLAIR-GOULD, John Anthony; s of Ralph Blair-Gould (d 1984), and Lydia, *née* Geneen (d 1974); *b* 25 Jan 1942; *Educ* Sherborne; *m* 11 Sept 1982, Margaret Anne, da of Joseph Lewis Bryan, of Oakham, Rutland; *Career* admitted slr 1965, called to the Bar Inner Temple 1970, rec 1986; memb Ctee Oxford and Cambridge Musical Club; *Recreations* music; *Style—* John Blair-Gould, Esq; 3 Raymond Buildings, Gray's Inn, London WC1R 5BH, (☎ 071 831 3833, fax 071 242 4221)

BLAIR-KERR, Sir Alastair; christened William Alexander but changed name by Declaration of change of name 1973; s of William Alexander Milne Kerr (d 1941), of Dunblane, Perthshire, and Annie, *née* Blair (d 1968); *b* 1 Dec 1911; *Educ* McLaren HS Callander, Univ of Edinburgh (MA, LLB); *m* 1942, Esther Margaret (d 1990), da of Sydney Fowler Wright (d 1947); 1s, 1 da; *Career* justice of appeal: Bermuda Court of Appeal 1975-79 (pres of Court 1979-89), Belize Court of Appeal 1975-79 (pres of Court 1979-81), justice of appeal Bahamas Court of Appeal 1975-78 (pres of Court 1978-81), Gibraltar Court of Appeal 1982-86; memb Gibraltar Court of Appeal 1982; kt 1973; *Recreations* music, walking; *Clubs* Royal Over-Seas League; *Style—* Sir Alastair Blair-Kerr; Gairn, Kinbuck, Dunblane, Perthshire FK15 0NQ (☎ 0786 823 377)

BLAIR OLIPHANT, Laurence Philip Kington; s of Maj Philip James Kington Blair Oliphant (d 1963), of Ardblair Castle, Blairgowrie, Perthshire, and Beatrice Mary Moore, *née* Carroll; *b* 26 Aug 1945; *Educ* Trinity Coll Glenalmond; *m* 11 Aug 1973, Jenny Caroline, da of Leonard Lockwood Anscombe, Taranaki, NZ; 1 s (Charles b 1976), 2 da (Amelia b 1977, Philippa b 1981); *Style—* Laurence Blair Oliphant of Ardblair and Gask, Esq; Ardblair Castle, Blairgowrie, Perthshire (☎ 0250 3155)

BLAKE, Sir Alfred Lapthorn; KCVO (1979, CVO 1975), MC (1945); s of late Leonard Nicholson Blake, and Nora Woodfall, *née* Lapthorn; *b* 6 Oct 1915; *Educ* Dauntsey's Sch, Univ of London (LLB); *m* 1, 1940, Beatrice Grace Nellthorp (d 1967); 2 s; m 2, 1969, Mrs Alison Kelsey Dick; *Career* slr and Notary Public; former ptnr Blake Lapthorn Slrs Portsmouth (conslt 1985-); Lord Mayor of Portsmouth 1958-59, dir The Duke of Edinburgh's Award Scheme 1967-78; lay canon Portsmouth Cathedral 1962-72, pres Portsmouth Youth Activities Ctee and other local community organisations; hon fell Portsmouth Poly; *Recreations* golf; *Style—* Sir Alfred Blake, KCVO, MC; 1 Kitnocks Cottages, Wickham Rd, Curdridge, Southampton SO3 2HG

BLAKE, Andrew Nicholas Hubert; s of John Berchmans Blake, of Clitheroe, Lancs, and Beryl Mary, *née* Murphy; *b* 18 Aug 1946; *Educ* Ampleforth, Hertford Coll Oxford (MA); *m* 7 July 1978, Joy Ruth, da of Ronald Shevloff (d 1986), of Southport; 1 s (Ben b 4 June 1980); *Career* called to the Bar Inner Temple 1971, rec Northern circuit 1988; *Recreations* skiing, the turf, fishing; *Style—* Andrew Blake, Esq; Brae House, 12 New Rd, Lymm, Cheshire; 18 St John St, Manchester (☎ 061 834 9843)

BLAKE, Anthony Martin; s of David Alick Blake, of Croydon, and Joan Irene, *née* Powell; *b* 18 Aug 1946; *Educ* Whitgift Sch; *m* 1 Aug 1970, Marion Celia Blake, da of Frederick George Davey; 2 da (Clare Elizabeth Blake b 9 Jan 1973, Sarah Louise Blake b 16 Jan 1975); *Career* articled clerk Jacob Cavenagh & Skeet Chartered Accountants 1964-68, ptnr Neville Russell 1974- (joined 1969); FCA 1978 (ACA 1968); *Recreations* chess, cricket, church work; *Clubs* City of London, Surrey CCC; *Style—* Anthony Blake, Esq; Neville Russell, 246 Bishopsgate, London EC2M 4PB(☎ 071 377 1000)

BLAKE, Anthony Teilo Bruce; s of Maj Charles Anthony Howell Bruce Blake (ka Korea 1951); h to baronetcy of kinsman, Sir Richard Valentine Blake, 17 Bt; *b* 5 May 1951; *Educ* Wellington, Lanchester Poly; *Career* engr; *Style—* Anthony Blake, Esq; 20 Lavender Gardens, Battersea, London SW11 1DL

BLAKE, Prof Christopher; s of George Blake (d 1961), of 75 Queen Margaret Drive, Glasgow, and Eliza Malcolm, *née* Lawson (d 1983); *b* 28 April 1926; *Educ* Dollar Acad, Univ of St Andrews (MA, PhD); *m* 25 July 1951, Elizabeth, da of John Easson McIntyre, of Embden House, Broughty Ferry (d 1947); 2 s (Duncan b 1952, Neil b 1954), 2 da (Catriona b 1959, Janet b 1960); *Career* Sub Lt RNVR, served Med 1944-47; Bonar professor applied economics Univ of Dundee 1974-88; dir Alliance Trust plc 1974-;, chm: William Low & Co plc 1985-, Glenrothes Devpt Corp 1987-; memb Royal Cmmn on Environmental Pollution 1980-85, treas Royal Soc of Edinburgh 1985-89; *Recreations* golf, reading; *Clubs* New (Edinburgh), Royal and Ancient St Andrews; *Style—* Prof Christopher Blake; Westlea, Wardlaw Gardens, St Andrews, Fife KY16 9DW

BLAKE, Prof David Leonard; s of Leonard Arthur Blake (d 1979), of London, and Dorothy Violet, *née* Briswor; *b* 2 Sept 1936; *Educ* Latymer Upper Sch Hammersmith, Gonville and Caius Coll Cambridge (BA, MA), Deutsche Akademie der Künste Berlin; *m* 24 Sept 1960, Rita Mary, da of Frank Adolphus Muir (d 1976); 2 s (Andrew b 23 Aug 1961, Daniel b 11 July 1964), 1 da (Claire b 24 Nov 1962); *Career* Nat Serv RAF 1955-57; teacher; prof of music Univ of York 1976- (lectr 1964, sr lectr 1971, head of dept 1981-84); composer: Chamber Symphony 1966, Lumina (cantata) 1969, Violin Concerto 1976, Toussaint Opera 3 acts 1977, From the Mattress Grave song cycle 1978, Clarinet Quintet 1980, Rise Dove for bass and orchestra 1983, The Plumber's Gift opera in two acts 1988; *Recreations* squash; *Style—* Prof David Blake; Mill Gill, Askrigg, Leyburn, N Yorks DL8 3HR (☎ 0969 50364), Dept of Music, University of York (☎ 0904 430000)

BLAKE, Dennis Arthur; MBE (1945), JP (1974); s of Lt-Col Terence Joseph Edward Blake, DSO (d 1921), of Hampstead, London, and Ethel Maud, *née* Moore (d 1986); *b* 13 April 1920; *Educ* The Hall Sch Hampstead, Douai Sch Woolhampton; *m* 10 July 1948, Helen Drake Milne, da of Capt Thomas Milne Swan (d 1977), of Kirkcaldy; 1 s (Terence b 1954), 1 da (Vanessa b 1949); *Career* WWII 1939-46, London Rifle Bde 1939, cmmnd Royal Fus 1940, IRE 1940-41, served 4 Indian Div Western Desert Eritrean and Syrian Campaigns (Croix de Guerre, despatches), GSO2 HQ 3 Corps and Force 140 1942-45, served Iraq, Italy, Greece, demob Hon Maj 1946; CA 1948-88; auditor accounts of the Chamberlain and Bridge Masters of Corp of London 1956-78, sr ptnr Baker Rooke 1970-78; hon memb BAFTA; chm Horsham Bench 1987-90, Gen Cmmr of Income Tax 1978 (chm Horsham Div), chm Lord Chllr's Advsy Ctee on Gen Cmmrs for W Sussex 1987; Freeman: City of London, Worshipful Co of Loriners 1956; FCA 1953; *Recreations* walking; *Clubs* Army and Navy, MCC; *Style—* Dennis Blake, Esq, MBE, JP; 13 Causeway, Horsham, W Sussex RH12 1HE (☎ 0403 53638)

BLAKE, Sir Francis Michael; 3 Bt (UK 1907); s of Sir (Francis) Edward Colquhoun Blake, 2 Bt (d 1950); *b* 11 July 1943; *Educ* Rugby; *m* 1968, Joan Ashbridge, o da of Frederic Cecil Ashbrige Miller, of Ramsay Lodge, Kelso; 2 s; *Heir* s, Francis Julian Blake b 17 Feb 1971; *Career* stockbroker; *Style—* Sir Francis Blake, Bt; The Dower

House, Tillmouth Park, Cornhill-on-Tweed, Northumberland (☎ 0890 2443)

BLAKE, Howard David; s of Horace Claude Blake (d 1985), of Brighton, and Grace, *née* Benson (d 1990); *b* 28 Oct 1938; *Educ* Brighton GS, RAM (LRAM); *m* 14 July 1990, Helen Mary, da of John Lloyd, of Bristol; *Career* composer, conductor, pianist; film scores incl: The Duellists 1977, The Riddle of the Sands 1978, The Snowman 1982, The Lords of Discipline 1983, A Month in the Country 1986, Granpa 1989; recordings: The Snowman 1982, Clarinet Concerto 1986, Benedictus 1988, Granpa 1988; theatre: Henry V RSC 1984, As You Like It RSC 1985; ballet: The Annunciation, Reflections, Diversions, Court of Love; orchestral works: Toccata 1976, The Snowman 1982, Concert Dances 1984, Concerto for Clarinet and Orchestra 1984, Nursery Rhyme Overture 1984; Suites: The Up And Down Man 1985, The Conquest of Space 1988, Granpa 1988, Diversions (1989); chamber music: Reflections 1974, The Up and Down Man 1974; piano and instrumental music: Penillion 1975, Eight character Pieces 1976, Dances for Two Pianos 1976, Prelude for Solo Viola 1979; brass ensemble and brass band: Sinfonietta 1981, Fusions 1986; Concert Dances (wind band) 1988; vocal music: Shakespeare Songs 1987, Three Sussex Songs 1973, A Toccata of Gallupi's 1978, Walking in the Air, Make Believe; choral music: The Song of St Francis 1976, The New National Songbook 1976, Benedictus 1979, Festival Mass 1987; stage works: The Annunciation 1979, The Station 1987; recent works incl: piano concerto (orchestral) commissioned by The Philarmonia for the birthday of HRH The Princess of Wales 1991, serenade for wind octet (chamber music) 1991, Four Songs of the Nativity (choral) 1991; dir Performing Right Soc 1978-87, fndr memb Assoc of Profesional Composers 1980; FRAM 1989; *Recreations* reading, walking, swimming; *Clubs* Savile, Groucho's; *Style—* Howard Blake, Esq; c/o Faber Music, 3 Queen Square, London WC1N 3AU (☎ 071 278 7436/3817, telex 299633); Sony Music Ltd, 17/19 Soho Square, London W1V 6HE (☎ 071 734 8181)

BLAKE, John Michael; s of Maj Edwin Francis Blake, MBE (d 1972), of London, and (Evelyn) Joyce, *née* Meadows; *b* 6 Nov 1948; *Educ* Westminster City GS, NW London Poly; *m* 29 June 1968, Diane Sutherland, da of Peter John Campbell (d 1973), of London,; 1 s (Adam b 1985), 2 da (Emma b 1969, Charlotte b 1971); *Career* reporter: Hackney Gazette 1965-68, Evening Post Luton 1968-69, Fleet Street News Agency 1969-71; columnist: London Evening News 1971-80, London Evening Standard 1980-82, The Sun 1982-84; asst ed Daily Mirror 1984-88, ed The People 1988; *Books* Up And Down With The Rolling Stones (1979), All You Needed Was Love (1981); *Recreations* sailing, skiing, distance running, travel; *Style—* John Blake, Esq; The People, 1 New Fetter Lane, London EC4A 1AR (☎ 01 822 3400, fax 01 353, telex 266888)

BLAKE, Jonathan Elazar; s of Asher Blake, of London, and Naomi, *née* Düm; *b* 7 July 1954; *Educ* Haberdashers' Aske's, Queens' Coll Cambridge (MA, LLM); *m* 3 Aug 1980, (Marion) Isabel, da of Joseph Horovitz, of London; 1 da (Lucy b 1984), 2 s (David b 1987, Simon b 1989); *Career* slr; Stephenson Harwood 1977-82, ptnr SJ Berwin Co 1982-; memb: Law Soc, Inst of Taxation, Br Venture Capital Assoc, Euro venture Capital Assoc; *Books* Terms and Conditions of Venture Capital Funds (contrib), Venture Capital in Europe (contrib); *Recreations* family, theatre, walking, skiing; *Style—* Jonathan Blake, Esq; SJ Berwin & Co, 236 Grays Inn Rd, London WC1X 8HB (☎ 071 278 0444, telex 8816928 WINLAWG, fax 071 833 2860)

BLAKE, Philip Haslewood; s of Robert Frederick Blake (d 1944), of Belfast, and Josephine Anne Isabella, *née* Sloss (d 1962); descended from all the sons of Edward III who left issue, all the like Magna Carta Barons, Sir Thomas More and William Haslewood, executor of Lord Nelson; Lordship of Barham Kent in family since 1597; *b* 3 May 1907; *Educ* Campbell Coll Belfast, Royal Coll of Music London; *Career* sub editor Northern Whig Belfast 1927-30, info offr Br Pavilion NY World's Fair 1939-40, temp admin offr Br Info Services NY, set up Govt exhibition serv in USA 1940-43, ed British topography Encyclopedia Britannica 1943-44; conductor Belfast Concerts for Sch Children and ENSA Orch 1944-45, music advsr ENSA in BLA 1945, PRO i/c visual publicity Min of Town and Country Planning 1946-48, Inland Revenue 1949-51; press offr: Fedn of Civil Engrg Contractors 1952-60, Royal Mint 1960-61; Soc of Genealogists: fndr Res Dept and first dir 1961-62, genealogist 1963-; memb: Cncl Br Record Soc 1949-, Kent Arch Soc 1982- (chm Records Ctee), Cncl Irish Genealogical Res Soc 1986-87 (fell and dir of res 1987); fndr: Assoc of Genealogists and Record Agents (AGRA) 1968, Kent Record Collections 1985 (chm); author of many articles in learned journals; *Books* History of Federation of Civil Engineering Contractors (1960), Canterbury Cathedral, Christ Church Gate (1965); *Recreations* chess, vintage cars; *Style—* Philip Blake, Esq; 5 Watkin Rd, Folkestone, Kent CT19 5EP (☎ 0303 41739)

BLAKE, Quentin Saxby; OBE (1988); s of William Blake, and Evelyn Blake; *b* 16 Dec 1932; *Educ* Downing Coll Cambridge (MA); *Career* freelance artist and illustrator; head of Dept of Illustration RCA 1978-86 (visiting prof 1989-); RDI, FCSD, sr fell RCA 1988; *Style—* Prof Quentin Blake, OBE; 30 Bramham Gardens, London SW5

BLAKE, Richard John Bowden; s of Frederick Milman Blake (d 1989), of Guildford, and Ida Mary (Mollie), *née* Wood; *b* 12 March 1936; *Educ* Aldenham Sch; *m* 1, 23 April 1960, Gillian Mary Wagner (d 11 July 1986); 1 s (Jonathan Rupert Bowden b 23 July 1962), 2 da (Annabelle Clare b 28 Feb 1965, Sophie Alexandra (twin) b 28 Feb 1965); m 2, 12 Aug 1988, Shirley Anne Virginia Edwards, da of Gerald Lee; *Career* Baker Todman (formerly part of Baker Tilly): articled clerk 1954, admitted slr 1960, ptnr 1964, chm London Mgmnt Ctee Baker Rooke 1981-82, staff ptnr 1973-76, sr ptnr 1986; chm Baker Tilly 1988; FCA; *Recreations* golf, theatre, tennis; *Clubs* MCC, Turf, Saints & Sinners, Lucifers, Surbiton Hockey; *Style—* Richard Blake, Esq; Baker Tilly, 2 Bloomsbury St, London WC1B 3ST (☎ 071 413 5100, fax 071 413 5101)

BLAKE, Sir (Thomas) Richard Valentine; 17 Bt (I 1622); s of Sir Ulick Temple Blake, 16 Bt, Saltergill, Yarm-on-Tees, Yorkshire (d 1963), and Elizabeth Longley-Cook (d 1978); *b* 7 Jan 1942; *Educ* Bradfield Coll; *m* 1, 1976, Jacqueline, da of late Desmond E Daroux, and formerly w of Peter Alers Hankey; m 2, 1982 (m dis 1986), as her 3 husband, the singer Bertice Reading; *Heir* kinsman, Anthony Teilo Bruce Blake; *Career* motor trade 1959; former car sales mangr Lavant Motor Centre; dir: Sir Richard Blake & Assocs 1967-75, City Chase Ltd 1980-84 (specialist in Rolls-Royce, Bentley, Gordon-Keeble cars); proprietor Autobart 1988-, md Axtell of Haslemere 1989-90; *Recreations* three day eventing, vintage cars; *Clubs* Gordon-Keeble Owners (hon life memb), Rolls-Royce Enthusiasts; *Style—* Sir Richard Blake, Bt; 74 Petersfield Rd, Midhurst, W Sussex GU29 9JR (☎ 0730 815010, mobile 0860 742766); Menlough Castle, Co Galway, Republic of Ireland

BLAKE, Baron (Life Peer UK 1971); Robert Norman William Blake; er s of William Joseph Blake (d 1964), of Brundall, Norfolk, and Norah Lindley Daynes; *b* 23 Dec 1916; *Educ* King Edward VI Sch Norwich, Magdalen Coll Oxford (DLitt, MA); *m* 1953, Patricia Mary, eldest da of Thomas Richard Waters (d 1983), of Great Plumstead, Norfolk; 3 da; *Career* sits as Conservative in House of Lords; served WWII Capt RA (POW Italy 1942-44, escaped 1944; despatches); student and tutor in politics Ch Ch Oxford 1947-68 (lecturer 1946-47, censor 1950-55, sr proctor 1969-60, Ford's lecturer in Eng history 1967-68); provost Queen's Coll Oxford 1968-87; pro-vice chllr Univ of Oxford 1971-87; memb City Cncl Oxford 1957-64; tstee Br Museum 1978-88; ed Dictionary of National Biography 1980-90; chm: Royal Cmmn Historical Manuscripts 1982-89, Rhodes Tst 1983-87; dir Channel Four Television Co 1983-87; high bailiff Westminster Abbey 1988-89 (high steward 1989-); JP Oxford 1964-86; FBA 1967; *Books* The Unknown Prime Minister, Bonar Law (1955), Disraeli (1966), The Conservative Party from Peel to Churchill (1970, 2nd edn The Conservative Party from Peel to Thatcher 1985), The Office of Prime Minister (1975), A History of Rhodesia (1977), The English World (editor, 1982) Disraeli's Grand Tour (1982), The Decline of Power 1915-1964 (1985); *Recreations* reading and writing; *Clubs* Beefsteak, Brooks's, United Oxford and Cambridge, Norfolk County, Pratt's; *Style—* The Rt Hon the Lord Blake; Riverview House, Brundall, Norwich (☎ 0603 712133)

BLAKE, (William) Seymour; TD (1965); s of William Harvey Blake, JP (d 1932), of Bridge, S Petherton, Somerset, and Gweneth Margaret, *née* Evans (d 1983); *b* 5 Feb 1919; *Educ* Uppingham, Univ of Oxford (MA); *m* 16 Sept 1950, (Ione) Daphne, da of Maj Charles Ion McKay, MC (d 1936), of Hythe, Kent; 4 s (John b 1951, Francis b 1953, Rodney b 1960, Andrew b 1963); *Career* RA 1940-46, Capt 1944, TA 1949-66, Maj 1959; slr Crewkerne Somerset 1949-88, Notary Public; chm S Petherton Village Hall Mgmnt Ctee 1968-90; *Recreations* family history, church architecture, walking, conjuring; *Clubs* ESU; *Style—* Seymour Blake, Esq, TD; Newbridge, 14 Palmer St, S Petherton, Somerset TA13 5DB (☎ 0460 40426)

BLAKEMORE, Prof Colin Brian; s of Cedric Norman Blakemore (d 1987), of Kidlington, Oxford, and Beryl Ann, *née* Smith; *b* 1 June 1944; *Educ* King Henry VIII Sch Coventry, Corpus Christi Coll Cambridge (BA, MA), Univ of California Berkeley (PhD), MA Oxon, ScD Cantab, DSc Oxon; *m* 28 Aug 1965, Andrée Elizabeth, da of Ronald George Washbourne, of Coventry; 3 da (Sarah Jayne b 1974, Sophie Ann b 1976, Jessica Katy b 1979); *Career* Harkness fell of the Cwlth Fund 1965-67; Univ of Cambridge: demonstrator in physiology 1967-72, lectr in physiology 1972-79, Royal Soc Locke res fell 1976-79, official fell and dir of med studies Downing Coll 1971-79; visiting prof: Dept of Psychology Univ of NY USA 1970, Dept of Psychology Mass Inst of Tech USA 1971; Lethaby prof RCA, visiting scientist Salk Inst San Diego California USA 1982-83, Waynflete prof of physiology Univ of Oxford and professorial fellow Magdalen Coll Oxford 1979-; dir McDonnell-Pew Centre for Cognitive Neuroscience 1990-, assoc dir of Med Res Cncl Research Centre for Brain and Behaviour 1990-; memb: BBC Sci Consultative Gp 1975-79, Sci Ctee of Bristol Exploratory 1983-, Professional Advsy Ctee Schizophrenia: A National Emergency (SANE) 1989-; patron of CORPAL (support gp for families affected by agentis of the callosum and Aicardi's Syndrome) 1989-; memb: Brain Res Assoc 1968 (memb Nat Ctee 1973-77), Physiological Soc 1968, Experimental Psychological Soc 1968, Euro Brain and Behaviour Soc 1972 (memb Ctee 1974-76), Int Brain Res Orgn 1973 (memb Governing Cncl and Exec Ctee 1973-), Cambridge Philosophical Soc 1975-79, Euro Neuroscience Assoc 1977 (memb Nominating Ctee 1988), Soc for Neuroscience 1981, Oxford Med Soc 1986, Child Vision Res Soc 1986 (memb Organising Ctee 1986-), Int Soc For Myochemistry 1989, Nat Conf of Univ Profs 1989; *Books* Handbook of Psychobiology (1975), Mechanics of the Mind (1977), Mindwaves (1987), The Mind Machine (1988), Images and Understanding (1990), Vision: Coding and Efficiency (1990); *Recreations* running, the arts; *Style—* Prof Colin Blakemore; University Laboratory of Physiology, Parks Rd, Oxford OX1 3PT (☎ 0865 272470, fax 0865 272488)

BLAKEMORE, Michael Howell; s of Dr Conrad Howel Blakemore (d 1976), and Una Mary, *née* Litchfield (later Mrs Heyworth, d 1982); related through American paternal gm Maud Howell to US presidents John Quincey Adams and John Adams; *b* 19 June 1928,Sydney, NSW; *Educ* Cranbrook Sch, The King's Sch, Univ of Sydney, RADA; *m* 1, 1960 (m dis 1986), Shirley Mary Bush; 1 s (Conrad); m 2, 1986, Tanya, da of Clement McCallin (actor, d 1978); 2 da (Beatrice b 1981, Clementine b 1984); *Career* stage and film dir (occasionally writer and actor); co-artistic dir Glasgow Citizen's Theatre 1966-68, assoc dir Nat Theatre 1971-76, resident dir Lyric Theatre Hammersmith 1980; freelance dir of prize winning prodns: A Day in the Death of Joe Egg 1968, Arturo Ui 1969, Forget-Me-Not-Lane 1971; also dir of: The National Health 1969, Plunder 1975, Long Day's Journey Into Night 1971, The Front Page 1972 (Plays and Players Best Dir award for the latter two prodns), The Wild Duck, Make and Break, Noises Off, Design for Living, Knuckle, Candida, Separate Tables, Privates on Parade, Deathtrap, All My Sons, Benefactors, Made in Bangkok, Lettice and Lovage (London and Broadway), Uncle Vanya, After The Fall; dir (abroad) of: City of Angels (Broadway), Noises Off (on Broadway and in Australia, received Drama Desk Award 1984); Films: A Personal History of the Australian Surf (also wrote and acted in the latter, Peter Seller's Award for Comedy in the Standard Film Awards); dir Privates on Parade 1982; actor drama documentary for Channel 10 television in Australia 1984; *Books* Next Season (1969); *Recreations* surfing, houses; *Clubs* RAC; *Style—* Michael Blakemore, Esq; 11A St Martin's Almshouses, Bayham St, London NW1 (☎ 071 267 3952)

BLAKENHAM, 2 Viscount (UK 1963); Michael John Hare; s of 1 Viscount Blakenham, OBE, PC (d 1982, 3 s of 4 E of Listowel), and Nancy, Viscountess Blakenham, *qv*; *b* 25 Jan 1938; *Educ* Eton, Harvard (AB Econ); *m* 12 Jan 1965, his 1 cous, Marcia Persephone, da of Maj Hon Alan Victor Hare, MC; 1 s, 2 da; *Career* 2 Lt The Life Gds 1956-57; English Electric 1958, Lazard Bros 1961-63, Standard Industrial Group 1963-71, Royal Doulton 1972-77, CE Pearson plc 1978; chm: Pearson plc 1983-, Financial Times 1983-; ptnr Lazard Ptnrs 1984-; dir: Sotheby's Holdings Inc 1987-, Elsevier NV 1988-, MEPC plc 1990-; memb: Int Advsy Bd Lafarge Coppée 1979-, House of Lords Select Ctee on Sci and Technol 1985-88, Nature Conservancy Cncl 1986-90; pres Sussex Wildlife Tst 1983-, chm Royal Soc for the Protection of Birds 1981-86; *Style—* The Rt Hon Viscount Blakenham; Pearson plc, 17th Floor, Millbank Tower, Millbank, London SW1P 4QZ (☎ 071 828 9020, telex 8953869)

BLAKENHAM, Nancy, Viscountess; Hon (Beryl) Nancy; *née* Pearson; da of 2nd Viscount Cowdray and Agnes, da of Lord Edward Spencer-Churchill; *b* 25 Feb 1908; *m* 1934, 1st Viscount Blakenham, OBE, PC (d 1982); 1 s (2nd Viscount), 2 da (Hon Mrs Sergison-Brooke, Hon Mrs Breyer); *Style—* The Rt Hon Nancy, Viscountess Blakenham; 10 Holland Park, London W11 3TH

BLAKER, Sir John; 3 Bt (UK 1919); s of Maj Sir Reginald Blaker, 2 Bt, TD (d 1975); *b* 22 March 1935; *m* 1, 1960 (m dis 1965), Catherine Ann, da of late Francis John Anselm Thorold; m 2, 1968, Elizabeth Katherine, da of Col John Tinsley Russell, DSO; *Style—* Sir John Blaker, Bt; Stantons Farm, E Chiltington, nr Lewes, Sussex

BLAKER, (Derek) John Renshaw; s of Col Cedric Blaker, CBE, MC (d 1965), of Town House, Scaynes Hill, Sussex, and Louise Douglas, *née* Chapple (d 1984); *b* 15 Oct 1924; *Educ* Haileybury, Ridley Coll Toronto Ontario, Univ of Toronto (BA), New Coll Oxford (Dip Econs); *m* 20 June 1956, Marie-Françoise Alice (d 1989), da of Guy Quoniam de Schompré; 3 da (Marie-Louise b 1958, Alexandra (Mrs Simon Finch) b 1961, Bettina (Countess de Ponteves) b 1964); *Career* Canadian Offrs Trg Corps TA 1942-44, Intelligence Corps Br Army 1944-46, Hong Kong Regt TA 1950-58; Gilman & Co Ltd Hong Kong: joined 1946, dir 1958-70, md 1967-70; dir 1967-70: The Hong Kong and Shanghai Banking Corporation, Union Insurance Soc of Canton Ltd, Hong Kong Television Broadcasts Ltd, Nan Yang Cotton Mill Ltd; memb Urban Cncl Hong Kong 1967-71, JP Hong Kong 1967-71; Freeman City of London 1945, Liveryman Worshipful Co of Vintners 1945; *Clubs* The Royal Hong-Kong Yacht; *Style—* John Blaker, Esq; Manoir de la Houbarderie, 35400 St Malo, France; 93 Eaton Place,

London SW1; Maison de Leoville, St Ouen, Jersey, CI

BLAKER, Rt Hon Sir Peter Allan Renshaw; KCMG (1983), PC (1983), MP (C) Blackpool S 1964-; s of Cedric Blaker, CBE, MC, ED (d 1965), of Scaynes Hill, Sussex, and Louise Douglas, *née* Chapple (d 1985); *b* 4 Oct 1922; *Educ* Shrewsbury, Trinity Coll Toronto, New Coll Oxford; *m* 1953, Jennifer, er da of Sir Pierson John Dixon, GCMG, CB (d 1965); 1 s, 2 da; *Career* WWII Capt Argyll and Sutherland Highlanders Canada (wounded); admitted slr 1948, barr 1952; Foreign Serv 1953-64; Parly under sec Army 1972-74 and FCO 1974, min of state FCO 1979-81, min of state for Armed Forces 1981-83; chm Cons Pty Foreign and Cwlth Affairs Ctee 1983- (vice chm 1974-79); *Recreations* tennis, sailing, swimming, opera; *Clubs* Garrick, RAC; *Style*— The Rt Hon Sir Peter Blaker, KCMG, PC, MP; House of Commons, London SW1A 0AA

BLAKER, Lt-Col (Guy) Peter; s of Guy Stewart Blaker (d 1969), of Rotherfield Greys, Henley-on-Thames, and Dawn Laetitia Prudence, *née* Watson; *b* 10 Nov 1936; *Educ* Lancing, Jesus Coll Cambridge (MA, LLB); *m* 18 Jan 1969, Hiltegund Maria, da of Dr Hermann Bastian (d 1945), of Freiburg-im-Breisgau; 2 s (Dominic b 1971, Nicholas b 1975), 1 da (Alexandra b 1970); *Career* Nat Serv, cmmnd W Yorks Regt 1957, Royal Green Jackets 1961-84, served Malaya, Borneo, Singapore, Cyprus, UK, Germany, Belgium (SHAPE); Army Aviation Pilot 1964-67, Staff Coll 1968, cmd Cambridge Univ Offrs Trg Corps 1979-82; Queen's Messenger 1984-85; gen mangr Newdata Publishing 1985-86, sec Gen Cncl and Register of Osteopaths 1987-; lay chm Rotherfield Greys PCC; chm Berkshire Automobile Club; *Recreations* classical music, history, languages, ornithology, fly-fishing, rowing; *Clubs* Naval and Military, MCC; *Style*— Lt-Col Peter Blaker; Greys Piece, Rotherfield Greys, Henley-on-Thames, Oxfordshire RG9 4QG (☎ 04917 308)

BLAKER, Sheila, Lady; Sheila Kellas; da of Alexander Cran, MB, of Little Court, Merrow, nr Guildford; *m* 1930, Maj Sir Reginald Blaker, 2 Bt, TD (d 1975); *Style*— Sheila, Lady Blaker; Knowles, Ardingly, Sussex

BLAKESLEY, Maj John Cadman; MBE (1958); s of Reginald Harry Blakesley (d 1978), of Ramsey, IOM, and Cassie Hilda, *née* Cadman (d 1978); *b* 28 July 1926; *Educ* Cheltenham; *m* 1, 5 July 1956 (m dis 1981), Selina Margaret (Patricia) Wynne-Eyton (d 1984); m 2, 19 March 1988, Mary (Robin) Ruane, da of C E Lucas-Phillips, OBE, MC, Croix de Guerre (d 1984), of Oxshott, Surrey; *Career* joined LG 1944, cmmd Kings Company Grenadier Gds 1946-53, transferred Royal Mil Police 1953, cmd 5 Units (despatches 1958), ret 1966; called to the Bar Middle Temple 1966; md RHB Holdings Ltd 1978-, dir Allen Power Equipment 1982-87; memb: Cons Pty 1966-, NFU 1973; sec Vale of Aylesbury Hunt 1982-86, memb County Gentleman's Assoc 1987-; memb Hon Soc of the Middle Temple 1966; *Recreations* foxhunting, cricket, music, breeding Hereford cattle and sheep; *Clubs* Naval & Military; *Style*— Maj John Blakesley, MBE; Shepherd's Hill House, Pinnock, Nr Winchcombe, Glos (☎ 0242 602620)

BLAKEWAY, (Arthur) John; s of Francis Lett Blakeway (d 1949), of Staverton, Cheltenham, Glos, and Bernice Marinda, *née* Matthews (d 1949); *b* 5 July 1925; *Educ* The Crypt GS Gloucester; *m* 1, 24 April 1946, Joyce Cynthia, da of Horace Forty; 3 s (Philip John b 1950, Francis Mark b 1952, Richard Clive b 1959), 1 da (Gillian Bridget b 1948); m 2, 8 April 1986, Rosemary Catherine de Courcy, da of Cdr Henry Leslie Spofforth Baker, RN, of Carrowduff House, Ballymacurley, Co Westmeath; *Career* served RN 1943-46; chm and md of family co started by father in 1925, Francis Blakeway Ltd, Fruit Merchants, formerly farmer; chm BSJA 1976-83 (currently vice pres); MFH: Croome 1961-68, Belvoir (Duke of Rutland's Hounds) 1983-; show dir Horse of Year Show 1987-; *Recreations* hunting; *Style*— John Blakeway, Esq; Blacklains Farm, Birdlip, Gloucester (☎ 0452 862355); 26 Eastbrooke Rd, Eastern Ave, Gloucester (☎ 0452 303376)

BLAKEY, Ian Johnston; s of Walter James Blakey, BEM, of 252 Northgate, Cottingham, N Humberside, and Freda Blakey, *née* Johnston; *b* 25 Aug 1932; *Educ* Hull GS; *m* 9 June 1956, Pamela Mary, da of late George Edward McMurran; 1 s (Jeremy Sean b 1961), 1 da (Zelda Rebecca b 1965); *Career* Nat Serv RN 1950-52; dir: Robertson Dale Transport Co Ltd 1952-62, Rediffusion Singapore (PTE) Ltd, Waste Paper Collections (Yorkshire) Ltd, Consultco Ltd, Nisa Today Ltd 1986-, Humberside Co Health Scheme 1987-; chm IJ Blakey Haulage Co Ltd 1962-, memb E Yorks Health Authy; govr Hull GS; chm: Humberside Wishing Well Appeal, Finance and Gen Purpose Ctee OStJ Humberside; FCIT 1981, FInstTA 1976, fell inst Tport 1981; *Recreations* golf, horse racing, charity fund raising; *Style*— Ian Blakey, Esq; Beech House, Northgate, Cottingham, North Humberside HU16 5QL (☎ 0482 846131); I J Blakey Haulage Co Ltd Fleet House, Woodhouse Street, Hedon Road, Hull HU 91AP North Humberside (☎ 0482 27359, telex 592649, fax 0482 216489)

BLAKEY, Richard John; s of Brian Blakey, of Huddersfield, and Anne Pauline; *b* 15 Jan 1967; *Educ* Rastrick GS; *Career* cricketer; Yorkshire CCC 1984- (debut 1985), Waverley CC Melbourne Australia 1985-86 and 1986-87, Mount Waverley CC Melbourne Australia 1987-88, Bionics CC Zimbabwe 1989-90; England A Team Tours: Zimbabwe 1990, Pakistan 1991; *Recreations* eating out, any sport, DIY, music; *Style*— Richard Blakey, Esq; c/o Yorkshire County Cricket Club, Headingley Cricket Ground, Headingley, Leeds LS6 3BU (☎ 0532 787394)

BLAKISTON, Ann, Lady; Ann Hope Percival; da of late Purcell Cooke Jeans, of Cortington Grange, Warminster, Wilts; *m* 1954, as his 2 w, Sir Arthur Frederick Blakiston, 7 Bt, MC (d 1974); *Style*— Ann, Lady Blakiston; Corton, Warminster, Wilts

BLAKISTON, Sir Ferguson Arthur James; 9 Bt (GB 1763); s of Sir (Arthur) Norman Hunter Blakiston, 8 Bt (d 1977); *b* 19 Feb 1963; *Educ* Lincoln Coll New Zealand (Dip Ag); *Heir* bro, Norman John Balfour Blakiston, *qv*; *Career* farmer; *Style*— Sir Ferguson Blakiston, Bt; 28 McKenzie St, Geraldine, S Canterbury, New Zealand

BLAKISTON, Lt-Col John Alan Cubitt; s of John Francis Blakiston, CIE (d 1965), of Anelog, Aberdaron, Pwllheli, Gwynedd, and Margaret Dora, *née* Ward-Jackson (d 1991); descended from Sir Matthew Blakiston, Lord Mayor of London 1760; *b* 15 July 1938; *Educ* Wellington, Univ of London; *m* 30 May 1975, Sally Ann, da of Lt-Col J D L Dickson, MC (d 1958); 1 s (Matthew b 11 Nov 1982), 2 da (Caroline b 22 Nov 1979, Emma b 1 July 1981); *Career* RNVR 1956-60, cmmnd 13/18 Royal Hussars (QMO) 1961, seconded to 4 Royal Tank Regt in Borneo 1964, seconded to UN Forces Cyprus 1966-67, Staff Coll RMCS and Camberley 1969-71, regtl duty in NI 1972, cmd Demonstration Sqdn Sch of Infantry 1972-74, SO2 (W) Def Intelligence Staff 1974-76, regtl duty in BAOR and NI 1976-78, German Staff Coll 1979-81, SO1 Def Intelligence Staff 1981-85; SO1 Ops HQ AFCENT 1985-88, sr mil rep AWE Aldermaston 1988, chm NATO and FINABEL (Euro) nuclear def ctees; *Recreations* riding, hunting; *Clubs* Cavalry and Guards'; *Style*— Lt-Col John A C Blakiston; c/o Coutts & Co, 1 Old Park Lane, London W1Y 4BS

BLAKISTON, Norman John Balfour; s of Sir (Arthur) Norman Hunter Blakiston, 8 Bt (d 1977); hp to baronetcy of bro, Sir Ferguson Blakiston, 9 Bt, *qv*; *b* 7 April 1964; *Style*— Norman Blakiston, Esq

BLAKSTAD, Michael Björn; s of Gabriel Clifford Clark Blakstad, and Alice Blakstad; *b* 18 April 1940; *Educ* Ampleforth, Oriel Coll Oxford (MA); *m* 1965, Patricia Marilyn, da of Robert Andrew Wotherspoon, DL (d 1977); 1 s, 2 da (twins); *Career* prodr; Papa Doc, The Black Sheep ITV 1970, Children in Crossfire BBC 1974; ed BBC 1974-80 (Tomorrow's World, The Risk Business), dir of progs Television South plc 1981-89; chm and chief exec 1988-90: Chrysalis Television Ltd, Workhouse Ltd; dir 1988-90: Chrysalis Group plc, Blackbird Interactive Servs; chm Workday Ltd 1988-90; dir 1990: London Wall Investments plc, Wonderland Ltd Quadrangle Ltd, Winchester Theatre Royal Ltd; chief exec Workhouse Ltd; prizes incl: BAFTA/Shell 1975, John Player 1975, RTS best science prog 1975, 1977 and 1979; Hon MSc Univ of Salford 1983; FRTS 1990, FRSA, FRI; *Books* The Risk Business, Tomorrow's World Looks to the Eighties; *Recreations* golf, squash, writing; *Clubs* Reform, RSA, Royal Inst; *Style*— Michael Blakstad, Esq; The Tudor House, Workhouse Lane, East Meon, Petersfield, Hants; Workhouse Prodns Ltd, Granville House, St Peter St, Winchester, Hants SO23 9AF; 10 Churton Place, London SW1

BLAKSTAD, Nigel Henry; s of Erick Blakstad (d 1978); *b* 8 April 1929; *Educ* Warwick Sch; *m* 1956, Patricia, *née* Hall; 1 s, 2 da; *Career* gp md Rendol Ltd 1979-86, Norstad Assocs Ltd mgmnt consits; *Style*— Nigel Blakstad, Esq; Greenmeadows, Withilee Road, Presbury, Cheshire

BLAMEY, Norman Charles; s of Charles Henry Blamey (d 1965), of London, and Ada, *née* Beacham (d 1980); *b* 16 Dec 1914; *Educ* Holloway Sch, Regent St Poly Sch of Art, Univ of London, Inst of Educn; *m* 26 Oct 1948, Margaret (d 1989), da of late Peter Kelly; 1 s (Stephen b 1950); *Career* Nat Serv Army 1941-46; art lectr and painter; lectr Regent St Poly Sch of Art 1946-63, sr lectr Chelsea Sch of Art 1963-79, painter mural cmmn Lutheran Church of St Andrew Ruislip Manor 1964 (Anglican Church of St Luke Leagrave 1956), visitor Ruskin Sch of Drawing and Fine Arts Univ of Oxford 1978; Royal Acad Summer Expo awards: Roy Miles 1978, Rowney Bi-centenary 1983, Charles Woolaston 1984; permanent collections incl: Municipal Gallery Port Elizabeth SA, Victoria and Albert Museum, Tate Gallery, Government Art Collection, Pennsylvania State Univ Museum of Art, Towner Art Gallery Eastbourne; cmmnd portraits incl: Sir Robert Bellinger, GBE 1984, Rt Hon Bernard Weatherill MP (Speaker House of Commons) 1988, Lord Rees-Mogg 1988; ARA 1970, RA 1975; *Recreations* walking; *Style*— Norman Blamey, Esq; 39 Lyncroft Gardens, London NW6 1LB (☎ 071 435 9250)

BLANC, Raymond Rene Alfred; s of Maurice Blanc, and Anne-Marie, *née* Tournier; *b* 19 Nov 1949; *Educ* Besançon Coll France (Dip BEPC); *m* 1, 14 Jan 1974 (m dis 1986), Jennifer Colbeck; 2 s (Olivier b 18 Oct 1974, Sebastien b 15 April 1980); *Career* chef; patron: Quat'Saisons Oxford 1977, Maison Blanc 1978, Manoir Aux Quat'Saisons 1988; TV appearances incl Food and Drink (1987), In At the Deep End (1989), Chef's Apprentice (1989); memb: Academie Culinaire de France, Syndicate de l'Haute Cuisine Française, Relais Chateaux Tradition Qualité; cdr of Gastronomie; *Books* Le Manoir Aux Quat'Saisons (1988); *Recreations* reading, music, tennis, walking; *Style*— Raymond Blanc, Esq; Le Manoir Aux Quat'Saisons, Church Rd, Great Milton, Oxon OX9 7PD (☎ 0844 278881, fax 0844 278847, telex 837552, car 0860 412691)

BLANCH, John William; s of Lt-Col John Blanch, of Betchworth, Surrey; *b* 10 May 1933; *Educ* Dulwich; *m* 1959, Nikola, da of William Thompson, of Dorking; 1 s, 1 da; *Career* dir Wasey Campbell-Ewald 1978-; *Recreations* travel, theatre, photography; *Style*— John Blanch, Esq

BLANCH, Baron (Life Peer UK 1983), of Bishopthorpe in the Co of N Yorks; Stuart Yarworth Blanch; PC (1975); s of late William Edwin and Elizabeth Blanch; *b* 2 Feb 1918; *Educ* Alleyns Sch Dulwich, St Catherine's Coll and Wycliffe Hall Oxford (DD); *m* 1943, Brenda Gertrude, da of William Arthur Coyte; 1 s, 4 da; *Career* served WWII navigator RAF, Tport Cmd India; vicar of Eynsham Oxon 1952-57, tutor and vice-princ Wycliffe Hall 1957-60 (chm Cncl 1967-); Oriel canon of Rochester and warden Rochester Theological Coll 1960-66, bishop of Liverpool 1966-75, 94 archbishop of York 1975-83, ret 1983; pro-chllr Hull Univ 1975-83, York Univ 1977-83; Hon DD Toronto, Hon Dr York; *Books* The World Our Orphanage (1972), For All Mankind (1976), The Christian Militant (1978), The Burning Bush (1978), The Trumpet in the Morning (1979), The Ten Commandments (1981), Living by Faith (1983), Way of Blessedness (1985), Encounters with Jesus (1988); *Recreations* squash, walking, music, meteorology; *Clubs* Royal Cwlth Soc; *Style*— The Rt Rev and Rt Hon the Lord Blanch, PC; Little Garth, Church Street, Bloxham, nr Banbury, Oxfordshire

BLANCH, Hon Timothy Julian Yarworth; s of Baron Blanch, *qv*; *b* 11 July 1953; *Educ* King's Sch Rochester, Keble Coll Oxford; *m* 1982, Monica Mary, da of late H M Keeble, of Cerne Abbas, Dorset; 1 da (Rosa Katherine b 1984); *Career* dir of a Housing Assoc; *Style*— Hon Timothy Blanch

BLANCO WHITE, Thomas Anthony; QC (1969); s of George Rivers Blanco White, QC (d 1966), of London, and Amber *née* Reeves, OBE, (d 1981); *b* 19 Jan 1915; *Educ* Gresham's Sch Holt, Trinity Coll Cambridge; *m* 20 Aug 1950, Anne Katherine, da of James Ironside-Smith, ICS (d 1929); 2 s (James b 1952, Henry b 1956), 1 da (Susan b 1955); *Career* RAFVR 1940-1946; called to the Bar Lincolns Inn 1937 (bencher); *Books* Patents for Inventions (1950, 1955, 1962, 1974, 1983 etc); *Recreations* gardening, photography; *Style*— Thomas A Blanco White, Esq, QC; Francis Taylor Building, Temple, London EC4Y 7BY (☎ 071 353 5657); 72 South Hill Park, London NW3 2SN; Mants, Bedham, Fittleworth, Pulborough, Sussex, RH20 1JR (☎ 079 882 421)

BLAND, (Francis) Christopher Buchan; eldest s of James Franklin MacMahon Bland, of Co Down, and Jess Buchan, *née* Brodie; *b* 29 May 1938; *Educ* Sedbergh, Queen's Coll Oxford; *m* 1981, Jennifer Mary Denise, elder da of late Rt Hon William Morrison May, MP, of Mertown Hall, Co Down, and formerly w of Viscount Enfield (now 8 Earl of Stafford); 1 s; *Career* chm: Sir Joseph Causton & Sons 1977-85, LWT Hldgs 1984-, Bow Gp 1970; dir Nat Provident Inst; *Recreations* fishing, skiing; *Clubs* Beefsteak, Flyfishers; *Style*— Christopher Bland, Esq; 10 Catherine Place, London SW1 (☎ 071 834 0021)

BLAND, Dr David Edward; s of Rev Albert Edward Bland, of Blackburn, and Lily, *née* Simmons; *b* 9 Dec 1940; *Educ* Queen Elizabeth GS Blackburn, Univ Coll Durham (BA, M Litt), Univ of Sheffield (PhD); *m* 27 Sept 1986, Christine, da of Keith Holliday, of King's Lynn, Norfolk; *Career* warden of Sorby Hall and pro vice chllr Univ of Sheffield, 1964-89, dir gen The Chartered Insurance Inst 1989-; fell Inst of Co Accountants 1970 (pres 1990-91), FSCA; *Books* Can Britain Survive? (with KW Watkins, 1971), Managing Higher Education (1990); *Recreations* walking, music; *Style*— Dr David Bland; 31 Dundee Court, 73 Wapping High St, London E1 9YG (☎ 071 481 8234); Western View, Sunny Bank, Great Longstone, Derbyshire DE4 1TL; The Chartered Insurance Institute, 20 Aldermanbury, London EC2V 7HY (☎ 071 606 3835, fax 071 726 0131, telex 957017)

BLAND, Hamilton Edwin; s of Herbert Bland, and Alice Bland; *b* 4 June 1943; *Educ* Folds Rd Sch Bolton, Hayward Sch Bolton, Loughborough Coll (DLC); *m* 1, 26 March 1967, Hazel, da of Leslie Gear; 1 da (Anna Danielle b 16 Aug 1978); m 2, 26 August 1989, Nicola Clare, da of Arthur May; *Career* master Rugby Sch 1965-67, nat tech offr Amateur Swimming Assoc 1967-72, dir of swimming Coventry 1972-81, chm and md Hamilton Bland (Prods) Ltd 1981-86, proprietor Hamilton Bland Consits 1987-, BBC TV swimming commentator 1975-; formerly: memb Coventry Round Table, chm Coventry Mentally Handicapped Soc; Winston Churchill fell 1969; *Books* Waterpolo, Swimming To Win; *Recreations* swimming; *Style*— Hamilton Bland, Esq; Chadwick Barns, Sparrowcock Lane, Chadwick End, Knowle, Warwicks (☎ 056 43 3920, car 0860 269340)

BLAND, Peter; s of Joseph Whalley Bland (d 1951), and Doris, *née* Simpson (d 1949); *b* 12 May 1934; *Educ* Alleynés GS Staffs, Victoria Univ of Wellington NZ; *m* 1956, Beryl Matilda, *née* Connolly; 1 s (Carl b 1960), 2 da (Karen b 1956, Joanna b 1958); *Career* freelance actor and writer; radio prodr NZ Bdcasting Co and journalist NZ Listener 1958-64, co-fndr and artistic dir Downstage Theatre Co Wellington 1964-68; actor: Bristol Old Vic Co 1969-72, Prahda Singh in Conduct Unbecoming (Queen's Theatre) 1970, Shut Your Eyes and Think of England (Apollo Theatre) 1974, Chichester Festival 1975, Peter Pan (London Palladium) 1976; TV appearances incl: Hammer House of Horror, The Les Dawson Show, The Old Curiosity Shop, Heart of the High Country, The Victoria Wood Show, Lazarus and Dingwall, Cribb; films: Don't Just Lie There, Say Something (1974), Came a Hot Friday (1984); poems: My Side of the Story (1964), The Man with the Carpet Bag (1972), Mr Maui (1976), Stone Tents (1981), The Crusoe Factor (1985), Selected Poems (1987), Paper Boats (1991); plays: Father's Day (1967), George the Mad Ad Man (1967); McMillan-Browne prize for Creative Writing Univ of NZ 1958, Melbourne Arts Festival Literary award 1960, Br Soc of Authors Cholmondely award for Poetry 1977, QEII Arts Cncl Drama fellowship 1968, Observer/Arvon Foundation Poetry Competition winner 1980 and 1990, Best Film Actor award Guild of Film and TV Arts 1986; memb PEN (NZ); *Recreations* tennis, travel, contemporary art; *Style*— Peter Bland, Esq; Fraser and Dunlop, 503 The Chambers, Chelsea Harbour, London SW10 OXF (☎ 071 352 4446, fax 071 352 7356)

BLAND, Lt-Col Sir Simon Claud Michael; KCVO (1982, CVO 1973, MVO 1967); s of Sir (George) Nevile Maltby Bland, KCMG, KCVO (d 1972), and Portia Christabel Irene, *née* Ottley (d 1968); *b* 4 Dec 1923; *Educ* Eton; *m* 1954, Beatrice Olivia, da of late Maj William Blackett, of Arbigland, Dumfries; 1 s, 3 da; *Career* WWII Scots Gds (served Italy), Br Jt Servs Mission Washington DC 1948-49, 2 Bn Scots Gds Malaya 1949-51, asst mil advsr UK High Cmmn Karachi 1959-60; comptroller and asst private sec to: HRH late Duke of Gloucester 1961-74, Private Sec to HRH late Prince William 1968-72; comptroller private sec and equerry to HRH Princess Alice, Duchess of Gloucester and to TRH the Duke and Duchess of Gloucester 1972-89 (extra equerry 1989-); conslt Operation Raleigh, Industl Metals Servs Ltd; dir West End Branch Commercial Union; pres: Friends of Edenbridge Hosp, Edenbridge Div St John Ambulance Bde, Edenbridge Players, Lingfield and Area Branch Riding for the Disabled; vice pres: Edenbridge Town Band, Nat Assoc of Boys Clubs; cncl memb: Distressed Gentlefolk's Aid Assoc, Pestalozzi Children's Village Tst, The Coll of St Barnabas; tstee Grant Maintained Schs Tst; CStJ 1978, KStJ 1987; *Recreations* shooting; *Clubs* Buck's; *Style*— Lt-Col Sir Simon Bland, KCVO; Gabriel's Manor, Edenbridge, Kent (☎ 0732 862340)

BLANDFORD, Marquess of; (Charles) James (Jamie) Spencer-Churchill; s and h (by 1 w, *see* Mrs John Gough), of 11 Duke of Marlborough, JP, DL; *b* 24 Nov 1955; *Educ* Pinewood, Harrow, RAC Cirencester; *m* 24 Feb 1990, Rebecca Mary, da of Peter Few Brown and Mrs John Winnington-Ingram; *Career* insurance broker and helicopter pilot; *Recreations* skiing, flying, shooting; *Clubs* Turf, Annabel's; *Style*— Marquess of Blandford

BLANDFORD, Prof Roger David; s of Jack George Blandford, and Janet Margaret Blandford; *b* 28 Aug 1949; *Educ* King Edward's Sch Birmingham, Magdalene Coll Cambridge (BA, Charles Kingsley Bye Fell, MA, PhD); *m* 1972, Elizabeth Denise Kellett; 2 s; *Career* res fell St John's Coll Cambridge 1973-76, memb Inst for Advanced Study Princeton 1974-75; Calif Inst of Technol: asst prof 1976-79, prof 1979-88, Richard Chace Tolman Prof of Theoretical Astrophysics 1989-; FRS, FRAS; Guggenheim fell 1988-89, Alfred P Sloan res fell 1980-84; *Style*— Prof Roger Blandford, FRS; 130-133 Caltech, Pasadena, California, 91125, USA (☎ 818 356 4200)

BLANDY, Prof John Peter; s of Sir Edmond Nicolas Blandy, KCIE, CSI, ICS (d 1942), of Calcutta, and Dorothy Kathleen, *née* Marshall (d 1985); *b* 11 Sept 1927; *Educ* Clifton, Balliol Coll Oxford (MA, DM, MCh), The London Hosp Med Coll; 6 Aug 1953, Anne, da of the late Henry Hugh Mathias, of Tenby; 4 da (Susan, Caroline, Nicola, Kitty); *Career* Nat Serv RAMC 1953-55 (Lt, Capt, Actg Maj), Maj 22 London Gen Hosp (TA), Maj RARO; conslt surgn: London Hosp 1964, St Peter's Hosp 1968; prof of urology Univ of London 1969, vice pres Urology Section RSM 1973; pres: Br Assoc of Urological Surgns 1985-86, Euro Assoc of Urology 1986-88, cncl memb RCS 1982; St Peters Medal 1982; FRCS 1956, FAC 1980; *Books* Tumours of the Testicles (1970), Transurethral Resection (1970), Lecture Notes on Urology (1976), The Prostate (1986), Operative Urology (1978); translations into Italian, Spanish, Portuguese; *Recreations* painting, sculpture; *Clubs* The Royal Society of Medicine; *Style*— Prof John Blandy; 61 Traps Hill, Loughton, Essex 1G10 1TD; The London Hospital, of London, Whitechapel E1 1BB (☎ 071 377 7000)

BLANE, Michael Lawrence; *b* 17 Aug 1938; *Educ* Washington and Lee Univ, Case Western Reserve Univ (BA, LLB); *Career* enforcement counsel US Securities and Exchange Cmmn 1967-70, vice pres and asst gen counsel Dean Witter Reynolds Inc 1973-81, sr counsel Merrill Lynch Europe Ltd 1981-90, dir Int Securities Regulatory Orgn 1985-86, gp compliance offr Banque Nationale de Paris 1990-; Securities Assoc memb 1986-88: Rules Ctee, Enforcement Ctee, Authorisation Ctee Bd; memb: 1992 Ctee Int Stock Exchange, Nat Assoc of Securities Dealers, American Arbitration Assoc, Commodity Futures Indust Assoc; *Style*— Michael L Blane, Esq; Banque Nationale de Paris London, 8-13 King William St, London EC4P 4HS (☎ 071 895 7216, fax 071 895 7013)

BLANEY, Roger Vaughan; *b* 30 May 1947; *Educ* Chester City GS, Fitzwilliam Coll Cambridge (MA); *m* 16 June 1978, Josephine Clare, da of Maj R Morgan, of Winscombe; 2 s (Robin b 1980, Timothy b 1983); *Career* Beecham Group plc 1968-85 (prod mangr, mktg mangr, nat account sales and mktg mangr); mktg dir: Stag Meredew Furniture Ltd 1985-, Stag Furniture Holdings plc 1988-; memb: Spelthorne Borough Cncl 1976-87, Newark & Sherwood Dist Cncl 1989-; *Recreations* gardening; *Style*— Roger Blaney, Esq; Morton Hall, Morton, Southwell, Nottinghamshire NG25 0UY; Stag Furniture Holdings plc, Haydn Rd, Nottingham NG5 1DU (☎ 0602 607121)

BLANK, Herbert; s of Alfred Blank; *b* 18 Dec 1923; *Educ* Dorking GS, Univ of Edinburgh; *m* 1952, Joyce, da of Alfred Pulfer; 1 s, 1 da; *Career* md and dep chm Polymark International Ltd (ret 1985); formed consultancy Co (Gate Lodge International Conservative Ltd); *Recreations* chess, bridge, tennis, squash, skiing; *Style*— Herbert Blank, Esq; Gate Lodge, 17 The Crescent, Hadley Common, Barnet, Herts EN5 5QQ

BLANK, (Maurice) Victor; s of Joseph Blank, and Ruth, *née* Levey; *b* 9 Nov 1942; *Educ* Stockport GS, St Catherine's Coll Oxford (MA); *m* 29 June 1977, Sylvia Helen, *née* Richford; 2 s (Simon b 1 May 1978, Robert b 23 June 1984), 1 da (Anna b 16 Sept 1979); *Career* slr; ptnr Clifford Turner 1969-81, dir Pentos plc 1979-, non-exec dir Coats Viyella plc 1989-, chm and chief exec Charterhouse Bank Ltd 1985-, chief exec Charterhouse plc; dir: The Royal Bank of Scotland Group plc 1985-, Porter Chadburn plc 1988-; memb: Business in the Community, Birthright, Childline, Campaign for Oxford, RSA, Great Ormond St Hosp Appeal; Freeman City of London, memb City of London Slrs Co; memb: Law Soc, CBIM; *Books* Weinberg and Blank on Takeovers and Mergers; *Recreations* family, tennis, cricket, theatre; *Clubs* IOD; *Style*— Victor Blank, Esq; 1 Paternoster Row, St Paul's, London EC4M 7DH, (☎ 071 248 8000, fax 071 248 6522)

BLANKSTONE, Michael David; s of Solomon Julius Blankstone (d 1981), of Liverpool, and Isobel, *née* Franklin (d 1979); *b* 20 Nov 1936; *Educ* Quarry Bank HS Liverpool; *m* 17 June 1963, Anne, *née* Harrison; 2 s (Mark Lewis b 13 April 1964, Neil Simon b 6 Jan 1968); *Career* joined family furniture mfrg business 1953-59, trainee then stockbroker Hornby Tobin & Ockleston 1959-66, memb Stock Exchange 1964, ptnr Neilson Hornby Crichton 1966-75, sr ptnr Blankstone Sington & Co 1975-89 (co-fndr); chm: Blankstone Investments Ltd, BS Advisory Services Ltd; chm and chief exec Blankstone Sington Ltd 1989-; chm The Stock Exchange Liverpool 1988-90 (vice chm 1986-88), memb Northern Stock Exchange Ctee, vice chm Liverpool Stock Exchange Benevolent Fund; tstee: Hillsborough Disaster Appeal, Liverpool Jewish Youth & Community Centre; MInstD 1975; *Recreations* golf, holidays in the sun, reading, charity work; *Clubs* Lee Park Golf; *Style*— Michael Blankstone, Esq; Blankstone Sington Ltd, Martins Buildings, 6 Water St, Liverpool L2 3SP (☎ 051 227 1881, fax 051 227 2912)

BLASHFORD-SNELL, Col John Nicholas; MBE (1969); s of Alderman The Rev Prebendary Leland John Blashford-Snell, MBE, TD (d 1978), of Angmering-on-Sea, Sussex, and Gwendolen Ives, *née* Sadler (d 1968); *b* 22 Oct 1936; *Educ* Victoria Coll Jersey, RMA Sandhurst, The Staff Coll Camberley; *m* 27 Aug 1960, Judith (Frances), da of Lt-Col Beresford Thomas Sherman, OBE (d 1982), of Tivoli Court, Westbourne, Dorset; 2 da (Emma b 1964, Victoria b 1967); *Career* cmmnd RE 1957, Trg Adj 33 Ind Field Sqdn RE Cyprus 1959-62 (Troop Cdr 1958-59), Troop Cdr Junior Leaders Regt RE 1962-63, Instr & Adventure Trg Offr RMA Sandhurst 1963-66, Adj 3 Div Engrs 1966-67, leader Gt Abbai (Blue Nile) Expdn 1968, Staff Coll (RMCS and Camberley) 1968-69, GSO2 MOD 1970-72, leader Br Trans-Americas Expdn 1972, OC 48 Field Sqdn RE (Belize, Oman, N Ireland) 1972-74, leader Zaire River Expdn 1974-75, GSO1 MOD 1975-76, CO Junior Leaders Regt RE 1976-78, Cdr Operation Drake 1978-81, ACPR MOD 1981-82, Cdr Fort George Volunteers 1983, Cdr Operation Raleigh 1984-89 (dir gen 1989-), leader Kalahari Quest Expdn 1990; chm: The Scientific Exploration Soc, Br Chapter Explorers Club; pres: Galley Hill Gun Club, Hereford Branch RE Assoc; Freeman the City of Hereford 1984; Hon DSc Durham 1986; FRSGS 1976; *Books* Weapons and Tactics (with Tom Wintringham, 1973), Where the Trails Run Out (1974), In the Steps of Stanley (1975), A Taste for Adventure (1978), Expedition the Experts Way (with Alistair Ballantine, 1977), In the Wake of Drake (with Mike Cable, 1980), Operation Drake (with Mike Cable, 1981), Mysteries, Encounters with the Unexplained (1983), Operation Raleigh the Start of an Adventure (1987), Operation Raleigh, Adventure Challenge (with Ann Tweedy, 1988), Operation Raleigh, Adventure Unlimited (with Ann Tweedy); *Recreations* shooting, diving, photography; *Clubs* RAC, Explorers, Wig and Pen; *Style*— Col John Blashford-Snell, MBE; c/o CHQ, Operation Raleigh, Alpha Place, Flood Street, London SW3 (☎ 071 351 7541, fax 071 351 9372)

BLATCH, Baroness (Life Peer UK 1987), of Hinchingbrooke in the county of Cambridgeshire; Emily May Blatch; *née* Triggs; CBE (1983); da of late Stephen Joseph Triggs, and late Sarah Ann, *née* Carpenter; *b* 24 July 1937; *Educ* Prenton Secdy Girls Sch, Huntingdonshire Coll; *m* 7 Sept 1963, John Richard Blatch, AFC, s of George Henry Blatch (d 1968); 3 s (David b 1964 d 1979, James b 1967, Andrew b 1968), 1 da (Elizabeth (twin) b 1968); *Career* WRAF 1955-59; govt whip 1990-, under sec of state for the Environment 1990-, cncllr Cambs 1977-89 (ldr of the Cncl 1981-85); pres Nat Benevolent Inst; memb: Euro Economic and Social Ctee, Assoc of Co Cncls 1981-85, Sch's Cncl 1981-; bd memb Peterborough Devpt Corp, chm Anglo American Community Relations Ctee RAF Alconbury; govr: Kimbolton Independent Sch, St Peter's Comprehensive Sch; Baroness in Waiting to HM The Queen 1990; FRSA 1983; *Recreations* reading, theatre, music; *Clubs* University Women's, RAF; *Style*— The Rt Hon the Lady Blatch, CBE; House of Lords, Westminster, London SW1 (☎ 071 219 3000)

BLATCHFORD, Brian; s of Brian Geoffrey Blatchford, MBE (d 1985), of Four Seasons, Cranes Rd, Sherborne St John, Basingstoke, and May Joyce, *née* Faulkner; *b* 7 Dec 1959; *Educ* St Edward's Sch Oxford, St Catherine's Coll Oxford (BA, MSc); *m* 22 March 1986, Caroline Mary, da of Colin Greenwood, of Brooklyn, Jarman Rd, Sutton, Macclesfield, Cheshire; *Career* IBM Laboratories Ltd Hursley 1979, tech offr in office automation ICL 1983-85, md Chas A Blatchford and Sons Ltd 1986- (mgmnt trainee 1985-86); govr London Sch of Prosthetics 1986-, chm Prosthetics Section British Surgical Trades Assoc 1988-; memb: Basingstoke C of C, Basingstoke and Andover Enterprise Centre, Biological Engrg Soc 1986-, Int Soc of Prosthetics and Orthotics 1986-; *Recreations* badminton, computers, wine tasting, reading; *Clubs* Basingstoke Rotary, IOD; *Style*— Brian Blatchford, Esq; Rondel, 1 Beaurepaire Close, Bramley, Basingstoke, Hampshire RG26 5DT (☎ 0256 881937); Chas A Blatchford and Sons Ltd, Lister Rd, Basingstoke, Hampshire RG22 4AH (☎ 0256 465771, fax 0256 479705)

BLATCHLY, Dr John Marcus; s of Alfred Ernest Blatchly (d 1982), and Edith Selina, *née* Giddings; *b* 7 Oct 1932; *Educ* Sutton GS Surrey, Christ's Coll Cambridge (MA, PhD); *m* 1955, Pamela Winifred Blatchly, JP, da of Maj Lawrence James Smith (d 1942); 1 s (Mark), 1 da (Janet); *Career* asst master and head of Sci Dept: King's Bruton 1957-62, Eastbourne Coll 1962-66, Charterhouse 1966-72; headmaster Ipswich Sch 1972; hon treas HMC 1990-; FSA 1975; *Books* Conference & Common Room (journal of HMC-ed), Eighty Ipswich Portraits (1980), Davy's Suffolk Journal (1983), The Town Library of Ipswich (1989); *Recreations* Suffolk countryside and history, all forms of music and music making; *Clubs* E India; *Style*— Dr John Blatchly; Headmaster's House, Ipswich School, Suffolk IP1 3QY (☎ 0473 259941); Ipswich School, Ipswich, Suffolk IP1 3SG (☎ 0473 255313)

BLATT, Nina Joy; da of Samuel Blatt (d 1980), of 50 Green Walk, Hendon, and Rose, *née* Meisler (d 1978); *b* 19 April 1934; *Educ* The Skinners Co Sch for Girls, City of London Coll Moorgate; *m* 17 Sept 1973 (m dis 1986), (Joseph) Peter Roden, s of Gregory Roden (d 1974), of Brinscall, Lancs; *Career* PA to head of publicity Hulton Press (Picture Post) 1949-56, freelance writer travel features for various magazines, PA to First Sec HM Embassy Paris 1956-58, prodr ATV Network Ltd 1958-71 (formerly: prodn asst, asst prodr, assoc prodr), dir Nina Blatt Ltd (representing prodrs and dirs in media); fndr memb The Samaritans, memb BAFTA 1971-; *Recreations* theatre, music, writing, literary pursuits; *Style*— Mrs Nina Roden; The Coach House, 1A Larpent Ave, Putney, London SW15 6UP (☎ 081 788 9971, 081 788 5602/3)

BLAU, Dr Joseph Norman; s of Abraham Moses Blau (d 1942), and Reisla, *née* Vogel (d 1942); *b* 5 Oct 1928; *Educ* Dame Alice Owens Sch, Bart's Hosp Univ of London (MB BS, MD); *m* 19 Dec 1968, Jill Elise, da of Geoffrey C Seligman; 2 s (Justin b 15 Jan 1970, Adrian b 27 April 1972), 1 da (Rosie b 9 Sept 1975); *Career* Nat Serv Lt and Capt RAMC 1953-55; med offr: SW Dist HQ Taunton 1954, Army Neurological Unit Wheatley Oxon 1955; sr registrar London and Maida Vale Hosp, Nuffield Med Res Fellowship Mass Gen Hosp Boston USA; conslt neurologist: Nat Hosps for Nervous Diseases Queen Square and Maida Vale 1962-, Royal Nat Throat Nose and Ear Hosp 1965-, Northwick Park Hosp Harrow Middx 1972-; hon sr lectr Histopathology Dept Guy's Med Sch 1970-89, jt hon dir and conslt neurologist City of London Migraine Clinic 1980-; chm Soc of Authors Writer Gp (Med Writers Gp) 1989-, former pres

London Jewish Med Soc, hon med advsr Br Migraine Assoc 1980-; memb: Scientific Advsy Ctee Migraine Tst 1982, Cncl Neurological Section RSM 1984-87, Assoc of Br Neurologists, Advsy Cncl Br Soc of Music Therapy; vice chm London Med Orch 1989; FRCP, FRCPath; *Publications* Headache and Migraine Handbook (1986), Migraine - Clinical, Therapeutic, Conceptual and Research Aspects (ed and contrib 1987), author of chapters in books and original articles on Headache, Migraine and other neurological topics; *Recreations* cello playing, philosophy; *Clubs* Royal Soc of Med; *Style—* Dr J N Blau; 5 Marlborough Hill, London NW8 0NN (☎ 071 586 3804); National Hospital for Nervous Diseases, Queen Square, London WC1N 3BG (☎ 071 829 8741)

BLAUG, Prof Mark; s of Bernard Blaug (d 1949), and Sarah, *née* Toeman (d 1974); *b* 3 April 1927; *Educ* Queen's Coll NY (BA), Univ of Columbia NY (MA, PhD); *m* 1, 1946 (m dis 1951), Rose Lapone; m 2, 1954 (m dis 1960), Brenda M Ellis; 1 s (David Ricardo b 1956); m 3, 26 March 1969, Ruth Marilyn, da of Ronald Towse (d 1971); 1 s (Tristan Bernard b 1971); *Career* asst prof Yale 1954-62, Univ of London Inst of Educn 1963-84 (sr lectr, reader, prof), lectr London Sch of Economics 1963-78, prof emeritus Univ of London 1984-, consIt prof Univ of Buckingham 1984-, visiting prof Univ of Exeter 1989-, consIt 1964-90 (World Bank, UNESCO, ILO, Ford Fndn), dir Edward Elgar Publishing 1986-; memb: American Econ Assoc, Royal Econ Soc; FBA 1989, FRSA 1990; foreign hon memb Royal Netherlands Acad of Arts and Scis 1986-; *Books* Ricardian Economics (1958), The Causes of Graduate Employment in India (1969), Education and The Employment Problem in Developing Countries (1973), The Methodology of Economics (1980), Economic Theory in Petrospect (1984), Economic History and the History of Economics (1986), John Maynard Keynes, Life, Ideas, Legacy (1990); *Recreations* talking, walking, sailing; *Style—* Prof Mark Blaug; Langsford Barn, Peter Tavy, Tavistock, Devon PL19 9LY (☎ 0822 810562); Dept of Economics, Univ of Exeter, Exeter EX4 4RJ (☎ 0392 263237, telex 42894)

BLAUHORN, Karl Max; s of Dr Josef Blauhorn; *b* 6 May 1912; *Educ* Real Gymnasium Vienna, Fed Inst of Technol Zurich (Dip Ing); *m* 1938, Kate, da of Julius Steiner; 1 da; *Career* formerly md J B Jackson & Partners; consultg engr 1967-; chm: Product Search & Devpt Ltd 1968-, Inst of Int Licensing Practitioners 1980-; CEng, FIMechE, FInstE, FCIBSE, FWeldI; *Recreations* reading; *Style—* Karl Blauhorn, Esq; 4 Wellington House, Eton Rd, London NW3 (☎ 071 586 1814)

BLAUSTEN, Cyril; JP; *b* 1916; *m* 1944, Norma Marion Cinnamon; 4 s (Richard, Douglas, Simon, Peter); *Career* surveyor; Lloyd's underwriter; dir: New Islington and Hackney Housing Assoc, JBG Housing Soc; cmmr of taxes; vice pres Jewish Care and Maccabi Assoc; Freeman City of London, Liveryman Worshipful Co of Glaziers and Painters of Glass; FZS; *Clubs* City Livery, United University, MCC; *Style—* Cyril Blausten, Esq, JP; 5 Linnell Close, Meadway, London NW11; office: 25 Gilbert Street, Grosvenor Square, London W1Y 2EJ

BLAXTER, Prof John Harry Savage; s of Kenneth William Blaxter, CMG (d 1964), and Janet Hollis (d 1981); *b* 6 Jan 1929; *Educ* Berkhamsted Sch, Oxford Univ (MA, DSc); *m* 20 Dec 1952, Valerie Ann, da of Gerald McElligott; 1 s (Timothy b 1958), 1 da (Julia b 1955); *Career* sci offr (then sr sci offr) Marine Lab Aberdeen 1952-64, lectr Zoology Dept Univ of Aberdeen 1964-69, princ sci offr Scot Marine Biological Assoc Dunstaffnage Marine Lab Oban 1969-74 (sr princ sci offr special merit 1974-85, dep chief sci offr special merit 1985-), hon prof Dept of Molecular and Biol Sci and Inst of Aquaculture Univ of Stirling 1986, hon prof Dept of Biology and Preclinical Med Univ of St Andrews 1990-; FIBiol, FRSE; *Books* Advances in Marine Biology (ed), over 130 papers in learned journals on fish behaviour and physiology, co-ed ICES Journal of Marine Science; *Recreations* sailing, gardening; *Style—* Prof John H S Blaxter; Letterwalton House, Ledaig, Oban, Argyll PA37 1RY (☎ 0631 72206); Scot Marine Biological Assoc, Dunstaffnage Marine Laboratory, Oban, Argyll PA34 4AD (☎ 0631 62244)

BLAXTER, Sir Kenneth Lyon; s of Gaspard Culling Blaxter, and Charlotte Ellen, *née* Lyon; *b* 19 June 1919; *Educ* City of Norwich Sch, Univs of Reading and Illinois (BSc, PhD, DSc, NDA); *m* 1957, Mildred Lillington Hall (memb Alcohol Educn & Research Cncl 1982-85); 2 s (Mark, Piers), 1 da (Alison); *Career* dir Rowett Res Inst 1965-82, consIt dir Cwlth Bureau of Nutrition 1965-82; visiting prof Agric Biochemistry & Nutrition Univ of Newcastle 1982-; pres: Nutrition Soc 1974-77, Royal Soc of Edinburgh 1979-83, Inst of Biology 1986-88; FRS, fell Royal Agric Socs; hon appts: memb Académie d'Agriculture de France, Lenin Acad of Agric Science USSR, Royal Dutch Acad; hon assoc Royal Coll Veterinary Surgns; Hon: DSc Queen's Univ Belfast, DSc Univ of Leeds, DSc Univ of Newcastle upon Tyne, LLD Univ of Aberdeen, DAgr Univ of Oslo; kt 1977; *Recreations* painting; *Clubs* Farmers; *Style—* Sir Kenneth Blaxter, FRS; Stradbroke Hall, Stradbroke, Suffolk IP21 5HH

BLAYNEY, Robert Hamilton; s of Lt-Col Owen Geoffrey Blayney, MC (d 1957), and Olive Agar, *née* Lazenby (d 1962); *b* 23 June 1934; *Educ* Uppingham; *m* 16 Jan 1965, Ann, da of James Francis Angus Turner; 2 s (Andrew Owen b 1966, David James b 1969); *Career* Lt Royal Northumberland Fusiliers TA; wine trade; dir: Blayney & Co Ltd 1956-68, Blayneys Park Hotels Ltd 1957-68, Leslie Rankin Ltd St Helier 1969-78; memb Cncl Wine and Spirit Assoc GB 1961-68; dir La Mare Vineyards Ltd Jersey; *Recreations* gardening, genealogy, wine with friends; *Clubs* Royal Over-Seas League; *Style—* Robert H Blayney, Esq; Elms Farm, St Mary, Jersey, CI (☎ 0534 81491); La Mare Vineyards, Jersey, CI (☎ 0534 81178)

BLEAKLEY, Rt Hon David Wylie; CBE (1984), PC (1971); s of John Wesley Bleakley, of Belfast, and Sarah, *née* Wylie; *b* 11 Jan 1925; *Educ* Ruskin Coll Oxford, Queen's Univ Belfast (MA); *m* 1949, Winifred, da of Alfred Wason (d 1931); 3 s; *Career* MP (Lab) Victoria (Belfast) NI Parly 1958-65, memb NI Assembly 1973-75, NI Convention 1975-76, min Community Rels NI Govt 1972, chm Standing Advsy Ctee on Human Rights 1980-; chief exec Irish Cncl of Churches 1980-, pres Church Missionary Soc London 1983-, lectr in industl rels Kivukoni Coll (Dar es Salaam) 1967-69; memb: Ctee of Inquiry on UK Police 1979, Press Cncl 1988-91; Hon MA Open Univ; *Books* Irish Peacemaker (1981), In Place of Work (1981), Work-Shadow & Substance (1983), Beyond Work Free to Be (1985), Peace Together (Symposium); *Recreations* reading, writing, travelling; *Style—* The Rt Hon David Bleakley, CBE; 8 Thornhill, Bangor, Co Down, N Ireland BT19 1RD (☎ 0247 454898); Church Missionary Society, 157 Waterloo Rd, London SE1 (☎ 071 928 8681)

BLEASDALE, Cyril; OBE (1988); s of Frederick Bleasdale, and Alice Bleasdale (d 1976); *b* 8 July 1934; *Educ* Stanford Business Sch; *m* 1970, Catherine Valerie; 2 da (Jane b 1970, Emma b 1972); *Career* md Freightliner 1975-82, dir BR Intercity 1982-86, gen mangr BR LM 1986-89, dir Scotrail 1990; FCIT, MBIM, FRSA; *Recreations* squash, keep fit; *Style—* Cyril Bleasdale, Esq, OBE; 40 Grieve Croft, Bothwell, Glasgow G71 8LU (☎ 0698 854008)

BLEASDALE, Prof John Kenneth Anthony; CBE (1988); s of John Henry Bleasdale (d 1958), and Helen, *née* Rushworth (d 1960); *b* 17 May 1928; *Educ* Manchester GS, Univ of Manchester (BSc, PhD); *m* 24 Sept 1953, Zoë Patricia, da of Frederick Vivian Wallis (d 1962); 2 s (Richard b 1956, Robert b 1959); *Career* cmmnd fighter controller RAF 1952-54; dir Nat Vegetable Res Station Wellesbourne Warwicks 1977-88 (joined 1954, head of Plant Physiology Section 1961-77), head of crop prodn Inst of Horticultural Res 1985-88; former nat pres: Assoc of Applied Biologists, Agric Section of Br Assoc for the Advancement of Sci, The Inst of Horticulture (cncl memb and chm Professional Affrs Standing Ctee); govr Pershore Coll, memb Horticultural Devpt and Educn Ctee NFU; special prof Univ of Nottingham 1977-, emeritus prof Univ of Birmingham 1988- (hon prof 1977-); Res Medal RASE 1973, Veitch Gold medal RHS 1989; FIBioL 1976, FIHort 1985; hon memb Assoc of Applied Biologists 1988; *Books* Plant Physiology in Relation to Horticulture (1973, 2 edn 1979), Know and Grow Vegetables vol 1 (co-ed and contrib vol 1 1979, vol 2 1982); *Style—* Prof John Bleasdale, CBE

BLEASE, Hon Maurice Caldwell; 2 s of Baron Blease, JP (Life Peer), *qv*; *b* 1944; *m* 1967, Mary, da of Philip Carrol; issue; *Style—* The Hon Maurice Blease; The Warden's Residence, Stranmillis College, Belfast BT9, Northern Ireland

BLEASE, Hon Paul Charles; yst s of Baron Blease, JP (Life Peer), *qv*; *b* 1953; *m* 1979, Ann, da of Howard Jennings; 1 s; *Style—* The Hon Paul Blease; Four Winds, 4 Lochinver Avenue, Holywood, Co Down, Northern Ireland

BLEASE, Baron (Life Peer UK 1978), of Cromac, City of Belfast; William John Blease; JP (Belfast 1974); s of late William John Blease, and Sarah Blease; *b* 28 May 1914; *Educ* Belfast Tech, New Univ of Ulster; *m* 1939, Sarah Evelyn, da of William Caldwell; 3 s, 1 da; *Career* industl rels consIt, former union official; memb IBA 1974-79; Hon DLitt Univ of Ulster 1972, Hon LLD Queen's Univ Belfast 1982; *Recreations* reading, DIY; *Style—* The Rt Hon Lord Blease; House of Lords, Westminster, London SW1

BLEASE, Hon William Victor; eldest s of Baron Blease, JP (Life Peer), *qv*; *b* 1942; *m* 1969, Rose Mary, da of Alan Seaton; issue; *Style—* The Hon William Blease; 26 Ormiston Park, Belfast BT4, Northern Ireland

BLECH, Harry; CBE (1984, OBE 1962); *b* 2 March 1910; *Educ* Trinity Coll of Music, Manchester Coll of Music; *m* 1, 1935, Enid Marion Lessing (d 1977); 1 s, 2 da; m 2, 1957, Marion Manley, pianist; 1 s, 3 da; *Career* musical dir Haydn-Mozart Soc; fndr and conductor London Mozart Players 1949-84, ret 1984; conductor laureate; *Style—* Harry Blech, Esq, CBE; The Owls, 70 Leopold Rd, London SW19 (☎ 081 946 8135)

BLECH, Neville Franklin; s of Samuel Blech (d 1982), and Lily, *née* Ziegenbaum; *b* 7 July 1937; *Educ* St Marylebone GS; *m* 16 April 1961, Sonia, da of Joseph Romano (d 1981); 2 da (Simonette Emanuelle b 8 May 1962, Mijanou b 23 Oct 1965); *Career* practising CA 1961-85; proprietor: The Crown Inn Whitebrook Monmouth 1972-79, Restaurant Mijanou 1980- (wine list of the year 1988); dir: Minale Tattersfield and Ptnrs 1985-, The Wine Treasurer Ltd 1989-; memb Worshipful Co of CAs 1978; FCA; *Recreations* opera, music, travel; *Clubs* Restauranteurs Assoc; *Style—* Neville Blech, Esq; 143 Ebury St, London SW1W 9QN (☎ 071 730 6774, 071 730 4099, fax 071 823 6402)

BLECHER, Dr Theodore (Ted); *Educ* King Edward VII Sch Johannesburg, Univ of Witwatersrand (MB BCh); *m* 20 March 1960, Avrille; 3 s (Ken b 1963, Brian b 1965, Derek b 1966); *Career* sr registrar in haematology Bristol Royal Infirmary 1964-68, consIt haematologist Univ Hosp Nottingham 1968-; FRCPath 1977 (MRCPath 1965), FRCP 1982 (MRCP 1962); *Books* contrib: Basic Immunology (1970), Treatment (1984); number of papers in med sci jls; *Recreations* squash, golf, chess, organ; *Style—* Dr Ted Blecher; Haematology Department, University Hospital, Nottingham (☎ 0602 421 421 ext 41188)

BLEDISLOE, 3 Viscount (1935 UK); Christopher Hiley Ludlow Bathurst; QC (1978); s of 2 Viscount Bledisloe, QC (d 1979); *b* 24 June 1934; *Educ* Eton, Trinity Coll Oxford; *m* 1962 (m dis 1986), Elizabeth Mary, da of late Sir Edward Thompson; 2 s (Hon Rupert, Hon Otto Benjamin Charles b 16 June 1971), 1 da (Hon Matilda Blanche b 16 Feb 1967); *Heir* s, Hon Rupert Bathurst, *qv*; *Career* called to the Bar Gray's Inn 1959; *Clubs* Garrick; *Style—* The Rt Hon the Viscount Bledisloe, QC; Fountain Court, Temple, London EC4 (☎ 071 583 3335)

BLEDISLOE, Joan, Viscountess; Joan Isobel; da of late Otto Krishaber, of 113 Mount St, W1; *m* 1933, 2 Viscount Bledisloe, QC (d 1979); 2 s; *Style—* The Rt Hon Joan, Viscountess Bledisloe; East Wing, Lydney Park, Glos (☎ 0594 843543); 14 Mulberry Walk, London SW3 6DY (☎ 071 352 7533)

BLEEHEN, Prof Norman Montague; s of Solomon Bleehen (d 1972), of London, and Lena, *née* Shlosberg; b 24 Feb 1930; *b* 24 Feb 1930; *Educ* Manchester GS, Haberdashers' Aske's, Univ of Oxford (MA, BSc, MB BCh), Middx Hosp Med Sch; *m* 14 Dec 1969, Tirza, da of Arnold Loeb, of Sydney, Aust; *Career* Nat Serv BAOR 1957-59, med specialist Br Military Hosp and Berlin MO to Spandau Military Gaol 1958-59; prof of radiotherapy Middx Hosp Med Sch 1969-75, prof of clinical oncology Univ of Cambridge 1975-, hon dir MRC Clinical Oncology and Radiotherapeutics Unit 1975-, chm Br Assoc Cancer Res 1977-80, pres Int Soc of Radiation Oncology 1985-89, vice-pres Int Assoc Study of Lung Cancer 1987-; hon fell American Coll of Radiologists 1973, hon doctorate Bologna 1990; Liveryman Worshipful Soc Apothecaries 1973; FRCR 1964, FRCP 1970; *Books* Tumours of the Brain (1986), Radiobiology in Radiotherapy (1988); *Recreations* reading, gardening; *Clubs* Athenaeum; *Style—* Prof Norman Bleehen; 21 Bentley Rd, Cambridge CB2 2AW (☎ 0223 354320); Univ of Cambridge Sch of Clinical Med, Dept of Clinical Oncology and Radiotherapeutics, Addenbrooke's Hosp, Hills Rd, Cambridge CB2 2QQ (☎ 0223 217158, fax 0223 412213, telex 81532)

BLEICHROEDER, Rudolf P J; s of Dr Fritz Bleichroeder, of Berlin (d 1938); *b* 9 March 1914; *Educ* Berlin and Holzminden (W Germany), Berlin and Madrid Univs; *m* 1940, Wera, da of Gustav Fuerstenberg, of Berlin (d 1931); 2 da; *Career* dir: Samuel Montagu & Co Ltd, City & Commercial Investmt plc, Drayton Consolidated plc, Drayton Premier Investmt plc, Dualvest Ltd, Fundinvest Ltd, Triplevest Ltd, G T Investmt Fund S A, Drayton Japan Tst plc (ret); *Recreations* bridge, swimming, walking; *Clubs* Brooks's; *Style—* Rudolf Bleichroeder, Esq; 58 Avenue Close, Avenue Rd, London NW8 (☎ 071 722 9933); 70 Les Oliviers, Beaulieu-sur-Mer, France (☎ 93 011342); Samuel Montagu & Co Ltd, 114 Old Broad St, London EC2P 2HY (☎ 071 588 6464)

BLENKINSOP, Henry Gerald; DL (Warwickshire 1970); s of late Henry Maxwell Blenkinsop, of Warwick; *b* 31 Jan 1925; *Educ* Marlborough; *m* 1957, Tessa Susan, da of Dr Eric Leonard Edmondson, of Leamington Spa; 1 s, 2 da; *Career* served WWII RAF Pilot 1943-47; admitted slr 1951-90; Under Sheriff Warwickshire 1951, W Midlands 1972-90, consIt 1981; pres Under Sheriffs Assoc 1984-87; *Recreations* sailing (yacht 'Callooh'); *Clubs* Island Sailing, Bentley Drivers, R-REC; *Style—* Gerald Blenkinsop, Esq, DL; 45 Mill St, Warwick (☎ 0926 491000); 13 Old Square, Warwick (☎ 0926 492407)

BLENKINSOPP, Robert John; s of Capt John Leslie Blenkinsopp, JP, of Sheriff Hutton Hall, York, and Judith Carol, *née* Cooper; *b* 12 May 1948; *Educ* Ampleforth; *Career* md Owen & Robinson plc 1975-87, Henry Hardcastle Ltd 1975-87, Murgatroyd & Horsfall Ltd 1975-87 (goldsmiths, silversmiths, jewellers and diamond merchants); *Recreations* fishing, shooting; *Clubs* Yorkshire; *Style—* Robert Blenkinsopp, Esq; Valley House, Scackleton, Hovingham, York (☎ 065382 339)

BLENNERHASSETT, Sir (Marmaduke) Adrian Francis William; 7 Bt (UK 1809); s of Lt Sir Marmaduke Charles Henry Joseph Casimir Blennerhassett, 6 Bt, RNVR (d 1940), and Gwenfra Mary, *née* Harrington-Morgan; *b* 25 May 1940; *Educ* Michael Hall, McGill Univ Montreal Canada (BSc), Imperial Coll London (MSc), Cranfield Business Sch (MBA); *m* 1972, Carolyn Margaret, da of late Gilbert Brown; 1 s (Charles b

1975), 1 da (Celina b 1973); *Heir* s, Charles Henry Marmaduke Blennerhassett b 18 July 1975; *Clubs* Royal Ocean Racing; *Style—* Sir Adrian Blennerhassett, Bt; 54 Staveley Rd, Chiswick, London W4 3ES (☎ 081 994 4908)

BLENNERHASSETT, His Hon Judge; Francis Alfred Blennerhassett; QC (1965); 2 s of John Blennerhassett, of Knowle, Warwicks, and Annie Elizabeth Blennerhassett; *b* 7 July 1916; *Educ* Solihull Sch; *m* 1946, Betty Muriel, da of Rex Bray, of Sheffield; 2 da; *Career* barr 1946, circuit judge 1978-; *Recreations* golf; *Clubs* Copt Heath Golf; *Style—* His Hon Judge Blennerhassett, QC; Manor Cottage, Hampton in Arden, Solihull, Warwicks

BLETHYN, Brenda; *Educ* Guildford Sch of Dance and Drama; *Career* actress; NT: Beaux Stratagem, Troilus and Cressida, Tambourlaine, Tales From the Vienna Woods, Madras House, The Passion, Bedroom Farce, The Double Dealer, Fruits of Enlightenment, Strife, A Midsummer Night's Dream, The Guardsman, The Provoked Wife, Dalliance; other theatre: Steaming (Comedy Theatre, Best Supporting Actress award), Benefactors (Vaudeville), Crimes of the Heart (Bush Theatre), A Doll's House (Royal Exchange), Born Yesterday (Manchester), The Amazing Adventures of Fanny Kemble (Southampton), Absent Friends (Manhattan Theatre NY); tv incl: The Labours of Erica, Death of An Expert Witness, A Chance in a Million (comedy award), Alas Smith and Jones, Tales of the Unexpected, The Shawl, The Roughest Way, Bedroom Farce, Play for Today (Grown Ups), Yes Minister, King Lear, Henry VI; film The Witches; *Style—* Miss Brenda Blethyn; c/o Ken McReddie Ltd, 91 Regent Street, London W1R 7TE

BLETSOE-BROWN, Maj Peter; TD (1949), DL (Northants 1983); s of James Harold Brown, DCM, MM (d 1965), and Mildred Alice Bletsoe (d 1958); *b* 11 Sept 1916; *Educ* Bilton Grange and Oakham; *m* 1950, Kathleen Cynthia Thelma, da of Col Murley, MC, of Devon; 3 s, 2 da; *Career* company dir and farmer; *Recreations* hunting; *Style—* Maj Peter Bletsoe-Brown, TD, DL; Sywell House, Sywell, Northants (☎ 0604 644156)

BLEWITT, Maj Sir Shane Gabriel Basil; KCVO (1989, CVO 1987, LVO 1981); s of late Col Basil Blewitt; *b* 25 March 1935; *Educ* Ampleforth, ChCh Oxford; *m* 1969, Julia, da of late Robert Henry Calvert, of Picts House, Horsham, Sussex; 1 s, 1 da (1 step s, 1 step da); *Career* Army Service Ir Gds 1956-74 (BAOR, Germany, Aden, Hong Kong); keeper of the privy purse and treasurer to HM The Queen 1988- (dep keeper 1985-87, asst keeper 1975-85); *Recreations* shooting, gardening; *Clubs* White's; *Style—* Maj Sir Shane Blewitt, KCVO

BLICKETT, Douglas Stanley; s of Walter Blickett (d 1958), of Hendon, and Ivy Beatrice, *née* Palmer (d 1970); *b* 24 Nov 1929; *Educ* Orange Hill GS Middx; *m* 6 March 1954, Ingeborg Hermine, da of Reginald George Gunton-Kendall, of Dulwich; 1 s (Philip b 2 Sept 1959), 1 da (Denise b 25 Feb 1955); *Career* Nat Serv RAF 1948-50; res offr GEC Res Laboratories 1957-59, pubn writer Marconi Co Ltd 1959-61, fndr and dir J & B Engrg Co (publication conslts) 1961-72, mgmnt trg GEC Marconi Coll 1972, chief author GEC Marconi Avionics 1972-85, tech pubns conslt Telub Inforum Ltd 1985-; memb Ctee EEA and BSI Tech Pubns Ctee (standards, procedures, symbols) 1972-80; CEng 1967, MIEE, MISTC; *Recreations* walking, writing; *Style—* Douglas Blickett, Esq; Telub Inforum, Inforum House, Know 1 Piece Wilbury Way, Hitchin, Herts (☎ 0462 420024, fax 0462 420 394)

BLIGH, (Peter) Robin; s of Barry Anstey Bligh, of 5 Ridgeway, Weston Favell, Northampton, and Mary Irene, *née* Floyd; *b* 1 Feb 1940; *Educ* Ardingly College Sussex, Bedford School; *m* 4 April 1964, Kathleen Mary, da of late John A Nicholson; 1 s (Andrew William Bligh b 3 Dec 1966, Helen Mary Bligh b 26 Sept 1968); *Career* Holloway, Blount, Duke slrs 1956; Spicer and Pegler Chartered Accountants: articled clerk 1957-62, Cambridge 1972, ptnr 1973-; ptnr Touche Ross & Co (following merger); dir Ely Diocesan Bd of Fin, govr The Perse Sch (chm Fin and Gen Purposes Ctee); Freeman City of London, Liveryman Worshipful Co of Wheelwrights 1986; ACA 1962; *Recreations* golf, skiing, wines, antiques; *Clubs* The Gog Magog Golf; *Style—* Robin Bligh, Esq; April House, 2 Penarth Place, Cambridge CB3 9LU (☎ 0223 66630); Touche Ross & Co, Leda House, Station Road, Cambridge CB1 2RN (☎ 0223 460222, 0223 350839)

BLIGHT, Catherine Montgomery; da of Murdo Montgomery (d 1969), and Catherine A Montgomery; *Educ* Laxdale Sch Isle of Lewis, George Watson's Coll Edinburgh, Univ of Edinburgh (BL, MSc); *m* 28 Oct 1961, David Philip Blight, *qv*, s of Frank Blight (d 1971); 2 da (Josephine b 1964, Charlotte b 1966); *Career* slr and economist Edinburgh Sch of Agric until 1990; cncllr for gas consumers Scotland 1988; memb MMC 1990; author of numerous pubns in learned jls; memb Commun na Gaidhlig, tstee and non-exec dir David Hume Inst, memb Mont Pelerin Soc, Euro Parly candidate Lothians 1989; memb: Club Gniomhachas nan Gaidheal, Scottish Crofters Union; memb: Law Soc of Scotland, Agric Law Assoc, Agric Econ Soc, Euro Assoc of Law and Economics; *Recreations* growing camellias, collecting books and maps; *Clubs* Farmers, Whitehall Court; *Style—* Mrs Catherine Blight; Parc Mead, Sticker, St Austell, Cornwall PL7 2HH (☎ 0726 73613)

BLIGHT, Dr David Philip; s of Frank Blight (d 1971), of Sticker, St Austell, Cornwall, and Phyllis Mary, *née* Tyack (d 1973); *b* 25 March 1930; *Educ* St Austell Co GS, Univ of Reading (BSc), Univ of Durham (MSc), Univ of Durham (PhD); *m* 28 Oct 1961, Catherine, *qv*, da of Murdo Montgomery (d 1969), of Edinburgh; 2 da (Josephine b 1964, Charlotte b 1966); *Career* Nat Inst of Agric Engrg: scientific offr 1955-58, sr scientific offr 1958-64, princ scientific offr 1964-71; Scottish Inst of Agric Engrg: sr princ scientific offr 1971-77, dir 1977-87; md C H Farms Ltd 1987-89; CEng, FIMechE, FIAgrE, FRSA; *Recreations* history of technology, genealogy, local history; *Clubs* Farmers'; *Style—* Dr David Blight; Parc Mead, Sticker, St Austell, Cornwall PL7 2HH (☎ 0726 73613)

BLIN-STOYLE, Roger John; FRS (1976); s of Cuthbert Basil St John Blin-Stoyle (d 1978), and Ada Mary, *née* Nash (d 1983); *b* 24 Dec 1924; *Educ* Alderman Newton's Boys' Sch Leicester, Wadham Coll Oxford (MA, DPhil); *m* 30 Aug 1949, Audrey Elizabeth, da of Joseph Clifford Balmford (d 1977); 1 s (Anthony b 1955), 1 da (Helena b 1952); *Career* WWII Served RCS 1943-46, cmmnd 1944; res fell Pressed Steel Co Univ of Oxford 1951-53, lectr in mathematical physics Birmingham Univ 1953-54, sr res offr in theoretical physics Univ of Oxford 1954-62, fell and lectr in physics Wadham Coll Oxford 1956-62 (hon fell 1987), visiting assoc prof of Physics MIT 1959-60; Sussex Univ: prof of theoretical physics 1962-90, Emeritus prof 1990, founding science dean 1962-68, pro-vice-chllr 1965-67, deputy vice-chllr 1970-72, pro-vice-chllr (science) 1977-79; chm Sch Curriculum Devpt Ctee 1983-88 memb or chm of various ctees incl SERC and Royal Soc; pres Inst of Physics 1990-92; Hon DSc Sussex 1990; FInstP 1962; *Books* Theories of Nuclear Moments (1957), Fundamental Interactions and the Nucleus (1973), Nuclear and Particle Physics (1991); *Recreations* making music; *Style—* Prof Roger Blin-Stoyle, FRS; 14 Hill Rd, Lewes, E Sussex BN7 1DB (☎ 0273 473640); Physics Building, The University of Sussex, Brighton, E Sussex BN1 9QH (☎ 0273 678088, fax 0273 678335)

BLISHEN, Edward William; s of William George Blishen, and Eliza Anne, *née* Pye; *b* 29 April 1920; *Educ* Queen Elizabeth's GS Barnet; *m* 4 Nov 1948, Nancy May, da of Geoffrey Smith; 2 s (Jonathan b 1949, Nicholas b 1952); *Career* weekly newspaper reporter 1938-40; teacher 1946-59, lectr Univ of York 1963-65; freelance writer and broadcaster 1959-; presented: Writers' Club (BBC African Serv) 1960-73, World of Books (BBC's Topical Tapes) 1973-89; FRSL 1989; *Books* Roaring Boys (1955), This Right Soft Lot (1969), A Cackhanded War (1971), Uncommon Entrance (1974), Sorry Dad (1978), A Nest of Teachers (1979), Shaky Relations (1981), Lizzie Pye (1982), Donkey Work (1983), A Second Skin (1984), The Outside Contributor (1986), The Disturbance Fee (1988), The Penny World (1990); *Recreations* reading, talking, photography; *Style—* Edward Blishen, Esq; 12 Bartrams Lane, Hadley Wood, Barnet, London EN4 0EH (☎ 081 449 3252)

BLISS, Dr Christopher John Emile; s of John Llwelyn Bliss of London (d 1978), founder of the BBC TV service from 1936, working as a "boffin" designer, etc, and Patricia Paula, *née* Dubern; *b* 17 Feb 1940; *Educ* Finchley Catholic GS, King's Coll Cambridge (BA, PhD); *m* 1, 1964, Heather, da of Cyril Midmer, of Dublin; 1 s (John Benet b 1966), 2 da (Anna Katharine b 1968, Madeline Frances b 1974); m 2, 1983, Ghada, da of Adel Saqf El Hait, of Kuwait; *Career* fellow Christ's College Cambridge 1965-71, asst lecturer 1965-67, lecturer 1967-71; prof of Economics Univ of Essex 1971-77; fell Econometric Soc 1978; ed Review of Economic Studies 1967-71; Nuffield reader in int economics and fell Nuffield Coll Oxford 1977-; *Books* Capital Theory of the Distribution of Income (1975), Palanpur: the Economy of an Indian Village (with N H Stern); *Recreations* music; *Style—* Dr Christopher Bliss; Tamarisk Cottage, South Street, Steeple Aston, Oxon OX5 3RT; Nuffield College, Oxford OX1 1NF (☎ 0865 278573)

BLISS, John Cordeux; QPM (1969); s of Herbert Bliss (d 1954), of Chipping Norton, Oxon, and Ida Muriel, *née* Hays (d 1969); *b* 16 March 1914; *Educ* Haileybury, Met Police Coll Hendon; *m* 18 Oct 1947, Elizabeth Mary, da of Charles Gordon Howard (d 1981), of Reigate; 1 s (Thomas John Cordeux b 1955), 2 da (Jane Katherine b 1949, Anne Elizabeth b 1951); *Career* WWII Flt Lt RAF 1942-45, served 227 Sqdn coastal cmd (Beaufighters), MEF; joined Met Police 1936, served CID in various divnl and HQ postings incl City & Met Co Fraud 1954-57, dir criminal law Police Staff Coll Bramshill 1961-63, seconded Home Office to set up Regnl Crime Squads, dep asst cmmr and nat co-ordinator Regnl Crime Squads England and Wales 1964-70; called to the Bar Middle Temple 1954, Parole Bd 1973-76 and 1978-81; Freeman City of London, Liveryman Worshipful Co of Merchant Taylors 1947; fell: Churchill Meml Tst 1967, Medico-Legal Soc 1948; *Recreations* Met Police RFC (vice pres), gardening; *Clubs* RAF; *Style—* John C Bliss, Esq, QPM; Foxhanger Down, Hurtmore, Godalming GU7 2RG

BLOCH, (Andrew Charles) Danby; s of late Prof Moishe Rudolf Bloch, and Mary Hall Bloch; *b* 19 Dec 1945; *Educ* Tonbridge, Wadham Coll Oxford (MA); *m* 1968, Sandra, da of late William Wilkinson; 1 s (Adam b 1972), 1 da (Hester b 1974); *Career* researcher Oxford Centre for Mgmnt Studies (now Templeton Coll) 1968-70; dir: Grosvenor Advsy Servs Ltd 1971-74, Oxford Fine Arts Ltd 1975-85, Raymond Godfrey & Ptnrs Ltd 1974-, Taxbriefs Ltd 1975-; regular weekly column on taxation: The Times 1979-82 and 1986-88, The Sunday Times (and related topics); regular fin column in The Daily Telegraph 1982-86; memb Bd Govrs Oxford Poly 1990, memb Cncl Museum of Modern Art Oxford 1990; *Style—* Danby Bloch, Esq; 17 Norham Rd, Oxford (☎ 0865 54971); 193 St John Street, London EC1 (☎ 071 251 4916)

BLOCK, Simon Anthony Allen; s of Gerald Allen Block (d 1969), of Little Park Farm, Battle, E Sussex, and Eileen Marjorie, *née* Handley (d 1982); *b* 19 July 1935; *Educ* Marlborough, Pembroke Coll Cambridge (MA); *m* 16 Aug 1958, Patricia Ann, da of Gen Sir Rodney Moore, GCVO, KCB, CBE, DSO (d 1985), Chief Steward of Hampton Court Palace; 3 s (Adam b 1960, Robert b 1962, Justin b 1964); *Career* 2 Lt 1 Bn Queen's Royal West Surrey Regt 1952-54; slr; sr ptnr Crossman Block and Keith 1977-88, ptnr Withers Crossman Block 1988-89, sr ptnr Crossman Block 1989-; memb Common Cncl City of London 1983-; Liveryman: Worshipful Co of Broderers 1958 (Master 1979-80), Worshipful Co of Weavers, City of London Solicitors Co 1988; Sheriff of the City of London 1988-89, pres The Embroiderers Guild 1986-; *Recreations* fine wines, field sports; *Clubs* Leander, City Livery, The Grannies; *Style—* Simon A A Block, Esq; Crossman Block, Aldwych House, Aldwych, London WC2B 4HN (☎ 071 836 2000, fax 071 240 2648, telex 21457)

BLOCKEY, Wing Cdr Robert Sandland (Robin); s of Air Vice-Marshal Paul Sandland Blockey, CB, CBE (d 1963), and Ella, *née* Temple (d 1987); *b* 16 July 1933; *Educ* Cranleigh, RAF Coll Cranwick; *m* 27 April 1957, Susan Rae, da of Hubert Arnold Pallant, DSO, MC (d 1977); 1 s (Charles b 1960), 2 da (Caroline b 1958, Fae b 1962); *Career* served RAF 1951-78; Sword of Honour Cranwell 1954; cmmnd Univ of Birmingham Air Sqdn 1962-65; chief flying instructor No 1 FTS 1972-73; Nat Defence Coll 1974; proprietor Tiroran County House Hotel Isle of Mull 1977-; *Recreations* portrait paintings (pastel), game shooting, gardening; *Clubs* RAF; *Style—* Wing Cdr Robin S Blockey; Tiroran House, Isle of Mull, Argyll, Scotland (☎ 068 15 232)

BLOFELD, The Hon Mr Justice; Sir John Christopher Calthorpe; s of late Thomas Robert Calthorpe Blofeld, CBE, JP (High Sheriff of Norfolk 1953, and chm CGA), and Grizel Blanche, *née* Turner; *b* 11 July 1932; *Educ* Eton, King's Coll Cambridge; *m* 1961, Judith Anne, elder da of late Dr Alan Mohun, and Mrs James Mitchell; 2 s, 1 da; *Career* called to the Bar Lincoln's Inn 1956, rec 1975, QC 1975, chllr Diocese of St Edmundbury 1973, chm CGA 1977, circuit judge (SE) 1982-90, judge High Court 1990-; kt 1990; *Recreations* gardening, antiques, pottering; *Clubs* Boodle's, Norfolk County; *Style—* The Hon Mr Justice Blofeld

BLOIS, Lady (Elizabeth) Caroline Elinor Evelyn; *née* Giffard; da of 3 Earl of Halsbury; *b* 4 March 1939; *m* 1968, Rodney John Derek Blois, 2 s of Capt Sir Gervase Ralph Edmund Blois, 10 Bt, MC (d 1968); 2 da (Camilla b 1970, Susanna b 1972); *Style—* Lady Caroline Blois; Cockfield Hall, Yoxford, Suffolk

BLOIS, Sir Charles Nicholas Gervase; 11 Bt (E 1686), of Grundisburgh Hall, Suffolk; elder s of Capt Sir Gervase Blois, 10 Bt, MC (d 1968); *b* 25 Dec 1939; *Educ* Harrow, Trinity Coll Dublin; *m* 8 July 1967, Celia Helen Mary, o da of Cyril George Francis Pritchett, CBE, of Aldburgh, Suffolk; 1 s, 1 da; *Heir* s, Andrew Charles David Blois b 7 Feb 1971; *Career* farmer and landowner; *Recreations* yacht cruising (yacht 'Caleta'), travel, shooting; *Clubs* Cruising Assoc, Ocean Cruising; *Style—* Sir Charles Blois, Bt; Red House, Westleton, Saxmundham, Suffolk (☎ 072 873 200)

BLOM-COOPER, Louis Jacques; QC (1970); s of Alfred Blom-Cooper (d 1964), of Los Angeles, California, USA, and Ella, *née* Flesseman (d 1932); *b* 27 March 1926; *Educ* Seaford Coll, King's Coll London (LLB), Municipal Univ of Amsterdam (Dr Juris), Fitzwilliam House Cambridge; *m* 1, 7 July 1952 (m dis 1970), Miriam Eve, da of Daniel Swift (d 1988); 2 s (Jeremy Rupert Louis b 25 Jan 1961, Keith Sebastian Daniel (twin) b 25 Jan 1961), 1 da (Alison Jeanette b 13 April 1958); m 2, 16 Oct 1970, Jane Elizabeth, da of Maurice Douglas Smither; 1 s ((Samuel) George Abbott b 8 July 1979), 2 da (Martha Clare Justine b 6 Jan 1971, Hannah Jane Notcutt b 13 Nov 1972); *Career* Nat Serv RCS 1944, cmmnd 2 Lt E Yorks Regt 1945, Capt 1946, demobbed 1947; called to the Bar Middle Temple 1952, bencher 1978, memb Home Sec's Advsy Cncl on the Penal System 1966-78; chm: Mental Health Act Cmmn 1988-, Press Cncl 1989-90, Ind Ctee for the Supervision of Standards of Telephone Info Servs 1986-, BBC London Local Radio Advsy Cncl 1970-73; vice pres Howard League for Penal Reform 1984- (chm 1973-84), jt dir Legal Res Unit Bedford Coll Univ of London 1967-82, visiting prof QMC Univ of London 1983-86, tstee Scott Tst (The Guardian

Newspaper) 1982-89; jt ed Common Market Law Reports; JP Inner London 1966-79 (transferred City of London 1969); FRSA 1964; *Books* Bankruptcy in Private International Law (1954), The Law as Literature (1962), The A6 Murder (A Semblance of Truth) (1963), A Calender of Murder (with TP Morris, 1964), Language of the Law (1965), Separated Spouses (with O R McGregor and Colin Gibson, 1970), Final Appeal: a study of the House of Lords in its judicial capacity (with G Drewry, 1972), Progress in Penal Reform (ed, 1975), Law and Morality (ed with G Drewry, 1976); *Recreations* watching and reporting on assoc football, reading, music, writing, broadcasting; *Clubs* MCC, Athenaeum; *Style*— Louis Blom-Cooper, Esq, QC; 2 Ripplevale Grove, London N1 1HU (☎ 071 607 8045); Glebe House, Montgomery, Powys SY15 6QA (☎ 068 681 458); Mental Health Act Commission, Maid Marion House, 56 Hounds Gate, Nottingham NG1 6BG (☎ 0602 50404, fax 0602 505998)

BLOMEFIELD, Sir (Thomas) Charles Peregrine; 6 Bt (UK 1807), of Attleborough, Co Norfolk; s of Sir Thomas Edward Peregrine Blomefield, 5 Bt (d 1984); *b* 24 July 1948; *Educ* Wellington, Mansfield Coll Oxford; *m* 1975, Georgina Geraldine, da of Cdr Charles Over, RN, of Lugger End, Portscatho, Cornwall; 1 s (William), 2 da (Emma, Harriet); *Heir* s, Thomas William Peregrine Blomefield b 16 July 1983; *Career* fine art dealer; Christies 1970-75, Wildenstein and Co 1975-76; dir: Lidchi Art Gallery Johannesburg 1976-78, Thomas Heneage and Co 1981-87, Fleetwood-Hesketh Ltd 1982-; md Charles Blomefield and Co 1980-; *Recreations* travel; *Style*— Sir Charles Blomefield, Bt; Clapton Manor, Cheltenham GL54 2LG

BLOMEFIELD, Ginette, Lady; Ginette; *née* Massart; da of late Dr Raphael Massart, of 15 Boulevard des Invalides, Paris; *m* 1, George Harting; *m* 2, 1947, Lt Cdr Sir Thomas Edward Peregrine Blomefield, 5 Bt, RNVR (d 1984); 1 s (Sir Charles Blomefield, 6 Bt, *qv*); *Style*— Ginette, Lady Blomefield; 1 Great Lane, Shaftesbury, Dorset

BLOMFIELD, Leslie Arthur Albert; s of Charles Harry Blomfield (d 1952), and Maud Clarissa, *née* Upson (d 1963); *b* 30 Aug 1920; *Educ* Sybourn Sch, Westminster Tech Coll, Southend Sch of Architecture; *m* 1 (m dis 1958), Alice Evelyn, *née* Howard; m 2, 18 July 1961, Elsa Mabel, da of Harold Piper (d 1956); 3 s (David, Simon, Ian), 1 da (Suzanne); *Career* Flying Offr RAFVR 1941-46, cmmnd Intelligence Branch 1943; architect; Premises Dept Barclays Bank London 1950-52, designed meml to Col Paul Van Lettow-Vorbeck Lusaka N Rhodesia 1952-, Port Elizabeth Schs for Retarded Children E Cape S Africa 1956-58, dir works & tech trg Nat Trg Orgn Ghana 1958-59, conslt 1959-62, prototype schs projects Perth Australia 1963-64, renovation & rebuilding conslt Lloyds Registrar of Shipping London 1 advsr Home Office 1972-77, architect Cape Town Civic Centre SA 1978, major works include: Secret Waters, The Little Red Boat, Beeches of Light; ret 1978, landscape and architectural watercolour artist 1978-; FRSA 1954, ARIBA 1955; *Recreations* history of art, fishing, wild flowers, the commonwealth; *Style*— Leslie Blomfield, Esq; Givendale Grange, Near Ripon, N Yorks HG4 5AD (☎ 0765 707977)

BLOOD, Peter Bindon; o s of Brig William Edmund Robarts Blood, CBE, MC (d 1976), and Eva Gwendoline Olive Clarisse Mends, *née* Harrison (d 1981); collateral descendant of Col Thomas Blood who attempted to steal the Crown Jewels on 9 May 1671, later pardoned and pensioned by Charles II; *b* 24 Sept 1920; *Educ* Imperial Service Coll, Windsor; *m* 20 June 1953, Elizabeth Ann, da of Harold Drummond Hillier, MC, of Sudbury, Suffolk; 1 s (Anthony b 1956), 1 da (Jennifer b 1954); *Career* served RE 1941-46 (despatches), regular cmmn RE 1948, Staff Coll Camberley 1951, sec Army Bd NATO Mil Agency for Standardisation 1952-53, invalided from serv 1953; intelligence co-ordination staff FO 1953-58; fndr and md: Isora Integrated Ceilings Ltd, Clean Room Construction Ltd, Mitchel and King Sales Ltd 1959-71; dir gen Inst of Marketing 1972-84, chm Industrial Market Research Ltd 1984-1987, govr and former chm Berks Coll of Art and Design 1981-89, cnsllr DTI Enterprise; FRSA, FInstM; *Recreations* local community activities, photography, travel, music, furniture restoration; *Style*— Peter Blood, Esq; The Malt Cottage, School Lane, Cookham Village, Berks SL6 9QN (☎ 062 85 25319)

BLOOM, Anthony Herbert; s of Joseph Bloom, and Margaret Roslyn Bloom; *b* 15 Feb 1939; *Educ* King Edward VII HS S Africa, Univ of Witwatersrand (BCom, LLB), Harvard Law Sch (LLM), Stanford Univ Graduate Sch of Business (Sloan fell); *m* 10 Jan 1972, Gisela; 2 s (Andrew Martin b 7 Sept 1965, Nicholas Peter b 10 Dec 1973), 2 da (Rosemary Claire b 24 Jan 1963, Alexis Monica b 27 May 1975); *Career* Hayman Godfrey & Sanderso 1960-64; Premier Group Ltd: joined 1966, dir 1969, dep chm 1975, chm 1975-87; Barclays Nat Bank and First Nat Bank of Southern Africa Ltd 1980-88, Liberty Life Association 1982-88, The South African Breweries Ltd 1983-89, CNA Gallo Ltd 1983-89, non-exec dir RIT Capital Partners plc, dir Rockridge Consolidated Ltd; involved: African Children's Feeding Scheme, Nat Devpt & Mgmnt Fndn of S Africa, Rhodes Scholarship Selection Ctee, Seshaba Tst (clinic in Soweto), S African Inst of Race Relations, S African Wildlife Fndn, The Nat Arts Fndn of S Africa, The Urban Fndn, Transvaal Assoc for the Care of Cerebral Palsy; *Recreations* karate, opera, ballet, theatre, music; *Style*— Anthony Bloom, Esq; Rockridge Consolidated Ltd, 8 Hanover Terrace, London NW1 4RJ (☎ 071 723 3422)

BLOOM, Bridget M; OBE (1989); da of Alan Bloom, and Dee, *née* Heavens (d 1990); *b* 29 June 1936; *Educ* Friends Sch Saffron Waldon, Crofton House Sch Vancouver Canada, Diss GS Norfolk, UCL (BA); *Career* researcher for Lord Stansgate and Wayland Young 1958-60, asst ed West Africa magazine 1960; former freelance BBC Radio and TV; Financial Times: Syndication Dept 1968-69, Africa corr 1969-80, def corr 1981-86, agric corr 1987-; *Recreations* theatre, opera, walking, gardening; *Style*— Ms Bridget Bloom, OBE; Rose Cottage, Pear Tree Green, Dunsfold, Surrey; Financial Times, 1 Southwark Bridge, London SE1 (☎ 071 873 3000)

BLOOM, Charles; QC (1987); s of Abraham Barnet Bloom (d 1973), of Manchester, and Freda, *née* Craft; *b* 6 Nov 1940; *Educ* Manchester Central GS, Manchester Univ (LLB); *m* 16 Aug 1967, Janice Rachelle, da of Reuben Goldberg, of Gwendor Ave, Crumpsal, Manchester; 1 s (David Benjamin b 31 Aug 1972), 1 da (Sarah Rebecca b 10 July 1969); *Career* called to the Bar Gray's Inn 1963, dep circuit judge 1979, rec Crown Court 1983; chm Med Appeal Tbnls 1979; *Recreations* theatre, tennis; *Clubs* Friedland Postmusaf Tennis; *Style*— Charles Bloom, Esq, QC; 10 Barcheston Road, Cheadle, Cheshire SH8 1LL (☎ 061 428 3725); 28 St John Street, Manchester M2 4DJ (☎ 061 834 8418, fax 061 835 3929)

BLOOM, Claire; da of late Edward Bloom and Elizabeth Bloom; *b* 15 Feb 1931; *Educ* Badminton, USA and privately; *m* 1, 1959 (m dis 1969), Rod Steiger; 1 da; m 2, 1969 (m dis 1976), Hillard Elkins; *Career* actress; has appeared in theatre, film and television productions; *Style*— Miss Claire Bloom; c/o Michael Linnitt, Globe Theatre, W1

BLOOM, Capt David Frederick Alfred; GM; s of Arthur Lionel Bloom (d 1983), of Leeds, and Jeanie Fraser, *née* Swan (d 1987); *b* 30 Oct 1924; *Educ* Caistor GS, Liverpool NC (Master Mariners Certificate); *m* 25 July 1953, Mary Iris May, da of Frederick William Singleton (d 1976), of Caerleon; 2 s (Peter b 1957, Robert b 1961), 2 da (Susan b 1955, Janet b 1959); *Career* served MN 1941-56, deck offr T&J Harrison Ltd 1941-56, supt Marine Police Trinidad and Tobago 1956-63, Trinidad and Tobago Def Force 1963-74, CO Trinidad and Tobago Coast Gd 1965-74, Queen's Messenger 1975-89; chm of numerous ctees concerned with security disaster relief and general marine matters in Trinidad; Trinidad Medal of Merit (Silver 1970, Gold 1971); *Recreations* golf, gardening; *Clubs* Merchant Navy (Lancaster Gate London); *Style*— Capt David Bloom, GM; Staubles, Western Rd, Wadhurst, E Sussex TN5 6TX (☎ 089 288 2483)

BLOOM, Patricia; da of Leonard Bloom (d 1988), of London, and Freda, *née* Myers; *b* 20 July 1940; *Educ* Maida Vale HS; *Career* account exec Alexander Butterfield 1964-67, launch team Mary Quant Cosmetics 1968-69, promotions ed Queen Magazine 1970, nat fund raiser Nat Fund Raising Charity 1971-79, fndr Pet Plan (providing comprehensive insur cover for cats, dogs and horses, underwritten by Lloyd's); finalist Veuve Clicqout Business Woman of the Year Award 1989; IBRC; *Recreations* bridge, tennis; *Style*— Patsy Bloom; Pet Plan Ltd, Pet Plan House, 10-13 Heathfield Terrace, London W4 4JE (☎ 081 995 1414, fax 081 994 7585)

BLOOM, Dr Victor Roy; s of Froim Bloom (d 1961), of Westbourne, and Jesse Selina Tomson, *née* Parker (d 1989); *b* 13 March 1932; *Educ* Bembridge Sch, Univ of Oxford (MA, BM BCh); *m* 4 April 1964 (m dis 1976), Chloe Ann, da of Frederick Jack Rick; 1 s (Marston), 1 da (Emma); *Career* UCH 1957-58, Bristol Royal Infirmary 1958-59, Hosp for Sick Children Gt Ormond St 1959-60, Nat Heart Hosp 1960, Hammersmith Hosp 1960-62, Central Middx Hosp 1962-64, physician Harley House 1964-; ed jl of RSM 1976-88; chm: Capital Diagnostic Centre plc, Harley Street Consultants Ltd, Harley Street Health Care Centre Ltd; dir Medical Investments Ltd; vice pres Hornsby Educnl Tst; memb: Nichiren Shoshu of the UK, advsy panel Pro-Dogs, Dartmoor Preservation Soc, Torquay Pottery Collectors Soc, Med Soc London, Assur Med Soc; Freeman City of London 1979, Liveryman Worshipful Soc of Apothecaries 1978; MRCP 1964, MFOM (RCP) 1982; *Recreations* opera, theatre, ceramics, cricket, assoc football; *Clubs* United Oxford & Cambridge; *Style*— Dr Victor Bloom; 40 Harley House, Marylebone Rd, London NW1 5HF (☎ 071 935 1411, fax 071 224 0178, car 0836 203783)

BLOOMER, Robin Howard; s of Arthur Hugh Bloomer (d 1972), of Mulberry House, The Avenue, Healing, Grimsby, Humberside, and Elizabeth Kathleen, *née* Watson (d 1964); *b* 6 May 1930; *Educ* Shrewsbury; *m* 24 May 1958, Edith Alice, da of Charles William Green (d 1954); 1 s (Charles b 1961), 1 da (Susan b 1966); *Career* admitted slr 1956, sr ptnr H K & H S Bloomer & Co slrs 1964-; pres Grimsby and Cleethorpes Law Soc 1978, jt vice chm No 10 Legal Aid Area 1988-; *Style*— Robin Bloomer, Esq; 1 Bargate Avenue, Great Grimsby (☎ 0472 43251); 28 Hainton Avenue, Great Grimsby, S Humberside DN32 9BG (☎ 0472 350711)

BLOOMFIELD, Barry Cambray; s of Clifford Wilson Bloomfield (d 1981), and Eileen Elizabeth Bloomfield (d 1953); *b* 1 June 1931; *Educ* East Ham GS, Univ Coll Exeter (BA), Birkbeck Coll London (MA); *m* 29 Dec 1958, Valerie Jean, da of George Philpot (d 1964); *Career* Nat Serv 1952-54; asst Nat Central Library 1955, librarian Coll of St Mark & St John 1956-61, asst librarian LSE 1961-63, librarian Sch of Oriental and African Studies 1972-78 (dep librarian 1963-72), dir India Office Library & Records FCO 1978-82, dir Collection Devpt 1990-, Dept of Oriental Manuscripts and Printed Books (keeper 1983-85), Br Library 1985-90; hon memb Darwin Coll Univ of Kent 1982-, fell Library Assoc 1965; memb: Cncl Britain-Burma Soc 1979-90, VP Bibliographical Soc 1979-90, Cncl Royal Asiatic Soc 1980-84, Cncl Br Assoc for Cemeteries in S Asia 1980-, Exec Ctee Friends of the Nat Libraries 1981-, Bibliographical Soc, Oxford Bibliographical Soc, Cambridge Bibliographical Soc; *Books* W H Auden: a bibliography (2 edn, with E Mendelson, 1972), An Author Index to Selected British Little Magazines (1976), Philip Larkin: a bibliography (1979), Middle East studies and Librarianship (1980); *Recreations* reading, music; *Clubs* Cwlth Tst, Civil Serv; *Style*— Barry Bloomfield, Esq; British Library, 14 Store St, London, WC1E 7DG (☎ 071 323 7637)

BLOOMFIELD, Ronald John; s of Ronald Henry Bloomfield (d 1973), of London, and Beatrice May Hewson (d 1959); *b* 12 Jan 1938; *Educ* Trinity College Cambridge (MA), Univ Coll Hosp (MB BChir); *Career* sr prodr BBC Continuing Educnl TV for leisure and environmental programes; series including: The Big E, The Wild Side of Town, Discovering Birds, Great Experiments, Better Than New; prodr Questors Theatre Ealing; memb BAFTA; *Recreations* theatre, food and wine, writing, art appreciation; *Style*— Ronald Bloomfield, Esq; 1 Selby Rd, Ealing, London W5 1LY (☎ 081 997 5806); BBC Continuing Education TV, Villiers House, Ealing Broadway, London W5 2PA (☎ 081 743 8000, fax 081 567 9356)

BLOOR, Hon Mrs (Giovanna); da of Baron Blackett, OM, CH (Life Peer); *b* 1926; *m* 1950, Kenneth Bloor; *Style*— The Hon Mrs Bloor; 9 Queenston Rd, West Didsbury, Manchester 20

BLOSSE; *see*: Lynch-Blosse

BLOUNT, Lt-Col Anthony Hubert; s of Col Hubert Blount, MC, TD, DL (d 1979), and Marion Emily, *née* Barclay (d 1990); *b* 13 March 1934; *Educ* Harrow, RMA Sandhurst; *m* 15 Jan 1966, Sarah Georgina da of Maj George Tunley Howard (d 1968); 3 da (Emma b 1967, Alice b 1968, Kitty b 1969); *Career* cmmnd 13/18 Royal Hussars 1954, resigned as Maj 1974; landowner and farmer; Cmdt Norfolk ACF 1988-; *Recreations* shooting, sailing; *Clubs* Norfolk; *Style*— Lt-Col A H Blount; Cley Old Rectory, Holt, Norfolk, NR25 7BA

BLOUNT, Hon Mrs (Susan Victoria); da of 1 Baron Cobbold, GCVO, PC, DL (d 1987), and Lady Hermione, da of 2 Earl of Lytton; *b* 24 May 1933; *m* 1957, Sqdn Ldr Christopher Charles Blount, (yr s of Air Vice-Marshal Charles Hubert Boulby Blount, CB, OBE, MC (d 1940); 2 s, 2 da; High Sheriff of the Country of Hertfordshire 1989-90; *Style*— The Hon Mrs Blount; Manor Farm, Barkway, nr Royston, Herts SG8 8EJ (☎ 076 384 550)

BLOUNT, Sir Walter Edward Alpin (Jasper); 12 Bt (E 1642), DSC (1943 and two bars 1945); s of Sir Edward Robert Blount, 11 Bt (d 1978), and Violet Ellen, *née* Fowler (d 1969); *b* 31 Oct 1917; *Educ* Beaumont Coll, Sidney Sussex Coll Cambridge; *m* 1954, Eileen Audrey, da of late Hugh Blasson Carritt; 1 da (Nicola Jane Eileen b 1955); *Heir* none; *Career* Lt RNVR; slr; farmer; Lloyds underwriter; *Recreations* sailing; *Clubs* Bembridge Sailing, Seaview Yacht, CUCC, RNVR Yacht, Law Soc Yacht; *Style*— Sir Walter Blount, Bt; 19 St Ann's Terrrace, St John's Wood, London NW8 (☎ 071 722 0802)

BLOW, Joyce (Mrs Anthony Darlington); da of Walter Blow (d 1962), and Phyllis, *née* Grainger (d 1961); *b* 4 May 1929; *Educ* Bell-Baxter Sch Cupar Fife, Univ of Edinburgh (MA); *m* 27 March 1974, (John) Anthony Basil Darlington (ret Lt-Col RE), s of Lt-Col Arthur James Darlington, DSO, JP (d 1960); *Career* princ Bd of Trade 1965-67, M & MC 1967-70, asst sec DTI 1972-77, under sec OFT 1977-80, under sec DTI 1980-84; memb Money Mgmnt Cncl 1985-90, chm Mail Order Publishers Authy 1985-, vice pres Inst of Trading Standards Admin 1985-, memb Bd Br Standards Inst (chm Consumer Policy Ctee) 1986-, dir Arts Club 1987-90, chm E Sussex Family Health Servs Authy 1990-, tstee Univ of Edinburgh Devpt Tst 1990-; Freeman City of London; FIPR 1964, FBIM 1977; *Recreations* music, the arts, travel, France; *Clubs* Arts, Reform; *Style*— Miss Joyce Blow; 17 Fentiman Rd, London SW8 1LD (☎ 071 735 4023); 9 Crouchfield Close, Seaford, E Sussex

BLOWER, Maria Tracey Michelle; da of Owen George Blower, and Mollie Doreen, *née* Forryan; *b* 21 Aug 1964; *Career* cyclist; 3 times jr champion 1981, nat 10 mile champion 1986, nat 25 mile champion 1989; Olympic Games 1984 and 1988, represented GB in 4 World championships, 22 nat medals; *Style*— Miss Maria Blower; Heatherfields, Priory Lane, Ulverscroft, Leicestershire (☎ 0509 890280)

BLOWER, Owen George; s of Frederick Blower (d 1967), and Clara Blower (d 1980); *b* 3 June 1932; *Educ* Loughborough Coll; *m* 1 Dec 1956, Mollie Doreen, da of Francis Victor Forryan, of Leicester; 2 da (Jacqueline Claire Yvonne b 1962, Maria Tracey Michelle b 1964); *Career* md: Owen Blower Knitwear (Leicester) Ltd 1967-, Owen Blower Int Cycles Ltd 1976-, Veloce Ital Ltd 1983-; British Best All Rounder Cycling Champion 1958, nat record holder, Multi GB International; *Recreations* cycling, ornithology; *Style*— Owen G Blower, Esq; Heatherfields, Priory Lane, Ulverscroft, Leicestershire LE6 0PA; Owen Blower Knitwear (Leicester) Ltd, Town Green Street, Rothley, Leicestershire LE7 7NW (☎ 0533 302459, telex 265451 MONREF G, ATT MAILBOX; 83:MI0170)

BLOWERS, Dr Anthony John; CBE 1985, JP (Surrey 1970), DL (Surrey 1986); s of Geoffrey Hathaway Blowers (d 1973), of Sunnymead Weir Rd, Chertsey, Surrey, and Louise, *née* Jux; *b* 11 Aug 1926; *Educ* Sloane GS Chelsea, Sir John Cass Coll Univ of London, Univ of Surrey (PhD); *m* 4 Sept 1948, Yvonne, da of Capt Alan Victor Boiteux-Buchanan (d 1986); 2 s (Colin b 1953, Christopher b 1955), 1 da (Anne (Mrs Ricketts) b 1951); *Career* RCS 1944-45, RAMC 1945-46, RWAFF (served Nigeria) 1946-48; experimental offr Miny of Agric 1953-59 (sr sci asst 1949-53), Sandoz Pharmaceuticals 1959- (sr res offr 1973-87, conslt psychopharmacology 1987-), conslt bacteriology Mansi Laboratories 1973-, dir corp affrs Magellan Medical Communications 1990-; numerous contribs to books and sci jls; NHS: vice chm SAHA 1976-77 (memb 1973-80), memb SW Thames RHA 1980-81, chm W Surrey and NE Hants Health Authy 1981-86, cmmr Mental Health Act Cmmn 1987-, memb Mental Health Review Tbnl 1975-; govr: Fullbrook Sch 1967-85 (chm 1981-85), Ottershaw Sch 1975-81 (chm 1979-81); memb: Cons Policy Gp on Mental Health 1978-81, Health Servs Ctee 1989-; pres Runnymede Scout Cncl 1970-84; chm: Runnymede and Elmbridge Police Community Liaison Ctee 1983-, SW Surrey Crime Prevention Ctee 1986-; vice chm Farnham Police Community Liaison Ctee 1985-; memb: Psychiatry Res Tst 1986-, Court Univ of Surrey 1986-, Cncl Magistrates Assoc 1986-; chm Surrey Magistrates Soc 1988-, asst dir gen St John Ambulance 1985- (cdr Surrey 1987-), vice chm Woking Duke of Edinburgh Award Ctee 1987- (chm SE Region 1990-, memb Nat Advsy Cncl), chm Surrey Ctee Police Convalescence and Rehabilitation Tst 1986-88, Runnymede and Elmbridge Ctee Wishing Well Appeal; Surrey Co Cncl 1970-85 (vice chm Social Servs Ctee 1973-77); chm: Chertsey Urban DC 1969-70 and 1973-74 (memb 1964-74), Runnymede Borough Cncl 1973-74 (memb 1973-84), Surrey Police Authy 1981-85 (memb 1973-90), memb Bd Visitors Coldingley Prison 1978-, High Sheriff of Surrey 1990-91; CStJ (OStJ 1986); Freeman: Borough of Runnymede 1985, City of London 1983; Liveryman Worshipful Soc of Apothecaries 1988 (Yeoman 1983-88); CBiol 1983, FIMLS 1983; *Books* numerous contributions to books and sci jls; *Recreations* fund raising, running, gardening; *Style*— Dr Anthony Blowers, CBE, JP, DL; Westward, 12 Birch Close, Boundstone, Farnham, Surrey GU10 4TJ (☎ 025 125 2769); Magellan Medical Communications, 40-42 Osnaburgh St, London NW1 3ND (☎ 071 465 8366, fax 071 465 8367)

BLOXHAM, John; s of John Bloxham (d 1953), of Doncaster, Yorks, and Lillian Mary, *née* Sherriff (d 1936); *b* 20 March 1917; *Educ* Doncaster GS, Doncaster Tech Coll, Architectural Assoc Sch of Architecture (AA Dip); *m* 29 Dec 1945, Peggy Lovell, da of Capt J O N Wood, RN; 1 s (Jeffrey St John b 1953), 1 da (Christine Gillian (Mrs Blanks) b 1948); *Career* 61 HAA Regt RA 1940, Battle of Br Essex RE 1942, cmmnd 2 Lt 1942, served 15 Scottish Div; 1 Br Inf Div: Tunis, Italy 1944, Anzio, Florence, Rome, Palestine, Egypt demobbed 1946; architect; pupilage 1932-37, Architectural Assoc Sch of Architecture 1937-40, Miners' Welfare Cmmn 1947, private office 1947-48, design architect Iraq Petroleum Co 1948-57, private practice 1957-; chm City of London Round Table 1956, hon sec Doncaster GS Old Boys Club, memb City Livery Club 1972 (chm Aero Section and Music Section, hon sec Aero Section), pres Lewisham C of C and Indust, ctee memb Catford Police Security Panel, cncl memb United Wards' Club of City of London Governing Body; Freeman City of London, Liveryman Worshipful Co of Basketmakers; memb: Architectural Assoc 1938-, RIBA, ARCUK; FSAI; *Recreations* walking, tennis, badminton, cricket; *Style*— John Bloxham, Esq; 36 Hall Drive, London SE26 6XB (☎ 081 778 8645)

BLUCK, Duncan Robert Yorke; CBE (1990, OBE 1984); s of Thomas Edward Bluck, and Ida Bluck; *b* 19 March 1927; *m* 1952, Stella Wardaw Murdoch; 1 s, 3 da; *Career* chm: Cathay Pacific Airways 1980-84 (dir 1970-, md 1971-84), Swire Pacific Ltd 1980-84 (dir 1970-), John Swire & Sons (HK) Ltd 1980-84 (dir 1970-84), Hong Kong Aircraft Engineering Co Ltd 1980-86, Br Tourist Authy 1984-90, English Tourist Bd 1984-90, Kent Econ Devpt Bd 1985-; dir Hong Kong and Shaighai Bank Corp 1980-84; JP Hong Kong 1976-84; chm English Schs Fndn (Hong Kong) 1976-84, memb Court Univ of Kent; *Recreations* sailing, swimming, tennis; *Clubs* Brooks's; *Style*— Duncan Bluck, Esq, CBE; Elfords, Hawkhurst, Kent TN18 4RP (☎ 0580 752153); John Swire & Sons Ltd, Swire House, 59 Buckingham Gate, London SW1E 6AJ (☎ 071 834 7717)

BLUE, Rabbi Lionel; s of Harry Blue (d 1965), and Hetty Blue; *b* 6 Feb 1930; *Educ* Westminster City Sch, Hendon Co Sch, Balliol Coll Oxford (MA), UCL (BA), Leo Baeck Coll (Rabbinical Dip); *Career* minister Settlement Synagogue 1957, rabbi Middx New Synagogue 1959, religious dir for Euro Bd World Union for Progressive Judaism 1963-66, lectr Leo Baeck Coll 1963-, convener Ecclesiastical Ct Reformed Synagogues of GB 1969-89; broadcaster: Prayer for the Day, Thought for the Day, Pause for Thought; writer, cookery columnist The Universe, co-ed Forms of Prayer 1969-, retreat leader; memb Rabbinical Assembly Reformed Synagogues of GB, vice chm Standing Conf of Jews, Christians and Moslems in Europe; memb Rabbinical Assemblies; *Books* To Heaven with Scribes and Pharisees (1975), Forms of Prayer Vols 1 and 2 (1977), A Backdoor to Heaven (1978), Kitchen Blues (1985), Bright Blue (1985), Blue Heaven (1987), Guide to Here and Hereafter (jtly, 1988), Blue Horizons (1989); *Recreations* monasteries, charity shops, painting, travelling; *Style*— Rabbi Lionel Blue; Leo Baeck College, 80 East End Rd, London N3 2SY (☎ 081 349 4525)

BLUETT, David Frederick; s of Frederick Dawson Bluett (d 1977), of 6 Fairleas Court, Courtdown Rd, Beckenham, Kent, and Muriel Emma, *née* Fells (d 1982); *b* 5 Dec 1937; *Educ* Cranleigh; *m* (m dis), Gillian Lalage, da of Richard Travis Harris; 2 s (James Edward Nutcombe b 3 Oct 1974, Charles Piers b 28 June 1978); *Career* CCF Artillery Section Cranleigh Sch 1951-55, HAC 1955-56, Nat Serv RA 1956-58, cmmnd 1957, Kent Yeo 1958-63; Royal Insurance Co 1955-56; chm: Bluett Smith & Co Ltd (and subsids of family co) 1972 (joined 1959, md 1968), Sunset Cleaning Gp 1975-89, subsids of TKM plc 1980-83, Saunders Abbott 1987; Old Cranleighan RFC: former Capt, sec, chm and vice pres; former chm Old Cranleighan Soc, former Capt Old Cranleighans Golf Soc; involved with St Christopher's Hospice; Liveryman: Worshipful Co of Skinners 1968 (Freeman 1961), Worshipful Co of Carmen 1979 (memb Court); FInstD 1960; *Recreations* tennis, golf, previously squash and rugby; *Clubs* City Livery, E India, RAC, IOD, HAC, Royal Cinque Ports, Old Cranleighan, Tower Ward, Offrs Dining (Kent), County of London Yeo; *Style*— David Bluett, Esq; Fairfield, Furze Hill, Kingwood, Tadworth, Surrey KT20 6HB (☎ 07373 51867); Bluett House, 189-195 High St, Beckenham, Kent BR3 1BA (☎ 081 658 2222, 081 658 0915, fax 081 650 1017, car 0860 300748, telex 946254)

BLUETT, Desmond; s of Montague Clarke Bluett (d 1942), and Elizabeth Stirling, *née* Gilliland (d 1957); *Educ* Guys Hosp and Univ of London (MB BS); *m* 12 Sept 1953, Elizabeth Jean Ward-Booth, da of Robert Christie, of Norfolk; 1 da (Anne Elizabeth b 22 Feb 1959); *Career* RN 1953-67, Surgn Cdr and sr conslt in obstetrics and gynaecology serv SA and Malta; gynaecologist Princess Margaret Hosp Nassau Bahamas, attending surgn Met and Fifth Ave Hosps NYC, lectr in obstetrics and gynaecology Royal Postgrad Med Sch Hammersmith Hosp London; Freeman City of London, Liveryman Worshipful Soc of Apothecaries; Hon MD Univ of NY; FRCOG, LRCP, MRCS, LMSSA, DObstRCOG; fell: Int Coll of Surgns, American Coll of Surgns; *Books* Resuscitation of The Neonate (1962), Update on Intrauterine Devices (1974); *Recreations* polo, sailing, travel; *Clubs* Royal Naval, RSM, Guards Polo Windsor; *Style*— Desmond Bluett, Esq; 21 Devonshire Place, London W1 (☎ 071 935 5979)

BLUGLASS, Prof Robert Saul; s of Henry Bluglass (d 1973), and Fay, *née* Griew; *b* 22 Sept 1930; *Educ* Warwick Sch, Univ of St Andrews (MB ChB, DPM, MD); *m* 24 Aug 1961, Dr Jean Margaret Kerry; 1 s (Charles Edward b 1963), 1 da (Amanda Clare b 1967); *Career* Nat Serv RAF 1948-49; house offr appts 1957-58, registrar in psychiatry Dundee 1958-61, sr registrar in psychiatry Royal Dundee Liff Hosp 1961-67, conslt in forensic psychiatry W Mids RHA and Hosp 1967-, prof of forensic psychiatry Univ of Birmingham 1979-, regnl advsr in psychiatry (formerly dep regnl advsr) 1986-, clinical dir Reaside Clinic 1986-; memb: Mental Health Review Tbnl 1979-, Mental Health Act Cmmn 1983-85; specialist advsr House of Commons Social Servs Ctee 1984-85; RCPsych: vice pres 1984-85, former chm Forensic Psychiatry Special Section, chm Midlands Div 1986-, Cncl memb; MRCPsych 1971, FRCPsych 1976, FRSM; memb: Br Acad of Forensic Sci, BHA, Soc of Authors; *Books* A Guide to the Mental Health Act 1983 (1983), Psychiatry, Human Rights and the Law (with Sir Martin Roth, 1985), Principles and Practice of Forensic Psychiatry (with Dr Paul Bowden, 1990, awarded highly commended category, Glaxo prize 1990); *Recreations* water colour painting, swimming, listening to music; *Clubs* RSM; *Style*— Prof Robert Bluglass; Reaside Clinic, Bristol Road South, Birmingham B45 9BE (☎ 021 453 6161)

BLUMBERG, Prof Baruch Samuel; s of Meyer Blumberg; *b* 28 July 1925; *Educ* Union Coll Schenectady NY (BS), Columbia Univ NY Graduate Sch, Coll of Physicians and Surgeons Columbia Univ (MD), Balliol Coll Oxford (DPhil); *m* 4 April 1954, Jean Liebesman; 2 s (George b 4 Aug 1958, Noah b 30 March 1965), 2 da (Anne b 18 April 1957, Jane b 9 Sept 1960); *Career* Nat Serv USN 1943-46, deck Ensign 1946, CO USS (L) 36 1945-46, Lt USNR 1946-55, Col med dir US Public Health Serv 1955-64, US Public Health Serv Res 1964-; intern and asst res First Columbia Med Div Bellevue Hosp NY 1951-53, fell Dept of Med Coll of Physicians and Surgns 1953-55; Univ of Oxford: Dept of Biochemistry 1955-57, visiting fell Trinity Coll 1972-73, George Eastman visiting prof Balliol Coll 1983-84, master Balliol Coll 1989-; chief Geographic Med and Genetics Section Nat Inst of Health Bethesda Maryland USA 1957-64, assoc prof in clinical med Georgetown Univ Sch of Med Washington DC 1962-64; Fox Chase Cancer Center Philadelphia USA: assoc dir for clinical res Inst for Cancer Res 1964-86, vice pres for population oncology 1986-89, sr advsr to the Pres 1989-, distinguished scientist 1989-; Univ of Pennsylvania Philadelphia USA: prof of human genetics 1970-75, attending physician (and Veterans Admin Hosp) 1965-82, prof of med and anthropology; sr attending physician Philadelphia Gen Hosp 1975-76, conslt Univ of Washington Med Res Unit Tapei Taiwan 1982-, Raman visiting prof Indian Acad of Sci Bangalore 1986, Ashland visiting prof Univ of Kentucky Lexington Kentucky USA 1986-87, clinical prof Dept of Epidemiology Sch of Public Health Univ of Washington Seattle USA 1983-88, conslt Office of Surgn Gen Office of Asst Sec for Health Rockville Maryland USA 1989-; hon fell: Balliol Coll Oxford 1976, Indian Acad of Sci Bangalore 1987; numerous awards incl: Grand Scientific Award of the Phi Lambda Kappa Med Fraternity 1971, Nobel Prize in Physiology of Med 1976, John P McGovern Award American Med Writers Assoc 1988; memb: Scientific Advsy Bd Leonard Wood Meml and Inst for Topical Health 1977-, Advsy Bd Vittal Mallya Scientific Res Fndn Bangalore India 1986-, Scientific Advsy Bd Stazione Zoologica Naples Italy 1987-, Scientific Advsy Bd Fogarty Int Centre Nat Inst of Health Bethesda Maryland USA 1989, John Morgan Soc Univ of Pennsylvania Interurban Clinical Club; hon fell: College of Physicians of Philadelphia, RCP, RSM, Gastroenterological Soc of the Dominican Republic, American Coll of Gastroenterology, Br Soc of Gastroenterology; Hon DSc: Univ of Pittsburgh 1977, Dickinson Coll Carlisle Pa 1977, Hahnemann Univ Philadelphia 1977, Franklin and Marshall Coll Lancaster Pa 1978, Albert Einstein Med Coll of Yeshiva Univ NY 1980, Ursinus Coll Pa 1982, Bard Coll Annandale on Hudson NY 1985, Elizabethtown Coll Pa 1988, Ball State Univ Muncie Indiana 1989; Hon Dr of Med Sci Med Coll of Pennsylvania Philadelphia 1977, Hon LLD Union Coll Schenectady NY 1977, Hon DLitt Jewish Theological Seminary of America NY 1977, Hon DUniv Univ of Paris VII France 1980, Hon LLD La Salle Univ Philadelphia 1982, Hon DHumane Litt Thomas Jefferson Univ Philadelphia Univ 1983, Hon DHumane Litt Rush Univ Chicago 1983, Hon MA Univ of Oxford 1984, La Laurea ad Honorem in Med e Chirurgia Univ Degli Studii de Firenze Florence Italy 1985, Hon DSc Columbia Univ; memb: Nat Acad of Scis USA (Inst of Med), American Philosophical Soc, American Acad of Arts and Scis, Assoc of American Physicians, American Soc for Clinical Investigation, American Soc of Human Genetics, Korean Med Assoc (hon); fell American Coll of Physicians; FRCP 1984; *Books* Proceedings of the Conference on Genetic Polymorphisms and Geographic Variations in Disease, February 23-25 1960 (ed, 1961), New Developments in Medicine (ed with HM Rawnsley, 1970), Australia Antigen and Hepatitis (jtly, 1972), Hepatitis B: The Virus, The Disease and the Vaccine (ed jtly, 1984); *Recreations* squash, canoeing, bicycle touring, cattle raising, trekking; *Clubs* Athenaeum, Utd Oxford and Cambridge; *Style*— Prof Baruch Blumberg; Balliol College, Oxford, Oxon OX1 3BJ (☎ 0865 277 710, fax 0865 277 803)

BLUMENTHAL, Dr Ivan; *b* 16 Jan 1947; *Educ* Queen's Coll Queenstown South Africa, Univ of Cape Town (MB ChB); *m* 16 Dec 1973, Janet Helen; 2 s (Morris b 4 Oct 1974, Toby b 3 Sept 1976); *Career* med trg in paediatrics: S Africa, UK, USA; currently conslt paediatrician Royal Oldham Hosp; contrib med jls; MRCP 1975, DCH 1974; *Books* Your Child's Health (1987); *Recreations* bridge; *Style*— Dr Ivan Blumenthal; 38 Norford Way, Bamford, Rochdale OL11 5QS (☎ 0706 358954); The Royal Oldham Hospital, Rochdale Rd, Oldham OL1 2JH (☎ 061 624 0420)

BLUMSOM, John David; TD (1964); s of Thomas George Blumsom, of Bosham, Sussex, and Joan, *née* Dixon; *b* 7 Dec 1932; *Educ* Merchant Taylors, London Business Sch; *m* 23 Feb 1957, Gillian Mary, da of Russell Paul, of Berkhamsted; 3 s (Giles, David, William), 2 da (Alexandra, Elizabeth); *Career* Nat Serv cmmnd Queens Royal Regt 1951-53; TA: Queens Royal Regt 1953-59, Beds and Herts Regt 1960-69, ret as Maj; articled clerk Moore Stephens & Co CAs 1953-59, commercial mangr Electrolux Ltd 1967-69, gen mangr Electrolux Commerical Equipment Ltd 1969-71 (joined 1959), dir Hambros Bank Ltd 1986- (joined 1971), non-exec dir Hemmington Scott Publishing Ltd 1986-; chm Herts Ctee Army Benevolent Fund 1986-; ICA, FCA; *Recreations* golf, squash, walking; *Style*— John Blumsom, Esq, TD; 25 Shrublands Rd, Berkhamsted, Herts HP4 3HX (☎ 0442 865 854); Hambros Bank Ltd, 41 Tower Hill, London EC3N 4HA (☎ 071 480 5000, telex 887465)

BLUNDELL, Prof Derek John; s of Frank Herbert Blundell (d 1978), and Irene Mary, *née* Davie (d 1963); *b* 30 June 1933; *Educ* East Grinstead GS, Univ of Birmingham (BSc), Imperial Coll London (PhD, DIC); *m* 15 Sept 1960, Mary Patricia, da of Archibald James Leonard (d 1968); *Career* lectr Univ of Birmingham 1959-70, reader Univ of Lancaster 1971-75 (sr lectr 1970-71), prof of environmental geology Univ of London 1975-; pres Geological Soc 1988-90; FGS 1956, MIGeol 1976; *Recreations* skiing, cycling, tennis, golf; *Clubs* Athenaeum; *Style—* Prof Derek Blundell; Geology Dept, Royal Holloway and Bedford New College, Egham, Surrey TW20 0EX (☎ 0784 443811, telex 935504)

BLUNDELL, Keith John; s of John Blundell (d 1945), and Bessie, *née* Jenner (d 1974); *b* 7 Jan 1936; *Educ* Maidstone GS, Medway Coll of Art; *m* 24 Sept 1960, Joan Ann, da of Albert Groves (d 1970); 1 s (John b 1963), 2 da (Karen b 1965, Kristin b 1969); *Career* architect; project architect Poltock and Associates 1960-72, dir Chapman and Hanson 1982- (sr architect 1972-82); MRIBA 1970; *Recreations* jazz musician; *Style—* Keith Blundell, Esq; Navarac, Stockett Lane, Coxheath, Maidstone, Kent ME17 4PS (☎ 0622 745347); Chapman and Hanson, 29 Widmore Rd, Bromley, Kent BR1 1RT (☎ 081 460 8834, 081 460 8838)

BLUNDELL, Sir Michael; KBE (1962, MBE 1943); s of Alfred Herbert Blundell, of Monks Hall, Appletreewick, Yorkshire, and Amelia Woodward, *née* Richardson; *b* 7 April 1907; *Educ* Wellington; *m* 1946, Geraldine Lötte (d 1983), da of Gerald Stanley Robarts; 1 da (Susan); *Career* 2nd Lt RE 1940, Maj 1940, Lt-Col 1941, Col 1944, Hon Col 3rd Kings African Rifles 1955-61; farmer in Kenya 1925-75; cmmr for Euro Settlement 1946-47, MLC Rift Valley Constituency Kenya 1948-63; ldr: Euro membs 1952, New Kenya Gp 1959-63; min Emergency War Cncl 1954-55, min of Agric 1955-59 and 1961-62; chm: Egerton Agric Coll 1962-72, EA Breweries Ltd 1964-77, Kenya Soc for the Blind 1978-81; dir Barclays Bank Kenya 1968-82, judge Guernsey Cattle RASE Show 1977; Freeman Worshipful Co of Goldsmiths 1953; *Publications* So Rough a Wind (1964), The Wild Flowers of Kenya (1982), Collins Guide To the Wild Flowers of East Africa (1987); *Recreations* music, gardening; *Clubs* Muthaiga (Nairobi), Landsdowne; *Style—* Sir Michael Blundell, KBE; Box 30181, Nairobi, Kenya (☎ 010 2542 512278)

BLUNDELL, Prof Thomas Leon (Tom); s of Horace Leon Blundell, of Sussex, and Marjorie, *née* Davis; *b* 7 July 1942; *Educ* Steyning GS, Brasenose Coll Oxford (BA, DPhil); *m* 1, 1964 (m dis 1973), Lesley; 1 s (Ricky b 19 Nov 1969); m 2, 1974 (m dis 1983), Reiko; m 3, 22 May 1987, Lynn Bancinyane, da of Phineas Sibanda, of Zimbabwe; 2 da (Sichelesile 5 Jan 1988, Samkeliso b 25 June 1989); *Career* Univ of Oxford: res fell Molecular Biophysics Laboratory 1967-72, jr res fell Linacre Coll 1968-70; lectr biological science Univ of Sussex 1973-76; Birkbeck Coll: prof Dept of Crystallography 1976-90, hon dir Imperial Cancer Research Fund Structural Molecular Biology Unit 1989; dir Int Sch of Crystallography Erice Italy 1982-, sec Agric & Food Res Cncl 1991-, chm Biological Sci Ctee SERC 1983-87 (memb Cncl 1989-), memb Cncl AFRC 1985-90; cncllr Oxford CBC 1970-73 (chm Planning Ctee 1972-73); FRS 1984; *Books* Protein Crystallography (1976); *Recreations* playing jazz, listening to opera, walking; *Style—* Prof Tom Blundell, FRS; ICRF Unit of Structural Molecular Biology, Dept of Crystallography, Birkbeck Coll, Malet St, London WC1E 7HX (☎ 071 631 6284, fax 071 436 8918)

BLUNDELL-HOLLINSHEAD-BLUNDELL, Brig Dermot Hugh; s of Maj Christian Victor Richard Blundell-Hollinshead-Blundell (d 1971), of 52 Kingston House North, London SW7, and Helen Kate, *née* Guthrie (d 1989); *b* 18 Oct 1935; *Educ* Eton, Sandhurst, Staff Coll Camberley; *m* 1, 16 Feb 1966 (m dis 1973), Princess Stephanie, da of Prince Franz Joseph Windischgraetz (d 1983); 2 s (Henry Victor William b 3 Nov 1967, Alexander Otto b 7 Aug 1969); m 2, 11 March 1976, Sally Anne Veronique, da of Victor Charles Hamish Creer, of Tilburys, Passfield, Liphook, Hampshire; 1 s (Victor Richard Dermot b 1 Dec 1978), 2 step s (Charles Donald Greville Leigh b 2 Nov 1969, Thomas William Elliot Leigh b 28 Nov 1971); *Career* cmmnd Grenadier Guards 1955, ADC to govr gen NZ 1960-62, cmd 2 Battalion Grenadier Guards 1976-78, COS London Dist 1984-86, cmd 56 London Brigade 1986-88, sec to COS SHAPE 1988; (despatches 1978); *Recreations* military history, country pursuits; *Clubs* Pratts, Army and Navy; *Style—* Brig Dermot Blundell-Hollinshead-Blundell; Laughern Hill, Wichenford, Worcester

BLUNDEN, George Patrick; s of Sir George Blunden, of Hindringham, Norfolk, and Anne, *née* Bulford; *b* 21 Feb 1952; *Educ* St Edwards Sch Oxford, Univ Coll Oxford (BA); *m* 8 July 1978, Jane Rosemary, da of Gp Capt Charles Eric Hunter (d 1986); 1 s (George Edward Paul b 4 Aug 1982), 2 da (Victoria Jane b 10 Sept 1980, Eleanor Louise b 18 Sept 1985); *Career* dir: Seccombe Marshall & Campion 1983-86, S G Warburg Securities 1986-, S G Warburg Discount 1989-; memb: Family Welfare Assoc Almshouse Ctee, Sir Abraham Dawes Almshouses; tstee Samuel Lewis Housing Tst; Freeman City of London 1988; *Recreations* tennis, cricket, charity work; *Clubs* Reform, MCC; *Style—* George Blunden, Esq; S G Warburg Securities, 1 Finsbury Avenue, London EC2M 2PA (☎ 071 606 1066)

BLUNDEN, Hubert Chisholm; er s and h of Sir Philip Overington Blunden, 7 Bt; *b* 9 Aug 1948; *Educ* Avoca Sch Blackrock; *Career* 1 Bn Irish Guards; *Style—* Hubert Blunden Esq

BLUNDEN, Pamela, Lady; Pamela Mary; *née* Purser; da of John Purser, of Merton House, Dublin 6; *m* 1945, Sir William Blunden, 6 Bt (d 1985); 6 da; *Career* formerly 2 Offr WRNS; *Style—* Pamela, Lady Blunden; Castle Blunden, Kilkenny

BLUNDEN, Sir Philip Overington; 7 Bt (I 1766), of Castle Blunden, Kilkenny; s of Sir John Blunden, 5 Bt (d 1923); suc bro Sir Wm Blunden, 6 Bt (d 1985); *b* 27 Jan 1922; *Educ* Repton; *m* 1945, Jeanette Francesca Alexandra (WRNS), da of Capt Duncan Macdonald, RNR, of Portree, Isle of Skye; 2 s, 1 da; *Heir* s, Hubert Chisholm, *qv*; *Career* WWII 1942-45 with RN; estate mangr Castle Blunden 1948-62, mktg indust plastics 1962-83; now engaged in fine art restoration and painting; *Recreations* gardening, fishing, field sports, reading, painting; *Clubs* Royal Dublin Soc (Life Memb); *Style—* Sir Philip Blunden, Bt; 66 Lucan Heights, Lucan, Co Dublin

BLUNKETT, David; MP (Lab) Sheffield Brightside 1987-; s of Arthur Blunkett (d 1960), and Doris Matilda Elizabeth, *née* Williams (d 1983); *b* 6 June 1947; *Educ* Univ of Sheffield (BA); *m* (m dis 1990); 3 s (Alastair Todd b 27 March 1977, Hugh Sanders b 13 July 1980, Andrew Keir b 31 Oct 1982); *Career* clerk typist 1967-69; lectr and tutor in Industl Rels and Politics 1973-81, seconded 1981-87; ldr Sheffield City Cncl 1980-87 (memb 1970-88); *Books* Building from the Bottom (1983), Democracy in Crisis (1987); *Recreations* poetry, walking, music, sailing, being with friends; *Style—* David Blunkett, Esq, MP; Room 1, St Paul's Chambers, St Paul's Parade, Sheffield S1 2LJ; House of Commons, London SW1A 0AA (☎ 071 219 4043)

BLUNT, Sir David Richard Reginald Harvey; 12 Bt (GB 1720); s of Sir Richard David Harvey Blunt, 11 Bt (d 1975); *b* 8 Nov 1938; *m* 1969, Sonia Tudor Rosemary, da of late Albert Edward Day; 1 da; *Heir* kinsman, Robin Anthony Blunt; *Style—* Sir David Blunt, Bt; 74 Kirkstall Rd, SW2 4HF

BLUNT, Margaret, Lady; Margaret Constance; *née* Dean; da of John H Dean, of Nutbeam, Cirencester, Glos; *b* 19 April 1912; *m* 1943, as his 2 w, Sir Richard David Harvey Blunt, 11 Bt (d 1975); 2 da (Georgina b 1945, m 1981 Martin Trotter; Caroline b 1947); *Style—* Margaret, Lady Blunt

BLUNT, Oliver Simon Peter; s of Maj-Gen Peter John Blunt, CB, MBE, GM, of Harefield House, Ramsbury, Wilts, and Adrienne, *née* Richardson; *b* 8 March 1951; *Educ* Bedford Sch, Univ of Southampton (LLB); *m* 29 Sept 1979, Joanna Margaret, da of Robert Dixon (d 1985); 1 s (Sebastian b 1989), 2 da (Felicity b 1981, Emily b 1983); *Career* called to the Bar Middle Temple 1974; *Recreations* cricket, squash; *Clubs* Roehampton, Barnes Sports; *Style—* Oliver Blunt, Esq; 39 Crestway, Roehampton, London SW15 (☎ 081 788 5122); 2 Garden Court, Temple, London EC4 (☎ 071 583 0434, fax 071 353 3987)

BLUNT, Maj-Gen Peter; CB (1978), MBE (1955), GM (1959); s of Albert George Blunt (d 1952), and Claudia Wintle (d 1972); *b* 18 Aug 1923; *m* 5 March 1949, Adrienne, da of General T W Richardson; 3 s (Oliver, Robin, Crispin); *Career* joined army 1937, cmmnd Royal Fus, served DCLI and Royal Scots Fus 1946, Foreign Serv 1946-49, Staff Coll 1957, Jt Serv Staff Coll 1963, cmd 26 Regt Bridging 1965, GSO 1 Def Plans FARELF 1968, Cdr RCT 1 Corps 1970, RCDS 1972, dep tport offr-in-chief (Army), later tport offr-in-chief 1973, Asst CPL (Army) MOD 1977-78, ACDS (Personnel and Logistics) MOD 1978-79; md Earls Court Ltd 1979-80, exec vice chm Brompton and Kensington Special Catering Co Ltd 1979-80, jt md Angex-Watson 1980-83, chm and md Angex Ltd 1983-88 (non-exec chm 1988-89), dir Assoc Newspaper Hldgs plc 1984-89, non-exec chm Angus Shield Ltd; Col cmd RCT 1974-89, specially appointed cmmr Royal Hosp Chelsea 1979-88; Liveryman Worshipful Co of Carmen 1973; *Recreations* sea fishing; *Style—* Maj-Gen Peter Blunt, CB, MBE, GM; Harefield House, Crowood Lane, Ramsbury, Marlborough, Wiltshire SN8 2PT

BLUNT, Robin Anthony; s of Capt Charles William Lockhart Blunt (d 1958, 3 s of 8 Bt), and Lilian (d 1958), da of late C Calcutt, of Goudhurst, Kent; hp of kinsman, Sir David Blunt, 12 Bt; *b* 2 Feb 1926; *Educ* Wellington, Derby Tech Coll; *m* 1, 1949 (m dis 1962), Sheila Stuart, da of C Stuart Brindley; 1 s; m 2, 1962, June Elizabeth, da of Charles Wigginton, of Heckington, Lincs; 1 s; *Career* engineer; exec dir Rolls Royce (France) Ltd Paris (ret); CEng, MIMechE; *Recreations* golf, sailing; *Clubs* The Sloane; *Style—* Robin Blunt, Esq; Little Paddock, Fairacre, Lea, Malmesbury, Wiltshire

BLYTH, Hon Adrian Ulrick Christopher David; yr s of 3 Baron Blyth (d 1977); *b* 23 Oct 1944; *Educ* Sebright Sch, Northants Coll of Agric; *m* 1966, Patricia Maureen, da of Desmond C Southey, of Northampton; 2 s (Mark Terence b 1969, Ian Christopher b 1975), 3 da (Sarah Ursula b 1967, Verena Rosemary b 1971, Natasha Rachael b 1973); *Career* engine reconditioner; *Recreations* sailing, flying, scuba diving; *Clubs* Galway Bay Sailing, Galway Flying, Galway Sub Aqua; *Style—* The Hon Adrian Blyth; Torwood, Maree, Oranmore, Co Galway, Eire

BLYTH, 4 Baron (1907 UK); Sir Anthony Audley Rupert Blyth; 4 Bt (1895); s of 3 Baron Blyth (d 1977); *b* 3 June 1931; *Educ* St Columba's Coll, Dublin; *m* 1, 1954 (m dis 1962), Elizabeth Dorothea, da of Robert T Sparrow, of Vancouver, BC, Canada; 1 s, 2 da; m 2, 1963, Oonagh Elizabeth Ann, yr da of late William Henry Conway, of Dundrum, Dublin; 1 s (Hon James Audley Ian b 1970), 1 da (Hon Lucinda Audley Jane b 1966); *Heir* s, Hon Riley Blyth; *Style—* The Rt Hon the Lord Blyth; Blythwood Estate, Athenry, Co Galway, Eire

BLYTH, Charles (Chay); CBE (1972), BEM (1967); s of Robert Blyth (d 1971), and Jessie Pat, *née* Patterson (d 1965); *b* 14 May 1940; *Educ* Hawick HS; *m* 1962, Maureen Margaret, da of Albert Morris (d 1956); 1 da (Samantha b 1967); *Career* Sgt Para Regt 1958-67; Cadbury Schweppes 1968-69; md: Rainbow Charters Ltd 1974-, South West Properties Ltd 1978-, Crownfields Ltd 1985-; chm Silk Cut Awards Ctee 1983-; conslt Hill & Knowlton Ltd 1983-; *Books* A Fighting Change (1966), Innocent Aboard (1968), The Impossible Voyage (1971), Theirs is the Glory (1974); *Sporting Achievements* rowed North Atlantic with Capt John Ridgway 1966, solo circumnavigated the world westwards in yacht British Steel 1970-71, competed in Whitbread Round the World yacht race with crew in Great Britain II 1973-74 (winning Elapsed Time Prize), won Round Britain Race in Great Britain IV 1978, won two handed trans-Atlantic Race and broke existing record 1981, number one to Blue Riband attempt in Virgin Atlantic Challenge I and II 1985 and 1986, chm The British Steel Challenge; *Recreations* horse riding, skiing; *Clubs* Royal Southern Yacht, Royal Western Yacht, Royal Ocean Racing, Caledonian, Special Forces; *Style—* Chay Blyth, Esq, CBE, BEM; Hill Farm Cottage, 18 Highlands Rd, Fareham, Hampshire PO16 7BN

BLYTH, Kenneth William; s of Rev Canon Arthur Cecil Blyth (d 1961), of Cambridge, and Lorna Marjorie Iveson, *née* Campbell; *b* 6 Sept 1933; *Educ* Marlborough, St Johns Coll Cambridge (MA, PhD); *m* 18 July 1964, Ena, da of Roy Franey (d 1959), of London; 2 s (Thomas b 1966, Stephen b 1967); *Career* DSIR res studentship 1958-61, scientific staff Nat Inst of Industl Psychology 1961-62, asst dir Nuffield Fndn 1964-72 (joined 1962); sec: IBA 1988-90 (joined 1972, chief asst to dir gen 1979-88), ITC 1990-; *Style—* Kenneth Blyth, Esq; ITC, 70 Brompton Rd, London SW3 1EY (☎ 071 584 7011, telex 24345, fax 071 823 9033)

BLYTH, Dr Nicola; da of Peter Eden Blyth, of Sheffield, and Rosemary, *née* Goodswen; *b* 6 Oct 1956; *Educ* Maltby GS, Univ of Newcastle on Tyne (BSc), Univ of Canterbury NZ (PhD); *Career* econ Agric Econ Res Unit Lincoln NZ 1980-83, ACM Trade Policy and Export Mktg AMLC Sydney Australia 1983-86, conslt Agripac Incorp USA 1986-; dir: Blyth & Co Ltd 1987-, Tricolor Line 1989-, Tricolor Line International 1990-; dir Trg and Enterprise Cncl 1990-; MBIM, memb LCOSA 1983, AAES 1983, AFUW 1984, AES 1986; *Recreations* outdoor sports, farming, arts, cinema; *Style—* Dr Nicola Blyth; Stone Mill, Maltby, S Yorks S66 8NU (☎ 0709 812321); Blyth & Co Ltd, Industrial Estate, Carlton, Notts S81 9LB (☎ 0909 730807, fax 0909 731573)

BLYTH, Peter Eden; s of Edward Eden Blyth (d 1978), of Doncaster, S Yorks, and Irene Gertrude, *née* Foster (d 1985); *b* 14 April 1927; *Educ* King Edward VII Sch Sheffield; *m* 6 Sept 1952, Rosemary, da of Herbert Goodswen (d 1933), of Booton, Norfolk; 1 s (Eden John b 1954), 1 da (Nicola Ellen b 1956); *Career* served Army Intelligence Corps in India 1944-54, Capt; md and chm: E E Blyth & Co Ltd, Blyth Metals Ltd, Blyth Marble Ltd, Blyth USA Inc, Blyth Asia Pte Ltd, Moriera Santos & Blyth LDA (formerly Blyth Portugal Ltd) 1962-89; chm Br Microlight Aircraft Assoc 1984-89; *Style—* Peter E Blyth, Esq; Stone Mill, Maltby, S Yorkshire; E E Blyth & Co Ltd, Industrial Estate, Callton in Lindrick, Worksop, Notts (☎ 0909 731666, fax 0409 731573)

BLYTH, Hon Riley Audley John; s and h of 4 Baron Blyth; *b* 4 March 1955; *Style—* The Hon Riley Blyth

BLYTHE, Hon Mrs (Rachel Georgiana); yst da of 2 Baron Rennell; *b* 1 Nov 1935; *Educ* MA (Oxon); *m* 1964 (m dis 1983), Richard Douglas Gordon Blythe, er s of L Gordon Blythe, of 7 Karoo St, S Perth, W Australia; 2 s (Joseph b 1968, Matthew b 1970); *Style—* The Hon Mrs Blythe; 43 McMaster Street, Victoria Park, Perth, W Australia

BLYTHE, Ronald George; s of Albert George Blythe (d 1957), of Sudbury, Suffolk, and Matilda Elizabeth Elkins (d 1976); *b* 6 Nov 1922; *Educ* St Peter's and St Gregory's Sch Sudbury Suffolk; *Career* writer; reference librarian until 1954, full-time writer 1954-; books incl: A Treasonable Growth (1960), The Age of Illusion (history, 1963), Components of the Scene: Poems, Essays and Stories of the Second World War (1965), Akenfield (1969), Aldeburgh Anthology (1972), The View in Winter (1979), From the Headlands (1982), The Stories of Ronald Blythe (1985), Private Words: Letters and Diaries of the Second World War (1991); essays, stories, poems and reviews in newspapers and magazines; critical studies of: Jane Austen, Leo Tolstoy, Henry James, J C Powys, William Hazlitt, Thomas Hardy; films: A Painter in the Country (BBC2) 1968, Constable Observed 1969, Akenfield 1974; awards: Heinemann award 1969, Angel prize 1985; memb Centre of E Anglian Studies UEA 1972-76, chm Essex Festival 1981-83, pres The John Clare Soc 1981-; Hon MA Univ of E Anglia 1990; memb Soc of Authors (memb Eastern Arts lit Panel, memb Mgmnt Ctee 1970-79), FRSL 1969; *Recreations* gardening, walking, looking at architecture, plants and landscape; *Style—* Ronald Blythe, Esq; Bottengoms Farm, Wormingford, Colchester, Essex (☎ 0206 271308); Deborah Rogers Literary Agency, 20 Powis Mews, London W11 1JN (☎ 071 221 3717, fax 071 229 9084)

BLYTON, Carey; s of Hanly Harrison Blyton, and Florence Maud, *née* Pullen; *b* 1932; *Educ* Beckenham GS Kent, UCL, Trinity Coll of Music London (BMus), Royal Danish Acad of Music Copenhagen; *m* Mary Josephine Mills; 2 s (Matthew James, Daniel Carey); *Career* music ed: Mills Music Ltd 1958-63, Faber & Faber Ltd (now Faber Music Ltd) 1964-74; music lectr 1963-; prof of harmony counterpoint and orchestration Trinity Coll of Music 1963-73, visiting prof of composition for film TV and radio GSM London 1972-83, short story writer and nonsense poet, composer; piano music incl: Six Epigrams (1951), Three Impressions (1963-64); madrigals and partsongs incl: What Then is Love (1956), The Silly Flea (1962), In Lighter Mood (1972), A Nursery Song Suite (1985); song cycles incl: The Poetry of Dress (1956), Prayers from the Ark (1964-65); voice and chamber ensemble: Moresques (1952), The Maiden Deceived (1982); music for schs: Mixed Bag (1962-63), Sweeney Todd the Barber (1977), Dracula! (1983), Frankenstein! (1987); chamber music: Scherzo (1949), For the Delight of Shiva (1986); music for saxophone quartet incl: In Memoriam Scott Fitzgerald (1971), Suite Carolina (1984); music for brass: Eilgut-Galopp (1980), Sweet and Sour Rag (1983), Pasticheries (1987); music for orchestra: Cinque Port (1957-58), The Birds of the Air (1971); Overture: The Hobbit (1967); *Books* The Faber Book of Nursery Songs (1968), Bananas in Pyjamas (1972), Noah & the Unicorns (1979); *Recreations* keeping tropical fish, reading; *Clubs* The Aborigine; *Style—* Carey Blyton, Esq; 55 Goldsel Rd, Swanley, Kent BR8 8HA (☎ 0322 664380)

BNINSKI, Dr Kazimierz Andrey; s of Count Charles Felix Bninski - Mizgalski (d 1983), of Sopot Poland, and Countess Sophie, *née* de Saryusz - Woyciechowska; *b* 28 Feb 1939; *Educ* Univ of Gdańsk Poland (MD); *m* 2 July 1988, Teresa Maria, da of Baron Adam Andrew Maria de Bisping; 1 s (Paul Charles b 11 Oct 1989); *Career* sr house offr: Nelson Hosp London 1967-68, St Mary Abbots Hosp London 1969-71; registrar in med St Mary's Hosp and St Charle's Hosp London 1972-76, physician 7 US Army Germany 1977-80, jr ptnr gen practice 1981-88; dir i/c Polish Clinic Harley St London 1988-; *Style—* Dr Kazimierz Bninski; The Polish Clinic, 131 Harley Street, London W1 (☎ 071 580 4693)

BOADEN, Prof Noel Thomas; s of William Alfred Boaden (d 1960), of York, and Mabel Gladys, *née* Winspear (d 1981); *b* 19 Dec 1934; *Educ* LSE (BSc), Univ of Essex (MA), Univ of Liverpool (PhD); *m* 1, 31 Dec 1955 (m dis 1984), June Margaret, da of Percy Till, of York; 1 da (Jane b 22 May 1959); *m* 2, 14 Dec 1985, Margaret Elizabet Hierons; *Career* Nat Serv RAPC 1956 -58; lectr: Ipswich Civic Coll 1959-63, Chesterfield Tech Coll 1963-65; prof of continuing educn Univ of Liverpool 1985- (res fell 1967-71, 1971-75, sr lectr 1975-85); memb Exec Ctee UCACE, chm Cooperative Devpt Servs (Liverpool) Ltd; FRSA 1988; *Books* Urban Policy Making (1971), Public Participation in Planning (1980), Participation in Local Services (1981); *Style—* Prof Noel Boaden; 7 Monksferry Walk, Beechwood Pk, Liverpool L19 0PR (☎ 051 494 0349); University of Liverpool, PO Box 147, Liverpool L69 3BX (☎ 051 794 2528, fax 051 708 6502, telex 627 UNILPL G)

BOAITEY KWARTENG, Charlotte; da of Kwaku Yentumi Boaitey (d 1944), and Lydia, *née* Sarpong (d 1989); *b* 21 March 1944; *Educ* Univ of London (LLB), Lady Margaret Hall Oxford (Dip Social Anthropology); *m* 19 Oct 1972, Alfred Kwasi Kwarteng, s of Kodua Kwarteng; 1 s (Kwasi Addob b 26 May 1975); *Career* called to the Bar Middle Temple 1976, practising barr; conslt Disappearing World Granada TV 1982; *Recreations* visiting friends, swimming; *Style—* Ms Charlotte Boaitey Kwarteng; 12 Old Sq, Lincolns Inn, London WC2 3TX (☎ 071 404 0875)

BOAL, (John) Graham; s of Surgn-Capt Jackson Graham Boal (d 1958), and Dorothy Kenley, *née* Hall (d 1984); *b* 24 Oct 1943; *Educ* Eastbourne Coll, Kings Coll London (LLB); *m* 28 June 1978, Elizabeth Mary, da of Col LC East, DSO, OBE; 1 s (Thomas Henry b 1980); *Career* called to the Bar Grays Inn 1966, sr prosecuting counsel to Crown at Central Criminal Ct 1985-, rec Crown Ct 1985-; *Clubs* Garrick, Royal Wimbledon Golf, MCC; *Style—* Graham Boal, Esq; Queen Elizabeth Building, Temple, London EC4 (☎ 071 583 5766, fax 071 353 0339)

BOAM, Maj-Gen (Thomas) Anthony; CB (1987), CBE (1978, OBE 1973); s of Lt-Col T S Boam, OBE; *b* 1932; *m* 1961, Penelope Christine Mary, da of Cyril Alfred Roberts, CBE, DL, *qv*; 1 s, 2 da; *Career* cmmnd Scots Gds 1952; served: NI, Canal Zone Egypt, Kenya, Malaysia, W Germany (BAOR); cmd Br Army Trg Team Nigeria 1976-78, Dep Cdr and COS Hong Kong 1979-81, head Br Def Staff Washington and def attaché 1981-84, cmd Br Forces Hong Kong, Maj-Gen Bde of Gurkhas; memb Hong Kong Exec Cncl 1985-87, dir Br Conslts Bureau 1988-; *Recreations* fishing, shooting, gardening, sport, bridge; *Clubs* MCC; *Style—* Maj-Gen Anthony Boam, CB, CBE; Bury Gate House, Pulborough, West Sussex RH20 1HA (☎ 0798 831 440)

BOARD, (Clinton) Julian; s of Frederick E Board (d 1966), and Eve, *née* Howson; *b* 19 April 1937; *Educ* Oundle; *m* 23 Aug 1980, Elizabeth Jennifer, da of Lt-Col F W Pywell; *Career* dir several UK and overseas cos; landowner; FICA; *Recreations* cresta run, bobsleigh, skiing, estate mgmnt; *Clubs* The Sheffield, St Moritz Tobogganing (hon treas 1973-); *Style—* Julian Board, Esq; Longwood Court, Darley Dale, Derbyshire DE4 2HE; 39 Cloth Fair, London EC1A 7JQ; Fountain House, Broomgrove Rd, Sheffield S10 2LS (☎ 0742 664491); 4 York House, Turks Row, London SW3, (☎ 071 730 8941)

BOARD, Prof Kenneth; s of George Herbert Board, of Llanelli, and Beryl, *née* Roberts; *b* 15 April 1941; *Educ* Llanelli Boys GS, Univ of Wales (BSc, MSc, DSc), Univ of Bangor (PhD); *m* 30 July 1966, Meriel, da of Gwilyn Leonard Jones, of Bynea, Llanelli, Dyfed; 2 s (Meirion b 1973, Alun b 1976); *Career* res scientist GEC Hirst Res Centre, res scientist Philips Res Laboratory 1969-75, Univ of Wales: lectr 1975-82, sr lectr 1982-84, reader 1984-86, prof 1986-; MIEE 1976, MIEEE 1982; *Books* Introduction to Semiconductor Microtechnology (1983); *Recreations* squash, running, music; *Clubs* Clyne Golf; *Style—* Prof Kenneth Board; Dept of Electrical Engineering, University of Wales, Singleton Park, Swansea SA2 8PP (☎ 0792 295, telex 0792 295532)

BOARDLEY, Hon Mrs (Katherine Susan); *née* FitzRoy; da of 2 Viscount Daventry (d 1986); *b* 24 Aug 1923; *Educ* private schs; *m* 1, 1945 (m dis 1958), Phil John Turner, eld s of Phil Turner; m 2, 1958, Anthony Woodington Boardley (d 1967), yr s of late Bertie Welton Boardley; 1 s (Kevan Anthony FitzRoy b 1961); *Career* late Cadet Ensign FANY, served Ceylon/Singapore 1943-46; prog asst Gen Overseas Service BBC 1953-61; ed Who's Who of Southern Africa 1979-85; *Recreations* gardening, music; *Style—* The Hon Mrs Boardley; PO Box 1284, Kelvin, 2054 Transvaal, South Africa (☎ 010 27 11 802 7911)

BOARDMAN, Hon Anthony Hubert Gray; s of Baron Boardman; *b* 6 May 1949; *Educ* Ampleforth; *m* 1977, Catherine, da of Thomas William Penn, of Manor Farm, Denton, Northampton; 3 da; *Style—* The Hon Anthony Boardman; Lodge Farm, Hall Lane, Welford, Northants NN6 7JB

BOARDMAN, Sir John; s of Federick Archibald Boardman (d 1938), and Clare, *née* Wells (d 1975); *b* 20 Aug 1927; *Educ* Chigwell Sch, Magdalene Coll Cambridge (BA, MA, Walston student); *m* 26 Oct 1952, Shelia Joan Lyndon Stanford; 2 c (Julia b 1955, Mark b 1957); *Career* Mil Serv 2 Lt Intelligence Corps 1950-52; asst dir Br Sch of Athens 1952-55 (tstee), asst keeper Ashmolean Museum Oxford 1955-59, reader in classical archaeology Univ of Oxford 1959-78; Merton Coll Oxford: fell 1963-78, subwarden 1975-78, hon fell 1978, Lincoln prof 1978-; Geddes-Harrower prof Univ of Aberdeen 1974; visiting prof: Columbia Univ 1965, Aust Inst of Archaeology 1987; prof of ancient history Royal Acad of Arts 1990-; ed: Jl of Hellenic Studies 1958-65; Lexicon Iconographicum 1972-; conducted excavations on: Chios 1953-55, Crete, Tocra in Libya 1964-65; del OUP 1979, corr fell Bavarian Acad of Sciences 1969; fell: Inst of Etruscan Studies Florence 1983, Austrian and German Archaeological Insts; hon fell Magdalene Coll Cambridge 1984; foreign memb: Royal Danish Acad 1979, Acad'emie des Inscriptions et Belles Lettres Institut de France 1985; hon MRIA 1986; FSA 1957, FBA 1969; *awards* Cromer Greek prize Br Acad 1959; *pubns incl* Cretan Collection in Oxford (1961), Island Gems (1963), Archaic Greek Gems (1968), Athenian Black Figure Vases (1974), Harari Collection of Finger Rings (jtly with D Scarisbrick, 1978), Escarabeos de Piedra de Ibiza (1984), The Oxford History of the Classical World (jtly 1986), Athenian Red Figure Vases, Classcial Period (1989), articles in various learned jls; *Clubs* Athenaeum; *Style—* Sir John Boardman, FSA; 11 Park Street, Woodstock, Oxford, Oxon (☎ 0993 811259, fax 0685 278082)

BOARDMAN, Hon Nigel Patrick Gray; s of Baron Boardman; *b* 1950; *Educ* Ampleforth, Univ of Bristol; *m* 1975, Sarah, da of T A Coslett, of Cambridge; 1 s (Hugo b 1990), 5 da (Tamsin b 1980, Charlotte b 1981, Rebecca b 1984, Victoria b 1985, Cordelia b 1987); *Career* admitted slr 1975; ptnr Slaughter and May; *Style—* The Hon Nigel Boardman; London

BOARDMAN, Peter Laird; s of Dr Hedley Boardman, of 49 Chatsworth Court, Pembroke Rd, London W8 6DH, and Patricia, *née* Laird (d 1954); *b* 24 Feb 1934; *Educ* Wrekin Coll Wellington Shropshire, Queens' Coll Cambridge (MA), Westminster Hosp Med Sch (MD); *m* 21 Sept 1963, Hilary Barbara, da of Dr Ronald Jones, of Thorndon Hill, nr Eye, Suffolk; 1 s (Alan b 1969), 2 da (Hannah b 1966, Laura b 1968); *Career* sr registrar Westminster Hosp 1964-67, Buswell fell and res instr in med State Univ of NY Buffalo 1967-68, conslt physician Royal Shrewsbury Hosp 1968-; ex pres Midland Rheumatology Soc, memb Br Soc of Rheumatology; FRCP; *Recreations* hill walking, golf, reading, wine; *Style—* Peter Boardman, Esq; 3 Mayfield Park, Shrewsbury SY2 6PD (☎ 0743 232768); Royal Shrewsbury Hospital, Shrewsbury (☎ 0743 231122)

BOARDMAN, Baron (Life Peer UK 1980); Thomas Gray Boardman; MC (1944), TD (1952), DL (Northants 1977); s of John Clayton Boardman (d 1944), of Daventry, Northants, and Janet, *née* Houston; *b* 12 Jan 1919; *Educ* Bromsgrove Sch; *m* 1948, (Norah Mary) Deirdre, da of Hubert Vincent Gough, of Pangbourne, and wid of John Henry Chaworth-Musters, of Annesley Park, Nottingham; 2 s, 1 da; *Career* sits as Conservative in House of Lords; served WW II Northants Yeo, cmdg 1956; MP (C) Leicester SW 1967-74 & Leicester S Feb-Sept 1974; min for Indust 1972-74, chief sec Treasy 1974; jt treas Cons Pty 1981-82; High Sheriff Northants 1979; chm Steetley Co 1978-83; pres Assoc of Br Chambers of Commerce 1977-80; dir: MEPC Ltd 1980-89, Nat West Bank 1979-89 (chm 1983-89); *Style—* The Rt Hon Lord Boardman, MC, TD, DL; The Manor House, Welford, Northants NN6 7HX (☎ 0858 575235); Flat 29, Tufton Court, Tufton St, London SW1P 3QH (☎ 071 222 6793); House of Lords, Westminster, London SW1A 0PW (☎ 071 219 3000)

BOAS, (John) Robert Sotheby; s of Edgar Henry Boas, of Teddington, Middx, and Mary Katherine, *née* Beattie; *b* 28 Feb 1937; *Educ* Clifton, Corpus Christi Coll Cambridge; *m* 25 Sept 1965, (Karen) Elisabeth, da of Gunnar Gersted, of Copenhagen; 2 s (Christopher b 1972, Nicholas b 1975), 1 da (Helena b 1970); *Career* 2 Lt Royal Signals 1955-57; merchant banker Price Waterhouse 1960-64, ICI 1964-65; vice chm S G Warburg & Co Ltd 1990- (joined 1965, dir 1971-), non-exec dir Chesterfield Properties 1978-; bd memb The Securities Assoc 1988-; cncl memb The English Stage Co 1978-83, dir ENO 1990-; FCA; *Recreations* opera, theatre, reading; *Style—* Robert Boas, Esq; 5 Longwood Drive, London SW15 5DL (☎ 071 788 9667); 2 Finsbury Ave, London EC2M 2PA

BOASE, Martin; s of Prof Alan Martin Boase (d 1982), of Inverleith Place, Edinburgh, and Elizabeth Grizelle, *née* Forster (d 1977); *b* 14 July 1932; *Educ* Rendcomb Coll, New Coll Oxford (MA); *m* 1, Dec 1960 (m dis 1971), Terry-Ann, *née* Moir; 1 s (Daniel b 1962), 1 da (Rachel b 1964); m 2, 1974, Pauline Valerie, da of Lt-Col Philip Henry Akerman Brownrigg, CMG, DSO, OBE, TD, of Wheelers, Checkendon, nr Reading, Berks; 1 s (Luke b 1981), 1 da (Hannah b 1976); *Career* Russian interpreter Intelligence Corps 1951-53; md Pritchard Wood & Ptnrs 1967-68; fndr ptnr later chm The Boase Massimi Pollitt Ptnrship 1968-83; chm: Boase Massimi Pollitt plc 1983-, Omnicom UK plc 1989, Advertising Assoc 1987-; FIPA; *Recreations* the Turf; *Style—* Martin Boase, Esq; Omnicom UK plc, 54 Baker St, London W1 (☎ 071 486 7200)

BOATENG, Paul; MP (Lab) Brent South 1987-; s of Kwaku Boateng, of Ghana and England, and Eleanor, *née* McCombie; *b* 14 June 1951; *Educ* Accra Acad, Apsley GS, Univ of Bristol (LLB); *m* 1980, Janet, da of Leonard Alleyne; 3 da (Mirabelle b 1980, Beth b 1982, Charlotte b 1983), 2 s (Benjamin b 1984, Seth b 1987); *Career* admited slr 1976, slr Paddington Law Centre 1976-79, slr and ptnr BM Birnberg & Co 1979-87; called to the Bar Gray's Inn 1989, legal advsr Scrap Sus Campaign 1977-81, memb (Lab) for Walthamstow GLC 1981-85 (chm Police Ctee 1981-85, vice chm Ethnic Minorities Ctee 1981-85); Labour Party: memb NEC Sub-Ctee Human Rights 1979-83, Jt Ctee on Crime and Policing 1984-85; Parly candidate (Lab) Hertfordshire West 1983, memb House of Commons Environment Ctee 1987-89, oppn spokesman Treasy and Economic Affairs 1989-; chm: Afro-Caribbean Educn Resource Project 1978-86, Westminster CRC 1979-81; vice pres Waltham Forest CRC 1981; memb: Home Sec's Advsy Cncl on Race Relations 1981-86, World Cncl of Churches Cmmn Prog to Combat Racism 1984-91, Police Training Cncl 1981-85, Exec NCCL 1980-86; chm Govrs Priory Park Sch 1978-84, govr Police Staff Coll Bramshill 1981-84, memb Bd ENO 1984-; *Recreations* escapism; *Clubs* Mangrove, Black and White Café (Bristol); *Style—* Paul Boateng, Esq, MP; House of Commons, London SW1A 0AA

BOBROWSKI, Dr Jan Jozef; s of Aleksander Bobrowski (d 1987), of Poland, and Antonina, *née* Kandefer (d 1978); *b* 31 March 1925; *Educ* Univ of London, Battersea Coll of Advanced Technol (BSc), ACT (Battersea), Univ of Surrey (PhD); *m* 28 Aug 1954, Zofia, da of Boleslaw Kowalski (d 1972), of Poland; 1 da (Izabella Cecylia Antonina b 3 June 1957); *Career* Polish Corps 1942-47, 2 Lt 1945; practical design training with Twisteel Reinforcement Ltd 1952-53, pt/t lectr Battersea Coll of Advanced Technol 1952-58, engrg asst CJ Pell & Ptnrs 1953-58 (asst); chief engr: Pierhead Engrg Div of Unit Construction Co 1958-59, Pierhead Ltd 1959-62, Unit Construction Co 1961-62, Jan Bobrowski and Ptnrs 1962-; medal for contributions to prestressed concrete 1978, currently holds record for longest span concrete shell constructed at the Olympic Saddledome Calgary; visiting prof Imperial Coll of Sci &

Technol 1981; vice pres Univ of Surrey Soc, pres Concrete Soc 1986/7; vice pres: Inst of Structural Engrs 1985-86, (UK) Fedn Internationale Precontrainte; memb Euro-Int Du Beton Econ Devpt ctee; Freedom City of London 1977, Liveryman Worshipful Co of Constructors 1977; FEng 1983, FICE 1962, FIStructE 1973, MCSCE, Hon FICT, MConsE, MSocIS (France), PEng (Alberta and BC); Sovereign Military Order of St John of Jerusalem Knights of Malta 1984, Polish Army Medal 1945, Cross of Monte Cassino 1945, Polish Defence Medal 1945; *Books* author of numerous articles to tech jls; *Recreations* equestrianism, fishing; *Style—* Dr Jan Bobrowski; Grosvenor House, Grosvenor Road, Twickenham, Middlesex TW1 4AA (☎ 081 892 7627, fax 081 891 3151, telex 8954665 VBSTLX G JBP); 1004-8 Avenue SE, Calgary, Alberta, Canada T2G OM4

BOCHMANN, Michael Paul Boulter; s of Martin Paul Bochmann (d 1983), and Mary Beatrice Consitt, *née* Boulter; *b* 30 Sept 1953; *Educ* Burford GS, Royal Acad of Music; *Career* violinist; finalist and winner for Best British Entrant Carl Flesch Prize 1972; prize winner Jacques Thibaud Prize Paris 1973; ldr of Bochmann Quartet 1976-87; frequent broadcaster on BBC Radio, also BBC2 TV; in residence Southampton Univ 1983-87; ARAM; *Recreations* drawing, ornithology, calligraphy; *Style—* Michael P B Bochmann, Esq; 8 King Charles Court, Bath Rd, Worcester WR5 3HF (☎ 0905 763071)

BOCKSTOCE, Lady Romayne Bryony; *née* Grimston; da of 6 Earl of Verulam; *b* 18 Aug 1946; *m* 1973, John Roberts Bockstoce; 1 s; *Style—* Lady Romayne Bockstoce; 1 Hill St, S Dartmouth, Mass 02748, USA

BODDEN, John; s of Harry Bodden (d 1954), of Oldham, Lancs, and Catherine, *née* Wood (d 1969); *b* 15 May 1923; *Educ* Felsted, Univ of Manchester (BSc, BA), Wadham Coll Oxford; *m* 30 April 1988, Patricia Anne, *née* Harrod; *Career* Lt RNVR, Anti Submarine Electrical Branch RN 1943-46; slr and Notary Public 1949, sr ptnr Platt Bodden & Co and Butcher & Barlow (Manchester & Bury), chm and dir Ernest Broadbelt Investments Ltd, underwriting memb of Lloyds; tstee Oldham Foundation, memb Manchester City Cncl 1959-62, pres Bury and Dist Law Soc 1989; FRSA; *Recreations* golf; *Clubs* St James's (Manchester), Manchester Tennis and Racquet, Hale Golf; *Style—* John Bodden, Esq; 10 Woodhead Drive, Park Rd, Hale, Altrincham, Cheshire WA15 9LG (☎ 061 980 6061); Kensham, Moat Hill, Totnes, S Devon TQ9 5ER (☎ 0803 863491); Butcher & Barlow, Bank Street, Bury, Lancs BL9 ODL (☎ 061 764 4062)

BODDINGTON, (Robert) Christopher Hance; s of Lt Robert Evelyn Boddington, RN (ka 1942), of Peterchurch, Herefordshire, and Heather Elizabeth Bryant, *née* Hance (d 1989); *b* 4 May 1941; *Educ* Rugby, The Queen's Coll Oxford (MA); *m* 21 Sept 1963 (m dis 1983), (Mary) Jane, da of John Baughn Wiggs (d 1973), of Bournemouth; 2 da (Naomi b 1964, Lucia b 1965); *Career* admitted slr 1966; slr: Western Sons & Neave 1966-69, McKenna & Co 1969-72; ptnr: Ziman and Co 1972-77, Nabarro Nathanson 1977-; commercial lawyer in field of corp fin; memb Law Soc 1966; *Recreations* travel, opera, food; *Clubs* Brooks's; *Style—* Christopher Boddington, Esq; 50 Stratton St, London W1X 5FL (☎ 071 493 9933, fax 071 629 7900, telex 8813144)

BODDINGTON, Ewart Agnew; JP (1955-); s of (Charles) Geoffrey Boddington (d 1982), and Edith Norah, MBE, *née* Agnew (d 1990); *b* 7 April 1927; *Educ* Stowe, Trinity Coll Cambridge (MA); *m* 1954, (Vine) Anne, da of Louis Arthur Hubert Clayton (d 1969); 2 s, 1 da; *Career* exec chm Boddingtons' Breweries plc 1970-88, chm Brewers Soc 1985-, pres Inst of Brewing 1972-74, dir Nat Westminster Bank (northern bd) 1977-; Hon MA Univ of Manchester; *Recreations* shooting, fishing, golf; *Style—* Ewart A Boddington, Esq, JP; Fanshawe Brook Farm, Henbury, Macclesfield, Cheshire SK11 9PP (☎ 0260 244387)

BODEN, John James (Jim); s of Dick Boden (d 1979), of Ashbourne, Derbyshire, and Betty, *née* Bayliss; *b* 11 July 1947; *Educ* Denstone Coll, Univ of Liverpool (LLB); *m* 21 July 1975, Patricia Jane, da of Dr Philip William Bowden, of Brailsford, Derbyshire; 1 s (Andrew b 1978), 1 da (Nicola b 1980); *Career* slr of the Supreme Court; dir Nottingham Conveyancers Ltd; former memb Ashbourne UDC; *Recreations* country sports; *Style—* Jim Boden, Esq; Brook Farm, Cubley, nr Ashbourne, Derbyshire DE6 2EZ (☎ 0335 23451); 158 High Rd, Beeston, Nottingham NG9 2LZ (☎ 0602 258277)

BODEN, Kenneth Henry Edmund; s of Henry James Randolph Boden (d 1982, formerly 4QOH and Inspr Palestine Police), and Ada Dorothy, *née* Hazle; *b* 15 Dec 1941; *Educ* Southend HS for Boys Southend on Sea; *m* 20 Sept 1969, June Irene, da of Harold Gibbs, of London; *Career* underwriters clerk Gardner Mountain D'Ambrumenil and Rennie Lloyds Insur Brokers 1958, marine cargo surveyor Insur Co of N America 1966-68, dep marine underwriter at Lloyds for Laurence Philipps Agencies 1968-80, active underwriter 1980-; memb: Round Table until 1982, Assoc of Ex-Tablers Club; ACII 1968; memb Lloyd's 1978; *Recreations* skiing, travel, gardening, cage birds; *Clubs* 41; *Style—* Kenneth Boden, Esq; Box 043, Lloyds, London (☎ 071 623 7100 ext 3765)

BODEN, Prof Margaret Ann; da of Leonard Forbes Boden, OBE, (d 1986), of London, and Violet Dorothy, *née* Dawson (d 1967); *b* 26 Nov 1936; *Educ* City of London Sch for Girls, Newnham Coll Cambridge (MA), Harvard Graduate Sch for Arts and Sciences (AM, PhD); *m* 24 June 1967 (m dis 1981), John Raymond Spiers; 1 s (Ruskin b 1968), 1 da (Jehane b 1972); *Career* lectr Univ of Birmingham 1959-65, prof in philosophy and psychology Univ of Sussex 1980- (lectr and reader 1959-65), founding dean Sch of Cognitive and Computing Sci Univ of Sussex 1987; co fndr Harvester Press Ltd 1969; memb: Cncl for Sci and Society, Mind Assoc, Aristotelian Soc, Royal Inst of Philosophy (memb Cncl 1988-), Br Psychological Soc, American Assoc for Artificial Intelligence, Br Soc for Philosophy of Science, advsy Bd Res Cncls 1989-; chm Cncl Science and Society Working Pty on Benefits and Dangers of Knowledge-Based Systems 1987-88; Hon ScD Univ of Cambridge 1990; FBA (1983, memb Cncl 1988-), vice pres Br Acad 1989; *Books* Purposive Explanation in Psychology (1972), Artificial Intelligence and Natural Man (1977), Piaget (1979), Minds and Mechanisms (1981), Computer Models of Mind (1988), Artificial Intelligence in Psychology (1989), The Philosophy of Artificial Intelligence (1990); *Recreations* dress-making, travel; *Clubs* Reform; *Style—* Prof Margaret Boden; School of Cognitive and Computing Sciences, Univ of Sussex, Brighton (☎ 0273 606755)

BODEN, Peter Horrox; s of Albert Boden (d 1931), of Romiley, Cheshire, and Lucy Isabel, *née* Horrox; *b* 19 April 1926; *Educ* Cheadle Hulme Sch, Univ of London (BSc, LLB), Univ of Manchester (cert of educn); *Career* called to the Bar Gray's Inn 1965; Miny of Labour 1943-57, lectr Coll of Commerce Birmingham Poly 1958-66, head of dept N Tyneside Coll 1966-88; pubns incl: Revision Notes in English Law; *Clubs* Whitley Bay Pantomime Soc, Playhouse Players; *Style—* P H Boden, Esq; 14 Kingston Drive, Whitley Bay, Tyne and Wear NE26 1JH (☎ 091 252 4660)

BODILLY, Lt Cdr Sir Jocelyn; VRD; s of Cdr Ralph Burland Bodilly, RN, of Trenarren, Alverton, Penzance, Cornwall, and Sybil Bodilly; *b* 15 Sept 1913; *Educ* Munro Coll Jamaica, Schloss Schule Salem Baden Germany, Wadham Coll Oxford; *m* 1, 1936, Phyllis Maureen (d 1963), da of Thomas Cooper Gotch; m 2, 1964, Marjorie, da of Walter Fogg, of St Helens, Lancs; *Career* RNVR 1937-56, Lt Cdr (S), served WWII; called to the Bar Inner Temple 1937; judge High Court Sudan 1946-55, crown counsel Hong Kong 1955, princ crown counsel Hong Kong 1961, law draftsman Hong Kong 1964, chief justice Western Pacific 1965-75, chm Industrial Tbnls for London (S) 1976-86; kt 1969; *Clubs* Royal Ocean Racing; *Style—* Lt Cdr Sir Jocelyn Bodilly, VRD, RNVR; Myrtle Cottage, St Peter's Hill, Newlyn, Penzance, Cornwall TR18 5EQ

BODIWALA, Gautam Govindlal; JP; s of Dr Govindlal R Bodiwala (d 1983), of Ahmedabad, India, and Sumanben, *née* Parikh; *b* 11 Oct 1943; *Educ* Univ of Gujarat (MB BS, MS); *m* 28 Dec 1969, Gita, da of Prabhulal G Thanawala, of Thana, India; 1 s (Dhaval b 1973), 1 da (Janki b 1977); *Career* conslt and head of Accident and Emergency Serv Leicester 1977-; hon treas Casualty Surgns Assoc, memb Rotary Int; memb: BMA, American Coll of Emergency Physicians; FRSM; fell: Int Coll of Surgns, Int Coll of Angiology; *Recreations* music and reading; *Clubs* Rotary (Oadby); *Style—* Gautam Bodiwala, Esq, JP; Lykkebo, 7 Blackthorn Lane, Oadby, Leicester LE2 4FA (☎ 0533 718899); Accident and Emergency Dept, Leicester Royal Infirmary, Infirmary Close, Leicester LE1 5WW (☎ 0533 541414)

BODMER, Sir Walter Fred; s of Dr Ernest Julius Bodmer (d 1968), and Sylvia Emily, *née* Bodmer; *b* 10 Jan 1936; *Educ* Manchester GS, Univ of Cambridge (BA, PhD); *m* 1956, Julia Gwynaeth, da of William Gwyn Pilkington (d 1976); 2 s (Mark, Charles), 1 da (Helen); *Career* Univ of Cambridge: res fell Clare Coll 1958-60, official fell 1961, demonstrator Dept of Genetics 1960-61; prof Dept of Genetics Stanford Univ Sch of Med 1968-70 (asst prof 1962-66, assoc prof 1966-68), prof of genetics Univ of Oxford 1970-79; dir of res Imperial Cancer Res Fund 1979-; pres: Br Soc for Histocompatibility and Immunogenetics 1990-91, Human Genome Orgn 1990-; chm: Ctee on Public Understanding of Sci 1990-, Science Consultative Gp BBC 1981-87; memb Advsy Bd for the Res Cncls 1983-88, Orgn of Euro Cancer Insts 1990; tstee: Br Museum (Nat History) 1983- (chm 1988-), Sir John Soane's Museum, Gtr Manchester Museum of Sci and Indust 1989-90; vice pres Royal Instn 1982-82; hon fell: Keble Coll Oxford, Clare Coll Cambridge 1989; pres: Royal Statistical Soc 1984-85, Br Assoc for the Advancement of Sci 1987-88, Assoc for Science Educn 1989; William Allan Meml Award 1980, Conway Evans Prize 1982, Rabbi Shai Shacknai Meml Prize Lectureship in Immunology and Cancer Res 1983, John Alexander Meml Prize Lectureship 1984, Rose Payne Distinguished Scientist Lectureship 1985; Laurea Honoris Causa in Medicine and Surgery Univ of Bologna 1987; Hon DSc: Univ of Bath 1988, Univ of Oxford 1988, Univ of Edinburgh 1990, Univ of Hull 1990; hon memb American Assoc of Immunologists; foreign memb: Czechoslovak Acad of Sciences 1988-, American Philisophical Soc USA 1989; foreign hon memb American Acad of Arts and Scis, foreign assoc US Nat Acad Scis, FRCPath, Hon FRCP, Hon FRCS, FRS; kt 1986; *Books* The Genetics of Human Populations (with L Cavalli-Sforza, 1971), Our Future Inheritance: Choice or Chance? (with A Jones, 1974), Genetics, Evolution and Man (with L Cavalli-Sforza, 1976); *Recreations* playing the piano, riding, swimming; *Clubs* Athenaeum; *Style—* Sir Walter Bodmer, FRS; 44 Lincoln's Inn Fields, London WC2A 3PX (☎ 071 242 0200); Imperial Cancer Res Fund, PO Box 123, Lincoln's Inn Fields, London WC2A 3PX (☎ 071 242 0200, telex 265107 ICRF G)

BODSWORTH, Prof Colin; s of George William Bodsworth (d 1971), of Sheffield, and Daisy Mary, *née* Gregory; *b* 10 Aug 1924; *Educ* Univ of Sheffield (BMet, MMet, PhD); *m* 9 July 1949, Muriel, da of William Henry Ashforth (d 1984); 1 s (David Gordon b 15 Nov 1957); *Career* WWII Somerset Light Inf and RCS 1944-47; mgmnt apprentice United Steel Cos Ltd 1940-44, lectr in metallurgy Univ of Liverpool 1950-64, chief physical metallurgist Richard Thomas & Baldwins Ltd 1964-65, res prof Brunel Univ 1988-90 (head Dept of Metallurgy 1965-82, vice-princ 1973-75, dean of technol 1982-88, prof emeritus 1990-); chm Accreditation Ctee of Inst of Metals 1987-90 (memb Cncl 1977-80, pres 1980-83), memb Engrg Ctee 4 and Ctee of Engrg Cncl; CEng, FIM 1958; *Books* Physical Chemistry of Iron and Steel Making (1963), Problems in Applied Thermodynamics (1965); *Recreations* gardening, walking, archeology; *Style—* Prof Colin Bodsworth; 52 Mayflower Way, Farnham Common, Bucks SL2 3UB (☎ 075364 3172); Department of Materials Technology, Brunel University, Uxbridge, Middx UB8 3PH (☎ 0895 74000, telex 261173 G, 0895 32806)

BODY, Sir Richard Bernard Frank Stewart; MP (C) Holland with Boston 1966-; s of Lt-Col Bernard Richard Body, of Donnington, Berkshire, and Daphne Mary Eleanor, *née* Corbett; *b* 18 May 1927; *Educ* Reading Sch; *m* 1959, (Doris) Marion, da of late Maj Harold John Graham, OBE, of Midhurst Sussex; 1 s, 1 da; *Career* called to the Bar 1949; MP (C) Billericay 1955-59, Lloyd's underwriter 1979-; kt 1986; *Books* Agriculture: The Triumph and the Shame (1982), Farming in the Clouds (1984), Red or Green for Farmers (and the Rest of Us) (1987), Europe of Many Circles (1990); *Recreations* hunting with own pack of bloodhounds; *Clubs* Carlton, Reform, Farmers'; *Style—* Sir Richard Body, MP; Jewell's Farm, Stanford Dingley, Reading, Berks (☎ 0734 744295)

BOE, Norman Wallace; s of Alexander Thomson Boe, of Edinburgh, and Margaret Wallace, *née* Revans; *b* 30 Aug 1943; *Educ* George Heriot's Sch, Univ of Edinburgh (LLB); *m* 9 Aug 1968, Margaret Irene, da of Alexander McKenzie; 1 s (Douglas), 1 da (Sheila); *Career* office of slr to Sec of State for Scotland: legal asst 1970-73, sr legal asst 1973-82, divnl slr 1982-87, dep slr 1987; *Recreations* golf, badminton, dog walking; *Clubs* Edinburgh Univ Staff; *Style—* Norman Boe, Esq; Solicitor's Office, Scottish Office, New St Andrew's House, Edinburgh, Lothian (☎ 031 244 4884)

BOEVEY; see Crawley-Boevey

BOGDANOR, Vernon; s of Harry Bogdanor (d 1971), of Oxford, and Rosa, *née* Weinger (d 1987); *b* 16 July 1943; *Educ* Queen's Coll Oxford (BA, MA); *m* 23 July 1972, Judith Evelyn, da of Frederick Beckett (d 1985), of Oxford; 2 s; *Career* sr tutor Brasenose Coll Oxford 1979-85 (fell 1966-), special advsr House of Lord's Select Ctee on Euro Communities 1982-83, reader in govt Univ of Oxford 1990-; memb: Political Studies Assoc 1966-, Cncl Hansard Soc for Parly Govt, Nat Ctee for Electoral Reform 1981-, Court Univ of Essex 1982-84; *Books* incl: The Age of Affluence 1951-64 (jt ed, 1970), Devolution (1979), The People and the Party System (1981), Liberal Party Politics (ed, 1983), Multi-Party Politics and the Constitution (1983), Science and Politics (ed, 1984), The Blackwell Encyclopaedia of Political Institutions (ed, 1987); *Recreations* music, walking, talking; *Style—* Vernon Bogdanor, Esq; Brasenose College, Oxford OX1 4AJ (☎ 0865 277830, fax 0865 277822)

BOGDANOV, Michael; s of Francis Benzion Bogdin (d 1962), and Rhoda, *née* Rees; *b* 15 Dec 1938; *Educ* Lower Sch of John Lyon, Harrow, Trinity Coll Dublin (MA), Univ of Munich, Sorbonne; *m* 17 Dec 1966, Patricia Ann, da of Walter Stanley Warwick (d 1985); 2 s (Jethro Rhys Warwick b 1968, Malachi Taplin b 1969), 1 da (Ffion b 1971); *Career* artistic dir: Phoenix Theatre Leicester 1973-77, Young Vic 1978-80; assoc dir National Theatre 1980-, artistic dir and fndr English Shakespeare Co 1986-; Intendant Deutsches Schauspielhaus Hamburg 1989-; Dir of the Year: SWET Award 1979, Laurence Olivier Awards 1989; outstanding achievement Drama Awards 1987, Melbourne Spoleto Golden Pegasus Award 1988; *Recreations* sport, music, Celtic languages, wine; *Clubs* Lord's Taverners; *Style—* Michael Bogdanov, Esq; The ESC, 369 St John St, London EC1V 4LB (☎ 071 278 7970)

BOGGIS-ROLFE, Richard; s of Paul Boggis-Rolfe (d 1988), of 54 Rue du Faubourg St Honoré, 75008 Paris, France, and (Anne) Verena, *née* Collins; *b* 5 April 1950; *Educ* Eton, Trinity Coll Cambridge (MA), London Business Sch; *m* 7 March 1987, Lucy Elisabeth, da of Lt-Col Stephen Jenkins, MC, DL, of Ballingers House, Hampnett,

Glos; 2 da (Elisabeth Verena b 1988, Alice Catherine b 1990); *Career* cmmnd Coldstream Gds 1970, ADC to Lt Gen Sir Richard Worsley (GOC 1 (Br) Corps) 1975-77, Co Cdr 1977-79, Staff Capt QMG MOD 1979-80, ret Hon Maj 1980; dir: Russell Reynolds Associates 1983, Norman Broadbent International Ltd 1984; md: Norman Broadbent (Hong Kong) 1986, NB Selection Ltd 1987-; Freeman City of London, Liveryman Worshipful Co of Pewterers; *Recreations* hunting, travel; *Clubs* Brooks's, Beefsteak, Pratt's; *Style*— Richard Boggis-Rolfe, Esq; The Glebe House, Shipton Moyne, Tetbury, Glos (☎ 0666 88441); 15 Brechin Place, London SW7 (☎ 071 373 5910); L'Hermitage, Basse Nouailette, Hautefort, Dordogne, France (☎ 010 33 53504371); 54 Jermyn St, London SW1 (☎ 071 493 6392, fax 071 409 1786)

BOGIE, Sheriff David Wilson; s of Robert T Bogie (d 1978), of Edinburgh, and Isobel, *née* Wilson; *b* 17 July 1946; *Educ* George Watson's Coll, Grenoble Univ, Edinburgh Univ (LLB), Balliol Coll Oxford (MA); *m* April 1983 (m dis 1987), Lady Lucinda Louise Mackay, da of 3 Earl of Inchcape; *Career* admitted memb of Faculty of Advocates 1972, temp Sheriff 1981; Sheriff of Grampian, Highland and Islands at Aberdeen and Stonehaven 1985; FSA Scot; *Clubs* Brooks's, New (Edinburgh), Royal Northern and Univ (Aberdeen); *Style*— Sheriff D W Bogie; 50 Whitehall Rd, Aberdeen; 31 Mortonhall Rd, Edinburgh; Sheriff's Chambers, Aberdeen

BOGLE, David Blyth; CBE (1967), WS (1927); s of late Very Rev Andrew Nisbet Bogle, and Helen Milne Bogle; *b* 22 Jan 1903; *Educ* George Watson's Coll Edinburgh, Univ of Edinburgh (MA, LLB); *m* 1955, Ruth Agnes, *née* Nicolson; *Career* cmmnd Queen's Own Cameron Highlanders 1940, served UK and ME 1942-45, demobbed Maj 1945; slr; former sr ptnr Lindsays WS Edinburgh; chm Scots Ctee 1962-70, memb Cncl on Tbnls 1958-70; *Recreations* RNIB, talking, books; *Clubs* New (Edinburgh); *Style*— David Bogle, Esq, CBE, WS; 3 Belgrave Cres, Edinburgh (☎ 031 332 0047)

BOGLE, Joanna Margaret; da of Herbert Eric Nash, of Wallington Surrey, and Ursula Mary, *née* Campbell; *b* 7 Sept 1952; *Educ* St Philomena's Sch Carshalton Surrey; *m* 20 Sept 1980, James Stewart Lockhart Bogle, s of Brig Bruce Lockhart Bogle; *Career* journalist author and broadcaster; cncllr London Borough of Sutton 1974-82, Conservative Res Dept 1978-79; reg contrib to: Daily Telegraph, Daily Mail, Universe, various US and Australian papers; lecture tours USA 1976, 1977, 1986 and 1987; Women of the Year speaker 1975 (as Britain's youngest borough cncllr); *Books* (1975-80): The First Croydon Airport, The Great Days Croydon Airport 1928-39, Croydon Airport and the Battle for Britain; A Book of Feasts and Seasons (1986), Celebrating Our Heritage (1988), Who Lies Where (1989), A Heart for Europe - a life of Emperor Charles and Empress Zita of Austria-Hungary (with James Bogle, 1991), numerous political and religious pamphlets; FRSA 1988; *Recreations* family life: nieces and nephews; eating chocolate cake, walking in rain; *Style*— Mrs Joanna Bogle

BOHM, Nicholas David Frederick; s of Franz Bohm, and Johanna Cecilia, *née* Bauer; *b* 12 July 1943; *Educ* Leighton Park Sch Reading, St John's Coll Cambridge (MA); *m* Carola Ann, *née* Freeman; 5 c; *Career* asst slr Gregory Rowcliffe & Co 1968-70 (articled clerk 1966-68); ptnr: Edward Moeran & Partners 1970-72, Norton Rose 1975- (asst slr 1972-75); Freeman City of London, memb City of London Solicitors' Co; *Recreations* rough gardening; *Style*— Nicholas Bohm, Esq; Salkyns, Great Canfield, Dunmow, Essex (☎ 0279 870285); Norton Rose, Kempson House, Camomile St, London EC3A 7AN (☎ 071 283 2434)

BOHT, Jean; da of Thomas Herbert Dance (d 1970), of Birkenhead, and Edna May, *née* McDonald (d 1989); *b* 6 March 1936; *Educ* Wirral GS for Girls Bebington, Hilary Burrow's Ballet Sch Liverpool; *m* 1 (m dis 1970), William P Boht (d 1975); m 2, 1971, Carl Davis; s of Irving Davis (d 1988); 2 da (Hannah Louise b 1 Jan 1972, Jessie Jo b 3 May 1974); *Career* actress; theatre work incl: Liverpool Playhouse 1962-64, Bristol Old Vic Co 1964, season Royal Ct Theatre 1965-66, seasons Library Theatre Manchester 1966-67, season NT 1968 and 1971, Lincoln Theatre Royal 1969, Joan Littlewood's Theatre Workshop 1969-71; roles incl: *West End* St Joan of the Stockyards (Queens Theatre London) 1964, Steel Magnolias (Lyric Theatre) 1990, Bread (Dominion Theatre) 1990-91, *Fringe Theatres* Kennedy's Children (Kings Head Islington) 1974, Mecca (Open Space) 1977, Wednesday (Bush Theatre) 1979, Touched and To Come Home To This (Royal Ct Theatre) 1980, Birds of Passage (Hampstead Theatre) 1983, Lost (Bush Theatre) 1986; TV plays incl: Where Adam Stood, Cranford, Eskimos Do It; films incl: Middle Not With Change, Distant Voices, Girl On A Swing, Arthur's Hallowed Ground; tv credits and series incl: Funny Man, Spyship, Sons and Lovers, Boys From The Black Stuff, Scully, I Woke Up One Morning, Bread; many guest appearances in comedy series, game shows, charity tv shows and radio plays; recorded The Pigeon (by Carla Lane) 1990; *Awards* BBC TV Personality 1988 (Variety Club of GB), Top Comedy Television Actress 1990 (The Br Comedy Awards), Top Television Personality 1990 (Whitbread Scouseology Awards); memb BAFTA; *Recreations* artistic dir of Barnes Theatre Co (an amateur gp for teenagers formed in 1985); *Style*— Miss Jean Boht

BOILEAU, Lt-Col Sir Guy Francis; 8 Bt (UK 1838); s of Sir Edmond Charles Boileau, 7 Bt (d 1980); *b* 23 Feb 1935; *Educ* Xavier Coll Melbourne, RMC Duntroon Aust; *m* 1962, Judith Frances, da of Sen George Conrad Hannan, of Glen Iris, Canberra; 2 s, 3 da; *Heir* s, Nicolas Boileau; *Career* Lt-Col Australian Army; co dir; *Style*— Lt-Col Sir Guy Boileau, Bt; 14 Faircroft Ave, Glen Iris, Victoria 3146, Australia

BOILEAU, Mary, Lady; Mary Catherine; da of late Lawrence Riordan, of Cradock, S Australia; *m* 1941, as his 2 w, Maj Sir Gilbert Boileau, 6 Bt (d 1978); 3 da; *Style*— Mary, Lady Boileau; Minto Lodge, 1480 Heatherston Rd, Dandenong, Victoria, Australia

BOILEAU, Nicolas Edmond George; s and h of Lt-Col Sir Guy Boileau, 8 Bt; *b* 17 Nov 1964; *Style*— Nicolas Boileau, Esq

BOISSIER, Roger Humphrey; 3 and yst s of Ernest Gabriel Boissier, DSC (d 1976), of Derby, and Doris Mary, *née* Bingham (d 1958); descended from Gaspard Boissier (d 1705), of Geneva, whose grandson Jean-Daniel Boissier (d 1770), settled in England at Lime Grove, Putney (*see* Burke's Landed Gentry, 18 edn, vol I, 1965); *b* 30 June 1930; *Educ* Harrow; *m* 30 Oct 1965, (Elizabeth) Bridget Rhoda, eldest da of Sir Gerald Gordon Ley, 3 Bt, TD (d 1980); (see Debrett's Peerage & Baronetage, 1980); 1 s (Rupert John b 25 May 1967), 1 da (Clare Louise b 16 Nov 1968); *Career* md Aiton & Co Ltd 1971-83; exec dir Whessoe plc 1976-83; dir: Derbyshire Building Society 1972-81, Ley's Foundries and Engineering plc 1977-82, Simmonds Precision NV (Holland), British Gas plc 1981-, Pressac Holdings plc 1984- (dep chm 1989, chm 1990), T & N plc 1987-, Edward Lumley Holdings Ltd 1988-, Severn-Trent plc 1989-, conslt Allott & Lomax 1984-, a vice pres Br Jr Chambers of Commerce 1961-64; High Sheriff of Derbyshire 1987-88; Master Worshipful Co of Tin Plate Workers (alias Wire Workers) 1988-89; govr Harrow Sch 1976- (dep chm 1988); *Clubs* City Livery, MCC, County (Derby); *Style*— Roger Boissier, Esq; Easton House, The Pastures, Repton, Derby DE6 6GG (☎ 0283 702274, fax 0283 701489)

BOIZOT, Peter James; MBE; s of Gaston Charles Boizot, and Susannah, *née* Culshaw; *b* 16 Nov 1929; *Educ* King's Sch Peterborough, St Catharine's Coll Cambridge (MA); *Career* Nat Serv 1948-50, commissioned RASC; fndr, chm and md Pizza Express Ltd 1965; fndr memb Soho Soc, pres Hampstead & Westminster Hockey Club, chm Soho Restauranteurs Assoc, vice chm Westminster Chamber of Commerce (former memb Cncl), former pres Eastern Region Liberal Party; dir Soho Jazz Festival 1986-91; FCHIMA 1989; Cavaliere Ufficiale Della Repubblica Italiana Al Ordine Del Merito (1983); *Books* Pizza Express Cook Book (1976); *Recreations* hockey, jazz; *Clubs* RAC, National Liberal; *Style*— Peter Boizot, Esq, MBE; 10 Lowndes Square London SW1X 9HA (☎ 01 235 9100); Kettners Restaurant, 29 Romilly Street, London W1V 6HP (☎ 071 437 6437, fax 071 434 1214, car 0836 209 142)

BOL, Lt-Col George Philip; s of Paulus Willem Bol (d 1963), and Petronella Johanna Jacoba van der Graaf (d 1962); *b* 3 Aug 1922; *Educ* Hogere Burger Sch (Leiden, Nijmegen), Mons, Aldershot; *m* 5 Oct 1963, Muriel Evelyn, da of Henry William Clarke (d 1954); *Career* Army Offr Royal Netherlands Army 1945-77; served UK 1945-46, Indonesia 1946-50, Netherlands 1950-62; SO HQN Army Gp Germany 1962-65, Netherlands 1965-70; SO HQ Chief GS 1970-77; *Style*— Lt-Col George P Bol; The Manor House, Worstead, Norfolk NR28 9SD (☎ 0692 536186)

BOLAND, John Anthony; s of Daniel Boland, MBE (d 1973), of Dublin, and Hannah, *née* Barton (d 1982); *b* 23 Jan 1931; *Educ* Castleknock Coll Co Dublin, Xavier Sch Dublin, Christian Brothers Dublin, Trinity Coll Dublin (MA, LLB); *m* 21 Oct 1972, Ann Mary, da of James C Doyle (d 1990); *Career* called to the Bar Middle Temple 1956; called to Irish Bar King's Inn Dublin 1967; Public Tstee Office London: joined 1956, chief admin offr 1974-79, asst public tstee 1979-80, public tstee 1980-87, public tstee and accountant gen 1987-; asst ed The Supreme Ct Practice, hon memb Coll Historical Soc Trinity Coll Dublin, tstee Trinity Coll Univ of Dublin Tst; chm: London Ctee Irish Sch of Ecumenics of Dublin, Tst Section Holborn Law Soc; *Recreations* walking, foreign travel, study of history; *Clubs* Kildare Street, University (Dublin); *Style*— John Boland, Esq; Stewart House, Kingsway, London WC2B 6JX (☎ 071 269 7010, fax 071 831 0060)

BOLD, Alan Norman; s of William Bold (d 1956), of Edinburgh, and Marjorie Urquhart Wilson (d 1983); *b* 20 April 1943; *Educ* Broughton Secdy Sch, Univ of Edinburgh; *m* 29 June 1963, Alice, *née* Howell; 1 da (Valentina b 5 April 1964); *Career* journalist The Times Educational Supplement Scotland 1965-66, full time writer and visual artist 1966-; reg contribs to The Sunday Times, currently reviewer The Glasgow Herald; exhibitions of illuminated poems: Univ of Boston, Nat Library of Scotland, Cheltenham Festival, Poetry Soc London, Demarco Gallery; illuminated poems in public collections incl: Scottish Nat Gallery of Modern Art, Scottish Arts Cncl; *poetry incl*: Society Inebrious (1965), A Perpetual Motion Machine (1969), The Auld Symie (1971), A Pint of Bitter (1971), This Fine Day (1979), Summoned by Knox (1985), Bright Lights Blaze Out (1986); stories: Hammer and Thistle (1975), The Edge of the Wood (1984); non-fiction incl: Thom Gunn & Ted Hughes (1976), The Sensual Scot (1982), MacDiarmid The Terrible Crystal (1983), MacDiarmid A Critical Biography (1988, awarded McVitie's Prize 1989, Scottish Writer of the Year), Scotland A Literary Guide (1989); ed incl: The Penguin Book of Socialist Verse (1970), Making Love The Picador Book of Erotic Verse (1978), The Sexual Dimension in Literature (1983), Byron Wrath and Rhyme (1983), The Poetry of Motion (1984), Auden The Far Interior (1985), The Quest for Le Carré (1988); *Recreations* gardening, playing the saxophone; *Style*— Alan Bold, Esq; Balbirnie Burns East Cottage, nr Markinch, Glenrothes, Fife KY7 6NE, (☎ 0592 757216)

BOLÉAT, Mark John; s of Paul John Boléat, and Edith Maud, *née* Still; *b* 21 Jan 1949; *Educ* Victoria Coll Jersey, Lanchester Poly (BA), Univ of Reading (MA); *Career* dir gen The Bldg Socs Assoc, vice-chm Circle 33 Housing Tst, bd memb Housing Corpn; *Books* The Building Society Industry (2 edn 1986), National Housing Finance Systems (1985), The Mortgage Market (with Adrian Coles, 1987), Housing in Britain (1989); *Recreations* squash, golf, reading; *Clubs* Carlton; *Style*— Mark Boléat, Esq; 26 Westbury Rd, Northwood, Middx HA6 3BU; BSA, 3 Savile Row, London W1X 1AF (☎ 071 437 0655, telex 24538 BSA G, fax 071 734 6416)

BOLES, Lady Anne Hermione; *née* Waldegrave; da of 12 Earl Waldegrave, KG; *b* 24 Dec 1937; *Educ* St Paul's Girls' Sch; *m* 1971, Sir Jack Boles, MBE, *qv*; *Style*— The Lady Anne Boles; Rydon House, Talaton, nr Exeter, Devon (☎ 0404 850225)

BOLES, Sir Jeremy John Fortescue; 3 Bt (UK 1922); s of Capt Sir Gerald Fortescue Boles, 2 Bt (d 1945); *b* 9 Jan 1932; *Educ* Stowe; *m* 1, 1955 (m dis 1970), Dorothy Jane, da of James Alexander Worswick; 2 s, 1 da; m 2, 1970 (m dis 1981), Elisabeth Gildroy, da of Edward Phillip Shaw, of Englefield Green, Surrey, and wid of Oliver Simon Willis Fleming; 1 da; m 3, 1982, Marigold Aspey, *née* Seckington; *Heir* s, Richard Boles; *Style*— Sir Jeremy Boles, Bt; Brook House, Stogumber, Taunton, Somerset TA4 3SZ

BOLES, Sir Jack John Dennis Jack; MBE (1960); s of Cdr Geoffrey Coleridge Boles (d 1976), and Hilda Frances, *née* Crofton; *b* 25 June 1925; *Educ* Winchester; *m* 1, Benita (d 1969), da of Maj Leslie Graham Wormald; 2 s, 3 da; m 2, 1971, Lady Anne Hermione, *qv*, da of 12 Earl Waldegrave; *Career* Colonial Serv N Borneo 1947-64; Nat Tst 1965-83 (dir gen 1975-83), regnl dir Lloyds Bank 1984-; kt 1983; *Clubs* Army and Navy; *Style*— Sir Jack Boles, MBE; Rydon House, Talaton, nr Exeter, Devon (☎ 0404 850225)

BOLES, Richard Fortescue; s and h of Sir Jeremy John Fortescue Boles, 3 Bt, and Dorothy Jane, *née* Worswick; *b* 12 Dec 1958; *m* 26 May 1990, Allison Beverly, *née* Donald; *Style*— Richard Boles, Esq; Paradise Farm, Crowcombe, Taunton, Somerset TA4 4BE (☎ 09848 234); Forestry Commission, Crown Offices, Coleford, Glos GL16 8BA (☎ 0594 33057)

BOLES, Timothy Coleridge; s of Vernon Coleridge Boles, and Elizabeth Ann, *née* Spence-Thomas; *b* 27 Nov 1959; *Educ* Eton, RMC Sandhurst; *Career* cmmnd into RHG 1 Dragoons 1978, Capt 1982-86, special reserve cmmn 1987; Sedgwick Underwriting Agencies 1986-88; dir: KC Webb (Underwriting) Ltd 1989, Edward Lumley and Sons (Underwriting Agencies) Ltd 1989, Gardner Mountain and Capel Cure Agencies Ltd 1989; FRGS 1983, memb Chartered Insurance Inst 1988; GSM Northern Ireland; *Recreations* winter sports, shooting, poetry, theatre (acting); *Clubs* Shikar, Cavalry & Guards, City; *Style*— Timothy Boles, Esq; Old Clune Lodge, Tomatin, Invernessshire (☎ 08082 208); 9 Cabul Rd, Battersea, London SW11 (☎ 081 228 7113); Gardner Mountain and Capel Cure Agencies Ltd, Underwriting Agents at Lloyd's

BOLIA, Ammanulla; s of Abdul Latif Bolia (d 1982), of Plantenstraat 24, B-3500 Hasselt, Belgium, and Sara Bai Bolia; *b* 8 Jan 1953; *Educ* Ntare Sch Mbarara Uganda, Univ of Glasgow (MB ChB); *m* 5 May 1979, Shamim, da of Essak Joossab, of Lobengula St, Bulawayo, Zimbabwe; 2 s (Nazim b 1986, Fayyaz b 1989); *Career* house offr 1979-80, sr house offr 1980-81, registrar in radiology 1981-83, sr registrar in radiology 1983-85, conslt radiologist 1986-; memb: Medical Protection Soc, Overseas Drs Assoc; FRCR, memb BMA; *Recreations* swimming, photography, Indian harmonium; *Style*— Ammanulla Bolia, Esq; 18 Grasmere Rd, Wigston, Leicester LE8 1RF (☎ 0533 884343); X-Ray Department, Leicester Royal Infirmary, Infirmary Square, Leicester LE1 5WW (☎ 0533 541414)

BOLINGBROKE AND ST JOHN, 7 Viscount (GB 1712); Sir Kenneth Oliver Musgrave St John; 11 Bt (E 1611); also Baron St John of Lydiard Tregoze (GB 1712), Viscount St John and Baron St John of Battersea (GB 1716); s of Capt Geoffrey

St John, MC (d 1972), gggs of 3 Viscount, by his 2 w, Isabella Charlotte Antoinette Sophia, Baroness Hompesch (d 1848); suc kinsman 1974; *b* 22 March 1927; *Educ* Eton; *m* 1, 1953 (m dis 1972), Patricia Mary, da of B J McKenna, of Christchurch, NZ; 1 s; m 2, 1972 (m dis 1987) Jainey Anne, da of late Alexander Duncan McRae, of Timaru, NZ; 2 s (Hon Oliver b 1972, Hon Nicholas b 1974); *Heir* s, Hon Henry St John; *Career* patron of one living; pres of Travel Agents Assoc of NZ 1966-68, dir of World Assoc of Travel Agencies 1967-75; chm: Atlantic & Pacific Travel Gp of Cos 1958-76, Australian Cncl of Tours Wholesalers 1972-75; dir Bolingbroke and Ptnrs Ltd; fell of Aust Inst of Travel; *Recreations* tennis, history, cricket; *Clubs* Christchurch Club (Christchurch); *Style—* The Rt Hon The Viscount Bolingbroke and St John; 15 Tonbridge Mews, Shrewsbury St, Christchurch, New Zealand

BOLLAND, Sir Edwin; KCMG (1981, CMG 1971); s of George Bolland, of Morley, Yorks; *b* 20 Oct 1922; *Educ* Morley GS, Univ Coll Oxford; *m* 1948, Winifred, da of William Mellor, of Morley, Yorks; 1 s, 3 da; *Career* joined Foreign Office 1947, head Far Eastern Dept 1965-67, cnsllr Washington 1967-71, ambass Bulgaria 1973-76, head Br Delgn to Negotiate Mutual and Balanced Force Reductions (MBFR) 1976-80, ambass Belgrade 1980-82; *Style—* Sir Edwin Bolland, KCMG; Lord's Spring Cottage, Godden Green, Sevenoaks, Kent

BOLLERS, Hon Sir Harold Brodie Smith; s of late John Bollers; *b* 5 Feb 1915; *Educ* Queen's Coll Guyana, London Univ; *m* 1, 1951, Irene Mahadeo (d 1965); 2 s, 1 da; m 2, 1968, Eileen Indrani, da of James Hanoman; 1 s; *Career* chief justice of Guyana 1966-81, chm Elections Cmmn 1982; kt 1969; *Style—* The Hon Sir Harold Bollers; c/o Chief Justice's Residence, 245 Vlissengen Rd, Georgetown, Guyana; 252 South Rd, Bounda, Georgetown

BOLLOM, Joseph; s of Ernest Bollom (d 1939), of Old St, London, and Sarah Myers, *née* Wilkins; *b* 7 Jan 1936; *Educ* Central Fndn London; *m* 6 Sept 1958, Sylvia Iris, da of John Green, of Virginia Water, Surrey; 1 s (Michael John b 10 Sept 1959), 2 da (Karen Sarah b 22 July 1963, Deborah Jane (twin) b 22 July 1963); *Career* chm: Arlington Printers Ltd 1959, Steelchrome Furniture Ltd 1963, Kewlox Furniture Ltd 1972, Ingersoll Watch Co plc 1970-75, Ingersoll Gp 1975-80, Arlington Leisure 1982, Blue Chip (UK) Ltd 1983; dir First Leisure plc 1983; chm Lady Mayoress Charity (Lady Gardener Thorpe) 1982 on behalf of Gt Ormond St Hosp for Sick Children, former ctee memb Prince Charles Charity; Freeman City of London 1973, Liveryman Worshipful Co of Watchmakers 1973, Liveryman Worshipful Co of Painters and Stainers 1983; *Style—* Joseph Bollom, Esq; The White House, Totteridge Common, London N20 (☎ 081 959 7555); Arlington Leisure Ltd, The Hawthorne Centre, Elmgrove Rd, Harrow, Middx (☎ 081 863 8311, fax 081 427 0240, car 0836 501 408/0836 610 064)

BOLONGARO, Michael Francis; s of Louis Harold Bolongaro (d 1969), of Tapley, Fleetwood Rd, Fleetwood, Lancs, and Millicent Dorcus, *née* Wrathall (d 1963); *b* 22 Feb 1930; *Educ* St Joseph's Coll Blackpool; *m* 30 Dec 1958, Anne June, da of John Frederick Dodding (d 1981), of The White Hart Hotel, Exeter; 3 s (Gregory John b 1966, Dominic Louis b 1972, Guy Francis b 1978), 4 da (Clare Celeste b 1962, Lucy Anne b 1965, Catherine Emma b 1968, Emma Louise b 1971); *Career* chartered surveyor; estates surveyor Shell-Mex and BP 1955-65, chief valuer of Dublin City & Co 1970-73, fine art conslt and connoisseur of old master paintings 1975-; FRICS; *Recreations* mountain walking, historical and art study; *Style—* Michael Bolongaro, Esq; Overbeck, 78 Greenside, Kendal, Cumbria LA9 5DT (☎ 0539 725435); Woodlands, Queens Rd, Kendal, Cumbria (☎ 0539 727934)

BOLSOVER, John Derrick; s of Dr G D Bolsover, MBE, of The Shrubbery, Eynsham, Oxford and Yoma Constance, *née* Stephens; *b* 21 June 1947; *Educ* Repton, McGill Univ Canada (BA); *m* 11 Sept 1971, Susan Elizabeth, da of Fletcher Peacock, of Gulfshore Boulevard, Naples, Florida; 2 s (Michael b 1976, Lincoln b 1978), 1 da (Jacqueline b 1974); *Career* chief exec & chief investmt offr Baring Int Investmt Mgmnt Ltd 1985-; *Recreations* sport; *Clubs* Boodles, City; *Style—* John Bolsover, Esq; 15 Hereford Square, London SW7 4TS; 9 Bishopsgate, London EC2N 3AQ (☎ 071 588 6133, telex 894989, fax 071 588 2591)

BOLT, Roderick Langston; s of Lt Cdr Geoffrey Peter Langston Bolt, of 20 Barneby Cl, Downton, Salisbury, Wilts, and Margaret Elmslie Ashley Hall, *née* Brebner; *b* 14 Oct 1943; *Educ* Sedbergh; *m* 20 July 1968, Gillian Rosamond, da of Lt-Col John Russell Palmer, MC, of Holly House, Carlton Hustwaite, Thirsk, Yorks; 1 s (Charles Henry Langston b 8 Jan 1971), 1 da (Annabel Margaret Langston b 27 May 1972); *Career* 13/18 Royal Hussars (Queen Mary's Own) 1962-67 medically discharged; asst agent for Earl of Harewood 1969-74, sr asst Cluttons 1974-77, resident agent for Lord St Oswald Wakefield 1977-79, princ land agent Hampshire CC 1979-82, factor for the Crown Estate Cmmrs Glenlivet and Auchindoun Estates with Smiths Gore 1983-86, def land agent Catterick 1986; FRICS 1986; *Recreations* shooting, fishing; *Style—* Roderick Bolt, Esq; Graystone Lodge, Maunby, N Thirsk, N Yorks; Defence Land Agent, Gough Rd, Catterick Garrison, N Yorks (☎ 0748 834208)

BOLTON, Anthony Hale; s of Eric Hale Bolton (d 1986), and Betty Maude (d 1986), of New Barnet, Herts; *b* 8 Aug 1942; *Educ* St Albans Sch, Herts; *m* 12 May 1962, Olive Muriel, da of Thomas Brian O'Loughlin, of Brookmans Park; 1 s (David b 1968), 1 da (Jenny b 1971); *Career* chm: Bowring Aviation 1981-, Bowring Int Insurance Brokers 1988-; dep chm C T Bowring & Co (Insurance) 1984-, a md Marsh & MacLennan Inc USA 1985-; memb Aviation Ctee Lloyds Insurance Brokers Ctee; *Recreations* golf, music, ballet; *Clubs* Brookmans Park Golf; *Style—* Anthony Bolton Esq; Brookmans Park, Herts; Bowring Aviation, The Bowring Building, Tower Place, London EC3

BOLTON, Archdeacon of; *see*: Brison, Ven William Stanley (Bill)

BOLTON, Bishop of 1984-; Rt Rev David George Galliford; s of late Alfred Edward Bruce Galliford, of Warneford Gardens, Withycombe Raleigh, Exmouth, Devon, and Amy Doris, *née* Pawley; *b* 20 June 1925; *Educ* Bede Coll Sunderland, Clare Coll Cambridge (MA); *m* 1, 27 May 1954, Enid May (d 1983), da of late Arthur Drax, of 219 Sewerby Road, Bridlington; 1 da (Clare Frances Hope b 1956); m 2, 21 April 1987, Mrs Claire Margaret Phoenix, da of late Alfred Henry Smalley, of 95 Edge Lane, Stretford, Manchester; *Career* curate St John's Newland Hull 1951-54, minor canon Windsor 1954-56, vicar St Oswald's Middlesbrough 1956-61, rector Bolton Percy and diocesan trg offr 1961-71, canon of York 1965-69, residentiary canon and treas of York Minster 1969-75, bishop of Hulme 1975-84; *Recreations* music, painting; *Clubs* Manchester; *Style—* The Rt Rev the Bishop of Bolton; Bishop's House, 4 Sandfield Drive, Lostock, Bolton BL6 4DU (☎ 0204 43400)

BOLTON, Eric James; CB (1987); s of James Bolton (d 1951), and Lilian Bolton (d 1983); *b* 11 Jan 1935; *Educ* Wigan GS, Chester Coll, Univ of Lancaster (MA); *m* 13 Aug 1960, Ann, da of late William Charles Edward Gregory; 1 s (Benjamin b 1962), 1 da (Emma b 1966, Charlotte (twin) b 1966); *Career* Nat Serv Loyal N Lancs Regt 1953-55; teacher of English Lancs Secdy Sch 1957-67, lectr in teacher trg Chorley Coll of Higher Educn 1967-70, LEA inspr of schs Outer London Borough of Croydon 1970-73; HM Inspectorate: HM inspr of schs 1973-, staff inspr educnl disadvantage 1979-81, chief inspr 1981-83, sr chief inspr and head 1983-; FRSA 1982; *Books* Verse Writing In Schools (1964); *Recreations* reading, music and opera, fly-fishing; *Style—* Eric Bolton, Esq, CB; Department of Education and Science, Elizabeth House, York Rd, London SE1 7PH (☎ 071 934 0722)

BOLTON, Frances Lawjua; da of John Aka Eqwu (d 1983), and Mercy Aqunyenwa Iweka; *b* 24 Nov 1950; *Educ* Queen's Coll Lagos Nigeria, The Collegiate Sch Winterbourne Bristol, Univ of Manchester (LLB); *m* 11 Feb 1976, Andrew John Bolton, s of John Edmund Bolton, of Hampton Court, Nelson St, Kings Lynn, Norfolk; 1 s (Lawrence Andrew John Bolton b 27 Sept 1989), 1 da (Fiona Samari Uchenna b 30 June 1977); *Career* called to the Bar 1981; Inn Rep for Muscular Distrophy Soc (Edward Bear Fndn), memb Hon Soc of Middle Temple; *Style—* Ms Frances Bolton; The White House, 42 Potter St, Harlow, Essex CM17 9AQ (☎ 0279 416496)

BOLTON, Sir Frederic Bernard; MC (1945); s of Louis Hamilton Bolton (d 1953), of Woodford Halse, nr Rugby, and Beryl (d 1977), da of Dr Bernard Shirley Dyer (d 1948); *b* 9 March 1921; *Educ* Rugby; *m* 1, 1950, Valerie Margaret (d 1970), da of George Short Barwick (d 1937); 2 s; m 2, 1971, Vanessa Mary Anne, da of Lt-Col Anthony Vere Cyprian Robarts (d 1981); 2 s, 2 da; *Career* served WW II Maj N Africa, Italy; shipowner; chm F Bolton Gp 1953-; pres: Chamber of Shipping 1966-67, Inst of Marine Engrs 1968-70, Br Shipping Fedn 1972-75, General Cncl of Br Shipping 1975-76, Int Shipping Fedn 1973-82; chm Dover Harbour Bd 1983-88, Br Ports Assoc 1985-88; pres British Maritime League 1985-; kt 1976; *Recreations* country sports; *Clubs* City of London, Cavalry & Guards; *Style—* Sir Frederic Bolton, MC; Pudlicote, nr Charlbury, Oxon (☎ 060 876 427)

BOLTON, James Douglas; TD (1962), DL (Herts 1968); s of Percy Bolton (d 1981), and Florence Madeleine, *née* Scott (d 1976), of Brabourne, Kimpton, nr Hitchin; *b* 4 Feb 1921; *Educ* Oundle, King's Coll Cambridge (BA); *m* 1959, Margaret Jean, da of James Forsyth (d 1959), of St Albans, Herts; 1 s, 1 da; *Career* slr, coroner E Herts Dist of Hertfordshire 1966-90, chm Lee Valley Water Co 1986-; memb Cncl Law Soc 1975-89; *Recreations* tennis, swimming; *Style—* James Bolton, Esq, TD, DL; Cox's, 23 Park Ave South, Harpenden, Herts AL5 2DZ (☎ 0582 712222)

BOLTON, John Eveleigh; CBE (1972), DSC (1945), DL (1974); s of Ernest Bolton (d 1933), of Burley in Wharfedale, and Edith Mary, *née* Duckhouse (d 1968); *b* 17 Oct 1920; *Educ* Ilkley Sch, Wolverhampton Sch, Trinity Coll Cambridge (MA), Harvard Business Sch (MBA); *m* 21 Aug 1948, Gabrielle Healey (Gay), da of Joseph Hall (d 1945), of Penn House, Penn, Wolverhampton, Staffs; 1 s (Nicholas b 1949), 1 da (Athalie b 1951); *Career* WWII ordinary seaman RN (later Lt RNVR); served: Atlantic, Arctic, Med; chm Solartron Laboratory Instruments Ltd 1953 (fin dir 1951-53), chm and md Solartron Electronic Group Ltd 1954-60 (dep chm 1960-65), chm and md Growth Capital Group Ltd 1968-, pres Development Capital Group Ltd 1984-88 (chm 1972-84); non-exec dir: Black & Decker Corporation USA, NCR Ltd, Plasmec plc, Hoskyns Group plc, Business Advisers Ltd; chm Cncl BIM 1964-66 (life vice pres), Advanced Mgmt Tst Int 1965- (fndr subscriber, chm tstees, chm emeritus), vice chm Royal Cmmn on Local Govt in England 1966-69, chm Ctee of Inquiry on Small Firms 1969-71, pres Engrg Industs Assoc 1981-84, memb Cncl IOD 1972-90, former chm Advsy Ctee Business Graduates Assoc, former pres W End Br Legion, vice pres Cobham CC, former treas and chm Cncl Univ of Surrey, High Sheriff of Surrey 1980-81; Bowie medal 1969; Hon DUniv of Surrey, Hon DSc Univ of Bath; FBIM 1966, CBIM 1976, life fell RSA 1967; *Recreations* shooting, swimming, the arts; *Clubs* IOD; *Style—* John Bolton, Esq, CBE, DSC, DL; Sunnymead, Tite Hill, Englefield Green, Surrey TW20 ONH (☎ 0784 435172, 0784 430523)

BOLTON, Hon Mrs (Lavinia Valerie); *née* Woodhouse; da of 4 Baron Terrington; *b* 29 Aug 1943; *Educ* Downham Herts, Montesano Gstaad; *m* 1974 (m dis), Nicholas George Bolton, s of Sir George Lewis French Bolton, KCMG; 2 da (Carina b 1976, Sophie b 1979); *Recreations* antique collecting, decorating, travelling; *Style—* The Hon Mrs Bolton; 13 Crail View, Northleach, Glos GL54 3QH

BOLTON, Lucinda Carol; da of Gordon Gustav-Adolf Winter, TD, of Noble Tree End, Hildenborough, Kent, and Elspeth Kerr, *née* Bone; *b* 3 Dec 1952; *Educ* Benenden Sch, St Hugh's Coll Oxford (MA); *m* 12 June 1982, (Francis) Edward Kennaway Bolton, s of Martin Alfred Butts Bolton, DL, JP, of Croxden Abbey, Nr Uttoxeter, Staffordshire; 1 da (Camilla b 1985); *Career* dir: Guinness Mahon & Co Ltd 1987-89, Lockton Superstores plc 1988-90, Lockton Retail Stores plc 1988-90, Lockton West Country Tenancies plc 1989-; cncllr London Borough of Hammersmith and Fulham 1980-82; *Style—* Mrs Lucinda Bolton; 33 St Maur Rd, London SW6

BOLTON, Martin Alfred Butts; JP (Staffs 1959), DL (1969); o s of Francis Alfred Bolton, JP (d 1951), of Moor Court, Oakmoor, Staffs; *b* 27 June 1923; *Educ* Shrewsbury, Magdalene Coll Cambridge (MA); *m* 1946, Margaret Hazel, da of C G Kennaway, WS, of Kenwood Park, Auchterarder, Perthshire; 2 s, 3 da; *Career* farmer; memb: Cncl NFU 1961-65, Int Egg Cmmn 1963-66; vice pres Staffordshire CLA 1988 (memb CLA Cncl 1962-82), chm: NFU Poultry Cmmn 1963-66, IFAP Poultry 1963-66, W Midlands Agric Land Tbnl 1974-; chm: Cmmn of Income Tax Staffs 1972-, Staffs Advsy Cmmn 1963-90; pres Staffs Agric Soc 1971, govr Harper Adams Agric Coll 1965-; High Sheriff Staffs 1960-61; *Recreations* shooting, golf, tennis; *Clubs* Farmers'; *Style—* Martin Bolton, Esq, JP, DL; Croxden Abbey, Uttoxeter, Staffs (☎ 088 926 225)

BOLTON, Lady; May (Maisie); da of Charles Amelia Howcroft; *b* 3 Sept 1900; *m* 1928, Sir George Lewis French Bolton, KCMG (d 1982), sometime chm Bank London & S America; 1 s (Nicholas), 2 da (Sheila, Gillian); *Style—* Lady Bolton; 305 Frobisher House, Dolphin Square, London SW1V 3LL (☎ 071 834 7278)

BOLTON, 7 Baron (GB 1797); Richard William Algar Orde-Powlett; s of 6 Baron Bolton (d 1963) and Victoria, da of late Henry Montagu Villiers, MVO, gn of 4 Earl of Clarendon; *b* 11 July 1929; *Educ* Eton, Trinty Coll Cambridge; *m* 1, 1951 (m dis 1981), Hon Christine Helena Weld Forester, da of 7 Baron Forester, and Marie, CStJ, da of Sir Herbert Perrott, 6 Bt, CH, CB; 2 s, 1 da; m 2, 1981, Masha Anne, da of Maj F E Hudson, of Winterfield House, Hornby, Bedale, Yorks; *Heir* s, Hon Harry Orde-Powlett; *Career* dir General Accident Life Assurance Ltd; former chm: Waterers Group, Yorks Soc of Agric, Yorks Branch Royal Forestry Soc 1963-64; JP N Riding of Yorks 1957-78; FRICS; *Style—* The Rt Hon the Lord Bolton; Park House, Wensley Leyburn, N Yorks (☎ 0969 22464 22303)

BOLTON, Roger John; s of Harold Bolton, and Olive Yarker, *née* Buck; *b* 13 Nov 1945; *Educ* Carlisle GS, Univ of Liverpool (BA); *m* 1 (m dis); 2 s (Alexander b 1970, Giles b 1973); m 2, 1987, Julia Helene McLaren; 2 da (Olivia b 1988, Jessica b 1989); *Career* BBC TV: gen trainee 1967, ed Tonight Prog 1977-79, ed Panorama 1979-81, ed Nationwide 1981-83, head of Manchester Network Prodn Centre 1983-86; Thames TV: ed This Week 1986-89, controller of network factual progs 1989-; *Books* Death on the Rock and other stories (1990); *Recreations* reading history, visiting churches, walking, 5-aside football; *Style—* Roger Bolton, Esq; Thames Television plc, 306-316 Euston Rd, London NW1 3BB (☎ 071 387 9494)

BOMFORD, Nicholas Raymond; s of Ernest Raymond Bomford (d 1962) and Patricia Clive, *née* Brooke; *b* 27 Jan 1939; *Educ* Kelly Coll, Trinity Coll Oxford (MA); *m* 1966, Gillian Mary, da of Maj Peter Beckingham Reynolds (ka 1943); 2 da (Kate b 1967, Rebecca b 1969); *Career* memb academic staff: BRNC Dartmouth 1964-68, Wellington Coll 1968-77; headmaster: Monmouth Sch 1977-82, Uppingham Sch 1982-; FRSA; *Books* Documents in World History 1914-70 (1973); *Recreations* shooting, fishing, music, gardening; *Style—* Nicholas Bomford, Esq; Headmaster's House, Uppingham

School, Rutland LE15 9TT (☎ 0572 822688)

BOMPAS, Donald George; CMG (1966); s of Rev Edward Anstie Bompas (d 1956), of London; *b* 20 Nov 1920; *Educ* Merchant Taylors', Oriel Coll Oxford; *m* 1946, Freda Vice, da of Fred Milner Smithyman (d 1969), of Malawi; 1 s, 1 da; *Career* formerly with Overseas Audit Serv; auditor-gen: Malaya 1960-63, Malaysia 1963-66; sec: Guy's Hosp Med and Dental Schs 1969-82, United Med and Dental Schs of Guy's and St Thomas's Hosps 1984-86; managing exec: Philip & Pauline Harris Charitable Tst 1986-; Liveryman Worshipful Co of Merchant Taylors' 1951; Hon JMN (Malaya) 1961; *Clubs* Royal Cwlth Soc; *Style—* Donald Bompas, Esq, CMG; 8 Birchwood Rd, Petts Wood, Kent (☎ 0689 821661)

BONALLACK, Michael Francis; OBE (1971); s of Col Sir Richard Frank Bonallack, CBE, *qv*, and (Winifred) Evelyn Mary, *née* Esplen (d 1986); *b* 31 Dec 1934; *Educ* Chigwell Sch, Haileybury; *m* 8 Feb 1958, Angela, da of Harry Vivian Ward, of Birchington, Kent; 1 s (Robert Richard Ward b 1967), 3 da (Glenna (Mrs Beasley) b 1959, Jane (Mrs Baker) b 1961, Sara b 1965); *Career* Nat Serv RASC 1953-55; joined Bonallack & Sons Ltd (later Freight Bonallack Ltd) 1955 (dir 1962-74), dir Miller Buckley and Buckley Investmts Ltd 1976-84; chm: Cotton (CK) Pennink & Ptnrs Ltd 1980-83, Miller Buckley Leisure Ltd 1980-83; sec Royal and Ancient Golf Club St Andrews 1983-; 5 times Br Amateur Golf Champion, 5 times Eng Amateur Golf Champion, 4 times Eng Amateur Stroke Play Champion, twice Leading Amateur in Open Golf Championship, played for Eng 1957-74 (Capt 1962-67), played for Br Walker Cup Team 1957-73 (Capt 1969-71), awarded Bobby Jones Trophy by US Golf Assoc 1972; chm: Golf Fndn 1977-83, PGA 1976-82; pres Eng Golf Union 1982; Freeman City of London, Liveryman Worshipful Co of Coachmakers and Coach Harness Makers 1962; *Recreations* all sports, reading; *Style—* Michael Bonallack, Esq, OBE; Clatto Lodge, Blebo Craigs, Cupar, Fife KY15 5UF (☎ 0334 85600); Royal and Ancient Golf Club, St Andrews, Fife KY16 9JD (☎ 0334 72112, fax 0334 77580, telex 76348)

BONALLACK, Sir Richard Frank; CBE (1955, OBE (mil) 1945); s of Francis Bonallack (d 1955), of Loughton, Essex, and Ada Frances, *née* Bateman (d 1963); *b* 2 June 1904; *Educ* Haileybury; *m* 1930, (Winifred) Evelyn Mary (d 1986), da of James Johnstone Esplen, OBE (d 1934), of Buckhurst Hill, Essex; 2 s (*see* Michael Bonallack), 1 da; *Career* served WWII Col ME; md Bonallack Gp 1946-71 (chm 1955-77), pres Freight Bonallack Ltd 1977-87, dir Alcan Transport Products 1979-85; memb Cncl SMT 1958-87, chm Working Pty Anglo-Soviet Ctee for Jt Tech collaboration 1971-78, memb Basildon Devpt Corp 1955-82; kt 1963; *Recreations* golf; *Style—* Sir Richard Bonallack, CBE; 4 The Willows, Thorpe Bay, Southend on Sea, Essex SS1 3SH (☎ 0702 588 180)

BONAPARTE WYSE, William Lucien; o s of Andrew Reginald Nicholas Duncan Bonaparte Wyse, CB, CBE (d 1940, gs of Rt Hon Sir Thomas Wyse, KCB, PC, DL, of a family settled in Waterford since *temp* Richard Earl of Pembroke and which provided Waterford with 36 Mayors and High Sheriffs 1452-1690; Sir Thomas m HH Laetizia Cristina, Princess Bonaparte, da of HIH Lucien Bonaparte, the bro of the Emperor, who nonetheless played a vital role in the 19 Brumaire coup and who was the last to support Napoleon during the tail end of the Hundred Days in 1815); Andrew m Countess Marie (d 1960), da of Count Dmitri Chiriponov, of Orel province, Russia; *b* 13 March 1908; *Educ* Downside, Pembroke Coll Cambridge; *m* 1, 1933 (m annulled 1946), Benedicta Madeleine Elizabeth Stephanie Marie Gabrielle (d 1969), o da of Charles Renfric Chichester, of Jersey; m 2, 1954, Olga Marie, da of Henry Clive Rollason, of Southsea, Hants; 1 s (Henry b 11 July 1950), 1 da (Frances b 28 Jan 1948); *Career* served WW II Lt Free Fr Navy, ADC to Adm Auboyneau (CIC 1942-45); *Style—* William Bonaparte Wyse, Esq; Beaumarchais, 22690 Pleudihen-sur-Rance, France

BONAR, Sir Herbert Vernon; CBE (1946); s of late George Bonar, of The Bughties, Broughty Ferry, Dundee, and Julia, *née* Seehusen; *b* 26 Feb 1907; *Educ* Fettes, Brasenose Coll Oxford (BA); *m* 1935, Marjory (d 1990), da of late Albert East, of Hill Rise, Dundee; 2 s; *Career* chm Low and Bonar Group 1949-74 (md 1938-73); vice pres WWF (UK); Hon LLD: Univ of St Andrew's, Univ of Birmingham, Univ of Dundee; TOT Commandant of the Golden Ark (Netherlands); kt 1967; *Style—* Sir Herbert Bonar, CBE; St Kitts, Albany Rd, Broughty Ferry, Dundee, Angus (☎ 0382 79947)

BONAS, Ian George; DL (Co Durham 1985); s of Harry Bonas (d 1984), and Winifred Bonas; *b* 13 July 1942; *Educ* Harrow, Univ of Oxford (MA, DipEcon); *m* 23 Sept 1967, Katharine Anne, *née* Steel; 2 s (James Henry b 19 April 1972, William Ian), 2 da (Anna Katharine b 25 May 1969, Sophie Katharine b 23 May 1971); *Career* Ferguson International Holdings plc 1988-; chm and md: Bonas Machine Co Ltd 1973-84 (md 1969-73), Bonas Griffith Ltd 1985-88; chm Bentley Group Ltd 1989-; memb: Northern Econ Planning Cncl 1973-79, Ctee in Fin for Indust NEDC 1978-, Cncl Univ of Durham 1983-89; dir Washington Devpt Corp 1979-83, chm Northern Region CBI 1981-83 (memb Nat Ctee 1973-84), dir Civic Tst for NE 1980-89, chm Durham FPC 1989-, cmmr of Income Tax 1973-; High Sheriff Co Durham 1987-88; *Recreations* music, books, painting, forestry, gardening, skiing, machine building, joinery; *Clubs* Oxford and Cambridge Univ, Northern Counties; *Style—* Ian Bonas, Esq, DL; Ferguson International Holdings plc, Appleby Castle, Appleby, Cumbria CA16 6XH (car 0836 613 439)

BONAS, Lady Mary Gaye Georgiana Lorna; *née* Curzon; da of 6 Earl Howe, CBE; *b* 21 Feb 1947; *m* 1, 1971 (m dis 1976), (Kevin) Esmond Peter Cooper-Key (d 1985), s of Sir Neil Cooper-Key, former MP; 1 da (Pandora b 1973); m 2, 1977 (m dis 1987), John Austen Anstruther-Gough-Calthorpe, s of Brig Sir Richard Anstruther-Gough-Calthorpe, 2 Bt, CBE (d 1985); 1 s (Jacobi b 1983), 2 da (Georgiana b 1978, Isabella b 1980); m 3, 29 Jan 1988, Jeffrey Bonas, s of late Harry Bonas, of Grangewood Hall, Netherseale, Burton-on-Trent; 1 da (Cressida b 1989); *Style—* Lady Mary Gaye Bonas; The Old Rectory, Ovington, Alresford, Hants (☎ 0962 732821)

BOND, Alan; AO (1984); s of late Frank Bond, and late Kathleen Bond; *b* 22 April 1939; *Educ* UK and Fremantle Boys' Sch Australia; *m* 1955, Eileen Teresa, da of W Hughes; 2 s, 2 da; *Career* chm: Bond Corpn Hldgs Ltd 1982- (formerly chief exec), Swan Brewery Co Ltd; dir: North Kalgurli Mines Ltd, Metals Exploration Ltd, Bond Media UK Ltd, Airship Industries UK, Bond Univ Ltd, Hampton Gold Mining Areas plc; winner Americas Cup 1983 (with 'Australia II'); memb: Australian Sports Cmmn, WA Business Advisory Gp, WA Devpt Corporation, Royal Blind Soc, Opera Fnd of Australia; *Recreations* yachting, tennis, swimming; *Clubs* Young Presidents Organisation, Royal Perth Yacht, RORC (UK); *Style—* Alan Bond, Esq, AO; Watkins Close, Dalkeith, 6009, W Australia

BOND, Anthony Hugh; s of Lt-Col James Hugh Bond, MC (d 1983), of Burford House, Shepton Mallet, Somerset, and Joan Winifred Dodman, *née* Turner (d 1989); *b* 7 July 1951; *Educ* Radley; *m* 27 July 1974, Caroline Mary, s of Brig Frederick Manus De Butts, CMG, OBE, DL, of The Old Vicarage, Great Gaddesden, Hemel Hempstead, Herts; 2 s (Jonathan James Hugh b 16 Aug 1977, Rupert Charles b 23 April 1980), 1 da (Victoria Jane b 3 Oct 1984); *Career* trainee CA Moore Stephens London, qualified CA 1977; KPMG Peat Marwick McLintock (formerly Peat Marwick Mitchell & Co): joined 1977, ptnr i/c Bahrain and Qatar 1982-84, ptnr London, nat co-ordinator for business servs 1987-89; ACA 1977, FCA 1983; *Recreations* golf, tennis, skiing; *Style—* Anthony Bond, Esq; The Granary, Reads Lane, Cublington, Leighton Buzzard, Beds LU7 OLE (☎ 0296 681 648); KPMG Peat Marwick McLintock, Norfolk House, 499 Silbury Boulevard, Central Milton Keynes MK9 2HA (☎ 0908 661 881, fax 0908 664 363)

BOND, Christopher Michael; s of Lt-Col James Hugh Bond, MC (d 1983), of Somerset, and Winifred Dodman, *née* Goodall (d 1989); *b* 28 June 1943; *Educ* Wellington, Trinity Hall Cambridge (BA); *m* 19 Feb 1966, Lindsay, da of late Arthur Lewis Cruickshank, of Bedford; 1 s (Neil Alexander), 1 da (Lara Marianne); *Career* admitted slr 1969, asst co sec Reuters Ltd 1972-76, ptnr Field Fisher Waterhouse 1979-; lectr int law confs in: America, Japan, Korea; UK memb BIEC missions to Korea and Taiwan; memb Law Soc 1969-; *Books* Investing in the United Kingdom (1986), Investing in the United Kingdom - The Basic Issues (1987); *Recreations* music, hill walking, reading, sailing; *Style—* Christopher Bond, Esq; Richmond, Surrey; Shepton Mallet, Somerset; 41 Vine Street, London EC3

BOND, (Charles) Derek; *see*: Bradwell, Bishop of

BOND, Edward; *b* 18 July 1934; *m* 1971, Elisabeth Pablé; *Career* playwright and dir; George Devine award 1968, John Whiting award 1968; *Style—* Edward Bond, Esq; c/o Margaret Ramsay, 14a Goodwins Court, St Martin's Lane, WC2

BOND, Prof Geoffrey Colin; s of Capt William Henry Bond, MC (d 1982), and Kate, *née* Digy; *b* 21 April 1927; *Educ* King Edward VI GS Stratford-upon-Avon, Univ of Birmingham (BSc, PhD, DSc); *m* 29 Aug 1953, (Angela) Mary, da of Arthur Lovatt Ingram (d 1981); 3 s (Richard b 1954, Martin b 1956, Andrew b 1959), 1 da (Rosemary b 1961); *Career* lectr Univ of Hull 1955-62, head Catalysis Res Gp Johnson Matthey & Co Ltd 1962-70; Brunel Univ: prof applied chemistry 1970-71, prof and head Dept Industl Chemistry 1971-82, vice princ 1979-81, dean Faculty Mathematics and Sci 1982-84, head Dept Chemistry 1984-; coordinator SERC initiative on interfaces and catalysis; FRSC, CChem; *Books* Catalysis by Metals (1962), Principles of Catalysis (1963), Heterogeneous Catalysis (2 edn, 1987); *Recreations* philately, gardening; *Style—* Prof Geoffrey Bond; Flint Cottage, Deadmans Ash Lane, Sarratt, Herts WD3 6AL (☎ 0923 263561); Department of Chemistry, Brunel University, Uxbridge UB8 3PH (☎ 0895 74000, fax 0895 56844, telex 261173 G)

BOND, Cdr Geoffrey Leonard; MBE (1970); *b* 5 Sept 1928; *Educ* Devizes GS, Univ of Bristol (BA, PGC); *m* 7 June 1952, Catherine Jean, *née* Healey; 2 s (Richard Patrick b 1959, Crispin Nicholas b 1964), 2 da (Caroline Nicola b 1956, Elizabeth May (Mrs De Lacey) b 1961); *Career* Nat Serv 2 Lt Wiltshire Regt 1950-52; extended serv cmmn to 1956; RN 1956-84: commando Trg Centre RM 1957-60, HMS Raleigh 1960-62, Depot RM 1962-64, HMS Ark Royal 1969-71, HMS St Angelo 1971-74, MOD 1965-69 and 1975-84; appointed first chief exec The English Vineyards Assoc 1985, ed The Grape Press, writer and lectr on history of wine in England, contrib works on landscape and English wine; Churchwarden St Andrew Mottingham, memb Greenwich Deanery Synod; *Recreations* exploring and studying the British land & townscape and their traditions; *Clubs* Royal British Legion, St James's; *Style—* Cdr Geoffrey Bond, MBE; 38 West Park, London SE9 4RH (☎ 081 857 3306/0452)

BOND, Godfrey William; s of William Niblock Bond (d 1955), and Emily Janet, *née* Godfrey (d 1955); *b* 24 July 1925; *Educ* Campbell Coll, Royal Belfast Acad Inst, Trinity Coll Dublin (scholar, BA, Berkeley medal, Classics Gold medal), St John's Coll Oxford (MA); *m* 19 Sept 1959, Shirley Alison, da of Mr Justice TC Kingsmill Moore (d 1979); 1 s (Kingsmill b 1967), 2 da (Catherine b 1960, Elwyn b 1962); *Career* Nat Serv and Foreign Office (GCHQ) 1943-45; fell and classical Tutor Pembroke Coll Oxford 1950-52, lectr in classics Univ of Oxford 1952-62, sr tutor Pembroke Coll 1962-72, sr proctor Univ of Oxford 1964-65, visitor of Ashmolean Museum 1972-81, dean of Pembroke Coll 1979-, public orator Univ of Oxford 1980-; memb: Inst for Advanced Study Princeton NJ 1969-70, Gen Bd of Faculties Univ of Oxford 1970-76; *Books* Euripides Hypsipyle (ed) 1963, Euripides Heracles (ed) 1981; *Recreations* opera, dining, swimming; *Clubs* Athenaeum, Kildare Street and University (Dublin); *Style—* Godfrey Bond, Esq; Masefield House, Boars Hill, Oxford OX1 5EY (☎ 0865 735373); Pembroke College, Oxford (☎ 0865 276465)

BOND, Graham; s of Thomas Carlile (d 1980), of Blackburn, and Mary, *née* Dixon; *Educ* Queen Elizabeth's GS Blackburn, RCM (exhibition scholar, various prizes); *Career* London Festival Ballet/Eng Nat Ballet: conductor 1970-76, princ conductor 1976-, music dir 1983-; tours incl: Aust, France, Spain, Italy, Germany, Yugoslavia, Greece, Denmark, Venezuela, Turkey, China, USA; orchs worked with incl: Monte Carol Philharmonic, Tivoli Symphony Copenhagen, Stanislavsky Theatre Moscow, Opera House Turin, Hong Kong Philharmonic 1987, Danish Radio 1988, Royal Opera Copenhagen 1988, Opera Teatro Massimo Sicily 1988, Cairo Symphony 1988; guest conductor: Stuttgart Ballet, San Carol Opera Orch Naples, Metropolitan Opera NY 1989, Deutsch Oper Berlin 1990, Royal Gala Orch Glasgow 1990, Bolshoi Ballet tour of Eng 1990; memb consulting staff RCM 1985-; *awards* incl: Worshipful Co of Musicians medal for a Distinguished Student RCM, Adrian Boult scholarship for study at the Accademia Chigiana Siena, repetiteur London Opera Centre 1970; *Recreations* theatre, reading, walkling; *Style—* Graham Bond, Esq; 21a Esmond Gardens, South Parade, London W4 1JT (☎ 081 995 8743); c/o English National Ballet, 39 Jay News, London SW7 (☎ 071 581 1245)

BOND, Ian Charles Winsor; s of Charles Walter Bond (d 1961), and Beryl Irene Bond (d 1961); *b* 15 June 1938; *Educ* King Edward VI Sch Camp Hill; *m* 28 July 1962, Audrey Kathleen, da of William Edward Robinson (d 1965), of Thornton Clevely, S Lancs; 2 s (Richard b 1965, Andrew b 1967), 2 da (Jane b 1963, Catherine b 1968); *Career* CA; managing ptnr Midlands Offices Baker Tilly 1988 (ptnr constituent firm 1964-), dir Baker Tilly Mgmnt Conslts Ltd 1988; farmer breeding Charolais cattle; memb Gen Cncl Stonehouse Gang; FCA 1960; *Recreations* shooting, farming; *Style—* Ian Bond, Esq; Baker Tilly, Tricorn House, Hagley Rd, Edgbaston, Birmingham B16 8TP (☎ 021 456 1483, fax 021 456 1485, car 0860 531103)

BOND, John David; MVO (1988); s of Arthur Henry Bond (d 1968), and Agnes Mary, *née* Peters (d 1984); *b* 14 June 1932; *Educ* St Mary's Welwyn; *m* 18 Jan 1958, Edna, da of William Samuel Reeves (d 1975); 1 s (Christopher John b 1962), 1 da (Susan Mary b 1959); *Career* keeper of the gardens The Gt Park Windsor 1970-; memb Cncl RHS 1985- (chm Rhododendron and Camelia Ctee 1987); Victoria medal of Hon in Horticulture RHS 1981; *Recreations* horticulture, natural history, travel, railways; *Style—* John Bond, Esq, MVO; Verderers, Wick Rd, Englefield Green, Egham, Surrey TW2 0HL (☎ 0784 432168); Crown Estate Office, The Great Park, Windsor, Berks (☎ 0753 860222)

BOND, Prof Michael Richard; s of Frederick Richard Bond, of 10 Falstone Ave, Newark on Trent, Notts, and Dorothy, *née* Gardner (d 1988); *b* 15 April 1936; *Educ* Magnus GS Newark Notts, Univ of Sheffield (MB ChB, MD, PhD); *m* 24 June 1961, Jane, da of Charles Issitt (d 1962); 1 s (Matthew b 9 Aug 1970), 1 da (Lucy b 2 June 1975); *Career* lectr in psychiatry Univ of Sheffield 1964-67 (asst lectr and res registrar surgery 1961-64); Univ of Glasgow: sr house offr, registrar, sr registrar neurosurgery 1967-71, lectr and sr lectr neurosurgery 1971-73, prof of psychological med 1973-, vice princ 1986-, admin dean Faculty of Med 1991-; govr Glasgow HS, chm Head Injury Tst Scotland; FRCSE 1969, FRCPsych 1981, FRCPS 1981; *Books* Pain: Its

Nature Analysis Treatment (2 edns 1979, 1984); *Recreations* painting, forest walking, physical fitness, antique book collecting; *Clubs* Atheneum; *Style—* Prof Michael R Bond; 33 Ralston Rd, Bearsden, Glasgow G61 3BA (☎ 041 942 4391); Dept of Psychological Medicine, 6 Whittinghame Gardens, Great Western Rd, Glasgow (☎ 041 334 9826)

BOND, Nigel Graham; s of (Peter) Graham Bond, of Matlock, Derbyshire, and Ann, *née* Marshall; *b* 15 Nov 1965; *Educ* Ernest Bailey GS Matlock, Chesterfield Coll of Technol; *Career* professional snooker player 1989-; represented England as amateur Home Int Championships 1987 and 1988, English Amateur champion 1989; best performances since turning professional: semi-finalist BCE Int 1989, quarter-finalist European Open 1990, finalist Rothmans Grand Prix 1990 (test v Stephen Hendry), quarter-finalist Stormseal UK Championship 1990; Best Newcomer of the Year (World Professional Billiards and Snooker Assoc) 1990; *Recreations* golf; *Clubs* Matlock Golf; *Style—* Nigel Bond, Esq; c/o Ian Doyle, Cuemasters Ltd, Kerse Rd, Stirling FK7 7SG (☎ 0786 6234, fax 0786 50068)

BOND, Richard Douglas; s of Douglas Charles Bond, and Vera Eileen, *née* Richards; *b* 23 July 1946; *Educ* Berkhamsted Sch, Guildford Coll of Law; *m* 27 Oct 1973, Anthea Mary, da of Harold Francis Charrington; 2 da (Charlotte Emma b 3 May 1976, Suzanne Claire b 1 Sept 1980); *Career* articled clerk Halsey Lightly & Hemsley 1964-69, ptnr Herbert Smith 1977- (joined as slr 1969), seconded to British National Oil Corporation 1976-78; memb Worshipful Co of Solicitors; memb: Law Soc, Int Bar Assoc; *Clubs* MCC, Lansdowne; *Style—* Richard Bond, Esq; Herbert Smith, Exchange House, Primrose St, London EC2R 2HS (☎ 071 374 8000, fax 071 496 0043)

BOND, Richard Henry; s of Lt-Col Ashley Raymond Bond, MBE, DL, JP (d 1975), of Creech Grange, Wareham, Dorset, and Mary, *née* Bowles (d 1952); *b* 15 April 1947; *Educ* Sherborne; *m* 25 April 1987, (Annabel) Susan, da of Brig John Henry Peter Curtis, MC, of Inshriach House, nr Aviemore, Invernessshire; 1 s (Henry b 30 Oct 1988), 1 da (Annabel b 27 Feb 1990); *Career* called to the Bar Inner Temple 1970; *Recreations* shooting, gardening, walking; *Clubs* Travellers', RAC; *Style—* Richard Bond, Esq; 1 Mitre Court Buildings, Temple, London EC4 (☎ 071 353 0434, fax 071 353 3988)

BOND GUNNING, Rufus Gordon; s of Col John Trehane Hamilton Gunning, and Beatrice Ibea Burton, *née* Todd (d 1973); the Gunnings are an old county family, and were seated at Tregonning in Cornwall during the reign of Henry IV, AD 1400; *b* 24 Sept 1940; *Educ* Harrow, RMA Sandhurst; *m* 1967, Lilah Mary, da of Capt John Bowen McKay, OBE (d 1971), of Laguna, Brightwalton Holt, nr Newbury, Berkshire; 1 s (Heyrick b 1971), 1 da (Annastasia b 1974); *Career* 9/12 Royal Lancers (POW) 1961, Capt, ret 1967; trg and personnel mangr Chubb Alarms Ltd 1967-72, dir and gen mangr Chubb Alarms Hong Kong Ltd 1972-74, md Chubb Hong Kong Ltd 1974-80, dir Chubb Cash 1980; chm: Chubb Alarms Ltd 1981-87, Guardal Ltd 1981-84, ICC Ltd 1981-82, Chubb Wardens Ltd 1981-87; exec memb Chubb & Son plc 1981-84, dir Chubb Racal Ltd 1986-87 (exec memb 1984-86), md Kalamazoo plc 1989 (resigned May 1989, md designate 1988-89); govr Tower Hamlets Coll of Further Educn 1970-72, tstee Royal Armouries 1989-; *Recreations* tennis, swimming, walking, skiing; *Clubs* Cavalry and Guards'; *Style—* R G Bond Gunning, Esq; Hopton Court, Alfrick, Worcestershire WR6 5HP

BOND-WILLIAMS, Noel Ignace; CBE (1979); s of late W H Williams; *b* 7 Nov 1914; *Educ* Oundle, Birmingham Univ; *m* 1939, Mary Gwendoline Tomey; 1 s, 2 da; *Career* dir Nat Exhibition Centre Ltd 1970-, vice chm Lucas Ltd 1979-84, chm Remploy Ltd 1979-82, pro chllr Univ of Aston in Birmingham 1970-82; *Style—* Noel Bond-Williams, Esq, CBE; Courtyard House, High Street, Lymington, Hampshire SO4 9AH (☎ 0590 72593)

BONDI, Prof Sir Hermann; KCB (1973); s of Samuel Bondi (d 1959), and Helene Bondi (d 1960); *b* 1 Nov 1919; *Educ* Realgymnasium Vienna, Trinity Coll Cambridge; *m* 1947, Christine M, da of Henry Watson Stockman, CBE (d 1982); 2 s, 3 da; *Career* former lectr maths Univ of Cambridge, prof mathematics King's Coll London 1954-85 (leave of absence 1967-71, honorary prof 1971-85, prof emeritus 1985-); chm Space Ctee MOD 1964-65, dir gen Euro Space Research Orgn 1967-71, chief scientific advsr MOD 1971-77, chief scientist Dept of Energy 1977-80; chm: Advsy Cncl Energy Conservation 1980-82, Natural Environment Research Cncl (and chief exec) 1980-84, Advsy Cncl Royal Naval Engrg Coll 1988-, Advsy Panel on Environmental Change, Commn of the Euro Communities and Euro Sience Fndn 1989-; pres: Inst of Mathematics & Its Applications 1974-75, Assoc of Br Science Writers 1981-83, Soc Research into Higher Educn 1981-, Br Humanist Assoc 1982-; master Churchill Coll Cambridge 1983-90; memb: Rationalist Press Assoc, Science Policy Fndn; fell: Trinity Coll Cambridge 1943-49 and 1952-54, KCL 1968-, Churchill Coll 1990-; Hon DSc: York, Sussex, Bath, Surrey, Southampton, Salford, Birmingham, St Andrews; G D Birla Award for Humanism New Delhi 1990; FRS 1959, FRAS, Hon FIEE; *Books* Cosmology, The Universe at Large, Assumption and Myth in Physical Theory, Relativity and Common Sense; *Recreations* walking, talking, skiing; *Style—* Prof Sir Hermann Bondi, KCB, FRS; 60 Mill Lane, Impington, Cambs CB4 4XN (☎ 0223 235075)

BONDS, William Arthur (Billy); MBE (1988); s of Arthur Edwin Bonds, and Barbara Ellen, *née* Robinson; *b* 17 Sept 1946; *Educ* Eltham Green Sr Sch; *m* 27 June 1970, Marilyn Teresa, da of John Charles Davis; 2 da (Claire Louise b 8 Nov 1974, Katie Elizabeth b 26 May 1979); *Career* professional footall manager; player: 95 appearances Charlton Athletic, 782 appearances West Ham Utd 1967-, 2 England under 23 caps (v Wales and Holland); honours as player West Ham Utd: FA Cup 1975 and 1980, runners up Euro Cup-Winners Cup 1976, runners up League Cup 1981; merit award Professional Footballers' Assoc 1988; *Style—* Billy Bonds, Esq; Manager, West Ham United FC, Upton Park, Green St, London E13 9AZ (☎ 071 472 2740)

BONE, Charles William Henry; s of William Stanley Bone (d 1966), and Elizabeth, *née* Burfoot; *b* 15 Sept 1926; *Educ* Farnham Coll of Art, Royal Coll of Art; *m* 1950, Sheila Mary, da of Lionel Mitchell (d 1956); 2 s (Richard, Sebastian); *Career* lectr Brighton Coll of Art 1950-86, conslt COSIRA 1952-70; craft advsr Malta Industs Assoc 1952-78, designer Stourhead Ball 1959-69, dir RI Galleries Piccadilly 1965-70; oils and water colours in exhibitions: Medici Gallery 1950-, London Gp, NEAC, RBA 1950-, RA 1950-; 29 one man exhibitions 1950; works in private collections: France, Italy, Malta, America, Canada, Japan, Aust, Norway, Sweden, Germany; produced Ceramic Mural on the History of Aerial Photography; critic for Arts Review; memb Cncl RI 1964 (vice pres 1974), govr Fedn of Br Artists 1976-81, 1983- and 1986-88 (memb Exec Cncl 1984-84), pres Royal Inst of Painters in Water Colours 1979-89 (vice pres 1974-79); Hunting Gp Prize for the Most Outstanding Watercolour by a Br Artist 1984; hon Botanical Artists, hon Medical Art Soc, hon memb Fedn of Canadian Artits, PPRI ARCA, FRSA, Hon FCA Canada; *Style—* Charles Bone, Esq; Winters Farm, Puttenham, Guildford, Surrey (☎ 0483 810226); 17 Carlton House Terrace, London

BONE, James (Jimmy); s of James Bone (d 1976), of Bilsthorpe, Notts, and Jean Syme (d 1986); *b* 22 Sept 1949; *Educ* Stirling HS; *m* 4 July 1970, Elizabeth Robina, da of Hugh Blair; 1 s (David Hugh b 29 June 1974); *Career* professional football manager; player: Partick Thistle 1968-72, Norwich City 1972-73, Sheffield Utd 1973-74, Celtic 1974-75, Arbroath 1975-78, St Mirren 1978-82, on-loan Toronto Blizzards Canada 1979 and 1980, Hong Kong Rangers 1982-83, Heart of Midlothian 1983-85; player-mangr Arbroath 1985-86, asst mangr St Mirren 1986-88, coach Dundee Utd 1988-89, mangr Airdrieonians 1989-; Scotland caps: 3 under 23, 2 full 1972-73; honours as player: Scot Div 2 Championship Partick Thistle 1971, Scot League Cup Partick Thistle 1972, Div 2 Championship Norwich City 1972, Anglo-Scot Cup St Mirren 1980; staff coach Scot Football Assoc, mining electrician 1966-72, branch mangr elecical wholesaler 1976-78, recreation asst 1985-86; *Recreations* reading; *Style—* Jimmy Bone, Esq; Airdrieonians FC, Broomfield Park, Airdre, Strathclyde (☎ 0236 68018)

BONE, John Bolam; s of John Bolam Bone (d 1945), of Redcar, Cleveland, and Adelaide, *née* Hobson (d 1936); *b* 20 March 1913; *Educ* privately, Sch of Architecture Univ of Durham, Univ of Newcastle; *m* 28 Aug 1943, Eleanor, da of William Alan Patterson (d 1968), of Saltburn-by-the-Sea, Cleveland; *Career* divnl architect Newcastle Regnl Hosp Bd 1948-52 (maj schemes for Teesside Div); sr architect: NCB Newcastle 1952-60 (large scale schemes incl workshops, pithead baths and med centres), Manchester Regnl Hosp Bd 1960-67, NW Metro Regnl Hosp Bd 1967-73; conslt architect Home Office involving prison establishments in N England 1973-87; chm Hampsthwaite Village Soc; ARIBA 1946, FRIBA 1970; *Recreations* music, water colours, conservation of amenity and improvement; *Clubs* Doric; *Style—* John Bone, Esq; 2 Thimbleby Cottages, Church Lane, Hampthswaite, Harrogate, North Yorkshire HG3 2HB (☎ 0423 771301)

BONE, Michael John Stuart; s of Cyril Bone (d 1983), and Ethel Florence; *b* 5 Feb 1937; *Educ* Framlingham Coll; *m* 20 April 1963, Valanda Penelope, da of Phillip Henry Lane, of Banstead, Surrey; 2 s (Timothy b 1964, Jason b 1972); *Career* admitted CA 1960; ptnrship practice 1960-86, md George Lines (Merchants) Ltd 1986-; Freeman: Worshipful Co of Horners, City of London; FCA; *Recreations* fly fishing, windsurfing; *Clubs* City Livery; *Style—* Michael Bone, Esq; Stradbroke House, Valley Way, Gerrards Cross, Bucks (☎ 0753 886410); Coln Industrial Estate, Old Bath Road, Colnbrook (☎ 0753 685354, fax : 0753 686031)

BONE, Dr Quentin; JP; s of Stephen Bone (d 1958), and Sylvia Mary, *née* Adshead; *b* 17 Aug 1931; *Educ* Warwick Sch, St John's Coll and Magdalen Coll Oxford (DPhil); *m* 9 Aug 1958, Susan Elizabeth, da of Sidney Smith (d 1963), of Merryfield House, Witney, Oxon; 4 s (Matthew b 5 June 1959, Oliver b 2 Jan 1961, Alexander b 13 Aug 1963, Daniel b 21 Nov 1965); *Career* zoologist Plymouth Lab of the Marine Biological Assoc UK 1959-; dep chief scientific offr 1987-; FRS 1984; *Books* Biology of Fishes (with N B Marshall, 1982); *Recreations* botany, travel, repairing machines; *Style—* Dr Quentin Bone, FRS, JP; Marchant House, Church Rd, Plymstock, Plymouth (☎ 0752 222772); The Marine Lab, Citadel Hill, Plymouth

BONE, Roger Bridgland; s of Horace Bridgland Bone (d 1979), and Dora Rose, *née* Tring; *b* 29 July 1944; *Educ* Palmer's Sch Grays Essex, St Peter's Coll Oxford (MA); *m* 3 July 1970, Lena Marianne, da of Georg Bergman (d 1975); 1 s (Christopher b 1977), 1 da (Marianne b 1980); *Career* HM Dip Serv: 3 sec Stockholm 1968-70, 1 sec Moscow 1973-75, 1 sec UK representation to the Euro Communities Brussels 1978-82, asst private sec to Sec of State for Foreign and Cwlth Affrs 1982-84, visiting fell Harvard Centre for Int Affrs 1984-85, chllr then head of Chancery Washington 1985-89, chllr FCO 1989-; *Recreations* wine, music; *Style—* Roger Bone, Esq; c/o Foreign and Commonwealth Office, London SW1A 2AH

BONE, Dr Thomas Renfrew (Tom); CBE (1987); s of James Renfrew Bone, of 64 Heather Court, Port Glasgow, and Mary, *née* Williams (d 1984); *b* 2 Jan 1935; *Educ* Port Glasgow HS, Greenock HS, Univ of Glasgow (MA, MEd, PhD); *m* 31 July 1959, Elizabeth, da of William Stewart (d 1972); 1 s (David James b 1960), 1 da (Hazel Jeanette b 1963); *Career* Eng teacher Paisley GS 1957-62, lectr educn Univ of Glasgow 1963-67; Jordanhill Coll: lectr educn 1962-63, head Dept of Educn 1967-71, princ 1972-; chm: Scottish Cncl for Educn Technology 1981-87, Standing Conf on Studies in Educn 1982-84, IBA's Educnl Advsy Cncl 1986-87, CNAA's Ctee for Teacher Educn 1987-89; vice chm: Scottish Examination Bd 1977-84, Scottish Tertiary Educn Advsy Cncl 1984-87, Gen Teaching Cncl 1987-90 and 1991- (chm 1990-91); fell Cwlth Cncl for Educnl Admin 1984; *Books* Studies in the History of Scottish Education 1872-1939 (ed, 1967), School Inspection in Scotland 1840-1966 (1968), The Changing Role of the Teacher Unesco (ed, 1987), Teacher Education in Europe: The Challenges Ahead (jt ed, 1990), contrib to various educnl books; *Recreations* golf; *Clubs* Western Gailes Golf, Paisly Burns; *Style—* Dr Tom Bone, CBE; Jordanhill College of Education, 76 Southbrae Drive, Jordanhill, Glasgow G13 1PP (☎ 041 950 320, fax 041 950 3268)

BONES, Dr Roger Alec; s of Stanley Frederick Bones (d 1953), and Ethel Kate, *née* Coles (d 1978); *b* 8 Feb 1928; *Educ* BSc, PhD; *m* 10 March 1955, Elizabeth, da of late William Richard Taylor; *Career* sci offr Govt Communications HQ 1952-55, lectr in physics Univ of Hong Kong 1955-58, econ advsr Nigerian Miny Commerce and Indust 1958-60, head trials assessment DeHavilland Propellors 1960, head govt contract laboratories Wayne Kerr Laboratories 1961-63; Standard Telephones and Cables Ltd (now STC plc) 1963-84: co tech ed 1963-64, mangr tech admin and coordination 1964-77, project asst to md STC plc 1977-79, mangr educnl liaison 1979-84, project dir Faraday Lecture 1981-84; dir industl projects City and Guilds of London Inst 1984-86 (hon memb), sr ptnr RAB Assocs consits 1987-; Freeman City of London, Liveryman Worshipful Co of Horners; ACIS, FIEE, CEng, CPhys, MInstP; *Books* Dictionary of Telecommunications (1973); *Recreations* classical music, photography, DIY, gardening; *Style—* Dr Roger Bones; White Jade, 5 Derwent Close, Claygate, Surrey KT10 ORF (☎ 0372 466018); RAB Assocs, 5 Derwent Close, Claygate, Surrey (☎ 0372 466018)

BONEY, Guy Thomas Knowles; QC (1990); s of Lt-Col Thomas Knowles Boney (d 1975), of Llandudno, and Muriel Hilary Eileen, *née* Long (d 1984); *b* 28 Dec 1944; *Educ* Winchester, New Coll Oxford (MA); *m* 4 Dec 1976, Jean Harris, da of Walter Ritchie, OBE (d 1979), of Solihull; 2 s (Oliver b 1979, Christian b 1981); *Career* called to the Bar Middle Temple 1968; rec 1985-, currently in practice Western Circuit; contrib to horological jls; *Books* The Road Safety Act 1967 (1971), Halsbury's Laws of England vol 40 (contrib); *Recreations* horology, music, amateur drama; *Clubs* Reform, Hampshire; *Style—* Guy Boney, Esq, QC; 3 Pump Ct, Temple, London EC4 (☎ 071 353 0711, fax 071 353 3319)

BONFIELD, Dr Peter Leahy; CBE (1989); s of George Robert Bonfield (d 1975), of Baldock, Herts, and Dora Patricia, *née* Talbot; *b* 3 June 1944; *Educ* Hitchin Boys' GS, Loughborough Univ of Technol (BTech, DTech); *m* 9 March 1968, Josephine, da of George Houghton, of Whitton, Humberside; *Career* div mangr Texas Instruments Inc Dallas USA 1966-81, exec dir and gp mktg dir Int Computers Ltd London 1981-84; chm STC Int Computers 1986-90 (md 1984-), dep chief exec STC plc 1987-90, chm and chief exec ICL plc 1990-; memb: Cncl CBI, Ct Cranfield Inst of Technol, Co of Technologists; CBIM; FIEE, FCIM, FBCS; *Recreations* music, sailing, jogging; *Clubs* RAC; *Style—* Dr Peter Bonfield, CBE; ICL plc, Putney, London SW15 1SW (☎ 081 788 7272, fax 081780 0158)

BONHAM, Sir Antony Lionel Thomas; 4 Bt (UK 1852); DL (Glos 1983); s of Maj Sir Eric Bonham, 3 Bt, CVO, JP (d 1937), and Ethel (d 1962), da of Lt-Col Leopold Seymour (s of Rt Hon Sir George Seymour, GCB, GCH, PC, and Hon Gertrude, da of 21 Baron Dacre; Sir George Seymour was s of Lord George Seymour, MP, s of 1 Marquess of Hertford); Sir Samuel George Bonham, 1 Bt, KCB, was govr and C-in-C Hong Kong and chief supt Br Trade in China 1847-53; *b* 21 Oct 1916; *Educ* Eton,

RMC Sandhurst; *m* 19 Feb 1944, Felicity, da of Col Frank Lionel Pardoe, DSO (d 1947), of Bartonbury, Cirencester; 3 s (Martin b 1945, Simon b 1947, Timothy b 1952); *Heir* s, (George) Martin Antony Bonham; *Career* serv Royal Scots Greys 1937-49, Maj; dir wine merchants 1950-70, ret; *Style*— Sir Antony Bonham, Bt, DL; Ash House, Ampney Crucis, Cirencester, Glos (☎ 028 585 391)

BONHAM, Hon Mrs (Caroline); *née* Hamilton; da of 2 Baron Holm Patrick, DSO, MC (d 1942); *b* 21 Oct 1926; *Educ* Lawnside Sch Malvern, Froebel Inst Roehampton; *m* 1951, Maj John Henry Hamilton Bonham, er s of Maj John Wroughton Bonham (d 1937), of Ballintaggart, Colbinstown, Co Kildare; 3 s; *Career* teacher Miss Ironside's Sch London 1948-50; *Recreations* reading, craftwork, languages; *Style*— The Hon Mrs Bonham; Trumroe, Castlepollard, Co Westmeath, Ireland (☎ 010353 44 61132)

BONHAM, (Arthur) Keith; s of George Bonham, of Plymouth, and Phyllis Ann, *née* Hammond; *b* 28 March 1939; *Educ* Plymouth Coll, Univ of Keele (BA); *m* 4 July 1964, Gillian Ann, da of William Ortelli Vokins (d 1981), of Bristol; 1 s (Adrian b 25 Sept 1970), 1 da (Tracy b 6 Aug 1968); *Career* CA 1966; ptnr Ernst and Whinney 1975 (managing ptnr Bristol office 1985-89, ptnr in charge of audit Ernst and Young 1989-90, managing ptnr Bristol office 1990-); pres W of Eng Soc of CAs 1987-88; treas and vice pres Clifton RFC 1967-; FCA; *Recreations* rugby, running, squash, swimming; *Clubs* Clifton RFC; *Style*— Keith Bonham, Esq; Ernst & Young, One Bridewell St, Bristol BS1 2AA

BONHAM, (George) Martin Antony; s and h of Sir Antony Bonham, 4 Bt, *qv*; *b* 18 Feb 1945; *Educ* Eton, Aston Univ; *m* 1979, Nenon Baillieu (b 1948), da of Robert Ruttan Wilson, of Petersfield (whose gggf in the male line, the Rev George Wilson, was bro of 9 and 10 Barons Berners), and Hon Yvette Baillieu, da of 1 Baron Baillieu; 1 s (Michael b 1980), 3 da (Lucie b 1982, Camilla b 1984, Sarah b 1987); *Career* sales mangr Calor Gas Ltd; *Recreations* sailing, skiing, golf, tennis, squash; *Clubs* Hurlingham, Bembridge Sailing; *Style*— Martin Bonham, Esq; The Old Vicarage, Gosfield, Halstead, Essex; Appleton Park, Riding Court Rd, Datchet, Slough, Berks (☎ 0753 40000)

BONHAM, Nicholas; s of the late Leonard Charles Bonham and Diana Maureen, *née* Magwood; *b* 7 Sept 1948; *Educ* Trent Coll; *m* 7 April 1977, Kaye Eleanor, da of John Robert Ivett, of Brisbane, Aust; 2 da (Katie b 1981, Jessica b 1982); *Career* dir Montpelier Properties 1970, dep chm W & FC Bonham & Sons Ltd 1987 (dir 1970, md 1975-87); Freeman City of London 1970, memb Worshipful Co of Pewterers; *Recreations* sailing, tobogganing, golf, skiing, elephant polo; *Clubs* South West Shingles Yacht, Acton Turville Bobsleigh, St Moritz Sporting, Royal Thames Yacht, Seaview Yacht, Kennel; *Style*— Nicholas Bonham, Esq; W & F C Bonham & Sons Ltd, Montpelier St, London SW7 IHH (☎ 071 584 9161, fax 071 589 4079)

BONHAM CARTER, Helena; da of The Hon Raymond Bonham Carter, and Elena, *née* Propper de Callejon; *b* 26 May 1966; *Educ* S Hampstead HS, Westminster; *Career* actress; films incl: Lady Jane 1985, A Room with a View 1986, A Hazard of Hearts 1987, Francesco 1988, Hamlet 1990, Where Angels Fear to Tread 1990; films for TV incl: The Vision 1987, Arms and the Man 1989; other work incl: theatre performances at Greenwich and Windsor, TV performances, BBC radio plays; *Recreations* going to the theatre and watching films; *Style*— Miss Helena Bonham Carter; c/o Jeremy Conway, Eagle House, 109 Jermyn St, Picadilly, London SW1 ☎ 071 839 2121

BONHAM-CARTER, Lady; Diane Anastasia; da of Mervyn Madden (d 1983); *m* 1973, as his 2 w, Sir (Arthur) Desmond Bonham-Carter, TD (former: dir Unilever, chm Bd of Govrs Univ Coll Hosp; d 1985), s of Gen Sir Charles Bonham-Carter, GCB, CMG, DSO (d 1955); *Career* hon sec The Nightingale Fund Cncl; assoc tstee Florence Nightingale Museum Tst, tstee W Sussex Nursing Benevolent Assoc, memb Chichester Community Health Cncl; *Style*— Lady Bonham-Carter; 15 Ashfield Close, Midhurst, Sussex GU29 9RP (☎ 073 081 2109)

BONHAM-CARTER, Baron (Life Peer UK 1986); Mark Raymond Bonham-Carter; eld s of Sir Maurice Bonham-Carter, KCB, KCVO (d 1960), and Baroness Asquith of Yarnbury, DBE (d 1969), *née* Lady Violet Asquith, da of 1 Earl of Oxford and Asquith, KG; *b* 11 Feb 1922; *Educ* Winchester, Balliol Coll Oxford, Univ of Chicago; *m* 1955, Leslie, da of late Condé Nast, of New York, and formerly w of 2 Baron St Just; 3 da (Jane b 1957, Virginia b 1959, Eliza b 1961) and 1 step-da; *Career* Capt Grenadier Gds; served WWII in N Africa and NW Europe (despatches, POW 1943, escape 1943); MP (Lib) Torrington 1958-59; chm: Race Rels Bd 1966-71, Community Rels Cmmn 1971-77; vice-chm and govr of BBC 1975-81; chm: Outer Circle Policy Unit 1976-81, Index on Censorship, Royal Ballet Govrs 1985-; dir Royal Opera House 1958-82; hon fell: Manchester Poly, Wolfson Coll Oxford 1990; Hon LLD Univ of Dundee 1978; *Clubs* Brooks's, MCC; *Style*— The Rt Hon the Lord Bonham-Carter; 13 Clarendon Rd, London W11 4JB; Collins Publishers, 8 Grafton St, London W1X 3LA (071 493 7070)

BONHAM-CARTER, Norman Albert; s of late Air Cdre David William Frederick Bonham-Carter, CB, DFC, AFC, and Joyce Angela Bonham-Carter; *b* 28 May 1928; *Educ* St Johns Coll and Gordon Bell HS Winnipeg Manitoba Canada, Charterhouse; *m* 1, 14 April 1956 (m dis 1974), Dorothy Lorna, da of late Samuel Harcombe; 2 s (David b 1963, Henry b 1965), 1 da (Miranda b 1962); m 2, 6 March 1974, Eirian Whittington, da of late Daniel Jenkins; *Career* National Provincial Bank (now National Westminster) 1946-49; admitted slr 1956; ptnr Thorold Brodie Bonham-Carter & Mason 1959-73, conslt Radcliffes & Co (following merger) 1974; hon slr Anglo Belgian Soc 1968-, vice pres Ctee Westminster Law Soc (former pres and sec), vice pres Slrs' Wine Soc (former chm) 1983-; memb Law Soc (memb Cncl 1980-89); officier Ordre de Coteaux de Champagne; *Recreations* wine, food, sport; *Clubs* Anglo Belgian; *Style*— Norman Bonham-Carter, Esq; (☎ 071 222 7040, fax 071 222 6208, telex 919302)

BONINGTON, Christian John Storey (Chris); CBE (1976); s of Charles Bonington (d 1983), and Helen Anne, *née* Storey; *b* 6 Aug 1934; *Educ* Univ Coll Sch London, RMA Sandhurst; *m* 1962, (Muriel) Wendy, da of Leslie Marchant; 2 s (and 1 s decd); *Career* cmmnd RTR 1956, served in N Germany, Army Outward Bound Sch (mountaineering instr); mgmnt trainee Unilever 1961-62; freelance writer, photographer and mountaineer 1962-; first ascent: Annapurna II (26,041 feet) Nepal with Dick Grant 1960, Nuptse (25,850 feet), third peak of Everest with Sherpa Ang Pemba 1961, Central Pillar of Freney Mont Blanc with Whillans, Clough and Djuclosz 1961; first Br ascent North Wall of the Eiger with Clough 1962; first ascent: Central Tower of Paine Patagonia with Whillans 1963, Old Man of Hoy with Patey and Bailey 1966; ascent Sangay in Ecuador (highest active volcano in the world) 1966; ldr: Annapurna South Face Expdn 1970, Br Everest Expdn 1972; first ascent: Brammah (21,036 feet) Kashmir with Estcourt 1973, Changabang Garhwal Himalaya with Boysen, Haston, Scott and Sandhu 1974; ldr Br K2 Expdn 1978, climbing ldr Br Mount Kongur Expdn 1981 (first ascent with Boardman, Rouse and Tasker 1981), ldr Br Everest Expdn NE Ridge 1982, first ascent W Summit of Shivling (21,330 feet) Gangotri with Fotheringham 1983, first Br ascent (solo) Mount Vinson (highest in Antarctica) 1983, ascent of Mount Everest (29,028 feet) as a memb of 1985 Norwegian Everest Expdn; ldr Norwegian - Br Menlungtse Expdn 1987; ldr Tibet Expdn 1988 which made first ascent West Summit Menlungtse; pres Lepra, dir Outward Bound Mountain Sch Eskdale; pres: Br Orienteering Fndn 1988, Br Mountaineering Cncl, Nat Tst Lake Dist Appeal; vice pres: Army Mountaineering Assoc, Young Explorers' Tst, Youth Hostels Assoc, Br Lung Fndn; Army Mountaineering Assoc, Young Explorer's Trust Youth Hostels Assoc, Br Lung Fndn; tstee Calvert Tst Outdoor Activity Centre for the Disabled, Himalayan Adventure Tst; Hon DSc: Sheffield, Lancaster; Hon MA Salford; Founder's medal RGS Lawrence of Arabia medal Royal Asian Soc; *Books* I Chose to Climb, Annapurna South Face, The Next Horizon, Everest South West Face, Changabang (jt author), Everest the Hard Way, Quest for Adventure, Kongur: China's Elusive Summit, Everest: The Unclimbed Ridge (with Dr Charles Clarke), The Everest Years, Mountaineer: Thirty Years of Climbing on the World's Great Peaks; *Clubs* Alpine, Climbers, Fell Rock, Climbing, Army & Navy; *Style*— Chris Bonington, Esq, CBE; Badger Hill, Hesket Newmarket, Wigton, Cumbria CA7 8LA (☎ 06998 286)

BONITTO, John Herbert Douglas; s of late Rudolph Erceldoune Bonitto, and late Violet May Bonitto; *Educ* Queen's Coll Oxford (Rhodes scholar, MA); *Career* navigator 2 Tactical Airforce RAF 1942-45, cmmnd offr 219 (Night Fighter) Sqdn; Colonial Devpt Corp 1949-53, memb Int Stock Exchange 1958 (joined 1954), memb Cncl Br Cwlth Ex-Servs League; AMSIA; *Recreations* reading, lawn tennis, racing; *Clubs* MCC, Royal Air Force, Queen's, Int Lawn Tennis Great Britain; *Style*— John Bonitto, Esq; 9 Donovan Court, Drayton Gardens, London SW10 9QS (☎ 071 370 3074)

BONN, Michael Walter; s of Maj Walter Basil Louis Bonn, DSO, MC (d 1973), of Oaklands, St Peter, Jersey, CI, and Lena Theodora, *née* Davidson; *b* 12 Jan 1927; *Educ* Eton; *m* 16 June 1951, Elizabeth Mary, da of Maj Anthony Buxton, DSO (d 1970), of Horsey Hall, Gt Yarmouth, Norfolk; 1 s (Simon b 1953), 3 da (Sara b 1952, Mary b 1956, Theresa b 1959); *Career* Lt Welsh Gds 1944-48, cmmnd 1945; joined Willis Faber & Dumas Ltd 1949 (dir 1965-76, md (Agencies) 196 dir: Morgan Grenfell (Jersey) Ltd 1960-, Anglo American Securities Ltd 1972-75, N Atlantic Securities Ltd 1972-75, Jersey Electricity Co Ltd 1980-, Fleming Ventures Ltd 1987-, Equity Capital for Indust Ltd 1987-, ECNG (Jersey) Ltd 1990-; memb: Men of the Trees Ctee 1976-88, Jersey Assoc of Youth & Friendship (treas 1976-78, chm 1984-88), Ctee Soc Jersiaise 1985-88, Cncl Int Dendrology Soc; dep of St Peter in States of Jersey 1978-84, Jurat of the Royal Court of Jersey 1985-; Kt of Magistral Grace, SMOM 1979; *Recreations* gardening; *Clubs* United; *Style*— Michael Bonn, Esq; Oaklands, St Peter, Jersey, CI (☎ 0534 814 81)

BONNAR, Douglas Kershaw; s of Thomas Bonnar; *b* 3 July 1931; *Educ* Edinburgh Acad, Melville Coll Edinburgh; *m* 1960, Suzanne, da of Charles Bettinson; 3 s, 1 da; *Career* memb ICA Scotland; md Chase Bank (Ireland) 1983-; *Recreations* bridge, snooker, golf; *Clubs* Caledonian, United (Jersey), Carrickmines Golf (Dublin), Fitzwilliam Lawn Tennis (Dublin); *Style*— Douglas Bonnar, Esq; Belmont, Kerrymount Ave, Foxrock, Co Dublin, Ireland

BONNAR, Joseph Hugh; s of Robert Bonnar (d 1978), of Dunfermline, and Jane Cant, *née* Paterson; *b* 31 Aug 1948; *Educ* Queen Anne Sch; *Career* md Joseph Bonnar Inc (specialising in antique and period jewellery); memb: Ctee Edinburgh and E Scot Assoc of Goldsmiths and Watchmakers, Nat Assoc of Goldsmiths, Soc of Jewellery Historians; *Recreations* foreign travel, the arts, good food; *Style*— Joseph Bonnar, Esq; 72 Thistle St, Edinburgh, Scotland (☎ 031 226 2811)

BONNELL, John Aubrey Luther; s of Thomas Luther Bonnell (d 1933), of Llanelli, and Ruth Griffiths (d 1982); *b* 2 March 1924; *Educ* Llanelli GS, King's Coll London, King's Coll Hosp (MB BS); *m* 1, June 1954 (m dis 1964), Joan Perham; 2 da (Sian Lesley b 2 April 1956, Amanda b 10 Oct 1957); m 2, 26 March 1966, Maureen Knowles (d 1990), da of Alfred Charles Warner (d 1985), of Ewell; *Career* asst physician Dept for Res in Industl Med MRC London Hosp 1950-58, chief med advsr CEGB 1978-86 (dep chief nuclear health and safety offr 1958-78), med advsr Electricity Cncl 1978-90 (Electricity Assoc 1990-), specialist advsr occupational med SW Thames RHA 1979-85; memb Bd Int Cmmn Occupational Health 1980-86; past pres: Soc Occupational Med 1976-77, Soc Radiological Protection 1972-74, Section of Occupational Med RSM 1982; Freeman: City of London 1968, Worshipful Soc of Apothecaries 1971 (chm Livery Ctee 1987-88); FFOM (RCP) 1979, FRCP 1987, FSRP 1989; *Books* Chapters in: Recent Advances in Occupational Medicine 3 (1987), Current Approaches in Occupational Health 3 (1987), Fitness For Work (1988), author of various scientific and med pubns on occupational med, radiological protection & toxicology; *Recreations* gardening, bridge; *Style*— Dr John Bonnell; 71 The Green, Ewell, Surrey KT17 3JX (☎ 081 393 1461); The Electricity Assoc, 30 Millbank, London SW1 (☎ 071 834 2333)

BONNER, Frederick Ernest; CBE (1974); s of George Frederick Bonner (d 1983), of London, and Edith May, *née* Luckhurst (d 1951); *b* 16 Sept 1923; *Educ* St Clement Danes Holborn Estate GS, Univ of London (BSc, DPA); *m* 1, 1957, Phyllis (d 1976), da of Henry Holder (d 1957), of Cobham, Surrey; m 2, 24 Sept 1977, Ethel Mary, da of John Beardon (d 1952), of Harberton, Devon; *Career* fin appts in local govt 1940-48, asst fin offr Central Electricity Authy 1950-58 (sr accountant 1949-), CEGB: asst chief fin offr 1958-61, dep chief fin offr 1961-65, chief fin offr 1965-69, bd memb 1969-75, dep chm 1975-86; memb Electricity Cncl 1969-86, pt/t memb UKAEA 1977-86, chm BA Helicopters 1983-85, memb of Monopolies and Mergers Cmmn 1987-, non exec dir Nuclear Electric plc 1990-; chm Uranium Inst 1987-88 (vice chm 1984-85), Bd memb Public Fin Fndn 1985-, memb Tech Advsy Ctee SE Soc CAs 1987-, hon treas BIEE 1989-; Freeman City of London 1983; memb IPFA 1946, FCA 1949, CBIM 1976, FRSA 1984; *Recreations* music, gardening, reading; *Style*— Frederick Bonner, Esq, CBE; Monopolies Mergers Commission, New Court, 48 Carey St, London WC2A 2JT (☎ 071 324 1467, fax 071 324 1400)

BONNER, Hilary Mary (Mrs Gunnell); da of Cecil Raymond Bawden (d 1980), of Bideford, North Devon, and Hilda May, *née* Keen; *b* 2 Aug 1949; *Educ* Edgehill Coll Bideford Devon; *m* 1969 (m dis), Geoff Bonner; m 2, 1987, Clive Gunnell; *Career* journalist; Daily Mirror Training Scheme Devon 1967-71, The Sun 1971-82 (news reporter, showbusiness reporter, feature writer and chief showbusiness writer); showbusiness ed: The Mail on Sunday 1982-86, The Daily Mirror 1986-90; asst ed and showbusiness ed The People 1990-; *Books* Rene and Me, The Story of Actor Gordon Kaye (1989); *Recreations* scuba diving, horse riding, films, gardening, backgammon, books, boats; *Clubs* Scribes; *Style*— Ms Hilary Bonner; The People, Holborn Circus, London EC1 (☎ 071 822 2519, fax 071 353 0922)

BONNER, Paul Max; s of Frank Max Bonner (d 1985), and Lily Elizabeth Marchant, *née* Jupp; *b* 30 Nov 1934; *Educ* Felsted; *m* 26 July 1956, (Nora) Jenifer, da of Dr George Raymond Hubbard; 2 s (Neil b 6 Jan 1957, Mark b 27 May 1959), 1 da (Alison b 27 June 1962); *Career* Nat Serv 1953-55, cmmnd 2 Lt RASC 1953, Acting Capt 1955, served in Egypt; radio studio mangr BBC 1955, asst producer 1957, BBC TV current affairs producer 1960, documentary producer 1965, head of sci and features 1977, controller of programmes Channel Four 1980 (exec dir 1983), dir Programme Planning Secretariat ITV 1987; memb Ctee for Public Understanding of Sci; dir Broadcast Support Services; FRTS 1989; *Books* The Third Age of Broadcasting (jtly); *Recreations* walking, photography, sailing; *Clubs* Reform; *Style*— Paul Bonner, Esq; Independent Television Association, Knighton House, 56 Mortimer St, London W1N 8AN (☎ 071 636 6866, telex 262988)

BONNET, Maj-Gen Peter Robert Frank; MBE (1975); s of James Robert Bonnet (d

1970), and Phyllis Elsie, *née* Lumsden (d 1985); *b* 12 Dec 1936; *Educ* RMA Sandhurst, Univ of London (BSc); *m* 29 Dec 1961, Sylvia Mary, da of George William Coy (d 1964); 2 s (Gavin b 21 Oct 1962, Timothy b 6 June 1964); *Career* cmmnd 2 Lt Royal Reg of Artillery 1958, regtl duty Parachute Bde 1962-64, Capt 17 Trg Regt RA 1964-66, 3 Regt RHA 1966-68, Maj Royal Mil Coll of Sci 1969, Staff Coll Camberley 1970, GS02 Intelligence Centre Ashford 1971-72, Battery Cdr 40 Field Regt RA 1973-75, Lt-Col HQ Dir RA 1975-78, CO 26 Regt RA 1978-81, Brig Cdr RA 2 Div 1982-84, Nat Def Coll New Delhi India 1984-85, Maj-Gen dir RA 1986-89, GOC Western Dist 1989; *Recreations* painting and sculpture; *Clubs* Army & Navy; *Style—* Maj-Gen Peter Bonnet, MBE

BONNETT, Ralph; s of William Herbert Bonnett (d 1961), of Bedford, and Mary Elizabeth, *née* Orpin (d 1975); *b* 6 Jan 1928; *Educ* Bedford Sch, Pembroke Coll Cambridge (BA); *m* 2 April 1964, Jean Sloss, da of Bertie Reginald Pearn, OBE (d 1976), of Norfolk; 1 s (Andrew James William b 17 Oct 1966); *Career* cmmnd Lt RA 1946-49; articled clerk Speechly Mumford & Craig 1952-55, admitted slr 1955, slr Long & Gardiner 1956-61, ptnr Linklaters & Paines 1967 (joined 1961); Liveryman Worshipful Co of Coachmakers & Coach Harness Makers (clerk 1957-58); memb: Law Soc, City of London Law Soc; *Recreations* gardening, walking; *Style—* Ralph Bonnett, Esq; 42 Hazlewell Rd, Putney, London, SW15 6LR (☎ 081 788 2832); Linklaters & Paines, Barrington Hse, 59/67 Gresham St, London, EC2V 7JA (☎ 071 606 7080, fax 071 606 5113)

BONNETT, Prof Raymond; s of Harry Bonnett (d 1955), of Lakenheath, and Maud, *née* Rolph; *b* 13 July 1931; *Educ* Bury St Edmunds Co GS, Imperial Coll London (BSc), Univ of Cambridge (PhD), Univ of London (DSc); *m* 24 Aug 1956, Shirley, da of Samuel James Rowe (d 1959), of Bewdley; 2 s (Paul b 1962, Alastair b 1964), 1 da (Helen b 1960); *Career* served RAF 1949-51, cmmnd PO 1950, RAF Lyneham 1950, RAF Mauripur 1951 (air movements); Salters fell Cambridge 1957-58, res fell Harvard 1958-59, assoc prof chemistry UBC 1959-61; QMC (now Queen Mary and Westfield Coll): lectr organic chemistry 1961-66, reader 1966-74, prof 1974-76, chm of organic chemistry 1976-, head Dept of Chemistry 1982-87; friend of: Tate, William Morris Gallery, Br Theatre; FRSC, CChem; *Clubs* Epping Soc; *Style—* Prof Raymond Bonnett; Chemistry Dept, Queen Mary and Westfield College, Mile End Rd, London E1 4NS (☎ 081 975 5024, fax 081 981 7517)

BONNEY, George Louis William; s of Dr Ernest Henry Bonney (d 1938), of 3 Vicarage Gardens, London and Gertrude Mary, *née* Williams; *b* 10 Jan 1920; *Educ* Eton, St Mary's Hosp Med Sch (MB, MS); *m* 26 Dec 1950, Margaret, da of Thomas William Morgan, of Nelson, Glamorgan; 2 da (Mary b 1952, Victoria b 1954); *Career* Surgn Lt RNVR 1945-47, RN Res 1949-53; travelling fellowship postgrad Med Fedn 1950-51, registrar and clinical res asst Inst of Orthopaedics 1947-54; orthopaedic surgn: Southend-on-Sea Gp of Hosps 1953-55, St Mary's Hosp Paddington 1954-84; Watson-Jones lectr RCS 1976, Henry Floyd lectr Inst Orthopaedics 1977; assoc ed Jl of Bone and Joint Surgery 1960-68; chm: St Mary's Hosp Med Ctee 1972-74, Dist Hosp Med Ctee Paddington and N Kensington Health Dist 1978-80, Mgmnt Team Paddington and N Kensington Health Dist 1978-80; memb: Cncl Med Def Union 1964-88 (Hon Fell), Bd of Govrs St Mary's Hosp 1972-74, SICOT; pres Old Etonian Med Soc 1989-; FRSM, FRCS; *chapters in*: British Surgical Practice (1957), Clinical Surgery (1966), Operative Surgery (ed), Clinical Orthopaedics (1983), Microreconstruction of Nerve Injuries (1987), Current Therapy in Neurologic Disease (1987), Medical Negligence (1990), Clinical Neurology (1990); *Recreations* fishing, reading, photography, listening to music; *Clubs* Leander; *Style—* G L W Bonney, Esq; 71 Porchester Terrace, London W2 3TT (☎ 071 262 4236); Wyeside Cottage, Fawley, Hereford HR1 4SP (☎ 0432 840219)

BONNOR-MAURICE, Maj Edward Arthur Trevor; DL (Powys 1983); s of Trevor Bonnor-Maurice (d 1959); *b* 24 April 1928; *Educ* Winchester; *m* 1958, Lavinia, eldest da of Sir Richard Leighton, 10 Bt, TD (d 1957); 2 da (Emma Mary b 1959, m 1987 Mark Fane, Frances Flavia b 1962); *Career* served Coldstream Gds 1946-61, Maj; MFH Tanatside Foxhounds 1971-, chm Br Horse Soc 1990-, memb CC Montgomeryshire 1961-74; High Sheriff 1975-76; *Clubs* Cavalry and Guards', MCC; *Style—* Maj Edward Bonnor-Maurice, DL; Bodynfoel Hall, Llanfechain, Powys (☎ 069 184 486)

BONO, (Paul Hewson); s of Robert (Bobby) Hewson, and Iris Hewson; *b* 10 May 1960; *Educ* Mount Temple Sch; *m* Alison (Ali); 1 da (Jordan b 10 May 1989); *Career* vocalist and fndr memb U2 1978-; U2 formed in Dublin with The Edge, *qv* (guitars, piano, vocals), Larry Mullen, *qv* (drums), and Adam Clayton, *qv* (bass); U2 played first London dates and released U23 (EP 1979, CBS Ireland) 1979, band signed to Island Records and released Boy (LP 1980) and three singles 1980, toured UK, US, Belguim and Holland 1980, released October (LP 1981, Silver disc) which entered UK charts at No 11 and three singles Fire, Gloria and A Celebration giving the band their first UK charts entries 1981-82, band toured extensively in UK, US, Ireland and Europe 1981-83, New Year's Day (single 1983) gave band their first UK Top Ten hit, War (LP 1983, US Gold disc) entered UK charts at No 1 and US Top Ten, band toured US and UK 1983, Under A Blood Red Sky (live album 1983, UK Platinum disc) entered UK charts at No 2, voted Band of the Year Rolling Stone Writers Poll 1984, Pride (In the Name of Love) single produced by Brian Eno and Daniel Lanois reached No 3 in UK charts gaining Silver disc 1984, band toured Aust, NZ and Europe, The Unforgettable Fire (LP 1984) entered UK charts at No 1, Unforgettable Fire (single 1985) entered UK charts at No 8; played: Madison Square Garden NY, Longest Day Festival Milton Keynes Bowl, Croke Park Dublin, Live Aid Wembley (Best Live Aid Performance Rolling Stone Readers Poll 1986) 1985; voted Best Band Rolling Stone Readers Poll 1986 (joint No 1 Critics Poll); played: Self Aid Dublin, A Conspiracy of Hope (Amnesty Int Tour) 1986; The Joshua Tree (LP 1987, Grammy award Album of the Year, 12 million worldwide sales) entered UK charts at No 1 as fastest selling album in Br music history and reached No 1 in US charts; With Or Without You (single 1987), I Still Haven't Found What I'm Looking For (single 1987), Where The Streets Have No Name (single 1987) released and entered UK charts; first three singles from The Joshua Tree reached No 1 in US charts; world tour opens Arizona 1987; 100 shows in US and Europe incl: Wembley Stadium, Madison Square Gardens NY, Sun Devil Stadium Arizona and Croke Park Dublin (winners Grammy award Best Rock Performance 1987-88); Desire (single 1988), gave U2 their first No 1 single, Rattle & Hum (LP 1988) entered UK charts at No 1, U2 play Smile Jamaica (Dominion Theatre) in aid of hurricane disaster relief 1988, world premiere U2 Rattle & Hum (film 1988) Dublin, Angel of Harlem (single 1988) entered UK charts at No 10; Grammy awards: Best Rock Performance (Desire) 1989, Best Video (Where The Streets Have No Name) 1989; When Love Comes to Town (single 1989), All I Want Is You (single 1989) released, band toured Aust 1989, New Year's Eve 1989 concert at Point Depot Dublin (broadcast live to Europe and USSR, 500 million estimated audience), recorded Night & Day for Aids benefit LP (Red, Hot & Blue) 1990; *Style—* Bono; c/o Principle Management, 30-32 Sir John Rogersons Quay, Dublin 2, Ireland (☎ 081 777 330, fax 071 777 276)

BONSALL, Sir Arthur Wilfred; KCMG (1977), CBE (1957); s of Wilfred Cook Bonsall (d 1963), of Beck House, Seathwaite, Broughton-in-Furness, and Sarah Bonsall; *b* 25 June 1917; *Educ* Bishop's Stortford Coll, St Catharine's Coll Cambridge; *m* 1941, Joan Isabel (d 1990), da of late G C Wingfield, of Bournemouth; 4 s, 3 da; *Career* joined Air Miny 1940, dir Govt Communications HQ 1975-78; *Style—* Sir Arthur Bonsall, KCMG, CBE; 1 Coxwell Court, Coxwell St, Cirencester, Gloucestershire GL7 2BQ

BONSALL, David Charles; s of Leonard Dale Bonsall (d 1984), and Nellie Bonsall; *b* 26 July 1956; *Educ* Winchester Coll, St John's Coll Cambridge (MA, LLM); *m* 11 Oct 1980, Margaret Ruth, da of Arthur George Shaw, OBE, of 15 Jennings Rd St Albans, Herts; 1 da (Philippa Ruth b 25 Sept 1989); *Career* admitted slr 1981; ptnr Freshfields 1987- (articled clerk 1979-81); Freeman Worshipful Co of Slrs; *Books* Securitisation (1990); *Recreations* golf, skiing, music; *Clubs* The Royal St George's Golf, Woking Golf, Rye Golf; *Style—* David Bonsall, Esq; 49 Scarsdale Villas, London W8 6PU (☎ 071 736 9343); Freshfields, Whitefriars, 65 Fleet St, London EC4Y 1HT (☎ 071 936 4000, fax 071 248 3487, car 0836 778404)

BONSALL, Richard James (Rick); s of Geoffrey Holtham (d 1972), and Gladys Elizabeth Catherine, *née* Tait; *b* 6 Nov 1955; *Educ* Westlake Boys HS Auckland NZ, Univ of Auckland (BA), Osaka Univ of Foreign Studies (postgrad dip), Tokyo Univ of Fine Arts (MA); *m* 1985, Julia, da of Roland Jesse; 1 s (James Joseph Holtham b 3 April 1990); *Career* press offr Japan Nat Tourist Orgn London 1979, mgmnt trainee and PR mangr Matsushita Electric London 1980-83, account dir Charles Barker Lyons 1983-85, assoc dir Roland Company London 1985, dir and head of International Business Unit Hill and Knowlton London 1986-; assoc Trinity Coll London (Dip Piano Teaching); memb Japan Soc (London), MIPR, MIOD; *Recreations* skiing, tennis, health and fitness, music, antiques; *Clubs* Holmes Place Fulham (health and fitness); *Style—* Richard Bonsall, Esq; 56 The Crescent, Chelsea Harbour, London SW10 0XB (☎ 071 352 2500); Hill and Knowlton (UK) Ltd, 11a West Halkin St, London SW1X 8JL (☎ 071 333 0333, fax 071 413 3223)

BONSER, Ven David; s of George Frederick Bonser (d 1981), of 123 Newsome Rd South, Huddersfield, and Alice, *née* Roe; *b* 1 Feb 1934; *Educ* Hillhouse Secdy Sch Huddersfield, Huddersfield Tech Coll, Kings Coll London (AKC), Univ of Manchester (MA); *m* 22 Aug 1960, Shirley, da of Irving Wilkinson (d 1965), of 24 Trinity St, Huddersfield; 1 s (Simon b 8 March 1965), 2 da (Jane b 21 June 1963, Elizabeth b 26 April 1967); *Career* Nat Serv SAC (RAF) 1955-57; textile mangr 1958; curate St James Heckmondwike 1962-65, asst chaplain Univ of Sheffield and curate St George's Sheffield 1965-68, rector St Clements Chorlton-cum-Hardy Manchester 1968-82, canon Manchester Cathedral 1980-, area dean Hulme 1981-82, vicar and archdeacon Rochdale 1982-86, archdeacon Rochdale 1986-; *Recreations* golf, tennis, reading, theatre; *Clubs* Commonwealth; *Style—* The Ven the Archdeacon of Rochdale; 21 Belmont Way, Rochdale, Lancs OL12 6HR (☎ 0706 486 40)

BONSOR, Elizabeth, Lady; Elizabeth; da of Capt Angus Valdimar Hambro, JP, DL (d 1957) of Milton Abbas, Dorset, and his 2 wife, Vanda Dorothy Julia, *née* Charlton (d 1981); *b* 22 Oct 1920; *m* 1942, Maj Sir Bryan Cosmo Bonsor, 3 Bt, MC, TD (d 1977); 2 s; *Style—* Elizabeth, Lady Bonsor; Ascot Lodge, London Road, Ascot, Berks

BONSOR, Hon Lady (Nadine Marisa); *née* Lampson; JP (Beds); da of 2 Baron Killearn; *b* 23 Aug 1948; *Educ* Francis Holland Sch, Univ of Oxford (MA); *m* 4 Sept 1969, Sir Nicholas Cosmo Bonsor, 4 Bt; 2 s (Alexander Cosmo, b 1976, James Charles b 1982), 3 da (Sacha Henrietta b 1975, Elizabeth Nadine b 1987, Mary Catherine b (twin) 1987); *Style—* The Hon Lady Bonsor, JP; Liscombe Park, Leighton Buzzard, Beds

BONSOR, Sir Nicholas Cosmo; 4 Bt (UK 1925), of Kingswood, Epsom, Surrey; MP (C) Upminster 1983-; s of Sir Bryan Bonsor, 3 Bt, MC, TD (d 1979), and Elizabeth, *née* Hambro, (*see* Bonsor, Elizabeth, Lady); *b* 9 Dec 1942; *Educ* Eton, Keble Coll Oxford; *m* 4 Sept 1969, Hon Nadine Marisa Lampson, da of 2 Baron Killearn; 2 s, 3 da; *Heir* s, (Alexander) Cosmo Bonsor b 8 Sept 1976; *Career* served The Royal Bucks Yeo (RA TA) 1964-69; called to the Bar Inner Temple; in practice 1967-75; MP (C) Nantwich 1979-83; vice-chm: Tourism Sub-Ctee 1980-83, Cons Parly Foreign Affrs Ctee 1981-83, Cons Parly Def Ctee 1987-90; chm: Food Hygiene Bureau Ltd 1986-, The Cyclotron Tst for Cancer Treatment 1984-, The Br Field Sports Soc 1988-; memb Cncl of Lloyd's 1987-; vice chm Standing Cncl of the Baronetage 1987-89 (chm 1990-); FRSA 1970; *Recreations* sailing, military history, sailing; *Clubs* White's, Royal Yacht Sqdn, House of Commons Yacht (commodore 1985-86), Pratt's, Beefsteak; *Style—* Sir Nicholas Bonsor, Bt, MP; Liscombe Park, Leighton Buzzard, Beds

BONSOR, (Angus) Richard; s of Sir Brian Bonsor, Bt, MC, TD (d 1977), of Liscombe, Leighton Buzzard, Beds, and Elizabeth, *née* Hambro; *b* 3 Feb 1947; *Educ* Eton, Keble Coll Oxford (BA); *m* 14 Jan 1971, Susan Anne, da of David Henry Lewis Wigan, of Thorpe Abbotts Race, Diss, Norfolk; 2 s (Rupert b 26 Sept 1974, Edward b 16 July 1976), 1 da (Clare b 3 Sept 1981); *Career* ptnr Rowe & Pitman 1978 (joined 1968), dir S G Warburg Securities 1986, associated to Matheson Securities 1989; memb Stock Exchange; *Recreations* golf, racquets; *Clubs* Whites, Turf, Royal West Norfolk Golf; *Style—* Richard Bonsor, Esq; Matheson Securities, 16 St Helens Place, London EC3A 6DE (☎ 071 638 1200, fax 071 638 9004, telex 885216, car 0860 212204)

BONYNGE, Richard; AO (1983), CBE (1977); s of C A Bonynge, of Epping, NSW; *b* 29 Sept 1930; *Educ* Sydney Conservatorium; *m* 1954, Dame Joan Sutherland, *qv*; 1 s; *Career* artistic dir Vancouver Opera Assoc 1975-; *Style—* Richard Bonynge, Esq, AO, CBE; c/o Australian Opera, PO Box 291, Strawberry Hills, NSW 2012, Australia

BOOBBYER, Hon Mrs ((Juliet) Honor); *née* Rodd; da of 2 Baron Rennell, KBE, CB (d 1978), and Lady Rennell of Rodd, Mary Constance Vivian Smith (d 1981); *b* 28 Oct 1930; *Educ* Westonbirt Sch; *m* 1957, Brian Boobbyer, s of Dr Philip Watson Boobbyer, WS (d 1960), of Ealing; 2 s (Philip, Mark); *Career* Moral Rearmament in Asia, US, Australia, Europe and S Africa; *Books* 'Columba', a play with music (1982); *Recreations* writing, painting; *Style—* The Hon Mrs Boobbyer; 2 The Paddock, Oxford OX2 7PN (☎ 0865 58624); Little Rodd, Presteigne, Powys LD8 2LL (☎ 0544 260 060)

BOODLE, John Victor; s of Rev John Boodle (d 1971); *b* 28 Oct 1926; *Educ* Wadham Coll Oxford (MA); *m* 1957, Lorna Eileen, da of James Vincent (d 1970); 1 da; *Career* md Br Fermentation Products 1981- (dir 1957-), dir G R Spinks & Co Ltd 1986; memb: Cncl CBI Eastern Region 1971-87, CBI Anglian Water & Enviroment Ctee 1972- (chm 1987,) Industl Rels Bd Chemical Industs Assoc 1972-, East Anglian Economic Devpt Cncl 1973-80, Anglian Water Authy 1977- 89; non-exec dir Anglian Water plc 1989-; *Recreations* shooting, fishing, music, lit; *Style—* John Boodle, Esq; 26 Graham Rd, Ipswich, Suffolk IP1 3QE (☎ 0473 254647)

BOOHAN, Michael Daniel; s of Daniel Ernest Boohan (d 1983), and Winifred Joan, *née* Tylee; *b* 9 Nov 1940; *Educ* Poole GS; *Career* ptnr Grant Thornton (London Office) 1967, non-exec vice chm Mornington Building Society (dir 1983-), appointed inspr to investigate affairs of Blue Arrow plc Dept of Trade and Indust; FCA; *Style—* Michael Boohan, Esq; Grant Thornton, Grant Thorton House, Melton St, Euston Square, London NW1 2EP (☎ 071 383 5100)

BOOK, Anthony; JP (1987); s of Alec Book (d 1987), of Newcastle upon Tyne, and Betty Book (d 1957); *b* 19 June 1946; *Educ* Newcastle Royal GS, Univ of Bristol (BSc); *m* 5 Aug 1969, Susan Lynn (d 1985), da of Irving Brand, of Long Beach,

California; 1 s (Jeffrey Adam b 1971), 2 da (Jennifer Beth b 1973, Juliette Hiliary b 1977); *Career* brand mangr and market res Lever Brothers Ltd 1969-78, dir of Consumer Servs American Express Europe Ltd 1978-84, managing ptnr Compass Consultancy 1984-; Awards: winner Br Computer Soc Award (for Applications) 1982, winner Int Direct Mktg Symposium (for Tech Innovation in Mktg) 1984; speaker on direct mktg and electronic media at major confs in UK and Overseas; govr Stanley Deason Sch; FBIM 1986; *Books* Database Marketing (1989); *Recreations* flying, DIY, gardening, philately, travel; *Style—* Anthony Book, Esq, JP; 50 Hill Dr, Hove BN3 6QL; Compass House, 13 Dover St, London W1X 3PH (☎ 071 491 9100)

BOOKER, Christopher John Penrice; s of the late John Mackarness Booker, of Shillingstone, Dorset, and Margaret Booker (d 1991); *b* 7 Oct 1937; *Educ* Shrewsbury, CCC Cambridge; *m* 1, 1963 (m dis), Hon Mrs Emma C Tennant, *qv*; m 2, 1972, Christine Verity (m dis); m 3, 1979, Valerie, da of late Dr M S Patrick, OBE; 2 s; *Career* author, journalist and broadcaster; *Style—* Christopher Booker, Esq; The Old Rectory, Litton, Bath, Somerset (☎ 076 121 263)

BOOKER, Russell Stuart; s of Wilfred Bryan Booker, of Maidstone, Kent, and Irene, *née* Netherton; *b* 21 Aug 1957; *Educ* Maidstone GS, Univ of Birmingham; *m* 23 March 1985 (m dis 1988), Hilary Margaret Curley; *Career* slr and ptnr Booth & Blackwell 1985-88, ptnr Masons 1988; *Books* Buying & Selling a Business (with L Kane, 1990); *Recreations* sailing, gardening; *Style—* Russell Booker, Esq; 30 Aylesbury St, London EC1R 0ER (☎ 071 490 4000, telex 8811117, fax 071 490 2545)

BOOME, Simon Adrian Kenneth; s of Lt-Col Kenneth Edward Boome (d 1973), and Leila Houssmayne, *née* Webb; *b* 7 Nov 1943; *Educ* Wellington; *m* 1968, Rosemary Georgina Patricia, da of Michael Thomas Barstow; 2 da (Helen Venetia b 1975, Laura Veronica b 1978); *Career* slr Markby Stewart & Wadesons, ptnr Cameron Markley Hewitt; memb Law Soc; *Recreations* golf, gardening; *Clubs* Royal Wimbledon Golf; *Style—* Simon Boome, Esq; 34 Dunstall Rd, London SW20 0HR (☎ 081 946 1830); Cameron Markby Hewitt, Sceptre Court, 40 Tower Hill, London EC3N 4BB (☎ 071 702 2345, fax 071 702 2303)

BOON, Maj John McMillan; OBE (1982); s of Percy Edmund Boon, of London (d 1916), and Lily Ellen, *née* Payne (d 1965); *b* 5 Oct 1914; *Educ* Great Yarmouth GS; *m* 16 April 1938, Barbara Olive, da of Charles George Wilkerson, of Great Yarmouth, Norfolk (d 1941); 2 s (Michael b 1942, Peter b 1945), 1 da (Susan b 1944); *Career* served WWII, Maj Norfolk Yeo (TA) (ret 1956); chartered sec and accountant; md: E Anglian Water Co 1961-84, dep chm 1985-; memb cncl of British Waterworks Assoc 1961-73 and Water Co's Assoc 1956- (chm 1979-84); memb: cncl of Water Research Centre 1965-82, E Suffolk & Norfolk River Authority 1963-73, cncl of River Authorities' Assoc 1963-73 (dep chm 1970-73); Liveryman Worshipful Co of Plumbers 1972, Freeman City of London; Hon Fell Inst of Water and Environmental Mgmnt 1984; *Recreations* fishing, shooting, golf; *Clubs* Royal Norfolk & Suffolk Yacht; *Style—* Major John Boon, OBE; Lyndhurst, Burgh Road, Gorleston, Great Yarmouth, Norfolk (☎ 0493 662811)

BOON, John Trevor; CBE (1968); s of Charles Boon (d 1943), of 42 Aylmer Road, London N2, and Mary Alice, *née* Cowpe (d 1964); *b* 21 Dec 1916; *Educ* Felsted, Trinity Hall Cambridge (MA); *m* 9 Sept 1943, Felicity Ann, da of Stewart Logan (d 1933), of Kuala Lumpur, Malaysia; 4 s (Christopher John b 1946, Nicholas Stewart b 1949, Charles Logan b 1955, Humphrey Fullerton b 1958); *Career* served WWII NW Europe (despatches); chm: Mills and Boon Ltd 1972-, Harlequin Overseas 1978-, Marshall Editions 1977-; dir Torstar Corp 1981-85; pres: Soc of Bookmen 1981-, Publishers' Assoc 1961-63, Int Publishers' Assoc 1972-76 (hon memb 1982); Hon MA Open Univ 1983; *Recreations* family and social life, walking, swimming, wine; *Clubs* Beefsteak, Garrick, Savile, RAC; *Style—* John Boon, Esq, CBE; Mills & Boon Ltd, Eton House, 18-24 Paradise Road, Richmond, Surrey TW9 1SR (☎ 081 948 0444, fax 081 940 5899, telex 24420)

BOON, Dr Nicholas Antony; s of Capt John Nicholas Boon, MC, of Cramond Lodge, Timber Ridge, Loudwater, nr Rickmansworth, Herts, and Doreen Myrtle, *née* Francke; *b* 31 Dec 1950; *Educ* Canford, Gonville and Caius Coll Cambridge (MA, MB BChir), Middx Hosp Med Sch (MD); *m* 19 May 1979, (Grace) Anne, da of Prof W B Robertson, of 3 Cambisgate, 109 Church Rd, Wimbledon, London; 2 da (Victoria b 11 Aug 1982, Sarah Jane b 15 March 1984); *Career* clinical lectr and sr registrar John Radcliffe Hosp Oxford 1983-86, conslt cardiologist Royal Infirmary of Edinburgh 1986-, hon sr lectr Univ of Edinburgh 1986-; FRCP 1988; *Books* author of numerous scientific pubns and contrib to various med textbooks, incl Davidson's Principles and Practice of Medicine; *Recreations* golf, skiing; *Clubs* Dalmahoy Country; *Style—* Dr Nicholas Boon; 7 Cobden Crescent, Edinburgh EH9 2BG (☎ 031 667 3917); Dept of Cardiology, Royal Infirmary of Edinburgh, Lauriston Place, Edinburgh (☎ 031 229 2477)

BOON, Sir Peter Coleman; s of Frank and Evelyn Clara Boon; *b* 2 Sept 1916; *Educ* Felsted; *m* 1940, Pamela; 1 s, 1 da; *Career* former chm and md Hoover (joined 1946, md (Australia) 1955-65, md 1965-75, chm 1975-78); chm: Highclere Investment Tst 1979-, Hoover Administrative Services Brussels 1978-; jt dep chm London Sound 1982-; Goodyear exec prof at Kent State Univ (USA); Hon LLD Strathclyde; Chevalier de l'Ordre de la Couronne (Belgium) 1976; FBIM, FRSA; kt 1979; *Clubs* Hurlingham, Western Racing (Ayr), Australia Jockey, American National (Sydney), Royal Sydney Yacht Sqdn; *Style—* Sir Peter Boon; 2969 Harriett Road, Cuyahoga Falls, Ohio 44224, USA; Goodyear Executive Professor, c/o Kent State University, Dept of Business Administration, Room 450, Kent, Ohio 44240, USA; c/o Hoover Ltd, PO Box 22, Perivale, Greenford, Middx

BOORD, Antony Andrew; s of Sqdn Ldr Sir Richard Boord, 3 Bt (d 1975), and bro and hp of Sir Nicolas Boord, 4 Bt; *b* 21 May 1938; *Educ* Charterhouse; *m* 1960, Anna Christina von Krogh; 1 s (Andrew Richard b 1962), 1 da (Tamsin Katrina b 1961); *Career* dir Planned Packaging Ltd; *Clubs* Special Forces; *Style—* Antony Boord, Esq; Darch House, Stogursey, Bridgwater, Somerset

BOORD, Sir Nicolas John Charles; 4 Bt (UK 1896); s of Sqdn-Ldr Sir Richard William Boord, 3 Bt (d 1975); *b* 10 June 1936; *Educ* Eton, Sorbonne, Societa Dante Alighieri (Italy), Univ of Santander (Spain); *m* 1, 1960 (m dis 1965), Françoise, da of Giuseppe Tempra; m 2, 1965, Françoise Renée Louise, da of Marcel Clovis Mouret, of Marseilles; *Heir* bro, Antony Andrew Boord; *Career* scientific translator/English trg specialist; jt translator of The History of Physics and The Philosophy of Science 1972, and of numerous scientific papers; *Style—* Sir Nicolas Boord, Bt; Résidence Les Aloadès, Bâtiment L, 94 Traverse Prat, 13008 Marseilles, France

BOORER, David Ian; s of Thomas Percy Boorer, of Sussex, and Edna Elsie, *née* Starkings; *b* 10 Sept 1948; *Educ* Worthing Tech HS, City of London Poly (BA); *m* 3 Nov 1973, Caroline Gail, da of John Graham Jackson, of France; 1 s (Nicholas b 1976), 3 da (Joanna b 1979, Emma b 1981, Louise b 1984); *Career* assoc dir Bank of Tokyo Int; *Recreations* rowing, music; *Style—* David I Boorer, Esq; The Old Manor House, Little Humby, Grantham, Lincolnshire NG33 4HW; 20/24 Moorgate, London EC2 (☎ 071 628 3000)

BOORMAN, Lt-Gen Sir Derek; KCB (1986, CB 1982); s of late N R Boorman, MBE, and Mrs A L Boorman, *née* Patman; *b* 13 Sept 1930; *Educ* Wolstanton, Sandhurst; *m* 1956, Jennifer Jane Skinner; 1 s, 2 da; *Career* Public Rels Army 1978-79, Dir Military Ops 1980-82, Cdr Br Forces Hong Kong 1982-85, Chief of Defence Intelligence 1985-88, Col The Staffordshire Regt (Prince of Wales) 1985-90, Col 6 Gurkha Rifles 1989-; chm Camberwell Health Authy 1989-; dir: Tarmac Construction Ltd 1988-, Crown House Engineering 1990-, Thai Holdings Ltd; *Recreations* gardening, music, shooting; *Clubs* Naval and Military; *Style—* Lt-Gen Sir Derek Boorman, KCB; c/o Lloyds Bank Ltd, Cox's and King's Branch, Pall Mall, London SW1

BOORMAN, Edwin Roy Pratt; s of Henry Roy Pratt Boorman, *qv*; *b* 7 Nov 1935; *Educ* Rydal Sch, Queens' Coll Cambridge (MA); *m* 1 (m dis 1982), Merrilyn Ruth Pettit; 4 da; m 2, 1983, Janine Mary, of William Craske, of Penenden Heath, Maidstone; 1 s; *Career* chm Kent Messenger Ltd 1986- (md 1965); chm Kent Assoc of Boys' Clubs, vice-chm St John for Kent, fin dir Royal British Legion Industries; *Recreations* sailing (yacht Messenger); *Clubs* Ocean Cruising, Medway Yacht; *Style—* Edwin Boorman, Esq; Redhill Farm, 339 Redhill, Wateringbury, Kent; Kent Messenger, Messenger House, New Hythe Lane, Larkfield, Kent ME20 6SG (☎ 717880)

BOORMAN, Henry Roy Pratt; CBE (1966, MBE 1945); s of Barham Pratt Boorman, JP, of Cedars, Maidstone (d 1928), and Elizabeth Rogers (d 1932); *b* 21 Sept 1900; *Educ* Leys Sch Cambridge, Queens' Coll Cambridge (BA, MA); *m* 1, 1933, Enid Margaret, da of Edgar E Starke; 1 s (Edwin Roy Pratt, *qv*); m 2, 1947, Evelyn Mary, da of Frederick G Clinch; 1 da (Mary Elizabeth); *Career* Dep County Welfare Offr 1941; Maj 1944 (served N Europe); Kent Messenger: journalist 1922-28, ed and proprietor 1928-52, chm 1952-82, pres 1982-; ed journal Kent 1931-62 (for which awarded Sir Edward Hardy Gold medal, Assoc of Men of Kent and Kentish Men 1964); FJI 1936, pres Newspaper Soc 1960-61; Kent CC 1933-46, Mayor of Maidstone 1962-63, Alderman Maidstone 1964-70, JP 1962-63, DL Kent 1968-82; tenor bell given to Canterbury Cathedral in H Boorman's name by Kent Messenger 1980; awarded medal of Honour American Biographical Inst; *Books* Merry America; *Recreations* travel; *Clubs* Royal Cwlth Soc; *Style—* Henry Boorman, Esq, CBE; St Augustine's Priory, Bilsington, Ashford, Kent TN25 7AU (☎ 0233 720252)

BOOSEY, Georgina Caroline; da of Dr Donald Harden, CBE, *qv*, and Cecil Ursula, *née* Harriss (d 1963); *b* 3 Jan 1936; *m* 1960, Anthony Leslie Marchant Boosey, vice pres The Hawk Tst, s of Leslie Boosey (d 1979), sometime chm of Boosey and Hawkes; *Career* managing ed Vogue Magazine, dir Friends of the Earth Tst, memb UK Ctee of Fndn Jules et Paul-Emile Léger of Quebec; *Style—* Mrs Anthony Boosey; Vogue, Vogue House, Hanover Sq, London W1R 0AD (☎ 071 499 9080)

BOOT, David Henry; s of Henry Matthews Boot (d 1974); *b* 15 Sept 1931; *Educ* Uppingham Sch, Loughborough Univ of Technol (DLC); *m* 1956, Gillian Mary, da of Reeves Charlesworth, OBE (d 1974); 4 s; *Career* chm Henry Boot & Sons; *Recreations* photography, golf, walking; *Style—* David Boot, Esq; Henry Boot & Sons PLC, Banner Cross Hall, Sheffield S11 9PD (☎ 0742 555444, fax 547453)

BOOT, Edward James (Jamie); s of (Edward) Hamer Boot, OBE, MM (d 1987), and Joan Margaret, *née* Denniff; *b* 19 Nov 1951; *Educ* Rossall Sch; *m* Susan Philippa (Sue), da of John Humphrey Gowers (d 1988); 2 s (Hamer b 1981, William b 1987), 1 da (Georgina b 1984); *Career* md Henry Boot & Sons plc 1986-; *Recreations* shooting; *Style—* Jamie Boot, Esq; Henry Boot & Sons plc, Banner Cross Hall, Ecclesall Road South, Sheffield S11 9PD (☎ 0742 555 444)

BOOTE, Barbara Mary; da of Arthur Boote (d 1989), of Colehill, Wimborne, Dorset, and Joan, *née* West (d 1980); *b* 8 June 1954; *Educ* Bromley GS; *Career* sec and editorial asst: Coronet Books 1973-77, Magnum Books 1977-80; publishing dir Sphere 1989- (ed mangr 1981-86, ed dir 1986-89); *Style—* Barbara Boote; Sphere Books Ltd, Orbit House, 1 New Fetter Lane, London EC4A 1AR (☎ 071 377 4618)

BOOTE, Charles Richard Michael; TD (1971, and two clasps 1978 and 1983), DL (Staffs 1988); s of Col (Charles Geoffrey) Michael Boote, MBE, TD, JP, DL, *qv*, and Elizabeth Gertrude, *née* Davies (d 1980); *b* 7 Aug 1939; *Educ* Cheltenham; *m* 9 Oct 1965, Alison Brookes, da of Charles Kenneth Stott (d 1979), of Tixall Lodge, Stafford; 1 s (James b 1974), 2 da (Vanessa b 1967, Emma b 1970); *Career* Maj TA cmd B (Staffs Yeo), The Queens Own Mercian Yeo 1974-78, 2 i/c The Queens Own Mercian Yeo 1978-80; md Armitage Shanks Integrated Systems 1988-90, corp devpt dir Home Products Div Blue Circle Industries plc 1987-89; chm Staffs Ctee of the Rural Devpt Cmmn 1984- (memb Cmmn's Econ Advsy Panel 1988-); dir Staffs Trg and Enterprise Cncl 1989-, dir Stafford Enterprise Ltd 1990-, memb Staffs Ctee Country Landowners Assoc 1988-, vice chm and treas Staffs Assoc of Boys Clubs 1976-, employers rep W Midlands TAVR Assoc Ctee 1983-; High Sheriff of Staffordshire 1990-91; FCA, FCMA, CMI; *Recreations* skiing, salmon fishing, stalking, tennis, squash, pedigree Suffolk sheep farming; *Clubs* Squash Raquets Assoc (life memb), Pointless (private dining); *Style—* Charles Boote, Esq, TD, DL; Enson Moor House, Sandon, Stafford ST18 9TA (☎ 088 97 223)

BOOTE, Gervase William Alexander; s of Col Charles Geoffrey Michael Boote, MBE, TD, JP, DL, *qv*, and Elizabeth Gertrude Boote, *née* Davies (d 1980); *b* 2 April 1944; *Educ* Cheltenham; *m* 1967 (m dis 1987), Janet Mary Pierrette, da of Alan Edward Stott, *qv*; 1 s (Richard b 1969), 1 da (Caroline b 1972); *Career* Peat Marwick Mitchell & Co 1962-72; dir Samuel Montagu & Co Ltd 1972-; FCA; *Recreations* tennis, golf, fishing; *Clubs* Hurlingham Worplesdon Golf; *Style—* Gervase W A Boote, Esq; 2A Hurlingham Court, Ranelagh Gardens, London SW6 3UL (☎ 071 736 6530); Samuel Montagu & Co Ltd, 10 Lower Thames Street, London EC3R 6AE (☎ 071 260 9000)

BOOTE, Robert Edward; CVO (1971); s of Ernest Haydn Boote (d 1983), and Helen Rose (d 1941); *b* 6 Feb 1920; *Educ* Hanley HS Stoke-on-Trent, Univ of London (BSc, DPA); *m* 2 April 1948, Vera, da of Ernest Badian; 1 s (Anthony Robert b 1953), 1 da (Karin Verli b 1949); *Career* Army 1939-46 actg Lt-Col, demob hon rank Maj; admin offr City of Stoke-on-Trent 1946-48, chief admin offr Staffs Co Planning and Devpt Dept 1948-54, first DG Nature Conservancy Cncl 1963-90 (princ 1954-64, dep dir 1964-73); chm Broadland Report 1965; memb: Govt Ctee on Pesticides 1958-73, UN Habitat Symposium 1970, Govt Countryside Review Ctee 1977-79; fndr and chm UK Ctee IUCN (treas and vice pres 1975-81, election offr 1984), UK del to Cncl of Europe Ctee for Conservation of Nature and Natural Resources 1963-71 (chm Euro Ctee 1969-71, Organising Ctee for Euro Conservation Conf 1970); various posts in meetings of UN, UNESCO, EEC and OECD 1968-81, Anglo American Environmental Gp Ditchley 1970; judge Agro Environmental TV and Films Berlin 1970, 1972, 1974 and 1980, speaker Eurogesprach Vienna 1970, IUCN rep Int Conf on Antarctica Marine Living Resources 1984 (chm Resolution 1981), advsr Euro Architectural Heritage Year 1975, advsr H&L Select Ctee on Euro Community 1980-81; chief Marshal to HM The Queen 1970; memb Cncl: FFPS 1979-83, BTCV (vice pres) 1980-, RSNC (vice pres) 1980-, WWF 1980-86, Ecological Parks Tst 1980-85, ctees for UK Conservation and Devpt Prog 1980-83, Friends of ENO 1980-87, Common Ground Int 1981-85, HGTAC Foresty Cmmn 1981-87, Age Concern (vice pres) 1990-; conservator Wimbledon and Putney Commons 1981-, Seychelles Appeal Ctee Royal Soc 1980-87, chm and initiator Age Resource 1988-; advsr: Macmillan Guide to Br Nature Reserves 1980-, Shell Better Br Campaign 1980-; memb editorial bds: International Journal of Environmental Studies 1975-, Town Planning Review 1979-85, International Journal of Environmental Education and Information 1981-83; helped to prepare and appeared in film Pacemaker 1970; BBC Man of Action 1977; Hon Assoc Landscape Inst 1971, Hon MRTPI 1978; FREconS 1953-61, AIPR 1957-61, FCIS 1960-81, FRSA 1971; Greek Distinguished Serv Medal 1946, van Tienhoven European Prize 1980, merit award IUCN 1984; *Books* Man and Environment (as Robert Arvill, 1967, 5 edn 1984); *Recreations* travel, theatre, music; *Style*— Robert Boote, Esq, CVO; 3 Leeward Gardens, Wimbledon, London SW19 7QR (☎ 081 946 1551)

BOOTH *see also*: Gore-Booth

BOOTH, Alan James; s of His Hon James Booth, of Worsley, Manchester, and Joyce Doreen, *née* Mather; *b* 18 Jan 1955; *Educ* Bolton Sch, Selwyn Coll Cambridge (MA); *m* 4 April 1983, Anne Lesley, da of Eric Binns, of Bramhall, Stockport, Cheshire; 1 s (Charles b 13 Nov 1988), 1 da (Jane b 29 March 1987); *Career* called to the Bar Grays Inn 1978; practising Northern circuit; *Recreations* athletics; *Clubs* Sale Harriers, Hawks Cambridge, Last Drop Bolton; *Style*— Alan Booth, Esq; Wayoh View House, Chapeltown, Turton, Lancs; Deans Court Chambers, Cumberland House, Crown Square, Manchester (☎ 061 834 4097, fax 061 834 4805)

BOOTH, His Hon Judge Alan Shore; QC (1975); 4 s of Parkin Stanley Booth, and Ethel Mary, *née* Shore; *b* 20 Aug 1922; *Educ* Shrewsbury, Univ of Liverpool; *m* 1954, Mary Gwendoline, da of John Hilton; 1 s, 1 da; *Career* called to the Bar 1949; circuit judge 1976-; *Recreations* golf; *Clubs* Royal Liverpool Golf, Royal and Ancient (St Andrews); *Style*— His Hon Judge Alan Booth, QC; 18 Abbey Rd, West Kirby, Wirral L48 7EW (☎ 051 625 5796)

BOOTH, Rt Hon Albert Edward; PC (1976); s of Albert Henry Booth, of Scarborough, and Janet, *née* Mathieson; *b* 28 May 1928; *Educ* St Thomas's Winchester, South Shields Marine Sch, Rutherford Coll of Technol; *m* 1957, Joan, da of Josiah Amis, of North Shields; 3 s; *Career* MP (Lab) Barrow-in-Furness 1966-83; election agent 1951, 1955; contested (Lab) Tynemouth 1964; Min State Employment 1974-76, Employment Sec 1976-79; oppn front bench spokesman Transport 1981; dir S Yorks Passenger Transport Exec 1983-; CIMechE; *Style*— The Rt Hon Albert Booth

BOOTH, Charles Leonard; CMG (1978), LVO (1961); s of Charles Leonard Booth (d 1987), and Marion, *née* Lawton (d 1981); *b* 7 March 1925; *Educ* Heywood GS, Pembroke Coll Oxford (MA); *m* 1 Aug 1958, Mary Gillian, da of Archibald George Emms (d 1978); 2 s (Charles b 1959, James b 1962), 2 da (Lydia b 1960, Rachel b 1964); *Career* WWII Capt RA 1943-47; Dip Serv; third sec (later second sec) Rangoon 1950-55, FO 1955-60 (private sec to Parly Under Sec 1958-60), first sec Rome 1960-63; head of chancery: Rangoon 1963-64, Bangkok 1964-67, FO 1967-69; Dep High Cmmr Kampala 1969-71; cnsllr and consul gen Washington 1971-73, cnsllr Belgrade 1973-77, ambass Burma 1978-82, high cmmr Malta 1982-85, FCO 1985-90; Offr of the Order of Merit of the Italian Republic 1961; *Recreations* opera, gardening, walking; *Clubs* Travellers'; *Style*— Charles Booth, Esq, CMG, LVO; 7 Queen St, Southwold, Suffolk IP18 6EQ

BOOTH, Sir Christopher Charles; s of Lionel Barton Booth and Phyllis Petley, *née* Duncan; *b* 22 June 1924; *Educ* Sedbergh Sch, St Andrew's Univ (MB, MD); *m* 1, 1959, Lavinia Loughridge, of Belfast; 1 s, 1 da; m 2, 1970, Soad Tabaqchali; 1 da; *Career* former sr lectr London Postgrad Medical Sch; prof and dir Dept Medicine RPMS London Univ 1966-77, dir Clinical Research Centre MRC 1978-; FRCP, FRCPEd, Hon FACP; kt 1982; *Style*— Sir Christopher Booth; 33 Dukes Ave, London W4 (☎ 081 994 4914)

BOOTH, Dr Clive; s of Henry Booth, of Poynton, Cheshire, and Freda Mary Booth; *b* 18 April 1943; *Educ* King's Sch Macclesfield, Trinity Coll Cambridge (MA), Univ of California Berkeley (PhD); *m* 28 June 1969, (Gwendolen) Margaret, da of George Sardeson (d 1967); *Career* Dept of Educn and Sci 1965 and 1975-81 (princ private sec to Sec of State 1975-77), Harkness fell Univ of Calif 1973-75, dep dir Plymouth Poly 1981-84, HM inspr of schs 1984-86, dir Oxford Poly 1986-; involved with: Cncl for Indust and Higher Educn, Cncl for Nat Academic Awards, Ctee of Dirs of Polys, Polys and Colls Funding Cncl, Oxford Sci Park, Oxford Tst; Thames Action Resource Gp for Educn and Trg, Oxford Consortium, First Oxfordshire Radio; memb: Computer Bd for Univs and Res Cncls, Fulbright Fellowship Scheme, Polys and Colls Employers Forum, Soc for Res into Higher Educn; *Recreations* walking, bridge, opera; *Style*— Dr Clive Booth; Oxford Polytechnic, Oxford OX3 0BP (☎ 0865 819001, fax 0865 819009, telex 83147 VIA)

BOOTH, Clive Antony; s of Reginald Frances Booth, MBE, and Irene, *née* Tonks; *b* 17 Dec 1951; *Educ* Worcester Sch, Univ of Aston (BSc); *m* 15 June 1979, Joan Patricia, da of John Owen, BEM (d 1986), of Rotherham; 2 s (Simon b 1982, Robin b 1985); *Career* md Pegasus Software Ltd 1988-90, dir of UK Ops Computerland Europe 1985-88, currently md Revelatio Technological (UK) Ltd and advsr to other computer cos; fndr memb and dir Br Microcomputer Fedn; memb Assoc of Accounting Technicians; *Recreations* flying; *Style*— Clive Booth, Esq; 17 Darlow Dr, Biddenham, Bedford MK40 4AX (☎ 0243 218368, office 0860 788630)

BOOTH, Rev Canon David Herbert; MBE (1944); s of Robert Booth (d 1941), of Milborne St Andrews, and Clara Annette, *née* Harvey; *b* 26 Jan 1907; *Educ* Bedford Sch, Pembroke Coll Cambridge (MA); *m* 2 May 1942, Diana Mary, da of Lt-Col William Wheaton Chard, MC (d 1953), of Brighton; 2 s (Peter b 1947, David b 1951), 1 da (Bridget b 1952); *Career* WWII RNVR 1939-45, served Chaplain HMS Orion, HMS Collingwood, advanced party Western Desert, 30 AV RM; asst curate Hampton Parish Church 1932-34, chaplain Tonbridge Sch 1935-39, rector of Stepney 1945-53, vicar of Brighton 1953-59, archdeacon of Lewes 1959-71, provost Shoreham Coll 1977- (headmaster 1972-77); chaplain to HM The Queen 1975-77; memb Local Educn Ctees; govr: Brighton Coll, Haileybury Coll; fndr and pres Nat Schools Jumping Championship 1963-; *Style*— The Rev Canon David Booth, MBE; Courtyard Cottage, School Rd, Charing, Ashford, Kent TN27 (☎ 023371 3349)

BOOTH, Dr Derek Blake; s of Sir Philip Booth, 2 Bt (d 1960); h to Btcy of bro, Sir Douglas Booth, 3 Bt, *qv*; *b* 7 April 1953; *Educ* Hampshire Coll, Univ of California, Stanford Univ, Univ of Washington; *m* 1981, Elizabeth Dreisbach; 1 s (Colin b 1982), 1 da (Rachel b 1986); *Career* geologist; *Style*— Dr Derek Booth

BOOTH, Sir Douglas Allen; 3 Bt (UK 1916); s of Sir Philip Booth, 2 Bt (d 1960); *b* 2 Dec 1949; *Educ* Gaspar de Portolà Junior HS, Beverly Hills HS California, Harvard Univ; *Heir* bro, Derek Blake Booth; *Career* TV and film writer; *Style*— Sir Douglas Booth, Bt; 438 South Cochran, Apt 108, Los Angeles, California 90036, USA

BOOTH, Sqdn-Ldr Frank; s of late William Booth, of Cheshire, and late Jessie Irene, *née* Dedman; *b* 27 Aug 1931; *Educ* Sir John Deanes GS Northwich; *m* 19 March 1955, Janice Ann, da of late Jack Clayton, of Hartford, Cheshire; 1 s (Jonathan Frank b 1965), 1 da (Heather Ann b 1957); *Career* served in RAF, Canada, Far East, Madagascar, Europe; flying appts with 12 and 210 Sqdn (Flt Cdr) Navigation Inst Cambridge Univ Air Sqdn, instr/flying duties RAF Flying Coll Manby, ops duties Wildenrath, Gp Navigation/Weapons Staff Offr, HQ 18 Gps/HQ Northern Maritime Air Region, Staff Offr Underwater Weapons Operational Requirements MOD (Air), RAF Exercise Co-ordinator MOD (Air), RAF Cdr RAF Lakenheath, Staff Offr Establishments, HQ RAF Support Cmd, ret 1986; bursar Forres Sch Swanage Dorset 1986-; *Recreations* sailing, walking, painting; *Style*— Sqdn Ldr Frank Booth; 24 Dacombe Close, Upton, Poole, Dorset (☎ 0202 623950); Forres School, Swanage, Dorset (☎ 0929 422 760)

BOOTH, Sir Gordon; KCMG (1980, CMG 1969), CVO (1976); s of Walter Booth, of Bolton, Lancs, and Grace Booth; *b* 22 Nov 1921; *Educ* Canon Slade Sch, Univ of London; *m* 1944, Jeanne Mary, da of James Herbert Kirkham, of Bolton; 1 s, 1 da; *Career* served WWII Capt RAC and 13/18 Royal Hussars; memb HM Dip Serv 1965-80; cnsllr Copenhagen 1965-69, consul gen Sydney 1971-74, NY 1975-80; advsr on Int Trade and Investmt, dir Hanson plc 1981-89, vice chm Bechtel Ltd 1986-, dir City of London Heliport Ltd 1989-; chm Simplification of Int Trade Procedures Bd 1980-86, memb Br Overseas Trade Bd 1981-85; *Clubs* Brooks's, Walton Heath Golf; *Style*— Sir Gordon Booth, KCMG, CVO; Pilgrims Corner, Ebbisham Lane, Walton on the Hill, Surrey KT20 5BT (☎ 073781 3788)

BOOTH, Dr (Vernon Edward) Hartley; s of Vernon William Hartley Booth, and Eilish, *née* Morrow; *b* 17 July 1946; *Educ* Queens Coll Taunton, Univ of Bristol (LLB), Downing Coll Cambridge (LLB, Dip Int Law, PhD); *m* 30 July 1977, Adrianne Claire Cranefield, da of Knivett Garton Cranefield, DFC; 2 s (Peter Toby Hartley b 1985, Thomas Edward Hartley b 1988), 1 da (Emily Claire Hartley b 1982); *Career* called to the Bar Inner Temple, practising 1970-84, special advsr to PM and memb 10 Downing St Policy Unit 1984-88, chief exec and md Br Urban Devpt Ltd 1988-90, chm Br Urban Regeneration Assoc 1990, dir Br Urban Devpt Ltd 1990; Parly candidate (C) Hackney and Stoke Newington 1983; vice pres OCU; advsr Royal Life Saving Soc, govr schs, chm Cncl Reference Norwich Drug Abuse Centre; FInstD; *Books* British Extradition Law and Procedure (volume I 1980, volume II 1981); *Clubs* Carlton; *Style*— Dr Hartley Booth; 21 Aldebert Terrace, London SW8 1BH (☎ 071 582 3270, fax 071 793 0595)

BOOTH, John Aidan; s of Sidney Booth (d 1953), and Ruth, *née* Traylor (d 1977); *b* 7 Dec 1926; *Educ* Selby Abbey Sch, Selby Tech Inst, Univ of Goettingen, Univ of Bristol; *m* 21 Oct 1947, Pamela Jean, *née* Olivant; 3 da (Dorinda b 1949, Kathryn b 1954, Joanne b 1961); *Career* WWII dep chief clerk RE 1944-48, chief engr 5 Div BAOR 1947; univ extramural lectr in fine art, freelance author, publisher Cambridge House Books; fndr: Univ of Bristol Bowman 1950, Royal Leamington Spa Canoe Club 1954; fndr memb West Wilts Youth Sailing Assoc 1966; FRSA 1977; *Books* Antique Maps of Wales (1977), Looking at Old Maps (1979), Looking at Old Prints (1983), Day War Broke Out (St Dunstan's Charity Book, 1984), Our Forgotton History (filmscript, 1986); *Recreations* collecting, chess, brassband music, power boating; *Style*— John Booth, Esq; 30 Edenvale, Westbury, Wiltshire BA13 3NY (☎ 0373 823 271)

BOOTH, John Barton; s of Capt (Percy) Leonard Booth (d 1972), of Bournemouth, and Mildred Amy, *née* Wilson (d 1975); *b* 19 Nov 1937; *Educ* Canford, King's Coll London, King's Coll Hosp Med Sch (MB BS, AKC); *m* 18 June 1966, Carroll, da of Lt-Col (James) Ivor Griffiths (d 1983), of Peel, IOM; 1 s (James b 29 Aug 1972); *Career* conslt ENT surgn London Hosp 1972-, conslt surgn Royal Nat Throat Nose and Ear Hosp 1973-78, Hunterian prof RCS 1980-81, conslt ENT surgn St Luke's Hosp for the Clergy 1983-, civil conslt otologist RAF; hon conslt laryngologist: Musicians Benevolent Fund 1974-, RCM 1974-, Newspaper Press Fund 1982-, Royal Opera House Covent Garden 1983-, Royal Soc of Musicians of GB 1987-; Fedn of Univ Cons: vice chm 1960-61, chm 1961-62, vice pres 1962-63; memb Gen Purposes and Exec Ctees Cons Pty 1961-62; ed Jl of Laryngology and Otology 1987- (asst ed 1979-87); memb Cncl RSM 1980-88 (memb Sci and Exec Ctee 1984-87); Freeman City of London 1972, Liveryman Worshipful Soc of Apothecaries 1969; MRAeS, assoc Zoological Soc of London, FRCS; *Books* The Ear (vol 3, ed 5 edn) Scott Brown's Otolaryngology (1987); *Recreations* golf, the arts; *Clubs* MCC, RAC, United and Cecil; *Style*— John Booth, Esq; 18 Upper Wimpole St, London W1M 7TB (☎ 071 935 5631)

BOOTH, John Sebastian Macaulay; 2 s of George Macaulay Booth (d 1970), sometime dir Bank of England (1 cous, through his f, Rt Hon Charles Booth, of Sir Alfred Booth, 1 Bt), and Margaret, aunt of Daniel Meinertzhagen, *qv*; *b* 26 April 1913; *Educ* Harrow, Trinity Coll Cambridge (BA); *m* 1957, Juno (d 1968), 2 da of Guy Maynard Liddell, CB, CBE, MC (d 1958; 2 cous once removed through his f Augustus of Alice Liddell, the model for Lewis Carroll's Alice, and gs of Hon George Liddell, 5 s of 1 Baron Ravensworth); 2 da (Georgina b 1959, Theresa b 1961); *Career* serv WWII Capt Dunkirk, 1 Army N Africa, 11 Armoured Divn Normandy; tanner; dir Garnar Booth; *Recreations* skiing; *Clubs* Reform; *Style*— John Booth, Esq; Bramley Tree Cottage, Manor Lane, West Hendred, Oxon OX12 8RP (☎ 0235 832436)

BOOTH, Laurie; *Educ* Dartington Sch of Arts; *Career* work with various experimental theatre gps incl Triple Action Theatre and Cardiff Laboratory Theatre 1979; ind choreographer and performer; works incl: Yip Yip Mix in the 20th Century 1985, Totally Successful Amnaesia 1986, Euroshima 1986, Andi (Deutsche Schauspielhas Hamburg) 1987, Suspect Terrain (NY) 1989, Terminus Terminux (Dance Umbrella London) 1989, Well-known Worlds (1990), Spatial Decay (1990); for TV: TV Dante (Channel 4) 1990, Dance House (BBC) 1991, work at Tate Gallery (BBC) 1991; awarded numerous public awards incl Greater London Arts Dance and Mime award 1984; *Style*— Laurie Booth, Esq; c/o Bolton & Quinn, Prebend Gardens, London W4 1TN

BOOTH, Hon Mrs Justice; Hon Dame Margaret Myfanwy Wood; DBE (1979); da of late Alec Wood Booth and Lillian May Booth; *b* 1933; *Educ* Northwood Coll UCL (LLM fell 1982); *m* 1982, Joseph Jackson, QC, s of Samuel Jackson (d 1987); *Career* called to the Bar Midlle and Inner Temples 1956, QC 1976, bencher Middle Temple 1979; govr Northwood Coll 1975-; memb Cncl UCL 1980-84; chm: Family Law Bar Assoc 1976-78, Lord Chllr's Advsy Ctee Inner London Justices 1990-; *Books* Rayden on Divorce (co-ed 10-13 and 15 edns),Clarke Hall and Morrison on Children (co-ed 9 edn, 1977); *Clubs* Reform; *Style*— Dame Margaret Booth, DBE; c/o Royal Courts of Justice, Strand, WC2A 2LL

BOOTH, Neil Douglas; s of Charles Douglas Booth, of Hartlepool, and Greta, *née* Sylvester (now Mrs Lawrence); *b* 11 Feb 1942; *Educ* Keighley Boys GS, St John's Coll Durham Univ; *m* 1, Barbara Ann, da of Edwin Cullerton, of Bradford; 2 da (Heidi Amanda b 1971, Christy Elizabeth b 1974); m 2, 22 July 1978, Yvonne Margaret, da of Peter Holdsworth Kennedy, of Bradford; *Career* CA; managing ptnr JWM Thompson & Co Keighley 1969-73, ordinand in trg for Anglican Miny 1973-76, various accountancy posts 1976-81, ptnr Rawlinsons Bradford 1981-83, sr ptnr Booth & Co Bradford 1983-89, ptnr Ernst & Young 1989-; ed Booth's NIC Brief; Inst of Taxation Thesis prize 1985; chm Nat Insur Ctee ICAEW; FCA 1964, FTII 1985; *Books* Social Security Contributions (1982), National Insurance Contributions (1984), DHSS Official Contribution Guides (1985), NIC Legislation and Cases (1986), Residence, Domicile and UK Taxation (1987); *Recreations* reading, water colour painting, video photography; *Style*— Neil Booth, Esq; Rivendell, 1114 Bolton Rd, Bradford, W Yorks BD2 4HS (☎ 0274 631154); Ernst & Young, Chartered Accountants, 1 Clifton House, 2 Clifton Villas, Bradford, W Yorks BD8 7DW (☎ 0274 498153, fax 0274 495867)

BOOTH, Peter John Richard; s of Eric Albert Booth, and Edith, *née* Brown; *b* 27 March 1949; *Educ* Benton Park Secdy Modern Sch; *m* 27 July 1970, Edwina Ivy; 3 s (Peter Tristran b 24 Jan 1971, Jonathen Richard b 11 Sept 1972, James Lee b 19 Sept 1978); *Career* Dyers Operative 1964; Nat Union of Dyers Bleachers and Textile Workers: dist offr 1973, nat res offr 1975, nat organiser 1980; nat sec TGWU 1986 (trade gp organiser 1982); vice pres Br Textile Confedn; dir: Apparel Knitting and

Textiles Alliance, Man-Made Fibres Indust Trg Advsy Bd; memb: Exec Ctee Int Textile Garment and Leather Workers Fedn, Presidium Euro Trade Union Ctee of Textiles Clothing and Leather, Textiles Clothing and Footwear Industs Ctee TUC, Confedn of Br Wool Textiles Trg Bd, Bd Carpet Indust Trg Cncl, Knitting and Lace Industs Resources Agency, Health and Safety Ctee Cotton and Allied Textiles Industs Advsy Ctee; *Books* The Old Dog Strike (1985); *Recreations* walking, gardening, dominoes, chess; *Clubs* Yeadon Trades Hall; *Style—* Peter Booth, Esq; Dye House, St John's Court, Yeadon, Leeds (☎ 0532 502182); TGWU Textile Trade Group, National House, Sunbridge Rd, Bradford (☎ 0274 725642, fax 0274 370282, telex 0274 51483 TGWTEX G)

BOOTH, Raymond Trygve; s of Douglas Edward Booth, of Brentwood, Essex, and Gerharda Jacoba, *née* Olsen (d 1965); *b* 14 July 1925; *Educ* Ilford Co HS, Middx Hosp London Univ (MB BS); *m* 8 Aug 1953, Enid, da of George Charles, Everitt (d 1982); 3 s (John b 1954, Andrew b 1956, Christopher b 1962), 1 da (Elizabeth b 1960); *Career* WW11 Sgt Navigator (air crew) RAF 1943-47; conslt obstetrician and gynaecologist SE Essex Gp of Hosps 1965-85; hon sec RCOG 1973-80; cncllr Brentwood DC; Freeman: City of London 1972, Worshipful Co of Apothecaries 1970; FRCOG 1974; *Recreations* aviation, music; *Style—* Raymond Booth, Esq; Friars, 192 Brentwood Rd, Herongate, Brentwood, Essex CM13 3PN (☎ 0277 810527)

BOOTH, Richard George William Pitt; *b* 12 Sept 1938; *Educ* Rugby, Univ of Oxford; *m* 12 Aug 1985, Hope Stuart, *née* Barrie; *Career* chm Richard Booth (Booksellers) Ltd 1961-; pres Welsh Booksellers Assoc; *Books* Country Life Book of Book Collecting (ed); *Style—* Richard Booth, Esq; Hay Castle, Hay-on-Wye, Herefordshire

BOOTH, Sir Robert Camm; CBE (1967), TD; s of Robert Wainhouse Booth (d 1955), of Bowdon, Cheshire, and Ann Gladys, *née* Taylor (d 1960); *b* 9 May 1916; *Educ* Altrincham GS, Univ of Manchester; *m* 1939, Veronica Courtenay, da of late F C Lamb, of Bowdon, Cheshire; 1 s (Nigel), 3 da (Anthea, Sarah, Joanna); *Career* WWII 8 (A) Bn Manchester Regt, Maj, served in France, Malta, ME and Italy 1939-46; called to the Bar Gray's Inn; Nat Exhibition Centre: fndr dir 1970-82, chm 1975-82, chief exec 1977-78; local non-exec dir Barclays Bank 1977-84; Birmingham Chamber of Indust and Commerce: sec 1958-65, dir 1965-78, pres 1977-78; Bd memb: Legal & General Assurance Soc 1979-87, BR (Midlands and NW) Bd 1979-87, Inst of Occupational Health 1980-; memb: W Midlands Econ Planning Cncl 1974-79, BOT Advsy Cncl 1975-82; tstee Nuffield Tst for the Forces of the Crown 1977-, life memb Ct of Govrs Univ of Birmingham (memb Cncl 1973-78), govr Sixth Form Coll Solihull 1974-77; winner Midland Man of the Year Press Radio and TV award 1970; travel with 20 Trade Missions and author of several mktg and econ pubns; Hon DSc Aston 1975, hon FInstM 1975, hon FRSA 1975, hon memb Br Exhibitions Promotions Cncl 1982; Officier de la Legion d'Honneur 1982; kt 1977; *Recreations* travel, writing, photography; *Style—* Sir Robert Booth, CBE, TD; White House, 7 Sandal Rise, Solihull, Warwickshire B19 3ET (☎ 021 705 5311)

BOOTH, Robin Godfrey; s of Frank Booth (d 1990), of York, and Dorothy, *née* Johnson; *b* 11 Aug 1942; *Educ* Winchester, King's Coll Cambridge (DipArch, MA), Univ of Edinburgh (MSc); *m* 10 July 1971, Katherine, da of Arthur Middleton, of Lynchburg, Virginia, USA; 1 s (Richard b 1977), 1 da (Emily b 1974); *Career* architect and town planner; GLC: master plan and job architect for Bletchley Town Devpt Dept of Architecture and Civic Design 1965-71, architect planner for South West Area Traffic and Devpt Branch 1971-72; project architect for New County HQ for Hereford-Worcester (RIBA commendation 1978) Robert Matthew Johnson-Marshall & Partners 1972-76, sr architect concerned with design of various projects overseas and in London John S Bonnington Partnership 1976-80, project architect then ptnr for Standard Chartered Bank's HQ (special award Marble Architectural Awards West Europe 1987) The Fitzroy Robinson Partnership 1980- (currently ptnr for Thames Exchange project and ptnr i/c of works on the Union Bank of Switzerland in London); author of various articles in Architects Journal and RIBA Journal; Br Assoc of Landscape Industries: Plaisterers' Trophy for fibrous Plasterwork 1985, Principal Award for interior landscaping 1986; memb: RIBA 1970 (memb Eastern Regions Competitions Ctee 1979-80), Royal Town Planning Inst 1978; *Books* Neufert: Architectural Data (contrib 1980 edn); *Recreations* music, theatre, travel, photography; *Clubs* Baconian Society (St Albans); *Style—* Robin Booth, Esq; The Fitzroy Robinson Partnership, 77 Portland Place, London W1N 4EP (☎ 071 636 8033, fax 071 580 3996)

BOOTH, Roger George; s of Spencer Banfield Booth (d 1975), of Stourbridge, W Midlands, and Ruth, *née* Wetters; *b* 11 Aug 1942; *Educ* King Edward VI GS Stourbridge, Univ of Sheffield (LLB); *m* 21 March 1964, Joan Muriel, da of James Connor (d 1985); 1 s (Dominic Miles b 10 Aug 1965), 1 da (Harriet Rachael b 23 Sept 1968); *Career* cmmnd TA 1975 (currently Maj with HQ 2 Inf Div); co-owner of philatelic investment and publishing business 1976-83; called to the Bar Gray's Inn 1966; adeundem Northern Circuit 1984- (head of Barristers' Chambers 1985-90); cncllr on Tyne and Wear Met County Cncl 1974-82, Parly candidate for South Shields 1979 (dep leader of opposition 1977-78), memb Royal Philatelic Soc 1985; *Books* A Catalogue of Revenue Stamps of GB, Ireland and Channel Islands (3 edn, 1989); *Recreations* TA, philately; *Clubs* RAC; *Style—* Roger Booth, Esq; 112 Deansgate, Manchester M3 3NW (☎ 061 833 1900, fax 061 832 5027)

BOOTH, Dr Victor Hubert Alexander; s of Alexander Booth (d 1949), of Glengormley, Co Antrim, and Laura Louisa Elizabeth Booth, *née* French (d 1985), descendant of William Booth of the London Drapers' Co, Architect of Draperstown, a model town in the Plantation of Ulster; *b* 18 April 1929; *Educ* Belfast HS, Trinity Coll (MA) Queen's Univ Belfast (MA) Univ of Southampton (PhD); *m* 17 July 1956, Lorna Jackaleen, da of Capt John Mann (d 1982), of Bangor, Co Down; 3 s (John b 1958, Christopher b 1962, Conor b 1965), 1 da (Karen b 1960); *Career* head of English Holywood County Secdy Sch 1959, sr remedial teacher Co Antrim 1966, advsr for special and remedial educn Worcestershire LEA 1972, county inspr for language, res and educnl devpt Hereford and Worcester LEA 1974-, specialist in learning disability; won scholarship Br Dyslexia Assoc to Texas 1972, visiting fell Queens Univ Belfast 1970; *Recreations* travel, squash, country pursuits; *Style—* Dr Victor H A Booth; Kinnersley House, 269 Wells Rd, Malvern Wells, Worcs WR14 4HH (☎ 0684 572970); c/o Education Office, Castle St, Worcester WR1 3AG (☎ 0905 765765)

BOOTH-CLIBBORN, Rt Rev Stanley Eric Francis; *see*: Manchester, Bishop of

BOOTH-JONES, Charles Vernon Colville; s of Major Thomas Vernon Booth-Jones JP, DL (d 1966), of Hale Park, Fordingbridge, Hampshire, and Margaret Wallace, *née* Colville (d 1984); *b* 5 Feb 1928; *Educ* Eton, Sandhurst; *m* 1, 2 Oct 1951 (m dis 1973), Louise Anne, 2 da of Col Guy Janion Edwards, DSO; 1 s (Roderick Vernon b 1954), 1 da (Thalia Jane b 1951); m 2, 19 Jan 1974, Pauline Celia, 3 da of Sir James Gunn, RA; *Career* RHG 1946, Sqdn Ldr 1957-64 (despatches 1959), 2 i/c 1965, Maj MOD HQ RAC 3 Div ret 1970; with Picture Gallery 1972, dealer in paintings 17-20 centuries, picture restorer; *Recreations* all country sports, painting; *Style—* Charles Booth-Jones, Esq; Hill Barn, Monkton Deverill, Wiltshire BA12 7EY; Fox Studio, Maiden Bradley (☎ 098 53 479)

BOOTHBY, Sir Brooke Charles; 16 Bt (1660), of Broadlow Ash; s of Sir Hugo Boothby, 15 Bt (d 1986); *b* 6 April 1949; *Educ* Eton, Trinity Coll Cambridge (BA); *m* 1976, Georgiana Alexandra, da of Sir John Wriothesley Russell, GCVO, CMG (d 1984), and Lady (Aliki) Russell, *qv*; 2 da; *Heir* kinsman, George William Boothby; *Career* High Sheriff S Glamorgan 1986-87; *Recreations* shooting; *Style—* Sir Brooke Boothby, Bt; Fonmon Castle, Barry, S Glam CF6 9ZN (☎ 0446 710206)

BOOTHBY, Baroness; Wanda; *née* Sanna; da of Giuseppe Sanna, of Sardinia; *m* 30 Aug 1967, Baron Boothby (Life Peer 1958) (d 1986); *Style—* The Rt Hon Lady Boothby; 1 Eaton Square, London SW1

BOOTHMAN, Clive Nicholas; s of Thomas Hague Boothman, and Margaret, *née* Knox; *b* 28 May 1955; *Educ* Charterhouse, Trinity Coll Oxford (BA); *m* 28 May 1983, Anne, da of Wace Philo; 2 s (Alexander b 4 July 1986, Harry b 9 July 1988), 1 da (Georgina b 1 Aug 1990); *Career* Arthur Young McClelland Moores Jersey CI 1976-81, qualified chartered accountant 1980, accountant Moore Stephens & Butterfield Bermuda 1982-83; Schroder Group: joined 1983, asst dir J Henry Schroder Wagg & Co Ltd 1986-87 (mangr 1985-86, investmt res 1983-85), md Schroder Unit Trusts Ltd 1988- (joined 1987, dir 1988); memb Soc Investmt Analysts 1984; ACA 1980; *Recreations* sailing, windsurfing, tennis, vintage cars; *Style—* Clive Boothman, Esq; Schroder Unit Trusts Limited, 33 Gutter Lane, London EC2V 6AS (☎ 071 382 6000)

BOOTHMAN, Philip Comrie; s of John Comrie Boothman, of Hartford, Cheshire, and Audrey Johnson, *née* Leather; *b* 25 April 1953; *Educ* Manchester GS, New Coll Oxford (MA); *Career* barr Inner Temple 1977, dir Kleinwort Benson Ltd 1989-; *Style—* Philip Boothman, Esq; Kleinwort Benson Ltd, 20 Fenchurch St, London EC3P 3DB (☎ 071 623 8000, fax 071 623 5535, telex 888531)

BOOTHROYD, Betty; MP (Lab) W Bromwich 1974-; da of Archibald Boothroyd (d 1948) of Dewsbury, Yorks, and Mary Boothroyd (d 1982); *b* 8 Oct 1929; *Educ* Dewsbury Tech Coll and Sch of Art; *Career* contested (Lab): Leicester SE (by-election) 1957, Peterborough 1959, Nelson and Colne (by-election) 1960, Rossendale 1970; memb Hammersmith Borough Cncl 1965-68, MP (Lab) W Bromwich 1973-74, asst govt whip 1974-75, UK memb Euro Parl 1975-77, Speaker's Panel of Chm 1980-87, Lab Pty Nat Exec Ctee 1981-87, House of Commons Cmmn 1983-87, second dep chm Ways and Means and dep speaker 1987; *Style—* Miss Betty Boothroyd, MP; House of Commons, London SW1A 0AA (☎ 071 219 4136)

BOOTLE, Roger Paul; s of David Bootle, MBE (d 1972), and Florence Ethel, *née* Denman (d 1982); *b* 22 June 1952; *Educ* Downer GS, Merton Coll Oxford (BA, MPhil); *Career* chief economist: Lloyds Merchant Bank 1986-88 (dir 1986-), Capel Cure Myers 1982-86, Greenwell Montagu Gilt Edged 1989- (exec dir); contrib: Financial Times, Times, numerous pubns; various TV and radio appearances as commentator on economic affairs; *Books* Theory of Money (jtly, 1978), Index - Linked Gilts (1986); *Recreations* bridge, squash, horseracing, classical music, theatre; *Style—* Roger Bootle, Esq; 98F Richmond Hill, Richmond, Surrey TW10 6RJ (☎ 081 948 4605); Greenwell Montagu Gilt Edged, 10 Lower Thames St, London EC3R 6AE (☎ 081 260 9664)

BOOTON, Dr Paul; s of Arthur Terence Booton, and Jean Brunhilde Mary, *née* Price; *b* 11 May 1955; *Educ* Hornchurch GS, The London Hosp Med Coll Univ of London (BSc, MB BS); *Career* physician to Prof J M Ledington London Hosp 1980, MO to Kaitak and Sham Shui Po refugee camps UN High Cmmn on Refugees 1981, sr house offr and registrar med Oldchurch Hosp Romford 1982-86, lectr gen practice United Med and Dental Schs 1988-90, lectr Dept of Gen Practice KCH Med Sch; memb: Lab Pty, CND, Med Campaign against Nuclear Weapons; MRCPUK 1984, MRCGP 1988; *Recreations* walking, skiing, sailing; *Style—* Dr Paul Booton; Dept of General Practice, Kings College Hospital Medical School, Denmark Hill, London SE5

BOOTYMAN, John Trevor; s of Walter Bootyman (d 1979), of Healing, and Gladys Mary, *née* Allenby (d 1980); *b* 14 March 1927; *Educ* Humberston Foundation Sch; *m* Helena Villette, da of John Thornton (d 1970), of London W14; 1 s (David b 1954), 1 da (Jane b 1958); *Career* RN 1945-48; CA 1954-; conslt Forrester Boyd 1989- (ptnr 1958-89); tstee: GF Sleight Settled Estates 1966-, May Watkinson Charity Tst 1971-; pres: Grimsby and N Lincs Soc of CAs 1968-69, Humberside & Dist Soc of CAs 1973-74, Rotary Club of Grimsby 1986-87; RI Paul Harris fell 1988; FCA; *Recreations* gardening, rotary activities; *Style—* J T Bootyman, Esq; Twigmoor, 51 Welholme Ave, Grimsby (☎ 0472 343588); 26 South St Mary's Gate, Grimsby DN31 1LW (☎ 0472 350601, fax 0472 241748)

BORALESSA, Harsha Shanta; *b* 1 July 1943; *Educ* Visakha Girls Sch Colombo Sri Lanka, Univ of Ceylon Sri Lanka (MB BS); *m* 2 Dec 1968, Harischandra Boralessa; 2 da (Harsha b 29 Oct 1970, Andosha b 5 march 1972); *Career* registrar in anaesthetics: St Mark's Hosp City Rd London 1974-75, UCH Golder St London 1975-77, Moorfields Eye Hosp City Rd London 1977-78; sr registrar in anaesthetics 1978-83: Eastman Dental Hosp Gray's Inn Rd London, Hammersmith Hosp, Royal Postgrad Med Sch; conslt in anaesthesia and intensive care Old Church Hosp Romford Essex 1983-; memb: BMA, Assoc of Anaesthetists GB, Intensive Care Soc; FFARCS; *Style—* Mrs Harsha Boralessa; Glensirae, 33 Priests Lane, Brentwood, Essex CM15 8BU (☎ 0277 210221); Oldchurch Hospital, Romford, Essex (☎ 0708 46090)

BORDASS, Dorothy Trotman; da of Reginald Wilson Foster (d 1963), and the late Alice, *née* Skinner; *b* 19 Nov 1905; *Educ* South Hampstead HS, Northwood Coll, Harrow Sch of Art, Academie Julian Paris, Heatherley Sch of Art; *m* 22 April 1930, Brig William Harrison Bordass, CBE, RA, s of William Bordass (d 1974); 1 s (William Trotman b 17 Nov 1943), 1 da (Jane (Mrs Shears) b 16 April 1931); *Career* painter, etcher and illuminator; 28 one man exhibitions since 1958 and many mixed exhibitions incl: RBA, RSA, Redfern Gallery, Nelson Art Gallery Kansas City, USA, Nat Gallery Kuala Lumpar, Contemporary Art Soc Sydney Gallery, on the Cam; purchasers incl: ILEA, F W Woolworth Manhattan, Usher Gallery Lincoln, Darlington City Art Centre, BR, UEA, Amstedamsche Beleggins Tst, Open Univ and many private collectors; prizes incl: Reeves E of Eng exhibition 1971 (for collage), Linton prize (for mixed media), silver medal Société des Artistés Francais Paris, Cambridge Drawing Soc Centenary prize; memb: Ctee Penwith Soc St Ives Cornwall, Art Soc; Cambridge Drawing Soc; former chm Singapore Art Soc; former memb Royal Soc Painter Etchers, former fell Freepainters and Sculptors; *Recreations* gardening, embroidery; *Style—* Mrs Dorothy Bordass; 30 Pretoria Rd, Cambridge CB4 1HE (☎ 0223 610 20)

BORDELL, Gerald Jacob; s of Gabriel Bordell, and Eve, *née* Gavelber (d 1980); *b* 3 April 1934; *Educ* City of London Sch; *m* 20 March 1960, Valerie Joyce, da of John Alick (d 1967); 2 s (Keith Stephen b 1963, Jonathan David b 1967); *Career* md Little Lady (London) Ltd 1967-1987; chm Mermaid Theatre Assoc 1977-81, fndr and hon organiser the Friends of the RSC 1982-87, memb Cncl of Mgmnt Royal Shakespeare Theatre Tst 1984-87; md London Theatre Tours Ltd 1987; admin Friends of the Br Theatre 1987, chm Friends of the Br Theatre (Charitable Tst) Ltd 1988-; Freeman City of London 1973, Liveryman Worshipful Co of Basketmakers 1975; *Recreations* theatre, gardening; *Clubs* The City Livery, ESU; *Style—* Gerald Bordell, Esq; 5 Abbotswood Gardens, Clayhall, Ilford, Essex IG5 0BG (☎ 081 550 0576)

BOREEL, Jonkheer Sir Francis David; 13 Bt (E 1645); s of Jonkheer Sir Alfred Boreel, 12 Bt (d 1964), and Countess Reiniera Adriana (d 1957), da of Count Francis David Schimmelpennick; *b* 14 June 1926; *Educ* Univ of Utrecht; *m* 1964, Suzanne, da of Willy Campagne; 3 da; *Heir* kinsman, Jonkheer Stephan Boreel; *Career* cncllr

Netherlands For Serv; *Style—* Jonkheer Sir Francis Boreel, Bt; Kapellestraat 25, 4351 AL Veere, Netherlands

BOREEL, Jonkheer Stephan Gerard; s of Jonkheer Gerard Lucas Cornelis Boreel (d 1970); h to Btcy of kinsman, Jonkheer Sir Francis Boreel, 13 Bt; *b* 9 Feb 1945; *m* Francien P Kooyman; 1 s; *Style—* Jonkheer Stephan Boreel; Elzenoord, 30, Vaassen, Holland

BOREHAM, Sir (Arthur) John; KCB (1980); 3 s of Ven Frederick Boreham (d 1966), Archdeacon of Cornwall and Chaplain to the Queen, and Caroline Mildred, *née* Slater (d 1943); *b* 30 July 1925; *Educ* Marlborough, Trinity Coll Oxford; *m* 1948, Heather, o da of Harold Edwin Horth (d 1952); 3 s (Stephen b 1949, Jonathan b 1951, Simon b 1955), 1 da (Deborah b 1959); *Career* served RAF Flt Lt 1943-46; dir Central Statistical Office and head Govt Statistics 1978-85; visiting fell Nuffield Coll Oxford 1979-88; pres Inst of Statisticians 1984-, conslt to CARICOM 1989-90, chm Weald of Kent Breast Cancer Tst; chm Editorial Ctee Royal Statistical Soc, pres Assoc of Social Res Orgns 1990-; *Recreations* music, golf; *Clubs* Knole Park Golf; *Style—* Sir John Boreham, KCB; Pipers Croft, Brittains Lane, Sevenoaks, Kent TN13 2NG (☎ 0732 454678)

BOREHAM, Hon Mr Justice; (Hon) Sir Leslie Kenneth; *m* ; 1 s, 1 da; *Career* barr 1947, QC 1965, judge of the High Court Queen's Bench Division 1972-, presiding judge North Eastern Circuit 1974-79; kt 1972; *Style—* The Hon Mr Justice Boreham; 1 Paper Buildings, Temple, London EC4

BOREHAM, Michael Bryant; s of Harold Leslie Boreham, of Beach Hotel, Worthing, Sussex (d 1971), and Irene Ethel, *née* Bryant (d 1967); *b* 7 June 1928; *Educ* Highgate Sch, Univ of London (LLB); *m* 21 Jan 1956, Alison Jane, da of Douglas Archibald Clarke, of 7 Middle Field, St John's Wood Park NW8, and Shardeloes, Old Amersham, Bucks; 2 da (Jane Caroline b 13 March 1959, Penelope Lucy b 18 Dec 1962); *Career* Lt 16/5 Lancers 1947; slr; sr ptnr Frere Cholmeley 1979-90; dir: Harris Int Fin NV, Knowles Electronics Co, Xomox Ltd, Polaroid (UK) Ltd (alternate), RCA Int Ltd, Warner Communications (UK) Hldgs; *Recreations* reading, theatre, shooting, fishing; *Clubs* Brooks's, Naval and Military; *Style—* Michael B Boreham, Esq; 314 Nell Gwynn House, Sloane Avenue, London SW3 3AX (☎ 071 581 3151); The Old Rectory, Sutton, nr Pulborough, W Sussex RH20 1PS (☎ 07987 258); 28 Lincoln's Inn Fields, London WC2A 3HH (☎ 071 405 7878, telex 27623, fax 071 405 9056, 071 242 7724)

BORG, Dr Alan Charles Nelson; s of Charles John Nelson Borg (d 1986), and Frances Mary Olive *née* Hughes (d 1985); *b* 21 Jan 1942; *Educ* Westminster, BNC Oxford (BA, MA, Fencing blue 1961 and 62), Courtauld Inst, Univ of London (MA, PhD); *m* 1, 1964; 1 s (Giles b 1965), 1 da (Emma b 1970); m 2, 1976, Caroline Sylvia, da of Lord Francis Hill; 2 da (Leonora b 1980, Helen b 1982); *Career* lectr of English Univ d'Aix-Marseille 1964-65, lectr history of art Univ of Indiana 1967-69; asst prof of history of art Princeton Univ 1969-70; asst keeper of the Armouries HM Tower of London 1970-78, keeper Sainsbury Centre for Visual Arts Univ of East Anglia 1978-82; dir-gen Imperial War Museum 1982-; FSA; *Books* Architectural Sculpture in Romanesque Provence (1972), European Swords and Daggers in the Tower of London (1974), Torture and Punishment (1975), Heads and Horses (1976), Arms and Armour in Britain (1979); *Recreations* music, travel; *Style—* Dr A C N Borg; Telegraph House, 36 West Square, London SE11 4SP (☎ 071 582 8122); Imperial War Museum (☎ 071 416 5000)

BORG, Colin David Nelson; s of Charles John Nelson Borg (d 1986), and Frances Mary Olive, *née* Hughes (d 1985); *b* 11 March 1936; *Educ* Westminster, Trinity Coll Cambridge (MA); *m* 16 April 1971, Amanda Portman, da of Paul Charles Lindo (d 1969); 2 s (Christopher Paul Nelson b 1973, Guy Charles Nelson b 1975); *Career* Nat Serv RAF 1954-56; copywriter: Benton & Bowles 1959-60, BBDO 1960-62, Masius Wynne-Williams 1962-66; dir Butler & Gardner 1966-77, managing ptnr Butler Dennis Garland 1977-85, fndr chm Butler Borg 1985-; govr Lanchester Poly 1975-80; Coronation medal 1953; MIPA 1974; *Recreations* transport history; *Clubs* Oriental, United Oxford and Cambridge University; *Style—* Colin Borg, Esq; Butler Borg, 4 Gee's Ct, London W1 (☎ 071 408 2301, fax 071 408 0382, telex 267529)

BORGES, Thomas William Alfred; s of Arthur Borges, of Prague, and Paula Borges; *b* 1 April 1923; *Educ* Dunstable GS, Luton Tech Coll; *m* 1, (m dis); m 2, 1966, Serena Katherine Stewart, *née* Jamieson; 2 s; *Career* served WWII 1941-45; trained in banking, shipping and indust 1945-49, dir Borges Law & Co Aust 1951, chm Smith Whitworth Ltd 1974-80; chm Royal Nat Orthopaedic Hosp 1980-82 (dep chm 1978-80, chm 1980-82), dir Inst of Orthopaedics Univ of London 1968- (dep chm 1978-80, chm 1980-82); memb: Grants Ctee King Edward VII Hosp Fund 1975-80, Cncl Professions Supplementary to Medicine 1980-88 (dep chm 1982-88); treas Riding for Disabled Assoc 1977-84, chm Australian Art Fndn 1984-, exec memb Sir Robert Menzies Tst 1981-; *Publications* Two Expeditions of Discovery in North West and Western Australia by George Grey (1969); *Recreations* collecting Australiana, riding, swimming; *Style—* Thomas Borges, Esq; Dorchester Lodge, 70 Westbourne Park Rd, London W2 5PJ

BORINGDON, Viscount; Mark Lionel Parker; s and h of 6 Earl of Morley, *qv*; *b* 22 Aug 1956; *Educ* Eton; *m* 12 Nov 1983, Carolyn Jill, da of Donald McVicar, of Meols, Wirral, Cheshire; 2 da (Alexandra b 1985, Olivia b 1987); *Career* Lieut (1982) Royal Green Jackets; *Style—* Viscount Boringdon; Pound House, Yelverton, South Devon

BORLAND, David Morton; s of David Borland, and Annie J Borland; *b* 17 Jan 1911; *Educ* Glasgow Acad, BNC Oxford; *m* 1947, Nessa Claire Helwig; 1 s, 1 da; *Career* dir Cadbury Schweppes Ltd 1968-76 and UBM Group Ltd 1976-81; Univ of Bristol: pro chancellor 1982-89, hon fell 1989; *Style—* David Borland, Esq; Garden Cottage, 3 Hollymead Lane, Stoke Bishop, Bristol (☎ 683978)

BORODALE, Viscount; Sean David Beatty; s and h of 3 E Beatty; *b* 12 June 1973; *Style—* Viscount Borodale

BORRETT, (Jack Geoffrey) Kingsley; s of Capt J T Borrett, OBE (d 1969), and Mary Edith Joy, *née* Symonds-Taylor (d 1981); *b* 25 April 1938; *Educ* Nautical Coll Pangbourne; *m* 1 May 1962 (m dis 1990), Caroline Ann, da of K P Herron (d 1961); 2 da (Juliette Patricia b 1964, Lucinda Jane b 1967); *Career* RNR 1951-56; broker Lloyd's 1956-; Bevington Vaizey and Foster Ltd 1956-80, Frizzell Gp Ltd 1980-, md Frizzell Professional Indemnity Ltd, dir Frizzell Gp Ltd; memb Lords Taverner Chiltern Region Ctee; Freeman: Worshipful Co of Insurers 1987, City of London 1987; ACII 1967, memb CIP 1989; *Recreations* golf, racing (horses and greyhounds), charity, travel; *Clubs* Royal & Ancient, Denham Golf, Quinta do Lago Golf, Lloyd's Golf; *Style—* Kingsley Borrett, Esq; Holmdale, Cokes Lane, Little Chalfont, Bucks HP8 4TX (☎ 0494 762010); Frizzell Group Ltd, 14/22 Elder St, London E1 6DF (☎ 071 247 6595, fax 071 247 7921)

BORRIE, Sir Gordon Johnson; QC (1986); s of Stanley Borrie; *b* 13 March 1931; *Educ* John Bright GS Llandudno, Univ of Manchester (LLB, LLM); *m* 1960, Dorene, da of Herbert Toland, of Toronto, Canada; *Career* called to the Bar Middle Temple 1952, bencher 1980, in practise 1954-57, lectr then sr lectr Coll of Law 1957-64; Univ of Birmingham: sr lectr 1965-68, prof Eng law and dir Inst Judicial Admin 1969-76, dean Law Faculty 1974-76; dir-gen of Fair Trading 1976-; memb Law Cmmn Advsy Panel Contract Law 1966-, former govr Birmingham Coll Commerce; former memb: Parole Bd, Consumers' Assoc Cncl, Equal Opportunities Cmmn; contested: (Lab) Croydon NE 1955, Ilford South 1959; Hon LLD Univ of Manchester; kt 1982; *Books* Commercial Law (6 ed, 1988), The Development of Consumer Law and Policy (1984), others in joint authorship; *Clubs* Reform, Garrick; *Style—* Sir Gordon Borrie, QC; Manor Farm, Abbots Morton, Worcestershire (☎ 0386 792330); 1 Plowden Buildings, Temple, London EC4 (☎ 071 353 4434)

BORRIE, Michael Anthony Frederick; s of Douglas Armitage Borrie (d 1964), of London, and Lucy Mary, *née* White (d 1981); *Educ* The Salesian Colls, London and Oxford, King's Coll London (BA), Inst of Historical Res; *m* 24 March 1974, Gillian Elizabeth, da of Clifford John Pollard, of Ipswich; 2 s (George b 1980, Thomas b 1981); *Career* asst keeper Dept of MSS Br Museum 1960, manuscripts librarian Br Library 1987; author of articles and reviews in: The Spectator, Journal of the British Archaeological Assoc, Journal of the Soc of Archivists, Library History, British Museum Quarterly; treas Plainsong and Medieval Music Soc 1966-79; First Div Assoc: sec Museums Sub Ctee 1968-75, nat exec memb 1971-79; memb: Cncl Br Records Assoc 1972, Cncl Friends of the Nat Libraries 1973, Ctee for Establishing the Museum of London 1973-76, Comité de Sigillographie Conseil International Des Archives 1974-88, Ctee Friends of the Geffrye Museum 1985; FRHistS 1969, FSA 1984; *Books* Magna Carta (1976), Vocabulaire International de Sigillographie (1984); *Recreations* gardening, reading, walking; *Style—* Michael Borrie, Esq; Department of Manuscripts, British Library, London WC1B 3DG (☎ 071 636 1544, fax 071 323 7745, telex 21462)

BORTHWICK, Antony Thomas; s and h of Sir John Borthwick, 3 Bt, MBE; *b* 12 Feb 1941; *Educ* Eton; *m* 1, 1966, Gillian Deirdre Broke, twin da of late Nigel Vere Broke Thurston, RN; 1 s, 2 da; m 2, 1985, Jenny, eldest da of George Lanning; *Style—* Antony Borthwick, Esq; c/o Midland Bank, 31 Holborn, London EC1

BORTHWICK, (William) Jason Maxwell; DSC (1942); s of Hon William Borthwick (d 1958), bro of 1 and last Baron Whitburgh (their f Thomas, chm and sr ptnr Thos Borthwick & Sons, was nominated a Peer 1912 but d before the patent passed the Great Seal); *b* 1 Nov 1910; *m* 1937, Elizabeth Cleveland, *née* Elworthy (d 1978); 1 s, 3 da; *Career* called to the Bar Inner Temple 1932, Thos Borthwick & Sons Ltd 1933 (dir 1946-76), International Commodity Clearing House 1952-83; Central Cncl of Physical Recreation 1950-, Cwlth Devpt Corpn 1971-77; *Recreations* shooting, sailing; *Clubs* United Oxford and Cambridge, Royal Thames Yacht; *Style—* Jason Borthwick, Esq, DSC; North House, Brancaster Staithe, King's Lynn, Norfolk PE31 8BY (☎ 0485 210475)

BORTHWICK, 23 Lord (S 1450) John Henry Stuart Borthwick of that Ilk; TD (1943), JP (Midlothian 1938), DL (Midlothian 1965); Baron (territorial) of Heriotmuir, Borthwick and Lockerwart, and as such was one of the four representative Scottish Barons at HM's post-coronation state visit to Edinburgh, carrying the crown canopy; Hereditary Falconer of Scotland to HM The Queen; o s of Henry Borthwick of Borthwick, *de jure* 22 Lord Borthwick (d 1937); claim as h male and 23 Lord Borthwick admitted by Lord Lyon 1986; *b* 13 Sept 1905; *Educ* Fettes, King's Coll Newcastle; *m* 8 Jan 1938, Margaret (d 1976), da of Alexander Campbell Cormack, of Leith; 2 s (twins); *Heir* s, John Borthwick, Master of Borthwick, *qv*; *Career* Lt-Col RATA, served WWII; chm Heriotmuir Properties Ltd 1965-, Heriotmuir Exporters 1972-; dir Ronald Morrison and Co 1972-; memb Lothians Area Ctee NFU Mutual Insur Soc 1969-87, chm Monitoring Ctee Scottish Tartans 1976, memb Standing Cncl Scottish Chiefs, vice pres Normandy Veterans' Assoc; Heraldry Master Gunner Scotland; *Recreations* shooting, travel, history; *Clubs* New (Edinburgh), Puffin's (Edinburgh), Royal Canadian Mil Inst; *Style—* The Rt Hon The Lord Borthwick, TD, JP, DL; Crookston, Heriot, Midlothian (☎ 087 535 232)

BORTHWICK, Master of; Hon John Hugh Borthwick; er (twin) s and h of 23 Lord Borthwick, TD, JP, DL, *qv*; *b* 14 Nov 1940; *Educ* Gordonstoun; *m* 1974, Adelaide, o da of Archy Birkmyre, of Lower Dalchonzie, Comrie, Perthshire; 2 da (Georgina b 1975, Alexandra b 1977); *Career* farmer, landlord; pres: N Country Cheviot Sheep Assoc 1988-89, Scotch Half Breed Sheep Soc 1988-; memb: Local SE Ctee Scottish Landowners Fedn, Local Ctee Wool Mktg Bd; *Recreations* trout fishing, stalking; *Clubs* Edinburgh New; *Style—* The Master of Borthwick; The Neuk, Heriot, Midlothian EH38 5YS (☎ 087 535 236)

BORTHWICK, Sir John Thomas; 3 Bt (UK 1908), MBE (1945); s of late Hon James Alexander Borthwick, 2 s of 1 Bt; suc to Btcy of unc, 1 Baron Whitburgh, formerly Sir Thomas Banks Borthwick, 2 Bt, who d 1967, when Barony became ext; *b* 5 Dec 1917; *Educ* Eton, Trinity Coll Oxford; *m* 1, 1939 (m dis 1961), Irene (d 1978), o da of Joseph Heller; 3 s; m 2, 1962, Irene, da of late Leo Fink, of Paris XVI; 2 s; *Heir* s, Antony Borthwick; *Career* late Major Rifle Bde (TA); dir Thomas Borthwick & Sons Ltd to 1983, vice chm 1979-83; *Style—* Sir John Borthwick, Bt, MBE; Virginia House, Belmont, Warwick, Bermuda (☎ 236 8481); 27 E65 Street, New York, NY 10021 (☎ 212 472 3881)

BORTHWICK, Kenneth White; CBE (1979), JP (1966), DL (Edinburgh 1980); s of Andrew Graham Borthwick; *b* 4 Nov 1915; *Educ* George Heriot Sch Edinburgh; *m* 1942, Irene Margaret, da of John Graham Wilson, of Aberdeen; 2 s, 1 da; *Career* Rt Hon Lord Provost of City of Edinburgh and Lord-Lt of City and Co of Edinburgh 1977-80; chm Cwlth Games Scotland 1986; Hon Consul for Malawi in Scotland; *Recreations* golf, gardening; *Style—* Kenneth Borthwick, Esq, CBE, JP, DL; 17 York Rd, Edinburgh EH5 3EJ (☎ 031 552 2519)

BORTHWICK OF GLENGELT, Hon James Henry Alexander; yr (twin) s of 23 Lord Borthwick, TD, JP, DL, *qv*; *b* 14 Nov 1940; *Educ* Gordonstoun, Heriot-Watt Univ; *m* 1972, Elspeth, da of Lt-Col Allan Dunn MacConachie, of Lauder, Berwickshire; 1 s (Malcolm Henry b 1973); *Style—* The Hon James Borthwick of Glengelt; Channelkirk Cottage, Oxton, Lauder, Berwickshire TD2 6PT

BORTON, Stephen James; s of John Charles Borton, of Porlock, Somerset, and Marion May, *née* Hadfield; *b* 21 April 1953; *Educ* All Saints' Choir Sch Margaret St London, Ellesmere Coll Shropshire, Royal Sch of Church Music; *Career* dir of music St Magnus London Bridge 1973-85, asst to dir of music All Saints Margaret St 1985-88, chief clerk and chief sealer Ct of Faculties of the Archbishop of Canterbury 1986-; Freeman City of London 1984-, Liveryman Worshipful Co of Musicians 1985 (asst clerk 1988); *Recreations* cooking, wine, books, looking at churches, victorian art; *Style—* Stephen J Borton, Esq; 6 Saint Barnabas St, London SW1W 8PE (☎ 071 730 4983); 1 The Sanctuary, Westminster, London SW1P 3JT (☎ 071 222 5381, fax 071 222 7502)

BORWICK, Hon George Sandbach; 2 s of 3 Baron Borwick (d 1961), but er s by his 2 w, Betty; half-bro and hp of 4 Baron Borwick, MC; *b* 18 Oct 1922; *Educ* Eton; *m* 1981, Esther (d 1985), wid of Sir John Ellerman, 2 and last Bt (d 1973, s of Sir John Ellerman, CH, 1 Bt), and yr da of Clarence de Sola, of Montreal, Canada; *Clubs* Garrick; *Style—* The Hon George Borwick

BORWICK, 4 Baron (UK 1922); Sir James Hugh Myles Borwick; 4 Bt (UK 1916), MC (1945); s of 3 Baron Borwick (d 1961), and his 1 w, Irene Phyllis, *née* Patterson; *b* 12 Dec 1917; *Educ* Eton, RMC Sandhurst; *m* 14 Sept 1954, Hyllarie Adalia Mary, yr da of late Lt-Col William Hamilton Hall Johnston, DSO, MC, DL, of Bryn-y-Groes, Bala, N Wales; 4 da; *Heir* half-bro, Hon George Borwick; *Career* Maj (ret) Highland Light Infantry; *Clubs* Royal Ocean Racing; *Style—* The Rt Hon the Lord

Borwick, MC; Lower Minchingdown, Black Dog, Crediton, Devon EX17 4QX (☎ 0884 860735)

BORWICK, (Geoffrey Robert) Jamie; s of Hon Robin Sandbach Borwick, of Guernsey, and Hon Patricia Garnet Borwick, *née* McAlpine; *b* 7 March 1955; *Educ* Eton Coll; *m* 1981, Victoria Lorne Peta, da of R Dennis Poore (d 1987), of London; 2 s (Edwin b 1984, Thomas b 1987), 1 da (Alexandra Victoria b 1990); *Career* md: Federated Tst Corp 1981-, Manganese Bronze Hldgs plc 1984-, Scottish and Mercantile Investment Tst plc 1985-, Stocklake Hldgs plc; chm London Taxis Int; *Recreations* travel; *Clubs* Caledonian; *Style*— Jamie Borwick, Esq; 22 Ilchester Place, London W14 8AA (☎ 071 603 0993); 1 Love Lane, London EC2V 7HJ (☎ 071 606 8744)

BORWICK, Hon Robin Sandbach; s of 3 Baron Borwick (d 1961); *b* 22 March 1927; *Educ* Eton; *m* 1950, Hon Patricia, only da of Baron McAlpine of Moffat (Life Peer, d 1990); 2 s (James, Richard) 1 da (Judith); *Career* memb Lloyd's 1958-; Lt The Life Gds 1946-52; fndr Donkey Breed Soc 1967 (former first chm, now vice pres), pres Br Mule Soc 1978-; *Books* People With Long Ears (1965), Donkeys (1970), Esel, Freunde der Kinder (1970), The Book of the Donkey (1981), Esel Halten (1984), A Brief Guide to Lihou Island (1986), Never At Half Moon (1989); *Recreations* horses, donkeys, all equines; *Clubs* Cavalry; *Style*— The Hon Robin Borwick; Lihou Island, nr Guernsey, Channel Islands (☎ 0481 65656)

BOSANQUET, (Samuel) Anthony John Pierre; JP (1982); s of Samuel John Anson Bosanquet (ka 1944), and Muriel Daphne, *née* Griffith; *b* 11 Jan 1944; *Educ* Eton, Keble Coll Oxford (MA); *m* 1975, Helen Margaret, da of William Hanbury Saumarez Smith, OBE; 2 s, 1 da; *Heir* Samuel David Saumarez Bosanquet (b 1977); *Career* landowner and sch master; music master Eton 1970-74, head of music King Henry VIII Sch Abergavenny 1974-79, asst music master Monmouth Sch 1979-; memb Welsh Rural Products Gp 1987-89, chm Gwent Branch Country Landowners Assoc 1988-90, chm Country Landowners Assoc Welsh Ctee 1990-, vice chm Historic Houses Assoc in Wales 1988-, chm Merlin Music Soc 1990-; *Recreations* gardening, country pursuits, music; *Style*— Anthony Bosanquet Esq, JP; Dingestow Court, Monmouth, Gwent NP5 4YD (☎ 060 083 238)

BOSANQUET, Dr Camilla; da of Sir Harry Ricardo (d 1974), of Woodside, Graffham, nr Petworth, Sussex, and Beatrice, *née* Hale (d 1975); *b* 18 Jan 1921; *Educ* Benenden Sch, Newnham Coll Cambridge, UCH (BA, MB BChir, DCH, DPM); *m* 23 Aug 1941, David Graham Bosanquet, s of Robert Carr Bosanquet (d 1935), of Rock Moor, Alnwick, Northumberland; 1 s (Robin b 1944), 2 da (Joanna b 1946, Annabel b 1950); *Career* house surgn and casualty offr Elizabeth Garret Anderson Hosp 1949, GP 1953-56, sr house offr Oakwood Mental Hosp 1956-58, clinical asst Bethlem Royal Maudsley Hosp 1959-60, UCH 1964-86, conslt psychiatrist Student Health Serv LSE 1969-87, trg analyst and former chm Soc of Analytical Psychology, fndr memb Guild of Psychotherapists 1973-, currently in private practice as analyst and psychotherapist, memb BMA, FRCPsych; *Recreations* animals, gardening, music; *Style*— Dr Camilla Bosanquet; 18 Montagu Square, London W1H 1RD (☎ 071 935 0119) Wyndside, Church Rd, Ryarsh, West Malling, Kent (☎ 0732 842351)

BOSANQUET, David Graham; s of Prof Robert Carr Bosanquet (d 1935), of Alnwick, Northumberland, and Ellen Sophia, *née* Hodgkin (d 1965); *b* 8 Oct 1916; *Educ* Winchester, Trinity Coll Cambridge (MA, LLM); *m* 23 Aug 1941, Camilla, da of Sir Harry Ralph Ricardo (d 1974), of Woodside, Graffham, Sussex; 1 s (Robin b 1944), 2 da (Joanna b 1946, Annabel b 1950); *Career* Maj RA 1940-46, served NW Europe; slr; dir: Fitzwilliam (Peterborough) Properties 1968-, Provincial Insur plc 1970-86, Provincial Gp plc 1986-90; conslt Currey & Co 1987- (ptnr 1951-87); *Recreations* gardening, painting, amateur dramatics; *Clubs* United Oxford and Cambridge; *Style*— David Bosanquet, Esq; Wyndside, Church Rd, Ryarsh, West Malling, Kent (☎ 0732 842351); 18 Montagu Square, London (☎ 071 935 0119); 21 Buckingham Gate, London SW1 (☎ 071 828 4091, fax 071 828 5049)

BOSANQUET, Prof Nicholas Francis Gustavus; s of Lt Col Neville Richard Gustavus Bosanquet, of Wiltshire, and Nancy Bosanquet, *née* Mason; *b* 17 Jan 1942; *Educ* Winchester, Clare Coll Cambridge, Yale Univ, LSE; *m* 31 Aug 1974, Connolly; 2 da (Kate b 1978, Helen b 1981); *Career* sr res fell Centre for Health Econ Univ of York, lectr in econs LSE and the City Univ, prof of health policy Royal Holloway and Bedford New Coll Univ of London 1988-; visiting prof St Mary's Med Sch; former special advsr to Social Servs Select Ctee of The House of Commons; econ advsr: Nat Bd for Prices and Incomes, Royal Cmmn on Distribution of Income and Wealth; conslt: World Bank, OECD, health authys and cos in Britain; arbitrator ACAS; contrib to Economic Journal, British Medical Journal; *Books* Industrial Relations in the NHS: The Search for a System (1980), After the New Right (1983), Family Doctors and Economic Incentives (1989); *Recreations* collecting books on WWI, running; *Style*— Prof Nicholas F G Bosanquet; RHBNC Univ of London, Egham Hill, Egham, Surrey TW20 0EX (☎ 0784 434455)

BOSCAWEN, Hon Charles Richard; s of 9 Viscount Falmouth; *b* 10 Oct 1958; *m* 1985, Frances Diana, yst da of late Maj Hon George Nathaniel Rous, of Dennington Hall, Woodbridge, Suffolk; 1 s (Arthur George b 25 Jan 1991), 1 da (Rosanna Frances b 3 Jan 1989); *Style*— The Hon Charles Boscawen

BOSCAWEN, Hon (Henry) Edward; s of 8 Viscount Falmouth (d 1962); *b* 4 Oct 1921; *Educ* Eton, Peterhouse Cambridge; *m* 1951, Anne Philippa, da of Sir Edward Warner, 2 Bt, DSO, MC; 1 s, 2 da; *Career* WWII Lt RE; chartered civil engr; High Sheriff W Sussex 1979-80; *Recreations* sailing, gardening; *Style*— The Hon Edward Boscawen; The High Beeches, Handcross, Sussex

BOSCAWEN, Hon Evelyn Arthur Hugh; s and h of 9 Viscount Falmouth; *b* 13 May 1955; *Educ* Eton, RAC Cirencester; *m* 1977, Lucia Caroline, da of Ralph Vivian-Neal, of Poundisford Park, Somerset; 1 s (b 1979), 1 da (b 1982); *Career* dir: Goonvean & Rostowrack China Clay Co 1979-, West Country Grain, Flt Wrigtey, Goonvcan Ceramic Materials; chm Cornish Grain; *Recreations* shooting, sailing; *Style*— The Hon Evelyn Boscawen; c/o Tregothnan Estate Office, Truro, Cornwall (☎ 087 252 310)

BOSCAWEN, Hon Nicholas John; 2 s of 9 Viscount Falmouth; *b* 14 Jan 1957; *Educ* Eton, RAC Cirencester; *m* 6 July 1985, Virginia M R, yr da of Robin Beare, of Scraggs Farm, Cowden, Kent; 1 da (Louisa Emily Chiara b 18 July 1990); *Career* land agent Cluttons 1980-85, institutional stockbroker Sheppards 1985-87; dir The Invisible Chef 1988-, Salcombe Dairy Ltd, St George plc; ARICS; *Recreations* shooting, fishing, skiing, sailing, gardening; *Clubs* Annabels; *Style*— The Hon Nicholas Boscawen; Peckham Place, Peckham Bush, Tonbridge, Kent TN12 5NA (☎ 0732 851 975)

BOSCAWEN, Hon Robert Thomas; MC (1944), MP (C) Somerton and Frome 1983-; s of 8 Viscount Falmouth; *b* 17 March 1923; *Educ* Eton, Trinity Coll Cambridge; *m* 1949, Mary Alice, JP (London), er da of Sir Geoffrey Codrington, KCVO, CB, CMG, DSO, OBE, TD; 1 s (Hugh), 2 da (Dozmary, Karenza); *Career* serv NW Euro 1941-45, Capt Coldstream Gds 1945; Lloyd's underwriter 1952-, memb London Exec Cncl NHS 1954-65; contested (C) Falmouth and Camborne 1964 and 1966, MP (C) Wells 1970-83, memb Select Ctee on Expenditure 1974, vice chm Cons Parly Health and Soc Security Ctee 1974, memb Parly Delgn to Soviet Union 1978 and to Nepal 1981, asst govt whip 1979-81, lord cmmr of the Treasy (govt whip) 1981-83, vice chamberlain of HM's Household 1983-86, comptroller HM Household 1986-88; *Clubs* Pratt's, Royal Yacht Sqdn; *Style*— The Hon Robert Boscawen, MC, MP; House of Commons, London SW1A 0AA

BOSEL, Charles Henry; s of Douglas Henry Bosel (d 1985), of Brisbane, Aust, and Edith May, *née* Bouel (d 1987); *b* 4 July 1937; *Educ* Univ of Queensland (BArch), Univ of Liverpool (Master of Civic Design), Academica Britannica Rome (Rome Scholar in Architecture); *m* 6 Feb 1960, (Betty) Eunice, da of Cyril Allan Asplin (d 1977), of Tully, Aust; 2 s (Michael Charles b 1964, Stuart Allan b 1966), 2 da (Juliet Ann b 1971, Nicole Betty b 1975); *Career* architect and town planner; chm: Claverton House (Avon) Ltd 1984, St George's Hill Ltd 1981, SSC Overseas Ltd 1986, Ecinue Holdings Ltd 1987; dir Al Marzouk and Abi Hanna 1980-; pres Cor-Dor Group Holdings NV 1986-; memb: Royal Town Planning Inst, RIBA, Royal Inst Aust Architects, Royal Aust Planning Inst, Soc of Rome Scholars, Soc of Kuwait Engrs; fell IOD; *Recreations* tennis, squash; *Style*— Charles Bosel, Esq; Arnolds, Nursery Lane, Fairwarp, East Sussex TN22 3BD (☎ 082571 2997, fax 082571 3444)

BOSOMWORTH, (Albert) John; s of John Bosomworth, of Beamsley, Skipton, and Agnes Mary, *née* Searle; *b* 28 Nov 1945; *m* 17 Sept 1977, Anne Caroline Mary, da of Charles Michael Dennison Roberts; *Career* farmer and landowner; dir: John Bosomworth (Holdings), J B Cara-Cars, CC Yacht Charter, Shooting Sch, Arms Dealing (JB); *Recreations* shooting (ex Br and English shooting teams), hunting, fishing, yachting, motor racing; *Clubs* CARYA, CPSA, CLA; *Style*— John Bosomworth, Esq; Beamsley Estate, Beamsley, Skipton, N Yorkshire (☎ 0756 71344, fax 0756 71554, car 0860 866662)

BOSSINGHAM, Dr David Hugh; s of Thomas Harry Hugh Bossingham (d 1971), of Harrow, and Vera Margaret, *née* Ingram; *b* 8 May 1948; *Educ* Downer County GS Harrow, St Mary's Hosp (MB BS); *m* 20 Feb 1971, Barbara, da of Charles Frederick Cawley (d 1987), of Manchester; 2 s (Thomas b 1973 d 1976, Patrick b 1980), 1 da (Claire b 1975); *Career* sr registrar in rheumatology Nuffield Orthopaedic Centre Oxford 1976-79, dir Mary Marlborough Lodge 1979-80, hon lectr in med Univ of Oxford 1976-80, conslt physician Nottingham Health Authy 1980-, clinical teacher Faculty of Med Univ of Nottingham; memb Ed Bd Annals of Rheumatic Diseases, sci pubns on arthritis and disability; pres: Trent Region Occupational Therapists 1982-84, Nottingham Branch Chartered Soc of Physiotherapists 1988-89; memb cncl Br Soc Rheumatology 1987-89; MRCS 1972, FRCP 1989 (MRCP 1975); *Recreations* angling, DIY; *Style*— Dr David Bossingham; Marlock Willows, Gunthorpe Rd, Lowdham, Nottingham NG14 7EN; Dept of Rheumatology, City Hospital, Hucknall Rd, Nottingham NG5 1PB (☎ 0602 691169 ext 46379)

BOSSOM, Lady Barbara Joan; *née* North; da of Maj Lord North (d 1940), and sis of 9 Earl of Guilford, JP, DL; raised to rank of Earl's da 1950; *b* 28 Sept 1928; *m* 1951, Maj The Hon Sir Clive Bossom, 2 Bt, *qv*; 3 s, 1 da; *Career* memb Bd of Habinteg (housing for handicapped) 1972-, dir exports and PR Vantona Viyella plc 1976-89; OStJ; *Style*— Lady Barbara Bossom; 97 Cadogan Lane, London SW1X 9DU (☎ 071 245 6531)

BOSSOM, Bruce Charles; s and h of Hon Sir Clive Bossom, 2 Bt, and Lady Barbara, *née* North, of 97 Cadogan Lane, London SW1; *b* 22 Aug 1952; *Educ* Eton, Coll of Estate Mgmnt, Harvard Business Sch; *m* 1985, Penelope Jane, da of Edward Holland-Martin (d 1981), of Overbury Court, Glos; 2 da (Rosanna Emily b 1986, Amanda Lucy b 1988); *Career* chartered surveyor; dir: Mountleigh Group plc, Phoenix Properties & Finance plc, New Court Property Fund; Liveryman Worshipful Co of Grocers; FRICS, FRSA; *Clubs* Bath & Racquet, Vanderbilt, Whites, Pilgrims; *Style*— Bruce Bossom, Esq; Overbury Court, nr Tewkesbury, Glos, GL20 7NP (☎ 038 689 303); 34, Princedale Rd, London W11 (☎ 071 727 5127) Mountleigh Group plc, 49 Grovenor St, London W1X 9FH (☎ 071 493 5555, fax 071 495 2977)

BOSSOM, Hon Sir Clive; 2 Bt (UK 1953), of Maidstone, Kent; s of Baron Bossom (Life Peer and 1 Bt) by his 1 w Emily, *née* Bayne (d 1932); Sir Clive suc to Btcy 1965; *b* 4 Feb 1918; *Educ* Eton; *m* 1951, Lady Barbara Joan, *qv*, *née* North, da of late Lord North and sis of 9 Earl of Guilford; 3 s, 1 da; *Heir* s, Bruce Charles Bossom; *Career* Maj Europe and Far East (regular soldier The Buffs 1939-48); CC Kent 1949-51; MP (C) Leominster 1959-74; PPS to: Jt Parly Secs of Mins of Pensions 1960, Sec of State for Air 1962-64, Home Sec 1970-72; chm Euro Assistance Ltd 1972-88, dir Vosper Ltd 1973-83; chm: Ex-Servs War Disabled Help Ctee 1973-88, Br Motor Sports Cncl 1975-82; vice chm Br Road Fedn 1975-82; int pres Int Social Service for Refugees 1984-89; pres: IFPA 1969-81, Anglo-Netherlands Soc 1978-89, Anglo-Belgian Soc 1983-85; vice pres: (d'honneur) FIA, Iran Soc (past pres); Cncl RGS 1971; Master Worshipful Co of Grocers 1979-80; vice chm Jt Ctee Red Cross and St John 1987-; almoner OStJ 1987-; FRSA; Cdr of Leopold II (Belgium), Cdr Order of Crown (Belgium), Kt Cdr Order of Orange Nassau (Netherlands), Order of Homayoun (Iran); KStJ (memb of Chapter Gen 1960-); *Recreations* travel; *Clubs* Carlton, RAC (chm 1975-78), BRDC, BARC (pres 1984-); *Style*— The Hon Sir Clive Bossom, Bt; 97 Cadogan Lane, London SW1X 9DU (☎ 071 245 6531)

BOSSONS, William Raymond; s of William Henry Bossons (d 1951), and Maude Bowers (d 1948); *b* 20 Oct 1918; *Educ* Wolstanton GS, Univ of Manchester; *m* 22 Dec 1943, Ruth, da of William Alexander Fraser (d 1948); 2 s (Richard b 1952, John b 1953 d 1978), 1 da (Jane b 1955); *Career* WWII 1940-46, cmmnd RA Capt/Adjt served Germany; md WH Bossons Ltd 1951 (dir 1948-), chm and governing dir WH Bossons (Sales) Ltd 1952-; chm Congleton Chamber of Indust 1972 (designed Congleton Borough Industrial Exhibition), fndr chm SE Cheshire Indust Liaison Gp 1974; ASIAD; *Recreations* sea sailing, photography, water colour painting; *Style*— W R Bossons, Esq; WH Bossons Ltd, Brook Mills, Mountbatten Way, Congleton Cheshire CW12 1DQ (☎ 0260 273693, fax 0260 270045)

BOSTELMANN, Michael John; s of Martin Horst Bostelmann; *b* 16 Nov 1947; *Educ* Bradfield; *m* 1973, Gillian, da of Allan Vickery; 2 s; *Career* CA; sr ptnr Arnold Hill; dir: Quadrem Hope Ltd, British Paper Co, Frogmore Mill Ltd, Stemmann Teckinic GmbH; *Recreations* long distance running, squash, tennis; *Clubs* Thames Hare and Hounds, Hurlingham; *Style*— Michael Bostelmann, Esq; 33 West Temple Sheen, East Sheen, London SW14 7AP

BOSTOCK; *see*: Ashton-Bostock

BOSTOCK, Edward; CBE (1975); s of Geoffrey Bostock (d 1961), of Hampstead; *b* 21 Aug 1908; *Educ* Charterhouse, Queen's Coll Oxford (MA); *m* 1934, Alice, da of George Smale; 3 s, 1 da; *Career* CA 1934; sr ptnr Annan Dexter & Co 1961-71, Dearden & Co 1972-75; FCA; *Recreations* gardening, opera, motoring; *Style*— Edward Bostock, Esq, CBE; 94 Richmond Hill, Richmond, Surrey TW10 6RJ (☎ 081 948 5834)

BOSTOCK, Godfrey Stafford; s of Henry John Bostock, CBE, JP (d 1956), of Shawms, Radford Bank, Stafford, and Eleanora, *née* Handley; *b* 23 June 1915; *Educ* Uppingham and Switzerland; *m* 1940, Diana, da of William Dickins Heywood (d 1922), of Little Onn Hall, Stafford; 2 s, 1 da; *Career* dir: The Claverley Co, Economic Estate Planning Co Ltd; High Sheriff Staffordshire 1958, Lord of the Manor of Kirkby Malzeard (and others); *Recreations* shooting, conservation, gardening; *Clubs* Boodle's; *Style*— Godfrey Bostock, Esq; Tixall, Stafford ST18 0XT (☎ 0785 661039); The Moor House Dallowgill, Ripon, Yorks HG4 3RH (☎ 076 583 371/491)

BOSTOCK, James Edward; s of William George Bostock (d 1948), and Amy, *née*

Titley (d 1976); *b* 11 June 1917; *Educ* Borden GS Sittingbourne, Medway Sch of Art, RCA London; *m* 20 Dec 1939, Gwladys Irene, *née* Griffiths; 3 s (Philip b 1946, Michael b 1950, Christopher b 1959); *Career* Durham LI and RCS 1940-46; sr lectr Ealing Sch of Art 1946-60, head of dip studies Stoke on Trent Coll of Art 1960-65, vice princ West of England Coll of Art 1965-70, academic devpt offr Bristol Poly 1970-78; has exhibited water colours engravings etchings and drawings worldwide; one-man shows in: Margate, Broadstairs, Deal, Folkestone, Canterbury; memb: Soc of Wood Engravers 1950, E Kent Art Soc, Ramsgate Arts Soc; hon ret fell Royal Soc of Painter - Etchers 1947; ARCA; *Books* Roman Lettering for Students (1959), Woodengraved Illustrations to Poems of Edward Thomas (1988); *Style*— James Bostock, Esq; 80 Lindenthorpe Rd, Broadstairs, Kent CT10 1DB (☎ 0843 69782)

BOSTOCK, Nicholas Stephen Godfrey; DL (Staffordshire 1989); s of Godfrey Stafford Bostock, of Tixall House, Tixall, Stafford, and Diana, *née* Heywood; *b* 8 July 1942; *Educ* Eton; *m* 9 Aug 1968, Marise Cynthia, da of Rupert Thomas Bebb; 1 s (Richard b 1969), 1 da (Tania b 1972); *Career* CA and farmer; dir: Econ Estate Planning Co Ltd 1978-, Glade Instruments Ltd 1988-; memb: CLA Co Ctee 1980-, Water Sub Ctee 1988-, Mid Staffordshire Health Authy 1989-; current chm Ingestre with Tixall Parish Cncl (cncl memb 1983); underwriting memb Lloyds 1968-; High Sheriff of Staffordshire 1987-88; FCA 1979; *Recreations* shooting, inland waterways; *Style*— Nicholas Bostock, Esq, DL; Tixall Lodge, Tixall, Stafford ST18 0XS (☎ 0785 661 713); Kennels Farm, Tixall, Stafford ST18 0XT (☎ 0785 662 626, fax 0785 660 780)

BOSTON, David Merrick; OBE (1976); s of Dr Hugh Merrick Boston (d 1980), of 86 Crane St, Salisbury, Wilts, and Jessie Mary, *née* Ingham (d 1979); *b* 15 May 1931; *Educ* Bishop Wordworth's Sch Salisbury Wilts, Selwyn Coll Cambridge (BA, MA), Univ of Cape Town; *m* 12 Aug 1961, Catharine Mary, da of Rev Prof E G S Parrinder, of Orpington, Kent; 1 s (Peter b 1966), 2 da (Janet b 1963, Andrea b 1969); *Career* Nat Serv 1950-51, Adj Marine Craft Trg Sch RAF Calshot, Flying Offr RAFRO 1951-55; Field Survey South African Inst of Race Relations 1955, keeper of ethnology (formerly special offr) Liverpool Museums 1956-62, asst keeper Dept of Ethnography Br Museum 1962-65, curator then dir Horiman Public Museum and Public Park Tst 1965- (formerly Horniman Museum and Library); visiting scientist: Nat Museum of Man Ottawa 1970, Japan Fndn Tokyo 1986; chm Br Nat Ctee of the Int Cncl of Museums 1976-80, hon sec Royal Anthropological Inst 1985-88 (vice pres 1972-75 and 1977-80), vice chm Int Ctee for Museums and Ethnography 1989-; vice pres Dulwich Decorative and Fine Arts Soc, tstee Photographers' Gallery; FMA, FRAI, FRAS, FRGS; Ordenom Jugoslavenske Zastave sa zlatnom zvezdom na ogrlici (Yugoslavia 1981); *Books* Pre-Columbian Pottery of the Americas (1980); *Recreations* travel; *Style*— David Boston, Esq, OBE; 10 Oakleigh Park Ave, Chislehurst, Kent (☎ 081 467 1049); Horniman Museum, London Road, Forest Hill, London SE23 (☎ 081 699 1872/2339)

BOSTON, George Louis; s of George Louis Boston, of Barnet, Herts, and Louisa May, *née* Chapman; *b* 16 Jan 1942; *Educ* Archbishop Tenison's GS Kennington Oval London; *m* 28 Sept 1968, Susan Jane, da of John Law (d 1973); 1 s (Matthew Luke b 1972), 1 da (Sarah Jane b 1971); *Career* joined BBC Radio London 1962, assist audio mangr BBC Manchester 1975 (joined 1967), mangr audio and cameras Open Univ Prodn Centre 1989 (appointed sound mangr 1982); memb Tech Ctee Int Assoc of Sound Archives 1985-, chm of Coordinating Ctee for the Tech Cmmns of the Int Orgns for Audio Film and TV Archives 1987-, chm Milton Keynes Cycle Users Gp; memb: Audio Engrg Soc 1987, RTS 1988; *Recreations* cycling; *Style*— George Boston, Esq; BBC Open University Production Centre, Walton Hall, Milton Keynes MK7 6BH (☎ 0908 655540, fax 0908 655300, telex 826485)

BOSTON, Richard; s of Frank and Janet Boston; *b* 29 Dec 1938; *Educ* Stowe, King's Coll Cambridge (MA); *Career* writer; author of Anatomy of Laughter, The Admirable Urquhart, Beer and Skittles, Baldness Be My Friend, Osbert: a Portrait of Osbert Lancaster; contributor to numerous newspapers and periodicals especially The Guardian, fndr and ed The Vole and Quarto magazines; *Style*— Richard Boston, Esq; The Old Sch, Aldworth, Reading, Berks (☎ 0635 578 587)

BOSTON, 10 Baron (GB 1761); Sir Timothy George Frank Boteler Irby; 11 Bt (E 1704); s of 9 Baron, MBE (d 1978), by his 2 w Erica; *b* 27 March 1939; *Educ* Clayesmore Sch Dorset, Southampton Univ (BSc); *m* 1967, Rhonda Anne, da of Ronald Albert Bate, of Balgowlah, NSW, Australia; 2 s (Hon George b 1971, Hon Jonathan b 1975), 1 da (Hon Rebecca b 1970); *Heir* s, Hon George William Eustace Boteler Irby b 1 Aug 1971; *Style*— The Rt Hon the Lord Boston; 135 Bishops Mansions, Stevenage Rd, Fulham SW6 6DX

BOSTON, William John (Billy); s of John Boston (d 1973), of Cardiff, and Ellen, *née* Lack (d 1980); *b* 6 Aug 1934; *Educ* South Church Street Sch Cardiff; *m* 28 Jan 1956, Joan, da of Walter Rudd; 1 s (William b 22 Nov 1966), 4 da (Christine b 19 Aug 1956, Lisa b 20 Sept 1957, Karen b 18 March 1959, Angela b 31 March 1964); *Career* Nat Serv Royal Signals 1952-54; former rugby player; rugby union: Cardiff Schoolboys 1948, Welsh Assoc of Boys Clubs 1950, Welsh Youth team 1951, Cardiff Int Rugby Club 1951, Cardiff Rugby Union Club 1952; rugby league Wigan 1953-68: debut 1953, 564 appearances, 571 tries; int rugby league: 31 GB caps, 24 tries, tour Aust 1954 and 1962, appeared in World Cup 1954 (France), 1957 (Aust), 1960 (Eng); honours: Challenge Cup 3 times (runners up 3 times), World Cup 1954 and 1960; highest try scorer on tour Aust, second highest try scorer in rugby league history; installed in Whitbread Trophy Hall of Fame Leeds and Welsh Sporting Hall of Fame Cardiff; *Recreations* cricket, table tennis, snooker, all sports; *Style*— Billy Boston, Esq; Griffin Hotel, 94 Standishgate, Wigan (☎ 0942 43898)

BOSTON OF FAVERSHAM, Baron (Life Peer UK 1976); Terence George; QC (1981); s of George Thomas Boston (d 1986), and Kate, *née* Bellati; *b* 21 March 1930; *Educ* Woolwich Polytechnic Sch, King's Coll London; *m* 1962, Margaret Joyce, da of Rowley Henry Jack Head (d 1932), of Toorak, Victoria, Aust; *Career* sits as Lab Peer in Lords; Flt Lt RAF 1950-52; called to the Bar Inner Temple 1960 (Gray's Inn 1973); former news sub-editor BBC External Services, sr prodr BBC (current affairs) 1960-64, chm TVS (now TVS Entertainment plc) 1981-; MP (Lab) Faversham Kent 1964-70; PPS to: Min of Public Bldg and Works 1964-66, Min of Power 1966-68, Min of Tport 1968-69; asst govt whip 1969-70, min of state Home Office 1979; oppn front bench spokesman on: Home Office Affrs 1979-84, Defence 1984-86; *Style*— The Rt Hon The Lord Boston of Faversham, QC; House of Lords, London SW1A 0AA

BOSVILLE MACDONALD OF SLEAT, Sir Ian Godfrey; 17 Bt (NS 1625); also 25 Chief of Sleat; s of Sir Somerled Bosville Macdonald of Sleat, 16 Bt, MC (24 Chief of Sleat, d 1958), and Mary, Lady Bosville Macdonald of Sleat, *qv*; *b* 18 July 1947; *Educ* Pinewood Sch, Eton, RAC Cirencester; *m* 1970, Juliet Fleury, o da of Maj-Gen John Ward-Harrison, OBE, MC; 1 s, 2 da; *Heir* s, Somerled Alexander Bosville Macdonald, yr of Sleat, b 30 Jan 1976; *Career* chartered surveyor 1972; memb: Royal Soc of Health 1972, Economic Research Cncl 1979; Co cncllr Bridlington S 1981-85; pres: Humberside Branch Br Red Cross 1988, Br Food and Farming Humberside 1989, Humberside Young Farmers; chm Rural Devpt Cmmn Humberside 1988, High Sheriff of Humberside 1988-89; *Recreations* ornithology; *Clubs* White's, Brooks's, Puffin's; *Style*— Sir Ian Bosville Macdonald of Sleat, Bt; Thorpe Hall, Rudston, Driffield, N Humberside (☎ 026 282 239); Upper Duntulm, Kilmuir, Isle of Skye (☎ 047 052 206)

BOSVILLE MACDONALD OF SLEAT, Mary, Lady; Mary Elizabeth; da of Lt-Col Ralph Crawley-Boevy Gibbs (1 cous of 1 Baron Wraxall); *b* 5 June 1919; *m* 1946, Sir (Alexander) Somerled Angus Bosville Macdonald of Sleat, 16 Bt, MC (d 1958); *Style*— Mary, Lady Bosville Macdonald of Sleat; Westcroft Farm, Rudston, Driffield, N Humberside (☎ 026 282 614)

BOSWALL; *see*: Houstoun-Boswall

BOSWELL, Timothy Eric; MP (C) Daventry 1987-; s of Eric New Boswell (d 1974), of Lower Aynho Grounds, Banbury, and Joan Winifred Caroline, *née* Jones; *b* 2 Dec 1942; *Educ* Marlborough, New Coll Oxford (Literae Humaniores post grad dip); *m* 2 Aug 1969, Helen Delahay, da of the Rev Arthur Delahay Rees (d 1956), of Pennard Vicarage, Swansea; 3 da (Victoria b 1971, Emily b 1975, Caroline b 1978); *Career* head of Econ Section Cons Res Dept 1970-73 (agric and economics advsr 1966-73); managed family farm from father's death in 1974; chm: Daventry Constituency Cons Assoc 1979-83 (treas 1976-79), Northants Leics and Rutland Counties branch NFU 1983; memb: Cncl Perry Fndn for Agric Res 1966-90 (pres 1984-90), Agric Select Ctee 1987-89, Agric and Foods Res Cncl 1988-90; chm Parly Charity Law Reform Panel 1988-90; PPS to fin sec to the Treasy 1989-90; asst govt whip 1990-; *Recreations* shooting; *Clubs* Farmers'; *Style*— Timothy Boswell, Esq, MP; Lower Aynho Grounds, Banbury, Oxon OX17 3BW (☎ 0869 810224); House of Commons, London SW1A 0AA (☎ 071 219 3000)

BOSWOOD, Anthony Richard; QC (1986); s of Noel Gordon Paul Boswood, of Radnage, Bucks, and Cicily Ann, *née* Watson; *b* 1 Oct 1947; *Educ* St Paul's, New Coll Oxford (BCL, MA); *m* 4 Jan 1973, Sarah Bridget, da of Sir John Lindsay Alexander; 3 da (Eleanor b 1976, Louise b 1978, Grace b 1983); *Career* called to the Bar Middle Temple 1970; *Recreations* opera, riding, tennis; *Clubs* Hurlingham; *Style*— Anthony Boswood, Esq, QC; Fountain Court, Temple, London EC4 (☎ 071 583 3335, fax 071 353 0329/1794, car 0860 419437, telex 8813408 FONLEG G); Podere Casanuova, Pieveasciata, Castelnuovo Berardenga (SI), Italy

BOSWORTH, Sir Neville Bruce Alfred; CBE (1982); s of late William Charles Neville Bosworth, of Birmingham, and late Nellie Ada Lawton, *née* Wheeler; *b* 18 April 1918; *Educ* King Edward's Sch Birmingham, Univ of Birmingham (LLB); *m* 22 Aug 1945, Charlotte Marian, da of late William Jacob Davis, of Birmingham; 1 s (Simon b 1946), 2 da (Jane b 1949, Josephine b 1950); *Career* admitted slr 1941; formerly sr ptnr Bosworth Bailey Cox & Co, currently conslt Grove Tompkins Bosworth, dir Nat Exhibition Centre and several private cos; memb (C) Birmingham CC since 1950 and held numerous offices, Lord Mayor 1969-70, ldr City Cncl 1976-80 and 1982-84; former govr King Edward's Sch (past tstee), chm and tstee Hook Memorial Homes, chm West Midlands Police Authy 1985-86, vice chm Assoc of Municipal Authorities 1979-80, pres Edgbaston Supper Club 1974-; Freeman City of Birmingham 1982; kt 1987; *Recreations* bridge, football; *Style*— Sir Neville Bosworth, CBE; Hollington, 8 Luttrell Rd, Four Oaks, Sutton Coldfield, Birmingham B74 2SR (☎ 021 308 0647); 54 Newhall Street, Birmingham B3 3QG (☎ 021 236 8091)

BOSWORTH, Simon Charles Neville; s of Sir Neville Bruce Alfred Bosworth, CBE, and Lady Charlotte Marian Bosworth, *née* Davis; *b* 6 Aug 1946; *Educ* Stouts Hill Gloucester, Bradfield; *m* 2 Feb 1979, Evelyn Fay, da of William Leslie Wallace (d 1984); 1 da (Claudia b 1984); *Career* dir: W H Cutler (Midlands) Ltd 1968-70, Sutton (Wine Bars) Ltd 1972-74, Hill Alveston & Co Ltd 1973-, Luttrell Park Investmts Ltd 1974-, Berkswell Properties Ltd 1983-, Berkswell Investments Ltd 1984-; *Recreations* football, gardening; *Clubs* St James's; *Style*— Simon C N Bosworth, Esq; The Thatched Cottage, Meriden Road, Berkswell, Coventry CV7 7BE; Hill Alveston Gp of Cos, Meriden Road, Berkswell, Coventry CV7 7BE (☎ 0676 33699)

BOTHAM, Brian William; s of William Botham (d 1979), of Staffs, and Ellen, *née* Burgess (d 1983); *b* 13 Feb 1932; *Educ* HS Newcastle-under-Lyme; *m* 14 Oct 1966, Christine, da of Wilfred Lord, of Bagnall Hall, Staffs; 1 s (Richard b 1968); *Career* slr; sr ptnr Clyde Chappell & Botham Slrs (Tunstall Meir and Biddulph Staffs); *Style*— Brian W Botham, Esq; The Retreat, Farley, nr Oakamoor, Staffs (☎ 0538 702 230); 84 Weston Rd, Meir, Stoke-on-Trent (☎ 0782 599 577); Inverdart, Kingswear, S Devon (☎ 080 425 465)

BOTT, Alan John; s of Albert Henry John Bott, and Eileen Mary, *née* Spiers; *b* 30 March 1935; *Educ* King's Coll Sch Wimbledon, Merton Coll Oxford (MA); *m* 10 Sept 1966, Caroline Gaenor, da of Frank Leslie Williams (d 1943); 2 s (Jonathan b 3 April 1968, Simon b 26 June 1970), 1 da (Alison b 24 March 1972); *Career* dir: The NZ Shipping Co 1971 (joined 1956), P & O Containers Ltd (formerly Overseas Containers Ltd) 1976-; chm: The Aust and NZ Shipping Confs 1978-, The Europe Southern Africa Shipping Conference 1990; dir ECSA and CENSA; churchwarden Godalming Parish Church 1979-, tstee Godalming Museum 1986-; FSA 1965; FCIT 1990; *Books* Monuments in Merton College Chapel (1964), Sailing Ships of the NZSCO (1973), Baptisms and Marriages at Merton College Oxford (1981), Godalming Parish Church (1988); *Recreations* tennis, gardening, writing and lecturing on the history of European architecture; *Clubs* Travellers'; *Style*— Alan Bott, Esq, FSA; Rake Court, Milford, Godalming, Surrey GU8 5AD (☎ 0483 416546); P & O Containers Ltd, Beagle House, Braham St, London E1 8EP (☎ 071 488 1313)

BOTT, (Charles) Harry Arden; s of Richard Harry Bott (d 1976), of Benington Lordship, Stevenage, Herts, and Esme' Blanche, *née* Brierley; *b* 26 Feb 1935; *Educ* Eton, Trinity Coll Cambridge (MA); *m* 4 April 1959, (Sarah) Naylor, da of late George Romney Fox, of Trewardreva, Constantine, Falmouth, Cornwall; 3 s (Richard b 6 Oct 1963, Andrew b 11 June 1965, Harry b 7 Dec 1966), 1 da (Susan b 12 April 1960); *Career* Nat Serv 2 Lt 4 QOH 1954; farmer 1959-; dir Lea Valley Water Co 1985-, chm Benington Parish Cncl, memb Ctee CLA; pres: county Young Farmers Club, memb Exec Ctee Herts Conservation Soc; JP Hertford & Ware 1965-86, High Sheriff of Herts 1987-88, gen cmmr for income tax 1964-; *Recreations* country sports, flying old light aircraft; *Style*— Harry Bott, Esq; Benington Lordship, Stevenage, Hertfordshire (☎ 043 885 668)

BOTT, Ian Bernard; s of Edwin Bernard Bott (d 1979), of Spain, and Agnes, *née* Hansell (d 1990); *b* 1 April 1932; *Educ* Nottingham HS, Southwell Minster GS, Stafford Tech Coll, Univ of Manchester (BSc); *m* 1955, Kathleen Mary, da of James Henry Broadbent; 1 s (Douglas James Bernard b 1961), 1 da (Mary Fiona b 1957); *Career* Nat Serv RAF 1953-55; Nottingham lace industry 1949-53, research laboratory English Electric (now part of GEC) 1955-57; MOD: research scientist Royal Radar Establishment Malvern (later head of Electronics Group) 1960-75, cnsllr defence research and devpt Br Embassy Washington (seconded to FCO) 1975-77, dep dir Underwater Weapon Systems Admty Underwater Weapon Establishment Dorset 1977-79, asst chief scientific advsr MOD HQ 1979-81, dir gen Guided Weapons and Electronics Army Controllerate 1981-82, princ dep dir Atomic Weapons Research Establishment Aldermaston 1982-84, dir Admty Research Establishment 1984-88; conslt engr 1988-; hon chm Portsmouth Area Hospice 1989; Freeman City of London 1985, Liveryman Worshipful Co of Engrs 1985; FInstP 1967 , FIEE 1972 , FEng 1985 (memb Cncl 1987-90); *Publications* Advances in Microwaves (vol 3, jtly), author of various articles in learned jls; *Recreations* horology, music, golf, computing, bricklaying; *Clubs* RAC; *Style*— Ian Bott, Esq

BOTT, Prof Martin Harold Phillips; s of Harold Bott (d 1958), and Dorothy, *née* Phillips (d 1970); *b* 12 July 1926; *Educ* Clayesmore Sch Dorset, Magdalene Coll Cambridge (MA, PhD); *m* 17 April 1961, Joyce Cynthia, da of Flying Offr John William Hughes (d 1969), of Lewes, Sussex; 2 s (Andrew Martin b 28 Aug 1962, Nicholas John b 6 Jan 1964), 1 da (Jacqueline Joyce Dorothy b 16 Jan 1966); *Career* Nat Serv Lt RCS 1945-48; Univ of Durham: Turner and Newall res fell Dept of Geology 1954-56, lectr in geophysics 1956-63, reader 1963-66, prof 1966-88, res prof pt/t 1988-; Anglican reader St Nicholas Church Durham; FRS 1977, FRAS, FGS; *Books* The Interior of the Earth (1982), ed of other pubns; *Recreations* mountain walking; *Style—* Prof Martin Bott, FRS; 11 St Mary's Close, Shincliffe, Durham DH1 2ND (☎ 091 386 4021); Department of Geological Sciences, Durham University, South Road, Durham DH1 3LE (☎ 091 374 2511)

BOTT, Rosemary Margaret; da of Brian Russell Thorpe, CBE, of 55 First Ave, Worthing, Sussex, and Ann Sinclair, *née* Raby; *b* 27 Nov 1956; *Educ* Convent of Our Lady of Sion Worthing, Univ of Southampton (LLB); *m* 1980 (m dis 1989), Adrian Bott; 1 s (Henry b 1985); *Career* admitted slr 1980; mktg ptnr Frere Cholmeley 1988- (ptnr 1986, articled 1978); memb: Law Soc, The Holborn Law Soc; *Recreations* skiing, swimming, sailing, theatre (dance and opera); *Style—* Ms Rosemary Bott; 28 Lincoln's Inn Fields, London WC2A 3HH (☎ 071 405 7878, fax 071 405 9056, telex 27623 FRERES G)

BOTTENHEIM, Michael Charles; s of Jack Charles Bottenheim (d 1972), and Caryl Rosemary Squires, *née* Baring-Gould (d 1978); *b* 1 Nov 1947; *Educ* Leiden Univ (Netherlands Doctoral in Law), Michigan State Univ (MBA); *m* 1981, Yvonne Maria Josephina, da of Edwin Eugen Meile; 2 c; *Career* Pierson Heldring & Pierson Amsterdam NL 1972-76; asst mangr: Citicorp Int Bank Ltd London UK 1976-79, Citicorp Int Finance SA Zurich- CH 1979-80; exec dir: Citicorp Int Bank Ltd, Lazard Bros & Co Ltd (London) 1980-85; *Style—* Michael C Bottenheim; Lazard Bros & Co Ltd, 21 Moorfields, London EC2P 2HT (☎ 071 588 2721, fax 071 920 0274)

BOTTERILL, Deryck; s of Cecil Botterill (d 1966), of St Austell, Cornwall, and Adela, *née* Salt (d 1978); *b* 31 May 1933; *Educ* St Austell GS; *m* 9 Aug 1958, Anne Fraser, da of Edward Fraser Treweek (d 1957), of St Austell, Cornwall; 1 s (Paul b 1964), 1 da (Hilary b 1961); *Career* CA; articled clerk Phillips Frith & Co St Austell, managing clerk Tribe Clerk & Co Bristol 1956-59, supervisor and sr mangr Cooper Bros & Co London 1959-64, mangr New Issue Dept W M Brandt's Sons & Co Ltd London 1964-66, asst to fin controller/fin dir (corp fin) Inchcape & Co Ltd 1966-71, dir Gray Dawes & Co Ltd 1966-71, ptnr Kidsons CA London 1971-90, chm Kidsons Assocs Ltd 1982-90, inspr DTI 1987-89, chm Kidsons Corporate Fin Ltd 1988-90, ptnr Kidsons Impry Chartered Accountants 1990-; reader licensed to Anglican Parish of St Nicolas Great Bookham; FCA 1956; *Books* The Creation and Protection of Capital (contrib 1974); *Recreations* flat green bowls, walking, cross country skiing, theology, family history; *Style—* Deryck Botterill, Esq; Kidsons, Russell Square House, 10-12 Russell Square, London WC1B 5AE (☎ 071 436 3636, fax 071 436 6603, telex 263901)

BOTTING, (Elizabeth) Louise; da of Robert Young, and Edith, *née* Roberts; *b* 19 Sept 1939; *Educ* Sutton Coldfield HS, LSE (BSc); *m* 1, 1964 (m dis 1986), Douglas Botting; 2 da (Catherine b 1966, Anna b 1967); m 2, 23 May 1989, Leslie Carpenter; *Career* broadcaster and financial journalist; investmt analyst Kleinwort Benson 1961-65, columnist Daily Mail 1970-76, chm Douglas Deakin Young 1974-, presenter Money Box BBC Radio 4 1977-; memb Top Salaries Review Body 1987; *Style—* Ms Louise Botting; Douglas Deakin Young Ltd, Empire House, 175 Piccadilly, London W1V 9DB (☎ 071 499 1206, fax 071 499 1017)

BOTTLE, Prof Robert Thomas; s of Edward James Bottle (d 1949), of Dial House, Harrietsham, Kent, and Hilda, *née* Tupper (d 1967); *b* 11 Feb 1929; *Educ* Ashford GS, Univ of London (BSc), Univ of Birmingham (PhD); *m* 7 Aug 1960, Margaret Joan, da of Samuel Horace Pilling (d 1989), of Wigan, Lancs; 1 s ((Robert) Alex b 1971), 2 da (Janet Margaret b 1961, Vanessa Anne b 1963); *Career* res assoc Indiana Univ 1954-55, sr res chemist Dunlop Res Centre 1955-56; lectr physical chemistry: Liverpool Coll of Technol 1956-60, Univ of Bradford 1960-71; prof Sch Library Sci Syracuse Univ 1968-70, lectr librarianship Univ of Strathclyde 1972-73; City Univ: dir Centre Info Sci 1973-83, prof info sci 1979-; memb Cncl Inst Info Scientists 1973-79, 1982-88 and 1990-; cncllr Harrietsham Parish Cncl 1976- (chm 1976-78, vice chm 1978-79 and 1987-), chm Noise Pollution Sub-Ctee N Downs Rail Concern 1988-; FLA 1973, fell Inst Info Sci 1977; *Books* Use of Chemical Literature (3 edn, 1979), Use of Biological Literature (2 edn, 1971), Gratis Controlled Circulation Jls for the Chemical and Allied Industs (1970); *Recreations* gardening, village life, bridge; *Style—* Prof Robert Bottle; Dial House, East St, Harrietsham, Maidstone, Kent ME17 1HJ (☎ 0622 859622); Dept of Information Science, City University, Northampton Square, London EC1V 0HB (☎ 071 253 4399, fax 071 250 0837)

BOTTOMLEY, Alan Ingham; TD; s of George R Bottomley (d 1980), and Olive, *née* Ingham (d 1989); *b* 14 Nov 1931; *Educ* Shrewsbury; *m* 25 March 1961, Jane Susan, da of Robert Werner (d 1973), of Harrogate; 1 s (Simon b 1962), 1 da (Anabel b 1964); *Career* Maj RA (TA), ret 1965; slr; jt sr ptnr Hammond Suddards Bradford Leeds and Brussels; *Recreations* sailing, opera, theatre, travel; *Clubs* Army and Navy; *Style—* Alan I Bottomley, Esq, TD; Dormy Lodge, Kent Rd, Harrogate, N Yorks; 68 Walton St, London SW3; Empire House, 10 Piccadilly, Bradford, W Yorks BD1 3LR

BOTTOMLEY, Baron (Life Peer UK 1984), of Middlesbrough in the Co of Cleveland; Rt Hon Arthur George Bottomley; OBE (1941), PC (1951); s of late George Howard Bottomley, and Alice Bottomley, of Tottenham, Middx; *b* 7 Feb 1907; *Educ* Gamuel Rd Cncl Sch, Toynbee Hall; *m* 1936, Dame Bessie Bottomley, DBE (*see* Bottomley, Baroness); *Career* delegate UN 1946, 1947, 1949; parly under sec Dominions 1946-47, overseas trade sec BOT 1947-51, cwlth affrs sec 1964-66, min Overseas Devpt 1966-67; MP (Lab): Chatham 1945-50, Rochester and Chatham 1950-59, Middlesbrough E 1962-74, Teesside Middlesbrough 1974-83; former London organiser NUPE; chm: Select Commons Ctee Race Rels and Immigration 1969-71, House of Commons Cmmn 1980-83; treas Cwlth Parly Assoc 1974-78; chm Attlee Fndn 1978-; Freeman City of: London, Chatham, Middlesbrough; Aung San Fagum Burma; *Books* Commonwealth Comrades and Friends, The Use and Abuse of Trade Unions; *Style—* The Rt Hon the Lord Bottomley, OBE, PC; 19 Lichfield Rd, Woodford Green, Essex

BOTTOMLEY, Baroness; Dame Bessie (Ellen) Bottomley; *née* Wiles; DBE (1970); da of Edward Charles Wiles, of Walthamstow, and Ellen, *née* Estall; *b* 28 Nov 1906; *Educ* Maynard Rd Girls' Sch, N Walthamstow Central Sch; *m* 1936, Rt Hon Arthur George Bottomley, OBE, MP (now Baron Bottomley, *qv*); no children; *Career* on staff of NUT 1925-36; memb Walthamstow Borough Cncl 1945-48, Essex CC 1962-65; chm Lab Party Women's Section: E Walthamstow 1946-71, Chingford 1973-; memb: Forest Group Hosp Mgmnt Ctee 1949-73, W Roding Community Health Cncl 1973-76; chm Walthamstow Nat Savings Ctee 1949-65, vice pres Waltham Forest Nat Savings Ctee 1965, chm 1975; Mayoress of Walthamstow 1945-46; memb WVS Regional Staff (SE England) 1941-45, past memb Home Office Advsy Ctee on Child Care, chm of govrs: of two secdy mod schs 1948-68, gp of primary and infant schs, of high schools, memb Whitefield Tst; JP 1955-76, Juvenile Bench 1955-71, dep chm Waltham Forest Bench; *Recreations* theatre, gardening; *Style—* The Rt Hon the Lady Bottomley, DBE; 19 Lichfield Rd, Woodford Green, Essex

BOTTOMLEY, Brian Rogers; s of Harry Bottomley (d 1958), of Sale, Cheshire, and Ivy, *née* Wragg (d 1974); *b* 14 Dec 1927; *Educ* Sale Central Sch; *m* 1950, Kathleen, da of Thomas Neville, of Altrincham; 1 s (Nigel Rogers); *Career* chartered engr; tech dir Churchill Machine Tool Co Ltd 1968-73; md: TI Matrix Ltd 1973-81, Staveley Machine Tools 1981-84; chm md and owner of Kearns-Richards Ltd and KRS Ltd 1984-89; mgmnt conslt; Eur-Ing, FIMechE, FIPiodE; *Recreations* sailing, shooting (Br short range pistol champion 1969); *Style—* Brian Bottomley, Esq; 7 The Dell, Southdowns Rd, Hale, Altrincham, Cheshire WA14 3HU (☎ 061 928 8623)

BOTTOMLEY, James Barry; s of Edgar Bottomley (d 1981), of The Towers, Lytham St Annes, and Elizabeth Pryce, *née* Thompson (d 1975); *b* 21 Feb 1940; *Educ* The Hulme GS for Boys Oldham, Univ of Manchester (LLB); *Career* slr 1968; NP 1984, Paul Harris fell appointed by the Rotary Club of Bredbury & Romiley 1975; *Recreations* ornithology, field studies; *Clubs* Manchester Literary and Philosophical Soc; *Style—* James Bottomley, Esq; The Gables, Stalybridge, Cheshire SK15 2RT (☎ 061 303 0578); Castle's, 61 Mottram Rd, Stalybridge, Cheshire SK15 2QP (☎ 061 338 2135)

BOTTOMLEY, Sir James Reginald Alfred; KCMG (1973, CMG 1965); s of Sir (William) Cecil Bottomley, KCMG, CB, OBE (d 1954), and Alice Thistle, *née* Robinson, JP; *b* 12 Jan 1920; *Educ* King's Coll Sch Wimbledon, Trinity Coll Cambridge; *m* 1941, Barbara Evelyn, da of Henry Vardon, of Market Drayton; 2 s (incl Peter Bottomley, MP, *qv*) and 1 s decd, 2 da; *Career* Inns of Court Regt NW Europe 1940-46; Cwlth Rels Office 1946, SA 1948-50, Pakistan 1953-55, USA 1955-59, UN NY 1959, dep high cmmr Malaysia 1963-67, dep under sec of state FCO 1970, ambass SA 1973-76, perm UK rep to UN at Geneva 1976-78; dir Johnson Matthey plc 1979-85; *Recreations* golf; *Style—* Sir James Bottomley, KCMG; 22 Beaufort Place, Thompson's Lane, Cambridge CB5 8AG

BOTTOMLEY, Jeffrey; s of George Henry Bottomley (d 1981), of Audenshaw, Manchester, Lancs, and Ada Lily, *née* Mathews (d 1985); *b* 29 March 1940; *Educ* St Margaret's Sch Manchester, Manchester Art Sch; *m* 14 Feb 1974, Beverley Ann, da of Henry Arthur Mantle, of Weston-super-Mare; *Career* art dir Image Arts Ltd 1973-78, chm Kingsley Cards Ltd 1980- (md 1979-80); *Recreations* collector of classic cars, antiques and silver; *Clubs* East India, Jaguar Drivers, Fleet St; *Style—* Jeffrey Bottomley, Esq; Horseshoes, High St, Nash, Milton Keynes MK17 0EP (☎ 0908 502 203); Kingsley Card Ltd, Catsbrain Farm, Oakley, Aylesbury, Bucks (☎ 08447 8874)

BOTTOMLEY, Dr Malcolm Brooke; s of John Reginald Bottomley (d 1988), of Sheffield, and Mary, *née* Evans; *b* 4 June 1933; *Educ* King Edward VII GS Sheffield, Univ of Sheffield (MB ChB); *m* 1, 1959 (m dis 1990), Paula Dorothy; 3 da (Caroline Mary b 1960, Sally Ann b 1962, Louisa Kate b 1965); m 2, 1991, Hilary Joyce; *Career* hon med offr: FA of Wales 1981-84, British Amateur Athletic Board 1984-; Bath Rugby Club 1989-; med offr to GB team: IAAF World Marathon Cup Seoul 1987, World Athletics Championships Rome 1987, Track and Field Squad Seoul Olympics 1988; GP Yorkshire and Shropshire 1960-83, med offr Univ of Bath 1984; *Books* Sports Injury Clinic (contrib, 1987), Medicine Sport and the Law (contrib, 1990); *Recreations* outdoor activities; *Style—* Dr Malcolm Bottomley; Brunswick Cottage, 42 Combe Rd, Combe Down, Bath BA2 5HY (☎ 0225 833757); University Medical Centre, Quarry House, North Rd, Bath BA2 7AY (☎ 0225 462395)

BOTTOMLEY, Peter James; MP (C) Eltham 1975-; s of Sir James Bottomley, *qv*; *b* 30 July 1944; *Educ* Westminster, Trinity Coll Cambridge; *m* 1967, Virginia Hilda Brunette Maxwell, MP, *qv*, da of John Garnett, CBE, *qv*; 1 s, 2 da; *Career* Parly under sec of state: Dept of Employment 1984-86, Dept of Transport (min for roads) 1986-89, to the NI Office 1989-90; chm: Br Union of Family Orgns 1973-80, Family Forum 1980-82, C of E Children's Soc 1983-84; tstee Christian Aid 1978-84; *Recreations* children; *Style—* Peter Bottomley Esq, MP; House of Commons, London SW1 (☎ 071 219 5060)

BOTTOMLEY, Stephen John; s of Frederick John Bottomley, of Barbican, London, and Jean Mary, *née* Moore; *b* 23 Oct 1954; *Educ* Sutton Valence, Univ of East Anglia (BA); *m* 8 June 1984, Gail Barbara, da of Grenville Herbert Ryder (d 1989), of Crosby, Liverpool; 2 da (Clare b 1987, Emma b 1989); *Career* admitted slr 1980; ptnr Bartletts De Reya 1984-88, dir Johnson Fry Corporation Finance Ltd 1988, ptnr Row and Maw 1988; treas Devas Youth Club Wandsworth; Freeman Worshipful Co of Slrs; memb Law Soc; *Recreations* squash, hockey, golf; *Style—* Stephen Bottomley, Esq; 39 Beauval Rd, London SE22 8UG (☎ 081 299 0501); Rowe & Maw, 20 Black Friars Lane, London EC4V 6HD (☎ 071 248 4282, fax 071 248 2009, telex 262787 MAWLAWG)

BOTTOMLEY, Virginia Hilda Brunette Maxwell; JP, MP (C) Surrey South-West 1984-; da of John Garnett, CBE, *qv*; *b* 12 March 1948; *Educ* Putney HS, Essex Univ (BA), LSE (MSc); *m* 1967, Peter James Bottomley, MP, *qv*; 1 s, 2 da; *Career* min of state Dept of Health 1989-; govt co chm Women's Nat Cmmn; *Style—* Mrs Virginia Bottomley, JP, MP; House of Commons, London SW1

BOUCH, Dr (Dennis) Clive; s of Tom Bouch (d 1967), of Aspatria, Cumbria, and Elizabeth Anderson, *née* Errington; *b* 12 Sept 1939; *Educ* Nelson Thomlinson GS, Wigton Cumbria, Univ of Edinburgh (BSc, MB ChB); *m* 12 Sept 1968, (Valerie Alexander) Sandra, da of Alexander Lamb (d 1983), of Edinburgh; 2 s (David Christopher b 1972, Jeremy Clive b 1973), 2 da (Caroline Anne b 1975, Katharine Mary b 1978); *Career* lectr in pathology Univ of Edinburgh 1966-75, conslt pathologist to Leicestershire Health Authy 1976-, head of dist pathology serv 1985-, Home Office pathologist 1984-; FRC Pathologists 1985; *Style—* Dr Clive Bouch; Dept of Pathology, The Leicester Royal Infirmary, Leicester LE1 5WW (☎ 0533 541414)

BOUCHER, Arthur James Kinnear; s of Frederick Boucher, OBE (d 1982); *b* 3 Oct 1934; *Educ* Campbell Coll, Queen's Univ Belfast (BSc); *m* 1962, Karen, da of William Andrew Leitch, CB, of Belfast; 4 da; *Career* chm Francis Curley Ltd; FCA Ireland; *Style—* Arthur Boucher, Esq; 9 Tweskard Park, Belfast BT4 2JY (☎ 0232 63153)

BOUCHERAT, Dr Rosemary; da of Joseph Hayes Fairweather (d 1959), of Clitheroe, and Mary Helen Fergusson, *née* Lawson, (d 1960); *b* 29 July 1936; *Educ* Clitheroe GS, Queenswood Sch Hatfield, St Mary's Hosp Univ of London (MB BS, DRCOG, DA, DCH, DPM); *m* 30 April 1966, Robert Jean-Marie Boucherat, s of Lucien Boucherat; 2 s (Ben b 28 May 1967, Mark b 11 Sept 1969); *Career* Civilian Med Offr RCAF 1965-66; sr registrar child psychiatry Sheffield Central Health Authy, conslt child psychiatrist Doncaster Royal Infirmary 1977-; memb: Amnesty Int, MIND, Greenpeace, People of Sheffield; MRCPsych 1975, Assoc Family Therapists 1980; *Recreations* walking, travelling, tennis, skiing; *Style—* Dr Rosemary Boucherat; 69 Church St, Bawtry, Doncaster, S Yorks DN10 6HR (☎ 0302 910951); Doncaster Royal Infirmary, Armthorpe Rd, Doncaster DN2 (☎ 0302 36666)

BOUCHIER, Lady; (Isabella) Dorothy Guyver; da of Frank Guyver Britton (d 1934), of Elmdon, Essex, and Alice Hiller (d 1966), of San Francisco; ggda of Count Johann Friedrich von Hillerscheidt, of Berlin; *b* 14 Feb 1922; *Educ* Claremont Sch England, Mills Coll California, San Francisco Conservatory of Music; *m* 1968, as his 2 w, Air Vice-Marshal Sir Cecil Arthur Bouchier, KBE, CB, DFC (d 1979), s of Arthur Couch Bouchier, of Chichester (d 1904); 1 step s; *Career* composer, author, poet (under maiden name); own TV programme NHK, Tokyo 1960-70; music pubns incl:

orchestral suites, Tokyo Impressions, Yedo Fantasy (Los Angeles, 1957), cantata, And Certain Women (New York 1957), 20 folksongs of Japan (Tokyo 1969); *Books* A Haiku Journey (Tokyo, 1975), National Parks of Japan (Tokyo, 1980), The Japanese Crane: Bird of Happiness (Tokyo, 1981), Totto-chan: the Little Girl at the Window (trans Tokyo, 1982); The Spider's Thread and other stories (trans Tokyo, 1987), The Girl with the White Flag (trans Tokyo, 1991); *Recreations* chess, shell collecting, birdwatching, watercolour painting; *Clubs* RAF, International House of Japan; *Style—* Lady Bouchier; 2275 Isshiki, Hayama, Kanagawa-ken 240-01, Japan (☎ 0468 75 1217); c/o Barclays Bank plc, 208 Kensington High St, London W8 7RJ

BOUCHIER, Prof Ian Arthur Dennis; CBE (1990); s of Edward Alfred Bouchier, of Cape Town, SA, and May, *née* Simons; *b* 7 Sept 1932; *Educ* Rondebosch Boys HS, Cape Town Univ, Univ of London, Boston Univ Med Sch USA (MB ChB, MD); *m* 5 Sept 1959, Patricia Norma, da of Thomas Henshilwood (d 1985), of Cape Town, SA; 2 s (Anthony James b 1962, David Ian b 1964); *Career* med registrar Groote Schuur Hosp 1958-61; various res posts 1961-65: Royal Free Hosp London, Boston Univ Med Sch; sr lectr in med Univ of London 1965-70 (reader 1970-73); prof of medicine: Univ of Dundee 1973-86, Univ of Edinburgh 1986-; memb: Chief Scientist Ctee in Scotland, Tenovus-Scotland Advsy Ctee, chm Health Serv Res Ctee; vice chm Scot AIDS Res Appeal, pres World Orgn of Gastroenterology, former memb MRC, former dean Faculty of Med Univ of Dundee; FRCP 1970, FRCPE 1973, FRSE 1985, FIBiol 1988; *Books* Gastroenterology (1973, 1977, 1982), Recent Advances in Gastroenterology (1976, 1980, 1983), Clinical Investigation of Gastrointestinal Function (1969, 1981, 1988), Textbook of Gastroenterology (1984); *Recreations* gardening, history of whaling, music; *Clubs* New, Edinburgh Angus; *Style—* Prof Ian Bouchier; Department of Medicine, Royal Infirmary, Edinburgh EH3 9YW (☎ 031 229 2477, fax 031 229 2948, telex 727 442 UNIVED G)

BOUCHIER HAYES, Col Prof Thomas Anthony Ivan; s of Thomas Adrian Bouchier Hayes (d 1962), of Dublin, and Mona, *née* Graham; *b* 10 June 1937; *Educ* Clongowes Wood Coll, RCSI (DObstRCOG); *m* 16 Sept 1964, Winifred Heather, da of Alfred Coulthard (d 1978); 1 s (Tommy Adrian b 5 Oct 1966), 1 da (Alexandra Siobhan b 29 Aug 1968); *Career* joined RAMC 1965; MO: Singapore 1965-70, BAOR 1970-73, Bridge of Guards 1975-80; tutor to Army Gen Practice 1975-80, SMO RMA Sandhurst 1980-83, Colchester 1983-85, Gp Practice Queen Elizabeth Mil Hosp B Woolwich 1985-87, prof Army Gen Practice RAMC Millbank 1987-; FRCGP 1980; fell London Soc of Med 1988, FRSM 1988, LAM; *Books* MRCGP tutor (1980), Beecham Manual of General Practice (1981), MRCGP Study Book (1892), MCQ Tutor (1982), Guide to PLAB (1983), Emergencies in General Practice (1983); *Recreations* tennis, bridge, watching sports; *Clubs* London Irish Rugby Football, Southfields Lawn Tennis; *Style—* Col Prof Thomas Bouchier Hayes; 9 Coldstream Gardens, Wandsworth, London SW18 (☎ 081 871 0614); Department of General Practice, Royal Army Medical College, Millbank, London SW1P 4RJ (☎ 071 930 4466 ext 8269, fax 071 821 6523)

BOUCKLEY, Christopher Paul Michael; s of John Gordon Bouckley, and Shelagh Mary, *née* McCrea; *b* 21 March 1956; *Educ* Colchester Royal GS, Corpus Christi Coll Cambridge (MA); *m* 16 April 1979, Alison Forster, da of Wilfred Walker (d 1972); 1 s (Timothy b 22 April 1987), 1 da (Stephanie b 15 May 1985); *Career* Euro res analyst Quilter Goodison & Co 1978-80, sr Euro fund mangr Hill Samuel Investment Managment 1980-83, md Carnegie International Ltd 1985- (dir 1983-), chm Carnegie Espana 1989-; *Recreations* tennis, country pursuits; *Style—* Christopher Bouckley, Esq; Carnegie International Ltd, Carthusian Court, 12 Carthusian St, London EC1M 6EB (☎ 071 606 0055, fax 071 796 2617, telex 892409)

BOUDARD, Robin; JP; s of Mark Victor Charles Boudard (d 1969), of Notts, and Isabel Helen, *née* Blurton (d 1979); *b* 29 March 1925; *Educ* Sedbergh, CCC Cambridge; *m* 1967, Elizabeth Isobel (d 1979), da of Noel William Radford (d 1977), of Notts; 1 s (Simon b 1970), 1 da (Lucinda b 1973); *Career* textile mfr; *Recreations* fishing; *Clubs* Brooks's; *Style—* Robin Boudard, Esq, JP; The Old Vicarage, Bleasby, Nottinghamshire (☎ 0636 830254); Christopher Day Ltd, Plumptre Place, Stoney St, Nottingham (☎ 0602 505505)

BOUGH, Francis Joseph (Frank); s of Austin Joseph Bough (d 1963), of Oswestry, Shropshire, and Annie Tyler, *née* Moulton; *b* 15 Jan 1933; *Educ* Oswestry Boys HS, Merton Coll Oxford (BA, soccer blue); *m* 25 July 1959, Nest, *née* Howells; 3 s (David b 1961, Stephen b 1963, Andrew b 1965); *Career* Nat Serv Cmmn 2 RTR 1955-57; ICI Billingham 1957-62; BBC presenter: joined 1962, Sportsview 1964-69, Grandstand 1969-82, 6 Olympic Games 1964-82, 6 world Cups, Nationwide 1972-83, Breakfast TV 1983-87, Holiday Prog 1986-88; The Frank Bough Interview Sky TV 1989-90; presenter Six O'Clock Live LWT 1989-, Moneywise TVS; Richard Dimbleby BAFTA award 1976, 3 awards for presenting sport, news, and current affairs TV and Radio Industs Club; *Books* Cue Frank (autobiography, 1980), The Frank Bough Breakfast Book (1984); *Recreations* cricket, football, hockey, drama; *Style—* Frank Bough, Esq; c/o Jon Roseman Associates Ltd, 103 Charing Cross Rd, London WC2 ODT (☎ 071 439 8245, fax 071 287 2977)

BOUGHEY, Lady; Gillian Claire; da of Maj Robert Moubray, DL, late 16th Lancers (d 1961), of Kelso, Roxburghshire; *b* 15 Oct 1933; *m* 1976, as his 2 w, Sir Richard Boughey, 10 Bt, JP, DL (d 1978); *Style—* Lady Boughey; The Old Rectory, Quarley, Andover, Hants SP11 8PZ (☎ 0264 88 245)

BOUGHEY, James Richard; s of Sir Richard Boughey, 10 Bt, JP, DL (d 1978); h to Btcy of bro, Sir John Boughey, 11 Bt; *b* 29 Aug 1960; *Educ* Eton, Royal Agricultural Coll Cirencester; *m* 1989, Katharine Mary, da of Warren Fenwick-Clennell; 1 da (Victoria Rose b 12 Nov 1990); *Career* agriculture; *Clubs* Cavalry & Guards; *Style—* James Boughey, Esq

BOUGHEY, Sir John George Fletcher; 11 Bt (GB 1798); s of Sir Richard Boughey, 10 Bt, JP, DL (d 1978); *b* 12 Aug 1959; *Educ* Eton, Univ of Harare; *Heir* bro, James Richard Boughey; *Career* medical; *Clubs* Boodle's; *Style—* Sir John Boughey, Bt; Bratton House, Westbury, Wilts

BOUGHTON, John Henry; OBE (1967); s of Thomas Trafford Boughton (d 1959), of Bucks, and Fanny, *née* Smith (d 1958); *b* 2 Sept 1918; *Educ* Dr Challoners GS Amersham; *m* 1949, Elisabeth Anne, da of Harold Hawgood (d 1970); 1 s (John b 1968), 4 da (Gillian b 1949, Ruth b 1952, Margaret b 1956, Pamela b 1960); *Career* dir: T T Boughton & Sons Ltd 1942-, Reynolds Boughton Ltd 1946-; chm: Agric Enterprises Ltd 1957-, Ulrich Mfrg Co (GB) Ltd 1965, Buckets Imports Ltd 1963-, TTB Fabrications Ltd 1966-; dir: Anchorpac Ltd 1966-, Scottom Trailers Ltd 1970-, Hearncrest Boughton Engrg Ltd 1974, Boughton Transmissions Ltd 1974-, Reynolds Boughton Chassis Ltd 1977-; govr: Dr Challoners GS Amersham 1983, Coll of Further Educn Amersham 1985, Counsel of Order of St John Bucks Div 1985; OStJ 1989; *Recreations* sailing, travelling, winter sports, reading, writing, painting; *Style—* John Boughton, Esq, OBE; 69 Amersham Road, Little Chalfont, Bucks HP6 6SP (☎ 0494 762480); T T Boughton & Sons Ltd, Bell Lane, Amersham, Bucks HP6 6PE (☎ 0494 764411, fax 0494 765218, telex 83132)

BOUGHTON, Michael Linnell Gerald; s of Edward Morley Westwood Boughton (d 1951), and Iris Dorothy, *née* Linnell; *b* 14 May 1925; *Educ* King Edwards Sch Birmingham (HND); *m* 1953, Barbara Janette, da of Sir Ivan Arthur Rice Stedeford, GBE (d 1975); 3 children; *Career* served WW II, Capt RE Middle East; co dir; dep gp md TI Gp 1982-84, dep chm 1984-86, md (operations) 1984-86; chm: TI Domestic Appliances 1974-83, Midland Aluminium 1975-, TI Raleigh Int 1981-85; dir: TI Gp 1964-86, Br Aluminium 1973-82, EIS Gp 1979-84 and 1986-; bd memb Port of London Authy 1986-; *Recreations* sailing, golf; *Clubs* Huntercombe Golf; *Style—* Michael Boughton, Esq; Little Heath, Crays Pond, nr Pangbourne, Berks RG8 7QG (☎ 0491 872622)

BOUGHTON, Stephen David; s of Gerald Leslie Grantham Boughton, and Marjorie Hilda, *née* Johns (d 1986); *b* 29 Sept 1955; *Educ* George Abbot Boys Sch Guildford, Trinity Hall Cambridge (MA); *Career* slr; assoc Sullivan & Cromwell NY 1982-83, ptnr Linklaters & Paines 1986- (slr 1980-82 and 1983-86); memb: Law Soc, City of London Slrs Co; *Recreations* sport, travel, theatre, cinema; *Style—* S D Boughton, Esq; Linklaters & Paines, Barrington House, 59-67 Gresham St, London EC2V 7JA (☎ 071 606 7080)

BOUGHTON, (Thomas) Trafford; s of T T Boughton (d 1959), of Amersham, and Fanny, *née* Smith (d 1958); *b* 25 Oct 1913; *m* 1, 25 Feb 1943, Barbara, *née* Langston; 3 s (Thomas b 1947, Richard b 1950, Stephen b 1952), 1 da (Bridget b 1944); m 2, 15 May 1968, Diana, da of William Southam Cox; 2 s (Robert b 1969, Edward b 1974); *Career* dir T T Boughton & Sons Ltd 1942 (chm 1959); *Style—* Trafford Boughton, Esq; Dodds Mill, Chenies, Bucks WD3 6EU (☎ 09278 2973); Boughton Gp, Bell Lane, Amersham, Bucks (☎ 0494 764411, fax 0494 765218, telex 83132)

BOUKAMEL, Bassam; s of Rafic Yusuf Boukamel (d 1989), and Vasima, *née* Cazou; *b* 2 June 1948; *Educ* International Coll Beirut, American Univ of Beirut (BA), Fordham Univ New York (MA); *Career* economist and investment advsr 1975-86, dir Raab Boukamel Galleries Limited 1986- (representing internationally recognized artists such as Rainer Fetting, Luciano Castelli, K M Hödicke, Peter Chevalier, Herman Albert, Ken Currie and Stephen Barclay); *Recreations* all racquet sports, skiing and reading; *Style—* Bassam Boukamel, Esq; Raab Boukamel Galleries Limited, 6 Vauxhall Bridge Rd, London SW1 2SD (☎ 071 828 2588, fax 071 976 5041)

BOULAY; *see*: Houssemayne du Boulay

BOULD, Stephen Andrew (Steve); s of Raymond Bould, of Blurton, Stoke-on-Trent, and Wendy May, *née* Taylor; *b* 16 Nov 1962; *Educ* Blurton HS Stoke-on-Trent; *Career* professional footballer; Stoke City 1982-88 (debut v Middlesbrough 1982, 183 league appearances), on loan Torquay Utd 1982 (9 league appearances), Arsenal 1988- (over 75 appearances); League Championship medal 1989; *Style—* Steve Bould, Esq; c/o Jerome Anderson Management, 248 Station Rd, Edgware, Middlesex HA8 7AU (☎ 081 958 7799, fax 081 958 2000)

BOULIS, Dr Zoser; s of Fouad Boulis (d 1976), and Irene Grais, *née* Wassif; *b* 1 Jan 1944; *Educ* Camboni Coll Khartoum Sudan, Univ of Khartoum (MB BS, ECFMG, DMRD), LRCP, MRCS; *m* 20 July 1974, Afaf Hanna, da of Ayoub Girgis (d 1989); 1 s (Michael Menes b 9 April 1975), 1 da (Sandra Anne b 23 April 1976); *Career* sr house offr Royal Marsden Hosp 1973, registrar in gen surgery Barking Hosp Essex 1973-76, sr registrar in diagnostic radiology Royal Free Hosp 1976-83, conslt radiologist Bromley Health Authy 1983-; contrib to Journal of Radiology; memb: BMA, Hosp Med Advsy Ctee; FRCS 1973, FRCSEd 1974, FRCSGlas 1975, FRCR 1982; *Style—* Dr Zoser Boulis; Consultant Radiologist, Farnborough Hospital (Ultrasound Department), Farnborough, Orpington, Kent (☎ 0689 53333 ext 471, 498)

BOULOS, Paul Bernard; s of Bernard Boulos (d 1964), of Khartoum, and Evelyn, *née* Haggar; *b* 10 March 1944; *Educ* Comboni Coll Khartoum Sudan, Univ of Khartoum (MB BS); *m* 1 March 1979, Marilyn Lesley, da of Ronald Robert Went, of Highgate, London; 1 s (Mark Ronald b 15 Aug 1980), 2 da (Sarah-Jane b 22 Sept 1981, Paula Louise b 28 Dec 1984); *Career* lectr in surgery Faculty of Med Univ of Khartoum 1973-76, res fell Dept of Surgical Studies Middx Hosp 1976-77, sr surgical registrar St Mark's Hosp 1977-81, sr lectr in surgery UCL 1981- (sr surgical registrar 1977-81), conslt surgn UCH 1981-; memb: RSM, Assoc of Surgns of GB and I, Br Soc of Gastroenterology, Assoc of Coloproctology of GB and I, Surgical Res Soc, BMA; MS, FRCS, FRCSE; *Style—* Paul Boulos, Esq; St Anne, 15 Richmond Road, New Barnet, Herts EN5 1SA (☎ 081 449 6552); Dept of Surgery, Faculty of Clinical Sciences, University College London, The Rayne Institute, University Street, London WC1E 6JJ (☎ 071 388 7176, fax 071 387 9300)

BOULT, David Luard; s of Maj Peter Boult, MC (d 1955), of Hoylake; *b* 6 Dec 1924; *Educ* Shrewsbury Sch; *m* 1957, Elizabeth Anne, da of David Collett, of Rickmansworth, Herts; 2 s, 1 da; *Career* serv WWII, Capt RE; dir: BICC Cables 1980-83, Community of St Helens Trust Ltd 1983-87; chm Merseyside Playing Fields Assoc 1978-84; bd memb Merseyside and N Wales Electricity Bd 1983-89; *Recreations* golf, gardening, Rugby Union admin; *Clubs* Delamere Forest Golf, Liverpool RUFC, Liverpool Racquets; *Style—* David Boult, Esq; Mariners, The Common, Southwold, Suffolk (☎ 0502 724921)

BOULT, Lt-Col Peter Walter Swinton; TD; s of Maj Peter Swinton Boult, MC (d 1955), of New Bunnee, Hoylake, Cheshire, and Rose Cawston, *née* Pattisson (d 1948); *b* 13 Sept 1919; *Educ* Shrewsbury; *m* 11 June 1949, (Elizabeth) Jane, da of Sir Frank Samuel Alexander, 1 Bt (d 1959); 2 s (Nigel b 1952 d 1984, Geoffrey b 1955), 2 da (Rosanne b 1950, Alison b 1953); *Career* WWII cmmnd 2 Lt RA (TA) 1939, served 149 RHA Regt Western Desert, instr RA OCTU Cairo, served 102 Regt Northumberland Hussars, instr Gunnery Sch of Artillery Salisbury Plain 1944, demob 1946; cmd Lt-Col 290 (City of London) FD Regt RA (TA) 1955-57; articled clerk Liverpool 1937-39, produce merchant and dir of cos trading in London Commodity Exchange 1946-64; dir: Symbol Biscuits Ltd (subsid of J Lyons & Co Ltd) 1964-68, Metlex Industs (chm 1980-82); dir of other cos within IS plc; pres Hardware Mfrs Assoc 1977-79, cncl memb CBI 1973-82 (chm Surrey area 1977-81), cncl chm Nat Artillery Assoc 1969-80, dep chm TA Sports Bd 1970-79; Liveryman: Worshipful Co of Distillers 1958, Worshipful Co of Tallow Chandlers 1960 (Warden 1987); *Recreations* watching sport, bridge, golf, golf course design; *Clubs* MCC, Aldeburgh Golf, Chislehurst Golf, Band of Brothers, Kent CCC; *Style—* Lt-Col Peter W S Boult, TD; Wellwood, Watts Lane, Chislehurst, Kent BR7 5PJ (☎ 081 467 3216)

BOULTER, Prof Donald; s of George Boulter (d 1953), and Vera Annabelle, *née* Medland; *b* 25 Aug 1926; *Educ* Portsmouth GS, ChCh Oxford (BA, MA, DPhil); *m* 1 Sept 1956, (Margaret) Eileen, da of William Kennedy (d 1952); 4 da (Susan (Mrs Stafford), Sara (Mrs Wilson), Catherine, Vanessa (Mrs Zhang)); *Career* RAF VR UT pilot, vocational advice offr RAF 1945-48; asst lectr King's Coll Univ of London 1955-57, sr lectr Univ of Liverpool 1957-66 (formerly lectr), prof and chm Dept of Biological Sciences Univ of Durham 1988- (prof and head Dept of Botany 1966-88); memb Plants and Environmental Res Ctee Agric and Food Res Cncl; govr: Scot Crop Res Inst, Inst of Plant Sci Res Cambridge; memb Exec Cmmn Horticulture Res Inst; FIBiol, FRSA; *Recreations* travel, reading; *Style—* Prof Donald Boulter; 5 Crossgate, Durham City DH1 4PS (☎ 091 386 1199) Department of Biological Sciences, University of Durham, South Rd, Durham DH1 3LE (☎ 091 374 2420, fax 091 374 3741, telex 537351 DURLIB G)

BOULTER, Prof Patrick Stewart; s of Frederick Charles Boulter, MC (d 1961), of Annan, Scotland, and Flora Victoria, *née* Black (d 1965); *b* 28 May 1927; *Educ* Kings Coll Sch, Carlisle GS, Guy's Hosp Med Sch (MB BS, Gold medal); *m* 7 March 1946, (Patricia) Mary Eckersley, da of Samuel Gordon Barlow (d 1966), of Lowton, Lancs; 2

da (Jennifer (Mrs Bond), Anne (Mrs Wood)); *Career* registrar Dept of Surgical Studies Middx Hosp 1957-59, sr surgical registrar Guy's Hosp 1959-62; conslt oncological and gen surgn 1962-: Royal Surrey Co Hosp, St Luke's Hosp, Regnl Cancer Unit Guildford; currently: regnl advsr, tutor in surgery Guy's Hosp Med Sch, Penrose-May teacher RCS, prof Univ of Surrey; numerous papers and book chapters on surgical subjects; vice pres and examiner RCSEd, fell and chm Educnl Ctee Assoc of Surgns of GB and I, hon fell Royal Aust Coll of Surgns 1984; memb Br Breast Gp; *Recreations* mountaineering, skiing, fishing; *Clubs* Alpine, Caledonian, Swiss Alpine; *Style—* Prof Patrick Boulter; Cairnsmore, Fairway, Merrow, Guildford, Surrey GU1 2XN (☎ 0483 504977); Quarry Cottage, Salkeld Dykes, Penrith, Cumbria CA11 9LL; 8 Waterden Rd, Guildford, Surrey; Department of Surgery, Royal Surrey County Hosp, Guildford, Surrey (☎ 0483 571122)

BOULTING, Roy A C; s of Walter Arthur Boulting (d 1957), and Rose Bennett (d 1980); twin bro of John Boulting, *qv*; *b* 21 Nov 1913; *Educ* HMS Worcester, Reading Sch; *m* 1, 1936 (m dis 1941), Angela, da of Rt Hon Edmond Warnock, KC, Home Sec NI (d 1971); m 2, 1942 (m dis 1951), Mrs Jean Capon, da of Eric Gamage; 2 s (Jonathan Eric Shaw b 1944, Laurence Roy Oliver b 1945); m 3, 1951 (m dis 1964), Mrs Enid Munnik, da of Pieter Groenwald, of S Africa (she m 1970, 9 Earl of Hardwicke); 3 s (Fitzroy Linde b 1951, Rupert Alan Francis David b 1952, Edmund Charles Alexander (twin) b 1952); common-law-wife (until 1967), Victoria, da of James Vaughan; 1 s (Fitzroy William Humphrey Rufus b 1965); m 4, 1971 (m dis 1978), Hayley Mills, the actress, da of Sir John Mills, CBE, *qv*; 1 s (Crispian b 1973); m 5, 1978 (m dis 1984), Sandra, da of Gilbert Spencer Payne; *Career* dir: Br Lion Films Ltd 1958-72, Shepperton Studios Ltd 1964-70; prodr and jt md Charter Film Prodns Ltd 1973-, formed ind film prodn co with late twin bro John 1937; prodr: Brighton Rock (1947), Seven Days to Noon (1950), Lucky Jim (1957), I'm All Right Jack, Heavens Above! (1962); dir: Thunder Rock (1942), Desert Victory (American Acad Award, 1942), Fame is the Spur (1946), The Guinea Pig (1948), Carlton-Browne of the FO (1958-59), Twisted Nerve (1968); memb: Exec Ctee Assoc of Cine Technicians 1946-47, Cncl Dirs' and Prodrs' Rights Soc 1987, Cncl Local Radio Assoc 1965; hon doctorate RCA 1990; *Recreations* film making; *Clubs* The Lord's Taverners; *Style—* Roy Boulting, Esq; Charter Film Productions Ltd, Twickenham Film Studios, St Margaret's, Twickenham, Middlesex

BOULTING, Sydney Arthur Rembrandt; *see*: Cotes, Peter

BOULTON, Dr Andrew James Michael; s of Prof James Thompson Boulton, and Margaret Helen, *née* Leary; *b* 21 Feb 1953; *Educ* Nottingham HS, Univ of Newcastle upon Tyne (MB BS, MD); *m* 3 July 1976, Helen Frances, da of Dr Mark Charlton Robson, of Maple House, The Green, Hurworth on Tees, County Durham; 1 s (Jonathan David b 1 July 1978), 2 da (Caroline Helen b 14 Sept 1979, Sarah Elizabeth b 24 July 1985); *Career* sr med registrar Royal Hallamshire Hosp 1981-86 (diabetes res fell 1979-81), visiting asst prof of med Univ of Miami Florida 1983-84, conslt and sr lectr in med Manchester Royal Infirmary 1986-; R D Lawrence lectr Br Diabetic Assoc 1990, Sri Prakash Endowment Lecture Madras 1990; dep ed Diabetic Medicine, author numerous papers on diabetic complications; memb Med and Sci Section Ctee and Patient Servs Ctee of Br Diabetic Assoc; MRCP 1979; *Books* The Foot In Diabetes (jtly, 1987), Diabetes In Practice (jtly, 1989); *Recreations* campanology, classical music; *Style—* Dr Andrew Boulton; Department of Medicine, Manchester Royal Infirmary, Oxford Rd, Manchester M13 9WL (☎ 061 276 4452, fax 061 273 5642)

BOULTON, Sir (Harold Hugh) Christian; 4 Bt (UK 1905); s of Sir (Denis Duncan) Harold Owen Boulton, 3 Bt (d 1968); *b* 29 Oct 1918; *Educ* Ampleforth; *m* 1944, Patricia Mary Maxwell-Scott, OBE (re-assumed her maiden name by deed poll 1951), da of late Maj-Gen Sir Walter Joseph Constable-Maxwell-Scott, 1 Bt, CB, DSO; *Career* late Capt Irish Gds (Sup Reserve); *Style—* Sir Christian Boulton, Bt; c/o Bank of Montreal, City View Branch, 1481 Merivale Rd, Ottawa, Ontario, Canada

BOULTON, Sir Clifford John; KCB (1990, CB 1985); s of Stanley Boulton, and Evelyn, *née* Hey, of Cocknage, Staffs; *b* 25 July 1930; *Educ* Newcastle-under-Lyme HS, St John's Coll Oxford (MA); *m* 1955, Anne, da of Rev E E Raven, of Cambridge; 1 adopted s, 1 adopted da; *Career* Nat Service RAC 1949-50, Lt Staffs Yeomanry TA; clerk in House of Commons 1953-: clerk of Select Ctees on Procedure 1964-68 and 1976-77, Public Accounts 1968-70, Parly Questions 1971-72, Privileges 1972-77; clerk Overseas Office 1977-79, princ clerk Table Office 1979-83, clerk asst 1983-87, clerk of the House of Commons 1987-; sch govr then bd memb Church Schs 1965-79; *Publications* Erskine May's Parliamentary Practice (ed 21 edn), contrib to Halsbury's Laws of England (4 edn), Parly jls; *Style—* Sir Clifford Boulton, KCB; The Elms, Lyddington, Oakham, Rutland, Leics LE15 9LT (☎ 0572 823487); House of Commons, London SW1A 0AA

BOULTON, Prof James Thomson; s of Harry Boulton, MM (d 1951), of Pickering, Yorks, and Annie Mary Penty, *née* Thompson (d 1974); *b* 17 Feb 1924; *Educ* Univ Coll Durham (BA), Lincoln Coll Oxford (BLitt), Univ of Nottingham (PhD); *m* 6 Aug 1949, Margaret Helen, da of Arthur Haydn Leary (d 1966), of Stockton-on-Tees; 1 s (Andrew Boulton b 1953), 1 da (Helen Wilcox b 1955); *Career* RAF Flt-Lt pilot 1943-46; Univ of Nottingham: lectr, sr lectr, reader in English 1951-64, prof 1964-75, dean of Faculty of Arts 1970-73; John Cranford Adams prof of English Hofstra Univ of NY 1967; Univ of Birmingham: prof of English Studies and head of Dept 1975-88, dean of Faculty of Arts 1981-84, public orator 1984-88, emeritus prof 1988-; chm of govrs Fircroft Coll of Adult Educn Selly Oak Birmingham; FRSL; *Books* Burke's Sublime And Beautiful (ed 1958, 1987), The Language of Politics In The Age of Wilkes and Burke (1963, 1975); ed Letters of D H Lawrence, Vols 1-6 (ed 1979-91); *Recreations* gardening; *Style—* Prof James Boulton; Inst For Advanced Res In The Humanities, Univ of Birmingham, PO Edgbaston, Birmingham B15 2TT (☎ 021 414 5850)

BOULTON, (Joseph) Sidney; s of Harry Boulton (d 1981), and Sarah, *née* Bithell (d 1981); *b* 15 May 1930; *Educ* Hawarden GS Flintshire; *m* 28 Aug 1954, Winifred Eileen, da of William James Wilson (d 1983); 2 da (Linda Joan b 1955, Elizabeth Anne b 1961); *Career* asst Chester Magisterial Serv 1946-53, sr asst Flintshire Magistrates Cts Ctee 1954-55, princ asst Salop Magistrates Cts Ctee 1956-64, dep clerk to the Justices Rochdale Magistrates Cts Ctee 1965-71, clerk to the Justices for 5 Divs in Herefordshire 1972-85, chief exec Hereford & Worcs Magistrates Cts Ctee 1986-; *Recreations* ballroom dancing, model railways; *Style—* Sidney Boulton, Esq; 91 Lichfield Avenue, Hereford HR1 2RL (☎ 0432 50458); The Court House, Worcester Rd, Ledbury, Herefordshire HRS 1DL (☎ 0531 4658)

BOULTON, Sir William Whytehead; 3 Bt (UK 1944), of Braxted Park, Co Essex, CBE (1958), TD (1949); 2 s of Sir William Boulton, 1 Bt, sometime MP (C) Sheffield Central and vice Chamberlain of HM's Household, by his w Rosalind (d 1969), herself da of Sir John Milburn, 1 Bt; suc bro, Sir Edward (Teddy) Boulton, 2 Bt, 1982; *b* 21 June 1912; *Educ* Eton (Capt Oppidans 1931), Trinity Coll Cambridge; *m* 30 Sept 1944, Margaret Elizabeth, da of late Brig Henry Noel Alexander Hunter, DSO; 1 s (John), 2 da (Julia, Susan); *Heir* s, John Gibson Boulton, b 1946; *Career* served WWII Middle East with 104 Regt RHA (Essex Yeo) and 14 Regt RHA 1940-44, Staff Coll Camberley 1944, Hon Lt-Col; called to the Bar Inner Temple 1936, practised 1937-39, Miny of Justice Control Branch Legal Div Control Cmmn Germany 1945-50; sec: Gen Cncl of the Bar 1950-74, Senate of the Inns of Ct and the Bar 1974-75; kt 1975; *Books* A Guide to Conduct and Etiquette at the Bar of England and Wales (6 edn 1975); *Style—* Sir William Boulton, Bt, CBE, TD; The Quarters House, Alresford, nr Colchester, Essex CO7 8AY (☎ 0206 822450)

BOURDEAUX, Rev Canon Michael Alan; s of Richard Edward Bourdeaux, and Lillian Myra, née Blair; *b* 19 March 1934; *Educ* Truro Sch, St Edmund Hall Oxford (MA, BD), Moscow State Univ; *m* 1, 1960, Gillian Mary Davies (d 1978); 1 s (Mark), 1 da (Karen); m 2, 1979, Lorna Elizabeth, da of John Waterton, of Birch House, Preston St Mary, Sudbury, Suffolk; 1 s (Adrian), 1 da (Lara Clare); *Career* ordained: deacon 1960, priest 1961; res assoc Centre de Recherches Geneva Switzerland 1965-68, London res fellow Univ of London 1968-70, visiting prof St Bernard's Seminary Rochester NY 1969, res fellow Royal Inst of Int Affairs 1970-72, Kathryn C Davis prof of Slavic studies Wellesley Mass 1981, Templeton prize 1984, sr assoc memb St Anthony's Coll Oxford and visiting fell St Edmund Hall Oxford 1989-90, Hon Canon Rochester Cathedral 1990; memb Philharmonia Chorus 1961-, fndr and gen dir Keston Coll 1969-, memb Br Tennis Umpires Assoc 1974-; *Books* Opium of the People (1965, 2 edn 1977), Religious Ferment in Russia (1968), Patriarch and Prophets (1970, 2 edn 1975), Faith on Trial in Russia (1971), Land of Crosses (1979), Risen Indeed (1983), Ten Growing Soviet Churches (1987), Gorbachev, Glasnost and the Gospel (1990); *Clubs* Athenaeum; *Style—* The Rev Canon Michael Bourdeaux; Bishopsdown, 34 Lubbock Rd, Chislehurst, Kent BR7 5JJ (☎ 081 467 3550); Keston Coll, Heathfield Rd, Keston, Kent BR2 6BA (☎ 0689 50116, telex KESCOL 897684)

BOURDILLON, Mervyn Leigh; JP (1970); s of Prebendary Gerard Leigh Bourdillon (d 1971), and Cara Phyllis Evan-Thomas (d 1971); *b* 9 Aug 1924; *Educ* Haileybury; *m* 1961, Penelope Anne, da of Peter Wellesbourne Kemp-Welch, OBE (d 1964); 1 s (Patrick), 3 da (Katherine, Sarah, Lucinda); *Career* served RNVR 1943-46; High Sheriff Breconshire 1970, memb Breconshire CC 1962-73, Forestry Cmmr 1973-76, Lord-Lt Powys 1986- (Vice Lord-Lt 1978-86, DL 1962-78); *Clubs* Army and Navy; *Style—* Mervyn Bourdillon, Esq, JP

BOURGEOIS, Mireille; da of Henri Bourgeois, of Marseille, and Marcelle Marti Bourgeois; *b* 2 Oct 1959; *Educ* Opéra de Marseille; *Career* Ballet National de Marseille 1975-81, roles incl: le loup, l'arlesienne, notre dame de Paris , le jeune-homme et la mort, á la memoire d'un ange (created for her), coppélia, casse-noisette, Proust; London Festival Ballet 1981-87, Northern Ballet Theatre 1987-89, Sadler's Wells Royal Ballet 1989-91; has danced some balanchine incl: symphonie in 3 movements divertimento no 15, 3 act from Sleeping Beauty, pas de deux from Don Quichotte, Odette-Odile in Swan Lake; from Sir MacMillan: les Hermanas elite syncopation, la fin du jour; has also danced roles from works by: Christopher Bruce, David Bintley, Sir Frederick Ashton (gypsy girl in Two Pigeons, Romeo and Juliette); additional ballets incl: Coppelia, Nutcracker, Les Sylphides, La Sylphide; *Style—* Miss Mireille Bourgeois

BOURKE, Dr Brian Eamonn; s of Edmund Egan Bourke (d 1961), of Lines End, Winchelsea, Sussex, and Joan Eileen, *née* Kiernan; *b* 29 April 1948; *Educ* Beaumont Coll, King's Coll and King's Coll Hosp Univ of London (MB BS); *m* 25 March 1972, Elisabeth Janie, da of Brig Christopher Percy Sibthorpe Bright, CBE (d 1988), of 31 New St, Henley-on-Thames, Oxfordshire; 2 s (Henry Edmund b 12 April 1976, Piers Christopher b 18 Aug 1978), 2 da (Serena Katherine b 15 March 1974, Imogen Elisabeth b 6 July 1984); *Career* house surgn KCH London 1972, house physician Royal Berks Hosp Reading 1972, sr house offr in med The London Hosp 1972-74, med registrar St Stephen's Hosp London 1974-76, registrar and sr registrar Charing Cross Hosp London 1976-81, conslt physician and hon sr lectr St George's Hosp and Med Sch London 1981-; MRCP 1974, FRCP 1989; hon sec: Br Soc for Rheumatology, BR Soc for Immunology; FRSM; *Recreations* tennis, swimming, skiing; *Clubs* Hurlingham; *Style—* Dr Brian Bourke; 152 Harley St, London W1 1HH (☎ 081 935 2477); St George's Hospital, London SW17 0QT (☎ 081 672 1255)

BOURKE, Christopher John; s of John Francis Bourke (d 1967), of Westwood House, Droitwich, and Eileen Winifred, *née* Beddoes (d 1976); *b* 31 March 1926; *Educ* Stonyhurst, Oriel Coll Oxford (MA); *m* 23 June 1956, Maureen, da of Gerald Antony Barron-Boshell (d 1935), of Trichinopoly, S India; 2 s (Rory b 20 May 1960, Toby b 7 Feb 1965), 1 da (Cressida b 31 July 1969); *Career* Nat Serv cmmnd Gloucestershire Regt 1946, ADC to Govr Sir John Huggins, served in BAOR and Jamaica; called to the Bar Gray's Inn 1953, Oxford circuit dir Public Prosecutions 1955-74, Metropolitan Stipendary Magistrate 1974-; *Recreations* painting; *Style—* Christopher Bourke, Esq; 61 Kingsmead Rd, London SW2 3HY (☎ 081 671 3977); Clerkenwell Magistrates Ct, London EC1

BOURKE, Hon Harry Richard; s of 10 E of Mayo; *b* 23 Sept 1960; *Style—* The Hon Harry Bourke; Doon House, Maam, Co Galway, Eire

BOURKE, Hon Mrs Geoffrey; Nancy Lisette; da of Douglas Theodore Thring (d 1931), estates bursar of Merton Coll Oxford; *m* 1926, Hon Geoffrey John Bourke (d 1982), FRICS; 4 s of 8 Earl of Mayo; 1 da (Elizabeth b 1928, m 1954 John Auden, of Switzerland; 1 s, 1 da) & 1 da decd 1956; *Style—* The Hon Mrs Geoffrey Bourke; 167 Russell Court, Woburn Pl, London WC1

BOURKE, Hon Mrs Bryan; Patricia May; *née* Dickinson; er da of late Harold Bertie Dickinson, of Tannachie, W Malvern, Worcs; *b* 29 July 1912; *Educ* Wycombe Abbey, London Univ (BA); *m* 1952, as his 2 w, Capt the Hon Bryan Longley Bourke, RIF (d 1961, f (by his 1 w) of 10 E of Mayo, *qv*), 3 s of 8 E of Mayo; *Career* section offr WAAF (served S Africa, Egypt, England); JP Glos 1959-61, govr Dursley Grammar and Mod Secdy Schs, dist cncllr Wadebridge Cornwall, memb Truro Diocesan Synod and Diocesan Bd of Educn; *Recreations* art (active and passive), musical appreciation; *Style—* The Hon Mrs Bryan Bourke; Dashells, Dog Village, Broadclyst, Exeter, Devon EX5 3AB (☎ 0392 61334)

BOURN, Dr John Bryant; CB (1986); s of Henry Thomas Bryant Bourne, of 65 Dawlish Avenue, Palmers Green, London N13, and Beatrice Grace, *née* Pope (d 1979); *b* 21 Feb 1934; *Educ* Southgate County GS, London Sch of Economics (BSc, PhD); *m* 21 March 1959, Ardita Ann, da of Maurice Wilfred Fleming (d 1940); 1 s (Jonathan b 1967), 1 da (Sherida b 1962); *Career* dep under sec of state (Defence Procurement) MOD 1985-, dep sec N Ireland Office 1982-85; visiting prof London Sch of Economics 1983-; *Recreations* swimming; *Style—* Dr John Bourn, CB; Ministry of Defence, Main Building, Whitehall, London SW1A 2HB

BOURN, Prof (Alan) Michael; s of Ernest James Bourn (d 1988), and Frances Mary, *née* Fones (d 1977); *b* 10 June 1934; *Educ* Southgate County GS London, LSE (BSc); *m* 4 April 1960 (m dis 1986), (Karoline) Sigrid, *née* Hegmann; 2 s (Alexander b 1961, Jeremy b 1962); *Career* Nat Serv 2 Lt RAPC 1958-60; professional accounting 1954-58, IBM UK Ltd 1960-61; various academic appts 1962-69: London, Liverpool, Manchester; prof of industl admin Univ of Canterbury NZ 1969-72, prof of business studies Univ of Liverpool 1972-80, dep vice chllr Univ of Southampton 1986-90 (prof of accounting 1980, faculty of social sciences 1983-86); pres Assoc of Univ Teachers of Accounting 1982-83, chm Conf of Profs of Accounting 1987-90; ACA 1958-68, FCA 1968; *Books* Shipping Enterprise And Management 1830-1939 (with F E Hyde and J R Harris, 1967), Studies In Accounting for Management Decision (1969), Favell's Book-keeping & Accounts (7 edn, 1980), Industrial Development In Merseyside (with P Stoney, 1984); *Recreations* trumpet-playing, jazz, racquet sports; *Style—* Prof Michael

Bourn; University of Southampton, Southampton SO9 5NH (☎ 0703 592545)

BOURNE, Lady; Heather Frances; da of Lt-Col F W Burbury, Royal W Kent Regt of Barnsley; *m* 1918, Sir Frederick Chalmers Bourne, KCSI, CIE (d 1977); *Career* awarded Kaisar-i-Hind Gold medal; *Style—* Lady Bourne; Fern Cottage, East Hoathly, nr Lewes, E Sussex BN8 6DP (☎ 082 584 386)

BOURNE, Henry; s of Prof Kenneth Bourne, of London, and Eleanor Anne, *née* Wells; *b* 10 May 1963; *Educ* City of London Sch, Crownwoods Sch; *Career* photographer; photographic asst to Michael Joseph 1982-84, freelance photographic asst 1984-86, freelance editorial photographer of portraits, fashion, interiors, still life and reportage; cmmns incl contribs to: Elle, Elle Decoration, The Guardian, The Independent, The Independent Magazine, Vogue, The World of Interiors; *Style—* Henry Bourne, Esq; 140 Camberwell Grove, London SE5 8RH (☎ 071 733 5504 and 081 852 6116)

BOURNE, Dr James Gerald; s of Walter William Bourne (d 1921), of Garston Manor, Herts, and Clara Louisa, *née* Hollingsworth (d 1941); *b* 6 March 1906; *Educ* Rugby, Univ of Cambridge (BA), St Thomas' Hosp (MA, MB BChir, DA, MD); *m* 1, Jenny Liddell (d 1967); 1 s (Michael b 18 Sept 1958); m 2, 18 May 1968, Susan Annette, da of Cdr William de Montigy Clarke (d 1966), of Stoke Poges; 2 s (William b 9 July 1969, Giles b 22 June 1970); *Career* WWII RAMC 1939-45: France 6 Casualty Clearing Station 1939-40, served Middle East (gen hosps, 1 Mobile Surgical Team Western Desert) 1941-45, ret Maj 1945; casualty offr and house physician St Thomas' Hosp 1937-38, house physician London Chest Hosp 1939; conslt anaesthetist: St Thomas' Hosp 1946-66, Salisbury Hosp Gp 1950-71; MRCS, LRCP, FFARCS, FDSRCS Eng; *Books* Nitrous Oxide in Dentistry: Its Danger and Alternatives (1960), Studies In Anaesthetics (1967); *Recreations* fishing, walking, music; *Clubs* RAC; *Style—* Dr James Bourne; Melstock, Nunton, Salisbury, Wilts SP5 4HN (☎ 0722 329734)

BOURNE, (Frederick) John; s of Sydney John Bourne (d 1960), of Evesham, Worcs, and Florence Beatrice, *née* Craven (d 1988); *b* 3 Jan 1937; *Educ* Prince Henry's GS Evesham, RVC (BVetMed), Univ of Bristol (PhD); *m* 12 Aug 1959, Mary Angela, da of William Reginald Minter; 2 s (Stephen b 1962, Nigel b 1964); *Career* private vet practice 1960-66; Univ of Bristol: lectr animal husbandry 1966-74, reader animal husbandry 1974-80, prof vet med 1980-88, prof animal health 1988-; visiting prof Univ of Reading 1990-; dir AFRC Inst Animal Health 1988-, memb Mgmnt Bd AFRC; MRCVS; *Books* Advances in Veterinary Immunology (1984 and 1985); *Recreations* gardening, fishing, cricket, golf, music; *Style—* John Bourne, Esq; Westlands, Jubilee Lane, Langford, Avon BS18 7EJ; Agriculture & Food Research Council, Institute for Animal Health, Compton, Newbury, Berks RG16 0NN (☎ 0635 578 411, telex 265871, fax 0635 578844)

BOURNE, Prof Kenneth; s of Clarence Arthur Bourne (d 1974), of Cheriton, Hants, and Doris, *née* English (d 1990); *b* 17 March 1930; *Educ* Southend-on-Sea HS, Univ of Exeter (BA), LSE (PhD); *m* 1 Jan 1955, Eleanor Anne, da of Ronald Edward Wells (d 1959), of Worthing; 1 s (Henry b 1963), 1 da (Joanna b 1959); *Career* res fell: Inst Historical Res London 1955-56, Univ of Reading 1956; LSE: lectr 1957-69, reader 1969-76, prof of internal history 1976-; visiting lectr Univ of California Davis 1966-67, Scaife distinguished lectr Kenyon Coll 1971, Kratter prof Stanford Univ 1979; visiting prof: Univ of S Miss 1981, Univ of S Alabama 1983; Harrison prof Coll of William & Mary 1984-85, distinguished visiting prof Univ of Colorado 1988, J Richardson Dilworth fell Inst for Advanced Study Princeton 1989; govr: Wilson's GS Camberwell 1964-74, Wilsons's Sch Sutton 1972-84, LSE 1986-90; memb Cncl List & Index Soc 1986-, sen Univ of London 1987-; memb: Br Nat Ctee Int Congress of Historical Sciences 1987-88, Cncl Sch of Slavonic and E Euro Studies 1987- (vice-chm 1989-), Archives and Manuscripts Ctee Univ of Southampton 1988-; FRHistS 1976, FBA 1984; *Books* Britain and the Balance of Power in North America, 1815-1908 (1967), Studies in International History (with D C Watt, 1967), The Foreign Policy of Victorian England (1970), The Blackmailing of the Chancellor (1975), Palmerston to Laurence and Elizabeth Sulivan, 1804-1863 (1979), Palmerston: The Early Years, 1784-1841 (1982), British Documents on Foreign Affairs: Reports and Papers from the Foreign Office Confidential Print (with D C Watt, 1983-); *Recreations* book collecting; *Style—* Prof Kenneth Bourne; 15 Oakcroft Rd, London SE13 7ED (☎ 081 852 6116); Dept of International History, LSE, Houghton St, London WC2A 2AE (☎ 071 955 7092, fax 071 242 0392, telex 24655 G)

BOURNE, Matthew Christopher; s of Harlod Jeffrey (Jim) Bourne, of London, and June Lilian, *née* Handley; *b* 13 Jan 1960; *Educ* Sir George Monoux Sch London, The Labon Centre (BA); *Career* dancer Transitions Dance Co 1986, fndr (artistic dir, resident choreographer and performer) Adventures In Motion Pictures 1987; choreography: Overlap Lovers 1987, Buck and Wing 1988, Spitfire 1988, The Infernal Gallop 1989, Green Fingers 1990, Town and Country 1991; performed with choreographers incl: Jacob Marley, Brigitte Farges, Ashley Page; fndr memb Lea Anderson's Featherstone Haughs 1988; choreography for theatre incl: As You Like It (RSC, Stratford, Barbican) 1989, Singer (RSC, Stratford, Barbican) 1989, Leonce and Lena (Crucible, Sheffield) 1989, Children of Eden (Prince Edward Theatre) 1991; awards: Place Portfolio award 1989, Bonnie Bird choreography award 1989, Barclays New Stages award 1990; *Recreations* theatre, cinema, the choreography of Frederick Ashton and Fred Astaire, the music of Percy Grainger, Ella Fitzgerald and most pre-1950 singers; *Style—* Matthew Bourne, Esq; Adventures In Motion Pictures, c/o Sadlers Well, Roseberry Avenue, London EC1R 4TN (☎ 071 278 6563 ext 208, fax 071 837 0965); agent John Wood, c/o Hope and Lyne, 108 Leonard St, London EC2A 4RH (☎ 071 739 6200, fax 071 739 4101)

BOURNE, Hon Michael Kemp; s of Gen Lord Bourne, GCB, KBE, CMG (Life Peer, d 1982); *b* 9 June 1937; *Educ* Harrow; *m* 1, 1963 (m dis 1980), Penelope Jane, da of Capt H W Blyth, of Wyncombe Hill, Fittleworth, Sussex; 1 s, 2 da; m 2, 1985, Marian Lockhart, eldest da of Maj John Francis Leetham Robinson, MC, of Bilbrough, Yorks; *Career* Nat Serv, 2 Lt 15/19 The King's Royal Hussars; *Clubs* Cavalry and Guards', City of London, MCC; *Style—* The Hon Michael Bourne; 50 Bradbourne St, London SW6 3TE

BOURNE, (Rowland) Richard; s of Arthur Brittan, and Edith Mary Bourne; *b* 27 July 1940; *Educ* Uppingham, BNC Oxford; *m* 1966, Juliet Mary, da of John Attenborough, CBE, *qv*; 2 s, 1 da; *Career* journalist and author; educn corr The Guardian 1968-72, asst ed New Society 1972-77, dep ed and columnist London Evening Standard 1977-78, ed Learn Magazine 1979, freelance and conslt 1980-83; dep dir Cwlth Inst 1983-89, dir Cwlth Human Rights Initiative; *Recreations* gardening, fishing, the theatre; *Clubs* RAC; *Style—* Richard Bourne, Esq; 36 Burney St, London SW10 8EX (☎ 081 853 0642)

BOURNE, Val; *Educ* Elmshurst Ballet Sch, Royal Ballet Sch (also with Cleo Nordi, Anna Heathcote and Andrew Hardie); *Career* performed with: Royal Ballet and Opera Ballet in final year at Royal Ballet Sch 1960-61, Sadlers Wells Opera Ballet 1961-63; Monsanto Chemicals Ltd 1963-64, Cyril Leonard & Co Estate Agents 1964-65, Wilfred Stiff Assocs PR (clients incl: Ballet Rambert, Owen Brannigan, Daniel Barenboim, John Ogden, Cyril and Phyllis Sellick); press and publicity offr: London Festival Ballet 1967, Ballet Rambert 1968-76; asst to offr i/c dance Music Dept Arts Cncl of GB 1976-77, dance offr Gtr London Arts 1977-80, artistic dir Dance Umbrella 1980- (organised first Dance Umbrella Festival 1978); *awards* Digital Dance Premier award 1989, Int Theatre Inst's award 1990; *Style—* Ms Val Bourne; Dance Umbrella, Riverside Studios, Crisp Rd, London W6 9RL (☎ 081 741 4040, fax 081 846 9039)

BOURNE, Sir (John) Wilfrid; KCB (1979, CB 1975), QC (1981); s of Capt the Rt Hon Robert Croft Bourne, MP (d 1938), and Lady Hester Margaret Bourne, *née* Cairns (d 1985); *b* 27 Jan 1922; *Educ* Eton, New Coll Oxford; *m* 2 Aug 1958, Elizabeth Juliet, da of George Romney Fox (d 1969), of Trewardreva, Constantine, Falmouth, Cornwall; 2 s (William b 1959, John b 1960); *Career* Rifle Bde 1941-45, Lt and Actg Capt Western Desert, Tunisia, Italy, NW Europe; called to the Bar Middle Temple 1948, Lord Chancellor's Office 1956- (dep clerk of crown 1975-77, clerk of crown and permanent sec 1977-82), bencher 1977; *Recreations* gardening; *Clubs* Leander; *Style—* Sir Wilfrid Bourne, KCB, QC; Povey's Farm, Ramsdell, Basingstoke, Hants (☎ 0256 850158)

BOUTFLOWER, John Charles; s of Charles Henry Boutflower (d 1969), and Jacqueline Marie, *née* Culverwell; *b* 26 Jan 1933; *Educ* Cheltenham, Univ of Bristol (BVSc); *m* 9 May 1964, Sheina Bridget, da of Lt-Col Douglas Bostock Duff (d 1976); 1 s (Robert Charles b 1965), 1 da (Kirstin Bridget b 1966); *Career* Nat Serv Royal Veterinary Corps, Capt Cyprus 1959-61; veterinary surgeon, ret; MRCVS; *Recreations* fishing, hunting, ornithology, rose growing; *Style—* John Boutflower, Esq; Woodcroft House, Woodcroft, Chepstow (☎ 02912 3518)

BOUTTELL, Brian; s of Robert Bouttell, of Middlesbrough, and Gertrude, *née* Page (d 1986); *b* 12 May 1944; *Educ* Middlesbrough HS; *m* 28 Sept 1963, Glenda Lee, *née* Jackson; 1 s (Gary b 19 Oct 1965 d 1990), 2 da (Janet b 6 May 1967, Laura b 4 Dec 1970); *Career* CA; articled clerk George C Wilkinson & Co 1960-66; Peat Marwick Mitchell Darlington: joined 1966, ptnr 1977, transfer to Leeds 1985, office managing ptnr Leeds 1987; sr regnl ptnr KPMG Peat Marwick McLintock 1990-; dir West Yorkshire Playhouse; FICA 1966; *Recreations* squash, running, bridge, theatre; *Style—* Brian Bouttell, Esq; Rockwell, 25 Margerison Rd, Ben Rhydding, Ilkley, W Yorks LS29 8QY (☎ 0943 602952); KPMG Peat Marwick McLintock, 1 The Embankment, Neville St, Leeds LS1 4DW (☎ 0532 313000, fax 0532 313200, car 0831 231088)

BOUTWOOD, Nigel Peter Ralph; s of Peter Ralph Wood Boutwood, of Holmes Farm, West Wittering, Sussex, and Roberta May, *née* Pool; *b* 12 May 1951; *Educ* Lancing; *m* 2 April 1977, Jeanette Elsma, da of Jeffery Warner Etherington; 2 da (Emma Jane Elsma b 27 March 1980, Tiffany Roberta b 7 April 1982); *Career* J Walter Thompson 1970, Thames TV 1971-78, Southern TV 1978-82, TVS 1982-85, chm and md Boutwood Advertising Ltd 1985-; *Recreations* sailing, skiing; *Style—* Nigel Boutwood, Esq; Boutwood Advertising Ltd, 37 Terminus Rd, Eastbourne, East Sussex BN21 3QL (☎ 0323 640212, fax 0323 411999)

BOVENIZER, John Gordon Fitzell; s of Vernon Gordon Fitzell Bovenizer, of 6 Cambanks, Union Lane, Cambridge, and Lilian Cherry, *née* Rowe (d 1970); family descended from resettled Huguenots from the Palatinate given land near Limerick Ireland in 1706; *b* 26 Jan 1945; *Educ* Tonbridge, Fitzwilliam Coll Cambridge (MA); *m* 1 April 1970, Helma, da of Jose Soares Limaverde, of Fortaleza, Ceara, Brazil (d 1985); 3 s (George b 1971, John b 1974, Ernest b 1976); *Career* banker; dir and treas Lloyds Merchant Bank 1986-87, dir Lloyds Bank Financial Futures Ltd, treas and exec vice pres Lloyds Bank plc in NY; *Recreations* sports, chess; *Style—* John Bovenizer, Esq; 35 Swifts Lane, Darien, Connecticut, USA

BOVEY, Barry William Vincent; OBE (1979); s of William Vincent Bovey (d 1965), of Worcester, and Irene Ida, *née* Holderness (d 1982); *b* 29 Oct 1929; *Educ* Haileybury, Univ of London; *m* 1, 23 June 1954 (m dis 1978), Daphne Joan, da of Cdr Arthur Gordon Marshall, RNR (d 1981), of Hampton Ct; 2 s (Michael b 1957, Nigel b 1961); m 2, 22 Dec 1979, Jean Christine, da of Ronald Yeardley Goddard, of Sheffield; *Career* Nat Serv cmmnd RA 1951-53, Capt RA (TA) 1953-57; gp sales dir Robert Jenkins Ltd 1967-72, md Orbit Valve Ltd 1972-, vice pres Energy Industs Cncl 1984 (chm 1980-84); Process Plant EDC: memb Nat Econ Devpt Office 1980-87, chm Int Mktg Gp 1981-87; Freeman: City of London, Worshipful Co of Glovers; FCIM 1980, FIEx 1987, FInstD 1979; *Recreations* yachting, golf; *Clubs* Royal Thames Yacht; *Style—* Barry Bovey, Esq, OBE; Chadmore House, Willersey, Broadway WR12 7PH (☎ 0386 858 922); Orbit Valve Ltd, Orbit House, Swallowfield Way, Hayes, Middx UB3 1DQ (☎ 081 561 8049, fax 081 561 2954, car 0860 746 630, telex 938171)

BOVEY, Dr Leonard; s of Alfred Bovey (d 1968, twice Mayor of Exeter), and Gladys, *née* Brereton; *b* 9 May 1924; *Educ* Hele's Sch Exeter, Emmanuel Coll Cambridge (BA, PhD); *m* Nov 1943, Constance (d 1987), da of Thomas Hudson (d 1970); 1 s (Christopher b 1951), 1 da (Jennifer b 1955); *Career* post doctoral fell Nat Res Cncl Ottawa 1950-52, AERE Harwell 1952-65; dir: W Midlands Regnl Office Miny of Tech 1966-70, Yorks & Humberside DTI 1970-73; cnsllr scientific and technol affrs High Cmmn Ottawa 1974-77, head technol requirements branch DTI 1977-84, ed Materials & Design 1985-; FInstP; *Recreations* theatre, music; *Clubs* Civil Service; *Style—* Dr Leonard Bovey; 32 Radnor Walk, London SW3 4BN (☎ 071 352 4142); Butterworth Heinemann, Guildford GU2 5BH (☎ 0483 300966, fax 0483 301563, telex 859556 SCITEC G)

BOVEY, Norman Henry; OBE (1957), DSC (1944), VRD (1960); s of Alfred Henry Bovey (d 1940), and Florence Emily, *née* Little (d 1962); *b* 16 Sept 1922; *Educ* St Dunstans Coll; *m* 21 Dec 1946, Dorothy Yvonne, da of Henry Williams (d 1938); 3 s (Philip Henry b 1948, Andrew John b 1952, William Evan Norman b 1956), 1 da (Susan Katherine b 1949); *Career* WWII Lt (A) RNVR 1940-46, Cdr (A) RNR and Pounding CO Channel Air Div RNVR 1948-62; sr contracts mangr Bovis Ltd 1946-60, gen mangr J Parnell & Son Ltd 1960-68; regnl mangr Midland Construction Indust Trg Bd 1968-87; vice pres Fleet Air Arm Offrs Assoc; MCIOB; *Recreations* gardening, house maintenance (listed building); *Clubs* Naval and Military; *Style—* Norman H Bovey, OBE, DSC, VRD; Killock House, Laughton, Lutterworth, Leicestershire LE17 6QD (☎ 0533 402278)

BOVEY, Philip Henry; s of Cdr Norman Henry Bovey, OBE, DSC, VRD, of Killock House, Laughton, Lutterworth, Leics, and Dorothy Yvonne, *née* Kent Williams; *b* 11 July 1948; *Educ* Rugby, Peterhouse Cambridge (BA, MA); *m* 14 Sept 1974, Jenet Alison, da of Canon James Mitchell McTear (d 1973); 2 c (Katherine b 1976, Stephen b 1978); *Career* FCO 1970-71; admitted slr 1974; Slaughter & May 1972-75, DTI 1976-77, Cabinet Office 1977-78, DTI 1978- (under sec 1985), inspr Companies Act 1984-88; *Recreations* photography; *Style—* Philip Bovey, Esq; 102 Cleveland Gdns, Barnes, London SW13 0AH (☎ 081 876 3710); 10-18 Victoria St, London SW1 (☎ 071 215 3452)

BOVILL, (William) Geoffrey; s of Edward William Bovill (d 1966), and Sylvia Mary Bovill, OBE, *née* Cheston; *b* 8 Oct 1926; *Educ* Eton; *m* 4 March 1957, Prudence Winifred Leonora, da of Maj-Gen Clifford Thomason Beckett, CB, CBE, MC, DL (d 1972); 3 s (Hugo b 1958, Desmond b 1960, Giles b 1965); *Career* Lt Grenadier Gds serv NW Europe 1945-48; chm Treatt plc 1963-, md Henry W Peabody Grain Ltd 1966-86; *Recreations* shooting, gardening, travel; *Style—* Geoffrey Bovill, Esq; Woodham Mortimer Grange, Maldon, Essex (☎ 024 541 2605)

BOWACK, Michael Hamilton; s of Norman Hamilton Bowack (ka 1942), and Vera Marion Ives, *née* Franklin; *b* 26 July 1942; *Educ* Uppingham; *m* 6 Aug 1983, Ann Jennifer, da of Frank Charles Sherwill (d 1988); 1 da (Claire b 1985); *Career* Blease

Lloyd & Co 1960-66, Touche Ross & Co 1966-67; various appts: Imperial Group plc 1967-74, The RTZ Corp plc 1974-85, The Plessey Co plc 1985-88, GEC Plessey Telecommunications Ltd 1988-90, Civil Serv 1990-; *Recreations* cricket, rugby football, gardening, music; *Clubs* MCC; *Style*— Michael Bowack, Esq; Pathways, 53 Fairmile Lane, Cobham, Surrey KT11 2DH (☎ 0932 865451)

BOWATER, Sir John Vansittart; 4 Bt (UK 1914); s of Capt Victor Spencer Bowater (d 1967), 3 s of 1 Bt; suc unc, Sir (Thomas) Dudley (Blennerhassett) Bowater, 3 Bt, 1972; *b* 6 April 1918; *m* 1943, Joan Kathleen (d 1982), da of Wilfrid Ernest Henry Scullard (d 1963), of Boscombe; 1 s, 1 da; *Heir* s, Michael Patrick Bowater; *Career* dir Oswald Bailey Gp of Cos; town cncllr Bournemouth 1983-; *Style*— Sir John Bowater, Bt; 214 Runnymede Ave, Bearwood, Bournemouth, Dorset (☎ 0202 571782)

BOWATER, Marina; da of Lt Alexandre Vassilievich Yakovleff (d 1975), and Nathalia Dmitrievna, *née* Palton (d 1959); *b* 11 May 1896; *Educ* Normanhurst Ct Sch Catsfield Sussex; *m* Dec 1945, Cdr William Henry Irving Bowater; *Career* WAAF 1941-45, special duties (ops), Fighter Cmd; entered commercial world of art with galleries in Kensington and St James's London, specialised in Imperial Russian Art (about which little was known at the time) 1959-78, currently conslt in Russian Art; memb: RSPCA, Royal Drawing Soc (full hons certificate 1935); former memb Br Antique Dealers Assoc; *Books* author of numerous articles on Russian art; The Serious Collecting of Russian Art (1990), The Decorative Arts of Russia (1990); *Recreations* writing; *Style*— Mrs Marina Bowater

BOWATER, Hon Lady (Ursula Margaret); *née* Dawson; da of 1 and last Viscount Dawson of Penn, GCVO, KCB, KCMG, PC (d 1945); *b* 1907; *m* 1927, Lt-Col Sir Ian Bowater, GBE, DSO, TD (d 1982), sometime Lord-Mayor of London 1969-70; 1 s, 2 da; *Style*— The Hon Lady Bowater; 38 Burton Court, Franklins Row, London SW3 4SZ (☎ 071 730 2963)

BOWDEN, Andrew; MBE (1961), MP (C) Brighton Kemptown 1970-; s of William Victor Bowden, of Brighton, and Francesa Wilson; *b* 8 April 1930; *Educ* Ardingly; *m* 1970, Benita, da of B A Napier, of Brighton; 1 s, 1 da; *Career* worked in paint indust 1955-68; personnel conslt 1967-; Parly candidate (C): N Hammersmith 1955, N Kensington 1964, Kemp Town Brighton 1966; jt chm All-Party Parly Gp for Pensioners 1971-; memb Select Ctee: Expenditure 1973-74, Abortion 1975, Employment 1979-; int chm People to People 1981-, memb Cncl of Europe 1987-; *Recreations* fishing, chess, golf; *Clubs* Carlton; *Style*— Andrew Bowden, Esq, MBE, MP; House of Commons, London SW1A 0AA (☎ 071 219 5047); Flat 11, 19-20 Sussex Square, Brighton, Sussex

BOWDEN, Francis William; s of Stanley Bowden (d 1951), of Stockport, and Ruth Grant, *née* Jenson; *b* 21 May 1944; *Educ* Manchester GS, Christ's Coll Cambridge (MA); *m* 2 May 1970, Bridget Elizabeth, da of Randle Leigh Smith (d 1975), of Solihull; 1 s (John b 1973), 1 da (Susanna b 1974); *Career* actuary Godwins Ltd 1970-73, actuary and dir Fenchurch Gp 1973-84; ptnr Hymans Robertson & Co 1985-; FIA 1968, FPMI 1978; *Recreations* gardening, philately; *Style*— Francis Bowden, Esq; 55 Somerset Rd, New Barnet, Herts (☎ 081 449 4268); Hymans Robertson & Co, 190 Fleet St, London EC4A 2AH (☎ 071 831 9561, fax 071 831 6800, telex 8813716)

BOWDEN, Sir Frank Houston; 3 Bt (UK 1915); s of Sir Harold Bowden, 2 Bt, GBE (d 1960), and his 1 w Vera, *née* Whitaker; *b* 10 Aug 1909; *Educ* Rugby, Merton Coll Oxford (MA); *m* 1, 28 April 1934 (m dis 1936), Marie-José, da of Charles Stiénon, of Paris, and Comtesse Laure de Messey; 1 s (Nicholas Richard); m 2, 3 March 1937, Lydia Eveline (d 1981), da of Jean Manolovici, of Bucharest; 3 s (Adrian, Aubrey, Gregory); m 3, 1989, Oriol Annette Mary, o da of Charles Hooper Bath, of London; *Heir* s, Nicholas Bowden; *Career* Paymaster Lt RNVR 1939-44; ret industrialist and landowner; vice chm Japan Soc (memb Exec Ctee); hon vice pres World Kendo Championships 1976, pres British Kendo Assoc 1969-; pres University Hall Buckland 1967-71; vice pres Oxfordshire County Scout Cncl; pres Thame branch Royal Naval Soc; has written collected and lectured on Japanese swords and armour; *Recreations* Kendo, bird-watching; *Clubs* White's, Royal Thames Yacht; *Style*— Sir Frank Bowden, Bt; The Old Vicarage, Winkfield, Windsor, Berks SL4 4SE (☎ 0344 886310)

BOWDEN, Geoffrey Anthony; s of James Benjamin Phillip Bowden (d 1986); *b* 5 June 1939; *Educ* Farnborough, Wimbledon; *m* 1; m 2, 1973, Wendy, da of Alfred Powell, of Richmond, Surrey; 1 s, 3 da; *Career* md Siebe Gorman & Co 1977-82; dep chm: Merryweather & Sons 1979-82, John Morris & Sons 1979-82; chm and md Glossmark Ltd 1982-84; chm Mainstay Computer Cover Ltd 1983-85, chm and md RJT 40 Ltd 1985-89 (business conslt), chief exec Mainstay Computer Cover NV and BV 1986-88, chief exec Accord Engineering Services Ltd 1988-90, business conslt Noble Associates 1990-; MinstM, FInstD, FBIM; *Recreations* golf, squash, theatre; *Clubs* St Pierre; *Style*— Geoffrey Bowden, Esq; Belair, Bryn Rhedyn, Llanfrechfa, Cwmbran, Gwent (☎ 063 33 60849); 42 Clifton Road, Richmond, Surrey (☎ 081 878 2647)

BOWDEN, Gerald Francis; TD, MP (C) Dulwich 1983-; s of Frank Albert Bowden, and Elsie, *née* Burrill; *b* 26 Aug 1935; *Educ* Battersea GS, Magdalen Coll Oxford, Coll of Estate Mgmnt; *m* 1967, Heather Elizabeth Hill, *née* Hall (d 1984); 2 da, 1 step s, 1 step da; *Career* memb Dulwich GLC 1977-81, barr Gray's Inn, chartered surveyor, princ lectr dept of estate mgmnt S Bank Poly; *Style*— Gerald Bowden, Esq, TD, MP

BOWDEN, Col (John Wallace) Guy; CBE (1962); s of Thomas Lake Bowden (d 1945), of Ranby Hall, Lincolnshire, and Margery Harnet, *née* Stack (d 1963); *b* 25 Sept 1915; *Educ* Westminster, Clare Coll Cambridge (MA); *m* 1, Jan 1947, Jean (d 1951), da of Sir John Humphrey Wise, KCMG, CBE (d 1984); m 2, July 1954, Countess Ilona, da of Count Edelsheim Gulyi (d 1984), of Cannes, France, and widow of HSH Stephen Horthy, Vice Regent of Hungary; *Career* cmmnd 3 King's Own Hussars 1939, served Falkland Islands 1939, Germany, Egypt, Pakistan, Burma (despatches); Military Attaché: British Embassy Lisbon 1952-54, British Embassy Iraq 1958-63 (Queen's Medal for Bravery); Inspr Staff Coll Quetta 1952-54; owner of Cicerone Properties Real Estate Agents Estoril Portugal; pres Royal British Legion (Lisbon) 1967-89 (life vice-pres 1989-); *Recreations* hunting, polo; *Clubs* Cavalry and Guards'; *Style*— Col Guy Bowden, CBE; Quinta de Janes, Malvera da Serra, 2750 Cascais, Portugal (☎ 010 351 2850 148); Cicerone Properties, 4 Av Bombieros Voluntarios, Estoril, Portugal (☎ 010 351 2860 387)

BOWDEN, Hon Mrs (Mary); *née* Bowden; da of Baron Bowden (Life Peer 1963, d 1989); *b* 6 May 1940; *Educ* McGill Univ Montreal (MEd), Concordia Univ Montreal (BA), Univ of Manchester England (Cert of teaching for Deaf); *m* 1964 (m dis), Dr Roger George Davey; 2 da (Lisa b 1969, Julie b 1971); has resumed her maiden name; *Career* integration teacher of hearing impaired children and assoc prof Dept of Communication Disorders McGill Univ Montreal, active presenter A G Bell Assoc for the Deaf, author of article in the Votla Review 1988; *Clubs* Toastmasters Organization; *Style*— The Hon Mrs Bowden; 4 Martin Avenue, Dorval, Québec H9S 3R3, Canada

BOWDEN, Nicholas Richard; s and h of Sir Frank Houston Bowden, 3 Bt; *b* 13 Aug 1935; *Educ* Millfield; *Career* Nat Serv, former trooper Life Gds; farmer; *Recreations* riding; *Style*— Nicholas Bowden, Esq; 4 Hensting Farm Cottages, Hensting Lane, Fishers Pond, nr Eastleigh, Hants SO5 7HH (☎ 096 274 260)

BOWDEN, Hon Robin Charles; only s of Baron Bowden (Life Peer, d 1989), by his 1 w Marjorie, *née* Browne (d 1956); *b* 22 Feb 1945; *Educ* Old Swinford Hosp Sch, Loughborough Univ; *m* 1, Jess, *née* MacPherson Duncan; 1 s (Alastair Robin b 1982), 1 da (Lindsay Catherine b 1979); *Career* cold store factory mangr; *Recreations* painting; *Style*— The Hon Robin Bowden; 12 Craigton Avenue, Mannofield, Aberdeen, Scotland

BOWDEN, Prof Ruth Elizabeth Mary; OBE (1980); da of Sqdn Ldr Frank Harold Bowden (d 1959), and Louise Ellen, *née* Flick (d 1976); *b* 21 Feb 1915; *Educ* St Paul's Girls' Sch, Univ of London (MB BS, DSc); *Career* graduate asst Nuffield Dept of Orthopaedic Surgery Peripheral Nerve Injury Unit 1942-45; Royal Free Hosp Sch of Med Univ of London: reader 1949 (formerly lectr), prof of anatomy 1951-80, emeritus prof 1980-; hon res fell Inst of Neurology 1980-, Sir William Collins prof of anatomy RCS 1984-89; WHO conslt in anatomy Sudan 1970, 1972 and 1974; former pres: Anatomical Soc of GB and Ireland, Med Women's Fedn, Inst of Sci and Technol; life vice pres Chartered Soc of Physiotherapy (former chm); N London Hospice Gp: cncl memb, exec ctee memb, chm professional sub ctee; convener Academic Awards Ctees of Br & Int Fedns of Univ Women; former memb exec ctee Women's Nat Cmmn, vice pres Riding For the Disabled, life memb Anatomical Soc GB and Ireland; memb: Zoological Soc, Royal Inst, Med Women's Fedn; Freeman by redemption City of London, Liveryman Worshipful Soc of Apothecaries; Jubilee Medal 1977, Wheatley Medal (jtly) Librarian's Assoc, Wood Jones Medal RCS; *Recreations* photography, painting, carpentry, reading; *Clubs* RSM, Br Fedn of Univ Women; *Style*— Prof Ruth Bowden, OBE; 6 Hartham Close, Hartham Rd, London N7 9JH (☎ 071 607 3464)

BOWE, David Robert; MEP (Lab) Cleveland and Yorkshire North 1989-; *b* 19 July 1955; *Educ* Heathfield Sr HS Gateshead, Sunderland Poly, Univ of Bath, Teesside Poly; *m* 1977, Helena Margaret; 1 s (James); *Career* sci teacher 1977-; memb Middlesborough Cncl 1983-89; EEC: Ctee on Environment Pub Health and Consumer Protection, substitute memb Ctee on Regnl Policy and Regnl Plannning and Ctee on Institutional Affairs, chm Working Party on Illicit Drugs; *Recreations* swimming, reading, walking; *Style*— David Bowe, Esq, MEP; 10 Harris St, Middlesborough, Cleveland TS1 5EF (☎ 0642 247722, fax 0642 247804)

BOWEN, Anthony James George; JP (1972); s of Howard James Bowen (d 1976), of Marina, The Strand, Saundersfoot, Dyfed, and Georgina Ann, *née* Morris; *b* 29 Jan 1941; *Educ* Narbeth GS, Loughborough Coll of Advanced Tech (DLC); *m* 1 June 1973, Patricia Ann, da of Douglas Edward Watson Hutchinson (d 1964), of Magdala Mount, Magdala Rd, Nottingham; 1 step s (Simon Miles Barrett b 30 April 1967), 1 step da (Lisa Ellen Barrett b 29 April 1970); *Career* dir J Bowen and Sons (LLawhaden) Ltd 1963-88, ptnr Bowens of Carmarthen 1975-87, chm and md Green Bower Garages Ltd (BMW main dealers Dyfed) 1963, ptnr Slebech Finance Co 1970-; sub prior Priory for Wales Order of St John HQ Cardiff, memb Management Bd Prince's Tst (chm Mid and W Wales Area Ctee), former memb Round Table, memb Rotary Int; FIMI 1984; KStJ 1988; *Recreations* golf, skiing, walking; *Style*— Anthony Bowen, Esq, JP; St Giles, Uzmaston Rd, Haverfordwest, Dyfed SA61 1TZ (☎ 0437 762792); Green Bower Garages Ltd, Slebech, Haverfordwest, Dyfed SA62 4PD (☎ 0437751 251, 0437757 373)

BOWEN, Prof David Aubrey Llewellyn; s of Thomas Rufus Bowen, JP (d 1946), and Catherine, *née* Llewellyn (d 1973); *b* 31 Jan 1924; *Educ* Caterham Sch Surrey, Univ of Wales, Univ of Cambridge (MA, MB); *m* 1, 1950, Joan Rosemary, *née* Davis (d 1973); 2 s (Mark b 1952, Roderic b 1966), 1 da (Diana b 1953); m 2, 21 Jan 1975, Helen Rosamund, da of Ralph Landcastle, of Haddenham, Bucks; *Career* Capt RAMC 1947-49; house offr: W Middx Hosp 1947, London Chest Hosp 1949-50, Bristol Royal Infirmary 1950-51; registrar: London Chest Hosp (Pathology) 1951-52, Nat Hosp for Nervous Diseases 1952-55, Royal Marsden Hosp 1955-56; forensic med lectr St Georges Hosp 1956-66, emeritus prof forensic med Univ of London, prof Charing Cross Hosp Med Sch 1977-90 (sr lectr 1966-73, reader 1973-77), lectr in forensic med Univ of Oxford 1974-90; chm Med Ctees Charing Cross Hosp and Med Sch; memb: Med Legal Soc (vice pres 1977-), Br Assoc Forensic Med (pres 1977-79), Int Academy Legal and Social Med 1976-, Br Academy Forensic Sci; vice pres Old Caterhamians Assoc 1987-88, pres W London Medico Chirurgical Soc 1987-88; Freeman City of London, Liveryman Worshipful Soc of Apothecaries; FRCP (London and Edinburgh), FRCPath, DPath, DMJ; *Recreations* hockey, running (jogging); *Style*— Prof D A L Bowen; 19 Letchmore Rd, Radlett, Herts WD7 8HU (☎ 092385 6936)

BOWEN, Prof David Quentin; s of William Esmond Bowen (d 1984), of Heddlys, Glasfryn, Llanelli, and Jane, *née* Wiliams; *b* 14 Feb 1938; *Educ* Llanelli GS, UCL (BSc, PhD); *m* 18 Sept 1965, Elizabeth, da of David Islwyn Williams (d 1989); 2 s (Huw b 1966, Wyn b 1969); *Career* prof: physical geography UCW Aberystwyth 1983, geography Univ of London Royal Holloway and Bedford New Coll 1985; prof and dir Inst Earth Studies UCW 1988; ed in chief Quaternary Sci Review 1982-, pres Quaternary Res Assoc (UK) 1979-81; memb: Natural Environment Res Cncl Ctees 1978-88, UGC Earth Sci Review 1988, Nature Conservancy Cncl 1986-91, Geological America 1987, Jt Nature Conservation Ctee (GB) 1990-, American Geophysical Union; dep chm Countryside Cncl for Wales 1990-; FRGS 1985, FGS 1988; *Books* Quaternary Geology (1978, Russian edn 1982, 1987), The Llanelli Landscape (1980), Glaciations in the Northern Hemisphere (1986); *Recreations* music, rugby, football, cricket; *Clubs* Athenaeum, Llanelli RFC Patrons; *Style*— Prof David Bowen; Castell Brychan, Aberystwyth SY23 2JD (☎ 0970 625 563); Inst of Earth Studies, UCW, Aberystwyth SY23 3DB (☎ 0970 622630, fax 0970 622659)

BOWEN, Duncan; s of William Henry Bowen, of Derbys, and Ivy, *née* Sanderson; *b* 6 June 1940; *Educ* Tupton Hall GS Chesterfield, Open Univ (BA); *m* 24 Aug 1963, Susan Elizabeth, da of late James Geoffrey Reynolds, of Derbyshire; *Career* admin Nat Tst, management and environmental ethicist; *Recreations* strolling; *Style*— Duncan Bowen, Esq; Laundry Cottage, Belton House, Grantham, Lincs NG32 2LS

BOWEN, Edward Farquharson; TD (1977); s of Stanley Bowen, CBE, *qv*; *b* 1 May 1945; *Educ* Melville Coll Edinburgh, Univ of Edinburgh (LLB); *m* 1975, Patricia Margaret, da of Rev Robert Russell Brown, of Gowanbank, Isla Rd, Perth; 2 s (James, David), 2 da (Helen, Alexandra); *Career* admitted slr 1968; advocate 1970, advocate depute 1979-83; Sheriff of Tayside Central and Fife at Dundee 1983-90; ptnr Thorntons WS 1990-; *Recreations* golf; *Clubs* New (Edinburgh), Hon Co of Edinburgh Golfers, Panmure Golf; *Style*— Edward Bowen, Esq, TD; Westgate, 12 Glamis Drive, Dundee; Whitehall Chambers, 11 Whitehall St, Dundee (☎ 0382 29111)

BOWEN, Rear Adm Frank; s of Alfred Bowen (d 1976), of St Helens, Lancs, and Lily, *née* Jenkins (d 1988); *b* 25 Jan 1930; *Educ* Cowley Sch St Helens, RNC Dartmouth, RNEC Manadon, RNC Greenwich, RCDS; *m* 1954, Elizabeth Lilian, da of Louis Charles Gibson Richards (d 1971) of Truro, Cornwall; 1 s (Peter), 2 da (Sarah, Emily); *Career* CSO to Chief Polaris Exec MOD 1974-76, special project rep (Navy) Washington DC 1976-78, dep chief Strategic Systems Exec 1980-81, Capt HMS Collingwood 1981-82, special project exec MOD 1982-84; dep chm (non-exec) Dowty Cap Ltd 1985-88, chm SALS Ltd 1989, ind def indust conslt 1988-; CEng, MIMechE, FBIM; *Recreations* golf, amateur theatre; *Clubs* IOD; *Style*— Rear Adm Frank Bowen; c/o Midland Bank plc, 102 High St, Lymington, Hants SO41 9ZP

BOWEN, Jill, Lady; Jill Claud Murray; *née* Evans; da of Cyril Lloyd Evans, of Prestea, Ghana; *m* 30 Aug 1947, Sir Thomas Frederic Charles Bowen, 4 Bt (d 1989); 1 s (Sir Mark, 5 Bt, *qv*), 2 da (Julia Rosemary b 10 July 1950, Margot Claire b 30

March 1952) and 1 da decd (b and d 13 Jan 1954); *Style*— Jill, Lady Bowen; 1 Barford Close, Fleet, Hants GU13 9HJ

BOWEN, John Griffith; s of Hugh Griffith Bowen (d 1988), and Ethel May, *née* Cooke; *b* 5 Nov 1924; *Educ* Queen Elizabeth's GS Crediton, Pembroke Coll Oxford (MA), St Anthony's Coll Oxford, Ohio State Univ; *Career* Capt Mahratha LI 1943-47; writer; novels: The Truth Will Not Help Us (1956), After the Rain (1958), The Centre of the Green (1959), Storyboard (1960), The Birdcage (1962), A World Elsewhere (1965), Squeak (1983), The MacGuffin (1984), The Girls (1986), Fighting Back (1988); plays incl: I Love You, Mrs Patterson (St Martin's Theatre) 1964, After the Rain (Duchess Theatre) 1966, The Waiting Room (Soho Poly) 1970, Heil, Caesar (Birmingham) 1974, Which Way Are You Facing? (Bristol Old Vic) 1976, The Inconstant Couple (adaptation of Marivaux, Chichester Festival Theatre) 1978, The Geordie Gentleman (adaptation of Molière, Newcastle Playhouse) 1987; TV plays for BBC, LWT, Associated Television, Yorkshire Television, Central Television (incl Heil, Caesar, winner of Tokyo prize); radio plays for BBC incl The False Diaghilev 1987, prodr of TV drama, dir of stage plays, author of various reviews and articles; *Style*— John Bowen, Esq; Old Lodge Farm, Sugarswell Lane, Edgehill, Banbury OX15 6HP (☎ 0295 88401)

BOWEN, Kenneth John; s of Hector John Bowen (d 1980), of Llanelli, Carmarthenshire, and Sarah Ann (Sally), *née* Davies (d 1939); *b* 3 Aug 1932; *Educ* Llanelli GS, Univ Coll of Wales Aberystwyth (BA), St John's Coll Cambridge (MA, MusB), Inst of Educn Univ of London; *m* 31 March 1959, Angela Mary, da of George Stanley Evenden, of Morecambe, Lancs; 2 s (Geraint, Meurig); *Career* Flying Offr Educn Branch RAF 1958-60; head of vocal studies RAM 1987-(prof singing 1967-); conductor: London Welsh Chorale 1983-, London Welsh Festival Chorus 1987-; former concert and operatic tenor (ret 1988); debut Tom Rakewell New Opera Co Sadlers Wells 1957; appeared: Promenade concerts, Three Choirs Festival, Aldeburgh, Bath, Swansea and Llandaff; performed at: Royal Opera, House ENO, WNO, Glyndebourne Touring Opera, English Opera Gp, English Music Theatre, Kent Opera, Handel Opera Soc; numerous recordings and int appearances, winner First prize Munich Int Competition and Queens prize; memb: Gorsedd of Bards, Royal Nat Eisteddfod of Wales, Cncl Br Youth Opera, vice pres Guild for Promotion of Welsh Music; hon memb RAM, FRSA; 1973; *Recreations* golf, fell walking, cinema, wine; *Style*— Kenneth Bowen, Esq; 12 Steeles Rd, London NW3 4SE; Royal Academy of Music, Marylebone Rd, London NW1 5HT (☎ 071 722 6279)

BOWEN, Sir Mark Edward Mortimer; 5 Bt (UK 1921), of Colworth, Co Bedford; o s of Sir Thomas Frederic Charles Bowen, 4 Bt (d 1989), and Jill Claud Murray, *née* Evans; *b* 17 Oct 1958; *Educ* Wellington Coll; *m* 1983, Kerry Tessa, da of Michael John Moriarty, of The Grey House, Links Road, Worthing, Sussex; 1 s (George Edward Michael), 1 da (Grace Francesca b 3 March 1989); *Heir* s, George Edward Michael Bowen b 27 Dec 1987; *Career* Lloyd's broker 1978-; *Recreations* swimming, golf; *Style*— Sir Mark Bowen, Bt; 14 Pendorves Road, West Wimbledon, London SW20 8RA; Minet House, 100 Leman Street, London E1 8HG

BOWEN, (Rosslyn) Mark; s of Rosslyn LLewelyn Bowen, of 12 New Henry St, Neath, W Glamorgan, and Mary, *née* Beynon; *b* 7 Dec 1963; *Educ* St Josephs RC Secdy Sch Port Talbot; *m* 5 July 1986, Karen Rose, da of Keith Hollingdale; 1 s (Joshua Thomas b 18 March 1990), 1 da (Daniella Rose b 29 July 1988); *Career* professional footballer; Tottenham Hotspur 1983-87 (23 appearances), Norwich City 1987- (over 200 appearances); Wales: 14 schoolboy caps, 12 youth caps, 6 under 21 caps, 12 full caps; UEFA Cup Winners medal (Tottenham Hotspur v Anderlecht) 1984, Norwich City player of the year 1989-90; *Recreations* horse racing; *Style*— Mark Bowen, Esq; c/o Norwich City FC, Carrow Road, Norwich, Norfolk NR1 1JE (☎ 0603 612131)

BOWEN, Dr (John) Myles; OBE (1977); s of Cdr Harold Townshend Bowen, OBE (d 1971), and Cicely Frances Anne, *née* Cooper; *b* 23 Aug 1928; *Educ* Sherborne, Lincoln Coll Oxford (BA), Univ of Edinburgh (PhD); *m* 7 Jan 1961, Margaret Compton, da of James Guthrie (d 1938); 3 da (Frances Belinda b 1963, Joanna Marion b 1964, Jennifer Isabel b 1968); *Career* cmmnd RA 1946; worked as exploration geologist for Royal Dutch/Shell Group 1954-84 (Africa, S America, Europe), exploration dir Enterprise Oil London 1984-88, dir N Sea exploration when 8 oil and 3 gas fields discovered; FGS, AAPG; *Recreations* sailing, skiing, rough shooting; *Clubs* Little Ship; *Style*— Dr Myles Bowen, OBE; 5 The Strand, London WC2 (☎ 071 930 1212, telex 895011 EPRISE G)

BOWEN, Maj-Gen (William) Neville; s of Maj-Gen William Oswald Bowen, CB, CBE (d 1961), of Winchester, and Ethel Gwenllian, *née* Davies; *b* 16 March 1935; *Educ* Shrewsbury, New York Univ Grad Sch of Business Admin; *m* 1960, Rosemary Rowena, da of Trevlyn Acheson-Williams-Flanagan; 2 da (Suzanne b 1963, Joanna b 1966); *Career* investment banker and advsr NY and Toronto 1957-72, md Hill Samuel Unit Tst Mangrs Ltd 1973-76, chief exec Bank von Ernst & Cie AG Switzerland 1976-80, dep chm Hill Samuel Life Assurance Co Ltd 1980-82; chm: Hill Samuel Investment Management Ltd 1982- (dep chm 1980-82), Investment Advisors Inc (USA) 1986-, Hill Samuel Investment Advisors Ltd 1987-, Hill Samuel Fagan Investment Management Ltd 1988-; chief exec Hill Samuel Investment Management Group Ltd 1986-; CBIM; *Recreations* skiing, swimming, gardening; *Clubs* Brooks's; *Style*— Maj-Gen Neville Bowen; Hill Samuel Investment Management Gp Ltd, 45 Beech St, London EC2P 2LX (☎ 071 638 1774, ext 2504)

BOWEN, Hon Sir Nigel Hubert; AC, KBE (1976); s of Otway P Bowen, of Ludlow; *b* 26 May 1911; *Educ* King's Sch Parramatta NSW, St Paul's Coll, Univ of Sydney; *m* 1, 1947, Eileen Cecily (d 1983), da of Francis J Mullens; 3 da; m 2, 1984, Ermyn Winifred Krippner; *Career* barr: NSW 1936, Victoria 1954; QC (Aust) 1953; MHR (Lib) Parramatta 1964-73, AG Aust 1966-69 and 1971, min for Educn and Science 1969-71, min Foreign Affrs 1971-72; chief justice Fed Court of Aust 1976-; *Recreations* swimming, music; *Clubs* Union (Sydney); *Style*— The Hon Sir Nigel Bowen, AC, KBE; Union Club, Bent St, Sydney, NSW 2000, Australia (☎ 010 612 230 8438)

BOWEN, Stanley; CBE (1972); s of Edward Bowen (d 1967), of Carnoustie, Angus, and Ellen Esther Powles (d 1967); *b* 4 Aug 1910; *Educ* Barry Sch Angus, Grove Acad Dundee, Univ Coll Dundee; *m* 1943, Mary Shepherd, da of Alexander Greig (d 1953), of Carnoustie, Angus; 2 s (Edward (*qv*), Douglas), 1 da (Mary); *Career* admitted slr 1932; memb Procurator Fiscal Serv 1933-41, princ asst Crown Edinburgh 1945-67, crown agent for Scotland 1967-74; Hon Sheriff Lothian and Borders 1975-; Coronation medal 1953; *Clubs* New and Press (Edinburgh); *Style*— Stanley Bowen, Esq, CBE; Achray, 20 Dovecot Rd, Corstorphine, Edinburgh EH12 7LE (☎ 031 334 4096)

BOWEN-SIMPKINS, Peter; s of Horace John Bowen-Simpkins (d 1969), and Christine Dulce, *née* Clarke; *b* 28 Oct 1941; *Educ* Malvern, Selwyn Coll Cambridge (MA), Guy's Hosp (MB BChir); *m* 19 Aug 1967, Kathrin, da of Karl Otto Ganguin (d 1987), of Chelmsford, Essex; 2 da (Emma Jane b 6 Nov 1969, Philippa b 28 Dec 1971); *Career* resident MO Queen Charlotte's Maternity Hosp London 1971, resident surgical offr Samaritan Hosp for Women London 1972, sr registrar and lectr in obstetrics and gynaecology Middx Hosp and Hosp for Women 1972-78, conslt gynaecologist and obstetrician Singleton Hosp Swansea 1979-, lectr in family planning Margaret Pyke Centre London; broadcaster and lectr; contrib chapters in various books on obstetrics and gynaecology, and author of papers and pubns in med jls incl: Br Med Jl, Br Jl of Obstetrics and Gynaecology; examiner: Royal Coll of Obstetricians and Gynaeologists, Univ of Wales, GMC; Handcock Prize for Surgery RCS 1966; co-fndr Victor Bonney Soc, ldr Cambridge Expedition to Eritrea 1963; Freeman City of London, Liveryman Worshipful Soc of Apothecaries 1976; LRCP 1966, MRCS 1966, MRCOG 1973, FRCOG 1985; *Books* Pocket Examiner in Obstetrics & Gynaecology (1983); *Recreations* fly fishing, skiing, golf, sailing, tennis; *Clubs* Royal Porthcawl Golf, Royal Overseas League; *Style*— Peter Bowen-Simpkins, Esq; Bosco's Knoll, 73 Pennard Rd, Southgate, Swansea SA3 2AJ; 38 Walter Rd, Swansea SA1 5NW (☎ 0792 655600)

BOWER, Hon Lady (Catherine Muriel); da of Capt Henry Edward Hotham (d 1912), and aunt of 8 Baron Hotham; raised to rank of Baron's da 1924; *b* 1908; *m* 12 April 1939, Lt-Gen Sir Roger Herbert Bower, KCB, KBE (d 1990); 1 adopted s (Michael b 1952) (and 1 s decd), 1 da (Anne b 1940); *Style*— The Hon Lady Bower; Cottage no 41, Headbourne Worthy House, Winchester, Hants SO23 7JG

BOWER, Michael James Eills Graham; s of James Graham Bower (d 1968), of Hants, and Sybil Galilee, *née* Eills (d 1971); *b* 14 June 1938; *Educ* Eton, Ch Ch Oxford (MA); *m* 23 June 1967, Carloyne Patricia Sherwell, da of Derek Frank Sherwell Clogg (d 1986), of London; 1 s (Michael b 3 Nov 1968); *Career* dir: Rea Bros 1974-(joined 1961), Rea Brothers Gp plc 1987-, Rea Bros Investmt Mgmnt 1988-; *Recreations* golf, bridge; *Clubs* Whites, The Brook, Royal and Ancient, Royal St Georges; *Style*— Michael Bower, Esq; 38 Chartfield Ave, London SW15; Aldermans House, Aldermans Walk, London EC2 (☎ 081 623 1155)

BOWER, Roger; s of Norman Franklin Bower, of Onchan, Isle of Man, and Dorothy Vera, *née* Lawson; *b* 30 March 1953; *Educ* Bootham Sch York, William Hulme's GS Manchester, Manchester Poly (BA); *m* 11 March 1979, Sonya Ruth, da of Dr Hyman Davies, of Prestwich, Manchester; 2 da (Anna Michelle b 1980, Jodie Samantha b 1982); *Career* admitted slr 1979; *Recreations* music appreciation, tennis, golf; *Style*— Roger Bower, Esq; West Winds, Hale Road, Hale Barns, Cheshire (☎ 061 980 7093); Bower Harris Solicitors, 211 Deansgate, Manchester (☎ 061 832 9404)

BOWERING, Christine; da of Kenneth Soper (d 1978), and Florence Evelyn Winifred, *née* Kruse (d 1982); *b* 30 June 1936; *Educ* St Bernard's Convent Westcliff, Newnham Coll Cambridge; *m* 23 July 1960, The Rev (John) Anthony Bowering, s of John Bowering; 1 s (John Robert b 1962), 1 da (Eleanor Jane (Mrs Wray) b 1964); *Career* teacher: St Bernard's Convent Westcliff 1959-60, Ursuline Convent Brentwood 1960-62; various pt/t occupations 1962-72, teacher then second mistress Sheffield HS for Girls GPDST 1972-84, headmistress Nottingham HS for Girls GPDST 1984-; memb: Engrg Cncl 1988-, Cncl GSA, Ind Schs Curriculum Ctee 1990-; govr Nottingham Poly 1989-, chm Educn Ctee GSA 1989; *Recreations* holidaying in France, church and family activities; *Clubs* University Women's; *Style*— Mrs Christine Bowering; The Vicarage, 2 Sunderland Street, Tickhill, Doncaster DN11 9QJ (☎ 0302 742224); Nottingham High Sch for Girls GPDST, 9 Arboretum St, Nottingham NG1 4JB (☎ 0602 417663)

BOWERING, Ven Michael Ernest; s of Hubert James Bowering (d 1961), of Barnstaple, and Mary Elizabeth, *née* Tucker (d 1982); *b* 25 June 1935; *Educ* Barnstaple GS, Kelham Theol Coll; *m* 18 Aug 1962, Aileen, da of James William Fox (d 1979), of Middlesbrough; 1 s (Paul b 1963), 2 da (Alice b 1965, Joanne b 1967); *Career* curate: St Oswald Middlesbrough 1959-62, All Saints Huntington 1962-64; vicar St Wilfrid Brayton with Barlow 1964-72, rural dean Selby 1971-72, vicar Emmanuel Saltburn By The Sea 1972-81, canon residentiary York Minster 1981-87, sec for Mission and Evangelism York Dio 1981-87, archdeacon of Lindisfarne 1987-; *Recreations* photography, walking; *Style*— The Ven the Archdeacon of Lindisfarne; 12 Rectory Park, Morpeth, Northumberland NE61 2SZ (☎ 0670 513 207)

BOWERMAN, David William; JP (1970); s of Alfred Hosegood Bowerman (d 1982), of Champs Hill, Coldwaltham, and Margaret, *née* Vellacott; *b* 9 Jan 1936; *Educ* Monkton Combe Sch, Univ of Reading (BSc); *m* 9 Sept 1961, (Clarice) Mary Bowerman, da of Prof William Melville Capper, of Clifton, Bristol (d 1975); 3 da (Janet (Mary) b 28 June 1962, Katharine (Emma) b 9 July 1964, Anna (Margaret) b 28 May 1966); *Career* farmer, property developer; chm: Arundel Bench 1985-89, bd of visitors HM Prison Ford 1979-82 (memb 1970-85), W Sussex Co Probation Ctee 1979-; High Sheriff W Sussex 1990-; *Recreations* music, fly fishing; *Style*— David Bowerman, Esq; Champs Hill, Coldwaltham, Pulborough, West Sussex (☎ 0798 831 868/831 205)

BOWERMAN, Ian Nicholas; s of Duncan Bowerman, and Olivia Irene, *née* Osborne; *b* 21 June 1921; *Educ* privately; *Career* qualified Army Staff Coll, ME 1944; dir: Louis Dreyfus & Co Ltd 1972-81, International Trade Development Co 1969-81; writer and lectr on philosophy; fndn fell Assoc of Corporate Treasurers; Liveryman Worshipful Co of Horner's, Freeman City of London, life memb Guild of Freemen of City of London; FRGS, FIOD; *Recreations* collecting oriental ceramics specialising in Chinese, Japanese and Tibetan artefacts; *Clubs* City Livery, Royal Overseas League, Royal Cwlth Soc; *Style*— Ian Bowerman, Esq; 6 Phoenix Lodge Mansions, Brook Green, London W6 7BG (☎ 071 603 9326)

BOWERS, (Frederick) John; s of Frederick Bowers (d 1971); *b* 23 Sept 1941; *Educ* Pembroke GS; *m* 1964, Sheila May, da of Hector Macdonald (d 1963); 2 s; *Career* dep md Johnston Construction; dir: Johnston Int Ltd (W Indies), Hadsphaltic Int (W Indies) Ltd; quantity surveyor; *Recreations* sailing, walking, scouting; *Clubs* Commonwealth; *Style*— F John Bowers, Esq; Hawkshaw, Eastbourne Rd, Blindley Heath, Lingfield, Surrey RH7 6JN (☎ 0342 833201)

BOWERS, (John) Michael; s of F G Bowers, CB (d 1937), of Surrey, and Frances Bowers (d 1982); *b* 24 April 1927; *Educ* Dauntsey's Sch, Balliol Coll Oxford (BA); *m* 13 Sept 1958, Rosalind, da of Percy Bourdon Smith; 2 s (Philip b 1960, Robert b 1963), 2 da (Joanna b 1961, Valery b 1965); *Career* ptnr McKenna & Co 1958-87; chm: CAB, CARE Br, Copyright Tbnl; dir London Sinfonietta, memb Hyde Housing Assoc, founding dir Greenwich Theatre; sailed across Atlantic 1982; *Recreations* sailing, music; *Clubs* Garrick; *Style*— Michael Bowers, Esq; 39 Cloudesley Rd, London N1 OEL; Yew Free Farm, Sweffling, Saxmundham, Suffolk

BOWERS, Michael John; s of Arthur Patrick Bowers (d 1961), and Lena Frances, *née* Maher (d 1983); *b* 1 Oct 1933; *Educ* Cardinal Vaughan Sch Kensington; *m* 29 Aug 1959, Caroline, da of William Joseph Clifford (d 1985); 2 da (Karen b 1963, Samantha b 1966); *Career* vice pres (and dir) BP N America Inc 1973-76, chief exec BP Gas Ltd 1976-81; regional co-ordinator Western Hemisphere BP Co plc 1981-83, chief exec The Int Petroleum Exchange of London Ltd 1983-85, md Two (UK) Ltd 1985-; *Recreations* gardening, bridge, chess, music; *Clubs* RAC, St James's; *Style*— Michael J Bowers, Esq; Wood End, Warren Drive, Kingswood, Surrey KT20 6PZ (☎ 0737 832629); 3 St James's Square, London SW1Y 4JF (telex 917831/881303)

BOWERS, Dr Peter John; s of Dr Arthur Clifford Bowers (d 1947), and Doris; *b* 2 June 1946; *Educ* Queen Elizabeth GS, Univ of London (BSc, AKC), Univ of Manchester (MB ChB, MSc); *m* 1 Aug 1970, (Patricia) Lesley, da of Philip Bethell, of Darlington, Co Durham; 2 s (Jonathan b 1975, Anthony b 1982), 1 da (Juliet b 1974); *Career* house physician and surgn Central Manchester Hosps 1973-74, sr house offr in paediatrics Booth Hall Hosp 1974-75, sr registrar in child psychiatry S Manchester Hosp 1978-81 (registra psychiatry 1975-78), tutor Dept of Child Psychiatry Univ of Manchester 1981-82; conslt in child and adolescent psychiatry 1983-: NW RHA, Tameside and Glossop Health Dist; expert witness for official slr in wardship cases in ct 1984-; chm: Local Hosp Med Staff Ctee, Dist Med Audit Ctee, Regnl Ctee of Child and Adolescent Psychiatrists; memb: Exec Ctee of Child and Adolescent Section of RCPsych, Manchester Med Soc, Assoc Family Therapists, Assoc Child Psychology and Psychiatry; MRCPsych 1978; *Recreations* amateur dramatics and operatics, theatre, jogging, travel; *Style*— Dr Peter Bowers; 6 Clifton Ave, Fallowfield, Manchester M14 6UB (☎ 061 224 9508); Springhill Dept of Child and Family Psychiatry, Tameside General Hospital, Fountain St, Ashton-Under-Lyne (☎ 061 330 8373)

BOWERS, Ronald Courtney; MBE (1959); s of Maj Stanley Bowers, TD (d 1938), of Warlingham, Surrey, and Mary, *née* Gadsdon (d 1938); *b* 18 May 1922; *Educ* Whitgift, RAF Apprentice Sch Halton; *Career* RAF Engrg Wing Cdr, SO HQ Air Support Cmd, mangr RAF Motor Sports Cyprus Rally Team 1972, cmd 103 MU Cyprus; family historian; CEng, MRAeS; *Books* Combs, Combmaking & the Combmakers Company (1987); *Recreations* bird watching, photography, oil painting, genealogy; *Clubs* RAF, Royal Aeronautical Soc; *Style*— Ronald Bowers, Esq, MBE; Road End Cottage, Stockland, Honiton, Devon EX14 9LJ (☎ 040 488 581)

BOWERS-BROADBENT, Christopher Joseph St George; s of Henry William Bowers-Broadbent (d 1965), of Ilfracombe, Devon, and Doris E, *née* Mizen; *b* 13 Jan 1945; *Educ* Kings Coll Cambridge, Berkhamsted Sch, Royal Acad of Music (Recital Dip); *m* 17 Oct 1970, Deirdre Ann, da of Norman Cape, of Kimbolton, Cambs; 1 s (Henry William b 10 Jan 1975), 1 da (Tabitha Jane b 2 May 1971); *Career* organist and choirmaster St Pancras Parish Church 1965-88, concert organist debut Camden Festival 1966, organist W London Synagogue 1973-, prof Royal Acad of Music 1976-, organist and choirmaster Grays Inn 1983-; many sacred and secular compositions; operas incl: The Pied Piper 1972, The Seacock Bane 1979, The Last Man 1983; FRAM; *Recreations* sketching; *Style*— Christopher Bowers-Broadbent, Esq; 94 Colney Hatch Lane, Muswell Hill, London N10 1EA (☎ 081 883 1933)

BOWERY, Leigh; s of Thomas Bradley Bowery, of 147 Morris Street, Sunshine, Victoria 3020 Australia, and Evelyn Joyce, *née* Griffiths; *b* 26 March 1955; *Educ* Sunshine West HS Sunshine Australia, Melbourne Boys HS; *Career* collections shown: New York 1983 and 1984, London (ICA) 1983 and 1984, Tokyo 1985, Vienna 1985 and 1986; subject of LWT documentary 1985, starred in Hail the New Puritan (film) 1985; with Michael Clark & Co: two seasons (Sadlers Wells), 1987 and 1988 touring Britain, Spain, Italy, Germany, Australia, Yugoslavia, America, Holland; exhibit at Anthony D'Offay Art Gallery 1988; *Recreations* Kung-Fu; *Clubs* Heaven; *Style*— Leigh Bowery, Esq; 43 Farrell House, Ronald St, London E1; 9-23 Dering Street, New Bond Street, London W1 (☎ 071 499 4100)

BOWERY, Prof Norman George; s of George Bowery (d 1971), and Olga, *née* Beevers; *b* 23 June 1944; *Educ* Christs Coll Finchley, Univ of London (PhD, DSc); *m* 14 Feb 1970, Barbara Joyce, da of Eric Norman Westcott, of Goring, Sussex; 1 s (Andrew James b 1975), 2 da (Nicole Louise b 1973, Annette Jane b 1977); *Career* sr lectr St Thomas Hosp London 1982-84 (lectr 1975-82), section ldr Neuroscience Res Centre MSD Harlow 1984-87, Wellcome prof of pharmacology Univ of London 1987-, memb and vice chm Biological Cncl 1988; memb: MRC Neuroscience Ctee 1983-87, SERC Link Ctee 1988-90, Br Pharmacological Soc, Royal Microscopical Soc, American Neuroscience Assoc, Soc Drug Res, Br Assoc Psychopharmacology; *Books* Actions and Interactions of GABA and Benzodiazepines (1984), GABAergic Mechanisms on the Periphery (1986), GABA Basic Research and Clinical Applications (1989), GABA receptors in mammalian function (1990); *Recreations* walking, gardening, socializing; *Style*— Prof Norman Bowery; Dept of Pharmacology, The School of Pharmacy, University of London, 29/39 Brunswick Square, London WC1N 1AX (☎ 071 837 7651)

BOWES LYON, Hon (Michael) Albemarle; s of late Capt the Hon Michael Claude Hamilton Bowes Lyon, 5 s of 14 E of Strathmore and Kinghorne; bro of 17 E; raised to the rank of an E's s 1974; *b* 29 May 1940; *Educ* Eton, Magdalen Coll Oxford; *Career* dir Coutts & Co 1969-, govr Peabody Tst 1982-, hon treas Family Serv Units 1976-; *Style*— The Hon Albemarle Bowes Lyon; c/o Coutts & Co, 440 Strand, London WC2R 0QS

BOWES LYON, Hon Lady; Rachel Pauline; da of late Col the Rt Hon Herbert Spender-Clay, CMG, MC, PC, MP, and Pauline, JP, da of 1 Viscount Astor and sis of 1 Baron Astor of Hever; *m* 1929, Hon Sir David Bowes Lyon, KCVO (d 1961), s of 14 E of Strathmore and Kinghorne; 1 s (*see* S A Bowes Lyon), 1 da (*see* 13 E of Stair, KCVO, MBE); *Style*— The Hon Lady Bowes Lyon; St Paul's Walden Bury, Hitchin, Herts (☎ 0438 871 225)

BOWES LYON, Simon Alexander; s of Hon Sir David Bowes Lyon, KCVO (d 1961), and Rachel Pauline, *née* Spender Clay (*see* Hon Lady Bowes Lyon); *b* 17 June 1932; *Educ* Eton, Magdalen Coll Oxford; *m* 11 April 1966, Caroline Mary Victoria, er da of Rt Rev Victor Joseph Pike, CB, CBE, MA, DD, Bishop of Sherborne 1959-76; 3 s (Fergus b 1970, David b 1973, Andrew b 1979), 1 da (Rosie b 1968); *Career* dir: Financial Insurance Gp Ltd, Dominion Insurance Co Ltd, Balfour Maclaine Int Ltd, WRVS Tstees Ltd and other cos; Lord Lieut of Hertfordshire 1986-; FCA 1959; *Recreations* shooting, gardening, walking, music; *Clubs* Brooks's; *Style*— Simon Bowes Lyon, Esq; St Paul's Walden Bury, Hitchin, Herts (☎ 0438 871218); 12 Morpeth Mansions, London SW1 (☎ 071 834 8057, fax 071 834 6597)

BOWES-LYON, David James; s of Maj-Gen Sir James Bowes-Lyon, KCVO, CB, OBE, MC (d 1977), and Mary, *née* De Trafford; *b* 21 July 1947; *Educ* Ampleforth; *m* 1976, Elizabeth Harriet, da of Sir John Colville, CB, CVO, of Broughton, nr Stockbridge, Hants; 2 s (James b 1979, Charles b 1989), 2 da (Georgina b 1977, Alexandra b 1986); *Career* Capt 14/20 Kings Hussars 1970-78 NI, W Germany, Cyprus, Zaire; The Union Discount Co of London 1979- (dir various subsid cos); dir: Scottish Business Achievement Tst 1981-, Aitken Campbell and Co Ltd 1987-, Lothian Racecourse Ltd (Edinburgh) 1987-; memb the Queen's Body Guard for Scotland (The Royal Company of Archers); *Recreations* shooting, fishing, racing; *Clubs* White's; *Style*— David Bowes-Lyon, Esq; Heriot Water, Heriot, Midlothian (☎ 087 535 281; work 031 226 3535)

BOWES-LYON, John Francis; s of Maj-Gen Sir James Bowes-Lyon, KCVO, CB, OBE, MC (d 1977), and Lady Bowes-Lyon, da of Sir Humphrey de Trafford (Bt); *b* 13 June 1942; *Educ* Ampleforth; *Career* dir: Sotheby's 1970-80, Direction UK Ltd 1989-; ed at large Condé Nast Publications Inc USA; *Clubs* Buck's, Pratt's; *Style*— John Bowes-Lyon, Esq; D5 Albany, Piccadilly, London W1 (☎ 071 494 1434)

BOWETT, Prof Derek William; CBE (1983), QC (1978); s of Arnold William Bowett (d 1960), of Sale, Cheshire, and Marion, *née* Wood (d 1948); *b* 20 April 1927; *Educ* William Hulme's GS, Downing Coll Cambridge (MA, LLB, PhD, LLD); *m* 29 Dec 1953, Betty, da of William Sidney Northall (d 1983), of Rhyl, N Wales; 2 s (Richard William b 1956, Adam Northall b 1958), 1 da (Louise Marion b 1961); *Career* AB RNVR 1945-47; barr Middle Temple 1953, bencher 1976; lectr in law Manchester Univ 1951-59; pres Queens' Coll Cambridge 1970-82 (fell 1960-70 and 1982-); Whewell prof of int law Cambridge 1981- (lectr then reader Law Faculty Cambridge Univ 1960-81); former memb Royal Cmmn Environmental Pollution; Hon PhD Manchester; FBA 1984; *Books* Self-Defence in International Law (1957), Law of International Institutions (1964), United Nations Forces (1964), Search for Peace (1970), Legal Regime of Islands (1978); *Recreations* music, walking, gardening; *Style*— Prof Derek Bowett, CBE, QC; 228 Hills Road, Cambridge CB2 2QE (☎ 0453 210688); Queens' College, Cambridge CB3 9ET (☎ 0453 335555, fax 0223 335533, telex 81240 CAM SPL-G)

BOWIE, Rev (Alexander) Glen; CBE (1984); s of Alexander Bowie (d 1983), of Stevenston, Ayrshire, and Annie Robertson, *née* McGhie (d 1977); *b* 10 May 1928; *Educ* Stevenston HS, Irvine Royal Acad, Univ of Glasgow (BSc), Univ of Glasgow Trinity Coll (Dip Theol), Open Univ (BA); *m* 15 March 1952, Mary, da of John McKillop (d 1945); 2 da (Alexandra b 8 March 1955, Jenifer b 12 Sept 1960); *Career* ordained minister Church of Scot 1954; chaplain RAF Henlow 1954, Padgate 1955-56, Akrotiri 1956-59, Stafford 1959-61, Butzweilerhof 1961-64, Halton 1964-67, Akrotiri 1967-70, RAF Coll Cranwell 1970-75, asst princ chaplain 1975, HQ Rheindahlen 1975-76, HQ RAFSC 1976-80, princ Chaplain Church of Scot and Free Churches 1980-84, Hon Chaplain to HM the Queen 1980-84, ret from RAF 1984; ed Scot Forces Bulletin 1985-, moderator of Presbytery of England 1988-89; hon chaplain Royal Scot Corp 1981-, pres Scot Chaplains Assoc 1987-88, memb Caledonian Soc of London; *Recreations* painting, boating and leading holy land pilgrimages; *Clubs* RAF; *Style*— The Rev Glen Bowie, CBE; 16 Weir Rd, Hemingford Grey, Huntingdon, Cambs (☎ 0480 632 69)

BOWIE, James; s of James Bowie, of 120 New Walk, Leicester and Olive May, *née* Elcock; *b* 22 Jan 1947; *Educ* Oakham Sch Rutland, Westminster Tech Coll London (HND Hotel Mgmnt); *m* 1, 1972 (m dis), Ann Margaret Stevens; 1 s (James b 15 Nov 1975); m 2, 1988, Susan Elizabeth, *née* Messenger; 1 s (Nicolas Edward b 24 June 1984), 1 da (Rosie Victoria b 27 Jan 1982); *Career* food service trg Hotel Normandie Le Havre 1964, food preparation and service Moëvenpick Zurich 1967; mgmnt trainee Plough & Harrow Birmingham 1968, Vendage Pommerol 1968; Belmont Hotel (family business): joined 1969, gen mangr 1971, md 1975; mangr Hathersage Inn Hathersage; chm: Leicester Hoteliers 1974, 1977 and 1985, Best Western Hotels 1988-90 (memb 1971-); vice chm Leicester Tourism TDAP 1989-; active in: BHRCA 1970-, Leicester Assoc of Hotels 1972-, FHCIMA 1980, Master Innholder 1986; *Recreations* hunting, eating, drinking, skiing, rugby, tennis; *Style*— James Bowie, Esq; Belmont BC, 124 New Walk, Leicester LE1 7GR(☎ 0533 544773, fax 0533 854151)

BOWIE, Norman Walter; s of Walter Stronach Bowie (d 1950) and Marion Louise, *née* Thomson (d 1956), of Beckenham; *b* 10 Oct 1914; *Educ* Stationers' Co's Sch, Coll of Estate Mgmnt; *m* 1947, Kathleen Cecelia, da of John Augustus Hannigan (d 1965), of Highgate; *Career* served WWII, Maj RE, 14 Army SE Asia Cmd; surveyor to Prudential Assurance Co 1934-59, ptnr Jones Lang Wootton (chartered surveyors) 1959-74 (conslt 1975-89), dir Town and City Properties 1962-73; memb of Ctee of Mgmnt The Pension Fund Property Unit Tst 1966-74, dir Es Court 1967-72; property conslt: British Land plc 1974-84, Nat River Authy Superannuation Fund 1974-, Crown Agents for Overseas Govts and Admins 1976-82; dir Imry Property Holdings 1965-86, chm Euro Gp of Valuers of Fixed Assets 1977-82, sec Int Assets Valuation Standards Ctee 1981-84, dir London Small Businesses Property Tst 1987-, memb Cncl Barnardo's 1981-89 (chm 1984-87), property conslt to chief exec Property Services Agency DOE 1982-83 and London Borough of Bromley 1982-84; hon fell Coll of Estate Mgmnt, chm Admin Bd Jones Lang Wootton Travelling Scholarship 1983-89 (memb 1983-), ed Statements of Asset Valuation Practice (RICS handbook); pres Chiswick Amateur Regatta; FRICS; *Recreations* rowing, writing on property investment and valuation; *Clubs* Ibis Rowing; *Style*— Norman Bowie, Esq; 1 Uplands Close, London SW14 7AS (☎ 081 876 1434); White Horses, 30 Coastal Rd, West Kingston, Littlehampton, W Sussex; office: 22 Hanover Square, London W1A 2BN (☎ 071 493 6040, telex 23858, fax 071 408 0220)

BOWIE, Ronald Stewart; s of Robert Hunter Bowie, of Greenock, and Jessie Dalziel, *née* Clark; *b* 23 Jan 1954; *Educ* Greenock Acad, Univ of St Andrews (BSc); *m* 23 June 1986, Stella Elizabeth Gordon, da of Dr John Goudie, of Greenock; 2 da (Audrey b 1988, Louise b 1989); *Career* ptnr Hymans Robertson & Co; FFA 1980; *Recreations* sport, family; *Clubs* RSAC; *Style*— Ronald Bowie, Esq; Hymans Robertson, 221 West George St, Glasgow (☎ 041 248 7007, fax 041 221 8426, telex 776 564)

BOWIER, Michael James Eills Graham; s of James Graham Bowier (d 1968), of Hants, and Sybil Gailee, *née* Eills (1971); *Educ* Eton, Ch Ch Oxford (MA); *m* 23 June 1967, Carolyne Patricia Sherwell, da of Derek Frank Sherwell Clogg (d 1986), of London; 1 s (Michael b 3 Nov 1968); *Career* joined Rea Bros- (dir 1974-), md Rea Bros Investmt Mgmnt 1988-; *Recreations* golf, bridge; *Clubs* Whites, The Brook, RA, Royal St Georges; *Style*— Michael Bowier, Esq

BOWIS, John Crocket; OBE (1981), MP (C) Battersea 1987-; s of Thomas Palin Bowis (d 1957), of Brighton, and Georgiana Joyce Bowis, *née* Crocket; *b* 2 Aug 1945; *Educ* Tonbridge Sch, BNC Oxford (MA); *m* 1968, Caroline Taylor, of Oxon; 2 s (Duncan b 1972, Alistair b 1978), 1 da (Imogen b 1970); *Career* Cons Central Office 1972-80, public affrs dir Br Insur Brokers' Assoc 1981-86, cnllr Royal Borough of Kingston upon Thames 1982-86 (chm of Educn 1984-86), memb Select Ctee on Membs Interests 1987-90, sec All Pty Social Sci Gp 1988-; PPS to: Min for Inner Cities and Local Govt 1989-90, Sec of State for Wales 1990; pres Br Youth Cncl 1987-; *Recreations* theatre, music, art, sport; *Style*— John Bowis, OBE, MP; House of Commons, London SW1A 0AA (☎ 071 219 3535/6214, 071 949 2555)

BOWKER, Alfred Johnstone (John); MC (1944); s of Alfred Bowker, of Winchester, and Isabel Florence, *née* Brett; *b* 9 April 1922; *Educ* Dragon Sch Oxford, Winchester, Ch Ch Oxford (MA); *m* 1947, Ann, da of John Christopher Fairweather (d 1978); 1 s (Robert b 1952), 1 da (Judith b 1954; actress known as Judi Bowker); *Career* Coldstream Gds, Capt Italian Campaign 1941-46; slr in Winchester 1949-57; master Meon Valley Beagles 1954-56, Winchester City Cncllr 1954-57, resident magistrate N Rhodesia 1957-65, slr in Salisbury Wilts 1965-72, joint master Hursley Foxhounds 1968-69 and 1970-71; chm Industl Tbnls Newcastle upon Tyne 1972, regnl chm Industl Tbnls Southampton 1982, ret 1987, memb Hants CC 1989; Liveryman Worshipful Co of Skinners; *Recreations* hunting, reading history; *Style*— John Bowker, Esq, MC

BOWKER, Robin Marsland; s of Joseph Maximilian Bowker, (d 1942), and Etheldreda Leonore Campbell, *née* Allen (d 1966); *b* 15 Feb 1920; *Educ* Charterhouse; *m* 11 Jan 1956, Mary Dora Elizabeth, da of Capt John Francis Pace, RN (d 1973); 2 s (Ian Patrick b 22 April 1958, Robin Charles Bowker b 11 July 1964), 2 da (Christina Elizabeth (Mrs Darby) b 4 Feb 1957, Dr Annabel Mary Audrey b 28 Nov 1960); *Career* md: Burnes Shipward Ltd, Bowker and Budd Ltd, Bowker Bertram Ltd; author of 100 articles in the sailing press of 15 countries; contrib: US News & World Report, The Daily Telegraph, The Times, The Sunday Times, The Guardian; *Books* A Boat of your Own, The Channel Handbook Vols I II and III, Historical Postcript to the Riddle of the Sands by Erskine Childers, MUTINY!! Aboard HM Transport Bounty in 1789 (with Lt Bligh in his official log), Make your own Sails (4 edn with S.A, Budd 1986); *Recreations* sailing, golf; *Clubs* Royal Ocean Racing, Royal London Yacht; *Style*— Robin M Bowker, Esq; Whitewalls, Harbour Way, Old Bosham, Chichester PO18 8QH (☎ 0243 572255)

BOWLAND, Ian Alexander; s of Alexander Hayburn Bowland, of Moseley, Birmingham, and Kathleen, *née* Hickinbotham (d 1988); *b* 14 Oct 1953; *Educ* Moseley GS, City of Birmingham Poly (BA); *Career* CA; Touche Ross 1976-80, Forward Tst Gp (Midland Bank) 1981-85, Peat Marwick McLintock 1985-89, Price Waterhouse 1989-; played: N Mids Rugby XV, English Univs Rugby XV; ACA 1980, FHD 1982;

Recreations sport, indoor games, walking, MENSA; *Clubs* Moseley Football; *Style—* Ian Bowland, Esq; 9 Keel Drive, Moseley, Birmingham B13 9XD (☎ 021 777 2959); Price Waterhouse, 169 Edmund St, Birmingham B3 2JB (☎ 021 200 300)

BOWLBY, Lady Ann Lavinia Maud Montagu Stuart-Wortley; da of 3 E of Wharncliffe (d 1953); *b* 25 Jan 1919; *m* 1939, as his 2 w, Cdr Vivian Russell Salvin Bowlby, RN (d 1972), s of Col Robert Russell Bowlby, of Tunbridge Wells; 1 s (Michael Robin Salvin b 1947); *Books* Maternal Care & Mental Health (1951), Attachment & Loss (3 vols, 1969-80); *Style—* Lady Ann Bowlby; Sutton Stables, Felixkirk Rd, Sutton-under-Whitestonecliffe, Thirsk, Yorks

BOWLBY, Sir Anthony Hugh Mostyn; 2 Bt (UK 1923); s of Sir Anthony Alfred Bowlby, 1 Bt, KCB, KCMG, KCVO, FRCS (d 1929); *b* 13 Jan 1906; *Educ* Wellington, New Coll Oxford; *m* 27 Jan 1930, Dora Evelyn, da of late John Charles Allen, of York; 2 da; *Heir* nephew, Richard Peregrine Longstaff Bowlby b 1941; *Style—* Sir Anthony Bowlby, Bt; The Old Rectory, Ozleworth, nr Wotton-under-Edge, Glos

BOWLBY, Hon Mrs (Dorothy Anne); da of Hon Dudley North, MC, JP (d 1936); sis and co-heiress of 13 Baron North (E 1554), ka 1941, since when the Barony has been in abeyance; *b* 4 May 1915; *m* 1, 1937 (m dis 1950), Clive Graham, Lt Sherwood Foresters; 1 da; m 2, 1950, Maj John Bowlby, 1 Royal Dragoons, s of Capt Geoffrey Bowlby, Royal Horse Gds (ka 1915), and Hon Mrs (Lettice) Bowlby, *qv*; 1 da; *Style—* The Hon Mrs Bowlby; 51 Shawfield St, London SW3 (☎ 071 352 0573)

BOWLBY, Hon Mrs (Penelope Isobel); da of 7 Viscount Portman (d 1948); *b* 21 July 1913; *m* 1, 1934 (m dis 1949), Brig Archer Francis Lawrence Clive, DSO, MC, s of Lt-Gen Sir George Sidney Clive, GCVO, KCB, CMG, DSO, of Perryshire Court, Hereford; 1 s, 1 da; m 2, 1949, David Arthur Salvin Bowlby (d 1985), 2 s of late Arthur Salvin Bowlby, of Gilston Park, Harlow, Essex; *Career* breeding racehorses; *Style—* The Hon Mrs Bowlby; Inverinate, Kyle of Lochalsh, Ross-shire; The Manor, Healing, Grimsby

BOWLBY, Rt Rev Ronald Oliver; *see*: Southwark, Bishop of

BOWLER, Geoffrey; s of James Henry and Hilda May Bowler; *b* 11 July 1924; *Educ* Sloane Sch Chelsea; *Career* chief gen mangr Sun Alliance and London Insurance Gp 1977-87; FCIS; *Style—* Geoffrey Bowler, Esq; 13 Green Lane, Purley, Surrey CR8 3PP (☎ 081 660 0756)

BOWLER, Ian John; CBE (1971, OBE 1957); s of Maj John Arthur Bowler; *b* 1920; *Educ* King's Sch Worcester, Oxford Univ; *m* 1963, Hamideh, da of Prince Yadollah Azodi, GCMG; 2 da; 1 step s, 1 step d; *Career* pres Iranian Mgmnt and Engrg Gp Ltd 1965-, chm Int Mgmnt and Engrg Gp Ltd 1973, dir Malaysian Mining Corpn (Gas) Sdn Bhd 1988, chm IMEG Malaysia Sdn Bhd 1989; *Style—* Ian Bowler, Esq, CBE; 4 Kucheh, Bagh Bank, Golhak, Tehran, Iran; 28 Mallord St, London SW3 (☎ 071 351 3322)

BOWLER, Philip; s of Albert Bowler, of Ashley Heath, Hants, and Eileen Alexandra, *née* Stanton; *b* 17 July 1950; *Educ* St Thomas More Tottenham London, Carshalton Coll; *m* 17 July 1971, Paula Jean, da of Derek Peter Pitfield, of 7 Plover Close, Edenbridge, Kent; 1 s (Stuart b 1974), 1 da (Victoria b 1972); *Career* computer serv mangr The Crown Agents Overseas Govts and Admins 1984- (computer operator 1971-75, ops mangr 1975-84); MIDPM 1985; *Recreations* reading, playing musical instruments, home computing; *Style—* Philip Bowler, Esq; 251 Malden Rd, Cheam, Surrey (☎ 081 644 2106); The Crown Agents for Overseas Governments and Administrations, St Nicholas House, Sutton, Surrey (☎ 081 643 3311, fax 081 643 8232, telex 916205)

BOWLES, Rt Rev Cyril William Johnston; s of late William C A Bowles, of Scotstoun, Glasgow; *b* 9 May 1916; *Educ* Brentwood Sch, Emmanuel Coll Cambridge, Jesus Coll Cambridge, Ridley Hall Cambridge; *m* 1965, Florence Joan, da of late John Eastaugh, of Windlesham, Surrey; *Career* ordained: deacon 1939, priest 1940; princ Ridley Hall 1951-63, hon canon of Ely Cathedral 1959-63, archdeacon of Swindon Dio of Bristol 1963-69, bishop of Derby 1969-87; memb House of Lords 1973-87, hon asst Bishop Dio of Glos 1987-; *Style—* The Rt Rev C W J Bowles; Rose Lodge, Tewkesbury Rd, Stow-on-the-Wold, Cheltenham, Glos GL54 1EN

BOWLES, Hamish Philip; s of David Victor Bowles, of London and Anne, *née* Burmester; *b* 23 July 1963; *Educ* Simon Langton Boys' GS Canterbury, William Ellis Sch Highgate, St Martin's Sch of Art; *Career* guest fashion ed Teenage Issue Harpers & Queen 1983, London and Paris ed Harpers' Bazaar Australia 1983-84, contributing ed 1983-84 (Harpers & Queen, The Face, Arena, GQ, Vanity Fair); Harpers & Queen: jr fashion ed 1985, Fashion dir 1987, style dir 1989-; memb The Costume Soc 1976; *Recreations* collecting vintage couture, travel, theatre; *Clubs* Freds, Quiet Storm; *Style—* Hamish Bowles, Esq; 221 Westbourne Park Rd, London W11 1EA; Harpers & Queen, National Magazine House, 72 Broadwick St, London W1V 2BP (☎ 071 439 5564, fax 071 437 6886)

BOWLES, Peter John; s of Herbert Reginald Bowles, and Sarah Jane, *née* Harrison; *b* 16 Oct 1936; *Educ* High Pavement GS Nottingham, RADA (scholar, winner Kendal prize); *m* 8 April 1961, Susan Alexandra, da of David Cyril Bennett; 2 s (Guy Rupert b 24 Sept 1962, Adam Peter b 26 Jan 1964); 1 da (Sasha Jane b 12 Oct 1966); *Career* actor; London debut in Romeo and Juliet (Old Vic) 1956; other work incl: Happy Haven and Platonov (Royal Court) 1960, Afternoon Men (Arts Theatre) 1961, Absent Friends (Garrick) 1975, Dirty Linen (Arts Theatre) 1976, Born In the Gardens (Globe) 1980, Some of My Best Friends are Husbands (Haymarket Leicester) 1985, The Entertainer (Shaftesbury) 1986, Canaries Sometimes Sing (Albery) 1987, Man of The Moment (Globe) 1990; TV series incl: Rumpole of The Bailey 1976-91, To The Manor Born 1979-82, Only When I Laugh 1979-82, The Bounder 1982-83, The Irish RM 1982-84, Lytton's Diary 1984-85, (Devised Series); Executive Stress 1987-88, Perfect Scoundrels 1989-91 (co-devised series); film work incl: Blow Up 1966, The Charge of the Light Brigade 1967, Laughter In The Dark 1968, A Day in the Death of Joe Egg 1970; *awards* Comedy Actor of the Year Pye awards 1984, ITV Personality of the Year Variety Club 1984; *Recreations* motoring and physical jerks; *Clubs* Garrick, Chelsea Arts, Groucho; *Style—* Peter Bowles, Esq; c/o London Management, 235-241 Regent Street, London W1 (☎ 071 493 1610)

BOWLES, Richard Douglas; s of Desmond Bowles (d 1975), and Glenys Doreen, *née* Isaacs; *b* 11 Feb 1949; *Educ* High Pavement GS, City of Westminster Coll; *m* 30 September 1972, Janice Brenda, da of Norman Derek Franklin; 1 s (Christopher Simon b 9 July 1976); *Career* BAT Industries 1969-79, Manulife Financial 1979- (vice pres int investments), md Manulife International Investment Management; ASIA 1974; *Recreations* most sports, bird watching, reading; *Style—* Richard Bowles, Esq; Manulife Financial, Broad St House, 55 Old Broad St, London EC2M 1TL (☎ 071 638 6611, fax 071 638 2059)

BOWLES, Sidney Theodore; s of Reginald Arthur Bowles (d 1988), of Norwich, and Elsie Maud, *née* Housego; *b* 11 May 1926; *Educ* Avenue Sch Norwich; *m* 7 Aug 1954, Ronalda Elizabeth, da of Cyril Joseph Coan (d 1979), of Hull, Yorks; 1 s (Andrew Theodore b 1961); *Career* FCA, FCCA; *Recreations* reading, music; *Style—* Sidney T Bowles, Esq; 6 Grange Road, Christchurch Road, Norwich NR2 3NH

BOWMAN, David; s of Andrew Bowman, of Edinburgh, and Sheila, *née* McDonald; *b* 10 March 1964; *Educ* Portobello HS; *m* Sept 1987, Helen Louise, da of Joe Wilkie; 2 da (Jemma b 27 March 1988, Rebecca b 15 August 1990); *Career* professional footballer; 155 appearances Hearts 1980-85, 44 appearances Coventry City 1985-86, 154 appearances Dundee Utd 1986-; Scotland: 30 youth caps, 6 under 21 caps; *Recreations* golf; *Style—* David Bowman, Esq; Dundee Utd FC, Tannadice Park, Dundee (☎ 0382 833 166)

BOWMAN, James Thomas; s of Benjamin and Cecilia Bowman; *b* 6 Nov 1941; *Educ* Ely Cathedral Choir Sch, King's Sch Ely, New Coll Oxford; *Career* counter-tenor; schoolmaster 1965-67; operatic performances with: Glyndebourne Festival Opera 1970-, Sydney Opera 1978, Opéra Comique Paris 1979, also Santa Fe, San Francisco, Dallas USA; Theatre du Châtelet Paris 1983-, Badisches Staatstheater, Karlsruhe 1984-, Royal Opera House 1972-, Eng Nat Opera 1985-, La Scala Milan 1987-, Scot Opera 1971-; prof of singing Guildhall Sch of Music; pres Hinckley Music Club; *Style—* James Bowman, Esq; 19a Wetherby Gardens, London SW5

BOWMAN, Jean, Lady; Jean; da of Henry Brooks, of Ashington, Northumberland; *m* 1922, Sir James Bowman, 1 Bt, KBE (d 1978); 1 s, 1 da; *Style—* Jean, Lady Bowman; Woodlands, Killingworth Station, Forest Hall, Newcastle upon Tyne

BOWMAN, Sir Jeffery Haverstock; s of Alfred Haverstock Bowman (d 1974), and Doris Gertrude, *née* Beck (d 1983); *b* 3 April 1935; *Educ* Winchester, Trinity Hall Cambridge (BA); *m* 15 June 1963, Susan Claudia, da of Dr Oliver Hays Bostock (d 1982), of Guernsey; 1 s (Mark b 1970), 2 da (Caroline b 1964, Victoria b 1967); *Career* 2 Lt RHG 1953-55; Price Waterhouse: articled 1958-61, mangr 1964, ptnr 1966, memb firm's Policy Ctee 1972-, dir Technical Servs 1973-76, dir London office 1979-81, sr ptnr 1982-; personal auditor Duchy of Cornwall 1971-; memb: ICAEW Accounting Standards Ctee 1982-87, ICAEW Cncl 1986-89, Cncl of the Industrial Soc 1985-, Cncl of Business in the Community 1985-; vice pres Union of Ind Companies 1983-, govr Brentwood Sch 1985-; FCA 1962; kt 1991; *Recreations* golf, opera, gardening, sailing; *Clubs* Garrick; *Style—* Sir Jeffery Bowman; The Old Rectory, Boreham, Chelmsford, Essex CM3 3EP (☎ 0245 467233); Price Waterhouse, Southwark Towers, 32 London Bridge St, London SE1 9SY (☎ 071 939 3000, fax 071 378 0647, telex 884657/8)

BOWMAN, Dr John Christopher; CBE (1986); s of Mark Christopher Bowman (d 1987), of Prestbury, and Clara Vera, *née* Simister; *b* 13 Aug 1933; *Educ* Manchester GS, Univ of Reading (BSc), Univ of Edinburgh (PhD), N Carolina State Univ; *m* 15 July 1961, Sheila Jean, da of James Lorimer (d 1953), of Bramhall; 3 da (Hilary b 1962, Jillian b 1964, Bernadette b 1968); *Career* geneticist rising to chief geneticist Thornber Bros Ltd 1958-66; Univ of Reading: prof of animal prodn (dir of Univ farms) 1966-81, dir Centre for Agric Strategy 1975-81; sec to NERC 1981-89, chief exec Nat Rivers Authy 1989-; chm Sonning Lawn Tennis Club, memb Sonning Parish Cncl; FIBioL 1970, FRSA 1976; Hon DSc, Cranfield Inst of Technol 1990; *Books* Introduction to Animal Breeding, Animals for Man, Future of Beef Production in the EEC (with P Susmel), Hammonds Farm Animals (with J Hammond Jr); *Recreations* gardening, tennis, golf; *Style—* Dr John Bowman, CBE; Farmhouse, Charvil Lane, Sonning, Reading RG4 0TH (☎ 0734 693224); National Rivers Authy, 30-34 Albert Embankment, London SE1 7TL (☎ 071 820 0101, fax 071 820 1603)

BOWMAN, Maj-Gen John Francis (Jack); CB (1986); s of Francis Bowman (d 1985), and Gladys Rose Bowman (d 1985); *b* 5 Feb 1927; *Educ* QEGS Penrith, Hertford Coll Oxford (MA); *m* 1956, Laura, da of John Moore (d 1952); 1 s (John b 1959), 1 da (Tessa b 1961); *Career* RN 1945-48 (Med, Atlantic and Antarctica), Army Maj-Gen; barr Grays Inn; dir Army Legal Services 1983-86 (served Africa, Far East, Near and MEast, UK, BAOR); life vice pres Army Boxing Assoc, memb Cncl Br Red Cross Soc; *Recreations* sailing, mountain walking, skiing; *Clubs* Royal Naval, Royal Albert Yacht; *Style—* Maj-Gen Jack Bowman, CB; c/o Midland Bank plc, Sloane Square Branch, London SW1X 9BN

BOWMAN, Sir John Paget; 4 Bt (UK 1884); s of Rev Sir Paget Mervyn Bowman, 3 Bt (d 1955); *b* 12 Feb 1904; *Educ* Eton; *m* 1, 1931, Countess Cajetana Hoyos (d 1948), da of Count Edgar Hoyos, of Schloss Soos, Lower Austria; 1 da (1 s decd); m 2, 1948, Frances Edith Marian, da of late Sir (James) Beethom Whitehead, KCMG; *Heir* kinsman, Paul Humphrey Armytage Bowman, *qv*; *Career* late 2 Lt 98 Surrey and Sussex Yeo, Field Bde RA; asst to chief accountant Western Electric London 1928-30, fin mangr Central Europe (Vienna) 1930-31, chief auditor London 1931-33, co sec Decca Record Co Ltd 1933-36, gen mangr Brymbo Steel Co Ltd 1936-40, fin mangr BSA Co Ltd 1940-43, commercial mangr Rolls-Royce Ltd (gas turbine engines) 1943-45, own business in Stoke-on-Trent 1945-48, gen mangr and dir Carter & Co Ltd Poole 1948-51, owner and mangr Purbeck Decorative Tile Co 1951-84; *Style—* Sir John Bowman, Bt; Bishops Green House, Greenham Common South, nr Newbury, Berks RG15 8HS (☎ 0635 268 202)

BOWMAN, Stephen Lindsay; s of Robert Lindsay Bowman, of 108 Fryent Way, Kingsbury, London NW9 9SE, and Violet Elizabeth, *née* Lovelock; *b* 14 Feb 1950; *Educ* Preston Manor GS; *m* 10 Oct 1980, Marion Grace, da of Stanley Edward Kisbee (d 1985); 1 s (Gavin Lindsay b 12 June 1983); *Career* ptnr Blackborn Graham (CAs) 1983-; ACA 1975, FCA 1981; *Clubs* IOD; *Style—* Stephen L Bowman, Esq; Blackborn Graham, Greencoat House, Francis St, London SW1P 1DH (☎ 071 834 9434, fax 071 834 1592, car 0836 204 222)

BOWMAN, William Archibald; s of Archibald George Bowman (d 1978), of Auchtermuchty, and Eleanor Little, *née* Ratcliff; *b* 30 May 1950; *Educ* George Watson's Coll Edinburgh, Univ of Edinburgh (BCom); *m* 10 April 1973, Helen Macaulay, da of Malcolm Macleod, of Strathkinness; *Career* CA, ptnr KPMG Peat Marwick McLintock; *Clubs* Royal Northern, University (Aberdeen); *Style—* William A Bowman, Esq; c/o KPMG Peat Marwick McLintock, Royfold House, Hill of Rubislaw, Anderson Drive, Aberdeen AB9 1JE (☎ 0224 208888, telex 739972, fax 0224 208027)

BOWMAN, William Cameron; s of John William Bowman (d 1976), of Carlisle, and Esther Reed, *née* Cameron (d 1980); *b* 26 April 1930; *Educ* Univ of London (BPharm, PhD, DSc); *m* 12 Aug 1972, Anne Wyllie, da of Frank Douglas Stafford (d 1968), of Sydney; 1 s (Ewen Cameron), 1 da (Alison); *Career* Nat Serv RAF 1955-57; lectr then reader Univ of London 1952-66; Univ of Strathclyde: prof pharmacology and head of dept 1966-86, dean Sch of Pharmaceutical Sciences 1974-77, dep princ then vice princ 1986-90; praelector Med Sch Univ of Dundee 1985, Litchfield lectr Med Sch Univ of Oxford 1986, visiting prof anaesthesia McGill Univ Montreal 1987, visiting Sterling prof pharmacology Cornell Univ NY 1989; author of numerous articles on res, served twelve editorial bds sci jnls (currently on seven); memb: Nomenclature Ctee Br Pharmacopoeia Cmmn 1964-67, Biology Ctee MOD 1966-75, TCT and SEAR Sub Ctees of CSM 1972-82, Biomedical Res Ctee SHHD 1980-85, Physiological Soc, Br Pharmacological Soc, NY Acad of Sciences, Br Toxicological Soc, Scot Soc of Experimental Med; fell: Royal Pharmaceutical Soc, RSM;Hon FFARCS 1986, FIBiol, FRSE, FRSA; *Books* ed of several books, author of Textbook of Pharmacology (with M J Rand, 1986, 2 edn 1980), Pharmacology of Neuromuscular Function (1980, 2 edn 1990), Dictionary of Pharmacology (with Anne Bowman and Alison Bowman, 1986); *Style—* Prof William C Bowman, FRSE; Dept of Physiology & Pharmacology, University of Strathclyde, Glasgow G1 1XW (☎ 041 552 4400, fax 041 552 0775, telex 77472 unslib g)

BOWMAN, William Powell; OBE (1972); s of George Edward Bowman (d 1977), and Isobel Conyers Dix (d 1971); *b* 22 Oct 1932; *Educ* Uppingham; *m* 26 April 1956,

Patricia Elizabeth, da of Wallace Normand McCoskrie, of Hemel Hempstead, Herts; 2 s (Jonathan b 1957, Edward b 1959); *Career* RAF 1951-53, Royal Aux Air Force 1953-58, Flying Offr (UK); gp personnel dir United Biscuits plc 1977-84 (md Int Div 1966-77, chm Van der Haas BV Holland 1987-89; dir: Twynam and Fishlock Advertising Ltd 1987-88, Harvey Bergenroth Ptnrs Ltd (mgmnt conslts) 1987-89, Right Assocs Ltd 1989-; chm: Trident Tst 1985-, Occupational Counselling and Unemployment Services Ltd 1986-89, Covent Garden Market Authy 1988-, Br Food and Farming (Bucks Ctee) 1987-89, Flowers and Plants Assoc 1989-, Gibbson Blackthorn Ltd 1989-90; dir Fresh Fruit Produce Assoc 1989-, tstee London Zoological Devpt Soc Cncl 1986-, chm St Peters Tst 1990-, fell London Zoological Soc; Freeman City of London 1989, memb Guild of Freeman 1989; FInstD, FInstM, MInstM, FIPM, Fell Royal Soc of Arts Manufacture and Sci 1989-; *Recreations* gardening, tennis, travel; *Clubs* RAF, White Elephant; *Style—* William Bowman, Esq, OBE; The Coach House, Shardeloes, Old Amersham, Bucks HP7 0RL (☎ 0494 724 187)

BOWMAN SHAW, Sir (George) Neville; s of George Bowman-Shaw; *b* 4 Oct 1930; *Educ* privately; *m* 1962, Georgina, da of G Blundell; 3 s, 1 da; *Career* chm: Lancer Boss Gp 1966-, Lancer Boss France 1967-, Lancer Boss Austria 1966-, Boss Trucks 1959-, Lancer Boss Int SA Lausanne 1962-, Boss Engrs 1961-, Boss Espana 1984-, Boss Trucks Espana 1984-, Steinbock GmbH Moosburg 1984-; memb: Design Cncl 1979-84, Br Overseas Trade Bd 1982-85; kt 1984; *Recreations* shooting, farming, rare breeds and vintage tractors collections; *Clubs* Cavalry & Guards, Carlton, Constitutional; *Style—* Sir Neville Bowman-Shaw; Toddington Manor, Toddington, Beds (☎ 052 55 2576); Lancer Boss Group Ltd, Grovebury Rd, Leighton Buzzard, Beds (☎ 0525 372031)

BOWMER, Christopher Kenneth John; s of Kenneth Claude Bowmer, of Farnham, Surrey, and Violet Audrey, *née* Appleton; *b* 13 Dec 1946; *Educ* Farnham GS, Univ of Leeds (BSc); *m* 28 March 1970, Rosalind Elizabeth Georgina, da of Kenneth Prosser, of Chester; 1 s (Simon b 1973), 1 da (Clare b 1971); *Career* fin dir Bowater Consumer Packaging Ltd 1980-85 (fin controller 1978-80), treas Bowater plc 1988-; memb London Treasurers Club; ACMA 1973; *Recreations* tennis, theatre, music; *Clubs* Surrey Tennis and Country; *Style—* Christopher Bowmer, Esq; 114 Burdon Lane, Cheam, Surrey SM2 7DA (☎ 081 643 7156); Bowater Industries plc, Bowater House, Knightsbridge, London SW1X 7NN (☎ 071 584 7070, fax 071 581 1149)

BOWMONT AND CESSFORD, Marquess of; Charles Robert George Innes-Ker; s and h of 10 Duke of Roxburghe by Lady Jane Grosvenor, da of 5 Duke of Westminster; *b* 18 Feb 1981; *Style—* Marquess of Bowmont and Cessford

BOWN, Prof Lalage Jean; OBE 1977; da of Arthur Mervyn Bown (d 1969), MC, of Woolstaston Hall, Shropshire, and Dorothy Ethel, *née* Watson; *b* 1 April 1927; *Educ* Wycombe Abbey, Cheltenham, Somerville Coll Oxford (BA, MA); *m*; 2 foster da (Taiwo b 1956, Kehinde (twin) b 1956); *Career* resident tutor Univ Coll of the Gold Coast (now Univ of Ghana) 1949-55, res tutor Makerere Univ Coll of Uganda 1955-59, assoc prof of the Extra-Mural Dept Univ of Ibadan Nigeria 1962-66 (tutorial advsr, asst dir and dep dir 1960-62), dir of extra-mural studies and prof Univ of Zambia 1966-70, prof of adult educn Ahmadu Bello Univ Nigeria 1971-76, dean of educn Univ of Lagos 1979-80 (prof of adult educn 1977-79), dir and titular prof Dept of Adult and Continuing Educn Univ of Glasgow 1981-; author of several academic books, monographs and articles; cwlth visiting prof Univ of Edinburgh, visiting fell Inst of Devpt Univ of Sussex and faculty fell Univ of Southampton 1977-79; hon life memb People's Educn Assoc Ghana 1973, hon life memb African Adult Educn Assoc 1976; memb bd Br cncl 1981-89; memb: Scottish Community Educn Cncl 1982-89, governing body Inst of Devpt Studies 1982-; pres Devpt Studies Assoc 1984-86; vice pres: Nat Union of Townswomens Guilds, Workers Educnls Assoc 1984-; pres Br Comparative Int Educn Soc 1985-86, memb bd of tstees of Nat Museums of Scotland 1987-, tstee Womankind Worldwide 1988-, Br memb Cwlth Standing Ctee for Student Mobility and Higher Educn 1989-; hon D Open Univ; FRSA 1984-; *Recreations* travel, entertaining friends; *Clubs* Royal Overseas League; *Style—* Prof Lalage Bown; Dept of Adult and Continuing Education, University of Glasgow, 57/61 Oakfield Ave, Glasgow, G12 8LW Scotland (☎ 041 339 8855 ext 4392, telex 777070 UNIGLA, fax 041 330 4808)

BOWN, Michael John David; s of Gordon Burley Bown (d 1979), of Leicester, and Sybil Charlotte, *née* Ellis (d 1973); *b* 22 May 1932; *Educ* Wyggeston Sch Leicester, Univ of Tubingen Germany, Queens' Coll Cambridge (BA, MA); *m* 2 July 1955, Dora Winifred, da of Wilfrid (d 1980), of Freckleton, Lancs; 2 s (Christopher b 1956, Jeremy b 1962), 1 da (Stephanie b 1959); *Career* Nat Serv RA 2 Lt 1954-56; euro mangr Unicam Instruments Ltd 1958-60, mgmnt conslt PA Mgmnt Conslts Ltd 1960-64, dir and gen mangr John Dale Ltd 1964-69, chief exec Sturtevant Engrg Co Ltd and subsids 1969-74, gp pres Peabody Int Corp 1974-82, chm Contessa Yachts Ltd 1982-85, dir UK Centre for Econ and Environmental Devpt 1984-86, dep chief exec Darchem Ltd 1986-88, business conslt 1988-; FRSA; *Recreations* sailing, hill walking, theatre, opera; *Clubs* United Oxford & Cambridge, Royal Lymington Yacht; *Style—* Michael Bown, Esq; 7 Kreisel Walk, Kew Green, Richmond, Surrey (☎ 081 940 6775); Les Merisiers, Avenue Marie-Louise, 62520 Le Touquet, France (☎ 010 33 21 05 01 23)

BOWN, Philip Arnold; MBE (1987); s of Ernest Bown (d 1984), and Gladys Bown; *b* 1 Sept 1934; *Educ* King Edwards Bath, Newport HS; *m* 28 April 1962, Diana, *née* Richards; 1 s (Damian), 3 da (Olivia, Tiffany, Coralie); *Career* Lt RA 1957-59; CA; Peat Marwick 1951-56, United Transport plc and subsids 1959-85 (dir 1977-85), chm and chief exec Brushes International 1979-; High Sheriff Co of Gwent 1989-90; gen cmmr of Income Tax; FCA, CBIM; *Recreations* sailing; *Clubs* Royal Yacht Sqdn, Royal Thames Yacht, Royal Soc Arts; *Style—* Philip A Bown, Esq; Uplands, Chepstow, Gwent NP6 6BQ (☎ 0291 622419); Brushes Int Ltd, Lower Church St, Chepstow, Gwent NP6 5XT (☎ 0291 279022, fax 0291 622356)

BOWN, Prof Stephen Glendening; s of Eric Inston Bown (d 1988), of Bexhill-on-Sea, and Olive Mary Kirkman, *née* Payne; *b* 13 Dec 1944; *Educ* St Dunstan's Coll Catford, Univ of Cambridge (MA, MB BChir, MD), Harvard Univ (AM); *m* 3 April 1982, Sheila Alyson, da of Peter Taylor, of Bexhill-on-Sea; 1 da (Philippa Lucy b 1989); *Career* dir Nat Med Laser Centre at UCL 1986-, conslt physician UCH 1987-, ICRF prof of laser med and surgery 1990-, past pres Br Med Laser Assoc; approximately 150 sci pubns on med applications of lasers, currently ed Lasers in Medical Science; Freeman City of London 1982; memb: Br Soc Gastroenterology 1977, BMA 1974; MRCP 1974; *Recreations* squash, sailing; *Style—* Prof Stephen Bown; 10 Watling St, St Albans, Herts AL1 2PX (☎ 0727 833701); National Medical Laser Centre, Dept of Surgery, Rayne Institute, 5 University St, London WC1E 6JJ (☎ 071 380 9801, fax 071 387 1710)

BOWNESS, Sir Alan; CBE (1976); er s of George Bowness (d 1951), and Kathleen, *née* Benton (d 1973); *b* 11 Jan 1928; *Educ* Univ Coll Sch Hampstead, Downing Coll Cambridge (MA), Courtauld Inst of Art Univ of London; *m* 1957, Sarah, da of Ben Nicholson, OM (d 1982), the painter, and Dame Barbara Hepworth, DBE (d 1975), the sculptor; 1 s (Paul), 1 da (Sophie); *Career* lectr, reader and finally prof & dep dir Courtauld Inst of Art (Univ of Lon 1957-79; dir Tate Gallery 1980-88; dir Henry Moore Fndn 1988-; kt 1988; *Clubs* Athenaeum; *Style—* Sir Alan Bowness, CBE; 91 Castelnau, London SW13 (☎ 081 748 9696)

BOWNESS, Sir Peter Spencer; CBE (1981), DL (Greater London 1982); s of Hubert Spencer Bowness (d 1981), and Doreen (Peggy) Blundell, *née* Davies; *b* 19 May 1943; *Educ* Whitgift Sch Croydon; *m* 1, 27 July 1969, Marianne Hall; 1 da (Caroline b 1978); m 2, 6 June 1984, Mrs Patricia Jane Cook; *Career* slr; chm London Boroughs Assoc 1978-; dep chm Assoc Metropolitan Authys 1978-80; ldr Croydon Cncl 1976-79 and 1980-; memb: Audit Cmmn England & Wales 1983-, London Residuary Body 1985-, govr Whitgift Fndn; ret 1986; Freeman City of London 1987; kt 1987; *Recreations* travel, theatre; *Clubs* Carlton; *Style—* Sir Peter Bowness, CBE, DL

BOWRING, Lt-Col (Henry) Christopher White; s of Henry Illingworth Bowring (d 1934), of Whelprigg, Barbon, Westmorland, and Margaret Hardcastle, *née* White (d 1973); *Educ* Marlborough, Univ Coll Oxford (BA); *m* 4 Sept 1939, Helen Lydia Victoria, da of Rev David Denholm Fraser (d 1948), of Kelso, Roxburghshire; 1 s (Henry Charles Fraser b 30 April 1949), 3 da (Victoria Ann b 25 July 1941, Priscilla Jane b 11 August 1943, Bridget Charlotte Helen b 21 Feb 1948); *Career* cmmnd 2 Bn Royal Fus 1932, 1 Bn Royal Fus Ahmednegar India 1933-35, sick leave due to typhoid fever 1935-37, rejoined 2 Bn 1937-39, BEF 1939-40 (evacuated Dunkirk), Staff Coll Camberley 1941, GSO 2 Corps Dist Newmarket, Staff Duties N Africa, ret 1948; qualified land agent, ptnr Davis & Bowring, ret 1971; High Sheriff of Westmorland 1955, JP Westmorland, DL Westmorland (subsequently Cumbria), lay reader Carlisle Dio, prison visitor (open prison Milnthrope), memb Carlisle Diocesan Dilapidation Bd; FLAS 1961, FRICS; *Recreations* shooting, fishing; *Clubs* Army & Navy; *Style—* Lt-Col Christopher Bowring; Willow Cottage, Arkholme, Carnforth, Lancs (☎ 05242 21 205)

BOWRING, Edgar Rennie Harvey; MC (1945); yst s of Arthur Bowring (d 1960), of Goudhurst, Kent, and Margaret Harvey, *née* Beakbane (d 1944); *b* 5 Nov 1915; *Educ* Eastbourne Coll, Clare Coll Cambridge (MA), Berkeley Coll Yale, Law Soc Sch of Law; *m* 6 April 1940, Margaret (Peggy) Grace, da of John Grant Brook (d 1938), of Goudhurst, Kent; 2 s (Anthony b 1941, Philip b 1942), 1 da (Clare b 1959); *Career* cmmnd Kent Yeo RA 1939, served in Iceland 1940-42, Capt 1941, served in UK 1942-44, Maj 1942, served in France and Germany 1944-45 (despatches 1944), demob 1946, acting Lt-Col; slr 1949; ptnr Cripps Harries Hall 1950-55; joined C T Bowring & Co (Insurance) Ltd 1956 (dir 1960), dir C T Bowring & Co Ltd 1962, chm English and American Insurance Co Ltd 1965-71, dep chm C T Bowring (Insurance) Holdings Ltd 1966-73, chm and chief exec C T Bowring & Co Ltd 1973-78; chm: C T Bowring Insurance Holdings, Bowmaker Ltd, Crusader Insurance Co Ltd and other cos 1973-77; dir Marsh & McLennan Cos Inc New York USA 1980-88 (advsy dir 1988-); Cmdt W Kent Special Constabulary 1965-71; tstee Memorial Univ of Newfoundland, Harlow Campus 1977-; pres Insurance Inst of London 1971-72 (dep pres 1970-71); vice pres Corporation of Insurance Brokers 1970-77; memb Insurance Brokers Registration Cncl 1979-81; chm City Ctee for Electoral Reform 1978-81; CBIM (FBIM 1970); *Recreations* golf, gardening; *Clubs* City Univ, Rye Golf, Piltdown Golf; *Style—* Edgar Bowring Esq, MC; Leopards Mill, Horam, Heathfield, East Sussex TN21 OPD (☎ 043 53 2687); The Bowring Building, Tower Place, London EC3 (☎ 071 283 3100)

BOWRING, Maj-Gen John Humphrey Stephen; CB (1968), OBE (1958), MC (1941); s of Maj Francis Stephen Bowring (ka 1915), and Helen Jessie, *née* McNabb (d 1945); *b* 13 Feb 1913; *Educ* Downside, RMA Woolwich, Trinity Coll Cambridge (MA); *m* 20 Oct 1956, Iona Margaret, da of Lenox Biggar Murray, OBE (d 1963), of Painswick Lodge, Painswick, Glos; 2 s (Charles b 1957, Michael b 1961), 2 da (Caroline (twin) b 1957, Camilla b 1959); *Career* 2 Lt RE 1933; served: Palestine 1936, India 1937-40; WWII: ME, Burma, BMM Greece 1947-49; GSO I Cabinet Offices 1949-51, CRE 17 Gurkha Div Malaya 1956-58, chief engr Farelf (Brig) 1961-64, Brig GS MOD 1964-65 (Col 1959-60), engr in chief (Army) 1965-68 (Maj-Gen), Col Gurkha Engrs 1966-71, Col Cmdt RE 1968-73; dir: Consolidated Gold Fields 1969-82, Amey Roadstone Corp 1971-82; High Sheriff Wilts 1984; FICE 1965; kt Sovereign Mil Order of Malta 1986; *Recreations* sailing, flying, riding; *Clubs* Army & Navy, Royal Ocean Racing; *Style—* Maj-Gen J H S Bowring, CB, OBE, MC; 4 The Manor, Coln St Aldwyns, Cirencester, Glos GL7 5AG (☎ 0285 75 492)

BOWRING, Rev Lyndon; s of Arthur Bowing, of Caerphilly, Mid Glam, and Ellen May, *née* Gardner; *b* 15 Feb 1948; *Educ* Caerphilly GS, London Bible Coll; *m* 25 May 1974, Celia Joan, da of Capt Edward Ernest Bartholomew (d 1983), of Shoreham-by-Sea; 2 s (Daniel Alexander, Andrew Gareth), 1 da (Emma Charlotte); *Career* Elim pentecostal minister Kensington Temple 1972-80, chm NFOL 1981-83, exec chm CARE 1983-; vice chm: Luis Palau's Mission 1984, Billy Graham's Mission 1989; chm Maranatha Christian Tst; dir Kingsway Pubns and Music, London and Nationwide Missions; public speaker; *Recreations* family, reading, walking, gardening, exploring London; *Style—* The Rev Lyndon Bowring; 22 Thornton Ave, Chiswick, London W4 (☎ 081 747 3796); CARE, 53 Romney St, London SW1 (☎ 071 233 0455, fax 07 233 0983)

BOWRING, Peter; eld s of Frederick Clive Bowring (d 1965), and Agnes Walker, *née* Cairns (d 1961); *b* 22 April 1923; *Educ* Shrewsbury; *m* 1, 1946 (m dis), Barbara Ekaterina Brewis; 1 s (Antony), 1 da (Thérèsa); m 2, 1979 (m dis), Carol Hutchings; m 3, 1986, Carole M Dear; *Career* served WWII 1941-46, cmmnd Rifle Brigade 1942, served Egypt, N Africa, Italy, Austria (despatches); chm: Help the Aged 1977-87 (pres 1988-), C T Bowring & Co 1978-82; vice chm Marsh & McLennan 1982-84 (dir 1980-84), dir Centre for Policy Studies 1983-88; memb of Lloyds; dir Ind Primary and Secdy Educn Tst; chm: Aldeburgh Fndn 1982-89, City Arts Tst 1987- (dep chm 1986-87), Inter-Action Social Enterprise Tst Ltd 1989-91, (chm 1977-1990) Bd of Govrs St Dunstan's Educnl Fndn (govr 1974-); memb Bd of Govrs Shrewsbury Sch; tstee: Ironbridge Gorge Museum Devpt Tst, Upper Severn Navigation Tst; memb Guild of Freemen of City of London, Liveryman Worshipful Co of Insurers, Master Guild of World Traders 1989-90 (sr warden 1988-89); FRSA, FlustD; *Recreations* sailing, motoring, listening to music, cooking, photography; *Clubs* Royal Thames Yacht, Royal Green Jackets; *Style—* Peter Bowring, Esq; 79 New Concordia Wharf, Mill St, London SE1 2BA (☎ 071 237 0818)

BOWRING, Prof Richard John; s of Richard Arthur Bowring (d 1987), and Mabel, *née* Eddy; *b* 6 Feb 1947; *Educ* Blundell's, Downing Coll Cambridge (BA, PhD); *m* 30 Jan 1970, Susan, da of Wilfred Raymond Povey, of Stoke-on-Trent; 1 da (Imogen Clare b 17 May 1977); *Career* mgmnt trainee Cathay Pacific Airways 1968-70, lectr in Japanese Monash Univ Melbourne Aust 1976-78, asst prof of Japanese Columbia Univ NY USA 1978-79, assoc prof of Japanese Princeton Univ New Jersey USA 1979-84, prof of mod Japanese studies Univ of Cambridge 1985- (lectr in Japanese 1984); *Books* Mori Oqai and the Modernisation of Japanese Culture (1979), Murasaki Shikibu: Her Diary and Poetic Memoirs (1982), Murasaki Shikibu: The Tale of Genji (1988); *Style—* Prof Richard Bowring; Faculty of Oriental Studies, University of Cambridge, Sidgwick Ave, Cambridge CB3 9DA (☎ 0223 335106, fax 0223 335110)

BOWRON, John Lewis; CBE (1986); s of John Henry Bowron (d 1944), and Lavinia, *née* Prosser (d 1967); *b* 1 Feb 1924; *Educ* Grangefield GS Stockton on Tees, King's Coll London (LLB); *m* 19 Aug 1950, Patricia, da of Arthur Cobby (d 1959) of Worthing; 2 da (Judith b 1952, Margaret b 1956); *Career* RAF 1943-46; slr 1950; ptnr Malcolm Wilson & Cobby, slrs, Worthing 1952 (sr ptnr 1964-74); sec general of The Law Society 1974, ret 1987; fell King's Coll London 1976; legal assessor Insur Brokers Registration Cncl 1987-; memb Disciplinary Appeals Ctee of the Stock

Exchange; pt/t chm Social Security Appeal Tbnl 1988-; *Recreations* golf, listening to music; *Style—* John Bowron, Esq; Wellington Cottage, Albourne, Hassocks, West Sussex BN6 9DE (☎ 0273 833345)

BOWSER OF ARGATY AND THE KING'S LUNDIES, David Stewart; JP (Perthshire 1956); s of Maj David Charles Bowser, CBE, (d 1979), and Maysie Murray, *née* Henderson (d 1974); in direct descent from William Bowser of Wharram le Street, Yorkshire, who lived in the mid 15 century; *b* 11 March 1926; *Educ* Harrow, Trinity Coll Cambridge (BA); *m* 1951, Judith, da of Col Sir John Gordon Crabbe, OBE, MC (d 1961), of Duncow, Dumfries; 1 s (Niall), 4 da (Emma, Susan, Fiona, Anna); *Career* Capt Scots Guards 1944-47; forestry cmmr 1974-82, tstee Scottish Forestry Tst 1983-89 (chm 1987-88); chm Scot Cncl The Br Deer Soc 1988-; memb Queen's Body Guard for Scotland (Royal Company of Archers); elder Killin and Ardeonaig Parish Church, convener Property Ctee of the Presbytery of Stirling; *Recreations* shooting, fishing, stalking; *Style—* David Bowser, Esq, JP; Auchlyne, Killin, Perthshire FK21 8RG (☎ 05672 506)

BOWSHER, Dr David Richard; s of Reginald William George Bowsher (d 1971), of Bishop's Cleeve, Glos, and Marion Bowsher, *née* Scott (d 1966); *b* 23 Feb 1925; *Educ* Haileybury, Gonville and Caius Coll Cambridge (MA, MD), Univ of Liverpool (PhD), UCH, Harvard Med Sch Boston USA; *m* 1, 1952 (m dis 1959), (Anna) Meryl, *née* Reid; 1 s (Julian Michael Charles b 1953); m 2, 1 April 1969, Doreen, da of Lawrence Arthur (d 1971); *Career* professeur associé Faculté des Sciences de Paris 1963-64, Cncl of Europe Res Fell Uppsala 1970 (Oslo and Leyden 1958), reader Faculty of Med Univ of Liverpool 1972- (res fell 1952-54, asst lectr 1954-56, lectr 1956-64, sr lectr 1964-72), Royal Soc Euro Fell Paris 1968-69, Marseilles 1974, professeur associé Facultié des Sciences de Marseille 1986, currently dir of res and tstee Pain Relief Fndn, author over 160 articles in med and scientific jls; hon conslt Mersey Regnl Centre for Pain Relief; former pres: Br and Irish Chapter Int Assoc for the Study of Pain, North of England Neurological Assoc, Liverpool div BMA; pres Burke and Hare Soc, ed Neuroscience Clinical Anatomy, chm Merseyside and N Wales Pain Gp; memb: Physiological Soc, Association des Physiologistes de Langue Française, Brain Res Assoc; memb: RCPEd, RCPath; *Books* Cerebrospinal Fluid Dynamics in Health and Disease (1960), Mechanisms of Nervous Disorder: An Introduction (1978), Introduction to the Anatomy and Physiology of the Nervous System (ed 1988) (ed, 1988), Pain: Management and Control in Physiotherapy (jtly, 1988), Neurological Emergencies in Medical Practice (1988); *Recreations* walking, language and languages, opera and music, history, uxoriousness; *Style—* Dr David Bowsher; Pain Research Institute, Walton Hospital, Liverpool L9 1AE (☎ 051 523 1486, fax 051 521 6155)

BOWSHER, His Hon Judge Peter Charles; QC (1978); s of Charles Bowsher, and Ellen Bowsher; *b* 9 Feb 1935; *Educ* Ardingly, Oriel Coll Oxford; *m* 1960, Deborah, da of Frederick Wilkins, of Vancouver; 2 s; *Career* barrister 1959, rec of Crown Ct SE circuit 1983-87, bencher of the Middle Temple 1985-, official referee and circuit judge 1987-; FCIArb 1990-; *Clubs* Brooks's, RAC; *Style—* His Hon Judge Bowsher, QC; Royal Courts of Justice, Strand, London WC2A 2LL

BOWSKILL, (Ronald) John; *b* 27 March 1944; *Educ* King Edward VII GS Retford; *Career* regnl admin trainee 1963-65, costing asst Sheffield Regnl Hosp Bd 1965-66, gen admin asst Gp HQ Nottingham Hosp Mgmnt Ctee 1966-68, hosp sec Nottingham Childrens' Hosp 1968-71, acting gp personnel offr Univ of Nottingham Hosp Mgmnt Ctee 1971; Sunderland Health Authy: hosp sec 1972-74, sector admin 1974-82, unit admin 1982-85, unit gen mangr 1985-; chm Sunderland Rotary Club Vocational Servs Ctee 1988-; *Recreations* all sports, walking; *Style—* John Bowskill, Esq; 1 Woodside, East Herrington, Sunderland, Tyne & Wear SR3 3SJ (☎ 091 5200595); (☎ business 091 5656256)

BOWTELL, Ann Elizabeth; *née* Kewell; CB (1989); da of John Albert Kewell, of Hove, and Olive Rose, *née* Sims; *b* 25 April 1938; *Educ* Kendrick Girls Sch Reading, Girton Coll Cambridge (BA); *m* 11 Feb 1961, Michael John Bowtell, s of Norman Bowtell; 2 s (Thomas, Samuel), 2 da (Sophie, Harriet); *Career* asst princ Nat Assistance Bd 1960-64; DHSS: princ 1964-73, asst sec 1973-80, under sec 1980-86, dep sec 1986-88; DSS 1988-90, Dept of Health 1990-; *Style—* Mrs Michael Bowtell, CB; DHSS, Richmond House, Whitehall (☎ 071 210 5459)

BOWYER, Barry Robert; s of Flt-Lt Frederick George Bowyer (d 1955), of Purley, Surrey, and Norah Margaret, *née* Bonwick (d 1966); *b* 31 July 1936; *Educ* Glenwood Sch Surrey; *m* 1962, Gillian Margaret, da of Walter Henry Mann (d 1948), of Suffolk; 3 s (Christopher b 1964, Jonathan b 1967, Robert b 1969); *Career* RAF 1956-59; tech advsr to electronics indust 1959-63, publishing and advtg accounts mangr 1963-67, founded Bowyer Design Consultancy Ltd 1967 (added BD Advtg 1978, BD PR in 1980); memb (Cons) Ashford Borough Cncl (representing Biddenden Ward); govr John Mayne Sch; MIPR; *Recreations* vintage cars, painting, sculpture, travel; *Clubs* Naval & Military, Bentley Drivers, Aston Martin Owners; *Style—* Barry Bowyer, Esq; Tollgate House, Biddenden, Ashford, Kent (☎ 0580 291830/291 560, fax 0580 292 080)

BOWYER, (Arthur) David; s of Sir Eric Blacklock Bowyer, KCB, KBE, (d 1964), and Elizabeth Crane, *née* Nicholls, now Lady Caine w of late Sir Sidney Caine, KCMG (d 1991); *b* 27 Aug 1940; *Educ* Tonbridge, Trinity Hall Cambridge (BA); *m* 6 Dec 1969, Ann Victoria, da of His Hon Judge Herbert Christopher Beaumont, MBE, *qv*, of Minskip Lodge, Minskip, Boroughbridge, Yorks; 2 s (Edward Christopher b 1972, Andrew Mark b 1975), 1 da (Katharine Sarah b 1971); *Career* admitted slr 1965; ptnr Clifford Chance (formerly Clifford-Turner) 1968-; memb: Law Society 1976, Int Acad of Estate and Tst Law (USA); *Recreations* skiing, golf, tennis, shooting; *Clubs* Boodles; *Style—* David Bowyer, Esq; Ashe Warren House, Ashe Warren, Overton, Basingstoke, Hants, RG25 3AW (☎ 0256 770 215); Clifford Chance, Blackfriars House, 19 New Bridge Street, London, EC4 (☎ 071 353 0211)

BOWYER, Hon Jocelyn Jane; o da of 2 Baron Denham; *b* 18 Oct 1957; *Educ* Riddlesworth Hall, Sherborne Sch for Girls; *Career* chartered physiotherapist; *Style—* The Hon Jocelyn Bowyer; The Farmhouse, 23 Broadhinton Rd, London SW4

BOWYER, (Arthur) William; s of Arthur Bowyer (d 1979), of Leek, Staffs, and Emma Bowyer (d 1983); *b* 25 May 1926; *Educ* Burslem Sch of Art, Royal Coll of Art; *m* Vera Mary, da of William Norman Small (d 1986); 2 s (Francis David b 1951, Jason Richard b 1957), 1 da (Emma Jane b 1966); *Career* Bevin Boy Sneyd Colliery Burslem 1942-44; teacher Gravesend Sch of Art, Central Sch of Art, Walthamstow Sch of Art, Sir John Cass head of fine art Maidstone Coll of Art 1971-81, ret to paint; work in collections: Royal Acad, Royal Soc of Painters in Watercolour, Nat Portrait Gallery, Graves Gallery Sheffield, Arts Cncl of GB; hon sec New English Art Club; ARA 1964; memb: Royal Soc of Painters in Watercolour 1969, Royal Acad 1973, Royal Soc of Portrait Painters; *Recreations* cricket, swimming; *Clubs* Arts; *Style—* William Bowyer, Esq; 12 Cleveland Avenue, Chiswick, London W4 (☎ 081 994 0346); Studio, 8 Gainsborough Rd, Chiswick, London W4

BOWYER-SMYTH, Sir Thomas Weyland; 15 Bt (E 1661); s of Capt Sir Philip Weyland Bowyer-Smyth, 14 Bt, RN (d 1978); *b* 25 June 1960; *Heir* kinsman, John Windham; *Style—* Sir Thomas Bowyer-Smyth, Bt

BOWYER-SMYTH, Lady; Veronica Mary; 2 da of Capt Cyril Whichelo Bower, DSC, RN (ret), of Rose Cottage, Fordwich, Kent; *m* 1951, as his 2 w, Capt Sir Philip Weyland Bowyer-Smyth, 14 Bt, RN (d 1978); 1 s, 1 da, (and 1 s decd); *Style—* Lady Bowyer-Smyth

BOX, Stephen Thomas; s of Thomas George, of Nuneaton, and Edith Helen, *née* Reid; *Educ* Queen Elizabeth GS Atherstone, Univ of Salford (BSc), Physical Electronics City Business Sch (DipBA); *m* 8 Jan 1988, Sarah, da of Dennis Grimwood Roscow; 2 da (Daisy Philippa b 24 Aug 1988, Imogen Poppy b 9 Aug 1990); *Career* sci offr AERE Harwell 1968-74, computer conslt CSI Ltd 1974-76, systems analyst Chase Manhattan Bank 1976-78, head int systems devpt Citicorp 1978-80, freelance mgmnt cnslt 1980-86, dir debt securities ops Kleinwort Benson Ltd 1987-89, mgmnt conslt and co fin Stephen Box & Co 1989-; *Recreations* shooting, tennis, golf, music, opera; *Style—* Stephen T Box, Esq; Woodmans Farm, Perrymans Lane, Burwash, East Sussex, TN19 7DN (☎ 0435 882 812, fax 0435 883443)

BOX-GRAINGER, Christopher Charles Walter; s of Walter Thomas Reginald Box (d 1970), of Rainham, Essex, and Olive Maud, *née* Henley (d 1976); *b* 18 April 1921; *Educ* Hugh Myddleton Sch, City and Guilds Inst, Victoria Coll Alexandria, El Azhar Univ Cairo (BA), Brunel Coll Technol (DipTech); *m* 23 Nov 1951, Jane Avril, da of George Kenneth Hampshire (d 1964), of Hallam Court, Hallam St, London; 1 s (Paul b Aug 1954), 2 da (Eve b Jan 1953, Jill b April 1957); *Career* GPO Film Unit and Crown Film Unit 1937-39; War serv 1939-46; Features and Outside Broadcasting Depts BBC and freelance radio and theatre work UK and N America 1946-54; dir: Hampshire Tutorials Ltd 1969-, Cricket Soc Ltd 1969-81, L'École Hampshire Sarl France 1977-, Telephone Rentals Gp 1979-88 (joined 1954); exec dir Telecommunications Engrg & Mfrg Assoc Ltd 1980-86 (joined 1967), dir Peter Nicholas & Co Ltd 1986-; chm Working Pty on Telecommunications for Disabled RNIB/TEMA, hon admin Hants Sch 50 Anniversary Educnl Tst; chm: Cricket Soc 1967-81 (joined 1953), MCC 1970-73, MCCU Sub ctees 1973-85, Cricket Welfare Fund 1986-; Freeman City of London 1985, Liveryman Worshipful Co Marketors 1982; FRGS (1953), MIProdE 1959, MBIM 1959, FInstBE 1981, FInstM 1981; Order of the Nile Egypt 1943, Silver Cross of Liberation Greece 1946; *Recreations* cricket, writing, reading, geographical survey, wine and food; *Clubs* MCC, The Cricket Soc, RAC, Jesters Lord's Taveners, Eccentric; *Style—* Christopher Box-Grainger, Esq; 23 Melton Court, Old Brompton Rd, London SW7 3JQ (☎ 071 584 0744); 42 Urbanización Doña Pillar, Mijas, Malaga, Spain; L'Éole Hampshire, SARL, Veyrines-de-Domme, 24250 Domme, Dordogne France (☎ 01033 53 29 53 15)

BOXALL, Bernard; CBE (1963); s of Arthur Sidney Boxall (d 1960), of Banstead, Surrey, and Maude Mary, *née* Mills (d 1974); *b* 17 Aug 1906; *Educ* King's Coll Sch Wimbledon, Imperial Coll London (BSc); *m* 11 July 1931, Marjorie Lilian, da of William George Emery (d 1959), of Deal, Kent; 1 s (Gerald b 27 May 1936), 1 da (Caroline Jill b 17 March 1939); *Career* gen mangr J A King & Co Ltd 1934-41, mgmnt cnslt P E Int 1942-59; dir: Export Packing Serv Ltd 1954-77, Booker Bros (Engineering Holdings) Ltd 1956-62; chm Scot Aviation Ltd 1957-66, memb SBAC 1959-65, dep chm Lindustries Ltd 1960-70, mgmnt cnslt Bernard Boxall CBE 1960-, dep chm Alvis Ltd 1963-67; memb: Highland Tport Bd 1963-66, Scot Advsy Ctee for Civil Aviation 1965-71; dir: Industl Reorganisation Corp 1966-71, Chrysler (UK) Ltd 1967-71; chm Br United Trawlers Ltd 1969-71; dir: A J Mills (Holdings) Ltd 1969-78, Erma Ltd 1972-85; dep chm Lancer Boss Group Ltd 1974-89; memb: Scottish Econ Planning Cncl 1967-71, Monopolies Cmmn 1969-74; Freeman City of London 1962, Master Worshipful Co of Coachmakers and Coach Harness Makers 1977; Imperial Coll London: FCGI 1969, FIC 1971; FIMechE, FIProdE, FIMC; *Recreations* golf, gardening; *Clubs* Walton Heath Golf; *Style—* Bernard Boxall, Esq, CBE

BOXALL, Richard George; s of Thomas Boxall, OBE, of Honiton, Devon; *b* 23 May 1936; *Educ* Bedford Sch, Christ's Coll Cambridge (MA); *m* 1960, Dorothy, da of Samuel Breeze, of Folkestone; 2 s, 1 da; *Career* mech engr, dir Ibstock Johnson plc; pres and chief exec offr Glen-Gery Corp Reading Pa USA; *Recreations* sailing, gardening; *Clubs* Naval; *Style—* Richard Boxall, Esq; Four Winds, S Tulpehocken Rd, Reading, Pa, USA; Rue du Commandant Charcot, Jard sur Mer, France 85520

BOXER, Stephen Stanley; s of Alfred Henry Boxer, Mosterton nr Beaminster Dorset and Muriel Dorothy Elizabeth, *née* Page; *b* 19 May 1950; *Educ* Magdalen Coll Sch Oxford, Rose Bruford Coll of Speech and Drama; *Career* actor; Zigger-Zagger (Nat Youth Theatre) 1966-68; repertory theatre: Lancaster, Leeds, Liverpool, Southampton, Sheffield; Paines Plough theatre co: fndr memb, Music to Murder By (Edinburgh Festival) 1976, Richard III pt 2 (Cottesloe) 1977; Empty Desk (Royal Court Theatre Upstairs) 1979, Young Vic 1979 (The Tempest, Hamlet) The Brothers Karamazov (Fortune Theatre Edinburgh, Soviet Union) 1981, The Devil and the Good Lord (Lyric Hammersmith) 1984, The Ass (Riverside Studios) 1985, The Cocktail Party (Phoenix Theatre) 1986, Portraits (Savoy Theatre) 1987, The Alchemist (Cambridge Theatre Co) 1988, Julius Caesar (Leicester Haymarket, India) 1988-89, Faith Hope and Charity (Lyric Hammersmith) 1989, Judgement Day (Old Red Lion) 1990; RSC: The Duchess of Malfi (Barbican Pit) 1990, Barbarians (Barbican Theatre) 1990; NT: Once in a While the Odd Thing Happens 1990, The Shape of the Table 1990, White Chameleon 1991; Rousseau's Tale (one man show Cockpit Theatre) 1990; TV: The Waterfall, co-presenter Mooncat and Co, Brookside, Virtuoso, The Best Man to Die; Caesar in South China (radio); composer of many pieces for theatre and radio; *Recreations* tennis, squash, walking, playing piano and guitar; *Style—* Stephen Boxer, Esq; Kerry Gardner Management, 15 Kensington High St, London W8 5NP (☎ 071 937 3142)

BOYARS, Marion Ursula; da of Johannes Asmus (d 1966), and Herta, *née* Feiner (d 1943); *b* 26 Oct 1929; *Educ* Ecole Les Rayons Gland Switzerland, Univ of NY, Univ of Keele (BA); *m* 1, 24 Nov 1950 (m dis 1962), George, s of Hans Lobbenberg (d 1969); 2 da (Susan (Mrs Quateman) b 13 March 1955, Catheryn (Mrs Kilgarriff) b 17 Jan 1957); m 2, 8 May 1964, Arthur Boyars; *Career* md Calder and Boyars publishers 1960-89: fiction (6 Nobel Prize winners), avant-garde poetry, music, theatre; md Marion Boyars Publishers London and NY 1975-: fiction (3 Nobel Prize Winners), music, film, theatre, social scis; memb: Publishers Assoc (memb various ctees), various anti-censorship orgns; *Recreations* all the arts, travel, cooking, food & wine; *Clubs* Hurlingham; *Style—* Mrs Marion Boyars; 4 Hollywood Mews, London SW10 9HU (☎ 071 352 6400); 24 Lacy Rd, London SW15 1NL (☎ 071 788 9522)

BOYCE, Graham Hugh; s of Cdr Hugh Boyce, DSC, RN, and Madeline Millicent, *née* Manley; *b* 6 Oct 1945; *Educ* Hurstpierpoint Coll, Jesus Coll Cambridge (MA); *m* 11 April 1970, Janet Elizabeth, da of Rev Gordon Charles Craig Spencer, of Bath; 1 s (James b 1971), 3 da (Rachel b 1974, Sara b 1980, Josephine b 1984); *Career* VSO Antigua 1967, HM Dip Serv 1968; 2 sec Ottawa 1971 (3 sec), MECAS Shemlan 1972-74, 1 sec Tripoli 1974-77, FCO 1977-81, 1 sec Kuwait 1981-85, asst head ME Dept FCO 1985-86, cnsllr and consul gen Stockholm 1987; *Recreations* squash, tennis, reading; *Clubs* Cannons; *Style—* Graham Boyce, Esq; c/o FCO, King Charles St, London SW1A 2AH

BOYCE, John Leslie; s of late Sir (Harold) Leslie Boyce, 1 Bt, KBE; hp of nephew, Sir Robert Boyce, 3 Bt; *b* 16 Nov 1934; *m* 1, 1957 (m dis 1975), Finola Mary, da of late James Patrick Maxwell, of Bansha, Co Tipperary; 1 s, 3 da; m 2, 1980, Fusako, da of Yonesaku Ishibashi, of Shinagawa-ku, Tokyo, Japan; 2 da; *Style—* John Boyce, Esq; 182 Huntingdon Rd, Mt Waverley, Victoria 3149, Australia

BOYCE, Joseph Frederick; JP 1975; s of Frederick Arthur Boyce (d 1976), and

Rosalie Mary Pinck (d 1987); *b* 10 Aug 1926; *Educ* Roundhay Sch Leeds, Leeds Poly; *m* 1953, Nina Margaret, da of Arthur Frederick Tebb (d 1956), of Leeds; 2 s (Nicholas Joseph b 1954, Jeremy Frederick b 1957); *Career* chartered surveyor 1947-, gen mangr Telford Devpt Corpn 1979-86 (chief quantity surveyor 1964-71, technical dir 1971-75, dep gen mangr 1975-79); mgmnt conslt (UK and France) 1986-; pres Ironbridge Rowing Club 1974-89; FRICS; *Recreations* reading, rugby, rowing, walking, water colour painting, travel; *Clubs* Ironbridge Rowing; *Style*— Joseph Boyce, Esq, JP; The Uplands, Port Hill Gdns, Shrewsbury

BOYCE, Sir Robert (Charles) Leslie; 3 Bt (UK 1952); s of Sir Richard (Leslie) Boyce, 2 Bt (d 1968), and Jacqueline Anne Boyce-Dennis, *née* Hill; *b* 2 May 1962; *Educ* Cheltenham Coll, Salford Univ; *m* 1985, Fiona Margaret, 2 da of John Savage, of Harborough Road, Coventry; *Heir* unc, John Leslie Boyce; *Career* electronics engr; *Clubs* IEE; *Style*— Sir Robert Boyce, Bt; 117 Derby Road, Northampton NN1 4JP; Plessy Research (Caswell) Ltd, Caswell, nr Towcester, Northants

BOYCE, Thomas Anthony John; s of John Boyce (d 1978), of Wellesley House, Broadstairs, Kent, and Barbara Maude, *née* Blackwell (d 1970); *b* 4 Dec 1942; *Educ* Eton, ChCh Oxford; *m* 7 April 1973, Lucy Caroline Penelope, only da of Capt Thomas Edward Harold Parsons (d 1950), of Ampney House, Cirencester, Glos; 1 s (Edward b 1975), 1 da (Caroline b 1978); *Career* banker; dir: Hambros Bank Ltd, Hambros Aust Ltd; Capt Royal Yeo; *Recreations* hunting, stalking; *Clubs* Boodles, Pratts; *Style*— Thomas Boyce, Esq; Downs Lodge, Shipton under Wychwood, Oxfordshire OX7 6HY (☎ 099 382 2269); 41 Tower Hill, London EC3N 4HA (☎ 071 480 5000, fax 071 702 0629, telex 883851)

BOYCOTT, Prof Brian Blundell; s of Percy Blundell Boycott (d 1953), of London, and Doris Eyton Boycott; *b* 10 Dec 1924; *Educ* Royal Masonic Sch for Boys Bushey, Birkbeck Coll Univ of London; *m* 7 May 1950, Marjorie Mabel, da of late George Edward Burchell, of Beaminster, Dorset; 2 s (Antony b 1 April 1951, Richard b 1956, d 1963); *Career* reserved occupation as res technician Nat Inst for Med Res 1942-46; UCL: asst in anatomy 1947-52, lectr zoology 1952-62, reader in zoology 1962-68, prof of zoology 1968-70; sr scientific staff MRC 1971-89, KCL: prof of biology 1971-89, dir Cell Biophysics Unit 1980-89; emeritus prof of biology and sr res fell Guys Hosp Med Sch 1990-; 61 pubns in learned jls; memb Cncl: Royal Soc 1976-78, Open Univ 1975-87; memb: Academic Advsy Ctee Open Univ 1990-, MRC Neuroscience and Mental Health Bd 1990-91; fell Kings Coll London 1990, HonD Open Univ; FIBiol 1967, FRS 1971; *Style*— Prof Brian Boycott; Department of Anatomy and Cell Biology, Guy's Hospital, London Bridge, London SE1 9RT (☎ 071 955 5000 ext 2991)

BOYCOTT, Geoffrey (Geoff); OBE (1981); s of late Thomas Wilfred Boycott, and Jane, *née* Speight; *b* 21 Oct 1940; *Educ* Kinsley Secdy Mod, Hemsworth GS; *Career* cricketer; played for: Yorks 1962-86 (Co Cap 1963, Capt 1971-78), England 1964-74 and 1977-82; scored one hundredth first class century 1977 (England v Australia), one hundred and fiftieth century 1986, exceeded world record no of runs scored in Test Matches Delhi 1981; memb Yorks CCC (memb Gen Ctee 1984-); *Books* Geoff Boycott's Book for Young Cricketers (1976), Put to the Test: England in Australia 1978-79 (1979), Geoff Boycott's Cricket Quiz (1979), Boycott On Batting (1980), Opening Up (1980), In the Fast Lane: Eng in WI (1981), Master Class (1982), Boycott, The Autobiography (1987), Boycott on Cricket (1990); *Videos* Boycott on Batting (1990), Geoff Boycott's Greatest England Team (1991); *Recreations* golf, tennis; *Style*— Geoff Boycott, Esq, OBE; Pear Tree Farm, Water Lane, Woolley, Wakefield, W Yorks WF4 2JQ

BOYD, Sir Alexander Walter; 3 Bt (UK 1916); s of late Maj Cecil Anderson Boyd, MC, MD, late RAMC, 2 s of 1 Bt; suc unc, Sir Walter Herbert Boyd, 2 Bt, 1948; *b* 16 June 1934; *m* 1958, Molly Madeline, da of late Ernest Arthur Rendell, of Vernon, Br Columbia; 2 s, 3 da; *Heir* s, Ian Walter Rendell Boyd (m 1986, Lee Ann Dillon; 1 s (Kyle Robert Rendell b 1987); *Style*— Sir Alexander Boyd, Bt; P.O. Box 261 Whistler, Br Columbia, Canada

BOYD, Hon Mrs (Catherine); *née* Jay; yr (twin) da of Baron Jay, PC (Life Peer), *qv*; *b* 1945; *Educ* North London Collegiate Sch, Sussex Univ (BA); *m* 1970, Stewart Boyd, QC; 1 s (Matthew b 1976), 3 da (Rachel b 1972, Emily b 1973, Hannah b 1987); *Books* The Br Way of Birth (jtly 1982); *Style*— The Hon Mrs Boyd; 1 Gayton Crescent, Hampstead, London NW3; Wraxall Manor, Higher Wraxall, Dorchester, Dorset DT2 OHP

BOYD, David Barclay; JP (Argyll and Bute); s of David Doyd, and Janet McLellan Barclay Boyd; *b* 23 July 1933; *Educ* Dunoon GS, Edinburgh Univ (BSc); *m* 8 Nov 1958, Emily Margaret, da of James Wilson, of Dunoon; 2 s (David James b 1960, Andrew Wilson b 1968), 2 da (Kirsty Allan b 1959, Bryony McFarlane b 1964); *Career* cmmnd 2 Lt RE 1957, active serv Cyprus 1957-58; dist offr Forestry Cmmn, asst regnl offr Argyll 1960-62, factor Glencruitten Estate Oban 1962-66, factor Islay Estate Islay of Islay 1966-; dir and former chm Islay Farmers Ltd; memb: Cncl Scottish Landowners Fedn, BBC Scottish Rural Affrs Advsy Ctee, Argyll and Bute Rating and Valuation Ctee; crew memb Sceptre America's Cup Challenge at Newport Rhode Island 1958; fell Inst of Chartered Foresters; *Recreations* shooting, sailing; *Clubs* Royal Socttish Automobile; *Style*— David Boyd, Esq, JP; 105 Hyndland Rd, Glasgow (☎ 041 339 7641); Ceannloch Hse, Bridgend, Islay, Argyll (☎ 049 681 464); Islay Estate Off, Bridgend, Isle of Islay, Argyll (☎ 049 681 221)

BOYD, Dennis Galt; CBE (1988); s of Thomas Ayre Boyd (d 1968), and Minnie, *née* Galt (d 1962); *b* 3 Feb 1931; *Educ* S Shields HS; *m* 1953, Pamela Mary, da of John Moore McLean (d 1980); 1 s (Simon), 1 da (Angela); *Career* dir Corporate Servs Health and Safety Exec 1975-80, chief conciliation offr Advsy Conciliation and Arbitration Serv 1980-; *Recreations* golf; *Clubs* Civil Serv; *Style*— Dennis Boyd, Esq, CBE; Dunelm, Silchester Rd, Little London, nr Basingstoke, Hants; Advsy Conciliation and Arbitration Serv, 27 Wilton St, London SW1X 7AZ

BOYD, Douglas; *Educ* RAM under Janet Craxton, studied with Maurice Bourgue in Paris; *Career* professional oboist; soloist in important musical centres of Europe, Far East and America; work with conductors incl: Claudio Abbado, Pavo Berglund, Sir Yehudi Menuhin, Alexander Schneider, Michael Tilson Thomas; int festivals incl: Berlin, City of London, Edinburgh, Korsholm, Charleston, Spoleto; debut Salzburg Festival 1990; recordings: Bach Oboe Concerto (dir and soloist, Deutsche Grammaphon) 1990; Strauss Oboe Concerto (ASV) 1990; co-fndr Chamber Orch of Europe (princ oboist, leading memb Wind Soloists); *Style*— Douglas Boyd, Esq

BOYD, Fionnuala; da of Joseph Douglas Allen Boyd (d 1990), and Doreen, *née* Wilson; *b* 13 April 1944; *Educ* The Grammar Sch Welwyn Garden City, St Albans Art Sch, Univ of Leeds (BA); *m* 1965, Leslie Douglas Evans, *qv*, s of Leslie Edward Evans; 1 s (Jack Luis b 1969), 1 da (Ruby Rose b 1971); *Career* artist; began working with Leslie Evans 1968, Bi-Centenial fell USA 1977-78; artist in residence: Milton Keynes Devpt Corp 1982-84, Brunei Rainforest Project 1991-92; solo exhibitions (with Evans): Angela Flowers Gallery 1972, 1974, 1977, 1979, 1980, 1982, 1984, 1986, 1988, Park Square Gallery Leeds 1972, Boyd and Evans 1970-75 (Turnpike Gallery Leigh) 1976, Fendrick Gallery Washington DC 1978, Graves Art Gallery Sheffield 1978, Spectro Arts Workshop Newcastle 1980, Ton Peek Utrecht 1981, A Decade of Paintings (Milton Keynes Exhibition Gallery) 1982-83, Drumcroon Art Centre Wigan 1985, Bird (Flowers East, London) 1990, English Paintings (Brendan Walter Gallery Santa Monica) 1990, Angela Flowers (Ireland) Inc Rosscarberry Ireland 1990, Flowers East London 1991; gp exhibitions incl: Postcards (Angela Flowers Gallery) 1970, British Drawing 1952-72 (Angela Flowers Gallery) 1972, Imagini Come Strumenta di Realta (Studio la Citta Verona) 1973, New Image Painting (First Tokyo Int Biennale of Figurative Art) 1974, Body and Soul (Peter Moores, Liverpool) 1975, British Realist Show (Ikon Gallery) 1976, Aspects of Realism (Rothmans of Pall Mall, Canada) 1976-78, The Real British (Fischer Fine Art) 1981, Black and White Show (Angela Flowers Gallery) 1985, Sixteen (Angela Flowers Gallery) 1986, State of the Nation (Herbert Gallery, Coventry) 1987, Contemporary Portraits (Flowers East) 1988, The Thatcher Years (Flowers East) 1989; Picturing People: British Figurative Art since 1945 (touring exhibition Far East) 1989-90, Art '90 London (Business Design Centre) 1990; work in public collections of: Arts Cncl of GB, Br Cncl, Museum of Modern Art NY, Sheffield City Art Gallery, Wolverhampton City Art Gallery, Leeds City Art Gallery, Contemporary Art Soc, Leicester Educn Authy, Manchester City Art Gallery, Unilever plc, Tate Gallery, Williamson Art Gallery, Borough of Milton Keynes; *awards* prizewinner Bradford Print Biennale, first prize 6th Festival Int de la Peinture Cagnes-sur-Mer; *Recreations* books, films, hills, friends, exercise, music; *Style*— Ms Fionnuala Boyd; Boyd & Evans, Flowers East, 199/205 Richmond Rd, London E8 3NJ (☎ 081 985 3333, fax 081 985 0067)

BOYD, Sir (John) Francis; s of John Crichton Dick Boyd, of Ilkley, and Kate Boyd; *b* 11 July 1910; *Educ* Ilkley GS, Silcoates Sch Wakefield; *m* 1946, Margaret, da of George Dobson, of Scarborough; 1 s, 2 da; *Career* served WWII 1939-45; The Guardian (prev Manchester Guardian): parly corr 1937-39, political corr 1945-72, political ed 1972-75; chm Lobby Journalists 1949-50; hon treas Commons Preservation Soc 1977-81 (vice pres 1981-90); Hon LLD Leeds 1973; kt 1976; *Style*— Sir Francis Boyd; 7 Summerlee Ave, London N2 9QP (☎ 081 444 8601)

BOYD, Iain Edward; s of John Edward Boyd (d 1982), of Glasgow, and Sheena Dunkeld, *née* Buchanan; *b* 4 March 1937; *Educ* The HS of Glasgow, Univ of Glasgow (MB ChB); *m* 26 March 1964, Una Barrie, da of John Cameron, of Glasgow; 1 da (Susan b 1967); *Career* Physiology Dept Univ of Glasgow 1962-64, Univ of Chicago clinics 1964-68, UCH London 1968-69, Queen Charlottes Maternity Hosp and Chelsea Hosp for Women 1969-73, Univ of Southampton Hosps 1974-; chm Specialist Sub Ctee Wessex Region, former sec S Western Obstetricians and Gynaecologists, memb Br Gynaecological Cancer Soc 1986; FRCS 1968, FRCOG 1982 (MRCOG 1968); *Recreations* skiing, dining out, theatre, sailing; *Clubs* Gynaecological Visiting Soc; *Style*— Iain Boyd, Esq; Forest Edge, Woodlands Crescent, Ashurst, Hants SO4 2AQ (☎ 0703 292324); Princess Anne Hospital, Coxford Rd, Southampton SO9 4HA (☎ 0703 777222)

BOYD, Ian Mair; s of John Telfer Boyd (d 1976), of Ayr, and Margaret Mair, *née* Murdoch; *b* 4 Sept 1944; *Educ* Ayr Acad, London Business Sch (MSc); *m* 20 Dec 1975, Theodora (Toody), da of Theodor Georgopoulos, of Athens; 2 s (Telfer, Fraser), 1 da (Amber); *Career* CA 1966, gp fin dir The Weir Group plc 1981-, memb Cncl Inst of CA's of Scotland 1987-; FICAS 1966; *Recreations* golf, hill-walking, skiing, bird watching, fishing; *Clubs* Prestwick Golf; *Style*— Ian Boyd, Esq; 34 Newark Dr, Glasgow G41 4PZ (☎ 041 429 1840); The Weir Group Plc, 149 Newlands Rd, Glasgow G44 4EX (☎ 041 637 7111, fax 041 637 2221, telex 77161 WPL CRT)

BOYD, Ian Walter Rendell; s and h of Sir Alexander Boyd, 3 Bt; *b* 14 March 1964; *m* 1986, Lee-Ann Dillon; 1 s (Kyle Robert Rendell b 1987); *Style*— Ian Boyd Esq

BOYD, James Edward; s of Robert Edward Boyd, and Elizabeth Reid Sinclair; *b* 14 Sept 1928; *Educ* Kelvinside Academy, The Leys Sch Cambridge; *m* Judy Ann Christey Scott; 2 s, 2 da; *Career* CA Scot (dist) 1951; ptnr McClelland Kerr & Co 1953-61; fin dir: Lithgows Ltd 1962-69, Scott Lithgow Ltd 1970-78; dir and fin advsr Denholm Gp of Cos 1968-; dir: Lithgows (Hldgs) Ltd 1962-87, Ayrshire Metal Products plc 1965- (dep chm 1989-), Invergordon Distillers (Hldgs) plc 1966-88 (md 1966-67), Nairn & Williamson (Hldgs) Ltd 1968-75, GB Papers plc 1977-87, Carlton Industries plc 1978-84, James River UK Hldgs Ltd 1987-, Jebsens Drilling plc 1978-85, Save & Prosper Gp Ltd 1987-89; Scottish Widows' Fund & Life Assurance Soc 1981- (dep chm 1988-), Br Linen Bank Ltd 1983- (govr 1986-), Shanks & McEwan Gp plc 1983-, Scottish Exhibition Centre 1983-89, Civil Aviation Authority 1984-85, Bank of Scotland 1984-, Bank of Wales 1986-88, dep chm BAA plc (formerly British Airports Authy) 1985-; chm: Fairfield Shipbuilding & Engrg Co Ltd 1964-65, Gartmore European Investmt Tst plc 1978-, English & Caledonian Investment plc 1981-, Yarrow plc 1984-86; memb: Clyde Port Authority 1974-80, Cncl Inst of Chartered Accountants of Scotland 1977-83 (vice pres 1980-82, pres 1982-83), Exec Ctee Accountants Jt Disciplinary Scheme 1979-81; memb Cncl Glenalmond Coll 1983-; *Recreations* tennis, golf, gardening; *Style*— James E Boyd, Esq; Dunard, Station Road, Rhu, Dunbartonshire G84 8LW (☎ 0436 820441); The Denholm Group, Inter-City House, 80 Oswald Street, Glasgow G1 4PX (☎ 041 204 1004)

BOYD, Dr James Ferguson; s of Andrew Boyd, JP (d 1965), of Glasgow, and Mary, *née* Somerville (d 1987); *b* 6 June 1925; *Educ* Hillhead HS Glasgow, Carrick Acad Maybole Ayrshire, Univ of Glasgow (MB ChB, MD); *m* 5 Jan 1951, Christina Maggie (Chris), da of Donald MacLeod (d 1956), of Isle of Harris; 2 s (Andrew Ferguson b 14 Jan 1952, Donald MacLeod b 22 Feb 1955), 2 da (Joan Rachel Somerville b 12 Feb 1957, Christine Margaret b 9 July 1963); *Career* RAMC 1949-51 (Lt 1949-50, Capt 1950-51); res: Hairmyres Hosp E Kilbride by Glasgow 1948-49, Royal Alexandra Infirmary Paisley 1949, Western Infirmary Glasgow 1951-52; trg posts in pathology 1952-61 (Western Infirmary Glasgow, Area Laboratory Serv Stirling, Res Dept Royal Maternity Hosp Glasgow, Pathology Dept Royal Hosp for Sick Children Glasgow), sr lectr in pathology of infectious diseases Univ of Glasgow and hon conslt pathologist Gtr Glasgow Health Bd 1961-, lectr in pathology Tulane Univ Med Sch New Orleans Louisiana USA 1970; pres Caledonian branch Assoc of Clinical Pathologists 1986-89; memb: BMA 1948, Pathological Soc of GB and I 1955, Assoc of Clinical Pathologists 1955, Royal Medico-Chirurgical Soc of Glasgow 1957, Res Def Soc 1963, Euro Soc of Pathology 1965, Int Soc for Study of Infectious and Parasitic Diseases 1966, Tulane Med Alumni Assoc 1972, Br Soc for Study of Infection 1974; FRCPE 1966, FRCPath 1973, FRCPG 1975; *Recreations* golf, walking; *Clubs* College (Univ of Glasgow); *Style*— Dr James Boyd; 44 Woodend Drive, Jordanhill, Glasgow G13 1TQ (☎ 041 959 2708); University of Glasgow, Glasgow G12 8QQ (☎ 041 339 8855)

BOYD, Prof (Thomas) James Morrow; s of Thomas James Boyd (d 1979), and Isobel Cameron, *née* Morrow; *b* 21 June 1932; *Educ* Larne GS, Queens Univ Belfast (BSc, PhD); *m* 5 Sept 1959, Marguerite Bridget, da of William Snelson (d 1980), of Drayton Manor, Dunston, Stafford; 2 da (Rebecca b 1964, Marguerite b 1968); *Career* res fell Univ of Birmingham 1957-59, asst res prof Univ of Maryland 1959-61, Ford fndn fell Princeton Univ 1962, sr res assoc UKAEA Culham Lab 1962-65, sr lectr Univ of St Andrews 1965-68, prof of applied mathematics 1968-82; Univ of Wales Bangor: prof of theoretical physics 1982-90, dean Faculty of Sci 1981-85; prof of physics Univ of Essex 1990-; visiting prof of physics Univ of British Columbia 1975, Fulbright sr fell and visiting prof of physics Dartmouth Coll USA 1987-88; memb NY Acad of Sciences 1987, FInstP 1987; *Books* Plasma Dynamics (1969), Electricity (1979); *Recreations* skiing, hill-walking, travel; *Style*— Prof James Boyd; 6 Frog Meadow, Brook St, Dedham, Colchester CO7 6AD (☎ 0206 323170); The Roddens, Larne, Co Antrim

BT40 1PN; Dept of Physics, University of Essex, Wivenhoe Park, Colchester CO4 3SQ (☎ 0206 872885)

BOYD, John; s of John Richardson Boyd, and Janet, *née* Anderson; *b* 5 April 1925; *Educ* Heriot Watt Edinburgh; *Career* WWII served RN 1942-45; Royal Milliner; *Style*— John Boyd, Esq; 93 Walton St, London SW3 2HP (☎ 071 589 7601); 91 Walton St, London SW3 2HP (☎ 071 589 7601)

BOYD, (David) John; QC (1982); s of David Boyd (d 1964), and Ellen Jane, *née* Gruer (d 1953); *b* 11 Feb 1935; *Educ* Eastbourne Coll, St George's Sch Newport USA, Gonville and Caius Coll Cambridge (MA); *m* 1960, Raija Sinikka, da of Onni Lindholm (d 1952), of Finland, 1 s (Roderick b 1972), 1 da (Karin b 1969); *Career* called to the Bar Gray's Inn 1963, bencher 1988; sec asst ICI 1957-62, legal asst Pfizer 1962-66, legal offr Henry Wiggin and Co 1966-68; joined Inco Europe Ltd 1968, sec and chief legal offr Inco Europe Ltd 1972-86 (dir 1984-86); in private practice at Bar 1986; dir legal servs Digital Equipment Co 1986-, chm Competition Panel CBI 1988-, dir Impala Platinum 1972-78, gen cmmr of Income Tax 1978-81, memb Senate of Inns of Ct and Bar 1978-81, chm Bar Assoc for Commerce Fin and Indust 1980-81, sec gen Assoc des Juristes d'Enterprise Européens 1983-84, legal advsr Review Bd for Govt Contracts 1984-; FCIArb; *Style*— John Boyd, Esq, QC; 44 Riverene, Grosvenor Drive, Maidenhead, Berks SL6 8PF (☎ 0628 75412); Beeches, Upton Bishop, Ross-on-Wye, Herefordshire (☎ 098985 214)

BOYD, John Dixon Iklé; CMG (1985); s of Prof James Dixon Boyd (d 1968), of Cambridge, and Amélie, *née* Lowenthal; *b* 17 Jan 1936; *Educ* Westminster, Clare Coll Cambridge (BA), Yale (MA); *m* 1, 28 Jan 1968 (m dis 1977), Gunilla Kristina Ingegerd, da of Gösta Rönngren, of Västeraås Sweden; 1 s (Jonathan b 1969), 1 da (Emily b 1971); m 2, 11 Nov 1977, Julia Daphne, da of Capt Antony Edward Montague Raynsford, of Milton Malsor Manor, Northampton; 3 da (Jessica b 1978, Alice b 1979, Olivia b 1981); *Career* FO: Hong Kong 1962-64, Peking 1965-67, FCO 1967-69, Washington 1969-73, Peking 1973-75, HM Treasy (on loan) 1976, Bonn 1977-81, UK Mission to UN 1981-84, political advsr Hong Kong 1985-87, dep under sec of state FCO 1987-89, chief clerk 1989-; *Recreations* music, fly fishing; *Clubs* Hawks', Hong Kong; *Style*— John Boyd, Esq, CMG; FCO, King Charles St, London SW1

BOYD, John George; s of John Boyd (d 1980), of Corby, Northampton, and Christina Blair, *née* Wood; *b* 7 April 1940; *Educ* Mackie Acad Stonehaven Kincardineshire, Gray's Sch of Art Aberdeen (DA), Hospitalfield Coll of Art Arbroath, Jordanhill Coll of Educn Glasgow; *m* 1, 23 Oct 1965 (m dis 1975), Janet, *née* Binns; m 2, 10 June 1980 (m dis 1985), Marilyn, *née* Apps; m 3, 11 Nov 1985, Estrild, *née* Macdougall; *Career* teacher 1963-78; pt/t lectr: Glasgow Sch of Art 1967-88, in further educn 1978-; artist exhibitions incl: New 57 Gallery Edinburgh 1967, Armstrong Gallery Glasgow 1970, Glasgow Art Club 1971, 1973, 1974, 1976 and 1980, Present Gallery Lanark 1975, Henderson's Gallery Edingburgh 1978 and 1980, Corners Gallery Glasgow 1985, Barclay Lennie Fine Art Glasgow 1988; regular exhibitor at: Royal Academy, RSA, RGI; works in private collections in: UK, USA, Earl of Moray, The Captain of Clanranald, Sir Norman McFarlane, Robert Fleming Hldgs, Bank of Ireland; public collections: People's Palace Glasgow, Paisley Art Gallery, Lillie Art Gallery Milngavie; Latimer award RSA 1972, Eastwood Publications award RGI 1990; memb Cncl RGI 1984-90 (elected 1982), elected RP 1989; *Recreations* reading, music, wine; *Clubs* Glasgow Art; *Style*— John Boyd, Esq; Hayston, 26 Cleveden Rd, Glasgow G12 OPX (☎ 041 357 2176)

BOYD, Hon Jonathan Aubrey Lewis; 3 s of 6 Baron Kilmarnock, MBE (d 1975); *b* 1 Oct 1956; *m* 20 March 1982, Annette Madeleine, er da of Joseph Constantine, FRICS, *qv*; 1 s (b 14 March 1989); *Style*— The Hon Jonathan Boyd

BOYD, Karen; da of William Boyd, of Carlisle Cumbria, and Irene, *née* Latimer; *b* 27 Jan 1962; *Educ* St Aidan's Camp, Newcastle Poly (BA); *Career* fashion designer; freelance illustration work with Drapers Record and Fashion Weekley; freelance design for: Laura Ashley, Next, Sock Shop and Mulberry Co Ltd; launched her own label with Amalgamated Talent 1984, showed three successful collections at the Br Designer Shows and the Coterie NY (first customers included Harrods and Joseph) 1985-86, jtly opened shop Boyd & Storey 1987, showed Spring/Summer collection at Br Designer Shows and La Mode Aux Tuilleries Paris 1987, ended partnership with Helen Storey and opened own studio in S London 1990 (stockists incl: Jones, Harvey Nichols, Harrods, Pellicano and others worldwide; clients incl: Madonna, Bananarama, Paula Yates, Basia, Paula Abdul, Pamella Bordes, Wendy James, Kylie Minogue, Miranda Richardson; *Awards* British Apparel Export award (with Helen Storey, 1989); *Style*— Ms Karen Boyd; Karen Boyd, Unit N301, Westminster Business Square, Durham St, London SE11 (☎ 071 582 0994, fax 071 582 2701)

BOYD, Lawrence David; s of William Robert Boyd, of Bothwell, Glasgow, and Agnes Jane, *née* Armstrong; *b* 25 May 1949; *Educ* Hamilton Acad Lanarkshire, Glasgow Univ (BSc), Imperial Coll London (MPhil, DIC); *m* 23 July 1977, Nicola Judith Ann, da of Norman Mahy, of Derby; 1 s (Neil b 30 Nov 1984), 1 da (Joanna b 16 April 1983); *Career* Alliance & Leicester Building Society: fin res offr 1976-80, corp planning mangr 1980-82, chief accountant 1982-83, mgmnt servs cncllr 1983-85, asst gen mangr mortgage admin 1985-87, asst gen mangr corp devpt 1987-90, gen mangr corp devpt and planning 1990-; ACBSI 1979, ACIS 1979, FCCA 1981; *Books* Accounting - Principles and Practice (1983); *Recreations* walking, fencing; *Style*— Lawrence Boyd, Esq; 28 Mallory Rd, Hove, E Sussex BN3 6TD (☎ 0273 504253); Alliance & Leicester Building Society, Hove Park, Hove, E Sussex BN3 7AZ (☎ 0273 775454)

BOYD, Michael Neil Murray; s of Lt Cdr Neil Kenneth Boyd, DSC, of New Milton, Hants, and Felicity Victoria, *née* Weston; *b* 17 Aug 1946; *Educ* Bryanston; *m* 30 May 1970, Belinda Rachel Elizabeth, da of Capt Basil Harry Lawrence (d 1973); 1 s (Ashleigh Boyd b 21 June 1980), 1 da (Zara Boyd b 18 Sept 1975); *Career* Ernst & Young: ptnr London 1975, NY 1979-82, London Audit Dept 1984-86, memb Exec and Firm's Cncl 1986-89, fin ptnr 1987-89, chm Int Extractive Industs Ctee 1988-, on merger with Arthur Young appt nat audit ptnr and ptnr with overall responsibility for E Europe 1989-; memb: Cncl Corps of Cranleigh Sch and St Catherine's Bromley 1975-, Cncl E Euro Trade Cncl 1989; govr Cranleigh Sch 1975-79 and 1985-; MInstPet 1983, FICA 1975 (memb 1969); *Recreations* tennis, skiing, opera; *Clubs* Gresham, Woking Lawn Tennis; *Style*— Michael Boyd, Esq; Pleasant Cottage, Chapel Lane, Pirbright, Surrey GU24 0LU (☎ 04867 5705); Ernst & Young, Becket House, 1 Lambeth Palace Rd, London SE1Y 7EU (☎ 071 928 2000, fax 071 928 9615/01 620 1612, telex 885234)

BOYD, Dr (John) Morton; CBE (1987); s of Thomas Pollock Boyd (d 1953), of Darvel, Ayrshire, and Jeanie Reid, *née* Morton (d 1955); *b* 31 Jan 1925; *Educ* Darvel Sch, Kilmarnock Acad, Univ of Glasgow (BSc 1953, PhD 1957, DSc 1964); *m* 18 Jan 1954, Winifred Isobel, da of John Rome (d 1971), of Kilmarnock, Ayrshire; 4 s (Alan Morton b 1955, Ian Lamont b 1957, Neil Rome b 1959, Keith John b 1963); *Career* Air Navigator, Station Adj RAF 1943-47, Flt Lt; regnl offr West Scotland Nature Conservancy 1957-68, asst dir Nature Conservancy (Scotland) 1968-70, dir (Scotland) Nature Conservancy Cncl 1971-85; ecological conslt: Forestry Cmmn 1985-, N Scotland Hydro Electric 1985-90, Scottish Hydro-Electric plc 1990-, Nat Tst for Scotland; editorial conslt: Edinburgh Univ Press 1985-, Mirror Publications Ltd 1989-90, guest lectr Swan (Hellenic) Ltd 1972-, Serenissima Travel Ltd 1990-; vice-pres Scottish Conservation Projects Tst; Nuffield travelling fell (ME and E Africa) 1964-65; FRSE 1968 (Neill prize 1983), CBiol, FIBiol, FRSA, Hon FRZSScot, Hon FRSGS; *Books* St Kilda Summer (with K Williamson, 1960), Mosaic of Islands (with K Williamson, 1963), The Highlands and Islands (with F F Darling, 1964), Travels in the Middle East and East Africa (1966), Island Survivors (with P A Jewell and C Milner, 1974), The Natural Environment of the Outer Hebrides (ed, 1979), The National Environment of the Inner Hebrides (ed with D R Bowes, 1983), Fraser Darling's Islands (1986), The Hebrides - A Natural History (with I L Boyd, 1990); *Recreations* travel, painting, photography; *Clubs* New (Edinburgh); *Style*— Dr J Morton Boyd, CBE, FRSE; 57 Hailes Gardens, Edinburgh EH13 0JH (☎ 031 441 3220); Balephuil, Isle of Tiree, Argyll PA77 6UE (☎ 08792 521)

BOYD, Prof Robert David Hugh; s of Prof James Dixon Boyd (d 1968), of Cambridge, and Dr Amélie Boyd; *b* 14 May 1938; *Educ* Univ of Cambridge, UCH London; *m* 1 April 1966, Meriel Cornelia, da of T G Talbot, CB, QC, of Falconhurst, Edenbridge, Kent; 1 s (Thomas b 1967), 2 da (Diana b 1969, Lucy b 1974); *Career* res med posts: UCH, Brompton Hosp, Gt Ormond St Hosp; res fell and sr lectr UCH 1967-80, dean Faculty of Med Univ of Manchester 1989- (prof of child health and paediatrics 1981-); pubns on child health, gen practice and foetal physiology; chm Academic Bd BPA, cncllr RCP, memb Standing Med Advsy Ctee Dept of Health; FRCP; *Books* Placental Transfer-Methods and Interpretations (co-ed, 1981), Perinatal Medicine (co-ed, 1983), Paediatric Problems in Gen Practice (jtly, 1989); *Style*— Prof Robert Boyd

BOYD, Prof Sir Robert Lewis Fullarton; CBE (1972); s of William John Boyd, of Sanderstead, Surrey; *b* 19 Oct 1922; *Educ* Whitgift Sch, Univ of London; *m* 1949, Mary, da of late John Higgins; 2 s, 1 da; *Career* dir (Mullard) Space Science Lab UCL 1954-83; prof of astronomy Royal Instn 1961-67, prof of physics Univ of London 1962-83; memb SRC 1977-81, tstee Nat Maritime Museum 1980-89; fell UCL 1989, FRS 1969; kt 1983; *Recreations* elderly Rolls Royce motor cars; *Style*— Prof Sir Robert Boyd, CBE, FRS; Roseneath, 41 Church St, Littlehampton, W Sussex BN17 5PU (☎ 0903 714438)

BOYD, Robert Nathaniel; CBE (1971); s of Peter Ferguson Boyd, and Annie Jane, *née* Newton; *b* 17 Nov 1918; *Educ* Boys' GS Suva Fiji, Churchers' Coll Petersfield; *m* 1947, Carrie, da of Harry Squires; 2 s; *Career* Lt-Col (ret) Br Somaliland 1940, Abyssinia, Madagascar and Burma, 30 years Territorial and Res served Central Africa; practising arbitrator, co dir and auditor gen Zambia 1966-68, sec and fin controller Air Tport and Travel Indust Trg Bd 1969-77; chm Dist Fin Ctee Wokingham Borough Cncl (later DC) 1974-77 (memb Cncl 1972-77); treas United Soc for Propagation of Gospel 1982- (vice chm 1982-90); Efficiency Decoration Zambia 1968, Order of the Epiphany Anglican Church in Central Africa 1968; FCIS, FCIArb, FBIM; *Recreations* bowls; *Clubs* Hurst Bowling, Royal Cwlth Soc; *Style*— Robert Boyd, Esq, CBE; 7 Acorn Drive, Wokingham, Berks RG11 1EQ (☎ 0734 781122)

BOYD, Dr Hon Robin Jordan; 2 s of 6 Baron Kilmarnock, MBE (d 1975), and hp of bro, 7 Baron; *b* 6 June 1941; *Educ* Eton, Strasbourg Univ, Keble Coll Oxford; *Career* page to Lord High Constable of Scotland at Coronation of HM the Queen, 1953; MB BS, LRCP, MRCS, DCH, MRCP, MRCPEd; *Style*— Dr The Hon Robin Boyd

BOYD, (Thomas) Rodney; s of Thomas Guthrie Boyd (d 1983), of Dumfries, and Mary Isabella Dunlop, *née* Irvine (d 1987); *b* 18 Aug 1944; *Educ* Dumfries Acad, Heriot-Watt Univ Edinburgh (BArch); *m* 1, 5 Sept 1968, Josephine Mary; 1 s (Rodney Alexander Guthrie b 1983), 4 da (Kirsty Robyn b 1972, Philippa Harriet b 1974, Tara Dunlop b 1979, Mandy McLeod b 1981); m 2, 14 Dec 1984, Maureen, da of Alexander Aitken, of Aberdeen; *Career* CA; design architect Melbourne Aust 1968-73, princ architect (late ptnr) Ian G Lindsay & Ptnrs 1973-81, own practice The Boyd Reid Gp 1981-; dir: Strathedin Properties Ltd 1984-, Criton Estates Ltd 1984-; tstee St Margaret's Sch (Edinburgh) Ltd Devpt Tst 1990-; *Style*— Rodney Boyd, Esq; c/o Slateford House, Lanark Rd, Edinburgh EH14 1TL (☎ 031 443 4467, fax 031 443 9442)

BOYD, Dr Roy Victor; s of Ernest Arthur Boyd (d 1965), and Olive, *née* Bachelor; *b* 14 Sept 1934; *Educ* Bromley Co GS, UCH London; *m* 1 (m dis 1966), Ann Esther, *née* Wright; 4 s (Andrew Charles b 22 Aug 1958, David John b 15 Jan 1960, Paul Nicholas (twin) b 15 Jan 1960, Simon James b 1 Sept 1965); m 2, Elizabeth Mary Jean, *née* Dalgleish (d 1986); 1 da (Rachel Jean b 1 Aug 1972); m 3, 12 July 1986, Jennifer; *Career* conslt in geriatric med: Greenwich 1964-73, Plymouth 1973-77, Nottingham 1977-; postgrad dean Univ of Nottingham Med Sch 1986; FRCP 1979, FRCPE 1980; *Recreations* bridge, music, theology; *Style*— Dr Roy Boyd; 133 Trowell Rd, Nottingham NG8 2EN (☎ 0602 288744); Queen's Medical Centre, Nottingham NG7 2UH (☎ 0602 709400)

BOYD, Stewart Craufurd; QC (1981); s of Leslie Balfour Boyd, OBE, of 2 Highbury Hill, London N1, and Wendy, *née* Blake; *b* 25 Oct 1943; *Educ* Winchester, Trinity Coll Cambridge (MA); *m* 1970, Catherine, da of The Rt Hon Lord Jay of Battersea; 1 s (Matthew b 1975), 3 da (Rachel b 1972, Emily b 1973, Hannah b 1987); *Career* barr; *Recreations* sailing, gardening, music; *Style*— Stewart Boyd, Esq, QC; 1 Gayton Crescent, London NW3 1TT (☎ 071 431 1581); Wraxall Manor, Higher Wraxall, Dorchester, Dorset (☎ 0935 83283); 4 Essex Court, Temple, London EC4Y 9AJ (☎ 071 583 9191, fax 071 583 2422)

BOYD, Hon Timothy Iain; s of 6 Baron Kilmarnock, MBE (d 1975); *b* 5 April 1959; *m* 1 July 1988, Lucy Teresa Emily, yr da of Michael Gray; *Style*— The Hon Timothy Boyd; Flat 2, 23 Ladbroke Crescent, London W11 1PS

BOYD, William Andrew Murray; s of Alexander Murray Boyd (d 1979), and Evelyn, *née* Smith; *b* 7 March 1952; *Educ* Gordonstoun, Univ of Nice (Dip), Univ of Glasgow (MA), Jesus Coll Oxford; *m* Susan Anne, da of David Leslie Wilson, of Maxwell Park, Glasgow; *Career* lectr in English lit St Hilda's Coll Oxford 1980-83, TV critic New Statesman 1981-83; author; novels: A Good Man in Africa (1981), On the Yankee Station (1981), An Ice-Cream War (1982), Stars and Bars (1984), School Ties (1985), The New Confessions (1987) Brazzaville Beach (1990); films: Good and Bad at Games (1983), Dutch Girls (1985), Scoop (1986), Stars and Bars (1988), Aunt Julia and the Scriptwriter (1990), Mr Johnson (1990); FRSL 1982; *Clubs* Chelsea Arts, Two Brydges Place, Groucho; *Style*— William Boyd, Esq; c/o Harvey Unna & Stephen Durbridge, 24 Pottery Lane, Holland Park, London W11

BOYD-CARPENTER, (Marsom) Henry; s of Francis Henry Boyd-Carpenter (d 1984), of East Lambrook Manor, Somerset, and Nina, *née* Townshend (d 1982); *b* 11 Oct 1939; *Educ* Charterhouse, Balliol Coll Oxford (BA, MA); *m* 18 Sept 1971, Lesley Ann, da of William Henry Davies (d 1986), of Billericay, Essex; 1 s (William Henry Francis b 28 July 1975), 1 da (Alexandra Mary b 28 June 1979); *Career* admitted slr 1966; ptnr Farrer & Co 1968-, slr Duchy of Cornwall 1976-; hon auditor Law Soc 1979-81, memb Governing Body Charterhouse Sch 1981-, hon steward Westminster Abbey 1980-, memb Cncl Chelsea Physic Garden 1983-; memb Law Soc 1966-; *Recreations* reading, listening to music, hill walking, gardening; *Clubs* Brooks's; *Style*— Henry Boyd-Carpenter, Esq; Guardswell House, Brockenhurst Road, South Ascot, Berkshire SL5 9HA (☎ 0344 23993); 66 Lincoln's Inn Fields, London WC2A 3LH (☎ 071 242 2022, fax 071 831 9748, tlx 24318)

BOYD-CARPENTER, Baron (Life Peer UK 1972) (of Crux Easton, co

Southampton); John Archibald Boyd-Carpenter; PC (1954), DL (Gtr London 1973); s of Maj Sir Archibald Boyd Boyd-Carpenter, MP (d 1937), of River House, Walton-on-Thames, and Annie, *née* Dugdale; gs of Rt Rev William Boyd-Carpenter, KCVO, DD, Bishop of Ripon (d 1918); *b* 2 June 1908; *Educ* Stowe, Balliol Coll Oxford (BA, pres Oxford Union Soc 1930); *m* 1937, Margaret Mary, da of Lt-Col George Leslie Hall, OBE, by his w, Dorothy, *née* Coventry, ggggda of 6 Earl of Coventry; 1 s, 2 da; *Career* WWII served Scots Gds 1939-45, Maj 1942; Harmsworth law scholar Middle Temple 1932, barr 1934, practiced London and SE Circuit 1934-39, jr SE Circuit 1939; MP (C) Kingston-upon-Thames 1945-72; fin sec Treasury 1951-54; Min of Transport and Civil Aviation 1954-55, Min of Pensions and Nat Insur 1955-62, chief sec Treasury and Paymaster-Gen 1962-64, opposition front bench spokesman on housing & land 1964-66, chm Public Accounts Ctee 1964-70, sits as Conservative in House of Lords, pres Assoc of Cons Peers 1990- (chm 1981-90); chm: Orion Insur Co and CLRP Investmt Tst 1968-72, Civil Aviation Authority 1972-77, Rugby Portland Cement Co 1976-84; dir of other cos, memb Cncl Trusthouse Forte 1977-; high steward The Royal Borough of Kingston-upon-Thames 1976-; *Books* Way of Life; *Recreations* swimming, tennis, walking, gardening; *Clubs* Carlton (chm 1979-86); *Style*— The Rt Hon Lord Boyd-Carpenter, PC, DL; 12 Eaton Terrace, London SW1 (☎ 071 730 7765); Crux Easton House, Crux Easton, Highclere, Newbury, Berks (☎ 0635 253037)

BOYD-CARPENTER, (Alan) Michael Haydon; VRD (1965); s of Gilbert Denys Ewart Boyd-Carpenter (d 1966), and Lydia Mary, *née* Cowan; *b* 19 Feb 1932; *Educ* Dragon Sch Oxford, Malvern; *m* 2 June 1956, Jennifer Ann, da of Arthur Alfred Prestwich (d 1986), of Edenbridge, Kent; 1 s, 4 da; *Career* Nat Serv RN, Midshipman submarine serv RNVR 1950-52; ret Lt Cdr 1976; Beecham Group 1952-53, Union Discount Co of London Ltd 1953-56, chm Joseph Sebag & Co 1980 (joined 1956, ptnr 1959), jt sr ptnr Carr Sebag & Co 1980-82; memb Stock Exchange 1956; *Clubs* Athenaeum, MCC; *Style*— Michael Boyd-Carpenter, Esq, VRD; c/o P M Boyd-Carpenter, 9 Queen's Gate, London SW7

BOYD-CARPENTER, Maj-Gen Thomas Patrick John; MBE (Mil 1973); s of Baron Boyd-Carpenter, PC, DL (Life Peer); *b* 1938; *Educ* Stowe; *m* 1972, Mary Jean, da of John Elwes Duffield; 3 c; *Career* Scots Gds, Col GSAT3 MOD 1981, Cmd 24 Inf Bde 1983-84, D DEF Pol MOD 1985-87; COS HQ BAOR 1988-89; ACDS (Prog) MOD 1989-; *Style*— Maj-Gen the Hon Thomas Boyd-Carpenter, MBE

BOYD MAUNSELL, Nevill Francis Wray; s of Col Cecil Robert Wray Boyd Maunsell (d 1961), of Worcester, and Elizabeth Frances, *née* Boyd; *b* 22 Dec 1930; *Educ* Winchester, Univ Coll Oxford (BA); *m* 5 Oct 1957, Lyghia, da of Dr Mihai Peterson (d 1954), of London; 1 s (Michael b 1958), 1 da (Indi b 1963); *Career* Nat Serv 2 Lt Royal Warwick Regt 1949-50; schoolmaster in UK and USA 1953-55; journalist: Reuters 1955-57, Financial Times 1957-60, Time and Tide 1960-61, Daily Sketch 1961-65, freelance 1965-73; city ed The Birmingham Post 1986- (dep city ed 1973-88); *Recreations* gardening, reading, idle chatter; *Style*— Nevill Boyd Maunsell, Esq; 19/21 Tudor Street, London EC4 (☎ 071 353 0811, fax 071 353 1762)

BOYD OF MERTON, Patricia, Viscountess; Lady Patricia Florence Susan; *née* Guinness; da of 2 Earl of Iveagh (d 1967); aunt of 3 Earl; *b* 3 March 1918; *m* 1938, 1 Viscount Boyd of Merton, CH, PC, DL (d 1983, sometime MP (C) Mid-Bedfordshire, Sec of State for the Colonies, dir ICI and jt vice-chm Arthur Guinness Son & Co); 3 s; *Style*— The Rt Hon Patricia, Viscountess Boyd of Merton; Ince Castle, Saltash, Cornwall PL12 4RA (☎ (075 55) 2274)

BOYD OF MERTON, 2 Viscount (UK 1960); Simon Donald Rupert Neville Lennox-Boyd; s of 1 Viscount Boyd of Merton, CH, PC, DL (d 1983), and Patricia, Viscountess Boyd of Merton, *qv*; *b* 7 Dec 1939; *Educ* Eton, ChCh Oxford (MA); *m* 1962, Alice Mary, JP (High Sheriff of Cornwall 1987), da of Maj Meysey George Dallas Clive (ka 1943); 2 s (Hon Benjamin b 21 Oct 1964, Hon Edward b 30 March 1968), 2 da (Hon Charlotte b 1963, Hon Philippa b 1970); *Heir* s, Hon Benjamin Alan Lennox-Boyd; *Career* dir The Iveagh Tstees Ltd; chm Save the Children Fund; *Recreations* planting trees; *Clubs* White's, Royal Yacht Sqdn; *Style*— The Rt Hon the Viscount Boyd of Mert; 9 Warwick Sq, London SW1V 2AA (☎ 071 821 1618); Wivelscombe, Saltash, Cornwall (☎ 0752 842672, fax 0752 849152); office: Iveagh House, 41 Harrington Gdns, London SW7 4JU (☎ 071 373 7261, telex 917935, fax 071 244 8281)

BOYD-ROCHFORT, Lady; (Elizabeth) Rohays Mary; da of Sir James Lauderdale Gilbert Burnett, of Leys, 13 Bt, CB, CMG, DSO, DL (d 1953); *b* 30 Aug 1916; *m* 1, 1938, Hon Henry Kerr Auchmuty Cecil (ka 1942), yr s of late Capt Hon William Amherst Cecil, MC (who was s of Baroness Amherst of Hackney, who succeeded her father, 1 Baron Amherst of Hackney); 4 s; m 2, 1944, Sir Cecil Charles Boyd-Rochfort, KCVO (d 1983), s of Maj R H Boyd-Rochfort, 15 Hussars; 1 s; *Style*— Lady Boyd-Rochfort; The Clydesdale Bank of Scotland, Banchory, Kincardineshire AB3 3QE

BOYDELL, Chancellor Peter Thomas Sherrington; QC (1965); s of late Frank Richard Boydell, JP, and late Frances Barton Boydell; *b* 20 Sept 1920; *Educ* Arnold Sch Blackpool, Univ of Manchester (LLB); *Career* Adj 17 Field Regt RA 1943, Bde Major RA 1 Armoured Div 1944, Bde Major RA 10 Indian Div 1945; admitted slr 1947, barr Middle Temple 1948, bencher 1970 (dep treas 1988, treas 1989); memb Legal Bd of Church Assembly 1958-71; Parly candidate (C) Carlisle 1964; chm Planning and Local Govt Ctee of the Bar 1973-86 (chm Local Govt and Planning Bar Assoc 1986-90), leader Parly Bar 1975-; chancellor Diocese of: Truro 1957-, Oxford 1958-, Worcester 1959-; ARICS 1982; *Recreations* mountaineering, travel, music; *Clubs* Garrick, RAC, Climbers'; *Style*— The Worshipful Chancellor Peter Boydell, QC; 45 Wilton Crescent, London SW1 (☎ 071 235 5505); 2 Harcourt Buildings, Temple, London EC4 (☎ 071 353 8415)

BOYER, Ernest Stanley; s of Walter Boyer (d 1981), of Holmstall, Quorn, Leics, and Evelyn, *née* Hudson (d 1976); *b* 30 Nov 1925; *Educ* Kingsbury GS, Regent St Sch of Arch; *m* 27 March 1954, Patricia, da of Montegue Cecil Cuthbertson (d 1950), of Hampstead, London; 1 s (Guy b 1959); *Career* architect, assoc ptnr Monro & Sons 1949-57, fndr E S Boyer & Ptnrs 1957, Boyer Design Gp 1974; dir: Boyer Professional Servs, Count Croft Properties; memb Cncl RIBA for Essex, Cambs and Herts 1961; memb: Worshipful Co of Bowyers, Worshipful Co of Constructors; FRIBA 1957, FFAS 1976; *Recreations* riding, painting, cricket; *Clubs* Les Ambassadeurs, Wig and Pen, MCC; *Style*— Ernest Boyer, Esq; Lone Pine, 100 Green Lane, Bovingdon, Herts HP3 OLA (☎ 0442 834 365); Boyer Design Group/E S Boyer & Ptnrs, Westminster House, High St, Egham, Surrey TW20 9HE (☎ 0784 39181, fax 0784 39242, car tel 0836 288149)

BOYER, John Leslie; OBE (1982); s of Albert Boyer, and Gladys Boyer; *b* 13 Nov 1926; *Educ* Nantwich and Acton GS; *m* 1953, Joyce Enid, *née* Thomasson; 1 s, 2 da; *Career* served Army 1944-48; dep chm Hong Kong and Shanghai Banking Corp 1977-81 (joined 1948, gen mangr Hong Kong 1973); chm: Wardley Ltd to 1981, Antony Gibbs Hldgs 1981-83; dir Anglo-Overseas Securities 1981-; former chm South China Morning Post; former dir: Eastern Asia Navigation Ltd, Mercantile Bank Ltd, British Bank of The Middle East, Swire Pacific Ltd, Mass Transit Railway Corp; *Recreations* bridge; *Style*— John Boyer, Esq, OBE; Friars Lawn, Norwood Green Rd, Norwood Green, Middx UB2 4LA (☎ 081 574 8489)

BOYES; *see*: Barratt-Boyes

BOYES, (Charles) Robin; s of Norman Frank Boyes, of Huntingdon, Cambs, and Rose Margaret, *née* Slingsby; *b* 16 Nov 1939; *Educ* Oundle; *m* 20 April 1968, Carroll Anne, da of Raymond Elkerton (d 1972), of St Albans, Herts; 1 s (Christopher b 1969); *Career* slr; dir Argyle Building Soc 1966-85; ptnr: Grover Humphreys & Boyes 1965-75, Warrens 1976-85, Warrens Boyes & Archer 1985-; hon slr Royal Photographic Soc of GB, Fenton Medal 1980; *Recreations* cricket, golf, collecting old toy soldiers; *Clubs* East India; *Style*— Robin Boyes, Esq; Punch's Grove, Hilton, Huntingdon, Cambs (☎ 0480 830335); 20 Hartford Road, Huntingdon, Cambs (☎ 0480 411331, fax 0480 59012)

BOYES, Roland; MP (Lab) Houghton and Washington 1983-; *b* 12 Feb 1937; *m* ; 2 s; *Career* former teacher and former asst dir Social Servs; memb GMB, chm Tribune Group 1985-86; Front Bench: environment spokesman 1985-88, defence spokesman 1988-; chm All Pty Photography Gp 1987-; vice pres Hartlepool Utd AFC; MEP (Lab) Durham 1979-84; *Recreations* photography, sports, brass bands; *Clubs* Peterlee CC (pres); *Style*— Roland Boyes, Esq, MP; 12 Spire Hollin, Peterlee, Co Durham (☎ 091 586 3917); Constituency Office (☎ 091 385 7825); House of Commons

BOYKO, Dr David Alexander; *b* 29 May 1954; *Educ* George Watson's Coll Edinburgh, Aberdeen Univ Med Sch (MB ChB, DipPharmMed, RCPUK); *m* 20 July 1979, Valerie Thomson, da of R Reid Jack, of E Lothian; *Career* physician, former sr med advsr Smith Kline and French Labs Ltd (Welwyn Garden City) 1984-87, dir clinical and med affrs and dep gen mangr ICI Pharmaceuticals (UK); memb Exec Ctee and treas Br Assoc of Pharmaceutical Physicians 1986-; memb BMA, FRSM; *Books* Dyspepsia and Cimetidine (Lancet), Cimetidine and the Critically Ill Patient (Br Journal of Hosp Medicine), Atenold and Pregnancy (Int Pharmacy Journal); *Recreations* skiing, physical fitness, food and wine, current affairs; *Clubs* Royal Soc of Medicine, Br Medical Assoc; *Style*— Dr David A Boyko; Glenmuir, Leicester Road, Hale, Cheshire WA14 9QA (☎ 061 927 7322); Stuart House, 50 Alderley Rd, Wilmslow, Cheshire (☎ 0625 535999, telex 668585)

BOYLE, Andrew Philip More; s of Andrew Boyle (d 1972), of Fenham, Newcastle upon Tyne, and Rose, *née* McCann (d 1964); *b* 27 May 1919; *Educ* Blair's Coll Aberdeen, Sorbonne (escaped as student from France 1940); *m* 1, 20 Nov 1943, Christina (d 1984), da of Thomas Galvin (d 1922); 1 s (Edmund Campion), 1 da (Diana Rosemary); m 2, 4 April 1986, Eleanor; *Career* RAFVR 1941-43, Maj (later Temp Col) Br Mil Intelligence served Far East, India and Burma 1943-47; BBC: prodr and scriptwriter Radio Newsreel, fndr ed The World At One 1965-76, head of news and current affrs Radio and TV BBC Scotland 1976, ret early to concentrate on writing; work published 1979 led to the exposure of Anthony Blunt as a spy; occasional contrib to newspapers including: Times, Spectator, Washington Post; memb Authors' Soc; *Books* No Passing Glory: The Authorised Biography of Group Capt Leonard Cheshire (1955), Trenchard: Man of Vision (1962), Montagu Norman: A Biography (1967), Only The Wind Will Listen: Reith of the BBC (1972), Poor Dear Brendan (1974, Whitbread award Biography of the Year), Erkine Childers: A Biography (1977), The Climate of Treason (1979), The Fourth Man: Anthony Blunt (1986), co-author of three other books; *Style*— Andrew Boyle, Esq; 39 Lansdowne Rd, London W11 2LQ (☎ 071 727 5758)

BOYLE, Billy; s of Bill Boyle (d 1983), of Dublin, Ireland, and Kathleen, *née* Noone; *b* 24 Feb 1948; *Educ* O'Connell's Sch Dublin Ireland; *Career* actor; TV appearances incl: Jackanory, The Professionals, Life at Stake, Frost Report, The Saturday Crowd, It's Billy Boyle, The Basil Brush Show, The Generation Game, Dance Crazy, The Kelly Monteith Show, The Bretts; theatre performances incl: Maggie May, Canterbury Tales, Hello Dolly, Billy, No Sex Please We're British, Playboy of the Western World, What's a Nice Country, The Fantastiks, The Rivals (NY), The Scheming Lieutenant (US), Parnell, The Grass Arena; theatre: Boots for the Footless, Merman; films: Barry Lyndon, Side by Side, Groupie Girl, Sean, The Scarlet and the Black, The Predator, Wild Geese II; *Style*— Billy Boyle, Esq; c/o Barry Brown Agency

BOYLE, Brian; s of Peter Joseph Boyle; *b* 24 Nov 1952; *Educ* Winchmore Sch; *Career* AV photographer; jtly ptnr photographic company; *Recreations* photography, music, sport, driving; *Style*— Brian Boyle Esq; 2 Haslemere Rd, Winchmore Hill, N21 (☎ 081 886 2026)

BOYLE, Marshal of the RAF Sir Dermot Alexander; GCB (1957, CB 1946), KCVO (1953), KBE (1953, CBE 1945), AFC (1939); s of Alexander Francis Boyle, JP, of Belmont House, Queen's Co, and Anna Maria, *née* Harpur; *b* 2 Oct 1904; *Educ* St Columba's Coll, RAF Coll Cranwell; *m* 1931, Una, da of Edward Valentine Carey, of Guernsey; 3 s (Timothy b and d 1933, Anthony Alexander b 1935, Christopher Patrick b 1937), 1 da (Penelope Susan b 1946); *Career* cmmnd RAF 1924, Air ADC to the King 1943, Air Cdre 1944, Dir-Gen of Personnel Air Miny 1948-49, Air Vice Marshal 1949, Dir-Gen of Manning 1949-51, AOC No 1 Gp Bomber Cmd 1951-53, AOCIC Fighter Cmd 1953-55, Air Marshal 1954, Air Chief Marshal 1956, Chief of Air Staff 1956-59, Marshal of the RAF 1958; vice-chm Br Aircraft Corporation 1962-71; *Style*— Marshal of RAF Sir Dermot Boyle, GCB, KCVO, KBE, AFC; Fair Gallop, Brighton Rd, Sway, Hants (☎ 0590 682322)

BOYLE, George Hamilton; DL (Leics 1980); s of Capt E M G L Boyle (d 1982), and Maida Cecil, *née* Evans-Freke; *b* 15 Sept 1928; *Educ* Canford, Univ of London (BSc); *m* 25 July 1953, Alathea Henriette Mary March Phillipps de Lisle; 3 s (Robert b 28 Sept 1954, Richard b 8 Jan 1959, Rupert b 19 Sept 1960); *Career* non-exec dir E Midland Electricity Bd 1980-90; memb Advsy Panel Environmental Devpt National Grid Co 1990-; pres Friends of Rutland Co Museum and Record Soc; High Sheriff Co of Rutland 1964 and Leics 1976; ARSM; *Style*— George Boyle, Esq, DL

BOYLE, Lady Georgina Susan; da of 9 Earl of Shannon; *b* 7 Feb 1961; *Career* artist, watercolourist; *Style*— Lady Georgina Boyle; 96 Wandsworth Bridge Road, London SW6

BOYLE, (Samuel) Gerald; s of Samuel Joseph Boyle, of Belfast (d 1972), and Mary Alice, *née* Edgar; *b* 23 May 1937; *Educ* St Patrick's HS Downpatrick Co Down; *m* 5 Oct 1965, Kathleen Bernadette, da of Hugh Blaney Crossey (d 1983); 3 s (Gary b 1966, Jonathan b 1968, Nicholas b 1972); *Career* chartered insurer dir: Shield Insurance Co Ltd Dublin 1984-, Euro Assistance Ltd Croydon 1987-89; divnl dir Eagle Star Insur Co Ltd 1987- (gen mangr 1985-87), dir Indust and Agric Safety Consits 1989-; *Recreations* golf and rugby; *Clubs* Effingham Golf (Surrey), Northern FC (Newcastle upon Tyne); *Style*— Gerald Boyle, Esq; Eaves Cottage, 42 Lower Rd, Fetcham, Surrey KT22 9ER (☎ 0372 373025); Eagle Star Insur Co Ltd, Eagle Star Hse, 9 Aldgate High St, London EC3N 1LD (tel 071 929 1111, fax 071 377 6180, telex 883018)

BOYLE, Lady Geraldine Lilian; da of Col Gerald Edmund Boyle (d 1927), and half sis of 12 Earl of Cork and Orrery, GCB, GCVO; *b* 1899; *Career* granted rank, title and precedence of an Earl's da which would have been hers had her father survived to succeed to the title; *Style*— Lady Geraldine Boyle; 38 Strand Court, Topsham, Exeter, Devon

BOYLE, Dr Iain Thomson; s of Dugald Thomson Boyle (d 1971), and Annie Ross, *née* MacPhail; *b* 7 Oct 1935; *Educ* Paisley GS, Univ of Glasgow; *m* 28 Aug 1964, Elizabeth Johnston, da of John Trew Carmichael, of Glasgow; 1 s (Douglas), 2 da (Catriona, Alison); *Career* Hartenstein res fell Univ of Wisconsin USA 1970-72, ed

Scottish Medical Journal 1978-83, reader in med Univ of Glasgow and Glasgow Royal Infirmary 1984-, dep med advsr Univ of Strathclyde; pres Caledonian Philatelic Soc 1983-84, chm Bd of Mgmnt Scottish Medical Journal 1987-, memb Exec Ctee Assoc of Physicians of GB and Ireland 1988-; FRCP Glasgow 1974, FRCP 1978, FSA Scotland 1985; *Recreations* angling, social history, philately, golf; *Style—* Dr Iain Boyle; Glasgow Royal Infirmary, 10 Alexandra Parade, Glasgow (☎ 041 552 3535)

BOYLE, John Godfrey (Geoff); OBE (1977); s of John Boyle (d 1980), of Edinburgh, and Maude Craven (d 1935); *b* 17 Nov 1928; *Educ* Daniel Stewart Coll Edinburgh; *m* 1955, Sarah, da of George Death Ward (d 1968), of Edinburgh; 1 s (Adrian), 1 da (Philippa); *Career* CA; fin conslt and enterprise cnsllr DTI, business cnsllr Scottish Devpt Agency, former fin dir Burmah Oil Exploration Ltd 1980-; dir: Burmah Oil Somalia Ltd 1982-, Burmah Shell Oil Storage & Distribution Co of India Ltd 1978-, Bladite Hldgs Ltd 1978-, Burmah Oil Co Pakistan Trading Ltd 1978-, PS & S (Personnel) Ltd 1983-, Assam Oil Co Ltd 1978-, Burmah Oil Kenya Ltd 1982-; *Recreations* literature, music, yachting; *Clubs* Sind, Karachi, East Lothian Yacht, North Berwick; *Style—* John Godfrey Boyle, Esq, OBE; Baltrenon, 22 Dirleton Ave, North Berwick, East Lothian EH39 4BQ (☎ 0620 2642)

BOYLE, Sheriff John Sebastian; s of Edward Joseph Boyle, of Glasgow (d 1960), and Constance Mary, *née* Hook (d 1983); *b* 29 March 1933; *Educ* St Aloysius Coll Glasgow, Univ of Glasgow (BL); *m* 1, 1955, Catherine Denise, da of John Croall, of Glasgow (d 1975); 1 s (Stephen b 1958), 2 da (Susan b 1957, Cecilia b 1960); m 2, 1978, Isobel Margaret, da of James Ryan (d 1984), of Ballytrent, Co Wexford, Ireland; 1 s (Edward b 1981, d 1989), 1 da (Elizabeth b 1979); *Career* slr Glasgow 1955-83; Sheriff of S Strathclyde Dumfries and Galloway at Airdrie 1983-; pres Glasgow Bar Assoc 1963; memb: Scot Arts Cncl 1966-72, Cncl Law Soc of Scotland 1968-75, Criminal Injuries Compensation Bd 1975-83; dir Scot Opera 1984-, chm Westbourne Music 1988-, govr Royal Scot Acad of Music and Drama 1989-; *Style—* Sheriff John Boyle; 5 Great Western Terrace, Glasgow G12 0UP (☎ 041 357 1459); Sheriff's Chambers, Airdrie Sheriff Court, Graham St, Airdrie ML6 6EE (☎ 02364 51121)

BOYLE, Hon John William; DSC (1945); s of Hon Reginald Courtenay Boyle, MBE, MC (d 1946), and Violet, *née* Flower (d 1974); bro and hp of 13 Earl of Cork and Orrery; granted title, rank and precedence of an Earl's son 1967; *b* 12 May 1916; *Educ* Harrow, King's Coll London (BSc Eng 1937); *m* 16 Oct 1943, Mary Leslie, da of Gen Sir Robert Gordon-Finlayson, KCB, CMG, DSO (d 1956); 3 s (John Richard b 1945, Robert William b 1948, (Charles) Reginald b 1957); *Career* served WWII (despatches twice), Lt Cdr RNVR, six years afloat with RN in most western theatres; FICE (ret), sometime MIMechE; *Recreations* country and family life, making and mending, reading; *Style—* The Hon John Boyle, DSC; Nether Craigantaggart, Dunkeld, Perthshire PH8 0HQ (☎ 073871 239)

BOYLE, Katie (Catherine Irene Helen Mary); da of Marchese Demetrio Imperiali dei Principi di Francavilla, and Dorothy Kate, *née* Ramsden; *b* 29 May 1926; *Educ* Switzerland and Italy; *m* 1, 1947 (m dis 1955), Viscount Boyle, now Earl of Shannon; m 2, 1955, Greville Baylis (d 1976); m 3, 1979, Sir Peter Saunders; *Career* author of "Dear Katie" column TV Times 1969-, frequent contributor to varied publications, permanent agony aunt for Daily Mail off shoot Dogs Today and for 8 years to Here's Health; broadcaster of wide variety of subjects (including Quite Contrary 1954, Golden Girl, Eurovision Song Contest, various Katie Boyle shows, currently on Radio 2 FM); stage and film work; dir: Peter Saunders Ltd 1979-, Peter Saunders Co Ltd 1979-; memb Ctee Battersea Dogs' Home; tstee: Peter Saunders Fndn, Katie Boyle Animal Welfare Fndn; *Recreations* animal welfare, dog training, gardening, jigsaw puzzles; *Style—* Miss Katie Boyle; 10 Maiden Lane, London WC2E 7NA (☎ 071 240 3177)

BOYLE, Leonard Butler; CBE (1976); s of Harold and Edith Boyle; *b* 13 Jan 1913; *Educ* Roundhay Sch Leeds; *m* 1938, late Alice Baldwin Yarborough; 2 s; *Career* dir and gen mangr Principality Building Society 1956-78; vice pres: Bldg Soc Assoc 1978 (chm 1973-75), Chartered Bldg Socs Inst 1978-; *Style—* Leonard Boyle Esq, CBE; Northwick Cottage, Marlpit Lane, Seaton, Devon (☎ 0297 22194)

BOYLE, Hon Mrs John; Marie; *née* Gibb; da of John Gibb, of Chillesford, Orford, Suffolk; *m* 1 (m dis), George Chettle; m 2, 1934, as his 2 w, Air Cdre the Hon John David Boyle, CBE, DSC (d 1974), yst s of 7 Earl of Glasgow, GCMG; *Career* JP and Co Cncllr for Wigtownshire; *Style—* The Hon Mrs John Boyle; Cushat Wood, Portpatrick, Stranraer, Wigtownshire

BOYLE, Capt Michael Patrick Radcliffe; DL (Hants 1982); s of Patrick Spencer Boyle (s of late Capt Hon E Spencer H Boyle, RN, 5 s of 5 Earl of Shannon, by his 2 w, Julia, da of Sir William Hartopp, 3 Bt); *b* 25 Jan 1934; *Educ* Eton; *m* 1962, Lady Nell Carleton Harris, da of 6 Earl of Malmesbury, TD, DL, and Hon Diana Carleton, da of 2 Baron Dorchester; 2 s, 1 da; *Career* cmmnd Irish Gds 1953, Capt 1961, ret 1966; High Sheriff Hants 1976-77, memb Hants CC 1970-, chm Hants Police Authority 1976-88; cmmnr St John's Ambulance Bde Hants 1969-75; Freeman City of London, Liveryman Worshipful Co of Gunmakers; CStJ; FBIM; *Recreations* shooting, sailing; *Clubs* Boodle's, Pratt's, Royal Yacht Sqdn; *Style—* Capt Michael Boyle, DL; Forest Lodge, Ashe Park, Basingstoke, Hants RG25 3AZ (☎ 0256 781611)

BOYLE, Ranald Hugh Montgomerie; DSC (1944); 2 s of David Hugh Montgomerie Boyle, CMG (d 1970), ggs of Rt Hon David Boyle, Lord Justice General and Pres of the Court of Session in Scotland, himself gs of 2 Earl of Glasgow, and of Laura Grant Tennant (d 1971), 3 da of James Tennant, of Fairlie, who was nephew of Sir Charles Tennant, 1 Bt, and 1 cous of 1 Baron Glenconner; *b* 19 Aug 1921; *Educ* Wellington, Exeter Coll Oxford (BA); *m* 27 April 1957, Norma, yst da of Alexander Gray (d 1932), merchant, of Calcutta and London; 5 s (Fergus b 1958, Alexander b 1959, Patrick b 1961, Jaikie b 1964, Hamish b 1970), 2 da (Laura b 1963, Beatrice b 1966); *Career* WWII Lt RNVR served: Channel Convoys, Dieppe Raid 1942 (wounded), Mediterranean, Far East (Br Pacific Fleet); Sudan Political Serv 1946-53, freelance journalist 1954, Iraq Petroleum Co 1955-56, HM Overseas Civil Service Kenya 1956-64, first sec HM Diplomatic Serv 1964-70, Hambros Bank 1970-81 (dir 1975-81), sr rep (London) Arab Banking Corp 1981-82, conslt Ranald Boyle Conslt 1982-; memb Royal Co of Archers (Queen's Body Guard for Scotland); *Recreations* field sports, tennis, reading, family life; *Clubs* United Oxford and Cambridge Univ, Puffin's (Edinburgh); *Style—* Ranald Boyle, Esq, DSC; 906 Beatty House, Dolphin Sq, London SW1V 3PN (☎ 071 821 8028); Downcraig Ferry, Millport, Isle of Cumbrae, Scotland (☎ 0475 530550); The Wooden House, Fairlie, Ayrshire, Scotland (☎ 0475 568284)

BOYLE, Hon Mrs (Rebecca Juliet); *née* Noble; da of Baron Glenkinglas (Life Peer, d 1984), and Baroness Glenkinglas, *qv*; *b* 1950; *m* 1973, Lt Cdr John Richard Boyle, RN, s of Hon John William Boyle, DSC, *qv*; 1 s (Rory Jonathan Courtenay b 10 Dec 1978), 2 da (Cara Mary Cecilia b 1976, Davina Claire Theresa (twin) b 1978); *Style—* The Hon Mrs Boyle; Lickfold House, Petworth, Sussex GU28 9EY

BOYLE, Viscount; Richard Henry John Boyle; s (by 2 m) and h of 9 Earl of Shannon; *b* 19 Jan 1960; *Educ* Northease Manor Sch; *Style—* Viscount Boyle; 96 Wandsworth Bridge Rd, London SW6 2TF

BOYLE, Sir Stephen Gurney; 5 Bt (UK 1904); er s of Sir Richard Gurney, 4 Bt (d 1983), s of Sir Edward Boyle, 2 Bt; suc to Btcy only of bro, Baron Boyle of Handsworth (1981), and Elizabeth Anne, yr da of Norman Dennes; *b* 15 Jan 1962; *Style—* Sir Stephen Boyle, Bt; 28 The Lawn, Harlow, Essex

BOYLE, William Russell; s of Charles Harry Boyle (d 1988), of Wimborne St Giles, Dorset, and Winifred Boyle (d 1967); *b* 15 Feb 1945; *m* 19 July 1969, Janet Elizabeth; 1 s (Matthew b 1974), 1 da (Joanne b 1971); *Career* insur broker; dir C T Bowring & Co (Insurance) Ltd, exec dir Bowring Marine & Energy Insur Brokers Ltd, md Marsh and McLennan Worldwide; *Style—* William R Boyle, Esq; C T Bowring & Co (Insurance) Ltd, The Bowring Building, Tower Place, London EC3 (☎ 071 357 5514)

BOYLSTON, Prof Arthur William; s of George Arthur Boylston, and Marie, *née* Showers; *b* 16 Nov 1942; *Educ* Phillips Exeter Acad, Yale Univ (BA), Harvard Univ (MD); *m* 1 July 1978, Anthea, da of John Murray Phelps; 2 s (Thomas Arthur b 1980, Nicholas John b 1984); *Career* sr asst surgn US Public Health Serv 1970-72, lectr, sr lectr then reader St Mary's Hosp Med Sch London 1972-88, prof pathology Univ of Leeds 1988; FRCPath 1988; *Recreations* walking; *Clubs* Atheneaum; *Style—* Prof Arthur Boylston; Pathology Department, University of Leeds, Leeds LS2 9JT (☎ 0532 333389, fax 0532 333404)

BOYNE, 10 Viscount (I 1717); Gustavus Michael George Hamilton-Russell; JP (Salop 1961), DL (Salop 1965); also Baron Hamilton of Stackallen (I 1715) and Baron Brancepeth (UK 1866); sits as Baron Brancepeth; s of Hon Gustavus Hamilton-Russell (ka 1940, s and h of 9 Viscount Boyne, JP, DL, by his w, Lady Margaret Lascelles, CBE, da of 5 Earl of Harewood) and Joan, da of Sir Harry Lloyd Verney, GCVO (gs of Sir Harry Verney, 2 Bt), by his w, Lady Joan Cuffe (da of 5 and last Earl of Desart, KP); suc gf 1942; *b* 10 Dec 1931; *Educ* Eton, Sandhurst, RAC Cirencester; *m* 11 April 1956, Rosemary Anne, 2 da of Sir Denis Stucley, 5 Bt (d 1983); 1 s, 3 da (1 decd); *Heir* s, Hon Gustavus Hamilton-Russell; *Career* formerly Lt Gren Gds (ret 1956); dir Nat West Bank 1976-90 (chm W Midland & Wales Regnl Bd); dep chm Telford Development Corporation 1976-82; Lord-in-waiting to HM The Queen 1981-; chm: Harper Adams Agric Coll, Ludlow Race Club Ltd; dir Private Patients Plan Ltd CStJ; *Recreations* skiing, shooting, fishing, motoring; *Clubs* White's; *Style—* The Rt Hon The Viscount Boyne, JP, DL; Burwarton House, Bridgnorth, Shropshire (☎ 074 633 203, office 207)

BOYNE, Sir Henry Brian (Harry); CBE (1969); 2 s of late Lockhart Alexander Boyne, of Inverness, and Elizabeth Jane Mactavish; *b* 29 July 1910; *Educ* HS and Royal Acad Inverness; *m* 1935, Margaret Little, da of John Templeton, of Dundee; 1 da; *Career* political corr: Glasgow Herald 1950-56, Daily Telegraph 1956-76; dir communications Cons Central Office 1980-82; kt 1976; *Books* The Houses of Parliament (1981), Scotland Rediscovered (1986); *Recreations* reading, walking; *Clubs* Victory; *Style—* Sir Harry Boyne, CBE; 122 Harefield Rd, Uxbridge, Middx UB8 1PN (☎ 0895 55211)

BOYNTON, Sir John Keyworth; MC (1944), DL (Cheshire 1975); s of Ernest Boynton (d 1940), of Hull; *b* 14 Feb 1918; *Educ* Dulwich Coll; *m* 1, 1947, Gabrielle (d 1978), da of G Stanglmaier, of Munich; 2 da; m 2, 1979, Edith Laane, of The Hague; *Career* slr; chief exec Cheshire CC 1974-79, election cmmr S Rhodesia 1979-80; kt 1979; *Books* Compulsory Puchase (6 edn, 1990), Job at the Top (1986); *Recreations* golf; *Clubs* Army and Navy; *Style—* Sir John Boynton, MC, DL; 1B Oakhill Ave, London NW3 7RD (☎ 071 435 0012)

BOYNTON-WOOD; *see*: Wood

BOYS, John Philip; s of late Rev Stephen Philip Boys, and late Constance Rhoda Towns; *Educ* Glasgow and Dundee Colls of Art (DA); *m* 29 June 1963 (m dis 1988), Christine Bridget, da of late Cdr Jorgen Svend Jensen; 2 s (Adam b 1967, Jamie b 1970), 1 da (Amanda Jo b 1974); *Career* RAEC Egypt and Kenya 1946-48; joined Boys Jarvis Partnership 1960 (now John Boys Architects); awards and commendations (with others) incl: finalist Sydney Opera House competition, finalist Financial Times Industl award, Assoc for the Protection of Rural Scotland award; Civic Tst and Saltire Soc Commendations RIBA/RIAS regnl award 1989; memb Royal Fine Art Cmmn for Scotland; ARSA, FRIBA, FRIAS; *Recreations* painting, curling, sailing; *Clubs* Glasgow Art; *Style—* John Boys, Esq; San Makessan, Gartocharn, Dunbartonshire G83 9LX (☎ 038 983 228); 19 Woodside Place, Glasgow G3 7QL (☎ 041 332 2228)

BOYSON, Rt Hon Sir Rhodes; MP (C) Brent North Feb 1974-; s of Alderman William Boyson, MBE, JP, of Haslingden, Lancs, and Bertha Boyson; *b* 11 May 1925; *Educ* Haslingden GS, Univ of Manchester, Univ Coll Cardiff, LSE, CCC Cambridge (BA, MA, PhD); *m* 1, 1946 (m dis), Violet Burletson; 2 da; m 2, 1971, Florette, *née* MacFarlane; *Career* headmaster: Lea Bank Secdy Modern Rossendale 1955-61, Robert Montefiore Secdy Sch Stepney 1961-66, Highbury GS 1966-67, Highbury Grove Sch 1967-74; contested (C) Eccles 1970, vice chm Cons Parly Educn Ctee 1975-76, oppn spokesman for educn 1976-79, Parly under-sec DES 1979-83, min for social security DHSS 1983-84, dep sec for NI 1984-86, min for local govt 1986-87; chm Nat Cncl Educnl Standards 1974-79; *Recreations* gardening, sport, writing, talking; *Clubs* St Stephen's, Carlton; *Style—* Rt Hon Sir Rhodes Boyson, MP; 71 Paines Lane, Pinner, Middx (☎ 081 866 2071)

BOZMAN, Michael Steven; s of John Michael Bozman (d 1988), and Ann Elizabeth, *née* Capper; *b* 2 Feb 1957; *Educ* Lancing; *m* 5 June 1982, Sally Ann, da of John Kimberley, of Hinksey Hill, Oxford; *Career* buyer Harrods Ltd 1975-84, mktg dir Totes 1984-; memb Mktg Soc 1988; *Recreations* cricket, tennis; *Clubs* MCC, Sussex Martlets; *Style—* Michael Bozman, Esq; 42 Gosberton Rd, London SW12 8LF (☎ 081 675 4991); Totes, Eastman House, Billericay, Essex (☎ 0277 630277)

BRABAZON, Hon David Geoffrey Normand; yr s of 14 Earl of Meath; *b* 9 Oct 1948; *Educ* Tabley House; *m* 1972, Gay Dorothea, da of late Cdr William (Jock) Whitworth, DSC, RN (d 1955, s of Adm Sir William Whitworth, KCB, DSO) by his w Dorothea (whose mother Sophia was sis of 8 Marquess of Ely's f, George); 1 s, 2 da; *Style—* The Hon David Brabazon; North Wing, Killruddery, Bray, Co Wicklow, Ireland

BRABAZON OF TARA, 3 Baron (UK 1942); Ivon Anthony Moore-Brabazon; s of 2 Baron Brabazon of Tara, CBE (d 1974, whose f, 1 Baron, was min of Aircraft Production after Beaverbrook; the Bristol-Brabazon airliner was named after him); *b* 20 Dec 1946; *Educ* Harrow; *m* 8 Sept 1979, Harriet, da of Mervyn de Courcy Hamilton, of Harare, Zimbabwe, by his w, Lovell Ann, da of Rowland Cullinan, of Olifantsfontein, Transvaal; 1 s (Hon Benjamin Ralph b 1983), 1 da (Hon Anabel Mary b 1985); *Heir* s, Hon Benjamin Ralph Moore-Brabazon b 15 March 1983; *Career* memb London Stock Exchange 1972-84; a Lord in Waiting (government whip) 1984-86; spokesman for Dept of Transport 1984-85, and for Treasy, Dept of Trade and Industry, Energy 1985-86; Parly under-sec of state for Transport and min for Aviation and Shipping 1986-89, min of state Foreign and Commonwealth Office 1989-90, min of state Dept of Tport 1990-; *Recreations* sailing; *Clubs* White's, Royal Yacht Sqdn; *Style—* The Rt Hon the Lord Brabazon of Tara; House of Lords, London SW1

BRABHAM, Sir John Arthur (Jack); OBE (1966); s of Cyril Thomas Brabham; *b* 2 April 1926; *Educ* Hurstville Tech Coll Sydney; *m* 1951, Betty Evelyn; 3 s; *Career* racing driver, ret 1970; md: Jack Brabham (Motors) Ltd, Jack Brabham (Worcester Park) Ltd, Engine Developements Ltd; three times World Motor Racing champion 1959, 1960 and 1966; kt 1979; *Books* When the Flag Drops; *Recreations* flying, boating, skindiving; *Clubs* BRDC, RAC; *Style—* Sir Jack Brabham, OBE; 33 Central Rd, Worcester Park, Surrey (☎ 081 337 0755)

BRABOURNE, 7 Baron (UK 1880); John Ulick Knatchbull; 16 Bt (E 1641); s of 5 Baron Brabourne, GCSI, GCIE, MC, JP, MP (d 1939, sometime viceroy and actg govr-gen India) by his w, Lady Doreen Browne (Dowager Lady Brabourne, d 1979, da of 6 Marquess of Sligo); suc er bro, 6 Baron (d 1943, shot by the Germans after escaping from a prison train in Italy and recaptured); *b* 9 Nov 1924; *Educ* Eton, BNC Oxford; *m* 1946, Lady Patricia Edwina Victoria Mountbatten (Countess Mountbatten of Burma, *qv*), da of 1 Earl Mountbatten of Burma; 4 s (and 1 s decd), 2 da; *Heir* s, Lord Romsey; *Career* chm Thames TV plc 1990-; dir Mersham Productions Ltd; producer/ co-producer feature films: Harry Black and the Tiger (1958), Sink the Bismarck (1960), HMS Defiant (1961), Othello (1966), Romeo and Juliet (1966), The Mikado (1967), Up the Junction (1968), The Dance of Death (1969), The Tales of Beatrix Potter (1971), Murder on the Orient Express (1974), Death on the Nile (1978), Stories from a Flying Trunk (1979), The Mirror Crack'd (1980), Evil Under the Sun (1982), A Passage to India (1984), Little Dorrit (1987); TV productions: The Life and Times of Lord Mountbatten (1968), Royal Family (1969, memb Advsy Ctee), Romantic Versus Classic Art (1973), The National Gallery - A Private View (1974), A Much Maligned Monarch (1976), Royal Heritage (1977, memb Advsy Ctee), Leontyne (1988); chm: Br Cncl Advsy Ctee on Film, TV and Video, Cncl Caldecott Community, Govrs of Norton Knatchbull Sch; govr: Gordonstoun, Nat Film Sch, Wye Coll, United World Coll of the Atlantic; tstee: BAFTA, Science Museum, Nat Museum of Photography; dep pro chllr Kent Univ; pres Kent Tst for Nature Conservation; memb Br Screen Advsy Cncl, pres The Producers Assoc; vice-pres Royal Soc of Nature Conservation; fell and govr BFI, memb Advsy Ctee Nat Sound Archivists; *Style—* The Rt Hon Lord Brabourne; Newhouse, Mersham, Ashford, Kent TN25 6NQ (☎ 0233 623466); 39/41 Montpelier Walk, London SW7 1JH (☎ 071 589 8829)

BRACEWELL, Hon Mrs Justice; Joyanne Winifred (Dame Joyanne Copeland); DBE (1990); da of Jack Bracewell, and Lilian Bracewell; *b* 5 July 1934; *Educ* Univ of Manchester (LLB, LLM); *m* 1963, Roy Copeland, s of late Jack Copeland; 1 s (Adam b 1965), 1 da (Philippa b 1967); *Career* rec of the Crown Court Northern Circuit 1975-83 (QC 1978), circuit judge Northern Circuit 1983-86, Western Circuit 1986-90, sworn in as Judge of High Court 1990-; *Recreations* antiques, cooking, reading, walking, bridge, wildlife conservation; *Style—* The Hon Mrs Justice Bracewell, DBE

BRACEWELL SMITH, Sir Charles; 4 Bt (UK 1947), of Keighley, Co York; s of Sir George Bracewell Smith, 2 Bt, MBE (d 1976); suc bro, Sir Guy Bracewell Smith 1983; *b* 13 Oct 1955; *Educ* Harrow; *Heir* none; *Style—* Sir Charles Bracewell Smith; Park Lane Hotel, Piccadilly, London W1

BRACEWELL-SMITH, Sir Charles; 5 Bt (UK 1947), of Keighley, Co York; suc bro Sir Guy Bracewell Smith, 4 Bt (d 1983); *b* 13 Oct 1955; *Educ* Harrow; *m* 1977, Carol Vivien, da of Norman Hough, of Cookham, Berks; *Style—* Sir Charles Bracewell-Smith, Bt; Park Lane Hotel, Piccadilly, London W1

BRACK, Peter Kenneth; s of Rev Martin Brack (d 1953), of Wolviston, Co Durham, and Dorothea, *née* Martin (d 1977); *b* 13 April 1922; *Educ* Trent Coll Derbyshire; *m* 1 April 1961, Nora, da of Francis Kilmartin, MM (d 1957), of Cheadle, Cheshire; *Career* Rolls Royce Ltd (Derby) 1940-71; engrg apprenticeship followed by various duties home and abroad: Cor Argentina 1950-52, Venezuela 1953-56, France and Italy 1957-59, md Rolls Royce De Espana SA 1963-71; dir: Bennett's Machine Co 1973-75, TTI Ltd (Translations Co) 1975-77; md Brack & Assoc Ltd 1977-; Derbyshire rep Int C of C 1975-, pres Br Club Barcelona 1966-71; CEng, FBIM; *Recreations* philately (recognised authority on Venezuelan stamps), golf, chess, natural history; *Clubs* Canning, Naval and Military; *Style—* Peter Brack, Esq; Chrysalis, Windley, Derbyshire DE5 2LP (☎ 077 389 364); Brack & Associates Ltd, 66-66A Friar Gate, Derby DE1 1DJ (☎ 0332 360242, fax 0332 291551)

BRACKENBURY, Mark Hereward; s of Charles Hereward Brackenbury (d 1979), of Tweedhill, Berwick-upon-Tweed, and Elise, *née* Cuming (d 1984); *b* 19 April 1931; *Educ* Ampleforth, New Coll Oxford; *m* 18 Sept 1956, Virginia Catherine, da of Gibson Stott (d 1985), of 100 Hobson St, Wellington, NZ; 1 s (David b 1961), 1 da (Claire b 1957); *Career* ptnr Sternberg Thomas Clarke & Co and predecessor firms 1964-76; memb London Stock Exchange; yachting author and journalist; *Books* incl: Norwegian Cruising Guide (1978), Scottish West Coast Pilot (1980), S W Baltic Pilot (1983), Normandy & Channel Island Pilot (1983); *Recreations* sailing (circumnavigated 1983-86), skiing, bridge; *Clubs* Garrick, Green Room, Royal Cruising; *Style—* Mark Brackenbury, Esq; Fallowfield, Stebbing, Dunmow, Essex CM6 3ST (☎ 037186 242)

BRACKENBURY, Michael Palmer; s of Frank Brackenbury (d 1959), and Constance Mary, *née* Palmer (d 1946); *b* 6 July 1930; *Educ* Norwich Sch, Lincoln Theol Coll; *m* 9 Apr 1953, Jean Margaret, da of Oscar Arnold Harrison (d 1966); *Career* RAF 1948-50; asst curate S Ormsby Gp 1966-69, rector Sudbrooke with Scothern 1969-77, rural dean Lawres 1973-78, diocesan dir of ordinands Lincoln 1977-87, personal asst to Bishop of Lincoln 1977-88, canon and prebendary of Lincoln 1979-, diocesan lay ministry advsr Lincoln 1986-87, archdeacon of Lincoln 1988-; memb Gen Synod 1989-; ACII 1956; *Recreations* music, reading, cricket, travel; *Style—* The Ven the Archdeacon of Lincoln; 2 Ashfield Rd, Sleaford, Lincolnshire NG34 7DZ (☎ 0529 307149)

BRACKFIELD, Peter; s of Julius Alexander Brackfield (d 1959); *b* 26 Sept 1922; *Educ* Berkhamsted Sch, Trinity Coll Cambridge (MA); *m* 1, 1954 (m dis), Odile, da of Louis de Koenigswarter, of Paris; 1 s; m 2, 1982, Beatrice, da of William Newton, of Kuala Lumpur; *Career* merchant banker; dir: Singer-Friedlander Ltd 1983-89 (md 1956-76, dep chm 1976-82), C T Bowring & Co 1971-80; chm Lavant Hill Devpt Ltd 1986-; cmmr Public Works Loans Bd; *Recreations* walking, tennis, skiing, gardening; *Style—* Peter Brackfield, Esq; Flat 6, 58 Rutland Gate, London SW7 (☎ 071 584 7432); Priory Stones, Lurgashall, Petworth, W Sussex (☎ 042 878 320)

BRADBEER, Sir (John) Derek Richardson; OBE (1973), TD (1964), DL (1988); s of William Bertram Bradbeer, of Hexham, Northumberland, and Winifred, *née* Richardson (d 1985); *b* 29 Oct 1931; *Educ* Canford, Sidney Sussex Coll Cambridge (MA); *m* 6 April 1962, Margaret Elizabeth, da of Gerald Frederick Chantler, TD, of Ponteland, Northumberland; 1 s (Jeremy b 1962), 1 da (Amanda b 1963); *Career* cmmnd RA 1951, CO 101 (N) Med Regt RA (V) 1970-73, Dep Cdr 21 and 23 Bdes 1973-77, Hon Col 101 (N) FD Regt RA (V) 1986-; chm TAVR Assoc North of England 1990-; admitted slr 1959; ptnr Wilkinson Maughan Newcastle 1961-; memb Cncl Law Soc 1973-, pres Newcastle Law Soc 1980, govr Coll of Law 1983-, chm Law Soc 1990- (vice pres 1986-87, pres 1987-88), memb Criminal Injuries Compensation Bd 1988-; dir: JT Dove Pensions Tst Ltd 1975-, Newcastle and Gateshead Water plc 1978-, Sunderland and South Shield Water plc 1990-, RB Bolton (Mining Engineers) Ltd 1990-; kt 1988; *Recreations* gardening, reading, tennis, general sport; *Clubs* Army & Navy, Northern Counties; *Style—* Sir Derek Bradbeer, OBE, TD, DL; Forge Cottage, Shilvington, Northumberland NE20 0AP (☎ 067 075 214); Wilkinson Maughan, Sun Alliance House, 35 Mosley St, Newcastle upon Tyne NE1 1XX (☎ 091 261 1841, fax 091 261 8267, telex 537477)

BRADBEER, Jonathan Linthorn; s of Leonard Harry Bradbeer (d 1983), and Grace Laura, *née* Whitting (d 1988); *b* 14 April 1938; *Educ* Clayesmore Sch Iwerne Minster Dorset, Guy's Hosp Dental Sch (BDS, LDS, RCS); *m* (m dis); *Career* Surgeon Lt (D) RN 1963-68; gen dental practice 1968-; memb: Br Dental Assoc, RSM; *Recreations* ocean racing, skiing, flying; *Clubs* Royal Yacht Sqdn, Royal Ocean Racing, Royal Lymington Yacht, Island Sailing, Royal Yachting Assoc; *Style—* Jonathan Bradbeer, Esq; 14 Ashley Ct, Morpeth Terr, London SW1 (☎ 071 828 4779); 7 Harcourt House, 19A Cavendish Square, London W1 (☎ 071 580 2551)

BRADBEER, Richard Neil; *b* 30 Oct 1936; *Educ* Burnham-on-Sea Secondary Sch; *m* 11 Dec 1986, Patricia Ann; *Career* professional golfer; clubs: Taunton and Pickeridge 1959-63, Bristol and Clifton 1963-69, Burnham and Berrow 1969-79, The Royal Birkdale 1979-; capt European PGA Cup Team (against USA) 1990, capt PGA 1990, sr instructor PGA, EGU Coach for the North West of England; *Books* 100 Golfing Tips (1990), Ahead of the Game (1990); *Recreations* travel, good food and wine; *Style—* Richard Bradbeer, Esq; 19 Harrod Drive, Birkdale Southport, Merseyside PR8 2HA (☎ 0704 68594); The Royal Birkdale Golf Club, Waterloo Rd, Birkdale Southport, Merseyside (☎ 0704 68857)

BRADBURN, Stephen Ernest; s of Ernest Bradburn, of Sheffield; *b* 24 Sept 1947; *Educ* Abbeydale Boys' GS Sheffield; *m* 1969, Geraldine, da of Albert Britton, of Woodley Berks; 1 s; *Career* dir: Hargreaves Tport Ltd 1976-, Hargreaves Vehicle Distributors Ltd 1978-; *Style—* Stephen Bradburn Esq; 10 Cottesmore Gdns, Hale Barns, Altrincham, Cheshire

BRADBURY, Surgn Vice Adm Sir Eric Blackburn; KBE (1971), CB (1968); s of late A B Bradbury, of Orchard House, Maze, Co Antrim; *b* 2 March 1911; *Educ* Royal Belfast Academical Instn, Queen's Univ Belfast; *m* 1939, Elizabeth Constance, da of late J C Austin, of Armagh; 3 da; *Career* RN Medical Service 1934, Surgn Capt 1959, Medical Offr i/c RN Hosp Haslar 1966, Surg Rear Adm 1966, Surgn Vice Adm 1969, Med Dir Gen of the Navy 1969-72; chm Tunbridge Wells DHA 1981-84; FRCS 1972, Hon LLD Queen's Univ Belfast, CStJ, former QHP; *Style—* Surgn Vice Adm Sir Eric Bradbury, KBE, CB; The Gate House, Nevill Park, Tunbridge Wells, Kent TN4 8NN (☎ 0892 27661)

BRADBURY, Hon John; s and h of 2 Baron Bradbury; *b* 17 March 1940; *Educ* Gresham's and Univ of Bristol; *m* 1968 Susan, da of late W Liddiard, of East Shefford, Berks; 2 s; *Style—* The Hon John Bradbury; 10 Clifton Hill, London NW8

BRADBURY, 2 Baron (UK 1925); John Bradbury; s of 1 Baron, GCB (d 1950); *b* 7 Jan 1914; *Educ* Westminster, BNC Oxford; *m* 1, 1939, Joan, o da of W D Knight, of Darley, Addlestone, Surrey; 1 s, 1 da; m 2, 1946, Gwerfyl, da of late E Stanton Roberts, of Gellifor, Ruthin, Denbigh; 1 da; *Heir* s, Hon John Bradbury; *Style—* The Rt Hon The Lord Bradbury; Wingham, Summerhays, Leigh Hill Rd, Cobham, Surrey (☎ 0932 867757)

BRADBURY, John Howard Hullah; CBE (1986); s of Prof Fred Bradbury (d 1948), and Florence Jane, *née* Ratcliffe (d 1982); *b* 26 Feb 1940; *Educ* Friends' Sch Saffron Walden, Pomfret Sch Pomfret Connecticut USA, Jesus Coll Cambridge; *m* 31 Aug 1963, Christine Annette J, da of Rev Christopher Augustine Kelly, of Gargrave, Skipton, Yorks; 1 s (Michael b 2 Jan 1973), 1 da (Elizabeth b 19 Mar 1970); *Career* factory supt AEI Rugby 1965-67 (prodn devpt engr 1964-65), raw materials buyer Mars Ltd 1968-75 (shift prodn mangr 1967-68), UK buying dir Utd Biscuits (UK) Ltd 1978-89 (dep buying dir 1975-78), dir euro indust policy and purchasing United Biscuits (UK) Ltd 1989- (gp dir of commodities and corporate Affrs 1991-); lay dir AFBD Ltd (non-exec dir); Tower Capt St Mary's Farnham Royal; former pres Cake and Biscuit Alliance; *Recreations* fell walking, flying, skiing, amateur radio, shooting, campanology; *Style—* John Bradbury, Esq, CBE; United Biscuits (UK) Ltd, Grant House, PO Box 40, Syon Lane, Isleworth, Middx TW7 5NN (☎ 081 560 3131, telex UBISLE 8954657, fax 081 568 3505)

BRADBURY, John Keith; s of Ronald Charles Bradbury, of Knowle, Warwicks, and Gladys Marjorie, *née* Green (d 1971); *b* 18 Feb 1932; *Educ* King Henry VIII Sch Coventry; *m* 6 March 1954, Molly, da of Horace Reginald Woodbridge, of Coventry (d 1973); 2 s (Andrew John b 1955, Richard Anthony b 1963), 1 da (Jennifer Ann 1958); *Career* Nat Serv RAF 1950-52; dep ed The Birmingham Post 1975-80; ed: Sandwell Evening Mail 1980-84, Birmingham Post and Mail Weeklies 1984-85, Sunday Mercury Birmingham 1985-90; hon sec Birmingham Dist Newspaper Press Fund 1972, chm Nat Cncl for the Trg of Journalists 1987-88; former chm Birmingham Press Club, vice pres Walmley CC, former pres Wylde Green Bowling Club; Guild Br Newspaper Eds: memb 1980, memb Cncl 1983, regnl chm 1983-84, sec 1990-; *Recreations* theatre, music, travel, gardening, railways; *Clubs* Birmingham Press; *Style—* John Bradbury, Esq; Farriers Cottage, Ebrington, Chipping Campden, Glos; and Eldon Dr, Sutton Coldfield, W Midlands (☎ 038 678 418); Sunday Mercury, Colmore Circus, Birmingham B4 6AZ (☎ 021 236 3366, fax 021 233 3958, telex 337 552)

BRADBURY, Prof Malcolm Stanley; CBE; s of Arthur Bradbury, and Doris, *née* Marshall; *b* 7 Sept 1932; *Educ* Leicester Univ, Queen Mary Coll London (MA, hon fell 1984), Manchester Univ (PhD), Indiana Univ, Yale Univ; *m* 1959, Elizabeth Salt; 2 s (Matthew, Dominic); *Career* staff tutor in lit and drama Dept of Adult Educn Univ of Hull 1959-61, lectr in English language and lit Dept of English Univ of Birmingham 1961-65; UEA: lectr, sr lectr, then reader in English and American lit Sch of English and American Studies 1965-70, prof of American studies 1970-; ed: Arnold Stratford upon Avon Studies series, Methuen Contemporary Writers series, The After Dinner (television plays, 1982); adapted for television: Tom Sharpe's Blott on the Landscape 1985, Tom Sharpe's Porterhouse Blue 1987 (winner of Int Emmy Award), Alison Lurie's, Imaginary Friends 1987, Kingsley Amis', The Green Man 1990; writer of: Anything More Would be Greedy (series for television), The Gravy Train (series for television); visiting prof to Univs of: Zurich, Washington, St Louis, Queensland; chm of judges Booker McConnell Prize 1981, hon fell Queen Mary and Westfield Coll London 1984; Hon DLitt: Leicester 1986, Birmingham 1989; FRSL; *Books* fiction incl: Eating People is Wrong (1959), Stepping Westward (1965), The History Man (1975), Who Do You Think You Are? (short stories, 1976), All Dressed Up and Nowhere To Go (1982), Rates of Exchange (shortlisted Booker Prize, 1982), Why Come to Slaka? (1986), Mensonge (1987), Cuts: a very short novel (1987); *Publications incl*: Evelyn Waugh (1962), What is a Novel? (1965), EM Forster: a collection of critical essays (ed 1965), A Passage to India: a Casebook (ed 1970), Penguin Companion to Literature Vol 3: American (with E Mottram, 1971), The Social Context of Modern English Literature (1972), Possibilities: essays on the state of the novel (1973), Modernism (with JW McFarlane, 1976), The Novel Today (ed 1977), An Introduction to American Studies (ed with H Temperley, 1981), Saul Bellow (1982), The Modern American Novel (1983), Penguin Book of Modern British Short Stories (ed 1987) The Modern World: Ten Great Writers (1987); *Clubs* Royal Over-Seas League; *Style—* Prof Malcolm Bradbury, CBE; School of English and American Studies, University of East Anglia, Norwich NR4 7TJ (☎ 0603 56161, telex UEANOR Norwich)

BRADBURY, Hon Paul; s of 1 Baron Bradbury, GCB (d 1950); *b* 28 Nov 1915; *Educ* Westminster, Brasenose Coll Oxford (MA); *m* 1940, Margaret Amy, da of John William Stammers; 3 s; *Career* company dir (now ret); *Style—* The Hon Paul Bradbury; Chelvey Batch, Brockley, Bristol BS19 3AP (☎ 0275 462813)

BRADBURY, Robert Henry; s of William Henry Bradbury (d 1950), and Edith Minnie, *née* Talboys (d 1985); family spent 25 yrs in India, with Balmer Lawrie & Co Ltd (dir for 12 years), returned to UK 1932; *b* 10 April 1919; *Educ* Oundle; *m* 1, 1942, Jean Margaret, *née* Watson; 1 s (John b 1943), 1 da (Suzanne b 1945); m 2, 24 March 1966, Enid Clement, da of William Vines (d 1965); *Career* RE 1939-46, ret as Maj; joined Crendon Concrete Co Ltd (family business founded by f 1933) 1948 (md

1950), exec chm Crendon Hldgs Ltd (chm of subsid cos and dir of Malaysian assoc cos); FInstD 1956; *Recreations* tennis, swimming, gardening, travel; *Clubs* IOD; *Style—* Robert Bradbury, Esq; The Old Crown, 97 Bicester Rd, Long Crendon, Aylesbury, Bucks HP18 9EF; Crendon Holdings Ltd, Long Crendon, Aylesbury, Bucks HP18 9BB (☎ 0844 208481, telex 83249G, fax 0844 201622)

BRADBURY, Rear Adm Thomas Henry; CB (1979); s of Thomas Henry Bradbury (d 1970), and Violet, *née* Buckingham; *b* 4 Dec 1922; *Educ* Christ's Hospital; *m* 1, 1945 (m dis 1979), Beryl Doreen Evans; 1 s, 1 da; m 2, 1979, Sarah Catherine, da of Harley Hillier; *Career* Flag Offr Admty Interview Bd 1977-79; gp personnel dir Inchcape Gp 1979-86, gp personnel exec Davy Corp 1987-; *Recreations* sailing, gardening; *Style—* Rear Adm Thomas Bradbury, CB; Padgham Down, Dallington, Heathfield, Sussex TN21 9NS (☎ 0435 830 657)

BRADBY, Hon Mrs (Josephine Julia Asquith); *née* Barber; yr da of Baron Barber, TD, PC (Life Peer), *qv*, and his 1 w, Jean Patricia, *née* Asquith (d 1983); *b* 1953; *m* 23 Sept 1989, William J L Bradby, s of James Bradby, of Spettisbury, Dorset; *Style—* The Hon Mrs Bradby; 43 Basuto Road, London SW6 4BL

BRADDON, Russell Reading; s of Henry Russell Braddon (d 1931), of Sydney, Australia, and Thelma Doris, *née* Reading (d 1964); *b* 25 Jan 1921; *Educ* Sydney C of E GS, Univ of Sydney (BA); *Career* Gunner AIF (POW in Malaya) Jan 1942-Sept 1945; author, scriptwriter for the BBC, broadcaster and lectr; various TV documentaries in UK and Australia; *Books* fiction includes: Those In Peril (1954), Gabriel Comes to 25 (1958), Proud American Boy (1960), When the Enemy is Tired (1968), Will You Walk a Little Faster (1969), End Play (1972), Funnelweb (1990); non fiction includes: The Piddingtons (1950), The Naked Island (1951), Joan Sutherland (1962), The Siege (1969), Hundred Days of Darien (1974), Thomas Baines (1986), Images of Australia (1988); *Style—* Russell Braddon, Esq; c/o John Farquharson Ltd, 162-168 Regent St, London W1R 5TB

BRADFIELD, Dr John Richard Grenfell; CBE (1986); s of Horace Bradfield (d 1959), of Cambridge, and Ada Sarah, *née* Houghton (d 1952); *b* 20 May 1925; *Educ* Cambridgeshire Co HS for Boys, Trinity Coll Cambridge (MA, PhD); *m* 23 June 1951, Jane, da of Capt Edgar W Wood, MC (d 1974); 1 s (Robert Andrew Richard b 1952); *Career* Univ of Cambridge: res fell in cell biology Trinity Coll 1947, sr bursar Trinity Coll 1956- (jr bursar 1951-56), hon fell Darwin Coll 1973-; Cwlth Harkness fell Chicago 1948; dir; Cambridge Water Co 1965-, Cambridge Bldg Soc 1968-; fndr Cambridge Sci Park 1970 and mangr since construction 1973-, bd memb Anglian Water Authy 1975-89, dir Anglian Water plc 1989-, chm Abbotstone Agric Property Unit Tst 1975-, dir Biotechnology Investments 1989-; former chm St Faith's Prep Sch Cambridge, govr Leys Sch; ASIA 1970-; *Recreations* walking, sailing, arboretum-visiting; *Style—* Dr John Bradfield, CBE; Trinity College, Cambridge CB2 ITQ (☎ 0223 338 400)

BRADFORD, Archdeacon of; *see*: Shreeve, The Ven David Herbert

BRADFORD, Barbara Taylor; da of Winston Taylor (d 1981), and Freda Walker Taylor (d 1981); *b* 10 May 1933; *Educ* Northcote Sch for Girls; *m* 24 Dec 1963, Robert Bradford; *Career* author and journalist; women's ed Yorkshire Evening Post 1951-53 (reported 1949-51), fashion ed Woman's Own 1953-54, columnist London Evening News 1955-57, exec ed The London American 1959-62, ed National Design Center Magazine USA 1965-69; nationally Syndicated columnist: Newsday (New York) 1968-70, Chicago Tribune New York Daily News Syndicate 1970-75, Los Angeles Times Syndicate (New York) 1975-81; work published in USA incl: Complete Encyclopedia Homemaking Ideas (1968), How To Be The Perfect Wife (1969), How to Solve Your Decorating Problems (1976), Luxury Designs for Apartment Living (1981); novels: A Woman of Substance (1980, Matrix award for books from New York Women in Communications 1985), Voice of the Heart (1983), Hold the Dream (1985, screen adaptation 1986), Act of Will (1986), To Be The Best (1988), The Women in his Life (1990); Hon DLitt Univ of Leeds 1990; memb: Cncl The Authors Guild Inc USA 1989, PEN USA; *Style—* Mrs Barbara Taylor Bradford; Bradford Enterprises, 450 Park Ave, New York, NY 10022, USA (☎ 010 1 212 308 7390, fax 010 1 212 935 1636)

BRADFORD, Christopher Mark Newens (Chris); s of Marcus Newens Bradford, of Great Shelford, Cambs, and Hilda Muriel Annie Bradford, JP; *b* 4 Nov 1934; *Educ* Bedford Sch, Sidney Sussex Coll Cambridge (MA); *m* 9 Aug 1958, Lesley June, *née* Harvey; 2 s, 4 da; *Career* 2 Lt Nat Serv 1952-54, TA 1954-60; admitted slr 1960; partnerships: Saffron Walden 1963-65, Gainsborough 1965-67, Cambridge 1967-80 (conslt 1980-); farmer; cncllr: Cambridge City Cncl 1970-74, Cambs CC 1973-; author of various booklets on educn issues ; memb Nat Advsy Body on Public Sector Higher Educn 1985-88, nat negotiating ctees on lectrs and teachers' pay and conditions of serv 1985-87, E Anglian Tourist Bd 1987-; SLD educn spokesman ACC 1987-89; Freeman Worshipful Co of Vitners; memb Law Soc 1960; *Recreations* cricket, walking, travelling; *Style—* Chris Bradford, Esq; 4 Cavendish Ave, Cambridge CB1 4US (☎ 0223 245796)

BRADFORD, (Sir) Edward Alexander Slade; (5 Bt, UK 1902); s of 3 Bt (d 1952); suc half-bro, Sir John Ridley Evelyn Bradford, 4 Bt, 1954, but does not use title; *b* 18 June 1952; *Heir* unc, Donald Bradford; *Style—* Edward Bradford Esq; Faith Cottage, Pett, Sussex

BRADFORD, Prof Henry Francis; s of Henry Bradford, and Rose Bradford; *b* 8 March 1938; *Educ* Dartford GS, Univ Coll London (MB BS), Univ of Birmingham (BSc), Inst of Psychiatry London (PhD, DSc); *m* 28 March 1964, Helen, da of Benjamin Caplan (d Nov 1985); 1 s (Daniel Benjamin Alexander b 24 Aug 1969), 1 da (Sonya Helen b 25 Jan 1968); *Career* Imp Coll London: lectr in biochemistry 1968-, reader in biochemistry 1975-, prof of neurochemistry 1979-, dir of undergraduate studies 1988-; ed The Journal of Neurochemistry 1973-81; silver jubilee lectr Indian Inst of Chemical Biology Calcutta 1982, Sandoz lectr Inst of Neurology London 1985, guest lectr Int Soc for Neurochemistry Japan 1985, Harold Chaffer Meml lectr Univ of Otago NZ 1987; gen ed The Biochemist 1988-, author of about 250 scientific papers, ed 3 vols of scientific reviews; chm MRC Epilepsy Res Coordinating Ctee 1978-88 (memb Neuroscience Ctee and Bd 1973-82), scientific advsr Brain Res Tst 1985-90, hon archivist The UK Biochemical Soc 1988- (hon sec 1973-81), Bronze medal for contrib to neurochemistry Univ of Okayama Japan 1985; memb: UK Biochemical Soc, Int Soc Neurochemistry, Brain Res Assoc; FRCPath; *Books* Chemical Neurobiology (1985); *Recreations* natural history, music; *Style—* Prof Henry Bradford; 5 Scotts Ave, Shortlands, Bromley, Kent BR2 0LG (☎ 081 464 4615); Department of Biochemistry, Imperial College, South Kensington, London SW7 2AZ (☎ 071 589 5111 ext 4134/71/40)

BRADFORD, 7 Earl of (UK 1815); The Rt Hon Richard Thomas Orlando Bridgeman; 12 Bt (E 1660); also Baron Bradford (GB 1794) and Viscount Newport (UK 1815); s of 6 Earl of Bradford, TD (d 1981); *b* 3 Oct 1947; *Educ* Harrow, Trinity Coll Cambridge (MA); *m* 1979, Joanne Elizabeth, da of Benjamin Miller, of 42 Pembroke Rd, W8; 3 s (Viscount Newport b 6 Sept 1980, Hon Henry Gerald Orlando b 18 April 1982, Hon Benjamin Thomas Orlando b 7 Feb 1987), 1 da (Lady Alicia Rose b 27 Dec 1990); *Heir* eld s, Viscount Newport; *Career* owner Porters Restaurant Covent Garden; chm: Expedier plc, Connect Training Group; dep chm Beacon Radio; chm: W Midlands Advsy Ctee Tidy Britain Group, Fundraising Ctee Birmingham Centre for Conductive Educn, Wrekin Heritage Assoc; pres: Wrekin Tourism Assoc, Telford and Dist Victims Support Scheme, Newport Branch RNLI, Wolverhampton Friends of the Samaritans, Master Chefs of GB, Assoc of Conf Execs; vice pres Re-Solv (The Campaign Against Solvent Abuse); *Recreations* shooting, cooking, gardening; *Style—* The Rt Hon the Earl of Bradford; Woodlands Hse, Weston-under-Lizard, Shifnal, Shropshire TF11 8PX

BRADFORD, Bishop of (cr 1920) 1984-; Rt Rev Robert (Roy) Kerr Williamson; s of late James Williamson, of Belfast, and late Elizabeth, *née* Kelly; *b* 18 Dec 1932; *Educ* Elmgrove Sch Belfast, Oak Hill Theol Coll London; *m* 1956, Anne Boyd, da of late John Smith, of Belfast; 3 s (Stephen b 1958, Jonathan b 1965, Andrew b 1966), 2 da (Gillian b 1959, Katharine b 1968); *Career* ordained: deacon 1963, priest 1964; curate of Crowborough Sussex 1963-66; vicar: Hyson Green Notts 1966-71, St Ann with Emmanuel Notts 1971-76, Bramcote 1976-79; archdeacon of Notts 1978-84; Hon DLitt Bradford; *Recreations* home, family, bird watching, music, watching TV sport, reading; *Style—* The Rt Rev the Bishop of Bradford; Bishopscroft, Ashwell Rd, Heaton, Bradford, W Yorks BD9 4AU (☎ 0274 545414)

BRADFORD, Hon Mrs (Tatiana Sonia); *née* Lucas; da of 1 Baron Lucas of Chilworth (d 1967); *b* 10 Jan 1933; *Educ* Convent HS Southampton, Eastbourne Sch of Domestic Economy; *m* 1964, Kenneth Bradford, s of Arthur Bradford (d 1961), of Charmouth, Dorset; 2 s (Adam, Justin); *Clubs* Royal Overseas League; *Style—* The Hon Mrs Bradford; Nashdom, 13 Woodlands Rd, Surbiton, Surrey KT6 6PR

BRADISH, Martyn Henry Stewart; s of Edward Henry Bradish, and Florence Gertrude, *née* Tidman; *b* 10 March 1951; *Educ* Queen Elizabeth's Sch Barnet; *m* 1 March 1975, Linda Kay, da of George Squires; 3 da (Kirsty Linda b 1979, Samantha Elizabeth b 1982, Sarah Louise b 1984); *Career* ptnr Wilkins Kennedy & Co CA 1977-83, managing ptnr Foster Squires 1984-; area chm Area 17 London NE Round Table; FCA 1973; *Clubs* Southgate Round Table; *Style—* Martyn Bradish, Esq; Rex House, 354 Ballards Lane, North Finchley, London N12 OEG (☎ 081 446 6055, fax 081 446 6964)

BRADISH-ELLAMES, Lt Col Simon Edward Mountague; OBE (1973); s of Maj John Edward Mountague Bradish-Ellames (d 1984), of Little Marlow, and Helen Chambers, *née* Lehmann (d 1985); *b* 17 Jan 1930; *Educ* Eton, Mons OCS; *m* 1960, Cynthia Mary, step da of Air Chief Marshal Sir Hubert Patch of Marbella; 2 s (Peter b 1963, Andrew b 1965, d 1970), 1 da (Jane b 1961); *Career* joined The Royal Dragoons 1948, 2i/c RHG/D (The Blues and Royals) 1969, CO The Life Gds 1971, ret 1974; dir Sabre Safety Ltd 1976; *Recreations* fishing, shooting, labradors; *Clubs* Cavalry and Guards'; *Style—* Lt-Col Simon Bradish-Ellames, OBE; Velhurst Farm, Alfold, Cranleigh, Surrey (☎ 0403 752 146); Sabre Safety Ltd, Matterson House, Aldershot, Hants (☎ 0252 344 141)

BRADLAW, Prof Sir Robert Vivian; CBE (1950); s of Philip Archibald Bradlaw, of Blackrock, Dublin; *b* 14 April 1905; *Educ* Cranleigh, Guy's Hosp Med Sch; *Career* conslt RN 1939-81; hon prof of oral pathology Royal Coll of Surgns of Eng 1948-, emeritus prof oral med Univ of London 1970-, chm Advsy Cncl on Misuse of Drugs Home Office 1976-82; hon degrees: Belfast, Birmingham, Boston, Durham, Leeds, Malta, Melbourne, Meshed, Montreal, Newcastle-upon-Tyne; Chevalier de la Santé Publique (France) 1950, Kt Order of St Olaf (Norway), Cdr Order of Homayoun (Iran); FRCS (England, Edinburgh, Glasgow, Ireland); kt 1965; *Recreations* golf, fishing, orchids, oriental ceramics; *Style—* Prof Sir Robert Bradlaw, CBE; The Manse, Stoke Goldington, Bucks (☎ 0908 55281)

BRADLEY, Anthony Wilfred; s of David Bradley (d 1970), of Dover, Kent, and Olive Margaret, *née* Bonsey (d 1964); *b* 6 Feb 1934; *Educ* Dover GS, Emmanuel Coll Cambridge (BA, LLB); *m* 5 Sept 1959, Kathleen, *née* Bryce; 1 s, 3 da; *Career* slr of the Supreme Ct 1960-89; Univ of Edinburgh: prof of constitutional law 1968-89, dean Faculty of Law 1979-82, emeritus prof 1990-; ed Public Law 1986-; called to the Bar Inner Temple 1989, in practice 1989-; fell of Trinity Hall Cambridge 1960-68; memb: Ctee of Inquiry into Local Govt in Scot 1980, Ctee to Review Local Govt in the Islands of Scot 1983-84; chm Edinburgh Cncl for Single Homeless 1984-88; Clifford's Inn Prize (Law Soc) 1960; *Books* Justice Discretion and Poverty (with M Adler, 1976), Constitutional and Administrative Law (ed, 10 edn 1985); *Recreations* music; *Style—* Prof Anthony Bradley; 19 Grosvenor Rd, Richmond, Surrey TW10 6PE (☎ 081 948 3127); Cloisters, 1 Pump Court, Temple, London EC4Y 7AA (☎ 071 583 0303, fax 071 583 5597)

BRADLEY, Clive; s of Alfred Bradley (d 1970), and Annie Kathleen, *née* Turner (d 1990); *b* 25 July 1934; *Educ* Felsted, Clare Coll Cambridge (MA), Yale Univ; *Career* PO RAF 1953-55; called to the Bar Middle Temple 1961; BBC 1961-63 and 1965, bdcasting offr Lab Party 1963-64, political ed and broadcaster 1965-67, gp lab advsr IPC 1967-69, dep gen mangr Daily and Sunday Mirror and controller of admin IPC Newspapers 1969-71, project dir IPC 1971-73, dir The Observer 1973-76, chief exec The Publishers Assoc 1976-, dir Confedn Info Communication Industries 1984-; author of various pubns on politics, econs, media, industl rels and law; dep chm Central London Valuation Panel; govr Felsted Sch Essex; Liveryman Worshipful Co of Stationers; FRSA; *Clubs* Reform, Groucho, Elizabethan; *Style—* Clive Bradley, Esq; 8 Northumberland Place, Richmond upon Thames, Surrey TW10 6TS (☎ 081 940 7172, fax 081 940 7603); 19 Bedford Square, London WC1B 3HJ (☎ 071 580 6321, fax 071 636 5375, telex 267160)

BRADLEY, Dr (Charles) Clive; s of Charles William Bradley, of Maidenhead, Berks, and Winifred, *née* Smith (d 1963); *b* 11 April 1937; *Educ* Longton HS, Univ of Birmingham (BSc), Univ of Cambridge (PhD); *m* 25 Sept 1965, Vivien Audrey, da of Charles Frederick Godley, of Hillsborough, Sheffield; 1 s (Daniel b 5 Sept 1969), 1 da (Abigail b 19 May 1973); *Career* res scientist MIT and Nat Bureau of Standards USA 1967-69, princ scientific offr Nat Physical Laboratory 1969-75, sr scientific offr 1961-67, sr princ scientific offr DTI 1975-82, cncllr in sci and technol and dep chief scientific offr Br Embassy Tokyo 1982-88, head Advsy Cncl on Sci and Technol Secretariat Cabinet Office 1988-90, md Sharp Laboratories of Europe 1990-; dep cmmr gen for UK Sci Expo Japan 1985, chm Industl Energy Conservation Ctee Int Energy Agency 1980-82, memb SERC and EC Ctees 1978-82 and 1989-; *Books* High Pressure Methods in Solid State Research (1969); *Recreations* tennis, gardening; *Style—* Dr Clive Bradley; 8 Montrose Gardens, Oxshott, Surrey KT22 0UU (☎ 0372 84 3664); Sharp Laboratories of Europe Ltd, Neave House, Winsmore Lane, Abingdon, Oxon OX14 5UD (☎ 0235 554572)

BRADLEY, Graham John; s of Norman Bradley, of Wetherby, West Yorkshire, and late Sheila, *née* Deacey; *b* 8 Sept 1960; *Educ* Wetherby HS; *Career* professional national hunt jockey 1979-; major races won: Hennessy Golo Cup 1982 (Bregawn), Sun Alliance Novice Hurdle 1983 (Sabin du Loir), Cheltenham Gold Cup 1983 (Bregawn), Welsh Grand Nat 1984 (Righthand Man), Irish Grand Nat 1985 (Rhyme n' Reason), Charlie Hall Chase 1985 (Wayward Lad), King George VI Chase 1985 (Wayward Lad), Grand Annual Chase 1986 (Pearlyman), Welsh Grand Nat 1987 (Stearsby), Sun Alliance Novice Chase 1987 (Kildimo), Long Walk Hurdle 1990 (Floyd); Nat Hunt jr champion 1981-82, memb Br Jockey's team 1984-91; Ritz Club Charity Trophy for leading rider at Cheltenham Festival 1983; *Recreations* Leeds Utd FC, golf, snooker, good films; *Style—* Graham Bradley, Esq; Brook House, West Street, Sparsholt, Wantage, Oxon OX12 9PS (☎ 023559 533, car 0860 722772); c/o

Chris Pimlott, Lacy's Cottage, Scrayingham, York YO41 1JD (☎ 0759 71586)

BRADLEY, Jenny; da of John Shannon Kean, of Oxford, and Jean Smith, *née* Coburn; *b* 2 June 1947; *Educ* Headington Sch Oxford, Oxford Poly; *Career* served indentures as journalist Bracknell News Berkshire 1966-69, PR exec Joan Chesney Frost Publicity Services London 1969-71, pubns mangr Marks & Spencer Ltd 1971-74; ed: Thames & Chilterns Tourist Bd Oxon 1974-77, Milk Producer 1977-82; pubns mangr Milk Mktg Bd 1977-82, communications dir Dairy Crest Ltd Surrey 1982-90, dir public affrs Heathrow Airport Ltd 1990-; memb: Int Assoc of Business Communicators 1987, Assoc of Women in PR 1988; *Style*— Ms Jenny Bradley; 20 Chestnut Road, Kingston, Surrey (☎ 081 456 3146); Room 107, D'Albiac House, Heathrow Airport Limited, Heathrow Airport, Hounslow, Middlesex TW6 1JH (☎ 081 745 4108, fax 081 745 6061)

BRADLEY, (David) John; s of David John Bradley (d 1954), of 33 Priestfields, Rochester, Kent, and Dorothy Frances Mary, *née* Black (d 1948); *b* 22 Aug 1924; *Educ* Rochester Cathedral Choir Sch, Kings Sch Rochester; *Career* RN 1942-46; dir Thomas Watson (Shipping) Ltd; consul for Sweden; tstee: Watts Charity (Rochester), Shatesbury Homes and Arethusa; memb Cnl and former chm Friends of Rochester Cathedral, govr Sir John Hawkins Hosp, chm Lord Chancellor's Advsy Ctee; Freeman: City of London 1971, Worshipful Co of Watermen & Lightermen of the River Thames; ICS 1965 (memb 1948); FInstFF; Knight Order of Vasa (Sweden 1965), Knight First Class Order of Polar Star (Sweden 1981); *Recreations* sailing, farming, fruit growing; *Clubs* Castle (Rochester), Danish; *Style*— John Bradley, Esq; Buck Hole Farm, High Halstow, Rochester, Kent ME3 8SE (☎ 0634 250 895); 252 High St, Rochester, Kent ME1 1HZ (☎ 0634 844632, telex 96109)

BRADLEY, Joseph Clyde; s of Joseph Richard Bradley, and Ada Beatrice Bradley; *b* 21 May 1940; *Educ* Gt Yarmouth GS, Univ Coll London (BA, BSc); *m* 1962, Ute Brunhilde; 1 s (Martin b 1968), 1 da (Karen b 1971); *Career* Unilever 1961-72; Nationwide Building Soc: gen mangr 1972-81, chief exec 1981-, md 1982-87; md Prudential Property Services 1988-; FICMA, FInstM, FRSA; *Recreations* music, chess, kayaking, cycling; *Style*— Joseph Bradley, Esq; Ravelston, 80 St Georges Rd West, Bickley, Bromley, Kent; Prudential Property Services Ltd, Winchmore House, 15 Fetter Lane, London EC4 1JJ (☎ 071 430 0176)

BRADLEY, Julia Anne (Mrs Keith Sharp); da of Herbert Bradley (d 1974), and Minnie Adelaide Amelia Doris, *née* King; *b* 22 Nov 1938; *Educ* Hove and Aldrington HS, Brighton Tech Coll; *m* 28 Sept 1963, Keith Lorenza Sharp, s of Frederick William Lorenza Sharp (d 1979); 2 s (Trevor b 1970, Martin b 1972); *Career* asst sec Atlas Homes Ltd 1959-64; ptnr: Bradley Kempton & Co 1966-69, WA Honey & Co 1977-85, Bradley Soni & Co 1987-; sec: Br Engineerium 1985, Fedn Sussex Industs 1986-87, Centre for RES and Educnl Trg and Energy, Brighton and Hove Business Enterprise Agency; cncl memb Inst Chartered Secs and Admins (former chm Sussex branch); govr: Davigdor First Sch, Hove Park Sch, Varndean Sch; former chm Sussex Branch Inst Taxation, chm Sussex Professional and Mgmnt Orgns; memb: Young Enterprise, Brighton and Hove Soc Miniature Locomotive Engrs; former memb: Brighton and Hove Camera Club, Sussex Car Club, Locomotive Club GB; Freeman City of London 1980, Liveryman Worshipful Co Chartered Secs and Admins 1980; FCIS, ATII; *Recreations* railways, photography, gardening, travel, bridge; *Style*— Miss Julia Bradley; 64 Palmeira Ave, Hove BN3 3GF (☎ 0273 734236); Bradley Soni & Co, 86 South Coast Rd, Peacehaven BN10 8SL (☎ 0273 582605, fax 0273 587745)

BRADLEY, Hon Mrs (Melissa Clare); *née* Remnant; da of 3 Baron Remnant, CVO; *b* 20 May 1963; *Educ* Wycombe Abbey; *m* 5 Jan 1990, David Wilson Bradley, yr s of J W A Bradley, of Halls Court, Chesterton, Cambridge; *Career* mgmnt information conslt; *Style*— The Hon Mrs Bradley

BRADLEY, Patrick James; s of Gerard Bradley (d 1967), of Dublin, and Nan, *née* O'Leary; *b* 10 May 1949; *Educ* Glenstal Abbey Sch Murroe Co Limerick Ireland, Univ Coll Dublin (MB BCh, BAO, DCH); *m* 17 May 1974, Sheena, da of Frank Kelly (d 1954), of Draperstown, Co Derry; 3 s (Darragh Francis b 19 Nov 1976, Cormac b 12 Dec 1978, Eoin Patrick b 16 Oct 1980), 2 da (Paula b 19 Nov 1975, Caithriona b 5 June 1984); *Career* conslt otolaryngologist and head and neck oncologist Nottingham Health Authy 1982-; author: pubns on head and neck cancer diagnosis and mgmnt, book of multiple choice questions on ENT disorders; hon sec and memb Assoc of Head and Neck Oncologists GB; memb: BASO, ESSO, ORL Res; memb BMA, FRCSI, FRCSEd; *Books* Ear, Nose and Throat Disease (with K P Gibbin, 1989); *Style*— Patrick Bradley, Esq; 32 The Ropewalk, Nottingham NG1 5DW (☎ 0602 472631)

BRADLEY, Philip Herbert Gilbert; s of Herbert Bradley (d 1981), of S Ireland, and Phyllis Eleanor Josephine, *née* Marshall; *b* 11 Nov 1949; *Educ* Charterhouse, Trinity Coll Dublin (BA, BAI); *m* 3 Sept 1977, Charlotte Knollys Olivia, da of Lt-Col John Clairmont Wood, of Coombe Down, Beaminster, Dorset; 3 s (William b 6 Oct 1980, Piers b 9 Dec 1982, Timothy b 14 March 1985); *Career* Coopers & Lybrand chartered accountants 1974-78, Robert Fleming & Co Ltd bankers 1978-79, Jardine Fleming & Co Ltd bankers Hong Kong 1979-81, dir Robert Fleming & Co bankers London 1981-; ACA; *Recreations* fishing, shooting, skiing; *Clubs* Kildare Street (Dublin), Lansdowne; *Style*— Philip Bradley, Esq; 25 Copthall Avenue, London EC2 (☎ 071 638 5858, fax 071 638 9110, telex 297451)

BRADLEY, Richard Alan; s of Capt Reginald Livingstone Bradley, MC, CBE (d 1976), of London, and Phyllis Mary, *née* Richardson (d 1974); *b* 6 Oct 1925; *Educ* Marlborough, Trinity Coll Oxford (scholar, BA, MA, Univ Greyhounds RFC, Univ Occasional Hockey Club); *m* 1, 1950 (m dis 1971), Meryll Joy; 1 s (Charles Richard b 1958), 2 da (Hilary Jane Patricia b 1953, Phillipa Mary b 1955); m 2, 1971, Mary Ann, da of Brig John Vicary, MC (d 1967); *Career* RM served India and Java 1944-46 (cmmnd Lt 1945), res offr and instr CCF 1950-61 (Maj 1961); asst master: Dulwich Coll London 1949-50, Tonbridge Sch Kent 1950-65; ESU exchange teacher Gilman Sch Baltimore 1954-55, Warden St Edward's Sch Oxford 1965-71; headmaster: Ridley Coll St Catherine's Ontario Canada 1971-81, The Rivers Sch Weston Mass USA 1981-91; memb: ESU (England) 1954-55, ESU (America) 1982- (dir Boston branch), Duke of Edinburgh's Awards Scheme (England and Canada) 1955-71, HMC, Canadian Assoc Ind Schs, Ind Sch Assoc Mass, New England Assoc Schs and Colls (USA); *Books* Tonbridge (1964), Canadian Association of Independent Schools Journal (ed, 1973-81); *Recreations* mountains, dogs, film, theatre, writing; *Clubs* Vincent's (Oxford), Univ Toronto; *Style*— Richard Bradley, Esq; 117 Pleasant St, South Natick, MA 01760, USA (☎ 508 655 8077); The Rivers School, 333 Winter St, Weston, MA 02193, USA (☎ 617 235 9300, fax 617 239 3614)

BRADLEY, Roger Thubron; s of Ivor Lewis Bradley (d 1972), of Bournemouth, and Elizabeth, *née* Thubron; *b* 5 July 1936; *Educ* Lancaster Royal GS, Univ of Oxford (MA); *m* 19 Sept 1959, Ailsa Mary, da of Eric Walkden, of Bromley Cross; 1 s (Mark b 1963), 1 da (Julia b 1960); *Career* dir Harvesting and Mktg 1983, forestry cmmr 1985; dist offr Argyll 1970, conservator N Wales 1977, sr offr Wales 1979; *Recreations* sailing, wind surfing, skiing, gardening; *Clubs* Cwlth Soc, Royal Overseas League; *Style*— Roger T Bradley, Esq; 231 Corstorphine Rd, Edinburgh (☎ 031 334 0303)

BRADLEY, Prof Ronald Duncan; s of Gerald Bradley (d 1973), and Helen Marr, *née* McKellar; *b* 8 July 1929; *Educ* Tonbridge, Univ of London (BSc, MB BS); *m* 22 Dec 1951, Betty Mary, da of Hubert Percival Gibbon (d 1978); 1 s (Giles b 14 May 1962), 2 da (Amanda b 16 Oct 1956, Vanessa b 9 Aug 1959); *Career* prof of intensive care med St Thomas' Hosp Univ of London 1989- (conslt physician and dir Intensive Care Unit 1965-, chm of physicians 1977-80, chm Dist Mgmnt Team 1980-81, chm of med and surgical offrs 1980-81); chm tstees Samaritan Fund; memb Assoc of Physicians 1984; FRCP; *Books* Studies of Acute Heart Failure (1977), The Oxford Textbook of Medicine (contrib, 1983); *Recreations* horseriding; *Style*— Prof Ronald Bradley; St Thomas' Hospital, London SE1 (☎ 071 928 9292)

BRADLEY, Stanley Walter; s of Walter Bradley (d 1955), and Laura, *née* Moss (d 1966); *b* 9 Sept 1966; *Educ* Boys' British Sch Saffron Walden; *m* 6 Aug 1955, Jean Margaret, da of Alfred Brewster, of Low Park Farm, Kirbymoorside, York; 3 s (Nigel b 1957, Mark b 1959, Paul b 1962), 1 da (Jane b 1969); *Career* RAF 1945-48; with Spicers Ltd 1948-83; md: Thorburn Bain & Co 1966-68, Spicers Stationery Co Ltd 1969-70 (personnel dir 1973-83); dir: Capital Spicers Ireland 1969-88, Harman Gp 1988-; dir gen Br Printing Industs Fedn 1983-88, pres E Anglian Printing Industs Alliance 1978-79; chm: Mfrg Stationery Indust Gp 1977-81, Printing Industs Sector Working Pty 1981-87; *Recreations* fly fishing, painting; *Style*— S W Bradley, Esq; Dale House, Hogs Lane, Chrishall, Royston, Herts SG8 8RB (☎ 0763 838820)

BRADLEY, (Charles) Stuart; CBE (1990); s of Capt Charles Bradley, OBE (d 1959), of Penarth, Glamorgan, and Amelia Jane, *née* Ryan; *b* 11 Jan 1936; *Educ* Penarth Co Sch, Univ of Southampton, Sch of Navigation; *m* 7 April 1959, Kathleen Marina (Kate); 2 s (Philip b 1962, Patrick b and d 1964), 1 da (Bridget b 1967); *Career* deck offr P&O SNCO 1952-54; Br Tport Docks Bd (then Assoc Br Ports) 1964: dock and harbour master Silloth 1968-70, dockmaster 1970-74, dock and marine supt Plymouth 1974-76, docks mangr Lowestoft 1976-78, port mangr Barry 1978-80, port mangr Hull 1980-87 (formerly dep port mangr), asst md resources 1987-88, md Assoc Br Ports 1988-, chm Red Funnel 1989-, dep chm NAPE 1986-89, memb NDLB 1987-90; master mariner FCIT 1978; *Recreations* cycling, walking, theatre, welsh rugby; *Clubs* Cardiff Athletic, Hon Co of Master Mariners; *Style*— Stuart Bradley, Esq, CBE; Associated British Ports Holdings plc, 150 Holborn, London EC1N 2LR (☎ 071 430 1177, fax 071 430 1384, telex 23913)

BRADLEY, Tom George; s of George Henry Bradley (d 1953), and Agnes Mason; *b* 13 April 1926; *Educ* Kettering Central Sch; *m* 15 Aug 1953, Joy Patricia, da of George Stramer (d 1964); 2 s (David b 1961, Peter b 1963); *Career* Northamptonshire Co Cncllr 1952-74, Co Alderman 1964-74, Kettering Borough Cncllr 1956-61, pres Tport Salaried Staffs Assoc 1964-76, actg gen sec 1977; memb Lab Pty Nat Exec Ctee 1966-81, chm Lab Pty 1976, MP Leicester E 1962-83 (Lab 1962-81, SDP 1981-83), fndr memb SDP, PPS to Roy Jenkins at Ministries of Aviation, Home Office and Treasy 1964-70, front bench oppn spokesman on Tport 1970-74, chm House of Commons Select Ctee on Tport 1979-83, dir Br section of the European League for Econ Co-operation 1979-; *Recreations* watching football, cricket; *Clubs* Savile; *Style*— Tom Bradley, Esq; The Orchard, 111 London Rd, Kettering, Northants (☎ 0536 513019)

BRADMAN, Godfrey Michael; s of William Isadore Bradman (d 1973), and Anne Brenda, *née* Goldsweig; *b* 9 Sept 1936; *m* 2, 1975, Susan, da of George Bennett, of Slough; 1 s (Daniel b 1977), 2 da (Camilla b 1976, Katherine b 1976); *Career* chm and jt chief exec Rosehaugh plc; FCA; *Recreations* riding; *Style*— Godfrey Bradman, Esq; 9 Marylebone Lane, London W1M 5FB (☎ 071 486 7100, fax 071 486 7600, telex 28167)

BRADSHAW, Hon Mrs (Alison Margaret); *née* Herbert; yst da of Baron Tangley, KBE (Life Peer, d 1973); *b* 25 May 1943; *m* 1965, John Michael Bradshaw, s of Norman William Bradshaw, of Westcott, Surrey; 3 da; *Career* LRAM, ARCM; *Style*— The Hon Mrs Bradshaw; Cherrydale, W Clandon, Surrey

BRADSHAW, Hon Mrs (Diana Mary); *née* Hepburne-Scott; 2 da of 10 Baron Polwarth, TD; *b* 30 June 1946; *m* 1977, Richard James Bradshaw, chief conductor and head of music Canadian Opera Co; 1 s, 1 da; *Style*— The Hon Mrs Bradshaw; 397 Wellesley Street East, Toronto, Ontario M4X 1H5, Canada

BRADSHAW, Dr John Richard; s of Robert Cecil Bradshaw (d 1974), of Bandon, Ireland, and Iris Arlene, *née* Lee; *b* 25 Aug 1944; *Educ* Midleton Coll, Co Cork, Trinity Coll Univ of Dublin (BA, MB BCh, BAO, DMRD); *m* 7 March 1970, Maria Loredana, da of Capt John Terence Gordon (d 1986), of Pillaton, Cornwall; 1 s (Jonathan b 1971), 1 da (Giulia b 1974); *Career* sr registrar in diagnostic radiology Univ Hosp of Wales Cardiff 1972-74, asst prof of radiology Meml Univ Newfoundland 1974-78, conslt radiologist St John's Gen Hosp 1974-78, conslt neuroradiologist South Western Regnl Health Authy and Frenchay Hosp Bristol 1978-; memb Mgmnt Ctee Wick Ct Centre Bristol, chm Unit Med Ctee Frenchay Hosp Bristol; FRCR 1974, Br Soc of Neuroradiologists, FRCP; *Books* Brain CT - An Introduction (1985), Brain Imaging - an Introduction (1989); *Recreations* photography, motor boating; *Style*— Dr John Bradshaw; Dept of Neuroradiology, Frenchay Hospital, Bristol BS16 6LE (☎ 0272 701212 ext 2341)

BRADSHAW, Sir Kenneth Anthony; KCB (1986, CB 1982); s of late Herbert Leo Bradshaw, and Gladys Margaret Bradshaw; *b* 1 Sept 1922; *Educ* Ampleforth, St Catharine's Coll Cambridge; *Career* clerk asst of House of Commons 1979-83, clerk of the House 1983-87 (ret); admin Compton Verney Opera Project 1988-; *Books* Parliament and Congress (with David Pring 1982); *Recreations* opera, theatre, golf; *Clubs* Garrick; *Style*— Sir Kenneth Bradshaw, KCB

BRADSHAW, Kenneth Morton; s of Leonard Walter Bradshaw (d 1956), of Rushden, Northants, and Dorothy Gwendoline, *née* Walters (d 1983); *b* 27 June 1932; *Educ* Wellingborough GS, Univ of Manchester (BA); *m* 29 Sept 1962, Veronica Ann, da of Sidney Arthur Steel Butcher, of Eastbourne; 1 s (Christopher b 1969), 3 da (Nicola b 1963, Carina b 1965, Deborah, b 1966); *Career* CA; sr ptnr Bradshaw & Co, dir Queens Hotel (Hastings) Ltd 1982-; FICA 1957; *Recreations* church and allied activities including Gideons Int, philately; *Style*— Kenneth M Bradshaw, Esq; 7 Hyde Tynings Close, Eastbourne BN20 7TQ (☎ 0323 411243); Bradshaw & Co, 2 Upperton Gardens, Eastbourne BN21 2AH (☎ 0323 25244)

BRADSHAW, Michael John; s of Harry Constantine Bradshaw (d 1979), original name Zalotynski, of Warsaw, and Gladys *née* Church (d 1985); *b* 7 June 1935; *Educ* Peckham Sch, Camberwell Coll of Art; *m* 5 July 1958, Joyce Mary, da of James Albert Reid (d 1960); 1 s (Neil Christian b 1960), 1 da (Gabrielle Louise b 1962); *Career* deputy creative dir Dorland Advertising 1970-81; creative dir Chetwynd Haddons 1981, exec creative dir 1987 (memb Creative Circle Cncl 1976-79), CLIO 1981 and 1982 (advertising award); Gold award Dubonnet 1971, designers and art directors award, gold awards (int) film and TV festival New York 1984 (silver awards 1981-83), Gold medal (New York Festival 1986); Freeman City of London 1983, MIPA, memb Creative Circle (1974); *Recreations* theatre, golf; *Clubs* Aquarius Golf, Le Beaujolais; *Style*— Michael Bradshaw, Esq; 75 Marmora Road, Dulwich, London SE22 0RY (☎ 081 693 6884); Chetwynd Haddons Ltd, 52-54 Broadwick St, London W1 (☎ 071 439 2288)

BRADSHAW, Paul Richard; s of Trevelyan William George Bradshaw, and Beryl Mary; *b* 18 Jan 1950; *Educ* Huntingdon GS, Nottingham Univ (BSc), FIA (Sir Joseph Burns prize); *m* 28 July 1971, Sheila Margaret, da of Andrew John Broodbank; 1 s (Christopher b 1976), 1 da (Laura b 1980); *Career* md Skandia Life Assurance Co Ltd;

dir: Skandia Investment Management Ltd, Skandia Financial Services Ltd, Skandia Life Business Services Ltd, Skandia Life Assurance (Hldgs) Ltd, Skandia Life (Pensions Tstee) Ltd, Skandia First Funding Ltd, Skandia Life America; *Recreations* chess; *Style—* Paul Bradshaw, Esq; 5 South End, Hursley, Nr Winchester, Hants; Frobisher House, Nelson Gate, Southampton SO9 7BX (☎ 0703 334411)

BRADSHAW, Roger Joseph; MBE (1987); s of Joseph Tarver Bradshaw (d 1970), of Bramhall, and Dorothy Marian, *née* Ratcliffe; *b* 22 Aug 1937; *Educ* William Hulmes GS, St Albans Sch, Imperial Coll London (BSc); *m* 28 April 1962 (m dis), Janet, da of George Wilkins (d 1972), of Bushey Heath; 2 s (Anthony Paul b 1963, Kevin Michael b 1968), 1 da (Helen Elizabeth b 1965); m 2, 29 June 1984, Ruth Margaret, *née* Akass; *Career* mgmnt devpt mangr Plastics Div ICI 1969 (Engrg Agric Div 1960), started own business Roger Bradshaw Assocs Mgmnt Conslts 1973-; co fndr: Refugee Childrens Holiday Fund 1959, Childrens Relief Int 1959; fndr: Eastern Ravens Tst Stockton-on-Tees 1961; *Recreations* painting, golf, walking, gardening, bird watching; *Style—* Roger J Bradshaw, Esq, MBE; Orchard Cottage, Stanningfield, Suffolk IP29 4RJ (☎ 0284 828436, fax 0284 828798)

BRADSHAW, Stephen Paul; s of Eric Douglas Bradshaw, and Victoria, *née* Gibbons; *b* 26 Nov 1948; *Educ* Nottingham HS, Queens' Coll Cambridge (MA); *m* 27 May 1972, Jenny, da of Michael Richards; 2 s (Nicholas b 4 Oct 1973, Rusty b 2 May 1977), 1 da (Mellisa b 17 Aug 1980); *Career* prodr BBC Radio London 1970-73; reporter and presenter: File on 4 BBC Radio Four 1977-80, Newsweek BBC2 1980-83, People and Power BBC1 1983, Newsnight BBC2 1984-87; corr Panorama BBC1 1987-90; *Books* Cafe Society (1978); *Recreations* work, children; *Style—* Stephen Bradshaw, Esq; 81 Charlotte St, London W1 (☎ 081 580 4886)

BRADSHAW, William Martin (Bill); s of Leslie Charles Bradshaw (d 1971), of Lobley Hill, Gateshead, and Vera, *née* Beadle; *b* 12 Dec 1955; *Educ* Gateshead GS and Saltwell HS, Darlington NCTJ Journalism Sch; *m* 13 June 1981, Fiona Judith, da of William MacBeth (d 1974); 1 s (Kit Leslie b 12 Nov 1990); *Career* jr then sr reporter Halifax Courier 1975-77, news reporter Newcastle Evening Chronicle 1977-79, sports reporter (coverning soccer and athletics) Newcastle Journal 1979-83; sports ed The People London 1990- (sports reporter Manchester 1983-85 and London 1985-89); memb: Football Writers' Assoc 1981, SWA 1985; *Recreations* cricket, soccer, water skiing, reading; *Style—* Bill Bradshaw, Esq; The People, Mirror Group Newspapers, Holborn Circus, London EC1 1DQ (☎ 071 822 3537, 071 353 0246, fax 071 822 3405)

BRADSHAW, Prof William Peter (Bill); s of Leonard Charles Bradshaw (d 1978), of Wargrave Berks, and Ivy Doris, *née* Steele (d 1980); *b* 9 Sept 1936; *Educ* Slough GS, Univ of Reading (BA, MA); *m* 30 Nov 1957, Jill Elsie, da of James Francis Hayward, of Plastow Green, Hampshire; 1 s (Robert William b 1966), 1 da (Joanna b 1968); *Career* Nat Serv 1957-59; gen mangr W Region BR 1983-85 (mgmnt trainee 1959, div movements mangr Bristol 1967, div mangr Liverpool 1973, chief ops mangr London Midland Region 1976, dep gen mangr London Midland Region 1977, dir of ops BR HQ 1978, dir Policy Unit BR HQ 1980); sr visiting res fell Centre for Socio Legal Studies Wolfson Coll Oxford 1985-, prof of tport mgmnt Univ of Salford 1986-, chm Ulsterbus 1987-; dir NI Tport Hldg Co 1988-; FCIT 1986; *Recreations* growing hardy perennial plants, playing memb of brass band; *Clubs* Nat Lib; *Style—* Prof Bill Bradshaw; Centre For Socio-Legal Studies, Wolfson College, Oxford OX2 6UD (☎ 0865 52967, fax 0865 274125)

BRADSTOCK, David Fitzherbert; MC (1944); s of Maj George Bradstock, DSO, MC (d 1976), and Ursula Mary, *née* Wright (d 1972); *b* 25 Nov 1923; *Educ* Eton, Sandhurst; *m* 5 Oct 1954, Philippa Mary, da of Col Bernard Alexander Wilson, DSO, MC (d 1978); 2 s (Mark Fitzherbert b 1958, Charles David Alexander b 1962), 1 da (Arabella Jane (Mrs Bridge) b 1956); *Career* Capt Royal Dragoons 1943-49; insurance broker: Hogg Robinson & Capel Cure, Burton Rowe & Viner; life pres Bradstock Gp plc 1989- (fndr 1959, chm 1959-88), fndr and ptnr Clanville Lodge Stud bloodstock breeders, underwriting memb Lloyds of London; *Recreations* hunting, skiing, fishing, shooting; *Clubs* White's, Pratt's, MCC; *Style—* David Bradstock, Esq, MC; Bradstock Group plc, 18 London St, London EC3R 7JP (☎ 071 436 7878, telex 884234)

BRADSTOCK, Hon Mrs (Sara Victoria); da of 4 Baron Trevethin and 2 Baron Oaksey; *b* 1962; *m* 8 Aug 1987, Mark Fitzherbert Bradstock, eldest s of David Fitzherbert Bradstock, MC, of Clanville Lodge, Andover, Hants; *Style—* The Hon Mrs Bradstock; Mabberleys, East Garston, nr Newbury, Berks

BRADSTREET, Philip Lionel Stanton; s of Arthur William Haywood Bradstreet (d 1987), and Catherine Margaret Patricia, *née* Brennan; *b* 14 Aug 1946; *Educ* Downside, Trinity Coll Cambridge (MA); *m* 5 June 1971, Marie Christine Francoise Dominique, da of Henri Coronat (d 1986); 3 s (Christophe b 1972, Matthieu b 1975, William b 1983), 1 da (Anne-Marie b 1976); *Career* expert Cmmn of the Euro Communities 1981-83, dir Euro Community Servs Price Waterhouse Brussels 1983-; memb: de L'Ordre des Experts Comptables France, de L'Institut des Experts-Comptables Belgium; Freeman City of London 1970; FCA; *Recreations* tennis, rugby, music; *Clubs* Hawks; *Style—* Philip Bradstreet, Esq; 38 Avenue Maurice, 1050 Brussels, Belgium (☎ 010 322 647 7394); Price Waterhouse, 135 Rue St Lambert, 1200 Brussels, Belgium (☎ 010 322 773 4911, fax 010 322 762 5100, telex 27184 PWECS)

BRADWELL, Bishop of 1976-; Rt Rev (Charles) Derek Bond; s of Flt Lt Charles Norman Bond, RAF (d 1985), and Doris, *née* Rosendale; *b* 4 July 1927; *Educ* Bournemouth Sch, King's Coll London (AKC); *m* 4 July 1951, (Joan) Valerie, da of Capt Ralph Meikle, RAOC (d 1988), of Bournemouth; 2 s (Stephen b 1957, Andrew b 1965), 2 da (Fiona b 1955, Elizabeth b 1963); *Career* Mids area sec SCM in Schs 1955-58; vicar: Harringay 1958-62, Harrow Weald 1962-71; archdeacon of Colchester 1971-76; *Recreations* travel; *Style—* The Rt Rev the Bishop of Bradwell; Bishop's House, 21 Elmhurst Ave, Benfleet, Essex SS7 5RY (☎ 0268 755 175)

BRADY, Hon Mrs (Charlotte Mary Thérèse); *née* Bingham; writes as Charlotte Bingham; da of 7 Baron Clanmorris; *b* 29 June 1942; *Educ* The Priory Hayward's Heath, The Sorbonne; *m* 1964, Terence Joseph Brady, *qv*, s of Frederick Arthur Noel Brady (d 1985), of Montacute, Somerset; 1 s (Matthew b 1972), 1 da (Candida b 1965); *Career* playwright, novelist; *Books* Coronet Among the Weeds (1963), Lucinda (1965), Coronet Among the Grass (1972), Rose's Story (with husb Terence Brady 1973), Yes Honestly (1977), Belgravia (1983), Country Life (1984), At Home, To Hear A Nightingale (1988), The Business (1989); *Stage Play* I wish, I wish; *tv series include* (with Terence Brady): Take Three Girls, Upstairs Downstairs, No Honestly, Yes Honestly, Play for Today, Thomas and Sarah, Nanny, Pig in the Middle; *tv films*: Love With A Perfect Stranger, This Magic Moment; *Recreations* horse breeding, riding, gardening, racing, swimming; *Style—* The Hon Mrs Brady; c/o Murray Pollinger, Literary Agent, 4 Garrick St, London WC2

BRADY, Janet Mary; *née* Mount; da of Allan Frederick Mount, of Oxford, and Doreen Margaret, *née* Hicks; *b* 26 Feb 1956; *Educ* Rochester GS, Medway and Maidstone Coll of Technol; *Career* legal asst Mobil Oil 1974-77, tax asst Marathon Oil 1977-81, account dir Sterling PR 1982-85, dir PR American Express (UK and Ireland) 1985-87, fndr dir Kinnear PR 1988-89, md Cadogan Management Ltd 1989-; voluntary trainer St John Cadets, publicity advsr Br Sports Assoc for the Disabled and Employers Forum on Disability; memb: Br Assoc Travel Eds 1987-91, Br Assoc for the Club of Rome; FIOD; *Recreations* ballooning, stonemasonry, landscape gardening, writing; *Clubs* Consul, IOD; *Style—* Ms Janet Brady; Barcheston Ho, Northside, Steeple Aston, Oxon OX5 3SE (☎ 0869 476 33); Cadogan Management Ltd, 27 Albemarle Street, Mayfair, London W1X 3FA (☎ 071 495 5040, fax 071 491 2551)

BRADY, Prof (John) Michael; s of John Brady, OBE, and Priscilla Mansfield, *née* Clark; *b* 30 April 1944; *Educ* Prescot GS, Univ of Manchester (BSc, MSc), Aust Nat Univ (PhD); *m* 2 Oct 1967, Naomi, da of Dr D Friedlander (d 1976), of NY; 2 da (Sharon b 1971, Carol b 1973); *Career* sr lectr Univ of Essex 1978-80 (lectr 1970-78), sr res scientist MIT 1980-85, prof Univ of Oxford 1985-; FRSA, MIEE, MIEEE; *Books* Theory of Computer Science (1975), Computer Vision (1981), Robot Motion (1983), Computational Models of Discourse (1983), Robotics (1985), Robotics Science (1989); *Recreations* windsurfing, squash, Dickens, wine, Everton; *Style—* Prof Michael Brady; Dept of Engineering Science, Univ of Oxford, Parks Rd, Oxford OX1 3PJ (☎ 0865 273002, telex NUCLOX G, fax 0865 273010)

BRADY, Terence Joseph; s of (Frederick Arthur) Noel Brady (d 1985), of Montacute, Somerset, and Elizabeth Mary Moore (d 1986); *b* 13 March 1939; *Educ* Merchant Taylors', Trinity Coll Dublin (BA); *m* 1964, Hon Charlotte Marie Thérèse, Brady, *qv*, da of Lord Clanmorris, of London; 1 s (Matthew), 1 da (Candida); *Career* writer and actor; television plays with Charlotte Bingham (spouse) incl: Take Three Girls, Upstairs Downstairs, Play for Today, 6 Plays of Marriage, No Honestly, Yes Honestly, Thomas and Sarah, Nanny, Pig in the Middle, Take Three Women, Love with A Perfect Stranger, Father Matthew's Daughter, This Magic Moment, Riders; other television incl: Dig This Rhubarb, Broad and Narrow, First Impressions, A Cars, My Name is Dora, Cribbins, A Man For Today, N F Simpson Series, Time For The Funny Walk, Boy Meets Girl; stage incl: I Wish I Wish, Glory Be!, The Dumb Waiter, Would Anyone Who Saw The Accident, Beyond The Fringe, In The Picture, A Present From The Corporation, Clope; films incl: Baby Love, Foreign Exchange; contrib: Daily Mail, Daily Express, Country Homes and Interiors, Punch; *Books* Rehearsal (1972), The Fight against Slavery (1976), Roses Story (1973), Yes Honestly (1977), Point-to-Point (1991); *Recreations* racing, training point-to-pointers, riding, music, painting; *Clubs* PEN; *Style—* Terence Brady, Esq; John Farquhason Ltd, 162-168 Regent St, London WIR 5JB

BRAGG, Henry John; s of Henry Bragg, of Torquay; *b* 28 Nov 1929; *Educ* Torquay GS, London Univ; *m* 1972, Anthea, da of Kew Shelley, QC; 3 children; *Career* md Calor Group Ltd 1980-, dir Imperial Continental Gas Ltd 1980; FCIT 1979; *Recreations* golf, hunting; *Clubs* Royal St George's Golf; *Style—* Henry Bragg Esq; 22 Thamespoint, Fairways, Teddington, Middx (☎ 081 977 9852); Hideway House, St George's Rd, Sandwich, Kent (☎ 0304 12364)

BRAGG, Melvyn; s of Stanley Bragg, of Wigton, Cumbria, and Mary Ethel, *née* Parks; *b* 6 Oct 1939; *Educ* Nelson-Thomlinson GS Wigton, Wadham Coll Oxford (MA); *m* 1, 1961, Marie-Elisabeth Roche (decd); 1 da; m 2, 1973, Catherine Mary, da of Eric Haste, of Crantock, Almondsbury, Avon; 1 s, 1 da; *Career* writer and broadcaster; began career on Monitor (BBC), presenter 2nd House 1973-77; presenter and ed: Read All About It (BBC) 1976-77, South Bank Show (ITV) 1978- (Prix Italia thrice); controller Arts Dept LWT 1990-, chm Border Television 1990-; memb RSL 1977-80, pres Nat Campaign for the Arts, BAFTA Richard Dimbleby Award 1987; Hon DUniv Open Univ 1988; Hon DLitt: Liverpool, Lancaster 1990, CNAA 1990; hon fell Lancashire Poly; Domus fell St Catherine's Coll Oxford 1990; FRSL; *Novels* For Want of a Nail (1965), The Second Inheritance (1966), Without a City Wall (1968), The Hired Man (1969), A Place in England (1970), The Nerve (1971), Josh Lawton (1972), The Silken Net (1974), Autumn Manoeuvres (1978), Kingdom Come (1980), Love and Glory (1983), The Maid of Buttermere (1987); *Non fiction* Land of the Lakes (1983), Laurence Olivier (1984), Rich (1988, biog of Richard Burton), Speak for England (oral history of England since 1900), A Time to Dance (1990); *Musicals*: Mardi Gras, Orion (TV, 1977), The Hired Man (W End 1984, Ivor Novello Award 1985); *Screenplays*: Isadora, Jesus Christ Superstar (with Ken Russell), The Music Lovers, Clouds of Glory; *Recreations* walking, books; *Clubs* Garrick; *Style—* Melvyn Bragg, Esq; 12 Hampstead Hill Gardens, London NW3; South Bank Television Centre, Kent House, Upper Ground, London SE1 9LT (☎ 071 261 3434, telex 918123)

BRAGG, Stephen Lawrence; eldest s of Sir (William) Lawrence Bragg, FRS (Nobel Laureate, d 1971), and Alice Grace Jenny Bragg, CBE, *née* Hopkinson (d 1989); *b* 17 Nov 1923; *Educ* Rugby, Trinity Coll Cambridge (MA), MIT (MSc); *m* 1951, Maureen Ann, da of Dr E Roberts (d 1953), of Darlington; 3 s; *Career* chartered engr, chief res engr Rolls-Royce 1963-70, vice-chllr Brunel Univ 1971-81, chm Cambridge Health Authy 1982-86, dir industl co-operation Univ of Cambridge 1984-87; admin American Friends of Cambridge Univ 1988-; FEng, FIMechE, FRAeS; *Books* Rocket Engines (1962); *Recreations* railway history; *Clubs* Athenaeum; *Style—* Stephen Bragg, Esq; 22 Brookside, Cambridge CB2 1JQ (☎ 0223 62208); American Friends of Cambridge Univ, The Pitt Building, Trumpington St, Cambridge CB2 1RP (☎ 0223 311201)

BRAGGE, Nicolas William; s of Norman Hugh Bragge, of The Towers, Brabourne, nr Ashford, Kent, and Nicolette Hilda, *née* Simms (d 1989); *b* 13 Dec 1948; *Educ* S Kent Coll of Technol Ashford, Holborn Coll of Law London (LLB), Inns of Court Sch of Law; *m* 23 Dec 1974, Pamela Elizabeth, da of Ronald Gordon Brett; 3 s (Thomas Hereward b 1976, Christopher Joseph b 1980, Alasdair Charles b 1986); *Career* called to the Bar Inner Temple 1972; in practice at Patent Bar 1973-, examiner of the Supreme Court 1978-88; pt/t chm Social Security Appeal Tbnls 1990-; author of various articles on legal and hist subjects; memb Br Gp AIPPI; Freeman City of London 1969, Liveryman Worshipful Co of Cutlers 1974; *Recreations* family; *Clubs* City Livery; *Style—* Nicolas Bragge, Esq; New Court, Temple, London EC4Y 9BE (☎ 071 353 1769/8719, fax 071 583 5885); The Towers, Brabourne, nr Ashford, Kent

BRAGGINS, Maj-Gen Derek Henry; CB (1986); s of Albert Edward Braggins (d 1988), of Pagham, Sussex, and Hilda Mary, *née* Pearce; *b* 19 April 1931; *Educ* Rothesay Acad, Hendon Tech Coll; *m* 10 April 1953, Sheila St Clair, da of George Stuart (d 1969), of Kirkwall, Orkney; 3 s (Geoffrey b 1953, Nigel b 1959, Mark b 1965); *Career* cmmnd RASC 1950, transferred RCT 1965; regtl and staff appts: Korea, Malaya, Singapore, Ghana, Aden, Germany, UK, Staff Coll Camberley 1962, Jt Servs Staff Coll Latimer 1970, CO 7 Regt RCT 1973-75, Col AQ Commando Forces RM 1977-80, cmd tport and movements BAOR 1981-83, dir gen tport and movements and head of RCT 1983-86; Col Cmdt RCT 1986 pres RASC and RCT Assoc 1988-; Freeman City of London 1983, Liveryman Worshipful Co of Carmen 1983-; FBIM 1979, FCIT 1983; *Recreations* running, shooting, fishing, gardening, country life; *Style—* Maj-Gen Derek Braggins, CB

BRAHAM, Philip John Cofty; s of Ronald Marcus Braham, of 65 Castlehill Road, Bearsden, and Dorothy May, *née* Cofty; *b* 8 April 1959; *Educ* Bearsden Acad, Duncan of Jordanstone Coll of Art Dundee (Br Cncl scholar, Dip Fin Art), Royal Acad of Fine Art The Hague (Greenshields award, special commendation for postgrad studies); *m* Barbara, *née* Campbell; 1 da (Robyn b 13 March 1987); *Career* artist, visiting artist, Univ of Calif LA 1981-82; solo exhibitions: Main Fine Art Glasgow 1984, The Scottish Gallery Edinburgh 1985, Glasgow Art Centre 1987, The Scottish Gallery 1988, The Raab Gallery London 1989 and 1991; gp exhibitions incl: The Human Touch (Fischer Fine Art, London) 1985, Artists at Work (Edinburgh Festival Event) 1986, The Vigorous Imagination (Nat Gallery of Modern Art, Edinburgh) 1987, Metamorphosis

(Raab Gallery, London & Berlin) 1989, Landscape and Cityscape (Raab Gallery, London) 1990, Cimal (Lucas Gallery, Valencia) 1990; works in the collections of: Scottish Arts Cncl, Scottish Nat Gallery of Modern Art, BBC, The Contemporary Arts Soc, RCP (Edinburgh), Life Assoc of Scotland, Educnl Inst of Scotland; *awards* EIS award 1985; subject of various exhibition catalogues; *Style—* Philip Braham, Esq; 20 Bryson Rd, Edinburgh, Scotland EH11 1EE; Raab Gallery, 6 Vauxhall Bridge Rd, London SW1V 2SD (☎ 071 828 2588, fax 071 976 5041)

BRAHAMS, Diana Joyce; da of Gustave Arnold, and Rita, *née* Rosenberg; *b* 18 Feb 1944; *Educ* Roedean SA, Queen's Coll Harley St London; *m* 14 June 1964, Malcolm Henry, Brahams s of Reginald Brahams; 2 s (Nigel Robert b 20 Aug 1966, Gareth Edmund b 25 April 1970), 1 da (Catherine Sophie b 16 July 1968); *Career* called to the Bar Middle Temple 1972, tenant to Ernest Scamell's chambers 1976, ed Medico-legal Jl 1983-, legal corr to The Lancet 1981-, currently practitioner free-lance writer and lectr specialising in med and the law; contrib to legal and property jls 1977-86 (Estates Gazette, Estates Times, Chartered Surveyors Weekly, Property Law Round-up, Law Society Gazette), contrib to medical and scientific jls 1981- (The Lancet, The Law Society Gazette, Anaesthesia, Dispensing Doctors' Journal, The Aids Letter, Independent Health News, Self Health, Journal of Medical Ethics, The Physician, The Practitioner, British Medical Bulletin, New Law Jl); responsible for up-dating section of loose-leaf work on Premises Management 1986-; memb working party on adverse consequences of med intervention and compensation RCP, fndr memb of Concern and Campaign; FRSM; *Books* A Casebook on Rent Review and Lease Renewal (with Mark Pawlowski, 1986); contrib: The Law and You (1987), Encyclopaedia Britannica's Medical and Health Annual (1985, 1986, 1989 and 1990), No Fault Compensation in Medicine (1989), Medical Malpractice Solutions (1989), Benzodiazepines - Current Concepts (1990), Human Genetic Information, Science Law and Ethics (1990); *Recreations* theatre, travel, reading, antiques, paintings (esp Victorian); *Style—* Mrs Diana Brahams; 15 Old Square, Lincoln's Inn, London WC2A 3UH (☎ 071 831 0801, fax 071 405 1387; home (☎ 081 458 8629, fax 081 458 8629)

BRAHMA, Dr Rupendra Kumar; s of Prof Nalini Kanta Brahma (d 1961), and Uma Rani Brahma (d 1985); *b* 18 May 1938; *Educ* Scot Church Sch, Scot Church Coll Calcutta, RG Kar Med Coll and Hosps Univ of Calcutta (MB BS), MRCP (Edinburgh), Inst of Psychiatry (DPM); *m* 28 Aug 1971, Mary, da of Harry Edwards (d 1960); *Career* conslt i/c Dept of psychological med Whipps Cross Hosp and conslt psychiatrist Claybury Hosp 1972-, clinical tutor in psychiatry Univ of London 1984-86 (sr registrar to Sir Desmond Pond 1969-72); chm: Sr Med Ctee Whipps Cross Hosp 1977-78, Dist Mental Health Care Planning Team 1980-82, Dist Psychiatric Div 1982-84; chm: Waltham Forest Div of BMA 1985-86 (1978-79), Regnl Cncl of BMA; memb Regnl Strategy Review Gp NE Thames 1988-, vice chm Regnl Conslts and Specialists Ctee 1979-, memb Regnl Med Advsy Ctee 1987-, memb Manpower Cmmn; lectr and advsr to: Alzheimers Soc, CRUSE and St John's Ambulance; memb Policy Planning Gp and Serv Devpt Gp Waltham Forest Social Serv Dept, memb Cncl Counsel and Care; MRCPsych, FRSM 1978, FRCPE 1986, FRCPsych 1986; *Recreations* travel, photography, gardening; *Style—* Dr Rupendra Brahma; Whipps Cross Hospital, Leytonstone, London E11 1NR (☎ 081 504 6923)

BRAIDEN, Prof Paul Mayo; s of Isaac Braiden (d 1966), and Lilian, *née* Mayo; *b* 7 Feb 1941; *Educ* Dudley GS, Univ of Sheffield (BEng, MEng, PhD); *Career* Speedicut res scholar Firth Brown Tool Ltd Sheffield 1965-68, asst prof and Ford Fndn fell Dept of Mechanical Engrg Carnegie-Mellon Univ Pittsburgh 1968-70, sr and princ sci offr AERE 1970-76; Univ of Durham 1976-83: lectr and sr lectr Dept of Engrg Sci, tutor Trevelyan Coll; Univ of Newcastle upon Tyne: Sir James Woodeson prof of mfrg engrg 1983-, John Holmes meml lectr 1989-; chm: NE Sector Working Pty on Advanced Mfr Technol DTI 1986-88, N Region IProdE 1988-90; chm Ctee of Design Mgnmt (memb Electro-Mechanical Ctee and memb Engrg Bd) SERC; memb Nat Ctee Methodist Hymn Book Revision 1979-82; CEng, MInstP 1976, FIMechE 1979, FIProdE 1981; *Recreations* music (especially opera and oratorio), trained tenor voice, cycling, talking; *Style—* Prof Paul Braiden; Dept of Mechanical Materials & Manufacturing Engineering, University of Newcastle upon Tyne, Stephenson Building, Claremont Rd, Newcastle upon Tyne NE1 7RU (☎ 091 222 6000, fax 091 261 1182, telex 53654 UNINEW G)

BRAILEY, Michael Carl; s of Walter Carl Brailey (formerly Schumacher) (d 1969), and Marguerite Brailey; *b* 7 June 1932; *Educ* St George's Coll Weybridge Surrey, Institut Auf Dem Rosenberg St Gallen Switzerland, Lausanne Univ Switzerland; *m* 1, 4 June 1960 (m dis 1976), Valerie Norma, da of Frederick Payne (d 1977); 1 s (Michael Anthony b 20 April 1961); m 2, 3 April 1979, Carol Ann, da of Robert Bithell, of Leven, Humberside; 1 s (James Ashley b 23 April 1980), 1 da (Camilla Rose b 9 July 1981); *Career* dir: Brailey GMBH and Co KG Erkrath W Germany 1955-, Brailey and Co Ltd Crawley Sussex 1969-, Gabro Engrg Ltd Crawley Sussex 1981-; FCIS 1969; *Recreations* classical music, tennis; *Style—* Michael Brailey, Esq; Fox Vane House, Sandpit Hall Rd, Cobham, Surrey GU24 8AN (☎ 09905 8559); Brailey and Co Ltd, 16 Royce Rd, Fleming Way, Crawley, Sussex RG10 2XN (☎ 0293 510227, fax 0293 31932, telex 878158)

BRAIN, Dr Anthony Thomas; s of Dr Reginald Thomas Brain (d 1971), of Rickmansworth, Herts, and Hallie Frances, *née* Weir; *b* 26 Feb 1932; *Educ* Highgate Sch, CCC Cambridge (MA, MB BChir), London Hosp Med Coll; *m* 23 Feb 1962, Cecilia, da of Sergio Cohen, of Santiago, Chile; *Career* London Hosp: house physician, house surgn, jr med registrar, med registrar; conslt geriatrician Hackney and St Andrews Hosp Bow, conslt in charge Dept Geriatric Med Bart's and Hackney Hosp (now City and Hackney AHA), until 1990, ret; FRCP 1978; *Recreations* writing, reading, studying natural history and human nature; *Clubs* Flyfishers, Bentley Drivers; *Style—* Dr Anthony Brain; 25 Southern Rd, London N2 9LH (☎ 081 883 6919)

BRAIN, 2 Baron (UK 1962); Sir Christopher Langdon Brain; 2 Bt (UK 1954); s of 1 Baron, DM, FRS, FRCP, FRCPI, FRCPE (d 1966); *b* 30 Aug 1926; *Educ* Leighton Park Sch, New Coll Oxford (MA); *m* 1953, Susan Mary, da of George Philip Morris; 3 da (Hon Nicola Dorothy b 1955, Hon Fiona Janice (Hon Mrs Proud) b 1958, Hon Naomi Melicent (Hon Mrs Kemp) b 1960); *Heir* bro, Hon Michael Brain; *Career* mgmnt conslt; various posts in photographic indust; Liveryman Worshipful Co of Weavers, Upper Bailiff 1984-85; *Recreations* sailing, fly fishing; *Clubs* Oxford and Cambridge Sailing Soc, Royal Photographic Soc (ARPS); *Style—* The Rt Hon The Lord Brain; The Old Rectory, Cross St, Moretonhampstead, Devon TQ13 8NL

BRAIN, Hon Mrs (Elizabeth Ann); *née* Herbert; da of Baron Tangley, KBE (Life Peer) (d 1973); *b* 17 Nov 1933; *Educ* Univ of Oxford (MA, BM BCh); *m* 10 Dec 1960, Hon Michael Cottrell Brain, *qv*, yr son of 1 Baron Brain (d 1966); 1 s, 2 da; *Career* assoc prof McMaster Univ Faculty of Health Sciences Canada, ret; *Books* Learning Resources (med ed 1970-); *Style—* The Hon Mrs Brain; 131 Northshore Blvd E, Burlington, Ontario, Canada L7T 4A4

BRAIN, Hon Michael Cottrell; s of 1 Baron Brain (d 1966), and hp of bro, 2 Baron; *b* 6 Aug 1928; *Educ* Leighton Park Sch, New Coll Oxford (MA, BCh, DM), London Hospital; *m* 1960, Hon Elizabeth Ann, da of Baron Tangley, KBE (Life Peer); 1 s (Thomas Russell b 1965), 2 da (Hilary Catherine (Mrs Guido Diro DeLuca) b 1961, Philippa Harriet b 1963); *Career* Capt RAMC 1956-58; physician Hammersmith Hosp 1966-69; prof of medicine McMaster Univ of Canada 1969-; FRCP, FRCP Canada; *Books* Current Therapy Hematology and Oncology (3 edn), Current Therapy of Internal Medicine (2 edn); *Recreations* tennis, sailing; *Style—* Dr Michael Brain; 131 North Shore Blvd E, Burlington, Ontario, Canada L7T 4A4

BRAIN, Dr the Hon Nicola Dorothy; eldest da of 2 Baron Brain, *qv*; *b* 26 Oct 1955; *Educ* Univ of Edinburgh (MB ChB 1979); *Style—* The Hon Nicola Brain; 74 Radbourne Street, Derby DE3 3HB

BRAIN, Sir (Henry) Norman; KBE (1963, OBE 1947), CMG (1953); s of Bert Brain, of Rushall, Staffs, and Ann Gertrude Swaffer; *b* 19 July 1907; *Educ* King Edward VI HS Birmingham, Queen's Coll Oxford; *m* 1939, Nuala Gertrude (d 1988), da of Capt Archibald W Butterworth, of Ryde, IOW; 1 s (and 1 s decd); *Career* ambass Cambodia 1956-58 and Uruguay 1961-66, pres Br-Uruguayan Soc 1973-; *Recreations* music, golf; *Clubs* Canning; *Style—* Sir Norman Brain, KBE, CMG; St Andrews, Abney Court, Bourne End, Bucks (☎ 20509)

BRAIN, Prof Paul Fredric; s of Frederick Ernest Brain, of Manchester, and Ada, *née* Squirell; *b* 1 July 1945; *Educ* Stretford Coll Manchester, Univ of Hull (BSc, PhD); *m* 4 July 1975, Sonja, da of Johannes Antonius Quirinus Strijbos, of Rotterdam, Holland; 2 s (Vincent Fredric b 1976, Daniel Robert b 1983); *Career* fellowship Univ of Sheffield 1970-71; Dept of Zoology Univ Coll Swansea: lectr 1971-78, sr lectr 1978-83, reader 1983-87, personal chair in zoology 1987-; visiting prof in psychology Univ of Hawaii 1986-, visiting prof in zoology Univ of Kebangsaan Malaysia 1987; memb: Soc for Endocrinology, Assoc for Study of Animal Behaviour; pres Int Soc for Res on Aggression; FIBiol; St Vincent (Italy) Int Prize for Med 1980; *Books* numerous incl: Hormones and Aggression Vol I (1977), Hormones and Aggression Vol II (1978), Hormones Drugs and Aggression Vol III (1979), Aggression: Functions and Causes (with JM Ramirez, 1985), Fear and Defence (1989); *Recreations* travel, reading, photography, marathon running; *Clubs* Glynneath Joggers, Sospan Road Runners; *Style—* Prof Paul Brain; Biological Sciences, University College Swansea, Swansea SA2 8PP (☎ 0792 295444, fax 0792 295447, telex 48358 ULSWAN G)

BRAINE, Rt Hon Sir Bernard Richard; PC (1985), DL (Essex 1978), MP (C) Castle Point 1983-; s of Arthur Ernest Braine (d 1933), of Kew Gdns; *b* 24 June 1914; *Educ* Hendon County GS; *m* 1935, Kathleen Mary (d 1982), da of late Herbert William Faun, of East Sheen; 3 s (Richard, Michael, Brendan); *Career* entered Civil Service 1931 (Inland Revenue); nat vice chm Jr Imp League (Cons youth movement) 1937-45; WWII 1939-45, cmmnd N Staffs Regt, served W Africa, NW Europe, SE Asia, Camberley Staff Coll; Temp Lt Col; Parly candidate (C) East Leyton 1945; MP (C): Billericay 1950-55, Essex SE 1955-83; Parly sec Miny of Pensions and Nat Insur 1960-61, under-sec of state Cwlth Rels 1961-62, Parly sec Miny of Health 1962-64; Cons front bench spokesman Cwlth Affairs and Overseas Aid 1967-70, chm Parly Select Ctee on Overseas Aid 1970-74; dep chm Cwlth Parly Assoc 1963-64 and 1970-74 (treas 1974-78); chm: Nat Cncl on Alcohol 1974-82, Br-German Parly Gp 1970, Br-Greek Parly Gp 1979-, UK Chapter Soc for Int Devpt; ldr Parly Missions to: India 1963, Mauritius 1971, Ethiopia 1971, W Germany 1973, Greece 1982, Poland 1986, Australia 1988; pres: UK Ctee Defence of the Unjustly Prosecuted, Gtr London Alcohol Advsy Service 1983-; chm Br 'Solidarity with Poland' Campaign 1981, tstee (and former govr) Cwlth Inst, assoc Inst of Devpt Studies Sussex Univ; chm: All Party Ctee on the Misuse of Drugs, All Party Pro-Life Ctee, Nat Cncl on Alcoholism 1974-82; vice-chm All Party Parly Human Rights Gp: Health Visitors Assoc; chm Tibet Parly Gp 1989; Father of the House of Commons 1987-; visiting prof Baylor Univ Texas USA; FRSA; kt 1972; Europe Peace Medal 1979, Cdr Polonia Restituta (Polish Govt in Exile) 1983, Kt Cdr Order of Merit (W Germany) 1984, KCSG 1987, Cdr Order of Honour (Greece) 1987; KStJ 1985; *Recreations* reading history, gardening; *Clubs* Beefsteak; *Style—* The Rt Hon Sir Bernard Braine, DL, MP; King's Wood, Great Wheatley Road, Rayleigh, Essex

BRAININ, Norbert; OBE (1960); s of Adolph and Sophie Brainin; *b* 12 March 1923,, Vienna; *Educ* High Sch Vienna; *m* 1948, Kathe Kottow; 1 da; *Career* leader of Amadeus String Quartet; prof of chamber music: Royal Acad of Music London, Hochschule fur Musik Cologne; hon doctorate: Univ of London, Univ of York; *Style—* Norbert Brainin Esq, OBE; 19 Prowse Ave, Bushey Heath, Herts (☎ 081 950 7379)

BRAINSBY, Anthony Thomas John (Tony); s of Thomas John Brainsby (d 1990), of Teesdale Gardens, Isleworth, Middx, and Kathleen Mary, *née* French (d 1985); *b* 6 March 1945; *Educ* Spring Grove GS; *m* 1980 (m dis 1984), Jane, *née* Abbott; 1 da (Miranda Jane Mary b 6 July 1979); *Career* PR co owner 1965-; clients incl: Jayne Mansfield 1966, Music Therapy Charity 1975-91, Thin Lizzy 1972-87, Queen 1974-79, Paul McCartney 1974-84, Steve Strange 1980-84, HMV Stores 1983-85, Virgin Atlantic Airline 1984-86, Me and My Girl 1985-88, Hippodrome Club, Limelight Club 1986-88, Montreal Comedy Festival 1988, Pink Floyd, Penthouse Magazine 1988-91, Chess, Knebworth Charity Concert 1990, David Essex 1991-, ELO part II 1991-, Arbiter Karaoke 1991-; Freeman City of London 1982; *Recreations* snooker, tennis, collector of music memorabilia, traveller; *Clubs* RAC, Pall Mall; *Style—* Tony Brainsby, Esq; 16B Edith Grove, London SW10 (☎ office 071 834 8341, home 071 352 3102, fax 071 352 9451, car 0836 333892)

BRAITHWAITE, Althea; da of Air Vice-Marshal Francis Joseph St George Braithwaite (d 1956), and Rosemary, *née* Harris (Lady Earle d 1978)); *b* 20 June 1940; *Educ* Felixtowe Coll; *m* 1, 1966 (m dis 1974), Malcolm Gordon Graham-Cameron; 1 s (Duncan Charles b 1968); m 2, 1979, Edward James Parker; *Career* writer and illustrator of about 200 books for children 1968-; specialises in information books covering numerous topics; fndr and managing ed Dinosaur Publications Ltd (sold to Collins 1984); *Style—* Ms Althea Braithwaite; Dinosaur Publications, Collins Publishers, 77 Fulham Palace Rd, London W6 8JB

BRAITHWAITE, His Hon Bernard Richard Braithwaite; s of Bernard Leigh Braithwaite, of Great House, Newchurch, Mon, and Emily Dora Ballard, *née* Thomas; *b* 20 Aug 1917; *Educ* Clifton, Peterhouse Cambridge; *Career* barr 1946, circuit judge 1971; ret; *Recreations* hunting, sailing; *Clubs* Boodle's; *Style—* His Hon B R Braithwaite; Summerfield House, Owlpen, Uley, Glos

BRAITHWAITE, Brian; s of Thomas Guy Braithwaite (d 1989), and Dorothea, *née* Swinbanks (d 1976); *b* 15 May 1927; *Educ* Mercers' Sch London; *m* 1, 6 June 1959 (m dis 1962), Patricia, *née* Moore; m 2, 1962, Gwendoline Phyllis, da of John Trevor Everson (d 1976); 2 s (Simon Guy b 1963, Christopher Brian b 1968), 1 da (Philippa Kate b 1964); *Career* Gordon Highlanders Trg Bn and Forces Broadcasting Serv, Italy and Austria 1945-48; Associated Newspapers 1948-53; advertisement exec: Hulton Press 1953-56, Harrison Raison 1956-64; advertisement and dir Bd Stevens Press 1964-69, joined Nat Magazine Co 1969; publisher: Harpers Bazaar 1969, Harper & Queen, Cosmopolitan 1972; publishing dir Good Housekeeping 1984 (dir Bd 1979); vice pres Publicity Club of London; *Books* Business of Women's Magazines (1978, 2 edn 1988), Ragtime to Wartime (1986), Home Front (1987), The Christmas Book (1988), Food Glorious Food (1990); *Recreations* golf, theatre, cinema; *Style—* Brian Braithwaite; 1 Narbonne Avenue, London SW4 (☎ 081 673 4100); National Magazine Co Ltd, National Magazine House, 72 Broadwick Street, London W1 (☎ 071 439 5259)

BRAITHWAITE, Sir (Joseph) Franklin Madders; DL (Cambs 1983); s of Sir John Braithwaite (d 1973, sometime chm Stock Exchange Cncl), and Martha Janette, *née*

Baker; *b* 6 April 1917; *Educ* Bootham Sch, King's Coll Cambridge; *m* 1939, (Charlotte) Isabel, da of Robert Elmer Baker, of NY; 1 s (Peter Franklin Braithwaite b 1942), 1 da (Virginia Louise b 1940); *Career* dir Baker Perkins 1950- (joined 1946), chm Baker Perkins Holdings plc 1980-84 (md 1971-79) pres Process Plant Assoc 1977-79, dir East Co Regnl Bd Lloyds Bank 1979-87, dep chm Peterborough Devpt Corp 1982-88, chm Peterborough Independent Hosp plc 1981-87; kt 1980; *Recreations* music, golf; *Clubs* Army and Navy; *Style*— Sir Franklin Braithwaite, DL; 7 Rutland Terrace, Stamford, Lincs PE9 2QD (☎ 0780 51244)

BRAITHWAITE, Mary Anne; da of Brig KW Hervey (d 1973), DSO, JP, of East Bilney Hall, Norfolk, and Hope Marian, *née* Barclay; *b* 16 Aug 1932; *Educ* Downham Sch Hatfield Heath Bishops Stortford Herts; *m* 1, 29 July 1952, Flt Lt James W Duff (d 1953); m 2, 12 July 1955, William Arthur (Jim) Drysdale (d 1970); 4 s (James (Jim) b 30 April 1956, William (Bill) b 27 Oct 1957, Keith (twin) b 27 Oct 1957, d 1989, Robert b 13 Nov 1960); m 3, 18 Dec 1975, Maj (Cecil) Geoffrey Braithwaite (d 1987); *Career* thoroughbred racehorse breeder 1970-, Jockey Club permit trainer 1976-86, dist cmmr Pony Club 1981-85; winner Horse and Hound Buccleuch Cup twice with homebred brother and sister horses; memb: BHS, Pony Club, Permit Trainers Assoc, Thoroughbred Breeders Assoc; *Recreations* hunting, fishing, stalking; *Style*— Mrs CG Braithwaite; Lochmalony, Cupar, Fife KY15 4QF (☎ 033 77 238)

BRAITHWAITE, Michael; *b* 10 Dec 1937; *Educ* City Univ (BSc); *m* 4 Feb 1967, (Pamela) Margaret; 1 s (James b 7 Jan 1971), 1 da (Sally b 4 Oct 1969); *Career* UKAEA 1958-69, ptnr responsible for info tech consulting Touche Ross & Co 1969-; Freeman Worshipful Co of Info Technologists 1988; CEng, MBCS, MInstMC; *Recreations* skiing, gardening; *Style*— Michael Braithwaite, Esq; The Manor House, Thriplow, Royston, Herts; Touche Ross and Co, 1 Little New St, London EC4A 3TR (☎ 071 936 3000)

BRAITHWAITE, Roderick Clive; s of Thomas Braithwaite (d 1965), and Winifred (d 1983); *b* 11 June 1932; *Educ* Mill Hill, Queens' Coll Cambridge (open scholar, MA); *m* 10 Aug 1956, Joan, da of Dr Francis Friend; 1 s (Nicholas b 1960), 1 da (Clare b 1959); *Career* Nat Serv Intelligence Corps 1954-56; chief exec Charles Barker Human Resources 1973-87; mgmnt conslt; memb Central Blood Laboratories Auth; *Books* How to Recruit (BIM), Communications and the Job-Seeker (Advertising Assoc); *Recreations* languages, geology; *Clubs* Reform, Old Millhillians; *Style*— Roderick Braithwaite, Esq; Vineyard Cottages, Cavendish, Suffolk

BRAITHWAITE, Sir Rodric Quentin; KCMG (1988); s of (Henry) Warwick Braithwaite (d 1971), and Lorna Constance, *née* Davies; *b* 17 May 1932; *Educ* Bedales Sch, Christ's Coll Cambridge (BA); *m* 1 April 1961, Gillian Mary, da of Patrick Robinson (d 1975); 4 s (Richard b 1962, Julian b 1968, Mark (twin) b 1968, d 1971, David b 1972), 1 da (Katharine b 1963); *Career* Nat Serv 1950-52; H M Dip Serv 1955-: Djakarta 1958-59, Warsaw 1959-61, FO 1961-63, Moscow 1963-66, Rome 1966-69, FO 1969-72, Oxford 1973-75, UK perm rep to Euro Community Brussels 1975-78, FO 1978-82, Washington 1982-84, FO 1984-88, Moscow 1988-; visiting fell All Souls Coll Oxford 1972-73; *Recreations* music, sailing, walking, reading, Russia; *Clubs* United Oxford and Cambridge Univ; *Style*— Sir Rodric Braithwaite, KCMG; c/o FCO, King Charles St, London SW1A 2AH

BRAMALL, Sir (Ernest) Ashley; DL (Gtr London 1982); er s of Maj Edmund Haselden Bramall, RA (d 1964), of 2 Symons St, Chelsea, and Katharine Bridget, *née* Westby (d 1985); bro of Field Marshal Lord Edwin Bramall; *b* 6 Jan 1916; *Educ* Westminster, Canford, Magdalen Coll Oxford (MA); *m* 1, 2 Sept 1939 (m dis 1950), Margaret Elaine, da of Raymond Taylor (d 1942), of Teddington, Middx; 2 s (Christopher b 1942, Richard b 1944); m 2, 23 Sept 1950, Germaine (Gery) Margaret, da of late Dr Victor Bloch (d 1968), of 48 Queen's Gate, London SW7; 1 s (Anthony b 1957); *Career* served WWII 1940-46, Maj RAC 1943, psc; called to the Bar Inner Temple 1949; MP (Lab) Bexley 1946-50; memb (Lab): Westminster City Cncl 1959-68, LCC Bethnal Green 1961-65, GLC Tower Hamlets 1964-73, Bethnal Green and Bow 1973-86; chm: GLC 1982-83, ILEA 1984-86 (ldr 1970-81), Nat Cncl for Drama Trg 1981-89; govr Museum of London, hon sec Theatres, Advsy Cncl; Freeman City of London, Liveryman Worshipful Co of Skinners 1951; Grand Offr Order of Orange Nassau (Netherlands) 1982; kt 1975; *Recreations* opera; *Style*— Sir Ashley Bramall, DL; 2 Egerton House, 59/63 Belgrave Rd, London SW1V 2BE (☎ 071 828 0973)

BRAMALL, Field Marshal Baron (Life Peer UK 1987) Edwin Noel Westby; KG (1990), GCB (1979, KCB 1974), OBE (1965), MC (1945) JP (1986); yr s of Maj Edmund Haselden Bramall, and Katherine Bridget, *née* Westby; bro of Sir Ashley Bramall, *qv*; *b* 18 Dec 1923; *Educ* Eton; *m* 1949, Dorothy Avril Wentworth, only da of Col Henry Albemarle Vernon, DSO, JP (ggggs of Henry Vernon by his w Lady Henrietta Wentworth, yst da of 1 Earl of Strafford, Henry Vernon being himself 2 cous of 1 Baron Vernon); 1 s, 1 da; *Career* 2 Lt KRRC 1943, served NW Europe WWII, Japan 1946-47, Middle East 1953-58, Instr Army Staff Coll 1958-61, involved in re-organising MOD 1963-64, served Malaysia during Indonesian confrontation 1965-66 (CO 2 Greenjackets KRRC), cmd 5 Airportable Bde 1967-69, IDC 1970, GOC 1 Div BAOR 1971-73, Lt-Gen 1973, Cdr Br Forces Hong Kong 1973-76, Gen 1976, C-in-C UKLF 1976-78, Vice-Chief Defence Staff (Personnel and Logistics) 1978-79, Chief General Staff 1979-82, ADC Gen to HM The Queen 1979-82, Field Marshal 1982, Chief of the Defence Staff 1982-85, Col Cmdt 3 Bn Roy Green Jackets 1973-84, Col 2 Gurkhas 1976-86; tstee Imperial War Museum 1983- (chm 1989); HM Lord Lt of Greater London 1986-; pres MCC 1988-89; pres Playing Fields Soc 1990-; *Recreations* MCC, Travellers, Pratt's; *Style*— Field Marshal the Rt Hon Lord Bramall, KG, GCB, OBE, MC, JP; c/o House of Lords, London SW1

BRAMBANI, Lisa; da of Peter Brambani, of Hartshead, Liversedge, and Patricia, *née* Nicholson; *b* 18 Aug 1967; *Educ* Liversedge Secdy Modern Sch, Heckmondwike GS Sixth Form; *Career* competitive cyclist; represented England and GB 1984-; Br Nat Road Race champion 1986-89, Br Nat 10 Mile Time Trial champion 1987-89, World Championship Road Race 1985-89, Olympic Games Road Race 1988, winner Ore-Ida Womens Challenge USA 1989, Cwlth Games Road Race 1990; rep sch and Yorks in swimming; Yorkshire Cycling Personality 1988; *Style*— Miss Lisa Brambani; Forte Hotel, Coal Pit Lane, Clifton Village, Brighouse, West Yorkshire HD6 4HW (☎ 0484 400400, fax 0484 400068)

BRAMBLE, Roger John Lawrence; DL (1986); s of Courtenay Parker Bramble, CIE (d 1987), of Childer Thornton, Cheshire, and Margaret Louise Bramble, MBE (d 1989), da of Sir Henry Lawrence, KCSI; *b* 3 April 1932; *Educ* Eton, King's Coll Cambridge (MA); *Career* dir: Richards Longstaff Ltd, ENO 1986-, English Nat Ballet 1986- (dep chm 1990-); chm Benesh Inst; tstee Serpentine Gallery 1990-; cncllr City of Westminster 1968-, Lord Mayor of Westminster 1985-86; FRSA 1989; Order Aztec Eagle Mexico 1985, Order of Merit Qatar 1985; *Recreations* music, farming, languages; *Clubs* Turf; *Style*— Roger Bramble, Esq, DL; 2 Sutherland St, London SW1V 4LB; Sutton Hosey Manor, Long Sutton, Langport, Somerset TA10 9NA; Battle Bridge Ho, 97 Tooley St, London SE1 2RF (☎ 071 407 4466, fax 071 403 3610)

BRAMLEY, Andrew; s of Peter Bramley (d 1989), of Ridgeway, Derbyshire, and Tessa, *née* Hardwick; *b* 18 Jan 1966; *Educ* Henry Fanshawe Sch Derbyshire; *Career* mangr family business until 1985; converted Old Vicarage (family home) into restaurant 1985-87; owner, mangr Old Vicarage 1987-; awarded: Good Food Guide Newcomer of the Year 1988, Derbyshire Restaurant of the Year award 1988-90, Clover Leaf award in Ackerman Guide 1990, Northern Restaurant of the Year award Chef Magazine 1991; featured in major Food and Wine Guides; TV and radio appearances; memb: Restaurant Assoc GB, Sheffield C of C; *Books* Women Chefs of Great Britain (with Tessa Bramley, 1990); *Recreations* cooking, writing, riding, shooting, cycling, interior design; *Style*— Andrew Bramley, Esq; The Old Vicarage, Ridgeway Moor, Ridgeway, Derbyshire, Nr Sheffield S12 3XW (☎ 0742 475814, fax 0742 477079)

BRAMLEY, Colin; s of John William Bramley (d 1965), of Pickering, N Yorks, and Charlotte Elizabeth, *née* Watson (d 1966); *b* 1 May 1932; *Educ* Malton GS N Yorks; *m* 11 May 1963, Christine, da of Duncan Nichol Watson (d 1947), of Scarborough, N Yorks; 1 da (Carol b 1964); *Career* CA 1955; ptnr Gardiners CAs N Yorks 1965-85, private practice 1985-; fndr memb and treas Scarborough and Dist Fuchsia Soc; FCA 1955, ATII 1956; *Recreations* horticulture; *Style*— Colin Bramley, Esq; 29 Westfield Ave, Newby, Scarborough, N Yorks (☎ 0723 365246)

BRAMLEY, Colin Ian Coulson; s of William Bramley, of Cawthorne, Barnsley, Yorks, and Violet, *née* Coulson; *b* 18 April 1944; *Educ* Ecclesfield GS Sheffield, Wadham Coll Oxford (MA, BCL), Univ of Pennsylvania USA; *m* Aug 1970, Janet Susan, da of William Thomas Wood (d 1976), of Chiswick, London; 2 s (Tom b 1971, Ben b 1974); *Career* admitted slr 1970; asst slr Slaughter and May 1970-76, ptnr Hepworth and Chadwick Leeds 1977-; sec Weston-with-Denton PCC Bradford, organist All Saints Church Weston; memb: Oxford Soc 1962-, Law Soc 1970-; *Recreations* music, gardening, walking, travel; *Clubs* The Leeds; *Style*— Ian Bramley, Esq; Hepworth and Chadwick Solicitors, Cloth Hall Court, Infirmary St, Leeds LS1 2JB (☎ 0532 430391, fax 0532 456188, telex 557917)

BRAMLEY, Dr John Vincent; s of George Vincent Bramley, and Kathleen Mary, *née* Phillips; *b* 4 July 1935; *Educ* Wyggeston GS Leicester, Imperial Coll London (BSc, PhD, DIC), ARSM; *m* 7 Jan 1961, Rosalind Mary Culhane, da of Maj George Pinckard Lathbury; 2 s (Robert George Vincent b 24 March 1964, Matthew John b 7 Nov 1967), 1 da (Katharine Susan b 31 Dec 1961); *Career* Laporte plc: joined 1959, mangr Glebe Mines 1969-76, gen mangr Laporte Minerals 1984-; govr Imperial Coll of Science Technol and Medicine; Inst of Mining and Metallurgy: memb 1961, fell 1972, memb Cncl 1986, chm Exec Ctee 1990; vice pres Mining Assoc of UK (chm Health & Safety Liaison Ctee); CEng, FEng 1988; *Recreations* choral singing, walking; *Style*— Dr John Bramley; Laporte Minerals, Cavendish Mill, Stoney Middleton, Sheffield S30 1TH (☎ 0433 30966, 0433 31736, fax 0433 31826)

BRAMLEY, Michael George; s of Arnold George Bramley (d 1973), and Violet, *née* White; *b* 9 July 1927; *Educ* Mountford House Neville Holt, Nottingham HS; *m* 17 Feb 1953, Kathleen Octavia, da of Robert Henry (d 1969); 1 s (Jonathan b 1967), 1 da (Jane b 1968); *Career* admitted slr 1951; life memb: Br Olympic Assoc, IEC Wine Soc; memb: The Nat Tst, The Woodland Tst, English Heritage; *Recreations* walking, swimming, theatre, travel, gardening; *Clubs* Notts CC; *Style*— Michael G Bramley, Esq; 420 Gedling Road, Arnold, Nottingham NG5 6PD (☎ 0602 269147); 1 Oxford St, Nottingham NG1 5BH (☎ 0602 475792, fax 0602 480853)

BRAMLEY, Prof Sir Paul Anthony; s of Charles Bramley (d 1962), and Constance Victoria Bramley (d 1983); *b* 24 May 1923; *Educ* Wyggeston Leicester, Univ of Birmingham (MB ChB, BDS); *m* 1952, Hazel Morag, da of Harold Arthur Boyd (d 1964), of Glasgow; 1 s, 3 da; *Career* Capt RADC 1946-48; conslt oral surgn Southwest Regnl Hosp Bd 1954-69; Univ of Sheffield: prof of Dental Surgery 1969-88, dean Dental Sch 1972-75; dean Faculty RCS 1980-83, chm Dental Protection Ltd, emeritus conslt RN; pres: Sands Cox Soc, BDA, memb Cncl Med Protection Soc; Hon DDS: Univ of Birmingham, Prince of Songkla; FDSRCS, FRCS, Hon FRACDS; Bronze medal Univ of Helsinki, Collier Gold medal RCS; kt 1984; *Style*— Prof Sir Paul Bramley; Greenhills, Back Lane, Hathersage S30 1AR (☎ 0433 50502)

BRAMLEY, Robin Thomas Todhunter; s of E A Bramley, of Boundary Farm, Gillingham, Norfolk, and M A M Bramley *née* Todhunter; *b* 16 June 1950; *Educ* Ampleforth, Univ of Exeter (LLB); *m* 20 Oct 1973, Patricia Anne, da of Maj E S L Mason of Dunburgh House, Geldeston, Beccles, Suffolk; 1 s (George b 1982), 1 da (Henrietta b 1979); *Career* Landowner and Farmer Gillingham Estate, ptnr Francis Hornor and Son chartered surveyors Norwich 1976-, md Norfolk Landfill Ltd; chm Broads Soc 1986-87 (and memb 1984-); memb: Ctee Norfolk Branch CLA, the Broads Authy; JP; FRICS 1978; *Recreations* shooting, riding; *Clubs* Norfolk; *Style*— Robin T T Bramley, Esq; Gillingham Hall, Norfolk (☎ 0502 717 247); Old Bank of England Court, Queen Street, Norwich (☎ 0603 629 871, fax 0502 716 856)

BRAMLEY, Tessa; da of Howard Hardwick (d 1990), of Coal Aston, nr Sheffield, and Irene, *née* Barber; *b* 3 April 1939; *Educ* Henry Fanshawe GS Derbyshire, High Storrs GS Sheffield, London Coll of Home Econ, Totley Hall Trg Coll Sheffield (Dip in Domestic Sci, Dip Ed); *m* 8 June 1965, Peter Bramley (d 1989), s of Francis Bramley; 1 s (Andrew b 18 Jan 1966); *Career* teacher and lectr in domestic sci 1963-75, sales and promotion in food business 1975-81, ran own restaurant (with husband) 1981-; opened Old Vicarage 1987: Good Food Guide's Newcomer of Year 1988, Egon Ronay Star 1988-90, Clover Leaf in Ackerman Guide 1990, Northern Restaurant of the Year award Chef Magazine 1991, Derbyshire Restaurant of the Year 1988-90; memb Restaurant Assoc of GB, Sheffield C of C, Inst of Master Chefs; *Books* Women Chefs of Great Britain (with Andrew Bramley, 1990); *Recreations* literature and music; *Style*— Ms Tessa Bramley; Old Vicarage, Ridgeway Moor, Ridgeway, Derbyshire, Sheffield S12 3XW (☎ 0742 475814, fax 0742 477079)

BRAMMA, Harry Wakefield; s of Fred Bramma (d 1983), of Guiseley, W Yorks, and Christine, *née* Wakefield; *b* 11 Nov 1936; *Educ* Bradford GS, Pembroke Coll Oxford (MA); *Career* master King Edward VI GS E Retford 1961-63, asst organist Worcester Cathedral 1963-76, dir of music The Kings Sch Worcester; organist: Three Chorus Festival in 1966, 1969, 1972, 1975, All Saints Margaret St London; conductor, Kidderminster Choral Soc 1972-79, organist and dir of music Southwark Cathedral 1976-89, hon treas Royal Coll of Organists 1987-, dir The Royal Sch of Church Music 1989-; Liveryman, Worshipful Co of Musicians; FRCO; *Style*— Harry Bramma, Esq; Addington Palace, Croydon, Surrey CR9 5AD (☎ 081 654 7676)

BRAMPTON, Sally Jane; da of Roy Reginald Brampton, of Sunbury on Thames, Middlesex, and Pamela Mary, *née* Ray; *b* 5 July 1955; *m* 1 (m dis 1990), Nigel Cole; m 2, 29 Dec 1990, Jonathan Powell; *Career* fashion writer Vogue 1978-81, fashion ed Observer 1981-85, ed-in-chief Elle 1985-89, assoc ed Mirabella 1990-, freelance journalist; *Recreations* writing; *Clubs* Groucho; *Style*— Miss Sally Brampton

BRANAGH, Kenneth Charles; s of William Branagh, and Frances Branagh; *b* 10 Dec 1960; *Educ* Meadway Comp Sch Reading, RADA; *Career* actor and dir; fndr Renaissance Theatre Co 1987; theatre performances incl: Another Country (Queen's Theatre) London 1982 (winner SWET Award and Plays and Players Award, Most Promising Newcomer), RSC 1984-85; films incl: A Month in the Country, Henry V (actor, author screenplay, dir); TV appearances incl: Fortunes of War, Boy in the Bush; author of play Public Enemy 1988; *Recreations* reading, playing the guitar; *Style*— Kenneth Branagh, Esq

BRANCH, Prof Michael Arthur; s of Arthur Frederick Branch (d 1986), of Hornchurch, Essex, and Mahala, *née* Parker; *b* 24 March 1940; *Educ* Shene London,

Univ of London Sch of Slavonic and E European Studies (BA, PhD), Univ of Helsinki; *m* 11 Aug 1963, (Ritva-Riitta) Hannele, da of Erkki Lauri Kari (d 1982), of Heinola, Finland; 3 da (Jane, Jean, Ann); *Career* Univ of London: lectr Finno-Ugrian Studies 1971-73 (asst lectr 1967-71), dir Sch of Slavonic and E Euro Studies 1980-, prof of Finnish 1986- (lectr 1973-77, reader 1977-86); chm Library Bd Univ of London; govr: Sch Oriental and African Studies, Warburg Inst, Br Inst Paris, GB-USSR Assoc, GB-E Euro Centre; Hon DPhil Univ of Oulu Finland 1983; Commander of the Finnish Lion Finland 1980; *Books* A J Sjögren: Travels in the North (1973), Finnish Folk Poetry: Epic (jtly, 1977), Student's Glossary of Finnish (jtly, 1981), Kalevala, translated W F Kirby (ed, 1985); *Recreations* walking, gardening; *Clubs* Athenaeum; *Style—* Prof M A Branch; 33 St Donatt's Rd, New Cross, London SE14 6NU; Hämeentie 28 A3, 00530 Helsinki, Finland; Sch of Slavonic and E Euro Studies, Univ of London, Senate Hse, Malet St, London WC1E 7NU (☎ 071 637 4934, fax 071 436 8916, telex 269400 SHULG)

BRANCH, Sir William Allan Patrick; *b* 17 Feb 1915; *m* Thelma, *née* Rapier; 1 s; *Career* md and Grenada rep Windward Islands Banana Assoc; kt 1977; *Style—* Sir William Branch; Dougaldston, Gouyave, St John's, Grenada

BRANCKER, Sir (John Eustace) Theodore; QC (1961); s of Jabel Eustace and Myra Enid Vivienne Brancker; *b* 9 Feb 1909; *Educ* Harrison Coll Barbados; *m* 1967, Esmé Gwendolyn, da of Victor Walcott, of Barbados; *Career* barr, pres Barbados Senate 1971-76; kt 1969; *Recreations* chess, classical music, drama; *Clubs* Rotary Barbados, Empire Barbados, Challoner (London), Bridgetown Barbados; *Style—* Sir John Brancker, QC; Valencia, St James, Barbados (☎ 04138)

BRAND, Colin Michael John; s of Herman Joseph Brand (d 1973), and Margaretta, *née* Shepherd (d 1976); *b* 7 Nov 1932; *Educ* John Fisher Sch Purley; *m* 5 Aug 1957, Joyce Margaret, da of John Young Minty; 2 s (Ian b 1963, Nigel b 1966), 1 da (Diana b 1969); *Career* Nat Serv RAF; co sec Lional Sage & Co Ltd 1975-80, dir Anton Underwriting Agencies Ltd 1980-90, md HG Poland (Agencies) Ltd 1990-; FInstD; *Recreations* philately (memb: India Study Circle for Philately, Nat Philatelic So); *Style—* Colin Brand, Esq; H G Poland (Agencies) Ltd, 10 Philpot Lane, London EC3M 8AA (☎ 071 626 8201, fax 071 283 2381, telex 9419440)

BRAND, Hon Lord; David William Robert; s of James Gordon Brand (d 1933), of Huntingdon, Dumfries, and Frances Jessie, *née* Bull (d 1955); *b* 21 Oct 1923; *Educ* Stonyhurst, Univ of Edinburgh (MA, LLB); *m* 1, 1948, Rose Josephine (d 1968), da of James Devlin, of Co Tyrone; 4 da; m 2, 1969, Brigid Veronica, da of Garrett Russell, of Co Limerick, and widow of Thomas Patrick Lynch; *Career* cmmnd in Argyll & Sutherland Highlanders 1942, Capt 1945; advocate 1948, QC (Scot) 1959, Sheriff Dumfries and Galloway 1968-70, slr-gen Scotland 1970-72, senator Coll of Justice Scotland (Lord of Session) 1972-89; Kt SMO Malta; *Recreations* golf; *Clubs* New (Edinburgh), Hon Co of Edinburgh Golfers; *Style—* The Hon Lord Brand; Ardgarten, 6 Marmion Rd, N Berwick, E Lothian (☎ 0620 3208)

BRAND, Hon Mrs (Laura Caroline Beatrice); *née* Smith; da of 3 Viscount Hambleden and Lady Patricia Herbert, da of 15 Earl of Pembroke; *b* 9 Sept 1931; *m* 1953, Michael Charles Brand, yr s of late Lt-Col John Charles Brand, DSO, MC, Coldstream Guards; 1 s, 2 da; *Style—* The Hon Mrs Brand; 6 Howley Place, London W2

BRAND, Terence Edwin; s of Edwin Albert Thomas Brand (d 1980), and Ethel Louise, *née* Stoneham; *b* 18 Oct 1924; *m* 6 Nov 1949 (m dis 1983), Linda Pasqualia Ceruti, step da of Maj Donald Thomas, of Sunbury on Thames; 2 s (Mark Edwin b 1959, Anthony Quentin b 1962); *Career* WWII RAF 1943-47: Flt Lt, navigator, Staff Coll, Coastal Transport and Trg Cmds; BA (formerly BOAC): pilot 1947-79, Sr Capt Boeing 747 1954-79, 3 Royal flights, involved trg and devpt VC10 and Concorde, dir and tstee Airways Pension Scheme, involved with TV and Advertising BA image in UK, USA and Australia (presentations and 3 films); business conslt 1979-, dep chm OPAS 1983-, dir Collins-Wilde plc 1984-; chm: Collins-Wilde Enterprises Ltd, tstee: BALPA Benevolent Ctee, Guild of Air Pilots Benevolent Ctee; govr Crossways Tst; Queens Commendation 1977; Freeman City of London 1970, Liveryman Guild of Air Pilots and Air Navigators 1970; FIN 1948, FRMETS 1948, ABAC 1988; *Recreations* squash, bridge; *Clubs* RAF, City Livery, MCC; *Style—* Terence Brand, Esq; 126 The Avenue, Sunbury on Thames, Middx TW16 5EA (☎ 09327 82704); 11 Belgrave Rd, SW1V 1RB (☎ 071 233 8080, fax 071 233 8016)

BRANDER, Lady Evelyn Jean Blanche; da of 3 Earl of Balfour (d 1968); *b* 22 March 1929; *m* 1948, Michael William Brander, yr s of Francis R Brander, of 80 Iverna Court, W8; 1 s, 2 da; *Style—* The Lady Evelyn Brander; Whittingehame Mains, Haddington, E Lothian

BRANDON, Michael; s of Sol Feldman, and Miriam, *née* Tumen; *b* 20 April 1945; *Educ* Central HS NY, Nassau Community Coll, NY Univ, American Acad of Dramatic Arts; *m* 1, Dec 1976 (m dis 1978), Lindsay Wagner; m 2, 18 Nov 1989, Glynis Barber; *Career* actor in films: Lovers and Strangers (with Diane Keaton), Jennifer On My Mind (with Robert De Niro), FM, Change of Seasons (with Shirley Mclaine and Anthony Hopkins), Richard and Famous (with Jacqueline Bisset), Four Flies on Grey Velvet, Promises in the Dark (with Marsha Mason); actor in four films of James Hadley Chase novels (Try This One for Size (with Robert Mitchum), Presumed Dangerous, Have a Nice Night, The Last Colt); TV films incl: James Dean, Queen of the Stardust Ballroom, Hitchike, Red Badge of Courage, Third Girl from the Left, Visitors (written by Dennis Potter), Rock and Roll Mum, Comedy Company; dir of: rock videos, Monsters TV series, documentary Ski Focus; dir and star (with Glynis Barber) of Dempsey and Makepeace; memb: Greenpeace, Children in Need; memb U12 Screen Actors Guild, Equity (American and Br), ACTT, Writers Guild, AFTRA, Academy of Motion Picture Arts and Sciences; *Recreations* skiing, scuba-diving, horseback riding, photography, photo exhibition in London 1986 for Prince's Trust; *Clubs* 190 Queens Gate, Mosiman's, Tramp, Rest; *Style—* Michael Brandon, Esq; c/o Jean Diamond London Management, 235-241 Regent St, London W1 (☎ 071 493 1610); Neil Koenigsberg Inc, 1033 Gayley Ave, Westwood, LA 90024 (☎ 010 1213 824 0133)

BRANDON, Hon Richard Henry; 2 s of Baron Brandon of Oakbrook, MC, PC (Life Peer); *b* 1961; *Educ* Winchester, Bristol Univ Drama Dept; *m* 15 May 1988, Jean Patricia, da of R B Horsfield, of Eccles, Manchester; 1 s (Henry Philip); *Career* theatre director; assoc dir Liverpool Playhouse 1984-85; artistic director, Hebden Bridge Festival Theatre 1987; *Style—* The Hon Richard Brandon

BRANDON, Hon Mrs (Signe Evelyn); *née* Gully; da of 2 Viscount Selby (d 1923); *b* 1909; *m* 1938, Max Brandenstein, who assumed the name Mark Leslie Brandon; 1 s, 1 da; *Style—* The Hon Mrs Brandon; 2 Tyrawley Rd, London SW6

BRANDON-BRAVO, Martin Maurice; MP (C) Nottingham South 1983-; s of Alfred (Issac) Brandon Bravo (d 1984), of London, and Phoebe Brandon Bravo (d 1967); of Sephardic origin with family records in Bevis Marks Synagogue dating back to late 1600s; *b* 25 March 1932; *Educ* Latymer Upper Sch, Trent Poly; *m* 1964, Sally Anne, da of Robert Wallwin, of Elton, Cambs; 2 s (Paul b 1967, Joel b 1971); *Career* md Richard Stump Ltd until 1983; contested Nottingham East 1979; PPS to: Min of State DOE 1985-87, Min of State Home Office 1987-89, Home Sec 1989-90, Lord Privy Seal and Leader House of Lords 1991; Nottingham City cncllr on Educn and Pub Works Ctees 1968-70 and 1976-87, chm County Local Govt Advsy Ctee Nottingham W; vice chm: City of Nottingham Fedn, Nottingham Cncl on City Fin and Tport Ctees Cncl 1976-87; pres Nottingham and Union Rowing Club, holder of FISA (int umpires' licence); FBIM; *Recreations* rowing; *Clubs* Leander, Nottingham and Union Rowing, Carlton; *Style—* Martin Brandon-Bravo Esq, MP; House of Commons, London SW1 (☎ 071 219 4429)

BRANDON OF OAKBROOK, Baron (Life Peer UK 1981); Sir Henry Vivian; MC (1942), PC (1978); yr s of Capt Vivian Ronald Brandon, CBE, RN (d 1944), of 33 Argyll Rd, Kensington, and Joan Elizabeth Maud, *née* Simpson (d 1979); *b* 3 June 1920; *Educ* Winchester, King's Coll Cambridge; *m* 1955, Jeanette Rosemary, da of Julian Vivian Breeze Janvrin, late Indian Police (d 1988); 3 s, 1 da; *Career* served WW II RA Madagascar 1942, India and Burma 1942-45; barr 1946; QC 1961; High Court Judge: Probate, Divorce and Admlty Div 1966-71, Family Div 1971-78; judge of Admiralty Court 1971-78, judge of Commercial Court 1977-78; Lord Justice of Appeal 1978-81; Lord of Appeal in Ordinary 1981-; kt 1966; *Recreations* watching cricket, travel, bridge; *Clubs* MCC; *Style—* The Rt Hon the Lord Brandon of Oakbrook, MC, PC; 6 Thackeray Close, Wimbledon, London SW19 (☎ 081 947 6344); House of Lords, London SW1 (☎ 071 219 3119)

BRANDRAM, Lady Katherine; HRH Princess Katherine of Greece and Denmark; yst da of HM King Constantine I of the Hellenes (d 1923), and HM Queen Sophie, *née* HRH Princess Sophie of Prussia (d 1932), 3 da of Friedrich III, German Emperor and King of Prussia; ggda of HM Queen Victoria; granted the style, title and precedence of a Duke's da in Great Britain by Royal Warrant of HM King George VI 9 Sept 1947; *b* 4 May 1913; *m* 21 April 1947, Maj Richard Campbell Andrew Brandram, MC, TD, RA, o s of late Richard Andrew Brandram, of The Well House, Bickley, Kent; 1 s (Paul); *Career* formerly HRH Princess Katherine of Greece and Denmark; Gd Cross Order of SS Olga and Sophia (Greece); *Style—* Lady Katherine Brandram; Croft Cottage, Pound Lane, Marlow, Bucks (☎ 062 84 3974)

BRANDRETH, Gyles Daubeney; s of Charles Daubeney Brandreth (d 1972), of London, and Alice, *née* Addison; *b* 8 March 1948; *Educ* Bedales, New Coll Oxford (MA); *m* 8 June 1973, Michele, da of Alec Brown; 1 s (Benet Xan b 1975), 2 da (Saethryd Charity b 1976, Aphra Kendal Alice b 1978); *Career* author, broadcaster, producer; journalist and TV presenter 1973-; chm: Victorama Ltd 1974-, Complete Editions Ltd; dir Newarke Wools Ltd, fndr Nat Teddy Bear Museum Stratford upon Avon; chm National Playing Fields Assoc 1989- appeals chm 1984-88); *Books* various incl Created in Captivity (1972), Everyman's Modern Phrase and Fable (1990); *Recreations* some time holder of world record for longest-ever after-dinner speech (12 1/2 hours); *Style—* Gyles Brandreth, Esq; Britannia House, Glenthorne Rd, London W6 0LF (☎ 081 741 2228, fax 081 748 3163, telex 619107)

BRANDSTRUP, Kim; s of Finn Brandstrup, of Denmark, and Tove Riis, *née* Mortensen; *b* 9 Jan 1957; *Educ* Univ of Copenhagen (BA), London Contemporary Dance Sch; *Career* Spiral Dance Company 1983, English Dance Theatre 1984; Arc Dance Company: fndr 1985, Les Noces 1985, Soldier's Tale 1986, The Dybbuk 1987, Peer Gynt 1990; London Contemporary Dance Theatre: Orfeo (Oliver award for most outstanding contrib to dance, 1989), The Dybbuk 1990, Life is a Dream 1991; *Style—* Kim Brandstrup, Esq; c/o Mark Ashman, 145a Kensington High St, London W8 (☎ 071 937 0746)

BRANDT, Peter Augustus; s of Walter Augustus Brandt, of Saffron Walden, and Dorothy Gray, *née* Crane; *b* 2 July 1931; *Educ* Eton, Trinity Coll Cambridge; *m* 1962, Elisabeth Margaret, da of Frans ten Bos, of Holland; 2 s, 1 da; *Career* chm Atkins Fulford Ltd 1977-, chief exec William Brandt's Sons & Co 1966-; dir: William Brandt's Sons & Co, London Life Assoc, Corp of Argentine Meat Producers' London Cos; *Recreations* rowing, sailing, watercolours; *Clubs* Carlton, Leander; *Style—* Peter Brandt, Esq; 13 Kensington Place, London W8 (☎ 071 727 8449); Spout Farm, Boxford, Colchester, Essex (☎ 0787 210297)

BRANDT, Richard; s of Edmund Hubert Brandt (d 1965), of London, and Norah, *née* Toole (d 1971); *b* 7 Aug 1929; *Educ* Downside, Lincoln Coll Oxford (BA, MA); *m* 4 July 1964, Margaret, da of Philip Archibald Campbell Adamson (d 1977), of Broadstairs; 2 s (Edmund Richard Adamson b 1967, William Robert Aldhelm b 1973), 1 da (Charlotte Louise b 1968); *Career* Nat Serv 1948-49; articled to Annan Dexter & Co 1953-57; ptnr: G Dixey & Co 1957-61, Dearden Harper Miller & Co 1962-68; mangr Arthur Andersen & Co 1969-72, ptnr Grant Thornton (formerly Thornton Baker & Co) 1972-; memb Cncl and Fin Ctee Save the Children Fund 1975-90 (treas 1982-87); ACA 1957, FCA 1962; *Recreations* sailing, collecting antiques (particularly drinking glasses); *Clubs* Sea View Yacht; *Style—* Richard Brandt, Esq; The Anchorage, Ryde Rd, Seaview, Isle of Wight PO34 5AB (☎ 0983 613 769); Grant Thornton House, Melton St, Euston Sq, London NW1 2EP (☎ 071 383 5100, fax 071 383 4715, telex 28984 GT LDNG)

BRANIGAN, Sir Patrick Francis; QC (Gold Coast 1949); eldest s of Daniel Branigan (d 1923) and Teresa Alice, *née* Clinton (d 1921); *b* 30 Aug 1906; *Educ* Newbridge Coll Co Kildare, Trinity Coll Dublin, Downing Coll Cambridge; *m* 1935, Prudence, da of Dr Arthur Avent (d 1953), of Seaton, Devon, 1 s, 1 da; *Career* barr; Colonial Legal Service 1931-54, attorney gen and minister of justice Gold Coast 1948-54, dep chm Devon QS, recorder Crown Ct; chm: Pensions Appeal Tbnl, Agric Land Tbnl, Med Appeal Tbnl, Mental Health Review Tbnl, ret 1978; chm Suflex Ltd, ret 1983; kt 1954; *Style—* Sir Patrick Branigan, QC; C'an San Juan, La Huerta de la Font, Pollensa, Mallorca (☎ 010 3471 530767)

BRANNAN, Anthony Victor Frederick (Tony); s of (Thomas) Martin Brannan, OBE, of Portinscale, Keswick, Cumbria, and Phillys May, *née* Venebles; *b* 21 Feb 1944; *Educ* St Bees Sch; *m* 27 Feb 1965, Irene Elizabeth, da of William Irving (Bill) Tolson, of High Harrington, Workington, Cumbria; 2 da (Juliet b 13 May 1966, Emma b 12 Oct 1968); *Career* Ward & Pridmore CAs 1951-53, S Brannan & Sons Ltd Thermometer Mfrg 1953- (dir 1970); *Recreations* spectator football, cooking; *Style—* Tony Brannan, Esq; Finkle Lodge, Portinscale, Keswick, Cumbria CA12 5RF (☎ 07687 73244); S Brannan & Sons Ltd, Cleator Moor, Cumbria CA25 5QE (☎ 0946 810413, telex 64248)

BRANSBY, Dr Peter Leigh; s of Dr Ernest Roy Bransby, of Warlingham, Surrey, and Nancy Barbara, *née* Leigh-Smith; *b* 9 Oct 1942; *Educ* Caterham, Trinity Coll Cambridge (scholar, BA, PhD); *m* July 1965, Jillian Elizabeth, da of R Eric Dobson; 1 s (Mark Fraser b 25 Oct 1969), 1 da (Hilda Jane b 21 April 1971); *Career* post doctoral fell Univ of British Columbia 1968-69, demonstrator (later lectr) Dept of Engineering Univ of Cambridge 1969-76, fell Christ's Coll Cambridge 1970-76, head materials handling then dep dir Warren Spring Laboratory (DTI) 1976-85, Policy Planning Unit DTI 1985-86, dir gen CIRIA 1986- ; Br Geotechnical Soc Prize 1970, author's prize Instn of Chemical Engrs 1982; MICE 1972, FICE 1987, FEng 1989; *Books* The Mechanics of Soils (with J H Atkinson, 1978); *Recreations* hill walking, tennis, folk dancing; *Style—* Dr Peter Bransby; CIRIA, 6 Storey's Gate, London SW1P 3AU (☎ 071 222 8891, fax 071 222 1708)

BRANSON, Lady Noreen; *née* Browne; yr da of late Lt-Col Lord Alfred Browne, DSO (ka 1918), s of 5 Marquess of Sligo; sis of 10 Marquess of Sligo; *b* 16 May 1910; *m* 1931, Clive Ali Chimmo Branson (ka 1944), s of Maj L H Branson; 1 da; *Career*

granted the style and precedence of a Marquess's da 1953; *Style—* Lady Noreen Branson; 46 Southwood Ave, N6

BRANSON, Richard Charles Nicholas; s of Edward James Branson, of Shamley Green, Surrey, and Evette Huntley, *née* Flindt; *b* 18 July 1950; *Educ* Stowe; *m* 1, 1969 (m dis); m 2, 17 March 1978 (m dis), Kristen Tomassi; m 3, 20 Dec 1989, Joan Sarah Drummond, da of John Templeman (d 1988), of Glasgow, Scotland; 1 s (Sam Edward Charles b 12 Aug 1985), 1 da (Holly Katy b 20 Nov 1981); *Career* ed Student magazine 1968-69; fndr: Student Advsy Centre (now Help) 1970, Virgin Mail-Order Co 1969, Virgin Retail 1970, Virgin Records 1973, Virgin Atlanta Airways 1984, Voyager Gp Ltd 1986; chm and chief exec: The Virgin Gp of Cos, Virgin Music Gp, Virgin Retail Gp, Virgin Communications, Virgin Hldgs; pres UK 2000 1988- (chm 1986-88), dir Intourist Moscow Ltd 1988-; tstee: Healthcare Fndn (fndr 1987), Charity Projects; patron: Nat Holiday Fund, Paul D'Gorman Fndn Trevor Jones Tst, London Sch for Performing Arts & Technol; pres Br Disabled Water Ski Assoc, hon vice pres Operation Raleigh, hon memb Ctee The Friends of the Earth; capt Atlantic Challenger II, winner Blue Riband for fastest crossing of the Atlantic by boat 1986, world record crossing of Atlantic by hot air balloon with Per Lindstrand 1987; Key to the City of NY; *Recreations* tennis, skiing, swimming, ballooning; *Clubs* Roof Garden, Br Balloon and Airship Club; *Style—* Richard Branson, Esq; 120 Campden Hill Rd, London W8 7AR (☎ 071 229 1282, fax 071 727 8200)

BRANSON, Hon Mrs (Stephana); *née* Warnock; da of Sir Geoffrey James Warnock, of Brick House, Axford, nr Marlborough, Wilts, and Baroness Warnock (Life Peeress), *qv*; *b* 9 July 1956; *Educ* Downe House, Oxford HS, Guildhall Sch of Music and Drama (GGSM); *m* 1 Aug 1987, David Ernest Branson, s of William Ernest Branson, of 53/54 High Street, Southill, nr Biggleswade, Beds; 1 da (Abigail Brigitte Edith b 16 April 1989); *Style—* Hon Mrs Branson; 7 St Ruald's Close, Wallingford, Oxon (☎ 0491 34983)

BRASH, Robert; CMG (1980); s of Frank Brash (d 1978), and Ida Brash; *b* 30 May 1924; *Educ* Portsmouth Southern GS, Trinity Coll Cambridge (BA); *m* 1954, Barbara Enid, da of Brig Frederick William Clarke (d 1966), of Bexhill; 3 s, 1 da; *Career* Lt Burma, served 1943-46; Foreign Serv 1949-84: consul gen Düsseldorf 1978-81, ambass to Jakarta 1981-84; chm Guildford Rambling Club; *Recreations* golf, walking, gardening, stained glass; *Clubs* RAC; *Style—* Robert Brash, Esq, CMG; Woodbrow, Woodham Lane, Woking, Surrey (☎ 0932 343874); c/o Foreign and Commonwealth Office, King Charles St, London SW1

BRASHER, Christopher William; s of (William) Kenneth Brasher, CBE (d 1972), and Katie, *née* Howe (d 1987); *b* 21 Aug 1928; *Educ* Rugby, St John's Coll Cambridge; *m* 1959, Shirley, *née* Bloomer; 1 s, 2 da; *Career* Olympic Gold medallist 1956; sports ed The Observer 1957-61, BBC TV reporter Tonight 1961-65, ed Time Out and Man Alive 1964-65; head Gen Features BBC TV 1969-72, columnist The Observer 1972-89; chm Brasher Leisure Ltd 1977-, md Fleetfoot Ltd 1979-, race dir London Marathon 1981-, chm Reebok UK Ltd 1990-; *Recreations* mountains, fly-fishing, orienteering, social running; *Clubs* Alpine, Hurlingham, Ranelagh Harriers, Travellers'; *Style—* Christopher Brasher Esq; The Navigator's House, River Lane, Richmond, Surrey TW10 7AG (☎ 081 940 0296/8822)

BRASSEY, Hon Edward; s and h of 3 Baron Brassey of Apethorpe; *b* 9 March 1964; *Educ* Eton, RMA Sandhurst; *Career* 2Lt Grenadier Guards 1985; *Style—* The Hon Edward Brassey; The Manor House, Apethorpe, Peterborough

BRASSEY, Lt-Col Hon Peter Esmé; JP (1947); yst s of 1 Baron Brassey of Apethorpe (d 1958), and Lady Violet Mary Gordon-Lennox (d 1946), da of 7 Duke of Richmond and Gordon; *b* 5 Dec 1907; *Educ* Eton, Magdalene Coll Cambridge; *m* 12 Dec 1944, Lady Romayne, *née* Cecil, da of 5 Marquess of Exeter, KG, CMG, TD; 2 s, 1 da; *Career* Northants Yeomanry 1938-46 (wounded 1944), control cmmn for Germany (legal div) 1945-46; barr 1930; chm Essex Water Co; High Sheriff Huntingdon and Peterborough 1966; Lord-Lt Cambs 1975-81; KStJ 1975; *Recreations* fishing; *Clubs* Carlton; *Style—* Lt-Col The Hon Peter Brassey, JP; Pond House, Barnack, Stamford, Lincs (☎ 0780 740238)

BRASSEY, Lady Romayne Elizabeth Algitha; *née* Cecil; OBE, ARRC; yr da of 5 Marquess of Exeter, KG, CMG, TD (d 1956), and Hon Myra Orde-Powlett (d 1973), o da of 4 Baron Bolton; *b* 22 March 1915; *m* 12 Dec 1944, Lt-Col Hon Peter Brassey, *qv*; *Style—* The Lady Romayne Brassey, OBE, ARRC; Pond House, Barnack, Stamford, Lincs (☎ 0780 740238)

BRASSEY, Hon Thomas Ian; s of 2 Baron Brassey of Apethorpe, MC, TD (d 1967); *b* 14 June 1934; *Educ* Stowe; *m* 1960, Valerie Christine Finlason, da of Mrs F F Powell (d 1964) and step da of F F Powell (d 1975), 1 s (Thomas b 1971), 3 da (Miranda b 1963, Louise b 1964, Davina b 1969); *Career* Lt Grenadier Gds 1953-58; company dir; *Clubs* Boodles; *Style—* The Hon Thomas Brassey; The Coach House, Duncote, Towcester, Northamptonshire NN12 8AQ (Tel: 0327 52855)

BRASSEY OF APETHORPE, Barbara, Lady; Barbara; da of late Leonard Jorgensen, of West Tytherley; *b* 19 Dec 1911; *m* 1, 1934 (m dis 1948), Lt-Col Herbert Campbell Westmorland, DSO, MC; m 2, 1963, 2 Baron Brassey of Apethorpe, MC, TD (d 1967); *Style—* The Rt Hon Barbara, Lady Brassey of Apethorpe; The Forge, 23 Bull Lane, Ketton, Stamford, Lincs PE9 3TB (☎ 0780 720920)

BRASSEY OF APETHORPE, 3 Baron (UK 1938); Sir David Henry Brassey; 3 Bt (UK 1922); JP (Northants 1970), DL (1972); s of 2 Baron Brassey of Apethorpe, MC, TD (d 1967, whose maternal gf was 7 Duke of Richmond and Gordon); *b* 16 Sept 1932; *Educ* Stowe; *m* 1, 15 Oct 1958, Myrna Elizabeth (d 1974), da of Lt-Col John Baskervyle-Glegg, of Withington Hall, Cheshire; 1 s; m 2, 17 Oct 1978, Caroline, da of Lt-Col Godfrey Evill, TD, of Chepstow; and step-da of Sir George Duntze, CMG, 6 Bt; 2 da (Hon Zara b 29 Feb 1980, Hon Chloe b 26 Feb 1982); *Heir* s, Hon Edward Brassey b 9 March 1964; *Style—* The Rt Hon the Lord Brassey of Apethorpe, JP, DL; The Manor House, Apethorpe, Peterborough PE8 5DL (☎ 0780 470231)

BRASSINGTON, (Alexander) Kim; s of Thomas Young Brassington (d 1947), and Catherine Marjorie St Clair, *née* Bower (d 1968); *b* 31 Dec 1943; *Educ* Lechampton Ct Sch, NGTC; *m* 21 March, Ruth; 1 s (Thomas b 1971); *Career* farmer and writer; author of History of Cruising serialized in Yachting Press; currently working on MS a biography of Sir Graham Bower (scapegoat for 1896 Jameson Raid); solo crossing Sahara 1964; London and Sydney marathon 1968, London and Mexico World Cup Rally 1970, Chelt Area Rep for Op Raleigh 1983- vice chm Whittington Parish 1988-; memb Cruising Assoc; *Recreations* books, gardening, yachting; *Style—* Kim Brassington, Esq; Court Farm House, Whittington, nr Cheltenham, Glos GL54 4HB (☎ 0242 820495)

BRATBY, John Randall; s of George Alfred Bratby (d 1948), and Lily Beryl Randall (d 1946); *b* 19 July 1928; *Educ* Tiffin Boys Sch, Royal Coll, Kingston Art Sch; *m* 1, 1953, Jean Esme Oregon, da of Alfred O Cooke (d 1960); 3 s (David b 1955, Jason b 1960, Dayan b 1968), 1 da (Wendy b 1970); m 2, 1977, Darling Patti, da of Laurence Prime (d 1960); *Career* artist & writer; painting Venice Bienalle 1956; Guggenheim Nat Award 1956 & 1958, won John Moore's junior section 1957, pictures for film 'Horses Mouth' 1958, works in Tate, Museum of Modern Art and countless public galleries, pictures for film Mistral's Daughter; Nat Portrait Gallery exhibition 1991; *Books* Breakdown (1960), Breakfast & Elevenses (1961), Brake-Pedal Down (1962), Break 50 Kill (1963), Stanley Spencer (1965); RA; *Recreations* gardening, walking, TV, photography, writing, traveling; *Style—* John Bratby, Esq; The Cupola & The Tower of the Winds, Belmont Road, Hastings, East Sussex TN35 5NR (☎ 0424 434037)

BRATZA, Nicolas Dušan; QC (1988); s of Milan Bratza (concert violinist, d 1964), and The Hon Margaret, *née* Russell (d 1981); *b* 3 March 1945; *Educ* Wimbledon Coll, Brasenose Coll Oxford (BA, MA); *Career* instr Univ of Pa Law Sch 1967-68, called to the Bar Lincoln's Inn 1969; jr counsel to the Crown, common law 1979-88, memb Cncl of Legal Educn 1988-; vice chm Br Inst of Human Rights 1989-; *Books* Halsbury's Laws of England (4 edn, jt contrib of titles Contempt of Court and Crown Proceedings); *Recreations* music, cricket; *Clubs* Garrick, MCC; *Style—* Nicolas Bratza, Esq, QC; 1 Hare Court, Temple, London EC4Y 7BE (☎ 071 353 3171, fax 071 583 9127, telex 8814348)

BRAUER, Irving; s of Jack Brauer (d 1972), of Hackney, London, and Lily, *née* Croll (d 1978); *b* 8 Aug 1939; *Educ* Davenant Fndn, Northern Poly (Dip Arch); *m* 21 April 1964, Stephanie Margaret, da of Edwin Sherwood, of Florida, 1 s (Marlow b 1975), 1 da (Amelia b 1965); *Career* architect and designer, worked in London and NY 1960-63, partnership Beryl Gollins 1963-76, princ Brauer Associates 1976-; elected memb Chartered Soc of Designers 1967 (elected fell 1976); visiting tutor: Canterbury Sch of Architecture 1967-70, Central London Poly 1968-71; RIBA; *Recreations* house renovation, theatre, reading, travel; *Style—* Irving Brauer, Esq; Mount Stuart, Westgrove Lane, Greenwich, London SE10 8QP (☎ 081 692 3210); Brauer Associates, 20 Dock St, London E1 8JP (☎ 071 481 2184, fax 071 481 3368)

BRAUN, Prof Edward; s of Cecil Arthur Braun (d 1952), of Bath, Somerset, and Stella Mabel, *née* Truscott (d 1956); *b* 28 Jan 1936; *Educ* City of Bath Boys' Sch, Univ of Cambridge (MA, PhD); *m* 18 Sept 1965, Sarah, da of John Brooke (d 1987), of Market Lavington, Wilts; 2 s (Felix b 1968, Joseph b 1970); *Career* Flying Offr RAF 1955-61; Univ of Bristol: lectr in drama 1969-, reader in drama 1980, head of Drama Dept 1985, appointed to chair in drama 1986; chm: Bristol Old Vic Tst 1987-, Gulbenkian Enquiry into dir trg in Br 1987-89; memb Assoc Univ Teachers; *Books* Meyerhold on Theatre (1969), The Theatre of Meyerhold (1979), The Director and the Stage (1982); *Recreations* cooking, wine, fishing on holiday; *Clubs* The Lab Party; *Style—* Prof Edward Braun; Department of Drama: Theatre, Film, Television, University of Bristol, 29 Park Row, Bristol BS1 5LT (☎ 0272 424601)

BRAUNE, Rudi Helmut; s of Wilhelm Friedrich Braune (d 1962), of E Germany, and Berta, *née* Riedel (d 1982); *b* 4 Sept 1925; *m* 23 July 1955, Diana, da of Harold Sheldon (d 1950), of Albert Rd, Southport, Lancs; 1 s (Jeremy b 1962), 3 da (Lindsey b 1956, Janet b 1958, Sara b 1961); *Career* dir Braune (Stroud) Ltd 1954-60, Wunda Machine Co Ltd 1955-57, Braune Batricar Ltd 1975-80; inventor of numerous patents worldwide; Int Riding and Driving (Bronze Medal 1942), Patent Expdn New York (Gold Medal 1975); memb RASE; *Recreations* driving, riding, landscaping; *Style—* Rudi Braune, Esq; R H Braune, Consultant, 113 Stratford Road, Stroud, Glos GL5 4AL (☎ 0453 765898)

BRAY, (Richard) Andrew; s of John Frederick Arthur Bray (d 1962), and Dorothy Agnes Bray (d 1981); *b* 5 Dec 1938; *Educ* Sandown Sch Bexhill-on-Sea Sussex, Canterbury Coll of Art (NDD), RCA Sch of Silversmithing and Jewellery Design (scholar); *m* 1965, Margaret Anne, da of James Norman Hope; 2 da (Emma Claire b 1970, Shuna Anne b 1974); *Career* silversmith; visiting tutor Dip AD Silversmithing: Canterbury Coll of Art 1965-67, Camberwell Sch of Art and Crafts 1963-73; head of Art Kent Coll Canterbury Kent 1976-77; Silversmithing and Metalwork Dept Camberwell Sch of Art and Crafts: lectr 1977, sr lectr 1983, princ lectr 1989-; design work 1965-89 (freelance for various firms, numerous cmmnd pieces of jewellery and silverplate for private and public bodies), involved in res 1983-85; participant in exhibitions at: The Commonwealth Institute London 1967, The Greewich Museum London 1968, Two Man Exhibitions Silver Plate London Wall 1969, The Fitzwilliam Museum Cambridge 1973, The Victoria and Albert Museum London 1977, The Goldsmiths Hall London 1982, The Rufford Craft Centre 1985; winner Ascot Gold Cup National Design Competition 1960; fell Soc Designer Craftsmen 1969, Freeman Worshipful Co of Goldsmiths 1989; *Style—* Andrew Bray, Esq

BRAY, Denis Campbell; CMG (1977), CVO (1975), JP (1960-84 Official, 1987 Non-Official); s of Rev Arthur Henry Bray, and Edith Muriel Bray; bro of J W Bray, MP, *qv*; *b* 24 Jan 1926; *Educ* Chefoo Sch China, Kingswood Sch Bath, Jesus Coll Cambridge; *m* 1952, Marjorie Elizabeth, da of John Hubert Bottomley; (1 s decd), 4 da; *Career* sec home affairs Hong Kong 1973-77 and 1980-84, Hong Kong cmmr London 1977-80; chm Denis Bray Consultants Ltd 1985; chm Eng Schs Fndn Hong Kong, pres Honk Kong Yachting Assoc; *Recreations* ocean cruising; *Clubs* Travellers', Royal Ocean Racing, Royal Hong Kong Yacht; *Style—* Denis Bray, Esq, CMG, CVO, JP; 8A-7 Borrett Mansions, 8-9 Bowen Rd, Hong Kong

BRAY, Derek William; s of Charles Bray, of Stratford House, Milford Haven; *b* 20 Sept 1926; *Educ* Milford Haven GS, Univ Coll Swansea (BSc); *m* 1948, Christina, da of Minard Hooper; 1 s, 1 da; *Career* chm: BICC Metals Ltd, BICC Connollys Ltd, Brookside Metal Co Ltd, Prescot Rod Rollers Ltd, Thomas Bolton & Sons (dir 1964-), Elsy & Gibbons 1979-; dir: BICC Industl Products 1980-82, BICC Cables Ltd, Br Kynoch Metals Ltd; pres Br Non-Ferrous Metals Fedn; *Recreations* work, golf; *Style—* Derek Bray Esq; Third Acre, Mottram Rd, Alderley Edge, Cheshire SK9 7JH (☎ 0625 582609); BICC Cables Ltd, PO Box 1, Prescot, Merseyside L34 5SZ (☎ 051 430 2202, telex 628811 BPILP)

BRAY, Dr Jeremy William; MP (Lab) Motherwell South 1983-; s of Rev Arthur Henry Bray and Edith Muriel Bray; bro of D C Bray, CMG, CVO, *qv*; *b* 29 June 1930; *Educ* Aberystwyth GS, Kingswood Sch, Jesus Coll Cambridge, Harvard Univ; *m* 1953, Elizabeth, da of Rev Dr Hubert Carey Trowell, OBE, MD, of Salisbury; 4 da; *Career* tech offr Wilton Works of ICI; contested (Lab) Thirsk and Malton 1959, MP (Lab): Middlesbrough West 1962-70, Motherwell and Wishaw 1974-83; memb select ctee: Nationalised Industs 1962-64, Treasury and Civil Service 1979-83 (chm sub-ctee 1981-82); chm: Lab Sci and Tech Gp 1964-66, Econ Affrs Estimates Sub-Ctee 1964-66; parly sec Miny of Power 1966-67, jt parly sec Miny of Tech 1967-69; chm Fabian Soc 1971-72, dir Mullard Ltd 1970-73, conslt Battle Res Centre Geneva 1973, visiting prof Univ of Strathclyde 1975-79 (sr res fell 1974); dep chm Christian Aid 1972-84, oppn front bench spokesman Sci and Technol 1983-; *Publications* Decision in Government (1970), Production Purpose and Structure (1982); *Recreations* sailing; *Style—* Dr Jeremy Bray, MP; House of Commons, London SW1A 0AA

BRAY, John Frederick; s of John Bray (d 1970), of Goosnargh, Lancs, and Doris Hilda, *née* Brewin, of Preston, Lancs; *b* 5 Sept 1934; *Educ* Preston GS, Victoria Univ of Manchester (BA, Dip Town and Country Planning), Univ of Illinois USA (MArch); *m* 1, 27 May 1958 (m dis 1988), Anne Christine Townley, da of Walter Kershaw, (d 1980), of Preston; 2 s (Andrew b 1962, Anthony b 1966), 1 da (Susan b 1961); m 2, 19 Aug 1989, Mary-Rew, da of George Bryce Robertson (d 1965); *Career* RNVR 1954-57, dep launching authy RNLI 1976-79 and 1985-87 (launching authy and asst sec 1979-85); asst architect and town planner London CC 1957-58; Central Mortgage and Housing Corpn (CMHC) Canada 1958-64; teaching asst Univ of Illinois USA 1959-60; sr architect and town planner private practice 1964-65, princ and ptnr architectural practice 1965-83, princ Bray Singleton Ptnrship 1983-; examiner: in Professional Practice Univ of Manchester, Architects Registration Cncl UK; lectr and dir Expert

Witness Course for CIArb (memb Cncl), former Cdre Ribble Cruising Club; Freeman City of London 1981, Liveryman Worshipful Co of Arbitrators 1982, Liveryman Worshipful Co of Chartered Architects 1990; FRIBA 1970, FRTPI 1972, FCIArb 1981, FBIM 1983; *Recreations* golf, fly-fishing, reading, music, photography; *Style*— John Bray, Esq; Tuesday Cottage, Church Lane, Mellor, nr Blackburn, Lancashire BB2 7JL (☎ 0254 81 2747); Bray Singleton Partnership, 50 Wood St, Lytham St Annes, Lancashire FY8 1QG (☎ 0253 712544, 0253 727769, fax 0253 723477, 0836 601177, telex 677457 FOSBY G)

BRAY, Julian Charles; s of Flt Lt Reginald Charles Julian Bray, and Irene Audrey, *née* Stewart; *b* 23 May 1945; *Educ* Ayr Acad Ayr Scotland; *m* 1, 1971 (m dis 1981), Judith Marina; 2 s (Dominic Julian b 13 Oct 1977, Oliver William b 13 June 1980), m 2, 1985, Vivienne Margaret, da of John Carlton; 1 s (William Charles b 18 Aug 1989); *Career* md Leadenhall Assocs Ltd 1986-; non exec dir CNS - City News Service 1986-; dir: NTN TV News Ltd 1988, DTI Eureka Information Bureau 1990; head of personal fin Granfield Rork Collins Fin, dir bus devpt Extel PR, dir corp servs Editorial Servs Ltd, head of media relations Welbeck PR Ltd; broadcaster and journalist for BBC radio; memb NUJ; *Books* Information Technology in the Corporate Environment (1980); *Recreations* theatre, travel, motor sport, radio; *Clubs* Bloggs, Scribes; *Style*— Julian Bray, Esq; Leadenhall Assocs (Conslts) Ltd, Lindsey House, 40-42 Charterhouse St, London EC1M 6JH (☎ 071 253 5523, fax 071 253 5523, ext 34)

BRAY, Kelvin Arthur; CBE (1990, OBE 1982); s of Arthur William Stretton Bray (d 1979), of Leicester, and Clarice May, *née* Perrin (d 1985); *b* 4 Feb 1935; *Educ* Leicester City Boys' Sch, King's Coll Cambridge (MA); *m* 1959, Grace Elizabeth, da of Dr Matthew Millar Tannahill (d 1981), of Lincoln; 2 s; *Career* sales mangr (Gas Turbine Div) Ruston & Hornsby Ltd 1963; md: Ruston Gas Turbines Ltd 1969- (Queen's Award for Export 1969, 1977, 1978 and 1982, Queens Award for Technol 1986), GEC Gas Turbines Ltd 1983-89; chm: GEC Diesels Ltd, Napier Turbochargers Ltd, Euro Gas Turbine Co NV 1989 (and chief exec offr); Royal Soc Esso Medal 1974; Mac Robert Award 1983; FEng, FIMechE; *Recreations* squash, swimming; *Style*— Kelvin Bray, Esq, CBE; 17 Cherry Tree Lane, Nettleham, Lincoln LN2 2PR; European Gas Turbine Co Ltd, PO Box 1, Lincoln LN2 5DJ (☎ 0522 512612)

BRAY, Michael Peter; s of Sqdn Ldr William Charles Thomas Bray, DFC (d 1985), and Ivy Isobel, *née* Ellison (d 1986); *b* 27 March 1947; *Educ* Caterham Sch, Univ of Liverpool (LLB); *m* 25 July 1970, Elizabeth-Ann, da of Hubert John Harrington (d 1981); 2 da (Natasha Jane b 13 April 1977, Samantha Louise b 13 April 1984); *Career* slr; Clifford Chance 1970-76 (ptnr 1976-); memb: Banking Law Sub Ctee City of London Slr's Co, Jt Working Pty on Banking Law of the Law Reform Ctees of the Law Soc Bar Soc; Freeman City of London Solicitors Co 1976; memb Law Soc; *Recreations* theatre, reading, skiing, photography; *Style*— Michael Bray, Esq; Blythe, Butlers Dene Rd, Woldingham, Surrey CR3 7HE (☎ 0883 652225); Clifford Chance, Royex House, Aldermanbury Sq, London EC2V 7LD (☎ 071 600 0808 ext 2104, fax 071 726 8561, tele COWARD G)

BRAY, Richard Winston Atherton; s of Winston Bray, CBE, and Betty Atherton, *née* Miller; *b* 10 April 1945; *Educ* Rugby, CCC Oxford; *m* 6 Jan 1978, Judith Elizabeth Margaret, da of Maj C B Ferguson (d 1980); 1 s (Edward b 2 Oct 1984), 3 da (Hester b 24 May 1981, Miranda b 12 Sept 1986, Rosalind b 23 Aug 1989); *Career* called to the Bar Middle Temple 1970; rec Midland and Oxford circuit 1987; *Recreations* cricket, real tennis, astronomy; *Clubs* MCC, Frogs, I Zingari; *Style*— Richard Bray, Esq; 1 Kings Bench Walk, Temple EC4 (☎ 071 353 8436)

BRAYBROOK, Nigel John Reginald; s of Edward Braybrook, CB, of North Harrow, and Rosalind, *née* Thomas; *b* 14 April 1939; *Educ* Merchant Taylors', Coll of Estate Mgmnt; *m* 14 Sept 1968, Lynne Christine, da of Leslie George Hardy (d 1987), of Mitcham; 1 s (Nicholas Edward b 1973), 1 da (Sarah Louise b 1970); *Career* chartered surveyor; Weatherall Green & Smith 1957-63, ptnr Montagu Evans & Son 1973 (joined 1963); Freeman City of London 1980, Liveryman Worshipful Co of Glass Sellers 1980; FRICS 1973, FRVA 1973; *Recreations* squash, photography; *Clubs* Bucks, Wig and Pen; *Style*— Nigel Braybrook, Esq; Tall Trees, Paines Lane, Pinner HA5 3BX; 11 Kingsway, London WC2B 6YE (☎ 071 240 2444)

BRAYBROOKE, Rev Marcus Christopher Rossi; s of Lt-Col Arthur Rossi Braybrooke, of Box Cottage, Cranleigh, Surrey, and Marcia Nona, *née* Leach; descended on female side from a brother of Robert Braybrooke, Bishop of London (d 1404); *b* 16 Nov 1938; *Educ* Cranleigh Sch, Magdalene Coll Cambridge (BA, MA), Univ of London (MPhil), Madras Christian Coll India, Wells Theological Coll; *m* 1964, Mary Elizabeth, da of George Walker, of 15 Sedley Taylor Rd, Cambridge; 1 s (Jeremy b 1966), 1 da (Rachel b 1965); *Career* curate St Michael's Highgate 1964-67, memb Strood Team Miny 1967-73, rector Swainswick with Langridge and Woolley 1973-79, dir of trg Dio of Bath and Wells 1979, prebendary Wells Cathedral 1990; chm: World Congress of Faiths 1978-1983, Int Ctee 1987-, int Interfaith Orgns Co-ordinating Ctee; exec dir Cncl of Christians and Jews 1984-87, priest i/c Christ Church Bath 1984-; *Books* Together to the Truth, The Unknown Christ of Hinduism, Interfaith Organisations, A Historical Directory, Time to Meet, Towards a Deeper Relationship of Jews, and Christians; ed (jls): World Faiths Insight, Common Ground; *Recreations* gardening, travel, tennis, swimming, home decorating, local history; *Style*— The Rev Marcus Braybrooke; Brookwalk, 2 The Bassetts, Box, Corsham, Wilts SN14 9ER (☎ 0225 742827)

BRAYBROOKE, Neville Patrick Bellairs; s of Patrick Philip William Braybrooke (d 1966), and Lettice Marjorie, *née* Bellairs (d 1986); *b* 30 May 1928; *Educ* Ampleforth; *m* 5 Dec 1953, June Guesdon, da of John Mayne Jolliffe (d 1962); 1 step da (Victoria Mary Guesdon Orr-Ewing b 1942); *Career* ed The Wind and the Rain Quarterly 1941-51, ed staff Chambers Encyclopaedia 1947-48, literary ed Catholic Herald 1964-66; *Books* This is London (1953), London Green: The Story of Kensington Gardens, Hyde Park, Green Park, and St James's Park (1959), London (1961), The Idler (1961), The Delicate Investigation BBC Play (1969), Four Poems for Christmas (1986), Dialogue with Judas (1989); ed: T S Eliot A Symposium for his 70th Birthday 1958, A Partridge in a Pear Tree: A Celebration for Christmas 1960, Pilgrim of the Future: Teilhard de Chardin Symposium 1966, The Letters of JR Ackerley 1975, Seeds in the Wind: 20th Century Juvenilia from W B Yeats to Ted Hughes 1989; *Recreations* little reviews, hats, animals; *Clubs* Island Sailing Cowes, Pen; *Style*— Neville Braybrooke, Esq; 10 Gardnor Rd, London NW3 1HA (☎ 071 435 1851); Grove House, Castle Rd, Cowes, Isle of Wight PO31 7QZ (☎ 0983 293950)

BRAYBROOKE, 10 Baron (GB 1788); Robin Henry Charles Neville; DL (Essex 1980); hereditary visitor Magdalene Coll Cambridge; s of 9 Baron Braybrooke, JP, DL (d 1990), and his 1 w, Muriel Evelyn, *née* Manning (d 1962); *b* 29 Jan 1932; *Educ* Eton, Magdalene Coll Cambridge (MA), RAC Cirencester; *m* 1, 1955 (m dis 1974), Robin Helen, o da of late T A Brockhoff, of Rose Bay, Sydney, NSW, Australia; 4 da (Hon Amanda Muriel Mary (Hon Mrs Murray) b 1962, Hon Caroline Emma b 1963, Hon Victoria b 1970, Hon Arabella b (twin) 1970), and 1 da decd (Henrietta Jane b 1965, d 1980); m 2, 1974, Linda, 2 da of Arthur Norman, of Robblyns, Saffron Walden, Essex; 3 da (Hon Sara Lucy b 1975, Hon Emma Charlotte b 1979, Hon Lucinda Octavia b 1984); *Heir* kinsman, George Neville b 1943; *Career* cmmnd Rifle Bde 1951, served with 3 Bn King's African Rifles in Kenya and Malaya 1951-52; farmer and landowner; RDC cncllr 1959-69, CC for Stansted 1969-72; memb: Cncl of CLA 1965-83, Agric Land Tbnl Eastern Area 1975-; chm: Price Tst 1983-, Rural Devpt Cmmn for Essex 1984-90; dir Essex and Suffolk Insur Co until taken over by Guardian Royal Ex; *Recreations* flying, railways, motorcycling; *Clubs* Boodle's; *Style*— The Rt Hon the Lord Braybrooke, DL; Abbey House, Audley End, Saffron Walden, Essex CB11 4JB (☎ 0799 22484, office 22354)

BRAYE, Baroness (8 holder of the title); Mary Penelope Aubrey-Fletcher; *née* Verney-Cave; JP (Northants); da of 7 Baron Braye, DL (d 1985); *b* 28 Sept 1941; *Educ* Assumption Convent, Hengrave Hall, Warwick Univ; *m* 1981, Lt-Col Edward Henry Lancelot Aubrey-Fletcher, DL, *qv* Gren Gds, s of Maj Sir Henry Lancelot Aubrey-Fletcher, 6 Bt, CVO, DSO, JP, HM Lord-Lieut for Bucks; *Heir* co-heiresses, Mrs Christopher Fothergill and Miss Tessa Browne; *Career* govr St Andrew's Hosp Northampton 1978-; JP South Northants 1981-86; High Sheriff Northants 1983; dep pres Northants Red Cross 1983-; govr Three Shires Hosp Northampton 1983-; pres Blaby Conservative Assoc 1986-; chm sch ctee St Andrew's Occupational Therapy Sch 1988-; *Style*— The Rt Hon Baroness Braye; Stanford Hall, Lutterworth, Leics LE17 6DH (☎ 0788 860250)

BRAYNE, Mark Lugard; s of Thomas Lugard Brayne, of Barney, Fakenham, Norfolk, and Audrey Diana, *née* Thompson; *b* 17 April 1950; *Educ* Gresham's, Wymondham Coll Norfolk, Univ of Leeds (BA); *m* 25 March 1977, Jutta, da of Fritz Hartung, of Ohlstadt, Germany; 2 s (Christopher b 1980, Alastair b 1982), 1 da (Katharine b 1987); *Career* Moscow and E Berlin Reuters News Agency 1973-78; BBC: German service corr Berlin 1979-81, Central Euro corr Vienna 1981-84, Peking corr China 1984-87, dip corr World Serv; *Recreations* family, singing, windsurfing, cycling; *Clubs* Reform; *Style*— Mark Brayne, Esq; BBC World Service, Bush House, Strand WC2B 4PH (☎ 071 257 2594, fax 071 836 0207)

BRAYNEN, Sir Alvin Rudolph; JP (Bahamas 1975); s of William Rudolph Braynen and Lulu Isabelle, *née* Griffin; *b* 6 Dec 1904; *Educ* in the Bahamas; *m* 1969, Ena Estelle, *née* Elden; (1 s, 1 da by a previous m); *Career* consultant to Shell Bahamas 1969-, Bahamas high cmmr in London 1973-77; kt 1975; *Style*— Sir Alvin Braynen, JP; PO Box N42, Nassau, Bahamas

BRAZEL, Hon Mrs (Lucinda Maria); *née* Stanley; only da of 8 Baron Stanley of Alderley; *b* 21 Feb 1958; *m* 1983, Peter Brazel, s of late Benedict Brazel, of Lyndhurst, S Australia; 3 s (Thomas Owen b 19 Feb 1984, Harry Jack b 19 Feb 1987, Jack Alexander b 26 Dec 1988); *Style*— The Hon Mrs Brazel

BRAZENDALE, Alan Courtenay; s of Capt George William Ernest Brazendale (d 1970), of 12 Hall Drive, Greasby, Wirral, and Alice Annie, *née* Courtenay (d 1981); *b* 15 Dec 1924; *Educ* Birkenhead Sch; *m* 13 July 1946, Elizabeth Ewan, da of William Stewart Carr (d 1969), of Shieldaig, Stanley, Perthshire; 1 da (Elizabeth Ann b 1953); *Career* Fleet Air Arm 1943-47; CA; mayor of Gateshead MBC 1980-81, chm Gateshead Educn Ctee 1982-; dir: N Regnl Examinations Bd, Alton Assocs Ltd; memb: Cncl of Local Educn Authorities, Assoc of Met Authorities Educn Ctee, Northern Cncl of Educn Ctees, Northern Cncl for Further Educn, Ct of Newcastle Univ, Cncl of Newcastle Poly; chm of govrs Gatehead Coll; FCA, MBIM, MInstAM, MIIM; *Recreations* golf, local history, reading, writing, gardening; *Style*— Alan Brazendale, Esq; 8 The Orchard, Whickham, Newcastle upon Tyne NE16 4HD (☎ 091 4881622); Gateshead Civic Centre, Gateshead, Tyne and Wear NE8 1HH (☎ 091 4771011)

BRAZIER, Julian William Hendy; MP (C) Canterbury 1987-; s of Lt-Col Peter Hendy Brazier, and Patricia Audrey Helen, *née* Stubbs, ggda of Bishop Stubbs of Oxford noted lectr an author of the Constitutional History of England; *b* 24 July 1953; *Educ* Dragon Sch Oxford, Wellington, BNC Oxford (scholar, MA), London Business Sch; *m* 21 July 1984, Katharine Elizabeth, da of Brig Patrick Blagden, CBE; 2 s (twins); *Career* SSLC with RE and Capt TA in Airborne Forces; Charter Consolidated Ltd 1975-84, H B Maynard Management Consultants 1984-87; *Recreations* cross country running, science, philosophy; *Style*— Julian W H Brazier, Esq, MP; c/o House of Commons, London SW1A 0AA

BRAZIER-CREAGH, Maj-Gen Sir (Kilner) Rupert; KBE (1962, CBE 1947), CB (1954), DSO (1944); s of Lt-Col Kilner Brazier-Creagh, TD (d 1956); *b* 12 Dec 1909; *Educ* Rugby, RMA Woolwich; *m* 1, 1938, Elizabeth Mary (d 1967), da of Edward Magor (d 1954); 1 s, 2 da; m 2, 1968, Marie, da of Edward O'Keeffe; *Career* served NW Europe 1944-45, Malayan Emergency 1952-55; Asst Cmdt Staff Coll 1955-57, COS E Cmd 1957-59, DSD War Office 1959-61; sec Horse Race Betting Levy Bd 1961-65; *Recreations* gardening, travel; *Style*— Maj-Gen Sir Rupert Brazier-Creagh, KBE, CB, DSO; Travis Corners Rd, Garrison, New York 10524, USA

BRAZINGTON, Edward Stanley; s of George T Brazington (d 1934); *b* 2 Oct 1926; *Educ* Hemel Hempstead GS, King's Coll London (BSc); *m* 1956, Jeanne Margaret; *Career* Lt RE served Palestine; dir Wiggins Teape Gp; chm: Wiggins Teape (Belgium) SA, Wiggins Teape (Europe) Ltd; chief exec Carbonless Papers Operations of Wiggins Teape 1981; Chev de L'Ordre de Leopold; *Recreations* landscape gardening, woodwork, painting, shooting, literature, music; *Style*— Edward Brazington Esq; c/o Wiggins Teape Group, PO Box 88, Gateway House, Basing View, Basingstoke, Hants RG21 2EE (☎ 0256 20262, telex 858031 WTBSTK G)

BREACH, Peter John Freeman; s of Andrew Breach, of Pensford, nr Bristol, and Christine Ruth, *née* Watson (d 1973); *b* 12 Jan 1942; *Educ* Clifton, Univ of Bristol (BA); *m* 17 Dec 1966, Joan, da of (William) Raymond Livesey, of Clitheroe, Lancashire; 3 s (Harry William Freeman b 1972, Christopher (Kit), Andrew Talbot b 1974, Alexander Robin Livesey b 1989); *Career* Coopers & Lybrand 1963-68, Hoare Govett 1968-69, County Bank Ltd 1969-70, JH Vavasseur & Co Ltd 1970-73, pres and chief exec offr Major Holdings & Developments Ltd 1972-73, divnl md Bath & Portland Gp Ltd 1974-78, md James Dixon/Viners Ltd 1978-82, fin dir Bristol & West Bldg Soc 1988- (dir 1976-, exec dir 1983-; dir: Principality Hldgs Gp, Thomas Silvey Gp, Hawksworth Securities plc; govr and chm Redland High Sch for Girls; Freeman: City of London, City of Bristol; Liveryman Worshipful Co of Basketmakers; FCA, ATII, ACT, ASIA; *Recreations* sailing, skiing; *Clubs* Royal Dart; *Style*— Peter Breach, Esq; Bristol & West Building Soc, Broad Quay, Bristol BS99 7AX (☎ 0272 294 271, fax 0272 211 632, car 0836 728 587, telex 44741)

BREADALBANE AND HOLLAND, 10 Earl of (S 1677); Sir John Romer Boreland Campbell; 14 Bt (NS 1625); also Viscount of Tay and Paintland (S 1677), and Lord Glenorchy, Benederaloch, Ormelie and Weick (S 1677); s of 9 Earl, MC (d 1959); *b* 28 April 1919; *Educ* Eton, RMC Sandhurst, Edinburgh Univ; *m* 1949 (m dis), Coralie, da of Charles Archer; *Heir* none known; *Career* formerly Lt Black Watch, served in France 1939-42 (despatches, invalided); *Style*— The Rt Hon The Earl of Breadalbane and Holland; 29 Mackeson Rd, NW3

BREADEN, Very Rev Robert William; s of Moses Breaden (d 1958), of Drummond, Magheracloone, Carrickmacross, Co Monaghan, and Martha Jane, *née* Hall; *b* 7 Nov 1937; *Educ* The King's Hosp Dublin, Edinburgh Theol Coll; *m* 3 July 1970, Glenice Sutton, da of Douglas Martin, of Dundee; 1 s (Patrick b 1971), 4 da (Sarah b 1973, Kathleen b 1979, Christina b 1981, Ann-Louise b 1987); *Career* ordained 1961, asst curate St Mary's Broughty Ferry 1961-65; rector: Church of the Holy Rood Carnoustie 1965-72, St Mary's Broughty Ferry 1972-; canon of St Paul's Cathedral

Dundee 1977, dean of the Diocese of Brechin 1984-; *Recreations* gardening, horse-riding; *Clubs* Rotary of Abertay (pres 1979-80); *Style*— The Very Rev the Dean of Brechin; 46 Seafield Road, Broughty Ferry, Dundee DD5 3AN (☎ 0382 77477)

BREAKS, Michael Lenox; s of Cdr John Lenox Breaks, OBE, RN, of Denmead, Portsmouth, and Madeleine Henrietta, *née* Page; *b* 12 Jan 1945; *Educ* St George's Coll Weybridge Surrey, Univ of Leeds (BA), Univ Coll Aberystwyth (Dip Lib); *m* 12 April 1970, Barbara Monica, da of Charles Lawson (d 1984); 1 s (Jeremy Lenox b 1 March 1973), 1 da (Sarah Jessica b 15 May 1975); *Career* asst librarian: Univ Coll Swansea 1971-72, Univ of York 1972-73; social scis librarian Univ Coll Cardiff 1977-81, dep librarian Univ Coll Dublin 1981-85, univ librarian Heriot-Watt Univ 1985-; LINC, SCONUL; MIInfSc 1986; *Recreations* gardening, walking; *Style*— Michael Breaks, Esq; 15 Corrennie Gardens, Edinburgh EH10 6DG (☎ 031 447 7193); Heriot-Watt University, Riccarton, Edinburgh EH14 4AS (☎ 031 449 5111)

BREALEY, Prof Richard Arthur; s of Albert Brealey (d 1974), and Irene Brealey; *b* 9 June 1936; *Educ* Queen Elizabeth's Sch Barnet, Exeter Coll Oxford (MA); *m* 10 Feb 1967, Diana Cecily, da of Derek Brown-Kelly, of Oddington, Glos; 2 s (David Andrew b 1970, Charles Richard b 1972); *Career* investmt mangr Sun Life Assurance Co of Canada 1959-66, mangr computer applications Keystone Custodian Funds of Boston 1966-68; London Business Sch: dir Inst Fin and Accounting 1974-84, memb Body Govrs, dep princ and academic dean 1984-88, currently Midland Bank prof of corporate fin; visiting prof: Univ of California, Berkeley, Univ of Br Colombia, Univ of Hawaii, Aust Graduate Sch of Mgmnt; dir Swiss Helvetia Fund Inc, pres European Fin Assoc, dir American Fin Assoc; *Books* incl: Introduction to Risk and Return from Common Stocks (2 edn, 1983), Principles of Corporate Finance (with S C Myers, 3 edn, 1988); *Recreations* rock climbing, skiing, pottery; *Style*— Prof Richard Brealey; Haydens Cottage, The Pound, Cookham, Berks (☎ 06285 20143); London Business Sch, Sussex Place, Regent's Park, London NW1 (☎ 071 262 5050, fax 071 724 7875, telex 27461 LOND IS KOL)

BREAM, Hon Mrs (Catherine Frances Lilian Berry); yst da of 2 Viscount Kemsley; *b* 9 June 1944; *m* 19 April 1969, Richard Douglas Fowler Bream, yr s of Clifford Ellett Bream, of The Manor Farm, Grace Dieu, Leics; 1 s, 1 da; *Career* co pres for St John Leicestershire; *Style*— The Hon Mrs Bream; The Manor Farm, Grace Dieu, Whitwick, Leics LE6 3UG

BREAM, Richard Douglas Fowler; TD, DL (Leicestershire 1984); 2 s of Clifford Ellett Bream (d 1987), of Grace Dieu, Leics, and Elaine Mary, *née* Fowler (d 1980); *b* 25 July 1936; *Educ* The Kings Sch Canterbury; *m* 19 April 1969, Catherine Francis Lilian, yst da of 2 Viscount Kemsley, *qv*, of Thorpe Lubenham, Market Harborough, Leics; 1 s (Tamerlane Douglas Fowler b 1972), 1 da (Atlanta Mary b 1971); *Career* TAVR 1970; dir D H Bream and Co Ltd 1963-; farmer; OStJ; High Sheriff Leics 1990; *Recreations* hunting, shooting, fishing; *Clubs* Naval and Military; *Style*— Richard D F Bream, Esq, DL; The Manor Farm, Grace Dieu, Leics LE6 3UG (☎ 0530 222277)

BREAM, Roland Ellett; TD (1967); s of Clifford Ellett Bream, MBE (d 1987), of Leics, and Elaine Mary, *née* Fowler (d 1980); *b* 15 Feb 1931; *Educ* Loughborough GS, Queens' Coll Cambridge (MA); *m* 8 Sept 1962, (Elizabeth) Gay, da of E L Whiteman, MC (d 1970), of Leics; 1 s (Charles b 1968), 2 da (Lindamina b 1964, Lucinda b 1966); *Career* Nat Serv cmmn RHA 1954, Maj S Notts Hussars Yeomanry 1955-67; mgmnt conslt logistics and distribution 1967-75, exec dir Harold Whitehead & Ptnrs 1970-75, dir and ptnr M M Distribution Conslts 1976-82, princ Roland Bream & Assocs; FIMC, FILDM; *Recreations* gardening, reading, classical music, fine wine, travel; *Clubs* Naval and Military; *Style*— Roland E Bream, Esq, TD; Cruck Meole House, Cruck Meole, Shrewsbury SY5 8JN (☎ 0743 860295)

BREARE, (William) Robert Ackrill; s of late Robert Ackrill Breare, and Emily, *née* Waddington; *b* 5 July 1916; *Educ* Charterhouse, Wadham Coll Oxford; *m* 1942, Sybella Jessie Macduff, da of John Roddick, of Annan; 1 s, 2 da; *Career* chm Ackrill Gp; memb: Press Cncl, Cncl of Newspaper Soc; *Recreations* music, sailing; *Style*— W Robert Ackrill Breare, Esq; Harrison Hill House, Starbeck, Harrogate, N Yorks (☎ 883302)

BREARLEY, Dr Arthur; TD (1960); s of Leonard Brearley, of Lancs, and Mary Brearley; *b* 31 Aug 1928; *Educ* Queen Elizabeth I GS Middleton, Univ of Manchester (BSc, MSc, PhD); *m* 1955, Margaret, da of Ben Lee, of Manchester; 2 s (John b 1961, Mark b 1963); *Career* professorial fell in mgmnt devpt Univ of Bradford; chm: R L Martindale Liverpool, George Nixon Manchester; dir: Lord Street Properties Southport, Anne Shaw Consultants Bollington, Sweater House Manchester, Toy and Hobby St Helens, Production Group Chelford; *Recreations* flying, fell walking; *Style*— Dr Arthur Brearley, TD; Sheringham House, Ladybrook Road, Bramhall, Stockport, Cheshire (☎ 061 485 3944); Ernst and Young, Commercial Union House Albert Sq, Manchester (☎ 061 831 7854)

BREARLEY, Christopher John Scott; s of Geoffrey William Brearley (d 1968), and Winifred Marion, *née* Scott; *b* 25 May 1943; *Educ* King Edward VII Sch Sheffield, Trinity Coll Oxford (MA, BPhil); *m* 1971, Rosemary Nanette, da of Lt-Col Wilfred Sydney Stockbridge; 2 s (Thomas b 1973, William b 1976); *Career* civil servant; former dir: Scottish Servs, Property Servs Agency 1981-83; under sec Cabinet Office 1983-85; DOE: dir Local Govt Fin 1985-88, dir Planning and Devpt Control 1988-89, dep sec Local Govt and Fin 1990-; *Recreations* walking, crosswords; *Clubs* New Club (Edinburgh); *Style*— Christopher Brearley, Esq; Dept of Environment, 2 Marsham St, London SW1 (☎ 071 276 3479)

BREARLEY-SMITH, Col Andrew Neville; OBE (1972); s of Andrew Smith (d 1969), and Vera Smith (now Mrs Copp); *b* 22 Oct 1928; *Educ* Bloxham Sch; *m* 4 Aug 1951, June Marguerite, da of John Richard Paterson (d 1984); 1 da (Jane 1953); *Career* RMA Sandhurst 1947-48, Lt RE 1948, AAG AG7 MOD 1973-76; DG Nat Fund Res into Crippling Diseases (incl Action Res for the Crippled Child and SPARKS) 1976-; memb and chm Assoc Med Res Charities 1983-87; memb Prince of Wales Advsy Gp on Disability 1982-; FBIM 1975, FRSM 1986; *Recreations* golf, music, garden; *Style*— Col Andrew Brearley-Smith, OBE; Nat Fund for Res into Crippling Diseases, Vincent House, N Parade, Horsham, West Sussex RH12 2DA (☎ 0403 210406, fax 0403 210541)

BREATHWICK, Leslie; s of R H Breathwick (d 1979), of Lincolnshire, and W M Breathwick (d 1973); *m* ; 2 s (Richard Eliot b 26 Nov 1962, Martin Leslie b 23 Dec 1964), 1 da (Katherine Juliet b 15 Dec 1971); *Career* qualified accountant 1956, ptnr (specialising in corp fin) Grant Thornton Leicester; FCA 1965, FCCA 1956; *Recreations* hill walking and rambling, golf, bridge; *Clubs* Leicestershire Golf, Leicestershire Aero; *Style*— Leslie Breathwick, Esq; 4 Springfield, 2 St Mary's Rd, Leicester LE2 1XA (☎ 0533 708054); Grant Thornton, 8 West Walk, Leicester LE1 7NH (☎ 0533 471234, fax 0533 471434)

BRECKENRIDGE, Prof Alasdair Muir; s of Thomas Breckenridge (d 1973), of Arbroath, Scotland, and Jane, *née* Mackay (d 1986); *b* 7 May 1937; *Educ* Bell Baxter Sch Fife, Univ of St Andrews (MB ChB, MD); *m* 28 Feb 1967, Jean Margaret, da of Trevor Charles William Boyle, of E London, SA; 2 s (Ross Alexander b 1969, Bruce Gordon b 1971); *Career* surgn Dundee Royal Infirmary 1961-62 (house physician); Hammersmith Hosp and Royal Postgrad Med Sch London 1962-74: house physician, res fell, registrar, sr registrar, lectr, sr lectr; prof of clinical pharmacology Univ of Liverpool 1974-; memb: Ctee on Safety of Medicines, Systems Bd MRC, Advsy Ctee on NHS drugs; foreign sec Br Pharmacological Soc; FRCP; *Recreations* golf, stock market; *Style*— Prof Alasdair Breckenridge; Cree Cottage, Feather Lane, Heswall, Wirral L60 4RL (☎ 051 342 1096); Dept of Pharmacology and Therapeutics, Univ of Liverpool, PO Box 147, Liverpool L69 3BX (☎ 051 794 5542, fax 051 794 5540)

BRECKNOCK, Earl of; James William John Pratt; s and h of 6 Marquess Camden; *b* 11 Dec 1965; *Educ* Eton, Edinburgh Univ; *Style*— Earl of Brecknock

BRECON, Baroness; Mabel Helen; CBE (1964), JP; da of John McColville (d 1946), of Abergavenny, and Martha McColville (d 1944); *b* 8 May 1910; *Educ* St Alban's Convent; *m* 1933, 1 and last Baron Brecon, PC (d 1976), s of Alfred William Lewis (d 1955); 2 da (Hon Mrs Price, Hon Mrs Foss, *qqv*); *Career* cncllr Brecknock RDC 1949-74 (chm 1972), magistrate 1957-80, High Sheriff Breconshire 1971-72; chm: Wales Women Cons Advsy Ctee 1955-62, Wales World Refugee Year 1959, Freedom from Hunger Campaign 1961-66; *Recreations* gardening, reading; *Style*— The Rt Hon the Lady Brecon, CBE, JP; Greenhill, Cross Oak, Brecon, Powys (☎ 087 487 247)

BREDIN, James John; s of John Francis Bredin (d 1981), and Margaret Bredin; *b* 18 Feb 1924; *Educ* Finchley Catholic GS, Univ of London; *m* 1958, Virginia, da of John Meddowes; 1 s, 2 da; *Career* served WWII Sub-Lt Fleet Air Arm RNVR Europe, ME, Far East; prodr: BBC TV 1950-55, ITN 1955-59, Associated TV (documentaries) 1959-64; chm Guild of Televison Prodrs and Dirs 1961-64, dir ITN 1970-72, md Border Television Ltd 1964-82; specialist in television archives 1982-; press fellow Wolfson Coll Cambridge 1987; FRTS 1983; *Clubs* Beefsteak; *Style*— James Bredin, Esq; 25 Stack House, Cundy St, London SW1W 9JS (☎ 071 730 2689)

BREEN, Geoffrey Brian; s of Ivor James Breen, of Cowbridge, S Wales, and Doreen Odessa Breen; *b* 3 June 1944; *Educ* Harrow HS, Coll of Law; *m* 8 April 1976, Lucy, da of Serafin Cabrera (d 1984), of Bogota, Colombia; 1 s (Christopher b 1977), 1 da (Deborah b 1979); *Career* Stiles Breen & Ptnrs 1962-67 (previously Stiles Wood Head & Co, formerly Stiles Wood & Co): articled clerk, admitted slr 1967, ptnr 1970-75, sr ptnr 1976-86; ptnr Blaser Mills & Newman 1976-86, asst rec of Crown Ct 1989-; former memb Ctee: Central and S Middx Law Soc, London Criminal Cts Slrs' Assoc; appointed metropolitan stipendary magistrate 1986; *Recreations* classical guitar, aviculture, reading; *Style*— Geoffrey Breen, Esq; Highbury Corner Magistrates Court, 51 Holloway Road, London N7 (☎ 071 607 66757)

BREEN, Dame Marie Freda; DBE (1979, OBE 1958); da of Frederick and Jeanne Chamberlin; *b* 3 Nov 1902; *Educ* St Michael's C of E Girls' GS; *m* 1928, Robert Tweedale Breen (d 1968); 3 da; *Career* senator for Victoria 1962-68; *see Debrett's Handbook of Australia and New Zealand for further details*; *Style*— Dame Marie Breen, DBE; 51 Carpenter St, Brighton, Victoria 3186, Australia (☎ 010 612 592 2314)

BREEZE, Alan Leonard; s of William John Richard Breeze, and Ivy Lorretta, *née* Bird; *b* 11 Nov 1950; *Educ* Eastbourne GS; *m* 7 July 1973, Barbara Caroline, da of Edwin Frederick Hope; 2 s (Jonathan b 1980, Thomas b 1983); *Career* CA 1973-, ptnr Breeze Ralph & Co; *Style*— Alan L Breeze, Esq; 36 Ratton Drive, Eastbourne, East Sussex; 69 Church Rd, Hove, (☎ 0273 739592); 5 Cornfield Terrace, Eastbourne (☎ 0323 411416)

BREMNER, Charles John Fraser; s of John Fraser Bremner, and Rosemary, *née* Ives; *b* 16 June 1951; *Educ* Blairmore Sch Aberdeenshire, St Peter's Coll South Australia, New Coll Oxford (BA), Univ Coll Cardiff (Dip in Journalism Studies); *m* 1, 1973 (m dis 1982), Valeria, *née* Gaidukowski; 1 da (Anna Lucy b 1977); m 2, 1987, Fariba, da of Abbas Shirdel, of Tehran; *Career* trainee Reuters 1975-77, corr Reuters: Moscow 1977-79, Mexico City 1979-80, Paris 1981-83, Moscow (bureau chief) 1983-86; corr The Times NY 1987-; *Recreations* flying, sailing; *Style*— Charles Bremner, Esq; The Times, 10 East 53rd St, New York, NY 10022, USA (☎ 212 527 2450, fax 212 371 8912)

BREMNER, Eric; s of Hamish Bremner, of Edinburgh, and Mary Wotherspoon Thomson, *née* Ross; *b* 9 July 1958; *Educ* Trinity Acad Edinburgh, Grays Sch of Art Aberdeen, Harrow Coll of Further Educn (Dip Fashion Design), RCA (MA); *m* 1 Sept 1979, Jane Catherine Mary, da of Donald Bruce Scott; 1 s (Hamish Scott b 10 May 1986); *Career* design asst Margaret Howell 1984; designer: Sportmax, Maxmara Italy 1984-; design conslt: Marina Rinaldi Italy 1986-, Prisma Commerciale Abbigliamento Italy 1987-; pt/t tutor Fashion Sch RCA 1987-; external assessor: fashion (MDes) Edinburgh Coll of Art 1989-, fashion (BA) Nat Coll of Art and Design Dublin 1989-; *Recreations* cooking, music; *Style*— Eric Bremner, Esq; The Old School, Garford, nr Abingdon, Oxon OX13 5PG (☎ 0865 391 341)

BREMNER, Rory Keith Ogilvy; s of Maj Donald Stuart Ogilvy Bremner (d 1979), of Merchiston, Edinburgh, and Anne Ulithorne, *née* Simpson; *b* 6 April 1961; *Educ* Wellington, King's Coll London (BA); *m* 8 Jan 1987, Susan Catherine, *née* Shackleton; *Career* satirical impressionist, writer and performer 1984-; tours and one-man shows 1985-89, BBC TV series incl Now Something Else 1986, 1987, own shows 1988-90, videos Rory Bremner 1988 and The Best of Rory Bremner 1989; winner press prize Montreux 1987; memb Lords Taverners 1986-, performance contrib to Friends of the Earth and Greenpeace; *Recreations* cricket, travel, tennis; *Clubs* Lord's Taverners; *Style*— Rory Bremner, Esq; c/o Richard Stone, 25 Whitehall, London SW1 (☎ 071 839 6421, fax 071 839 5002)

BREMRIDGE, Sir John Henry; KBE (1983, OBE 1976); s of Godfrey Bremridge, and Monica, *née* Bennett; *b* 12 July 1925; *Educ* Dragon Sch Cheltenham, St John's Coll Oxford (MA); *m* 1956, Jacqueline Everard; 2 s, 2 da; *Career* served Rifle Bde; chm John Swire & Sons (Hong Kong) Ltd 1973-80, fin sec Hong Kong 1981-86, dir Swire Gp 1986-89; Hon DSc Chinese Univ of Hong Kong, Hon DCL Univ of Hong Kong; *Style*— Sir John Bremridge, KBE; Church House, Bradford-on-Avon, Wiltshire (☎ 02216 6136)

BRENCHLEY, (Thomas) Frank; CMG (1964); s of Robert Ballard Brenchley (d 1967), and Alice, *née* Brough (d 1974); *b* 9 April 1918; *Educ* Univ of Oxford (MA), Open Univ (BA); *m* 1946, Edith Helen (d 1980), da of Moritz Helfand (d 1938), of Vienna, Austria; 3 da (Hilary, Victoria, Clare); *Career* RCS 1939-46, ME cmd, Actg Lt-Col; first sec: Singapore 1950-53, Cairo 1953-56, FO 1956-58, MECAS 1958-60; cnsllr Khartoum 1960-63, charge d'affaires Jedda 1963, head of Arabian Dept FO 1963-67, under sec FCO 1967-68; ambass: Norway 1968-72, Poland 1972-74; dep sec (head of Oversea and def sec) Cabinet Office 1975-76, ret HM Dip Serv 1976; chm: Inst for Study of Conflict 1984-89, Res Inst for Study of Conflict and Terrorism 1989-; dir Center for Security Studies Washington DC 1988-, pres Int Inst for Study of Conflict Geneva 1989-; *Recreations* collecting books; *Clubs* Travellers; *Style*— Frank Brenchley, Esq, CMG; 19 Ennismore Gdns, London SW7 1AA (☎ 071 584 7981)

BRENDEL, Alfred; KBE (1989); s of Albert Brendel, of Graz, and Ida, *née* Wieltschnig; *b* 5 Jan 1931; *m* 1, 1960 (m dis 1972), Iris Heymann-Gonzala; 1 da (Doris); m 2, 1975, Irene, da of Dr Johannes Semler, of Munich; 1 s (Adrian), 2 da (Anna-Sophie, Katharina); *Career* pianist and writer; concert career since 1949; recordings for Vox, Turnabout, Vanguard, Philips; Hon RAM; Hon DMus: London 1978, Sussex 1980, Oxford 1983; Cdr of Arts and Letters (France) 1985; *Books* Musical Thoughts and Afterthoughts (essays, 1976); *Recreations* reading, theatre, films, unintentional humour, kitsch; *Style*— Alfred Brendel, Esq, KBE; c/o Ingpen &

Williams, 14 Kensington Court, London W8 (☎ 071 937 5158)

BRENNAN, Daniel Joseph; QC (1985); s of Daniel Brennan, of Bradford (d 1969), and Mary, *née* Ahearne (d 1966); *b* 19 March 1942; *Educ* St Bede's GS Bradford, Univ of Manchester (LLB); *m* 21 Aug 1968, Pilar, da of Luis Sanchez Hernandez, of Madrid (d 1980), and Nieves Moya Dominguez; 4 s (Daniel b 1971, Patrick b 1972, Michael b 1977, Alexander b 1980); *Career* called to the Bar: Gray's Inn 1967, King's Inn Dublin 1990; rec Crown Ct 1982, memb Criminal Injuries Compensation Bd 1989; *Publications* Provisional Damages (1986), Bullen & Leake on Pleadings (contrib 13 edn); *Style—* Daniel J Brennan, Esq, QC; Brook House, Brook Lane, Alderley Edge, Cheshire SK9 7RU; 39 Essex St, London WC1R 3AT (☎ 071 583 1111, fax 071 353 3978)

BRENNAN, Thomas Gabriel; s of Michael Brennan, of 30 Anne St, Dundalk, Eirè, and Mary, *née* McDaniel; *b* 25 March 1939; *Educ* CBS Dundalk, Univ Coll Dublin (MB BCh, BAO, BSc); *m* 14 June 1974, Mary, da of Lt Derek Hunt, of 62 Parlington Meadows, Barwick in Elmet, Leeds; 1 s (Michael b 25 Sept 1978), 3 da (Jessica b 31 May 1975, Jennifer b 7 July 1977, Catherine b 3 April 1980); *Career* sr registrar Yorks Region 1969-71, conslt gen surgn Leeds DHA 1975-, hon sr lectr in surgery Univ of Leeds 1986- (lectr 1971-75); memb Cncl in surgery RSM, tutor in surgery RCS (memb Ct of Examiners); FRCS, FRCSEd, FRCSI; *Books* Lateral Paramedian Incision in Abdominal Operations; *Recreations* squash, golf; *Clubs* RSM; *Style—* Thomas Brennan, Esq; Butts Garth House, Butts Garth, Thorner, Leeds LS14 3DA Yorkshire (☎ 0532 893051); St James's Univ Teaching Hospital, Beckett Street, Leeds 9, Yorkshire (☎ 0532 443144); BUPA Hospital Leeds, Jackson Avenue, Leeds 8 (☎ 0532 693939)

BRENNAND-ROPER, Dr David Andrew; s of Dr John Hanson Brennand-Roper (d 1974), of Guernsey, CI, and Joyce Brennand-Roper, *née* Deans; *b* 22 Aug 1946; *Educ* Bryanston, BNC Oxford (MA), Guy's Hosp Med Sch (BM BCh); *Career* Sir Phillip Oppenheimer res fell in nuclear cardiology 1979-81, sr registrar in cardiology Guy's Hosp 1981-82, conslt cardiologist Guy's and West Hill Hosps 1982-; lectr of the Br Heart Fndn, memb Br Cardiac Assoc; Freeman City of London 1977, former Freeman Worshipful Co of Tobacco Pipe Makers 1977-82; memb BMA; FRCP; *Recreations* golf, photography, oenology; *Style—* Dr David Brennand-Roper; 97 Harley St, London W1N 1DF (☎ 071 486 9318, car 0860 836 748)

BRENNER, Sydney; CH (1987); *b* 13 Jan 1927; *Educ* Univ of Witwatersrand S Africa (MSc, MB BCh), Univ of Oxford (DPhil); *m* 3 c, 1 step s; *Career* Carnegie Corp fell USA 1954, Virus laboratory Univ of Calif Berkeley USA 1954, lectr in physiology Univ of Witwatersrand S Africa 1955-56, fell King's Coll Cambridge 1959; MRC: memb scientific staff 1957-, dir Laboratory of Molecular Biology Cambridge 1979-86, dir Molecular Genetics Unit 1986-; non-resident fell The Salk Inst San Diego Calif USA 1981-85, visiting fell Central Res and Devpt Dept E I du Pont de Nenours & Co Wilmington Delaware USA 1985-, visiting prof in med Royal Free Hosp Sch of Med Univ of London 1987-, hon prof of genetic med Univ of Cambridge Clinical Sch 1989-, scholar in residence The Res Inst of Scripps Clinic La Jolla USA 1989-; awards: Warren Triennial prize 1968, Royal medal (Royal Soc of London) 1974, Ciba medal (Biochemical Soc) 1981, Neil Hamilton Fairley medal (RCP) 1985, Prix Louis Jeantet de Medicine (Fndn Louis Jeantet de Medicine, Switzerland) 1987, Hughlings Jackson medal (Royal Soc of Med London) 1987, Waterfords Bio-Medical Sci award (The Res Inst of Scripps Clinic, La Jolla, USA) 1988, Kyoto prize 1990; foreign hon memb American Acad of Arts and Scis 1965; Hon DSc: Trinity Coll Dublin 1967, Univ of Witwatersrand 1972, Univ of Chicago 1976, Univ of London 1982, Univ of Leicester 1983, Univ of Oxford; hon memb: Deutsche Akademie der Natursforscher Leopoldine Germany 1975, Soc for Biological Chemists 1975, The Chinese Soc of Genetics (Taiwan) 1989; hon FRSE 1979; Hon LLD Univ of Glasgow 1981; hon fell: Exeter Coll Oxford 1985, Indian Acad of Scis 1989; hon FRCP 1990; foreign assoc: US Nat Acad of Scis 1977, Royal Soc of S Africa 1983; foreign memb: American Philosophical Soc 1979, Real Academia de Ciencias (Spain) 1985; external scientific memb Max-Planck Soc 1988, memb Academia Europaea 1989; FRS 1965, FRCP 1979; *Style—* Dr Sydney Brenner, CH

BRENT, Allan Arthur; s of Lawrence Arthur Brent (d 1975); *b* 10 Aug 1931; *Educ* Woodhouse Sch, City of London Coll; *m* 1, 1963 (m dis 1980), Sheila Moira, da of James Patrick Caird MacKinlay; 3 s, 1 da; m 2, 1983, Alberta Joy, da of Albert Coisant; *Career* md Grendon Tst Ltd 1969-71, chm Camco (Machinery) Ltd 1975-80, sr conslt Alpha Beta Consultants Ltd 1975-, pres Dania Securities Inc 1983-; FCIS (memb Cncl 1974-80), FCIArb, FTII (memb Cncl 1966-8l, pres 1969-70); *Recreations* tennis, sailing, bridge, travel; *Clubs* Athenaeum, City Livery, Balboa Bay (USA); *Style—* Allan Brent Esq; c/o David Moate Esq, Moate Thorpe & Co, CA, 40 Curzon St, W1; 1221 West Coast Highway, Newport Beach, CA 9266C, USA; 10 Old Burlington St, London W1

BRENT, Prof Leslie; s of late Arthur Baruch, of Köslin Germany, and late Charlotte, *née* Rosenthal; *b* 5 July 1925; *Educ* Bunce Court Sch Kent, Birmingham Central Tech Coll, Univ of Birmingham (BSc), UCL (PhD); *m* 16 April 1955, Joanne Elisabeth, da of Oates Manley, of Todmorden, Lancs; 1 s (Simon b 1956), 2 da (Susanna b 1958, Jennifer b 1963); *Career* Served Inf UK, Italy and Germany 1943-47 (acting Capt); lectr in zoology UCL 1954-62; Rockefeller res fell 1956-57, scientist Nat Inst for Med Res 1962-65, prof zoology Univ of Southampton 1965-69, prof immunology St Mary's Hosp Med Sch London 1969-90, emeritus prof; ed: Transplantation 1962-67, Immunology Letters 1983-90; fndr chm Wessex Branch Inst of Biology 1966-68, memb WHO Expert Advsy Ctee on Immunology 1970-90, fndr sec Br Transplantation Soc 1972-75 (pres 1976-78); chm: Organising Ctee of 9 Int Transplantation Congress 1982, Fellowship Cmmn Inst of Biol 1979-85, Univ of London Jt Advsy Cmmn in Immunology 1987-90, British Univ Vietnam Orphans Appeal Fund 1967-69; convenor Res and Action Gp of the Social Serv Haringey Lab Pty 1970-79, treas Haringey Community Rels Cncl 1974-79 (chm 1979-80), fndr memb and vice chm Exec Ctee Haringey Cncl for Voluntary Serv 1974-79; fndr chm Haringey SDP 1981-83; memb SLD 1987; Vice Chllr Prize 1951, Scientific Medal Zoological Soc of London 1964; memb: Br Soc for Immunology, Br Transplantation Soc (hon memb 1988), Hon MRCP 1986; FIBiol 1964; *Books* Progress in Immunology II (ed, 1974), Proceedings of the 9 Int Congress of The Transplantation Soc (2 vols ed, 1983), Organ Transplantation - Current Clinical and Immunological Concepts (ed, 1989); *Recreations* formerly hockey (Br Univs and Staffs); fell walking, cricket, music, novels, singing (Crouch End Festival Chorus); *Style—* Emeritus Prof Leslie Brent; 30 Hugo Road, London N9; 4th Floor, Clarence Wing, St Mary's Hospital, London W2

BRENT, Lucy Elizabeth; da of Allan Henry David George Brent (d 1978), and Irene Dorothy, *née* Jameson; *b* 7 Jan 1947; *Educ* Oak Hall; *Career* dep chm Trimite Ltd; FBIM; *Recreations* skiing, bridge, golf, theatre, opera; *Clubs* Wentworth Golf; *Style—* Miss Lucy Brent; c/o Midland Bank, 28 High St, PO Box 41, Uxbridge, Middx

BRENT, Michael Hamilton; s of Allan Henry David George Brent, (d 1978), and Irene Dorothy, *née* Jameson; *b* 18 March 1943; *Educ* Charterhouse; *m* 1973, Janet, da of Irvine McBeath; 1 s, 2 da; *Career* chm and md Trimite Ltd 1974-; FCA; *Recreations* bridge, chess, golf, sailing, skiing, tennis; *Clubs* Carlton, Wentworth Golf; *Style—* Michael Brent, Esq; Trimite Ltd, Arundel Rd, Uxbridge, Middx UB8 2SD (☎ 0895 51234, telex 934444 TRIMIT G); c/o Midland Bank, 28 High St, PO Box 41, Uxbridge, Middx

BRENT, Michael Leon; QC (1983); *b* 8 June 1936; *Educ* Manchester GS, Univ of Manchester (LLB); *m* 22 Aug 1965, Rosalind, *née* Keller; 2 da (Sasha b 1970, Ella b 1972); *Career* called to the Bar Gray's Inn 1961; practised: Northern Circuit 1961-67 (Circuit Jr 1964), Midland & Oxford Circuit 1967-; rec Crown Court 1990-; *Style—* Michael Brent, Esq, QC; 2 Dr Johnson's Bldgs, Temple, London EC4Y 7AY (☎ 071 353 5371, fax 071 353 1344)

BRENTFORD, 4 Viscount (UK 1929), of Newick, Sussex; Sir Crispin William Joynson-Hicks; 4 Bt of Holmbury (UK 1919), 2 Bt of Newick (UK 1956); s of 3 Viscount Brentford, DL (d 1983) and Phyllis, *née* Allfrey (d 1979); *b* 7 April 1933; *Educ* Eton, New Coll Oxford; *m* 1964, Gillian Evelyn, er da of late Gerald Edward Schluter, OBE, of Nairobi, Kenya; 1 s, 3 da (Hon Emma b 1966, Hon Rowena (Hon Mrs Banks) b 1967, Hon Amy b 1978); *Heir* s, Hon Paul William Joynson-Hicks b 1971; *Career* late Lt 9 Lancers; slr 1960; ptnr in legal firm of Taylor Joynson Garrett 1961-; Master Worshipful Co of Girdlers 1983-84; *Style—* The Rt Hon the Viscount Brentford; Cousley Place, Wadhurst, East Sussex TN5 8HF (☎ 089 288 3737)

BRENTON, Annabel Louisa; da of Alan Harry Robson of Curlew Cottage Sharrington, Norfolk, and Eileen Marie, *née* Hayward; *b* 17 Oct 1958; *Educ* Loughton Co HS, Univ of London (LLB), Univ of Oxford (BCL); *m* 29 Aug 1981, Timothy Deane Brenton, *qv*, s of Cdr Ronald William Brenton, MBE (d 1982); 1 da (Louisa Elizabeth b 8 April 1990); *Career* admitted slr 1984; ptnr of Messrs Withers 1988-; AKC; memb Law Soc; *Recreations* golf, gardening, needlepoint; *Clubs* Fakenham Golf; *Style—* Mrs Annabel Brenton; 20 Essex St, London WC2R 3AL (☎ 071 836 8400)

BRENTON, Howard John; s of Donald Henry Brenton, and Rose Lilian, *née* Lewis; *b* 13 Dec 1942; *Educ* Chichester HS for Boys, St Catherine's Coll Cambridge (BA); *m* 31 Jan 1970, Jane Margaret, da of William Alfred Fry; 2 s (Samuel John b 23 Sept 1974, Harry William Donald b 6 Sept 1976); *Career* plays incl: Christie in Love (Portable Theatre) 1969, Revenge (Royal Court Theatre Upstairs) 1969, Hitler Dances (Traverse Theatre Workshop Edinburgh) 1972, Measure for Measure, after Shakespeare (Northcott Theatre Exeter) 1972, Magnificence (Royal Ct Theatre) 1973, Brassneck (with David Hare, Nottingham Playhouse) 1973, The Churchill Play (Nottingham Playhouse) 1974 and twice revived by the RSC in 1978 and 1988, Government Property (Aarhus Theatre Denmark) 1975, Weapons of Happiness (NT) 1976 (winner of the Evening Standard Best Play of the Year award), Epsom Downs (Jt Stock Theatre Co) 1977, Sore Throats (RSC) 1979, The Romans in Britain (NT) 1980, Thirteenth Night (RSC) 1981, The Genius (Royal Ct Theatre) 1983, Bloody Poetry (Folo Novo Theatre) 1984 and revived by the Royal Ct Theatre 1988, Pravda, (with David Hare, NT) 1985 (winner of the Evening Standard Best Play of the Year award), Greenland (Royal Ct Theatre) 1988, Irania Nights (with Tariq Ali, Royal Ct Theatre) 1989, HID - Hess is Dead (RSC and Mickery Theatre Amsterdam) 1989, Moscow Gold (with Tarig Ah, 1990); TV plays incl: A Saliva Milkshake BBC 1975, The Paradise Run Thames 1976, Desert of Lies BBC 1984, the four part series Dead Head BBC 1986; Freeman City of Buffalo NY State USA; *Books* Diving for Pearls (1989); *Recreations* painting; *Clubs* Crystal Palace Football; *Style—* Howard Brenton, Esq; c/o Margaret Ramsay Ltd, 14A Goodwin's Ct, St Martin's Lane, London WC2N 4LL

BRENTON, Timothy Deane; s of Cdr Ronald William Brenton, MBE (d 1982), and Peggy Cecilia Deane, *née* Biggs; *b* 4 Nov 1957; *Educ* Kings Sch Rochester, Britannia RNC, Univ of Bristol (LLB); *m* 29 Aug 1981, Annabel Louisa, *qv*, da of Alan Harry Robson, of Curlew Cottage, Sharrington, Norfolk; 1 da (Louisa Elizabeth b 8 April 1990); *Career* RN 1975-79; lectr in law King's Coll London 1980, called to the Bar Middle Temple 1981; *Recreations* golf, windsurfing, fishing; *Clubs* Fakenham Golf; *Style—* Timothy Brenton, Esq; 2 Essex Court, Temple, London EC4 (☎ 071 583 8381, fax 071 353 0998, telex 8812528 ADROIT G)

BRERETON, Donald; s of Clarence Vivian Brereton (d 1965), and Alice Gwendolin, *née* Galpin; *b* 18 July 1945; *Educ* Plymouth Coll, Univ of Newcastle upon Tyne (BA); *m* 12 April 1969, Mary Frances, da of William Turley (d 1967); 1 s (Samuel Edward b 21 Feb 1977), 2 da (Kathryn Vivian b 15 Nov 1972, Sally Clare b 21 Dec 1974); *Career* VSO Malaysia 1963-64, asst princ Miny of Health 1968-71, asst private sec to Sec of State for Social Servs 1971-72, private sec to Permanent Sec DHSS 1972-73, princ Health Servs Planning 1973-79, princ private sec to Sec of State for Social Servs 1979-82; asst sec: DHSS Policy Strategy Unit 1982-84, Housing Benefit 1984-89; under sec and head PM's Efficiency Unit 1989-; selector VSO; *Recreations* squash, holidays, books, bridge; *Style—* Donald Brereton, Esq; 70 Whitehall, London SW1A 2AS (☎ 071 270 0527, fax 071 270 0099)

BRESLAND, Richard Charles; s of Charles William Bresland (d 1941), and Frances Ellen, *née* Fisher (d 1968); *b* 7 April 1926; *Educ* Bristol GS, Wadham Coll Oxford (MA); *Career* staff dir (London) NCB 1981-86, dir Coal Trade Benevolent Assoc 1972; Freeman City of London 1986, Liveryman Worshipful Company of Fuellers 1986; FIPM; *Recreations* walking, music, reading; *Style—* Richard Bresland, Esq; 3 Cedar Falls, Bishop's Lydeard, Taunton, Somerset TA4 3HR (☎ 0823 433487)

BRESLER, Fenton Shea; s of Herman Bresler (d 1972), and Bronia, *née* Tannenholtz (d 1968); *b* 22 Aug 1929; *Educ* Brighton Hove & Sussex GS, Sorbonne, King's Coll Univ of London (LIB); *m* Georgina Mary Bell (Gina), da of Capt George Bell Potts (d 1985); 1 s (Nicholas Joseph b 24 April 1961), 1 da (Katherine Celia (Mrs Sheppard) b 10 Aug 1959); *Career* called to the Bar Middle Temple 1951; journalist and author, extensive TV and radio work 1955-, investigations into unsolved crimes, investigations for Daily Express on Marilyn Monroe and Natalie Wood, conslt to US Justice Dept 1984, memb Medico-Legal Soc London; *Books* 16 books incl The Murder of John Lennon (1989), currently working on a major new book on Interpol; *Recreations* geriatric but hopefully still effective squash, reading and music; *Clubs* Reform, Savage; *Style—* Fenton Bresler, Esq; 2 Cavaye House, Cavaye Place, London SW10 9PT (☎ 071 373 2871); 3 Paper Buildings, Temple, London EC4Y 7EU (☎ 071 583 1183, fax 071 583 2037)

BRESSLAW, Bernard; s of Maurice Bresslaw (d 1970), of London, and Clara, *née* Davis (d 1973); *b* 25 Feb 1934; *Educ* The Coopers' Company Sch London, RADA; *m* 8 Aug 1959, Mary Elizabeth, da of James Wright, of Formby, Lancs; 3 s (James Harris b 7 Jan 1961, Mark Anthony b 9 June 1963, Jonathan Damon b 29 June 1968); *Career* actor; began career touring with Strand Repertory Company: Alf Donklin in It Won't Be a Stylish Marriage 1953, Lachie in The Nasty Heart; West End performances: debuted as Rory McRory in The McRory Whirl (Duchess Theatre) 1953, Leroy in The Bad Seed (Aldwych Theatre) 1955, Jenkins in The Good Sailor (Lyric Hammersmith) 1956, Chuchie in Hatful of Rain (Princes Theatre) 1957; appearances in 22 pantomimes (debuted in The Sleeping Beauty (London Palladium) 1958), toured with own variety show 1958; played with: RSC, NT, Pop Theatre, The Young Vic, The English Stage Co; awards: Emile Littler award at RADA public show, Most Promising Newcomer award Variety Club of GB 1958, Personality of the Year Daily Sketch 1958, Comic of the Year award Weekend Magazine 1958, Lifetime Comedy award ITV & Writers Guild of GB 1990; *Recreations* books; *Clubs* Grand Order of Water Rats (King in 1988), Lords Taverner's; *Style—* Bernard Bresslaw, Esq; c/o Harbour & Coffey, 9 Blenheim St, New Bond St, London W1 (☎ 071 499 5548)

BRET DAY, Robin Carew; s of Lawrence Bret Day (d 1963), and Marguerite Jeanne, *née* Cros (d 1979); *b* 20 Aug 1926; *Educ* St Paul Sch France, Sorbonne; *m* 29 March 1952, Joan Hannah, da of Charles Henry Harding (d 1943); 2 s (Philip b 1954, Timothy b 1959), 1 da (Joanna b 1968); *Career* conslt oral and maxillofacial surgn: Edgware and Hillingdon Hosps, Guy's Hosp 1966; chm: Med and Dental Ctee Guy's Hosp, Academic Bd United Med and Dental Schs of Guy's and St Thomas' Hosp; govr: United Med and Dental Schs of Guy's and St Thomas' Hosp; FDS RCS, LRCP, MRCS; memb: BMA, BDA; *Recreations* tennis, shooting, reading; *Style—* Robin Bret-Day, Esq; Oakwood, 12 North Park, Iver, Bucks (☎ 0753 3653 226); 84 Harley St, London W1N 1AE (☎ 071 935 8084, 071 486 2109); Guy's Hospital Dental School, St Thomas St, London SE1

BRETT, Hon Christopher Lionel Baliol; el s, and h of 4 Viscount Esher; *b* 23 Dec 1936; *Educ* Eton, Magdalen Coll Oxford; *m* 1, 1962 (m dis 1970), Camilla Charlotte, da of Sir (Horace) Anthony Claude Rumbold, 10 Bt, KCMG, CB; 1 s (Matthew b 1963), 2 da (Miranda b 1964, Rebecca b 1966); m 2, 1971, F Valerie, da of Maxwell Maurice Harrington; 2 s (Oliver b 1972, William b 1982), twin da (Susannah and Clare b 1973); *Style—* The Hon Christopher Brett; Watlington Park, Watlington, Oxon (☎ 049 161 2302)

BRETT, (Peter) Jeremy William Huggins; s of Col HW Huggins, DSO, MC, DL (d 1964), and Elizabeth, *née* Cadbury Butler (d 1959); *b* 3 Nov 1935; *Educ* Abberley Hall, Eton; *m* 1, 28 May 1958 (m dis 1962), Anna, da of Raymond Massey; 1 s (David b 1959); m 2, Joan Wilson (d 1985); 1 step s (Caleb), 1 step da (Rebekah); *Career* actor; *theatre*: Hamlet (Strand) 1961, The Kitchen (Royal Court and Broadway) 1964, A Month In The Country (Cambridge Theatre) 1965, Any Just Cause (Adeline Green Theatre) 1967; NT: As You Like It 1967, Tartuffe 1967, Edward II 1968, Much Ado About Nothing 1968, Love's Labours Lost 1969, The Merchant of Venice 1970, Hedda Gabler 1970; A Voyage Round My Father (Haymarket) 1971, Traveller Without Luggage (Thorndicke Theatre) 1972, Design for Living (Phoenix) 1973-74; Stratford Festival Theatre Canada: A Midsummer Night's Dream 1976, The Way Of The World 1976; Robert & Elizabeth (England and Canada) 1976-77, Dracula 1978-79, The Crucifer of Blood (Ahmanson Theatre) 1981, Noel (Goodspeed Opera House Connecticut) 1981, The Tempest 1982, The Secret of Sherlock Holmes (Wyndham); *film*: War and Peace (1956), My Fair Lady (1964), Seagull Island (1980); *TV*: The Typewriter 1962, The Three Musketeers 1967, The Incantation of Casanova 1967, An Ideal Husband 1969, A Portrait of Katherine Mansfield 1973, A Legacy 1974, Jennie 1974, The Picture of Dorian Gray 1976, Piccadilly Circus 1976-77, Rebecca 1979, Madame X 1981, Macbeth 1982, Number 10 1982, Sherlock Holmes 1983-90; *Recreations* archery; *Style—* Jeremy Brett, Esq; The Penthouse, 47 Clapham Common, London SW4(☎ 071 622 7745)

BRETT, Hon Michael Jeremy Baliol; 2 s of 4 Viscount Esher, CBE; *b* 26 April 1939; *Educ* Eton, Architectural Assoc London; *m* 1971, Sarah Calloway; *Career* architect in private practice; ARIBA; *Style—* The Hon Michael Brett; Shelbyville, Kentucky, USA

BRETT, Michael John Lee; s of John Brett and Margaret, *née* Lee; *b* 23 May 1939; *Educ* King's Coll Sch Wimbledon, Wadham Oxford; *Career* dir Throgmorton Publications and Financial Times Business Publishing Div; ed Investors Chronicle 1977-; *Style—* Michael Brett Esq; 134 Offord Rd, N1 (☎ 071 609 2362)

BRETT, Hon (Maurice) Sebastian Baliol; 4 s of 4 Viscount Esher; *b* 16 May 1944; *Educ* Eton, Trinity Coll Oxford; *m* 1968 (m dis), Pauline, da of Lt-Cdr Paul Murray-Jones, RN (ret); *Style—* The Hon Maurice Brett; Cordwainers, Titchfield, Hants

BRETT, Simon Anthony Lee; s of Alan John Brett (d 1979), and Margaret, *née* Lee; *b* 28 Oct 1945; *Educ* Dulwich, Wadham Coll Oxford (maj scholar, BA, pres OUDS); *m* 27 Nov 1971, Lucy Victoria, da of late Alastair Dixon McLaren; 2 s (Alastair b 22 July 1977, Jack b 11 March 1981), 1 da (Sophie b 9 Oct 1974); *Career* writer; Father Christmas Toy Dept Shinners of Sutton Nov-Dec 1967; prodr light entertainment: BBC Radio 1968-77 (progs worked on incl: Week Ending, Frank Muir Goes Into..., The News Huddlines, Lord Peter Wimsey, The Hitch-Hikers Guide to the Galaxy), LWT 1977-79 (progs worked on incl: End of Part One, Maggie and Her, The Glums); full time writer 1979-; pubns incl: 14 crime novels featuring actor-detective Charles Paris (Cast, In Order of Disappearance, So Much Blood, Star Trap, An Amateur Corpse, A Comedian Dies, The Dead Side of The Mike, Situation Tragedy, Murder Unprompted, Murder in the Title, Not Dead Only Resting, Dead Giveaway, What Bloody Man is That?, A Series of Murders, Corporate Bodies), 5 other crime novels (A Shock to the System (Best Novel award nomination by Mystery Writers of America), Dead Romantic, A Nice Class of Corpse, Mrs Presumed Dead, Mrs Pargeter's Package), 2 crime novels for children (The Three Detectives and the Missing Superstar, The Three Detectives and the Knight-in-Armour), 1 volume of crime short stories (A Box of Tricks), various humorous books; writing for TV incl After Henry (nominated for 1988 and 1989 BAFTA awards); writing for radio incl: Afternoon Theatre, Frank Muir Goes Into..., Semicircles, Molesworth, After Henry (BPG award for Outstanding Radio Programme 1987); Writers Guild award for Best Radio Feature Script (with Frank Muir) 1973; chm Crime Writers' Assoc 1986-87; *Style—* Simon Brett, Esq; c/o Michael Motley, 78 Gloucester Terrace, London W2 3HH (☎ 071 723 2973)

BRETT, Simon Baliol; s of Antony Reginald Forbes Baliol, MBE (d 1981), and Bay Helen, *née* Brownell (d 1989); *b* 27 May 1943; *Educ* Ampleforth, St Martins Sch of Art; *m* 31 Aug 1974, Juliet Anne, da of Paul Hamilton Wood, OBE (d 1962); 1 da (Emily b 1977); *Career* wood engraver and artist illustrator; pt/t teacher Marlborough Coll Art Sch 1971-89, proprietor Paulinus Press 1981-; Francis Williams illustration award for The Animals of St Gregory, chm Soc of Wood Engravers 1987- (memb 1984); ARE 1987; *Books* Engravers - A Handbook for the Nineties (1987), Forty Nudes (1988), The Wood Engravings of Gwen Raverat (ed, 1989), Reader's Digest Illustrated Bible (contrib, 1990); *Recreations* For a freelance artist? You must be joking!; *Style—* Simon Brett, Esq; 12 Blowhorn St, Marlborough, Wilts SN8 1BT (☎ 0672 512905)

BRETT-JONES, Antony Tom (Tony); CBE (1979); s of Lt David Tom Jones, DCM (d 1969), of London, and Mary, *née* Brett Needham; *b* 4 March 1922; *Educ* Cranbrook Sch; *m* 30 Aug 1952, Ann, da of Sir Lionel Wray Fox, MC (d 1961); 1 s (Harry Anthony Lionel b 1964), 3 da (Lucy Katharine b 1955, Sarah Josephine b 1956, Jane Rosalind b 1959); *Career* WWII Flt Offr RAF Bomber Cmd 1942-46; chartered Quantity Surveyor, ptnr Dearle & Henderson 1957-87; RICS: memb Cncl 1952-90, memb Div Cncl 1955- (pres 1969-70), govr Coll of Estate Mgmnt 1964-90 (chm govrs 1980-85), chm Educn Ctee 1973-78; vice pres Cruising Assoc 1985-88, ed Cruising Assoc Handbook 1982-; Freeman City of London 1977, memb Worshipful Co of Chartered Surveyors 1977; ARICS 1947, FRICS 1962, FCIArb, FRSA; *Books* 4 Aqua books (contrib 1960-); *Recreations* sailing; *Clubs* Reform; *Style—* Tony Brett-Jones, Esq, CBE; 13 Cumberland St, London SW1V 4LS (☎ 071 834 7885)

BRETTEN, (George) Rex; QC (1980); s of Horace Victor Bretten (d 1954), and Kathleen Edna Betty Bretten; *b* 21 Feb 1942; *Educ* King Edward VII Sch, King's Lynn, Sidney Sussex Coll Cambridge (MA, LLB); *m* 1965, Maureen Gillian, *née* Crowhurst; 1 da; *Career* Called to the Bar 1970; *Style—* Rex Bretten Esq, QC; Church Farm, Great Eversden, Cambs (☎ 0223 263538)

BRETTLE, Robert Harvey Linton; s of Robert Edward Brettle (d 1974), and Mabel, *née* Linton, of Willingdon, nr Eastbourne, Sussex; *b* 3 April 1935; *Educ* Highgate Sch London, Ch Ch Oxford (MA); *m* 27 May 1964, Lindsay Mary, da of the late Sydney Howson; 3 s (Thomas b 1966, Oliver b 1969, Adrian b 1972); *Career* Nat Serv: cmmnd Middx Regt 1955, Royal West Africa Frontier Force 3 Bn Nigeria Regt (later Queen's Own Nigeria Regt) 1955-56, Intelligence and Recruitment Offr asst adj; admitted slr 1963, ptnr Peard Son and Webster of Croydon 1966 (sr ptnr 1983), sr ptnr Peard Webster Pringle and John 1986-, insolvency practitioner; memb London Legal Aid Area Appeals Ctee, pres Croydon and Dist Law Soc 1972-73, chm of Govrs St Margaret's Sch for Spastics and Physically Handicapped Children 1972-84; memb Law Soc 1963-; *Recreations* bridge, gardening, travel; *Clubs* RAC; *Style—* Robert Brettle, Esq; 42 Brownlow Rd, Croydon, Surrey, CRO 5JT (☎ 081 688 3307); Peard Webster Pringle and John, Suffolk House, College Rd, Croydon CR9 1DR (☎ 081 680 5262, fax 081 686 4560, telex 9180263 PWPJ G)

BREW, Richard Maddock; CBE (1981), DL (Greater London 1989); s of late Leslie Maddock Brew, of Suffolk, and Phyllis Evelyn, *née* Huntsman (d 1949); *b* 13 Dec 1930; *Educ* Rugby, Magdalene Coll Cambridge (BA); *m* 1953, Judith Anne, da of Dr Percy Ellis Thompson Hancock; 2 s (Antony b 1957, Timothy b 1961), 2 da (Charlotte b 1955, Sophie b 1967); *Career* called to the Bar Inner Temple 1955; dep chm Brew Bros Ltd 1955-72 chm Monks Dormitory Ltd 1979-, Budget Boilers Ltd 1984- regnl dir (Eastern counties) Lloyds Bank plc 1988-; memb: NE Thames RHA 1982- (vice chm 1982-86), Royal Borough of Kensington Cncl 1959-65, Royal Borough of Kensington and Chelsea Cncl 1964-70; GLC 1968-86: alderman 1968-73, vice chm Strategic Planning Ctee 1969-71, memb for Chingford 1973-86, dep ldr of Cncl and ldr Policy and Resources Ctee 1977-81, dep ldr Cons Pty and oppn spokesman on finance 1974-77 and 1981-82, ldr of the oppn 1982-83; memb Nat Theatre Bd 1982-86, High Sheriff Greater London 1988-89; memb Cncl Pony Club 1975-; *Recreations* The Pony Club, gardening; *Clubs* Carlton, MCC; *Style—* Richard Brew, Esq, CBE, DL; The Abbey, Coggeshall, Essex CO6 1RD (☎ 0376 561246)

BREWER, David; s of William Watson Brewer (d 1968), and Eileen, *née* Hall; *b* 24 July 1946; *Educ* Brigg GS, Emmanuel Coll Cambridge (BA); *m* 26 May 1973, Elizabeth Margaret, da of John William Ferguson (d 1986); 1 da (Jane b 1975); *Career* British Coal Corporation: area chief accountant South Midlands 1979-85, chief accountant 1985-87, head of fin servs 1987-; ACMA 1978; *Style—* David Brewer, Esq; Westwinds, 2 Church Hill, Aspley Guise, Milton Keynes, Bucks MK17 8HW (☎ 0908 585 700); British Coal Corporation, Hobart House, Grosvenor Place, London SW1X 7AE (☎ 071 235 2020/0302 366 611, fax 0302 34682, 0302 36144, telex 882161 HOB)

BREWER, David John; s of Raymond Bennett (d 1982), of Padstow, Cornwall, and Patricia Mary, *née* Key; *b* 29 Jan 1949; *Educ* Bodmin Co GS, Univ of Bath (BSc); *m* 31 Mar 1973, Kate, da of Mitchell Scatterty Milne; 1 da (Rebecca b 1977); *Career* CA; Deloitte Haskins and Sells: London 1970-78, Dubai UAE 1978-86 ptnr 1980-, ptnr in charge Arabian Gulf Practice 1982-, sr ptnr (CI Firm) 1986-; tres: Assoc Jersey Charities, Jersey Amateur Swimming Assoc; MInstD (Jersey Branch), FCA, memb ICAEW 1974; *Recreations* bridge, sailing, supporting amateur swimming; *Clubs* United, St Helier; *Style—* David Brewer, Esq; Clos du Coin, La Haule, St Brelade, Jersey (☎ 0534 46432); Deloitte Haskins and Sells, Whiteley Chambers, 41 Don St, St Helier, Jersey (☎ 0534 75151, fax 0534 24321, telex 4192035)

BREWER, Prof Derek Stanley; s of Stanley Leonard Brewer, and Winifred Helen, *née* Forbes; *b* 13 July 1923; *Educ* The Crypt GS, Magdalen Coll Oxford; *m* 1951, Lucie Elisabeth Hoole; 3 s, 2 da; *Career* academic publisher; master Emmanuel Coll Cambridge 1977-90, prof of English 1983-90 (emeritus 1990-); FSA; *Style—* Prof Derek Brewer, FSA; Emmanuel College, Cambridge (☎ 0223 334200)

BREWER, Rear Adm George Maxted Kenneth; CB (1981); s of Capt George Maxted Brewer (d 1954), of Dover, Kent, and Cecilia Victoria Jessie, *née* Clark (d 1987); paternal gf served in HMS Basilisk under the then Capt Moresby during his discoveries in New Guinea in 1873, hence Brewer Island shown on Admiralty Chart 1873; *b* 4 March 1930; *Educ* The Nautical Coll Pangbourne; *m* 1989, Betty Mary, o da of Cdr Claude Harold Welton, RN; *Career* cmd: HMS Carysfort (Home, Med and Far E) 1964-65, HMS Agincourt (Home) 1967, HMS Grenville (Home, Med and Far E) 1967-69, HMS Juno and Capt Fourth Frigate Sqdn (Home and Med) 1973-74; course student RCDS 1975; cmd: HMS Tiger (Far E deployment) and Flag Capt to the Flag Offr Second Flotilla 1978, appointed ADC to HM The Queen 1980, HMS Bulwark (NATO area) 1978-80; Flag Offr Medway and Port Adm Chatham 1980-82; *Recreations* watercolour painting; *Clubs* Naval and Military, Royal Navy Club of 1765 and 1785; *Style—* Rear Adm George Brewer, CB; c/o Nat Westminster Bank, Portchester, Fareham, Hants

BREWER, Rt Rev John; *see*: Lancaster, Bishop of

BREWERTON, David Robert; s of Ernest John Brewerton (d 1980), and Violet Florence, *née* Smith; *b* 25 Feb 1943; *Educ* Coopers Company's Sch; *m* 25 May 1963, Patricia Ann, da of James Albert Driscoll, OBE; 2 s (Benjamin David b 27 March 1968, Jake David b 14 April 1970), 1 da (Sarah Ann Jane b 14 Sept 1973); *Career* Stock Exchange red button with Grieveson Grant 1959; sub ed: Extel Statistics 1964, Financial Times 1965; commercial property corr Daily Telegraph 1971 (reporter 1969), ed Policy Holder Insurance News 1977, Questor Daily Telegraph 1978, city ed The Independent 1986, exec ed fin and indust The Times 1988, dir Brunswick PR Ltd 1991; *Awards* Financial Journalist of the Year 1986; *Recreations* sailing, cooking, travel; *Style—* David Brewerton, Esq; 88 London Rd, Brentwood, Essex CM14 4NJ (☎ 0277 227073); Brunswick Public Relations Ltd, 15 Lincoln's Inn Fields, London WC2A 3ED (☎ 071 404 5959, fax 071 831 2823, car 0831 216378)

BREWIN, Hon Mrs (Anne Sheridan); *née* Walston; resumed use of former married name, Brewin; da of Baron Walston (Life Peer); *b* 4 Nov 1937; *m* 1, 6 Aug 1960 (m dis 1972), Charles Edward Brewin, s of late Maj Clement Noel Brewin, MC, RA; 1 s, 4 da; m 2, 1978 (m dis 1982), Edward McCririe-Hallman; *Style—* The Hon Mrs Brewin; Clare Cottage, 30 Northfield End, Henley on Thames, Oxon RG9 2JL (☎ 0491 572910)

BREWIN, Daniel Robert (Dan); s of John Stuart Brewin (d 1968), of Sheffield, and Elsie Mary Brewin, *née* Timm; *b* 22 Aug 1946; *Educ* King Edward VII Sch Sheffield, Univ of Salford (BSc), Cranfield Sch of Mgmnt (MBA 1977); *m* 1974, Sylvia Mary Frances (separated), da of Roland Jones Sale Cheshire; 2 s (John b 1976, Timothy b 1980), 1 da (Anna b 1978); *Career* British Airways - various 1964-81; dir of operations Manchester Airport 1981-84; gen mangr UK Sales British Caledonian 1984-87; snr gen mangr Commerical British Caledonian 1987; *Recreations* tennis, cinema; *Style—* Daniel Brewin, Esq; 5 Old Martyrs, Crawley, W Sussex (☎ 0293 511980); British Caledonian, Caledonian House, Crawley (☎ 0293 583694)

BREWIS, Dr (Robert) Alistair Livingston; s of Dr Ernest George Brewis, and Jean Elizabeth, *née* Livingston; *b* 16 Oct 1937; *Educ* Royal GS Newcastle, Univ of Durham, Univ of Newcastle upon Tyne (MB BS, MD); *m* 3 Nov 1962, Dr Mary Brewis, da of John William Burdus; 3 s (George b 1964, Robert b 1965, John b 1966); *Career* house offr: Royal Victoria Infirmary Newcastle, Hammersmith and Brompton Hosps London; registrar Charing Cross Hosp London, lectr in med Univ of

Manchester 1966-70, currently conslt physician and sr lectr in med Royal Victoria Infirm Newcastle upon Tyne; vice pres Br Thoracic Soc, chm Res Ctee Nat Asthma Campaign; FRCP 1974; *Books* Lecture Notes on Respiratory Disease (4 edn, 1990), Respiratory Medicine (jt ed, 1990), Classic Papers in Asthma (1990); *Recreations* painting; *Style—* Dr Alistair Brewis; 1 Oaklands Ave, Gosforth, Newcastle upon Tyne NE3 4YJ (☎ 091 285 3655); Royal Victoria Infirmary, Newcastle upon Tyne NE1 4LP (☎ 091 232 5131)

BREWIS, Lady Anne Beatrice Mary; *née* Palmer; da of 3 Earl of Selborne, CH, PC (d 1971); *b* 26 March 1911; *Educ* Queen's Coll Harley St, Somerville Coll Oxford; *m* 3 July 1935, Rev John Salusbury Brewis (d 1972), s of George Robert Brewis, of Oxford; 2 s, 2 da; *Recreations* nature conservation, botany, flora writing; *Style—* The Lady Anne Brewis; Benham's House, Benham's Lane, Greatham, Hants GU33 6BE (☎ 042 07 348)

BREWIS, Pearl Paulina; *née* Beaumont-Thomas; da of Col Lionel Beaumont-Thomas, MC (d 1942), of Great Brampton House, Madley, Herefordshire, and Pauline Grace, *née* Marriott (d 1954); *b* 21 June 1921; *Educ* Downe House Sch nr Newbury Berks; *m* 1, 17 Aug 1940, Capt Peter Robert Sandham Bankes, MC (d 1943), s of Rev Conrad Douglas Richard Oakley Bankes (d 1940), of Morningthorpe, Long Stratton, Norfolk; 1 s (Peter b 14 July 1944); m 2, 9 Aug 1947 (m dis 1955), Richard Henry Ridgway (d 1985), s of Henry Ridgway, JP (d 1955), of Rossmore, Mallow, Co Cork, Eire; m 3, 13 Oct 1956 (m dis 1960), Lt-Col Charles Richard Wynn Brewis, DSO, MC, s of Capt Charles Richard Wynn Brewis, CBE, RN (d 1953), of Tuffs Hard, Bosham, nr Chichester; 1 s (Samuel Charles b 19 Nov 1957), 1 da (Susan Pauline b 30 Aug 1959); *Career* cmmnd 2 Lt Womens Aux Serv Burma, promoted 1 Lt 1943 (despatches 1945); farmer 1958-88; memb Lloyds 1978-; alternately hon sec and chm New Forest and Dist Cancer Relief Macmillan Fund 1973-89, fndr local gp to raise funds for various charities 1989-; memb PC and New Forest Consultative Panel 1979-83; *Recreations* equestrian, sailing, painting, sculpture, gardening, music; *Clubs* Royal Lymington Yacht; *Style—* Mrs Pearl P Brewis; Arnewood Manor, Arnewood Bridge Rd, Sway, nr Lymington, Hampshire SO41 6ER (☎ 0590 682 214)

BREWSTER, David John; s of Dr Leslie George Brewster (d 1974), and Evangeline, *née* Creed (d 1976); *b* 16 June 1936; *Educ* Whitgift Sch, St John's Coll Cambridge (MA); *m* 9 May 1964, Christine, *née* Booth; 1 s (Jonathan b 27 March 1967), 3 da (Sarah b 6 March 1965, Louise b 10 Jan 1969, Emma b 22 Dec 1971); *Career* called to the Bar Gray's Inn 1961; practising barr in England 1961-63, ptnr Appleby Spurling and Kempe (barristers and attorneys) Bermuda 1964-74, dir Tyndall Gp 1974-86, legal dir Investmt Mgmnt Regulatory Orgn 1986-; chm St Peters Hospice Bristol 1984-88; *Style—* David Brewster, Esq; Investmt Mgmnt Regulatory Orgn Ltd, Broadwalk House, 5 Appold St, London EC2A 2LL

BREWSTER, Martyn Robert; s of Robert Richard Frederick Brewster of Watford, Herts, and Doreen Violet, *née* Lilburn; *b* 24 Jan 1952; *Educ* Watford Boys GS, Hertfordshire Coll of Art, Brighton Poly (BA, Dip Painting and Printmaking, Art Teachers Cert); *m* 1988, Hilary Joy, da of Peter John Carter; 1 da (Sophie Roberta b 19 Aug 1988); *Career* artist; lectr in art East Herts Coll 1980-89; visiting lectr various arts schs 1980-89 incl: Winchester, Bournemouth, London Coll of Furniture; Space Studio in London 1983, studio in Dorset 1990; two-man exhibition Thumb Gallery Soho 1987-; one-man exhibitions incl: Peterborough City Museum and Art Gallery 1983, London Coll of Furniture 1984, Warwick Arts Tst London 1986, Winchester Gallery Hampshire 1986, Minories Essex 1986, Woodlands Gallery London 1987, Thumb Gallery (Shadows and Light 1987, Light Falls 1990); group exhibitions incl: Spirit of London (Festival Hall) 1983, English Expression (Warwick Arts Tst) 1984, Int Art Fair London 1985, Angela Flowers Gallery 1985-86, Int Art Fairs LA 1987-90, London Group (RCA) 1988, Art London (Thumb Gallery) 1989-90, Critics Choice (Air Gallery London and Ianetti Lanzone Gallery San Francisco) 1989; works in collection of: Warwick Arts Tst, The Open Univ, Wiltshire Educn Authy, various Hosps, Peterborough Museum, various private collections worldwide; Eastern Arts award 1977, awarded various Regnl Arts Association grants 1979-86; memb Brighton Open Studios 1975-79; *Recreations* reading, jogging; *Style—* Martyn Brewster, Esq; c/o Thumb Gallery Ltd, 38 Lexington St, Soho, London W1R 3HR (☎ 071 439 7319/ 7343); Studio ☎ 0202 423300)

BREWSTER, Richard David; s of David Edward Brewster; *b* 5 Jan 1946; *Educ* Highgate; *m* Susan Ann; 2 s (Edward, William), 2 da (Emily, Rachel); *Career* CA; fin dir Giltspur plc to 1983, chief exec David S Smith (Holdings) plc 1983-; Liveryman Worshipful Co of Stationers and Newspaper Makers; FCA 1968; FInstD; *Recreations* sailing, tennis, skiing; *Clubs* Island Cruising, IOD, Richmond Cricket and Tennis; *Style—* Richard Brewster, Esq; c/o David S Smith (Holdings) plc, 16 Great Peter St, London SW1 (☎ 071 222 8855)

BREYER, Hon Mrs (Joanna Freda); da of 1 Viscount Blakenham, OBE, PC, and Hon Beryl Nancy Pearson, da of 2 Viscount Cowdray; *b* 27 July 1942; *m* 1967, Judge Stephen Breyer, prof Harvard Law Sch 1967-, of San Francisco, California, USA; 1 s (Michael b 1974), 2 da (Chloe b 1969, Nell b 1971); *Style—* The Hon Mrs Breyer; 12 Dunstable Rd, Cambridge, Mass, USA

BRIANCE, Richard Henry; o s of John Albert Perceval Briance, CMG (d 1989), and Prunella Mary *née* Chapman; *b* 23 Aug 1953; *Educ* Eton, Jesus Coll Cambridge (BA); *m* 13 Oct 1979, Lucille, *née* de Zalduondo; 2 s (Henry b 1984, Frederick b 1989), 2 da (Zoe b 1982, Clementine b 1987); *Career* merchant banker; exec dir Credit Suisse First Boston Ltd; *Clubs* Hawks, Hurlingham, Royal Automobile; *Style—* Richard Briance, Esq; The Old House, Holland St, London W8 4NA (☎ 071 937 2113); Credit Suisse First Boston, 2A Great Titchfield St, London W1

BRIANT, Bernard Christian; CVO (1977), MBE (1945); s of Bernard Briant, of London (d 1977), and Cecily, *née* Christian (d 1971); *b* 11 April 1917; *Educ* Stowe, Univ of Oxford (MA); *m* 22 Oct 1942, Margaret Emslie, da of Arthur Strong Rawle, of Walton Heath (d 1964); 1 s (Richard b 1952), 2 da (Sarah b 1947, Elizabeth b 1949); *Career* 1940-45 Maj Intelligence Corps (despatches) Tunisia, Italy, Austria; conslt Daniel Smith Chartered Surveyors 1952- (sr ptnr 1976-82); land steward Manor of Kennington of the Duchy of Cornwall 1963-76; agent All Souls Coll Oxford 1966-79, dir Church of Eng Building Soc 1953-87, Anglia Building Soc 1983-87, Nationwide Anglia Building Soc 1987-; memb: various RICS Ctees 1948-70, RICS Cncl 1962-70; clerk Co of Chartered Surveyors 1980-85, memb Ctee Mgmnt Lambeth Southwark Housing Soc 1971-; *Recreations* golf, reading, walking; *Clubs* United Oxford and Cambridge Univ, Aldeburgh Golf, Rye Golf; *Style—* Bernard C Briant, Esq, CVO, MBE; c/o 32 St James's St SW1A HT

BRIANT, (Anne) Gillian; da of Sir John Fletcher-Cooke, CMG (d 1989), and Alice Elizabeth, *née* Egner; *b* 12 Nov 1953; *Educ* Cheltenham, Univ of Bristol (BA), Univ of Oxford (PGCE); *m* 30 Sept 1978, Nicholas Adrian Briant, s of Donald William Briant, of Thickets, Holt Wood, Aylesford, Nr Maidstone, Kent; 2 da (Genevieve Elizabeth b Sept 1985, Catherine Diane b Dec 1989); *Career* admitted slr 1979; ptnr Denton Hall Burgin & Warrens 1984-, legal trg ptnr 1988-; memb: IBA, Law Soc; *Recreations* squash, cooking; *Clubs* Hurlingham, Wimbledon Squash & Badminton; *Style—* Mrs Gillian Briant; Denton Hall Burgin & Warrens, 5 Chancery Lane, Cliffords Inn, London EC4 (☎ 071 242 1212, fax 071 404 0087, telex 263567 BURGI)

BRIARS, Colin Hubert; s of Hubert Alfred Briars (d 1958); *b* 8 July 1926; *Educ* Christ's Hosp; *m* 2, 1975, Susan, da of James Douglas Frail, CBE; 1 s, 1 da; *Career* conslt Pirbic Orgn Ltd; dir: Brush Switchgear Ltd 1960-70, Allenwest Ltd 1970-79, Westinghouse Electric MK Ltd 1979-83, Ottermill Ltd; chm Control and Automation Manufacturers Assoc; CEng; *Recreations* squash, tennis, skiing; *Clubs* RAC; *Style—* Colin Briars Esq; Shannon House, Kings Rd, Sunninghill, Berks (☎ Ascot (0990) 22448)

BRIAULT, Dr Eric William Henry; CBE (1976); s of Henry George Briault (d 1932), of Brighton, Sussex, and Beatrice Mary Emmaline, *née* Day (d 1961); *b* 24 Dec 1911; *Educ* Brighton Hove and Sussex GS, Peterhouse Cambridge (BA, MA); Univ of London (PhD); *m* 3 Aug 1935, (Alice) Marie, da of Arthur Ernest Knight (d 1948), of Brighton; 2 s (Timothy b 1938, Stephen b 1952), 1 da (Anthea b 1943); *Career* sch teacher 1933-47; London CC: inspr of Schs 1948-56, dep educn offr 1956-71, educn offr ILEA 1971-76, visiting prof Univ of Sussex 1977-80 and 1984-85; chm of govrs: Storrington First Sch, Rydon Community Sch; Freeman City of London, Liveryman Worshipful Co of Goldsmiths; Hon DLitt Univ of Sussex 1975; FRGS (hon sec 1953-63); *Books* Introduction to Advanced Geography (jtly, 1957), Geography in and out of School (jtly, 1960 and 1963), Falling Rolls in Secondary Schools (jtly, 1980), Primary School Management: Learning from Experience (jtly, 1990); *Recreations* theatre, ballet, travel; *Style—* Dr Eric Briault CBE; Woodedge, Hampers Lane, Storrington, W Sussex, (☎ 0903 74 3919)

BRICE, Edward St John; er s of W Brice, OBE, TD, DL, of Highover Hoo, Rochester (d 1990); *b* 15 Feb 1936; *Educ* Tonbridge, Clare Coll Cambridge (MA); *m* 1960, Elizabeth, da of G Grieve; 1 s, 1 da; *Career* farmer, underwriter Lloyd's; memb Kent CC 1977, High Sheriff Kent 1980-81, chm Kent Co Agric Soc 1984-; Master Worshipful Co of Skinners 1990; *Recreations* golf, tennis; *Clubs* Royal and Ancient, Royal St George's Golf, MCC; *Style—* Edward Brice, Esq; Hoo Lodge, Hoo, Rochester, Kent (☎ 0634 251078)

BRICE, Geoffrey James Barrington Groves; QC (1979); s of Lt Cdr John Edgar Leonard Brice, MBE (d 1971), and Winifried Ivy, *née* Field; *b* 21 April 1938; *Educ* Magdalen Coll Sch Brackley, UCL; *m* 1963, Ann Nuala, da of William Connor (d 1958); 1 s (Paul); *Career* called to the Bar Middle Temple 1960; arbitrator Lloyd's 1978-, Wreck cmmr 1979-, rec of Crown Ct 1980-, master of the Bench 1986; visiting prof of maritime law Tulane Univ New Orleans USA 1989-90; memb Gen Cncl of the Bar 1988; chm: London Common Law and Commercial Bar Assoc 1988-89, Direct Professional Access Ctee 1988-89; *Books* Maritime Law of Salvage (1983); *Recreations* listening to music; *Clubs* Athenaeum; *Style—* Geoffrey Brice, Esq, QC; 15 Gayfere St, Smith Square, London SW1P 3HP (☎ 071 799 3807); Queen Elizabeth Building, Temple, London EC4Y 9BS (☎ 071 353 9153, telex 262762 INREMG)

BRICE, (Ann) Nuala; *née* Connor; da of William Connor (d 1957), of Manchester, and Rosaleen Gertrude, *née* Gilmartin; *b* 22 Dec 1937; *Educ* Loreto Convent Manchester, UCL (LLB, LLM, PhD); *m* 1 June 1963, Geoffrey James Barrington Groves Brice, QC, s of Lt Cdr John Edgar Leonard Brice, MBE; 1 s (Paul Francis b 17 March 1964); *Career* admitted slr 1963 (awarded Stephen Herlis prize and John Peacock conveyancing prize); asst sec-gen The Law Society 1987- (asst slr 1963, asst sec 1964, sr asst sec 1973, deptl sec 1982); visiting prof of law Tulane Univ New Orleans 1990; Freedom City of London, Liveryman City of London Solicitors Co; memb Law Soc 1963; *Recreations* reading, music, gardening; *Style—* Mrs Nuala Brice; Yew Tree House, Spring Coppice, Lane End, Bucks HP14 3NU (☎ 0494 881810); 15 Gayfere Street, Smith Square, London SW1P 3HP (☎ 071 794 3807); The Law Society, 113 Chancery Lane, London WC2 1PL (☎ 071 242 1222)

BRICKWOOD, Sir Basil Greame; 3 Bt (UK 1927); s of Sir John Brickwood, 1 Bt; suc half bro, Sir Rupert Brickwood, 2 Bt, 1974; *b* 21 May 1923; *Educ* King Edward's GS Stratford, Clifton; *m* 1, 1947 (m dis), Betty Cooper; m 2, 1956, Shirley Anne, da of Richard Wallace Brown; 2 da; *Heir* none; *Career* served WWII in RAF 1940-46; *Clubs* RAF; *Style—* Sir Basil Brickwood, Bt; c/o RAF Club, 128 Piccadilly, London W1V OPY

BRICKWOOD, Richard Ian; s of Basil Arthur Brickwood (d 1979) and Hilary Joan; *b* 22 Dec 1947; *Educ* Wesley Coll Dublin, Hele's GS Exeter Devon; *m* 6 March 1971, Susan Vanessa Mary, da of Donald Hugh Galpin (d 1971); 1 s (Stephen James b 1979), 1 da (Sarah Louise b 1977); *Career* Lloyds broker, memb Lloyds 1986; md Marsh & McLennan Inc 1989; dir: CT Bowring (Insurance) Ltd 1985, Bowring Financial, Professional Insurance Brokers Ltd 1988; *Recreations* sailing, canoeing, fishing; *Clubs* Lloyds Yacht, Junior Offshore Group; *Style—* Richard I Brickwood, Esq; Swan House, Widford, Nr Ware, Herts SG12 8SJ (☎ 027 984 2425, 071 283 3100)

BRIDEN, Prof James Christopher; s of Henry Charles Timberlake Briden, of High Wycombe, and Gladys Elizabeth *née* Jefkins; *b* 30 Dec 1938; *Educ* Royal GS High Wycombe, St Catherine's Coll Oxford (MA), Aust Nat Univ Canberra (PhD); *m* 20 July 1968, Caroline, da of Kenneth Gillmore (d 1988); 1 s (Benjamin b 1977), 1 da (Hannah b 1974); *Career* res fell Univ of: Rhodesia 1965-66, Oxford 1966-67, Birmingham 1967-68; Univ of Leeds: lectr 1968-73, reader 1973-75, prof of geophysics 1975-86, hon prof 1986-; Canadian Cwlth fell and visiting prof Univ of W Ontario 1977-80, dir of Earth Sciences NERC 1986-; contrib of over 70 geological and geophysical papers to learned jls; memb: Cncl Euro Geophysical Soc 1976-84, RAS Cncl 1978-79, Governing Cncl In Seismological Centre 1979-83, NERC 1980; awarded Murchison medal of Geological Soc 1984; FGS (1961), FRAS (1963); *Books* jt author of 2 books on past position of the continents; *Style—* Prof James Briden; Natural Environment Research Council, Polaris House, North Star Ave, Swindon, Wilts, SN2 1EU (fax 0793 411584, telex 444293 ENVRE G)

BRIDGE, Very Rev Antony Cyprian (Tony); s of Cdr Cyprian Dunscomb Charles Bridge (d 1938), and Gladys, *née* Steel (d 1969); *b* 5 Sept 1914; *Educ* Marlborough, Royal Acad Sch of Art; *m* 10 May 1937, Brenda Lois, da of Dr Raymond Streatfeild; 1 s (Cyprian b 1955), 2 da (Victoria b 1944, Charlotte b 1946); *Career* served WWII, demobbed Maj 1945; artist and painter; ordained: deacon 1955, priest 1956; curate Hythe Kent 1955-58, vicar Christ Church Lancaster Gate London 1958-68, dean of Guildford 1968-86, dean emeritus 1986-; FSA 1980; *Books* Images of God (1960), Theodora: Portrait in a Byzantine Landscape (1978), The Crusades (1980), Suleiman the Magnificent (1983), One Man's Advent (1985), Richard the Lionheart (1989); *Recreations* bird watching; *Style—* The Very Rev Tony Bridge, FSA; 34 London Rd, Deal, Kent CT14 9TE (☎ 0304 366792)

BRIDGE, Christopher Charles Cyprian; ERD, DL (E Sussex 1983); s of Brig Charles Edward Dunscombe Bridge, CMG, DSO, MC (d 1961), of Hale House, De Vere Gardens, Kensington, and Georgena Canning, *née* Hall (d 1970); gs of Brig-Gen Sir Charles Henry Bridge, KCMG, CB; *b* 23 Oct 1918; *Educ* Eton, Trinity Coll Cambridge; *m* 1953, Hon Dinah, yr da of 1 and last Baron Brand, CMG (d 1963, s of 2 Visc Hampden), of Eydon Hall, Daventry, and former wife of Lyttelton Fox; 1 s (Charles), 1 da (Joanna), 1 step s, 1 step da; *Career* Maj Coldstream Gds 1939-45; ptnr Akroyd & Smithers 1953-66; md Seccombe Marshall & Campion 1967-79, dir Hambros Investment Trust 1979-89; High Sheriff of E Sussex 1979-80; *Recreations* gardening, racing, reading; *Clubs* Buck's, Beefsteak; *Style—* Christopher Bridge Esq, ERD, DL; 18 The Street, Firle, Lewes, E Sussex BN8 6NR (☎ 0730 858507); 74

Melton Court, Old Brompton Rd, London SW7 3JH (☎ 071 581 4166)

BRIDGE, Christopher John; s of Lt-Col J E Bridge, OBE, TD (d 1983), and Jeanne, *née* Pryor; *b* 30 April 1948; *Educ* Mount House Sch Tavistock, Prior Park Coll Bath, Univ of Aberdeen (LLB); *m* 1976, Caroline, da of John Perchard; 2 da (Claire b 7 Aug 1981, Helen b 13 Aug 1984); *Career* industl rels asst Rolls Royce Glasgow 1968-71, sr personnel offr BBC 1971-77; dist personnel offr: Kensington Chelsea and Westminster AHA 1977-82, Victoria Health Authy 1982-86; assoc gen mangr Charing Cross Hosp 1986-88, gen mangr Mental Health Unit North East Essex Health Authy 1988-; MIPM 1971, govr Colchester Inst of Higher and Further Educn 1990; *Recreations* cricket, rugby (referee), sailing, local charities; *Style—* Christopher Bridge, Esq; North East Essex Health Authority, Severalls Hospital, Boxted Rd, Colchester, Essex CO4 5HG (☎ 0206 852271, fax 0206 844435, car 0831 216527)

BRIDGE, Hon Mrs (Dinah); yr da of 1 and last Baron Brand, CMG (d 1963); *b* 1920; *m* 1, 1943 (m dis 1950), Lyttleton Fox; 1 s, 1 da; m 2, 1953, Christopher Charles Cyprian Bridge, *qv*; 1 s, 1 da; *Style—* The Hon Mrs Bridge; 18 The Street, Firle, East Sussex BN8 6NR (☎ 0730 858507); 74 Melton Court, Old Brompton Rd, London SW7 3JH (☎ 071 581 4166)

BRIDGE, (Walter) John Blencowe; DL; s of Walter Bridge (d 1969), of Bury St Edmunds, Suffolk; *b* 8 March 1920; *Educ* Repton; *m* 1948, Susan Mary, da of Capt Robert Basil Wyndham Rushbrooke (d 1972), of Bury St Edmunds, Suffolk; 2 s, 1 da; *Career* former chm Greene King and Sons (brewers) 1979; *Style—* John Bridge, Esq, DL; Broom Hall, Bradfield St George, Bury St Edmunds, Suffolk IP30 0AY (☎ 028486 289)

BRIDGE, Prof John William; s of Harry Bridge (d 1985), of Crewkerne, Somerset, and Rebecca, *née* Lilley (d 1983); *b* 2 Feb 1937; *Educ* Crewkerne Sch Somerset, Univ of Bristol (LLB, LLM, PhD); *m* 28 July 1962, Janet Faith, da of Horace George Attew Hearn (d 1985), of Crewkerne, Somerset; 1 da (Susan b 1968); *Career* visiting prof and sr Fulbright scholar Coll of William and Mary 1977-78; Univ of Exeter: lectr then sr lectr 1961-74, prof of public law 1974-, dean faculty of law 1979-82, head of Dept of Law 1983-88; visiting prof: Univ of Connecticut 1985, Univ of Fribourg/Suisse 1990, Univ of Mauritius 1987; visiting fell All Souls Coll Oxford 1988-89; memb: Cncl of UK Nat Ctee for Comparative Law, Ed Bd Euro Law Review; pres Exeter Musical Soc 1983-88; memb Soc of Public Teachers of Law 1961; *Books* European Legislation (with E Freeman, 1975), Law and Institutions of the European Communities (with D Lasok, 4 edn 1987); *Recreations* singing in choirs, local history, gardening; *Style—* Prof John Bridge; 8 Pennsylvania Close, Exeter, Devon EX4 6DJ (☎ 0392 54576); Faculty of Law, University of Exeter, Amory Building, Rennes Drive, Exeter, Devon EX4 4RJ (☎ 0392 263370, fax 0392 263108, telex 42894 EXUNIV G)

BRIDGE, Nicholas Anthony; s of Herbert Charles Bridge, of Essex, and Josephine Maisie Evelyn, *née* Mackee (d 1974); *b* 16 Jan 1948; *Educ* Southend and Southchurch Hall HS; *m* 2 Sept 1972, Valerie Christine, da of Joseph James Smith (d 1990), of Leigh-on-Sea, Essex; 1 s (Andrew b 1975), 1 da (Lianne b 1977); *Career* dir: Alexander Howden Reinsurance Brokers Ltd 1985, Bain Clarkson Reinsurance Brokers Ltd 1990; *Recreations* angling; *Style—* Nicholas Bridge, Esq; 32 Glebelands, Benfleet, Essex SS7 4LT (☎ 0268 751944); 15 Minories, London EC3N 1NJ (fax 071 480 6137)

BRIDGE OF HARWICH, Baron (Life Peer UK 1980); Nigel Cyprian Bridge; PC (1975); s of Cdr Cyprian Dunscombe Charles Bridge, RN (d 1938); bro of Very Rev Antony Cyprian Bridge, Dean of Guildford, *qv*; *b* 26 Feb 1917; *Educ* Marlborough; *m* 1944, Margaret, da of Leonard Heseltine Swinbank, of Weybridge, Surrey; 1 s, 2 da; *Career* barr 1947-68, High Court judge 1968-75, Lord Justice of Appeal 1975-80, Lord of Appeal in Ordinary 1980-; chm Permanent Security Cmmn 1982-85; kt 1968; *Style—* The Rt Hon Lord Bridge of Harwich, PC; c/o House of Lords, London SW1

BRIDGEHOUSE, Edward; s of Joseph Bridgehouse (d 1965); *b* 19 May 1939; *Educ* Audenshaw GS; *m* 1, 1962, Brenda Elizabeth (d 1979); 1 s, 1 da; m 2, 1981, Muriel Winifred; *Career* CA; managing ptnr Boardman Woolrich 1964-89; co sec United Engineering Industries plc 1970-82, dir and co sec Br Thornton Industries Ltd 1983-89, owner Bridgehouse & Co 1990-; *Recreations* golf; *Style—* Edward Bridgehouse, Esq; Trefin, Hilda Road, Gee Cross, Hyde, Cheshire (☎ 061 368 3649)

BRIDGEMAN, Hon Charles Gerald Orlando; 2 s of 6 Earl of Bradford (d 1981), and Mary Willoughby, *née* Montgomery; *b* 25 June 1954; *Educ* Harrow, Univ of Warwick (BA), RAC Cirencester (MRAC); *m* 1982, Nicola Marie-Thérèse, only da of Brian Denyer Sales (d 1989), of Congleton; 2 s (James b 1978, Robert b 1983); *Career* landowner, rural surveyor; *Style—* The Hon Charles Bridgeman; Albion Hayes Farm, Bomere Heath, Shrewsbury, Shropshire (☎ 0939 290246)

BRIDGEMAN, Viscountess; (Victoria) Harriet Lucy; da of Ralph Merydith Turton, TD (d 1988), of Kildale Hall, Whitby, N Yorks, and Mary Blanche, *née* Chetwynd-Stapylton; *b* 30 March 1942; *Educ* St Mary's Sch Wantage, Trinity Coll Dublin (MA); *m* 10 Dec 1966, 3 Viscount Bridgeman, *qv*; 4 s; *Career* exec ed The Masters 1966-68; ed: Discovering Antiques 1970-72, series Going, Going, Gone Sunday Times Colour Magazine 1973; ed and dir The Bridgeman Art Library 1971-, author and ed of numerous books incl The Encyclopedia of Victoriana and Guide to Gardens of Europe; *Recreations* reading, work, family, travelling; *Style—* The Rt Hon the Viscountess Bridgeman; 19 Chepstow Rd, London W2 5BP (☎ 071 727 4065, fax 071 792 8509)

BRIDGEMAN, Hon Mrs Henry; Joan; da of late Hon Bernard Constable-Maxwell; *m* 1930, Col Hon Henry George Orlando Bridgeman, DSO, MC (d 1972); 2 s, 2 da; *Style—* The Hon Mrs Henry Bridgeman; 50 Lennox Gdns, London SW1

BRIDGEMAN, John Stuart; DL (Oxon 1989); s of James Alfred George Bridgeman (d 1961), of Whitchurch, Cardiff, and Edith Celia, *née* Watkins; *b* 5 Oct 1944; *Educ* Whitchurch Sch Cardiff, Univ Coll Swansea (BSc); *m* 1967, Lindy Jane, da of Sidney Wesley Fillmore, of Gidea Park, Essex; 3 da (Victoria b 1972, Philippa b 1974, Annabel b 1980); *Career* cmmnd TA 1978, QOY 1981-84, Maj REME (V) 1985-90; commercial dir Alcan (UK) Ltd 1977-80, vice pres (Europe) Alcan Basic Raw Materials 1978-82, divnl md Alcan Aluminium (UK) Ltd 1981-82, md Extrusion Div British Alcan Aluminium plc 1983-87, md British Alcan Enterprises 1987-; chm: Aluminium Corporation Ltd, Alcan Building Products Ltd, Alcan Ekco Packaging Ltd, British Alcan Conductor Ltd, British Alcan Consumer Products Ltd, British Alcan Extrusions Ltd, British Alcan Wire Ltd, Luxfer Holdings Ltd, Pentagon Radiator Ltd; memb: Magnesium Indust Cncl 1976-80, Cncl Aluminium Extruders Assoc 1982-, Bauxite Advsy Gp Aluminium Fedn (memb Cncl 1987-88, memb Educn Sub Ctee 1989-), British Airways Consumer Cncl 1978-, TAVRA Oxon and E Wessex 1985- (memb Employer Liaison Ctees 1987-); chm: Aluminium Extruders Assoc 1987-88, Banbury Business & Indust Gp 1984-, Enterprise Cherwell Ltd 1985-, Banbury & Dist Appeal for Katherine House Hospice 1986-; vice chm Heart of England Trg and Enterprise Cncl 1989-; FBIM; AMIPM; *Recreations* shooting, gardening, public affairs, education; *Clubs* Glamorgan County Cricket; *Style—* John Bridgeman, Esq, DL; British Alcan Aluminium plc, Enterprises Division, Southam Rd, Banbury, Oxon OX16 7SN (☎ 0295 264444, telex 83645)

BRIDGEMAN, 3 Viscount (UK 1929); Robin John Orlando Bridgeman; s of Brigadier Hon Geoffrey John Orlando Bridgeman, MC (d 1974, 2 s of 1 Viscount Bridgeman, sometime Home Sec & First Ld of the Admlty & gs of 2 Earl of Bradford), and Mary Meriel Gertrude (d 1974), da of Rt Hon Sir George Talbot, a High Court Judge and gs of John Chetwynd Talbot, QC (4 s of 2 Earl Talbot); suc his uncle, 2 Viscount 1982; *b* 5 Dec 1930; *Educ* Eton; *m* 10 Dec 1966, (Victoria) Harriet Lucy; 3 da of Ralph Meredyth Turton, TD (d 1988), of Kildale Hall, Whitby, by his w Mary Blanche, da of Brig-Gen Bryan Chetwynd Stapylton, CBE; 4 s (Hon William Caspar Orlando, Hon Luke Robinson Orlando b 1 May 1971, Hon Esmond Francis Ralph Orlando b 3 Oct 1974, Hon Orlando Henry Geoffrey b 11 April 1983); *Heir* s, Hon William Caspar Orlando b 15 Aug 1968; *Career* 2 Lt Rifle Bde 1950-51; CA 1958; ptnr Henderson Crosthwaite & Co Stockbrokers 1973-86; dir: Guinness Mahon & Co Ltd 1988-90, Nestor-BNA plc; tstee Hammersmith and Queen Charlotte's Special Health Authority; *Recreations* gardening, skiing, shooting, music; *Clubs* MCC, Beefsteak; *Style—* The Rt Hon the Viscount Bridgeman; 19 Chepstow Rd, London W2 5BP (☎ 071 727 4065); Watley House, Sparsholt, Winchester SO21 2LU (☎ 096 272 297)

BRIDGEMAN, Lady Serena Mary; da of 6 Earl of Bradford, TD, JP, DL (d 1981), and Mary, Countess of Bradford (d 1986); has reverted to maiden name of Bridgeman; *b* 1 July 1949; *Educ* Benenden; *m* 1978 (m dis 1989), Richard Arnold Andrew; *Style—* The Lady Serena Bridgeman; Flat 1, 3 Westgate Terrace, London SW10 9BT (☎ 071 373 9345); Dell House, Whitebridge, Inverness-shire IV1 2UP (☎ 045 63 278)

BRIDGER, David Wilson; s of Marcus Bridger, and Rosemary, *née* Wilson; *b* 15 Oct 1944; *Educ* Wy Ggeston Boys Sch, Univ of Bristol (BA); *m* 6 Jan 1968, Elizabeth Ann, da of Ernest Tapson; 1 s (Thomas Wilson b 6 Aug 1986), 2 da (Katherine Jane b 19 Sept 1982, Susanne Mary b 18 April 1985); *Career* accountant; Price Waterhouse: joined 1966, mangr 1972, ptnr 1978, ptnr i/c Euro Computer Security Div 1988-; auditing prize in ACA final exams; FCA 1970 (ACA 1969); *Recreations* church, watching sport; *Style—* David Bridger, Esq; Price Waterhouse, Milton Gate, 1 Moor Lane, London EC2Y 9PB (☎ 071 939 3000, fax 071 638 1358)

BRIDGER, Rev Canon Gordon Frederick; s of Dr John Dell Bridger (d 1955), and Hilda, *née* Piddington (d 1968); *b* 5 Feb 1932; *Educ* Christ's Hosp Horsham, Selwyn Coll Cambridge (BA, MA), Ridley Hall Cambridge; *m* 29 Sept 1962, Elizabeth Doris, da of Rev Canon Thomas Francis Cecil Bewes, of 10 Farm Lane, Chase Side, Southgate, London; 3 da (Rachel b 1963, Sarah b 1965, Mary b 1969); *Career* curate: Islington Parish Church 1956-60, Holy Sepulchre Church Cambridge 1960-62; vicar St Mary North End Fulham 1962-69, chaplain St Thomas's Episcopal Church Edinburgh 1969-76, rector Holy Trinity Church Heigham Norwich 1976-87, rural dean Norwich (south) 1981-86, examining chaplain to Bishop of Norwich 1981-86, hon canon Norwich Cathedral 1984-87 (emeritus 1988-), princ Oak Hill Theol Coll 1987-; memb Principal's Conf 1987-; *Books* The Man from Outside (1969), A Day that Changed the World (1975), A Bible Study Commentary (1985); *Recreations* music, sport, reading, walking; *Clubs* Christ's Hosp; *Style—* The Rev Canon Gordon Bridger; 10 Farm Lane, Chase Side, Southgate, London N14 4PP (☎ 081 441 7091); Oak Hill Theological College, Chase Side, Southgate, London N14 (☎ 081 449 0467)

BRIDGES, Alan James Stuart; *b* 28 Sept 1927; *Educ* Holt HS Shrewsbury, Rhyl GS, RADA London (Dip RADA); *m* 31 July 1954, Eileen Middleton, da of Ridgeway Proctor Morton Brown (d 1965), of Newcastle and London; 1 s (Adam Patrick Ridgeway b 1965), 1 da (Emma Ann b 1962); *Career* Army serv Capt; film, theatre and TV dir; work incl The Edwardians (West End), Ghosts (RSC), Come As You Are (West End), The Father (BBC TV), The Intrigue, The Idiot, Great Expectations, Les Miserables, Let's Murder Vivaldi, The Lie (BAFTA Award), Traitor (BAFTA Award), Crown Matrimonial (BAFTA Award), Saturday Sunday Monday; films incl: The Hireling (Gold Palm Cannes Film Festival 1973), The Return of the Soldier, Golden Globe (USA), Puddinhead Wilson, Displaced Person (Emmy Award, USA), The Shooting Party, Pig Robinson (TV film); *Recreations* reading, music, theatre, film and sport; *Clubs* Garrick; *Style—* Alan Bridges, Esq; The Old Manor Farm, Church Street, Sunbury-on-Thames, Middlesex TW16 6RG (☎ 0932 780166)

BRIDGES, Christopher Jeffrey; s of Jeffrey Israel Bridges, of 12 Carshalton Rd, Gwain Miskin, Beddau, and Jennifer Mary, *née* Jones; *b* 31 Aug 1968; *Educ* Llywncrwn Jr Sch Beddau, Bryncelynnog Comp Sch Beddau; *m* 17 Sept 1989, Sarah Louise, da of Carole Margaret John; 1 s (Daniel Christopher b 19 March 1990); *Career* Rugby Union scrum half Neath and Wales (4 caps); capt: Pontypridd under 15 1983, Welsh Youth 1986-87; memb: Wales under 19 tour NZ 1987, Wales under 20, Wales under 21, Wales B tour Canada 1989; Neath RFC record points scored 1988-89; Wales: debut v Namibia 1990 (2 test appearances), replacement v England 1991; *Recreations* cricket, golf; *Style—* Christopher Bridges, Esq; Neath RFC, Gnoll Park Rd, Neath, W Glamorgan

BRIDGES, Ian Scott; s of Joseph Edward Bridges, and Margaret Mackintosh, *née* McCarue; *b* 24 April 1947; *Educ* Lenzie Acad, Univ of Glasgow, Mackintosh Sch of Architecture (Dip Arch Glasgow); *m* 12 Nov 1976, June Margaret; *Career* architect; dir Ian Bridges (Architects); RIBA; ARIAS; *Clubs* Glasgow Arts; *Style—* Ian S Bridges, Esq; 13 Ruskin Terrace, Glasgow G12 8DY; 4 Royal Terrace, Glasgow G3 7NT (☎ 041 332 9838, car 0860 414000)

BRIDGES, Prof James Wilfrid; s of Wilfrid Edward Seymour Bridges, of Cuxton, nr Rochester, Kent, and Winifred Mary, *née* Cameron (d 1986); *b* 9 Aug 1938; *Educ* Bromley GS, King's College Univ of London (BSc), St Mary's Hosp Med Sch Univ of London (PhD); *m* 2 Feb 1962, Daphne, da of Langston Rose Hammond, of Exmouth, Devon; 1 s (Jonathan Michael b 15 April 1964), 1 da (Lynne Fiona b 3 April 1966); *Career* res asst St Mary's Hosp Med Sch Univ of London 1960-62 (lectr 1962-68), sr lectr and reader Univ of Surrey 1968-78; visiting prof: Univ of Texas 1973 and 1979, Univ of Rochester NY 1974; visiting sr scientist Nat Inst of Environmental Health Sciences USA 1976, founding dir Robens Inst of Industl and Environmental Health and Safety 1978-, prof of toxicology Univ of Surrey 1978-, dean Faculty of Sci Univ of Surrey 1988-; chm Br Toxicology Soc 1980-81, first pres Fedn of Euro Socs of Toxicology 1985-88, memb Exec Ctee of Euro Soc of Biochemical Pharmacology 1983-, fndr Euro Drug Metabolisms Workshops; memb: Veterinary Products Ctee (MAFF) 1982-, Advsy Ctee on Toxic Substances (HSE) 1986-89, Air Soil and Water Contaminants Ctee (DHSS, DOE) 1984-, UK Shadow GP on Toxicology (DHSS) 1984-, Watch Ctee (HSE) 1987-, Food Safety and Applied Res Consultative Ctee 1989-, Advsy Ctee on Irradiated and Novel Foods (MAFF) 1982-88, Maj Hazards Ctee (HSE) 1982-84; chm Food Policy Gp Inst of Biology 1990-; MRCPath 1984, CChem, FRSC, FIBiol, CBiol 1981, MInstEnvSci 1980, FRSA; *Books* Progress in Drug Metabolism (ed with Dr L Chasseaud, Vols 1-10); *Recreations* running, theatre going; *Style—* Prof James Bridges; Robens Institute of Industrial and Environmental Health and Safety, University of Surrey, Guildford, GU2 5XH (☎ 0483 509203, telex 859331)

BRIDGES, Hon Mark Thomas; er s and h of 2 Baron Bridges, GCMG, *qv*; *b* 25 July 1954; *Educ* Eton, Corpus Christi Coll Cambridge; *m* 1978, Angela Margaret, da of J L Collinson, of Mansfield, Notts; 3 da (Venetia Rachel Lucy b 1982, Camilla Frances Iona b 1985, Drusilla Katharine Anne b 1988); *Career* slr; dir Abinger Hall Estate Company 1984-, ptnr Farrer & Co 1985-; memb Cncl Royal Sch of Church Music 1989-; *Recreations* walking, sailing (yacht 'Bitter Sweet'), reading, music; *Clubs* Brooks's, House of Lords' Yacht; *Style—* The Hon Mark Bridges; 66 Lincoln's Inn

Fields, London WC2

BRIDGES, Dame Mary Patricia; DBE (1981); *m* 1951, Bertram Marsdin (d 1988); 1 s (1 da decd); *Career* dir Home Care Trust; tstee: Exmouth Lympstone Hospice Care, Exmouth Adventure Tst for Girls; fndr chm Exmouth Cncl of Voluntary Serv, county chm and nat vice chm; Royal Br Legion Womans Section: memb Central Ctee (NAT), Cons Pty worker, memb Exec St Loyes Coll Exeter, fndr pres Exmouth Ctee of Br Heart Fndn, pres The Abbeyfield (Exmouth) Soc Ltd; *Recreations* cricket; *Clubs* Exmouth CC, Retford CC; *Style—* Dame Mary Bridges, DBE; Walton House, 3 Fairfield Close, Exmouth, Devon EX8 2BN (☎ 0395 265317)

BRIDGES, Hon Nicholas Edward; yr s of 2 Baron Bridges, GCMG, *qv*; *b* 29 March 1956; *Educ* Eton, Univ of Bath (BSc, BArch); *m* 1985, Susan, da of Peter Guggenheim, of Woodbury Salterton, Devon; 1 s (Matthew b 1988), 1 da (Alice b 1986); *Career* architect, memb RIBA; *Style—* The Hon Nicholas Bridges; 103 Hemingford Rd, London N1 1BY

BRIDGES, Dr Paul Kenneth; TD (1977); s of Albert Charles Bridges (d 1955), of Stroud, Glos, and Alice Elizabeth, *née* Paul (d 1973); *b* 24 July 1931; *Educ* Marling Sch Stroud Glos, UCL, UCH (MB BS, MD, PhD, DPM, LRCP); *Career* RAMC 1957-60: Lt, Capt, Maj; sr psychiatric registrar KCH 1963-65, sr lectr in psychiatry The Royal Free Hosp 1965-70 (res fell and psychiatric registrar 1960-63), conslt psychiatrist Guy's Hosp 1970-, sr lectr in psychiatry UMDS Guy's and St Thomas' Hosp Unvi of London 1970-; conslt psychiatrist: The Geoffrey Knight Nat Unit for Affective Disorders, Regnl Neurosurgical and Neurological Units Brook Gen Hosp London, Bexley Hosp Kent; Liveryman Worshipful Soc of Apothecaries 1980, Freeman City of London 1986; memb BMA, FRSM 1961 (pres Section of Psychiatry 1983-84), memb Br Assoc for Psychopharmacology (hon treas 1974-79, hon sec 1981-83), MRCS, FRCPsych; *Books* Psychiatric Emergencies: Diagnosis and Management (1971), Psychiatry for Students (1989); *Recreations* visiting british country houses and classical sites abroad; *Clubs* Royal Automobile; *Style—* Dr Paul Bridges, TD; York Clinic, Guy's Hospital, London SE1 9RT (☎ 071 955 5000)

BRIDGES, Sir Phillip Rodney; CMG (1967); eldest s of Capt Sir Ernest Arthur Bridges (d 1953), of Bedford, and Agnes Ida, *née* Conyers; *b* 9 July 1922; *Educ* Bedford Sch; *m* 1, 1951 (m dis 1961), Rosemary Ann, da of late Rev Canon Arthur Herbert Streeten, MC, of Bury St Edmunds; 2 s, 1 da; m 2, 1962, Angela Mary, da of Frederick George Dearden, of Appledore, and wid of James Huyton; *Career* RA; served: UK, W Africa, India, Burma 1941-47; Capt, acting Maj TA (Beds Yeo) 1947-54; slr (England) 1951, barr (Gambia) 1954, slr gen Gambia 1961, QC (Gambia) 1964, attorney gen Gambia 1964, chief justice Gambia 1968-83; kt 1973; *Clubs* Travellers'; *Style—* Sir Phillip Bridges, CMG; Weavers, Coney Weston, Bury St Edmunds, Suffolk IP31 1HG (☎ 035 921 316)

BRIDGES, Captain Richard Antony Yeoward; RN; s of Antony Gifford Bridges (d 1976), of Bow Hall, Castletownsend, Co Cork, Ireland, and Margaret Champernoune Denny, *née* Townsend (d 1976); *b* 14 Nov 1942; *Educ* Gordonstoun; *m* 23 Jan 1976, Helen Macgregor, da of James Gardner Struthers (d 1979), of Ardmaddy Castle, by Oban, Argyll; 1 s (Tom b 1977), 1 da (Lucy b 1979); *Career* joined RN 1960, HMS Eastbourne Far East Fleet 1962-64, HMS London 1964, Lt 1965, flying trg 1965, gained wings and joined 848 Naval Air Sqdn seeing serv in Aden 1966, qualified as helicopter instr 1968, Lt Cdr HMS Endurance 1972, RN Staff Course 1974, CO Univ of Aberdeen RN Unit 1975, CO 845 Naval Air Sqdn 1977-78, Cdr 1982, SO Ops FOST 1980-82, desk offr MOD 1982, CO HMS Jupiter involved in evacuation of UK and foreign nationals from Aden 1986, Capt 1986, asst dir Central Staff MOD, CO HMS Intrepid 1988-90, RCDS 1991-; memb IISS 1976; *Recreations* equestrian (eventing), sailing, fishing; *Clubs* Farmers; *Style—* Capt Richard Bridges, RN; RCDS, Seaford House, Belgrave Square, London SW1X 8NS

BRIDGES, Hon Mrs (Susan Constance); da of 6 Baron Auckland (d 1941); *b* 5 Sept 1918; *m* 1 (m dis 1956), 1942, Jose Diaz de Rivera; 1 s; m 2, 1957, Guillermo Pakenham Bridges, OBE (d 1980), HM Hon Vice-Consul at Rio Grande, Argentina; *Style—* The Hon Mrs Bridges

BRIDGES, 2 Baron (UK 1957), of Headley, Co Surrey and of St Nicholas-at-Wade, Co Kent; Sir Thomas Edward Bridges; GCMG (1988, KCMG 1983, CMG 1975); s of 1 Baron Bridges, KG, GCB, GCVO, MC (d 1969), and Hon Katherine, da of 2 Baron Farrer (d 1986); *b* 27 Nov 1927; *Educ* Eton, New Coll Oxford (MA); *m* 1953, Rachel Mary, da of Sir Henry Bunbury, KCB (d 1968), of Ewell, Surrey; 2 s, 1 da; *Heir* s, Hon Mark Bridges; *Career* entered HM Foreign Serv 1951; served: Bonn, Berlin, Rio de Janiero, Athens, Moscow, Foreign Office; private sec (overseas affrs) to PM 1972-74, min (commercial) Washington 1975-79, dep sec FCO 1979-83, ambass to Italy 1983-87, ret 1987; memb: Select Ctee on Euro Communities House of Lords 1988-, Ind Bd The Securities Association Limited 1989-; *Style—* The Rt Hon the Lord Bridges, GCMG; 57 Church St Orford, Woodbridge, Suffolk 1P12 2NT

BRIDGES-ADAMS, (John) Nicholas William; s of William Bridges-Adams, CBE (d 1965), of Stratford-upon-Avon, and Marguerite Doris Wellsted (d 1963); *b* 16 Sept 1930; *Educ* Stowe, Oriel Coll Oxford (MA, DipEd); *m* 1962, Jenifer Celia Emily, da of David Hugh Sandell; *Career* cmmnd RA 1949, RAFVR 1951; called to the Bar Lincoln's Inn 1958 (Gray's Inn 1979); head of chambers 1979; memb: Exec Ctee Soc of Cons Lawyers 1967-69 (chm Criminal Law Sub Ctee 1983-86), House of Lords Reform Ctee 1982-; contested (C) West Bromwich West Oct 1974; govr St Benedicts Upper Sch 1980-83; memb: RIIA, IISS; FCIArb; *Recreations* shooting, sailing, skiing; *Clubs* Savile, Garrick; *Style—* Nicholas Bridges-Adams, Esq; Fornham Cottage, Fornham St Martin, Bury St Edmunds, Suffolk; 4 Verulam Buildings, Grays Inn, London WC1

BRIDGETT, John Alan Charles; s of Eric Bridgett (d 1987), of Rickmansworth, and Gwendoline, *née* Powell; *b* 13 Feb 1948; *Educ* Watford GS; *m* 28 June 1973, Christine Jennifer, da of Willen Arie Verkerk, of London; 1 s (Mark Peter John b 27 Oct 1969), 1 da (Claire b 2 May 1972); *Career* Br Movietone News 1965-68, Attos Film & TV Prodns 1968-84, BBC TV 1984-; BAFTA Sound Award Dubbing Ed for The Duty Men 1987; *Recreations* music, gardening; *Clubs* BBC; *Style—* John Bridgett, Esq; Chalklands, Bourne End, Bucks SL8 5TJ (☎ 06285 22336); BBC Film Dept, Ealing Studios, Ealing W5

BRIDGEWATER, Adrian Alexander; s of Maj Philip Alexander Clement Bridgewater (d 1980), of Southdown, Crease Lane, Tavistock, Devon, and Hon Ursula Vanda Maud Vivian (d 1984); *b* 24 July 1936; *Educ* Eton, Magdalene Coll Cambridge (BA); *m* 1, 11 April 1958 (m dis 1968), Charlotte, da of Rev Michael Ernest Christopher Pumphrey (d 1982); 1 s (Thomas Michael George b 12 Nov 1964), 2 da (Emma Mary b 23 Dec 1960, Sophy Charlotte b 31 July 1962); m 2, 7 Nov 1969, Lucy Le Breton, da of Sir Basil Bartlett, 2 Bt (d 1986); 1 s (Benjamin Hardington b 20 March 1979), 2 da (Nancy Le Breton b 10 Aug 1971, Daisy Maud b 27 Jan 1973); *Career* dir CRAC 1963-74; chm: Hobsons Press Ltd 1974-87, Hobsons Publishing PLC 1987-, Johansens Ltd 1987-; dir Papworth Industries 1989; memb Cncl: Inst for Manpower Studies 1966-67, Open Univ 1974-80, RCA 1979-81, Nat Inst Careers Education and Counselling 1966-, VSO 1980-82, Br Sch Osteopathy 1989-; govr Kings Coll Choir Sch Cambridge 1988-; *Recreations* walking, surfing, racing; *Clubs* Garrick; *Style—* Adrian Bridgewater, Esq; Manor Farm, Great Eversden, Cambs CB3 7HW (☎ 0223 263229); 9 Abbey Gardens, London NW8; Hobsons Publishing PLC, Bateman St, Cambridge CB2 1LZ (☎ 0223 354551)

BRIDGEWATER, Allan; *b* 26 Aug 1936; *Educ* Wyggeston GS Leicester; *m* Janet; 3 da; *Career* Norwich Union Insurance Group 1979-: dep gen mangr Norwich Union Fire Insurance Society Ltd 1983- (gen mangr 1984-89), dir Main Group Bds 1985, gp chief exec 1989-; dir Riggs A P Bank Ltd; chm Endeavour Trg, govr Norwich HS, pres Chartered Insur Inst 1989-90; *Style—* Allan Bridgewater, Esq; Norwich Union Insurance Group, PO Box 6, Surrey St, Norwich (☎ 0603 622200)

BRIDGEWATER, Geraldine Diana Noelle; da of William Reay Bridgewater, of London, and Sheila Rosemary, *née* Burke; *b* 26 Dec 1952; *Educ* Holland Park Comprehensive; *Career* first woman dealer on Floor London Metal Exchange (ring dealer) 1976, first women individual subscriber London Metal Exchange 1986, commodity broker; Freeman City of London; *Recreations* metaphysics, philosophy, alternative medicine, reading; *Clubs* CND, Greenpeace, UNICEF, Action Aid, Network: Financial Initiative; *Style—* Miss Geraldine Bridgewater; 48 New River Crescent, Palmers Green, London N13; London Metal Exchange, Plantation House, Fenchurst St, London EC3

BRIDGMAN, Peter Thomas; s of Thomas William Bridgman; *b* 11 Nov 1924; *m* 1950, Eileen Mary, da of Albert Alexander Free (d 1956); 4 s; *Career* Nat Serv WWII Sub-Lt RNVR Far East; accountant; md: Urwick Dynamics 1970-81, Urwick Orr & Ptnrs (mgmnt conslts) 1981-84; The Urwick Gp, Price Waterhouse 1984-86 (ret); *Recreations* gardening, golf, fishing, music; *Style—* Peter Bridgman, Esq; Baysham Cottage, Sellack, Ross-on-Wye, Herefordshire HR9 6QP (☎ 0989 64990)

BRIDGWATER, Arthur Brian; MBE (1971); s of Arthur John Bridgwater, OBE (d 1975), and Kathleen, *née* Burton (d 1950); *b* 20 Nov 1923; *Educ* Bristol GS, Univ of Bristol (BSc Eng); *m* 1949, Olive, da of William Edward Bracher (d 1929); 1 s (Nicholas b 1953), 1 da (Jennifer b 1956); *Career* Flt Lt RAFVR, coastal cmd 1941-45; chm London & South Eastern Section Fedn of Civil Engrg Contractors 1968; chartered civil engr, chm Bridgwater Bros Hldgs Ltd 1982-88; *Recreations* philately, geology, golf, calligraphy; *Clubs* RAC; *Style—* Brian Bridgwater, Esq, MBE; Merlin, Pleasure Pit Rd, Ashtead, Surrey KT21 1HR (☎ 0372 274 290)

BRIDGWATER, Prof John; s of Eric Bridgwater, of Solihull, and Mabel Mary, *née* Thornley; *b* 10 Jan 1938; *Educ* Solihull Sch, Univ of Cambridge (MA, PhD, ScD), Princeton Univ (MSE); *m* 29 Dec 1962, Diane, da of Arthur Edgarton Tucker (d 1965); 1 s (Eric Arthur b 1966), 1 da (Caroline Mary b 1967); *Career* chemical engr Courtaulds Ltd 1961-64; Univ of Cambridge 1964-71: demonstrator and lectr in chemical engrg, fell St Catharine's Coll; visiting assoc prof Univ of BC 1970-71; Univ of Oxford 1971-80: fell Balliol Coll (former fell Hertford Coll), lectr in engrg sci; dean Faculty of Engrg Univ of Birmingham 1989- (prof 1980-, head Sch of Chemical Engrg 1983-89); exec ed Chemical Engrg Sci 1983-; memb: Governing Body Solihull Sch, Cncl Inst of Chemical Engrs, Engrg Bd SERC 1986-89; FIChemE 1974, FEng 1987; *Recreations* running, Relate Marriage Guidance, travel; *Style—* Prof John Bridgwater; School of Chemical Engineering, University of Birmingham, Edgbaston, Birmingham B15 2TT, (☎ 021 414 5322, fax 021 414 5324)

BRIDPORT, 4 Viscount (UK 1868); Alexander Nelson Hood; also Baron Bridport (I 1794) and 7 Duke of Brontë in Sicily (cr 1799 by Ferdinand IV, the 'Lazzarone' King of the Two Sicilies, largely for Nelson's role in exterminating the Parthenopean Republic). In 1801 a Br Royal Licence was issued to Admiral Lord Nelson allowing him to accept for himself and his heirs the Dukedom of Brontë; s of 3 Viscount (d 1969, fourth in descent from the union of 2 Baron Bridport (2 s of 2 Viscount Hood) and Lady Charlotte Nelson, da of 1 Earl and niece of the great Admiral); *b* 17 March 1948; *Educ* Eton, Sorbonne; *m* 1, 1972 (m dis 1979), Linda Jacqueline, da of Lt-Col Vincent Rudolph Paravicini, of Nutley Manor, Basingstoke; 1 s; m 2, 1979, Mrs Nina Rindt; 1 s (Hon Anthony Nelson b 7 Jan 1983); *Heir* s, Hon Peregrine Alexander Nelson Hood; *Career* Kleinwort Benson Ltd 1967-80; Robert Fraser & Ptnrs 1980-83; exec dir Chase Manhattan Ltd 1983-85 (gen mangr 1985-86); dir Chase Manhattan Bank (Suisse); md Shearman Lehman Hutton Fin (Switzerland) 1986-; *Recreations* skiing, sailing; *Clubs* Brooks's; *Style—* The Rt Hon the Viscount Bridport; Villa Jonin, 1261 Le Muids, Vaud, Switzerland (☎ 022 66 17 05, fax 022 661898)

BRIEN, Alan; s of late Ernest Brien, and Isabella, *née* Patterson; *b* 12 March 1925; *Educ* Bede GS Sunderland, Jesus Coll Oxford (BA); 2 previous m; m 3, 1973, Jill Sheila, da of Patrick Graeme Tweedie, CBE (d 1990); *Career* served WWII Air Gunner RAF 1943-46; novelist and journlist; assoc ed Mini-Cinema 1950-52, courier 1952-53, film critic and columnist Truth 1953-54, TV critic The Observer 1954-55; film critic: New York Correspondent 1954-56, Evening Standard 1956-58; drama critic and features ed The Spectator 1958-61; columnist: Daily Mail 1958-62, Sunday Dispatch 1962-63, Spectator 1963-65, New Statesman 1966-72, Punch 1972-84; political columnist Sunday Pictorial 1963-64, film critic Sunday Times 1976-84 (diarist 1967-75); regular broadcaster: radio 1952-, TV 1955-; IPC Critic of the Year 1966 and 1967; *Books* Domes of Fortune (essays, 1979), Lenin: The Novel (1988), And When Rome Falls (1991); *Clubs* Garrick; *Style—* Alan Brien; 15 Marlborough Yard, Holloway Road London N19 4ND (☎ 071 281 9640); Blaen-y-Glyn, Pont Hyndwr, Llandrillo, Clwyd (☎ 0490 084 291)

BRIER, James Allan; s of James George Brier (d 1951), of Chesterfield, and Clara Annie, *née* Booth (d 1969); *b* 17 April 1925; *Educ* Chesterfield GS; *Career* WWII RN served coastal forces UK and Far East Sub Lt RNVSR 1943-46, Lt RNR 1962-72, Lt RNVR 1972-; CA, sr ptnr S E Short & Co; *Recreations* tennis, badminton, mountain walking, skiing, member of jazz band; *Clubs* Royal Over-seas League; *Style—* James Brier, Esq; S E Short & Co, Chartered Accountants, 6 Fairfield Rd, Chesterfield S40 4TP

BRIERLEY, Andrew Duncan; s of Dennis Brierley, of the Old Rectory, St Mark's Rd, Torquay, Devon, and Dorothy Lorna, *née* Turner; *b* 30 Sept 1961; *Educ* King Edward VI Macclesfield, Torquay Boys GS, Kingston Poly (LLB); *Career* called to the Bar Middle Temple 1984, crown prosecutor City of London 1986-87, private practice 1988-; nat vice chm Fedn of Cons Students 1984-85, memb Nat Union Exec Ctee Cons Pty 1984-88, dep chm Fulham Cons Assoc 1988-, Sec Nat Young Cons Tst Fund; *Clubs* Lansdowne; *Style—* Andrew Brierley, Esq; 6 Kings Bench Walk, Temple EC4Y (☎ 071 583 0410)

BRIERLEY, Hon Mrs (Caroline); *née* Gordon Walker; da of Baron Gordon-Walker, CH, PC (d 1980); *b* 22 Dec 1937; *Educ* Cheltenham Ladies Coll, Lady Margaret Hall Oxford (BA); *m* 23 April 1960, David Brierley, *qv*, s of John Brierley (d 1965), of Durban, South Africa; 1 da (Margaret b 1970); *Career* economist Int Sugar Cncl, Political and Economic Planning, head of Food and Services Unit Nat Economic Devpt Office, Henley Centre for Forecasting; *Books* Food Prices and The Common Market, The Making of European Policy, Textiles Industrial Review, Lifting Barriers to Trade, Work in the Countryside; *Recreations* travel, gardening; *Style—* The Hon Mrs Brierley; Old Farm, Harthall Lane, Kings Langley, Herts WD4 8JW (☎ 0923 262507); Henley Centre for Forecasting, 2-4 Tudor St, London EC4Y OAA (☎ 071 353 9961)

BRIERLEY, Christopher Wadsworth; CBE (1987); s of Eric Brierley (d 1978), and Edna Mary, *née* Lister (d 1980); *b* 1 June 1929; *Educ* Whitgift Middle Sch Croydon; *m* 1, 24 Aug 1951 (m dis), Dorothy, da of Jack Scott (d 1987); 2 da (Lesley Jeanne b

1956, Alison Jane b 1958); m 2, 20 Nov 1984, Dilwen Marie, da of John Morgan (d 1969); *Career* Nat Serv 1947-49, Sgt RAEC, serv UK and BAOR; chief accountant: EMI Records Ltd 1960-68, Br Gas E Midlands Region 1970-74; dir of fin: Br Gas Eastern Reg 1974-77, Br Gas Corp 1977-80; dir of econ planning Br Gas Corp 1980-82 (md 1982-87); dir: Br Gas Corp 1984-86, Br Gas plc 1986-90 (md resources and new business 1987-89); conslt World Bank; *Recreations* music; *Clubs* RAC; *Style*— Christopher W Brierley, Esq, CBE; 6 Stobarts Close, Knebworth, Herts SG3 6ND (☎ 0438 814 988)

BRIERLEY, David; s of John Paul Brierley (d 1965), of SA, and Ruth Mary, *née* Richmond; *b* 30 July 1936; *Educ* Hilton Coll SA, Univ of Natal, Oxford Univ (BA); *m* 23 April 1960, Caroline, *qv*, da of Baron Patrick Gordon Walker (Life Baron 1974, d 1980); 1 da (Margaret b 1970); *Career* teacher in France 1958-59, advertising 1960-75, author 1975-; *Books* Cold War (1979), Blood Group O (1980), Big Bear Little Bear (1981), Shooting Star (1983), Cjechmate (1984), Skorpion's Death (1985), Snowline (1986), One Lives One Dies (1987); *Style*— David Brierley, Esq; Old Farm, Harthall Lane, Kings Langley, Herts WD4 8JW (☎ 0923 262507)

BRIERLEY, David; CBE (1986); s of Ernest William Brierley (d 1982), of Romiley, Stockport, Cheshire, and Jessie, *née* Stanway; *b* 26 July 1936; *Educ* Stockport GS, Clare Coll Cambridge (MA, CertEd); *m* 7 Dec 1962, Ann, da of Charles Rossell Fosbrooke Potter; 2 s (Benedict b 1964, Crispin b 1966); *Career* teacher 1959-61; Royal Shakespeare Theatre: stage mangr 1961, gen stage mangr 1963, asst to the dir 1966, gen mangr 1968; *Recreations* reading; *Style*— David Brierley, Esq, CBE; The Chestnuts, Upper Quinton, Stratford-upon-Avon, Warwicks CV37 8SX (☎ 0789 720 423); Royal Shakespeare Theatre, Stratford-upon- Avon, Warwicks CV37 6BB (☎ 0789 296 655, fax 0789 294 810)

BRIERLEY, Ronald; OBE (1984), MM (1944), JP (Manchester 1961); s of Thomas Brierley, of Oldham, and Matilda, *née* Fothergill; *b* 31 July 1921; *Educ* Oldham HS; *m* 30 Aug 1950, Mary, da of Albert Edward Barlow; 1 s (Jonathan b 1 Oct 1954); *Career* Mil Serv Border Regt, RTR and SOE (despatches 3 times); Alliance Insurance 1938-48, started own broking firm 1948 (mergers ending in Lowndes Lambert Ltd), dep chm in indust 1969-71; Sedgwick Collins: joined 1971, dir North region, dep chm Sedgwick UK Ltd 1977, ret 1981; dir Manchester Science Park Ltd, gen cmmnr of Income Tax Altrincham, industl advsr Design Cncl; formerly: hon treas Manchester C of C, pres Manchester Jr C of C (and Nat Sec), Manchester luncheon club; lay memb: CA's Disciplinary Ctee, Gtr Manchester and Lancs Rent Assesment Ctee; fndr chm Gtr Manchester Outward Bound Assoc, treas Univ of Manchester 1983-88, memb Cncl and chm Fin Ctee St Ann's Hospice; memb Corp of Insur Brokers (sec 1950-58, chm 1962-64); IRBC: nat memb 1981-, memb Disciplinary Ctee, treas 1986, chm Cncl 1987-90; Hon LLD Manchester 1989; ACII; *Recreations* working, gardening; *Clubs* Lansdowne, Special Forces; *Style*— Ronald Brierley, Esq, OBE, MM, JP; 52 Trafford Road, Alderley Edge, Cheshire SK9 7DN (☎ 0625 585273)

BRIERLEY, Sir Zachry; CBE (1978, MBE 1969); s of late Zachry Brierley, of Rhos, and Nellie, *née* Ashworth; *b* 16 April 1920; *Educ* Rydal Sch Colwyn Bay N Wales; *m* 1946, Iris, da of Arnold Macara; 1 da; *Career* chm: Z Brierley Ltd 1972-90 (dir 1952-90, chm and md 1957-72), Australia Pty 1973-90; pres Z Brierley USA Inc 1972-90; memb: CBI Central Cncl 1970-82, Welsh Devpt Agency 1975-86, Design Cncl 1976-86, Nat Bdcasting Cncl Wales 1981-85; pres Cons Political Centre Wales 1981-89; chm: Small and Medium Firms Cmmn Union des Industries de la Communauté Européenne Brussels 1975-77, Wales Cons and Unionist Assoc 1982-86 (pres 1987-89); vice chm Mostyn Art Gallery 1979-85; kt 1987; *Recreations* philately, reading, sketching; *Clubs* Carlton; *Style*— Sir Zachry Brierley, CBE; West Point, Gloddaeth Ave, Llandudno, Gwynedd (☎ 0492 76970)

BRIERS, Nigel Edwin; s of Leonard Arthur Roger Briers, of 16 Biddle Rd, Littlethorpe, Leicester, and Evelyn, *née* Measures; *b* 15 Jan 1955; *Educ* Lutterworth GS, Borough Rd Coll (BEd); *m* 3 Sept 1977, Suzanne Mary Tudor; 2 s (Michael Edward Tudor b 25 March 1983, Andrew James Tudor b 30 June 1986); *Career* professional cricketer; Leicestershire CCC: debut 1971, awarded county cap 1981, vice capt 1988-89, capt 1990-, benefit 1990, 287 first class appearances, 13,120 first class runs; former capt: England young cricketers, England schoolboys, Br colls; youngest player to represent Leicestershire aged 16 1971, shares Leics record with Roger Tolchard for highest fifth wicket stand of 233 v Somerset 1979; winner's medal Benson & Hedges Cup 1985; advanced cricket coach, lectr in physical educn Leicester Poly 1980, head of physical educn and history teacher Ludgrove Sch Wokingham; *Recreations* watching Leicester Tigers, music, swimming, keep fit; *Style*— Nigel Briers, Esq; Leicestershire CCC, Grace Road, Leicester (☎ 0533 832128, fax 0533 440363)

BRIERS, Richard David; OBE (1989); s of Joseph Benjamin Briers (d 1980), and Morna Phyllis, *née* Richardson; *b* 14 Jan 1934; *Educ* Rokeby Prep Sch, Ridgeways Co-Educational Sch Wimbledon; *m* 24 Feb 1957, Ann Cuerton, da of Ronald Horace Davies (d 1980); 2 da (Katy Ann b 10 Aug 1963, Lucy Jane b 19 Aug 1967); *Career* Nat Serv with RAF 1951-53; actor on stage and television; *Style*— Richard Briers, Esq, OBE; c/o ICM Ltd, 388-396, Oxford St, London W1N 9HE (☎ 071 629 8080)

BRIGGS, Prof Anthony David Peach; s of Horace Briggs (d 1972), and Doris Lily, *née* Peach; *b* 4 March 1938; *Educ* King Edward VII Sch Sheffield, Trinity Hall Cambridge (BA, MA), Univ of London (PhD); *m* 28 July 1962, Pamela Anne, da of Harry Metcalfe, of Cookridge, Leeds; 1 s (Julian b 2 Jan 1974), 2 da (Fiona b 4 Nov 1966, Antonia 15 Aug 1970); *Career* Nat Serv 1956-58, trained as Russian interpreter CSC interpretership 1958; Univ of Bristol 1968-87: lectr in Russian, sr lectr, reader, head Russian Dept; prof of Russian language and lit Univ of Birmingham 1987-; memb Br Assoc for Soviet Slavonic and E Euro Studies; *Books* Mayakovsky, A Tragedy (1979), Alexander Pushkin: A Critical Study (1983), A Wicked Irony (Lermontov's A Hero of Our Time) (with Andrew Barratt, 1989), The Wild World (Pushkin, Nekrasov, Blok) (1990); *Recreations* Mozart, housebuilding and restoration, country walking with large dogs; *Style*— Prof Anthony Briggs; Over Moreton, Breach Hill, Nempnett Thrubwell, Chew Stoke, Bristol BS18 8YA (☎ 0761 62143); Dept of Russian Language & Literature, University of Birmingham, Edgbaston, Birmingham (☎ 021 414 6043)

BRIGGS, Baron (Life Peer UK 1976); Asa Briggs; o s of William Walker Briggs (d 1952), of Keighley, and Jane Briggs; *b* 7 May 1921; *Educ* Keighley GS, Sidney Sussex Coll Cambridge (BA), LSE (BSc); *m* 1955, Susan Anne, da of Donald Ivor Banwell (d 1980), of Keevil, Wilts; 2 s, 2 da; *Career* serv Intelligence Corps (Bletchley) 1942-45; historian and writer; prof of history Univ of Sussex 1961-76 (vice-chllr 1967-76), provost Worcester Coll Oxford 1976-; chm Cwlth of Learning 1988-; fell Br Acad; recipient: Marconi Medal, French Academy of Architecture's Medal for formation and teaching 1982; *Recreations* travel; *Clubs* Beefsteak, Oxford and Cambridge; *Style*— The Rt Hon the Lord Briggs; The Provost's Lodgings, Worcester College, Oxford (☎ 0865 278362); The Caprons, Keere St, Lewes, Sussex (☎ 0273 474704)

BRIGGS, Hon Daniel Nicholas; s of Rt Hon Lord Briggs of Lewes, *qv*; *b* 13 Dec 1958; *Educ* Lancing Coll, Univ of Bristol (BA); *m* 7 Oct 1989, Anabel E M, yst da of Harvey Ziegler, of Little Barsden, Chiddingfold, Surrey; *Career* co dir The Flower Corpn Ltd; *Publications* The Bristol Post Office in The Age of Rowland Hill (1984); *Style*— The Hon Daniel Briggs; 132 Bennerley Road, London SW11 6DY; Elms Gardens, Glaziers Lane, Normandy, Guildford GU3

BRIGGS, David Muir; s of Maj Brian Ridsdale Briggs (d 1966), of Allt-Grianach Lochearnhead, and Elizabeth Hope, *née* Greenlees (d 1946); *b* 18 June 1944; *Educ* Ardvreck Sch Crieff Perthshire, Loretto Sch Musselburgh Midlothian; *m* 5 July 1974, Julie Marilyn, da of Milton George Webber, of 10 Sortie Port, Castlecrag, Sydney, Australia; 1 s (Ian b 6 Jan 1979), 1 da (Alison b 15 Nov 1976); *Career* qualified CA 1967, Peat Marwick Mitchell (Paris) 1967-70, ptnr Messrs Turner Hutton & Lawson 1977-77; dir: GN Fund Management Ltd 1977-82, J Rothschild Investment Management Ltd 1982-84, Murray Johnstone Ltd 1987; auditor Gartocarn CC; *Recreations* fishing, golf, hill-walking, gardening, reading; *Clubs* Prestwick GC; *Style*— David Briggs, Esq; Claddoch, Gartocharn, Dunbartonshire, G83 8NQ (☎ 038 983 210); Murray Johnstone Ltd, 7 West Nile St, Glasgow (☎ 041 226 3131, fax 041 248 5420, telex 778667)

BRIGGS, Sir Geoffrey Gould; 2 s of late Rev C E Briggs, of Amersham, Bucks; *b* 6 May 1914; *Career* called to the Bar 1938; QC (Nigeria) 1955; former Puisne judge: Sarawak, N Borneo and Brunei; chief justice W Pacific 1962-65, Puisne judge Hong Kong 1965-73; chief justice: Hong Kong 1973-79, Brunei 1973-79; pres: Brunei Ct of Appeal 1979-87, Pensions Appeal Tbnls for England and Wales 1980-86; kt 1974; *Clubs* Wig & Pen; *Style*— Sir Geoffrey Briggs; 1 Farley Court, Melbury Rd, Kensington, London W14 8LJ (☎ 071 602 2541)

BRIGGS, Dr James Charles; s of Dering Thomas Briggs (d 1964), and Ivy Grace, *née* Muench; *b* 5 May 1933; *Educ* East Ham GS, St Thomas' Hosp Med Sch; *m* 14 Jan 1961, Waltraud Charlotte, da of Walter Schreck (d 1976), of Germany; 1 s (Robert James b 1963), 1 da (Nicola Charlotte d 1961); *Career* Nat Serv RAF 1951-53; lectr in clinical pathology St Thomas' Hosp 1960-66, conslt histopathologist Frenchay Hosp Bristol 1966-, clinical teacher in pathology Univ of Bristol 1966-; med referee City of Bristol 1985-; author of numerous pubns in jls; nat vice pres Hosp Conslts and Specialists Assoc, hon sec UK Melanoma Study Gp, fndr and coordinator UK Melanoma Histology Gp; memb: Int Acad of Pathology, Assoc of Clinical Pathologists; *Recreations* flying radio controlled model aircraft; *Style*— Dr James Briggs; 194 Stoke Lane, Bristol BS9 3RU (☎ 0272 681415); Dept of Pathology, Frenchay Hospital, Bristol BS16 1LE (☎ 0272 701212 ext 2766)

BRIGGS, John; s of John Briggs (d 1990), of Bolton, and Mabel, *née* Edwar; *b* 30 May 1933; *Educ* Stowe, Selwyn Coll Cambridge (MA, LLM); *m* 21 May 1960, Celia Rosalind, da of Henry Cecil Wild (d 1975), of Bury; 1 s (Paul Dudley John b 30 June 1964), 2 da (Nicola Rosalind b 6 July 1961, Angela Rosemary b 2 Aug 1965); *Career* admitted slr 1960, Notary Public 1965; princ: Claude Leatham & Co Wakefield, Brown Wilkin & Scott Wakefield, Owen & Briggs Huddersfield, Cartwright Cliffe & Co Huddersfield; past pres: Huddersfield Inc Law Soc, Union Discussion Soc, Huddersfield Borough Club; hon sec The Royal Soc of St George Huddersfield Branch; memb: Law Soc, Provincial Notaries Soc; *Recreations* fell walking, stock rearing (Blonde d'Aquitaine cattle and Texel sheep); *Clubs* Huddersfield Borough; *Style*— John Briggs, Esq; office: 13 Railway St, Huddersfield, W Yorks HD1 1JX (☎ 0484 519999, fax 0484 544099)

BRIGGS, (Frederick) John; s of Frederick John Briggs (d 1969), of Bournemouth, and Jessie Catherine, *née* Creighton; *b* 24 Oct 1923; *Educ* Christ Coll Finchley, William Hulme GS Manchester; *m* 1949, Margaret Jessie, da of Maj Percy Libbis Smout, MC (d 1960); 3 s (John, Norman, Stewart); *Career* served RAF 1942-46; chm: Manston Development Group Ltd 1978-81, Duckry Ltd 1980-, Wiljay plc 1981-84, Pavion International plc 1982-87, Bullers plc 1983-89; dep chm: Wheway plc 1984-, Reece plc 1986-; dir: Norcros plc 1966-83, Reading FC Ltd 1978-83, Bunzl plc 1978-88, Blagden Ind plc 1980-89, Tudor plc 1982-, Erskine House plc 1983-; memb BR Western Bd 1981-88; fndr pres World Packaging Orgn 1968-72; chm Organising Ctee: Pakex '77, Pakex '80, Pakex '83; memb: Cncl PIRA 1971-81, Euro Trade Ctee 1974-83; memb Ct and Liveryman: Worshipful Co of Tylers and Bricklayers 1954- (Master 1982-83), Worshipful Co of Marketors 1973-; FCIM (nat chm 1976, pres 1978-81), FInstPkg (nat chm 1970, pres 1972-81), CBIM (pres Reading Branch 1978-81, dir BIM Fndn 1980-83), FInstD, FRSA; *Recreations* tennis; *Clubs* Carlton, City Livery, RAF, MCC; *Style*— John Briggs, Esq; Huish Cross, Finchampstead, Berks RG11 3SU (☎ 0734 733156, fax 0734 733182)

BRIGGS, (Peter) John; s of Percy Briggs, CBE (d 1980), of Wansford, Peterborough, and Annie Maud (Topsy), *née* Folker; *b* 15 May 1928; *Educ* Kings Sch Peterborough, Balliol Coll Oxford (MA, BCL); *m* 24 July 1956, Sheila Phyllis, da of George Walton (d 1981), of Grimsby, Lincs; 1 s (Simon b 1963), 3 da (Ann b 1957, Abigail b 1960, Helen b 1961); *Career* RA and RAEC 1946-48, Warrant Offr; barr 1953-, dep circuit judge 1973, rec Crown Ct 1978-, chm Mersey Mental Health Review Tbnl 1979- (legal memb 1969, dep chm 1971-79); *Recreations* music, especially amateur operatics, golf; *Style*— John Briggs, Esq; Peel House, Harrington St, Liverpool L2 9XN (☎ 051 236 0718, fax 051 255 1085); Park Lodge, 107 Tarbock Rd, Huyton, Liverpool L36 5TD (☎ 051 489 2664)

BRIGGS, Raymond Redvers; s of Ernest Redvers Briggs, and Ethel, *née* Bowyer; *b* 18 Jan 1934; *Educ* Rutlish Sch Merton, Wimbledon Sch of Art, Slade Sch of Fine Art London Univ (DFA); *m* 1963, Jean Patricia (d 1973), da of Arthur Taprell Clark; *Career* book illustrator, designer, author; *Publications incl*: Father Christmas (1973), Fungus the Bogeyman (1977), The Snowman (1978), When the Wind Blows (book, radio play and stage play (1982-83)); *Clubs* Groucho's; *Style*— Raymond Briggs, Esq; Weston, Underhill Lane, Westmeston, nr Hassocks, Sussex

BRIGHAM, Peter; s of Arthur Peter Donald Brigham (d 1964), of Scarborough, and Florence Drusilla, *née* Robson (d 1973); *b* 4 Nov 1928; *Educ* Bootham Sch York, Univ of Liverpool; *m* 5 Sept 1953, Sheila Margaret, da of Henry John Riding (d 1971), of Ormskirk; 2 da (Catherine b 1957, Erica b 1960); *Career* lectr, former mgmnt conslt and architect; former conslt to OECD Paris; memb Nat Cncl Chartered Inst of Marketing; memb RIBA, MCIM, FCIOB; *Recreations* riding, travel, conservation of historic houses and gardens; *Style*— Peter Brigham, Esq; Redcliff, 9 Lower Park Road, Chester CH4 7BB (☎ 0224 679276)

BRIGHT, Andrew John; s of Joseph Henry Bright (d 1970), of Wells, Somerset, and Freda Madeleine Phyllis, *née* Cotton; *b* 12 April 1951; *Educ* Wells Cathedral Sch, UCL (LLB); *m* 3 Jan, 1976, Sally Elizabeth, da of Charles Carter, of Rochester, Kent; 2 s (Daniel b 1980, Charles b 1981); *Career* called to the Bar Middle Temple 1973, practised from the chambers of Louis Blom-Cooper QC 1974-86; in practice from chambers of H Michael Self QC 1986-; memb Criminal Bar Assoc; *Recreations* music; *Clubs* Chorleywood Round Table; *Style*— Andrew Bright, Esq; Gayfield, Loudhams Wood Lane, Chalfont St Giles, Bucks HP8 4AR (☎ 02404 2302); 4 Brick Court, Temple, London EC4 (☎ 071 583 8455)

BRIGHT, Brig Douglas Richard Lucas; OBE (1960); s of Maj Richard George Tyndall Bright, CMG (d 1944), of Arnewood Ct, Sway, Hants, and Murielle Dorothea, *née* Lucas-Tooth (d 1968); *b* 4 Sept 1918; *Educ* Eton, RMC Sandhurst; *m* 6 Nov 1948, (Charlotte) Rosemary, da of Hon Mr Justice P A Farrer Manby (d 1938), of Manorfield, Lower Pennington, Lymington, Hants; 1 s (Richard b 1954), 1 da (Rosamond b 1951); *Career* cmmnd 1938 Oxfordshire & Buckinghamshire LI; WWII serv: France, Belgium, India, Burma; subsequent serv: Far E, ME, USA, Kenya, Italy, UK; cmd Kenya Regt 1961-63, cmd 143 Inf Bde 1965-67, COS UK mil rep NATO 1967-69, ret 1971; chm Lymington RNLI Branch 1981-85, cdre Royal Lymington Yacht Club 1983-86; *Recreations* bird watching, natural history, sailing, field sports; *Clubs* Army & Navy, Royal Lymington Yacht; *Style*— Brig Douglas Bright, OBE; Willow Tree Cottage, Barnes Lane, Milford-on-Sea, Hants SO41 0RR

BRIGHT, Graham Frank James; MP (C) Luton South 1983-; s of late Robert Frank Bright, and Agnes Mary, *née* Graham; *b* 2 April 1942; *Educ* Hassenbrook Comp Sch, Thurrock Tech Coll; *m* 16 Dec 1972, Valerie, da of late Ernest Henry Wooliams; 1 s (Rupert b 1984); *Career* chm and md Dietary Foods Ltd 1977-; MP (C) Luton East 1979-83; PPS to: David Waddington, QC, MP and Patrick Mayhew, QC, MP, (Mins of State) Home Office March 1983 - June 1983, David Waddington, QC, MP, and Douglas Hurd, MP (Mins of State) Home Office June 1983 - July 1983, David Waddington, QC, MP, and Giles Shaw, MP, 1984-86, Earl of Caithness as paymaster gen July 1989- (at DOE Oct 1988 - July 1989), John Major (as Chllr and now PM) 1990-; dir Small Business Bureau Ltd 1989-; Parly candidate (C): Thurrock 1970 and 1973, Dartford 1974; memb: Thurrock Borough Cncl 1966-79, Essex CC 1967-70; sec back bench Cons Smaller Business Ctee 1979-80 (vice chm 1980-83), sec back bench Aviation Ctee 1980-83, memb Select Ctee on House of Commons Servs 1982-84, chm Cons Smaller Businesses Ctee 1983-84 and 1987-88, vice chm Cons Aviation Ctee 1983-85, sec back bench Food and Drink Sub Ctee 1983-85; introduced Private Members Bills: Video Recordings Act 1984, Entertainments (Increased Penalties) Act; jt sec Parly Aviation Gp 1984, vice chm Aviation Ctee 1987-88, nat vice chm Young Cons; *Recreations* gardening and golf; *Clubs* Carlton; *Style*— Graham Bright, Esq, MP; House of Commons, London SW1A 0AA (☎ 071 219 5156)

BRIGHT, Sir Keith; s of Ernest William Bright, and Lilian Mary Bright; *b* 30 Aug 1931; *Educ* Univ of London (BSc, PhD); *m* 1, 1959 (m dis), Patricia Anne; 1 s, 1 da; m 2, 1985, Margot Joan Norman; 1 da; *Career* former scientist, chm and co dir, gp chief exec Huntley & Palmer Foods until 1982; dir: Extel Gp Ltd, London & Continental Advertising Hldgs; formerly with: De La Rue (md of Formica), Hill Samuel, Sime Darby (Singapore trading house); chm and chief exec London Regnl Tport 1982-88, non-exec chm Thomas Goode & Co Ltd, chm Electrocomponents plc 1989-; FRSC, FCIT; kt 1987; *Style*— Sir Keith Bright; Electrocomponents plc, 21 Knightsbridge, London SW1X 7LY (☎ 071 245 1277)

BRIGHT, Michael John; s of John Thomas Bright (d 1984), and Alice Hearne; *b* 10 Aug 1944; *Educ* Bromley GS Kent; *m* 15 July 1967, Catherine Ellen, da of Clifford Brown (ret silversmith of Sheffield); 1 s (James Michael b 1972), 1 da (Victoria Jane b 1970); *Career* chief exec and md New Scotland Insurance Group plc, dep chm Independent Insurance Co Ltd 1988- (chief exec and md 1987-) dir Lambert Smith Hampton 1990-, dir and gen mangr Lombard Elizabethan Insurance Co plc (subsequently Lombard Continental Insurance plc) 1982-87, Orion Insurance Co Ltd 1967-82 (gp asst gen mangr 1980); memb: Lloyds of London, The Worshipful Co of Insurers; Freeman City of London; ACII; *Recreations* gardening, reading, holidays; *Clubs* MCC; *Style*— Michael J Bright, Esq; The Oasts, Biddenden Rd, Smarden, Kent (☎ 0233 77289); Independent Insurance Co Ltd, 12th Floor, Fountain House, 130 Fenchurch St, London, EC3M 5AU (☎ 071 623 8877, fax 071 283 8275)

BRIGHTMAN, Dr The Christopher Anthony John; s of Baron Brightman, PC (Life Peer), *qv*; *b* 18 March 1948; *Educ* Marlborough Coll, St John's Coll Cambridge, Middlesex Hosp (MA, MB BChir, MSc, MRC Path); *m* 1975, Elisabeth Justina, yr da of Jonkheer I R Willem Egbert Justinus de Beyer; 3 da (Louisa b 1978, Justina b 1980, Eugenie b 1982); *Career* medical practitioner and conslt bacteriologist The Public Health Laboratory Lincoln; memb BMA; *Recreations* woodwork, Tudor and Stuart history, egyptology; *Style*— Dr the Hon Christopher Brightman; c/o The Public Health Laboratory, The County Hospital, Lincoln, Lincs LN2 5RF

BRIGHTMAN, Baron (Life Peer UK 1982); John Anson Brightman; PC (1979); 2 s of William Henry Brightman (d 1951), of St Albans, Herts; *b* 20 June 1911; *Educ* Marlborough, St John's Coll Cambridge (MA, hon fellow 1982); *m* 1945, Roxane Gilda Hyacinth, da of Gerasimo Ambatielo (d 1958), of Cephalonia; 1 s (Hon Christopher, *qv*); *Career* served WWII Able Seaman MN 1939-40; Lt Cdr RNVR Mediterranean and Atlantic, asst naval attaché Ankara, staff SEAC 1940-46; barr Lincoln's Inn 1932, attorney-gen Duchy Lancaster and attorney and serjeant within Co Palatine of Lancaster 1969-70, high court judge (Chancery Div) 1970-79, judge Nat Industl Relations Court 1971-74, Lord Justice of Appeal 1979-82, Lord of Appeal in Ordinary 1982-86, QC 1961; govr Tancred's Fndn 1982-; kt 1970; *Recreations* sailing, skiing; *Style*— The Rt Hon the Lord Brightman, PC; Ibthorpe, Hants SP11 OBY

BRIGHTMORE, Neil James John; s of James Joseph Edmund Brightmore (d 1964), of Stoke-on-Trent, Staffs, and Ethel Lettice, *née* Goode, MBE (d 1986); *b* 21 Jan 1937; *Educ* The Lymes Sch, Newcastle-under-Lyme, Stoke-on-Trent Coll of Art; *m* 1, m 1961 (m dis), Sheila Charsley; 2 s (Adrian Neil b 1963, Roger Jason b 1967); m 2, 5 Sept 1979, Vivienne Brenda Margaret, da of John Anthony Augustus Ireson; 1 da (Verity Abigail b 1981); *Career* Nat Serv, RAF trained in photography; press photographer; BIPP Fellow of the Year 1985, Peter Grugeon Jubilee award 1985, Patrick Lichfield Portfolio award 1985, Nat BIPP Portrait Photographer of the Year 1985, Kodak Portrait Photographer 1986 and 1988; winner: Gold and Silver awards World Cncl of Professional Photographers 1989, World Travelling Exhibition three Kodak Gold awards 1989; 5 time winner Curzon Regnl BIPP Trophy; memb: Nat Cncl BIPP 1984-86, Qualification Bd RPS 1986-; chm: BIPP NW Regn 1987-88, Qualifications for the MPA; FBIPP 1985, FRPS 1986, FRSA 1987, FMPA 1988; *Style*— Neil Brightmore, Esq; Elm Tree House, Garden St, Penkhull, Stoke-on-Trent, Staffs (☎ 0782 621839); 25 Ironmarket, Newcastle, Stafs ST5 1RH (☎ 0782 621 839, fax 0782 611 957)

BRIGHTON, Wing Cdr Peter; s of Henry Charles Brighton (d 1983), and Ivy Irene, *née* Crane (d 1987); *b* 26 March 1933; *Educ* Wisbech GS, Univ of Reading (BSc), RAF Tech Coll (RAF pilot with special distinction), RAF Staff Coll; *m* 6 June 1959, (Anne) Maureen Lewis, da of Joseph Llewelyn Jones (d 1977); 1 s (Simon Peter b 1968, d 1970), 1 da (Amanda Jane b 1963); *Career* RAF 1955-71 (pilot 26 Sqdn, Engr Offr and Attache South Vietham, ret as Wing Cdr); md: Rockwell-Collins UK 1974-77, Plessey ME 1977-78, Cossor Electronics 1978-85; ops dir British Aerospace 1988 (divnl md 1985), dir gen Engrg Employers Fedn 1989-; pres Electronic Engrg Assoc 1984-85 (memb Cncl 1979-87); memb: Cncl British Aerospace Cos 1988, RoundTable (Watton, Norfolk & Wokingham, Berks); Freeman City of London 1989, Liveryman Worshipful Co of Coachmakers and Coach Harness Makers 1989, CEng 1967, FRAeS 1979 (AFRAeS 1962), CBIM 1982, FIEE 1983; *Recreations* flying, bridge, golf; *Clubs* Athenaeum, Royal Air Force; *Style*— Wing Cdr Peter Brighton; St Andrew's Cottage, Church Lane, Much Hadham, Hertfordshire SG10 6DH (☎ 0279 842309); Engineering Employers' Federation, Broadway House, Tothill St, London SW1H 9NR (☎ 071 222 7777, fax 071 222 2782)

BRIGHTWELL, Ann Elizabeth; *née* Packer; MBE (1965); da of Hector Frederick George Packer (d 1977), and Lilian Rosina, *née* Deacon; *b* 8 March 1942; *Educ* Moulsfield C of E Sch, Wallingford Co GS, Didcot Girls' GS, Dartford Coll of Physical Educn; *m* 19 Dec 1964, Robbie Ian Brightwell, s of William Stanley Brightwell; 3 s (Gary Scott b 6 Oct 1965, Ian Robert, *qv*, b 9 April 1968, David John b 7 Jan 1971); *Career* former international athlete; represented GB: long jump, 100m, 4 x 100m, 200m, 400m, 800m, 80m hurdles; achievements incl: Bronze medal 4 x 100m Euro Championships Belgrade 1962, Silver medal 4 x 100m Cwlth Games Perth Aust 1962, Gold medal 800m Olympic Games Tokyo 1964 (Silver 400m); records: world 800m 1964, Euro 400m 1964, first Br woman to win track Gold medal Olympic Games; former hockey player: Southern Cos, Berks, Leics; teacher: Lady Edridge GS South Norwood 1962-64, New Malden Girls' Sch Croydon 1964-65; *Recreations* jogging, gardening, cooking, watching sons play football for Manchester City; *Style*— Mrs Anne Brightwell, MBE

BRIGHTWELL, Ian Robert; s of Robbie Ian Brightwell, and Ann Elizabeth Brightwell, *qv*, *née* Packer; *b* 9 April 1968; *Educ* Westlands HS Congleton Cheshire; *Career* professional footballer; schoolboy player Cheshire, amateur Congleton Town; Manchester City 1985-: youth team 1985-86, professional 1986-, league debut v Wimbledon 1986, 0ver 150 appearances; England caps: 3 under 19, 4 under 21 1989-90 (2 goals); played in every outfield position Manchester City; honours: FA Youth Cup 1986, Central League 1987; Cheshire 800m youth champion 1984; *Recreations* golf, tennis, all sports; *Style*— Ian Brightwell, Esq; Manchester City FC, Maine Road, Moss Side, Manchester M14 7WN (☎ 061 226 1191)

BRIGHTY, (Anthony) David; CMG (1984), CVO (1985); s of C P J Brighty and Winifred, *née* Turner; *b* 7 Feb 1939; *Educ* Northgate GS Ipswich, Clare Coll Cambridge (BA); *m* 1, 1963 (m dis 1979), Diana Porteous; 2 s, 2 da; m 2, 1982, Jane Docherty; *Career* entered Foreign Office 1961, Brussels 1962-63, Havana 1964-66, FO 1968-69, resigned; joined S G Warburg & Co 1969, rejoined FCO 1971, Saigon 1973-74, UK Mission to UN NY 1975-78, RCDS 1979, head of Personnel Operations Dept FCO 1980-83, cnsllr Lisbon 1983-86; dir of private office of Sec Gen of NATO 1986-87, HM ambass to Cuba 1989-; res chm Civil Serv Selection Bd 1988; *Style*— David Brighty, Esq, CMG, CVO; c/o Foreign and Commonwealth Office, London SW1

BRIGINSHAW, Baron (Life Peer UK 1974); Richard William Briginshaw; *b* 1910; married; *Career* gen sec Nat Soc of Operative Printers, Graphical and Media Personnel 1951-75, memb Gen Cncl TUC 1965-75, memb ACAS 1974-76, former memb Br Nat Oil Corp; *Style*— The Rt Hon The Lord Briginshaw; House of Lords, SW1

BRIGNELL, Prof John Ernest; s of Patrick John Brignell, and Marjorie Beatrice, *née* Acock; *b* 13 July 1937; *Educ* Stationers' Company's Sch Hornsey, Univ of London (BSc, PhD); *m* 1 July 1965, Gillian, da of Harry Wright (d 1985), of Nether Wallop; 1 da (Penelope b 1971); *Career* student apprentice STC Ltd 1955-59; City Univ London: res asst Northampton Coll 1959-64, res fell and res tutor 1964-67, lectr 1967-70, reader in electronics 1970-80; Louis Newmark prof of industrial instrumentation Univ of Southampton 1985- (prof of electronics 1980-85); Goldsmiths travelling fell 1969: Grenoble, Gdansk, Geneva; Chm Broughton Cons Br; memb IOD, FIEE, FInstP, FInstMC, FRSA; *Books* Laboratory on-line computing (1975); *Recreations* fly-fishing, horticulture; *Clubs* Andover Cons, Romsey Fly-Fishers; *Style*— Prof John Brignell; Chalk Bank Cottage, Broughton, Stockbridge, Hants SO20 8AN (☎ 0794 301420); Department of Electronics and Computer Science, University of Southampton, Highfield, Southampton SO9 5NH (☎ 0703 593580, fax 0703 592865, car 0836 500982)

BRIGNELL, Roger John; *b* 24 Aug 1946; *Educ* Soham GS, Univ of Manchester (BSc); *Career* Phillips & Drew 1967-70, Fielding Newson Smith 1970-73, Rowe & Pitman 1973-79, md Eagle Star Pension Funds 1979-, dir Eagle Star Investment Management 1979-; *Style*— Roger Brignell, Esq; Eagle Star, 60 St Mary Ave, London EC3A 8JQ (☎ 071 929 1111, fax 071 283 2187)

BRIGSTOCKE, Alexander Julian (Sandy); DL (Surrey 1990); s of Major Arthur Montagu Brigstocke (d 1928), and Doris Mamie, *née* Butler (d 1982); *b* 11 Nov 1922; *Educ* Wellington, Univ of London (BA); *m* 14 Dec 1949, Diana Mavis, da of John Arundel Evershed (d 1984); 1 s (Timothy b 1951), 2 da (Jennifer b 1953, Juliet b 1962); *Career* WWII Capt Rifle Bde served N Africa, Italy 1941-45; jt headmaster Boxgrove Sch Guildford 1953-64; Surrey CC: elected 1970, vice chm Social Servs Ctee 1977-81, chm Planning 1981-85, vice chm Educn Ctee 1987-89, vice chm 1987-90, chm 1990-; memb Exec Cncl Assoc of CCs 1989-; chm: Guildford Cons Assoc 1978-81, Nat Tst Winkworth Arboretum Mgmnt Ctee 1981-89, W Surrey Centre Nat Tst 1985-89, Surrey Historic Bldgs Tst 1985-; govr: Kingston Poly, Guildford Coll of Technol, W Surrey Coll of Art and Design 1973-89; *Recreations* music, sport, travel; *Clubs* MCC, Surrey CCC; *Style*— Sandy Brigstocke, Esq, DL; Granton House, Shackleford, Godalming, Surrey GU8 6AX (☎ 0483 422545); County Hall, Kingston upon Thames (☎ 081 541 9009)

BRIGSTOCKE, Baroness (Life Peer UK 1990), of Kensington, in the Royal Borough of Kensington and Chelsea; Heather Renwick Brigstocke; Baroness (Life Peer 1990); da of Sqdn Ldr John Renwick Brown, DFC, and Mrs May Brown; *b* 2 Sept 1929; *Educ* Abbey Sch Reading, Girton Coll Cambridge; *m* 1952, Geoffrey Brigstocke (d 1974); 3 s, 1 da; *Career* classics mistress Francis Holland Sch (Graham Terrace), Godolphin & Latymer Sch; Latin teacher Nat Cathedral Sch Washington DC, headmistress Francis Holland (Clarence Gate) 1965-74, high mistress St Pauls' Girls' Sch 1974-89; former memb: Cncl of Middlesex Hosp Med, Cncl of the City Univ, Cncl of the Royal Holloway Coll; former memb Ctee Automobile Assoc; former tstee: Nat Gallery, Kennedy Meml Tst; former govr Wellington Coll; former Cncl of the Royal Soc of Arts; memb: Cncl London House for Overseas Graduates, Health Educn Authy, Programme Advsy Bd; govr: The Royal Ballet Sch, Museum of London; chm: Autistic Care and Trg Devpt Appeal, Tstees of Geffrye Museum, Thames LWT Telethon Tst; tstee City Technol Colls Tst, special advsr Burberry's, ind nat dir Bd of Times Newspapers Holdings, pres Bishop Creighton Sch Settlement Fulham; *Style*— Baroness Brigstocke; House of Lords, London SW1A 0PW

BRIGSTOCKE, Rear Adm John Richard; s of Canon G E Brigstocke (d 1971), and Mollie, *née* Sandford; *b* 30 July 1945; *Educ* Marlborough, Britannia Royal Naval Coll Dartmouth, Royal Naval Coll Greenwich, RCDS; *m* 21 April 1979, Heather, da of Dennis Day and Muriel Day, of Oxshott, Surrey; 2 s (Tom b 1981, Jamie b 1984); *Career* RN: joined 1962, Cdr 1977, Capt 1982, Rear Adm 1991; sea cmnds HMS: Upton 1970-71, Bacchante 1978-79, York and 3 Destroyer Sqdn 1986-87, Ark Royal 1989-90, Flag Offr 2 Flotilla 1991-; shore appts: MOD Naval Plans 1980-81 and 1982-84,, Capt Britannia RNC Dartmouth 1987-88; younger bro Trinity House; *Recreations* skiing, riding; *Style*— Capt John Brigstocke, RN; Ministry of Defence (c/o Naval Secretary), Old Admiralty Building, Spring Gardens, London SW1A 2BE

BRIGSTOCKE, Nicholas Owen; s of Mervyn Owen Brigstocke, 12 Deep Acres, Chesham Bois, Amersham, Bucks, and Janet Mary, *née* Singleton; *b* 25 June 1942; *Educ* Summerfields Oxford, Epsom Coll; *m* 17 May 1969, Carol Barbara, da of Air Marshal Sir Walter Philip George Pretty, CB, KBE (d 1975), 2 s (Marcus b 1973, Henry b 1981), 1 da (Lucinda b 1971); *Career* Shell Mex and BP Ltd 1961-69, de Zoete and Gorton Ltd 1969-78, ptnr de Zoete and Bevan Ltd 1978-86; Barclays de Zoete Wedd Securities Ltd: dir and head of UK equity sales 1986-89, md corporate broking 1987; dir de Zoete and Bevan Ltd 1991; *Recreations* tennis, cricket; *Clubs* MCC, City of London, Escorts SRC Twelve; *Style*— Nicholas Brigstocke, Esq;

Linchmere House, Linchmere, nr Haslemere, Surrey GU27 3NG (☎ 0428 722 134); Barclays De Zoete Wedd Ltd, Ebbgate House, 2 Swan Lane, London EC4R 3TS (☎ 071 623 2323, fax 071 956 3286, car 0860 telex 888221)

BRILL, John; s of late Eric William Brill, of Bramhall, Cheshire, and Barbara Brill; *b* 21 Aug 1935; *Educ* King's Sch Macclesfield, Jesus Coll Cambridge (MA); *m* 10 Sept 1960, Elizabeth, da of late David James Hughes-Morgan; 3 s (Timothy, Jonathon, James); *Career* nat serv RN 1956-59; mgmnt trainee and dep PR mangr Rank Organisation 1959-64, account exec London Press Exchange 1964-66, md Brian Dowling Ltd 1966-76; chm 1976-90: Sterling Public Relations, GCI Group, McAvoy Bayley; FIPR; *Recreations* golf, tennis; *Clubs* Savile; *Style—* John Brill, Esq; Rookhurst, Coast Hill Lane, Westcott, Dorking, Surrey (☎ (0306) 882344); GCI Sterling Public Relations, 1 Chelsea Manor Gardens, London SW3 5PN (☎ 071 351 2400, fax 071 352 6244)

BRIMACOMBE, Michael William; s of Lt-Col Winston Brimacombe, OBE, *qv*, of Marine Lodge, Cliff Rd, Livermead, Torquay, S Devon, and Marjorie Gertrude, *née* Ling; bro of Rodney J Brimacombe, *qv*; *b* 6 March 1944; *Educ* Kelly Coll Univ of London (LLB); *m* 8 April 1968, Pamela Jean, da of Charles Mark Stone, of Choisie, Mont Cochon, St Helier, Jersey, CI; 1 s (John Mark b 1969), 2 da (Ruth Michelle b 1972, Helen Marie-Anne b 1976); *Career* ptnr: Norman Allport & Co 1972-, Price Waterhouse (UK and Jersey) 1975-85; md Legal Tstees (Jersey) Ltd 1985-, non-exec dir The CI Knitwear Co Ltd trading as Pierre Sangan Int 1986; FID, FCA 1968, FRSA 1987; *Recreations* reading, travelling, walking; *Clubs* Royal Western YC of Eng; *Style—* Michael Brimacombe, Esq; Temple View, Rue des Marettes, Faldouet, St Martin, Jersey, Channel Islands (☎ 0534 51087); Norman Allport & Co, Hill Street Chambers, 6 Hill St, St Helier, Jersey C1 (☎ 0534 75544, fax 0534 78118, telex 4192123)

BRIMACOMBE, Rodney John; s of Lt-Col Winston Brimacombe, OBE, *qv*, of Marine Lodge, Cliff Rd, Livermead, Torquay, and Majorie Gertrude (*née* Ling); bro of Michael W Brimacombe, *qv*; *b* 22 Dec 1940; *Educ* Kelly Coll Tavistock; *m* 16 Nov 1968, Susan Jane, da of John Stredwick, of Burrow Cottage, Livermead, Torquay; 2 s (Simon Rodney b 28 Jan 1970, Justin John b 22 May 1972); *Career* gen mangr Pophams Ltd Plymouth 1964-69, md Jolly Ltd Bath 1970-72, gp asst md E Dingle Co Plymouth 1972-79, non-exec dir Westward TV Ltd 1979-81, dir and gen mangr sales and devpt Harrods Ltd 1979-86; chm Knightsbridge Gp 1985-86, md MOR Advertising Ltd 1989-; vice pres and cncllr French C of C 1986, sec 20 Club 1986, cncllr Plymouth C of C and Indust 1990; MIPA; *Recreations* sailing; *Clubs* Royal Western Yacht, Itchenor Sailing; *Style—* Rodney Brimacombe, Esq; The Penthouse, 25 Dolphin House, Sutton Harbour, Plymouth PL4 0DW (☎ 0752 222 852); MOR Advertising Ltd, 18 Addison Rd, North Hill, Plymouth PL4 8LL (☎ 0752 661643, fax 0752 667613)

BRIMACOMBE, Winston; OBE (1959); s of John Brimacombe (d 1947), of Penradden, Lifton, Devon, and Louisa Beatrice, *née* Tubb (d 1956); *b* 23 Dec 1908; *Educ* Dunheved Coll Launceston Cornwall; *m* 8 June 1935, Marjorie Gertrude, da of Herbert Stephen Ling (d 1955), of Leamington Spa; 3 s (Peter b 1936, Rodney b 1940, Michael b 1944, *qqv*); *Career* Army Serv 1940-45 (Lt-Col 1943); chm: Nat Savings Ctee Plymouth 1955-74, Commercial Union Assurance Gp Plymouth and Cornwall 1959-83, SW Regn and Nat Indust Ctees of Nat Savings 1960-74; memb and nat chm Assoc Retail Distributors Cncl 1958-82, gen cmmr Income Tax Plymouth 1970-85, chm and md E Dingle Gp 1954-76; founder memb Bd Westward TV 1961-80; chm: Chiesman Gp plc, Army & Navy Stores plc; Main Bd dir House of Fraser (90 stores in UK incl Harrods) 1971- (re 1981); life pres: E Dingle Gp Cos 1981-, Mayflower Tst Ltd; chm FH Dingle Tst Ltd; govr Kelly Coll Tavistock 1960-85; FRSA 1972; *Recreations* golf, gardening; *Clubs* Royal Western Yacht; *Style—* Winston Brimacombe, Esq, OBE; Marine Lodge, Cliff Road, Livermead, Torquay, Devon (☎ Torquay 24000)

BRIMBLECOMBE, Prof Frederic Stanley William; CBE (1975); s of Dr Stanley Leemore Brimblecombe (d 1963), of Stoke Sub Hamdon, Somerset, and Mary Noel, *née* Gill (d 1971); *b* 10 Sept 1919; *Educ* Blundells, St Mary's Hosp London (MD); *m* 25 Sept 1948, Esther Mary, da of Arthur James Stone, MBE (d 1942); 1 s (Nicholas William b 1950), 1 da (Sarah Lee b 1952); *Career* conslt paediatrician Royal Devon and Exeter Hosp 1954-79, WHO prof of paediatrics Univ of Khartoum 1968-72, hon prof of child health Univ of Exeter 1978-; visiting prof: Univ of Southern California, Univ of Baghdad, Univ of Basrah; examiner RCP 1965-81; external examiner: Univ of Liverpool, Univ of Manchester, Univ of Bristol, Univ of Khartoum, Univ of Baghdad; memb Cncl Nat Children's Bureau 1982-87, chm Children's Ctee DHSS 1978-81; pres: Devon and Exeter Med Soc 1984-85, League of Friends Exeter Hosp 1988-; hon memb Br Paediatric Assoc 1985-; FRCP (London 1962), DCH(Eng) 1950; *Books* Sick Children (1971), Children in Health and Disease (1978), Early Separation and Special Care Baby Units (1978), The Story of Honeylands (1988); *Recreations* classical music, cricket, golf; *Style—* Prof Frederic Brimblecombe, CBE; Coxes Farm, Clyst St Mary, Exeter EX5 1DN (☎ 0392 873633); Department of Child Health, Postgraduate Medical School, Royal Devon and Exeter Hospital (Wonford), Barrack Road, Exeter EX2 5DW (☎ 0392 411611, fax 0392 402390)

BRIMELOW, Baron (Life Peer UK 1976); Thomas Brimelow; GCMG (1975, KCMG 1968, CMG 1959), OBE (1954); s of William Brimelow (d 1951), of New Mills, Derbys, and Hannah, *née* Smith; *b* 25 Oct 1915; *Educ* New Mills GS, Oriel Coll Oxford; *m* 1945, Jean E, da of late John William Underwood Cull, of Glasgow; 2 da; *Career* FO 1938; cnsllr Washington 1960-63, min Br Embassy Moscow 1963-66, ambass to Poland 1966-69, dep under sec of state FCO 1969-73, perm under sec of state FO and head of Diplomatic Service 1973-75; MEP 1977-78; chm Occupational Pensions Bd 1978-82; *Style—* The Rt Hon the Lord Brimelow, GCMG, OBE; 12 West Hill Court, Millfield Lane, London N6 (☎ 081 340 8722)

BRIMS, Charles David; s of David Vaughan Brims, of Northumberland, and Eve Georgina Mary, *née* Barrett; *b* 5 May 1950; *Educ* Winchester, Brasenose Coll Oxford; *m* 1973, Patricia Catherine, da of John Desmond Henderson, of Berks; 2 s (David b 1980, Edward b 1982); *Career* dir: Courage (Western) Ltd 1980-83, Imperial Inns and Taverns Ltd 1983-86, Imperial Leisure and Retailing Ltd 1985-86; chief exec Portsmouth and Sunderland Newspapers plc 1986, chm Portsmouth News Shops Ltd-; govr Portsmouth Poly; *Recreations* cricket, tennis, golf, shooting; *Clubs* MCC, Vincent's Oxford; *Style—* Charles Brims, Esq; Pond House, Ramsdell, nr Basingstoke, Hants RG26 5PR; Buckton House, 37 Abingdon Rd, London W8 6AH (☎ 071 938 3039, fax 071 937 1479)

BRIMSON LEWIS, Stephen John; s of David Raymond Lewis (d 1969), and Doris Agnes, *née* West; *b* 15 Feb 1963; *Educ* The Barclay Sch Herts, The Hertfordshire Coll of Art and Design, The Central Sch of Art and Design (BA); *Career* theatre designer; designer: Once in a While the Odd Thing Happens (NT), Encounters (NT Studio) Young Writer's Festival 1991 (Royal Court); Costume designer: Bookends (West End), Vanilla (Lyric), Jeffrey Bernard is Unwell (Apollo), Mrs Klein (NT and West End), American Clock (NT), The Barber of Seville (Royal Opera House); set designer: Otello (Vienna State Opera), Turn of the Screw (Aust Opera); asst designer: Orpheus Descending (Haymarket), The Tempest (NT), A Winter's Tale (NT), Cymbeline (NT), New Year (Glyndebourne), The Threepenny Opera (NT); tv and film costume designer The Nightmare Years (TTN Cable US); exhibition Making Their Mark; memb Equity; *Style—* Stephen Brimson Lewis, Esq; c/o Stephen Hatton Management, 26 Danbury Street, Islington, London N1 8JU (☎ 071 359 3593)

BRINCKMAN, Hon Lady; (Greta) Sheira Bernadette; *née* Grant-Ferris; da of Baron Harvington, PC (Life Peer); *b* 1937; *m* 1, 1956, John Frederick Edward Trehearne; 1 s (Edward b 1963), 2 da (Lucinda b 1957, Petrina b 1959); m 2, 1970 (m dis), Christopher Mark Henry Murray; m 3, 1983, as his 2 w, Sir Theodore (George Roderick) Brinckman, Bt, *qv*; *Style—* The Hon Lady Brinckman; Somerford Keynes House, Cirencester, Glos GL7 6DN

BRINCKMAN, Sir Theodore (George Roderick); 6 Bt (UK 1831); s of Col Sir Roderick Brinckman, 5 Bt, DSO, MC, Grenadier Guards (d 1985), and his 1 w, Margaret Wilson (d 1977), da of Wilson Southam, of Ottawa, Canada; *b* 20 March 1932; *Educ* Millfield, Trinity Coll Sch Port Hope Ontario, ChCh Oxford, Trinity Coll Toronto Univ; *m* 1, 11 June 1958 (m dis 1983), Helen Mary Anne, da of late Arnold Elliot Cook, of Toronto, Canada; 2 s (Theodore, Nicholas), 1 da (Sophia); m 2, 1983, Hon (Greta) Sheira Bernadette Grant-Ferris, *qv*, da of Baron Harvington; *Heir* s, Theodore Jonathan Brinckman; *Career* publisher and antiquarian bookseller; *Clubs* White's, University (Toronto); *Style—* Sir Theodore Brinckman, Bt; Somerford Keynes House, Cirencester, Glos GL7 6DN (☎ 0285 861562); office (☎ 0285 860554)

BRIND, Bryony Jane Susan St John; da of Maj Roger Michael Atchley Brind, and Jenifer Mary St John, *née* Grey; *b* 27 May 1960; *Educ* Royal Ballet Sch White Lodge and Sr Sch; *Career* ballerina; Royal Ballet Co: joined 1978, soloist 1981, princ 1984; winner Prix de Lausanne 1977, winner Olivier Award 1981; repertory of major classical ballets and created roles during career; *Style—* Miss Bryony Brind; The Royal Opera House, Covent Garden, Floral St, London WC2 (☎ 071 240 1200)

BRIND, (Arthur) Henry; CMG (1973); o s of late Thomas Henry Brind, of Barry, and N W B Brind; *b* 4 July 1927; *Educ* St John's Coll Cambridge (MA); *m* 1954, Barbara, da of late George Frederick Harrison, of Bedford; 1 s, 1 da; *Career* HMOCS 1950-60; joined Dip Serv 1960; actg high cmmr Uganda 1972-73, high cmmr Mauritius 1974-77, ambass Somalia 1977-80, high cmmr Malawi 1983-87; *Clubs* Reform; *Style—* Henry Brind Esq, CMG; 20 Grove Terrace, London NW5 1PH (☎ 071 267 1190)

BRIND, Brigadier (ret) James Lindesay; DSO (1946); s of Gen Sir John Brind KCB, KBE, CMG, DSO (d 1954), and Dorothey Swire Frodsham (d 1924); descended from Walter Brind, prime warden of Goldsmith's Co (1820) and his s Gen Sir James Brind, GCB (1808-88) whose descendants were mostly Naval and Military; *b* 29 Aug 1909; *Educ* Wellington and RMA Sandhurst; *m* 21 Aug 1946, Evelyn Elizabeth, da of Stanley Lake Mann, of Leamington Spa (d 1972); 1 s (Christopher Markham b 1949); *Career* cmmnd Somerset LI 1929, Adj Depot Somerset LI (UK) 1936, Staff Coll Camberley 1943-44, staff and regimental offr France, Belgium and Holland 1944-45, CO 5 Wiltshire Regt Germany 1945-45, CO 4 Devonshire Regt Austria 1945-46, staff offr Sch of Infantry 1946-48, staff offr Middle East GHQ Egypt 1948-52, CO 1 Somerset LI Germany and Malaya 1952-55, bde cdr 159 TA Inf Bde UK 1955-58, Cdr Rhine Area Germany 1958-61, ret from regular Army 1961; appointed Ret Offr II i/c training areas East Midlands 1963-75; *Recreations* music, fishing, writing; *Clubs* Army and Navy, Pall Mall London; *Style—* Brigadier J L Brind, DSO; The Manor, East Markham, Newark, Notts NG22 0SA

BRINDLE, Hon Mrs (Joan Kathleen); *née* Davies; da of 1 Baron Darwen (d 1950); *b* 26 Oct 1917; *m* 1940, Walter Higham Brindle, MBE, TD, s of Walter Brindle, of St Annes-on-Sea; 1 s, 1 da; *Style—* The Hon Mrs Brindle; 27 Abbotsford Court, Colinton Road, Edinburgh EH10 5EH

BRINDLEY, Rev Canon Brian Dominick Frederick Titus; s of Frederick Benjamin Brindley (d 1973) of Wood Way, Bushey Heath, and Violet, *née* Williams (d 1975); *Educ* Stowe, Exeter Coll Oxford (BA, MA); *Career* ordained: deacon 1962, priest 1963; asst curate Clewer St Andrew 1962-67, parish priest Most Holy Trinity Reading 1967-89, pastoral sec Dio of Chichester 1989-, sec Chichester Diocesan Advsy Ctee 1989-, hon canon Christ Church Oxford 1986-89 (canon emeritus 1989-), proctor in convocation 1975-89; memb: Standing Ctee of Gen Synod 1980-89, Policy Sub Ctee 1980-85, (chm Business Sub-Ctee), Exec Ctee and Gen Cncl Church Union; former chm Church Literature Assoc and Soc of St Peter and St Paul; *Books* Porci Ante Margaritam (1954); *Recreations* cooking, garden design and history, bridge, opera, sacred music; *Clubs* Athenaeum; *Style—* The Rev Canon Brian Brindley; 9 Brunswick Square, Hove, E Sussex BN3 1EN (☎ 0273 29023); Flat 1, 17 Devonshire Place, Brighton BN2 1QA (☎ 0273 608 895)

BRINE, Roger Ernest William; s of Ernest Albert Brine, of Bexhill-on-sea, E Sussex, and Ivy, *née* Funnell; *b* 13 Nov 1943; *Educ* Purley GS; *m* 12 May 1973, Monica, da of Erich Bredenbrucher (d 1945), of Herdecke Germany; 1 s (Martin b 1974), 1 da (Katharine b 1977); *Career* admitted slr 1969; ptnr: Vallis and Struthers 1971-87, Amhurst Brown Colombotti 1988-; memb: Law Soc, City of Westminster Law Soc, Soc for Computers and Law, Sevenoaks Round Table 1974-84; *Style—* Roger Brine, Esq; 2 Duke St, St James's, London SW1Y 6BJ (☎ 071 930 2366, telex 261857, fax 071 930 225)

BRINK, Prof André Philippus; s of Daniel Brink, of Potchefstroom, South Africa, and Aletta Wilhelmina, *née* Wolmarans; *b* 29 May 1935; *Educ* Rhodes University (DLitt); *m* 1, 3 Oct 1959 (m dis 1965), Estelle, da of David Naudé (d 1950), of Durban; 1 s (Anton b 1962); m 2, 28 Nov 1965 (m dis 1966), Salomina Louw; 1 s (Gustav b 1966); m 3, 17 July 1970 (m dis 1987), Sophia Albertina Miller; 1 s (Daniel b 1971), 1 da (Sonja b 1973); *Career* Rhodes University: lectr 1961-73, sr lectr 1973-75, assoc prof 1976-79, prof 1980-; memb Dutch Soc of Letters 1964-, pres Afrikaans Writers' Giild 1980-82; D Litt Univ of the Witwatersrand 1986; Chevalier de la Legion d'Honneur France 1982, Officier de l'Ordre des Arts et des Lettres France 1987; *Books* An Instant in the Wind (1976), A Dry White Season (1979), A Chain of Voices (1982), States of Emergency (1988); *Style—* Prof André Brink; Rhodes University, Grahamstown, S Africa (☎ 0461 22023, fax 0461 25049)

BRINSMEAD, Barry Michael; s of Lt Cdr Alfred Charles Brinsmead RN (d 1965), and Gladys Ella, *née* Knight; *b* 13 Feb 1954; *Educ* Royal Hosp Sch Holbrook; *m* 20 July 1974, Deborah, da of Wing Cdr Owen Leslie Hardy, DFC, AFC, RAF; 1 s (Simon b 1980), 1 da (Jennifer b 1983); *Career* ptnr Hunt and Partners (Portsmouth, Chichester, IOW, Newbury, Bournemouth); dir Cawley Financial Services Ltd 1989; private pilot (PPL); FCA; *Style—* Barry Brinsmead, Esq; Park Farm Barn, East Street, Hambledon, Hants (☎ 070132 625); Holbrook Court, Northumberland Rd, Portsmouth (☎ 0705 815342, fax 0705 291019, telex 86475)

BRINTON, Michael Ashley Cecil; s of Maj Sir (Esme) Tatton Cecil Brinton, DL (d 1985), of Queen's Gate, London SW7, and his 1 wife Mary Elizabeth, *née* Fahnestock (d 1960); bro of C Topham C Brinton, *qv*; *b* 6 Oct 1941; *Educ* Eton, Vienna, Perugia, Aix-en-Provence; *m* 1966, Angela, da of John Ludlow, of High Wycombe; 2 s, 1 da; *Career* dir Brintons Ltd 1970- (mktg and sales dir 1988-); pres Confedn Int des Tapis et Tissus D'Ameublement; *Recreations* shooting, fishing; *Style—* Michael Brinton, Esq; Park Hall, nr Kidderminster, Worcs (☎ 0562 700268)

BRINTON, Timothy Denis (Tim); s of Dr Denis Hubert Brinton (d 1986) (whose mother was Dorothea, gda of Sir William Bowman, 1 Bt; the Dr's 1 cousins include late Sir Tatton Brinton and late Lady (Life Baroness) Stocks), and his 1 wife Joan Violet, *née* Hood (d 1971); *b* 24 Dec 1929; *Educ* Eton, Geneva Univ, Central Sch of Speech and Drama; *m* 1, 1954 (m dis), Jane-Mari, da of Air-Marshal Sir Arthur Coningham; 1 s, 3 da; m 2, 1965, Jeanne Frances Wedge; 2 da; *Career* 2 Lt Royal Scots (UK); broadcaster: BBC 1951-59, ITN 1959-62; media conslt, presenter and commentator, memb Kent CC 1974-81, MP (C) Gravesend 1979-87, memb Select Ctee Educn 1979-83, chm Cons Pty Media Cmmn 1983-87; memb Court London Univ 1979-; *Recreations* fishing; *Style—* Tim Brinton, Esq; Westwell House, Tenterden, Kent TN30 6TT (☎ 058 06 3030)

BRINTON, (Charles) Topham Cecil; s of Maj Sir (Esme) Tatton Cecil Brinton (d 1985), and Mary Elizabeth, *née* Fahnestock (d 1960); bro of Michael A C Brinton, *qv*; *b* 10 Sept 1939; *Educ* Eton, Brown Univ USA (BA); *m* 26 June 1965, Rosemary Anna, da of Alfred Peter Wilson, 2 da (Catharine Elizabeth b 18 Aug 1966, Annabelle Mary b 4 Feb 1968); *Career* Brintons Ltd: dir 1966, asst md 1977, vice chm 1978, chm 1981, chm and jt md 1988; memb Carpet Indust Trg Bd 1969-71; memb Jt Advsy Cncl for the Carpet Indust 1971-83: chm Dist Jt Cncl 1972-84, chm Nat Jt Cncl 1972-; pres Kidderminster and Dist C of C 1977-78, memb Br Carpet Mfr's Assoc Ltd 1978- (pres 1981-86); chm: Kidderminster Area Bd Young Enterprise 1981-83, Kidderminster Dist Carpet Mfrs and Spinners Assoc 1981-83 (tax cmmr 1983-); chm W Mids Region CBI 1986-88 (vice chm 1988-); Fell Royal Soc of Arts and Mfrs; *Recreations* squash, shooting, tennis; *Style—* Topham Brinton, Esq; Gothersley Hall, Stourton, Stourbridge, Worcs (☎ 0384 873974); Brintons Ltd, PO Box 16 Exchange St, Kidderminster, Worcs DY10 1AG (☎ 0562 820000, fax 0562 515597, car 0860 747934, telex 338586)

BRISBOURNE, Richard; OBE (1971); s of Percy George Brisbourne (d 1957), of Uttoxeter, Staffs, and Beatrice Mabel, *née* Smith (d 1969); *b* 8 June 1920; *Educ* Alleynes GS Uttoxeter; *m* 17 June 1942, Joan, da of William Henry Smith (d 1959), of Uttoxeter, Staffs; 2 s (Richard Paul b 19 Nov 1943, Giles b 20 July 1948); *Career* Lt Leics Yeo 1942-46, served NW Europe; chm: Africa Timber and Plywood 1961-70, Ghana Timber Assoc 1961-65, pres Nigeria Timber Fedn 1965-70; conslt on tropical timber industs (Ind) to World Bank, FAO etc 1970-79, advsr on forest concessions (Sarawak Govt) and timber industs 1979-80; Bucks CC rep Chalfont St Giles 1981- (vice chm Bucks CC 1989-), memb Thames Valley Police Authy; author: Sawmilling in the Tropics, Forest Development in Midwest Nigeria; Liveryman Worshipful Co of Loriners, Freeman City of London; *Recreations* golf, bridge, travel; *Clubs* Beaconsfield Golf; *Style—* Richard Brisbourne, OBE; c/o Lloyds Bank Plc, The Broadway, Wycombe End, Beaconfield, Bucks

BRISBY, John Constant Shannon McBurney; s of Michael Douglas James McBurney Brisby (d 1965), of London, and Liliana, *née* Daneva, *qv*; *b* 8 May 1956; *Educ* Westminster, Christ Church Oxford (MA); *m* 20 April 1985, Claire Alexandra Anne, da of Sir Donald Arthur Logan, KCMG, of 6 Thurloe St, London SW7; *Career* 2 Lt 5 Royal Inniskilling Dragoon Gds 1974, transferred Res 1975-77; called to the Bar Lincoln's Inn 1978; *Style—* John Brisby, Esq; 40 St Dunstan's Rd, Baron's Court, London; Stockings Farm, nr Helmdon, South Northamptonshire; 4 Stone Bldgs, Lincoln's Inn, London WC2A 3XT

BRISBY, Stephen James Michael; s of Michael Douglas James Brisby (d 1965), and Liliana, *née* Daneva; *b* 31 Dec 1950; *Educ* Westminster, Trinity Hall Cambridge (BA); *m* 26 Jan 1989, Fritze, da of Hans Ole Klingenberg; 1 s (Michael Douglas James b 12 Jan 1990); *Career* dir: J Henry Schroder Wagg & Co Ltd 1983-85 (joined 1971), Salomon Bros International Ltd 1985-88; vice chm UBS Phillips & Drew Securities Ltd 1988-; Freeman City of London, memb Worshipful Co of Blacksmiths; *Recreations* hunting, opera, music; *Style—* Stephen Brisby, Esq; UBS Phillips & Drew Ltd, 100 Liverpool St, London EC2M 2RH (☎ 071 901 4958, fax 071 901 2912)

BRISCO, Sir Donald Gilfrid; 8 Bt (GB 1782), JP (1967); s of Sir Hylton Musgrave Campbell Brisco, 7 Bt (d 1968); *b* 15 Sept 1920; *Educ* Wairapa Coll New Zealand; *m* 5 Aug 1945, Irene, o da of Henry John Gage, of Ermine Park, Brockworth, Glos; 3 da; *Heir* cousin, Campbell Howard Brisco b 1947; *Career* served WW II, pilot RNZAF and RAF; sheep farmer (ret); *Style—* Sir Donald Brisco, Bt, JP; PO Box 165, Havelock North, Hawke's Bay, New Zealand

BRISCOE, Prof Eric Merrington; OBE; s of William Merrington Briscoe (d 1961), of Shrewsbury, and Gertrude Violet, *née* Edwards (d 1963); *b* 15 Nov 1924; *Educ* Coalbrookdale County HS, UCL (BSc, county scholarship); *m* 24 March 1951, Honor Mary, da of Col Theodore Browning; 3 s (Simon Jeremy b 27 Dec 1951, Charles William b 6 April 1954, Nigel James b 18 Sept 1955); *Career* postgrad trg A Reyrolle 1945-47, devpt engr Elecrical Res Assoc 1947-50, chief res devpt engr Crompton Parkinson 1950-57, dir of devpt Mawson Taylor 1957-62; Doulton Group 1962-86: divnl dir Doulton Industl Porcelains 1962-68, fndr md Doulton Industl Products, md Doulton Insulators, divnl dir Doulton Engineering Group, dir Advanced Materials Engineering, chm Doulton Aerospace Inc (USA), chm Hopyard Foundries, chm Fairey Tecramics; proprietor Briscoe Assocs (consultancy) 1987-; chm: Ceramic Indust Certification Scheme 1989-, Staffordshire CBI, various govt ctees (DTI); ldr various export missions (DTI), pres Inst of Ceramics, memb Ct Univ of Keele; hon prof Univ of Sheffield 1989; FEng 1985, FIEE 1960, MIMechE 1960, FICeram 1985; *Recreations* sailing; *Clubs* Sloane, Br Pottery Mfrs; *Style—* Prof Eric Briscoe, OBE; Watersmeet, Fradley Junction, Alrewas, Nr Burton on Trent, Staffs DE13 7DN (☎ 0283 790256)

BRISCOE, (John) James; s and h of Sir John Leigh Charlton Briscoe, 4 Bt, DFC; *b* 15 July 1951; *Educ* Oratory Sch, UCL; *m* 1985, Felicity Mary, eldest da of D M Watkinson, of Gowthorpe Manor, Swardeston, nr Norwich, Norfolk; *Career* Newman Sumpter & Co Diss Norfolk; ACA 1978, FCA 1988; *Recreations* vintage cars, ocean racing; *Clubs* Royal Ocean Racing; *Style—* James Briscoe, Esq; 10 Hopgood St, London W12; Hall Barn, Swainsthorpe, nr Norwich, Norfolk NR14 8QA

BRISCOE, Dr John Hubert Daly; s of Dr Arnold Daly Briscoe, TD, of Seckford Lodge, Woodbridge, Suffolk, and Doris Winifred, *née* Nicholson (d 1985); *b* 19 March 1933; *Educ* Winchester, St John's Coll Cambridge, St Thomas's Hosp London (BA, MB BChir, MA); *m* 1 Feb 1958, Janet Anne, da of James Douglas Earlam (d 1958), of Bayfield, Warlingham, Surrey; 1 s (James b 1964), 4 da (Sarah b 1959, Emma b 1960, Lucy b 1961, Martha b 1967); *Career* MO Overseas Civil Serv Basutoland 1959-62, asst in gen practice Aldeburgh Suffolk 1963-65, princ in gen practice Eton Berkshire 1965-; MO: Eton Coll 1965-, St George's Sch Windsor Castle 1976-; apothecary to: HM Household Windsor, HM The Queen Mother's Household Royal Lodge 1986-; memb Windsor and Dist Med Soc 1965-, Hon MO The Gds Polo Club 1966-83, bridgemaster Baldwin's Bridge Tst Eton 1988, pres MOs of Schools Assoc 1989- (hon sec 1980-85); hon auditor Euro Union of Sch and Univ Health and Med 1981-89; Liveryman City of London 1966, asst Worshipful Soc of Apothecaries of London 1984- (apprentice 1952, Yeoman 1956, Liveryman 1966); DObstRCOG 1959, MRCGP 1968; *Recreations* growing vegetables; *Clubs* Omar Khayyam; *Style—* Dr John Briscoe; Eton Court House, Eton, Windsor, Berkshire SL4 6AQ

BRISCOE, Sir John Leigh Charlton; 4 Bt (UK 1910), of Bourn Hall, Bourn, Co of Cambridge, DFC (1945); s of Sir J Charlton Briscoe, 3 Bt (d 1960), of Lakenheath Hall, Suffolk; *b* 3 Dec 1911; *Educ* Harrow, Magdalen Coll Oxford (MA); *m* 1948, Teresa Mary Violet, da of Brig-Gen Sir Archibald Home, KCVO, CB, CMG, DSO; 2 s, 1 da; *Heir* s, James Briscoe; *Career* served RAFVR 1942-46; dir of aerodromes Miny of Aviation 1961-66, dir ops BAA 1966-73; ACA, FCIT; *Recreations* old cars; *Clubs* RAF, Royal Ocean Racing; *Style—* Sir John Briscoe, Bt, DFC; Little Acres, Stoke Poges, Bucks (☎ 02814 2394)

BRISE; *see*: Ruggles-Brise

BRISON, Ven William Stanley (Bill); s of William P Brison (d 1967), of Glen Rock, New Jersey, USA, and Marion, *née* Wilber (d 1953); *b* 20 Nov 1929; *Educ* Ridgewood New Jersey HS, Alfred Univ NY (BSc), Berkeley Divinity Sch New Haven Conn (now Berkeley with Yale Divinity Sch) (MDiv, STM); *m* 16 June 1951, Marguerite (Peggy), da of Leroy Nettleton; 2 s (Paul b 1958, Daniel b 1961), 2 da (Sarah b 1964, Martha b 1965); *Career* Active Serv US Marine Corps 1951-53, Capt; engr Norton Co Mass USA 1953-54, rector Christ Episcopal Church Bethany Conn USA 1957-69, archdeacon of New Haven Dio of Conn 1967-69, rector Emmanuel Episcopal Church Stamford Conn 1969-72, vicar Christ Church Davyhulme Dio of Manchester 1972-81, rector All Saints Newton Heath Manchester and area dean N Manchester Deanery 1981-85, archdeacon of Bolton 1985-; *Recreations* squash, gardening; *Style—* The Ven the Archdeacon of Bolton; 2 Myrrh St, Bolton BL1 8XE (☎ 0204 27269)

BRISTER, Graeme Roy; s of Royston George Brister, of Loughton, Essex, and Eileen Gladys Brister; *b* 5 May 1955; *Educ* Forest Sch Essex, Phillips Exeter Academy Exter New Hampshire USA, Brasenose Coll Oxford (MA); *m* 26 July 1986, Ashley Fiona, da of Frank Michael Ashley Hines (Wing Cdr RAF retd), of Welton, Lincolnshire; 1 da (Leander b 1988); *Career* slr 1979, ptnr Linklaters and Paines 1985-; memb Law Soc 1979; *Recreations* buying country houses, sport, travel, wine; *Style—* Graeme R Brister, Esq; 19 Denning Road, Hampstead, London, NW3 1ST (☎ 071 435 0626); Linklaters & Paines, Mitre House, 160 Aldersgate Street, London, EC1A 4LP (☎ 071 606 7080, fax 071 606 5113, telex 884 349)

BRISTER, William Arthur Francis; CB (1984); s of Gp Capt Arthur John Brister, OBE (d 1984), and Velda Mirandoli (d 1974); *b* 10 Feb 1925; *Educ* Douai Sch, Brasenose Coll Oxford (MA); *m* 1949, Mary, da of John Speakman (d 1936); 1 s (and 1 s decd), 1 da; *Career* asst govr class II HM Borstal Lowdham Grange 1949-52, asst princ Imperial Training Sch Wakefield 1952-55, asst govr HM Prison Parkhurst 1955-57; dep govr HM Prison: Camp Hill 1957-60, Manchester 1960-62; govr HM Borstal: Morton Hall 1962-67, Dover 1967-69; govr: II Prison Dept HQ 1969-71, HM Remand Centre Ashford 1971-73, I Prison Dept HQ 1973-75 (asst controller 1975-79); chief inspr of the Prison Service 1979-81, HM dep chief inspr of Prisons 1981-82, dep dir gen Prison Service 1982-85; Nuffield travelling fell Canada and Mexico 1966-67; memb Parole Bd 1986-90; memb Bd of Govrs: New Hall Sch 1986, Farnborough Hill Sch 1989-; *Recreations* shooting, music, venetian history; *Clubs* United Oxford & Cambridge University, English-Speaking Union; *Style—* William Brister, Esq, CB

BRISTOL, Archdeacon of; *see*: Balmforth, Ven Anthony James

BRISTOL, Bishop of 1985-; Rt Rev Barry Rogerson; s of Eric Rogerson (d 1986), and Olive Hooper; *b* 25 July 1936; *Educ* Magnus GS Newark Notts, Univ of Leeds (BA); *m* 1961, Olga May, da of Wilfred Gibson (d 1982); 2 da (Susan Claire b 1963, Deborah Jane b 1966); *Career* Nat Serv RAF 1955-57, Corpl; Midland Bank 1952-57; curate: St Hilda with St Thomas South Shields 1962-65, St Nicholas Bishopwearmouth 1965-67; lectr Lichfield Theol Coll 1967-71, vice princ Lichfield Theol Coll 1971-72, lectr Salisbury/Wells Theol Coll 1972-75, vicar St Thomas Wednesfield 1975-79, team rector Wednesfield Team 1979, bishop Wolverhampton dio of Lichfield 1979-85; chm Advsy Cncl for the Church's Min 1987-; *Recreations* cinema, stained glass, photography; *Clubs* Royal Cwlth Soc; *Style—* The Rt Rev the Lord Bishop of Bristol; Bishop's House, Clifton Hill, Clifton, Bristol BS8 1BW

BRISTOL, 7 Marquess of (UK 1826); (Frederick William) John Augustus Hervey; also Baron Hervey of Ickworth (E 1703), Earl of Bristol (GB 1714) and Earl Jermyn (UK 1826); Hereditary High Steward of the Liberty of St Edmund; patron of thirty livings; s of 6 Marquess of Bristol (d 1985), and his 1 w, Pauline Mary (now Mrs Edward G Lambton), da of late Herbert Coxton Bolton; *b* 15 Sept 1954; *Educ* Harrow, Univ of Neuchâtel Switzerland; *m* 1984, Francesca, formerly w of Phillip Jones, of USA, and da of Douglas H Fisher, of Marbella, Spain; *Heir* half-bro, Lord Nicholas Hervey; *Career* governing ptnr Jermyn Shipping; MInstD; *Recreations* horse racing, flying helicopters, snooker; *Clubs* Royal Thames Yacht, House of Lords Yacht, Travellers (Paris); *Style—* The Most Hon the Marquess of Bristol; Ickworth, Bury St Edmunds, Suffolk (☎ 028 488 285)

BRISTOL, Paul Lanfear Harold; s of Arnold Charles Verity Bristol (d 1984); *b* 10 Nov 1937; *Educ* Wellington; *m* 1968, Polly Elizabeth, da of Gen Sir George Watkin Eban James Erskine, GCB, KBE, DSO; 3 children; *Career* short serv cmmn King's Own Scottish Borderers; chief exec Brompton Holdings plc; *Recreations* work, reading; *Clubs* Buck's; *Style—* Paul Bristol, Esq; Chateau de la Rouagere, 03370, St Sauvier, France (70 07 01 38)

BRISTOL, Timothy Arnold Neil; s of Arnold Charles Verity Bristol (d 1984), of Wotton, Surrey, and Lillias Nina Maud, *née* Francis-Hawkins; *b* 21 Feb 1941; *Educ* Cranleigh Sch, Guildford Art Sch, RMA Sandhurst; *m* 7 Sept 1968, Elizabeth Olivia, da of John Gurney, *qv* of Walsingham Abbey, Norfolk; 2 s (Benjamin T F b 7 Nov 1972, Samuel F J b 3 Sept 1983), 1 da (Arabella F A b 19 Aug 1970); *Career* 1 Bn KSOB 1960-67, service in the Radfan, Borneo, S Arabia and Dhofar campaigns, seconded to the Sultan of Muscat's Forces 1966-67, ret as capt; diamond valuer De Beers, seconded to the Sierra Leone Govt Diamond Office 1967-70; publishing mangr Medici Society Ltd 1970-73, chm and chief exec Eastern Counties Printers and Publishing Gp 1972-85, dir Marlar International Ltd 1986-90, chief exec Sheffield International Ltd 1990-; *Recreations* riding, flying, travel; *Style—* Timothy Bristol, Esq; 14-18 Copthall Avenue, London EC2 7DJ (☎ 071 628 4208)

BRISTOL, Dowager Marchioness of; Yvonne Marie; *née* Sutton; only da of Anthony Sutton, of Woodstock, The Glen, Farnborough Park, Kent; *m* 1974, as his 3 w, 6 Marquess of Bristol (d 1985); 1 s (Lord Frederick b 19 Oct 1979), 2 da (Lady Victoria b 6 Oct 1976, Lady Isabella b 9 March 1982); *Style—* The Most Hon the Dowager Marchioness; Sun Tower, Square Beaumarchais, Monte Carlo, Principality of Monaco

BRISTOW, Alan Edgar; OBE (1966); *b* 3 Sept 1923; *Educ* Portsmouth GS; *m* 1945, Jean Catherine; 1 s, 1 da; *Career* chm: Bristow Helicopters Ltd 1953-85; Briway Transit Systems 1985-; FRAeS; Croix de Guerre; *Recreations* flying, shooting, sailing, farming, four-in-hand driving; *Style—* Alan Bristow Esq, OBE; Baynards Park Estate, Cranleigh, Surrey (☎ 0483 277170)

BRISTOW, Hon Mrs (Caroline Jean); da of 2 Baron Luke, KCVO, TD, JP, DL; *b* 25 Dec 1935; *m* 1958, James Bristow, *qv*; 3 s, 1 da; *Clubs* Sea View Yacht (IOW); *Style—* The Hon Mrs Bristow; Penmorfa, Sea View, IOW PO34 5HE (☎ 0983 613248)

BRISTOW, Eric John; MBE (1988); s of George Bristow, and Pamela Helen, *née* McEvoy; *b* 25 April 1957; *Educ* Hackney Down GS; *m* 2 Sept 1989, Jane Bristow, da of Leslie Higginbotham; *Career* darts player; World Masters champion 1977, 1979, 1981, 1983, 1984, N American Open champion 1979, 1983, 1984, 1986, World Professional champion 1980, 1981, 1984, 1985, 1986, World singles champion 1983,

1985, 1987, 1989, currently ranked world number 1; *Books* The Crafty Cockney (1985), Darts The Crafty Cockney Way (1986); *Recreations* golf; *Style—* Eric Bristow, Esq; c/o Dick Allix, McLeod Holden Enterprises Ltd, priory House, 1133 Hessle High Rd, Hull HU4 6SB (☎ 0482 565444, fax 0482 53635)

BRISTOW, (Sylla) Hazel; da of Kenneth Bernard Bristow (d 1976), and Sylla Mabel Florence, *née* Nash (d 1981); *b* 23 July 1932; *Educ* Oak Hall Haselmere Surrey, Tochter Institut Klosters Switzerland (German Dip), Univ of Geneva Switzerland (French Dip); *m* 12 Aug 1988, Ernst Gorge, s of Oskar Gorge (d 1931); *Career* head of PR Br Diabetic Assoc 1966-; charity rep on Examining Bd for CAM dip; Charity Forum: hon life memb, memb Cncl, former chm; judge Charity Annual Report and Accounts Awards; MIPR; *Recreations* tennis, bridge; *Style—* Ms Hazel Bristow; 15 Earls Terrace, London W8 6LP (☎ 071 602 6653); British Diabetic Assoc, 10 Queen Anne St, London W1M 0BD (☎ 071 323 1531, fax 071 637 3644)

BRISTOW, James; s of James Percy Bristow, of Aldeburgh; *b* 25 May 1934; *Educ* Oakham Sch; *m* 1958, Hon Caroline Jean, *qv*, da of 2 Baron Luke, KCVO, TD, JP, DL; 3 s, 1 da; *Career* High Sheriff Beds 1982-83; horologist; Queen's Silver Jubilee Medal; *Recreations* music, sailing; *Clubs* Seaview Yacht; *Style—* James Bristow Esq; Penmorfa, Sea View, Isle of Wight PO34 5HE (☎ 0983 613248)

BRISTOW, Kate; da of Kenneth James Bristow, of Hertfordshire, and Pauline Theresa, *née* Barrett (d 1990); *b* 11 March 1963; *Educ* Sacred Heart GS, St Dominic's Sixth Form Coll, New Coll Oxford (BA, MA, Volleyball half blue); partner JHE Griffith; *Career* advertising exec, graduate trainee and account exec Grandfield Rork Collins 1984-86, account supervisor Saatchi and Saatchi 1986-87, sr account mangr Gold Greenlees Trott 1987-89 memb Bd Leagas Shafron Davis Chick 1990- (account dir 1989-); *Recreations* keeping fit, eating and drinking well with friends; *Style—* Miss Kate Bristow; leagas Shafron Davis Chick, 1 Star Street, London W2 1QD (☎ 071 262 0874, fax 071 706 1549)

BRISTOW, Air Cdre Nicholas Roger Lyell; s of Edward Lyell Bristow (d 1949), of London, and Margaret Emily, *née* Ekin (d 1963); *b* 13 April 1924; *Educ* Wellington; *m* 29 July 1950, Una Claire Margaret, da of Sir Anthony Francis Vincent, 14 Bt (d 1936); 2 s (Robert b 1954, Edward b 1954), 2 da (Clare b 1951, Jane b 1953); *Career* RAF 1944-79, ret; *Recreations* riding, walking, garden, travel; *Clubs* RAF; *Style—* Air Cdre N R L Bristow, RAF

BRISTOW, Hon Sir Peter Henry Rowley; s of Walter Rowley Bristow (d 1947), of London, and Florence, *née* White; *b* 1 June 1913; *Educ* Eton, Trinity Coll Cambridge (MA); *m* 1, 1940, Josephine Noel (d 1969), da of Bertram Leney, of Wateringbury, Kent; 1 s, 1 da; m 2, 1975, Elsa, da of Edwin Reynolds (d 1949), of Warwick, and wid of H B Leney; *Career* served WWII Sqdn Ldr RAF; called to the Bar Middle Temple 1936, QC 1964, dep chm Hants QS 1964-70, judge of Courts of Appeal of Guernsey and Jersey 1965-70, judge of the High Court Queen's Bench Div 1970-85, presiding judge Western Circuit 1979-82; kt 1970; *Books* Judge for Yourself; *Recreations* fishing, gardening; *Style—* The Hon Sir Peter Bristow; The Folly, Membury, Axminster, Devon EX13 7AG

BRISTOW, Richard Lindsay; OBE (1984), VRD (1951); s of Percy Alfred Bristow (d 1963), and Emily Edith Lord, *née* Bernard (d 1934); *Educ* Radley, Christ's Coll Cambridge (MA); *m* 29 April 1939, (Jean) Elizabeth, da of Maj Harold Graham Paris, MC (ka 1918); 2 s (Alan b 1940, Brian b 1947), 3 da (Susan b 1943, Jean b 1948, Anne b 1957); *Career* RNVR 1939-62 (Cdr RNR 1957), joined RN Aux Serv 1962, ret 1971; dir various private companies; non-exec dir Folkestone and Dist Water Co 1976-84; JP Borough of Folkestone 1961-81 (chm of Bench 1977-81), chm Gen Cmmrs for Taxes Folkestone 1979-80, pres Cons Assoc Folkestone and Hythe 1988- (chm 1979-81), pres Euro Cons Constituency Cncl E Kent 1988-; govr Dover Coll, former chm Folkestone Girls GS (presently Folkestone Sch for Girls); *Recreations* cricket, bridge, politics, gardening, walking; *Clubs* Naval; *Style—* Richard Bristow, Esq, OBE, VRD, JP

BRITTAIN, Clive Edward; s of Edward John Brittain (d 1948), of Calne, Wilts, and Priscilla Rosalind, *née* Winzer (d 1990); *b* 15 Dec 1933; *Educ* Calne Secdy Mod Sch; *m* 23 Feb 1957, Maureen Helen, da of Percy Russell Robinson (d 1987); *Career* Nat Serv 1954-56; racehorse trainer 1972-; won 1000 Gns 1984, Eclipse Stakes, Dubai Champion Stakes and Breeders Cup Turf USA 1985 with Pebbles, won Japan Cup Tokyo 1986 with Jupiter Island, won St Leger 1988 with Julio Mariner; *Recreations* shooting; *Clubs* Jockey Club Rooms; *Style—* Clive Brittain, Esq; Carlburg, 49 Bury Rd, Newmarket, Suffolk CB8 7BY (☎ 0638 663739); Carlburg Stables, 49 Bury Road, Newmarket, Suffolk CB8 7BY (☎ 0638 664347, fax 0638 661744, car 0860 327118)

BRITTAIN, Dr John; s of Patrick Brittain (d 1962), of Warlingham, Surrey, and Anne, *née* Daly (d 1965); *b* 25 May 1923; *Educ* Slough GS, St Mary's Hosp and Univ of London (MB BS); *m* 29 Oct 1955, Sheila Farnham, da of Albert George Wick (d 1961), of E Sheen; 2 s (Paul John b 1956, Jonathan b 1961), 1 da (Wendy Frances b 1958); *Career* RCS transferred RAMC Res; gen practice 1954-78, chief med offr Fred Olsen Shipping 1974-, attending physician Sus Allen Memorial Hosp Eldorado Kansas USA 1977; med advsr: Laporte Fluorides 1984, Wendstone Chemicals (Laporte) 1985-88, Laporte Industs R & D Div 1988, Laporte Interox 1988; memb: Sub Ctee Gen Cncl for Shipping Code of Practice Hygiene of Food and Fresh Water Supplies in Passenger Ships 1979, Comité Technique Européan Du Fluor 1987-; Freeman Worshipful Soc of Apothecaries (Liveryman 1963); MRCS, LRCP, AFOM, DIH, FRSM; memb: Medical Soc of London, BMA, Br Toxicology Soc, Soc Occupational Medicine; *Recreations* golf, reading; *Clubs* Savile, RSM, Tandridge Golf; *Style—* Dr John Brittain; Research Division, Laporte Industries, P O Box 2, Moorfield Rd, Widnes, Cheshire WA8 0JU (☎ 051 495 2222,ext 2425, fax 051 420 4089, tel 82221)

BRITTAIN, Nicholas John; s of Denis Jack Brittain, MBE (d 1977), of Hungerford, Berks, and Irene Jane Williams (d 1945); *b* 8 Sept 1938; *Educ* Lord Wandsworth Coll, Jesus Coll Oxford (MA); *m* 1964, Patricia Mary, da of Alan Francis John Hopewell (d 1957); 1 s (James b 1969), 2 da (Charlotte b 1971, Rebecca b 1973); *Career* Unilever plc 1960-82, head of gp fin and dir of various subsid cos Legal and General plc 1983-86, chief accountant Barclays plc and Barclays Bank plc 1986-, chm Limebank Property Co Ltd and Bardco Property Investmts Ltd 1986-; pres SW Surrey Cons Political Centre 1988- (chm 1984-87), govr Alexandra Tst 1980-, dir Fullemploy Gp; memb: Cncl GP and Educn Ctee CACA 1988-, Mgmnt Ctee Providence Row Housing Assoc (chm Fin Ctee 1986-); chm Accounting Ctee Br Bankers Assoc 1987-; FCCA; *Recreations* politics, singing, cricket, gardening; *Clubs* Cannons, Brook CC, Privateers CC, 59, Warbrook Ward; *Style—* Nicholas J Brittain, Esq; Churchfields, Church Lane, Witley, Godalming, Surrey GU8 5PP; Barclays Bank plc, Johnson Smirke Building, 4, Royal Mint Court, London EC3N 4AJ (☎ 071 626 1567)

BRITTAIN, Peter John; s of John Arthur Brittain, of 76 Norfolk Road, Erdington, Birmingham, and Joyce Barbara, *née* Dayman; *b* 29 June 1952; *Educ* King Edward's GS Birmingham; *m* 15 Sept 1984, Sally, da of David Hamilton Jacob, of 3 Dunchurch Close, Balsall Common, Coventry; 2 da (Samantha, Stephanie); *Career* CA 1978-; Hacker Young Chartered Accountants Birmingham; memb Birmingham Chamber of Commerce; FCA 1975; *Recreations* sports generally, stamp collecting; *Clubs* Birmingham Welsh RFC; *Style—* Peter Brittain, Esq; 43 Vesey Road, Wylde Green, Sutton Coldfield, West Midlands (☎ 021 355 3217); 18th Floor, Metropolitan House, 1 Hagley Road, Birmingham (☎ 021 456 4010, fax 021 456 3842)

BRITTAN, Rt Hon Sir Leon; PC (1981), QC (1978); s of Dr Joseph Brittan, and Rebecca, *née* Lipetz; yr bro of Samuel Brittan *qv*; *b* 25 Sept 1939; *Educ* Haberdashers' Aske's, Trinity Coll Cambridge (MA), Yale Univ; *m* 1980, Diana Peterson; *Career* called to the Bar Inner Temple 1962, bencher 1983; chm Bow Gp 1964-65; editor Crossbow 1966-68; Parly candidate (C) Kensington N 1966 and 1970; MP (C): Cleveland and Whitby Feb 1974-83, Richmond Yorks 1983-88; oppn spokesman: Devolution 1976-79, House of Commons Affrs 1976-78, Employment 1978-79; min of state Home Office 1979-81, chief sec to Treasy 1981-83, sec of state for the Home Dept 1983-85; sec of state for Trade and Indust 1985-86; chm Soc of Cons Lawyers 1986-88, vice pres Cmmn of Euro Communities 1989-; kt 1989; *Clubs* Carlton, MCC; *Style—* The Rt Hon Sir Leon Brittan, QC; Commission of European Communities, Rue de la Loi, 200, 1049 Brussels, Belgium

BRITTAN, Samuel; s of Dr Joseph Brittan and Rebecca, *née* Lipetz; er bro of Rt Hon Sir Leon Brittan, QC, *qv*; *b* 29 Dec 1933; *Educ* Kilburn GS, Jesus Coll Cambridge; *Career* with Financial Times 1955-61, economics ed Observer 1961-64, advsr Dept of Econ Affairs 1965, princ econ commentator Financial Times 1966-, asst ed Financial Times 1978-, visiting fell Nuffield Coll 1974, visiting prof Chicago Law Sch 1978; hon prof of politics Univ of Warwick 1987-, hon fell Jesus Coll Cambridge 1988-; memb: Peacock Ctee on the Finance of the BBC 1985-86; awards: Wincott Prize for Financial Journalism 1971, George Orwell Prize for 1980, Ludwig Erhard Prize for Econ Writing 1988; Hon DLitt Heriot Watt Univ 1985; *Books* Left or Right: The Bogus Dilemma (1968), The Price of Economic Freedom: A Guide to Flexible Rates (1970), Steering the Economy (1971), Is There an Economic Consensus? (1973), Capitalism and the New Permissive Society (1973, revised edn 1988) The Delusion of Incomes Policy (with Peter Lilley, 1977), The Economic Consequences of Democracy (1977), The Role and Limits of Government: Essays in Political Economy (1983), A Restatment of Economic Liberalism (revised edn, 1988); *Style—* Samuel Brittan, Esq; The Financial Times, Number One, Southwark Bridge, London SE1 9HL (☎ 071 873 3000)

BRITTEN, Alan Edward Marsh; s of Robert Harry Marsh Britten (d 1987), and Helen Marjorie, *née* Goldson; *b* 26 Feb 1938; *Educ* Radley, Emmanuel Coll Cambridge (MA), Williams Coll Massachusetts, Princeton Univ NJ USA; *m* 23 Sept 1967, Judith Clare, da of Cdr Anthony Charles Akerman, OBE, DSC, RN, of Edinburgh; 2 da (Tamara b 22 July 1970, Sophie b 29 Feb 1972); *Career* Northamptonshire Regt 1956-57, 2 Lt Cheshire Regt 1957-58, served Malaya; md Mobil Oil Co Ltd UK 1987- (joined 1961), vice pres Mobil Europe Centre of Operations 1990-, co assignments USA and Italy; md: Mobil Oil Kenya Group, Mobil Oil A/S Denmark, Mobil Oil Portuguesa SARL, Mobil Oil BV Group Rotterdam; memb: Cncl Aldeburgh Fndn, Cncl Royal Warrant Holders Assoc, Advsy Bd 10 Days At Princeton; *Recreations* music, travel, gardening; *Clubs* Garrick; *Style—* Alan Britten, Esq; Mobil Oil Co Ltd, Mobil House, 54-60 Victoria St, London SW1E 6QB (☎ 071 828 9777, fax 071 828 9777 ext 2659, telex 8812411 MOBIL (A-J) G)

BRITTEN, Maj-Gen Robert Wallace Tudor (Bob); CB (1977), MC; s of Lt-Col Wallace Ernest Britten, OBE (d 1947), of Spindlestone, Belford, Northumberland, and Elizabeth Jane, *née* Thorp (d 1971); *b* 28 Feb 1922; *Educ* Wellington, Trinity Coll Cambridge; *m* 1947, Elizabeth Mary (Jane), da of Edward H Davies, of Pentre, Rhondda; 1 s (Simon), 1 da (Sian); *Career* served WWII, 2 Lt RE 1941, Madras Sappers and Miners, 19 Indian Div in India and Burma, Cmd 21 FD Pk Sqdn and 5 FD Sqdn RE 1947-50, WO 1951-53, Br liaison offr to US Corps of Engrs 1953-56, cmd 50 FD Sqdn RE 1956-58, WO 1958-61, on staff 1 (BR) Corps BAOR 1961-64, Lt-Col i/c 1 Trg Regt RE 1964-65, GSO1 (DS) JSSC 1965-67, Brig 1967, Cmd 30 Engr Bde (v) and chief engr Western Cmd 1967, dir equipment mgmnt MOD (Army) 1970-71, Maj-Gen 1971, DQMG 1971-73, GOC W Midlands Dist 1973-76, ret 1976; Col Cmdt RE 1977-82, chm RE Assoc 1978-83; Hon Col Birmingham Univ OTC 1978-87; dir R and E Coordination Ltd; CBIM, Companion Inst of Civil Engrs; *Recreations* bridge building, fishing, dowsing (vice pres Br Soc of Dowsers); *Clubs* Army & Navy; *Style—* Maj-Gen Robert Britten, CB, MC; Birch Trees, Fernden Lane, Haslemere, Surrey GU27 3LA (☎ 0428 2261)

BRITTENDEN, (Charles) Arthur; s of late Tom Edwin Brittenden and Caroline, *née* Scrivener; *b* 23 Oct 1924; *Educ* Leeds GS; *m* 1, 1953 (m dis 1960), Sylvia Penelope Cadman; m 2, 1966 (m dis 1972), Ann Patricia Kenny; m 3, 1975, Valerie Arnison; *Career* northern ed Daily Express 1962-63, dep ed Sunday Express 1963-64, ed Daily Mail 1966-71, dep ed The Sun 1972-81; dir: corp relations News International plc 1982-87, Times Newspapers Ltd 1982-87; sr conslt Lowe Bell Communications Ltd 1988-; dir Dowson-Shurman Associates Ltd 1990-; memb Press Cncl 1982-86 (jt vice chm 1983-86); *Style—* Arthur Brittenden, Esq; 22 Park St, Woodstock, Oxfordshire OX7 1SP (☎ 0993 811425)

BRITTON, David George; *b* 3 Aug 1946; *Educ* The GS For Boys Weston-super-Mare; *m* 4 Nov 1967, Linda Diana; 1 s (Stephen b 7 May 1973), 1 da (Rachel b 11 Sept 1970); *Career* chief dealer: American Express International Banking Corporation London 1967-74, Nordic Bank Ltd 1975-78; dir: Banque Belge Ltd 1978-90, Quin Cope Ltd 1985-90, Belgian & Generale Investments 1989; Euro treas AGM Union Bank of Finland; memb: of Membership and Rules Ctee London Int Fin Futures Exchange, Euro Advsy Ctee The Chicago Mercantile Exchange; chm Foreign Banks and Securities Houses Assoc Foreign Exchange Ctee; *Recreations* fell walking, oriental antiques, sport; *Clubs* Anglo Belgian, Knightsbridge; *Style—* David Britton, Esq; Union Bank of Finland Ltd, 46 Cannon St, London EC4N 6JJ (☎ 071 248 3333, telex 888328)

BRITTON, Sir Edward Louis; CBE (1967); s of George Edwin Britton (d 1956), and Ellen Alice Britton; *b* 4 Dec 1909; *Educ* Bromley GS, Trinity Coll Cambridge (MA); *m* 1936, Nora, da of Thomas Gregory Arnald (d 1912); *Career* headmaster Warlingham Co Secdy Sch 1952-60; gen sec: Assoc of Teachers in Tech Instns 1960-68, Nat Union of Teachers 1969-75; sr res fell Univ of Sheffield 1975-79, lectr Christ Church Coll Canterbury 1979-86; memb TUC General Cncl; Hon DEd (CNAA); kt 1975; *Style—* Sir Edward Britton, CBE; 40 Nightingale Rd, Guildford, Surrey GU1 1ER (☎ 0483 572084)

BRITTON, Jeremy Elliott; s of Timothy Davis Britton, JP, of 28 West Temple Sheen, E Sheen, London SW14 7AP, and Elizabeth Helen Theo, *née* Elliott; *b* 6 Dec 1954; *Educ* Bearwood Coll Royal Merchant Navy Sch; *m* 1, Janet Fiona Woodhouse (d 1980); m 2, 19 June 1982, Anne, da of John Rowland Davies, of Bell Cottage, Llanwysg, nr Crickhowell, Powys; 1 s (James Edward b 4 Feb 1987), 2 da (Katherine Anne b 29 Dec 1983, Emma Jane b 9 May 1985); *Career* five years in RMR; jt md Cockade Ltd 1988- (jr designer 1971-73, salesman 1973-82, sales 1982-84, sales and mktg dir 1984-87, md 1987-); *Style—* Jeremy Britton, Esq; Cockade Ltd, Waterway House, The Ham, Brentford, Middx (☎ 081 569 9696, fax 081 569 8869, tlx 267583)

BRITTON, Jonathan; s of Gerald Percy Britton (d 1978), and Jean, *née* Bowler; *b* 23 May 1954; *Educ* King's Sch Worcester, Keble Coll Oxford (MA); *m* 21 Sept 1985, Dr Helen Florence Britton, da of Reginald George Drake; 1 s (Thomas b 1987), 1 da (Emma Katherine b 6 March 1990); *Career* CA; Peat Marwick Mitchell & Co 1977-80, Financial Training Ltd 1980-82; mgmnt conslt: Arthur Andersen & Co 1982-84, Morgan Stanley International 1984-86; fin dir Swiss Bank Corporation London 1986-; memb ICAEW; *Recreations* opera, golf, sailing, running, DIY, wine; *Clubs* Vincents,

Salcombe Yacht, Malden Golf, Royal Ocean Racing; *Style—* Jonathan Britton, Esq; Upper Burrells, Chiltington Lane, East Chiltington, nr Lewes, East Sussex BN7 3QT (☎ 0273 890703); Swiss Bank House, 1 High Timber St, London (☎ 071 329 0329, fax 071 329 8700, telex 887434)

BRITTON, (Berry) Julian; s of Capt Gordon Berry Cowley Britton, CBE, RN (d 1979), of Southampton, and Vera, *née* Hyman (d 1988); *b* 9 Nov 1941; *Educ* Taunton Sch Southampton, St Barts Hosp Med Sch (MB BS, FRCS, MS, MA); *m* 20 April 1968, (Edith) Mona, da of Robert Cowans (d 1967), of Gateshead; 1 s (Jonathan b 1972), 1 da (Rachel b 1970); *Career* lectr in surgery St Bart's Hosp 1972-74, reader in surgery Univ of Oxford 1976-80, conslt surgn Oxfordshire Health Authy 1980-; Green Coll Oxford: fell 1979-, sr tutor 1979-83, vice warden 1989-; dir clinical studies Univ of Oxford 1985-88; memb Int Hepatobilary and Pancreatic Soc; memb: BMA, RSM; *Recreations* fly-fishing, carpentry; *Style—* Julian Britton, Esq; 89 Lonsdale Rd, Oxford OX2 7ET (☎ 0865 515404); Department of Surgery, John Radcliffe Hospital, Headington, Oxford OX3 9DU (☎ 0865 220929)

BRITTON, Robert Alexander; s of Thomas Bellew Britton, of Sully, S Glamorgan, and Majorie Alexandra, *née* Miller; *b* 4 July 1945; *Educ* Monkton House Sch Cardiff; *m* 14 Sept 1968, Pamela Harbour, da of Frank Eric Broadfield (d 1987); 2 s (Lloyd Anthony b 4 Jan 1977, Tudor Kevin b 30 Sept 1979); *Career* Called to the Bar Inner Temple 1973; memb Lord Hooson QC's chambers; memb: GB and E Europe Centre, Lib Democrats; *Recreations* tennis, squash; *Clubs* London Welsh Rugby, Gerrards Cross Lawn Tennis; *Style—* Robert Britton, Esq; 1 Dr Johnson's Buildings, Temple, London EC4 (☎ 071 353 9328, fax 071 353 4410)

BRIXWORTH, Bishop of (First) 1989-; Rt Rev Paul Everard Barber; s of Cecil Arthur Barber (d 1981), and Marye (Mollie), *née* Hardingham; *b* 16 Sept 1935; *Educ* Sherborne, Univ of Cambridge (MA), Wells Theol Coll; *m* 1959, Patricia Jayne, da of Hubert Jack Walford, of Penygroes, Pen y Lan, Bassaleg, Gwent; 3 s (Andrew, Philip (decd), David), 2 da (Jane, Thi Lien Clare (adopted)); *Career* ordained: deacon 1960, priest 1961; asst curate St Francis Westborough Guildford 1960-66; vicar: St Michael's Yorktown Camberley 1966-73, St Thomas-on-the-Bourne Farnham 1973-80; rural dean of Farnham 1974-79, archdeacon of Surrey 1980-89; *Recreations* cricket, theatre, walking; *Style—* The Rt Rev the Bishop of Brixworth; 4 The Avenue, Dallington, Northampton NN5 7NA

BROACKES, Sir Nigel; s of late Donald Broackes, and Nan Alford; *b* 21 July 1934; *Educ* Stowe; *m* 1956, Joyce Edith Horne; 2 s, 1 da; *Career* Nat Serv, cmmnd 3rd Hussars 1953-54; chm: Trafalgar Ho Ltd, London Docklands Devpt Corp 1981-84; tstee Royal Opera House Tst, dir Horserace Totalisator Bd 1976-81, Guardian Young Businessman of the Year 1978, Stewart & Hughman Ltd Lloyds under-writing agents 1952-55, various property devpt 1955-57, Trafalgar House Investmts Ltd (md 1958, dep chm and jt md 1968, chm 1969), Ship and Marine Technol Requirements Bd 1972-77, dep chm Offshore Energy Technol Bd 1975-77; hon treas Kensington Ho Tst 1963-69; vice-chm: Mulberry Housing Tst 1965-69, London Housing Tst 1967-70; memb Cncl Nat Assoc of Property Owners 1967-73; govr Stowe Sch 1974-81; memb Advisory Cncl Victoria and Albert Museum 1980-83; chm Crafts Cncl 1991-; kt 1984; *Books* A Growing Concern (1979); *Recreations* silversmith; *Style—* Sir Nigel Broackes; 41 Chelsea Square, London SW3; Checkendon Court, Checkendon, Oxon

BROACKES, Simon Nigel; s of Sir Nigel Broackes, *qv*, of Berkley St, London W1, and Joyce Edith, *née* Horn; *b* 31 July 1966; *Educ* Eton; *Career* published two ephemeral magazines proceeds going to charity and produced first Door-Door distribution pubns (forerunners of London Portrait) 1981-82, quantity surveyor with Trollop and Colls Ltd and awarded BEC mgmnt trg prize 1985, formed property devpt and investment co Made in England Ltd 1986, sr conslt to Sir Robert McAlpine & Sons Ltd inc admin of all property devpt activity; memb: Gen Cncl Westminster Property Owners Assoc, Lime St Ward Club 1986, Land Inst 1988; offr in Met Special Constabulary; *Recreations* classic cars, tennis; *Clubs* Harrys Bar, Riverside; *Style—* Simon Broakes, Esq; 41 Chelsea Square, London SW3; Checkendon Court, Checkendon, Oxon; La Bastide de la Roquette, La Roquette sur Siagne, France, Alpes Maritimes; 40 Bernard St, London WC1N ILG (☎ 071 837 3377, tlx 22308, fax 071 833 4102, car 0860 256 739)

BROAD, (Brian) Christopher; s of Kenneth Brian Broad, of Burnt House Farm, Long Lane, Wrington, nr Bristol, and Nancy Pamela Jane, *née* Thomson; *b* 29 Sept 1957; *Educ* Colston's Sch Bristol, St Paul's Coll Cheltenham; *m* 14 July 1979, Carole Ann; 1 s (Stuart Christopher John b 24 June 1986), 1 da (Gemma Joanne b 4 Jan 1984); *Career* cricketer; Gloucestershire CCC 1979-83 (capped 1981), Nottinghamshire CCC 1984- (capped 1984); 25 England Caps (average of just under 40), debut v West Indies 1984; tours: Australia 1986-87, Pakistan/New Zealand 1987-88, South Africa (for an invitation England side) 1990; also played: One Day Internationals, MCC v Rest of World Centenary game (Lords) 1987, England v Australia Bicentenary game (Sydney) 1988; awards: South-West Sports Personality 1986, Int Cricketer of the Year 1986-87; Books: Home Truths from Abroad!! (1987); *Recreations* DIY, music - playing the piano; *Style—* Christopher Broad, Esq; c/o Notts CCC, Trent Bridge, Nottingham NG2 6AG (☎ 0602 821525)

BROAD, (Charles) Peter; s of Charles Frederick Herbert Broad (d 1984), of Wimbledon, and Hilda Evelyn, *née* Cook; *b* 24 July 1930; *Educ* St Paul's Sch, King's Coll London, Westminster Med Sch (MB BS); *m* 25 April 1959, Dr Patricia Broad, da of David Ian Laird, of Keston, Kent; 1 s (Andrew St John), 2 da (Katharine Lucy, Rachel Victoria); *Career* house surgn Westminster Hosp 1956-57, lectr and tutor Dept of Anatomy King's Coll London 1959-62, registrar in orthopaedics Hammersmith Hosp and Postgrad Med Sch 1962-63, first asst in orthopaedics St Georges Hosp and The Rowley Bristow Orthopaedic Hosp, currently sr conslt orthopaedic surgn Bournemouth Dorset; author of several articles on surgery and orthopaedics in med pubns; memb: Cons Party, Cons Med Soc; memb BMA, fell Br Orthopaedic Assoc, FRSM, FRCS; *Recreations* shooting and sailing; *Clubs* Old Pauline, Poole Harbour Yacht; *Style—* Peter Broad, Esq; Midwood, 14 Martello Rd, Canford Cliffs, Poole, Dorset BH13 7DH (☎ 0202 708550); Lansdowne Private Clinic, 65 Lansdowne Rd, Bournemouth, Dorset BM1 1RN (☎ 0202 291866)

BROADBENT, Dr Donald Eric; CBE 1974; s of Herbert Arthur Broadbent (d 1963), and Hannah Elizabeth, *née* Williams (d 1965); *b* 6 May 1926; *Educ* Winchester, Pembroke Coll Cambridge (BA, ScD); *m* 1, 1949, Margaret Elizabeth, da of Frederick Holden Wright (d 1952); 2 da (Patricia b 1951, Judith (d 1979)); m 2, 1972, Margaret Hope, da of Romney Moncrief Pattison Muir (d 1963); *Career* experimental psychologist; sci staff MRC 1949-, memb Applied Psychology Unit Cambridge 1949-50, dir Apu 1958-74, memb external staff Oxford Univ, author 200 papers in scientific jls; hon doctorate: Univ of Southampton 1973, Univ of York 1979, City Univ 1983, Free Univ of Brussels 1985; hon fell: FOM (Royal Coll of Physicians) 1981, Royal Coll of Psychiatrists 1985, Br Psychological Soc 1986 (pres 1965); *Books* Perception and Communication (1958), Behaviour (1961), Decision and Stress (1971), In Defence of Empirical Psychology (1973); *Recreations* reading, camping, photography, motor-cycling; *Style—* Dr Donald Broadbent, CBE; Dept of Experimental Psychology, South Parks Rd, Oxford OX1 3UD (☎ 0865 27444)

BROADBENT, Prof Edward Granville; s of Joseph Charles Fletcher Broadbent (d 1963), and Lucetta, *née* Riley (d 1968); *b* 27 June 1923; *Educ* Huddersfield Coll, St Catharine's Coll Cambridge (MA, ScD); *m* 7 Sept 1949, Elizabeth Barbara, da of Percy Charles Puttick (d 1975); *Career* dep CSO RAE 1969-83 (govt scientist 1943-83), visiting prof Mathematics Dept Imperial Coll 1983-; author numerous scientific papers in learned jls on theory of: aero-elasticity, aerodynamics, magneto hydrodynamics, acoustics propulsion; FRAeS 1959, FIMA 1965, FRS 1977, FEng 1978, FRSA 1984; *Books* The Elementary Theory of Aeroelasticity (1953); *Recreations* gardening, theatre, concerts, bridge, chess; *Style—* Prof Edward Broadbent, FRS; 11 Three Stiles Rd, Farnham, Surrey GU9 7DE (☎ 0252 714 621); Mathematics Dept, Imperial Coll, Huxley Building, Queens Gate, London SW7 2BZ (☎ 071 589 5111, ext 5733)

BROADBENT, Sir Ewen; KCB (1984, CB 1973), CMG (1965); s of Rev Wilfred Broadbent (d 1945), of London, and Mary, *née* Ewen (d 1972); *b* 9 Aug 1924; *Educ* King Edward VI Sch Nuneaton, St John's Coll Cambridge (MA); *m* 1951, Barbara, da of F A David (d 1974), of Weston Super Mare; 1 s (Christopher); *Career* Capt Gordon Highlanders 1943-47; civil servant Air Miny and Miny of Def 1949-84, second perm sec 1982-84; dir Int Mil Servs 1984-; Carroll Indust Corp, vice chm Farnborough Aerospace Devpt Corp, tstee RAF Museum 1985-; chm: Look Ahead Housing Assoc 1987-, Cncl Vol Welfare Work 1989-; *Books* The Military and Government, from Macmillan to Heseltine (1988); *Recreations* golf; *Clubs* Royal Cwlth, Army & Navy; *Style—* Sir Ewen Broadbent KCB, CMG; c/o Carroll House, 2-6 Catherine Place, Westminster, London SW1E 6HF (☎ 071 828 6842)

BROADBENT, Prof Geoffrey Haigh; s of Albert Broadbent (d 1962), and Florence, *née* Haigh (d 1962); *b* 11 June 1929; *Educ* Holme Valley GS, Huddersfield Sch of Art, Univ of Manchester (BA); *m* 25 June 1955, Anne Barbara (d 1985), da of Edgar Sheard; 2 s (Mark b 22 April 1960, Antony b 27 Feb 1962); *Career* asst architect Harry S Fairhurst & Sons 1956-69, lectr Univ of Manchester 1959-61, sec Inst of Advanced Architectural Studies Univ of York 1961-62, lectr Univ of Sheffield 1963-67, head Sch of Architecture Portsmouth Poly 1967-88, prof of architecture Portsmouth Poly 1980-; Br Cncl and other lecture tours to: USA, Canada, Central America, S America, Middle East, S Africa, Europe, SE Asia, Australasia, China; pres Portsmouth Soc 1973-88, memb Cncl ARCUK 1974-79 and 1981-86; Br Sch at Rome: memb Faculty of Architecture 1969-85, memb Appointing Bd Rome Scholar in Architecture 1985-; memb Cirque Int des Critiques d'Architecture 1986-; Prof Honorario Universidad Antonoma de Santo Domingo 1975, Huespedad de Honor Universidad Nacional di Rosario Argentina 1981, Dr Honoris Causa Universidad di Tucuman Argentina 1981; Prof Visitante Univ Nac de Ingeniera Lima 1989, Dip de Honor Univ de Arequipa 1989, Prof Honorario Univ de Cusco 1989; FRIBA 1955, FRSA 1983; *Books* Design in Architecture (1973, 1987), Emerging Concepts in Urban Space Design (1990); co-ed and contrib: Design Methods in Architecture (with A Ward, 1969), Signs, Symbols and Architecture (with C Jencks and R Bunt, 1980), Meaning and Behaviour in the Built Environment (with T Llorens and R Bunt, 1980); *Recreations* music, fine arts, travel, photography; *Clubs* Architectural Assoc; *Style—* Prof Geoffrey Broadbent; 11 Hereford Rd, Southsea, Hants PO5 2DH (☎ 0705 828 787)

BROADBENT, Sir George Walter; 4 Bt (UK 1893); AFC; s of John Graham Monroe Broadbent (d 1967), and Elizabeth Mary Beatrice, *née* Dendy (d 1976); suc kinsman Sir William Francis Broadbent, 3 Bt (d 1987); *b* 23 April 1935; *m* 1962, Valerie Anne, only da of (Cecil) Frank Ward, of York; 1 s, 1 da; *Heir* s, Andrew George Broadbent b 26 Jan 1963; *Career* Sqdn Ldr RAF; *Style—* Sir George Broadbent, Bt, AFC; 98 Heworth Green, York YO3 7TQ

BROADBENT, Col (Herbert) Henry; OBE (1955), TD (1945) DL (Gtr Manchester 1974, Lancs 1973); s of Harry Broadbent (d 1942), and Dorothy, *née* Hatchman (d 1978); *b* 26 April 1914; *Educ* Ashton under Lyne GS; *m* 17 Aug 1938, Mary, *née* Clark; 1 da (Jillian b 1942); *Career* Manchester Regt TA 1933, served WWII Africa (Sudan Def Force 1940-42), India and Burma 1942-45 (Despatches), Col (TA REME) 1957-62; foundryman; chm: Triangle International Ltd 1975-79, Dewramet Ltd 1975-1985, Asco (UK) Ltd 1975-85, Trind Pension Tst Ltd 1975-; chm: Steel Castings Res and Trade Assoc 1975-77, Gtr Manchester ACF Welfare Ctee; pres Prestbury branch Br Legion 1989-; Liveryman Worshipful Co of Founders; *Style—* Col Henry Broadbent, OBE, TD, DL; Glebe House, Prestbury Village, Cheshire SK10 4DG (☎ 0625 827 734)

BROADBENT, John Michael (Mike); s of Ronald William Percy Broadbent (d 1979), of Huddersfield Yorks and Timperley Cheshire, and Marion, *née* White (d 1963); *b* 24 Nov 1933; *Educ* Manchester GS; *m* 29 July 1961, Sandra Elizabeth, da of Lewis Phillips (d 1966), of Runcorn, Cheshire; 2 s (Adam b 1971, Simon b and d 1967), 3 da (Maryan b 1965, Jane b 1969, Philippa b 1971 d 1972); *Career* Nat Serv Bombardier RA 1953-55; journalist: Kemsley Newspapers 1950-57, Star Newspaper 1957-59; with BBC 1959-: scriptwriter TV News, prodr (later ed) Westminster 1968-72, ed Nine O'Clock News, ed Sixty Minutes, founding ed One O'Clock News, former ed Commons TV, Currently Asst Head BBC Westminster; fndr sec and former chm Whitehill Ave Luton Res Assoc, memb Luton Town Supporters Club; *Recreations* supporting Luton Town FC everywhere; *Style—* Mike Broadbent, Esq; 1 Whitehill Ave, Luton, Beds (☎ 0582 20494); c/o 1, Bridge Street, Westminster, London SW1A 2JR (☎ 071 973 6108)

BROADBENT, (John) Michael; s of John Fred Broadbent (d 1973), of Westington House, Chipping Camden, Glos, and Hilary Louise, *née* Batty; *b* 2 May 1927; *Educ* Rishworth Sch, Bartlett Sch of Architecture, UCL (Certificate in Architecture); *m* 8 June 1954, Mary Daphne, da of Edgar Lionel Joste (d 1985), of High Gate, Dousland, Devon; 1 s (Bartholomew b 11 Jan 1962), 1 da (Emma b 9 Jan 1959); *Career* Nat Serv; RA 1945-48 (2 Lt and asst adj Dover Castle 1947-48); trainee Laytons Wine Merchants London 1952-53, Saccone and Speed London 1953-55, dir and UK sales mangr John Harvey and Sons Ltd 1963-66 (London Office 1955-57, NW region 1957-61, local dir London 1961-63), dir Christie Manson and Woods Ltd 1967- (head of Wine Dept 1966-); pres Northern Wine Soc 1962-67, chm Wine Trade Art Soc 1972-, pres Int Wine and Food Soc 1985-; Freeman City of London, Upper Warden Worshipful Company of Distillers 1989 (Liveryman 1964, Cncl 1969), Master of Wine 1960; Memb Inst Masters of Wine (chm 1971-72); Commander d'Honneur Bontemps du Médoc et des Graves (1965), Prodhome de la Jurade de St Emilion (1965), Membre d'Honneur l'Académie du Vin de Bordeaux (1973), Chevalier de l'Ordre National du Mérite (1979), Confrère d'Honneur St Etienne d'Alsace (1985), La Medaille de la Ville de Paris Echelon Vermeil; *Books* Wine Tasting (1968), The Great Vintage Wine Book (1980); ed: Christie's Wine Review (1972-80), Price Index of Vintage Wines (1982-84), Christie's Wine Pubns (1982-); *Recreations* drawing, piano playing, talking and writing about wine; *Clubs* Brooks's; *Style—* Michael Broadbent, Esq; 87 Rosebank, London SW6 (☎ 071 381 0858); Chippenham Lodge, Old Sodbury, Avon BS17 6RQ (☎ 0454 315712); Christie's, 8 King Street, St James's, London SW1 (☎ 071 839 9060, fax 071 839 7869, tlx 916429)

BROADBENT, Simon Hope; s of Edmund Urquhart Broadbent, CBE, of Broughton, Hants, and Doris, *née* Hope; *b* 4 June 1942; *Educ* Univ Coll Sch, Hatfield Coll Durham (BA), Magdalen Coll Oxford (BPhil); *m* 2 Dec 1966, Margaret Ann, da of Herbert Franklin Taylor of Thornbury, Avon; 2 s (Matthew b 1968, William b 1972), 1 da (Victoria b 1971); *Career* Malawi Civil Serv 1964, first sec UK Treasy and Supply

Delegation Washington 1974, seconded to Bank of England 1977, visiting scholar IUHEI Geneva 1984, chief economic advsr FCO 1988- (economic advsr 1971, jt head of Economists Dept 1978, head of economic advsrs 1984); *Style—* Simon Broadbent, Esq; Foreign and Commonwealth Office, London SW1 2AH (☎ 071 270 2721, fax 071 270 3369)

BROADBENT, William Benedict; ERD (1959); s of William Keighley Benedict Broadbent (d 1948), of Huddersfield; *b* 10 Jan 1924; *Educ* Rugby; *m* 1954 (m dis 1980), Joy Valerie, da of Ernest Wilkinson, CBE; 4 da; *Career* Capt TA and Army Emergency Reserve UK; chm Severn Valley Railway Hldgs plc 1975-87 (dir 1972-); dir: Festiniog Railway Co 1954-86, Sales Ltd, Staveley Industs Ltd 1968-71; chm: Staveley Lime Ltd 1966-71 (dir 1962-71), RD Nicol & Co Ltd 1966-71 (md 1960-66); md Br Salt Ltd 1966-71; chief ops exec Greater Manchester PTE 1972-76; engr, mgmnt conslt and florist/nurseryman; *Recreations* hill climbing, cruise sailing; *Clubs* Mountain Rangers Assoc; *Style—* William Broadbent, Esq, ERD; Pembroke Cottage, Long Compton, Warwicks CV36 5JN

BROADBRIDGE, Hon Mrs Ralph - Emma Rose Hancock; da of Henry Van der Weyden, of London; *m* 1925, Hon Ralph George Cameron Broadbridge (d 1983), s of 1 Baron Broadbridge; 3 da; *Style—* The Hon Mrs Ralph Broadbridge

BROADBRIDGE, Hon Howard Eustace; 4 s of 1 Baron Broadbridge, KCVO (d 1952); *b* 17 Nov 1904; *m* 1935, Margaret Ada Marion, da of Capt H H Witherington, of St Michaels, Natal; 1 da; *Style—* The Hon Howard Broadbridge; 12 Texel, Alexandra Rd, Pietermaritzburg, Natal, S Africa

BROADBRIDGE, 3 Baron (UK 1945); Sir Peter Hewett Broadbridge; o s of 2 Baron Broadbridge (d 1972), and Mabel Daisy, *née* Clarke (d 1966); *b* 19 Aug 1938; *Educ* Hurstpierpoint, St Catherine's Coll Oxford (MA, BSc); *m* 1, 1 April 1967 (m dis 1980), Mary, o da of Wilhelm Otto Busch; 2 da (Hon Jemima Louise b 1970, Hon Sophie Mary b 1972); m 2, 14 Jan 1989, Sally Frances Finn; *Heir* cousin, Martin Broadbridge; *Career* dir The London Venture Capital Market Ltd; formerly conslt Coopers & Lybrand, Peat Marwick Mitchell & Co; mktg appts with Gallaher, Colgate-Palmolive, Unilever; Liveryman Worshipful Co of Goldsmiths; pres Nat Assoc of Allotment Gardeners 1977-80; FRSA; *Recreations* early English watercolours, old English silver, silversmithing, tennis, squash; *Style—* The Rt Hon the Lord Broadbridge

BROADHEAD, Neil; s of Henry Broadhead (d 1988), of Dridlington, and Eleanor Broadhead, *née* Hope (d 1986); *b* 30 Oct 1954; *Educ* St James Sch Knaresborough, Univ of Hull (BSc); *m* 1, 30 Sept 1979 (m dis 1986), Anna Marie D'Orazio, of Chieti, Italy; m 2, 12 July 1986, Elizabeth, da of Raymond Baldam, of Sheffield; 1 s (Grant b 14 June 1988), 1 da (Laura b 13 March 1987); *Career* BA 1985-: software project mangr 1985, support integrity mangr; *Recreations* real ale sampling, rugby league; *Style—* Neil Broadhead, Esq; British Airways, Comet House (S45), PO Box 10, Hounslow, Middx TW6 2JA (☎ 081 562 2112, fax 081 562 8810)

BROADHURST, Dr Alan Desmond; s of Sydney Broadhurst (d 1980), of Thurmaston, Leicestershire, and Grace Ellen, *née* Kettle; *b* 24 Feb 1926; *Educ* Wyggeston Sch Leicester, Univ of London, Univ of Sheffield, Univ of Cambridge (MB ChB); *m* 11 Oct 1969, Lotte, da of Hans Zingrich, of Villigen, Kt Aargau, Switzerland; 2 s (Mark b 2 July 1970, Peter b 28 Dec 1971); *Career* staff Capt ME Forces 1947-49; clinical pharmacologist 1955-60 (Geigy, Manchester, Basle), registrar in psychological med Fulbourn Hosp Cambridge 1960-62, sr res in med American Hosp of Paris 1963-64, med registrar Papworth Hosp Cambridge 1964-66, sr registrar in psychiatry and medicine Addenbroke's Hosp Cambridge 1966-70, sr conslt psychiatrist W Suffolk Hosp Bury St Edmunds 1970-, conslt physician Addenbrooke's Hosp Cambridge 1970-89; Univ of Cambridge: memb Faculty of Clinical Med 1970-, clinical teacher in psychopharmacology 1984-; author of papers psychopharmacology and the effects of drugs on human performance and in aviation medicine; memb: Exec Ctee Eastern Div RCPsych 1984-89, E Anglian Thoracic Soc, BMA, Aero-Med Int, Oxford Postgraduate Inst of Psychiatry; fndr memb British Assoc for Psychopharmacology; MRCS, LRCP 1955, DPM 1963, MRCPsych 1971, MIBiol 1983, FRCPsych 1984; *Recreations* motor cruising, sailing, travelling; *Style—* Dr Alan Broadhurst; The Park, Great Barton, Suffolk (☎ 0284 87 288)

BROADHURST, Air Chief Marshal Sir Harry; GCB (1960, KCB 1955, CB 1944), KBE (1945), DSO and bar (1941), DFC (1940, and bar 1942), AFC (1937); s of Capt Harry Broadhurst, of Emsworth, Hants; *b* 28 Oct 1905; *Educ* various Serv Colls; *m* 1, 1931 (m dis 1945), Doris Kathleen French; 1 da; m 2, 1946, Jean Elizabeth, da of Dr J E Townley, MC, of Kinnersley, Hereford, 1 da; *Career* C-in-C 2 Tactical Air Force Germany 1954-56, Air Offr C-in-C Bomber Cmd 1956-59, Cdr Allied Forces Central Europe 1959-61; md AVROE and Co 1961-66; dir Hawkley Siddeley Gp Ltd 1968-76 (dir and dep md Hawker Siddeley Aviation Ltd 1966-76), pres SBAC 1974-75; American Legion of Merit 1943, Kt Gd Cross Order of Orange Nassau 1948; *Recreations* music, sailing; *Clubs* RAF; *Style—* Air Chief Marshal Sir Harry Broadhurst, GCB, KBE, DSO, DFC, AFC; Lock's End House, Birdham, Chichester, W Sussex PO20 7BB (☎ 0243 512717)

BROADHURST, (Ian) Kevan Averill; s of Samuel Broadhurst (d 1974), of Stoke-on-Trent, and Gladys, *née* Averill; *b* 30 Dec 1935; *Educ* Coll of Commerce Stoke-on-Trent; *m* 18 June 1966, Maureen, da of James Haddon, of Stoke-on-Trent; *Career* CA; Bourner Bullock and Co CAs 1951-67, Statham and Co CA's 1967-70, sr ptnr Harding Higgins Ptnrship (formerly Geo E Harding and Co Cert Accountants) 1971-89, md Harding Servs Ltd until 1989, consltg CA 1989-, chm Langenfeld Ltd; FCA 1962, FCCA 1971, ATII 1957, FRSA 1962; *Recreations* film making, photography, travel; *Style—* Kevan Broadhurst, Esq; Langenfeld, Meadow Way, Church Lawton, Stoke-on-Trent, Staffs (☎ 0270 873 832); c/o 6 Marsh Parade, Newcastle-under-Lyme, Staffs ST5 1DU (☎ 0782 617 868)

BROADHURST, Paul Andrew; s of Malcolm Thomas Henry Broadhurst, of Tamforth, Staffs, and Denise Evelyn Mary, *née* Bartlam (d 1982); *b* 14 Aug 1965; *Educ* Atherstone North Middle Sch, Atherstone Comp Sch; *m* 12 Jan 1991, Lorraine Mary, da of John Cyril Masefield; *Career* professional golfer; English Sch champion 1983, Lytham Trophy (amateur) 1988, memb English Amateur team 1985-88; turned professional 1988, winner Cannes Open 1989 and Motorola Classic 1990, Eng int 1987-89 (GB & Ireland 1989), runner up Euro Team Championship 1988; rookie of the year 1989, equalled lowest ever round Br Open 1990 (63); former employment: landscape gardner, delivery driver, glass fibre laminator; *Recreations* rock music, supporting Leeds Utd FC and Atherstone Utd FC; *Style—* Paul Broadhurst, Esq; c/o PGA European Tour, Wentworth Club, Virginia Water, Surrey GU25 4LS (☎ 09904 2881)

BROADLEY, Lady; Kathleen May; da of late Alfred J Moore, of Camden Sq, London; *m* 1927, Sir Herbert Broadley, KBE (d 1983); *Style—* Lady Broadley; Hollingsworth, Redlands Lane, Ewshot, Farnham, Surrey

BROADWAY, (Robert) Patrick Plewman; s of Col Philip Robert Broadway, OBE (d 1979), and Olive Eileen, *née* Plewman (d 1934); *b* 30 July 1929; *Educ* Dauntsey's Sch, Northern Poly (Dip Arch); *m* 17 July 1965, Sheila Marion Lillian, da of Clement Alexander Francis (d 1951); 1 s (Robert Francis b 15 March 1970), 1 da (Joy Marion Olive b 23 Oct 1972); *Career* Nat Serv 1947-49, craftsman REME; architect; Bridgewater and Shepheard 1956-58, Michael Lyell Assocs 1958-63, Elidir LW Davies and Partners 1963-65, Fisk and Fisk 1965-71, Aslan and Freeman 1971-72, assoc WS Hattrell and Partners 1972-76, started own practice 1976-; ARIBA 1956; *Recreations* tennis, golf, skiing, windsurfing, fishing, philately; *Clubs* Cumberland Lawn Tennis, Wembley Sailing; *Style—* Patrick Broadway, Esq; 19 Chesterford Gardens, London NW3 7DD (☎ 071 435 2950)

BROATCH, (Michael) Donald; s of Dr Alexander Donaldson Broatch (d 1982), of Folkestone, Kent; *b* 28 May 1948; *Educ* Felsted, QMC London (LLB, LLM); *m* 1 June 1974, Catherine Margaret, *née* Block, da of Barry John Block (d 1968), of Shirley, Croydon; 2 s (Neil b 1978, Ian b 19; *Career* called to the Bar 1971, in practice 1972-; *Style—* Donald Broatch, Esq; 5 Paper Buildings, Temple, London EC4 (☎ 071 353 8494, 071 583 4555, fax 071 583 1926, telex 8956431 Anton G LDE Box 415)

BROCAS, Viscount; Patrick John Bernard Jellicoe; s (by 1 m) and h of 2 Earl Jellicoe, DSO, MC, PC; *b* 29 Aug 1950; *Educ* Eton; *m* 1971 (m dis 1981), Geraldine Ann FitzGerald Jackson; 1 s (Hon Justin Amadeus b 1970); *Heir* bro, Hon Nicholas Charles; *Career* engineer; *Style—* Viscount Brocas; Pantglas, Llanwoda, Dyfed

BROCK, Baroness; Chrissie Palmer; *née* Jones; da of John Alfred Jones, of Leeds; *b* 1 June 1903; *Educ* Leeds Girls' HS, Royal Sch Needlework; *m* 1979, as his 2 w, Baron Brock (d 1980); 2 step da; *Career* private sec; *Style—* The Rt Hon the Lady Brock; 39 Chancellor House, Tunbridge Wells TN4 8BT

BROCK, Prof David John Henry; s of John Fleming Brock (d 1983), of Cape Town, SA, and Ruth Mary, *née* Lomberg (d 1990); *b* 5 June 1936; *Educ* Univ of Oxford (BA), Univ of Cape Town (PhD); *m* 30 July 1959, Sheila Margaret, da of Norman J Abercromby (d 1976), of Edinburgh; 4 s (Andrew b 1962, Graham b 1963, James b 1966, Martin b 1974); *Career* Univ of Edinburgh 1968-: lectr 1968-76, reader 1976-85, prof 1985-; FIBiol, FRCPE, FRSE, FRCPath; *Books* Early Diagnosis of Foetal Defects (1982); *Recreations* walking; *Style—* Prof David Brock; Human Genetics Unit, Western General Hospital, Edinburgh EH4 2XU (☎ 031 332 7917)

BROCK, John Hedley; OBE (1976); s of John Brock, JP (d 1949), of Kelly Bray, Cornwall, and Mary, *née* Priest (d 1960); *b* 18 Jan 1912; *Educ* Callington Sch; *m* 1, Vera Wonnacott (d 1972); 1 s; m 2, 1973, Ann Felicity, da of Harry Laity, JP (d 1980); *Career* served RN 1940-46, Lt-Cdr; mangr Lloyds Bank plc 1950-74, dir South Crofty Ltd 1972-85; chm: China Clay Cncl 1972-, Cornwall Indust Devpt Assoc 1975-83; pres Cornish Mining Devpt Assoc 1972-; *Recreations* music; *Style—* John Brock, Esq, OBE; Chy an Mor, Coverack, Helston, Cornwall TR12 6SZ (☎ 0326 280417)

BROCK, Dr Michael George; CBE (1981); s of Sir Laurence George Brock, CB (d 1949), and Ellen Margery, *née* Williams; *b* 9 March 1920; *Educ* Wellington, Corpus Christi Coll Oxford; *m* 1949, Eleanor Hope Morrison; 3 s; *Career* historian; pro vice chllr Univ of Oxford 1980-88; warden: Nuffield Coll Oxford 1978-88, St George's House Windsor Castle 1988-; hon fell: Wolfson Coll Oxford 1977, Corpus Christi Coll Oxford 1982, Nuffield Coll; Hon DLitt Univ of Exeter 1982; FRHistS, FRSL, FRSA; *Style—* Dr Michael Brock, CBE; 24 The Cloisters, Windsor Castle SL4 1NJ (☎ 0753 866 444); St George's House, Windsor Castle SL4 1NJ (☎ 0753 861 341)

BROCKBANK, Mark Ellwood; s of John Ellwood Brockbank, of Westward Pk, Wigton, Cumbria, and Elizabeth, *née* Allen; *b* 2 April 1952; *Educ* Bootham Sch York; *Career* appointed Lloyd's Underwriter 1983; dir: Alston Brockbank Agencies Ltd 1982, Energy Entertainment Co Ltd 1987, Hayter Brockbank plc 1988, Hayter Brockbank Agencies Ltd 1988, John Hayter Motor Underwriting Agencies Ltd 1988, Charles Howard Underwriting Ltd 1988; *Recreations* the arts, cinema, shooting, bridge; *Style—* Mark Brockbank, Esq; 18 Rood Lane, London EC3M 8AP (☎ 071 283 6977, fax 071 283 5124, telex 8951858)

BROCKBANK, Thomas Frederick; s of John Bowman Brockbank (d 1990), of Hilton, and Alice Margaret, *née* Parker (d 1987); *b* 6 March 1938; *Educ* Bootham Sch York, Loughborough Coll (DLC Mech Engrg); *m* 16 Dec 1967, Joan Emma, da of Martin Israelski, of Leamington; 3 da (Eleanor Clare b 1970, Laura Katherine b 1973, Harriet Elisabeth b 1975); *Career* merchant banker; Courtaulds Ltd 1960-65, mgmnt conslt Arthur Andersen & Co London 1965-68, RTZ Consultants (part of RTZ Corporation) 1968-73, Hill Samuel & Co Ltd 1973-87 (dir of corp fin 1985-, jt head of Smallers Cos Team); mechanical engr Internal Consultancy Operational Research; author of numerous lectures and articles, particularly on finance for growing companies, flotation and general strategy; FRSA 1986; *Recreations* music, theatre, art, photography, travel; *Style—* Thomas Brockbank, Esq; Hill Samuel Bank Ltd, 100 Wood St, London EC2P 2AJ (☎ 071 628 8011)

BROCKBANK, (James) Tyrrell; DL (Durham 1970); *b* 14 Dec 1920; *Educ* St Peter's York, St John's Coll Cambridge; *m* 1950, Pamela Margaret Oxley, *née* Parker; 4 s; *Career* clerk of the peace Durham 1961-71, clerk of Durham CC 1961-74, clerk to Durham Ltcy 1964-88; memb Local Govt Boundary Cmmn Eng 1976-85, High Sheriff Durham 1989, Vice Lord-Lieut Durham 1990-; *Recreations* fishing, shooting, golf; *Clubs* Travellers', Durham County; *Style—* Tyrrell Brockbank, Esq, DL; The Orange Tree, Shincliffe Village, Durham DH1 2NN (☎ 091 386 5569)

BROCKET, 3 Baron (UK 1933); Sir Charles Ronald George Nall-Cain; 3 Bt (UK 1921); s of late Hon Ronald Charles Manus Nall-Cain, er s of 2 Baron; suc gf 1967; *b* 12 Feb 1952; *Educ* Eton; *m* 1982, Isabell (Isa) Maria, only da of Gustavo Lorenzo, of Whaleneck Drive, Merrick, Long Island, NY, USA; 1 s; *Heir* s, Hon Alexander Christopher Charles b 30 Sept 1984; *Career* late 14/20 King's Hussars; Gen Service Medal, UN Medal; *Style—* The Rt Hon The Lord Brocket; Brocket Hall, Welwyn, Herts

BROCKHURST, Rowan Benford; s of Geoffrey Thomas Brockhurst, of 1 Lumby Drive, Ringwood, Hants, and Barbara, *née* Wickens; *b* 23 June 1936; *Educ* Sutton Valence, Coll of Law London; *m* 1, 8 April 1961 (m dis 1984), Eve, da of Maj William Tristram (d 1942); 1 s (Nicholas b 1965), 1 da (Harriet b 1963); m 2, 13 May 1987, Fiona Daphne, da of John Cunningham (d 1985); *Career* Nat Serv 2 Lt RASC 1959-60, Capt Army Emergency Res of Offrs; admitted slr 1958; sr ptnr Meesons Ringwood & Fordingbridge Hants; pres Hants Inc Law Soc 1978-79, dir Slrs Benevolent Assoc 1982; chm: Ringwood and Dist Community Assoc, Ringwood and Fordingbridge Footpath Soc; pres Ringwood Philatelic Soc, vice chm Ringwood Meeting House Assoc, govr Moyles Ct Sch Ringwood and Holme Grange Sch Wokingham; memb Law Soc 1958; *Recreations* walking, gardening, reading, inland waterways; *Style—* Rowan Brockhurst, Esq; 78 Allen Water Drive, Fordingbridge, Hants (☎ 0425 53748); New House Market Place, Ringwood, Hants (☎ 0425 472 315, fax 0425 470 912)

BROCKINGTON, Prof Ian Fraser; s of Prof Colin Fraser Brockington, of Ballasalla, IOM, and Joyce Margaret, *née* Furze; *b* 12 Dec 1935; *Educ* Winchester, Gonville and Caius Coll Cambridge, Univ of Manchester Med Sch; *m* 1 Aug 1969, Diana Hilary, da of Wilfred Joy Pink (d 1984); 2 s (Daniel b 1970, Samuel Fraser b 1978), 2 da (Alice Rose b 1972, Grace Ellen b 1976); *Career* house physician Hammersmith Hosp 1964, sr registrar UCH Ibadan 1964, Wellcome res fell Royal Postgrad Med Sch and Univ of Ibadan 1966, sr lectr Univ of Manchester 1975; visiting prof: Univ of Chicago 1980, Univ of Washington St Louis 1981; prof of psychiatry Univ of Birmingham 1983; pres Marcé Soc 1982; *Books* Motherhood and Mental Illness (vol 1 1982, vol 2 1988); *Recreations* choral singing, French & Italian literature, family activities, house restoration; *Style—* Prof Ian Brockington

BROCKINGTON, Dr John Leonard; s of Rev Leonard Herbert Brockington (d 1978), and Florence Edith, *née* Woodward; *b* 5 Dec 1940; *Educ* Mill Hill Sch, Corpus Christi Coll Oxford (MA, DPhil); *m* 2 Aug 1966, Mary, da of Joseph Gascoigne Fairweather (d 1988); 1 s (Michael b 1971), 1 da (Anne b 1967); *Career* reader Univ of Edinburgh 1989- (lectr in Sanskrit 1965-82,head of dept 1975, sr lectr 1982-89); *Books* The Sacred Thread: Hinduism in its Continuity and Diversity (1981), Righteous Rama: The Evolution of an Epic (1985); *Style—* Dr John Brockington; 99 Cluny Gardens, Edinburgh EH10 6BW (☎ 031 447 7580); Department of Sanskrit, University of Edinburgh, 7 Buccleuch Place, Edinburgh EH8 9LW (☎ 031 650 4174)

BROCKLEBANK, Sir Aubrey Thomas; 6 Bt (UK 1885); s of Sir John Montague Brocklebank, 5 Bt, TD (d 1974), and Pamela, *née* Pierce; *b* 29 Jan 1952; *Educ* Eton, Univ Coll Durham (BSc); *m* 1979, Dr Anna-Marie, da of Dr William Dunnet; 2 s (Aubrey William b 1980), Hamish John b 1987); *Heir* s, Aubrey William b 15 Dec 1980; *Career* dir Augill Castle Antiques Ltd; ACA; *Style—* Sir Aubrey Brocklebank, Bt; 37 Kyrle Rd, London SW11

BROCKLEBANK, Edward; s of Flt Lt Fred Brocklebank, of Ballater, Grampian, and Agnes Mitchell, *née* Ainslie (d 1969); *b* 24 Sept 1942; *Educ* Madras Coll St Andrews Fife; *m* 21 Aug 1965 (m dis 1979), Lesley Beverley, da of Dr Ronald Beverley Davidson (d 1975), of Dundee; 2 s (Andrew Edward b 4 Feb 1967, Jonathan Ainslie b 31 Dec 1967); *Career* trainee journalist DC Thomson & Co Ltd Dundee 1960-63, freelance 1963-65, journalist Scot TV Glasgow 1965-70, in vision journalist/presenter Grampian TV Aberdeen 1970-77, head of News and Current Affrs 1977-85, head of documentaries 1985-; prodns incl: What Price Oil? (BAFTA Award 1974), Tale of Two Cities (TRICS Award 1977), Oil (8 pt series for Channel 4, AMANDA Award 1988); *Recreations* rugby football, golf, oil painting; *Clubs* New Golf (St Andrews), Aberdeen Petroleum; *Style—* Edward Brocklebank, Esq; Grampian Television, Queen's Cross, Aberdeen AB9 2XJ (☎ 0224 646464)

BROCKLEBANK, Pamela, Lady; Pamela Sue; da of late William Harold Pierce, OBE, of Bidston, Cheshire; *m* 1 (m dis), Maj Leslie Forshaw-Wilson; m 2, 1950, Maj Sir John Montague Brocklebank, 5 Bt, TD (d 1974); 1 s (Sir Aubrey Thomas, 6 Bt, *qv*); *Style—* Pamela, Lady Brocklebank; Il Palazz, Zejtun, Malta

BROCKLEBANK, Ralph Wilfrid; s of Cdr Denys Royds Brocklebank, RN (d 1947), of Longbridge House, Warminster, Wilts, and Kathleen, *née* Lindsay (d 1985); *b* 18 July 1927; *Educ* Lakefield Sch Ontario, Michael Hall Sch Sussex, Millfield Sch Somerset, Trinity Coll Cambridge (MA); *m* 8 Feb 1954, Beryl, *née* Seabury; 1 s (Guy (Lt Cdr RN) b 1954), 2 adopted s (Mark b 1959, Leo b 1965), 2 adopted da (Susan b 1956, Keren b 1960); *Career* Goethean Science Foundation 1951- (now tstee); chm: The Colour Group (GB) 1971-73, Sunfield Children's Homes 1985- (dir 1973-85); *Recreations* heraldry; *Clubs* English-Speaking Union; *Style—* Ralph Brocklebank, Esq; Orland, Clent, Stourbridge, West Midlands DY9 9QS (☎ 0562 730285); Sunfield Childrens Homes, Clent Grove, Clent, Stourbridge, West Midlands DY9 9PB (☎ 0562 882253)

BROCKLEBANK, Roger James; s of Frederick James Brocklebank (d 1979), of Bexhill-on-Sea, and Gladys Clara, *née* Shaw; *b* 18 June 1938; *m* 1964, Alana; 3 c (Justin b 3 March 1969, Quentin b 25 Nov 1970, Hannah b 8 Aug 1975); *Career* cmmnd Royal Signals served W Germany 1956-59; STC 1959-68 (trained engr and accountant), Economist Intelligence Unit 1968-69; Gallaher Limited 1969-77: various fin and gen mgmnt positions, md subsid; fin dir Jermyn Holdings 1978-82, Unitech plc 1982-84, dir Schroder Securities 1985-; FCMA (ACMA 1968), ACIS 1966, MBIM 1968; *Recreations* country pursuits, second home in Spain, family; *Style—* Roger Brocklebank, Esq; Schroder Securities Ltd, 120 Cheapside, London EC2V 6DS (☎ 071 382 3214, fax 071 382 3079)

BROCKLEBANK, (John) Trevor; s of Henry Pearson Brocklebank (d 1975), and Eva Mary, *née* Wood; *b* 25 Sept 1938; *Educ* Barnard Castle Sch, Univ of Durham (MB BS); *m* 9 Aug 1969, Susan Hall, da of Earnest Kinghorn, of Beckwithshaw, Harrogate, N Yorks; 1 s (Simon Pearson b 1970), 2 da (Emma b 1976, Sophie b 1984); *Career* registrar in paediatrics Royal Victoria Infirmary Newcastle 1968-73, res fell Div Paediatric Nephrology Washington Univ St Louis USA 1973-76, sr lectr in paediatrics and hon conslt paediatrician Univ of Leeds 1981- (lectr 1976-81); FRCPE; *Recreations* sailing; *Style—* Trevor Brocklebank, Esq; 5 Woodbourne, Leeds LS8 2JW (☎ 0532 653592); Department of Paediatrics, St James' University Hospital, Leeds LS9 7TF (☎ 0532 433144)

BROCKLEBANK-FOWLER, Christopher; s of Sidney Straton Brocklebank Fowler (d 1954), of Oakham, Rutland; *b* 13 Jan 1934; *Educ* Perse Sch Cambridge; *m* 1, 1957 (m dis 1975), Joan, da of Louis Raymond Nowland (d 1961), of Kalgoorlie, W Australia; 2 s; m 2, 1975 (m dis 1985), Mary Berry; 1 step da; *Career* served RN (submarines) 1952-54, Sub-Lt RNVR; farm mangr Kenya 1954-57; md: ACP Devpt Agency Ltd 1984-, Cambridge Corp Conslts Ltd 1985-87; dir: Creative Conslts Ltd 1966-, Bow Publications 1968-71, SOS Children's Villages UK Trading 1981-84 (chm SOS Children's Villages UK 1978-84); contested (C) West Ham N 1964, MP (C) King's Lynn 1970-74, MP (C then SDP from 1981) Norfolk NW 1974-83; contested (SDP) Norfolk NW 1983 and 1987; memb Bow Gp 1961-81 (chm 1968-69); vice chm: Cons Parly Foreign and Cwlth Affrs Sub Ctee 1979-81, Cons Parly Trade Ctee 1979-81; chm: UN Parly Gp 1979-83; Overseas Devpt Sub Ctee 1979-83, memb Select Parly Ctee on Foreign Affrs 1979-83; SDP spokesman Agric and Foreign Affrs 1981-83, chm SDP Overseas Devpt Policy Ctee 1981-83; vice chm: SDP Agric Policy Ctee 1981-83, SDP Communications Ctee 1982-83; memb Cncl for Social Democracy 1982-; fndr and non exec chm Overseas Trade and Devpt Agency Ltd 1979-83, govr Inst of Devpt Studies Univ of Sussex 1978-81 (hon fellow), memb Cncl Centre for World Devpt 1979-88; MCAM MCIM, FInstD, FRGS; *Recreations* swimming, shooting, fishing, painting; *Clubs* Royal Cwlth Soc; *Style—* Christopher Brocklebank-Fowler Esq; The Long Cottage, Flitcham, King's Lynn, Norfolk PE31 6BU (☎ Hillington (0485) 600255)

BROCKLEHURST, Aubrey Bernard; s of Clement George Bernard Brocklehurst (d 1937), of Chorlton-cum-Hardy, Manchester, and Ellen, *née* Davies (d 1943); *b* 29 June 1913; *Educ* Chorlton HS Manchester; *m* 1, 23 Nov 1940 (m dis 1983), Joan, da of James Rowbotton (d 1945), of Woodland Way, Middleton, Lancs; 2 s (Kevin b 7 Nov 1943, Edwin (twin) b 7 Nov 1943), 1 da (Ruth b 14 Jan 1955); m 2, Hazel Victoria (d 1984), da of Henry James Bryan (d 1931), of Liverpool; m 3, 11 Dec 1987, Helen, da of Charles Lawrence Pryal (d 1940), of San Francisco; *Career* lab asst and observer in an experimental machinery lab Br Cotton Indust Res Assoc 1931-37, calculator in drawing office Henry Wallwork & Co Ltd 1937-38, mechanical designer Ferguson Pailin Ltd 1938-42, travel organiser for overseas workers Friend's Relief Serv 1946-49, self employed watch and clock repairer 1950-63, proprietor (retailing and repairing) antique clock shop 1963-; chm London Section Fell and Rock Climbing Club 1986-88, chm North London Branch Br Horological Inst 1978-, memb Ctee Nat Benevolent Soc of Watch and Clockmakers 1985-; Freeman City of London 1970, Liveryman Worshipful Co of Clockmakers 1973; FBHI 1960, memb Br Antique Dealers Assoc 1973; *Recreations* walking, mountaineering, skiing, travel; *Clubs* Ski, Fell & Rock Climbing; *Style—* Aubrey Brocklehurst, Esq; Flat 1, 124 Cromwell Rd, S Kensington, London SW7 4ET (☎ 071 373 0319); 12 Beaconsfield Rd, Hastings, E Sussex TN34 3TN

BROCKLEHURST, Ben Gilbert; s of Ernest (d 1935), and Kathleen (d 1965); *b* 18 Feb 1922; *Educ* Bradfield Coll 1935-40; *m* 1, March 1947 (m dis 1957), Mary; m 2, June 1962, Belinda, da of William S Bristowe; 3 s, 1 da; *Career* 10 Devon Regt 1940, Maj 13 FF Rifles Indian Army 1942, Lt-Col 4/12 FF Regt LA 1946 served Burma; dairy farmer Berks 1947, joined Advertisement Dept Country Life 1957, advertisement mangr Tothill Press 1961, advertisement dir Mercury House Pubns (md 24 Magazines Mercury House), proprietor The Cricketer 1972, fndr Cricketer Holidays; co cricketer: Somerset 2 XI 1951, Somerset 1XI 1952-54 (Capt 1953 and 1954); *Recreations* cricket, golf, tennis, squash; *Clubs* Naval and Military, Piccadilly, MCC, Free Foresters, IZ; *Style—* Ben Brocklehurst, Esq; Beech Hanger, Ashurst, nr Tunbridge Wells, Kent (☎ 089274 0256)

BROCKLEHURST, Prof John Charles; CBE (1988); s of Harold John Brocklehurst (d 1981), and Dorothy, *née* Harrison; *b* 31 May 1924; *Educ* Glasgow HS, Ayr Acad, Univ of Glasgow (MB ChB, MD); *m* 27 July 1956, Gladys Florence (Susan); 2 s (Paul Harrison b 20 Aug 1958, Neil John b 20 June 1961), 1 da (Morag Jane b 1 May 1957); *Career* Maj RAMC 1949-51; Christine Hansen res fell Univ of Glasgow 1948- 49, med offr Grenfell Mission N Newfoundland and Labrador 1955-57, jr hosp appts 1957-61 (1951-55), conslt geriatrician Bromley Hosp Gp 1961-69, conslt geriatric gen med Guys Hosp 1969-70, hon conslt geriatrician NW Regnl Health Authy 1970-, prof of geriatric med Univ of Manchester 1970- (dir Unit for Biological Ageing Res 1974-), visiting prof and head of Div of Geriatric Med Univ of Saskatchewan 1978-79; tstee CIBA Geigy Educnl Tst 1977-, govr Res into Ageing 1980-, vice pres Age Concern England 1980- (vice-chm 1971-73, chm 1973-77); pres: Age Concern Lancs 1977 (chm 1972-77), Manchester and Salford Med Engrg Club 1976-77, Soc of Chiropodists 1977-83, Br Geriatrics Soc 1983-85; chm Age Concern Macclesfield 1988-; Hon MSc Univ of Manchester 1974; MRCPS (Glasgow) 1959, FRCPS (Glasgow) 1972, MRCPE 1961, FRCPE 1970, FRCP 1984; *Books* Incontinence in Old People (1951), The Geriatric Day Hospital (1971), Textbook of Geriatric Medicine and Gerontology (jtly 1973, 1978, 1985), Geriatric Care in Advanced Societies (jtly 1975), Geriatric Medicine For Students (jtly 1976, 1981, 1985), Progress in Geriatric Day Care (1980), Atlas of Geriatric Medicine (jtly 1983), Urology in Old Age (jtly 1984), Geriatric Pharmocology and Therapeutics (jtly 1984), British Geriatric Medicine in the 1980's (jtly 1987), Case Studies in Medicine for the Elderly (jtly 1987); *Recreations* painting; *Clubs* East India and Devonshire; *Style—* Prof John Brocklehurst, CBE; 59 Stanneylands Rd, Wilmslow, Cheshire SK9 4EX (☎ 0625 526795)

BROCKLEHURST, (John) Michael; s of John Mark Brocklehurst (d 1946), and Emily Victoria, *née* Burnet (d 1983); *b* 21 Nov 1929; *Educ* Ripon GS, Manchester Coll of Technol; *m* 1, 18 July 1959 (m dis 1984), Maureen Palles, da of Robert Bulloch Waddell; 1 s (Andrew b 1964), 1 da (Catherine b 1961); m 2, 18 April 1985, Lieselotte Tozer, da of Engelbert Jeibmann; *Career* cmmnd RASC; dir: Loch Long Estates Ltd 1972-81, Quarnford Estates Ltd 1987; chm: Craven DC 1979-80, Skipton Cons Assoc 1980-83; MBIM; *Clubs* Royal Scottish Automobile; *Style—* Michael Brocklehurst, Esq

BROCKLEHURST, Peter James; s of late John Gleave Brocklehurst, and Blanche Brocklehurst, *née* Hampson; *b* 30 Jan 1923; *Educ* Uppingham, RMA Sandhurst; *m* 17 June 1950, Dinah Millicent, da of the late George Oldham, of Cheshire; 1 s (John George David Brocklehurst b 1953); *Career* WWII Capt Grenadier Gds; chartered loss adjuster, memb Lloyds, High Sheriff of Cheshire 1986-87; *Recreations* gardening, opera, riding; *Clubs* City of London & Guards; *Style—* Peter J Brocklehurst, Esq; Peover Cottage, Peover Superior, Knutsford, Cheshire WA16 9HG (☎ 056 581 2210); Suite 655, Lloyds, 1 Lime Street, London EC3 7DQ (☎ 071 626 5243)

BROCKLESBY, Donald Ian; s of William Brocklesby, of Hull, N Humberside, and Brenda Margaret, *née* Russell; *b* 8 Sept 1948; *Educ* Cottingham Co Secdy Sch Hull, Bradford Univ (Post Graduate Dip in Fin & Ind Admin) 1973-74; *m* 21 Sept 1974, Gillian, da of James Alexander Sutherland, of Whitley Bay, Tyne & Wear; 1 s (Mark Russell b 1979), 2 da (Laura Jayne b 1977, Hannah Gillian 1983); *Career* CA 1972; ptnr White & Hoggard 1979-89, sr mangr Ernst & Young 1989-; chm St Peters Church Boys Club 1985-; FCA, FCCA; *Recreations* assoc football (Hull City Supporter), Cricket (Yorkshire); *Style—* Donald Brocklesby, Esq; 91 Westella Rd, Kirk Ella, Hull, N Humberside (☎ 0482 25531)

BROCKLESBY, Ian; s of Harold Brocklesby (d 1967), of Doncaster, and Eleanor May Berry; *b* 5 March 1944; *Educ* Pocklington, Univ of Durham (BA), Univ of Liverpool; *m* 1978, Anna-Kay Elizabeth, da of Peter Eversley Evelyn, of Florida; 3 s (Benjamin b 1979, Matthew Ian b 1981, Joshua b 1989; *Career* dir Ogilvy & Mather Ltd 1984-; *Recreations* golf, opera; *Style—* Ian Brocklesby, Esq; The Nines, Village Way, Little Chalfont, Buckinghamshire HP7 9PX (☎ 02404 2868); Ogilvy & Mather Ltd, Brettenham House, Lancaster Place, London WC2E 7EZ (☎ 071 836 2466, fax 071 836 9899)

BROCKMAN; *see*: Drake-Brockman

BROCKMAN, Vice Adm Sir Ronald Vernon; KCB (1965), CSI (1947), CIE (1946), CVO (1979), CBE (1943), DL (Devon 1968); er s of Rear Adm Henry Stafford Brockman, CB (d 1958), and Edith Mary, *née* Sheppard (d 1974); *b* 8 March 1909; *Educ* Weymouth Coll; *m* 1932, Marjorie Jean, da of Charles James Butt; 1 s, 3 da; *Career* served RN 1927-65: private sec to Govr Gen of India 1947-48, princ SO to Chief of Def Staff Adm of The Fleet The Earl Mountbatten of Burma 1959-65; extra gentleman usher to HM The Queen 1979- (gentleman usher 1967-79); KstJ 1984; *Recreations* sailing; *Clubs* White's, MCC, Royal Western Yacht of England, Naval (London); *Style—* Vice Adm Sir Ronald Brockman, KCB, CSI, CIE, CVO, CBE, DL; 3 Court House, Basil St, London SW3 1AJ (☎ 071 584 1023)

BROCKWAY, Hon Christopher Fenner; s of Baron Brockway (Life Peer, d 1988), and his 2 w, Edith Violet, *née* King; *b* 24 Nov 1946; *Educ* Magdalen Coll Oxford; *Style—* The Hon Christopher Brockway; 42 Chemin d'Eysins, CH-1260 Nyon, Switzerland

BROCKWAY, Baroness; Edith Violet; *née* King; da of late Archibald Herbert King, of Catford, London SE6; *m* 5 April 1946, as his 2 w, Baron Brockway (Life Peer, d 1988); 1 s (Hon Christopher Fenner, *qv*); 31 Ashlyn Close, Bushey, Herts (☎ 0923 43592)

BRODIE, Alan; s of Maxwell Brodie, of Glasgow, Scotland, and Judy, *née* Jacobson; *b* 11 Jan 1955; *Educ* HS of Glasgow, Univ of Edinburgh (BA, LLB); *m* 15 Nov 1982, Rosemary Anne, da of Donald H Squire (d 1985); 1 s (Daniel Henry b 1987), 1 da (Jennifer b 1986); *Career* dir Michael Imison Playwrights Ltd (Literary Agents) 1981-89, fndr Alan Brodie Representation 1989-; memb Down's Syndrome Assoc; *Style—* Alan Brodie, Esq; 91 Regent Street, London W1R 7TB

BRODIE, Sir Benjamin David Ross; 5 Bt (UK 1834); s of Sir Benjamin Collins Brodie, 4 Bt, MC (d 1971); *b* 29 May 1925; *Educ* Eton; *m* ; 1 s, 1 da; *Heir* s, Alan Brodie; *Style—* Sir Benjamin Brodie, Bt

BRODIE, (James) Bruce; s of John Hobson Brodie (d 1979), of Graaff-Reinet, S A, and Edith Florence, *née* Murray; *b* 19 March 1937; *Educ* Union HS S A, Univ of Natal (BA), Fitzwilliam Coll Cambridge (MA); *m* 15 Dec 1962, (Amie) Louise, da of Kenneth Turner James, MBE (d 1964), of Fetcham, Surrey; 2 da (Sarah b 1964, Nicola b 1966); *Career* slr; Frere Cholmeley: ptnr, chm 1990-; memb The Law Soc;

Recreations cricket, fishing; *Clubs* Hawks (Cambridge), MCC; *Style—* Bruce Brodie, Esq; Frere Cholmeley, 28 Lincoln's Inn Fields, London WC2A 3HH (☎ 071 405 7878, fax 071 405 9056, telex 27623 FRERES G)

BRODIE, Colin Alexander; QC (1980); s of Sir Benjamin Collins Brodie, MC, 4 Bt (d 1971); *b* 19 April 1929; *Educ* Eton, Magdalen Oxford; *m* 1955, Julia Anne Irene, da of late Norman E Wates, of Elmore, Chipstead, Surrey; 2 s (Christian Norman, Alexander Colin); *Career* called to the Bar 1953, bencher Lincoln's Inn 1988, memb Bar Cncl 1989; *Recreations* polo; *Style—* C A Brodie, Esq, QC; 24 Old Bldgs, Lincoln's Inn, London WC2

BRODIE, Philip Hope; QC (Scot 1987); s of Very Rev Dr Peter Philip Brodie (d 1990), of 13 Victoria Square, Stirling, and Constance Lindsay, *née* Hope; *b* 14 July 1950; *Educ* Dollar Acad, Univ of Edinburgh (LLB), Univ of Virginia (LLM); *m* 16 April 1983, Carol Dora, da of Dr Ian Stanley McLeish, of 4 Grange Rd, Bearsden, Glasgow; 2 s (Alexander b 1984, Peter b 1986), 1 da (Alice b 1988); *Career* admitted Faculty of Advocates 1976; standing jr counsel (Scot)MOD (Procurement) Health and Safety at Work Exec 1983, pt/t chm industl tbnls 1987, memb Mental Welfare Cmmn for Scot 1985-, memb Faculty of Advocates; *Style—* Philip H Brodie, Esq, QC; 2 Cobden Crescent, Edinburgh EH9 2BG (☎ 031 667 2651); Advocates Library, Parliament House, Edinburgh (☎ 031 226 5071)

BRODIE, Robert; CB (1990); s of Robert Brodie, MBE (d 1966), and Helen Ford Bayne, *née* Grieve; *b* 9 April 1938; *Educ* Morgan Acad Dundee, Univ of St Andrew's (MA, LLB); *m* 26 Sept 1970, Jean Margaret, da of Sheriff Princ Thomas Pringle McDonald, QC (d 1969); 2 s (Robert b 1971, James b 1980), 2 da (Alison b 1973, Ruth b 1978); *Career* legal asst to Sec of State for Scotland 1965 (dep slr 1984-87, slr 1987-), dep dir of Scottish Cts admin 1975-82; memb: Sheriff Ct Rules Cncl 1975-82, Scottish Ctee on Jurisdiction and Enforcement 1977-80, Working Party on Divorce Procedure 1979-80; session clerk Wardie Parish Church; memb Law Soc of Scotland; *Recreations* music, hill walking, making jam; *Style—* Robert Brodie, Esq, CB; 45 Stirling Rd, Edinburgh EH5 3JB (☎ 031 552 2028); Solicitors Office, New St Andrews House, Edinburgh EH1 3TE (☎ 031 244 5247)

BRODIE, Stanley Eric; QC (1975); s of Dr Abraham Brodie, of Allerton Bradford (d 1978), and Cissie Rachel Garstein; uncle Sir Israel Brodie, former chief rabbi of GB and The Cwlth; *b* 2 July 1930; *Educ* Bradford GS, Balliol Coll Oxford (MA); *m* 1, 31 July 1956, Gillian Rosemary, da of Sir Maxwell Joseph; 2 da (Henrietta b 1957, Charlotte b 1960); m 2, 29 Oct 1973, Elizabeth, da of Peter Gloster; 1 da (Sophie b 1978), 1 s (Samuel b 1981); *Career* called to the Bar Inner Temple 1954, recorder Crown Court 1975, bencher Inner Temple 1984, Bar Cncl 1987; *Recreations* fishing, boating, opera, holidays; *Clubs* Flyfishers; *Style—* Stanley Brodie, Esq, QC; Skeldon House, Dalrymple, Ayrshire; 39 Clarendon St, London SW1V 4RE; 2 Hare Ct, Temple, London EC4 (☎ 071 583 1770)

BRODIE, Hon Mrs (Vanessa Nathalie Mary); *née* Hawke; da of 10 Baron Hawke; *b* 20 June 1957; *m* 1985, (Peter) Adam William Brodie, s of Maj-Gen Thomas Brodie, CB, CBE, DSO, of Camberley, Surrey; 2 da (Nathalie Jane b 30 July 1986, Elizabeth Sarah b 17 Aug 1989); *Style—* The Hon Mrs Brodie; The Old Rectory, Tallarn Green, Malpas, Cheshire

BRODIE COOPER, Cristina; *Career* asst to Dir of Appeals The Forces Help Soc & Lord Roberts Workshops 1985-86, exec fund raiser for Royal Acad of Arts 1986-88, dir Devpt Fund RCM 1988-; *Style—* Miss Cristina Brodie Cooper; Director Development Fund, Royal College of Music, Prince Consort Rd, London SW7 2BS (☎ 071 589 3643, fax 071 589 7740)

BRODIE-HALL, Sir Laurence Charles; CMG (1976); *b* 10 June 1910; *Educ* Sch of Mines Kalgoorlie (Dip Metallurgy, DipME); *m* 1, 1940, Dorothy Jolly (decd); 3 s, 2 da; m 2, 1978, Jean Verschuer; *Career* RAE; tech asst to md Western Mining Corporation 1950-51, gen supt Great Western Consolidated 1951-58; dir: Western Mining Corporation 1962-82 (gen supt 1958-62), Alcoa of Aust 1972-82; pres: Chamber of Mines WA 1970-75, AIMM 1974; chm: CSIRO State Ctee 1971-78, Central Norseman Gold Corporation 1974-82 (geologist 1948-49), Three Springs Talc 1974-82, Kalgoorlie Mining Associates, Gold Mines of Kalgoorlie 1974-85, Westintech Innovation Corporation 1984-87, Bd of Mgmnt W Aust Sch of Mines 1982-, fndn for Sci and Technol; dir: Ansett WA 1983-, Coolgardie Gold NL; cncllr Curtin Univ of Technol; Freemason of the City of Kalgoorlie/Boulder 1989; Hon DTech WA Inst Technol 1978; Inst Medal Aust Inst of Mining and Metallurgy 1977 (former pres); fell Curtin Univ, Citizen of the Year award WA 1975; life memb: AIMM, Chamber of Mines WA, WASM Graduates Assoc, Agricola Coll; kt 1982; *Style—* Sir Laurence Brodie-Hall, CMG; 2 Cliff St, Perth, WA 6000, Australia

BRODIE OF BRODIE, (Montagu) Ninian Alexander; JP (Morayshire 1958), DL (Nairn 1970); 25 Chief of Clan Brodie; s of Ian Brodie of Brodie (d 1943); *b* 12 June 1912; *Educ* Eton; *m* 1939, Helena, da of Janssen Budgen, of Wendover; 1 s, 1 da (d 1972); *Heir* Alastair Brodie, younger of Brodie, *qv*; *Career* professional actor 1935-40 and 1945-50; market gardener and landowner 1953-80, ret; now involved in voluntary work (as a guide etc) at Brodie castle which has been owned by the Nat Tst for Scot since 1980; *Recreations* shooting, bridge, backgammon, bird watching; *Style—* Ninian Brodie of Brodie, JP, DL; Brodie Castle, Forres, Moray IV36 0TE (☎ 03094 202)

BRODIE, YOUNGER OF BRODIE, Alastair Ian Ninian; s and h of Ninian Brodie of Brodie, JP, DL, *qv*; *b* 7 Sept 1943; *Educ* Eton, Balliol Coll Oxford; *m* 1968 (m dis 1986), Mary Louise Johnson; 2 s, 1 da; *Career* Turnkey Systems Pty, Sydney, Australia; *Recreations* squash, chess; *Style—* Alastair Brodie, yr of Brodie; c/o Ninian Brodie of Brodie, JP, DL, Brodie Castle, Forres, Moray IV36 OTE

BRODRIBB, Dr Arthur Gerald Norcott; s of Dr Arthur Williamson Brodribb, JP (d 1950), and Violet Sybil Swainson (d 1970); *b* 21 May 1915; *Educ* Eastbourne Coll, Univ Coll Oxford (MA, DipEd), Univ of London (PhD); *m* 3 April 1954, Jessica (d 1986), da of Col Henry Vere Barr (d 1968); 1 s (Michael Bryan b 1955); *Career* master Canford Sch, Headmaster Hydneye House Sch, writer, archaeologist; co-dir Excavations at Beauport Park 1966-; FSA; *Books* The English Game (1947), Cricket in Fiction (1950), All Round The Wicket (1951), Next Man In (1952), The Bay and Other Poems (1953), Hastings and the Men of Letters (1954), Hit for Six (1960), Felix on the Bat (1962), The Croucher (1974), Maurice Tate (1976), The Art of Nicholas Felix (1985), Roman Brick and Tile (1987), Cricket at Hastings (1989); *Recreations* cricket, golf, Royal tennis, mangr Ewhurst Utd FC, music, archaeology; *Clubs* Marylebone Cricket, Rye Golf, Cricket Writers; *Style—* Dr Gerald Brodribb, FSA; Stubbles, Ewhurst Green, E Sussex TN32 5TD (☎ 058 0830 510)

BRODRICK, His Hon Judge; Michael John Lee; s of His Hon (Norman John Lee) Brodrick, QC, *qv*; *b* 12 Oct 1941; *Educ* Charterhouse, Merton Coll Oxford; *m* 1969, Valerie Lois, da of Gerald Max Stroud 2 C; *Career* called to the Bar Lincoln's Inn 1965; Western Circuit; elected to Senate of Inns of Court and the Bar 1979, served 1979-82, rec 1981-87; memb Wine Ctee Western Circuit 1982-86, judicial memb Tport Tbnl 1986, circuit judge 1987; *Recreations* gardening; *Clubs* Hampshire; *Style—* His Hon Judge Brodrick

BRODRICK, His Hon Norman John Lee; QC (1960), JP; 4 s of (William John) Henry Brodrick, OBE (d 1964), of 12 Frognal Gdns, Hampstead, NW3; *b* 4 Feb 1912; *Educ* Charterhouse, Merton Coll Oxford; *m* Ruth Severn, da of Sir Stanley Unwin, KCMG; 3 s (*see* Brodrick, Michael), 1 da; *Career* circuit judge, (ret); *Style—* His Hon N J L Brodrick, QC, JP; Slade Lane Cottage, Slade Lane, Rogate, Petersfield, Hants GU31 5BL

BRODTMAN, Robert Maurice; OBE (1977); s of Harris Brodtman (d 1942), and Marguerite, *née* Lippmann (d 1953); *b* 15 April 1917; *Educ* St Pauls; *m* 28 Feb 1978, Anne Madeleine, da of John Jacob Carter (d 1980); *Career* admitted slr 1939; chm: Hampstead Cncl Christians and Jews 1956-77, Camden CAB 1960-75, Hampstead Nat Savings Ctee; memb Tstees Savings Ctee South East, Camden Cncl of Social Serv, Camden Cncl of Community Rels Veridian Hosp Management Ctee; alderman Hampstead Borough Cncl 1962-65 (cncllr 1949-62), JP Inner London 1965-87, pres B'Nai B'rith 1st Lodge 1970-72, former memb Hampstead Old Peoples Housing Tst 1952-89; memb: Nat Heart & Chest Hosps 1972-88, Cardiothoracic Inst 1972-88; vice pres Hampstead Cons Assoc, tstee Hampstead Wells Campden Tst; *Recreations* gardening, crossword puzzles; *Clubs* Institute Directors; *Style—* Robert M Brodtman, Esq, OBE; 20 Beaufort Drive, London NW11 6BU (☎ 081 455 0086)

BRODWELL, John Shenton; s of Joseph Brodwell (d 1964), and Blanche Brodwell, *née* Shenton (d 1984); *b* 3 May 1945; *Educ* Woodhouse Grove Sch, Univ of Southampton (LLB); *Career* admitted slr 1970; ptnr: Harrisons 1973-87, Harrison Jobbings 1987-89, Blacks 1989; asst dep coroner W Yorks (Eastern Dist) 1990-; Immigration Appeal adjudicator 1976-; govr: Woodhouse Grove Sch 1980-, Horsforth Sch 1974-80 and 1988 (vice chm 1978-80); chm Horsforth Civic Soc 1973-, hon sec Leeds Philharmonic Soc 1982-, memb Bd Mgmnt of Methodist Schs 1987-91; *Recreations* music, choral singing, conservation of the environment; *Clubs* East India, Wig & Pen, Horsforth; *Style—* J S Brodwell, Esq; 30 Jackman Drive, Horsforth, Leeds LS18 4HS (☎ 0532 582744); 28 Park Square, Leeds LS1 2PH (☎ 0532 433311)

BROERS, Prof Alec Nigel; s of Alec William Broers (d 1987), of Melbourne, Victoria, Aust, and Constance Amy, *née* Cox; *b* 17 Sept 1938; *Educ* Geelong GS, Melbourne Univ (BSc), Caius Coll Cambridge (BA, PhD); *m* 1964, Mary Therese, da of Michael Phelan (d 1944); 2 s (Mark b 1965, Christopher b 1967); *Career* numerous managerial positions incl mangr Photon and Electron Optics IBM T J Watson Res Lab 1965-81; mangr: Lithography and Technology Tools 1981-82, Advanced Devpt IBM E Fishkill Lab 1983-84; prof of Electrical Energy and head Electrical Div Univ of Cambridge Engrg Dept 1984-, Master Churchill Coll Cambridge 1990-; IBM fell 1977, fell Trinity Coll 1985-90, memb IBM Corp Tech Ctee 1984; IEEE Cledo Brunetti award 1985, American Inst of Physics prize for Industl Applications of Physics 1982; FIEE, FEng, FRS; author of numerous papers, book chapters and patents on integrated circuit microfabrication and related subjects; *Recreations* music, sailing, skiing, tennis; *Style—* Prof Alec Broers, FRS; Master's Lodge, Churchill College, Cambridge CB3 0DS (☎ 0223 336226); Univ Engineering Dept, Trumpington St, Cambridge CB2 1PZ (☎ 0223 332675, fax 0223 332662, telex 81239)

BROGDEN, John Patrick Newton; s of Lt Alban Thomas Brogden, RFC (1948), and Mabel Le Butt, *née* Newton (d 1976); *Educ* Hull GS; *m* 7 June 1952, Eileen Norah Mary, da of Henry Mahony (d 1975), of 16 St Colman's Ave, Cosham, Portsmouth; 1 s (Richard b 1956), 2 da (Teresa b 1953, Veronica b 1962); *Career* Nat Serv RN 1946-48; CA 1952; ptnr Jones Avens Portsmouth 1956-, chm Radio victory Ltd 1974-84; dir: Day Hartley & Pembroke Bishops Walthan (fin planning conslts), Hants Bldg Soc 1989-; city cncllr Portsmouth 1967-76, Lord Mayor City of Portsmouth 1973-74; chm: Cncl Community Serv Portsmouth 1977-82, Mgmnt Ctee Citizens Advice Bureau Portsmouth 1983-; Freeman City of London, Liveryman Worshipful Co of Carmen; FCA 1952; *Recreations* bridge; *Style—* John Brogden, Esq; 70 Links Lane, Rowlands Castle, Hants (☎ 0705 41 2990); 53 Kent Rd, Southsea, Portsmouth, Hants (☎ 0705 820726, fax 0705 291224)

BROKE, Adam Vere Balfour; s of Charles Vere Broke (d 1944), and Violet Rosemary, *née* Balfour; *b* 16 April 1941; *Educ* Eton; *m* 27 March 1965, Sarah Penelope, da of Norman Lanyon, DSC (d 1981); 3 da; *Career* CA; former pres Inst of Taxation; Freeman Worshipful Co of CAs; FCA 1964, FTII 1971; *Recreations* music, gardening, shooting; *Clubs* Boodles; *Style—* Adam Broke, Esq; Adam Broke & Co, 29 Maiden Lane, London WC2E 7JS (☎ 071 497 0105)

BROKE, Michael Haviland Adlington; s of Philip Adlington Broke, of 167 Broadway, Peterborough, and Jean, *née* Hiley; *b* 9 March 1936; *Educ* Eton, Corpus Christi Coll Cambridge (MA), London Business Sch; *m* 1961, Vera Antonjeta, da of Nikola Gjuracic (d 1972); 1 s (Philip b 9 Sept 1962), 1 da (Nicola b 17 June 1964); *Career* dir J Rothschild & Co Ltd 1975-84, chief exec Stockley plc 1984-87, dep chm Chelsfield plc 1987-; *Recreations* cricket, theatre, music; *Clubs* Buck's, Cavalry & Guards, MCC; *Style—* Michael Broke, Esq; 67 Brook St, London W1

BROKE, Maj-Gen Robert Straton; CB (1967), OBE (1946), MC (1940); s of Rev Horatio George Broke (d 1931), and Mary Campbell, *née* Adlington (d 1949); *b* 15 March 1913; *Educ* Eton, Magdalene Coll Cambridge; *m* 1939, Ernine Susan Margaret, da of Rev William Henry Bonsey (d 1951); 2 s (*see* Lt-Col George Broke); *Career* RA 1933-66, served ME, N Africa, Europe, Maj-Gen 1964, Northern Army Gp 1964-66; Col Cmdt RA 1968-78; farmer; dir Wellman plc 1968-88; pres Metallurgical Plantmakers Fedn 1977-79; *Recreations* country sports; *Clubs* Army and Navy; *Style—* Maj-Gen Robert Broke, CB, OBE, MC; Ivy Farm, Holme Hale, Thetford, Norfolk IP25 7DJ (☎ 0760 440225)

BROKE, Lt-Col (George) Robin Straton; LVO (1977); s of Maj-Gen Robert Straton Broke, CB, OBE, MC, *qv*, and (Ernine) Susan Margaret, *née* Bonsey; *b* 31 March 1946; *Educ* Eton (Capt of Tennis, memb The Eton Soc); *m* 20 Dec 1978, Patricia Thornhill, da of Thomas Thornhill Shann (d 1983), of Trenoweth, Feock, Cornwall; 1 s (George Straton b 1981); *Career* cmmnd RA 1965; Equerry-in-Waiting to HM The Queen 1974-77; attended Army Staff Coll 1979; attended US Army Staff Coll 1985; cmd 3 Regt RHA 1987-89; *Recreations* country sports, photography; *Clubs* Lansdowne; *Style—* Lt-Col Robin Broke, LVO; Ivy Farm, Holme Hale, Thetford, Norfolk IP25 7DJ (☎ 0760 440225)

BROLLY, Brian Thomas; s of late Thomas Henry Brolly, and Winifred Louise, *née* Christie; *b* 21 Oct 1936; *Educ* St Dunstan's Coll London; *m* 1 June 1963, Gillian, da of late William Adams; 2 s (Sarsfield Kean b 1967, Tristan Patrick b 1970); *Career* with MCA Inc (USA); md & fndr MCA UK & Europe: Records Ltd, Films Ltd, Universal Pictures Ltd; sr vice pres MCA TV, exec asst to dir gen Radio Telefis Eireann 1961-63, dir Universal Pictures Ltd 1963-73 (1957-61), md MPL Communications Ltd (Paul McCartney: recording, TV, films, music, photography, books; Wings: recording, world concert tour) 1973-78; md The Really Useful Co (now The Really Useful Gp plc, Andrew Lloyd Webber's company) 1978-; *Recreations* sport, rugby (London Irish), Surrey; *Clubs* Hurlingham; *Style—* Brian T Brolly, Esq; The Really Useful Group, 20 Greek Street, London W1V 5LF (☎ 01 734 2114, telex 8953151, fax 01 734 6230)

BROMAGE, Dr (James) David; s of James Richard Vincent Arthur Bromage, CBE, and Dr Frances Charlotte Kerr (d 1989); *b* 23 Sept 1949; *Educ* Sedbergh, St Mary's Hosp Univ of London (MB BS); *m* 24 Jan 1981, Elizabeth Eugenie Margaret, da of Richard Wordsworth Hamilton Raikes; 2 da (Julia b 1983, Isabelle b 1986); *Career* conslt orthopaedic surgn; FRCS, FRCSEd 1979; memb: RSM 1979, Br Orthopaedic Assoc 1980; *Style—* Dr David Bromage; District General Hospital, Kettering, Northants (☎ 0536 410666); The Clinic, 71 Park St, London W1

BROMAGE, Hon Mrs (Jaqumine); *née* Thellusson; da of 8 Baron Rendlesham by his 2 w, Clare; *b* 21 Aug 1960; *m* 11 June 1987, Charles N Bromage, s of Col Nigel Bromage, of Powys; *Style*— The Hon Mrs Bromage; c/o Colonel Nigel Bromage, Barland House, Presteigne, Powys

BROME, Vincent; s of Nathaniel Gregory Brome, and Emily Brome; *Educ* Streatham GS, Elleston Sch; *Career* feature writer Daily Chronicle, ed Menu Magazines, Miny of Info, asst ed Medical World, memb for Library Advsy Ctee 1975-82; play The Sleepless One 1962 and six plays for TV and radio; pubns: Anthology (1936), Clement Atlee (1947), H G Wells (1951), Aneurin Bevan (1953), The Last Surrender (1954), The Way Back (1956), Six Studies in Quarrelling (1958), Sometimes at Night (1959), Frank Harris (1959), Acquaintance With Grief (1961), We Have Come A Long Way (1962), The Problem of Progress (1963), Love in Our Time (1964), Four Realist Novelists (1964), The International Brigades (1965), The World by Luke Jympson (1966), Freud and His Early Circle (1967), The Surgeon (1967), Diary of a Revolution (1968), The Revolution (1969), The Imaginary Crime (1969), Confessions of a Writer (1970), The Brain Operators (1970), Private Prosecutions (1971), Reverse Your Verdict (1971), London Consequences (1972), The Embassy (1972), The Day of Destruction (1975), The Happy Hostage (1976), Jung - Man and Myth (1978), Havelock Ellis - philospher of Sex (1981), Ernest Jones: Freud's Alter Ego (1983), The Day of the Fifth Moon (1984), J B Priestley (1989); contrib: The Times, Sunday Times, Observer, Manchester Guardian, New Statesman, New Society, Encounter, Spectator, TLS; *Recreations* writing plays, talking; *Clubs* Savile; *Style*— Vincent Brome, Esq; 45 Great Ormond Street, London WC1 (☎ 071 405 0550)

BROMET, Lady; *see*: Conan Doyle, Dame Jean

BROMHEAD, Col David de Gonville; LVO (1984), OBE (1988); 2 s of Lt-Col Edmund de Gonville Hosking Bromhead (d 1977, himself yr bro of Sir Benjamin Bromhead, 5 Bt, OBE, and great nephew of Lt-Col Gonville Bromhead, VC, who defended Rorke's Drift in the Zulu War of 1879) and Joan, da of late Brig Sir Henry Scott, CB, DSO, MC; bro of John Bromhead, *qv*; *b* 16 Sept 1944; *Educ* St Andrew's Grahamstown SA, RMA; *m* 1970, Susan, da of Cdr Richard Furley Fyson, DSC, JP, RN; 1 s (James b 1974), 2 da (Annabel b 1973, Antonia b 1978); *Career* Royal Regt of Wales, Gen Serv Medal (Clasps) S Arabia and NI; has taken part in expeditions under John Blashford-Snell down Blue Nile (1968) and led reconnaissance party through Darien Gap during Trans-America Expedition 1971; equerry to HRH The Prince of Wales 1982-84, Lt-Col 1983, cmd 1 Bn Royal of Wales, Col 1987; *Recreations* fishing; *Style*— Col David Bromhead, LVO, OBE; c/o Cox's & King's Lloyds, 6 Pall Mall, London SW1

BROMHEAD, Sir John Desmond Gonville; 6 Bt (UK 1806), of Thurlby Lincs; s of Sir Benjamin Bromhead, 5 Bt, OBE (d 1981); *b* 21 Dec 1943; *Educ* Wellington; *Heir* cous, John Bromhead; *Style*— Sir John Bromhead, Bt; Thurlby Hall, Thurlby, nr Lincoln LN5 9EG

BROMHEAD, John Edmund de Gonville; s of late Lt-Col Edmund de Gonville Hosking Bromhead (d 1973), and Joan, da of late Brig Sir Henry Scott, CB, DSO, MC; bro of Lt-Col David Bromhead, *qv*; first cous and hp of Sir John Bromhead, 6 Bt; *b* 10 Oct 1939; *Educ* St Andrew's Coll Grahamstown S Africa, RAF Coll Cranwell; *m* 1965, Janet, da of Henry Brotherton, of Moreton-in-Marsh, Glos; 1 s, 1 da; *Career* Capt Br Airways, served RAF to 1964 (when ret); *Style*— John Bromhead Esq; Duiker House, Fencott, Islip, Oxford

BROMHEAD, Lady; Nancy Mary; da of late T S Lough, of Buenos Aires; *m* 1938, Sir Benjamin Bromhead, 5 Bt, OBE (d 1981); 1 s, 2 da; *Style*— Lady Bromhead; Thurlby Hall, Lincoln

BROMLEY, Archdeacon of; *see*: Francis, Edward Reginald

BROMLEY, Charles Howard; s and h of Sir Rupert Bromley, 10 Bt, *qv*; *b* 31 July 1963; *Style*— Charles Bromley Esq; PO Box 249, Rivonia 2128, Transvaal

BROMLEY, (Amey) Ida; MBE; da of William Gordon Bromley (d 1967), and Amy Elizabeth, *née* Marsden (d 1973); *b* 18 July 1929; *Educ* Saxonholme Sch Birkdale Lancs, Royal Liverpool Hosps Sch of Physiotherapy; *Career* appts in various hosps in England and Royal N Shore Hosp Sydney Aust 1952-65; supt physiotherapist: Stoke Mandeville Hosp Aylesbury 1966-77, King's Coll Hosp London 1977-79; dir of physiotherapy services Hampstead Health Dist 1979-86; memb NHS Health Advsy Serv 1983-; memb: Br Sports Assoc for the Disabled 1973-76, Soc for Res in Rehabilitation 1978 (fndr memb and former pres), Cncl Western Cerebral Palsy Centre 1980-, Cncl Mobility for the Disabled, Int Soc of Paraplegia; chm Cncl of Chartered Soc of Phsiotherapy 1978-82 (memb 1952); memb editorial bds: Paraplegia, Physiotherapy Practice; accompanied Br team to Olympic Games for the paralysed in Japan, Israel, Germany; frequent lectr at nat and int confs; FCSP 1986; *Books* Paraplegia and Tetraplegia (1976), International Perspectives in Physical Therapy (series ed 1984-); *Recreations* music, bridge, country pursuits, conservation, foreign travel, entertaining, bird watching; *Style*— Miss Ida Bromley, MBE; 6 Belsize Grove, London NW3 4UN (☎ 071 722 1794)

BROMLEY, Sir Rupert Charles; 10 Bt (GB 1757), of East Stoke, Nottinghamshire; s of Maj Sir Rupert Bromley, 9 Bt, MC (d 1966, fifth in descent from Sir George Bromley, 2 Bt, who changed his name to Bromley from Smith); *b* 2 April 1936; *Educ* Rhodes Univ, Ch Ch Oxford; *m* 26 April 1962, Priscilla Hazel, o da of late Maj Howard Bourne, HAC; 3 s; *Heir* s, Charles Howard Bromley, *qv*, b 31 July 1963; *Career* co exec Murray & Roberts Ltd; diocesan registrar Dio of Johannesburg; *Recreations* golf; *Clubs* Western Province Sports, Johannesburg Country; *Style*— Sir Rupert Bromley, Bt; PO Box 249, Rivonia 2128, Transvaal

BROMLEY-DAVENPORT, William Arthur; DL (Cheshire 1982); only s of Lt-Col Sir Walter Bromley-Davenport (d 1989), and Lenette, *née* Jeanes (d 1989); *b* 7 March 1935; *Educ* Eton, Cornel Univ; *m* 1962, Elizabeth Boies, da of John Watts, of Oldwick, NJ, USA; 1 s; *Career* Lord Lt of Cheshire 1990-; *Style*— William Bromley-Davenport, Esq, DL; The Kennels, Capesthorne, Macclesfield, Cheshire

BROMLEY GARDNER, Lt-Col Richard; MC (1944); s of Richard Bromley Gardner (d 1934), and Evelyn Doris, *née* Walker (d 1977); *b* 21 June 1921; *Educ* Wrekin Coll, RMA Sandhurst; *m* 11 June 1949, Jean Dorothy, da of Theodore Bower (d 1967); 2 s (Michael b 1952, Charles b 1960), 1 da (Caroline b 1950); *Career* 2 Lt Highland LI 1939, war serv Western Desert, Sicily, Italy, Greece, Dalmation Islands (MC, despatches), instr RMA Sandhurst 1947-49, Capt King's Guard Balmoral 1949, Staff Coll 1950, serv Korea, Malaya 1954-56 (despatches), Lt-Col 1961, ret 1968; steward's sec Jockey Club 1969-87, (sr steward's sec 1987), pres Jockey Club Officials' Assoc, steward Bath and Salisbury racecourses; *Recreations* fox hunting, bloodstock breeding, music; *Clubs* Army and Navy; *Style*— Lt-Col Richard Bromley Gardner, MC; Kingscote Park, Tetbury, Glos (☎ 0453 860223)

BROMLEY-MARTIN, Michael Granville; s of Capt David Eliot Bromley-Martin, of Tuffs Hard, Bovham Hoe, Chichester, Sussex, and Angela Felicity, *née* Hampden-Ross; *b* 27 April 1955; *Educ* Eton, Univ of Southampton (BSc); *m* Anna Frances, da of Maj Peter Rouse Addison Birley, of Church Farm House, Frampton, Dorchester, Dorset; 1 s (Charles b 28 May 1989), 1 da (Alexandra Anne b 22 May 1990); *Career* called to the Bar Grays' Inn 1979; joined chambers of Victor Durand, QC 1981; *Recreations* sailing, fishing; *Clubs* Royal Ocean Racing; *Style*— Michael Bromley-Martin, Esq; 3 Raymond Buildings, Grays Inn, London WC1R 5BH (☎ 071 831 3833, fax 071 242 4221)

BRON, Eleanor; da of Sydney Bron and Fagah Bron (d 1990); *Educ* North London Collegiate Sch, Newnham Coll Cambridge (BA); *Career* actress and writer; De La Rue Co 1961; appearances incl: revue, Establishment Nightclub Soho 1962, NY 1963, Not So Much a Programme More a Way of Life BBC TV 1964, several TV series written with John Fortune; also TV series incl: Making Faces (by Michael Frayn) 1976, Pinkerton's Progress 1983; TV plays incl: Nina 1978, My Dear Palestrina 1980, A Month in the Country 1985, Quatermaine's Terms 1987, changing step 1989; stage performances incl: The Doctor's Dilemma (Jennifer Dubedat) 1966, The Prime of Miss Jean Brodie (Jean Brodie) 1967 and 1984, Hedda Gabler (title role) 1969, The Merchant of Venice (Portia) 1975, Private Lives (Amanda) 1976, Uncle Vanya (Elena) 1977, The Cherry Orchard (Charlotte 1978 and Vanya 1985), A Family (Margaret) 1978, On Her Own 1980, The Amusing Spectacle of Cinderella and her Naughty, Naughty Sisters 1980, Goody Biddy Bean, Betrayal 1981, Heartbreak House 1981, Duet for One 1982, The Duchess of Malfi 1985, The Real Inspector Hound and The Critic (double bill) 1985, Oedipus and Oedipus at Colonus (Jocasta and Ismene) 1987, Infidelities 1987, The Chalk Garden 1989; films incl: Help!, Alfie, Two for the Road, Bedazzled, Women in Love, The National Health, The Day That Christ Died 1980, Turtle Diary 1985, Little Dorrit; composer of song-cycle with John Dankworth 1973, also verses for Saint - Saens' Carnival of the Animals 1975; publications: Is Your Marriage Really Necessary (with John Fortune 1972), My Cambridge (contrib 1976), More Words (contrib 1977), Life and Other Punctures (1978), The Pillow Book of Eleanor Bron (1985); performances incl: Facade by Walton, Almeida Festival of Contempary Music ORAL TREASON - by Kagel 1987; *Style*— Miss Eleanor Bron; c/o Jeremy Conway, 18-21 Jermyn St, London SW1 (☎ 071 287 0077)

BRONDER, Peter; s of Johann Bronder, and Gertrude, *née* Kastl; *b* 22 Oct 1953; *Educ* Letchworth GS, RAM; *Career* tenor; Bayreuth Festival Chorus 1983, Glyndebourne Festival Chorus 1985, princ tenor WNO 1986-90 (performances for WNO in NY and Milan 1989, Tokyo 1990); debut: Royal Opera Covent Garden 1986, ENO 1989, Glyndebourne Festival 1990, in Europe as guest at Netherlands Opera 1989; live on BBC Radio 3: Snape Maltings Concert 1987, Salome R Strauss 1988, Sonnambula Bellini 1989; recordings: Kiri Te Kanawa recital 1988, Adriana Lecouvreur Citea 1988, Osuol Janacek 1989; many appearances on TV and radio incl: BBC TV Laurence Oliver Awards 1985, BBC TV Falstaff Verdi WNO 1989, Wozzeck Berg ENO 1990; ARAM, LRAM, LGSM; *Recreations* sports, photography, electronics, motorcyling; *Style*— Peter Bronder, Esq; c/o Allied Artists, 42 Montpelier Sq, London SW7 1JZ (☎ 071 589 6243)

BROOK, Anthony Donald; s of Donald Charles Brook (d 1976), and Doris Ellen, *née* Emmett (d 1987); *b* 24 Sept 1936; *Educ* Eastbourne Coll; *m* 18 March 1964, Ann Mary, da of Edwin Reeves, of 51 Albert Road, New Milton, Hampshire BH25 6SP; 2 da (Claire b 30 June 1966, Joanne b 24 April 1970); *Career* joined Assoc Television Ltd 1966, fin controller ATV Network Ltd 1966-74, dir external fin IBA 1974-78, fin dir/gen mangr ITC Entertainment Ltd 1978-81, md TVS Television Ltd and dir TVS Entertainment plc 1981-; dir: Invicta Sound plc, TVS Telethon Tst; govr The Out of Town Centre; FCA 1970; *Recreations* sailing, golf; *Clubs* Royal Southern Yacht; *Style*— Anthony Donald Brook, Esq; TVS Television Ltd, Television Centre, Southampton SO9 9HZ (☎ 0703 634211, fax 0703 636570)

BROOK, Hon Mrs (Catherine Mary); *née* Hawke; da of 10 Baron Hawke, and Angela Margaret Griselda, *née* Bury (d 1984); *b* 11 July 1940; *Educ* Tudor Hall, London Univ (BEd); *m* 16 March 1963, Charles Groves Darville Brook, s of Air Vice-Marshal William Arthur Darville Brook, CB, CBE (d 1953); 2 da (Charlotte b 1965, Henrietta b 1968); *Career* teacher now working as a volunteer organiser for Richmond upon Thames; *Style*— The Hon Mrs Brook; 7 The Hermitage, Richmond, Surrey TW10 6SH

BROOK, Prof Charles Groves Darville; s of Air Vice-Marshal William Arthur Darville Brook, CB, CBE (d 1953), and Marjorie Jean Hamilton, *née* Grant; *b* 15 Jan 1940; *Educ* Rugby, Magdalene Coll Cambridge (BA, MA, MD), St Thomas's Hosp Med Sch (MB BChir); *m* 16 March 1963, Hon Catherine Mary, da of Lord Hawke, of Old Mill House, Cuddington, Northwich, Cheshire; 2 da (Charlotte b 1965, Henrietta b 1968); *Career* resident posts: St Thomas's Hosp 1964-68, Hosp for Sick Children Gt Ormond St 1968-74; Wellcome travelling res fell Kinderspital Zurich 1972-73, conslt paediatrician Middx Hosp 1974-, prof of paediatric endocrinology Univ of London 1989-; chm Richmond Soc 1968-74, special tstee The Middx Hosp 1984-, tstee Richmond Parish Land Charity 1988-; memb Ctee of Mgmnt: Royal Med Benevolent Fund 1976- (treas 1989), RSM; MRCP London 1967, FRCP 1979, DCH 1968; *Books* Practical Paediatric Endocrinology (1978), Clinical Paediatric Endocrinology (2 edn, 1989), Growth Assessment in Childhood & Adolescence (1982), All about Adolescence (1985), Current Concepts in Paediatric Endocrinology (1988); *Recreations* DIY, gardening, fishing; *Style*— Prof Charles Brook; 7 The Hermitage Richmond, Surrey TW10 6SH (☎ 081 940 2581); The Middlesex Hospital, Mortimer St, London W1N 8AA (☎ 071 380 9455, fax 071 636 9941)

BROOK, Air Vice-Marshal David Conway Grant; CB (1990), CBE 1983); s of Air Vice Marshal William Arthur Darville Brook CB, CBE (d 1953), and Marjorie Jean Hamilton, *née* Grant; *b* 23 Dec 1935; *Educ* Marlborough, RAF Coll Cranwell; *m* 14 Jan 1961, Jessica Rose, da of Col Michael Ronald Lubbock (d 1989), of Ottawa; 1 s (William b 1965), 1 da (Julie b 1961); *Career* Pilot- Nos 263, 1 (Fighter) and 14 Sqdns (Hunter aircraft) 1957-62, ADC to AOC-in-C Near East Air Force 1962-64, CO No 1 (Fighter) Sqdn (Hunter MK 9) 1964-66, RN Staff Course 1967, RAF Advsr to Dir Land/Air Warfare (MOD Army) 1968-69, Wing Cdr Offensive Support (Jt Warfare Estab) 1970-72, CO No 20 (Army Cooperation) Sqdn (Harrier) 1974-76, Station Cdr RAF Wittering (Harrier) 1976-78, Royal Coll of Def Studies 1979, princ Staff Offr to Chief of Def Staff 1980-82, SASO HQ RAF Germany 1982-85, Air Offr Scot and NI 1986-89, ret 1989; appt civil emergencies advsr Home Office 1989; *Recreations* golf, music, hill-walking; *Clubs* RAF; *Style*— Air Vice-Marshal D C G Brook, CB, CBE; Cherry Orchard Cottage, Broad Campden, Glos GL55 6UU (☎ 0386 840352)

BROOK, Greville Bertram; s of Bertram Frederick Brook (d 1979), and Frances Emily Weldon (d 1975); *b* 30 July 1926; *Educ* Hipperholme GS, Scunthorpe GS, Univ of Sheffield (BMet); *m* 12 Sept 1953, Mary Rose, da of William Owen Saunders; 2 s (Adrian Kevin b 13 June 1958, Julian Simon William b 9 Jan 1963), 1 da (Deborah Clare Amanda b 2 Jan 1961); *Career* bursar Br Non-Ferrous Metals Res Assoc 1947-49; Fulmer Research Institute Ltd: investigator 1949-54, section head 1954-68, princ metallurgist 1968-75; dir: Fulmer Research Laboratories Ltd 1975-90, Yarsley Tech Centre Ltd 1982-90; visiting reader Dept of Metallurgy Univ of Surrey 1974-86, metallurgical conslt 1990-; *Awards* Sir Robert Hadfield medal prize Inst of Metals 1988, TB Marsden award Inst of Metals 1989; M Univ Surrey 1980; fell Inst of Metals 1970 (memb 1946, memb Cncl 1983-87), FEng 1987; FRSA 1988, London Metallurgical Soc (chm 1980-81); *Publications* Die Casting Handbook (contrib), Advanced Materials Technology (ed 1990, 2 edn 1991); *Recreations* theatre, opera, photography, gardening, travel, music, wine; *Style*— Greville Brook, Esq; 9 Whitfield Rd, Hughenden Valley, High Wycombe, Bucks HP14 4NZ (☎ 024024 3570, 049456

3570)

BROOK, Lady; Helen; eldest da of John and Helen Knewstub, of Chelsea, SW3; *b* 12 Oct 1907; *Educ* Convent of Holy Child Jesus Mark Cross Sussex; *m* 2, 1937, Sir Robin Brook, CMG, OBE, *qv*; 2 da (and 1 da of previous m); *Career* opened the first birth control sessions for the unmarried woman in 1960 in the Marie Stopes Centre; fndr and pres The Brook Advsy Centres for young people 1963; vice pres Family Planning Assoc, chm Family Planning Sales 1974-80; *Style*— Lady Brook; 31 Acacia Rd, London NW8 6AS (☎ 071 722 5844); Claydene Garden Cottage, Cowden, Kent (☎ 0342 367)

BROOK, Leopold; s of Albert and Kate Brook, of Hampstead; *b* 2 Jan 1912; *Educ* Univ Coll London (BSc); *m* 1, 1940, Susan (d 1970), da of David Rose, of Hampstead; 2 s; m 2, 1974, Elly, wid of Gilbert G Rhodes; 2 step s, 1 step da; *Career* chm: Simon Engineering plc 1970-77, Associated Nuclear Services Ltd 1977-90, Brown & Sharpe Group Ltd 1979-88; dir Renishaw plc 1981-; fell UCL 1970; FICE, FIMechE; *Clubs* Athenaeum, Hurlingham; *Style*— Leopold Brook, Esq; 55 Kingston House North, Prince's Gate, London SW7 1LW (☎ 071 584 2041)

BROOK, Michael; s of John Brook (d 1981), and Mary, *née* Gilpin; *b* 1 Sept 1949; *Educ* Batley GS, Leeds Poly Faculty of Mgmnt Studies (BA); *m* 21 April 1973, Lynn, da of Leonard Sargeant Allan; 2 da (Alison Judith b 7 Feb 1976, Joanne Elizabeth b 25 May 1977); *Career* asst sales mangr British Jeffrey Diamond Wakefield 1972-73, asst mktg controller Yorkshire Electricity Bd 1974-76, brands mangr Thomas Eastham & Sons 1976-79; Graham Poulter Partnership: account mangr 1979-80, account dir 1980-82, assoc dir 1982-83, dir and ptnr 1983-91; md Geddes Advertising and Marketing 1991-; MCIM 1976; *Recreations* golf, cricket, photography, music; *Clubs* South Leeds Golf, Gildersome Taverners and Cricket; *Style*— Michael Brook, Esq; 3 Woodkirk Gardens, Leeds Rd, Dewsbury, W Yorks WF12 7HZ (☎ 0924 475544); Geddes Advertising & Marketing, Linden House, 34 Moorgate Rd, Rotherham, S Yorks S60 2AG (☎ 0709 375184, fax 0709 379367, car 0860 488198)

BROOK, Peter; s of Ernest John Brook, and Jenny, *née* Waters; *b* 17 Jan 1947; *Educ* Barry GS, Swansea Univ (BSc), London Univ (MSc); *m* 2 June 1978, Deirdrie Teresa, da of T Handley (d 1983); 2 da (Jessica b 1982, Elizabeth b 1987); *Career* Services Electronics Res Laboratory 1967-76; Royal Signals & Radar Estab 1976-87: head Air Def ATC 1985-87, dir sci Land Systems 1987-89; *Recreations* singing (choral and solo), DIY, family; *Style*— Peter Brook, Esq; Riversmead, Pankridge St, Crondall, Farmham GU10 5RA

BROOK, Sir Robin (Ralph Ellis); CMG (1954), OBE (1945); s of Francis Brook, of Harley St, London W1; *b* 19 June 1908; *Educ* Eton, King's Coll Cambridge; *m* 1937, Helen, *qv*; 2 da; *Career* WWII Brig served W Europe 1945; former dir Bank of England; former chm: Gordon Woodroffe & Co, Leda Investment Tst, Ionian Bank Ltd, Carclo Engineering Group; dir BP 1970-73; vice pres Assoc of Br Cs of C (formerly pres), président d'honneur Conf Permanente of EEC Cs of C; vice pres London C of C and Indust (formerly chm then pres); memb City and Hackney Health Authy (formerly City and E London HA) 1974-85; govr St Bartholomew's Hosp 1962-74 (treas and chm 1969-74), chm Special Tstees 1974-88, pres Medical Coll 1969-88, chm Res Tst; vice pres: Family Planning Assoc, Brook Advsy Centres; former chm Sports Cncl and Sport Devpt Ctee; govr Exec Ctee Sports Aid Fund; chm Colson Tst; memb: Cncl and Fin Ctee City Univ, Cncl and Mgmnt Ctee King's Fund, Cncl Festival of Britain; pres London Homes for the Elderly; high sheriff London 1950; past master and wine warden Worshipful Co of Haberdashers; Br sabre champion 1936 (Olympic Games 1936 and 1948); Hon DSc City Univ; Cdr Legion of Merit, Legion of Honour, Croix de Guerre and bars, Offr Order of Leopold, Belgian Croix de Guerre; kt 1974; *Style*— Sir Robin Brook, CMG, OBE; 31 Acacia Rd, London NW8 (☎ 071 722 5844); Claydene Garden Cottage, Cowden, Kent (☎ 034 286367)

BROOK, Rosemary Helen; da of Charles Rex Brook (d 1971), and Nellie Beatrice, *née* Yare; *b* 7 Feb 1946; *Educ* Gravesend Sch for Girls, Newnham Coll Cambridge (MA); *m* 1, 1970 (m dis 1979), Roger John Gross; m 2, 22 Sept 1984, Richard Winston Arbiter; 1 step da (Victoria b 1974); *Career* account mangr McCann Erickson Ltd 1975-77; head of public affrs Wiggins Teape Gp Ltd 1977-82 (Euro mktg coordinator 1968-75); dep chm and chief exec Daniel J Edelman (UK) Ltd 1982-; Freeman City of London 1985; FIPR 1977, MIPRA 1979; *Recreations* opera, ballet, reading, gardening, swimming; *Clubs* Reform; *Style*— Miss Rosemary Brook; Kingsgate House, 536 King's Road, London SW1O OTE (☎ 071 835 1222, fax 071 351 7676, telex 929478)

BROOK-PARTRIDGE, Bernard; s of Leslie Brook-Partridge (d 1933), and Gladys Vere, *née* Brooks (later Mrs Burchell) (d 1989); *Educ* Selsdon Co GS, Cambs Tech Coll, Univ of Cambridge, Univ of London; *m* 1, 3 Nov 1951 (m dis 1965), (Enid) Elizabeth, da of Frederick Edmund Hatfield (d 1951), of Sanderstead; 2 da (Eva Katherine Helen (Mrs New) b 6 Dec 1952, Katrina Elizabeth Jane (Mrs Gannon) b 18 Aug 1954); m 2, 14 Oct 1967, Carol Devonald, da of Arnold Devonald Francis Lewis (d 1989), of Gower, S Wales; 2 s (Charles Gareth Devonald b 21 Dec 1969, James Edward Devonald b 4 June 1974); *Career* Nat Serv 1944-48; called to the Bar Gray's Inn 1950, cashier and accountant Dominion Rubber Co Ltd 1950-51, asst export mangr Br & Gen Tube Co Ltd 1951-52, asst sec Assoc of Int Accountants 1952-59, sec gen Inst of Linguists 1959-62, various teaching posts FDR 1962-66, special asst to md M G Scott Ltd 1966-68, business conslt (incl various directorships) 1968-72, memb Peterborough Devpt Corp 1972-88, ptnr Carsons Brook-Partridge & Co 1972-, dir and sec Roban Engrg Ltd 1975-, chm Queensgate Mgmnt Servs Ltd 1981-87; dir: Brompton Troika Ltd 1985-, Pugh Carmichael Conslts Ltd 1988-, Alan Wooff Assocs Ltd 1986-, Edmund Nuttall Ltd 1986-, MKL Consltg Engrs 1988-, PEG Mgmnt Conslts plc 1988-, Kyle Stewart Ltd 1989-; local govt and political advsr Transmanche-Link 1988-89; contested (C) St Pancras N LCC 1958, memb (C) St Pancras Met Borough Cncl 1959-62, prospective parly candidate (C) Shoreditch and Finsbury 1960-62, contested (C) Nottingham Central 1970; GLC: memb for Havering 1967-73, memb for Havering (Romford) 1973-85 (chm 1980-81); chm: Enviromental Planning (NE) Area Ctee 1967-71, Town Devpt Ctee 1971-73, Arts Ctee 1977-79, Public Servs and Safety Ctee 1978-79; opposition spokesman: for Arts and Recreation 1973-74, for Policy matters 1983-85; memb: Exec Ctee Greater London Arts Assoc 1973-78, Exec Cncl Area Museums serv for SE Eng 1977-78, Cncl and Exec Greater London and SE Cncl for Sport and Recreation 1977-78, GLC Leaders Ctee with special responsibility for law and order and police liaison matters 1977-79; dep ldr Recreation and Community Servs Policy Ctee 1977-79; memb: Exec Ctee Exmoor Soc 1974-79, BBC Radio London Advsy Cncl 1974-79, Gen Cncl Poetry Soc 1977-86 (treas 1982-); tstee: London Festival Ballet 1977-79, Sadler's Wells Fndn 1977-79; chm: London Symphony Chorus Devpt Ctee 1981-88, The Young Vic Theatre 1983-87 (dir 1977-88), London Music Hall Tst Ltd 1983-, Samuel Lewis Housing Tst 1985- (tstee 1976-), St George's Housing Assoc Ltd 1985-, Shipworkers Jubilee Housing Tst 1985-, Spearhead Housing Tst 1986-; memb London Orchestral Concert Bd Ltd 1977-78, dir ENO 1977-79, memb LCDT 1979-84, govr and tstee SPCK 1976-, vice chm London Music Hall Protection Soc Ltd (Wilton's Music Hall) 1983- (bd memb 1978-, chm 1981-83); pres: Br Sch of Osteopathy Appeal Fund 1980-84, Witan Rifle Club 1979-, City of London Rifle League 1980-, Gtr London Horse Show 1982-86, Gtr London Co Hall branch of the Royal Br Legion 1988-; Hon FIET, hon fell and Hon PhD Columbia Pacific Univ USA 1984; FCIS 1970, FCPU, MBIM 1978, FRSA; Order of Gorkha Dakshina Bahu (2 class, Nepal) 1981; *Books* Europe - Power and Responsible: Direct Elections to the European Parliament (with David Baker, 1972), author of numerous contribs to learned jls and periodicals on various subjects; *Recreations* conversation, opera, ballet, classical music, being difficult; *Clubs* Athenaeum, United and Cecil, Nikaean, Sette of Odd Volumes, Surrey Co Cricket; *Style*— Bernard Brook-Partridge, Esq; 14 Redcliffe St, London SW10 9DT (☎ 071 373 1223, 071 244 7541, fax 071 835 1335, telex 946918 (A/B: LIQUID G)

BROOKE, Sir Alistair Weston; 4 Bt (UK 1919), of Almondbury, W Riding of Yorkshire; s of Sir John Weston Brooke, 3 Bt (d 1983), by 1 w Rosemary (m dis 1963), da of late Percy Llewelyn Nevill (gs of 4 Earl of Abergavenny); *b* 12 Sept 1947; *Educ* Repton, RAC Cirencester; *m* 1982, Susan Mary, only da of Barry Griffiths, of Church House, Norton, Powys; 1 da (Lorna b 1983); *Heir* bro, Charles Weston Brooke, *qv*; *Style*— Sir Alistair Brooke, Bt; Wootton Farm, Pencombe, Hereford; Fearn Lodge, Ardgay, Ross-shire

BROOKE, Prof Bryan Nicholas; s of George Cyril Brooke (d 1934), of Croydon, and Margaret Florence, *née* Parsons; *b* 21 Feb 1915; *Educ* Bradfield, Corpus Christi Coll Cambridge, St Bartholomew's Hosp London (MB BChir), Univ of Cambridge (MChir), Univ of Birmingham (MD, MRCP); *m* 23 Dec 1940, Naomi Winefride, da of Charles E Mills (d 1972), of Richmond; 3 da (Marian Esther b 5 May 1942, Nicola Sarah b 23 July 1943, Penelope Frances b 16 April 1947); *Career* RAMC 1943-46: Capt 1943, Maj surgical specialist 1944, Lt-Col 1945; sr lectr in surgery Univ of Aberdeen 1946, reader in surgery Univ of Birmingham 1947-63 (sr lectr), prof of surgery Univ of London at St George's and St James's Hosps 1976-80; ed Clinics in Gastroenterology 1972-86, conslt ed World Medicine 1980-82; awards: Copeman Medal for Sci Res, Award of NY Soc of Colon and Rectal surgns, AB Graham Award of American Soc of Colon and Rectal surgns; memb Med Appeals Tbnl for Industl Injury Benefit, pres Med Art Soc 1979-83; memb Cncl: C of E Coll for Girls Birmingham 1948-65, Malvern Girls Coll 1959-87 (chm 1972-82), Malvern Coll 1983-87; fndr and pres Ileostomy Assoc of GB and Ireland; hon fell: Philadelphia Proctologic Soc, American Soc of Colon and Rectal Surgns, Hong Kong Surgical Soc, Royal Aust Coll of Surgns (Proctology Section), RSM (Coloproctology Section); MRCS 1939, LRCP 1939, FRCS 1942, FRACS (hon) 1977; *Books* You and Your Operation (1955), Understanding Cancer and Ulcerative Colitis (1972), The Troubled Gut (1986), A Garden of Roses (1987), various books on Crohn's Disease; *Clubs* Athenaeum; *Style*— Prof Bryan N Brooke; 112 Balham Park Road, London SW12 8EA (☎ 081 767 0130)

BROOKE, Charles Weston; s (by 1 m) of Sir John Weston Brooke, 3 Bt; hp of bro, Sir Alistair Brooke, 4 Bt, *qv*; *b* 27 Jan 1951; *Educ* Repton; *m* 1984, Tanya Elizabeth, da of Anthony Thelwell Maurice, of Lloran, Robertson, NSW, Aust; 2 da (Nicola Margery b 1985, Emily Grace b 1988); *Style*— Charles Brooke, Esq; Midfearn, Ardgay, Ross-shire

BROOKE, Hon Christopher Arthur; yr s of 2 Viscount Brookeborough, PC, DL; *b* 16 May 1954; *Educ* Gordonstoun; *Career* served with 5 Inniskilling Dragoon Guards, ret Capt 1980; served Sultans Special Forces 1980-83; md Int Real Estate Dubai and Al Madfai Trading 1983-88; *Recreations* shooting, fishing, riding, diving, photography; *Clubs* Special Forces, Cavalry and Guards; *Style*— The Hon Christopher Brooke; Ashbrooke, Brookeborough, Co Fermanagh, N Ireland

BROOKE, Prof Christopher Nugent Lawrence; s of Prof Zachary Nugent Brooke (d 1946), of Cambridge, and Rosa Grace Stanton (d 1964); *b* 23 June 1927; *Educ* Gonville and Caius Coll Cambridge (BA, MA, DLitt); *m* 18 Aug 1951, Dr Rosalind Beckford Clark, da of Leslie Herman Septimus Clark; 3 s (Francis Christopher b 23 July 1953, Philip David Beckford b 19 April 1956, Patrick Lawrence Harvey b 23 May 1959); *Career* Nat Serv 1948-50 RAEC temp Capt 1949-50; Dixie prof of ecclesiastical history Univ of Cambridge 1977- (asst lectr 1953-54, lectr 1954-56) prof of mediaeval history Univ of Liverpool 1956-67, prof of history Westfield Coll Univ of London 1967-77; vice pres Royal Historical Soc 1971-74, memb Royal Cmmn on Historical Monuments 1977-84, fell of Gonville and Caius Coll 1977- (1949-56), Reviewing Cmmn on Export of Works of Art 1979-82, corresponding fell Medieval Acad of America 1981, pres of the Soc of Antiquaries 1981-84, vice pres Cumberland and Westmorland Antiquarian and Archaeological Soc 1985-89, memb Northants Record Soc 1987-, corresponding memb Monumenta Germaiae Historica 1988, fell Società Internazionale di Studi francescani; Hon DUniv of York; FSA, FBA, FRHistS; *Books* The Letters of John Salisbury (with W J Millor and H E Butler, 1955 and 1959), Carte Nativorum: a Peterborough Abbey Cartulary of the fourteenth Century (1960), The Saxon and Norman Kings (1963), Gilbert Foliot and his Letters (with A Morey, 1965), Letters and Charters of Gilbert Foliot (with A Morey, 1967), The Twelfth Century Renaissance (1969-70), The Heads of Religious Houses, England and Wales, 940-1216 (with D Knowles and VCM London, 1972), The Monastic World 1000-1300 (with Wim Swaan, 1974), A History of Gonville and Caius Coll (1985), Oxford and Cambridge (with Roger Highfield and Wim Swaan, 1988), The Medieval Idea of Marriage (1989); *Style*— Prof Christopher Brooke, FSA; Gonville and Caius College, Cambridge CB2 1TA

BROOKE, David; s of Alec Brooke, of Huddersfield (d 1959); *b* 18 Dec 1940; *Educ* Uppingham, Univ of Leeds, Sorbonne; *m* 1967, Ann Margaret, da of William Stork, of Kirkburton, W Yorks; 1 s, 1 da; *Career* dir: C & J Hirst & Sons 1977, Market Devpt Int Ltd 1983-, Scandinavian Selections Ltd 1983-; sole trader David Brooke Int marketing and cmmn agent 1983-; *Style*— David Brooke, Esq; Mount Annan, Annan, Dumfriesshire DG12 5LN (☎ 0461 202186)

BROOKE, (Richard) David Christopher; s and h of Sir Richard Neville Brooke, 10 Bt, by his 1 w, Lady Mabel, *née* Jocelyn, da of 8 Earl of Roden; *b* 23 Oct 1938; *Educ* Eton; *m* 1963 (m dis 1978), Carola Marion (*see* Stormonth-Darling, R A), da of Sir Robert Erskine-Hill, 2 Bt, *qv*; 2 s; *Style*— David Brooke Esq; Cedar House, Shurlock Row, Twyford, Berks

BROOKE, Sir Francis George Windham; 4 Bt (UK 1903), of Summerton, Co Dublin; s of Sir George Brooke, 3 Bt, MBE (d 1982), and Lady Melissa Brooke, *qv*; *b* 15 Oct 1963; *Educ* Eton, Edinburgh Univ (MA); *m* 8 April 1989, Katharine Elizabeth, o da of Marmaduke James Hussey and Lady Susan Katharine Hussey, DCVO, *qqv*; *Heir* kinsman, Geoffrey A G Brooke, *qv*; *Clubs* Turf, Kildare Street (Dublin); *Style*— Sir Francis Brooke, Bt; 49 Masbro Rd, London W14 0LU

BROOKE, Lt Cdr Geoffrey Arthur George; DSC; s of Capt John Brooke, DSC (d 1974, 6 s of Sir George Frederick Brooke, 1 Bt, who was govr of Bank of Ireland); hp of kinsman, Sir Francis Brooke, 4 Bt; *b* 25 April 1920; *Educ* RNC Dartmouth; *m* 1956, Venetia Mabel, o da of late Capt Hon Oswald Wykeham Cornwallis, OBE, RN; 3 da; *Career* Lt Cdr RN (ret); press offr Racal, ret 1985; currently conslt; *Books* Alarm Starboard! (with Patrick Stephens, 1982), Radar Mate (with Adlard Coles, 1986), Singapore's Dunkirk (with Leo Cooper, 1989); *Recreations* shooting, fishing, painting, photography, gardening; *Clubs* Army and Navy; *Style*— Lt Cdr Geoffrey Brooke, DSC; Beech House, Balcombe, Sussex RH17 6PS

BROOKE, Lord; Guy David Greville; s and h of 8 Earl of Warwick, JP; *b* 30 Jan 1957; *Educ* Eton, Ecole des Roches; *m* 1981, Susan (Susie) Cobbold, formerly w of

Nicholas Cobbold; 1 s, 2 step c; *Heir* s, Hon Charles Fulke Chester Greville, b 27 July 1982; *Style*— Lord Brooke; 4 Walter Street, Claremont, Perth, W Australia 6010

BROOKE, Hon Mr Justice; Hon Sir Henry; yr s of Baron Brooke of Cumnor, CH, PC (Life Peer) (d 1984), and Baroness Brooke of Ystradfellte, DBE (Life Peeress, *qv*); br of Rt Hon Peter Brooke, MP, *qv*; *b* 19 July 1936; *Educ* Marlborough, Balliol Coll Oxford (MA); *m* 16 April 1966, Bridget Mary, da of Wilfrid George Kalaugher, of Jesmond, Newcastle upon Tyne; 3 s (Michael John b 1967, Nicholas George b 1968, Christopher Robert b 1973), 1 da (Caroline Mary b 1973); *Career* Nat Serv 2 Lt RE 1955-57; called to the Bar Inner Temple 1963; jr counsel to the Crown (Common Law) 1978-81, QC 1981, counsel to Sizewell B Nuclear Reactor Inquiry 1983-85, recorder SE circuit 1983-88, DTI inspr into the affairs of House of Fraser Holdings plc 1987-88, Master of the Bench (Inner Temple) 1987, chm Professional Standards Ctee Bar Cncl 1987-88, Justice of the High Court (Queen's Bench Div) 1988-; *Clubs* Brooks's; *Style*— The Hon Sir Henry Brooke; Royal Courts of Justice, Strand, London WC2A 2LL

BROOKE, Martin Montague; s of Montague Brooke (d 1957), of Kew Gardens, Surrey, and Sybil Katharine, *née* Martin (d 1959); *b* 25 Aug 1923; *Educ* Eastbourne Coll, Magdalene Coll Cambridge (MA); *m* 1950, Judith Mary, da of Rev Truman Tanqueray (d 1960), of Peaslake, Surrey; 2 s (Anthony, Samuel), 1 da (Katharine); *Career* Lt RNVR, served Atlantic and Indian Oceans 1942-45; banker; dir: Guinness Mahon 1963-72, Emperor Fund NV 1968-, Cannon Assurance 1969-84; chm Druidale Securities 1972-; memb Cncl Distressed Gentlefolk's Aid Assoc 1969-; *Recreations* gardening, walking; *Clubs* Naval; *Style*— Martin Brooke, Esq; Duxbury House, 53 Chantry View Rd, Guildford, Surrey GU1 3XT (☎ 0483 504777); Johnson's Cottage, Druidale, Michael, Isle of Man; 41/42 King William Street, London EC4R 9ET (☎ 071 623 6064, telex 888542)

BROOKE, Lady Melissa Eva Caroline; *née* Wyndham-Quin; da of 6 Earl of Dunraven, CB, MBE, MC (d 1965); *b* 16 Feb 1935; *m* 25 June 1959, Maj Sir George Cecil Francis Brooke, 3 Bt, MBE (d 1982); 1 s, 1 da; *Style*— Lady Melissa Brooke

BROOKE, Michael Eccles Macklin; s of Reginald Eccles Joseph Brooke (d 1978), and of Beryl Cicely, *née* Riggs (d 1988); *b* 8 May 1942; *Educ* Lycée Francais de Londres, Univ of Edinburgh (LLB); *m* 21 Oct 1972 (m dis 1985), Annie Sophie, da of André Vautier; 3 s (Nicholas b 1975, Anthony b 1977, Benjamin b 1979); *Career* called to the Bar of England and Wales and in practice 1968-; admitted avocat a la Cour d'Appel de Paris and in practice 1987-; *Recreations* boating, England and France; *Style*— Michael Brooke, Esq; 46 Molyneux St, London W1 (☎ 071 723 8652); 2 Crown Office Row, Temple, London EC4 (☎ 071 583 8155, fax 071 583 1205); 250 Bis Blvd St Germain, Paris 75007 (☎ 1 4954 6464, fax 1 4544 6226)

BROOKE, Hon Mrs (Nancy Marion); *née* Allsopp; da of 3 Baron Hindlip (d 1931); *b* 15 Oct 1910; *m* 1936, Peter Geoffrey Brooke, s of Maj-Gen Geoffrey Francis Hereman Brooke, CB, DSO, MC (d 1966); 1 s; *Style*— The Hon Mrs Brooke; Dial House, Chilmark, Wilts

BROOKE, Patrick Thomas Joseph; s of Robert Samuel Brooke (d 1974), of Ross-on-Wye, and Mary Agnes, *née* Coleman (d 1987); *b* 4 Feb 1947; *Educ* Ross GS; partner Rosemary Elizabeth Joyce, *née* Brooke; 2 s (Daniel Patrick Coleman b 31 Oct 1983, Lewis Samuel Joseph b 9 Oct 1985); *Career* qualified CA 1970; ptnr Waugh Haines Rigby 1974 (merged Cheltenham office with Grant Thornton 1986), managing ptnr 1986, nat ptnr responsible for Single Euro Market Servs 1989-; chm Tstees Cotswold Hosp Radio 1988-, memb Local Advsy Ctee of Cotswold Nuffield Hosp 1988-, non-exec dir Glos Trg and Enterprise Cncl 1990-; ATII 1972, FCA 1979 (ACA 1970); *Recreations* golf, squash, tennis, music, reading; *Clubs* The New Cheltenham, East Gloucestershire, Cotswold Hills Golf; *Style*— Patrick Brooke, Esq; Grant Thornton, Chartered Accountants, The Quadrangle, Imperial Square, Cheltenham, Glos GL50 1PZ (☎ 0242 222900, fax 0242 222330, car 0860 315880)

BROOKE, Rt Hon Peter Leonard; PC (1988), MP (C) City of London and Westminster S 1977-; s of Baron Brooke of Cumnor, CH, PC (Life Peer) (d 1984), and Baroness Brooke of Ystradfellte, DBE (Life Peeress, *qv*); br of Hon Sir Henry Brooke, *qv*; *b* 3 March 1934; *Educ* Marlborough, Balliol Coll Oxford, Harvard Business Sch (MBA); *m* 1, 1964, Joan (d 1985), da of Frederick Smith, of São Paulo, Brazil; 3 s (and 1 s decd); m 2, 25 Jan 1991, Mrs Lindsay Allinson; *Career* formerly with RE (invalided out); res assoc IMEDE Lausanne and Swiss corr Financial Times 1960-61; chm Spencer Stuart Management Consultants 1974-79; asst govt whip 1979-81, lord cmmr Treasy (govt whip) 1981-83, under sec of state Educn and Sci 1983-85, min of state Treasy 1985-87, paymaster gen 1987-89, chm Cons Pty 1987-89, sec of state for NI 1989-; *Recreations* cricket, walking; *Clubs* Brooks's, City Livery, I Zingari, MCC, St George's, Conservative; *Style*— The Rt Hon Peter Brooke, MP; House of Commons, London SW1

BROOKE, Piers Leighton; s of Sir Richard Brooke, Bt and Lady Mabel Cheetham, *née* Jocelyn (da of Lord Roden) (d 1985); *b* 28 Dec 1940; *Educ* Eton; *m* 15 July 1967, Susan W, da of John Davenport of Middletown, New Jersey, USA (d 1987); 1 s (Sebastian b 1974), 1 da (Arabella b 1973); *Career* Lt Scots Gds 1960-63; regnl dir S E Asia Chase Manhattan Bank 1978-79 (dir USA 1979-82), exec dir Lloyds Bank Int 1982-85, md Lloyds Merchant Bank 1985-88, gp asset and liability Midland Bank plc 1988-; *Recreations* fishing, skiing, bridge, shooting; *Clubs* Boodle's; *Style*— Piers Brooke Esq; 37 Yeomans Row, London SW3 (☎ 071 584 7823); Midland Bank plc, 10 Lower Thames Street, London EC3R GAE (☎ 071 260 9252)

BROOKE, Sir Richard Neville; 10 Bt (E 1662), of Norton Priory, Cheshire; s of Sir Richard Christopher Brooke, 9 Bt (d 1981) by his 1 w, Marian Dorothea (d 1965), da of late Arthur Charles Innes-Cross; *b* 1 May 1915; *Educ* Eton; *m* 1, 1937 (m dis 1959), Lady Mabel Kathleen Jocelyn, da of 8 Earl of Roden; 2 s; m 2, 1960, Jean Evison, da of late Lt-Col Arthur Cecil Corfe, DSO, and formerly w of Sir Nicolas John Cheetham, KCMG; *Heir* s, (Richard) David Christopher Brooke; *Career* former Lt Scots Gds, serv WWII (POW escaped); sr ptnr Price Waterhouse & Co European Firms 1969-75, ret; FCA; *Recreations* racing, fishing; *Clubs* Boodle's; *Style*— Sir Richard Brooke, Bt; Pond Cottage, Crawley, nr Winchester, Hants (☎ 096 272 272)

BROOKE, Rodney George; DL (1989); s of George Sidney Brooke (d 1967), of Morley, Yorks, and Amy, *née* Grant; *b* 22 Oct 1939; *Educ* Queen Elizabeth's GS Wakefield; *m* 2 Sept 1967, Clare Margaret, da of William Martin Cox (d 1985), of Windermere Rd, Moseley, Birmingham; 1 s (Magnus b 1971), 1 da (Antonia b 1973); *Career* asst slr: Rochdale CBC 1962-63, Leicester City Cncl 1963-65; dir of admin Stockport CBC 1971-73 (sr asst slr 1965-67, asst town clerk 1967-69, dep town clerk 1969-71), chief exec and clerk W Yorks CC 1981-84 (dir of admin 1973-81), clerk to W Yorks Lieutenancy 1981-84, chief exec Westminster City Cncl 1984-89, clerk to Gtr London Lieutenancy 1987-89, hon sec London Boroughs Assoc 1984-90, chm Bradford Health Authy 1989-90, assoc Ernst and Young 1989-90, advsr Longman Gp 1989-90, sec Assoc of Metropolitan Authorities 1990; visiting res fell: Royal Inst of Public Admin 1989-, Nuffield Inst for Health Service Studies Univ of Leeds 1989-; hon fell Inst of Local Govt Studies Univ of Birmingham 1987-; OM (France) 1984, Order of Aztec Eagle (Mexico) 1985, Medal of Merit (Qatar) 1985, Order of Merit (Germany) 1986, Order of Merit (Senegal) 1988; *Books* Managing the Enabling Authority (1989), The Environmental Role of Local Government (1990); *Recreations* skiing, opera, Byzantium; *Clubs* Athenaeum, Ski of GB; *Style*— Rodney Brooke Esq; Stubham Lodge, Middleton, Ilkley, W Yorks LS29 0AX (☎ 0943 601869); 706 Grenville Ho, Dolphin Sq, SW1V 3LR (☎ 071 798 8086); 35 Great Smith Street, London SW1P 3BJ (☎ 071 222 8100, fax 071 222 0878)

BROOKE, (Christopher) Roger Ettrick; s of Maj Ralph Brooke, RAMC; *b* 2 Feb 1931; *Educ* Tonbridge, Trinity Coll Oxford; *m* 1958, Nancy; 3 s, 1 da; *Career* HM Dip Serv 1955-66; dep md IRC 1966-69, vice chm Pearson Longman Ltd 1976-79, gp md EMI Ltd 1979-1980, chief exec Candover Investments plc 1981-, dir Slough Estates plc; *Recreations* tennis, theatre, golf; *Style*— Roger Brooke, Esq; c/o Candover Investments plc, 20 Old Bailey, London EC4M 7LN (☎ 071 489 9848, telex 928035, fax 071 248 5483); 99 Flood St, London SW3 5TD (☎ 071 352 3232)

BROOKE, (Christopher) Roger Ettrick; s of Ralph Brooke (d 1985), and Marjorie Lee; *b* 2 Feb 1931; *Educ* Tonbridge, Univ of Oxford (MA); *m* 1958, Nancy Belle, da of Eugene M Lowenthal (d 1985); 3 s (Christopher b 1962, Kenneth b 1966, Stephen b 1973), 1 da (Jenny b 1960); *Career* HM Dip Serv 1955-61, served at HM Embassies Bonn, Washington, Tel Aviv and at the FO London 1966-69; dep md Industl Reorganization Corp London 1969-71, md Scienta SA Brussels 1971-79, cncllr Royal Borough of Kensington and Chelsea 1973-79, exec dir Pearson Gp, vice chm Pearson Longman, chm Longman 1979-80, gp md EMI, chief exec Candover Investmts plc 1980-, dir Slough Estates plc 1980-; *Recreations* golf, tennis, music, theatre; *Clubs* Brooks's, Woking Golf; *Style*— Roger Brooke, Esq; Water Meadow, Swarraton, nr Alresford, Hants (☎ 0962 732259); Candover Investmts plc, Cedric House, 8/9 East Harding St, London EC4A 3AS (☎ 071 583 5091, telex 928035, fax 071 583 0717)

BROOKE-HITCHING, Hon Mrs (Emma Caroline); *née* Blades; da of 2 Baron Ebbisham, TD; *b* 28 May 1954; *Educ* St Mary's Calne, Univ of Tours France; *m* 1977, Franklin Brooke-Hitching; 3 s (Edward Robert b 1982, Matthew Thomas b 1985, William Franklin b 1987); *Style*— The Hon Mrs Brooke-Hitching; Osmington House, Kintbury, Newbury, Berks

BROOKE-LITTLE, John Philip Brooke; CVO (1984, MVO 1969); s of Raymond Brooke-Little (d 1961), late of Unicorns House, Swalcliffe, Oxon, and Constance Marie, *née* Egan; *b* 6 April 1927; *Educ* Clayesmore Sch, New Coll Oxford (MA); *m* 1960, Mary Lee, o da of late John Raymond Pierce; 3 s, 1 da; *Career* fndr Heraldry Soc (chm 1947-), hon ed The Coat of Arms 1950-, on Earl Marshal's Staff 1952-53, served as Gold Staff Offr Coronation 1953, Bluemantle Pursuivant 1956-67, Richmond Herald 1967-80, Norroy and Ulster King of Arms 1980-, Registrar and Knight Attendant on the Order of St Patrick 1980-; Coll of Arms: registrar 1974-82, librarian 1974-, treas 1978-; an advsr on Heraldry to Nat Tst 1983-, dep dir Herald's Museum 1983-; fell Soc of Genealogists 1969, hon fell Inst of Heraldic and Genealogical Studies, pres English Language Literary Tst 1985-, govr Clayesmore Sch 1960- (chm 1961-83); Freeman and Liveryman Scriveners' Co (Master 1985-86); FSA; Kt of Malta 1955 (chllr 1973-77), Cdr Cross of Merit Order of Malta 1964, Cruz Distinguida (1st class) Order of San Raimundo de Penafort (Spain) 1955, Grand Cross of Grace Constantinian Order of St George 1975; *Books* Royal London, Pictorial History of Oxford, Boutell's Heraldry, Knights of the Middle Ages, Prince of Wales, Fox-Davies' Complete Guide to Heraldry, Kings and Queens of Great Britain, An Heraldic Alphabet, Beasts in Heraldry (co-author), The British Monarchy in Colour, Royal Arms, Beasts and Badges, Royal Ceremonies of State; *Clubs* City Livery, Chelsea Arts; *Style*— John Brooke-Little, Esq, CVO, FSA; Norroy and Ulster King of Arms, Heyford House, Lower Heyford, Oxford OX5 3NZ (☎ 0869 40337); College of Arms, Queen Victoria St, EC4V 4BT (☎ 071 248 1310)

BROOKE OF YSTRADFELLTE, Baroness (Life Peeress 1964); Barbara Muriel Brooke; *née* Mathews; DBE (1960); yst da of Rev Canon Alfred Augustus Mathews (d 1946), of Llanwern, Gwent, and Ethel Frances, *née* Evans (d 1951); *b* 14 Jan 1908; *Educ* Queen Anne's Sch Caversham, Glos Training Coll of Domestic Sci; *m* 1933, Baron Brooke of Cumnor, CH, PC (d 1984); 2 s (The Rt Hon Peter Brooke, PC, MP, *qv*, The Hon Sir Henry Brooke, Kt, QC, *qv*), 2 da; *Career* memb Hampstead Borough Cncl 1948-65, vice-chm Cons Pty Orgn 1954-64, memb N W Met Regnl Hosp Bd 1955-66; chm: Governing Body of Godolphin and Latymer Sch 1960-78, Exec Ctee Queen's Inst of Dist Nursing 1961-71; memb Mgmnt Ctee King Edward's Hosp Fund for London 1967-70; *Style*— The Rt Hon The Lady Brooke of Ystradfellte, DBE; Romans Halt, Mildenhall, Marlborough, Wilts

BROOKE-ROSE, Prof Christine; da of Alfred Northbrook Rose (d 1934), and Evelyn Brooke (d 1984); *b* 16 Jan 1923; *Educ* St Stephen's Coll Folkestone (now Broadstairs), Univ of Oxford (BA, MA); London (PhD); *m* 1948 (m dis 1975), Jerzy Peterkiewicz; *Career* Flt Offr WAAF 1941-45; freelance journalist 1955-68; prof of lit theory Univ of Paris 8 1968-; author; *Books* A Grammar of Metaphor (1958), A ZBC of Ezra Pound (1971), A Rhetoric of the Unreal (1981), The Languages of Love (1957), The Sycamore Tree (1958), The Dear Deceit (1960), The Middlemen (1961), Out (1964), Such (1965), Between (1968), Thru (1975), Amalgamemnon (1984), Xorandor (1986), Brooke-Rose Omnibus (1986), also short stories and essays; *Style*— Prof Christine Brooke-Rose; c/o Carcanet Press Ltd, 208 Corn Exchange Buildings, Manchester M4 3BQ

BROOKE TURNER, Alan; CMG (1980); s of Capt Arthur Brooke Turner, MC (d 1953), of Bournemouth, and Ella Gladys, *née* Jackson, formerly Ella Gladys Rabone (d 1978); *b* 4 Jan 1926; *Educ* Marlborough, Balliol Coll Oxford; *m* 9 Oct 1954, Hazel Alexandra Rowan, da of Wilfred Alexander Henderson, CIE (d 1958), of Argyll; 2 s (Peter b 1958, James b 1960), 2 da (Prudence b 1955, Clarissa b 1964); *Career* served in RAF 1944-48 (pilot offr); head of Southern European Dept FCO 1972-73, cnsllr HM Embassy Rome 1973-76, dir of studies and Dep Cmdt NATO Defence Coll Rome 1976-78, min HM Embassy Moscow 1979-82; ambass to Finland 1983-86, dir GB/E Europe Centre 1987-; fell of Center for Int Affairs Harvard Univ 1968-69; res assoc Int Inst for Strategic Studies 1978-79; memb: Working Gp on Peacemaking in a Nuclear Age (C of E Bd for Social Responsibility) 1986-88, Cncl of Anglican Centre Rome 1976-77; chm Cncl of Sch of Slavonic and E European Studies (Univ of London) (memb 1987-); *Recreations* skiing, sailing; *Clubs* Travellers'; *Style*— Alan Brooke Turner, CMG; Poultons, Moor Lane, Dormansland, Lingfield, Surrey RH7 6NX (☎ 0342 832079); Great Britain/East Europe Centre, 31 Knightsbridge, London SW1X 7NH (☎ 071 245 9771)

BROOKEBOROUGH, 3 Viscount (UK 1952); Sir Alan Henry Brooke; 7 Bt (UK 1822), DL (Co Fermanagh 1987); er s of 2 Viscount Brookeborough, PC, DL (d 1987), and Rosemary, Viscountess Brookeborough, *qv*; *b* 30 June 1952; *Educ* Harrow, Millfield; *m* 12 April 1980, Janet Elizabeth, o da of John Cooke, of Ballyvoy Lodge, Doagh, Co Antrim; *Heir* bro, Hon Christopher Arthur Brooke, *qv*; *Career* cmmnd 17/21 Lancers 1972, transferred to UDR part-time 1977, Capt Permanent Cadre 4 Bn UDR 1980-83, transfer UDR pt/t 1983, Maj-Co Cdr 1988-; farmer; *Recreations* riding, fishing, shooting, skiing; *Clubs* Cavalry and Guards; *Style*— The Rt Hon the Viscount Brookeborough; Colebrooke, Brookeborough, Co Fermanagh, NI (☎ 036 553 402)

BROOKEBOROUGH, Rosemary, Viscountess; Rosemary Hilda; eldest da of Lt-Col Arthur O'Neill Cubitt Chichester, OBE, MC (d 1972), and Hilda Grace, *née* Young; *b* 12 Feb 1926; *m* 4 March 1949, 2 Viscount Brookeborough, PC, DL (d 1987); 2 s, 3 da; *Style*— The Rt Hon Rosemary, Viscountess Brookeborough; Ashbrooke,

Brookborough, Co Fermanagh, N Ireland

BROOKER, Alan Bernard; JP (Essex 1972), DL (Essex 1982); s of Bernard John Brooker (d 1958), and Gwendoline Ada, *née* Launchbury (d 1974); *b* 24 Aug 1931; *Educ* Chigwell Sch Essex; *m* 23 March 1957, Diana, da of Colin Raymond Coles (d 1956); 1 s, 2 da; *Career* Nat Serv 2 Lt 2 RHA 1954-56; mangr Cole Dickin & Hills (chartered accountants) 1956-58 (articled clerk 1949-54), accountant Independent Dairies 1958-59, asst accountant Exchange Telegraph Co 1959-64, dir Extel Group plc 1964-87 (chm and chief exec 1980-87); vice chm: Provident Financial plc 1983-, James Martin Associates 1987-89; non-exec dir: Pauls plc 1984-85, Aukett Associates plc 1988-, Plysu plc 1988-, PNA Holdings plc 1988-89, Addison Worldwide Ltd 1990-, East Anglian Daily Times Ltd 1990-; chm: Kode International plc 1988-, Seriff Cowells plc 1990-; memb Cncl CPU 1975-88; CBI: memb Companies Ctee 1979-83, memb Cncl London Region 1980-83, appeal chm Newspaper Press Fund 1985-86; govr: Chigwell Sch 1968-(chm 1978-), Felixstowe Coll 1986-; Churchwarden St Bride's Fleet Street 1986-; Freeman City of London, Liveryman Worshipful Co of Stationers and Newspapermakers (Court Assoc 1985-); FCA, FInstD, FRSA 1980; *Recreations* golf, cricket; *Clubs* East India, MCC, Royal Worlington and Newmarket Golf; *Style*— Alan Brooker, Esq, JP, DL; Kode International plc, Drakes Way, Swindon, Wiltshire

BROOKER, Dr Arthur Edward William; s of Edward John Brooker (d 1963), of London, and Mary Harriett, *née* Fuller (d 1953); *b* 12 Dec 1912; *Educ* Roan Sch Greenwich, Univ of London, St Bartholomew's Hosp Med Coll (jr scholar, MRCS, LRCP, MB BS, MD, FRCGP 1970); *m* 14 Nov 1942, Kathleen Elma, da of George Alexander Raw (d 1973), of Isle of Wight; 2 s (John b 1946, Stephen b 1956), 1 da (Catherine b 1950); *Career* Capt RAMC 1939-45; extern-intern St Bartholomew's Hosp 1938, sr med registrar RPMS 1946-47, asst Med Professorial Unit Royal Hosp Sheffield 1947-48, GP princ Cliftonville 1948-76, locum conslt rheumatology S E Thames RHA 1976-85, examining MO DHSS 1978-87, occasional ship's surgn for various shipping lines; sometime memb Kent Local Med Ctee, life memb Assoc of Men of Kent and Kentish Men, veteran memb Royal Temple YC, memb Br Soc for Rheumatology 1958-; Freeman City of London 1970, Liveryman Worshipful Soc of Apothecaries 1970; life memb BMA 1937; *Books* Cervical Spondylosis (thesis in two volumes, 1963), Cervical Spondylosis - A Clinical Study with Comparative Radiology (jtly, in Brain, 1965); *Recreations* photography and videography, motoring, sailing; *Clubs* Royal Temple Yacht; *Style*— Dr Arthur Brooker; Six Elms, Lanthorne Rd, Broadstairs, Kent CT10 3NA (☎ 0843 68741)

BROOKER, Margaret Anne; da of James Gibson Wood (d 1977), Ashurst, Hants, and Joan Ivy Grace, *née* Young; *b* 19 March 1946; *Educ* Brockenhurst Co HS, Univ of Texas at Austin (BSc), Univ of Pennsylvania (MSc); *m* 23 June 1965, Robin Christopher Brooker, s of Harry Frederick Brooker (d 1974), of Spinney Cottage, Chestfield, Kent; 1 da (Joanna Marta b 1966); *Career* botanical advsr Anglo American Expedition to Mount Roraima Venezuela 1970, botanist Estacion Central de Ecologia Madrid 1971-74, ldr Univ of Texas Botanical Expdn to Mount Tacaha Guatemala 1975, dir Nat Survey of Flora Ecuador 1975-77, conslt botanist Servicios Parques Nacionales de Costa Rica 1978-83, botanical advsr Int Union for Conservation of Nature and Natural Resources 1984-; memb: Real Sociedad Espanola de Historia Natural Madrid, Portuguese League for Protection of Nature Lisbon, Fedn Francaise des Sociétés de Protection de la Nature Paris, Nat Geographic Soc, Sociedad de Ciencias Naturales Aranzadi San Sebastian; *Books* Alpine Flora of Iberia (1975), Insect Pollinators at High Altitudes (1978), Flora of the High Andes (1980), The Conservation of Alpine Habitats in Europe (1985); *Recreations* travel, entomology, hot air ballooning, rock climbing; *Style*— Mrs Margaret Brooker

BROOKES, Beata Ann; MEP (EDG) N Wales 1979-; da of George Brookes, JP (d 1983), of Cwybr Farm, Rhyl, and Gwen Brookes; *b* 21 Jan 1931; *Educ* Lowther Coll Abergele, Univ of Wales Bangor, USA scholarship; *m* (m dis 1963); *Career* former social worker; farmer and company secretary; *Recreations* swimming, working; *Style*— Ms Beata Brookes, MEP; The Cottage, Wayside Acres, Bodelwyddan, N Wales

BROOKES, Brian Sydney; MBE (1982); s of Sydney Herbert Brookes (d 1967), and Edith, *née* Walker (d 1965); *b* 4 May 1936; *Educ* Beckenham GS, Kings Coll London (BSc, PGCE), Univ of Dundee (MSc); *m* 30 Aug 1962 (m dis 1989), Margaret Mary; 3 s (David b 1967, Stephen b 1968, James b 1972), 1 da (Mary b 1970); *Career* teacher Forest Hill Sch and Sloane Sch 1958-65, asst warden Slapton Ley Field Centre Devon 1965-67, warden Kindrogan Field Centre Perthshire 1967-85, freelance biologist and environmental conslt 1985-, author scientific papers; memb: Nat Botanical Soc's Cncls and Ctees, various ctees Scottish Wildlife Tst, local community cncl, regnl advsy ctees Forestry Cmmn; memb Inst of Biol, Chartered Biologist; *Books* British Naturalists' Guide to Mountains and Moorlands (1985); *Recreations* beekeeping; *Style*— Brian Brookes, Esq, MBE; Borelick, Trochry, Dunkeld, Perthshire PH8 0BX (☎ 03503 222)

BROOKES, James Robert (Jim); s of James Brookes, of Worsley, Lancs, and Hettie, *née* Colley; *b* 2 Sept 1941; *Educ* Manchester GS, Corpus Christi Coll Oxford (MA); *m* 30 May 1964, Patricia, da of John Gaskell, MBE, of Knutsford, Cheshire; 3 da (Diane Chambers b 9 Oct 1965, Gail b 28 June 1967, Maura b 8 July 1969); *Career* various posts in UK and USA as systems and applications programmer in devpt, tech support and sales; then branch mangr Univ and Nat Res Region Ferranti Int Computers 1962-67, computer servs mangr Queens Univ Belfast 1967-69, mangr Univ of Manchester Regnl Computer Centre 1969-75, dir SW Univs Regnl Computer Centre 1975-87, dir Univ of Bath Computer Servs 1983-87, chief exec Br Computer Soc 1987-, chm BISL 1988-; CEng, FBCS 1971, FRSA; memb Worshipful Co of Info Technologists 1988, Freeman City of London 1989; *Recreations* sailing, fellwalking, cycling, bridge, squash, badminton; *Clubs* United Oxford & Cambridge Univ, Cannons Country (Bath); *Style*— Jim Brookes, Esq; 29 High St, Marshfield, Chippenham, Wilts SN14 8LR (☎ 0225 891294); The British Computer Society, 13 Mansfield St, London W1M 0BP (☎ 071 637 0471, fax 071 631 1049)

BROOKES, Hon John David; s of Baron Brookes (Life Peer); *b* 22 Sept 1940; *Educ* Malvern, Oriel Coll Oxford; *m* 1, 1970 (m dis 1982), Faith, da of late John Redman, of Bidford on Avon, Warwicks; 2 s; m 2, 1986, Susan Nemeth; *Career* md GKN Transmissions 1974-78, vice pres GKN Automotive Components (USA) 1978-; *Recreations* fishing, conflict simulation; *Clubs* Lansdowne; *Style*— The Hon John Brookes; 30425 S Greenbriar, Franklin, Mich 48025, USA (☎ 313 626 7738)

BROOKES, Nicola; da of Leon Bernard (d 1954), of Ruislip, and Violet Charlotte, *née* Farrar; *b* 25 Dec 1951; *Educ* Wycombe HS, Univ of Warwick (BSc); *m* 27 Sept 1980, Ian Thomas Burns, s of Thomas George Burns, of W Kirby Wirral; 1 s (Thomas Leon Phillip b 1990), 1 da (Laura Kathryn b 1988; *Career* trainee accountant Arthur Andersen & Co 1973-76; Amari plc 1976-89: US controller 1978-79, mgmnt buyout mangr 1983, corporate devpt dir 1984, fin dir 1986; fin dir Dent Lee Witte plc 1989-, mgmnt conslt Harrison Brookes; selected by Business magazine as one of Britain's Top 40 Young Ldrs finalist Business Woman of the Year 1988; FCA 1981; *Recreations* swimming, skiing, reading, music and opera; *Style*— Ms Nicola Brookes; Amadeus, 26A Holloway Lane, Chesham Bois, Amersham, Bucks HP6 6DJ (☎ 0494 728 520); Dent Lee Witte plc, Bechtel House, 245 Hammersmith Rd, London W6 8DP (☎ 081 528 9873, fax 081 895 1163)

BROOKES, Baron (Life Peer UK 1975); Raymond Percival Brookes; s of William Percival Brookes, of W Bromwich, Staffs, and Ursula Brookes; *b* 10 April 1909; *Educ* Kenrick Tech Coll W Bromwich; *m* 1937, Florence Edna, da of Isaac William Sharman; 1 s; *Career* former memb Cncl CBI; chm and chief exec Guest Keen & Nettlefolds Ltd 1965-74 (life pres 1975-); dir Plessey Co to 1989, memb Dubai Aluminium Authy 1981-86; kt 1971; *Style*— The Rt Hon the Lord Brookes; Mallards, Santon, Isle of Man (☎ 0624 822451)

BROOKES, Sir Wilfred Deakin; CBE (1972), DSO (1944), AEA (1945); s of Herbert Robinson Brookes, and Ivy, *née* Deakin; *b* 17 April 1906; *Educ* Melbourne GS, Melbourne Univ; *m* 1928, Bertha (Betty) (d 1968), da of Albert Henry Heal; 1 s; *Career* former chm and dir various industrial, commercial and mining cos, ret; patron Deakin Univ Fndn, chm Edwards Charitable Tst; former govr Corps of Commissionaires; DLitt (hc Deakin); kt 1979; *Style*— Sir Wilfred Brookes, CBE, DSO, AEA; 20 Heyington pla, Toorak, Victoria 3142, Australia (☎ 20 4553)

BROOKHOUSE, Graham Raymond; s of Raymond Nuttall Brookhouse, and Phyliss Adeline Teresa, *née* Hart; *b* 19 June 1962; *Educ* King Edward VI Camphill Sch for Boys Birmingham, Coll of St Paul and St Mary Cheltenham (BEd), LSSM (Dip); *Career* teacher of swimming Stowe Sch 1985-87, Br Modern Pentathlon champion 1987-89, Bronze medal Team Modern Pentathlon Seoul Olympics 1988; pt/t coach Cheltenham Swimming Club, active memb Cheltenham Harriers; *Recreations* horses, coaching, running, swimming; *Clubs* Spartan Modern Penthatlon; *Style*— Graham Brookhouse, Esq; 137 Village Rd, Cheltenham, Gloucs (☎ 0242 572 930)

BROOKING, Maj-Gen Patrick Guy; CB (1988), MBE (1975); s of Capt C A H Brooking, CBE, RN, and G M J White, *née* Coleridge; *b* 4 April 1937; *Educ* Charterhouse, Alliance Francaise Paris (Dip French Lang); *m* 11 April 1964, Pamela Mary, da of the late Lt-Col J E S Walford, MBE; 1 s (Jonathan b 1967), 1 da (Samantha b 1965); *Career* cmmnd 5 Royal Inniskilling Dragoon Gds 1956; served: Eng, W Germany, NI, Cyprus; Camberley Staff Coll 1969, Maj 39 Bde Belfast 1974-75, Regtl Cdr 1975-77, instr Army Staff Coll 1978, COS 4 Armd Div 1979-80, RCDS 1981, Cdr 33 Armd Bde 1982-83, asst COS UK Land Forces 1984-85, Cmdt and GOC Br sector Berlin 1986-88, dir gen Army Manning and Recruiting 1988-89, sr exec worldwide subsidiaries of Krone AG 1990-; Freeman City of London 1979, memb Worshipful Co of Broderers; *Recreations* tennis, skiing, golf, music; *Clubs* Cavalry and Guards; *Style*— Maj-Gen P G Brooking, CB, MBE; c/o National Westminster Bank, 26 Haymarket, London, SW1

BROOKNER, Dr Anita; da of Newson Brookner, and Maude, *née* Schiska; *b* 16 July 1928; *Educ* James Allen's Girls' Sch, King's Coll London (BA); *Career* lectr then reader Courtauld Inst of Art 1964-88; Hon PhD Courtauld Inst; FRSL; *Books* Watteau (1964), J B Greuze (1971), The Genius of the Future (1972), J L David (1980); has also written twelve novels incl Hotel du Lac (1984, Booker-McCon prize, filmed for TV 1986), A Friend from England (1987), many articles in Apollo, Burlington Magazine,TLS; *Recreations* walking, reading; *Style*— Dr Anita Brookner; 68 Elm Park Gardens, London SW10 (☎ 071 352 6894)

BROOKS, Alastair Groves; s of Rev Ronald Groves Brooks (d 1979), of The Rectory, Bow Brickhill, Milton Keynes, Bucks, and Mabel MacNair, *née* Melvin; *b* 23 Aug 1947; *Educ* Swanbourne House Sch Bucks, St Edward's Sch Oxford; *m* 27 July 1974, Nora Elizabeth, da of John Brendan Browne; 4 s (Sean Nicholas b 18 March 1966, Simon David b 6 March 1967, Robert Groves b 2 Oct 1976, Richard Ronald b 21 July 1979); *Career* slr and NP, sr ptnr Brooks and Co Slrs Milton Keynes; rotarian; memb Law Soc; *Recreations* golf; *Clubs* The Rugby, Woburn Golf; *Style*— Alastair Brooks, Esq; Fairview, 63 Church Rd, Aspley Heath, Milton Keynes MK17 8TJ (☎ 0908 582207); Sovereign Ct, 209 Witan Game East, Central Milton Keynes MK9 2HP (☎ 0908 665968, fax 0908 678722, car 0836 244922, telex 827542)

BROOKS, Hon Mrs (Ann); *née* Fremantle; da of 4 Baron Cottesloe, GBE, TD, and his 1 w, Lady Elizabeth Berwick (d 1983), da of 5 Earl of Malmesbury; *b* 21 Oct 1930; *m* 29 Nov 1951, Timothy Gerald Martin Brooks, JP, s of Hon Herbert Brooks (s of 2 Baron Crawshaw); 3 s (Richard m 1985, Diana, yr da of Sir Michael Thomas, 11 Bt; 1 s, Char Andrew b 1966, Michael b 1969), 2 da (Lucy m 1978, Keith Charlton; 2 s, 2 da, Nicola m 1978, Gerald Michel; 2 da); *Style*— The Hon Mrs Brooks; Wistow Hall, Leicester (☎ 053 759 2000)

BROOKS, Charles Patrick Evelyn; s of Robert Noel Brand Brooks (d 1978), and Caroline Diana, *née* Todd; *b* 3 March 1963; *Educ* Cothill House, Eton; *Career* racehorse trainer; trained one hundred winners in first two seasons when England's youngest trainer; *Style*— Charles Brooks, Esq; Uplands, Lambourn, Newbury, Berks RG16 7QH (☎ 0488 72077, fax 0488 71206)

BROOKS, (Kathleen) Claire; OBE (1986); da of Arthur Graham (d 1969), of The Mains, Giggleswick, Settle, N Yorks, and Clara Grace, *née* Grisedale; *b* 20 June 1931; *Educ* Settle PS, Abraham Lincoln Sch NJ, Settle Girls HS, Skipton Girls HS, UCL (LLB); *m* 28 Sept 1963 (m dis 1971) Herbert Berwick, s of Herbert Berwick Brooks Sr (d 1959), of Superior, Wisconsin, and Louisville, Kentucky; *Career* admitted slr 1956; S Kitching Walker & Co 1956-61, Medley Drawbridge & Co 1961-64, Victor D Zermansky & Co 1973-75; proprietor K Claire Brooks & Co Solicitors 1975-; dir former Settle Carlisle Joint Action Committee Ltd; tstee: Skipton & Craven Assoc for Disabled (pres 1988- 89), Craven Museum, Petyt Library, Heap Parkinson Homes; memb Ct and Cncl Univ of Lancaster; govr Skipton GHS and others; lifelong lib; memb: Craven DC 1976- (chm 1988-89), Skipton Town Cncl 1976- (Mayor 1985-86); Parly candidate: 6 nat elections (4 Lib, 2 Alliance), 2 Euro elections; memb: Lib Pty Nat Exec Ctee 1975-88, Lib Pty Cncl 1973-88, Nat Exec Ctee Lib Movement 1988-90; memb: Law Soc, Br Legal Assoc; *Recreations* local history and archaeology, genealogy; *Clubs* Nat Lib; *Style*— Mrs Claire Brooks, OBE; The Mains, Giggleswick, Settle, N Yorks (☎ 0729 823709); Mesdames K Claire Brooks & Co Solicitors, 43 Otley Street, Skipton, N Yorks BD23 1EL (☎ 0756 795069 & 793328, fax 0756 798243)

BROOKS, Hon David Gerald; s of 3 Baron Crawshaw (d 1946); hp of bro, 4 Baron; *b* 14 Sept 1934; *Educ* Eton; RAC, Cirencester; *m* 1970, Belinda Mary, da of G P H Burgess, of Sandringham, Melbourne, Australia; 4 da (Susanna b 1974, Amanda b 1975, Elisabeth b 1976, Katharine b 1978); *Style*— The Hon David Brooks; Little Riste Farm, Long Whatton, Loughborough, Leics (☎ 0509 842392)

BROOKS, Donal Meredith; s of Edward Clive Brooks, of Dublin, and Kathleen Purdon, *née* Pollock; *b* 10 April 1917; *Educ* Repton, Trinity Coll Dublin; *m* 1947, Stephanie, da of Cyril W Mackworth-Praed, CBE; *Career* conslt orthopaedic surgn King Edward VII Hosp of Offrs London, emeritus civilian conslt orthopaedic surgn in hand surgery to RN, hon civilian conslt orthopaedic surgn in hand surgery RAF; conslt orthopaedic surgn: UCH, Royal Nat Orthopaedic Hosp London (surgn i/c of peripheral nerve injury and hand unit); former chm of the Ct of Examiners RCS; former pres: orthopaedic section RSM, Chelsea Clinical Soc, Combined Servs Orthopaedic Soc; fell Br Orthopaedic Assoc (travelling fell 1954-), former memb Hand Club; memb: Br Soc for Surgery of the Hand, Groupe d'Etude de la Main; guest lectr: American Assoc of Neurosurgeons 1977, S African Soc for Surgery of the Hand 1978; Wattie visiting prof New Zealand 1983, Robert Jones lectr RCS 1979, fndr lectr of American Soc for Surgery of the Hand 1983; Jackson Burrows Lecture and Medal Award 1983; papers on peripheral nerve injuries and hand surgery in books and jls; *Recreations* farming, gardening, travelling; *Clubs* Landsdowne, Royal Irish Yacht; *Style—* Donal Brooks, Esq; Errislannan Manor, Clifden, Co Galway

BROOKS, Douglas; s of Oliver James Brooks (d 1977), and Olive, *née* Davies (d 1980); *b* 3 Sept 1928; *Educ* Newbridge GS, Univ Coll Cardiff; *m* 1952, June Anne, da of Hedley Branch (d 1965); 1 s, 1 da; *Career* assoc dir Hoover Ltd 1972-78, memb Cncl Econ and Social Res Cncl 1976-82, chief personnel exec Tarmac Ltd 1978-79, chm Wooburn Festival Soc Ltd 1978-86; dir: Walker Brooks and Ptnrs Ltd 1980-90, Flexello Castors & Wheels plc 1987-; memb BBC Consultative Gp on Social Effect of TV, visiting sr fell Policy Studies Inst 1982-84; *Recreations* talking, cooking, music, gardening; *Clubs* Reform; *Style—* Douglas Brooks, Esq; Old Court, Winforton, Hereford HR3 6EA (☎ 0544 68425)

BROOKS, Harry; eldest s of Harry Brooks Sr (d 1978), of Peover Hall, Knutsford, Cheshire, and Norah Brooks (d 1991); *b* 16 Feb 1936; *Educ* Macclesfield GS, St John HS Canada; *m* 23 July 1977, Mileva, da of Capt Dušan Babic, of Yugoslavia; 1 da (Milanka b 12 Sept 1983); *Career* actor, photographer, prodr and writer; appeared Liverpool Playhouse 1958 before appearing in many productions in theatre/television and films; prodr The Lady of Light, writer of an original screenplay (Disguise), fndr and chm MIDAS (Manufacturers and Industrialists Devpt Agency Servs Ltd), tstee Quality in the Community 1991-, chm and chief exec prodr Hamlet Prodns Ltd; *Style—* Harry Brooks, Esq; Hamlet Productions Ltd; c/o Wright Webb Syrett, 10 Soho Square, London W1V 6EE (☎ 0565 633051, 071 235 1811)

BROOKS, John; s of Lewis Russell Brooks of Norfolk and Alice Evelyn *née* Boast (d 1978); *b* 25 Oct 1939; *Educ* Norwich Sch, Gonville Caius Coll Cambridge (MA); *m* 1 July 1966, Francine Andrée, da of Rémi Tridon of Auxerre France (d 1977); 2 da (Sylvie b 1969, Stephanie b 1972); *Career* chm Phonographic Performance Ltd, Video Performance Ltd 1986; *Recreations* messing about in boats; *Clubs* RAC, ARA; *Style—* John Brooks Esq; Glenwood, River Avenue, Thames Ditton; 17/19 Soho Square, London W1V 6HE (☎ 071 734 8181)

BROOKS, Hon John Patrick; yst s of 3 Baron Crawshaw (d 1946); *b* 17 March 1938; *Educ* Loughborough Coll; *m* 1967, Rosemary Vans Agnew, da of C Vans Agnew Frank, of Hunmanby, E Yorks; 1 s, 1 da; *Style—* The Hon John Brooks; 25 Cadogan St, SW3

BROOKS, Hon Mary Aletheia; da of 3 Baron Crawshaw (d 1946); *b* 12 March 1931; *Style—* The Hon Mary Brooks; Whatton, nr Loughborough, Leics

BROOKS, Dr Nicholas Hugh; s of Lt-Col A Brooks, of Great Missenden, Bucks, and Mary, *née* Gerrard; *b* 6 July 1947; *Educ* Perse Sch Cambridge, St Bartholomews Hosp, Med Coll Univ of London (MB BS, MD, MRCP); *m* 16 March 1974, Barbara Mary, da of Dr Robert Boal, of Southampton; 1 s (Alexander James b 1977), 1 da (Victoria Jane b 1979); *Career* St Bartholomew's Hosp: house surgn Surgical Professional Unit 1971, house surgn in cardiothoracic surgery, sr house offr gen med 1972, registrar in cardiology 1973-74; house physician Southampton Gen Hosp 1971, Br Heart Fndn res fell St Georges Hosp 1976-77 (registrar in med 1975), clinical lectr and hon sr registrar London Chest Hosp and London Hosp 1977, conslt cardiologist Wythenshawe Hosp Manchester 1984; hon sec Cardiology Ctee RCP; chm Audit Ctee: Br Cardiac Soc, RCP; FRCP 1990; *Books* Diseases of the Heart (contrib, 1989); *Recreations* tennis, skiing, music; *Style—* Dr Nicholas Brooks; Oldcroft House, Elm Grove, Alderley Edge, Cheshire SK9 7PD (☎ 0625 582853); Regional Cardiac Centre, Wythenshawe Hospital, Manchester M23 9LT (☎ 061 998 7070

BROOKS, Prof Nicholas Peter; s of Dr (William) Donald Wykeham Brooks, CBE, of Storrington, W Sussex, and Phyllis Kathleen, *née* Juler (d 1988); *b* 14 Jan 1941; *Educ* Winchester, Magdalen Coll Oxford (BA, MA, DPhil); *m* 16 Sept 1967, Chloë Carolyn, da of Rev Sidney C Willis (d 1978); 1 s (Crispin b 29 Dec 1970), 1 da (Ebba b 31 Jan 1969); *Career* sr lectr in medieval history Univ of St Andrews 1978-85 (lectr 1964-78), prof Univ of Birmingham 1985-; chm St Andrews Preservation Tst 1977-83; FBA, FRHistS, FSA; *Books* Latin and the Vernacular Languages in Early Medieval Britain (1982), The Early History of the Church of Canterbury (1984); *Recreations* gardening, golf, squash; *Style—* Prof Nicholas Brooks; Department of Medieval History, University of Birmingham, PO Box 363, Birmingham B15 2TT (☎ 021 414 5744)

BROOKS, Nigel John; s of Norman John Leslie Brooks, of Southfield, Helens Bay, Co Down, and Sheila, *née* Mercer; *b* 20 March 1959; *Educ* Campbell Coll Belfast, Pembroke Coll Cambridge (MA); *Career* Price Waterhouse 1980-84, merchant banker asst dir Charterhouse Bank 1984-; ACA; *Recreations* swimming, skiing, travel; *Clubs* Oriental; *Style—* Nigel Brooks, Esq; 91 Warwick Rd, London SW5 (☎ 071 244 9738); 1 Paternoster Row, St Paul's, London EC4 (☎ 071 248 4000)

BROOKS, Peter Malcolm; s of Roger Morrison Brooks (d 1968), of Winchester, and Phyllis Fuller, *née* Hopkinson; *b* 12 Feb 1947; *Educ* Marlborough, Univ of Southampton (LLB, Eng and Br Univs squash team rep); *m* 1, 1974 (m dis); 1 s (Matthew Harry Morrison b 21 July 1980); m 2, 1987, Patricia Margaret; 1 s (Nicholas John Morrison b 27 Nov 1987); *Career* VSO Sarawak 1965-66; slr; ptnr: MacFarlanes 1977-84 (articled clerk 1969-71), Clifford Turner (now Clifford Chance) 1984-; memb: City of London Slrs Co, Law Soc 1971; *Recreations* real tennis, cricket, opera, theatre, travel; *Clubs* MCC; *Style—* Peter Brooks, Esq; Clifford Chance, Royex House, Aldermanbury Square, London EC2 (☎ 071 600 0808, car 0831 342765, fax 071 956 0103)

BROOKS, Robert; s of William Frederick Brooks, of Bishopswood House, Bishopswood, Herefordshire, and Joan Patricia, *née* Marshall; *b* 1 Oct 1956; *Educ* St Benedict's Sch Ealing; *m* 30 May 1981, Evelyn Rachel, da of Prof John William Durnford; 2 s (Charles b 24 Aug 1984, John b 21 June 1987), 1 da (Sarah b 11 May 1983); *Career* dir Christie's S Kensington Ltd 1984-87 (joined 1975), dir Christie Manson and Woods Ltd 1987-89; *Recreations* flying; *Style—* Robert Brooks, Esq; Robert Brooks' (Auctioneers) Ltd, 81 Westside, London SW4 9AY (☎ 071 228 8000)

BROOKS, Robert Anthony (Bobby); s of Ronald Clifton Brooks (d 1980), and Iris Winifred, *née* Payne (d 1978); *b* 12 April 1931; *Educ* Eton; *m* 1955, Sally, da of Richard Burnie Armistead; 3 da (Amanda (Mrs Keegan) b 1956, Sarah b 1959, Lucy b 1966); *Career* articled clerk Viney Price & Goodyear 1951-57; CA: Coopers & Lybrand 1957-60, Robert Benson Lonsdale (amalgamated to become Kleinwort, Benson Ltd) 1960- (dir 1967-); dir: Commercial Union plc 1977-, M&G Group plc 1979-, Kleinwort Development Fund plc 1983-, The Securities Association Ltd 1989-; Freeman City of London, Liveryman Worshipful Co of Grocers; FCA; *Recreations* fishing, gardening, golf; *Clubs* City of London; *Style—* Bobby Brooks, Esq; Kleinwort Benson Limited, 20 Fenchurch St, London EC3 (☎ 071 623 8000)

BROOKS, (Richard) Simon; s of Maj Richard Clement Brooks, TD, JP (d 1980), of Wrington, Nr Bristol, and Edith Mary, *née* Shellard (d 1950); *b* 29 March 1931; *Educ* Radley; *m* 8 Aug 1959, Helen Rosemary, da of Frederick James Weeks, of Wrington, Bristol; 1 s (Adam b 1965), 2 da (Victoria (Mrs Botsford) b 1961, Emma (Mrs Thompson) b 1962); *Career* Nat Serv RAF, PO Royal Auxiliary Air Force 1955 (Flying Offr 1959); CA 1954, former pres Br Textile Rental Assoc, chm and md Brooks Serv Gp plc; former memb W Eng Ctee IOD, tstee Clifton Suspension Bridge, govr Clifton Coll, former chm Clifton Club, treas Anchor Soc; Freeman City of: Bristol 1969, London 1971; Liveryman Worshipful Co of: Dyers, Launderers, Merchant Venturers; FCA 1965, (ACA 1954); *Recreations* reading, music, food and drink, motor sport, occasional squash, skiing, riding, sailing, golf, tennis, bridge, travel; *Clubs* Clifton; *Style—* Simon Brooks, Esq; Aztec West, Almondsbury, Bristol, Avon BS12 4SN (☎ 0454 614668)

BROOKS OF TREMORFA, Baron (Life Peer UK 1979); John Edward Brooks; s of Edward George Brooks, and Rachel, *née* White; *b* 12 April 1927; *m* 1, 1948 (m dis 1956); 1 s, 1 da; m 2, 1958, Margaret Pringle; 2 s; *Career* parliamentary agent to Rt Hon James Callaghan, MP, 1970 and 1979 gen elections; *Style—* The Rt Hon the Lord Brooks of Tremorfa; 57 Janet St, Slott, Cardiff (☎ 40709)

BROOKSBANK, Lady; Ann; da of Col Thomas Claud Clitherow, DSO, of Hotham Hall, Brough, Yorks; *m* 1943, Sir (Edward) William Brooksbank, 2 Bt, TD, JP, DL (d 1983); 1 s; *Style—* Ann, Lady Brooksbank; Menethorpe Hall, Malton, N Yorks

BROOKSBANK, Sir (Edward) Nicholas; 3 Bt (UK 1919), of Healaugh Manor, Healaugh, W Riding of Yorks; Lord of the Manor of Healaugh; s of Sir William Brooksbank, 2 Bt, TD, JP, DL (d 1983), and Ann, Lady Brooksbank, *qv*; *b* 4 Oct 1944; *Educ* Eton; *m* 1970, Hon Emma Myrtle Mary Anne, da of Baron Holderness, PC, DL, *qv*; 1 s, 1 da; *Heir* s, Florian Tom Charles b 9 Aug 1982; *Career* Capt the Blues and Royals, ret; Christie's rep York; *Style—* Sir Nicholas Brooksbank, Bt; Ryton Grange, Malton, N Yorks (☎ Kirby Misperton (065 386) 270)

BROOKSHAW, Sarah Caroline (Sally); da of John Latter Barratt (d 1988), of Minsterley Hall, Shrewsbury, Shropshire, and Pauline Monica, *née* Gapp; *b* 10 Jan 1956; *Educ* Shrewsbury HS, Univ of Aberystwyth (LLB); *m* 6 June 1987, Oliver Chitty Brookshaw, s of Herbert Philip Brookshaw MC, of Old House Farm, Saunderton, Princes Risborough, Buckinghamshire; *Career* slr, ptnr William Sturges and Co 1986-90; *Recreations* riding and hunting; *Clubs* HAC Saddle, South Shropshire Hunt, Lansdowne; *Style—* Mrs Sally Brookshaw; Thorpe Underwood Farm, Northampton (☎ 0536 713446); Shoosmiths & Harrison, 3 Victoria St, Northampton (☎ 0604 31747, fax 0604 234109)

BROOM, Prof Donald Maurice; s of Donald Edward Broom (d 1971), of Tatsfield, Surrey, and Mavis Edith Rose, *née* Thompson; *b* 14 July 1942; *Educ* Whitgift Sch, St Catharine's Coll Cambridge (MA, PhD); *m* 31 May 1971, Sally Elizabeth Mary, da of Thomas Edward Fisher (d 1969), of Ufton Nervet, Berkshire; 3 s (Oliver b 1973, Tom b 1976, Giles b 1981); *Career* lectr (later reader) Dept of Pure and Applied Zoology Univ of Reading 1967-86, Colleen Macleod prof of Animal Welfare Dept of Clinical Veterinary Med Univ of Cambridge 1986-; visiting asst prof Dept of Zoology Univ of Calif 1969, visiting lectr Dept of Biology Univ of WI Trinidad 1972; invited expert: Cncl of Euro Standing Ctee on Welfare of Animals Kept for Farming Purposes 1987, Cmmn of Europe Communities Farm Animal Welfare Expert Gp 1981; visiting scientist Div of Animal Prodn Cwlth Sci and Industl Res Orgn Perth 1983, hon res assoc Animal and Grassland Res Inst 1985, tstee Farm Animal Care Tst 1986, fell St Catharine's Coll Cambridge 1987-, hon treas Assoc for the Study of Animal Behaviour 1971-80 (cncl memb 1980-83); pres Soc for Veterinary Ethology 1987-89 (cncl memb 1981-84, vice pres 1986-87 and 1989-); memb: Int Ethological Ctee 1976-79, Br Tst for Ornithology, Br Soc of Animal Prodn, Zoological Soc of London, Assoc of Veterinary Teachers and Res Workers; winner of George Fleming prize for best paper in Br Veterinary Jl (1990); FIBioL 1986; *Books* Birds and their Behaviour (1977) Biology of Behaviour (1981), Encyclopaedia of Domestic Animals (ed, with P A Messent, 1986), Farmed Animals (ed, 1986), Farm Animal Behaviour and Welfare (with A F Fraser 1990); *Recreations* squash, modern pentathlon, ornithology; *Clubs* Hawks (Cambridge); *Style—* Prof Donald Broom; Department of Clinical Veterinary Medicine, Univ of Cambridge, Madingley Rd, Cambridge CB3 0ES; St Catharine's College, Cambridge (☎ 0223 337 697, fax 0223 337 610)

BROOM, Air Marshal Sir Ivor Gordon; KCB (1975, CB 1972), CBE (1969), DSO (1945), DFC (1942 and two bars 1944 and 1945), AFC (1956); s of Alfred Godfrey Broom, of Southport, and Janet Broom; *b* 2 June 1920; *Educ* W Monmouth Sch, Pontypridd GS; *m* 1942, Jess Irene, da of William Joseph Cooper, of Ipswich; 2 s, 1 da; *Career* served WWII bomber pilot, Cmdt Central Flying Sch 1968-70, controller of Nat Air Traffic Servs and Bd Memb CAA 1974-77, ret RAF 1977; int aerospace conslt 1977-; chm Gatwick Handling Ltd 1982-, dir Plessey Airports Ltd 1982-86, chm Farnborough Aerospace Devpt Corpn 1985-; *Recreations* golf; *Clubs* RAF, Moor Park Golf; *Style—* Air Marshal Sir Ivor Broom, KCB, CBE, DSO, DFC, AFC; Cherry Lawn, Bridle Lane, Loudwater, Rickmansworth, Herts WD3 4JB (☎ 0923 778878)

BROOME, David; OBE (1970); s of Fred and Amelia Broome, of Chepstow; *b* 1 March 1940; *Educ* Monmouth GS; *m* 1976, Elizabeth, da of K W Fletcher, of Thirk, N Yorkshire; 1 s; *Career* show jumper and farmer; World Show Jumping Champion 1970; MFH; *Style—* David Broome Esq, OBE; Mount Ballan Manor, Crick, Chepstow, Gwent (☎ Caldicot 42077)

BROOME, Ronald Frederick; OBE (1983), QPM (1989); s of Edgar Broome (d 1977), and Ida, *née* Richardson (d 1975); *b* 29 Dec 1932; *Educ* Hemsworth GS; *m* 2 Oct 1954, Kathleen, da of Jack Lyon (d 1962); 3 s (Christopher b 31 Oct 1956, Graham Mark b 21 Nov 1957, Michael Antony b 2 May 1964) 2 da (Deborah Elizabeth b 4 Aug 1960, Helen Lucy b 7 June 1968); *Career* RAF police 1950-54; W Riding Constabulory 1954, dep chief constable W Midlands Police 1980 (asst chief constable 1977), chief constable Avon and Somerset Constabulory 1983-89; vice pres: Police Athletic Assoc, Royal Life-Saving Soc, memb Cncl of St John in Avon; *Recreations* tennis, badminton; *Clubs* Bristol Savages, Shakespeare; *Style—* Ronald Broome, Esq, OBE, QPM

BROOMER, James Vincent; s of Vincent Walter Mason Broomer (d 1951), and Christina, *née* Joyce (d 1974); *b* 27 Feb 1927; *Educ* Lancaster Royal GS, Univ of Manchester (LLB); *m* 24 March 1955, Averil Mary, da of Frank Crapper, of Goole, N Yorkshire; 2 s (Charles b 1961, Jason b 1968), 1 da (Alison b 1964); *Career* RN 1946-49; asst to legal aid offr 1947-49; admitted slr 1951, dep clerk to magistrates Howden 1952-63, ptnr Taylor Broomer & Co Goole; fndr pres Rotary Club of Howden; memb Law Soc; *Recreations* law, music; *Style—* James Broomer, Esq; 20 Riversdale Drive, Goole DN14 5LJ (☎ 0405 2219); 157 Boothferry Rd, Goole DN14 6AL (☎ 0405 3853, fax 0405 720246)

BROOMFIELD, Graham Martin; s of Herbert Broomfield (d 1989), of W Sussex, and Muriel Joyce, *née* Robinson; *b* 12 Feb 1945; *Educ* Dorking County GS, Chelsea Coll, Univ of London (BSc); *m* 5 Oct 1974, Wai Yu (Miranda), da of Leung Fu Ping (d 1972); 1 s (Lee b 1978), 1 da (Amy b 1981); *Career* CA; Charles Comins & Co 1967-72, Peat Marwick Mitchell & Co 1972-76, Warner Communications Inc 1977-81, Prager & Fenton 1981-87, Broomfield & Co 1983-; treas Friends of St James Norlands, govr St Clements & St James Sch; *Recreations* politics, squash; *Style—* Graham M Broomfield, Esq; 17 Cromwell Grove, London W6 (☎ 071 603 4487, fax 071 371 4908)

BROOMFIELD, Nigel Hugh Robert Allen; CMG (1986); s of Col Arthur Allen Broomfield, OBE, MC (d 1970), and Ruth Sheilagh, *née* Anderson (d 1974); *b* 19 March 1937; *Educ* Haileybury, Trinity Coll Cambridge (BA); *m* 8 June 1963, Valerie, da of G Fenton, of Garden Court, Noirmont, Jersey, CI; 2 s (Alexander Allen b 29 April 1970, Nicholas Richard Allen b 2 Oct 1976); *Career* Maj 17/21 Lancers 1958-68; first sec: FCO 1969, Bonn 1970, Moscow 1973, FCO 1975; RCDS 1978, cnsllr and head of Chancery BMG Berlin 1979, head E Euro and Soviet Dept FCO 1981, dep high cmmr New Delhi 1986, ambass to GDR E Berlin 1988, dep under sec of state (Defence) FCO 1990; Br Amateur Squash Champion 1957-58; *Recreations* reading, music, sport; *Clubs* MCC, RAC; *Style—* Nigel Broomfield, Esq, CMG; c/o FCO, Whitehall, London SW1A 2AA

BROOMHEAD, Ivor William; s of Frederick William Broomhead (d 1970), and Florence Elizabeth, *née* Percival (d 1989); *b* 7 Dec 1924; *Educ* Doncaster GS, St John's Coll Cambridge (MA, MChir), UCH London (MB); *m* 18 Dec 1950, Dorothea Primrose, da of John Edward Pretty Wagstaff (d 1963); 1 s (Anthony b 1954), 2 da (Amanda b 1951, Susan b 1963); *Career* Nat Serv, med offr RAF 1950-52; conslt plastic surgn: The Hosp for Sick Children 1964-87, Guy's Hosp 1968-87, Royal Masonic Hosp 1974-86; specialist pubns on cleft lip and palate, and other congenital malformations; conslt advsr in plastic surgery to DHSS Chief Med Offr; pres: Royal Soc of Med (plastic surgery section) 1981, Br Assoc of Plastic Surgns 1985; FRCS; *Recreations* horology (skeleton clocks); *Clubs* Athenaeum; *Style—* Ivor Broomhead, Esq; 7 Saxon Place, Lower Buckland Rd, Lymington, Hants (☎ 0590 671975)

BROOMHEAD, Philip; s of James Robert Broomhead (d 1985), and Marion, *née* Mather; *b* 17 Nov 1935; *Educ* Heckmondwike GS; *m* 1, Denise Fogarty (d 1970); 3 s (Howard b 4 Sept 1963, Paul b 17 Nov 1964, Alan b 26 March 1966); m 2, 7th Aug 1971, Mary Teed, da of late Joseph Everingham; 1 step s (Edward John b 15 Oct 1963), 1 step da (Philippa b 7 Jan 1966); *Career* Nat Serv RAF 1960-62; articled clerk TN Steel & Co 1954-59, qualified 1959, sr clerk Beevers & Adgie Chartered Accountants Cleckheaton and Leeds 1962-65, mangr Peat Marwick Mitchell & Co Cleckheaton 1965-68; ptnr: Binns Martindale Chartered Accountants Mirfield and Cleckheaton 1968-69, Revell Ward Chartered Accountants Huddersfield Leeds; Cleckheaton Dewsbury & Halifax 1969-, Moore Stephens Huddersfield 1980-1990; Huddersfield Soc of CAs 1987-88, vice chm Bd of Govrs Castle Hall grant maintained Sch Mirfield; FCA (ACA 1959); *Recreations* gardening, travel, photography, collecting phonographs/vintage gramophones; *Clubs* Rotary Club of Mirfield (pres 1985-86), Northern Phonograph and Gramaphone Soc; *Style—* Philip Broomhead, Esq; The White House, 26 Crowless Road, Mirfield, West Yorkshire WF14 9PJ (☎ 0924 492575); Revel Ward, Chartered Accountants, Cross Lane House, Crown St, Cleckheaton, West Yorkshire BD19 3NF (☎ 0274 874867, fax 0274 851242)

BROPHY, Brigid Antonia; o da of John Brophy (d 1965, author), and Charis Weare, *née* Grundy; *b* 12 June 1929; *Educ* St Paul's Girls' Sch, St Hugh's Coll Oxford; *m* 1954, Sir Michael Levey, *qv*; 1 da; *Career* author and playwright; FRSL; *Books* 11 fiction volumes and 10 non-fiction; *Style—* Miss Brigid Brophy; Flat 3, 185 Old Brompton Rd, London SW5 0AN (☎ 071 373 9335)

BROPHY, Michael John Mary; s of Gerald Mary Brophy, and Mary Brophy; *b* 24 June 1937; *Educ* Ampleforth, RN Coll Dartmouth; *m* 1962, Sarah Myrtle, da of Capt G B Rowe RN; 3 s (James, Jonathan, Thomas), 1 da (Lucy); *Career* RN (Lt Cdr) 1953-66; assoc dir J Walter Thompson 1962-74, appeals dir The Spastics Soc 1975-81, dir Charities Aid Fndn 1982-; *Recreations* travel, walking; *Clubs* Athenaeum; *Style—* Michael Brophy Esq; Pond House, Isfield, E Sussex

BROSSFIELD, Sir Norman Eugene; s of Eric Stanley Brossfield (d 1953), and Joy, *née* Bilben (d 1958); *b* 11 Feb 1942; *Educ* Stanmore Hill GS, Penn State Univ USA (Masters in business studies); *Career* Jelbing-Ren NV: started as sales trainee, rising to sales mangr of Euro then dir of sales, dep chm Exec Bd 1983-, dep chm Exec Bd 1983-; awarded Charity/Fund Raiser Plate Br Inst of Tech Management 1980; pres Nat Cncl of Federated Texturisers 1980-, memb Br Cncl of Low Country Traders 1985; kt (1982); *Recreations* model-making, philately; *Clubs* Pennsylvania Floreat (USA), Clubmans; *Style—* Sir Norman Brossfield; Jelbingren NV, 2 Bishop's Row, London EC4A 4EJ

BROSTER, Brenda Maeve; *née* Shaw; da of Col F O J Shaw, of Wingham, Kent, and Catherine Maeve Power, *née* McCaul, of Guildford, Surrey; *b* 11 Nov 1944; *Educ* St Mary's Priory Warwicks, St Godric's Coll Hampstead; *m* 9 Oct 1965, David George, s of H F Broster (d 1973), of Bursledon, Hants; 2 s (Oliver b 1971, Humphrey b 1979), 2 da (Natalie b 1974, Georgette b 1975); *Career* md: Sales Promotions Agency, Powergirls Ltd Int Agency; *Recreations* horses, gemology, astronomy, the arts; *Style—* Mrs Brenda M Broster; The Hermitage, 193 Lower Road, Gt Bookham, Surrey; Powergirls Ltd, 59d Church Road, Gt Bookham, Surrey KT23 3JJ

BROTHERHOOD, James; s of Frederick Arthur Brotherhood (d 1974), and Isabel, *née* Bradley; *b* 5 June 1946,,; *Educ* King's Sch Chester; *m* 1, 2 Aug 1969, Susan Elizabeth, da of Thomas Ian Jodrell Toler, of Cheshire; 3 s (Jonathan Alexander Jodrell b 1973, Philip Richard Thomas b 1975, Michael Rupert Benjamin b 1981), 2 da (Katherine Mary b 1978, Eleanor Elizabeth b 1984); m 2, March 1989, Rosalind Ann, da of late Dr Robert Alan Blyth, of Cheshire; *Career* architect; pres Cheshire Soc of Architects 1978-80, chm NW region RIBA 1983; dip arch (Hons) 1973, RIBA 1974; *Recreations* shooting, fishing; *Clubs* City (Chester), St James (Manchester), Pitt; *Style—* James Brotherhood, Esq; 7 Selkirk Road, Curzon Park, Chester CH4 OHU (☎ 0244 683983); Steam Mill, Chester, CH3 5AN (☎ 0244 347557)

BROTHERHOOD, Peter; s of Albert J Brotherhood, of 6 Spa Rd, Gainford, nr Darlington, Co Durham, and Lily, *née* Woolford; *b* 28 June 1945; *Educ* Open Univ (BA); *m* Sandra; 1 s (Mark b 6 May 1976); *Career* Student 1966-69 (RMN), postgrad student 1969-71 (RGN), staff nurse 1971-72, charge nurse 1972-75, postgrad student 1975-76 (registered nurse in Mental Handicap), charge nurse 1976-77, nursing offr 1977-79, sr nursing offr 1979-81, dir nursing servs 1981-84, chief nursing offr 1984-85, unit gen mangr 1985-, appointed Mental Health Act cmmr 1985; various achievements in the field of Mental Health Care; memb: Royal Coll of Nursing, Manchester Business Sch Assoc; *Recreations* sailing, motoring, gardening; *Style—* Peter Brotherhood, Esq; Station House, Piercebridge, nr Darlington, Co Durham PL2 3TS (☎ 0325 374342); Winterton Hospital, Sedgefield, Stockton on Tees TS21 3EJ (fax 0740 20521/3067, car 0860 470188)

BROTHERS, Brian Peter; s of Ernest Norman (d 1988), and Frances Ruth (d 1987); *b* 18 May 1929; *Educ* Dauntsey's Sch, King's Coll; *m* 1, 1950, Diana Elizabeth, da of Edward J Tucker (d 1986); 3 s (Timothy b 1951, Jeremy b 1955, Toby b 1961), 1 da (Anne b 1956); m 2, 1974, Jacquelin Ann; 1 da (Katharine b 1975); *Career* fin advsr; arranged fin for over 50 Hosps/Health Schemes mainly S America some with Economist Intelligence Unit 1975-80; dir: W Sussex Area Enterprise Centre Ltd, Voice of Progress, Seacourt Press, Oxford Initiative Investments, Individual Finance, Individual Television; FID (memb S Ctee); *Recreations* talking newspaper for the blind; *Clubs* Worthing: Golf, Rotary, Tennis; *Style—* Brian P Brothers, Esq; 4 Parklands Ave, Goring-By-Sea, Worthing BN12 4NH

BROTHERS, Air Cdre Peter Malam; CBE (1964), DSO (1944), DFC (1940, bar 1943); s of John Malam Brothers (d 1953), of Prestwich, Lancs, and Maude Elizabeth Owen (d 1969); *b* 30 Sept 1917; *Educ* North Manchester Sch; *m* 1939, Annette, da of James Wilson (d 1959), of Hutton House, Birmingham; 3 da (Caroline, Wendy, Hilary); *Career* Pilot Offr RAF 1936, Flt Lt 1939, served WW II, Battle of Britain 1940, Sqdn Ldr 1941, Wing Cdr 1942, Tangmere Wing Ldr 1942-43, Staff HQ No 10 Gp 1943, Exeter Wing Ldr 1944, US Cmd and Gen Staff Sch 1944-45, Central Fighter Estab 1945-46; joined HM Colonial Serv 1947 (dist offr: Meru 1947-48, Kisumu 1948-49); rejoined RAF 1949, cmd Bomber Sqdn 1949-52, HQ No 3 Gp 1952-54, RAF Staff Coll 1954, HQ Fighter Cmd 1955-57, Bomber Stn 1957-59, Gp Capt and staff offr SHAPE Paris 1959-62, Dir of Ops (overseas) Air Miny 1962-65, Air Cdre and AOC Mil Air Traffic Ops 1965-68, dir PR (RAF) MOD (AIR) 1968-73, ret 1973; chm and md Peter Brothers Consultants Ltd 1973-86; Master Guild Air Pilots & Air Navigators 1974-75 (Freeman 1966, Liveryman 1968, Warden 1971), Freeman City of London 1967; patron Spitfire Assoc Aust; vice pres: Spitfire Soc, Devon Emergency Vols; *Recreations* flying, fishing, swimming; *Clubs* RAF, Honiton Golf; *Style—* Air Cdre Peter Brothers, CBE, DSO, DFC; c/o National Westminster Bank, Topsham, Devon

BROTHERTON, Ian Dryhurst; TD (1964), DL (Middx 1964, Greater London 1967); s of Thomas D Brotherton, of Hampton, Middx; *b* 16 Nov 1920; *Educ* Hampton Sch, Univ of London; *m* 1943, Margaret, da of Sidney F Ponting, of Shepperton; 3 da; *Career* Middx Regt 1939-46 (despatches), Bt Col 1962, ADC (TA&VR) to HM The Queen 1968-73; md: S Daval & Sons 1968-69, British American Optical Co 1970-72, Hadley Co 1972-85, princ Cruise Training 1985-89; Croix de Guerre; *Recreations* photography, yachting; *Clubs* Army & Navy, Royal Lymington Yacht; *Style—* Ian Brotherton, Esq, TD, DL; The Moorings, 6 Cranfield Ave, Wimborne, Dorset BH21 1DE (☎ 0202 886887)

BROTHERTON, Michael Lewis; s of late Capt John Basil Brotherton, and Maud Brotherton; *b* 26 May 1931; *Educ* RNC Dartmouth; *m* 1968, Julia, da of Austin Gerald Comyn King, of Bath; 3 s, 1 da; *Career* Lt Cdr RN until 1964 (despatches Cyprus, 1957); Times Newspapers 1967-74; MP (C) Louth 1974-83; proprietor Michael Brotherton Assocs (PR conslts) 1986; pres Hyde Park Tories 1975; *Recreations* cricket, cooking; *Clubs* Army and Navy; *Style—* Michael Brotherton, Esq; The Old Vicarage, Wrangle, Boston, Lincs (☎ 0205 870 688)

BROUCHER, David Stuart; s of Clifford Broucher, of Ewenny, Glamorgan, and Betty Elma, *née* Jordan; *b* 5 Oct 1944; *Educ* Manchester GS, Trinity Hall Cambridge (BA); *m* 25 Nov 1971, Marion Monika, da of Mr Wilkinson Gill, of Stagshaw, Northumberland; 1 s (Nicholas David b 1972); *Career* Foreign Office 1966-68, Br Mil Govt Berlin 1968-72, Cabinet Office 1972-75, Br Embassy Prague 1975-78, FCO 1978-83, UK perm rep to the EC 1983-85, Br Embassy: Jakarta 1985-89, Bonn 1989; *Recreations* golf, music, sailing; *Style—* David Broucher, Esq

BROUGH, Dr Colin; s of Peter Brough (d 1964), and Elizabeth Cassels Collison, *née* Chalmers; *b* 4 Jan 1932; *Educ* Bell Baxter Sch Cupar Fife, Univ of Edinburgh (MB ChB, DPH, DIH); *m* 28 Dec 1957, Maureen (Jenny), da of late William Frederick Jennings; 4 s (Hamish b 1960, Ewan b 1963, Angus b 1967, Dugald b 1969), 1 da (Catriona b 1959); *Career* Surgn Lt RN 1957-60; house offr Leicester Gen Hosp 1956-57, GP Leith and Fife 1960-64, dep superintendent Royal Infirmary Edinburgh 1965-67 (house offr 1956-57); S Eastern Regnl Hosp Bd Scotland 1967-74: ASMO, PASMO, dep SAMO; chief admin MO Lothian Health Bd 1980-88 (community medicine specialist 1974-80); FFCM 1978, FRCPE 1982; *Recreations* golf, shooting, fishing; *Style—* Dr Colin Brough; The Saughs, Gullane, E Lothian EH31 2AL (☎ 0620 842179)

BROUGH, Michael David; s of (Kenneth) David Brough (d 1990), of Highgate, London, and Frances Elizabeth, *née* Davies; *b* 4 July 1942; *Educ* Westminster, Christ's Coll Cambridge, Middx Hosp Med Sch (MA, MB BChir); *m* 8 June 1974, Dr Geraldine Moira, da of Ernest Alfred Sleigh, of Sutton Coldfield; 2 s (Jonathan b 1977, Nicholas b 1983), 2 da (Charlotte b 1978, Veronica b 1981); *Career* med post 1968-71: Middx Hosp, Central Middx Hosp; surgical trg posts Birmingham hosps 1971-74; plastic surgeon trg posts 1975-80: Mt Vernon Hosp London, Odstock Hosp Salisbury, Withington Hosp Manchester; conslt in plastic surgery 1980-82: St Andrews Hosp Billericay, Queen Elizabeth Hosp Hackney, Whipps Cross Hosp; conslt plastic surgery 1982-: UCH, Royal Free Hosp, Whittington Hosp, Royal Northern Hosp; Freeman City of London 1974; Liveryman: Worshipful Co of Tin Plate Workers (memb Ct of Assts), Worshipful Co of Apothecaries; FRCS; *Recreations* family, skiing; *Clubs* Hawks (Cambridge); *Style—* Michael Brough, Esq; 6 Stormont Rd, London N6 4NL; The Consulting Suite, 82 Portland Place, London WIN 3DH (☎ 071 935 8910)

BROUGHAM, Hon Charles William; s and h of 5 Baron Brougham and Vaux; *b* 9 Nov 1971; *Style—* The Hon Charles Brougham; Highleaze House, Oare, nr Marlborough, Wilts

BROUGHAM, Hon David Peter; s of 4 Baron Brougham and Vaux (d 1967); *b* 22 Aug 1940; *Educ* Sedbergh; *m* 1, 1969, Moussie Christina Margareta Hallström, da of Sven Hörnblad, of Stockholm, Sweden; 1 s (Henry, b 1971); m 2, 1977, Caroline Susan, only da of Lt-Col James Michael Heigham Royce Tomkin, MC, of Red House, Wissett, Halesworth, Suffolk (by his w Margaret Elinor, da of Sir Charles Henry Napier Bunbury, 11 B), and former w of Julian Dixon; 1 s (Oliver, b 1978); *Style—* The Hon David Brougham; Flat D, 10 Girdlers Rd, London W14

BROUGHAM, Hon Henrietta Louise; da of 5 Baron Brougham and Vaux and Olivia Hicks, *née* Gray; *b* 23 Feb 1965; *Educ* Cranborne Chase Sch, Cambridgeshire Coll of Arts & Technology; *Style—* The Hon Henrietta Brougham; 6 Bedford Court, Grena Rd, Richmond, Surrey TW9 1XT

BROUGHAM AND VAUX, 5 Baron (UK 1860); Michael John Brougham; s of 4 Baron (d 1967) by his 2 w, Jean, da of late Brig-Gen Gilbert Follett, DSO, MVO, and Lady Mildred, *née* Murray, da of 7 Earl of Dunmore, DL; *b* 2 Aug 1938; *Educ* Lycée Jaccard Lausanne, Millfield, Northampton Inst of Agric; *m* 1, 1963 (m dis 1968), Olivia Susan, da of Rear Adm Gordon Thomas Seccombe Gray, DSC, of Midhurst; 1 da; m 2, 1969 (m dis 1981), Catherine (who m 1981 Rupert Edward Odo Russell, gs of Sir Odo Russell, KCMG, KCVO, CB, himself 2 s of 1 Baron Ampthill), da of William Gulliver; 1 s; *Heir* s, Hon Charles Brougham; *Career* Parly conslt and co dir; former pres ROSPA; chm Tax Payers Soc; *Recreations* rugger, tennis, photography; *Style—* The Rt Hon the Lord Brougham and Vaux; 11 Westminster Gardens, Marsham St, London SW1P 4JA

BROUGHSHANE, 2 Baron (UK 1945); Patrick Owen Alexander Davison; s of 1 Baron, KBE (d 1953), by his 1 w, Beatrice Mary, da of late Sir Owen Roberts, DCL, LLD, FSA, DL; *b* 18 June 1903; *Educ* Winchester, Magdalen Coll Oxford; *m* 1929, Bettine, da of late Sir Arthur Edward Montague Russell, 6 Bt (cr 1812); 1 s decd; *Heir* bro, Hon Kensington Davison; *Career* Irish Gds 1939-42, asst sec (mil) War Cabinet 1942-45; barr Inner Temple 1926; Legion of Merit (USA); *Clubs* White's; *Style—* The Rt Hon The Lord Broughshane; 21 Eaton Sq, London SW1; 28 Fisher St, Sandwich, Kent

BROUGHTON, Alan William; *b* 22 May 1944; *Career* National Provincal Bank (later Nat West) 1960-70; Orion Bank: seconded to Orion Termbank 1971, treasy mangr 1972-76, asst dir 1976-78, dir 1978-80, md and memb Exec Ctee 1980-81, md Orion Royal Bank 1981-83; vice pres and euro treas Royal Bank of Canada 1983-85; Guiness Mation & Co Ltd: exec dir 1985-86, memb Exec Ctee 1986-89, md 1989-; *Clubs* Overseas Bankers; *Style—* Alan Broughton, Esq; Guinness Mahon & Co Limited, 32 St Mary at Hill, London EC3P 3AJ (☎ 071 623 9333, fax 071 528 0846)

BROUGHTON, Air Marshal Sir Charles; KBE (1965, CBE 1952), CB (1961); s of Charles and Florence Gertrude Broughton, of Christchurch, NZ; *b* 27 April 1911; *Educ* New Zealand, RAF Coll Cranwell; *m* 1939, Sylvia Dorothy Mary, da of late Col C H de St P Bunbury; 1 da (and 1 da decd); *Career* cmmnd RAF 1932; DG Orgn Air Miny

1961-64, UK rep in Ankara, perm mil Deputies Gp of Central Treaty Orgn 1965-66, air memb for Supply and Orgn Miny of Defence 1966-68; *Style*— Air Marshal Sir Charles Broughton, KBE, CB; c/o Shrewsbury House, Cheyne Walk, London SW3

BROUGHTON, David Delves; s of Lt Cdr Peter John Delves Broughton, RN (d 1963); hp to Btcy of kinsman, Sir Evelyn Delves Broughton 12 Bt; *b* 7 May 1942; *Style*— David Broughton Esq

BROUGHTON, Sir (Evelyn) Delves; 12 Bt (E 1660), of Broughton, Staffs; s of Sir John Delves Broughton, 11 Bt (d 1942), and Vera Edyth, *née* Boscawen (d 1966); *b* 2 Oct 1915; *Educ* Eton, Trinity Coll Cambridge; *m* 1, 28 Jan 1947 (m dis 1953), Hon Elizabeth Florence Marion Cholmondeley, da of 4 Baron Delamere, JP, by his 1 w, Phyllis, da of Lord George Montagu-Douglas-Scott, OBE, 3 s of 6 Duke of Buccleuch, KG, KT, PC; m 2, 1955 (m dis 1974), Helen Mary, da of J Shore, of Wilmslow; 1 s (John b 12 July 1963 d 1965), 3 da (Isabella Delves (Mrs Detmar Blow) b 19 Nov 1958, Julia Helen Delves b 11 Feb 1961, Lavinia Mary b 14 Feb 1965); m 3, 1974, Rona, da of E Clifford Johns, of Wargrave, and formerly w of Donald Crammond, of Bodiham, Sussex; *Heir* kinsman, David Delves Broughton; *Career* farmer and landowner; former 2 Lt Irish Gds; *Recreations* shooting, travel; *Clubs* Brooks's, White's, Tarporley Hunt; *Style*— Sir Delves Broughton, Bt; 37 Kensington Square, London W8 5HP (☎ 071 937 8883); Doddington Cottage, Nantwich, Cheshire (☎ 0270 841 258)

BROUGHTON, Hon James Henry Ailwyn; s and h of 3 Baron Fairhaven, JP; *b* 25 May 1963; *Educ* Sunningdale, Harrow; *m* 22 March 1990, Sarah Olivia, da of Harold Digby Fitzgerald Creighton, *qv*, of Upper Brook St, London W1; *Career* Capt Blues and Royals; *Recreations* polo, shooting, skiing, hunting; *Clubs* Cavalry and Guards; *Style*— The Hon James Broughton

BROUN, Sir Lionel John Law; 12 Bt (NS 1686), of Colstoun, Haddingtonshire; s of Sir (James) Lionel Law 11 Bt (d 1962), and Lady Broun, *qv*; *b* 25 April 1927; *Style*— Sir Lionel Broun, Bt; 89 Penshurst St, Willoughby, NSW 2068, Australia

BROUN, William Windsor; s of William Arthur Broun (d 1925); hp to Btcy of kinsman, Sir Lionel Broun, 12 Bt; *b* 1917; *m* 1952, D'Hrie, da of Frank R King, of Bingara, NSW; 2 da; *Style*— William Broun Esq; 23 Clanalpine St, Mosman, NSW, Australia

BROUWER, Egbert; CBE (1980); s of Jan Hendrick Brouwer, and Margaretha M E Dyjers; *b* 14 Feb 1927; *Educ* Nederlands Lyceum, The Netherlands Beatrix Coll Switzerland; *m* 14 Oct 1953, Dorine, da of Cornelis van Holst Pellekaan (d 1952); 3 s, 1 da; *Career* dapt Dutch Army 1947-49; branch mangr: Internatio NV in SE Asia 1949-56, Roosendaal Commodity Brokers Rotterdam 1957-65; gen mangr BP Nederland BV Amsterdam 1965-80, md BP Nutrition Ltd London 1978-87; memb: Cncl VNO 1973-78, Bd Govrs Maritime Ryksmuseum 1972-80; chm Supervisory Bd Atlas COPCO Amsterdam 1975-80; memb Bd: Atlas Copco (GB) Hemel Hempstead 1980-, Purina Mills Inc 1986-89, BP Nutrition Ltd 1987-89; memb Supervisory Bd: Merrem and Laporte 1974-80, JP Morgan Nederland 1977-90, BP Nederland 1980-89; chm Supervisory Bd Hendrix International 1979-89; Knight Netherlands Lion (1987); *Recreations* sailing, skiing; *Clubs* Royal Netherlands Yacht; *Style*— Egbert Brouwer, Esq, CBE; Howick Farm, Balls Cross, nr Petworth GU28 9JY (☎ 040 377 548)

BROW, John David Bromfield; s of Keith Phorson Brow, MBE, (d 1979), of 71 Albert Rd, Caversham, Reading, Berks, and Mary Brow, *née* Bromfield (d 1989); *b* 8 Oct 1930; *Educ* Aldenham; *m* 19 July 1958, Loelia Alfreda, da of Alfred Douglas Lewis (d 1962), of 20 Priest Hill, Caversham, Reading, Berks; 3 s (Jeremy b 1960, Robert b 1963, Alastair b 1966), 1 da (Elizabeth b 1978); *Career* Mil Serv Lt RNVR; CA, ptnr of Ensors CA's of Ipswich 1966-88, sec Bury Engrg Co Ltd Suffolk; chm: Bridget Collett Educnl Fndn, Ipswich Suzuki Assoc; hon treas: Aldeburgh Poetry Tst, Suffolk Wildlife Tst; sec Orwell Investmt Club; *Recreations* gardening, the arts, local history; *Clubs* MCC, The Naval; *Style*— J D B Brow, Esq; Lea Bank, Westerfield, Ipswich, Suffolk IP6 9AJ (☎ 0473 251207)

BROWELL, Col Jasper Miles; MBE (1968); s of Capt Jasper Geoffrey Browell, MC (d 1960), of Silanchia, Norham-on-Tweed, and Eleanor Mary, *née* Faulkner (d 1985); *b* 4 June 1928; *Educ* Loretto; *m* 9 March 1957 (m dis 1979), Elizabeth Pamela Anne, da of Rev Canon T E G Morris, of Llanfrynach, nr Brecon, Powys; 2 s (Quentin b 1958, Marcus b 1959); *Career* cmmnd RA 1948, RA Trg Bde 1948-51, IFD Battery RWAFF Nigeria 1951-53, Capt ADC to GOC-in-C W Africa 1953-56, Adj 20 FD Regt 1956-59, 3 Regt RHA 1959-61, Maj instr gunnery Larkhill 1961-65, CO Kings Troop RHA 1965-68, 2 i/c 40 FD Regt RA 1968-70, Lt-Col CO 42 Regt RA 1970-73, sr instr gunnery UKLF 1973-76, chief instr gunnery Larkhill 1977, Col Dep Cmdt Larkhill 1978-83; *Recreations* shooting, walking; *Clubs* Army and Navy; *Style*— Col Jasper Browell, MBE; Sandway House, Bourton, Nr Gillingham, Dorset (☎ 0747 840 538); Delgaty Ranch, Bellevue, Idaho, USA

BROWETT, John Peter; s of Peter Harry James Browett, and Florence Margaret, *née* Kingdom; *b* 12 June 1946; *Educ* Wyggeston Boys' GS Leicester, St Bart's Med Coll London; *m* 6 Sept 1969, Penelope Ann, da of Alan Ross Land; 1 s (Oliver Peter Ross), 1 da (Deborah Louise); *Career* conslt orthopaedic surgn Bart's 1980-; orthopaedic conslt to Tottenham Hotspur FC; Liveryman Worshipful Co of Barber Surgns 1989; memb: Br Orthopaedic Assoc, BMA; *Recreations* skiing, wildlife, shooting; *Style*— John Browett, Esq; 95 Harley Street, London W1 (☎ 071 486 9323, fax 0836 223281)

BROWN; *see*: Crichton-Brown, Holden-Brown, Pigott-Brown, Richmond Brown

BROWN, (Francis) Adam; s of David Brown, of Flayosc, France, and Mrs R Y Preston-Jones, *née* Auckland; *b* 13 March 1955; *Educ* Harrow, Univ of Oxford (MA); *Career* dir David Brown Hldgs Ltd 1978, dep chm David Brown Corp plc 1986, exec search consultancy in assoc with Sotherby Sanders & Ptnrs 1990; *Recreations* foxhunting; *Style*— Adam Brown, Esq; Saddlers House, Upper Denby, Huddersfield HD8 8UN (☎ 0484 861519)

BROWN, Adrian James; s of Rev Stanley George Brown, of 134 Lynn Rd, Ely, Cambridge, and Gabrielle Mary, *née* Holmes; *b* 25 Nov 1946; *Educ* The Friends' Sch Saffron Walden Essex, Univ of Birmingham (BSc); *m* 21 Feb 1976, Jill, da of George Charles Harmsworth, of Crossways, Hullbridge Rd, Rayleigh, Essex; 1 s (Gregory b 1985), 2 da (Hilary b 1980, Fiona b 1984); *Career* dir: MIM Ltd 1986-88, Britannia Asset Management Ltd 1985-86; sr investmt mangr Refuge Assurance plc 1988-; *Recreations* reading; *Style*— Adrian Brown, Esq; Colts Pightle, Post Office Rd, Woodham Mortimer, Maldon, Essex (☎ 024541 5381); 66 Gresham St, London EC2V 7PQ (☎ 071 600 0339, telex 295958)

BROWN, Alan Edward; s of Edward George Brown, and Irene Frances, *née* Blower; *b* 8 Jan 1946; *Educ* St Peter's Coll Oxford (MA); *m* 7 Sept 1968, Diane June, da of Walter Oakley, of 3 Wolverhampton Rd, Bridgnorth, Shropshire; 2 da (Michelle b 1974, Alison b 1976); *Career* dir Barclays Merchant Bank Ltd 1981-86, corp dir Barclays Bank plc 1986- (corp fin dir 1982-86), dir Barclays Devpt Capital Ltd 1987-; Freeman Town of Bridgenorth; ACIB; *Recreations* golf, windsurfing; *Clubs* Pinner Hill Golf, Rickmansworth Windsurfing, Oxford & Cambridge Golfing Soc; *Style*— Alan Brown, Esq; Grasmere, 12 Moor Lane, Rickmansworth, Herts WD3 1LG; Barclays Bank plc, 54 Lombard St, London EC3P 3AH (☎ 071 626 1567, telex 894076, fax 071 621 0386)

BROWN, Prof Alan Geoffrey; s of Roy Brown (d 1943), and Edith Lillian, *née* Swift; *b* 20 April 1940; *Educ* Mundella GS Nottingham, Univ of Edinburgh (BSC, MB ChB, PhD); *m* 13 April 1963, Judith, da of Leonard Thomas Allen (d 1987); 1 s (Jeremy David b 1967), 1 da (Jessica Anne b 1968); *Career* Univ of Edinburgh: asst lectr in veterinary physiology 1964-65, lectr 1965-76, Beit meml fell for Medres 1968-71, res fell supported by MRC 1971-74, reader in veterinary physiology 1976-84, prof 1984-; memb Physiological Soc 1968; FRSE 1984, FIBiol 1987; *Books* Organization in the Spinal Cord (1981), Intracellular Staining of Mammalian Neurones (with REW Fyffe, 1984); *Recreations* music, gardening; *Style*— Prof Alan Brown, FRSE; The Hitchell, 5c St Margaret's Rd, Edinburgh EH9 1AZ (☎ 031 447 1316); Dept of Preclinical Veterinary Sciences, University of Edinburgh, Summerhall, Edinburgh EH9 1QH (☎ 031 667 1011 ext 5274, telex 727442 UNIVED G)

BROWN, Alan Reginald; *b* 10 Jan 1932; *m* 2 June 1962, Rosemary Evelyn; 2 s (David b 1966, Peter b 1972), 2 da (Fiona b 1967, Clare b 1970); *Career* 2 Lt RE 1953-55; dir Matthew Hall PLC 1974-, dir and chm Matthew Hall Pension Tstees Ltd 1980-; Matthew Hall Mechanical and Electrical Engineers Ltd: chief exec 1974-90, chm 1987-90, dep chm 1990-; dir: Amec Pensions Trustee Ltd 1989-, Amec International Construction Ltd 1989-, Travel Places (International) Ltd 1989-, business devpt AMEC plc 1990-; tstee Matthew Hall Staff Trust Fund 1975-; govr: S Bank Poly, Vauxhall Coll, St Hilary's Sch Godalming; Liveryman Worshipful Co of Plumbers (memb Ct of Assts); FRSH, MASHRAE, CCIBSE; *Recreations* sailing, fly fishing; *Clubs* East India, Royal Corinthian Yacht; *Style*— Alan Brown, Esq; AMEC plc, 7 Baker Street, London W1M 1AB (☎ 071 224 6664, fax 071 224 3584, telex 291441)

BROWN, Alan Thomas; CBE (1978), DL (Oxon 1978); s of Thomas Henry Brown, of Cromer, and Lucy Lilian, *née* Betts; *b* 18 April 1928; *Educ* Wyggeston GS Leicester, Sidney Sussex Coll Cambridge; *m* 1962, Marie Christine, da of Hubert York East, late of Blackburn; 2 da; *Career* chief exec Oxon CC 1973-88; *Recreations* reading, chess, cliff walking; *Style*— Alan Brown, Esq, CBE, DL; 7 Field House Drive, Oxford

BROWN, Hon Mrs (Alison de Bois); da of 2 Baron Clwyd, JP (d 1987); *b* 24 Feb 1939; *m* 1, 1965 (m dis 1972), George Stricevic; 1 s (Milorad b 1967); m 2, 1972, Anthony H Brown; 3 s (Barnaby Joseph b 1973, Benedict Joseph b 1975, Lionel Trevor b 1978); *Style*— The Hon Mrs Brown; 9 Royal Terrace, Glasgow G3 7NT

BROWN, Allen Roger; MVO (1980); s of Arthur William Brown (d 1970), of Maidstone, Kent, and Cicie, *née* Rogers (d 1937); *b* 29 Dec 1934; *m* 24 March 1956, Brenda, da of John Thomas Breakwell (d 1974), of Birmingham; 2 s (Mark b 1960, Richard (twin) b 1960), 1 da (Judy Catherine b 1956); *Career* RN 1953-65; diplomat; Br Embassy postings: Brussels 1967-69, Benghazi 1969-71, Kuwait 1973-75, Berne 1978-81, Amman 1981-85, first sec (commercial) Baghdad 1987-90, head Br Interests Section Tripoli; ME Centre for Arab Studies Lebanon 1971-73; *Recreations* good husbandry; *Style*— Allen Brown, Esq, MVO; c/o Foreign and Commonwealth Office, King Charles St, London SW1

BROWN, Andrew David; s of Frank Brown, of Prestwich, Manchester, and Marion Evelyn, *née* Brown; *b* 1 March 1953; *Educ* Stand GS Whitefield Manchester; *m* 18 April 1981, Pamela Edith, da of Eric Howarth, of Bury, Lancs; 2 s (Christopher Gary Howarth b 15 May 1975, Dominic David Howarth b 7 July 1982); *Career* ptnr Thomson Morley Jackson & Co (incorporating Neild Hulme & Co) 1981-; FCA 1979, FCCA 1986; *Recreations* golf; *Clubs* Prestwich Golf; *Style*— Andrew Brown, Esq; 9 Royston Close, Greenmount, Bury BL8 4BZ (☎ 0204 88 6312); Brook House, 64/72 Spring Gdns, Manchester M2 2BQ (☎ 061 236 8880, fax 061 236 9921)

BROWN, Hon Angus John Duncan; yst s of Baron Brown, PC, MBE (Life Peer) (d 1985); *b* 13 Jan 1951; *Educ* Bryanston, Newcastle Univ (BA); *m* 1974, Polonca, da of Janez Baloh, of Ljubljana; 2 children (Maya, Alesh); *Career* architect; AADipl; *Style*— The Hon Angus Brown; 39 Clifton Road, London N8 8JA

BROWN, Anthony Cecil; OBE (1984); s of Cecil Philip Brown, of Dartmouth, Devon, and Bronwen Delia Llewella, *née* Lloyd-Griffiths (d 1980); *b* 16 Feb 1928; *Educ* Whitgift, Imperial Coll London (BSc); *m* 1974, Lesley Ann, da of Frederick Collings, of Broxbourne, Herts; 4 s (Simon (twin) b 1965, Matthew b 1968, Patrick b 1978), 2 da (Katherine b 1966, Genevieve b 1971); *Career* chm and md Spirax-Sarco Engineering plc 1971-, dep chm Turriff Corporation plc 1978-83, dir Sale Tilney plc 1982-83, local dir (Bristol) Barclays Bank 1977-; ACGI, FCIBS, CBIM; *Recreations* skiing, sailing, motor racing, reading, travel; *Clubs* St Stephen's, MCC; *Style*— Anthony Brown Esq, OBE; Longwood House, Bishops Cleeve, Glos; Avonmouth, Bigbury-on-Sea, Devon; Spirax-Sarco Engineering plc, Charlton House, 14 Cirencester Rd, Cheltenham, Glos GL53 8ER (☎ (0242) 521361, telex 43123)

BROWN, Anthony Nigel; s of Sydney Brown, of Birmingham, and Gene, *née* Laitner; *b* 12 June 1955; *Educ* Clifton Coll Bristol, Univ of Manchester (LLB); *m* 16 April 1989, Gail Denise, da of Dr Nathaniel Rifkind, of Glasgow; *Career* admitted slr 1980; asst slr Janners 1980-84, voluntary asst Artlaw 1978-81; fndr and md Connaught Brown 1984-; exhibitions: Northern Spirit 1986, work of Oleg Tselkov 1990; organised Artlaw auction Royal Acad 1981 and Dulwich Art '90; memb Soc of London Art Dealers; *Recreations* looking at art, reading, swimming; *Clubs* RAC; *Style*— Anthony Brown, Esq; Connaught Brown, 2 Albemarle St, London W1X 3HF (☎ 071 408 0362, fax 071 495 3137)

BROWN, Prof Arthur Joseph; CBE (1974); s of Joseph Brown (d 1957), of Meliden, Prestatyn, Flintshire, and Adelene, *née* Lyles (d 1960); *b* 8 Aug 1914; *Educ* Bradford GS, Queen's Coll Oxford (BA, MA, DPhil); *m* 28 Dec 1938, Joan Hannah Margaret, da of Rev Canon Bertham Eustace Taylor (d 1961), of Walton Breck, Liverpool; 3 s (John Richard b 1940, d 1959, Henry Joseph b 1942, William Arthur b 1945); *Career* fell All Souls Coll Oxford 1937-46, lectr Hertford Coll Oxford 1937- 40, Foreign Res and Press Serv 1940-43, FO Res Dept 1943-45, Cabinet Office economic section 1945-47, prof of economics Univ of Leeds 1947-79 (emeritus 1979); visiting prof: Columbia Univ NY 1950, Aust Nat Univ Canberra 1963; memb: East Africa Econ and Fiscal Cmmn 1960, Central Africa Office Sec of State's Advsy Gp 1962, Hunt Ctee on Intermediate Areas 1967-69, Univ Grants Ctee 1968-78 (vice chm 1977-78); memb: Thoresby Soc, Leeds Civic Tst, Art Collections Fund; Hon DLitt: Univ of Bradford 1975, Univ of Kent 1979, Univ of Sheffield 1979; Hon LLD Univ of Aberdeen 1978, hon fell Queen's Coll Oxford 1985; FBA 1972, pres Royal Econ Soc 1976-78, memb RSS 1940; *Books* Applied Economics (1948), The Great Inflation 1939-51 (1955), The Framework of Regional Economics in the UK (1972), World Inflation Since 1950 (1985); *Recreations* gardening, walking; *Clubs* Athenaeum; *Style*— Prof Arthur Brown; 24 Moor Dr, Leeds LS6 4BY (☎ 0532 755 799)

BROWN, Arthur Robert (Bob); s of Arthur Brown, of Gawsworth, Macclesfield, Cheshire (d 1973), and Winifred, *née* Poulson (d 1975); *b* 18 July 1945; *Educ* Sandbach GS; *m* 1, Dec 1966 (m dis 1977), Kim, *née* Mahoney; 2 s (Philip b 1964, Michael b 1968), 4 da (Fenella b 1963, Samantha b 1965, Claire b 1967, Justine b 1970); m 2, 22 July 1977, Maureen, da of Percy Valentine Law; *Career* formerly with: Thames TV Ltd, William Cory & Sons Ltd, Int Computers Ltd; gen mangr computer mktg Cable & Wireless plc 1970-76, assoc ptnr Touche Ross & Co 1976-82, mktg dir Software Sciences Ltd 1982- (currently dir i/c Tokyo subsid); *Books* Optimum Packing and Depletion (1971), VAT for the Computer User (1972), Program Debugging (1973); *Recreations* music (the twentieth century symphony); *Style*— Bob Brown, Esq; 103

Ishikawa Homes, Rokubancho 2, Chiyoda-ku, Tokyo 102, Japan (☎ 03 261 1346); Software Sciences Japan, Kowa Bldg No 1, 1-11-41 Akasaka, Minato-ku, Tokyo 107, Japan (☎ 03 583 9601, fax 03 582 1176)

BROWN, Dr Aubrey; MBE (1975); s of Robert Brown (d 1963), of Dunmurry Co Antrim, and Emily, *née* Dillon; *b* 4 Dec 1927; *Educ* Huddersfield Tech Teachers Trg Coll (pres Student Body), Univ of Leeds (Cert Ed), Queen's Univ Belfast (BSc), Univ of Northern Colorado (MA), Columbia Pacific Univ (PhD); *m* 30 June 1962, Catherine, da of Francis McHugh (d 1973), of Blackrock, Co Louth; *Career* Colombo plan advsr on tech educn Pakistan 1963-65, sr inspr of schs (tech and commercial) Swaziland 1971-78, inspr of educn (tech) Transkei SA 1979, educn offr Southern Educn and Library Bd NI 1979-81, conslt on tech educn Univ of Papua New Guinea 1986-88; elected to Who's Who among students in American Univs and Colleges; memb coll of Handicraft 1952, fell Coll of Craft Educn 1966; *Books* A Technical Teachers' Training Manual (1988), The Training of Technical Teachers by Competency-Based Methods in Papua New Guinea; *Recreations* woodworking and history of furniture; *Style*— Dr Aubrey Brown, MBE; Tornabodagh Cottage, Drumaroan Rd, Ballycastle, County Antrim, NI, BT54 6QU (☎ 02657 63 685)

BROWN, Dr (James) Barry Conway; OBE (1978); s of Frederick Clarence Brown, of Stroud, Glos, and Alys Brown, *née* Bleackley; *b* 3 July 1937; *Educ* King's Coll Taunton, Clare Coll Cambridge (MA), Univ of Birmingham (MSc, PhD); *m* 7 Sept 1963, Anne Rosemary, da of Frederick Clough (d 1970); 2 s (Andrew b 1964, Phillip b 1967), 1 da (Clare b 1971); *Career* res offr CEGB 1963-67; sci offr Br Cncl: London 1967-69, Spain 1969-72, France 1972-78; head Sci and Tech Gp Br Cncl London 1978-81, rep (head) Br Cncl and cultural cnsllr Br Embassy Mexico 1981-85, dep controller Higher Educn Div Br Cncl London 1985-89, dir Euro Cmmn Liaison Unit (Higher Educn) Br Cncl Brussels 1989-; memb: Thames Vale Singers, GB USSR Assoc 1960-; *Recreations* singing, reading, foreign travel; *Style*— Dr Barry Brown, OBE; 42 Hazel Rd, Purley-on-Thames, Reading RG8 8BB (☎ 0734 417 581); British Council, 10 Spring Gardens, London SW1A 2BN (☎ 071 930 8466, telex 8952201 BRICON G)

BROWN, Bernard Joseph (Joe); CBE (1981), JP (1970); s of William Goulson Brown (d 1935), and Kate Alice Brown (d 1960); *b* 27 Feb 1916; *Educ* Ealing Co Sch, Southall Tech Coll; *m* 9 Sept 1939, Vera, da of Clarence Douglass (d 1918); 4 s (Peter b 1941, Christopher b 1945, Roger b 1949, Philip b 1955), 1 da (Felicity b 1947); *Career* WWII vol RA 1939 (cmmnd Survey 1941), Staff Capt Combined Ops 1942-46; asst Barry and Vernon Estate Agents London 1933-39, lands offr Air Miny Lands Branch 1946-49, fndr BJ Brown and Ptnrs Chartered Auctioneers and Estate Agents 1949-84; pres Ruislip Round Table 1961-63 (vice chm 1947, chm 1948), chm Ruislip Cons 1955-60 and 1965-70; memb Ruislip Northwood UDC 1949-55, Mayor London Borough of Hillingdon 1969-70 (Alderman 1964-74), vice chm GLC 1970-71 (memb 1967-77), memb Ct of Common Cncl City of London 1972-86, Sheriff City of London 1977-78, chief commoner Corp of London 1981, govr Christs Hospital, pres City Livery Club 1984-85, former pres W Middx and S Bucks Assoc of Surveyors and Estate Agents; Freedom City of Quito Equador 1981, Master Worshipful Co of Fletchers 1986-87 (memb 1970); FAI 1939, FRICS 1970; Order of King Abdul al Aziz (Class 2) 1981; *Recreations* gardening, music; *Clubs* City Livery, United Wards, Royal Soc of St George; *Style*— Joe Brown, Esq, CBE, JP; 1 Lunsford Manor, Ninfield Rd, Bexhill-on-Sea, E Sussex (☎ 0424 892 513)

BROWN, Brian Michael John; s of Arthur John Frederick Brown (d 1978), and Ethel Louise, *née* Redsull (d 1982); *b* 11 Feb 1937; *Educ* Sir Roger Manwoods GS Kent; *m* 1, 22 Feb 1960 (m dis 1989), Maureen Ivy Ticehurt; 2 s (Mark Stephen John b 12 March 1964, Timothy John Michael b 18 Jan 1967), 1 da (Rachel Suzanne b 17 March 1961); m 2, 20 April 1989, Elizabeth Charlotte, da of Maj Thomas John Saywell; *Career* serv Royal Hampshire Regt 1955-57, Intelligence Corps 1957-58; Trustee Savings Bank: London 1959-60, South Eastern 1960-67; TSB Trust Company Ltd: mktg mangr 1967-71, gen mangr 1971-83, dir 1976, md 1983-88, chief exec 1988-; memb: Unit Trust Assoc Exec Ctee 1980-88, Lautro Selling Practices Ctee 1989-; govr Cricklade Coll Andover 1989, FBIM 1976, FCIB 1977; *Recreations* railways, coin and stamp collecting, walking, reading, eating out; *Style*— Brian Brown, Esq; Darvra House, Foxcotte Road, Charlton, Andover, Hampshire SP10 4AR (☎ 0264 359657); TSB Trust Company Limited, Keens House, Andover, Hampshire

BROWN, Adm Sir Brian Thomas; KCB (1989), CBE (1983); s of Walter Thomas Brown (d 1984), and Gladys, *née* Baddeley (d 1989); *b* 31 Aug 1934; *Educ* Peter Symonds' Sch; *m* 1 Aug 1959, Veronica Mary Elizabeth, da of Wing Cdr J D Bird (d 1982); 2 s (Mark b 1960, Matthew b 1962); *Career* joined RN (Dartmouth) 1952, pilot 898 and 848 sqdns 1958-62, dep supply offr HMY Britannia 1966-68, supply offr HMS Tiger 1973-75; secretary to: VCNS 1975-78, First Sea Lord 1979-82; RCDS 1983, Capt HMS Raleigh 1984-86, DGNPS 1986, DGNMT 1987-88; Second Sea Lord and Adm Pres RNC Greenwich 1988; Freeman City of London 1989; Hon DEd 1990; CBIM 1989; *Recreations* cricket, gardening, ornithology; *Clubs* Army and Navy; *Style*— Adm Sir Brian Brown, KCB, CBE; c/o Lloyds Bank, High St, Winchester, Hants

BROWN, Bryan William; s of William James Brown (d 1958), and Beatrice Cutugno (d 1980); *b* 7 Oct 1938; *Educ* Salesian Coll; *m* 12 April 1975, Florie Therese, da of Anthony Stravens, of Seychelles; 3 s (Paul b 1976, Colin b 1977, Ian b 1979), 1 da (Lisa b 1986); *Career* CA; dir Joe Smith (conslts) Ltd; memb MICA Tax Legislation Ctee; *Recreations* gardening, walking, entertaining; *Clubs* Gresham; *Style*— Bryan Brown, Esq; 68 Hill View Court, Woking, Surrey GU22 7QW (☎ 0483 722597)

BROWN, Cedric Harold; s of late William Herbert Brown, and Constance Dorothy, *née* Frances; *b* 7 March 1935; *Educ* Sheffield, Rotherham and Derby Coll of Technol; *m* 1956, Joan Hendry; 1 s, 3 da; *Career* East Midlands Gas Bd: pupil gas distribution engr 1953-58, various engrg posts 1958-75; engr asst Tunbridge Wells Borough Cncl 1959-60, dir engr E Midlands Gas 1975-78; British Gas Corporation: asst dir ops and dir construction 1978-79, dir Morecombe Bay Project 1980-87, regnl chm British Gas West Midlands 1987-88; gp exec memb exploration and prodn British Gas plc 1989-90, memb Bd and md British Gas plc 1989; Freeman City of London, 1989 dir Bow Valley Industries 1988; Freeman City of London, Liveryman Worshipful Co of Engrs 1988; FEng, CEng, FIGasE, FICE; *publications* author of various tech papers to professional bodies; *Recreations* sport, countryside, places of historic interest; *Style*— Cedric Brown, Esq; British Gas plc, Rivermill House, 152 Grosvenor Road, London SW1V 3JL (☎ 071 821 1444, fax 071 821 8522, telex 938529)

BROWN, Lt-Col Sir Charles Frederick Richmond; 4 Bt (UK 1863), TD, DL (N R Yorks 1962); s of late Frederick Richmond Brown, 2 s of 2 Bt; suc unc, Sir Melville Richmond Brown, 3 Bt, 1944; *b* 6 Dec 1902; *Educ* Eton; *m* 1, 1933 (m dis 1948), Audrey, da of late Brig-Gen the Hon Everard Baring, CVO, CBE; 1 s, 2 da; m 2, 1951 (m dis 1968), Hon Gwendolin Carlis Meysey-Thompson, da of 1 Baron Knaresborough; m 3, 1969, Pauline Emily Gwyneth Mansel, da of late Arden Henry William Llewelyn Morgan, and wid of Edward John Westgarth Hildyard, FSA, FRES, of Middleton Hall, Pickering, Yorks; *Heir* s, George Francis Richmond Brown; *Career* Capt (ret) Welsh Gds, and Lt-Col cmdg 7 Bn Green Howards (TA); *Style*— Lt-Col Sir Charles Richmond Brown, Bt, TD, DL; Middleton Hall, Pickering

BROWN, Prof Charles Malcolm; s of Capt Charles Brown (d 1978), of Durham, and Beatrice Lily, *née* Haddrick (d 1988); *b* 21 Sept 1941; *Educ* Houghton-Le-Spring GS, Univ of Birmingham (BSc, PhD, DSc); *m* 16 July 1966, Diane Mary, da of Joseph Bryant (d 1962), of Birmingham; 3 da (Sara b 1969, Ann b 1971, Liz b 1976); *Career* lectr Univ of Newcastle upon Tyne 1966-73, sr lectr Univ of Dundee 1973-79; dir S Marine Biological Assoc 1975-81, Bioscot Ltd 1982-86, Fermentech Ltd 1983-85; prof Heriot Watt Univ 1979- (head of Dept of Biological Sciences 1988-); dir ICBD; FIBiol 1979, FRSA 1980, FRSE 1982; *Books* Sediment Microbiology (jtly, 1981), Introduction to Biotechnology (jtly, 1987); *Recreations* music, walking, gardening; *Style*— Prof Charles Brown, FRSE; 19 Burnside Park, Balerno, Edinburgh EH14 7LY (☎ 031 449 7125); The International Centre for Brewing and Distilling, Heriot-Watt University, Riccarton, Edinburgh EH14 4AS (☎ 031 451 3181, fax 031 451 3009)

BROWN, Rev Christopher; s of Reginald Frank Greenwood Brown (d 1970), and Margaret Eleanor, *née* Simmons (d 1988); *b* 21 June 1938; *Educ* Hertford GS, Kings Coll London (AKC), St Boniface Coll Warminster, Green Coll Oxford; *m* 28 Sept 1968, Helen Margaret, da of George Arthur Woolsey, of Winchester; 3 s (Ian b 1974, Timothy b 1976, Joseph b 1984), 1 da (Lucy b 1973); *Career* ordained: deacon 1963, priest 1964; asst curate Diocese of Southwark 1963-67, probation offr Nottingham 1968-72, sr probation offr W Midlands 1972-74, asst dir Social Servs Dept Solihull 1974-76, asst chief probation offr Hereford and Worcester 1976-79; chief probation offr: Oxfordshire 1979-86, Essex 1986-89; dir NSPCC 1989-; memb Parole Bd England and Wales 1984-87, chm Social Issues Ctee Assoc of Chief Offrs of Probation 1985-88; memb: Br Assoc of Social Workers 1973, Cwlth Soc 1989; *Recreations* walking, conversation, gardening; *Clubs* Commonwealth Trust; *Style*— The Rev Christopher Brown; NSPCC, 67 Saffron Hill, London EC1N 8RS (☎ 071 242 1626)

BROWN, Christopher David; s of Edward Kenneth Brown and Iris, *née* Hoddell; *b* 8 July 1944; *Educ* Plymouth Coll, Fitzwilliam Coll Cambridge (MA); *m* 1972, Caroline, da of Dr Arthur Dunkerley (d 1980); 2 da (Katharine b 1979, Jennifer b 1981); *Career* head of Eng Radley Coll 1975-84, headmaster Norwich Sch 1984-; *Style*— Christopher Brown, Esq; 70 The Close, Norwich

BROWN, Claude Read; s of Gilbert Brown (d 1971), and Sarah Hanson, *née* Read (d 1988); *b* 12 Nov 1939; *Educ* Carlisle GS, Yeovil Sch, Univ of Manchester (BA); *m* Juliette Olivia; 1 da (Olivia Frances b 1975); *Career* chartered accountant; Charles Comins & Co 1962-66; Pannell Kerr Forster: nat chm 1984-90, Euro Region chm 1987-, sr ptnr London 1988-, vice chm Int Assoc 1990-; Freeman City of London, Liveryman Worshipful Co of Carmen 1988; FCA 1964; *Recreations* water-skiing, golf, theatre and music, the country; *Style*— Claude Brown, Esq; Pannell Kerr Forster, New Garden House, 78 Hatton Garden, London EC1N 8JA (☎ 071 831 7393, fax 071 405 6736)

BROWN, Colin Bertram; s of Prof Leslie Julius Brown (d 1981), of SA, and Adolfinna Anna, *née* Rose (d 1985); *b* 24 May 1942; *Educ* King David HS SA, Guy's Univ of London (BSc, MB BS, MRCS, LRCP); *m* 22 Sept 1975, Jacquelynne Anne, *née* Baldwin; 2 s (Nicholas Daniel b 1966, Jason Peter b 1971), 2 da (Kate Victoria b 1978, Hannah Camilla Lester b 1982); *Career* res fell Harvard Med Sch Boston USA 1974-75, sr registrar Guy's 1973-78, conslt renal physician Royal Hallamshire Hosp Sheffield 1979-; chm Pub Cmmn of Peritoneal Dialysis; memb: Ctee on Renal Diseases RCP, Section on Renal Disease MRC, Int Soc of Nephrology, Euro Dialysis and Transplant Assoc, Int Soc of Peritoneal Dialysis, Exec Ctee Renal Assoc of GB; FRCP 1985; *Books* Manual of Renal Disease (1984); contrib incl: Guy's Hospital Reports (1965), Lancet (1970), British Journal of Urology (1972), American Journal of Physiology (1977), Cornell Seminars in Nephrology (1978), Journal of Infection (1983), British Medical Journal (1984), Transplantation (1986), Bone (1981), Clinica Chimica Acta (1988), Nephron (1989), Nephrology (1990); *Recreations* sailing, tennis, golf; *Clubs* Royal Yachting Assoc; *Style*— Colin Brown, Esq; Sheffield Kidney Institute, Regional Renal Unit, Northern General Hospital, University of Sheffield Medical School, Herries Rd, Sheffield, S Yorks S5 7AU (☎ 0742 434343, fax 0742 720260)

BROWN, Colin Ian; s of Sidney Brown (d 1986), and Marion Esther, *née* Surrey; *b* 3 Dec 1933; *Educ* Raynes Park Co GS; *m* 15 May 1965, Lorna Louise, da of Albert Jarrett (d 1975); 3 da (Philippa b 8 April 1967, Rachel b 14 Dec 1968, Hilary b 17 June 1970); *Career* Nat Serv RAPC 1956-58; CA; trg James Worley and Sons 1951-56, fin dir and ptnr Price Waterhouse 1987- (joined 1958, nat recruitment ptnr 1966-72, ptnr i/c Audit Tax Gp and memb UK Policy Ctee 1972-79, seconded to PW World Firm 1979-87); chm: IASC Steering Gp, IFAC Jt Sub Ctee; ICA (chm Audit Registration Ctee); *Books* The Institute Guide on Accounting and Auditing for Banks (jtly); *Recreations* golf, sailing, skiing and photography; *Clubs* Royal Lymington Yacht, North Downs Golf; *Style*— Colin Brown, Esq; Gabilan House, Park View Road, Woldingham, Surrey CR3 7DN (☎ 088 365 2005); Price Waterhouse, Southwark Towers, 32 London Bridge Street, London SE1 9SY (☎ 071 939 3000, fax 071 3780647, telex 884657/8)

BROWN, (William) Colin; JP; s of James Chalmers Brown, MC, and Annie Oman, *née* Shaw; *b* 20 Feb 1923; *Educ* Imperial Serv Coll (now Haileybury); *m* 25 July 1952, Mary Elizabeth, da of Sir Charles G Connell, WS, of Edinburgh; 3 s (Peter b 24 Oct 1953, Timothy b 14 Dec 1955, Roy b 26 April 1961); *Career* Capt Parachute Regt 1943-52; dir Dunfermline Bldg Soc 1964, md Furnishing Co 1968-88, dir Ski Sch 1970; chm: investmt co 1979, property co 1982, dir Cairngorm Chairlift Tst 1982, Br Ski Fedn 1980-84; former ctee memb Fedn Internationale de Ski; memb: Co Merchants Edinburgh, Magistrates Ctee and Ct; former FNAEA; Croix de Guerre (Silver); *Recreations* skiing, fishing; *Clubs* New (Edinburgh); *Style*— Colin Brown, Esq, JP; 4 Blackbarony Rd, Edinburgh (☎ 031 667 1894); Bruach, Carrbridge, Inverness-shire

BROWN, Hon Mrs; Hon Cordelia; *née* Fraser; er da of late 2 Baron Strathalmond, CMG, OBE, TD; *b* 12 Dec 1949; *m* 1981, (m dis 1986), Ralph Lyman Brown, s of Ralph Lyman Brown (d 1978); *Style*— The Hon Mrs Brown; 47 Aynhoe Road, London W14 0QA. (☎ 071) 603 3551)

BROWN, Craig Edward Moncrieff; s of Edward Peter Moncrieff Brown, of Duncton, W Sussex, and Jennifer Mary, *née* Bethell; *b* 23 May 1957; *Educ* Eton, Univ of Bristol; *m* Frances, da of Colin Welch; 1 s (Silas b 1990), 1 da (Tallulah b 1988); *Career* freelance journalist and columnist; articles for numerous newspapers and magazines incl: New Statesman, The Observer, TLS, Mail on Sunday, New York, Stern, Corriere della Sevre; Parly sketch writer The Times 1987-88, columnist The Times 1988-, restaurant critic Sunday Times 1988-; columnist (as Wallace Arnold): The Spectator 1987, Private Eye 1989-; *Books* The Marsh Marlowe Letters (1983), A Year Inside (1988), The Agreeable World of Wallace Arnold (1990); *Recreations* flower arrangement, needlework, tidying, deportment, mecrame; *Clubs* The Academy; *Style*— Craig Brown, Esq

BROWN, Sir Cyril Maxwell Palmer (Max); KCB (1969, CB 1965), CMG (1957); s of Cyril Palmer Brown, of Wanganui, NZ; *b* 30 June 1914; *Educ* Wanganui Collegiate Sch, Victoria Univ NZ, Clare Coll Cambridge; *m* 1940, Margaret May, da of late W Edward Gillhespy, of Hathersage, Derbyshire; 3 s, 1 da; *Career* second perm sec BOT 1968-70, DTI 1970-74; dir: ERA Technol Ltd 1974-86, John Brown & Co 1975-82, Ransome Hoffman Pollard (later RHP Gp) 1975-88; dep chm MMC 1976-81; *Style*— Sir Max Brown, KCB, CMG; 20 Cottenham Park Rd, London SW20 (☎ 081

946 7237)

BROWN, Sir David; s of Francis (Frank) Edwin Brown (d 1941), of Huddersfield, and Caroline Brown; *b* 10 May 1904; *Educ* Rossall, Huddersfield Tech Coll; *m* 1, 1926 (m dis 1955), Daisie Muriel Firth; 1 s, 1 da; m 2, 1955 (m dis 1980), Marjorie, da of Frederick Herbert Deans, of Leeds; m 3, 1980, Paula Elizabeth, da of John Benjamin Stone (d 1974); *Career* chm David Brown Holdings and Vosper Ltd until 1978; chm: David Brown International Ltd, David Brown Gear Industries Ltd Aust, David Brown Gear Industries (PTY) Ltd SA; dir T-craft Ltd SA; Grand Cdr of Royal Crown of Johor; made 'Chief Flying Sun' of the Iroquois Tribe, Mohawk Nation 1959; FIMechE; kt 1968; *Recreations* tennis, yachting (My Flying Sun); *Clubs* Monte Carlo Country, Yacht Club de Monaco, Club International des Anciens Pilotes de Grand Prix, Automobile Club de Monaco; *Style—* Sir David Brown; L'Estoril, 31 Avenue Princesse Grace, Monte Carlo, MC98000 Monaco

BROWN, Prof David Clifford; s of Bertram Critchley Brown (d 1973), and Constance Mabel, *née* Nicholls, of Gravesend, Kent; *b* 8 July 1929; *Educ* Gravesend GS, Univ of Sheffield (BA, BMus, MA), Univ of Southampton (PhD); *m* 24 Dec 1953, Elizabeth, da of William Henry Valentine (d 1948); 2 da (Gabrielle b 1955, Hilary b 1957); *Career* Nat Serv, RAF 1952-54; schoolmaster 1954-59, music librarian Univ of London 1959-62; Univ of Southampton: lectr 1962-70, sr lectr 1970-75, reader 1975-83, prof of musicology 1983-89, now ret; freelance writer and broadcaster on music; memb Editorial Ctee Musica Britannica; memb: RMA 1959, RSA 1987; *Books* Thomas Weelkes (1969), Mikhail Glinka (1973), John Wilbye (1974), Tchaikovsky: 4 vols (vol 1 1978, vol 2 1982, vol 3 1986); *Recreations* Walking; *Style—* Prof David Brown; Braishfield Lodge West, Braishfield, Romsey, Hants SO51 0PS (☎ 0794 68163)

BROWN, David John Bowes; CBE (1982); s of Matthew Brown (d 1973), and Adelaide Helene, *née* Bowes (d 1990); *b* 2 Aug 1925; *Educ* King James Sch Knaresborough, Leeds Coll of Technol; *m* 1, 1954 (m dis 1982) Patricia; 2 s (David Patrick b 27 March 1955, John Bowes b 9 June 1958), 2 da (Angela (now Mrs Hall) b 31 July 1956, Janet (now Mrs Tough) b 9 April 1962); m 2, 24 Jan 1986, Eve Rose Watkinson; *Career* logging contractor UK and West Africa 1946-60, design draftsman Hunslet Engine Co 1960-62, chief designer Chaseside 1962-65, md Muir Hill Ltd 1965-73, started DJB Engineering Ltd 1973, sold DJB Engineering Ltd product rights and formed Artix Ltd 1985, purchased Bedford trucks and formed AWD Ltd 1987, purchased Luton Design Centre and formed Automotive Development Centre Ltd; memb: CBI, Prince's Youth Business Trust; *Recreations* rally driving, shooting, horse riding; *Clubs* Mossimann's; *Style—* David J B Brown, Esq, CBE; Artix Ltd, Peterlee, Co Durham SR8 2HX (☎ 091 586 333, fax 091 586 1208); AWD Ltd, Boscombe Rd, Dunstable, Bedfordshire LUS 4SE (☎ 0582 472244, fax 0582 604920)

BROWN, Vice Adm Sir David Worthington; KCB (1984); s of Capt John Ronald Stewart Brown, RN (d 1989), of Cheltenham, and Mrs D M E Brown (d 1988); *b* 28 Nov 1927; *Educ* HMS Conway; *m* 1958, Etienne Hester, da of Col Dick Boileau, DSO (d 1978), of Bradford on Avon; 3 da; *Career* joined RN 1945; cmd HM Ships: MGB 5036, MTB 5020, Dalswinton, Chailey, Cavendish, Falmouth, Hermione, Bristol; dir Naval Ops and Trade 1971-72, dir of Offr Appts (Exec) 1976-78, ACDS (Ops) 1980-82, Vice Adm 1982, Flag Offr Plymouth, Port Admiral Devonport, Cdr Plymouth Sub Area Channel 1982-85; devpt conslt Mayne Nickless (UK) Ltd, Hogg Group; Fell Inst of Personnel Mgmnt 1985; *Clubs* Army & Navy; *Style—* Vice Adm Sir David Brown, KCB; c/o Barclays Bank, 69 West St, Fareham, Hants PO16 0AW

BROWN, Maj Denis Frederick Spence; MC (1945), TD (1950); s of Frederick William Brown (d 1965), of Woodhall Spa, Lincs, and Violet Spence Brown, *née* Hubbard (d 1976); *b* 24 Feb 1917; *Educ* Trent Coll; *m* 13 Jan 1945, Margaret, da of Frederick Harry Shutler (d 1973), of London; 2 s (Nigel Denis Spence b 1946, Peter Frederick Spence b 1951), 1 da (Rosemary Spence b 1949); *Career* cmmnd TA 1939, served RA, field and anti-tank, France, ME, Western Desert, Sicily, Italy, Maj 1944 (despatches 1945); with family firm (now Brown Butlin Group) 1933-: dir and chm 1965, resigned as chm 1987 and appointed pres; FInstD; *Recreations* travel, gardening, reading; *Style—* Maj Denis Brown, MC, TD; The Close, Dorrington, Lincoln LN4 3PX (☎ 0526 832 282); Brown Butlin Group, Brook House, Ruskington, Sleaford, Lincs (☎ 0526 834200)

BROWN, Denise Jeanne Marie Lebreton (Mrs F Waters); da of Lt Frederick Peter Brown (d of wounds 1918), and Jeanne Marie Louise Lebreton (d 1974); *b* 8 Jan 1911; *Educ* Lyzeum Nonnenwerth im Rhein, RCA (ARCA); *m* 1938, Frank William Eric Waters (d 1986), s of Frank Waters (d 1922); 1 s (Peter); *Career* Br Inst scholarship in engraving 1932, Rome scholarship in engraving 1936, RCA travelling scholarship 1936; has exhibited regularly: Royal Acad 1934-, Royal Soc of Painter-Etchers & Engravers 1941-, Royal West of England Acad 1979-; has also exhibited in Canada, USA and S Africa; works represented: Br Museum, V&A, Ashmolean Museum, Sheffield Art Gallery, perm collection RWA; RE 1959 (ARE 1941), ARWA 1980 (elected cncl memb 1984), RWA 1986; *Books illustrated* many in the Famous Childhoods series, several gardening books; also illustrations for Farmers Weekly and designs for book jackets; *Recreations* music, gardening; *Clubs* RAF; *Style—* Miss Denise L Brown; 7 Priory Lodge, Nightingale Place, Rickmansworth, Herts WD3 2DG (☎ 0923 773515)

BROWN, Sir Douglas Denison; s of Robert Brown (d 1968), and Alice Mary Brown; *b* 8 July 1917; *Educ* Bablake Sch Coventry; *m* 1941, Marion Cruickshanks, da of James Emmerson (d 1935); 1 s, 1 da; *Career* served WWII RA: ME, N Africa, Italy, ret Maj; chm James Corson Co (ret 1988); chm: NW Leeds Cons Assoc 1961-74, Leeds and Northern Clothing Assoc 1975-77, Yorkshire Area Cons Assoc 1978-83 (treas 1971-78), Jacob Kramer Coll of Further Educn 1978-; vice chm PCC St Edmund's Church Roundhay 1980-, memb: Wool Textiles and Clothing Action Ctee Wooltac 1982, Bd Yorkshire Water Authy 1983-1986; pres Water ALD Yorks 1988, vice pres Leeds Allotment and Gardens Assoc 1989; hon memb Br Clothing Industs Assoc 1990 (memb Exec Bd until 1989); kt 1983; *Recreations* gardening, golf, rugby, cricket; *Style—* Sir Douglas Brown; Bankfield, 6 North Park Rd, Roundhay, Leeds LS8 1JD (☎ 0532 66 2151)

BROWN, Sir Edward Joseph; MBE (1958), JP; s of Edward Brown (d 1932), of Camberwell; *b* 15 April 1913; *Educ* Morley Coll; *m* 1940, Rosa, da of Samuel Feldman, of Stepney; 1 s, 1 da; *Career* co dir; chm Nat Union of Cons and Unionist Assocs 1959 and 1960, chm Cons Pty Conf 1960, MP (C) for Bath 1964-79 (contested Stalybridge and Hyde 1959); kt 1961; *Style—* Sir Edward Brown, MBE, JP; 71 Holly Walk, Enfield, Middx (☎ 081 363 3450)

BROWN, Hon Mrs (Emily Rose); da of Baron Eden of Winton (Life Peer); *b* 26 Feb 1959; *m* 30 June 1984, Ronald Etienne Brown, s of James Brown; 1 s (Nicholas James b 1986), 1 da (Charlotte Lucy b 1985); *Style—* Hon Mrs Brown; Combebelle le Haut, Villespassons, St Chinian 34360, Herault, France

BROWN, Prof Eric Herbert; s of Samuel Brown (d 1970), and Ada, *née* Hewes (d 1966); *b* 8 Dec 1922; *Educ* King Edward VII GS Melton Mowbray, Kings Coll London (BSc), UCW Aberstwyth (MSc), Univ of London (PhD); *m* 30 Oct 1945, Eileen (d 1984), da of Phillip ap John Reynolds (d 1946); 2 da (Jane, Megan); *Career* pilot Coastal Cmd 517 Sqdn RAF 1940-45; lectr in geography Univ Coll of Wales Aberystwyth 1947-50; UCL 1950-91: lectr, reader, prof of geography, Alumni dir; chm Governing Body Longdean Sch Hemel Hempstead, church warden St Peter's Berkhamsted; FRGS 1947, hon fell Geographic Soc Argentina 1968, hon fell RGS 1989 (hon vice pres 1989); *Books* Relief and Drainage of Wales (1961); *Recreations* travel, rugby, wine; *Clubs* Athenaeum, Geographical; *Style—* Prof Eric Brown; Monterey, Castle Hill, Berkhamsted, Herts HP4 1HE (☎ 0442 864 077); Department of Geography, University College, 26 Bedford Way, London WC1H 0AP (☎ 071 380 7050, fax 071 380 7565)

BROWN, Capt Eric Melrose; CBE (1970, OBE 1945, MBE 1944), DSC (1942), AFC (1947); s of Robert John Brown (d 1947), of Edinburgh, and Euphemia Dorothy, *née* Melrose (d 1933); *b* 21 Jan 1919; *Educ* Royal HS Edinburgh, Univ of Edinburgh (MA 1947); *m* 17 Jan 1942, Evelyn Jean Margaret, da of Robert Macrory (d 1946), of Belfast; 1 s (Glenn b 1 March 1948); *Career* Capt RN; serv WWII, Fleet Air Arm Fighter Pilot 1939-42, Naval Test Pilot 1942-44, Chief Naval Test Pilot 1944-49, resident Br Naval Test Pilot in USA 1951-52, CO No 804 (F) Sqdn 1953-54, Cdr (Air) RN Air Station Brawdy 1954-56, Head Br Naval Air Mission to Germany 1958-60, dep dir Gunnery Div Admiralty 1961, Naval Air Warfare Admiralty 1962-64, Naval Attaché Bonn 1965-67, CO RN Air Station Lossiemouth 1967-70; ADC to HM The Queen 1969-70; chief exec: Br Helicopter Advsy Bd 1970-87 (vice pres 1988-), European Helicopter Assoc 1980-; pres: Royal Aeronautical Soc 1982-83, Royal Naval Assoc (E Grinstead Branch); chm Exec Ctee Br Aviation Bicentenary 1983-84, hon fell Soc of Experimental Test Pilots 1984; Freeman City of London 1975, Liveryman Guild of Air Pilots and Air Navigators 1978; Hon FEng Inst of Engrs Pakistan, FRAeS 1964; *Books* Wings on My Sleeve (1961, 2 edn 1978, paperback 1984), Aircraft Carriers (jtly, 1969), Wings of the Luftwaffe (1977, 2 edn 1979, 3 edn 1987), Wings of the Navy (1980, 2 edn 1987), The Helicopter in Civil Operations (1981), Wings of the Weird and Wonderful Vol I (1982), Vol II (1985), Duels in the Sky (1989); *Recreations* golf, skiing, bridge; *Clubs* Naval and Military, Explorers' (New York), City Livery; *Style—* Capt Eric Brown, CBE, DSC, AFC, RN; Carousel, New Domewood, nr Copthorne, Sussex RH10 3HF (☎ 0342 712 610)

BROWN, Prof Ewan; s of John Moir Brown (d 1971), of Perth, and Isobel, *née* Crerar; *b* 23 March 1942; *Educ* Perth Acad, Univ of St Andrews (MA, LLB); *m* 1966, Christine Robertson, da of Hugh Douglas Robertson Lindsay; 1 s (Philip b 1968), 1 da (Kirsty b 1971); *Career* CA and merchant banker; exec dir Noble Grossart Ltd 1970; princ dir: Scottish Business Sch 1972-80 (memb Exec Ctee 1974-80), Church of Scotland Tst 1981-87; dir: Pict Petroleum plc 1974-, Scottish Development Finance 1982-, John Wood Gp plc 1982-, Aberdeen Trust plc 1982-85, Scottish Transport Group 1983-87, Stagecoach Hldgs Ltd 1988-; govr Edinburgh Coll of Art 1986-88, asst Merchant Co of Edinburgh 1988-, session clerk Mayfield Church 1983-88, memb Cncl Inst of CA's of Scotland 1989-; Hon Prof Heriot Watt Univ 1989-; *Recreations* skiing, golf, music, mah jongg, family; *Clubs* Royal and Ancient (St Andrews) New (Edinburgh); *Style—* Prof Ewan Brown; 48 Queen St, Edinburgh EH2 3NR (☎ 031 226 7011, fax 031 226 6032)

BROWN, Prof Fred; s of Fred Brown (d 1982), of Burnley, Lancs, and Jane Ellen, *née* Fielding (d 1975); *b* 31 Jan 1925; *Educ* Burnley GS, Univ of Manchester (BSc, MSc, PhD); *m* 1 May 1948, Audrey Alice, da of Ernest Doherty (d 1954); 2 s (Roger b 21 Nov 1949, David b 17 Oct 1953); *Career* asst lectr in chemistry Univ of Manchester 1946-48, lectr Univ of Bristol 1948-50, sr sci offr Hannah Dairy Res Inst 1950-53, sr sci offr Christie Hosp Manchester 1953-55; Animal Virus Res Inst Pirbright: sr sci offr 1955-58, princ scientific offr 1958-64, sr princ scientific offr 1964-71, dep chief scientific offr 1971-83, dep dir 1980-83; head of Virology Dept Wellcome Biotechnology 1983-90, adjunct prof Dept of Epidemiology and Pub Health Yale; memb Soc for Gen Microbiology, vice pres Inst of Biology 1988-90; FRS 1981; *Recreations* fell walking, watching cricket and association football; *Style—* Prof Fred Brown, FRS; Syndal, Glaziers Lane, Normandy, Guildford, Surrey GU3 2DF (☎ 0483 811107)

BROWN, Prof Geoffrey; s of William Henry Brown (d 1981), of Kingston upon Hull, and Dorothy, *née* Shaw; *b* 26 June 1935; *Educ* Kingston HS, Univ of Leicester (MEd), Univ of Lancaster (PhD); *m* Christine Ann, da of William Bath (d 1982), of Stoke-on-Trent; 2 da (Helen b 21 May 1963, Clare 28 Dec 1965); *Career* Nat Serv RAF 1953-55; lectr educnl psychology Anstey Coll of Physical Educn 1966-70, sr lectr educnl psychology Univ of Lancaster 1970-81, prof educn UEA 1981- (dean educn 1986-); chm Bd Studies Br Dyslexia Assoc; FBPsS; *Books* Experiments in the Social Sciences (1975), Child Development (1977), Piaget's Theory: A Psychological Critique (1981); *Recreations* walking, music, woodturning; *Clubs* Liberal; *Style—* Prof Geoffrey Brown; School of Education, University of East Anglia, Norwich, NR4 7TJ, (☎ 0603 56161, fax 0603 58553)

BROWN, Rev Canon Geoffrey Harold; s of Harry Charles Brown, MBE (d 1972), and Ada Ethel, *née* Holliday; *b* 1 April 1930; *Educ* Monmouth, Trinity Hall Cambridge (MA); *m* 24 Aug 1963, (Elizabeth) Jane, da of Jack Watson Williams (d 1981), of Dudley, Worcs; 2 da (Frances b 14 May 1964, Alison (twin)); *Career* RA 1949-51; asst curate: St Andrew's Plaistow London 1956-60, St Peter's Spring Hill Birmingham 1960-63; rector: St George's Birmingham 1963-73, Grimsby 1973-85; vicar St Martin in the Fields 1985-; chm Humberside Cncl on Alcoholism 1977-87, vice chm Humberside Local Radio Cncl 1983, exec memb Nat Cncl on Alcoholism 1980-83; *Recreations* theatre, photography, the countryside; *Style—* The Rev Canon Geoffrey Brown; St Martin in the Fields, Trafalgar Square, London WC2N 4JJ (☎ 071 930 1862)

BROWN, George Francis Richmond; s and h of Sir Charles Brown, 4 Bt; *b* 3 Feb 1938; *Career* Lt Welsh Guards, extra equerry to HRH Duke of Edinburgh 1961-3, ADC to Gov of Queensland 1963-5; *Style—* George Brown Esq

BROWN, Maj George Gordon; s of Capt Arthur Frederick Brown (d 1963), and Evelyn Maude, *née* Lee (d 1974); *b* 17 Feb 1925; *Educ* Eastbourne Coll, Queen's Coll Oxford; *m* 16 Aug 1968, Wendy Margaret, da of Capt Thomas George Clark (d 1986) (see Peerage and Baronetage, Clark, Bt, cr 1886, colls), of 16 Melville Cres, Edinburgh; 1 s (Richard b 9 March 1973), 1 da (Melanie b 5 Oct 1969); *Career* 2 Lt 27 Lancers 1945, 1 RGH Austria 1945-46, ADC to Gen McCreery Germany 1946-68, 12 Royal Lancers Germany and Malaya 1948-60, 9/12 Royal Lancers Aden and Trucial Oman 1960-65, Staff Coll 1958, Maj 1964, ret 1965; called to the Bar Inner Temple 1966, divorce and family law practice in London and Western Circuit 1966-, dep judge 1978-85; chm res reports: Case for Family Courts (CPC, 1978), The Future of Marriage (CPC, 1981), Reconcilliation and Conciliation in Divorce (Order of Christian Unity, 1982); chm Family Courts Ctee Soc of Cons Lawyers; memb Exec Ctee: Cons Family Campaign, Nat Campaign for Family; Freeman City of London 1946, Master Worshipful Co of Tylers and Bricklayers 1973; memb Family Law Bar Assoc; *Books* Getting a Divorce (1971), The New Divorce Laws (1971), Brown on Divorce (1974, 2 edn 1986), Brown on Separation (1981), Finding Fault in Divorce (1989); *Recreations* golf, skiing, cricket; *Clubs* Cavalry and Guards, Hampshire; *Style—* Major George Brown; 2 Kings Benchwalk, Temple, London EC4Y 7DE (☎ 071 353 1746, fax 071 583 2051)

BROWN, George Mackay; OBE (1974); s of John Brown (d 1940), of Stromness, Orkney, and Mary Jane, *née* Mackay (d 1967); *b* 17 Oct 1921; *Educ* Stromness Acad, Newbattle Abbey Coll, Univ of Edinburgh (MA); *Career* poet and writer; Hon MA

Open Univ 1973, Hon LLD Univ of Dundee 1974, Hon DLitt Univ of Glasgow 1985; *Books* Fiction: A Time To Keep (1969), Greenvoe (1972), Magnus (1973), Hawkfall (1974), The Two Fiddlers (1975), Andrina (1983), The Golden Bird (1987), The Masked Fisherman (1989); plays: A Spell for Green Corn (1970), Three Plays (1984); poetry: Fisherman With Ploughs (1971), Selected Poems (1976), Christmas Poems (1984), The Wreck of the Archangel (1989); *Recreations* watching TV, reading; *Style—* George Mackay Brown, Esq, OBE; 3 Mayburn Court, Stromness, Orkney KW16 3DH

BROWN, Prof Gillian; da of Geoffrey Rencher Read (d 1969), and Elsie Olive Read; *b* 23 Jan 1937; *Educ* Perse Sch for Girls Cambridge, Girton Coll Cambridge (exhibition, BA, MA), Univ of Edinburgh (PhD); *m* 21 Aug 1959, Prof (Edward) Keith Brown, s of Rev Reginald John Brown (d 1978); 3 da (Jane Caroline (Mrs Whitgift) b 1960, Katherine Victoria (Mrs Ruttle) b 1961, Sarah Harriett (Mrs Fleming) b 1962); *Career* lectr Univ Coll of Cape Coast Ghana 1962-64, reader Dept of Linguistics Univ of Edinburgh 1981-83 (lectr 1965-81), prof of Applied Linguistics Univ of Essex 1983-88; Univ of Cambridge: prof of English as an int language 1988-, dir Res Centre for English and Applied Linguistics 1988-, fell Clare Coll 1988-; memb: Ctee for Linguistics in Educn 1985-88, Kingman Ctee of Inquiry Into the Teaching of English Language 1987-88, ESRC Council 1987-90, Br Cncl English Teaching Advsy Ctee 1987-, Univ Grants Ctee 1987-89, Univ Funding Cncl 1989-, Cncl of the Philological Soc; chm ESRC Res Grants Bd 1987-90; Doctorate hc Univ of Lyon 1987; *Books* Phonological Rules and Dialect Variation (1972), Listening to Spoken English (1977), Discourse Analysis (with G Yule, 1983), Teaching the Spoken Language (with G Yule, 1983); *Style—* Prof Gillian Brown

BROWN, Prof Godfrey Norman; s of Percy Charles Brown (d 1957), of Croydon, Surrey, and Margaret Elizabeth, *née* Weller (d 1954); *b* 13 July 1926; *Educ* Whitgift Sch, Merton Coll Oxford (MA, DPhil); *m* 11 Jan 1960, Dr Freda Bowyer, da of Thomas Willis Bowyer (d 1976), of Huddersfield; 3 s (Denton Charles b 1961, Nigel Willis b 1963, Martin Giles b 1965); *Career* RAC Lt Intelligence Corps 1944-48; social affairs offr UN HQ NY 1953-54, sr history master Barking Abbey Sch Essex 1954-57, lectr in educn Univ Coll of Ghana 1958-61, visiting prof Univ Coll of Rhodesia and Nyasaland 1963, prof Univ of Ibadan Nigeria 1963-67 (sr lectr 1961), dir Inst of Educn Univ of Keele 1967-80, emeritus prof; dir Betley Court Gallery 1980-, ed West African Journal of Education 1962-66; memb Exec Ctee and Bd of Dirs World Cncl for Curriculum and Instruction 1974-77, chm Assoc for Recurrent Educn 1976-77; vice pres: Cncl for Educn in World Citizenship, Community Cncl of Staffs; Newcastle under Lyme Civic award for Conservation 1990; *Books* An Active History of Ghana (2 vols, 1961 and 1964), Africa in the 19th and 20th Centuries (ed with J C Anene, 1966), Living History (1967), Towards a Learning Community (ed, 1971), Conflict and Harmony in Education in Tropical Africa (ed with M Hiskett, 1975), Apartheid, A Teacher's Guide (1981), Betley Through the Centuries (1985), This Old House - A Domestic Biography (1987); *Recreations* family life, art history, conservation; *Style—* Prof Godfrey Brown; Betley Court Gallery, Betley, nr Crewe, Cheshire CW3 9BH (☎ 0270 820652)

BROWN, (James) Gordon; MP (Lab) Dunfermline East 1983-; s of Rev Dr John Brown, and J Elizabeth Brown; *b* 20 Feb 1951; *Educ* Kirkcaldy HS, Edinburgh Univ (PhD); *Career* journalist Scottish TV, chm Scottish Lab Pty (memb Exec Ctee 1977-); memb Shadow Cabinet 1987-, shadow chief sec to the Treasy 1987-, oppn spokesman regnl affrs 1985-87; rector Univ of Edinburgh 1972-85; *Books* Maxton (1986); *Recreations* golf, tennis, reading; *Style—* Gordon Brown, Esq, MP; House of Commons, London SW1

BROWN, Gordon Lamont; s of John Bell Brown, of 23 Academy St, Troon, Ayrshire, and Mary, *née* McFadyen; *b* 1 Nov 1947; *Educ* Marr Coll Troon; *m* Linda Jean, da of William McKenzie Hastings, of 49 Dundonald Rd, Troon, Ayrshire; 1 s (Rory b 27 Nov 1978), 1 da (Mardi b 7 Aug 1975); *Career* rugby footballer; British Linen Bank 1964-70, Leicester Building Society 1970-76, Bristol & West Building Society 1976-; 30 int caps for Scotland; 3 Br Lions tours: New Zealand 1971 and 1977, SA 1974; holder of world record number of tries by a forward on tour (8 in SA sr vice chm Stars Orgn for Spastics (Scotland), memb Fin Ctee Nat Playing Fields Assoc (Scotland); *Books* Broon from Troon (1983), Rugby is a Funny Game (contrib, 1987); *Recreations* after dinner speaker, golf, real tennis; *Clubs* Wig & Pen, Royal Troon Golf, Old Prestwick Golf, Sun Court Tennis Troon; *Style—* Gordon Brown, Esq; 65 Bentinck Drive, Troon, Ayrshire, Scotland (☎ 0292 314070); Bristol & West Building Society, 78 Union St, Glasgow, Scotland (☎ 041 226 3173)

BROWN, Hon Mrs (Gweneth Mary); da of 1 and last Baron Williams (d 1966); *b* 22 June 1927; *m* 1, 1947 (m dis 1958), Hugh Sharp Eadie, s of David Anderson Eadie, of Markinch; 1 s, 1 da; m 2, 1961, Donald Walker Alexander Brown, o son of Archibald Donald Brown (d 1958); *Style—* The Hon Mrs Brown

BROWN, Hamish Macmillan; s of William Dick Brown (d 1968), of Dollar, and Kinghorn, and Effie Grace, *née* Swanson (d 1988); *b* 13 Aug 1934; *Educ* Dollar Acad; *Career* Nat Serv RAF Egypt and E Africa; asst Martyrs Meml Church Paisley 1958-59, outdoor educn Braehead Sch 1960-71, Fife Outdoor Activities Adviser 1972-73; freelance author, photographer, lectr, poet, mountaineer and traveller 1974-; served SMLTB, dir SROW, creator Ultimate Challenge event; expeditions to: Andes, Himalayas, Arctic, Africa, etc; contribs in over 100 pubns; *Books* Hamish's Mountain Walk (1978, SAC Award), Hamish's Groats End Walk (1981, shortlist for W H Smith Travel Prize), Poems of the Scottish Hills (1982), Speak to the Hills (1985), The Great Walking Adventure (1986), Travels (1986), Hamish Brown's Scotland (1988), The Island of Rhum (1988), Climbing the Corbetts (1988), Scotland Coast to Coast (1990); *Recreations* skiing, canoeing, alpine flowers, gardening, bird philately, music, books; *Clubs* Alpine, Swiss Alpine, Scottish Mountaineering; *Style—* Hamish Brown, Esq; 21 Carlin Craig, Kinghorn, Fife KY3 9RX (☎ 0592 890422)

BROWN, Harold Arthur Neville; CMG (1963), CVO (1961); s of Stanley Raymond Brown, of Penarth, and Gladys Maud Brown; *b* 13 Dec 1914; *Educ* Cardiff HS, Univ Coll Cardiff; *m* 1939, Mary McBeath, da of late Alan Urquhart, of Cardiff; 1 s, 1 da; *Career* entered Miny of Labour 1939; FO: joined 1955, ambass Liberia 1960-63, FO 1963, ambass Cambodia 1966-70, consul-gen Johannesburg 1970-73, min Pretoria/Cape Town 1973-74, ret 1975; *Style—* Harold Brown, Esq, CMG, CVO; 14 Embassy Court, King's Rd, Brighton, Sussex BN1 2PX (☎ 0273 734623)

BROWN, (Arthur) Hedley; s of Thomas Baden Brown (d 1972), and Ann, *née* Summerskill (d 1977); *b* 8 April 1934; *Educ* Newcastle Royal GS, Univ of Durham (MB BS, MS); *m* 12 Sept 1964, Dr Ann Elizabeth Brown, da of Dr Eion Richard Howell Davies (d 1964), of Harrogate; 1 s (Richard Hedley b 1971), 1 da (Amanda b 1966); *Career* Nat Serv Maj RAMC surgical specialist Far East 1959-61; house surgn and physican Newcastle 1957-58, demonstrator in anatomy Newcastle 1958-59; registrar: in gen and cardiothoracic surgery Newcastle 1961-63, in cardiothoracic surgery Hammersmith Hosp 1963-66; sr registrar St Thomas's Hosp 1966-68; fell in cardiac surgery 1968-71: Presbyterian San Francisco, Massachusetts Gen Hosp; sr registrar Brook Guy's, St Thomas' Hosps 1971-73; conslt cardiac surgn: St Thomas' 1973, Wellington Hosp NZ; 1973-78; conslt cardiothoracic surgn Freeman Hosp Newcastle 1978-; memb: Cardiothoracic Surgns Soc of GB and Europe, N of Eng Surgical Soc, Br cardiac soc, N of Eng Thoracic Soc, Forum for Prevention of Coronary Heart Disease; FRCS 1963, FRACS (NZ) 1975; *Books* Cardiothoracic Handbook (1988), Manual of Cardiothoracic Critical Care (1989); *Recreations* cycling, running; *Clubs* Blue Funnel, Dave's, Bats; *Style—* Hedley Brown, Esq; Cardiothoracic Surgery, Freeman Hospital, Newcastle upon tyne (☎ 091 284 3111)

BROWN, Hon Mrs (Helen Jean); er da of Baron Todd, OM, *qv*; *b* 13 July 1941; *Educ* Westonbirt Glos, Somerville Coll Oxford (MA, BSc); *m* 21 Sept 1963, Philip Edgar Brown, s of Lawrence Felix Brown, of Stretford, Lancs; 2 s, 1 da; *Style—* The Hon Mrs Brown; 124 Edge Hill, Darras Hall, Ponteland, Newcastle-upon-Tyne (☎ 0661 24533)

BROWN, Sir (Ernest) Henry Phelps; MBE (1945); o son of Edgar William Brown, of Calne, Wilts; *b* 10 Feb 1906; *Educ* Taunton Sch, Wadham Coll Oxford; *m* 1932, Dorothy Evelyn Mostyn, yst da of Sir Anthony Alfred Bowlby, 1 Bt, KCB, KCMG, KCVO (d 1929); 2 s, 1 da; *Career* prof of econs of labour, later emeritus prof Univ of London 1947-68; kt 1976; *Style—* Sir Henry Phelps Brown, MBE; 16 Bradmore Rd, Oxford (☎ 0865 56320)

BROWN, Hilary Neilson; da of James Wilson Stanley, of Glasgow, and Irene Mignon Stanley; *b* 6 June 1952; *Educ* Hutchesons Girls' GS, Glasgow and W of Scotland Coll of Domestic Sci (Dip Dom Sci), Jordanhill Coll (Dip Ed); *m* 27 Dec 1973, David Richard Brown, s of James Alexander Brown; *Career* restaurateur; teacher Bellarmine Sch Glasgow 1973-75, chef and proprietor La Potiniere Gullane 1975-; awards: Good Food Guide Mortar & Pestle 1979-, AA Rosette 1977-, Egon Ronay star 1985-, Michelin star 1991; *Books* La Potiniere and Friends (1990); *Recreations* France, Italy, cookery, films, health and nutrition, art; *Style—* Ms Hilary Brown; La Potinière, Gullane, East Lothian, Scotland (☎ 0620 843214)

BROWN, Howard Roger; s of Leslie John Brown (d 1975), of Portsmouth, and Ruth Ethel, *née* Smith; *b* 25 Feb 1945; *Educ* Portsmouth GS; *m* 17 Oct 1977, Elizabeth Jane, da of Sidney Douglas Hillyar (d 1985), of Emsworth Hants; 3 da (Sally b 1974, Judith b 1976, Helen b 1979); *Career* trainee accountant Grant Thornton 1963-69, ptnr and sr prtnr Ernst & Young 1969-, dir UK Banking GP Ernst & Young 1985-, chm Int Banking Ctee Ernst & Young 1986-; FCA 1969; Deacon Bloomsbury Central Church London 1981-; *Books* Leasing, Accounting & Tax Implications (1978), International Bank Accounting (1987); *Recreations* badminton, tennis, reading; *Style—* Howard Brown, Esq; Ernst & Young, 1 Lambeth Palace Rd, London, SE1 7EU (☎ 071 928 2000, fax 071 928 1345)

BROWN, Col Hugh Goundry; TD (1968), DL (1986); s of Charles Franc Brown, of Newcastle, and Edith Temple, *née* Smithson (d 1952); *b* 25 Feb 1927; *Educ* St Peter's Sch York, Univ of Durham (MB BS); *m* 26 Aug 1961, Ann Mary, da of Thomas Coburn Crump (d 1982); 1 s (Andrew b 1963), 2 da (Catherine b 1962, Elizabeth b 1967); *Career* Nat Serv RMO ATT 1(NY) BN KAR 1950-52; TA 1 (N) Gen Hosp 1952-75, OC 201 (N) Gen Hosp 1970-73, Hon Col 201 (N) Gen Hosp 1982-87; conslt plastic surgn and sr lectr 1968-; QHS 1972; pres: Br Soc for Surgery of the Hand 1985, Br Assoc of Plastic Surgns 1988, Br Assoc of Clinical Anatomists 1989; FRCS 1958; *Style—* Col Hugh Brown, TD, DL; Royal Victoria Infirmary, Newcastle (☎ 091 232 5131)

BROWN, Ian James Morris; s of Bruce Beveridge Brown (d 1957), of Alloa, Scotland, and Eileen Frances, *née* Carnegie (d 1986); *b* 28 Feb 1945; *Educ* Dollar Acad, Univ of Edinburgh (MA, DipEd, MLitt); *m* 8 June 1968, Judith Ellen, da of George Woodall Sidaway, of Adelaide; 1 s (Joshua b 1977), 1 da (Emily b 1972); *Career* playwright 1967-; sch teacher 1967-69 and 1970-71; lectr in drama: Dunfermline Coll Edinburgh 1971-76, Br Cncl Edinburgh and Istanbul 1976-78; princ lectr Crewe and Alsager Coll 1978-86 (seconded as sec Cork Enq into Professional Theatre 1985-86); drama dir Arts Cncl of GB 1986-, programme dir Alsager Arts Centre 1980-86; chm Scot Soc of Playwrights 1973-75 and 1984-87, convenor N W Playwrights' Workshop 1982-85, chm British Theatre Inst 1985-87 (vice chm 1983-85); *plays incl* Mother Earth 1970, The Bacchae 1972, Positively the Last Final Farewell Performance (ballet scenario) 197 Carnegie 1973, Rune (choral work) 1973, The Knife 1973, Rabelais 1973, The Fork 1976, New Reekie 1977, Mary 1977, Runners 1978, Mary Queen and the Loch Tower 1979, Pottersville 1982, Joker in the Pack 1983, Beatrice 1989, First Strike 1990, The Scotch Play 1991; *Recreations* theatre, sport, travel; *Style—* I J M Brown, Esq; Arts Council, 14 Gt Peter St, London SW1P 3NQ (☎ 071 333 0100)

BROWN, Dr Ian Lamont; s of James Brown, of 13 Wright Street, Renfrew, and Marion Goudie Roberts, *née* Annan; *b* 22 Oct 1948; *Educ* Paisley GS, Univ of Glasgow (BSc, MB, ChB); *m* 11 July 1974, Janice Margaret, da of Thomas Barr, of 205 Whitehaugh Avenue, Paisley; 1 s (Paul b 1978), 2 da (Gyda b 1976, Kathryn b 1982); *Career* lectr in pathology Univ of Glasgow 1978, hon conslt pathologist Greater Glasgow Health Bd 1983; Res and Pubns Ctee CARE; MRCPath 1982, Memb Int Acad of Pathologists 1984; *Books* Multiple Choice Questions in Pathology (1985), Medicine in Crisis (1988); *Style—* Dr Ian Brown; Univ Dept of Pathology, Western Infirmary, Glasgow, (☎ 041 339 8822)

BROWN, Jack; MBE 1985, JP (Lancaster 1967-); s of Maurice Brown (d 1979), of Leigh, Lancs, and Edith, *née* Horrocks (d 1977); *b* 10 Nov 1929; *Educ* Pennington C of E Sch Leigh Lancs; *m* 2 April 1952, Alice, da of John Brown (d 1958), of Atherton, Manchester; 1 s (David b 4 Aug 1953); *Career* Nat Serv gunner RA 1949-51, Sgt TA 1951-54; textile worker 1943-49 and 1951-54, various appts Trade Union 1954-76, dir and vice chm Fielden House Productivity Centre Ltd 1975-90, gen sec Amalgamated Textile Workers Union 1976-86, non-exec memb N Western Electricity Bd 1984-90, sec Textile Div Gen Municipal Boilermakers and Allied Trade Union 1986-87; cncllr Atherton Urban Dist Cncl 1958-61, memb Industl Tribunals 1975-90; former branch sec: Atherton Trades Cncl and Labour Party, The Workers Educnl Assoc and Fabian Soc; *Recreations* reading, rugby league football, politics, current affairs; *Clubs* Atherton Discharged Soldiers and Sailors; *Style—* Jack Brown, Esq, MBE, JP; 11 Thomas St, Atherton, Manchester (☎ 0942 870218)

BROWN, Maj-Gen James; CB (1982); s of late James Brown; *b* 12 Nov 1928; *Educ* Methodist Coll Belfast, RMA Sandhurst; *m* 1952, Lilian May Johnson; 2 s; *Career* dir gen Ordnance Servs 1980-83, current dir Mgmnt Info Servs Div London Univ; *Style—* Maj-Gen James Brown, CB; c/o Royal Bank of Scotland, Holt's Branch, Kirkland House, Whitehall, London SW1

BROWN, James Alan; s of Douglas R Brown, of 14 Riverside, Windsor Rd, Surrey, and Dulcie M Brown; *b* 4 Dec 1940; *Educ* Kingsbury Co GS London, Acton Hotel & Catering Sch Acton (HCIMA); *m* 28 Sept 1968, M Louise, da of Dudley James; 2 s (Rupert James Heathcliffe b 10 Feb 1970, Oliver James Quentin b 24 July 1972); *Career* trainee mangr Grand Metropolitan Hotels Ltd 1962-64, mangr 1964-66, advsr Cunard Line Ltd 1966-68; mangr: Rank Hotels Ltd 1968-70, Skyway Hotels (London) Ltd 1970-72; gen mangr Royal Garden Hotel 1975- (involved in bldg 1972-75); Freeman City of London, Master Innholder; FMCIMA 1962; *Style—* James Brown, Esq; 15 Riverside, Windsor Road, Egham, Surrey TW20 OAA; Royal Garden Hotel, Kensington High St, London W8 (☎ 071 937 8000)

BROWN, James Clifford; s of Henry John Brown (d 1933), of Ipswich, Suffolk, and Loïs, *née* Smith (d 1973); *b* 18 Aug 1923; *Educ* Northgate GS Ipswich, St John's Coll Cambridge (MA, MusB); *Career* Dept of Music Univ of Leeds: lectr 1948-72, univ organist 1948-83, sr lectr 1972-83, acting head of dept 1982; composed: piano sonata 1950, sonata for violin and piano 1956, serenade for chamber orch 1969, scena for organ The Burning Bush 1973, oratorio The Baptism of Christ 1979, cello concerto 1980, piano trio 1982, cantata The World of Light 1988; ctee memb Leeds Philharmonic Soc 1972-, pres Ipswich Choral Soc 1989-; FRCO 1948, memb Leeds Organists Assoc 1963-; *Recreations* meeting friends; *Style*— James Brown, Esq; 29 Vesper Gate Drive, Leeds LS5 3NH

BROWN, James David Denholm (Tim); s of Lt-Col Robert Louis Brown (d 1988), of Torwood, Kilmacolm, Renfrewshire, Scotland, and Katherine Lang, *née* Denholm (d 1983); *b* 9 Oct 1932; *Educ* St Marys Melrose, Merchiston Castle Sch Edinburgh; *m* 2 Oct 1965, Judith Elaine, da of Roland Edmund Dangerfield (d 1964), of Hoe Farm, Peaslake, Surrey; 1 s (Duncan b 1969), 3 da (Diana b 1966, Camilla b 1968, Kirsty b 1974); *Career* Nat Serv Pilot Offr RAF 1951-53; dir Denholm Gp of Cos in London (joined Denholms Glasgow 1953, based London as Denholm Coates 1954-); FICS 1962; *Recreations* bridge; *Clubs* Baltic Exchange; *Style*— Tim Brown, Esq; Swains, Bonfire Hill, Southwater, Horsham, Sussex; Denholm Coates & Co Ltd, 26 Great Tower St, London EC3R 5AQ (☎ 071 626 0816, fax 071 283 9509, telex 885337)

BROWN, Janet; *Educ* Gallowflat Sch, Rutherglen Acad; *m* Peter Butterworth (decd); 1 s (Tyler), 1 da (Emma); *Career* actress/impressionist; began career with amateur concerts in Glasgow, first engagement Children's Hour BBC Radio; tv work incl: Who Do You Do, Special for Thames TV, Janet and Company 1983; guest appearances on: The Val Doonican Show, Parkinson, Aspel & Co, Thats Life, The Johnny Carson Show (USA); subject of This is Your Life; best known impression that of Margaret Thatcher MP; appeared on two Royal Command performances; theatre work incl: Mr Gillie (Garrick), The Bargain (St Martin's), Plaza Suite (Australia and Nottingham Playhouse); *Books* Prime Mimicker (autobiog, 1986); *Style*— Ms Janet Brown; (cabaret and personal appearances) Bernard Lee Management, Moorcroft Lodge, Farleigh Common, Warlingham, Surrey CR3 9PE (☎ 0883 625667); (acting) Marina Martin Management, 6a Danbury St, London N1 8JU (☎ 071 359 3646)

BROWN, Hon Mrs (Jennifer Mary); *née* Bethell; da of 2 Baron Bethell (d 1965), and Veronica (d 1981), da of Hon Sir James Connolly; *b* 26 Aug 1930; *Educ* St Mary's Convent Ascot; *m* 1954, Edward Peter Moncrieff Brown (ret stockbroker), s of Andrew Moncrieff Brown, of Wooder Manor, Widecombe, Devon; 4 s (Alistair, Craig, Jamie, David); *Recreations* tennis, sailing; *Style*— The Hon Mrs Brown; St Anthony's Cottage, Duncton, Petworth, W Sussex GU28 0JY (☎ 0798 42559)

BROWN, Jeremy Ronald Coventry; s of Kenneth Coventry Brown, MBE (d 1987), of Durban, SA, and Mavis Kathleen, *née* Keal; *b* 2 May 1948; *Educ* Westville Boys HS SA, Univ of Natal (MSc, Chem Eng), Univ of SA (B Iuris); *Career* Spoor and Fisher (patent attorneys) South Africa 1971-78, Linklaters & Paines (solicitors) London 1978-; memb: Licensing Execs Soc Br and Ireland (vice pres 1990-91), Cncl AIPPI (British gp);; *Recreations* tennis, travel, the Arts; *Clubs* Roehampton; *Style*— Jeremy Brown, Esq; Linklaters & Paines, Barrington House, 59/67 Gresham St, London EC2V 7JA (☎ 071 606 7080)

BROWN, Joe; MBE (1975); s of Joseph Brown (d 1930), and Mary, *née* Attwell (d 1983); *b* 26 Sept 1930; *Educ* Stanley Grove Sch Manchester; *m* 17 Feb 1957, Valerie Melville, da of Melville Gray (d 1947); 2 da (Helen Josephine b 1960, Zoe Melville b 1966); *Career* Nat Serv 1948-50; mountaineer; ascents: west face Petit Dru 1954, first ascent Kunchenjunga 1955, Mustagh Tower 1956, Mount Communism USSR 1962, Trango Tower 1976, Cataphaxi 1979, Mount Kenya 1984, Mount McInley 1986; other expdns: El Torro 1970, Bramah 1979, Thalaysaga 1982, north east ridge Mount Everest 1986 and 1988; retailer of climbing equipment Llanberis & Capel Curig North Wales 1965; film maker for cinema and TV; hon memb Climers Club (memb 1961-65); hon fell Manchester Poly 1970; *Recreations* mountaineering, fishing; *Style*— Joe Brown, Esq, MBE; Menai Hall, Llanberis, Gwynedd (☎ 0286 870327)

BROWN, John David; s of Alfred Stanley Brown, 24 Valley Rd, Little Billing, Northampton, and Joan Mary, *née* Ogle; *b* 13 Oct 1942; *Educ* Northampton GS, Univ of Nottingham (BSc); *m* 24 Sept 1967, Diane Elaine, da of Eric Edmund Hatton (d 1987); *Career* entered patent agent profession 1964, qualified patent agent 1969, ptnr Forrester Ketley & Co London 1972, fndr ptnr Forrester & Boehmert London, Munich, Bremen 1977; memb: Kiwanis Club Welwyn, Cncl of the Chartered Inst of Patent Agents (chm Parey Ctee), Parey & Scientific Ctee; substitute memb Cncl of Euro Patent Inst; memb: SCL 1964, RSC 1964, CIPA 1969; *Recreations* walking, skiing, squash; *Style*— John D Brown, Esq; Forrester Ketley & Co, Forrester House, 52 Bounds Green Rd, London N11 2EY (☎ 081 889 6622, fax 081 881 1088)

BROWN, Sir John Douglas Keith; er s of Ralph Douglas Brown (d 1972), of Manor Hotel, Hindhead, and Rhoda Miller Keith; *b* 8 Sept 1913; *Educ* Glasgow Acad; *m* 1940, Margaret Eleanor, da of William Alexander Burnet (d 1942); 2 s; *Career* former CA; chm: Jardine Henderson Ltd Calcutta 1957-63, McLeod Russel & Co Ltd London 1972-79; chm and dir other cos; kt 1960; *Style*— Sir John Brown; Glenyra, 60 Kingswood Firs, Grayshott, Hindhead, Surrey GU26 6ER (☎ 0428 604173)

BROWN, Sir John Gilbert Newton; CBE (1966); s of John Brown, of Kent (d 1986) and Mary Edith, *née* Purchas (d 1974); *b* 7 July 1916; *Educ* Lancing, Hertford Coll Oxford (MA); *m* 1946, Virginia, da of late Darcy Braddell, of Holland Park, London W11; 1 s, 2 da; *Career* 2 Lt RA Malaya; publisher OUP 1956-80; chm: B H Blackwell 1980-83, Basil Blackwell Publishers 1983-85 (dep chm 1983-87); dir: John Brown Publicity Ltd, Blackwell Gp, Basil Blackwell Publishers, Book Tokens; chm Univ Bookshop Oxford; kt 1974; *Clubs* Garrick; *Style*— Sir John Brown, CBE; Milton Lodge, Great Milton, Oxford (☎ 0844 279217)

BROWN, Dr John Graham; s of Malcolm Brown, of York, and Doreen Ethel, *née* Calpin; *b* 3 March 1957; *Educ* Nunthorpe GS York, Queen Elizabeth Coll London (BSc, Helen R White prize in microbiology), Sch of Hygiene and Tropical Med London (PhD); *Career* MRC res fell Sch of Hygiene and Tropical Med London 1981-84, res and devpt offr Health Educn Cncl 1984-87; Burson-Marsteller Ltd (pr/public affrs) 1987-: initially account dir currently mangr Healthcare Unit, Exec Ctee sr dirs 1990- (dir 1989-); memb: Steering Ctee Food and Health Forum RSM, Fin and Gen Purposes Ctee Coronary Prevention Gp, Cncl Br Nutrition Soc 1986-89 (memb 1975), MBIM 1988, MIPR 1990; *Recreations* foreign travel, good food, numismatics; *Style*— Dr John Brown; Burson-Marsteller Ltd, 24-28 Bloomsbury Way, London WC1A 2PX (☎ 071 831 6262, fax 071 430 1033, car 0836 762 633)

BROWN, John Granger; s of Frank Brown, of Birkenhead; *b* 24 Nov 1939; *Educ* Birkenhead Sch, Univ of Birmingham; *m* 1964, Averil, da of Arthur Jones, of Birkenhead; 2 da; *Career* CA; corp dir and sec Bernard Matthews plc 1977-; *Recreations* squash, cricket, golf, bridge; *Style*— John Brown, Esq; Rose Cottage, West End, Old Costessey, Norwich (☎ 0603 744477)

BROWN, John Neville; s of Alfred Herbert Brown (d 1978), of Tutbury, Staffordshire, and Jessie Wright; *b* 18 Nov 1935; *Educ* Denstone Coll, Selwyn Coll Cambridge (MA); *m* 3 April 1965, Ann Hilliar, da of George William Hubert Edmonds; 1 s (Hamish John Benedict b 19 Dec 1968), 1 da (Sara Elizabeth Hilliar b 2 July 1966); *Career* articled clerk Shipley Blackburn Sutton & Co (Chartered Accountants) 1960-63; Ernst & Young (and predecessors): sr 1965, mangr 1968, ptnr 1986; nat chm VAT Practioners' Gp; hon treas World Pheasant Assoc; FCA 1964, AInsT 1966, FRGS 1988; *Recreations* photography, travel, running, beagling, reading, ornithology, conservation; *Clubs* United Oxford and Cambridge University; *Style*— John Brown, Esq; Ernst & Young, Rolls House, Fetter Lane, London EC4A 1NH (☎ 071 928 2000)

BROWN, John Stevenson; s of Stanley Brown (d 1978), of Sanderstead, Surrey, and Agnes Campbell, *née* Stevenson; *b* 28 Dec 1929; *Educ* Whitgift Middle Sch Croydon, Coll of Estate Mgmnt; *m* 1953, Catherine Mary, da of Maurice Ludlam-Taylor (d 1981); 1 s, 1 da; *Career* Nat Serv RE UK, served E Africa 1948-49; vice chm and md Artagen Properties Ltd 1966-76, md Peachey Property Corporation plc 1977-; dir: A Peachey plc, Frankswood Property Co Ltd and subsids; non-exec dir Property Servs Agency DOE; pres: Br Chapter FIABCI 1975-76, Br Property Fedn 1986-87; Liveryman Worshipful Cos of: Basketmakers, Paviors; FRICS; *Recreations* sailing (sloop Conclusion); *Clubs* Royal Thames Yacht, Royal Lymington Yacht; *Style*— John Brown, Esq; Peachey Property Corporation plc, 19 Sloane St, London SW1X 9NE (☎ 071 235 2080)

BROWN, Joseph Lawler; CBE (1977), TD (1953), DL (W Midlands 1975); s of Neil Brown, of Peebles; *b* 22 March 1921; *Educ* Peebles, Heriot-Watt Coll Edinburgh, Open Univ (BA); *m* 1950, Mabel, da of Alderman Pearson Smith, BEM; 1 s, 1 da; *Career* served WWII, Europe, Maj 7/9 The Royal Scots, TA 1946-57; dir: Coventry Newspapers 1960-69 (md 1964-69), BPM Hldgs 1971-81, Reuters 1972-75; chm & md Birmingham Post and Mail 1971-77; memb Press Assoc 1968-75 (chm 1971); pres: Newspaper Soc 1976-77, Birmingham Chamber of Industry & Commerce 1979; warden Neidpath Castle Peebles 1983, bailiff The Schs of King Edward VI in Birmingham 1987; Cdr Order of Merit (Italy) 1973, Kt of Mark Twain Soc (USA) 1979; *Books* History of Peebles: 1850-1990 (1990); *Recreations* Japanese woodcuts; *Style*— Joseph Brown, Esq, CBE, TD, DL; 37 Mearse Lane, Barnt Green, Birmingham B45 8HH (☎ 021 445 1234)

BROWN, Hon Mrs (Juliet); yst da of Dr Geoffrey Tyndale Young and Baroness Young, PC (Life Peer); *b* 1962; *m* 7 June 1986, Stephen P Brown, er s of Dr Stanley Brown, of Harborne, Birmingham; 1 s (Simon Richard b 9 Nov 1989); *Style*— The Hon Mrs Brown

BROWN, Karen; da of Leslie Gordon Brown, of High Trees, Westerham Rd, Oxted, Surrey, and Valerie Elizabeth, *née* Blyth; *b* 9 Jan 1963; *Educ* Oxted Co Sch; *Career* hockey player; Orpington Ladies Hockey Club 1977-87, Slough Ladies Hockey Club 1987-; England: jr 1979-81, under 21 1981-83, 69 full caps 1984-, 79 full caps GB 1984-; honours incl: Silver medal Euro Championships 1987, Bronze medal Euro Indoor Championships 1982 and 1987, fourth place Olympic Games 1988, fourth place World Cup 1990; UK palyer of the Year 1984; official National Westminster Bank 1982-; *Recreations* Manchester United FC; *Style*— Miss Karen Brown; 12 Parklands, Lynwood Rd, Redhill, Surrey (☎ 0737 778790); c/o All England Women's Hockey Assoc, 51 High St, Shrewsbury, Shropshire SY1 1ST

BROWN, Keith Clark; s of George Harold Brown (d 1970), and Sophie Eleanor, *née* Clark; *b* 14 Jan 1943; *Educ* Forest Sch, City of London Coll; *m* 16 April 1972, Rita Hildegard, da of Jack Stanley Rolfe (d 1977); 1 s (Timothy b 1979), 1 da (Lucy b 1976); *Career* stockbroker and investmt banker; ptnr W Greenwell & Co 1978-86; md: Greenwell Montagu Securities 1987, Morgan Stanley International 1988-; govt dir Br Aerospace 1989; cncllr: London Borough Havering 1968-74, Brentwood DC 1976-86; chm Brentwood DC 1983-84, memb Bd London Regnl Tport 1984-; Liveryman Worshipful Co of Coopers; *Recreations* public and charitable affairs, memb Racehorse Owners Assoc; *Clubs* Cordwainer; *Style*— Keith C Brown, Esq; Fryerning House, Ingatestone, Essex CM4 0PF (☎ 0277 352959); Morgan Stanley International, 1A Wimpole Street, London W1 (☎ 071 709 3000)

BROWN, Keith John; JP (1979); s of Frederick Charles Brown, and Doris Lilian, *née* French; *b* 21 June 1949; *Educ* Forest Hill Sch, City and East London Coll, Univ of London; *Career* ocularist: Moorfields Eye Hosp 1970, Kent Co Ophthalmic and Aural Hosp Maidstone 1973, Kent and Sussex Hosp Tunbridge Well 1975; private practice ownership: Brown Poole & Ptnrs Tunbridge Wells 1972, Brown and Gimpel Southborough 1979; ind private practice: Southborough, Maidstone, W Malling 1981; conslt oculist: Keelers (Cromwell Hosp) 1984, Trotters Edinburgh 1986, Dolland and Aitchison Group 1987, Chaucer Hosp Canterbury 1988; chm Lib Democrat Pty Cranbrook and dist; Freeman: City of London, Worshipful Co of Spectacle Makers; fndn fell Br Assoc Dispensing Opticians 1986; *Recreations* cooking, walking, shooting; *Clubs* Nat Lib; *Style*— Keith Brown, Esq, JP; Linnet House, Hawkhurst, Kent (☎ 0580 753 668); 23-27 Swan St, West Malling, Kent (☎ 0732 848 384); 100 London Rd, Southborough Tunbridge Wells, Kent (☎ 0892 31004/ 35683)

BROWN, Kenneth Edward Lindsay; s of Col Thomas Pyne Brown, OBE (d 1957); *b* 17 Oct 1940; *Educ* Sherborne; *m* 1968, Mary Ruth, da of Thomas Forrester (d 1969); 3 s; *Career* chm A R Brown McFarlane & Co Ltd 1972- (dir 1967-); FCA; *Recreations* sailing, skiing; *Clubs* Royal Ocean Racing; *Style*— Kenneth Brown Esq; 65 St Andrews Drive, Glasgow G41 4HP (☎ 041 423 8381); A R Brown McFarlane & Co Ltd, 239 Myreside St, Glasgow G32 6DR (☎ 041 551 8281, telex 779595)

BROWN, Prof Lawrence Michael (Mick); s of Bertson Waterworth Brown, of Central Park Lodge, Riverside Drive, Windsor, Ontario, Canada, and Edith, *née* Waghorne (d 1989); *b* 18 March 1936; *Educ* Univ of Toronto (BASc), Univ of Cambridge (MA), Univ of Birmingham (PhD); *m* Dr Susan Drucker Brown, da of David Drucker, of 164B Bison Lane, Oronoque Village, Stratford, WNN 06497, USA; 1 s (Toby Solomon b 1974), 2 da (Sarah May b 1969, Isabel b 1972); *Career* Univ of Cambridge: W H Tapp fellowship Gonville and Caius Coll 1963, demonstrator 1965, lectr 1970, fndr fell and dir of studies in physical sci Robinson Coll 1977, reader 1982, prof 1990; awarded: Rosenhain Medal (Inst of Metals), R F Mehl Medal (Metals Soc and Inst of Metals); FRS 1981, FInstP, FIM; *Style*— Prof Mick Brown; Cavendish Laboratory, Madingley Rd, Cambridge CB3 0HE (☎ 0223 337291, fax 0223 63261)

BROWN, Leith Roy Thomas; s of Russell John Brown (d 1982), of New Plymouth, New Zealand, and Heather Valmae Campbell, *née* Smith; *b* 25 Oct 1955; *Educ* Highlands Intermediate Sch, New Plymouth Boys HS NZ, Univ of Otago NZ, NZ Sch of Physiotherapy (Dip Physiotherapy), W Aust Inst of Technology (Kellogs scholar, BASc, post graduate dip Manipulative Therapy); *m* 2 July 1983, Kathryn Janis, da of Frederick Louise Warren; 3 s (Michael James Edward b 21 May 1984, Nicholas Warren Andrew b 1 June 1987, Alexander Russell Thomas b 13 Oct 1989); *Career* memb NZ Soc Physiotherapy and State Registration 1977, private practice L G Geden Esq New Plymouth NZ 1977-79, managed private practice Albany WA 1982, arrived UK 1983; fndr: Rayleigh Physiotherapy Clinic 1983, South Woodham Ferrers Physiotherapy Clinic 1986 (sold 1987); public relations offr Manipulation Assoc of Chartered Physiotherapists 1986-89 (elected to Nat Exec Ctee 1986), took over Sarah Key Physiotherapy Clinic 1988-; lectured throughout UK; MNZSP 1977, MAPA (Aust) 1980, SRP, MCSP 1986; *Publications* author of articles on combined movements (Physiotherapy jnl, 1988 and 1989); *Recreations* skiing, squash, jogging, walking, swimming, tennis, polo, reading; *Clubs* Rayleigh & Dist Round Table, Survival; *Style*— Leith Brown, Esq; The Sarah Key Physiotherapy Clinic, 27 Weymouth St, London W1N 3FJ (☎ 071 636 3433, 071 636 7280, fax 071 255 1522)

BROWN, Maggie; da of Cecil Walter Brown and Marian, *née* Evans; *b* 7 Sept 1950;

Educ Colston's Girls' Sch, Univ of Sussex, Univ of Bristol (BA), Univ of Cardiff (Dip in Journalism); *m* 22 June 1979, Charles John Giuseppe Harvey, s of Hon John Wynn Harvey, of Coed-y-Maen, Meifod, Powys (s of 1 Baron Harvey of Tasburgh); 2 da (Elena b 27 Dec 1982, Nina b 11 Aug 1985); *Career* trainee journalist Birmingham Post & Mail 1972-74; staff writer: Birmingham Post 1974-77, Reuters 1977-78; news editor: Financial Weekly 1979-80, The Guardian 1980-86; media editor The Independent 1986-; contributor to magazines and BBC radio; memb Victorian Soc; *Recreations* reading, gardening, being a mother; *Style—* Ms Maggie Brown; 162 East Dulwich Grove, London SE22 (☎ 081 693 5838); office, The Independent, 40 City Rd, London EC1Y 2DB (☎ 081 253 1222)

BROWN, Malcolm Carey; s of Rev William George Brown (d 1978), and Bernice Nellie Cordelia, *née* Radcliffe (d 1978); *b* 7 May 1930; *Educ* Nelson GS Lancashire, Poole GS Dorset, St John's Coll Oxford (scholar, BA); *m* 1953, Beatrice Elsie Rose, da of Austin Albert George Light; 2 s (Martin John Carey b 1959, Michael Paul b 1961), 1 da (Catherine Mary b 1963); *Career* Nat Serv midshipman RNVR 1952-54; BBC: gen trainee 1955-57, TV prodn asst 1957-60, documentary film prodr 1960-86; Freelance writer 1986- (pt/t freelance writer 1968-86); TV documentary films (prodr/dir): T E Lawrence 1962, Horseman Pass By 1966, Scapa Flow 1966, The World Turned Upside Down 1967, The Chalfont Profiles 1970-75, Battle of the Some (short-listed Int Emmy) 1976, Armistice and After 1978, Graf Spee 1979, Gordon of Khartoum 1983; *Books* Scapa Flow (jtly, 1968), Tommy Goes To War (1978), Christmas Truce (jtly, 1984), A Touch of Genius (jtly, 1988, short-listed NCR Non-Fiction Book award 1989 and Nelson Hurst and Marsh Biography award 1989), The Letters of T E Lawrence (ed, 1988), A Touch of Genius; *Recreations* walking, the making and keeping of friends; *Style—* Malcolm Brown, Esq; 4 Northbury Avenue, Ruscombe, Twyford, Reading, Berkshire RG10 9LG (☎ 0734 340370)

BROWN, Prof Sir (George) Malcolm; s of George Arthur Brown (d 1937), and Anne Brown (d 1987); *b* 5 Oct 1925; *Educ* Coatham Sch Redcar, Univ of Durham (BSc, DSc), Univ of Oxford (MA, DPhil), Princeton Univ, Univ of California, Univ of Berne; *m* 1, 1963 (m dis 1977); m 2, Sally Jane Marston, er da of Alan Douglas Spencer, *qv*; 2 step da (Polly Marston b 1969, Verna Marston b 1971); *Career* served RAF (aircrew) 1944-47; univ lectr; Cwlth fell (Harkness) Princeton Univ 1954-55, coll lectr Lincoln New Coll, fell St Cross Coll Univ of Oxford 1955-66, sr res fell Geophysical Laboratory Washington DC USA 1966-67; Univ of Durham 1967-79: prof of geology, dean of sci and pro vice chllr; princ investigator NASA Apollo Moon Exploration Prog 1967-75; dir: Br Geological Survey, Geological Museum, Geological Survey of NI 1979-85; conslt geologist 1985-, geological advsr MOD 1979-85; Hon DSc Univ of Leicester, HonD Open Univ; FRS, FGS; kt 1985; *Books* Layered Igneous Rocks (1968), Origin of the Solar System (contrib, 1978), Planet Earth (contrib, 1977); *Recreations* exploration, classical guitar; *Clubs* Royal Overseas League; *Style—* Prof Sir Malcolm Brown, FRS; Coral Spring House, Curbridge Rd, Witney, Oxon OX8 7NR (☎ 0993 772915)

BROWN, Malcolm Ronald; s of Ronald Ernest Charles Brown, MBE (d 1988), of Orpington, Kent, and Peggy Elizabeth, *née* Mitchener; *b* 2 Aug 1946; *Educ* Quintin GS, Univ of London (BSc); *m* 3 Oct 1970, Lyntina Sydnie, da of Clinton Sydney Squire; 1 s (Philip Clinton b 18 May 1975), 1 da (Samantha Anne b 13 Feb 1972); *Career* construction analyst: de Zoete & Gorton 1968-72, James Capel & Co 1972- (ptnr 1981, sr exec 1984); chm Repair and Maintenance Gp Construction Indust Forecasting Body Nat Econ Devpt Office; treas E Berks Cons Assoc; author numerous specialist papers and pubns; ASIA; *Recreations* ocean racing, chess, gardening; *Style—* Malcolm Brown, Esq; Carbery House, Carbery Lane, Ascot, Berks (☎ 0344 22620); James Capel House, 6 Bevis Marks, London EC3A 7JQ (☎ 071 621 0011 ext 2644)

BROWN, Hon Mrs (Marjorie Elizabeth); *née* Palmer; da of 2 Baron Palmer (d 1950); *b* 24 April 1910; *m* 1945, Frederick Richard Brown, CBE, s of Roger Grounds Brown (d 1947), of Liverpool; 3 s, 1 da; *Style—* The Hon Mrs Brown; 13 Islescourt, Ramsbury, nr Marlborough, Wilts SN8 2QW (☎ 0672 20740)

BROWN, (Laurence Frederick) Mark; s of Rt Rev Ronald Brown, Lord Bishop Suffragan of Birkenhead, of Trafford House, Victoria Crescent, Chester, and Joyce, *née* Hymers (d 1987); *b* 16 March 1953; *Educ* Bolton Sch, Univ of Durham (BA); *m* 5 Aug 1978, Jane Margaret, da of Rev Dr F H Boardman, RD, of Woodside Burton Wood Rd, Gt Sankey, Cheshire; 1 s (Nicholas b 29 April 1984); *Career* called to the Bar Inner Temple 1975; in practice Northern Circuit 1976-, pt/t tutor in law Univ of Liverpool 1976-83; *Recreations* golf, gardening; *Clubs* The Royal Liverpool Golf; *Style—* Mark Brown, Esq; Holly Bank, Gayton Rd, Heswall Lower Village, Wirral (☎ 051 342 2939); The Corn Exchange, Fenwick St, Liverpool (☎ 051 227 1081, fax 051 236 1120); 5 Essex Court, Temple, London

BROWN, Sir Mervyn; KCMG (1981, CMG 1975), OBE (1963); s of William Brown, of Murton, Co Durham; *b* 24 Sept 1923; *Educ* Ryhope GS Sunderland, St John's Coll Oxford (MA); *m* 1949, Elizabeth, da of Harry Gittings, of Shipley, Derby; *Career* HM Foreign Serv 1949-83: ambass to Madagascar 1967-70 (non resident 1976-78), high cmmr Tanzania 1975-78, min and dep perm rep to UN 1978, high cmmr Nigeria and ambass to Benin 1979-83; chm: Visiting Arts 1983-89, and Anglo-Malagasy Soc; *Books* Madagascar Rediscovered (1978); *Recreations* music, tennis, history; *Clubs* Royal Cwlth Soc, Hurlingham, All England Lawn Tennis; *Style—* Sir Mervyn Brown, KCMG, OBE; 195 Queen's Gate, London SW7 5EU

BROWN, Maj-Gen Michael; s of Erick Charles Brown (d 1983), and Winifred Ellen, *née* Kemp (d 1979); *b* 17 Jan 1931; *Educ* Bedford Sch, Univ of London (BSc), UCH (MB BS); *m* 3 Dec 1955, Jill Evelyn, da of John Henry Grace (d 1943); 2 s (Richard James b 22 Aug 1958, Peter Michael b 21 April 1960); *Career* joined RAMC 1956, conslt physician 1966, jt prof of mil med 1981, conslt physician BAOR 1985, dir Army Med 1988-90; QHP 1988-90; FRCPE 1971 (MRCPE 1959), FRCP 1976 (MRCP 1960), FRSTM & H 1982 (DTM&H 1963); *Recreations* golf, photography; *Style—* Maj-Gen Michael Brown; 5 Cheswell Gardens, Chruch Crookham, Aldershot, Hants GU13 0NJ

BROWN, (Charles) Michael; s of Richard Charles Brown (d 1982), of Minchinhampton, Glos; *b* 11 June 1930; *Educ* Clifton; *m* 1, 1954, Sonia Teresa, da of Harvey Valency Schwalm (d 1959), of Angmering, Sussex; 3 s, 1 da; m 2, 1977, (Pauline) Anne, da of John Robinson (d 1981), of Allanton, Berwicks; *Career* chm Vinten Group plc 1975-87; dir: Pauls plc 1980-85, Domino Printing Sciences plc 1985-88; memb Ctee of Mgmnt The Fleming Property Unit Tst 1986-; FCA; *Recreations* shooting; *Style—* Michael Brown, Esq; 301 Lonsdale Rd, Barnes, London SW13 9PY (☎ 081 878 7783); Fort Fredrick, Port Royal, Roatan Island, Honduras

BROWN, Hon Michael Colin Duncan; s of Baron Brown, PC, MBE (Life Peer) (d 1985); *b* 11 July 1944; *Educ* Bryanston, Architectural Assoc; *m* 1970, Fenella, da of Peter Barnard, of Dorking; 1 s (Jago), 2 da (Merrilees, Clio); *Career* ptnr Brown Ibbotson Charnley (architects and urban designers); *Style—* The Hon Michael Brown

BROWN, Michael John; s of Lt Cdr S R Brown (d 1976), of Aylesbury, and Ada Phyllis, *née* Evett; *b* 23 Sept 1932; *Educ* Berkhamsted Sch, New Coll Oxford (MA); *m* 20 Sept 1963, Margaret Jordan, JP (d 1988), da of William C Jordan; 4 s (Edward b 1964, Thomas b 1966, Robert b and d 1968, Adam b 1970); *Career* admitted slr 1957; ptnr Denton Hall and Burgin 1959-80; dir: Urwick Orr and Partners Ltd (chm 1981-84), Channel TV 1972-77, Purcell Graham and Co 1978-88, Paulstra Ltd 1977-; sr ptnr Brown Cooper 1981-, hon slr Variety Club of GB 1966-; chm Pooh Properties Trust 1972-, pres Soc Eng and American Lawyers 1989- (chm 1985-88); *Recreations* diverse; *Clubs* Garrick; *Style—* Michael Brown, Esq; The Master's House, The Common, Chorleywood, Herts; 7 Southampton Place, London WC1 (☎ 071 404 0422, fax 071 831 9856, telex 265471)

BROWN, Air Vice-Marshal Michael John Douglas; s of Norman Hillier Barnes Brown (d 1969), of Esher, Surrey, and Margaret Mary, *née* Nisbet (d 1981); *b* 9 May 1936; *Educ* Drayton Manor Sch, Trinity Hall Cambridge (BA, MA); *m* 8 Sept 1961, Audrey Florence, da of Leslie James Woodward (d 1983), of Frinton-on-Sea, Essex; 1 s (Stephen b 1964); *Career* RAF: cadet entry Tech Coll Henlow 1953, cmmnd Tech (now Engr) branch 1954, pilot trg 1958-59, engrg duties Bomber Cmd 1959-61, signals duties Kenya 1961-64, advanced weapons course 1965-66, ops analyst MOD 1966-69, Staff Coll 1970, operational requirements MOD 1970-73, chief engr RAF Boulmer Radar Station 1973-75, USAF War Coll 1975-76, Gp Capt engrg co-ordination and plans HQ RAF Strike Cmd 1976-78, CO RAF North Luffenham 1978-80, RCDS 1981, dir air guided weapons MOD (PE) 1983-86, dir gen strategic electronic systems MOD (PE); CEng 1968, MRAeS 1968, AFIMA 1968, MRIN 1981; *Recreations* gardening, reading, music, archaeology; *Clubs* RAF; *Style—* Air Vice-Marshal M J D Brown; c/o Lloyds Bank Ltd, Cox's & Kings Branch, 7 Pall Mall, London SW1Y 5NA; MOD, Dir-Gen of Strategic Electronic Systems, Room 632, Turnstile House, Holborn, London WC1V 6LL (☎ 071 430 5226)

BROWN, Michael Russell; MP (C) Brigg and Cleethorpes 1983-; s of Frederick Alfred Brown, and Greta Mary Brown, OBE, *née* Russell; *b* 3 July 1951; *Educ* Littlehampton, Univ of York; *Career* memb Middle Temple; mgmnt trainee Barclays Bank 1972-74; lectr Swinton Cons Coll 1974-76, res asst to Michael Marshall MP 1975-77, Parly res asst to Nicholas Winterton MP 1977-79; MP (C) Brigg and Scunthorpe 1979-83; sec Parly NI Ctee 1981-87 (vice chm 1987), PPS to Hon Douglas Hogg MP, min of state DTI 1989-90, min of state FCO 1990-; *Style—* Michael Brown, Esq, MP; House of Commons, London SW1

BROWN, Prof (Lionel) Neville; OBE; s of Reginald Percy Neville Brown (d 1978), of York Crescent, Wolverhampton, and Fanny, *née* Carver (d 1980); *b* 29 July 1923; *Educ* Wolverhampton GS, Pembroke Coll Cambridge (MA, LLM), Lyons Univ France (Dr en Droit); *m* da of Charles Dennis Vowles (d 1984), of Heathcote, Great Barr, West Bromwich; 3 s (Roger b 1961, Simon b 1963, Adrian b 1965), 1 da (Rachel b 1967); *Career* WWII RAF 1942-45; admitted slr 1951; lectr in law Univ of Sheffield 1953-55; Univ of Birmingham: lectr 1955-57, sr lectr 1957-64, reader 1964-66, prof of comparative law 1966-90 (emeritus prof 1990-), dean Faculty of Law 1970-74; sr res fell Univ of Michigan 1960; visiting prof: Tulane Univ New Orleans 1968, Nairobi Univ 1974, Laval Univ Quebec 1975, 1979, 1983, 1987 and 1990, Limoges Univ 1987-88, Univ of Mauritius 1988-89; Cwlth Fndn Lectureship Caribbean 1976; memb Cncl on Tbnls 1982-88, chm Birmingham Social Security Appeal Tbnl 1988-; reader C of E Lichfield Dio 1972-; Leverhume fellowship 1990-92; memb Law Soc 1951 Docteur Honoris Causa Limoges Univ France 1988, Officier Dans L'Ordre Des Palmes Academiques France 1987; *Books* Amos & Walton's Introduction to French Law (3rd edn with FH Lawson & Anton, 1967), French Administrative Law (3 edn with JF Garner, 1983), Court of Justice of European Communities (3 edn with FG Jacobs, 1989; *Recreations* landscape gardening, country walking, music; *Clubs* United Oxford and Cambridge; *Style—* Prof Neville Brown, OBE; 14 Waterdale, Compton, Wolverhampton WV3 9DY (☎ 0902 26 666); Faculty of Law, University of Birmingham, Edgbaston, Birmingham B15 2TT (☎ 021 414 6284)

BROWN, Nicholas (Anthony) Phelps; s of Prof Sir Henry Phelps Brown, of 16 Bradmore Rd, Oxford, and Dorothy Evevelyn Mostyn, *née* Bowlby; *b* 5 May 1936; *Educ* Westminster, Trinity Coll Cambridge (Exhibition, MA, MD), Middlesex Hosp (DO); *m* 12 Dec 1960, Heather Mary, da of Ronald Hubert White; 1 s (Giles Nicholas b 22 May 1972), 2 da (Emily Sarah b 1 June 1967, Lucy Kate b 8 Oct 1969); *Career* Nat Serv 1955-57 (cmmnd RA); The Middlesex Hosp: house surgn 1964, house physician 1964, house offr 1965, clinical asst Univ Coll Hosp 1966-67; Moorfields Eye Hosp: out patient offr 1966-67, resident surgical offr 1967-70, chief clinical asst 1970-71, res fellow to Contact Lens Dept 1971-73, lectr then sr lectr Depts of Clinical Ophthalmology and Experimental Ophthalmology 1971-76 (and Inst of Ophthalmology), hon conslt 1975-76; clinical asst The Hammersmith Hosp 1971-75, private practice 1977-, pt/t teaching at Inst of Ophthalmology and with Univ Examination Postal Inst 1977-, hon conslt The Redcliffe Infirmary Oxford 1983-, dir Clinical Cataract Res Unit Nuffield Laboratory of Ophthalmology Oxford 1989- (res assoc 1983-); Kodak Res Award: slit-image camera devpt 1971, MRC Res Grant: study of the Diabetic lens 1974-75, Nuffield Fndn Res Award: computerised analysis of the image of the lens of the eye 1987, Iris Fund for Eye Res: Glaucoma disc assessment by computerised image analysis 1989, Violt M Richards Charity: spoke cataract study 1990; FRCS 1969, FCOph; memb: RSM, BMA, Assoc for Eye Res, Oxford Ophthalmological Congress, Ophthalmological Soc of UK; *Publications* author of numerous papers and articles in ophthalmology journals; chapters in: Medical Ophthalmology, (ed Clifford Rose, 1975), Scientific Foundations of Ophthalmology (1977); *Recreations* natural history, photography; *Style—* Nicholas Phelps Brown, Esq; 25 Gordon PLace, London W8 4JE (☎ 071 938 4065); 69 Harley St, London W1 (☎ 071 636 7153)

BROWN, Nicholas Hugh; MP (Lab) Newcastle upon Tyne, East 1983-; s of late R C Brown, and G K Brown, *née* Tester; *b* 13 June 1950; *Educ* Tunbridge Wells Tech HS, Univ of Manchester; *Career* memb: Newcastle upon Tyne Cncl 1980-, Housing Sub Ctee on Slum Clearance; *Style—* Nicholas Brown, Esq, MP; House of Commons, London SW1

BROWN, Nicholas Warriner; s of Byron Warriner George Brown, and Constance Louise, *née* Austin; *b* 5 Nov 1938; *Educ* Oundle; *m* 13 July 1962, Margaret Joan, da of Charles Robert Smurthwaite; 1 s (David b 1964), 1 da (Sophia b 1963); *Career* fndr and chm Wallcoverings Int Ltd, chm and chief exec Walker Greenbank plc; *Recreations* golf, art; *Style—* Nicholas W Brown, Esq; Walker Greenbank plc, Zoffany Hse, 74-78 Wood Lane End, Hemel Hempstead, Herts HP2 4RF

BROWN, Nigel Denis Spence; s of Denis Frederick Spence Brown, MC, of Dorrington, Lincoln, and Margaret, *née* Shutler; *b* 6 May 1946; *Educ* Uppingham, Manchester Business Sch; *m* 18 Sept 1971, Gillian Elizabeth Ann, da of Dr G H P Drake, of Appleshaw, Hants; 2 s (Thomas b 1980, James b 1982), 1 da (Juliet b 1986); *Career* CA 1966-71, merchant banker 1971-74, joined Brown Butlin Group 1974 (gp chm 1987-); FCA 1968; *Style—* Nigel Brown, Esq; The Old Rectory, Fulbeck, Grantham, Lincs NG32 3JS (☎ 0400 73101); Brown Butlin Group Ltd, Brook House, Lincs (☎ 0526 834200)

BROWN, Prof Nigel Leslie; s of Leslie Charles Brown (d 1983), of Beverley, and Beryl, *née* Brown; *b* 19 Dec 1948; *Educ* Beverley GS, Univ of Leeds (BSc, PhD); *m* 7 Aug 1971, Gayle Lynnette, da of John Wallace Blackah, of Beverley; 2 da (Sally b 1975, Katie b 1977); *Career* lectr in biochemistry Univ of Bristol 1976-81, Royal Soc sr res fell 1981-88, visiting fell in genetics Univ of Melbourne Aust 1987-88, prof of molecular genetics and microbiology Univ of Birmingham 1988- memb: Soc Gen

Microbiology, Biochemical Soc, Genetical Soc, Inst of Biology, American Soc Microbiology; FIBiol 1989, FRSC 1990; *Recreations* science, travel, folk dance; *Style*— Prof Nigel Brown; 12 The Vale, Edgbaston, Birmingham B15 2RP; School of Biological Sciences, University of Birmingham, PO Box 363, Birmingham B15 2TT (☎ 021 414 6556, fax 021 414 5925, telex 33893

BROWN, Dr Norman John; s of William John Brown (d 1983), of Bristol, and Lilian Rose, *née* Hackney (d 1935); *b* 2 March 1918; *Educ* Bristol GS, Univ of Bristol (MB ChB); *m* 7 March 1942, Enid Rhoda, da of Samuel Gale (d 1961), of Portishead, Avon; 2 s (Christopher b 1943, Peter b 1952), 2 da (Pamela b 1947, Catherine b 1955); *Career* RAMC Lt 1942, Capt 1943-47, served M East, Italy, Regtl MO RA 1943-45, specialist in pathology 1946-47; house physician casualty offr Bristol Royal Infirmary 1941-42, registrar in pathology Utd Bristol Hosps 1947-49, lectr in pathology Univ of Bristol 1949-51; conslt pathologist: Southmead Hosp Bristol 1951-83, Bristol Royal Hosp Sick Children 1971-83; clinical teacher in pathology Univ of Bristol 1955-83, temp advsr WHO 1971-74; ed Bristol Medico-Chirurgical Jl 1961-74, pres Bristol Medico-Chirurgical Soc 1980-81; chm: SW Regnl Lab Med Ctee 1979-82, Med Educn Ctee Southmead Hosp Bristol 1958-82; parish cncllr Portbury Avon 1966-76, chm Parish Cncl 1973-76; memb: Cncl Int Acad of Pathology 1973-76, Br Paediatric Assoc 1977-; pres Paediatric Pathology Soc 1980-81; FRCP, FRCPath; *Books* Pathology of Testis (jtly, 1975), Tumours of Children (jtly, 1968, second edn 1975), Prematurity By Corner (1960); *Recreations* music (french horn player 40 years), gardening, photography; *Style*— Dr Norman Brown; The Old Vicarage, Harford Square, Chew Magna, Bristol BS18 8RA (☎ 0272 333 126)

BROWN, Paul Ray Beck; s of Sqdn Ldr Frederick Beck Brown, of Malvern, Worcestershire, and Kathleen, *née* May; *b* 20 July 1944; *Educ* Churchers Coll Petersfield Hants; *m* 1964, Maureen Ellen Ann, da of Joseph Archibald McMillan (d 1982); 2 da (Lucy Elizabeth Beck b 10 Feb 1965, Clara Louise Beck b 20 Jan 1968); *Career* indentured: East Grinstead Courier 1963-65, Lincolnshire Standard 1965-66, Leicester Mercury 1966-68; investigative reporter Birmingham Post 1968-74, news ed Evening Post-Echo Hemel Hempstead 1980-81 (joined 1974), The Sun 1981-82, environment correspondent The Guardian 1989- (joined 1982); Midlands Journalist of the Year 1974; *Books* The Last Wilderness, 80 Days in Antarctica (1991); *Recreations* badminton, travel; *Style*— Paul Brown, Esq; The Guardian, 119 Farringdon Rd, London EC1R 3FR (☎ 071 239 9803)

BROWN, Peter Eric; s of Eric Henry Ibbetson Brown (d 1951), of Yoxford House, Kings Lynn, Norfolk, and Violet Mary, *née* Phipps (d 1931); *b* 3 Oct 1931; *Educ* Cheltenham; *m* 23 Aug 1958, Sylvia Mary Ethel, da of Rev Charles Henry Watson (d 1949), of Lilleshall Vicarage, Lilleshall, Shropshire; 1 s (Richard Henry b 1967), 3 da (Vanessa Mary (Mrs Perkins) b 1960, Melanie Lucy b 1963, Camilla Susan b 1964); *Career* Nat Serv Capt 1952, RAOC 1950-52; mktg dir Martin Cadbury Ltd 1966-70, dep chief exec Andercroft Ltd 1970-73, md Brown Knight & Truscott Ltd 1977-79, chm and md Claremont Press Ltd 1979-; Freeman City of London 1974, Liveryman Worshipful Co of Stationers and Newspaper Makers 1975; memb Inst of Printing 1977, FInstM 1985; *Recreations* golf, tennis, badminton, theatre; *Clubs* City Livery; *Style*— Peter Brown, Esq; Claremont Press, Foundry Close, Horsham, W Sussex (☎ 0403 61387, fax 0403 55593)

BROWN, Peter John; s of John Jesse Brown (d 1942), of London, and Alice Irene, *née* Magnus (d 1978); *b* 12 April 1934; *Educ* Finchley GS, Harrow, City Lit Inst; *m* 8 Feb 1963, Marie-France, da of Stephanie Albert Chasles (d 1958), of France; 2 s (Philippe John b 3 Dec 1967, Christopher Mark b 5 Oct 1974), 1 da (Natalie Christina b 17 March 1964); *Career* Nat Serv RAF 1953-55; COI 1951-52, HMSO 1952-53, United Africa Co 1955-59, Lintas Ltd 1959-61, Greenlys 1961-63, The Times 1963-65, J Walter Thompson 1965-67, The Leslie Bishop Co 1967-68, Harris and Hunter 1968-69, chief exec PB Communications International PR and mktg consultancy; MIPR, memb PRCA; *Recreations* classical music, skiing, cricket, tennis; *Clubs* MCC; *Style*— Peter Brown, Esq; 13 Colinette Rd, Putney SW15 6QG; 2 Lansdowne House, Lansdowne Rd (☎ 071 229 8225, fax 071 221 3446)

BROWN, Peter Michael; s of Michael George Harold Brown (d 1969), of Sussex, and Dorothy Margaret, *née* Douty; *b* 11 July 1934; *Educ* Rugby; *m* 1963, Rosemary Anne, da of Hubert Simon Baden-Baden (d 1979), of Geneva; 2 s (Hugo Michael Hubert b 1964, Dominic Peter b 1965); *Career* Nat Serv 2 Lt Somerset Light Infantry; chm and dir: Associated British Industries plc, ABI Inc (USA), Synergy Holdings Ltd, The Reward Group, William Dawson Holdings plc, Stag Jointings, Stag (USA); charity appts Davis Laing & Dick; pres: Thomas Coram Fndn, Thames Help Tst, Charities Effectiveness Review Tst; *Recreations* charity work, squash; *Clubs* Carlton, Lansdowne; *Style*— Peter Michael Brown, Esq; 12 Hyde Park Place, London W2 2LH; 1 Lancaster Place, London WC2E 7EB (☎ 071 836 5831)

BROWN, Peter Wilfred Henry; s of Rev Wilfred George Brown (d 1968), and Joan Margaret, *née* Adams; *b* 6 June 1941; *Educ* Marlborough, Jesus Coll Cambridge (MA); *m* 29 March 1969 (m dis), Kathleen, da of Hugh Clarke, of Freetown (d 1982); 1 da (Sonya b 1971); *Career* asst master in classics Birkenhead Sch 1963-66, lectr in classics Fourah Bay Coll Univ of Sierra Leone 1966-68, asst sec SOAS Univ of London 1968-75, sec Br Acad 1983- (dep sec 1975-83, acting sec 1976-77); memb: Br Library Advsy Cncl 1983-89, Cncl Sch of Slavonic and E European Studies Univ of London 1984-, Warburg Inst Univ of London 1987-; *Recreations* sedentary pursuits, musical, bookish; *Style*— Peter Brown, Esq; 34 Victoria Rd, London NW6 6PX; The British Academy, 20-21 Cornwall Terrace, London NW1 4QP (☎ 071 487 5966, fax 071 224 3807)

BROWN, Philip Nicholas; s of Reginald F Brown (d 1970), and Margaret E Gladwell, *née* Simmons (d 1988); *b* 24 June 1942; *Educ* Cheshunt GS, Albion HS, Hobart Coll (BA), Columbia Univ (LLB); *m* 27 Dec 1975, Geraldine Lynn, da of Frederick Grover, of New Malden, Surrey; 2 da (Naomi b 1982, Emily b 1983); *Career* Vol Serv Peace Corps 1966-68; worked on New Jersey Law Reform Project 1969-71, managing ptnr Wilde Sapte 1988- (ptnr 1975); memb: Law Soc 1975, NY Bar 1966, New Jersey Bar 1969; *Recreations* pottery; *Style*— Philip Brown, Esq; Wilde Sapte, Queensbridge House, 60 Upper Thames St, London EC4V 3BD (☎ 071 236 3050, fax 071 236 9624, telex 88773)

BROWN, Ralph; s of Walter Wesley Brown, and Minnie, *née* Clay; *b* 24 April 1928; *Educ* Leeds GS, Leeds Sch of Art, Hammersmith Sch of Art, RCA; *m* 1, 1952 (m dis 1962), Margaret Elizabeth Taylor; 1 s (Matthew b 1953), 1 da (Sara b 1955); m 2, Feb 1964, Caroline Ann, da of Graham Clifton-Trigg (d 1983), of Jersey; 1 s (Jasper b 1965); *Career* sculptor; exhibited widely in UK and Europe 1953-, pt/t tutor RCA 1958-69; work purchased by many public collections incl: Tate Gallery, Leeds, Liverpool, Bristol, Arts Cncl of GB, RCA, Cardiff, Rijksmuseum, Kröller-Müller, Stuyvesant Fndn SA, Art Gallery of NSW, Contemporary Art Soc; ARA 1968, RA 1972; *Style*— Ralph Brown, Esq; Seynckley House, Amberley, Stroud, Glos GL5 5BB

BROWN, Rt Rev Mgr Ralph; s of John William Brown, and Elizabeth Josephine Brown; *b* 30 June 1931; *Educ* Highgate Sch, St Edmund's Coll, Old Hall Green Herts, Pontifical Gregorian Univ Rome; *Career* Middx Regt 1949, served Korea 1950; ordained priest Westminster Cathedral 1959; Dio of Westminster: vice chllr, vice officialis 1964-69, officialis 1969-76 and 1987-, vicar gen 1976-; papal chamberlain 1972, sec Canon Law Soc of GB and I 1986-89 (pres 1980-86), nat coordinator for Papal visit to England and Wales 1982, prelate of honour to HH the Pope 1987, canonical advsr to Br Mil Ordinariate 1987-; memb Old Brotherhood of English Secular Clergy 1987; appointed Knight of the Holy Sepulchre 1984; hon memb Canon Law Soc of: Aust and NZ 1975, Canada 1979, America 1979; *Books* Marriage Annulment (1969, 3 edn 1990), Matrimonial Decisions of Great Britain and Ireland (ed, 1969), The Code of Canon Law in English Translation (co-translator, 1983), various articles in Heythrop Jl, Studia Canonica, Theological Digest, The Jurist; *Clubs* Anglo-Belgian; *Style*— The Rt Rev Mgr Ralph Brown; 42 Francis Street, London SW1P 1QW (☎ 071 828 3255, 071 828 5380)

BROWN, Hon Sir Ralph Kilner; OBE (1945), TD (1952), DL (Warwicks 1956); s of Rev Arthur Ernest Brown, CIE (d 1952), of The Manor House, Churchdown, Glos, and E Gertrude, *née* Parsons (d 1971); *b* 28 Aug 1909; *Educ* Kingswood Sch, Trinity Hall Cambridge; *m* 1943, Cynthia Rosemary, da of Lt-Col George Vernon Breffit, MC; 1 s, 2 da; *Career* served WWII Brig HQ 21 Army Gp 1945; called to the Bar Middle Temple 1934, QC 1958, judge of the High Ct, Queen's Bench Div 1970-84, judge Employment Appeal Tbnl 1976-84; kt 1970; *Recreations* watching cricket and athletics (rep Camb Univ, England and Great Britain); *Clubs* Naval and Military, Hawks (Cambridge); *Style*— The Hon Sir Ralph Kilner Brown, OBE, TD, DL; 174 Defoe House, Barbican, London EC2Y 8DN

BROWN, Ralph William John; s of John F W Brown, and Heather R Laming; *b* 18 June 1957; *Educ* LSE (LLB); *Career* actor; films: Withnail and I 1986, Buster 1987, Diamond Skulls 1988, Impromptu 1989, Alien 3 1991; tv: West 1986, Christabel 1988, Rules of Engagement 1989, The Black & Blue Lamp 1989, Say Hello to the Real Dr Snide 1990; stage: West 1985, Deadlines 1986, Panic 1987, Macbeth 1987, Earwig 1990; playwright Sanctuary (winner Samuel Beckett award for best first play) 1987; *Style*— Ralph Brown, Esq; ICM/Duncan Heath, Paramount House, 162/170 Wardour Street, London W1 (☎ 071 439 1471)

BROWN, Sir Raymond Frederick; OBE (1966); s of Frederick Brown (d 1944), and Susan Evelyn Brown; *b* 19 July 1920; *Educ* Morden Terrace LCC Sch, SE London Tech Coll, Morley Coll; *m* 1, 1942 (m dis 1949), Evelyn Jennings; 1 da (decd); m 2, 1953, Carol Jacquelin Elizabeth, da of Henry Robert Sprinks, of Paris; 2 s, 1 da; *Career* jt fndr Racal Electronics 1950 (chm, md and pres 1950-66), head of def sales Miny of Technol and Def 1966-69, conslt advsr (commercial policy and exports) to Sec of State DHSS 1969-72; chm: Racecourse Technical Services 1970-85, Muirhead plc 1970-85 (chief exec and md 1970-82); indust advsr to NEDC 1976-85, dir National Westminster Bank Outer London Region 1978-85, exec dir STC plc 1985-90; memb Soc of Pilgrims; Liveryman Worshipful Co of: Scriveners, Scientific Instrument Makers; Hon DSc Univ of Bath 1980; kt 1969; *Recreations* polo, farming, shooting, golf; *Clubs* Sunningdale Golf, Guards' Polo (life memb), Swinley Forest Golf, City Livery, Travellers' (Canada, Australia, Ends of the Earth); *Style*— Sir Raymond Brown, OBE

BROWN, Hon Richard Banks Duncan; s of Baron Brown, MBE (Life Peer, d 1985), and Marjorie Hershel Skinner; *b* 31 May 1942; *Educ* Bryanston, Brunel Univ (BTech); *m* 1968, Gillian Mary, da of John Kennedy Carter; 1 s (Cameron b 6 June 1974), 1 da (Emma 3 Aug 1971); *Style*— The Hon Richard Brown; Alderholt Lodge, Alderholt, Fordingbridge, Hants

BROWN, Richard Francis; s of Francis Edwin Brown (d 1981), and Eileen Margaret Edith, *née* Searle; *b* 5 June 1949; *Educ* Chingford Co HS, Poly of Central London (Dip Arch); *m* 10 Sept 1977, Sally Elizabeth, da of Ernest James Little (d 1967); 2 s (Timothy b 1979, Matthew b 1981); *Career* architect; ptnr ATP Group Partnership 1985 (joined 1973); chm W Essex Chapter RIBA 1986-87, pres Lions Club Chingford 1984-85 (memb 1975-88), memb Lions Club Billericay 1988-; memb RIBA 1975, AFAS 1984; *Recreations* photography, archery; *Style*— Richard Brown, Esq; 28 Carson Rd, Billericay, Essex CM11 1SA (☎ 0277 631020); ATP Group Partnership, Mayflower House, The Walk, Billericay, Essex CM12 9YB (☎ 0277 658662, fax 0277 652312, car 0860 350251)

BROWN, (James) Richard; s of James Leonard Brown, MD (d 1972), of Lenham Kent, and Kathleen Mary, *née* Wild; *b* 28 Aug 1940; *Educ* Mill Hill Sch; *m* 20 April 1985, Sally Karen, da of (Percival) Richard Day, of West Meon, Hants; *Career* CA: Arthur Young 1959-68, NM Rothschild 1969-71, Rothschild Investment Trust and successor cos 1971-86, Electra Management Services Ltd 1987-; tstee Childrens' Med Charity; Freeman City of London 1985; FCA; *Recreations* golf, swimming; *Clubs* RAC; *Style*— Richard Brown, Esq; The Oast House, Dale Hill, Ticehurst, E Sussex; Electra Management Services Ltd, 65 Kingsway, London WC2B 6QT (☎ 071 831 6464, fax 071 404 5388, telex 265525)

BROWN, His Hon Judge Robert; s of Robert Brown (d 1966), and Mary Lily, *née* Pullen; *b* 21 June 1943; *Educ* Downing Coll Cambridge (BA, LLB); *m* 1, 1964 (m dis 1971) Susan; 1 s (Andrew Juston b 20 June 1964), 1 da (Jocelyn Fiona 15 Sept 1970), m 2, 3 Nov 1973 Carole, *née* Tait; 2 step s (James Francis b 12 May 1965, Benjamin William b 1 May 1967); *Career* barr Inner Temple 1968, standing counsel to DHSS Northern Circuit 1983-88, recorder Crown Ct 1983-88, circuit judge 1988; *Recreations* golf; *Clubs* Royal Lytham St Annes Golf; *Style*— His Hon Judge Robert Brown; Chambers, 2 Old Bank St, Manchester M2 7PE (☎ 061 832 3791)

BROWN, Robert Crofton; DL (Tyne and Wear 1988); s of William Brown (d 1954), of Newcastle upon Tyne; *b* 16 May 1921; *Educ* Atkinson Rd Tech Sch, Rutherford Tech Coll; *m* 1945, Marjorie, da of Anne Hogg, of Slaithwaite, Yorks; 1 s, 1 da; *Career* served in Royal Signals 1942-46; Gas Bd official; memb Newcastle Corp 1958-68; sec constituency Lab Pty and election agent 1950-66, sponsored by GMWU; MP (Lab): Newcastle upon Tyne West 1966-83, Newcastle upon Tyne North 1983-87; PPS to Min of Tport 1968-70; vice chm: Trade Union Gp of Lab MPs 1970, Parly Lab Pty Tport Gp 1970; Parly under sec of state: DHSS 1974, Def (Army) 1974-79; memb (Newburn Ward) Newcastle upon Tyne CC; *Style*— Robert Brown, Esq; 1 Newsham Close, The Boltons, N Walbottle, Newcastle upon Tyne, NE5 1QD

BROWN, Robert Glencairn; s of William Brown (d 1958), of Glasgow, and Marion, *née* Cockburn (d 1965); *b* 19 July 1930; *Educ* Hillhead HS Glasgow; *m* 25 May 1957, Florence May, da of William Stalker (d 1967), of Glasgow; 2 s (Gordon b 1959, Stewart b 1960); *Career* cmmnd 2 Lt Royal Signals 1949-51, serv Austria; Forestry Cmmn 1947-63, seconded Civil Serv Pay Res Unit 1963-64; princ: Miny of Land and Natural Resources 1964-67, Miny Housing and Local Govt 1968-71; seconded Nat Whitley Cncl 1969, asst dir Countryside Cmmn 1971-77, asst sec DOE 1977-83 (under sec 1983-86), dir Housing Corp 1986-; chm W Middx Centre Nat Tst; *Recreations* gardening, skiing, reading; *Clubs* Ski Club of GB; *Style*— Robert Glencairn Brown, Esq; 2 The Squirrels, Pinner, Middx HA5 3BD (☎ 081 866 8713); Housing Corporation, 149 Tottenham Court Rd, London W1P 0BN (☎ 071 387 9466)

BROWN, Roger Garrett; s of Norman Garrett Brown (d 1945), of Ipswich, Suffolk, and Molly Beryl, *née* Powlyn; *b* 24 Feb 1943; *Educ* Ipswich Sch; *m* 1971, Bridget, *née* O'Sullivan; 1 s (Michael b 31 March 1975), 1 da (Laura b 22 Nov 1979); *Career* CA; articled clerk Ballam and Partners Ipswich 1962-67, Cooper Brothers 1967-76, Dearden Farrow 1976-87, BDO Binder Hamlyn (following merger with Dearden Farrow) 1987-; treas Nat Shearwater Club, former memb First Team YMCA Rugby

Club Ipswich; FCA (ACA 1968); *Recreations* sailing, classic cars, photography; *Clubs* Elite and Reliant Scimitar Car, Stone Sailing, Nat Shearwater; *Style—* Roger Brown, Esq; 20 Old Bailey, London EC4 (☎ 071 489 9000, car 0860 213658)

BROWN, Roger Glendenning; s of Charles Henry Brown, of Cuddington, Northwich, Cheshire, and Gwendoline Irene, *née* Evans (d 1980); *b* 10 Oct 1932; *Educ* Bemrose Sch, Univ of Manchester (BA); *m* 8 Aug 1956, Betty Joy, da of Wilfred Rimmington (d 1964), of Derby; 1 s (Andrew Ashleigh b 26 Sept 1957), 1 da (Rosamund Lindsey b 30 Jan 1961); *Career* dep regnl architect to Liverpool RHB 1971-75, regnl architect to North Western RHA 1975-87, private practice 1987-; chm Component Devpt Gp DHSS 1975-87, pres Manchester Soc of Architects 1989-90; MRIBA 1957 (memb Cncl 1983-86); *Recreations* walking, sketching; *Style—* Roger Brown, Esq; Norley, Warrington, Cheshire

BROWN, Roland; s of Fred Brown (d 1982), of 14 Park Ave, Burnley, Lancs, and Jane Ellen, *née* Fielden (d 1975); *b* 16 Nov 1922; *Educ* Burnley Municipal Coll; *m* 24 Sept 1949, Anne, da of Owen Taylor (d 1975), of 39 Milville St, Burnley, Lancs; 1 s (Peter Anthony b 20 April 1951), 1 da (Wendy Elizabeth b 11 Dec 1956); *Career* WWII RAF 1942-46, Corpl 1946; CA; gp accountant Bury & Mosco Industries Ltd 1961-66, fin dir Coloroll Ltd 1966-76, md Learoyd Packaging Ltd 1976-; memb: Burnley Enterprise Tst, Burnley C of C; FCA 1959 (ACA 1949); *Recreations* golf; *Style—* Roland Brown, Esq; 14 Park Ave, Burnley, Lancs (☎ 0282 380 16); Learoyd Packaging Ltd, Heasandford Mill, Queen Victoria Rd, Burnley, Lancs (☎ 0282 38016, fax 0282 30289)

BROWN, Rt Rev Ronald; *see*: Birkenhead, Bishop of

BROWN, Ronald (Ron); MP (Lab) Edinburgh Leith 1979-; s of James Brown and Margaret McLaren; *b* 1940; *Educ* Ainslie Park HS Edinburgh, Bristo Engrg Inst Edinburgh; *m* 1963, May Smart; 2 s; *Career* formerly served Royal Signals; former AUEW branch chm and shop stewards' convener; memb Campaign Gp Lab MPs 1982-; *Style—* Ron Brown Esq, MP; House of Commons, London SW1

BROWN, Ronald Hedley; OBE (1945); s of Reginald Hedley Brown (d 1967), and Lilian, *née* Howard (d 1963); *b* 2 Feb 1914; *Educ* Cambridgeshire HS, Univ of London (BSc, DipEd); *m* 1, 12 Aug 1939, Margaret Caroline Linforth (d 1982), da of Edward Clifford Pitman (d 1963), of Alpheton, Suffolk; 1 s (Richard Hedley b 1951), 1 da (Patricia Carol b 1947); m 2, Rosemary Dorothy, *née* Carter; *Career* RAF: educn offr 1938-39, intelligence offr 1939-46, Flt-Lt Bircham Newton 1939-41, Sqdn Ldr Iceland 1941-42, Staff Coll 1942, Sqdn Ldr N Russia 1943, Gibraltar 1943-45 (despatches 4 times); Colonial Serv 1947-63 (dir educn N Rhodesia 1959-63); chief examiner Univ of Cambridge Syndicate GCE A Level (general studies) 1979-89; pres Devon Beekeepers Assoc, former ed Beekeeping; *Books* 1000 Years of Devon Beekeeping (1973), Beeswax (1981), Beekeeping - A Seasonal Guide (1985), Honey Bees - A Guide to Management (1988); *Recreations* beekeeping, foreign travel; *Style—* Ronald Brown, Esq, OBE; 20 Parkhurst Rd, Torquay, Devon (☎ 0803 327563)

BROWN, Ronald William; JP (London 1961); s of George Brown; yr bro of late Lord George Brown; *b* 7 Sept 1921; *Educ* Borough Poly; *m* 1944, Mary, *née* Munn; 1 s, 2 da; *Career* MP (Lab) Shoreditch and Finsbury 1964-74, Hackney S and Shoreditch 1974-83 (resigned from Lab Pty 1981, SDP MP from 1981), asst govt whip 1966-67, former chm London Gp Parly Lab Pty, former memb House of Commons Select Ctee Sci & Technol, alderman and ldr Southwark 1964, ldr Camberwell Borough Cncl 1956, former memb Gtr London Labour Pty Exec; former sr lectr in electrical engrg and princ Industl Training Sch; memb Cncl of Europe Assembly & WEU 1965-68, 1970-73, 1975-77 and 1980-83, memb Euro Parl 1977-79; rapporteur on Econ Affrs, Sci and Technol, Tport, Nuclear Power, Environment and Public Health, Data Protection, and Def; memb Bd of Estate Govrs Alleyn's Coll of God's Gift (chm 1976-78), former memb Bd of Govrs Bart's, memb Bd of Govrs and treas Bart's Med Coll, memb NW Thames RHA 1974-; memb Policy Ctee, Nat Ctee and Cncl for Social Democracy 1981-83, Parly advsr to Furniture Timber & Allied Trades Union 1968-81, former Parly conslt to nat and local govt offrs; dep DG Fedn of Master Builders; FBIM; *Style—* Ronald Brown, Esq, JP; 45 Innings Drive, Pevensey Bay, East Sussex BN24 6BH (☎ 0323 764808)

BROWN, Russell Milton; s of Harry Louis Brown (d 1974), and Murielle Katherine, *née* Wartski (d 1983); *b* 20 May 1929; *Educ* Stowe; *Career* Nat Serv RAPC 1951-53; fin offr and clerk to the Govrs Sadlers Wells Theatre 1956-63, chief accountant and prodn controller RSC 1963-66, bursar RCA 1966-86; dir Scottish Ballet; tstee: Royal Ballet Benevolent Fund, Dancers Resettlement Fund, Areopagitica Educnl Tst; hon fell RCA 1986, FCA; Chevalier de L'Ordre Nationale de Merite 1970; *Books* Sadlers Wells Theatre Ballet (ed, 1955); *Recreations* ballet, opera, music, theatre, foreign travel; *Style—* Russell Brown, Esq; Flat 8, 284 Old Brompton Rd, London SW5 9HR; Oak Tree Cottage, Thornborough, Bucks (☎ 071 373 3141)

BROWN, The Hon Mr Justice; Sir Simon Denis; s of Denis Baer Brown (d 1981), and Edna Elizabeth, *née* Abrahams; *b* 9 April 1937; *Educ* Stowe Sch, Worcester Coll Oxford (BA); *m* 31 May 1963, Jennifer, da of (Robert) Prosper Gedye Buddicom (d 1968); 1 da (Abigail b 1964), 2 s (Daniel b 1966, Benedict 1969); *Career* called to the Bar Middle Temple 1961 (Harmsworth Scholar), rec 1979-84, first jr treas counsel Common Law 1979-84, master of the Bench Hon Soc of Middle Temple 1980-, judge of the High Ct of Justice (Queen's Bench Div) 1984-; kt 1984; *Recreations* golf, skiing, theatre, reading; *Clubs* Denham Golf; *Style—* The Hon Mr Justice Simon Brown; Royal Courts of Justice, Strand, London WC2

BROWN, Sir (Frederick Herbert) Stanley; CBE (1959); s of Clement Brown, of Birmingham, and Annie S Brown; *b* 9 Dec 1910; *Educ* King Edward's Sch Birmingham, Univ of Birmingham; *m* 1937, Marjorie Nancy (d 1989), da of William Astell Brown, of Sutton Coldfield; 2 da; *Career* chm CEGB 1965-72; FEng, FIEE, FIMechE; kt 1967; *Style—* Sir Stanley Brown, CBE; Cobbler's Hill, Compton Abdale, Glos GL54 4DR (☎ 024 289 233)

BROWN, Rt Hon Sir Stephen; PC (1983); s of Wilfrid Brown (d 1972), of Longdon Green, Staffs, and Nora Elizabeth Brown; *b* 3 Oct 1924; *Educ* Malvern, Queens' Coll Cambridge; *m* 1951, Patricia Ann, da of Richard Good, of Tenbury Wells, Worcs; 2 s (twins), 3 da; *Career* served WWII as Lt RNVR; called to the Bar Inner Temple 1949; 1974, dep chm Staffs QS 1963-71, QC 1966, rec W Bromwich 1965-71, rec and hon rec 1972-75, bencher 1974, judge High Ct (Queen's Bench) 1977-83 (Family Div 1975-77), presiding judge Midland and Oxford Circuit 1977-81, former memb Parole Bd England & Wales, Lord Justice of Appeal 1983-88, pres Family Div 1988-; memb Advsy Cncl on Penal System 1977, chm Cncl Malvern Coll 1976-; kt 1975; *Recreations* sailing; *Clubs* Garrick, Birmingham; *Style—* The Rt Hon Sir Stephen Brown; President's Chambers, Royal Courts of Justice, Strand, London WC2A 2LL

BROWN, Sir (Arthur James) Stephen; KBE (1967); s of Arthur Mogg Brown, and Ada Kelk, *née* Upton; *b* 15 Feb 1906; *Educ* Taunton, Univ of Bristol; *m* 1935, Margaret Alexandra, da of late D L McArthur; 1 s, 1 da; *Career* former dir Fairey Co; dep chm Chloride Group 1965-73; chm: Stone-Platt Industries Ltd 1968-73, Molins Ltd 1971-78; dir Porvair Ltd 1971-78; fndr memb Export Cncl for Europe 1960; pres: Engrg Employers Fedn 1964-65, CBI 1966-68; memb Nat Econ Devpt Cncl 1969-71; *Style—* Sir Stephen Brown, KBE; Flat 20, Danny House, Hurstpierpoint, W Sussex (☎ 0278 833755)

BROWN, Stephen Kenneth (Steve); s of Kenneth Alan Thomas Brown, of Wimbledon, London, and Valerie Ellen May, *née* Phillips; *b* 15 July 1962; *Educ* Wallington HS; *Career* darts; county player: Surrey 1978-80, London 1981-; championships incl: BDO Mayday Festival champion 1986 and 1987, Thames TV Cockney Classic champion 1986 and 1987, Turnhout Open champion 1987, Antwerp Open champion 1988 and 1989, Dutch Open champion 1988, N American Open champion 1988 and 1989, Winmau Dutch Masters champion 1989, Rotterdam Open champion 1989, Flanders Open champion 1989, NDAGB Nat Pairs champion 1989, USA Int Challenge of Champions Champion 1989, Malta Open Pairs champion 1989 and 1990, Dutch Open Pairs champion 1990, Swiss Open champion 1990, Texas Open champion 1990, London Champion of Champions champion 1990; ranked number 4 by World Darts Fedn 1990; memb: Br Darts Orgn, World Darts Fedn, Dutch Darts Fedn; *Recreations* astronomy, the music of Wagner, first world war poetry; *Style—* Steve Brown, Esq; 95 Welbeck Rd, Carshalton, Surrey SM5 1TB (☎ 081 644 0585); Sports Administration Services, 14 Melrose Tudor, Plough Lane, Wallington, Surrey SM6 8LR (☎ 081 669 0471)

BROWN, Prof Stewart Jay; s of Vernon George Brown, of St Charles, Illinois, USA, and Marion Eleanor, *née* Little; *b* 8 July 1951; *Educ* Glenbard West HS, Univ of Illinois (BA), Univ of Chicago (MA, PhD); *m* 2 Sept 1972, Teri Beth, da of Thomas Dorsey Hopkins (d 1982); 1 s (Adam b 1977), 1 da (Elizabeth b 1980); *Career* Whiting fell in humanities Univ of Chicago 1979-80, asst to Dean and lectr in history N Western Univ 1980-82, assoc prof and asst head Dept of History Univ of Georgia 1982-88, prof of ecclesiastical history Univ of Edinburgh 1988-; memb Cncl: Scot Church History Soc, Scot Catholic Historical Assoc; *Books* Thomas Chalmers and the Godly Commonwealth In Scotland (1982); *Recreations* swimming, hill-walking; *Style—* Prof Stewart Brown; 160 Craigleith Hill Ave, Edinburgh EH4 2NB (☎ 031 343 1712); Department of Ecclesiastical History, University of Edinburgh, New College, Mound Place, Edinburgh EH1 2LU (☎ 031 225 8400)

BROWN, Stuart William; s of Ronald John Brown, and Madelaine Delia, *née* Emery; *b* 19 Sept 1971; *Educ* Newnham Croft; *Career* professional footballer; Luton Town 1990- (apprentice 1988-90); 2 caps E of England under 14, former capt Cambridge City Schoolboys under 14 and under 15; *Recreations* other sports, cars, technical drawing, computers, TV; *Style—* Stuart Brown, Esq; 32 Grantchester St, Newnham, Cambridge CB3 9HY (☎ 0223 63412); Luton Town FC, Kenilworth Stadium, 1 Maple Rd, Luton, Beds LU4 8AW (☎ 0582 411622)

BROWN, Sue; da of George Hockham, of London, and Myrtle Violet, *née* McKelvie; *b* 27 April 1956; *Educ* Clapham Co GS for Girls, Univ Coll London (BA), Kingston Regnl Mgmnt Centre (CNAA Dip); *m* 1, 3 March 1979 (m dis 1986), Michael Thomas Brown; m 2, 2 April 1988, Anthony Danaher, s of Michael Danaher; 1 da (Katie b 7 Feb 1989); *Career* graduate mgmnt trainee London Borough of Wandsworth 1978-89, exec asst to Dame Shirley Porter City of Westminster 1979-82, London Docklands Development Corporation 1982-86 (exec asst to Chief Exec, head of admin, controller High Technol Sales Team), exec dir MSP Communications; memb Bristol Inst of Mgmnt; *Recreations* cooking, travel, films, reading; *Clubs* Women's Network; *Style—* Ms Sue Brown; MSP Communications, Third Floor, South Quay Plaza II, 183 Marsh Wall, London E14 (☎ 071 538 0022, fax 071 538 3849)

BROWN, Sir Thomas; s of Ephraim Hugh and Elizabeth Brown; *b* 11 Oct 1915; *Educ* Royal Belfast Academical Inst; *m* 2 Sept 1988, Dr Eleanor A Thompson; *Career* slr 1938; chm Eastern Health and Social Servs Bd NI 1973-84; kt 1974; *Style—* Sir Thomas Brown; Westgate, Portaferry, Co Down, Northern Ireland (☎ 024 77 28309)

BROWN, Timothy Colin; s of Peter Brindley Brown, of Isles Court, Ramsbury, Wilts, and Margaret Jean, *née* McIntosh; *b* 20 Sept 1957; *Educ* Eton, RMA Sandhurst; *m* 24 Jan 1987, Lady Vanessa Petronel Pelham, yst da of 7 Earl of Yarborough; *Career* 4/7 Royal Dragoon Gds 1976-82 (A/Capt 1980); dir City & Commercial Communications plc; *Recreations* skiing, shooting, backgammon; *Clubs* Cavalry and Gds', Lansdowne; *Style—* Timothy Brown, Esq; 56 Hugh St, London SW1V 4ER (☎ 071 630 1194); Bell Court House, 11 Blomfield St, London EC2 (☎ 071 588 6050, fax 071 628 1861)

BROWN, Timothy Frank (Tim); s of Frank Steel Brown, of The Furrows, Borstal, Rochester, Kent, and Katherine Mary, *née* Osenton; *b* 7 Nov 1944; *Educ* Sir Joseph Williamson's Mathematical Sch; *m* 1 July 1967, Kathleen Patricia, da of Frederick Geoffrey Smith (d 1975); 2 s (Matthew Philip b 1975, Michael James b 1980), 2 da (Karen Patricia b 1971, Amy Clare b 1978); *Career* CA; Larking & Larking 1963-68, Deloite's 1968-69, md UBS Philips & Drew (joined 1969); FCA 1968, ATII 1969; *Style—* Tim Brown, Esq; Angley Lake, Cranbrook, Kent TN17 2PR (☎ 0580 714248); UBS Phillips & Drew, 100 Liverpool St, London (☎ 071 901 3333)

BROWN, Lady Vanessa Petronel; 3 da of 7 Earl of Yarborough, JP; *b* 21 Sept 1961; *m* 24 Jan 1987, Timothy C Brown, o s of Peter Brown; *Style—* Lady Vanessa Brown

BROWN, (Harold) Vivian Bigley; s of Alec Sidney Brown, of Leeds, and Joyce, *née* Bigley; *b* 20 Aug 1945; *Educ* Leeds GS, St John's Coll Oxford (BA), St Cross Coll Oxford (BPhil); *m* 25 July 1970, Jean Josephine, da of Sir Eric Blacklock Bowyer, KCB (d 1963); 2 s (Matthew b 1973, Oliver b 1974); *Career* entered Miny of Technol 1970, private sec to Perm Sec DTI 1972-74; commercial sec: Br Embassy Jedda 1975-79, DTI 1979-86; Cabinet Office 1986-89; head of competition policy dir DTI 1989; *Books* Islamic Philosophy and The Classical Tradition (with S M Stern and A Hourani, 1972); *Recreations* cycling, canoeing, piano; *Style—* Vivian Brown, Esq; Room 620, DTI, 1 Victoria St, London SW1H 0ET

BROWN, William; CBE (1971); s of Robert Brown, of Ayr; *b* 24 June 1929; *Educ* Ayr Acad, Univ of Edinburgh; *m* 1955, Nancy Jennifer, da of Prof George Hunter, of Edmonton, Alberta; 1 s, 3 da; *Career* Scottish TV: London sales mangr 1958, sales dir 1961, dep md 1963, md 1966-90, dep chm 1974-; dir: Radio Clyde Ltd, Scottish Opera Theatre Royal Ltd, Scottish Amicable Life Assur Soc (chm 1989-); Gold medallist Royal TV Soc 1984, Hon DUniv Edinburgh 1990; *Recreations* golf, gardening, films; *Clubs* Caledonian, Prestwick Golf, Royal & Ancient Golf of St Andrews; *Style—* William Brown, Esq, CBE; Scottish Television plc, Cowcaddens, Glasgow G2 3PR (☎ 041 332 9999, telex 77388)

BROWN, Dr William Aiken; TD (1972); s of William Aiken Brown (d 1973), and Gladys Hester, *née* Small; *b* 18 Dec 1933; *Educ* Campbell Coll Belfast, Queen's Univ Belfast (MB BCh, BAO); *m* 1 April 1959, Margaret Elisabeth, da of Edward Churchill Tuke (d 1985); 2 s (Michael William Tuke b 1964, Peter Aiken Edward b 1966), 1 da (Helen Margaret b 1962); *Career* Maj TA 1960-72; conslt radiologist Belfast City Hosp 1965-; FRCR; *Recreations* golf; *Clubs* Royal Co Down, Newcastle (Co Down); *Style—* Dr William Brown, TD; 38 Malone View Rd, Belfast BT9 5PH (☎ 0232 61387); 2 Royal Court, Dundrum Rd, Newcastle, Co Down; X-Ray Dept, Belfast City Hosp, Lisburn Rd, Belfast (☎ 0232 329241)

BROWN, Prof William Arthur; s of Prof Arthur Joseph Brown, of Leeds, and Joan Hannah Margaret Brown; *b* 22 April 1945; *Educ* Leeds GS, Wadham Coll Oxford (BA); *Career* dir Industl Rels Res Unit of the ESRC; prof Univ of Warwick, Montague Burton prof of industl rels Univ of Cambridge 1985-; *Books* Piecework Bargaining (1973), The Changing Contours of British Industrial Relations (1981); *Recreations* gardening, walking; *Style—* Prof William A Brown; Wolfson Coll, Cambridge CB3 9BB (☎ 0223 335900); Faculty of Economics & Politics, Cambridge CB3 9DD (☎ 0223 334236)

BROWN, William Charles Langdon; OBE (1982); s of Charles Leonard Brown (d 1952), and Kathleen May, *née* Tizzard (d 1988); *b* 9 Sept 1931; *Educ* John Ruskin Sch Croydon, Ashbourne GS Derbyshire; *m* 14 Feb 1959, Nachiko, da of Dr Eiji Sagawa (d 1952), of Tokyo, Japan; 1 s (Carl b 1959), 2 da (Lillian b 1963, Naomi b 1967); *Career* Nat Serv RAF 1949-51; Westminster Bank 1947-54; Standard Chartered Bank (formerly Chartered Bank of India, Aust and China): Tokyo 1954-59, Bangkok 1959-62, Hong Kong 1962-69, Singapore 1969-72, Bangkok 1972-75, area gen mangr Hong Kong 1975-87, sr gen mangr (London) for Asia Pacific Region 1987; SC plc: exec dir 1987, md 1988, dep gp chief exec 1988; dep chm SC Bank 1989; unofficial memb of Legislative Cncl of Hong Kong 1980-85; Hon Doctorate in Social Science Chinese Univ Hong Kong 1987; FCIB; *Recreations* mountain walking, skiing, yoga, philately, photography, clasical music; *Clubs* Oriental, RAC; *Style—* William Brown, Esq, OBE; 38 Bishopsgate, London EC2N 4DE (☎ 071 280 7500, fax 071 280 7112); Flat 4, 19 Inverness Terrace, Kensington Gardens, London W2 3TJ; Appleshaw, 11 Central Ave, Findon Valley, Worthing, Sussex BN14 ODS

BROWN, William Ernest; s of William Brown (d 1941); *b* 9 Dec 1923; *Educ* Christ's Hospital and Grocers' Company Sch; *m* 1950, Catherine, *née* McColgan; 1 s, 1 da; *Career* md E G Cornelius and Co Ltd, dir Cornelius Chemical Co Ltd; *Style—* William Brown, Esq; 8 Elm Grove, Hornchurch, Essex

BROWNE; *see*: Gore Browne

BROWNE, Anthony George; s of Aloysious Browne, of London, and Frances, *née* Gurney; *b* 18 June 1950; *Educ* Downside, BNC Oxford (MA); *m* 15 Nov 1969, Monique Odette, da of Maxime Marnat (d 1965), of Paris; 2 da (Geraldine b 1970, Emily b 1972); *Career* CA 1974; Price Waterhouse: joined 1971, Exechequer and Audit Dept 1980-82, ptnr i/c privatisation servs 1983-; treas Wimbledon House Res Assoc; FCA 1975; *Books* Guide to Evaluating Policy Effectiveness; *Recreations* sailing, opera, art, literature; *Clubs* Reform, Royal Cruising, Royal Southern Yacht; *Style—* Anthony Browne, Esq; Caley House, 74 Leopold Rd, Wimbledon, London SW19 7JQ (☎ 081 946 8196); Price Waterhouse, Southwark Towers, 32 London Bridge St, London SE1 9SY (☎ 071 939 2006, fax 071 403 0733)

BROWNE, Benjamin Chapman; s of Benjamin Chapman Browne (d 1968), of Park House, Balsham, Cambs, and Marjorie Grace Hope, *née* Hope-Gill; *b* 18 May 1953; *Educ* Eton, Trinity Coll Cambridge (BA); *m* 28 July 1979, Sara Katharine, da of Brian Pangbourne, of Hythe, Hants; 2 s (Benjamin Chapman b 22 Dec 1982, Edward Pangbourne b 1 April 1985), 1 da (Rebecca Katharine b 24 April 1989); *Career* admitted slr 1978; Morrell Peel and Gamlen Oxford 1979-89, ptnr Clyde and Co London 1985 (joined 1981), res ptnr Clyde and Co Dubai 1989-90; *Recreations* walking, sailing, tennis, gardening, family; *Style—* Benjamin Browne, Esq; Hillside House, Petersfield House, Petersfield Rd, Ropley, nr Alresford, Hants SO24 0EE (☎ 0962 773690); Clyde and Co, Beaufort House, Chertsey St, Guildford GU1 4HA (☎ 0483 31161, fax 0483 67330, telex 859477 CLYDE G)

BROWNE, Charles Egerton; s of John Charles David Browne (d 1952), of Isle of Wight, and Emmie Marie, *née* Egerton (d 1922); *b* 15 Jan 1910; *Educ* Heatherley Sch of Art, Herts Coll of Art and Design; *m* 28 May 1941, Violet Mary Ellen (d 1977), da of Francis William James Squire (d 1947), of Luton, Beds; 1 s (Nicholas Egerton b 1949); *Career* aerospace engr; chm The Egerton Gp of Cos 1941-88; sculptor; distinctions incl: hon mention Paris Salon 1969, Bronze medal Paris Salon 1970, Silver medal Paris Salon 1971, Gold medal Paris Salon 1984, Diplome d'Honneur Galerie Vallombreuse Biarritz, Halliday prize for Portraiture; works exhibited: Whitbread & Co London, Shire Horse Soc Peterborough, Farmers Club London, Watford Museum, Lucy Kemp-Welch Meml St James's Church Bushey; princ Frobisher Sch of Art, govr The Heatherley Sch of Art; Freeman City of London, Liveryman Worshipful Co of Gunmakers 1963; MIProdE, CEng, memb Societe des Artistes Francais; *Recreations* fishing, shooting; *Clubs* Fly Fishers; *Style—* Charles Browne, Esq; Haydon Dell, Merry Hill Rd, Bushey, Herts (☎ 081 950 2035); Egerton Fine Art, The Gallery, Haydon Dell Farm, Merry Hill Rd, Bushey, Herts (☎ 081 950 4769)

BROWNE, (John) Colin Clarke; s of Ernest Browne, JP (d 1964), of Lisburn, Co Antrim, N Ireland, and Isobel Sarah, *née* McVitie; *b* 25 Oct 1945; *Educ* Wallace HS Lisburn, Trinity Coll Dublin (BA); *m* 3 March 1984, Karen Lesley, da of Ian Barr, of Edinburgh; 1 s; *Career* BT: dir Chm's Office 1981-85 (PO 1980-81), chief exec Broadband Servs 1985-86, dir corp rels 1986-; memb Inst of PR; *Recreations* sport, music, reading; *Clubs* Tulse Hill Hockey; *Style—* Colin Browne, Esq; Wandsworth Bridge Rd, London SW6; British Telecom Centre, 81 Newgate St, London EC1A 7AJ (☎ 071 356 5350, fax 071 356 6630, telex 8811510

BROWNE, Coral Edith; *née* Browne; da of Leslie Clarence Browne, and Victoria Elizabeth, *née* Bennett; *b* 23 July 1913; *Educ* Claremont Ladies' Coll Melbourne; *m* 1, 1950, Philip Westrope Pearman (d 1964); m 2, 1974, Vincent Price; *Career* actress; *Style—* Miss Coral Browne; c/o Duncan Heath Associates Ltd, Paramount House, 162/170 Wardour Street, London W1V 3AT

BROWNE, Desmond John Michael; QC (1990); s of Sir Denis Browne, KCVO (d 1967), of London, and Lady Moyra Browne, *née* Ponsonby, DBE; *b* 5 April 1947; *Educ* Eton, New Coll Oxford; *m* 1 Sept 1973, Jennifer Mary, da of Frank Wilmore, of Brierfield, Lancs; 2 da (Natasha b 1974, Harriet b 1976); *Career* called to the Bar Gray's Inn 1969; *Recreations* British prints, Australiana, the South Downs; *Clubs* Brooks's, Beefsteak; *Style—* Desmond Browne, Esq, QC; 10 South Square, Gray's Inn, London WC1R 5EU (☎ 071 242 2902, fax 071 831 2686)

BROWNE, Hon Dominick Geoffrey Thomas; s and h of 4 Baron Oranmore and Browne, *qv*, and his 1 w Mildred Helen (d 1980), da of Hon Thomas Egerton; *b* 1 July 1929; *m* 25 Oct 1957 (m dis 1974), Sara Margaret, da of late Dr Herbert Wright, of 59 Merrion Sq, Dublin; *Career* poet, author; *Style—* The Hon Dominick Browne; 6 Kensington Square, London W8 5EB

BROWNE, Donald John Woodthorpe; JP (1977); s of Harold Browne; *b* 1 Dec 1924; *Educ* Dulwich, Hertford Coll Oxford; *m* 1965, Dinah, da of Arthur Gurling, MC, of London W1; 1 s, 2 da; *Career* Sub Lt RNVR; chm Hays Oils & Chemicals and assoc cos 1980-; *Recreations* penal matters, country living; *Clubs* Western, Ulster; *Style—* Donald Browne, Esq, JP; Hays Oils & Chemicals Ltd, Redding-Muirhead, Falkirk FK2 9TS (☎ 0324 712712, telex 779314)

BROWNE, Lady Ulick; Fiona; *née* Glenn; *m* 1962, as his 2 w, Lord Ulick Browne, s of late Lt-Col Lord Alfred Eden Browne, DSO, s of 5 Marquess of Sligo, who was raised to the rank of a Marquess' son (1953) and who d 1980; 1 s, 1 da,; *Style—* Lady Ulick Browne; 32 The Little Boltons, London SW10

BROWNE, Hon Garech Domnagh; s of 4 Baron Oranmore and Browne, and Oonagh Lady Oranmore and Browne, *née* Guinness; *b* 25 June 1939; *Educ* Castle Park Dublin, Le Rosey Switzerland; *m* 1980, Princess Harshad Purna Devi, *née* Jadeja, da of HH Sri Mahendra Sinhji, Maharaja of Morvi (d 1957), and HH Sri Vijaykuverba, Maharani of Morvi, *née* Jhala; *Career* chm: Claddagh Records Ltd, Woodtown Music Publications Ltd; landowner (6,000 acres); *Style—* The Hon Garech Browne; 13 Rue de la Douzaine, Fort George, St Peter Port, Guernsey; Luggala, Rundwood, Co Wicklow, Ireland (☎ 81 81 50); Claddagh Records Ltd, Dame House, Dame St, Dublin 2 (☎ 77 80 34)

BROWNE, (Harold) Godfree Rodan; s of Robert Hugh Browne, of Augusta, Western Australia, and Jean Eleanor Douglas, *née* Rodan (d 1984); *b* 19 Sept 1940; *Educ* Uppingham, Univ of London (LLB); *m* 18 Dec 1965 (m dis 1989), Frances Mary, da of late Francis Joseph Woods, of Luton; 1 s (Christopher), 1 da (Mary (Mrs Wood)); *Career* magistrates' cts S Rhodesian Civil Serv 1958-68, advocate Rhodesia 1968-70 (Botswana 1969), lectr Herts Educn Ctee 1970-71, practising barr 1972-; former chm Luton Churches Housing Ltd, memb Ctee Family Housing Assoc; FBIM 1981, MRIN 1981; *Recreations* cruising and offshore racing; *Clubs* Royal Ocean Racing; *Style—* Godfree Browne, Esq; 1 Middle Temple Lane, London EC4Y 9AA (☎ 071 583 0659)

BROWNE, Henry; s of Henry Clarence Browne (d 1974), and Veva Helen, Symons (d 1978); *b* 11 July 1944; *Educ* Felsted, Gstaad Int Switzerland; *m* 30 May 1969, Marion Carole, da of Charles Andrew Wenninger, of Poole, Dorset; 1 s (Stephen Henry b 15 Dec 1975), 1 da (Juliette Caroline b 30 Nov 1971); *Career* memb Lloyds 1972, chm Walker and Staff Holdings plc 1974; *Recreations* golf; *Clubs* Moor Park Golf, RAC; *Style—* Henry Browne, Esq; Walker & Staff Holdings plc, Walker House, Boundary St, London E2 7JG (☎ 071 739 8456, fax 071 729 5695, tlx 21394)

BROWNE, Henry Buxton; s of Richard Buxton Browne (d 1922), of Durban, S Africa, and Mary Hill Ryrie (d 1949); kinsman of Barons Brocket, Croft and Denman; *b* 28 Oct 1919; *Educ* private sch; *m* 4 April 1953, Enid Dorothy, da of George Cuthbert Jarvis (d 1965), of Petts Wood, Kent; *Career* served 1940-46 RA, RAOC and REME in UK, France and Germany; FCA; *Recreations* golf, genealogical research; *Clubs* Chislehurst Golf; *Style—* H Buxton Browne, Esq; 1 Moorlands, Wilderness Rd, Chislehurst, Kent BR7 5HB

BROWNE, John Ernest Douglas de la Valette; MP (C) Winchester 1979-; s of Col Ernest Coigny de la Valette Browne, OBE, of Woodside House, Freshford, nr Bath, and late Victoria Mary Eugene, *née* Douglas; *b* 17 Oct 1938; *Educ* Malvern, RMA Sandhurst, Cranfield Inst of Technol (MSc), Harvard Business Sch (MBA); *m* 1965 (m dis 1983), Elizabeth Jeannette Marguerite, *née* Garthwaite; m 2, 1986, Elaine Boylen, *née* Schmidt; *Career* served Grenadier Gds Br Guyana (bn pilot), Cyprus, BAOR 1959-67, Capt 1963, TA Grenadier Gds (Vol) 1981-, Maj 1986; assoc: Morgan Stanley & Co NY 1969-72, Pember & Boyle London 1972-74; dir ME ops Euro Banking Co Ltd 1974-78, md Falcon Finance Management 1978-, advsr Barclays Bank 1978-83; dir: The Churchill Clinic 1980-, Worms Investment Ltd 1981-83, Scan Sat Broadcasting Ltd 1987-, Int Bd of World Paper 1988-, Tijari Finance Ltd 1989-; memb: Westminster City Cncl 1974-78, Ct Univ of Southampton 1979-; govr Malvern Coll 1981-; memb: Treasy Select Ctee 1982-87, Social Security Select Ctee; chm Cons Backbench Smaller Business Ctee 1984-87 (vice-chm 1983-84); sec: Cons Backbench Fin Ctee 1981-84, Cons Backbench Def Ctee 1982-84; UK del N Atlantic Assembly 1986-, elected rapporteur on human rights 1989-; Liveryman Worshipful Co of Goldsmiths 1982; OStJ; *Recreations* riding, sailing, skiing, shooting, golf; *Clubs* Boodle's, Turf; *Style—* John Browne, Esq, MP; House of Commons, London SW1A 0AA

BROWNE, Lady Karen Lavinia; 2 da of Earl of Altamont; *b* 3 July 1964; *Style—* Lady Karen Browne

BROWNE, (Matthew) Kennedy; s of John Browne (d 1954), of Glasgow, and Mary Kennedy, *née* Goslan (d 1969); *b* 21 Nov 1929; *Educ* Whitehill Sr Secdy Sch, Univ of Glasgow (BSc, MB ChB, MD); *m* 15 July 1954, (Elspet Mary) Elma, da of Joseph Henry Walter Wood (d 1975), of Bothwell; 1 s (David b 29 Jan 1970), 2 da (Katy b 1964, Mandy b 1966); *Career* Flt Lt RAF Inst of Aviation Med Farnborough 1955-58; conslt surgn Glasgow Royal Infirmary 1963-77, hon clinical lectr Univ of Glasgow 1963-, surgn Belvedere Hosp 1970-77, conslt surgn Monklands Dist Gen Hosp Airdrie; clinical sub-dean Faculty of Med Univ of Glasgow, memb W of Scotland Postgrad Med Ctee; FRCS Edinburgh 1961, FRCS Glasgow 1978; *Books* Clinical Gastroenterology (1972), Adult Surgery (1973), Taurolin, Ein Neues Konzept Zur Antimikrobiellen. Chemotherapie Chirugischer Infektionen (contrib, 1985); *Recreations* wandering in Europe, Spanish studies; *Clubs* RAF, Piccadilly; *Style—* Kennedy Browne, Esq; 7 Winton Drive, Glasgow G12 0PZ (☎ 041 339 4926); 9 Finca La Nayca, Javea, Alicante, Spain; Kelvingrove Consulting Rooms, 901 Sauchiehall St, Glasgow G3 7TD (☎ 041 339 5550/339 5260)

BROWNE, Lady Lucinda Jane; yst da of Earl of Altamont; *b* 18 May 1969; *Style—* The Lady Lucinda Browne

BROWNE, Hon Martin Michael Dominick; s of 4 Baron Oranmore and Browne by his 1 w, Mildred, da of Hon Thomas Egerton, s of 3 Earl of Ellesmere, JP, DL; *b* 27 Oct 1931; *Educ* Eton; *m* 1958, Alison, Margaret, o da of John Bradford; 1 s (Shaun), 1 da (Cara); *Career* stockbroker; *Clubs* White's; *Style—* The Hon Martin Browne; Berghane Hall, Castle Camps, Cambridge CB1 6TN (☎ 079 984 304)

BROWNE, (Edward) Michael Andrew; QC (1970); yr s of Prof Edward Granville Browne (d 1926), of Cambridge, and Alice Caroline, *née* Blackburne Daniell (d 1925); bro of Rt Hon Sir Patrick Browne, *qv*; *b* 29 Nov 1910; *Educ* Eton, Pembroke Coll Cambridge (MA); *m* 1937, Anna Florence Augusta, da of James Little Luddington (d 1935), of Wallington, King's Lynn; 2 da (Maria, Alice); *Career* served WWII 1939-45, Capt RA, Adjt 82 HAA Regt Gibraltar, GSO III Directorate of Mil Ops War Office; called to the Bar Inner Temple 1934, bencher 1964; *Clubs* Athenaeum; *Style—* Michael Browne, Esq, QC; 19 Wallgrave Rd, London SW5 0RF

BROWNE, Brig Michael Edward; TD (and two Bars), DL (1989); s of John Edward Stevenson Browne, CBE (d 1976), and Muriel May, *née* Lambert (d 1965); *b* 6 Dec 1942; *Educ* Uppingham; *m* 11 Dec 1970, Susan Elizabeth, da of James Hugh Neill, CBE; 2 da (Anna Jane b 27 April 1974, Nicola Catherine b 1975); *Career* TA 1961-, cmd 3 WFR 1982-84, currently Brig TA UKLF; admitted slr 1966, dep coroner Retford Dist 1970-80, dep registrar Supreme Ct of Judicature 1986-; former chm Bassetlaw Cons Assoc; memb Law Soc 1966; *Recreations* squash, tennis, golf; *Clubs* Army and Navy; *Style—* Brig Michael Browne, TD, DL; Eel Pie Farm, Markham Moor, Retford, Notts DN22 0QX (☎ 0777 83 581); 19 Churchgate, Retford, Notts DN22 6PF (☎ 0777 707401, 0777 707407, 0836 739391)

BROWNE, Lady Moyra Blanche Madeleine; *née* Ponsonby; DBE (1977, OBE 1962); o da of 9 Earl of Bessborough, GCMG, PC (d 1956); *b* 2 March 1918; *Educ* privately; *m* 10 Dec 1945, as his 2 w, Sir Denis John Wolko Browne, KCVO, FRCS (d 1967), s of late Sylvester Browne, of Australia; 1 s, 1 da; *Career* SEN 1946; chm Hospitality Ctee Victoria League 1956-62, vice-chm Central Cncl Victoria League 1961-65; supt-in-chief St John Ambulance Bde 1970-83 (dep supt-in-chief 1964-70), vice pres Royal Coll of Nursing 1970-85; nat chm Support Gps and govr Res into Ageing 1987; DGStJ 1984 (DSJ 1970, CSJ 1968); hon memb Br Assoc of Paediatric Surgeons; *Recreations* music, fishing, travel; *Style—* The Lady Moyra Browne, DBE; 16 Wilton St, London SW1 (☎ 071 235 1419)

BROWNE, Nicholas Egerton; s of Charles Egerton Browne, of Bushey, Herts, and Violet Mary Ellen, *née* Squire (d 1977); *b* 12 April 1949; *Educ* Rugby, Univ of Edinburgh (BSc); *Career* CA; Arthur Andersen & Co 1972-80, ptnr Egerton Browne & Co 1980-81, md Egerton Gp of Companies 1984-88 (dir 1981-83); mgmnt conslt; sr ptnr Egerton Browne & Co 1988-; art dealer; managing ptnr Egerton Fine Art 1988-, dir Bushey Museum Tst 1985-, chm Bushey Museum Services Ltd 1988-; Freeman City of London, Liveryman Worshipful Co of Gunmakers 1975; FCA 1982; *Recreations* skiing, fishing, shooting; *Clubs* Flyfishers', Farmers', City Livery, SCGB; *Style—* Nicholas Browne, Esq; Haydon Dell, Merry Hill Rd, Bushey, Herts (☎ 081 950

2035); Haydon Dell Farm, Merry Hill Rd, Bushey, Herts (☎ 081 950 4769)

BROWNE, Hon Mrs Tara; Noreen Anne; da of Sean MacSherry, of Co Down; *m* 1963, Hon Tara Browne (d 1966), s of 4 Baron of Oranmore and Browne; 2 s; *Style*— The Hon Mrs Tara Browne; 19 Eaton Row, SW1

BROWNE, Rt Hon Sir Patrick (Reginald Evelyn); OBE (1945), TD (1945), PC (1974); er s of Prof Edward Granville Browne, Arabic and Persian scholar at Cambridge (d 1926, himself s of Sir Benjamin Browne, JP, DL, an engr & sometime Mayor Newcastle), and Alice Caroline, *née* Blackburne Daniell; bro of Michael Browne, QC, *qv*; *b* 28 May 1907; *Educ* Eton, Pembroke Coll Cambridge (hon fell 1975-); *m* 1, 1931, Evelyn Sophie Alexandra (d 1966), o da of Sir Charles Walston and sis of Baron Walston; 2 da (*see* Sir Peter Swinnerton-Dyer); m 2, 1977, Lena, da of James Atkinson; *Career* served Army 1939-45, GSOI, Lt-Col; called to the Bar Inner Temple 1931, QC 1960, bencher 1962, High Ct Judge Queen's Bench Div 1965-74, Lord Justice of Appeal 1974-80; controller Royal Opera House Devpt Land Tst 1981-84; kt 1965; *Clubs* Garrick, Cambridge County; *Style*— The Rt Hon Sir Patrick Browne, OBE, TD; Thriplow Bury, Thriplow, Cambs (☎ 076 317 208 234)

BROWNE, Percy Basil; DL (Devon 1984); s of Capt W P Browne, MC, of Higher Hougton, Blandford, Dorset (d 1970), and M R Hoare (d 1953); *b* 2 May 1923; *Educ* Eton; *m* 1, 1947, Pamela Iwerne (d 1951), da of late Lt-Col Harold Exham, DSO, of Iwerne Minster, Dorset; 1 s (Anthony b 1949); m 2, 1953, Jenefer Mary, da of late Major Gerald Petherick, of The Mill House, St Cross, Winchester, Hants; 2 s (Benjamin b 1954, Toby b 1955), 1 da (Mary Alice b 1959); *Career* served WWII Italy and NW Europe (cmmnd Royal Dragoons); MP (C) Torrington Div of Devon 1959-64; dir Aggledore Shipbuilders 1965-72 (former chm), N Devon district cncllr 1973-79 (vice chm 1978-79); memb SW Regnl Hosp Bd 1967-70, vice chm N Devon Hosp Mgmnt Ctee 1967-74, chm N Devon Meat Ltd 1982-86, Miny of Agric's SW Regnl Panel 1985-; chm West of England Building Society 1986- (vice chm 1985-86, dir Western Counties Building Society 1965-85); farmer; rode in Grand Nat 1953; High Sheriff Devon 1978; *Style*— Percy B Browne, Esq, DL; Wheatley House, Dunsford, Exeter (☎ 0647 52037)

BROWNE, Peter Kilmaine; s of Noël Francis Howe Browne (d 1943), and hp of 7 Baron Kilmaine; *b* 1920; *m* 1948, Grace Dorothy Robson, of Nakuru, Kenya; 2 da; *Style*— Peter Browne Esq; Morningside Farm, P O Box 692, Rustenburg, Transvaal

BROWNE, Prof Roger Michael; s of Arthur Leslie Browne (d 1974), of Birmingham, and Phyllis Maud, *née* Baker (d 1942); *b* 19 June 1934; *Educ* Berkhamsted Sch, Univ of Birmingham (BSc, BDS, PhD, DDS); *m* 31 May 1958, Lilah Hilda, da of Issac Harold Manning (d 1960), of Leek; 1 s (Andrew b 1963), 1 da (Nicola b 1960); *Career* Univ of Birmingham: lectr in dental surgery 1960-64, lectr in dental pathology 1964-67, sr lectr in oral pathology 1967-77, prof 1977-, head Dept of Oral Pathology 1979-, dir of Dental Sch 1986-89, postgrad advsr in dentistry 1977-82; visiting prof Univ of Lagos Nigeria 1969; pres: Br Dental Assoc Hosps Gp 1986-87, Br Soc for Oral Pathology 1985-86 and 1990-, Section of Odontology Birmingham Med Inst 1975-76; FDS RCS 1962, FRCPath 1979; *Books* Colour Atlas of Oral Histopathology (with E A Marsland, 1975), A Radiological Atlas of Diseases of the Teeth and Jaws (with H D Edmondson and P G J Rout, 1983); *Recreations* walking, rugby football; *Style*— Prof Roger Browne; Dept of Oral Pathology, Dental School, St Chad's Queensway, Birmingham B4 6NN (☎ 021 236 8611)

BROWNE, Sheila Jeanne; CB (1977); da of Edward Elliott Browne; *b* 25 Dec 1924; *Educ* Lady Margaret Hall Oxford, Ecole des Chartes Paris; *Career* asst lectr Royal Holloway Coll Univ of London, tutor and fell St Hilda's Coll Oxford and lectr in French 1951-61; sr chief inspr DES 1974-83 (formerly staff inspr and chief inspr Secondary Educn, dep sr chief inspr DES 1972-74), princ Newnham Coll Cambridge 1983- (succeeding Mrs J E Floud); memb: CNAA 1984-, Marshall Aid Cmmn 1987-, Franco-British Cncl 1987-; hon fell: St Hilda's Coll Oxford 1978, Lady Margaret Hall Oxford 1978; Hon DLitt Warwick 1981; Hon LLD: Exeter 1984, Birmingham 1987; *Style*— Miss Sheila Browne, CB; Newnham College, Cambridge

BROWNE-CLAYTON, Capt Robert Bruce; s of Lt-Col William Patrick Browne-Clayton (d 1971), of 13 Nutley Rd, Dublin, and Janet Maitland Broce, *née* Jardine; direct descendant of Robert Browne of Browne's Hill, Carlow (d 1677) and of James Bruce, who discovered source of Blue Nile; *b* 25 April 1940; *Educ* Loretto, RMA Sandhurst, Royal Agric Coll Cirencester; *m* 1 March 1969, Jane Evelyn Reine, da of Eric Peter Butler, of Orchard Close, Blagdon, nr Bristol; 1 s (Benedict John (Ben) b 1970), 1 da (Clare Louise b 1973); *Career* Capt Royal Green Jackets KRRC, served Germany and Br Guiana 1960-68; dir and co sec Economy Car Hire Ltd 1968-71, fin conslt 1971-74; desk offr responsible for agric, fisheries, food, forestry and rural affrs Cons Res Dept 1976-84; dir economic and public affairs The Building Employers Conf; fndr and first sec Nat Agric and Countryside Forum; cncllr London Borough of Greenwich 1978-82, vice chm Greenwich Cons Assoc 1983-84 and 1987-; *Recreations* shooting, fishing, painting, music, reading, tennis, golf; *Clubs* University and Kildare Street; *Style*— Robert Browne-Clayton, Esq; 34 Park Vista, Greenwich, London SE10 9LZ

BROWNE-WILKINSON, Rt Hon Sir Nicolas Christopher Henry; PC (1983); s of late Canon Arthur R Browne-Wilkinson, and Molly Browne-Wilkinson; *b* 30 March 1930; *Educ* Lancing, Magdalen Coll Oxford; *m* 1, 1955, Ursula, da of Cedric de Lacy Bacon (d 1987); 3 s, 2 da; m 2, 20 April 1990, Mrs Hilary Tuckwell; *Career* QC 1972; judge Ct of Appeal Jersey & Guernsey 1976-77, High Ct judge (Chancery) 1977, Lord Justice of Appeal 1983-85, vice chllr Supreme Ct 1985; *Recreations* gardening, music; *Style*— The Rt Hon Sir Nicolas Browne-Wilkinson; Royal Courts of Justice, The Strand, WC2

BROWNING, Frank Sacheverel (Chips); s of Frank Sacheverel Browning, of 5 Canonbury St, Berkeley, Gloucester, and Ivy Mary Jean, *née* Spice (d 1967); *b* 28 Oct 1941; *Educ* Dulwich, Univ of St Andrews (MB ChB); *m* 9 July 1966, (Carol) Angela, da of George Sutcliffe Seed (d 1958); 1 s (Benjamin Sacheverel b 1968), 2 da (Georgina Mary b 1970, Rebecca Louise b 1973); *Career* sr registrar in plastic surgery Leeds and Bradford 1971-80, conslt plastic surgn The Gen Infirmary at Leeds and St James's Univ Hosp 1980-; microsurgery res fell St Vincent's Hosp Melbourne 1975-76; contrib to chapter in book; Hon MO Headingly Rugby Football Club, med dir Bramham Three Day Event; Freeman City of London; memb: BAPS, BAAPS, Med Equestrian Assoc; FRCS; *Style*— Chips Browning, Esq; The General Infirmary at Leeds, Great George St, Leeds LS1 3EX (☎ 0532 432799 ext 3403)

BROWNING, (Walter) Geoffrey; s of Lt Walter Samuel Browning, of Highleaden, Mere, Knutsford, Cheshire, and Dorothy Gwendoline, *née* Hill (d 1987); *b* 6 Nov 1938; *Educ* Burnage GS Manchester; *m* 1, 20 June 1964 (m dis 1982), Barbara; 1 s (Matthew b 18 Sept 1967), 2 da (Helen b 11 May 1965, Claire b 22 April 1969), 1 adopted s (Jon b 16 March 1972); m 2, 17 Aug 1983, Pauline Ann, da of William Wilkinson, of Lockgate, West Runcorn, Cheshire; 2 da (Alexandra b 7 June 1984, Danielle b 9 Sept 1985); *Career* CA, asst gp slr Peat Marwick Mitchell and Co 1961-63 (articled clerk 1955-60), div co sec The Steetly Co Ltd 1963-64, fin dir Syd Abrams Ltd 1964-69, jt md Boaloy Ltd 1969-90, dir Marling Industs plc 1990; underwriting memb Lloyds 1980-; FCA; *Recreations* sailing, golf; *Clubs* Duquesa Golf (Spain), Duquesa Sailing; *Style*— Geoffrey Browning, Esq; Cherry Rise, Lynwood, Hale, Cheshire WA15 ONF (☎ 061 980 5884)

BROWNING, Michael Lovelace; s of Harold Louis Browning (d 1963), of Exmouth; *b* 18 March 1937; *Educ* Kelly Coll Tavistock; *m* 1965, Anna Lynne, da of late Lawrence Clifford White, of Sampford Peverell; 3 da; *Career* dir HAT Group plc 1976-89 (ret); FCA; *Style*— Michael L Browning, Esq; Elm Tree Farm, Harts Lane, Hallatrow, Bristol BS18 5EA (☎ 0761 52218)

BROWNING, (David) Peter James; CBE (1984); s of Frank Browning (d 1950), and Lucie Audrey, *née* Hiscock (d 1986); *b* 29 May 1927; *Educ* Christ's Coll Cambridge (MA), Sorbonne, Univ of Strasbourg, Univ of Perugia; *m* 1953, Eleanor Berry, da of John Henry Forshaw, CB, MC (d 1973); 3 s (Paul, Jonathan, Nicholas); *Career* educator; asst dir of educn Cumberland LEA 1962-66, dep chief educn offr Southampton LEA 1966-69; chief educn offr: Southampton 1969-73, Beds 1973-89; memb: Schs Cncl Governing Cncl and 5-13 Steering Ctee 1969-75, Cncl Univ of Southampton 1970-73, C of E Bd of Educn Schs Ctee 1970-75, Cncl Nat Youth Orch 1972-77, Br Educnl Admin Soc (chm 1974-78, fndr memb Cncl of Mgmnt), UGC 1974-79, Taylor Ctee of Enquiry into Mgmnt and Govt of Schs 1975-77, Governing Body Centre for Info on Language Teaching and Res 1975-80, Euro Forum for Educnl Admin (fndr chm 1977-84), Library Advsy Cncl (England) 1978-81, Cambridge Inst of Educn Govrs (vice chm 1980-89), Univ of Cambridge Faculty Bd of Educn 1983-, Br Sch Technol Cncl of Mgmnt 1984-88, Univ of Lancaster Cncl 1988-; govr: Gordonstoun Sch 1985-, Lakes Sch Windermere 1988-, Charlotte Mason Coll of Higher Educn Ambleside 1988-; conslt Miny of Educn: Sudan 1976, Cyprus 1977, Italy 1981; Sir James Matthews Memorial Lecture (Univ of Southampton) 1983; Cavaliere Order of Merit (Italy) 1985, Cdr Order of Palmes Académiques (France) 1989; FRSA 1981; *Publications* Julius Caesar for German Students (ed 1957), Macbeth for German Students (ed 1959); *Recreations* music, travel, gardening; *Style*— Peter Browning, Esq, CBE; Park Fell, Skelwith, nr Ambleside, Cumbria LA22 9NP (☎ 05394 33978)

BROWNING, Ralph Morgan; s of Lt-Col John Morgan Browning (d 1974), of Coventry, Warwicks, and Anne, *née* Chalker (d 1971); *b* 9 Aug 1925; *Educ* Cheltenham, Queen's Coll Oxford (MA); *m* 6 Dec 1950, Mary Louise, da of Capt Martinelle McLachlin (d 1925), of St Thomas, Ontario, Canada; *Career* Lt 1/7 Rajput IA 1945-47; mktg mangr The Procter and Gamble Co (UK, France, Italy, USA) 1950-66, mktg dir Reynolds Tobacco Co (Europe and ME) 1967-70, dir L'Orèal (UK) 1970-75, jt md Rèmy and Associés 1976-90, chm Rèmy and Associès 1990-, md Reid Pye and Campbell Ltd 1982-; memb Chelsea Cons Assoc; Freeman Worshipful Co of Distillers 1987; *Recreations* fishing, stalking, tennis; *Clubs* Turf, Hurlingham, Carlton, Oxford & Cambridge; *Style*— Ralph M Browning, Esq; 14 Curzon St, London W1Y 7FH (☎ 071 499 8701, fax 071 409 2988)

BROWNJOHN, John Nevil Maxwell; s of Gen Sir Nevil Charles Dowell Brownjohn (d 1973), and Isabelle, *née* White (d 1984); *b* 11 April 1929; *Educ* Sherborne, Lincoln Coll Oxford (MA); *m* 19 Nov 1968, Jacqueline Sally; 1 s (Jonathan b 1971), 1 da (Emma b 1969); *Career* cmmnd Somersetshire LI 1948, served Royal W African Frontier Force 1948-49; author; chm Exec Ctee Translators Assoc Soc of Authors 1976; Schlegel-Tieck Special Award 1979; US PEN Goethe-House Prize 1981; *Books incl:* The Night of the Generals (1962), Memories of Teilhard de Chardin (1964), Klemperer Recollections (1964), Brothers in Arms (1965), Goya (1965), Rodin (1967), The Interpreter (1967), Alexander the Great (1968), The Poisoned Stream (1969), The Human Animal (1971), Hero in the Tower (1972), Strength Through Joy (1973), Madam Kitty (1973), A Time for Truth (1974), The Boat (1974), A Direct Flight to Allah (1975), The Manipulation Game (1976), The Night of the Long Knives (1976), The Hittites (1977), Willy Brandt Memoirs (1978), Canaris (1979), Life with the Enemy (1979), A German Love Story (1980), Richard Wagner (1983), The Middle Kingdom (1983), Solo Run (1984), Momo (1985), The Last Spring in Paris (1985), Invisible Walls (1986), Mirror in the Mirror (1986), Assassin (1987), The Battle of Wagram (1988), Daddy (1989), The Marquis of Bolibar (1989), Eunuchs for Heaven (1990), Little Apple (1990), Jaguar (1990); *screen credits*: Tess (in collaboration with Roman Polanski and Gérard Brach, 1980), The Boat (1981), Pirates (1986), The Name of the Rose (1986), The Bea (1989); *Recreations* music; *Style*— John Brownjohn, Esq; The Vine House, Nether Compton, Sherborne, Dorset DT9 4QA (☎ 0935 814553)

BROWNLIE, Alistair Rutherford; OBE (1987); s of James Rutherford Brownlie (d 1966), of Edinburgh, and Muriel, *née* Dickson (d 1971); ancestors were dependents of the Dukes of Hamilton and Brandon; *b* 5 April 1924; *Educ* George Watson's Coll, Univ of Edinburgh (MA, LLB, Dip Admin Law); *m* 20 June 1970, Martha Barron Mounsey, da of Thomas Mounsey (d 1964); *Career* served WWII as bombardier RA and radio op with 658 Air Op Sqdn RAF in Europe and India; slr in private practice; memb Lord Merthyr's Ctee of House of Lords on the Bastardy (Blood Tests) Bill and thereafter of Lord Amulree's Ctee, memb Cncl of Law Soc of Scot 1966-78, slr for the poor in High Ct (immediately prior to introduction of Criminal Legal Aid in Scot), served Legal Aid Central Ctee 1970-86; fndr memb and sometime pres Forensic Sci Soc (Silver medal 1977); lectr and author on legal aspects of Forensic Sci, co-author Drink Drugs and Driving; elder Morningside Utd Church Edinburgh; sec Soc of Slrs in Supreme Courts of Scot, memb Scot Legal Aid Bd 1986-90; *Recreations* the spade, the pen and the saw; *Style*— Alistair R Brownlie, Esq, OBE; Cherrytrees, 8 Braid Mount, Edinburgh EH10 6JP (☎ 031 447 4255); 2 Abercromby Place, Edinburgh EH3 6JZ (☎ 031 556 4116)

BROWNLIE, Prof Ian; QC (1979); s of John Nason Brownlie (d 1952), and Amy Isabella, *née* Atherton (d 1975); *b* 19 Sept 1932; *Educ* Alsop HS Liverpool, Oxford (MA, DPhil, DCL); *m* 1, 1957, Jocelyn Gale; 1 s, 2 da; m 2, 1978, Christine Apperley; *Career* called to the Bar Gray's Inn 1958, in practice 1967-, bencher Gray's Inn 1988; fell Wadham Coll Oxford 1963-76, prof of int law LSE 1976-80, Chichele prof of public int law Oxford 1980-; co-ed Br Year Book of International Law, dir of studies Int Law Assoc; author of various works on public int law; fell All Souls Coll Oxford 1980-; FBA (1979); *Style*— Prof Ian Brownlie, QC; 43 Fairfax Rd, Chiswick, London W4 1EN (☎ 081 995 3647); 2 Hare Court, Temple London EC4Y 7BM (☎ 071 583 1770); All Souls Coll, Oxford (☎ 0865 279 342)

BROWNLOW, Air Vice-Marshal Bertrand; CB (1982), OBE (1967), AFC (1962); s of Robert John Brownlow, and Helen Louise Brownlow; *b* 13 Jan 1929; *Educ* Beaufort Lodge Sch; *m* 1958, Kathleen Shannon; 2 s, 1 da; *Career* joined RAF 1947, def and air attaché Stockholm 1969-71, CO Experimental Flying (Royal Aircraft Estab) Farnborough 1971-73, Dir Flying (Research and Devpt) MOD 1974-77, Cmdt Aeroplane and Armament Experimental Estab Boscombe Down 1977-80, RAF Coll Cranwell (AOC 1980-82, Asst Cmdt, Offr and Flying Training 1973-74), Dir-Gen Training RAF 1982-83, ret 1984; dir Marshall of Cambridge (Engineering) Ltd (joined 1984); awarded Silver medal of the Royal Aero Club for services to gliding FRAeS; *Style*— Air Vice-Marshal Bertrand Brownlow, CB, OBE, AFC; Woodside, Abbotsley Rd, Croxton, Huntingdon, Cambridgeshire (☎ 048087 663)

BROWNLOW, (Andrew) Claude; s of Lt-Col Andrew L'Estrange Brownlow (d 1972), and Jean Kennedy, *née* Risk (d 1962); *b* 23 Oct 1935; *Educ* Marlborough; *m* 2 June 1964, Kathleen Morag, da of Lt-Col John Meiklejohn Bannerman, MBE, ED (d 1988); 1 s (Patrick Andrew John b 15 Aug 1970), 1 da (Catriona Jean b 8 Aug 1965); *Career* Nat Serv A&SH 1955-56; British Aluminium Co Ltd 1962-64, PA Management

Consultants Ltd 1964-65, McLintock Moores and Murray Management Consultants 1965-67, gp fin controller Anglo Thai Corp 1967-74, fin dir Guthrie Berhad 1975-76, self employed mgmnt and fin conslt 1977-81, chm Winsec Financial Services Ltd 1981-, chm Winsec Management Services Ltd 1988-; hon treas Tiptree Cons Assoc, govr Thurstable Sch; MICAS; *Recreations* squash (15 caps Scotland), golf, shooting, fishing, Scottish dance music; *Clubs* New (Edinburgh), Tanglin, Singapore Island Country, Royal Bangkok Sports; *Style*— Claude Brownlow, Esq; 33 Chapel Rd, Tiptree, Colchester, Essex CO5 0RA (☎ 0621 815268); Brownlows (Chartered Accountants), 1 The Centre, Church Rd, Tiptree, Colchester, Essex CO5 0HF (☎ 0621 815047, fax 0621 817965, car 0836 7348

BROWNLOW, 7 Baron (1776 GB), of Belton; Sir Edward John Peregrine Cust; 10 Bt (1677 E); s of 6 Baron Brownlow (d 1978), by his 1 w, Katherine, da of Brig-Gen Sir David Kinloch, 11 Bt, CB, MVO; *b* 25 March 1936; *Educ* Eton; *m* 1964, Shirlie, da of late John Yeomans, of The Manor Farm, Hill Croome, Upton-on-Severn; 1 s; *Heir* s, Hon Peregrine Edward Quintin Cust b 9 July 1974; *Career* memb Lloyd's; dir Hand-in-Hand Fire and Life Insur Soc (branch of Commercial Union Assur Co Ltd) 1962-82, md Harris & Dixon (Underwriting Agencies) Ltd 1976-82, High Sheriff of Lincs 1978-79; *Clubs* White's, Pratt's; *Style*— The Rt Hon the Lord Brownlow; La Maison des Prés, St Peter, Jersey, CI

BROWNLOW, James Christy; s of Col Guy James Brownlow, DSO, DL (d 1960), of Ballywhite, Portaferry, Co Down, NI, and Elinor Hope Georgina, *née* Scott (d 1978); *b* 12 Dec 1922; *Educ* Eton; *m* 28 July 1951, Susan Honor Rushton, da of James Parkinson Barnes (d 1975), of Springfield, Alderley Edge, Cheshire; 1 s (William James b 1952), 2 da (Elisabeth Susan b 1955, Joanna Sarah b 1957); *Career* 60 Rifles 1941-47 (served Western Desert, Italy and Greece), Cheshire Yeomanry 1947-53; dir: W M Christy and Sons Ltd 1950-55, Christy and Co 1951-72; High Sheriff Co Down 1971; *Clubs* Army & Navy; *Style*— James Brownlow, Esq; The Old Rectory, Kelling, Holt, Norfolk NR25 7EW (☎ 0263 713657)

BROWNLOW, James Hilton; CBE (1984), QPM (1978); s of late Ernest Cuthbert Brownlow, and Beatrice Annie Elizabeth Brownlow; *b* 19 Oct 1925; *Educ* Worksop Central Sch; *m* 1947, Joyce Key; 2 da; *Career* served WW II RAF Flt-Sgt 1943-47; slr's clerk 1941-43, Police Constable Leicester City Police 1947, from Police Constable to Detective Chief Supt with Kent County Constabulary 1947-69, Asst Chief Constable Hertfordshire Constabulary 1969-75, asst to HM Chief Inspector of Constabulary Home Office 1975-76, Dep Chief Constable Greater Manchester Police 1976-79, Chief Constable S Yorks Police 1979-82, HM Inspector of Constabulary for NE England 1983-; *Recreations* golf, music, gardening, travel; *Clubs* Sheffield Club; *Style*— James Brownlow, Esq, CBE, QPM

BROWNLOW, Jeremy Taylor; *b* 4 Dec 1945; *Educ* Heversham Sch, St Catharine's Coll Cambridge; *m* 1971, Lynden, *née* Snape, 3 s, 1 da; *Career* Clifford-Turner 1968-73 (articled clerk and asst slr), ptnr Company Dept Clifford Chance 1973; *Style*— Jeremy Brownlow, Esq; Clifford Chance, Royex House, Aldermanbury Square, London EC4V 7LD

BROWNLOW, Peter; s of Frederick Brownlow, of Leeds, and Margaret Brownlow (d 1985); *b* 4 June 1945; *Educ* Rothwell GS; *m* 1971, Judith Margaret, da of Douglas Alton, of Leeds; 2 s (Nicholas Simon b 1975, James Mark b 1978); *Career* accountant; fin dir Border Television plc; *Recreations* sports; *Style*— Peter Brownlow; Quarry Bank, Capon Hill, Brampton, Cumbria CA8 1QN; Border Television plc, The Television Centre, Carlisle CA1 3NT (fax 0228 511193)

BROWNLOW, Maj William Stephen; JP (Co Down 1956), DL (Co Down 1961); er s of Col Guy James Brownlow, DSO, DL (d 1960), of Ballywhite, Portaferry, Co Down, and Elinor Hope Georgina (d 1978), 2 da of Col George John Scott, DSO; descended from a jr branch of Lord Lurgan's family (*see* Burke's Irish Family Records 1976); *b* 9 Oct 1921; *Educ* Eton; *m* 11 Jan 1961, Eveleigh Finola Margaret, o da of Lt-Col George William Panter, MBE (d 1946), of Enniskeen, Newcastle, Co Down; 1 s (James George Christy b 20 Sept 1962), 2 da (Camilla Jane b 29 July 1964, Melissa Anne b 8 May 1968); *Career* Maj RB 1940-54 (wounded, despatches), Staff Coll Camberley 1951, Hon Col 4 Bn Royal Irish Rangers TAVR 1973-78; High Sheriff Co Down 1959; memb: Irish Nat Hunt Ctee 1956, Down CC 1969-72, NI Assembly 1973-75, Irish Turf Club 1982; master E Down Foxhounds 1959-62; chm: Downpatrick Race Club 1960-, NI Region Br Field Sports Soc 1971-; *Recreations* field sports; *Clubs* Army and Navy; *Style*— Maj William Brownlow, JP, DL; Ballywhite House, Portaferry, Co Down, N Ireland BT22 1PB (☎ 02477 28325)

BROWNRIGG, Deva; da of Charles William Cayzer, Bt (d 1940), of Kinpurnie Castle, Newtye, Angus, Scotland, and Lady Cayzer, OBE (d 1980); *b* 22 Jan 1923; *Educ* Miss Spalding's Queensgate London, Queen's Secretarial Coll; *m* 20 July 1946, John Studholme, s of late Lt Cdr John Studholme Brownrigg RN, RTD, DSC; 1 s (Henry John Studholme b 20 May 1961); *Career* 3 Offr WRNS 1943-46, Hove HMS Lizard Staff of C in C Plymouth, Staff of FOLEM Leiut Egypt, Staff of C in C Med, Italy and Malta; *Recreations* painting, pottery, gardening; *Clubs* The Lansdowne, Royal Lymington Yacht, Royal Yachting Assoc, RNSA Island Sailing (Cowes); *Style*— Mrs Deva Brownrigg; Badgers Wood, Lymore Lane, Milford-on-Sea, Lymington, Hants SO4 10TX (☎ 42063)

BROWNRIGG, Michael Gawen; s and h of Sir Nicholas Brownrigg, 5 Bt; *b* 11 Oct 1961; *Style*— Michael Brownrigg, Esq

BROWNRIGG, Sir Nicholas Gawen; 5 Bt (UK 1816); s of late Gawen Egremont Brownrigg, 2 s of 4 Bt; suc gf, Rear Adm Sir Douglas Egremont Robert Brownrigg, 4 Bt, CB, 1939; *b* 22 Dec 1932; *m* 1, 1959 (m dis 1965), Linda Louise, da of Jonathan B Lovelace, of Beverly Hills, California, USA; 1 s, 1 da; m 2, 1971, Valerie Ann, da of Julia A Arden, of Livonia, Michigan, USA; *Heir* s, Michael Gawen Brownrigg; *Style*— Sir Nicholas Brownrigg, Bt; PO Box 548, Ukiah, Calif 95482, USA

BROWNRIGG, Philip Henry Akerman; CMG (1964), DSO (1945), OBE (1953), TD (1945); s of Charles Edward Brownrigg (d 1942), of Oxford, and Valerie, *née* Akerman (d 1929); *b* 3 June 1911; *Educ* Eton, Magdalen Coll Oxford; *m* 1936, Marguerite Doreen, da of Capt C R Ottley (d 1936); 3 da; *Career* served WWII Reconnaissance Corps (RAC) NW Europe, Lt-Col 1944; journalist 1934-52, ed Sunday Graphic 1952; Anglo American Corp of SA 1953; dir in: Rhodesia 1961-63, Zambia 1964-65; dir Nchanga Consolidated Copper Mines Ltd and Roan Consolidated Mines Ltd 1969-80; pres Zambia Soc 1980-; Insignia of Honour (Zambia) 1981; *Books* Biography of Kenneth Kaunda (1989); *Recreations* golf, sport on TV; *Style*— Philip Brownrigg, Esq, CMG, DSO, OBE, TD; Wheeler's, Checkendon, nr Reading, Berks (☎ 0491 680328)

BROWNSDON, Susannah Clare; s of John F Brownsdon, and Caroly, *née* Stevenson; *b* 16 Oct 1965; *Educ* Millfield, Univ of Calgary; *Career* int swimmer; Olympic Games 1980-88; Cwlth Games: 1982 Bronze medal 100m breaststroke, Silver medal medley relay 1986, Gold medal medley relay; Euro Championships 1981-89 (100m breaststroke Silver medal 1981), World Championships 1982 and 1986, World Cup and Br Grand Prix Champion 1988 and 1989, Capt Br Women's team 1989, Alberta Achievement award 1988; Cwlth Games 1990 Bronze medal 100m breaststroke, Silver medal medley relay; *Recreations* wine tasting; *Style*— Ms Susannah Brownsdon

BROWSE, Prof Norman Leslie; s of late Reginald Dederic Browse, BEM, and late Margaret Louise, *née* Gillis; *b* 1 Dec 1931; *Educ* East Ham GS, St Bart's Hosp Med Coll (MB BS), Bristol Univ Med Sch (MD); *m* 6 May 1957, Jeanne Audrey, da of Lt-Col Victor Richard Menage, RE (d 1952); 1 s (Dominic James b 1962), 1 da (Sarah Lesley b 1960); *Career* Capt RAMC 1957-59; lectr in surgery Westminster Hosp 1962-64, res assoc Harkness Cwlth fell Mayo Clinic 1964-65, prof of surgery St Thomas' Hosp London 1982- (conslt surgn and reader in surgery 1965-72, prof of vascular surgery 1972-82); pres: Euro Soc for Cardiovascular Surgery 1982-84, Surgical Res Soc 1990-, Venous Forum RSM 1990-; chm: Assoc of Profs of Surgery 1983-87, Specialist Advsy Ctee in Surgery 1985-88, Br Atherosclerosis Discussion Gp 1988-; cncl memb: Assoc of Surgns of GB & Ireland 1985-88, Royal Coll of Surgns 1986-, Marlborough Coll 1989-; hon memb: American Soc for Vascular Surgery, Australian Vascular Soc; pres elect Surgical Res Soc; *Books* Physiology and Pathology of Bed Rest (1964), Symptoms and Signs of Surgical Disease (1978), Reducing Operations for Lymphoedema (1987), Diseases of the Veins (1988); *Recreations* golf, sailing, marine painting; *Style*— Prof Norman Browse; Blaye House, 8 Home Farm Close, Esher, Surrey KT10 9HA; Dept of Surgery, St Thomas' Hospital, London SE1 (☎ 071 928 9292 ext 2516)

BROXBOURNE, Baron (Life Peer UK 1983), of Broxbourne, Co Herts; Sir Derek Colclough Walker-Smith; 1 Bt (UK 1960), of Broxbourne, Co Herts, TD, PC (1957), QC (1955); s of late Sir Jonah Walker-Smith; *b* 13 April 1910; *Educ* Rossall, Ch Ch Oxford (BA); *m* 1938, Dorothy, da of Capt Louis John Walpole Etherton, of Rowlands Castle, Hants; 1 s, 2 da; *Heir* (to btcy only) s, John Jonah Walker-Smith; *Career* served WW II Lt-Col RA (TA); called to the Bar Middle Temple 1934, bencher 1963; MP (C): Hertford 1945-55, Hertfordshire East 1955-83; chm: Cons Members (1922) Ctee 1951-55, Cons Advsy Ctee on Local Govt 1954-55, parly sec to Bd of Trade 1955-56, econ sec to HM Treasury 1956-57, min state Bd of Trade Jan to Sept 1957, min Health 1957-60; *Clubs* Carlton; *Style*— The Rt Hon the Lord Broxbourne, TD, PC, QC; 25 Cavendish Close, London NW8 (☎ 071 286 1441)

BROZOVIC, Dr Milica; da of Filip Vasic (d 1973), of Beograd, Yugoslavia, and Jelisaveta Vukovic (d 1958); *b* 30 Sept 1937; *Educ* Univ of Belgrade (MD); *m* 12 Aug 1958, Branko Brozovic, s of Ivan Brozovic (d 1981), of Salzburg; 1 s (Nicholas b 10 April 1972); *Career* res asst Royal Postgraduate Med Sch 1964-66, registrar on haematologist St Bart's 1966-69, scientific staff Nat Inst for Med Res 1969-74, conslt haematologist Northwick Park Hosp 1974-75, head haematology Central Middx Hosp 1975-; fndr and med advsr Sickle Cell Soc, ctee memb Br Soc for Haematology, memb Br Ctee for Standards in Haematology; MRCPath 1968, FRCPath 1980; *Books* Manual of Clinical Blood Transfusion (with B Brozovic, 1987); co-author of many standard reference books incl: Blood and its Diseases, Practical Haematology, Bleeding Disorders; *Recreations* hill walking, reading, embroidery; *Style*— Dr Milica Brozovic; Department of Haematology, Central Middlesex Hosptial, Acton Lane, London NW10 7NS (☎ 081 965 5733 ext 2111)

BRUCE; *see*: Cumming-Bruce, Hovell-Thurlow-Cumming-Bruce

BRUCE, Hon Alastair John Lyndhurst; s and h of 4 Baron Aberdare, PC; *b* 2 May 1947; *Educ* Eton, Ch Ch Oxford; *m* 1971, Elizabeth Mary Culbert, da of John F Foulkes; 1 s, 1 da; *Style*— The Hon Alastair Bruce; 16 Beverley Road, London SW13 0LX

BRUCE, (Robert) Alister Peel; AFC (1943); s of Col Kenneth Hope Bruce, DSO (d 1968), and Lorna, *née* Burn-Murdoch (d 1948), of Trevereux Hill, Limpsfield; *b* 27 Aug 1915; *Educ* Eton; *m* 1941, Monica, da of R H A Jeff (lost at sea 1941), of Kuala Lumpur; 3 da (Claudia, Linda, Claire); *Career* WWII RAF Trg Cmd, 2 TAF, served Canada, Europe and USA; dir: Practical Investmt Co plc 1953-, London & St Lawrence Investmts plc 1954-, Pennant Properties plc 1961-, Tst of Property Shares plc 1980-; FCA; *Recreations* tennis, golf, shooting, fishing; *Clubs* Army & Navy; *Style*— Alister Bruce, Esq, AFC; Cinderhill, Chailey, E Sussex (☎ 0825 72 2603)

BRUCE, Hon Charles Benjamin; yst s of 4 Baron Aberdare, PC; *b* 29 May 1965; *Educ* Eton; *m* 7 April 1990, Anna, da of late Bo Brannerydh, of Gävle, Sweden; *Career* chartered accountant; *Clubs* Queen's; *Style*— The Hon Charles Bruce

BRUCE, Lord; Charles Edward Bruce; s and h of 11 Earl of Elgin, and Kincardine, Broomhall, Dunfermline KY11 3DU; *b* 19 Oct 1961; *Educ* Eton, St Andrew's Univ (MA); *m* in Alaska 29 July 1990, Amanda L Movius; *Career* page of honour to HM Queen Elizabeth, The Queen Mother 1975-77; *Style*— Lord Bruce

BRUCE, Hon (Edward) David; yst s of 10 Earl of Elgin (d 1968); *b* 29 Feb 1936; *Educ* Eton, Balliol Coll Oxford; *m* 1960, Sara Elizabeth Wallop, yr da of Capt Newton James Wallop William-Powlett, DSC, RN, of Cadhay, Ottery St Mary, Devon; 1 s, 1 da; *Career* formerly Lt Intelligence Corps; *Style*— The Hon Edward Bruce; Blairhill, Rumbling Bridge, Kinross

BRUCE, David Ian Rehbinder; s of Ian Stuart Rae Bruce, MC (d 1967), and Reinhildt Hilda Henriette Reinholdtsdotter, *née* Baroness Rehbinder; *b* 16 Aug 1946; *Educ* Eton, Oriel Coll Oxford (MA); *m* 4 Dec 1976, Anne Margaret Turquand, da of Col David Frank Turquand Colbeck, OBE; 2 s (Edward b 1984, Ian (twin) b 1984); *Career* CA; Peat Marwick Mitchell & Co 1968-72; Cazenove & Co: investmt analyst 1972-79, conslt Ctee to Review the Functioning of Fin Inst 1977-79; Royal Dutch/Shell Gp: asst treas advsr Shell Int Petroleum Co Ltd 1979-80, mangr fin planning Shell Canada Ltd 1980-83, treas & controller Shell UK Ltd 1983-86; exec dir fin and admin The Int Stock Exchange 1986-90; gp fin dir Guinness Mahon Holdings plc 1990-; memb The Hundred Gp, memb 1992 Membership and Tech Ctees of the Assoc of Corporate Treasurers 1988-; Freeman City of London 1977, Liveryman Worshipful Co of Merchant Taylors 1980; FCA, ASIA, FCT; *Recreations* shooting, fishing; *Clubs* Turf, Pratt's, City of London, White's; *Style*— David Bruce, Esq; 5 Bolingbroke Grove, London SW11 6ES (☎ 081 673 1434); Guinness Mahon Holdings plc, 32 St Mary at Hill, London EC3P 3AJ (☎ 071 623 6222, fax 071 626 7007, telex 893065)

BRUCE, Hon George John Done; yr s of 11 Baron Balfour of Burleigh (d 1967), and Violet Dorothy Done; *b* 28 March 1930; *Educ* Westminster, Byam Shaw Sch of Drawing and Painting; *Career* vice pres Royal Soc of Portrait Painters 1984-90 (memb 1959-); cmmnd works incl: three portraits of Archbishop Ramsey for the Church of England, Baron Lane as Lord Chief Justice, speaker George Thomas for the House of Commons, Baron Butler of Saffron Walden for Trinity Coll Cambridge, Sir Alan Cottrell vice chllr Cambridge; RP; *Recreations* windsurfing, skiing, hang gliding; *Clubs* Athenaeum; *Style*— The Hon George Bruce, JD; 6 Pembroke Walk, London W8 6PQ (☎ 071 937 1493)

BRUCE, Hon Henry Adam Francis; s of 4 Baron Aberdare, KBE, PC, DL; *b* 5 Feb 1962; *Educ* Eton, Trinity Coll Oxford; *Career* serving bro to order of St John 1990, slr 1988; *Clubs* Royal Tennis Court, Hampton Court, Lansdowne; *Style*— The Hon Henry Bruce; 23 Campana Rd, London SW6 4AT

BRUCE, Sir Hervey James Hugh; 7 Bt (UK 1804); s of Sir Hervey John William Bruce, 6 Bt (d 1971); *b* 3 Sept 1952; *Educ* Eton, Mons Officer Cadet Sch; *m* 1979, Charlotte Sara Jane, da of John Temple Gore (s of late Capt Christopher Gore and Lady Barbara, da of 16 Earl of Eglinton); 1 s (Hervey Hamis Peter Bruce b 1984), 1 da (Laura Crista b 1984); *Career* Maj Gren Gds; *Recreations* tapestry, polo; *Clubs* Cavalry and Guards; *Style*— Sir Hervey Bruce, Bt

BRUCE, Ian Cameron; MP (C) South Dorset 1987-; s of Henry Bruce (d 1970), and

(Ellen) Flora, *née* Bingham, of Frinton, Essex; *b* 14 March 1947; *Educ* Chelmsford Tech HS, Univ of Bradford, Mid-Essex Tech Coll; *m* 6 Sept 1969, Hazel, da of Edward Sidney Roberts (d 1981); 1 s (James b 1974), 3 da (Kathleen b 1975, Maxine b 1977, Tasmin b 1978); *Career* apprentice Marconi; work study engr: Sainsbury's, Pye & Marconi; work study mangr: Pye (factory mangr Pye), ESI, Sinclair; md Ian Bruce Assocs Ltd, employment & mgmnt conslt, formerly md BOS Recruitment Gp; Parly candidate (C) Burnley 1983, Euro Parly candidate (C) Yorkshire West 1984; chm Cons Candidates Assoc 1986-87; *Recreations* badminton, sailing, hill walking, scouting, camping; *Style—* Ian C Bruce, Esq, MP; House of Commons, London SW1A 0AA (☎ 071 219 5086)

BRUCE, Capt Ian Norton Eyre; s of Lt-Col Eyre Bruce, MC (d 1961), of Norton-Sub-Hamdon, Somerset, and Nona Elland, *née* Norton (d 1944); *b* 28 Feb 1928; *Educ* Wellington, RMA Sandhurst; *m* 10 July 1959, Elizabeth Mary, da of J D Lyon-Smith (d 1986), of Inkberrow, Worcestershire; 2 s (Andrew b 1961, Rupert b 1963); *Career* 11 Hussars (PAO) 1948-58, served BAOR, Malaya and UK, ADC to HE The Govr Gen of NZ 1953-55; dir: J Walter Thompson Co Ltd 1969-79 (exec 1958-59), J Walter Thompson Group Ltd 1974-81; chm: Lexington International PR Ltd 1974-81 (md 1969-74), JWT Recruitment Advertising Ltd 1977-81; dir PR Conslts Assoc 1970-80, regnl dir The British Horse Soc 1982-; MIPR 1969, MIPA 1974; *Recreations* painting, field sports, photography; *Clubs* Cavalry and Guard's; *Style—* Capt Ian Bruce; Netherwood Hse, Dumfries DG1 4TY (☎ 0387 53 090)

BRUCE, Ian Waugh; s of Thomas Waugh Bruce (d 1980), and Una Nellie, *née* Eagle (d 1987); *b* 21 April 1945; *Educ* King Edward VI Sch Southampton, Central HS Arizona, Univ of Birmingham (BA); *m* 19 June 1971, Anthea Christine (Tina), da of Dr P R Rowland, of London; 1 s (William Waugh (Tom) b 18 May 1976), 1 da (Hannah b 20 Dec 1970); *Career* apprentice chem engr Courtaulds 1964-65, mktg trainee then mangr Unilever 1968-70; chm Coventry Int Centre 1964, memb Arts Cncl of GB (Art Panel, Art Film Ctee, New Activities Ctee) 1967-71; Sir Raymond Priestley Expeditionary Award Univ of Birmingham 1968; conslt UN Div of Social Affrs 1970-72, appeals and PR offr then asst dir Age Concern Eng 1970-74, spokesman Artists Now 1973-77, dir Nat Volunteer Centre 1975-81, Nat Good Neighbour Campaign 1977-79; memb: Exec Ctee Nat Cncl for Voluntary Orgns 1978-81, Cncl Ret Execs Action Clearing House 1978-83; sec Volunteurope Brussels 1979-81, advsr BBC Community Progs Unit 1979-81, memb advsy cncl Centre for Policies on Ageing 1979-83, controller of secretariat then asst chief exec Borough of Hammersmith and Fulham 1981-83, memb Educn Advsy Cncl IBA 1981-83, dir gen RNIB 1983-; memb: Steering Ctee Disability Alliance 1985-, Exec Ctee Age Concern Eng 1986-, Nat Advsy Cncl on Employment of Disabled People 1987-; co chm Disability Benefits Assoc; memb ICA, MBIM 1975, FBIM 1981; *Books* Public Relations and the Social Services (1972), Patronage of the Creative artist (jtly, 1974, 2 edn 1975); papers on: visual handicap, voluntary and community work, old people, contemporary art and marketing; *Recreations* the arts, the countryside; *Style—* Ian Bruce, Esq; 54 Mall Road, London W6

BRUCE, Hon James Michael Edward; JP (Perthshire 1962); 2 s of 10 Earl of Elgin and 14 of Kincardine (d 1968); *b* 26 Aug 1927; *Educ* Eton, RMC, RAC Cirencester; *m* 1, 1950, Hon (Margaret) Jean Dagbjørt Coats, da of 2 Baron Glentanar, KBE (d 1971); 2 s (and 1 s decd), 1 da; m 2, 1975, Morven-Anne, da of Alistair Macdonald; 2 s, 2 da; *Career* served Scots Gds; chm: SWOAC Hldgs Ltd, Scottish Woodlands Ltd, Flintshire Woodlands Ltd; memb Home Grown Timber Advsy Ctee, vice pres Scottish Opera, chm RSA in Scotland; FRSA, FInstD; *Clubs* New (Edinburgh), Pratt's; *Style—* The Hon James Bruce, JP; Dron House, Balmanno, by Perth PH2 9HG (☎ 073881 2786)

BRUCE, Hon Katherine Gordon; *née* Bruce; da of late 7 Lord Balfour of Burleigh; *b* 27 Nov 1922; *Educ* Univ of Oxford; *m* 1946 (m dis 1961), Thomas Riviere Bland, MC; 1 s, 2 da; reverted by deed poll 1975 to surname of Bruce; *Style—* The Hon Katherine Bruce; 25 Kew Green, Kew, Richmond, Surrey TW9 3AA

BRUCE, Malcolm Gray; MP (Lib Democrat) Gordon 1983-; s of David Stewart Bruce, of White Wold, Mere Lane, Heswall, Wirral, and Kathleen Elmslie, *née* Delf; *b* 17 Nov 1944; *Educ* Wrekin Coll Shropshire, St Andrew's and Strathclyde Univs (MA, MSc); *m* 1969, Veronica Jane, da of Henry Coxon Wilson, of West Kirby, Wirral; 1 s (Alexander b 1974), 1 da (Caroline b 1976); *Career* contested (Lib): North Angus and Mearns Oct 1974, West Aberdeenshire 1979; ldr Scot Lib Democrats 1988-, vice pres Nat Deaf Childrens' Soc; rector Univ of Dundee 1986-89; *Clubs* Nat Lib; *Style—* Malcolm Bruce, Esq, MP; House of Commons, London SW1

BRUCE, Hon Mrs Victor; Margaret Charlotte; da of Alfred Ernest Beechey, of Hilgay, Downham Market, Norfolk; *m* 1941, as his 2 w, Hon Victor Austin Bruce (d 1978), yst s of Col 2 Baron Aberdare (d 1929); 1 s, 2 da; *Style—* The Hon Mrs Victor Bruce; Cranmore, 1 Frog Grove Lane, Wood Street Village, Guildford, Surrey

BRUCE, Marie Louise; da of Sir Stanley Gordon Irving, KBE, CMG (d 1972), of Well Place, Ipsden, Oxon, and Lady Irene Hazel Irving, MBE, *née* Maclean (d 1986); *b* 27 July 1931; *Educ* Downham Herts, St George's Ascot, Panama Co-ed, St Anne's Coll Oxford (BA, MA); *m* 17 Sept 1959, George Ludgate Bruce, s of George Bruce (d 1942), of Thurso, Scotland; 2 s (Rupert b 1964, Hugo b 1969), 1 da (Tessa b 1965); *Career* author historical biographies; *Books* Anne Boleyn (1972), The Making of Henry VIII (1977), The Usurper King (1986); *Recreations* art; *Style—* Mrs Marie Louise Bruce

BRUCE, Lady Martha Veronica; OBE (1958), TD, DL (Fife 1987); da of late 10 Earl of Elgin and (14 of) Kincardine, KT, CMG, TD, CD, and Hon Dame Katherine Cochrane, DBE, da of late 1 Baron Cochrane of Cults, and Lady Gertrude Boyle, OBE, da of 6 Earl of Glasgow; *b* 7 Nov 1921; *Educ* Downham; *Career* Lt-Col WRAC (TA) CWRAC 51 Highland Div (TA); lady-in-waiting to HRH the late Princess Royal Jan to March 1965; govr: Greenock Prison 1969-75 (asst govr 1967-69), HM Instn Cornton Vale 1975-83; *Recreations* gardening, hill walking; *Style—* Lady Martha Bruce, OBE, TD, DL; Gardener's Cottage, The Old Orchard, Limekilns, Dunfermline KY11 3HS

BRUCE, Hon Mrs Bernard; Mary Patricia; *née* Macdonald; da of Maj Donald Ramsay Macdonald, DSO, MC, of Hollymount, Co Carlow (d 1934), and Helen, *née* McMahon; *m* 1 (m dis), Gerald Francis Annesley, of Castlewellan, Co Down; 2 s (Francis Rory, William Richard); m 2, 1976, as his 3 w, Hon Bernard Bruce, MC (d 1983), yst s of 9 Earl of Elgin and (13 Earl of) Kincardine, KG, PC, GCSI, GCIE; *Style—* The Hon Mrs Bernard Bruce; Culross Abbey House, Culross, By Dunfermline, Fife KY12 8JB

BRUCE, Sir (Francis) Michael Ian; 12 Bt (NS 1628); s of Sir Michael William Selby Bruce, 11 Bt (d 1957); discontinued use of Christian name Francis; *b* 3 April 1926; *m* 1, 1947 (m dis 1957), Barbara Stevens, da of Francis J Lynch; 2 s; m 2, 1961 (m dis 1963), Frances Keegan; m 3, 1966 (m dis 1976), Marilyn Anne, da of Carter Mullaly; *Heir* s, Michael Ian Richard Bruce; *Career* US Marine Corps 1943-46, memb Sqdn A 7 Regt NY 1948 (ret); Master's Ticket 1968; pres: Newport Sailing Club and Academy of Sail 1977-, American Maritime Co 1980-; *Clubs* Balboa Bay, Vikings of Orange (both Newport Beach); *Style—* Sir Michael Bruce, Bt; 106 Via Antibes, Lido Isle, Newport Beach, Calif 92663, USA; Newport Sailing Club and Academy of Sail, 3432 Via Oporto, Suite 204, Newport Beach, Calif 92663, USA (☎ 714 675 7100)

BRUCE, Michael Ian Richard; s (by 1 m) and h of Sir (Francis) Michael Bruce, 12 Bt; *b* 10 Dec 1950; *Style—* Michael Bruce, Esq

BRUCE, Michael Jonathan; s of Oliver Bruce (d 1954), and Helen Marjorie, *née* King-Stephens; *b* 22 March 1920; *Educ* Sherborne; *m* 26 April 1942, Joyce Irene, da of George John Pepper (d 1984); 2 s (Colin b 1948, Timothy b 1951); *Career* WWII gunner RA 1940, cmmnd 2 Lt 1941, Lt 1943, invalided out 1944; admitted slr 1946; joined a family firm of slrs 1949, sole proprieter 1951-85 (until amalgamation with Halsey Lightly London 1985), conslt 1987-; memb Royal Br Legion Droxford Hants; memb Law Soc; *Recreations* jazz music, collection of nostalgia, cinema organs, theatre, TV, railways; *Style—* Michael Bruce, Esq; Harvestgate, Meonstoke, Hampshire SO3; c/o 10 Cartaret St, Queen Anne's Gate, London SW1 (☎ 071 222 8844, fax 071 222 4123)

BRUCE, Robert Bryson; s of Robert Bruce (d 1952), of Pinnacle, Ancrum, Jedburgh, and Mary Bryson, *née* MacTaggart; *b* 18 June 1930; *Educ* Loretto, Edinburgh Coll of Agriculture (DIP); *m* 19 July 1955, Maureen Rough, da of Dr Andrew Simpson (d 1973), of 19 Bridge St, Hawick, Roxburghshire; 1 s (Robert Simpson b 21 May 1960), 2 da ((Elizabeth) Susan b 17 May 1957, Katrina Mary b 23 Nov 1962); *Career* farmer and landowner; elder Ancrum Church, govr Loretto Sch, chm BFSS Borders Region, former MFH Duke of Buccleuchs Hunt; *Recreations* golf, fishing, shooting, fox hunting; *Clubs* Hon Co of Edinburgh Golfers (Muirfield Gullane), Royal and Ancient Golf (St Andrews); *Style—* Robert Bruce, Esq; Pinnacle, Ancrum, Jedburgh, Roxburghshire TD8 6UP (☎ 08353 232)

BRUCE, Robert Charles; s of Maj James Charles, MC (and bar), of Morpeth, Northumberland, and Enid Lilian, *née* Brown; *b* 5 May 1948; *Educ* Belmont House, Solihull Sch, City of London Coll (BSc); *Career* trainee accountant Edward Moore and Sons 1971-75, ed Accountancy Age 1981- (staff writer and news ed 1976-81); memb: Indust Soc Employee Involvement Working Pty, Indust Achievement Award Judging Panel; *Books* Winners - how small businesses achieve excellence (1986); *Recreations* cricket, buying books; *Clubs* Surrey Cricket, Ronnie Scott's; *Style—* Robert Bruce, Esq; 87 Marylands Rd, London W9 2DS (☎ 071 286 0211); Accountancy Age, 32-34 Broadwick St, London W1A 2HG (☎ 071 439 4242, fax 071 437 7001)

BRUCE, Col Robert Nigel Beresford Dalrymple; CBE (1972, OBE Mil 1946), TD (and Clasp 1946); s of Maj Robert Nigel Dunlop Bruce (d 1921), of Hampstead, and Adelaide Frances, *née* Firth (d 1921); *b* 21 May 1907; *Educ* Harrow, Magdalen Coll Oxford (BA, BSc); *m* 1945, Elizabeth Brogden, da of John Gage Moore; 2 s (Patrick, Kenneth, twins), 2 da (Jane, Susan); *Career* 2 Lt The Rangers (KRRC) TA 1931, WWII Maj 1939 cmd 9 KRRC, Greece 1941, Western Desert 1941-42, Lt-Col 1942, dir of materials MEF GHQ Cairo ME Supply Centre, Col 1942-45; staff controller Gas Light & Coke Co 1945-49 (res chemist 1929-35, asst to gen mangr 1936-39), dep chm N Thames Gas Bd 1956-60 (staff controller 1949-56); chm: SE Gas Bd 1960-72, Cncl Engrg Inst 1968-78; pres Inst Gas Engrs 1968; sec Tennis and Rackets Assoc 1974-81, govr Westminster Coll 1946-70 (chm of Governing Body 1957-70); CEng; *Recreations* walking, golf, fly fishing; *Clubs* The Queen's; *Style—* Col Robert Bruce, CBE, TD; Fairway, 57 Woodland Grove, Weybridge, Surrey

BRUCE, Steve Roger; s of Joseph Bruce, of Newcastle upon Tyne, and Sheenagh, *née* Creed; *b* 31 Dec 1960; *Educ* Benfield Comp Sch Newcastle upon Tyne; *m* Janet, da of Lesley Smith; 1 s (Alex b 23 Sept 1984), 1 da (Amy b 24 May 1987); *Career* professional footballer; Gillingham 1978-84: league debut 1979, 205 league appearances, 28 goals; Norwich City 1984-87: joined for a fee of £135,000, 141 league appearances, 14 goals; transferred for a fee of £825,000 to Manchester Utd 1987- (over 100 appearances); England: 8 youth caps, 1 B cap (capt); honours: League Cup Norwich City 1985, FA Cup Manchester Utd 1990; *Style—* Steve Bruce, Esq; Manchester United FC, Old Trafford, Manchester M16 ORA (☎ 061 872 1661)

BRUCE, William Henry; JP; s of William Bruce, of Grangewood, Ellon; *b* 17 Sept 1933; *Educ* Ellon Acad; *m* 1957, Margaret, da of Albert Wyness; 1 s, 2 da; *Career* chm: Biocure Holdings plc, Gordon Enterprises Trust; dir: Scotia Homes Ltd, Bruce and Partners (Ellon) Ltd; ptnr Bruce and Partners Estate Agents and Property Consultants; *Recreations* golf, country pursuits; *Clubs* Gleneagles, Cruden Bay Golf, Br Horse Soc (steward), Royal Over-Seas League; *Style—* William Bruce, Esq, JP; Logie House, Ellon, Aberdeenshire (☎ 0358 20531)

BRUCE-GARDNER, Bryan Charles; s of Sir Charles Bruce-Gardner, 1 Bt (d 1960); bro of Sir Douglas Bruce-Gardner, 2 Bt; *b* 4 July 1924; *Educ* Uppingham, Trinity Coll Cambridge (MA); *m* 1952, Rosemary, da of Digby Sowerby (d 1974), of Kirmington House, Kirmington, Lincs; 4 s; *Career* md Patent Shaft Steel Works 1961-81, dir Laird Group 1963-81; *Recreations* golf; *Style—* Bryan Bruce-Gardner, Esq; Stedefield, Church Lane, Flyford Flavell, Worcester (☎ 038 682 451)

BRUCE-GARDNER, Sir Douglas Bruce; 2 Bt (UK 1945); s of Sir Charles Bruce-Gardner, 1 Bt (d 1960); *b* 27 Jan 1917; *Educ* Uppingham, Trinity Coll Cambridge; *m* 1, 27 July 1940 (m dis 1964), Monica Flumerfelt, o da of late Prof Sir Geoffrey Jefferson, CBE, FRS; 1 s, 2 da; m 2, 18 March 1964, Sheila Jane, da of late Roger Stilliard, of Seer Green, Bucks; 1 s, 1 da; *Heir* s, Robert Henry Bruce-Gardner, *qv*; *Career* chm: GKN Steel 1965-67, GKN Rolled and Bright Steel 1968-72, GKN (S Wales), Miles Druce & Co 1974-77; dep chm GKN Gp 1974-77; dir: BHP GKN Hldgs 1977-78, GKN Ltd 1960-82, Iron Trades Employers Insur Assoc, Iron Trades Mutual Insur Co 1977-87; Prime Warden Worshipful Co of Blacksmiths 1983-84; *Style—* Sir Douglas Bruce-Gardner, Bt; Stocklands, Lewstone, Ganarew, nr Monmouth (☎ 0600 890 216)

BRUCE-GARDNER, Robert Henry; s & h of Sir Douglas Bruce-Gardner, 2 Bt, by his 1 w, Monica; *b* 10 June 1943; *Educ* Uppingham, Reading Univ; *m* 1979, Veronica Hand-Oxborrow, da of late Rev W E Hand; 1 s (Thomas Edmund Peter b 28 Jan 1982); *Style—* Robert Bruce-Gardner, Esq; 6/11 Sinclair Rd, London W14 (☎ 071 602 3690)

BRUCE-GARDYNE, Hon Adam George John; yr s of Baron Bruce-Gardyne (Life Peer); *b* 7 Sept 1967; *Educ* Marlborough; *Style—* The Hon Adam Bruce-Gardyne; 13 Kelso Place, London W8

BRUCE-GARDYNE, Baroness; Sarah Louisa Mary; *née* Maitland; o da of Cdr Sir John Francis Whitaker Maitland, RN (d 1977), of Harrington Hall, nr Spilsby, Lincs, and Bridget, *née* Denny (d 1988); *b* 26 July 1932; *m* 24 Jan 1959, Baron Bruce-Gardyne (Life Peer, d 1990); 2 s, 1 da; *Style—* The Rt Hon Lady Bruce-Gardyne; 13 Kelso Place, London W8 (☎ 071 937 6953); The Old Rectory, Aswardby, Spilsby, Lincolnshire (☎ 0790 52652)

BRUCE-GARDYNE, Hon Thomas Andrew; er s of Baron Bruce-Gardyne (Life Peer); *b* 22 March 1962; *Educ* Marlborough; *Style—* The Hon Thomas Bruce-Gardyne; 13 Kelso Place, London W8

BRUCE-JONES, Tom Allan; s of Tom Bruce-Jones (d 1984), of Blairlogie, Stirlingshire, and Rachel Inglis, *née* Dunlop; *b* 28 Aug 1941; *Educ* Charterhouse, Lincoln Coll Oxford (BA); *m* 1, 1965 (m dis 1980), R Normand; 1 s (Tom b 8 Sept 1968), 1 da (Caroline b 23 Nov 1966); m 2, 6 March 1981, Stina Birgitta, da of Harry Ossian Ahlgren (d 1982), of Helsinki; *Career* dir Price and Pierce (Woodpulp) Ltd 1973-77, vice pres Georgia-Pacific International Inc 1977-79, md James Jones and Sons Ltd 1987 (jt md 1979-87); dir: Jones and Campbell (Hldgs) Ltd 1988-, Jones Buckie

Shipyard Ltd 1988-, Timber Processors plc, Highland Sawmillers plc 1988-; *Recreations* fishing, golf, music; *Clubs* Hon Co of Edinburgh Golfers; *Style—* Tom Bruce-Jones, Esq; 15 Queen's Gate, Dowanhill St, Glasgow; The Glebe, Killin, Perthshire; James Jones & Sons Ltd, Broomage Ave, Larbert, Stirlingshire (☎ 0324 562 241, fax 0324 558 755)

BRUCE LOCKHART, John Macgregor; CB (1960), CMG (1951), OBE (1944); s of John Harold Bruce Lockhart (d 1956; headmaster Sedbergh Sch, Yorkshire), and Mona Alwine, *née* Brougham (d 1980); *b* 9 May 1914; *Educ* Rugby, St Andrew's Univ (MA); *m* 1939, Margaret Evelyn, da of Rt Rev Bishop Campbell Hone (d 1967; Bishop of Wakefield 1938-45); 2 s (James, Alexander), 1 da (Sarah); *Career* TA cmmn Seaforth Highlanders, served UK, ME, Italy, master Rugby Sch 1937-39, Lt-Col 1944; HM Foreign Service 1945-65, served Paris, Germany, Washington and FO; dir staff personnel Courtaulds 1966-71, advsr Post Exp Prog City Univ 1971-80, chm Business Educn Cncl 1974-80; visiting fell: St Andrew's Univ 1981, Rand Afrikaans Univ 1983; *Recreations* golf, real tennis, fishing; *Clubs* Reform; *Style—* John Bruce Lockhart, Esq, CB, CMG, OBE; 37 Fair Meadow, Rye, Sussex, (☎ 0797 223410)

BRUCE LOCKHART, Logie; s of John Harold Bruce Lockhart (d 1956), of Drum Mor, Bemersyde, and Mona Alwine, *née* Brougham (d 1981); *b* 12 Oct 1921; *Educ* Sedbergh, St John's Coll Cambridge (MA); *m* 6 Oct 1944, Josephine, da of Reginald Colville Agnew (d 1970), of Boscombe, Hants; 2 s (Rhuraidh Agnew b 1949, Duncan Roderick McGregor b 1961), 3 da (Jennifer Morag b 1945, Kirsty Amanda b 1953, d 1960, Fiona Jacqueline (Mrs Drye) b 1957); *Career* WWII served RMC Sandhurst 1941, Lt 9 Sherwood Foresters 1942-43, 2 Household Cav 1944 (invasion NW Europe); asst master Tonbridge Sch 1948-55, headmaster Gresham's Sch 1955-82; former chm Eastern Div HMC; memb: RAF Educn Ctee, Int Educnl Sub Ctee; played: rugby football for Scotland 1948, 1950 and 1953, squash for Cambridge; *Books* Pleasures of Fishing (1981), Tribute to a Norfolk Naturalist (1987); *Recreations* writing, painting, fishing, sport, France; *Clubs* East India, Public Schools; *Style—* Logie Bruce Lockhart, Esq; Church Farm Hse, Lower Bodham, Nr Holt, Norfolk NR25 6PS (☎ 0263 712137)

BRUCE LOCKHART, Robin Norman; s of Sir Robert Hamilton Bruce Lockhart, KCMG (d 1970), and late Jean Haslewood, *née* Turner; paternal grandmother descended from King James II of Scotland; *b* 13 April 1920; *Educ* RNC Dartmouth, Pembroke Coll Cambridge (BEcon); *m* 1, 1941, Margaret Crookdake; 1 da (Sheila Margaret b 1951); m 2, 1955, Ginette de Noyelle (d 1985); m 3, 1987, Eila Owen; *Career* WWII Lt RNVR 1939-46; asst to Br Naval Attaché Paris, naval intelligence Admty, Flag Lt to C in C China, Eastern Fleet, Ceylon, staff C in C Plymouth; foreign mangr Financial Times 1946-53; memb London Stock Exchange 1962-; dep chm Central Wagon Co Ltd 1965-69; chm: Moorgill Properties Ltd 1967-72, Chasebrook Ltd 1967-72, 37/38 Adelaide Cres (Hove) Ltd 1983-; *Books* Reilly Ace of Spies (1967-, TV series 1984-85), Halfway to Heaven (1985), Reilly the First Man (1967); *Recreations* salmon fishing, travel; *Clubs* MCC, Royal Scot Automobile; *Style—* Robin Bruce Lockhart, Esq; 37 Adelaide Crescent, Hove, Sussex (☎ 0273 777962; Quand Meme, Rue Romain Rolland, Collioure, Pyrénées Orientales, France (☎ 01033 68 82 29 14)

BRUCE OF DONINGTON, Baron (Life Peer UK 1974); Donald William Trevor Bruce; s of William Trevor Bruce (d 1934), of Norbury, Surrey; *b* 3 Oct 1912; *Educ* The GS Donington Lincs; *m* 1, 1939 (m dis 1980), Joan Letitia, da of late H C Butcher, of London; 1 s, 2 da (and 1 da decd); m 2, 1981, Cyrena Heard, *née* Shaw; *Career* served WWII UK and France in rank of Maj; CA 1936-; economist and author; MP (Lab) Portsmouth N 1945-50, PPS to Min of Health 1945-50; memb Euro Parl 1975-79, sits as Lab Peer; oppn spokesman on: Trade and Industl matters 1983-87, Treasy matters 1979-83 and 1987-90; *Recreations* swimming; *Style—* The Rt Hon the Lord Bruce of Donington; 310/305 Euston Rd, London NW1 (☎ 071 388 2456)

BRUCE-RADCLIFFE, Godfrey Martin; s of Roy Bruce-Radcliffe (d 1976), of Surrey, and Joyce Evelyn, *née* Shewring; *b* 19 June 1945; *Educ* King's Coll Taunton, Guildford Coll of Law; *m* 5 Oct 1974, Anita Claire, da of Maj Charles Ronald Miller; 1 s (Edward Charles b 9 Aug 1976), 1 da (Helen Victoria b 2 Nov 1982); *Career* articled clerk Trower Still & Keeling (now Trowers and Hamlins) 1964, slr 1970, ptnr D J Freeman & Co 1978 (joined 1977); Freeman City of London 1986; memb Law Soc 1970; *Recreations* sailing, walking, gardening, music; *Style—* Godfrey Bruce-Radcliffe, Esq; Ellacombe, 21 Anstey Lane, Alton, Hants GU34 2NB (☎ 0420 83343); D J Freeman & Co, 1 Fetter Lane, London EC4A 1BR (☎ 071 583 5555, fax 071 583 3232)

BRUCE-SMYTHE, Simon Carrington; s of Capt Reginald Oliver Bruce-Smythe (d 1969), and Jane Bruce-Smythe (d 1976); *b* 1 Aug 1942; *Educ* Downside; *m* 22 Oct 1966, Caroline Ann, da of Derek Godfrey Leach; 2 s (Charles Oliver b 19 Feb 1971, Peter Carrington b 30 Sept 1976); *Career* CA 1966; currently ptnr i/c Price Waterhouse SE at Redhill (joined 1965); memb ICAEW; *Recreations* horse racing, shooting, fishing; *Style—* Simon Bruce-Smythe, Esq; Bridge Gate, High St, Redhill, Surrey (☎ 0737 766 300)

BRUCE-WHITE, Frank; s of Bernard Frank White (d 1979), and Amy Beatrice, *née* Pitt (d 1970); *b* 16 Jan 1917; *Educ* Pembroke Lodge, Cheltenham, Univ of Southampton; *m* 1, 2 Oct 1948, Olive (d 1983), da of late John Russell; 2 s (Bernard Roger b 1949, Richard Stuart b 1951); m 2, 27 Sept 1990, Pamela Dorothy, da of A B Curtis Quick (d 1980); *Career* WWII Capt RE served: France, Assam, Burma, Punjab, Maldive Islands; articled city engr Salisbury 1935-38, jr engr Southampton 1938-39 and 1945-46, dist engr Sudan 1947-49, farmer 1949-51, dist engr Tanganyika 1951-53, farmer 1953-; competed in motor sports 1949-; CEng, MRSI, AMICE, AMISE; *Recreations* motor sport, cricket; *Clubs* BARC Vintage Sports Car, Vintage Motor Cycle, Tanganyika Cricket, Wilts Queries Cricket; *Style—* Frank Bruce-White, Esq; Ivy Cottage, Garters Lane, Winterbourne Dauntsey, Salisbury, Wilts SP4 6ER

BRUCK, Steven Mark; s of Herbert Martin Bruck, of London, and Kathe Margot Bruck; *b* 30 Sept 1947; *Educ* Hendon GS, Univ of Southampton (BSc), LSE (MSc); *m* 1 July 1971, Mirela, da of Alexander Izsak; 1 s (Jonathan b 1977), 1 da (Tamara b 1974); *Career* articled clerk Chalmers Impey CAs 1969-72, gp accountant Halma plc 1972-73, special projects accountant Overseas Containers Ltd 1973-75, Pannell Fitzpatrick 1975-78, ptnr Mercers Bryant 1978-84, ptnr and nat dir Pannell Kerr Forster 1984-; bd memb Belsize Square Synagogue; FCA 1972; *Recreations* family, theatre, eating; *Style—* Steven Bruck, Esq; Pannell Kerr Forster, New Garden House, 78 Hatton Garden, London EC1N 8JI (☎ 071 831 7393, fax 071 405 6736, telex 295928)

BRUCKHEIMER, Nathan Norbert; s of Simon Bruckheimer; *b* 6 Nov 1933; *Educ* Alleyne's Stevenage, Holloway Sch London, Univ of Edinburgh (MA); *Career* jt md Jacob Metals Ltd (A Cohen group); *Recreations* theatre, music (particularly opera); *Style—* Nathan Bruckheimer, Esq; c/o Jacob Metals Ltd, Clareville House, 25-27 Oxendon St, London SW1Y 4EL (☎ 071 930 6953, telex 918034/23 111)

BRUCKNER, Dr Felix Ernest; s of William Bruckner, of London, and Anna, *née* Hahn; *b* 18 April 1937; *Educ* London Hosp Med Coll, Univ of London (MB BS); *m* 24 June 1967, Rosalind Dorothy, da of George Edward Farley Bailey, of Herts; 2 s (James b 1974, Thomas b 1976), 1 da (Catherine b 1981); *Career* conslt physician and rheumatologist St George's Hosp London 1970-; FRCP; *Books* numerous papers on rheumatology; *Recreations* chess, music; *Clubs* Royal Society of Medicine; *Style—* Dr Felix Bruckner; 12 Southwood Ave, Kingston upon Thames, Surrey KT2 7HD (☎ 081 949 3955); 152 Harley St, London W1N 1HH (☎ 081 935 1858)

BRUDENELL, Edmund Crispin Stephen James George; DL (Northants 1977); s of George Brudenell (2 s of Cdr Lord Robert Brudenell-Bruce, RN, 4 s of 3 Marquess of Ailesbury); *b* 24 Oct 1928; *Educ* Harrow, RAC Cirencester; *m* 8 Nov 1955, Hon Marian Cynthia, *née* Manningham-Buller, eldest da of 1 Viscount Dilhorne, PC; 2 s (Robert b 1956, Thomas (twin) b 1956), 1 da (Anna Maria b 1960); *Career* contested (C) Whitehaven 1964; High Sheriff of Leics 1969, High Sheriff of Northants 1987; landowner and farmer; *Recreations* shooting, deer stalking, travelling; *Clubs* Carlton, Pratt's; *Style—* Edmund Brudenell, Esq, DL; 18 Laxford House, Ebury St, London SW1 (☎ 071 730 8715); Deene Park, Corby, Northants (☎ 078 085 223)

BRUDENELL, Hon Mrs (Marian Cynthia); *née* Manningham-Buller; JP; eldest da of 1 Viscount Dilhorne, PC (d 1980); *b* 26 Nov 1934; *m* 8 Nov 1955, Edmund Brudenell, *qv*; 2 s (twin), 1 da; *Style—* The Hon Mrs Brudenell; Deene Park, Corby, Northamptonshire (☎ 078 085 223); 18 Laxford House, Ebury St, London SW1 (☎ 071 730 8715)

BRUDENELL, (John) Michael; s of Clement Shenstone Brudenell (d 1964), of Ashford, Middx, and Elizabeth Marjery, *née* James; *b* 13 April 1925; *Educ* Hampton Sch, Kings Coll London and Kings Coll Hosp London (MB BS); *m* 6 April 1957, Mollie, da of Arthur Herbert Rothwell (d 1974), of Audenshaw, Lancs; 4 s (Timothy b 1958, Jeremy b 1960, Marcus b 1962, Edward b 1967); *Career* Capt RAMC 1950-52, Maj AER field surgical team 1953-63; conslt obstetrician and gynaecologist: Bradford Royal Infirmary Yorks 1961-64, King's Coll Hosp London 1964-90; conslt gynaecologist King Edward VIII Hosp London 1980-, sr conslt gynaecologist Queen Victoria Hosp 1964-90; fell RSM (former pres section of obstetrics and gynaecology); Freeman City of London 1974, Liveryman Worshipful Soc of Apothecaries 1967; hon fell Royal Soc of Med Barcelona 1979; FRCS 1956 (memb Cncl 1985-90), FRCOG 1973 (memb Cncl 1973-89, hon treas 1980-87); *Recreations* reading, tennis, skiing; *Clubs* Gynaecological Travellers; *Style—* Michael Brudenell, Esq; The Barn, Station Rd, Hever, Kent TN8 7ER (☎ 0732 863086); 73 Harley St, London W1N 1DE (☎ 071 935 5098)

BRUDENELL, Thomas Mervyn; s of Edmund Crispin Stephen James George Brudenell, of Deene Park, Corby, Northamptonshire, and Marian Cynthia, *née* Manningham Buller; *b* 12 Aug 1956; *Educ* Eton; *m* 5 May 1984, Venetia Jane, da of Maj Robert Patricius Chaworth Musters, of Felley Priory, Jacksdale, Notts; 2 da (Sophia b 12 April 1985, Victoria b 11 Feb 1987); *Career* called to the Bar Inner Temple 1977; *Recreations* hunting, fishing, shooting, stalking, rackets, racing; *Clubs* Pratt's; *Style—* Thomas Brudenell, Esq; 23 Caroline Terrace, London SW1 (☎ 071 730 4305); Queen Elizabeth Building, Temple, London EC4 (☎ 071 583 7837)

BRUDENELL-BRUCE, Lord Charles Adam; s of 7 Marquess of Ailesbury (d 1974), and his 3 w, Jean, *née* Wilson; *b* 23 March 1951; *Educ* Eton; *Career* former Lt Royal Hussars, with COI 1976; formerly with Chestertons (until 1987), subsequently self-employed property advsr; *Recreations* tennis, squash, shooting; *Clubs* Cavalry and Guards'; *Style—* The Lord Charles Brudenell-Bruce; Little Lye Hill, Savernake Forest, Marlborough, Wilts (☎ 0672 810261)

BRUDENELL-BRUCE, Lady Kathryn Juliet; da of 8 Marquess of Ailesbury, of Sturmy House, Durley, Nr Marlborough, Wiltshire; *b* 24 Aug 1965; *Educ* St Mary's Sch Calne, Bristol Univ; *Style—* The Lady Kathryn Brudenell-Bruce

BRUDENELL-BRUCE, Lady Louise; da of 8 Marquess of Ailesbury, of Sturmy House, Durley, Nr Marlborough, Wiltshire; *b* 13 July 1964; *Educ* St Mary's Sch Calne; *Style—* The Lady Louise Brudenell-Bruce

BRUDENELL-BRUCE, Lady Piers; Nelida Garcia Otero; da of Mariano Garcia Villalba, of Madrid; *m* 1958, as his 2 w, Lord (Chandos Gerald) Piers Brudenell-Bruce (d 1980; 2 s of 7 Marquess of Ailesbury); 2 da; *Style—* The Lady Piers Brudenell-Bruce; Cortijo de la Plata, Zahara de los Atunes, Cadiz, Spain

BRUEN, Eleanor Mary (Nell); da of Dr William Cornelious Cremin, of 120 St Stephen's Green, Dublin, Ireland, and Eleanor, *née* O'Gorman; *b* 29 July 1918; *Educ* Sacred Heart Convent Roehampton, Univ Coll Dublin (BSc); *m* 6 June 1945, James Joseph Bruen, s of James Bruen, of Lake View, Blackrock, Cork, Ireland; 3 s (Christopher b 20 March 1948, David b 27 Oct 1955, Michael b 18 Oct 1961), 3 da (Rosemary b 30 March 1946, Daphne b 30 Nov 1950, Barbara b 6 June 1953); *Career* chm James Bruen & Sons Inc Insurance Brokers 1972-; pres Irish Ladies' Golf Union 1985-86, pres Ladies Golf Union 1989-; *Recreations* golf; *Clubs* Cork Golf, Muskerry, Killarney; *Style—* Mrs Nell Bruen; Birkdale, Kilcoolishall, Glanmire, Co Cork, Ireland; 45 South Mall, Cork, Ireland

BRUFORD, Dr Alan James; s of Prof Walter Horace Bruford (d 1988), and Gertrude Elisabeth Clara (Gerda), *née* Hendrick (d 1976); *b* 10 May 1937; *Educ* Edinburgh Acad, Winchester, St John's Coll Cambridge (BA), Univ of Edinburgh (PhD); *m* 17 April 1969, Morag Bartleman, da of James Denholm Wood (d 1978); 1 da (Elspeth b 1971); *Career* archivist Sch of Scot Studies Univ of Edinburgh 1965-, ed Tocher 1971-; treas Scottish Assoc of Magazine Publishers 1974-79, chm Scottish Oral History Gp 1987- (memb Ctee 1983-87); *Books* Gaelic Folk-Tales and Mediaeval Romances (1969), The Green Man of Knowledge and Other Scots Traditional Tales (ed 198; *Recreations* music (traditional, baroque, composition), exploring Scotland, quizzes; *Clubs* Edinburgh Univ Staff, Speculative Soc; *Style—* Dr Alan Bruford; S Mains, W Linton, Peeblesshire EH46 7AY (☎ 0968 60562); School of Scottish Studies, University of Edinburgh, 27 George Square, Edinburgh EH8 9LD (☎ 031 650 4160 ext 6692)

BRUFORD-DAVIES, Maj (Edmund) Robin; s of Brig Edmund Davies; *b* 29 June 1928; *Educ* Radley, Sandhurst; *m* 1969, Sheelagh, da of Dr Norman Patterson; *Career* Royal Ulster Rifles 1948-69; dir W M Bruford & Sons, Gowland Bros; *Recreations* tennis, skiing; *Clubs* Special Forces; *Style—* Maj Robin Bruford-Davies; 13A Marlborough Rd, Exeter, Devon EX2 4TJ

BRUGES, (Charles) James Long; s of Maj (Charles) Eric Lond Bruges (d 1967), of Brook House, Semington, Trowbridge, Wilts, and Beatrice Rose Campbell, *née* Leighton Stevens; *b* 25 Aug 1933; *Educ* Sheikh Bagh Kashmir, Kelly Coll Devon, Architectural Assoc London (AA Dip); *m* 4 June 1971, Anthea, da of (Oliver) Maldwyn Davies, of Bath; 1 s (Benedict b 1961), 3 da (Clare b 1963, Kate b 1972, Beatrice b 1974); *Career* asst architect Trevor Dannatt Assocs 1958-60, resident architect Khartoum Univ 1960-63, assoc Whicheloe Macfarlane 1963-69, ptnr Towning Hill and Ptnrs 1969-73, princ Brugers Tozer Architects 1973-; fndr memb Concept Planning Gp 1988, advsr on urban design Br Devpt Corp 1989; memb: Bristol City Docks Gp, Civic Soc, Bristol Visual & Environmental Gp, RIBA; *Recreations* painting, tennis, music; *Style—* James Bruges, Esq; 40 Cornwallis Crescent, Bristol, Avon BS8 4PH (☎ 0272 738634); Bruges Tozer Partnership, 7 Unity St, Bristol, Avon BS1 5HH (☎ 0272 279797)

BRUGGEMEYER, (William) James; s of Lt William Charles Bruggemeyer (d 1972), of London, and Kathleen, *née* Mangan (d 1983); *b* 16 June 1934; *Educ* St Joseph's Coll Beulah Hill, British Sch of Osteopathy (DO, MRO); *Career* Nat Serv 1952-54, Malaya 1953, GSM and Clasp; *Recreations* music (singing), gardening, travel; *Style—* James Bruggemeyer, Esq; 99 Herne Hill, London SE24 9LY

BRUGHA, Dr Traolach Seán; s of Ruairi Brugha, of Dublin, and Maire, *née* MacSwiney; *b* 6 Jan 1953; *Educ* Gonzaga Coll Dublin, Univ Coll Dublin (MB BCh, MD); *m* 3 April 1976, Máire Eoghain; 3 da (Rossa Eoghain, Lia Patricia, Cillian Traolach); *Career* registrar in psychiatry St Vincents Hosp Elm Park Dublin 1979-80, registrar then sr registrar Bethlem and Maudsley Hosp London 1980-87 clinical scientist MRC Social Psychiatry Unit London 1982-87, hon lectr in psychiatry Inst of Psychiatry London 1984-87, sr lectr Univ of Leicester 1987-, hon conslt psychiatrist Leicester Health Authy 1987-; MRC Psych 1981-; *Recreations* photography, cycling, music; *Style—* Dr Traolach Brugha; Department of Psychiatry, University of Leicester, Leicester (☎ 0533 52340)

BRUINVELS, Peter Nigel Edward; er s of Capt Stanley Bruinvels, of Dorking, Surrey, and Ninette Maud, *née* Kibblewhite; *b* 30 March 1950; *Educ* St John's Sch Leatherhead, Univ of London (LLB), Cncl of Legal Educn; *m* 20 Sept 1980, Alison Margaret, da of Maj David Gilmore Bacon, of Lymington, Hants; 2 da (Alexandra Caroline Jane b 6 April 1986, Georgina Emma Kate b 20 Oct 1988); *Career* news broadcaster, political columnist, freelance journalist, author, media mgmnt and public affrs advsr; dir Aalco Nottingham 1983-88, public affrs dir Abel Gp Ltd 1988-89, princ Peter Bruinvels Assocs (media mgmnt corporate communications and public affrs consits) 1986-; non-exec dir: 3i plc; co sec BPC Publishing Ltd 1978-81; MP (C) Leicester East 1983-87, memb Cons Home Off & NI Ctees 1983-87; jt vice chm: Cons Urban Affrs and New Towns Ctee 1984-87, Cons Educn Ctee 1985-87; chm Br-Malta Parly Gp 1984-87, fndr jt chm Br Parly Lighting Gp 1983-87, promoter Crossbows Act 1987, chm Law Students Cons Assoc of GB 1974-76, memb Cons NUEC 1976-81, vice chm Dorking Cons Assoc 1979-83, chm Dorking Cons Political Centre 1979-83, fndr sponsor Cons Family Campaign 1984-; chm SE Area Young Conservatives 1977-79; memb: Guildford Diocesan Synod Gen Synod C of E 1985-, Bishops Cncl and Bd of Patrons 1985-; Freeman City of London 1980; FRSA, MJI, MCIM, MIPR, Fell Indust and Parl Tst; *Books* Zoning in on Enterprise (1982), Light up the Roads (1984), Sharing in Britains Success: A Study in Widening Share Ownership Through Privatisation (1987), Investing in Enterprise: A Comprehensive Guide to Inner City Regeneration and Urban Renewal (1989); *Recreations* politics in the C of E, lawn tennis umpire, cricket, political campaigning, the media; *Clubs* Carlton, Inner Temple, Corporation of Church House; *Style—* Peter Bruinvels, Esq; 14 High Meadow Close, Dorking, Surrey RH4 2LG (☎ 0306 887082)

BRUMMER, Alexander; s of Michael Brummer, of Brighton, and Hilda Brummer; *b* 25 May 1949; *Educ* Brighton Hove & Sussex GS, Univ of Southampton (BSc), Univ of Bradford Mgmnt Centre (MBA); *m* 26 Oct 1975, Patricia Lyndsey, da of Saul Leopold Magrill; 2 s (Justin Adam b 29 Sept 1980, Gabriel Joseph b 30 Dec 1981), 1 da (Jessica Rachel b 5 Jan 1978); *Career* journalist; De La Rue Company 1971-72, Haymarket Publishing 1972-73; The Guardian: fin corr 1973-79, Washington corr 1979-85, Washington bureau chief 1985-89, foreign ed 1989, fin ed 1990-; winner Best Foreign Corr in US (Overseas Press Club) 1989; *Books* American Destiny (jt author, 1985); *Recreations* reading, antiques; *Style—* Alexander Brummer, Esq; The Guardian, 119 Farringdon Rd, London EC1 3ER

BRUMMER, Malcolm Howard; s of David Brummer, of London, and Sylvia, *née* Miller; *b* 21 March 1948; *Educ* Haberdashers' Aske's, Downing Coll Cambridge (MA); *m* 12 March 1980, Yvonne Simy, *née* Labos; 1 s (Richard Joseph b 16 Feb 1982), 1 da (Natasha Nina b 1 Dec 1985); *Career* Berwin Leighton: articled clerk 1970-72, ptnr 1975-, head Property Dept 1983-89, chm Fin Ctee 1987-, chm Bd 1990-; memb Law Soc 1972; *Recreations* family, opera; *Style—* Malcolm Brummer, Esq; 3 Milton Close, Hampstead Garden Suburb, London N2 OQH (☎ 081 209 0213); Berwin Leighton Solicitors, Adelaide House, London Bridge, London EC4R 9HA (☎ 071 623 3144, fax 071 623 4416)

BRUNNER, Elizabeth, Lady; (Dorothea) Elizabeth; OBE (1965), JP (Oxon 1946); o da of Henry Brodribb Irving (d 1919), and Dorothea, *née* Baird; gda of Sir Henry Irving, the actor; *m* 1926, Sir Felix Brunner, 3 Bt (d 1982); 3 s (and 2 s decd); *Career* chm: Nat Fedn of Women's Insts 1951-56, Keep Britain Tidy Gp 1958-67 (pres 1967-85), the Women's Gp on Pub Welfare The Nat Cncl of Social Servs 1960-70; *Style—* Elizabeth, Lady Brunner, OBE, JP; Greys Court, Henley-on-Thames, Oxon RG9 4PG (☎ 049 17 296)

BRUNNER, Hugo Laurence Joseph; s of Sir Felix John Morgan Brunner, 3 Bt (d 1982), of Greys Court, nr Henley-on-Thames, Oxon, and Elizabeth, Lady Brunner OBE, *qv*; *b* 17 Aug 1935; *Educ* Eton, Trinity Coll Oxford (MA); *m* 7 Jan 1967, Mary Rose Catherine, da of Arthur Joseph Lawrence Pollen (d 1968), of Harpsden Wood, Henley-on-Thames, Oxon; 5 s (Joseph b 1967, Samuel b 1972, Magnus b 1974, Philip b 1977, Francis b 1982), 1 da (Isabel b 1969); *Career* publisher, various appts Oxford Univ Press 1958-65 and 1977-79, dir Chatto and Windus 1967-76 and 1979-85 (md 1979-82, chm 1982-85); dir Caithness Glass 1966- (chm 1985-), dir Brunner Investmt Tst 1987-; Parly candidate (Lib) for Torquay 1964 and 1966, chm Oxford Diocesan Advsy Ctee for Care of Churches 1985-; High Sheriff Oxfordshire 1988-89; *Recreations* hill walking, church crawling; *Clubs* Reform; *Style—* Hugo Brunner, Esq; 26 Norham Rd, Oxford OX2 6SF (☎ 0865 54821)

BRUNNER, Sir John Henry Kilian; 4 Bt (UK 1895), of Druids Cross, Little Woolton, Lancashire; Winnington Old Hall, Winnington, Cheshire; and Ennismore Gardens, Westminster, Co London; s of Sir Felix Brunner, 3 Bt (d 1982); *b* 1 June 1927; *Educ* Eton, Trinity Coll Oxford; *m* 1955, Jasmine Cicely, da of late John Wardrop-Moore by his w Janet (da of Sir James Erskine, JP, MP, himself gs of Sir David Erskine, 1 Bt, of Cambo); 2 s, 1 da; *Heir* s, Nicholas Felix Minturn, b 16 Jan 1960; *Career* formerly Lt RA & ADC to GOC 2 Infantry Div; with Political & Economic Planning (now Policy Studies Inst) 1950-53, talks producer BBC 1953, econ advsr with HM Treasury 1958-61, asst mangr with Observer (UK) 1961; formerly Lt RA & ADC to GOC 2 Infantry Div; *Style—* Sir John Brunner, Bt; 13 Glyndon Ave, Brighton, Victoria, Australia 3186

BRUNNING, His Hon Judge David Wilfrid; s of Wilfred George Brunning (d 1983) of Burton on Trent, and Marion, *née* Humphries; *b* 10 April 1943; *Educ* Burton-upon-Trent GS, Worcester Coll Oxford (BA, DPA); *m* 8 July 1967, Deidre Ann Shotton; 3 s (b 1972, 1974, 1977); *Career* articled clerk Leicester CC 1966-67, called to the Bar Middle Temple 1969, in practice Midland and Oxford Circuit 1970-88, Circuit Judge 1988-; chm: Kirk Lodge Probation Hostel Mgmnt Ctee 1973-88, Leicester Anchor Club 1983-89; *Recreations* squash, campanology, music, good food and wine; *Style—* His Honour Judge Brunning; Nottingham Combined Court Centre, Canal St, Nottingham

BRUNO, Franklin Roy (Frank); MBE (1990); s of Robert Bruno (d 1977), and Lynette, *née* Cambell; *b* 16 Nov 1961; *Educ* Oak Hall Sch Sussex; *m* 5 Feb 1990, Laura Frances, da of Peter James Mooney; 2 da (Nicola Frances b 24 July 1982, Rachel Lynette b 28 Aug 1986); *Career* professional boxer; began boxing with Wandsworth Boys Club 1970, memb Sir Philip Game Amateur Boxing Club 1977-80, turned professional 1982; achievements as amateur: 21 contests, 20 victories, represented Young England 1980, winner nat and London ABA heavyweight titles 1980; achievements as professional: 35 contests, 32 victories (31 inside the distance), Euro heavyweight champion 1985-86 (relinquished title), world heavyweight title challenges v Tim Witherspoon 1986 and Mike Tyson 1989; memb Equity, appeared in pantomime Dominion Theatre 1990 and Nottingham 1991, former presenter People (BBC), guest appearances on numerous TV shows; TV Times Sports Personality of the Year 1990, SOS Sports Personality of the Year 1990; *Recreations* swimming, training, driving, eating, shopping for good clothes, listening to jazz-funk and soul records, watching old boxing videos; *Style—* Frank Bruno, Esq, MBE; c/o PO Box 38, Hornchurch, Essex RM11 3NQ (fax 04024 37033)

BRUNSKILL, Dr Ronald William; OBE (1990); s of late William Brunskill (d 1986), of Morecambe, Lancs, and Eliza Hannah, *née* Gowling; *b* 3 Jan 1929; *Educ* Bury HS, Univ of Manchester (BA, MA, PhD); *m* 20 June 1960, Miriam, s of late Joseph Allsopp, of Weirsdale, Florida, USA; 2 da (Lesley (Mrs Glass) b 27 Oct 1961, Robin b 9 Sept 1963); *Career* Nat Serv 1953-55, 2 Lt RE served in Suez Canal zone; studio asst in architecture Univ of Manchester 1951-53; architectural asst: London CC 1955, Univ of Manchester 1955-56, Cwlth Fund Harkness fell and visiting fell Massachusetts Inst of Technol Boston Mass USA 1956-57, architect to Williams Deacon's Bank Manchester 1957-60, reader in architecture Univ of Manchester 1983-89 (lectr 1960-73, sr lectr 1973-83, hon fell 1989-), visiting prof Univ of Florida Gainesville Florida USA 1969-70; architect in private practice, ptnr Carter Brunskill Assocs 1965-70; memb: Royal Cmmn on Ancient and Historical Monuments of Wales 1983-, Ctee Historic Bldgs Cncl for Eng 1978-84, Historic Buildings and Monuments Cmmn for Eng 1984-89; cmmr and chm Churches and Historic Bldgs Advsy Ctee, Eng Heritage 1989-, Cathedrals Advsy Cmmn for Eng 1981-, Cathedral Fabric Ctees Manchester, Blackburn, Chester, Diocesan Advsy Ctee Manchester, govr Bolton Inst for Higher Education 1982-89; pres Cumberland and Westmorland Archaeological and Antiquarian Soc 1 vice pres Weald and Downland Museum Tst; tstee Br Historic Bldgs Tst; chm Ancient Monuments Soc 1990-, chm Friends of Friendless Churches 1990-; RIBA 1951, FSA 1975; *Books* Illustrated Handbook of Vernacular Architecture (1971, 3 edn 1987), Vernacular Architecture of the Lake Counties (1974), English Brick Building (with Alec Clifton-Taylor, 1978), Houses (1982), Traditional Buildings of Britain (1981), Traditional Farm Buildings of Britain, (1982, 2 edn 1987), Timber Building in Britain (1985), Brickwork in Britain (1990); *Recreations* enjoying the countryside; *Style—* Dr Ronald Brunskill, OBE; Three Trees, 8 Overhill Rd, Wilmslow, SK9 2BE (☎ 0625 522099); Glan Gors, Harlech, Gwynedd; School of Architecture, University of Manchester, Manchester M13 9PL (☎ 061 275 6934)

BRUNT, Harry Edwin; s of (Edwin) Alfred Brunt (d 1964), of Hale, Cheshire, and Hilda Mary, *née* Cannon; *b* 16 Jan 1931; *Educ* Manchester GS, Downing Coll Cambridge (MA); *m* 3 Sept 1960, Myra Jean, da of Alfred James Woodley (d 1956), of St Neots, Huntingdonshire; 2 s (Michael b 1964, Philip b 1965), 2 da (Susan b 1961, Margaret b 1968); *Career* Corpl RASC 1949-50, Flt Lt RAF 1956-64; mgmnt trainee WS Shuttleworth & Co Ltd chocolate manufacturers Bermondsey, admitted slr 1967; Eversherd & Tomkinson Birmingham 1965-89: articled clerk 1965-67, asst slr 1967-70, assoc 1970-74, ptnr 1974-89; conslt to Eversherd Wells & Hind Slrs Birmingham 1989-; memb Law Soc 1967; *Books* contrib Tolley's Tax Planning (annually 1979-88); *Recreations* walking, crosswords, DIY; *Style—* Harry Brunt, Esq; Eversherd Wells & Hind, 10 Newhall St, Birmingham B3 3LX (☎ 021 233 2001, fax 021 236 1583, telex 336688)

BRUNT, Dr Peter William; s of Harry Brunt, of Prestatyn, Clwyd, and Florence Jane Josephine, *née* Airey; *b* 18 Jan 1936; *Educ* Manchester GS, King George V Sch, Univ of Liverpool; *m* 1961, (Marina Evelyn) Anne, da of Rev Reginald Henry Lewis (d 1974), of Liverpool; 3 da (Kristin, Nicola, Coralie); *Career* house surgn and house physician Liverpool Royal Infirmary 1959-60, med registrar hosps in Liverpool region 1960-64, res fell Dept of Med Genetics John Hopkins Hosp and Sch of Med Baltimore USA 1965-66, lectr in med Univ of Edinburgh 1967-68, sr registrar in gastroenterology Western Gen Hosp Edinburgh 1968-69, hon lectr in med Univ of London 1969-70, conslt physician and gastroenterologist Aberdeen Royal Infirmary, clinical sr lectr in med Univ of Aberdeen, physician to HM The Queen (in Scotland); author of numerous chapters in books and articles mainly on liver an alimentary diseases; *Books* Diseases of Liver and Biliary System (1984), Gastroenterology (1984); *Recreations* mountaineering, music; *Clubs* Association of Physicians; *Style—* Dr Peter Brunt; 17 Kingshill Rd, Aberdeen AB2 4JY (☎ 0224 314204); Aberdeen Royal Infirmary, Forsterhill, Aberdeen

BRUNTISFIELD, 1 Baron (UK 1942); Sir Victor Alexander George Anthony Warrender; 8 Bt (GB 1715), MC (1918); s of Vice Adm Sir George John Scott, 7 Bt, KCB, KCVO (d 1917) and Lady Ethel Maud Ashley-Cooper, da of 8 Earl of Shaftesbury; *b* 23 June 1899,Queen Victoria stood sponsor at christening; *Educ* Eton; *m* 1, 1920 (m dis 1946), Dorothy Etta (d 1975), da of late Col Richard Hamilton Rawson, MP, by his w Lady Beatrice, *née* Anson (da of 2 Earl of Lichfield); 3 s; m 2, 1948, Tania, da of Dr M Kolin, of St Jacob, Dubrovnik, Yugoslavia; 1 s, 1 da; *Heir* s, Hon John Warrender, OBE, MC, TD; *Career* private sec to Sir Robert S Horne, GBE, KC, MP 1920-22; MP (Cons) Kesteven and Rutland Grantham Div 1923-42, PPS (unpaid) to Parly Under Sec of State for India 1924, asst Cons whip 1928-31, chm Young Cons Union 1929-30, jr lord of the Treasury 1931-32, vice chamberlain of the Household 1932-35, comptroller of HM's Household 1935, Parly and fin sec to Admiralty 1935, fin sec to War Dept and memb Army Cncl 1935-40, Parly sec to Admiralty 1940-45; *Clubs* Turf; *Style—* The Rt Hon The Lord Bruntisfield, MC; Residence le Village 1B, 1837 Chateau-d'Oex, Switzerland (☎ 010 41 029 47117)

BRUNTON, Sir Gordon Charles; s of late Charles Arthur Brunton and Hylda Pritchard; *b* 27 Dec 1921; *Educ* Cranleigh Sch, LSE; *m* 1, 1946 (m dis 1965), Nadine Lucile Paula Sohr; 1 s, 2 da (and 1 s decd); m 2, 1966, Gillian Agnes Kirk; 1 s, 1 da; *Career* cmmnd RA 1942, joined IA 1942, served in India, Assam and Burma 1942-46; joined Tothill Press (appointed to bd 1954), md Tower Press Gp of Cos 1958-61, PA to md Odhams Press Ltd 1961, md Thomson Pubns Ltd 1961, dir Thomson Orgn Ltd 1963, md and chief exec Thomson Orgn 1968, pres Int Thomson Orgn Ltd, md and chief exec Int Thomson Orgn plc, ret 1984; chm: Bemrose Corp plc, Martin Currie Pacific Tst plc 1985-, The Racing Post plc 1985-, Euram Consltg Ltd 1985-, Community Ind Ltd, Ingersoll Pubns Ltd; chm Racing International Ltd dir: Cable and Wireless plc, Yattendon Investmt Tst Ltd; dir Arts Cncl South Bank Bd, memb Fin Ctee OUP; fell LSE; former pres: Nat Advertising Benevolent Soc, Periodical Publishers Assoc Ltd, Printers' Charitable Corp; patron History of Advertising Tst; kt 1985; *Recreations* breeding horses, books; *Style—* Sir Gordon Brunton; North Munstead, Godalming, Surrey

BRUNTON, Dr James Lauder; s and h of Sir (Edward Francis) Lauder Brunton, 3 Bt; *b* 24 Sept 1947; *Educ* Selwyn House Sch Montreal, Bishops Coll Sch Lennoxville, McGill Univ (BSc 1968, MDCM 1972); *m* 1, 1 July 1967 (m dis 1983), Susan Elizabeth, da of Charles Hons; 1 s (Douglas Lauder b 1968), 1 da (Jennifer Anne b 1971); m 2, 1984, Beverly Anne Freedman; 1 s (Robert James b 1987); *Career* assoc prof of medicine Univ of Toronto; staff physician Mount Sinai Hosp Toronto; FRCP (Canada); *Style—* Dr James Brunton; 7 Blaine Drive, Don Mills, Ontario, Canada M3B 2G3 (☎ 0101 416 447 0441); Suite 435, Mount Sinai Hospital, 600 University Ave, Toronto, Canada M5G 1X5 (☎ 0101 416 586 5175)

BRUNTON, Sir (Edward Francis) Lauder; 3 Bt (UK 1908), of Stratford Place, St

Marylebone; s of Sir (James) Stopford (Lauder) Brunton, 2 Bt (d 1943); *b* 10 Nov 1916; *Educ* Trinity Coll Sch Port Hope Ontario, Bryanston Sch, McGill Univ; *m* 1946, Marjorie Grant, only da of David Sclater Lewis, MSc, MD, FRCP (Canada), of Montreal; 1 s, 1 da; *Heir* s, James Brunton; *Career* hon attending physician: Royal Victoria Hosp Montreal, St Martha's Hosp; fell: Int Soc of Hematology, American Coll of Physicians; memb American Soc of Hematology; *Style—* Sir Lauder Brunton, Bt; PO Box 140, Guysborough, Nova Scotia, Canada

BRUNTON, Ronald (Ron); s of John White Brunton, of Town Green, Whitfield, Northumberland, and Magaret, *née* Snowball; *b* 8 May 1949; *m* 20 Oct 1979, Helen Deira, da of Frederick William Hutchinson; 2 s (James Ronald b 5 July 1985, Andrew Ian b 31 Aug 1988); *Career* gen and sales mgmnt Mills & Allen plc 1974-85; jt md: Brunton Curtis Outdoor Advertising Ltd 1986-90, Poster Power Outdoor Advertising Ltd 1990-, R&S Advertising Consultants Ltd 1990-; *Style—* Ron Brunton, Esq; 4/6 Peterborough Rd, Harrow HA11 2BQ (☎ 081 864 3644, fax 081 423 8562)

BRUTON, Dr Dudley Malcolm; s of David Idris Bruton (d 1979), and Catherine, *née* Jones (d 1977); *b* 26 June 1933; *Educ* Aberdare County Sch, Reading Sch Berks, The London Hosp Med Coll, Univ of London, The London Sch of Hygiene and Tropical Med, Univ of London (MB BS, MSc); *m* 5 May 1956, Joan, da of Cyril David Lewis (d 1977); 2 s (David b 1960, James b 1963), 1 da (Elizabeth b 1958); *Career* Flt Lt RAF Med Branch UK and Malta 1957-60; princ med offr BEA BOAC and BA 1969-79, dir med servs Rothmans International Tobacco (UK) Ltd 1979-; hon sec Soc of Occupational Med 1976-79, memb Bd Faculty of Occupational Med RCP 1978-83, memb Cncl RSM 1981-86, memb Specialist Advsy Ctee on Occupational Med Jt Ctee on Higher Med Trg 1982-86, regnl specialty advsr occupational med NW Thames Region 1986-; area surgn St John Ambulance Bde (Bucks) 1984-89; memb Bucks Cncl on Alcohol and Drug Abuse 1984-89; DIH 1964, MFOM 1978, FFOM 1979; *Recreations* art, music, various sports; *Clubs* Leander; *Style—* Dr Dudley M Bruton; Wildwood, Rotherfield Rd, Henley-on-Thames, Oxon RG9 1NN, (☎ 0491 575143)

BRUTON, Prof Michael John; s of (Patrick) John Bruton, of Hertford, and Louise Ann, *née* Roberts; *b* 28 March 1938; *Educ* Richard Hale Sch Hertford, Univ Coll London (BA), Imperial Coll London (MSc, DIC), Regent St Poly (Dip TP); *m* 2 March 1963, Sheila Grace, da of Alexander Kyle Harrison; 2 da (Suzy b 1969, Catherine b 1972); *Career* princ planning offr Bucks CC 1966-67 (Lanarkshire CC 1965-66), princ lectr town planning Oxford Poly 1967-72, head school planning and landscape Birmingham Poly 1972-77, dep princ and registrar UWIST 1985-88 (prof town planning 1977-85), registrar Univ of Wales Coll of Cardiff 1988-; govr Centre for Environmental Studies 1978-81, chm CNAA town planning bd 1978-84; memb: Countryside Cmmn for Wales 1981-85, Univ Grants Ctee Social Studies Sub-Ctee 1985-, ESRC Post Graduate Bd 1985-; chm Regnl Rivers Advsy Ctee for Wales 1989-, planning advsr to Univ Funding Cncl 1989-; MRTPI, MCIT, MIHT; *Books* Introduction to Transportation Planning (3 edn, 1985), Spirit and Purpose of Planning (2 edn, 1984), Local Planning in Practice (1987); *Recreations* watching rugby and cricket, travel; *Clubs* Royal Commonwealth; *Style—* Prof Michael Bruton; Univ of Wales, College of Cardiff, PO Box 920, Cardiff CF1 3XP (☎ 0222 874792, fax 0222 874792, telex 497368)

BRYAN, Sir Arthur; s of William Woodall Bryan, and Isobel Alan, *née* Tweedie; *b* 4 March 1923; *Educ* Longton HS Stoke-on-Trent; *m* 1947, Betty, da of F G Ratford, of Essex; 1 s (Lawrence), 1 da; *Career* pres and dir Waterford Wedgwood 1986-88; Wedgwood: joined Wedgwood 1947, gen sales mangr 1959, dir 1960, md 1963, chm 1968-86; dir: Friends' Provident Life Office 1985-, UK Fund Inc (USA), Rank Orgn plc, JCB Inc of America; HM Lord Lt Staffs 1968; memb Ct Univ of Keele; Hon MUniv Keele 1978; CBIM, FInstM, CICeram, FRSA 1964; KStJ; kt 1976; *Recreations* walking, tennis, reading; *Style—* Sir Arthur Bryan; Parkfields Cottage, Tittensor, Stoke-on-Trent, Staffs (☎ 078 139 2686)

BRYAN, Dora (Mrs William Lawton); da of Albert Broadbent, and Georgina, *née* Hill; *b* 7 Feb 1923; *Educ* Hathershaw Council Sch; *m* 1954, William Lawton; 2 s (David b 1959, William b 1962), 1 da (Georgina b 1960); *Career* WWII ENSA Italy and England; pantomimes: London Hippodrome 1936, Manchester Palace 1937, Alhambra Glasgow 1938, Oldham Reperatory 1939-44; West End Theatres: Travellers' Joy, Accolade, Lyric Review, Simon and Laura, The Water Gypsies, Gentlemen Prefer Blondes, Six of One, Too True to be Good, Hello Dolly!, They Don't Grow on Trees (Her Majesty's) 1979, The Merry Wives of Windsor (Regents Park) 1984, She Stoops to Conquer (Nat Theatre) 1985, The Apple Cart (Haymarket) 1986, Charlie Girl (Victoria Palace) 1986 (Birmingham) 1988; Pygmalion (Plymouth, NY) 1987, Chichester Festival Seasons 1971-74, London Palladium Season 1971, London Palladium Pantomime Season 1973-74; films incl: The Fallen Idol 1949, Two A Penny 1968; TV appearances: Sunday Night at the London Palladium, According to Dora 1968, Both Ends Meet 1972; Awards: Br Acad Best Actress for A Taste of Honey, Variety Club of GB and Manchester Evening News Best Actress for She Stoops to Conquer (Nat Theatre); a vice pres Assoc of Lancastrians in London 1991; *Books* According to Dora (autobiography); *Recreations* patchwork quilts, reading, cats, dogs; *Style—* Ms Dora Bryan; Clarges, 118 Marine Parade, Brighton, E Sussex (☎ 0273 603235)

BRYAN, Prof Eric Reginald; s of Reginald Harold Bryan, of Kingston upon Thames, and Elizabeth Ellen, *née* Cowlard (d 1980); *b* 20 Dec 1927; *Educ* Tiffin Boys' Sch Kingston upon Thames, Univ of London (MSc, PhD); *m* 31 March 1951, Jean, da of Walter Cyril Wrigley; 2 s (Roger Stephen b 5 March 1952, Julian Simon b 13 July 1958), 1 da (Lydia Catharine b 1 Oct 1953); *Career* Alkali Div ICI 1948-60 (civil engrg designer, construction mangr, design engr); sr lectr Dept of Engrg Univ of Manchester 1965-70 (DSc, lectr 1960-65); Dept of Civil Engrg Univ of Salford: prof of structural engrg 1970-85, pro vice chancellor 1979-82, prof of civil engrg and chm of dept 1985-88, res prof of civil engrg 1988-; former chm Sub Ctees Br and Euro Standards, chm Constructional Steel Quality Assurance Scheme; Sir Arnold Waters medal Inst of Structural Engrs, Distinguished Serv medal Euro Convention for Constructional Steelwork; FIStructE 1969, FICE 1970, FEng 1988; *Books* The Stressed Skin Design of Steel Buildings (1973), Manual of Stressed Skin Diaphragm Design (with J M Davies, 1982); *Recreations* travel, historic properties, woodwork; *Style—* Prof Eric Bryan; Department of Civil Engineering, University of Salford, Salford M5 4WT (☎ 061 745 5000, fax 061 745 5060)

BRYAN, Felicity Anne (Mrs Alexander Duncan); da of Sir Paul Bryan, DSO, MC, and Betty Mary, *née* Hoyle (d 1968); *b* 16 Oct 1945; *Educ* Courtauld Inst of Art, Univ of London; *m* 23 Oct 1981, Alexander Duncan, s of Patrick Duncan (d 1967); 2 s (Maxim Paul b 1983, Benjamin Patrick b 1987), 1 da (Alice Mary b 1982); *Career* journalist: Financial Times 1968-70, The Economist 1970-72; literary agent and dir Curtis Brown Ltd 1972-88, fndr The Felicity Bryan Agency 1988; *Books* The Town Gardener's Companion (1982), A Garden for Children (1986), Nursery Style (1989); *Recreations* opera, gardening, travel, entertaining; *Clubs* Groucho; *Style—* Ms Felicity Bryan; The Old Rectory, Mill St, Kidlington, Oxford OX5 2EE (☎ 08675 2355); 2 A North Parade, Banbury Rd, Oxford OX2 6PE (☎ 0865 513 816, fax 0865 310055)

BRYAN, Gerald Jackson; CMG (1964), CVO (1966), OBE (1960), MC (1941); s of George Bryan, OBE, of Belfast (d 1929), and Ruby Evelyn, *née* Pollexfen (d 1975); *b* 2 April 1921; *Educ* Wrekin, RMA Woolwich, New Coll Oxford; *m* 1947, Georgiana Wendy Cockburn, da of William Barraud Hull (d 1967), of Mbabane, Swaziland; 1 s (Caesar), 2 da (Diana, Mary); *Career* Maj RE, served with 11 (Scot) Commando in M East; Colonial Serv 1944-67: Swaziland, Barbados, Mauritius; admin: Virgin Is 1959-62, St Lucia 1962-67, ret 1967; govt sec and head of Civil Serv IOM 1967-69; gen mangr Londonderry Devpt Cmmn 1969-73, Bracknell Devpt Corpn 1973-82, memb Lord Chllr's Panel 1982; dir: Lovaux Engrg Co 1982-88, MDSL Co 1988-; sec gen Assoc of Contact Lens Mfrs 1983-88; memb (C) Berks CC 1983-85; FBIM 1969; CStJ 1964, KStJ 1985; *Recreations* walking, swimming; *Style—* Gerald Bryan, Esq, CMG, CVO, OBE, MC; Whitehouse, Murrell Hill Lane, Binfield, Berks RG12 5BY (☎ 0344 425 447)

BRYAN, (James) Howard; s of (Albert) Marriott Bryan (d 1984), of Leeds, and Theresa Edna Gwendolyn (Gwen); *b* 24 April 1944; *Educ* Silcoates Sch Wakefield, Univ of Leeds (LLB); *m* 18 March 1972, Jacquelyn Sarah, da of Percy Herbert Stanley Pilcher; 1 s (Ross James b 11 Feb 1979), 1 da (Louise Victoria b 5 July 1983); *Career* admitted slr 1968; ptnr Hepworth & Chadwick 1971-; govr Silcoates Sch 1978; Liveryman Worshipful Co of Wheelwrights; memb: Law Soc, Anglo-German Jurists Assoc, Industl Law Soc; *Recreations* sailing, skiing, tennis; *Clubs* Royal Northern and Clyde Yacht, Clyde Cruising, Leeds; *Style—* Howard Bryan, Esq; Hepworth & Chadwick, Cloth Hall Court, Leeds LS1 2JB (☎ 0532 430391, fax 0532 456188)

BRYAN, James Robert Emmett; s of James Edward Bryan (d 1985), of Bristol, and Florence May, *née* Miller (d 1960); *b* 27 Jan 1913; *Educ* St Mary-on-the-Quay Bristol, St Brendan's Coll Bristol; *m* 31 Aug 1936, Kathleen Alice (d 1966), da of James Joseph McNally (d 1969), of Bristol; 1 s (Michael James b 1937), 2 da (Jaqueline Mary b 1939, Valerie Jean b 1942); *Career* chm and md: family firm of Bryan Bros motor distributors Bristol 1929 (dir 1941), Bryan Bros Holdings Ltd; controlling: Bryan Bros Ltd, Bryan Bros Trucks Ltd, Bryan Bros (Hanham) Ltd, Bryan Bros (St Austell) Ltd, Bristol Auto Centre Ltd, Bryan Bros (Contract Hire) Ltd; main Ford dealer 1933; chm Bristol Football Club (RU) 1956-74 (pres 1975-84); FIMI; *Recreations* rugby, cricket; *Clubs* Bristol Football (RFU), Glos Co Cricket; *Style—* James R E Bryan, Esq; The Grange, Tytherington, Wotton-under-Edge, Glos GL12 8QB (☎ 0454 412255); Bryan Bros Ltd, College Green, Bristol BS1 5XN (☎ 0272 293881, fax 225839, telex 449662, car 0860 357381)

BRYAN, Sir Paul Elmore Oliver; DSO (1943), MC (1943); s of Rev John Thomas Ingram Bryan (d 1953), of Milton Ernest, Bedford; *b* 3 Aug 1913; *Educ* St John's Sch Leatherhead, Gonville and Caius Coll Cambridge; *m* 1, 1939, Betty Mary (d 1968), da of James Cars Hoyle; 3 da; m 2, 1971, Cynthia Duncan, da of late Sir Patrick Ashley Cooper, of Hexton Manor, Herts; *Career* MP (C): Howden 1955-83, Boothferry 1983-87; min of state Dept of Employment 1970-72; dir: Granada Television, Granada Theatres, Greater Manchester Independent Radio Ltd 1972-83, Furness Withy Ltd 1983-89, The Scot Lion Insurance Co Ltd 1984-; dep chm Furness Withy Ltd 1984-89, chm United Cable TV (London S) 1985-; *Style—* Sir Paul Bryan, DSO, MC; 5 Westminster Gardens, Marsham St, London SW1 (☎ 071 834 2050); Park Farm, Sawdon, nr Scarborough, N Yorks (☎ 0723 85370)

BRYAN, (Percival Charles) Rex; s of Percival George Bryan (d 1962), of Suffolk, and Lilian Georgina Bryan (d 1983); *b* 25 Feb 1924; *Educ* Coll of Technol Cambridge, Northampton Coll of Art, Coll of Preceptors; *m* 20 May 1944, Vera; 2 s (Peter b 1944, Alan b 1946); *Career* CA; sr ptnr Rex Bryan Son and Pennock; formerly with Dept of Arch & Planning Cambridge City and Northants Borough Cncl; memb RIBA; *Recreations* golf; *Clubs* Northamptonshire Co Golf, Cheyne Walk (Northampton), Northampton and Co, Farmers; *Style—* Rex Bryan, Esq; The Lodge, 50 High St, Great Houghton, Northampton; Great Houghton House, Great Houghton, Northampton (☎ 0604 764051)

BRYAN, Rex Victor; s of Bertram Henry Bryan (d 1970), of Purley, Surrey, and Annie Ella Margaret, *née* King; *b* 2 Dec 1946; *Educ* Wallington GS, Jesus Coll Oxford (MA); *m* 1, 31 July 1971 (m dis 1981), Catherine, da of Samuel Carbery, of Ballymena, Co Antrim, NI; 1 s (Roland Patrick b 1977); m 2, 9 Aug 1982, Mary Elizabeth, da of Brendan Joseph O'Toole, of Woodford Green, Essex; 2 s (Adam Francis b 1985, Thomas Edward b 1988), 1 da (Victoria Louise b 1986); *Career* called to the Bar Lincolns Inn 1971, barr 1978-, head of chambers 1986-; *Recreations* carpentry, languages; *Style—* Rex Bryan, Esq; 5 Pump Ct, Temple, London EC4 (☎ 071 353 2532, fax 071 353 5321)

BRYAN, Robert Hedley; s of Joseph William Bryan (d 1976), and Gladys, *née* Bacon; *b* 25 Aug 1934; *Educ* Derby GS, Univ of Hull (BSc, DipEd); *m* 1 March 1963, Ann Mollie, da of Alfred Edgar Daly (d 1971); 2 da (Joanna b 1968, Emma b 1970); *Career* theatre and TV lighting designer and theatre lighting conslt; fndr team memb Theatre Projects Lighting Ltd 1960-78; designed lighting for extensive number of prodns incl: Royal Opera House, ENO, Glyndebourne Festival Opera, NT, RSC, Staatsoper Vienna, Paris Opera, Geneva, Nice; memb: Soc of Br Theatre Lighting Designers 1970, Soc of TV Lightning Dirs 1980; *Recreations* reading, walking, squash, film & television; *Style—* Robert Bryan, Esq; 19 Blatchington Hill, Seaford, E Sussex BN25 2AH (☎ 0323 89 2308); Royal Opera House, Covent Garden, London (☎ 071 240 1200)

BRYAN, William Alexander (Bill); s of Andrew Bryan (d 1928), and Margaret Ann Bryan (d 1965); *b* 21 July 1924; *Educ* Newton Park Higher Grade Sch Ayr Scotland; *m* 30 June 1950, Margaret Aitken Jess, da of William Muir Morton (d 1951); 2 s (David b 1956, Gordon b 1959); *Career* accountant; co sec Tennant Budd and Roderick Pratt Ltd 1970-73; dir The Builders Accident Insur Ltd 1984- (co sec 1972-83, gen mangr 1984-88); FICAS; *Recreations* golf, reading; *Clubs* Caledonian; *Style—* Bill Bryan, Esq; 9 Paddock Way, Wivenhoe, Colchester, Essex CO7 9HL (☎ 0206 824038); 31/33 Bedford St, Strand, London WC2E 9EL (☎ 071 836 9885, telex 297311, fax 010 379 5329)

BRYANS, Dame Anne Margaret; *née* Gilmour; DBE (1957, CBE 1945); da of Col Rt Hon Sir John Gilmour, 2 Bt, GCVO, DSO, MP (d 1940); *b* 29 Oct 1909; *Educ* private; *m* 1932, Lt Cdr John Reginald Bryans, RN (d 1990), s of Rev R du F Brya 1922); 1 s; *Career* HQ Staff 1938; Br Red Cross and St John War Orgn: dep cmmr, M East cmmn 1943, cmmr Jan-June 1945, dep chm 1953-64, vice chm 1964-76; memb Exec Ctee BRCS, lay memb Cncl for Professions Supplementary to Med until 1979; memb: Ethical Practices Sub Ctee Royal Free Hosp 1974-, Royal Free Hosp Sch Cncl 1968-83, Bd of Govrs Eastman Dental Hosp 1973-79, Camden and Islington AHA 1974-79; vice pres Open Sect RSM 1975 (pres 1980-82), former memb ITA (later IBA); memb: Govt Anglo-Egyptian Resettlement Bd, BBC/ITA Appeals Ctee Med Sch St George's Hosp; special tstee and former chm Royal Free Hosp and Friends of Royal Free Hosp, former chm Bd of Govrs Royal Free Hosp; memb Cncl Florence Nightingale Hosp, tstee Florence Nightingale Aid in Sickness Tst 1979-; govr Royal Star and Garter Home 1975-87; memb Exec Ctee Royal Soc of Medicine 1982-84, vice pres Royal Coll of Nursing, former govr Westminster Hosp; FRSM 1976; chm Order of St John of Jerusalem and BRCS Service Hosp Welfare Ctee and VAD Ctee 1960-89, vice chm Jt Ctee and BRCS 1976-81, chm Grants Ctee Nations Fund for Nurses; DStJ; *Clubs* Royal Lymington Yacht, New Cavendish; *Style—* Dame Anne Bryans, DBE; 57 Elm Park House, Elm Park Gardens, London SW10 9QD (☎ 071 352 7436)

BRYANT, Christopher Gordon Alastair; s of Gordon Douglas Clifford Bryant (d

1975), of Bristol, and Edna Mollie, *née* Shrubb; *b* 14 April 1944; *Educ* Kingston GS, Univ of Leicester (BA, MA), Univ of Southampton (PhD); *m* Elizabeth Mary, da of George Thomas Martyn Peters; 2 da (Catherine Elizabeth, Lucy Ann); *Career* tutorial asst in sociology Univ of Leicester 1965-66, lectr Dept of Sociology and Social Admin 1968-72 (asst lectr 1966-68), prof Dept of Sociology Univ of Salford 1982- (sr lectr 1976-82, chm 1982-90); guest prof Goethe Univ of Frankfurt am Main 1973; visiting fell: Ohio State Univ Columbus 1981, Univ of Utrecht 1986-; memb: Br Sociological Assoc 1966-, Exec Ctee of Br Sociological Assoc 1987-; chm Pubns Ctee 1989-; *Books* Sociology in Action (1976), Positivism in Social Theory and Research (1985), What Has Sociology Achieved? (1990); *Recreations* theatre, concerts, walking, seeing friends; *Style—* Prof Christopher Bryant; 104 Brooklands Rd, Sale, Cheshire M33 3QL (☎ 061 962 6081); Dept of Sociology, University of Salford, Salford M5 4WT (☎ 061 745 5000, fax 061 745 5999, telex 668680 SULIB)

BRYANT, David John; CBE (1980, MBE 1969); s of Reginald Samuel Harold Bryant (d 1978), of Avon, and Evelyn Clair, *née* Weaver (d 1987); *b* 27 Oct 1931; *Educ* Weston-super-Mare GS, St Paul's Coll Cheltenham, Redland Coll Bristol; *m* 2 April 1960, Ruth Georgina, da of George Roberts (d 1971), of Avon; 2 da (Jacqueline Anne b 7 May 1962, Carole Jayne b 6 Jan 1965); *Career* schoolmaster 1955-71; dir: Sporting Boutiques 1971-78, Drakelite Ltd (bowls consits) 1978-; professional bowler 1980-; Cwlth Games Singles Gold Medallist 1962, 1970, 1974 and 1978, World Outdoor Bowls Singles Champion 1966, 1980 and 1988, World Indoor Bowles Singles Champion 1979, 1980 and 1981, English Outdoor Singles Champion 6 times, English Indoor Singles Champion 9 times, British Isles Singles Outdoor Champion 4 times, British Isles Singles Indoor Champion 4 times, Int Invitation Masters Singles Champion 9 times; *Books* Bryant on Bowls (1966), Bowl with Bryant (1984), The Game of Bowls (1990); *Recreations* gardening, angling; *Clubs* Clevedon Bowling, Clevedon Conservative; *Style—* David Bryant, Esq, CBE; 47 Esmond Grove, Clevedon, Avon BS21 7HP (☎ 0272 875423); Drakelite Ltd, 81 High Street, Southwold, Suffolk IP18 6DS (☎ 0502 722002)

BRYANT, His Hon Judge David Michael Arton; s of Lt-Col Arthur Denis Bryant, of Tanfield House, W Tanfield, Ripon, N Yorks, and Dorothy Alice, *née* Arton; *b* 27 Jan 1942; *Educ* Wellington, Oriel Coll Oxford (scholar, BA); *m* (Diana) Caroline, da of Brig Charles Walker Sloan, CBE, of Lady's Walk, Hutton Conyers, Ripon, North Yorkshire; 2 s (Edward Denis Charles b 1971, William Robert b 1982), 1 da (Lucinda Mary b 1972); *Career* called to the Bar Inner Temple 1964, practised North Eastern Circuit 1965-89, rec 1985-89, circuit judge 1989-; memb Ripon Deanery Synod; *Recreations* gardening, shooting, medieval history; *Clubs* Carlton; *Style—* His Hon Judge Bryant; Middlesborough Combined Court Centre, Middlesborough, Cleveland

BRYANT, Air Vice-Marshal Derek Thomas; CB (1987), OBE (1974); s of (Joseph) Thomas Bryant (d 1957), and (Daisy Elizabeth) Mary, *née* Thurley; *b* 1 Nov 1933; *Educ* Latymer Upper GS Hammersmith; *m* 4 Aug 1956, Patricia, da of William Dodge (d 1977); 1 s (Iain David b 1957), 1 da (Janine b 1960); *Career* fighter pilot 1953, flying instr 1957, Sqdn Cdr 228-OCU and 14 Sqdn 1968-74, Station Cdr RAF Coningsby 1976-78, Sr ASO Offr (SASO) 38 Gp 1982-84, Dep Cdr RAF Germany 1984-87, Cmdt RAF Staff Coll 1987-88; *Recreations* gardening, golf; *Clubs* RAF; *Style—* Air Vice-Marshal D T Bryant, CB, OBE; Manor Stables, Lower Swell, Fivehead, Taunton, Somerset TA3 6PH (☎ 04608 209)

BRYANT, Edward James; s of Edward Bryant, of Minister House, Shaw, Wilts, and Alma Mary, *née* James (d 1955); *b* 24 April 1910; *Educ* The Abbey Portishead, Leamington Coll Warwicks; *m* 16 Aug 1948, Suzanne, da of Gp Capt John de Courcy, MC, Croix de Guerre oak leaves (despatches) (ka 1940), of The Manor House, Barton, Cambridge; 2 s (Edward b 1951, David b 1955); *Career* RAFVR 1940-46, Actg Wing Cdr; elected: W Suffolk CC 1963-73, St Edmunds Bury Borough Cncl 1979-87; min's rep on Eastern Regn Sports Cncl 1972-76, chm W Suffolk Marriage Guidance Cncl to 1976; volunteer memb Probation After Care Serv Bury St Edmunds, community emergency advsr Hundon Centre, vice-chm Suffolk War Pensioners Ctee; *Recreations* shooting, cricket, tennis; *Clubs* Royal Overseas League; *Style—* Edward Bryant, Esq; Marsh Morgen House, Stradishall, Newmarket, Suffolk (☎ 0440 820 287); Priory Cottage, Stogursey, Somerset (☎ 0278 732492)

BRYANT, Prof Greyham Frank; s of Ernest Noel Bryant (d 1981), and Florence Ivy, *née* Russell (d 1974); *b* 3 June 1931; *Educ* Univ of Reading (BSc), Imperial Coll London (PhD); *m* 2 July 1955, Iris Sybil, da of Albert Edward Jardine (d 1980); 2 s (Mark Greyham b 2 Jan 1963, David Nicholas b 18 Aug 1966); *Career* sr scientific offr Br Iron and Steel Res 1959-64; Imperial Coll London: res fell 1964-67, reader in industl control 1975-82, prof of control 1982-, dep dir Interdisciplinary Res Centre in Systems Engrg 1989-; chm Broner Consits 1979-88, md Greycon Consits 1985-, dir Circulation Res 1989-; MIEE, FIMA, FEng; *Books* Automation of Tandem Mills (jtly); *Recreations* music; *Style—* Prof Greyham Bryant; 18 Wimborne Ave, Norwood Green, Middx (☎ 081 574 5648); Dept Electrical Engineering, Imperial College, London SW7 (☎ 071 589 5111)

BRYANT, Prof John Allen; s of Joseph Samuel Bryant, of Croydon, Surrey, and (Beatrice Maud), Patricia, *née* Wallace-Page (d 1990); *b* 14 April 1944; *Educ* Whitgift Sch Croydon, Queens' Coll Cambridge (BA, MA, PhD); *m* 27 July 1968, Marjorie Joan, da of Maj Gerald C G Hatch (d 1983), of Hingham, Norfolk; 2 s (Mark b 1 Jan 1972, Simon b 3 Jan 1974); *Career* res fell Univ of East Anglia 1969-70, lectr Univ of Nottingham 1970-74, reader Univ Coll Cardiff 1982-85 (lectr 1974-77, sr lectr 1977-82), head of biological sciences Univ of Exeter 1986- (prof 1985-); chm Biotechnology South West, memb Cell Biology Ctee Soc for Experimental Biology 1988-89 (cncl memb 1981-87, hon sec 1983-87), memb SERC Plant Sci and Microbiology Ctee; C Biol 1984, FIBiol 1986 (MIBiol 1970), FRSA 1989; *Recreations* cross-country (formerly at intercounty level) & road running, birdwatching, walking, sailing; *Style—* Prof John Bryant; Dept of Biological Sciences, University of Exeter, Exeter EX4 4QG (☎ 0392 264672, fax 0392 263700)

BRYANT, Col John Hamlyn; s of Lt-Col Leslie George Hamlyn Bryant, OBE (d 1974), of Stoulton, Worcs, and Evelyn Doreen, *née* Devereux (d 1982); *b* 14 Aug 1933; *Educ* Wellington, RMA Sandhurst; *m* 8 March 1969, (Dorothea) Leslie Perceval, da of Col Perceval Clayton Marsden Hingston, MBE, of Upton upon Severn, Worcs; 2 s (Oliver b 1973, Mark 1974), 2 da (Penelope b 1971, Joanna b 1973); *Career* cmmnd 1954, Worcs Regt 1954-68, 3 Bn KAR 1960-64, Staff Coll Camberley 1965 Worcs and Sherwood Foresters Regt 1968-74, chief instr RMA Sandhurst 1969-71, BM 3 Inf Bde 1971-74 (despatches 1973), CO Depot Prince of Wales Div 1974-76, Queen's Medal (Bisley) 1975; Br Army Advsy Team: Dubai (UAE) 1977-79), Nigeria 1979-81; def attaché Montevideo 1982-85, Cmdt Cadet Trg Centre 1985-88, ret 1988; bursar Hawford Lodge Sch 1989-; FBIM 1988; *Recreations* jewellery making, photography, gardening; *Style—* Col John Bryant; c/o Barclays Bank, Pershore, Worcs WR10 1AN

BRYANT, Judith Marie (Mrs H M Hodkinson); da of John Frederick Bryant (d 1945), and Joan Marion Summerfield (d 1948); *b* 31 Dec 1942; *Educ* City of London Sch for Girls, Hove County GS, Brunel Univ (MPhil), The London Hosp Whitechapel (RGN); *m* 22 Nov 1986, Professor (Henry) Malcolm Hodkinson; *Career* staff nurse Paediatric Ward The London Hosp Whitechapel 1964-65, staff nurse and word sister Intensive Therapy Unit Univ Coll Hosp London 1965-69, nursing offr Intensive Therapy Unit Northwick Park Hosp Harrow 1969-71 (sr nursing offr Personnel Dept 1971-75), divnl nursing offr Community and Geriatrics Harrow Health Dist 1975-78, dist nursing offr Enfield Health Authy 1978-82, chief nursing offr Victoria Health Authy 1982-85, chief nursing offr and dir quality assur Riverside health Authy 1985-86, regnl nursing offr N East Thames Regnl Health Authy 1986-90, fell in clinical servs mgmnt King's Fund Coll 1990-; fndr memb RCN ITU Gp 1968-71, Florence Nightingale meml scholar USA and Canada 1970, serv advsr to DHSS Res Liaison Gp for the Elderly 1977-83, memb Royal Coll of Nursing Mgmnt Gp 1980-, memb S West Hertfordshire Dist Health Authy 1981-87, memb NHS Trg Authy Nursing and Midwives Staff Trg Ctee 1986, memb Bd 1930 Fund for Dist Nurses 1986-, memb Epsom Cluster Working Gp; memb Working Pty of King's Fund Pubn Commissioning Hospital Buildings (2 edn, 1981); *Recreations* opera, gardening, ceramics; *Style—* Ms Judith Bryant; The Kings Fund Coll, 2 Palace Court, London W2 4HS (☎ 071 727 0581)

BRYANT, Kenneth Marrable; s of Philip Harry Bryant (d 1979), of Guildford, Surrey, and Hilda Gertrude, *née* Linch (d 1988); *b* 13 June 1927; *Educ* Latymer Upper Sch, King's Coll London, Charing Cross Hosp Med Sch (MB BS); *m* 26 July 1952, Rosemary, da of Thomas Hawkins (d 1962), of Ealing, London; 1 s (Richard b 1962), 2 da (Elizabeth b 1957, Angela b 1959); *Career* Flt Lt 1952-55 RAF Orthopaedic Serv, RAF Hosp Ely; conslt orthopaedic surgn: St James Hosp 1965, Bolingbroke Hosp 1972, St George's Hosp 1980; hon sr lectr St George's Hosp Med Sch 1976, hon orthopaedic surgn Cheyne Centre for Spastic Children 1978, visiting orthopaedic surgn HM Prison Serv 1979; former lay chm Deanery Synod, churchwarden; Freeman City of London 1966, Liveryman Worshipful Soc of Apothecaries 1966; FRSM, FBOA, FRCS, AKC; *Recreations* gardening, fine bookbinding, pottering about in churches; *Style—* Kenneth Bryant, Esq; Orthopaedic Dept, St George's Hosp, London SW17 0QT (☎ 081 672 1255); Mitchell Mews, Truro, Cornwall

BRYANT, Martin Warwick; s of Douglas William Bryant, of Chichester, Sussex, and Elsie Marjorie Sylvia, *née* Simpkins; *b* 30 June 1952; *Educ* Chichester HS, ChCh Oxford (MA), Univ of Leeds (MA), Cranfield Sch of Mgmnt (MBA); *m* 26 May 1979, Hilary May, da of Philip Readhead Southall, of Rednal, Worcs; 1 s (Laurence Michael b 1984), 2 da (Emily Anna b 1981, Madeleine Rose b 1989); *Career* Swaziland ODI 1975-77, business analyst Foster Wheeler Ltd 1978-82, planning mangr BOC Gp plc 1983-86, dir of corporate devpt: Charles Barker plc 1986-89, Boots Co plc 1989-; ctee memb Village CC; *Recreations* golf, skiing; *Clubs* Ski (GB); *Style—* Martin Bryant, Esq; Boots Co plc, Head Office, Nottingham, NG3AA (☎ 0602 592935)

BRYANT, Michael Dennis; CBE (1988); s of William Frederick Bryant (d 1954), of London, and Ann Mary Kerrigan, *née* Jackson (d 1965); *b* 5 April 1928; *Educ* Battersea GS; *m* 1, 1958 (m dis 1980), Josephine Martin; 2 s (Kerrigan, Simon), 2 da (Sarah, Josephine); m 2, 1990, Judith Mary Coke; *Career* ordinary seaman MN 1945, 2 Lt 7 Queen's Own Hussars 1947-49; actor; RSC 1964-65, Nat Theatre player 1977-; assoc of Nat Theatre 1984-, memb Cncl RADA 1982-; *Recreations* walking; *Style—* Michael Bryant, Esq, CBE; The Nat Theatre, South Bank, London SE1 9PX

BRYANT, Michael Sydney; s of Sydney Cecil Bryant (d 1977), of Keynsham, Avon, and Lily May, *née* Jefferies; *b* 16 March 1944; *Educ* Bristol GS, Univ of Exeter, City of London Coll; *Career* estate duty off Inland Revenue 1965-70, assoc dir Bevington Lowndes Ltd 1970-75, dir Rathbone Bros plc (formerly Comprehensive Financial Services plc) 1975; contrib: Daily Telegraph, Sunday Times, Money Mktg; memb Cncl FIMBRA 1986-88 and 1990-, chm Insur and Compensation Ctee FIMBRA, memb Tax Ctee BIIBA; IBRC 1977; *Recreations* food, wine, travel; *Clubs* Carlton; *Style—* Michael Bryant, Esq; 50 Hans Place, London SW1X 0LA (☎ 071 225 0759); University House, Lower Grosvenor Place, London SW1W 0EX (☎ 071 630 5611, fax 071 821 1437, telex 262257)

BRYANT, William Wells; s of Frank Wells Bryant, and Helen Muff, *née* Doe; *b* 24 May 1931; *Educ* Bungay GS, Univ of Durham (BSc); *m* 31 March 1956, Patricia Margaret, da of James Wesley Davison; 2 da (Karen Anne (Dr Bryant-Mole) b 1957, Rachel Jane (Mrs Waugh) b 1959); *Career* Nat Serv, RAF 1949-51; dep dir NU Philips Gloeilampenfabrieken 1972-76, tech dir Polygram Record Ops Ltd 1977-87; cncllr Reigate and Banstead Borough Cncl, lay chm Epsom Deanery Synod, memb Mid Surrey DHA, fell Inst of Statisticians 1959; *Style—* William Bryant, Esq; 10 Bolters Lane, Banstead, Surrey SM7 2AR (☎ 0737 357053)

BRYARS, Donald Leonard; s of Leonard Bryars (d 1961), of Goole, Yorks, and Marie, *née* Purcell (d 1977); *b* 31 March 1929; *Educ* Goole GS, Univ of Leeds (BA); *m* 18 July 1953, Joan, da of Jonathan Charles Noble Yealand (d 1967), of Goole, Yorks; 1 da (Anne b 1954); *Career* Nat Serv Royal Signals 1951-52; HM Customs and Excise 1953-84: princ 1964, asst sec 1971, on loan to Cabinet Off 1976-78, cmmr 1978-84, dir Customs 1978, dir personnel 1979-84, ret 1984; dir Customs Annuity and Benevolent Fund 1986-; memb: Editorial Ctee Focus Magazine, Chalfont St Giles Res Assoc; *Clubs* Civil Service (chm 1981-85); *Style—* Donald Bryars, Esq; 15 Ellwood Rise, Chalfont St Giles, Bucks HP8 4SU (☎ 02407 5466)

BRYCE, Andrew John; s of John Robert Murray Bryce, of Lymington, Hampshire, and Eileen Josephine, *née* Denham; *b* 31 Aug 1947; *Educ* Thorpe GS Norwich, Univ of Newcastle (LLB), Coll of Law Lancaster Gate; *m* 1972 (sep 1985), Karalee Frances Lovegrove; 1 s (Alexander Henry b 22 June 1977), 1 da (Lucy Charlotte b 21 May 1980), partner, Rosalind Beverly Hardy; 1 s (Matthew Cameron b 2 Oct 1986); *Career* Cameron KEMM Norden (now Cameron Markby Hewitt): articled clerk 1969-71, admitted slr 1971, ptnr 1973-; memb Law Soc 1973; UK Environmental Law Assoc: fndr memb 1986, vice chm 1987-88, chm 1988-; vice chm Planning and Environmental Sub Ctee City of London Solicitors Co; *Recreations* birdwatching, tennis, travel; *Clubs* David Lloyds Rackets, RSPB; *Style—* Andrew Bryce, Esq; Cameron Markby Hewitt, Sceptre Court, 40 Tower Hill, London EC3N 4BB (☎ 071 702 2345, fax 071 702 2303)

BRYCE, Sir (William) Gordon; CBE (1963); s of late James Chisholm Bryce, and Emily Susan, *née* Lees; *b* 2 Feb 1913; *Educ* Bromsgrove, Hertford Coll Oxford (MA); *m* 1940, Molly Mary, da of late Arthur Cranch Drake; 2 da; *Career* chief justice of the Bahamas 1970-73 (formerly attorney gen Gibraltar, Aden, Bahamas); kt 1971; *Style—* Sir Gordon Bryce, CBE; Broom Croft, Lydeard St Lawrence, Taunton, Somerset

BRYCE, Iain Ross; TD, DL (Humberside) 1977; s of William James Noel Bryce (d 1972), and Jessie (Jerry) Fleming, *née* Ross (d 1973); *b* 19 March 1936; *Educ* Bridlington GS; *m* 13 Jan 1962, Janet Elizabeth, da of Reginald Wilfred Arro; 2 da (Alison Jane (now Mrs Jonathan Peacock) b 26 Jan 1963, Alexandra Helen b 14 Feb 1968); *Career* Nat Serv 1959-61; TA and Vol Reserve 1961-83: 131 Para Engr Regt, cmd 72 Engr Regt (Tynes) 1974-76, dep cdr 29 Engr Brigade 1976-79, Col RE ret; articled clerk JC Beauvais & Co 1953-58, qualified chartered accountant 1959, ptnr: Buckley Hall Devlin & Co 1966-73 (asst 1961-66), Whinney Murray & Co (following merger) 1973-80, Ernst & Whinney (name change) 1980-89; Managing ptnr Hull Ernst & Young (following merger) 1989-; Prov Grand Master Yorks N & E Ridings United Grand Lodge of Eng 1984; memb Worshipful Co of Merchant Adventurers of York; FCA (ACA 1959); *Recreations* golf, yacht racing, freemasonry; *Clubs* Army & Navy, Ganton Golf (Scarborough), Royal Yorkshire Yacht (Bridlington); *Style—* Iain R Bryce, Esq; Managing Partner, Ernst & Young, PO Box 3, Lowgate House, Lowgate, Hull, Humberside HU1 1JJ (☎ 0482 25531, fax 0482 20284)

BRYCE-SMITH, Prof Derek; s of Charles Philip Smith (d 1938), of Wanstead, London, and Amelia, *née* Thick (d 1962); *b* 29 April 1926; *Educ* Bancrofts Sch Woodford Wells, SW Essex Tech Coll, West Ham Municipal Coll, Bedford Coll London (BSc, PhD, DSc); *m* 1, 5 Sept 1956, Marjorie Mary Anne (d 1966), da of Maj Eric Stewart, MC (d 1937), of London; 2 s (Duncan b 1959, David b 1963), 2 da (Madeleine b 1957, Hazel b 1961); m 2, 21 June 1969, Pamela Joyce Morgan, da of Marius Andreas Thorndahl (d 1942), of Denmark; 2 step da (Pamela b 1948, Diana b 1953); *Career* ICI postdoctoral fell King's Coll 1951-55 (asst lectr 1955-56); Univ of Reading: lectr 1956-63, reader 1963-65, prof 1965-89, pt/t prof 1989-; sr reporter Royal Soc Chem; formerly conslt to: Shell, Esso, EI Du Pont de Nemours (USA), Dutch State Mines; currently conslt: Lamberts Health Prods Natural Justice Ltd; dir Nature's Own Ltd; endowed lectureship Royal Soc Chem 1984 (John Jeyes Silver Medal); numerous radio and television broadcasts in UK and abroad largely on environmental chemistry topics; FRSC (chm Photochemistry Subject Gp), CChem, memb American Chem Soc; *Publications* Lead or Health (with R Stephens, 1980), The Zinc Solution (with L Hodgkinson, 1986) Photochemistry Vols 1-21 (sr reporter); *Recreations* singing, piano playing, gardening, debating; *Style*— Prof Derek Bryce-Smith; Chemistry Dept, University of Reading, Whiteknights Park, Reading, Berks, (☎ 0734 875123)

BRYCESON, Dr Anthony David Malcolm; s of Lt Col Donald John Bryceson (d 1978), and Muriel Gertrude, *née* Hutton (d 1979); *b* 16 Nov 1934; *Educ* Winchester, Univ of Cambridge (MB, BChir, MD), Westminster Hosp Med Sch; *m* 25 Oct 1969, Ulla, da of Axel Skalts; 1 s (William b 16 Aug 1972), 1 da (Maia b 16 Dec 1974); *Career* MO Columbo Plan Laos 1961-63, med registrar Hosp for Tropical Diseases London 1964, asst prof Harte Salasse I Univ Addis Abeba Ehiopia 1965-67, Wellcome res fell 1968, external scientific staff MRC Ahmadu Bello Univ Zaria Nigeria 1970-74, conslt physician Hosp for Tropical Diseases 1974-, sr lectr London Sch of Hygiene and Tropical Med 1974, seconded as WHO conslt Clinical Res Centre Nairobi 1980-82, hon conslt in tropical diseases for the Army 1982-; memb Royal Soc of Tropical Med and Hygiene (hon sec 1984-89); DTM & H (Eng) 1961; FRCP: Edinburgh 1972, London 1984; *Books* Leprosy (with R E Pfaltzgraff, 3 edn 1990); *Recreations* ornithology, photography, travel; *Style*— Dr Anthony Bryceson; Hospital for Tropical Diseases, 4 St Pancras Way, London NW1 0PE (☎ 071 580 2475, 071 387 4411, fax 071 383 0041)

BRYDEN, Hon Mrs ((Monica) Deborah); *née* Morris; da of 3 Baron Killanin, MBE, TD; *b* 24 Feb 1950; *Educ* Convent of the Assumption Hengrave, Byam Shaw Sch of Drawing and Painting; *m* 1970, Bill Bryden, *qv*; 1 s (Dillon), 1 da (Mary); *Style*— The Hon Mrs Bryden

BRYDEN, William Campbell Rough (Bill); s of late George Bryden and Catherine Bryden; *b* 12 April 1942; *Educ* Greenock HS, Univ of Glasgow; *m* 1970, Hon (Monica) Deborah, *née* Morris, *qv*, da of 3 Baron Killanin, MBE, TD; 1 s (Dillon Michael George b 1976), 1 da (Mary Kate b 1975); *Career* tv and theatre dir; documentary writer Scottish TV 1963-64; asst dir: Belgrade Theatre Coventry 1965-67, Royal Court Theatre London 1967-69; assoc dir Royal Lyceum Theatre Edinburgh 1971-74; dir: Cottesloe Theatre (Nat Theatre) 1978-80, Royal Opera House Covent Garden (productions include; Parsifal 1988, The Cunning Little Vixen 1990), Bernstein's Mass GSMD 1987, A Life in the Theatre Haymarket 1989, The Ship Glasgow 1990; exec producer BBC TV: Tutti Frutti (by John Byrne) 1987 (best series BAFTA awards), The Play on One (series) 1989; dir The Shawl (by David Mamet) BBC TV 1989; winner: Dir of the Year (Laurence Olivier Awards) 1985, Best Dir Award (Evening Standard) for The Mysteries Nat Theatre 1985, Assoc and Drama Magazine Awards 1986, Gulliver Award; Hon DUniv Queen Margaret Coll Edinburgh 1989; memb bd Scottish TV 1979-85; plays: Willie Rough (1972), Benny Lynch (1974), Old Movies (1977); *Recreations* music; *Style*— Bill Bryden, Esq; National Theatre, South Bank, London SE1 9PX (☎ 071 928 2033); BBC, Queen Margaret Drive, Glasgow G12 8DG (☎ 041 330 2520, fax 041 334 0614)

BRYDON, Donald Hood; s of James Hood Brydon (d 1975), of Edinburgh, and Mary Duncanson, *née* Young; *b* 25 May 1945; *Educ* George Watson's Coll Edinburgh, Univ of Edinburgh (BSc); *m* 16 April 1971, Joan Victoria Rea; 1 s (Angus b 1977), 1 da (Fiona b 1975); *Career* res asst Dept of Economics Univ of Edinburgh; investmt mangr: Airways Pension Scheme (British Airways), Barclays Bank; dir Barclays Investment Management, chief exec BZW Investmt Mgmt; ldr Bracknell DC 1977-80, vice chm Nat Assoc of Pension Funds 1988-90, chm Inst Shareholders Ctee 1989-90; AMSIA 1972; *Books* Economics of Technical Information Services (jtly, 1972), Pension Fund Investment (jtly, 1988); *Recreations* golf; *Clubs* Caledonian; *Style*— Donald Brydon, Esq; BZW Investment Management Ltd, Seal House, 1 Swan Lane, London EC4R 3UD (☎ 071 623 7777, fax 071 621 9411)

BRYENTON, Michael John; s of Benjamin Bryenton (d 1958), of Heveningham, and Hilda, *née* Roberts, of Wenhaston, Suffolk; *b* 3 April 1946; *Educ* Walpole, Halesworth; *Career* fndr treas Halesworth Cancer Res Campaign Ctee 1977, church warden and church treas St Margaret's Church Heveningham, sch govr Walpole 1988; Citizen of the Year for Halesworth and Dist for work on cancer res; *Recreations* reading, the countryside, fund raising for charities; *Style*— Michael Byenton, Esq; Rose Cottage, Heveningham, Halesworth, Suffolk

BRYER, Prof Anthony Applemore Mornington; s of Gp Capt Gerald Mornington Bryer, OBE, AFC, of Little Applemore, Pilley Bailey, Lymington, Hants, and Joan Evelyn, *née* Grigsby; *b* 31 Oct 1937; *Educ* Canford, Sorbonne (diploma), Balliol Coll Oxford (MA, DPhil); *m* 2 Aug 1961, Elizabeth, da of John Milman Lipscomb, of Cumberland Cottage, Chilham, Canterbury, Kent; 3 da (Theodora Jane b 3 Feb 1965, Anna Caroline b 2 Sept 1966, Sarah Katherine b 19 March 1971); *Career* Nat Serv RAF Adjutant 1956-58; prof of Byzantine studies Univ of Birmingham 1980- (res fell, lectr, sr lectr, reader 1964-80, first dir of Centre for Byzantine Studies 1976-); res fell Univ of Athens 1961-62, Hellenic Cruise guest lectr 1967-, five times visiting fell Dumbarton Oaks Harvard Univ 1970-, Loeb lectr Harvard Univ 1980, visitng Byzantinist Medieval Acad of America 1984, visitor Merton Coll Oxford 1985, humanities res advsr to Govt of Cyprus 1988, visiting lectr Australian Byzantine Assoc 1989, Wiles lectr Belfast 1990; chm: Br Nat Ctee of Int Byzantine Assoc, Soc for The Promotion of Byzantine Studies 1989-; memb: Ctee Br Inst of Archaeology at Ankara, Ctee Br School at Athens; FSA 1973; *Books* Iconoclasm (1977), The Empire of Trebizond and the Pontos (1980), The Byzantine Monuments and Topography of the Pontos (2 vols, 1985), Continuity and Change in Late Byzantine and Early Ottoman Society (1986), Peoples and Settlement in Anatolia and the Caucasus 800-1900 (1988); *Recreations* travel, trying to find the Third Programme; *Clubs* Buckland (Birmingham), Lochaline Social (Morvern), Black Sea (Trebizond); *Style*— Prof Anthony Bryer; 33 Crosbie Rd, Harborne, Birmingham B17 9BG (☎ 021 427 1207); Centre for Byzantine, Ottoman and Modern Greek Studies, University of Birmingham, Birmingham B15 2TT (☎ 021 414 5777)

BRYER, (Alastair) Robin Mornington; s of Gp Capt Gerald Mornington Bryer, OBE, AFC, and Joan Evelyn, *née* Grigsby; *b* 13 May 1944; *Educ* Dauntsey's Sch, King's Coll Univ of Durham (BA); *m* 16 Sept 1976, Jennifer Sheridan, da of Lt Col Richard Sheridan Skelton, OBE; 1 s (William b 1977); *Career* sr planning asst Hampshire CC 1967-73, ptnr Inland and Waterside Planners 1973-77, ind chartered town planner (one of the first in private practice) assisting landowners, developers, MPs, conservation bodies and govt depts 1977-; has exhibited in architectural section of RA 1980, guest lectr Hellenic Travellers Club 1980-, chm PEST (Tory pressure gp) 1966-68, memb Consultancy Bd Royal Town Planning Inst 1980-83, chm Old Dauntseians Assoc 1985-86, guildsman City Guild of Old Mercers 1985; Freeman City of London 1987; MRTPI 1973; *Books* Jolie Brise, A Tall Ships Tale (1982), Roving Commissions (ed 1983-86); *Recreations* sailing; *Clubs* Royal Cruising, Royal Lymington Yacht; *Style*— Robin Bryer, Esq; Princes Place, Closworth, Yeovil, Somerset BA22 9RH (☎ 0935 782268)

BRYERS, Brig Richard Hugh Castellain; CBE (1963); s of Rev John Shaw Bryers (d 1945), of Bowers Gifford Rectory, Essex, and Charlotte Susan, *née* Newman (d 1959); *b* 12 Sept 1911; *Educ* Harrow, St John's Coll Cambridge (BA); *m* 1, July 1938, Phyllis (d 1964), da of Major David Lewis Hankin (d 1949), of N Rhodesia; 2 s (Humphrey b and d 1941, John Richard Feneran b 1944), 1 da (Eliane Susan Gray b 1942); m 2, 22 May 1965, Isabella Marjorie, da of Percy Cromwell Clark (d 1928), of Wallington, Surrey; *Career* Kings Own Royal Regt 1933-63, served WWII India, Iraq, Burma, Instr Staff Coll 1942-44, Staff Appts War Office 1945-48 and 1957-60, BJSM Washington 1950-52, served Korea 1953-54, cmd 5 Bn Malay Regt Malayan Emergency 1954-56, Cdr Land Forces Persian Gulf 1960-63; dep pres Red Cross Suffolk Branch 1977-89 (memb 1968-89, branch dir 1974-76); *Recreations* shooting, gardening; *Clubs* Army and Navy, Western India; *Style*— Brig Richard Bryers, CBE; Thorndon Old Rectory, nr Eye, Suffolk IP23 7LX (☎ 037 971 284)

BRYMER, Jack; OBE (1960); s of Jack Brymer, of South Shields, Co Durham (d 1975), and Mary, *née* Dixon (d 1960); *b* 27 Jan 1915; *Educ* South Shields GS, Goldsmiths Coll Univ of London (Dip Ed); *m* 21 Oct 1939, Joan, da of Jack Richardson (d 1924), of Lancaster, Lancs; 1 s (Timothy b 1951); *Career* princ clarinet: RPO 1947-63, BBC Symphony Orchestra 1963-71, London Symphony Orchestra 1971-86; prof: Royal Acad 1952-58, Kneller Hall 1963-67, Guildhall Sch of Music (1981-89); dir Shell LSO Scholarship 1982-, London Wind Soloists; broadcaster: On a Personal Note, Music you love, At Home J B Presents; has recorded complete wind works of: Mozart, Bach, Haydn, Beethoven; presenter in Play the Clarinet Video; Hon MA Univ of Newcastle; Hon RAM, Hon FGSM; awarded Corbbett medal by Worshipful Soc of Musicians 1989; *Books* The Clarinet (Menuhin Guides), From Where I Sit (autobiography), In The Orchestra; *Recreations* golf, gardening; *Clubs* Croham Hurst Golf; *Style*— Jack Brymer, Esq, OBE; Underwood, Ballards Farm Rd, South Croydon, Surrey CR2 7JA (☎ 081 657 1698)

BRYNING, Charles Frederick; s of Frederick Bryning (d 1982), of 58 Mossom Lane, Norbreck, Blackpool, and Dorothy Edith Bryning; *b* 17 July 1946; *Educ* Arnold Sch, Blackpool Lancs; *m* 29 April 1983, Katrina Carol, da of John Carol Boris Ely, of 52 Worsley Rd, Lytham St Annes; 1 s (Simon b 1983); *Career* CA; ptnr Jones Harris & Co 1972-, chief exec the Alexander Walker Gp of cos 1987-; FCA, FCCA, FInstD; *Style*— Charles Bryning, Esq; 17 St Peters Place, Fleetwood, Lancs FY7 6EB (☎ 0253 87 4255)

BRYSON, Col (James) Graeme; OBE (1954), TD (1949), JP (Liverpool 1956), DL (1968); s of John Conway Bryson, slr (d 1959), of Liverpool, and Oletta, *née* Olsen; *b* 4 Feb 1913; *Educ* St Edward's Coll Liverpool, Univ of Liverpool (LLM); *m* 1938, Jean (d 1981), da of Walter Cook Glendinning, of Liverpool; 2 s (and 1 s decd), 4 da; *Career* slr 1935, sr dist registrar High Ct of Justice Liverpool 1947-78, dep circuit judge 1978-82; chm Med Appeal Tbnl 1978-86; pres Royal Br Legion NW England 1979-90 (City of Liverpool 1950-); HM Vice Lord-Lieut Merseyside 1979-89; Queen's Commendation for Brave Conduct 1961; Knight of Holy Sepulchre 1974; FRSA 1989; *Books* Execution in Halsbury's Laws of England (jtly, 3 edn 1976); *Recreations* ex-service interests, local history, boating; *Clubs* Athenaeum (Liverpool, pres 1969); *Style*— Col Graeme Bryson, OBE, TD, JP, DL; Sunwards, Thirlmere Rd, Hightown, Liverpool L38 3RQ (☎ 051 929 2652)

BRYSON, Adm Sir Lindsay Sutherland; KCB (1981); s of James McAuslan Bryson (d 1976), and Margaret, *née* Whyte (d 1946); *b* 22 Jan 1925; *Educ* Allan Glen's Sch Glasgow, Univ of London (BSc); *m* 1951, Averil, da of W T Curtis-Willson (d 1957); 1 s, 2 da; *Career* joined RN 1945, dir Naval Guided Weapons 1973, dir Surface Weapons Project (Navy) 1974-77, dir gen Weapons (Naval) 1977-81, Chief Naval Engr Offr 1979-81, controller of the Navy 1981-84; pres IEE 1985-86; dir ERA Technol Ltd (non exec) 1985 (chm 1990-), chm Marine Technol Directorate Ltd 1987, dep chm GEC Marconi Ltd 1987-90, non exec dir Molins plc 1988; hon fell Paisley Coll of Technol 1987; cncl chm Univ of Sussex 1989-, pres Soc of Underwater Technol 1989-, chm Bd of Govs Brighton Coll 1990, pres Sussex SATRO 1990; Lord Lt E Sussex 1989-; Hon DSc: Univ of Strathclyde 1987, Univ of Bristol 1988; FEng, FRSE, FRAeS, FIEE; *Recreations* sailing, opera; *Clubs* Army and Navy, MCC, Royal Yacht Sqdn; *Style*— Adm Sir Lindsay Bryson, KCB; 74 Dyke Road Ave, Brighton, Sussex BN1 5LE (☎ 0273 553638)

BUBB, Nicholas Henry (Nick); s of John William Edward Bubb, of Orsett, Essex, and Diana Rosemary, *née* Willetts; *b* 24 March 1955; *Educ* Gillingham GS, Ch Ch Oxford (MA); *m* 10 April 1982, Susan Mary, da of Francis Dare, of Chichester, Sussex; 1 s (Alexander Benjamin Thomas b 1985), 1 da (Amy Louise Harriet b 1988); *Career* retailing analyst: Rowe & Pitman & Co 1977-79, Citicorp Scrimgeour Vickers (formerly Kemp-Gee & Co and Scrimgeour Kemp-Gee) 1979-88 (ptnr 1983), Morgan Stanley since 1988 (exec dir); memb Stock Exchange, British Cncl of Shopping Centres; AMSIA; *Recreations* cricket, running, gym, travel, golf, reading, films, wine; *Clubs* Oriental, Riverside Sports Chiswick, MCC; *Style*— Nick Bubb, Esq; 6 Orchard Rise, Richmond, Surrey TW10 5BX (☎ 081 878 1155); Kingsley House, 1 A Wimpole St, London W1M 7AA (☎ 071 709 3707, fax 071 709 3907, telex 8812564)

BUCCLEUCH AND QUEENSBERRY, Mary, Duchess of; (Vreda Esther) Mary; da of Maj William Frank Lascelles (gn of 3 Earl of Harewood), and Lady Sybil de Vere Beauclerk (2 da of 10 Duke of St Albans); *b* 17 Sept 1900; *m* 1921, 8 Duke of Buccleuch and (10 of) Queensberry, KT, GCVO, TD, PC (d 1973); 1 s (9 Duke), 2 da (Duchess of Northumberland, w of 10 Duke; Lady Caroline Gilmour, w of Sir Ian Gilmour, 3 Bt, MP); *Career* held the Queen's (now HM Queen Elizabeth The Queen Mother) canopy at the Coronation in 1937; *Style*— Her Grace Mary, Duchess of Buccleuch and Queensberry; Boughton Manor, Kettering, Northants

BUCCLEUCH AND QUEENSBERRY, 9 and 11 Duke of (S 1663 and 1684); Walter Francis John Montagu Douglas Scott; KT (1978), VRD (1959), JP (Roxburgh 1975), DL (Selkirk 1955, Midlothian 1960, Roxburgh 1962, Dumfries 1974); also Lord Scott of Buccleuch (S 1606), Lord Scott of Whitchester and Eskdaill, Earl of Buccleuch (both S 1619), Earl of Dalkeith (S 1663), Earl of Doncaster, Baron Scott of Tynedale (both E 1663), Lord Douglas of Kinmont, Middlebie and Dornoch, Viscount of Nith, Thorthorwald and Ross, Earl of Drumlanrig and Sanquhar, and Marquess of Dumfriesshire (all S 1706); s of 8 and 10 Duke of Buccleuch and Queensberry, KT, GCVO, TD, PC (d 1973), and Mary, da of Maj William Lascelles (ggs of 2 Earl of Harewood); *b* 28 Sept 1923; *Educ* Eton, Christ Church Oxford; *m* 1953, Jane, da of John McNeill, QC, of Drumavuic, Argyll; 3 s, 1 da; *Heir* s, Earl of Dalkeith, DL; *Career* served RNVR & RNR 1942-71 Lt Cdr; Hon Capt RNR 1988; Roxburgh CC

1958-; MP (C) Edinburgh N 1960-73, PPS Sec of State Scotland 1961-64; Lord-Lt: Roxburghshire 1974-75, Selkirk 1975, Roxburgh, Ettrick and Lauderdale 1975-; pres Royal Highland & Agricultural Soc for Scotland 1969, St Andrews Ambulance Assoc 1973-; Royal Blind Asylum & Sch, chm Royal Assoc for Disability & Rehabilitation 1973-, pres E of England Ag Soc 1976, Royal Scot Agric Benevolent Inst, Scot Nat Inst for War Blinded; chm Cwlth Forestry Assoc 1979-; Capt Royal Co Archers (Queen's Body Guard for Scotland); chm Buccleuch Heritage Tst 1985-, chm Living Landscape Tst 1986-; *Recreations* music, painting, field sports, photography, travel; *Clubs* New (Edinburgh); *Style—* His Grace the Duke of Buccleuch and Queensberry, KT, VRD, JP; Drumlanrig Castle, Thornhill, Dumfriesshire (☎ 0848 30248); Boughton House, Kettering, Northants; Bowhill, Selkirk (☎ 0750 20732)

BUCHAN, Dr Alexander Stewart; s of Samuel Buchan, of Carnoustie, and Mary, *née* Steward (d 1982); *b* 7 Sept 1942; *Educ* Loretto, Univ of Edinburgh (MB ChB); *m* 24 Feb 1968, Henrietta Young, da of William Constable Dalrymple, of Edinburgh; 1 s (Alexander b 1969); *Career* conslt anaesthetist 1975-: Royal Infirmary Edinburgh, Royal Hosp for Sick Children, Princess Margaret Rose Orthopaedic Hosp; admin conslt for obstetric anaesthesia Simpson Memorial Maternity Pavilion 1988-; memb: Scottish Soc of Anaesthetists, Edinburgh and East of Scotland Soc of Anaesthetists; FFARCS 1970; *Recreations* fishing, sailing, golf; *Style—* Dr Alexander Buchan; 21 Chalmers Crescent, Edinburgh EH9 1TS (☎ 031 667 1127); Department of Anaesthetics, Royal Infirmary, Edinburgh (☎ 031 229 2477)

BUCHAN, (James Alexander) Bruce; s of James Welsh Ross Buchan, and Phyllis Clare, *née* Buckle; *b* 4 May 1947; *Educ* Fulneck Boys Sch, Univ of Birmingham (LLB); *m* 24 July 1982, Felicité Jacqueline; *Career* slr: ptnr Dibb Lupton Broomhead & Prior 1975-; nat chm Young Slrs' Gp of The Law Soc 1982-83, dep registrar of High Ct of Justice and Co Ct 1986-; memb: Ctee Leeds Law Soc, Law Soc; govr Fulneck Boys' Sch; *Recreations* walking, golf; *Clubs* The Leeds, Headingly Golf; *Style—* Bruce Buchan, Esq; 8 St Helen's Croft, Adel, Leeds LS16 8JY (☎ 0532 679780); 117 The Headrow, Leeds LS1 5JX (☎ 0532 439301, fax 0532 452632)

BUCHAN, Edward Meldrum (Ted); s of Gavin Struthers Muir Buchan (d 1965), of Edinburgh, and Sarah Davidson, *née* Burnside; *b* 1 Nov 1920; *Educ* Boroughmuir Sch Edinburgh, Heriot Watt Coll Edinburgh, Dundee Sch of Econs; *m* 19 Feb 1947, Janet Kirkland, da of John Kirkland Wilson, of Kilmarnock, Ayrshire; 2 da ((Laura) Louise b 1948, Lorna Mary b 1950); *Career* WWII 1941-46; trainee exec Crudens Ltd Midlothian 1947-49; Rentokil Group plc: joined 1950, jt md 1956-73, chief exec 1974-78, non-exec dir 1978-86; hon treas Br Wood Preserving Assoc; *Recreations* forestry, travel, family; *Clubs* Caledonian; *Style—* Ted Buchan, Esq

BUCHAN, (Charles Walter) Edward Ralph; s of the Hon William James De L'Aigle Buchan, and Barbara Howard, *née* Ensor (d 1969); *b* 5 Aug 1951; *Educ* Magdalen Coll Sch Oxford, Univ of Southampton (BSc); *m* 27 Nov 1982, Fiona Jane, da of Capt E P Carlisle, of Llanigon, Hay-on-Wye; 1 s (William b 1984), 2 da (Annabel b 1986, Laura b 1988); *Career* dir Hill Samuel Bank Ltd 1985- (joined 1977); FCA 1976; *Clubs* Travellers'; *Style—* Edward Buchan, Esq; Hill Samuel Bank Ltd, 100 Wood St, London EC2P 2AJ (☎ 071 628 8011, fax 071 588 5111)

BUCHAN, Lady Evelyn Rose; *née* Phipps; da of 4 Marquess of Normanby, CBE; *b* 1955; *m* 1986, James Buchan, s of Hon William Buchan, of Hornton, Oxon, *qv*; *Style—* Lady Evelyn Buchan; 5 Clover Mews, London SW3

BUCHAN, Hon Mrs Alastair; Hope; da of late David Gordon Gilmour, of Ottawa, Canada; *m* 1942, Prof the Hon Alastair Francis Buchan, CBE (d 1976); 2 s, 1 da; *Style—* The Hon Mrs Alastair Buchan; 10, The Firs, Brill, Bucks

BUCHAN, Janey (Jane O'Neil); MEP (Lab) Glasgow 1979-; da of Joseph Kent, of Glasgow, and Christina Kent; *b* 30 April 1926; *m* 1945, Norman Findlay Buchan, MP (Lab) Paisley South 1983-90 (d 1990), s of John Buchan, of Fraserburgh, Aberdeenshire; 1 s (Alasdair); *Career* former chm: Scottish Gas Consumers' Cncl, Scottish Cncl of Lab Pty; former memb Scottish Arts Cncl; *Style—* Mrs Janey Buchan, MEP; 72 Peel St, Glasgow G11 5LR (☎ 041 339 2583)

BUCHAN, 17 Earl of (S 1469); Malcolm Harry Erskine; JP (Westminster 1972); also Lord Auchterhouse (S 1469), Lord Cardross (S 1610), and Baron Erskine (UK 1806); s of 16 Earl of Buchan, and Christina, *née* Woolner; *b* 4 July 1930; *Educ* Eton; *m* 1957, Hilary Diana Cecil, da of late Sir Ivan McLannahan Cecil Power, 2 Bt; 2 s (Henry Thomas Alexander (Lord Cardross) b 1960, Hon Montagu John b 1966), 2 da (Lady Seraphina Mary b 1961, Lady Arabella Fleur b 1969); *Heir* s, Lord Cardross; *Style—* The Rt Hon The Earl of Buchan, JP; Newnham House, Newnham, Basingstoke, Hants

BUCHAN, Hon William James De L'Aigle; s of 1 Baron Tweedsmuir, PC, GCMG, GCVO, CH (d 1940; the author John Buchan), and hp of bro, 2 Baron Tweedsmuir, CBE, CD; *b* 10 Jan 1916; *Educ* Eton, New Coll Oxford; *m* 1, 1939 (m dis 1946), Nesta Irene, da of Lt-Col C D Crozier; 1 da; m 2, 1946 (m dis 1960), Barbara Howard (d 1969), da of Ernest Nash Ensor, of Wimbledon; 3 s, 3 da (of whom 2 are twins); m 3, 1960, Sauré Cynthia Mary, da of late Maj G E Tatchell, Royal Lincs Regt; 1 s; *Career* Sqdn-Ldr RAF Vol Reserve; *Books* John Buchan, a Memoir (biography of father, 1982), The Rags of Time (autobiography), three novels; *Clubs* Travellers'; *Style—* The Hon William Buchan; West End House, Hornton, Banbury, Oxon OX15 6DA (☎ 029 587 608)

BUCHAN-HEPBURN, (John) Alastair Trant Kidd; s of John Trant Buchan-Hepburn (d 1953), and Edith Margaret (Mitchell), *née* Robb, hp of kinsman, Sir Ninian Buchan-Hepburn of Smeaton-Hepburn, 6 Bt; *b* 27 June 1931; *Educ* Charterhouse, Univ of St Andrews, RMA Sandhurst; *m* 1957, Georgina Elizabeth, SRN, da of Oswald Morris Turner, MC (d 1953), of Armathwaite, Cumberland; 1 s (John Christopher Alastair b 1963), 3 da (Caroline Georgina (Mrs A W P Thompson) b 1958, Sarah Elizabeth (Mrs D A Cox) b 1960, Louise Mary (Mrs A D S Kinnear) b 1966); *Career* Capt 1 King's Dragoon Gds, ADC to GOC-in-C Malaya Cmd 1956-57, attached to Swiss Army Cav, served BAOR and Far East, attached Household Cav; brewing sr exec Arthur Guinness & Co Ltd 1958-86, ret; agent Royal Insur Co, divnl dir Broughton Brewery Ltd; memb: Inst of Brewing, Burgess and Guild Bros of Glasgow, Incorporation of Maltmen; life memb St Andrew Preservation Tst; Freeman Citizen of Glasgow; *Recreations* gardening, shooting, fishing, walking, old china and glass, golf, tennis, travel in Scottish Islands; *Clubs* New (Edinburgh), Royal and Ancient Golf, St Andrews; *Style—* Capt Alastair Buchan-Hepburn; Chagford, 60 Argyle St, St Andrews, Fife KY16 9BU; (☎ 0334 72161); office: Broughton Brewery Ltd, Broughton, By Biggar, Lanarkshire ML12 6HQ (☎ 08994 345)

BUCHAN-HEPBURN, Sir Ninian Buchan Archibald John; 6 Bt (UK 1815), of Smeaton Hepburn, Haddingtonshire; s of Sir John Karslake Thomas Buchan-Hepburn, 5 Bt (d 1961); *b* 8 Oct 1922; *Educ* Canford; *m* 1958, Bridget (d 1976), da of Sir Louis (Leisler) Greig, KBE, CVO (d 1952); *Heir* kinsman, John Alistair Buchan-Hepburn; *Career* served Burma 1943-46 with Queen's Own Cameron Highlanders (wounded 1944); painter (RA and RSA exhibitor); memb Queen's Body Gd for Scotland (Royal Co of Archers); *Recreations* opera, gardening, shooting; *Clubs* New (Edinburgh), Puffin's (Edinburgh); *Style—* Sir Ninian Buchan Hepburn of Smeaton-Hepburn, Bt; Logan, by Stranraer, Scotland DG9 9ND

BUCHAN OF AUCHMACOY, Capt David William Sinclair; JP (Aberdeenshire 1959-, Westminster 1972-); s of Capt Stephen Lloyd Trevor, JP (d 1959), and Lady Olivia, *née* Sinclair, da of 18 Earl of Caithness, CBE (d 1947); suc maternal gf (18 Earl) as Chief of the Name of Buchan and recognised as such by Lord Lyon 1949; *b* 18 Sept 1929; *Educ* Eton, RMA Sandhurst; *m* 1961, Hon (Blanche) Susan Fionodhbar, *née* Scott-Ellis, da and co-heiress of 9 Baron Howard de Walden; 4 s, 1 d; *Heir* s, Charles Buchan of Auchmacoy the younger; *Career* cmmnd Gordon Highlanders 1949, served Berlin, BAOR and Malaya, Capt and ADC to GOC-in-C Singapore 1951-53, ret 1955; memb London Stock Exchange, sr ptnr Gow & Parsons 1961-68; memb: Queen's Body Guard for Scotland, The Pilgrims, Friends of Malta GC, Alexandra Rose Day Cncl, Cook's Soc (Australia), Cncl Royal Sch of Needlework 1987, Cons Industl Fund Ctee 1988; govr London Clinic 1988; vice pres: Aberdeenshire CCC 1962, Bucks CCC 1984-; memb Worshipful Co of Broderers (renter warden 1990), Freeman City of London; KStJ 1987 (OStJ 1981), memb Cncl for London Order of St John; FIOD; *Recreations* cricket, tennis, squash; *Clubs* White's, Turf, City of London, Pratt's, RAC, MCC, Puffin's (Edinburgh), Canada; *Style—* Capt David Buchan of Auchmacoy, JP; Auchmacoy House, Ellon, Aberdeenshire (☎ 0358 20229); 28 Little Boltons, London SW10 (☎ 071 373 0654) and D-310, Puenta Romana, Marbella, Spain

BUCHAN OF AUCHMACOY, Hon Mrs ((Blanche) Susan Fionodhbar); *née* Scott-Ellis; da of 9 Baron Howard de Walden and (5 Baron) Seaford; co-heiress to Barony of Howard de Walden; *b* 6 Oct 1937; *m* 1961, Capt David William Sinclair Buchan of Auchmacoy; 4 s, 1 da; *Style—* The Hon Mrs Buchan of Auchmacoy; Auchmacoy House, Ellon, Aberdeenshire; 28 The Little Boltons, London SW10 9LP

BUCHAN OF AUCHMACOY YR, (John) Charles Augustus David; s and h of Capt David Buchan of Auchmacoy, JP, and Hon Susan, *née* Scott-Ellis, da of 9 Baron Howard de Walden, to which Barony he is in remainder through his m; *b* 1 March 1963; *Educ* Ampleforth, RAC Cirencester; *Career* investmt banker; CIBC 1986-89, estate agent Mellersh & Harding 1990-; Liveryman: Worshipful Co of Shipwrights, Worshipful Co of Borderers; *Recreations* cricket, tennis, shooting; *Clubs* RAC; *Style—* Charles Buchan of Auchmacoy Yr

BUCHANAN; *see*: Leith-Buchanan, Macdonald-Buchanan

BUCHANAN, Alistair John; s of John James Buchanan (d 1983), and Phoebe Leonora, *née* Messel (d 1952), of Grosvenor Square, London; *b* 13 Dec 1935; *Educ* Eton, New Coll Oxford; *m* 1963, Ann Hermione, da of Raymond Alexander Baring (d 1967); 3 da (Katie, Tessa, Helen); *Career* 2 Lt 2 Bn Coldstream Guards 1954-56; Layton-Bennett Billingham & Co 1959-62, Allen Harvey & Ross Ltd 1962-81, A Sarasin & Co Ltd 1980-87, Cater Allen Hldgs plc 1981-85, LIFFE 1981-84, Heritage of London Trust Ltd 1982, md Morgan Grenfell Govt Securities 1985-87, dep chm and md Mees & Hope Securities Holdings Ltd 1987, Mannin Industries Ltd, Feathercombe Farm Ltd; MInstD, FCA; *Recreations* golf, gardening, shooting, stalking; *Clubs* White's, Swinley Forest Golf; *Style—* Alistair Buchanan, Esq; Hillbarn House, Great Bedwyn, Marlborough, Wilts

BUCHANAN, Sir Andrew George; 5 Bt (UK 1878), of Dunburgh, Stirlingshire; s of Maj Sir Charles Buchanan, 4 Bt (d 1984), and Barbara Helen (d 1986), da of Lt-Col Rt Hon Sir George Frederick Stanley, GCSI, GCIE, CMG; *b* 21 July 1937; *Educ* Eton, Trinity Coll Cambridge, Wye Coll London; *m* 26 April 1966, Belinda Jane Virginia, JP Notts, da of Donald Colquhoun Maclean, of Thurloe Sq, London SW7, and widow of Gresham Vaughan (d 1964); 1 s (George), 1 da (Laura b 1967), 1 step s, 1 step da; *Heir* s, George Charles Mellish, *qv*; *Career* 2 Lt Coldstream Guards 1956-58, Major cmd A Sqdn Sherwood Rangers Yeo (TA) 1971-74, Hon Col B Sqdn (Sherwood Rangers Yeo) Royal Yeo 1989; farmer, chartered surveyor, land agent; High Sheriff Nottinghamshire 1976-77; chm Bd of Visitors HM Prison Ranby 1983-84; dir Bucentaur Gallery Ltd 1982-; DL Notts 1985; Lord-Lieut of Nottinghamshire 1991-; *Recreations* skiing, shooting; *Clubs* Boodle's; *Style—* Sir Andrew Buchanan, Bt; Hodsock Priory, Blyth, Worksop, Notts S81 0TY (☎ 0909 591204)

BUCHANAN, Dr (Alexander) Angus; s of Andrew Buchanan (d 1988), and Edith, *née* Rudd (d 1980); *b* 1 March 1926; *Educ* Brentwood Sch, St Mary's Hosp London (MB BS, BSc); *m* 24 May 1958, Mary Winifred (Mollie), da of Eric Durdle (d 1961); 1 da (Alexandrina Caroline b 1968); *Career* Capt Argyll and Sutherland Highlanders 1943-47; assoc prof physiology Duke Univ N Carolina USA 1955; St Mary's Hosp London: house physician 1954-55, registrar Med Unit 1957-59, res worker MRC 1959-62, sr registrar 1962-66; sr physician Bedford Gen Hosp 1966-90; former memb Bedford AHA, memb Bedford DHA, regnl advsr RCP; memb: Med Res Soc 1954, Br Diabetic Assoc; memb: BMA 1950, RSM 1950; MRCS, FRCP; *Recreations* gardening, fishing, DIY; *Style—* Dr Angus Buchanan; Longacre, 67 Putnoe Lane, Bedford MK41 9AE (☎ 0234 353718); Bedford General Hospital, Kempston Rd, Bedford (☎ 0234 355122)

BUCHANAN, Prof (Robert) Angus; s of Robert Graham Buchanan (d 1975), of Sheffield, and Bertha, *née* Davis, MBE, JP (d 1975); *b* 5 June 1930; *Educ* High Storrs GS Sheffield, St Catharine's Coll Cambridge (BA, MA, PhD); *m* 10 Aug 1955, Brenda June, da of George Henry Wade (d 1955), of Sheffield; 2 s (Andrew Nassau b 1958, Thomas Claridge b 1960); *Career* Nat Serv RAOC 1948-50, GHQ FARELF 1949-50; educn offr Royal Fndn of St Katharine Stepney 1956-60, co-opted memb London CC Educn Ctee 1958-60; Univ of Bath: lectr, sr lectr, reader, prof (1990); dir Centre for the History of Technol Sci & Soc 1964-, royal cmmr Royal Cmmn for Historical Monuments 1979-; properties ctee memb Nat Tst 1974-; pres: Assoc for Industl Archaeology 1975-77, Newcomen Soc for History of Engrg and Technol 1981-83; visiting prof Aust Nat Univ 1981, Jubilee prof Chalmers Univ Sweden 1984, visiting lectr Wuhan Peoples Repub of China 1983, chm Bath branch Historical Assoc 1987-90, dir Nat Cataloguing Unit for the Archives of Contemporary Scientists 1987-; Hon DSc Chalmers Univ Sweden 1986; Leonardo da Vinci medal Soc for the History of Technol 1989; FRHists 1978; FSA 1990; *Books* Technology and Social Progress (1965), Industrial Archaeology in Britain (1972), History and Industrial Civilisation (1979), The Engineers - A History of the Engineering Profession in Britain 1750-1914 (1989); *Recreations* walking, rambling, travelling; *Style—* Prof Angus Buchanan, FSA; Centre for the History of Technology Science and Society, University of Bath, Claverton Down, Bath BA2 7AY, (☎ 0225 826826, telex 449097)

BUCHANAN, Archie; s of James Adams Buchanan, of Broadmayne, Dorset, and Aileen Elizabeth, *née* Thompson (d 1940); *b* 5 July 1928; *Educ* Winchester, St Peter's Coll Oxford (BA); *m* 7 Jun 1952, Margaret Jean; 1 s (Jamie b 1955), 1 da (Maggie b 1953); *Career* served RTR 1946-48, 2 Lt; Foote Cone and Belding Ltd 1951-63, dir David Williams and Ptnrs Ltd 1963-68, md Rodway Smith Advertising Ltd 1969-83, chm Buchanan and Ptnrs 1983-; former chm Royal Counties Branch Inst of Mkting; former Liveryman Worshipful Co of Marketors; FInstD, memb Chartered Inst of Mktg; *Style—* Archie Buchanan, Esq; Buchanan & Partners Ltd, Buchanan House, Church Square, Princes Risborough, Bucks, HP17 9AQ, (☎ 08444 2033 fax 08444 2997)

BUCHANAN, Cameron Roy Marchand; s of Maj Alexander Bell Watson Buchanan, MC, TD, of Woking, Surrey, and Katharine Norma, *née* Stiles; *b* 17 Sept 1946; *Educ* St Edwards Sch Oxford, Sorbonne Paris; *m* 12 May 1973, Diana Frances, da of Hugh Wilson Jones (d 1979); 1 s (Alexander Cameron b 4 April 1977), 1 da (Tanya Katharine b 18 Sept 1974); *Career* md George Harrison & Co Edinburgh Ltd 1985, dir Br Knitting and Clothing Export Cncl (chm Menswear Ctee); Freeman Worshipful Co of Merchants Edinburgh, Liveryman Worshipful Co of Glovers 1987; *Recreations* skiing, squash, tennis; *Clubs* New (Edinburgh), DHO Muren Switzerland; *Style—* Cameron Buchanan, Esq; Gateside, Old Church Lane, Duddingston Village, Edinburgh EH15 3PX (☎ 031 661 1889); Lawhill House, Auchterarder, Perthshire PH3 1LJ; George Harrison & Co (Edinburgh) Ltd, 24 Forth St, Edinburgh EH1 3LP (☎ 031 557 2540, fax 031 557 5128, telex 72464)

BUCHANAN, Prof Dennis Langston; s of Langston Llewellyn Buchanan (d 1954), and Georgina Vera, *née* Wheatley; *b* 15 April 1947; *Educ* Cambridge High, Rhodes Univ (BSc), Univ of Pretoria (MSc), Univ of London (PhD), Imperial Coll London (DIC); *m* 17 Dec 1970, Vaughan Elizabeth, da of Fritz Reitz Hayward, of Port Elizabeth; 1 s (James George), 1 da (Alexandra Claire); *Career* Union Corp Ltd SA 1969-73, res fell Univ of Witwatersrand SA 1978-79 (res asst 1976-77), prof of mining geology Royal Sch of Mines Imp Coll 1984- (res asst 1976-77, lectr 1980-83); CEng 1976, FGSSA 1986, FIMM 1989; *Books* Platinum Group Element Exploration (1988); *Recreations* jogging; *Clubs* Royal Sch of Mines Assoc; *Style—* Prof Dennis Buchanan; Department of Geology, Imperial College, London SW7 2BP (☎ 071 589 5111 ext 5615, fax 071 584 7596, telex 929484)

BUCHANAN, Gary Church; s of Robert Smith Buchanan, of Kirkcaldy, and Winifred Margery, *née* Church; *b* 30 June 1954; *Educ* George Watsons' Coll Edinburgh, Univ of Aberdeen (BSc); *Career* conslt to travel orgns inc BA; travel writer and contributor to numerous pubns, specialist lectr including on board QE2; dir: Jersey Artists 1984-, Communecosse 1983-; FRGS; *Books* Night Ferry (with George Behrend, 1985), Dream Voyages (1989), Luxury Train Cruises (1991); *Recreations* travel, food and wine; *Style—* Gary Buchanan, Esq; 18 Raith Gardens, Kirkcaldy, Fife KY2 5NJ Scotland (☎ 0592 264 964)

BUCHANAN, George Charles Mellish; s and h of Sir Andrew George Buchanan, 5 Bt, and Belinda Jane Virginia, JP, da of Donald C Maclean; *b* 27 Jan 1975; *Style—* George Buchanan, Esq; c/o Hodsock Priory, Blyth, Worksop, Notts

BUCHANAN, Prof (John) Grant; s of Robert Downie Buchanan (d 1937), of Dumbarton, and Mary Hobson, *née* Wilson; *b* 26 Sept 1926; *Educ* Dumbarton Acad, Glasgow Acad, Christ's Coll Cambridge (MA, PhD, ScD); *m* 14 July 1956, Sheila Elena, da of Reginald Lugg (d 1961), of Highgate, London; 3 s (Andrew b 1959, John b 1962, Neil b 1965); *Career* res fell Univ of California at Berkeley 1951-52, res asst Lister Inst of Preventive Med London 1952-54; Univ of Newcastle upon Tyne: lectr in organic chemistry Kings Coll 1955, sr lectr 1962, reader in organic chemistry 1965; Heriot-Watt Univ: prof of organic chemistry 1969, head of Dept of Chemistry 1987; pres Euro Carbohydrate Orgns 1991; FRSC 1981 (memb Cncl 1982-85), FRSE 1972 (memb Cncl 1980-83), CChem 1981; *Publications* over 160 original papers and reviews on organic a bioorganic chemistry; *Recreations* golf; *Clubs* Bruntsfield Links Golfing Soc; *Style—* Prof Grant Buchanan; Evergreen, 61 South Barnton Avenue, Edinburgh EH4 6AN (☎ 031 312 6296); Chemistry Department, Heriot-Watt University, Riccarton, Edinburgh EH14 4AS (☎ 031 451 3102, fax 031 451 3180)

BUCHANAN, Hugh Charles Stanley; s of Maj Sir Charles Buchanan Bart (d 1984), of Nottinghamshire, and Barbara Helen, *née* Stanley; *b* 26 Aug 1942; *Educ* Eton, McGill University (BA); *m* 10 Dec 1969, Nony Caroline Vatcher, da of Lt-Col John Johnston Dingwall, DSO, of Lyford Grange, Wantage, Oxfordshire; 1 s (James Iain Stanley b 6 March 1974), 2 da (Clarissa Victoria Rosamond b 9 Oct 1972, Arabella Patricia Dingwall b 9 Sept 1981); *Career* admitted slr 1980; currently ptnr: Cole & Cole, Morland & Son; memb Oxon CC 1985-89; *Recreations* gardening, photography; *Style—* Hugh Buchanan, Esq; The Manor House, Little Milton, Oxford OX9 7RB (☎ 0844 279368); Larriberau, Loubersan, Gascony, France; Morland & Son, Bath St, Abingdon OX14 3RL (☎ 0235 520204, fax 0235 532954)

BUCHANAN, James Meredith; s of Donald Geoffrey Buchanan (d 1978), and Violet Hetherington, *née* Bell; *b* 4 March 1943; *Educ* Haberdasher's Aske's, St George's Hosp Med Sch Univ of London (MB BS, AKC); *m* 4 May 1974, Judith, da of James Edward Spence, of 2 Claremont Grove, Sedgefield, Co Durham; 3 da (Helen, Charlotte, Sarah); *Career* registrar: Norfolk and Norwich Hosp 1972, St Mary's Hosp Portsmouth 1973; sr registrar St George's Hosp London 1974-77 (house offr posts 1967), conslt orthopaedic surgn Sunderland Gp of Hosps 1977-; hon clinical lectr Univ of Newcastle upon Tyne 1979; author of paper in RCS annals; LRCP 1967, FRCS 1972, fell Br Orthopaedic Assoc 1977; *Recreations* marathon running, rugby football; *Clubs* Chester-Le-Street A/C, Blaydon RUFC; *Style—* James Buchanan, Esq; 8 Grange Terrace, Stockton Rd, Sunderland, Tyne and Wear SR2 7DF (☎ 091 5100 555)

BUCHANAN, John David; MBE (1944), ERD (1989), DL (Leicestershire 1980); s of John Nevile Buchanan, DSO, MC (d 1969) of 17 Cavendish Ave, London, and Nancy Isobel, *née* Bevan (d 1981); *b* 26 Oct 1916; *Educ* Stowe, Trinity Coll Cambridge (MA), Staff Coll Camberley; *m* 9 Nov 1946, Janet Marjorie (d 1990), da of Brig JAC Pennycuick, DSO (d 1965), of Little London, Horam, E Sussex; 4 s (John b 20 March 1954 d 1962, James b 23 Aug 1956, Jonathan b 13 April 1964, Jocelyn b 19 March 1967), 4 da (Judith b 15 Nov 1947, Joanna b 6 Oct 1949, Jenny b 19 Jan 1953, Josephine b 21 March 1958); *Career* Nat Serv Grenadier Gds 1938, Adj 3 Bn 1941-43 (despatches 1943), Bde Maj 1 Gds Bde 1943-45, demobbed Actg Lt-Col 1946; private sec Security Cncl UN 1946, asst master Sherborne 1948-57 (Westminster Under-Sch 1947), headmaster Oakham Sch 1958-77, admin Scholarship Scheme Inchcape plc 1978-; govr: Haileybury, Kimbolton Sch, Royal Russell Sch; tstee Jerwood Fndn 1978, chm Owston and Newbold Village Meeting, hon treas St Andrews Church Owston; *Books* Operation Oakham (1980), Oakham Overture to Poetry; *Recreations* gardening, golf; *Style—* John Buchanan, Esq, MBE, ERD, DL; Rose Cottage, Owston, Oakham, Leics LE15 8DN (☎ 066 477 545)

BUCHANAN, Maj John Edward (Ian); s of Dr John Vassie Buchanan (d 1966), of Creed Lodge, Grampound, Cornwall, and Marion Waiata, *née* Godsal (d 1978); *b* 24 Oct 1926; *Educ* Wellington, Univ of Edinburgh (PhD); *m* 12 April 1957, Fiona Margaret Houstoun, da of Archibald Hugh Houstoun Ross, CBE (d 1969), of The Dowery House, Ford, Midlothian; 2 s (Hugh Ross b 29 April 1958, Fergus Andrew John b 3 Aug 1963), 1 da (Victoria Waiata b 18 Aug 1960); *Career* served 1 Bn Black Watch BAOR (Berlin, Kenya, UK, Cyprus); 2 Lt Black Watch 1945, instr Eaton Hall Offr Cadet Sch 1951-52, Capt commanding trg co Black Watch Perth 1956-58, GSO2 HQ offensive support wing RAF 1958-59, Directorate of Mil Ops Min of Def 1960-62, Co Cdr Demo Bn Sch of Infantry 1962-63, trg Maj 4/5 Black Watch 1963-65; gp admin mangr and sec to Mgmnt Ctee Scot & Newcastle Breweries 1982-86 (asst to md wines and spirits subsids 1965, gen sales mangr 1971, gen mangr regions 1974, beer co admin mangr 1978), ret 1986; Univ of Edinburgh 1986-89 (PhD thesis The Colleton Family and the Early History of South Carolina and Barbados: 1646-1775); pres Buchanan Soc 1985-87; FRSA 1990; *Recreations* writing, historical research; *Style—* Maj J E Buchanan; Woodhall, Pencaitland, East Lothian EH34 5DH (☎ 0875 340 243)

BUCHANAN, Prof Keith; s of James Deans Buchanan (d 1976), of Thornliebank, Glasgow, and Helen Parker, *née* Watson; *b* 24 July 1934; *Educ* Shawlands Sch, Univ of Glasgow (MB ChB); *m* 21 March 1961, Maureen, da of James Bryans (d 1982); 2 s (Fraser James b 10 July 1965, Neil Bryans b 16 May 1972), 2 da (Carol Elizabeth b 2 Sept 1963, Kirsty Anne b 19 Jan 1970); *Career* sr registrar in med Glasgow Royal Infirmary 1962-68, prof of metabolic med Queens Univ of Belfast 1976- (sr lectr in med 1969-76); over 200 pubns in jls; *Recreations* golf, gardening, swimming; *Style—* Prof Keith Buchanan; 30 North Circular Rd, Lisburn, Co Antrim, N Ireland BT28 3AH (☎ 0846 601207); Wellcome Research Laboratories, Dept of Medicine, Mulhouse, Grosvenor Rd, Belfast BT12 6BJ (☎ 0232 240503)

BUCHANAN, Nigel James Cubitt; s of Rev Basil Roberts Buchanan, (d 1987), of Cambridge, and Elene, *née* Cubitt; *b* 13 Nov 1943; *Educ* Denstone Coll; *m* 6 July 1968, (Katherine) Mary, da of Prof Sir Arthur Llewellyn Armitage (d 1984); 1 s (James b 20 Nov 1979), 2 da (Katherine Lucy b 21 Sept 1975, Elizabeth Mary b 15 May 1978); *Career* Price Waterhouse: ptnr 1978-, Euro dir of fin servs practice 1988-; vice chm World Financial Services Practice 1989-; FCA; *Books* Accounting for Pensions (jtly), Pw/Euromoney Debt Equity Swap Guide (jtly); *Recreations* tennis, golf; *Clubs* Carlton; *Style—* Nigel Buchanan, Esq; Longwood, 16 Park Ave, Harpenden, Herts AL5 2EA (☎ 0582 763076); Southwark Towers, 32 London Bridge St, London SE1 9SY (☎ 071 939 3000, fax 071 378 0647)

BUCHANAN-BARROW, Paul M; s of Rev Dr H R Buchanan-Barrow, of Henley, Oxon; *b* 23 April 1945; *Educ* Univ of St Andrews (MA); *m* 12 July 1969, Eithne A, da of G W M O'Shea, of Richmond, Surrey; 2 da (Perdita b 1972, Jessica b 1974); *Career* merchant banker and dir County Bank Ltd 1981-86, exec search conslt and md Goddard Kay Rogers & Assocs 1986-; govr Royal Star & Garter Home 1989-; *Recreations* politics, squash, chess; *Clubs* Reform, Honourable Artillery Co, MCC; *Style—* Paul Buchanan-Barrow, Esq; 127 Queens Rd, Richmond, Surrey; Newhouse Cottages, Luxborough, Somerset; Old London House, 32 St James's Square, London SW1Y 4JR

BUCHANAN-DUNLOP, Brig (Archibald) Ian; CBE (1959), DSO (1944); 2 s of Lt-Col Archibald Henry Buchanan-Dunlop, 18 Laird of Drumhead, Dunbartonshire (d 1947), and Mary Agnes, *née* Kennedy (d 1964); *b* 3 March 1908; *Educ* Loretto, RMC Sandhurst; *m* 1938, Renée Caroline Frances, da of John Charles Serjeant, of Hextable, Kent; 1 s, 1 da; *Career* psc, jssc, idc; cmd 6 Cameronians (SR) 1944-45, 1 Royal Scots Fus 1946-47, 2 Royal Scots Fus 1947-48 (N W Europe); DAG FARELF 1956-58, Col Royal Scots Fus 1958-59, dir Boys' Trg WO 1958-60; princ Scottish Office 1960-75; professional artist 1975-; CStJ 1968; *Recreations* gardening, reading, writing; *Clubs* British Water Colour Soc; *Style—* Brig Ian Buchanan-Dunlop, CBE, DSO; Broughton Place, Broughton, by Biggar, Lanarks ML12 6HJ

BUCHANAN-JARDINE, John Christopher Rupert; s and h of Sir Andrew Rupert John Buchanan-Jardine, 4 Bt, MC, JP, DL; *b* 20 March 1952; *Educ* Harrow, RAC Cirencester; *m* 1975, Pandora, da of Peter Murray Lee; 5 da (Tessa b 1979, Katie b 1980, Lorna b 1984, Juliet b 1986, Alice b 1988); *Style—* John Buchanan-Jardine, Esq

BUCHANAN-JARDINE, Prudence, Lady; Prudence Audrey; da of William Haggie, of Knayton, Thirsk, Yorks; *m* 1944, as his 2 wife, Capt Sir John William Buchanan-Jardine, 3 Bt (d 1969); 1 s (Charles James), 1 da (Caroline Anne); *Style—* Prudence, Lady Buchanan-Jardine; Moulin de la Mourachonne, 06370 Mouans Sartoux, France

BUCHANAN-JARDINE, Sir (Andrew) Rupert John; 4 Bt (UK 1885), MC (1945), JP (Dumfriesshire 1957), DL (1978); s of Sir John Buchanan-Jardine, 3 Bt, JP (d 1969), by his 1 w, Jean (d 1989), da of Lord Ernest Hamilton, sometime MP N Tyrone (7 s of 1 Duke of Abercorn, KG, PC, and Lady Louisa Russell, 2 da of 6 Duke of Bedford, KG); *b* 2 Feb 1923; *Educ* Harrow, RAC Cirencester; *m* 1950 (m dis 1975), Jane, da of Sir Archibald Edmonstone, 6 Bt, and Gwendolyn, da of Marshall Field, of Chicago; 1 s, 1 da; *Heir* s, John Buchanan-Jardine; *Career* farmer and landowner, formerly Maj RHG; master Dumfriesshire Foxhounds 1950-; KASG; *Recreations* country pursuits; *Clubs* MCC; *Style—* Sir Rupert Buchanan-Jardine, Bt, MC, JP, DL; Dixons, Lockerbie, Dumfriesshire (☎ 05762 2508)

BUCHANAN-SMITH, Rt Hon Alick Laidlaw; PC (1981), MP (C Kincardine and Deeside 1983-); 2 s of late Baron Balerno, CBE, TD, JP, DL (Life Peer); *b* 8 April 1932; *Educ* Edinburgh Acad, Trinity Coll Glenalmond, Pembroke Coll Cambridge, Univ of Edinburgh; *m* 1956, Janet, da of Thomas Lawrie, CBE; 1 s (James b 1962), 3 da (Jean b 1957, Margaret b 1960, Fenella b 1965); *Career* Nat Serv in Gordon Highlanders, later Capt 5/6 Gordon Highlanders (TA); farmer; contested (C) West Fife, 1959; MP (C) N Angus and Mearns 1964-83, parly under-sec Scot Office 1970-74, oppn spokesman Scot Affrs and memb Shadow Cabinet from which he resigned over devolution issue 1977, Min of State Agric Fish and Food 1979-83, Min of State Energy 1983-87; chm Parly Gp for Energy Studies 1987-; *Style—* The Rt Hon Alick Buchanan-Smith, MP; House of Commons, London SW1A 0AA

BUCHANAN-SMITH, Hon Jock Gordon; 4 s of late Baron Balerno (Life Peer); *b* 3 March 1940; *Educ* Trinity Coll Glenalmond, Aberdeen Univ, Iowa State Univ USA, Texas Tech Coll, Oklahoma State Univ (PhD); *m* 1964, Virginia Lee, el da of John S Maxson, of Dallas, Texas, 1 s (Peter b 1972), 1 da (Rachel b 1975); *Career* Lt Gordon Highlanders 1963; prof Univ of Guelph, Ontario; *Style—* The Hon Jock Buchanan-Smith; Pitcaple Farm, RR22, Cambridge, Ontario N3C 2V4, Canada

BUCHANAN-SMITH, Hon Mrs George; (Isobel Angela) Margaret; da of Edward Bowden, of Oxshott, Surrey; *m* 1, Stuart McIntosh (decd); m 2, 1961, Rev Hon George Adam Buchanan-Smith (d 1983, sometime housemaster Fettes Coll Edinburgh), eldest s of Baron Balerno (Life Peer); 2 s, 1 da; *Style—* The Hon Mrs George Buchanan-Smith; Woodhouselee, Easter Howgate, Midlothian EH26 0PF

BUCHANAN-SMITH, Rev the Hon Robin Dunlop; 3 s of Brig Baron Balerno, CBE, TD (Life Peer; d 1984), and Mary Kathleen, *née* Smith (d 1947); *b* 1 Feb 1936; *Educ* Edinburgh Acad, Trinity Coll Glenalmond, Pembroke Coll Cambridge (BA), New Coll Edinburgh, Princeton Theol Seminary USA (ThM); *m* 13 July 1966, Sheena Mary, da of Alexander Edwards (d 1951), of Oban; 2 s (Beppo, Chay); *Career* minister Christ's Church Dunollie Oban 1962-66; chaplain: 8 Bn Argyll and Sutherland Highlanders 1962-66, St Andrews Univ and St Andrews Univ OTC 1966-73, Highland Volunteers 1966-68; chllr's assessor St Andrews Univ 1981-85; dir Scottish Television plc 1982-, chm Scotland's Heritage Hotels 1988-; *Recreations* sailing, country; *Clubs* Caledonian, Royal Highland Yacht; *Style—* The Rev the Hon Robin Buchanan-Smith; Isle of Eriska, Ledaig, Oban, Argyll PA37 1SD (☎ 0631 72 371, fax 0631 72 531, telex 777040)

BUCK, Sir (Philip) Antony (Fyson); QC (1974), MP (C) Colchester N 1983-; yr s of late A F Buck, of Ely; *b* 19 Dec 1928; *Educ* King's Sch Ely, Trinity Hall Cambridge; *m* 1, 1955 (m dis 1989), Judy Elaine, o da of late Dr C A Grant, of Cottesloe, Perth, W Australia; 1 da; m 2, 22 March 1990, Bienvenida Perez-Blanco; *Career* MP (C) Colchester 1961-83, min for RN 1972-74; chm Cons Pty Def Ctee until 1988; chm Select Ctee on Parly Cmmn for Admin (Ombudsman) 1977-; kt 1983; *Recreations* most sports, reading; *Clubs* Oxford & Cambridge; *Style—* Sir Antony Buck, QC, MP; House of Commons (☎ 071 219 4011/4171)

BUCK, Antony Charles; s of Stephan Frank Buck, of London NW7 and Rosemary, *née* Tyoran; *b* 8 Aug 1963; *Educ* Haberdashers' Aske's, Univ of Warwick (BSc, Hockey and Tennis First teams); *m* 2 July 1989, Jane Amanda, da of Anthony Halperin; *Career* advertising exec; currently bd account planning dir BMP DDB Needham (joined 1985); winner first prize IPA Advertising Effectiveness awards for: Kia-Ora 1988, Clarks Desert Boots 1988, Alliance & Leicester 1990; *Recreations* antique collecting, big game photography, fishing, tennis, golf; *Style—* Antony Buck, Esq; BMP DDB Needham, 12 Bishops Bridge Rd, London W2 6AA (☎ 071 258 3979)

BUCK, Arthur John; s of Arthur Buck (d 1979), of Mill Lane, Amersham, Bucks, and

Lucy Mary, *née* Hart (d 1966); *b* 10 June 1924; *Educ* Ilford Co HS; *m* 1, 1952, Mary (d 1980), da of Sydney John Thompson; 2 s (Michael b 1954, Richard b 1956), 1 da (Rosemary b 1962); m 2, 1984, Mary Ida Lowe, *née* Fewster; *Career* Lt RA 1943-47; civil serv Miny of Works 1941-43, articled clerk Hamilton-Hill & Evershed 1948-50, slr legal Dept Nat Film Finance Corp 1950-62; ptnr: Oswald Hickson Collier & Co London and Amersham 1962-67, Denton Hall Burgin & Warrens London 1967-90 (conslt 1990-); memb: Law Soc 1950, Copinger Soc of Arts and Entertainment Lawyers 1980 (pres 1990-91); *Recreations* theatre, music, gardening, walking; *Style—* Arthur Buck, Esq; 1 Old Palace Place, The Green, Richmond, Surrey TW9 1NQ (☎ 081 948 6327); Denton Hall Burgin & Warrens, 5 Chancery Lane, Cliffords Inn, London EC4A 1BU (☎ 071 320 6502, fax 071 404 0087)

BUCK, Charles Gerard; JP (1966); s of Walter Gerard Buck (d 1934); *b* 21 Sept 1910; *Educ* Trent Coll; *m* 1946, Georgette Forrest, da of John Hamilton Shepherd Raeside (d 1957); 1 da (and 1 da decd); *Career* served Maj RA in UK, India, Africa; CA 1934-; chm: Buck & Lloyd (Sheffield) Ltd 1969-87, Sheffield Brick Group plc 1975-80; pres Sheffield Amateur Sports Club Ltd; gen cmmr Taxes 1970-82; High Sheriff S Yorks 1980-81; *Recreations* cricket, hockey, golf; *Clubs* MCC, Sheffield (pres); *Style—* Charles Buck, Esq, JP; The Grange, Bradway Road, Sheffield S17 4PF (☎ 0742 363585)

BUCK, David Howard; s of Maj Glyn Howard Buck (d 1977), of Ipswich, Suffolk and Snape, Suffolk, and Mary Elizabeth, *née* Blackburn; *b* 16 Oct 1946; *Educ* St Edmunds Sch Kesgrave Suffolk, Greshams Sch; *m* 10 July 1971, Doreen Jeannette, da of Henry John Slater Wright, of Ispwich, Suffolk; 3 da (Rachel b 1977, Sarah b 1978, Heather b 1980); *Career* articled Ensor Son & Goult Ipswich 1966, qualified chartered accountant and joined Peat Marwick Mitchell Norwich 1972, mangr Ensor Son & Goult Felixstowe 1975-78 (joined 1973); ptnr: Stoy Hayward Norwich (formerly Hemming Graham & Poole) 1979-, Stoy Hayward Management Services 1988-; chm and former treas Gt Plumstead New Village Hall Assoc 1980-88 (Hall opened 1988); FCA; *Recreations* tennis, swimming; *Clubs* Oasis Sports, Felixstowe Lawn Tennis (vice pres, former treas), Strangers (Norwich); *Style—* David Buck, Esq; Low Farm, Cox Hill Road, Beighton, Norfolk NR13 3JX (☎ 0493 750351) ; 58 Thorpe Rd, Norwich, Norfolk NR1 1RY (☎ 0603 620 241, fax 0603 630 224); 12 The Close, Norwich NR1 4DH (☎ 0603 619719)

BUCK, David Shuttleworth; s of Douglas Shuttleworth Buck (d 1960), and Gladys May, (Pearl) (d 1988); *b* 8 April 1934; *Educ* Ashville Coll Harrogate N Yorks, Queen Elizabeth GS Gainsborough Lincs, Emmanuel Coll Cambridge (BA); *m* 16 Aug 1958, Jennifer, da of Clifford Kenneth Boundy, of Stratford-upon-Avon; 1 s (Stephen b 1963), 3 da (Vanessa b 1961, Katherine b 1964, Margaret b 1969); *Career* Nat Serv FEAF Hong Kong 1952-54, PO RAF Fighter Control; mktg mangr Fibres Div ICI Ltd 1957-76, commercial mangr J Bibby & Sons Henry Cooke 1976-77, assoc ptnr textile analyst Laing & Cruickshank 1978-83, ptnr textile analyst De Zoete and Bevan 1983-86, dir res Barclays de Zoete Wedd 1986-, leading city textile analyst 1984-88, fndr own co DB Research 1990; Star Analyst 1986, 1987, and 88, Top Star Analyst 1987 and 1988, memb Stock Exchange 1982; ASIA 1981, FTI 1985, FCFI 1986; *Recreations* golf, fell walking, bridge, travel; *Clubs* Welwyn Garden City Golf; *Style—* David S Buck, Esq; D B Research, 124 Parkway, Welwyn Garden City, Herts AL8 6HN (☎ 0707 336 827, fax 0707 335946); Barclays De Zoete Wedd, Ebbgate House, 2 Swan Lane, London EC4R 3TS (☎ 071 623 2323)

BUCK, (Harry) Grant; s of Harry Reuben Buck, OBE, JP (d 1970), of Newmarket; *b* 17 June 1921; *Educ* Perse Sch, Clare Coll Cambridge (MA); *m* 1950, Nancy Elizabeth, da of Frederick Boyton Taylor (d 1959), of Dullingham House, Newmarket; 3 da; *Career* Maj Royal Inniskilling Fusiliers 1941-46; N Africa and Europe Royal Dutch Shell Group 1947-79 (dir Shell Venezuela 1964-66), chm Star Offshore Serv plc 1979-81, int oil conslt and memb Bd of Advsrs Northville Industrial Corp USA 1981-; *Recreations* travel, swimming, horseracing; *Style—* Grant Buck, Esq; Plovers, Hadstock, nr Cambridge CBI 6PF (☎ 0223 891027)

BUCK, Louisa; da of Sir Antony Buck, QC, MP, and Judy, *née* Grant; *b* 10 July 1960; *Educ* Queensgate Sch London, Girton Coll Cambridge (BA), Courtauld Inst of Art Univ of London (MA); partner, Tom Deew Mathews; *Career* freelance lectr and journalist, freelance lectr on Twentieth Century Art 1983-84 (Tate Gallery, Sotheby's fine art courses, art courses in London and Europe), Tate Gallery 1984-85 (cataloguer of John Banting and Edward Burra material, curator of exhibition of Bantings graphic work, public lectr), Ran Bonhams Modern Pictures Dept 1985; freelance journalist, broadcaster lectr and researcher 1986-; arts correspondent GQ magazine; contrib to: Arena Magazine, New Statesman & Society, Mirabella magazine, City Limits, Guardian arts pages, Tatler, Vogue, Marie Claire, The Evening Standard, Sunday Correspondent; radio 1988-90: visual arts critic LBC, currently presenter Kaleidoscope BBC Radio 4 (arts, design and book reviewer); lectr on Twentieth Century art design and culture: Tate Gallery, RCA, Saatchi Collection, Univ of Reading; *Books* author of catalogue essays for: A Salute to British Surrealism (Minories Gallery Colchester) 1985, The Surrealist Spirit in Britain (Whitford & Huges) 1988, Sylvia Ziranek: Ici Villa Moi (Watermans Arts Centre) 1989, Jacqueline Morreau: Paradise Now (Odette Gilbert Gallery) 1990, Meret Oppenheim retrospective Barcelona, Relative Values: Or What's Art Worth? (jtly, 1990); *Recreations* gardening, swimming, travelling; *Clubs* Chelsea Arts, Kennington Weightwatchers; *Style—* Ms Louisa Buck

BUCKINGHAM, Prof (Amyand) David; s of Reginald Joslin Buckingham (d 1956), and Florence Grace, *née* Elliot (d 1977); *b* 28 Jan 1930; *Educ* Barker Coll Hornsby NSW, Univ of Sydney (BSc, MSc), Corpus Christi Coll Cambridge (PhD, ScD); *m* 24 July 1965, Jillian, da of Harold Vincent Bowles, OBE (d 1965); 1 s (Mark b 1968), 2 da (Lucy b 1967, Alice b 1971); *Career* jr censor ChCh Oxford 1963-65 (lectr 1955-57, student 1957-65), lectr in inorganic chemistry Univ of Oxford 1958-65, prof of theoretical chemistry Univ of Bristol 1965-69, prof of chemistry Univ of Cambridge 1969-, fell Pembroke Coll Cambridge 1970-; pres Faraday Div Royal Soc of Chemistry 1987-89; docteur honoris causa Univ de Nancy 1979, FRS; *Books* The Laws and Applications of Thermodynamics (1964), Molecular Physics (ed 1968-72), Organic Liquids (ed, 1978), int reviews in Physical Chemistry (ed 1981-89), Chemical Physics Letters (ed 1978-); *Recreations* cricket, tennis, travel; *Clubs* ESU; *Style—* Prof David Buckingham; University Chemical Laboratory, Lensfield Rd, Cambridge CB2 1EW (☎ 0223 336376, fax 0223 336362)

BUCKINGHAM, Ven Hugh Fletcher; s of Rev Christopher Leigh Buckingham (d 1963), of Alciston, Sussex, and Gladys Margaret, *née* Shellabear (d 1984); *b* 13 Sept 1932; *Educ* Lancing, Hertford Coll Oxford (MA), Westcott House Cambridge; *m* 7 Jan 1967, Alison Mary, da of John Heywood Cock, of Norwich; 1 s (William Hugh b 28 Sept 1971), 1 da (Harriet Jane b 10 Dec 1969); *Career* curate: Halliwell St Thomas Bolton 1957-60, St Silas Sheffield 1960-65; incumbent: Hindolveston and Guestwick Norfolk 1965-70, Fakenham Norfolk 1970-88; rural dean Burnham Walsingham Norfolk 1981-87, chm Diocesan Bd for Social Responsibility Diocese of Norwich 1981-88, hon canon Norwich Cath 1985, archdeacon of the East Riding and canon York Minster 1988-; *Books* How To Be A Christian In Trying Circumstances (1985), Feeling Good (1989); *Recreations* pottery, gardening; *Style—* The Ven the Archdeacon of the East Riding; Brimley Lodge, Beverley, N Humberside HU17 7DX (☎ 0482 881659)

BUCKINGHAM, Michael Simm; s of Maurice William Buckingham (d 1989), of Aylesbury, Bucks, and Edith Gwendolin, *née* Simm; *b* 6 Feb 1944; *Educ* Berkhamsted Sch, St Bartholomew's Hosp Med Sch (MB BS), Univ of Southampton (DM); *m* 10 Oct 1970, Hazel Diana, da of Thomas William White, of Meranti Lodge, Clifton, Rugby; 1 s (Timothy b 1976), 1 da (Susannah b 1974); *Career* conslt obstetrician and gynaecologist Royal Hampshire Co Hosp 1981-; memb BMA, FRCOG (1987, MRCOG 1974); *Recreations* fly fishing; *Style—* Michael Buckingham, Esq; Smoke Acre, Crossway, Shawford, Winchester, Hants SO21 2BZ (☎ 0962 712227); Royal Hampshire County Hospital, Romsey Rd, Winchester, Hants (☎ 0962 863535)

BUCKINGHAMSHIRE, Margot, Countess of; Margot Macrae; da of John Storey Rodger, of NSW, Australia, landowner and timber mill owner; *Educ* privately in Australia and Noumea, New Caledonia; *m* 1, F C Bruce Hittman, MD, FRACS (decd), of Sydney, Australia; m 2, 1972, 9 Earl of Buckinghamshire (d 1983); *Career* Int columnist for Australian gp and various int newspapers (fashion, social, famous people) 1960-70; public relations rep Nina Ricci UK 1971-87; charity work with Cancer Research and Leukemia Research Fund and Royal Manor Hosp; *Recreations* writing poetry, collecting memorabilia; *Clubs* English Speaking Union (UK and USA); *Style—* The Rt Hon Margot, Countess of Buckinghamshire; c/o Barclays Bank, 160 Piccadilly, London W1; 21a Hanover Sq, London W1

BUCKINGHAMSHIRE, 10 Earl of (GB 1746); Sir (George) Miles Hobart-Hampden; 14 Bt (E 1611); Baron Hobart (GB 1728); s of Cyril Langel Hobart-Hampden (d 1972), ggs of 6 Earl of Buckinghamshire; suc kinsman 1983; *b* 15 Dec 1944; *Educ* Clifton, Univ of Exeter (BA), Univ of London (MA); *m* 1, 1968 (m dis), Susan Jennifer, o da of Raymond W Adams, of Halesowen, Worcs; m 2, 1975, Alison Wightman, da of late William Forrest, of Edinburgh; 2 step s; *Heir* kinsman, Sir John Hobart, 3 Bt *qv*; *Career* dir: Hong Kong and Shanghai Banking Corporation 1963-64, Hudsons Bay Co 1968-70, Noble Lowndes & Partners Ltd 1970-81, Scottish Pension Trustees Ltd 1979-81, Anthony Gibbs Pension Services 1981-86, The Angel Trustee Co 1983-86, Wish Nominees Ltd 1986-, Wardley Investment Services (Luxembourg) SA 1988-, Wardly Global Selection 1988-, Gota Global Selection (Sicav) 1988, WISL Bahamas; md Wardley Investment Services International Ltd; chm: Wardley Unit Trust Managers Ltd 1988-, Wardley Fund Managers (Jersey) Ltd 1988-; memb House of Lords Select Ctee EC Sub Ctee on Fin Trade and External Relations, patron Hobart Town (1804) Early Settlers Assoc (Tasmania); FInstD; *Recreations* squash, fishing, music, reading, walking, rugby football; *Clubs* Western (Glasgow), West of Scotland Football; *Style—* The Rt Hon the Earl of Buckinghamshire; House of Lords, London SW1; Wardley Investment Services International Ltd, 3 Harbour Exchange Square, London E14 9GJ

BUCKLAND, Gerald David; s of Francis G Buckland, of Cheshunt, Hertfordshire, and Elizabeth, *née* Hamilton-Allen; *b* 22 March 1948; *Educ* St Ignatius' Coll, E Herts Coll; *m* 27 May 1975, Paula, da of Mark Gandy (d 1989); 1 s (Anthony Francis Gerald b 3 Jan 1988), 2 da (Marianne Paula Elizabeth b 10 Feb 1980, Isabella Louise Geraldine b 9 June 1983); *Career* press offr BP Chemicals Ltd 1977-80, PR coordinator BP Int Ltd 1980-82, PR mangr Marathan Int Petroleum Inc 1982-88, corporate rels dir TVS Entertainment plc 1988-; *Recreations* music, travel, languages; *Style—* Gerald Buckland, Esq; TVS Entertainment plc, 84 Buckingham Gate, London SW1E 6PD (☎ 071 976 7199, fax 071 233 0903)

BUCKLAND, Ross; s of William Arthur Haverfield Buckland, and Elizabeth, *née* Schmitzer; *b* 19 Dec 1942; *Educ* Sydney Boys' HS; *m* 22 Jan 1966, Patricia Ann, da of William Stephen Bubb, of Warriewood, NSW, Aust; 2 s (Sean William b 1968, Mark Charles b 1970); *Career* held various positions in companies engaged in banking, engrg, office equipment and food indust 1958-66; dir fin and admin Elizabeth Arden Pty Ltd 1966-73, md Kellogg (Aust) Pty Ltd 1978 (various positions 1973-77), pres and chief exec offr Kellogg Salads Canada Inc 1979-80, vice pres Kellogg Co USA, chm Kellogg Co of GB Ltd, dir euro operations Kellogg Co 1981; pres Food & Drink Fedn 1987-89; CBIM, FICSA, FASA, FIGD; *Recreations* walking; *Style—* Ross Buckland, Esq; Beam House, 8 Bucklow View, Bowdon, Cheshire WA14 3JP (☎ 061 941 1319); Kellogg Company of Great Britain Ltd, Park Road, Stretford, Manchester M32 8RA (☎ 061 869 2202, fax 061 869 2795)

BUCKLAND-WRIGHT, Dr (John) Christopher; s of John Buckland-Wright (d 1954), of Dunedin, NZ, and Mary Elizabeth, *née* Anderson (d 1976); *b* 19 Nov 1945; *Educ* Lycée Francais De Londres, Kings Coll London (BSc, AKC, PhD); *m* 11 Nov 1975, Rosalin, da of Charles W G T Kirk, OBE (d 1986), of Hemel Hempstead; 2 da (Helen b 1977, Alexandra b 1978); *Career* asst head Dept of Comparative Osteology Centre of Prehistory and Paleontology Nairobi Kenya 1966-67, teacher Lycée Francais de Londres 1971-72, anatomy lectr St Mary's Hosp Med Sch of London 1973-76, sr lectr Guy's Hosp Med Sch London Univ 1980-89 (lectr 1976-80, reader in radiological anatomy 1989-), head of Macroradiographic Res Unit Guy's Hosp 1981-; memb Int Cmmn on Radiation Units and Measurements 1987, author of over 70 scientific pubns on Microfocal Radiography and its application to the study of bone and arthritis; Freeman City of London 1980, Liveryman (and Hon Librarian) Worshipful Co of Barbers 1980; FZS 1971, memb Anat Soc 1974, memb Br Soc Rheumatology 1984; *Books* Cockerel Cavalcade (1988), The Engravings of John Buckland-Wright (1990); *Recreations* fine art and antiquarian books, drawing, painting, walking, sailing; *Clubs* City Livery, Upper Thames Sailing; *Style—* Dr Christopher Buckland-Wright; 50 Beechwood Ave, Kew, Richmond, Surrey TW9 4DE (☎ 081 876 2011); Anatomy Dept, Utd Medical and Dental Sch of Guys' and St Thomas' Hosp, London SE1 9RT (☎ 071 955 4364, fax 071 407 3913)

BUCKLE, Roger Nicholas; s of Leslie Grieves Buckle, of Old Priest's House, Church Street, Kidlington, Oxford (d 1981), and Rachel Joan, *née* McLaren (d 1987); *b* 19 Oct 1942; *Educ* Pocklington Sch; *m* 9 Sept 1972, Evelyn, da of Leonard Alfred Douglas Fenton (d 1960), of Earlwood, Sydney, Australia; *Career* articled clerk Critchley Ward and Pigott Oxford 1961-65, Thomson McLintock & Co London 1966-72, treasy mangr The Boots Co plc; hon treas The Vale of Belvoir Protection Gp, memb the Georgian Gp; FCA 1976 (ACA 1966); *Clubs* Ski Club of GB; *Style—* Roger Buckle, Esq; The Boots Company plc, Nottingham NG2 3AA

BUCKLER, Dr John Michael Heslington; s of Thomas Arnold Buckler (d 1974), and Dorothy, *née* Hargreaves (d 1987); *b* 13 July 1935; *Educ* King Edwards Sch Birmingham, Brasenose Coll Oxford (MA, DM, BM BCh), St Bartholomew's Hosp London (DCH, MRCP); *m* 21 May 1966, Janet Brimley, da of Roger Spencer Spong (d 1982); 3 s (Andrew Jonathan Heslington b 1968, Timothy James Granville b 1970, Christopher Mark Spencer b 1971); *Career* various jr hosp med appts London 1960-65, asst chief res Children's Hosp of Philadelphia USA 1966-67, res asst Gt Ormond St Hosp London 1967-70, sr lectr in child health Univ of Leeds 1970-, hon conslt paediatrician United Leeds Hosps then Leeds Western Healt and Leeds Gen Infirmary 1972-; memb: BMA, Br Paediatric Assoc; Yorkshire reg paediatric advsr RCP; fell BMA, FRCP 1977; *Books* A Reference Manual of Growth and Development (1979), The Adolescent Years (1987), A Longitudinal Study of Adolescent Growth (1990); *Style—* Dr John Buckler; 4 Grosvenor Terrace, Grosvenor Rd, Leeds LS6 2DY (☎ 0532 759578); Department of Paediatrics, D Floor, Clarendon Wing, Leeds General Infirmary, Belmont Grove, Leeds LS2 9NS (☎ 0532 432799 ext 3904)

BUCKLEY, Prof Adrian Arthur; s of Arthur Penketh Buckley (d 1977), and Beatrice May Buckley (d 1953); *b* 28 Dec 1940; *Educ* Poole GS, Univ of Sheffield (BA), Univ of Bradford (MSc); *m* 6 June 1966, Jenny Rosalie Buckley (d 1977); 2 s (Peter James Scott b 24 Dec 1971, David John Scott b 4 April 1974); *Career* Corp Fin Charterhouse Bank 1971-73, gp treas Redland plc 1973-79, prof Cranfield Sch of Mgmnt 1986- (joined 1980); FCA 1963, FCCA 1980, FCT 1985; *Books* Multinational Finance (1986), The Essence of International Money (1990); *Recreations* skiing, walking, theatre; *Style*— Prof Adrian Buckley; Cranfield School of Management, Cranfield, Bedford MK43 0AL (☎ 0234 751122)

BUCKLEY, Anthony James Henthorne; s of William Buckley (d 1956), and Nancy, *née* Stott; *b* 22 May 1934; *Educ* Haileybury, ISC, St John's Coll Cambridge (MA, LLB); *m* 9 March 1964, Celia Rosamund, da of Charles Sanderson (d 1971); 1 s (William b 9 Aug 1964), 2 da (Anna b 24 April 1966, Camilla b 25 Nov 1970); *Career* CA 1959; Peat Marwick Mitchell & Co 1959-62, Rank Orgn Ltd 1962-62, conslt Slater Walker Securities Ltd 1975- (joined 1966, md 1972-75), memb Worshipful Co of Makers of Playing Cards; *Clubs* MCC; *Style*— Anthony Buckley, Esq; 2 St Mary's Grove, Barnes, London SW13 0JA

BUCKLEY, Rt Hon Sir Denys Burton; MBE (Mil 1945), PC (1970); 4 s of 1 Baron Wrenbury (d 1935); *b* 6 Feb 1906; *Educ* Eton (OS), Trinity Coll Oxford (BA, MA, hon fell); *m* 1932, Gwendolen Jane, yr da of Sir Robert Armstrong-Jones, CBE, JP, DL (d 1943); 3 da (Jane, Catherine, Miranda); *Career* served 1939-45 in RAOC (temp Maj GSOII, Sigs Directorate, War Office); called to the Bar Lincolns Inn 1928 (bencher 1949, pro-treasurer 1967, treasurer 1969), High Court Judge (Chancery) 1960-70, Lord Justice of Appeal 1970-81; master Merchant Taylors' Co 1972-73; pres: Senate of Inns of Court 1970-72; Treasury Jr Counsel (Chancery) 1949-60; hon fell American Coll of Trial Lawyers 1970; CStJ 1966, Medal of Freedom (USA) 1945, kt 1960; *Clubs* Brooks's, Beefsteak; *Style*— Rt Hon Sir Denys Buckley, MBE; Stream Farm, Dallington, E Sussex (☎ Rushlake Green 0435 830223); 105 Onslow Square, London SW7 (☎ 071 584 4735)

BUCKLEY, James; s of Harold Buckley (d 1966), and Mabel, *née* Taylor; *b* 5 April 1944; *Educ* Sheffield City GS, Imperial Coll of Sci & Technol (BSc, ARCS); *m* 15 Aug 1972, Valerie (Elizabeth), da of Ivor Powles, of Newport, Gwent; 1 da (Louise b 1976); *Career* scientific offr RAF Coastal Cmd MOD 1965, princ CSD 1971, private sec to Min for Civil Service and Ldr House of Lords successively Lord Peart, Lord Soames and Baroness Young 1979-82, private sec to govr Rhodesia 1979-80, sec Civil Service Coll 1982-85, chief exec BVA 1985-87; dep dir-gen Gen Cncl Br Shipping 1987-; *Recreations* photography, squash, tennis; *Style*— James Buckley, Esq; 29 Spenser Ave, Weybridge, Surrey KT13 0ST (☎ 0932 843 893); General Council of British Shipping, 30-32 St Mary Axe, London EC3A 8ET (☎ 071 283 2922, fax 071 626 8135, telex 884008)

BUCKLEY, Sir John William; s of John William Buckley, and Florence Buckley; *b* 9 Jan 1913; *m* 1, 1935 (m dis 1967), Bertha Bagnall; 2 s; m 2, 1967, Molly Neville-Clarke, chm MENCAP (Royal Soc for Mentally Handicapped Children and Adults); 1 step s, and 1 step s decd; *Career* gen mangr George Kent 1945-50 (joined 1934); md: Emmco Party 1950-55, BMC Party 1955-60; vice chm and dep chm Winget Gloucester Ltd 1961-68, chm Alfred Herbert 1975-79; memb BSC 1978-, pres Anglo-Soviet C of C 1977-83, former dir BOTB; chm: Alfred Herbert 1975-79, Davy Corp (formerly Davy International) 1973-82 (md and dep chm 1968-73), Oppenheimer International 1983-; FRSA, Hon FIChemE, FIProdE; kt 1977; *Style*— Sir John Buckley; Fuerst Day Lawson, St Clare House, 30-33 Minories, London EC3N 1LN (☎ 071 488 0777)

BUCKLEY, Dr Richard Anthony; s of Alfred Buckley, of Southampton, and Dorothy Iris, *née* Neale; *b* 16 April 1947; *Educ* Queen Elizabeth GS Wakefield, Merton Coll Oxford (MA DPhil); *Career* called to the Bar Lincoln's Inn 1969; lectr in law King's Coll London 1970-75, fell and tutor in law Mansfield Coll Oxford 1975-; writer of various articles for legal periodicals; *Books* The Law of Nuisance (1981), Salmond and Heuston on Torts (19 edn with RFV Heuston, 1987), The Modern Law of Negligence (1988); *Recreations* walking, swimming, working; *Clubs* United Oxford and Cambridge; *Style*— Dr Richard Buckley; 14 Hobson Rd, Oxford OX2 7JX (☎ 0865 510537); Mansfield Coll, Mansfield Rd, Oxford OX1 3TF (☎ 0865 270999)

BUCKLEY, Lt Cdr Sir (Peter) Richard; KCVO (1982, CVO 1973, MVO 1968); 2 s of Alfred Buckley (d 1952), and Elsie Gwendoline Buckley (d 1987); *b* 31 Jan 1928; *Educ* Wellington; *m* 1958, Theresa Mary, da of Charles Peter Neve, OBE (d 1990); 2 s, 1 d; *Career* joined RN as cadet 1945, invalided 1961, Lt Cdr; private sec to TRH The Duke and Duchess of Kent 1961-89, dir Malcolm McIntyre Consultancy 1989-; govr Wellington Coll 1989-; *Recreations* sailing, fishing, beekeeping; *Clubs* Army and Navy, Royal Dart Yacht, Royal Yacht Sqdn, All England Lawn Tennis; *Style*— Lt Cdr Sir Richard Buckley, KCVO; Coppins Cottages, Iver, Bucks (☎ 0753 653004)

BUCKLEY, Roger John; s of Frederick William Buckley, of Mersham, Kent, and Eileen, *née* Street; *b* 11 Jan 1945; *Educ* Plymouth Coll, Exeter College Oxford, St Thomas' Hosp Med Sch (MA, BM BCh); *m* 30 Jan 1971, Elizabeth Arnold, da of William Joseph Arnold Sykes (d 1986), of Speldhurst, Kent; 1 s (Adam b 1978), 1 da (Harriet b 1974); *Career* house surgn St Thomas' Hosp London 1970, sr registrar Westminster Hosp 1978, conslt ophthalmologist and dir Contact Lens and Prosthesis Dept Moorfields Eye Hosp 1981 (res surgical offr 1975); memb: Br Standards Instn Contact Lens Ctee 1984-89, Ctee on Dental and Surgical Materials DHSS 1983-, Gen Optical Cncl 1988-; pres Med Contact Lens Assoc 1989-; author of a number of papers and chapters on the cornea contact lenses and ocular allergy; ATCL 1964, FRCS 1978, FCOphth 1989; *Recreations* music, hill walking; *Clubs* RSM; *Style*— Mr Roger Buckley; 57A Wimpole St, London W1M 7DF (☎ 071 486 8959); Moorfields Eye Hospital, City Road, London EC1V 2PD (☎ 071 253 3411, fax 071 253 4696, telex 266129)

BUCKLEY, Stephen; s of Leslie Buckley (d 1972), of Leicester and Nancy Throsby (d 1989); *b* 5 April 1944; *Educ* City of Leicester Boys' GS, Univ of Newcastle upon Tyne (BA), Univ of Reading (MA); *m* 1973, Stephanie James; 1 s (Felix Rupert b 1978), 1 da (Scarlet Matilda b 1973); *Career* artist in residence King's Coll Cambridge 1972-74, ind work 1974-; over 60 one man shows worldwide to date incl retrospective Museum of Modern Art Oxford 1985 and Yale Center for British Art Newhaven Connecticut 1986; contrib to: John Moores Liverpool Exhibition 1974 and 1985, Chichester National Art Exhibition 1975, Tolly Cobbold Exhibition 1977; work in collections of: Arts Cncl GB, British Cncl, Tate Gallery, V & A Museum Contemporary Arts Soc, Aberdeen Art Gallery, City Art Gallery Bristol Eastern Arts Assoc, Walker Art Gallery Liverpool, Whitworth Art Gallery Manchester, Southampton City Art Gallery, Metropolitian Museum NY, Museum of Modern Art Caracas, Australian National Gallery Canberra, National Gallery Wellington NZ, Kettles Yard Gallery Univ of Cambridge; in collaboration with Rambert Dance Co 1987 and 1989; *Style*— Stephen Buckley, Esq; c/o Knoedler Gallery, 22 Cork St, London W1X 1HB (☎ 071 439 1096)

BUCKLEY, Thomas George McLean; s of John McLean Buckley (d 1972), of London, and Oonah Pamela, *née* Thesiger (d 1982); *b* 14 Jan 1932; *Educ* Eton, Magdalen Coll Oxford (MA); *m* 1963, Valerie Frances, da of E Donald R Shearer; 3 s (William Donald McLean b 31 March 1965, Edward John McLean b 20 June 1967, Thomas Fitzpatrick McLean b 18 June 1971); *Career* Slaughter and May: articled clerk 1955-58 (City Slrs Co prize 1958), ptnr 1966-; memb Worshipful Co of Skinners 1955; memb Law Soc; *Recreations* sailing; *Clubs* West Mersea Yacht; *Style*— Thomas Buckley, Esq; Slaughter and May, 35 Basinghall St, London EC2V 5DB (☎ 071 600 1200)

BUCKLEY, Maj William Kemmis; MBE (1959), DL (Carmarthenshire, latterly Dyfed 1969); o s of Lt-Col William Howell Buckley, DL, of Castell Gorfod, Dyfed, and Karolie Kathleen, *née* Kemmis; *b* 18 Oct 1921; *Educ* Radley, New Coll Oxford; *Career* served WWII, Lt-Col Welsh Gds (despatches) and Suez 1956, mil asst to vice-CIGS 1958-59; dir: Rhymney Brewery (now Whitbread) 1962, Felinfoel Brewery 1975; pres Buckley's Brewery 1983-86 (chm 1972-83); High Sheriff Carmarthenshire 1966-67, vice Lord Lt Dyfed 1989; KStJ 1983; *Recreations* gardening; *Clubs* Brooks's, Cardiff and County; *Style*— Maj William Buckley, MBE, DL; Briar Cottage, Ferryside, Dyfed (☎ 026 785 359)

BUCKMAN, Hon Mrs (Griselda Rosalind); *née* Eden; 2 da of 6 Baron Henley (d 1962); *b* 16 Jan 1917; *m* 1939 (m dis 1964), John Buckman, late Sqdn-Ldr RAFVR, 3 s of late Isaac Buckman; 1 s, 1 da; *Style*— The Hon Mrs Buckman; 8 High St, West Haddon, Northampton NN6 7AP

BUCKMASTER, Hon Colin John; s of late 2 Viscount Buckmaster, and his 1 w, Joan, da of Dr Garry Simpson; hp of bro, 3 Viscount; *b* 17 April 1923; *Educ* Winchester; *m* 1946, May, da of late Charles Henry Gibbon, of The Lodge, Great Bentley, Essex; 3 s, 2 da; *Career* late Flt-Lt RAF; *Clubs* Brooks's; *Style*— The Hon Colin Buckmaster; Ryece Hall, Brettenham, Ipswich, Suffolk

BUCKMASTER, 3 Viscount (UK 1933); Martin Stanley Buckmaster; OBE (1979); also Baron Buckmaster (UK 1915); s of 2 Viscount (d 1974), and his 1 w, Joan, da of Dr Garry Simpson; *b* 11 April 1921; *Educ* Stowe; *Heir* bro, Hon Colin Buckmaster; *Career* FO 1946, first sec Br High Cmmr Kampala 1969-71, Beirut 1971-73, FCO 1973-77, head of chancery Yemen Arab Republic 1977-; FRGS; *Style*— The Rt Hon The Viscount Buckmaster, OBE; 8 Redcliffe Square, London SW10

BUCKNALL, Dr Clifford Adrian; s of Eric Bucknall, of Berkswell W Midlands, and Elsie Constance, *née* Whittaker; *b* 25 Feb 1956; *Educ* Leamington Coll, Kings Coll London, Westminster Med sch London (MB, BS, MD); *m* 30 July 1983, Sarah Anne, da of Dudleigh Oscar Topp, of Scaynes Hill, Sussex; 2 s (Sam b 1984, Tom b 1986); *Career* house surgn Warwick 1979-80, house physician Westminster 1980, sr house physician Nottingham 1980-82, registrar Brighton 1984-85, sr registrar in cardiology Guys 1987-89 (res fell 1982-84), conslt cardiologist Kings Coll Hosp 1989- (registrar 1985-86, locum sr registrar 1986-87), conslt cardiologist Dulwich Hosps 1989-; FRSM 1979, LRCP 1979, MRCS 1979, MRCP 1982, memb Br Cardial soc; *Books* Horizons In Medicine no 1 (contrib, 1989); *Recreations* hockey, tennis, swimming; *Style*— Dr Clifford Bucknall; Cardial Dept, Kings College Hospital, Denmark Hill, London SE5 (☎ 071 733 9069)

BUCKNALL, Derek Edwin; s of William Ralph Bucknall, of Norton House, Vision Hill Rd, Budleigh Salterton, Devon, and Nellie, *née* Aston (d 1938); *b* 23 Sept 1936; *Educ* Durham Sch, St John's Coll Cambridge (MA); *m* 26 June 1965, Pamela Marianne, da of James Chalmers Miller (d 1967), of Orchard Brae, Edinburgh; 1 s (Graham b 1970), 1 da (Jane b 1967); *Career* ICI Fibres 1961-77, personnel dir ICI Plastics 1978-83; dir Weston-Hyde Ltd 1983-86, gen mangr ICI Petrochemicals and Plastics 1984-86, personnel dir Br Aerospace plc 1986-90, chm Br Aerospace Enterprises 1990-; *Recreations* golf, gardening, enjoying a developing family, watching cricket and rugby; *Clubs* Utd Oxford and Cambridge Univ; *Style*— Derek Bucknall, Esq; Allerton, 27 Orchard Rd, Tewin, Herts AL6 0HL (☎ 043 879 228); Br Aerospace plc, 11 Strand, London WC2N 5JT (☎ 071 930 1020, telex 919221, fax 071 389 3983)

BUCKNER, Jack Richard; s of Rev Richard Pentland Buckner, of Northumberland, and Anne Margaret, *née* Ferguson; *b* 22 Sept 1961; *Educ* St Petroc's Sch Bude, Worksop Coll, Loughborough Univ (BSc); *m* 10 Sept 1983, Kerin, da of Anthony John Wilson; *Career* 5000m runner; Silver medal Cwlth Games 1986, Gold medal Euro Championships 1986, Bronze medal World Championships 1987, sixth place Olympic Games 1988; *Recreations* reading, theatre, cinema, walking, writing; *Style*— Jack Buckner, Esq

BUCKS, David; s of Michael Bucks (d 1984), of London, and Phyllis, *née* Rosenthal (d 1971); *b* 25 Oct 1934; *Educ* Highgate Sch; *m* 19 Jan 1962, Ann Starr, da of Richard Starr Jukes, CBE (d 1987), of London; 2 s (Michael b 2 March 1963, Richard b 22 Dec 1964), 1 da (Romola (twin) b 22 Dec 1964); *Career* 2 Lt RCS 1958-59; CA; Peat Marwick Mitchell & Co 1952-66, exec Industrial Reorganisation Corpn 1966-68, dir Samuel Montagu & Co Ltd 1968-75, dep chm Hill Samuel & Co Ltd 1987- (dir 1975-86, vice chm 1986); current directorships incl: Dobson Park Industries plc, First Leisure Corporation plc, Hill Samuel Bank Ltd, St Helen's Sch Northwood Ltd, NW Thames RHA, Merchant Bank of Central Africa Ltd, chm Hillingdon FHSA 1989; FCA 1957; *Recreations* tennis, skiing, opera; *Clubs* Oriental; *Style*— David Bucks, Esq; Hill Samuel Bank Ltd, 100 Wood St, London EC2P 2AJ (☎ 071 628 8011, fax 071 726 2818, telex 888822)

BUCKS, Peter; s of Nathan Bucks (d 1959), and Winifred José Beryl, *née* Hooper (d 1959); *b* 30 Sept 1947; *Educ* Sevenoaks Sch, Univ of Southampton (BSc); *m* 1973, Sarah Ann, da of Leslie Bernard Dobson (d 1983); 2 s (Oliver b 1978, Toby b 1982), 1 da (Eleanor b 1980); *Career* merchant banker; dir Hill Samuel Bank Ltd 1987; *Style*— Peter Bucks, Esq; 104 Addison Gardens, London W14 0DS (☎ 071 603 9629); 100 Wood St, London EC2P 2AJ (☎ 071 628 8011)

BUCKWELL, Prof Allan Edgar; s of George Alfred Donald Buckwell, of Timsbury, Avon, and Jessie Ethel Neave (d 1989); *b* 10 April 1947; *Educ* Gillingham GS, Univ of London (BSc), Univ of Manchester (MA); *m* 1, (m dis 1990); 2 s (Andrew Simon b 1967, Timothy James b 1971); *Career* lectr Univ of Newcastle upon Tyne 1973-84, prof agric econs Univ of London 1984-; memb: Agric Econs Soc, Euro Assoc of Agric Economists; *Books* Costs of the Common Agricultural Policy (with D R Harley, K Parton and K J Thompson, 1982), Chinese Grain Economy and Policy (with Cheng Liang Yu, 1990); *Style*— Prof Allan Buckwell; 57 Oxenturn Rd, Wye, Ashford, Kent TN25 5AY (☎ 0233 813106); Department of Agricultural Economics, Wye College, University of London, Wye, Ashford, Kent TN25 5AH (☎ 0233 812401, fax 0233 813320)

BUCKWELL, Anthony Basil; s of Maj B A Buckwell, DSO, MC, of Biddestone, Wiltshire, and Y E S Buckwell, *née* Tomlin; *b* 23 July 1946; *Educ* Winchester, RAC Cirencester; *m* 27 April 1968, Henrietta Judith, da of Ronald K Watson, WS, of Ham, Marlborough, Wilts; 2 da (Tara b 1970, Alexia b 1971); *Career* merchant banker, dir Kleinwort Benson Ltd London 1985; dir: Centro Internationale Handelsbank AG Vienna 1985, Absentminders Ltd London 1976; *Recreations* fishing, riding; *Clubs* Brooks's; *Style*— Anthony B Buckwell, Esq; Craven Keep, Hamstead Marshall, Newbury, Berkshire; 20 Fenchurch St, London EC3 (☎ 071 623 8000)

BUCKWELL, (John) Jeremy Beaumont; s of John Beaumont Buckwell (d 1987), and Margaret Elaine, *née* Lindsay; *b* 12 April 1934; *Educ* Bedford Sch, Univ of Cambridge (MA); *m* 1, 30 Mar 1964 (m dis 1977), Cynthia Jane, da of William Denis Heymanson (d 1988); 2 s (Oliver Charles Beaumont b 1966, William Dominic Heymanson b 1970), 1 da (Rebecca Geraldine b 1967); m 2, 19 Sept 1990, Gilda, da of William Hyde Clarke; *Career* Nat Serv Sub Lt RNVR 1952-54; admitted slr 1960; sr ptnr: Gates &

Co 1986-88 (ptnr 1961-86), Fitzhugh Gates 1988-; chm: Brighton Round Table 1972-73, Dist Nursing Assoc Tst 1974-85, Somerset Day Centre Brighton 1978-85; pres Brighton & Hove Chamber of Commerce and Trade 1985-86; memb Nat Chamber of Trade Legislation and Taxation Ctee 1984-89; Freeman City of London 1960, Liveryman Worshipful Co of Skinners 1960; sec Nat Young Slrs 1967-69; memb: Law Soc 1960- (memb Planning Ctee 1988-), RTPI 1964- (memb Cncl 1978-); *Recreations* skiing, sailing, golf; *Clubs* Itchenor Sailing, W Sussex Golf, SCOGB, Kandahar Ski, Dyke Golf; *Style*— Jeremy Buckwell, Esq; 19 Cornwall Gardens, Brighton BN1 6RH (☎ 0273 552000); 3 Pavilion Parade, Brighton BN2 1RY (☎ 0273 686811, fax 0273 676837)

BUCKWORTH-HERNE-SOAME, Sir Charles John; 12 Bt (E 1697) of Sheen, Surrey; s of Sir Charles Burnett Buckworth-Herne-Soame, 11 Bt (d 1977), and Elsie May, *née* Lloyd (d 1972); *b* 28 May 1932; *m* 1958, Eileen Margaret Mary, da of late Leonard Minton, of Caughley, Shrops; 1 s (Richard b 1970); *Heir* s, Richard John Buckworth-Herne-Soame b 17 Aug 1970; *Career* Nat Serv 4 Regt RHA, RA (TA) (30 years); *Style*— Sir Charles Buckworth-Herne-Soame, Bt; Sheen Cottage, Coalbrookdale, Shropshire

BUDD, Prof Alan Peter; s of Ernest Frank Budd (d 1981), and Elsie Nora, *née* Hambling (d 1985); *b* 16 Nov 1937; *Educ* Oundle, LSE (BSc), Churchill Coll Cambridge (PhD); *m* 18 July 1964, Susan, da of Prof Norman Millott, of Millport, Isle of Cumbrae; 3 s (Joel b 1973, Nathaniel b 1976, Saul b 1978); *Career* lectr Univ of Southampton 1966-69, Ford visiting prof Carnegie-Mellon Univ of Pittsburgh 1969-70, sr econ advsr HM Treasy 1970-74, high level conslt OECD 1976, prof of economics London Business Sch 1981-88 (sr res fell 1974), Res Bank of Australia res prof Univ of NSW 1983, memb Securities and Investmts Bd 1987-88, econ advsr 1988-; memb Bloomsbury DHA 1986-88; *Books* The Politics of Economic Planning (1976); *Recreations* music, gardening; *Clubs* Reform; *Style*— Professor Alan P Budd; 30 Laurier Rd, London NW5 1SG (☎ 071 485 3779); Barclays Bank, 54 Lombard St, London EC3P 3AH (☎ 071 626 1567)

BUDD, Bernard Wilfred; s of Rev William Robert Arscott Budd (d 1955), of Elham, and Florence Daisy, *née* Hewson (d 1970); *b* 18 Dec 1912; *Educ* Cardiff HS, W Leeds HS, Pembroke Coll Cambridge (MA); *m* 29 April 1944, Margaret Alison (Meg), da of Rt Hon E Leslie Burgin, MP, of Harpenden, Herts; 2 s (Colin b 1945, Robert Andrew b 1952); *Career* Indian Civil Serv 1935-47, Pakistan Admin Serv 1947-51, called to the Bar 1952, appointed QC 1969, ret 1982; Lib Party Candidate Folkstone 1974 and 1979 (Dover 1964 and 1966), chm Assoc of Lib Lawyers 1978-82, vice pres Int Assoc for the Protection of Industl Property (Br Gp), lay preacher Methodist Church; *Recreations* bird watching, hill walking, gardening; *Clubs* United Oxford and Cambridge, Nat Lib; *Style*— Bernard Budd, Esq, QC; Highlands, Elham, Canterbury, Kent CT4 6UG (☎ 0303 840350)

BUDD, Rachel; *b* 1960; *Educ* Univ of Newcastle upon Tyne, Royal Coll of Art; *Career* artist; exhibitions: Painters at the RCA (Gloucestershire Coll of Art and Technol) 1986, Platform (Axiom Gallery Cheltenham) 1986, Contemporary Arts Soc Market (Covent Garden) 1986 and 1987, Groucho Club Soho 1986, Christies Fine Arts Course common room 1987, The London Gp Show (RCA Henry Moore Gallery) 1987, Athena Art Awards (The Barbican Arts Centre) 1987, Art for the City (Lloyds Bldg) 1987, Pomeroy Purdy Gallery 1988 and 1990, Mary Somerville Art Fair (Smiths Gallery Covent Garden) 1988, Bath Art Fair 1988 and 1989, Al Fresco (Royal Acad) 1988, Olympia Art Fair 1989, Whitechapel Open (Eastend Open Studios) 1989, Summer Show (Pomeroy Purdy Gallery) 1989, 3 Ways (Br Cncl RCA Travelling Show, Hungary, Poland, Czechoslovakia) 1990, My Favourite Tree (Financial Times) 1990, Imagination Bldg (Gallery of Design and Communications Bldg) 1990, Moods and Spaces (Young Gallery Salisbury) 1990; work in various public and private collections; awards: A W Smiles Travel Scholarship, Northern Arts Purchase award, Jeffrey Archer prize GLC Painting Competition, Picker fellowship Kingston Poly, Henry Moore prize The London Gp Show RCA, Mark Rothko Meml Tst Fund travel bursarship for USA; *Style*— Ms Rachel Budd; Vyner Street Arts, 23 Vyner St, Bethnal Green, London E2 (☎ 081 980 1224)

BUDD, Robert Fleming; s of Hal Fleming Budd (d 1976), of Brighton, and Eva, *née* Smith (d 1940); *b* 20 Dec 1930; *Educ* Varndean GS, LSE (BSc); *m* 26 April 1954, Margaret Irene, da of Harold Stenning (d 1976), of Brighton; 3 s (Kevin Robert b 1956 d 1959, Melvin Robert b 1959, Colin Robert b 1961), 1 da (Trudi Lisa b 1961); *Career* 3 Trg Bn RAOC: asst adj and trg offr, 2 Lt 1952-54, 1 Lt 1954; Frank Wright & Son Ltd: trainee mangr 1955-, branch mangr 1957, dir 1967, md 1968; Freeman City of London 1977, Liveryman Worshipful Co Builders Merchants 1977; memb Inst Builders Merchants; *Recreations* golf, squash; *Clubs* Naval; *Style*— Robert Budd, Esq; 3 Hillbrow Rd, Brighton BN1 5JP (☎ 0273 607 044); 124 Lewes Rd, Brighton BN2 3LU (☎ 0273 607 044, fax 0273 685 208)

BUDDEN, Julian Medforth; s of Prof Lionel Bailey Budden (d 1956), of Heswall, Merseyside, and Dora Magdalene, *née* Fraser (d 1976); *b* 9 April 1924; *Educ* Stowe Sch, Bucks, Queen's Coll Oxford (MA), RCM, Trinity Coll of Music London (BMus); *Career* Friends Ambulance Unit 1943-6; music prodr BBC 1956, chief prodr opera BBC radio 1970, external servs music organiser 1976, ret 1983; FBA 1987; *Books* The Operas of Verdi (vol I 1973, vol II 1978, vol III 1981), Verdi (1985); *Style*— Julian Budden, Esq; 94 Station Rd, London N3 2SG (☎ 081 349 2954); Via Fratelli Bandiera, 9, 50137 Firenze, Italy (☎ 010 39 55 678471)

BUDDS, Alan Roy; s of Leonard Frederick George Budds, of Hants, and Olive Miriam, *née* Bone (d 1964); *b* 26 April 1934; *Educ* Luton GS; *m* 28 June 1958, Dorothy Blanche, da of Stephen John Lower, of Luton (d 1980); 2 s (Jonathan Paul b 1963, Richard Mark b 1965), 1 da (Andrea Lorraine b 1960); *Career* admitted slr 1957; cmmr for Oaths 1962, dep registrar Co Ct SE circuit 1985; pres Luton and Dunstable Law Soc 1983, memb Nat Exec British Legal Assoc; *Recreations* tennis, ecology, gardening, travel; *Style*— Alan R Budds, Esq; 6 Salisbury Ave, Harpenden, Herts AL5 2QG; Alan Budds & Co, Solicitors, 29 King St, Luton LU1 2DW (☎ 0582 22194)

BUDGE, Anthony Frederick; OBE (1985); s of Frederick Thomas Frank Budge (d 1985), and Charlotte Constance Annie (d 1990), *née* Parker; *b* 9 Aug 1939; *Educ* Boston GS; *m* 1960, Janet, da of Harry Cropley (d 1983); 1 s (Karl), 3 da (Elizabeth, Karen, Lindsay); *Career* UK chm and md A F Budge Ltd and group cos 1962-; FICE, FIHT; *Clubs* Carlton, Turf; *Style*— Tony Budge, Esq, OBE; Osberton Hall, Worksop, Notts S81 0UF; A F Budge Ltd, West Carr Rd, Retford, Notts DN22 7SW (☎ 0777 706 789, telex 56347)

BUDGE, David; s of Alistair Budge, of Wick, and Elizabeth, *née* Henderson; *b* 18 Oct 1957; *Educ* Wick HS, Glasgow Coll (SHND, Dip Indust Admin); *m* 5 Aug 1983, Christine Margaret, da of James Deans Rankin (d 1970); 1 da (Alexandra); *Career* res exec Consensus Res Pty Brisbane 1979-80, pres offr Wolf Electric Tools Ltd London 1980-81, dir PR Conslts Scotland 1987- (joined 1982); Winner IPR Sword of Excellence 1986; memb Glasgow Publicity Club; MIPR; Dip Cam; *Recreations* tennis, badminton; *Clubs* Blantyre Sports, Glasgow Publicity; *Style*— David Budge, Esq; 4 Lytham Meadows Bothwell G71 8ED (☎ 0698 852900); PR Consultants Scotland, 9 Lynedoch Crescent, Glasgow G3 6EQ (☎ 041 333 0557, fax 041 332 7990)

BUDGE, Prof Ian; s of John Elder Budge (d 1985), of Edinburgh, and Elizabeth, *née* Barnet (d 1979); *b* 21 Oct 1936; *Educ* Wardie and George Heriot's Schs Edinburgh, Univ of Edinburgh, Univ of Yale; *m* 17 July 1964, Judith Beatrice Ruth, da of Richard Franklin Harrison (d 1973), of Preston Lancs; 1 s (Gavin b 1965), 1 da (Eileen Elizabeth b 1968); *Career* lectr Univ of Strathclyde 1963-66, prof Univ of Essex 1977- (formerly lectr, sr lectr, reader); visiting prof: Univ of Wisconsin Madison USA 1969-70, Euro Univ Inst Florence 1982-85, Univ of California Irvine 1989, Wissenscaftzentrum Berlin 1990; memb Political Studies Assoc of UK, exec dir Euro Consortium for Political Res 1979-83; FRSA; *Books* jtly: Scottish Political Behaviour (1966), Belfast: Approach to Crisis (1973), Voting and Party Competition (1978), Explaining and Predicting Elections (1983), The New British Political System (1988); Parties and Democracy (1990); *Recreations* gardening, walking, travel, Italy; *Style*— Prof Ian Budge; 4 Oxford Rd, Colchester, Essex CO3 3HW (☎ 0206 46622); Dept of Government, University of Essex, Colchester CO4 35Q (☎ 0206 87 2128, fax 0206 843 598)

BUDGEN, Nicholas William; MP (C) Wolverhampton S W Feb 1974-; s of Capt G N Budgen (d 1942), of Lichfield; *b* 3 Nov 1937; *Educ* St Edward's Oxford, Corpus Christi Coll Cambridge; *m* 1964, Madeleine Elizabeth, only da of Col Raymond Kittoe, OBE, by his w Rosalind, *née* Arbuthnot (a distant cousin of the Viscounts of Arbuthnott); 1 s, 1 da; *Career* barr Gray's Inn 1962; asst govt whip 1981-82; *Recreations* farming, hunting; *Style*— Nicholas Budgen, Esq, MP; Malt House Farm, Colton, nr Rugeley, Staffs (☎ 088 94 77059)

BUDGEN, Hon Mrs ((Anne) Patricia Rosamund); *née* Wynn; er da of 7 Baron Newborough, DSC; *b* 14 Sept 1947; *Educ* St Mary's Sch Wantage; *m* 1970, Anthony George Budgen; 1 s, 1 da; *Style*— The Hon Mrs Budgen; Boreatton House, Baschurch, Shrewsbury, Shropshire SY4 2EP

BUENO, Antonio de Padua Jose Maria; s of Antonio de Padua Bueno (d 1987), and Ana Teresa de Jesus, *née* Zuloaga; *b* 28 June 1942; *Educ* Downside, Salamanca Univ; *m* 22 July 1966, Christine Mary, da of Michael Lees, of Milton Abbas, Dorset; 3 da (Nicola b 20 July 1967, Julia b 3 April 1972, Emily b 28 Dec 1988); *Career* called to the Bar Middle Temple 1984, asst rec 1984, rec 1989, QC 1989; *Books* Atkin's Court Forms: Banking (jt ed, 1976), Byleson Bills of Exchange (asst ed 1979, jt ed, 1988), Paget's Law of Banking (asst ed, 1982); *Recreations* fishing, shooting and flying; *Clubs* Flyfishers, East India; *Style*— Antonio Bueno, Esq; 7 Pitt St, London W8 4NX (☎ 071 937 0403); 5 Paper Bldgs, Temple, London EC4Y 7HB (☎ 071 353 8494, fax 071 583 1926, car 0836 216634)

BUENO DE MESQUITA, Lt-Col Patrick David; OBE (1983); s of Reginald David Bueno de Mesquita (d 1977), and Joyce Court; *b* 17 March 1934; *Educ* Wellington Coll, RMA Sandhurst; *m* 1 April 1961, Gillian Anne, da of Lt Cdr Dermot Grove White (d 1941); 3 s (Nicholas b 27 May 1962, Charles b 23 July 1964, Philip b 15 July 1966), 1 da (Rosanna b 23 July 1964); *Career* cmmnd Tenth Royal Hussars 1954, commanded Regt 1 Br Corps Hq 1981-84, ret 1986; dir med res charity, memb Nat Garden Scheme; memb Assoc of Med Res Charities; *Recreations* golf, tennis, bridge, gardening; *Clubs* Naval & Military; *Style*— Lt-Col Patrick Bueno De Mesquita, OBE; The Old Rectory, Stanton Prior, Bath BA2 9HT (☎ 0761 71942)

BUERK, Michael Duncan; s of Capt Gordon Charles Buerk (d 1974), and Betty Mary Buerk (d 1960); *b* 18 Feb 1946; *Educ* Solihull Sch, Warwickshire; *m* 9 Sept 1968, Christine, da of late Bernard Joseph Lilley, of Hereford; 2 s (Simon, Roland (twins) b 30 Nov 1973); *Career* BBC TV News Corr 1973-: Energy 1976-79, Scotland 1979-81, special 1981-82, Africa 1983-87; corr/presenter BBC TV News 1987- (1982-83); awards: Royal Television Soc Television Journalist of the Year 1984, Royal Television Soc Int News Award 1984, George Polk Award (US) Foreign TV Reporting 1984, Nat Headlines Award (US) 1984, Int News/Documentary Award Monte Carlo Festival 1984, BAFTA News & Documentary Award 1985, James Cameron Meml Award 1987, Glaxo Science Writer of the Year Award 1989; *Recreations* oenophily; *Style*— Michael Buerk, Esq; c/o BBC TV News, London W12 (☎ 081 576 7779)

BUFFHAM, Prof Bryan Austin; s of William Austin Buffham (d 1979), of Ilford, and Florence Ethel Mary, *née* London (d 1957); *b* 2 Nov 1936; *Educ* County HS Ilford, UCL (BSc), Yale (MEng), Loughborough Univ of Technol (PhD), Univ of London (DSc); *m* 12 Nov 1960, Dolores Marie, da of Alfred Lane (d 1986), of Allentown Pa, USA; 1 s (Timothy b 1967), 2 da (Robin b 1961, Christi 1962); *Career* chemical engr Air Products and Chemicals Inc Allentown Pa USA 1959-6 prof Loughborough Univ of Technol: res fell 1964-65, lectr 1965-71, sr lectr 1971-81, reader 1982-86, prof 1986-); ed Chemical Engineering Journal; FIChemE 1979; *Books* Mixing in Continuous Flow Systems (with E B Nauman, 1983); *Recreations* cycling; *Style*— Prof Bryan Buffham; 21 Springfield, Kegworth, Derby DE7 2DP (☎ 0509 672938); Department of Chemical Engineering, Loughborough University of Technology, Loughborough, Leics LE11 3TU (☎ 0509 222503)

BULFIELD, Peter William; s of Wilfred Irving Roden Bulfield (d 1969), of Midhurst, and Doris Margaret, *née* Bedford (d 1974); *b* 14 June 1930; *Educ* Beaumont Sch; *m* 21 June 1958, Pamela June, da of Arthur Henry Frederick Beckett (d 1963), of Buenos Aires; 2 da (Julia Therese b 1960, Marion Louise b 1963); *Career* CA Scotland 1953; dir: Newsphere Trading Co 1963, J Henry Schroder Wagg 1967-86, Darling Holdings Aust 1973-82; vice-chm Mitsubishi Trust and Banking Corporation (Euro) SA 1973-84, jt dep chm Schroder Int 1977, exec dir Yamaichi Int (Euro) Ltd 1986-88, md and chief exec Yamaichi Bank (UK) plc 1988-, dir London Italian Bank Ltd 1989-; dep chm Crown Agents for Overseas Govts and Admins 1982-85 (memb 1978-85); memb: Overseas Projects Bd 1983-86, Export Guarantees Advsy Cncl 1986-88; *Recreations* music, sailing (yacht 'Keiko IV'), shooting, painting; *Clubs* Royal Thames Yacht; *Style*— Peter Bulfield, Esq; 14 Lower Sloane St, London SW1W 8BJ (☎ 071 730 2493); The Mill Hse, Merrieweathers, Mayfield, Sussex TN20 6RJ (☎ 0435 872177); Yamaichi Bank (UK) plc, Guildhall Hse, Gresham St, London EC2V 7NQ (☎ 071 600 1188, fax 071 600 1169, telex 919549 YBKLDN)

BULGIN, Ronald Arthur; s of Wing Cdr Arthur Bulgin, OBE, of Essex; *b* 20 Aug 1935; *Educ* Westminster, Merton Coll Oxford; *m* 1, 1958 (m dis), Margaret Gray; 2 s, 1 da; m 2, 1969, Elaine Harvey; 1 s, 1 da; *Career* chm Bulgin Group; *Recreations* riding, golf; *Clubs* Essex Farmers Hunt, Chigwell Golf, RAC; *Style*— Ronald Bulgin Esq; AF Bulgin & Co plc, Barking, Essex

BULKELEY; see Williams-Bulkeley

BULL, Anthony; CBE (1968, OBE Mil 1944); s of Rt Hon Sir William Bull, MP, JP (d 1931), of London, and Lady Bull, *née* Lilian Hester Brandon (d 1963); *b* 18 July 1908; *Educ* Gresham's Sch Holt Norfolk, Magdalene Coll Cambridge (MA); *m* 5 Oct 1946, Barbara (d 1947), da of Peter Donovan (d 1962), of Yonder, Rye, Sussex; 1 da (Caroline (m 1974, Sir Robin Chichester-Clark) b 11 July 1947); *Career* RE 1939-45, staff Capt, Maj WO 1939-42, Lt-Col trans African lines of communication 1942-43, Lt-Col GHQ ME 1943, staff of Supreme Cdr SE Asia 1943-45, Col Tport Div Berlin 1945-46; London Underground Gp of Cos: joined 1929, serv in Staff Publicity and P/R Depts and in chms office 1929-36, sec to Vice Chm London Passenger Tport Bd 1936-39; war serv 1939-46; chief staff and welfare offr LPTB 1946; memb: London Tport Exec 1955-62, London Tport Bd 1962-65, vice chm London Tport 1965-71; tport conslt 1971-89, advsr to House of Commons Tport Ctee 1981-82; chm London Regnl Cncl for Technol Educn 1953-62; FCIT (pres 1969-70); Bronze Star (USA);

Recreations travel; *Clubs* United Oxford and Cambridge; *Style—* Anthony Bull, Esq, CBE; 35 Clareville Grove, London SW7 5AU (☎ 071 373 5647)

BULL, Christopher; s of William Albert Bull (d 1984), of Taunton, Somerset, and Norah Bull; *b* 6 Sept 1936; *Educ* Taunton Sch; *m* Patricia Marcelline Barbara, da of Henry John Gardner (d 1983), of Paris; 1 s (James b 1965), 2 da (Helen b 1963, Fiona b 1974); *Career* CA, Goodland Bull & Co Taunton 1957-68, Price Waterhouse Trinidad 1968-71, Price Waterhouse London 1971- (ptnr 1974-); memb: Florence Nightingale Museum Tst Appeals Ctee 1987-88, Guildford Diocesan Bd of Fin 1988; memb ICAEW 1962 (fell 1972); *Recreations* golf, choral singing; *Clubs* Carlton, North Hants Golf; *Style—* Christopher Bull, Esq; Kantara, Reading Road North, Fleet, Hampshire GU13 8AQ (☎ 0252 615 008); Price Waterhouse, Southwark Towers, 32 London Bridge St, London SE1 9SY (☎ 071 407 8989, fax 071 378 0647)

BULL, Christopher Robert Howard; s of Robert Golden Bull, of Settle, N Yorks, and Audrey, *née* Ineson; *b* 14 May 1942; *Educ* Christ's Hosp, Corpus Christi Coll Cambridge (MA); *m* 1 April 1967, Rosemary Anne, da of Frank Coltman (d 1979), of Bromley, Kent; 2 s (Jeremy b 1969, Andrew b 1972), 1 da (Stephanie b 1976); *Career* CA; Whinney Murray & Co 1964-68, Centre for Interfirm Comparison 1968-71, industl gas div controller Air Products Ltd 1971-75, head of gp fin analysis BICC plc 1975-80, fin dir BICC Technologies Ltd 1981-84, corp treas BT 1984-88, fin dir BTR plc 1988-; FCA 1968; *Recreations* music, sailing; *Style—* Christopher Bull, Esq; BTR plc, Silvertown House, Vincent Square, London SW1P 2PL (☎ 071 821 3752, fax 071 834 2279, telex 22524)

BULL, Wing Cdr Constance Patricia Irene; da of Leslie John Bull (d 1984), and Constance Nellie, *née* Smith; *b* 22 Dec 1935; *Educ* Huntingdon GS; *Career* Flying Offr Princess Mary's RAF Nursing Serv 1966, Flt Offr 1968, Sqdn Ldr 1976, Wing Cdr 1984; qualified as SRN Addenbrooke's Hosp Cambridge 1957 and state certified midwife at Plymouth and Hitchin 1959, nursing sister Mombasa Kenya 1960-62, night nursing supt Huntingdon Co Hosp 1962-65; ward sister PMRAFNS 1966-: Germany 1966-68, ME 1970-71, exchange serv RAAF 1975-77; matron RAF Hosps 1980-88: UK, Germany, Cyprus; admin nursing offr (RAF) Inst of Community and Occupational Med Halton 1988-; memb RCN; ARRC 1972 memb RCN; *Style—* Wing Cdr Constance Bull; Royal Air Force Institute of Community and Occupational Medicine, Halton, Aylesbury, Buckinghamshire HP22 5PG (☎ 0296 623535 ext 7596)

BULL, Deborah Clare; s of Rev (Michael) John Bull, of Surrey, and Doreen Audrey, *née* Plumb; *b* 22 March 1963; *Educ* The Royal Ballet Sch, Academie de Danse Classique de Monte Carlo; *m* 26 Jan 1991, Charles Richard Biss, s of Dr Gerald Claverton Biss; *Career* Royal Ballet: joined 1981, soloist 1986, first soloist 1989; major dance roles incl: Rite of Spring, Layadere, Prince of the Pagodas, Violin Concerto, Agon, Giselle, Le Baiser de la Fee, Swan Lake; created major roles in still life at: The Penguin Café, Pursuit, Piano, The Planets; danced in Italy, Canada and N America with Wayne Eagling's Co (Principals of the Royal Ballet); winner Prix de Lausanne 1980; *Recreations* literature, Mozart, food, wine and alpine air; *Style—* Miss Deborah Bull

BULL, George Anthony; OBE (1990); s of George Thomas Bull (d 1937), and Bridget Philomena, *née* Nugent (d 1983); *b* 23 Aug 1929; *Educ* Wimbledon Coll, Brasenose Coll Oxford (MA); *m* 2 March 1957, Dido Marjorie, *née* Griffin; 2 s (Julian, Simon), 2 da (Catherine, Jennifer); *Career* Nat Serv Royal Fus 1947-49; foreign news ed Financial Times 1956-59, news ed McGraw Hill World News 1959-60, The Director magazine 1960-84 (dep ed, ed in chief), dir Anglo-Japanese Economic Institute 1986-, ed International Minds 1989; pres Central Banking Publications Limited; author; memb Soc of Art Historians; FRSL, FRSA; *Books incl* translations for Penguin Classics and OUP, Inside the Vatican (1982); *Style—* George A Bull, Esq; 19 Hugh St, London SW1V 1QJ; Morley House, 314-322 Upper Regent St, London W1R 5AD (☎ 071 637 7872)

BULL, George Jeffrey; s of Michael Herbert Perkins Bull (d 1965), and Hon Noreen Madeleine Hennessy, da of 1 Baron Windlesham; *b* 16 July 1936; *Educ* Ampleforth; *m* 7 Jan 1960, Jane Fleur Thérèse, da of Patrick Freeland (d 1977); 4 s (Sebastian b 1960, Rupert b 1963, Justin b 1964, Cassian b 1966), 1 da (Tamsin b 1972); *Career* Lt Coldstream Gds 1954-57, served in Germany and UK; joined Dorland Advertising Ltd 1957, joined Twiss Browning & Hallowes wine merchants 1958, md Gilbey Vintners Ltd 1970, dir IDV (Home Trade) and IDV Ltd (Int Distillers and Vintners) 1973, md IDV Europe Ltd 1977, dep md IDV Ltd 1982, dir Grand Metropolitan Ltd 1985, chief exec IDV Ltd 1987, chm and chief exec IDV Ltd and chm Grand Metropolitan plc drinks section; *Recreations* golf; *Clubs* Cavalry and Guards', Royal Worlington Golf; *Style—* George Bull, Esq; The Old Vicarage, Arkesden, Saffron Walden, Essex (☎ 0799 550 445); IDV Ltd, 1 York Gate, Regent's Park, London NW1 (☎ 071 935 4446, fax 071 486 2583, telex 261161 INDIS

BULL, John Michael; QC (1983); s of John Godfrey Bull (d 1969), and Eleanor, *née* Nicholson; *b* 31 Jan 1934; *Educ* Norwich Sch, Corpus Christi Coll Cambridge (Parker exhibitioner, MA, LLM); *m* 20 Dec 1959, Sonia Maureen, da of Frank Edward Woodcock, of 82 Brian Ave, Norwich; 1 s ((John) Michael Curties b 14 March 1968), 3 da (Caroline Elisabeth b 15 Dec 1961, Rachel Clare b 26 Feb 1963, Francesca Margaret b 23 Nov 1964); *Career* called to Bar Gray's Inn 1960, rec Crown Ct 1980-; *Style—* John Bull, Esq, QC; Gosden End, Bramley, Surrey GU5 OAE (☎ 0483 893733); 2 Crown Office Row, The Temple, London EC4Y 7HJ (☎ 071 583 8155, fax 071 583 1205)

BULL, Hon Mrs (Judith Florence); *née* Gurdon; DL (1980 Suffolk); yr da of late 2 Baron Cranworth, KG, MC; *b* 8 May 1914; *m* 1943, Maj Thomas Henry Bull, TD, late Lt RA (d 1984), yst s of late William Perkins Bull, KC, of Toronto, Canada; *Style—* The Hon Mrs Bull, DL; Park Farm, Grundisburgh, Suffolk

BULL, Lady; Megan Patricia; OBE (1982); da of Dr Thomas Jones (d 1954), and Letitia Jones; *b* 17 March 1922,Naanpoort S Africa; *Educ* Good Hope Seminary Cape Town, Cape Town Univ (MB ChB), Queen's Univ Belfast (MSc); *m* 1947, Sir Graham MacGregor Bull (d 1987); 3 s, 1 da; *Career* medical offr Holloway Prison 1966-71, govr 1971-82, ret; DCH, DPM, MRCP; *Recreations* book collecting; *Style—* Lady Bull, OBE; 29 Heath Drive, London NW3 7SB (☎ 01 435 1624)

BULL, Hon Mrs (Noreen Madeleine Mary); *née* Hennessy; 3 da of 1 Baron Windlesham, OBE, JP; *b* 1910; *m* 1931 (m dis 1948), Michael Bull (d 1962), 3 s of late William Perkins Bull, KC, of Lorne Hall, Rosedale, Toronto, Canada; 2 s; *Style—* The Hon Mrs Bull; Flat 25, Belgravia Court, 33 Ebury St, London SW1

BULL, (Oliver) Richard Silvester; s of Walter Haverson Bull, of Shilling Orchard, Lavenham, Suffolk (d 1975), and Margaret Bridget, *née* Horne (d 1983); *b* 30 June 1930; *Educ* Rugby, Univ of Oxford (MA); *m* 18 Aug 1956, Anne Hay, da of Hubert Fife, of 19 Bloxam Gardens, Rugby; 2 s (Matthew b 1970, Leroy b 1973), 4 da (Kate b 1960, Alice b 1962, Philippa b 1964, Hannah b 1964); *Career* asst master Eton 1955-77 (housemaster 1967-77); headmaster: Oakham Sch 1977-84, Rugby 1985-90; *Recreations* music, reading, walking, sport; *Style—* Richard Bull, Esq; The Cwm, Gladestry, Kington, Herefordshire (☎ 054 422 235)

BULL, Sir Simeon George; 4 Bt (UK 1922), of Hammersmith, Co London; s of Sir George Bull, 3 Bt (d 1987), and Gabrielle Muriel, *née* Jackson (d 1989); *b* 1 Aug 1934; *Educ* Eton, Innsbruck (Law Faculty), Ecole de Notariat Paris; *m* 17 June 1961, Annick Elisabeth Geneviève Renée, da of late Louis Bresson (d 1960), of Château des Masselins, Chandai, Orne, France; 1 s (Stephen Louis), 2 da (Jacqueline Hester b 15 Oct 1964, Sophia Ann b 2 March 1971); *Heir* s, Stephen Louis Bull b 5 April 1966; *Career* admitted slr 1959; sr ptnr legal firm of Bull & Bull; Cdre London Corinthian Sailing Club 1968-71, fndr hon sec Assoc of Thames Valley Sailing Clubs 1972-78, memb Cncl Royal Yachting Assoc 1977- 79; Freeman of City of London 1955, Liveryman of Worshipful Co of Fishmongers; *Recreations* sailing, foreign travel, gardening, carpentry, reading; *Clubs* Royal Thames Yacht, MCC; *Style—* Sir Simeon Bull, Bt; Beech Hanger, Shepherd's Hill, Merstham, Surrey RH1 3AE (☎ 07374 5041); Pen Enez, Pont l'Abbé, S Finistère, France; 199 Piccadilly, London W1V 9LE (☎ 071 405 7474, fax 071 734 9107)

BULL, Tony Raymond; s of Henry Albert Bull (d 1963), and Phyllis Rosalie, *née* Webber; *b* 21 Dec 1934; *Educ* Monkton Combe Sch, London Hosp Med Coll; *m* June 1959, Jill Rosemary Beresford, da of Air Vice-Marshal Albert Frederick Cook, CBE; 1 s (Antony b 1965), 2 da (Amanda b 1960, Karen b 1962); *Career* conslt surgn: Charing Cross Hosp, Royal Nat Throat Nose & Ear Hosp; FRCS; *Recreations* tennis (Somerset County) hockey (Essex County); *Clubs* MCC, Queens, Hurlingham; *Style—* Tony Bull, Esq; 26 Scarsdale Villas, London W8 (☎ 071 937 3411); 107 Harley Street, London W1 (☎ 071 935 3171)

BULL, Sir Walter Edward Avenon; KCVO (1977, CVO 1964); s of Walter Bull, of Walton-on-Thames, Surrey, and Florence Bull; *b* 17 March 1902; *Educ* Gresham's, Aldenham; *m* 1933, Moira Christian, da of William John Irwin, of N Ireland; 1 s; *Career* chartered surveyor; sr ptnr Vigers 1942-74, dir City of London Building Soc 1957-74, conslt Walter Bull and Co chartered surveyors 1987; memb Cncl Duchy of Lancaster 1957-74; Liveryman Worshipful Co of Merchant Taylors; pres RICS 1956; *Recreations* music, bowls, golf; *Clubs* Naval & Military, Gresham; *Style—* Sir Walter Bull, KCVO; The Garden House, 1 Park Crescent, Brighton, Sussex BN2 3HA (☎ 0273 681196)

BULLARD, Sir Giles Lionel; KCVO (1985), CMG (1981); 2 s of Sir Reader Bullard, KCB, KCMG, CIE (d 1976), and Miriam, *née* Smith (d 1973); bro of Sir Julian Bullard, *qv*; *b* 24 Aug 1926; *Educ* Blundell's Sch, Balliol Coll Oxford; *m* 1, 1952, Hilary Chadwick Brooks (d 1978); 2 s, 2 da; m 2, 1982, Linda Rannells Lewis; *Career* Foreign Serv: entered 1955, consul-gen Boston 1977-80, ambass Bulgaria 1980-83, high cmmr Barbados 1983-86; *Style—* Sir Giles Bullard, KCVO, CMG; Manor House, West Hendred, Wantage, Oxon OX12 8RP

BULLARD, Julian Leonard; GCMG (1987, KCMG 1982, CMG 1975); s of Sir Reader Bullard, KCB, KCMG, CIE (d 1976), sometime ambass Teheran, and Miriam (d 1973), da of late A L Smith, sometime Master Balliol Coll Oxford; bro of Sir Giles Bullard, *qv*; *b* 8 March 1928; *Educ* Rugby, Magdalen Coll Oxford; *m* 1954, Margaret Stephens; 2 s, 2 da; *Career* served HM Forces 1950-52; FO 1953-88, served: Vienna, Amman, Bonn, Moscow, Dubai; head E Euro and Soviet Dept 1971-75, min Bonn 1975-79, dep under-sec and political dir FCO 1979- and dep to Perm Under-Sec and political dir 1982-84, ambass Bonn 1984-88; fell All Souls Coll Oxford, hon fell St Antony's Coll Oxford; chm Cncl Univ of Birmingham; *Style—* HE Sir Julian Bullard, GCMG; 18 Northmoor Rd, Oxford OX2 6UR

BULLEID, (Henry) Anthony Vaughan; s of Oliver Vaughan Snell Bulleid, CBE (d 1970), of Boxhurst, Dorking, Surrey, and Marjorie Campbell, *née* Ivatt (d 1985); *b* 23 Dec 1912; *Educ* Ampleforth, Univ of Cambridge (MA); *m* 11 April 1942, Margery Ann Mary, da of Laurence Dorian McCann (d 1931), of Sutton, Surrey; 1 s (David b 1945), 2 da (Susan b 1948, Hilary b 1958); *Career* prodn and engrg dir ICI Fibres Ltd 1965-72; FIMechE 1949, ARPS 1946, FRPSL 1985; *Books* Special Effects in Cinematography (1954), Master Builders of Steam (1963), The Aspinall Era (1967), Bulleid of the Southern (1977), Brief Cases (1977), Cylinder Musical Box Design and Repair (1987); *Clubs* Athenaeum; *Style—* Anthony Bulleid, Esq; Cherrymead, Ifold, Billingshurst, West Sussex RH14 0TA (☎ 0403 752 309)

BULLEN, Christopher Keith (Chris); s of Keith Thomas Bullen, of Morden, Surrey, and Joan, *née* Casley; *b* 5 Nov 1962; *Educ* Rutlish Sch Merton Park; *Career* professional cricketer; Surrey CCC 1983-, debut v Oxford Univ 1983 whilst still an amateur, awarded county cap June 1990; represented Young England v W Indies under 19 1982; man of the match NatWest Bank Trophy v Wiltshire 1990 (scored 93 not out); *Recreations* soccer, golf, cinema, shopping; *Style—* Christopher Bullen, Esq; Surrey CCC, The Oval, Kennington, London (☎ 071 582 6660)

BULLEN, James Edward; s of Albert Edward Bullen (d 1977), and Doris Josephine, *née* McHale; *b* 26 March 1943; *Educ* Univ of London (LLB); *m* 1, 1973 (m dis 1984); m 2, 27 Sept 1985, Mary, da of late Patrick Keane, 1 s (William James b 1986); *Career* called to the Bar Gray's Inn 1966, senate of Inns of Ct and Bar 1979-82; *Recreations* music, reading, walking; *Clubs* Garrick, RAC; *Style—* James Bullen, Esq; 5 Kings Bench Walk, Temple, London EC4 (☎ 071 353 2882)

BULLEN, Michael Fitzherbert Symes; s of Lt-Col John Fitzherbert Symes Bullen (d 1966), and Anne, *née* St John (d 1963); *b* 20 May 1937; *Educ* Millfield; *m* 28 April 1962, Sally Elizabeth, da of Frank Forbes Beazley, of Broncroft Parks, Craven Arms, Shropshire; 2 s (Edward b 1966, Henry b 1970), 1 da (Lucinda b 1963); *Career* Nat Serv 3rd Hussars later Queen's Own Hussars 1955-58 (ret as Capt); Olympic Rider Three Day Event Rome 1960, Tokyo 1964; dir Int Bloodstock Shipping Co 1961-; *Recreations* riding, shooting, stalking, skiing, motor racing; *Clubs* Cavalry and Guards'; *Style—* Michael Bullen, Esq; Borough Court, Hartley Wintney, Hampshire RG27 8JA (☎ 025126 2592); Peden International, Orchard Garage, Chievely, Newbury, Berks (☎ 0635 24 8911)

BULLEN, Air Vice-Marshal Reginald; CB (1975), GM (1945); s of Henry Arthur Bullen (d 1932), of London, and Alice May, *née* Quaife (d 1947); *b* 19 Oct 1920; *Educ* Grocers' Co Sch, Gonville and Caius Coll Cambridge (MA); *m* 12 March 1952, (Doreen) Christiane, da of Eric Kenneth Phillips (d 1958), of Marseilles, France; 1 s (Michael b 1958), 1 da (Danielle b 1953); *Career* 39 Sqdn Malta and 458 Sqdn N Africa 1942-44, Air Miny 1945-50, RAF Coll Cranwell 1952-54, RAF Staff Coll Bracknell 1955, exchange USAF Washington DC 1956-58, DSD RAF Staff Coll 1959-61, admin Staff Coll Henley 1962, PSO to CAS 1962-64, NATO Def Coll Paris 1965, Adj-Gen AAFCE 1965-68, dir of personnel RAF 1968-69, IDC 1970, Dep AOA Maintenance Cmd 1971, AOA RAF Trg Cmd 1972-75; fell and sr bursar Gonville and Caius Coll Cambridge 1975-87, life fell and property devpts conslt Gonville and Gaius Coll Cambridge 1987-; chm Huntingdon Health Authy 1981-; FBIM 1979 (MBIM 1971); *Recreations* work, travel; *Clubs* RAF; *Style—* Air Vice-Marshal Reginald Bullen, CB, GM; Gonville and Caius Coll, Cambridge CB2 1TA (☎ 0223 332437 or 332455)

BULLEN, Dr William Alexander (Bill); s of Francis Lisle Bullen, and Amelia, *née* Morgan; *b* 22 Sept 1918; *Educ* Merchant Taylors', London Hosp Med Coll; *m* 1 (m dis); m 2 (m dis); m 3, 10 June 1983, Rosaling Margaret, da of Lawrence Reginald Gates; *Career* WWII cmmnd RTR (SR) 1939, resigned Maj 1946; med dir Boehringer-Pfizer 1957-62; pres: Pfizer Canada 1962-64, GM Pfizer Consumer Options UK 1964-66; md Scribbans Kemp 1966-67; chm: Coty (England) 1965-66, Thos Borthwick & Sons plc 1975-81 (md 1967-77), Whitburgh Investments 1976-80; président Boucherie Bernard Paris 1977-81; memb Canterbury Wine Growers, assoc memb English Vineyards Assoc; Freeman City of London 1975, Liveryman Worshipful Co of Butchers 1975; FBIM 1976, MRCS, LRCP, MRCGP; *Recreations* sailing, music, viticulture; *Clubs* Royal Thames Yacht; *Style—* Dr Bill Bullen

BULLEY, Philip Marshall; s of Alfred Whishaw Bulley (d 1976), of Carpenters, Udimore, nr Rye, Sussex, and Eileen Mary, *née* Prentice; *b* 1 Aug 1934; *Educ* Radley, CCC (MA); *m* 11 Dec 1963, Anne Dione, step da of Samuel Carson Fitzwilliam Allen (d 1984), of Lathbury Park, Newport Pagnell, Bucks; 2 da (Charlotte b 1965, Isabel b 1967); *Career* Nat Serv Intelligence Corps 1953, cmmnd 2 Lt 1954, SMIS served in Malaya 1954-55; dir: J Weiner Ltd 1962-69 (md 1967-69), City Magazines 1963-69, Berrows of Worcester Ltd 1963-69, Bees Ltd 1967-73; ptnr Theodore Goddard 1987-; *Recreations* golf, opera; *Clubs* Rye Golf; *Style—* Philip Bulley, Esq; Sackville Court, Kennington Park Rd, London SE11 4JS (☎ 071 735 0503); Theodore Goddard, 150 Aldersgate St, London EC1A 4EJ (☎ 071 606 8855, fax 071 606 4390)

BULLMORE, George Hilary Lanyon; s of Edward Augustus Bullmore (d 1948), of Wisbech and Falmouth, and Hilda Maud, *née* Lanyon (d 1922); *b* 23 March 1912; *Educ* Oundle, Oriel Coll Oxford (MA, BM BCh), UCH London (LMSSA, DPM); *m* 25 May 1948, Kitty, *née* Dedman; 2 s (Christopher b 1949, Theodore b 1950); *Career* Capt 1941-45 RAMC (Lt 1940-41) served India 1943-45; memb Med Advsy Ctee Br Epilepsy Assoc 1951-77 (chm Employment Ctee), sec PsychoEndocrine Assoc 1957-62, dep physician supt St Ebba's Hosp Epsom 1957-77; pres Kingston Numismatic Soc; Freeman City of London, Liveryman Worshipful Soc of Apothecaries; *Recreations* numismatics; *Clubs* City Livery; *Style—* George Bullmore, Esq; 12 Portsmouth Rd, Kingston, Surrey KT1 2LU (☎ 081 546 9262)

BULLMORE, (John) Jeremy David; CBE (1985); s of Francis Edward Bullmore, and Adeline Gabrielle, *née* Roscow; *b* 21 Nov 1929; *Educ* Harrow, Ch Ch Oxford; *m* 1958, Pamela Audrey Green; 2 s, 1 da; *Career* chm J Walter Thompson 1976- (joined 1954, dir 1964, dep chm 1975), dir J Walter Thompson (USA) 1980-; chm Advertising Assoc; memb Nat Ctee Electoral Reform 1978-; *Style—* Jeremy Bullmore, Esq, CBE; 20 Embankment Gdns, SW3 (☎ 071 351 2197)

BULLOCH, Brig Gavin; MBE (1973); s of David Carnie Bulloch (d 1974), and Maud Alice, *née* Knowles (d 1951); *b* 2 Oct 1938; *Educ* Kings Coll Taunton; *m* 18 April 1964, Sandra Valerie, da of Roy Francis Powys Malise Speer (d 1966); 1 s (James b 1965); *Career* cmmnd Middx Regt 1957, transfd Queen's Regt 1967, staff appts in UK and Germany, CO 3 Bn Queen's Regt 1979-81 (despatches 1979), MOD Central Staff 1984-86, NATO HQ (Strategic Plans) 1987-89, def and mil attaché Athens; *Recreations* country sports, travel; *Style—* Brig Gavin Bulloch, MBE

BULLOCK, Hon Adrian Charles Sebastian; 2 s of Baron Bullock (Life Peer); *b* 1944; *m* 1970 (m dis 1984), Susan Elizabeth Swindlehurst; 1 da (Hannah b 1977); *Style—* The Hon Adrian Bullock; 46 Walton Crescent, Oxford OX1 2JQ

BULLOCK, Baron (Life Peer UK 1976); Sir Alan Louis Charles Bullock; s of Rev Frank Allen Bullock, of Bradford, Yorks; *b* 13 Dec 1914; *Educ* Bradford Sch, Wadham Coll Oxford (MA, DLitt); *m* 1940, Hilda Yates, da of Edwin Handy, of Bradford; 3 s, 2 da; *Career* historian and writer; fell, dean and tutor New Coll Oxford 1945-52, founding master St Catherine's Coll Oxford 1960-80, vice-chllr Oxford Univ 1969-73; chm of tstees Tate Gallery 1973-80; FBA; kt 1972; *Books* Hitler, A Study in Tyranny (1952), The Life and Times of Ernest Bevin (Vol I 1960, Vol II 1967), Ernest Bevin, Foreign Secretary (1983), The Humanist Tradition (1955); *Style—* The Rt Hon The Lord Bullock; Gable End, 30 Godstow Rd, Oxford OX2 8AJ

BULLOCK, David Graham; s of late Ernest Cyril Bullock, of Shropshire, and Joyce Eliza Grace, *née* Bailey; *b* 21 July 1941; *Educ* Coalbrookdale HS, Univ of Nottingham (BA); *m* 4 April 1970, Georgina Alexandra Elizabeth, da of Michael Edward Fawcus, of Kenya; 2 s (Piers b 1974, Miles b 1981), 1 da (Romayne b 1977); *Career* dist admin and sec Trade and Econ Relations Ctee (TERC) Southern Rhodesia Govt 1963-64, with Unilever 1965-81, Lever Bros SA 1967-73; dir: Unilever Indonesia 1973-78, Batchelors Foods 1978-81, BP Int 1982-84, PA Consulting Gp 1986-87; chm David Bullock Assocs 1984, formed Warmington Gp 1984; exec memb Cons Foreign and Cwlth Cncl, Br Atlantic Ctee, Peace Through NATO; FInstD; memb: Royal Inst of Int Affrs, RASE, Anglo Indonesian Soc, Br Philippines Soc; *Recreations* eastern culture, old motor cars, fishing, falconry; *Clubs* Oriental, RREC, Millbank, Hall's Croft; *Style—* David Bullock, Esq; Warmington Manor, South Warwickshire OX17 1BU (☎ 029 589 239); Warmington Group, nr Banbury OX17 1BU (☎ 029 589 302)

BULLOCK, Prof Frederick William; s of Frederic Bullock (d 1936), of Bramshott Hants, and Elizabeth May, *née* Kent (d 1979); *b* 24 April 1932; *Educ* GS, UCL (BSc, PhD); *m* 1, 1 s (Ross b 7 July 1958); m 2, 30 Oct 1964, Margaret Ann, da of Robert Francis Tully (d 1973), of Dunstable Beds; 2 s (Iain Robert b 22 Feb 1966, Andrew b 20 May 1967); *Career* dean of Faculty of Mathematical and Physical Sciences UCL 1989- (res asst 1958-63, lectr 1963-74, reader in physics 1978-88, prof 1988-); memb: Nuclear Physics Bd of the SERC, Particle Physics Ctee of the SERC; chm Particle Physics Grants Sub-Ctee of the SERC; FInstP, CPhys; *Recreations* golf, watching Luton Town FC; *Style—* Prof Frederick Bullock; Dept of Physics and Astronomy, University College London, Gower St, London WC1E 6BT (☎ 071 380 7149)

BULLOCK, Gareth Richard; s of George Haydn Bullock, of Richmond, Surrey, and Veronica, *née* Jackson; *b* 20 Nov 1953; *Educ* Marling Sch Stroud, St Catharine's Coll Cambridge (MA); *m* 3 Sept 1983, Juliet Lucy Emma, da of Maj Cyril Vivian Eagleson Gordon, MC, of Winterbourne Gunner, Wilts; 2 s (Joshua b 1985, Marcus b 1987); *Career* vice pres Citibank NA London 1984 (joined 1977), exec dir Swiss Bank Corp Investment Banking Ltd 1984-90, dep md UBS Phillips & Drew (Securities) Ltd 1990; memb: Ctee St Catharine's Coll Soc, RSPB; *Books* Euronotes and Euro-Commercial paper (1987); *Recreations* second-hand book collecting, ornithology; *Style—* Gareth Bullock, Esq; 47 Kingston Lane, Teddington, Middlesex TW11 9HN

BULLOCK, Hazel Isabel; *née* MacNaughton-Jones; da of Henry MacNaughton-Jones, MD (d 1950), and Isabel Jessie, *née* Pownceby (d 1929); *b* 12 June 1919; *Educ* Kingsley Sch Hampstead, RADA, St Martin's Sch of Art, Sir John Cass Coll of Art; *m* 1, 8 March 1945 (m dis 1950), Vernon Kelso (d 1959); m 2, 13 Feb 1951, Ernest Edgar Bullock, s of Ernest Peter Bullock (d 1962); *Career* actress and painter (stage name Hazel Lawrence); BBC TV and London Stage 1943-51; exhibitions in London at: Loggia Gallery 1973, Judd St Gallery 1985, Phoenix Gallery 1989; gp exhibitions in London at: Browse and D'Arby, Whitechapel Art Gallery, Nat Soc, RBA, HAC, FPS; memb Free Painters & Sculptors Soc; *Recreations* travel; *Clubs* Arts; *Style—* Mrs Hazel Bullock; 32 Devonshire Place, London W1N 1PE (☎ 071 935 6409); Las Cancelas, La Herradura, Granada, Spain

BULLOCK, John; s of Robert Arthur Bullock (d 1960), of London, and Doris Edith Jane, *née* Thomas; *b* 12 July 1933; *Educ* Latymer Upper Sch; *m* 3 Sept 1960, Ruth Jennifer, da of Vernon William Bullock (d 1979), of Coulsdon, Surrey; 3 s (Mark b 1965 d 1982, Alastair b 1967, Robert b 1969); *Career* cmmnd RAF 1956-58; Smallfield Fitzhugh Tillet & Co 1949-56 and 1958-61; Robson Morrow: joined 1961, ptnr 1965-70 (Robson Morrow merged with Deloitte Haskins & Sells); ptnr i/c Deloitte Haskins & Sells Management Consultants 1971-79; Deloitte Haskins & Sells: managing ptnr 1979-85, dep sr ptnr 1984-85, sr ptnr 1985-90; vice chm Deloitte Haskins & Sells Int 1985-89, chm Deloitte Europe 1985-89, dep chm Coopers & Lybrand Deloitte (jt sr ptnr), chm Coopers & Lybrand Europe 1990-; pt/t memb UK Energy Authy; Liveryman Worshipful Co of Chartered Accountants 1989; FCA, FCMA, FIMC; *Recreations* opera, theatre, ballet, skiing, tennis; *Style—* John Bullock, Esq; Coopers & Lybrand Deloitte, 128 Queen Victoria St, London EC4P 4JX (☎ 071 248 3913, fax 071 248 3623, telex 894941)

BULLOCK, John Angel (aka Bulloch); s of William Percy George Bullock (d 1938), and Dorothy, *née* Motyer (d 1985); *b* 15 April 1928; *Educ* Penarth Co Sch, HMS Conway; *m* 1, 1951 (m dis 1971), Hazel Maxeen Campbell; 1 s; m 2, 1972 (m dis 1985), Susan Olivia Birkett; 1 s, 1 da; m 3, 1986, Jill Valerie Brown; 1 s (adopted), 1 da (adopted); *Career* served in MN; journalist; worked on local papers in S Wales and NE Eng before joining Press Assoc in 1955; Daily Telegraph: joined 1958, Central Africa corr 1960-69, ME corr 1969-76, memb Dip Staff 1978-86; dip corr BBC World Service 1977; dip ed: The Independent 1988-90 (ME ed 1986-88), The Independent on Sunday 1990-; *Books* Spy Ring (1961), MI5 (1963), Akin to Treason (1966), Death of a Country (1977), The Making of a War (1979), Final Conflict (1983), The Gulf (1984), The Gulf War (with Harvey Morris, 1989), Saddam's War (with Harvey Morris, 1991); *Recreations* growing vegetables, brewing beer; *Style—* John Bullock, Esq; The Independent on Sunday, 40 City Rd, London EC1Y 2DB (☎ 071 415 1329, fax 071 415 1333)

BULLOCK, John Charles Ernest; s of Ernest Henry Bullock (d 1957), of Kingston upon Hull, and Emily, *née* Boodie (d 1974); *b* 15 Aug 1942; *Educ* Hymers Coll Hull; *m* 23 May 1969, Dilys Rosalyn Cross, da of Francis Robert Metcalfe (d 1970), of Kirk Ella; 1 s (Richard), 1 da (Amanda); *Career* admitted slr 1969; clerk to Justices S Hunsley Beacon Div 1971-72; dir: Derwent Valley Railway Co 1976-86, Derwent Valley Hldgs plc 1984-86; underwriting memb of Lloyds 1981-; cncl memb Hull Incorporated Law Soc 1979-85; memb Law Soc 1969; *Recreations* sailing, golf, walking; *Clubs* Royal Yorkshire Yacht, Lloyds Yacht; *Style—* John Bullock, Esq; Westwood Hall, Westwood Rd, Beverley, Humberside HU17 8EN; Wilston House, Manor St, Kingston Upon Hull HU1 1YX, (☎ 0482 23697, fax 0482 28132)

BULLOCK, Hon Matthew Peter Dominic; yst s of Baron Bullock (Life Peer); *b* 9 Sept 1949; *Educ* Magdalen Coll Sch Oxford, Peterhouse Cambridge; *m* 1970, Anna-Lena Margareta, da of Sven Hansson, of Uppsala, Sweden; 1 s, 2 da; *Career* banker; regnl dir Leeds Barclays Bank; *Recreations* gardening, reading, walking; *Clubs* Oxford and Cambridge; *Style—* The Hon Matthew Bullock; Fern Dale, Parish Ghyll Drive, Ilkley, West Yorkshire LS29 9ND (☎ 0532 440232); Barclays Bank plc, Leeds Regional Office, 6 East Parade, Leeds LS1 1HA (☎ 0532 440232)

BULLOCK, Hon (Oliver) Nicholas Alan; eldest s of Baron Bullock (Life Peer); *b* 28 April 1942; *Educ* King's Coll Cambridge (MA, PhD, DipArch); *m* 1, 1967 (m dis); m 2, 1972 (m dis), Ellen J Blatt; 2 children, 2 step children; m 3, 1984 Sally Todd, da of late Sinclair Holmes, of Bolden; *Career* fell and tutor King's Coll Cambridge, lectr and dir of studies in architecture Cambridge Univ; *Recreations* squash, cycling (competitive), guitar; *Style—* The Hon Nicholas Bullock; King's College, Cambridge

BULLOCK, Peter Bradley; s of William H Bradley Bullock, of Benson, Oxon; *b* 9 June 1934; *Educ* Dudley GS, QMC London (BSc); *m* 1958, Joyce Frances Muriel, da of Horace Rea (d 1957); 2 children; *Career* md Flymo Ltd (memb of Electrolux Gp of Sweden mfr of lawnmowers), jt md Electrolux Gp UK to 1983; chief exec: James Neill Hldgs plc 1983-89, Spear & Jackson Int plc 1985-89; chm Henley Business Consultants Ltd 1990-; non-exec dir 600 Gp plc, Syltone plc, Weatherby Consultants Ltd; Queen's Award: for Export 1966 and 1982, for Technol 1979 and 1983; CEng, MInstE; *Recreations* sailing; *Clubs* Arts (London), Phyllis Court, Leander (Henley on Thames); *Style—* Peter Bullock, Esq; The Cottage, Queenwood, Christmas Common, Watlington, Oxford OX9 5HW (☎ 049161 2406); The Mill Cottage, Edale, Via Sheffield, Derbyshire S30 2ZE (☎ 0433 670231)

BULLOCK, Richard Henry Watson; CB (1971); er s of Sir Christopher Llewellyn Bullock, KCB, CBE (d 1972), of Kensington, London, and Barbara May, *née* Lupton (d 1974); *b* 12 Nov 1920; *Educ* Rugby, Trinity Coll Cambridge; *m* 20 Dec 1946, Beryl, da of John Haddan Markes (d 1950), of Ipoh, Federated Malay States, and Shripney; 1 s (Osmund Haddan Watson b 1951), 1 da (Susan Amaryllis Watson b 1947); *Career* served WWII 1940-46: 102 OCTU RAC 1940-41, cmmnd 2 Co of London Yeo (Westminster Dragoons) 1941, served England, NW Europe, Italy, Germany 1941-45, instr Armd Corps Offr Trg Sch India 1945-46, demob 1947 (Maj); joined Civil Serv 1947: asst sec Miny of Supply 1956-60 (asst princ 1947-49, princ 1949-56), on loan to WO 1960-61, Miny of Aviation 1961-64 (under sec 1963), Miny of Technol 1964-70 (head of space divn 1969-70), dep sec DTI 1970-80, ret 1980; dir-gen Electronic Components Indust Fedn 1984-90 (conslt dir 1981-84); dir: Berkeley Seventh Round Ltd 1981-87, Grosvenor Place Amalgamations Ltd 1982-; conslt Falkbourn Consulting Services 1981-; vice pres Westminster Dragoons Assoc 1972- (welfare offr 1950-72, chm 1978-82), dir Rugby Sch Devpt Campaign 1981-86, pres Old Rugbeian Soc 1984-86 (memb Exec Ctee 1950-), vice pres CS Hockey Ctee 1984-90 (pres 1978-84); pres: Rugby Alternatives Hockey Club 1976-, Dulwich Hockey Club 1962-; *Recreations* watching cricket, playing tennis, administrating hockey, fly fishing; *Clubs* Army & Navy, MCC, Hurlingham, Cambridge Union, Dulwich Hockey; *Style—* Richard Bullock, Esq, CB; 12 Peterborough Villas, London SW6 2AT (☎ 071 736 5132); Electronic Components Industry Federation, Romano House, 399-401 Strand, London WC2 (☎ 071 497 2311)

BULLOCK, (James) Rodney; s of James Mayou Bullock (d 1986), of Worcester, and Evelyn Maxine Buckley Bullock; *b* 3 Dec 1945; *Educ* Cheltenham Coll; *m* 1 s (John James b 1979), 1 da (Miriam Catherine b 1983); *Career* slr; *Recreations* squash, racing; *Style—* Rodney Bullock, Esq; 22 College Mews, Stratford-on-Avon, Warwickshire CV37 6FF (☎ 0985 298715); R J Evans Bullock Co, 1206 Stratford Road, Hall Green, Birmingham B28 8HN (☎ 021 777 7222)

BULLOUGH, Prof Donald Auberon; s of William Bullough (d 1961), and Edith Shirley, *née* Norman (d 1974); *b* 13 June 1928; *Educ* Newcastle-under-Lyme HS, Univ of Oxford (BA); *m* 12 Dec 1963, Belinda Jane, da of John Turland (d 1955); 2 da (Caroline b 1965, Elizabeth b 1968); *Career* Nat Serv RA 1947, transferred TA, seconded OTC 1956, Maj RA 1961, res list 1967; Fereday res fell St John's Coll Oxford 1952-55, lectr Univ of Edinburgh 1955-66, visiting prof Southern Methodist Univ of Dallas 1965-66, prof Univ of Nottingham 1966-73, dean Faculty of Arts Univ of St Andrews 1984-88 (prof 1973-); acting dir Br Sch at Rome 1984; fndr Gunner Heritage Appeal Fndn 1991; FRHistS 1958, FSA 1968; Korrespondierende Mitglied, Monumenta Germaniae Historica 1983; *Books* The Age of Charlemagne (1965, new edn 1973), Caroline Renewal: Sources and Heritage (1991); *Recreations* talk, looking at buildings, postal history, cooking; *Clubs* Athenaeum; *Style—* Prof Donald Bullough, FSA; 23 South St, St Andrews, Fife KY16 9QS (☎ 0334 72932); Dept of Medieval History, 71 South St, St Andrews KY16 9QW (☎ 0334 76161)

BULLOUGH, Dr Ronald; s of Ronald Bullough (d 1953), of The Bungalow, Larkhill, Kearsley, Lancs, and Edna, *née* Morrow (d 1937); *b* 6 April 1931; *Educ* Farnworth GS, Univ of Sheffield (BSc, PhD, DSc); *m* 31 July 1954, Ruth, da of late Joseph Corbett, of 15 School St, Newton le Willows, Warrington, Merseyside; 4 s (David Andrew, Timothy John, Mark Adrian, Neil Philip); *Career* res scientist Fundamental Res Laboratory Assoc Electrical Industs 1956-63, head Material Devpt Div Harwell Laboratory 1984-87 (gp ldr Theoretical Physics Div 1963-84), dir res and chief scientist AEA 1987-; visiting prof: Rensselaer Poly Inst USA 1968, Univ of Wisconsin USA 1978, Univ of Illinois USA 1979 (1964, 1973); visiting scientist Oak Ridge Nat

Laboratory 1969 and 1979 (Nat Bureau of Standards 1965), memb Res and Devpt Ctee CBI; author of several books; hon citizen of Tennessee 1967; FInstP 1963, FIM 1964, FRS 1985, FRSA 1986; *Recreations* walking, reading, music; *Style*— Dr Ronald Bullough, FRS; 4 Long Meadow, Manor Rd, Goring, Reading, Berks RG8 9EQ; Directorate, AEA Technology, Harwell Laboratory, Bldg 329, Didcot, Oxon OX11 0RA (☎ 0235 432861, telex 83135 ATOMHA G, fax 0235 433945)

BULMER, (James) Esmond; s of Edward Bulmer and Margaret, *née* Rye; *b* 19 May 1935; *Educ* Rugby, King's Coll Cambridge; *m* 1959, Morella Kearton; 3 s, 1 da; *Career* cmmnd Scots Gds 1954; H P Bulmer Hldgs: dir 1962-, dep chm 1980-82, chm 1982-; dir Nat West Bank (W Midlands and Wales Regnl Bd) July 1982-; memb Exec Ctee National Tst 1977-87; MP (C) Kidderminster Feb 1974-83, MP (C) Wyre Forest 1983-87; *Clubs* Boodle's; *Style*— Esmond Bulmer, Esq; 56 Warwick Square, London SW1

BULMER, Ian Lowes; s of Maj Eric Lowes Bulmer, MBE, TD (d 1980), and Monica Evelyn, *née* Head; *b* 16 Oct 1948; *Career* chm Bulmer Travel Associates 1977-; involved various charity works; IATA 1979; *Recreations* art in general, the art of living in particular; *Clubs* Windermere Island (Bahamas); *Style*— Ian Bulmer, Esq; residences in London and New York; 110 Strand, London WC2R 0AA (☎ 071 836 5244, fax 071 497 9106, telex 916 933)

BULMER, Lady Marcia Rose Aileen; *née* Leveson Gower; da of 5 Earl Granville, MC; *b* 10 Feb 1961; *m* 15 Oct 1986, Jonathan C Bulmer, yst s of late Edward Charles Bulmer; *Style*— Lady Marcia Bulmer

BULMER, Oliver Frederick; s of Robert Harold Bulmer (d 1985), of Hereford, and Pamela Mary Pleasance, *née* Dudding; *b* 29 Oct 1948; *Educ* Hereford Cathedral Sch, Univ of Bristol (BA); *m* 8 Sept 1980, Mary Rose, da of Ian Francis Henry Sconce, OBE, of Westerham, Kent; 3 da (Claire Olivia b 23 July 1981, Felicity Helena b 21 Oct 1982, Alison Rosemary b 2 Aug 1984); *Career* ptnr Pannell Kerr Forster 1979; vice chm Cottered and Throcking Cons Assoc; FCA 1974, MBCS; *Recreations* tennis, skiing; *Style*— Oliver Bulmer, Esq; Wilding, Cottered, Buntingford, Herts SG9 9QB (☎ 076 381 249); Pannell Kerr Forster, 78 Hatton Garden, London (☎ 071 831 7393)

BULMER-THOMAS, Ivor; CBE (1984); s of Alfred Ernest Thomas (d 1918), of Cwmbran, Gwent, and Zipporah, *née* Jones (d 1952); assumed the additional surname of Bulmer by Deed Poll 1952; *b* 30 Nov 1905; *Educ* W Monmouthshire Sch Pontypool, St John's Coll Oxford, Magdalen Coll Oxford; *m* 1, 5 April 1932, Dilys Primrose (d 1938), da of Dr William Llewelyn Jones (d 1931), of Merthyr Tydfil; 1 s (Michael Alcuin); m 2, 26 Dec 1940, (Margaret) Joan, da of Edward Frederick Bulmer (d 1941), of Breinton, Herefordshire; 1 s (Victor Gerald), 2 da (Jennifer Elizabeth (Mrs Patten), Miranda (Mrs Wilson)); *Career* WWII served: Royal Fusiliers 1939-40, Royal Norfolk Regt 1940-45, Capt 1941; sub-ed The Times 1930-37, leader writer News Chronicle 1937-39, leader writer and acting dep ed Daily Telegraph 1952-56; MP Keighley 1942-50, Parly sec for Civil Aviation 1945-46, Parly under-sec state for the Colonies 1946-47, delegate to Gen Assembly of UN 1946, first UK memb of Trusteeship Cncl 1947; hon dir Friends of Friendless Churches 1957-; chm Ancient Monuments Soc 1978-90; memb Parish Clerks' Co 1963; hon fell St John's Coll Oxford 1985, Hon DSc Warwick Univ 1979; FSA 1970; Stella della Solidarietà Italiana 1948; *Books* Coal in the New Era (1934), Gladstone of Hawarden (1936), Top Sawyer (1938), Greek Mathematical Works (Loeb Library 1939, 1942), Warfare By Words (1942), The Problem of Italy (1946), The Socialist Tragedy (1949), The Party System in Great Britain (1953), The Growth of the British Party System (1965), Dilysia: A Threnody (1987); *Recreations* ski-ing; *Clubs* Athenaeum, Vincent's (Oxford); *Style*— Ivor Bulmer-Thomas, Esq, CBE; 12 Edwardes Square, London W8 6HG (☎ 071 602 6267); The Old School House, Farnborough, Wantage, Oxon

BULTEEL, Christopher Harris; MC (1943); s of Maj Walter Bulteel (d 1965), of Charlestown, Cornwall, and Constance, *née* Gaunt (d 1976); *b* 29 July 1921; *Educ* Wellington, Merton Coll Oxford (MA); *m* 1958, Jennifer Anne, da of Lt-Col Kenneth Previté (d 1974), of Marnhull, Dorset; 1 s (James), 2 da (Cynthia, Nicola); *Career* Coldstream Gds 1940-46, Capt, served in N Africa and Italy; sr history teacher and head of dept Wellington Coll 1949-54 and 1956-61, chm Abbeyfield Soc 1956-59, headmaster Ardingly Coll Sussex 1962-80; GAP Activity Projects dir 1982-88; *Recreations* sailing, natural history, collecting antiques; *Style*— Christopher Bulteel, Esq, MC; 3 Coastguard Cottages, Mevagissey, St Austell, Cornwall PL26 6QP (☎ 0726 843928); Street Farm Cottage, Charlton, nr Malmesbury, Wilts SN16 9DF (☎ 0666 823764)

BULTEEL, Kenneth Michael; s of Gerald Melville Bulteel, of Stansted, and Nancy Georgina Bulteel; *b* 4 Nov 1947; *Educ* Birkenhead Sch, Fitzwilliam Coll Cambridge (MA); *m* 29 Jan 1972, Lynda, da of Frank Milner; 3 s (Simon Courtenay b 2 March 1974, Peter Hillesden b 8 April 1975, Paul Bellenden b 6 Feb 1978); *Career* L Messel & Co Stockbrokers: jr analyst 1969-70, analyst 1970-72, sr analyst/proj ldr 1972-74; Hill Samuel Group: proj ldr 1974-75, proj mangr 1975-77, systems and programming mangr 1977-78 asst to md Hill Samuel International 1978-79, business devpt mangr Hill Samuel Registrars 1979-80, data processing conslt 1980-81, mgmnt servs dir Noble Lowndes Group 1990- (systems dir 1981-90); *Recreations* Buxted Park CC, East Grinstead Hockey, Piltdown Golf; *Style*— Kenneth Bulteel, Esq; Noble Lowndes & Partners, PO Box 144, Norfolk House, Wellesley Rd, Croydon CR9 3EB (☎ 081 686 2466, fax 081 681 1458)

BULWER-LONG, Capt William Hanslip; s of Brig Hetherington Bulwer-Long, OBE, MC (d 1989), of Heydon Grange, and Mary Elizabeth Earle Bulwer-Long; *b* 9 May 1937; *Educ* Wellington, RMA Sandhurst; *m* 26 May 1962, Sarah Jane, da of Sir Frederick Rawlinson, Bt (d 1964); 2 s (Edward Hanslip b 1966, Benjamin Earle b 1970), 1 da (Daisy Lydia b 1974); *Career* 9 Queens Royal Lancers (9 and 12 Queens Royal Lancers), ADC GOC Northern Cmd 61/62 1957-67; served: BAOR, NI, ADEN, UK; farmer and landowner, contrib to Eastern Daily Press 1979-; winner Norfolk farmland conservation award 1984; cncl memb CLA 1976-85, vice chm FWAG Norfolk 1981-83, chm CLA Norfolk 1983-85, memb Jockey club 1986, High Sheriff Norfolk 1988-89, memb Exec Ctee RNAA 1989- (cncl memb 1988-); racing steward at: Liverpool, Cheltenham, Fakenham, Newmarket, Yarmouth; dir: Newmarket Racecourse Tst, Fakenham Racecourse Co; *Recreations* hunting, racing, country houses, antiques, literature, social history; *Clubs* Whites, Cavalry, Overseas League; *Style*— Capt William Bulwer-Long; Heydon Hall, Norwich NR11 6RE (☎ 026 387343)

BUMPUS, Bernard Sydney Graham; s of John Graham Bumpus (d 1949), of Sidmouth, Devon, and Gladys Louise, *née* White (d 1976); *b* 10 May 1921; *Educ* Oundle; *m* 30 July 1966, Judith Harriet, da of Robert Collison, of Budleigh Salterton, Devon; 2 da (Nicola b 1967, Francesca b 1968); *Career* RCS 1940-46, T/Maj on Demobilisation Burma; admin offr Colonial Admin Serv Gold Coast/Ghana 1946-, head Int Bdcasting and Audience Res Dept BBC 1973-82; ceramic historian 1982-; organizer Rhead Artists and Potters Exhibition 1986-87; *Books* Charlotte Rhead Potter and Designer; *Style*— Bernard S G Bumpus, Esq

BUNBURY; *see*: Richardson-Bunbury

BUNBURY, Sir Michael William; 13 Bt (E 1681); s of Sir (John) William Napier Bunbury, 12 Bt (d 1985), and Margaret Pamela, *née* Sutton; *b* 29 Dec 1946; *Educ* Eton, Trinity Coll Cambridge (MA); *m* 1976, Caroline Anne, da of Col Anthony Derek Swift Mangnall, OBE, of Bradley Court, Chieveley, Berks; 2 s (Henry b 1980, Edward b 1986), 1 da (Katherine b 1978); *Heir* s, Henry Michael Napier Bunbury b 4 March 1980; *Career* farmer and company director; chm Smith and Williamson; landowner (1100 acres); *Recreations* shooting; *Clubs* Boodle's; *Style*— Sir Michael Bunbury, Bt; Naunton Hall, Rendlesham, Woodbridge, Suffolk IP12 2RD (☎ (0394) 460235); No1 Riding House Street, London W1 (☎ 071 637 5377)

BUNBURY, Pamela, Lady; (Margaret) Pamela; *née* Sutton; da of Thomas Alexander Sutton (gs of Sir Richard Sutton, 4 Bt); *b* 22 April 1919; *m* 1940, Sir (John) William Napier Bunbury, 12 Bt (d 1985); 4 s (Sir Michael William, 13 Bt (*qv*), Charles Thomas b 1950, Christopher Henry b 1950 (twin), Peter Charles Napier b 1941, d 1964); *Style*— Pamela, Lady Bunbury; 9, Lee Rd Aldeburgh, Suffolk (☎ 0728 452196)

BUNCE, Michael John; s of Roland John Bunce (d 1977), and Dorie, *née* Woods; *b* 24 April 1935; *Educ* St Paul's, Kingston Coll; *m* 1 April 1961, Tina, da of Capt Sims (d 1939); 2 s (Charles b 1962, Rupert b 1966), 2 da (Miranda b 1968, Arabella b 1970); *Career* Nat Serv RAF; joined BBC as engr, subsequently studio mangr; prodr: People and Politics World Service, A Man Apart-The Murderer 1965, Minorities in Britain, The Younger Generation, Italy and the Italians; dir Gallery; ed: The Money Programme 1968-70, BBC Nationwide 1970-75; BBC chief asst Current Affairs 1976-78 (also ed Tonight), head of Information Servs TV 1978-82, head of Information Div 1982-83, controller Information Services 1983-, visiting ed in residence Univ of Alabama 1987-; memb: EMU Working Pty 1978, Francis Ctee 1977; chm Nat Industs PR Offrs 1991; Shell International TV award 1969; Marshall Fund fell USA 1975; FRTS 1989 (chm PR Ctee, memb Cncl); *Recreations* gardening, visiting interesting buildings, fishing; *Clubs* Reform; *Style*— Michael Bunce, Esq; BBC, Broadcasting House, London W1A 1AA (☎ 071 580 4468)

BUNCE, Dr Ross John; s of Ross Frederick Bunce, DFC, of Gerrards Cross, Bucks, and Gwendoline Janet, *née* Fox; *b* 28 March 1948; *Educ* Kingsbury County GS, Univ Coll London (BSc, PhD); *m* 29 Dec 1972, Monique Irene, da of Pierre Roy; 2 s (Philippe Ross b 27 Oct 1978, John Marc Alexander b 26 April 1980); *Career* asst vice pres Investmt Mgmnt Bankers Tst Co London 1974-81, Mercury Asset Mgmnt 1981- (dep chm 1989); dir: Mercury Asset Mgmnt Ltd 1983, Mercury Asset Mgmnt Hldgs 1987, Mercury Asset Mgmnt plc 1987; assoc memb Soc of Investmt Analysts; *Recreations* squash, tennis, golf; *Clubs* Radlett Tennis and Squash, Porters Park Golf; *Style*— Dr Ross Bunce; 6 Lamorna Close, Radlett, Hertfordshire; 33 King William St, London EC4R 9AS (☎ 071 280 2800)

BUNCH, Sir Austin Wyeth; CBE (1978, MBE 1974); s of Horace William Bunch (d 1953), and Winifred Ada Bunch; *b* 20 March 1918; *Educ* Christ's Hosp; *m* 1944, Joan Mary, *née* Peryer; 4 da; *Career* Lt Essex Regt 1940-44; Deloite Plender Griffiths 1935-48, with Southern Electricity Bd 1949-76 (chm 1974-76), chm The Electricity Cncl 1981-83 (dep chm 1976-81); nat pres Br Limbless Ex-Serv Men's Assoc 1983-; kt 1983; *Recreations* sports for the disabled; *Clubs* Victory (Services); *Style*— Sir Austin Bunch, CBE; Sumner, School Lane, Cookham, Berks

BUNDY, Christopher; *b* 7 Oct 1945; *Educ* Cheshunt GS; *m* 8 Aug 1970, Wendy Constance; 1 s (Dominic b 1973), 2 da (Phillipa b 1975, Prudence b 1979); *Career* CA; fin accountant Caravans Int Ltd, fin dir subsidiary co Lex Service Gp, chm and md E J Arnold and Son, indust advsr, dir Griffin International (GIVK Ltd); chm: A1 Security & Electrical Ltd, Glastics Ltd; FCA; *Recreations* wine, computers; *Style*— Christopher Bundy, Esq; Brook House, Elvington, York YD4 5AA (☎ 0904 85 297, fax 0904 85 256)

BUNKER, Albert Rowland; CB (1966); s of Alfred Francis Bunker (d 1961), and Ethel, *née* Trudgian (d 1938); *b* 5 Nov 1913; *Educ* Ealing GS; *m* 19 Aug 1939, Irene Ruth Ella, da of Walter Henry Lacey (d 1930); 2 s (Richard b 1942, Robert b 1945); *Career* RAF 1943-45, cmmnd air crew 1944; Home Office: asst sec 1948-61, asst under sec of state 1961-72, dep under sec of state 1972-75; also served: Cabinet Office, HM Treasy, Miny of Home Security; *Recreations* golf; *Clubs* RAF, Denham Golf; *Style*— Albert Bunker, Esq, CB; 35 Park Ave, Ruislip, Middx HA4 7UQ (☎ 0895 635331)

BUNKER, Christopher Jonathan; s of Jonathan William Bunker, and Beryl Kathleen Rose, *née* Wood; *b* 16 Dec 1946; *Educ* Ilford County HS, King's Coll London; *m* 9 Sept 1972, Julia Doris, da of Arthur James Seymour Russell (d 1954); 2 da (Jennifer b 1978, Elizabeth b 1982); *Career* accountant; finance dir Westland Group plc; *Style*— Christopher Bunker, Esq; Westland Group plc, Yeovil, Somerset

BUNKER, Peter John; OBE (1988); s of Leslie John Daniel Bunker (d 1985), of Hove, and Rosa Amelia, *née* Sands (d 1961); *b* 26 Feb 1928; *Educ* Brighton Hove and Sussex GS, Gonville and Caius Coll Cambridge (MA, LLM); *m* 31 May 1952, Angela Elizabeth, da of David Higham (d 1957), of Brighton; 1 s (John b 1957), 3 da (Elizabeth b 1955, Margaret b 1960, Catherine b 1965); *Career* Nat Serv Acting Petty Offr (radio electrician) Fleet Air Arm 1946-48; admitted slr 1954; pres Sussex Law Soc 1979-80, memb Law Soc's Solicitors' Assistance Panel, fndr chm PACT; past chm of govrs: Goldstone Junior Sch Hove, Blatchington Mill Comprehensive Sch Hove; fndr chm: Martlet Housing Assoc, E Sussex Cncl on Alcoholism; chm Frederick Soddy Tst; memb Nat Exec United Reformed Church; awarded Law Soc Broderip and Mellersh prizes; FRGS 1978; *Recreations* gardening, skiing, listening to music; *Style*— Peter Bunker, Esq, OBE; 38 Shirley Drive, Hove, East Sussex (☎ 0273 503729); Bunker & Co, Solicitors, 9 The Drive, Hove, East Sussex (☎ 0273 29797)

BUNKER, Richard David Charles; s of Albert Rowland Bunker, CB, of 35 Park Ave, Ruislip, Middx, and Irene Ruth Ella, *née* Lacey; *b* 1 May 1942; *Educ* Ealing GS, St Peter's Coll Oxford (MA), Univ of Nottingham (PGCE); *m* 5 Aug 1967, Jennifer, da of George Calow (d 1986); 2 s (Andrew b 1971, Jonathan b 1973); *Career* English language asst 1963-64, personnel offr Unilever 1965-66; languages teacher: Drayton Manor GS Ealing 1966, Haberdashers' Aske's 1967-70, asst educn offr London Borough of Hillingdon 1970-74, asst educn offr then sr asst educn offr Bedfordshire CC 1974-80, dir of educn W Sussex CC 1985- (dep dir 1980-85); hon treas Nat Fndn for Educnl Res, dir Nfer-Nelson Ltd, memb of Cncl Univ of Sussex, tstee Chichester Festival Theatre; FBIM 1984, FRSA 1984, FIL 1989; *Recreations* travel, languages; *Clubs* Royal Over-Seas League; *Style*— Richard Bunker, Esq; 15 Stanton Drive, Summersdale, Chichester, W Sussex PO19 4QN; Education Department, W Sussex County Council, County Hall, West St, Chichester, W Sussex PO19 1RF (☎ 0243 777750, fax 0243 777229, telex 86279 CHILIB G)

BUNN, Douglas Henry David; s of George Henry Charles Honeybunn (d 1967), of Selsey, Nr Chichester, W Sussex, and Alice Ann, *née* Philpot (d 1986); *b* 1 March 1928; *Educ* Chichester HS, Trinity Coll Cambridge (MA); *m* 1, 26 June 1952, Rosemary Heather (d 1959), da of John Pares Wilson, of Formby, Lancs; 3 da (Claudia b 27 Sept 1953, Lavinia b 6 June 1956, Theresa b 24 Sept 1958); m 2, 16 March 1960 (m dis 1979), Diane Susan Beverley, da of Archie Dennis-Smith; 2 s (Edward b 22 Jan 1961, John b 18 May 1966), 1 da (Elizabeth b 8 Nov 1963); m 3, 12 March 1979, Lorna Margaret, da of Joseph Kirk, of Cambridge; 2 s (Douglas b 6 Oct 1981 d 1981), Charles b 30 March 1987), 2 da (Chloe b 3 April 1980, Daisy b 24 Jan 1983); *Career* called to the Bar Lincoln's Inn, practised as barrister 1953-59; Br Show Jumping Team 1957-58; founded: White Horse Caravan Co Ltd 1958, All England Jumping Course Hickstead 1960; chm: Southern Aero Club 1968-72, Br Show Jumping Assoc 1969;

memb Br Equestrian Fedn, joint master of Mid-Surrey Draghounds 1976; *Recreations* horses, flying, books, wine; *Clubs* Saints & Sinners, Bucks, Turf; *Style—* Douglas Bunn, Esq; Hickstead Place, Hickstead, Sussex RH17 5NU (☎ 0273 834666); All England Jumping Course, Hickstead, Sussex RH17 5NU (☎ 0273 834315, fax 0273 834452, telex 877159, 0831 473858)

BUNN, Richard Herbert; s of Herbert Cecil Bunn (d 1966), of Croydon, and Mabel Eveline Bunn; *b* 17 Feb 1936; *Educ* Whitgift Sch Croydon; *m* 1, 20 June 1964 (m dis 1982); 4 s (Nicholas Richard b 26 Feb 1968, Jonathan James b 22 Aug 1970, Timothy William b 5 Dec 1971, Philip Edward b 24 May 1974); m 2, 21 Sept 1984, Kitrina Elizabeth; *Career* actuarial student Law Union and Rock Insurance Co Ltd 1954-58; Hoare & Co Stockbrokers (became Hoare Govett Ltd 1970): joined 1958, ptnr 1968, currently dir corporate fin; memb Stock Exchange; FIA 1965; *Recreations* golf, bridge, walking, travelling, reading; *Clubs* City of London, Old Whitgiftians, Woodcote Park Golf, St Mellion's Golf; *Style—* Richard Bunn, Esq; Woodlands, Farm Drive, Purley, Surrey CR8 3LP (☎ 081 660 3628); Hoare Govett Ltd, 4 Broadgate, London EC2N 7LE (☎ 071 374 1781, mobile 0831 451 316)

BUNNEY, Elliot John; s of David Lindsay Bunney, of Edinburgh, and Elizabeth Ann, *née* Ridgway; *b* 11 Dec 1966; *Educ* Bathgate Acad; *Career* athlete; 10 Scot sr caps (4 jr), 10 Br sr caps (8 jr); Scot Schs 100, and 200, champion 1982, 1984, 1985, sch co 100m and 200m champion 1984; Scot AAA: jr 100m and 200m champion 1982, under 20 100m and 200m champion 1983, 1984, 1985, sr 100m champion 1985 and 1986; AAA: indoor 60m youth champion 1983, 100m under 20 champion 1983, 1984, 1985, 60 m under 20 champion 1984, 1985, 1987; int honours: Gold medal 100m and 4 x 100m Euro Jr Championships 1985 (Bronze 4 x 100m 1983), Bronze medal 4 x 100m Cwlth Games 1986, Bronze medal 4 x 100m Euro Championships 1986, Silver medal 4 x 100m Olympic Games 1988; records: Scot jr 100m 1984, equalled UK jr 60m 1985, Scot and UK all-comers 60m 1987, Br and Celth 4 x 100m 1988; *Recreations* soccer, reading, tv; *Clubs* Caledon Park Harriers; *Style—* Elliot Bunney, Esq; 29 Mansefield Court, Bathgate, W Lothian EH48 4HE (☎ 0506 633058)

BUNNEY, John Herrick; *b* 2 June 1945; *m* 1970, Pamela Anne Simcock; 1 s, 1 da; *Career* 2 Sec FCO 1971, MECAS 1971, 1 sec Damascus 1974-78, consul Sana'a 1981-; *Style—* John Bunney, Esq; c/o Foreign & Commonwealth Office, King Charles St, London SW1

BUNTING, Gerald Leeson; DL (1988); s of Charles Gilbert Bunting (d 1967), of Northbrook, Hartlepool, and Edith Joyce, *née* Hopkinson; Landed Gentry family long resident in Kent until 17 Century from thence onwards found as Landed Woolcombers in Northants and Durham. Thomas Bunting of Lydd mentioned in Chamberlains Account Books of Lydd 1429. His gs John (attainted of High Treason for supporting Duke of Buckingham's Rebellion 1493), landed with Henry Tudor at Milford Haven and fought at Bosworth receiving a manor as reward. John Bunting (b 1490, d 1546) was Jurat and MP for New Romney as was his eld s Richard (d 1574); *b* 1 March 1928; *Educ* Uppingham; *m* 16 June 1956, Diana, da of late Richard Henry Middleton, of Friars Lodge, Bamburgh; 2 s ((Gerald) Nigel b 1957, Mark Charles b 1959), 1 da ((Diana) Jane (Countess of Hillsborough) b 1962); *Career* cmmnd 1947, served Mid East; TA Capt 508 field sqn RE TA 1952-60; slr; sr ptnr Gilbert Bunting & Co; dep Coroner Cleveland N 1968, pres Hartlepool Law Soc 1972-73; pres Durham and N Yorks Law Soc 1988-89; memb: Hartlepool Hosp Mgmnt Ctee 1969-74, Hartlepool Community Health Cncl 1974-82; vice chm Hartlepool Health Authy 1982-90, Cleveland Family Practitioner Ctee 1985-90; *Recreations* golf, shooting; *Style—* Gerald Bunting, Esq, DL; Otterington House, Northallerton, N Yorks DL7 9EP (☎ 0609 772545); Gilbert Bunting & Co, Solicitors, Exchange Building, Church St, Hartlepool (☎ 0429 267032)

BUNTING, Dr John Stanton; s of Sqdn Ldr Stanton William Morrison Bunting (d 1984), of Milford on Sea, Hants, and Beatrice, *née* White; *b* 27 Nov 1924; *Educ* King's Sch Chester, Bart's (MB BS, DMRT); *m* 24 Sept 1949, Pauline Helen, da of Herbert Roy Boswell (d 1945), of Mill Hill; 2 s (Christopher John Stanton b 1955, Anthony David Stanton b 1961); *Career* serv RAC 1942-46, cmmnd 1945, IA 1945-46, Capt RAMC TA 1957; house physician Addenbrooks Hosp Cambridge 1954, MO Alexandra MH Millbank 1955, registrar radiotherapy Guy's 1956, sr registrar Bart's 1961-63, conslt radiotherapist Colchester 1964-67, conslt radiotherapist and oncologist Royal Berkshire Hosp Reading 1967-, hon conslt Sue Ryder Fndn 1980-, hon conslt and chm Sue Ryder Home Nettlebed; Liveryman Worshipful Soc Apothecaries, Freeman City of London 1982; vice pres Section of Radiology RSM 1990; FFR 1963, FRCR 1972; *Books* various pubns in med press incl: British Journal of Radiology (1965), Clinical Radiology (1974); *Recreations* painting; *Clubs* Phyllis Court (Henley on Thames); *Style—* Dr John Bunting; Autumn Cottage, 10 Watlington Rd, Nettlebed, Henley on Thames, Oxon (☎ 0491 641217); 13 Bath Rd, Reading, Berks (☎ 0734 584711)

BUNTING, Martin Brian; s of Thomas Brian Bunting (d 1988), of Maidstone, and Renee Conworth, *née* Fish; *b* 28 Feb 1934; *Educ* Rugby; *m* 11 July 1959, Veronica Mary, da of Bertam Harold Cope, of Wolverhampton; 2 s (Timothy, Nigel), 1 da (Caroline (Countess of Macduff, see Macduff, Earl of); *Career* 2 Lt 1952-54 8 Kings Royal Irish Hussars; md Courage (Central) Ltd 1969-71; Courage Ltd: asst md 1972, gp md 1975; Imperial Group Ltd: joined 1961, dir 1975, dep chm Imperial Brewing & Leisure Ltd, ret 1986; non-exec dir: Horndean Hotels Ltd 1984-, George Gale & Co Ltd 1984-, Longman Cartermill Ltd 1985-90, Norcros plc 1986-, Shepherd Neame Ltd 1986-; chief exec Clifford Foods plc 1990 (non-exec dir 1989-90); Gen Cmmr of Income Tax 1986-; memb MMC 1982-88, Freeman Worshipful Co of Brewers; FCA 1960; *Clubs* Travellers'; *Style—* Martin Bunting, Esq; The Lodge, Riseley, Berks RG7 1QD (☎ 0734 883234)

BUNTING, Michael Geoffrey; s of James Norman Bunting, of 88 Kenilworth Rd, St Anne's on Sea, Lancs, and Dorothy, *née* Lowndes; *b* 20 May 1947; *Educ* King Edward VII Sch Lytham, Trinity Coll Cambridge (BA, MA), Manchester Business Sch (MBA); *m* 18 Feb 1984, Sheila Carolyn, da of George Herbert Booth, of Haxby, York; 2 s (Adrian b 1986, Richard b 1988), 1 da (Julia b 1984); *Career* gp treas: Tootal Gp plc 1982-84, The Boots Co plc 1984-; *Recreations* mountaineering; *Style—* Michael Bunting, Esq; 7 Highgrove Gdns, Edwalton, Nottingham, NG12 4DF (☎ 0602 231 406); The Boots Co plc, Head Office, Notts NG2 3AA (☎ 0602 506 111, fax 0602 592 727)

BUNTON, Christopher John; s of John Bunton, and Marion Helen, *née* Gotobed; *b* 22 Feb 1948; *Educ* Charterhouse, Trinity Coll Cambridge (MA), London Graduate Sch of Business Studies (MSc); *m* 10 May 1975, Jane Melanie, da of Antony J S Cartmell; 2 s (Anthony, Michael); *Career* with Gulf Oil Corpn 1973-1985, gp treas Saatchi & Saatchi plc 1986-; *Recreations* music; *Clubs* Hawks; *Style—* Christopher Bunton, Esq; Saatchi & Saatchi Co plc, Berkeley Square, London W1X 5DH (☎ 071 495 5000)

BUNYARD, Robert Sidney; CBE (1986), QPM (1978); s of Albert Percy Bunyard, and Nellie Maria, *née* Mount; *b* 20 May 1930; *Educ* Queen Elizabeth GS Faversham, Regent Street Poly Mgmnt Sch (DMS), Open Univ (BA); *m* 1948, Ruth; 2 da (Anne, Christine); *Career* joined Met Police 1952; chief superintendent: Lewisham 1969-71, Greenwich 1971-72; asst chief constable Leics 1972-77; RCDS 1977, dep chief constable Essex 1977 (chief constable 1978); chm: ACPO Computer Ctee 1980-82, ACPO Training Ctee 1984-87, No 5 Regional Crime Squad Ctee 1980-87; HM Inspector of Constabulary 1988-, Cmdt Police Staff Coll 1988-; MIPM, CBIM; *Books* Police Organisation and Command (1978), Police Management Handbook (1979); *Recreations* music, opera, painting; *Style—* Robert Bunyard, Esq, CBE, QPM; The Police Staff College, Bramshill, Bramshill House, Hartley Wintney, Hampshire RG27 0JW (☎ 025 126 2931)

BUNZL, Thomas F; s of Dr Max Bunzl; *b* 13 Dec 1934; *Educ* Bembridge Sch IOW, Univ of Glasgow, Univ of California; *m* 1959, Marian, da of Walter Strauss; 2 da; *Career* md Electrautom Ltd 1965-89; chm and md Robots Ltd; MIEE, MIEEE, FISM, FIPM, Eur Ing 1989; *Style—* Eur Ing Thomas Bunzl; 126 West Heath Rd, London NW3 (☎ 081 458 2691)

BURBIDGE, Sir Herbert Dudley; 5 Bt (UK 1916); s of late Herbert Edward Burbidge, 2 s of 1 Bt; suc kinsman, Sir John Richard Woodman Burbidge, 4 Bt, 1974; *b* 13 Nov 1904; *Educ* University Sch Victoria BC Canada; *m* 1933, Ruby, da of Charles Ethelbert Taylor, of Comox, Vancouver 1, BC; 1 s; *Heir* s, Peter Burbidge; *Career* mangr Silverwood Industries (Vancouver) 1931-70; *Style—* Sir Herbert Burbidge, Bt; 3809 West 24th Avenue, Vancouver, British Columbia, Canada

BURBIDGE, Peter Dudley; s and h of Sir Herbert Burbidge, 5 Bt; *b* 20 June 1942; *m* 1967, Peggy Marilyn, da of Kenneth Anderson, of Ladner, BC; 1 s, 1 da; *Style—* Peter Burbidge, Esq; 3809 West 24th Ave, Vancouver, BC, Canada

BURBRIDGE, Very Rev (John) Paul; s of John Henry Gray Burbridge (d 1980), of Warninglid, Sussex, and Dorothy Vera, *née* Pratt (d 1981); *b* 21 May 1932; *Educ* King's Sch Canterbury, King's Coll Cambridge (MA), New Coll Oxford (MA), Wells Theol Coll; *m* 7 July 1956, Olive Denise, da of Denis Arthur Grenfell, of Holcombe, Dawlish, S Devon; 4 da (Rachel (Mrs Howgego) b 1960, Deborah (Mrs Johnson) b 1962, Sarah (Mrs Bourne) b 1966, Felicity b 1969); *Career* Nat Serv cmmn RA 1957, Asst Adj 80 LAA Regt RA; curate Eastbourne Parish Church 1959-62, chamberlain York Minster 1962-76 (canon residentiary and precentor 1966-76), archdeacon of Richmond 1976-83, dean of Norwich 1983-; FSA; *Style—* The Very Rev the Dean of Norwich; The Deanery, Norwich, Norfolk (☎ 0603 760140)

BURBRIDGE, Stephen Nigel; s of John Henry Gray Burbridge (d 1980), and Dorothy Vera, *née* Pratt (d 1981); *b* 18 July 1934; *Educ* King's Sch Canterbury, ChCh Oxford (MA); *Career* Nat Serv 2 Lt RA 1953-55; asst princ BOT 1958; first sec: commercial Karachi 1963, econ Rawalpindi 1965; DTI: princ 1967, asst sec 1971, under sec 1980; sec to the MMC 1986; *Recreations* sport, collecting; *Clubs* Rye Golf, West Sussex Golf; *Style—* Stephen Burbridge, Esq; Monopolies and Mergers Commission, New Court, 48 Carey St, London WC2A 2JT (☎ 071 324 1427, fax 071 324 1400)

BURBURY, Hon Mrs (Sarah Dingle); *née* Foot; o da of Baron Caradon, GCMG, KCVO, OBE, PC (Life Peer, d 1990); *b* 24 Sept 1939; *m* 1961, Maj Timothy Nicholas Percival Winter Burbury, The Blues and Royals, s of Surg-Col Dermot Roland Winter Burbury; 1 s (Charles Alexander Winter b 1964), 1 da (Camilla Jane Winter (Mrs Mark Lindfield) b 1962); *Career* author, journalist and editor of Cornish Scene magazine under maiden name Sarah Foot; now involved in social work Derriford Hosp Plymouth; *Books Incl:* Following the River Fowey, Following the Tamar, My Grandfather Isaac Foot, The Cornish Countryside; *Style—* The Hon Mrs Burbury; Ince Barton, Saltash, Cornwall (☎ 0752 847709)

BURBURY, Hon Sir Stanley Charles; KCMG (1981), KCVO (1977), KBE (1958), QC (1950); s of Daniel Charles Burbury and Mary, *née* Cunningham; *b* 2 Dec 1909; *Educ* Hutchins Sch Tasmania, Univ of Tasmania (LLB); *m* 1934, Pearl Christine, da of late Wallace Barren; *Career* barr 1934, slr-gen Tasmania 1952, chief justice Supreme Ct of Tasmania 1956-73, governor of Tasmania 1973-82; Hon LLD Univ of Tasmania; KStJ 1974; *Recreations* lawn bowls, music; *Clubs* Roy Hobart Bowls; *Style—* Hon Sir Stanley Burbury, KCMG, KCVO, KBE; 3 Mona St, Kingston, Tas 7150, Australia

BURCH, Maj-Gen Keith; CB (1985), CBE (1977, MBE 1965); s of Christopher Burch, of Saltdean, Sussex, and Gwendoline Ada, *née* James; *b* 31 May 1931; *Educ* Bedford Modern Sch, RMA Sandhurst; *m* 12 June 1957, Sara Vivette, da of Reginald Thomas Hales (d 1974); 1 s (Giles St John b 1966), 2 da (Amanda b 1958, Emma b 1960); *Career* cmmnd Essex Regt 1951, dir staff Staff Coll Camberley 1968-69, cmd 3 Bn The Royal Anglian Regt 1969-71, asst sec Chiefs of Staff Ctee MOD 1972-75, Col GS HQ 2 Armoured Div 1975-78, dir Admin Planning (Army) MOD 1978-80, Indian Nat Def Coll New Delhi 1981, dep dir Army Staff Duties MOD 1981-83, asst chief of the Def Staff (personnel and logistics) MOD 1984, dir personnel MOD 1985; chapter clerk York Minster 1985; *Recreations* country pursuits; *Clubs* Yorkshire (York); *Style—* Maj-Gen Keith Burch, CB, CBE

BURCHFIELD, Dr Robert William; CBE (1975); s of Frederick Burchfield (d 1979), and Mary Lauder, *née* Blair (d 1974); *b* 27 Jan 1923; *Educ* Wanganui Tech Coll NZ, Victoria Univ Coll Wellington NZ, Magdalen Coll Oxford; *m* 1, 1949 (m dis 1976), Ethel May Yates; 1 s (Jonathan), 2 da (Jennifer, Elizabeth); m 2, 1976, Elizabeth Austen, da of Cedric Hankinson Knight (d 1983); *Career* RNZA 1941-46, NZ and Italy, Sgt 1941-44; lectr in English language Ch Ch Oxford 1953-57, fell and tutor in English language St Peter's Coll Oxford 1963-79 (sr res fell 1979-90, emeritus fell 1990-); ed A Supplement to the Oxford English Dictionary 1957-86; *Books* The Oxford Dictionary of English Etymology (with C T Onions and G W S Friedrichsen, 1966), A Supplement to the Oxford English Dictionary Vol 1 A-G (1972), Vol 2 H-N (1976), Vol 3 O-Scz (1982), Vol 4 Se-Z (1986), The Spoken Word (1981), The English Language (1985), The New Zealand Pocket Oxford Dictionary (1986), Studies in Lexicography (1987), Unlocking the English Language (1989); *Recreations* investigating English grammar, travelling; *Style—* Dr Robert Burchfield, CBE; 14 The Green, Sutton Courtenay, Oxfordshire OX14 4AE (☎ 0235 848645); St Peter's College Oxford OX1 2DL

BURDEN, Clive Albert; s of Albert Henry Burden (d 1964), and Alice Louise, *née* Lowton (d 1976); *b* 1 June 1934; *Educ* Drayton Manor GS, Univ Coll of SW (BSc); *m* Pauline Elaine, da of Fredrick Charles Dean (d 1988); 1 s (Philip Dean b 26 Dec 1960), 1 da (Jacqueline (Mrs Watson) b 15 Feb 1963); *Career* Flying Offr RAF 1955-58; Br Oxygen Co: res scientist 1958, mangr Automatic Welding Dept 1959, asst mangr Welding Dept 1962, trainee mangr production 1965, equipment sales mangr Eastern Region 1968, nat sales mangr welding equipment 1971, gen sales mangr 1971; dir Irish Industl Gases 1971 (gen mangr Automatic Welding Equipment Prodn and gen sales mangr Welding Prodn Div); started antiquarian book and print business 1973; author of several tech papers, received Harvey Shacklock award for best tech paper at Rand Exhibition 1964; sr MWeld 1959, MInstP 1965, memb ABA 1980; *Recreations* sports in general; *Clubs* Moor Park Golf; *Style—* Clive Burden, Esq; 26 Sandy Lodge Rd, Moor Park, Rickmansworth, Herts WD3 1LJ (☎ 0923 772387); 10 Tio Charles, Benalmadena Pueblo, Spain; 46 Talbot Rd, Rickmansworth, Herts WD3 1HE; 93 Lower Sloane St, London; PO Box 2792, Naples, Florida, USA 33939 (☎ 0923 778097, fax 0923 896 520)

BURDEN, Norman; s of Walter Burden (d 1975), of Sefton Park, Liverpool, and Margaret Jane, *née* Thomas (d 1979); *b* 24 Sept 1934; *Educ* Liverpool Collegiate Sch, Christ's Coll Cambridge (MA); *m* 29 March 1958, Margot Asquith, da of George Lowe Tennant (d 1947); 3 da (Sarah b 1960, Xanthe b 1963, Celia b 1965); *Career* RAF 1956-58, Pilot Offr 1956, Flying Offr 1957; dir gp mktg Compair Ltd 1971-77, int chief exec Burmah Indust Prods Ltd 1979-81, chief exec The Rawlplug Gp 1981-85, ptnr Templewood Assocs 1985-, dir Dzus International Ltd 1990-, chm Vitalograph Ltd

1990-; nat chm Chartered Inst of Mktg 1985 and 1986 (former vice chm and treas), Br rep Euro Mktg Cncl 1980-86; memb Governing Bd Mktg Quality Assurance 1990-; singing memb The Windsor and Eton Choral Soc; Freeman City of London 1982, Liveryman Worshipful Co of Marketors 1982; FCIM 1974, FRSA 1984, FInstD 1986; *Recreations* choral music, running; *Style—* Norman Burden, Esq; Penwern, 23 Mayflower Way, Farnham Common, Bucks SL2 3TU (☎ 02814 2325)

BURDER, (John) Robert; s of Edward Russell Burder (d 1965), and Elspeth Anne, *née* Little; *b* 27 Dec 1929; *Educ* Ashbury Coll Ottawa Canada, Tonbridge; *m* 30 Oct 1954, Diana Mary, da of Thomas Henry Beckett (d 1954); 1 s (Simon), 1 da (Susie); *Career* Nat Serv 1948-49, 4 Royal Tank Regt Egypt and Jordan; admitted slr 1955, ptnr Batchelor Fry Coulson and Burder 1960, sr ptnr Batchelor Street Longstaffe (now Batchelors) 1986-; govr St Christopher's Sch Farnham Surrey, churchwarden Seale and Sands Parish Surrey; Liveryman City of London Slrs Co 1964; *Recreations* watercolour painting, dinghy sailing, gardening, walking; *Style—* Robert Burder, Esq; Point House, Lynch Road, Farnham, Surrey GU9 8BT (☎ 0252 713717); Batchelors, The Outer Temple, 222-225 Strand, London WC2R 1BG (☎ 071 353 5134, fax 071 353 2766, telex 262363)

BURDETT, Crispin Peter; s and h of Sir Savile Burdett, 11 Bt; *b* 8 Feb 1967; *m* Aug 1988, Julia Winifred Gresham, *née* Copeland; *Style—* Crispin Burdett, Esq

BURDETT, Noel Henry; OBE (1986); s of Frederick Deane Burdett, of Philippine Islands (bro of Sir Henry Burdett KCB, K CVO, fndr of Nat Pension Fund for Nurses), and Janet Grant, *née* Chavasse (d 1959) (great niece of the writer George Eliot (Mary Ann Evans)); *b* 24 March 1920; *Educ* Christ's Hosp Horsham, Peterhouse Cambridge (BA, MA); *m* 17 May 1941, Rachel Mary, da of Capt William Dobson Womersley, of Westwick, Cambs; 1 s (Francis b 1952), 2 da (Christina b 1955, Jane b 1956); *Career* Capt RA 1940-45, served in N Africa and W Euro (despatches); dir of Richard Haworth & Co Ltd 1951-53, md of Cluett Peabody and Co (UK) Ltd 1959-65 (dir of Euro servs 1954-59, 1965-85), chm Abbeyfield Cambs Soc 1961, vice pres Abbeyfield (Nat) Soc 1985 (chm 1977-85, dir 1972); dep chm The Housing Corpn 1983-86 (bd memb 1980), chm First Cambridge Assured Properties plc 1988, jt chm Abbeyfield International 1988, chm First Stansted Assured Properties plc; *Recreations* painting, reading, travelling, voluntary housing; *Clubs* Savile, Pitt; *Style—* Noel H Burdett, Esq, OBE; Westwick Hall, Oakington, Cambridgeshire CB4 5AR (☎ 0223 234477, office ☎ 0223 232240, fax 0223 235248)

BURDETT, Robert Pierpoint; s of Scott Langshaw Burdett, CBE, MC (d 1961), and Frances Eileen Davis, *née* Workman (d 1976); *b* 23 May 1935; *Educ* Marlborough; *m* 11 April 1959, Robina Clare Lindsay, da of Rear Adm Ralph Lindsay Fisher, CB, DSO, OBE, DSC (d 1988); 2 s (John b 1962, James b 1967), 2 da (Clare b 1961, Helen b 1965); *Career* RN 1953-72, ret as Lt Cdr; admitted slr 1975; in private practice 1975-80, ptnr Dyer Burdett & Co 1980-; *Recreations* sailing; *Clubs* Royal Cruising, RN Sailing Assoc; *Style—* Robert P Burdett, Esq; 64 West St, Havant PO9 1PA (☎ 0705 492472)

BURDETT, Sir Savile Aylmer; 11 Bt (E 1665); s of Sir Henry Aylmer Burdett, 10 Bt, MC (d 1943); *b* 24 Sept 1931; *Educ* Wellington, Imperial Coll London; *m* 1962, June Elizabeth Campbell, o da of late Dr James Mackay Rutherford, of Knowl Hill, Woking, Surrey; 1 s, 1 da (Felicity Susan b 1963); *Heir* s, Crispin Peter Burdett b 8 Feb 1967; *Career* late temporary Sub-Lt RNVR; md: Rapaway Energy Ltd 1977-, Hydraulic Compressors Ltd 1979-; *Style—* Sir Savile Burdett, Bt; Farthings, 35 Park Ave, Solihull, W Midlands

BURDITT, Geoffrey Boulter; s of Col Howard Burditt, MC, TD (d 1963), and Norah Consitt, *née* Boulter, LRAM (d 1972); *b* 2 Feb 1924; *Educ* Kimbolton Sch; *m* 5 April 1951, Cynthia Mary, da of Leslie John Wright (d 1972); 1 s (Philip b 1956), 1 da (Susan b 1954); *Career* served WW II 56 Reconnaissance Regt 1943-47; chm: Rigid Containers Holdings Ltd 1973- (md 1965-73), Market Harborough Building Society 1990- (dir 1974-); FCA; *Recreations* music, bowls; *Clubs* Rotary; *Style—* Geoffrey B Burditt, Esq; Steeping House, Glendon, Kettering, Northants NN14 1QE (☎ 0536 712255); Rigid Containers Holdings Ltd, Rushton Road, Desborough, Kettering

BURDON, Prof Roy Hunter; s of Ian Murray Burdon (d 1956), and Rose Carnegie Burdon (d 1962); *b* 27 April 1938; *Educ* Glasgow Acad, Univ of St Andrews (BSc), Univ of Glasgow (PhD); *m* 4 Sept 1962, Margery Grace; 2 s (Ian J, Keith A); *Career* Univ of Glasgow: asst lectr 1959-63, lectr 1964-68, sr lectr 1968-74, reader in biochemistry 1974-77, titular prof in biochemistry 1977-89; post doctorate and res fell Univ of NY 1963-64, guest prof of microbiology Polytechnical Univ of Denmark Copenhagen 1977-78, prof of molecular biology Univ of Strathclyde 1985- (chm Dept of Bioscience and Biochemistry 1986-88), vice chm Br Coordinating Ctee Biotechnol 1990, The Biochemical Soc: hon meetings sec 1981-85, hon gen sec 1985-89, chm 1989; govr W of Scotland Coll of Agric; FIBiol 1987, FRSE 1975; *Books* RNA Biosynthesis (1976), Molecular Biology of DNA Methylation (1985); *Recreations* painting, golf, clarinet/saxophone playing; *Style—* Prof Roy Burdon; 144 Mugdock Rd, Milngavie, Glasgow G62 8NP (☎ 041 956 1689); Dept of Bioscience & Biotechnology, Todd Centre, University of Strathclyde, Glasgow G4 0HR (☎ 041 552 4400 ext 3536)

BURDON-COOPER, Alan Ruthven; s of Sqdn-Ldr Ruthven Hayne Burdon-Cooper (d 1970), of Radlett, and Anna Kathleen Beverley, *née* Farquharson; *b* 27 June 1942; *Educ* Oundle, Emmanuel Coll Cambridge (MA, LLB); *m* 2 Sept 1967, Virginia Louise, da of Archibald George Mobsby (d 1989), of Radlett; 1 s (John b 1968), 1 da (Sarah b 1970); *Career* admitted slr 1968; sr ptnr Collyer-Bristow 1985-; life memb Cambridge Union; Liveryman Worshipful Co of Dyers; memb Law Soc 1968; *Recreations* sport, music, gardening, philately; *Style—* Alan Burdon-Cooper, Esq; 30 Newlands Ave, Radlett, Herts (☎ 09276 5719); 4 Bedford Row, London WC1R 4DF (☎ 071 242 7363, fax 071 405 0555, telex 21615)

BURDUS, (Julia) Ann; da of Gladstone Beaty (d 1966), of Alnwick, Northumberland, and Julia Wilhamena Charlton, *née* Booth (d 1988); *b* 4 Sept 1933; *Educ* Univ of Durham (BA); *m* 1, 1956 (m dis 1961), William Ramsay Burdus; m 2, 11 June 1981, Ian Buchanan Robertson; *Career* clinical psychologist 1956-60, res exec Mather & Crowther 1961-67, res dir Garland Compton (later Compton Partners) 1967-71, res dir McCann Erickson 1971-75, vice chm McCann UK 1975-77, sr vice pres McCann International 1977-79, chm McCann & Co 1979-81, dir strategic planning Interpublic Group of Cos 1981-83, dir AGB Research plc 1983-89, sr vice pres mktg and communications Olympia & York Canary Wharf Ltd 1989-; chm Advertising Assoc 1980-81; memb: NEDC 1984-88, Top Salaries Review Bd 1990-; *Recreations* home building; *Style—* Miss Ann Burdus; Olympia & York, 10 Great George Street, London SW1P 3AE (☎ 071 222 8878, fax 071 233 1110)

BURFORD, Earl of; Charles Francis Topham de Vere Beauclerk; s and h of 14 Duke of St Albans, *qv*; *b* 22 Feb 1965; *Educ* Sherborne, Hertford Coll Oxford; *Career* apptd Brig-Gen of Louisiana by Governor Edwin Edwards 1986; chm and fndr De Vere Soc, tstee Shakespearian Authorship Tst, apptd a vice-chm The Royal Stuart Soc 1989; Liveryman Worshipful Co of Drapers 1990; *Clubs* Brooks's; *Style—* Earl of Burford; c/o Viscount Exmouth, Canonteign House, nr Exeter, Devon EX6 7RH

BURFORD, Jeremy Michael Joseph; QC (1987); s of Major Alexander Joseph Burford, and Constance Grace Arlene, *née* Blakeley; *b* 3 June 1942; *Educ* Rondebosch Boys HS S Africa, Diocesan Coll S Africa, Univ of Cape Town (BA), Emmanuel Coll Cambridge (MA, LLB), Harvard Law Sch (LLM); *Career* called to the Bar Inner Temple 1968; *Style—* Jeremy Burford, Esq, QC; 2 Mitre Court Building, Temple, London EC4 (☎ 071 583 1355)

BURFORD, Dr Robert John; s of Robert John Burford, of Welham Green, Herts, and Grace Violet, *née* Piacentini; *b* 29 Jan 1941; *Educ* East Barnet GS, King's Coll London (BSc, PhD); *m* 2 March 1968, (Stephanie) Kaye, da of Ernest James Woodley, of Rugby, Warwicks; 2 s (David b 1970, Paul b 1972), 1 da (Tracey b 1969); *Career* OR analyst NCB 1965-66, conslt GPS Sciences Ltd 1966-71, divnl dir Software Sciences Ltd 1980-82 (princ conslt 1971-80), dir ASYST Systems Conslts Ltd 1982-83, sr mangr Perkin-Elmer Data Systems 1983-85, tech dir Data Logic Ltd 1985-; MBCS 1974, MORS 1968; *Recreations* American square and round dancing, travelling; *Style—* Dr Robert J Burford; 8 Winding Wood Drive, Camberley, Surrey GU15 1ER (☎ 0276 28397); Data Logic Ltd, Queens House, Greenhill Way, Harrow, Middx HA1 1YR (☎ 081 863 0383, fax 081 861 2010)

BURG, Gisela Elisabeth; Hon CBE (1987); da of Oberstudiendirektor Friedrich Schlüsselburg, of Langen, Germany, and Gerda Schlusselburg; *b* 12 Oct 1939; *Educ* Gymnasium Philippinum Weilburg Germany, Ladies' Coll Wetzlar Germany; *Career* fndr and md Expotus Ltd; chm Fedn of Br Audio 1976-78 (vice-pres 1978-82); memb: NEDO Electronic SWP 1979-82, Br Overseas Trade Bd 1982-87; named Times/ Clicquot Businesswoman of the Year 1981; *Recreations* golf, horseracing; *Style—* Ms Gisela Burg; 82 Kensington Heights, Campden Hill Rd, London W8 7BD; Expotus Ltd, 95 Grays Inn Rd, London WC1 8TX (☎ 071 405 9665)

BURGE, Dr (Peter) Sherwood; s of Graham Mowbray Burge (d 1974), of Shiplake, and Anne Elizabeth, *née* Batt; *b* 8 July 1944; *Educ* Lancing, Royal Free Hosp Sch of Med, London Sch of Hygiene & Tropical Med (MB BS, MSc, MD); *m* 18 Aug 1968, Dr Anne Willard, da of Canon James Stanley Willard (d 1988) of Holland-on-Sea, Essex; 2 s (Cedd b 1974, Chad b 1977); *Career* lectr in Dept of Clinical Immunology Cardiothoracic Inst London 1976-80, conslt physician Solihull Hosp 1980-, conslt chest physician East Birmingham Health Authy 1980-, dir Occupational Lung Disease Unit Birmingham 1980-; numerous sci pubns on: occupational lung diseases, indoor air quality and sick building syndrome, asthma and bronchitis; Br rep and cncl memb Euro Respiratory Soc, temporary advsr to WHO on indoor air quality; MRCS 1969, MFOM 1984, FRCP 1985; *Recreations* punting, racing, skiing, brass rubbing, playing the recorder; *Style—* Dr Sherwood Burge; Solihull Hospital, Lode Lane, Solihull, West Midlands B91 2JL (☎ 021 711 4455, fax 021 766 6611)

BURGE, Stuart; CBE (1974); s of Henry Ormsby Burge (d 1968), and Kathleen, *née* Haig; *b* 15 Jan 1918; *Educ* Felsted; *m* 22 Dec 1949, Josephine, da of Alan Parker (d 1965); 3 s (Stephen, Nicholas, Matthew), 2 da (Lucy, Emma); *Career* artistic dir: Nottingham Playhouse 1968-73, Royal Court 1978-81; assoc Stratford ONT 1964; recent screen: Naming the Names, The Rainbow, Circles of Deceit; recent theatre: The Black Prince, Sunsets and Glories; memb bd English Stage Co Royal Court; *Clubs* Garrick; *Style—* Stuart Burge, Esq, CBE; Harriet Cruickshank, 97 Old South Lambeth Rd, London SW8 1XU (☎ 081 735 2933)

BURGEN, Sir Arnold Stanley Vincent; s of late Peter Burgen, and Elizabeth, *née* Wolfers; *b* 20 March 1922; *Educ* Christ's Coll Finchley, Univ of London; *m* 1946, Judith, da of Frederick Browne; 2 s, 1 da; *Career* med scientist, dir Nat Inst Med Res 1971-82, master Darwin Coll Cambridge 1982-89; pres Academia Europaea 1988-; FRS; kt 1976; *Recreations* sculpture, music; *Style—* Sir Arnold Burgen, FRS; 2 Stukeley Close, Cambridge CB3 9LT (☎ 0223 323014)

BURGESS, Dr Anthony; s of Joseph Wilson (d 1938), of Manchester, and Elizabeth, *née* Burgess (d 1918); *b* 25 Feb 1917; *Educ* Xaverian Coll Manchester, Univ of Manchester (BA); *m* 1, 12 Jan 1942, Llewela Isherwood (d 1968), da of Maj Edward Jones, MC (d 1963), of Leicester; 1 s (Paolo Andrea b 9 Aug 1964); m 2, 9 Oct 1968, Liliana Macellaro, da of Contessa Lucrezia Maria Pasi Piani della Pergola; *Career* RAMC 1940-42, warrant offr Army Educnl Corps 1942-46; lectr: Univ of Birmingham 1946-49, Bamber Bridge Trg Coll 1949-51; master Banbury GS 1951-54, educn offr Malaya and Borneo 1954-59, prof Princeton Univ 1969-70, distinguished prof City Coll of NY 1971-73; Hon DLitt Univ of Manchester 1979, Hon LLD Univ of Birmingham 1986; FRSL 1964, memb ASCAP 1970; Foreign Orders: Commandeur des Arts et des Lettres 1983, Commandeur de Merite Cultural Monaco 1982; *Books* incl: Time for a Tiger (1956), The Enemy in the Blanket (1958), The Worm and The Ring (1961), A Clockwork Orange (1961, filmed 1971), The Wanting Seed (1962), Nothing Like The Sun (1964), A Shorter Finnegan's Wake, Enderby Outside (1968), Shakespeare (1970), Joysprice (1973), The Clockwork Testament (1974), Moses (1976), Ernest Hemingway and His World (1978), The Land Where the Ice Cream Grows (1979), Enderby's Dark Lady (1984), The Kingdom of the Wicked (1985), Little Wilson and Big God (autobiog 1987); translation of stage plays incl: Cyrano de Bergerac (1971), Oedipus the King (1973); as Joseph Kell: One Hand Clapping (1961), Inside Mr Enderby (1963); as John Burgess Wilson: English Literature: A Survey for Students (1958); TV Scripts: Moses the Lawgiver (1977), Jesus of Nazareth (1977), Blooms of Dublin (radio musical 1982); contrib to: Observer, Spectator, Listener, Queen, Times Literary Supplement, Playboy, Le Monde; *Recreations* music, philosophy, motoring; *Clubs* Monaco Automobile; *Style—* Dr Anthony Burgess; 44 Rue Grimaldi, Monaco; 63 Via Cantonale, Savosa, Switzerland

BURGESS, Anthony Jack; s of late Edgar Jack Burgess, and late Emma Marie, *née* Shafe; *b* 27 June 1925; *Educ* Lewes Co GS, Hertford Coll Oxford (MA); *m* 24 Sept 1949, Barbara Evelyn, da of late Bertram Tofts; 3 s (Quentin b 1950, Rupert b 1958, Jeremy b 1963), 2 da (Charlotte b 1954, Emma b 1961); *Career* Capt RA 1943-48; Notary Public and sr ptnr Cheeswright Murly & Co 1958, memb Baltic Exchange 1987, cncllr Colchester Borough Cncl 1962-65; Freeman Worshipful Co of Scriveners 1958 (Master 1969-70); *Recreations* reading, history, music, theatre (Shakespeare), wine, golf; *Style—* Anthony Burgess, Esq; 33 Riverside Court, Nine Elms Lane, London SW8; Henpools House, Lower Littleworth, Stroud, Gloucestershire; Los Limoneros, Mijas Costa, Malaga, Spain; Cheeswright, Murly & Co, Baltic Exchange Chambers, 24 St Mary Axe, London EC4 (☎ 071 623 9477, fax 071 623 5428, car 0860 330 4 330 481, telex 883 806)

BURGESS, Anthony Reginald Frank (Tony); CVO (1983); *b* 27 Jan 1932; *Educ* Ealing GS, Univ Coll London (BSc); *m* 21 May 1960, Carlyn, da of Harold Samuel Shawyer (d 1942); 1 s (Paul b 1971); *Career* Nat Serv 1953-55 cmmnd RAOC, parachutist, TA 16 Airborne Div 1955-57; journalist 1955-62, Euro Community Civil Serv 1962-65; HM Dip Serv 1966-90: first sec Euro Econ Orgn Dept FCO 1966-67, first sec (Political) Dhaka 1967-69, first sec SE Asia Dept FCO 1970-72, first sec (Econ) Ottawa 1972-76, head of Chancery HM Consul Bogota 1976-79, first sec Rhodesia Dept FCO 1979-80, asst hd of Info Dept FCO 1980-82, dep high cmmr Dhaka 1982-86, (cnsllr) hd of Chancery Havana 1986-90; business conslt specialising in S Asia and Latin America 1990-; *Books* The Common Market and the Treaty of Rome Explained (jtly, 1967); *Recreations* travel, photography, shooting, scuba diving; *Clubs* Brooks's; *Style—* Tony Burgess, Esq, CVO; c/o Barclays Bank plc, 23 St James's St, London SW1A 1HE

BURGESS, (Dilys) Averil; da of David Evans, of Berthlwyd, Nantmor, Nantgwynant, Gwynedd, and Dorothy, *née* Owen; *b* 8 July 1938; *Educ* Ashby de la Zouch Girls' GS

Leics, Queen Mary Coll London (BA); *m* 5 Dec 1959 (m dis 1973), Clifford Charles Antony Burgess, s of Sidney Burgess, of Boreham Wood, Herts; *Career* Fulham Co Sch 1965-69, head of history and second mistress Wimbledon HS GPDST 1969-74, headmistress South Hampstead HS GPDST 1975-; memb: Bursaries Mgmnt Ctee GPDST 1979-86, Exec Ctee GS Assoc 1984- (chm Edcn Sub Ctee 1986-87, pres 1988-89); govr Central Sch of Speech and Drama; memb: Secdy Heads Assoc, GS Assoc 1975, Cncl For Accreditation of Teacher Educn; chm Ind Schs Jt Cncl Policy Gp; *Recreations* reading, mountain walking, cross-country skiing; *Style—* Mrs Averil Burgess; South Hampstead High School, 3 Maresfield Gardens, London NW3 5SS (☎ 071 435 2899)

BURGESS, Claude Bramall; CMG (1958), OBE (1954); s of George Herbert Burgess (d 1956), of Weaverham, Cheshire, and Martha Elizabeth, *née* Gilbert (d 1966); *b* 25 Feb 1910; *Educ* Epworth Coll, Ch Ch Oxford (MA); *m* 1, 1952 (m dis 1965), Margaret Joan, da of Reginald Charles Webb; 1 s (Tobias); *m* 2, 1969, Linda Nettleton, da of William Grothier Beilby (d 1973), of New York, USA; *Career* cmmnd RA 1940 (POW 1941-45), demobbed as Lt-Col 1946; Colonial Office 1946-48; IDC 1951; govt posts in Hong Kong 1952-57, colonial sec (and actg govr on various occasions) Hong Kong 1958-63; head of Co-ordination and Devpt Dept Euro Free Trade Assoc Geneva 1964-73, min for Hong Kong Commercial Rels with Euro Communities and Memb States Br Embassy Brussels 1974-82; *Style—* Claude Burgess, Esq, CMG, OBE; 75 Chester Row, London SW1W 8JL (☎ 071 730 8758)

BURGESS, Dr Colin Gordon; s of Ernest Arthur Walter Burgess (d 1976), of Henfield, Sussex, and Evie, *née* Evans (d 1983); *b* 2 Feb 1940; *Educ* Epsom Coll, South Bank Poly (BSc, PhD); *m* 10 Aug 1963, Rosalind Ann, da of Sydney George Gray (d 1964), of 6 Springhead Rd, North Fleet, Kent; 1 s (Alastair Mark b 5 May 1973), 1 da (Claire Louise b 11 Dec 1969); *Career* tech mangr Castrol Plastics Ltd 1966-69, export mangr Cray Valley Products (Coates Inks Ltd) 1969-72, tech dir Swan Plastics 1972-76, md Kent Chemical Co 1980- (commercial and tech dir 1977-80), chm Ian Young Aerosols Ltd 1988; Freeman City of London 1981, Liveryman Worshipful Co of Horners 1981; FRSC, MPI, FInstD; *Style—* Dr Colin Burgess; Kent Chemical Co, George House, Bridewell Lane, Tenterden, Kent TN3 9DL (☎ 05806 4244, fax 05806 5652, telex 95508)

BURGESS, David Charles William; s of Leonard Cecil Burgess (d 1970), and Comfort, *née* Horler; *b* 25 Sept 1947; *Educ* Ermysted GS Skipton Yorks, St Catharine's Coll Cambridge (MA); *m* 4 July 1987, Youdon, *née* Lhamo; 1 s (Tenzin b 21 May 1981), 2 da (Dechen b 21 June 1978, Kusang b 7 Aug 1985); *Career* admitted slr 1972, ptnr Winstanley-Burgess 1975; *Style—* David Burgess, Esq; Winstanley-Burgess, 378 City Rd, London EC1V 2QA (☎ 071 278 7911, fax 071 833 2135)

BURGESS, Rev David John; s of Albert Burgess, of the Pinfold, Ailsworth, Cambs, and Mary, *née* Kelsey; *b* 4 Aug 1939; *Educ* The King's Sch Peterborough, Trinity Hall Cambridge (MA), Cuddesdon Theol Coll Oxford, Halki Studentship Istanbul; *m* 17 Feb 1976, Katherine Lousie, da of Lindsay Costeloe (d 1978); 1 s ((Patrick) Rollo Lindsay b 25 May 1978), 1 da (Frances Mary (Fanny) b 26 July 1981); *Career* curate All Saints Maidstone 1965-66; Univ Coll Oxford: asst chaplain 1966, chaplain and fell 1969, domestic bursar 1971; canon Windsor 1978-87, treas Coll of St George, guild vicar St Lawrence Jewry Next Guildhall 1987; Chaplain to HM the Queen 1987; govr Pangbourne Coll; Freeman City of London; hon chaplain to Worshipful Cos of: Haberdashers, Loriners, Distillers, Insurers, Constructors, Actuaries, Archtects, Surveyors; hon Fell Inst of Clerks of Works; *Books* Signs of Faith, Hope, and Love (contrib, 1988); *Recreations* The Aula, The Omar Khayyam; *Style—* The Rev David Burgess; The Vicarage, St Lawrence Jewry Next Guildhall, London EC2V 5AA (☎ 071 600 9478)

BURGESS, Gen Sir Edward Arthur; KCB (1982), OBE (1972); s of Edward Burgess and Alice Burgess; *b* 30 Sept 1927; *Educ* All Saints Sch Bloxham, Lincoln Coll Oxford, RMA Sandhurst; *m* 1954, Jean Angelique Leslie Henderson; 1 s, 1 da; *Career* cmmnd 1948 RA, served BAOR, Far East and M East, GSO 1 Staff Coll 1968-70, CO 25 Light Regt RA 1970-72, Cdr RA 4 Div 1972-74; dir: Army Recruiting 1975-77, Combat Devpt 1977-79; GOC Artillery Div 1979-82, Cdr UK FD Army and Inspr Gen TA 1982-84, Col Cmdt RA 1982-, Dep Supreme Allied Cdr Europe 1984-87; ADC Gen 1985-87; Gentleman Usher to the Sword of State 1988-; pres: Army Football Assoc 1982-88, Royal Br Legion 1987-; *Recreations* sailing, fishing, music, wines; *Clubs* Army & Navy; *Style—* Gen Sir Edward Burgess, KCB, OBE; c/o Lloyds Bank, Haslemere, Surrey

BURGESS, Rear Adm John; CB (1987), LVO (1975); s of Albert Burgess (d 1957), of Styvechale, Coventry, and Winifred, *née* Evans; *b* 13 July 1929; *Educ* RNEC, advanced engrg RNC Greenwich; *m* 21 June 1952, Avis, da of William Johnson-Morgan (d 1953), of Coventry; 2 da (Sara b 14 Jan 1958, Jenny (Mrs Andersson) 6 Aug 1960; *Career* RN Serv 1945-; HMS: Aisne, Maidstone, Theseus, Implacable, Cumberland, Caprice; commnd 1952, lectr in Thermodynamic RNEC 1962-65, HMS Victorious, appt Cdr 1968, nuclear design and manufacture Rolls Royce 1968-70, naval staff Washington DC 1970-72, Royal Yacht Britannia 1972-75, head Forward Design Gp Ship Dept 1975-77, appt Capt 1976, naval asst to controller RN 1977-79, HMS Defiance 1979-81, OC HMS Sultan 1981-83, appt Adm 1983, md HM Docky Rosyth 1984-87; dir Rolls Royce 1987-: special projects, business devpt; contrib various papers for professional socs and periodicals; memb: naval charities, local church socs, conservation socs; Hon Freeman New Orleans 1974; CEng, FIMechE, FIMarE; *Recreations* sailing, golf, music, theatre; *Style—* Rear Adm John Burgess, CB, LVO; Rolls Royce and Associates Ltd, Raynesway, Derby (☎ 0332 661461)

BURGESS, Michael John Clement; s of David Clement Burgess (d 1966), and Dr Ethne Nannette Moira Barnwall, *née* Ryan, of Kingston Upon Thames; *b* 31 March 1946; *Educ* Beaumont Coll Old Windsor Berks, King's Coll London; *m* 31 July 1971, Catherine Vivian, da of Vivian John Du Veluz Gout, of Mulhausen, W Germany; 1 s (Peter b 1980), 2 da (Alexandra b 1974, Nicola b 1976); *Career* admitted slr 1970, conslt McNamara Ryan Weybridge 1986- (ptnr 1972-86), coroner Surrey 1986- (asst dep coroner 1979-86); pres West Surrey Law Soc 1985-86 (hon treas 1979-84), memb Catholic Union 1974-, chm fin ctee and parish cncl memb St Francis de Sales RC Church Hampton, helper (ex gp ldr and regnl chm) Handicapped Children's Pilgrimage Tst, advsr to several local charities and trusts; Freeman: City of London, Worshipful Co of Feltmakers 1967; memb: Law Soc 1970, Coroner's Soc; *Recreations* reading, art, music, gardening; *Clubs* Surrey Law; *Style—* Michael Burgess, Esq; c/o McNamara Ryan, Ashburton House, 3 Monument Green, Wembridge, Surrey KT13 8QR (☎ 0932 846041, fax 0932 857709)

BURGESS, Paul Graham; s of James Cooke Burgess (d 1987), and Marian, *née* Ellison (d 1987); *b* 5 May 1953; *Educ* Wallasey GS; *m* 11 Oct 1975, Christine Anne, da of Derek Sidney Carey, of 6 Redcar Rd, Wallasey, Wirral; 2 s (Graham John b 1983, Jonathan Paul b 1988), 1 da (Anne Marie b 1980); *Career* ACA 1979, sr ptnr and fndr of Paul G Burgess & Co 1982; dir: Life Cycles (Biorhythms) Ltd 1982-, Rinksport plc 1985-, Rinksport (Wirral) Ltd 1985-, Bontrane Ltd 1988-, BKN International Ltd 1988-; *Recreations* sailing; *Style—* Paul G Burgess, Esq; 259 Wallasey Village, Wallasey, Wirral L45 3LR (☎ 051 630 6404, fax 051 691 2846)

BURGESS, (Ian) Peter; s of Samuel Richard Burgess (d 1985), and Gladys Eugenie, *née* Blake; *b* 27 Aug 1923; *Educ* Ellesmere Coll; *m* 22 May 1948, Roberta Helen, da of Mark Stott (d 1970); 2 da (Eugenie b 1949, Victoria b 1952); *Career* RN 1942-45; gen cmmr of Income Tax 1971, former chm McCartneys Livestock Auctioneers 1977; surveyor and farmer; *Recreations* shooting; *Style—* Peter Burgess, Esq; Whitcliffe Lodge, Ludlow, Shropshire; 19 Britannia House, Marina Bay, Gibraltar; 25 Corve St, Ludlow (☎ 0584 872659)

BURGESS, (Robert Lawie Frederick) Robin; s of Sir John Burgess (d 1987), of Carlisle, and Lady Burgess, *née* Gilleron; *b* 31 Jan 1951; *Educ* Trinity Coll Glenalmond; *m* 20 Sept 1986, Alexandra Rosemary, da of W A Twiston-Davies, of Herefordshire; *Career* 2 Lt The Kings Royal Border Regt 1969-72; md Cumbrian Newspapers Gp Ltd 1985-; dir: Cumberland and Westmorland Herald Printing Co Ltd 1985-, Border TV plc 1987-; *Clubs* Army and Navy, Pall Mall, Border and County (Carlisle); *Style—* R L F Burgess, Esq; Cumbrian Newspapers Gp Ltd, Dalston Rd, Carlisle, Cumbria CA2 5UA (☎ 0228 23488)

BURGESS, Sydney; s of Charles Ernest Burgess (d 1935), and Dorothy Iris Burgess; *b* 14 Oct 1926; *Educ* Wrangle Co Sch, Kings Sch Peterborough; *m* 7 June 1947, Christine Rose, da of James Harper (d 1948), of Hubberts Bridge, Boston, Lincolnshire; 1 s (Maxwell b 1948); *Career* memb Farm Animal Welfare Cncl 1979-; md Buitelaar Gp of Cos 1968; Queens Award for Exports 1978; dir: Frans Buitelaar Ltd and various subsidiary companies, Bands of Perth Ltd, Lincolnshire Rabbits Ltd, Sydney Burgess & Ptnrs Ltd, Sydney Burgess (Life & Pensions) Ltd, Community Guarantee Insur Co Ltd (Guernsey), GB Biomedical Prods Ltd, Societie Transformation Viandes (Tunis), Boston United FC Ltd, Br Meat Exporters Consortium Ltd, Bury St Edmunds Meat Co Ltd, Bonecosse Viande Ltd, Colelle Skin Care Products Ltd, Snacks and Treats Ltd, Karim SA (Panama); *Recreations* all sports; *Clubs* Co Farmers (Boston), Wig and Pen; *Style—* Sydney Burgess, Esq; Beck Lodge, Wyberton Fen, Boston, Lincs (☎ 0205 363104); Buitelaar Gp of Companies, Wyberton Fen; Boston, Lincs (☎ 0205 52020, car ☎ 0860 413 574)

BURGH, 7 Baron (E 1529); Alexander Peter Willoughby Leith; s of 6 Baron (d 1959); *b* 20 March 1935; *Educ* Harrow, Magdalene Coll Cambridge; *m* 29 Aug 1957, Anita Lorna, da of Frederick Charles Eldridge, of Gillingham, Kent; 2 s, 1 da; *Heir* s, Hon Gregory Leith; *Career* formerly RAF Pilot Offr; *Style—* The Rt Hon The Lord Burgh; c/o The Hon Gregory Leith, 28 High Street, Nettlebed, Henley-on- Thames, Oxon

BURGH, Sir John Charles; KCMG (1981), CB (1975); *b* 9 Dec 1925; *Educ* Friends' Sch Sibford, LSE; *m* 1957, Ann Sturge; 2 da; *Career* under sec Employment Dept 1968-71 (formerly with BOT, Colonial Office, DEA), dep chm Community Rels Cmmn 1971-72; dep sec: CPRS 1972-74, Prices and Consumer Protection 1974-79, Dept of Trade 1979-80, dir gen Br Cncl 1980-87, pres Trinity Coll Oxford 1987-; chm: Associated Bd The Royal Sch of Music 1987-, Int Student House 1987-90; dir Eng Shakespeare Co 1989-; sec: Nat Opera Coordinating Ctee 1972-, Opera Ctee Royal Opera House Covent Garden 1972-80; chm of govrs LSE 1985-87 (govr 1980-, hon fell 1982), exec memb Political and Econ Planning 1970-78; memb cncl: Policy Studies Inst 1978-85, VSO 1980-87, RSA 1982-86; FRSA; Hon LLD Bath, Hon RNCM; *Style—* Sir John Burgh, KCMG, CB; Trinity College, Oxford OX1 3BH (☎ 0865 279900)

BURGHERSH, Lord; Anthony David Francis Henry Fane; s and h of 15 Earl of Westmorland, KCVO; *b* 1 Aug 1951; *Educ* Eton; *m* 1985, Mrs Caroline E Fairey, da of Keon Hughes; 1 da (Daisy Caroline b 18 Jan 1989); *Career* sports conslt; life pres St Moritz Sporting Club, govr Guild of Veteran Pilots and Racing Drivers; *Style—* Lord Burghersh; 10 Peterborough Villas, London SW6

BURGHES, Prof David Noel; s of Edmund Noel Burghes (d 1944), and Lilian Mary, *née* Luckhurst; *b* 21 March 1944; *Educ* Christ's Coll Finchley, Univ of Sheffield (BSc, PhD); *m* 21 Sept 1968, Jennifer Jean, da of Dr Donald Harry Smith (d 1971); 4 s (Andrew b 1970, Christopher b 1972, Jamie b 1974, Timothy b 1975); *Career* asst lectr Dept of Applied Mathematics Univ of Sheffield 1970-71 (jr res fell 1968-70), lectr Sch of Mathematics Univ of Newcastle 1972-75, dir Cranfield Centre for Teacher Servs Cranfield Inst of Technol 1980-81 (lectr 1975-79), dir Centre for Innovation in Mathematics Teaching Univ of Exeter 1986- (prof of educn 1981-); author and co-author of over twenty books on mathematics and educn mathematics dir Spode Group 1980-; chm Indust and Educn Maths Ctee DTI 1985-88, founding ed jl Teaching Mathematics and its Applications 1985-; FIMA 1970; *Recreations* reading train timetables, travelling; *Style—* Prof David Burghes; Centre for Innovation in Mathematics Teaching, Exeter University, Exeter, Devon (☎ 0392 217113, 0392 264772)

BURGHLEY, Lord; Anthony John Cecil; s and h of 8 Marquess of Exeter; *b* 9 Aug 1970; *Style—* Lord Burghley; 100 Mile House, PO Box 8, Br Columbia V0K 2E0, Canada (☎ 0101 604 395 2767)

BURGIN, Adrian Gwyn John; s of Arthur Carver Burgin (d 1985), of Lincs, and Anne Mary, *née* Hassall; *b* 23 Sept 1950; *Educ* St James Sch Peterborough; *m* 8 Sept 1973, Susan Georgina, da of George Falconer McLean (d 1980), of Lincs; 2 s (John b 1979, Thomas b 1982), 1 da (Holly b 1981); *Career* CA; princ Burgin and Co; treas Stamford Festival Assoc Ltd 1983; FICA; *Recreations* mountaineering, cricket, literature; *Clubs* Daniel Lamberts, Lyke Wake, Motley Crew Cricket; *Style—* Adrian Burgin, Esq; The Warden's House, 4 Broad St, Stamford, Lincs (☎ 0780 51315)

BURGIN, Patrick Leslie; s of The Rt Hon Edward Leslie Burgin, MP the first Min of Supply (d 1945), of South Beds, and Dorothy Theresa, *née* Cooper (d 1975); *b* 28 Nov 1919; *Educ* St George's Sch Harpenden, Le Rosey Rolle Gstaad Switzerland, Gonville & Caius Coll Cambridge; *m* 27 April 1950, Elizabeth Lavender, da of Benjamin John Uren (d 1972), of St Ives, Cornwall; 1 s (Mark b 1954), 2 da (Caroline b 1952, Rosemary b 1957); *Career* WWII joined The Beds & Herts (Pte) 1940, Northamptonshire Regt (2/Lt) 1941, Intelligence Sch Karachi India (Capt Instructor) 1941-42, GIII(I) Lucknow Dist HQ 1943, GIII(I) Army HQ New Delhi (major in security intelligence planning s 1943, Burma E Gp 1944 45 (despatches), repatriated UK GII(I) Scottish Cmd HQ Edinburgh until June 1946; admitted slr, ptnr Denton Hall & Burgin 1948; chm Rentokil Gp plc 1969-81 (dir 1953-85), dir Assoc Br Picture Corp 1964-72, chm Dentsply Ltd (formerly Amalgamated Dental Co) 1970-85, chm Val de Travers Asphalte Ltd (alternate dir Iraq, Basrah, Mosul & Petrol Cos) 1970-73; dir: Total Oil Holdings Ltd, Total Oil Marine plc, Total Oil Great Britain Ltd; sr ptnr Dental Hall and Burgin (now Denton Hall Burgin & Warrens) 19 conslt; chm Govrs St George's Sch Harpenden; memb: Herts County Cncl 1966-76, Law Soc 1948; Order of Dannebrog Denmark 1967, Legion d'Honneur France 1988; *Recreations* hunting, gardening, skiing, reading; *Clubs* Oriental, RAC; *Style—* Patrick Burgin, Esq; 10 Park Ave South, Harpenden, Herts (☎ 058 27 2035); Denton Hall Burgin & Warrens, 5 Chancery Lane, Clifford's Inn, London EC4A 1BU (☎ 071 242 1212, fax 071 404 0087, telex 263567

BURGIN, Peter Brinton; s of George Burgin, of Huddersfield; *b* 3 Aug 1934; *Educ* Holme Valley GS Holmfirth; *m* 1960, Jean, da of Donovan Hartshorne, of Tamerton Foliat; 1 s, 1 da; *Career* mktg dir: Crittall Windows 1974-78, Dow-Mac Concrete 1985-88; dir and sec Dow-Mac Concrete 1978-81, md Lion Foundry Co Ltd 1981-85; practice mangr Landscape Design Assocs 1988-; ACMA, MBCS, MCIM; *Recreations* golf, gardening; *Style—* Peter Burgin, Esq; 4 Briar Walk, Bourne, Lincs PE10 9TG

(☎ 0778 425 361); Landscape Design Associate, 17 Minster Precincts, Peterborough PE1 1XX (☎ 0733 310471)

BURGNER, Thomas Ulric; s of John Henry Burgner (d 1974), of London, and Doerte, *née* Wolf; *b* 6 March 1932; *Educ* Haberdashers' Aske's Hampstead, St Catharine's Coll Cambridge (BA, MA); *m* 5 June 1958, Marion; 2 s (David Paul b 1964, Steven Alexander b 1968); *Career* Flying Offr RAF 1953-55; Nat Cncl Bd 1955-61, Assoc of Chemical and Allied Employers 1961-64, Dept of Econ Affrs 1965-69, head Gen Aid Div HM Treasy 1974-76 (head Exchange Control 1972-74), sec NEDC 1976-80, head Indust, Agric and Employment Gp 1984-89 (head Pub Enterprises Gp 1980-84), sec Ctee of Vice Chllrs and Princs of Univs of UK 1989-; FRSA 1990; *Style—* Thomas Burgner, Esq; CVCP, 29 Tavistock Square, London WC1H 9EZ (☎ 071 387 9231)

BURGON, Geoffrey Alan; s of Alan Wybert Burgon (d 1983), and Ada Vera Isom; Huguenot descent; *b* 15 July 1941; *Educ* Pewley Sch Guildford, Guildhall Sch of Music and Drama; *m* 1963 (m dis), Janice Elizabeth, da of Frank Garwood; 1 s (Matthew b 1967), 1 da (Hannah b 1965); *Career* composer and conductor; dramatic works include: Joan of Arc 1970, Orpheus 1982, Hard Times 1990; orchestral music includes: Concerto for String Orchestra 1963, Gending 1968; orchestral music with voices includes Requiem 1976, The World Again 1983, Revelations 1984, Mass 1984, Title Divine 1986; ballet music includes: The Golden Fish 1964, Running Figures 1975, Songs Lamentations and Praises 1979, The Trials of Prometheus 1988; choral music includes: Three Elegies 1964, Short Mass 1965, Two Hymns to Mary 1967, Mai Hamama 1970, A Prayer to the Trinity 1972, The Fire of Heaven 1973, Noche Oscura 1974, Dos Coros 1975, This World From 1974, Laudate Dominum 1980, But Have Been Found Again 1983, The Song of the Creatures 1987; chamber music includes: Gloria 1973, Six Studies 1980; chamber music with voices includes: Five Sonnets of John Donne 1967, Worldës Blissë 1971, Lunar Beauty 1986; film and tv scores include: The Changeling 1973, Dr Who and the Terror of the Zygons 1975, Monty Python's Life of Brian 1979, Tinker Tailor Soldier Spy 1979, The Dogs of War 1980, Brideshead Revisited 1981, Turtle Diary 1985, The Death of the Heart 1985, Bleak House 1986, The Chronicles of Narnia 1988, Children of the North 1990; *Recreations* cricket, jazz, wasting money on Bristol cars; *Style—* Geoffrey Burgon, Esq; 8-9 Frith St, London W1V 5TZ (☎ 071 434 0066)

BURGOYNE, Rev Geoffrey; s of Edward Godfrey Burgoyne (d 1968), and Florence Mildred, *née* Lloyd (d 1968); *b* 18 Nov 1927; *Educ* UC of Wales Aberystwyth (BA), St Michael's Coll Llandaff; *Career* asst priest: Aberavon 1951-55, Ynyshir 1955-63; vicar Bockleton with Leysters and Hatfield 1963-70, housemaster The Bishops Bluecoat School Hereford 1970-, licensed under seal of Bishop of Hereford; *Recreations* game fishing, pottery; *Style—* The Rev Geoffrey Burgoyne; Lawnswood, Tupsley, Hereford HR1 1UT (☎ 0432 268860); Bluecoat School, Hereford (☎ 0432 57481, ext 215)

BURGOYNE, Dr John Henry; CBE (1980); s of Sir John Burgoyne, OBE, JP (d 1969), of Luton, and Florence Emily Burgoyne, *née* Farrow (d 1964); *b* 4 Aug 1913; *Educ* Luton Modern GS, Univ of London (BSc, PhD, DSc); *m* 8 March 1944, Margaret Graves, da of Herbert Beeston Tupholme (d 1963), of Sheffield; 1 s (John b 1944); *Career* lectr in chem engrg Imp Coll London 1946-64 (latterly sr lectr, and reader), ind conslt 1964-68, sr ptnr Dr J H Burgoyne ptnrs 1968-78, conslt Burgoyne Gp 1978-; visiting prof and sr fell City Univ 1972-83, visiting prof Univ of Sheffield 1986-; chm Safety in Mines Res Advsy Bd Miny of Fuel & Power 1970-75, memb Advsy Ctee on Major Hazards Health and Safety Cmmn 1976-83, chm Inquiry into Offshore Safety Dept of Energy 1979-80, pres Assoc of Consulting Scientists 1987-; CChem 1948, FEng 1982, FCGI 1984; *Recreations* music, photography, travel; *Style—* Dr J H Burgoyne, CBE; The Lodge, 2 Silverdale Rd, Sheffield S11 9JL, (☎ 0742 352600); The Burgoyne Group, 39A Bartholomew Close, London EC1A 7JN, (☎ 071 726 4951, fax 071 726 8980, telex 884957 BGOYNE G)

BURJA'N, Imre Josef; s of Imre Burja'n (d 1986), of Hungary, and Vilma, *née* Szebik (d 1956); descendent of old Hungarian family, arrived England 1956, naturalised Br 1968; *b* 24 March 1935; *Educ* Technical Univ Budapest (DipArch), Coll of Art Manchester (awarded distinction by RIBA); *m* 20 Nov 1956, Julianna, da of Imre Teilinger (d 1980), of Hungary; 1 s (Attila Imre Winston b 1958); *Career* chartered architect; former ptnr Turner Buttres Architects, now solo practitioner architect; memb: ARCUK, RIBA; *Recreations* general drawing, water colours; *Style—* Imre J Burja'n, Esq; 51 South Drive, Chorlton Ville, Manchester

BURKE, Chief Constable David Michael; QPM; s of Desmond Francis Burke (d 1963), of Newcastle, and Lois Mary, *née* Stephenson; *b* 18 Jan 1939; *Educ* Open Univ (BA), Yorks Coll of Agric (NCA); *m* 18 April 1960, Eleanor Elizabeth (Betty), da of George Leslie Lister (d 1979), of Pickering; 1 s ((John) Stephen b 1961); *Career* Nat Serv RAF 1958-60; constable to asst chief constable: N Riding constabulary, York and NE Yorks Police, N Yorks Police 1963-83, dep chief constable Warwickshire 1983-89, chief constable N Yorks 1989-; vice pres and NE regnl chm RLSS; Queens Silver Jubilee Medal 1977, Police Long Service Medal 1985, Pro Ecclesia Et Pontifice by The Pope 1983; *Recreations* riding, driving horses, shooting, swimming; *Clubs* St Johns; *Style—* Chief Constable David Burke, QPM; Police HQ, Newby Wiske Hall, Northallerton, N Yorks (☎ 0609 773131, fax 0609 773131251, telex 58565)

BURKE, David Thomas (Tom); s of Jeremiah Vincent Burke, DSM, of Nazareth House, Plymouth, Devon, and Mary, *née* Bradley; *b* 5 Jan 1947; *Educ* St Boniface's Coll Plymouth, Univ of Liverpool (BA); *Career* lectr: W Cheshire Coll 1970-71, Old Swan Tech Coll 1971-73; Friends of the Earth: local gps coordinator 1973-75, exec dir 1975-79, dir special projects 1979-80, vice chm 1980-81; non-exec dir Earth Resources Res 1975-87, memb Waste Mgmnt Advsy Cncl 1976-80, memb Packaging Cncl 1978-82, memb Exec Ctee Euro Environment Bureau 1987- (policy advsr 1978-86), dir Green Alliance 1982- (memb Exec Ctee 1979-83), memb Exec Ctee and chm Planning and Environment Gp NCVO 1984-89, memb UK Nat Ctee Euro Year of the Environment 1986-88, dir Sustain Ability 1987-89; contested (SDP): Brighton Kemptown Gen Election 1983, Surbiton Gen Election 1987; Royal Humane Soc Testimonial Parchment 1969 (Vellum 1966); hon visiting fell Manchester Business Sch 1984-86; memb Cncl RSA 1990; FRSA; *Books* Euro Environment (jtly, 1981), Pressure Groups in the Global System (1982), Ecology 2000 (jtly, 1984), The Gaia Atlas of Planetary Management (contrib, 1984), The Green Capitalists (jtly, 1987), Green Pages (jtly, 1988); *Recreations* birdwatching, photography; *Clubs* Reform; *Style—* Tom Burke, Esq; 36 Crewdson Road, London SW9 OLJ (☎ 071 735 9019); The Green Alliance, 49 Wollington St, London WC2 (☎ 071 836 0341, fax 071 240 9205)

BURKE, Prof Derek Clissold; s of Harold Burke (d 1973), of Avon, Warwickshire, and Ivy Ruby, *née* Clissold (d 1973); *b* 13 Feb 1930; *Educ* Bishop Vesey's GS Sutton Coldfield, Univ of Birmingham (BSc PhD); *m* 21 May 1955, Mary Elizabeth, da of Theodore Tines Dukeshire; 1 s (Stephen Dukeshire b 1952), 3 da (Elizabeth Anne b 1957, Rosemary Margaret b 1962, Virginia Ruth b 1964); *Career* res fell in chemistry Yale 1953-55, scientist Nat Inst for Medical Res London 1955-60, lectr and sr lectr Dept of Biological Chem Univ of Aberdeen 1960-69, prof of biological scis Univ of Warwick 1969-82 Eleanor Roosevelt fell Univ of Colorado USA 1975-76, vice pres and scientific dir Allelix Inc Toronto Canada 1982-87, vice chllr UEA 1987-; pres Soc of Gen Microbiology 1987-90, dir Cancer Res Campaign 1989-, chm Advsy Ctee on Novel Foods and Processes 1988-, memb Advsy Ctee on Genetic Modification 1987-, tstee Norfolk and Norwich Triennial Festival 1988-; Hon LLD Univ of Aberdeen (1982); Soc for Gen Microbiology, memb Euro Molecular Biology Orgn; *Books* Creation and Evolution (1985), numerous scientific and popular articles on interferon and viruses; *Recreations* music, opera, walking; *Clubs* Royal Cwlth Soc; *Style—* Prof Derek Burke; Wood Hall, Hethersett, Norwich NR9 3DE (☎ 0603 810 203); Sea-Green Cottage, Walberswick, Suffolk IP18 6TU (☎ 0502 723607); Vice Chancellor's Office, University of East Anglia, Norwich NR4 7TJ (☎ 0603 56161, fax 0603 507753)

BURKE, Frank Desmond; *b* 23 March 1944; *Educ* Newcastle (MB BS); *m* Linda Margaret; 2 s (Richard b 1972, Timothy b 1979), 1 da (Sarah b 1975); *Career* fell in hand surgery: Louisville Kentucky 1976, Iowa City 1977; conslt hand surgn Derbyshire Royal Infirmary 1981-; sec Br Soc For Surgery Of The Hand 1989, pres Br Assoc Of Hand Therapists 1989; FRCS 1972, memb American Soc Of Surgery Of The Hand 1989; *Books* Principles of Hand Surgery (with D A McGrougher and P J Smith, 1990); *Style—* Frank Burke, Esq; 28 Midland Place, Derby DE1 2RR (☎ 0332 290480); The Hand Unit, Derbyshire Royal Infirmary, London Rd, Derby (☎ 0332 47141 ext 727)

BURKE, Sir James Stanley Gilbert; 9 Bt (I 1797), of Marble Hill, Galway; s of Sir Thomas Stanley Burke, 8 Bt (d 1989), and Susanne Margaretha, *née* Salvisberg (d 1983); *b* 1 July 1956; *m* 1980, Laura, da of Domingo Branzuela, of Philippines; 1 s (Martin b 1980), 1 da (Catherine); *Heir* s, Martin James Burke b 22 July 1980; *Style—* Sir James Burke, Bt; Lindenbergstr 231, CH-5618 Bettwil, Switzerland (☎ 057 273124)

BURKE, John Kenneth; QC (1985); s of Kenneth Burke (d 1960), of Stockport, and Madeline Lorina, *née* Eastwood; *b* 4 Aug 1939; *Educ* Stockport GS; *m* 30 March 1962, Margaret Anne, da of Frank Scattergood, of Nottingham; 3 da (Virginia b 1963, Joanna b 1967, Geraldine b 1969); *Career* Nat Serv with Cheshire Regt in Far E 1958-60, Capt 12/13 Bn The Parachute Regt (TA) 1962-67, Capt/Actg Maj 4 Bn The Parachute Regt (TAVR) 1974; called to the Bar Middle Temple 1965; rec of Crown Ct 1980-; *Recreations* walking, drawing, painting; *Style—* John Burke, Esq, QC; 1 Hawthorn View Cottage, Knutsford Road, Mobberley, Cheshire WA16 7BA (☎ 0565 872627); 18 St John Street, Manchester M3 4EA (☎ 061 834 9843, fax 061 835 2051); 14 Grays Inn Square, Grays Inn WC1R 5JP (☎ 071 242 0858)

BURKE, Sir Joseph Terence Anthony; KBE (1980, CBE 1973, OBE 1946); s of late R M J Burke; *b* 14 July 1913; *Educ* Ealing Priory Sch, King's Coll London (MA), Courtauld Inst of Art, Yale Univ; *m* 1940, Agnes, da of late Rev James Middleton; 1 s; *Career* private sec to PM Rt Hon C R Attlee 1945-46, Herald prof of fine arts Univ of Melbourne 1947-79, prof emeritus Univ of Melbourne 1979-; *Books* various art publications; *Recreations* golf, swimming; *Clubs* Melbourne, Athenaeum; *Style—* Sir Joseph Burke, KBE; Dormers, Falls Rd, Mt Dandenong, Victoria 3766, Australia

BURKE, Michael John; s of Ulick Burke (d 1986), and Dorothy Margaret, *née* Clark; *b* 22 June 1934; *Educ* Westcliff HS, Univ of Nottingham (LLB); *m* 9 Nov 1959, Margaret, da of Harry Charles (d 1987), of 43 Leasway, Westcliff; 1 s (Anthony b 1961), 3 da (Jane b 1962, Henrietta b 1965, Sophia b 1970); *Career* admitted slr 1958; Layton & Co: assoc slr 1962-64, ptnr 1967- (merged to become Cameron Markby 1981, merged 1989 to become Cameron Markby Hewitt); govr Westcliff Girls Sch 1966-, hon slr Essex Yacht Club 1978-; memb: City Livery Club Cncl 1976-, City Slrs Co, Livery Consultative Ctee 1981-; dep clerk Carmen's Co 1974-; clerk: Farriers Co 1962-70, Downgate Ward 1974-; Freeman City of London 1962, Liveryman Worshipful Co of: Solicitors 1962, Farriers 1963, Carmen 1984; *Recreations* sailing, golf, walking; *Clubs* Essex Yacht, City Livery; *Style—* Michael Burke, Esq; 66 Undercliff Gardens, Leigh on Sea, Essex (☎ 0702 79 871); Sceptre Ct, 40 Tower Hill, London EC3N 4BB (☎ 071 702 2345, fax 071 702 2303, telex 925779)

BURKE, Prof Philip George; s of Henry Burke (d 1969), of Woodford, London, and Frances Mary, *née* Sprague (d 1980); *b* 18 Oct 1932; *Educ* Wanstead GS London, Univ of Exeter (BSc), UCL (PhD); *m* 29 Aug 1959, Valerie Mona, da of Harold William Martin (d 1987), of Eastbourne, Sussex; 4 da (Helen Frances b 1961, Susan Valerie b 1963, Pamela Jean b 1964, Alice Charlotte b 1973); *Career* asst lectr Computer Unit Univ of London 1957-59; Univ of California Berkeley 1959-62: res fell, princ sci offr, sr princ sci offr; UK Atomic Energy Authy Harwell 1962-67, prof of mathematical physics Queens Univ Belfast NI 1967-, head of Theory and Computational Sci Div Daresbury Lab (jt appt) 1978-82, fell UCL 1986 (res fell 1956-57); over 200 pubns in learned jls; memb: Physics Ctee Sci Res Cncl 1967-71, Jt Policy Ctee on Advanced Res Computing 1988-, Sci and Engrg Res Cncl 1989-, Cncl Royal Soc 1990-; chm: Sci Bd Computer Ctee Sci Res Cncl 1976-77 and 1984-86, Computer Bd Computer Conslt Cncl 1983-85, Atlas Centre Supercomputer Ctee 1988-89; Hon DSc Univ of Exeter 1981; FInstP 1970, MRIA 1974, FRS 1978; *Books* Atomic Processes and Applications (1976), Potential Scattering in Atomic Physics (1977), Atoms in Astrophysics (1983), Electron Molecule Scattering and Photoionisation (1988); *Recreations* swimming, walking, reading, tennis; *Style—* Prof Philip Burke; 33 Leverogue Rd, Lisburn, N Ireland BT27 5PP (☎ 0232 826416); Brook House, Crowton, nr Northwich, Cheshire CW8 2RR (☎ 0928 88301); Dept of Applied Mathematics and Theoretical Physics, Queens University, Belfast, N Ireland BT7 1NN (☎ 0232 245133, fax 0232 247895, telex 74487)

BURKE, Richard Sylvester; s of David Burke (d 1948), and Elizabeth, *née* Kelly (d 1987); *b* 29 March 1932; *Educ* Christian Brothers Sch Thurles and Dublin Ireland, Nat Univ of Ireland (BA, MA, HDipEd); *m* 1961, Mary Josephine, da of John J Freeley (d 1934); 3 s (Joseph (d 1962), David Joseph b 1964, Richard Anthony b 1969), 3 da (Mary Carmel b 1963, Audrey Elisabeth b 1966, Avila Therese b 1971); *Career* taught at: Presentation Coll 1953-55, Blackrock Coll 1955-72; govr Univ Coll Dublin 1967-70; memb Dublin CC 1967-73 (chm 1972-73); barr at law King's Inns 1973-; TD 1969-77 and 1981-82, opposition chief whip and spokesman on Posts and Telegraphs 1969-73, Min for Educn 1973-76; memb and vice pres Cmmn of Euro Communities 1977-81 and 1982-85; chm Player and Wills 1981-82; dir: Abbey Life 1981-82, Sedgwick Europe BV 1985-86; special advsr Euro Community Off Ernst and Young 1985-; assoc fell Harvard Univ Centre for Int Affairs 1980-81; Pro Merito Europa medal (European Parliament 1980), Order of Leopold II (Grand-Cross) Belgium 1981, Order of Phoenix (Grand-Cross) Greece 1983; *Books* Anthology of Prose (ed, 1967); *Recreations* golf, music, travel; *Clubs* Royal Golf De Belgique (Brussels), Portmarnock Golf (Dublin), Elm Park Golf (Dublin), Hibernian United Services (Dublin); *Style—* Richard Burke, Esq; 67 Ailesbury Rd, Dublin 4 (☎ 0001 1692520); 1443 Strawinskylaan, 1077 XX Amsterdam, Netherlands (☎ 31 20 575 3209, fax 31 20 575 3167)

BURKE, Sheila; da of Maurice Burke, and Eileen, *née* McKenna; *b* 26 May 1956; *Educ* Notre Dame RC GS for Girls; *Career* dir of studies KMG Thomson McLintock 1980-86; recruitment mangr Binder Hamlyn BDO 1987-88, md SB Business Services Ltd 1989-; *Recreations* art, music, antiques, photography, theatre, tennis, badminton; *Clubs* Country Gentleman's Assoc, Cognac, International Teddy Bear; *Style—* Ms Sheila Burke; Ridley Hall, Honington, Suffolk (☎ 0359 269666)

BURKE-GAFFNEY, John Campion; s of Dr Henry Joseph O'Donnell Burke-Gaffney, tropical medicine expert (d 1973), and Constance Mary, *née* Bishop (d 1986); *b* 27 Feb 1932; *Educ* Douai Sch; *m* 7 July 1956, Margaret Mary Jennifer, da of Lt-Col

Humphrey Herbert Stacpoole (d 1971); 2 s (Jonathan b 1959, Rupert b 1962), 2 da (Sarah b 1957, Frances b 1964); *Career* Nat Serv cmmnd RAC 1950-52, TA East Riding Yeo (Lieut-Actg Capt) 1952-56; called to the Bar Gray's Inn 1956; Shell Mex & BP Ltd 1956-75, Shell UK Ltd 1975-77, md Shell & BP Zambia Ltd 1977-81, Shell Int Petroleum Co Ltd 1981-85; dir gen Br Red Cross Soc 1985-; *Style—* John Burke-Gaffney, Esq; c/o Lloyds Bank, Aldwych, London WC2R 0HR; 9 Grosvenor Crescent, London SW1 (☎ 071 235 5454)

BURKE-GAFFNEY, Michael Anthony Bowes; QC; s of Henry Joseph O'Donnell Burke-Gaffney (d 1978), of Bagshot, Surrey, and Constance May, *née* Bishop (d 1985); *b* 1 Aug 1928; *Educ* Douai Sch, RMA Sandhurst, SOAS; *m* 1961, Constance Caroline, da of Lt-Col Alan Murdoch; 2 s (Timothy Henry James b 6 Sept 1966, Giles Peter Anthony b 26 April 1978), 1 da (Constance Emma Mary b 12 Jan 1968); *Career* served 1 Bn RIF Akaba, Gibraltar, Rhine, cmmnd 1948; served 1 Bn Royal Ulster Rifles Korea and Hong Kong 1951-52, Capt on Staff 44 Inf Div 1957-58, ret; called to the Bar Gray's Inn 1959, rec Crown Court 1986-, bencher Gray's Inn 1988; *Recreations* cricket, wine, family, plants; *Clubs* Naval and Military; *Style—* Michael Burke-Gaffney, Esq, QC; Lamb Building, Temple, London EC4Y 7AS (☎ 071 353 6701, fax 071 353 4686, car 0836 200462)

BURKETT, John; s of Alfred Burkett, MC (d 1986), of Stoke Bishop, Bristol, and Marjorie, *née* Wingfield (d 1972); *b* 17 Feb 1926; *Educ* Eltham Coll, Jesus Coll Cambridge, Architectural Assoc Sch (AA Dip); *m* 24 April 1948, Patricia Ann (d 1988), da of Stanley Walter Mack (d 1985), of Chislehurst, Kent; 2 da (Deborah Jane b 1953, Sarah Louise b 1955); *Career* Flt Lt RAF 1944-48; lectr Architectural Assoc Sch of Architecture 1955-57; ptnr: D J Mclennan & Ptnrs, John Burkett Assocs, Scarlett Burkett Assoc 1971-78; sr ptnr Scarlett Burkett Griffiths 1987 (ptnr 1979-87); Winner: Civic Tst awards 1968 and 1972, Financial Times Indust Architecture award 1971, Heritage Landscape Award 1976; memb Cncl and hon sec Assoc of Conslt Architects; FRIBA, FCIArb; *Recreations* gardening, skiing; *Clubs* Architectural Assoc, SCGB; *Style—* John Burkett, Esq; Scarlett Burkett Griffiths, 14 Clerkenwell Close, Clerkenwell, London EC1R 0PQ (☎ 071 490 5002, fax 071 490 2160)

BURKETT, Mary Elizabeth; OBE (1978); da of Ridley Burkett (d 1965), of Canet Place, PO, France, and Mary Alice Gaussen (d 1965); The Gaussens were a Huguenot family from Lunel, this branch settled at Loughneagh; *Educ* Musgrave Sch, Univ of Durham (BA); *Career* art teacher Wroxall Abbey 1942-55, art lectr Charlotte Mason Coll Ambleside 1955-62, dir Abbot Hall Art Gallery and Museums Kendal 1967-86; memb Bd Border TV 1982-; memb: N Western Museums and Art Gallery Servs Area Cncl 1975-86, Cumbria and West Moreland Fedn of WI's Art Sub Ctee 1977, Arts Cncl Art Fin Ctee 1978-80, Nat Tst NW Regional Exec Ctee 1978-85; Cumbria CC: Museums Advsy Gp 1975, Museums Offrs Working Pty 1975-87; judge: Scot Museum of the Year award 1977-, Eng Museum of the Year award 1986-; Br Tourist Authy Museums Mission to USA 1981, Hawkshead GS Ctee 1981; tstee: Carlisle Cathedral Appeal 1981-, Armitt Tst 1982-86, Senhouse Tst 1985-; pres Feltmakers Assoc 1984; FRSA, FMA, FRGS; *Books* William Green of Ambleside (1984), Kurt Schwitters and the Art of the Feltmaker; *Recreations* travelling, writing, photography; *Style—* Miss Mary Burkett, OBE; Isel Hall, Cockermouth, Cumbria

BURKHARDT, Prof (George) Hugh; s of Dr George Norman Burkhardt, of 18 Macefin Ave, Manchester, and Caroline Mary, *née* Bell; *b* 4 April 1935; *Educ* Manchester GS, Balliol Coll Oxford (BA), Univ of Birmingham (PhD); *m* 21 Dec 1955, Diana Jeanette, da of Stapley Farmer (d 1970); 2 s (Roger b 1960, Ian b 1963), 1 da (Jan b 1962); *Career* res fell: Columbia Univ 1958-59, California Inst of Technol 1959-60; lectr then sr lectr in mathematical physics Univ of Birmingham 1960-76, prof of mathematical educn Univ of Nottingham 1976-; dir Shell Centre for Mathematical Educn; visiting prof: UCLA 1968-69, CERN 1964-66 and 1973-74; memb Jt Mathematical Cncl of Nat Curriculum Mathematical Working Gp 1976-79, nat memb Int Cmmn on Mathematics Instruction 1980-88 (treas 1982-85); *Books* Dispersion Relation Dynamics (1969), The Real World and Mathematics (1981), Problem Solving - A World View (1988); *Recreations* oboe, theatre, dance; *Style—* Prof Hugh Burkhardt; Schell Centre for Mathematical Education, University of Nottingham, University Park, Nottingham NG7 2RD (☎ 0602 484848 ext 3271, fax 0602 420825)

BURLAND, Prof John Boscawen; s of John Whitmore Burland, and Margaret Irene, *née* Boscawen (d 1986); *b* 4 March 1936; *Educ* Parktown Boys HS Johannesburg, Univ of the Witwatersrand (BSc, MSc, DSc), Emmanuel Coll Cambridge (PhD); *m* 30 March 1963, Gillian Margaret, da of John Kenneth Miller (d 1981); 2 s (David 1965, Timothy 1967), 1 da (Tamsin 1969); *Career* engr Ove Arup and ptnrs London 1961-63, Building Res Estab: SSO, PSO 1966-72, SPSO head Geotechnics Div 1972-79, asst dir DCSO 1979-80; visiting prof Univ of Strathclyde 1973-82, prof of soil mechanics Imp Coll of Sci Technol and Med 1980-; MICE 1969, MIStructE 1976, FEng 1981, FICE 1982; *Recreations* golf, sailing, painting; *Style—* Prof John Burland; Department of Civil Engineering, Imperial College of Science, Technology and Medicine, Imperial College Rd, London SW7 2BU (☎ 071 589 5111, telex 918351, fax 071 823 8525)

BURLEIGH, Robert Haydon; s of Thomas Haydon Burleigh, of Kirkgate, Holme, Hunstanton, Norfolk PE36 6LH, and Kathleen Mary Lenthall Eager; *b* 16 Aug 1941; *Educ* Dragon Sch Oxford, Repton, Trinity Coll Oxford (MA, Golf blue); *m* 31 May 1969, Ann Elizabeth Lea, da of Cecil George Steddy; 1 s (Edward Thomas Haydon b 5 July 1980), 1 da (Emma Susan Lenthall b 16 Sept 1977); *Career* articled clerk Robert Gray Clegg & Sons Sheffield 1964-66, admitted slr 1966; Clifford-Turner (became Clifford Chance 1988): joined 1968, ptnr 1971, Amsterdam 1972-73, assigned Salah Hejailan Riyadh Saudi Arabia 1978-80; memb: Worshipful Co of Slrs, Law Soc; *Recreations* golf, skiing, fishing, music; *Clubs* City of London, Royal and Ancient, Moles GS, Vincent's; *Style—* Robert Burleigh, Esq; 33 Burnsall St, London SW3 3SS (☎ 071 584 5158); Clifford Chance, Royex House, Aldermanbury Square, London EC2V 7LD (☎ 071 600 0808, fax 071 6009319, direct line: 071 600 1060)

BURLETSON, Bryan Richard; s of Bryan Burletson (ka 1941, Fleet Air Arm), and Evelyn Loveday Sharp, *née* Bradshaw; *b* 28 June 1941; *Educ* Harrow, Univ of Dublin (MA); *m* 20 March 1965, Prudence Margaret, da of Henry Wheatley Ridsdale; 1 s (Richard b 1966), 1 da (Louise b 1968); *Career* chm and chief exec Clayform Properties plc; *Recreations* sailing, skiing, tennis, riding; *Style—* Bryan Burletson, Esq; 24 Bruton Street, Mayfair, London W1X 7DA (☎ 071 491 8400, fax 071 499 1053)

BURLEY, Dr Jeffery; s of Jack Burley (d 1978), and Eliza Nellie Victoria, *née* Creese (d 1949); *b* 16 Oct 1936; *Educ* Portsmouth GS, Univ of Oxford (BA, MA, Basketball blue), Yale Univ (MF, PhD); *m* 26 Aug 1961, Jean Shirley, da of Douglas MacDonald Palmer (d 1989); 2 s (Jeremy Andrew b 1963, Timothy John b 1966); *Career* Lt Royal Signals short serv cmmn 1954-57; UNESCO expert offr i/c Forest Genetics Res Laboratory Agric Res Cncl of Central Africa 1965-68, sr res offr Cwlth Forestry Inst Oxford 1968-76, lectr in forestry Univ of Oxford 1976-83, head Dept of Forestry and dir Cwlth Forestry Inst 1983-84, dir Oxford Forestry Inst and professional fell Green Coll 1985-; forty consultancies with int devpt agencies; advsr, sponsor and memb Ctee: Earthwatch (UK), Tree Aid, Cwlth Forestry Assoc, Br Cncl, Nat Environment Res Cncl; *Books* Tropical Trees: variation, breeding and conservation (ed with B T Styles, 1976); *Style—* Dr Jeffery Burley; Woodside, Frilford Heath, Abingdon, Oxon OX13 5QG (☎ 0865 390754); Oxford Forestry Inst, Department of Plant Scis, Oxford Univ, South Parks Rd, Oxford OX1 3RB (☎ 0865 275050, fax 0865 275074, telex 83147)

BURLEY, (William) John; s of William John Rule Burley, (d 1935), of Falmouth, and Annie, *née* Curnow (d 1956); *b* 1 May 1914; *Educ* Cornwall Tech Schs (Keam scholar), Balliol Coll Oxford (BA, Herbertson prize); *m* 10 April 1938, Muriel, da of Edward Wolsey; 2 s (Alan John b 13 June 1940, Nigel Philip b 4 Aug 1943); *Career* writer; student engr in gas engrg 1931-36, asst mangr Truro Gas Undertaking 1936-40, mangr several small gas undertakings South West Gas and Water Corp 1940-50, head of biology Richmond and East Sheen GS 1953-55, head of biology and sixth form tutor Newquay Sch 1955-74; full time writer 1974-; works incl: A Taste of Power 1966, Three-Toed Pussy 1968, Death in Willow Pattern 1969, To Kill a Cat 1970, Guilt Edged 1971, Death in a Salubrious Place 1973, Death in Stanley Street 1974, Wycliffe and Pea-green Boat 1975, Wycliffe and the Schoolgirls 1976, The Schoolmaster 1977, Wycliffe and the Scapegoat 1978, The Sixth Day 1978, Charles and Elizabeth 1979, Wycliffe in Paul's Court 1980, The House of Care 1981, Wycliffe's Wild Goose Chase 1982, Wycliffe and the Beales 1983, Wycliffe and the Four Jacks 1985, Wycliffe and the Quiet Virgin 1986, Wycliffe and the Winsor Blue 1987, Wycliffe and the Tangled Wed 1988, Wycliffe and the Cycle of Death 1990, Wycliffe and the Dead Flautist 1991; memb: Crime Writers' Assoc, South West Writers, Authors' Licensing and Collecting Soc; *Recreations* gardening and watercolour painting; *Style—* John Burley, Esq; St Patrick's, Holywell, Newquay, Cornwall TR8 5PT (☎ 0637 830362); Victor Gollancz, 14 Henrietta St, London WC2E 8QJ

BURLEY, Hon Mrs (Laura Blackstock); *née* Butterworth; yr da of Baron Butterworth, CBE (Life Peer); *Educ* Benenden, Westfield Coll London; *m* 1985, John Laughton Burley, s of John Burley, of Pocklington, York; *Style—* Hon Mrs Burley; The Coffee House, Everingham, York

BURLEY, Cdr Malcolm Keith; MBE (1966); s of Leonard Lancelot Burley (d 1976), and Edythe Emmeline Hasluck, *née* Baker (d 1968); *b* 28 Sept 1927; *Educ* Solihull Sch, RNC Dartmouth; *m* 29 May 1965, Fiona Mairi, da of Rev James Fergus Macdonald, TD, of Carnoustie, Angus; 3 da (Ailsa b 1966, Leonie b 1969, Erica b 1972); *Career* served RN, Med, Far E (Korean War), East Indies, Antarctic and S Atlantic 1945-73; ldr 2 Arctic expdns 1958-60; ldr jt servs expdns: S Georgia 1964-65, Elephant Island, British Antarctica 1970-71; bursar Stowe Sch 1973-86, mgmnt Anchor Estate 1986-; vice chm Br Schs Exploring Soc, former pres RN Assoc (Buckingham), chm Peasenhall and Sibton Cons Assoc, pres Saxmundham Rotary Club, former pres Buckingham Rotary Club; Freeman City of London 1986; FRGS, FRSA; *Recreations* offshore sailing (Navy Colours), travelling, gardening; *Style—* Cdr Malcolm Burley, MBE; Bay House, Peasenhall, Suffolk IP17 2NQ (☎ 072 879 221); The Anchorage, Iken, Suffolk IP12 2ER (☎ 072 888 262)

BURLEY, Stephen Rodney; s of Ronald Gordon Burley, of Beckenham, Kent, and Marjorie, *née* Methuen; *b* 9 July 1947; *m* 1 June 1974, Katherine Mary, da of Stanley Dransfield; 1 s (Robert b 1979), 1 da (Elizabeth b 1977); *Career* Commerical Union Assurance 1971-82, investmt mangr RTZ Pension Investments Ltd, non-exec dir Strata Investments plc 1985; hon treas Ranfurly Library 1985; *Recreations* riding, walking; *Style—* Stephen Burley, Esq; 6 St James's Square, London SW1Y 4LD

BURLIN, Prof Terence Eric; s of Eric Jonas Burlin, and Winifred Kate, *née* Thomas; *b* 24 Sept 1931; *Educ* Acton Co Sch, Univ of Southampton (BSc), Univ of London (BSc, PhD, DSc); *m* 23 March 1957, Plessey Pamela, da of John William Carpenter; 1 s (Adrian b 1962), 1 da (Helen b 1965); *Career* physicist Mount Vernon Hosp and Radium Inst 1953-57, sr physicist Hammersmith Hosp 1957-62, pt/t princ physicist St John's Hosp for Diseases of Skin 1960-90, sr lectr Poly of Central London 1969-71 (reader 1969-71, pro dir 1971-74, sr pro rector 1974-82, rector 1982-); govr: Quintin Kynaston Sch 1971-73, Central Sch of Speech and Drama 1980-; memb: Longfield Sch Managing Body 1973-76, Cncl Inst for Study of Drug Dependence 1974-86, Academic Bd Harrow Coll of Higher Educn 1979-84, Sci Bd SERC 1986-89 (Polys Ctee 1976-78), Paddington Coll Governing Body 1986-90, Br Cncl Ctee for Int Co-operation in Higher Educn 1988-; hon treas Ctee of Dirs of Polys 1985-; FInstP 1969, CPhys 1976, FIPSM 1988, FIEE 1976; Hon FCP 1990-; *Recreations* tennis, music; *Clubs* Athenaeum; *Style—* Prof Terence Burlin; Polytechnic of Central London, 309 Regent St, London W1 (☎ 071 911 5000, fax 071 911 5103)

BURLINGTON, Earl of; William Cavendish; s of Marquess of Hartington, *qv*; *b* 6 June 1969; *Clubs* Arsenal FC; *Style—* Earl of Burlington

BURMAN, Sir (John) Charles; JP (Birmingham 1942), DL (Warwicks 1967); s of Sir John Bedford Burman, JP (d 1941), of Tibbington House, Edgbaston, and Elizabeth Vernon, *née* Pugh; *b* 30 Aug 1908; *Educ* Rugby; *m* 1936, Ursula, *qv*, da of John Herbert Hesketh-Wright, and Millicent Ella, *née* Pickering, of Bournemouth; 2 s, 2 da; *Career* Lord Mayor Birmingham 1947-49; chm: S Staffs Waterworks Co 1959-79, Tarmac Ltd 1961-71; memb: Govt Ctee on Admin Tbnls 1955, Royal Commn on Police 1960; chm: Birmingham Cons Assoc 1963-72, Tstees Barber Inst of Fine Arts 1970-90 (tstee 1936-90); High Sheriff Warwicks 1958-59; Hon LLD Univ of Birmingham 1986; KStJ 1961; kt 1961; *Recreations* gardening; *Style—* Sir Charles Burman, JP, DL; Little Bickerscourt, Danzey Green, Tanworth-in-Arden, Warwicks B94 5BL (☎ 056 44 2711)

BURMAN, Richard; s of Robert Burman (d 1938), of Alvechurch, Worcs, and Margaret Harriet, *née* Shaw (d 1960); *b* 22 Jan 1916; *Educ* Bromsgrove Sch; *m* 5 April 1947, Joan Edith, da of James Louis Dearne (d 1972), of Hunnington, Worcs; 2 s (Paul Robert James b 12 June 1948, David Richard b 27 Sept 1951); *Career* HG; CA 1951, ptnr Burman and Co 1939- (sr ptnr formerly Roberts Hall and Co); chm: Darby and Co Holdings 1960-, Worcestershire Metal Holdings Ltd 1970-; further overseas directorships in USA, Singapore, Nigeria and formerly in Aust and NZ; trade missions to: Hong Kong, Malaysia, Kenya, Zimbabwe; ldr Birmingham C of C, clerk Alvechurch PC 1945-; former dir: Birmingham City FC, Worcs Co Cricket 2 XI, Barnt Green CC, Alvechurch CC, Hopwood CC; FICA; *Style—* Richard Burman, Esq; Shepley Gables, Barnt Green, Worcs (☎ 021 445 1988); Golg-Y-Mor, Llwylgwrill, Gwynedd; Burman House, 39 George Rd, Edgbaston, Birmingham B15 1PL (☎ 021 454 3894, fax 021 454 4529, telex 337820)

BURMAN, Sir Stephen France; CBE (1954, MBE 1943); s of Henry Burman, of 103 Harborne Rd, Edgbaston, Birmingham; *b* 27 Dec 1904; *Educ* Oundle; *m* 1931, Joan Margaret, da of John Henry Rogers, of Edgbaston; 2 s (1 decd); *Career* former dir: Midland Bank Ltd, Averys Ltd, ICI Ltd, Imperial Metal Industries Ltd, J Lucas Industries Ltd; chm Serck Ltd Birmingham 1962-70; kt 1973; *Style—* Sir Stephen Burman, CBE; 12 Cherry Hill Rd, Barnt Green, Birmingham B45 8LJ (☎ 021 445 1529)

BURMAN, Lady; Ursula; JP (1949-); da of John Herbert Hesketh-Wright (d 1967), and Ella Millicent, *née* Pickering (d 1959); *b* 26 Feb 1914; *Educ* Benenden Sch Kent; *m* 26 Sept 1936, Sir (John) Charles Burman, JP, DL, *qv*, s of Sir John Bedford Burman, JP (d 1941); 2 s (John Hesketh b 8 Sept 1939, Michael Charles b 16 June 1944), 2 da (Elizabeth Ursula (Mrs Landale) b 22 Dec 1937, Rosanne Margaret (Mrs Corben) b 26 Nov 1941); *Career* WWII Civil Nursing Res (St John) and WVS 1939-46; chm (formerly memb, chm and vice chm) Juvenile Ct Panel 1949-79, memb Nat Cncl Magistrates Assoc 1957-75, pres Birmingham Branch Magistrates Assoc 1975-84 (chm 1970-75);

memb: Bd of Visitors Winson Green Prison, Home Office Ctee Legal Aid in Criminal Proceedings 1964-66, Cncl Benenden Sch 1972-83; Lady Mayoress Birmingham 1947-49; *Recreations* riding, reading; *Style—* Lady Burman, JP; Little Bickerscourt, Danzey Green, Tanworth-in-Arden, Warwicks B94 5BL (☎ 05644 2711)

BURN, (Bryan) Adrian Falconer; s of Reginald Falconer Burn (d 1981), and Kathleen Ruth, *née* Davis; *b* 23 May 1945; *Educ* Abingdon Sch; *m* 1968, Jeanette Carol; 4 c (Clare b 1976, Victoria b 1979, Katharine b 1983, James b 1985); *Career* chartered accountant Whinney Murray 1968-72 (articled clerk 1964-68); BDO Binder Hamlyn: joined 1973, ptnr 1977, London Region managing ptnr 1988-; FCA (ACA 1968); *Style—* Adrian Burn, Esq; BDO Binder Hamlyn, 20 Old Bailey, London EC4M 7BH (☎ 071 489 9000/6012, fax 071 489 6280, car 0860 392 732)

BURN, Hon Mrs (Anne Catherine); *née* Wilberforce; da of Baron Wilberforce, CMG, OBE, PC; *b* 5 Sept 1948; *m* 1975, Lindsay Stuart Burn; *Style—* The Hon Mrs Burn

BURN, David; s of Maurice Burn, and Mary, *née* Urwin; *b* 23 Sept 1943; *Educ* Dartington Hall, Univ of Exeter (BA), RCM (ARCM), Open Univ (BA) Trinity Coll (LTCL); *Career* actor professional name David Urwin; West End prodns 1965-89 incl: Black and White Minstrels, Trelawney, Jesus Christ Superstar, Irene, Beyond the Rainbow, Oliver!, Sweeney Todd, Oklahoma, Cats; theatrical agent; ptnr The Singers Agency and Hill Urwin Assocs; *Recreations* golf, travel, music; *Style—* David Burn, Esq; Caversham House, Harris Lane, Shenley, Radlett, Herts WD7 9EB (☎ 0923 852175); 22 Inverness St, London NW17HJ (☎ 071 267 6845, fax 071 267 7188)

BURN, Edward Hector; s of Edward Burn (d 1982), and Bertha Maud, *née* Hector (d 1976); *b* 20 Nov 1922; *Educ* St Edward's Oxford, Wadham Coll Oxford (BCL, MA); *m* 21 Dec 1948, Helen Joyce, da of Maj Merrick Hugh McConnel, RHA (ka 1917); *Career* cmmnd 1 Bucks Bn, Oxford Bucks, Capt GSO 3 1 Airborne Corps, Maj GSO 2 26 Indian Div (despatches Normandy 1944 and Sumatra 1946); called to the Bar Lincoln's Inn 1951; student and tutor in jurisprudence Christ Church Oxford 1954-90, Censor of Christ Church 1959-64, lectr in law Inns of Ct 1965-80, Hon Master of the Bench Lincoln's Inn 1980, prof City Univ 1983-, lectr in law St Hugh's Coll Oxford 1990-; govr St Edward's Sch Oxford; Hon DCL City Univ 1990; *Books* Maudsley and Burn Land Law (5 edn, 1986), Cheshire and Burn Modern Law of Real Property (14 edn, 1988), Maudsley and Burn Trusts and Trustees (4 edn, 1990); *Clubs* Athenaeum, MCC; *Style—* Edward Burn, Esq; Christ Church, Oxford

BURN, Geoffrey Robert Hale; s of George Robert Burn (d 1974), and Grace, *née* Downs; *b* 19 Nov 1945; *Educ* St Peter's Coll Birmingham, RMA, Pacific Western Univ (BSc, MBA); *m* 29 Dec 1985, Judith Irene, da of John William Palmieri, of Windsor; 1 s (Hale, decd), 2 da (Sacha b 1987, Vita b 1990); *Career* Lt RA 1967-71; sales exec Prentice Hall 1971-72, managing ed McGraw Hill 1971-72, publishing and mktg dir Methuen Publications 1975-82, pres Butterworth Canada 1982-87, md Butterworth Sci 1987-90; dir publishing BMA 1990-; lay minister Hosp Chaplaincy; FInstD; *Recreations* gardening, reading, golf, skiing; *Clubs* Athenaeum; *Style—* Geoffrey R H Burn, Esq; British Medical Association, BMA House, Tavistock Square, London WC1H 9JR (☎ 071 387 4499)

BURN, (John) Ian; s of Cecil Walter Burn (d 1983), and Margaret Hannah, *née* Cawthorne (d 1988); *b* 19 Feb 1927; *Educ* Taunton Sch, St Bartholomew's Hosp Med Coll (MB BS, capt athletics team and United Hosps Cross Country team); *m* 1951, Fiona May, da of late Alexander Allan; 2 s (Alastair James b 1952, Jonathan Mark b 1964), 2 da (Hilary Kathryn (Mrs Stevens) b 1954, Lindsay Margaret (Mrs O'Kelly) b 1958); *Career* RAF Med Serv 1952-54; Anatomy Dept Univ of Cambridge 1954-55, training posts in surgery St Bartholomew's Hosp and Hammersmith Hosp 1955-65, cancer res scholarship USA 1961-62; conslt surgn: Hammersmith Hosp 1965-73, Charing Cross Hosp Fulham 1973-87 (hon consltg surgn 1987-), Harley St Clinic 1973-; visiting conslt surgn King Edward VII Hosp Midhurst 1988-, specialist in malignant disease (surgical oncology); Hunterian prof RCS 1967; pres: Br Assoc of Surgical Oncology 1980-83 (fndr memb 1973), Euro Soc of Surgical Oncology 1987-90 (fndr memb 1983); vice pres RSM 1989- (hon sec 1981-87), chm Treatment of Cancer Project Ctee Int Union Against Cancer 1989-; Freeman City of London 1986, Liveryman Worshipful Co of Barbers of London 1986, hon assoc memb Belgian Royal Soc for Surgery 1987; FRCS 1956, memb Assoc of Surgeons of GB 1963-; *Books* Systematic Surgery (1965), Surgical Oncology (co-ed, 1989), Breast Cancer (co-ed, 1989); sr ed European Jl of Surgical Oncology, author of numerous chapters and articles on cancer; *Recreations* opera, visiting islands, history of medicine; *Style—* Ian Burn, Esq; 134 Harley St, London W1N 1AH (☎ 071 935 0482)

BURN, Dr John; s of Henry Burn, of Bishop Auckland, Co Durham, and Margaret, *née* Wilkinson; *b* 6 Feb 1952; *Educ* Barnard Castle GS, Univ of Newcastle upon Tyne (BMedSci, MB BS); *m* 5 Aug 1973, Linda Marjorie, da of Charles Frederick Wilson, of Winston, Darlington, Co Durham; 1 s (James Richard David b 20 Sept 1981), 1 da (Danielle Louise b 17 Aug 1977); *Career* jr med trg Newcastle teaching hosps 1976-80, hon sr registrar in clinical genetics Gt Ormond St Hosp 1981-84, conslt clinical geneticist Royal Victoria Infirmary Newcastle 1984-, clinical lectr Univ of Newcastle upon Tyne 1984-; gen sec Clinical Genetics Soc of GB, memb Ctee on Clinical Genetics RCP; MRCP 1978, FRCP 1989; *Recreations* running, snooker; *Style—* Dr John Burn; Northern Region Genetics Advisory Service, 19-20 Claremont Place, Newcastle upon Tyne NE2 4AA (☎ 091 232 5131)

BURNABY-ATKINS, Maj Andrew Graham; MC (and bar 1945); s of John Burnaby-Atkins (d 1946), of Halstead Place, Kent, and Dorothy Dalrymple, *née* Graham-Watson (d 1982); *b* 29 Dec 1922; *Educ* Eton; *m* 8 Jan 1966 (Anne) Caroline, da of Christopher Thomas Dalgety, of Broomy Lodge, Ringwood, Hants; 1 s (Hugh b 5 Jan 1968), 1 da (Joanna b 17 Aug 1969); *Career* WWII enlisted Green Jackets 1941, cmmnd KRRC 1942, served 12 Bn Normandy Landings to the Baltic, Adj 2 Bn 1946, ADC to Field Marshal Viscount Montgomery 1947-49; Adj Eton Cadet Force 1951-53; dir Whitbread & Co 1960 (joined 1953), ret 1974; dir Burghley Horse Trials 1976-78; *Style—* Maj Andrew Burnaby-Atkins, MC; Manton Lodge Farm, Oakham, Rutland LE15 8SS (☎ 057285 269)

BURNABY-ATKINS, Hon Mrs; Hon (Anne) Jennifer; *née* Lawrence; da of 3 Baron Trevethin and 1 Oaksey, DSO, TD, PC (d 1971); *b* 1926; *m* 1951, Lt-Col Frederick John Burnaby-Atkins, er s of John Burnaby-Atkins (d 1946), of Tolethorpe Hall, Stamford, Rutland; 1 s, 3 da; *Style—* The Hon Mrs Burnaby-Atkins; 11 Rupert House, Nevern Sq, London SW5; 3 The Street, Oaksey, Malmesbury, Wilts

BURNAND, Paul William; s of Guy Matthew Burnand (d 1985), and Mary Veronica (d 1986); *b* 24 Nov 1944; *Educ* Downside, RMA Sandhurst; *m* 13 May 1967 (m dis 1979), Fiona Mary, da of late Anthony Kenneth Forbes; 1 s (Edward b 1969), 1 da (Louise Mary b 1970); *Career* cmmnd KRRC (60 Rifles) 1964, res 1968; insur broker Sedgwick Collins & Co Ltd 1968-69; Astley & Pearce Ltd: joined 1969, dir Hong Kong 1977, gen mangr Japan 1978; dir Exco Int Plc 1982-; *Recreations* book collecting, clock and watch collecting, skiing; *Clubs* Travellers', MCC, RAC; *Style—* Paul W Burnand, Esq; Exco Int Plc, 80 Cannon St, London EC4N 6LJ (☎ 071 623 4040)

BURNELL, Digby McLaren; s of Charles McLaren Burnell; *b* 25 Feb 1920; *Educ* Stoneyhurst, Harvard USA; *m* 1958, Maureen, da of Dr Moray Melvin, of Fraserburgh; 3 s; *Career* served RN 1939-46, N Atlantic, Mediterranean and Br Admiralty Delgn to Washington DC; chm: AAA Industs Ltd, Agil Hldgs Ltd, London Leisure Ltd, TVL Ltd and other companies; Liveryman Worshipful Co of Coachmakers and Coach Harness Makers, Freeman City of London; *Recreations* reading, music; *Clubs* Army & Navy; *Style—* Digby Burnell Esq; AAA Industries, Wokingham, Berkshire RG11 2QL

BURNELL, Dr (Susan) Jocelyn Bell; da of George Philip Bell (d 1982), of Solitude, Lurgan, N Ireland, and Margaret Allison Bell, MBE, JP, *née* Kennedy; *b* 15 July 1943; *Educ* The Mount Sch York, Univ of Glasgow (BSc), New Hall Cambridge (PhD); *m* 21 Dec 1968 (m dis 1989), Martin Burnell, s of Arnold Burnell, of London; 1 s (Gavin b 1973); *Career* Univ of Southampton: SRC fell 1968-70, jr teaching fell 1970-73; Mullard Space Sci Lab UCL: pt/t graduate programmer 1974-76, pt/t assoc res fell 1976-82; Royal Observatory Edinburgh: pt/t sr res fell 1982-86, astronomer i/c of Visitor Centre 1985-86, pt/t sr sci offr and head of James Clerk Maxwell Telescope Section 1986-89, pt/t grade 7 and head of James Clerk Maxwell Telescope Section 1989-; Open Univ 1973-88: tutor, conslt, guest lectr; ed The Ovservatory 1973-76; memb Cncl RAS 1978-81, memb various ctees and panels SERC 1978- (incl vice chm Astronomy 1 Ctee 1983-84), hon fell Univ of Edinburgh 1988-; memb: Br Cncl of Churches Assembly 1978-90, Scottish Churches Cncl 1982-90 (Exec Ctee 1984-88); Michelson medal Franklin Inst Philadelphia 1973, J Robert Oppenheimer Meml prize Center for Theoretial Studies Miami 1978, Beatrice Tinsley prize American Astronomical Soc (first recipient) 1987, Herschel medal RAS London 1989; FRAS 1969, memb Int Astronomical Union 1979; *Recreations* swimming, learning Dutch, knitting and sewing, ecumenical activities; *Style—* Dr Jocelyn Burnell; Royal Observatory, Blackford Hill, Edinburgh EH9 3HJ (☎ 031 668 8100, fax 031 668 8264, telex 72383 G)

BURNESS, Hon Mrs (Marie Louise); *née* Forte; 2 da of Baron Forte (Life Peer), *qv*; *b* 16 Sept 1950; *m* 3 May 1975, Robert Alexander Burness; 2 da (Georgina Gerda b 21 Sept 1976, Julia Irene b 6 Oct 1978); *Style—* The Hon Mrs Burness; 4 Clarendon Close, London W2 4NS

BURNET, David Stewart; s of Alexander James Findlay Burnet, of Ilfracombe, Queensland, Aust (ka 1944), and Bonnie Jean McNair, *née* Stewart (d 1974); *b* 7 April 1927; *Educ* Scotch Coll Melbourne Victoria Australia, Univ of Melbourne (B Com); *m* 2 Feb 1951, Elizabeth Joan Phyllis, da of Frederick William Haig, AFC, of Portsea, Victoria, Australia (d 1984); 2 s (Gregory b 1953, John b 1958), 2 da (Sue b 1957, Katarina b 1964); *Career* chm: Testlink Holdings Ltd, CMR Ltd; non-exec dir Vikingate Ltd; *Recreations* tennis, swimming, skiing, farming; *Style—* David Burnet, Esq; Westland Farm, Ewhurst, Surrey

BURNET, George Wardlaw; LVO (1981), DL (Midlothian 1975); s of Sheriff John Rudolph Wardlaw Burnet, KC (d 1941), and Lucy Margaret Ord, *née* Wallace (d 1962); *b* 26 Dec 1927; *Educ* Edinburgh Acad, Lincoln Coll Oxford (BA), Univ of Edinburgh (LLB); *m* 26 July 1951, Jane Elena Moncrieff, da of Malcolm Moncrieff Stuart, CIE, OBE, of Smeaton Dower, Inveresk, Midlothian; 2 s (Peter b 1957, Andrew b 1962), 1 da (Sarah b 1955); *Career* Served Black Watch (RHR) TA, ret Capt 1957; WS 1954; sr ptnr Murray Beith & Murray WS, chm The Life Assoc of Scotland Ltd, dir Hibernian Life Assoc Ltd and other cos; cncllr Midlothian 1967-76; convener Church of Scotland Fin Ctee 1980-83; Brig Royal Company of Archers (HM The Queen's Bodyguard for Scotland); legal advsr RIAS 1962- (hon fell 1980); KStJ; *Recreations* shooting, gardening, architecture; *Clubs* New (Edinburgh); *Style—* George Burnet, Esq, LVO, DL; Rose Court, Inveresk, Midlothian; 39 Castle St, Edinburgh (☎ 031 225 1200)

BURNET, Sir James William Alexander (Alastair); s of late Alexander and Schonaid Burnet, of Edinburgh; *b* 12 July 1928; *Educ* The Leys Sch Cambridge, Worcester Coll Oxford; *m* 1958, Maureen Campbell Sinclair; *Career* former editor: The Economist, Daily Express; news presenter ITN 1976- (News at Ten), assoc ed News at Ten 1982-; dir Times Newspaper Hldgs; kt 1984; *Style—* Sir Alastair Burnet; 43 Hornton Court, Campden Hill Rd, London W8

BURNET, Pauline Ruth; CBE (1970), JP (1957); da of Rev Edmund Willis (d 1946), and Constance Marjorie, *née* Bostock (d 1968); *b* 23 Aug 1920; *Educ* St Stephen's Coll Kent; *m* 1940, John Forbes Burnet (d 1989), s of William Hodgson Burnet (d 1932); 2 s (David, Martin (decd)), 1 da (Susan); *Career* housewife, memb Windsor & Eton HMC 1948, Fulbourn & Ida Darwin HMC 1951-74; chm: Cambridgeshire AHA (Teaching) 1974-82, Cambridge Mencap; pres Cambridgeshire Mental Welfare Assoc; *Recreations* walking, swimming; *Style—* Mrs Pauline Burnet, CBE, JP; Grange House, Selwyn Gardens, Cambridge CB3 9AZ (☎ 0223 350726)

BURNETT, (Robert) Andrew; s of Wing-Cdr Robert Leslie Burnett, AFC, of Barton-on-Sea, and Barbara Noel, *née* Pink; *b* 20 Feb 1942; *Educ* St Lawrence Coll Kent; *m* 8 Feb 1964, Patricia, da of John Holden, of Bournemouth; 2 s (Robert Gwyer b 27 Nov 1966, Richard John b 14 April 1969), 2 da (Sarah Louise b 6 Sept 1965, Ann-Marie Frances b 23 Aug 1970); *Career* served HAC 1960-65; joined Price Waterhouse 1960 (ptnr 1974, nat dir of Info Technol); dir American C of C; FCA 1965; *Recreations* computers, skiing, golf, jogging; *Clubs* North Hants Golf (Fleet), Hon Artillery Co; *Style—* Andrew Burnett, Esq; Sutherland, 75 Elvetham Rd, Fleet, Hants GU13 8HL (☎ 0252 621 419); Price Waterhouse, Southwark Towers, 32 London Bridge St, London SE1 9GY (car 0836 525 432, telex 884657/8)

BURNETT, Lt Cdr Arthur Noel Stuart; RN; s of Alexander Douglas Gilbert Burnett (d 1962), of Kemnay, Aberdeenshire, Ceylon and London, and Margaret Irene, *née* Kennedy (d 1978); *b* 16 Dec 1922; *Educ* Cheltenham, RN Engrg Coll Devonport; *m* 6 Sept 1952, Elizabeth Gwynne, da of Rev Arthur Molony (d 1976), of Cragg, Co Clare, Eire; 2 s (Andrew (Andy), Robin), 2 da (Penelope (Penny), Joanna (Joey)); *Career* cadet 1941; midshipman (E) RN Russian Convoy 1943: HMS Belfast, HMS Duke of York; HMS Manxman (Far E Pacific Fleet) 1944-45, HMS Duke of York (Flagship Far E Fleet) 1945-6; RN Sch of Physical Trg Portsmouth 1947; PT and Recreational Trg Offr: HMS Imperieuse, HMS Raleigh 1946-49, HMS Devonshire (cadet trg cruiser) 1949-50; engr in chief Admty Bath 1950-52-, chief engr HMS Cygnet 1952-54, PT and Recreational Trg Offr HMS Thunderer and RN Engrg Coll Plymouth 1955-57, sqdn engr offr MTBS HMS Hornet (Gosport) 1958, chief engr HMS Puma (S Atlantic Sqdn) 1958-60, dir Gen Ship Dept Admty Bath 1960-63, ret 1963; sales mangr Elliott Marine Automation Greenwich 1963-65, marine mangr FA Hughes & Son (Epsom) 1965-69; pres and chief exec: Int Marine Servs 1970-81, offshore & Marine Int Servs & Assoc 1981; Devon CCC 1949-57, Rugby Union referee Somerset Co 1960-63, memb: MCC (playing) 1957, MCC Main Ctee 1983-86, MCC Bicentenary Sub Ctee 1985-87, Soc of Petroleum Engrs, Soc of Underwater Technol; C Eng, FIMarE, MIMechE, MRINA, MCIM; *Clubs* RAC; *Style—* Lt Cdr Arthur Burnett, RN; Castleton, Hookwood Park, Limpsfield, Surrey RH8 0DU (☎ 0883 712637); Inst of Directors, 116 Pall Mall, London (☎ 071 839 1233, fax 071 930 1949, telex 21614 IOD G)

BURNETT, Air Chief Marshal Sir Brian Kenyon; GCB (1970, KCB 1965, CB 1961), DFC (1942), AFC (1939); s of Kenneth Burnett (d 1959), of Hurley, Maidenhead, Berks, and Anita Catherine, *née* Evans (d 1964); *b* 10 March 1913; *Educ* Charterhouse, Wadham Coll Oxford (BA); *m* 4 Nov 1944, Valerie Mary, da of Joseph St Ludger (d 1952), of Bromsgrove, Worcs; 2 s; *Career* joined RAF 1934, Long Distance Record Flight 7158 miles Egypt to Australia Nov 1938, served WWII, dir Bomber and Reconnaissance Ops Air Miny 1956-57, IDC 1958, air offr Admin HQ Bomber Command 1959-61, AOC No 3 Gp Bomber Cmd 1961-64, vice chief of Air Staff 1964-67, air sec MOD 1967-70, C-in-C Far East Cmd Singapore 1970-71, ret

1972; ADC to HM The Queen 1953-57 and Air ADC 1969-72; hon fell Wadham Coll Oxford 1974; pres Squash Racquets Assoc 1972-75; chm All England Lawn Tennis Club Wimbledon 1974-83 (vice pres 1984-); *Recreations* lawn tennis, golf, skiing; *Clubs* RAF, Int Lawn Tennis of GB, Hankley Common Golf; *Style*— Air Chief Marshal Sir Brian Burnett, GCB, DFC, AFC; Heather Hill, Littleworth Cross, Seale, Farnham, Surrey GU10 1JN (☎ 025 18 2165)

BURNETT, Carl Joseph; s of Carl Joseph Burnett, Sr, and Elizabeth, *née* Smith (d 1976); *b* 4 Jan 1927; *Educ* US Naval Acad, Harvard Sch of Mgmnt; *m* 1; 1 s (Michael), 1 da (Kathryn); m 2, 1980, Patricia, da of Percy B Cooke; *Career* served US Navy WWII, Lieut, Atlantic and Euro theatre, Pacific; chm and pres Mobil N Sea 1985-88, chm Burnett Assocs and Stena Offshore Ltd; dir: Hardy Oil and Gas, J P Kenny Partners Ltd; FIOD, Fell Nigerian Mining and Geoscience Soc; MInstPet; *Recreations* golf, tennis; *Clubs* Highgate, RAC; *Style*— Carl J Burnett, Jr; 1A Akenside Rd, London NW3; office: 108 New Bond St, London W1

BURNETT, Charles David; s and h of Sir David Burnett, 3 Bt, MBE, TD; *b* 18 May 1951; *Educ* Harrow, Lincoln Coll Oxford; *m* 21 Oct 1989, Victoria Joan, er da of James Simpson, of Rye, Sussex; *Career* underwriting memb of Lloyd's; *Recreations* wine, fishing, travel; *Clubs* Brooks's, Turf, 106 (pres); *Style*— Charles Burnett, Esq

BURNETT, Charles John; s of Charles Alexander Urquhart Burnett (d 1977), of Fraserburgh, Aberdeenshire, and Agnes, *née* Watt; *b* 6 Nov 1940; *Educ* Fraserburgh Acad, Gray's Sch of Art Aberdeen (DA), Aberdeen Coll of Educn; *m* 29 April 1967, Aileen Elizabeth, da of Alexander Robb McIntyre (d 1982), of Portsoy, Banffshire; 2 s (Sandy b 1972, John b 1976), 1 da (Sara b 1969); *Career* Advertising Dept House of Fraser 1963-64, Exhibitions Div Central Office of Information 1964-68, asst curator Letchworth Museum and Art Gallery 1968-71, head of design Nat Museum of Antiquities of Scotland 1971-85, curator of fine art Scot United Servs Museum Edinburgh Castle 1985-; heraldic advsr Girl Guide Assoc Scotland 1978-, vice patron Genealogical Soc of Queensland Aust 1986-, cncl memb Soc of Antiquaries of Scot 1986-88, memb Advsy Bd Heraldry Soc of Ireland 1986-, vice pres Heraldry Soc of Scot 1987-, librarian Priory of the Order of St John in Scot 1987-; numerous pubns on Scottish history and heraldry; HM Offr of Arms: Dingwall Pursuivant 1983, Ross Herald 1988; hon citizen State of Oklahoma USA 1989; FSA Scot 1964, AMA 1972, FHSS 1989; KStJ 1991 (CStJ 1982, OStJ 1974, SBStJ 1972); *Recreations* reading, visiting places of historic interest; *Style*— Charles J Burnett, Esq; 3 Hermitage Terrace, Morningside, Edinburgh EH10 4RP (☎ 031 447 5472); Scottish United Services Museum, Edinburgh Castle EH1 2NG (☎ 031 225 7534); Court of the Lord Lyon, HM New Register House, Edinburgh EH1 3YT (☎ 031 556 7255)

BURNETT, David Henry; s of George Dawson Burnett, CBE, TD, of Surrey, and Ferdinanda Anna Van Den Brandeler; *b* 16 Dec 1951; *Educ* Tonbridge, Churchill Coll Cambridge (MA); *Career* dir Capital Markets - New Issues, Samuel Montagu & Co Ltd; *Style*— David H Burnett, Esq; Faircroft, Vale of Health, London NW3 1AN; Samuel Montagu & Co Ltd, 10 Lower Thames St, London EC3R 6AE (☎ 071 260 9000, telex 889213)

BURNETT, Sir David Humphery; 3 Bt (UK 1913), of Selborne House, Co Borough of Croydon; MBE (1945), TD; s of Col Sir Leslie Trew Burnett, 2 Bt, CBE, TD, DL (d 1955), and Joan, Lady Burnett, *qv*; *b* 27 Jan 1918; *Educ* Harrow, St John's Coll Cambridge (MA); *m* 21 July 1948, Geraldine Elizabeth Mortimer, da of late Sir Godfrey Arthur Fisher, KCMG; 2 s (and 1 s decd); *Heir* s, Charles David Burnett b 18 May 1951; *Career* served WWII (despatches) in France N Africa Sicily and Italy, temp Lt-Col GSO1 1945; ptnr David Burnett & Son (chartered surveyors) 1947-50; dir: Proprietors of Hay's Wharf Ltd 1950-80 (chm 1964-80), Gaurdian Royal Echange Assurance Ltd 1967-88; memb Port of London Authy 1962-75; one of HM Lieuts of City of London; chm: London Wharfingers Assoc 1964-71, S London Botanical Inst 1976-81 (pres 1985); memb Cncl Brighton Coll; Master: Co of Watermen and Lightermen of the River Thames 1964, Worshipful Co of Gridlers 1970; FRICS, FLS; *Style*— Sir David Burnett, Bt, MBE, TD; Tandridge Hall, nr Oxted, Surrey; Tillmouth Park, Cornhill-on-Tweed, Northumberland

BURNETT, David John Stuart; s of J E Burnett; *b* 6 Feb 1958; *Educ* Oundle, Peterhouse Cambridge; *m* 1988, Anne, da of C J C Humfrey; 1 s (Joe Alexander Stuart b 9 Aug 1990); *Career* stockbroker; former ptnr Rowe & Pitman, dir Warburg Securities; *Style*— David Burnett, Esq; The Old Rectory, Steeple Gidding, Huntingdon, Cambs (☎ 08323 488); 70 Holland Park, London W11 (☎ 071 243 0887)

BURNETT, George Dawson; CBE (1985), TD; s of George Alexander Burnett (d 1952), of Belsay, Northumberland, and Fanny Louisa Evelyn, *née* Dawson; *b* 30 Sept 1917; *Educ* Pocklington Sch; *m* 20 Jan 1951, Ferdinanda Anna (Nan), da of Jonkheer Bastiaan van den Brandeler (d 1970), of Zeist, The Netherlands; 2 s (David Henry b 1951, Daniel George b 1954); *Career* WWII 2 Lt 1939 (POW 1942, escaped 1943, despatches), demob Maj RA 1946; gen mangr: Nat Provincial Bank Ltd 1967-68 (sec 1963-67), Nat West Bank Ltd 1969-77 (dir 1973-77); chm Jt Ctee on Gilt Edged Settlements 1977-79; dir: TSB (England and Wales) plc 1979-87 (dep chm 1983-87), London Italian Bank Ltd 1989-; FCIB 1970; *Recreations* fishing, golf; *Clubs* Richmond Golf; *Style*— George Burnett, Esq, CBE, TD; The Warren, Fitzgeorge Ave, New Malden, Surrey KT3 4SH (☎ 081 949 2245)

BURNETT, Joan, Lady; Joan; da of late Lt-Col Sir John Humphery (d 1938), and his 1 wife, Amy Constance, *née* Rixon; *m* 1917, Col Sir Leslie Trew Burnett, 2 Bt, CBE, TD, DL (d 1955); 2 s, 2 da (and 1 da decd); *Style*— Joan, Lady Burnett; Stratton Cottage, Godstone, Surrey

BURNETT, Prof John; s of Arthur Burnett (d 1971), of Nottingham, and Evelyn, *née* Thornton (d 1961); *b* 20 Dec 1925; *Educ* High Pavement Sch Nottingham, Emmanuel Coll Cambridge (BA, MA, LLB), LSE (PhD); *m* 2 Aug 1951, Denise, da of Frank Brayshaw (d 1973), of Morecambe, Lancs; 1 s (Mark Thornton b 1961); *Career* lectr Guildford Tech Coll 1948-59, head of liberal studies Poly of South Bank 1959-63, head of general studies Brunel Coll 1963-66, pro vice chllr Brunel Univ 1980-83 (reader in social history 1966-72, prof 1972-), author 9 books and numerous papers articles and reviews; chm Social History Soc of the UK 1985-; *Books* Destiny Obscure (1982), Useful Toil (1984), A Social History of Housing (1986), Plenty and Want. A Social History of Food (1989); *Recreations* writing, architecture, antiques, jazz (clarinet); *Style*— Prof John Burnett; Dept of Government, Brunel University, Uxbridge, Middx (☎ 0895 56461)

BURNETT, (Ernest) John; s of Ernest Burnett, MBE, of Staplehurst Manor, Staplehurst, Kent, and Norah Agnes, *née* Davis (d 1982); *b* 7 Oct 1931; *Educ* Liverpool Collegiate Sch, Colfe's GS; *m* 17 Dec 1955, Anne, da of Walter Hazell (d 1946), of IOW; 2 s (Jonathan b 1959, David b 1963), 1 da (Brigitte b 1956); *Career* CA 1955; ptnr Victor Stewart & Co 1959-69, princ John Burnett & Co (later John Burnett McMahon & Co) 1969-; cncllr Maidstone Borough 1972-84; Freeman City of London, memb Court of Assts Worshipful Co of Bowyers; FCA, FCCA, ATII; *Recreations* philosophy, restoration of Elizabethan timbered house; *Style*— John Burnett, Esq; Chequers, High St, Headcorn, Ashford, Kent TN27 9NE (☎ 0622 890 052); 103 Newgate St, London EC1A 7AP (☎ 071 606 4861, fax 071 606 4862)

BURNETT, Sir John Harrison; s of Rev T Harrison Burnett, of Paisley; *b* 21 Jan 1922; *Educ* Kingswood Sch Bath, Merton Coll Oxford; *m* 1945, Enid Margaret, er da of Rev Dr Edgar W Bishop; 2 s; *Career* served WWII Lt RNVR (despatches) Atlantic, Channel, Mediterranean; fell Magdalen Coll Oxford 1949-54; prof of Botany: Univ of St Andrews 1955-60, Univ of Newcastle 1960-68; Regius prof of Botany Univ of Glasgow 1968-70, Sibthorpian prof of rural economy and fellow St John's Oxford 1970-79, princ and vice chllr Univ of Edinburgh 1979-87; Hon FRSC Edin 1983, Dr hc Edin 1988; Hon LLD: Dundee 1982, Strathclyde 1983 Glasgow 1987; Hon DSc: Buckingham 1981, Pennsylvania 1983; exec sec World Cncl for the Biosphere 1987-; chm Coordinating Cmmn for Biological Recording 1988; kt 1987; *Books* Vegetation of Scotland (1964), Fundamentals of Mycology (1968, 1976), Mycogenetics (1975), Edinburgh Univ Portaits II (1985), Speciation in Fungi (1988); *Recreations* writing, walking, gardening; *Clubs* Athenaeum (London); *Style*— Sir John Burnett; c/o Agricultural Science Building, Department of Plant Sciences, Parks Road, Oxford OX1 3PR (☎ 0865 270880)

BURNETT, Paul Arthur Brian; s of Brian Walter Burnett, of Wittersham, Kent, and Eve Catherine Anne, JP, *née* McHaffie; *b* 24 June 1957; *Educ* Tonbridge, RCM (GRSM, ARCM); *Career* freelance conductor, horn player, organist and harpsichordist; professional homoeopath; asst dir of music Downside 1980-, hornplayer BBC Symphony Orch, English Chamber Orch, English Wind Ensemble 1980-; fndr and music dir Purley Philharmonic Soc 1980-, conductor Dulwich Orch 1982-, don Winchester Coll 1983-87; Freeman City of London 1982-, Liveryman Worshipful Co of Musicians 1982-; memb Royal Coll of Organists 1981-; *Recreations* tennis, squash; *Style*— Paul Burnett, Esq; Flat 3, Arndell House, 48 Benhill Wood Road, Sutton Surrey SM1 4HN (☎ 081 642 7484)

BURNETT, Dr Rodney Alister; s of Ronald Andrew Burnett (d 1961), of Congleton, Cheshire, and Agnes Shirlaw, *née* McGauchie (d 1988); *b* 6 June 1947; *Educ* Sandbach Sch Cheshire, Univ of St Andrews (MB ChB); *m* 1974, Maureen Elizabeth, da of William Patrick Dunn (d 1982), of Burnside, Glasgow; 2 da (Claire Marie b 15 April 1975, Katharine Victoria b 2 June 1981); *Career* lectr in pathology Univ of Glasgow 1974-79, conslt pathologist and head admin Dept of Pathology Stobhill Hosp Glasgow 1979-85, conslt pathologist with responsibility for diagnostic servs Univ Dept of Pathology Western Infirmary Glasgow 1985-; sec Caledonian Branch ACP; FRCPath; *Recreations* golf; *Style*— Dr Rodney Burnett; Department of Pathology, Western Infirmary, Glasgow (☎ 041 339 8822 ext 4343)

BURNETT, Timothy Adrian John; s of late Lt-Col Maurice John Brownless Burnett, DSO, DL, of Dunsa Manor, Dalton, Richmond, North Yorks, and Crystal Henrietta Deschamps, *née* Chamier; *b* 12 April 1937; *Educ* Eton, Trinity Coll Cambridge (BA); *m* 15 Jul 1961, (Catherine Barbara) Jean, da of Dr Julius Harald Beilby (d 1978), of Aiskew House, Bedale, North Yorks; 1 s (James b 1964), 1 da (Henrietta b 1962); *Career* 2 Lt Coldstream Gds 1956-58; asst keeper Dept of Manuscripts Br Museum 1961, Manuscripts Librarian Br Library 1986; owner Dunsa Manor Estate; *Books* The Rise and Fall of a Regency Dandy, The Life and Times of Scrope Berdmore Davies (1981), Byron, Childe Harold Canto III (1988); *Recreations* architectural history, travel, sailing, shooting, fishing; *Clubs* Beefsteak, Pratts, Royal Yacht Sqdn; *Style*— Timothy Burnett, Esq; 11 Highbury Place, London N5 (☎ 071 226 6234); Dunsa Manor, Dalton, Richmond, North Yorks; Dept of Manuscripts, British Library, Great Russell Street, London WC1 (☎ 071 323 7523)

BURNETT ARMSTRONG, Lady (Christine) Caroline Catherine; *née* Rous; eld da of 5 Earl of Stradbroke (d 1983), and Hon Mrs Mary April Rous, *née* Asquith, *qv*; *b* 27 April 1946; *Educ* Stella Maris Convent Bideford, Croft House Sch Dorset, Cranborne Chase Sch Wiltshire, Univ of Zambia, Inst of Educ, Univ of London (BSc, PGCE, DipEd); *m* 1978, John Francis Burnett Armstrong, of Dalby, Terrington, N Yorks, s of Capt George Burnett Armstrong, MC (d 1982); 2 s (Henry b 1978, George b 1982), 1 da (Catherine Julia b 1986); *Career* ptnr in JF Armstrong Farms; *Recreations* riding; *Clubs* The Yorkshire; *Style*— The Lady Caroline Burnett Armstrong; Dalby, Terrington, N Yorks (☎ 034 75 666)

BURNETT-HALL, Richard Hamilton; s of Basil Burnett-Hall (d 1982), and Kathleen Ruth, *née* Wilson; *b* 5 Aug 1935; *Educ* Marlborough, Trinity Hall Cambridge (MA); *m* 25 April 1964, Judith Diana (Judy), da of Robert Newton, CMG (d 1983); 2 s (John b 1967, Graham b 1970), 1 da (Louisa b 1965); *Career* Nat Serv RCS 1954-56, 2 Lt 1955; Carpmaels & Ransford 1960-68, Int Synthetic Rubber Co Ltd 1968-71; McKenna & Co Slrs 1971-: admitted slr 1974, ptnr 1974-; cncl memb UK Environmental Law Assoc, chartered patent agent 1966; Freeman Berwick-upon-Tweed 1965; memb Law Soc; *Recreations* music; *Clubs* United Oxford & Cambridge; *Style*— Richard Burnett-Hall, Esq; McKenna & Co, Mitre House, 160 Aldersgate St, London EC1A 4DD (☎ 071 606 9000, fax 071 606 9100, telex 27251)

BURNETT-HURST, Clive Robert; s of Lt Alexander Robert Burnett-Hurst (d 1973), of Parbold, and Winifred Gladys, *née* Thompson (d 1983); *b* 21 June 1932; *Educ* Clitheroe Royal GS; *m* 30 July 1966, Marjorie, da of Thomas Allen, of Wigan; 1 s (Peter Robert b 1970) 2 da (Caroline Ann b 1973, Alexandra Jill b 1974); *Career* princ managing clerk Wilkinson & Freeman CAs Preston 1957-60, ptnr CR Burnett Hurst & Co CAs Parbold 1959-, lectr on accountancy Wigan and Dist Mining and Tech Coll 1960-74, Stubbs Parkin CAs Formby 1979-; chm Kingswood Parents Assoc Birkdale Southport, rep for Merseyside and Sefton on Ind Schs Action Ctees, memb Liverpool Soc of CAs Educn Ctee; FCA 1958, ATII 1958, ACIS; *Recreations* photography, philately, railway preservation, numismatism; *Style*— Clive R Burnett-Hurst, Esq; 5A The Common, Parbold, Nr Wigan, Lancs WN8 7HA (☎ 0257 462482/ 464403)

BURNETT OF KEMNAY, Madam Susan Letitia; da of Arthur Moubray Burnett (d 1948), of Kemnay, and Muriel, *née* Andrew Speed (d 1963); family granted charter for Kemnay by James VII 1688, Baronage of Scotland; *b* 16 Oct 1922; *Educ* Heatherley, Inverness and Kemnay Secondary Sch; *m* 19 Aug 1946, Fredrick James Milton, s of Edwin Barnes Milton (d 1959), of S Africa; *Career* leading Wren, WRNS Rosyth Cmd; *Recreations* music, drama, gardening, art; *Style*— Madam Burnett of Kemnay; Kemnay House, Kemnay, Aberdeenshire AB5 9LH (☎ 0467 42220)

BURNEY, Sir Cecil Denniston; 3 Bt (UK 1921), of Preston House, Preston Candover, Co Southampton; s of Sir Charles Dennistoun Burney, 2 Bt, CMG (d 1968), and Gladys, *née* High (d 1982); *b* 8 Jan 1923; *Educ* Eton, Trinity Coll Cambridge; *m* 5 Sept 1957, Hazel Marguerite, yr da of Thurman Coleman (d 1939), of Weymouth, Dorset, and former w of Trevor de Hamel; 2 s; *Heir* s, Nigel Dennistoun Burney; *Career* served WWII Special Branch RNVR, Lt; chm: JMD Group plc, Hampton Trust plc 1975-87; memb Legislative Cncl of N Rhodesia 1959-64, MP Zambia 1964-68; chm Public Accounts Ctee Zambia 1964-67; *Recreations* tennis, skiing; *Clubs* White's, Turf, Carlton, Buck's, Leander, Harare, Ndola; *Style*— Sir Cecil Burney, Bt; 5 Lyall St, London SW1X 8DW (☎ 071 235 4014); The Plaza, 535 King's Road, London SW10 0SZ (☎ 071 352 4001, fax 071 376 8966)

BURNEY, Nigel Dennistoun; s and h of Sir Cecil Burney, 3 Bt; *b* 6 Sept 1959; *Educ* Eton, Trinity Coll Cambridge; *Clubs* Turf, Annabels; *Style*— Nigel Burney, Esq; 5 Lyall St, London SW1 (☎ 01 235 4014)

BURNHAM, Peter Michael; s of Frank Burnham (d 1980), of Chislehurst, and Winifred Eileen, *née* Fyson (d 1972); *b* 13 May 1935; *Educ* Eltham Coll, Univ of Bristol (BA); *m* 6 Feb 1963, Jill, da of Langton Gowlland, of Godalming, Surrey; 2 da (Sarah Jane Reily b 6 June 1964, Emma Elizabeth Reily b 6 April 1965); *Career* Nat

Serv Pilot Offr RAF 1959-61 (Sword of Honour 1960); Sturges, Fraser, Cave & Co 1956-59; Coopers & Lybrand: joined 1961, dir 1970, dep md 1983-88, sr dir key accounts 1988-; dir London E Trg and Enterprise Cncl 1989-, cmmr Historic Bldgs & Monuments Cmmn 1984-88, dir UK Cncl for Computing Devpt 1984-88; memb Ctee Royal Thames Yacht Club 1988-; Freeman City of London, memb Worshipful Co of Information Technologists; FCA 1969 (ACA 1959), FCMA 1963; *Recreations* sailing; *Clubs* Reform, Royal Thames Yacht, RAF; *Style—* Peter Burnham, Esq; Tilthams House, Meadrow, Godalming, Surrey GU7 3BX (☎ 04868 4889); Jardinas de la Bahia, No 3, La Herradura, Grenada, Spain (☎ 010 34 5882 7426); Plumtree Ct, London EC4A 4HT (☎ 071 583 5000, 071 822 4520, fax 071 822 4652, telex 887470)

BURNHAM, 5 Baron (UK 1903); Sir William Edward Harry Lawson; 5 Bt (UK 1892), JP (Bucks 1970), DL (1977); s of Maj-Gen 4 Baron Burnham, CB, DSO, MC, TD (d 1963, he was ggs of Joseph Moses Levy, fndr proprietor of The Daily Telegraph as the first London penny daily), and Marie Enid, CBE, *née* Scott-Robson; *b* 22 Oct 1920; *Educ* Eton; *m* 1942, Anne (a DL for Bucks 1985-), da of Maj George Gerald Petherick, of St Cross, Winchester; 1 s (decd), 3 da; *Heir* bro, Hon Hugh Lawson; *Career* landowner; served Royal Bucks Yeomanry 1939-41, Scots Gds 1941-68 (cmd 1 Bn 1959-62), ret as Lt-Col 1968; chm: Sail Trg Assoc 1977-, Masonic Housing Assoc 1979-; *Recreations* sailing, shooting; *Clubs* Royal Yacht Sqdn, Turf, Garrick; *Style—* The Rt Hon the Lord Burnham, Bt, JP, DL; Hall Barn, Beaconsfield, Bucks (☎ 0494 673315)

BURNS, David Allan; s of Lt Col Allan Robert Desmond Burns, GM (d 1968), of New Station House, Bagshot, Surrey, and Gladys Frances, *née* Dine; *b* 20 Sept 1937; *Educ* Brentwood Sch, Sch of E Euro and Slavonic Studies Univ of London; *m* 15 June 1971, Inger Ellen, da of Nils Gustav Kristiansson, of Stockholm, Sweden; 1 s (Paul b 1971), 1 da (Anna b 1974); *Career* 2 Lt RCS 1956-58; jr appts FO Belgrade and Bangkok 1959-71, head of chancery Br Embassy Belgrade 1972-75, asst head Arms Control Dept FCO 1976-79, political cnsllr Br Embassy Bangkok 1979-83, HM consul gen Boston 1983-87, head N America Dept FCO 1988-; memb Marshall Scholarships Selection Ctee for New Eng 1983-87; Freedom City of Lowell Massachusetts 1987; *Recreations* fell walking, sport; *Clubs* Travellers, Royal Bangkok Sports; *Style—* David Burns, Esq; Foreign and Commonwealth Office, King Charles St, London SW1A 2AH (☎ 071 270 2661)

BURNS, Maj-Gen Sir (Walter Arthur) George; GCVO (1991, KCVO 1962), CB (1961), DSO (1944), OBE (1953), MC (1940); s of Walter Spencer Morgan Burns (d 1929) (whose mother was Mary, sister of J Pierpont Morgan, the celebrated American financier), of North Mymms Park, Hatfield, Herts, by his w Ruth (herself 2 da of William Cavendish-Bentinck, MP, who was in his turn ggs of 3 Duke of Portland); *b* 29 Jan 1911; *Educ* Eton, Trinity Coll Cambridge; *Career* served Coldstream Gds from 1932: CO 3 Bn (Italy) 1943-44 and Palestine 1947-50, Bde Maj Household Bde 1945-47, CO 3 Bn 1948-50, DAG London Dist 1950-52, Regtl Lt-Col 1952-55, cdr 4 Gds Bde 1955-59, GOC London Dist and Household Bde 1959-62, Col 1966-; Lord-Lieut Herts 1961-1986; also served as ADC to Viceroy India 1938-40 and Staff Coll Camberley 1945; steward Jockey Club 1964-67; *Style—* Major-General Sir George Burns, GCVO, CB, DSO, OBE, MC; (☎ 0707 45117)

BURNS, Graham Gordon; s of Gordon Burns, of Bebington, Merseyside, and Freda, *née* Bayley; *b* 9 Aug 1958; *Educ* King's Sch Chester, Univ of Durham (BA); *Career* admitted slr 1983; ptnr Stephenson Harwood 1988- (articled clerk 1981-83, asst slr 1983-88); Freeman City of London Slrs Co 1989; memb Law Soc 1983; *Recreations* hockey, skiing, cricket, walking; *Clubs* Wimbledon Hockey; *Style—* Graham Burns, Esq; 7 Strachan Place, Crooked Billet, Wimbledon, London SW19 4RH; Stephenson Harwood, One St Paul's Churchyard, London EC4M 8SM (☎ 071 329 4422, fax 071 606 0822, telex 886789 SHSPC G)

BURNS, Iain Keatings; s of Edward Burns (d 1962), and Mary Ann, *née* Keatings; *b* 6 April 1948; *Educ* St Mungos Acad Glasgow, Univ of Glasgow (BSc); *m* 1972, Adrienne Mary Elizabeth, *née* Kelly; 2 s (Jonathan b 1975, Nicholas b 1981), 1 da (Jennifer b 1977); *Career* dir: Glasses Guide Service Ltd 1982-85, William Collins plc 1973-82, Pan Books Ltd 1986-; finance dir: Octopus Publishing Gp, Int Thomson Publishing Ltd; ACMA; *Recreations* music, reading, painting; *Style—* Iain Burns, Esq; 30 Greystone Gdns, Kenton, Middx HA3 0EG (☎ 01 907 8585); 59 Grosvenor Street, London W1X 9DA (☎ 01 493 5841)

BURNS, James; JP (Motherwell 1972), DL (1989); s of James Burns (d 1980), and Mary, *née* Magee; *b* 8 Feb 1931; *Educ* St Patrick's Sch Shotts, Coatbridge Tech Coll; *m* 1959, Jean, da of John Ward (d 1951); 2 s (James, Colin); *Career* engr NCB 1948-71; memb: Lanark CC 1967-75, Lanarkshire Health Bd 1973-77, Strathclyde Regnl Cncl 1974-; vice-convener 1978-82, convenor Strathclyde Regnl Cncl 1982-86; chm: Gen Purposes Ctee 1975-82, Visiting Ctee HM Prison Shotts 1980-86; memb: Cwlth Games Cncl for Scotland 1982-86, Main Organising Ctee Cwlth Games 1982-86; hon pres: Strathclyde Community Rels Cncl 1982-, The Princess Louise Scottish Hosp (Erskine Hosp) 1982-86; vice pres St Andrew's Ambulance Assoc 1984-; patron: Strathclyde Youth Club 1982-, The Scottish Pakistani Assoc 1984-, Scottish Retirement Cncl 1984-; *Recreations* fishing, golf; *Style—* James Burns, Esq, JP, DL; 57 Springhill Rd, Shotts ML7 5JA (☎ 0501 20187); Strathclyde Regional Council, Strathclyde House, India St, Glasgow G2 4PF (☎ 041 227 3395, telex 777237)

BURNS, Dr James; s of John Burns (d 1971), of Liverpool, and Margaret, *née* Eales (d 1945); *b* 20 May 1937; *Educ* St Francis Xavier's Coll Liverpool, Univ of Liverpool (MB ChB, MD); *m* 28 July 1964, Noreen Susan, da of John Dudley Pauling (d 1988), of Liverpool; 2 s (John b 1966, Michael b 1968), 1 da (Sally b 1969); *Career* lectr in forensic pathology Univ of Liverpool 1969-73, conslt pathologist St John Gen Hosp New Brunswick Canada and hon lectr Dalhousie Univ of Nova Scotia Canada 1973-78, home office pathologist City of Birmingham (1978-81), conslt pathologist Selly Oak Hosp Birmingham 1978-81, home office pathologist Merseyside 1981-, sr lectr in forensic pathology Univ of Liverpool 1981-, hon conslt histopathologist Royal Liverpool Hosp 1981-; author of papers on pathology and forensic pathology in various jls; memb Bd of Examiners RCPath, cncl memb Br Assoc in Forensic Med, meetings sec Merseyside Medico-Legal Soc; FRCPath 1980 (MRCPath 1969); *Recreations* golf, music, literature; *Clubs* The Xaverian, Birch House; *Style—* Dr James Burns; 5 Sinclair Drive, Liverpool L18 0HN (☎ 051 722 6266); Sub-Department of Forensic Pathology, Duncan Building, Royal Liverpool Hospital, PO Box 147, Liverpool L69 3BX (☎ 051 706 4300, fax 051 722 6266, telex 627095 UNILPL G)

BURNS, Sir John Crawford; s of William Barr Burns, and Elizabeth Crawford; *b* 29 Aug 1903; *Educ* Glasgow HS; *m* 1941, Eleanor Margaret Haughton, da of late Rev Montague G James; 1 s, 3 da; *Career* served WW II, Capt; dir James Finlay & Co 1957-74; kt 1957; *Recreations* golf, fishing; *Clubs* Oriental; *Style—* Sir John Burns; Blairalan, Dargai Terrace, Dunblane, Perthshire (☎ 0786 822367)

BURNS, Keith John; s of Brian Brendan Burns, of Leigh, Lancashire, and Veronica Josephine, *née* Renton; *b* 1 Dec 1962; *Educ* St Aelred's HS Newton Merseyside, Manchester Youth Theatre, Mountview Theatre Sch London (singing scholar); *Career* actor; theatre roles incl: Narrator in The Threepenny Opera (Sweden) 1984, Riff-Raff in The Rocky Horror Show (Nat tour) 1984-85, Montparnasse in Les Miserables (Barbican) 1985-86, Marius in Les Miserables (Palace) 1986, princ performer in Merrily We Roll Along (The Canery Shaftesbury) 1988, Duncaire in Carmen (Vienna Kammeroper) 1988-89, Thuy in Miss Saigon (Drury Lane) 1989-, Judas' in Jesus Christ Superstar The Concert (Barbican) 1990, princ performer in Sondheim Masterclasses (Univ of Oxford) 1990; TV work incl: Royal Variety Performance 1987, Oliver Awards 1987, Stage by Stage 1988, the Heat Is On (The Making of Thames) 1989; prodr: Kiss of the Spider Woman, Friday Night Tears (musical) 1988, Man in the Moon; original cast recordings incl: Miss Saigon, Les Miserables (also symphonic recording); *Recreations* travel, walking, records, tennis, Coronation St, reading (crime); *Clubs* Browns, Great Queen St; *Style—* Keith Burns, Esq; c/o Mr Richard Grenville, London Management, 235 Regent St, London W1A 2JT (☎ 071 493 1610)

BURNS, Kevin Francis Xavier; CMG (1984); *b* 18 Dec 1930; *Educ* Finchley GS, Trinity Coll Cambridge (BA); *m* 1963, Nan Pinto (d 1984); 1 s , 1 da; *Career* Br high cmmr to Ghana and ambass (non-resident) to Togo 1983-86, Br high cmmr to Barbados and E Caribbean 1986-90; *Style—* Kevin Burns, Esq, CMG; Foreign and Commonwealth Office, King Charles St, London SW1

BURNS, Hon Mrs (Mary Margaret); *née* Addington; da of 7 Viscount Sidmouth; *b* 27 July 1956; *m* 1978, James Alexander Burns; 1 da (Julia b 1985); *Style—* The Hon Mrs Burns; Travessa da Portugesa No 5, Lisbon, Portugal

BURNS, Michael James; s of William James Burns (d 1977), and Belle Evelyn, *née* Harrison (d 1970); *b* 18 June 1925; *Educ* St Paul's, Hertford Coll Oxford (MA); *Career* gen mangr and dir Equity & Law Life Assur Soc 1974-86 (joined 1948); non exec dir: Nat Home Loans 1985-91, Ecclesiastical Insur Office 1987-; memb Cncl Inst Actuaries 1973-82 (treas 1979-81); hon treas: Nat Fedn Music Socs 1981-88, Insur Benevolent Fund 1987-; Freeman City of London 1979; Liveryman: Worshipful Co of Musicians 1981, Worshipful Co of Actuaries 1984; FIA 1955; *Recreations* music, travel; *Style—* Michael Burns, Esq; 7 Laverton Mews, London SW5 0PB (☎ 071 370 4709)

BURNS, Neil David; s of (Edmund) Roy Burns, of Chelmsford, Essex, and (Rose) Marie, *née* Cordery; *b* 19 Sept 1965; *Educ* Moulsham HS; *m* 26 Sept 1987, Susan Anne, da of Brian Arthur Laurence Clark; *Career* Essex CCC 1982-86 (first class debut v Surrey 1986), Somerset CCC 1987-, advanced cricket coach; rep: Eng Young Cricketers WI tour 1985; Essex CCC Young Player of the Year 1984; chm and dir NBC Ltd 1988-; *Recreations* playing & watching most sports, photography; *Style—* Neil Burns, Esq; NBC Ltd, B W Estate, Olnmixon Crescent, Weston-super-Mare, Avon BS24 9BA (☎ 0934 417576, fax 0934 635264)

BURNS, Paul; s of Edward Burns, of Hamilton, and Gertrude, *née* Press; *b* 28 May 1947; *Educ* St Aloysius Coll Glasgow, Univ of Glasgow (LLB); *m* 11 Sept 1977, Diana Mary, da of Thomas Taylor (d 1986); 1 da (Madeleine Kirsty b 1985); *Career* Lieut RCT; slr; sr ptnr Hamilton Burns Moore 1987-; fndr and chm Legal Defence Union 1986-, fndr and ed Glasgow Legal Review, memb Cncl Law Soc; *Recreations* flying, fencing, writing, philosophy, archaeology; *Clubs* RSAC, Royal Cwlth Soc; *Style—* Paul Burns, Esq; 17 Winton Drive, Glasgow; Hamilton Burns & Moore, 111 Union Street, Glasgow (☎ 041 248 6668)

BURNS, Sandra Pauline; CB (1989); da of John Burns, and Edith Maud, *née* Manning; *b* 19 June 1938; *Educ* Manchester Central HS for Girls, Somerville Coll Oxford (BA, BCL); *Career* called to the Bar Middle Temple 1964, parliamentary counsel 1980-; *Recreations* computer programming; *Style—* Miss Sandra Burns, CB; Office of the Parliamentary Counsel, 36 Whitehall, London SW1 (☎ 071 210 6630)

BURNS, Simon Hugh McGuigan; s of Maj Brian Stanley Burns, MC, of Wilts, and Shelagh Mary, *née* Nash; *b* 6 Sept 1952; *Educ* Christ the King Sch Accra Ghana, Stamford Sch, Worcester Coll Oxford (BA); *m* 1982, Emma Mary, da of David Clifford, of London; 1 da (Amelia b 1987); *Career* political asst to Rt Hon Mrs Sally Oppenheim MP 1975-81, dir What to Buy Ltd 1981-83, conf organiser IOD 1983-87, PPS to Tim Eggar MP Min of State Dept of Education 1990- (Dept of Employment 1989-90); *Recreations* photography, travelling, swimming, antiques; *Clubs* Chelmsford Cons (patron); *Style—* Simon Burns, Esq; House of Commons, London SW1 (☎ 01 219 3000)

BURNS, Sir Terence; s of Patrick Owen Burns, and Doris Burns; *b* 13 March 1944; *Educ* Houghton-le-Spring GS, Univ of Manchester (BA Econ), London Business Sch; *m* 1969, Anne Elizabeth Powell; 1 s, 2 da; *Career* chief econ advsr to Treasy and head Govt Econ Serv 1980-; vice pres Soc of Business Economists 1985-; memb Cncl Royal Econ Soc 1986-; kt 1983; *Recreations* soccer spectator, golf, music; *Clubs* Reform; *Style—* Sir Terence Burns; c/o HM Treasury, Parliament St, London SW1P 3AG (☎ 071 270 5203)

BURNS, Prof (Duncan) Thorburn; s of James Thorburn Burns (d 1953), and Olive Mary Constance, *née* Waugh (d 1987); *b* 30 May 1934; *Educ* Whitcliffe Mount Sch, Univ of Leeds (BSc, PhD); *m* 16 Dec 1961, Valerie Mary, *née* Vinten; 1 s (James Fredrick Thorburn b 1979), 2 da (Mary Jane Thorburn b 1963, Susan Jean Thorburn b 1967); *Career* lectr in physical chemistry Medway Coll of Technol 1959-63 (asst lectr 1958-59), sr lectr in analytical chemistry Woolwich Poly 1965-66, reader Loughborough Univ of Technol 1971-75 (sr lectr 1966-71), prof of analytical chemistry Queens Univ Belfast 1975-; author of numerous papers and reviews; chm Cmmn V/IUPAC 1987-89, pres Analytical Div RSC 1988-90, memb Poisons Bd of NI 1989-; Theophilus Redwood Lecture RSC 1982, Analytical Reactions and Analytical Reagents Medal and Award RSC 1984, Boyle-Higgins Gold Medal, Inst of Chemistry of Ireland 1990, Annual Gold medal and lecture BDH/RSC 1990, Erhen Gold medal Analytical Inst, Tech Univ Vienna; FRSC 1976, MRIA 1984, FRSE 1984; *Recreations* history of chemistry, walking; *Clubs* Savage, Irish; *Style—* Prof Thorburn Burns; Dept of Chemistry, Queens University, Belfast, Northern Ireland BT9 5FG (☎ 0232 661111, fax 0232 247895, telex QUBADM 74487)

BURNSIDE, Dame Edith; DBE (1976, OBE 1957); *m* W K Burnside; 1 s, 1 da; *Career* pres Prince Henry's Hosp Central Cncl of Auxiliary 1952; awarded DBE for services to hospitals and the community; *Style—* Dame Edith Burnside, DBE; Flat 6-1, 9 Struan St, Toorak, Vic 3142, Australia

BURNSTOCK, Prof Geoffrey; FRS (1986); s of James Burnstock (d 1947), and Nancy, *née* Green (d 1978); *b* 10 May 1929; *Educ* Greenford Co GS, King's Coll London (BSc), King's Coll and UCL (PhD), Melbourne Univ (DSc); *m* 9 April 1957, Nomi, da of Sigmund Hirschfeld (d 1988); 3 da (Aviva b 1959, Tamara b 1960, Dina b 1964); *Career* Nat Serv 1947-48; Nat Inst for Med Res London 1956-57, Dept of Pharmacology Univ of Oxford 1957-59, Dept of Physiology Univ of Illinois (Rockefeller travelling fellowship) 1959; Univ of Melbourne Aust: sr lectr Dept of Zoology 1959-62, reader in physiological zoology 1962-64, prof of zoology and chm of dept 1964-75, assoc dean (biological sci) 1969-72; visiting prof Dept of Pharmacology UCLA 1970; UCL: prof of anatomy and head of Dept of Anatomy and Developmental Biology 1975-, convenor centre for neuroscience 1979-, vice dean (Faculty of Med Sci) 1980-83; visiting prof RSM Fndn New York; author of over 600 pubns in scientific and med jls and books; memb Gt Barrier Reef Ctee, fndr memb Int Cncl for Scientific Devpt and Int Acad of Sci; memb Cncl: The Bayliss and Starling Soc, Royal Postgrad Med Sch; memb Int Cncl Neuronegative Res; memb: Bd MRC vice pres Anatomical Society of Great Britain and Ireland 1990-, Br Physiological Soc, Aust Physiological and Pharmacological Soc, Int Soc for Biochemical Pharmacology, Br Pharmacological Soc, Br Anatomical Soc, Euro Artery Club, Int Brain Res Orgn, Int Soc for Devptal

Neuroscience, Euro Neuroscience Assoc, Clinical Autonomic Res Soc; ed in chief Journal of the Autonomic Nervous System, memb Ed Bd of 20 other Journals; Hon MSc 1962; FAA 1971, FRS 1986, Hon MRCP 1987; *Books* How Cells Work (1972), Adrenergic Neurons: Their Organisation, Function and Development in the Peripheral Nervous System (jtly, 1975); An Atlas of the Fine Structure of Muscle and its Innervation (jtly, 1976), Vascular Neuroeffector Mechanisms (jt ed, 1976), Purinergic Receptors (ed, 1981), Somatic and Autonomic Nerve-Muscle Interactions (jt ed, 1983), Nonadrenergic Innervation of Blood Vessels (jt ed, 1988), Peptides: A Target for New Drug Development (jt ed, 1990), The Automatic Nervous System, Vols I-III (ed, 1991); *Recreations* wood sculpture and tennis; *Style*— Prof Geoffrey Burnstock, FRS; Dept of Anatomy and Developmental Biology, UCL, Gower St, London WC1E 6BT (☎ 071 387 7050 ext 3344, fax 071 380 7349)

BURNTON, Stanley Jeffrey; QC (1982); s of Harry Burnton, of London, and Fay, *née* Levy; *b* 25 Oct 1942; *Educ* Hackney Downs GS, St Edmund Hall Oxford (MA); *m* 26 Feb 1971, Gwenyth, da of Frank Castle, of Aust; 1 s (Simon b 1974), 2 da (Abigail b 1972, Rebecca b 1976); *Career* called to the Bar Middle Temple 1965; *Recreations* theatre, wine, travel, reading, music; *Style*— Stanley Burnton, Esq, QC; 9 Kidderpore Ave, London NW3 7SX (☎ 071 431 2819); 1 Essex Court, Temple, London EC4Y 9AR (☎ 071 583 2000, fax 071 583 0118, telex 889109 Essex G)

BURR, John Perry Underwood; MBE (1944); s of John Perry Burr (d 1929), of St Neots, Cambs, and Evelyn Mabel, *née* Underwood (d 1945); *b* 18 July 1918; *Educ* Bedford Sch; *m* 2 June 1945, Kathleen Mary (Billie), da of Arnold Gladstone Palmer (d 1967), of Great Paxton, Cambs; 2 s (David John b 17 Jan 1947, Christopher Stephen b 10 Aug 1951); *Career* served WWII BEF, MEF, Eighth Army (despatches 1943), BAOR, Lt-Col RAOC; brewer; dir Bass Ltd; chm: Bass Products, Bass Europe, Charrington & Co, Crest Hotels, ret 1982; dir Carling-O'Keefe (Toronto) Canada 1977-83; pres Common Market Brewers Cncl 1980-84, vice chm Food and Drinks Ind Cncl 1981-83, chm Sidney C Banks Ltd 1980-, Brewing Research Fndn Cncl 1980-84, memb Inst of Brewing; Bronze Star (USA) 1944; Royal Warrant Holder (1975-78); *Recreations* racing, music; *Style*— John Burr, Esq, MBE; Greenacres, Cleat Hill, Ravensden, Bedford MK41 8AN (☎ 0234 771245); Sidney C Banks plc, St Neots Road, Sandy, Beds (☎ 0767 680351)

BURR, Martin John; s of Bertram John Burr, and Margaret, *née* Mapleson; *b* 19 Feb 1953; *Educ* Berkhamstead Sch, Pembroke Coll Oxford (BA, MA, Dip Comp Phil); *Career* called to the Bar Middle Temple 1978; joined: Lincoln's Inn 1980, Inner Temple 1988; joint head of chambers 1989-; oratorios composed incl: Vita Sci Bonifati, Vita Sci Justi, Vita Sci Cuthberti, Vita Sci Ceddis, Vita Sci Dunstani, Vita Sci Edwardi, Vita Sci Bedae, Vita Moysis, Vita Eliae, Vita Sci Iohannis Baptistae, Vita Sci Pirani; memb: Sion Coll, Henry Sweet Soc, Int Arthurian Soc, Philological Soc, Br Archeological Assoc ACIArb 1990; *Publications* The Law and Health Visitors (1982), papers incl: Legal Punctuation - Past and Present (1986), Anglo-Saxon Wills their Beginnings and Continuations but not their Ends (1989);; *Recreations* theology, liturgiology, opera, plainsong, singing, composing music, neumology, philology, writing poetry, railways; *Style*— Martin Burr, Esq; 2 Temple Gardens, Temple, London EC4Y 9AY (☎ 071 353 4636, fax 071 583 3455)

BURR, Michael Rodney; s of Frank Edward Burr, of Mayals Rd, Swansea, and Aileen Maud, *née* May; *b* 31 Jan 1941; *Educ* Brecon Boys GS, King Edward VI Sch Chelmsford; *m* 30 March 1963, Rhoda, da of Ernest Rule, of Aberdare, Mid Glamorgan; 4 s (David b 1964, Richard b 1965, Andrew b 1967, Edwin b 1973), 1 da (Elizabeth b 1970); *Career* admitted slr 1964; asst slr Hilliard and Ward Chelmsford 1964-69, sr ptnr Peter Williams and Co Swansea 1972-, asst rec 1983, rec 1988; sec Inc Law Soc of Swansea and Dist 1980-83; non cncl memb of Law Soc ctees: Professional Purposes Ctee 1985-86, Adjudication Ctee 1986-89; memb Law Soc; *Recreations* flying; *Style*— Michael Burr, Esq; 93 Walter Rd, Swansea SA1 5QA (☎ 0792 465597, fax 0792 467390)

BURRELL, Denis James; CBE (1982); s of Edwin Charles Merrick Burrell (d 1950); *b* 25 May 1930; *Educ* Rugby, Clare Coll Cambridge (MA); *m* 1977, Susan, da of Eric Alwyn Ingham (d 1978); 1 child; *Career* chm and md Martin Baker Aircraft Co Ltd 1981- (mfr of ejection seats for use in mil aircraft); winner of Queen's Award for Export 1969 and 1982; *Recreations* squash, tennis; *Style*— Denis Burrell Esq, CBE; Denham Mount, Denham, nr Uxbridge, Middx; Martin-Baker Aircraft Co Ltd, Higher Denham, nr Uxbridge, Middx UB9 5AJ (☎ 0895 832214)

BURRELL, Derek William; s of Thomas Richard Burrell (d 1960), and Flora Frances (d 1986), *née* Nash; *b* 4 Nov 1925; *Educ* Tottenham GS, Queens' Coll Cambridge (MA); *Career* asst master Solihull Sch 1948-52, head of Eng Dollar Acad 1952-59, headmaster Truro Sch 1959-86; memb: Headmaster's Conf Secondary Heads Assoc; fully accredited local preacher (Methodist) 1948-; vice chm: Cornwall Ctee of VSO, Govrs of Luton Industl Coll, Mid Cornwall Branch of Leprosy Mission, Methodist Day Sch Ctee; vice pres Br Methodist Conf 1987-88; FRSA; *Recreations* music, drama, walking in London or deep countryside; *Clubs* East India, Devonshire, Sports & Public School; *Style*— Derek Burrell Esq; 2 Strangways Terrace, Truro, Cornwall TR1 2NY (☎ 0872 77733)

BURRELL, Mark William; yr s of Sir Walter Burrell, 8 Bt, CBE, TD, DL (d 1985); *b* 9 April 1937; *Educ* Eton, Pembroke Coll Cambridge (BA); *m* 1966, Margot Rosemary, yr da of Westray Pearce, of Killara, NSW, Aust, and former w of Mackenzie Munro; 2 s, 1 da; *Career* dir: Pearson plc, Lazard Bros & Co. Ltd, Yorkshire Television Holdings Ltd; *Style*— Mark Burrell, Esq; c/o Pearson plc, Millbank Tower London SW1P 4QZ (☎ 071 828 9020)

BURRELL, Michael Ian; s of Sidney Burrell, of Haslemere, Surrey, and Mary, *née* Smith; *b* 25 June 1950; *Educ* Godalming Co GS Surrey, St Peter's Coll Oxford (MA); *Career* journalist Durham Advertiser 1971-72, local govt corr Evening Argus Brighton 1972-73, lobby corr Westminster Press 1973-83, Profile PR 1983-86, md Westminster Strategy 1986-, chm and chief exec R & M European Strategy 1990-; author of various articles on lobbying Westminster, Whitehall and the Euro Community; *Recreations* doing nothing in the sunshine; *Style*— Michael Burrell, Esq; Westminster Strategy, 1 Dean's Yard, London SW1P 3NR (☎ 071 799 9811, fax 071 233 0124); R & M European Strategy, 10 Rue Breydel, 1040 Brussels, Belgium (☎ 010 32 2 230 29 29, fax 010 32 2 230 10 96)

BURRELL, Sir (John) Raymond; 9 Bt (GB 1774), of Valentine House, Essex; s of Lt-Col Sir Walter Burrell, 8 Bt, CBE, TD, DL (d 1985), by his w, Hon Anne Judith, OBE, da of 3 Baron Denman, GCMG, KCVO, PC, JP; *b* 20 Feb 1934; *Educ* Eton; *m* 1, 1959 (m dis 1971), Rowena Frances, da of Michael H Pearce; 1 s ; m 2, 1971, Margot Lucy, da of F E Thatcher, of Sydney; 1 s (Andrew b 1974), 1 da (Catherine b 1977); *Heir* s, Charles Raymond Burrell b 27 Aug 1962; *Style*— Sir Raymond Burrell, Bt; Rosemont House, Sydney, NSW, Australia

BURRETT, (Frederick) Gordon; CB (1974), FSA (1985); s of Frederick Harold John Burrett, of London (d 1957), and Marion, *née* Knowles (d 1956); *b* 31 Oct 1921; *Educ* Emmanuel Sch, St Catharine's Coll Cambridge (BA); *m* 17 April 1943, Margaret Joan, da of Edward George Giddins of Petersfield, Hants (d 1969); 1 s (John b 1954), 2 da (Ann b 1948, Jill b 1949); *Career* served in RE, N Africa, Italy, Yugoslavia, Greece 1942-45 Capt (despatches); Dip Serv 1946: 3 sec Budapest 1946-49, FO 1949-51, vice consul NY 1951-54, FO 1954-57, 1 sec Rome 1957-60; transferred to HM Treasy 1960; private sec to chief sec Treasy 1963-64, asst sec HM Treasy 1964; Cabinet Office 1967-68; sec Review Body on Doctors' and Dentists' Remuneration 1967-68, sec Review Body on Pay of Higher Civil Serv 1967-68, under sec Civil Serv Dept 1969, memb of Civil Serv Pay Res Unit Bd 1978-81, dep sec Civil Serv Dept 1972-81; conducted Govt Scrutiny of V & A and Science Museums 1982; advsr to Govt of Oman on Civil Serv reorganisation 1984, led Govt review of policies and operations of Cwlth Inst 1987, leader of review team on responsibilities of the dirs of the nat museums and galleries 1987, led review of grading of sr Arts Cncl and Br Film Inst posts 1988, chm Ctee of Inquiry into Civil Serv Pay Hong Kong 1988-89, chm Wagner Soc 1984-87; FSA 1985; *Books* article on the watercolours of J M Wright (1777-1866) in vol 54 Old Water Colour Society's Club Annual; *Recreations* reading, music, walking; *Clubs* Athenaeum; *Style*— Gordon Burrett, Esq, CB, FSA; Trinity Cottage, Church Rd, Claygate, Surrey (☎ 0372 462783)

BURRETT, John Arthur; s of Albert Arthur Burrett, of Melbourne, Aust, and Gladys, *née* Green; *b* 23 Oct 1947; *Educ* Eliot Coll Univ of Kent (BA); *m* 17 Aug 1979, Jennifer Ann; *Career* cmmnd RAOC 1970 (ret 1974); called to the Bar Middle Temple 1979; dir: Canterbury Chambers Ltd, Manston Aviation Ltd; *Recreations* private pilot; *Clubs* Thanet Flying; *Style*— John Burrett, Esq; The Canterbury Chambers Ltd, Watling St, Canterbury, Kent CT1 2UD (☎ 0227 456865, fax 0227 456890)

BURRIDGE, Simon St Paul; s of James Dugdale Burridge, of Ab Kettleby, nr Melton Mowbray, Leics, and Anne Henrietta-Maria St Paul, *née* Butler; *b* 20 March 1956; *Educ* Sherborne, The Queen's Coll Oxford; *m* 13 Sept 1986, Camilla Rose, da of Bryan Rogerson Barkes; 1 da (Felicity Rose St Paul b 3 May 1989); *Career* advertising exec; graduate trainee Ayer Barker Hegemann Feb-July 1979, account exec Minden Luby & Associates 1979-1981; Dewe Rogerson: account exec 1981-82, account dir 1982-84, dir 1984-87; dir J Walter Thompson 1988- (sr assoc dir 1987-88); *Recreations* horse racing (family owns: Desert Orchid, Peacework, Tudor Orchid, Irish Orchid), literature; *Style*— Simon Burridge, Esq; J Walter Thompson Company Ltd, 40 Berkeley Square, London W1 (☎ 071 499 4040, fax 071 493 3432/3418, car 0860 493373)

BURRILL, Timothy Peckover; yr s of Lyonel Peckover Burrill, OBE (d 1983), and Marjorie Sybil, *née* Hurlbutt (d 1976); *b* 8 June 1931; *Educ* Eton, Sorbonne; *m* 1, 1959 (m dis 1966) Philippa, o da of Maurice Hare; 1 da (Rebecca Nina b 1961); m 2, 1968 (m dis 1989), Santa, er da of John Raymond; 1 s (Joshua Hal Peckover b 1973), 2 da (Jemima Lucy b 1970, Tabitha Sara b 1974); *Career* served Grenadier Gds 1949-52, 2 Bn 1950-52; jr mgmnt Cayzer Irvine & Co 1952-56; entered film indust 1956, joined Brookfield Productions 1965, md Burrill Productions 1966-, dir World Film Services 1967-69, first prodn admin Nat Film Sch 1972, md Allied Stars (responsible for Chariots of Fire) 1979-80; dir: Dovemead Ltd 1977-, Artistry Ltd (responsible for Superman and Supergirl films) 1982, Central Casting 1988-; conslt Nat Film Devpt Fund 1980-81, chm Film Asset Devpt plc 1987-; chm: BAFTA 1981-83 (vice chm 1979-81), First Film Fndn 1989-; prodr memb: Cinematograph Films Cncl 1980-83, gen Cncl ACTT 1975-76, Exec Ctee Br Film and TV Prodrs Assoc 1981-90; govr: Nat Film and TV Sch 1981-, Nat Theatre 1982-88; memb Exec Ctee The Producers Assoc 1990-; *Recreations* theatre; *Style*— Timothy P Burrill, Esq; 19 Cranbury Rd, London SW6 2NS (☎ 071 736 8673, fax 071 731 3921, mobile tel 0860 576134)

BURRINGTON, Ernest; s of Harold Burrington (d 1978), of Chadderton, Lancs, and Laura, *née* Slater; *b* 13 Dec 1926; *m* 5 Jan 1950, Nancy, da of Fred Crossley (d 1988), of Lees, Oldham; 1 s (Peter), 1 da (Jill); *Career* Army 1943-47; reporter and sub ed Oldham Chronicle 1947-49 (reporter 1941-43), sub ed Bristol Evening World 1950; Daily Herald: sub ed Manchester 1950, night ed 1955, London night ed 1957; asst ed IPC Sun 1965 (night ed 1964), asst ed and night ed News International Sun 1969, dep night ed Daily Mirror 1970, assoc ed Sunday People 1972 (dep ed 1971), ed The People 1985-88 and 1989-90, md Mirror Group Newspapers 1990 (dep chm and asst publisher 1988); dir: MGN Magazine and Newsday Ltd 1989-, Sygma Photo Agency Paris 1990-, The European Ltd 1990-, IQ Newsgraphics Ltd 1990-; chm: Syndication International 1989-, Sunday Correspondent 1990; memb: Int Press Inst, Foreign Press Assoc; tstee: Int Inst of Child Studies, Youthscan; *Recreations* travel, tennis, bridge; *Style*— Ernest Burrington, Esq; Mirror Group Newspapers, Holborn Circus, London EC4A 1AR (☎ 071 822 2599, fax 071 882 2144, telex 896713)

BURROUGH, (Anthony) Paul; s of Evan Jerome Ridgway Burrough (d 1987), of Oxford, and Elaine Shelton, *née* Bliss; *b* 14 Dec 1943; *Educ* Beaumont Coll, RAC Cirencester; *m* 1, 7 June 1968, Veronica Ann, da of Lt-Col Reginald Walter (d 1982); 1 s (Daniel b 7 March 1969), 1 da (Kirsty b 19 Feb 1971); m 2, Gillian Olivia Courtenay, da of Alfred Edward Courtenay Snell (d 1985); *Career* fndr Burrough & Co Estate Agents 1979; MICAC; *Recreations* shooting, riding, racing; *Style*— Paul Burrough, Esq; Rose Cottage, Marten, Marlborough, Wilts (☎ 0264 89 279); Kennet House, High St, Hungerford, Berks (☎ 0488 682349, car 0836 292 976)

BURROUGHS, Dr Andrew Kenneth; s of Kenneth Douglas Burroughs, of Via Montello 30, 00195 Rome, Italy, and Vidia, *née* Sfredda; *b* 26 May 1953; *Educ* Kent Coll Canterbury, Univ of Liverpool (MB ChB, MRCP); *m* 19 Aug 1979, Rajesvarie, da of Govindarajoloo Kamalason Nulliah, of 31 Alexander Drive, Lydiate, Liverpool; 1 da (Natasha b 1983); *Career* registrar in gen med and gastroenterology Royal Free Hosp London 1979-81, hon clinical lectr Royal Free Hosp Sch of Med 1981-83, lectr in med and hon sr registrar Royal Free Hosp and Sch of Med 1983-87 (sr lectr and hon conslt physician 1988-); ctee memb Br Assoc for the Study of the Liver, press offr Br Digestive Fndn; Cavaliere Ufficiale al Ordine del Merito della Repubblica Italiana 1989; *Recreations* philately, tourism; *Style*— Dr Andrew Burroughs; Hepato-biliary and Liver Transplantation Unit, Royal Free Hospital and School of Medicine, Pond St, Hampstead, London NW3 2QG (☎ 01 794 0500, fax 01 435 5803)

BURROUGHS, Philip Anthony; s of Anthony John Burroughs, of 7 Arden Close, Bovington, Herts, and Brenda Mabel, *née* Downing; *b* 2 Oct 1955; *Educ* Hemel Hempstead GS, Univ of Bristol (LLB); *m* 23 July 1977, Katharine Mary, da of Douglas Campbell Doughty, of 21 Dundale Rd, Tring, Herts; 1 s (Alastair b 1984), 1 da (Rebecca b 1982); *Career* admitted slr 1980; asst slr Freshfields 1980-83, ptnr Lawrence Graham 1985 (asst slr 1983-85); chm Langleys Round Table 1988-89 (memb 1984); Freeman Worshipful Co of Solicitors; memb: Law Soc, City London Law Soc, Westminster Law Soc; affiliate Br Cncl Shopping Centres; *Recreations* Round Table, reading, wine, gardening; *Style*— Philip Burroughs, Esq; Messrs Lawrence Graham, 190 Strand, London WC2R 1JN (☎ 071 379 0000, fax 071 379 6854)

BURROW, Dr Charles Thomas; s of Richard Burrow, of 42 Slyne Rd, Lancaster, and Ivy Reta *née* Coates; *b* 22 Sept 1945; *Educ* Lancaster Royal GS, Univ of Liverpool (MB ChB); *m* Ann Jane, da of William George Frederick Gunstone (d 1977); 1 s (Michael b 1987), 2 da (Katharine b 1976, Lucy b 1977); *Career* lectr Univ of Liverpool 1975-77, conslt pathologist Walton Hosp Liverpool 1978-; FRCPath 1988 (MRCPath 1976); *Style*— Dr Charles Burrow; Walton Hospital, Rice Lane, Liverpool (☎ 051 525 3611)

BURROW, Francis Andrew; *b* 29 Aug 1936; *m* 1959, Pearl Frances Agnes; 2 s (Kevin, Lee), 1 da (Julie); *Career* md: Simpson Wright & Lowe 1974-82, Nicholls & Wileman 1982-85, Pex Ltd 1985-; *Recreations* sport, gardening; *Style*— Francis

Burrow, Esq; 16 Beggars Lane, Leicester Forest East, Leicester LE3 3NQ (☎ 0533 387577); Pex Limited, 577 Aylestone Rd, Leicester LE2 8TD (☎ 0533 833461, telex 34688, fax 0533 440008)

BURROW, Prof John Wyon; s of Charles Wyon Burrow, of Exeter, and Amy Alice, *née* Vosper; *b* 4 June 1935; *Educ* Exeter Sch, Christ's Coll Cambridge (MA, PhD); *m* 11 Oct 1958, Diane Margaret, da of Harold William Dunnington (d 1983), of Cambridge; 1 s (Laurence b 1961), 1 da (Francesca b 1968); *Career* res fell Christ's Coll Cambridge 1959-62, fell Downing Coll Cambridge 1962-65, lectr Univ of East Anglia 1965-69, reader in history Univ of Sussex 1969-82, prof University of Sussex 1982-; Dr in Scienze Politiche (Bologna) 1988; FRHistS, FBA; *Books* Evolution and Society (1966), A Liberal Descent (1981), Gibbon (1985), Whigs and Liberals (1988); *Style*— Prof John Burrow; 7 Ranelagh Villas, Hove, East Sussex (☎ 0273 731296); Arts Building, Univ of Sussex, Falmer, Brighton, East Sussex (☎ 0273 606755)

BURROW, Richard John; s of Capt John Hilton Burrow, of 9 Windsor Drive, Caistor, Lincs, and Ellen Elizabeth Burdett, *née* Marshall; *b* 19 April 1947; *Educ* Mountgrace Sch Potters Bar; *Career* admitted slr 1975; currently ptnr Berwin Leighton London; memb City of London Slrs Co 1989, Freeman City of London 1989; memb Law Soc 1975; *Recreations* horse breeding, theatre, relaxation; *Style*— Richard Burrow, Esq; Tower Wood, Burwash Rd, Heathfield, East Sussex TN21 8QX (☎ 0435 86 4759); Berwin Leighton, Adelaide House, London Bridge, London EC4R 9HA (☎ 071 623 3144, fax 071 623 4416, telex 886420)

BURROW, Robert Philip; s of Robert F Burrow, Market Harbrough, Leics, and Rosalind, *née* Hughes; *b* 24 March 1951; *Educ* St Georges Coll Weybridge, Fitzwilliam Coll Cambridge (MA); *m* 21 July 1984, Angela Mary, da of Henry Cornelius Bourne Hill, of London SW19; 2 s (Matthew Robert Henry b 5 June 1985, Simon Richard Philip b 20 July 1987); *Career* admitted slr 1975; articled clerk Clifford Turner 1973-75 (slr 1975-76), slr Linklater & Paines 1976-78, dir RIT Mgmnt Ltd 1979; md: J Rothschild & Co 1981-85, Transcontinental Serv Gp NV (dir 1983-88); non-exec dir: Control Components Ltd 1983, Wickes plc 1989-; ptnr S J Berwin & Co 1985-; memb Law Soc; *Style*— Robert P Burrow, Esq; 11 Lambourne Ave, London, SW19 7DW; 236 Grays Inn Rd, London, WC1 (☎ 071 278 0444, fax 071 833 2860)

BURROWES, Norma Elizabeth (Mrs Emile Belcourt); da of Henry Burrowes (d 1973), of Bangor, Co Down, N Ireland, and Caroline Mathers, *née* Irwin (d 1987); *b* 24 April 1946; *Educ* Sullivan Upper Sch Holywood Co Down, Queen's Univ Belfast (BA), Royal Acad of Music (ARAM); *m* 23 Dec 1969 (m dis 1979), Stuart John Rudolph Bedford, s of Leslie Herbert Bedford; m 2, 27 Feb 1987, Emile Adrien Belcourt, s of Adrien Joseph Belcourt; 1 s (Sébastien), 1 da (Romilly); *Career* opera and concert singer (soprano); debut: Glyndebourne 1970, ENO 1971, Royal Opera House Covent Garden 1970, Salzburg Fesival 1973, Paris Opera 1975, Met Opera New York 1979, La Scala Milan 1982; numerous other performances world wide incl: Berlin, Buenos Aires, Geneva, Lyons; recording incl: Die Entführing alls dern Serail, Die Schöpfung, Carmina Burana, Fauré Requiem, Sernele, Acis and Galatea; Hon Doctor of Music Queen's Univ Belfast 1979; *Recreations* swimming, needlework; *Style*— Miss Norma Burrowes

BURROWS, Sir Bernard Alexander Brocas; GCMG (1970, KCMG 1955, CMG 1950); s of Edward Henry Burrows (d 1910), and Ione, *née* MacDonald; *b* 3 July 1910; *Educ* Eton, Univ of Oxford (BA); *m* 1944, Ines, da of late John Walter, of St Catherines, Bear Wood, Wokingham, Berks; 1 s (Rupert), 1 da, (Antonia); *Career* Foreign Serv 1934: ambass to Turkey 1958-62, dep under sec of state FO 1963-66, perm Br rep N Atlantic Cncl 1966-70; conslt Fed Tst for Educn and Res (former dir gen); *Style*— Sir Bernard Burrows, GCMG; Rubens West, East Dean, Chichester, W Sussex

BURROWS, (Joseph) Brian; s of Joseph Ronald Burrows, of Bramhope, Leeds (d 1976), and Lady Joyce Doreen Woodeson, *née* Haste, of Overcliffe Foxton, Northumberland; step f Sir James Brewis Woodeson, OBE (d 1980, chm NEI plc Engineers); *b* 12 May 1943; *Educ* Oundle, Univ of Leeds (Dip Textiles Industs); *m* 1, 14 Sept 1968 (m dis Nov 1982), Suzanne, da of Charles Henry Vince (d 1982); 1 s (Neil b 1975), 2 da (Vanessa b 1971, Georgina b 1972); m 2, 6 March 1986, Linda Louise, da of John Duncan Raper, of Dunstran Farm, Leeds; 1 da (Nicola b 1988); *Career* dir: J & F Burrows Ltd, R & B Textiles Ltd (and co fndr) 1965-73; chm Burmatex Group (formerly R & B Textiles 1973-87); *Recreations* golf, cricket, rugby; *Clubs* Alwoodley Golf, Ganton Golf, Headingley Taverners; *Style*— Brian Burrows, Esq; Hallcroft Hall, Addingham, Ilkley, W Yorks LS29 0QN (☎ 0943 830349)

BURROWS, Prof Clifford Robert; s of Edward Stephen Burrows (d 1969), and Edith Mable, *née* Aspland; *b* 20 July 1937; *Educ* West Cliff HS for Boys, Univ of Wales (BSc), Univ of London (PhD, DSc); *m* 8 July 1961, Margaret Evelyn, da of Harry Percy Mathews (d 1983); 3 s (Stephen Peter b 1 Jan 1963, Paul Robert b 8 March 1965, John Alastair b 11 March 1967), 1 da (Rachael Elizabeth b 8 June 1974); *Career* reader Univ of Sussex 1980 (lectr 1969), prof of dynamics and control Univ of Strathclyde 1982, prof of systems engrg and dir of the Fluid Power Centre Univ of Bath author of over 70 res papers; chm IMechE Fluid Power Systems Ctee (vice chm Solid Applied Mechanic and Machine Systems Ctee), non stipendiary priest C of E 1977; FIMechE 1982, FRSA 1988; *Books* Fluid Power Control (1972); *Recreations* digging potatoes, rugby football; *Style*— Prof Clifford Burrows; School of Mechanical Engineering, University of Bath, Claverton Down, Bath BA2 7AY (☎ 0225 826935, fax 0225 826928, telex 449097)

BURROWS, (Robert) David; s of Sir Robert Burrows (d 1961); *b* 12 May 1929; *Educ* Shrewsbury; *m* 1973, Erica, da of Louis Simonds; 1 s, 3 da; *Career* formerly 2 Lt 9 Lancers; chm and md Fieldgrove Developments Ltd; *Recreations* shooting; *Style*— David Burrows, Esq; Waste Barn, Knockdown, Tetbury GL8 8QY (☎ 066 6890 361)

BURROWS, General Eva Evelyn; AO; da of Robert John Burrows (d 1970), and Ella Maria Watson (d 1967); *b* 15 Sept 1929; *Educ* Queensland Univ (BA), Univ of London (Cert Ed), Sydney Univ (MEd); *Career* Zimbabwe - missionary educator Howard Inst 1952-57, princ Usher Inst 1967-69, vice princ Int Coll for Officers 1970-73 (princ 1974-75), ldr Women's Social Servs in GB and Ireland 1975-77; Territorial Cdr: Sri Lanka 1977-79, Scot 1979-82, Australia 1982-86; General (International Ldr) of the Salvation Army 1986; Hon Doctorate of Liberal Arts EHWA Women's Univ Seoul Korea 1988, Hon LLD Asbury Coll USA 1988; *Recreations* classical music, reading, travelling; *Style*— General Eva Burrows, AO; Salvation Army International Headquarters, 101 Queen Victoria St, London EC4P 4EP (telex 8954847, fax 071 236 3424)

BURROWS, John Hedley; OBE (1991); s of Charles Edward Burrows (d 1970), of Sutton in Ashfield, Nottinghamshire, and Madge, *née* Fletcher (d 1966); *b* 18 Sept 1939; *Educ* Magnus GS Newark on Trent Notts; *m* 1, 1968 (m dis 1985); 1 s (Adam Charles), 1 da (Laura Ann); *Career* prodr TV Commercials 1964-68, dir prodr and concert promotor Howard and Wyndham Theatres 1968-78, dir Capital Radio Music Festival 1983-90 (controller of promotions 1980-90); memb RCM Devpt Tst, chm The Wren Orchestra of London 1989- (formerly dir); hon degree RCM 1986; hon memb RCM; *Recreations* music, tennis, photography; *Clubs* Royal Automobile; *Style*— John Burrows, Esq, OBE; 60 St Helens Gardens, London W10 6LH (☎ 081 960 5572); Capital Radio, Euston Tower, London NW1 3DR (☎ 071 388 1288, fax 387 2345, tlx 21365, car 367135)

BURROWS, Reginald Arthur; CMG (1964); s of Arthur Richard Burrows (d 1947), and Nellie Gertrude, *née* Oxley (d 1963); f was first dir of programmes of BBC in 1923, subsequently sec gen The Int Broadcasting Union Geneva; *b* 31 Aug 1918; *Educ* Mill Hill Sch, St Catharine's Coll Cambridge (MA); *m* 1952, Jenny Louisa Henriette (d 1985), da of Maurice Campiche, of Lausanne, Switzerland; 1 s (Stephen), 1 da (Susan); *Career* WWII served RAF in Europe and SE Asia, cmmnd 13 Sqdn, Wing Cdr; Dip Serv 1947-78; served: France, Pakistan (twice), Iran, Vietnam, Netherlands, Turkey; asst under sec of state 1976-78; *Recreations* skiing, tennis, mountain walking; *Style*— Reginald Burrows, Esq, CMG; 9 Summer Court, Summer Hill, Harbledown, Canterbury, Kent, CT2 8NP (☎ 0227 457394)

BURROWS, (Anthony) Richard Brocas; s of Lt Gen Montagu Brocas Burrows (d 1966), and Molly Rose, *née* Le Bas; *b* 27 Jan 1939; *Educ* Eton; *m* 6 Oct 1966, Angela Margaret, da of John Vincent Sheffield; 1 s (Brocas b 1975), 3 da (Carey b 1968, Joanna b 1969, Petra b 1972); *Career* chm: Le Bas Investmt Tst, Tex Hldgs, I S & G Steel Stock Holders; *Recreations* golf, tennis, travel; *Clubs* White's; *Style*— Richard Burrows, Esq; Barham Hall, Ipswich, Suffolk (☎ 0473 830315); Le Bas Investment Trust Ltd, Claydon Industrial Park, Gripping Rd, Great Blakenham, Ipswich IP6 0JD (☎ 0473 830055)

BURROWS, Rt Rev Simon Hedley; s of Very Reverend Hedley Robert Burrows (d 1983), and Joan Lumsden, *née* Lovett; *b* 8 Nov 1928; *Educ* Eton, Kings Scholar, Kings Coll Cambridge (MA); *m* 25 June 1960, Janet, da of Rev Canon Frederick Hampden Basil Woodd (d 1986); 2 s (Giles b 1965, Jeremy b 1969), 3 da (Philippa b 1961, Frances b 1962, Rebecca b 1967); *Career* clerk Holy Orders, curate St John's Wood 1954-57, chaplain Jesus Coll Cambridge 1957-60, vicar Wyken Coventry 1960-67, vicar Holy Trinity Fareham 1967-74; suffragan bishop of Buckingham 1974-; *Style*— Right Reverend Simon H Burrows; Sheridan, Grimms Hill, Great Missenden, Bucks HP16 9BD

BURSELL, His Hon Judge Rupert David Hingston; QC (1986); s of Rev Henry Bursell (d 1983), and Cicely Mary, *née* Pawson (d 1977); *b* 10 Nov 1942; *Educ* St John's Sch Leatherhead, St Edmund Hall Oxford (MA, DPhil), Univ of Exeter (LLB), St Stephen House Oxford; *m* 1 July 1967, Joanna Ruth, da of Maj Robert Peter Davies Gibb, of Arbutus, 2 The Chestnuts, Winscombe; 2 s (Michael Hingston b 1970, James David Hingston b 1972), 1 da (Polly Joanna Hingston b 1976); *Career* called to the Bar Lincoln's Inn 1968, circuit judge 1988-; ordained deacon 1968, priest 1969; hon curate: St Marylebone 1968-69, St Mary The Virgin Almondsbury 1969-71, St Francis Bedminster 1971-83, Christ Church and St Stephen Bristol 1983-88; chllr, vicar gen and official princ Dio of Durham 1989-; *Books* Atkins Court Forms (contrib Ecclesiastical Law), Halsbury's Laws of England: Cremation and Burial (contrib Ecclesiastical Law), Principles of Dermatitis Legislation (contrib), Crown Court Practice (jtly); *Recreations* church music, military history, archaeology of Greece and the Holy Land; *Clubs* MCC; *Style*— His Hon Judge Bursell, QC; The Crown Court, The Guildhall, Bristol BS1 2HL (☎ 0272 211681)

BURSTALL, Dr Clare; da of Alfred Wells (d 1958), and Lily, *née* Humphreys (d 1988); *b* 3 Sept 1931; *Educ* Ribston Hall HS for Girls Gloucester, Univ of London (BA, PhD); *m* 1955 (m dis 1977), Michael Lyle Burstall, s of Dr Francis Hereward Burstall (d 1956); 1 s (Francis), 1 da (Lindsay); *Career* psychologist; dir: Nat Fndn for Educnl Res 1983- (dep dir 1972-83), Nfer-Nelson Publishing Co 1983-; *Books* French in the Primary School (1970), Primary French in the Balance (1974); *Recreations* art collection, sailing, needlework; *Clubs* IOD, Royal Over-Seas League; *Style*— Dr Clare Burstall; 26 Lennox Gardens, London SW1X 0DQ (☎ 071 584 3127); National Foundation for Educational Research, The Mere, Upton Park, Slough, Berks SL1 2DQ (☎ 0753 74123)

BURSTALL, Prof Rodney Martineau; s of Alfred Reginald Burstall, and Annie, *née* Lammie; *b* 11 Nov 1934; *Educ* King George V GS Southport, Univ of Cambridge (BA, MSc), Univ of Birmingham (PhD); *m* Seija-Leena (d 1990), da of Anton Ilmari Ihalainen (d 1975), of Kotka, Finland; 3 da (Kaija b 27 Feb 1961, Taru b 5 July 1962, Taina b Nov 1963); *Career* Nat Serv Flying Offr RAF Radar Servicing 1956-58; Univ of Edinburgh: lectr Experimental Programming Unit 1967-70, prof Dept of Artificial Intelligence 1977-79 (reader 1970-77), prof Dept of Computer Sci 1979-, co-dir Laboratory for the Fndns of Computer Sci; memb: Vajradhatu Buddhist Soc, Academia Europda; *Books* Computational Category Theory (1988); *Style*— Prof Rodney Burstall; Department of Computer Science, University of Edinburgh, The King's Buildings, Mayfield Rd, Edinburgh EH9 3JZ (☎ 031 667 1081 ext 2782, fax 031 662 4712, telex 727442 UNIVED G)

BURSTEIN, Joan; da of Ashley Harvey Jotner (d 1956), Mary, *née* Pleeth (d 1956); *b* 21 Feb 1926; *Educ* Henrietta Barnet Sch, Hampstead Garden Suburb; *m* Sidney Burstein, s of Barnet Burstein; 1 s (Simon b 1951), 1 da (Caroline b 1949); *Career* opened Browns on South Molton St 1970, introduced many designers to London, Donna Karan, Giorgio Amarni, Ralph Lauren, Calvin Klein, Romeo Gigli; *Style*— Mrs Joan Burstein; Browns, 27 South Molton St, London W1Y 1DA

BURSTIN, Nicholas Ernest; s of Capt Oswald Burstin, of London, and Lydia, *née* Hammerschmid; *b* 29 April 1957; *Educ* Univ Coll School London, Jesus Coll Cambridge, Harvard Business Sch; *m* 3 Aug 1988, (Sarah) Anne, da of Lt James William Roylance, of Melbourne, Aust; *Career* dir J Walter Thompson Co Ltd 1989; *Recreations* sailing, music; *Style*— Nicholas Burstin, Esq; J Walter Thompson Co Ltd, 40 Berkeley Square, London W1 (☎ 071 499 4040, fax 071 493 8432/8418, car 0836 314944)

BURT, Alistair James Hendrie; MP (C) Bury North 1983-; s of James Hendrie Burt and Mina Christie Robertson; *b* 25 May 1955; *Educ* Bury GS, St John's Coll Oxford, Chester Coll of Law; *m* 1983, Eve Alexandra Twite; 1 s, 1 da; *Career* slr; memb Haringey Borough Cncl 1982-84; vice-pres Tory Reform Gp, patron Lawyers Assoc working for Soviet Jewry; memb: All Party Paper Ind Gp, All Party Textile Gp; sec: Parly Christian Fellowship, All Party Safety In The Home Gp; PPS to Rt Hon Kenneth Baker, MP 1985-90; *Recreations* family, modern art, music, sport, church and religious affairs; *Style*— Alistair Burt, Esq, MP; House of Commons, London SW1

BURT, David Lyndon; s of Maj Robert Frederick Burt (d 1969); *b* 13 Jan 1930; *Educ* Tonbridge; *m* 1961, Prunella Mary, *née* Antrobus, of Johannesburg, SA; 1 s, 1 da; *Career* joined Lewis & Peat Group 1958, former dep chm Guinness Peat Group; dir: Lewis & Peat Ltd, Wilson Smithett & Cope Ltd, Multigerm Int Ltd; *Recreations* skiing, shooting, gardening, farming, horses; *Clubs* Cavalry; *Style*— David Burt, Esq; Silton, Peaslake, Surrey GU5 9SR (☎ 0306 730792, fax 0306 730027)

BURT, Hilary Rose; *née* Garnett; da of Onslow Garnett (d 1958), of Wainstalls, Yorkshire (whose maternal gf was Maj-Gen Reginald Onslow Farmer, RA, bro of William Francis Gamul Farmer, High Sheriff of Surrey 1849, owner of Nonsuch Palace, Surrey, a former royal residence, *see* Burke's Visitation of Seats and Arms, vol I, p 214), and Elaine Mary (who m 2, Brig Percival de Courcy Jones, OBE, *qv*), da of Harry Charles Connatty, of Co Cork (whose mother was Amelia Lovejoy, a Gaiety Girl); *b* 4 Dec 1943; *Educ* Byam-Shaw Sch of Art, BA (Hon) Leeds 1990; *m* 1966, Timothy Lyndon Burt, writer, linguist, economist and Restauranteur, s of Oliver Burt, actor, and first cousin of David Lyndon Burt, *qv*; 2 da (Sophie Jane Caroline b 1967,

Olivia Lucy b 1972); *Career* artist and sculptor, work exhibited in York, Thirsk and London; *Recreations* tennis, riding, music, theatre, arts; *Style—* Mrs Timothy Burt; Jack's Cottage, West Tanfield, Ripon, N Yorkshire; 349 Portobello Rd, London W10 5SA

BURT, Terence William; s of Terence William Burt, of Walgrave, Northants, and Dorothy Evelyn, *née* Jones; *b* 21 June 1956; *Educ* Pilgrim GS, Hatfield Poly; *m* 20 Sept 1980, Susan, da of John Hudson of Bedford; 4 s (Michael b 1983, Philip b 1984, Nicholas b 1986, Darren b 1989); *Career* md Star Computers Ltd 1985-, sec & gp fin dir Star Computer Gp plc 1985-; ret 1988, formed K2 Systems plc; ACMA; *Style—* Terence Burt, Esq; 17 Farnham Way, Bedford, (☎ 0234 58919); 70 Bells Rd, Gorleston, Norfolk (☎ 0923 816266, fax : 0923 816260); 4 Colonial Business Park, Colonial Way, Watford WD2 4PT

BURT, Hon Mrs (Vanessa Mary Linda); *née* Russell; only da of 4 Baron Ampthill; *b* 18 Sept 1960; *m* 24 June 1983, Charles Burt, elder s of Ivor Burt; 1 s (James Ivor Geoffrey b 1984), 1 da (Emma Louise Victoria b 1986); *Style—* The Hon Mrs Burt; 21 Macaulay Road, London SW4 0QP

BURTCH, Mervyn Arthur; s of Walter James Powell Burtch (d 1956), and Mary Ann, *née* Jones; *b* 7 Nov 1929; *Educ* Lewis Sch Pengam, Univ Coll Cardiff; *Career* composer; operas incl: Alice in Wonderland 1981, Canterville Ghost 1984, various smaller operas; other works incl: I Saw a Child for choir and orchestra 1985, String Quartet number 3 1987 (number 1 1985, number 2 1986); large quantity of smaller chamber, vocal and choral works; *Style—* Mervyn Burtch, Esq; 5 Oakfield St, Ystrad Mynach, Hengoed, Mid Glam CF8 7AF (☎ 0443 812100); Welsh College of Music and Drama, North Rd, Cardiff, S Glam (☎ 0222 342854)

BURTON, Anthony George Graham; s of Donald Graham Burton (d 1960), and Irene, *née* Trotter; *b* 24 Dec 1934; *Educ* King James's GS Knaresborough, Univ of Leeds; *m* 28 March 1959, Pip, da of Walter Sharman (d 1961); 2 s (Jonathan b 1961, Nicholas b 1964), 1 da (Jenny b 1963); *Career* freelance writer and broadcaster; books incl: The Canal Builders (1972, 2 edn 1981), The Reluctant Musketeer (1973), Remains of a Revolution (1975), Josiah Wedgwood (1976), Industrial Archaeological Sites of Britain (1977), The Past at Work (1980), The National Trust Guide to Our Industrial Past (1983), The Rise and Fall of King Cotton (1984), Wilderness Britain (1985), Britain Revisited (1986), Steaming Through Britain (1987), Walking Through History (1988), The Yorkshire Dales and York (1989), Astonishing Britain (1990); *Recreations* steam engines, boats, walking, beer; *Style—* Anthony Burton, Esq; 7A Belgrave Rd, Clifton, Bristol BS8 2AA

BURTON, Anthony Philip; s of Frank Burton (d 1975), and Lottie, *née* Lax; *b* 25 Oct 1942; *Educ* The King's Sch Macclesfield, Wadham Coll Oxford (MA, BLitt); *m* 21 Sept 1985, Carol Deborah, da of Adrian Hilary Baker; *Career* asst keeper in the directorate V & A Museum 1979-81 (asst keeper of the library 1968-79), head Bethnal Green Museum of Childhood 1981-; *Style—* Anthony Burton, Esq; 59 Arlington Ave, London N1 7BA (☎ 071 226 0394); The Bethnal Green Museum of Childhood, Cambridge Heath Rd, London E2 9PA (☎ 081 981 1711)

BURTON, Sir Carlisle Archibald; OBE (1968); *b* 29 July 1921; *Educ* Harrison Coll Barbados, Univ of London (BA), Sch of Librarianship Leeds (ALA), Univ of Pittsburgh (MS); *m* 1946, Hyacinth Marjorie Adelle Barker; *Career* perm sec PM's Office and head of Civil Service Barbados 1972-81; chm: Public Serv Cmmn Barbados 1981-88, Public Servs Cmmn Turks & Caicos Islands 1988-90; chm Cave Hill Campus Cncl, Univ of the W Indies 1984-; co dir; kt 1979; *Style—* Sir Carlisle Burton, OBE; Caradelle, Mountjoy Avenue, Pine Gardens, St Michael, Barbados, West Indies

BURTON, Charles Philip Henry; s of Sir George Vernon Kennedy Burton, KT, CBE, DL, of Aldham, Hadleigh, Suffolk, and Sarah Katherine, *née* Tcherniavsky; *b* 6 Dec 1952; *Educ* Charterhouse, Univ of Exeter (BA); *m* 2 Nov 1985, Susanna Louise, da of Peter Henry Buller, of Bramley, Surrey; *Career* economist Beecham Pharmaceuticals Ltd 1974-75; CBI 1975-85: head industl trends and economic forecasting, dep dir economic directorate; business devpt mangr Wharton Econometric Forecasting Assocs Ltd 1985-88, jt md Business Strategies Ltd 1988-; FRSA, memb Soc of Business Economists; *Books* Competition and Markets (1990); *Recreations* music, history, photography; *Clubs* RAC; *Style—* Charles Burton, Esq; 33 Anselm Rd, London SW6 1LH (☎ 071 381 8736); Business Strategies Ltd, 10 Kendrick Mews, London SW7 3HG (☎ 071 823 071 589 9004)

BURTON, (Anthony) David; s of Leslie Mitchell Burton (d 1967) and Marion, *née* Marsh (d 1976); *b* 2 April 1937; *Educ* Arnold Sch Blackpool; *m* 30 May 1964, Valerie, da of Harry Swire, of Burnley, Lancs; 1 s (Michael John b 1971), 2 da (Judith Alison b 1966, Anne Louise b 1968); *Career* Nat Serv RAPC 1955-57; chief dealer Bank of America NT & SA 1967-72, exec dir S G Warburg & Co Ltd 1979 (chief dealer 1972-79); LIFFE: Fndr memb Working Party 1979, dir 1980-85, chm Membership & Rules Ctee 1982-88, dep chm 1985-88, chm 1988-; chm: S G Warburg Futures & Options Ltd 1988-, Marshalls Finance Ltd (int money brokers) 1989-; fndr memb Assoc of Futures Brokers and Dealers 1986-88; memb: Br Invisible Exports Cncl 1988-90, Euro Ctee Br Invisibles 1990-, Governing Body City Research Project 1990-; Freeman City of London 1984, Liveryman Worshipful Co of Glass Sellers 1984; FCIB, FCT; *Books* collector, lectr and writer on: early English glass c 1600-1800, English blackjacks and leather bottles c 1550-1700, early German Rhenish pottery c 1500-1650; *Recreations* fine wine, sport, music, opera; *Clubs* MCC; *Style—* David Burton, Esq; S G Warburg & Co Ltd, 2 Finsbury Avenue, London EC2M 2PA (☎ 071 860 0499, fax 071 382 4800, direct fax 071 860 0480, car 0836 279854)

BURTON, David Gowan; s of Reginald Frank Burton (d 1967), of Woodford Green, Essex, and Nellie Erwin, *née* Biggs; *b* 3 April 1943; *Educ* McEntree Tech Sch; *m* 8 Aug 1970, Hilary Kathleen, da of Canon Robert Smith; 2 s (Matthew Edward Gowan b 21 Oct 1972, Simon James b 19 May 1983), 1 da (Emma Clare b 8 Sept 1975); *Career* articles with Keens Shay Keens & Co 1960-65, Thomson McLintock 1965-73 (latterly sr mangr), sr mangr Neville Russell & Co 1973-75; Touche Ross & Co: sr mangr 1975-83, ptnr 1979-, seconded to IOM 1983, established green field office IOM 1985-; FCA 1976 (ACA 1965); *Recreations* family, golf, walking, gardening, farming (Scotland); *Clubs* Castletown Golf IOM; *Style—* David Burton, Esq; Bridge House, W Baldwin, Isle of Man (☎ 0624 851997); 41 Chigwell Park Drive, Chigwell, Essex IG7 5BD (☎ 081 500 5770); Touche Ross & Co, Bank of Scotland House, Prospect Hill, Douglas, IOM (☎ 0624 672332); Touche Ross & Co, Hill House, 1 Little New St, London EC4A 3TR (☎ 071 936 3000)

BURTON, Frances Rosemary; da of Maj Richard Francis Heveningham Pughe, DFC, ERD, of Ridlington, Norfolk (d 1990), and Pamela Margaret, *née* Coates (d 1978); *b* 19 June 1941; *Educ* St Mary's Convent Bishops Stortford Herts, Tortington Park Arundel Sussex, Lady Margaret House Cambridge, St Anne's Coll Oxford, Univ of London (LLB); *m* 1, 26 Oct 1963 (m dis 1973), Robert Scott Alexander (now Lord Alexander of Weedon, QC), s of Samuel James Alexander (d 1965), of Fleet, Hants; 2 s (Hon David Robert James b 1964, William Richard Scott b 1969), 1 da (Mary Frances Anne b 1966); m 2, 28 Nov 1975, David Michael Burton, s of Frank Raymond Burton (d 1965), of Wellington, Shropshire; 2 da (Jane Richenda Frances b 1979, Charlotte Alice Octavia b 1981); *Career* called to the Bar Middle Temple 1970 (ad eundem Lincoln's Inn 1972), practised Chancery Bar until 1975, tutor for Bar and Law Soc examinations, lectr and tutor Dept of Law and Faculty of Business City of London Poly 1989-, author of legal text books; govr Westminster Coll until 1973; numerous fundraising activities incl: justice Br section Int Cmmn of Jurists 1963-, Peckham Settlement 1973-, Jubilee Sailing Tst 1985-, Cancer Res Campaign 1986-, Duke of Edinburgh's Award Scheme 1987; chm Ctee Justice Ball 1983 and 1985, memb Exec Ctee Big Bang City Ball 1986; memb Soc of Cons Lawyers; *Books* Family Law Textbook (1988, revised edn 1990), Bar Final General Paper Textbook (1990); *Recreations* opera, history, archaeology; *Clubs* RAF (assoc memb); *Style—* Mrs Frances Burton; 41 Crescent Wood Rd, Sydenham Hill, London SE26 6SA (☎ 081 299 2154); 10 Old Square, Lincoln's Inn, London WC2A 3SU (☎ 071 405 0758, fax 071 831 8237)

BURTON, Sir George Vernon Kennedy; CBE (1972, MBE 1945), DL (Suffolk) 1980; s of George Ethelbert Earnshaw Burton, and Francesca, *née* Holden-White; *b* 21 April 1916; *Educ* Charterhouse, Weimar Univ; *m* 1, 1945 (m dis), Sarah Katherine Tcherniavsky; 2 s; m 2, 1975, Priscilla Margaret, da of Cecil Harmsworth King *qv*, and formerly w of St John Gore *qv*; *Career* formerly Capt RA WW II; chm Fisons 1973-86; dir: Barclays Bank International 1976-82, Thomas Tilling 1976-82, Rolls-Royce 1976-83; memb Cncl CBI 1970-84, chm CBI Overseas Ctee 1975-83; memb: BOTB 1972-82, NEDC 1975-79, Assoc Br Sponsorship of the Arts 1978-84; FRSA; Br Nat Ctee of Int C of C 1979-86, govr Suttons Hosp in Charterhouse 1979-; Cdr Order of Ouissam Alaovite Morroco 1968, Cdr Order of Leopold II, Belgium 1974; FRSA; kt 1977; *Recreations* music; *Clubs* Farmers, Oriental; *Style—* Sir George Burton, CBE, DL; Aldham Mill, Hadleigh, Suffolk IP7 6LE

BURTON, Gerald; s of Edward Neville Burton (d 1985), of Kelsall, nr Chester, and Mary Elizabeth, *née* Bull (d 1977); *b* 12 Aug 1938; *Educ* Liverpool Collegiate GS; *m* 4 May 1963, Gillian Margaret, da of John Dean Wilson (d 1986), of West Kirby, Cheshire; 3 s (John, James, Andrew), 1 da (Deborah); *Career* sr ptnr Kidsons Impey CAs 1989- (joined 1961, ptnr 1965); auditor Corporation of London; Freeman City of London 1980, Liveryman Worshipful Co of Basketmakers 1982; FCA; *Recreations* golf, music; *Clubs* City Livery, Wig & Pen, Cricketers, Vagabonds; *Style—* Gerald Burton, Esq; Hilbre, Old Farm Close, Knotty Green, Beaconsfield, Bucks (☎ 0494 671560); Kidsons Impey CAs, Spectrum House, 20-26 Cursitor St, London EC4A 1HY (☎ 071 405 2088, fax 071 831 2206)

BURTON, Graham Stuart; CMG (1987); s of Cyril Stanley Richard Burton (d 1982), and Jessie Blythe Burton; *b* 8 April 1941; *Educ* Sir William Borlase's Sch Marlow; *m* 30 Jan 1965, Julia Margaret Lappin; 1 da (b 1966), 1 s (b 1967); *Career* HM Dip Serv; FO 1961, Abu Dhabi 1964, ME Centre for Arabic Studies 1967, Kuwait 1969, FCO 1972, Tunis 1975, UK Mission to UN 1978, cnsllr Tripoli 1981, FCO 1984-87, consul-gen San Francisco 1987-90, HM ambass Utd Arab Emirates Abu Dhabi 1990-; *Recreations* golf, watching all sports, opera; *Clubs* MCC; *Style—* Graham Burton, Esq, CMG; c/o Foreign and Commonwealth Office, London SW1

BURTON, Air Marshal Sir Harry; KCB (1971, CB 1970), CBE (1963, MBE 1943), DSO (1941); s of Robert Reid Burton (d 1975), of Rutherglen, Lanarkshire; *b* 2 May 1919; *Educ* Glasgow HS; *m* 1945, Jean (d 1987), da of Tom Dobie (d 1930), of Whitehaven, Cumberland; 1 s, 1 da; m 2, 1988, Sandra, da of Thomas McGlashan, of Clydebank, Renfrewshire; *Career* RAF 1937, served Europe, Burma, Pacific (despatches 1942); CO RAF Scampton 1960-63, SASO 3 Bomber Group, air exec to Dep for Nuclear Affrs SHAPE NATO 1965-67, AOC 23 Gp RAF 1968-70, AOC-in-C Air Support Command 1970-73; co dir; *Recreations* golf, squash; *Clubs* RAF; *Style—* Air Marshal Sir Harry Burton, KCB, CBE, DSO; Mayfield, West Drive, Middleton-on-Sea, Sussex PO22 7TS (☎ 024 369 2976)

BURTON, Humphrey McGuire; s of Harry Philip Burton (d 1980), and Kathleen Alice, *née* Henwood (d 1982); *b* 25 March 1931; *Educ* Long Dene Sch Chiddingstone Kent, The Judd Sch Tonbridge, Univ of Cambridge (BA); *m* 1, 1957 (m dis), Gretel, *née* Davis; 1 s (Matthew), 1 da (Clare); m 2, 1970, Christina, da of Svante Hellstedt; 1 s (Lukas), 1 da (Helena); *Career* former head Music and Arts BBC-TV 1965-67 and 1975-81, TV presenter BBC Young Musician of the Year 1978-90, TV dir Operas and Concerts Worldwide, currently art advsr Barbican Centre (former artistic dir 1988-90); chm TV Music Working Pty Euro Broadcasting Union 1976-85, memb Barbican Arts Bd, prodr Omnibus Bernstein's West Side Story; Chevalier de l'ordre des Arts et Lettres France; *Recreations* tennis, travel; *Clubs* Garrick; *Style—* Humphrey Burton, Esq; 123 Oakwood Court, London W14 8LA; BBC-TV Kensington House, Richmond Way, London W14 0AX (☎ 081 743 1272)

BURTON, Iris Grace; da of Arthur Robert Burton, of Lewisham, London, and Alice Elizabeth Burton (d 1980); *Educ* Roan Girls GS, City of London Coll; *m* Joseph Thomas Lucas, s of Elio Lucas (d 1987), of Spain; 1 s (Joseph b 8 Aug 1976), 1 da (Rachel b 12 April 1971); *Career* asst ed TV Times 1978-80; ed: Woman's Own Magazine 1980-86, Prima Magazine 1986-87, Best Magazine 1987-88; ed dir and publisher G & J UK 1988-; *Recreations* walking, gardening; *Style—* Ms Iris Burton; G & J of the UK, Portland House, Stag Place, Victoria, London SW1 (☎ 071 245 8700, fax 071 630 5509)

BURTON, (Sara) Jocelyn Margarita Elissa; da of Wing Cdr Roland Louis Ernest Burton, AFC (ret), of La Grange, La Garedie, Correze, France, and Sian Joan, *née* Gwilliam Evans (d 1980); *b* 10 Jan 1946; *Educ* St Clare's Sch Devon, Lady Margaret House Cambridge, Sir John Cass Coll Central Sch of Art; *Career* Diamonds Int award 1968, first one man exhibition Archer Gallery Dover St 1971, modern silver collection for Jean Renet Bond St 1970-75; pieces in many pub and private collections throughout world; works incl: silver table fountain for Worshipful co of Fishmongers 1975, Fitzwilliam Cup 1984, centrepiece for Sir Roy Strong V & A; Freeman: City of London 1974, Worshipful Co of Goldsmiths; *Recreations* playing harpsichord, travel, reading; *Clubs* Arts Dover Street; *Style—* Miss Jocelyn Burton; 50C Red Lion Street, Holborn, London WC1 R4PF (☎ 071 405 3042, fax 071 405 0972)

BURTON, Dr John Lloyd; s of Maj Lloyd Burton (d 1986), of Loscoe, Derbyshire, and Dorothy Mary, *née* Pacey; *b* 29 Aug 1938; *Educ* Heanor GS, Univ of Manchester (BSc, MD); *m* 12 Sept 1964, Dr Patricia Anne Burton, da of Walter Crankshaw; 1 s (Ben b 1969), 2 da (Jane b 1967, Helena b 1977); *Career* jr med trg 1964-68: Manchester, London, Edinburgh; sr registrar and res fell Dept of Dermatology Newcastle upon Tyne 1968-73, conslt dermatologist Bristol Royal Infirmary 1973-, reader in dermatology Univ of Bristol 1982-; Dowling Orator RSM 1980, ed British Journal Dermatology 1981-85 (asst ed 1977-81), MRCP examiner RCP, advsr in dermatology to Chief Med Offr DHSS, Parkes Weber lectr RCP 1988; contrib over 200 articles to med and scientific jls; memb ctee: Br Assoc of Dermatologists, CCSC, RSM, BMA, RCP, ESDR; *Books* Essential Medicine (1976), Aids to Medicine for Nurses (1981), Aids to Medicine for Dental Students (with R Matthews, 1983), Textbook of Dermatology 3 vols (jt ed, 4 edn, 1986), Aids to Postgraduate Medicine (5 edn, 1988), Aids to Undergraduate Medicine (5 edn, 1990), Essentials of Dermatology (3 edn, 1990); *Recreations* bookbinding, painting; *Style—* Dr John Burton; Norland House, Canynge Rd, Clifton, Bristol BS8 3LD (☎ 0272 733933); Dept of Dermatology, Bristol Royal Infirmary, Bristol BS2 8HW (☎ 0272 230000 ext 2770)

BURTON, John Michael; s of Gerald Victor Burton, of Northampton, and Kathleen Blodwyn, *née* Harper; *b* 21 May 1945; *Educ* Oxford Sch of Architecture; *m* 11 Sept

1971, Sally, da of Norman Donaby Bason (d 1987), of Northampton; 1 s (Thomas Donaby b 19 April 1977), 1 da (Amy Victoria b 17 Jan 1975); *Career* architect; conservation of: Wingfield Coll 1972-74, Lavenham Guildhall 1973-, Holy Trinity Church Long Melford 1974-, Melford Hall 1975-, Flatford Mill for Nat Tst 1979-85, Colchester Castle 1980-, Newnham Coll Cambridge 1984-, St Marys Thaxted 1988-, Manor House Bury St Edmunds 1990-, Hunsdon House Herts 1990-; chm: Colchester Arts Centre 1985-90, Redundant Churches Uses Ctee Chelmsford; memb Diocesan Advsy Ctees: Chelmsford, St Edmundsbury, Ipswich; MRIBA; *Recreations* sail boarding, archaeology; *Clubs* Trinity Rotary; *Style—* John Burton, Esq; St Marys Hall, Rawstorn Road, Colchester, Essex CO3 3JH (☎ 0206 549487, car 0836 330580)

BURTON, John Nelson; s of John Burton (d 1947), and Veronica, *née* Parle (d 1932); *b* 12 Oct 1923; *Educ* RC Church Schs Carlisle, Univ of Bristol, Mills Coll Calif; *m* (m dis); 1 s (Christopher John b 27 Oct 1962), 1 da (Kathryn Elizabeth b 29 Oct 1965); *Career* Lieut RNVR 1942-46; fellowship in drama Mills Coll Oakland CA 1950-51, prodr then dir of prodns Arts Cncl's W of England Theatre Co 1952-55, drama prodr BBC TV 1955-56, freelance writer, prodr and dir 1956-; has adapted plays for TV and has written numerous originals; dir films incl: Never Mention Murder 1964, Fade Out 1970; winner: Leonard Brett Best Producer award 1960, Silver medal for Original Screenplay (Drake's Venture) NY Int Film and TV Festival 1980; memb: Dirs Guild of GB, Writers Guild of GB; *Recreations* sailing, climbing, walking; *Style—* John Burton, Esq

BURTON, 3 Baron (UK 1897); Michael Evan Victor Baillie; s of Brig Hon George Evan Michael Baillie, MC, TD (s of Baroness Burton, to whom Barony passed from 1 Baron by special remainder, and her 1 husband, Col James Baillie, MVO, JP, DL, sometime MP Inverness-shire), by his w, Lady Maud, *née* Cavendish, CBE, JP, widow of Capt Angus Mackintosh, RHG, and da of 9 Duke of Devonshire, KG; through Lady Maud Lord Burton is 1 cous to late Maurice Macmillan, MP, and 2 Viscount Stuart of Findhorn; suc grandmother 1962; *b* 27 June 1924; *Educ* Eton; *m* 1, 1948 (m dis 1977), Elizabeth, da of late Capt Anthony Wise; 2 s, 4 da; m 2, 1978, Coralie, da of Claude Cliffe, of S Africa; *Heir* s, Hon Evan Baillie; *Career* sits as Conservative in House of Lords; formerly Lt Lovat Scouts and Scots Gds; landowner and farmer; memb Inverness CC 1948-75, JP 1961-75, DL 1963-65; *Recreations* stalking, shooting, fishing, hunting; *Clubs* Cavalry and Guards', Pratt's, New (Edinburgh); *Style—* The Rt Hon the Lord Burton; Dochfour, Inverness IV3 6JY (☎ 046 386 252)

BURTON, Michael John; QC (1984); s of Henry Burton, QC (d 1952), and Hilda, *née* Shaffer (d 1986); *b* 12 Nov 1946; *Educ* Eton, Balliol Coll Oxford (MA); *m* 17 Dec 1972, Corinne Ruth, da of Dr Jack Cowan, MC, of Putney; 4 da (Josephine b 1977, Isabel b 1979, Genevieve b 1982, Henrietta b 1986); *Career* called to the Bar Gray's Inn 1970, lectr in law Balliol Coll 1972-74; candidate (L) Kensington Cncl 1971, parly candidate (L) Stratford-on-Avon 1974, cand (SD) GLC Putney 1981; recorder of Crown Ct 1989; *Recreations* amateur theatricals, lyric writing, singing, bridge, watching Wimbledon FC; *Style—* Michael Burton, Esq, QC; High Trees, 63 Murray Rd, Wimbledon, London SW19; 2 Crown Office Row, Temple, London EC4 (☎ 071 583 2681, fax 071 583 2850)

BURTON, Michael St Edmund; CMG, CVO; s of Brig G W S Burton, DSO (d 1981), and Barbara, *née* Kemmis Betty; *b* 18 Oct 1937; *Educ* Bedford Sch, Magdalen Coll Oxford (MA); *m* 1 April 1967, Henrietta Jindra, da of Joseph Hones, of Nicosia, Cyprus; 1 s (Nicholas b 1969), 2 da (Samantha b 1968 d 1971, Amanda b 1971); *Career* FCO: joined 1960, asst political agent Dubai Trucial States 1962-64; served: Khartoum 1967-69, Paris 1969-72, Amman 1975-77, Kuwait 1977-79; secondment to BP as head of Policy Review Unit 1984-85, Br minister and dep cmdt Berlin 1985-; *Recreations* tennis, travel, opera; *Clubs* United Oxford and Cambridge Univ, Hurlingham; *Style—* M St E Burton, Esq, CMG, CVO; c/o Foreign & Commonwealth Office, King Charles St, London SW1

BURTON, Nigel Foster; s of Kenneth Burton, of Nottingham, and Margaret Valerie, *née* Foster; *b* 20 Sept 1951; *Educ* Leeds GS, Cheltenham GS, Pembroke Coll Oxford (MA); *m* 17 Aug 1973, Alwyn, da of Brian Robson, of Cheltenham; 3 s (Thomas b 1978, William b 1980, Edward b 1984); *Career* dep actuary Lloyds Life Assurance Ltd (now Royal Heritage) until 1983, currently exec dir Allied Dunbar Assurance plc; dir Allied Dunbar: Insurance and Investment Servs Ltd, International Funds Ltd, International Ltd; FIA 1977; *Style—* Nigel Burton, Esq; Manor Farmhouse, Broad Blunsdon, nr Swindon, Wilts (☎ 0793 721 260); Allied Dunbar Assurance plc, Allied Dunbar Centre, Station Rd, Swindon, Wilts SN1 1EL (☎ 0793 514 514, fax 0793 512 371)

BURTON, Richard Hilary; s of Robert Claud Burton (d 1971), of Sussex, and Theodora Constance Helen, *née* Hill (d 1957); *b* 28 Dec 1923; *Educ* Lancing, Brasenose Coll Oxford (MA); *m* 1962, Priscilla Jane, da of Geoffrey Coode-Adams (d 1985), of Essex; 1 s (Edward David Fowler b 1963), 1 da (Sarah Catherine b 1964); *Career* WWII Capt 60 Rifles 1942-46 (despatches), memb the Mil Courts Palestine; called to the Bar Inner Temple 1951, barr 1951-54; mangr Legal Dept Gillette Industries Ltd 1954-65 (legal dir 1965-78, chm 1978-84), dir to Chm The Gillette Co (USA) 1984-88; chm: Cable Authy 1984-90, Nestor-BNA 1986-89; chm West Middx Arts Devpt Tst 1978-86, memb Ctee MCC 1989; Freeman City of London; FRSA; *Recreations* cricket, real tennis, shooting, ornithology, lepidoptery; *Clubs* Boodle's; *Style—* Richard Burton, Esq; Danmoor House, Heckfield, Basingstoke, Hants (☎ 0734 326233)

BURTON, Col Richard Michael; TD; s of Dr Rennie Cooksey Burton (d 1970), of Sheffield, and Elsie Jane, *née* Laycock (d 1967); *b* 28 July 1926; *Educ* King Edward VII Sch Sheffield, Newton HS Newtonville Mass USA, Phillips Acad Andover Mass USA, Univ of Durham, RAF Coll Cranwell, Univ of Sheffield (MB ChB), Univ of Cambridge (MA), Univ of London (BSc); *m* 1 (m dis 1984), Jillian Elisabeth, *née* Creber; 1 s (Tom b 1966), 2 da (Margaret Elisabeth (Mrs Rodwell) b 1962, Nancy Harriet Edith b 1971); m 2, 26 July 1985, Antoinette Brenda, da of Arthur Christiansen (d 1964), of Holland-on-Sea, Essex; 1 step da (Sharon Elizabeth (Mrs Duce) b 1951); *Career* RAF 1945-48, pilot, RAFRO 1948-64 (flying doctor RAF Inst of Aviation Med Farnborough 1955-64), TA 257 Southern Gen Hosp 1964-, CO RAMC (Vols) 1980-84, conslt in surgery to the army; conslt in obstetrics and gynaecology Ealing and Hillingdon Health Inst 1968-88, hon clinical teacher UCH and Middx Hosp, authorised med examiner CAA; area surgn St John Ambulance Bde, MO Br Red Cross Soc, asst co cmmr Scout Assoc; Freeman City of London; Liveryman: Worshipful Soc of Apothecaries, Worshipful Co of Barbers, Guild of Air Pilots and Air Navigators; OStJ; *Recreations* swimming, bowls; *Clubs* United Oxford & Cambridge Univ; *Style—* Col Michael Burton, TD; Briar Close, 16 Latchmoor Ave, Gerrards Cross, Bucks SL9 8LJ (☎ 0753 886979); Penwig ISAF, South John St, New Quay, Dyfed SA45 9NN (☎ 0545 560333)

BURTON, Richard St John Vladimir; s of Percy Basil Harmsworth Burton, and Vera, *née* Poliakoff Russell; *b* 3 Nov 1933; *Educ* Bryanston, AA Sch of Architecture (AA Dipl); *m* 3 April 1956, Mireille, da of Joseph Dernbach-Mayen; 3 s (Mark b 24 April 1957, David b 25 Oct 1958, Jonathan b 2 Jan 1960), 1 da (Catherine b 7 Jan 1962); *Career* ptnr & dir Ahrends Burton & Koralek Architects 1961-; princ works incl: Trinity Coll Dublin (Berkeley library 1972, Arts F Bldg 1979), residential bldg Keble Coll 1976, Templeton Coll Oxford 1969-88, St Mary's Hosp Newport IOW, British Embassy Moscow 1988-, stations for extension Docklands Railway Hooke Park Coll Dorset; govr Bldg Centre Tst, chm Percent for Art Steering Gp Arts Cncl of GB 1989; memb RIBA 1957, FRSA 1980; *Recreations* building, writing; *Style—* Richard Burton, Esq; Ahrends Burton and Koralek, Unit 1, 7 Chalcot Rd, London NW1 8LH (☎ 071 586 3311)

BURTON-CHADWICK; *see*: Chadwick

BURTON OF COVENTRY, Baroness (Life Peeress UK 1962); Elaine Frances Burton; da of late Leslie Aubrey Burton, of Harrogate, and Frances Burton; *b* 2 March 1904; *Educ* Leeds Modern Sch, Leeds Trg Coll; *Career* joined SDP 1981; teacher Leeds 1924-35; memb: S Wales Cncl of Social Welfare 1935-37, of Nat Fitness Cncl 1938-39, MP (L) Coventry S 1950-59; former conslt John Waddington Ltd, Courtaulds Ltd; memb: ITA 1964-69, Cncl of Industrial Design 1963-68, Sports Cncl 1965-71; chm Mail Order Publishers' Authy 1970, pres Inst of Travel Managers in Industry and Commerce; *Style—* The Rt Hon The Lady Burton of Coventry; 18 Vincent Court, Seymour Place, London W1

BURTON-RACE, John William; s of Denys Arthur Race, and Shirley, *née* Manning; *b* 1 May 1957; *Educ* St Mary's Coll Southampton, Highbury Tech Coll (City Guilds 706/1, 706/2), Portsmouth Poly (HCITB Cert of Apprenticeship), Westminster Coll; *m* 15 July 1978, Marie-Christine Jeanne Germaine, da of Andre Rene Germaine Bourdeau; 1 da (Naomi Lea May b 5 June 1989); *Career* apprentice Wessex Hotel Winchester 1973-75, commis Quaglino's Hotel Meurice London 1975-76, first commis Chewton Glen Hotel 1976-78, chef Olivers Midhurst 1978-79, chef tournant La Sorbonne Oxford 1979-82, private chef MacKenzie-Hill Property Development International 1982-83, sous chef Les Quat Saisons Oxford 1983-84, head chef and mangr Le Petit Blanc Oxford 1984-86, chef dir L'Ortolan Shinfield 1986-; three star Egon Ronay 1989 (Restaurant of the Year 1991), two star AA, five out of five Good Food Guide 1990 and 1991, seventeen out of twenty Gault Millau three Red Toques, one star Michelin 1987-, Personnalite De L'annee Chef Laureat (Paris) 1991, Relais Gourmand 1990-, Mumm prize winner 1987, Caterer Hotelkeeper Acorn, Best in Br Ackerman Guide; memb: Academic Culinare Fillale Grande Bretagne, Chambre Syndicate de Haute Cusine Francaise, Restaurateurs Assoc of GB; contrib to: Best Fish, Best Game, Best Chocolate series 1987, Master Chefs of Europe 1988, Great British Chefs 1989, Great European Chefs 1990; *Recreations* very little; *Clubs* 190 Queen's Gate, Acorn Club; *Style—* John Burton-Race, Esq; L'Ortolan, The Old Vicarage, Church Lane, Shinfield, nr Reading, Berks RG2 9BY (☎ 0734 883783, 0734 884498, fax 0734 885391)

BURTON STEWART, Colin; s of Gavin Burton Stewart, CBE (d 1973), of Appin, Argyll, and Joyce Irene, *née* Middleton, MBE (d 1977); *b* 21 Jan 1948; *Educ* Milton Abbey, Univ of Paris; *m* March 1985, Avril, da of Capt John Ogilvie Munro (d 1980), of Banchory, Aberdeenshire; 1 s (John b 1985); *Career* dir: Anglo-Swiss Reinsur Brokers Ltd 1977-85, The Number Two Oil Co Ltd 1985-; chm: The Stewart Transport & Trading Co Ltd 1984-; *Recreations* travelling, fishing, shooting, reading, model railways; *Clubs* Caledonian, Special Forces; *Style—* Colin Burton Stewart, Esq; c/o Bank of Scotland plc, 16-18 Piccadilly, London W1; 7 Westminster Palace Gardens, London SW1

BURWELL, Prof (Richard) Geoffrey; s of Capt Arthur Reginald Burwell (d 1960), from Leeds, and Mabel Walker, *née* Robinson (d 1988); *b* 1 July 1928; *Educ* Leeds GS, Harrogate GS, Univ of Leeds (BSc, MB ChB, MD); *m* 19 Jan 1963, Helen Mary, *née* Petty, da of Capt Frank Petty (d 1952); 1 s (Matthew b 30 Dec 1963), 1 da (Jane b 8 Dec 1965); *Career* Capt RAMC jr surgical specialist Gibraltar Hosps 1955-57; orthopaedic registrar Gen Infirmary Leeds 1957-58 (house surgn 1952), lectr in surgery Univ of Leeds 1963-65 (lectr in Anatomy 1958-63), sr registrar in traumatic and orthopaedic surgery Robert Jones and Agnes Hunt Orthopaedic Hosp Oswestry 1965-68; prof: of Orthopaedics Univ of London 1968-72, of human morphology and experimental orthopaedics Univ of Nottingham 1974-; hon conslt in orthopaedics Nottingham Health Authy; pres Br Orthopaedic Res Soc 1982-84, tstee Br Scoliosis Soc 1989-93 (pres 1982-84); FRCS 1955; *Recreations* family, history, travel, archeology; *Clubs* Old Oswestrians (pres 1989-91); *Style—* Prof Geoffrey Burwell; 63 Rodney Rd, W Bridgford, Nottingham NG2 6JH (☎ 0602 232745); Department of Human Morphology, Queens Medical Centre, Clifton Boulevard, Nottingham NG7 2UH (☎ 0602 421421 ext 41417, fax 0602 709259, telex 37346 (Uninot G))

BURY, Diana Mary; *née* Incledon-Webber; Lady of the Manors of Croyde and Putsborough, Devon; eldest da of Lt-Col Godfrey Sturdy Incledon-Webber, TD, DL (d 1986), of Buckland Manor, Braunton, N Devon, and Angela Florence, 4 da of Sir Pierce Thomas Lacy, 1 Bt; descended from John Webber, Mayor of Barnstaple (17 cent), ggs Philip Rogers Webber, JP, DL; m 1759, Mary, er da and co-heir of John Incledon, of Buckland, Braunton, Devon (*see* Burke's Landed Gentry, 18 edn, vol I, 1965, Incledon-Webber of Buckland); *b* 27 Sept 1932; *Educ* Stoodley Knowle Convent Torquay; *m* 28 June 1961, John Edward Bury, DL, o s of Col John Bury, OBE (d 1969), of Berden Lodge, Berden, Herts; 1 s (Henry Incledon b 5 May 1962), 5 da (Mary Helen b 1964 (m 1987, Marc Cumberlege), Anne b 1965, Eleanor b 1967, Jane b 1971, Clare b 1972); *Career* sec in Foreign Office 1955-60; pres N Devon Branch DGAA; ctee memb: NADFAS, St Brannoc's RC Church; *Recreations* tennis, swimming; *Clubs* Lansdowne; *Style—* Mrs Diana Bury; Buckland Manor, Braunton, N Devon EX33 1HN (☎ 0271 812016)

BURY, John Edward; DL (1989); s of Col John Bury, OBE (d 1969), of Berden Lodge, Berden, Herts, and Ruth Alice, *née* Le Marchant (d 1982), eld da of Brig Gen Sir E T Le Marchant (4 Bart) KCB, CBE, JP, DL; *b* 26 Sept 1927; *Educ* Prince of Wales Nairobi Kenya, Exeter Coll Oxford (MA); *m* 28 June 1961, Diana Mary, da of Lt Col Godfrey Sturdy Incledon-Webber, TD, DL (d 1986), of Buckland Manor, Braunton; 1 s (Henry b 5 May 1962), 5 da (Mary Helen (Mrs Cumberlege) b 1964, Anne b 1965, Eleanor b 1967, Jane b 1971, Clare b 1972); *Career* London Stock Exchange 1952-80, ptnr Pidgeon de Smitt and Predecessor firms, chm Croyde Bay Holidays Ltd 1986-88 (md 1981-86), chm Incledon Estates Ltd 1988; memb Devon Cncl NFU 1983, dir Br Holiday and Home Park Assoc Ltd 1983-89, vice pres Devon Agric Assoc 1984, memb Exec Ctee West Country Tourist Bd 1985-88, dep pres Devon branch BRCS 1985; memb: TAVRA W Wessex 1986, Agric Land Tbnl SW Area 1987, Ctee Devon branch Country Landowners 1987; pres: Braunton and Dist Museum 1988, Gt Torrington Hort Soc 1988; govr Grenville Coll Bideford 1989; Freeman City of London 1964, Liveryman Worshipful Co of Clothworkers 1966; *Recreations* gardening; *Clubs* Army and Navy; *Style—* John Bury, Esq, DL; Buckland Manor, Braunton, N Devon EX33 1HN (☎ 0271 812016)

BURY, Lady Mairi Elizabeth; *née* Vane-Tempest-Stewart; JP (Co Down); da of 7 Marquess of Londonderry, KG, MVO, TD, PC (d 1949); *b* 25 March 1921; *Educ* private; *m* 10 Dec 1940 (m dis 1958), Lt-Col Viscount Bury (d 1968), s of 9 Earl of Albemarle, 2 da (Elizabeth, Rose); *Career* former farmer and estate owner; pres Co Down branch Br Red Cross Soc, former pres and chm of Ards Womens Unionist Assoc N Ireland; Liveryman Worshipful Co of Air Pilots and Air Navigators; fell Royal Philatelic Soc London; *Recreations* philately; *Style—* The Lady Mairi Bury, JP; Mount Stewart, Newtownards, Co Down, NI BT22 2AD (☎ 024 774 217)

BURY, Viscountess; Marina; *née* Orloff-Davidoff; da of Count Serge Orloff-Davidoff, and Hon Elisabeth, *née* Scott-Ellis, da of 8 Baron Howard de Walden and 4 Baron Seaford; *b* 30 Dec 1937; *m* 1964, as his 2 w, Viscount Bury (d 1968), s and h of 9 Earl of Albemarle, MC (d 1979); 1 s (10 Earl of Albemarle, *qv*); *Career* RIBA, AA Dip; *Style—* Viscountess Bury; Piazza di Bellosguardo 10, Florence 50124, Italy (☎ 055 222055)

BURY, Dr Robert Frederick; s of William George Bury, and Evelyn Winifred, *née* Liggins; *b* 10 Aug 1948; *Educ* Kettering GS, Univ of London (BSc), Middx Hosp Sch (MB BS); *m* 18 Nov 1972, Linda Joyce, da of Samuel Hart; 3 s (Nicholas b 1974, Mathew b 1977, Tom b 1984), 1 da (Kate b 1976); *Career* MO RAF Med Branch 1971-88: med cadetship 1971-73, surgn PMRAF Hosp 1974-79 (55 Field Surgical Team 1976-77), radiologist 1979-88; conslt radiologist nuclear med 1988-; FRCS 1978, FRCR 1983; *Books* Radiology: A Practical Guide (1988), and various pubn in Radiology; *Recreations* hill walking, fishing, writing; *Style—* Dr Robert Bury; Dept of Nuclear Medicine, Leeds General Infirmary, Great George St, Leeds LS1 3EX (☎ 0532 432799 ext 7171)

BURY, Thomas Edmund Oswell; s of Michael Oswell Bury, of Springfields, Blackmore, Ingatestone, Essex, and Jean Threlkeld, *née* Wood; *b* 14 May 1958; *Educ* Charterhouse, St Edmund Hall Oxford (BA); *Career* Young & Rubican Ltd London 1980-85: graduate trainee, account mangr 1982, account supervisor 1983; Ogilvy & Mather: account supervisor 1985, account dir 1985, bd dir 1987, mgmnt supervisor 1988, new business dir 1988, head of client services 1989-, gp dir 1990- (responsible for the accounts of Ford UK, Guinness UK, Brooke Bond, Coley Porter Bell, Worldwide Fund for Nature); MIPA; *Recreations* cricket, golf, squash, racquets, books; *Clubs* United Oxford and Cambridge Univ, RAC, MCC, Arabs, I Zingari, Old Carthusians; *Style—* Thomas Bury, Esq; Flat 5, 44 Cornwall Gardens, London SW7 4AA (☎ 071 937 2868); Ogilvy and Mather Advertising Ltd, Brettenham House, Lancaster Place, London WC2E 7EZ (☎ 071 836 2466, fax 071 497 2731, car 0836 323031)

BUSBRIDGE, Raymond John; s of John Charles Busbridge (d 1968), and Marie Ida, *née* Stratton; *b* 11 Dec 1946; *Educ* Woodside Secdy Sch; *m* 1, June 1966 (m dis 1979), Dianne Rosemary, *née* Webster; 1 s (Phillip James b 8 May 1970), 1 da (Claire Nanette b 21 Nov 1974); m 2, 13 March 1982, Mary Claire, da of Paul Fennelly, of Kilkenny, Ireland; *Career* Leslie & Godwin 1963-64, aviation asst underwriter RW Sturge 1964-75, aviation underwriter: Assicurazioni Generali 1975-80, JFC Dugdale (later Octavian Underwriting), fndr AJM Drake (later Busbridge Aviation Syndicate), exec dir Octavian Gp plc; exec memb Lloyd's Ctee for Lloyds Aviation Claims Centre, memb Lloyd's 1985-; *Recreations* shooting, fishing, painting; *Style—* Raymond Busbridge, Esq; 84 Fenchurch St, London EC3M 4BY (☎ 071 265 0071, telex 8951200)

BUSBY, (Thomas Samuel) Charles; CBE (1977 OBE 1971), AE (1946), DL (Kent 1981); s of Thomas William Busby (d 1974), and Alice, *née* Feaver (d 1972); *b* 28 July 1919; *Educ* Cranbrook Sch Kent; *m* 1949, Diana Daun, da of William Cruickshank Dalgarno (d 1954); *Career* joined 500 Sqdn (Co Kent) AAF 1939, served Coastal Cmd Sqdns as Flt Lt (demobilised 1946); FSVA incorporated surveyor, auctioneer and estate agent (ret 1984); chm Royal Br Legion Village and Industries 1965-, life vice pres Kent Br Legion 1967- (vice chm 1952, chm 1962-67), vice chm Central Kent Hosp Mgmnt Ctee 1970-72 (memb 1964), chm Preston Hosp Ctee 1970-74, memb Cncl Br Cwlth Ex-Services League 1971-, memb Maidstone and Dist Hosp Mgmnt Ctee 1972-74, memb Kent Family Practitioner Ctee 1974-75, nat chm Royal Br Legion 1975-78 (nat vice chm 1972-75), chm Brith, memb Cncl World Veterans Fedn 1977- (lay memb Med Advsy Ctee), memb Maidstone Health Authy 1984-88, pres SE Area Royal Br Legion 1986; *Recreations* gardening, rugby football and cricket; *Clubs* RAF, Royal Overseas League; *Style—* Charles Busby, Esq, CBE, AE, DL; Willow Cottage, Benenden, Cranbrook, Kent TN17 4DB (☎ 0580 240466)

BUSBY, John Philip; s of Eric Alfred Busby, MBE (d 1983), and Margaret Elizabeth, *née* Ware; *b* 2 Feb 1928; *Educ* Ilkley GS, Leeds Coll of Art (NDD), Edinburgh Coll of Art (DA Edin); *m* 18 July 1959, Joan, da of Fred Warriner, of Cleveland; 1 s (Philip b 1960), 2 da (Rachel b 1962, Sarah b 1966); *Career* Nat Serv RAF 1946-48; lectr Edinburgh Coll of Art 1956-88; pres Soc of Scottish Artists 1973-76, fndr memb Soc of Wildlife Artists; memb RSW 1983, ARSA 1987; *Books* The Living Birds of Eric Ennion (1982), Drawing Birds (1986), Birds in Mallorca (1988); *Recreations* ornithology, travel, music; *Style—* John P Busby, Esq; Easter Haining, Ormiston Hall, Ormiston, E Lothian EH35 5NJ (☎ 0875 340512)

BUSBY, Richard Anthony; s of Ronald Arthur Busby, of Bromley, Kent, and Sheila Annora, *née* Fitzherbert; *b* 4 June 1950; *Educ* St Dunstan's Coll S E London, Univ of Essex (BA); *m* 1, 24 July 1977 (m dis 1983), Karen, da of Ian Barr, of Edinburgh; m 2, 5 July 1985, Kathleen, da of Daniel Henebury (d 1984); 2 step s (Nicholas b 1961, Richard b 1964); *Career* articled clerk Touche Ross 1968-69, asst prodn mangr Hodder & Stoughton 1973-76, mktg mangr Futura Pubns 1976-77; md C & C Communications 1977-85, chm and chief exec offr Strategic Sponsorship 1985-; involved various environmental and charitable orgns; *Recreations* reading, current affairs, art, theatre, opera, jazz and cinema; *Style—* Richard Busby, Esq; 11 Blackstock Mews, London N4 2BT (☎ 071 354 5000, fax 071 359 2202)

BUSCALL, Robert Edmond; JP (Norfolk 1971), DL (Norfolk 1989); s of Lt-Col V H Buscall (d 1979), of Carbrooke Hall, Thetford, Norfolk, and Gwendolene Mary Angela, *née* Mahony; *b* 2 April 1935; *Educ* Downside, RAC Cirencester (MRAC); *m* 7 Oct 1961, Livia, da of Sir Stephen Lycett Green, Bt, CBE, DL, of Ken Hill, Snettisham, Kings Lynn; 2 s (Harry Charles b 1963, Patrick Edward b 1965); *Career* Lt Irish Guards 1953-56; farmer; cncllr Breckland DC 1983-, gen cmmr of income tax 1983-; memb: Bd of Visitors Wayland Prison 1984-87, Agric Land Tbnl (E Area) 1983; *Recreations* country pursuits, gardening; *Clubs* Whites, Allsorts; *Style—* Robert Buscall, Esq, JP, DL; Carbrooke Hall, Thetford, Norfolk (☎ 0953 881 274)

BUSH; *see*: de L'Isle Bush

BUSH, Dr Alan Dudley; s of Alfred Walter Bush, (d 1966), and Alice Maud, *née* Brinsley (d 1987); *b* 22 Dec 1900; *Educ* Highgate Sch, RAM (ARAM), Univ of Berlin; *m* 1931, Nancy Rachel, da of Frederick D Head; 3 da (Rachel b 1931, Catherine b 1937, Alice (twin) b 1937 d 1952); *Career* WWII served RAMC 1941-45; prof of composition RAM 1925-30 and 1946-78; concert pianist, orchestral and operatic conductor 1925-84; examiner Assoc Bd RSM 1947-78; musical compositions incl: four full length operas (libretti for Wat Tyler, Men of Blackmoor and The Sugar Reapers aka Guyana Johnny written by his w Nancy Bush), numerous orchestral, solo and instrumental works reaching Opus 121; Hon DMus: Univ of London, Dunelm Dunedin 1965; RSA 1960, FRAM; *Books* In my eighth decade and other essays (1980), Strict Counterpoint in the Style of Palestrina; *Recreations* chess, walking; *Style—* Dr Alan Bush; 25 Christchurch Crescent, Radlett, Hertfordshire (☎ 0923 856 422)

BUSH, Geoffrey Hubert; s of Sidney Arthur Bush, of Bristol, and Dorothy Elizabeth, *née* Rowlands (d 1990); *b* 5 April 1942; *Educ* Cotham GS Bristol; *m* Sylvia Mary, da of Walter Frank Squibb, of Whimple, Devon; 1 s (Jonathan Mark b 1966), 1 da (Sarah Jane Mary b 1968); *Career* Inland Revenue: tax offr 1959, inspr of taxes 1968, dist inspr 1973, princ inspr 1981, under sec 1988, dir of info technol 1990; *Recreations* tennis, golf, sailing, country pursuits; *Clubs* Knowle Lawn Tennis, Topsham Sailing; *Style—* Geoffrey Bush, Esq; Somerset House, London WC2R 1LB (☎ 071 438 6120)

BUSH, Hon George Walker; 41 President of the United States of America; 2 s of Senator Prescott Sheldon Bush (d 1972), and Dorothy, *née* Walker; *b* 12 June 1924; *Educ* Greenwich Country Day Sch Greenwich Conn, Phillips Acad Andover Mass, Yale Univ; *m* 6 Jan 1945, Barbara, da of Marvin Pierce, of Rye, NY; 4 s (George Walker b 6 July 1946, John Ellis b 11 Feb 1953, Neil Mallon b 22 Jan 1955, Marvin Pierce b 22 Oct 1956), 2 da (Robin d 1953, Dorothy Walker (Mrs LeBlond) b 18 Aug 1959); *Career* enlisted US Navy as Seaman 2 cl 1942, Lt 1943, served WW II 1942-45 (DFC, 3 Air Medals); oil field supply salesman for Dresser Industries W Texas and Cal 1948-51; co-fndr: Bush-Overbey Development Corporation Midland Texas 1951-53, Zapata Petroleum Midland Texas 1953-59, Zapata Offshore Co Houston Texas 1959-66; chm Exec Ctee First International Bank of Houston 1977-78; Adjunct Prof of Business Rice Univ 1977-78; US Representative Texas 7th Dist 1967-71 (memb Ways and Means Ctee); US Ambass to UN 1971-73; chief US liaison offr in People's Republic of China 1974-75; dir Central Intelligence Agency 1976-77; Vice-Pres of USA 1981-89; Pres of USA 1989-; chm Republican Nat Ctee 1973-74; memb Bd Episcopal Church Fndn; *Books* Looking Forward (autobiography, with Victor Gold, 1987); *Recreations* fishing, tennis, golf, jogging, horseshoes, boating; *Style—* The President of the United States of America; The White House, Pennsylvania Avenue, Washington, DC, USA; Walker's Point, Kennebunkport, Maine, USA; North Post Oak Lane, Houston, Texas

BUSH, Prof John Farrall; s of John Thomas Bush (d 1954), and Alida Josephine Bush (d 1979); *b* 6 April 1924; *Educ* Leyton County HS, King's Coll Newcastle upon Tyne, Univ of Durham (BSc); *m* 1949, Maisry Joan, da of late Robert Simpson; *Career* Rolls Royce Ltd: stress engr Barnoldswick 1944-46, stress engr Derby 1946-56, chief stress engr 1956-58, devpt engr 1958-61, project engr 1961-63, sr project engr 1963-65, chief engr 1965-67, engrg dir 1967-71, chief engr 1971-83, corp head of mechanical technol 1983-86, ret; engrg conslt to Rolls Royce plc 1986-90, chm Turbo-Kinetic Design Ltd 1990- (joined 1986); special prof Mechanical Engrg Dept Univ of Nottingham 1987-; RAeS Silver medal for outstanding achievement in aeronautical engrg 1990; FEng 1989, FRAeS 1965, FBIM; *Recreations* geology, music, walking, flying; *Style—* Prof John Bush; 36 Vauxhall Ave, Derby DE3 4DZ (☎ 0332 42536); Turbo-Kinetic Design Ltd, Power Engineering Consultants, 50 Friargate, Derby DE1 1DF

BUSH, Adm Sir John Fitzroy Duyland; GCB (1970, KCB 1965, CB 1963), DSC (1941, and two bars 1941 and 1944); s of Fitzroy Bush (d 1949), of Beach, Bitton, Glos; *b* 1 Nov 1914; *Educ* Clifton; *m* 1938, Ruth Kennedy, da of Capt Herbert K Horsey, RN, of Fareham, Hants; 3 s, 2 da; *Career* RN; formerly: C-in-C Western Fleet, Allied C-in-C Channel, Allied C-in-C E Atlantic 1967-70, Vice-Adm of UK and Lt of Admiralty 1979-84; Clifton Coll Cncl: memb 1971-87, chm 1978-81, pres 1982-87; *Recreations* fishing, gardening; *Style—* Adm Sir John Bush, GCB, DSC; Becksteddle House, Colemore, nr Alton, Hants (☎ 042 058367)

BUSH, Prof Stephen Frederick; s of Albert Edward Bush (d 1982), and Winifred May, *née* Maltby; *b* 6 May 1939; *Educ* Isleworth GS, Trinity Coll Cambridge (MA, PhD), Mass Inst of Technol (MSc); *m* 26 Oct 1963, Gillian Mary, da of Reginald Charles Layton, of Thorpe Bay, Essex; 1 s (James Henry b 1970), 1 da (Jane Elizabeth b 1972); *Career* gp mangr of chem engrg ICI Corporate Laboratory 1969-72, mangr Systems Technol Dept ICI Europa Ltd 1972-79, chair of polymer engrg Univ of Manchester 1979; md Prosyma Research Ltd 1987, chm and co-fndr N of England Plastic Processors Consortium 1990; awarded: Moulton medal 1969, Sir George Beilby medal and prize 1979; MIMechE (memb Cncl 1978-81), MIChemE; FRPI (memb Cncl 1985-87), chm Applied Mechanics Ctee SERC 1985-87; *Books* Chemical Reaction Engineering (contrib, 1972), Macromolecular Chemistry Reports (contrib, 1980), Polymer Engineering (contrib, 1984), Synthetic and Biological Networks (contrib, 1988); *Recreations* mountain walking, British Imperial history, music, tennis; *Style—* Prof Stephen Bush; University of Manchester Institute of Science and Technology, PO Box 88, Manchester M60 1QD (☎ 061 200 3760, fax 061 200 37)

BUSHBY, Alan Fennell; s of Henry Fennell Bushby (d 1965), and Catherine Bell (d 1982); *b* 21 Dec 1926; *Educ* Portsmouth GS, Univ of Edinburgh; *m* 17 May 1958, Annelise Pachnicke, da of Ove Bernhard Nielsen (d 1977); 1 s (Robert b 12 July 1961), 1 da (Jean Kirsten b 31 Oct 1959); *Career* Capt RAMC 1952-54; house surgn Edinburgh Royal Infirmary, registrar and tutor Hammersmith Hosp, sr registrar and tutor Jessop Hosp Sheffield, conslt obstetrition and gynaecologyist Derby Hosps 1964-; former memb DHA, fell Birmingham Obstetrics and Gynaecology Soc, FRCOG; *Recreations* sailing, golf; *Clubs* Army & Navy; *Style—* Alan Bushby, Esq; 120 Belper Rd, Derby (☎ 0332 40819); City Hospital, Uttoxeter Rd, Derby (☎ 0332 40131)

BUSHE, Peter Dalwyn Scott; s of Louis Alfred Bushe (d 1986), of Surrey, and Marion Howard, *née* Wing (d 1970); *b* 17 Aug 1924; *Educ* Lodge Sch Barbados, Lancing Coll; *m* 14 April 1951, Margaret, da of Major Frank Walter Mace (d 1975), of Surrey; 2 s (Andrew b 1952, David b 1956); *Career* RNVR Sub Lt Normandy and Far East 1943-46, Royal Sch of Mines 1946-47; Trinidad Petroleum Devpt Ltd 1948-60, BP (Trinidad) Ltd 1960-68, BP Libya 1968-71, technical co-ordinator BP London 1971-76, co-ordinator Abu Dhabi Marine Areas 1976-83; dir: Ilex Lubricants Ltd 1968-, Cadmuir Devpts Ltd 1983-, Headston Contracts Ltd 1985-; FInstPet; *Recreations* tennis, golf; *Clubs* Naval; *Style—* Peter Bushe, Esq; Little Fairhall, Colley Lane, Reigate, Surrey RH2 9JA (☎ 0737 245193); Headston Contracts Ltd, Little Fairhall, Colley Lane, Reigate, Surrey RH2 9JA (☎ 0737 240001)

BUSHELL, Garry Llewellyn; s of George Frederick Henry Bushell, BEM, of Greenhill, Kent, and Evelyn May Mary, *née* Barker (d 1987); *b* 13 May 1955; *Educ* Colfe's GS, NE London Poly (BA), London Coll of Printing (NCTJ); *m* 31 July 1976, Carol Ann Cousins, da of Francis Cousins; 2 s (Danny John b 25 Aug 1980, Robert Llewellyn b 1 April 1988), 1 da (Julie Ann b 23 Nov 1978); *Career* messenger Shell, clerk London Fire Brigade; journalist; trainee Socialist Worker (block release from Coll) 1976, publisher and ed Nepalm (punk fanzine) 1976-78, features ed Sounds 1980-84 (rock journalist 1978-84), freelance author 1984-85; temp shifts 1984-85 (The Sun, London Evening Standard, Daily Mirror); The Sun: casual contract 1985-87, staff journalist 1987, ed Bizarre column 1987, TV critic 1987, TV ed and showbusiness ed 1988; singer The Gonads (punk rock band) 1976-82; mangr: The Cockney Rejects (punk rock band) 1979-80, The Blood (shock rock band) 1985-86; compiler of rock albums: Oi - The Album 1980, Strength thru Oi 1981, Carry on Oi! 1981, Oi Oi Thats Yer Lot 1982, The Beerdrop Explodes 1982, Total Noise 1982, Son of Oi 1983; conceived and organised The Sun's number one single by Ferry Aid 1987, conceived and wrote successful one-off magazines: Dance Craze (The 2-Tone Story) 1981, Punk's Not Dead 1981; MENSA 1989-; *Books* Running Free, The Biography of Iron Maiden (1984, reprinted 1985, 1986, 1987), Twisted Sister 'The Official Book' (1985), Diary of a Madman (jtly, 1986); *Recreations* beer drinking, curry eating, rock music, sitcom writing, boxing (spectator), Beethoven and Wagner (listening), politics (discussing), nationalism (advocating), swimming, collecting military prints, Bernard Manning videos, comedy videos, books, guitar playing, history (reading), live club comics; *Clubs* Blackheath and Newbridge Working Man's, Charlton Conservative; *Style—* Garry Bushell, Esq; The Sun News International, 1 Virginia St, London E1 9XP (☎ 071 782 4000, fax 071 488 3253)

BUSHELL, John Hudson; s of (Charles) Harold Bushell, OBE, of Reigate, Surrey, and Bessie Mary, *née* Smith; *b* 13 Oct 1941; *Educ* Haileybury; *m* 8 Oct 1966, Marian Elisabeth, da of Eric Percival Marsh, of Woking, Surrey; 1 s (Alistair b 1970), 2 da (Emma b 1968, Heather b 1978); *Career* dir J Henry Schroder Wagg & Co Ltd 1975-85, chm and chief exec London Shop plc 1986-89 (dir 1982-89, exec vice chm 1985-86); FCA 1964; *Recreations* cricket, tennis; *Clubs* Walton Strollers Cricket, Inst of Dirs; *Style*— John Bushell, Esq

BUSK, Maj-Gen Leslie Francis Harry; CB (1989); s of Lt-Col Charles William Francis Busk (d 1959), and Alice Van Bergen; *b* 12 Sept 1937; *Educ* Wellington, RMCS Shrivenham (BSc); *m* 9 Jan 1960, Jennifer Helen Busk; 3 s (Jonathan b 1963, Edward b 1966, Crispin b 1974); *Career* cmmnd RE 1957, cmdg offr 35 Engr Regt 1977-79, Cdr II Engr Brigade 1981-83, RCDS 1984, dir Army Air Corps 1987-89; DG Br Heart Fndn; *Recreations* tennis, gardening, golf, framing watercolours; *Clubs* Army and Navy; *Style*— Maj-Gen Leslie Busk, CB; Director General, British Heart Foundation, 14 Fitzhardinge Street, London W1H 4DH (☎ 071 935 0185)

BUSSE, Hon Mrs (Susan Anne); er da of Baron Trevelyan (Life Peer; d 1985); *b* 10 Jan 1941; *m* 1961, Harald Busse, s of Gerhard Busse, of Cologne; 2 s, 1 da; *Style*— The Hon Mrs Busse; Zukunftsweg 22B, 5307 Wachtberg-Villiprott, W Germany

BUSSELL, Darcey Andrea; da of Philip Michael Bussell, and Andrea Pemberton, *née* Williams; *b* 27 April 1969; *Educ* Arts Educnl Sch, Royal Ballet Sch; *Career* ballerina; appeared in 1986 and 1987 Royal Ballet Sch performances, joined Sadlers Wells Royal Ballet (now Birmingham Royal Ballet) 1987; Royal Ballet: joined as soloist 1988, first soloist 1989, princ 1989 (currently Royal Ballet's youngest princ dancer); leading roles incl: Myrthe in Giselle (first professional leading role), Odette/Odile in Swan Lake, the Lilac Fairy in The Sleeping Beauty, Gamzatti in La Bayadere, princ girl Chaboukiani's Laurentia pas de six, princ girl Song of the Earth, Agnus Dei Girl in Requiem, leading role Galanteries, leading role The Spirit of Fugue (created on her by David Bintley), leading role Pursuit, leading role in first Royal Ballet performance of Balanchine's Rubies, the Winter Fairy in Cinderella, Lady Mary in Enigma Variations, second solo shade La Bayadere; pas de deux (Farewell for Bussell) created for her and Irek Mukhamedov by Kenneth MacMillan (performed at the Queen Mother's 90th Birthday Tribute London Palladium and The Royal Opera House); The Prince of the Pagodas and the Queen Mother's 90th Birthday Tribute televised in 1990; 1990 season: debut as Sugar Plum Fairy in The Nutcracker, Bethena Waltz Girl in MacMillan's Elite Syncopations, Raymonda in Raymonda Act III, creator of leading role in Ashley Page's Bloodlines, leading (Aria 1) Girl in first performance by Royal Ballet of Balanchine's Stravinsky Violin Concerto; winner Prix de Lausanne 1986, Dancer of the Year Dance and Dancers Magazine 1990; *Style*— Miss Darcey Bussell; The Royal Opera House, Covent Garden, London WC2 (☎ 01 240 1200)

BUSTON, Maj Roger; TD (1985); s of Russell Buston, of Parkstone, Dorset, and Kathleen, *née* Williams (d 1955); *b* 24 May 1953; *Educ* Colchester RGS, Poole GS, Queen Mary Coll London (LLB); *Career* Univ of London OTC 1971-74; 36 Signal Regt (TA): Troop Cdr 1974, Sqdn Cdr 1986-87, Regtl Ops Offr 1988-90; admitted slr 1977; sole practitioner Asher Prior & Son 1981-86, ptnr Asher Prior Bates and Bates Group 1986-; MBIM; *Recreations* skiing; *Style*— Maj Roger Buston, TD; New House, Wellesley Rd, Colchester CO3 3HF (☎ 0206 45986); Asher Prior Bates (Solicitors), Blackburn House, 32 Crouch St, Colchester, Essex CO3 3HH (☎ 0206 573089, fax 0206 760096, car tel 0860 833483)

BUSUTTIL, Prof Anthony; s of Anthony Busuttil (d 1973), of Malta, and Maria, *née* Vassallo; *b* 30 Dec 1945; *Educ* St Aloysius' Coll Malta; *m* 31 Aug 1969, Angela, da of Angelo Bonello (d 1979), of Gozo; 3 s (Godwin b 1970, Christopher b 1973, Joseph b 1978); *Career* lectr in pathology Univ of Glasgow 1971-76, conslt pathologist Lothian Health Bd 1976-87, regius prof forensic med Univ of Edinburgh (sr lectr pathology 1976-87), contrib to several books on gastroenterology and genitourinary pathology; memb: BMA, Assoc of Clinical Pathology; DMJ(Path); fell Br Assoc of Forensic Med, MRCPath, FRCPath, FRCPE; *Recreations* classical music, reading; *Style*— Prof Anthony Busuttil; 78 Hillpark Ave, Edinburgh EH4 7AL (☎ 031 336 3241); Forensic Medicine Unit, Medical School, University of Edinburgh, Teviot Place, Edinburgh EH8 9AG (☎ 031 6620294)

BUSWELL, Hon Mrs (Barbara); *née* Fisher; yr da of 2 Baron Fisher (d 1955); *b* 1 Oct 1925; *m* 1961, Leslie Charles Croft Buswell, s of Gerald Buswell (d 1959), of Johannesburg, S Africa ; 1 s, 1 da; *Style*— The Hon Mrs Buswell; Jersey, CI; Normandie Farm, PO Box 6, Firgrove, Cape 7110 S Africa

BUTCHER, Alan Raymond; s of Raymond Earnest Butcher, of 58 Shirley Way, Shirley, Croydon, Surrey, and Rose Marina, *née* Webbey; *b* 7 Jan 1954; *Educ* Heath Clark GS Croydon; *m* Oct 1972 (m dis 1985), Elaine; 2 s (Mark Alan b 23 Aug 1972, Gary Paul b 11 March 1975), 1 da (Lisa Marie b 29 July 1979); partner, Madeleine Dunlop; *Career* professional cricketer; Surrey CCC 1972-86: first class debut 1972, awarded county cap 1975, benefit 1985; Glamorgan CCC: debut 1987, awarded county cap 1987, capt 1989-; represented Aust under 15 1968; England: schs tour India 1970-71, 1 Test Match v India Oval 1979, 1 one day Int v Aust Oval 1980; football coach Cumnor House Sch Croydon 1973-90; *Recreations* sport, music, reading; *Style*— Alan Butcher, Esq; Glamorgan CCC, Sophia Gardens, Cardiff, S Glamorgan (☎ 0222 343478)

BUTCHER, Anthony Edward William Hugh (Tony); s of Humphrey George Herbert Butcher, and Mary Josephine, *née* McCaffrey; *b* 6 Nov 1940; *Educ* Ampleforth; *m* 18 Sept 1965, Sarah, da of Raymond Stuart Harwood; 3 da (Louise b 18 July 1966, Katherine b 14 Feb 1969, Clare b 23 Nov 1974); *Career* CA; articled clerk J S Streets & Co Lincoln 1959-64, Turquand Youngs & Co London 1964-65, Selincourt Group 1965-67, Price Waterhouse 1967-85; Pannell Kerr Forster: dir of fin and admin 1985, ptnr professional resources 1988, managing ptnr Central Region 1990-; FCA, MInstD; *Recreations* rugby, board sailing, travel, gardening; *Clubs* Nottingham Rugby Football (chm of rugby); *Style*— Tony Butcher, Esq; Pannell Kerr Forster, Harby Lodge, 13 Pelham Road, Nottingham NG5 1AP (☎ 0602 606260, fax 0602 622229)

BUTCHER, Ian George; s of George Wilfred Robert Butcher, of Winchmore Hill, London, and Joyce Patricia, *née* Payne; *b* 13 April 1950; *Educ* Winchmore Sch, City of London Coll; *m* 15 Sept 1978, Sarah Jane, da of Donald Percy Jeffery, of Aston Hill Farmhouse, Halton, Bucks; 1 s (Harry b 1987), 2 da (Emma b 1981, Kellie b 1984); *Career* exec dir County Bank Ltd 1974-84, fin dir Addison Page plc 1984-86, corp devpt dir Addison Conslt Group plc 1986-87, gp fin dir Charles Baker plc 1987-89, chm Lefax Publishing Ltd 1984-88, dir Whitehead Mann plc 1989-; FCA; *Recreations* hockey, cricket, tennis, music, reading; *Clubs* MCC, RAC; *Style*— Ian G Butcher, Esq; Aston Hill Farmhouse, Aston Hill, Halton, nr Aylesbury, Bucks HP22 5NQ (☎ 0296 630643); Whitehead Mann Group plc, 50 Welbeck St, London W1 (☎ 071 224 4444)

BUTCHER, Michael Joseph Edward; s of Edward Harry Butcher (d 1985), of France, and Margaret Enid, *née* Camp; *b* 9 Aug 1951; *Educ* Haywards Heath GS, Univ of Keele (BA); *Career* called to the Bar Gray's Inn 1975; memb Legal Dept ESSO UK plc and Exxon USA 1976-88, legal dir and sec Eurotunnel Gp 1989 (legal advsr 1988); *Recreations* chess, cinema, reading, skiing; *Style*— Michael Butcher, Esq; Eurotunnel, Victoria Plaza, 111 Buckingham Palace Rd, London SW1W 0ST (☎ 071 834 7575)

BUTCHER, Nicholas Andrew Christopher; s of Reginald Herbert Butcher, of Norwich, and Elsie May, *née* Balls; *b* 11 Nov 1945; *Educ* City of Norwich Sch, Trinity Hall Cambridge (MA, LLM); *m* 12 May 1973, Pamela Ann, da of Harry Roberts (d 1987), of Coventry; 1 s (David Simon b 27 May 1980); *Career* slr 1971; memb Nat Exec Nat Assoc of Round Tables GB and Ireland 1982-84; *Recreations* gastronomy, sport (squash, hockey), music; *Clubs* Strangers', Norwich, Rotary; *Style*— Nicholas Butcher, Esq; The Weavers' Barn, Squires Rd, Halvergate, Norfolk BR13 3PZ (☎ 0493 701122); 4 Cathedral St, Norwich (☎ 0603 660701, fax 0603 616302, telex 975649)

BUTCHER, Prof Paul Newman; s of Henry Butcher (d 1970), of Ashford, Kent, and Beatrice Ada, *née* Bridges (d 1968); *b* 11 Aug 1929; *Educ* Ashford GS, Imperial Coll London (BSc, DIC, PhD); *m* 2 Aug 1952, Alfreda (Freda), da of Frederick Stone (d 1929); *Career* scientific civil serv 1951-67, head Theoretical Physics Group RSRE Malvern 1964-67, prof theoretical physics Univ of Warwick 1967-; visiting prof: Ohio State Univ 1963-64, Danish Tech Univ Copenhagen 1970; 175 pubns on topics incl: microwave tubes, nonlinear optics and electronics, amorphous and crystalline semiconductors, electronic microstructures; ARCS, FIEE, former fell Physical Soc; *Books* The Principles of Nonlinear Optics (1990); *Recreations* walking, music; *Style*— Prof Paul N Butcher; Physics Dept, University of Warwick, Coventry CV4 7AL (☎ 0203 523989, telex 312331 UNIWARG, fax 020 692016)

BUTCHER, Roland Orlando; s of Robert Butcher, of Barclay Crescent, Stevenage, Herts, and Doreen, *née* Parris; *b* 14 Oct 1953; *Educ* Shephalbury Secondary Sch, Hitchin Coll of Further Education; *m* 7 Feb 1980, Cheryl Denise, da of Kenneth Hubert Hurley; 1 s (Paul Nicholas Roland b 2 Jan 1979), 1 da (Michelle Denise b 11 Nov 1982); *Career* cricketer: Middlesex CCC: joined 1972, debut 1974, capped 1979, toured Zimbabwe 1980-81, highest first class score 197 vs Yorkshire 1982; England: capped 1980, 3 Tests vs W1 1980-81, 3 One Day Ints 1980-81; fastest first class century of season 1987; semi-pro footballer; coach: FA, Advance Cricket; biography Rising To The Challenge (1989); *Recreations* horse racing, charity work; *Style*— Roland Butcher, Esq; Cricket Match Ltd, EMP House, Pembroke Rd, London N10 2HR (☎ 081 442 0596, fax 081 883 9504)

BUTCHER, Terry Ian; s of Leonard Charles Butcher, of Lowestoft, Suffolk, and Valerie May, *née* Flowers; *b* 28 Dec 1958; *Educ* Lowestoft GS; *m* 20 Jan 1980, Rita Mary, da of Ernest Charles Adams; 3 s (Christopher Charles b 7 April 1982, Edward John b 19 July 1985, Alistair Ian b 16 January 1990); *Career* professional football player; Ipswich Town FC 1976 (winner UEFA Cup 1981), transferred to Glasgow Rangers FC 1986-90 (winners Skol League Cup 1986 and 1988, winners Premier League Championship 1987, 1989 and 1990), player/manager Coventry City FC 1990-; England Team: 7 Under-21 Caps, 1 B Cap, 77 Full Caps, 6 times capt National Team; memb Scot Stars for Spastics Charity, involved with Leukaemia & Cancer Children's Fund Scotland; *Books* Both Sides of the Border (1987); *Recreations* golf, tennis, cricket, snooker, fishing; *Style*— Terry Butcher, Esq; c/o Coventry City Football Club, Highfield Road Stadium, King Richard Street, Coventry CV2 4FW (☎ 0203 257171)

BUTCHER, Thomas Edmund; s of Lt-Col Osborne Arthur Butcher (d 1934), and Beatrice Viola, *née* Hodgson (d 1968); *b* 28 May 1924; *Educ* Oundle; *m* 8 June 1957, Jean Audrey (d 1963), da of Ernest Leonard Warren (d 1986); 2 da (Alison (Mrs Huntrods) b 1959, Fiona (Mrs Fraser) b 1962); *Career* Lt RNVR 1942-46; slr; *Style*— Thomas Butcher, Esq; 19 Lee Grove, Chigwell, Essex (☎ 081 500 2587); 20 Queen Anne St, London W1 (☎ 071 580 8021)

BUTE, Dowager Marchioness of; Lady Eileen Beatrice; *née* Forbes; da of 8 Earl of Granard; *b* 1 July 1912; *m* 1932, 5 Marquess of Bute (d 1956); 3 s (incl 6 Marquess), 1 da; *Style*— The Most Hon the Dowager Marchioness of Bute; Dumfries House, Cumnock, Ayrshire

BUTE, 6 Marquess of (GB 1796); Sir John Crichton-Stuart; 11 Bt (S 1627), JP (Bute 1967); Lord Crichton (S 1488), Earl of Dumfries, Viscount of Air, Lord Crichton of Sanquhar and Cumnock (S 1633), Earl of Bute, Viscount Kingarth, Lord Mountstuart, Cumra(e) and Inchmarnock (S 1703), Baron Mountstuart of Wortley (GB 1761), Baron Cardiff of Cardiff Castle (GB 1776), Earl of Windsor and Viscount Mountjoy (GB 1796); Hereditary Sheriff and Coroner of Co Bute, Hereditary Keeper of Rothesay Castle; patron of 9 livings (but being a Roman Catholic cannot present); s (twin) of 5 Marquess (d 1956), and Lady Eileen, *née* Forbes, da of 8 Earl of Granard; *b* 27 Feb 1933; *Educ* Ampleforth, Trinity Coll Cambridge; *m* 1, 1955 (m dis 1977), (Beatrice) Nicola Grace, da of late Lt-Cdr Wolstan Beaumont Charles Weld-Forester, CBE, RN, gs of 5 Baron Forester; 2 s, 2 da; m 2, 1978, Jennifer, da of J B Home-Rigg and former w of Gerald Percy (of the family of the Duke of Northumberland); *Heir* s, Earl of Dumfries; *Career* Lord-Lieut: Bute 1967-75 (DL 1961), Argyll and Bute 1990-; chm Nat Tst for Scotland Exec Ctee 1969-84; convenor Buteshire CC 1967-70; memb: Countryside Cmmn for Scotland 1970-78, Devpt Cmmn 1973-78, Oil Devpt Cncl for Scotland 1973-78, Cncl RSA 1990-, Bd of Brit Cncl 1987-; chm: Historic Buildings Cncl Scotland 1983-88, Nat Museums of Scotland 1985-; tstee Nat Galleries Scotland 1980-87; Hon LLD Glasgow, Hon FRIAS; *Clubs* Turf, White's, New (Edinburgh); *Style*— The Most Hon the Marquess of Bute, JP; Mount Stuart, Rothesay, Isle of Bute PA20 9LR (☎ 0700 502730)

BUTLER, Sir Adam Courtauld; PC (1984); s of Baron Butler of Saffron Walden, KG, CH, PC (d 1982), by his 1 w, Sydney, da of Samuel Courtauld; *b* 11 Oct 1931; *Educ* Eton, Pembroke Coll Cambridge; *m* 1955, Felicity, da of Kemyel Molesworth-St Aubyn (s of Sir Hugh Molesworth-St Aubyn, 13 Bt, JP, by his w, Emma, da of Adm Charles Wake, 2 s of Sir Charles Wake, 10 Bt; Adm Charles Wake m Emma, da of Sir Edward St Aubyn, 1 Bt, and sis of 1 Baron St Levan); 2 s, 1 da; *Career* Nat Serv 2 Lt KRRC 1950-51; dir: Kayser Bondor 1966-73, Aristoc Ltd 1966-73, Capital & Counties Property Co Ltd 1973-79, HP Bulmer Hldgs 1988-; pres Br Noise Soc, dep chm CMW Gp plc, chm Samuel Courtauld Tst; MP (C) Bosworth 1970-87, Cons whip 1974-75, PPS to Rt Hon Margaret Thatcher 1975-79; min of state: Indust 1979-81, NI 1981-4, Def 1984-5; chm Airey Neave Tst 1990-; farmer; kt 1986; *Recreations* field sports, music, pictures; *Style*— The Rt Hon Sir Adam Butler; The Old Rectory, Lighthorne, Warwick (☎ 0926 651214)

BUTLER, Alan Edward; s of Albert Frederick Butler (d 1978), of Clacton on Sea, and Lillian Elizabeth, *née* Carlson (d 1969); *b* 6 Dec 1940; *Educ* Raine's Fndn GS, UCL (BSc); *m* 27 Nov 1981, Gail Katharine; 1 s (Richard b 1984); *Career* md: Carl Byoir and Assocs Ltd 1975- (dir 1970), Communications Strategy Ltd 1985-, Countrywide Communications Ltd 1987-; former chm and memb Strangers Gallery NW Surrey House of Commons Dining Club, former chm PR Conslts Assoc; Freeman City of London; Liveryman: Worshipful Co of Gold and Silver Wyre Drawers 1982, Worshipful Co of Marketors 1988; MBCS, MIPRA, FIPR; *Recreations* most sports; *Clubs* Wentworth, Wig and Pen; *Style*— Alan Butler, Esq; Greenway Cottage, Abbey Rd, Virginia Water, Surrey (☎ 0344 842385); Countrywide Communications Ltd, Bowater House East, 68 Knightsbridge, London SW1 (☎ 071 584 0122, fax 071 584 6655)

BUTLER, Rt Rev Arthur Hamilton Butler; MBE (1944); s of George Booker, of Dublin, and Anne Maude Butler; *b* 8 March 1912; *Educ* Friars Sch Bangor, Trinity

Coll Dublin; *m* 1, 1938, Betty Pringle (d 1976), da of Seton Pringle, of Dublin; 1 s; m 2, 1979, Dr Elizabeth Mayne; *Career* ordained 1935, bishop Tuam Killala and Achonry 1958-69, bishop Connor 1969-81, ret; *Style—* The Rt Rev Arthur Butler, MBE; 1 Spa Grange, Ballynahinch, Co Down, N Ireland BT24 8PD (☎ 0238 562966)

BUTLER, Arthur William; ERD (1964); s of Frederick Butler (d 1975), and Elizina, *née* Bond; *b* 20 Jan 1929; *Educ* Wanstead HS, LSE (BSc); *m* 3 May 1958, Evelyn Mary, da of Thomas Alexander Luetchford (d 1988), of South Island Place, London SW9; 1 da (Caroline b 7 May 1966); *Career* Offr Cadet India Cadet Co 1946, 2 Lt RAOC 1947-48, Capt AER 1957-64 (Lt 1953); trainee Kemsley Newpapers Graduate Trg Course 1951-55, political corr News Chronicle 1956-60, political ed Reynolds News 1960-62, political corr Daily Express 1963-69, political ed Daily Sketch 1969-71, md Partnerplan Public Affrs 1971-74, dir Public Affrs Div John Addey Assocs 1974-77, vice chm Charles Barker Watney and Powell 1987-89 (jt md 1978-87); conslt on parly relations McAvoy Wreford Bayley 1989-; jt ed Eng edn The Free Romanian Newspaper 1985-; sec: Middlesborough Trades Cncl 1952-55 (memb), Parly All Party Roads Study Gp 1974-86, Roads Campaign Cncl 1974-86, Parly Scientific Ctee 1978; govr Sch for Disabled Putney 1975-79, fndr sec Parly Info Technol Ctee 1981-84; Liveryman Worshipful Co of Tobacco Pipe Makers, Freeman City of London 1976; memb: The Royal Institution of Great Britain 1980; *Books* No Feet to Drag (with Alfred Morris MP, 1972), The First Forty Years- A History of the Parliamentary and Scientific Committee (1980), Lobbying in the British Parliament (with Douglas Smith, 1986); *Recreations* walking, gardening, collecting books and militaria, travel; *Style—* Arthur Butler, Esq, ERD; 30 Chester Way, Kennington, London SE11 4UR (☎ 071 582 5170); McAvoy Wreford Bayley, 36 Grosvenor Gardens, London SW1W OEB (☎ 071 730 4500, fax 071 730 9364)

BUTLER, Audrey Maude Beman; da of Robert Beman Minchin (d 1972), and Vivien Florence Fraser, *née* Scott (d 1976); *b* 31 May 1936; *Educ* Queenswood Sch Herts, Univ of St Andrews (MA); *m* 1959 (m dis 1981), Anthony Michael Butler, s of Michael John Butler; 2 da (Clare, Siobhan); *Career* geography teacher; head of geography St Michael's Burton Park 1970-73 and 1976-78, housemistress Manor House Lancing Coll 1978-81, headmistress Queenswood Hatfield Herts 1981-; govr: Aldenham Sch Tockington Manor, Duncombe Sch, Maltman's Green Sch; memb: Girls Schs Assoc, memb and chm Boarding Schs Assoc 1989-; FRGS, MInstD; *Recreations* golf, tennis, swimming, walking, theatre; *Style—* Mrs Audrey Butler; Queenswood, Shepherd's Way, Brookmans Park, Hatfield, Herts AL9 6NS

BUTLER, Auriol Lilian Evelyn; da of Alexander Ross Biddle (d 1927), of Temple Hill, East Budleigh, Devon, and Margaret Louise, *née* Allfrey (d 1958); *Educ* Byam Shaw Sch of Art, Slade Sch London; *m* 30 April 1940, Maj Richard S Butler (d 1988), s of Col Charles Walter Butler, OBE (d 1942), of Longham, Cornwood, Devon; 1 s (Patrick James Richard b 1944), 1 da (Penelope Eve); *Career* artist; portraits incl Sir William Scott and The Princess Royal; landscapes shown in: Paris Salon, RBA London, Nat Soc, United Soc; gold and silver medallist Academia Internaziale Rome, certificate of merit 1974, Diploma di Distinzione di Premio d'Italia, Slade Certificate of Fine Art, Diploma Academia Internaziale; FRSA, Fell Int Inst of Art; *Recreations* archaeology; *Style—* Mrs Auriol Butler; Glebe Studio, Longham, Cornwood, Ivybridge, Devon PL21 9QZ (☎ 075 537 229)

BUTLER, Basil Richard Ryland; OBE (1976); s of Hugh Montagu Butler, (d 1971), of Churchdown, Glos, and Annie Isabelle, *née* Wiltshire (d 1969); *b* 1 March 1930; *Educ* Denstone Coll Staffs, St John's Coll Cambridge (MA); *m* 26 June 1954, Lilian Joyce, da of Reginald Merryweather Haswell (d 1989), of Amersham, Bucks; 1 s (Richard b 1957), 2 da (Clare b 1960, Helen b 1964); *Career* 2 Lt 5th Royal Inniskilling Dragoon Gds 1948-50; reservoir engr Trinidad Leaseholds Ltd 1954, petroleum engr to Chief Petroleum Engr and Supt Prodn Planning Div Kuwait Oil Co 1958-68, ops mangr BP (Colombia) 1968, ops mangr and gen mangr BP Alaska Inc 1970, seconded to Kuwait Oil Co as gen mangr ops 1972; mangr: Ninian Developments, BP Petroleum Development Co Ltd (London) 1975, Sullom Voe Terminal Shetland Islands 1976; BP Petroleum Development Ltd: gen mangr exploration and prod (Aberdeen) 1978, chief exec (London) 1980; international dir BP International Ltd, md and chief exec BP Exploration Co Ltd 1981, md The BP Co plc 1986, chm BP Exploration Co Ltd 1986-89; pres Inst of Petroleum, chm Environment Ctee of the Business and Indust Advsy Ctee to the OECD in Paris; memb: CBI Environment Ctee, Ctee for ME Trade, Offshore Indust Advsy Bd, Cncl of the Centre for Exploitation of Sci and Technol; Freeman: City of London, Worshipful Co of Shipwrights 1988; FEng 1985, FIMM 1985; *Recreations* sailing, music; *Clubs* IOD; *Style—* Basil Butler, Esq, OBE; The British Petroleum Co plc, Britannic House, Moor Lane, London EC2Y 9BU (☎ 071 920 6165, fax 071 920 4232)

BUTLER, Charles Alfred Edward; s of William Charles Valentine Butler (d 1976), and Ivy, *née* Payne (d 1975); *b* 30 Nov 1929; *Educ* Enfield GS; *m* 31 Oct 1953, Rosemary Patricia, da of Henry John Patten, of Hullbridge, Essex; 1 s (Keith Charles b 25 Dec 1960 d 1982), 1 da (Jacqueline Anne b 9 Sept 1962); *Career* Nat Serv Corpl RAF 1948-50; audit mangr Harmood Banner 1956-60, co sec Arks Publicity Ltd 1960-72, dep md Warwick Parsons Advertising Ltd 1972-79, dir Graham & Gillies & Warwick Ltd 1979-82, chief accountant The Order of St John 1982-89; comptroller St John Ambulance London (Prince of Wales's) Dist; hon treas Professional Classes Aid Cncl, memb Mgmnt Ctee The Guild of Aid for Gentlepeople, sec Br Humane Assoc; FCA 1956; *Recreations* bowls, photography, theatre; *Style—* Charles Butler, Esq; 24 Craddocks Ave, Ashtead, Surrey KT21 1PB (☎ 0372 275222); St John Ambulance, London (Prince of Wales's) District, 63 York St, London W1H 1PS (☎ 071 258 3456, fax 071 258 3793)

BUTLER, Christopher John; MP (C) Warrington South 1987-; s of Dr John Lynn Butler, of Cardiff, and late Eileen Patricia Butler; *b* 12 Aug 1950; *Educ* Cardiff HS, Emmanuel Coll Cambridge (MA); *m* 25 March 1989, Jacqueline Clair, *née* Harper; *Career* market res consIt 1972-77, Cons Res Dept 1977-80, Political Office 10 Downing St 1980-83, special advsr to Sec of State for Wales 1983-85, market res consIt 1985-86, special advsr to Min for Arts 1986-87; *Recreations* writing, tennis; *Style—* Christopher J Butler, Esq, MP; Flat 2, 48 Clifton Gardens, London W9 1AU (☎ 071 219 3000); 27 Kildonan Rd, Grappenhall, Warrington, Cheshire; Conservative Hall, Grappenhall Rd, Stockton Heath, Warrington, Cheshire (☎ 0925 601 534, car 0860 419611)

BUTLER, Sir Clifford Charles; s of C H J Butler, of Earley, Reading; *b* 20 May 1922; *Educ* Reading Sch, Univ of Reading (BSc, PhD); *m* 1947, Kathleen Betty Collins; 2 da; *Career* former physics lectr Univ of Manchester, prof physics and head Physics Dept Imperial Coll London 1963-70, dean Royal Coll Sci 1966-69, dir Nuffield Fndn 1970-75; vice-chllr Loughborough Univ of Technol 1975-85; memb: Schs Cncl 1965-84, Univ Grants Ctee 1966-71, Univ of Oxford Cncl 1971-, Br Cncl Sci Advsy Ctee 1980-85; chm: Cncl Educn & Trg Health Visitors 1977-83, Advsy Ctee Supply & Educn Teachers 1980-85; Steering Ctee DES Educnl Counselling & Credit Transfer Info Serv Project 1983-89, ABRC/NERC study into Geological Surveying 1985-87; Hon DSc Univ of Reading, Hon DUniv Open Univ, Hon DTech Loughborough Univ of Technol; FRS; kt 1983; *Clubs* Athenaeum; *Style—* Sir Clifford Butler, FRS; Low Woods Farm House, Low Woods Lane, Belton, Loughborough, Leics LE12 9TR (☎ 0530 223125)

BUTLER, Dr David Edgeworth; s of Prof Harold Edgeworth Butler (d 1951), and Margaret Lucy, *née* Pollard (d 1982); *b* 17 Oct 1924; *Educ* St Pauls, New Coll Oxford, Princeton Univ, Nuffield Coll Oxford (BA, MA, DPhil); *m* 1962, Prof Marilyn Speers, da of Sir Trevor Evans (d 1981); 3 s (Daniel b 1963, Gareth b 1965, Edmund b 1967); *Career* Lt Staffs Yeo 1943-45; fell Nuffield Coll Oxford 1951-, PA to HM Ambass Washington 1955-56; Hon DUniv Paris 1978, Hon DSSc Univ of Belfast 1985; *Books* British General Election Studies (contrib, 1951-87), Political Change in Britain (1974), British Political Facts 1900-1985 (1986); *Clubs* Oxford & Cambridge; *Style—* Dr David Butler; Nuffield College, Oxford OX1 1NF (☎ 0865 278516, fax 0865 278621)

BUTLER, David John; s of Sidney James Butler, and Sylvia Joan, *née* Board; *b* 23 Feb 1953; *Educ* Sir John Cass Sch; *m* 8 June 1974, Bernadette Sheila, *née* Teahan; 2 s (Daniel David b 5 Sept 1981, Sean Francis b 18 March 1984); *Career* stockbroker; dealer Spencer Thornton 1972-80, int salesman Fielding Newson Smith 1980-82, head Int Dept Credit Suisse Buckmaster & Moore 1982-87, head of UK and Euro equity sales and exec dir Yamaichi Int 1987-; Freeman City of London; memb London Stock Exchange; *Style—* David Butler, Esq; Finsbury Court, 111-117 Finsbury Pavement, London EC2 (☎ 071 638 5599, fax 071 588 3134)

BUTLER, David John; s of John Carrol Butler (d 1979), of Sunderland, and Doris, *née* Stockdale; *b* 28 Sept 1952; *Educ* Bede Sch Sunderland, Sunderland Coll of Art; *Career* painter, printmaker and community artist 1985; ed: Making Ways 1985, Artists Newsletter 1985-; freelance writer and ed 1985-; *Style—* David Butler, Esq; 15 Shakespeare Terrace, Sunderland SR2 7JG (☎ 091 510 9144)

BUTLER, Denis William Langford; s of William Henry Butler (d 1965), and Kitty Langford, *née* Sweeney; *b* 26 Oct 1926; *Educ* Repton; *m* 17 Oct 1953, Margaret (Marna), da of Charles Donald Taylor (d 1962); 3 da (Wendy b 1955, Susan b 1957, Katharine b 1957); *Career* comptroller and city solicitor to the City of London 1981-, solicitor 1951, asst solicitor Norfolk CC 1953-54, asst solicitor Shropshire CC 1954-57, asst solicitor Lindsey (Lincs) CC 1957-60, dep clerk Wiltshire CC 1960-74, county solicitor and clerk Wiltshire CC 1974-81, chm County Secretaries Soc 1974-76; Freeman City of London 1981, Liveryman Worshipful Co of Slrs 1983; *Recreations* gardening and travel; *Style—* Denis Butler, Esq; 5 Stone House, 9 Weymouth Street, London W1N 3FF (☎ 071 580 2707; Guildhall, London EC2P 2EJ (telex : 265608 London G; fax : 071 260 1119)

BUTLER, Lady Denyne Gillian Patricia; only surv da of 9 Earl of Lanesborough, TD, DL; *b* 23 Feb 1945; *Style—* The Lady Denyne Butler; 1850 W 11th Avenue, Vancouver, BC V6J 2C5, Canada

BUTLER, Hon Edmund Henry Richard; s of 17 Viscount Mountgarret; *b* 1 Sept 1962; *Educ* Stowe; *m* 7 May 1988 (m dis 1990), Adelle, only da of M Lloyd, of New York; *Style—* The Hon Edmund Butler; RR 2S 12C 26, Gibsons Landing, VON IVO, British Columbia, Canada (☎ 0101 604 886 9196)

BUTLER, Hon Mrs (Elizabeth Olson); *née* Erskine; da of 1 Baron Erskine of Rerrick, GBE (d 1980); *b* 2 July 1923; *m* 1944, Gilbert Butler, s of Harry John Butler, of 39 Duffryn Av, Cardiff; 2 s, 1 da; *Career* WWII Subaltern ATS 1939-45; *Style—* The Hon Mrs Butler; Gatehouse, 8b Churchfields Ave, Weybridge, Surrey KT13 9YA

BUTLER, His Hon Judge Gerald Norman; QC (1975); s of Joshua Butler (d 1978), and Esther, *née* Lampel; *b* 15 Sept 1930; *Educ* County HS Ilford, LSE (LLB), Magdalen Coll Oxford (BCL); *m* 2 April 1959, Stella, da of Harris Isaacs (d 1975); 1 s (Mark b 28 Feb 1963), 2 da (Jane b 26 Oct 1960, Charlotte b 29 April 1967); *Career* 2 Lt RASC 1954-56; called to the Bar Middle Temple 1955, rec of Crown Ct 1977-82, Circuit Judge 1982, sr Judge of Southwark Crown Court 1984-; *Recreations* opera, rugby, reading; *Clubs* MCC; *Style—* His Honour Judge Butler, QC; Southwark Crown Ct, London SE1 (☎ 071 403 4141)

BUTLER, Hon Henrietta Elizabeth Alexandra; da of 17 Viscount Mountgarret; *b* 4 Nov 1964; *Style—* The Hon Henrietta Butler

BUTLER, Hubert Arthur James; s of Charles Butler, MBE, of Newport, Essex; *b* 24 Sept 1937; *Educ* Eton, RAC Cirencester; *m* 1968 (m dis 1984), Anne, da of Capt Peter Robert Churchward, of Devon; 1 s, 2 da; *Career* formerly Lt 17/21 Lancers; dir Winchmore plc 1963; ARICS; *Recreations* shooting, cricket; *Clubs* Cavalry & Guards, Farmers; *Style—* Hubert Butler, Esq; Le Pavillon, Newport, Essex (☎ 0799 40225)

BUTLER, Ian Geoffrey; CBE; s of Hubert Desramaux Butler, of Cumbria; *b* 12 April 1925; *Educ* Stowe, Trinity Coll Oxford; *m* 1973, Anne, da of James Robertson, of Dunbartonshire; 2 da; *Career* Lt Coldstream Gds 1945-47; ptnr Tansley Witt 1951-55; chm: Cookson Gp plc (formerly Lead Industries Gp, mfr of specialist industl materials) 1976- (md 1973-84), Barclays Bank plc, Nurdin & Peacock plc; FCA; *Recreations* yachting (National Swallow Skua), skiing; *Clubs* Royal Yacht Sqdn, Royal Thames Yacht, Itchenor Sailing; *Style—* Ian Butler, Esq, CBE; Wyke Hse, Ellanore Lane, W Wittering, Sussex (☎ 0243 513269); 105 Abingdon Rd, London W8 (☎ 071 937 5220)

BUTLER, Dr James Morris; s of Frederick Thomas Butler; *b* 15 June 1926; *Educ* Hull GS, Univ of Cambridge; *m* 1950, Freda; 1 s, 2 da; *Career* chm: McKechnie plc, Cronite Gp plc; dir Johnson & Firth Brown plc; former pres Br Non-Ferrous Metals Fedn, former chm Int Wrought Copper Cncl; *Recreations* golf; *Style—* Dr James Butler; 2 Old Hall, Whittington, Staffs (☎ 0543 432323)

BUTLER, (Percy) James; CBE; s of Percy Ernest Butler (d 1942), of The Hill, Batheaston, Bath, and Phyllis Mary Butler (d 1950); *b* 15 March 1929; *Educ* Marlborough, Clare Coll Cambridge (MA); *m* 26 June 1954, Margaret Prudence, da of Percy Copland (d 1968); 1 s (David James b 1961), 2 da (Elizabeth Anne b 1957, Susan Margaret b 1958); *Career* Nat Serv 1947-49, 2 Lt RA; qualified CA 1955; KPMG Peat Marwick McLintock 1952- (ptnr 1967, managing ptnr 1980, dep sr ptnr 1985, sr ptnr 1986-); tstee Winchester Cathedral Tst, memb Marlborough Coll Cncl, chm Winchester Cath Appeal; dep chm Mersey Docks & Harbour Co (govt dir 1972-90) memb Govt Ctee on British Rail Fin; memb Court Worshipful Co of Cutlers, memb Worshipful Co of Chartered Accountants; *Recreations* bridge, shooting; *Clubs* Carlton; *Style—* James Butler, Esq, CBE; KPMG Peat Marwick McLintock, 1 Puddle Dock, Blackfriars, London EC4V 3PD (☎ 071 236 8000, fax 071 248 6552)

BUTLER, Hon (Samuel) James; yst s of Baron Butler of Saffron Walden, KG, CH, PC (Life Peer) (d 1982) by his 1 w, Sydney, da of Samuel Courtauld; *b* 13 Dec 1936; *Educ* Eton, Pembroke Coll Cambridge; *m* 1, 24 June 1960 (m dis 1977), Lucilla Blanche, yr da of late Algernon Malcolm Borthwick, MC, TD, of Wethersfield Place, Braintree, Essex; 2 s, 4 da; m2, 4 July 1986, Jennifer, only da of Dr George Gladston of Almeria NY State, USA; *Career* late 2 Lt RHG; head of Features Rediffusion 1966-68, exec producer Granada TV 1968-70, Freeland TV Producer 1970-, memb of Cncl Univ of Essex, chm Arts Ctee Univ of Essex; *Recreations* talking, walking; *Style—* The Hon James Butler; Gladfen Hall, Halstead, Essex

BUTLER, James Walter; s of Walter Arthur Butler (d 1942), and Rosina Harriet, *née* Kingman (d 1967); *b* 25 July 1931; *Educ* Maidstone GS, Maidstone Sch of Art, St Martins Sch of Art; *m* 1 (m dis); 1 da (Kate b 12 Dec 1966); m 2, 1975, Angela Elizabeth, da of Col Roger Berry; 4 da (Rosie b 23 Aug 1975, Saskia b 12 April 1977, Candida b 24 April 1979, Aurelia b 11 Aug 1983); *Career* sculptor; tutor of sculpture and drawing City and Guilds London Art Sch 1960-75; works in pub places: portrait statue Pres Kenyatta Nairobi 1973, Momument to Freedom Fighters of Zambia Lusaka 1975, sculpture of Burton Cooper Staffs 1977, Meml to King Richard III Leicester 1980, portrait statue Field Marshall Earl Alexander of Tunis Wellington Barracks 1985, bronze sculpture Skipping Girl Harrow 1985, Dolphin Fountain Dolphin Square London 1987, portrait statue Sir John Moore and Figures of Rifleman and Bugler Sir John Moore Barracks Winchester 1986; portrait statue John Wilkes New Fetter Lane London 1988, bronze sculpture The Leicester Seamstress Leicester 1990, portrait head Sir Hugh Wontner Savoy Hotel 1990; RA 1964, fell RBS, memb Royal W of Eng Acad; *Recreations* golf, astronomy; *Clubs* The Arts; *Style*— James Butler, Esq; Valley Farm, Radway, Warwickshire CV35 OUJ (☎ 0296 641938, fax 0926 640624)

BUTLER, Hon John Fitzwalter; s and h of 28 Baron Dunboyne; *b* 31 July 1951; *Educ* Winchester, Trinity Cambridge (MA), London Business Sch (Sloan Fellow); *m* 1975, (Diana) Caroline, da of Sir Michael Sanigear Williams, KCMG (d 1984); 1 s (Richard b 1983), 3 da (Genevieve b 1977, Imogen b 1979, Cleone b 1986); *Style*— The Hon John Butler; c/o C Hoare & Co, 37 Fleet Street, London, EC4P 4DQ

BUTLER, John Sherburne; s of Thomas George Butler (d 1961), of Oswaldtwistle, Lancashire, and Isabella, *née* Lord (d 1972); *b* 7 Dec 1931; *Educ* Accrington GS, Manchester Municipal Sch of Art (Goadsby medal for architecture 1960); *m* 19 May 1956, (Beryl) Eurwen, da of Richard Jones (d 1963), of Oswaldtwistle; 1 da (Ursula Anne b 1959); *Career* sr ptnr Grimshaw and Townsend Chartered Architects 1975- (joined as ptnr 1962); The Methodist Church N Lancs Dist 1962-73: sec Home Missions and Redundancy Cmmn, memb Home Missions Bd, Exec Ctee Connechional Property Div Bd; memb Round Table and Rotary Clubs of Accrington; JP Accrington Bench 1976-86; FAMS, FRIBA 1971 (Assoc 1961), FCI Arb 1978 (Assoc 1977), FRSA 1979; *Recreations* gardening, painting, reading, birdwatching, walking; *Style*— John Butler, Esq; Grimshaw and Townsend, 24 Willow St, Accrington, Lancashire BB5 1LS (☎ 0254 320 07/320 30)

BUTLER, Lady Juliana Mary Philomena; da of 9 Earl of Carrick, and Belinda, da of Maj David Turville-Constable-Maxwell , TD (s of Hon Bernard Constable-Maxwell, 4 s of 10 Lord Herries of Terregles, by his 2 w, Hon Alice, *née* Fraser, da of 15 Lord Lovat), by his w, Mary, da of Lt-Col Oswald Turville-Petre, TD, JP, DL (gggs of 9 Baron Petre); *b* 20 Dec 1960; *Educ* Univ of Sussex, St Andrew's Coll Cambridge; *Career* neurobiologist; *Clubs* IAM (elected memb), Mensa, BSAC, BAPC; *Style*— The Lady Juliana Butler; 10 Netherton Grove, London SW10

BUTLER, Keith Stephenson; CMG (1977); s of Raymond Renard Butler (d 1972), of St Leonards on Sea, Sussex, and Gertrude, *née* Stephenson (d 1972); *b* 3 Sept 1917; *Educ* Liverpool Coll, Univ of Oxford (MA), Canadian Nat Def Coll; *m* 1, 1952, Geraldine Marjorie Clark (d 1979); m 2, 1979, Mrs Priscilla Wittels, da of Cdr John Boldero, DSC (and Bar), RN (d 1984), of Bridport, Dorset; *Career* HM Forces 1939-46: Maj RA, N Africa, Greece and Crete, POW in Germany 1941-45 (despatches); HM Dip Serv 1950-77 (HM consul gen: Seville 1968-69, Bordeaux 1969-74, Naples 1974-77); appeal dir for charities 1978-; *Recreations* historical res; *Clubs* Oxford Union Soc; *Style*— Keith Butler, Esq, CMG; Easter Cottage, Westbrook, Boxford, Newbury, Berks RG16 8DN (☎ 048838 557)

BUTLER, Prof Marilyn Speers; da of Sir Trevor Maldwyn Evans, CBE (d 1981), of Kingston-on-Thames, and Margaret Speers, *née* Gribbin; *b* 11 Feb 1937; *Educ* Wimbledon HS, St Hilda's Coll Oxford (MA, DPhil); *m* 3 March 1962, David Edgeworth, s of Harold Edgeworth Butler (d 1951); 3 s (Daniel b 1963, Gareth b 1965, Edmund b 1967); *Career* trainee and talks producer BBC 1960-62; Univ of Oxford: res and teaching 1962-70, jr res fell St Hilda's Coll 1970-73, fell and tutor St Hugh's Coll 1973-85; King Edward VII prof of Eng lit Univ of Cambridge 1986-; fell Kings Coll Cambridge 1988-; *Books* Maria Edgeworth, a Literary Biography (1972), Jane Austen and the War of Ideas (1975), Peacock Displayed (1979), Romantics Rebels and Reactionaries (1981, 1985), Burke Paine Godwin and the Revolution Controversy (1984), The Works of Mary Wollstonecraft (ed); *Style*— Prof Marilyn Butler; 151 Woodstock Rd, Oxford OX2 7NA (☎ 0865 58323); Kings Coll, Cambridge (☎ 0223 350411)

BUTLER, Michael (Mike); s of Humphrey Daniel Butler, of Eglwysbach, Clywd, and Lucy, *née* Mills; *b* 15 Nov 1952; *Educ* Ellesmere Coll Shrop; *m* 6 March 1974, Jennifer Catherine (Jenny), da of Thomas Ramsey Sharpe; 1 s (Ben b 2 May 1977), 1 da (Anna b 1 March 1979); *Career* RN 1972-82; offr i/c Devonport Field Gun Crew 1981; served Sultan of Oman's Navy 1982-85, security conslt and md SECON Ltd 1985-87, md Thompson Butler Assocs Ltd, (exec search and mgmnt conslts) 1988-; memb Int Pro Security Assoc; Sultan of Oman Peace Medal (1983); *Recreations* shooting, sailing; *Style*— Mike Butler, Esq; Thompson Butler Associates Ltd, Minster Chambers, Church St, Southwell, Notts (☎ 0636 815 277, fax 0636 815 657, car 0860 810 038)

BUTLER, Sir Michael Dacres; GCMG (1984, KCMG 1979, CMG 1975); s of T D Butler, of Almer, Blandford, Dorset, and Beryl May, *née* Lambert; *b* 27 Feb 1927; *Educ* Winchester, Trinity Coll Oxford; *m* 1951, (Margaret) Ann, da of Rt Hon Lord Clyde, (d 1975, MP (C) North Edinburgh 1950-54, Lord Justice-Gen of Scotland 1954-72); 2 s, 2 da; *Career* Diplomatic Service 1950: under sec in charge of EEC Affairs FCO 1974-76, dep under sec of state FCO 1976-79, UK perm rep to EEC 1979-85, dep chm Bd of Tstees Victoria & Albert Museum 1985-; exec dir Hambros Bank 1986-; dir: Wellcome Fndn 1986-, Oriental Aut Mag 1987-; advsr Euro Affairs to chm ICL 1986-; *Books* Europe More Than a Continent (1986); *Recreations* collecting Chinese porcelain, tennis, skiing; *Clubs* Brooks; *Style*— Sir Michael Butler, GCMG; 36A Elm Park Rd, London SW3 6AX; 6 Rond-Point Robert Schumann, Brussels, Belgium

BUTLER, Prof Michael Gregory; s of Maurice Gregory Butler (d 1973), and Winifred May, *née* Barker; *b* 1 Nov 1935; *Educ* High Pavement Sch Nottingham, Univ of Cambridge (BA, MA), Univ of Oxford (DipEd) CNAA (PhD); *m* 31 Dec 1960, Jean Mary, da of William John Griffith (d 1966); 1 s (Julian Michael b 1964), 1 da (Emma Catherine b 1967); *Career* asst master: Kings Sch Worcs 1958-61, Reuchlin Gymnasium Pforzheim FRG 1961-62; head of German Ipswich Sch 1962-70; Univ of Birmingham: lectr 1970, sr lectr 1980-86, head Dept of German Studies 1984, prof of Mod German Lit 1986, head Sch of Mod Languages 1988-; ed Samphire 1972-83; FIL 1967; *Books* The Novels of Max Frisch (1975), Englische Lyrik der Gegenwart (ed,1981), The Plays of Max Frisch (1985), Frisch: Andorra (1985), Rejection and Emancipation German-Swiss Writing 1945-91 (ed, 1991); *Recreations* walking, talking; *Style*— Prof Michael Butler; 45 Westfields, Catshill, Bromsgrove, Worcs B61 9JH (☎ 0527 74189); Dept of German Studies, University of Birmingham, PO Box 363, Birmingham B15 2TT (☎ 021 414 6173)

BUTLER, Michael Howard; s of Howard Butler, of Beech Ct, Mapperley, Notts, and Constance Gertrude, *née* King; *b* 13 Feb 1936; *Educ* Nottingham HS; *m* 27 July 1961, Christine Elizabeth, da of Sidney Frank Killer, of West Bridgeford, Notts; 2 s (Ian Michael b 1965, Andrew John b 1967), 1 da (Ruth Elizabeth b 1971); *Career* dir gen of fin NCB 1980- (treas 1978), fin dir Br Coal Corp 1985- (corp memb 1986-); FCA 1958, CBIM 1987; *Recreations* tennis, music, gardening assoc, football; *Style*— Michael Butler, Esq; British Coal Corporation, Hobart House, Grosvenor Place, London, (☎ 071 235 2020)

BUTLER, Michael James; s of late Lt-Col James Dighton Butler (1987), formerly of Bath, and Pamela Elizabeth, *née* Pickwoad (d 1987); *b* 7 July 1944; *Educ* Eastbourne Coll, RMA Sandhurst, RAC Cirencester; *m* 1981, Jennifer, da of late Percy Williams, of Dundee; 1 da (Elizabeth b 1985); *Career* cmmnd 15/19 The King's Royal Hussars 1965, now sole princ Axworthy Chartered Surveyors Tiverton, Devon; memb Royal Forestry Soc; FAAV 1978, FRICS 1980; *Recreations* singing, work; *Clubs* Farmers; *Style*— James Butler, Esq; Axworthy Chartered Surveyors, 32 St Peter St, Tiverton, Devon EX16 6NR (☎ 0884 258010, fax 0884 258344)

BUTLER, Sir (Reginald) Michael Thomas; 3 Bt (UK 1922), of Old Park, Devizes, Wilts; QC (Can 1967); s of Sir (Reginald) Thomas Butler, 2 Bt (d 1959); *b* 22 April 1928; *Educ* Brentwood Coll Victoria BC, Univ of BC (BA), Osgoode Hall Sch of Law Toronto; *m* 1, 1952 (m dis 1967), Marja Margaret Elizabeth, da of Ewen H McLean, of Toronto; 3 s; m 2, 1968 (m dis 1974), Barbara Anne, da of Kevin Cahill, of Dublin; 1 s (adopted); *Heir* s, (Reginald) Richard Michael Butler; *Career* barr and slr Ontario 1954 and BC 1967; ptnr Messrs Butler, Angus (Victoria, BC); *Clubs* Vancouver; *Style*— Sir Michael Butler, Bt, QC; (☎ 604 388 6155); 736 Broughton St, Victoria, Br Columbia V8W 1E1, Canada

BUTLER, Prof Neville Roy; s of Dr Cuthbert John Butler (d 1937), of Harrow, Middx, and Ida Margaret, *née* Soman (d 1959); *b* 6 July 1920; *Educ* Epsom Coll, Charing Cross Hosp Med Sch (MB BS, DCH); *m* 14 May 1954 (m dis 1979), Jean Ogilvie, da of John McCormack (d 1983); 2 da (Claire b 1957, Fiona b 1959); *Career* Capt RAMC; first asst Paediatric Unit UCH 1950, med registrar and pathologist Hosp for Sick Children Gt Ormond St 1953, conslt paediatrician Oxford and Wessex RHB 1957-63, dir Perinatal Morality Survey (Birthday Tst Fund 1958), conslt physician Hosp for Sick Children Gt Ormond St and sr lectr Inst of Child Health Univ of London 1963-65, co-dir Nat Child Devpt Study (1958 Cohort) 1965-75, prof of child health Univ of Bristol 1965-85 (emeritus prof 1985-); dir: Child Health and Educn Study (1970 Cohort) 1970-85, Int Centre for Child Studies 1982-, Youthscan UK 1985-; vice pres: RCM 1972-, HVA 1975-; memb: BPA 1958, Neonatal Soc 1961-, Cuban Paediatric Soc 1973, Hungarian Paediatric Soc 1979-; FRCP, FRCOG; *Books* Perinatal Mortality (jtly, 1963), 11,000 Seven Year Olds (1966), Perinatal Problems (1969), From Birth to Seven (1972), ABO Haemolytic Disease of the Newborn (1972), The Social Life of Britain's Five Year Olds (1984), From Birth to Five (1986); *Recreations* running a charity; *Style*— Prof Neville Butler; Vine Cottage, Seagry Road, Sutton Benger, Chippenham, Wilts

BUTLER, Norman Frank Paul; s of Paul Butler (d 1981), of Tipperary and Oak Brook, Illinois, USA, and Adèle Josephine Rooney (d 1975); *Educ* Hodder, Stoneyhurst, Downside, Univ of Oxford, Colombia Univ Graduate Sch of Law USA; *m* 1, 28 Oct 1948 (m dis 1958), Pauline Katherine (d 1983), da of Hon Charles Winn (s of 2 Baron St Oswald), and former w of Hon Edward Ward (twin s of 2 Earl of Dudley); 2 da (Sandra Whitney Butler b 1949 (m 1972, m dis, Timothy Heise), Paget b 1953 (m 1970 Baron Ernst von Wedel)); m 2, 1959 (m dis 1978), Hon Penelope Cynthia, da of 3 Baron Forteviot; 2 s (Paul b 1960 d 1988, Sean b 1963), 1 da (Tracey b 1961); m 3, 1981, Baroness Gabriella Gröger von Sontag, of Cracow, Poland; 1 s (Patrick); *Career* served WWII, volunteer US Marines (inventor of radar life raft); dir and vice pres Butler Co Illinois; dir: Butler Aviation, Butler Int, Butler Nat Golf Club; fndr and chm Butler Co SA; fndr Old Oak Brook and Kilboy Estates Stud Farms Ireland; breeder and horse owner; horses incl: Pabui, Pidget (winner of Irish Oakes and St Leger), Kilboy; 2 Air Medals, 2 Presidential Citations 1945; *Recreations* gardening, polo, sailing, surfing, breeding horses and Irish Wolf Hounds; *Clubs* Union, Buck's, Oxford & Cambridge, Boojums, Oak Brook Polo, Butler Int Golf, River (NY), Bath & Tennis, Everglades, Seminole Polo (Palm Beach), Lansdowne, Union League, Royal Cornwall Yacht, Chicago, Arts (Dublin), Royal Cornwall Yacht Club; *Style*— Norman de Butler Esq; Barclays Bank, Monte Carlo; 1637 Charmey, Switzerland; Glen Mawnan, Mawnan Smith, Cornwall TR11 5LL; Old Oak Brook, Oak Brook, Illinois 60521; Le Bon Accueil, Chąteau D'Oex 1837, Suisse

BUTLER, Dr Paul; s of Frank William Butler (d 1966), and Elizabeth, *née* Wright; *b* 4 June 1952; *Educ* Cotham GS, UCL (BSc), Westminster Med Sch (MB BS, MRCP); *m* 28 Jan 1978, Janet Ann Butler, da of Percival Jack Barber, of Marissal Road, Henbury, Bristol; 1 s (David b Oct 20 1982), 1 da (Claire b Dec 19 1980); *Career* med registrar rotation Leicester AHA 1979, trainee in radiodiagnosis Manchester RHA 1983, sr registrar neuroradiology Manchester Royal Infirmary, currently conslt neuroradiologist The Royal London Hosp, conslt and hon sr lectr The Royal Free Hosp; conslt neuroradiologist: London Ind Hosp, Churchill Clinic, Harley St Clinic; Freeman City of London, Yeoman Worshipful Soc of Apothecaries; memb Br Soc of Neuroradiologists, DMRD 1983, FRCR 1983; *Books* Imaging of the Nervous System (ed, 1990); *Recreations* classical music, opera; *Style*— Dr Paul Butler; Department of Neuroradiology, The Royal London Hospital, Whitechapel, London E1 1BB (☎ 071 377 7164, car 0523 523523 no 602417)

BUTLER, Hon Mrs (Penelope Cynthia); *née* Dewar; yr da of Maj 3 Baron Forteviot, MBE; *b* 29 April 1935; *m* 1959 (m dis 1978), Norman Frank Paul Butler; 2 s (1 decd), 1 da; *Style*— The Hon Mrs Butler; 73 Duchess Drive, Newmarket, Suffolk

BUTLER, Hon Piers James Richard; s and h of 17 Viscount Mountgarret; *b* 15 April 1961; *Educ* Eton, Univ of St Andrews; *Style*— The Hon Piers Butler

BUTLER, Hon Sir Richard Clive; DL (Essex 1972); s of late Baron Butler of Saffron Walden, KG, CH, PC (Life Peer), by his 1 w, Sydney, da of Samuel Courtauld; *b* 12 Jan 1929; *Educ* Eton, Pembroke Coll Cambridge; *m* 1952, Susan Anne Maud, da of Maj Patrick Walker, MBE (s of Sir James Walker, 3 Bt); 2 s, 1 da; *Career* 2 Lt RHG BAOR 1948-49; farmer; pres NFU 1979-86 (memb cncl 1962-); dir: National Westminster Bank plc 1986-, NatWest Investment Bank Ltd 1989-, County Nat West Investment Management Ltd 1989- (chm), Ferruzzi Trading (UK) Ltd 1986- (chm), The National Farmers' Union Mutual Insurance Soc 1985-; chm The Butler Tst; kt 1981; *Recreations* hunting, shooting, tennis; *Clubs* Farmers'; *Style*— The Hon Sir Richard Butler, DL; Penny Pot, Halstead, Essex (☎ 0787 472828)

BUTLER, Richard Pierce; s and h of Sir Thomas Pierce Butler, 12 Bt, CVO, DSO, OBE; *b* 22 July 1940; *Educ* Eton, NY Univ, Inst of CA in England and Wales; *m* 21 Oct 1965, Diana Anne, yr da of Col Stephen John Borg (d 1971); 3 s (Thomas b 1966, Stephen b 1968, Rupert b 1971), 1 da (Anne b 1973); *Career* ptnr Charles Wakeling & Co 1964-66; dir: The First Boston Corp (NY) 1967-78, Paine Webber Int Bank 1978-89, European Industrial Equity Company SA 1987-, TTG Co (UK) Ltd 1989-, Ibercapital SA 1990-; memb Cncl Pestalozzi Children's Village Trust 1983-, govr Summer Fields Sch Oxford 1984-; MBA, FCA; *Style*— Richard Butler, Esq; 18 Chapel St, London SW1X 7BY

BUTLER, Capt Robert George Danhaive (Bob); s of George Keating Butler (d 1967), of Brussels, and Germaine Helene Caroline, *née* Danhaive (d 1966); *b* 27 Jan 1916; *Educ* Coll St Micheal Brussels, Ecole Abbat Maredsous Belgium, Sch of Law; *m* 14 July 1951, (Dorothy) Elyzabeth, da of Walter James Keates (d 1958), of Hong Kong; 1 s (Alan b 4 April 1955), 1 da (Carole (Mrs Coulson-Gilmaur) b 28 Nov 1956); *Career* Trooper Inns of Ct Regt TA 1937, Sandhurst 1939, cmmnd RAC 1940, 47 RTR, seconded Hobsons Horse IA 1940, Capt and Tech Adj served Iraq and Persia 1941, offr i/c D & M Wing Abbassia Egypt 1942, seconded Spears Mission in Syria and Lebanon 1943-45, UK and demob 1945; Hedleys (originally A M Longhurst & Butler): articled clerk 1935-39, asst slr 1948-51, ptnr 1951, sr ptnr 1978-85, ret 1985, conslt 1985-; NP 1974; sec chartered shipbrokers Protection and Indemnity Assoc Ltd 1961, fndr chm and md Int Shipbrokers and Agents P & I Club Ltd 1983-86 (hon life memb 1986-); memb Cncl Notaries Soc 1988; Liveryman Worshipful Co of Slrs of the City of London; memb: Law Soc 1948, Baltic Exchange 1963-85; assoc Lloyds, fell Inst of Linguists 1963, FCIArb, FICS 1986; *Recreations* piano, organ, DIY, languages, geneology; *Clubs* Victory Serv, Anglo Belgian Soc; *Style—* Capt Bob Butler; Merrilea, Ivy Lane, Woking, Surrey GU22 7BY, (☎ 04862 60493)

BUTLER, Robin Christopher (Chris); s of Thomas George Butler (d 1988), and Gladys Elsie Irene, *née* Packwood (d 1975); *b* 8 Aug 1948; *Educ* Atlantic Sixth Form Coll, Univ of Nottingham (BSc); *m* 1974, Ruth Margaret, *née* Owen; 2 da (Kathryn Sarah b 1978, Laura Jane b 1979); *Career* dir Financial Dynamics Ltd; *Style—* Chris Butler, Esq; Financial Dynamics Ltd, 30 Furnival Street, London EC4A 1JE

BUTLER, Sir (Frederick Edward) Robin; KCB (1988), CVO; s of Bernard Daft Butler, and Nora, *née* Jones, of St Annes on Sea, Lancs; *b* 3 Jan 1938; *Educ* Harrow, Univ Coll Oxford (BA); *m* 1962, Gillian Lois, da of Dr Robert Galley, of Teddington, Middlesex; 1 s (Andrew b 1968), 2 da (Sophie b 1964, Nell b 1967); *Career* private sec: Rt Hon Edward Heath 1972-74, Rt Hon Harold Wilson 1974-75; princ private sec to Rt Hon Margaret Thatcher 1982-85, second perm sec HM Treasy 1985-87, sec to the Cabinet and head of the Home Civil Service 1988-; *Recreations* competitive games, opera; *Clubs* Anglo-Belgian, Athenaeum, Brooks's, United Oxford and Cambridge Univ; *Style—* Sir Robin Butler, KCB, CVO; Cabinet Office, 70 Whitehall, London SW1 (☎ 071 233 3000)

BUTLER, Robin Noel Holman; s of George Noël Butler (d 1969), of Honiton, and Marjorie Blanche, *née* Dunn; *b* 26 April 1943; *Educ* Allhallows Sch; *Career* schoolmaster 1961-63, family antiques business 1963-, memb Br Antique Dealers Assoc 1970- (cncl 1984-87); *Books* Arthur Negus Guide to English Furniture (1978), Book of Wine Antiques (1986); *Recreations* photography, cooking and playing snooker badly; *Clubs* Clifton; *Style—* Robin Butler, Esq; 20 Clifton Road, Bristol BS8 1AQ (☎ 0272 733017); 20 Clifton Rd, Bristol BS8 1AQ (☎ 0272 733017)

BUTLER, Roger John; *b* 19 June 1947; *Educ* Cheltenham GS; *m* 31 Aug 1968, Kathleen Teresa, 1 s (David b 1983) 1 da (Caroline b 1979); *Career* ptnr Fryer Whitehill & Co 1971-80; Arthur Young: ptnr 1981-89, regnl managing ptnr London; chief exec Butler Corporate Finance Ltd 1989-; FCA 1969; *Recreations* golf, tennis; *Style—* Roger Butler, Esq; Far End, Wagon Way, Loudwater, Herts WD3 4JE (☎ 0923 774 110); 17 Devonshire Street, London W1N 1FS (☎ 071 323 0186, fax 071 323 9504)

BUTLER, Dr Rohan D'Olier; CMG (1966); s of Sir Harold (Beresford) Butler , KCMG, CB (d 1951), of Little Court, Sonning, Berks, and Olive Augusta Newnham, *née* Waters; *b* 21 Jan 1917; *Educ* Eton, Balliol Coll Oxford (BA, MA, DLitt); *m* Lucy Rosemary, da of Eric Byron, Lord of The Manor of White Notley (d 1964), of White Notley Hall, nr Witham, Essex; *Career* WWII RAPC 1941-42, HG 1942-44; All Souls Coll Oxford: fell 1938-84, sub warden 1961-63, fell emeritus 1984-; staff Min of Info 1939-41 and 1942-44, special ops exec 1941, FO 1944-45; sr ed: Documents on Br Foreign Policy (1919-39) 1955-65 (ed 1945-55), Documents on Br Policy Overseas 1973-82; historical advsr: sec of state for Foreign Affrs 1963-68, for Foreign and Cwlth Affrs 1968-82; govr Felsted Sch 1959-77 (rep GBA 1964-77), tstee Felsted Almshouses 1961-77, memb Ct Univ of Essex 1971-; FRHistS 1966; Laureate of Instit de France 1982; *Books* The Roots of National Socialism 1783-1933 (1941), Choiseul (1980); *Recreations* idling; *Clubs* Beefsteak, The Lunch; *Style—* Dr Rohan Butler, CMG; White Notley Hall, nr Witham, Essex

BUTLER, (Stanley) Roy; s of Harry Butler (d 1950) of Epsom, and Emily, *née* Whiteing (d 1950); *b* 16 Feb 1923; *m* 14 July 1951, Jessie, da of Edward James Fletcher (d 1966), of Brixton; 1 s (Glenn b 1961), 1 da (Deborah b 1958); *Career* departmental administrator Hawker Aircraft 1940-42, RA ordnance corps 1942-47, serv ME 1943-46; ptnr Wallis & Wallis The Militaria Arms and Armour auctioneers 1962- dir Arms Fairs Ltd 1967-; fndr The Military Heritage Museum (Lewes) 1977; TV appearances: Going for a Song (1973), BBC Antiques Roadshow (arms and militaria expert, 1977-90), ITV Heirlooms (1987 and 1988), BBC Heirs and Graces (1988); conslt ed Miller's Annual Antiques Guide, pres St John Ambulance (Lewes div), benefactor and life memb Soc of Friends of RN Museum, life memb HMS Warrior Assoc, memb Rotary Club of Lewes; Freeman City of London 1981, memb Worshipful Co of Pipemakers 1979; *Recreations* swimming, snooker, gardening; *Clubs* IOD; *Style—* Roy Butler, Esq; Wallis & Wallis, West Street, Auction Galleries, Lewes, Sussex BN7 2NJ (☎ 0273 480208, fax 0273 476562, telex 896691 TLX

BUTLER, Col Sir Thomas Pierce; 12 Bt (I 1628), CVO (1970), DSO (1944), OBE (1954); s of Lt-Col Sir Richard Pierce Butler, 11 Bt, OBE (d 1955); *b* 18 Sept 1910; *Educ* Harrow, Trinity Coll Cambridge (BA); *m* 1937, Rosemary Liège Woodgate, da of late Maj James Hamilton Davidson-Houston (d 1961), of Pembury Hall, Kent and of Thurloe Sq, SW7; 1 s, 2 da (Caroline m Maj-Gen Richard Keightley, *qv*); *Heir* s, Richard Pierce Butler; *Career* Army 1933-61, cmd Gds Composite Bn Norway 1945-46, cmd 2 Bn Grenadier Gds BAOR 1949-52, AQMG London Dist 1952-55, Col, Lt-Col Cmdg Grenadier Gds 1955-59, mil advsr to High Cmmr for UK in New Zealand 1959-61, Maj and res govr of HM Tower of London 1961-70, Keeper of Jewel House Tower of London 1968-70, pres London (Prince of Wales's) Dist St John Ambulance Bde 1967-70; CStJ 1969; former JP Co London; *Recreations* fishing, gardening, travel, sketching; *Clubs* Cavalry and Guards; *Style—* Col Sir Thomas Butler, Bt, CVO, DSO, OBE; 6 Thurloe Sq, London SW7 2TA (☎ 071 584 1225); Ballin Temple, Ardattin, Co Carlow, Eire (☎ 0503 56662)

BUTLER, Vincent Frederick; *b* 27 Oct 1933; *Educ* St Bedes Coll Manchester, Edinburgh Coll of Art (DA), Acad of Fine Art Milan; *m* 21 Aug 1961, Camilla Luisa, da of Cavaliere Giuseppe Meazza (d 1971), of Milan; 2 s (Angus, Adam); *Career* language tutor Milan 1956-60, head Sculpture Dept Univ of N Nigeria 1960-63, lectr in sculpture and art history Edinburgh Coll of Art 1960-89; leading Scottish figurative sculptor; SSA 1966, RSA 1971, RGI 1989; *Recreations* hillwalking, travel; *Style—* Vincent Butler, Esq; 17 Deanpark Cres, Edinburgh EH4 1PH (☎ 031 332 5884)

BUTLER, Prof William Elliott; s of William Elliott Butler, of Black Mountain, N Carolina, US, and Maxine Swan Elmberg; *b* 20 Oct 1939; *Educ* The American Univ (BA), The Johns Hopkins Univ (MA), Harvard Law Sch (JD), The Johns Hopkins Univ (PhD), Univ of London (LLD); *m* 2 Sept 1961, Darlene Mae Johnson (d 1989); 2 s (William Elliott III, Bradley Newman); *Career* res asst Washington Centre of Foreign Policy Res John Hopkins Univ 1966-68, res assoc in law Harvard Law Sch and Assoc 1968-70, reader in comparative law Univ of London 1970-76; visiting scholar: Moscow State Univ 1972(1980), USSR Acad of Sci 1976 (1981, 1983, 1984, 1988), Mongolian State Univ 1979; memb cncl SSEES 1973-88 (vice chm 1983-88 and 1989-), prof of comparative law Univ of London 1976-, dean Faculty of Laws Univ Coll London 1977-79; visiting prof: NY Univ Law Sch 1978, Ritsumeikan Univ 1985, Harvard Law Sch 1986-87; coordinator UCL-USSR Acad of Sci Protocol on Co-operation in Socl Sci 1981-, dir Centre for Study of Socialist Legal systems Univ coll London 1982-, lectr Hague Acad of Int Law 1985, memb Ctee of Mgmnt Inst of Advanced Legal Studies Univ of London 1985-88, govr City of London Poly 1985-89, dean Faculty of Laws Univ of London 1988-90, author of more than 60 books, 450 articles, reviews, and translations on int and comparitive law, especially Soviet Law and other socialist legal systems, bookplates, and bibliography; sec The Bookplate Soc 1978-86 (foreign sec 1988-), fndr ed The Bookplate Jl 1983-86 (co-ed 1989-), VP Fed Int des Sociétés d'Amateurs d'Ex-Libris 1984-86 (exec sec 1988-); memb: Dist of Columbia Bar, Bar of US Ct of Appeals for Dist of Columbia, Bar of US Supreme Ct, hon memb: All Union Soc of the Book (USSR) 1989 Soviet Maritime Law Assoc (Ussr) 1990, USSR Union of Jurists 1990; memb Associé Int Acad of Comparative Law 1986; FRSA 1986, FSA 1989; *Recreations* book collecting, bookplate collecting; *Clubs* Cosmos; *Style—* Prof William Butler; 20 Ainger Rd, London NW3 3AS (☎ 071 586 2454); Faculty of Laws, Univ College London, Bentham House, Endsleigh Gdns, London WC1H OEG (☎ 071 380 7017, fax 071 387 9597, telex 28722 UCPHYS G)

BUTLER-ADAMS, Richard; s of Derek Butler-Adams, and Beatrice Margaret, *née* Baker; *Educ* Eton, Worchester Coll Oxford (MA); *m* 11 July 1968, Carol Ann Janet, da of Roland Dermott Scott Hebeler (d 1985); 3 da (Louise b 26 Nov 1970, Clare b 22 Aug 1973, Melissa b 15 Oct 1974); *Career* qualified CA 1969; ptnr Dixon Wilson 1973- (joined 1966); treas CPRE 1988-; Liveryman Vintners Co; FCA 1969, ATII; *Recreations* fishing, skiing, shooting, reading; *Clubs* Boodle's; *Style—* Richard Butler-Adams, Esq; Dixon Wilson, Chartered Accountants, PO Box 900, Rotherwick House, 3 Thomas More St, London E1 9YX (☎ 071 628 4321, fax 071 702 7969)

BUTLER-HENDERSON, Edward; 3 s of Hon Eric Brand Butler-Henderson (d 1953, 6 s of 1 Baron Faringdon, CH, JP), of Faccombe Manor, Andover, and Hon Sophia Isabelle Massey (2 da of 5 Baron Clarina, DL); *b* 9 June 1916; *Educ* Eton, Trinity Coll Cambridge; *m* 1939, Elizabeth Marjorie (d 1988), da of Henry George Dacres Dixon (d 1948), of Ireland; 1 s, 1 da; *Career* formerly Lt-Col 99 Bucks Yeo RA (TA); md Henderson Administration Ltd 1951-69, chm Naydale Services; *Recreations* shooting, escapism; *Clubs* City of London; *Style—* Edward Butler-Henderson, Esq; Flat 11, 3 West Halkin St, London SW1X 9JX (☎ 071 235 5888, 071 235 9308)

BUTLER-HENDERSON, Kenneth; yst s of late Capt Hon Eric Brand Butler-Henderson (6 s of 1 Baron Faringdon, CH, JP), and Hon Sophia Isabelle Massey (da of 5 Baron Clarina, DL); *b* 19 May 1929; *Educ* Eton; *m* 1952, Phyllis Daphne, da of late Lt-Col Alfred Edward Cartmel, CIE, MM, of Hertford; 2 s, 1 da; *Career* memb Stock Exchange, Societe Generale Turnbull Securities Ltd; *Recreations* shooting, golf; *Clubs* City of London, Farmer's, Frilford Heath Golf; *Style—* Kenneth Butler-Henderson, Esq; 11 Egerton Place, London SW3 2EF (☎ 071 589 2648); Societe Generale Turnbull Securities Ltd Stockbrokers, Exchange House, Broadgate, London EC2A 2DD (☎ 071 638 5699)

BUTLER-SLOSS, Rt Hon Lord Justice; Rt Hon Dame (Ann) Elizabeth Oldfield Butler-Sloss; DBE (1979), PC (1987); da of Sir Cecil Havers, QC (d 1977), and Enid, *née* Snelling (d 1956), and sister of Baron Havers, *qv*; *b* 10 Aug 1933; *Educ* Wycombe Abbey; *m* 1958, Joseph William Alexander Butler-Sloss, *qv*; *Career* called to the Bar Inner Temple 1955, registrar Principal Registry, Probate Div (subsequently Family Div) 1970-79, High Court Judge (Family Div) 1979-88, a Lord Justice of Appeal 1988-; Parly candidate (Cons) Lambeth Vauxhall 1959; sometime vice pres Medico-Legal Soc, memb Judicial Studies Bd 1985-89, chm Cleveland Child Abuse Inquiry 1987-88; hon fell St Hilda's Coll Oxford, Hon LLD Univ of Hull 1989; *Style—* The Rt Hon Lord Justice Butler-Sloss, DBE; Royal Courts of Justice, Strand, London WC2

BUTLER-SLOSS, Joseph William Alexander; s of Francis Alexander Sloss (d 1952); *b* 16 Nov 1926; *Educ* Bangor GS Co Down, Hertford Coll Oxford; *m* 1958, Dame (Ann) Elizabeth Oldfield, DBE, *qv*; 2 s, 1 da; *Career* Sub Lt RNVR; barr 1952, rec Crown Ct 1972-, Judge High Ct Kenya 1984-90; *Recreations* violin, hunting; *Clubs* Carlton, Muthaiga (Nairobi); *Style—* Joseph Butler-Sloss, Esq; Higher Marsh Farm, Marsh Green, Rockbeare, nr Exeter, Devon

BUTLIN, Martin Richard Fletcher; CBE (1990); s of Kenneth Rupert Butlin (d 1965), and Helen Mary, *née* Fletcher, MBE; *b* 7 June 1929; *Educ* Rendcomb Coll, Trinity Coll Cambridge (MA), Courtauld Inst of Art Univ of London (DLit); *m* 31 Jan 1969, Frances Caroline, da of Michael Anthony Chodzko, of France; *Career* Nat Serv RAMC; asst keeper Tate Gallery 1955-67, keeper Historic Br Collection Tate Gallery 1967-89; pubns incl: A Catalogue of the Works of William Blake in the Tate Gallery (1957, 2 edn 1971, 3 edn 1990), Samuel Palmer's Sketchbook of 1824 (1962), Turner Watercolours (1962), Turner (with Sir John Rothenstein 1964); with Mary Chamot and Dennis Farr: Tate Gallery Catalogues, The Modern British Paintings, Drawings and Sculpture (1964); The Later Works of JMW Turner (1965), William Blake (1966), The Blake-Varley Sketchbook of 1819 (1969); The Paintings of JMW Turner (co wrote with Evelyn Joll 1977), The Paintings and Drawings of William Blake (1981), Aspects of British Painting 1550-1800 from the collection of the Sarah Campbell Blaffer Foundation (1988); William Blake in the collection of the National Gallery of Victoria (with Tedd Gott, 1989), Turner at Petworth (with Mollie Luther and Ian Warrell, 1989), involved in selection and cataloguing of exhibitions on Blake and Turner, author of numerous articles and reviews for magazines; FBA 1984; *Recreations* opera, ballet, travel; *Style—* Martin Butlin, Esq, CBE; 74C Eccleston Sq, London SW1V 1PJ

BUTLIN, Robert Frank (Bobbie); s of Sir William (Billy) Butlin (d 1980, pioneer of holiday camps in the 1930s); *b* 30 April 1934; *Educ* Stowe; *Career* chm and md Butlin's Ltd 1968-; dir Rank Organisation, md Rank Hotels and Holiday Div; CStJ; *Style—* Bobbie Butlin, Esq; c/o Butlin's Ltd, 441 Oxford St, London W1A 1BH (☎ 071 629 6616)

BUTT, Geoffrey Frank; s of Frank Thomas Woodman Butt (d 1946), of Exeter, and Dorothy Rosamond, *née* Graseman (d 1968); *b* 5 May 1943; *Educ* Royal Masonic Sch Bushey, Univ of Reading (BA); *m* 8 July 1972, Lee Anne, da of Frederick Arthur Davey, of Exmouth; 2 s (David b 1973, Richard b 1976 twin), 1 da (Anne b 1976 twin); *Career* joined Office Slr for Customs and Excise 1971 (qualified slr, sr legal asst 1974, asst slr 1982, princ asst slr 1986); memb Law Soc 1970; *Recreations* family life, gardening, classical music, literature and art; *Style—* Geoffrey Butt, Esq; Office of the Solicitor for the Customs and Excise, New King's Beam House, 22 Upper Ground, London SE1 9PJ (☎ 071 382 5126)

BUTT, Henry Arthur; s of Capt Robert Arthur Butt (d 1963),of South Rd, Weston-super-Mare, and Annee Matilda, *née* Willis; gs of Robert Henry Coate Butt, Charter Mayor and first Freeman, Borough of Weston-super-Mare; *b* 8 March 1928; *Educ* Dulwich; *m* 5 Sept 1953, Barbara Mary, da of Arthur MacDonald Perks (d 1976), of Chipping Sodbury; 2 da (Patricia b 1960, Ann b 1964); *Career* CA; articled J & W Sully & Co 1948-51; nat dir local govt servs Price Waterhouse 1983-88 (ind 1952, ptnr 19 ind memb Econ Devpt Ctee for Shipbuilding and Repairing 1972-74; FCA, FIMC, MCIM, MBCS; *Recreations* travel, gardening, DIY; *Style—* Henry Butt, Esq; Court Barn, Upton Snodsbury, Worcester WR7 4NN (☎ 090 560 557)

BUTT, Sir (Alfred) Kenneth Dudley; 2 Bt (UK 1929), of Westminster, Co London; s of Sir Alfred Butt, 1 Bt (d 1962); *b* 7 July 1908; *Educ* Rugby, BNC Oxford; *m* 1, 1938 (m dis 1948), Kathleen Breen, da of E Farmer, of Shanklin, IOW; m 2, 1948, Marie Josephine, da of John Bain, of Wadhurst, and wid of Lt-Col Ivor Watkins Birts; *Career* bloodstock breeder and farmer; Lloyd's underwriter 1931-74, dir Brook Stud Co 1949 (md and chm 1962-81); chm Thoroughbred Breeders Assoc 1973; pres Aberdeen

Angus Cattle Soc 1967-68; *Recreations* shooting, paintings, racing; *Clubs* Carlton; *Style—* Sir Kenneth Butt, Bt; Wheat Hill, Sandon, Buntingford, Herts SG9 0RB (☎ 076 387 203); Flat 29, 1 Hyde Park Square, London W2 (☎ 071 262 3988)

BUTT, Michael Acton; s of late Gp-Capt Leslie Butt; *b* 25 May 1942; *Educ* Rugby, Magdalen Coll Oxford, INSEAD Fontainebleau France (MBA); *m* 1, 1965 (m dis 1986), Diana Lorraine, da of Sir Robin Brook, *qv*; m 2, 1986, Zoe Bennett; *Career* dir Bland Payne Hldgs 1970, chm Sedgwick Ltd 1983, dep chm Sedgwick Gp 1985, chm and chief exec Eagle Star Hldgs; memb of bd of BAT Industs 1987; *Recreations* opera, skiing; *Style—* Michael Butt, Esq; 4 Maida Ave, Little Venice, London W2 (☎ 071 723 9657); Eagle Star Insurance Co Ltd, 60 St Mary Ave, London EC3A 8JQ (☎ 071 929 1111, telex 914962)

BUTT, Richard Bevan; s of Roger William Bevan Butt, of Latimer, Winchester Close, Esher, Surrey, and Jean Mary, *née* Carter; *b* 27 Feb 1943; *Educ* Magdalen Coll Oxford (BA), Univ of Lancaster (MA); *m* 25 July 1976, Amanda Jane, da of late Hon Judge John Finlay; 2 s (Matthew b 1979, Nicholas b 1983); *Career* asst sec HM Treasy 1978-86 on secondment to Dip Serv as fin cnsllr, UK rep to Euro Community 1981-84, head of conservation English Heritage 1986-89, currently chief exec Rural Devpt Cmmn; *Recreations* ceramics, music, travel, books; *Style—* Richard Butt, Esq; 11 Cowley St, London SW1P 3NA

BUTT, Ronald Herbert; CBE (1987); s of Herbert Butt (d 1965), and Elizabeth Clare, *née* Morley (d 1948); *b* 17 Feb 1920; *Educ* St Dunstan's Coll, St Catherine's Coll Oxford (BA, MA); *m* 20 Oct 1956,(Daphne) Margaret Forfar, da of Theodore William Chaundy (d 1966), of Oxford; 2 s (Oliver b 1960, Edmund b 1963), 2 da (Bridget b 1959, Elizabeth b 1966); *Career* Army Intelligence Corps; The Financial Times 1951-67: ldr writer, political corr, political ed; res fell Nuffield Coll Oxford 1964-65, asst ed and political commentator Sunday Times 1967-83, assoc ed The Times 1983-85 (columnist on public affrs 1968-); memb: Butler Ctee on Mentally Abnormal Offenders 1972-75, cncl Westfield Coll Univ of London 1971-89; *Books* The Power of Parliament (1967), A History of Parliament: The Middle Ages (1989); *Recreations* music, reading, walking, history; *Clubs* Carlton; *Style—* Ronald Butt, Esq, CBE; The Times, 1 Pennington St, London E1 9XN (☎ 071 782 5038)

BUTTENSHAW, Brig Cedric George; CBE (1967, OBE 1953, MBE 1943), DSO (1945); s of late Brig Alfred Sidney Buttenshaw, DSO, Dorset, and late Constance Mary, *née* Garlick; *b* 17 June 1912; *Educ* Sherborne, RMA Woolwich; *m* 1939, Barbara Burnett, da of late Hubert de Burgh Wooldridge, of Chiswick; 3 da; *Career* served WWII, CO 142 Field Regt Royal Devon Yeomanry 1944-45, Brig 1961, dep fortress cdr Gibraltar 1959-62, provost marshal War Office 1962-65, cmmnd Salisbury Plain Sub-Dist 1965-67; *Recreations* following hounds, gardening; *Style—* Brig Cedric Buttenshaw, CBE, DSO; The Coach House, Worton, Devizes, Wilts

BUTTER, Maj David Henry; MC (1942); s of Col Charles Adrian James Butter, OBE, JP, DL (d 1944), of Cluniemore, Pitlochry, Perth, and Agnes Marguerite, *née* Clark, of New Jersey, USA (d 1972); *b* 18 March 1920; *Educ* Eton, Oxford; *m* 1946, Myra Alice, yr da of Maj-Gen Sir Harold Augustus Wernher, 3 Bt, GCVO, of Luton Hoo, Luton, Beds, and Lady Zia Wernher, da of HIH Grand Duke Michael of Russia and his morganatic wife Countess Torby; 1 s, 4 da; *Career* landowner, farmer, co dir; 2 Lt Scots Gds 1940, served WWII in N Africa, Italy and Sicily, Temp Maj 1946; Brigadier Queen's Body Guard for Scotland (Royal Co of Archers); DL Perthshire 1956, vice Lt 1960, HM Lt Perthshire 1971-75, Kinross 1974-75, Lord-Lt Perth and Kinross 1975-; pres Highland TAVR 1979-1984, co cncllr Perthshire 1955-74; *Clubs* R&A St Andrews, Turf Club; *Style—* Major David Butter, MC; Cluniemore, Pitlochry, Perthshire (☎ 0796 2006); 64 Rutland Gate, London SW7 (☎ 071 589 6731)

BUTTER, His Hon Judge (Neil McLaren); QC (1976); s of late Andrew Butter, MD, of London, and late Ena Butter; *b* 10 May 1933; *Educ* The Leys Sch, Queens Coll Cambridge; *m* 1974, Claire Marianne, da of A Miskin, of Ifield Court Farm, Ifield, Kent; *Career* barr 1955, asst and dep recorder Bournemouth 1971, Crown Court recorder 1972-, Circuit judge 1982-; tstee Kingdon-Ward Speech Therapy Tst 1980-; *Recreations* holidays, motoring; *Clubs* Oxford & Cambridge, Hampshire (Winchester); *Style—* His Honour Judge Butter, QC; Carpmael Building, Temple, EC4 (☎ 071 353 5537)

BUTTER, Prof Peter Herbert; s of Capt Archibald Edward Butter, CMG (d 1928), of Newton Hall, Gifford, E Lothian, and Helen Cicely, *née* Kerr (d 1976); *b* 7 April 1921; *Educ* Charterhouse, Balliol Coll Oxford (MA); *m* 30 Aug 1958, Bridget Hope, da of Lt-Col Henry Johnson Younger (d 1940), of Baro, Haddington, E Lothian; 1 s (Archibald b 1962), 2 da (Rachel b 1965, Helen b 1970); *Career* WWII, RA 1941-46 (Capt 1945); lectr in English Univ of Edinburgh 1948-58, prof of English Queen's Univ Belfast 1958-65, regius prof of English language and lit Univ of Glasgow 1965-86; various articles in periodicals; memb Int Assoc Univ Profs of English (sec and treas 1962-70); *Books* Shelley's Idols of the Cave (1954), Francis Thomson (1961), Edwin Muir (1962), Edwin Muir: Man and Poet (1966), Shelley's Alastor and other Poems (ed, 1971), Selected Letters of Edwin Muir (ed, 1974), Selected Poems of William Blake (ed, 1982), The Truth of Imagination: Uncollected Prose of Edwin Muir (ed, 1988); *Recreations* gardening, hill walking; *Clubs* New (Edinburgh); *Style—* Prof Peter Butter; Ashfield, Prieston Rd, Bridge of Weir, Renfrewshire PA11 3AW (☎ 0505 613139)

BUTTERFIELD, Baron (Life Peer UK 1988), of Stechford in the Co of W Midlands; Sir (William) John Hughes Butterfield; OBE (1953); s of late William Hughes Butterfield, of Hampton-in-Arden, Warwicks, and Mrs Doris North; *b* 28 March 1920; *Educ* Solihull Sch, Exeter Coll Oxford, Johns Hopkins Univ USA; *m* 1, 1946, Ann (d 1948), da of late Robert Sanders, of New York, USA; 1 s (Hon Jonathan West Sanders b 23 Oct 1948); m 2, 1950, Isabel-Ann, da of Dr Foster Kennedy (d 1952), neurologist, of New York City; 2 s (Hon Jeremy John Nicholas b 23 Dec 1954, Hon Toby Michael John b 6 Dec 1965), 1 da (Hon Sarah Harriet Ann (Hon Mrs Willetts) b 28 Aug 1953); *Career* Maj RAMC; Regius prof of Physics Cambridge 1975-87, master Downing Coll Cambridge 1978-87, vice chllr Univ of Cambridge 1983-85; chm: E Midlands Econ Devpt Cncl 1973-75, Medicines Cmmn 1976-81, Health Promotion Res Tst 1982-; kt 1978; *Recreations* real tennis, cricket; *Clubs* Athenaeum, Beefsteak, MCC, Oxford & Cambridge, Vincents; *Style—* The Rt Hon the Lord Butterfield, OBE; 39 Clarendon St, Cambridge CB1 1JX (☎ 0223 328854)

BUTTERFIELD, Keith Oldham; s of Edwin Butterfield (d 1966), and Edna Mary Oldham (d 1986); *b* 1 July 1931; *Educ* Merchant Taylors', Lincoln Coll Oxford (MA); *m* 1 Sept 1962, Susan Felicity, da of Alwyn Rigby Hughes (d 1981); 1 s (John Charles b 1969), 1 da (Ann Mary b 1966); *Career* admitted slr 1958; asst slr Bd of Inland Revenue 1981-; *Books* under pen name Charles Fox: The Law and You (1967), The Countryside and the Law (1971); *Recreations* reading, writing, travel; *Clubs* United Oxford and Cambridge Univs; *Style—* Keith Butterfield, Esq; 6 Priors Barton, Kingsgate Rd, Winchester SO23 9QF (☎ 0962 863297); Solicitors Office, Inland Revenue, Somerset House, Strand, London WC2R 1LB (☎ 071 438 7087)

BUTTERFIELD, Leslie Paul; s of Leslie John Butterfield (d 1983), and Ruth, *née* Andräs; *b* 31 Aug 1952; *Educ* N East London Poly (BA), Univ of Lancaster (MA); *m* 14 May 1988, Judy Mary Tombleson; *Career* advertising exec; account planner and assoc dir Boase Massimi Pollitt Ltd 1975-80, planning dir Abbott Mead Vickers/SMS Ltd 1980-87, chm and planning dir Butterfield Day Devito Hockney 1987-; chm Account Planning Gp 1987-89; IPA 1990- (chm Educn and Trg Ctee and memb Cncl); *awards* IPA Advertising Effectiveness Award 1984; FIPA (1988); *Books* How to Plan Advertising (1987); *Style—* Leslie Butterfield, Esq; Butterfield Day Devito Hockney, 47 Marylebone Lane, London W1M 5FN (☎ 071 224 3000, fax 071 935 9865)

BUTTERFIELD, (John) Michael; s of John Leslie Butterfield (d 1962), of Headingley Leeds, and Hilda Mary, *née* Judson (d 1971); *b* 2 July 1926; *Educ* Leeds Modern Sch, Univ of Leeds Textiles Dept; *m* 7 May 1955, Mary Maureen, da of John Martin (d 1976), of Helton, Penrith, Cumbria; 2 s (Peter John b 1 July 1956 d 1963, David Michael b 6 July 1958), 2 da (Helen Mary b 8 Feb 1964, Pamela Jean (twin) 8 Feb 1964); *Career* Army Serv RA and Army Educn (UK and India) 1944-47; woollen textile indust W Yorkshire 1949-61: mfrs agent John Butterfield & Son 1949-59, sales exec John Atkinson (Sowerby Bridge) Ltd 1959-61; youth offr Coventry Cathedral 1961-68, asst sec then ops dir Liverpool Cncl of Social Serv 1961-68, chief exec Nat Assoc of Youth Clubs 1975-86, self-employed 1986-; advsr Merseyside Baring Fndn, UK rep American Youthwork Center, vice chm Nat Cncl for Voluntary Youth Servs 1977-83, chm Youthaid 1985-90, chm Leicestershire Cncl for Voluntary Youth Servs 1985-, memb Cncl and vice chm UK Advsy Ctee Save The Children Fund, chm Youth Clubs Leicestershire 1990-; *Recreations* music especially opera, hillwalking; *Clubs* Cwlth Tst; *Style—* Michael Butterfield, Esq; 4 Church Farm Court, Aston Flamville, nr Hinckley, Leics LE10 3AF (☎ 0455 611027)

BUTTERFIELD, Hon Sarah Harriet Anne (Hon Mrs Willetts); da of Baron Butterfield, OBE, *qv*, of 39 Clarendon St, Cambridge, and Isabel Ann Foster, *née* Kennedy; *b* 28 Aug 1953; *Educ* Sherborne Sch for Girls, Univ of Edinburgh (BA), Ruskin Sch of Fine Art and Drawing Oxford Univ, Univ of Bristol (Dip Arch); *m* 19 April 1986, David Lindsay Willetts, s of John Roland Willetts, of West Midlands; 1 da (Imogen Anna b 12 June 1988); *Career* architect 1978-86: California, Bristol, London; illustrator for Experimental Psychology Dept Cambridge Univ 1976-78, art critic Oxford Mail 1978; artist; exhibitions incl: RCA 1978, Mall Galleries 1980, 1984 and 1986, Royal Soc of Br Artists 1988, Young Comtemporaries Agnews 1988, Richmond Gallery, Cork Street, London 1990; Egerton Coghill Landscape Award 1976, Winsor & Newton Award 1978, finalist Hunting Gp Art Competition 1987, commended Spector Three Cities Competition 1988; painting purchased by Wimbledon Lawn Tennis Museum (All England Club) 1989; ARCUK; *Books* Word Order Comprehension Test (with Dr Gillian Fenn); *Clubs* Queen's; *Style—* The Hon Sarah Butterfield

BUTTERFILL, John Valentine; MP (C) Bournemouth W 1983-; s of George Thomas Butterfill (d 1980), and Elsie Amelia, *née* Watts (d 1974); *b* 14 Feb 1941; *Educ* Caterham Sch, Coll of Estate Mgmnt London; *m* 1965, Pamela Ross, da of Frederick Ross-Symons; 1 s (James b 1975), 3 da (Natasha b 1969, Samara b 1974, Jemima b 1976); *Career* chartered surveyor; valuer Jones Lang Wooton 1962-64, sr exec Hammerson Gp 1964-69, dir Audley Properties Ltd (Bovis Gp) 1969-71, md St Paul's Securities Gp 1971-76, sr ptnr Churchod & Co Chartered Surveyors 1977-; contested (C) London S Inner in Euro Parl 1979, vice chm Guildford Cons Assoc 1980-82, contested Croydon NW by-election 1981, dep chm Euro Democrat Forum 1981-, vice chm Foreign Affairs Forum 1983-, chm Cons Gp for Europe; sec: Backbench Tourism Ctee 1983-85 (vice chm 1985-88), Backbench Trade and Indust Ctee 1987-88; PPS Sec of State for Tport 1988-89 and 1989-90; FRICS 1974; *Recreations* skiing, tennis, riding, bridge, music; *Clubs* Carlton; *Style—* John Butterfill, Esq, MP; House of Commons, London SW1; Churchod & Co, Chartered Surveyors, Portmore House, 54 Church Street, Weybridge, Surrey KT13 8DP (☎ 0932 854370)

BUTTERICK, Peter Stephen; s of Stephen Butterick (d 1987), of Epsom, and Josephine Kathleen, *née* Ansell (d 1958); *b* 1 Dec 1933; *Educ* Ealing GS; *m* 1958, Audrey, da of Raymond St Quintin Bates (d 1986), of Watford; 2 s (Ian, Howard); *Career* dir and sec Macmillan Bloedel Containers Ltd 1975-1983, dir UK Corrugated Ltd 1983-89, accounting and pro retirement conslt 1989-; FCA; *Recreations* church, gardening, motoring, DIY; *Style—* Peter Butterick, Esq; Openfields, Love Lane, King's Langley, Herts WD4 9HW (☎ 0923 264085)

BUTTERS, Francis Arthur; s of Arthur Butters (d 1968), of Westcliff-on-Sea, Essex, and Elsie Beatrice Annie, *née* Wood (d 1975); *b* 4 March 1920; *Educ* Lindisfarne Coll; *m* 20 July 1946, Heather Margaret, JP, da of Gilbert Harris (d 1969), of Stone, Staffs; 1 s (Richard b 8 Jan 1948), 3 da (Margaret (Mrs Grieve) b 20 Dec 1949, Rosalind (Mrs Southworth) b 9 Aug 1952, Veronica (Mrs Kempton) b 14 Sept 1957); *Career* mobilised RNV (W) (R) telegraphist, served minesweeping trawlers, cmmnd 1940, served armed merchant cruisers coastal forces ops dir Admty 1941, ADC and private sec (Lt RNVR) to Lord Swinton res min W Africa 1942, Miny of Civil Aviation 1944-45 (memb UK Delegation Int Civil Aviation Confs Chicago 1944, Cape Town 1945), i/c PR private offr Civil Aviation Miny 1945, info work HQ Miny Civil Aviation 1945, 1 PR Offr Heathrow Airport 1949; joined firm PR Conslts 1950, fndr own PR cos 1957; Berks CC 1956-89 (former ldr Cncl and vice chm Cncl, former chm Gen Purpose Ctee); chm Educn and Social Servs Thames Valley Police Authy; memb: Ct and Cncl Univ of Reading 1973-89, Industl Tbnls 1976-88, ACC 1962-77 and 1984-89 (former chm Police Ctee); chm PDSA 1987-(memb Cncl Mgmnt 1976-) former chm Police Cncl UK, served various Home Office Working Parties (incl Miny Tport); dir Thames Valley Broadcasting, various int radio appearances; FIPR 1969 (MIPR 1949, chm Educn Ctee), memb Soc Tech Analysts 1988; *Books* The Government Explains (with study gp Royal Inst Pub Admin, 1965); various pubns incl articles and photographs (Encyclopaedia Britannica, world exclusive pictures of Prince of Wales Crown); *Recreations* still and video photography, music, information technol, travel; *Clubs* Carlton; *Style—* Francis Butters, Esq; Cornerstone, Fifield, Maidenhead, Berks SL6 2PF (☎ 0628 27112)

BUTTERS, Guy; s of James David Butters, and Pauline Ann, *née* Cook; *b* 30 Oct 1969; *Educ* Mellow Lane Comp Sch Hayes; partner, Angela Fowkes; 1 da (Frankii Holly Mia Skye b 11 March 1990); *Career* professional footballer; Tottenham Hotspur 1988-90: scored own goal on cup debut v Blackburn, scored goal on league debut v Wimbledon, 40 appearances; transferred to Portsmouth 1990-; 3 England under 21 caps 1989; former Barclays Young Eagle of the Month for London; *Style—* Guy Butters, Esq; Portsmouth FC, Fratton Park, Frogmore Rd, Portsmouth PO4 8RA (☎ 0705 731204)

BUTTERWICK, Antony James; s of (James) Cyril Butterwick (d 1966), and Hon (Agnes) Désirée Butterwick, OBE (d 1986), da of 1 Baron Dickinson, KBE; *b* 27 Sept 1930; *Educ* Eton, Trinity Coll Oxford (BA); *m* 8 Oct 1958, Joanna Vivien, yr da of Col Hugh A G Vanderfelt (d 1982); 2 s (James Hugo b 1962, (Antony) Guy b 1966), 1 da (Henrietta b 1960); *Career* Nat Serv cmmn Rifle Bde; with Grieveson Grant & Co stockbrokers 1953-58, chief passenger mangr Union Castle Line 1958-65, jt md P & O Containers Ltd (formerly Overseas Containers Ltd) 1965-; govr: Gresham's Sch Holt, North Foreland Lodge Sch; chm local ctee Nat Tst; Warden Fishmongers' Co; *Recreations* golf, shooting; *Style—* Antony Butterwick, Esq; Pinkneys House, Pinkneys Green, Berks SL6 6QD (☎ 0628 21726); P & O Containers Ltd, Beagle House, Braham St, London E1 8EP (☎ 071 488 1313, fax 071 481 3459, telex 883947)

BUTTERWICK, John Newton; TD (1961); s of (James) Cyril Butterwick (d 1966), of Old Park, Beaconsfield, and Hon (Agnes) Desirée Butterwick, OBE (d 1986), da of 1 Baron Dickinson, KBE; *b* 3 March 1923; *Educ* Eton, Trinity Coll Oxford; *m* 1956,

Marcia, o da of John Scott, of Pittsburgh, USA (d 1969); 3 s (Nicholas Scott b 1959, Christopher Hugh b 1963, William Toby b 1965), 1 da (Sarah b 1958); *Career* Capt WWII NW Europe 1942-46, TA 1949-62, ret with rank Bt-Col; vice chm Lazard Bros & Co 1981-83 (dir 1972-80); dir: Glyn Mills & Co (later Williams & Glyn's Bank) 1961-72, London Merchant Securities plc 1963-, Duncan Lawrie Ltd 1987-; *Recreations* golf, gardening; *Clubs* Boodle's, Royal West Norfolk Golf; *Style*— John Butterwick, Esq, TD; Danyells, Sandon, Buntingford, Herts (☎ 0763 87 312); The Gables, Brancaster, King's Lynn, Norfolk (☎ 0485 210242)

BUTTERWORTH, Arthur Eckersley; s of Harold Butterworth (d 1945), and Maria, *née* Nelson (d 1935); *b* 4 Aug 1923; *Educ* N Manchester GS, Royal Manchester Coll of Music; *m* 12 July 1952, Diana, da of Charles Stewart, OBE (d 1967); 2 da (Nicola Diana b 1960, Carolin Ann b 1962); *Career* RE attached 51 Highland Div 1942-47; composer: Symphony No 1 op 15 Cheltenham Festival 1957 and BBC Proms 1958, Symphony No 2 op 25 Bradford 1965, Organ Concerto 1973, Violin Concerto 1978, Symphony No 3 op 52 Manchester 1979, Piano Trio Cheltenham Festival Cmmn 1983, Symphony No 4 op 72 Manchester 1986, Odin Symphony for Brass Op 76 (National Brass Band Festival) London 1989; conductor Huddersfield Philharmonic Soc 1964-, various guest conductor appearances 1965-; *Recreations* country-living, animal welfare; *Style*— Arthur Butterworth, Esq; Pohjola, Dales Ave, Embsay, Skipton, N Yorks BD23 6PE 0756 792968

BUTTERWORTH, Bevil; s of Percy Howard Butterworth (d 1973), of Maidstone, Kent, and Lilian Beatrice, *née* Thompson (d 1982); *b* 11 Aug 1931; *Educ* Maidstone and Wallasey GS, Central London Sch of Architecture, Canterbury Coll of Art; *m* 1, 8 July 1959 (m dis 1963), Anne, da of John Berkeley (d 1961), of Durham; 1 s (Christopher b 1960), 1 da (Jane b 1962); m 2, 7 Oct 1972, Dorothey Joyce, da of John Mathieson-Rae (d 1980), of Ecclefechan; 1 s (Alan b 1981), 1 da (Natalie b 1979); *Career* team leader Chapman Taylor & Ptnrs 1964-66, assoc ptnr Meers Pring Wager & Ptnrs 1966-69, fndr TA Bevil Butterworth Assoc Chartered Architects 1969-, elected name at Lloyds 1981; ARIBA 1969, FRSH 1968, MCIOB 1979, FFB 1984, FBIM 1984; *Recreations* golf, marathons, antiquarian horology, 18 century glassware; *Clubs* Neville & La Manga Golf; *Style*— Bevil Butterworth, Esq; Hunters Farm, Nutley, E Sussex TN22 3LS (☎ 082 571 2161); 265 Los Miradores, La Manga Club, Los Belones, Cartagena, Spain; 12 Wellington Square, Hastings, Sussex TN34 1PB (☎ 0424 425904, fax 0424 720633, car 0836 516955)

BUTTERWORTH, Christopher Roger; s of Harold Earnshaw Butterworth (d 1988), of Cowes, IOW, and Matilda Earnshaw Butterworth (d 1983); *b* 19 Nov 1935; *Educ* Heywood GS, Sch of Architecture Portsmouth; *m* 19 Sept 1959, Margaret Day, da of James Ridgway (d 1987), of Newport, IOW; 3 s (Miles Christopher b 20 Sept 1963, Timothy James b 20 June 1965, Nicholas Mark b 17 Dec 1967); *Career* princ Christopher Butterworth Assocs (CAs); govr Burwood Park Sch; corp memb: RIBA 1966, Br Acad of Experts 1989; *Recreations* field sports; *Clubs* MCC, Flyfishers; *Style*— Christopher Butterworth, Esq; 3 The Quadrant, 80 Church Street, Weybridge, Surrey KT13 8DL (☎ 0932 852292)

BUTTERWORTH, Henry; s of Henry Butterworth (d 1955), and Wilhelmena Butterworth (d 1931); *b* 21 Jan 1926; *Educ* St Mary's Leyland Lancs, Preston Tech Coll, Univ of Birmingham; *m* 28 Oct 1948, Ann, da of late Patrick Joseph Smith; 2 s (Peter b 1951, James b 1956); *Career* engr; md Royal Ordnance Factories MOD 1984-86 (dir gen 1979-84), md Royal Ordnance plc 1986-88, ret; CEng, MIMechE; *Recreations* fishing, dancing, boating; *Style*— Henry Butterworth, Esq; 5 Vicarsfield Rd, Worden Park, Leyland, Lancs (☎ 0772 436073)

BUTTERWORTH, Prof Ian; CBE (1984); s of Harry Butterworth, and Beatrice, *née* Worsley; *b* 3 Dec 1930; *Educ* Bolton Co GS, Univ of Manchester (BSc, PhD); *m* 9 May 1964, Mary Therese Butterworth; 1 da (Jody); *Career* scientific offr and sr scientific offr UKAEA AERE Harwell 1954-58, visiting physicist Lawrence Berkeley Laboratory Univ of California 1964-65, gp leader Bubble Chamber Res Gp Rutherford Laboratory as sr princ scientific offr 1968-71, visiting prof Univ of California Riverside 1970, prof of physics Univ of London 1971, head of physics Imperial Coll 1980 (lectr 1958-64, sr lectr 1965-68, head of High Energy Nuclear Physics Gp 1971), res dir Euro Organisation for Nuclear Res 1983-86, princ QMC Univ of London 1986-89, princ QMW Univ of London 1989-; author of numerous papers in learned jls; hon fell Imperial Coll 1988; FRS; *Recreations* reading, art history; *Clubs* Athenaeum; *Style*— Prof Ian Butterworth, CBE, FRS; Queen Mary and Westfield College, University of London, Mile End Rd, London E1 4NS (☎ 071 975 5555, telex 893750, fax 071 975 5500)

BUTTERWORTH, Ian Stuart; s of John Derek Butterworth, of Crewe, Cheshire, and Doreen, *née* Bickerton; *b* 25 Jan 1964; *Educ* Ruskin County High School Crewe; *m* 30 May 1986, Kathryn Ann, da of Alfred George Garrathy; 1 s (Harrison George b 13 June 1990), 1 da (Olivia Marie b 17 Nov 1987); *Career* professional footballer; Coventry City 1981-85 (91 appearances), Nottingham Forest 1985-86 (27 appearances); Norwich City 1986-: on loan from Nottingham Forest Oct 1986-Nov 1986, signed Dec 1986, capt 1989-, over 180 appearances; 9 England under 21 caps 1984-86; *Recreations* most other sports, music; *Style*— Ian Butterworth, Esq; Norwich City FC, Carrow Rd, Norwich, Norfolk NR1 1JE (☎ 0603 612131)

BUTTERWORTH, Baron (Life Peer UK 1985), of Warwick, Co Warwick; John Blackstock Butterworth; CBE (1982), JP (City of Oxford 1962, Coventry 1963-), DL (Warwicks 1967-74, W Midlands 1974-); only s of John William Butterworth, by his wife, Florence, da of John Blackstock, of Dumfries; *b* 13 March 1918; *Educ* Queen Elizabeth's GS Mansfield, Queen's Coll Oxford; *m* 1948, Doris Crawford, da of George Elder, of Edinburgh; 1 s (Hon John William Blackstock b 1952), 2 da (Hon Anna Elizabeth Blackstock (Hon Mrs Walker) b 1951, Hon Laura Blackstock (Hon Mrs Burley) b 1959); *Career* Maj RA 1939-46; called to the Bar Lincoln's Inn 1947, hon bencher 1988; fell New Coll Oxford 1946-63, bursar 1956-63, managing tstee Nuffield Fndn 1964-85 (tstee 1985-); vice chllr Univ of Warwick 1963-85; govr Royal Shakespeare Theatre 1964-, memb Bd of Br Cncl 1981-86; chm Melapraxis Ltd 1990- (dir 1986-); memb: Jarratt Ctee on Univ Efficiency 1986, Croham Ctee on Review of UGC 1987, Fulbright Cmmn 1988; chm Fndn for Sci and Technol 1990-; univ cmmr (under Educn Reform Act 1988) 1988-; Hon DCL Sierra Leone 1976, Hon DSc Univ of Aston 1985, Hon LLD Univ of Warwick 1986; *Clubs* Athenaeum; *Style*— The Rt Hon Baron Butterworth, CBE, JP, DL; The Barn, Barton, Guiting Power, Glos GL54 5US

BUTTERWORTH, Sir (George) Neville; DL (Gtr Manchester 1974); s of (George) Richard Butterworth, and Hannah, *née* Wright; *b* 27 Dec 1911; *Educ* Malvern, St John's Coll Cambridge (MA); *m* 1947, Barbara Mary, da of Frank William Briggs; 2 s; *Career* former chm: NW Cncl CBI, Tootal Ltd (previously chm English Sewing Cotton Co Ltd, merged with The Calico Printers' Assoc); former memb Royal Cmmn on the Distribution of Income Wealth; High Sheriff Gtr Manchester 1974; kt 1973; *Style*— Sir Neville Butterworth, DL; Oak Farm, Ollerton, Knutsford, Cheshire (☎ 0565 3150)

BUTTERWORTH, Peter John; s of John Bielby Butterworth (d 1981), of Bridgwater, Somerset, and Olive Gwendoline, *née* Stevens (d 1978); *b* 12 Nov 1927; *Educ* Monkton Combe Sch Bath; *m* 25 Aug 1956, Carolyn Mary, da of Antony Squibbs (d 1971), of Bridgwater; 2 s (Philip b 30 May 1957, Michael John b 12 Aug 1960), 1 da (Gillian Mary Jane b 28 Aug 1963); *Career* KRRC 1945, REME 1946-48 (WOII 1948); sr ptnr Butterworth Jones & Co Bridgwater 1983- (ptnr 1953-83); treas: Bridgwater Cancer Res Campaign 1954-84, County Club Bridgwater 1955-75 (chm 1977-80); sec Bridgwater C of C 1956-; ACA 1951, FCA 1956, ACCA 1968, FCCA 1973; *Recreations* golf, philately, local history res; *Clubs* County Club (Bridgwater), Ivel (Yeovil), Rotary (Sedgemoor); *Style*— Peter Butterworth, Esq; 20 King Square, Bridgwater, Somerset (☎ 0278 423948); 7 Castle St, Bridgwater, Somerset (☎ 0278 428251, fax 0278 428 358)

BUTTFIELD, Dame Nancy Eileen; *née* Wheewall Holden; DBE (1972); da of Sir Edward Wheewall Holden (d 1947), and Hilda May Lavis; *b* 12 Nov 1912; *Educ* Woodlands C of E Girls' GS Adelaide, Adelaide Univ, Cauposenea Paris; *m* 1936, Frank Charles Buttfield; 2 s; *Career* senator for S Australia 1955-65 and 1968-74; emeritus dir Co-op Gp of Companies; *Books* So Great a Change (Story of Holden Family); *Recreations* embroidery, wood carving and polishing; *Clubs* Queen Adelaide; *Style*— Dame Nancy Buttfield, DBE; 52 Strangways Terrace, N Adelaide, S Australia 5006

BUTTON, Air Vice-Marshal Arthur Daniel; CB (1976), OBE (1959); s of Leonard Victor Daniel Button (d 1966), of Eastbourne, and Agnes Ann, *née* Derbyshire (d 1981); *b* 26 May 1916; *Educ* Co HS for Boys Ilford Essex, Univ of Southampton (BSc London); *m* 1944, Eira Guelph, da of Reginald Waterhouse Jones (d 1955); 1 s (John Daniel b and d 1945); *Career* RAF offr in GD 1941-46 (Educn 1938-41 and 1946-76); dir: RAF Educn Branch 1972-76, ARELS Examinations Tst 1976-86; pres Assoc of Recognised Eng Lang Schs - Fedn of Eng Lang Course Organisers; active in RAF and other Serv charities; *Recreations* music; *Clubs* RAF; *Style*— Air Vice-Marshal Arthur D Button, CB, OBE; 7 Parsonage Ct, Tring, Herts HP23 5BG (☎ 044 282 6017)

BUTTON, Roger Martin; s of Frederick Charles Button, of High Dell, Harrow-on-the-Hill, Middx (d 1970), and Una Florence, *née* Martin; *b* 7 Feb 1931; *Educ* Winchester Coll, Pembroke Coll Cambridge (MA Arch); *m* 2 April 1955, Shirley Gwynfryd, da of Dr Rodney Howell Holt, of Eastbourne, Sussex (d 1970); 2 s (Rupert b 1959, Benjamin b 1962, d 1978), 1 da (Myfanwy b 1969); *Career* Lt RE 1949-51; ptnr: Adie Button & Ptnrs 1963-, Waterhouse Ripley 1968-; asst architect to Sir Basil Spence for Coventry Cathedral Reconstruction 1955-62; *Recreations* sailing, swimming, gardening; *Clubs* Royal Ocean Racing, Royal Engineer Yacht, Artworkers Guild; *Style*— Roger M Button, Esq; The Old Stores, Ashampstead, Reading, Berkshire RG8 8RT (☎ 0635 578 559); 50 Charlotte St, London W1P 1LW (☎ 071 637 0881)

BUTTRESS, Donald Reeve; s of Edward Crossley Buttress, of Manchester, and Evelyn Edna, *née* Reeve-Whaley; *b* 27 April 1932; *Educ* Stockport Sch, Univ of Manchester (MA); *m* 15 Dec 1956, Elsa Mary, da of Herbert Bardsley, of Bramhall (d 1964); 2 s (Richard b 1960, John b 1966), 3 da (Helen b 1958, Fiona b 1962, Lucy b 1973); *Career* Flying Offr RAF 1958-61; architect and ecclesiastical surveyor; architect: Sheffield and Bangor Cathedrals 1978-88, Llandaff Cathedral 1986; surveyor Chichester Cathedral 1985, surveyor of the fabric Westminster Abbey 1988; FSA, FRIBA; *Recreations* walking, countryside conservation, books; *Clubs* RAF; *Style*— Donald Buttress, Esq; 2B Little Cloister, Westminster Abbey, London SW1P 3PL; 176 Oxford Rd, Manchester M13 9QQ (☎ 061 273 5405)

BUXTON, Andrew Edward; s of Desmond Gurney Buxton (d 1987), of Hoveton Hall, Norfolk, and gggs of Sir Edward Buxton, 2 Bt, MP; *b* 3 March 1935; *Educ* Eton, Magdalene Coll Cambridge; *m* 1967, Barbara, da of Capt Cyril Gascoigne Lloyd; 1 s, 2 da; *Career* dir RTZ Corpn plc; *Recreations* shooting, tennis, cricket; *Clubs* Boodle's; *Style*— Andrew Buxton, Esq; 36 Burnsall St, London SW3 3SP; Hoveton Hall, Norwich, Norfolk NR12 8RJ

BUXTON, Andrew Robert Fowell; s of Capt Joseph Gurney Fowell Buxton, Grenadier Gds (ka 1943, gggs of Sir Thomas Buxton, 1 Bt), and Elizabeth (da of late Maj Robert Barbour, of Bolesworth Castle, Tattenhall, Chester) who m subsequently Alexander Grant (half-bro of Lt-Col Ian Grant - *see below*); *b* 5 April 1939; *Educ* Winchester, Pembroke Coll Oxford; *m* 1965, Jane Margery, da of Lt-Col Ian (John Peter) Grant, MBE, of Rothiemurchus, and Lady Katherine Grant, *qv*; 2 da; *Career* 2 Lt Grenadier Gds; vice chm Barclays Bank; *Style*— Andrew Buxton, Esq; Bentley Park, Ipswich, Suffolk

BUXTON, Gervase Michael; s of Lt Cdr Michael Buxton, RNVR (d 1990), sometime High Sheriff Rutland (himself s of Henry Fowell Buxton, 7 ggs of Sir Thomas Buxton, 1 Bt), by his 1 w, Katharine, da of Rt Hon James Round, JP, DL; *b* 2 Jan 1939; *Educ* Harrow, Trinity Coll Cambridge; *m* 1965, Susan Margaret, er da of Kenneth Malcolm McKenzie, of Kensington; 2 s (Matthew b 1967, Jocelyn b 1972), 2 da (Lucy b 1966, Cara b 1969); *Career* 2 Lt Royal Scots Greys; exec dir Barclays Merchant Bank, on secondment int finance dir Barclays Bank Int 1982-; *Style*— Gervase Buxton, Esq; Swangles Farm, Cold Christmas, Ware, Herts

BUXTON, James Anthony Fowell; s of Robert James Buxton (d 1968), of Galhampton Manor, Yeovil, Somerset, and Lilla Mary Alyson, *née* Pumphrey (d 1979); *Educ* Harrow, Trinity Coll Cambridge (MA); *m* 4 Nov 1975, Margaret Elizabeth, da of Adm The Hon Sir Guy Russell, GBE, KCB, DSO; 2 s (Edward b 1978, Charles b 1986), 2 da (Harriet b 1976, Meriel b 1980); *Career* called to the Bar 1971, Chambers of Joseph Jackson QC 1972-78, Chambers of David Calcutt QC 1978-82; admitted slr 1984, ptnr Burges Salmon Bristol 1984-; memb Law Soc; *Books* contrib: Law of Agricultural Holdings (1989), Halsburys Laws of England; *Recreations* shooting, fishing, tennis, walking; *Clubs* Brooks's, St James's; *Style*— James Buxton, Esq; Galhampton Manor, Yeovil, Somerset BA22 7AL (☎ 0963 40297); Narrow Quay House, Prince St, Bristol BS1 4AH (☎ 0272 276567, telex 44736, fax 0272 294705, car 0836 605694)

BUXTON, James Desmond; s of Desmond Gurney Buxton (d 1987), and Rachel Mary, *née* Morse; *b* 20 Aug 1947; *Educ* Eton, Magdalene Coll Cambridge (MA); *m* 1975, Annabella, yr da of Douglas Collins; 2 c (Jasper Francis b 10 April 1979, Oliver Desmond b 10 Sept 1980); *Career* Evening Echo Hemel Hempstead 1969-72; Financial Times: joined 1972, foreign staff ME and N Africa 1973-80, Rome corr 1980-86, Scottish corr 1986-; winner Ischia prize Italy 1986; *Recreations* sailing, reading, travel; *Clubs* Norfolk; *Style*— James Buxton, Esq; Redcroft, 23 Murrayfield Road, Edinburgh EH12 6EP; Financial Times, 37 George St, Edinburgh EH2 2HN (☎ 031 220 1420, fax 031 220 1578)

BUXTON, Hon (Aubrey) James Francis; yr s of Baron Buxton of Alsa; *b* 20 March 1956; *Educ* Ampleforth, Royal Agricultural Coll Cirencester; *m* 1981, Melinda, da of Peter Henry Samuelson, of Ugley Hall, Essex; 1 s (Henry b 19 May 1988), 2 da (Emma Lucy Maria b 1984, Olivia Louise b 1986); *Career* ptnr Bidwells Chartered Surveyors Cambridge; *Recreations* shooting, painting, music; *Clubs* White's; *Style*— The Hon James Buxton; Church Farm, Carlton, Newmarket, Suffolk (☎ 0223 290 511)

BUXTON, James Geoffrey Pease; s of Maj Peter Stapleton Buxton (ka 1944), and Julia Victoria, *née* Pease; *b* 24 Oct 1939; *Educ* Eton, Trinity Coll Cambridge (MA); *m* 20 June 1970, Meriel Jessica, da of Maj Denis Joseph Cowen, OBE (d 1986), of E Farndon Manor, Market Harborough, Leics; 1 s (Hugh b 1975), 1 da (Rose b 1973); *Career* local dir Barclays Bank: Peterborough 1970-79, Norwich 1979-87; fin admin Shuttleworth Agric Coll 1988-89, sr exec Br Horse Soc 1989-; AIB 1967; *Recreations* hunting, stalking, beekeeping; *Style*— James Buxton, Esq; Manor Farm House, Lubenham, Market Harborough, Leicestershire LE16 9TD (☎ 0858 431758); The British Horse Society, Stoneleigh, Kenilworth, Warwickshire CV8 2LR (☎ 0203

696697, fax 0203 696685)

BUXTON, Hon Jane Elizabeth Noel; da of 1 Baron Noel-Buxton, PC (d 1948); *b* 22 May 1925; *Career* relinquished surname of Noel by public declaration, 1957; *Style—* The Hon Jane Buxton; 27 Redington Rd, Hampstead, NW3

BUXTON, Joanna Margaret Reader; da of Capt Godfrey Buxton, MBE, MC (d 1986), of Woodend, Crawley Ridge, Camberley, Surrey, and Dorothea, *née* Reader Harris (d 1967); *b* 17 July 1927; *Educ* Sherborne Sch for Girls, Univ of Edinburgh (Social Studies Dip), LSE; *Career* psychiatric social worker 1950-62 (work with child adoption, delinquency and 6 years in Westminster Hosp), market res conslt 1962-; memb: N Westminster Victim Support Scheme, Westminster Volunteer Bureau, Prison Fellowship, Market Res Soc; FRSA; *Recreations* travel: China, USA, Malaysia, India, Nigeria, Middle East, Europe, Australia; *Style—* Miss Joanna Buxton; 21A Porchester Terrace, Bayswater, London W2 3TS (☎ 071 262 1060)

BUXTON, Jocelyn Charles Roden; VRD; s of late Capt Roden Buxton, CBE, RN, 2 s of 4 Bt, by 1 w, Dorothy, da of late Col Charles St John, RE; hp of kinsman, Sir Thomas Buxton, 6 Bt; *b* 8 Aug 1924; *m* 1960, Ann Frances, da of Frank Smitherman, MBE; 3 da; *Career* WWII Lt Cdr RNVR (despatches); *Style—* Jocelyn Buxton, Esq, VRD; Rodwell House, Loddon, Norwich

BUXTON, John Joseph; s of Anthony Buxton (d 1970), of Horsley Hall, Norfolk, and Mary Philomena Constable, *née* Maxwell (d 1953); *b* 9 Dec 1927; *Educ* Ampleforth, Univ of Cambridge (BA); *m* 11 Sept 1958, Bridget, da of late Charles de Bunsen, of Reepham, Norfolk; 1 s (Robin Anthony b 1963), 3 da (Jane Mary b 1959, Clare Margaret b 1960, Caroline Mary b 1965); *Career* RMA Sandhurst 1946, Lt Royal Norfolk Regt 1946-48; landowner, film maker, wildlife cameraman; cncl memb Norfolk Naturalist Tst 1965-; *Recreations* wildlife, photography, fishing, shooting; *Style—* John Buxton, Esq

BUXTON, Prof John Noel; s of John William Buxton (d 1971), and Laura Frances, *née* Whitehead; *b* 25 Dec 1933; *Educ* Bradford GS, Trinity Coll Cambridge (MA); *m* 8 Feb 1958, Moira Jean, da of William E C O'Brien (d 1972); 2 s (Nigel b 1961, Patrick b 1965), 2 da (Jocelyn b 1959, Delia b 1963); *Career* flight trials engr de Havilland Propellers 1955-59, ops res scientist Br Iron & Steel Res Assoc 1959-60, applied sci rep IBM UK 1960-62, lectr Inst of Computer Sci Univ of London 1962-66, chief software conslt SCICON (formerly CEIR) 1966-68, prof of computer sci Univ of Warwick 1968-84, prof of info technol King's Coll London 1984-; visiting scholar Harvard Univ 1979-80; UNDP project mangr Int Computer Educn Centre Budapest 1975-77, memb various SERC Ctees 1987-; FBCS 1968; *Books* Simulation Programming Languages (ed, 1968), Proceedings of NATO Software Engineering Conf (jt ed, 1970), The Craft of Software Engineering (jtly, 1987); *Recreations* mountaineering, music, restoration of medieval homes; *Clubs* Climbers; *Style—* Prof John Buxton; Bull's Hall, Yaxley, Eye, Suffolk IP23 8BZ; Kings College, Univ of London, Strand, London WC2R 2LS

BUXTON, Jonathan James; s of Cdr Michael Buxton (s of Henry Fowell Buxton, by his 1 w, Katharine, da of Rt Hon James Round, of Birch Hall, Essex; Henry Buxton was 1 s of John Henry Buxton, DL, by his w, Emma, da of Capt Richard Pelly, DL, RN, 5 s of Sir John Pelly, 1 Bt; John Henry Buxton was 1 s of Thomas Buxton, JP, 2 s of Sir Thomas Buxton, 1 Bt); *b* 2 July 1943; *Educ* Harrow; *m* 1972, Rosaleen, da of Sir John Bagge, 6 Bt; 3 da; *Career* formerly Maj 17/21 Lancers; co dir; *Recreations* sailing, skiing; *Clubs* Cavalry; *Style—* Jonathan Buxton, Esq; 62 Endlesham Rd, London SW12 8JL (☎ 081 675 4242)

BUXTON, Hon Lucinda Catherine; 2 da of Baron Buxton of Alsa, and Pamela Mary, *née* Birkin; *b* 21 Aug 1950; *Educ* New Hall Sch Chelmsford; *Career* wildlife photographer; has made 17 tv films for survival wildlife series tstee Falkland Islands Appeal, wildlife advsr Falkland Islands Fndn; Media Award 1982, The Cherry Kearton Award (RGS) 1983; ctee memb United Kingdom Falkland Islands Ctee; FRGS; *Books* Survival in the Wild (1980), Survival - South Atlantic (1983); *Recreations* tennis, flying, diving; *Style—* The Hon Lucinda Buxton; The Old House, Langham, Holt, Norfolk (☎ 0328 830352); 69 Archel Rd, London W14 (☎ 071 381 9922)

BUXTON, Hon Mrs (Margaret Evelyn); *née* Bridges; da of 1 Baron Bridges, KG, GCB, GCVO, MC (d 1969), and Hon Katharine, da of 2 Baron Farrer; *b* 9 Oct 1932; *Educ* Downe House Newbury, Lady Margaret Hall Oxford (MA, DPhil); *m* 1, 1954 (m dis 1969), Trevor Aston; m 2, 1971, as his 2 w, Paul William Jex Buxton, s of Denis Alfred Jex Buxton (d 1964), and gggs of Sir Thomas Buxton, 1 Bt; 2 da; *Career* lectr St Anne's Coll Oxford 1956-59, res fell Newnham Coll Cambridge 1961-66, hon sr res fell Queen's Univ Belfast 1984-85; FRHS, FSA; *Books* (under name of Margaret Aston) Thomas Arundel (1967), The Fifteenth Century (1968), Lollards and Reformers (1984), England's Iconoclasts (1988); *Style—* The Hon Mrs Buxton, FSA; Castle House, Chipping Ongar, Essex (☎ 0277 362642)

BUXTON, Dr Paul Kenneth; s of Kenneth Buxton, of Swallowfield Park, Reading, Berks, and Agnes, *née* Bragg; *b* 28 Feb 1936; *Educ* Trinity Coll Cambridge, St Thomas's Hosp London; *m* 22 Dec 1962, Heather Clive, da of Lt-Col J C Edlmann; 1 s (Jonathan Charles b 30 June 1965), 1 da (Joanna Rachel b 12 April 1967); *Career* staff Royal Jubilee Hosp Victoria 1971-81, conslt dermatologist Royal Infirmary Edinburgh and Fife Health Bd 1981-, vice chm Fife Branch Scot Wildlife Tst 1986-, pres Fife Branch BMA 1986-87; FRSM, FRCPEd 1985; *Books* ABC Dermatology (1988); *Recreations* seafaring, books, farming; *Clubs* New (Edinburgh); *Style—* Dr Paul Buxton; Old Inzievar House, By Dunfermline, Fife KY12 8HA (☎ 0383 880297); University Dept of Dermatology, Royal Infirmary, Edinburgh EH3 9YW (☎ 031 229 2477)

BUXTON, Paul William Jex; s of Denis Buxton (d 1964), of Gt Yarmouth, and Emily, *née* Hollins (d 1970); gggs of Sir Thomas Fowell Buxton who carried Bill abolishing slavery through Commons 1835; *b* 20 Sept 1925; *Educ* Rugby, Balliol Coll Oxford (BA, MA); *m* 1, 1950 (m dis 1971), Katharine (d 1977); 2 s (Charles b 1951, Toby b 1953), 1 da (Mary b 1956); m 2, 1971, Margaret, *qv*, da of Rt Hon Lord Bridges, KG (d 1969), of Headley, Surrey; 2 da (Sophie b 1972, Hero b 1974); *Career* Capt Coldstream Gds Germany 1945-47; Foreign and Diplomatic Service 1950-71, served: India, United Nations New York, Guatemala, United States; cnsllr Washington 1967-70, Northern Ireland Office 1974-85, under sec Belfast 1981-85; staff memb MMC 1985-, hon treas Anti-Slavery Int, memb cncl Howard League for Penal Reform; *Recreations* forestry, gardening; *Clubs* Brooks's; *Style—* Paul Buxton, Esq; Castle House, Chipping Ongar, Essex CM5 9JT

BUXTON, Dr Roger St John; s of Brig Noel St John Grey Dudley Buxton (d 1980), of Shanklin, IOW; *b* 16 July 1924; *Educ* Cheltenham, King's Coll London, King's Coll Hosp London (MB BS, PhD, DCH); *m* 29 April 1950, Diana Margaret, da of William Gladstone Borrow, of London; 3 s (Clive b 1952, Nigel b 1953, Julian b 1963), 1 da (Angela b 1960); *Career* Univ of Bristol: sr lectr Dept of Physiology 1958-73, preclinical dean Faculty of Med 1967-72; PMO DHSS 1973-82, chm EC Ctee on Health Servs Res 1978-81, specialist in community med SE Thames RHA 1982-88; dep CMO St John Ambulance Assoc 1976-; church warden: St Albans Westbury Park Bristol 1966-70, St Marys Aldingbourne Chichester; memb: Faculty of Community Med, Soc for Social Med, Assoc for Study Med Educn, Br Diabetic Assoc, Faculty of Public Health Med; Freeman City of London 1949, Liveryman Worshipful Soc of Apothecaries 1948; KStJ; *Recreations* travel, theatre; *Clubs* St John House, Civil Service; *Style—* Dr Roger Buxton; Borrowdale, Arundel Rd, Norton, Chichester PO18 0JX (☎ 0243 543930)

BUXTON, Ronald Carlile; s of Murray Barclay Buxton, and Janet Mary Muriel, *née* Carlile; *b* 20 Aug 1923; *Educ* Eton, Trinity Coll Cambridge (MA); *m* 1959, Phyllida Dorothy Roden; 2 s, 2 da; *Career* dir H Young & Co London and assoc cos; MP(C) Leyton 1955-66; FIStructE; *Recreations* travel, music, riding; *Clubs* Carlton; *Style—* Ronald Buxton, Esq; Kimberley Hall, Wymondham, Norfolk; 67 Ashley Gdns, London SW1

BUXTON, Hon Simon Campden; 2 s of 2 Baron Noel-Buxton (d 1980); *b* 9 April 1943; *Educ* Bryanston, Balliol Coll Oxford; *m* 1981, Alison, da of S J Liddle, of Exmouth; 1 s (Christopher John Noel b 11 June 1988), 1 da (Katherine Helen b 1983); *Career* editor social action programmes Thames Television; tstee Noel-Buxton Tst, govr Kingsway Coll, memb Arts Access Ctee; *Clubs* MCC; *Style—* The Hon Simon Buxton

BUXTON, Hon Timothy Leland; er s of Baron Buxton of Alsa; *b* 20 Nov 1948; *Educ* Ampleforth; *m* 1972, Julie Mary, da of Lt Cdr (John) Michael Avison Parker, CVO; 1 s (Edward Leland b 1976), 1 da (Alexandra Louise b 1973); *Style—* The Hon Timothy Buxton; The Dower House, Heydon, Norfolk

BUXTON, Hon Victoria Jane; 4 da of Baron Buxton of Alsa, *qv*; *b* 4 June 1960; *Educ* St Mary's Convent Ascot; *Career* commercial pilot; *Style—* The Hon Victoria Buxton; Burntwalls Farm, Daventry, Northants

BUXTON OF ALSA, Baron (Life Peer UK 1978), of Stiffkey, Co Norfolk; Aubrey Leland Oakes Buxton; MC (1943), DL (Essex 1975); s of late Leland William Wilberforce Buxton, s of Sir Thomas Fowell Buxton, 3 Bt, GCMG, JP, DL; *b* 15 July 1918; *Educ* Ampleforth, Trinity Coll Cambridge; *m* 1946, Pamela Mary (d 1983), da of Sir Henry Ralph Stanley Birkin, 3 Bt, and widow of Maj Samuel Luckyn Buxton, MC, 17/21 Lancers; 2 s, 4 da; m 2, 16 July 1988, Mrs Kathleen Peterson, of Maine, USA; *Career* Maj Supplementary Reserves; chief exec Anglia TV Group (dir 1955-88, chm 1986-88), chm ITN 1981-86; vice pres Royal TV Soc 1973-77, treas London Zoological Soc 1977-83, chm Survival Anglia 1986-; memb: Countryside Cmmn, Royal Cmmn on Pollution, Nature Conservancy Cncl 1988-90; prodr of television and wildlife films; Queens award for Industry 1974; Extra Equerry to HRH The Duke of Edinburgh 1964-, High Sheriff of Essex 1972; *Style—* The Rt Hon the Lord Buxton of Alsa, MC, DL; Old Hall Farm, Stiffkey, Wells-next-the-Sea, Norfolk NR23 1QJ (☎ 032 875 347)

BUZZARD, Sir Anthony Farquhar; 3 Bt (UK 1929), of Munstead Grange, Godalming, Surrey; s of Rear Adm Sir Anthony Wass Buzzard, 2 Bt, CB, DSO, OBE (d 1972), and Margaret (d 1989), da of Sir Arthur Knapp, KCIE, CSI, CBE; *b* 28 June 1935; *Educ* Charterhouse, Ch Ch Oxford, Bethany Theological Coll (MA); *m* 1970, Barbara Jean, da of Gordon Arnold, of Michigan; 3 da (Sarah b 1971, Claire b 1974, Heather b 1988); *Heir bro* Timothy MacDonnell; *Career* modern languages teacher at American School in London 1974-81, lectr in theology Oregon Bible Coll Illinois 1982-; articles on Christology & Eschatology in various theological journals, fndr of Restoration Fellowship; *Books* The Coming Kingdom of the Messiah: A Solution to the Riddle of the New Testament (1987); *Recreations* music, tennis; *Style—* Sir Anthony Buzzard, Bt; Box 100, Oregon, Illinois 61061, USA (☎ 815 734 4344, 815 732 7991)

BUZZARD, Timothy Macdonnell; s of Rear Adm Sir Anthony Wass Buzzard, 2 Bt, CB, DSO, OBE (d 1972); hp of bro, Sir Anthony Buzzard, 3 Bt; *b* 28 Jan 1939; *Educ* Royal Acad of Music; *m* 1970, Jennifer, da of Peter Patching (d 1971); 1 s, 1 da; *Career* dir of music; LRAM, GRSM; *Style—* Timothy Buzzard, Esq; Kennel Cottage, East Mascalls, Lindfield, West Sussex (☎ 0444 483420)

BYAM SHAW, (John) James; CBE; s of John Byam Liston Shaw (d 1919), of London, and Caroline Evelyn Eunice, *née* Pyke-Nott (d 1960); *b* 12 Jan 1903; *Educ* Westminster, Christ Church Oxford (MA); *m* 1, 1929 (m dis 1938), Eveline, da of Capt Arthur Dodgson, RN; m 2, 1945, Margaret (d 1965), da of Arthur Saunders; 1 adopted s (James Frederick b 1950); m 3, 1967, Christine Pamela, wid of W P Gibson; *Career* WWII The Royal Scots 1940-46: cmmnd 2 Lt, Capt 1941, Maj 1944, served UK, India, Burma; lectr and asst to dir Courtauld Inst of Art 1933-34, dir P & D Colnaghi & Co 1937-68 (joined 1934); Christ Church Oxford: lectr 1964-73, assoc curator of pictures 1973-74, hon student fell 1976; Hon DLitt Oxford Univ; hon fell: Pierpont Morgan Library New York, Ateneo Veneto Venice; FSA, FRSA; Grande Ufficiale (Order of Merit of the Rep of Italy) 1982; *Books* The Drawings of Francesco Guardi (1951), The Drawings of Domenico Tiepolo (1962), Catalogue of Paintings at Christ Church Oxford (1967), Catalogue of Drawings at Christ Church (1976), Catalogue of Italian Drawings in the Lugt Collection Fondation Custodia Institut Néerlandais Paris (1983), Catalogue of Italian 18th Century Drawings in the Robert Lehman Collection Metro Museum New York (with George Knox, 1987); *Clubs* Athenaeum; *Style—* James Byam Shaw, Esq, CBE, FSA; 4 Abingdon Villas, London W8 6BX (☎ 071 937 6128)

BYAM SHAW, Nicholas Glencairn; s of Lt Cdr David Byam Shaw, OBE, RN (ka 1941), and Clarita Pamela Clarke; gf, a painter who started the Byam Shaw Art Sch early in 20 century (John Byam Liston Shaw, d 1919); *b* 28 March 1934; *Educ* RNC Dartmouth; *m* 1, 1956, Joan, da of Major Hedley Edmund Dennis Elliott, of Roundabout, West Chiltington, Sussex (d 1958); 2 s (Justin b 1960, Matthew b 1963), 1 da (Clare b 1957); m 2, 1987, Constance, da of Rev Serson Clarke, of Ottawa, Canada (d 1979); *Career* Lt RN (cmmnd 1953), promoted 1956; publisher; md: Macmillan Publishers Ltd 1969-, Macmillan Ltd 1983-; chm: Pan Books Ltd 1986-, Macmillan Ltd 1990-; dir St Martins Press NY and other Macmillan cos; *Recreations* gardening, music, theatre; *Style—* Nicholas Byam Shaw, Esq; Macmillan Ltd, 4 Little Essex St, London WC2 (☎ 071 836 6633)

BYATT, Antonia Susan; CBE (1990); da of His Hon Judge John Frederick Drabble, QC (d 1983), of Martlesham, Suffolk, and Kathleen Marie Bloor (d 1984); *b* 24 Aug 1936; *m* 1959 (m dis 1969), I C R Byatt; 1 s (Charles b 1961, d 1972), 1 da (Antonia b 1960); m 2, 1969, Peter John Duffy; 2 da (Isabel b 1 Miranda b 1973); *Career* teacher: Westminster Tutors 1962-65, Extra-mural Dept Univ of London 1962-71; pt/t lectr Dept of Lib Studies Central Sch of Art and Design 1965-69, lectr Dept of Eng UCL 1972-, tutor for admissions Dept of Eng UCL 1980-82 (asst tutor 1977-80), sr lectr Dept of Eng UCL 1981-83; full-time writer 1983-; regular reviewer: various newspapers, The Times Literary Supplement, BBC Kaleidoscope; external assessor in lit Central Sch of Art and Design, external examiner UEA; judge Booker Prize 1973; memb: panel of judges Hawthornden Prize, Communications and Cultural Studies Bd CNAA 1978-83, Creative and Performing Arts Bd 1984, BBC's Social Effects of TV Advsy Gp 1974-77, Kingman Ctee on Eng Language 1987-88, Lit Advsy Panel Br Cncl 1990-, London Library Ctee 1990-, Advsy Bd Harold Hyam Wingate Fellowship 1988-; assoc Newnham Coll Cambridge, chm Ctee of Mgmnt Soc of Authors 1986-88 (dep chm 1985-); Hon DLitt: Bradford 1987, Durham 1991, York 1991; FRSL; *Books* Shadow of a Sun (1964), Degrees of Freedom (1965), The Game (1967), The Virgin in the Garden (1978), Still Life (1985), Sugar and Other Stories (1987), Unruly Times (1989), Posession: A Romance (Booker Prize, Aer Lingus Int Fiction Prize Irish Times, 1990), Passions of The Mind (essays, 1991); author of varied literary criticism, articles, prefaces, reviews and broadcasts; *Style*— Mrs A S Byatt, CBE; 37 Rusholme Rd, London SW15 3LF (☎ 081 789 3109)

BYATT, Sir Hugh Campbell; KCVO (1985), CMG (1979); s of Sir Horace Archer Byatt, GCMG (d 1933), and Lady Byatt, MBE, *née* Olga Margaret Campbell (d 1943); *b* 27 Aug 1927; *Educ* Gordonstoun, New Coll Oxford (MA); *m* 1954, Fiona, da of Ian Pountney Coats, DL; 2 s, 1 da; *Career* Nat Serv RNVR 1945-48; Nigerian Political Serv 1952-57, CRO India and Cabinet Office 1957-67, head of chancery Lisbon 1967, asst head Asia Dept FCO 1970, consul gen Mozambique 1971-73, inspr HM Dip Serv 1973-75, RCDS 1976, dep high cmmr Kenya 1977-78, first ambass to Angola 1978-81, Portugal 1981-86; chm of governors Centre for Info of Language Teaching and Res (CILT) 1986-90, dir Dragon Tst plc (Edinburgh Fund Managers), chm Java Trust plc (Edinburgh Fund Managers); KtGCMO of Christ (Portugal 1985); *Recreations* sailing, fishing, gardening; *Clubs* New (Edinburgh), Royal Ocean Racing; *Style*— Sir Hugh Campbell Byatt, KCVO, CMG; Leargnahension, By Tarbert, Argyll

BYATT, Dr Ian Charles Rayner; s of Charles Rayner Byatt (d 1944), and Enid Marjorie Annie, *née* Howat (d 1977); *b* 11 March 1932; *Educ* Kirkham GS, St Edmund Hall Oxford, Nuffield Coll Oxford (BA, DPhil), Harvard Univ; *m* 4 July 1959 (m dis 1969), Antonia Susan, da of His Hon Judge J F Drabble, QC (d 1982); 1 s (Charles Nicholas John b 1961, d 1972), 1 da ((Helen) Antonia b 1960); *Career* serv RAF 1950-52; lectr in econs Univ of Durham 1958-62, econ conslt HM Treasy 1962-64, lectr LSE 1964-67, sr econ advsr DES 1967-69, dir of econs and statistics Miny of Housing (later DOE) 1969-72, dep chief econ advsr HM Treasy 1978-89 (head of pub sector 1972-78), dir gen of Water Servs 1989-; memb: Holy Cross Church, Holy Cross Centre Tst, Cncl Royal Econ Soc; FRSA; *Books* British Electrical Industry 1875-1914 (1979); *Recreations* painting; *Clubs* Oxford and Cambridge; *Style*— Dr Ian Byatt; 17 Thanet St, London WC1H 9QL (☎ 071 388 3888); Office of Water Services, 13-15 Floor, Centre City Tower, 7 Hill St, Birmingham B5 4UA (☎ 021 625 1350, fax 021 625 1311)

BYATT, Ronald Archer Campbell (Robin); CMG (1980); s of Sir Horace Archer Byatt, GCMG (d 1933), of Megsdon Hall, Buntingford, Herts, and Olga Margaret Byatt, MBE, *née* Campbell (d 1943); *b* 14 Nov 1930; *Educ* Gordonstoun, New Coll Oxford (BA), King's Coll Cambridge; *m* 10 July 1954, Ann Brereton (Jilly), da of C B Sharpe, of Field Cottage, Terrington, N Yorks; 1 s (Andrew b 1959), 1 da (Ann b 1957); *Career* Nat Serv RNVR 1949-50; admin offr HMOCS Nyasaland 1954-59; HM Dip Serv: Havana 1961-63, FO 1963-66 (and 1959-61), Kampala 1970-71, cnsllr to Head of Rhodesia Dept FCO 1972-75, memb UK Delgn to Rhodesian Constitutional Conf Geneva 1976, head of Chancery UK Mission to UN NY 1977-79 (and 1966-70), asst under sec of state FCO 1979-80, memb Directional Staff RCDS London 1983-84, ambass to Rabat Morocco 1985-87, high cmmr to NZ and Western Samoa 1987-90 (Harare Zimbabwe 1983), govr of Pitcairn Islands 1987-; visiting fell Univ of Glasgow 1975-76; tstee Beit Tst 1987-; Order of the Thorne Morocco 1987; *Recreations* sailing, bird watching, gardening; *Clubs* United Oxford and Cambridge Univ, Leander; *Style*— Robin Byatt, Esq, CMG; Drim Na Vullin, Lochgilphead, Argyll PA31 8LE (☎ 0546 2615)

BYERS, Hon Charles William; o s of Baron Byers, OBE, PC, DL (Life Peer, d 1984), and Baroness Byers, *qv*; *b* 24 March 1949; *Educ* Westminster, Ch Ch Oxford; *m* 8 July 1972, Suzan Mary, o da of Aubrey Kefford Stone (d 1980); 2 s (Jonathan Charles b 11 April 1975, George William b 19 Nov 1977); *Career* called to the Bar Gray's Inn 1973; *Style*— The Hon Charles Byers; 3 Clayford, Dormansland, Surrey

BYERS, Baroness; Joan Elizabeth; da of late William Oliver, of Alfriston, Wayside, Golders Green, London NW11; *m* 1939, Baron Byers, OBE, PC, DL (Lib Life Peer, cr 1964, a former chief whip, chm of the pty, and ldr of Libs in House of Lords, d 1984); 1 s (Charles, *qv*), 3 da (Elizabeth Gaff, Luise Nandy, Sara Somers, *qqv*); *Style*— The Rt Hon Lady Byers; Hunters Hill, Blindley Heath, Lingfield, Surrey

BYERS, Sir Maurice Hearne; CBE (1978), QC (1960); s of Arthur Tolhurst Byers (d 1950), and Mabel Florence, *née* Hearne (d 1950); *b* 10 Nov 1917; *Educ* St Aloysius Coll Sydney, Sydney Univ (LLB); *m* 1949, Patricia Therese, da of Henry Gilbert Davis (d 1947); 2 s, 1 da; *Career* barr, slr-gen of Aust 1973-83, ldr Aust Delgn to UN Cmmn on Int Trade Law 1974, 1976-81; chm: Police Bd of NSW 1984-88, Aust Constitutional Cmmn 1985-88; kt 1982; *see Debrett's Handbook of Australia and New Zealand for further details*; *Style*— Sir Maurice Byers, CBE, QC; 14 Morella Rd, Clifton Gdns, NSW 2088, Australia (☎ 969 8257, 6/180 Phillip St, Sydney (☎ 232 4766)

BYFORD, Sir Lawrence; CBE (1979), QPM (1974), DL (1987); s of George Byford (d 1949), of Normanton, Yorks, and Monica Irene Byford; *b* 10 Aug 1925; *Educ* Univ of Leeds; *m* 1950, Muriel Campbell Massey; 2 s, 1 da; *Career* barr; joined W Riding Police 1947, divnl cdr Huddersfield 1966-68, chief constable Lincs 1973-77 (asst chief constable 1968-70, dep chief constable 1970-73), HM Inspr of Constabulary for SE region 1977-78, for NE region 1978-83, HM Chief Inspr of Constabulary 1983-87; Hon LLD Univ of Leeds 1987; now engaged as mgmnt and security conslt; kt 1984; *Clubs* MCC, Royal Overseas League, Yorkshire CC (pres 1991-); *Style*— Sir Lawrence Byford, CBE, QPM, DL; Royal Overseas League, Park Place, St James's St, London SW1A 1LR

BYGRAVE, Clifford; s of Fred Bygrave, of Caddington, nr Luton, and Beatrice Rose Bygrave; *b* 24 May 1934; *Educ* Luton GS; *m* 15 July 1961, Jean Elizabeth, da of Edward Neale (d 1986); 3 da (Angela Joy b 1964, Paula Jane b 1968, Heather Alison b 1972); *Career* RNVR 1955-59; CA; ptnr Hillier Hills Frary & Co 1962, ptnr Arthur Young (now Ernst & Young) 1981; chm Bd of Govrs Ashton Middle Sch, vice chm Ashton Schs Fndn Dunstable, pres Beds Bucks and Herts Soc of Chartered Accountants 1975-76 (memb Mgmnt Ctee 1971-), tstee and treas Friends of Luton Parish Church, vice pres Luton Town FC; memb Worshipful Co of Chartered Accountants, Freeman City of London; FCA 1958, ATII 1964, memb Cncl Inst of CAs 1980-; *Recreations* golf, soccer; *Clubs* Farmers, Dunstable Downs Rotary, Ashridge Golf; *Style*— Clifford Bygrave, Esq; The Rustlings, Valley Close, Studham, Dunstable, Beds (☎ 0582 872 070); 400 Capability Green, Luton, Beds (☎ 0582 400700, fax 0582 484121)

BYGRAVES, Max Walter William; OBE (1983); s of Henry Walter Bygraves (d 1974), and Lilian Mary Bygraves (d 1985); *b* 16 Oct 1922; *Educ* St Joseph's London; *m* 1942, Blossom Mary; 1 s (Anthony b 1947), 2 da (Christine b 1943, Maxine b 1953); *Career* fitter RAF 1940-45; performed as entertainer in shows for troops; turned professional 1946, has appeared all over world; 19 Royal Command Performances; 31 Gold Disc recordings; host Family Fortunes TV show; *Books* I Wanna Tell You a Story (1976), The Milkman's on his Way (1977), After Thoughts (1988); *Recreations* golf, travel, short story writing; *Clubs* St James, East India, RAC; *Style*— Max Bygraves, Esq, OBE; 32 Stafford Mansions Place, London SW1 (☎ 071 828 4595)

BYLES, David Warner; s of Charles Humphrey Gilbert Byles (d 1970), of Kemsing, Kent, and Pamela Beatrice Byles; *b* 6 April 1954; *Educ* Sevenoaks Sch, Univ of Kent (BA); *m* 1981, Susan Jane, da of Edward Fowles; 1 s (Thomas Edward b 1988), 1 da (Jennifer Mary b 1985); *Career* advtg exec; asst to Co Sec HP Drewry (Shipping Consultants) Ltd 1976-77; Benton & Bowles: graduate trainee 1977-78, media exec 1978-79, media gp head 1979-81; J Walter Thompson: dep media gp mangr 1981-82, media gp mangr 1982-83, asst media dir 1983-87, bd dir media 1987-89, media dir 1989-; accounts handled for JWT incl: Rowntree Mackintosh, NatWest, Thomson Holidays, St Ivel, Kellogg; RAF Special Flying award 1970-71; memb RSPB 1985, MIPA 1988; *Recreations* orinithology, motorcycling; *Clubs* RAC; *Style*— David Byles, Esq; J Walter Thompson Co Ltd, 40 Berkeley Square, London W1X 6AD (☎ 071 499 4040, fax 071 493 8432/8418)

BYLLAM-BARNES, Joseph Charles Felix Byllam; s of Cyril Charles Byllam-Barnes (d 1976), of Boothby House, Ashtead, Surrey, and Barbara Isabel Mary, *née* Walls; *b* 30 Aug 1928; *Educ* The Modern Sch Streatham, Shaftesbury, City of London Freemen's Sch; *m* 1 April 1978, Maureen Margaret Mary, da of Maj Claude Montague Castle, MC (d 1940), of Hampstead, London; *Career* RAMC 1946-49, i/c Mil and Public Health Servs Eritrea 1948-49; with Barclays Bank plc 1945- (Head Office inspr 1976-); pres Farringdon Ward Club; memb: Cncl City Livery Club, Cncl Royal Soc of St George City of London Branch, Governing Body United Wards Club of the City of London, Ward of Cheap Club, Guild of Freemen of the City of London (Ct of Assts 1990), Ctee Friends of Guildhall Sch of Music and Drama; local covenant organiser RC Diocese of Arundel and Brighton, Oblate of Quarr Abbey 1963; fell: Chartered Inst of Bankers, Inst of Financial Accountants; Freeman: City of London 1983, Worshipful Co of Upholders 1984 (treas 1985, Ct of Assts 1986); *Recreations* music, opera, walking, study of law and theology; *Clubs* Guards Polo, City Livery Yacht, Surrey County Cricket; *Style*— Joseph Byllam-Barnes, Esq; Walsingham House, Oldfield Gardens, Ashtead, Surrey; 25 Farringdon St, London EC4A 4LD (☎ 071 489 1995, fax 071 248 5875, telex 884670 INSPBB G)

BYNG, Hon Julian Francis; yr s of 7 Earl of Strafford (d 1984), and his 1 w Maria, *née* Cloete; *b* 3 May 1938; *Educ* Eton; *m* 1, 1966 (m dis 1983), Ingela Brita, da of Axel Berglund, of Stockholm; 2 s (Francis b 1968, Alexander b 1973); *m* 2, 1984, Prudence Mary, da of Albert Edward Delany (d 1980), of Queensland, Australia, and former w of David Kent; *Career* Capt Queen's Royal Rifles (TA); *Clubs* Boodle's; *Style*— The Hon Julian Byng; 8 Elm Park Rd, London SW3 6BB (☎ 071 351 4750)

BYNG, Julian Michael Edmund; assumed surname of Byng by Deed Poll 1952 in lieu of his patronymic, and was granted Royal Licence to bear the arms of Byng 1969 in accordance with the will of his grandfather the 6th Earl of Stafford; s of Capt Michael William Millicent Lafone (d 1966), of Lusaka Turf Club, N Rhodesia, by his first w, Lady (Florence) Elizabeth Alice Byng (resumed her maiden surname by Deed Poll 1952, in accordance with her father's will and d 1987), da of 6 Earl of Strafford; descended from Adm Sir George Byng (1 Viscount Torrington), Hon Robert Byng (Govr of Barbados), and FM Sir John Byng (1 Earl of Strafford, Col of Coldstream Gds and Cdr of Gds Bde at Waterloo); *b* 20 Oct 1928; *Educ* Eton, Lausanne Univ, King's Coll Cambridge; *m* 28 Oct 1960, Eve Finola, da of Captain Michael St Maur Wellesley-Wesley (d 1982), of Doon, Tahilla, Co Kerry; 3 s (Robert b 1962, Patrick b 1965, Thomas b 1970), 1 da (Georgiana (Mrs Piers Monckton) b 1964); *Career* called to the Bar Inner Temple 1954; farmer, thoroughbred breeder; landowner (in excess of 1000 acres); chm Herts branch Country Landowners' Assoc 1970-73; *Recreations* shooting, skiing, flying, racing; *Clubs* Brooks's, Pratt's, Jockey (Paris); *Style*— Julian Byng, Esq; Wrotham Park, Barnet, Herts EN5 4SB (☎ 081 449 1499); Flat J, 42 Eaton Square, London SW1 (☎ 071 235 7512)

BYNG, Rupert Wingfield; s of Leonard Harold Robert Byng (d 1974), of The Salutation, Sandwich, Kent, and Lady Mary Anne Denham, *née* Stuart; *b* 5 June 1946; *Educ* Harrow, New Coll Oxford (MA), Sorbonne; *m* 28 April 1987, Francesca, da of Arthur Ivor Stewart Liberty, MC, TD, of The Lee, Bucks; *Career* mangr int dept Joseph Sebag 1969-75, W I Carr & Sons (Overseas) 1981-86, dir int equities Barclays De Zoete Wedd 1986-; Br Camelia Owners & Breeders Assoc; *Recreations* tennis, sailing, Alpaca breeding; *Clubs* Annabels; *Style*— Rupert Byng, Esq; Langley Farm, Cowden, Kent

BYRNE, Anthony John; s of Benjamin James Byrne, of Dublin, and Ruby Anne, *née* O'Brien (d 1975); *b* 9 Aug 1947; *Educ* Oakham Sch Rutland, Univ of Lancaster, Univ of Colorado, Sidney Sussex Coll Cambridge; *m* 5 Sept 1971, Kathy, da of Carl Strain, of Denver, Colorado; 2 da (Rachel, Jenny); *Career* PA to gen mangr Central Lancs Devpt Corpn 1973-77, Inst of Advanced Architectural Studies Univ of York 1977-78; dir: Bicentenary of the Iron Bridge Ironbridge Gorge Museum Tst 1978, Bristol Mktg Bd 1983-87, BAFTA; project dir Watershed Media Centre Bristol 1980-83, chm Sci-Tech Film and TV Festivals 1987 and 1989; tstee: Brunel Tst Temple Meads Bristol, Vivat Tst, Wildscreen Tst; Parly candidate (Lab) Rutland and Stamford 1972-74; *Style*— Anthony Byrne, Esq; 6 Kensington Place, Clifton, Bristol BS8 3AH; BAFTA, 195 Piccadilly, London W1V 9LG (☎ 071 734 0022)

BYRNE, Derek Cyril; s of Noel Byrne, of Beauparc, Navan, Co Meath, Eire, and Christine, *née* Fitzsimons; *b* 10 March 1966; *Educ* St Patrick's Classical Sch Navan Co Meath; *Career* national hunt jockey 1984-; formerly apprentice flat racing jockey Ireland; represented England at World Jump Jockey's Championship Aust 1990; runner-up Irish Unidare Apprentice Championship 1986, Conditional Jump Jockey champion 1989 and 1990; winner Scottish Nat 1990 (Four Trix), rode a double at Aintree 1990, rode four winners Boxing Day 1989; *Recreations* fishing, playing football and pool; *Style*— Derek Byrne, Esq; 39 Dickens Road, Malton, North Yorkshire YO17 OFE (☎ 0653 600461)

BYRNE, John Edward Thomas; s of John Byrne (d 1979), and Violet Mary, *née* Harris; *b* 16 Feb 1935; *Educ* Kilkenny Coll, Mountjoy Sch Dublin, Trinity Coll Dublin (BA, MB BCh, BAO); *m* 23 Nov 1963, Margaret Elizabeth Ross, da of William Albert Wilson (d 1975); 2 da (Katharine b 1969, Johanna b 1971); *Career* house surgn and house physician Dr Steevens Hosp Dublin 1961-62, fell in otology Wayne State Univ Detroit 1973, conslt in otolaryngology Belfast City Hosp 1974-, hon ed Proceedings of the Irish Otolaryngological Soc 1974-, external examiner to constituent colls Nat Univ of I, examiner RCSI (Otolaryngology), author of various pubns on blast injury to ears; memb: ORS, Irish Otolaryngological Soc, Ulster Med Soc, Br Cochlea Implant Gp, TCD Assoc; FRCSI 1970; *Books* Scott/Brown's Otolaryngology (contrib, 1987); *Recreations* sailing, maritime history, gardening, theatre; *Clubs* Strangford Lough Yacht; *Style*— John Byrne, Esq; Mulroy Lodge, Ballymenoch Park, Holywood, N Ireland BT18 0LP (☎ 02317 3374); Belfast City Hospital, Belfast BT9 7AB (☎ 0232 329241)

BYRNE, John Napier; s of Christopher Thomas Byrne (d 1973), and Christian McDougall, *née* Napier; *b* 28 Aug 1953; *Educ* Bangor GS, Gonville and Caius Coll Cambridge (MA); *m* 16 May 1981, (Birgit) Marita, da of Arne Gotthard Westberg; 1 s (Daniel b 1986); *Career* admitted slr 1978; ptnr Freshfields 1985 (joined 1978); Freeman City of London Slrs Co; *Clubs* Landsdowne; *Style*— John Byrne, Esq; Whitefriars, 65 Fleet St, London EC4Y 1HT (☎ 071 936 4000, fax 071 248 3487/8/9)

BYRNE, Hon Mrs (Nona Georgette); *née* Lawrence; yst da of 3 Baron Lawrence (d 1947); *b* 10 Sept 1922; *Educ* F H S Graham Ter; *m* 8 Feb 1945, Wing Cdr Vincent George Byrne (d 1978), yst s of late James Byrne, of Malahide, Co Dublin; 5 s (Nicholas, James, Patrick, Dominic, Rory), 4 da (Teresa, Deirdre (decd), Clare, Fiona); *Career* chm Catholic Building Society; *Clubs* RAF; *Style*— The Hon Mrs Byrne; Blackberry Cottage, Rookwood Road, West Wittering, West Sussex PO20 8LT (☎ 0243 513057)

BYROM, Richard John; JP (1973); s of Richard Byrom (d 1961), of Bury, and Bessie, *née* Jardin; *b* 12 Oct 1939; *Educ* Denstone Coll, Univ of Manchester (BA); *m* 4 April 1964, Susan Hope, da of Richard Clegg (d 1984), of Gwydir; 2 s (Peter b 1965, David b 1967), 1 da (Joy b 1968); *Career* ptnr in private architectural practice 1964-, dir Byrom Clark Roberts Architects Surveyors and Consulting Engrs Manchester 1989-; practicing arbitrator; memb Cncl Incorporated Soc of Valuers and Auctioneers (chm Building Surveying Ctee 1986-); memb Gen Synod of The Church of England 1970-75; reader Hawkshaw Parish Church 1964-; memb Manchester Soc of Architects; RIBA 1965, FCIArb 1977, FSVA 1976, FBIM; *Books* The Building Society Valuer (1979); *Recreations* industrial archaeology, antiquarian books; *Style—* Richard J Byrom, Esq, JP; 3 Hawkshaw Lane, Bury, Lancs BL8 4JL (☎ 020 488 3110); Byrom Clark Roberts Ltd, The Building Centre, 115 Portland St, Manchester M1 6DW (☎ 061 236 9601, fax 061 236 8675, car 0836 603521)

BYRON, Kathleen Elizabeth; *née* Fell; da of Richard John Fell (d 1981), of Herne Bay, Kent, and Eleanor Mary, *née* Macaree; *b* 11 Jan 1922; *Educ* GS, Old Vic Theatre Sch; *m* 1, 1944 (m dis 1951), Daniel John Bowen, s of D J Bowen (d 1955), of Atlanta, Georgia; m 2, 23 Sept 1953, Alaric Jacob, s of Col Harold Jacob, CSI (d 1937), of Aden; 1 s (Jasper Alexander b 2 July 1958), 1 da (Harriet Christina Mary b 20 April 1954); *Career* actress; entered profession 1946; films incl: Matter of Life and Death 1946, Black Narcissus 1947, Small Back Room 1948; TV incl: Emergency Ward 10 1961-64, Portrait of a Lady 1969, The Golden Bowl 1971, Dearly Beloved 1983, Casualty, Portrait of a Marriage; The Mousetrap (theatre) 1988-89; *Recreations* pottery; *Style—* Ms Kathleen Byron; 30 Glengall Rd, London SE15 6NN (☎ 071 231 9316)

BYRON, Pauline, Baroness; Pauline Augusta; *née* Cornwall; da of late T J Cornwall, of Wagin, W Australia; *m* 1931, 11 Baron Byron (d 1983); 1 da; *Style—* The Rt Hon Pauline, Lady Byron; 1/12 Mount Street, Claremont, WA

BYRON, 13 Baron (E 1643); Robert James Byron; 2 (but only surviving) s of 12 Baron Byron (d 1989), and his 2 w, Dorigen Margaret, *née* Esdaile (d 1985); *b* 5 April 1950; *Educ* Wellington Coll, Trinity Coll Cambridge; *m* 1979, Robyn Margaret, da of John McLean, of Hamilton, NZ; 1 s (Hon Charles Richard Gordon b 1990), 3 da (Hon Caroline b 1981, Hon Emily b 1984, Hon Sophie b 1986); *Heir* s, Hon Charles Richard Gordon Byron b 28 July 1990; *Career* barr 1974; admitted slr 1978; ptnr Holman Fenwick & Willan 1984-; *Style—* The Rt Hon the Lord Byron; 19 Spencer Park, London SW18; Holman Fenwick & Willan, Marlow House, Lloyds Avenue, London EC3

BYRT, His Hon Judge (Henry) John; QC (1976); s of Albert Henry Byrt, CBE (d 1966), and Dorothy Muriel Thorne (d 1972); *b* 5 March 1929; *Educ* Charterhouse, Merton Coll Oxford; *m* 1957, Eve Hermione, da of Lt-Col Gordon McLaurin Bartlett (d 1964); 1 s (Charles b 1966), 2 da (Frances b 1962, Hermione b 1964); *Career* called to the Bar 1953, in practice SE Circuit, circuit judge 1983; vice princ The Working Mens Coll 1978-82 (princ 1982-87, memb Corp 1978-); memb Cncl Queens Coll Harley St 1981-; pres Social Security Appeal Tbnls and Med Appeal Tbnls 1983-89; *Clubs* Leander; *Style—* His Hon Judge John Byrt, QC; 65 Gloucester Crescent, London NW1 7EG (☎ 071 485 0341)

BYSTRAM, Charles Anthony; s of Baron Cyprian Bystram, sometime Col in Polish Army (d 1961), of London, and Sophia, *née* Smolicz (d 1978); *b* 23 Dec 1929; *Educ* Douai Sch, Univ of Cambridge (BA); *m* 11 Jan 1958, Jean Denise, da of Col Ian Hardie, DSO, RA (d 1977); 1 s (Michael b 1967), 2 da (Nicola b 1960, Antonia b 1963); *Career* dir United Biscuits Hldgs 1972-85, md United Biscuits Int 1978-85 (dir gp corporate devpt 1980-83, dir external affrs 1983-85); chm Ortiz SA 1975-85; dir: Lewmar plc 1985-87, Stakis plc 1987- (dep chm 1987), chm Geest plc 1986-90; *Recreations* travel, food and wine, various sports; *Style—* Charles Bystram, Esq

BYWATER, James Edward; s of Elam Bywater; *b* 22 May 1921; *Educ* Morley GS Yorks; *m* Margaret, da of Leonard Fry; 1 da; *Career* engineering; dir Ford of Britain 1965, chm and chief exec Sime Darby Holdings 1975, chm Thermal Syndicate 1980; dir: Associated Biscuits 1979-83, Varity Holdings Ltd 1983-; chm Nesbit Evans Group 1990-; *Recreations* archaeology, prehistory; *Clubs* Oriental; *Style—* James Bywater, Esq; 27 Park Close, Old Hatfield, Herts

C

CABARRUS; *see*: de Cabarrus

CABBELL MANNERS, Hon Richard Neville; s of 4 Baron Manners, MC (d 1972), and Mary Edith, *née* Gascoyne-Cecil; *b* 4 April 1924; *Educ* Eton; *m* 14 July 1945, Juliet Mary, eldest da of Lt-Col Sir Edward Hulton Preston, 5 Bt, DSO, MC (d 1963), of Beeston Hall, Neatishead, Norwich; 3 s, 1 da; *Career* farmer; *Recreations* hunting; *Style—* The Hon Richard Cabbell Manners; Cromer Hall, Cromer, Norfolk (☎ 0263 2506)

CABLE, Sir James Eric; KCVO (1976), CMG (1967); s of Eric Grant Cable, CMG (d 1970), and Nellie Margaret, *née* Skelton; *b* 15 Nov 1920; *Educ* Stowe, Corpus Christi Coll, Cambridge; *m* 1954, Viveca, da of Dr Ragnar Hollmerus, of Helsinki; 1 s; *Career* entered Foreign Office 1947, asst under sec of state FCO 1972-75, ambassador to Finland 1975-80, ret; writer on International Relations and Naval Affairs; *Style—* Sir James Cable, KCVO, CMG; c/o Lloyds Bank, 16 St James's St, London SW1A 1EY

CABLE-ALEXANDER, Margaret, Lady; Margaret Mabel; da of late John Leopold Burnett, of Dublin; *m* 1942, as his 2 w, Sir Desmond William Lionel Cable-Alexander, 7 Bt (d 1988); 2 da (Jacqueline (Mrs Dillon Godfrey Welchman) b 1942, Susan (Mrs Richard Humphrey Hardwicke) b 1948); *Style—* Margaret, Lady Cable-Alexander; Denne Park House, Horsham, W Sussex

CABLE-ALEXANDER, Lt-Col Sir Patrick Desmond William; 8 Bt (UK 1809), of the City of Dublin; s of Sir Desmond William Lionel Cable-Alexander, 7 Bt (d 1988), and his 1 w Mary Jane, *née* O'Brien; *b* 19 April 1936; *Educ* Downside, RMA Sandhurst; *m* 1, 1961 (m dis 1976), Diana Frances, eld da of late Col Paul Heberden Rogers, of Bushey, Herts; 2 da (Melanie Jane b 1963, Louise Fenella b 1967); m 2, 1976, Jane Mary, da of Dr Anthony Arthur Gough Lewis, MD, of Benson, Oxon; 1 s (Fergus William Antony b 1981); *Heir* s, Fergus William Antony Cable-Alexander b 19 June 1981; *Career* former Lt-Col Royal Scots Dragoon Guards (Carabiniers and Greys), cmmnd 1956, serv BAOR, UK, Aden, Army Staff Coll 1967, asst mil attaché Saigon 1968-70, BAOR, MOD, Nat Def Coll 1975-76, cmd Duke of Lancaster's Own Yeo 1978-80, COS HQ NW Dist 1981-83, ret 1984; bursar and clerk Cncl Lancing Coll 1984-; *Recreations* the arts, painting, gardening, cricket, reading; *Style—* Lt-Col Sir Patrick Cable-Alexander; Windrush House, Hoe Court, Lancing, W Sussex BN15 0QX

CABORN, Richard George; MP (Lab) Sheffield Central 1983-, MEP (Lab) Sheffield 1979-; s of George and Mary Caborn; *b* 6 Oct 1943; *Educ* Hurlfield Comprehensive Sch, Granville Coll of Further Education, Sheffield Polytechnic; *m* 1966, Margaret; 1 s, 1 da; *Career* engineer; convenor of shop stewards Firth Brown Ltd 1967-79; *Style—* Richard Caborn, Esq, MP, MEP; 29 Quarry Vale Rd, Sheffield (☎ 0742 393802); office: 54 Pinstone St, Sheffield S1 2HN (☎ 0742 737947)

CABOT, (Richard) Murray de Quetteville; s of Dr Philippe Sidney de Quetteville Cabot, of Totnes, Devon; *b* 20 June 1936; *Educ* Dartington Hall, Emmanuel Coll Cambridge (BA); *m* 1960, Janet, da of James MacGibbon, of Manningtree; 1 s, 2 da; *Career* vice chm W & A Gilbey Ltd 1976-82; dir IDV Export Ltd 1976-82, dir mktg London Business Sch 1982-85; asst vice pres Brown-Forman Int Ltd 1985-; Freeman Worshipful Co of Distillers; *Recreations* tennis, sailing, skiing; *Clubs* Royal Harwich Yacht, MCC, The Globe; *Style—* Murray Cabot, Esq; 44 Courthope Rd, London NW3 2LD (☎ 071 485 2755, work 071 323 9332)

CACCIA, Hon Mrs (Antonia Catherine); yr da of Baron Caccia, GCMG, GCVO (Life Peer, d 1990), and Anne Catherine, *née* Barstow; has resumed her maiden name; *b* 25 Feb 1947; *m* 1970 (m dis 1974), Barton Midwood, 1 s (Jacob b 1972); *Style—* The Hon Mrs Caccia; 21 Westwood Rd, Barnes, SW13

CACOYANNIS, Michael; s of Sir Panayotis Cacoyannis (d 1980), and Angeliki, *née* Efthyvoulou (d 1982); *b* 11 June 1922; *Educ* Greek Gymnasium Limassol Cyprus, Central Sch of Dramatic Art; *Career* director stage and screen; called to the Bar Gray's Inn 1943, actor on English stage 1946-51; dir films: Windfall in Athens 1954, Stella 1955, A Girl in Black 1956 (Golden Globe Award, Silver Bear Award), A Matter of Dignity 1958, Our Last Spring 1960, The Wastrel 1961, Electra 1962, Zorba the Greek 1964 (3 Oscars, Golden Globes), The Day The Fish Came Out 1967, The Trojan Women 1972, Attila '74 1975, Iphiqenia 1977, Sweet Country 1986; dir plays NY: The Trojan Women 1964, Things that go Bump in the Night 1965, The Devils 1966, Iphiqenia in Aulis 1968, Lysistrata 1972, The Bacchae 1980, Zorba (musical) 1985; dir Oedipus Rex (Abbey Theatre Dublin); dir plays Paris: The Trojan Women 1965, Romeo and Juliet 1968, 7 + 7 1970, The Bacchae 1977; dir plays Greece incl: Miss Marqarita 1975, The Glass Menagerie 1977, Antony and Cleopatra 1979, The Three Sisters 1981, Electra 1983, Naked 1989, Henceforward 1990; dir opera: Mourning Becomes Electra (Met Opera NY) 1967, La Boheme (Juilliard NY) 1972, Clemenza di Tito (Aix-en-Provence, Strasbourg, Orleans 1988-89), La Traviata (Greece) 1983, Iphiqenia in Aulis and in Tauris (Frankfurt State Opera) 1987; choreographed full length ballet to Theodorakis music (Greece) 1989; Order of Golden Phoenix (Greece) 1965, Commandeur Des Arts Et Des Lettres (France) 1986; Hon DUniv Columbia Coll Chicago 1975, hon citizen Limassol Cyprus 1976; *Publications* translations into Greek incl: Antony and Cleopatra, Hamlet, Coriolanus; translation into English of Euripides' The Bacchae; *Recreations* swimming, painting; *Style—* Michael Cacoyannis, Esq; 15 Mouson St, Athens, 117-41, Greece (☎ 301 9222054); 96 BD Montparnasse, Paris 75014, France (☎ 331 43354533)

CADBURY, Sir (George) Adrian Hayhurst; s of Laurence John Cadbury, OBE (d 1982), of Birmingham, and Joyce, *née* Mathews, OBE; *b* 15 April 1929; *Educ* Eton, King's Coll Cambridge (MA); *m* 1956, Gillian Mary, da of Edmund Drane Skepper (d 1962), of Neuilly-sur-Seine, France; 2 s, 1 da; *Career* chm: Cadbury Gp 1965-69, Cadbury Schweppes plc 1975-89 (dep chm and md 1969-74); dir: Bank of England 1970-, IBM (UK) Ltd 1975-; memb Covent Garden Market Authy 1974-89; chm: W Mids Econ Planning Ctee 1967-70, CBI Econ and Fin Policy Ctee 1974-80, Food and Drink Industs Cncl 1981-83; chllr Aston Univ 1979-; chm PRO NED (promotion of non-exec dirs) 1984-, pres Birmingham Chamber of Indust and Commerce 1988-89; Freeman City of Birmingham 1982; Hon DSc Aston Univ 1973, Hon DSc Cranfield 1985, Hon LLD Bristol 1986, Hon LLD Birmingham 1989; CBIM, FIPM, Hon FInstM; kt 1977; *Clubs* Athenaeum, Boodle's, Hawks, Leander; *Style—* Sir Adrian Cadbury; Rising Sun House, Baker's Lane, Knowle, Solihull, W Midlands B93 8PT (☎ 021 458 2000)

CADBURY, Kenneth Hotham; CBE (1974), MC (1944); s of Joel Hotham Cadbury, of Birmingham; bro of Michael Hotham Cadbury, *qv*; *b* 19 Feb 1919; *Educ* Bootham Sch York, Birmingham Univ; *m* 1, 1944 (m dis 1964), Margaret Rosamund King; 1 s, 1 da; m 2, Marjorie Iris Lille; 3 da; *Career* asst princ Post Office 1946, princ Cabinet Office 1950-53, sr dir Planning and Purchasing Post Office 1970, asst md Telecommunications 1976-; *Style—* Kenneth Cadbury, Esq, CBE, MC; Pendle, Burdenshott Hill, Worplesdon, Surrey (☎ 0483 2084)

CADBURY, Michael Hotham; DL (W Midlands 1975); s of Joel Hotham Cadbury, of Birmingham; bro of Kenneth Hotham Cadbury, *qv*; *b* 16 Dec 1915; *Educ* Leighton Park Sch Reading, Univs of Munich and Freiburg; *m* 1939, Margaret Heather, *née* Chambers; 2 s, 1 da; *Career* former dir Cadbury Bros Ltd; High Sheriff W Midlands 1974; memb Friends Ambulance Unit 1940-46, American Relief for France 1945-46, dir Friends Provident Life Office 1950-75, elected memb Cncl Nat Tst 1978-90, vice pres Birmingham Branch English Speaking Union 1975, pres Scout Assoc Birmingham 1981-90, tstee Selly Oak Colleges 1975, chm Friends of Birmingham Museum and Art Gallery 1983, Cncl Winston Churchill Memorial Tst 1975-90, pres Birmingham Assoc Youth Clubs 1987; Freeman City of London 1987; Gold medal Birmingham Civic Soc 1984; *Style—* Michael H Cadbury, Esq, DL; 54 Ramsden Close, Selly Oak, Birmingham B29 4JX

CADBURY, Peter Egbert; s of Sir Egbert Cadbury, DSC, DFC, JP, DL (d 1967), and Mary Forbes, *née* Phillips (d 1968); gs of George Cadbury, founder of Cadbury Bros, Bournville; *b* 6 Feb 1918; *Educ* Leighton Park Sch, Trinity Coll Cambridge (MA); *m* 1, 13 Dec 1947 (m dis 1968), (Eugenie) Benedicta, da of late Maj Ewen Cameron Bruce, DSO, MC, of Montpelier Gardens, Cheltenham, and former w of St John Donn-Byrne; 1 s (Justin Peter b 13 April 1951), 1 da ((Eugenie Mary) Felicity (Mrs Michael Wigan) b 14 Dec 1948); m 2, 1970 (m dis 1976), Jennifer Victoria (now Mrs Jennifer d'Abo, *qv*), da of Maj Michael William Vernon Hammond-Maude, of Amerdale House, Arncliffe, Yorks, and former w of Capt David Gwyn Morgan-Jones, The Life Guards; 1 s (Joel Michael b 28 July 1971); m 3, 1976, Angela Jane, *née* Thoyts, former w of Humphrey Mead, of Moyaux, Normandy; 2 s (George, James); *Career* experimental test pilot 1941-45; Parly candidate (Lib) Stroud 1945; called to the Bar Inner Temple 1946-54; exec chm of various cos: Keith Prowse Ltd, Ashton & Mitchell, Alfred Hays 1954-71, Westward TV 1960-80, Air Westward 1976-78, Prowest Ltd, Preston Estates, George Cadbury Trust 1979- (chm), Westward Travel Ltd 1981-84, Educational Video Index Ltd 1982-85; Freeman City of London 1946, Liveryman Worshipful Co of Curriers 1946; *Recreations* flying (Cessna 340 'G-Pete', Helicopter (Squirrell) 'G-Jany'), sailing (express 55' motor cruiser 'Colinette VI'), golf, tennis, shooting, travelling; owner of racehorses (Cool Million, Egbert, Westward Lad, Westward Ho); *Clubs* MCC, Buck's, Royal Motor Yacht, RAF Yacht, Island Sailing, The Acad, Special Forces, Hawks (Cambridge), Lords Taverner's; *Style—* Peter Cadbury, Esq; Armsworth Hill, Alresford, Hampshire SO24 9RJ (☎ 0962 734656, fax 0962 734757); 42 Cadogan Square, London SW1 (☎ 071 589 8755)

CADBURY, Peter Hugh George; 3 s of (John) Christopher Cadbury, of Beaconwood, Rednal, nr Birmingham, by his 1 w, Honor Mary, *née* Milward (d 1957); *b* 8 June 1943; *Educ* Rugby; *m* 1969, Sally, er da of Peter Frederick Strouvelle, of Cape Town, S Africa; 1 s (Simon b 1975), 1 da (Eleanor b 1973); *Career* slr; dir Morgan Grenfell, chm TR Smaller Companies Investment Trust plc, non-exec dir Cannon Lincoln plc; *Clubs* City of London; *Style—* Peter Cadbury, Esq; Morgan Grenfell & Co Ltd, 23 Great Winchester St, London EC2 (☎ 071 588 4545, fax 0962 734757)

CADDY, David Henry Arnold Courtenay; s of Colonel John Caddy, of Ivy House, Highgate Village, London N6, and Elizabeth, *née* Day; *b* 22 June 1944; *Educ* Eton; *m* 24 July 1971, Valerie Elizabeth Margaret, da of Dr Kelly Swanston, of Tillypronie, Mill Lane, Helmsley, N Yorks; 1 s (Julian b 1972), 1 da (Henrietta b 1978); *Career* articled to Layton Bennett Billingham and Co London 1962-68, CA 1968; Coopers & Lybrand Deloitte: joined 1968, ptnr Liberia 1974, managing ptnr Liberia 1974-77, ptnr UK 1977-; memb Ctee: London Soc of CAs 1980, ICAEW 1968-, ICA (Ghana) 1983-, Cncl of Partners Coopers Deloitte 1989, ICA (Nigeria) 1983-; *Recreations* golf, swimming, walking, reading, theatre; *Clubs* Boodle's, Leander; *Style—* David Caddy, Esq; Ivy House, Highgate Hill, London N6 5HD (☎ 081 340 9067); Coopers and Lybrand Deloitte, Harman House, 1 George St, Uxbridge UB8 1QA (☎ 0895 73305, fax 0895 56413, car 0860 710730, telex 887470)

CADE, David Patrick Gordon; s of Richard William Poole Cade, of Lyme Regis, Devon, and Mabel, *née* Lamb; *b* 17 Nov 1942; *Educ* The Leys Sch, Queens' Coll Univ of Cambridge (MA); *m* 18 June 1966, Julia Christine, da of Cdr William Percy Cooper, OBE, of Guildford, Surrey; 2 da (Heather b 1969, Angela b 1973); *Career* ptnr Arthur Andersen & Co Chartered Accountants 1976-; FICA 1967; *Recreations* sailing, music; *Clubs* RAC; *Style—* David Cade, Esq

CADELL, Alan Henry; s of Lt-Col John George Cadell, DSO (d 1950), of South Ct, Finchamstead, Berks, and Muddlebridge Hse, Fremington, Barnstaple, Devon, and Clara Margaret Annie, *née* Hunt (d 1963); *b* 2 Feb 1926; *Educ* Marlborough, Clare Coll Cambridge; *m* 27 Aug 1960, Valentine Frances, da of Charles Ernest St John Evers, OBE, of Bell Cottage, Bury Gate, nr Pulborough, Sussex; 1 s (Andrew b July 1966), 1 da (Iona b Feb 1969); *Career* Lt The Royal Scots 1945-48; trainee accountant McClelland Kerr 1950, CA 1952, Peat Marwick Mitchell & Co 1952-55 (a year spent in Singapore), Scruttons plc 1955-86 (fin dir 1971-86); Freeman City of London, Liveryman of the Worshipful Co of Gunmakers 1966; *Recreations* shooting, dog handling, beagling, sailing; *Clubs* Utd Oxford and Cambridge, Keyhaven Yacht; *Style—* Alan Cadell, Esq; Heatherside, Bennetts Lane, Burley, nr Ringwood, Hants BH24 4AT

CADELL, Air Cdre Colin Simson; CBE (1944); s of late Lt-Col John Macfarlane Cadell, DL, JP, of Foxhall, Kirkliston, W Lothian, and Avoncrook, Stirling; *b* 7 Aug 1905; *Educ* Merchiston, Univ of Edinburgh, Ecole Supérieur de l'Electricité Paris (MA, AMIEE); *m* 1939, Rosemary Elizabeth, da of Thomas Edward Pooley, of Victoria, BC, Canada; 2 s (*see* Ian Victor Cadell), 1 da; *Career* Air Cdre RAF, ret; md International Aeradio Ltd 1947-58, chm Edinburgh Airport Consultative Ctee 1972-83; DL Linlithgowshire 1963-82, Vice Lieut W Lothian 1972-82; memb Royal Co of Archers (HM The Queen's Body Guard for Scotland); Legion of Merit (USA) 1943;

Clubs New Club; *Style*— Air Cdre Colin Cadell, CBE; 2 Upper Coltbridge Terrace, Edinburgh EH12 6AD

CADELL, Ian Victor; s of Air Cdre Colin S Cadell, CBE, *qv*; *b* 3 July 1940; *Educ* Eton; *m* 11 Oct 1966, Teresa, da of Philip German-Ribon; 2 s (Piers b 1970, Charlie b 1978), 2 da (Olivia b 1968, Lucy b 1981); *Career* chm: MCP Group; memb Royal Co of Archers (The Queen's Body Guard for Scot); *Clubs* New (Edinburgh); *Style*— Ian Cadell, Esq; MCP Group, Alperton, Wembley, Middx HA0 4PE (☎ 081 902 1191)

CADELL, Vice Adm Sir John Frederick; s of Henry Dunlop Mallock Cadell (d 1936), of York, and Elizabeth, *née* Vandyke (d 1989), of Faversham; *b* 6 Dec 1929; *Educ* BRNC Dartmouth, RNC Greenwich; *m* 15 Feb 1958, Jaquetta Bridget, da of Paterick Gould Nolan (d 1968); 1 s (Charles Henry b 1965), 2 da (Caroline Elizabeth b 1959, Alexandra Jane b 1961); *Career* Capt 3 Frigate Sqdn 1975, DG Naval Personal Servs 1980, COS to Cdr Naval Forces South 1982; dist and gen mangr Canterbury & Thanet Authy 1986; *Recreations* skiing, tennis, chess; *Style*— Vice Adm Sir John Cadell; Great Mongeham House, nr Deal, Kent CT14 0HD (☎ 0304 373658); Canterbury & Thanet Health Authority, Regency Buildings, Ramsgate, Kent CT11 9PF (☎ 0843 594592)

CADELL OF GRANGE, William Archibald; DL (W Lothian 1982); eld s of Col Henry Moubray Cadell, OBE, RE (d 1967), HM Lord-Lt for W Lothian 1952-64, and Christina Rose, *née* Nimmo; descended from William Cadell, burgess of Haddington, b 1668 and sr rep of the family of Cadell of Grange and Banton and formerly of Banton and Cockenzie; *b* 9 March 1933; *Educ* Merchiston, Trinity Coll Cambridge (MA), London Poly (Dip Arch); *m* 1960, Mary-Jean, da of Cdr Arthur Harold Carmichael, RN, of Gozo, Malta; 3 s (John, Patrick, Benjamin); *Career* architect in private practice with related occupation of estate mgmnt; RIBA, FRIAS; *Style*— William Cadell of Grange, DL; Grange, Linlithgow, W Lothian EH49 7RH (☎ 0506 842946)

CADMAN, 3 Baron (1937 UK); John Anthony Cadman; s of 2 Baron Cadman (d 1966); *b* 3 July 1938; *Educ* Harrow, Selwyn Coll Cambridge, RAC Cirencester; *m* 1975, Janet, da of Arthur Hayes, of Morecambe; 2 s Hon Giles Oliver Richard b 5 Feb 1979); *Heir* s Hon Nicholas Anthony James Cadman b 18 Nov 1977; *Career* farmer; *Style*— The Rt Hon The Lord Cadman; Heathcourt House, Ironmould Lane, Brislington, Bristol, Avon BS4 5RS (☎ 0272 775706)

CADMAN, Kenneth John; o s of Herbert Cadman (d 1957), and Phyllis, *née* Knaggs (d 1990); nephew of 1 Baron Cadman; *b* 31 Aug 1925; *Educ* Berkhamsted Sch, Queens Univ Belfast (BSc); *m* 1, 12 March 1953, Marie, da of David R Bates, JP; 1 s (James b 1964), 1 da (Janet b 1960); m 2, 23 May 1980, Inger, da of Dr Med Erik Mogensen (d 1957); *Career* flying offr RAF WWII; dir Robert M Douglas Holdings plc 1978-88, md Rapid Metal Developments Ltd, ret 1988; MICE; *Recreations* gliding; *Clubs* Priory Tennis, Coventry Gliding (pres), Edgbaston Golf; *Style*— Kenneth J Cadman, Esq; 27 Barlows Rd, Edgbaston, Birmingham 15 (☎ 021 455 7433); Rapid Metal Developments Ltd, Stubbers Green Rd, Aldridge, Staffs (☎ 0922 743 743)

CADMAN, Marjorie, Baroness; Marjorie Elizabeth; *née* Bunnis; da of Byron William Bunnis; *m* 1936, 2 Baron Cadman (d 1966); 2 s (3 Baron, Hon James Cadman); *Style*— The Rt Hon Marjorie, Lady Cadman; Overlands, 157 Church Rd, Combe Down, Bath, Somerset

CADMAN, Hon Mrs (Sybil Mary); yr da of 1 Baron Cadman, GCMG, FRS (d 1941); *b* 1916; *m* 1, 1938, Maj-Gen William Pat Arthur Bradshaw, CB, DSO, late Scots Gds (d 1966), s of Arthur Bradshaw; 3 s, 2 da; m 2, 1968, as his 2 w, her 1 cousin, James Simon Cadman (d 1986), o son of James Cadman, DSC, JP, DL (d 1947), of Walton Hall, Staffs; *Style*— The Hon Mrs Cadman; Bryn-Dedwydd, Maerdy, Corwen, Clwyd LL21 9NY

CADOGAN, Col Henry Michael Edward; OBE (1986); s of Col Edward H Cadogan, CBE, of Sway, Lymington, Hampshire, and Lady Mary Veronica, *née* Lambart (d 1989); *b* 18 Jan 1935; *Educ* Winchester, RMA Sandhurst, Staff Coll Camberley; *m* 17 Dec 1966, Daphne Jane Richards, da of H Ashley Mason (d 1956); 1 s (Edward b 2 March 1970), 1 da (Camilla b 4 Nov 1968); *Career* ammnd RWF 1955, (Vol) Bn RWF 1978-80, def naval mil and air attaché Damascus and Beirut, mil advsr to Min of Def UAE and sr Br liaison offr 1985-87, ret 1990; Hon Col 3rd (Vol) Bn RWF 1989; schs liaison offr N Wales dist 1990-, chm Clwyd N Wales Appeal Ctee of Army Benevolent Fund; *Recreations* sailing, shooting; *Clubs* Army and Navy; *Style*— Col Henry Cadogan; Fron Isaf, Pentrecelyn, Ruthin, Clwyd LL15 2HR (☎ 097 888 651)

CADOGAN, Peter William; s of Archibald Douglas Cadogan (d 1947), of Newcastle upon Tyne, and Audrey, *née* Wannop (d 1978); *b* 26 Jan 1921; *Educ* King's Sch Tynemouth, King's Coll Newcastle upon Tyne, University of Newcastle upon Tyne (BA, Dip Ed); *m* 1949 (m dis 1969), Joyce, da of late William Stones, MP for Consett; 1 da (Claire b 1950); *Career* WWII, Coxswain RAF Air Sea Rescue Serv served Orkneys D Day, Arnhem 1941-46; with Atlas Assurance Co Ltd 1936-40, undergraduate 1946-51; history teacher: Kettering 1951-53, Cambridge 1953-65; sec Nat Ctee of 100 1965-68, fndn sec Save Biafra Campaign 1968-70, gen sec South Place Ethical Soc 1970-81; extra mural lectr Univ of London 1981-; fndr E W Peace People 1978, co-chm Anglo-Afghan circle 1986, memb Cncl of the Gandhi Fndn, chm Blake Soc 1989; *Books* Early Radical Newcastle (1975), Direct Democracy (1976), writer of many acad and polemical papers; *Recreations* gardening, social invention; *Style*— Peter Cadogan, Esq; 3 Hinchinbrook House, Greville Rd, London NW6 5UP (☎ 071 328 3709)

CADOGAN, 7 Earl (1800 GB) William Gerald Charles Cadogan; MC (1943), DL (County of London 1958); also Baron Cadogan of Oakley (GB 1718), Viscount Chelsea (GB 1800), and Baron Oakley of Caversham (UK 1831); s of 6 Earl (d 1933), and Lilian (d 1973), *née* Coxon, who m 2, 1941, Lt-Col H E Hambro; the name Cadogan, of Welsh origin, was spelt Cadwgan to *c* 1600; *b* 13 Feb 1914; *Educ* Eton, Sandhurst; *m* 1, 1936 (m dis 1959), Hon Primrose Yarde-Buller, da of 3 Baron Churston and sis of Viscountess Camrose, Denise Lady Ebury (ex-w of 5 Baron) and Lydia, Duchess of Bedford (ex-w of 13 Duke); 1 s, 3 da; m 2, 1961, Cecilia, da of Lt-Col Henry K Hamilton-Wedderburn, OBE; *Heir* s, Viscount Chelsea; *Career* Capt Coldstream Guards (ret), Lt Col Royal Wiltshire Yeomanry (TA); patron of four livings; pro grand master of United Grand Lodge of Freemasons 1969-82; landowner, Mayor of Chelsea 1964, chm Cadogan Estates Ltd and subsidiaries 1935-; *Style*— The Rt Hon the Earl Cadogan, MC, DL; 28 Cadogan Sq, London SW3 2RP (☎ 071 730 4567); Snaigow, Dunkeld, Perthshire (☎ 073 871 223)

CADWALLADER, Anthony Robin; s of F A Cadwallader, and M K Cadwallader, *née* Stone; *b* 16 June 1944; *Educ* King Edward II GS Lichfield; *m* 26 May 1973, Mary Gwendoline, da of Rev Kenneth C Sawyer (d 1986); 1 s (Martin Anthony b 1976), 1 da (Tina Mary b 1974); *Career* md Cadwallader Ltd 1971-; dir: Cadwallader (Metal Fittings) Ltd 1979-, Dragon Merchandising Ltd past pres Midland Reg Assoc of Shopfitters, exec memb Nat Assoc of Shopfitters; ACIS, FIOS; *Recreations* family, computer programming; *Style*— Anthony Cadwallader, Esq; 119 Beacon Street, Lichfield, Staffs WS13 7BG (☎ 0543 254494); Cadwallader Ltd, 400 Aldridge Rd, Perry Barr, Birmingham B44 8BJ (☎ 021 356 6211, fax 021 3566212)

CAESAR, Rev Canon Anthony Douglass; LVO (1987); s of Rev Canon Harold Douglass Caesar (d 1961), and Winifred Kathleen Caesar; *b* 3 April 1924; *Educ* Cranleigh Sch, Magdalene Coll Cambridge (MA, MusB), St Stephen's House Oxford; *Career* Flying Offr RAF 1943-46; asst music master Eton 1948-51, precentor Radley 1952-59, asst curate St Mary Abbots Kensington 1961-65, asst sec ACCM 1965-70, chaplain Royal Sch of Church Music 1965-70, dep priest-in-ordinary to HM The Queen 1967-68 (priest-in-ordinary 1968-70), resident priest St Stephen's Church Bournemouth 1970-73, precentor and sacrist Winchester 1974-79, (residentiary canon 1976-79, hon canon 1979-); sub dean of HM Chapels Royal, dep clerk of the Closet and sub-almoner, domestic chaplain to HM The Queen 1979-; FRCO; *Style*— The Rev Canon Anthony Caesar, LVO; Marlborough Gate, St James's Palace, London SW1 (☎ 071 930 6609)

CAFFYN, Robert James Morris; s of Sir Sydney Morris Caffyn, CBE (d 1976), and Annie, *née* Dawson (d 1989); *b* 1 June 1935; *Educ* Eastbourne Coll, Peterhouse Cambridge (MA); *m* 1961, Gillian Mabel Ann, *née* Bailey; 1 s, 2 da; *Career* jt md Caffyns plc 1972-; hon treas: Free Church Federal Cncl 1976-82, Br Cncl of Churches 1982-; FCA; *Style*— Robert Caffyn, Esq; Field House, Old Willingdon Rd, Friston, nr Eastbourne, E Sussex (☎ 032 15 3100)

CAHILL, Christina Tracy; *née* Boxer; da of Raymond Walter Boxer, and Joan Eleanor, *née* Almond; *b* 25 March 1957; *Educ* Yateley Comprehensive, Loughborough Univ of Technol (BSc, PGCE); *m* 27 Sept 1986, Séan Cahill, s of Robert Cahill, of Leeds; *Career* middle distance runner, Cwlth Games 1982 Gold Medallist 1500m, Olympic Games 1984 6 place 1500m, Europa Cup 1985 Silver Medallist 1500m, Olympic Games 1988 4 place 1500m; formerly Br record holder: 800m, 1500, mile; hon life memb Br Sports Assoc for the Disabled, Cwlth Games 1990 Silver Medallist 1500m, former ministers' nominee for Northern Sports Cncl; *Recreations* athletics, gardening, birdwatching, walking, countryside pubs; *Clubs* Gateshead Harriers; *Style*— Mrs Christina Cahill

CAHILL, John Conway; s of Francis Conway Cahill (d 1969), of London, and Dorothy Winifred, *née* Mills; *b* 8 Jan 1930; *Educ* St Pauls; *m* 5 July 1956, Giovanna Caterina (Vanna), da of Riccardo Lenardon (d 1972), of Valvasone, Italy; 3 da (Karen Lavina b 5 May 1961, Ann Catherine b 6 Dec 1963, Mary Elizabeth b 24 March 1965); *Career* Nat Serv 1948-50; BTR Industs Ltd: joined 1955, dep overseas gen mangr 1963, dir 1968, dep md 1975, vice pres BTR Inc USA 1976, pres and chief exec BTR Inc 1976, chm BTR Pan American Ops 1979, chief exec BTR plc 1987-90; *Recreations* tennis, reading, walking, music; *Style*— John Cahill, Esq; BIR Inc, 1000, 1 Main Place, 750 Main St, Stamford, Connecticut 06901 FOREIGN (☎ 0101 203 352 0001)

CAHILL, Michael Leo; s of John Cahill, MBE (d 1980), and Josephine, *née* Bergonzi (d 1964); *b* 4 April 1928; *Educ* Beaumont Coll, Magdalen Coll Oxford (MA); *m* 1961, Harriette Emma Clemency, da of Christopher Gilbert Eastwood, CMG (d 1983), of Oxfordshire; 2 da (Lydia b 1964, Jessica b 1967); *Career* civil servant FO Colonial Office and Overseas Devpt Admin; UK permanent delegate to UNESCO 1972-74, head of Central and Southern Africa Dept, overseas devpt admin 1983-88; chm Woldingham Sch Parents' Assoc 1981-83; *Recreations* history of art, pianism; *Style*— Michael M Cahill, Esq; 9 Murray Rd, London SW19 4PD (☎ 081 947 0568)

CAHILL, Teresa Mary; da of Henry Daniel Cahill, of Rotherhithe (d 1948), and Florence, *née* Dallimore (d 1964); *b* 30 July 1944; *Educ* Notre Dame HS Southwark, Guildhall Sch of Music & Drama, London Opera Centre; *m* 1971 (m dis 1978), John Anthony Kiernander; *Career* opera and concert singer; Glyndebourne debut 1969, Covent Garden debut 1970, La Scala Milan 1976, Philadelphia Opera 1981, specialising in Mozart & Strauss; concerts: all the London orchestras, Boston Symphony Orch, Chicago Symphony Orch, Vienna Festival 1983, Berlin Festival 1987, Rotterdam Philharmonic 1984, Hamburg Philharmonic 1985, West Deutscher Rundfunk Cologne 1985; promenade concerts BBC Radio & TV; recordings incl Elgar, Strauss and Mahler for all major cos; recitals and concerts throughout Europe, USA and the Far East; Silver medal Worshipful Co of Musicians, John Christie award 1970; AGSM, LRAM; *Recreations* cinema, theatre, travel, reading, collecting antique furniture; *Clubs* Royal Over-Seas League; *Style*— Miss Teresa Cahill; 65 Leyland Rd, London SE12 8DW

CAHN, Sir Albert Jonas; 2 Bt (UK 1934), of Stanford-upon-Soar, Co Nottingham; s of Sir Julien Cahn, 1 Bt (d 1944); *b* 27 June 1924; *Educ* Harrow; *m* 1948, Malka, da of Reuben Bluestone (d 1961); 2 s, 2 da; *Heir* s, Julien Cahn; *Career* clinical dir The Elm Therapy Centre, New Malden, Surrey; *Style*— Sir Albert Cahn, Bt; 10 Edgecombe Close, Warren Rd, Kingston upon Thames, Surrey (☎ 081 942 6956)

CAHN, Julien Michael; s and h of Sir Albert Cahn, 2 Bt; *b* 15 Jan 1951; *Educ* Harrow; *Style*— Julien Cahn, Esq

CAILLARD, Air Vice-Marshal (Hugh) Anthony; CB (1981); s of Col Felix Caillard, MC (d 1955), and Monica Yoland, yr da of Count Riccardi-Cubitt; *b* 16 April 1927; *Educ* Downside, Oriel Coll Oxford, RAF Coll Cranwell; *m* 20 Aug 1957, Margaret Ann, da of late Kenneth Malcolm Crawford, of Palm Beach, NSW, Australia; 4 s (Richard b 1958, Andrew b 1959, Davi 1961, John b 1963); *Career* RAF 1945-82, ret as dir of Ops Central Region Air Forces NATO; dir gen Br Australia Soc 1982-89; air advsr House of Commons Defence Ctee 1985; chm: Ex-Servs Fellowship Centres 1987, Ex-Servs Mental Welfare Soc 1990; memb Grants and Appeals Ctee RAF Benevolent Fund 1990; *Recreations* gardening, travel; *Clubs* RAF; *Style*— Air Vice-Marshal Anthony Caillard, CB; 114 Ashley Rd, Walton on Thames KT12 1HW

CAIN, John Clifford; s of William John Cain (d 1940), and Florence Jessie, *née* Wood (d 1975); *b* 2 April 1924; *Educ* Emanuel Sch, Univ of London (BSc, MSc), Open Univ (BA); *m* 1954, Shirley Jean, da of Edward Arthur Roberts, of Amblecote, Brierley Hill, W Midlands; 2 da (Charlotte, Susannah); *Career* RAF Aircrew Flt Sgt 1943-47; mathematics and sci teacher 1950-59, sci museum lectr 1959-61, asst head Sch of Bdcasting Assoc Rediffusion 1961-63, prodr and sr prodr BBC 1963-71, asst head Further Educn Television BBC 1971-72 (head 1972-77), asst controller Educnl Broadcasting 1977-80, controller Public Affrs BBC 1981-84, res historian BBC 1984-; Bdcasting Support Servs: chm 1980-85 tstee 1980-89, hon vice pres 1989-; memb Health Educn Cncl 1977-83, dir Bdcasters Audience Res Bd 1982-84; memb: Royal Television Soc, BAFTA; FRSA; *Books* Talking Machines (1961), Mathematics Miscellany (jtly, 1966), Culture, Education and the State (1988), numerous articles and reviews; *Recreations* reading, music, gardening, theatre, study; *Style*— John Cain, Esq; 63 Park Rd, London W4 3EY (☎ 081 994 2712); BBC Bdcasting House, London W1 (☎ 071 927 4956)

CAIN, (Thomas) William; QC (1989); s of James Arthur Cain (d 1956), of IOM, and Mary Edith Cunningham Robertson, *née* Lamb (d 1965); *b* 1 June 1935; *Educ* Marlborough, Worcester Coll Oxford (BA, MA); *m* 25 Nov 1961, Felicity Jane, da of Rev Arthur Stephen Gregory (d 1989); 2 s (Patrick Arthur b 18 June 1964, Simon Thomas Hugh b 10 July 1966), 1 da (Joanna Penelope b 14 Jan 1963); *Career* Nat Serv RAC 1953-55, cmmnd 2 Lt 1954, served Middle East 1954-55; called to the Bar Gray's Inn 1959, advocate Manx Bar with TW Cain & Sons Douglas IOM 1961-79, HM Attorney Gen IOM 1980-; pres IOM Law Soc 1985-89, chm Manx Nature Conservation Tst 1973-, pres Friends of Manx Youth Orchestra; *Recreations* sailing; *Clubs* Ellan Vannin; *Style*— William Cain, Esq, QC; Ivie Cottage, Kirk Michael, IOM (☎ 0624 878 266); Attorney General's Chambers, Government Office, Douglas IOM (☎ 0624 26 262 ext 2000)

CAINE, Francesca Mary; da of David Campbell Thomas, of Radcliffe-on-Trent, and

Doris, *née* Hunter; *b* 12 Dec 1956; *Educ* Nottingham HS for Girls, Churchill Coll Cambridge (MA); *m* 11 June 1988, Philip Michael Caine, s of Charles William Caine (d 1962), of Douglas, IOM; 1 da (Eleanor b 1989); *Career* mangr SCYP and Magazine Progs BBC Radio 1988-91, admin mangr Toshiba Europe 1991-; *Recreations* singing, music, house renovation; *Style—* Mrs Francesca Caine; Toshiba Corporation, Europe Office, Audrey House, Ely Place, London EC1N 6SN (☎ 071 242 7295, fax 071 405 1489, telex 894906 TSBLDN G)

CAINE, Michael (né Maurice Joseph Micklewhite); s of late Maurice Micklewhite, and Ellen Frances Marie Micklewhite; *b* 14 March 1933; *Educ* Wilson's GS Peckham; *m* 1, 1955 (m dis), Patricia Haines; 1 da; m 2, 1973, Shakira Baksh; 1 da; *Career* actor in TV, theatre, films; *Style—* Michael Caine, Esq; Dennis Selinger, ICM, 388-396 Oxford St, London W1N 9HE

CAINE, Sir Michael Harris; o s of Sir Sydney Caine, KCMG (d 1991), and his 1 w, Muriel Ann, *née* Harris (d 1962); *b* 17 June 1927; *Educ* Bedales Sch, Lincoln Coll Oxford (BA), George Washington Univ Washington DC; *m* 1, 30 Aug 1952 (m dis 1987), Janice Denise, *née* Mercer; 1 s (Richard Jonathan Harris b 24 Nov 1955), 1 da (Amanda b 7 Feb 1954); m 2, 9 May 1987, Emma Harriet Nicholson, MP (*qv*), da of Sir Godfrey Nicholson, 1 Bt; *Career* RNAS 1945-47; chm Booker plc 1979- (joined 1952, dir 1964, chief exec 1975-79); chm: Mgmnt Ctee Booker Prize for Fiction 1972-, Cncl for Tech Educn and Trg for Overseas Countries (TETOC) 1973-75, UK Cncl for Overseas Student Affrs 1979-86, Cncl Royal African Soc 1984-, Cwlth Scholarship Cmmn in UK 1987-, The One World Bdcasting Tst 1987-; dep chm Cwlth Devpt Corp 1989- (dir 1985-), The Cwlth Equity Fund 1990-; memb: Governing Body Inst of Devpt Studies Sussex 1975, Nat Inst of Econ and Social Res 1979-, Queen Elizabeth House Oxford 1983-, IBA 1984-89; CBIM, FRSA; kt 1988; *Recreations* reading, gardening; *Clubs* Reform; *Style—* Sir Michael Caine; c/o Booker plc, Portland House, Stag Place, London SW1E 5AY (☎ 071 828 9850, fax 071 630 8029, telex 888169)

CAIRD, John Newport; s of late Rev George Bradford Caird and Viola Mary, *née* Newport; *b* 22 Sept 1948; *Educ* Selwyn House Sch Montreal, Magdalen Coll Sch Oxford, Bristol Old Vic Theatre Sch; *m* 1, 1972 (m dis 1982), Helen Frances Brammer; m 2, 1982 (m dis 1990), Ann Dorzynski; 2 s, 1 da; m 3, 1990, Frances Ruffelle; 1 s 1 da; *Career* theatre director; assoc dir Contact Theatre Manchester 1974-76: Look Back in Anger, Downright Hooligan, Twelfth Night; resident dir RSC 1977-82: Dance of Death 1977, Savage Amusement 1978, Look Out Here Comes Trouble 1978, Caucasian Chalk Circle 1979, Nicholas Nickleby (co-dir with Trevor Nunn in London, NY and Los Angeles) 1980, 1982 and 1986, Naked Robots 1981, Twin Rivals 1981, Our Friends in the North 1982, Pete Pan (co-dir with Trevor Nunn) 1982-84, Twelfth Night 1983, Romeo and Juliet 1983, The Merchant of Venice 1984, Red Star 1984, Philistines 1985, Les Miserables (co-dir with Trevor Nunn in London, Washington, NY, Boston, Oslo, LA, Tokyo and Sydney) 1985-88, Every Man in His Humour 1986, Misalliance 1986, A Question of Geography 1987, The New Inn 1987, As You Like it 1989, A Midsummer Night's Dream 1989; dir: Song and Dance (London) 1982, As You Like It (Stockholm) 1984 (also for TV, 1985), Siegfried & Roy Show (Las Vegas) 1989; script writer: Beethoven, The Kingdom of the Spirit (a concert for a actor and string quartet) 1986, Children of Eden (with music and lyrics by Stephen Schuwartz) 1991; *Awards* (for Nicholas Nickleby) SWET award 1980 and Tony award for Best Director 1982, (for Les Miserables) Tony award for Best Director 1986 and 1987; *Style—* John Caird, Esq; 3rd Floor, Gloucester Mansions, Cambridge Circus, London WC2H 8HD (☎ 071 240 0027, fax 071 240 1945)

CAIRNCROSS, Sir Alexander Kirkland (Alec); KCMG (1967, CMG 1950); 3 s of Alexander Kirkland Cairncross (d 1948), of Lesmahagow, Lanark, and Elizabeth Andrew Cairncross; *b* 11 Feb 1911; *Educ* Hamilton Acad, Univ of Glasgow, Univ of Cambridge (PhD); *m* 1943, Mary Frances, da of Maj Edward Francis Glynn, TD (d 1948), of Ilkley; 3 s, 2 da; *Career* econ advsr to HM Govt 1961-64, head Govt Econ Serv 1964-69; master St Peter's Coll Oxford 1969-78, chllr Univ of Glasgow 1972-; *Recreations* travelling, writing; *Style—* Sir Alec Cairncross, KCMG; 14 Staverton Rd, Oxford (☎ 0865 52358)

CAIRNCROSS, Neil Francis; CB (1971); s of James Cairncross (d 1964), and Olive Hunter, *née* Amner (d 1969); *b* 29 July 1920; *Educ* Charterhouse, Oriel Coll Oxford (MA); *m* 26 July 1947, Eleanor Elizabeth, da of Herbert Walter Leisten (d 1927); 2 s (Ian b 1950, David b 1951), 1 da (Julia (Mrs Pearce) b 1948); *Career* serv in Royal Sussex Regt 1940-45; called to the Bar Lincoln's Inn 1948; joined Home Office 1948, a private sec to Prime Minister 1955-58, sec Royal Cmmn on the Press 1961-62, dep sec Cabinet Office 1970-72, dep sec NI Office 1972, dep under sec of state Home Office 1972-80; memb: Parole Bd 1982-85, Home Grown Timber Advsy Ctee 1981-90, Avon Probation Ctee (co-opted) 1983-89; *Recreations* painting; *Clubs* Utd Oxford and Cambridge Univ; *Style—* Neil Cairncross, Esq, CB; Little Grange, The Green, Olveston, Bristol BS12 3EJ (☎ 0454 613060)

CAIRNES, (Simon) Paul Steven; s of Edward Michael Hornby Cairnes, and Audrey Mary, *née* Stevens; *b* 19 Dec 1957; *Educ* UCW Aberyswyth (LLB), Christ Coll Brelon; *m* 6 July 1985 (m dis 1989), Elizabeth Gaynor, da of Llew Hughes, of Aberyswyth; *Career* called to the Bar Gray's Inn 1980 (NSW Aust 1989); memb Barrs Euro Gp 1989; *Recreations* sailing, music, travelling, socialising; *Clubs* RAC; *Style—* Paul Cairnes, Esq; Francis Taylor Bldg, Temple, London EC4Y 7BY (☎ 071 353 2182, fax 071 583 1727)

CAIRNS, Hon (Hugh) Andrew David; yr s of 5 Earl Cairns, GCVO, CB (d 1989); *b* 27 Aug 1942; *Educ* Wellington, Trinity Coll Dublin (BA); *m* 1966, (Celia) Elizabeth Mary, da of Lt-Col Francis Cecil Leonard Bell, DSO, MC, TD, of Cross Glades, Chiddingfold, Surrey; 1 s, 1 da; *Career* banker; regnl dir Barclays Bank plc; dir United Services Tstee; *Recreations* shooting, fishing, golf; *Clubs* Pratt's, Royal St George's Golf; *Style—* The Hon Andrew Cairns; Knowle Hill Farm, Ulcombe, nr Maidstone, Kent (☎ 0622 850240)

CAIRNS, Dowager Countess; Barbara Jeanne Harrison; yst da of late Sydney Harrisson Burgess, of Heathfield, Bowden, Cheshire; *m* 1936, Rear Adm 5 Earl Cairns, GCVO, CB (d 1989); 2 s (6 Earl, Hon (Hugh) Andrew David, *qqv*), 1 da (Lady Elisabeth Lowe, *qv*); *Style—* The Rt Hon the Dowager Countess Cairns; The Red House, Clopton, Woodbridge, Suffolk

CAIRNS, David Howard; s of David Lauder Cairns, of Mulberry Rd, Birmingham, and Edith, *née* Rose; *b* 4 June 1946; *Educ* Cheadle Hulme Sch, LSE (MSc); *m* 1 May 1980, Stella Jane, da of Stanley Cecil Askew, DSO, DFC; *Career* CA; Pannell Kerr Forster 1964-71, Carlsberg Brewery Ltd 1971-72, Black & Decker Ltd 1972-75, PD Leake fell LSE 1973-75, ptnr Stoy Hayward 1975-85, sec gen Int Accounting Standards Ctee 1985-; pres Thames Valley Soc CA's 1979-80; FCA 1974 (ACA), FBIM 1982; *Books* Current Cost Accounting after Sandilands (1976), Financial Times Survey of 100 Major European Companies Reports and Accounts (1979), Financial Times World Survey of Annual Reports (1980), Survey of Accounts and Accountants (1983-84); *Recreations* cricket, cycling, music; *Clubs* RAC; *Style—* David Cairns, Esq; Bramblewood, Turville Heath, Henley-on-Thames, Oxon RG9 6JY (☎ 049 163 296); International Accounting Standards Committee, 41 Kingsway, London WC2B 6YU (☎ 071 240 8781, fax 071 379 0048, telex 295177

CAIRNS, The Hon Mrs Andrew Cairns (Cecilia) Elizabeth Mary; da of Lt-Col Francis Cecil Leonard Bell, DSO, MC, TD, of Cross Glades, Chiddingfold, Surrey, and Mary Wynne, *née* Jacob; *b* 14 Sept 1943; *Educ* Priors Field Godalming Surrey, Trinity Coll Dublin (BA); *m* 22 Oct 1966, Hon (Hugh) Andrew David, s of Rear Adm The Earl Cairns, KCVO (d 1989); 1 s (Bertie b 28 Jan 1972), 1 da (Katherine b 27 June 1974); *Career* sr legal asst Charity Commission 1972-78, admitted slr 1978; ptnr Jaques and Lewis 1984-90 (asst slr 1979-84); specialist in charity law; memb Wills and Equity Ctee Law Soc; *Books* Charities: Law and Practice (1988); *Recreations* gardening, fishing; *Style—* The Hon Mrs Andrew Cairns; Knowle Hill Farm, Ulcombe, Maidstone, Kent ME17 1ES (☎ 0622 850240)

CAIRNS, Air Vice-Marshal Geoffrey Crerar; CBE (1970), AFC (1960); s of James William Cairns (d 1949), and Marion, *née* Crerar; *b* 21 May 1926; *Educ* Loretto, Gonville and Caius Coll Cambridge; *m* 1948, Carol (d 1985), da of Ivan Evernden (d 1979); 4 da (Madeline b 1949, Claudia b 1952, Catherine b 1960, Eliza b 1964); *Career* RAF 1944-80 (AVM), Cmdt A & AEE Boscombe Down 1971-74, asst chief of Air Staff (Operational Requirements) 1975-76, Cmdt Southern Maritime Air Region 1976-77, chief of Staff 18 Gp 1978-80; def conslt Marconi Avionics Ltd 1980-81; dir: Trago Aircraft Ltd 1982-88, ORCA Aircraft Ltd 1988-89; FRAes 1979, FBIM; *Recreations* golf, music, railways; *Clubs* RAF; *Style—* Air Vice-Marshal Geoffrey Cairns, CBE, AFC

CAIRNS, Lady; Helena; da of George McCullough; *m* 1944, Sir Joseph Foster Cairns, JP (d 1981, former Lord Mayor of Belfast and memb Senate of Northern Ireland); 1 s, 1 da; *Style—* Lady Cairns; Amaranth, Craigdarragh Rd, Helens Bay, Northern Ireland

CAIRNS, Prof John Harper; s of John Cairns (d 1984), of Colwyn Bay, and Edith, *née* Harper (d 1962); *b* 20 Jan 1932; *Educ* William Hulme's Sch Manchester, Univ of Manchester (BSc, MSc, PhD); *m* 17 Aug 1957, Monica Mary, da of Lawrence Lonnon (d 1976), of Zeals, Wiltshire; 1 s (Ian b 1963), 2 da (Rosemary b 1958, Stephanie b 1961); *Career* asst lectr and lectr in metallurgy UMIST 1956-60, co tech exec Yorkshire Imperial Metals Ltd 1964-71 (former head of res 1960-64), md Anson Cast Products Ltd 1971-79, dep vice chllr Univ of Bradford 1988- (prof of industl tech 1979-85, pro vice chllr 1985-88); FIM 1967, CEng 1977; *Books* Technology of Heavy Non Ferrous Metals (1967); *Recreations* sailing, fell walking; *Style—* Prof John Cairns; Crest Hill House, Shadwell Ring Rd, Leeds LS17 8NJ (☎ 0532 650684); University of Bradford, Bradford, West Yorks BD7 1DP (☎ 0274 733466, fax 0274 305340, telex 51309 UNIBFDG)

CAIRNS, Peter Granville; s of Maj H W Cairns, MC (gs of 1 Earl Cairns); *b* 3 Sept 1940; *Educ* Eton; *Career* Lt Royal Scots Greys, ret; banker; dir: Cater Ryder 1976-81, Cater Allen 1981-; *Recreations* fox-hunting; *Clubs* Turf, White's; *Style—* Peter Cairns, Esq; 11 St Mary Abbots Court, London W14 (☎ 071 603 7356)

CAIRNS, Robert James; s of Robert Mons Cairns, of Birkenhead, and Rita Mary, *née* Crocker (d 1985); *b* 1 June 1951; *Educ* Wirral County GS, Univ of Sussex (BA); *m* 4 Nov 1971, Julia Ann, da of Leslie Miles Richardson, of Whickham, Newcastle Upon Tyne; 2 da (Rebecca b 1972, Abby-Louise b 1979); *Career* branch mangr Britannia Building Society 1980-83, dep gen mangr Cumberland Building Society 1987- (asst sec 1983-86, asst gen mangr of admin and sec 1987), dir Funds Transfer Sharing Ltd 1989; chm Carlisle Area Bd of Young Enterprise; memb: Ctee Cumberland Centre and Northern Gp Chartered Bldg Socs Inst, Round Table; FCBSI 1985; *Recreations* sport, music; *Style—* Robert Cairns, Esq; Allendale House, Armathwaite, Carlisle (☎ 06992 239); Cumberland Building Society, Cumberland House, 38 Fisher St, Carlisle (☎ 0228 41341, fax 0228 25309)

CAIRNS, Dr Roger John Russell; s of Arthur John Cairns (d 1982), and Edith Ann, *née* Russell (d 1979); *b* 8 March 1943; *Educ* Ranelagh Sch Berks, Univ of Durham (BSc), Univ of Bristol (MSc, PhD); *m* 20 July 1966, Zara Corry, da of Herbert Bolton (d 1970); 2 s (Nigel b 1969, Alistair b 1973), 1 da (Kirsten b 1975); *Career* oilfield water mgmnt BP 1978-81, planner Qatar General Petroleum Corp 1981-83; md: Trafalgar House Oil and Gas Ltd (tech and commercial dir 1983-89), Hardy Oil and Gas plc 1989-; FRCS, CChem, MInstPet; memb SPE, IOD, MENSA; *Recreations* theatre and music, wine making, tennis, reading, chess; *Style—* Dr Roger Cairns; High Larch, Lewis Lane, Chalfont Heights, Gerrard's Cross, Bucks SL9 9TS; 2 Chalkhill Rd, London W6 SW (☎ 081 741 7373)

CAIRNS, 6 Earl (UK 1878); Simon Dallas Cairns; also Baron Cairns (UK 1867) and Viscount Garmoyle (UK 1878); s of 5 Earl Cairns, GCVO, CB (d 1989); *b* 27 May 1939; *Educ* Eton, Trinity Coll Cambridge; *m* 4 Feb 1964, Amanda Mary, o da of late Maj Edgar Fitzgerald Heathcoat-Amory, RA; 3 s (Viscount Garmoyle, Hon David Patrick b 1967, Hon Alistair Benedict b 1969); *Heir* s, Viscount Garmoyle b 26 March 1965; *Career* jt chm S G Warburg & Co Ltd, jt vice chm S G Warburg Gp 1987 (formerly with J A Scrimgeour), dir BAT Industries plc 1990, chm Voluntary Servs Overseas 1981; Receiver Gen Duchy of Cornwall 1990-; *Clubs* Turf; *Style—* The Rt Hon the Earl Cairns; Bolehyde Manor, Allington, Chippenham, Wilts (☎ 0249 652105)

CAIRNS, William James; s of Lt-Col Robert William Cairns, MBE, TD, MA (d 1972), of Edinburgh, and Marjory Helen, *née* Dickson (d 1983); *b* 13 March 1936; *Educ* Heriot's, King's Coll, Univ of Durham (DLD), MIT (MCP); *m* 3 Oct 1962, Barbara Marjory, da of Lt-Col George Stuart Russell, OBE, WS; 1 s (Alastair b 1966), 1 da (Sarah b 1966 (twin); *Career* Nat Serv: RMP, Cyprus 1954-56; TA 7/9 & 8/9 Bn The Royal Scots 1958-62 (Lt); landscape architect, environmental conslt, urban & rengl planner, fndr chief exec and chm W J Cairns & Ptnrs Ltd environmental consIts (Edinburgh and Belfast) 1972-, assoc princ Land Use Consultants 1968-72, princ landscape architect Craigavon Devpt Cmmn 1966-68, res assoc Jt Centre Urban Studies MIT & Harvard 1964-66, asst prof of landscape architecture Univ of Georgia 1962-64; pres Int Prof Assoc for Environmental Affrs, chm ICOE, ed in chief North Sea Oil and the Environment; chm: Standing Ctee for Environment, Int Soc of City and Regnl Planners, RAPP Gen 26 World Congress on Planning Warsaw 1990; memb Int Ctee for the Int Univ for the Bio-Environment; FLI, FRSA, FInstPet, PIRE, FID; *Recreations* golf, hill walking, gardening, skiing; *Clubs* New (Edinburgh), Scottish Arts, Bruntsfield Golfing Soc; *Style—* William Cairns, Esq; 37 Heriot Row, Edinburgh BH3 6ES; 16 Randolph Crescent, Edinburgh EH3 7TT (☎ 031 225 3241, fax 031 225 5016)

CAITHNESS, 20 Earl of (S 1455); Malcolm Ian Sinclair; 15 Bt (S 1631), PC (1990); also Lord Berriedale (S 1592); s of 19 Earl of Caithness (d 1965), and his 2 w Madeleine Gabrielle, *née* de Pury (d 1990); *b* 3 Nov 1948; *Educ* Marlborough, RAC Cirencester; *m* 1975, Diana Caroline, da of Maj Richard Coke, DSO, MC, DL (gs of 2 Earl of Leicester); 1 s, 1 da (Lady Iona b 1978); *Heir* s, Lord Berriedale, *qv*; *Career* a Lord in Waiting and Government Whip 1984-85, under sec for transport 1985-86, Minister of State Home Office 1986-88, Minister of State Dept of the Environment 1988-89, Paymaster Gen 1989-90, Minister of State FCO 1990-; FRICS; *Style—* The Rt Hon the Earl of Caithness; c/o The House of Lords, London SW1

CALAM, Dr Derek Harold; s of Richard Hellyer Calam, of Northwood, and Winifred Ella, *née* Nortier (d 1986); *b* 11 May 1936; *Educ* Christ's Hosp, Wadham Coll Oxford (MA, DPhil); *m* 15 Sept 1965, Claudia, da of Gerald Marcus Summers (d 1967); 2 s (Duncan b 1969, Douglas b 1973), 1 da (Josephine b 1971); *Career* Nat Serv 2 Lt RA 1954-56; Nat Inst for Med Res 1962-66 and 1969-72, Rothamsted Experimental Station 1966-69, head Chemistry Dept Nat Inst for Biological Standards and Control

1975- (joined 1972), author of numerous pubns in jls; memb: Br Pharmacopoeia Cmmn 1982-, Euro Pharmacopoeia Cmmn 1988-; expert advsr WHO 1984-; CChem, FRSC 1977; *Recreations* walking, travel; *Style—* Dr Derek Calam; National Institute for Biological Standards and Control, Blanche Lane, South Mimms, Potters Bar, Herts EN6 3QG (☎ 0707 54753, fax 0707 46730, telex 21911)

CALAM, Dr John; s of Christopher Towers Calam, of Alderley Edge, Cheshire, and Irene May Calam; *b* 17 Feb 1948; *Educ* The King's Sch Macclesfield, Univ of Liverpool Med Sch (MD); *m* 15 Aug 1973, Joyce Elizabeth, da of Harold Cecil Rooney, of Nuneaton, Warwickshire; 1 s (Jeffrey), 2 da (Amy, Molly); *Career* sr med lectr and conslt physician Royal Postgraduate Med Sch and Hammersmith Hosp 1983-, first to demonstrate a causal link between gastric helicobacter bacteria and excessive acid secretion in patients with duodenal ulcers, reported in the Lancet and The Sunday Times 1989; FRCP 1988; *Recreations* sailing; *Clubs* The Physiological Soc of London; *Style—* Dr John Calam; 16 Cranbourne Dr, Pinner, Middx HA5 1BZ (☎ 081 868 8263), Department of Medicine, Royal Postgrad Medical School, Hammersmith Hospital, DU Cane Road, London W12 0NN (☎ 081 740 3169)

CALBRADE, Rodney David; s of Joseph Calbrade, of Manchester, and Edna, *née* Massey; *b* 27 July 1947; *Educ* Queen Elizabeth's GS Middleton Manchester; *m* Jean Calbrade, *née* Birrell; 1 s (Neil Andrew b 10 June 1975), 2 da (Dawn Louise b 1 Sept 1970, Fiona Jayne b 6 Sept 1973); *Career* prodn asst: Co-operative Wholesale Soc (Co-op) 1965-67, MacDonald Advertising Manchester 1967-72; media mangr Yeoward Taylor & Bonner (subsequently became J Walter Thomson) 1972-77, fndr All Media Services North (bought by TMD Holdings PLC 1988) 1977, TMD Holdings PLC 1988-; MInstM 1971-; *Recreations* angling, bird watching; *Style—* Rodney Calbrade, Esq; TMD Advertising (Manchester) Ltd, Adamson House, Market Place, Manchester M3 1RE (☎ 061 834 9793, fax 061 835 1363)

CALCUTT, David Charles; QC (1972); s of Henry Calcutt (d 1972); *b* 2 Nov 1930; *Educ* Cranleigh, King's Coll Cambridge, Stewart of Rannoch Sch; *m* 1969, Barbara Ann, da of Vivian Walker (d 1965); *Career* barr 1955, dep chm Somerset QS 1970-71, rec 1972-89, Dept of Trade inspr Cornhill Consolidated 1974-77; chm: Civil Serv Arbitration Tbnl 1979-, Inst of Actuaries' Appeal Bd 1985-, Falklands Islands Cmmn of Enquiry 1984, Cyprus Servicemen Inquiry 1985-86; master Magdalene Coll Cambridge 1986-; chllr dioceses of Exeter and Bristol 1971, Europe 1983; chm Cncl Cranleigh and Bramley Schs 1987-; dir Edington Music Festival 1956-64; memb: Criminal Injuries Compensation Bd 1977-, Cncl of Tbnls 1980-86, Gen Cncl of the Bar 1968-72, Senate of the Inns of Court and the Bar 1979-85 (chm of the Senate 1984-85, chm of the Bar 1984-85), UK Delgn Consultative Ctee Bars and Law Socs EEC 1979-83; Colliery Ind Review Body 1985-88; hon memb: American Bar Assoc 1985-, Canadian Bar Assoc 1985-; fell Int Acad of Trial Lawyers (NY); *Recreations* living on Exmoor; *Clubs* Athenaeum, New (Edinburgh); *Style—* David Calcutt, Esq, QC; Magdalene Coll, Cambridge; Lamb Building, Temple, London EC4

CALDECOTE, 2 Viscount (UK 1939); Sir Robert Andrew Inskip (Robin); KBE (1987), DSC (1941); s of 1 Viscount Caldecote (Rt Hon Sir Thomas Walker Hobart Inskip, CBE, d 1947), and Lady Augusta Orr Ewing (d 1967), wid of Charles Orr Ewing, MP, and er da of 7 Earl of Glasgow; *b* 8 Oct 1917; *Educ* Eton, King's Coll Cambridge (MA), RNC Greenwich; *m* 22 July 1942, Jean Hamilla, da of Rear Adm Hugh Dundas Hamilton (d 1963); 1 s, 2 da; *Heir* s, Hon Piers James Hampden Inskip; *Career* served RNVR 1939-45; asst mangr Vockes Naval Yard 1947-48, lectr in engrg Engrg Dept Univ of Cambridge 1948-54; dir: English Electric Co 1953-69, British Aircraft Corporation 1960-69 (dep md 1961-67); chm: EDC Movement of Exports 1965-72, Export Cncl for Europe 1970-71, Design Cncl 1972-80, Legal and General Group 1977-80, BBC Gen Advsy Cncl 1982-85, Investors in Industry Group plc 1980-87, Mary Rose Tst 1983-; dir: Consolidated Gold Fields 1969-78, Delta Group plc 1970-82 (chm 1972-82), Lloyds Bank 1975-88, W S Atkins Ltd 1982-; chm Industries Ventures Ltd 1989-; pres: Parly and Scientific Ctee 1966-69, Fellowship of Engrg 1981-86, Royal Inst Naval Architects 1987-90; memb: Review Bd for Govt Contracts 1969-76, Inflation Accounting Ctee 1974-75, Engrg Industs Cncl 1975-82, BR Bd 1979-85, Advsy Cncl for Applied Research and Devpt 1981-84, Engrg Cncl 1982-85; pro chllr Cranfield Inst of Technol 1976-84; fell: King's Coll Cambridge 1948-55 (and lectr in engrg), Eton Coll 1953-72; tstee: Princess Youth Business Tst 1986-90, Church Urban Fund 1987-; FEng, Hon FIEE, Hon FICE, Hon FIMechE, FRINA, Hon FSIAD 1976; Hon DSc: Cranfield, Aston, Bristol, City; Hon LLD: London, Cambridge; *Recreations* sailing (yacht 'Citara III'), shooting, golf; *Clubs* Pratt's, Royal Yacht Sqdn, Royal Ocean Racing, Royal Cruising, Athenaeum; *Style—* The Rt Hon the Viscount Caldecote, KBE, DSC; Orchard Cottage, South Harting, Petersfield, Hants (☎ 0730 825529)

CALDER, Dr Allan Balfour; s of Alexander Angus Calder (d 1986), of Crewe, and Jane Calder, *née* Balfour (d 1973); *b* 13 Sept 1920; *Educ* Montrose Acad, Univ of St Andrews (Bsc), Univ of Edinburgh (PhD); *m* 6 Nov 1954, (Janet) Netta Kerr, da of William Law Cockburn Scullion (d 1969), of Linlithgow; 2 da (Mary b 1955, Jane b 1955); *Career* metallurgical chemist Colvilles Ltd Motherwell 1943-47, sr spectroscopist Edinburgh and E of Scot Coll of Agric 1947-56, sr analyst British Titan Products Co Ltd Billingham 1956-57, sr lectr in inorganic chemistry Newcastle upon Tyne Poly 1957-81; former elder and lay preacher Jesmond Utd Reform Church; fell Victoria Inst; CChem, FRSC 1954, FIS 1959; *Books* Photometric Methods of Analysis (1969), Statistics from Modern Methods of Geo-chemical Analysis (contrib, 1971); papers: Operational Statistics in Instrumental Analysis (1961), The Use of Discriminant Functions in Biological Sampling (1961), How Substances are Formed (1966), The Use of Nomograms in Purity Control Analysis (1968); *Recreations* walking, listening to music; *Style—* Dr Allan Calder; 8 Crossway, Jesmond, Newcastle upon Tyne NE2 3QH (☎ 091 281 4424)

CALDER, Hon Allan Graham Ritchie; 3 s of Baron Ritchie-Calder, CBE (d 1982); *b* 4 Jan 1944; *Educ* Ewell Tech Coll, Birkbeck Coll London (BSc, PhD); *m* 1, 1967, Anne Margaret, da of Robert Allan Wood; 1 s; m 2, 1983, Lilian Lydia, da of Edward Godfrey; *Career* commercial balloon pilot and mathematician; asst prof: Carlton Univ Ottawa 1970-71, Louisiana State Univ 1971-72, Univ of Missouri 1975-76; lecturer in mathematics: Univ of Essex 1972-73, Birkbeck Coll 1972-83; assoc prof New Mexico State Univ 1979-81; chief pilot: Sunrise Balloons California 1981-82, Bombard Soc France 1983- (sr pilot 1982); *Recreations* classic cars, sailing, hot air ballooning; *Clubs* Savile, Bentley Drivers, Porsche GB, Br Balloon and Airship; *Style—* The Hon Allan Calder; c/o Royal Bank of Scotland, 15 Kingsway, London WC2

CALDER, Col Anthony John Kennion; OBE (1985); s of William John Calder, of Melbourn, Royston, Herts, and Louise Forbes, *née* Morton; *b* 22 Oct 1943; *Educ* Millfield, RMA Sandhurst; *m* 29 July 1967, Caroline Melesina, da of Lt-Col Anthony Richard Reeve, MBE, TD, of Langlands, Netherhampton, Sailsbury, Wilts; 3 s (Charles b 26 Sept 1968, Jason b 23 Oct 1969, Nicholas b 7 Sept 1973), 1 da (Melesina b 5 May 1982); *Career* cmmnd IE Anglian Regt 1963 (later R Anglian Regt), cmd IR Anglian 1982-85, promoted Col 1986, currently serving HQ Afnorth Norway; *Recreations* cricket, sailing, skiing, shooting; *Style—* Col Anthony Calder, OBE; Seccos, HQ Afnorth, BFPO 50 (☎ 010 472 02 472453)

CALDER, Finlay; OBE (1990); s of Robin Calder, of Haddington, East Lothian, and Elizabeth Guthrie, *née* Hamilton; *b* 20 Aug 1957; *Educ* Daniel Stewarts and Melville Coll Edinburgh; *m* 22 July 1978, Elizabeth Agnes, da of Alexander George Lyal; 1 s (David Alexander Finlay b 4 Oct 1983), 1 da (Hazel Elizabeth Spottiswoode b 5 Aug 1985); *Career* Rugby Union flanker Stewart's Melville FP RFC and Scotland (28 caps); clubs: Melrose RFC 1975-80 (135 appearances), Stewart's Melville FP 1981-, Edinburgh 1982-90 (43 appearances); Scottish Schs 1974 (3 caps); for Scotland: Aust tour (5 appearances) 1982, Romania tour (1 appearance) 1984, debut v France Murrayfield 1986, World Cup squad 1987, capt 1989, Championship Winners 1990, NZ tour 1990; capt British Lions Aust tour (3 test appearances, won series 2-1) 1989; memb: Scotland Seven Aust tour 1988, Barbarians Seven HK 1989; winner Middx Sevens 1982; Ceres (UK) Ltd 1985-; *Style—* Finlay Calder, Esq, OBE

CALDER, Hon Isla Elizabeth Ritchie; *née* Calder; resumed surname of Calder by deed poll; yr da of Baron Ritchie-Calder (Life Peer), CBE (d 1982); *b* 7 Sept 1947; *Educ* Nonsuch Co Sch Cheam, St George's Edinburgh, Froebel Inst of Education; *m* 1971 (m dis 1983), Alan Evans; *Career* business consultant; *Style—* The Hon Isla Calder

CALDER, Dr John Forbes; s of Alexander Beattie Calder, of Glasgow, and Annie Scott, *née* Milne; *b* 13 May 1942; *Educ* The HS of Glasgow, Univ of Glasgow (MB ChB); *m* 28 March 1967, Marion, da of John Anderson Miller (d 1964), of Kirkintilloch; 1 s (Nicholas b 1972), 1 da (Lorna b 1975); *Career* govt MO Malawi 1968-70, sr registrar radiology Glasgow 1973-76 (registrar radiology 1971-73); sr lectr radiology: Univ of Nairobi 1976-80, Univ of Aberdeen 1980-86; conslt radiologist Victoria Infirmary Glasgow 1986-; elder Church of Scotland, sec Scottish Radiological Soc; memb RCR 1975, FRCR; *Books* An Atlas of Radiological Interpretation The Bones (1988); *Recreations* music, hill walking, soccer; *Clubs* Cwlth; *Style—* Dr John Calder; 145 Clober Rd, Milngavie, Glasgow, G62 7LS (☎ 041 956 3535); Dept of Radiology, Victoria Infirmary, Glasgow G42 9TY (☎ 041 649 4545)

CALDER, John Mackenzie; s of James Calder, of Ardargie, Forgandenny, Perthshire, and Lucianne Wilson; *b* 25 Jan 1927; *Educ* McGill Univ, Sir George Williams Coll, Univ of Zürich; *m* 1, 1949, Mary Ann Simmonds; 1 da; m 2, 1960 (m dis 1975), Bettina Jonic; 1 da; *Career* publisher, ed, author; fndr and md John Calder (Publishers) Ltd 1950-, dir of other associated publishing and opera cos; co-fndr Def of Lit and the Arts Soc, chm Fedn of Scot Theatres 1972-74; contested (Lib): Kinross and W Perthshire 1970, Hamilton 1974, Centl Scot (Euro election) 1979; Chev des Arts et des Lettres, Chev Ordre de Mérite Nat; FRSA; *Books* ed: A Samuel Beckett Reader, Beckett at 60, The Nouveau Roman Reader, Gambit International Drama Review, William Burroughs Reader, Henry Miller Reader As No Other Dare Fail: For Samuel Beckett on his Birthday; author The Defence of Literature; fiction and plays; *Clubs* Caledonian, Scottish Arts; *Style—* John Calder, Esq; John Calder (Publishers) Ltd, 9-15 Neal St, London WC2H 9TU (☎ 071 497 1741)

CALDER, Michael John; s of Geoffrey Charles Calder (d 1974), of Dulwich, and Mary Patricia Calder (d 1982); *b* 28 Nov 1931; *Educ* Dulwich, ChCh Oxford (MA); *m* 10 June 1965, Sheila, da of Herbert Maughan (d 1962), of Sunderland; 2 s (James b 1966, Andrew b 1968); *Career* Lt RA 1950-56; Shell 1956-57; CA 1959-; sr ptnr W J Calder Sons & Co (gs of fndr); FCA; *Recreations* music, travel, cricket; *Clubs* Travellers'; *Style—* Michael Calder, Esq; 42 Carson Rd, Dulwich, London SE21 8HU (☎ 071 670 6207); W J Calder Sons & Co, 25 Lower Belgrave St, London SW1W 0LS (☎ 071 730 8632, fax 071 730 7372)

CALDER, Hon Nigel David Ritchie; eldest s of Baron Ritchie-Calder, CBE (Life Peer, d 1982); *b* 2 Dec 1931; *Educ* Merchant Taylors', Sidney Sussex Coll Cambridge (MA); *m* 1954, Elisabeth, da of Alfred James Palmer; 2 s, 3 da; *Career* writer New Scientist 1956-66 (ed 1962-66); freelance author and TV scriptwriter; author of over 20 books; *Books Incl:* Einstein's Universe (1979), Nuclear Nightmares (1979), The Comet is Coming (1980), Timescale (1983), The English Channel (1986), Spaceship Earth (1990); *Recreations* sailing (ketch, 'Charmed'); *Clubs* Athenaeum, Cruising Assoc; *Style—* The Hon Nigel Calder; 8 The Chase, Furnace Green, Crawley, Sussex (☎ 0293 26693)

CALDERWOOD, James William; s of Rev James W Calderwood (d 1971), of The Manse, Bready, Strabane, Co Tyrone, and Kathleen Calderwood; *b* 3 Dec 1936; *Educ* Foyle Coll Londonderry, Queen's Univ Belfast (MB BCh, BAO); *m* 29 Aug 1967, Dr (Catherine) Lesley Crozier, da of George Crozier, of Belfast Bank House, Enniskillen (d 1963); 2 da (Catherine, Claire); *Career* conslt orthopaedic surgn Belfast City and Musgrave Park Hosp 1975, Royal Victoria Hosp 1977; examiner of RCSEd 1986-; memb: Br Soc for Surgery of the Hand 1980, Ulster Surgeons Travelling Club 1990-; fell Br Orthopaedic Assoc, FRCS 1970, FRSM 1986; *Recreations* skiing, jogging, golf; *Style—* James Calderwood, Esq; 8 Broomhill Park, Belfast BT9 5JB (☎ 0232 666940); Belfast City Hospital, Lisburn Rd, Belfast (☎ 0232 32941)

CALDERWOOD, Richard Johnston; s of Alistair Lawton Calderwood, DFC, AFC, of Bulawayo, Zimbabwe, and Inex Annandale, *née* Johnston; *b* 18 April 1946; *Educ* St Stephen's Coll Bulawayo Rhodesia; *m* 10 Sept 1976, Susan Elizabeth, da of David Basil Jones (d 1988), of Sevenoaks, Kent; 3 s (Alistair b 1977, William b 1978, Peter b 1982); *Career* articled Coopers & Lybrand London, chief accountant and head of corp fin Standard Merchant Bank of Rhodesia 1973-76, ptnr Waring & Partners (CAs) 1983-; FCA (ACA 1970); *Recreations* sailing, flying; *Style—* Richard Calderwood, Esq; c/o Roper Yard, Roper Rd, Canterbury, Kent CT2 7EX (☎ 0227 766666, fax 0227 766667)

CALDERWOOD, Robert; s of Robert Calderwood (d 1952), and Jessie Reid, *née* Marshall; *b* 1 March 1932; *Educ* Darrel HG Sch, William Hulme's Sch Manchester, Univ of Manchester (LLB); *m* 6 Sept 1958, Meryl Anne, da of David Walter Fleming (d 1977); 3 s (Robert b 1959, David b 1965, Iain b 1968), 1 da (Lyn b 1962); *Career* slr Supreme Ct of Judicature 1956; town clerk and cheif exec: Salford 1966-69, Bolton 1969-73, Manchester 1973-79; chief exec Strathclyde Regnl Cncl 1980-; UN Assocs, Discharged Pensioners Aid Orgns; dep pres NUS 1954; memb Parole Bd (England) 1971-73, advsy ctees on community rels and crime prevention for Sec of State for Scot; memb Glasgow Trades House, Indust Soc 1981; CBIM 1981, companion Inst of Water and Enviornmental Mgmnt 1987; *Recreations* walking, swimming, garden, reading, theatre; *Style—* Robert Calderwood, Esq; 6 Mosspark Ave, Milngavie, Glasgow G62 8NL (☎ 041 956 4585); Strathclyde Regional Council, 20 India St, Glasgow G2 4PF (☎ 041 227 3415, fax 041 227 2870, telex 77428)

CALDICOTT, Dr Fiona; da of Joseph Maurice Soesan, of Coventry, and Elizabeth Jane, *née* Ransley; *b* 12 Jan 1941; *Educ* City of London Sch for Girls, St Hilda's Coll Oxford (MA, MB BCh); *m* 5 June 1965, Robert Gordon Caldicott, s of Capt Gordon Ezra Woodruff Caldicott (d 1941), of Louisville, Kentucky; 1 s (Richard Woodruff b 1971, d 1990), 1 da (Lucy Woodruff b 1968); *Career* conslt psychiatrist Univ of Warwick 1979-85, sr clinical lectr in psychotherapy Univ of Birmingham 1982-, unit gen mangr Mental Health Unit Central Birmingham Health Authy 1998- (conslt psychotherapist Uffculme Clinic 1979-); memb Central Manpower Ctee BMA 1977-89, dean RCPsych 1990- (sub dean 1987-90, chm Manpower Ctee 1981-89); FRCPsych 1985; *Style—* Dr Fiona Caldicott; Kings Hill, Kings Hill Lane, Finham, Coventry CV3 6PS; Uffculme Clinic, Queensbridge Rd, Moseley, Birmingham B13 8QD (☎ 021 442 4545)

CALDIN, Prof Edward Francis Hussey; s of Edward Caldin (d 1951), and Agnes Mary, *née* Hussey (d 1948); *b* 5 Aug 1914; *Educ* St Paul's, Queen's Coll Oxford (MA, DPhil, DSc); *m* 17 April 1944, Mary, da of Joseph Francis Parker (d 1960); 2 s (Hugh b 1946, Giles b 1948); *Career* jr res fell Queen's Coll Oxford 1939; Armaments Res Dept Miny of Supply 1941-45; Univ of Leeds: lectr 1945-54, sr lectr 1954-64, reader 1964-65; Univ of Kent: reader 1965-66, prof of physical chemistry 1966-79, emeritus prof 1979-; memb Royal Soc of Chemistry; *Books* The Power and Limits of Science (1949), Science and Christian Apologetic (1953), Chemical Thermodynamics (1958), Fast Reactions in Solution (1964), The Structure of Physical Science (1961), Proton - Transfer Reactions (ed with V Gold, 1975); *Style—* Prof E F Caldin; c/o University Chemical Laboratory, Canterbury, Kent CT2 7NH

CALDWELL, Edward George; CB (1990); s of Prof A F Caldwell, of Herts, and Olive Gertrude, *née* Riddle; *b* 21 Aug 1941; *Educ* St Andrew's Singapore, Clifton, Worcester Coll Oxford; *m* 1965, Bronwen Anne, da of Dr J A Crockett, of Oxford; 2 da (Bronwen Lucy b 1968, Sophie b 1971); *Career* slr Fisher Dowson & Wasbrough 1966; Law Cmmn 1967, Office of the Parly Counsel, Law Cmmn 1974-76 and 1987-88; *Style—* Edward Caldwell, Esq, CB; Office of the Parliamentary Counsel, 36 Whitehall, London SW1

CALDWELL, Dr James Richard (Dick); s of late James Caldwell, JP, of The White House of Speen, Aylesbury, Bucks, and late Anne Blanche, *née* Young; *b* 25 Feb 1916; *Educ* Uppingham, St Thomas's Hosp London (MB BS); *m* 14 Feb 1948, Phyllis Doreen, da of late Geofrey Reynolds, of Nakuru, Kenya; 4 da (Janet, Nancy, Helen, Carol); *Career* WWII RAFVR 1939-45, served Europe, ME and Far E (despatches); med practioner 1946-83; Hunterian Gold medal 1963; memb: Mid-Sussex Hosp Mgmnt Ctee, E Sussex Local Med Ctee, E Sussex Family Practioner Ctee, Gen Med Ctee of BMA; Freeman City of London, Liveryman Worshipful Co of Shipwrights; FRCGP, BMA; *Recreations* gardening, being a grandfather; *Style—* Dr Dick Caldwell; Silver Birches, 26 Newick Hill, Newick, Sussex BN8 4QR (☎ 02572 2572)

CALDWELL, Prof John Bernard; OBE (1979); s of Dr John Revie Caldwell (d 1968), of Barkbooth, Winster, Cumbria, and Doris, *née* Bolland (d 1929); *b* 26 Sept 1926; *Educ* Bootham Sch York, Univ of Liverpool (BEng), Univ of Bristol (PhD); *m* 12 Aug 1955, Jean Muriel Frances, da of Leonard Francis Duddridge, of 6 Dene Garth, Ovingham, Northumberland; 2 s (Philip b 1959, Michael b 1961); *Career* shipbuilding apprentice Vickers-Armstrong 1943-48 (ship tech draughtsman 1948-49), res fell in naval architecture Univ of Bristol 1953-55, sr sci offr then princ sci offr RN Scientific Serv 1955-60, asst prof of applied mechanics RNC Greenwich 1960-66, visiting prof MIT 1962-63; Univ of Newcastle Upon Tyne: prof of naval architecture 1966-, head of dept 1966-83, dean Faculty of Engrg 1983-86, head Sch of Marine Technol 1975-80 and 1986-88; visiting lectr: Norway 1969, Singapore 1970, Brazil 1973, SA 1974, Hong Kong 1975, Canada 1976, Egypt 1979, China 1980, Malaysia 1981, Yugoslavia 1985, Aust 1986, USA, Holland, Italy, Poland, Indonesia, Japan; visting prof Univ of Br Columbia Canada 1989; David Taylor medal from the American Soc of Naval Architects and Marine Engrs 1987; memb Tyne Port Authy 1973-75; non exec dir: Nat Maritime Institute Ltd 1983-85, Marine Design Consultants Ltd 1985-89, Newcastle Technol Centre 1985-90, Marine Technology Technol Directorate Ltd 1986-90; memb Engrg Cncl 1988-, chm Bd for Engrs Registration 1990-; memb of various ctees for: MOD Def of Sci Advsy Cncl, Dept of Energy, Offshore Energy Technol Bd, Dept of Indust, Dept of Tport, DES SERC; memb Tech Ctee Lloyds Register of Shiping; memb Br Ship Res Assoc: Naval Architecture Ctee, Co-ordinating Ctee on Ship Structures; RINA: memb Cncl, Gen Purposes and Fin Ctee, chm Educn and Trg Ctee; Int Ship and Ocean Structures Congress: UK memb of Standing Ctee 1967-76, chm Ctees on Design Philosphy, Superstructures and Plastic Analysis; chm W Euro Grad Educn in Marine Technol: Exec Ctee, annual conference; memb Ed Bd: Jl of Soc of Underwater Technol, Euro Shipbuilding Progress, Int Jl of Marine Structures; conslt for various marine orgns incl: Br Shipbuilders, MOD; author of numerous papers and articles on marine matters; Hon DSc Tech Univ of Gdansk Poland 1985; FRINA 1966 (Froude medal 1984, pres 1984-87), MIStructE 1966, FEng (fndr memb) 1976, FNECInst 1977 (Gold medal 1973, pres 1976-78), hon memb Soc of Naval Architects and Marine Engrs Singapore 1978; *Recreations* reading, listening, seeing, thinking; *Clubs* Nat Lib; *Style—* Prof John Caldwell, OBE; The White House, 18 Cadehill Rd, Stocksfield, Northumberland NE43 7PT (☎ 0661 843 445); University of Newcastle Upon Tyne, Newcastle Upon Tyne, Tyne and Wear NE1 7RU (☎ 091 222 6722 ext 6722, fax 091 261 1182, telex 563654 UNINEW G)

CALDWELL, Wilfrid Moores (Bill); s of Col Wilfrid Caldwell (d 1935), and Mabel Gertrude, *née* Moores; *b* 14 Oct 1935; *Educ* Marlborough, Magdalene Coll Cambridge (MA); *m* 8 April 1972, Linda Louise, da of Robert Ian Hamish Sievwright (d 1978); 2 s (William b 1978, James b 1981), 1 da (Fiona b 1976); *Career* Nat Serv 2 Lt RA 1954-56, Lt (TA) 1956-59; CA, ptnr Price Waterhouse 1970- (joined 1959); chm of govrs: Redcliffe Sch Fulham 1979-89, Arundale Sch Pulborough 1985-; FCA 1963; *Recreations* golf, skiing, bridge, philately; *Clubs* Carlton; *Style—* Bill Caldwell, Esq; The Grange, Hesworth Lane, Fittleworth, Pulborough, W Sussex (☎ 079 882 384); Price Waterhouse, Southwark Towers, 32 London Bridge St, London SE1 9SY (☎ 071 939 3000, fax 071 378 0647, telex 884657/8)

CALEDON, Elisabeth, Countess of; Marie Elisabeth Burton; *née* Allen; da of Maj Richard Burton Allen, 3 Dragoon Guards, of Benvheir House, Ballachulish, Argyll; *m* 1, 1955 (m dis 1964), Maj Hon Iain Maxwell Erskine, later 2 Baron Erskine of Rerrick; m 2, 1964, as his 3 w, 6 Earl of Caledon (d 1980); *Style—* The Rt Hon Elisabeth, Countess of Caledon; The Gate House, Hunsdon, nr Ware, Hertfordshire

CALEDON, 7 Earl of (I 1800); Nicholas James Alexander; JP; Baron Caledon (I 1790), Viscount (I 1797); s of 6 Earl of Caledon (d 1980), by his 2 w, Baroness Anne (d 1963), da of Baron Nicolai de Graevenitz (Dukedom of Mecklenburg-Schwerin 1847, Russia (Tsar Nicholas I) 1851); *b* 6 May 1955; *Educ* Gordonstoun; *m* 1, 1979 (m dis 1985), Wendy Catherine, da of Spiro Nicholas Coumantaros, of Athens; m 2, 19 Dec 1989, Henrietta Mary Alison, er da of John Newman, of Compton Park, Compton Chamberlayne, Wilts; 1 s (Frederick James b 15 Oct 1990); *Heir* s, Viscount Alexander b 15 Oct 1990; *Career* HM Lord Lieutenant for Co Armagh 1989-; chm Caledon Estates; *Recreations* travel, skiing, flying; *Clubs* Corviglia Ski, Helicopter Club of Ireland; *Style—* The Rt Hon the Earl of Caledon, JP; Caledon Castle, Co Tyrone, Northern Ireland (☎ 568 232)

CALIGARI, Prof Peter Douglas Savaria; s of Flt Lt Kenneth Vane Savaria Caligari, DFM, RAF, of Roselle Cottage, Sinton Green, nr Hallow, Worcester, and Mary Annetta, *née* Rock; *b* 10 Nov 1949; *Educ* Hereford Cathedral Sch, Univ of Birmingham (BSc, PhD, DSc); *m* 23 June 1973, Patricia Ann, da of John Feeley (d 1988); 2 da (Louise b 13 Jan 1978, Helena b 26 Sept 1980); *Career* res fell Univ of Birmingham 1974-81 (res asst 1971-74), princ sci offr Scottish Crop Res Inst 1984-86 (sr sci offr 1981-84), head Dept Agric Botany Univ of Reading 1987- (chair 1986-); author of numerous sci articles and reports; FRSA 1990; *Style—* Prof Peter Caligari; Department of Agricultural Botany, School of Plant Sciences, University of Reading, Whiteknights, PO Box 221, Reading RG6 2AS (☎ 0734 318091, fax 0734 750630, telex 847813 RULIBG)

CALLADINE, Prof Christopher Reuben; s of Reuben Calladine (d 1968), of Stapleford, Nottingham, and Mabel, *née* Boam (d 1963); *b* 19 Jan 1935; *Educ* Nottingham HS, Peterhouse Cambridge (BA), MIT (SM), Univ of Cambridge (ScD); *m* 4 Jan 1964, Mary Ruth Howard, da of Alan Howard Webb, of Bengeo, Hertford; 2 s (Robert James b 1964, Daniel Edward b 1967), 1 da (Rachel Margaret b 1966); *Career* devpt engr English Electric Co 1958-60; Univ of Cambridge: univ demonstrator 1960-63, univ lectr 1963-78, reader in structural mechanics 1978-86, prof of structural mechanics 1986-; fell Peterhouse 1960-; fndn govr Cherry Hinton Infants Sch, former govr Richard Hale Sch Hertford, memb Gen Bd Univ of Cambridge 1984-88; FRS 1984; *Style—* Prof Christopher Calladine, FRS; Peterhouse, Cambridge CB2 1RD (☎ 0223 338 200, fax 0223 337 578)

CALLAGHAN, Sir Bede Bertrand; CBE (1968); s of Stanislaus Callaghan (d 1950), of Sydney, NSW, and Amy Ryan; *b* 16 March 1912; *Educ* Newcastle HS Australia; *m* 1940, Mary T (Mollie), da of late G F Brewer; 3 da; *Career* exec dir IMF and IBRD 1954-59; gen mangr Commonwealth Development Bank of Australia 1959-65, md Commonwealth Banking Corp 1965-76, chllr Newcastle Univ 1977-88 (dep chllr 1973-77); kt 1976; *Clubs* Union (Sydney); *Style—* Sir Bede Callaghan, CBE; 69 Darnley St, Gordon, NSW 2072, Australia (☎ 010 61498 7583)

CALLAGHAN, James; MP (Lab) Heywood and Middleton 1983-; s of James Callaghan; *b* 28 Jan 1927; *Career* lectr St John's Coll Manchester 1959-74; former borough councillor Middleton; MP (Lab) Middleton and Prestwich 1974-1983, oppn front bench spokesman on Euro and Community Affairs 1983-; *Style—* James Callaghan, Esq, MP; 17 Towncroft Ave, Middleton, Manchester M24 3LA (☎ 061 643 8108)

CALLAGHAN, Hon Michael James; s of Baron Callaghan of Cardiff, KG, PC (Life Peer), *qv*; b 1945; *b* 1945; *Educ* Dulwich, Univ of Wales Cardiff, Manchester Business Sch; *m* 1968, Jennifer Mary, *née* Morris; 1 s (Joseph Edwin James b 1981), 2 da (Kate Elizabeth b 1970, Sarah Jane b 1972); *Career* assoc dir of business strategy Ford Automotive Group 1990-; fell Assoc of Corporate Treasurers; *Style—* The Hon Michael Callaghan; 3515 Maxwell Court, Birmingham, Michigan 48010, USA

CALLAGHAN, Dr (Thomas) Stanley; s of Thomas Callaghan, of Wyncroft, Killane Rd, Limavady, NI, and Marion, *née* Whyte; *b* 11 Feb 1948; *Educ* Limavady GS NI, The Queen's Univ Belfast (MB BCh, MRCP, MD); *m* 12 July 1973, Irene Helen, da of R Bowie, of Stenhouse, Edinburgh; 1 s (Gavin b 29 March 1979), 1 da (Rhona b 29 Jan 1975); *Career* resident Royal Victoria Hosp Belfast 1972-73, registrar in med, cardiology and metabolic med, sr registrar in med and cardiology Royal Victoria Hosp Belfast and Belfast City Hosp, conslt physician Stracathro Hosp Brechin Angus 1982-; memb: MRS, Br Hyperlipidaemia Soc; fell Ulster Soc of Internal Med; memb: Aberdeen Medicoi-Chirological Soc, Scottish Soc Physicians, Forfarshire Med Soc; *Recreations* walking, shooting, photography, music; *Clubs* Edinburgh Angus; *Style—* Dr Stanley Callaghan; The Mary Acre, Argyll St, Brechin, Angus DD9 6JL Scotland (☎ 03562 4725); Department of Medicine, Stracathro Hospital, Brechin, Angus DD9 7QA (☎ 03564 7291)

CALLAGHAN OF CARDIFF, Baron (Life Peer UK 1987), of the City of Cardiff, Co S Glamorgan; Sir (Leonard) James Callaghan; KG (1987), PC (1964); s of James Callaghan, Chief Petty Offr RN, of Portsmouth; *b* 27 March 1912; *Educ* Portsmouth Northern Secondary Sch; *m* 1938, Audrey Elizabeth, da of Frank Moulton, of Loose, Kent; 1 s, 2 da; *Career* joined Civil Service 1929, asst sec Inland Revenue Staff Fedn 1936-47; MP (Lab) South Cardiff 1945-50, South East Cardiff 1950-83, Cardiff South and Penarth 1983-87; Parly sec Min of Transport 1947-50, Parly and fin sec Admiralty 1950-51, Chllr of the Exchequer 1964-67, home sec 1967-70, sec of state for Foreign and Cwlth Affairs 1974-76, min of Overseas Devpt 1975-76, Prime Minister and first lord of the Treasury 1976-79, leader of Oppn 1979-80, father of the House (of Commons) 1983-87; pres Univ Coll Swansea 1985-; *Books* A House Divided: the dilemma of Northern Ireland (1973), Time and Chance (memoirs, 1987); *Style—* The Rt Hon Lord Callaghan of Cardiff, KG, PC; House of Lords, London SW1A 0PW

CALLAHAN, J Loughlin; s of John G P Callahan, Lt-Col US Air Force (ret), of 661 Garden Road, Dayton Ohio 45419, and Marie, *née* Loughlin; *b* 18 Jan 1948; *Educ* Holy Cross Coll Worcester Massachusetts (BA), Harvard Law Sch Cambridge Massachusetts (Juris Dr, cum laude); *m* 5 May 1973, Mary, da of Vincent Reilly (d 1969), of 25 Lennox Drive, Tinton Falls, New Jersey, USA; 1 s (Christopher b 1974), 1 da (Denise b 1976); *Career* lawyer Davis Polk & Wardwell New York 1972-80, investment banker S G Warburg Securities (London) 1980-; dir: S G Warburg & Co Ltd 1983-86, International Primary Market Association 1986- (vice chm 1988-); jt head of Fixed Interest Div S G Warburg Securities (dir 1986-); *Recreations* art collecting and tennis; *Style—* J L Callahan, Esq; 7 Spencer Hill, London SW19 4PA (☎ 081 947 7726); S G Warburg Securities, 1 Finsbury Ave, London EC2 (☎ 071 280 4218)

CALLAN, Maj-Gen Michael; CB (1979); s of Maj John Callan, and Elsie Dorothy, *née* Fordham; *b* 27 Nov 1925; *Educ* Farnborough GS, Army Staff Coll, JSSC, RCDS; *m* 1948, Marie Evelyn, *née* Farthing; 2 s; *Career* 1 Gurkhas IA 1944-47, RAOC 1948-80, DDOS 1972-73, Cmmnd Rhine Area BAOR 1975-76, dir gen Ordnance Servs (MOD) 1976-80, Col Cmdt RAOC 1981-89 (Rep Col Cmdt 1982, 1985, 1988), Hon Col SW London ACF 1982-89; *Recreations* jogging, sailing, gardening, DIY; *Style—* Maj-Gen Michael Callan, CB; c/o Royal Bank of Scotland Ltd, Kirkland House, Whitehall, London SW1A 2EB

CALLANDER, Lady Mary Pamela; *née* Douglas; da of 21 Earl of Morton; *b* 12 Nov 1950; *m* 1973, Richard Callander; 1 s (James Edward b 1979), 2 da (Sarah Mary b 1977, Emma Louise b 1981); *Style—* The Lady Mary Callander; Saughland House, Pathhead, Midlothian

CALLARD, Sir Jack (Eric John); s of Frank Callard (d 1951), of Torquay; *b* 15 March 1913; *Educ* Queen's Coll Taunton, St John's Coll Cambridge (MA); *m* 1938, Pauline Mary, da of Rev Charles Pengelly (d 1941); 3 da; *Career* chartered mechanical engr; chm: ICI Ltd 1971-75, British Home Stores 1976-82; dir: Midland Bank 1971-87, Commercial Union Assurance 1975-83, Ferguson Industrial Holdings 1975-86, Equity Capital for Industry 1976-84; Hon DSc Cranfield Inst of Technol; FEng, Hon FIMechE; kt 1974; *Recreations* fly fishing, gardening; *Clubs* Fly Fishers; *Style—* Sir Jack Callard; Crookwath Cottage, High Row, Dockray, nr Penrith, Cumbria CA11 0LG

CALLAWAY-FITTALL, Betty Daphne; *née* Roberts; MBE (1984); da of William Arthur Roberts (d 1965), and Elizabeth Theobald, *née* Hayward (d 1972); *b* 22 March 1928; *Educ* St Pauls Convent, Graycoat Sch London; *m* 1, 1949, E Roy Callaway; m 2, 1978, late Capt William Percival Fitta; *Career* ice skating trainer; nat trainer W Germany 1969-72; pupils include: Angelika and Erich Buck (Euro Champions and second in World Championships 1972), Chrisztine Recoczy and Andras Sally (Hungarian and World Champions and Olympic Silver medallists 1980), Jayne Torvill and Christopher Dean (World and Euro Champions 1981, 1982, 1983-84, also Olympic Champions 1984); Hon citizen Ravensburg Germany 1972, Gold medal Nat Skating Assoc 1955, Hungarian Olympic medal 1980, now skating dir International Ice Dance Acad Slough; *Recreations* water skiing, music, gardening; *Style—* Betty Callaway-Fittall, MBE; 35 Long Grove, Seer Green, Beaconsfield, Bucks (☎ 0494 67 6370)

CALLENDER, Ronald Montgomery (Ron); s of Peter Callender (d 1958), of Lanarkshire, and Isabella, *née* Montgomery; *b* 12 July 1933; *Educ* Dalziel HS Motherwell, Poly of Central London; *m* 5 April 1958, Margaret, da of James

Beveridge, of Burnbank; 2 s (Andrew b 7 Jan 1970, Paul b 6 May 1972); *Career* Nat Serv Cameronians Scot Rifles Suez Canal Zone 1951-53; clerical officer Mechanical Engrg Res Laboratory E Kilbride 1953-57; scientific photographer GEC Hirst Research Centre 1957-64, mangr Photographic Unit Unilever Research Laboratory 1964-90; Euro ed Modern Gold Miner; RPS: Lancet award Med Gp 1973 and 1978, Tech medal Med Gp 1974, Hood medal 1976, Kodak bursary 1978, 50th Anniversary Travel Award Br Cncl 1984; delivered Hurter and Driffield Meml lecture RPS 1979, hon memb Reading Soc of the Miner's Library Wanlockhead 1977; FRPS 1960, FBIPP 1961 (pres 1975-76); *Books* Gold in Britain (1990); *Recreations* travel, exploration, pictorial photography, recreational gold prospecting; *Clubs* Kildonan Prospecting; *Style*— Ron Callender, Esq; 36 Broadlake, Willaston, South Wirral, Cheshire L64 2XB (☎ 051 327 6747)

CALLENDER, Stephen; *b* 30 Aug 1950; *Style*— Stephen Callender, Esq; 9 Elles Ave, Merrow, Guildford, Surrey (☎ 0483 505206); KLP Ltd, 1 Craven Hill, London W2 3EW (☎ 071 723 4388, fax 071 262 7955)

CALLEY, Sir Henry Algernon; DSO (1945), DFC (1943), DL (Wilts 1968); yst s of Rev Algernon Charles Mainwaring Langton (d 1948), and Elizabeth Ina, *née* Calley (d 1960); assumed the surname of Calley in lieu of Langton 1974; *b* 9 Feb 1914; *Educ* St John's Sch Leatherhead; *Career* RAF 1941-48, actg Wing Cdr Bomber Cmd 1944-; Met Police 1938-41; former teacher; former chm: Cncl and Fin Ctee Wilts CC, Wessex Area Cons Assoc; stud owner and mangr: kt 1964; *Style*— Sir Henry Calley, DSO, DFC, DL; Overtown House, Wroughton, Swindon, Wilts (☎ 0793 812208)

CALLICOTT, Richard Kenneth; s of Ernest Victor Callicott, of Bristol, and Joan Alfreda, *née* Furley (d 1968); *b* 18 Sept 1946; *Educ* Colston Sch Bristol, Univ of Birmingham (BPhil Ed); *m* 4 July 1985, Jacqueline Eleanor Elizabeth, da of John Charles Fenton (d 1985), of Sydney, Aust; 3 s (Benjamin Richard b 20 Jan 1976, Daniel Joseph b 26 Sept 1979, Thomas Fenton b 5 Feb 1985); *Career* project coordinator Birmingham bid to host 1992 Olympics 1985, devpt mangr sport and leisure City of Birmingham 1989-90, account dir (sport) National Indoor Arena, chm Tech Ctee World Student Games Sheffield 1991; played cricket for Gloucester 2 XI 1963-64; chm English Volleyball Assoc 1980, pres Cwlth Volleyball Assoc 1988, memb Bd of Admin Euro Volleyball Confedn 1988; tstee Kaleidoscope Theatre; memb Inst of Leisure and Amenity Mgmnt 1988; *Recreations* theatre, jogging, golf; *Style*— Richard Callicott, Esq; 46 Streetley Lane, Four Oaks, Sutton Coldfield, W Midlands B74 4TX; National Indoor Arena, PO Box 4040, Birmingham B40 1P2 (☎ 021 782 8888, fax 021 780 3929)

CALLINAN, Raymond Clive; s of Jeremiah Callinan (d 1959); *b* 13 March 1934; *Educ* Clifton Coll, BNC Oxford; *m* 1962 (m dis 1977), Gita, da of Satish Gore, of Calcutta; 1 s, 1 da; *Career* banker; md Singer & Friedlander Ltd 1970-; *Recreations* cricket, motor racing, reading; *Style*— Raymond Callinan, Esq; 19 Westbourne St, London W2

CALLINICOS, Hon Mrs (Aedgyth Bertha Milburg Mary Antonia Frances); *née* Lyon-Dalberg-Acton; OBE (1986); decorated by Greek Govt (1961) for work in connection with Ionian Islands Earthquakes 1953; 7 da of 2 Baron Acton, KCVO (d 1924); *b* 15 Dec 1920; *Educ* various convents and finishing schs in the United Kingdom and Europe; *m* 1949, John Alexander Callinicos, yst s of Alexander Theodore Callinicos, of Ithaca, Greece; 2 s; *Career* FO 1942-49; PR and hotel mgmnt Zimbabwe; engaged in political and welfare work Zimbabwe; chm Prankerd Jones Memorial Fund, hon sec and co fndr Br Zimbabwe Soc, hon sec Zimbabwe Leprosy Assoc; *Style*— The Hon Mrs Callinicos; Villa Ithaki, Hatfield, Harare, Zimbabwe (☎ 50065)

CALLMAN, His Hon Judge; Clive Vernon Callman; o s of Felix Callman, and Edith Callman; *b* 21 June 1927; *Educ* Ottershaw Coll, St George's Coll Weybridge, LSE (BSc); *m* 1967, Judith Helen, o da of Gus Hines, OBE, JP, of Adelaide, S Aust; 1 s, 1 da; *Career* called to the Bar Middle Temple 1951, practiced in London and Norwich 1951-73, dep circuit judge in Civil and Criminal Jurisdiction 1971-73, circuit judge (SE Circuit) 1973-; sitting: Royal Cts of Justice, Family Div, Mayor's and City of London Ct, Crown Cts Univ of London; senator 1978-; memb: Standing Ctee of Convocation 1958-79, Cncl Anglo-Jewish Assoc 1956-, Careers Advsy Bd 1979-, Advsy Ctee for Magistrates Courses 1979-; memb Ed Bd: Media Law and Practice, Professional Negligence, Jl of Child Law; govr: Birbeck Coll London, LSE; *Recreations* the arts, travel, reading; *Clubs* Bar Yacht; *Style*— His Hon Judge Callman; 11 Constable Close, London NW11 6UA (☎ 081 458 3010)

CALMADY-HAMLYN, Lt-Col (Vincent) Warwick; o s of Maj Charles Hamlyn Hunt Calmady-Hamlyn, TD, JP (d 1963), of Leawood and Paschoe, Devon, and Grace (d 1948), yst da of Rev Sabine Baring-Gould (the author of Onward Christian Soldiers); descended from an Exeter family which acquired Paschoe early 15 cent and Leawood by the marriage of Christopher Hamlyn to Elizabeth Mary Calmady in the 18 cent (*see* Burke's Landed Gentry, 18 ed, vol III, 1972); *b* 5 Dec 1915; *Educ* Cheltenham, RMC Sandhurst; *m* 1, 25 Jan 1945 (m dis 1957), (Marguerite) Kilmeny Sarah, o da of Lt-Col Peter Calvert Lord, OBE, RE (d 1960); m 2, 20 Nov 1958, Madeleine Joan, o da of Henry Albert Moulden, of New Malden, Surrey; 2 da (Laura Dawn b 16 April 1960, Angela Grace b 6 July 1961); *Career* cmmnd Royal Sussex Regt 1936, served in Palestine, Cyprus, Egypt, Iraq, 8 Army, (despatches India), ret 1951; memb Bridestowe Parish Cncl (sometime chm), former memb Okehampton RDC, former dist cmmr Lamerton Hunt (Devon) Pony Club, former Master Delhi and Meerut (India) Hunts; *Recreations* steeple chasing, hurdle racing, polo, hunting; *Clubs* Delhi Gymkhana; *Style*— Lt-Col Calmady-Hamlyn; Leawood, Bridestowe, Okehampton, Devon EX20 4ET (☎ 083 786 203)

CALMAN, Mel; s of Clement Calman, and Anna Calman; *b* 19 May 1931; *Educ* Perse Sch Cambridge, St Martins Sch of Art (NDD), Goldsmiths Coll London (ATD); *m* 1, 1957 (m dis) Pat MvNeill; 2 da; m 2 (m dis) Karen Usborne; *Career* cartoonist: Daily Express 1957-63, BBC Tonight Programme 1963-64, Sunday Telegraph 1964-65, Observer 1965-66, Sunday Times 1969-84, The Times 1979-; freelance cartoonist for various magazines and nespapers 1957-, designer of book jackets, advertising campaigns, illustrator, fndr The Workshop (now The Cartoon Gallery) 1970, prodr The Arrow (animated cartoon), Men & Women (syndicated feature USA 1976-82), radio play Sweet Tooth BBC Radio 3 1987; FRSA, FSIA, AGI; *Books* Help! (1982), Calman Revisited (1983), The Big Novel (1983, dramatised for radio 1986), It's Only You That's Incompatible (1984), What Else Do You Do? (autobiography, 1986), Modern Times; *Recreations* brooding and worrying; *Style*— Mel Calman, Esq; 83 Lambs Conduit Street, London WC1

CALMAN, Montague; s of Clement Calman (d 1946), and Anna Marcus (d 1961); *b* 18 June 1917; *Educ* Grocers' Co Sch; *m* 24 Oct 1957, Deecie Campbell, da of Gordon Lyall (d 1960); *Career* served WWII 1940-46; asst press offr Miny of Supply 1947, press offr NCB 1947; ballet, music and opera critic London Evening Standard, columnist LA Times, feature columnist Ballet Today; PR conslt; FRSA 1947, MJI 1947, MIPR 1956; *Clubs* Royal Cwlth Soc; *Style*— Montague Calman, Esq; 1E Carlisle Place, London SW1P 1NP (☎ 071 828 6665)

CALNE, Prof Sir Roy Yorke; s of Joseph Robert Calne (d 1984), and Eileen Calne (d 1989); *b* 30 Dec 1930; *Educ* Lancing, Guy's Hosp Med Sch; *m* 2 March 1956, Patricia Doreen; 2 s (Russell b 1964, Richard b 1970), 4 da (Jane b 1958, Sarah b 1959, Deborah b 1962, Suzanne b 1963); *Career* Nat Serv RAMC BMH Singapore RMO to KEO 2 Gurkhas 1954-56; conslt and sr lectr (surgery) Westminster Hosp London 1962-65, prof of surgery Univ of Cambridge 1965-, conslt surgn Cambridge Health Authy 1965-; kt 1986; *Books* Renal Transplantation (1963), Lecture Notes in Surgery (with H Ellis, 1965), A Gift of Life (1970), Clinical Organ Transplantation (ed 1971), Organ Grafts (1974), Liver Transplantation (ed & contrib 1983), A Colour Atlas of Transplatation (Renal (1984), Pancreas (1985), Liver (1985)), Transplant Immunology (ed & contrib 1984), Living Surgical Anatomy of the Abdomen (1988); *Recreations* squash, tennis, painting; *Style*— Prof Sir Roy Calne; 22 Barrow Rd, Cambridge (☎ 0223 242708); Dept of Surgery, Addenbrooke's Hills Rd, Cambridge CB2 2QQ (☎ 0223 336975)

CALNE AND CALSTONE, Viscount; Simon Henry George Petty-Fitzmaurice; s and h of Earl of Shelburne and gs of 8 Marquess of Lansdowne, PC; *b* 24 Nov 1970; *Style*— Viscount Calne and Calstone

CALTHORPE; *see*: Anstruther-Gough-Calthorpe

CALTHORPE, 10 Baron (GB 1796); Sir Peter Waldo Somerset Gough-Calthorpe; 11 Bt (1728); s of Hon Frederick Gough-Calthorpe (d 1935), and Dorothy, *née* Vernon-Harcourt (d 1985); suc bro, 9 Baron, 1945; *b* 13 July 1927; *Educ* Stowe; *m* 1, June 1956 (m dis 1971), Saranne Frances (d 1984), o da of James Harold Alexander, of Dublin; m 2, 1979, Elizabeth, da of James Young, of Guildford, Surrey; *Career* late Lt Welsh Gds Palestine; airline pilot (freelance, later for Aer Lingus, then Jersey Airlines) 1951-59; md Mercury Airlines 1960-65; author of two novels published under pseudonym Peter Somerset 1966-67; gp investment mangr 1970-81; *Recreations* theatre, paintings (not modern); *Style*— The Rt Hon the Lord Calthorpe; c/o IOM Bank Ltd, 2 Athol St, Douglas, Isle of Man

CALTON, (Frederick) George; s of Harold Percy Calton (d 1968), of Waterlooville, Hants, and Ethel May, *née* Ching; *b* 11 July 1925; *Educ* Price's Sch Fareham, Queen's Univ Belfast; *m* 28 March 1956, Pamela Margaret, da of Clarence Thomas Church, CBE (d 1963), of Goring-by-Sea; 1 s (Grant b 8 April 1960); *Career* RAF 1944-47; CA; Joseph Lucas Ltd 1951-53, chm Cross and Herbert Ltd 1953-; memb Cncl Br Retailer's Assoc, dir Co Chemists' Assoc; FCA 1951; *Recreations* reading, music, walking; *Style*— George Calton, Esq; Hangmoor, Callow Hill, Virginia Water, Surrey GU25 4LD (☎ 09904 3246); 41 High St Egham, Surrey TW20 9DS (☎ 0784 34244)

CALVERLEY, 3 Baron (UK 1945) Charles Rodney Muff; s of 2 Baron Calverley (d 1971); *b* 2 Oct 1946; *Educ* Moravian Boys' Sch Fulneck; *m* 1972, Barbara Ann, da of Jonathan Brown, of Colne, Lancs; 2 s (Hon Jonathan, Hon Andrew b 1978); *Heir* s, Hon Jonathan Edward Muff b 16 April 1975; *Career* memb W Yorkshire Police; formerly with City of Bradford Police; *Style*— The Rt Hon the Lord Calverley; 110 Buttershaw Lane, Wibsey, Bradford, W Yorkshire BD6 2DA (tel 0274 676414)

CALVERLEY, Dr Peter Martin Anthony; s of Peter Calverley, and Jennifer, *née* Taylor; *b* 27 Nov 1949; *Educ* Queen Elizabeth GS Blackburn, Univ of Edinburgh (MB ChB); *m* 27 June 1973, Margaret Elizabeth, da of William Tatam, of Grantham, Lincs; 4 s (Adam Richard b 1977, James Iain (twin) b 1977, Robert Andrew b 1979, Thomas Peter b 1981); *Career* house offr Edinburgh 1973-74, sr house offr Dept of Med Leicester 1975-76, clinical fell MRC 1977-79, sr registrar Dept of Med Univ of Edinburgh 1979-85, MRC (Can) travelling fell McGill Univ Montreal 1982-83; currently: conslt physician Walton and Fazakerley Hosps Liverpool, hon clinical lectr Univ of Liverpool (sr fell Dept of Med); assoc ed Thorax; memb Br Thoracic Soc (memb Scientific Ctee), sec NW Thoracic Soc, memb American Thoracic Soc; FRCP, FRCPE, FCCP; *Recreations* travel, skiing and talking; *Style*— Dr Peter Calverley; 17 Eshe Rd North, Blundellsands, Liverpool L23 8UE (☎ 051 924 3286); Regional Thoracic Unit, Fazakerley Hospital, Longmoor Lane, Liverpool L9 7AL (☎ 051 525 5980, fax 051 525 6086)

CALVERT, Barbara Adamson; *née* Parker; QC (1975); da of Albert Parker, CBE (d 1980), and Lilian Maud, *née* Midgley (d 1972); *b* 30 April 1926; *Educ* St Helen's Northwood, Univ of London (BSc Econ); *m* 1948, John Thornton Calvert, CBE (d 1987), s of Harry Thornton Calvert, MBE (d 1947); 1 s, 1 da; *Career* called to the Bar Middle Temple 1959, rec SE Circuit 1980, bencher Middle Temple 1982, memb Matrimonial Causes Rule Ctee 1983-86, full-time chm Industl Tbnl 1986- (pt/t chm 1974-); *Recreations* swimming, gardening, poetry; *Clubs* Royal Fowey Yacht; *Style*— Mrs John Calvert, QC; 4 Brick Court, Temple, London EC4 (☎ 071 353 5392); 158 Ashley Gdns, London SW1P 1HW (☎ 071 828 0530)

CALVERT, Denis George; s of Thomas George Calvert (d 1985), Sutton Place, Abinger Hammer, Surrey, and Isabel; *b* 23 April 1928; *Educ* Epsom Coll, Middlesex Hosp Univ of London (MB BS); *m* 7 Sept 1962, Penelope Edith Dorothy, da of Peter Vince, of Clacton on Sea, Essex; 2 s (David b 22 March 1964, Ian b 14 Aug 1966), 1 da (Sarah b 26 May 1965); *Career* sr surgn Gloucester Royal Hosp 1967, conslt surgn Stroud Hosp 1970-; memb: Gloucestershire Health Authy, of Cncl Br Assoc of Urological Surgns; author of multiple surgical papers in various surgical jls; FRCS (England) 1960, FRCS (Edinburgh) 1960; *Recreations* golf, fine wines; *Clubs* Army and Navy; *Style*— Denis Calvert, Esq; Old Weavers, Pitchcombe, Stroud, Gloucestershire (☎ 0452 812580); 9 College Green, Gloucester (☎ 0452 27348)

CALVERT, (Louis Victor) Denis; CB (1985); s of late Louis Victor Calvert, of Belfast, and Gertrude Cherry, *née* Hobson (d 1985); *b* 20 April 1924; *Educ* Belfast Royal Acad, Queen,s Univ Belfast (BSc), Administative Staff Coll Henley-on-Thames; *m* 24 Aug 1949, Vivien Millicent, da of George Albert Lawson (d 1958); 2 s (David b 1951, Steven b 1952), 1 da (Jacqueline b 1961); *Career* RAF 1943-47, FO navigator (UK, Europe, S Africa); NI Civil Serv 1947-80: min of Agriculture 1947-56, dep princ 1951, princ min of Finance 1956-63, min of Health and Local Govt 1963-65, asst sec 1964, min of Devpt 1965-73, sr asst sec 1970, dep sec 1971, min of Housing Local Govt and Planning 1973-76, DOE for NI 1976-80; comptroller and auditor gen for NI 1980-89; *Recreations* gardening, golf, reading, television; *Style*— Denis Calvert, Esq, CB; Northern Ireland Audit Office, Rosepark House, Upper Newtownards Road, Belfast BT4 2NS

CALVERT, Margaret Ada Tomsett; JP; da of Donald Arthur Hodge, of 69 Stratheden Court, Seaford, Sussex, and Ada Constance Janette, *née* Tomsett (d 1973); *b* 8 Jan 1924; *Educ* Haberdashers' Aske's, UCL (BA); *m* 4 July 1953, Dr Jack Maxwell Calvert, s of Albert Henry Calvert (d 1978), of Selby, Yorks; 4 s (David b 1955, Ian b 1956, Jonathan b 1958, Alastair b 1967); *Career* WWII WRNS 1942-46; CA; princ accountant (first woman) Univ of Oxford 1952-53, public practice as int tax specialist 1954-, lectr comparative taxation Univ of Manchester 1958-88, memb Taxation Advsy Panel ICEAW 1984-89; memb and one time div pres Br Red Cross Cheshire Branch, cmmr and memb Cncl Girl Guides Assoc, pres Br Fedn of Univ Women 1987-90; former treas: Int Fedn Univ Women, World Assoc of Girl Guides and Girl Scouts; memb: VAT Tbnl, Nat Insur Tbnl, Community Health Cncl, Women's Nat Commission 1990-; FCA 1959; *Recreations* travel, photography; *Clubs* University Womens; *Style*— Mrs Margaret Calvert, JP; 3 Chyngton Place, Seaford, E Sussex BN25 4HQ (☎ 0323 490 685)

CALVERT, Michael John; JP (1972), DL (Surrey 1974); s of John Charles Calvert (d 1974); *b* 15 Sept 1930; *Educ* Eton, RMA Sandhurst; *m* 1963, Sally Noel, da of Noel Victor Sharpe Cannon (d 1958); 3 da (Clare, Nicola, Celia); *Career* 60 Rifles 1949-62, Adjt Queen's Royal Rifles 1962-64; farmer and market gardener 1964-; chm: Surrey

TAVRA 1980-87, Surrey Community Devpt Tst 1982-; High Sheriff Surrey 1979-80; non-exec dir Seeboard 1985-90; *Recreations* shooting, cricket, golf; *Clubs* Farmers'; *Style—* Michael J Calvert, Esq, JP, DL; Ockley Court, Ockley, nr Dorking, Surrey (☎ 0306 711160)

CALVERT, Paul Thornton; s of John Thornton Calvert, CBE (d 1987), of London, and Barbara Adamson, *née* Parker, QC; *b* 17 March 1949; *Educ* Rugby, Univ of Cambridge (MA, MB BChir); *m* 20 July 1972, Deborah Deidre Anne, da of Maj Bruce Merivale-Austin, of London; 1 s (Dominic b 1979), 1 da (Natasha b 1976); *Career* conslt orthopaedic and traumatic surgn: Hinchingbrooke Hosp Huntingdon 1985-86, St George's Hospital 1986-; author of scientific papers related to shoulder injury and children's orthopaedics; FRCS 1977, FRSM 1983, fell Br Orthopaedic Assoc 1985; *Recreations* squash, tennis; *Clubs* Hawks; *Style—* Paul Calvert, Esq; 27 Woodwarde Rd, Dulwich, London SE22 8UN (☎ 081 693 3998), Consultant Orthopaedic Surgeon, St Georges Hospital, Blackshaw Rd, London SW17 0QT (☎ 081 672 1255)

CALVERT, Peter Anthony Richard; *b* 19 Nov 1936

CALVERT, Phyllis (Mrs Hill); da of Frederick Bickle (d 1964), and Annie Williams (d 1957); *b* 18 Feb 1915; *Educ* French Lycee, Margaret Morris Sch Dancing and Acting; *m* 1941, Peter Auriol Murray Hill (d 1957), s of George Murray Hill (d 1941); 1 s (Piers), 1 da (Auriol); *Career* actress; theatre appearances incl: A Woman's Privilege (Kingsway Theatre) 1939, Punch without Judy (Embassy) 1939, Flare Path (Apollo) 1942, Escapade (St James's) 1953, It's Never Too Late (Strand) 1954, River Breeze (Phoenix) 1956, The Complaisant Lover (Globe) 1959, The Rehearsal (Globe) 1981, Ménage à Trois (Lyric) 1963, Portrait of Murder (Savoy and Vauderville) 1963, A Scent of Flowers (Duke of York's) 1964, Present Laughter (Queen's) 1965, A Woman of No Importance (Vauderville) 1967, Blithe Spirit (Globe) 1970, Crown Matrimonial (Haymarket) 1973, Dear Daddy (Ambassadors) 1976, Mrs Warren's Profession (Worcester) 1977, She Stoops to Conquer (Old World Exeter) 1978, Suite in Two Keys (tour) 1978, Before the Party (Queen's) 1980, The Heiress (Chichester Festival) 1989; films 1939-; Kipps, The Young Mr Pitt, Man in Grey, Fanny by Gaslight, Madonna of the Seven Moons, They were Sisters, Time out of Mind, Broken Journey, My Own True Love, The Golden Madonna, A Woman with No Name, Mr Denning Drives North, Mandy, The Net, It's Never too Late, Child in the House, Indiscreet, The Young and The Guilty, Oscar Wilde, Twisted Nerve, Oh! What a Lovely War, The Walking Stick; tv series incl: Kate 1970, Month in the Country 1984, PD James' Cover Her Face 1984; *Style—* Phyllis Calvert; Hill House, Waddesdon, Bucks (☎ 0296 651291); agent Jeremy Conway (☎ 071 839 2121)

CALVERT, (William) Roger Spencer; s of Charles Gilbert Calvert (d 1983), of Hale, Cheshire, and Eva, *née* Rathbone; *b* 18 May 1938; *Educ* Liverpool Coll, Rossall Sch, Selwyn Coll Cambridge (MA, LLM); *m* 11 Jan 1973, Evelyn Moira, da of Kenneth Harland Wilson (d 1967); 1 s (Simon Harland Spencer b 5 April 1974), 1 da (Nicola Eve b 7 June 1977); *Career* Nat Serv Cmmnd (active serv Aden and Kenya) 1958-59; articled clerk Maxwell Batley 1963-66, admitted slr 1966-; asst slr Slaughter & May 1966-69; ptnr: North Kirk & Co Liverpool 1971-82 (asst slr 1969-71), Cuff Roberts North Kirk (following merger) 1982-; sec Pool Promoters Assoc 1983-; memb Law Soc 1966-; *Recreations* golf, rugby (watching now!), music, gardening; *Clubs* Liverpool Racquet, Waterloo RFC, Northern Cricket, Formby Golf, Liverpool Rotary; *Style—* Roger Calvert, Esq; Sandfield, 52 Dowhills Rd, Blundellsands, Liverpool L23 8SW (☎ 051 924 9412); Messrs Cuff Roberts North Kirk Solicitors, 25 Castle St, Liverpool L2 4TD (☎ 051 227 4181, fax 051 227 2584)

CALVERT-SMITH, David; s of Arthur Eustace Calvert-Smith, of Bury, W Sussex, and Stella Margaret, *née* Tilling; *b* 6 April 1945; *Educ* Eton, Kings Coll Cambridge (MA); *m* 4 Dec 1971, Marianthe; 1 s (Richard b 1972), 1 da (Stella b 1975); *Career* called to the Bar 1969, rec 1986, treasy counsel 1986; *Style—* David Calvert-Smith; Queen Elizabeth Bldg, Temple, London EC4 (☎ 071 583 5766, fax 071 353 0339)

CALVIN-THOMAS, Joseph Wyndham (known as Wyn Calvin); MBE (1989); s of John Calvin-Thomas (d 1959), and Ethel Mary, *née* Griffiths (d 1974); *b* 28 Aug 1927; *Educ* Canton HS Cardiff; *m* 1975, Eileen Carole Jones; *Career* served RASC 1944-45; theatre and broadcasting 1945-; memb Ctee Entertainment Artistes Benevolent Fund 1960-, chm Wales Ctee Variety Club of GB 1980-82 and 1984-86, dir and govr Monkton House Educnl Tst, vice pres Cor Meibion de Cymru (Massed Male Choir of S Wales), hon prodr Wales Festival of Remembrance (Royal Br Legion); barker Variety Club of GB 1963-, "King" Grand Order of Water Rats 1990-91; *Recreations* writing, reading, world-wandering; *Style—* Wyn Calvin, Esq, MBE; 121 Cathedral Rd, Cardiff CF1 9PH (☎ 0222 232777)

CALVO-PLATERO, Hon Mrs (Ariadne Grace); *née* Beaumont; yr da of Baron Beaumont of Whitley (Life Peer), *qv*; *b* 22 April 1963; *Educ* Ch Ch Oxford; *m* 1990, Mario Calvo-Platero, yr s of late Guido Calvo-Platero, of Milan; *Career* investment banking; *Style—* The Hon Ariadne Beaumont

CALVOCORESSI, Hon Mrs (Barbara Dorothy); *née* Eden; da of 6 Baron Henley (d 1962); *b* 1915; *m* 1938, Peter John Ambrose Calvocoressi, s of Pandia Calvocoressi (d 1965), of 31 Albion Gate, London W2; 2 s; *Style—* The Hon Mrs Calvocoressi; 1 Queen's Parade, Bath, Avon BA1 2NJ

CALVOCORESSI, Maj Ion Melville; MBE (1945), MC (1942); s of Matthew John Calvocoressi, and Agnes Hermione, da of late Judge Robert Melville, of Sussex and Salop; *b* 12 April 1919; *Educ* Eton, Magdalen Coll Oxford (MA); *m* 1947, Katherine, da of Capt Edward Coverley Kennedy, RN (ka 1939, ggs of Hon Robert Kennedy, bro of 1 Marquess of Ailsa and 3 s of 11 Earl of Cassillis), and Rosalind, da of Sir Ludovic Grant, 11 Bt; 3 s, 1 da; *Career* Scots Gds 1939-46: Middle East, Sicily, Italy, SE Asia 1941-45, ADC, GOC 8 Army 1944, Mil Asst; CGS ALFSEA 1945; memb London Stock Exchange 1949; High Sheriff Kent 1978-79; *Recreations* cricket, gardening; *Clubs* Cavalry & Guards, City of London, Pratt's, MCC, Kent CCC; *Style—* Maj Ion Calvocoressi, MBE, MC; Court Lodge, Westerham, Kent (☎ 0959 63358)

CALVOCORESSI, Peter John Ambrose; s of Pandia John Calvocoressi (d 1965), of 31 Albion Gate, London W2, and Irene, *née* Ralli; *b* 17 Nov 1912,Karachi; *Educ* Eton, Balliol Coll Oxford; *m* 1938, Hon Barbara Dorothy Eden, da of late 6 Baron Henley; 2 s; *Career* serv WWII Wing Cdr RAFVR (Air Intelligence); called to the Bar Inner Temple 1935; contested (Lib) Warwicks (Nuneaton Div) 1945; author; dir Chatto & Windus Ltd and The Hogarth Press Ltd 1954-65; reader in Int Relations Univ of Sussex 1966-71, editorial dir and chief exec Penguin Books 1972-76, chm Open Univ Educnl Enterprises 1979-89; memb cncl: Royal Inst of Int Affairs, Inst of Strategic Studies; *Clubs* Garrick; *Style—* Peter Calvocoressi, Esq; 1 Queen's Parade, Bath, Avon

CAMBER, Hon Mrs (Angela Felicity); *née* Birk; JP; only da of Baroness Birk (Life Peeress) by her husband Ellis Samuel Birk; *b* Jul 1947; *Educ* Camden Sch for Girls, London Univ; *m* 1970, Richard Camber (*qv*); *Style—* The Hon Mrs Camber

CAMBER, Richard Monash; s of Maurice Camber, of Glasgow, and Libby Camber (d 1981); *b* 22 July 1944; *Educ* Glasgow HS, Univ of Edinburgh (MA), Univ of Paris, Univ of London; *m* 26 Oct 1970, The Hon Angela Felicity, da of Ellis Birk, of London; 1 s (Thomas b 1980), 2 da (Alice b 1974, Chloe b 1980); *Career* asst keeper Dept of Medieval and later antiquities Br Museum 1970-78; dir: Sotheby's London 1983-87, Sotheby's, Sotheby's Int; conslt Euro Works of Art 1988-; FSA; *Recreations* reading, listening to music (particularly opera); *Style—* Richard Camber, Esq, FSA; 28 Heath Drive, Hampstead, London NW3 7SB (☎ 071 435 5250, 071 431 4553)

CAMBRIDGE, Alan John; s of Thomas David Cambridge (d 1969), and Winifred Elizabeth, *née* Jarret (d 1970); *b* 1 July 1925; *Educ* Beckenham GS; *m* 1947, Thelma, da of Francis Elliot (d 1960); 3 s, 1 da; *Career* RAF 1943-47, Flt Sgt rear gunner, 150 Sqdn Bomber Cmd; War Pensions Office and MPNI 1948-55; joined Cwlth Rels Office 1955, Madras 1956-58, Kuala Lumpur 1959-62, Rhodesia and Nyasaland 1962-65; HM Dip Serv 1965, 1 sec UN Dept FCO 1966-69, del UN Gen Assembly 1968, 1 sec Prague 1969, 1 sec (consular aid) Suva 1970-72, consul Milan 1972-74, asst head Info Dept FCO 1974-78, 1 sec (info) Ankara 1978-81, asst head then head Migration and Visa Dept FCO 1981-85, ret 1985; assessor FCO 1985-89; *Recreations* photography, tennis, swimming; *Clubs* Civil Service; *Style—* Alan Cambridge, Esq; 9 The Ferns, Carlton Rd, Tunbridge Wells, Kent TN1 2JT (☎ 0892 31223)

CAMDEN, 6 Marquess (UK 1812); David George Edward Henry Pratt; also Baron Camden (GB 1765), Earl Camden and Viscount Bayham (GB 1786), and Earl of Brecknock (UK 1812); s of 5 Marquess Camden, JP, DL (d 1983), and his 1 w, Marjorie Minna, DBE (d 1989), da of late Col Atherton Edward Jenkins; *b* 13 Aug 1930; *Educ* Eton; *m* 1961 (m dis 1985), Virginia Ann, only da of late Francis Harry Hume Finlaison, of Windsor; 2 s (1 decd), 1 da; *Heir* s, Earl of Brecknock; *Career* late 2 Lt Scots Gds; *Style—* The Most Hon the Marquess Camden; Cowdown Farm House, Andover, Hants SP11 6LE (☎ 0264 352085)

CAMERON, Maj Allan John; MBE (1988), JP (Ross and Cromarty 1960), DL; s of Col Sir Donald Cameron of Lochiel, KT, CMG (d 1951), and Lady Hermione Graham (d 1978), da of 5 Duke of Montrose; *b* 25 March 1917; *Educ* Harrow, RMC Sandhurst; *m* 1945, (Mary) Elizabeth, da of Col Arthur Vaughan-Lee, MVO (d 1933), of Dillington, Somerset; 2 s (and 1 s decd), 2 da; *Career* Regular Offr Queen's Own Cameron Highlanders 1936, served WWII Maj (POW 1942), ret 1948; landowner and farmer; served on: BBC Cncl for Scot, Countryside Cmmn of Scot, Red Deer Cmmn, Ross-shire CC 1955- (chm County Educn Ctee 1962-75); pres Royal Caledonian Curling Club 1963-64, Vice Lord-Lieut Ross and Cromarty Highland Region 1977-; *Recreations* shooting, fishing, curling, golf, gardening; *Clubs* Naval and Military; *Style—* Maj Allan Cameron, MBE, JP, DL; Allangrange, Munlochy, Ross and Cromarty (☎ 046 381 249)

CAMERON, Lt-Col Charles Alexander; MC (1944), TD (1947), JP (1961), DL (1956); s of Sir Donald Walter Cameron of Lochiel, KT, CMG (d 1951); bro of Col Sir Donald Cameron of Lochiel and of Maj Allan John Cameron, *qv*; *b* 29 Sept 1920; *Educ* Loretto; *m* 1953, Felicia Margaret, er da of Col Kenneth Macdonald, of Tote, Skye; 1 s, 1 da; *Career* served 1939-45 Cameron Highlander TA, Maj 1944, Lt-Col 1957; memb: Inverness-shire CC 1952-75, Highland Regnl Cncl 1975-82; highland regnl rep Nat Tst for Scotland 1982-86; *Style—* Lt-Col Charles Cameron, MC, TD, JP, DL; 3 Marine Cottages, Nairn, Scotland

CAMERON, Donald Allan; s of David Stuart Cameron (d 1956), and Madge Kay, *née* Murphy (d 1942); *b* 16 July 1939; *Educ* Allan Glens Sch, Univ of Glasgow (BSc), Cornell Univ USA (MIE); *m* 1, 1968 (m dis 1980), Dorothy Ann, *née* Golding; m 2, 23 Oct 1981, Margaret Louise, da of James Tobin, of Avon; 4 s (James, Allan, Thomas, David), 2 da (Hannah, Louise); *Career* Univ Air Sqdn RAFVR 1957-60; Bristol Aeroplane Co 1963-65, Richard Thomas & Baldwins 1965-67, RTZ 1967-70, Cameron Balloons Ltd 1970-; vice pres Federation Aeronautique Internationale Int Ballooning Cmmn, ctee memb Br Balloon and Airship Club, tstee dir Bristol Balloon Fiesta, memb of Tech Ctee Airship Assoc, Chm of govrs High Down Infant Sch; Hon MA Univ of Bristol 1990; MRAeS; *Books* The Ballooning Handbook (1980), Zanussi Transatlantic Balloon (1983); *Clubs* Br Balloon and Airship; *Style—* Donald Cameron, Esq; 3 The Knoll, Woodhill Road, Portishead BS20 9NU (☎ 0272 845033); Cameron Balloons Ltd, St Johns St, Bristol BS3 4NH (☎ 0272 637216, fax 0272 661168, telex 444825 GASBA G, car 0836 788162)

CAMERON, Dr Douglas; s of Dr Robert Cameron (d 1949), of Cambridge, and Louise Patricia, *née* Smith; *b* 2 Aug 1943; *Educ* The Leys Sch Cambridge, Univ of Glasgow (BSc, MB ChB); *m* 5 July 1969, Catherine Love, da of William Leslie Bews (d 1971), of Glasgow; 2 da (Esther b 1970, Sarah b 1972); *Career* conslt psychiatrist specialising in alcohol problems Leicestershire Health Authy 1976-, fndr and currently involved with Leicestershire Community Alcohol and Drugs Servs 1978-; fndr memb and currently chm New Directions in the Study of Alcohol Gp 1976-, memb DHSS Steering Gp on the Future of Nat Voluntary Alcohol Agencies 1982-83, interim then full exec memb Alcohol Concern 1983-87 (chair of Policy Ctee 1984-87); memb: Exec Ctee The Griffins Soc 1985-, Faculty of Community Meds Working Pty on Alcohol and other drugs 1987-89; ind scientific advsr to the Portman Gp 1989; FRCPsych 1988 (MRCPsych 1974); *papers incl*: Lessons from an out-patient controlled Drinking Group, Journal of Alcoholism (with M T Spence, 1976), Teenage Drinking in South West Scotland, British Journal of Addiction (with R J McKechnie, I A Cameron, J Drewery, 1977), Rate of Onset of Drunkenness, Journal of Studies on Alcohol (with M T Spence, J Drewery, 1978); contrib: Alcoholism, A Multidisciplinary Approach (eds Kenyon Madden Walker, 1977), Aspects of Alcohol and Drug Dependence (eds Madden Walker Kenyon, 1980), The Misuse of Alcohol, Crucial Issues in Dependence, Treatment and Prevention (ed Heather Robertson Davies, 1985); *Recreations* participant observation of public house culture!; *Style—* Dr Douglas Cameron; Drury House, 50 Leicester Rd, Narborough, Leicestershire LE9 5DF (☎ 0533 863267)

CAMERON, Ewen William; OBE, JP; s of William Tulloch Cameron (d 1955), of Lochearnhead Hotel, Perthshire, and Christine Mabon (d 1944); *b* 23 Dec 1926; *Educ* Trinity Coll Glenalmond; *m* 27 April 1955, Davina Anne, da of Morton Frew (d 1983), of the Shieling, Race Course Rd, Ayr; 1 s (Angus James b 1957), 1 da (Elaine Tootie b 1959); *Career* South East Asia RNVR 1944-47; md: Lochearn Devpt Co 1951-, Lochearnhead Hotel 1955, Lochearnhead Water Sports Co 1970-; vice chm: Cumbernauld New Town Devpt Corp 1963-77, Royal Highland Shaw 1981; chm Br Water Ski Fedn 1966-70; pres: Edinchip Curling Club 1950-82, Lochearnhead Highland Games 1978-; govr: Morrisons Acad Crieff, Ardvreck Sch Criett; memb: Perth CC 1963-75, Stirling DC 1974-77, Perth and Kinross DC 1980- (dep provost 1982-84), Scottish Sports Cncl 1980-88, Perth Prison Bd 1980-, Scottish Electricity Cncl 1981-87, Tayside Health Bd 1982-, Scottish Tourist Bd, Highlands Islands Advsy Bd; Scottish champion Highland Games Field Events 1953; *Recreations* shooting, golf, curling, dominoes; *Clubs* Kandahar, Royal Perth, Saints and Sinners (Scotland), Elie Golf; *Style—* Ewen Cameron, Esq, OBE, JP; Ben Ouhr Lochearnhead, Perthshire FK19 8PT (☎ 05673 231); Admiralty House, Elie, Fife (☎ 033 3330 686)

CAMERON, George Edmund; CBE (1970); s of William Cameron and Margaret, *née* Craig; *b* 2 July 1911; *Educ* Ballymena Acad; *m* 1939, Winifred Audrey, da of James Brown; 2 s; *Career* sr ptnr Wright Fitzsimmons and Cameron (CA), chm Northern Ireland Carriers Ltd, dir Cameron Investmts Ltd, Lombard & Ulster Banking Ltd, Ulster Bank Unit Tst Mangrs Ltd; *Style—* George Cameron, Esq, CBE; Ardavon, Glen Rd, Craigavad, Co Down, N Ireland

CAMERON, Ian Donald; s of Ewen Donald Cameron, and Enid Agnes Maud Levita; *b* 12 Oct 1932; *Educ* Eton; *m* 1962, Mary Fleur, *née* Mount; 2 s (Allan b 1963, David b 1966), 2 da (Tania b 1963, Clare b 1971); *Career* memb Stock Exchange 1955, sr ptnr

Panmure Gordon and Co (stockbrokers); High Sheriff of Berkshire 1978-79; *Clubs* White's; *Style*— Ian Cameron, Esq; The Old Rectory, Peasemore, Newbury, Berks; Panmure Gordon & Co, 9 Moorfields Highwalk, London EC2Y 9DS (☎ 017 638 4010; telex 883832)

CAMERON, Prof Ian Rennell; s of James Cameron (d 1985), of London, and Frances Mary, *née* Little (d 1959); *b* 20 May 1936; *Educ* Westminster, CCC Oxford (MA), St Thomas's Hosp Med Sch (BM BCh, DM); *m* 1, 1 Feb 1964 (m dis 1980), Jayne Heather, da of Lt-Col Frank Bustard, OBE (d 1974), of Haslemere, Surrey; 1 s (Hugh Nicholas b 1968), 1 da (Lucinda Emma b 1970); m 2, 24 Dec 1980, Jennifer Jane, da of George Stewart Cowin (d 1978), of IOM; *Career* res fell Cedars - Sinai Med Center LA, asst prof Dept of Physiology Univ of California LA 1968-69; St Thomas's Hosp Med Sch: med registrar and lectr 1963-68, sr lectr 1969-75, reader in med 1975-79, prof of med 1979-; princ UMDS 1989-; chm W Lambeth DHA mgmnt team 1982-83, memb Medway Health Authy 1981-86; Freeman City of London 1984, Liveryman Worshipful Soc of Apothecaries 1985 (Yeoman 1976); FRCP 1976; *Books* Respiratory Disorders (with NT Bateman, 1983); *Recreations* collecting books, china, paintings; *Clubs* Athenaeum; *Style*— Prof Ian Cameron; 52 Beaconsfield Rd, Blackheath, London SE3 7LG (☎ 081 853 1921); United Med and Dental Schs of Guys and St Thomas's Hosps, Lambeth Palace Rd, London SE1 7EH (☎ 071 928 9292 ext 2546)

CAMERON, Sir James Clark; CBE (1969), TD (1947); s of Malcolm Clark Cameron, of Rannoch, Perthshire; *b* 8 April 1905; *Educ* Perth Acad, Univ of St Andrews (MB ChB); *m* 1933, Irene Maud (d 1986), da of Arthur Ferguson, of Perth; 1 s, 2 da; *Career* serv WWII Capt RAMC attached 1 Bn The Rifle Bde, Calais (POW 1940, despatches 1945); chm Gen Med Services Ctee BMA 1964-74 (hon life memb); chm Cncl BMA 1976-79; hon memb Cncl Cameron Fund Ltd; FRCGP; Gold medal for distinguished merit BMA 1974; kt 1979; *Recreations* medical politics; *Style*— Sir James Cameron, CBE, TD; 62 Haven Green Court, Haven Green, Ealing W5 2UY (☎ 081 997 8262)

CAMERON, Prof James Kerr; s of Joseph Hepburn Cameron (d 1973), of Ilkley, Yorkshire, and Amelia Edgar Crackston, *née* Kerr (d 1951); *b* 5 March 1924; *Educ* Oban HS, Univ of St Andrews (MA, BD), Hartford Theol Seminary (PhD, SCL); *m* 28 Sept 1956, (Emma) Leslie, da of George Sherrett Birse (d 1953); 1 s (Euan Kerr b 15 July 1958); *Career* asst min Church of the Holy Rude Stirling 1952-55, lectr Univ of Aberdeen 1955-56, prof of ecclesiastical history Univ of St Andrews 1970-89 (lectr, sr lectr 1956-70); pres Ecclesiastical History Soc 1976, pres Br Sub-Cmmn Cmmn Internationale d'Histoire Ecclèstiastique Comparée 1980-; FRHistS; *Books* Letters of John Johnston and Robert Howie (1963), The First Book of Discipline (1972); *Recreations* gardening; *Style*— Prof James K Cameron; Priorscroft, 71 Hepburn Gdns, St Andrews KY16 9LS (☎ 0334 73996)

CAMERON, John Alastair; QC (Scotland 1979); s of William Philip Legerwood Cameron (d 1977), of Edinburgh, and Kathleen Milthorpe, *née* Parker (d 1966); *b* 1 Feb 1938; *Educ* Glenalmond Coll Perth, Pembroke Coll Oxford (MA); *m* 1968, Elspeth Mary Dunlop, da of James Bowie Miller, of E Lothian; 3 s (Hamish b 1970, Neil b 1972, Iain b 1975); *Career* Nat Serv, 2 Lt RASC Aldershot & Malta 1956-58; called to the Bar Inner Temple 1963; advocate 1966, advocate depute 1972-75; standing jr counsel Dept of Energy 1976-79, Scot Devpt Dept 1978-79; vice dean Faculty of Advocates 1983-; pres Pensions Appeal Tbnls for Scotland 1985-(legal chm 1979-), chm Faculty Services Ltd 1983-89, (dir 1979-89); *Publications* Medical Negligence: An Introduction (1983); *Recreations* sport, travel, Africana; *Style*— Alastair Cameron, Esq; 4 Garscube Terrace, Edinburgh EH12 6BQ (☎ 031 337 3460); Advocates' Library, Parliament House, Edinburgh EH1 1RF (☎ 031 226 5071)

CAMERON, John Bell; CBE; s of Capt John Archibald, MC (d 1960), and Margaret (d 1974); *b* 14 June 1939; *Educ* Dollar Acad; *m* 24 July 1964, Margaret, da of James Clapperton, OBE (d 1977); *Career* pres NFU of Scotland 1979-84 (first long term pres); chm: EEC Sheepmeat Ctee 1983-90, World Meats Gp 1983-, UK Sheep Consultative Ctee 1984-86, BR (Scotland) Bd 1988-, United Auctions Ltd 1988-; memb BR Bd 1988-; chm Bd of Govrs Dollar Acad; FRAgS; *Recreations* flying, shooting, swimming; *Style*— John Cameron, Esq, CBE; Balbuthie Farm, Leven, Fife, Scotland (☎ 03337210)

CAMERON, Hon Lord; Sir John Cameron; KT (1978), DSC (1944), DL (Edinburgh 1953); s of John Cameron, SSC (d 1943), of Edinburgh; *b* 8 Feb 1900; *Educ* Edinburgh Acad, Edinburgh Univ; *m* 1, 1927, Eileen Dorothea (d 1943), da of Harry Milburn Burrell; 1 s (Rt Hon Lord Cameron of Lochbroom, PC, *qv*), 2 da; m 2, 1944, Iris Eunice, da of late Eric Alfred Henry, Indian Police, and wid of Lambert C Shepherd; *Career* advocate Scotland 1924, KC 1936, appointed a lord of session with title Lord Cameron 1955, ret from bench 1985; former Sheriff of Inverness Elgin and Nairn and of Inverness Moray Nairn and Ross and Cromarty; Hon: RSA, FRSE, FBA; Hon LLD: Edinburgh, Aberdeen, Glasgow; Hon DLitt Heriot-Watt, Hon DUniv Edinburgh; kt 1954; *Style*— The Hon Lord Cameron, KT, DSC, DL; 28 Moray Place, Edinburgh (☎ 031 225 7585)

CAMERON, Prof John Robinson (Robin); s of Rev Dr George Gordon Cameron (d 1981), of Edinburgh, and Mary Levering, *née* Robinson (d 1989); *b* 24 June 1936; *Educ* Dundee HS, Univ of St Andrews (MA, BPhil); *m* 1, 19 Aug 1959, Mary Elizabeth (d 1984), da of Rev Dr Charles Wesley Ranson (d 1988), of Lakeville, USA; 1 s (Ian b 1967), 2 da (Margaret b 1962, Catherine b 1965); m 2, 25 June 1987, Barbara Elizabeth, da of James Moncur (d 1967), of Newport-on-Tay; *Career* lectr in philosophy Queen's Coll Dundee 1963-67 (asst lectr 1962-63), sr lectr Univ of Dundee 1973-78 (lectr 1967-72); regius prof of logic Univ of Aberdeen 1979-; elder Church of Scotland; *Recreations* bricolage; *Style*— Prof Robin Cameron; 70 Cornhill Rd, Aberdeen AB2 5DH (☎ 0224 486700); Dept of Philosophy, Univ of Aberdeen, King's Coll, Old Aberdeen AB9 2UB (☎ 0224 272365)

CAMERON, Sir John Watson; OBE (1960); s of Capt Watson Cameron and Isabel Mann; *b* 16 Nov 1901; *Educ* Lancing; *m* Lilian Florence, *née* Sanderson; 1 s, 2 da; *Career* cmmd Durham RGA 1920; memb Northern Area Econ League 1950-80; (chm 1964-69), pres J W Cameron & Co Brewery 1977- (joined 1922, md 1940, chm 1943-75); treas Northern Area Cons Pty 1967-72; pres and patron Hartlepool Cons Pty 1978- (chm 1942-45, pres 1945-76, patron 1976-78); kt 1981; *Style*— Sir John Cameron

CAMERON, Joseph Gordon Stuart; WS; s of James Douglas Cameron (d 1973), of Edinburgh, and Josephine Gordon Cameron, *née* Stuart (d 1955); *b* 4 Feb 1927; *Educ* George Watson's Boys' Coll, Univ of Edinburgh (MA, LLB); *m* 24 July 1956, Celia Margaret, da of Hugh Alexander Russell Niven (d 1981), of Rugby; 3 s (Gordon b 1957, Hugh b 1960, James b 1962), 1 da (Lucy b 1965); *Career* Nat Serv Corpl Wilts Regt 1948-49; ptnr Stewart & Stewart W S 1953-90; lectr in conveyancing Edinburgh Univ 1955-60; govr St Leonards Sch 1969-88; *Books* Paton and Cameron Law of Landlord and Tenant in Scotland (jtly 1967); *Recreations* arboriculture, hillwalking; *Clubs* New (Edinburgh), Univ of Edinburgh Staff; *Style*— J G S Cameron, Esq, WS; 23 Rutland St, Edinburgh EH1 2RN (☎ 031 228 6449)

CAMERON, Hon Mrs (Judith Evelyn Maud); *née* Baillie; o da of Brig the Hon George Evan Michael Baillie, MC, TD, RA (ka 1941), by his wife, Lady Maud, CBE, JP (d 1975), wid of Capt Angus Alexander Mackintosh, RHG, and er da of 9 Duke of Devonshire, KG; sis of 3 Baron Burton; raised to rank of a Baron's da 1964; *b* 12 Nov 1925; *m* 1949, Lt-Col Angus Ewen Cameron, MC, Scots Gds, *qv*, gs of late Donald Cameron of Lochiel, 24 Chief of Clan Cameron; 1 s, 1 da; *Career* in ATS 1944-47; *Style*— The Hon Mrs Cameron; Aldourie Castle, Inverness (☎ 046 375 309)

CAMERON, Dr Keith Colwyn; s of Leonard George Cameron (d 1969), of Cwmbran, Gwent, and Ethel Cameron; *b* 1 April 1939; *Educ* Jones' West Monmouth Sch, Univ of Exeter (BA), Univ of Cambridge (Cert Ed), Université de Rennes (LèsL, Doct de l'univ); *m* 4 Aug 1962, Marie-Edith Françoise, da of Francis Marie-Joseph Briens (d 1978), of I et V, France; 3 da (Anne b 1963, Cécilia, b 1964, Virginia b 1968); *Career* asst lectr Univ of Aberdeen 1964-66, reader Univ of Exeter 1988- (lectr 1966-76, sr lectr 1976-88); gen ed: Exeter Textes littéraires 1970-, CALL 1989-; dir: Exeter Tapes 1974-, Elm Bank Pubns 1977-; chm Euro Movement Devon branch; *Books* Montaigne et l'humour (1966), Agrippa d'Aubigné (1977), Henri III - a Maligned or Malignant King? (1978), Montaigne and his Age (1981), René Maran (1985), B Palissy, Recepte véritable (1988), Concordance de Du Bellay (1988), Computer Assisted Language Learning (1989), From Valois to Bourbon (1989); *Recreations* theatre, walking, travel; *Style*— Dr Keith Cameron; Dept of French, Queen's Building, The University, Exeter EX4 4QH (☎ 0392 264221, fax 0392 263108, tlx 42894 EXUNI

CAMERON, Prof Kenneth; CBE (1987); s of Angus Whittaker Cameron (d 1948), of Habergham, Burnley, Lancs, and Elizabeth Alice, *née* Hargreaves (d 1989); *b* 21 May 1922; *Educ* Burnley GS, Univ of Leeds (BA), Univ of Sheffield (PhD); *m* 8 Dec 1948, Kathleen (d 1977), da of Frank Ewart Heap, of Burnley, Lancs; 1 s (Iain b 1955), 1 da (Susan (Mrs Cole) b 1949); *Career* WWII Fst Lt RAF 1941-45;Univ of Nottingham: sr lectr 1959-62, reader 1962-63, prof of Eng lang 1963-67, head Dept Eng Studies 1984-87, prof emeritus 1988; external prof Univ of Loughborough 1990-93; Sahlgren prize Royal gustav Adolfs Acad 1990; hon dir English Place Name Soc; Hon Fil Dr Univ of Uppsala 1977; FBA 1976, FRHS 1970, FSA 1984; *Books* The Place-Names of Derbyshire (3 vols 1959), English Place-Names (1961,1988), The Place-Names of Lincolnshire (1985), Studies in Honour of Kenneth Cameron (1987), Place-Name Evidence for the Anglo-Saxon Invasion and Scandinavian Settlements (1975); *Recreations* sports (supporting); *Style*— Prof Kenneth Cameron, CBE, FSA; 292 Queens Road, Beeston, Nottingham NG9 1JA (☎ 0602 254 503); The University of Nottingham, Nottingham, NG5 2RD (☎ 0602 484 848, ext 2892)

CAMERON, Malcolm Maben; s of Charles Cameron, of Waikanae, NZ, and Margaret Isabella Jean, *née* Brash (d 1976); *b* 10 July 1941; *Educ* Rongotai Coll Wellington NZ, Victoria Univ Wellington NZ (BSc), Otago Med Sch NZ (MB ChB); *m* 12 Dec 1987, Cecily Anne, da of John Honeyford; 1 s (Jody Brent Alexander b 3 Aug 1981); *Career* Capt TA NZ 1967-72; sr registrar neurosuregy Salford 1976-, conslt neurosurgn Wakefield 1979-; 23 articles neurosurgical lit 1974-89; surgical assessor Int Soc Paediatriconcology, chm Local Div Surgery, memb Cncl N of England Neurological Assoc; memb: SIOP, SBNS, NENA; FRCS (Ed) 1973; *Books* Complications of Paediatric Surgery (contrib, 1982), Complications In Spinal Surgery (jtly, 1989), Spinal Surgery-Science and Practice (jtly, 1989); *Recreations* swimming, shooting, reading, writing; *Style*— Malcolm Cameron, Esq; Liley Beck, Clough Lane, Upper Hopton, Mirfield, W Yorks WF14 8EQ (☎ 0924 480588); Dept of Neurosurgery, Pinderfields Gen Hosp, Wakefield, W Yorks WF1 4DG (☎ 0924 375217)

CAMERON, Michael David; s of Alec Leslie Cameron (d 1950), of Calcutta, and Evelyn Grace, *née* Sandifer (d 1979); *b* 1 Aug 1928; *Educ* Rottingdean Sch, Michaelhouse S Africa, Pembroke Coll Cambridge (MA,MB BChir); *m* 2 Aug 1952, Enid Mary, da of Frank Burge; 1 s (Ian Sandifer b 1953), 2 da (Patsy b 1958, Nicola (twin)); *Career* Nat Serv Flt Lt RAF 1952-54; sr obstetrician and gynaecologist: St Thomas's London 1967-79, Royal Masonic Hosp 1979-; FRCS, FRCOG, memb RSM; *Recreations* fishing, shooting, egyptology; *Clubs* Oriental; *Style*— Michael Cameron, Esq; 15 Melcombe Regis Court, 59 Weymouth St, London W1N 3LL (☎ 071 486 9494)

CAMERON, Peter John; MBE; s of John Gordon Cameron (d 1945), of Cheadle Hulme, and Beatrice, *née* Ward (d 1955); *b* 28 Sept 1926; *Educ* Xaverian Coll Manchester, Univ of Manchester Inst of Sci and Technol (BSc); *m* 1957, Helen Cecilia, da of Daniel Whealing; 2 s (John Gordon b 1958, Adrian Peter b 1960), 3 da (Ann Elizabeth b 1959, Margaret Bernadette b 1962, Catherine Cecilia b 1964); *Career* served Army rising to the rank of Capt REME 1946-48; jr engr Steam Turbine Dept Metropolitan Vickers 1951-54 (coll apprentice 1949-51); NNC Ltd (formerly AEI John Thompson Nuclear Energy Company): engr 1955-60, gp head Projects 1961-69, chief engr Heysham II and Torness Power Stations 1981-87, projects gen mangr Gas Reactor Construction 1987-89; conslt for Nuclear Safety and Station Decommissioning Scottish Nuclear Ltd 1989-; FIMechE 1970, CEng 1970, FEng 1990; *Recreations* walking, swimming, reading; *Style*— Peter Cameron, Esq, MBE; 42 Edenbridge Road, Cheadle Hulme, Cheadle, Cheshire SK8 5PX (☎ 061 485 1408)

CAMERON, Prof Robert Andrew Duncan; s of late George Duncan Cameron, of 21 Stirling Rd, Chichester, Sussex, and Margaret Mary, *née* Walker; *b* 7 April 1943; *Educ* Marlborough, St John's Coll Oxford (BA), Univ of Manchester (PhD); *m* 12 April 1969, Margaret, da of Romilly Ingram Redfern, of Ipswich; 1 s (Alexander b 1974), 1 da (Harriet b 1976); *Career* res fell and lectr Portsmouth Poly 1967-73; Univ of Birmingham: lectr in zoology 1973-80, sr lectr 1980-86, dep head of the Sch of Continuing Studies 1984-, reader in ecological genetics 1986-89, prof of evolutionary biology 1989-; memb: SDLP, Br Ecological Soc, Malacological Soc of London, The Conchological Soc of GB and Ireland; FLS 1969-; *Books* British Land Snails (with M Redfern, 1976), A Field Guide to the Land Snails of Britain and NW Europe (with M P Kerney, 1979); *Recreations* reading, photography, politics; *Style*— Prof Robert Cameron; School of Continuing Studies, University of Birmingham, Edgbaston, Birmingham B15 2TT (☎ 021 414 5598)

CAMERON, Sheila Morag Clark; QC (1983); da of Sir James Clark Cameron, CBE, TD, of 62 Haven Green Court, Ealing, London, and Lady Irene Maud, *née* Ferguson (d 1986); *b* 22 March 1934; *Educ* Commonwealth Lodge Sch Purley Surrey, St Hugh's Coll Oxford (MA); *m* 3 Dec 1960, Gerard Charles Ryan; 2 s (Andrew b 21 Aug 1965, Nicholas b 6 Dec 1967); *Career* called to the Bar Middle Temple 1957, Harmsworth law scholar 1958, pt/t lectr law Univ of Southampton 1960-64, pt/t tutor Cncl of Legal Educn, rec Crown Court, bencher Middle Temple 1988; memb: Bar Cncl 1967-70, Cncl on Tbnls 1986-90; boundary Cmmn for England 1989-; chllr Diocese of Chelmsford 1969; memb: Cncl Wycombe Abbey Sch 1972-76, Legal Advsy Cmmn Gen Synod C of E 1975; vicar Gen Province of Canterbury 1983; *Style*— Miss Sheila Cameron, QC; 2 Harcourt Buildings, Temple, London EC4Y 9DB (☎ 071 353 8415, fax 071 353 7622)

CAMERON, Stuart Gordon; MC (1943); s of James Cameron, and Dora Sylvia, *née* Godsell; *b* 8 Jan 1924; *Educ* Chigwell; *m* 1946, Joyce Alice, da of Roland Ashley Wood; 3 s, 1 da; *Career* chm and chief exec Gallaher Ltd 1980-89 (md 1976-78, dep chm 1978-80); dir American Brands Inc 1980-; *Style*— Stuart Cameron, Esq, MC; Gallaher Ltd, 65 Kingsway, London WC2B 6TG (☎ 071 242 1290, tlx 25505)

CAMERON-HAYES, Col John; MVO; s of Hugh Cameron-Hayes (d 1967), and Mabel Henrietta, *née* Jones (d 1971); *b* 30 July 1925; *Educ* Clifton; *m* 11 Aug 1951, Patricia Mary, da of Lt-Col Geoffrey Hartley Yates, OBE (d 1983); 1 s (Jonathan b 1953), 1 da

(Nicola b 1957; *Career* RHA, active serv ME and Far E The Kings Troop RHA, i/c Gun carriage funeral HM King George VI, first army offr instr Britannia RNC 1964-, cmd Regt BAOR 1966-68, RAF Staff Coll Bracknell 1969, asst dir def policy MOD 1970-72, ret 1972; amateur rider Nat Hunt Steeplechases, hurdle and flat races, competitor Badminton; show jumping, Prince of Wales Cup winner Earls Court; chief exec Racecourse Assoc 1972-89, conslt worldwide basis to firms building racecourses and polo grounds, fund raiser Home Farm Tst; *Recreations* racing, polo, three-day events; *Style—* Col John Cameron-Hayes, MVO; Worplesdon Chase, Worplesdon, Surrey GU3 3LA

CAMERON-HEAD OF INVERAILORT, Mrs (Lucretia Pauline Rebecca Ann); *née* Farrell; CBE, JP (Inverness-shire), DL (1974); elder da of late Charles Bennett Farrell, of Archargle, Argyll; *m* 1942, Francis Somerville Cameron-Head of Inverailort (decd); *Style—* Mrs Cameron-Head of Inverailort, CBE, JP, DL; Inverailort, Lochailort, Inverness

CAMERON OF BALHOUSIE, Lady; Patricia Louise; *née* Asprey; da of late Maj Edward Asprey, RE; *m* 1947, Marshal of the RAF Baron Cameron of Balhousie, KT, GCB, CBE, DSO, DFC, AE (Life Peer) (d 1985); 1 s, 1 da; *Style—* The Rt Hon Lady Cameron of Balhousie; c/o King's College, Strand, London WC2

CAMERON OF LOCHBROOM, Baron (Life Peer UK 1984), of Lochbroom, in the District of Ross and Cromarty; Kenneth John Cameron; PC (1984), QC (1972); s of Hon Lord (John) Cameron, KT, DSC, *qv*, and his 1 w, Eileen Dorothea, *née* Burrell (d 1943); *b* 11 June 1931; *Educ* Edinburgh Acad, Oxford Univ (MA), Edinburgh Univ (LLB); *m* 1964, Jean Pamela, da of late Col Granville Murray; 2 da (Hon Victoria Christian b 1965, Hon Camilla Louise b 1967); *Career* served RN 1950-52; advocate 1958; chm Indust Tbnls (Scotland) 1966-81, pres Pensions Appeal Tbnl (Scotland) 1976-84 (chm 1975), chm Ctee for Investigation in Scotland of Agric Mktg Schemes 1980-84; Lord Advocate of Scotland 1984-89; senator of the Coll of Justice 1989-; *Clubs* Scottish Arts, New (Edinburgh), Beefsteak; *Style—* The Rt Hon the Lord Cameron of Lochbroom, PC, QC; 10 Belford Terrace, Edinburgh EH4 3DQ (☎ 031 332 6636)

CAMERON OF LOCHIEL, Col Sir Donald Hamish; KT (1973), CVO (1970), TD (1944), JP; 26 Chief of the Clan Cameron; s of Col Sir Donald Walter Cameron of Lochiel, KT, CMG, 25 Chief of the Clan of Cameron (d 1951), and Lady Hermione Graham (d 1978), da of 5 Duke of Montrose; *b* 12 Sept 1910; *Educ* Harrow, Balliol Coll Oxford; *m* 1939, Margaret, da of Lt-Col Hon Nigel Gathorne-Hardy, DSO; 2 s, 2 da; *Heir* s, Donald Angus Cameron yr of Lochiel b 1946; *Career* dir: Royal Bank of Scotland 1954-80 (vice chm 1969-80), Scottish Widows Fund 1955-81, Save & Prosper Securities 1968-85; Lt-Col cmdg Lovat Scouts 1945; Hon Col: 4/5th Bn QO Cameron Highlanders 1958-69, 2 Bn 51 Highland Volunteers 1970-75; Scottish Railways Bd 1964-72 (chm Scottish Area Bd 1959-64); pt/t memb BR Bd 1962-64; Crown Estate Cmmr 1957-69, govr Harrow Sch 1967-77, pres Royal Highland Agric Soc of Scotland 1971, 1979, 1987; Lord-Lt of County of Inverness 1971-85 (formerly Vice-Lt); FCA; *Clubs* New (Edinburgh), Pratt's; *Style—* Col Sir Donald Cameron of Lochiel, KT, CVO, TD, JP; Achnacarry, Spean Bridge, Inverness-shire (☎ 039 781 708)

CAMERON OF LOCHIEL, yr, Donald Angus; DL (Lochaber, Inverness and Badenoch and Strathspey, 1986); s and h of Col Sir Donald Cameron of Lochiel, KT, CVO, TD, Chief of Clan *qv*, and Margaret, *née* Gathorne-Hardy; *b* 2 Aug 1946; *Educ* Harrow, ChCh Oxford (MA); *m* 1 June 1974, Lady Cecil Nennella Therese Kerr, da of 12 Marquess of Lothian, KCVO, *qv*; 1 s (Donald Andrew John b 26 Nov 1976), 3 da (Catherine Mary b 1 March 1975, a bridesmaid to HRH The Princess of Wales, Lucy Margot Therese b 5 July 1980, Emily Frances b 18 Jan 1986); *Career* 2 Lt 4/5 Queen's Own Cameron Highlanders (TA) 1966-68; dir J Henry Schroder Wagg & Co Ltd 1984-; FCA 1971; *Clubs* Pratt's; *Style—* Donald Cameron of Lochiel, yr, DL; 26 The Little Boltons, London SW10 (☎ 071 373 0999); c/o J Henry Schroder Wagg & Co Ltd, 120 Cheapside, London EC2 (☎ 071 382 6000)

CAMERON WATT, Prof Donald; s of Robert Cameron Watt (d 1982), and Barbara, *née* Bidwell (d 1977); *b* 17 May 1928; *Educ* Rugby, Oriel Coll Oxford (BA, MA); *m* 1, 1951, Marianne Ruth, *née* Grau (d 1962); 1 s (Ewen b 24 June 1956); m 2, 29 Dec 1962, Felicia Cobb Stanley, *née* Cobb; 1 step da (Cathy); *Career* Nat Serv Sgt BTA 1946-48; FO Res Dept 1951-54, lectr LSE 1956-62 (asst lectr 1954-56), Rockefeller res fell Washington Centre for Policy Res 1960-61; LSE: sr lectr 1962-65, reader 1966-71, titular prof of int history 1972-82, Stevenson prof of int history 1982-; official historian Cabinet Office 1977-; sec and chm Assoc of Contemporary Historians 1966-85, chm Greenwich Forum 1974-84, sec and treas Int Cmmn for the History of Int Rels; memb Ed Bd: Political Quarterly, International History Review, Review International Studies, Marine Policy, Intelligence and National Security; FBA, FRHistS, FRSA; *Books* Britain and the Suez Canal (1956), Britain Looks to Germany (1965), Personalities and Policies (1965), Survey in International Affairs 1961-63 (ed, 1965-71), A History of the World in the Twentieth Century Part 1 (1967), Contemporary History of Europe (ed, 1969), Hitler's Mein Kampf (ed, 1969), Current British Foreign Policy (annual vols, 1970-72), Too Serious a Business (1975), Succeeding John Bull: America in Britain's Place 1900-1975 (1984), How War Came (1989); *Recreations* exploring London; *Clubs* Players Theatre; *Style—* Prof Donald Cameron Watt; c/o London School of Economics, London WC2A 2AE (☎ 071 405 7686, fax 071 242 0392, telex 24655 B

CAMERON WATT, Ewen; s of Prof Donald Cameron Watt, *qv*, and Marianne Ruth Grau; *b* 24 June 1956; *Educ* St Pauls, Oriel Coll Oxford (BA); *m* 8 Jan 1983, Penelope Ann, *qv*, da of Robert Henry Weldon, of Stone, Bucks; *Career* ptnr E B Savory Milln 1979-85, divnl dir Warburg Securities (formerly Rowe & Pitman) 1986-90 (dir 1990-); memb Int Stock Exchange; *Recreations* walking, travel, Scottish watercolours; *Clubs* Vincent's (Oxford); *Style—* Ewen Cameron Watt, Esq; A2 Banyan Villas, 9 Stanley Village Rd, Hong Kong (☎ 0852 8130736, fax 0852 8139074); SG Warburg Securities Far East Ltd, 20 Floor, Alexander House, 16-20 Chater Rd, Central Hong Kong (☎ 0852 5246113, fax 0852 8452075)

CAMERON WATT, Penelope Ann; *née* Weldon; da of Robert Henry Weldon, and Brenda Marianne, *née* Jones; *b* 10 May 1959; *Educ* Clifton HS Bristol, St Hugh's Coll Oxford (BA); *m* 8 Jan 1983, Ewen Cameron Watt, *qv*, s of Prof Donald Cameron Watt, *qv*, of London; *Career* EB Savory Milln 1980-82, Wico Galloway and Pearson 1982-84, Kleinwort Benson 1984-87, investmt mangr Robert Fleming 1987-, investmt mangr Indosuez Asia Investment Services 1990-; *Recreations* travel, walking, Japanese language; *Style—* Mrs Ewen Cameron Watt; A2 Banyan Villas, 9 Stanley Village Rd, Hong Kong (☎ 0852 8130736, fax 0852 8139074); Indosuez Asia Investment Services, Suite 2606/2608, One Exchange Square, Central Hong Kong (☎ 0852 5214231, fax 0852 8681447)

CAMILLERI, His Hon Sir Luigi Antonio; s of late Notary Giuseppe Camilleri, and Matilde, *née* Bonello; *b* 7 Dec 1892; *Educ* Gozo Seminary, Malta Univ; *m* 1914, Erminia, da of Prof G Cali'; 5 s, 3 da; *Career* Malta Legislative Assembly 1921-24; magistrate 1924-30; one of HM judges in Malta 1930-52; chief justice and pres Court of Appeal 1952-57; examiner in civil, criminal and roman law at Malta Univ 1931-70; Kt SMO Malta 1952; kt 1954; *Style—* His Hon Sir Luigi Camilleri; 27 Victoria Ave, Sliema, Malta (☎ 513532)

CAMOYS, 7 Baron (E 1264; called out of abeyance 1839); (Ralph) Thomas Campion George Sherman Stonor; s of 6 Baron Camoys (d 1976), and Mary Jeanne, *née* Stourton (d 1987); the Stonors inherited the Barony through a Mary Biddulph who m Thomas Stonor 1732, descended from an earlier Thomas Stonor and Jeanne, da of John de la Pole, Duke of Suffolk, thus descending from Geoffrey Chaucer, the poet; *b* 16 April 1940; *Educ* Balliol Coll Oxford; *m* 11 June 1966, Elisabeth Mary Hyde, o da of Sir William Hyde Parker, 11 Bt; 1 s, 3 da (Alina b 1967, Emily b 1969, Sophia b 1971); *Heir* s, Hon (Ralph) William Robert Thomas Stonor b 10 Sept 1974; *Career* sits as Cons Peer in House of Lords; chm: Robert Jackson & Co Ltd 1968-85, Amex Bank 1977-78 (md 1975-77); dir: National Provident Institution 1981-, Barclays Bank International Ltd, Mercantile Credit Co Ltd; vice chm Barclays Merchant Bank Ltd 1985-86 (md 1978-85), dir Barclays plc 1985-, dep chm Barclays de Zoete Wedd Holdings Ltd 1988- (chief exec 1986-88); cmmr Eng Heritage 1984-87, memb Royal Cmmn Historical MSS 1987-; memb Court of Assts Fishmongers' Co; 1 cl Order of Gorkha Dakshina Bahu (Nepal) 1980; *Recreations* the arts, shooting; *Clubs* Boodle's, Pratt's, Leander; *Style—* The Rt Hon the Lord Camoys; Stonor Park, Henley-on-Thames, Oxon RG9 6HF (☎ 049 163 644); Barclays de Zoete Wedd Ltd, Ebbgate House, Swan Lane, London (☎ 071 623 2323)

CAMP, Anthony John; s of Henry Victor Camp (d 1954), of Walkern Lodge, Hertfords, and Alice Emma, *née* Doidge (d 1973); *b* 27 Nov 1937; *Educ* Alleyne's Sch Stevenage, UCL (BA); *m* 24 Aug 1976 (m dis 1978), Deborah Mary, da of Joseph Donald Jeavons, of Bristol; 1 s (Gavin b 1977); *Career* Soc Genealogists: res asst 1957, librarian 1959, dir res 1962, dir 1979, hon fell 1982; lectr: English Genealogical Confs 1975-, yearly Nat Genealogical Confs USA 1981-, Australasian Congress Canberra 1986, Sesquicentennial Conference Auckland 1990; contrib daily Diary Family Tree Magazine 1984-; award of Merit Nat Genealogical Soc 1984, fell Utah Genealogical Assoc 1989; hon genealogical advsr Assoc to Combat Huntington's Chorea 1974-; Assoc Genealogists and Record Agents: fndr memb 1968, memb Cncl 1968-75, chm 1973-75, vice pres 1980-; memb Cncl: Br Record Soc 1967-71 and 1983-, Br Archaeology 1973-, English Genealogical Congress 1975-90, Br Records Assoc (Records Preservation Section) 1980-83 and 1985-88, Friends of Public Record Office 1988-; pres Hertfords Family History and Population Soc 1982-; Freeman City of London 1984; *Books* Genealogists Handbook (1964), Tracing Your Ancestors (1964), Wills and Their Whereabouts (2 edn, 1974), Everyone Has Roots (1978), Index to Wills Proved in Prerogative Court of Canterbury 1750-1800 (1976-88), My Ancestor was a Migrant (1987), My Ancestors came with the Conqueror (1988); *Style—* Anthony Camp, Esq; 65 Fursecroft, George St, London W1H 5LG (☎ 071 723 3758); 14 Charterhouse Bldgs, Goswell Rd, London EC1M 7BA (☎ 071 251 8799)

CAMP, Clarence Victor (Larry); JP (City of London 1974); s of George Camp (d 1955), of Colless Rd, London, and Marjorie Minnie, *née* Salmon (d 1977); *b* 7 May 1920; *Educ* Down Lane Sch London; *m* 17 Nov 1945, Kathleen, da of Walter Moody (d 1948), of Shouldham St, London; 2 s (Stuart b 26 March 1949, Stephen b 8 Feb 1954); *Career* RAOC 1940-46: 8 Army 1941-44, served Malta 1944-45, NI 1946; Bank of England 1947-80: Econ Intelligence Dept 1952-63, mangr Mgmnt Servs Dept 1963-74, memb delegation to Aust and NZ 1967, princ Job Evaluation Div 1974-80; dep chm City of London Magistrates 1981-90, vice chm Cts Ctee 1984; chm: Probation Ctee 1980-82, Licensing Ctee; dep chm Ct User Gp; Freeman City of London 1957, Liveryman Worshipful Co Carmen 1976; *Books* Bankers Management Handbook (contrib, 1976); *Recreations* reading, theatre, gardening, walking; *Clubs* City Livery, Aldgate Ward, Probus; *Style—* Larry Camp, Esq, JP; Headley Cottage, Grays Lane, Ashtead, Surrey KT21 1BZ (☎ 0372 274000)

CAMP, Jeffery Bruce; s of George and Caroline Camp; *b* 17 April 1923; *Educ* Lowestoft and Ipswich Art Schs, Edinburgh Coll of Art; *m* 1963, Laetitia, *née* Yhap; *Career* artist; pt/t lectr Slade Sch of Fine Art Univ of London; public collections incl: Arts Cncl of GB, City Art Gallery Bradford, Br Cncl, Contemporary Arts Soc, DOE, Fermoy Art Gallery King's Lynn, Univ of London, Manchester Educn Dept, Norwich Castle Museum, The Nuffield Orgn, Tate Gallery, Towner Art Gallery Eastbourne, Harris Museum and Art Gallery Preston, RA; one man exhibitions: Edinburgh Festival 1950, Galerie de Seine London 1958, Beaux Arts Gallery London 1959/61/63, New Art Centre London 1968, Fermoy Art Gallery Kings Lynn 1970, South London Art Gallery (Retrospective) 1973, Royal Shakespeare Theatre Stratford 1974, Serpentine Gallery (Arts Cncl) 1978, Bradford City Art Gallery 1979, Browse and Darby 1984, The 29 Aldeburgh Festival in assoc with the Arts Cncl of GB 1986, Nigel Greenwood Gallery 1986-87 and 1990, The Library Gallery Univ of Surrey 1988, Royal Albert Museum Exeter (Retrospective) 1988, Royal Acad of Arts London 1988, Manchester City Art Gallery 1988, Laing Art Gallery Newcastle 1988; group exhibitions incl: Aldeburgh Festival 1958/61/63, Cafe Royal Centenary 1965, Marlborough Gallery London 1968, Br Painting 1974, Hayward Gallery London 1974, Br Painting 1952-77, Royal Acad Drawings at Burlington House 1977, Drawing and Watercolours for China (Edinburgh, Br Cncl Touring) 1982, Br Cncl Exhibition Delhi and Bombay 1985, Proud and Prejudiced Twining Gallery NY 1985, The Self Portrait A Modern View Artsite Gallery Bath and tour 1987, Small is Beautiful Angela Flowers Gallery London 1988, Picturing People - Figurative Painting from Britain 1945-89 (Br exhib, Kuala Lumpar) 1988-89, Salute to Turner (Thos Agnew & Sons) London 1989, Images of Paradise Harewood House 1989, Nine Comntemporary Painters Bristol Art Gallery 1990, For a Wider World (Br Cncl), RA Summer Exhib 1990; ARA 1974, RA 1984; *Style—* Jeffery Camp, Esq; 27 Stirling Rd, London, SW9 9EF (☎ 071 737 8272)

CAMPBELL; *see*: Cockburn-Campbell, Montgomery Campbell

CAMPBELL, Agnes, Lady; Agnes Louise; da of late William Henry Gerhardi; *m* 1, Victor Vsevolod Watson, MBE; m 2, 1941, as his 3 wife Sir Ian Vincent Hamilton Campbell, 7 Bt, CB (d 1978); 1 s; *Style—* Agnes, Lady Campbell; Barcaldine Castle, Ledaig, Argyllshire; White Rose, Hawkhurst, Kent

CAMPBELL, Sir Alan Hugh; GCMG (1979, KCMG 1976, CMG 1964); s of late Hugh Elphinstone Campbell, of Bantham, S Devon, and Ethel, *née* Warren; *b* 1 July 1919; *Educ* Sherborne, Gonville and Caius Coll Cambridge; *m* 1947, Margaret Jean, da of Gilbert Taylor, of Sydney, NSW; 3 da; *Career* Dip Serv 1946-: ambass to Ethiopia 1969-72, dep under sec of state FO 1973-76, ambass to Italy 1976-79, ret; *Books* Colleagues and Friends (1988); *Clubs* Beefsteak, Brooks's; *Style—* Sir Alan Campbell, GCMG; 45 Carlisle Mansions, Carlisle Place, London SW1

CAMPBELL, Hon Alastair Colin Leckie; s (by 1 m) and h of 3 Baron Colgrain; *b* 16 Sept 1951; *Educ* Eton, Trinity Coll Cambridge; *m* 1979, Annabel Rose, da of Hon Robin Hugh Warrender (s of 1 Baron Bruntisfield, MC); 2 s (Thomas Colin Donald b 9 Feb 1984, Nicholas Robin b 12 Dec 1986); *Style—* The Hon Alastair Campbell; The Stables, Everlands, Sevenoaks, Kent

CAMPBELL, Hon Alastair James Calthrop; yr s of Baron Campbell of Croy, MC, PC (Life Peer); *b* 6 Jan 1952; *Educ* Eton, Oxford (BA); *Career* cmmnd Queen's Own Highlanders 1973, Capt 1976, Maj 1984; FRGS; Sultan of Oman's Commendation medal; *Recreations* bagpipes, squash, skiing; *Style—* The Hon Alastair Campbell

CAMPBELL, Alastair John; s of Donald Campbell, of Embsay, Yorks, and Elizabeth Howie, *née* Caldwell; *b* 25 May 1957; *Educ* City of Leicester Boys Sch, Gonville and Caius Coll Cambridge (MA); partner, Fiona Millar; 2 s (Rory b 23 Oct 1987, Calum b

29 July 1989); *Career* trainee reporter Tavistock Times and Sunday Independent Truro Mirror Group Training Scheme 1980-82, freelance reporter London 1982-83, reporter Daily Mirror 1983-85, news ed Sunday Today 1985-86, reporter Daily Mirror 1986; Sunday Mirror: politcal corr 1986-87, politcal ed 1987-89, columnist 1989-; political ed Daily Mirror 1989-; *Recreations* children, bagpipes, Burnley Football Club; *Style—* Alastair Campbell, Esq; Mirror Group Newspapers, 33 Holborn, London EC1P 1DQ (☎ 071 353 0246, fax 071 233 0470)

CAMPBELL, Prof Alexander George Macpherson (Alex); s of Alexander McCorkindale Campbell, DSO, OBE, TD, of Skipton, Yorks, and Isabel Catherine, *née* Macpherson (d 1990); *b* 3 Feb 1931; *Educ* Dollar Acad, Univ of Glasgow (MB ChB); *m* 19 Sept 1959, Sheila Mary, da of Sir Peter George Macdonald (d 1983), of Edinburgh; 1 s (Andrew Alexander Macdonald b 1965), 2 da (Fiona Ann b 1960, Patricia Mary b 1963); *Career* Nat Serv Parachute Field Ambulance 16 Ind Parachute Bde 1956-58; registrar paediatrics Royal Hosp for Sick Children Edinburgh 1959-61 res house offr Gt Ormond St Hosp 1961-62, asst chief res physician Children's Hosp of Philadelphia USA 1962-63; fell: paediatric cardiology Hosp for Sick Children Toronto Canada 1963-64, perinatal physiology Nuffield Inst for Med Res Oxford 1964-66; lectr child health Univ of St Andrews 1966-67, asst (later assoc prof) paediatrics Yale Univ Sch of Med Connecticut USA 1967-73, prof child health Univ of Aberdeen 1973-; chm Jt Ctee for Vaccination and Immunisation Dept Health; FRCPE; *Style—* Prof Alex Campbell; 34 Woodburn Crescent, Aberdeen (☎ 0224 319152); Univ of Aberdeen, Department of Child Health, Medical School, Foresterhill, Aberdeen (☎ 0224 681818)

CAMPBELL, Alexander Rennie; s of Alexander Rennie Campbell (d 1959), of Edgware, Middx, and Mary Isobel, *née* Hayes (d 1976); *b* 2 Sept 1936; *Educ* Univ Coll Sch Hampstead, Gonville and Caius Coll Cambridge (BA, MA); *m* 1 May 1970, Marilyn Daphne, da of Capt Robert Cyril Kerfoot, of Cheshire; 1 s (Rennie b 1972), 2 da (Kate b 1972, Anna b 1976); *Career* dir London Midland & Scottish Contractors Ltd 1974-77, chm and md AR Campbell Construction Ltd 1977-; pres Forth Valley Bldg Trades Employers Assoc, vice pres Airthey Castle Curling Club, govr and vice chm Beaconhurst Grange Sch; memb Area Manpower Bd Central Scotland and Fife 1986-88; MICE 1963; *Recreations* curling; *Clubs* Stirling and County, Naval; *Style—* Alexander Campbell, Esq; Old Farm, Blair Drummond, By Stirling FK9 4UP (☎ 0786 841601); Burghmuir Industrial Estate, Stirling FK7 7PY (☎ 0786 50500, fax 0786 50413, car 0860 734446)

CAMPBELL, Alida, Lady; Alida Virginie Lilian; da of Augustus Peeters van Nieuwenrode, of Pachtof, Nieuwenrode, Belgium; *m* 1, F A S Allan (decd); m 2, 1955, as his 2nd wife, Maj Sir Guy Colin Campbell, 4 Bt (d 1960); *Style—* Alida, Lady Campbell; c/o Cavalry & Guards Club, 127 Piccadilly W1

CAMPBELL, Dr Angus Scott; s of Archiebald Campbell, CBE (d 1978), and Jane, *née* Russell (d 1976); *b* 16 June 1929; *Educ* Wallington Co GS, Royal Sch of Mines Imperial Coll, London Univ (BSc, ARSM), Kings Coll Univ of Durham (PhD); *m* 1, 15 March 1952 (m dis 1977), May Ethel Campbell, da of Harold Slight (d 1976), of Carlisle, Cumbria; 1 s (Ian b 1956), 2 da (Susan b 1952, Alison b 1960); m 2, 5 Feb 1977, Anne, da of William Heslam (d 1982) of North Shields, Tyne and Wear; *Career* RAF: Pilot Offr 1954, Flying Offr 1955; geologist Conorada Petroleum Corpn Somaliland 1956-58; Oasis Oil: sr geologist Tripoli Libya 1958-62, dir geological lab 1962-66, mangr geology Libya 1967-72; staff geologist Continental Oil Stamford USA 1974-76; Conoco Inc: mangr exploration Houston Texas 1976-82, md (UK Ltd) London 1982-87, area mangr (Euro, Asia) Houston Texas 1987-88; memb Amercan Assoc Petroleum Geologists; *Recreations* travel, jogging, theatre; *Clubs* RAC; *Style—* Dr Angus Campbell; c/o Conoco (UK) Ltd, 116 Park St, London, W1Y 4NN (☎ 071 408 6000)

CAMPBELL, The Hon Mr Justice; Hon Sir (William) Anthony; s of Harold Ernest Campbell, CBE (d 1980), of Rockmore, Newcastle, Co Down, and Marion Fordyce, *née* Wheeler; *b* 30 Oct 1936; *Educ* Campbell Coll Belfast, Queens' Coll Cambridge (BA); *m* 8 July 1960, (Isobel Rosemary) Gail, da of Frederick Malcolm McKibbin, JP, of Redene Cottage, Bangor Rd, Holywood, Co Down; 3 da (Fiona (Mrs Chamberlain) b 1961, Nicola b 1963, Susan b 1964); *Career* called to the Bar Gray's Inn 1960, Inn of Court NI 1960; QC 1974, sr crown counsel NI 1984-88, judge of the High Court of Justice NI 1988; memb Cncl St Leonards Sch St Andrews, govr Campbell Coll Belfast; kt 1988; *Recreations* hill walking, sailing; *Clubs* Royal Ulster Yacht; *Style—* The Hon Mr Justice Campbell; Royal Courts of Justice, Belfast BT1 3JY (☎ 0232 235111)

CAMPBELL, (Mary Lorimer) Beatrix; da of James William Barnes, of Carlisle, Cumbria, and Catharina Johana, *née* Lorier; *b* 3 Feb 1947; *Educ* Harraby Secdy Mod Sch, Carlisle HS, AA; *m* 28 Oct 1968 (m dis 1978), Bobby Campbell; *Career* journalist: Morning Star 1967-76, Time Out 1979, City Limits 1981-87; freelance reporter: New Statesman, Guardian, Marxism Today; broadcaster: I Shot My Husband and No One Asked Me Why (documentary) Channel 4 TV, Listening to the Children (documentary) Channel 4 TV; memb : Communist Pty, Women's Liberation Movement, Bd Marxism Today; *Books* Sweet Freedom (with Anna Coote, 1981), Wigan Pier Revisited (1984, winner of Cheltenham Literary Festival), The Iron Ladies: Why Women Vote Tory (1987, winner of Fawcett Prize), Unofficial Secrets - The Cleveland Child Sex Abuse Case (1988); *Style—* Ms Beatrix Campbell

CAMPBELL, Col (George) Bryan; OBE (1977, MBE 1968); s of Capt Ian Bryan Campbell, OBE (d 1951), and Anne Baron, *née* Black (d 1949); *b* 22 Dec 1935; *Educ* The Edinburgh Acad, Royal Military Acad Sandhurst; *m* 22 Dec 1959, (Loyola Megan) Tui, da of Frederick Godrey Vaughan-Morgan (d 1972); 1 s (Nicholas Bryan Vaughan); *Career* cmmnd 1955, served: Malaya, Cyprus, Aden, Malta, Singapore, NI; cmd 1 Bn The Royal Highland Fusiliers 1974-77 (dispatches 1978), Dep Cdr 39 Infantry Bde 1983-85, Col gen staff AFSE 1985-89 (dispatches 1986), Army HQ Scotland 1990-; *Recreations* gardening, shooting; *Style—* Col Bryan Campbell, OBE; Oaklea, Athelstaneford, North Berwick, East Lothian EH39 5BE (☎ 062 088 280, 031 310 2315)

CAMPBELL, Bryn; s of Brinley Campbell, (d 1990), and Dorothy Irene, *née* Hughes; *b* 20 May 1933; *Educ* Mountain Ash GS (awarded Viscount Hall travel scholarship), Univ of Manchester; *m* 1960, Audrey Campbell, da of late Thomas Idris Berryman; *Career* Nat Serv photographer RAF 1951-53, industl photographer London 1956-57, agency photographer Fleet St 1957-58, asst ed Practical Photography and Photo News Weekly 1959-60, ed Cameras 1960-61, assoc ed British Journal of Photography 1962-63, redesigned and picture edited BJ Annual 1964, picture ed The Observer and helped to launch The Observer Colour Magazine 1964-66, freelance photographer retained by The Observer 1966-72, offical photographer Br Headless Valley Expedition (which carried out first ever N-S transnavigation of Canada by water) 1972, named photographer Magnum Photos 1972-73, external examiner in photography to eight polys and art colls 1974-, first foreign photographer to lecture to Guild of Finnish Photographers Univ of Vaasa Finland 1974-, photographed final stages of Vietnam War 1975, travelled widely on assignment for maj magazines 1975-77, wrote and presented BBC TV series and book Exploring Photography 1978, offical photographer Transglobe Expedition (which carried out first ever transnavigation of the world's surface on its polar axis) 1979-82, ed World Photography (UK, USA and Japan) 1981; conslt picture ed: Sunday Express Magazine 1984-85, The Illustrated London News 1985-87, Daily Telegraph Magazine 1987-88; occasional appearances Saturday Review BBC TV 1985-86; memb: Photography Bd CNAA 1977-78, Arts Panel Arts Cncl of GB 1980-83 (memb Photography Ctee 1978-80); chm Sports Pictures of the Year Judging Panel 1984-88; Br judge: World Press Photo competition 1985, Int Center for Photography annual awards NY 1989-; tstee The Photographers' Gallery London 1974-84; solo exhibitions incl: Reports and Rumours (The Photographers' Gallery London and tour) 1973, Village School (Chichester 900 festival Sussex and tour) 1975, Caring and Concern (Kodak Gallery London) 1976, Sports View (Watford and tour) 1977, retrospective (Salzburg Coll Austria) 1978, Antarctic Expedition (Olympus Gallery London) 1980, colour retrospective (The Photographers' Gallery London then tour) 1981; gp exhibitions incl: The Camera and the Craftsman (Crafts Centre London) 1975, Personal View (Br Cncl London and tour) 1977, European Colour Photography (The Photographers' Gallery London) 1978, Kindness: The Keflex Collection (Hamiltons Gallery London) 1982, The Other Britain (Nat Theatre London) 1983; numerous books on photography; *awards* 1st prize (News) Br Press Pictures of the Year 1969; FBIPP 1969, FRPS 1971; *Style—* Bryn Campbell, Esq; 11 Belsize Park Mews, London NW3 5BL (☎ 071 435 4312)

CAMPBELL, Christopher James; s of Dr David Heggie Campbell (d 1979), and Nettie Phyllis, *née* Burgess (d 1944); *b* 2 Jan 1936; *Educ* Epsom Coll Surrey; *Career* Nat Serv 2 Lt RAPC 1958-60; dir: Harvey Nichols Ltd 1973-78, Lotus Ltd 1973-78; md Hardy Amies Ltd 1979-81; dir: Debenhams Fashion Div 1981-84, Debenhams Dept Store Bd 1984-86, Debenhams Finance Ltd 1984-86; exec memb National Business Co 1986-88 (non-exec memb 1988-), fin dir Nat Rivers Authy Advsy Ctee 1988-89, chm British Shipbuilders 1989-; treas Bow Gp 1966; FCA 1959; *Recreations* reading, current affairs, listening to music, entertaining, indifferent bridge; *Clubs* Brooks's; *Style—* Christopher Campbell, Esq; 19 Morpeth Mansions, Morpeth Terrace, London SW1P 1ER (☎ 071 630 7527); 197 Knightsbridge, London SW7 1RB (☎ 071 581 1393)

CAMPBELL, Lord Colin Ivar; yr s of 11 Duke of Argyll (d 1973), by his 2 w, Louise (d 1970), only da of late Henry Clews, of Château de la Napoule, AM, France; *b* 14 May 1946; *Educ* in USA, Trinity Coll Glenalmond; *m* 1974 (m dis 1975), Georgia Ariana, da of Michael Ziadie; *Style—* The Lord Colin Campbell; c/o Inveraray Castle, Inveraray, Argyll

CAMPBELL, Colin John Bruce; s of Capt Richard Galbraith Campbell (d 1975), and Margaret Kathleen, (*née* Spoor (d 1970); *b* 6 April 1939; *Educ* Gordonstoun, Royal Marines; *m* 15 Aug 1964, Angela Rosemary, da of the late Lt-Col Colin Gordon Irving-Bell; 2 da (Shuna Catherine Islay b 1965, Ffyona Jane Alison b 1967); *Career* Nat Serv cmmnd RM 1959-61, regular cmmn 1961, Troop Cdr 45 commando Aden 42 Commando Borneo 1962-63, flying trg RAF Linton on Ouse and RNAS Culdrose 1964-65, Fleet Air Arm Helicopter Pilot 845 NACS HMS Bulwark 1965-67, qualified Helicopter Flying Instr 1967, Flying Instr RNAS Culdrose 1967-69, exchange appt USMC New River N Carolina 1969-71, display pilot 1971-72, Helicopter Standards instr RAE Farnborough 1972-74, VIP Pilot RNAS Lee-on-Solent 1974-76; capt Br Airways Helicopters 1976, hotelier 1989; memb Rotary Int; *Recreations* sailing, hill walking, skiing; *Clubs* Argyllshire Gathering; *Style—* Colin J P Campbell, Esq; Pitcairn House, Baileys Meadow, Stoke Fleming, Dartmouth, Devon (☎ 0803 770500)

CAMPBELL, Sir Colin Moffat; 8 Bt (NS *ca*1668), of Aberuchill, Perthshire; MC (1945); s of Sir John Campbell, 7 Bt (d 1960); *b* 4 Aug 1925; *Educ* Stowe; *m* 1952, Mary Anne Chichester, da of Brig George Alexander Bain, OBE (d 1982); 2 s, (and 1 da decd); *Heir* James Alexander Moffat Bain; *Career* James Finlay and Co Ltd: Calcutta 1948-58, Nairobi 1958-71, dir 1971-, dep chm 1973-75; chm James Finlay and associated cos 1975-90; pres Fedn of Kenya Employers 1962-70; chm: Tea Bd of Kenya 1961-71, E African Tea Trade Assoc 1960-61, 1962-63 and 1966-67; memb: Scottish Cncl CBI 1979-85, Cncl CBI 1981-, Commonwealth Devpt Corpn 1981-89 (dep chm 1983-89); FRSA; *Recreations* gardening, racing, travel, cards; *Clubs* Boodle's, Western (Glasgow), Royal Calcutta Turf, Tollygunge (Calcutta), Nairobi, Muthaiga (Kenya); *Style—* Sir Colin Campbell, Bt, MC; Kilbryde Castle, Dunblane, Perthshire (☎ 0786 823104)

CAMPBELL, Prof Colin Murray; s of Donald Campbell, and Isobel Campbell; *b* 26 Dec 1944; *Educ* Robert Gordons Coll Aberdeen, Univ of Aberdeen (LLB); *m* 15 Aug 1974, Elaine, da of Roger Carlisle; 1 s (Andrew William Roger b 1983), 1 da (Victoria Louise b 1979); *Career* lectr: Faculty of Law Univ of Dundee 1967-69, Dept of Public Law Univ of Edinburgh; Queen's Univ of Belfast: prof of jurisprudence 1974-88, dean Faculty of Law 1977-80, pro vice chllr 1983-87; chm Qubis Ltd 1983-88, vice chllr Univ of Nottingham 1988-; memb: Cncl Soc for Computers and Law 1973-88, Standing Advsy Cmmn on Human Rights for NI 1977-80, Legal Aid Advsy Ctee NI 1978-82, Mental Health Legislation Review Ctee NI 1978-82, UGC 1987-88, Nottingham Devpt Enterprize 1988-, UFC Scottish Ctee 1989-; chm: Ind Advice Gp on Consumer Protection in NI 1984, NI Econ Cncl 1987-, Lacemarket Devpt Co 1989-, Human Fertilization and Embryology Authy 1990-; *Books* Law & Society (co-ed, 1979), Do We Need a Bill of Rights? (ed, 1980), Data Processing and the Law (ed, 1984); contrib numerous articles in books and periodicals; *Recreations* sport, walking, music, reading; *Style—* Prof Colin Campbell; University of Nottingham, University Park, Nottingham NG7 2RD (☎ 0602 484848, fax 0602 227554, telex 37346)

CAMPBELL, Sir (Bruce) Colin Patrick; 3 Bt (UK 1913, with precedence of 1804), of Ardnamurchan, Argyllshire; name does not, at time of going to press, appear on the Official Roll of Baronets; s of Lt-Col Sir John Bruce Stuart, 2 Bt, DSO (d 1943, whilst prisoner in Palembang Camp, Sumatra); *b* 2 July 1904; *Educ* Edinburgh Acad, Glenalmond and Pangbourne Nautical Colls; *Career* no information concerning this baronet has been received since 1943; *Style—* Sir Colin Campbell, Bt

CAMPBELL, Hon David Anthony; o s and h of 6 Baron Stratheden and Campbell, *qv*; *b* 13 Feb 1963; *Style—* The Hon David Campbell; c/o The Rt Hon Lord Stratheden and Campbell, Ridgewood, M5 1064, Cooroy, Queensland 4563, Australia

CAMPBELL, Prof Donald; CBE (1987); s of Archibald Peter Campbell, DCM (d 1949), of Glasgow, and Mary Campbell (d 1947); *b* 8 March 1930; *Educ* Pitlochry HS, Hutchesons' Boys GS, Univ of Glasgow; *m* 1, Nancy Rebecca (d 1974); 1 s (Alistair Mackintosh b 18 May 1954), 1 da (Kirsteen Mary b 26 Aug 1956); m 2, 29 Nov 1975, Catherine Conway, da of George Bradburn, of Glasgow; 2 da (Barbara Jane b 1 Sept 1976, Pamela Margaret b 13 April 1978); *Career* aonslt anaesthetist Glasgow Royal Infirmary 1961-76, prof of anaesthesia Univ of Glasgow 1976- (dean Faculty of Med 1987-); dean Faculty of Anaesthetists RCS 1982-85 (vice dean 1981-82), vice pres RCS 1985-87, visitor RCPS (Glas) 1990-; chm Scot Cncl for Postgrad Med Educn 1985-90, chm Steering Ctee Nat Enquiry into Postoperative Deaths 1988-; fell Coll of Anaesthetists 1959, FFARCS (Ireland) 1979, FRCP (Glasgow) 1983, FRCS (Eng) 1985; *Books* A Nurse's Guide to Anaesthetics, Resuscitation and Intensive Care (jtly, 7 edn 1983), Anaesthetics, Resuscitation and Intensive Care (jtly, 7 edn 1988); *Recreations* curling, angling, game-shooting; *Style—* Prof Donald Campbell, CBE; 27 Tannoch Drive, Milngavie, Glasgow G62 8AR (☎ 041 956 1736); Medical Faculty Office, University of Glasgow, Glasgow G12 8QQ (☎ 041 339 8855, fax 041 330 4808)

CAMPBELL, Donald Angus; s of William Alexander Campbell, of Elgin, Moray, and

Williamina Scott, *née* Allan; *b* 10 April 1948; *Educ* Elgin Acad, Univ of Edinburgh (BSc, MB ChB); *m* 9 Sept 1972, Görrel Anna Kristina, da of (Stig Ture) Olof Sahlberg, of Sweden; 1 s (Alasdair Olof b 7 Oct 1981); *Career* neurosurgn: Karolinska Sjukhuset 1972, Royal Infirmary of Edinburgh 1972-73 and 1978-78; surgn: Köpings Lasarett 1973-76, King's Coll London 1976-77, Royal Marsden Hosp 1977-78; neurosurgn Walton Hosp Liverpool 1981-84, conslt neurosurgn to W Midlands RHA 1984-; res papers on: chronic pain, epilepsy, head injury, meningiomas, stereotactic surgery; hon pres Headway Staffs; FRCS 1977, FRCSE 1977, FRSM 1977; *Recreations* model aircraft engineering, parachuting, photography; *Clubs* Soc of Model Aeronautical Engrs; *Style*— Donald Campgell, Esq; Camrose Hall, Rudyard, Staffordshire Moorlands ST13 8RL (☎ 0538 33 627); Nuffield Hospital, Clayton Rd, Newcastle-under-Lyme ST5 4DB (☎ 0782 625431)

CAMPBELL, Donald le Strange; MC (1944); s of Donald Fraser Campbell (d 1964), of Summerhill, Heacham, Norfolk, and Caroline, *née* Henry; *b* 16 June 1919; *Educ* Winchester, Clare Coll Cambridge (BSc); *m* 6 Sept 1952, Hon Shona Catherine Greig, da of 1 Baron Macpherson of Drumochter (d 1965); 1 s (Bruce Donald le Strange b 10 July 1956), 1 da (Victoria Louise b 3 April 1959); *Career* 2 Lt RA 1939, Maj 1944, demobilised 1945; dir: Project Servs Overseas Ltd, Hovair Int Ltd, Beechdean Farms Ltd; md and dep chm Davy Ashmore Ltd; Liveryman Worshipful Co of Blacksmiths 1968; *Recreations* field sports, sailing, countryside conservation; *Clubs* Boodle's, Royal Yacht Sqdn; *Style*— Donald Campbell, Esq, MC; Little Dartmouth House, Dartmouth, Devon TQ6 0JP (☎ 0803 832120)

CAMPBELL, Hon Mrs (Elisabeth Joan); *née* Adderley; da of 6 Baron Norton (d 1961) and Elizabeth, *née* Birkbeck (d 1952); *b* 12 June 1919; *m* 1943, Prof (Alexander) Colin Patton Campbell, FRCP, FRCPath, s of Alexander Callender Campbell (d 1952), of Edinburgh; 2 s, (Andrew, Richard d 1990), 1 da (Rosamund); *Career* served VAD RAF Hosp Ely 1940-43; *Style*— The Hon Mrs Campbell; The Priory House, Ascott-under-Wychwood, Oxon (☎ 0993 830626)

CAMPBELL, Hon Mrs (Elizabeth Janet); *née* Mackay; da of Baron Mackay of Clashfern (Life Peer), *qv*; *b* 1961; *m* 1982, James Campbell; 2 s, 1 da; *Style*— The Hon Mrs Campbell; Milton of Ness Side, Inverness

CAMPBELL, Lady Fiona; *née* Erskine; da of 13 Earl of Mar and 15 of Kellie, *qv*; *b* 5 April 1956, (twin with Hon Michael Erskine); *Educ* St Leonards Sch, St Andrews Fife; *m* 30 Aug 1980, Maj Andrew P W Campbell, Argyll & Sutherland Highlanders, yr s of late Prof Wilson Campbell, of Coquet House, Warkworth, Northumberland; 1 s (Barnabas b 1983), 2 da (Poppy b 1985, Rosanna b 1986); *Style*— The Lady Fiona Campbell; c/o Claremont House, Alloa, Scotland FK10 2JF (☎ 0259 212020)

CAMPBELL, Graham Gordon; CB (1984); s of late Lt-Col P H Campbell; *b* 12 Dec 1924; *Educ* Cheltenham, Gonville and Caius Coll Cambridge (BA); *m* 1955, Margaret Rosamond Busby; 1 da; *Career* WWII, RA 1943-46; Miny of Fuel and Power: asst princ 1949, private sec to Parly Sec 1953-54, princ 1954; asst sec Miny of Power 1965, under sec DTI 1973, under sec Dept of Energy 1974-84; *Style*— Graham Campbell, Esq, CB; 3 Clovelly Ave, Warlingham, Surrey CR6 9HZ (☎ 0883 62 4671)

CAMPBELL, Col Sir Guy Theophilus Halswell; 5 Bt (UK 1815), OBE (1954), MC (1941); s of Maj Sir Guy Colin Campbell, 4 Bt (d 1960), and Mary Arabella Swinnerton Kemeys-Tynte (d 1948), sis of 8 Baron Wharton; *b* 18 Jan 1910; *Educ* Eton, St Andrew's Univ; *m* 1956, Elizabeth (stage name Lizbeth Webb), da of Frederick Holton (d 1956); 2 s (Lachlan, Rory); *Heir* s, Lachlan Philip Kemeys Campbell; *Career* KOYLI and Col late 60 Rifles, Camel Corps, Sudan Defence Force, served WW II (wounded), A/Brig 1945, Palestine 1948, mil advsr to Count Folke Bernadotte and Dr Ralph Bunche UN Mediation Force of Advsrs Mediation of Palestine in Cairo, Civil Affairs Office Cairo, British Mil Mission to Ethiopia 1948-52, Mau Mau 1952-56 (cmd Kenya Regt), head British Mil Mission to Libya 1956-60, ret 1960; former chm Anglo-Sudanese Soc in UK; *Books* The Charging Buffalo (a history of the Kenya Regt, 1986); *Recreations* writing, heraldry, painting; *Clubs* Army & Navy, Special Forces, Puffin's, Royal and Ancient; *Style*— Col Sir Guy Campbell, Bt, OBE, MC; 18 Lansdown Terrace, Malvern Road, Cheltenham, Glos GL50 2JT (☎ 0242 43320)

CAMPBELL, Maj-Gen The Rev Sir Hamish Manus; KBE (1963), CB (1961); s of late Maj Arthur Crawford Julian Campbell (d 1940), and Alice, *née* O'Keeffe; *b* 6 Jan 1905; *Educ* Downside, New Coll Oxford; *m* 1929, Marcelle Amelie Alice (d 1983), da of Charles Ortlieb (d 1922), of Neuchâtel, Switzerland; 1 s; *Career* cmmnd Argyll and Sutherland Highlanders 1927, transfd RAPC 1937, Maj-Gen 1959, Paymaster-in-Chief 1959-63, ret 1963; Col Cmdt RAPC 1963-70; professed in Order of Canons Regular of Prémontré 1984, ordained priest 1988; *Style*— Maj-Gen The Rev Sir Hamish Campbell, KBE, CB; Our Lady of England Priory, Storrington, Pulborough, W Sussex RH20 4LN (☎ 090 66 2150)

CAMPBELL, Hugh Hall; QC (1983); s of William Wright Campbell, of Cambuslang, Lanarkshire, and Marianne Doris Stewart, *née* Hutchison; *b* 18 Feb 1944; *Educ* Glasgow Acad, Glenalmond Coll, Exeter Coll Oxford (BA), Univ of Edinburgh (LLB); *m* 1969, Eleanor Jane, da of Sydney Charles Hare, of Stoke Poges; 3 s (Benjamin b 1972, Timothy b 1975, Thomas b 1978); *Career* advocate Scottish Bar 1969, standing jr counsel to Admty 1976; dir Scottish Ensemble; FCIArb 1986; *Recreations* music, hill-walking, golf; *Clubs* Hon Co of Edinburgh Golfers; *Style*— H H Campbell, Esq, QC; 12 Ainslie Place, Edinburgh EH3 6AS (☎ 031 225 2067)

CAMPBELL, Iain; s of Joeseph Love Campbell, of Bangor, and Helen Mae, *née* Lyons; *b* 9 Nov 1953; *Educ* Sullivan Upper GS Holywood Co Down, Univ of Edinburgh (BSc); *m* 14 May 1977, Linda Jaeanne, da of James Walter Stanley; 1 s (Jamie Ross Ewan b 8 Dec 1988), 2 da (Nicola Jane b 10 Nov 1980, Donna Melanie b 6 June 1984); *Career* asst engr Fairhurst and Partners 1976-78 (projects incl: Motherwell New Town Centre, Gorgie Abbattoir, Sloch Beag Bridge), site engr Balfour Beatty Construction (Scotland) Ltd 1979-81 (supervised various aspects of Colinton Section of Edinburgh Bypass); Freeman Fox Ltd 1981-87: conslt engr 1981-84 (projects incl Musselburgh and Tranent Bypasses, structural design in timber, steel and masonry), sr structures engr involved in design of civil and structural elements for devpt of a naval depot 1985-87; civil and structural engr ptnr Building Design Partnership 1988- (responsible for design of civil check-in facility and parking and traffic facilities at Belfast Int Airport); MICE 1982, MIStructE 1984; *Style*— Iain Campbell, Esq; 12 Maralin Avenue, Bangor, N Ireland BT20 4RQ (☎ 0247 455673); Building Design Partnership, 2 Bruce St, Belfast BT2 7JD (☎ 0232 243394, fax 0232 329 337)

CAMPBELL, Iain Chalmers; s of Peter Campbell (d 1988), and Janet McVey Milton Fraser Lauder; *b* 27 May 1951; *Educ* Ringwood GS, Manchester Poly (BA); *m* 7 Sept 1974, Valerie, da of Alfred Neville Downer (d 1957); 1 s (James b 1978), 2 da (Anna b 1976, Beth b 1984); *Career* slr; princ Bowen Symes Weymouth; *Recreations* windsurfing; *Style*— Iain Campbell, Esq; Rowans, Osmington, Weymouth DT3 6EE; 7 Frederick Place, Weymouth DT4 8DP (☎ 0305 783555)

CAMPBELL, Ian; s of William Campbell (d 1968), and Helen, *née* Crockett (d 1986); *b* 26 April 1926; *Educ* Dumbarton Acad, Royal Tech Coll Glasgow; *m* 1950, Mary, da of late Alexander Millar; 2 s, 3 da; *Career* test engr for power stations S of Scotland Electricity Bd Local Auth 1958-70, ptnr C & W Consltants; provost of Dumbarton 1962-70, dir Dumbarton District Enterprise Trust, memb Strathclyde Regnl Cncl Valuation Appeal Ctee; MP (Lab) W Dunbartonshire 1970-83 and Dunbarton 1983-87; PPS to Sec of State for Scotland 1976-79; MIMechE, CEng; *Recreations* family; *Style*— Ian Campbell, Esq; The Shanacles, Gartocharn, Alexandria, Dunbartonshire (☎ 0389 52286)

CAMPBELL, Col Ian Clement; OBE (1962), DFC (1944), TD (1951), JP (1980), DL (Renfrewshire 1970); s of S Campbell, MC, of Glasgow; *b* 26 April 1922; *Educ* Hurst Grange, The Leys Sch; *m* 1, 1945, Nadine Lilian (decd), da of H Wesley Steel, of Glasgow; 3 da; m 2, 1972, Kathleen Mary, *née* Bagot; *Career* RAF 1940-46, TA 1947-68; dir Scotcros plc; *Style*— Col Ian Campbell, OBE, DFC, TD, JP, DL; Scotcros plc, 3 Woodside Place, Glasgow (☎ 041 248 5822); Barcapel Holm Farm, Newton Mearns, Renfrewshire (☎ 041 639 3735)

CAMPBELL, Ian James; s of Allan Campbell (d 1968), and Elizabeth, *née* Gamble (d 1986); *b* 9 June 1923; *Educ* George Heriot's Sch, Univ of Edinburgh (MA); *m* 14 Dec 1946, Stella Margaret, da of Matthew Baird Smith (d 1924); *Career* scientist; head of Torpedo Res Div Admty Underwater Weapons Estab 1961-68, chief scientist Naval Construction Res Estab 1969-73, head of Weapons Dept and dep dir AUWE 1973-76; MOD: dir of res (Ships) 1976-78, scientific advsr to Ship Dept 1976-81, dir gen res (Maritime) 1978-81; tech dir CAP Scientific 1983-87, dir of studies Centre for Operational Res and Def Analysis 1987-88; dir: Defence Science Sema Scientific 1987-, Defence Analysis Yard Ltd 1989-; chm Res Advsy Ctee Electronic Engrg Assoc 1989-; author of various res pubns and numerous MOD internal reports; *Style*— I J Campbell, Esq; Claremont, North St, Charminster, Dorchester, Dorset DT2 9QZ (☎ 0305 264270); Sema Gp plc 233 High Holborn, London WC1V 7DJ (☎ 071 831 6144)

CAMPBELL, Ian Matthew; s of John Strange Campbell (d 1978), and Mary Brown, *née* Wright; *b* 4 April 1952; *Educ* Coatbridge HS, Univ of Glasgow (BSc); *m* 1975, Carolyn Jean, da of Robin Dalziel Vanstone, of Coatbridge; 2 s (Andrew b 1978, Jamie b 1985), 1 da (Deborah b 1980); *Career* actuary (life assur, pensions and investmt); sr asst gen mangr of FS Assurance Ltd 1987-89, Sedgwick Financial Services 1989-; dir: FS Investment Services Ltd 1987-89, FS Investment Managers 1984-89, FS Assurance Tstees Ltd 1986-89; Northern Mortgage Corp 1986-89, Sedgwick Actuarial Services Ltd 1990-; *Recreations* golf, gardening; *Clubs* Royal Scottish Automobile, Lenzie Golf; *Style*— Ian Campbell, Esq; 6 Grove Park, Lenzie, Glasgow G66 5AH (☎ 041 775 0481); Sedgwick Actuarial Services Ltd, 178 Bath St, Glasgow G2 4S2 (☎ 041 332 2900, fax 041 332 7827)

CAMPBELL, Air Vice-Marshal Ian Robert; CB (1976), CBE (1964), AFC (1948); s of late Maj Duncan Elidor Campbell, DSO (gs of 2 Earl Cawdor) and Hon Florence Evelyn, *née* Willey, da of 1 Baron Barnby; *b* 5 Oct 1920; *Educ* Eton, RAF Coll Cranwell; *m* 1, 1953, Beryl Evelyn (d 1982), da of Brig Thomas Kennedy Newbigging, MC (d 1968), of Thaxted, Essex; 1 s; m 2, 1984, Elisabeth Lingard-Guthrie; *Career* joined RAF 1939, air attaché Bonn 1968-70, DMSI MOD 1970-72, Air Cdre 1965, Air Vice-Marshal 1970, Chief of Staff No 18 (Maritime) Gp 1973-75; *Clubs* Boodle's, Royal Air Force; *Style*— Air Vice-Marshal Ian Campbell, CB, CBE, AFC; Pike Farm, Fossebridge, Cheltenham, Glos GL54 3JR (☎ 0285 720537)

CAMPBELL, Cdr Sir Ian Tofts; CBE (1984), VRD (1961), JP (1987); s of Capt John Walter Campbell (d 1982), and Mary Hardie, *née* Scott (d 1982); *b* 3 Feb 1923; *Educ* Daniel Stewart's Coll Edinburgh; *m* 7 March 1961, Marion, da of Archibald Shiel (d 1943); *Career* RN 1942-46, Cdr RNR 1946-65; md MacGregor Wallcoverings Ltd 1966-78, dep chm Heath Collins Halden (Scotland) Ltd 1987-, dir Travel Systems Ltd 1987-89, chm Select Assured Properties plc 1988-, dir Hermiston Securities 1990; fin dir Cons Bd of Fin 1977-90, cncllr City of Edinburgh Dist Cncl 1984-88; memb Inst Sales Mgmnt 1954, FInstD 1960; OStJ 1987; *Recreations* golf, water colour painting, vintage cars; *Clubs* Caledonian, Royal Overseas League, Murrayfield Golf; *Style*— Cdr Sir Ian Campbell, CBE, VRD, JP; Merleton, Boswall Rd, Edinburgh EH5 3RH (☎ 031 552 4825); Heath Collins Halden (Scotland) Ltd, 9 Melville Crescent, Edinburgh EH3 (☎ 031 226 7699, fax 031 226 7698)

CAMPBELL, Sir Ilay Mark; 7 Bt (UK 1808), of Succoth, Dunbartonshire; s of Capt Sir George Ilay Campbell, 6 Bt, JP, DL (d 1967), and Clematis Elizabeth Denys, *née* Waring (d 1986); *b* 29 May 1927; *Educ* Eton, Ch Ch Oxford (MA); *m* 22 July 1961, (Margaret Minette) Rohais, da of (James) Alasdair Anderson of Tullichewan (d 1982); 2 da (Cecilia (Mrs MacGregor, younger of MacGregor) b 1963, Candida b 1964); *Career* Christies: Scottish agent 1968, jt Scottish agent 1973-, chm Scotland 1978-; pres Assoc for the Protection of Rural Scotland 1978-90, convener Church of Scotland Ctee for Artistic Matters 1987-, hon vice pres Scotland's Garden Scheme 1983-, Scottish rep Nat Art Collections Fund 1972-83; dir: High Craigton Farming Co Castle Fisheries Ltd, memb Historic Buildings Cncl for Scotland 1989-; FRSA 1986; *Recreations* heraldry, family history, collecting heraldic bookplates; *Clubs* Turf, Arts (Glasgow); *Style*— Sir Ilay Campbell, Bt; Crarae Lodge, Inveraray, Argyll PA32 8YA (☎ 0546 86274); Cumlodden Estate Office, Inveraray, Argyll PA32 8YA (☎ 0546 86633)

CAMPBELL, Hon James Alexander; yr s of 5 Earl Cawdor (d 1970), and his 1 wife Wilma Mairie, *née* Vickers; *b* 21 July 1942; *Educ* Eton, Royal Coll of Art; *m* 1, 1964 (m dis 1973), Brigid Carol Dolben, da of late Maj Patrick Owen Lyons, RA; 2 da (Slaine Catherine b 1966, Cara Jenny b 1968); m 2, 1973 (m dis 1986), Ann Elizabeth, da of late Col Argyle Henry Gillmore, OBE; 2 da (Lucy Georgia Elizabeth b 1973, Sarah Ann b 1977); *Career* designer/maker of ceramics; draughtsman; work exhibited and in private and public collections in UK, USA, Europe and Japan; lectr; ARCA; *Style*— The Hon James Campbell; 141 Bath Rd, Cheltenham, Glos

CAMPBELL, James Alexander Moffat Bain; s and h of Sir Colin Moffat Campbell, 8 Bt; *b* 23 Sept 1956; *Educ* Stowe; *Career* Capt Scots Gds ret 1983, Capt London Scottish 1/51 Highlanders 1984-87; insurance broker 1983-; *Recreations* motorcycling, gliding; *Clubs* Boodle's; *Style*— James Campbell, Esq; Kilbryde Castle, Dunblane, Perthshire (☎ 0786 823104)

CAMPBELL, Hon Mrs (Jennet Parker); da of 1 Baron Adrian, OM; *b* 16 Oct 1927; *m* 1953, Peter Watson Campbell, s of Peter Watson Campbell (d 1959), of W Kensington; 1 s (Richard), 2 da (Sally, Emma); *Style*— The Hon Mrs Campbell; St Anthony in Roseland, Portscatho, Truro, Cornwall, TR2 5EY (☎ 087 258 229)

CAMPBELL, Hon Mrs Angus; Joan Esther Sybella; JP (Cheshire); da of late Col Hercules Arthur Pakenham, CMG (d 1937), and Lilian Blanche Georgiana, *née* Ashley (d 1939); *b* 2 Feb 1904; *m* 1926, Hon Angus Dudley Campbell, CBE, JP (d 1967), yr s of 1 Baron Colgrain; 3 da; *Style*— The Hon Mrs Angus Campbell, JP; Doddington Cottage, Nantwich, Cheshire

CAMPBELL, John; OBE (1988); s of John Brown Campbell (d 1976), of Durham, and Christiana Weightman (d 1973); *b* 3 Dec 1932; *Educ* Univ of Wales Bangor (BSc); *m* 20 Aug 1955, (Jessie) May, da of Edward Davies, of Llanfyllin; 1 s (Ian b 1956), 1 da (Heather Dawn b 1958); *Career* Economic Forestry Gp: fndr memb 1957-, gp chief exec 1968-, dep chm 1986-; memb: Advsy Bd Oxford Univ 1968-, EEC Forestry Advsy Ctee 1983-, Cncl IOD 1983-, Advsy Bd Univ of Aberdeen 1986-, Rotary Club High Wycombe 1974 (pres 1989); FICF, FInstD, FRSA 1990; *Books* European Forestry - A Global Perspective (S J Hall Lecture, Univ of California, Berkeley, 1989); *Recreations* nature conservation; *Clubs* Caledonian, Phyllis Court; *Style*— John Campbell, Esq, OBE; Nethercote, Totteridge Lane, High Wycombe, Bucks HP13 7PH (☎ 0494 20442); Economic Forestry Group plc, Forestry House, Great Haseley, Oxford 0X9 7PG (☎ 0844 279571, fax 0844 279541)

CAMPBELL, Hon John Charles Middleton; er s (by 1 m) of Baron Campbell of Eskan (Life Peer), *qv*; *b* 3 July 1940; *Educ* Eton; *m* 1 Jan 1965, Patricia Ann, er da of late Tom Webster, of Bishopwood, Highgate, London N6; 2 da and 1 adopted da; *Style—* The Hon John Campbell; 39 Gondar Gardens, London NW6

CAMPBELL, John Davies; CVO (1980), CBE (1981, MBE 1957), MC and Bar (1945); s of late Maj William Hastings Campbell, and Hon Eugenie Anne Westenra, *née* Plunkett, da of 14 Baron Louth; *b* 11 Nov 1921; *Educ* Cheltenham, Univ of St Andrews; *m* 1959, Shirley Bouch; 1 s, 2 da; *Career* (despatches 1957); joined HM Dip Serv 1961 (formerly with Col Serv), cnsllr Ottawa 1972-77, consul-gen Naples 1977-81; Commendatore dell'Ordine al Merito della Repubblica Italiana 1980; *Style—* John Campbell, Esq, CVO, CBE, MC; Ridgeway, Ludlow Road, Leominster, Herefordshire HR6 0DH

CAMPBELL, John Donington; s of Maj John Donington Campbell, of Heathfield, Sussex, and Edith Jean, *née* Crick; *b* 23 April 1959; *Educ* Harrow, RMA Sandhurst; *m* 4 June 1988, Catriona Helen Cecelia, da of John Spence Swan, of Letham, Fife; *Career* cmmnd Royal Scots Dragoon Guards 1979, ADC to General Offr Cmd Scot and Govr of Edinburgh Castle 1985-87; Phoenix Burners Ltd 1977-79, Ivory and Sime plc 1987-89, dir Instate plc 1989-; *Recreations* country pursuits, tobogganing, tennis; *Clubs* Carlton, St Moritz Tobogganing; *Style—* John Campbell, Esq; Currburn, Yetholm, Roxburghshire; Instate plc, 4a Glenfinlas St, Edinburgh EH3 6AQ (☎ 031 220 6688, fax 031 220 6788)

CAMPBELL, John Lorne; OBE (1990); s of Lt-Col Duncan Campbell of Inverneill (d 1954), by his 1 w Ethel Harriet, *née* Waterbury; *b* 1 Oct 1906; *Educ* Rugby, abroad, St John's Coll Oxford (MA, DLitt); *m* 1935, Margaret Fay, da of late Henry Clay Shaw, of Glenshaw, Pennsylvania, USA; *Career* ret farmer; presented Isle of Canna to the Nat Trust for Scotland 1981; author; pres Folklore Inst Scotland 1947-51; chief Inverness Gaelic Soc 1965; Hon LLD St Francis Xavier NS 1953, DLitt Glasgow 1965, DLitt Oxford 1965; FRSE 1989; *Books* Canna, the Story of a Hebridean Island (1984), Songs Remembered In Exile; Gaelic Songs From Nova Scotia (1990); *Recreations* entomology, music, sea fishing, listening to old Gaelic stories; *Style—* John L Campbell, Esq, OBE, FRSE; Canna House, Isle of Canna, Scotland PH44 4RS

CAMPBELL, John Park; JP; s of Keith Campbell (d 1950), and Joan Rankin, *née* Park (d 1985); *b* 1 April 1934; *Educ* Strachur Public Sch Argyll, Strathallan Sch Perth; *m* 3 April 1957, Catherine Mary Sutherland; 3 s (Ian b 1960, Keith b 1962, Colin b 1968), 1 da (Karen b 1958); *Career* farmer; chm and md Glenrath (Farms) Ltd; convener Tweeddale DC 1979-88; FRAgS; *Style—* John Campbell, JP; Glenrath Manor, Peeblesshire (☎ 07214 221); The Whim Poultry Farm, Lamancha, West Linton, Peeblesshire (☎ 0968 75596)

CAMPBELL, John Quentin; s of John McKnight Campbell, OBE, MC (d 1959), and Katharine Margaret, *née* Grant (d 1983); *b* 5 March 1939; *Educ* Loretto, Wadham Coll Oxford (MA); *m* 1, 1960, Penelope Jane Redman; 3 s (James Alistair b 1962, John Marcus b 1964, Matthew b 1967), 1 da (Jessica Louise b 1970); m 2, 1977, Ann Rosemary, da of Sqdn Ldr Richard Henry Beeching (ret); 1 s (Frederick b 1982), 1 da (Anabella b 1977); *Career* rec, met stipendiary magistrate 1981-; chm Govrs Bessels Leigh Sch Oxford 1977-; *Clubs* Chelsea Arts, Frewen (Oxford); *Style—* J Q Campbell, Esq; 12 Park Town, Oxford; Marlborough St Magistrates Court, 21 Great Marlborough St W1A 4EY

CAMPBELL, John Townsend; s of John Townson Campbell (d 1979), of 6 Ballacurry Ave, Onchan, Isle of Man, and Elsie, *née* Heaton; *b* 14 July 1944; *Educ* Blackley Tech HS Manchester; *m* Patricia, da of Frank Leach, of 90 Sumerton Court, Blackley Manchester; 1 s (John b 21 Oct 1969), 2 da (Wendy 21 Aug 1971, Penny 8 Nov 1979); *Career* asst mangr McFisheries 1961, mangr Scotts Fine Fare 1962, property conslt 1963-76, md Tudor Homes Ltd 1976-87, chm Campbell Gp 1987; chm Isle of Man Freepost; *Recreations* golf, squash; *Clubs* Castletown Golf Isle of Man; *Style—* John Campbell, Esq; 72 King Edward Rd, Onchan, Isle of Man (☎ 0624 22060); Harbour Rd, Onchan, Isle of Man (☎ 0624 22060, fax 0624 72661, car 0860 640 212); Freeport Building, Ronaldsway, Isle of Man

CAMPBELL, (Alastair) John Wilson; s of Wilson William Campbell (d 1975), of Warkworth, Northumberland, and Pearl Gray, *née* Ackrill; *b* 18 Feb 1947; *Educ* Kings Sch Canterbury, Sidney Sussex Coll Cambridge (MA); *m* 25 Feb 1972, Sarah Jane, da of Patrick Phillip Shellard (d 1982); 2 s (Milo b 1974, Rollo b 1978), 1 da (Coco b 1976); *Career* exec NM Rothschild & Sons Ltd 1969-72, dir Noble Grossart Ltd 1973-88, md McLeod Russel 1979-82, dir Campbell Lutyens Hudson & Co Ltd 1988-; *Clubs* Reform, New (Edinburgh); *Style—* John Campbell, Esq; 25 Lansdowne Rd, London W11 3AG (☎ 071 229 6768); Campbell Lutyens Hudson & Co Ltd, 4 Clifford St, London W1X 1RB (☎ 071 439 7191, fax 071 437 0153)

CAMPBELL, Juliet Jeanne d'Auvergne; CMG (1988); da of Maj-Gen W D'Auvergne Collings, CB, CBE (d 1984), of St Peter Port, Guernsey, and Harriet Nancy Draper, *née* Bishop (d 1983); *b* 23 May 1935; *Educ* Lady Margaret Hall Oxford (BA); *m* 28 July 1983, Alexander Elmslie (Alec) Campbell; *Career* FCO: joined 1957, Brussels Conf 1961-63, Bangkok 1964-66, News Dept 1967-70, The Hague 1971-74, Euro Integration Dept 1974-77, press cnsllr Paris 1977-80, RCDS 1981, cnsllr Jakarta 1982-83, head Trg Dept 1984-88, ambass Luxembourg 1988-; *Style—* Mrs Juliet Campbell, CMG; British Embassy, 14 BD Roosevelt, Luxembourg (☎ 010 352 29864)

CAMPBELL, Lachlan Philip Kemeys; s and h of Sir Guy Campbell, 5 Bt, OBE, MC, *qv*; *b* 9 Oct 1958; *m* 1986, Harriet Jane Sarah, o da of F E Jex Girling, of W Malvern, Worcs; *Career* The Royal Green Jackets, served in N Ireland (short service cmmn), Queen Victoria's Rifles (TA); *Style—* Lachlan Campbell, Esq

CAMPBELL, Louis Auchinbreck; s and h of Sir Robin Auchinbreck Campbell, 15 Bt; *b* 17 Jan 1953; *Style—* Louis Campbell, Esq

CAMPBELL, Lucy B; *née* Barnett; da of James Allen Barnett, of Portland, Oregan, USA, and Jane, *née* Dodge (d 1952); *b* 26 Jan 1940; *Educ* Nightingale Bamford Sch NYC, The Garland Coll Boston Mass; *m* 1, 1959 (m dis 1963), Clifford Smith Jr, s of Clifford Smith (d 1961), of Rockpart, Maine, USA; 2 s (Cifford Allen b 24 Aug 1960, Grafton Dodge b 3 Dec 1961); m 2, 1965 (m dis 1981), Colin Guy Napier Campbell, s of Archibald Campbell (d 1975), of London; 2 da (Georgina Dorothy b 24 Jan 1969, Tessa Sylvia b 3 April 1971); m 3, 1990, Peter Henry Arthur Stanley; *Career* art dealer in antiquarian prints and watercolours; owner of Lucy B Campbell Gallery London (founded 1984) and Lucy B Campbell Ltd NY; *Style—* Mrs Lucy B Campbell; 43 Clabon Mews, London SW1X 0EQ (☎ 071 589 4295); 123 Kensington Church St, London W8 7LP (☎ 071 727 2205, fax 071 229 4252)

CAMPBELL, Malcolm; s of Malcolm Brown Campbell (d 1940), and Helen Munro, *née* Carruthers; *b* 3 Jan 1934; *Educ* Glenalmond Coll; *m* 1, 25 Sept 1960 (m dis 1977), Fiona, *née* McLaren; 3 s (Colin b 30 Sept 1961, David b 19 April 1963, Graham b 6 March 1967); m 2, 18 Feb 1983, Susan Elizabeth Patten, da of Sydney David (d 1965), of Mid Glamorgan; 1 s (James b 29 June 1984), 1 step da (Elizabeth b 7 Oct 1975); *Career* Nat Serv RA 1953-55; chm Malcolm Campbell Ltd 1969-(joined 1955, sales mangr 1959, sales dir 1961, md 1966); dir: Glasgow C of C, Br Retailers Assoc (memb Cncl); winner Scottish Special Free Enterprise Award by Aims of Indust 1988; memb Bd of Govrs Queen's Coll Glasgow 1989-; Freeman City of London 1978, Liveryman Worshipful Co of Fruiterers 1978; *Recreations* golf, sailing (Western Gailes capt 1974); *Clubs* Royal and Ancient St Andrews, Prestwick Western; *Style—* Malcolm Campbell, Esq; Malcolm Campbell Ltd, 24 George Square, Glasgow G2 1EG (☎ 041 204 4455, fax 041 204 4360)

CAMPBELL, Malcolm Godfrey Wilson; s of Wilson William Campbell (d 1975), of Northumberland, and Pearl Gray, *née* Ackrill; *b* 30 July 1945; *Educ* The King's Sch Canterbury, Jesus Coll Oxford (MA); *Career* Oxford Univ Air Sqdn 1963-66; slr, ptnr Linklaters & Paines 1977-; memb Law Soc 1970; *Recreations* sport, flying, travel, photography; *Style—* Malcolm Campbell, Esq; Barrington House, 59-67 Gresham Street, London EC2V 7JA (☎ 071 606 7080, fax 071 606 5113, telex 884349)

CAMPBELL, Margaret Jane (Mrs Margaret Bain); da of Dr Colin Campbell, of Waddesdon, Aylesbury, Bucks, and Daphne EM, *née* Robbins; *b* 15 June 1957; *Educ* Aylesbury HS, RCM; *m* 22 Dec 1990, Christopher Bain; *Career* princ flute: City of Birmingham Symphony Orchestra 1977-86, Orchestra of the Royal Opera House Covent Gdn 1986; winner Nat Fedn of Music Socs award for young concert artists 1981; memb ISM, ARCM; *Style—* Ms Margaret Campbell; 59 Chandos Ave, Ealing, London W5 4EP (☎ 081 568 3605)

CAMPBELL, Hon Mrs (Margaret Taylor Young); *née* Westwood; MBE; yr da of 1 Baron Westwood, OBE (d 1953); *b* 15 Dec 1913; *m* 1, 1934 (m dis 1943), William Blackbird Lynn, s of John Lynn, of S Shields; m 2, 1945 (m dis 1974), John Bruce Campbell, s of George Howard Campbell, of Port Hope, Ontario, Canada; 1 s (Robert b 1948), 1 da (Helen b 1946); *Style—* The Hon Mrs Campbell, MBE; 2 Ethorpe Crescent, Gerrards Cross, Bucks

CAMPBELL, Sir Matthew; KBE (1963), CB (1959); s of Matthew Campbell (d 1952), of High Blantyre, Lanarkshire; *b* 23 May 1907; *Educ* Hamilton Acad, Univ of Glasgow; *m* 1939, Isabella, da of late John Wilson, of St Conans, Rutherglen, Lanarkshire; 2 s (Colin, John); *Career* Civil Serv 1928-: sec Dept of Agric and Fisheries 1958-68 (under-sec 1953-58); dep chm White Fish Authy 1968-78; *Style—* Sir Matthew Campbell, KBE, CB; 10 Craigleith View, Edinburgh (☎ 031 337 5168)

CAMPBELL, Michael David Colin Craven; s of Bruce Colin Campbell (d 1980), and Doris, *née* Craven-Ellis; *b* 12 Dec 1942; *Educ* Radley; *m* 6 April 1967, Linda Frances, da of Charles Brownrigg (d 1982); 1 s (Jamie Loudoun Craven b 1970), 2 da (Alexandra Jane b 1968, Laura Grace b 1977); *Career* chm Ellis Campbell Gp 1987-(md 1977-); dir Authority Investmts plc 1986-; govr and tstee The Treloar Tst; tstee Hampshire Gardens Tst; patron Small Business Bureau 1983-, memb Hampshire CC 1983-87; tstee Hampshire Buildings Preservation Tst; *Recreations* shooting, sailing, skiing, cars; *Clubs* Boodle's, Royal Yacht Sqdn; *Style—* Michael Campbell, Esq; c/o Craven House, Arundell Place, West Street, Farnham, Surrey (☎ 0252 722333, fax 0252 714189)

CAMPBELL, Lady Moyra Kathleen; *née* Hamilton; CVO (1963); only da of 4 Duke of Abercorn (d 1979); *b* 22 July 1930; *m* 1966, Cdr Peter Colin Drummond Campbell, LVO, DL *qv*, s of Maj-Gen Sir Douglas Campbell, KBE, CB, DSO, MC (d 1980); 2 s; *Career* a train bearer to HM The Queen at Coronation 1953, lady-in-waiting (temp) to HRH Princess Alexandra of Kent 1954-64, a lady-in-waiting 1964-66, and an extra lady-in-waiting 1966-69; *Style—* The Lady Moyra Campbell, CVO; Hollybrook House, Randalstown, Co Antrim, N Ireland BT41 2PB (☎ 084 94 72224)

CAMPBELL, Hon Neil Donald; DSC (1945); yst s of 2 Baron Colgrain (d 1973); *b* 24 Aug 1922; *Educ* RNC Dartmouth; *m* 1951, Angela Louise Vereker, da of Rt Hon Sir Ronald Hibbert Cross, 1 Bt, KCMG, KCVO; 2 s (and 1 s decd), 1 da; *Career* late Lt RN, ret 1947; dir: Geo & R Dewhurst 1947-56, James Capel 1970-77; *Style—* The Hon Neil Campbell, DSC; Yorks Hill Farm, Ide Hill, Sevenoaks, Kent

CAMPBELL, Neville Stuart; s of Neville Campbell, and Mary, *née* Robinson (d 1987); *b* 5 Nov 1960; *Educ* Harehills Middle Sch, Intake HS, London Sch of Contemporary Dance; partner, Penny Rae; 1 da (Scarlett Rae Campbell b 6 Nov 1988), 1 adopted s (Mark Rae Campbell b 26 April 1986); *Career* dancer and choreographer English Dance Theatre 1980-83, dancer Moves Afoot 1983-84, dance artist in res Strathclyde Regnl Cncl 1984-86, artistic dir Phoenix Dance Co 1987-; choreographies: Human Scandals (Phoenix) 1989, Solo (Phoenix) 1990, over 14 pieces for Br youth and community gps; teaching in colls and gps in Br, France, Holland and Zimbabwe; *Recreations* travel, family, carpentry, music; *Style—* Neville Campbell, Esq; Phoenix Dance Company, 3 St Peter's Buildings, St Peter's Square, Leeds LS9 8AH (☎ 0532 423486, fax 0532 444736)

CAMPBELL, Sir Niall Alexander Hamilton; 8 Bt (UK 1831), of Barcaldine and Glenure, Argyllshire; 15 Chieftain, Hereditary Keeper of Barcaldine Castle; s of Sir Ian Campbell, 7 Bt, CB (d 1978), and Madeline Lowe Reid, *née* Whitelocke (d 1929); *b* 7 Jan 1925; *Educ* Cheltenham, CCC Oxford; *m* 1949 (m dis 1956), *née* Turner; m 2, 1957, Norma Joyce, da of W N Wiggin; 2 s, 2 da; *Heir* s, Roderick Duncan Hamilton; *Career* barr 1951, hospital administrator 1953-70, dep chief clerk Inner London Magistrates' Courts 1970-76, clerk to Justices of Barnstaple, Bideford and Great Torrington and S Molton (N Devon Divs) 1976-; *Style—* Sir Niall Campbell, Bt; The Old Mill, Milltown, Muddiford, Barnstaple, Devon (☎ 0271 341); The Law Courts, Civic Centre, Barnstaple, Devon (☎ 0271 72511); Barcaldine Castle, Benderloch via Connel, Argyllshire

CAMPBELL, Maj-Gen (Charles) Peter; CBE (1977); s of Charles Alfred Campbell (d 1975), and Blanche, *née* Appleton (d 1983); *b* 25 Aug 1926; *Educ* Gillingham GS, Emmanuel Coll Cambridge; *m* 1, 11 May 1949, Lucy (d 1986), da of William David Kitching (d 1960); 2 s (Murray b 2 July 1951, Colin b 16 May 1954); m 2, 22 Nov 1986, Elizabeth Barbara, da of Maj William Barington Tristram (ka 1942); *Career* cmmnd RE 1945; army staff course 1957; OC 11 Ind Field Sqdn RE in Far East 1960-62, Jt Servs Staff Course 1963, Co Cdr RMA Sandhurst 1965-67, CRE 1 Divn BAOR 1967-70, GSO1 Plans MOD 1970-71, CRE 3 Div UK 1971, cmd 12 Engrg Bde UK 1972-73, RCDS 1974, COS in HQ UK 1975-77, Engr-in-Chief (Army) 1977-80; Col Cmdt RE 1981-86; Hon Col 101 (London) Engr Regt (EOD) 1986-; chm RE Assoc 1983-89, dir Quicks Gp plc 1982-, conslt Terex Equipment 1983-89; FBIM 1971; *Recreations* painting, collecting militaria; *Clubs* Naval and Military; *Style—* Maj-Gen Peter Campbell, CBE; c/o Lloyds Bank plc, 6 Pall Mall, London SW1

CAMPBELL, Cdr Peter Colin Drummond; LVO (1960), DL (Antrim 1984); s of Maj-Gen Sir (Alexander) Douglas Campbell, KBE, CB, DSO, MC (d 1980), and Patience Loveday, *née* Carlyon; *b* 24 Oct 1927; *Educ* Cheltenham, RNC Dartmouth; *m* 1966, Lady Moyra Kathleen, *qv*, da of 4 Duke of Abercorn (d 1979); 2 s; *Career* late Cdr RN; equerry to HM the Queen 1957-60; farmer; Ireland rep Irish Soc 1974-; memb NI Advsy Bd Abbey Nat Bldg Soc 1982-; life vice pres RN Assoc 1979-, High Sheriff Co Antrim 1985, Freeman City of London 1975; *Recreations* field sports, boating; *Clubs* Army & Navy; *Style—* Cdr Peter Campbell, LVO, DL; Hollybrook House, Randalstown, Co Antrim, NI (☎ 084 94 72224); Rathlin Island, Co Antrim (☎ 02657 63911)

CAMPBELL, Hon Peter Mark Middleton; yr s (by 1 m) of Baron Campbell of Eskan (Life Peer), *qv*; *b* 4 March 1946; *Educ* Eton; *m* 1972, Anne Susan, da of John E Cuthbert, of Mudeford, Dorset; 2 s, 1 da (d 1980); *Style—* The Hon Peter Campbell; Hampton House, 7 Grays Hill, Henley-on-Thames, Oxfordshire RG9 1SL

CAMPBELL, Prof Peter Walter; s of Walter Clement Howard Campbell (d 1958), of Bournemouth, and Lillian Muriel, *née* Locke (d 1978); *b* 17 June 1926; *Educ*

Bournemouth Sch, New Coll Oxford (MA), Nuffield Coll Oxford; *Career* lectr in govt Univ of Manchester 1949-60; Univ of Reading: prof of political economy 1960-64, prof of politics 1964-91, dean of Faculty of Letters and Social Scis 1966-69, chm Graduate Sch of Contemp Euro Studies 1971-73; vice chm Social Serv Reading DC 1966-71, chm Reading Romilly Assoc 1965-69, Berks Electoral Reform Gp 1979-80, Reading Campaign for Homosexual Equality 1979-80, sec treas Political Studies Assoc of UK 1955-58, chm Inst of Electoral Res 1958-65, memb Cncl Hansard Soc for Parliamentary Govt 1962-77, ed Political Studies 1963-69; memb: Cwlth Scholarship Cmmn's Advsy Panel 1964-73, Soc Sci Res Cncl's Political Sci Ctee 1968-72, CNAA Bds and Panels 1969-78; UGC's Soc Studies Sub Ctee 1973-83, vice pres Electoral Reform Soc 1973-, chm Cons Gp for Homosexual Equality 1982-88 (vice pres 1988-); treas Conservative Action for Electoral Reform 1990-; *Books* Encyclopaedia of World Politics (with W Theimer, 1950), French Electoral Systems and Elections 1789-1957 (1958), The Constitution of the Fifth Republic (1958); *Recreations* idling, ambling; *Clubs* Athenaeum, Oxford and Cambridge, English-Speaking Union; *Style*— Prof Peter Campbell; Department of Politics, The University of Reading, Reading, Berkshire RG6 2AA (☎ 0734 875 123)

CAMPBELL, Philip Arthur Cockburn; s of Lt-Col George Campbell (d 1951), and Mrs Helen Hossack, *née* Jackson (d 1990); *b* 4 May 1947; *Educ* Gordonstoun, Moray Sch, Pembroke Coll Cambridge (MA); *m* 22 July 1972, Sarah Elizabeth, da of Thomas Alfred Graham Charlton, CB, of Penn, Buckinghamshire; 2 da (Katie b 1977, Georgina b 1980); *Career* BBC writer, prodr, reporter; ed progs: TV News, News Extra, Westminster, Newsnight, This Week Next Week, Week in Lords; ed live coverage Party Conf, now managing ed politics BBC News and Current Affrs TV and radio; *Recreations* family, tennis, walking, theatre, opera; *Style*— Philip Campbell, Esq; 20 Ashchurch Terrace, London W12; BBC News and Current Affairs, Television Centre, Wood Lane, London W12

CAMPBELL, Hon Mrs (Phyllis Audrey); *née* Thomson; er da of 1 Baron Thomson of Fleet, GBE (d 1976); *b* 6 July 1917; *m* 1947, Clarence Elwood Campbell, s of late George Brown Campbell; 3 da; *Style*— The Hon Mrs Campbell; c/o Thomson Organisation Ltd, PO Box 4YG, 4 Stratford Place, W1A 4YG

CAMPBELL, Robert; s of Robert Stewart Campbell (d 1966), of Booking Hall, Coughton, Warwickshire, and Isobella Frances, *née* Nettleton (d 1957); *b* 18 May 1929; *Educ* Loughborough Univ (DLC, MSc); *m* 1950, Edna Maud, da of Thomas Henry Evans (d 1949); *Career* chartered engr 1954-69, various appts in water industry, miny inspr 1969-74, asst dir Anglian Water 1974-77; chief exec Epping Forest Dist Cncl 1977-79, md Thomas Telford Ltd, chm REM Campbell Int Mgmnt Conslts 1982-; sec Inst of Civil Engrs (tstee Benevolent Fund 1979-82), dir Watt Ctee Energy Ltd; FICE; *Recreations* music, gardening, watching cricket; *Clubs* MCC; *Style*— Robert Campbell, Esq; 8 Tansy Close, Northampton NN4 9XW; Jubilee House, Weston Favell, Northampton NH3 4HW (☎ 0604 414500, fax 411192)

CAMPBELL, Hon Robert Dudley (Robin); 2 s of late 2 Baron Colgrain (d 1973); *b* 6 July 1921; *Educ* Eton, Trinity Coll Cambridge; *m* 1, 1954 (m dis 1978), Cecilia Barbara, da of late Cdr Alexander Leslie, RN; 2 da; m 2, 1983, Mrs Muriel Anne Kandal, da of George Tuson, RN (ka 1941), of Loughborough, Leics; *Career* Scots Gds 1940-46, Capt, wounded ME; dir Forbes Forbes Campbell & Co Ltd Bombay 1946-89 (dep chm 1953-60); md: Balfour Williamson & Co Ltd 1962-76, Baltic Investments (London) Ltd 1977-81; dep chm C E Coates & Co Ltd 1981-83; chm Br Exports Houses Assoc 1966-67, memb Advsy Cncl ECGD 1972-76; MIEx; *Clubs* Cavalry and Guards', Willingdon (Bombay); *Style*— The Hon Robin Campbell; Sharp's Place, Boughbeech, Edenbridge, Kent

CAMPBELL, (Alistair) Robert Macbrair; s of Dr Bruce Campbell, OBE, of West End Barn, Wootton, Woodstock, Oxon, and Margaret Campbell; *b* 9 May 1946; *Educ* Marlborough, Univ of Aberdeen (BSc); *m* 7 Sept 1968, Frances Rosemary, da of Prof Kenneth Kirkwood, of 233 Woodstock Rd, Oxford; 1 s (Tomas b 11 Aug 1971), 2 da (Chloe b 5 July 1973, Nancy b 15 May 1977); *Career* chm ADONIS Consortium of Int Publishers 1980-, md Blackwell Scientific Pubns 1987- (ed 1968-76, ed dir 1976-87); pres: Blackwell Scientific Pubns Inc (USA) 1988-, Arnette (France) 1989-; chm Blackwell Wissenschafts (FRG) 1989-; MIBiol 1975, memb Br Ecological Soc; *Books* A Guide to the Birds of the Coast (1976), Microform Publishing (1979), Journal Publishing (1987); *Recreations* fly fishing, writing, wine; *Clubs* Groucho's; *Style*— Robert Campbell, Esq; Blackwell Scientific Publications Ltd, Osney Mead, Oxford OX2 0EL (☎ 0865 240201, fax 0865 721205)

CAMPBELL, Robin Alexander; s of Robert Campbell (d 1986), of Sway, Hants, and Marion Steele, *née* Davidson; *Educ* Aldenham, Wadham Coll Oxford (MA); *m* 1968, Heather-Ann, da of Gordon Henderson Munro, TD (d 1980), of Inverness; 1 s (Alexander b 1972), 1 da (Fiona b 1974); *Career* Nat Serv 2 Lt: Gordon Highlanders, 4 King's African Rifles (Kenya and Uganda); dist offr HM Overseas Civil Serv N Rhodesia 1961-64, magistrate Zambia 1964-65, called to the Bar Middle Temple 1967; *Books* Seneca: Letters from a Stoic (translation, 1969), Lumley's Public Health Acts (jt ed, 1970-72); *Recreations* mountain walking, sea canoeing, drawing and watercolours, wildlife; *Style*— Robin Campbell, Esq; 5 Arlington Sq, London N1 7DS (☎ 071 359 2334); Pollanaich, Nedd, Drumbeg by Lairg, Sutherland IV27 4NN (☎ 05 713 292); 4-5 Gray's Inn Sq, Gray's Inn, London WC1R 5AY (☎ 071 404 5252, fax 071 242 7803)

CAMPBELL, Sir Robin Auchinbreck; 15 Bt (NS 1628), of Auchinbreck; s of Sir Louis Hamilton Campbell, 14 Bt (d 1970), and Margaret Elizabeth Patricia (d 1985), da of Patrick Campbell; *b* 7 June 1922; *Educ* Eton; *m* 1, 1948, Rosemary (Sally) (d 1978), da of Ashley Dean, of Christchurch, New Zealand; 1 s, 2 da; m 2, 1978, Elizabeth, da of Sir Arthur Colegate, MP, and formerly w of Richard Wellesley Gunston; *Heir* s, Louis Auchinbreck Campbell; *Career* late Lt (A) RNVR; *Style*— Sir Robin Campbell, Bt; Greta Valley, RMD, N Canterbury, New Zealand

CAMPBELL, Roderick Duncan Hamilton; Yr of Barcaldine and Glenure; s and h of Sir Niall Campbell, 8 Bt, *qv*; *b* 24 Feb 1961; *m* 15 April 1989, Jean Caroline, da of L H Bicknell, of Tom's Hill, Lobb, Braunton, N Devon; 1 da (Kate b 25 Feb 1990); *Style*— Roderick Campbell, Esq; East Almer Farmhouse, Almer, Blandford, Dorset DT11 9EL

CAMPBELL, Prof Ronald William Fearnley; s of Robert Walter Campbell, of Brightons, Falkirk, Stirlingshire, Scotland, and Mary Campbell Dawson, *née* Jack; *b* 11 Oct 1946; *Educ* Dollar Acad Scotland, Univ of Edinburgh (MRCP); *m* 18 July 1969, Agnes Margaret, da of Charles Struth, of Grangemouth, Stirlingshire, Scotland; 1 da (Xanthe b 3 Nov 1974); *Career* med positions Edinburgh Teaching Gp Hosps 1969-75, Sir Henry Wellcome Fellowship of MRC Duke Univ Durham N Carolina USA 1975-76, sr lectr in academic cardiology Newcastle Gp Hosps 1976-86, Br Heart Fndn prof of cardiology Univ of Newcastle and hon conslt cardiologist Freeman Hosp Newcastle 1986-, UCCA selector Univ of Newcastle, med advsr Northumbria Ambulance Serv; memb: Ctees Br Heart Fndn, Ball Ctee Newcastle Annual Heart Ball, Br Cardiac Soc 1979; FRCPE 1981, FRCP 1984, fell Euro Soc of Cardiology; *Books* Dynamic Electrocardiography (1985); *Recreations* skiing, fell walking, videography; *Style*— Prof Ronald Campbell; Academic Cardiology, Freeman Hospital, Newcastle upon Tyne NE7 7DN (☎ 091 2843111, fax 091 2130498)

CAMPBELL, Ronnie; MP (Lab Blyth Valley 1987-); s of Ronald Campbell, and Edna, *née* Howes; *b* 14 Aug 1943; *Educ* Ridley HS; *m* 17 July 1967, Deirdre, da of Edward McHale (d 1976); 5 s (Edward b 1968, Barry b 1971, Shaun b 1973, Brendan b 1973, Aiden b 1977), 1 da (Sharon b 1969); *Career* former miner; memb: Blyth Borough Cncl 1969-74, Blyth Valley Cncl 1974-; dist cncllr 1969-88; chm Bates NUM; *Style*— Mr Ronnie Campbell, Esq, MP; House of Commons, London SW1A OAA

CAMPBELL, Hon Rosalind Leonora Middleton; er da (by 1 m) of Baron Campbell of Eskan (Life Peer), *qv*; *b* 8 July 1942; *Educ* Down House Newbury; *Career* bookbinder and restorer; *Style*— The Hon Rosalind Campbell; 13 Alma Green, Stoke Row, Oxon (☎ 0491 681349)

CAMPBELL, Hon Mrs (Shona Catherine Greig); *née* Macpherson; da of 1 Baron Macpherson of Drumochter (d 1965); *b* 31 July 1929; *m* 1952, Donald le Strange Campbell, MC, *qv*; 1 s, 1 da; *Recreations* home, country life, charities; *Clubs* Boodle's; *Style*— The Hon Mrs Campbell; Little Dartmouth House, Dartmouth, Devon TQ6 0JP (☎ 0803 832120)

CAMPBELL, Steven MacMillan; s of George Campbell, of Rutherglen, Glasgow, and Martha Dallas McKenzie, *née* MacMillan; *b* 19 March 1953; *Educ* Rutherglen Acad, Glasgow Sch of Art (BA), Pratt Inst NY; *m* 4 July 1975, Carol Ann, da of Andrew Crossan Thompson, of Glasgow, Scotland; 1 s (Rory Thompson b 6 June 1988), 2 da (Lauren Holly b 22 May 1984, Greer Caitlin b 25 Feb 1987); *Career* artist; solo exhibitions incl: Barbara Toll Fine Arts NY 1983, John Webber Gallery NY 1983, Dart Gallery Chicago 1983, Rona Hoffman Gallery Chicago 1984, Galerie Six Freidrich Munich Germany 1984, Riverside Studios London 1984, Fruitmarket Gallery Edinburgh 1985, Barbara Toll Fine Arts NY 1985, Walker Art Center Minneapolis 1985, Middendorf Gallery Washington DC 1985, Galerie Pierre Huber Geneva 1986, John Berggruen Gallery San Francisco 1986, Marlborough Fine Art London 1987, Marlborough Fine Art NY 1988, Riva Yares Gallery Scotsdale Arizona 1989, The Third Eye Centre Glasgow 1990, Rex Irwin Gallery Sydney Australia 1990, Marlborough Fine Art Tokyo 1990, Oriel Mostyn Llandudno Wales 1990, Aberdeen Art Gallery 1990, Whitworth Art Gallery Manchester 1990, Southampton City Art Gallery 1991; public collections incl: Arts Cncl of GB, Art Inst of Chicago, City Art Gallery Southampton, Glasgow Art Gallery and Museum, Contemporary Art Soc London, Tamayo Museum Mexico City, Walker Arts Center Minneapolis, Aberdeen Art Gallery and Museum, Danheiser Fndn NY, Metropolitan Museum NY, Leeds City Art Gallery, Tate Gallery London, Tate Gallery Liverpool, Br Cncl, Scottish Arts Cncl, Phoenix Art Museum, Hirshorn Museum Washington DC, Chase Manhattan Bank NY, Southampton Gallery, High Museum of Art Atlanta Georgia; awarded Fulbright scholarship 1982-83; *Recreations* angling, reading, mathematics, detective novels; *Style*— Steven Campbell, Esq; Ballochleam Farm, Kippen, Stirlingshire FK8 3JM (☎ 078 687 526); Marlborough Fine Art (UK) Ltd, 6 Albemarle St, London W1X 4BY (☎ 071 629 5161, fax 071 629 6338)

CAMPBELL, Thomas; s of Thomas Campbell (d 1965), of Edinburgh, and Mary Frances, *née* Young (d 1971); *b* 13 Aug 1924; *Educ* Melville Coll Edinburgh, Manchester Univ; *m* 19 Nov 1955, Sheila Margaret, da of Sir George Campbell, KCIE (d 1965); 3 s (Hamish and Niall b 1957 (twins), Iain b 1958); *Career* served W Africa 1954-69; sr exec Unilever Gp of Cos 1954-74, chm George Campbell and Sons 1983-, Cons cncllr Perth and Kinross Dist Cncl, ldr Cons Gp, chm Perthshire Tourist Bd; *Recreations* golf, gardening; *Clubs* Royal Perth Golfing Soc, Perth Hunt; *Style*— Thomas Campbell, Esq; Balnabeggan, Bridge of Cally, Perthshire (☎ 025 086 305)

CAMPBELL, Maj-Gen William Tait; CBE (1945, OBE 1944); s of late Dr Robert B Campbell, of Edinburgh; *b* 8 Oct 1912; *Educ* Fettes Coll, RMC Sandhurst; *m* 1942, Rhoda Alice, da of late Adm Algernon Walker-Heneage-Vivian, CB, MVO; 2 da; *Career* 2 Lt Royal Scots (Royal Regt) 1933; Lt-Col cmdg 1 Bn Royal Scots 1954-57 (despatches), Brig i/c admin Malaya 1962, Maj-Gen 1964, DQMG MOD (Army Dept) 1964-67, ret 1967; Col Royal Scots 1964-74; dir Fairbridge Soc 1969-78; *Style*— Maj-Gen William T Campbell, CBE; Ashwood, Boarhills, St Andrews, Fife KY16 8PR

CAMPBELL GOLDING, (Frederick) Keith; s of Dr Frederick Campbell Golding (d 1984), of The Barn, Hursley, Winchester, Hants, and Barbara, *née* Hubbard; *b* 17 May 1947; *Educ* Mill Hill Sch; *m* 26 July 1980, Davina, da of Sir David Lancaster Nicolson, of Howicks, Dunsfold, Godalming, Surrey; 1 s (Angus b 1987), 3 da (Amy b 1981, Tania b 1981, Juliette b 1984); *Career* md Campbell Golding Assocs Ltd 1977-84, exec dir EBC AMRO Bank Ltd 1986-89, md EBC AMRO Asset Mgmnt Ltd 1986-89; *Recreations* field sports, wine collecting; *Clubs* Bucks; *Style*— Keith Campbell Golding, Esq; Queens Court, Tockenham, Wootton Bassett, Wilts (☎ 0793 853186); EBC AMRO Asset Mgmnt Ltd, 10 Devonshire Sq, London EC2M 4HS (☎ 071 621 0101, fax 071 626 7915, telex 8811001)

CAMPBELL-GRAY, Hon Andrew Godfrey Diarmid Stuart; *see*: Gray, Master of

CAMPBELL-GRAY, Hon Cailain Douglas; yr s of late Maj Hon Lindsay Stuart Campbell-Gray (Master of Gray), MC (d 1945); bro of 22 Lord; raised to rank of a Baron's son, 1950; *b* 14 July 1934; *Educ* Eton; *m* 1963, Wendy Helen Katharine, yr da of late William Herbert Dunlop, of Doonside, Ayr; 1 s, 1 da; *Style*— The Hon Cailain Campbell-Gray; Fanamor, Taynuilt, Argyll PA35 1HR

CAMPBELL-HARRIS, Alastair Neil; s of Maj Arthur Edward Campbell-Harris, MC, of London (d 1970), and Doris Marie, *née* Robson (d 1964); *b* 9 Feb 1926; *Educ* Sunningdale Sch, RNC Dartmouth; *m* 9 Jan 1962, Zara Carolyn, da of William Herbert Harrison, of Staffs (d 1975); 1 s (James Neil b 1966), 2 da (Clare Louise b 1963, Lucinda Zara b 1968); *Career* RN 1943-55: midshipman in Atlantic and East Indies 1943, Sub Lt in Med 1945, Lt Far East 1947-50, home waters 1950-52, ADC to Govr Gen of NZ 1952-55, ret as Lt 1955; fin PR conslt, chm Citigate Communications Gp Ltd 1987, dep chm Streets Fin Strategy Ltd 1986 (dir Streets Financial Ltd 1975-86); *Recreations* shooting, fishing, golf, gardening; *Style*— Alastair Campbell-Harris, Esq; Gattendon Lodge, Goring-on-Thames, nr Reading, Berks RG8 9LU (☎ 0491 872292); Citigate Communications Group Ltd, 7 Birchin Lane, London EC3M 2PA (☎ 071 623 2737)

CAMPBELL-JOHNSON, Alan; CIE (1947), OBE (1946); s of Lt-Col James Alexander Campbell-Johnson (ka 1918), of S Aust, and Gladys Susanna, *née* Geering (d 1976); *b* 16 July 1913; *Educ* Westminster, ChCh Oxford (BA, MA); *m* 8 Oct 1938, (Imogen) Fay de la Tour, da of Ernest Alexander Dunlap (d 1923), of Jacksonville, Illinois, USA; 1 s (Keith b 1945 d 1970), 1 da (Virginia b 1942); *Career* Nat Serv RAFVR 1941-46, combined ops HQ 1942-43, HQ Supreme Allied Cdr SE Asia (Wing Cdr i/c Inter Allied Records Section) 1943-46; political sec to Rt Hon Sir Archibald Sinclair Ldr of the Lib Pty 1937-39; Parly candidate (Lib) Salisbury and S Wilts 1945 and 1950; press attaché to Viceroy and Govr Gen of India 1947-48; PR conslt; fndr and chm Campbell-Johnson Ltd 1953-78; dir Hill and Knowlton (UK) Ltd 1978-85; former pres Inst of PR; US Legion of Merit 1947; Hon DLitt Univ of Southampton; MIPR 1948, FIPR 1954, Hon FIPR 1988, MRI 1956, FRSA 1957; *Books* Growing Opinions (ed, 1935), Peace Offering (1936), Anthony Eden - A Biography (1938, revised 1955), Viscount Halifax - A Biography (1941), Mission with Mountbatten (1951, republished 1971 and 1985); *Recreations* cricket, mountaineering; *Clubs* Brooks's, Nat Lib, MCC; *Style*— Alan Campbell-Johnson, Esq, CIE, OBE; 21 Ashley Gdns, Ambrosden Avenue, London SW1P 1QD (☎ 071 834 1532, office 071 630 1653, fax 071 828 6633)

CAMPBELL-JOHNSTON, Rev Michael Alexander Ninian; *b* 27 Sept 1931; *Educ*

Beaumont Coll Old Windsor, Séminaire des Missions Chantilly (LicPhil), LSE (BSc), Instituto Libre de Filosofia Mexico City (STL); *Career* entered Jesuits Roehampton 1949, teacher Beaumont and Stonyhurst Coll 1958-60, tertianship Volta Redonda Brazil 1965, involved with sociological survey Guyana and Barbados 1966-67, dir Guyana Inst of Social Res and Action 1967-75, exec sec Jesuit Social Secretariat Rome 1975-84, regnl coordinator Jesuit Refugee Serv in Central America 1984-87, prov superior British Province of Jesuits 1987-; *Style*— The Rev Michael Campbell-Johnston, SJ; 114 Mount St, London W1Y 6AH (☎ 071 499 0285)

CAMPBELL OF AIRDS, Alastair Lorne; s of Brig Lorne Campbell of Airds, VC, DSO, OBE, TD, *qv*, and Amy Muriel Jordan, *née* Campbell (d 1950); *b* 11 July 1937; *Educ* Eton, Sandhurst; *m* 1960, Mary Ann, da of Lt-Col (George) Patrick Campbell-Preston, MBE; 4c; *Career* md Waverley Vintners Ltd 1977-83; chm Christopher and Co Ltd 1975-83, chief exec Clan Campbell 1984-, dir Beinn Bhuidhe Holdings Ltd 1983-; HM Unicorn Pursuivant of Arms, memb Ct of the Lord Lyon 1987-; *Style*— Alastair Campbell of Airds

CAMPBELL OF AIRDS, Brig Lorne Maclaine; VC (1943), DSO (1940, and Bar 1943), OBE (1968), TD (1941); s of Col Ian Maxwell Campbell, CBE, TD (d 1954), and Hilda Mary Wade (d 1969); *b* 22 July 1902; *Educ* Dulwich, Merton Coll Oxford (MA); *m* 1935, Amy Muriel Jordan (d 1950), da of Alastair Magnus Campbell of Auchendarroch; 2 s (Alastair, *qv*, Patrick); *Career* 8 (Argyllshire) Bn Argyll and Sutherland Highlanders 1921-42, Hon Col 1954-67, cmd 7 Bn 1942-43, cmd 13 Inf Bde 1943-44, BGS Br Army Staff Washington 1944-45, WWII 1939-45 (despatches four times); wine shipper; Master Worshipful Co of Vintners 1958-59 (Liveryman); Lieutenancy City of London 1958-68; Offr US Legion of Merit (1945); *Clubs* New (Edinburgh); *Style*— Brig Lorne Campbell of Airds, VC, DSO, OBE, TD; 95 Trinity Rd, Edinburgh EH5 3JX (☎ 031 552 6851)

CAMPBELL OF AIRDS BAY, Maj Michael McNeil; yr twin s of Rear Adm Keith McNeil Campbell-Walter, CB (d 1976), and Frances Henriette, eldest da of Sir Edward Campbell of Airds Bay, 1 Bt, MP (d 1945); *b* 3 March 1941; *Educ* Wellington, RMA Sandhurst; *m* 1963, Anne Catriona, da of late Capt Ian Andrew Tait, Queen's Own Cameron Highlanders; 1 s, 2 da; *Career* 2 Lt Scots Gds 1961, Adjt 1 Bn 1967-69, Maj 1970, ret 1971; recognized by Lord Lyon 1954 as representor of family of Campbells of Airds Bay and matriculated as successor and representor to his uncle Sir Duncan Campbell of Airds Bay, 2 and last Bt (d 1954); memb Queen's Body Guard for Scotland (Royal Co of Archers); Hon ADC to Lt-Govr of Jersey 1973-80; sec-gen Confedn of Jersey Indust 1976-85; *Style*— Major Michael Campbell; Fonthill, Trinity Hill, St Helier, Jersey, CI (☎ 0534 70 681)

CAMPBELL OF ALLOWAY, Baron (Life Peer UK 1981), of Ayr, in the District of Kyle and Carrick; Alan Robertson Campbell; QC (1965); s of late John Kenneth Campbell; *b* 24 May 1917; *Educ* Aldenham, Trinity Hall Cambridge, Ecole des Sciences Politiques Paris; *m* 1957, Vivien, yr da of late Cdr A H de Kantzow, DSO, RN; *Career* sits as Cons in House of Lords; late Lt RA supp reserve, served in BEF France during WWII, POW; called to the Bar Inner Temple 1939, bencher 1972; Western Circuit; conslt to Sub-Ctee of Legal Ctee of Cncl of Europe on Industl Espionage 1965-74; chm: Legal Res Ctee, Soc Cons Lawyers 1968-80; memb: Law Advsy Ctee Br Cncl 1974-80, Mgmnt Ctee Assoc for European Law 1975-90; memb of Old Carlton Club Political Ctee 1967-79; memb House of Lords Select Ctee on: Murder and Life Imprisonment 1988-89, Privileges 1982-, Personal Bills 1987-; rec of Crown Court 1976-89; *Clubs* Carlton, Pratt's, Beefsteak; *Style*— The Rt Hon Lord Campbell of Alloway, QC; 2 King's Bench Walk, Temple, London EC4 7DE (☎ 071 353 9276)

CAMPBELL OF CROY, Baron (Life Peer UK 1974), of Croy, Co Nairn; Gordon Thomas Calthrop Campbell; MC (1944 and Bar 1945), PC (1970); s of Maj-Gen James Alexander Campbell, DSO (d 1964), and Violet Constance Madeline Calthrop (d 1978); *b* 8 June 1921; *Educ* Wellington; *m* 1949, Nicola Elizabeth Gina, da of Capt Geoffrey Spencer Madan, and Marjorie, er da of Sir Saxton Noble, 3 Bt; 2 s, 1 da; *Career* regular army 1939-46, Major 1942 (wounded and disabled); HM Dip Serv 1946-57; MP Moray and Nairn 1959-74, lord cmmr of the Treasury 1962-63, parly under-sec of state for Scotland 1963-64, oppn spokesman on Defence and Scottish Affairs 1966-70, sec of state for Scotland 1970-74; chm Alliance Bldg Soc (Scottish Bd), dir Alliance and Leicester Bldg Soc (formerly Alliance Bldg Soc) 1983-; ptnr Holme Rose Farms and Estate; conslt Chevron Cos; chm: Scottish Cncl of Independent Schs 1974-78, Stoic Insur Services 1979-, Advsy Ctee on Pollution of the Sea 1979-81 and 1987-89; tstee Thomson Fndn 1978-; chm Int Year of Disabled People in Scotland 1981; pres Anglo-Austrian Soc 1991-; first fell Nuffield Provincial Hosp Tst, Queen Elizabeth the Queen Mother fellowship 1981; DL Nairnshire 1985; Vice Lieut Nairnshire 1988; *Books* Disablement: Problems and Prospects in the United Kingdom; *Style*— The Rt Hon the Lord Campbell of Croy, PC, MC; Holme Rose, Cawdor, Nairn (☎ 066 78 223)

CAMPBELL OF DUNSTAFFNAGE, Michael John Alexander; 22 Hereditary Capt and Maor of Dunstaffnage; s of Michael Eadon Campbell of Dunstaffnage, and Kathleen Weddall, *née* Lundon; *b* 22 Nov 1953; *Educ* Stowe; *m* 1977 (m dis 1988), Anne Ingrid, da of Charles Arthur McIntyre; 1 s (Angus Arthur Eadon b 1983), 1 da (Claire Ingrid b 1981); m 2, 1989 Elizabeth, da of Capt David MacCall; *Career* yacht Capt 1973-77; chm Bencamp Ltd, dir Halfway House Enterprises Ltd, proprietor Dunstaffnage Seafoods; *Recreations* sailing, shooting; *Style*— The Captain of Dunstaffnage; Dunstaffnage, Connel, Argyll, Scotland

CAMPBELL OF ESKAN, Baron (Life Peer UK 1966), of Camis Eskan, Co Dunbarton; John (Jock) Middleton Campbell; s of Colin Algernon Campbell (d 1957), 4th of Colgrain, Dunbartonshire, and late of Underriver House, Sevenoaks, Kent, and Mary Charlotte Gladys, *née* Barrington; *b* 8 Aug 1912; *Educ* Eton, Exeter Coll Oxford (hon fell 1973); *m* 1, 8 Jan 1938 (m dis 1948), Barbara Noel, da of late Leslie Arden Roffey, of Hayesden House, nr Tonbridge, Kent; 2 s, 2 da; m 2, 7 May 1949, Phyllis Jacqueline Gilmour (d 1983), da of late Henry Boyd, CBE, of St Germain-en-Laye, France, and formerly w of James Edward John Taylor; *Career* former chm Booker McConnell Ltd and Statesman and Nation Publishing Co Ltd; former dir London Weekend TV Ltd; chm Commonwealth Sugar Exporters' Assoc 1950-84; dir Commonwealth Devpt Corp 1968-81, chm Milton Keynes Devpt Corp 1967-83, pres Town and Country Planning Assoc 1980-; first freeman of Milton Keynes 1982; D Open Univ 1973; kt 1957; *Style*— The Rt Hon Lord Campbell of Eskan; 15 Eaton Sq, London SW1 (☎ 071 235 5695); Lawers, Crocker End, Nettlebed, Oxon (☎ 0491 641202)

CAMPBELL OF STRACHUR, (Ian) Niall Macarthur; 24 Chief of the Macarthur Campbells of Strachur and Representor of Baronial House of Campbell of Strachur, who held their Barony of Strachur direct from the Crown, for galley service; s of Lt-Col Kenneth John Campbell of Strachur (d 1965); *b* 23 Nov 1916; *Educ* Beaumont Coll; *m* 1947, Diana Susan, da of of Ernest Albert Sursham, JP, Lord of the Manor of Markyate, Herts; 1 s, 1 da; *Career* 2 Lt Black Watch 1939-45, Maj 1945; GRA Property Trust 1951-64; hon sec Br Field Sports Soc (Berwickshire) 1980-; memb Scot Ctee 1984-; *Recreations* fishing, shooting, skiing; *Clubs* Puffin's (Edinburgh); *Style*— Niall Campbell of Strachur; Newtonlees, Kelso, Roxburghshire (☎ 057 37 229)

CAMPBELL OF STRACHUR yr, David Niall MacArthur; s of (Ian) Niall MacArthur Campbell of Strachur, and Diana, *née* Sursham; *b* 15 April 1948; *Educ* Eton, Exeter Coll Oxford; *m* 1974, Alexandra Wiggin, Marquesa de Muros, da of Sir Charles Wiggin, KCMG, Marques de Muros (d 1977); 1 s (Charles Alexander b 25 May 1977), 1 da (Iona Margot b 15 Jan 1979); *Career* int publishing dir of Hachette, Paris; *Clubs* White's; *Style*— David Campbell of Strachur yr; 8 Rue Garanciere, Paris 6e, France; Barbreck House, By Lochgilphead, Argyll PA31 8QW (☎ 08525 293)

CAMPBELL-ORDE, Eleanor, Lady; Eleanor Hyde; *née* Watts; da of late Col Humphrey Watts, OBE, TD, and G Mary Parkes; *b* 25 Aug 1908; *Educ* St Winifred's Eastbourne, Lady Margaret Hall Oxford; *m* 1938, Maj Sir Simon Campbell-Orde, 5 Bt, TD (d 1969); 2 s, 1 da; *Career* decorator with de Basil's Russian Ballet, Festival Ballet etc; painter; exhibited RA and RWS etc as 'E Watts'; memb Arts Educational Sch Tst (former memb Cncl of Mgmnt), dir Royal Caledonian Sch; Hon Citizen Tennessee US; *Recreations* gardening, travel; *Clubs* Caledonian; *Style*— Eleanor, Lady Campbell-Orde; Westgate House, Dedham, Colchester, Essex CO7 6HJ (☎ 0206 322496)

CAMPBELL-ORDE, Sir John Alexander; 6 Bt (GB 1790), of Morpeth, Northumberland; s of Maj Sir Simon Arthur Campbell-Orde, 5 Bt, TD (d 1969) and Eleanor, Lady Campbell-Orde, *qv*; *b* 11 May 1943; *Educ* Gordonstoun; *m* 1973, Lacy Rals, da of T Grady Gallant, of Nashville, Tennessee, USA; 1 s, 3 da; *Heir* s, John Simon Arthur Campbell-Orde, b 15 Aug 1981; *Career* art dealer; *Clubs* Caledonian, Lansdowne; *Style*— Sir John Campbell-Orde, Bt; Beeswing Farm, Box 380, Route 2, Kingston Road, Fairview, TN 37062, USA

CAMPBELL-PRESTON OF ARDCHATTAN, Lt-Col Robert Modan Thorne; OBE (1955), MC (1943), TD, JP (1950), DL (Argyll and Bute 1951); s of Col Robert William Piggott Clark-Campbell-Preston, JP, DL (d 1929), of Ardchattan and Valleyfield, Fife, and Mary Augusta, *née* Thorne, MBE (d 1964); *b* 7 Jan 1909; *Educ* Eton, Ch Ch Oxford; *m* 1950, Hon Angela, *née* Pearson (d 1981), 3 da of 2 Viscount Cowdray (d 1933) and wid of Lt-Col George Murray, OBE, RA; 1 da, 1 step s (*see* Duke of Atholl); *Career* Lt Scottish Horse, Lt-Col 1945; Hon Col Fife and Forfar Yeo/ Scottish Horse 1962-67; memb Royal Co of Archers (Queen's Body Guard for Scotland), vice Lord Lt Argyll and Bute 1976-90; Silver Star (USA) 1945; *Recreations* fishing, shooting, gardening; *Clubs* Puffins; *Style*— Lt-Col Robert Campbell-Preston of Ardchattan, OBE, MC, TD, JP; 31 Marlborough Hill, London NW8 (☎ 071 586 2291); Ardchattan Priory Connel, Argyll (☎ 063 175274)

CAMPBELL-PRESTON, Lt-Col Robert Modan Thorne; OBE (1955), MC (1943), TD and 2 Bars (1944), JP (1950), DL (1951); s of Lt-Col R W P Clarke Campbell-Preston, JP, DL (d 1929), of Ardchattan Priory, by Oban, Argyll, and Mary Augusta Margaret, *née* Nicol Thorne, MBE (d 1964); *b* 7 Jan 1909; *Educ* Eton, Christ Church Oxford (MA); *m* 6 June 1950, Hon Angela Murray, wid of Lt-Col G A Murray, OBE, TD (ka Italy 1945), and da of 2 Viscount Cowdray, DL (d 1933); 1 da (Sarah Hope (Mrs Troughton) b 7 March 1951); *Career* 2 Lt Scottish Horse 1927, Lt-Col 1945, Hon Col Fife Forfar Yeo/Scottish Horse 1962-67; md Alginate Indust Ltd 1949-74; former memb CBI Scotland; chm Argyll and Bute Tst, Vice Lord Lieut Argyll and Bute 1976, memb (retired list) Royal Co of Archers (The Queen's Body Guard for Scotland); American Silver Star 1945; *Recreations* shooting, fishing, gardening; *Clubs* Puffins; *Style*— Lt-Col Robert Campbell-Preston, OBE, MC, TD, JP, DL; Ardchattan Priory, by Oban, Argyll (☎ 063 175 274)

CAMPBELL REGAN, (Maurice David) Brian; s of Flt Lt Maurice O'Regan, RAFMS, and Margaret, *née* McElerney; *b* 7 Nov 1936; *Educ* Ampleforth, Sorbonne Paris; *m* 1 Aug 1970, Jasmine, da of Ivor Elystan Campbell-Davys, JP (d 1965), of Neuaddfawr, Llandovery, Dyfed, and Askomel, Campbelltown, Argyll; 1 s (Justin), 2 da (Ciaran, Alice); *Career* CA; ptnr Buzzacott & Co; FICA; *Recreations* fishing, shooting, reading, painting; *Clubs* Reform; *Style*— Brian Campbell Regan, Esq; Beauchamps, Wyddial, Buntingford, Herts SG9 OEP (☎ 0763 71382); Buzzacott & Co, 4 Wood St, London EC2V 4JJ (☎ 071 600 0336)

CAMPBELL-SAVOURS, Dale Norman; MP (Lab) Workington 1979-; s of John Lawrence, and Cynthia Lorraine Campbell-Savours; *b* 23 Aug 1943; *Educ* Keswick Sch, Sorbonne; *m* 1970, Gudrun Kristin Runolfsdottir; 3 s; *Career* former co dir; contested (Lab) Darwen Lancs 1974, Workington Cumbria 1976; *Style*— Dale Campbell-Savours Esq, MP; House of Commons, London SW1A 0AA

CAMPBELL-SHARP, Noelle; *b* 24 Dec 1943; *m* (m dis 1987), Neil Campbell-Sharp; 1 da (Tara b 1 May 1971); *Career* clerk typist, moved into PR, freelance fashion writer for Irish newspapers, bought half share in Irish Tatler 1977 (bought out ptnrs 1979), fndr Success magazine 1981, bought Social and Personal 1985; prodr on board magazines for: Ryan Air 1986, Swansea-Cork Ferries 1988, Irish Rail 1989, Irish Ferries 1989, Aer Rianta 1989; regular appearances on Irish TV and radio, estab ptnrship (with Robert Maxwell's magazine publishing arm, 1989) to work with local community group on pre-famine village Cill Rialáing (International Artists Retreat) 1990; *Recreations* collecting antique cars, collecting Napoleonic paraphenalia; *Style*— Miss Noelle Campbell-Sharp; Campanella, Marino Ave West, Killiney, Co Dublin

CAMPBELL-WALTER, Richard Keith; s of Rear Adm Keith McNiel Campbell-Walter, CB (d 1976), of 19a Princes Gate Mews, London SW7, and Frances Henriette, da of Sir Edward Taswell Campbell, 1 Bt, MP (d 1945); *b* 3 March 1941; *Educ* Milton Abbey, RAC Cirencester; *m* 1, 1963 (m dis), Marion Clare, o da of F G Minter, MBE; 2 da (Lavinia b 1964, Petrina b 1967); m 2, Dorothy Ann, yst da of late T W Oliver; 1 s (Jamie Oliver b 1972); *Career* 2 Lt Argyll and Sutherland Highlanders 1958-1964 TA; dir Simpson Piccadilly Ltd 1982 (retail dir 1990-); *Style*— Richard K Campbell-Walter, Esq; 9 Passmore Street, London SW21 (☎ 071 823 4299); Simpson Piccadilly Ltd, 203 Piccadilly, London W1 (☎ 071 734 2002)

CAMPDEN, Viscount; Anthony Baptist Noel; s and h of 5 Earl of Gainsborough; *b* 16 Jan 1950; *Educ* Ampleforth, RAC Cirencester; *m* 1972, Sarah Rose, er da of Col Thomas Foley Churchill Winnington, MBE; 1 s; *Heir* s, Hon Henry Robert Anthony Noel b 1 July 1977; *Style*— Viscount Campden; 105 Earls Court Rd, London W8 (☎ 071 370 5650); Exton Park, Oakham, Rutland, Leics. (☎ Oakham (0572) 812209)

CAMPION, Barry David Bardsley; s of Norman Campion (d 1987), of Southport, Lancs, and Enid Mary, *née* Bardsley; *b* 20 March 1938; *Educ* Shrewsbury; *m* 1, 1962 (m dis 1972), Victoria Wild; 1 s (Mark), 1 da (Sarah); m 2, 1979, Sally, da of Frank Walter Manning Arkle; *Career* dir: Wheatsheaf Distribution and Trading 1968-78, BAF Securities Ltd 1972- (chm), Linfood Holdings 1978-81; chm Food Div CWS Ltd 1982-87, chief exec Monarchy Foods Ltd 1987-90; chm: Meridian Foods 1990-, Freshfield Foods 1990-; dir: Bensons Crisps plc 1990-, North Wales Seafoods 1991-, Monach Seafoods 1991-; *Recreations* golf, cricket; *Clubs* MCC, Delamere Forest Golf, Royal Birkdale Golf; *Style*— Barry Campion, Esq; Monarchy Hall Farm, Utkinton, Tarporley, Cheshire CW6 0JZ (☎ 0829 51363); Meridian Foods Ltd, Corwen, Clwyd, North Wales LL21 9RT

CAMPION, David Gifford; CBE (1985), TD (1963); s of Charles Aldworth Gifford Campion (d 1963), of Brasted, Kent and Margery Frances Mary, *née* Farrington (d 1956); *b* 9 Nov 1924; *Educ* Stowe, Trinity Coll Cambridge (MA); *m* 26 April 1958, Elisabeth Mary, da of Cdr Aubery Richmond Bishop Phelp, OBE, RN, of Bath, Avon; 1 s (Charles Richmond Gifford b 29 June 1963), 1 da (Alexandra Mary b 15 April 1959); *Career* WWII Lt Rifle Bde 1943-47, Maj London Rifle Bde Rangers 1951-65;

called to the Bar Inner Temple 1950; Seccombe Marshal & Campion Ltd (billbroker) 1950-85: dir 1951-56, md 1956-77, chm 1977-85 (Bank of England broker 1975-85); *Recreations* fishing, travel, gardening; *Clubs* Army and Navy, Green Jacket; *Style*— David Campion, Esq, CBE, TD; Littleworth Cottage, Milton Lilbourne, Pewsey, Wilts SN9 5LF

CAMPION, Sir Harry; CB (1949), CBE (1945); s of John Henry Campion, of Worsley, Lancs; *b* 20 May 1905; *Educ* Farnworth GS Manchester; *Career* former dir Central Statistical Office Cabinet Office; pres Int Statistical Inst 1963-67; kt 1957; *Style*— Sir Harry Campion, CB, CBE; Rima, Priory Close, Stanmore, Middx (☎ 081 954 3267)

CAMPION-SMITH, (William) Nigel; s of H R A Campion-Smith, of Gerrards Cross, Bucks, and Moyra, *née* Campion; *b* 10 July 1954; *Educ* King George V Sch Southport, Royal GS High Wycombe, St John's Coll Cambridge (MA); *m* 31 July 1976, Andrea Jean, da of Edward Willacy, of Hale Barns, Cheshire; 2 s (Jonathan b 1985, Timothy b 1990), 1 da (Joanna b 1983); *Career* admitted slr 1978; ptnr Travers Smith Braithwaite 1982-; memb Law Soc 1978; *Style*— Nigel Campion-Smith, Esq; Travers Smith Braithwaite, 10 Snow Hill, London EC1A 2AL (☎ 071 248 9133, fax 071 236 3728, telex 887117)

CAMPLING, The Very Reverend Christopher Russell; s of Rev Canon William Charles Campling (d 1972), and Phyllis Russell, *née* Webb; *b* 4 July 1925; *Educ* Lancing, St Edmund Hall Oxford (MA); *m* 1953, Juliet Marian, *née* Hughes; 1 s, 2 da; *Career* temp Sub Lt (special cypher) RNVR 1943-47; curate Basingstoke 1951-55; chaplain: King's Sch Ely and minor canon Ely 1955-60, Lancing Coll 1960-67; vicar Pershore 1968-76, rural dean Pershore 1970-76, hon canon Worcs Cathedral 1974-84, archdeacon Dudley 1976-84, priest i/c St Augustine's Church Dodderhill and dir religious educn Worcs Dio 1976-84, dean Ripon 1984-; memb Gen Synod 1970-, chm Cncl for Care of Churches 1988; *Books* The Way, the Truth and the Life (6 volumes: a series for schools), Words for Worship, The Fourth Lesson (ed); *Recreations* music, golf, theatre; *Clubs* Naval; *Style*— The Very Rev the Dean of Ripon; The Minster House, Ripon, North Yorkshire HG4 1PE (☎ 0765 3615)

CAMPLING, Dr Graham Ewart George; s of Reginald Ewart Campling, of Lindfield, Sussex, and Elsie Clara, *née* Wodhams; *b* 27 Aug 1938; *Educ* Birkbeck and Imperial Colls Univ of London (BSc, PhD); *m* 1 April 1961, Zena Margaret, da of George William Birkbeck (d 1969); 2 s (Noel b 1963, Jeremy b 1969); *Career* Lt TA 1959-62; Bank of England 1956-63, Selfridges Ltd 1963-65; lectr and sr lectr in computing Brighton Poly 1965-69, head of Dept of Mgmnt S Bank Poly 1969-72, vice princ Kilburn Poly 1973-77, princ Dacorum Coll Hemel Hempstead 1978-89; gp trg mangr BAA plc 1989-; memb: Cuckfield UDC 1968-74 (chm Ctee 1969-73, vice chm Cncl 1971-72), Mid Sussex DC 1974-76; chm of govrs: Lindfield Primary Sch's 1971-79, Oathall Comp Sch 1972-81; pres Assoc of Princ's of Colls 1989 (hon sec 1985-88, vice pres 1988-89), chm Educn Ctee Inst of Admin Mgmnt 1973-81 (Inst medal 1982); Freeman City of London; MBCS 1970, FBIM 1980, CEng 1990; *Books* Can You Manage Statistics? (1968); *Recreations* transport organisation, music, film-making; *Style*— Dr Graham Campling; 46 Hickmans Lane, Lindfield, Haywards Heath, Sussex RH16 2BY (☎ 0444 483539); BAA plc Management Centre, Pease Pottage, Crawley, Sussex RH11 9AD (☎ 0293 523271)

CAMROSE, Viscountess; Joan Barbara; *née* Yarde-Buller; e da of 3 Baron Churston, MVO, OBE (d 1930); *b* 22 April 1908; *m* 1, 1927 (m dis 1936), Gp Capt Loel Guinness, OBE (d 1988); 1 s; m 2, 1936 (m dis 1949), Prince Aly Khan (d 1960), s of HH Aga Khan, GCSI, GCIE, GCVO, PC; 2 s (HH Aga Khan, Prince Amyn Aga Khan); m 3, 1986, 2 Viscount Camrose, *qv*; *Style*— The Rt Hon the Viscountess Camrose; Hackwood Park, Basingstoke, Hants (☎ 0256 464630)

CAMROSE, 2 Viscount (UK 1941); Sir (John) Seymour Berry; TD; 2 Bt (UK 1921), also Baron Camrose (UK 1929); eldest s of 1 Viscount Camrose (d 1954), and Mary Agnes (d 1962), eldest da of Thomas Corns, of Bolton Street, London; *b* 12 July 1909; *Educ* Eton, Ch Ch Oxford; *m* 1986, Hon Joan Yarde-Buller, eldest da of 3 Baron Churston, MVO, OBE (d 1930), formerly w of (i) Gp Capt Loel Guinness (d 1988), and (ii) Prince Aly Khan (d 1960); *Heir* bro, Baron Hartwell, *qv*; *Career* served WW II as Maj City of London Yeo (despatches), N Africa and Italian Campaigns 1942-45; MP (C) Hitchin 1941-45; dep chm The Daily Telegraph Ltd 1939-87, vice-chm Amalgamated Press Ltd 1942-59, dir Daily Telegraph plc; a Younger Brother of Trinity House; memb Cncl Maritime Trust; *Clubs* White's, Buck's, Beefsteak, Pratt's, MCC, Royal Yacht Sqdn (tstee); *Style*— The Rt Hon the Viscount Camrose, TD; Hackwood Park, Basingstoke, Hants RG25 2JY (☎ 0256 464630); 8a Hobart Place, London SW1W 0HH (☎ 071 235 9900)

CAMROUX-OLIVER, Timothy Patrick; s of Wing Cdr George Leonard, DFC, AFC (d 1984), and Patricia Rosamund, *née* Douglas; *b* 2 March 1944; *Educ* Christs Hosp; *m* 18 July 1966, Susan Elizabeth, da of Maj Frederick Wilson Hanham, of The Cottage, Chipps Manor Lane End, Bucks; 2 s (James Richard b Sept 1967, Charles Guy b 1 April 1970), 1 da (Alexa Kate Louise b 25 Dec 1974); *Career* asst gen mangr IGI (SA) 1969-71; dir: Manson Byng Group 1971-, Hampden Russell plc 1987-; chm: Hampden Insurance Holdings Ltd 1973-, Market Run-Off Services Ltd 1984-; memb Lloyds 1977; Freeman City of London 1966, memb Worshipful Co of Ironmongers 1966; FRGS 1963; *Style*— Timothy Camroux-Oliver, Esq; Hampden House, Great Hampden, Bucks HP16 9RD (☎ 0494 488888); Gallery Ten, Lloyd's of London, 1 Lime St, London EC3M 7DQ (☎ 071 626 3036, fax 071 929 0044, telex 83688 Market G, car 0860 515 552)

CANAVAN, Dennis Andrew; MP (Lab) Falkirk West 1983-; s of Thomas Canavan (d 1974), of Cowdenbeath, and Agnes Canavan; *b* 8 Aug 1942; *Educ* St Columba's HS Cowdenbeath, Edinburgh Univ (BSc, DipEd); *m* 1964, Elnor, da of late Charles Stewart, of Montrose; 3 s, 1 da; *Career* former head of maths dept, former assistant head Holyrood HS Edinburgh; MP (Lab) West Stirlingshire 1974-83, chm Scottish Parly Lab Gp 1980-81 (Educn convener 1976-80, Convener of Devolution Ctee 1985-87); memb House of Commons Select Ctee on Foreign Affairs, Scottish chm of Liberation; hon pres Milton Amateurs Football Club; *Recreations* walking, marathon running, swimming, football; *Clubs* Camelon Labour, Bannockburn Miners' Welfare; *Style*— Dennis Canavan, Esq, MP; 15 Margaret Road, Bannockburn, Stirlingshire (☎ 0786 812581); House of Commons, London SW1A 0AA (☎ 071 219 3000)

CANBY, Guy Richard; JP (Rotherham 1990); s of Arthur John Canby (d 1985), of Cottingham, Humberside, and Ivy Gladys, *née* Hutton; *b* 13 April 1950; *Educ* Hymers Coll Hull, RAC; *m* 19 July 1975, Diana Mary, da of Capt John Buckingham Segrott, of E Lothian; 2 s (Michael John b 1978, James Guy b 1981), 1 da (Charlotte Mary b 1984); *Career* asst factor Lothian Estates 1973-83; resident land agent: Thonock and Somerby Estates 1983-86, Fitzwilliam (Wentworth) Estates 1986-; FRICS, MRAC; *Recreations* shooting, fishing, squash, tennis, golf; *Style*— Guy Canby, Esq, JP; Cortworth House, Wentworth, Rotherham, S Yorks (☎ 0226 742288); Estate Office, Clayfields Lane, Wentworth, Rotherham, S Yorks (☎ 0226 742041)

CANBY, Michael William; s of Clarence Canby, and Mary Frances, *née* Drake; *b* 11 Jan 1955; *Educ* Buckhurst Hill County HS, Univ of Cambridge (MA, LLB); *m* 6 Sept 1980, Sarah, da of John Houghton Masters (d 1965); 1 s (Philip Charles Houghton b 1988); *Career* admitted slr 1980, ptnr Linklaters & Ptnrs 1986-; memb Law Soc; *Style*— Michael Canby, Esq; Barrington House, 59/67 Gresham St, London EC2V 7JA

CANDLER, Janet Elizabeth; da of Col Kenneth David Treasure, CB, CBE, TD, DL (d 1983), and Jean, *née* Mitchell, of Gwent; *b* 3 Aug 1942; *Educ* Norfolk House Sch Cardiff, Alice Ottley Sch Worcester; *m* 1, 5 Nov 1966 (m dis 1977); 1 da (Kate b 1972); m 2, 30 Jan 1988, Nicolas John Pycock Candler; *Career* slr and ptnr Treasures Blackwood; clerk to Gen Cmmrs of Income Tax 1983-; *Recreations* theatre, sea watching, domesticity; *Style*— Mrs N J P Candler; 1 Chesterholme, Stow, Park Ave, Newport, Gwent (☎ 0633 213915); 114A High Street, Blackwood, Gwent (☎ 0495 223328)

CANDY, Prof David Charles Alexander; s of Arthur Edward Candy, of 24 Brunswick Rd, Hove, and Gwen May, *née* Chatfield; *b* 5 Dec 1947; *Educ* Pulteney GS Adelaide S Aust, Univ of Adelaide (MB BS), Univ of London (MSc), Univ of Birmingham (MD); *m* 16 Aug 1979, Christine Elizabeth, da of Charles Walter Stannett, of 25 Culver Parade, Sandown, IOW; 1 s (Rupert b 5 Oct 1980), 1 da (Felicity b 22 June 1987); *Career* Wellcome sr lectr Dept of Child Health Univ of Birmingham 1984-88; hon conslt paediatrician 1984-88: The Children's Hosp Birmingham, Dept of Communicable and Tropical Diseases E Birmingham Hosp, prof and dir Dept of Child Health Kings Coll Sch of Med and Dentistry; treas Immunology and Infectious Disease Gp Br Paediatric Assoc; FRCP 1989; *Books* Manual of Paediatric Gastroenterology (with J H Tripp, 1985); *Recreations* my family, dining out; *Style*— Prof David C A Candy; 516 Ben Jonson House, Barbican, London EC2Y 8DL; Dept of Child Health, King's College School of Medicine and Dentistry, Bessemer Rd, London SE5 8RX (☎ 071 326 3215)

CANDY, Thomas Frank; s of Frank Patrick Candy, and Jacqueline Honoreen, *née* Vroome; *b* 18 Dec 1955; *Educ* Eastbourne Coll, Univ of Surrey; *m* Emma, *née* Bishop; 1 s (Peter b 12 April 1990); *Career* banker; dir Eurobond Dept Hambros Bank Ltd; *Recreations* tennis, squash, windsurfing, skiing; *Clubs* Queen's; *Style*— Thomas Candy, Esq; Fairlawn, Parkfield, Sevenoaks, Kent; Hambros Bank Ltd, 41 Tower Hill, London (☎ 071 480 5000)

CANE, Alison; da of Ronald Cane, of Longfellow Drive, Hutton Mount, Essex, and Jeanne, *née* Snow; *b* 18 Aug 1960; *Educ* Ongar Comprehensive Sch Essex, Loughton Coll of Further Educn Essex, St Martins Sch of Art; *Career* freelance designer 1982, Michael Peters plc 1982-86 (jr designer, sr designer), asst creative dir Coley Porter Bell (joined as sr designer); clients incl: Prestige, Boots, Corgi Toys, Marks and Spencers, Jacksons, Masterchoice; several D&AD nominations, several Clio nominations, winner Foods Design Effectiveness Award CLIO, highly commended Int Design Annual Award 1990; *Recreations* all general sports, trying golf!!!; *Clubs* Flames Health, Streatham Squash; Coley Porter Bell, 4 Flitcroft Street, London WC2H 8DJ (☎ 071 379 4355, fax 071 379 5164)

CAÑEDO, Lady Rosemary Millicent; *née* Ward; da (twin, by 1 m), 4 Earl of Dudley, and Stella Carcano; *b* 26 May 1955; *m* 1980, Castor Cañedo, s of Castor Cañedo Pidal (d 1974); 1 da (Gabriela b 1982); *Style*— The Lady Rosemary Cañedo

CANHAM, (Bryan Frederick) Peter; MC (1943); s of Frederick William Canham (d 1961), and Emma Louisa, *née* Martin (d 1971); *b* 11 April 1920; *Educ* Trinity Co Sch; *m* 1944, Rita Gwendoline, *née* Huggett, 1 s (Richard); *Career* Capt 1 RTR, N Africa, Italy, NW Europe 1939-46; controller S Europe and N Africa Shell International Petroleum 1956-; fin dir: Shell Co Philippines and assoc cos 1960-63, Shell Co Malaysia and assoc cos 1963-68; div head Loans Directorate Dir Gen XVIII EEC 1973-76 (dir investmt a loans 1976-80); chm Eurofi (UK) Ltd 1980-; FCIS, ACIS; *Style*— Peter Canham, Esq, MC; The Old Laundry, Penshurst, Kent (☎ 0892 870 239); The Cottage, Stedhamhall, nr Midhurst, W Sussex (☎ 073081 2947); Eurofi plc, Guildgate House, Newbury Berks (☎ 0635 31900)

CANN, (John William) Anthony; s of Dr John Cann, of 1 Meadowhead Rd, Southampton, and Enid Grace, *née* Long; *b* 21 July 1947; *Educ* Old Malthouse Sch Swanage, Shrewsbury, Southampton Univ (LLB); *m* 6 Jan 1973, Anne, da of Harold Thorswald Clausen, of Johannesburg; 2 s (John Harold b 25 Nov 1973, Robert Charles b 13 Aug 1984), 1 da (Sally Elizabeth b 10 Jan 1978); *Career* admitted slr 1972; Linklaters & Paines 1970-: asst slr 1972-78, New York office 1975-82, ptnr 1978-; memb Advsy Ctee CAB (Battersea) 1973-75; Freeman City of London Slrs Co 1978; memb Law Soc; *Books* Mergers & Acquisitions Handbook (Part D), Mergers and Acquisitions in Europe (United Kingdom); *Recreations* photography, sports; *Clubs* MCC, Wimbledon, Wimbledon Squash and Badminton; *Style*— Anthony Cann, Esq; Langrick, 13 Murray Rd, Wimbledon, London SW19 4PD (☎ 081 946 6731); Linklaters & Paines, Barrington Ho, 59-67 Gresham St, London EC2V 7JA (☎ 071 606 7080, fax 071 606 5113, telex 884349

CANN, Prof Johnson Robin (Joe); s of late Johnson Ralph Cann, and Ethel Mary, *née* Northmore; *b* 18 Oct 1937; *Educ* St Alban's Sch, St John's Coll Cambridge (BA, MA, PhD, ScD); *m* 10 Aug 1963, Janet Mary Teresa, da of Prof Charles John Hamson (d 1987), of Trinity Coll Cambridge; 2 s (John b 1964, David b 1966); *Career* res fell St Johns Coll Cambridge 1962-65, post doctoral res Cambridge 1962-66, Br Museum (Natural History) 1966-68, lectr then reader Sch of Enviromental Sciences UEA 1968-77, J B Simpson prof of geology Univ of Newcastle upon Tyne 1977-89, adjunct scientist Woods Hole Oceanographic Instn 1987-, prof of earth sciences Univ of Leeds 1989-; chm UK Ocean Drilling Program Grants Ctee 1987-; memb, Bridge Coordinating Ctee 1988-; FGS; *Style*— Prof Joe Cann; 12 Oakfield Terrace, Leeds LS6 4EQ, Department of Earth Sciences, University of Leeds, Leeds LS6 9JT (☎ 0532 335200)

CANNAN, Rt Rev Edward Alexander Capparis; s of Alexander Capparis, and Mabel, *née* Harris (d 1973); *b* 25 Dec 1920; *Educ* St Marylebone GS, King's Coll London (BD, AKC); *m* 31 May 1941, Eunice Mary, da of Arthur Blandford, (d 1964); 3 s (Jeremy b 1943, Stephen b 1949, Nigel b 1951); *Career* RAF 1937-46 (despatches 1941), cmmnd Tech Branch 1942, RAF Chaplains' Branch 1953-74, RAF Cosford 1953-54, RAF Padgate 1954-57, HQ 2 Gp Germany 1957-58, lectr RAF Chaplains' Sch 1958-60, RAF Gan Maldive Is 1960-61, RAF Halton 1961-62, RAF Hereford 1962-64, RAF Khormaksar Aden 1964-66, vice princ RAF Chaplains' Sch 1966-69, asst chaplain-in-chief 1969-74, FEAF Singapore 1969-72, HQ Trg Cmd 1972-73, princ RAF Chaplains' Sch 1973-74, hon chaplain to HM The Queen 1972-74; ordained: deacon 1950, priest 1951; curate Blandford Forum Dorset 1950-53, chaplain St Margaret's Sch Bushey 1974-79, bishop of St Helena (S Atlantic) 1979-85, asst bishop Diocese of Hereford 1986-; *Books* A History of the Diocese of St Helena 1502-1984 (1985); *Recreations* house maintenance, gardening; *Clubs* RAF; *Style*— The Rt Rev Edward Cannan; Church Cottage, Allensmore, Hereford HR2 9AQ (☎ 0432 277357)

CANNELL, Dr Lewis Bernard; *b* 10 June 1926; *Educ* Droitwich, Northampton GS, Lincoln Coll Oxford, St Marys Hosp, St Georges's Hosp, Bart's; *Career* doctor of med and conslt radiologist Stoke Mandeville Hosp; Freeman Worshipful Soc of Apothecaries; memb: BMA, Br Royal Coll of Radiology, Br Inst of Radiology, BMUS; *Clubs* Vincent's; *Style*— Dr Lewis Cannell; Rye Cottage, Butler's Cross, Aylesbury, Bucks HP17 0XA; Dept of Radiology, Stoke Mandeville Hosp, Aylesbury, Bucks

CANNING, Prof Elizabeth Ursula; da of Maj Miles Howell Canning MC, TD (d 1950), and Winifred, *née* Jenkins (d 1980); *b* 29 Sept 1928; *Educ* Truro HS, Imperial Coll London (BSc, DSc), London Sch of Hygiene and Tropical Med (PhD); *m* 15 Aug 1953, Christopher Maynard Wilson, s of George Henry Cyril Wilson (d 1973); 1 s

(Miles Richard Guy b 29 April 1966), 2 da (Victoria Jane (Mrs M J Harvey) b 16 March 1958, Catherine Alexandra (Mrs J P Williams) b 3 March 1960); *Career* Imperial Coll London: lectr 1951-70, sr lectr 1970-71, reader 1971-81, prof of protozoology 1981-; former pres, vice pres and sec Br Section Soc of Protozoologists, vice pres Int Soc of Protozoologist, memb Royal Soc of Tropical Med and Hygiene; ARCS, FIBiol; *Books* The Microsporidia of Vertebrates (1986); *Recreations* sport, crossword puzzles, bridge; *Style—* Prof Elizabeth Canning; Tiles Cottage, Forest Rd, Winkfield Row, nr Bracknell, Berks RG12 6NR; Imperial College at Silwood Park, Garden Wood Laboratories (West), Ascot Berks SL5 7PY (☎ 0344 23911, fax 0344 294339)

CANNING, Hon Spencer George Stratford de Redcliffe; s and h of 5 Baron Garvagh; *b* 12 Feb 1953; *m* 1979, Julia Margery Morison, da of Col F C E Bye, of Twickenham, Middx; 1 s (Stratford George Edward de Redcliffe b 7 Feb 1990), 2 da (Cordelia Louise Morison b 1985, Florence b 1988); *Style—* The Hon Spencer Canning; 24 Cobbold Rd, London W12 (☎ 081 749 4360)

CANNINGS-BUSHELL, David John; s of Thomas Meredith Cannings-Bushell, of Cirencester, Glos, and Julia Dorothy, *née* Dawe; *b* 8 April 1949; *Educ* Cirencester GS; *m* 31 July 1971 (sep 1981, m dis 1990), Jennifer Ann, da of Meurig Jone of Meifod, Powys; 2 da (Catherine Sarah b 5 Feb 1974, Louisa Frances 24 Nov 1976); m 2, 29 Dec 1990, Monica Anne Goddard, *née* Trinder; *Career* lighting dir TV drama Pebble Mill BBC 1983 (engr 1968, lectr 1978); maj prodns: Deadhead 1985, Lizzies Pictures 1986, Vanity Fair 1987, Franchise Affair 1988, Shalom, Salaam 1989, Debut on Two, Bingo 1990; BAFTA nomination Video Lighting 1987; tenor singer Pershore Choral Soc, memb Soc of TV Lighting Dirs 1981; *Recreations* choral singing, photography, painting, walking; *Style—* David Cannings-Bushell, Esq; Tanglewood, Bridge St, Lower Moor, Pershore, Worcs (☎ 0386 860 922); BBC, Pebble Mill, Birmingham (☎ 021 414 8418)

CANNON, George Anthony; s of Lt-Col Douglas Rabbetts Cannon, of Poole, Dorset (d 1973), and Olivia Lumley, *née* Robinson (d 1963); *b* 9 Feb 1925; *Educ* Westminster, ChCh Oxford (MA); *m* 9 Sept 1950, Jacqueline Hélène Edmée Charlotte, da of Dr Werner Hoedemakers, of Brussels (d 1975); 1 s (Robin b 1953), 3 da (Joy b 1955, Carolyn b 1960, Alison b 1962); *Career* dir: Portsmouth and Sunderland plc, Hemsworth Photo Processing Ltd, Resources Int plc, Esk Food Hldgs Ltd; *Style—* George Cannon, Esq; Princhetts, Chelsworth, Ipswich IP7 7HU; 1 Smyrna Mansions, Smyrna Rd, London NW6 4LU (☎ 071 328 3552)

CANNON, Prof John Ashton; CBE (1985); s of George Ashton Cannon, and Gladys Violet Cannon; *b* 8 Oct 1926; *Educ* Hertford GS, Peterhouse Cambridge (BA, MA), Univ of Bristol (PhD); *m* 1, 1948 (m dis 1953), Audrey Elizabeth, da of G R Caple, of Bristol; 1 s (Marcus b 1948), 1 da (Hilary b 1952); m 2, 1953, Minna Sofie, da of Frederick Pedersen, of Denmark; 1 s (Martin b 1966), 2 da (Susan b 1955, Annelise b 1962); *Career* RAF Flt Lt 1947-49 and 1952-55; reader Univ of Bristol 1970-75 (lectr 1961-67, sr lectr 1967-69), pro vice chllr Univ of Newcastle upon Tyne 1983-86 (prof modern history 1976-, dean Faculty of Arts 1979-82), chm Radio Bristol 1970-74; memb Univ Grants Ctee 1983-89 (vice chm 1986-89, chm Arts Sub Ctee 1983-89); FRHistS, FRSA; *Books* The Fox-North Coalition (1970), Parliamentary Reform (1973), The Letters of Junius (ed 1978), The Historian at Work (1980), The Whig Ascendancy (1981), Aristocratic Century (1984), Dictionary of Historians (ed 1988), Oxford Illustrated History of The Monarchy (with R Griffiths, 1988); *Recreations* music, sailing, tennis; *Style—* Prof John Cannon, CBE; 17 Haldane Terrace, Jesmond, Newcastle upon Tyne (☎ 091 281 5186); Alma House, Grosmont, Gwent; Dept of History, University of Newcastle upon Tyne (☎ 091 232 8511, ext 6694)

CANNON, Nicholas Charles; s of Dr Ronald Cannon, of W Sussex, and Anita, *née* Foux; *b* 21 April 1951; *Educ* Northease Manor Lewes Sussex, Davies's Tutors Hove Sussex, King's Coll London (LLB), Inns of Court Sch of Law; *Career* called to the Bar Gray's Inn 1973, lectr Inns of Court Sch of Law 1974-77, barr in the Chamber of R A K Wright QC 1977-78, legal advsr Br Bankers Assoc 1978-80; author of various articles on int fin law; memb Legal Ctee EEC Banking Cmmn, legal advsr Scandinavian Bank Group plc 1980-89 (gp legal advsr and exec dir 1987), conslt Canadian Inst 1990-; memb: Inst of Strategic Studies London, Bar Assoc of Commerce and Indust; *Recreations* opera, art history, international politics and relations, tennis, travel; *Clubs* St James's; *Style—* Nicholas C Cannon, Esq; 13 Wilton Mews, London SW1X 7AT; Scandinavian Bank Group plc, Scandinavian House, 2/6 Cannon St, London EC4M 6XX (☎ 071 236 6090, fax 071 248 6612, telex 889093)

CANNON, (Jack) Philip; s of William George Cannon (d 1973), of Hope Cottage, Rose, Perranporth, Cornwall, and Charlotte Loraine, *née* Renoir (d 1984); *b* 21 Dec 1929; *Educ* Falmouth GS, Dartington Hall, RCM; *m* 15 July 1950, Jacqueline Playfair Laidlaw (d 1984), da of Hugh Alexander Lyon Laidlaw; 1 da (Virginia Shona Playfair b 29 June 1953); *Career* dep prof RCM 1953-59, lectr in music Univ of Sydney 1959-60, prof of composition RCM 1960-, author of many articles for music jls; compositions incl: Morvoven (opera) 1964, String Quartet winner of Grand Prix de la Critique Paris 1965, Oraison Funèbre de L'Ame Humaine (symphony cmmnd by ORTF) 1971, Son of Man (symphony cmmnd by BBC) 1973, Te Deum (cmmnd by HM Queen for St Georges Day) 1975, Logos (clarinet quintet cmmnd by BBC for Silver Jubilee) 1977, Lord of Light (requiem) 1980, Dr Jekyll and Mr Hyde (cmmnd by BBC); memb Royal Philharmonic Soc, FRCM 1971; memb: ISM, Composers' Guild of GB; *Recreations* exploring comparative philosophies, travel, swimming; *Clubs* Savile, Chelsea Arts; *Style—* Philip Cannon, Esq; Royal College of Music, Prince Consort Rd, S Kensington, London SW7 (☎ 071 589 3643)

CANNON, Simon Adrian; s of Henry Leigh Cannon (d 1987), of Bristol, and Frances Mary; *b* 5 June 1952; *Educ* Clifton, Nottingham Univ (LLB, MIL); *m* Aug 1978, Gunda, da of Paul Kern, of Remscheid, W Germany; *Career* dir John Martin Publishing Ltd 1978-, dir and co sec Planning Research and System plc 1983-; *Recreations* languages (translations), script writing, music; *Style—* Simon A Cannon, Esq; PRS plc, 44-48 Dover Street, London W1 (☎ 071 409 1635, fax (071 629 0221)

CANNON, Prof Thomas; s of Albert Edward Cannon (d 1986), and Bridget, *née* Ryan, of Liverpool; *b* 20 Nov 1945; *Educ* St Francis Xavier's GS, South Bank Poly; *m* Frances, da of Bernard Constable; 2s (Robin, Rowland); *Career* res assoc Univ of Warwick 1968-71, lectr Enfield Coll of Tech 1971-72, brand mangr Imperial Group 1973-76, lectr Univ of Durham 1973-81, prof Univ of Stirling 1981-89, dir Manchester Business Sch 1989-; memb: Indust Employment & Environment Ctee (ESRC) jt Ctee ESRC/SERC, C of C & Indust (Manchester), exec Br Acad of Mgmnt; chm Jt Working Pty Scottish Examinations Bd; pres North Cheshire Branch BIM; fell: Inst of Physical Distribution Mgmnt, Inst of Export; FRSA; *Books* Advertising Research (1972), Distribution Research (1973), Advertising: The Economic Implications (1975), How to Win Profitable Business (1984), How to Win Business Overseas (1985), Small Business Development (1987); *Recreations* supporting Everton, computing; *Style—* Prof Thomas Cannon; Manchester Business School, Booth Street West, Manchester M15 6PB (☎ 061 275 6412, fax 061 273 7732, telex 668354)

CANNON-BROOKES, Dr Peter; s of Victor Montgomery Cannon-Brookes, and Nancy Margaret, *née* Markham Carter; *b* 23 Aug 1938; *Educ* Bryanston, Trinity Hall Cambridge (MA), Courtauld Inst of Art Univ of London (PhD); *m* 13 April 1966, Caroline Aylmer, da of Lt Col John Aylmer Christie-Miller, CBE, TD, DL, of Manor House, Bourton-on-the-Hill, Gloucs; 1 s (Stephen William Aylmer b 1966), 1 da (Emma Wilbraham Montgomery b 1968); *Career* keeper Dept of Art: City Museum and Art Gallery Birmingham 1965-78, Nat Museum of Wales 1978-86; Int Cncl of Museums: memb Exec Bd UK Ctee 1973-81, pres Int Art Exhibitions Ctee 1977-79 (Exec Bd 1975-81), vice pres Conservation Ctee 1978-81 (Exec Bd 1975-81); Welsh Arts Cncl 1978-87: Art Ctee 1978-84, Craft Ctee 1983-87; Projects and Orgns Ctee Crafts Cncl 1985-87, pres Welsh Fedn of Museums 1980-82, pres S Wales Art Soc 1980-87, ed International Journal of Museum Management and Curatorship 1981-, dir museum servs Stipple Database Services Ltd 1986-89, conslt curator The Tabley House Collection 1988-; Town Twinning Ctee Birmingham Int Cncl 1968-78, Birmingham Dio Synod 1970-78, Birmingham Dio ADU Ctee for Care of Churches 1972-78, Edgbaston Deanery Synod 1970-78 (lay jt chm 1975-78); JP: Birmingham 1973-78, Cardiff 1978-82; Liveryman Worshipful Co of Goldsmiths 1974 (Freeman 1969); FMA, FIIC, FRSA; *Books* European Sculpture (with H D Molesworth, 1964), Baroque Churches (with C A Cannon-Brookes, 1969), Lombard Painting (1974), After Gulbenkian (1976), The Cornbury Park Bellini (1977), Michael Ayrton (1978), Emile Antoine Bourdelle (1983), Ivor Roberts-Jones (1983), Czech Sculpture 1800-1938 (1983), Paintings from Tabley (1989); *Recreations* cooking, growing vegetables, photography; *Clubs* Athenaeum, Birmingham (Birmingham); *Style—* Dr Peter Cannon-Brookes; Thrupp House, Abingdon, Oxon OX14 3NE (☎ 0235 5205 95)

CANOSA MONTORO, Francisco Octavio (Frank); s of Dr Francisco Canosa Lorenzo, and Elisa, *née* Montoro de la Torre; *b* 28 May 1951; *Educ* Columbia Univ NY (BA), Fordham Univ NY (JD); *m* 1, Dec 1972 (m dis 1975), Gloria de Aragón; m 2, 15 Sept 1979, Belinda Mary, da of Lt-Col Charles Reginald Clayton Albrecht, OBE, TA, of Pulborough, Sussex; 2 da (Alexandra Elisa b 12 Jan 1983, Isabel Christina b 20 June 1985); *Career* asst to pres Bank of America NY 1975, asst vice pres Manufacturers Hanover Trust Co NY 1978; Bank of America International Ltd London: vice pres 1980, exec dir 1985, head corporate fin UK and Europe 1987-89; *Clubs* RAC; *Style—* Frank Canosa Montoro, Esq; 38 St Mary's Grove, London W4 (☎ 081 994 6827); Bankers Trust Company, 1 Appold Street, London EC2A 2HE (☎ 071 982 3750 fax 071 982 3380 telex 883341)

CANSDALE, George Soper; yst s of George William Cansdale (d 1973), of Paignton, Devon, and Alice Louisa Cansdale (d 1948); *b* 29 Nov 1909; *Educ* Brentwood Sch, Univ of Oxford (BA, BSc); *m* 1940, Margaret Sheila, o da of Robert Marshall Williamson, Indian Forest Serv; 2 s (David, Richard); *Career* Colonial Forest Serv Ghana 1934-48, supt Zoological Soc of London 1948-53, TV presenter 1948-89; TV Soc Silver Medal 1952; *Books* Animals of West Africa (1946), West African Snakes (1960), Animals of Bible Lands (1970); *Recreations* gardening, birdwatching, fishing; *Clubs* Royal Cwlth Soc; *Style—* George Cansdale, Esq; Dove Cottage, Great Chesterford, Essex CB10 1PL (☎ 0799 30274)

CANTACUZINO, Sherban; CBE (1988); s of Prince Georges Matei Cantacuzino (d 1960), and Princess Alexandra, *née* Princess Stirbey; *b* 6 Sept 1928; *Educ* Winchester, Magdalene Coll Cambridge (MA); *m* 29 Jan 1954, Anne Mary, da of Maj Cecil Edward Trafford, MC (d 1948); 1 s (Sherban d 1978), 2 da (Ilinca, Marina); *Career* ptnr Steane Shipman & Cantacuzino Chartered Architects 1956-65, in private practice as Sherban Cantacuzino Assocs 1965-73, exec ed Architectural Review 1973-79 (asst ed 1967-73), sr lectr Dept of Architecture Coll of Art Canterbury 1967-70; sec Royal Fine Art Cmmn 1979-; tstee: Thomas Cubitt Tst 1978-, Design Museum (Conran Fndn) 1981-; memb: Arts Panel Arts Cncl 1977-80, Steering Ctee Aga Khan Award for Architecture 1980-83 (memb of Maste 1980), Cncl RSA 1980-85, Design Ctee London Tport 1981-82, Advsy Panel Railway Heritage Tst 1986-; memb Exec Ctee and chm UK Ctee Int Cncl of Monuments and Sites (ICOM memb Fabric Ctee Canterbury Cathedral 1987; Freeman City of London 1988, Liveryman Worshipful Co of Chartered Architects 1990; ARIBA 1956, FRIBA 1969; *Books* Modern Houses of the World (1964, 3 edn 1966), Great Modern Architecture (1966, 2 edn 1968), European Domestic Architecture (1969), New Uses for Old Buildings (1975), Architectural Conservation in Europe (ed, 1975), Wells Coates, a monograph (1978), Saving Old Buildings (with Susan Brandt, 1980), The Architecture of Howell, Killick, Partridge and Amis (1981), Charles Correa (1984), Architecture in Continuity: building in the Islamic world today (ed, 1985), Re/Architecture: old buildings, new uses (1989), articles in Architectural Review; *Clubs* Garrick; *Style—* Sherban Cantacuzino, Esq, CBE; 140 Iffley Rd, London W6 0PE (☎ 081 748 0415); Royal Fine Art Commission, 7 St James's Square, London SW1Y 4JU, (☎ 071 839 6537)

CANTER, Prof David Victor; s of Chaim Yizchak (Harry) Canter (d 1959), and Coralie Lilian, *née* Hyam (d 1970); *b* 5 Jan 1944; *Educ* Liverpool Collegiate GS, Univ of Liverpool (BA, PhD); *m* 10 Nov 1967, Sandra Lorraine, da of late Alfred Smith; 1 s (Daniel b 1972), 2 da (Hana b 1970, Lily b 1979); *Career* visiting lectr Birmingham Sch of Architecture 1967-70, visiting res fell Tokyo Univ 1970-71, lectr Univ of Strathclyde 1970-71 (res fell Building Performance Res Unit 1965-70), chair of psychology and head of dept Univ of Surrey 1987- (lectr 1972-78, reader 1978-83, personal chair in applied psychology 1983-87); managing ed Journal of Environmental Psychology 1981-; numerous contribs to jls, TV and radio; chm Psychologists for Peace 1985-88, memb CND; Freeman City of Quito 1985; Hon MD 1987, hon memb Japanese Inst of Architects 1970; FBPs 1975, FAPA 1985, FBIM 1985, CPsychol 1988; *Books* Architectural Psychology (1970), Psychology and the Built Environment (1974), The Psychology of Place (1977), Designing for Therapeutic Environments (1979), Fire and Human Behaviour (1980, revised 1990), Psychology in Practice (with S Canter, 1982), Facet Theory: Approaches to Social Research (1985), The Research Interview: Uses and Approaches (1985), Environmental Perspectives (1988), Environmental Policy Assessment and Communication (1988), New Directions in Environmental Participation (1988), Football In Its Place (with M Comber and D Uzell, 1989); *Recreations* clarinet, collage, horse riding; *Style—* David Canter, Esq; Department of Psychology, University of Surrey, Guildford, Surrey GU2 5XH (☎ 0483 509176, fax 0483 32813)

CANTERBURY, Archdeacon of; *see*: Till, Ven Michael Stanley

CANTLAY, Charles Peter Thrale; s of Peter Allen Cantlay, and Elizabeth Ann Cantlay; *b* 4 Feb 1954; *Educ* Radley Coll, Oriel Coll Oxford (BA); *m* 1985, Sandra Jane; *Career* Alexander Howden Reinsurance Brokers Ltd 1976-: dir Marine Div 1983-86, md Marine Div 1986; *Recreations* golf, hockey, skiing; *Clubs* Tandridge Golf, Oxted Hockey; *Style—* Charles P T Cantlay, Esq; 10 Killieser Ave, London SW2 4NT (☎ 081 674 1136); Alexander Howden Reinsurance Brokers Ltd, 8 Devonshire Square, London EC2M 4PL (☎ 071 623 5500, telex 882171, fax 071 621 1511)

CANTLAY, George Thomson; CBE (1973); s of George Thomson Cantlay (d 1939); *b* 2 Aug 1907; *Educ* HS Glasgow; *m* 1934, Sibyl Gwendoline Alsop, da of John Alsop Stoker (d 1965); 1 s, 1 da; *Career* stockbroker; memb Stock Exchange, former ptnr Murray and Co; dir: AB Electronic Products Gp plc, Welsh Nat Opera (now ret); *Recreations* opera; *Clubs* Cardiff and County; *Style—* George Cantlay, Esq, CBE; 8 Park Road, Penarth, S Glamorgan CF6 2BD (☎ 0222 704588)

CANTLEY, Sir Joseph Donaldson; OBE (1945); s of Dr Joseph Cantley (d 1926), of Crumpsall, Manchester, and Georgina, *née* Kean (d 1968); *b* 8 Aug 1910; *Educ* Manchester GS, Univ of Manchester; *m* 1966, Hilda Goodwin, da of Arthur George Jones (d 1954), of Fyling Hall, Robin Hood's Bay, Yorks, and wid of Sir (Albert) Denis

Gerrard (d 1965); 1 step s; *Career* serv WWII Lt-Col N Africa and Italy; barr 1933, QC 1954, rec of Oldham 1959-60, judge of the Court of Record for the Hundred of Salford 1960-65, judge of appeal IOM 1962-65, a judge of the High Court of Justice (Queen's Bench Div) 1965-85, presiding judge of the Northern Circuit 1970-74, presiding judge of the South Eastern Circuit 1980; Hon Col OTC Univ of Manchester and Univ of Salford 1971-77; Hon LLD Univ of Manchester; kt 1965; *Recreations* music, golf, reading books; *Clubs* Travellers'; *Style—* Sir Joseph Cantley, OBE

CANTRELL, Dr (Winifred Dorothy) Jane; da of William Harvey Cantrell (d 1974), and Ethel May, *née* Anderson; *b* 29 Nov 1944; *Educ* Blackheath HS, St Bartholomews Hosp Med Sch (MB BS); *m* 20 Jan 1979, David John Cooper, s of John Alec Cooper, of 22 Marcus St, Stratford, London; 1 da (Laura b 1982); *Career* various appts in anaesthetics 1970-74: London Hosp, Hadassah Med Centre Jerusalem, Whipps Cross Hosp; sr registrar: Royal Free, Nat Hosp for Nervous Diseases, Brompton Hosp 1975-77; conslt anaesthetist Whipps Cross Hosp 1977, faculty tutor and dep regnl advsr Faculty of Anaesthetists 1978-87, fndr and organiser Basic Anaesthesia Course Whipps Cross Hosp (later residential N E Thames Trg Centre); involved with C of E Urban Fund; memb: Coll of Anaesthetists, RSM, BMA, History of Anaesthesia Soc; LRCP, MRCS, FFARCS; *Recreations* sailing, shooting, music, wine growing, opera, ballet, 15-17 century European history; *Clubs* Lansdowne; *Style—* Dr Jane Cantrell; 3 Fairlawn Drive, Woodford Green, Essex IG8 9AW (☎ 081 504 1272); Lou Cantou, Ceps, Cessenon Herault, France (☎ 010 3367895499); Dept of Anaesthesia, Whipps Cross Hospital, Leytonstone, London E11 (☎ 081 539 5522)

CANTY, Brian George John; OBE (1988); s of George Robert Canty (d 1971), of Chingford, London, and Phoebe Charlotte, *née* Cobb (d 1984); *b* 23 Oct 1931; *Educ* S W Essex Tech Coll, Univ of London (external); *m* 4 Sept 1954, Maureen Kathleen (Kenny), da of William George Kenny (d 1982), of IOW; 1 s (Nigel b 1959), 1 da (Elaine b 1957); *Career* RN 1950-57; civil serv: Air Miny 1957, Fin Advsr's Office Cyprus 1960, Air Force Dept MOD 1963, RAF Staff Coll Bracknell 1970; entered Dip Serv 1971, Br Embassy Oslo 1973, Br High Cmmn Kingston 1977, consul Vienna 1979, FCO London 1984, dep govr Bermuda 1986, govr Anguilla 1989; *Recreations* sailing, skiing, DIY; *Clubs* RAC, Beefsteak Vienna, Royal Bermuda Yacht; *Style—* Brian Canty, Esq, OBE, JP; Government House, Old Ta, The Valley, Anguilla, British West Indies (☎ 010 1 809 497 2292); c/o Foreign and Commonwealth Office, King Charles' St, London SW1 2AH

CAPARROS, Miguel; s of Miguel Caparros, of Fuengirola, Spain, and Francisca; *b* 7 April 1944; *Educ* Ecole des Hautes Etudes Commerciales France (HEG), Graduate Sch of Business Univ of Chicago (MBA); *m* 2 Dec 1967, Nancy, da of Paul Vogeler, of Chicago, USA; 1 s (Alexander b 1978), 2 da (Elizabeth b 1968, Marie-Laure b 1972); *Career* Continental Illinois Nat Bank 1970-83, md Morgan Stanley Int 1985-, involved banking in France and Spain; *Clubs* Queen's Tennis; *Style—* Miguel Caparros, Esq; Morgan Stanley Int, Kingsley House, 1A Wimpole St, London W1M 7AA (☎ 071 709 3039, fax 071 709 3944, telex 8812 564)

CAPE, Donald Paul Montagu Stewart; CMG (1977); s of late John Scarvell Cape and Olivia Millicent Cape; *b* 6 Jan 1923; *Educ* Ampleforth, BNC Oxford; *m* 1948, Cathune Agnes Johnston; 4 s, 1 da; *Career* entered FO 1946; cnsllr: Washington 1970-73, Brasilia 1973-75; ambass to Laos 1976-78, ambass and UK permanent rep Cncl of Europe 1978-83; admin Anglo-Irish Encounter; chm Anglo- Portuguese Soc; *Style—* Donald Cape, Esq, CMG; Hilltop, Wonersh, Guildford GU5 0QT (☎ 0483 893407)

CAPEL, David John; s of John Capel and Angela Janet Capel; *b* 6 Feb 1963; *Educ* Roade Comprehensive Sch; *m* 1985, Deborah Jane; *Career* pro-cricketer Northants CCC and England; *Style—* David Capel, Esq; c/o Northants CCC, County Ground, Wantage Rd, Northampton

CAPEL, Dr John Philip; s of Henry Capel (d 1985), of Newport Mon, and Gwendoline Maud, *née* Gower; *b* 21 Aug 1926; *Educ* Univ of Edinburgh (LRCP); *m* 24 March 1954, Jeanne Hatton, da of John Simmonds (d 1981), of Chepstow, Gwent; 1 s (Nigel John b 24 June 1956); *Career* conslt in accident and emergency med 1972, clinical lectr in traumatic surgery Univ of Bristol 1972; pres Br Red Cross Soc Avon, fell Br Orthopaedic Assoc; memb: Casualty Surgns Assoc, BMA; LRCS, LRFP, LRFS; *Recreations* gardening, swimming, antiques; *Style—* Dr John Capel; Hatters Cottage, 66 School Road, Frampton, Cotterell, Bristol BS17 2DH (☎ 0454 778396), Frenchay Hospital, Bristol (☎ 0454 701212)

CAPEL CURE, George Ronald (Ronnie); s of George Nigel Capel Cure, *qv*; *b* 21 Oct 1936; *Educ* Eton; *m* 1968, Caroline Ann (d 1986), o da of Giles Yarnton Mills, of Puys sur Dieppe, France; 3 s; *Career* dir CT Bowring and Co (Insur) Ltd 1985; *Style—* Ronnie Capel Cure, Esq; Blake Hall, Ongar, Essex (☎ 0277 362652)

CAPEL CURE, (George) Nigel; TD, JP (1947), DL (1947); s of late Maj George Edward Capel Cure, JP (d 1943); the family, Capel Cure of Blake Hall, descends from Thomas Cure, of Southwark, Surrey, saddler to Edward VI, Mary I and Elizabeth I, arms granted 1588; *b* 28 Sept 1908; *Educ* Eton, Trinity Coll Cambridge; *m* 1935, Nancy Elizabeth, da of William James Barry (d 1952), of Great Witchingham Hall, Norwich; 2 s, 1 da; *Career* insur broker ret; landowner and farmer; High Sheriff of Essex 1951-52, Vice Lord-Lt of Essex 1958-78; *Clubs* City University, MCC; *Style—* G Nigel Capel Cure, Esq, TD, JP, DL; Ashlings, Moreton Rd, Ongar, Essex CM5 0EZ (☎ 0277 362634)

CAPES, Geoffrey Lewis (Geoff); s of George William Capes, of Washway Road, Holbeach, Spalding, Lincs, and Eileen Nelie, *née* Newham; *b* 23 Aug 1949; *Educ* George Farmer Comp Sch; partner, Kashmiro Davy Bhatti; 1 s (Lewis Leonard), 1 da (Emma Jane); *Career* GB shot put international 1967-80: 17 nat titles, twice Cwlth champion, 2 Gold, 2 Silver and 1 Bronze medal Euro Indoor Championships, Bronze medal Euro Championships, 3 times Euro Cup champion, 3 times Olympian; turned professional Highland Games and strong man competitor 1980-: 6 times World Highland Games champion, 2 times World's Strongest Man, 3 times Br Strongest Man, 3 times Euro Strongest Man; physical training instructor Police Force 1979-90, dir Geoff Capes Promotions 1980-, proprietor Creative Bodies Gymnasiums 1980-; record of 67 int caps for male UK athlete, record of 35 wins; Churchill scholar 1974, Queen's Jubilee medal 1977; *Books* Big Shot (autobiography); *Recreations* fishing, gardening, breeding budgerigars; *Clubs* Enfield Harriers; *Style—* Geoff Capes, Esq; c/o Bagnall Harvey, 141-142 Drury Lane, London (☎ 071 379 4625)

CAPIE, Prof Forrest Hunter; s of Daniel Forrest Capie (d 1975), and Isabella Ferguson, *née* Doughty; *b* 1 Dec 1940; *Educ* Nelson Coll NZ, Univ of Auckland NZ (BA), LSE (MSc, PhD); *m* 11 Feb 1967, Dianna Dix, da of William John Harvey, of Auckland, NZ; *Career* economics tutor LSE 1970-72; lectr: Dept of Economics Univ of Warwick 1972-74, Sch of Economics Univ of Leeds 1974-79; Centre for Banking and Int Fin City Univ London: lectr 1979-82, sr lectr 1982-83, reader 1983-86, prof of econ history 1986-, head of dept 1988-; memb: Econ Hist Soc 1970- (memb Cncl 1986-); Econ Hist Assoc 1972-, Cliometric Soc 1986-, Western Economics Assoc of the USA 1987; assoc Centre for Metropolitan History Univ of London 1986-; *Books* The British Economy Between the Wars (with M Collins, 1983), Depression and Protectionism, Britain Between the Wars (1983), Monetary History of the United Kingdom 1870-1970: Data Sources and Methods (with A Webber, 1985), Financial Crises of the World Banking System (ed with GE Wood, 1986) Monetary Economics in the 1980's: Some Themes from Henry Thornton (ed with GE Wood, 1988), A Directory of Economic Institutions (ed, 1990); *Recreations* golf, watching sport, classical music, opera, theatre; *Clubs* Hampstead Golf, Middx Cricket; *Style—* Prof Forrest Capie; 2 Fitzroy Rd, Primrose Hill, London NW1 8TZ ☎ 071 722 7456); Department of Banking and Finance, City University Business School, Frobisher Crescent, Barbican, London EC2 (☎ 071 920 0111)

CAPLAN, Harold; s of Samuel Caplan (d 1980), and Gertrude Caplan (d 1972); *b* 13 March 1927; *Educ* Queen Elizabeth's Hosp Bristol, The Coll of Aeronautics Cranfield (MSc); *m* 22 Nov 1968, Isabel, da of Stephen Randall (d 1981); *Career* chartered insurance practitioner; called to the Bar Middle Temple 1955; head Legal Dept The British Aviation Insurance Co Ltd 1960-69 (chief tech offr 1955), md International Insurance Services Ltd 1981- (jt gen mangr 1970-81) dir Airclaims Insurance Services Ltd 1987-; legal advsr Int Union of Aviation Insurers 1985-, fndr memb Air Law Gp Royal Aeronautical Soc, memb Bar Assoc for Commerce Finance and Indust; CEng, FRAeS, FCIArb; *Recreations* iconoclasm; *Clubs* Athenaeum, City of London; *Style—* Harold Caplan, Esq; International Insurance Services Ltd, 15 St Helen's Place, Bishopsgate, London EC3A 6DE (☎ 071 638 7208, fax 071 374 0460, telex 887857 115G)

CAPLAN, The Hon Lord; Philip Isaac Caplan; QC (Scot 1970); s of Hyman Caplan (d 1962), of Glasgow, and Rosalena Silverstone (d 1985); *b* 24 Feb 1929; *Educ* Eastwood Secdy Sch, Univ of Glasgow (MA, LLB); *m* 1, 1953, Elaine Marcia, da of Abraham Gelfer, of Glasgow; 2 s, 1 da; m 2, 1974, Joyce Ethel, da of Walter Stone, of London; 1 da; *Career* admitted Faculty of Advocates 1957-, former standing jr counsel to the Accountant of Ct, former chm Plant and Seeds Tbnl (Scot); Sheriff of Lothian and Borders at Edinburgh 1979-83, Sheriff Princ of N Strathclyde 1983-88, Sheriff Ct Rules Cncl 1984-88, senator Coll of Justice 1980; cmmr Northern Lighthouse Bd 1983-88; chm: Scottish Assoc for the Study of Deliquency 1985-89 (hon vice pres 1989), Scot Assoc of Family Conciliation Servs 1989-; FRPS, AFIAP; *Recreations* photography, music, reading; *Clubs* New (Edinburgh); *Style—* The Hon Lord Caplan, QC; Court of Session, Parliament Square, Edinburgh (☎ 031 225 2595)

CAPLAN, Simon Anthony; JP (1986); s of Malcolm Denis Caplan and Jean Hilary, *née* Winroope (d 1984); *b* 13 Dec 1946; *Educ* Carmel Coll Wallingford; *m* 6 Sept 1970, Yolande Anne, da of Simon Albert (d 1978); 1 s (Benjamin b 1974), 1 da (Amanda b 1971); *Career* Touche Ross 1970; jt fndr Fin Advice Panels (within CAB); fndr Caplan Montagu Assoc, chm and md of Stagestruck Gp of Cos; Barker of the Variety Club of GB; memb: BAFTA, Soc of W End Theatre, Royal TV Soc, Royal Inst; fndr dir Criterion Fund Mgmnt Ltd, Gen Cmmr Income Tax 1988; Freeman City of London 1980; FCA, FTII; *Recreations* art and antique collecting, theatre; *Clubs* Reform, IOD; *Style—* Simon A Caplan, Esq, JP; Stowe March, Barnet Lane, Elstree, Herts; 57 Duke St, Grosvenor Square, London W1 (☎ 071 629 2334, fax 071 493 3808)

CAPNER, Gareth Roger John; s of John Hammond Capner (d 1973), and Clarice May, *née* Gibbins (d 1971); *b* 14 May 1947; *Educ* Taunton Sch Somerset, Univ of Sheffield (BA, MA); *m* 2 Jan 1971, Susan Mary, da of Arthur Snell, of S Humberside; *Career* princ planning offr Berkshire CC 1973-79; Barton Willmore Planning Partnership: assoc 1979-81, ptnr 1981-85, sr ptnr 1985-; MBIM 1978; FRTPI 1983 (MRTPI 1974); *Recreations* sailing, skiing, shooting and gourmet dining; *Style—* Gareth Capner, Esq; Shepherds Hill House, Boxford, Newbury, Berks RG16 8DX (☎ 048 838 222); 2 The Old Mill, Mill Lane, Lymington, Hants (☎ 0590 671551); The Barton Willmore Planning Partnership, Beansheaf Farmhouse, Bourne Close, Calcot, Reading, Berks RG3 7BW (☎ 0734 425577, fax 0734 418410, car 0860 793364)

CAPON, Timothy Wills Hugh; s of Rev Martin Gedge Capon, of Exmouth, Devon, and Mary Wills Hamlyn (d 1978); *b* 26 Oct 1940; *Educ* Prince of Wales Sch Nairobi Kenya, Magdalene Coll Cambridge (BA, LLB); *m* 3 Sept 1966, Elizabeth Fleming, da of Henry Campbell McAusland, OBE; 1 s (Oliver Fleming b 1 Aug 1970), 2 da (Sarah Elizabeth b 19 March 1969, Lucy Jane b 10 July 1972); *Career* admitted slr 1965; res ptnr NY office Linklaters and Paines 1974-77 (ptnr 1970), exec dir The Diamond Trading Co (Pty) Ltd 1977-; dir: Bank Leumi UK plc, Union Bank of Israel Ltd, De Beers Consolidated Mines Ltd, De Beers Centenary AG; *Clubs* Hurlingham; *Style—* Timothy Capon, Esq; 17 Charterhouse Street, London EC1 (☎ 071 404 4444, fax 071 405 7020)

CAPPER, Rt Rev Edmund Michael Hubert; OBE (1961); s of Arthur Charles Capper (d 1958), of Torquay, and Mabel Lavinia, *née* Barnett (d 1961); *b* 12 March 1908; *Educ* St Joseph's Acad Blackheath, St Augustine's Coll Canterbury, LTh (Durham); *Career* ordained: deacon 1932, priest 1933; RA Chaplains Dept (EA) 1942-46, HCF 1946-, officiating chaplain to King's African Rifles 1954-62; memb Univs Mission to Central Africa 1936-62, archdeacon of Lindi and canon of Masasi Cathedral 1947-54, archdeacon of Dar es Salaam and canon of Zanzibar Cathedral 1954-58, provost Collegiate Church of St Alban the Martyr Dar es Salaam 1957-62, bishop St Helena 1967-73; chaplain: Palma de Mallorca 1962-67, St Georges Malaga 1973-76; auxiliary bishop in the Dio of Gibraltar in Europe 1973-, asst bishop Southwark 1981-; chm Tanganyika Br Legion Benevolent Fund 1956-62, pres Tanganyika Br Legion 1960-62; *Clubs* Travellers'; *Style—* The Rt Rev Edmund Capper, OBE; Morden Coll, Blackheath, London SE3 0PW (☎ 081 858 9169)

CAPPI, Graham Vincent; s of Vincent Ronald Cappi, of Frinton-on-Sea, Essex, and Margaret W Cappi; *b* 1 Aug 1968; *Educ* Framlingham Coll, Hounslow Borough Coll (HND); *Career* copywriter and D & ADA course tutor Gold Greenlees Trott 1988-89, art dir and D & ADA course tutor Leagas Shafron Davis Chick; *awards* two D & ADA nominations 1990, Creative Circle Silver award 1990, Campaign Poster Silver award 1990; memb D & ADA; *Recreations* films, art galleries, opera, theatre; *Clubs* Subterrania; *Style—* Graham Cappi, Esq; Leagas, Shafron, Davis, Chick, 1 Star St, London W2 1QD (☎ 071 262 0874)

CAPPIN, John Michael; s of Louis Cappin, of 4 Abbey Court, Abbey Rd, London NW4, and Yetta Cappin; *b* 7 Dec 1938; *Educ* Mercers Sch, Univ of Cambridge (MA, MB BChir, DO); *m* 2 April 1967, Marion Kay, da of Ernest Clifford Stammers (d 1967), of Tunbridge Wells; 2 s (Simon James b 7 July 1969, Matthew Jonathen b 25 Nov 1978), 1 da (Melissa Catherine b 1 Nov 1972); *Career* conslt ophthalmic surgn Leicester Health Authy 1975-; FRCS, fell Coll of Ophthalmology 1989; *Recreations* pianist, choral conductor, tennis; *Style—* John Cappin, Esq; Leicester Clinic, Scraptoft Lane, Leicester (☎ 0533 769502)

CAPRON, (George) Christopher; s of Lt-Col George Theodore Herbert Capron (d 1970), of Southwick Hall, Peterborough, and Hon Edith Christian Hepburne-Scott, 3 da of 9 Baron Polwarth (d 1989); *b* 17 Dec 1935; *Educ* Wellington, Trinity Hall Cambridge (BA); *m* 1958, Edna Naomi, da of Chanania Goldrei (d 1973); 1 s (David), 1 da (Naomi); *Career* 2 Lt 12 Royal Lancers (POW) 1954-56; BBC TV 1959-87: ed Tonight 1976-77, Panorama 1977-79, asst head current affrs programmes 1979-81 (head 1981-85), head of Parly bdcasting 1985-87; ind TV prodr Capron Prodns Ltd 1987-; memb: BAFTA, Royal TV Soc; *Recreations* tennis, village cricket; *Clubs* Northamptonshire CCC, Hurlingham; *Style—* Christopher Capron, Esq; 32 Amerland Rd, London SW18 (☎ 081 874 4829)

CAPSTICK, Brian Eric; QC (1973); o s of (Norman) Eric and Betty Capstick; *b* 12

Feb 1927; *Educ* Sedbergh, Queen's Coll Oxford; *m* 1960, Margaret Elizabeth Harrison; 1 s, 1 da; *Career* barr 1952, recorder of the Crown Court 1980-; dir Hartley Main Farms Ltd 1950-; *Style*— Brian Capstick, Esq, QC; 2 Crown Office Row, Temple, London EC4 (☎ 071 583 2681); 71 Sout End Rd, NW3 (☎ 071 435 3540)

CAPSTICK, Charles William; CMG (1972); s of William Capstick and Janet Frankland; *b* 18 Dec 1934; *Educ* King's Coll Durham Univ, Kentucky Univ; *m* 1962, Joyce Alma, da of William Dodsworth; 2 s; *Career* former under-sec Milk and Milk Products MAFF; dir Economics and Statistics 1977-89; dep sec (Fisheries and Food) Miny of Agric, Fisheries and Food 1989-; *Style*— Charles Capstick, Esq, CMG; 7 Dellfield Clo, Radlett, Herts (☎ Radlett 7640)

CAPSTICK-DALE, (John) Rodney; s of E J Capstick-Dale, of Bristol, and Norah, *née* Airey (d 1987); *b* 26 Oct 1934; *Educ* St Brendans Coll Bristol; *m* 1; 4 s (Simon Rodney b 1962, Nicholas John (twin) b 1962, Marcus Jack b 1966, Daniel Joseph b 1969); m 2, 1984, Diana Suzanne, da of late Alan Leon, of Johannesburg; 1 step s (Jeremy Cohen); *Career* admitted slr 1961; articled clerk Bush and Bush Bristol, fndr and ptnr Capstick-Dale & Co Essex (ret 1974); dir property co and property investmt co (owners of Great Western Antique Centre Bath); dir: Grosvenor Gallery of London 1983-86, Fine Art Aquisitions Inc NY 1984-85; fndr and jt md Albemarle Gallery London; memb Law Soc; *Recreations* travel, collecting twentieth century paintings; *Clubs* Chelsea Arts; *Style*— Rodney Capstick Dale, Esq; Albemarle Gallery, 18 Albemarle St, London W1X 3HA (☎ 071 355 1880, fax 071 491 9272)

CARANCI, Lady Georgina Joceleyn; da of late 8 Earl of Chichester; *b* 7 June 1942; *m* 27 June 1974, Halios Alberto, s of Helios Jorge Caranci, of Buenos Aires, Argentina; 1 s (Helios Nicolás b 1983), 2 da (Cecilia Catalina b 1976, Ursula Claudia b 1978); *Style*— The Lady Georgina Caranci; La Catalina, Diego de Alvear, Santa Fe, Argentina

CARBERRY, Debbie Claire; da of Robert John Stephens, of Horsham Sussex, and Sylvia Marie, *née* Mogford; *b* 11 Aug 1960; *Educ* Holy Trinity C of E Sch Sussex, Crawley Coll of Further Educn; *Career* PR exec; sec Int Mktg Div EMI Music Ltd 1978-79, PR asst Constructors John Brown Ltd 1979-80, jr then sr account exec Max Redlich Ltd 1980-81; account mangr: Imprimatur (PR) Ltd 1981-82, Peter Walker Associates 1982-83; sr account dir Genesis (acquired by Daniel J Edelman Ltd 1985) 1983-85, assoc dir then main bd dir Daniel J Edelman Ltd 1985-87, dir Biss Lancaster plc 1988; *Recreations* fitness training, riding, gardening, wine appreciation, reading; *Style*— Mrs Debbie Carberry; Biss Lancaster plc, 69 Monmouth St, London WC2H 9DG (☎ 071 497 3001, fax 071 497 8915, car 0860 303615)

CARBERRY, (Hon) Juanita Virginia Sistare; *née* Carberry; da of 10 Baron Carbery (d 1970), and his 2 wife, Maïa Ivy, *née* Anderson (d 1928); *b* 7 May 1925; *Educ* Roedean Johannesburg, Wickham Pietermaritzburg Switzerland; *Career* seaman; *Style*— Ms Juanita Carberry; PO Box 96094, Likoni, via Mombasa, Kenya, East Africa

CARBERY, 11 Baron (I 1715); Sir Peter Ralfe Harrington Evans-Freke; 7 Bt (I 1768); s of Maj the Hon Ralfe Evans-Freke, MBE (d 1969), 2 s of 9 Baron; suc unc, 10 Baron, 1970; *b* 20 March 1920; *Educ* Downside; *m* 1941, Joyzelle Mary, o da of late Herbert Binnie, of Sydney, NSW; 3 s, 2 da; *Heir* Hon Michael Evans-Freke; *Career* served WWII 1939-45 as Capt RE in India and Burma; former memb London Stock Exchange; author of novels, plays and poetry; MICE; *Clubs* Kennel, Ski Club of Great Britain; *Style*— The Rt Hon the Lord Carbery; 2 Hayes Court, Sunnyside, Wimbledon, London SW19 4SH (☎ 081 946 6615)

CARBUTT, Billy (Francis); s of George H Carbutt (d 1956), and Ann, *née* de Montmorency (now Mrs E W Swanton); *b* 16 July 1936; *Educ* Eton Coll; *m* 19 July 1958, Sally Fenella, da of James C Harris of Ampfield, Hants; 1 s, (George Henry de Montmorency b 1963), 1 da (Emma Louise (Mrs Swinton) b 1961); *Career* Nat Serv Lt Rifle Bde 1954-56; CA; ptnr Ernst & Young 1967- (joined 1956); chm Ct of the Mary Rose; memb Ct Worshipful Co of Grocers (Master 1990/91); FCA (1961); *Recreations* swimming, photography, gardening, all kinds of music; *Clubs* Boodles, City of London, MCC; *Style*— Billy Carbutt, Esq; The White House, Langham, Colchester, Essex CO4 5PY (☎ 0206 323182); Ernst & Young, Becket House, 1 Lambeth Palace Rd, London SE1 7EU (☎ 071 931 3626 and 071 928 2000, fax 071 928 1345, telex 885234)

CARD, Philip Haven; s of Oliver Card (d 1962), of Caldicot, Gwent, and Alice Mary, *née* Summerfield (d 1982); *b* 12 Aug 1933; *Educ* Latymer Fndn Sch Hammersmith; *m* 19 Sept 1959, Barbara Rose, da of Charles William Hanslow (d 1987), of Barnes; 1 da (Christine Judith b 10 May 1972); *Career* Nat Serv RAF 1951-53; Morris Ashby Ltd 1948-79, chm and md Panmond Ltd 1980-; special constable City of London Police 1966-88; Liveryman Worshipful Co of Pattenmakers; FRMS; *Recreations* shooting, clockmaking and restoration; *Clubs* Hitchin Cons, Victory Servs; *Style*— Philip Card, Esq; Panmond Ltd, 10a Bucklersbury, Hitchin, Herts SG5 1BB (☎ 0462 434281, fax 0462 422595)

CARDALE, David Michael; s of Brig W J Cardale, OBE (d 1986), of West Lodge, Bradfield St George, Bury St Edmunds, Suffolk, and Audrey Vere, *née* Parry-Crooke; *b* 26 Dec 1947; *Educ* Eton, Univ of Essex (BA), INSEAD (MBA); *m* 31 Aug 1985, Fionna, *née* MacCormick; 1 s (Hugo William b 7 March 1989), 1 da (Natasha Lucy Vere b 19 Dec 1990); *Career* County Bank: exec 1972-78, asst dir 1978-81, N American Rep 1981-83, dir 1983-87; exec dir County Nat West 1987-, dir Sphere Investment Trust Plc 1988- (currently non exec dir); *Recreations* hunting, tennis, windsurfing; *Style*— David Cardale, Esq; County Nat West, 135 Bishopsgate, London EC2M 3UR (☎ 071 375 5000)

CARDALE, William Tyndale; s of Brig W J Cardale, OBE, ADC (d 1986), and Vere Audrey, *née* Parry-Crooke; *b* 10 Dec 1945; *Educ* Eton; *m* 13 Aug 1988, Lynn Meriel, da of Alan Thomas Brown, CBE, DL, *qv*; 1 s (Thomas William b 24 Feb 1990); *Career* CA; managing tax conslt Tst Dept Price Waterhouse Birmingham W Midlands and S of England; lectr in taxation Univ of Birmingham (on secondment from Price Waterhouse and at various Insts of CA's courses); FCA, ATII; *Recreations* riding (hunter trials and events), tennis; *Style*— William T Cardale, Esq; West Lodge, Bradfield St George, Bury St Edmunds, Suffolk; 71 Ravenhurst Rd, Harborne, Birmingham B17 9TB

CARDEN, Christopher Robert; s (by 1 m) and h of Sir Henry Carden, 4 Bt, OBE; *b* 24 Nov 1946; *Educ* Eton, Univ of Aberdeen (BSc); *m* 1, 1972 (m dis 1979), Sainimere Rokotuibau, of Suva, Fiji; m 2, 1981, Clarita Peralta Eriksen, of Manila, Philippines; 1 step s (Johnny Eriksen b 1975); *Career* forestry 1970; Govt of Papua New Guinea 1970-74; Fiji Pine Cmmn 1976-79, dir C R Forestry Services 1979-82, Usutu Pulp Co Swaziland 1982-86; Cwlth Fund for Tech Co-operation Solomon Is 1986-88; forestry conslt 1989-; *Recreations* tennis, squash, bowls, travel, philately, ufology; *Style*— Christopher Carden Esq; 39 St Cuthbert St, Wells, Somerset BA5 2AW (☎ 0749 679282, fax 0749 75096)

CARDEN, Lt-Col Sir Henry Christopher; 4 Bt (UK 1887), of Wimpole Street, Middlesex, and of Mole Lodge, Surrey; OBE (1945); s of Maj Sir Frederick Henry Walter Carden, 3 Bt (d 1966), and Winifred Mary, *née* Wroughton (d 1972); *b* 16 Oct 1908; *Educ* Eton, RMC Sandhurst; *m* 1, 5 June 1943 (m dis 1961), Jane St Clare, da of late Thomas Edward St Clare Daniell, OBE, MC; 1 s, 1 da (Melinda Jane (Mrs A J Wilson) b 1950); m 2, 8 Nov 1962, Gwyneth Sybil, da of late Herbert Arthur Dyke Acland, and widow of Flt Lt Roderick Stanley Emerson, RAFVR (ka 1944); *Heir* s, Christopher Robert Carden, *qv*; *Career* cmmnd 17/21 Lancers 1928, serv Egypt and India 1930-39, Staff Coll 1941, cmd 2 Armoured Delivery Regt France 1944-45, CO 17/21 Lancers in Greece and Palestine 1947-48, WO 1948-51, mil attaché Stockholm 1951-55, ret 1956; Order of the Sword (Sweden) 1954; *Recreations* most field sports (incl polo), cricket; *Clubs* Cavalry and Guards'; *Style*— Lt-Col Sir Henry Carden, Bt, OBE; Moongrove, East Woodhay, Newbury, Berks (☎ 0635 253661)

CARDEN, Sir John Craven; 7 Bt (I 1787), of Templemore, Tipperary; s of Capt Sir John V Carden, 6 Bt, MBE (d 1935); *b* 11 March 1926; *Educ* Eton; *m* 1947, Isabel Georgette, yst da of late Robert de Hart; 1 da; *Heir* kinsman, Derrick Charles Carden, *qv*; *Style*— Sir John Carden, Bt; PO Box N7776, Lyford Cay, Nassau, Bahamas

CARDEN, Peter Maurice Arthur; s of Paul Carden (d 1985), and Lilias Kathleen, *née* Wills (d 1989); *b* 18 June 1931; *Educ* Harrow; *m* 3 Dec 1966, Sheila Joan, da of Richard Vevers Matson (d 1957); 1 s (Tom b 1972), 2 da (Alice b 1968, Kate b 1969); *Career* Nat Serv 1949-51, 2 Lt RHA 1950; dir: Thos and Jas Harrison Ltd 1967 (Caribbean rep 1953-60, mangr Liverpool 1960), Charente Steam-Ship Co Ltd 1971; chm: Caribbean Overseas Lines (CAROL) 1975, Prentice Service & Henderson Ltd 1980 (dir 1965); dir Associated Container Transportation Ltd (ACT) 1985; govr Liverpool Sch of Tropical Med 1962-72, chm Assoc of W India Trans Atlantic Steamship Lines (WITASS) 1971-; *Recreations* sailing, tennis, gardening; *Clubs* Liverpool Racquet; *Style*— Peter Carden, Esq; Croughton Ho, Chester CH2 4DA (☎ 0244 383 162); Thos & Jas Harrison Ltd, Mersey Chambers, Liverpool L2 8UF (☎ 051 236 5611, fax 051 236 1200, telex 628 404)

CARDEN, Philippe O'Neill; s of Dick Guy Carden, of London, and Françoise Jeanne, *née* Domerc; *b* 22 Sept 1950; *Educ* Wimbledon Coll, Bellarmine Coll (Kentucky), St John's Coll Cambridge (BA); *m* 20 Sept 1975, Julia Francesca, da of Austin Raymond Lindon, of London; 2 da (Mondane b 1979, Genevieve b 1981); *Career* CA; dir and vice chm London Bubble (Bubble Theatre Co Ltd) 1990-; *Recreations* theatre, music, gastronomy; *Style*— Philippe Carden, Esq; 12 Lintons Lane, Epsom, Surrey KT17 1DD; 38A High St, Ewell, Epsom, Surrey KT17 1RW

CARDEN, Simon Dennis; s of Dennis Leek Carden, of St Annes on Sea, Lancashire, and Jean Dorothy, *née* Holland; *b* 10 June 1955; *Educ* Arnold Sch, Manchester Poly (BA, DipArch); *m* 25 April 1981, Anna Patricia Carden, da of Capt Ronald Hubert Paul Holt RASC (d 1968); 2 da (Lucy b 1984, Gabriella b 1987); *Career* dir John Brunton Ptnrship 1989; patron Manchester City Art Gallery, memb RIBA; *Recreations* shooting, skiing; *Style*— Simon Carden, Esq; John Bruton PLC, Waterfront Quay, Waterfront 2000, Salford Quays, Manchester M5 2XW (☎ 061 872 4556, fax 061 848 0041)

CARDEN, (Graham) Stephen Paul; CBE (1986), TD (1968) DL (Greater London 1983); s of Paul Carden (d 1985), and Lilias Kathleen, *née* Wills (d 1989); *b* 14 May 1935; *Educ* Harrow; *Career* 9 Lancers 1954-56, City of London Yeo (Rough Riders) and on amalgamation Inns of Ct and City Yeo 1956-74, TA Col 1976-78; stockbroker Cazenove & Co 1956, ptnr 1964-; dir Greenfriar Investment 1966-; Hon Col 71 (Yeo) Signal Regt 1989-; vice pres Greater London TAVRA 1988- (vice chm Cncl TAVRAs 1984-88), vice chm ACF Assoc 1989-, cmmr Royal Hosp Chelsea 1986-, vice pres Yeo Benevolent Fund 1986-, vice chm and hon treas Fairbridge Drake Soc 1987- (hon treas Fairbridge Soc 1964-87), govr vice-chm London House for Overseas Graduates (chm 1990-); *Recreations* Equestrian (mainly hunting), fishing, sailing, watching cricket; *Clubs* Cavalry and Guards, White's, City of London, MCC, Royal Yacht Squadron; *Style*— Stephen Carden, Esq, CBE, TD, DL; 12 Warwick Square, London SW1V 2AA (☎ 071 834 8919); 12 Tokenhouse Yard, London EC2R 7AN (☎ 071 588 2828, telex 886758, fax 071 606 9205)

CARDEW, Anthony John; s of Lt-Col Martin Philip Cardew, of Rookley Manor, Rookley, IOW, and Anne Elizabeth, *née* Foster; *b* 8 Sept 1949; *Educ* Bishop Wordsworth's Sch Salisbury Wilts, Marlborough; *m* 10 Dec 1971, Janice Frances, da of Alec Anthony Smallwood (d 1985); 1 s (James), 1 da (Sarah); *Career* chief reporter Surrey Mirror 1968-70, news reporter UPI 1970-71, fin corr Reuters 1972-74, dir then head of fin PR Charles Barker Ltd 1974-83, chm Grandfield Rork Collins 1985- (dir 1983-); *Recreations* book collecting, walking; *Clubs* Reform, Thunderers; *Style*— Anthony Cardew, Esq; Horns Farm House, Eversley, Hampshire (☎ 0734 732 200); Grandfield Rork Collins Ltd, Prestige House, 14-18 Holborn, London EC1 (☎ 071 242 2002, fax 071 405 2208, telex 8956158)

CARDEW, Lt Cdr Philip Peel; s of Evelyn Philip Cardew (d 1978), of Middleton on Sea, Sussex, and Dorothy Lilian Cardew, *née* Nuttall (d 1946); *b* 5 June 1929; *Educ* Dragon Sch, Reigate GS; *m* 5 Oct 1957, Anne Florence, da of Lt-Col Henry Baker (d 1975), of Hartley Wintney; 1 s (Geoffrey b 1958), 1 da (Caroline b 1965); *Career* RN Fleet Air Arm 1947-69, Lt-Cdr; professional pilot: BEA 1969-72, Corporate Aviation 1972-; md Br Car Auctions (Aviation) 1976-, airport dir Blackbushe 1984-, chm Farnham Fleet Aldershot Sea-Cadets 1977-; memb Cncl: GAMTA, ATOA, BAUA; Freeman Worshipful Co of Air Pilots and Navigators; *Recreations* golf, tennis, sailing, squash, riding; *Clubs* Offs (Aldershot); *Style*— Lt Cdr Philip Cardew; Woodside, Broad Oak, Odiham, Basingstoke, Hants (☎ 0420 64030, fax 0252 874444, telex 858858 BLKBG); Terminal Bldg, Blackbushe Airport, Camberley, Surrey (☎ 0252 879 449, car 0836 281641)

CARDIFF, Archbishop of (RC), 1983-; Most Rev John Aloysius Ward; OFMCap; s of Eugene Ward and Hannah, *née* Cheetham; *b* 24 Jan 1929; *Educ* Prior Park Coll Bath; *Career* OFM Cap 1945-, ordained priest 1953, guardian and parish priest Peckham 1960-66, provincial definitor 1963-69, minister provincial 1969-70, gen definitor Rome 1970-80, Bishop Coadjutor of Menevia 1980-81, Bishop of Menevia 1981-83; *Style*— His Grace the Archbishop of Cardiff, OFMCap; Archbishop's House, 41-43 Cathedral Road, Cardiff, South Glamorgan CF1 9HD (☎ 0222 20411)

CARDIGAN, Earl of; David Michael James Brudenell-Bruce; s and h of 8 Marquess of Ailesbury; *b* 12 Nov 1952; *Educ* Eton, Rannoch, RAC Cirencester; *m* 1980, Rosamond Jane, er da of Capt W R M Winkley, of Wyke Champflower Manor, Wyke Champflower, Bruton, Somerset; 1 s (Thomas b 1982), 1 da (Catherine b 1984); *Heir* s, Viscount Savernake; *Career* owner mangr Savernake Forest; *Style*— Earl of Cardigan; Savernake Lodge, Savernake Forest, Marlborough, Wilts (☎ 0672 512161)

CARDOZO, Linda Dolores; da of Felix Elia Cardozo (d 1971), of London, and Olga Annette, *née* Schwatz; *b* 15 Sept 1950; *Educ* Haberdashers Aske's, Acton Tech Coll, Univ of Liverpool (MB ChB, MD); *m* 13 July 1974, Stuart Ian Hutcheson, s of Ian Steen Hutcheson; 1 s (Marins b 27 July 1990), 2 da (Melissa b 27 Feb 1989, Juliet (twin) b 27 July 1990); *Career* house offr and sr house offr obstetrics and gynaecology Liverpool, res registrar in urodynamics St George's Hosp London 1976-78, conslt obstetrician and gynaecologist specialising in female urinary incontinence King's Coll Hosp 1985- (registrar then sr registrar 1979-85); memb Int Continence Soc; memb: RSM, BMA, ICS, IUGA, IMS; MRCOG 1980; *Recreations* flying, diving, skiing, riding; *Style*— Ms Linda Cardozo; The Sloes, Potter St Hill, Pinner, Middlesex HA5 3YH; King's College Hospital, Flying Hill, London SE5 (☎ 071 274 6222); 8 Devonshire Place, London W1 (☎ 071 935 2357)

CARDROSS, Lord; Henry Thomas Alexander Erskine; s and h of 17 Earl of Buchan, JP, *qv*; *b* 31 May 1960; *Educ* Eton, Central Sch of Art and Design; *m* 28 Feb 1987, Charlotte Catherine Lucinda, da of Hon Matthew Beaumont, *qv*; 1 s (Alexander

Henry David John b 26 April 1990); *Career* stained glass designer and photographer; *Recreations* cars, photography, video, travel; *Style*— Lord Cardross

CARDWELL, Jennifer Lesley Winter; *b* 14 Feb 1943; *Educ* Tottenham Co Sch, Nevilles Cross Coll Durham; *m* 7 April 1966, Benjamin Jon Cardwell; 1 s (Angus Blair b 18 Dec 1975), 1 da (Joanna Emily b 2 Jan 1973); *Career* hockey coach and manager; player: Ipswich Ladies Hockey Club 1968-82, counties second XI 1962-68 (Durham, Essex, Sussex), Suffolk first XI 1968-82, East territory 1968-72, 1973-75, 1976-80, 30 caps England 1970-72 and 1973-74 (England B 1970); coach: East Srs 1985-91 (jrs 1982), Ealing Ladies Hockey Club 1987-89, Essex Ladies 1985-90; mangr England Sr Womens team 1989- (coach 1983-86); achievements as coach: East Srs champions 3 times, Ealing nat champions 3 times, Essex territorial champions 3 times, England fourth place Euro Cup 1983 and fifth place World Cup 1986 (fourth 1990 as mangr); *Recreations* golf (two holes-in-one), keeping fit, learning to play bridge; *Style*— Mrs Jennifer Cardwell; Little Dene, 13 Manor Rise, Bearsted, Maidstone, Kent ME14 4DB (☎ 0622 37736); All England Womens Hockey Association, 51 High St, Shrewsbury, Shropshire SY1 1ST (☎ 0743 233572, fax 0743 233583)

CARDWELL, Prof Richard Andrew; s of Lt-Cdr Albert Cardwell RN, of Marlborough, Hillcrest, Helston, Cornwall, and Mary Margarethe, *née* Knight; *b* 16 July 1938; *Educ* Helston GS, Univ of Southampton (BA, DipEd), Univ of Nottingham (PhD); *m* 29 July 1961, Oithona Shaguine (Bunty), da of Edgar Treadwell (d 1968); *Career* lectr UCW Aberystwyth 1965-67 (asst lectr 1964-65); Univ of Nottingham: lectr 1967-74, sr lectr 1974-78, reader 1978-83, prof of modern Spanish lit and head of Dept of Hispanic Studies 1983-; author of numerous articles; memb: Assoc of Br Hispanists, Anglo-Catalan Soc, Assoc of Teachers of Spanish and Portuguese, memb Real Academia Sevillana de Buenas Letras Seville Spain; Boy Scout's Assoc Silver Cross for Gallantry and Royal Humane Soc Testimonial on Vellum for Gallantry 1958; *Books* Blasco Ibanez's La Barraca (1972), Juan Ramón Jimenez: The Modernist Apprenticeship (1977), Espronceda (1981), Gabriel Garcia Marquez: New Readings (1987), Virgil: Essays for the Bimillenium (1987), Literature and Language (1989); Espronceda: Student of Salamanca (1990); *Recreations* gardening, garden design, walking, conversation with intelligent women; *Style*— Prof Richard A Cardwell; The Yews, 6 Town St, Sandiacre, Nottingham NG10 5DP (☎ 0602 397316), Dept of Hispanic Studies, University of Nottingham, University Park, Nottingham NG7 2RD (☎ 0602 484848, telex 37346 (UNINOT G), fax 0602 420825)

CARDY, Peter John Stubbings; s of Gordon Douglas Stubbings, of Gosport, Hants, and Eva, *née* Walker; assumed the surname of Cardy by deed poll 1987; *b* 4 April 1947; *Educ* Price's Sch, Univ Coll Durham (BA), Cranfield Inst of Technol (MSc); *m* 5 Sept 1987, Christine Mary, da of Ronald Edward Francis Doyle, of Manchester; *Career* dist sec WEA N of Scotland 1971-77, dep dir Volunteer Centre UK 1977-87, dir Motor Neurone Disease Assoc 1987-; memb: Carnegy Ctee Community Educn in Scotland 1976-77, Conseille de Rédaction Aménagement et Nature Paris 1979-84; visiting lectr Australian Red Cross Soc 1981, treas Volonteurope 1981-84, Socio de Honor Assoc Geriatrica Valenciana Spain 1983, res assoc Policy Studies Inst London 1984, memb Morrison Ctee Broadcasting and Voluntary Action 1986-87, chm Nat Assoc Volunteer Bureaux 1988-91; panellist Charities Effectiveness Review Tst 1990-; *Recreations* sailing, conversation, travel; *Clubs* Reform, Royal Cwlth Soc; *Style*— Peter Cardy, Esq; Motor Neurone Disease Association, PO Box 246, Northampton NN1 2PR (☎ 0582 794824, 0604 250505)

CARE, Prof Anthony Deuchar; s of Clarence Deuchar Care (d 1984), and Florence Edith, *née* Wills (d 1987); *b* 28 Sept 1928; *Educ* Ilkley GS, Downing Coll Cambridge (MA), Univ of Leeds (PhD, DSc), Univ of Edinburgh (BVMS); *m* 12 July 1958, and Grizel Rosemary Frances, da of Sir John Taylor, KBE, CMG (d 1973); 1 s (Ian Colin Deuchar b 1 May 1960), 2 da (Fiona b 19 Feb 1962, Ailsa b 29 May 1966); *Career* princ scientific offr ARC Inst of Animal Physiology Babraham Cambridge 1961, sr princ scientific offr Rowett Res Inst Bucksburn Aberdeen 1968, prof and head of Dept of Animal Physiology and Nutrition Univ of Leeds 1971; MRCVS 1959; *Recreations* squash, hill walking, gardening; *Style*— Prof Anthony Care; Mill Farm, Mandrowen, Fishguard, Dyfed SA65 9PT; Department of Biochemistry, University College Wales, Aberystwyth SY23 3DD (☎ 0970 828 236, fax 0970 617 172, telex 35181 ABYUCW G)

CARE, Jeffrey; s of David Banfield Care, and Alice Elizabeth, *née* Smart; *b* 2 July 1948; *Educ* Gravesend GS; *m* 1972, Margaret Alacoque, da of late Martin Murray, of Gallanstown House, Chapelizod, Eire; *Career* civil servant Miny of Works 1966-68, librarian Daily Mail 1968-77, civil servant Boundary Commission 1979, chief librarian Observer 1980-; *Books* Observer Sayings of the Eighties (ed, 1989); *Recreations* Dante Studies; *Style*— Jeffrey Care, Esq; Cherry Tree Cottage, Pine Walk, East Horsley, Surrey; Observer, Chelsea Bridge House, Queenstown Rd, London SW8 4NN (☎ 071 350 3420, fax 071 627 5570/1/2)

CAREW, Hon Gavin George; MBE (1945), TD; 2 s of late 5 Baron Carew (d 1927); *b* 21 Sept 1906; *Educ* Clifton; *m* 1932, Aileen Hilda Frances (d 1974), o da of late Ean Francis Cecil, of Hilltop, Sunningdale, Berks; 1 da; *Career* late Maj Co London Yeo; *Style*— The Hon Gavin Carew, MBE, TD; Gellillyndu, Llanio, Tregaron, Dyfed

CAREW, Sir Rivers Verain; 11 Bt (E 1661), of Haccombe, Devon; s of Sir Thomas Palk Carew, 10 Bt (d 1976), and his 2 wife, Phyllis Evelyn, *née* Mayman; *b* 17 Oct 1935; *Educ* St Columba's Coll, Univ of Dublin (MA, BAgrSc Hort); *m* 1968, Susan Babington, yr da of late Harold Babington Hill, of London; 1 s (and 1 s decd), 3 da; *Heir* s, Gerald de Redvers Carew b 24 May 1975; *Career* ed, journalist and author; asst ed Ireland of The Welcomes (Irish Tourist Bd magazine) 1964-67, jt ed The Dublin Magazine 1964-69, journalist Irish TV 1967-, BBC World Serv 1987-; *Books* Figures out of Mist (poems with T Brownlow, 1966); *Recreations* reading, music, reflection; *Style*— Sir Rivers Carew, Bt

CAREW, 6 Baron (I 1834 and UK 1838); William Francis Conolly-Carew; CBE (1966); s of 5 Baron Carew (d 1927); *b* 23 April 1905; *Educ* Wellington, Sandhurst; *m* 1937, Lady Sylvia Gwendoline Eva Maitland, da of 15 Earl of Lauderdale; 2 s, 2 da; *Heir* Hon Patrick Thomas Conolly-Carew; *Career* assumed by Deed Poll 1938 additional surname of Conolly; Maj Duke of Cornwall's LI (ret); former ADC to Govr and C-in-C of Bermuda; former nat chm Br Legion; CStJ; *Clubs* Armyand and Navy, Kildine Street Dublin; *Style*— The Rt Hon the Lord Carew, CBE; Oakville, Donadea, Co Kildare, Eire (☎ 45 69171)

CAREW POLE, Col Sir John Gawen; 12 Bt (E 1628), DSO (1944), TD, JP (Cornwall 1939), DL (1947); s of late Lt-Gen Sir Reginald Pole-Carew, KCB, *qv*, and Lady Beatrice, *née* Butler, er da of 3 Marquess of Ormonde, and kinsman of Sir Frederick Arundell de la Pole, 11 Bt (d 1926); assumed by deed poll 1926 the name of John Gawen Carew Pole in lieu of John Gawen Pole-Carew; *b* 4 March 1902; *Educ* Eton, RMC Sandhurst; *m* 1, 1928, Cynthia Mary Burns, OBE (d 1977), da of Walter Spencer Morgan Burns, of North Mymms Park, Hatfield, Herts; 1 s, 2 da; m 2, 1979, Joan Shirley, da of Rear Adm Charles Maurice Blackman, DSO, of Peak Cottage, Bishop's Waltham, Hants, and wid of Lt-Col (Francis Edgar) Anthony Fulford, and previously of Maj Jocelyn Arthur Persse, Rifle Bde; *Heir* s (John) Richard Walter Reginald Carew Pole; *Career* Coldstream Gds 1923-39, ADC to C-in-C India 1924-25, cmd 5 Bn Duke of Cornwall's Light Infantry TA 1939-43, cmd 2 Devonshire Regt 1944 (Normandy, Belgium, Holland, Germany), Col Second Army HQ 1944-45 (despatches 1945), raised and cmd post-war TA Bn 4/5 Bn DCLI 1946-47, Hon Col 4/5 Bn DCLI (TA) 1958-60, Hon Col DCLI (TA) 1960-67; comptroller to Govr-Gen Union of SA 1935-36; former dir: Lloyds Bank Ltd (and chm Devon and Cornwall Regnl Bd), English China Clays, Keith Prowse, Westward TV Ltd (vice chm); memb Western Region BR; chm Cornwall CC 1946-57, CA 1954-66 Cornwall, High Sheriff 1947-48, Vice-Lt 1950-62, Ld-Lt 1962-77, a Gentleman of HM Bodyguard of the Hon Corps of Gentlemen-at-Arms 1950-72, Standard Bearer 1968-72, memb Prince of Wales's Cncl 1952-68, steward Nat Hunt Ctee 1953-56, memb Jockey Club 1969-; Prime Warden Worshipful Co of Fishmongers' 1969-70; KStJ 1972; Hon LLD Exeter 1979; *Clubs* Army and Navy, Pratt's, MCC; *Style*— Col Sir John Carew Pole, Bt, DSO, TD, DL; Horson House, Torpoint, Cornwall PL11 2PE (☎ 0752 812406)

CAREW POLE, (John) Richard Walter Reginald; s and h of Sir John Gawen Carew Pole, DSO, TD, 12 Bt; *b* 2 Dec 1938; *Educ* Eton, RAC Cirencester; *m* 1, 1966 (m dis 1973), Hon Victoria Marion Ann Lever, da of 3 Viscount Leverhulme; m 2, 1974, Mary, LVO, JP, da of Lt-Col Ronald Dawnay (d 1990); 2 s; *Heir* s Tremayne John Carew Pole; *Career* late Coldstream Gds; memb: Cornwall CC, Devon and Cornwall Ctee, Nat Tst 1978-83; pres Surf Life Saving Assoc of GB 1978-87; High Sheriff of Cornwall 1979; part-time dir SW Electricity Bd 1981-90, regnl dir West of England Building Soc 1989-; pres Royal Cornwall Agric Show 1981, chm Devon and Cornwall Police Authy 1985-87; govr: Seale Hayne Agric Coll 1979-89, Plymouth Coll 1981-; dir Theatre Royal Plymouth 1985-; Cornwall CC: chm Planning and Employment Ctee 1980-84, chm Finance Cmmn 1985-89, chm Property Ctee 1989-; Liveryman Worshipful Co of Fishmongers; *Recreations* walking, travelling, contemporary pictures, gardening; *Clubs* White's, Pratt's; *Style*— Richard Carew Pole, Esq; Antony House, Torpoint, Cornwall PL11 2QA (☎ 0752 814914)

CAREY, Brig Conan Jerome; s of Dr James J Carey (d 1982), and Marion, *née* O'Sullivan (d 1979); *b* 8 Aug 1936; *Educ* Belvedere Coll Dublin, RMA Sandhurst; *m* 27 May 1966, (Elizabeth) Gay, da of Col L R Docker, OBE, MC, TD (d 1980); 1 s (James b 1970), 2 da (Verna b 1967, Philippa b 1981); *Career* cmmnd RASC 1956-: Army Air Corps 1960-65, RCT 1965, RMCS 1967, Staff Coll Camberley 1968, CO 155 RCT (TA) 1976-78, Def Staff Br Embassy Washington DC USA 1979-82, Col 1982, Brig 1985, Dep DG Tport Movements 1985-88; DG Home Farm Tst 1988-; MInstD; FCIT FIPM, FBIM; *Recreations* tennis, golf; *Clubs* Army and Navy, Tracy Park Golf (Bath); *Style*— Brig Conan Carey; The Home Farm Trust Ltd, Merchants House, Wapping Rd, Bristol BS1 4RW (☎ 0272 273746, fax 0272 225938)

CAREY, de Vic Graham; QC (1989); s of Michael Carey (d 1964), of Guernsey, and Jean, *née* Bullen (d 1975); *b* 15 June 1940; *Educ* Cheam Sch, Bryanston, Trinity Hall Cambridge (BA, MA), Caen Univ; *m* 22 June 1968, Bridget, da of Maj John Lindsay Smith (ka 1943); 2 s (Perrin b 1971, Julius b 1980), 2 da (Jenette b 1974, Henrietta b 1979); *Career* slr Supreme Ct of Judicuture 1965, advocate Royal Ct of Guernsey 1966, in private practice 1966-76; Guernsey: HM Slr-Gen 1977-82, HM Attorney-Gen 1982-, HM Receiver-Gen 1985-; people's dep States of Guernsey April-Dec 1976, memb Gen Synod C of E 1982-; *Style*— de Vic Graham Carey, Esq, QC; Les Padins, St Saviours, Guernsey, Channel Islands (☎ 0481 64587); St James Chambers, Guernsey, Channel Islands (☎ 0481 723355)

CAREY, Dennis Charles Peter; *b* 28 July 1931; *Educ* Sherborne, Univ of Cambridge (MA); *m* 1, 1957 (m dis), Ann; m 2, 1972 (m dis), Michele; 1 s, 2 da; *Career* industrialist; md Coates Brothers and Co Ltd 1972-74, Euro vice pres Morton Chemical Co Inc 1975-80; dir: Borthwicks plc 1989- (chief exec 1981-89), Burton Son and Sanders Ltd 1981-, Broadland Foods Ltd; *Recreations* travel, languages; *Style*— D C P Carey, Esq; Borthwicks plc, Priory House, St John's Lane, London EC1M 4BX (☎ 071 253 8661, telex 23716 BOWSTRING)

CAREY, George Leonard; *see*: Bath and Wells, Bishop of

CAREY, Godfrey Mohun Cecil; s of Dr Godfrey Fraser Carey, MVO (d 1972), of Connaught Sq, London, and Prudence Loveday, *née* Webb (d 1977); *b* 31 Oct 1941; *Educ* Eton; *m* 1, 10 July 1965 (m dis 1975), Caroline; 2 s (Sebastian b 1969, d 1971, Hugo b 1972), 1 da (Miranda b 1967); m 2, 1978 (m dis 1985), Dorothy, da of Harold Sturgeon, of Essex; 1 da (Lucy 1 1978); *Career* legal asst Rolls Royce 1966-70; called to the Bar Inner Temple 1969, rec SE Circuit 1986-; *Recreations* tennis, jazz, woodruff; *Clubs* Lansdowne, Annabel's; *Style*— Godfrey Carey, Esq; 40 Walton Street, London SW3 1RD (☎ 071 584 0160); 5 Paper Buildings, Temple, London EC4Y 7HB (☎ 071 583 6117)

CAREY, Prof John; s of Charles William Carey (d 1965), of Barnes, London, and Winifred Ethel, *née* Cook (d 1967); *b* 5 April 1934; *Educ* Richmond and E Sheen County GS, St John's Coll Oxford (MA, DPhil); *m* 1960, Gillian Mary Florence, da of Reginald Booth (d 1968), of Wilmslow, Cheshire; 2 s (Leo b 1974, Thomas b 1977); *Career* 2 Lt E Surrey Regt 1953-54; Harmsworth sr scholar Merton Coll Oxford 1957-58, lectr ChCh Oxford 1958-59, Andrew Bradley jr res fell Balliol Oxford 1959-60; tutorial fell: Keble Coll Oxford 1960-64, St John's Coll Oxford 1964-75; Merton prof of English literature Univ of Oxford 1975-; princ book reviewer Sunday Times 1977-, author of articles in Modern Language Review, Review of English Studies etc; chm judges Booker Prize 1982; FRSL; *Books* The Poems of John Milton (ed with Alastair Fowler, 1968), Milton (1969), The Violent Effigy: a Study of Dickens' Imagination (1973), Thackeray: Prodigal Genius (1977), John Donne: Life, Mind and Art (1981), The Private Memoirs and Confessions of a Justified Sinner (ed, 1981), Original Copy: Selected Reviews and Journalism 1969-1986 (1987), The Faber Book of Reportage (ed, 1987); *Recreations* swimming, gardening, beekeeping; *Style*— Prof John Carey; Brasenose Cottage, Lyneham, Oxon; 57 Stapleton Rd, Headington, Oxford (☎ 0865 64304); Merton Coll, Oxford (☎ 0865 276389)

CAREY, Peter John; s of Percival William (d 1974), and Mollie, *née* Griffin; *b* 17 Aug 1946; *Educ* Haverstock Hill Hampstead, Poly of Central London (Dip in Photography); *m* 1967, Lena Margaret, da of Ernest Sailor; 1 s (Timothy Patrick b 15 Jan 1975), 1 da (Catherine Blossom b 24 July 1972); *Career* freelance photographer 1965-66, sr photographer Summit Studies London 1966-68, estab studio (with Stephen Ward) Carey Ward Ltd Camden London 1968-76 (specialising in advtg photography for maj clients), visiting lectr PCL 1970, freelance photographer 1976-; fndr Photography Summer Sch Swansea 1989-; winner D&AD Poster award Simple as Blinking Kodak; ABIPP 1967, FBIPP 1972, FRPS 1984; *Recreations* to liaise with students on indust to facilitate new blood, volunteer advsr on drug abuse help; *Style*— Peter Carey, Esq; Instantaneous Photographist, 157 Junction Rd, Islington, London N19 5PZ (☎ 071 272 6516)

CAREY, Peter Philip; s of Percival Stanley Carey (d 1984), and Helen Jean Carey; *b* 7 May 1943; *Educ* Geelory GS Australia; *m* 1, (m dis) Leish Westman; m 2, 16 March 1985, Alison Margaret, da of Stanley Newnham Summers (d 1987); 2 s (Sam Summers Carey b 1986, Charley Carey Summers b 1990); *Career* writer; *Books* The Fat Man in History (1979), Bliss (1980), Illywhacker (1985), Oscar and Lucinda (1988), The Tax Inspector (1991); awards: NSW Premier award for Lit 1979, 1980, Miles Franklin award 1980 and 1989, Nat Book Cncl award 1980, 1985, Victorian Premier award 1985, Age Book of the Year award 1985, Booker Prize 1988; DLitt Univ of Queensland 1989; FRSL; *Recreations* swimming; *Style*— Peter Carey, Esq

CAREY, Sir Peter Willoughby; GCB (1982, KCB 1976, CB 1972); s of Jack Delves Carey, of Portsmouth, Hants, and Sophie Carey; *b* 26 July 1923; *Educ* Portsmouth GS, Oriel Coll Oxford; *m* 1946, Thelma, da of John Brigham Young, of Portsmouth; 3 da; *Career* dep sec Cabinet Office 1971; DTI: joined 1972, second perm sec 1973-76, perm sec 1976-83; chm: Dalgety 1986, Morgan Grenfell Group plc 1987-89; *Clubs* United Oxford and Cambridge Univs; *Style—* Sir Peter Carey, GCB; Rose Cottage, 67 Church Rd, Wimbledon, London SW19 (☎ 081 947 5222)

CAREY-EVANS, David Lloyd; OBE (1983), JP (1969), DL (1988); s of Sir Thomas John Carey-Evans MC, FRCS (d 1947), and Lady Olwen Elizabeth, DBE, *née* Lloyd George (d 1990), da of 1 Earl Lloyd George of Dwyfor; *b* 14 Aug 1925; *Educ* Oundle, Univ of Wales (BSc); *m* 14 Nov 1959, Annwen, da of William Williams, of Craig, Llanerchymedd, Anglesey; 3 s (Thomas Robert b 1961, William Lloyd b 1962, Richard Huw b 1968), 1 da (Davina b 1964); *Career* WWII Sub Lt RNVR 1943-46; farmer 1947-; chm: Welsh Cncl NFU 1978-81, Cncl WAOS 1984-; *Clubs* Sloane; *Style—* D L Carey-Evans, Esq, OBE, JP, DL; Eisteddfa, Criccieth, Gwynedd

CAREY-JONES, Norman Stewart; CMG (1965); s of Samuel Carey-Jones (d 1963), of Swansea, and Jessie Isabella Stewart; *b* 11 Dec 1911; *Educ* Monmouth Sch, Merton Coll Oxford (MA); *m* 1946, Stella (d 1990), da of Maj Claud Myles (d 1961), of Cape Town, SA; 2 s (David, Owen); *Career* Colonial Audit Serv 1934-54, Colonial Admin Serv 1954-65, perm sec Miny of Lands and Settlement Kenya 1962-65, dir in devpt admin Univ of Leeds 1965-77; *Books* The Pattern of a Dependent Economy, The Anatomy of Uhuru Politics, Public Enterprise and the Industrial Development Agency; *Clubs* Royal Cwlth Soc; *Style—* Norman Carey-Jones, Esq, CMG; Mawingo, Welsh St Donats, nr Cowbridge, S Glamorgan CF7 7SS (☎ 04463 2841)

CARGILL, Kenneth George; s of George Reid Cargill, of 56 Annfield Drive, Arbroath, Angus, Scotland, and Florence Jean, *née* Mitchell; *b* 17 Feb 1947; *Educ* Arbroath HS, Univ of Edinburgh (MA, LLB); *m* 17 Feb 1987, Una, da of James Gallacher, of Glasgow; *Career* BBC Scotland: researcher 1972-73, TV reporter Current Account 1973-78, film dir current affrs 1978-79, dep ed TV news and current affrs 1984-88 (prodr 1979-84), ed Scotland 2000 1986-87, ed TV news and current affrs 1988-90, head TV news, current affrs and sport 1990; *Clubs* Caledonian; *Style—* Kenneth Cargill, Esq; 1 Victoria Park Corner, Glasgow G14 9NZ (☎ 041 959 3171); BBC Scotland, Broadcasting House, Queen Margaret Drive, Glasgow G12 8DG (☎ 041 330 2250, fax 041 334 0614)

CARINE, Rear Adm James; s of Amos Carine (d 1953), of Castletown, IOM, and Kathleen Prudence, *née* Kelly (d 1986); *b* 14 Sept 1934; *Educ* Victoria Rd Sch Castletown IOM, King William's Coll IOM; *m* 26 Aug 1961, (Carolyn) Sally, da of Surgn Capt Wilfred Bertram Taylor (d 1990), of Alverstoke, Hants; 5 s (Andrew b 1963, Patri b and d 1964, David (twin) b and d 1964, Malcolm b 1965, Gregory b 1984 1 da (Catriona b 1970); *Career* joined RN 1951, sec Second Sea Lord 1979-82, Capt 1980, Saclant HQ Norfolk VA 1982-85, Naval Home Cmd 1985-88, Cdre 1988, in cmd HMS Drake 1988-89, Rear Adm 1989, COS to C in C Naval Home Cmd; Freeman City of London 1988, memb Ct of Assts Worshipful Co of Chartered Secs and Admins; FCIS 1971; Kt of the Order of St Gregory the Great (Civil Div) Rome 1983; *Recreations* dinghy sailing, horse racing; *Clubs* Royal Naval, Royal Albert Sailing (Portsmouth); *Style—* Rear Adm James Carine; Trinity House, HM Naval Base, Portsmouth, Hampshire PO1 3LR (☎ 0705 818370)

CARINGTON, Hon Rupert Francis John; s and h of 6 Baron Carrington; *b* 2 Dec 1948; *Educ* Eton, Univ of Bristol; *m* 12 Sept 1989, Daniela, da of Flavio Diotallevi; 1 s (Robert b 7 Dec 1990); *Style—* The Hon Rupert Carington; 16 Mallord St, London SW3 6DU (☎ 071 376 5626)

CARLESS, Hugh Michael; CMG (1976); s of Henry Alfred Carless, CIE (d 1975), and Gwendolen Mary, *née* Pattullo (d 1989); *b* 22 April 1925; *Educ* Sherborne, SOAS, Trinity Hall Cambridge; *m* 1957, Rosa Maria, da of Martino Frontini, of São Paulo, Brazil; 2 s; *Career* Dip Serv 1950-85; served: Kabul, Rio de Janeiro, Tehran, Budapest, Luanda, Bonn; head of Latin America Dept FCO 1973-77, chargé d'affaires Buenos Aires 1977-80, seconded to Northern Engrg Industs Int 1980-82, ambass to Caracas 1982-85; currently int conslt; exec vice pres Hinduja Fndn, dep chm S Atlantic Cncl; *Recreations* golf; *Clubs* Travellers', Royal Mid Surrey; *Style—* Hugh Carless, Esq, CMG; 15 Bryanston Square, London W1H 7FF

CARLETON-SMITH INGLIS, Lt-Col Dudley Guy; DL (Ayrshire 1972); s of Lt-Col Dudley Lancelot Guy Carleton-Smith; bro of Maj-Gen Michael Edward Carleton-Smith, *qv*; *b* 8 Sept 1918; *Educ* Lancing, Sandhurst and Camberley; *m* 1947, Barbara Anne, da of Air Cdre Henry Le Marchant Brock, CBE (d 1964); 1 s, 1 da; *Career* cmmnd Royal Scots Fusiliers 1939, Lt-Col Madagascar, N Africa, Sicily, Italy and Palestine; served 2 and 4/5 Bns RSF and on staff XIII Corps HQ 8 Army, War Office and MOD as memb personal staff of CDS; cmd 4/5 Bn RSF (TA) 1960-62; cncllr: Royal Burgh of Ayr 1967, Baillie 1968; ret 1972; *Style—* Lt-Col Dudley Carleton-Smith Inglis, DL; Dooncroft, Doonfoot, Ayrshire

CARLETON-SMITH, Maj Gen Michael Edward; CBE (1979, MBE 1966); s of Lt-Col Dudley Lancelot Guy Carleton-Smith (himself gggs (through female line) of Gen Sir Guy Carleton, KB, 1 Baron Dorchester who was first Lt-Govr of Canada 1766-70) and Barbara Leticia Camilla, *née* Popham (d 1980), descended from Rear Adm Sir Home Popham, who captured Buenos Aires 1807 (with William Beresford, later Viscount Beresford), becoming C-in-C on the Jamaica Station until his death in 1820; *b* 5 May 1931; *Educ* Radley, RMA Sandhurst (psc, jssc), NDC, RCDS; *m* 1963, Helga Katja, da of Josef Stoss (d 1973); 3 s; *Career* Cdr Gurkha Field Force Hong Kong 1977-79, dep dir staff duties MOD 1981-82, Maj-Gen def advsr and mil advsr Canberra Aust and mil advsr Wellington NZ 1982-85; DG Marie Curie Fndn 1985-; chm Marie Curie Trading Co Ltd; *Recreations* riding, gardening; *Style—* Maj-Gen Michael Carleton-Smith, CBE; 28 Belgrave Square, London SW1

CARLIER, Maj-Gen (Anthony) Neil; OBE (1982); s of Geoffrey Anthony George Carlier (d 1966), and Sylvia Maude, *née* Emerson; *b* 11 Jan 1937; *Educ* Highgate Sch, RMA Sandhurst, RMCS (BSc), RCDS; *m* 18 May 1974, Daphne Kathleen, da of Capt Langley Humphreys, of Church View, Coombe Cross, Bovey Tracey, S Devon; 1 s (Christopher b 18 May 1975), 1 da (Donna b 27 June 1980); *Career* cmmnd RE 1957, RMCS 1958-61, Troop Cdr RE 1961-63, GS03 1964-65, instr RMA Sandhurst 1966-69, RNC and Army Staff Coll Shrivenham 1970-71, GS02 RN 1972-73, Sqdn Cdr 50 Field Sqdn 1974-75, 2 i/c 2 Armd Div Engr Regt 1976-77, CO 39 Engr Regt 1978-79, MA to Army Bd Memb (MGO) 1980-82, Col ASD 2 MOD 1982-83, Cdr 11 Engr Gp 1984-85, RCDS 1986, Cdr Br Forces Falkland Islands 1987-88, Chief Jt Servs Liaison Orgn Bonn 1989-90, head Logistic Support Review 1991; Capt Army Team Round the World Yacht Race 1977-78, Flag Offr Army Sailing Assoc 1978-87, Cdre RE YC 1984-87; MIRE of RE 1958; *Recreations* sailing (offshore), fly fishing, DIY, gardening; *Clubs* Int Soc of Cape Horners, RHS; *Style—* Maj-Gen Neil Carlier, OBE; Warren House, Doras Green, Ewshot, Farnham, Surrey GU10 5BL (☎ 0252 850 303)

CARLILE, Alexander Charles; QC, MP (Lib) Montgomery 1983-; s of Erwin Falik, MD, and Sabina Falik; *b* 12 Feb 1948; *Educ* Epsom Coll Surrey, King's Coll London (LLB), Inns of Court Sch of Law; *m* 1968, Frances, da of Michael Soley; 3 da; *Career* Parly candidate (Lib) Flintshire E: Feb 1974, 1979; chm Welsh Lib Pty 1980-82, Lib Democrats spokesman on Trade and Indust; rec Crown Ct, lay memb GMC, memb Advsy Cncl on Pub Records, vice chm GB E Europe Centre; AKC; *Clubs* Reform, National Liberal, Bristol Channel Yacht; *Style—* Alexander Carlile Esq, QC, MP; House of Commons, London SW1

CARLILE, Lady; Katharine Elizabeth Mary; *née* Field; o da of Rev George Hawkes Field (d 1954), Rector of Milton Keynes, Bletchley, Bucks, and Frances Georgiana, *née* Cadogan (d 1970); *b* 11 Nov 1908; *m* 1, 30 Nov 1940, as his 2 w, Sir (William) Walter Carlile, 1 and last Bt (d 1950); m 2, 24 April 1973, as his 2 w, Geoffrey Dover (d 1984), s of Thomas Dover; has reverted to her former style; *Career* JP Bucks 1948-78; *Recreations* natural history; *Style—* Lady Carlile; The Old Cottage, Gayhurst, Newport Pagnell, Bucks MK16 8LG (☎ 0908 55248)

CARLILL, Rear Adm John Hildred; OBE (1969); s of Dr Hildred Bertram Carlill (d 1942), and Mildred Constance, *née* Godfrey (d 1984); *b* 24 Oct 1925; *Educ* RNC Dartmouth; *m* 1955, (Elizabeth) Ann, da of Lt-Col Willis Southern (d 1968), of Guildford, Surrey; 3 da (Jennifer, Gale, Joanne); *Career* RN 1939-82; serv WWII: HMS Mauritius 1943-45, Med, Normandy, N Atlantic, Arctic; psc 1961, jssc 1967, Capt 1972, sec to Flag Offr Naval Air Cmd, dir Naval Manning and Trg (S) MOD, sec to Second Sea Lord MOD, pres Admty Interview Bd, Cdre HMS Drake, Rear Adm 1980, Adm Pres RN Coll Greenwich; sec The Engrg Cncl 1983-87; *Recreations* walking, skiing, DIY, gardening, water colour painting; *Style—* Rear Adm John Carlill, OBE; Crownpits Barn, Crownpits Lane, Godalming, Surrey GU7 1NY (☎ 0483 415022)

CARLINE, Gordon David; s of David Smith Carline (d 1961), and Helen Louise, *née* Carpenter (d 1941); *b* 25 June 1933; *Educ* BEC GS, Westminster Tech Coll London; *m* 14 Aug 1954, Doreen Margaret, da of Albert Edward Brown (d 1941); 1 s (David Stuart b 1961), 1 da (Denise Elizabeth b 1959); *Career* trainee draughtsman Laidlaw Smith 1949-51; draughtsman/designer: Johnson Ireton 1951-54, Moore and Tucker 1954-55; engr John F Farquharson and Ptnrs 1955-61, ptnr Andrews Kent and Stone 1972- (engr 1961-65, assoc 1965-72); FIStructE 1959, FICE 1966, FCIOB 1979, FFS 1963 (pres 1986-87), MWeldI 1959, ACIArB 1977, FRS 1987, FIHospE 1972; *Recreations* reading; *Clubs* Clarendon (Oxford); *Style—* Gordon Carline, Esq, FRS; Chaumont, 55 Clifden Rd, Worminghall, nr Aylesbury, Bucks HP18 9JR (☎ 0844 339209); Andrews Kent & Stone, Seacourt Tower, West Way, Botley, Oxford OX2 0JJ (☎ 0865 240071, fax 0865 248 006, car 0860 531 586)

CARLING, William David Charles (Will); *b* 12 Dec 1965; *Educ* Univ of Durham; *Career* Rugby Union centre three quarter Harlequins FC and England (21 caps); clubs: Durham Univ RFC, Harlequins FC; England: debut v France 1988, tour Aust and Fiji (3 test appearances) 1988-89; *Recreations* painting, sketching; *Style—* Will Carling, Esq; Harlequins FC, Stoop Memorial Ground, Craneford Way, Twickenham, Middlesex (☎ 081 892 0822)

CARLISLE, Anthony Edwin Charles Glen; s of George Geddes Glen Carlisle (d 1980), and Dorothy Louise, *née* Pickering; *b* 10 March 1947; *Educ* Charterhouse, Univ of Sussex (BA); *m* Nancy Susan, *née* Hayward; *Career* Lintas Advertising 1968-70, dir, chief exec and dep chm Dewe Rogerson Ltd 1986 (joined 1970); Freeman: City of London, Worshipful Co of Glovers; MIPA, memb PRCA; *Recreations* travel, books, music, wine; *Style—* Anthony Carlisle, Esq; Dewe Rogerson Ltd, 3 1/2 London Wall Building, London Wall, London EC2M 5SY (☎ 071 638 9571)

CARLISLE, Brian Apcar ; CBE (1974), DSC (1945); 2 s of Capt Frederick Montagu Methven Carlisle, MC (d 1973); *b* 27 Dec 1919; *Educ* Harrow, CCC Cambridge; *m* 1953, Elizabeth Hazel Mary, da of Cdr J A Binnie, RN (d 1945); 1 s, 3 da; *Career* served WWII Lt RNVR (HMS Hood and subsequently destroyers); Sudan Political Serv 1946-54, Royal Dutch/Shell Gp 1955-74, regnl co-ordinator Oil and Gas ME, conslt Lloyds Bank 1975-80, dir Home Oil UK Ltd 1977-80, chm Saxon Oil plc 1980-85; chm Govrs Gordons Sch W End Woking; *Clubs* Athenaeum; *Style—* Brian Carlisle Esq, CBE, DSC; Heath Cottage, Hartley Wintney, Hants (☎ 025 126 2224)

CARLISLE, 12 Earl of (E 1661); Charles James Ruthven Howard; MC (1945), DL (Cumbria 1984); also Viscount Howard of Morpeth, Baron Dacre of Gillesland (both E 1661) and 12 Lord Ruthven of Freeland (S 1651) (suc mother, Lady Ruthven of Freeland, who m as her 2 husb 1 Viscount Monckton of Brenchley and d 1982); s of 11 Earl (d 1963, whose ancestor, 1 Earl, was gggs of 4 Duke of Norfolk), and Lady Ruthven of Freeland; *b* 21 Feb 1923; *Educ* Eton; *m* 3 Oct 1945, Hon Ela Hilda Aline, *née* Beaumont (*see* Carlisle, Countess of); 2 s, 2 da; *Heir* Viscount Morpeth; *Career* late Lt Rifle Bde; former forestry cmmr; chartered surveyor; FRICS; *Clubs* Boodle's, Pratt's; *Style—* The Rt Hon the Earl of Carlisle, MC; Naworth Castle, Brampton, Cumberland (☎ 06977 2621)

CARLISLE, Countess of; Hon Ela Hilda Aline; *née* Beaumont; da of 2 Viscount Allendale, KG, CB, CBE, MC (d 1956); *b* 27 May 1925; *m* 1945, 12 Earl of Carlisle, *qv*; 2 s, 2 da; *Career* OStJ; *Style—* The Rt Hon the Countess of Carlisle; Naworth Castle, Brampton, Cumberland

CARLISLE, Hon Mrs (Elizabeth Mary); *née* McLaren; er da of 2 Baron Aberconway, CBE (d 1953); *b* 31 May 1911; *m* 9 June 1938, Maj Kenneth Ralph Malcolm Carlisle (d 1983); 1 s (Kenneth Carlisle, MP, *qv*), 3 da (Christabel b 1939, m 1965 Sir James Watson, Bt, *qv*; Katharine (twin with Kenneth) b 1941, m 1970 Victor Newell; Barbara b 1951); *Career* over fifty years in St John Ambulance Bde; SSStJ 1974; *Style—* The Hon Mrs Carlisle; 7 Laurie House, Airlie Gdns, London W8 (☎ 071 229 1714); Wyken Hall, Stanton, Bury St Edmunds, Suffolk IP31 2DW (☎ 0359 50240)

CARLISLE, Esmé, Countess of; Esmé Mary Shrubb; da of Charles Edward Iredell; *b* 7 Feb 1914; *Educ* St Paul's Girls Sch, Bedford Coll London; *m* 1947, as his 2 w, 11 Earl of Carlisle (d 1963); 1 da (Lady Susan Ankaret de Meyer); *Career* special duties Civil Service (London, Aden, Athens, Cairo, Algiers and Rome) 1936-44, Western Dept Foreign Office 1944-46, conslt and sec to Working Parties Museums and Galleries Cmmn 1971-86 (actg sec to Cmmn Feb-July 1976); *Style—* The Rt Hon Esmé, Countess of Carlisle; West Wing, Duns Tew Manor, Oxford OX5 4JS (☎ 0869 40721)

CARLISLE, Hugh Bernard Harwood; QC (1978); s of William Harwood Carlisle (d 1979), and Joyce Carlisle; *b* 14 March 1937; *Educ* Oundle, Downing Coll Cambridge (MA); *m* 1964, Veronica Marjorie, da of George Arthur Worth, MBE, DL, of Manton, Rutland; 1 s, 1 da; *Career* Nat Serv 2 Lt RA; called to the Bar Middle Temple 1961, jr treasy counsel (personal injuries cases) 1975-78, inspr Dept of Trade Inquiry into Bryanston Finance Ltd 1978-87, memb Criminal Injuries Bd 1982-, rec S E Circuit 1983-, inspr Dept of Trade Inquiry into Milbury plc 1985-87; *Recreations* fishing, croquet; *Clubs* Garrick, Hurlingham (chm 1982-85); *Style—* Hugh Carlisle Esq, QC; 1 Temple Gardens, London EC4Y 9BB (☎ 071 583 1315)

CARLISLE, John Russell; MP (C) North Luton 1987-; s of Andrew Russell Carlisle (d 1967), and Edith Carlisle (d 1964); *b* 28 Aug 1942; *Educ* Bedford Sch, St Lawrence Coll Ramsgate, Univ of London; *m* 1964, Anthea Jane Lindsay, da of Cedric May; 2 da; *Career* memb London Corn Exchange 1970-, former treas Br/Gibraltar Gp, sec SA Gp (chm 1987-); dir Granfin Agriculture Ltd 1979-86; MP (C): Luton W 1979-87, Luton N 1983-; vice chm Parly All Party Football Ctee, non-exec dir Bletchley Motor Group plc, chm Cons Back Bench Sports Ctee 1981-; pres: Luton 100 Club, Luton Band; govr Sports Aid Fndn (Eastern Area), memb Select Ctee on Agric 1986-88;

Recreations watching sport; *Clubs* Farmers', Rugby, MCC, XL; *Style*— John Carlisle, Esq, MP; House of Commons, London SW1A 0AA

CARLISLE, Kenneth Melville; MP (C) Lincoln 1979-; s of Maj Kenneth Ralph Malcolm Carlisle, TD (d 1983), and Hon Mrs Carlisle, *qv*; *b* 25 March 1941; *Educ* Harrow, Magdalen Coll Oxford; *m* July 1986, Carla, da of A W Heffner, of Maryland USA; 1 s (Sam Fenimore Cooper b 28 Jan 1989); *Career* with Brooke Bond Liebig 1966-74; called to the Bar 1965; farmer; government whip 1987; Parly under-sec Miny of Defence 1990-; *Style*— Kenneth Carlisle, Esq, MP; Wyken Hall, Stanton, Bury St Edmunds, Suffolk (☎ 0359 50240)

CARLISLE, Sir (John) Michael; s of John Hugh Carlisle (d 1958), and Lilian Amy, *née* Smith (d 1990); *b* 16 Dec 1929; *Educ* King Edward VII Sch Sheffield, Univ of Sheffield (BEng); *m* 1957, Mary Scott, da of Robert Magnus Young (d 1972); 1 s (Andrew b 1962), 1 da (Janet b 1960); *Career* pres Sheffield Jr C of C 1967-68; memb Cncl: Sheffield C of C 1967-79, Prodn Engrg Res Assoc 1968-73; chm: Sheffield Productivity Assoc 1970, N Sheffield Univ Hosp Mgmnt Ctee 1971-74, Sheffield Area Health Authy (teaching) 1974-82, Sheffield Health Authy 1982; memb: Bd of Govrs Utd Sheffield Hosps 1972-74, Sheffield Univ Careers Advsy Bd 1973-82; govr: Sheffield City Poly 1979-82 (hon fell 1977), Sheffield HS 1980-87; dir Torday and Carlisle plc; non-exec dir: Fenchurch (Midlands), Norhomes plc; former dir: Diesel Marine Int and gp subsid cos (Norway, Holland, Greece, Singapore, and Hong Kong), Eric Woodward (Electrical) Ltd; memb Cncl and Ct Univ of York 1990-; memb Ct: Univ of Sheffield, Univ of Nottingham; chm Trent Regnl Health Authy 1982; Hon LLD Univ of Sheffield 1988; Freeman Worshipful Co of Cutlers Hallamshire; FRSA, FIMechE, FIMarE, CBIM; kt 1985; *Recreations* golf, walking in N Yorkshire, watercolour painting; *Clubs* Sickleholme Golf, Kirbymoorside Golf; *Style*— Sir Michael Carlisle; 7 Rushley Ave, Dore, Sheffield S17 3EP; St Ovins, Lastingham, N Yorks YO6 6TL; Trent RHA, Fulwood House, Sheffield S10 3TH (☎ 0742 630300, fax 0742 306956)

CARLISLE OF BUCKLOW, Baron (Life Peer UK 1987), of Mobberley, Co Cheshire; Mark Carlisle; PC (1979), QC (1971), DL (Cheshire 1983); 2 s of late Philip Edmund Carlisle, of Alderley Edge, Cheshire, and Mary Carlisle; *b* 7 July 1929; *Educ* Radley, Univ of Manchester (LLB); *m* 1959, Sandra Joyce, da of John Hamilton Des Voeux (d 1963), of St Ives, Cornwall; 1 da (Hon Vanessa Lucy); *Career* called to the Bar Gray's Inn 1954, bencher 1980; rec of the Crown Court 1976-79 and 1981-; Parly under sec of state Home Office 1970-72, min of state Home Office 1972-74, sec of state for Educn and Science 1979-81; chm: Criminal Injuries Compensation Bd 1989-, Review Ctee on the Parole System in England and Wales 1988; *Style*— The Rt Hon Lord Carlisle of Bucklow, PC, QC, DL; Queen Elizabeth Building, Temple, London EC4 (☎ 071 583 5766); 3 Holt Gardens, Mobberley, Cheshire (☎ 056 587 2275)

CARLOW, Viscount; Charles George Yuill Seymour Dawson-Damer; eldest s and h of 7 Earl of Portarlington; *b* 6 Oct 1965; *Educ* Eton, Univ of Edinburgh (MA); *Career* page of honour to HM The Queen 1979-81; *Style*— Viscount Carlow; 19 Coolong Rd, Vaucluse, NSW 2030, Aust; c/o Yuills Ltd, Bride House, 18-20 Bride Lane, London EC4Y 8DX; c/o John Swire & Sons Ltd, GPO Box 1, Hong Kong

CARLTON, Vivienne Margaret; da of John Carlton, and Phyllis Florence Kaye, *née* Minchin; *b* 28 Sept 1947; *Educ* Herts & Essex HS Bishop's Stortford, Trent Park Coll, Univ of London; *m* 1985, Julian Charles Bray; 1 s (William Charles b 18 Aug 1989); *Career* account dir: Biss Lancaster plc 1980-82, Opus PR Ltd 1982-84; dir: Osca plc 1985-86, Leadenhall Assoc Ltd 1986-, ITN Television News Ltd 1988-; MIPR, MInstD; *Recreations* theatre, interior design, reading; *Style*— Ms Vivienne Carlton; Leadenhall Associates Ltd, Lindsey House, 40/42 Charterhouse Street, London, EC1M 6JH (☎ 071 253 5523)

CARLTON-PORTER, Robert William; s of Francis William Porter, of Derbyshire, and Cyrilla, *née* Carlton; *b* 29 Nov 1944; *Educ* St Helens Derby; *m* 9 Oct 1987, Angela, da of William Jenkins, of Ledbury, Herefordshire; 1 s (Alexander William b 8 Aug 1988); *Career* fin dir: Hoechst UK Ltd 1973-83, EEC Group plc 1983-; chm ECC Overseas Investments Ltd 1983-, pres English China Clays Inc (USA) 1983-, dir and chm Assoc of Corp Treas, non-exec dir Western Trust & Savings Ltd, non-exec dir Cornwall Enterprise Board Ltd; memb Stock Exchange Pre-emption Ctee; ACIB 1968, MInstM 1973, FBIM 1976, FCT 1979 (fndn fell); *Recreations* antiques, philately, gardening, Nat Kidney Res Fund; *Style*— Robert Carlton-Porter, Esq; ECC Group plc, 125 Wood St, London EC2V 7AQ (☎ 071 696 9229, fax 071 696 9269)

CARLYLE, Nigel Stewart; s of Thomas Edward Carlyle (d 1982), of Scothern, Lincoln, and Gertrude Ellen, *née* Strutt; *b* 14 July 1938; *Educ* Queen Elizabeth Boys' GS Mansfield, Univ of Leeds (LLB); *m* 22 Sept 1962, Susan Margaret, da of Capt John Hugh Storey (d 1975), of Harrogate; 2 s (Nicholas Stuart b 1963, Jonathan Stuart b 1967), 2 da (Helen Margaret b 1965, Kathryn Margaret b 1970); *Career* slr; John Barran Ltd 1968-69, mangr of fin analysis Rolls Royce Motors Ltd 1971-73, sr ptnr Hodgson Carlyle and Co Slrs 1979-; memb Cncl Lincolnshire Law Soc 1985-89, chm Lincoln Ramblers Assoc, Scothern CC, treas Lincoln Branch Gideons Int 1985-; FICA; *Recreations* rambling, badminton, classical music; *Style*— Nigel S Carlyle, Esq; Churchside House, Scothern, Lincoln LN2 2UA (☎ 0673 62412); Epton & Co, Slrs, 2 Bank St, Lincoln LN2 1DR

CARMAN, George Alfred; QC (1971); o s of Alfred George Carman, of Blackpool, and late Evelyn Carman; *b* 6 Oct 1929; *Educ* St Joseph's Coll Blackpool, Balliol Coll Oxford (BA); *m* 1, 1960 (m dis 1976), Cecilia Sparrow; 1 s; m 2, 1976 (m dis 1984), Frances Elizabeth, da of Thomas Venning, MBE, of Ilkley, N Yorks; *Career* acting Capt RAEC 1948-49; called to the Bar Lincoln's Inn 1953, recorder of the Crown Court 1972, bencher Lincoln's Inn 1978; *Clubs* Garrick; *Style*— George Carman, Esq, QC; chambers: New Court, Temple, London EC4 (☎ 071 583 6166)

CARMICHAEL; *see*: Gibson-Craig-Carmichael

CARMICHAEL, Andrew James; s of James Horsfall Elliott Carmichael, MD, FRCR, DMRD, of Liverpool, and Maureen Catherine McGowan, JP, *née* McGowan; *b* 8 Aug 1957; *Educ* St Edwards Coll Liverpool, Downing Coll Cambridge (MA); *Career* articled clerk Linklaters & Paines 1979, slr 1981, ptnr Linklaters & Paines 1987; special min of St Thomas More Catholic Church; *Recreations* cooking, theatre; *Style*— Andrew Carmichael, Esq; 69 Therapia Rd, London SE22 0SD (☎ 081 693 4432); Linklaters & Paines, Barrington House, 59-67 Gresham St, London EC2V 7JA

CARMICHAEL, Ian Gillett; s of Arthur Denholm Carmichael (d 1958), of North Ferriby, N Humberside, and Kate, *née* Gillett (d 1962); *b* 18 June 1920; *Educ* Scarborough Coll, Bromsgrove Sch, RADA; *m* 6 Oct 1943, Jean Pyman (d 1983), da of Donald Pyman MacLean (d 1970), of Sleights, Yorks; 2 da (Carol Lee (Mrs West) b 2 April 1946, Sally Maclean (Mrs Hennen) b 9 Sept 1949); *Career* WWII served 22 Dragoons, Maj NW Europe (despatches); film, theatre, TV and radio actor; TV performances incl: The World of Wooster, Lord Peter Wimsey; Hon DLitt Univ of Hull 1987; *Books* Will the Real Ian Carmichael...(autobiography, 1979); *Recreations* gardening, walking, reading; *Clubs* MCC; *Style*— Ian Carmichael, Esq; c/o London Management, 235/241 Regent St, London W1A 2JT (☎ 071 493 1610)

CARMICHAEL, Ian Leslie; s of Henry Carmichael (d 1972), of Hilton House, Claines, Worcester, and Alice Muriel, *née* Brown; *b* 4 Oct 1941; *Educ* Oundle, Univ of Wales (BSc); *m* 29 Jan 1966, Myra Phillips, da of Myrfyn Reginald Jones (d 1980), of 10A Mount Pleasant, Troedyrhiw, Mid Glam, South Wales; 1 s (Edward), 2 da (Annabel, Camilla); *Career* graduate trainee Rootes Group 1963-64, pa to MD Dodge Trucks (UK) Ltd 1964-66, pa to Prodn Dir Commercial Vehicle Div Chrysler (UK) Ltd 1966-67 (pa to Dir Diversified Prods 1967-69), dir and gen mangr Mfrg Div Carmichael & Sons Ltd 1975-77 (sales mangr 1969-75), chm and md Carmichael Holdings Ltd 1977-; govr and a six master Royal GS Worcester, chm Worcs Assoc, treas Worcs Hunt, vice prodr Worcs Horses; MIMechE 1964; *Recreations* skiing, riding, tennis; *Clubs* Ski Club of GB, Worcestershire Hunt; *Style*— Ian Carmichael, Esq; Morton Hall, Holberrow Green, Redditch, Worcs B96 6SJ (☎ 0386 792244); Carmichael Holdings Ltd, Gregory's Mill St, Worcester WR3 8BE (☎ 0905 21381, fax 0905 20596, car 0836 28 telex 0905 338039)

CARMICHAEL, James; s of James Carmichael (d 1976), of Glasgow, and Margaret, *née* Pettigrew (d 1970); *b* 14 July 1933; *Educ* Whitehill Sch Glasgow, Glasgow Coll of Printing, London Coll of Printing; *m* 28 June 1958, Isabelle Pettigrew, da of William Barr (d 1979), of Glasgow; 3 s (Alistair James b 1959, Gordon William b 1962, Andrew David b 1965); *Career* md: The Cavendish Press Ltd 1972-, The Cavendish Collection Ltd 1977-; chm Fotofit Ltd 1987; dir: Clondalkin Group (UK) Ltd 1988-, A & P Burt & Sons Ltd 1988-; chm Leicester Guild of Printers, past pres Publicity Assoc of Leicester 1984; *Recreations* golf, bridge, gardening; *Clubs* National Liberal; *Style*— James Carmichael, Esq; Linwood House, Willoughby Waterleys, Leicestershire LE8 3UD (☎ 0533 478 313); Gibson Place, St Andrews, Fife (☎ 0334 76240)

CARMICHAEL, Sir John; KBE (1955); s of late Thomas Carmichael, of Kinburn Terrace, St Andrews, and Margaret Doig Coupar; *b* 22 April 1910; *Educ* Madras Coll St Andrews, Univ of St Andrews, Michigan Univ; *m* 1940, Cecilia Macdonald, da of late Joseph Edwards, of Kingask, St Andrews; 1 s, 3 da; *Career* entered Sudan Civil Serv 1936, under sec Min of Fin Sudan Govt 1955-59, memb Br delegation to 19 UN 1959, chm Herring Advsy Bd 1960-63, dep chm Ind TV Authy (acting chm 1963), former dep chm and chief exec Fison's 1961-68; dir: Royal Bank of Scot 1960-80, Abbey National Building Soc 1968-81; chm Sidlaw Industry Ltd 1970-80, memb Scot Devpt Advsy Bd 1972-82, cncllr EEC Social and Econ Ctee 1972-74; capt Royal and Ancient Golf Club 1974-75, chm St Andrews Link Tst 1983-88; *Clubs* Royal and Ancient Golf, Augusta Nat Golf, Pine Valley Golf, Hon Co of Edinburgh Golfers; *Style*— Sir John Carmichael, KBE; Hayston Park, Balmullo, St Andrews, Fife (☎ 0334 870 268)

CARMICHAEL, Keith Stanley; CBE (1981); s of Stanley Carmichael (d 1949), of Bristol, and Ruby Dorothy, *née* Fox (d 1980); *b* 5 Oct 1929; *Educ* Charlton House Sch, Bristol GS; *m* 1958, Cynthia Mary, da of John David Robert Jones (d 1971); 1 s (Richard John Carmichael b 1968); *Career* qualified CA 1951, ptnr Wilson Bigg and Co 1957-69; dir: H Foulks Lynch & Co Ltd 1957-69, Radio Rentals Ltd 1967-69; sole practitioner 1968-81 and firm 1990, managing partner Longcrofts 1981-90; memb Monopolies and Merger Cmmn 1983-, Lloyd's underwriter 1979-90; pres Hertsmere Cons Assoc; chm Bd of Govrs and Tstees of Rickmansworth Masonic Sch; memb Editorial Bd Simons Taxes 1970-82; FCA, FInstD, FTII; *Books* Spicer and Peglers Income Tax (1965), Corporation Tax (1966), Capital Gains Tax (1966); Ranking Spicer and Peglers Executorship Law and Accounts (ed, 1965-87), Taxation of Lloyds Underwriters (with P Wolstenholme, 1988), Strategic Tax Planning (contrib, 1989); *Recreations* gardening, reading, golf, tennis; *Clubs* Carlton, MCC, Lord's Taveners, City of London; *Style*— Keith Carmichael, Esq, CBE; 117 Newberries Ave, Radlett, Herts WD7 7EN (☎ 0293 855098); 26 Great Queen St, London WC2B 5BP (☎ 071 404 1255, fax 071 404 1256)

CARMICHAEL, Peter; CBE (1981); s of Robert Carmichael (d 1986), of Perthshire, and Elizabeth Paterson (d 1987); *b* 26 March 1933; *Educ* Univ of Glasgow (BSc, DSc); *m* 1 (m dis); 2 s (Colin David b 1957, Angus Robert b 1961), 4 da (Sheena Elizabeth b 1956, Fiona Helen b 1959, Morag Isobel b 1964, Heather Jane b 1967); m 2, June 1980, da of Ronald D Philip, of Perthshire; *Career* design engr Ferranti Ltd 1958-65; Hewlett-Packard: project ldr 1965-68, prodn engrg mangr 1968-69, quality assur mangr 1969-72, R and D mangr 1972-74, mfrg mangr 1974-75, gen mangr 1975-78, jt md 1978-81; dir of small business and electronics Scottish Devpt Agency 1981-87, exec dir for E of Scotland Scottish Devpt Agency i/c instrument design (which won Queen's award to Indust 1967) 1987-89, non-exec chm Hillhouse Holdings 1989-; chm: Wolfson Microelectronics 1990-, Esmée Fairbairn Res Centre Heriot-Watt Univ 1990-; specialist in antique clocks and barometers 1989-; *Recreations* music, gardening, antique clock restoration; *Style*— Peter Carmichael, Esq, CBE; 86 Craiglea Drive, Edinburgh EH10 5PH (☎ 031 447 6334); Craiglea Clocks, 88 Comiston Rd, Edinburgh EH10 5QJ (☎ 031 452 8568)

CARMICHAEL, Maj Peter Oliphant; JP (Perthshire 1962), DL (1966); s of late Col James Louis Carmichael, TD, JP (d 1953), of Arthurstone, Perthshire; *b* 25 Aug 1921; *Educ* Stowe, Peterhouse Cambridge, RAC Cirencester; *m* 1948, Pamela Muriel, da of Col Maurice James Hartley Wilson, OBE (d 1977), of Ashmore; 3 s, 1 da; *Career* served with 79 (Scottish Horse) Medium Regt RA 1942-45, with Scottish Horse RAC TA 1951-61; *Clubs* New (Edinburgh); *Style*— Maj Peter Carmichael, JP, DL; Little Arthurstone, Coupar Angus, Blairgowrie, Perthshire PH13 9EV (☎ 0828 27430)

CARMICHAEL OF KELVINGROVE, Baron (Life Peer UK 1983), of Camlachie in the Dist of the City of Glasgow; Neil George Carmichael; s of James Carmichael (d 1966, former MP Glasgow Bridgeton); *b* 1921,Oct; *Educ* Eastbank Acad Glasgow, Royal Coll of Science and Technology Glasgow; *m* 1948, Catherine McIntosh, da of John Dawson Rankin, of Glasgow; 1 da (Hon Mrs Sharpe); *Career* memb Glasgow Corp 1962; MP (Lab): Glasgow Woodside 1962-74, Glasgow Kelvingrove 1974-83; PPS to Min of Technol 1966-67; Parly sec to Min of Technol and Power 1969-70; Parly under-sec of state: Miny of Tport 1967-69, DOE 1974-75, DOI 1975-76; memb Select Ctee on Tport 1980-83; *Style*— The Rt Hon the Lord Carmichael of Kelvingrove; 53 Partick Hill Rd, Glasgow G11 5AB (☎ 041 334 1718)

CARNAC; see Rivett-Carnac

CARNARVON, 7 Earl of (GB 1793); Henry George Reginald Molyneux Herbert; KCVO (1982), KBE (1976), DL (Hants 1965); also Baron Porchester (GB 1780); o s of 6 Earl (d 1987) and his 1 w Anne Catherine Tredick, *née* Wendell; *b* 19 Jan 1924; *Educ* Eton, RAC Cirencester (DipAg); *m* 7 Jan 1956, Jean Margaret, er da of Hon Oliver Malcolm Wallop (s of 8 Earl of Portsmouth); 2 s (Lord Porchester, Hon Henry Malcolm b 1959), 1 da (Lady Carolyn Penelope b 1962); *Heir* s, Lord Porchester, *qv*; *Career* late Lt Royal Horse Gds, Hon Col 115 (Hants Fortress) Engineer Regt (TA) 1963-67; appointed racing mangr to HM The Queen 1969; pres Thoroughbred Breeders' Assoc 1969-74 and 1986- (chm 1964-66), chm Agric Res Cncl 1978-82, vice pres Game Res Assoc 1967 (chm and fndr memb 1960-67), memb Game Conservancy 1967-, chm Stallion Advsy Ctee to Betting Levy Bd 1974-, memb Nat Stud Advsy Panel 1986, pres Royal Agric Soc 1980-81; CC Hants 1954: Alderman 1965-74, vice chm 1971-74, chm 1973-77; vice chm CC's Assoc 1972-74; chm: S E Econ Planning Cncl 1971-79, Sports Cncl Planning Ctee 1965-70; pres Hants and IOW Naturalist Tst 1987-; chm: Newbury Racecourse plc 1985-, Equine Virology Res Fndn 1986-, Basingstoke and N Hants Med Tst 1981-; memb: Nature Conservancy Cncl 1953-66, Forestry Cmmn 1967-70; Verderer of the New Forest 1961-65, High

Steward of Winchester 1977; memb Jockey Club (chm Race Planning Ctee 1967-84); pres: Amateur Riders Assoc 1970-76, Hants Assoc for the Care of the Blind 1975-, Bas Sports Tst 1983-86 (chm 1970-82); hon fell Portsmouth Poly 1976; Hon DSc Reading 1980; *Clubs* White's, Portland, Hants CC (pres 1966-68), S Wales Hunts Cricket (hon memb); *Style—* The Rt Hon the Earl of Carnarvon, KCVO, KBE, DL; Milford Lake House, Burghclere, Newbury, Berks RG15 9EL (☎ 0635 253387)

CARNE, Dr Christopher Alan; s of Colin Ewing Carne, of London, and Philippa, *née* Trouton; *b* 31 Oct 1953; *Educ* Bryanston, Middx Hosp Med Sch (MB BS), Univ of London (MD, MRCP); *Career* lectr genito-urinary med Middx Hosp Medical Sch 1984-87, conslt genito-urinary med Addenbrooke's Hosp Cambridge 1987-, assoc lectr Faculty Clinical Med Cambridge 1988-; asst ed Genito-Urinary Medicine; memb BMA 1978, MSSVD 1983; *Books* Aids (1987, 3 edn 1989); *Recreations* tennis, golf; *Style—* Dr Christopher Carne; Genitomedical Clinic, Addenbrooke's Hosp, Hills Rd, Cambridge CB2 2QQ (☎ 0223 217774)

CARNE, Dr Stuart John; CBE (1986, OBE 1977); s of late Bernard Carne, and Millicent, *née* Chaikin; *b* 19 June 1926; *Educ* Willesden County GS, Middx Hosp Med Sch (MB BS, MRCS, LRCP, DCH); *m* 16 Dec 1951, Yolande Judith, da of Michael Cooper; 2 s (Simon b 1966, Charles b 1972), 2 da (Victoria b 1964, Emma b 1974); *Career* RAF Flt Lt Med Branch 1952-54, hon civil conslt in gen practice to RAF 1974-; house surgn Middlesex Hosp 1950-51; Queen Elizabeth Hosp for Children 1951-52: house physician, house surgeon, casualty offr; in gen practice London 1954-, sr ptnr Grove Health Centre 1967-, sr tutor in gen practice Royal Postgrad Med Sch 1970-; DHSS: memb Central Health Servs Cncl 1976-79, memb Personal Social Servs Cncl 1976-80, memb Children's Ctee 1978-81, chm Standing Med Advsy Ctee 1982-86 (memb 1974-86), chm Jt Ctee on Contraception 1983-86 (memb 1975-86); RCGP: memb 1958, memb Cncl 1961-, hon treas 1964-81, fell 1970, pres 1988-91; pres World Orgn of Nat Colls and Acads of Gen Practice and Family Med 1976-78 (memb Cncl 1970-80), memb Exec Cncl Br Diabetic Assoc 1981-87; hon med offr Queen's Park Rangers FC 1960-90; examiner in medicine Soc of Apothecaries 1980-88; chm St Mary Abbots Court Ltd 1981-; vice pres Queen's Park Rangers FC; Freeman City of London 1984; FRSM; fell: Royal NZ Coll of GPs 1990, Coll of GPs (Pakistan) 1991; memb Irish Coll of Gen Practioners; hon memb BPA 1982; *Publications* Paediatric Care (1976), DHSS Handbook on Contraceptive Practice (jtly, 4 edn, 1988); contribs to Lancet, British Medical Journal and other learned jls; *Recreations* music, photography, philately; *Clubs* Royal Air Force; *Style—* Dr Stuart Carne, CBE; 5 St Mary Abbots Court, Warwick Gardens, London W14 8RA (☎ 071 602 1970); The Grove Health Centre, Goldhawk Rd, London W12 8EJ (☎ 081 743 7153)

CARNEGIE, Lady Alexandra Clare; da of 3 Duke of Fife and Hon Lady Worsley; *b* 20 June 1959; *Recreations* tennis, skiing, travel; *Clubs* Queen's; *Style—* The Lady Alexandra Carnegie

CARNEGIE, Hon James Duthac; TD (1944), JP (Perthshire); yst s of 10 Earl of Southesk (d 1941); *b* 26 Sept 1910; *Educ* Eton, Trinity Coll Cambridge (BA); *m* 1935, Claudia Katharine Angela, da of Hon Lord Blackburn (d 1941), Scottish Lord of Session, and Lady Constance, da of 13 Earl of Strathmore and Kinghorne; 1 s (Robin Andrew Duthac b 24 March 1937); *Career* Maj 4/5 Bn Black Watch RHR (TA); *Style—* The Hon James Carnegie, TD, JP; Balloch, Alyth, Perths PH11 8JN (☎ 082 83 2339)

CARNEGIE, Hon Jocelyn Jacek Alexander Bannerman; s of Countess of Erroll (d 1978), and 2 husband, Maj Raymond Alexander Carnegie, gs of late 10 Earl of Southesk; half-bro of Earl of Erroll; *b* 21 Nov 1966; *Educ* Glenalmond; *m* 5 Jan 1990, Susie Mhairi, o da of Thomas Mitchell Hastie Butler, of Garvald, E Lothian; *Recreations* skiing, shooting, sailing, photography, literature; *Style—* The Hon Jocelyn Carnegie; Crimonmogate, Lonmay, Aberdeenshire

CARNEGIE, Maj Raymond Alexander; o s of Hon Alexander Bannerman Carnegie (d 1989; s of 10 Earl of Southesk), and his 1 w, Susan Ottilia (d 1968), da of Maj Ernest Rodakowski, and Lady Dora Susan, *née* Carnegie, da of 9 Ear of Southesk; *b* 9 July 1920; *Educ* Eton; *m* 1, 1943 (m dis 1953), Patricia Elinor Trevor, da of Cdr Sir Hugh Trevor Dawson, 2 Bt (cr 1920), RN; 2 da; m 2, 1964, Diana Denyse Hay, Countess of Erroll (who m 1 (m dis), Capt Sir (Rupert) Iain Kay Moncreiffe of that Ilk, 11 Bt (d 1985), and who d 1978); 1 s (*see* Carnegie, Hon Jocelyn); m 3, 1989, Maria Congreve, da of Maj Ian Stafford Alexander, Royal Irish Fus, and former w of Richard Anthony Bamford; *Career* late Scots Gds, wounded 3 times and despatches WWII; *Books* author of 19 published books (1954-71); *Style—* Maj Raymond Carnegie; Crimonmogate, Lonmay, Aberdeenshire

CARNEGIE, Lt-Gen Sir Robin Macdonald; KCB (1979), OBE (1968), DL (1990); yr s of Sir Francis Carnegie, CBE (d 1946), and Theodora, *née* Matthews; *b* 22 June 1926; *Educ* Rugby; *m* 1955, Iona, da of Maj-Gen Sir John Sinclair, KCMG, CB, OBE (d 1977); 1 s, 2 da; *Career* cmmnd QOH 1946, cmd 1967-69, cmd 11 Armd Bde 1971-72, student RCDS 1973, GOC 3 Div (Maj-Gen) 1974-76, COS HQ BAOR 1976-78, mil sec 1978-80, DG Army Trg MOD 1981-82, Col QOH 1981-87, non-serving memb Home Office Selection Bd 1987-; *Style—* Lt-Gen Sir Robin Carnegie, KCB, OBE, DL

CARNEGY, Colin David; s of Rev Canon Patrick Charles Alexander Carnegy (d 1969), of Spalding, Lincs, and Joyce Eleanor, *née* Townsley; *b* 16 Aug 1942; *Educ* Rugby, Univ of Oxford (MA); *m* 1 Sept 1973, Rosemary Frances Deschamps, da of Saunders Edward Chamier, MC (d 1990), of Wadhurst, Sussex; 3 s (Charles b 15 Aug 1975, Edward b 3 Oct 1977, Francis b 10 Oct 1981), 1 da Henrietta b 18 Oct 1983); *Career* admitted slr 1968, ptnr Parker Bullen Salisbury 1974-; NP; pres Salisbury Slrs Assoc 1990; chm Govrs Berwick St James First Sch Salisbury; memb: Law Soc; *Recreations* music and skiing; *Style—* Colin Carnegy, Esq; The Parsonage, Stapleford, Salisbury, Wilts SP3 4LJ (☎ 0722 790334); Parker Bullen, 45 Castle St, Salisbury, Wilts SP1 3SS (☎ 0722 412000, telex 477019, fax 0722 411822)

CARNEGY, Derek Francis; s of Francis Anthony Roberts Carnegy; *b* 23 Aug 1928; *Educ* Pangbourne Coll; *m* 1961, Judith Frances; 2 s; *Career* submarine specialist RN 1946-68; Hambros Bank 1968-89; *Style—* Derek Carnegy, Esq; 14 Ranelagh Rd, Winchester, Hants (☎ 0962 866077)

CARNEGY, Patrick Charles; s of Canon P C A Carnegy (d 1969), and Joyce Eleanor, *née* Townsley; *b* 23 Sept 1940; *Educ* Trinity Hall Cambridge (MA); *Career* writer, lectr, broadcaster on music, theatre and lit; journalist TES 1964-69, asst ed TLS 1969-78, ed music books Faber and Faber Ltd 1978-88, dir Faber Music Ltd 1979-88, dramaturg Royal Opera House 1988-; broadcasting incl contribs to BBC Radio 4's arts magazine Kaleidoscope; documentaries on: Kafka, Thomas Mann, Wagner's Ring; founding memb Bayreuth Int Arts Centre; memb: BBC Central Music Advsy Ctee 1986-89, BBC Gen Advsy Ctee 1990-; *Books* Faust as Musician: A Study of Thomas Mann's novel 'Doctor Faustus' (1973), Christianity Revalued (ed, 1974); *Recreations* mountains, wine; *Style—* Patrick Carnegy, Esq; The Royal Opera House, Covent Garden, London WC2E 9DD (☎ 071 240 1200, fax 071 836 1762, telex 27988 COVGAR G)

CARNEGY-ARBUTHNOTT, Bt-Col David; TD (1969), DL (Co of City of Dundee 1973-89, Co of Angus 1989-); s of Lt-Col Wilmot Boys Carnegy-Arbuthnott (d 1973), and Enid Carnegy-Arbuthnott, *née* Carnegy-Arbuthnott (d 1986), thirteenth of Balnamoon and thirteenth of Findowrie; Alexander Carnegy, 5 of Balnamoon, took part in 1715 rebellion, captured, imprisoned, pardoned 1721, estates forfeited, repurchased 1728. James Carnegy, subsequently 6 of Balnamoon, took part in 1745 rebellion, captured, tried but not convicted, because of misnomer - he had married Margaret Arbuthnott who became 5 of Findowrie and added her name to his; *b* 17 July 1925; *Educ* Stowe; *m* 1949, Helen Adamson, da of Capt David Collier Lyell, MC (d 1970); 2 s (James, Hugh), 2 da (Sarah, Bridget); *Career* emergency cmmn Black Watch 1944-47, TA 1955-69, Bt-Col 1969, Hon Col First Bn 51 Highland Volunteers (TA) 1980-89; CA 1953, in practice Dundee 1956-89; landowner through family cos (3000 acres); pres Dundee C of C 1971-72, memb Ct Univ of Dundee 1977-85, govr Dundee Coll of Educn 1985-87 and Northern Coll of Educn 1987-91, convener Standing Ctee of Gen Synod of Episcopal Church in Scotland 1987-; DL Co of City of Dundee 1973-89; memb Royal Co of Archers (Queen's Body Gd for Scotland) 1959-; Hon LLD Univ of Dundee 1982; *Recreations* shooting, country pursuits; *Clubs* New (Edinburgh), Army and Navy, Puffins (Edinburgh); *Style—* Bt-Col David Carnegy-Arbuthnott of Balnamoon, TD, DL; Balnamoon, Brechin, Angus DD9 7RH (☎ 035 66 208)

CARNEGY OF LOUR, Baroness (Life Peer UK 1982), of Lour in the District of Angus; Elizabeth Patricia Carnegy of Lour; DL (Angus 1988); eld da of Lt-Col Ughtred Elliott Carnegy of Lour, 12 of Lour, DSO, MC, JP, DL (d 1973), and Violet, MBE, *née* Henderson (d 1965); *b* 28 April 1925; *Educ* Downham Sch Essex; *Career* worked in Cavendish Laboratory Cambridge 1943-46; Girl Guide Assoc: joined 1947, co cmmr Angus 1956-63, trg advsr Scotland 1958-62, trg advsr Cwlth HQ 1963-65, pres Angus 1971-84, pres Scotland 1979-89; coopted onto Angus CC Educn Ctee 1967-75; chm: Working Pty on Professional Trg for Community Educn in Scotland 1975-77, Scottish Cncl Community Educn 1981-88 (memb 1978-88), MSC for Scotland 1981-83, Tayside Ctee on Med Res Ethuis 1990-; memb: Cncl Tertiary Educn Scotland 1979-83, MSC 1979-82, Scottish Econ Cncl 1981-; cncllr Tayside Regnl Cncl 1974-82 (convener: Recreation and Tourism 1974-76, Educn Ctee 1977-81); Hon Sheriff 1969-84; memb: Cncl Open Univ 1984-88, Admin Cncl Royal Jubilee Tsts 1984-; tstee Nat Museums of Scotland 1987-, hon pres Scottish Library Assoc 1989-; FRSA; *Clubs* Lansdowne; *Style—* The Rt Hon the Lady Carnegy of Lour, DL; Lour, Forfar, Angus DD8 2LR (☎ 0307 82 237); House of Lords, Westminster SW1A OPW

CARNELL, Rev Canon Geoffrey Gordon; *b* 5 July 1918; *Educ* City of Norwich Sch, St John's Coll Cambridge (Lightfoot scholar, BA, MA); *m* 1945, Mary Elizabeth Boucher, da of John Smith (d 1946), of Abington, Northampton; 2 s (Martin, Andrew); *Career* asst curate Abington Northampton 1942-48, chaplain and lectr St Gabriel's Coll Camberwell 1949-53; rector: Isham with Gt and Little Harrowden 1953-71, Boughton Northampton 1971-85; chaplain to the High Sheriff of Northants 1972, dir post-ordination trg, examining chaplain to the Bishop Peterborough 1962-86, non-residentiary canon of Peterborough Cathedral 1965-85, chaplain to HM The Queen 1981-88, canon emeritus 1986-, chaplain to the Mayor of Kettering 1988-89; librarian Ecton House Conf and Retreat Centre 1968-, memb Ecclesiastical History Soc 1978-, vice chm Northamptonshire Record Soc 1981-89; *Recreations* walking, music, reading (especially biography), visiting art collections; *Style—* The Rev Canon Geoffrey Carnell; 52 Walsingham Ave, Barton Woods, Kettering, Northants NN15 5ER (☎ 0536 511415)

CARNELLEY, Ven Desmond; *b* 29 Nov 1929; *Educ* St John's Coll York (CertEd), Univ Coll of Southwest Exeter (CertRelEd), William Temple Coll Rugby, Ripon Hall Oxford, Open Univ (BA); *m* 1, 6 June 1954, Dorothy (d 1986); 3 s (Philip b 1957, John b 1961, David b 1965), 1 da (Elizabeth Amy b 1964); m 2, 2 May 1988, Marjorie; *Career* teacher 1951-59; curate Aston Sheffield 1960, priest i/c St Paul Ecclesfield 1963, vicar of Balby Doncaster 1967, priest i/c (later vicar) of Mosborough Sheffield 1973, archdeacon of Doncaster 1985-; *Recreations* reading, theatre, walking in Derbyshire; *Style—* The Ven the Archdeacon of Doncaster; 1 Balmoral Road, Town Moor, Doncaster DN2 5BZ

CARNEY, Michael; s of Bernard Patrick Carney (d 1988), of Panton Place, Holywell, Clwyd, and Gwyneth, *née* Ellis; *b* 19 Oct 1937; *Educ* The Grammar Sch Holywell, Univ Coll of N Wales Bangor (BA); *m* 22 Apr 1963, Mary Patricia Carney, da of Robert Ingmam Davies (d 1983), of Wern Isaf, Llanfairfechan, Gwynedd; 2 s (Owen, Gwyn), 1 da (Bethan); *Career* staff offr to Dep Chm NCB 1963-67, asst sec Electricity Cncl 1971-74 (admin offr 1968-71), personnel mangr Midlands Region CEGB 1980-82 (sec SW Region 1974-82), personnel dir Oxfam 1982-87, sec Water Servs Assoc 1987-; MIPM; *Recreations* book collecting, reading; *Style—* Michael Carney, Esq; 16 Brodrick Rd, London SW17 7DZ (☎ 081 682 2830); WSA, 1 Queen Anne's Gate, London SW1H 9BT (☎ 071 222 8111, fax 071 222 1811, telex 918518)

CARNEY, Dr Michael William Patrick; s of Major Patrick Leo Carney, Croix de Guerre (d 1984), of 19 Meadway Close, Staines, and Gladys Louise Carney; *b* 8 Jan 1931; *Educ* St Joseph's Acad Blackheath London, Univ Coll Dublin (MB BCh, BAO, MD, DPM); *m* 19 Sept 1963, Dr (Margaret) Meg Carney, da of Dr Andrew Bell Hamilton Irvine, of Rectory Park, Morpeth, Northumberland; 3 s (John Niall b 25 Sept 1964, Andrew Patrick b 30 April 1966, Peter Michael b 21 March 1969); *Career* med offr RAMC 1956-60 (trainee in psychiatry 1956-58, MELF 1959-60), house physician St Vincents Hosp Dublin 1954, sr registrar to Sir Martin Roth Royal Victoria Infirmary Newcastle upon Tyne 1960-63; conslt psychiatrist: Blackpool and Fylde Hosps 1963-74, Northwick Park Hosp and Clinical Res Centre Harrow 1974-; 121 published papers in med and scientific jls, contrib to med text books, author of med book reviews, referee of original papers for British Journal of Psychiatry; assessor and examiner: GMC Health Ctee NW Thames Regn, Gen Dental Cncl Health Ctee NW Thames Regn; Gen Nursing Cncl Health Ctee examiner for nurses midwives and health visitors; memb Nat Counselling and Welfare Serv for Sick Drs; FRCPI 1971, FRCPsych 1974; *Recreations* walking, jogging, swimming, reading, amateur antiquary; *Clubs* 71 Club, Northwick Park Hosp; *Style—* Dr Michael Carney; Hill House, Mount Park Rd, Harrow on the Hill, Middx HA1 3JY (☎ 081 864 6946); Northwick Park Hosp & Clinical Res Centre, Harrow, Middx HA1 3UJ (☎ 081 864 3232); Clementine Churchill Hosp, Sudbury Hill, Harrow, Middx (☎ 081 422 3464); Visiting Conslt Priory Hosp, Roehampton; Surrey Visiting Conslt Bowden House Clinic, Harrow on the Hill HA1 3JL; Visiting Conslt Royal Masonic Hosp, Ravenscourt Park, London W6 0TN (☎ 081 741 9000)

CARNOCK, 4 Baron (UK 1916); Sir David Henry Arthur Nicolson; 14 Bt (NS 1637), of Carnock, Co Stirling; recognised by Lord Lyon 1984 as holder of the Baronetcy of Lasswade (NS 1629) and as chief of the Clan Nicolson and Nicolson of that Ilk; s of Captain 3 Baron Carnock, DSO, JP, RN (d 1982), by his w, Hon Katharine Lopes (d 1968), da of 1 Baron Roborough; *b* 10 July 1920; *Educ* Winchester, Balliol Coll Oxford; *Heir* 1 cous, Nigel Nicolson, MBE; *Career* served 1940-46 Royal Devon Yeo Staff, DAQMG HQ Land Forces Hong Kong, Maj 1945; admitted slr 1949, ptnr Clifford-Turner Slrs 1955-86; *Recreations* shooting, fishing, gardening, foreign travel; *Clubs* Travellers', Beefsteak; *Style—* The Rt Hon the Lord Carnock; 90 Whitehall Court, London SW1A 2EL (☎ 071 839 5544); Ermewood House, Harford, Ivybridge, Devon PL21 0JE (☎ 0752 892519)

CARNWATH, Sir Andrew Hunter; KCVO (1975), DL (Essex 1972); s of Dr Thomas Carnwath, DSO (Dep CMO, Min of Health, d 1954), and Margaret Ethel, *née* McKee; *b* 26 Oct 1909; *Educ* Eton (King's scholar); *m* 1, 1939, Kathleen Marianne (d 1968), da of late William Anderson Armstrong, of Westoe, Co Durham; 5 s, 1 da (Felicity, now Hon Mrs Diarmid Guinness, *qv*); m 2, 1973, Joan Gertrude (author, writing as Joan Alexander), da of Maj-Gen Henry Lethbridge Alexander, CB, CMG, DSO (d 1944), and widow of D S Wetherell-Pepper; *Career* served WWII Flt Lt RAF; ret merchant banker; with Baring Bros and Co Ltd 1928-74 (md 1955-74); chm: Save and Prosper Group 1961-80, London Multinational Bank 1971-74; dir Equity and Law Life Assurance Society 1955-83, Scottish Agricultural Industries 1969-75, Great Portland Estates 1977-89; chm: Manor Charitable Tstees 1969-88, Baring Fndn 1982-85; memb London Ctee Hongkong Shanghai Bank 1967-74, pres Inst of Bankers 1970-72; chm: Central Bd of Fin C of E Investmt Mgmnt Ctee 1960-74, Chelmsford Dio Bd of Fin 1969-75; govr: King Edward's Hosp Fund for London 1976-85 (treas 1965-74), Felsted Sch 1965-81; tstee Imperial War Graves Endowment Fund 1963-74 (chm 1964-74), memb Royal Cmmn for Exhibition of 1851 1964-85; treas: Friends of Tate Gallery 1966-82, Univ of Essex 1973-82; High Sheriff of Essex 1965, memb CC 1973-77 Master Worshipful Co of Musicians 1981-82; hon fell Eton 1981, Hon DUniv Essex 1983; *Recreations* music (playing the piano), pictures; *Clubs* Athenaeum, Essex; *Style*— Sir Andrew Carnwath, KCVO, DL; Garden Flat, 39 Palace Gardens Terrace, London W8 4SB (☎ 071 727 9145)

CARNWATH, Francis Anthony Armstrong; s of Sir Andrew Hunter Carnwath, KCVO, DL, and Kathleen Marianne, *née* Armstrong (d 1968); *b* 26 May 1940; *Educ* Eton (Oppidan Scholar), Trinity Coll Cambridge; *m* 1 March 1975, Penelope Clare, da of Sir Charles Henry Rose, 3 Bt (d 1965), of Hardwick House, Whitchurch-on-Thames, Oxon; 1 s (Alexander Patrick b 1980), 2 da (Flora Helen b 1976, Catriona Rose b 1978 (d 1985)); *Career* dir Baring Bros and Co Ltd 1979-89, chm Ravensbourne Registration Servs Ltd 1981-89, dep dir The Tate Gallery 1990-; Shelter Nat Campaign for the Homeless: treas, later dep chm and chm Exec Ctee 1968-76; treas VSO 1979-84; chm: Spitalfields Historic Bldg Tst 1984-, Henley Soc (Civic Amenity Tst Soc) 1984-88; memb Exec Ctee Friends of Tate Gallery (treas 1985-), dir Foreign Anglican Church and Educational Association Ltd 1973- (co sec 1973-85); *Recreations* music, gardening, walking; *Clubs* Royal Commonwealth Soc; *Style*— Francis Carnwath, Esq; Southernhay, Nettlebed, Henley-on-Thames, Oxon RG9 5BD (☎ 0491 641357); The Tate Gallery, Millbank, London SW1P 4RG (☎ 071 821 1313)

CARNWATH, Robert John Anderson; QC (1985); s of Sir Andrew Carnwath, KCVO, and Kathleen Marianne, *née* Armstrong (d 1968); *b* 15 March 1945; *Educ* Eton, Trinity Coll Cambridge (MA, LLB); *m* 18 May 1974, Bambina, da of G D'Adda, of Bergamo, Italy; *Career* called to the Bar 1969; jr counsel to Revenue 1980-85, attorney gen to Prince of Wales 1988-; author of various legal pubns; memb Governing Body RAM, chm Shepherds Bush Housing Assoc, Musicians Co; *Recreations* violin, singing, tennis; *Clubs* Garrick; *Style*— Robert Carnwath, Esq, QC; 2 Paper Building, Temple, London, EC4 (☎ 071 353 5835)

CARO, Sir Anthony Alfred; CBE (1969); s of Alfred and Mary Caro; *b* 8 March 1924; *Educ* Charterhouse, Christ's Coll Cambridge, Regent St Poly, Royal Acad Schs; *m* 1949, Sheila May Girling; 2 s; *Career* pt/t asst to Henry Moore 1951-53, pt/t teacher St Martin's Sch of Art 1953-79, teacher of sculpture Bennington Coll Vermont USA 1963-65, memb Cncl Royal Coll of Art London 1981-83; teacher Triangle Artist's Workshop in: US 1982-90 (fndr), Maastricht Holland 1985, Barcelona Spain 1987; visiting artist: workshop in Berlin 1987, Univ of Alberta Canada 1989, Red Deer Coll Alberta 1989; museum shows held at: Washington Gallery of Modern Art Washington DC 1965, Rijksmuseum Kroller-Muller Otterlo Holland 1967, Museum of Modern Art NY USA 1975, Museum of Fine Arts Houston 1975, Walker Art Centre Minneapolis 1975, Museum of Fine Arts Boston 1976, Tel Aviv Museum (extensive travelling show) 1977, York Sculptures Museum of Fine Arts Boston 1980, Moderne Galerie im Saarland-Museum Sarbrucken 1982, Kunstmuseum Dusseldorf 1985, Walker Hill Arts Centre Seoul Korea 1989, Musée des Beaux Arts Calais France 1990; tstee Tate Gallery 1982-89, memb Cncl Slade Sch of Art London 1982-89; hon fell: Christ's Coll Cambridge 1981, RCA 1986; hon memb American Acad of Arts and Sci's 1988; Freeman City of NY 1974; Hon DLitt: York Univ Toronto 1974, UEA 1979, Brandeis Univ Mass 1981; Hon LittD Cambridge 1985, Hon DUniv Surrey 1987, Hon DFA Yale Univ Conn 1989, Hon DFA Univ of Alberta 1990; kt 1987; *Recreations* listening to music; *Style*— Sir Anthony Caro, CBE; 111 Frognal, Hampstead, London NW3 6XR

CAROE, Martin Bragg; s of Alban Douglas Rendall Caroe, OBE, of 15 Campden Hill Square, London, and Gwendolen Mary, *née* Bragg (d 1984); *b* 15 Nov 1933; *Educ* Winchester, Trinity Coll Cambridge (BA), Kingston upon Thames Sch of Architecture (DipArch); *m* 15 Sept 1962, Mary Elizabeth, da of Capt Stephen Wentworth Roskill, CBE, DSC, RN (d 1982), of Frostlake Cottage, Malting Lane, Cambridge; 2 s (William b 1967, d 1974, Oliver b 1968), 3 da (Rebecca b 1965, Ruth b 1972, Emily b 1976); *Career* Lance Corpl KRRC 1952, 2 Lt 1 Royal Fus 1952-53, Capt 8 Royal Fus 1954-62; ptnr Caroe and Martin 1962; third generation conservation architect specialising in care of historic bldgs; work incl: St David's Cathedral 1966, Wells Cathedral West Front Sculpture Conservation 1981-86, repair on accession to Nat Tst Kingston Lacy 1982-84, surveyor Rochester Cathedral 1982-; Civic Tst Award Wells Vicars Close 1984; pres EASA (Ecclesiastical Architects & Surveyors Assoc) 1978-79; memb: Faculty Jurisdiction Cmmn 1980-84, Exec Ctee Cncl for the Care of Churches 1986-; Freeman Worshipful Co of Plumbers (Master 1986); ARIBA 1960, FSA 1988; UN medal Korea; *Recreations* gardening, punting; *Style*— Martin Caroe, Esq; Vann, Hambledon, nr Godalming, Surrey GU8 4EF (☎ 042 868 3413); 1 Greenland Place, London NW1 0AP (☎ 071 267 9348, car 0836 211 142)

CARPENTER, David Iain; s of Jeffrey Frank Carpenter, of Epsom, Surrey, and Joyce Cumming, *née* Mitchell; *b* 14 Oct 1951; *Educ* Sutton GS, Kingston upon Thames Sch of Architecture, Britannia RN Coll, Heriot-Watt Sch of Architecture Edinburgh (Dip Arch); *m* 20 Jan 1979, Anne Richmond, da of Dr Norman John McQueen, of Appin, Argyll; 4 s (Angus b 1980, Edward b 1981, Alexander b and d 1983, Simon b 1984); *Career* supply and secretariat offr RN 1974-78, RNR 1979-, architect J & F Johnston & Ptnrs 1982, sr architect 1986, assoc dir 1987, estab own practice David Carpenter Architect Edinburgh 1988, dir Plan Shop (Edinburgh) Ltd 1989; *Recreations* sailing, sketching, reading; *Clubs* Royal Scots (Edinburgh); *Style*— David Carpenter, Esq; David Carpenter Architect, 9-14 Maritime St, Edinburgh EH6 6SB (☎ 031 554 3041, fax 031 553 5358)

CARPENTER, Harry Leonard; s of Harry Carpenter (d 1974), and Adelaide May, *née* Lascelles; *b* 17 Oct 1925; *Educ* Ashburton Sch Shirley Surrey, Selhurst GS Croydon Surrey; *m* 22 Sept 1950, Phyllis Barbara, da of William Matthews; 1 s (Clive Harry b 20 Sept 1954); *Career* sports commentator; journalist: Greyhound Express 1941-43, Greyhound Owner 1946-48, Speedway Gazette 1949-50, Sporting Record 1950-54, Daily Mail 1954-62; sports commentator: BBC TV 1949-, BBC radio 1951-; DAVI award (Best Sports Prog on Video) 1983, TRIC award (Sports Personality of the Year) 1989, American Sportscasters Assoc award (Int Sportscaster of the Year) 1989; *Books* Masters of Boxing (1964), History of Boxing (1975), The Hardest Game (1981); *Recreations* golf; *Clubs* Royal & Ancient Golf (Scotland), Royal St George's Golf (Kent); *Style*— Harry Carpenter, Esq; BBC Television, Kensington House, London W14 0AX (☎ 081 895 6611)

CARPENTER, Humphrey William Bouverie; s of Rt Rev Harry James Carpenter; *b* 29 April 1946; *Educ* Dragon Sch Oxford, Marlborough, Keble Coll Oxford (MA, DipEd); *m* 1973, Mari Christina, *née* Prichard; 2 da; *Career* author, broadcaster, musician; BBC gen trainee 1968-70, staff prodr BBC Radio Oxford 1970-74, freelance writer and broadcaster 1975-; fndr of band Vile Bodies (1920s and 1930s jazz and dance music) resident Ritz Hotel London 1986-; *Books* A Thames Companion (with Mari Prichard, 1975), J R R Tolkien: A Biography 1977, The Inklings 1978, Jesus 1980, The Letters of J R R Tolkien (co-ed Christopher Tolkien, 1981), W H Auden: A Biography 1981, The Oxford Companion to Children's Literature (with Mari Pritchard, 1984), OUDS: a centenary history of the Oxford University Dramatic Society 1985, Secret Gardens: the golden age of children's literature 1985, Geniuses Together: American writers in Paris 1987, A Serious Character: the life of Ezra Pound 1988, The Brideshead Generation: Evelyn Waugh and His Friends 1989; Children's Books: The Joshers 1977, The Captain Hook Affair 1979, Mr Majeika 1984, Mr Majeika and the Music Teacher 1986, Mr Majeika and the Haunted Hotel 1987, The Television Adventures of Mr Majeika 1987, More Television Adventures of Mr Majeika 1988, Mr Majeika and the Dinner Lady 1989, Further Television Adventures of Mr Majeika 1990; Mr Majeika books serialized on television 1988-90; winner: Somerset Maugham award 1978, E M Forster award American Acad of Arts and Letters 1984, Duff Cooper Meml prize 1988; FRSL 1983; *Recreations* sleep; *Style*— Humphrey Carpenter, Esq; 6 Farnon Rd, Oxford OX2 6RS (☎ 0865 56673)

CARPENTER, Dr (George) Iain; s of George Anthony Carpenter (d 1967), of Horsmonden, Kent, and Dr Annie Pack MacKinnon; *b* 2 June 1950; *Educ* Christ's Hospital Horsham Sussex, Univ of Edinburgh (BSc, MB ChB); *m* 1, 22 Feb 1970 (m dis 1982), (Marie) Catrine, da of Gaston Bauer, of Le Verger, Rte de Lamonly, Anglet, Bayonne, France; 1 s (Edward b 24 May 1979), 1 da (Violaine b 1 May 1976); m 2, 11 June 1983, Bridget Mary, da of Robert Charles Combley, of Headington, Oxford; 1 s (James b 30 Jan 1986), 1 da (Annie b 18 Aug 1984); *Career* sr registrar in geriatric med: Brighton Gen Hosp 1978-80, Bolingbroke 1980-81, St George's Hosp 1980-81; conslt geriatrician 1981- and conslt in rehabilitation medicine 1990: Royal Hants Co Hosp, St Paul's Hosp Winchester; regnl med advsr and dir of screening Beaumont Med Serv 1986-89, dir ICS Med Ltd 1989-; memb: Br Geriatric Soc, BMA; MRCP 1978; *Books* All Of Us - Strategies For Health Promotion for Old People (jtly, 1989), Housing, Care and Frailty (jtly, 1990); *Recreations* walking, swimming, scuba diving, windsurfing, radio controlled model aircraft; *Style*— Dr Iain Carpenter; Windy Willows, Potters Heron Close, Ampfield, Nr Romsey Hants SO51 9BX; St Paul's Hospital, Winchester, Hants SO22 5AA (☎ 0962 60661)

CARPENTER, James Montagu; s of Edward Harry Osmund Carpenter (d 1974), of Holbeache, Trimpley, Worcs; *b* 28 Dec 1924; *Educ* Eton; *m* 1961, Mary Morris, o da of Brig Geoffrey William Auten, OBE (d 1981), of Knockholt, Kent; 3 s; *Career* served WWII Sub Lt RNVR Far East and Med; High Sheriff of Worcestershire 1965; chm Hereford and Worcs Ctee of COSIRA 1983-88; dir South Staffordshire Waterworks Co 1983-; *Recreations* farming, tennis, shooting; *Style*— James Carpenter, Esq; Holbeache House, Trimpley, nr Bewdley, Worcs (☎ 029 97 256)

CARPENTER, Maj-Gen (Victor Harry) John; CB (1975), MBE (1945); s of Harry Carpenter, and Amelia Carpenter; *b* 21 June 1921; *m* 1946, Theresa McCulloch; 1 s, 1 da; *Career* 2 Lt RASC 1939, Maj-Gen 1971; tport offr in chief MOD 1971-73, dir of movements (Army) MOD 1973-75, ret; chm Traffic Cmmrs Yorks Traffic Area 1975-, traffic cmmr Western Traffic Area Bristol 1985-; *Style*— Maj-Gen John Carpenter, CB, MBE; Traffic Commissioners, Western Traffic Area, The Gaunts House, Denmark St, Bristol BS1 5DR

CARPENTER, Leslie Arthur; s of William and Rose Carpenter; *b* 26 June 1927; *Educ* Hackney Tech Coll; *m* 1952, Stella Louise Bozza; 1 da; *Career* chm and chief exec International Publishing Corpn Ltd, chief exec Reed International plc 1982-; dir IPC Investmts (Pty) Ltd; *Style*— Leslie Carpenter, Esq; Reed House, Piccadilly, London W1A 1GJ

CARPENTER, Percival Benjamin; s of Harold Percival Carpenter, of 8 Streets lane, Cheslyn Way, Walsall, West Midlands, and Ida, *née* Baker; *b* 4 Aug 1932; *Educ* Queen Mary's GS Walsall, Univ of Birmingham (MB ChB); *m* 8 Sept 1956, Janet Elizabeth, da of Arthur James Bourne; 2 s (David Bryan b 15 Jan 1958, Michael Anthony b 7 Sept 1960), 2 da (Gillian b 1 Oct 1962, Petra Jane b 12 Jan 1969); *Career* Nat Serv Capt RAMC 1958-60; house offr St Chad's Hosp Birmingham 1957-58, sr registrar in radiology United Birmingham and other Birmingham Hosps 1963-65 (registrar 1960-63); conslt radiologist: West Birmingham Hosps 1966-85, Walsall Hosps 1975-; unit gen mangr Acute Services Walsall Hosp 1985-90 (chm Med Exec Ctee 1982-85), med dir Walsall NHS Trust Hosps 1990-; FRCR 1965; *Recreations* model engineering, DIY, music; *Style*— Percival Carpenter, Esq; 6 Sandra Close, Aldridge, West Midlands (☎ 0922 53214); Manor Hospital, Moat Rd, Walsall, West Midlands

CARPENTER, Robert David Evans; s of Ernest Henry Carpenter (d 1973), of Reading, and Muriel Carpenter; *b* 22 Jan 1940; *Educ* Mill Hill; *m* 16 Sept 1967, Gloria Faith Davies, da of Gordon Stuart Clarke (d 1980); 1 s (James Nicholas b 9 June 1970), 1 da (Caroline Claire b 18 Dec 1972); *Career* ptnr Montagu Loebl Stanley & Co 1979-85 (joined 1968), dir of investmt res Kitcat & Aitken 1985-90, dir Carr Kitcat & Aitken 1990-; AIB 1962; *Recreations* squash; *Style*— Robert Carpenter, Esq; 86 Manor Way, Beckenham, Kent BR3 3LR (☎ 081 650 0358); Carr Kitcat & Aitken, 1 London Bridge, London SE1 9TJ (☎ 071 378 7050, fax 071 403 0755, telex 8956121)

CARR; *see*: Baker-Carr

CARR, Lady Anne Mary; *née* Somerset; da of 11 Duke of Beaufort; *b* 21 Jan 1955; *m* 26 March 1988, Matthew Carr, yr s of Sir Raymond Carr, of Burch, N Molton, Devon; *Style*— The Lady Anne Carr

CARR, Very Rev Dr Arthur Wesley; s of Arthur Eugene Carr, and Irene Alice, *née* Cummins; *b* 26 July 1941; *Educ* Dulwich, Jesus Coll Oxford (MA), Jesus Coll Cambridge (MA), Ridley Hall Cambridge, Sch of Ecumenical Studies Geneva, Univ of Sheffield (PhD); *m* 20 April 1967, Natalie Gay, da of Norman Robert Gill; 1 da (Helga b 1973); *Career* curate Luton Parish Church 1967-71, tutor Ridley Hall 1970-71 (chaplain 1971-72), Sir Henry Stephenson fell in biblical studies Univ of Sheffield 1972-74, hon curate Ranmoor Parish Church Sheffield 1972-74, chaplain Chelmsford Cathedral 1974-78 (canon residentiary 1978-87), dep dir and programme dir Chelmsford Cathedral Centre for Research and Trg 1974-82, Bishop of Chelmsford's dir of trg 1976-84, examining chaplain to Bishop of Chelmsford 1976-86, hon fell Dept of Christian Ethics and Applied Theology New Coll Edinburgh 1986-; dean of Bristol 1987-; *Books* Angels and Principalities (1981), 'Angels' and 'The Devil' in A Dictionary of Christian Spirituality (1983), The Priestlike Task (1985), Brief Encounters, Pastoral Ministry through the Occasional Offices (1985), The Pastor as Theologian (1989), articles in various jls; *Recreations* reading, writing, music, gardening; *Style*— The Very Rev the Dean of Bristol; The Deanery, 20 Charlotte St, Bristol BS1 5PZ (☎ 0272 262443); Bristol Cathedral, College Green, Bristol BS1 5TJ (☎ 0272 264879)

CARR, David; s of Samuel Carr (d 1940), of Liverpool, and Lily, *née* Marks (d 1958); *b* 20 June 1922; *Educ* Oulton HS, Univ of Liverpool; *m* 13 Jan 1954, Adèle, da of Israel Karp (d 1980), of Liverpool; 3 s (Nigel b 1955, Colin b 1957, Timothy b 1964); *Career* Sgt wireless operator (serv Normandy 1944) RCS 1942-47; admitted slr 1949, sr ptnr David Carr & Roe Birkenhead 1949-; chm Social Security Appeal Tbnl 1980, sr warden Liverpool Old Hebrew Congregation 1972-74, life govr Imperial Cancer Res Fund; memb: Law Soc 1949, Slrs Benevolent Assoc; *Recreations* bridge, swimming, travel; *Style—* David Carr, Esq; 1 Merrilocks Green, Blundellsands, Liverpool L23 6XR (☎ 051 924 4883); 34 Hamilton St, Birkenhead, Merseyside L41 5AJ (☎ 051 647 7401)

CARR, Donald Bryce; OBE (1985); s of Col John Lillingston Carr (d 1963), and Constance Ruth, *née* Smith (d 1987); *b* 28 Dec 1926; *Educ* Repton, Worcester Coll Oxford (MA); *m* 1953, Stella Alice Vaughan, da of Rev Francis Vaughan Simpkinson; 1 da (Diana b 1958), 1 s (John b 1963); *Career* Lt Royal Berks Regt; Derbyshire CCC: asst sec 1953-59, sec 1959-62, capt; asst sec MCC 1962-74, sec Test and Co Cricket Bd 1974-86; played cricket for England; Soccer blue Oxford; *Recreations* golf, gardening; *Clubs* MCC, Vincents, Porters Park Golf; *Style—* Donald B Carr, Esq, OBE; 28 Aldenham Ave, Radlett, Herts (☎ 0923 855602)

CARR, Dorothy; da of Daniel Greenwood (d 1976), of Harrow, Middx, and Elvina, *née* Stanworth (d 1968); *b* 8 Feb 1921; *Educ* Harrow Co Sch for Girls, LSE (BA); *m* 1948, David Carr (d 1990), s of Alfred Edward Carr (d 1958), of Bath; 1 da (Susan b 1951); *Career* historian; lectr and adult educn tutor (ret); tutorial studentship King's Coll London 1965-69, corr tutor London Region Open Univ 1970-71, memb Panel of Tutors Dept of Extra-mural Studies Univ of London 1970-85; *Books* The Reformation in England to the Accession of Elizabeth I (co-ed A G Dickens, 1967); *Recreations* music, reading, walking, travel; *Style—* Mrs Dorothy Carr; 18 Roundwood View, Banstead, Surrey SM7 1EQ (☎ 0737 355267)

CARR, Dr Eric Francis; s of Edward Francis Carr (d 1963), and Maude Mary Carr (d 1954); *b* 23 Sept 1919; *Educ* Mill Hill Sch, Emmanuel Coll Cambridge (BA), London Hosp (MB BCh Cantab 1943, MA Cantab 1946, DPM 1952); *m* 23 Jan 1954 (m dis 1980), Janet Gould, da of Rev Trevor Gilfillan; 2 s (Anthony James b 1955, Nicholas Francis b 1956), 1 da (Sara Jane b 1958); *Career* Nat Serv 1944-46, Capt RAMC, Regnl MO 1 RTR, serv India, W Africa; conslt psychiatrist: St Ebba's Hosp 1955-61, KCH 1961-70, Epsom Dist and KCH 1970-76, sr princ MO DHSS 1976-78, Lord Chllrs visitor 1978-89, Mental Health Act cmmr 1983-89; memb: Mental Review Health Tbnl, Parole Bd 1988-; MRCP 1948, FRCP 1971, FRCPsych 1972; *Recreations* music, french language; *Style—* Dr Eric Carr; 116 Holly Lane East, Banstead, Surrey SM7 2BE (☎ 0737 353 675)

CARR, Frank George Griffith; CB (1967), CBE (1954); s of Dr Frank Carr (d 1957), and Agnes Maud, *née* Todd (d 1956); *b* 23 April 1903; *Educ* Perse Sch, Trinity Hall Cambridge (BA, LLB); *m* 20 July 1932, Ruth, da of Harold Hamilton Burkitt (d 1961), of Ballycastle, Co Antrim; *Career* Actg Lt-Cdr RNVR, WWII RN N Atlantic Convoys and Coastal Forces; Yacht Master's (deep sea) Certificate BOT 1927, mate of Thames sailing barge 1928, asst librarian House of Lords 1929-47, dir Nat Maritime Museum Greenwich 1947-66, chm Cutty Sark Ship Mgmnt Ctee 1953-72, int chm American Ship Tst Ctee 1978-, chm World Ship Tst 1979-89 ; FSA, FRAS, ARINA, FRInstNav; *Books* Sailing Barges (1931), Vanishing Craft (1934), A Yachtsman's Log (1935), The Yachtsman's England (1936), The Yacht Master's Guide (1940), The Medley of Mast and Sail (1976), Leslie A Wilcox, RI, RSMA (1977); *Recreations* yacht cruising, nautical research; *Clubs* Royal Cruising, Cruising Assoc; *Style—* Frank Carr, Esq, CB, CBE, FSA; 10 Park Gate, Blackheath, London SE3 9XB (☎ 081 852 5181)

CARR, Henry James; s of Malcolm Lester Carr (d 1984), of Liverpool, and Dr Sara, *née* Leigh; *b* 31 March 1958; *Educ* King David Sch Liverpool, Hertford Coll Oxford (BA), Univ of British Columbia (LLM); *m* 22 Sept 1988, Jan Mary, da of Maj Richard Alfred Dawson, of Harrogate; 1 s (Oliver b 1989); *Career* called to the Bar Gray's Inn 1982; memb London Computer Lawyers Gp; *Books* Protection of Computer Software in the United Kingdom (1986); *Recreations* squash, tennis, swimming, skiing; *Clubs* RAC, Vanderbilt Racquet; *Style—* Henry Carr, Esq; 11 South Square, Gray's Inn, London WC1R 5EU (☎ 071 405 1222, fax 071 242 4282)

CARR, Ian Cufaude; DL (Cumbria 1988); s of Laurence Carr (d 1938), and Beryl, *née* Cufaude (d 1979); *b* 12 Aug 1928; *Educ* Rugby; *m* 1, 24 May 1952 (m dis 1975), Doreen, *née* Hindle; 2 s (Jonathan Michael Ian b 12 April 1954, Dominic David b 11 Oct 1966), 2 da (Melanie Elizabeth b 3 Nov 1956, Stephanie Clare b 31 May 1960); m 2, 1976, Mrs Rilla Cameron Diggle, *née* Carr; 1 step s (Peter), 1 step da (Alison); *Career* chm Carr's Milling Industries plc 1964-; chm E Cumbria Health Authy 1986-; chm Penrith and Border Conservative Assoc 1970-75; *Recreations* shooting, golf; *Clubs* Royal and Ancient Golf, Silloth Golf, Southerness Golf, Border and County (Carlisle); *Style—* Ian Carr, Esq, DL; Brown Hill, Walton, Brampton, Cumbria CA8 2JW (☎ 06977 2540); Carr's Milling Industries plc, Stanwix, Carlisle (☎ 0228 28291)

CARR, Ian Henry Randell; s of Thomas Randell Carr (d 1979), of Gosforth, Newcastle upon Tyne, and Phyllis Harriet Carr (d 1985); *b* 21 April 1933; *Educ* Barnard Castle Sch, Kings Coll Newcastle Upon Tyne (BA, DipEd); *m* 1, 28 June 1963, Margaret Blackburn (d 1967), da of John Lowery Bell (missing presumed dead 1943), of Annfield Plain, Co Durham; 1 da (Selina b 29 July 1967); m 2, 9 Dec 1972 (m dis 1989), Sandra Louise, *née* Major; *Career* Nat Serv 2 Lt Royal Northumberland Fusiliers 1956-58 served NI and W Germany; performer: Emcee Five Quintet 1960-62, Rendell-Carr Quintet 1963-69, Ian Carr's Nucleus 1969-89, The Utd Jazz and Rock Ensemble 1975- (worldwide tours); composed: Solar Plexus 1970, Labyrinth 1973, Will's Birthday Suite (for the Globe theatre Tst) 1974, Out of the Long Dark 1978, Northumbrian Sketches 1988; assoc prof Guildhall Sch of Music and Drama; many presentations BBC Radio 3; memb: Gtr London Arts Assoc 1975-80; patron: live Theatre Co Newcastle upon Tyne 1985-, Art at the Whittington Hosp Appeal Islington; PRS 1970, Royal Soc of Musicians of GB 1982, Assoc of Professional Composers 1983, Central Music Advsy Ctee BBC Radio and TV 1987-89; Italian Calabria award 1982; *Books* Music Outside (1973), Miles Davis: A Critical Biography (1982), Jazz: The Essential Companion (jtly, 1987), Keith Jarrett: The Man and his Music (1991); *Recreations* music, the visual arts, world literature, travel; *Style—* Ian Carr, Esq; 34 Brailsford Rd, London SW2 2TE, (☎ 081 671 7195)

CARR, James Lloyd; s of Joseph Carr (d 1949), of Sherburn-in-Elmet, Yorks, and Elizabeth, *née* Welbourn (d 1947); *b* 20 May 1912; *Educ* Castleford Secondary Sch; *m* Sally, da of William Sexton, of Frating Hall, Essex (d 1945); 1 s (Robert b 1947); *Career* Intelligence Offr RAF 1940-46; school teacher: Hedge End Hampshire 1933, Birmingham 1935, Huron S Dakota 1938, Birmingham 1946; headmaster Kettering 1951; novels: A Day in Summer also TV film (1964), A Season in Sinji (1967), The Harpole Report (1971), How Steeple Sinderby Wonderers won the FA Cup (also play, 1975), A Month in the Country (also cinema film, 1980), The Battle of Pollocks Crossing (1985), What Hetty Did (1987), Harpole & Foxberrow (1991); *Recreations* stone carving; *Style—* James Carr, Esq

CARR, Marian Jane; da of David Fitzroy Ashmore (d 1974), and Marigold Vaugham, *née* Wilkes (d 1964); *b* 13 Dec 1946; *Educ* Wycombe Abbey Sch High Wycombe; *m* 22 March 1975 (m dis 1987), Kenneth; *Career* Midland Ladies golf champion 1979, admin sec Ladies Golf Union 1986-87, sec Eng Ladies Golf Assoc 1987; *Recreations* golf; *Clubs* Edgbaston Golf, Royal St David's Golf (Harlech); *Style—* Mrs Marian Carr; Coal Cottage, 87 Northfield Road, Harborne, Birmingham B17 0ST (☎ 021 427 6118), English Ladies Golf Association, Edgbaston Golf Club, Church Rd, Birmingham B15 3TB (☎ 021 456 2088)

CARR, Michael Derek; s of Horace Osmond Carr (d 1949), and Lady Althea Florence Williams, *née* Partridge; *b* 14 Aug 1925; *Educ* Dover Coll, Univ of Aberdeen; *m* 3 June 1950, Gillian Enid, *née* Brock; 2 s (Jonathan Nigel b 31 Dec 1953, Simon Michael b 19 June 1957); *Career* CA; sr ptnr Sturges Fraser Cave and Co 1968-71 (ptnr 1953), sr tax ptnr Price Waterhouse 1976-86 (ptnr 1971); ACA 1951; *Recreations* music; *Style—* Michael Carr, Esq; Rentokil Group plc, Felcourt, East Grinstead, W Sussex RH19 2JY (☎ 0342 833022, fax 0342 326229, telex 95456 RNTKILG)

CARR, Peter Derek; CBE (1989); s of George William (d 1972), of Mexborough, Yorkshire, and Marjorie, *née* Tailby; *b* 12 July 1930; *Educ* Fircroft Coll Birmingham, Ruskin Coll Oxford, Garnett Coll London; *m* 12 April 1958, Geraldine Pamela, da of Alexander Quarrier Ward, of Babbacombe; 1 s (Steven John b 1959), 1 da (Alyce b 1963); *Career* Nat Serv Mountain Rescue Serv RAF 1951-53; site mangr Construction Indust 1944-60, sr lectr in mgmnt Thurrock Coll Essex 1964-69, dir Cmmn on Industl Rels 1969-74, section dir ACAS 1974-78, dip serv cncllr Br Embassy Washington DC 1978-83, regnl dir DOE Northern and ldr Govt City Action Team 1983-89; chm: Northern Regnl Health Authy, Co Durham Devpt Co; sr ptnr Peter D Carr and Assocs, visiting fell Univ of Durham, chm Northern Media Forum; *Books* Worker Participation and Collective Bargaining in Europe, Industrial Relations in the National Newspaper Industry; *Recreations* cabinet making, walking, cooking; *Style—* Peter D Carr, Esq, CBE; Corchester Towers, Corbridge, Northumberland NE45 5NR (☎ 0434 632841, fax 0434 63 3726)

CARR, Peter John; s of John Carr, of The Oaks, 23 Warning Tongue Lane, Bessacarr, Doncaster DN4 6TB, and Mrs Hilda Mawdsley, *née* Dillon; *b* 1 Jan 1941; *Educ* Oundle; *m* 1 June 1963, Pirjo Kristiina, da of Unto Savunen, of Rauma, Finland; 1 s (Steven b 26 Dec 1965), 1 da (Tiina b 25 Sept 1964); *Career* md John Carr Doncaster Ltd 1978 (dir 1963, jt md 1967), gp md Rugby Gp plc 1990- (dir 1985-90); dir: Addison Corp Atlanta USA 1988, VP Winter Taunton USA 1988, Stegbar Pty Ltd Aus 1988; memb: British Woodworking Fedn, Doncaster C of C; *Recreations* golf, game shooting; *Clubs* Wheatley Golf, Lindrick Golf; *Style—* Peter Carr, Esq; John Carr Gp plc, Watch House Lane, Doncaster, S Yorks DN5 9LR (☎ 0302 783333, fax 0302 787383, telex 547160, 0836 713073)

CARR, Sir (Albert) Raymond Maillard; s of Reginald Maillard Carr, of Bath; *b* 11 April 1919; *Educ* Brockenhurst Sch, Christ Church Oxford; *m* 1950, Sara, da of Algernon Strickland, of Apperley, Glos; 3 s, 1 da; *Career* former fell of All Souls' and New Coll Oxford, prof of Latin American history Oxford 1967-68, warden of St Antony's Coll Oxford 1968-1987; author; D Litt Oxford; FBA; kt 1987; *Recreations* foxhunting; *Style—* Sir Raymond Carr; Burch, North Molton, South Bolton, Devon EX36 3JU (☎ 07697 267)

CARR, Rodney Paul (Rod); s of Capt George Paul Carr, of Whatton-in-the-Vale, Nottingham, and Alma, *née* Walker (d 1960); *b* 10 March 1950; *Educ* Carlton Le Willows GS Nottingham, Univ of Birmingham (BSc); *m* 21 July 1971, Lynne Alison, da of Charles Wilfred Ashwell; 1 s (David b 15 Feb 1982), 1 da (Joanne b 17 Oct 1979); *Career* yachtsman; instr London Borough of Haringey 1972-75, chief instr and dep dir Nat Sailing Centre Cowes IOW 1979-81 (instr 1975-79, memb winning Br Admirals Cup team 1981, chief racing coach (yachting) Royal Yachting Assoc 1984- (olympic coach 1981-84); coach to J Richards and P Allan Flying Dutchman Class Bronze medal Olympics 1984, M McIntyre and B Vaile Star Dutchman Class Gold medal Olympics 1988; *Recreations* sailing, music; *Style—* Rod Carr, Esq; 14 Spring Way, Alresford, Hampshire S024 9LN (☎ 0962 734148); Royal Yachting Association, RYA House, Romsey Rd, Eastleigh, Hants (☎ 0703 629962, fax 0703 629924, telex 47393)

CARR, Dr Stephen Paul; s of Denis Carr, and Muriel Betty, *née* Jamieson; *b* 1 May 1955; *Educ* Marple Hall GS, Univ of Warwick (BA), Univ of Oxford (DPhil); *m* 9 July 1977, Pamela Susan, da of Prof Harold Leslie Rosenthal; 1 s (Jonathan Gilbert b 1989); *Career* food mfrg analyst Rowe and Pitman 1979-89, head of UK res and dir Warburg Securities Ltd 1989- (divnl dir 1986-89); memb Woolhampton Parish Cncl 1982-83; *Style—* Dr Stephen Carr; 4 Sandford House Cottages, Knowl Hill, Kingsclere, Newbury RG15 (☎ 0635 298 817); Warburg Securities, 1 Finsbury Ave, London EC2 (☎ 071 606 1066)

CARR, Dr Thomas Ernest Ashdown (Tommy); CB (1977); s of Laurence Hudson Ashdown Carr (d 1959), and Norah E V, *née* Taylor; *b* 21 June 1915; *Educ* Co HS for Boys Altrincham, Victoria Univ Manchester (BSc, MB ChB); *m* 1940, Mary Sybil, da of Percy Harold Enoch Dunkey (d 1979); 1 s, 2 da; *Career* served WWII Maj RAMC NW Europe; RCGP: provost SE England Faculty 1962-64, memb Cncl 1964-66; princ med offr DHSS 1966, sr princ med offr GP and Regnl Med Serv 1967-79, pt/t med referee 1979-87; chm: QUIT (Nat Soc of Non-Smokers) 1982-1986 (vice pres 1986-), Guildford Div BMA 1988-89; DObstRCOG, FRCGP, FFCM; *Recreations* music, photography, foreign travel, country walks; *Clubs* Civil Service, RSM; *Style—* Dr Tommy Carr, CB; 17 Westpoint, Putney Hill, London SW15 6RU (☎ 081 788 9969)

CARR, Air Cdre William George; CBE; s of William George Carr (d 1937); *b* 12 Nov 1916; *Educ* Freemantle and Univ Coll Southampton; *m* 1949, Marion Ethel, da of late Capt Joseph Archibald Martin Hislop; 1 s (Martin b 1952), 1 da (Rosemary b 1955); *Career* entered RAF 1939, served in maintenance, trg, tport, air support, Far East and ME Cmds, RAF Coll Cranwell MOD, dir of movements RAF; ret 1972; Br Tport Hotels 1972-81; *Recreations* gardening, bridge, travel; *Clubs* RAF; *Style—* Air Cdre W G Carr, CBE; High Oaks, Wonersh Park, nr Guildford, Surrey GU5 0QS (☎ 0483 892289)

CARR-ELLISON, Col Sir Ralph Harry; TD (1962), ED (TAVR 1974); s of Maj John Campbell Carr-Ellison (d 1956), of Hedgeley Hall, and his 1 wife, Daphne Hermione Indica, *née* Cradock (m dis 1946, d 1984); *b* 8 Dec 1925; *Educ* Eton; *m* 1951, Mary Clare McMorrough, da of Maj Arthur Thomas McMorrough Kavanagh, MC (d 1953), of Borris House, Co Carlow; 3 s, 1 da; *Career* served CMF 1945-46, BAOR 1946-49, TA and TAVR 1949-73; Lt-Col cmdg Northumberland Hussars 1966-69, Territorial Col (TAVR) NE Dist 1969-73, Hon Col Northumbrian Univs OTC 1982-86, Northumberland Hussar Sqdns 1986-88, Col Cmdt Queens Own Yeo 1990- (Hon Col 1988-90), ADC (TAVR) to HM The Queen 1970-75; chm: Northumbrian Water Authy 1973-82, Tyne Tees TV Ltd 1974- (dir 1966-), N Tyne Area Manpower Bd MSC 1983-84, N of England Territorial Assoc 1976-80 (pres until 1990), AA 1986- (vice chm 1985-86), Univ of Newcastle Devpt Tst 1979-81; dir: Newcastle and Gateshead Water Co 1964-73, Trident TV 1972-81 (dep chm 1976-81); memb Ct Univ of Newcastle 1979-, vice chm nat Union of Cons and Unionist Assoc 1969-71, govr Swinton Cons Coll 1967-81, pres Northern Area Cons Cncl 1974-78 (treas 1961-66, chm 1966-69), memb Cncl Scout Assoc 1982- (co cmmr Northumberland 1958-68, pres 1989-); former JP Northumberland, High Sheriff 1972, DL 1981-85, Vice Lord Lt 1984 Northumberland, Lord Lt for County of Tyne and Wear 1984-; Hon DCL Univ of Newcastle upon Tyne 1989; FRSA 1983; KStJ 1984; kt 1973; *Recreations* jt master West Percy Foxhounds 1950-90; *Clubs* Cavalry and Guards, Pratt's, White's, Northern Counties (Newcastle); *Style—* Col Sir Ralph Carr-Ellison, TD, ED; Hedgeley Hall, Powburn, Alnwick, Northumberland (☎ 066 578273 091 2610181)

CARR-GOMM, Richard Culling; OBE (1985); s of Mark Culling Carr-Gomm (d 1965) and Thea, *née* Heming (d 1961); *b* 2 Jan 1922; *Educ* Stowe; *m* 21 Oct 1957, Susan, da of Ralph Gibbs (d 1957); 2 s (Adam b 1965, David b 1967), 3 da (Anna b 1958, Elizabeth b 1959, Harriet b 1964); *Career* cmmnd Coldstream Gds 1941; served with 6 Gds Tank Bde in NW Europe (twice wounded, despatches), Palestine 1945, Cyprus, Canal Zone and Tripoli, Maj resigned cmmn 1955; fndr: Abbeyfield Soc 1956, Carr-Gomm Soc 1965, Morpeth Soc 1972; Croix de Guerre (Silver star) France 1944, KStJ 1981, Templeton UK Project award 1984; *Books* Push on the Door (autobiog, 1979), Loneliness - The Wider Scene (1987); *Recreations* golf, drawing; *Style*— Richard Carr-Gomm, Esq, OBE; 9 The Batch, Batheaston, Avon BA1 7DR (☎ 0225 858 434); Telegraph Hill Centre, Kitto Road, Brockley, London SE14 5TX (☎ 071 277 5050)

CARR-LOCKE, Prof David Leslie; s of Dennis Charlton Carr-Locke, of Melksham, Wilts, and Ruby Marjorie, *née* Gibbs; *b* 19 Aug 1948; *Educ* Hardenhuish GS Chippenham, Gonville and Caius Coll Cambridge (MA, MB BChir); *m* 19 June 1971, Caroline Elizabeth Scott, da of Dr Adam Scott Smith, MBE, of Melrose, Roxburghshire; 1 s (Alexander Charles Scott b 26 Nov 1974), 1 da (Antonia Louise Papworth b 26 Nov 1974); *Career* med and surgical house offr Kettering Gen Hosp 1972-73; sr house offr: obstetrics and gynaecology Orsett Hosp Essex 1973-74, med specialities Leicester Gp of Hosps 1974-75; lectr in med (gastroenterology) Univ of Leicester 1975-83, res fell in gastroenterology New England and Baptist Hosp Boston USA 1978-79, conslt physician in gastroenterology Royal Infirmary 1983-89, dir of endoscopy and dir of clinical gastroenterology Brigham and Women's Hosp 1989-, assoc prof of med Harvard Med Sch 1989-; FRCP 1988; *Books* Endoscopy (1990); *Recreations* music, tennis, skiing, travel; *Clubs* Harvard (Boston USA); *Style*— Prof David Carr-Locke; Dir of Endoscopy, Division of Gastroentrology, Brigham and Women's Hospital, 75 Francis St, Boston, MA 02115, USA (☎ 0101 617 732 7414, fax 0101 617 732 7407)

CARR OF HADLEY, Baron (Life Peer UK 1975), of Hadley in Greater London; (Leonard) Robert Carr; PC (1963); s of late Ralph Edward Carr and Katie Elizabeth Carr, of Totteridge, Herts; *b* 11 Nov 1916; *Educ* Westminster, Gonville and Caius Coll Cambridge; *m* 1943, Joan Kathleen, da of Dr E W Twining, of Cheadle, Cheshire; 1 s (decd), 2 da (Hon Susan Elizabeth (Hon Mrs Rhodri Bradley-Jones), Hon Virginia Sarah (Hon Mrs Michael Fox)); *Career* MP (C) Mitcham 1950-74, Sutton (Carshalton) 1974-75; former PPS to Sir Anthony Eden; Parly sec to Min of Lab and Nat Serv 1955-59, sec for Tech Co-operation 1963-64, sec of state for Employment 1970-72, Lord Pres of the Cncl and ldr of the House of Commons 1972, sec of state for Home Affairs 1972-74; former dir: Prudential Corpn plc (chm 1980-85), Prudential Assur Co Ltd (chm 1980-85), Securicor Ltd 1961-63, 1965-70 and 1974-85, SGB Gp Ltd 1974-86, Cadbury Schweppes Gp plc 1979-87; former govr and dep chm of governing body Imperial Coll of Science and Technol (fell 1985), chm Business in the Community 1984-87; *Recreations* tennis, music, gardening; *Clubs* Brooks, Surrey County Cricket (pres 1985-86), All England Lawn Tennis and Croquet; *Style*— The Rt Hon the Lord Carr of Hadley, PC; 14 North Court, Great Peter St, London SW1

CARRATU, Nicholas Francis Ralph; s of L Mario Carratu, and L Anna, *née* Abate Deceased 1971; *b* 9 Jan 1937; *Educ* St Lawrence Coll Ramsgate; *m* 12 July 1964, Judith Anne, da of G Talbot-Spence; 2 s (Matthew b 2 March 1966, Benedict b 9 Aug 1969), 1 da (Charlotte b 27 Dec 1967); *Career* articled clerk Mann Judd & Co 1959-64; McLintock & Whinney Murray: joined 1965, conslt, ptnr 1971-76; Ernst & Young (and predecessor firms) 1976-: ptnr, ptnr i/c Fin Mgmnt Consultancy; FCA (ACA 1964), FIMC; *Recreations* sailing, mountaineering, painting; *Clubs* Gresham, Little Ship; *Style*— Nicholas Carratu, Esq; Ernst Young, Becket House, 1 Lambeth Palace Rd, London SE1 7EU (☎ 071 928 2000, fax 071 928 1345, car 0860 840057)

CARRELL, Prof Robin Wayne; s of Ruane George Carrell, of Christchurch, NZ, and Constance Gwendoline, *née* Rowe; *b* 5 April 1936; *Educ* Christchurch Boys HS NZ, Univ of Otago (MB ChB), Univ of Canterbury (BSc), Univ of Cambridge (MA, PhD); *m* 27 Jan 1962, Susan Wyatt, da of John Leonard Rogers (d 1975), Christchurch, NZ; 2 s (Thomas Wyatt George b 1968, Edward Robin William b 1970), 2 da (Sarah Anne b 1963, Rebecca Susan b 1964); *Career* MRC Abnormal Haemoglobin Unit Cambridge 1965-68, dir clinical Biochemistry Christchurch NZ 1968-75, lectr and conslt Addenbrookes Hosp and Univ of Cambridge 1976-78, prof of pathology Christchurch Clinical Sch Univ of Otago 1978-86, prof of haematology Univ of Cambridge 1986-; Cwlth fell St John's Coll Cambridge 1985-86, fell Trinity Coll Cambridge 1987-; memb Gen Bd Univ of Cambridge 1989; FRACP 1973, FRCPath 1976, FRCP 1990, FRSNZ 1980; *Recreations* gardening, walking; *Style*— Prof Robin Carrell; 19 Madingley Rd, Cambridge CB3 0EG (☎ 0223 312 970); Haematology Dept, Univ of Cambridge, MRC Centre, Hills Rd, Cambridge CB2 2QL (☎ 0223 336 788, fax 0223 336 709, telex 81240 G)

CARRENO, Josè Manuel; s of Lorenzp Torres, of Habana Cuba, and Caridad Carreno; *b* 25 May 1968; *Educ* Escuela Cubana de Ballet; ptnr Lourdes Novoa; *Career* dancer; with Ballet Nacional de Cuba pas de deux: Diana Y Acteon 1986, Corsaire 1987, White Swan 1988, Black Swan 1989, Tchaikowsky 1990; other work incl: Flower Festival 1987, Joseph Legend 1988, Apollo 1988, Fille Mal Gardeé 1988, Coppelia 1989, In The Night 1989, Flames of Paris 1989, Don Quijote 1989, Giselle 1990; with Eng Nat Ballet pas de deux: Don Quijote 1991, Nutcracker 1990-91, Nuestros Valses 1991; *Awards* winner: Gold medal New York Competition, Grand Prix Jackson Competition (Mississippi); *Recreations* listening to music, (especially Latin), movie watching; *Style*— Josè Manuel Carreno, Esq

CARRICK, 9 Earl of (I 1748); Brian Stuart Theobald Somerset Caher Butler; also Viscount Ikerrin (I 1629) and (sits as) Baron Butler of Mount Juliet (UK 1912); s of 8 Earl (d 1957), by his 1 w Marion; *b* 17 Aug 1931; *Educ* Downside; *m* 1, 1951 (m dis 1976), (Mary) Belinda, da of Maj David Constable-Maxwell, TD; 1 s, 1 da; m 2, 4 June 1986, Gillian, da of Leonard Grimes; *Heir* s, Viscount Ikerrin; *Career* dir: Balfour Maclaine Corporation, Cargill UK Ltd, Ralli Bros & Coney Ltd, Bowater Indust plc, Bowater Inc; *Recreations* bridge, racing; *Clubs* Brooks's, Pratt's, White's; *Style*— The Rt Hon the Earl of Carrick; 10 Netherton Grove, London SW10 (☎ 071 352 6328)

CARRICK, Phillip; s of Arthur Carrick (d 1969), of Leeds, and Ivy, *née* Kennedy; *b* 16 July 1952; *Educ* Bramley Co Sch, Intake Co Sch, Park Lane Coll; *m* 2 April 1977, Elspeth Campbell; 2 da (Emma b 6 May 1980, Pippa b 11 Jan 1982); *Career* cricketer; York CCC: debut 1970, benefit year 1985, capt 1987-89, scorer of over 9000 runs, taker of over 900 wickets, winner Benson & Hedges Cup 1987; played for: E Province SA 1976-77, N Transvaal SA 1982; proprietor Phil Carrick Enterprises (promotional product business); *Recreations* golf; *Style*— Phillip Carrick, Esq; Yorkshire CCC, Headingley Cricket Ground, Leeds LS6 3BU (☎ 0532 787394)

CARRICK, Roger John; CMG (1983), LVO (1972); s of John Horwood Carrick, of Whitchurch Hants, and Florence May, *née* Pudner; *b* 13 Oct 1937; *Educ* Isleworth GS, London Univ Sch of Slavonic and Euro Studies; *m* 1962, Hilary Elizabeth, da of Terence Verdun Blinman; 2 s (John, Charles); *Career* RN 1956-58; HM Diplomatic Serv FO 1958-61, Br Legation Sofia 1962-65, FO 1965-67, Br Embassy Paris 1967-71, Head of Chancery Br High Cmmn Singapore 1971-73, FCO 1973, cnsllr and dep head Personnel Ops Dept 1976, visiting fell Inst of Int Studies Univ of California Berkeley 1977-78, cnsllr Br Embassy Washington 1978-82, head Overseas Estate Dept, FCO 1982-85, HM consul gen Chicago 1985-; *Books* East-West Technology Transfer in Perspective (1978); *Recreations* sailing, some racquet games, music, reading, avoiding gardening, collecting walking sticks; *Clubs* Royal Cwlth Soc, Univ (Chicago), Tavern, Cliff Dwellers' (Chicago); *Style*— Roger Carrick, Esq, CMG, LVO; 1260 N Astor St, Chicago, Illinois 60610; c/o FCO (Chicago), King Charles St, London SW1A 2AH; Br Consulate Gen, 33 N Dearborn St, Chicago, Illinois 60602, USA (☎ 312 346 1810, telex 254432 a/b Britain GGO)

CARRICK, Ruth, Countess of; Ruth; *née* McEnery; da of Francis T M McEnery, of Chicago, Ill, USA; *b* 1918; *m* 1954, as his 3 w, 8 Earl of Carrick (d 1957); *Style*— The Rt Hon Ruth Countess of Carrick; PO Box 1190, Pinehurst, N Carolina 28374, USA (☎ 919 295 6337)

CARRINGTON, Prof Alan; s of Albert Carrington (d 1971), of 45 Ashdown Rd, Chandler's Ford, and Constance, *née* Nelson; *b* 6 Jan 1934; *Educ* Colfes GS, Univ of Southampton (BSc, PhD); *m* 7 Nov 1959, (Noreen) Hilary, da of Patrick Ferraby Taylor (d 1981); 1 s (Simon Francis b 1966), 2 da (Sarah Elizabeth b 1962, Rebecca Anne b 1964); *Career* res fell Univ of Minnesota 1957-58, asst dir res and official fell Downing Coll Cambridge 1963-67 (GEC res fell 1959-60, asst res and res fell Downing Coll 1960-63), royal soc res prof Univ of Southampton 1979-84 and 1987- (prof chemistry 1967-76, SERC sr res fell 1976-79), royal soc res prof and professorial fell Jesus Coll Oxford 1984-87; awards: Harrison Meml medal and prize Chem Soc 1962, Meldola medal Royal Inst Chem 1963, Marlow medal Faraday Soc 1966, Corday-Morgan medal and Prize Chem Soc 1967, award and medal Structural Chemistry Chem Soc 1970, Tilden medal and Lectureship Chem Soc 1972; Faraday medal Royal Soc of Chemistry 1985; Hon DSc Southampton 1985; FRS 1971 (memb Ctees), for hon memb American Acad Arts and Scis 1987, FRSC 1989, CChem 1989; *Books* Introduction to Magnetic Resonance (with A D McLachlan, 1967), Microwave Spectroscopy of Free Radicals (1974); *Recreations* music; *Style*— Prof Alan Carrington, FRS; 46 Lakewood Rd, Chandler's Ford, Hants SO5 1EX (☎ 0703 265092); Dept of Chemistry, Univ of Southampton, Hants SO9 5HN (☎ 0703 593431, telex 37661)

CARRINGTON, Maj-Gen Colin Edward George; CB (1991), CBE (1983); s of Edgar John Carrington (d 1988), and Ruth, *née* West (d 1990); *b* 19 Jan 1936; *Educ* Royal Liberty Sch, RMA Sandhurst, Army Staff Coll, Nat Def Coll, RCDS; *m* 5 Aug 1967, Joy, da of Albert Louis Bracknell (d 1987); 1 s (Damian Edward Colin b 21 Oct 1970), 1 da (Hannah Jane b 17 April 1974); *Career* Troop Cdr BAOR 1956-59, Air Despatch duties 1960-64, instr RMA Sandhurst 1964-68, Sqdn Cdr BAOR 1972-74, Directing Staff Staff Coll 1976-78, CO 1 Armd Div Tport Regt 1978-80, Dep COS 1 Armd Div 1980-82, dir Manning Policy (Army) 1984-86, Cdr Tport 1 (BR) Corps 1986-88, dir gen Tport and Movements (Army) 1988-; memb RCT Benevolent fund; Freeman: City of London, Worshipful Co of Carmen; FCIT 1988, FILDM 1989; *Recreations* gardening, golf, reading; *Style*— Maj-Gen Colin Carrington, CB, CBE; LE(A) Andover, Portway, Monton Rd, Andover, Hants (☎ 0264 2308)

CARRINGTON, Hon Mrs (Jennifer Michelle); *née* Souter; da and co-hp of 25 Baron Audley; *b* 23 May 1948; *m* Michael Carrington; 2 s (Jesse Michael b 1978, Jonah David b 1980), 1 da (Holly b 1975); *Style*— The Hon Mrs Carrington; 4766 Soquel Creek Road, Soquel, California 95073, USA

CARRINGTON, Matthew Hadrian Marshall; MP (C) Fulham 1987-; s of Walter Hadrian Marshall Carrington, of 18 Lansdowne Rd, London W11, and Dilys Mary Gwyneth Carrington; *b* 19 Oct 1947; *Educ* French Lycee London, Imperial Coll Univ of London (BSc), London Business Sch (MSc); *m* 29 March 1975, Mary Lou, da of Robert Darrow, of Columbus, Ohio, USA; 1 da (Victoria b 11 June 1981); *Career* prodn foreman GKN Sankey 1969-72; banker: The First National Bank of Chicago 1974-78, Saudi Int Bank 1978-87; *Recreations* cooking, political history; *Style*— Matthew H M Carrington, Esq, MP; 34 Ladbroke Square, London W11 3NB (☎ 071 221 4243); House of Commons London SW1A 0AA (☎ 071 219 6855)

CARRINGTON, 6 Baron (I 1796, GB 1797); Peter Alexander Rupert Carington; KG (1985), CH (1983), GCMG (1988, KCMG 1958), MC (1945), PC (1959), JP (Bucks 1948), DL (1951); s of 5 Baron Carrington, JP, DL (d 1938, n of 3 Baron, KG, GCMG, PC, JP, DL, sometime MP High Wycombe, and also 1 and last Marquess of Lincolnshire, govr of New South Wales, Lord Great Chamberlain of England and Lord Privy Seal) by his w, Hon Sybil, da of 2 Viscount Colville of Culross; *b* 6 June 1919; *Educ* Eton, RMC Sandhurst; *m* 1942, Iona, yr da of Sir Francis Kennedy McClean, AFC (d 1955); 1 s, 2 da (Hon Mrs de Bunsen, Hon Virginia); *Heir* s, Hon Rupert Carrington; *Career* served as Maj Gren Gds NW Europe; Parly sec Miny of Agric and Fisheries 1951-54, MOD 1954-56; high cmmr Australia 1956-59; first lord of Admiralty 1959-63; min without portfolio and ldr of House of Lords 1963-64, ldr of oppn House of Lords 1964-70 and 1974-79; sec of state: for Defence 1970-74, Dept of Energy 1974, for Foreign and Cwlth Affrs and min of Overseas Devpt 1979-82; Min of Aviation Supply 1971-74, chm Cons Party 1972-74, sec gen NATO 1984-88; chm: GEC 1983-84 (dir 1982-84), Christie's 1988-; fell Eton 1966-81; hon fell St Antony's Coll Oxford 1982-; memb Int Bd United World Colls 1982-84; chm of tstees V&A Museum 1983-88; Chllr of the Order of St Michael and St John 1984; Hon Bencher of Middle Temple 1983; Hon Elder Brother Trinity House 1984; Hon LLD: Leeds, Cambridge 1981, Philippines, S Carolina, Aberdeen 1985, Sussex 1989, Reading 1989, Buckingham 1989; Hon DSc Cranfield 1983, Hon DUniv Essex; *Clubs* Pratt's, White's, Melbourne; *Style*— The Rt Hon the Lord Carrington, KG, CH, GCMG, MC, PC, JP, DL; 32A Ovington Sq, London SW3 1LR (☎ 071 584 1476); The Manor House, Bledlow, nr Aylesbury, Bucks (☎ 084 44 3499)

CARRINGTON, Simon Robert; s of Robert Carrington, of Suffolk, and Jean, *née* Hill, of Wilts; *b* 23 Oct 1942; *Educ* ChCh Cathedral Choir Sch Oxford, The King's Sch Canterbury, King's Coll Cambridge, New Coll Oxford; *m* 2 Aug 1969, Hilary Elizabeth, da of Leslie Stott (d 1964); 1 s (Jamie b 1973), 1 da (Rebecca b 1971); *Career* dir The King's Singers 1968-; teacher and adjudicator Double Bass, dir Choral Summer Sch Marlborough Coll Wilts and Berwang Austria; with The King's Singers: 40 LP's for EMI, tours worldwide, concerts, workshops and master classes; regular TV appearances worldwide incl: Live at the Boston Pops 1983, BC TV Series The King's Singers Madrigal History Tour 1984, ABC TV (USA) The Sound of Christmas from Salzburgh 1987, 8 appearances on the Johnny Carson Tonight Show (NBC TV, USA) 1983-90; festival dir Barbican Summer in the City Festivals 1988-89, 20 Anniversary Concerts Worldwide 1988, Grammy nomination USA 1986; FRSA; *Books* The King's Singers - a Self Portrait (1981), choral arrangements for pubn; *Recreations* vintage cars, inland waterways, gardens, trees, walking, jogging; *Clubs* Royal Soc of Musicians, Inc Soc of Musicians; *Style*— Simon Carrington, Esq; The Old House, Rushall, Pewsey, Wiltshire SN9 6EN (☎ 0980 630 477); The King's Singers Management, Gillian Newson Associates, 13 Norfolk Mansions, Prince of Wales Drive, London SW11 4HL (☎ 071 720 7678)

CARRO, Hon Mrs (Alice Louise); *née* Walpole; er da of 10 Baron Walpole, JP, and Mrs Michael Chaplin; *b* 1 Sept 1963; *m* 16 Feb 1990, Dr Angel Cesar Carro Castrillo, yr s of Sr Herminio Carro Sanz, and Sra Esther Castrillo Del Pozo, of Geneva; 2 da (Hester Nancy b 8 Dec 1990, Beatrice Maud (twin)); *Career* HM Dip Serv; *Style*— The Hon Mrs Carro

CARROL, Charles Gordon; s of Charles Muir Carrol (d 1974), of Edinburgh, and Catherine Gray, *née* Napier; *b* 21 March 1935; *Educ* Melville Coll Edinburgh, Univ of Edinburgh (MA, DipEd); *m* 1970, Frances Anne, da of John A Sinclair, of Edinburgh; 3

s (Simon b 1971, Christopher b 1974, David b 1979); *Career* educn offr: Govt Northern Nigeria 1959-65, Cwlth Inst Scotland 1965-71; dir Cwlth Inst Scotland 1971-; lay memb Press Cncl 1978-83; *Recreations* hill walking, angling; *Clubs* Rotary (Edinburgh); *Style—* Charles Carrol Esq; 11 Dukehaugh, Peebles, EH45 9DN (☎ 0721 21296); Commonwealth Institute Scotland, 8 Rutland Square, Edinburgh EH1 2AS (☎ 031 229 6668)

CARROLL, Ben; s of Joseph Carroll, of Harrow, Middx, and Margaret, *née* O'Carroll; *b* 5 May 1945; *Educ* London Oratory; *m* 13 May 1967, Rosemary-Anne, da of Morris Tucker; *Career* Scottish Widows Fund & Life Assurance Soc 1964-66, Keith Shipton (Life & Pensions) Ltd 1966-68; Noble Lowndes & Partners Ltd: joined as legal and revenue mangr 1968, regnl dir London West End Region 1975, regnl dir London City Region 1980, md Noble Lowndes International Ltd 1986, md Employee Benefits 1988, md Personal Fin Servs 1990-; author of papers on behalf of firm; FPMI (pres 1987-89), FCII; *Recreations* fine wine, travel, theatre, modern films, art; *Style—* Ben Carroll, Esq; Noble Lowndes & Partners Limited, Norfolk House, Wellesley Rd, Croydon CR9 3EB (☎ 081 686 2466, fax 081 680 7998)

CARROLL, Gerald John Howard; s of John Robert Carroll, of London and Frinton-on-Sea, Essex, and Catherine Florence Howard; lineal descendant of ancient Sept O'Carroll, Princes of Ely, Barons of Ely O'Carroll, Co Offaly, Ireland; *b* 9 Oct 1951; *Educ* Herrington House, Ipswich Sch; *Career* chm The Carroll Group and Associated Cos 1972-, chief exec Farnborough Aerospace Development Corporation Ltd 1985-; dir: Longfield Investment Co Ltd 1972-, Westbury Investment Co Ltd 1972-, Soild State Securities Ltd 1973-, Dukes Park Industrial Estates Ltd 1974-75, Culver Developments 1980-, London and Central Properties Ltd 1980-, Automated Machine Industries Ltd 1980-, Strategic R & D Corporation Ltd 1985-, Carroll Australia Corporation 1989-, Carroll Global Corporation 1989-, The Manchester Canal and Business Park Development Corportaion, Carroll Aircraft Corporation Ltd 1985-, PYBT Development Fund (Yorkshire) Ltd; tstee: Carroll Fndn 1972-, Carroll Inst, Carroll Art Collection 1990-; memb: Br Helicopter Advsy Bd 1985-, Royal United Servs Inst 1988-, Chllr's Court of Benefactors Univ of Oxford 1990-, Capital Historical Soc Washington DC; *Recreations* racing, sailing, shooting; *Clubs* Royal Thames Yacht, Cirencester Park Polo, Race Horse Owners Assoc, Old Ipswichian, Cavalry and Guards (hon memb); *Style—* Gerald Carroll, Esq; 29 Eaton Sq, Belgravia, London SW1W 9DF; Warren Park, Newmarket, Suffolk CB8 8QL; Carroll House, 2-6 Catherine Place, Westminster, London SW1E 6HF

CARROLL, John; s of Sean Carroll, of 63 Winnipeg Rd, Bentley, nr Doncaster, and Norah, *née* Coombes; *b* 15 April 1964; *Educ* St Peter's HS Doncaster; *m* 17 Nov 1989, Tracy, da of John Hunter; 1 da (Danielle b 29 Oct 1990); *Career* flat race jockey 1981-, best season 62 winners 1989; achievements: winner Molecomb Stakes Group Three Goodwood 1988, runner up Heinz 57 Group One Phoenix Park; *Recreations* shooting, fishing, playing football; *Style—* John Carroll, Esq; 1 Rectory Gardens, Cockerham, nr Lancaster LA2 0ED (☎ 0524 791697, car 0836 238602); c/o Joe Rowntree, Esq (☎ 03476 482, car 0836 326084)

CARROLL, Prof John Edward; s of Sidney Wentworth Carroll (d 1959), and May Doris, *née* Brand; *b* 15 Feb 1934; *Educ* Oundle, Queens' Coll Cambridge (BA, MA, PhD, ScD); *m* Vera Mary, *née* Jordan; *Career* princ scientific offr Servs Electronic Res Laboratory 1961-67; Univ of Cambridge Engrg Dept: lectr 1967-76, reader 1976-83, prof 1983-; fell Queens' Coll Cambridge 1961-; FIEE 1965, FEng 1980; *Books* Hot Electron Microwave Generators (1970), Semiconductor Devices (1974), Rate Equations in Semiconductor Electronics (1985); *Recreations* carpentry, walking, reading; *Style—* Prof John Carroll; Dept of Engineering, University of Cambridge, Trumpington St, Cambridge CB2 1PZ (☎ 0223 332799, fax 0223 332662)

CARROLL, Robin David; s of William George Carroll, of Putney and Mary Jenny, *née* Crane; *b* 29 Feb 1948; *Educ* Elliot Sch, Kingston Coll of Art (BA); *Career* sr art dir: Ogilvy and Mather 1972-79, Mathers Allders and Marchant 1979-84; creative dir Bastable Dailey 1984-; memb Creative Circle 1986; memb D&AD 1984-; *Recreations* antique collecting, writing; *Style—* Robin Carroll, Esq; Bastable Advertising, 4 Bouverie St, London EC4 (☎ 071 353 5272, fax 071 583 3997)

CARROLL, Stuart Paul; s of John James Carroll, and Sadie June Carroll; *b* 24 July 1951; *Educ* Univ of London (LLB); *Career* admitted slr 1977; sr litigation ptnr and head Litigation Dept Nabarro Nathanson 1982-; memb Law Soc; *Style—* Stuart Carroll, Esq; Nabarro Nathanson, 50 Stratton St, London W1X 5FL (☎ 071 493 9933, fax 071 629 7900, telex 8813144 NABAROG)

CARROLL, Terence Patrick (Terry); s of George Daniel Carroll, of Upchurch, Kent, and Betty Doreen, *née* Holmes; *b* 24 Nov 1948; *Educ* Gillingham GS, Univ of Bradford Mgmnt Centre (BSc); *m* 1, 4 April 1971 (m dis 1984), Louise Mary, da of Leslie Charles Smith; 1 s (Mark George b 1979); m 2, 12 Oct 1984, Penelope Julia (Penny), da of Walter John Berry; *Career* auditor and computer auditor Armitage & Norton 1970-76, mgmnt accountant Bradford & Bingley Bldg Soc 1976-80, exec and memb of stock exchange Sheppards & Chase 1980-82, treas Halifax Bldg Soc 1982-85, chm Bradford Breakthrough Ltd 1989-90, gp treasy dir Nat and Provincial Bldg Soc 1990 (fin dir 1985-89); MBIM 1979, FCA 1980, MCT 1985, FCBSI 1986; *Recreations* golf, hockey, bridge; *Clubs* Bradford, Ilkley Golf; *Style—* Terry Carroll, Esq; National & Provincial BS, Provincial House, Bradford, W Yorks BD1 1NL (☎ 0274 842 502, fax 0274 733 858, car 0836 789 336)

CARRON, Byron Richard; s of Arthur Carron (d 1966), and Gladys Irene, *née* Richards; *b* 18 March 1942; *Educ* Swindon HS; *m* 1965, Joan Olive, da of Archibald John Scott (d 1973); 1 s (Richard b 1967), 4 da (Louise b 1968, Annette b 1970, Rebecca b 1971, Sarah (twin) b 1971); *Career* admitted slr 1965; ptnr Messrs Townsends Swindon; former memb Nat Young Slrs Gp; former chm Glos and Wilts Young Slrs; former chm Devizes Constituency Lib Assoc; Wilts CC: memb 1981-89, former vice chm, chm of fin 1985-89; *Recreations* gardening, walking, music; *Clubs* Swindon Rotary; *Style—* Byron R Carron, Esq; The Gables, Lower Wanborough, Swindon, Wilts (☎ 0793 790294); Townsends, 42 Cricklade St, Swindon, Wilts (☎ 0793 354231)

CARRUTHERS, Dr (George) Barry; s of George Harry Carruthers, CBE (d 1979), and Mary, *née* Barry (d 1990); *b* 22 Dec 1924; *Educ* St Paul's Sch Hammersmith, The Middx Hosp London (MD, MB BS); *m* 4 s (Graeme David Barry b 2 June 1956, Stephen Robert b 3 Jan 1958, Richard Barry b 7 Jan 1965, Simon b 13 May 1967), 1 da (Nicola Jane Mary b 8 April 1971); *Career* med offr RAF 1949-57; med offr: Bank of England Printing Works 1956-71, Nat Heart Hosp 1960-, Royal Northern Hosp 1966-83; conslt in male infertility and dir of laboratories Royal Northern Hosp 1968-75, hon conslt Dept of Urology St Thomas' Hosp 1971-, med dir Wimpole St Med Centre 1981-; memb RSM 1971; *Books* Virility Diet (1973), Infertility (1981); *Recreations* antiquarian books and prints, golf, bridge; *Clubs* Reform; *Style—* Dr Barry Carruthers; London Wimpole Clinic, 55 Wimpole St, London W1M 7DF (☎ 071 486 4646)

CARRUTHERS, James Edwin; s of James Carruthers (d 1964), and Dollie Carruthers (d 1968); *b* 19 March 1928; *Educ* George Heriot's Sch, Univ of Edinburgh (MA); *m* 5 March 1955, Phyllis May, *née* Williams; 1 s (James Alexander b 1964); *Career* Queen's Own Cameron Highlanders 1949-57; Air Miny 1951-60, Miny of Aviation 1960-62, MOD 1962-68, chief offr Sovereign Base Areas Admin Cyprus 1968-71, MOD 1971-73, Cabinet Office 1973-74, Br Aerospace 1975-79, Royal Ordnance Factories 1980-83, chm Civil Serv Selection Bd 1983-84, asst under sec of state MOD 1984-88, asst sec Royal Hosp Chelsea; *Style—* James Carruthers, Esq

CARRUTHERS, Philip Anthony (Tony); s of Donald Carruthers (d 1983), of Torquay, Devon, and Beatrice Ada, *née* Tremain (d 1987); *b* 29 Nov 1934; *Educ* Homelands Tech HS Torquay, S Devon Tech Coll Torquay; *m* 4 April 1964, Sheila Mary, da of Rowdon Atkins (d 1956), of St Marychurch, Torquay, Devon; 1 da (Anne-Marie Carole b 1966); *Career* RN 1951-54, RNR 1954-59; dir: Charles Moxham & Co Ltd 1960 (joined 1954), Moxhams of Torquay Ltd (Barlow Group) 1968, Thos Barlow Motors Ltd 1970, Barlow Handling Ltd 1972 (co sec 1975), Thos Barlow Holdings Ltd (Materials Handling Div of J Bibby & Sons plc) 1985, DD Lamson plc 1990-; supporter: Henley Royal Regatta, Henley Festival of Music and Art; FID 1968; *Recreations* theatre, opera; *Clubs* Leander, Phyllis Court (Henley); *Style—* Tony Carruthers, Esq; St Marymead, Wargrave, Berks (☎ 0734 402693); Moongates, Torquay, Devon; Thos Barlow Holdings Ltd, Airfield Estate, Maidenhead, Berks SL6 3QN (☎ 062 882 6401, fax 062 882 5745, telex 848191)

CARSBERG, Sir Bryan Victor; s of Alfred Victor Carsberg, of Chesham Bois, Bucks, and Maryllia Cicely, *née* Collins; *b* 3 Jan 1939; *Educ* Berkhamsted, LSE (MSc), Univ of Manchester (MA); *m* 1960, Margaret Linda, da of Capt Neil McKenzie Graham (d 1966); 2 da (Debbie, Sarah); *Career* CA, sole practice 1962-64, lectr in accounting LSE 1964-68, visiting lectr Graduate Sch of Business Univ of Chicago 1968-69, prof of accounting Univ of Manchester 1969-81 (dean Faculty of Econ and Social Studies 1977-78), visiting prof of business admin Univ of California Berkeley 1974, Arthur Anderson prof of accounting LSE 1981-87, dir of research (pt/t) ICA 1981-87, visiting prof of accounting LSE 1987-89; asst dir of res and technical activities Financial Accounting Standards Bd USA 1978-81, memb Cncl ICA 1975-79; dir: Economists Advsy Gp 1976-84, Economist Bookshop 1981-, Philip Allan Publishers 1981-; dir gen of telecommunication OFTEL 1984-, vice chm Accounting Standards Bd 1990-; memb: Bd Radiocommunications Agency 1990-, Cncl Univ of Surrey 1990-; Cas Founding Socs' Centenary award 1988; hon fell LSE 1990; kt 1989; *Books* An Introduction to Mathematical Programming for Accountants (1969), Modern Financial Management (with H C Edey, 1969), Analysis for Investment Decisions (1974), Indexation and Inflation (with E V Morgan and M Parkin, 1975), Economics of Business Decisions (1975), Investment Decisions under Inflation (with A Hope, 1976), Current Issues in Accountancy (with A Hope, 1977), Topics in Management Accounting (with J Arnold and R Scapens, 1980), Current Cost Acccounting (with M Page, 1983), Small Company Financial Reporting (with M Page and others, 1985); *Recreations* road running, theatre, opera, music; *Style—* Sir Bryan Carsberg; Office of Telecommunications, Export House, Ludgate Hill, London EC4M 7SJ (☎ 071 822 1601)

CARSON, Ciaran Gerard; s of William Carson, of Belfast, and Mary Ellen, *née* Maginn; *b* 9 Oct 1948; *Educ* St Mary's Christian Brothers' Sch, Queens Univ Belfast (BA); *m* 16 Oct 1982, Deirdre, da of Patrick Shannon; 2 s (Manus b 5 April 1986, Gerard 29 Oct 1987), 1 da (Mary Ellen b 3 Oct 1990); *Career* traditional arts offr Arts Cncl of NI 1975-; The New Estate (1976), The Irish for No (1988), Belfast Confetti (1990), The Pocket Guide to Irish Traditional Music (1986); Gregory award 1976, Alice Hunt Bartlett award 1988, Irish Times/Aer Lingus award 1990; *Recreations* playing traditional music; *Style—* Ciaran Carson, Esq; Arts Council of Northern Ireland, 181A Stranmillis Rd, Belfast BT9 5DU (☎ 0232 381591)

CARSON, (Thomas) Richard; s of Johnston Carson, and Rebecca, *née* Farrell; *Educ* Portora Royal Sch, Queen's Univ Belfast (BSc, PhD); *m* Ursula Margaret Mary, *née* Davies; 1 s (David b 1973); *Career* sr scientific offr Atomic Weapons Res Estab Aldermaston, sr lectr and reader in astrophysics Univ of St Andrews; sometime: visiting fell and prof Univ of Colorado, sr res assoc NASA Inst for Space Studies NY, visiting staff memb Los Alamos Nat Laboratory Univ of California; memb: Int Astronomical Union 1966, American Astronomical Soc 1968, NY Acad of Scis 1989; FRAS 1959; *Books* Atoms and Molecules in Astrophysics (ed with M J Roberts, 1972); *Recreations* skiing, tennis, swimming; *Style—* Richard Carson, Esq; 7 Cairnsden Gardens, St Andrews, Fife KY16 8SQ (☎ 0334 73813); Dept of Physics and Astronomy, University of St Andrews, N Haugh, St Andrews KY16 9SS (☎ 0334 76161 ext 8359)

CARSON, Air Cdre Robert John; CBE (1974), AFC (1964), QC (1962); er s of Robert George Carson, and Margaret Etta Carson; *b* 3 Aug 1924; *Educ* Regent House Sch Newtownards, RAF; *m* 1945, Jane, *née* Bailie; 3 da; *Career* Air Cdre; served in Far East, ME, Europe, NATO, Rhodesia, Africa, Canada, USA; Air Advsr Br High Cmmn Ottawa 1974-75, Def Advsr to Br High Cmmr in Canada 1975-78; mangr (Panavia Office) Grumman Aerospace Corp Bethpage 1978-80, dir Leics Medical Res Fndn Univ of Leicester 1980-; MRAeS, MBIM, memb Inst of Admin Mgmnt; *Recreations* golf, tennis, rugby, gardening; *Clubs* RAF, Royal Ottawa, Leicestershire Golf; *Style—* Air Cdre Robert J Carson, CBE, AFC, QC; 20 Meadow Drive, Scruton, Nr Northallerton, N Yorks DL7 0QW (☎ 0609 748 656); Leicestershire Medical Research Foundation, Leicester University, Leicester LE1 7RH (☎ 0533 556 662 or 556 665)

CARSON, (Edward) Rory; s of The Hon Edward Carson, MP (d 1987), of Hastings, Sussex, and Hon Mrs Heather Carson, *née* Sclater; *b* 25 May 1949; *Educ* Radley; *m* 19 April 1975, Araminta, da of Sir John Horlick, Bt, of Scotland; 4 s (Toby b 1977, Jonathen b 1979, Oliver b 1982, Bartholomew b 1988); *Career* dir: Swift 103 Ltd 1984-, London Motorentals Ltd 1984-; *Recreations* tennis, walking, exotic pets; *Clubs* Raffles; *Style—* Rory Carson, Esq; Perseverance Cottage, Harpsden, Henley-on-Thames, Oxon R59 4AS; Bank Messrs Coutts and Co, 15 Lombard Street, London EC3; 1 Shortlands, Hammersmith, London W6 (☎ 071 741 4981)

CARSON, Stuart Crosbie; s of Douglas Carson, and Anna, *née* Murray; *b* 1 April 1951; *Educ* Solihull Pub Sch, Univ of Wales (LLB), UCL (LLM); *m* Linda Joy, da of Frank Bailey; 2 da (Sally b 7 Sept 1976, Dawn b 27 May 1979); *Career* called to the Bar Inner Temple; practising barr 1980-81, slr and exec sec Assoc of Br Insurers 1982-86, asst dir Inst of CA 1986-88, legal advsr Lautro 1988-90, co sec First Tokyo Index Trust 1990-, dir and legal counsel London & Bishopsgate International Investment Management plc 1990-; legal counsel and compliance dir London & Bishopsgate Trading plc 1990-; *Recreations* fly-fishing, photography, squash, sailing; *Style—* Stuart Carson, Esq; Legal Counsel, London & Bishopsgate International Investment Management plc, 12th Floor, 76 Shoe Lane, London EC4A 3JB (☎ 071 583 1978, fax 071 353 0040)

CARSON, William Hunter Fisher (Willie); OBE (1983); s of Thomas Whelan Carson, and Mary Hay; *b* 16 Nov 1942; *Educ* Riverside Sch Sterling; *m* 1, 1963 (m dis 1979), Carole Jane Sutton; 3 s (Antony Thomas, Neil John, Ross William); m 2, 5 May 1982, Elaine, do of John B Williams; *Career* racehorse jockey; apprentice to: Capt G Armstrong 1957-63 (first winner Catterick 1962), Fred Armstrong 1963-66; first jockey to: Lord Derby 1967, Dick Hern 1977-; appointed Royal jockey 1977; major races won: 2000 Guineas 4 times (High Top 1972, Known Fact 1980, Don't Forget Me 1987, Nashawn 1989), Oaks 4 times (Dunfermline 1977 for HM The Queen, Bireme 1980, Sun Princess 1983, Salsabil 1990), Derby 3 times (Troy 1979, Henbit

1980, Nashwan 1989), King George VI and Queen Elizabeth Diamond Stakes 4 times (Troy 1979, Ela-Mana-Mov 1980, Petoski 1985, Nashwan 1989), St Leger 3 times (Dunfermline 1977 for HM The Queen, Sun Princes 1983, Minster Son 1988), the Eclipse twice (Nashwan 1989, Elmaamul 1990), Ascot Gold Cup 1983 (Little Wolf), 1000 Guineas 1990 (Salsabil); champion jockey 1972, 1973, 1978, 1980, 1983, ridden over 100 winners every season 1972- (except 1984 when injured), became third most successful Br jockey with 3,112 wins Aug 1990 (incl over 50 group one races), jt record holder with six wins at one meeting Newcastle 1990; *Recreations* hunting; *Style—* Willie Carson, Esq, OBE; Minster House, Barnsley, Cirencester, Gloucs

CARSS, Gordon; s of Herbert Jackson Carss, of Seaham, Co Durham, and Florence May Carss; *b* 12 March 1931; *Educ* Argyle House Sch, Sunderland; *m* 31 March 1954, Doreen; 1 da (Amanda Jayne b 1966); *Career* gen mangr and sec Mid Sussex Bldg Soc (sec 1972); asst sec: Harrow Bldg Soc 1970-, Chesham Bldg Soc 1971; chm Brighton and Dist CBSI 1983-84 and 1990-91; FCIS, FCBSI, MBIM; *Clubs* Rotary, Burgess Hill and Dist; *Style—* Gordon Carss, Esq; Hurzanmyne, 70C Ferndale Rd, Burgess Hill, W Sussex RH15 0HD (☎ 0444 242330); 66 Church Rd, Burgess Hill, W Sussex RH15 9AU

CARSTAIRS, Ian Andrew; s of Alexander Gordon Carstairs, of Leics, and Dorothy Mary, *née* Carr; *b* 13 Feb 1951; *Educ* Hinckley GS (now John Cleveland Coll), St John's Coll Cambridge (MA); *m* 1973, Kay, da of Keith Reginald Muggleton, of Leics; 3 s (Thomas Andrew b 1979, Benjamin James b 1980, Joseph William b 1983); *Career* Sun Life Assurance Society Ltd 1972-80, J Rothschild Investment Management Ltd 1980-84, Target Investment Management Ltd 1984-89, Target Residential Property Fund SA 1986-89, The Bike Chain Ltd 1989-; *Recreations* tennis, squash, swimming, fine food and wine, crosswords; *Style—* Ian Carstairs, Esq; Mercury Asset Management Ltd, 33 King William St, London EC4 (☎ 071 280 2800)

CARSWELL, John Patrick; CB (1977); s of Donald Carswell (d 1940), and Catherine Roxburgh Macfarlane (d 1946); *b* 30 May 1918; *Educ* Merchant Taylors' Sch, St John's Coll Oxford (MA); *m* 1945, Ianthe, da of Capt Eric Bramley Elstob, RN (d 1946); 2 da; *Career* serv WWII Maj India and E Bengal; Civil Serv 1946-77, Miny of Pensions Nat Insur 1946-60, HM Treasy 1960-64, under sec DES 1964-74, sec UGC 1974-77; sec Br Acad 1978-83; author; FRSL; *Recreations* writing, war on a small scale; *Clubs* Garrick; *Style—* John Carswell, Esq, CB; 5 Prince Arthur Rd, London NW3 (☎ 071 794 6527); Berins Hill, Ipsden, Oxfordshire

CARSWELL, Richard John; s of Ronald Alec Carswell, of Oulton, Suffolk, and Lada Josipa, *née* Kalebic; *b* 4 Feb 1947; *Educ* Anglo-American Sch Kuwait, Taunton Sch Somerset, Univ of London (BA); *Career* European Movement London 1974-75, Cmmn of Euro Communities, Brussels 1975-78, Euro Parliament London 1979, CSM Parliamentary and European Consultants London 1980-86, Profile Politicial and Public Relations London 1986-87, Traverse-Healy & Regester London 1987, Charles Barker London 1987-; RSA preliminary cert in TEFL; MIPR (chm IPR Govt Affairs Gp 1989-91); *Recreations* travel, reading, languages, walking, table tennis; *Style—* Richard Carswell, Esq; Charles Barker, 30 Farringdon St, London EC4A 4EA (☎ 071 634 1102, fax 071 236 0170)

CARSWELL, Hon Mr Justice; Sir Robert Douglas; s of Alan Edward Carswell (d 1972), of Belfast, and Nance Eileen, *née* Corlett; *b* 28 June 1934; *Educ* Royal Belfast Academical Inst, Pembroke Coll Oxford (MA), Univ of Chicago Law Sch; *m* 1961, Romayne Winifred, da of James Ferris, JP, of Co Down; 2 da (Catherine, Patricia); *Career* called to the Bar NI 1957, English Bar (Gray's Inn) 1972, counsel to Attorney Gen for NI 1970-71, QC 1971, sr Crown counsel in NI 1979-84, bencher Inn of Ct of NI 1979, judge of the High Court of NI 1984; pro chllr and chm Cncl Univ of Ulster 1984, chm Law Reform Advsy Ctee NI 1989, chllr Dioceses of Armagh and of Down and Dromore 1990; kt 1988; *Recreations* golf; *Clubs* Ulster Reform (Belfast); *Style—* The Hon Mr Justice Carswell; c/o Royal Cts of Justice, Belfast BT1 3JF (☎ 0232 235111)

CARTE, Brian Addison; TD (1976); s of late James Carte; *b* 7 Aug 1943; *Educ* St Lawrence Coll Ramsgate; *m* 1969, Shirley Anne, da of Lt-Col W H Brinkley; 2 da; *Career* Co Cdr Queen's Regt TA, Maj GSO II HQ London Dist, asst project offr DTA and C, RARO 1987; chief exec Lombard North Central plc; former pres Assoc of Corp Treasurers; govr St Lawrence Coll; Freeman and Liveryman Co of Scriveners; FCIB, FCT, FRSA; *Recreations* golf, opera; *Clubs* New Zealand Golf, RAC; *Style—* Brian Carte, Esq, TD; Fairfield Lodge, Hardwick Close, Knott Park, Oxshott, Surrey KT22 0HZ

CARTER, Adrian Ross Grant; s of Rear Adm Simon Lorris Ian Carter (d 1982), and Agnes Gwndolyn Doris Lack, OBE (d 1987); *b* 4 May 1940; *Educ* Harrow, Univ of Oxford (BA), Univ of Moscow (Int Law), Nuffield Coll Oxford (PhD); *m* 1, 11 April 1971 (m dis 1973), Laura Edna, da of Lt-Col Claude Clarence King (d 1980); m 2, 6 Aug 1975, Ziba, *née* Decorri (d 1976); m 3, 3 Dec 1979 (m dis 1982), Maira Lolita, *née* Gormez; m 4, 20 Feb 1983, Ludmilla Olga, *née* Lobchesky (d 1985); *Career* slr; articled clerk Mayo & Perkins Eastbourne 1976-80, jr ptnr Smart & Spicer 1980-83, ptnr Cooper Carter & Odhams Eastbourne 1983-; vice chm Elvis Presley Fan Club 1983-85, chm E Sussex branch Comm Pty 1985- (press offr 1981-85); memb ctee Law Soc 1985-89); *Books* A Trip though Northern Siberia (1984), All You Need to Know about Ferrets (1986), White Mice in Sickness and Health (1987), How to go Bankrupt the Easy Way (1988), Russian Law Made Easy (1989); *Recreations* ferret-keeping, pearl fishing, judo, flower-arranging, taxidermy; *Style—* Adrian Carter, Esq; 62 Baldwin Ave, Eastbourne (☎ 0323 23873; Cooper Cartier & Odhams, 25 Hyde Gardens, Eastbourne, E Sussex BN21 4PX (☎ 0323 410933, fax 0323 410683, telex 6919)

CARTER, Alan Owen; s of Arthur Henry Carter (d 1958), of Cardiff, and Lily May, *née* Jones (d 1983); *b* 28 July 1932; *Educ* Penarth GS, Univ of Wales Cardiff (BA Hons, Hockey blue); *m* July 1962, Wendy Barbara, da of Sidney Clifford Page; 1 s (Matthew Christian Alan b June 1967), 1 da (Emma Siân b Aug 1971); *Career* educn offr RAF 1955-58; Stanwell Sch 1959-91: teacher of history, head of sixth form; pres: Welsh Hockey Assoc 1986-, Welsh Hockey Umpires Assoc 1985-; memb: Euro Hockey Fedn 1988-, Euro Club Championship Ctee (Hockey) 1988-, Int Hockey Fedn (and int umpire) 1979-85; Welsh nat umpire (indoor) 1979-83; Euro hockey official at tournaments in: Moscow 1984, Finland 1988, Sardinia 1989, Sweden 1990, Gibraltar 1991; *Recreations* reading, theatre, art, music, cricket; *Style—* A O Carter, Esq; 48 Minehead Avenue, Sully, Penarth, South Glamorgan CF6 2TJ (☎ 0222 530 561)

CARTER, Alan Ponsford; s of William Howard Carter (d 1971), of Bishop's Cannings, Devizes, Wilts, and Brenda, *née* Ponsford; *b* 10 Dec 1941; *Educ* Devizes GS, RVC London; *m* 28 Dec 1968, Margaret Lyon, da of Col Thomas Henry Band, of Stratford Upon Avon; 1 s (Benjamin b 1978), 2 da (Clare b 1972, Lucy b 1974); *Career* vet surgn gen practice 1967-70, dep regnl offr Milk Mktg Bd 1979-81 (vet offr 1970-81), ptnr in gen practice Longmead 1981-; memb local PCC; memb BVA, memb ctee SCVS; *Style—* Alan Carter, Esq; Castleton House, Breach Lane, Shaftesbury, Dorset (☎ 0747 52820); Longmead Vet Practice, Shaftesbury, Dorset (☎ 0747 52064)

CARTER, Andrew; s of Eric Harry Carter (d 1988), and Margaret Elizabeth, *née* Maycock; *b* 4 Dec 1943; *Educ* Latymer Upper Sch, Jesus Coll Cambridge (MA), RCM; *m* 1, 1973 (m dis 1986), Anne Caroline Morgan; 1 da (Catherine b 1978); m 2, 21 May 1988, Catherine Mary, da of Peter Haswell Tyler, of Torcross, S Devon; 1 da (Alice b 1989); *Career* asst master Marlborough 1965-70; HM Diplomatic Service 1971-; Warsaw 1972-74, Geneva 1975, Bonn 1975-78, FCO 1978-86, UK delegation to NATO Brussels 1986-90, dep govr of Gibraltar 1990-; FRCO 1979, ARCM 1962, LRAM 1979; *Recreations* music; *Style—* Andrew Carter, Esq; c/o Foreign and Commonwealth Office, London SW1

CARTER, (Alan) Barham; s of Edwin Carter (d 1953), of Belvedere, Kent, and Laura Emily Edith, *née* Mead (d 1960); *b* 5 Feb 1907; *Educ* Tonbridge Sch, St Olave's GS London, Gonville and Caius Coll Cambridge (MA, MD, BCH), St Thomas's Hosp London; *m* 10 June 1937, Mollie Christina, da of Alderman Sidney Sanders, JP (d 1942), of Streatham, London; 2 s (Clive b 1942, Stephen b 1953), 2 da (Clare b 1946, Jane b 1949); *Career* RAMC, Maj 1947, Lt-Col 1949, conslt neurologist mil hosps and advsr neurology WO 1950, Hon Col, civilian conslt neurologist Cambridge Mil Hosp 1960; conslt physician: Middx Hosp 1938-43, Ashford Hosp 1943-74; hon conslt: Atkinson Morleys Hosp 1960-76, St Georges Hosp 1976-80; Freeman City of London 1965, Liveryman Worshipful Co of Clockmakers 1965; Coronation Medal 1936; FRCP 1961, FRSM (cncllr 1950-60); *Books* Cerebral Infarction (1964), All About Strokes (1968), The Art of Ageing (1983); *Recreations* cricket, golf; *Clubs* Royal Soc Medicine; *Style—* Dr Barham Carter; The Bracken, St Georges Hill, Weybridge, Surrey KT13 0NU (☎ 0932 864422); Nuffield Hosp, Woking, Surrey (☎ 048 62763511)

CARTER, Bernard Thomas; s of Cecil Carter (d 1962), and Ethel, *née* Darby (d 1961); *b* 6 April 1920; *Educ* Haberdashers' Aske's, Goldsmiths Coll of Art London (NDD, ATD); *m* 1952, Eugenie Mary, da of Capt David William Alexander, RNR (d 1952); 1 s (John); *Career* RAF 1939-46; art lectr 1952-68; Nat Maritime Museum: asst keeper prints and drawings 1968, dep keeper and head of Picture Dept 1970, keeper and head of Dept of Pictures and Conservation 1972-77; full time artist 1977-; one man exhibitions: Arthur Jeffress Gallery 1955, eleven one man exhibitions Portal Gallery Grafton St W1; pictures in many public collections in UK and abroad; memb Advsy Cncl on Export of Works of Art 1970-77; Hon RE; *Recreations* music, theatre, restaurants, gardening, travel, reading, TV; *Style—* Bernard Carter, Esq; 56 King George St, Greenwich, London SE10 8QD (☎ 081 858 4281)

CARTER, Hon Mrs (Brenda Ruby); *née* Pearson; 4 da of 2 Viscount Cowdray (d 1933), and Agnes Beryl (d 1948), da of Lord Edward Spencer-Churchill; *b* 15 Nov 1912; *m* 1, 1934 (m dis 1948), Gp-Capt Paul Willert, RAF, o s of Sir Arthur Willert, KBE; 2 da (Pauline m John, s of Sir Maurice Dorman, *qv*, Wanda m John Rix); m 2, 1948, Hugh Carter; 1 s (Harold m Theresa Silkstone); *Style—* The Hon Mrs Carter; Mallards, Duck Lane, Midhurst, W Sussex GU29 9DE

CARTER, His Hon Judge (Frederick) Brian; QC (1980); s of late Arthur Carter, and late Minnie Carter; *b* 11 May 1933; *Educ* Stretford GS, Kings Coll London (LLB); *m* 1960, Elizabeth Hughes, JP, da of late W B Hughes; 1 s (and 1 s decd); *Career* called to the Bar Gray's Inn 1955; practised Northern Circuit 1957-85, prosecuting counsel for Inland Revenue Northern circuit 1973-80, rec of The Crown Ct 1978-85, circuit judge 1985-; *Recreations* golf, travel; *Clubs* Chorlton-cum-Hardy Golf, Big Four (Manchester); *Style—* His Hon Judge Brian Carter, QC

CARTER, Sir Charles Frederick; yst s of Frederick William Carter, FRS (d 1950), of Rugby; *b* 15 Aug 1919; *Educ* Rugby, St John's Coll Cambridge (MA); *m* 1944, Janet, da of Edward Shea (d 1923), of Newcastle; 1 s, 2 da; *Career* lectr in statistics Univ of Cambridge 1947-51, fell Emmanuel Coll Cambridge 1947-51 (now hon fell); prof of economics: Queen's Univ Belfast 1950-59, Univ of Manchester 1959-63; vice chllr Univ of Lancaster 1963-79, pres Policy Studies Inst 1989-; vice chm Joseph Rowntree Foundation 1981- (tstee 1966-); chm: Sir Halley Stewart Tst 1986-, N Ireland Econ Cncl 1977-87; former jt ed Economic Journal and Journal of Industrial Economics; former pres Manchester Statistical Soc and Br Assoc for Advancement former chm Schools' Broadcasting Cncl, NW Econ Planning Cncl, Centre for Studies in Social Policy; Hon DSc: Univ of Lancaster, Queen's Belfast, New Univ Ulster; Hon LLD: Univ of Liverpool, Trinity Coll Dublin; Hon DEconSc National Univ Ireland; FBA; kt 1978; *Recreations* gardening; *Style—* Sir Charles Carter; 1 Gosforth Rd, Seascale, Cumbria CA20 1PU (☎ 09467 28359)

CARTER, Christopher John; s of Wilfred Lawrence Carter, of Broadwater House, Burwood Park, Walton-on-Thames, Surrey, and Betty Mary, *née* Vavasour; *b* 7 Aug 1945; *Educ* Uppingham, Interpreters's Inst Munich; *m* 17 June 1978, Emma Caroline, da of Sir Robin Kinahan, ERD, JP, of Castle Upton, Templepatrick, Co Antrim, NI; 4 s (Thomas b 7 Jan 1981, Alastair b 14 March 1983, Nicholas b 16 March 1987, Rory b 3 July 1989); *Career* HAC 1964-66; ED & F Man Gp of Co's 1964-85 (NY 1969-71, Hong Kong 1974-76, dir (London) 1976-85); dir: London Int Fin Futures Exchanges 1982-85, Channel Island Money Brokers Ltd 1985-; md GNI (Jersey) Ltd 1986-, regnl coordinator Assoc of Lloyd's Members; Liveryman Worshipful Co of Grocers 1977-; *Recreations* tennis, fishing, skiing; *Clubs* United, St Helier; *Style—* Christopher Carter, Esq; Maufant Manor, St Saviour's, Jersey, CI (☎ office 0534 210 86); Hameau Coimbot, Teurtheville Bocage, Normandy, France (☎ 010 33 33 44 1566)

CARTER, Clive; s of Eric Carter (d 1965), of London, and Jacqueline, *née* Digby; *b* 12 Jan 1953; *Educ* Sir William Collins School London, LAMDA; *m* 5 Oct 1975, Anita Helen, da of Lt-Col Harry Beresford Richards; 1 s (Richard Nigel Beresford b 7 Sept 19850, 1 da (Louise Erica Beresford b 21 Sept 1987); *Career* actor; repertory work: York, Leicester, Exeter, Nottingham, Cambridge; Rocky Horror Show (Euro tour), Oklahoma! (Nat tour); London theatre incl: Julius Caesar (Mermaid), Otello (Mermaid); New Shakespeare Co: A Midsummer Night's Dream, O'Flaherty VC; Marilyn (Adelphi), Wild Wild Woman (Astoria), Sister Mary Ignatius Explains It All For You (Ambassadors), Two Into One (Shaftesbury), Les Miserables (Barbican, Palace Theatre), Someone Like You (Strand Theatre), Into the Woods (Phoenix); performed in many concerts and one-off charity shows; TV: Mitch, Never the Twain, Robin's Nest; Films: Death on the Nile, Officer; *Recreations* keep fit workouts, running, swimming and skin diving, modern and classical music, reading, collecting vintage ports & champagne, antique clocks; *Clubs* The Groucho, Arts, Metropolitan; *Style—* Clive Carter, Esq; Richard Grenville, London Management, 235/241 Regent St, London W1R 7AG (☎ 071 493 1610, fax 071 408 0065, telex 27498)

CARTER, (William) David Antony; s of William Henry Newton Carter, CBE (d 1981) and Joan Stuart Carter (d 1983); *b* 21 Feb 1938; *Educ* Oundle, Oriel Coll Oxford (MA); *m* 27 April 1963, Angela Mary, da of Archibald Elliot Peel; 2 s (Justin Mark b 1964, Dominic William b 1967), 3 da (Catherine Sarah (Kate) b 1965, Emma Rachel b 1971, (Mary) Jessica b 1975); *Career* 2 Lt RA 1956-58; CA 1964, ptnr Peat Marwick Mitchell & Co 1975, head of corporate fin serv Peat Marwick McLintock 1986- (mgmnt buyout specialist 1981-); memb Fin Ctee Ampleforth Abbey; FCA 1974; *Recreations* opera, cricket, redundant Devon farmhouse; *Clubs* Oxford & Cambridge; *Style—* David Carter, Esq; 7 Bois Ave, Amersham, Bucks HP6 5NS (☎ 0494 727 109); Peat Marwick McLintock, 1 Puddle Dock, London EC4V 3PD (☎ 071 236 8000)

CARTER, Prof David Craig; s of Horace Ramsay Carter, and Mary Florence, *née* Lister; *b* 1 Sept 1940; *Educ* Univ of St Andrews (MB ChB), Univ of Dundee (MD); *m* 23 Sept 1967, Ilske Ursula, da of Wolfgang August Luth (d 1945), of Riga, Latvia; 2 s (Adrian b 5 Jan 1969, Ben b 3 Nov 1970); *Career* St Mungo prof of surgery Univ of Glasgow 1979-88, regius prof of clinical surgery Univ of Edinburgh 1988-; memb: Br

Broadcasting Cncl Scot, Biomedical Res Ctee Scot Home and Health Dept, Cncl of RCSEd, Int Surgical Gp; chm: Scottish Fndn for Surgery in Nepal 1987-, seat Cncl for Postgrad Med Educn 1990-, pres Int Hepato-Biliary and Pancreatic Assoc 1988-89; FRCSEd, FRCPS (Glas); *Books* Peptic Ulcer (1983), Principles and Practice of Surgery (1985), Atlas of General Surgery (1986), British Journal of Surgery (co ed 1986), Perioperative Care (1988), Pancreatitis (1989); *Recreations* golf, music; *Clubs* Royal and Ancient, New (Edinburgh); *Style*— Prof David Carter; 19 Buckingham Terrace, Edinburgh EH4 3AD (☎ 031 332 5554); University Dept of Surgery, Royal Infirmary, Edinburgh EH3 9YW (☎ 031 229 2477 ext 2266, fax 031 228 2661, telex 727442 (UNIVED G)

CARTER, David Ewart; s of Maj Ewart Grattan Carter, MC, TD (d 1978), of The Hollins, Ilkley, W Yorks, and Joan Elizabeth, *née* Harrison; *b* 4 Feb 1946; *Educ* The Leys Sch Cambridge, Univ of Leeds (BA); *m* 29 Aug 1978, Claire Noel Raffles, da of Alexander Maben (d 1981), of Chalfont Court, Leeds; 1 da (Alice Eleanor Louisa b 9 Sept 1980), 1 step s (Christian Alexander Henry b 25 March 1974); *Career* joined Bd of Carter & Parker Ltd 1974 (chm 1978-); chm Sharow and Copt Hewick Cons Assoc, memb Constituency Exec Ctee; *Recreations* shooting, politics, billiards and snooker; *Style*— David Carter, Esq; Sharow Close, Ripon, N Yorks HG4 5BQ (☎ 0765 701474); Carter & Parker Ltd, Netherfield Road, Guiseley, W Yorkshire LS20 9PD (☎ 0943 72264, fax 0943 78689, telex 51234 WENDY G)

CARTER, Baron (Life Peer UK 1987), of Devizes, Co Wilts; Denis Victor Carter; s of Albert William Carter (d 1973), of Sussex, and Annie Julia, *née* Tynan (d 1972); *b* 17 Jan 1932; *Educ* Xaverian Coll Brighton, East Sussex Coll of Agric, Essex Coll of Agric (Nat Dip in Agric), Worcester Coll Oxford (BLitt); *m* 1957, Teresa Mary, da of Cecil William Walter Greengoe (d 1972), of Sussex; 1 s (Andrew Peter b 1963 d 1982), 1 da (Hon Catherine Mary b 1959); *Career* Sgt Army, Suez Canal zone; farmer and agricultural conslt; dir: AKC Ltd (Agricultural Accounting and Mgmnt) 1957- (and fndr), United Oilseeds Ltd 1968-, Cave Holdings/W E and D T Cave Ltd 1976-; oppn spokesman on agric 1988-, oppn spokesman on social security agric and health 1989-; *Recreations* reading, walking, supporting Southampton FC; *Clubs* Farmers, Turners, Grasshoppers; *Style*— The Rt Hon Lord Carter; c/o House of Lords, London SW1

CARTER, Sir Derrick Hunton; TD (1952); s of Dr Arthur Hunton Carter (d 1961), of Sedbergh, and Winifred *née* MacMeikan (d 1947); *b* 7 April 1906; *Educ* Haileybury, St John's Coll Cambridge (MA); *m* 1, 1933, Phyllis, da of Denis Best, of Worcester; 1 s, 1 da; m 2, 1948, Madeline, da of Col Denis Moriarty O'Callaghan, CMG, DSO; 1 da; *Career* served WWII RA Lt-Col 1942; civil engr Dominion Bridge Co (Canada) 1927-28, res engr ICI 1928-33 (sales mangr 1933-39, md 1953); chm: Gen Chem Div ICI 1961, Mond Div ICI Ltd 1963-67, Remplo Ltd 1972-76; Freeman City of London 1973; kt 1975; *Recreations* gardening, woodworking; *Clubs* Army and Navy; *Style*— Sir Derrick Carter, TD; Withington House, Withington, Cheltenham, Glos GL54 4BB (☎ 024 289 286)

CARTER, Eric Stephen; CBE (1986); s of Albert Harry Carter, MBE (d 1973), of Cheltenham, Dep Chief Constable of Glos, and Doris Margaret, *née* Mann (d 1983); *b* 23 June 1923; *Educ* Lydney GS Glos, Univ of Reading (BSc 1945); *m* 23 Oct 1948, Audrey, da of Joseph Windsor (d 1970), of Bream, Glos; 1 s (Michael b 1958); *Career* dist agric offr Nat Agric Advsy Serv Glos 1946-57, sr dist agric advsr Lincs 1957-63, co agric offr Lincs 1963-69, dep regnl dir Yorks/Lancs Region and regnl agric offr 1969-74, chief regnl offr MAFF 1974-75, dep dir gen Agric Devpt and Advsy Serv MAFF 1975-81; advsr Farming and Wildlife Tst 1981-88; memb: Royal Agric Soc of England 1976- (ed of jl 1985-), Governing Body Grassland Res Inst 1976-87, Governing Body Inst for Grassland & Environmental Res 1989-; Selection Ctee Nuffield Farming Scholarship Tst 1981-, Long Ashton Res Station Agric Ctee 1984-90, Cncl Assoc of Agric 1985-, Welsh Plant Breeding Station Advsy Ctee 1987-; convener Standing Conference on Country Sports 1988-; visiting lectr Univ of Nottingham 1984-; FBiol 1974, FRAgS 1985, hon fell RASE 1988; *Books* Modern Farming and the Countryside (with M H Soper, OBE 1985); *Recreations* gardening, walking, reading, music; *Clubs* Farmers'; *Style*— Eric Carter, Esq, CBE; 15 Farrs Lane, East Hyde, Luton, Beds LU2 9PY (☎ 0582 760504)

CARTER, Lady Frances Elizabeth; *née* Bernard; yr da of Air Chief Marshal 5 and last Earl of Bandon, GBE, CB, CVO, (d 1979), and his 1 w, (Maybel) Elizabeth (*see* Holcroft, Elizabeth, Lady); *b* 4 Feb 1943; *m* 1967, Paul Mark Carter, o s of Flt Lt Mark Carter, DFC (d 1940); 1 s (Philip b 1979), 2 da (Emma b 1969, Annabelle b 1971); *Style*— Lady Frances Carter; Woodsprings, Snelsmore Common, Newbury, Berks

CARTER, Frederick Brian; QC (1980); s of late Arthur Carter, and Minnie Carter; *b* 11 May 1933; *Educ* Stretford GS, King's Coll London (LLB); *m* 1960, Elizabeth, da of late WB Hughes; 1 s, 3 da; *Career* called to the Bar Gray's Inn 1955, prosecuting counsel for the Inland Revenue Northern Circuit 1973-80, circuit judge 1985-; *Style*— His Hon Judge Carter, QC; 23 Lynton Park Road, Cheadle Hulme, Cheadle, Cheshire SK8 6JA

CARTER, (William) George Key; s of Lt-Col William Tom Carter, OBE, JP (d 1956), and Georgina Margaret, *née* Key (d 1986); *b* 29 Jan 1934; *Educ* Warwick Sch; *m* 30 June 1965, Anne Rosalie Mary, da of Trevor Acheson-Williams Flamagan (d 1987); 1 s (Alexander Corfield b 1971), 1 da (Louisa Mary-Anne b 1968); *Career* 2 Lt 16/5 The Queens Royal Lancers 1958-60 (asst Adj 1959); qualified CA 1957; Price Waterhouse: joined 1956, mangr 1963, ptnr 1966, sr ptnr (W Midlands) 1982-; vice chm W Midlands Devpt Agency; memb Cncl: Birmingham Chamber of Indust and Commerce (memb Gen Purposes Ctee), W Midlands CBI; judge W Midlands Business of the Year award; memb: Ferrous Foundry Indust Advsy Ctee, Pharmacist Review Bd; feoffee and govr Old Swinford Hosp Sch; FCA 1957; *Books* The Work of the Investigating Accountant; *Recreations* golf, shooting, sailing, gardening; *Clubs* Cavalry and Guards; *Style*— George Carter, Esq; The Old Rectory, Elmley Lovett, Droitwich, Worcs WR9 OPS; 28 Westmorland Terr, London SW1 (☎ 029 923 251); Price Waterhouse, Livery House, 169 Edmund St, Birmingham B32 (☎ 021 200 3000, fax 200 2464, car 0836 245 455, telex 338684)

CARTER, Godfrey James; CBE (1984); s of Capt James Shuckburgh Carter, Grenadier Gds (ka 1918), and Diana Violet Gladys, *née* Cavendish (d 1962); *b* 1 June 1919; *Educ* Eton, Magdalene Coll Cambridge (MA, LLM); *m* 15 June 1946, Cynthia, da of Eric Strickland Mason, of Park Farm, Iden, Rye, Sussex; 3 s (James b 1948, Simon b 1953, Hugh b 1960); *Career* WWII Capt Rifle Bde 1940-45, served 8 Army ME (twice wounded); called to the Bar Inner Temple 1946; Parly Counsel Office 1949-56 and 1964-79 (ret); Commercial Depts Bristol Aeroplane Co and Bristol Siddeley Engines 1 draftsman of: Companies Act 1985, Insolvency Act 1986, Insolvency Rules 1986; *Clubs* Travellers'; *Style*— Godfrey J Carter Esq, CBE; Old Bournstream House, Wotton-under-Edge, Glos GL12 7PA (☎ 0453 843246)

CARTER, Jeffrey Alan; s of George Thomas Carter and Frances Lily Carter, of London; *b* 9 April 1938; *Educ* Whitgift Sch, Imperial Coll Univ of London (BSc), Harvard Graduate Sch; *m* 1962, Diana Shirley, da of Harry Aukett; 1 s, 2 da (1 decd); *Career* md: Babcock Woodall Duckham Ltd 1978-, Babcock Engineering Contractos (Pty) Ltd Johannesburg SA 1980-; dir: Coal Processing Consultants Ltd 1979-, Fluidised Combustion Contractors Ltd 1979-, Babcock Contractors Ltd 1979-, Babcock Africa (Pty) Johannesburg 1980-, GEC Diesels Ltd 1983-; MIMechE, CEng; *Recreations* ornithology, music; *Style*— Jeffrey Carter Esq; 36 Hurst View Rd, Croham Hurst, South Croydon, Surrey CR2 7AG (☎ 081 688 6203, work 09252 5151, telex 627131 GECDUK G)

CARTER, John Graham; s of Eric Gordon Carter, of Shropshire, and Mercia Gertrude, *née* Edmonds; *b* 3 March 1942; *Educ* Twickenham Sch of Art, Kingston Sch of Art, British Sch in Rome; *m* 11 July 1986, Belinda Juliet, da of Alan Cadbury; *Career* artist; one person exhibitions incl: Redfern Gallery 1968, 1971, 1974 and 1977, Univ of Reading 1979, Nicola Jacobs Gallery 1980, Retrospective (1965-83) 1983, Paintings Structures and Drawings (Warwick Arts Tst) 1983, Nicola Jacobs Gallery 1983 and 1987, Moris Gallery Tokyo 1987 and 1989, Gallery Yamaguchi (Osaka Sumi Gallery Okayama) 1989, Galerie Hoffman (Friedberg) 1990; contribs to group exhibitions incl: New Generation (Whitechapel Art Gallery) 1966, New British Painting and Sculpture (UCLA Art Galleries Los Angeles and touring USA), British Painting (Hayward Gallery) 1974, British Art Show (Mappin Art Gallery Sheffield and touring) 1979, The British Cncl Collection (Serpentine Gallery) 1980, British Art 1940-80 (The Arts Cncl Collection Hayward Gallery) 1981, British Art Show (Birmingham Museum and touring) 1984, New Works on Paper (British Cncl and World tour), Contemporary British Art (Warwick Arts Tst) 1984, Die Ecke (Galerie Hoffmann Friedberg) 1986, 1000 Cubic Centimetres (Galerie de Sluis Leidschendam) 1987, Null Dimension (New Space Fulda) 1988, Britannica: 30 ans de Sculpture (Musée André Malraux Le Havre) 1988, The Presence of Painting Aspects of British Abstraction 1957-88 (Mappin Art Gallery Sheffield and touring) 1988, Britse Sculptuur 1960-88 (Museum van Hedendaagse Kunst Antwerp) 1989, Arte Constructivo y Sistematico (Centro Cultural de la Villa Madrid) 1989, 10 Years (Nicola Jacobs Gallery) 1989, 1000 Kubikzentimeter Geom Minituren (Wilhem Hack Museum Ludwigshafen) 1990, Between Dimensions (Curwen Gallery) 1990, Universal Progression (Manege Moscow) 1990, Konstruktive Tendenzen (Messer Ladwig Galerie Berlin) 1990; works in collections incl: Arts Cncl of GB, Arthur Andersen & Co, British Cncl, Chemical Bank NY, Chase Manhattan Bank, Contemporary Art Soc; awards: Leverhulme travelling scholarship to Italy 1963, Peter Stuyvesant Fndn travel bursary fo USA 1966, Arts Cncl awards 1977 and 1979; *Style*— John Carter, Esq; 71A Westbourne Park Road, London W2 5QH (☎ 071 229 3242); Nicola Jacobs Gallery, 9 Cork St, London W1X 1DD (☎ 071 437 3868)

CARTER, Dr John Timothy (Tim); *b* 12 Feb 1944; *Educ* Dulwich Coll, CCC Cambridge (MA, BA, BChir), UCH, London Sch of Hygiene and Tropical Med (MSc); *Career* lectr London Sch of Hygiene 1974-75, med advsr BP 1975-83, dir health policy Health and Safety Exec 1989- (dir med servs 1983-); FRCP, FFOM; *Style*— Dr Tim Carter; Health and Safety Executive, Baynards House, 1 Chepstow Place, London W2 4TF (☎ 071 243 6100)

CARTER, (Thomas) Mark; JP (1971), DL (Staffs 1983); s of William Edward Carter, JP (d 1965), of Eccleshall Castle, Staffs, and Rose Margaret Eleanor, *née* Morris-Eyton (d 1982); *b* 20 May 1936; *Educ* Harrow, RAC Cirencester; *m* 3 July 1965, Cecilia Catherine, da of Maj Henry Cecil Wenger, of Staffs; 2 da (Melissa Margaret b 1966, Catherine Elizabeth b 1973); *Career* Lt Grenadier Gds Suez Canal Zone and Kenya 1954-56; chartered surveyor, then farmer and landowner; High Sheriff Staffs 1974-75; hunt sec and master N Staffs Hunt 1963-76, gen cmmr Inland Revenue; memb: Agric Lands Tbnl, Bd of Mgmnt Heart of Eng Tourist Bd 1985-88, Cncl Historic Houses Assoc 1986-; engaged in opening Eccleshall Castle to the public; Kt SMO Malta; *Recreations* hunting, tennis, shooting; *Clubs* Cavalry and Guards, MCC; *Style*— Mark Carter, Esq, JP, DL; Eccleshall Castle, Stafford ST21 6LS (☎ 0785 850204); Estates Office, Eccleshall Castle, Stafford ST21 6LS (☎ 0785 850204)

CARTER, Michael James Frederick; CBE (1987); s of Dr David Michael Frederick Carter (Surgn Lt RN, d 1975), and Alice, *née* McNally (d 1981); *b* 23 March 1941; *Educ* Downside; *m* 29 April 1967, Camilla Gillian Carter, JP, da of Arthur Gordon Taylor; 2 s (James Gordon Frederick b 15 Nov 1968, David John b 29 Dec 1971), 1 da (Rachel Jane b 16 April 1970); *Career* dir: Olives Hldgs plc, Altsprung Furniture Gp plc; chm E Somerset NHS Hosp Tst; memb: Somerset Health Authy 1978-90, Nat Union of Cons and Unionist Assocs 1979-, Royal Bath and West Show Arts Ctee; High Sheriff of Somerset 1987-88; *Books* Modern British Painters 1900-40 (1978); *Recreations* gardening; *Style*— Michael Carter, Esq, CBE

CARTER, Lady Nichola Jane Eleanora (Minervina); *née* Boyle; da of Rear Adm 9 Earl of Glasgow, CB, DSC (d 1984); *b* 21 Dec 1946; *m* 1976, Thomas G Carter, 1 s (Matthew b 1978); *Style*— The Lady Nichola Carter

CARTER, Peers Lee; CMG (1965); s of Peers Owen Carter (d 1966), and Edith, *née* Lee (d 1982), of Bolton, Lancs; *b* 5 Dec 1916; *Educ* Radley, Ch Ch Oxford (MA); *m* 1940, Joan Eleanor, da of Capt Alfred Victor Robertson Lovegrove, DSO, RD, RNR, of Vancouver; 1 s; *Career* serv WWII Fezzan and N Africa, Southern Europe, Maj; entered HM Foreign Serv 1939, 2 then 1 sec Baghdad 1945-49, 1 sec cmmr gen's office Singapore 1951-54, cnsllr Washington 1958-61, head Perm Delgn to UN Geneva 1961-63, inspr then chief inspr HM Dip Serv 1963-68, ambass Afghanistan 1968-72, asst under sec of state and ministerial interpreter FCO 1973-76, ret; memb Int Assoc of Conf Interpreters, chm AFGHANAID; Sardar-e A'ala 1971; *Recreations* mountain walking, beekeeping, photography; *Clubs* Special Forces, Travellers'; *Style*— Peers Carter, Esq, CMG; Dean Land Shaw, by Jobes, Balcombe, Haywards Heath, W Sussex RH17 6HZ (☎ 0444 811205)

CARTER, Peter Basil; QC (1990); s of Albert George Carter (d 1961), and Amy Kathleen FitzGerald Carter (d 1973); *b* 10 April 1921; *Educ* Loughborough, Oriel Coll Oxford (BCL, MA); *m* 1, 1960, the late Elizabeth Maxwell Ely; m 2, 1982, Lorna Jean Sinclair; *Career* Serv WWII Capt; called to the Bar Middle Temple 1947, hon bencher Middle Temple 1981; jt ed Int and Comparative Law Quarterly 1961-; fell Wadham Coll Oxford 1949-88 (emeritus fell 1988-), former visiting prof various Cwlth and United States Univs; chm Univ Life Assur Soc 1980- (dir 1969-); JP 1959-88; Croix de Guerre 1944; FInstD 1984; *Recreations* criticising bad architecture; *Clubs* United Oxford and Cambridge University; *Style*— Peter Carter, Esq, QC; Wadham College, Oxford (☎ 0865 277900)

CARTER, Philip David; CBE (1981); s of Percival Carter and Isobell, *née* Stirrup; *b* 8 May 1927; *Educ* Waterloo GS Liverpool; *m* 1946, Harriet Rita, *née* Evans; *Career* Fleet Air Arm 1945-; Littlewoods Orgn 1944-83 (chief exec 1976-83), ret; chm: Empire Trust 1986, Merseyside Tourism Bd 1986, Liverpool Cons Assoc 1985, Merseyside Devpt Corp 1987 (memb 1981-); pres Football League 1986-88, chm Everton FC 1977; *Style*— Philip Carter, Esq, CBE; Oak Cottage, Noctorum Rd, Noctorum, Wirral, Merseyside L43 9UQ

CARTER, Air Cdre Robert Alfred Copsey; CB (1956), DSO (1942), DFC (1943); s of late Sidney Herbert Carter (d 1961), and S Carter, *née* Copsey (d 1949); *b* 15 Sept 1910; *Educ* Portsmouth GS, RAF Coll Cranwell; *m* 1947, Sarah Ann, da of Florence Booker Peters, of Hampton, Va, USA; 2 s, 1 da; *Career* joined RAF 1927, SASO Tport Cmd 1955-58, Air Cdre 1956, DPS (A) Air Min 1958-61, AOA RAF Germany 1961-64, ret; CEng, MRAeS; *Clubs* RAF; *Style*— Air Commodore R A C Carter, CB, DSO, DFC; The Old Cottage, Castle Lane, Whaddon, Salisbury, Wilts SP5 3EQ

CARTER, Prof Robert Lewis; s of Edwin Christopher Carter (d 1964); *b* 23 Aug 1932; *Educ* Univ of London (BSc), Univ of Sussex (DPhil); *m* 1954, Pearl Rita Carter;

1 s, 2 da; *Career* prof of Insurance Studies Univ of Nottingham (holds Britain's only chair of insur studies); govt nominee to Insur Brokers Registration Cncl 1979-82 and 1986-, memb Cncl Insur Ombudsman Bureau 1981-, govr Inst of Risk Mgmnt 1986-90; visiting prof of insur American Graduate Sch of Int Mgmnt 1982-83; FCII, FIRM, FRSA; *Recreations* reading, pottering in the garden, travelling, walking; *Style*— Prof Robert Carter; 4 Bramcote Lane, Beeston, Nottingham NG9 5EN; Department of Industrial Economics Accounting and Insurance, Univ of Nottingham, Nottingham NG7 2RD (☎ 0602 484848)

CARTER, Roger Hayward; s of Harry Edgar Carter (d 1964), of London, and Hannah Carter; *b* 28 Aug 1936,1; *Educ* Glendale GS; *m* 1958, Jeanne Florence; 1 s (Antony b 1967), 1 da (Jacqueline b 1970); *Career* RN - able seaman; dir weekly newspaper; publishers and printers; *Recreations* squash, football, cricket; *Style*— Roger Carter; 8 New Farm Drive, Abridge, Essex (☎ 037 881 3290); London and Essex Guardian Newspapers Ltd, News Centre, Fulbourne Road, Walthamstow, London E17 (☎ 081 531 4141, fax 081 527 3696)

CARTER, Roger James; s of Frank William Carter (d 1959), of Finchley, London, and Eva Grace, *née* Howard (d 1968); *b* 29 Nov 1941; *Educ* Christs Coll Finchley, Northern Poly Sch of Architecture (Dip Arch); *m* 5 Oct 1963, Margaret, da of Frederick Walker (d 1990), of Mill Hill; 1 s (Jeffrey Richard b 1972), 1 da (Victoria Eve); *Career* registered architect ARCUK 1965, assoc memb RIBA 1966, fell faculty of Architects and Surveyors 1984, princ Roger Carter Architects; asst dir of architecture London Borough of Newham 1979-84; memb Nat Assoc of Round Tables 1972-82, chm Hornsey Round Table 1976, vice chm London NW NSPCC Centenary Appeal Ctee 1983, memb Hatfield Rotary Club 1990-; *Recreations* flat green bowls; *Clubs* Hatfield Bowls, Hertfordshire Indoor Bowls Assoc; *Style*— Roger J Carter, Esq; 47 The Ryde, Hatfield, Hertfordshire AL9 5DQ

CARTER, Roy John; OBE (1985), MBE (1979); s of William Henry Carter (d 1948), and Ellen Frances, *née* Kirby (d 1968); *b* 6 Jan 1931; *Educ* Dover GS; *m* 28 March 1955, Ann Mary Cameron, da of John Cameron Robertson, of Folkestone, Kent; 1 s (Nigel b 30 Aug 1956); *Career* RA 1949-51: The Nigeria Police 1954-66, HMDip Serv 1966-; *Style*— Roy Carter, Esq, OBE; 19 Glen Atkinson St, St Heliers, Auckland, New Zealand; British Consulate-General, 151 Queen St, Private Bag, Auckland, NZ (☎ 010 649 303 2973, fax 010 649 303 1836, telex NZ 2412)

CARTER, Stephen McCart; s of Dr Ralph Harlan Carter (d 1962), of Burwash Common, East Sussex, and Dorothy Maud, *née* Williams, of Vain Cottage, Burwash Common, East Sussex; *b* 3 July 1935; *Educ* Clayesmore Sch Iwerne Minster Dorset, Cranfield Mgmnt Coll 1971, Harvard Business Sch 1977; *m* 13 Oct 1962, Diana Mary, da of Eric James Foice, of Station Lane, Tewkesbury, Glos; 1 s (Julian b 1964), 1 da (Philippa b 1966); *Career* gen mangr P & O Bulk Shipping 1976-77, head of P & O Deep Sea Cargo Div, md P & O Bulk Shipping Ltd 1981-83, md Boyle Fin Services 1984-, chief exec Biffex Ltd 1985-87, sec gen The Baltic Futures Exchange Ltd 1987-; FICS 1960, The Baltic Exchange 1972; *Recreations* golf, shooting, fishing; *Style*— Stephen Carter, Esq; 19A The Vale, Coulsdon, Surrey CR5 2AU, (☎ 081 660 9010); 24/28 St Mary Axe, London EC3A 8EP (☎ 071 626 7985, fax 071 623 2917, telex 916434 BALFUT G)

CARTER, Air Vice-Marshal Wilfred; CB (1963), DFC (1943); s of Samuel Carter (d 1943), of Nottingham; *b* 5 Nov 1912; *Educ* Witney GS; *m* 1950, Margaret Enid, da of Herbert Jones Bray, of Gainsborough, Lincs; 1 s (decd), 1 da; *Career* joined RAF 1929, Air Cdre 1960, AOA Bomber Command 1965-67, Air Vice-Marshal 1965, ret 1967; dir Australian Counter Disaster Coll 1969-78, int disaster conslt 1978-; Officer of Order of Cedars of Lebanon (1954); *Books* Disaster Preparedness and Response, Disaster Management; *Recreations* swimming, walking; *Style*— Air Vice-Marshal Wilfred Carter, CB, DFC; Blue Range, Macedon, Vic 3440, Australia

CARTER, Sir William Oscar ; s of Oscar Carter (d 1952), of Norwich, and Alice Carter; *b* 12 Jan 1905; *Educ* Swaffham GS, City of Norwich Sch; *m* 1934, Winifred Rose, da of Sidney Charles Thompson (d 1952), of Wymondham, Norfolk; *Career* served WWII Wing Cdr RAF; slr 1931; conslt Daynes Hill and Perks (Slrs) Norwich, memb Cncl Law Soc 1954-75 (vice pres 1970, pres 1971-72); pres: East Anglian Law Soc 1952-80, Norfolk and Norwich Inc Law Soc 1959, Int Legal Aid Assoc 1974-80; life memb Cncl Int Bar Assoc (first vice pres 1976-78); memb: C Ct Rules Ctee 1956-60, Supreme Ct Rules Ctee 1960-75, Criminal Injuries Compensation Bd 1967-82 (dep chm 1977-82); hon memb The Fellows of the American Bar Fndn; Liveryman Worshipful Co of Glaziers (Master 1985); kt 1972; *Recreations* swimming, foreign travel; *Clubs* Army and Navy, Norfolk (Norwich); *Style*— Sir William Carter; 83 Newmarket Rd, Norwich (☎ 0603 53772); Holland Court, The Close, Norwich NR1 4DX (☎ 0603 611212, telex 97197)

CARTER-CAMPBELL OF POSSIL, Lt-Col Duncan MacLachlan; OBE (1958); o s of Maj-Gen George Tupper Campbell Carter Campbell, CB, DSO (d 1921), of Fascadale, Ardrishaig, Argyllshire, and Frances Elizabeth, *née* Ward (d 1960) (see Burkes Landed Gentry, 18 edn, Vol III, 1972); *b* 6 Dec 1911; *Educ* Malvern, RMC Sandhurst; *m* 31 July 1948, Margaret Elliot (Peggie), yr da of Norman Thain Davidson (d 1940), of Ashstead, Surrey; 2 s (Lorne George Tupper b 20 May 1951, Colin Duncan b 17 May 1958), 3 da (Jean Frances b 10 Aug 1949, Mary Elizabeth b 21 Jan 1953, Anne Catherine b 28 May 1954); *Career* cmmnd The Cameronians (Scottish Rifles) 1932, served WWII Italy and NW Europe, cmd 1 Bn The Cameronians 1956-58, ret 1960; dist cmmr Linlithgow and Stirling Pony Club 1967-72, treas Dumfries Br Red Cross 1979-83; *Recreations* gardening, horses; *Style*— Lt-Col Duncan Carter-Campbell of Possil, OBE; The Clachan, Dumfriesshire (☎ 038 782 340)

CARTER-CLOUT, Derrick Gilbert; s of Leslie Douglas Carter-Clout (d 1969), of 20 Saffrons Court, Compton Place Rd, Eastbourne, Sussex, and Hilda Elizabeth, *née* Kendall; *b* 13 Aug 1920; *Educ* Cranleigh, Sch of Bldg Brixton; *m* 1, 8 April 1945 (m dis), Joyce Elizabeth (d 1975), da of Percy Welford Davidson (d 1961), of Cloverlands, Birthwaite Rd, Windermere; 1 s (Anthony b 1948), 1 da (Catherine b 1946); m 2, 1964, Joan Dane, da of George Robert Gummery (d 1929); *Career* HAC 1938, RE OCTU 1939, cmmnd 2 Lt RE 1940, India Royal Bombay Sappers & Miners 1940, Maj RBS Malaya 9 India Div 1941, India Co Cmd 1941, invalided out of serv 1944; jt pres G & S Allgood Ltd (Architectural Ironmongers) 1980 (propentor 1947, md 1948-80); pres Execs Assoc of GB 1979-84 (dir 1967-69, chm 1969-70), chm Local Cons Branch Ashford Kent 1984, memb Ctee E Ashford Rural Tst; fell Faculty of Bldg; memb Cncl City Livery Club 1988; Freeman Worshipful Co of Ironmongers 1979, memb Guild of Freeman City of London 1984 (Freeman 1960); *Recreations* golf; *Clubs* Ashford Golf, City Livery, Rugger, Wellington, IOD, Henley Royal Regatta; *Style*— Derrick Carter-Clout, Esq; The Grange, Mersham, nr Ashford, Kent (☎ 023 3720314); Flat 30, Silsoe House, 50 Park Village East, London NW1 (☎ 071 388 0645); G & S Allgood Ltd, Carterville House, Euston Rd, London NW1 (☎ 071 387 9951, fax 071 380 1232, telex 261817)

CARTER-PEGG, Hallam; s of Carter Pegg (d 1970), of Manor Way, S Croydon, Surrey, and Helen Elise, *née* Johnson (d 1975); f played cricket for the London Counties with W G Grace; *b* 7 May 1932; *Educ* Whitgift Sch, Croydon; *m* 16 April 1960, Margaret Edith, da of Norman Dale Mant (d 1957), of Hurst Way, S Croydon, Surrey; 2 s (Nicholas Hallam b 1964, Christopher Norman b 1973), 1 da (Karen Margaret b 1967); *Career* sr ptnr Pegg Robertson CAs; chm and dir: Peckham Building Society, dir Lizzard & Co Ltd; awards for serv to scouting: Medal of Merit, Silver Acorn; FCA; *Recreations* scouting, gardening, shooting; *Style*— Hallam Carter-Pegg, Esq; 47 Wandle Rd, Croydon, Surrey CR0 1DF (☎ 081 686 8011, fax 081 681 8993, car 0860 516 793)

CARTER-RUCK, Peter Frederick; s of Frederick Henry Carter-Ruck (d 1968), of Gerrards Cross, Bucks, and Nell Mabel, *née* Allen; *b* 1914; *Educ* St Edward's Oxford; *m* 6 July 1940, Pamela Ann, only da of Gp Capt Reginald Stuart Maxwell, MC, DFC (d 1960), of Thorney Island, Emsworth; 1 s (Brian b 1943 d 1973), 1 da (Julie b 1941); *Career* served RA 1939-44, Capt Instr in Gunnery; admitted slr 1937; sr ptnr: Oswald Hickson Collier & Co 1945-81, Peter Carter Ruck & Ptnrs 1981-; Carlton Mansions Property Co Ltd 1990; specialist memb Cncl Law Soc 1971-84; pres: City of Westminster Law Soc 1976, Media Soc 1981-82 and 1984-86; chm: Law Soc Law Reform Ctee 1980-83, Media Ctee Int Bar Assoc 1983-85; memb: Cncl of Justice, Intellectual Property Ctee of Law Soc; hon conslt slr: Inst of Journalists, Media Soc; Lloyd's Underwriter; govr St Edward's Sch Oxford 1950-78, past chm and fndr govr Shiplake Coll Henley; memb City of London Solicitors' Co 1949; *Books* Libel and Slander (3 edn 1985), The Cyclist and the Law (with Ian Mackrill, 1953), Copyright: Modern Law and Practice (with Edmund Skone James, 1965), Memoirs of a Libel Lawyer (1990); *Recreations* writing, cinematography, wood-turning, ocean racing and cruising; *Clubs* Carlton, Garrick, Press, Royal Yacht Sqdn, Law Soc Yacht, (past Cdre) Royal Ocean Racing, Ocean Cruising (past Cdre); *Style*— Peter Carter-Ruck, Esq; Latchmore Cottage, Great Hallingbury, Bishop's Stortford, Herts (☎ 0279 654357); Eilagadale, N Ardnamurchan, Argyll (☎ 097 23 267); 75 Shoe Lane, London EC4A 3BQ (☎ 071 379 3456, fax 071 240 1486/071 583 2115/071 583 6225, telex 265277 Libel G)

CARTLAND, Dame Barbara (Hamilton); DBE (1991); da of late Maj Bertram Cartland, Worcs Regt; *b* 9 July 1901; *m* 1, 1927 (m dis 1932), Alexander George McCorquodale (d 1964); 1 da (Countess Spencer); m 2, 1936, Hugh McCorquodale (d 1963), 2 son of Harold McCorquodale, of Forest Hall, Ongar, Essex; 2 s (*see* Ian McCorquodale); *Career* best selling authoress in the World (Guinness Book of Records 1983) has also published plays, poems, biography and autobiography; former chm St John Ambulance Exhibition Ctee, fndr Barbara Cartland Onslow Romany Gypsy Fund, pres Nat Assoc of Health 1966; awarded Woman of Achievement by Nat Home Fashions League 1981, received Bishop Wright Air Ind award for the development of aviation 1984; chm St John Cncl for Herts (first woman on Chapter General for 1000 yrs); La Medaille de Vermeil de la Ville de Paris 1988; FRSA; DStJ 1972; *Books* 530; *Style*— Dame Barbara Cartland, DBE; Camfield Place, Essendon, Nr Hatfield, Herts (☎ 0707 42612, 42657)

CARTLAND, John Barrington; s of Sir George Barrington Cartland, CMG, of Sandy Bay, Hobart, Tas, and Dorothy, *née* Rayton; *b* 4 March 1941; *Educ* Rossall Sch, Balliol Coll Oxford (MA); *m* 11 March 1967, Gillian Margaret Campbell, da of Alastair Robert Campbell Cunningham; 2 da (Claire Louise b 4 April 1968, Nicola Janet b 5 Jan 1972); *Career* CA 1966; KPMG Peat Marwick McLintock (formerly Peat Marwick Mitchell & Co): articled clerk 1963-66, ptnr 1969-73 (Peat Marwick Mitchell & Co Uganda, Lawrie Prophet & Co, E H Shelton & Co), sr mangr in charge of trg and recruitment Birmingham 1976, sr mangr in charge of computer devpt 1983, ptnr 1984-; treas and memb Cncl Outward Bound Tst of Uganda 1967-73; vice pres Birmingham and W Midlands Soc of CAs 1990 (memb Ctee 1984-, treas 1988-90); FCA; *Style*— John Cartland, Esq; Broomhall Grange, Norton Road, Worcester WR5 2PD (☎ 0905 356111); KPMG Peat Marwick McLintock, Peat House, 2 Cornwall St, Birmingham B3 2DL (☎ 021 233 1666, car 0836 605 104, fax 021 233 4390)

CARTLEDGE, Sir Bryan George; KCMG (1985, CMG 1980); s of Eric Montague George Cartledge, and Phyllis, *née* Shaw; *b* 10 June 1931; *Educ* Hurstpierpoint Coll, St John's Coll Cambridge, St Antony's Coll Oxford; *m* 1960, Ruth Hylton, da of John Gass; 1 s, 1 da; *Career* Lt Queen's Royal Regt 1950-52; Dip Serv 1960-: private sec overseas affrs to PM 1977-79, ambass to Hungary 1980-83, asst under sec of state Def 1983-84, dep sec of the Cabinet 1984-85, ambass to Soviet Union 1985-88; princ Linacre Coll Oxford 1988-; hon fell: St John's Coll Cambridge 1985, St Antony's Coll Oxford 1987; *Clubs* Utd Oxford and Cambridge Univ; *Style*— Sir Bryan Cartledge, KCMG; Linacre College, Oxford OX1 3JA

CARTLEDGE, Stanley; s of Henry Cartledge (d 1965), of Southport, and Ivy, *née* Green (d 1978); *b* 30 Sept 1917; *Educ* King George V Sch Southport; *m* 1, 28 Jan 1946 (m dis 1983), Yvonne Hilda, da of William Piercy (d 1918); 1 s (Stephen b 1952); m 2, 26 March 1983, Brenda Amy, *née* Johnson, da of late Francis Dennett; *Career* WWII Lt RA 1942-46, Burma; Metropolitan Police 1936-38, Staffordshire Police 1938-63, Dep Chief Constable Bath City Police 1963-67 (ret); called to the Bar Gray's Inn 1957 (practising since 1973, recent Head Assize Ct Chambers Bristol), memb Western Circuit of the Bar; Bristol Polytechnic 1963-82 (ret as Head of Law Degree Sch); author of various articles for learned jls; memb Bristol Medico-Legal Soc; *Recreations* gardening, holidays in Menorca; *Style*— Stanley Cartledge, Esq; St John's Chambers, Small Street, Bristol BS1 1DW (☎ 0272 294821)

CARTLIDGE, Hon Mrs (Mary Cecilia); *née* Wigg; eld da of Baron Wigg, PC (d 1983), and Florence, *née* Veal; *b* 25 June 1930; *m* 1958, Robert George Cartlidge; 3 da; *Style*— The Hon Mrs Cartlidge; Abilene, 2 Princes' St, Huntly, Aberdeenshsire AB54 5HB (☎ 0466 793445)

CARTTISS, Michael Reginald Harry; MP (C) Great Yarmouth 1983-; s of Reginald Carttiss and Doris Culling; *b* 11 March 1938; *Educ* Great Yarmouth Tech HS, Goldsmith's Coll Univ of London, LSE; *Career* teacher 1961-69, former constituency agent for Yarmouth, memb Norfolk CC 1966-, memb Gt Yarmouth Borough Cncl 1973-82; *Style*— Michael Carttiss Esq, MP; House of Commons, London SW1

CARTWRIGHT, Christopher Egerton; s of Herbert Edward Cartwright (d 1978), and Ruth, *née* Collins; *b* 19 Oct 1944; *Educ* Kings Sch Worcester, Univ of Bristol; *m* 30 Dec 1967, Susan Lois, da of Anthony John Mindham, of Brighton, Sussex; 1 s (James Egerton b 1971), 1 da (Sarah Elizabeth b 1974); *Career* stockbroker; formerly ptnr and dir Wood MacKenzie & Co, Paribas Ltd; memb Stock Exchange, FCA 1969; *Recreations* gardening, microcomputing, angling, guitar; *Clubs* Chiselhurst Golf; *Style*— Christopher Cartwright, Esq; Hostye Farm, Cudham Lane North, Cudham, Kent TN14 7QT (☎ 0959 73163, car 0831 514 336); Paribas Ltd, 33 Wigmore St, London W1H 0BN (☎ 071 355 2000)

CARTWRIGHT, Rt Rev (Edward) David; o s of John Edward Cartwright (d 1957), of Grimsby, and Gertrude, *née* Lusby (d 1962); *b* 15 July 1920; *Educ* St James's Choir Sch Grimsby, Lincoln Sch, Selwyn Coll and Westcott House Cambridge (BA, MA); *m* 12 June 1946, Elsie Irene, o da of Walter Rogers (d 1930), of Grimsby; 1 s (Roger Edward Henry b 1948), 2 da (Sarah Elizabeth (Mrs Thornton) b 1952, Rachel Mary (Mrs Robinson) b 1958); *Career* curate of Boston Lincs 1943-48, mayor's chaplain 1945-48; vicar: St Leonard's Redfield Bristol 1948-52, Olveston with Aust 1952-60, Bishopston 1960-73; hon canon: Bristol 1970, Winchester 1973; archdeacon of Winchester 1973-84, vicar of Sparsholt 1973-84, bishop of Southampton 1984-88; memb: Church Assembly and General Synod 1956-83, C of E Pensions Bd 1980-84; church cmmr 1973-83; *Recreations* books, music, roses; *Style*— The Rt Rev David

Cartwright; Bargate House, 25 Newport, Warminster, Wilts BA12 8RH (☎ 0985 216298)

CARTWRIGHT, Harry; CBE (1979, MBE Mil 1946); s of Edwin Harry Cartwright, and Agnes Alice, *née* Gillibrand; *b* 16 Sept 1919; *Educ* William Hulme's GS, St John's Coll Cambridge; *m* 1950, Catharine Margaret Carson Bradbury; 2 s; *Career* Dept of Atomic Energy 1949: chief engr 1955, dir Industl Power 1960-64, dir Water Reactors 1964-70, dir Fast Reactor Systems 1970-73; dir Atomic Energy Estab Winfrith 1973-83; pres Euro Nuclear Soc 1983-85; *Style—* Harry Cartwright, Esq, CBE; Tabbit's Hill House, Corfe Castle, Wareham, Dorset (☎ 0929 480582)

CARTWRIGHT, Ian David; s of Cyril Cartwright, of Pistyll, Gwynedd, and Doreen Cartwright; *b* 28 March 1952; *Educ* The County GS Hyde Cheshire, Ashton-under-Lyne Coll of Further Educn, Leeds Poly (BA); *m* 1976, Christine May, da of William Robertson Lennie; 1 s (Lewis Edward b 15 April 1983); *Career* asst photographer Technical Public Relations and Graham Powell Studios 1975-78; photographer: Woburn Studios 1978-82, Montage 1982-87; photographer and md Avalon 1987-; FBIPP 1989; memb Assoc of Photographers; *Recreations* skiing, tai chi, painting, drawing; *Clubs* The Ski Club of Manchester (chm 1990-91), The Ski Club of GB; *Style—* Ian Cartwright, Esq; Avalon Photography Limited, 5 Pittbrook St, Ardwick, Manchester M12 6LR (☎ 061 274 3313, fax 061 273 2752)

CARTWRIGHT, Jim; s of Jim Cartwright, of Farnworth, Lancs, and Edna, *née* Main; *b* 27 June 1958; *Educ* Harper Green Secdy Sch Farnworth; *m* Angela Louise, da of Sam Jones; 1 s (James Lewis b 22 Oct 1984); *Career* writer; plays: Road (performed Royal Court Theatre 1986-87, adapted for BBC TV 1987), Baths (Radio 1988), Bed (NT 1989), Wedded (BBC TV 1990), TO (Octagon Bolton and Young Vic London 1989-90), Vroom (film 1988); *awards* for Road: Samuel Beckett award, BTA Drama Magazine award, George Devine award, Plays and Players Best New Play, Golden Nymph award for Best Film at Monte Carlo TV and Film Festival; *Style—* Jim Cartwright, Esq; Judy Daish Associates, 83 Eastbourne Mews, London W2 6LQ (☎ 071 262 1101, fax 071 706 1027)

CARTWRIGHT, John Cameron; MP (SDP) Woolwich 1983-; JP (1970); s of late Aubrey John Randolph Cartwright and Ivy Adeline Billie Cartwright; *b* 29 Nov 1933; *Educ* Woking Co GS; *m* 1959, Iris June Tant; 1 s, 1 da; *Career* exec civil servant 1952-55; Lab Pty agent 1955-67; dir Royal Arsenal Co-op Society Ltd 1972-74 (political sec 1967-72); MP (Lab changed to SDP 1981) Greenwich Woolwich E 1974-83, Woolwich 1983-, PPS to Sec of State for Educn and Sci 1976-77, fndr memb SDP March 1981, parly spokesman on housing local govt and the environment, SDP Whip 1983-, SDP spokesman on def 1983, SDP pres 1988- (vice pres 1987-88); former tstee Nat Maritime Museum; *Books* Cruise, Pershing and SS20 (jtly, 1985), View from the House (jtly, 1986); *Style—* John Cartwright, Esq, JP, MP; 17 Commonwealth Way, London SE2 (☎ 081 311 4394)

CARTWRIGHT, Capt John Cecil; DSC (1942, and bar 1953); s of Edward Cartwright (d 1948), of Bristol, and Gertrude, *née* Ellershaw (d 1953); *b* 22 May 1914; *Educ* RNC Dartmouth; *m* 17 Aug 1946, Alice Susan Gillespie, da of John Jagoe, of Liskeard and Buenos Aires; 2 da (Elizabeth b 1949, Charlotte Mary b 1956); *Career* entered RNC Dartmouth 1928, served RN mainly in destroyers (despatches 1940 and 1942); cmd HM Ships: Puckeridge 1942-43, Raider 1944-45, Contest 1946-47, Consort 1947-48, Opossum 1952-53, Plymouth and 4 Frigate Sqn 1960-63, Sea Eagle as dir of Jt Anti-Submarine Sch and Sr Naval Offr NI 1963-65, ret 1965; Bursar Portora Royal Sch 1965-69, Gentleman Usher of the Black Rd (NI Parl) 1969-73; *Recreations* shooting, fishing; *Style—* Capt J C Cartwright, DSC; 29 High St, Sydling St Nicholas, Dorset (☎ 030 03 357)

CARTWRIGHT, John Wallace; s of Reginald Cartwright (d 1982), of Cambridge, and Iris Marion, *née* Dear; *b* 10 March 1946; *Educ* Bedford Sch, Cranfield Mgmnt Sch (MBA); *m* 1973, Christine Elise, da of Jack Whitaker, of Newbury; 1 s (Timothy b 1975), 2 da (Genevieve b 1978, Bethany b 1980); *Career* merchant banker; dir: devpt capital ANZ Merchant Bank Ltd 1989- (formerly dir risk placement and syndication), ANZ Grindlays, 3i Investment Services td 1989, Second Indian Investment Fund Ltd 1990, Transatlantic Capital Ltd 1989; FCIB; *Recreations* gardening, golf; *Style—* John Cartwright, Esq; 16 Millfield, Berkhamsted HP4 2PB (☎ 0442 864984); Palace House, 3 Cathedral St, London SE1 9AN (☎ 071 378 2864)

CARTWRIGHT, Dr Keith Anthony Vincent; s of Albert George Frank Cartwright (d 1983), and Jean Cartwright; *b* 21 Sept 1946; *Educ* Mill Hill Sch, Univ of Oxford (BA, BM Bch); *m* 13 Sept 1969, Prudence Lilian, da of John Edward Serby, CB, CBE, of Farnham, Surrey; 1 s (Julian b 1975), 2 da (Katharine b 1973, Victoria b 1976); *Career* conslt microbiologist Western Gen Hosp Edinburgh 1978-80, dir Gloucester Public Health Laboratory Gloucester 1981-; res advsr Mennigitis Tst; FRCPath 1988 (MRCPath 1978); *Recreations* mountaineering, rock climbing; *Clubs* Oxford Alpine, Climbers; *Style—* Dr Keith Cartwright; Public Health Laboratory, Gloucestershire Royal Hospital, Great Western Road, Gloucester GL1 3NN (☎ 0452 305334)

CARTWRIGHT, Dame Mary Lucy; DBE (1969); da of Rev William Digby Cartwright (d c1926), sometime Rector of Aynho, and Lucy Harriette Maud, *née* Bury (d 1950); *b* 17 Dec 1900; *Educ* Godolphin Sch Salisbury, St Hugh's Coll Oxford (MA, DPhil), (ScD Cantab); *Career* Cambridge Univ: lectr mathematics 1935-59 (reader 1959-68, emeritus reader 1968), mistress Girton Coll 1946-68 (former staff fell, life fell 1968); Hon LLD Edinburgh 1953; Hon DSc: Leeds 1958, Hull 1959, Wales 1962, Oxford 1966, (Brown) USA 1969; Cdr Order of the Dannebrog 1961; FRS; *Style—* Dame Mary Cartwright, DBE; 38 Sherlock Close, Cambridge (☎ 0223 352 574)

CARTWRIGHT, Nigel John Frederick; *b* 12 Aug 1939; *Style—* Nigel Cartwright, Esq; Trotton Place, Petersfield, Hampshire GU3 15EN (☎ 0730 813 672); City Merchants Investment Managment Ltd, 9 Devonshire Square, London EC2 M4YL (☎ 071 929 5269, fax 071 929 5889/8, telex 883621/886108)

CARTWRIGHT, Rt Rev Richard Fox; s of Rev George Frederick Cartwright (vicar of Plumstead, d 1938), and Constance Margaret, *née* Clark (d 1975); *b* 10 Nov 1913; *Educ* The King's Sch Canterbury, Pembroke Coll Cambridge (BA, MA), Cuddesdon Theol Coll; *m* 6 Sept 1947, Rosemary Magdalen, da of Francis Evelyn Bray (d 1973), of Woodham Grange, Surrey; 1 s (Andrew Martin b 1948), 3 da (Rosemary Jane (Mrs Turner) b 1951, Mary Katharine (Mrs Bradley) b 1953, Susan Margaret (Mrs Meikle) b 1958); *Career* curate St Anselm Kennington Cross 1936-40, princ Lower Kingswood 1940-45; vicar: St Andrew Surbiton 1945-52, St Mary Redcliffe Bristol (with Temple 1956- and St John Bedminster 1965-) 1952-72; hon canon Bristol 1960-72, suffragan bishop of Plymouth 1972-81; asst bishop: Diocese of Truro 1982-, Diocese of Exeter 1988-; proctor in convocation 1950-52, memb Gen Synod 1976-80; chm Govrs Kelly Coll Tavistock 1973-88, govr Summer Fields Oxford 1964-88; dir: Ecclesiastical Insurance Gp 1964-85, All Churches Tst 1985-; Grand Chaplain Utd Grand Lodge of England 1973-75; Hon DD Univ of the South Tennesee 1969; OStJ 1957; *Recreations* fly fishing, gardening, water colour painting; *Clubs* Army and Navy; *Style—* The Rt Rev Richard Cartwright; 5 Old Vicarage Close, Ide, nr Exeter, Devon EX2 9RT (☎ 0392 211 270)

CARTWRIGHT, Ronald Casper; s of late Joseph William Cartwright; *b* 21 Nov 1919; *Educ* King's Coll Sch Wimbledon; *m* 1, 1947, Ella Margaret, *née* Trinnear (d 1978); 1 s, 1 da; m 2, 1980, Isobel Andrews, *née* Stevenson; *Career* chartered sec; chm Martonair Int plc 1980-86; *Clubs* Burhill Golf, RAC; *Style—* Ronald Cartwright, Esq; Tanglewood, 27 Sandown Rd, Esher, Surrey

CARTWRIGHT, Sally Amanda; da of Dennis Cartwright (d 1990), and Eileen Sergeant Cartwright (d 1979); *b* 8 May 1944; *Educ* Merton House Sch Keymer Sussex; *m* 1, 23 Feb 1973, John William Robinson; m 2, 29 Feb 1980, John Brian Hutchings; *Career* secretary 1961-69; IPC Magazines: merchandising exec 1970, promotions exec 1971-76, publicity mangr 1976-79, asst publisher 1979-82, publisher (responsible for Woman's Journal and Ideal Home Magazines) 1983-86; md: Capital Magazine 1987, Harmsworth Publications (pt of Assoc Newspapers) 1988-90; publishing dir Hello! magazine 1990-; memb Women's Advtg Club of London 1985-, chm Advtg Ctee Women of the Year Luncheon 1990-; *Recreations* reading, embroidery, skiing, swimming, opera, theatre; *Style—* Ms Sally Cartwright; Hello Limited, 30/34 New Bridge Street, London EC4V 6HH (☎ 071 489 9064, fax 071 236 6072, car 0831 176268)

CARTWRIGHT, Stephen John; s of Cyril Cartwright, of Dorset; *b* 5 Dec 1953; *Educ* King's Coll London (BSC, AKC), Univ of Oxford, Cncl of Legal Educn; *Career* writer and photographer; winner of William Stebbing prize 1975; joined Hon Soc Gray's Inn 1974, chm and md Bloomsbury Times Ltd 1987-; *Recreations* ballet, attempting to ingratiate self with misanthropic Persian cat; *Style—* Stephen J Cartwright, Esq; 103 Warwick Rd, London SW5 9EZ

CARTY, Dr Austin Timothy; s of Dr Thomas James Augustine (Gus) Carty (d 1975), of Lindsay Rd, Glasnevin, Dublin, and Dr Catherine Anne Carty, *née* Quinn (d 1981); *b* 22 June 1941; *Educ* Belvedere Coll Dublin, University College Dublin (MB BCh, BAO); *m* 23 Sept 1967, Helen Marie-Louise, da of Roland Moloney (d 1971), of Dun Laoghaire, Co Dublin and Dungarvan, Co Waterford; 1 s (Timothy b 1968), 2 da (Jennifer b 1970, Sarah b 1973); *Career* conslt radiologist Liverpool Health Authy 1974, clinical sub-dean Univ of Liverpool at Royal Liverpool Hosp 1987-90, chm Dist Med Advsy Ctee Liverpool Health Authy 1989-90, med dir Royal Liverpool Univ Hosp Tst 1991-, pres Liverpool Med Inst 1990-; FRCR, FRCPI, FFR RCSI; *Recreations* dinghy sailing, opera, wine; *Clubs* Twenty (Liverpool) (pres 1990-91), Innominate (Liverpool), Artists (Liverpool); *Style—* Dr Austin Carty; 6 Grosvenor Rd, Cressington Park, Liverpool L19 0PL (☎ 051 427 6727); X-Ray Department, Royal Liverpool Hospital, Prescot St, Liverpool L7 8XP (☎ 051 706 2751)

CARTY, James Patrick; s of James Patrick Carty (d 1958), and Phyllis Elizabeth Carty; *b* 3 March 1937; *Educ* Cotton Coll, Univ of London (BSc), Univ of Lancaster (MA); *Career* Price Waterhouse 1965-72 (articled clerk, asst mangr), lectr in accounting and fin Univ of Lancaster 1972-74, sec Accounting Standards Ctee 1974-81, accountant in public practice James Carty & Co 1981-87, ptnr Robson Rhodes 1987-; FCA 1975, FCCA 1983; *Books* Practical Financial Management (ed 1984); *Style—* James Carty, Esq; Robson Rhodes, 186 City Rd, London EC1V 2NU (☎ 071 251 1644, fax 071 250 0801)

CARUS, Louis Revell; s of Lt-Col Martin MacDowall Carus-Wilson, RAEC (d 1969), and Enid Madeleine Thaxter, *née* Revell (d 1973); *b* 22 Oct 1927; *Educ* Rugby, Brussels Conservatoire of Music, Peabody Conservatory of Music (USA); *m* 11 July 1951, Nancy Reade, da of Percival Edward Noell (d 1981), of Durham, N Carolina, USA; 2 s (Kenneth Edward b 20 Feb 1953, Colin Martin b 4 Sept 1956), 1 da (Alison Noell (Mrs L J Du Cane) b 29 May 1955); *Career* violinist, teacher and admin; memb Scot Nat Orch 1950-55, head of strings Royal Scot Acad of Music and Drama 1955-75, dean of faculty Birmingham Sch of Music 1975-87, artistic dir Int String Quartet Week 1987-, admin Benslow Tst Musical Instrument Loan Scheme 1987-; former pres ISM, chm Euro String Teachers Assoc (Br Branch); FRCM, FRSAMD, FBSM, Hon RAM; *Recreations* gardening, walking, painting; *Style—* Louis Carus, Esq; 15 Kings End Rd, Powick, Worcs WR2 4RA (☎ 0905 831715)

CARUTH, David Alexander; s of Maj Robert Alexander Caruth (d 1939), and Ruby Duncan, *née* Hodgson (d 1980); *b* 31 July 1931; *Educ* Wekington Coll, Univ of Southampton; *m* 1, 1963; 3 da (Sophie b 1964, Melissa b 1966, Julia Jill b 1968); m 2, 1987, Ann Thomas, da of Col Alan Clarence Langford; *Career* slr 1956, advocate Kenya 1958, New York Bar Assoc 1983; Linklatar & Paines: joined 1960, corp ptnr 1966, ptnr i/c New York 1983-86, left 1990; dir J Henry Schroder Wagg & Co Ltd 1990-; non-exec dir Bradbury Wilkinson & Co Ltd 1972-83, Matthew Hall & Co Ltd 1978-83, Allstate Insurance Ltd 1979-83; inspr DTI 1988-89; memb Oxfordshire Co Cncl 1977-814; govr: Walingford Sch 1977-81, St Mary's Sch Calne 1978-83; memb Newtonian Soc 1972-; memb Law Soc 1956; *Recreations* racing, swimming, shooting; *Clubs* Boodles, The 1900, The 65; *Style—* David Caruth, Esq; 169 Queens Gate, London SW7 5HE; J Henry Schroder Wagg & Co Ltd, 120 Cheapside, London EC2V 6DS (☎ 071 382 6447, car 0831 308 699)

CARUTH, Maj Michael James; s of Maj R A Caruth (d 1939), and Ruby Duncal Hodgson (d 1980); *b* 23 Nov 1928; *Educ* Wellington, RMA Sandhurst; *m* 7 June 1958, Anne, da of Brig J N Lumley (d 1965); 1 s (Patrick b 1959), 1 da ((Camilla b 1962); *Career* 4/7 Royal Dragoon Gds 1949-66; md Wightman-Mountain Co 1975-; MFH Weser Hunt 1957-59; *Recreations* hunting, shooting; *Clubs* Cavalry and Guards; *Style—* Maj Michael J Caruth; Hardington Lodge, Hardington-Mandeville, Yeovil, Somerset; Arklow Rd, London SE14 6EB (☎ 081 694 8682, fax 081 694 8380, car 0860 343738)

CARVELL, John Edward; s of Robert Charles Carvell (d 1984), of Perth, Scotland, and Ivy, *née* Dutch (d 1987); *b* 30 May 1946; *Educ* Perth Acad, Univ of St Andrews (MB ChB), Univ of Dundee (MMSc); *m* 22 July 1972, Carol, da of Gilbert D Ritchie, of Broughty Ferry, Dundee; 1 s (Robin b 1979), 1 da (Claire b 1976); *Career* registrar orthopaedics Royal Utd Hosps Bath 1976-77, sr registrar orthopaedics Nuffield Orthopaedic Centre Oxford and John Radcliffe Hosp Oxford 1978-83, conslt orthopaedic surgn Odstock Hosp Salisbury 1983-; regnl and dist pres Arthritis and Rheumatology Cncl; FRCSE 1976, fell Br Orthopaedic Assoc 1983; *Recreations* music, gardening, squash, tennis; *Clubs* Moonrakers (Salisbury); *Style—* John Carvell, Esq; Newstead, 143 Bouverie Avenue S, Salisbury, Wilts SP2 8EB (☎ 0722 330519); New Hall Hosp, The Lodge, Bodenham, Salisbury (☎ 0722 331021)

CARVER, Hon Andrew Richard; er s of Field Marshal Baron Carver, GCB, CBE, DSO, MC (Life Peer), *qv*; *b* 1950; *m* 1973, Anne Rosamunde, da of Brian Stewart, of The Broich, Crief, Perthshire; *Style—* The Hon Andrew Carver; 18 Hayter Rd, London SW2

CARVER, Hon John Anthony; s of Baron Carver (Life Peer); *b* 1961; *Educ* Winchester Coll, Durham Univ (BA); *Career* financial management; *Style—* The Hon John Carver

CARVER, (James) John; s of James Carver, and Jean Mary, *née* Kerry; *b* 28 Sept 1957; *Educ* Dulwich, Canterbury Coll of Art; *m* Jan 1987, Susan Jane, *née* Silvester; *Career* md designate J Carver & Co 1977-79, account exec International Marketing & Promotions (pt of the Masius Gp) 1979-81, creative exec Promotional Marketing Limited (pt of O & M) 1981-82, freelance art dir and writer 1982-85, creative dir and fndr ptnr The Leisure Process 1985-; winner various advtg prizes and awards from the music indust and mktg/advtg sector 1985-91; memb: ITV Assoc Zoo Check; *Books* Duran Duran (1985), Michael Jackson (1985); *Recreations* marlin fishing, hot air ballooning, historic car racing, classic car collecting, angling, aerobics, Thai boxing, travel; *Clubs* Fred's, Mercedes-Benz, Maserati Club of GB; *Style—* John Carver, Esq; 9 Airlie Gardens, Campden Hill Rd, Holland Park, London W8 (☎ 071 792 3375); The Leisure Process Ltd, 126 Great Portland St, London W1 (☎ 071 631 0666, fax 071 631 3753, car 0836 768422)

CARVER, Prof Martin Oswald Hugh; s of Lt-Col John Hobart Carver, of Shapley Hill, Winchfield, Hants, and Jocelyn Louisa Grace, *née* Tweedie; *b* 8 July 1941; *Educ* Wellington, RMA Sandhurst, RMC of Science Shrivenham (BSc), Univ of Durham; *m* 1, 5 April 1964 (m dis), Carolyn Rose, da of John Wolsely Haig; 1 s (Justin John), 1 da (Emma Rose); m 2, 2 April 1981, Madeleine Rose Hummler; 3 s (Frédéric Hugh, Jacques Francis, Louis Alexandre), 1 da (Geneviève Louise); *Career* adj 4 RTR 1968-70 (cmmnd RTR 1960), ret as Capt 1972; freelance archaeologist 1972-78, dir Field Archaeology Unit Univ of Birmingham 1978-86, prof and head Dept of Archaeology Univ of York 1986-; presenter and scriptwriter on Sutton Hoo BBC Films 1984, 1986, and 1988; dir Sutton Hoo Res Project 1983-; FSA, MIFA; *Books* Medieval Worcester (1980), Underneath English Towns (1987); *Style—* Prof Martin Carver, FSA; Dept of Archaeology, University of York, Micklegate House, York YO1 1JZ (☎ 0904 636731)

CARVER, Baron (Life Peer 1977), of Shackleford, Co Surrey; Field Marshal Sir (Richard) Michael Power Carver; GCB (1970, KCB 1966, CB 1957), CBE (1945), DSO (1943) and Bar (1943), MC (1941); 2 s of late Harold Power Carver, of Ticklerton, Salop, and Winifred Anne Gabrielle, *née* Wellesley; *b* 24 April 1915; *Educ* Winchester, RMA Sandhurst; *m* 1947, Edith, da of Lt-Col Sir Henry Lowry-Corry, MC (gs of 3 Earl Belmore); 2 s (Hon Andrew Richard, *qv*, b 1950, Hon John Antony, *qv*, b 1961), 2 da (Hon Susanna Mary b 1948, Hon Alice Elizabeth (Hon Mrs Walters) b 1954); *Career* sits as Ind peer in House of Lords; 2 Lt RTC 1935, cmd 4 Armd Bde 1944-47, Lt-Col 1942, Brig 1944; GOC 3 Div (Maj-Gen) 1962-64, Dep Cdr UN Force in Cyprus 1964, DSD MOD 1964-66, C-in-C Far East 1967-69, GOCIC Southern Cmd 1969-71, CGS 1971-73, Field-Marshal 1973, CDS 1973-76; Col Cmdt: REME 1966-76, RAC 1973-77; British Resident Cmmr (Designate) in Rhodesia 1977-78; *Books* El Alamein (1962), Tobruk (1964), The War Lords (ed, 1976), Harding of Petherton (1978), The Apostles of Mobility (1979), War Since 1945 (1980), A Policy for Peace (1982), The Seven Ages of The British Army (1984), Dilemmas of the Desert War (1986), Twentieth Century Warriors (1987), Out of Step (1989); *Recreations* sailing, tennis, gardening; *Clubs* Anglo-Belgian, Cavalry and Guards; *Style—* Field Marshal The Rt Hon Lord Carver, GCB, CBE, DSO, MC; Wood End House, Wickham, Fareham, Hants (☎ 0329 832143)

CARVER, Gp Capt Neville John; OBE (1986), AFC (1961); s of Bertie John Carver (d 1952), of Norfolk, and Rose Harriett, *née* Bloom (d 1970); *b* 5 Aug 1922; *Educ* Norwich Sch; *m* 1950, Caroline Mary, da of Arthur Henry Whewell (d 1966), of Lincs; 1 s (Michael Christopher b 1955), 2 da (Sarah Jane b 1953, Carolyn Rebecca b 1963); *Career* RAF 1941, cmmnd 1942; flying operations: Mediterranean, North Africa, Atlantic 1943-46; ret 1963 Gp Capt; joined: Ford Motor Co 1963, British Leyland 1969; former dir: Rover Gp plc (exec), ISTEL Ltd, BLMC Ltd, Lloyds Register Quality Assur Ltd, Br Motor Heritage Ltd; dir UGC Ltd; *Recreations* golf, gardening, squash, reading; *Clubs* RAF; *Style—* Gp Capt Neville Carver, OBE, AFC; Weirdown, Blackthorn, Bicester, Oxon OX6 0TH (☎ 0869 244 911)

CARVER, Peter William John; JP (1973), DL (Humberside 1983); 23 patron of North Cave living; s of Maj John Henton Carver, JP, TD (d 1968), and Juliet (d 1969), er da of Col T C Clitherow, DSO (d 1963), of Hotham Hall, York; *b* 18 June 1938; *Educ* Uppingham; *m* 1963, Jacqueline Sarah, da of James Boyce, of Fornham All Saints, Suffolk (d 1984); 1 s (Christian Henton James); *Career* Nat Serv 2 Lt DCLI; staff broadcaster with Br Forces Network Germany 1959-62, Radio Luxembourg 1962-64; farmer and landowner; underwriting memb of Lloyd's 1971-; cncllr E Riding Yorks CC 1971-74; contested (C) Hull Central 1974 (twice), pres Humberside Euro Constituency 1983-88 (chm 1978-83), chm Humberside Scout Assoc 1978-83 (co cmmr 1983-90); memb Ctee of the Cncl Scout Assoc 1986-90; dir: Hull City AFC 1981, Viking Radio; memb Yorks Regnl Ctee Nat Tst, landowner (1500 acres), dep chm S Hunsley Magistrates, memb Cncl of St John (Humberside); *Recreations* shooting, gardening, historic houses; *Clubs* Royal Over-Seas; *Style—* Peter Carver, Esq, JP, DL; The Croft, North Cave, East Yorks (☎ 0430 422203); Hotham Estate Farms, North Cave, East Yorks HV15 2NG

CARVER, Wyndham Houssemayne; s of Capt Edmund Squarey Carver, DSC, RN, and Freda Wilmot Houssemayne, *née* Du Boulay (d 1970); *b* 4 May 1943; *Educ* Malvern Coll, Harvard Business Sch (PMD); *m* 11 May 1974 (m dis 1984), Jocelyn Mary Anne, da of Graham Rogers, of Hungerford House, Hyde, Fordingbridge, Hants; m 2, Shona Leslie, da of Maj Ian McKillop, of Ladys Walk, East Cholderton, nr Andover, Hants; 1 da (Tamsin b 7 Sept 1985); *Career* md Wyvern International (subsidiary of International Distillers & Vintners Ltd of Grand Met plc) 1982- (joined 1965); *Recreations* squash, tennis, golf, forestry, travel; *Clubs* Annabels, Lansdowne; *Style—* Wyndham Carver, Esq; Rondle Wood House, nr Milland, Liphook, Hants (☎ 0730 821 397); 151 Marylebone Rd, London NW1 5QE (☎ 071 258 5100, fax 071 258 5151, telex 262548 SPIRIT G)

CARY, Hon Mrs (Clare Louise Katharine); o da of Baron Elworthy, KG, GCB, CBE, DSO, LVO, DFC, AFC (Life Peer); *b* 1950; *m* 1975, Anthony Joyce Cary, s of Sir (Arthur Lucius) Michael Cary, GCB; 3 s (Sam Michael b 1978, Thomas Joyce b 1980, Arthur Lucius b 1983), 1 da (Harriet Maude b 1985); *Style—* The Hon Mrs Cary

CARY, Hon Mrs Byron; Daphne Helen; *née* King; er da of late Capt Edward Westcott King, RA; *m* 1932, Hon Byron Godfrey Plantagenet Cary (d 1971), 2nd s of 13 Viscount Falkland, OBE; 1 s, 2 da; *Style—* The Hon Mrs Byron Cary; The Cottage, 26 Dorset Rd South, Bexhill-on-Sea, E Sussex

CARY, Nicolas Robert Hugh; s and h of Sir Roger Cary, 2 Bt, *qv*; *b* 17 April 1955; *Educ* St Paul's, London Univ (BA); *m* 1979, Pauline Jean, da of Thomas Ian Boyd, of Grays, Essex; 2 s (Alexander b 1981, Nathaniel b 1983); *Career* with Sotheby's 1977-82, production asst Catalogue Dept 1979-82; city print rep Westerham Press 1982-; *Recreations* book collecting, typography, cookery; *Style—* Nicolas Cary Esq; 232 Ongar Rd, Brentwood, Essex CM15 9DX (☎ 0277 225424)

CARY, Sir Roger Hugh; 2 Bt (UK 1955); s of Sir Robert Cary, 1 Bt, sometime MP for Eccles and Manchester (Withington), PPS to Capt Harry Crookshank 1951-55; *b* 8 Jan 1926; *Educ* Ludgrove, Eton, New Coll Oxford; *m* 1, 1948 (m dis 1951), Marilda, da of Maj Philip Pearson-Gregory, MC; 1 da; m 2, 1953, Ann Helen Katharine, da of Blair Brenan, OBE; 2 s, 1 da; *Heir* s, Nicolas Cary, *qv*; *Career* former sub ed and leader writer The Times and dep ed The Listener, sr asst then special asst (public affairs) BBC 1972-77, special asst to md BBC TV 1977-82, chief asst to dir of programming BBC TV 1983-86, conslt to dir gen BBC 1986-; tstee Kedleston 1989-; *Recreations* looking at pictures; *Clubs* Pratt's; *Style—* Sir Roger Cary, Bt; 23 Bath Rd, London W4 (☎ 071 994 7293); BBC, Broadcasting House, London W1A 1AA (☎ 071 580 4468 ext 3838)

CARY-ELWES, Charles Gervase Rundle; s of Lt-Col Oswald Aloysius Joseph Cary-Elwes, and Elizabeth Pamela, *née* Brendon; *b* 8 Nov 1939; *Educ* Ampleforth, Sorbonne, Trinity Coll Oxford (MA); *m* 2 April 1972, Angela Jean, da of Maj Eric Rowland, TD, TA (d 1960); 1 s (James b 1976), 1 da (Lucy b 1974); *Career* stockjobber Durlacher Oldham Mordaunt Godson 1962-65, self-employed 1965-74, Peat Marwick Mitchell & Co CA 1975-79, corporate fin exec Grieveson Grant & Co 1980-83, Exco Int plc 1983-85; dir: British & Commonwealth Holdings plc 1986-89, Broomhill Securities Ltd 1991-; FCA, ATII; *Recreations* golf, music, theatre, travel; *Clubs* Dulwich and Sydenham Hill Golf; *Style—* Charles Cary-Elwes, Esq; 112 Court Lane, Dulwich, London SE21 7EA (☎ 081 693 1743)

CASE, Anthea Fiendley; da of Thomas Fiendley Stones, OBE, of London, and Bessie Mackie (d 1985); *b* 7 Feb 1945; *Educ* Christ's Hosp, St Anne's Coll Oxford (BA); *m* David Charles Case, s of Charles Kendall Case, of Essex; 2 da (Melissa b 1977, Laura b 1983); *Career* HM Treasy: various posts 1967-70, private sec to Fin Sec 1970-71, princ 1971-80, asst sec 1980-88, under sec Home Educn Gp 1988-90, under sec Pay and Industl Rels Gp 1990-; *Style—* Mrs Anthea Case; HM Treasury, Parliament St, London SW1 (☎ 071 270 4400)

CASE, David Charles; s of Charles Kendal Case, and Grace Tennent, *née* Smith; *b* 18 Oct 1943; *Educ* Oakham Sch, Univ of Oxford (MA); *m* 3 June 1967, Anthea Fiendley, da of Thomas Fiendly Stones, OBE; 2 da (Melissa Katherine b 1977, Laura Alexandra b 1983); *Career* ICI 1967-68, export mangr British Sidac 1968-72, dir CCA Galleries plc (formerly Christie's Contemporary Art) 1972-89, md Marlborough Graphics Ltd; *Clubs* Arts, Chelsea Arts; *Style—* David Case Esq; Marlborough Graphics Ltd, 42 Dover St, London W1 (☎ 071 495 2642)

CASE, David James; s of James Henry Case (d 1935), and Kathleen Nora Savory (d 1971); *b* 1 Sept 1923; *Educ* King Edward VII King's Lynn, Paston Sch; *m* 16 Oct 1956, Ruth; 1 s (James b 1958, 1 da (Gillian b 1957); *Career* RN 1941-46, Lt RNVR; lifeboatman 1953-, station hon sec Wells Station Branch RNLI 1969-; past pres Norfolk Assoc of Agric Valuers, harbour cmmr Wells-next-the-Sea Norfolk; FRICS, FAAV; *Recreations* shooting, sea fishing, gardening; *Style—* David J Case, Esq; Saxons, Northfield, Wells-next-the Sea, Norfolk NR23 1JZ (☎ 0328 710234); Case and Dewing, Church St, Dereham, Norfolk NR19 2DJ (☎ 0362 692004)

CASE, David Winston; s of Stanley Herbert George Case, of Broadstairs, Kent, and Doreen, *née* Jeans; *b* 10 June 1952; *Educ* Dane Court GS, St Martin's Sch of Art (BA); *m* 7 March 1987, Deborah Jane, da of Harold Pratt; 1 s (James Alexander b 9 Sept 1986), 1 da (Rachael Mary Louise b 2 July 1988); *Career* graphic artist: The Sunday Times 1975-78, TV Times magazine 1978-79; head of graphics Now! magazine 1979-81, asst art ed The Mail on Sunday 1981-84, art ed Which? magazine (Consumer Association) 1984-86, design dir Financial Times 1986-; awards: Best Design award Daily Nat Newspaper (Financial Times) 1990, Best Design award (with Andrew Chappin) Sunday Nat Newspaper (The Sunday Correspondent) 1990, awards for illustration by Soc for News Design USA 1990; fndr memb and vice pres Euro Soc for News Design; *Style—* David Case, Esq; 39 Cossington Rd, Canterbury, Kent CT1 3HU (☎ 0227 765510); Financial Times, Number One, Southwark Bridge, London SE1 9HL (☎ 071 873 3000, fax 071 407 5700)

CASE, Janet Ruth; da of James Anthony Simpson, of Exeter, and Cathleen, *née* King; *b* 29 June 1943; *Educ* Bishop Blackall Sch Exeter, Univ of Durham (LLB); *m* 1965 (m dis 1982), Jeremy David Michael Case, s of Glyn Pryce (d 1980), of Gunley; 1 s (Edwin b 1969), 1 da (Charlotte b 1966); *Career* called to the Bar Inner Temple 1975, Wales and Chester Circuit 1975; chm Med Appeals Tbnl; *Recreations* gardening; *Clubs* Lansdowne; *Style—* Mrs Janet Case; Croeswylan, Oswestry, Shropshire (☎ 0691 653726); 40 King St, Chester (☎ 0244 323886)

CASE, Hon Mrs (Pauline Marian); yr da of 3 Viscount Astor (d 1966) by his 3 w; *b* 26 March 1964; *Educ* Downside, Sarah Lawrence Coll; *m* 13 Oct 1990, George C V Case, s of late Denis Case; *Clubs* Women's Univ; *Style—* The Hon Mrs Case; 34 Talbot Rd, London W2

CASEWELL, Prof Mark William; s of William John Ivor Casewell (d 1951), of Hants, and Phyllis Rebecca, *née* Raymond (d 1976); *b* 17 Aug 1940; *Educ* Royal Masonic Sch, Univ of London (BSc, MB BS, MD); *m* 8 July 1967 (m dis 1972), Carolle Anne, da of Richard Eaton, of Portsmouth, Hants; *Career* house physician St Bartholomew's Hosp 1965-66, asst pathologist Univ of Cambridge 1967-70, sr lectr in microbiology (former lectr) St Thomas' Hosp 1971-81, reader and hon conslt in microbiology The London Hosp 1982-84, prof of med microbiology King's Coll Sch of Med and Dentistry 1984-; memb: AIDS Advsy Gp Camberwell Health Authy, Ed Bd of Jl of Hosp Infection; chm Hosp Infection Soc 1987- (fndr memb 1979); MRCS 1965, LRCP 1965, MRCPath 1975 (memb Cncl), FRCPath 1986; *Books* numerous contribs incl: British Medical Students Association Annual Educational Report (1963), Journal of Clinical Pathology (1973), Journal of Hospital Infection (1980), Skin Microbiology: Relevance to Cervical Infection (1981), Recent Advances in Infection (1982), Journal of Antimicrobial Chemotherapy (1984), Journal of Dental Research (1988); *Recreations* cooking, Italy and very fast cars; *Clubs* Wig & Pen, Fountain (Barts), Zanzibar; *Style—* Prof Mark Casewell; 43 Primrose Gardens, London NW3 4UL; Dept of Medical Mircobiology, King's College School of Medicine and Dentistry, Bessemer Rd, London SE5 9PJ, (☎ 071 326 3213, fax 071 326 3404, car 0860 625611)

CASEY, Lady Arabella; 2 da of 7 Earl of Yarborough, JP; *b* 20 Jan 1960; *Educ* Heathfield, L'Institut Alpin Videmanette Switzerland; *m* 2 June 1984, Christopher Casey, o s of Ronald Casey, of Pecklands, Stansted, Kent; 2 da (Laura Alexandra b 1 Aug 1986, Emma Olivia b 13 April 1988); *Style—* The Lady Arabella Casey

CASEY, Gavin Frank; *b* 18 Oct 1946; *Career* chartered accountant; Harmood Banner & Co 1965-69, Cooper Brothers & Co 1970-71, County Natwest Ltd 1972-89, Smith New Court plc 1989-; Freeman City of London, memb Worshipful Co of Chartered Accountants in England and Wales; FCA 1970; *Recreations* horse racing, theatre; *Clubs* City of London; *Style—* Gavin Casey, Esq; Smith New Court plc, PO Box 293, 20 Farringdon Rd, London EC1M 3NH (☎ 071 772 2327, fax 071 772 2903)

CASEY, Jayne; da of John Casey (d 1988), of Bidston, Wirral, and Sonia Georgette, *née* Burden-Green (d 1963); *b* 12 Sept 1956; *Educ* Wallasey Tech HS; 1 s (Ra Jojo Cole); *Career* singer and songwriter; work incl: Big in Japan 1977, Pink Military 1980, Pink Industry 1980; dir Zulu Records 1981-87; assessor Merseyside Arts (memb Asian Music Panel); dir: Liverpool Festival of Comedy 1991, performing arts Bluecoat Arts Centre Liverpool; *Clubs* Arts; *Style—* Ms Jayne Casey; Bluecoat Arts Centre, Bluecoat Chambers, School Lane, Liverpool L1 3BX (☎ 051 708 8877)

CASEY, Kevin Lawrence; s of James Casey, of Hillingdon, and Theresa, *née* Daly; *b* 2 Oct 1949; *Educ* Gunnersbury GS; *m* 5 Aug 1972, Theresa Margaret, da of Patrick Rooney, of Galway, Eire; 2 da (Emma b 1977, Claire b 1979); *Career* serv 10 Bn (V) Para Regt 1970-74; qualified CA 1973, Price Waterhouse: ptnr 1984-, ptnr i/c UK Customs and VAT 1985, chm world customs specialists 1988, ptnr i/c Euro VAT 1989; fndr VAT Practitioners Gp 1982; former memb: London Soc of CAs VAT Ctee, ICAEW VAT Ctee; govr St Bernadette's PS Hillingdon; FCA; *Recreations* shooting, marathon running, cooking; *Style—* K L Casey, Esq; Sneppenlaan 24, Tervuren 3080, Brussels, Belgium; Price Waterhouse, Rue St Lambert 135, B-1200, Brussels, Belgium (☎ 32 2 773 4972)

CASEY, Michael Bernard; s of Joseph Bernard Casey, OBE (d 1985), and Dorothy, *née* Love (d 1949); *b* 1 Sept 1928; *Educ* Colwyn Bay GS, LSE (LLB); *m* 1963, Sally Louise, da of James Stuart Smith; 2 s (James Dominic b 1966, Matthew Damian b 1967), 2 da (Louise Dorothy b 1964, Charlotte Hanna b 1971); *Career* offr: MAFF

1954-63, Miny of Sci 1963-64, Dept Econ Affrs 1964-69, Miny of Technol 1969-71; asst sec DTI 1971-72, under sec to head Shipbuilding Policy Div Dept Indust 1975-77; chief exec and dep chm Br Shipbuilders 1977-80, chm and md Mather and Platt Ltd 1980-82, dir Marlar Int Ltd 1982-87, chm and chief exec Sallingbury Casey Ltd 1986-; *Recreations* golf, chess, bridge; *Clubs* Reform; *Style—* Michael B Casey, Esq; 3 Barkston Gardens, London SW5 (☎ 071 244 6124); 25 Victoria St, London SW1 (☎ 071 222 1566, fax 071 222 3220, telex 268456)

CASEY, Michael Vince; OBE; s of Charles John Casey (d 1966), of Exmouth, Devon, and May Louise, *née* Yeulett (d 1981); *b* 25 May 1927; *Educ* Glossop GS, Univ of London (BSc); *m* 1954, Elinor Jane (d 1987), da of Alfred George Harris (d 1982), of Purton, Wilts; 2 s (William, Edward), 2 da (Annabel, Angela); *Career* various engrg posts with BR 1944-78, engrg dir BR Engrg Ltd 1978-82, dir of mech and electrical engrg BR Ltd 1982-87, project dir BREL Privatisation 1987-89; chief engr Channel Tunnel Rail Link Gp 1989-90; ret; FEng, FIMechE; *Recreations* gardening, philately; *Style—* M V Casey, Esq, OBE; Hunters Ride, Stoke Row Rd, Peppard, Henley-on-Thames, Oxon (☎ 0734 722 653)

CASH, Prof John David; s of John Henry Cash (d 1982), and May Annie, *née* Taylor (d 1986); *b* 3 April 1936; *Educ* Ashville Coll, Univ of Edinburgh (BSc, PhD, MB ChB); *m* 22 Sept 1962, Angela Mary, da of Robert David Thomson (d 1980); 1 s (Michael Peter b 1965), 1 da (Julie Suzanna b 1967); *Career* dir Regnl Blood Transfusion Serv Edinburgh and S E Scotland 1974-79, nat med dir Scot Nat Blood Transfusion Serv 1979-; FRCPE, FRCPath; *Recreations* fishing, gardening; *Style—* Prof John Cash; Scottish Nat Blood Transfusion Serv, Headquarters' Unit, Ellen's Glen Rd, Edinburgh 17 7QT (☎ 031 664 2317, fax 031 658 1639)

CASH, William Nigel Paul; MP (C) Stafford 1984-; s of Capt Paul Trevor Cash, MC (ka Normandy 1944), and Moyra Margaret Elizabeth, *née* Morrison; *b* 10 May 1940; *Educ* Stonyhurst, Lincoln Coll Oxford (MA); *m* 1965, Bridget Mary, da of James Rupert Lee; 2 s (William, Samuel), 1 da (Letitia); *Career* slr William Cash and Co; chm Cons Backbench Ctee Euro Affrs 1989-; vice chm: Cons Constitutional Ctee 1986, Cons Small Business Bureau 1984, Backbench Ctee on Smaller Business 1988; memb Select Ctee on Euro Legislation; chm All Pty Parly Ctee: on Widows 1984, on E Africa 1988; hon sec Lords and Commons Cricket, bd memb Ironbridge Gorge Tst; contrib to The Times 1986- *Publications* A Democratic Way to European Unity Against Federation (1990); *Recreations* cricket, tennis, the heritage, cutting lawns, cutting red tape; *Clubs* Carlton, Vincent's (Oxford), Free Foresters CC; *Style—* William Cash, Esq, MP; Upton Cressett Hall, nr Bridgnorth, Shropshire (☎ 074 631 307); 37 St George's Square, London SW1 (☎ 071 821 6237); William Cash & Co, 5 Great College St, London SW1 (☎ 071 222 7040, telex 919302)

CASHEL AND OSSORY, Bishop of (901) 1980-; Rt Rev Noel Vincent Willoughby; 58 Bp of Cashel (901), 89 Bp of Ossory (441), 63 Bp of Waterford (1096), 70 Bp of Lismore (631); s of George Willoughby, and Mary Jane Willoughby; *b* 15 Dec 1926; *Educ* Tate Sch Wexford, Trinity Coll Dublin; *m* 1959, Valerie Moore, of Dungannon, Tyrone; 2 s, 1 da; *Career* deacon 1950, ordained Armagh Cathedral 1951; curate: Drumglass Parish 1950-53, St Catherine's Dublin 1953-55, Bray Parish 1955-59; rector: Delgany Parish 1959-69, Glenageary Parish 1969-80; hon sec General Synod 1976-80, treas St Patrick's Cathedral Dublin 1976-80, archdeacon of Dublin 1979-80; *Books* What We Believe (1985); *Style—* The Rt Rev the Bishop of Cashel and Ossory; The Palace, Kilkenny, Ireland (☎ 056 21560)

CASHMAN, Dr Michael David; s of Lt-Col John David Cashman (d 1977), and Jenet Ann, *née* Neville; *b* 19 Nov 1930; *Educ* St Cuthberts GS Newcastle, Univ of Durham (MB BS); *m* 4 Feb 1956, Sheila, da of Matthew McHale (d 1964); 2 s (John b 1963, Damien b 1965), 3 da (Patricia b 1955, Ann b 1960, Clare b 1964); *Career* RAMC: Lt 1954, Capt 1955, Maj 1955-57; asst psychiatrist Lancaster Moor Hosp 1959-63; conslt psychiatrist: S Shields Gen Hosp 1963-66, Blackpool and Fylde Hosps 1966-; former examiner GNC; advsr and assessor GMC, assessor Mental Health Review Tbnl and Mental Health Act Cmmn, advsr Lancaster Diocesan Marriage Tbnl, memb Cons Med Soc; former: fell Cncl RCPsych, Convenor of Accreditation All Ireland; FRCPEd, FRCPsych, DIPM; *Recreations* music (piano, organ, french horn, flute, piccolo), church organist; *Clubs* Royal Lytham St Anne's Golf; *Style—* Dr Michael Cashman; 1 Windor Rd, St Anne's on Sea, Lancs FY8 1ET (☎ 0253 721876); Victoria Hospital, Blackpool, Lancs FY3 8NR (☎ 0253 303689)

CASHMAN, Michael Maurice; s of John Cashman, of London, and Mary Alvena, *née* Clayton; *b* 17 Dec 1950; *Educ* Cardinal Griffin Secdy Modern, Gladys Dare's Sch; *Career* actor; in theatre, musical theatre, TV, films and radio; first role in Oliver 1963, Colin in Eastenders (BBC TV), Horst in Royal Nat Theatre prodn of Bent; patron: Frontliners, London Lighthouse, London Friend, Family Welfare Assoc; chm Stonewall Lobbying Gp, memb Lab Pty; special serv award from American Assoc of Physicians for Human Rights; *Style—* Michael Cashman, Esq; Royal National Theatre, South Bank, London SE1 (☎ 071 928 2033)

CASKIE, Don William; s of Donald John Caskie, of Wychbold, and Christine, *née* Harris; *b* 12 Dec 1965; *Educ* Rednock Sch Dursley, W London Inst of Higher Educn (BEd); *Career* Rugby Union centre Gloucester RFC and Scotland (no caps awarded); Bristol RFC 1984-85, London Scottish RFC 1986-89, joined Gloucester RFC 1989-; debut Anglo Scots dist championships 1989-90; Scotland under 21: v Italy 1985-86 and 1986-87, reserve v Wales 1986-87; memb Scotland Students at inaugural Students World Cup 1988; Scotland debut Spain Seville 1990; qualified PE teacher, sport mktg, lease and finance servs Reading; *Recreations* golf, fishing; *Style—* Don Caskie, Esq; Gloucester Rugby Club, Kingsholm, Worcester St, Glos

CASS, Alain Jules; s of Edouard Catzeflis (d 1985), and Irene Lempicka (d 1986); *b* 6 Oct 1944; *Educ* Victoria Coll Alexandria Egypt, Athens Coll Greece, Bradfield Coll Berkshire; *m* 1, 8 March 1968 (m dis 1978), Susan Jean Freeman; 1 s (Julian b 7 Feb 1976), 1 da (Claudia b 18 Nov 1972); m 2, 18 Dec 1985, Caroline Jane Pritchard; *Career* Daily Express 1967-74: reporter, feature writer, foreign corr (assignments incl: NI 1969-71, Oct M East War 1973); Financial Times: foreign staff M East specialist 1974-76, foreign news ed 1976-82, Asia ed and asst foreign ed 1982-86, asst ed of the Financial Times and ed International Edition 1986-89, asst ed (news) and news ed 1989-; *Recreations* journalism, music, travel and journalism; *Style—* Alain Cass, Esq; The Financial Times, Horseshoe Court, 1 Southwark Bridge, London SE1 9HL (☎ 071 873 3000, fax 071 407 5700)

CASS, David; s of Flt Lt Zbigniew Henryk Czarnecki, of Hereford, and Betty, *née* Mitchell; *b* 4 April 1946; *Educ* The Paston Sch Norfolk; *m* 1, 6 Oct 1971 (m dis 1982), (Doris) Jill, da of Edward Russell (d 1984), of Poole, Dorset; 1 s (Russell b 19 Feb 1973); m 2, 16 July 1983, Buddug Rhiannon, da of John Philip Williams (d 1970) of Hereford, and Catherine Ann, *née* Morgan; 1 s (William b 7 Feb 1989); *Career* BBC Local Radio 1970-72, sports corr BBC TV News 1978-84, prog controller Screensport 1984-86, newscaster ITN 1986- (incl Into the Night 1988); memb: Lord's Taverners, RTS; *Recreations* gardening, golf, charity cricket; *Style—* David Cass, Esq; 1726 M ST NW, Suite 703, Washington DC 20036, USA (☎ 010 1 202 429 9080, fax 010 1 202 429 8948)

CASS, Geoffrey Arthur; s of Arthur Cass (d 1982), of Darlington and Oxford, and Jessie, *née* Simpson (d 1967); *b* 11 Aug 1932; *Educ* Queen Elizabeth GS Darlington, Jesus Coll Oxford, (BA, MA, Tennis and Badminton blues), Dept of Social and Administrative Studies Oxford, Nuffield Coll Oxford, Jesus Coll Cambridge, Clare Hall Cambridge (MA); *m* 1957, Olwen Mary, JP, da of late William Leslie Richards, of Brecon; 4 da (Fiona b 1961, Karen b 1962, Miranda b 1965, Fleur b 1969); *Career* cmmnd PO RAFVR (Oxford Univ Air Sqdn) 1954, Nat Serv PO 1958, Flying Offr 1960, Air Min Directorate Work Study RAF 1958-60; conslt PA Mgmnt Conslts 1960-65; private mgmnt conslt: British Communications Corporation, Controls and Communications Ltd 1965; md George Allen & Unwin 1967-71 (dir 1965-67); dir: Controls and Communications Ltd 1966-69, Chicago Univ Press (UK) Ltd 1971-86; chief exec Cambridge Univ Press 1972-, dir Weidenfeld Publishers Ltd 1972-74; dir: Newcastle Theatre Royal Tst 1984-89, American Friends Royal Shakespeare Theatre 1985-, Cambridge Theatre Co 1986-; tstee and guardian Shakespeare Birthplace Tst 1982-; chm: Royal Shakespeare Theatre Tst 1983- (dir 1967-), Royal Shakespeare Co 1985- (govr 1975-), Br Int Tennis and Nat Trg 1985-90; memb: Bd Lawn Tennis Assoc GB 1985-90 (memb Cncl 1976-), Wimbledon Championships Ctee of Mgmnt 1990- (memb Jt Fin Bd 1989), Governing Syndicate Fitzwilliam Museum Cambridge 1977-78; chm of govrs Perse Sch for Girls Cambridge 1978-88, memb: Univ of Cambridge Ctee and Exec Sub Ctee Mgmnt Fenners 1976-, Exec Ctee Univ of Cambridge Careers Service Syndicate 1982- (memb 1977-); County tennis singles champion: Durham 1951, Cambridgeshire 1975; chm Cambridge Univ Lawn Tennis Club 1977-, pres Cambridgeshire Lawn Tennis Assoc 1980-82; played Wimbledon Championships: 1954, 1955, 1956, 1959; Br Veterans Singles champion Wimbledon 1978, Hon Cambridge Tennis Blue 1980; hon fell of Clare Hall Camb 1979; FInstD 1968, FIWM 1979, FIIM 1979, CBIM 1980; Chevalier de L'Ordre des Arts et des Lettres France 1982; *Recreations* lawn tennis, theatre, running; *Clubs* Hurlingham, Queen's, Int Lawn Tennis of GB, The 45, Cambridge Univ Lawn Tennis, Veterans Lawn Tennis GB; *Style—* Geoffrey Cass Esq; Middlefield, Huntingdon Rd, Cambridge CB3 0LH; The Edinburgh Building, Shaftesbury Rd, Cambridge CB2 2RU (☎ 0223 312393)

CASS, (Edward) Geoffrey; CB (1974), OBE (1951); s of Edward Charles Cass (d 1974), and Florence Mary, *née* Tailby (d 1990); *b* 10 Sept 1916; *Educ* St Olave's Sch, Univ Coll London (BScEcon), The Queen's Coll Oxford (MA); *m* 2 June 1941, Ruth Mary, da of Robert Powley (d 1953); 4 da (Jenifer b 1943, Sally b 1946, Lesley b 1949, Harriet b 1952); *Career* economist and statistician; asst under sec of state MOD 1965-72, dep under sec of state 1972-76, govr Reserve Bank of Rhodesia 1988-89; *Style—* Geoffrey Cass, Esq, CB, OBE; 60 Rotherwick Rd, London NW11 7DB (☎ 081 455 1664)

CASS, Richard Martin; s of Edward Charles Cass, of Cheshire, and Hazel Rosemary; *b* 25 May 1946; *Educ* High Wycombe GS, Sheffield Univ (BArch, MA); *m* 1977, Judith Claire, da of Dr Linton Morris Snaith, of Newcastle upon Tyne; 2 s (Simon b 1983, Alexander b 1986); *Career* architect and landscape architect; dir Brian Clouston and Ptnrs 1979-82, princ Cass Assoc 1982-; *Recreations* music, theatre, gardening, sailing, reading; *Style—* Richard M Cass, Esq; Osborne House, Fullwood Park, Liverpool (☎ 051 727 7614); Cass Associates, Albion House, 30 James St, Liverpool (☎ 051 236 9074, fax 051 236 1582)

CASSAR, Dr Joseph; s of Charles George Cassar, and Sabina, *née* Debono; *b* 22 Sept 1940; *Educ* Royal Univ of Malta (MD), Imperial Coll of Science and Technol (DIC), Univ of London (PhD); *m* 21 Feb 1976, Carol Anne, da of William Richmond Wilson; 1 s (Christopher b 8 June 1979), 1 da (Claire b 19 Nov 1977); *Career* rotating intern: Middlesex Meml Hosp Middletown Connecticut USA 1966, sr house offr Westminster Med Sch 1966-67, Cwlth scholar 1967-70; registrar: KCH 1970-71, Royal Free Hosp 1971-73; sr registrar Royal Postgrad Med Sch 1973-79, conslt physician W Middlesex Univ Hosp 1979-; author of papers on diabetes endocrinology and gen med; memb: BDA, BMA, RSM; MRCP, FRCP; *Recreations* tennis, sail boarding, walking, chess, reading; *Style—* Dr Joseph Cassar; 16 Queens Gardens, Ealing, London W5 1SF (☎ 081 998 2576); W Middlesex University Hospital, Isleworth, London TW7 6AF (☎ 081 565 5390); 22 Harley St, London W1 (☎ 081 637 0491)

CASSEL, His Hon Sir Harold Felix; 3 Bt (1920 UK), TD (1975), QC (1970); s of Sir Felix Cassel, 1 Bt, PC, QC (d 1953); suc bro, Sir Francis Cassel, 2 Bt 1969; *b* 8 Nov 1916; *Educ* Stowe, CCC Oxford; *m* 1, 1940 (m dis 1963), Ione Jean, *née* Barclay; 3 s, 1 da; m 2, 1963, Mrs Eileen Elfrida Smedley, *née* Faulkner; *Heir* s, Timothy Cassel; *Career* called to the Bar 1946, dep chm Herts 1959-62, rec Great Yarmouth 1968-71, rec Crown Court 1972-76, circuit judge 1976-88; JP Herts 1959-62; *Style—* His Hon Judge Sir Harold Cassel, Bt, TD, QC; 49 Lennox Gdns, London SW1 (☎ 071 584 2721)

CASSEL, Jeremy James; s of Sir Harold Cassel, Bt, QC, TD, of 49 Lennox Gardens, London SW1, and Ione Jean, *née* Barclay; *b* 7 June 1950; *Educ* Eton, Sorbonne; *m* 7 June 1982, Vivien Helen, da of David John Hayter, of Kinghams Farm, Highclere, Berks; 2 s (Hugo b 1982, Felix b 1988), 1 da (Sieglinde b 1984); *Career* trained Savoy Hotel Gp 1970, gen mangr Compleat Angler Marlow 1978, hotels and restaurants conslt 1982, md Cassel Hotels and Restaurants plc 1989; tstee King Edward VII Br-German Fndn; *Recreations* racing; *Style—* Jeremy Cassel, Esq; Manor House, Kirby Underdale, York (☎ 075 96 519); The Grange Hotel, Clifton, Yorks (☎ 0904 644744)

CASSEL, Timothy Felix Harold; QC (1988); s and h of His Hon Judge Sir Harold Cassel, Bt, TD, QC; *b* 30 April 1942; *Educ* Eton; *m* 1971 (m dis 1975), Mrs Jenifer Samuel; 1 s, 1 da; m 2, 1979, Ann, only da of Sir William Mallalieu; 2 da; *Career* called to the Bar Lincoln's Inn 1965; jr prosecutor for the Crown of the Central Criminal Ct 1978, asst boundary cmmr 1979, sr prosecutor for the Crown 1986; *Style—* Timothy Cassel, Esq, QC; Studdridge Farm, Stokenchurch, Bucks

CASSELLS-SMITH, Dr Alan James; s of James Smith (d 1976), and Margaret Cooper, *née* Cassells (d 1984); *b* 13 May 1925; *Educ* South Shields HS, Trinity Hall Cambridge, Univ of Durham Med Sch; *m* 23 Aug 1952, Rosamond, da of Jack Turndull; 1 s (Richard Alan b 1960), 1 da (Rosalynne Anne b 1958); *Career* tech offr: A&AEE 1945-46, WDOL Industs Res Assoc 1946-47; South Shields Gen Hosp: house physician 1952, demonstrator in pathology Univ of Durham 1953-57, lectr chemical pathology 1957-60, conslt chemical pathologist Newcastle Gen Hosp 1960-78, conslt chemical pathologist Freeman Hosp Newcastle upon Tyne 1977-; memb: Bio Chemistry Soc 1947-90, Assoc Clinical BioChemistry 1953-90, Assoc Clinical Pathology 1961-90; *Recreations* baking, gardening; *Style—* Dr Alan Cassells-Smith; 26 Bents Park Rd, South Shields NE33 2NL (☎ 091 455 3734); Clinical Biochemistry, Freeman Hospital, Freeman Rd, High Heaton, Newcastle upon Tyne NE7 7DN (☎ 091 284 3111)

CASSELS, Field Marshal Sir (Archibald) James Halkett; GCB (1961, CB 1950), KBE (1952, CBE 1944), DSO (1944); s of late Gen Sir Robert Archibald Cassels, GCB, GCSI, DSO (d 1959), and Florence Emily, *née* Jackson; *b* 28 Feb 1907; *Educ* Rugby, Sandhurst; *m* 1, 1935, Joyce (d 1978), da of late Brig-Gen Henry Kirk; 1 s; m 2, 1978, Joy, wid of Kenneth Dickson; *Career* 2 Lt Seaforth Highlanders 1926 (Col 1957-61), cmd Bde Normandy (to VE Day); cmd: 51 Highland, 6 Airborne, 1 Cwlth Korea, 1 Br Corps Br Army of the Rhine, N Army Gp NATO; Adj-Gen to Forces 1963-64, CGS 1965-68, FM 1968; Col Cmdt: Corps of Royal Mil Police 1957-68, Army Physical Trg Corps 1961-66; Col Queen's Own Highlanders (Seaforth and Camerons)

1961-66; ADC (Gen) to HM the Queen 1960-63; *Style*— Field Marshal Sir James Cassels, GCB, KBE, DSO; Hamble End, Higham Rd, Barrow, Bury St Edmunds, Suffolk IP29 5BE (☎ 0284 810895)

CASSELS, John Seton; CB (1978); s of Alastair Macdonald Cassels, and Ada White, *née* Scott; *b* 10 Oct 1928; *Educ* Sedbergh Sch Yorks, Trinity Coll Cambridge; *m* 1956, Mary Whittington; 2 s, 2 da; *Career* min of labour 1954, former under sec Nat Bd for Prices and Incomes, chief exec Training Services Agency 1972-75, dir Manpower Services Cmmn 1975-81, 2 perm sec 1981-83, dir gen NEDO 1983-; *Style*— John Cassels, Esq, CB; 10 Beverley Rd, Barnes, London SW13 (☎ 081 876 6270)

CASSIDI, Adm Sir (Arthur) Desmond; GCB (1982, KCB 1978); s of Cdr Robert Alexander Cassidi, RN (d 1966), and his 1 wife Clare Florinda, *née* Alexander (d 1925); *b* 26 Jan 1925; *Educ* RNC Dartmouth; *m* 1, 1950, (Dorothy) Sheelagh Marie Scott (d 1974), da of Rev Canon Robert Francis Scott, of Garvagh, Co Derry; 1 s, 2 da; *m* 2, 1982, Deborah Marion, *née* Bliss; *Career* War Serv as Midshipman and Sub Lt 1942-45, CO HMS Ark Royal 1972-73, Flag Offr Carriers and Amphibious Ships 1974-75, dir gen Naval Manpower Trg 1975-77, Flag Offr Naval Air Cmd 1978-79, Chief of Naval Personnel and Second Sea Lord 1979-82, C-in-C Naval Home Command 1982-85; Flag ADC to HM The Queen 1982-85; pres: FAA Museum Yeovilton, Royal Naval Assoc; tstee Science Museum S Kensington, dep grand pres Br Cwlth Ex Services League; *Recreations* country pursuits; *Style*— Adm Sir Desmond Cassidi, GCB; c/o Barclays Bank Ltd, 16 Whitehall, London SW1

CASSIDY, Bryan Michael Deece; MEP (C) Dorset E and Hants W 1984-; s of William Francis Deece Cassidy (d 1986), and Kathleen Selina Patricia, *née* Geraghty (d 1989); *b* 17 Feb 1934; *Educ* Ratcliffe Coll Leicester, Sidney Sussex Coll Cambridge (MA); *m* 27 Aug 1960, Gillian Mary, da of Austen Patrick Bohane (d 1988); 1 s (Dominic b 1964), 2 da (Katherine b 1961, Siobhan b 1962); *Career* Cmmnd RA, 1955-57 (Malta and Libya), HAC 1957-62; with Ever Ready, Beechams and Reed Int; memb Cncl CBI 1981-84, dir gen Cosmetic Toiletry and Perfumery Assoc 1981-84; Parly candiddate Wandsworth Central 1966, memb GLC (Hendon North) 1977-85 (oppn spokesman on indust and employment 1983-84); *Recreations* country pursuits; *Clubs* Carlton; *Style*— Bryan Cassidy, Esq, MEP; 11 Esmond Court, Thackeray St, London W8 5HB; Constituency HQ, The Stables, White Cliff Gardens, Blandford Forum, Dorset DT11 7BU (☎ 0258 452 420)

CASSIDY, Ven George Henry; s of Joseph Abram Cassidy (d 1979), and Ethel, *née* McDonald (d 1973); *b* 17 Oct 1942; *Educ* Belfast HS, Queen's Univ Belfast (BSc), UCL (MPhil), Oak Hill Theol Coll (MRTPI); *m* 17 Dec 1966, Jane Barling, da of Rev Frank Hayman Stevens; 2 da (Sarah, Gael); *Career* civil servant: NI 1967-68, Govt of Kenya 1968-70; curate Christ Church Clifton Bristol 1972-75; vicar: St Edyth's Sea Mills Bristol 1975-82, St Paul's Portman Sq W1 1982-87; archdeacon of London and canon residentiary of St Paul's Cathedral 1987-; Freedom of the City of London 1988, Liveryman Worshipful Co of Tylers and Bricklayers 1988, Hon Chaplain Worshipful Co of CAs 1989; *Recreations* rugby football, art, chamber music; *Clubs* National; *Style*— The Ven the Archdeacon of London; 2 Amen Court, Warwick Lane, London EC4M 7BU (☎ 071 248 3312, fax 071 489 8579)

CASSIDY, Mark Anthony; s of Anthony Roland Richard Jessie Patrick Cassidy, of Fownehope, Herefordshire, and Pauline Joyce Cassidy; *b* 27 March 1953; *Educ* King Edward VI Sch Bath, Univ of York (BA); *m* 25 Sept 1982, Lynne Kezia, da of Herbert Reginald Grainger (d 1978); 1 s (David b 1983), 1 da (Sarah b 1985); *Career* slr to the Bromyard and Winslow Town Cncl 1982-, sr ptnr Rutter & Senior (slrs), Bromyard, Ledbury and Malvern; *Recreations* rugby; *Style*— Mark A Cassidy, Esq; The Old Rectory, Putley, Ledbury, Herefordshire (☎ 0531 83 288); 38 High St, Bromyard, Herefordshire (☎ 0885 82323)

CASSIDY, Michael John; s of Francis Cassidy, and Vera Rosina, *née* Valler; *b* 14 Jan 1947; *Educ* Downing Coll Cambridge (BA), City Univ Business Sch (MBA); *m* 7 Sept 1974 (m dis 1988), Amanda, da of Richard George Fitzgerald (d 1981); 1 s (Thomas b 1981), 2 da (Kate b 1977, Annabel b 1979); *Career* ptnr Maxwell Batley Slrs 1971; dir: Cannon Assurance Ltd 1979-84, Conrad Ritblat Residential Properties Ltd 1989, Baker Harris Saunders plc 1990; chm Planning and Communications Ctee Corp of London 1986-89 (memb Cncl 1980-); Liveryman Worshipful Co of: Slrs (memb Court of Assts), Fletchers; memb Law Soc 1971; *Recreations* archery, swimming; *Clubs* The Broadgate; *Style*— Michael Cassidy, Esq; 202 Cromwell Tower, Barbican, London EC2 8AB (☎ 071 628 5687); 27 Chancery Lane, London WC2A 1PA (☎ 071 405 7888, fax 071 242 7133, car 0836 2068)

CASSIDY, Michael Warren Arkinstall; s of George Edward Cassidy, of Kew, Richmond, Surrey, and Kathleen Mary, *née* Roberts; *b* 22 March 1939; *Educ* Latymer Upper Sch Hammersmith, UCL (BA Arch), Univ of California (Harkness fell 1968, MCP); *m* 1, 5 Jan 1963 (m dis), Mary Madeline, da of Joseph Burnhill; m 2, 13 Nov 1981, Marianthi, da of Constantino P Constantinu (d 1969); 1 da (Melina b 1982); *Career* architect and town planner; head planner Environmental Studies Gp GLC 1970-75, ptnr Cassidy Taggart Ptnrship; work includes until 1983: Univ of Warwick, John Radcliffe Hosp, teaching hosp Enugu Nigeria, med coll Basrah Univ Iraq (large commissions Bahrain, Hong Kong, Jordan); work includes 1983-: residences for heads of state, Govt Conf Centre Kuwait, maj ind commercial and planning projects UK, Middle and Far East; visiting prof (arch) Washington Univ St Louis, lectr Univ Coll, dir Mantra Ltd; RIBA (chm NE Thames Architectural Soc), MRTPI; *Books* frequent tech papers in architectural jls; *Recreations* walking, travelling; *Style*— Michael Cassidy, Esq; 47 Highpoint, North Hill, London N6 4BA (☎ 081 341 4884); Cassidy Taggart Partnership, 22 Little Portland St, London W1N 5AF (☎ 071 580 5791, telex 23152, fax 071 323 0630)

CASSIDY, (Michael) Stuart; s of John Michael Cassidy, of Tunbridge Wells, Kent, and Jacqueline Eleanor, *née* Allison; *b* 26 Sept 1968; *Educ* White Lodge, Royal Ballet Sch; *Career* ballet dancer; Royal Ballet: Romeo in Romeo and Juliet, Blue Bird in Sleeping Beauty, Prince in Prince of The Pagodas, Colas, Gloria, Song of the Earth, Galantries, Persuit, Pas De Six, Nutcracker, Raymonda, Bayadere, Elite Syncopations; cr roles in David Bintley's Spirit of Fugue and Ashley Page's Piano; Ashton's pas de deux in the opera Die Fledermaus (BBC2) 1990; Nora Roche award 1984, Prix de Lausanne professional prize 1987; *Recreations* classic cars, music (all types), computers, pasta, cakes; *Style*— Stuart Cassidy, Esq; c/o Rashna Homji-Jefferies, DACS Management, 14 Rusthall Ave, Chiswick, London W4 1BP (☎ 081 995 1995)

CASSIDY, Thomas Daniel; s of Joseph Cassidy (d 1963), and Mary, *née* Gilligan (d 1974); *b* 3 May 1920; *Educ* St Dunstan's RC Elementary Sch Manchester; *m* 16 Sept 1944, Bridget Mary (Bridie), da of the late Joseph Donnelly, of Belfast, NI; 2 s (Paul b 1945, Timothy b 1958), 4 da (Bernadette b 1949, Patsy b 1951, Frances b 1961, Michelle b 1963); *Career* fndr Cassidy Brothers 1946 (currently chm and md); former memb Lions Club and Rotary Club; former chm and vice pres Br Toy and Hobby Assoc, former sr master Vale of Lune Harriers; current memb: Catenian Assoc (past pres), Blackpool and Fylde Soc for the Blind; *Recreations* hunting, shooting, fishing, photography; *Style*— Thomas Cassidy, Esq; Calder House, Garstang, nr Preston, Lancs PR3 1ZE (☎ 09952 3345); Cassidy Brothers plc, Casdon Works Mitcham Road, Blackpool, Lancs FY4 4QW (☎ 0253 66411, fax 0253 691486, telex 67293 CASDON G)

CASSILLIS, Earl of; Archibald Angus Charles Kennedy; s and h of 7 Marquess of Ailsa, OBE, DL, *qv*; *b* 13 Sept 1956; *m* 1979 (m dis 1989), Dawn Leslie Anne, o da of David A Keen, of Paris; 2 da (Lady Rosemary Margaret b 1980, Lady Alicia-Jane Lesley b 1981); *Heir* bro, Lord David Kennedy; *Recreations* shooting, skiing, youth work; *Clubs* New (Edinburgh); *Style*— Earl of Cassillis; Cassillis House, Maybole, Ayrshire (☎ 029 256 310)

CASSON, Sir Hugh Maxwell; CH (1985), KCVO (1978); s of late Randal Casson, and late May Caroline, *née* Man; *b* 23 May 1910; *Educ* Eastbourne Coll, St John's Coll Cambridge; *m* 1938, Margaret MacDonald, da of Dr James MacDonald Troup, of Pretoria; 3 da; *Career* architect; dir of architecture Festival of Britain 1948-51, prof RCA 1953-75, memb Royal Fine Art Cmmn 1960-83, pres Royal Acad 1976-84, architectural advsr to Commons Servs Ctee 1983-; hon fell UCL 1983; kt 1952; *Books* Hugh Casson's Diary (1980), Hugh Casson's London, Hugh Casson's Oxford (1987); *Style*— Sir Hugh Casson, CH, KCVO; 6 Hereford Mansions, Hereford Rd, London W2 5BA; office: 35 Thurloe Place, London SW7 (☎ 071 584 4581)

CASSON, Prof Mark Christopher; s of Rev Stanley Christopher Casson (d 1988), and Dorothy Nowell, *née* Barlow (d 1974); *b* 17 Dec 1945; *Educ* Manchester GS, Univ of Bristol, Churchill Coll Cambridge; *m* 26 July 1975, Janet Penelope, da of William Louis Close (d 1961); 1 da (Catherine Mary b 1984); *Career* head Dept of Econs Univ of Reading 1987- (lectr 1969-77, reader 1977-81, prof 1981-); memb Cncl Royal Economic Soc 1985-90; *Books* Introduction to Mathematical Economics (1973), The Future of the Multinational Enterprise (1976), Alternatives to the Multinational Enterprise (1979), Youth Unemployment (1979), The Entrepreneur: An Economic Theory (1982), Unemployment: A Disequilibrium Approach (1981), Economics of Unemployment: An Historical Perspective (1983), Growth of International Business (1983), Economic Theory of the Multinational Enterprise: selected papers (1985), Multinationals and World Trade (1986), The Firm and the Market: Studies in Multinational Enterprise and the of the Firm (1987), Enterprise and Competitiveness: A Systems View of International Business (1990), Multinational Corporations (1990), Entrepreneurship (1990); *Recreations* book collecting; *Style*— Prof Mark Casson; 6 Wayside Green, Woodcote, Reading RG8 0QJ (☎ 0491 681483); Department of Economics, University of Reading, Box 218, Reading RG6 2AA (☎ 0734 318227, telex 847813, fax 0734 750236)

CASSON, (Frederick) Michael; OBE (1983); s of William Casson (d 1953), of London, and Dorothy, *née* Miller; *b* 2 April 1925; *Educ* Tollington GS, Hornsey Coll of Art (NDD, ATD); *m* 2 April 1955, Sheila, *née* Wilmot; 1 s (Ben b 1966), 2 da (Clare b 1958, Lucy b 1960); *Career* potter; pt/t teacher 1952-73; Harrow Sch of Art: jt fndr (with Victor Magrie) Studio Pottery Course 1963, head Ceramics Dept 1971-73; awarded Craft Cncl bursary to develop own work 1973, presenter The Crafts of the Potter (BBC) 1975; pt/t teacher history of ceramics Cardiff Coll of Art 1983, visiting lectr Banff Centre Canada 1986, presenter workshops and lectures USA 1984-, speaker Aust Bicentenniel Ceramics 88 Conference Sydney 1988, artist in residence Chisholm Melbourne May-June 1988; solo exhibitions incl: Heals London 1959, 10 Years at Wobage Farm 1988, Oxford Gallery and Craftman Potters Assoc London 1990-91; winner Gold medal Int Acad of Ceramics Prague 1964; Craftsman Potters Assoc: fndr memb 1958, memb Cncl 1958-70, chm 1963-66, vice chm Br Crafts Cncl 1985; *Books* Pottery in Britain Today (1967), The Craft of the Potter (1976); *Recreations* historical research especially ceramic; *Style*— Michael Casson, Esq, OBE; Wobage Farm, Upton Bishop, nr Ross-on-Wye, Herefordshire HR9 7QP (☎ 098 985 233)

CASSTLES, Col David Stewart; TD, DL (Essex 1983); s of Joseph Cecil Casstles (d 1956); *b* 5 March 1936; *Educ* Brentwood Sch, Univ of Cambridge; *m* 1964, Lynne Frances, *née* Alexandre; 1 s (Andrew b 1969), 1 da (Amanda b 1966); *Career* TA 1957-83, Col 1983; investment banker; *Recreations* opera-going, dining, sailing, shooting, volunteer soldiering; *Clubs* Army and Navy; *Style*— Col David Casstles, TD, DL; Sandylay House, Great Leighs, Essex CM3 1PS (☎ 0245 361258)

CASSWELL, Hon Mrs (Helen Jennifer Frances); *née* Annesley; yst da of 14 Viscount Valentia, MC, MRCS, LRCP; *b* 13 Oct 1935; *m* 1957, Simon Fitzroy Casswell, yst s of His Honour Joshua David Casswell, QC (d 1963); 1 s, 2 da; *Style*— The Hon Mrs Casswell; The Limes Farm, Smarden, nr Ashford, Kent

CASTENSKIOLD, Holger; s of Ludvig Helmuth Frederik Holger Castenskiold (d 1957), of Gyllingnaes, Denmark, and Gudrun, *née* Thorsen; *b* 5 April 1931; *Educ* Oester Farimagsgade Sch Oester Borgerdyd Copenhagen, Commercial HS Copenhagen, City of London Coll; *m* 27 Oct 1962, Gurli Bering, da of Capt Arthur Hermann Franz Pittelkow (d 1964), of Copenhagen; 1 s (Erik b 1 Feb 1967), 1 da (Birgitte b 14 Dec 1963); *Career* Royal Danish Navy 1951-52; The E Asiatic Co Ltd (Copenhagen, London, Manila, Singapore) 1949-72; md: Utd Baltic Corporation Ltd 1972-, MacAndrews & Co Ltd 1973-, Bank Line Ltd 1989- (dir 1977-), Andrew Weir Shipping Ltd 1989-; dir Andrew Weir & Co Ltd 1989-; actg hon Royal Danish Consul Manila 1960-61; chm: Philippines Euro Conf Manila 1957-59, Assoc of Int Steamship Lines Manila 1961, London Steamship Owners Mutual Insur Assoc 1985-; memb Baltic Exchange 1972-; *Recreations* golf, gardening, travels, reading; *Clubs* MCC, Moor Park Golf, Wig and Pen; *Style*— Holger Castenskiold, Esq; 1 The Broad Walk, Northwood, Middx HA6 5AU (☎ 09274 22875); Dexter House, 2 Royal Mint Court, London EC3N 4XX (☎ 071 265 0808, fax 071 481 4784, telex 887392)

CASTLE, Andrew Nicholas; s of Frank James Castle (d 1985), and Lyn Mathers, *née* Pollock; *b* 15 Nov 1963; *Educ* Huish's GS Taunton, Millfield, Wichita State Univ USA (BA); *Career* tennis player; GB Davis Cup team 1986-90, European Cup team 1986-90, nat singles champion 1987 and 1989, nat doubles champion 1987-89, reached third round US Open (lost to Boris Becker) 1987, memb Olympic team 1988, finalist Korean Open Grand Prix 1988, won Dunlop Masters of Japan 1988; doubles champion: Rye, NY, Madeira, Cherbourg, Singapore, Nagoya, Adelaide, Korea; *Style*— Andrew Castle, Esq; c/o The Lawn Tennis Association, Barons Court, West Kensington, London W4 (☎ 071 385 2366)

CASTLE, Enid; *b* 28 Jan 1936; *Educ* Hulme GS for Girls Oldham, Royal Holloway Coll London (BA), Dept of Educn Univ of London; *Career* teacher Colne Valley HS Linthwaite Huddersfield 1958-62, head of History Dept of Kenya HS Nairobi 1962-65, head of History Dept and sr mistress Queens Coll Nassau Bahamas 1965-68, dep head Roundhill HS Thurmaston Leicester 1969-72; headmistress: HS for Girls Denmark Rd Gloucester 1973-81, The Red Maids' Sch Bristol 1982-87; princ The Cheltenham Ladies Coll 1987-; memb: Girls' Schs' Assoc (pres 1990-91), Secdy Heads' Assoc (former pres Area 7), Boarding Schs' Assoc, Girls' Common Entrance Examinations Bd; govr St Alban's HS Hertfordshire; former chm: Gloucester Careers Advsy Ctee, conference of Gloucestershire Secdy Heads 1977-80; pres Gloucester Soroptimist Club 1979-80; *Recreations* tennis, squash, bridge, choral music, travel; *Clubs* Univ Women's; *Style*— Miss Enid Castle; The Cheltenham Ladies' Coll, Bayshill Rd, Cheltenham, Glos GL50 3EP (☎ 0242 520691, fax 0242 227882)

CASTLE, Geoffrey Ellis Trevor; s of Richard Basil Trevor Castle, OBE (d 1986), of Cuckfield, West Sussex, and Geraldine Therese, *née* Ellis; *b* 12 Aug 1936; *Educ* Uppingham, Coll of Estate Mgmnt; *m* 5 Oct 1963, Sarah Margaret Sherwin, da of Francis (Frank) Neville (d 1986), of Cookham, Berks; 2 da (Frances b 1966, Helen b

1968); *Career* asst surveyor Jones Lang Wootton 1961-69, ptnr B A James and Co 1970-72, dir Herring Daw 1972-76, ptnr Dron and Wright 1976- (sr ptnr since 1984); Freeman City of London, memb Worshipful Co of Chartered Surveyors 1984, FRICS 1973 (ARICS 1961); *Recreations* gardening, arts; *Style—* Geoffrey Castle, Esq; St George's House, 12a St George St, London W1 (☎ 071 491 7332)

CASTLE, Roy; *Career* Nat Serv RAF; TV presenter, singer, dancer, actor, comedian and musician; first worked with various comedians incl: Norman Teale, Jimmy Clitheroe, Jimmy Jones; gained own slot on Dickie Valentine's Show; first Royal Command Performance 1958 (of five to date); major theatre appearances incl: Sam Weller in Pickwick on Broadway NY 1966, Cosmo Brown in Singin' In The Rain London Palladium 1983-85; TV presenter: Show Castle, Feeling Great, Record Breakers 1972-, Marchin as to War, The Hymn Makers, Castle's in Europe, All Star Record Breakers 1977; holder of two World Records: tap dancing (completing one million taps in 23 hours and 45 minutes), wing walking from Gatwick to Paris (in 3 hours and 23 minutes); nomination Best Supporting Actor in Pickwick 1966, BAFTA award for the Best Children's Light Entertainment or Drama Programme for the Year 1977; *Style—* Roy Castle, Esq; Television Centre, Wood Lane, London W12 7RJ (☎ 081 743 8000)

CASTLE OF BLACKBURN, Baroness (Life Peer UK 1990), of Ibstone in the Co·· .ty of Buckinghamshire; Barbara Anne Castle; PC (1964); MEP (Lab): Gtr Manchester N 1979-84, Gtr Manchester W 1984-89; Baroness Castle; da of Frank Betts, and Annie Rebecca Betts; *b* 6 Oct 1910; *Educ* Bradford Girls' GS, St Hugh's Coll Oxford; *m* 1944, Edward Cyril (Ted) Castle (d 1979), cr Baron Castle (Life Peer) 1974; *Career* MP (Lab): Blackburn 1945-50, Blackburn E 1950-55, Blackburn 1955-79; memb Nat Exec Ctee of Labour Party 1950-85, chm Labour Party 1959, min of Overseas Devpt 1964-65, min of Transport 1965-68, first sec of state and sec of state for Employment and Productivity 1968-70, oppn spokesman on employment 1971, sec of state for Social Servs 1974-76, vice chm Socialist Gp in European Parl 1979-85; *Books* The Castle Diaries 1974-76 (1981), The Castle Diaries 1964-70 (1984), Sylvia and Christabel Pankhurst (1987); *Style—* The Rt Hon Lady Castle of Blackburn, PC; Hell Corner Farm, Ibstone, High Wycombe, Bucks HP14 3XX

CASTLE STEWART, 8 Earl (I 1800) Arthur Patrick Avondale Stuart; 15 Bt (S 1628); also Baron Castle Stuart (I 1619), and Viscount Castle Stuart (I 1793); s of 7 Earl Castle Stewart, MC (d 1961), and Eleanor, *qv*, da of Solomon R Guggenheim; *b* 18 Aug 1928; *Educ* Eton, Trinity Coll Cambridge; *m* 1952, Edna, da of William Edward Fowler; 1 s, 1 da; *Heir* s, Viscount Stuart; *Career* late Lt Scots Gds; farmer; FBIM; *Clubs* Carlton; *Style—* The Rt Hon the Earl Castle Stewart; Stone House, East Pennard, nr Shepton Mallet, Somerset BA4 6RZ (☎ : 074 986 240); Stuart Hall, Stewartstown, Co Tyrone (☎ 086 873 208)

CASTLE STEWART, Eleanor, Countess; Eleanor May; er da of Solomon R Guggenheim, of New York; *b* 1896; *m* 1920, 7 Earl Castle Stewart (d 1961); 2 s; *Style—* The Rt Hon Eleanor, Countess Castle Stewart; Windyridge, Wych Cross, Forest Row, Sussex RH18 5JP

CASTLEDEN, Prof (Christopher) Mark; s of Dr Leslie Ivan Mark Castleden (d 1984), and Joan, *née* Plumbe; *b* 22 July 1944; *Educ* UCS, Bart's and Univ of London (MB BS, MD); *m* ; 3 da (Emily Jayne b 1972, Lorraine b 1974, Caroline b 1975); *Career* prof RCP 1987 (memb 1972, memb Geriatrics Ctee 1979-85, fell 1984); chm Advsy Sub Ctee Geriatrics Med Tst 1981, memb Ctee Safety of Meds 1984-86; memb Br Geriatrics Soc; *Recreations* sailing, gardening, antiques, reading; *Clubs* Univ of Leicester Sailing; *Style—* Prof Mark Castleden; 10 Milton Gardens, Oadby, Leicestershire LE2 5SA; Leicester General Hosp, Dept of Medicine for the Elderly, Gwendolen Rd, Leicester LE5 4PW (☎ 0533 490490)

CASTLEMAINE, 8 Baron (I 1812); Roland Thomas John Handcock; MBE; s of late 7 Baron (1973); *b* 22 April 1943; *Educ* Campbell Coll Belfast; *m* 1988, Lynne Christine, eldest da of Maj J M Gurney, RAEC; 1 s; *Heir* s, Hon Ronan Michael Edward Handcock b 27 March 1989; *Career* Lt-Col Army Air Corps; *Style—* The Rt Hon the Lord Castlemaine; c/o Lloyds Bank, Aldershot, Hants

CASTLEMAN, Christopher Norman Anthony; s of James Stanley Phillips (d 1969), and Joan Doris (now) Pyper; *b* 23 June 1941; *Educ* Harrow, Clare Coll Cambridge (MA); *m* 1, 1967, Sarah Victoria (d 1979), da of Judge Frank Alleyne Stockdale, of Sussex; 1 s (Jonathan b 1971), 1 da (Amanda b 1967); m 2, 1980, Caroline Clare, da of Thomas Norman Westcott, of S Africa; 2 da (Alexandra b 1982, Georgia b 1984); m 3, 1990, Susan Mary, da of Geoffrey Michael Twycross, of S Africa; *Career* corp fin dept Hill Samuel & Co Ltd (formerly M Samuel & Co Ltd) 1965-69, gen mangr Hill Samuel Aust Ltd 1970-72, corporate fin dir Hill Samuel & Co Ltd 1973-75, md Hill Samuel Int Ltd 1976-77; chief exec: Hill Samuel Gp (SA) Ltd 1978-80, Hill Samuel Gp plc 1980 (resigned 1987), Blue Arrow plc 1987 (resigned 1988), LIT Hldgs plc 1989-; fin advsr Christopher Castleman & Co 1988-89; *Recreations* travel, sports; *Clubs* MCC (Associate); *Style—* Christopher Castleman, Esq; 182 Kensington Park Rd, London W11 2ER (☎ 071 727 8284)

CASTONGUAY, Lady Marina June; da of 7 Marquess of Exeter by his 2 w, Lillian; *b* 16 June 1956; *Educ* Vancouver City Coll; *m* 1980, Peter Castonguay, s of Nelson Castonguay, of Ottawa; 1 s (Dylan b 1984), 1 da (Majessa b 1983); *Career* shop owner, mangr and mother; *Recreations* tennis, cross-country skiing, swimming; *Style—* The Lady Marina Castonguay; PO Box 8, 100 Mile House, Br Columbia V0K 2E0, Canada (☎ 604 395 3717 or 395 4311)

CASTRO, Dr John Edward; s of Edward George Castro, of Norfolk, and Ivy Leuze Castro; *b* 10 Aug 1940; *Educ* Barnet GS, UCL (scholar, BSc, Suckling Prize for Anatomy), UCH Med Sch (Fanny Magrath scholar in surgery, MRCS, LRCP, MB BS, MS, PhD, Sir Frances Walshe prize in neurology, Erichson prize for practical surgery); *m* 1 (m dis), Sylvia Rosemary Barber; 1 s (Ashley John b 1967), 2 da (Naomi Jane b 1970, Rebecca Elizabeth b 1973); m 2, Pamela Elizabeth, da of Rev Preb John Clifford Dale; *Career* house surgn UCH July-Dec 1965 (house physician Jan-June 1965), GP 1966; sr house surgn: Accident Service Luton and Dunstable Hosp Jan-June 1967, Hammersmith Hosp July-Dec 1967; res fell and hon urological registrar RPMS 1968-69, rotating surgical registrar Norfolk and Norwich Hosp 1969-71, scientific worker 1971-73 (Nat Inst for Med Res Mill Hill and Clinical Res Centre Harrow), res grant Cancer Res Campaign 1975, Arris-Gale lectr RCS 1975, hon conslt urologist Hammersmith Hosp 1975-79 (sr surgical registrar urology 1973-75), sr lectr in urology RPMS 1975-79 (tutor in surgery and lectr in immunology 1973-75), conslt urologist and transplant surgn 1979-; Patey Prize Surgical Res Soc 1973 and 1975, Univ Medal Univ of Hiroshima 1975, Ethicon Travel fellowship 1977; memb: Int Transplant Soc, BMA, Br Assoc of Urological Surgeons, European Dialysis and Transplantation Assoc, Euro Assoc of Urology; fndr memb Br Transplantation Soc, FRSM, FRCS (Edin) 1968, FRCS (Eng) 1970; *Books* Treatment of Benign Prostate Hypertrophy and Neoplasia (1974), Immunology for Surgeons (1976), Immunological Aspects of Cancer (1978), Treatment of Renal Failure (1980); *Recreations* gardening, cooking, collecting card cases; *Clubs* Chelsea Clinical Soc; *Style—* Dr John Castro; 9 Lammas Park Gardens, Ealing, London W5 5HZ (☎ 081 587 0578); Suite 8, 103 Harley Street, London W1N 1HD (☎ 071 487 4899, fax 071 224 3975, car 0860 319194)

CASWELL, Gp Capt Arthur William; CBE 1961 (OBE 1946); s of late William George Caswell; *b* 8 Aug 1906; *Educ* Swindon & North Wilts Secdy Sch and Tech Inst (Swindon Coll); *m* 7 July 1934, Rhoda Mary; 1 s (Alan Godfrey); *Career* third Entry Halton Aircraft Apprentices 1923-25; Fleet Air Arm 1927-29 and 1935-37, WWII 1939-45, MID 1945, dep chm W Euro Est Cmmn 1947-48, Asst Commandant No 2 S of TT RAF Cosford 1956-59 (Commandant and Station Cdr 1959-61), dio sec and sec Bd of Fin Hereford Dio 1961-74; hon admin Hereford Cathedral 1974-82 (emeritus 1982); Memb Gen Synod C of E 1965-80; life vice pres Hereford Branch RAF Assoc; CEng, MRAeS, FInstBE; *Clubs* RAF; *Style—* Gp Capt Arthur Caswell, CBE; Tralohr, 5 Pentaloe Close, Mordiford, Hereford HR1 4LS

CASWELL, (Fuad) Matthew; *b* 18 Aug 1931; *Educ* King's Coll Univ of London (MA), Sch of Oriental and African Studies Univ of London, St Catherine's Coll Oxford; *m* 21 Aug 1957, Hilda (Helen); 2 s (John Cecil b 29 Jan 1963, Benjamin Cecil b 7 Nov 1969), 1 da (Rebecca Mary (Mrs Gent) b 27 Aug 1961); *Career* called to the Bar Middle Temple 1968; in practice NE circuit; *Recreations* walking, chess, watching cricket; *Style—* Matthew Caswell, Esq; 11 King's Bench Walk, Temple, London EC4Y 7EQ (☎ 071 353 3337/8)

CATCHPOLE, Prof David Ridley; s of Rev Cyril Walter John Catchpole (d 1973), and Winifred Patricia Mary, *née* Critchell; *b* 1 May 1938; *Educ* Cheltenham GS, Queen's Coll Oxford (BA, MA), Pembroke Coll Cambridge (PhD); *m* 21 Aug 1963, Dorothy Ann, da of Lt-Col Charles Alexander Scott (d 1960); 2 da (Helen Margaret b 1966, Catherine Ailsa b 1970); *Career* tutor Clifton Theol Coll Bristol 1966-69, lectr and sr lectr Dept of Religious Studies Univ of Lancaster 1969-84, prof theological studies Univ of Exeter 1984-; sec Soc for New Testament Study 1983-88, memb Gen Synod C of E 1970-75 (reader C of E 1970-); *Books* The Trial of Jesus (1971); *Recreations* gardening, cricket, croquet, theatre; *Style—* Prof David Catchpole; 9 Uplowman Rd, Tiverton, Devon EX16 4LU (☎ 0884 252100); Dept of Theology, Univ of Exeter, Queen's Bldg, The Queen's Drive, Exeter EX4 4QH (☎ 0392 264242)

CATCHPOLE, Nancy Mona; OBE (1987); da of George William Page (d 1980), of New Eltham, and Mona Dorothy, *née* Cowin (d 1979); *b* 6 Aug 1929; *Educ* Haberdashers' Aske's Hatchman Girls Sch, Bedford Coll London Univ (BA); *m* 1959, Geoffrey David Arthur Catchpole; 1 s, 1 da; *Career* pres Br Fedn of Univ Women 1981-84, jt sec Womans Nat Cmmn 1985-88 (co chm 1983-85), conslt Women's Trg Roadshow Prog RSA Womans Working Gp 1990- (vice chm 1985-); memb of Wessex Regnl Health Authy 1986-90; FRSA 1986; *Clubs* Crosby Hall; *Style—* Nancy Catchpole, OBE; 66 Leighton Rd, Weston, Bath BA1 4NG (☎ 0225 423338); Royal Society for Arts, 8 John Adam St, London WC2N 6EZ (☎ 071 930 5115)

CATER, Sir Jack; KBE (1979, CBE 1973, MBE 1956); yr s of Alfred Francis Cater and Pamela Elizabeth Dukes; *b* 21 Feb 1922; *Educ* Sir George Monoux GS Walthamstow; *m* 1950, Peggy Gwenda Richards; 1 s, 2 da; *Career* Colonial Admin Service Hong Kong 1946, dir Commerce and Industry 1970-72, sec for Information 1972 (Home Affairs and Information 1973), chief secretary 1978-; *Style—* Sir Jack Cater, KBE; Victoria House, Hong Kong (☎ 5 96696)

CATER, Sir Robin John Robert; s of Sir John James Cater (d 1962), of Edinburgh, and Jessie Sheila MacDonald, *née* Moodie (d 1948); *b* 25 April 1919; *Educ* George Watson's Coll Edinburgh, Jesus Coll Cambridge (MA); *m* 1945, Isobel Calder Ritchie; 1 da; *Career* chm: The Distillers Co 1976-83, The Scotch Whisky Assoc 1976-1983; kt 1984; *Style—* Sir Robin Cater; Avernish, Elie, Fife, Scotland KY9 1DA (☎ 0333 330 667)

CATES, Armel Conyers; s of Conyers Seely Cates (d 1965), of Guildford, and Jacqueline Maude, *née* Geoffroy (d 1988); *b* 3 May 1943; *Educ* Charterhouse, Univ of Southampton (LLB); *m* 8 July 1967, Pamela Susan, da of Colin Huson Walker, of Barrington, Cambs; 2s (Tom b 1974, Sam b 1978), 1 da (Ilaria b 1980); *Career* articled to Theodore Goddard (London) and Vinters (Cambridge) 1967-69, admitted slr 1969; asst slr Coward Chance 1970-72, Clifford-Turner 1972-76, ptnr Clifford Chance 1976-; ed advsr International Financial Law Review; tstee Charterhouse Mission in Southwark, memb of City of London Slrs Co; memb: Law Soc 1969, Int Bar Assoc; *Recreations* golf, tennis, photography; *Style—* Armel Cates, Esq; Graves Farm, Catmere End, Saffron Walden, Essex CB11 4XG; Clifford Chance, Royex House, Aldermanbury Square, London EC2V 7LD (☎ 071 600 0808, fax 071 726 8561, telex 8959991 G)

CATES, Dr Joseph Elmhirst; s of Dr Henry Joseph Cates (d 1969), and Rosa, *née* Elmhirst; *b* 22 June 1914; *Educ* Clifton, Bart's Hosp London (MD); *m* 6 Aug 1955, Dr Mary Elizabeth Cates, da of Frank Willoughby Moore (d 1953); 4 s (Christopher, Robert, Michael, Andrew), 2 da (Anne, Kathleen); *Career* RNVR Surgn Lt 1940, Lt Cdr 1943-46; house physician and chief asst Bart's 1936-40 and 1946-50, conslt physician Bristol Royal Infirmary 1951-79, med postgrad dean Univ of Bristol 1957-80, emeritus conslt physician Avon AHA; Hon MD Univ of Bristol 1981; FRCP; *Style—* Dr Joseph Cates; 11 Cedar Park, Bristol BS9 1BW

CATFORD, Gordon Vivian; s of Harry George Bascombe (d 1984), of 19 Uphill Rd North, Weston-super-Mare, and Gladys Annie, *née* Horton (d 1951); *b* 23 Nov 1927; *Educ* Clifton, Univ of Bristol (MB ChB); *m* 10 June 1955, June Crichton, da of Robert Baxter (d 1983), of 8 Craigleith View, Edinburgh 4; 2 s (Gordon Baxter b 1958, Paul Nicholas b 1961); *Career* Nat Serv, Sqdn Ldr RAF Med Br CME 1954-56; house appts: Bristol Infirmary 1951-52, Bristol Eye Hosp 1952-54; chief clinical asst Moorfields Eye Hosp 1960-64 (house appt 1958-60); conslt ophthalmic surgn: St George's Hosp London 1963-88 (first asst 1961-63), Royal London Homoeopathic Hosp 1969-88, Royal Masonic Hosp London 1973-, St Luke's Hosp for the Clergy 1988-; ophthalmologist: Linden Lodge Sch for the Blind 1978-89, Greenmead Sch for Multiple Handicapped 1978-89, John Aird Sch 1978-; memb Med Appeals Tbnl London South 1988-, advsr Br Orthoptic Soc; govr Linden Lodge Sch 1978-89, memb Cncl Clifton Coll 1982-; hon fell of orthoptics Br Orthoptic Soc 1988; Freeman City of London 1963, Liveryman Worshipful Soc of Apothecaries 1963; memb BMA 1952, FRSM 1961, FRCS 1961, fell Coll of Ophthalmology 1988-; *Recreations* gardening; *Style—* Gordon Catford, Esq; 9 St Johns Wood Park, London NW8 6QP; 11 Devonshire Place, London W1N 1PB (☎ 071 935 9523)

CATFORD, (John) Robin; CBE (1990); er s of Adrian Leslie Catford (d 1979), and Ethel Augusta, *née* Rolfe (d 1988); *b* 11 Jan 1923; *Educ* Hampton GS, Univ of St Andrews (BSc), St John's Coll Cambridge (Dip Agric); *m* 21 Aug 1948, Daphne Georgina, da of Col John Francis Darby, CBE, TD (d 1951); 3 s (John Charles b 1949, Simon Leslie b 1956, Francis James Robin b 1959), 1 da (Lucy Georgina b 1952); *Career* Sudan CS Dept of Agric and Forests 1946-55; commercial appts in UK 1955-66; MAFF 1966-82 (princ 1966, asst sec 1972, under sec 1979); transfered to PM's office 1982, sec for appts to PM and ecclesiastical sec to Lord Chllr 1982-; *Recreations* sailing, travel, theatre, arts; *Clubs* United Oxford and Cambridge University; *Style—* Robin Catford, Esq, CBE; 10 Downing St, London SW1A 2AA

CATHCART, 6 Earl (UK 1814); Alan Cathcart; CB (1973), DSO (1945), MC (1944); also 15 Lord Cathcart (S *circa* 1447), Baron Greenock and Viscount Cathcart (both UK 1807); s of 5 Earl Cathcart (d 1927), and Vera Estelle, *née* Fraser (now Dowager Lady Hodge); *b* 22 Aug 1919; *Educ* Eton, Magdalene Coll Cambridge; *m* 1, 1946, Rosemary Clare Marie Gabrielle (d 1980), da of late Air-Cdre Sir Henry Smyth-Osborne, CMG, CBE; 1 s, 2 da; m 2, 1984, Marie Isobel, da of late Hon William

Joseph French (3 s of 4 Baron de Freyne), and widow of Sir Thomas Brian Weldon, 8 Bt; *Heir* s, Lord Greenock (*qv*); *Career* sits as Cons in House of Lords; 2 Lt Scots Gds 1939, Brig Ops Div SHAPE 1967-69, Maj-Gen 1969, GOC Yorks Dist 1969-70, GOC Berlin (Br Sector) 1970-73, ret; dep speaker House of Lords 1976-89; pres ROSPA 1982-86; Brig Queen's Body Guard for Scotland (Royal Co of Archers), Commodore Royal Yacht Sqdn 1974-80; dep grand pres Br Cwlth Ex-Services League 1975-86, pres Army Cadet Force Assoc 1976-82; Lord Prior Order of St John of Jerusalem 1985-88; *Clubs* Brooks's, Royal Yacht Squadron; *Style*— The Rt Hon the Earl Cathcart, CB, DSO, MC; Moor Hatches, West Amesbury, Salisbury, Wilts SP4 7BH (☎ 0980 623839)

CATHCART, Brian John; s of (Hektor) Rex Cathcart, of Coleraine, N Ireland, and Hazel Jane, *née* Storey (d 1988); *b* 26 Oct 1956; *Educ* Sandford Park Sch Dublin, Campbell Coll Belfast, Trinity Coll Dublin (BA); *m* 1 Nov 1985, Ruth, da of Thomas William Griffiths; 1 s (Thomas William Cathcart b 25 June 1989); *Career* Reuters News Agency: trainee journalist 1978-81, corr Paris 1981-85, diplomatic corr London 1985-86, corr Netherlands 1986; The Independent: sub ed (foreign) 1986-88, asst foreign ed 1988-89; foreign ed The Independent on Sunday 1989-; *Style*— Brian Cathcart, Esq; Foreign Editor, The Independent on Sunday, 40 City Rd, London EC1Y 2DB (☎ 071 253 1222, fax 071 415 1366)

CATHERWOOD, (Elizabeth Walkinshaw) Adare; da of late John Adair McClelland, and late Jean, *née* Gilmere; *b* 30 Jan 1934; *Educ* Ballyclare HS, Belfast Coll of Technol; *m* 5 April 1957, Harold Matthew Stewart Catherwood, s of late Herbert Alexander Courtney Catherwood; 3 da (Jayne b 8 April 1959, Suzanne b 27 Feb 1961, Sarah b 12 June 1974); *Career* showjumper and sidesaddle rider; appeared at: Dublin Horse Show, Royal Ulster Agric Soc (won championship on numerous occasions); fndr of a Riding for the Disabled Gp, owner of racehorses; best horses owned: Littel Bay, FlaxenKing, Four Trix (winner of Scot Nat), Dark Ivy; *Recreations* horse racing; *Style*— Mrs Adare Catherwood

CATHERWOOD, Sir (Henry) Frederick Ross (Fred); MEP (EDG) Cambridgeshire 1979-; s of late Harold Matthew Stuart, and late Jean Catherwood, of Co Londonderry; *b* 30 Jan 1925; *Educ* Shrewsbury, Clare Coll Cambridge; *m* 1954, Elizabeth, er da of Rev Dr D Martyn Lloyd-Jones, of Westminster Chapel, London; 2 s, 1 da; *Career* chm: Br Inst of Mgmnt 1974-76, Br Overseas Trade Bd 1975-79, Euro Parl Ctee on External Economic Relations 1979-84; dep ldr Cons Euro MPs 1983-87, vice pres Euro Parl 1989-; kt 1971; FCA 1951; *Books* The Christian in Industrial Society (1964), The Christian Citizen (1969), A Better Way (1976), First Things First (1979), God's Time God's Money; *Recreations* music, gardening, reading; *Clubs* United Oxford and Cambridge Univ; *Style*— Sir Fred Catherwood, MEP; Sutton Hall, Balsham, Cambridgeshire

CATHIE, Kyle Anne Bewley (Mrs Charles Simon); yst da of Dr Ian Aysgarth Bewley Cathie, DL (d 1989), of Barton House, Barton-on-the-Heath, Moreton-in-Marsh, Glos, and Dr Marian Josephine Cunning (d 1982); *b* 10 Oct 1948; *Educ* Chipping Norton GS, Cheltenham; *m* 21 April 1973, (David) Charles Simon; 2 s (Thomas b 1978, Nicholas b 1980), 1 da (Josephine b 1985); *Career* sr ed Pan Books 1983, editorial dir Elm Tree Books 1983-86, Papermac publisher and editorial dir Macmillan London Ltd 1986-89, md and publisher Kyle Cathie Ltd 1989-; *Books* Complete Calorie Counter (1978), Complete Carbohydrate Counter (1980), The Corgi Calorie Counter (1989); *Recreations* bee keeping, opera, theatre; *Style*— Ms Kyle Cathie; 3 Vincent Square, London SW1P 2LX (☎ 071 834 8027)

CATLING, Brian David; s of Leonard Frederick Catling, of London, and Lilian Alice Catling; *b* 23 Oct 1948; *Educ* N East London Poly, RCA London; *m* 1; 1 s (Jack Ishmael b 19 Dec 1983); m 2; Clare Carswell; 1 s (Finn Bell b 23 Nov 1990), 1 da (Florence Pike b 13 April 1989); *Career* artist, solo exhibitions incl: Air Gallery 1977, Camden Arts Centre 1979, Anolfini Gallery 1980, Norwich Sch of Art Gallery 1982-84, Atlantis Gallery 1984, South Hill Park Gallery 1984, Liefsgade 22 Copenhagen 1986, Hordaland Kunstnercentrum Bergen Norway 1987, Matts Gallery 1987, Neuw Gallerie (Sammlung Ludwig Aachen) 1988, Museum of Modern Art Oxford 1989; gp exhibitions incl: Sculptors Attitude to Drawing 1974, Albion Island Vortex (Whitechapel Gallery) 1974, Imagination is the Venom (Ikon Gallery) 1981, Art and the Sea (Anolfini and ICA) 1982, Nordic Winter Symposium (Geilo Norway) 1982, Licence and Device (Herbert Read Gallery) 1985, Edel Smeldelgroep (Valkenberg & Stolberg) 1987, Bookworks (V & A Museum) 1988, Torben Grondael Gallery Copenhagen 1989, MOBSHOP IV (Viborg and Malmo Kunsthaller Sweden) 1989, Upturned Art (Pitt Rivers Museum Oxford) 1990, Nylistasfnid (The Living Art Museum Iceland) 1990; performance works incl: Miltonian Ghost Dance (Whitechapel Gallery) 1980, Spogelsemasse (Leifscade 22 Copenhagen) 1986, Readings from the Gamble Room (Bookworks project, V & A Museum) 1987, 5 performances cmmnd by Museum of Modern Art Oxford 1989, Two Works for Trondheim (Trondelac Arts Centre Trondheim Norway) 1990; visiting lectr: Jan Van Eyck Akademie Maastricht Netherlands 1980-84, Chelsea Sch of Art, Royal Acad, Vestlandets Kunsteakademi Berger Norway, Kunsteakademi Trondheim Norway; Henry Moore fell in sculpture Norwich Sch of Art 1982-85, tutor in sculpture RCA 1983-90, princ lectr in sculpture Brighton Poly, external examiner for Newcastle Poly; FRCA; poet; *Publications* The First Electron Heresy (1977), Vorticegargen (1979), Pleides in Nine (1981), Vox Humana (1984), Das Kranke Tier (1984), The Tulpa Index (1986), Lair (1987), Boschlog (1988), Boschlog (1989), The Stumbling Block (1990); *Style*— Brian Catling, Esq; Matts Gallery, 10 Martello St, London Fields E8

CATO, Brian Hudson; s of Thomas Cato (d 1972), and Edith Willis Hudson (d 1976); *b* 6 June 1928; *Educ* LEA Elementary and GS, Trinity Coll Oxford (MA), Univ of London (LLB); *m* 1963, Barbara Edith, da of Harry Myles (d 1977); 1 s (Paul Marcus b 1964); *Career* pilot offr RAF 1952-54; barr NE Circuit 1954-75, rec Crown Ct 1974-75; industl tbnl chm 1975-, regnl chm No 9 Region 1989-; Freeman: Newcastle upon Tyne 1950, City of London 1985; *Recreations* bibliomania, antiquarian studies and family life; *Style*— Brian Cato, Esq; 46 Bemersyde Drive, Jesmond, Newcastle upon Tyne NE2 2HJ (☎ 091 281 4226); 2 Croft Place, High Newton-by-the-Sea, Alnwick, Northumberland (☎ 066 576 334); Plummer House, Market St East, Newcastle upon Tyne NE1 6NF

CATO, Michael John; s of William Henry Cato (d 1978), and Cladys Annie Hayes; *b* 13 Dec 1933; *Educ* Mercers Sch London; *m* 1, 1959, Rosemary (d 1978), da of Thomas Tapping; 2 s (Timothy b 1961, Alastair b 1963), 2 da (Jane Rosalind b 1960, Catherine b 1966); m 2, 1985, Helen Peeples, da of Col Leonard Frederick Butler (d 1968); 1 step s (Benson b 1977), 2 step da (Lesley b 1976, Emily b 1979); *Career* chm and md William Cato and Sons Ltd 1971- (dir 1961); chm and dir Br Hardware Fedn Merchandising Co 1981-85, memb Nat Ctee Br Hardware Fedn 1974- (memb Bd of Mgmnt 1976-85, chm Marketing Gp 1981-85); memb Royal Metal Trades Bd of Mgmnt 1982-87; churchwarden Benefice of Farnham Royal St Mary's Hedgerley 1974-84, Burnham Deanery Synod 1970-84; fell Nat Inst of Hardware; *Recreations* cricket, sailing, association football; *Clubs* MCC, Farnham Cricket, Old Mercers' (pres 1988-89); *Style*— Michael Cato, Esq; Lawday House Farm, Follyhill, Farnham, Surrey GU10 5AB (☎ Farnham 715562); William Cato and Sons Ltd, 6 Alexandra Terrace, Alexandra Rd, Aldershot, Hants (☎ Aldershot 334871)

CATOR, Albemarle John; s of John Cator, of Woodbastwick, Norfolk, and Elizabeth Jane, *née* Kerrison; *b* 23 Aug 1953; *Educ* Harrow; *m* 29 Nov 1980, Fiona Mary, da of Robert Edgar Atheling Drummond; 2 s (John b 1983, Robert Henry b 1985); *Career* Lt Scots Guards 1971-74; with Samuel Montagu 1975-84, exec dir Chemical Bank International Ltd 1984-88, exec dir Chemical Securities Ltd 1988-, vice pres Chemical Bank 1988-; *Recreations* sailing, shooting, skiing; *Clubs* RYS, Pratts; *Style*— Albemarle Cator, Esq; Whitehouse Farm, Woodbastwick, Norwich, Norfolk; Chemical Bank House, 180 Strand, London WC2R 1EX (☎ 071 379 7474)

CATOR, Hon Mrs (Jacquetta); *née* Storey; only da of Baron Buckton (Life Peer), who d 1978, and sis of the Hon Sir Richard Storey, 2 Bt *qv*; *b* 19 April 1930; *m* 1956, Francis Cator, yr s of Lt-Col Henry John Cator, OBE, MC (d 1965), of Woodbastick Hall, Norwich, Norfolk; 3 s, 1 da; *Style*— The Hon Mrs Cator; 12 Warwick Square Mews, London SW1 (☎ 071 821 0920); The Old House, Ranworth, Norfolk (☎ 060 549 300)

CATOR, Lady (Wilhelmina) Joan Mary; *née* Fitz-Clarence; raised to rank of an Earl's da 1928; da of late Maj the Hon Harold Edward Fitz-Clarence, MC and sis of 5 Earl of Munster (d 1975); *b* 1904; *m* 1, 1928, Oliver Birkbeck (d 1952); 2 s (*see* Birkbeck Edward Harold, John Oliver), 1 da; m 2, 1961, Lt-Col Henry John Cator, OBE, MC (d 1965); *Style*— The Lady Joan Cator; Little Massingham House, King's Lynn, Norfolk

CATOR, Peter John; s of Sir Geoffrey Cator, CMG (d 1973), and Elizabeth Margaret Wynne, *née* Mostyn; *b* 26 Oct 1924; *Educ* Shrewsbury, CCC Cambridge; *m* 23 Jan 1951, Katharine Vera, da of Capt Honble Reginald Coke, DSO (d 1969); 1 s (Charles Henry b 1952), 1 da (Caroline Sarah (Mrs de la Force) b 1954); *Career* WWII RAFVR and Welsh Gds (Lt) 1943-47; HM Overseas Civil Serv 1949-62; sr dist offr Nigeria Petroleum Indust Trg Bd 1967-82; *Style*— Peter J Cator, Esq; Paxton Hse, Blockley, Moreton Marsh, Glos GL56 9BA (☎ 0386 700213)

CATTANACH, Bruce Macintosh; s of James Cattanach (d 1970), and Margaretta May, *née* Fyfe (d 1970); *b* 5 Nov 1932; *Educ* Heaton GS Newcastle upon Tyne, King's Coll Durham (BSc), Inst of Animal Genetics Univ of Edinburgh (PhD, DSc); *m* 17 Sept 1966, Margaret Bouchier, da of Percival Bouchier Crewe (d 1972); 2 da (Jean Margaret b 3 June 1967, Susan Elizabeth b 4 Jan 1969); *Career* scientific staff MRC Induced Mutagenesis Unit Edinburgh 1959-62, NIH post doctoral res fell Biology Div Oak Ridge Nat Laboratory Tennessee USA 1962-64, sr scientist City of Hope Med Centre Duarte Calif 1966-69; MRC Radiology Unit Chilton Oxfordshire: scientific staff 1969-, head Genetics Div 1987-; FRS 1987; *Recreations* squash, breeding, showing and judging of pedigree dogs; *Style*— Dr Bruce Cattanach, FRS; Down's Edge, Reading Road, Harwell, Oxon OX11 0JJ (☎ 0235 835410); Genetics Division, MRC Radiobiology Unit, Chilton, Didcot, Oxfordshire OX11 ORD (☎ 0235 834393, fax 0235 834918)

CATTANACH, Capt John Harkness; JP (1974); s of Capt Donald Cattanach (d 1944), of The Lodge, Kingussie, Inverness-shire, and Helen, *née* Macgregor (d 1964); *b* 19 Jan 1919; *Educ* Sherry's Coll Glasgow, Anderson Coll of Medicine; *m* 21 May 1949, Williamina, da of George Fraser (d 1955), of Glenbanchor, Newtonmore, Inverness-shire; 1 s (James Maccoll b 6 March 1951); *Career* cmmnd Cameronians (Scottish Rifles) 1938, served on active list until 1946; proprietor own business 1946-50, accountant 1950-55, proprietor own business 1956-74; memb: Highland Regnl Cncl 1982-86, Nairn DC 1974-; awarded Order of Virtuti Militari by Polish Govt in exile 1982, apptd Hon Lt-Col in Polish Armed Forces by Polish Govt in exile 1981; *Books* The Jeep Track (1990); *Recreations* photography, sailing, salmon fishing on Loch Ness; *Clubs* Cameronians, Scottish Rifles (Glasgow); *Style*— Capt John Cattanach, JP; Lorne House, Geddes, by Nairn, Scotland IV12 5SB (☎ 06677 279); Nairn District Council, Courthouse, Nairn, Nairnshire (☎ 0667 53207)

CATTELL, George Harold Bernard; s of Harold William Kingston Cattell (d 1955); *b* 23 March 1920; *Educ* Royal GS Colchester, Staff Coll Camberley, Royal Mil Coll of Sci; *m* 1951, Agnes Jean, da of Brig John Hardy (d 1969); 3 s (Jonathan, Jeremy, Simon), 1 da (Sarah); *Career* served with RA Maj; asst dir London Engrg Employers Fedn 1958-60, with Rootes Gp and Chrysler Organisation 1960-68 (former dir of manufacturing UK Chrysler), dir of manpower and productivity servs Dept of Employment and Productivity 1968-70, dir gen NFU 1970-78, chief exec (former gp md) FMC Gp plc (meat wholesalers) 1978-, chief exec NFU Hldgs Ltd 1978-84; FBIM, FRSA; *Recreations* tennis, fishing; *Clubs* IOD; *Style*— George Cattell, Esq; Little Cheveney, Yalding, Kent

CATTELL, Dr William Ross; s of William Ross Cattell (d 1961), of Gollanfield, Inverness-shire, and Elizabeth, *née* Fraser (d 1960); *b* 25 March 1928; *Educ* Inverness Royal Acad, Univ of Edinburgh (MB ChB, MD); *m* 1, 12 Oct 1956 (m dis 1976), (Norma) Ann, da of Frederick Beardwell (d 1974), of Cheam, Surrey; 1 s (Ross b 1957), 2 da (Sarah b 1960, Caroline b 1962); m 2, 2 April 1977, Patricia Margaret, da of Frank Gordon, of Drymen, Strathclyde; 2 da (Katherine b 1978, Alexandra b 1981); *Career* MO RAMC 1952-54; cmmnd Lt later Capt MELF BMH Fayid Egypt; house physician: Royal Infirmary and Assoc Hosps Edinburgh 1954-56, Brompton Hosp 1956; med registrar UCH 1956-59, sr lectr Bart's 1963-66 (lectr 1959-63), Rockefeller travelling fell Boston USA 1963-64, conslt physician Bart's 1966- (sr physician 1986-); memb: conslt City and Hackney DHA, Cncl and sec Renal Assoc, Cncl Renal Assoc, Cncl Euro Dialysis Assoc; former govr Med Coll Barts; RSM, Assoc of Physicians GB, FRCPE 1969, FRCP 1971; *Publications* Clinical Gynaecological Urology (contrib, 1984), British Textbook Genito-Urinary Surgery (contrib, 1985), Clinical Medicine (contrib, 1987), Clinical Renal Imaging (1989); *Recreations* gardening, DIY; *Style*— Dr William Cattell; Dept of Nephrology, St Bartholomew's Hosp, London EC1 (☎ 071 601 8787); 99 Harley St, London W1 (☎ 071 935 7258)

CATTERALL, John Stewart; s of John Bernard Catterall (d 1965), and Eliza, *née* Whitiker; *b* 13 Jan 1939; *Educ* Blackpool Tech Coll Sch of Art; *m* 18 Sept 1965, (Ann) Beryl, da of Edgar Watkin Hughes; 2 s (Andrew b 4 Aug 1969, Stewart b 3 Feb 1971); *Career* Nat Serv band memb 12 Royal Lancers 1958-60; dep auditor Preston CBC 1966-68, sr accountant Derby CBC 1968-70, mgmnt and chief accountant Cambs and Isle of Ely CC 1970-73, asst co treas Cambs CC 1973-76, dist treas Southampton & SW Hants Health Authy 1976-78, area treas Hants AHA 1978-82, regnl treas NE Thames RHA 1982-85; CIPFA: dep dir fin mgmnt and head health serv 1985-88, dir consultancy for health 1988-89; md and chief exec C International Ltd; *Recreations* golf, tennis; *Style*— John Catterall, Esq; Birkdale, Green Lane, Chilworth, Hants (☎ 0703 769 402); Heron House, 10 Dean Farrar Street, London SW1H 0DX (☎ 071 222 3433, fax 071 222 2988, car 0860 523068)

CATTLE, Walter Edmund (Tony); s of Lt-Col Edward Arthur Cattle (d 1969), of Pinner, and Margaret Doris Williams (d 1952); *b* 12 July 1937; *Educ* Westminster Tech Coll, Regent St Poly; *m* 1, 4 May 1963 (m dis 1988), Linda, da of Sidney James Theobold (d 1970); 2 da (Joy Dawn b 22 May 1968, Anne Julia b 7 Sept 1970); m 2, 10 Aug 1988, Catriona McLean, da of John Challen (d 1988); *Career* RAF marine engr Air Sea Rescue 1955-60, PO Volunteer Res Trg 1961-63; dir (later chm) Higgins & Cattle (SW) Ltd (int building servs) 1960-; capt of Br Flight Team 1977, set world record for the greatest number of landings at different airports in a day 1976, holder world speed record London to Spitzburgh 1977; memb Runnymede Borough Cncl:

former chm Enviromental Health and Gen Purposes Ctees, vice chm Highway Ctee, chm Housing and Elderly Servs Ctees; pres League of Friends of St Peter's Hosp Chertsey; Freeman City of London 1970; memb: Worshipful Co of Glaziers, Worshipful Co of Lightmongers (Master 1975); FIAA 1987, FIEEE 1969; *Recreations* clay pigeon shooting; *Style—* Tony Cattle, Esq; Linton Lodge, Fan Court Gardens, Longcross Rd, Longcross, Chertsey, Surrey KT16 0DJ (☎ 0932 872571); 12 Guildford St, Chertsey, Surrey KT16 9DA (☎ 0932 568 666, fax 0932 567 882, car 0836 584 021)

CATTO, Hon Alexander Gordon; 2 s (by 1 m) of 2 Baron Catto; *b* 22 June 1952; *Educ* Westminster, Trinity Coll Cambridge; *m* 1981, Elizabeth Scott, da of the late Maj T P Boyes, MC, of Brookval Cottage, Whitford, Devon; 2 s (Thomas Innes Gordon b 18 Oct 1983, Al Gordon b 1986), 1 da (Charlotte Gordon b 1988); *Career* vice pres Morgan Guaranty Trust Co of New York 1980-85; dir: Yule Catto & Co 1981-, Morgan Grenfell & Co Ltd 1986-88; md Lazard Bros & Co 1988-; *Style—* The Hon Alexander Catto; c/o Yule Catto and Co, Central Road, Templefields, Harlow, Essex CM20 2BH

CATTO, Prof Graeme Robertson Dawson; s of Dr William Dawson Catto, of Aberdeen, and Dora Elizabeth, *née* Spiby (d 1978); *b* 24 April 1945; *Educ* Robert Gordons Coll Aberdeen, Univ of Aberdeen (MB, CHB, MD, DSc), Harvard Univ; *m* 14 July 1967, Joan, da of James Alexander Sievewright (d 1958), of Aberdeen; 1 s (Simon b 1972), 1 da (Sarah b 1970); *Career* house offr Aberdeen Royal Infirmary 1969-70, Harkness fell in med Harvard Med Sch USA 1975-77; Univ of Aberdeen: lectr in med 1970-75, sr lectr in med 1977-88, prof in med and therapeutics 1988-; co-ordinator of clinical services Acute Services Unit Grampian Health Board 1988-; hon conslt physician nephrologist Grampian Health Board 1977-, memb: Assoc of Physicians of GB and I, Rotary Club of Aberdeen; burgess of guild City of Aberdeen; FRCP, FRCPE, FRCPG; *Books* Clinical Nephrology (1988); *Recreations* hill walking, curling; *Clubs* Royal Northern and University; *Style—* Prof Graeme R D Catto; 4 Woodend Ave, Aberdeen AB2 6YL (☎ 0224 310509); Dept of Medicine and Therapeutics, University of Aberdeen, Foresterhill, Aberdeen AB9 2ZD (☎ 0224 681818, fax 0224 685307)

CATTO, Hon Innes Gordon; s (by 1 m) and h of 2 Baron Catto, *qv*; *b* 7 Aug 1950; *Educ* Grenville Coll, Shuttleworth Agric Coll; *Style—* The Hon Innes Catto; House of Schivas, Ythanbank, Ellon, Aberdeenshire (☎ 03587 224)

CATTO, Hon Isabel Ida Gordon; OBE (1952); da of late 1 Baron Catto; *b* 1912; *Career* govr PNEU Schs; world pres YWCA 1955-63, pres YWCA of GB 1966-72; *Clubs* Oriental; *Style—* The Hon Isabel Catto, OBE; Holmdale, Holmbury St Mary, Surrey; 61 Cadogan Gdns, London SW3

CATTO, 2 Baron (UK 1936); Sir Stephen Gordon Catto; 2 Bt (UK 1921); s of 1 Baron Catto, CBE, PC (d 1959), and Gladys Forbes, *née* Gordon (d 1980); *b* 14 Jan 1923; *Educ* Eton, Trinity Coll Cambridge; *m* 1, 28 July 1948 (m dis 1965), Josephine Innes, er da of late George Herbert Packer, of Alexandria, Egypt; 2 s, 2 da; m 2, 27 Jan 1966, Margaret, da of James Stuart Forrest, of Dilston, Tasmania; 1 s, 1 da (Hon Georgina Lucinda Gordon b 21 May 1969); *Heir* s, Hon Innes G Catto; *Career* served RAFVR 1943-47; chm: Yule Catto & Co 1971-, Australian Mutual Provident Society (UK Branch) 1973-90, Pearl Group plc 1989-90; Morgan Grenfell & Co Ltd 1948-79 (dir 1957, chm 1973-79), pres Morgan Grenfell Group plc 1987- (chm 1980-87); dir: GEC plc 1959-, News International plc 1969-, The News Corporation Ltd 1979-89, Times Newspaper Holdings Ltd 1981-; memb: Advsy Cncl ECGD 1959-65, London Transport Bd (pt/t) 1962-68, London Advsy Ctee Hong Kong and Shanghai Banking Corporation 1966-80; chm Cncl RAF Benevolent Fund 1978-, tstee and chm Exec Ctee Westminster Abbey Tst 1973-; FCIB; *Recreations* music, gardening; *Clubs* Oriental, Melbourne (Australia); *Style—* The Rt Hon the Lord Catto; 41 William Mews, Lowndes Square, London SW1X 9HQ; Morgan Grenfell Group plc, 23 Great Winchester St, London EC2P 2AX (☎ 071 588 4545, fax 071 826 6155, telex 8953511 G)

CATTRALL, Peter Jeremy; s of Ralph W Cattrall, of Westwood, Old Green Road, Cliftonville, Margate, Kent, and Sally, *née* Lunn; *b* 8 Jan 1947; *Educ* King's Sch Canterbury, Trinity Coll Oxford (MA); *m* 26 April 1975, Amanda Jane Maria, da of Maj Gen W N J Withall, CB, of Wiltshire; 1 s (Charles David b 1 March 1980), 1 da (Sarah Louise b 21 Sept 1982); *Career* sch master Holmewood House Kent; admitted slr 1974, asst slr Knocker and Foskett Kent 1974-77, slr to Esso UK plc (formerly Esso Petroleum Co Ltd) 1977-91; memb: Kent Co Squash Side, Beckenham Cricket Club, Oxford Union; memb: Law Soc, IBA; *Recreations* cricket, squash, golf, tennis, swimming, cycling, reading, music, current affairs; *Clubs* United Oxford and Cambridge University, MCC, Rye Golf, Free Foresters, Izingari, Arabs, Jesters, Band of Brothers, Harlequins, Vincent's; *Style—* Peter Cattrall, Esq; 21 Whitmore Road, Beckenham, Kent (☎ 081 658 7265, 071 245 2150)

CAUGHEY, Sir (Thomas) Harcourt Clarke; KBE (1972), JP; s of James Marsden Caughey; *b* 4 July 1911; *Educ* King's Coll Auckland, Univ of Auckland; *m* 1939, Patricia Mary, da of Hon Sir George Finlay; 1 s, 2 da; *Career* dep chm: South British Insurance Co Ltd 1978-81, NZ Insurance Co 1981-86; exec chm Smith and Caughey Ltd 1975- (md 1962-85); former chm: Auckland Hosps Bd, Social Cncl of NZ, NZ Med Res Cncl, Caughey Preston Tst Bd, All Blacks (Rugby) 1932-37; pres Auckland Med Res Fndn 1978-84; Hon LLD Auckland 1986, CStJ; *Recreations* gardening, walking; *Clubs* Northern; *Style—* Sir Harcourt Caughey, KBE, JP; 7 Judges Bay Rd, Auckland, New Zealand

CAULFEILD, James Alexander Toby; s of Wade Toby Caulfeild, of Honeysuckle Cottage, Redford, Midhurst, Sussex, and Philippa Mary, *née* Brocklebank; *b* 30 March 1937; *Educ* Eton, New Coll Oxford (MA); *m* 20 March 1976, (Diana) Penelope, da of Col Martin Pound, of Duke House, Robert St, Deal, Kent; 4 da (Harriet Katharine, Victoria Louise, (Charlotte) Frances, Sophie Elizabeth); *Career* Nat Serv 2 Lt KRRC; asst investment mangr Provincial Insur 1967-70; dir M & G Investment Mgmnt 1970-89; FCA; *Recreations* skiing; *Clubs* Ski; *Style—* James Caulfeild, Esq; Hookland, Redford, Midhurst, Sussex (☎ 042 876 415); 3 Quays, Tower Hill, London EC3 (☎ 071 626 4588)

CAULFEILD, John Day; s of Eric St George Caulfeild (d 1975), and hp of uncle, 13 Viscount Charlemont; *b* 19 March 1934; *m* 1, 1964, Judith Ann (d 1971), da of James Dodd; 1 s, 1 da; m 2, 1972, Janet Evelyn, da of Orville Nancekivell; *Style—* John Caulfeild, Esq; 39 Rossburn Drive, Etobicoke, Ontario M9C 2P9, Canada

CAULFEILD, Hon Patricia St George; da of 9 Visc Charlemont (d 1964); *b* 17 Sept 1920; *Career* 3 Officer WRNS 1939-45; *Style—* The Hon Patricia Caulfeild; 55 New Rd, Lewes, E Sussex

CAULFIELD, Hon Mr Justice; Hon Sir Bernard; QC (1961); s of late John Caulfield, of St Helens, Lancs, and Catherine Quinn; *b* 24 April 1914; *Educ* St Francis Xavier's Coll, Liverpool Univ; *m* 1953, Sheila Mary, da of Dr John F J Herbert, of London; 3 s, 1 da; *Career* slr 1940, called to the Bar Lincoln's Inn 1947; rec Coventry 1964-68, judge High Court of Justice (Queen's Bench Div) 1968-89, presiding judge N Circuit 1976-80; master of the walks Lincoln's Inn 1984, treas and dean Lincoln's Inn Chapel 1987; kt 1968; *Style—* Sir Bernard Caulfield; 10 Old Square, Lincoln's Inn, London WC2A 3SU

CAUSLEY, Charles; CBE (1986); s of Charles Causley, and Laura, *née* Bartlett; *b* 24 Aug 1917; *Educ* Launceston Nat Sch, Horwell GS, Launceston Coll, Peterborough Trg Coll; *Career* RN, served WWII; poet; hon visiting fell in Poetry Univ of Exeter; former literary ed Signature and Apollo BBC W Region Radio; Queen's Gold Medal for Poetry 1967, Cholmondeley Award 1971, Signal Poetry Award 1986, Kurt Maschler Award 1987, Ingersoll Award (USA) 1990; has contributed to numerous anthologies of verse UK, USA; Hon DLitt Univ of Exeter, Hon MA Open Univ; FRSL; *Publications include* Hands to Dance (1951), Union Street (1957), Underneath the Water (1968), The Puffin Book of Magic Verse (ed, 1974), Collected Poems 1951-75 (1975), The Last King of Cornwall (1978), The Puffin Book of Salt-Sea Verse (ed, 1978), 25 Poems by Hamdija Demirovic (trans, 1980), The Ballad of Aucassin and Nicolette (1981), The Sun, Dancing (ed, 1982), Secret Destinations (1984), 21 Poems (1986), Kings' Children (trans, 1986), Early in the Morning (1986), Jack the Treacle Eater (1987), A Field of Vision (1988), Figgie Hobbin (poetry collection, 1990); *Recreations* travel, piano, the re-discovery of native town; *Style—* Charles Causley, Esq, CBE; 2 Cyprus Well, Launceston, Cornwall (☎ 0566 2731)

CAUTE, (John) David; *b* 16 Dec 1936; *Educ* Edinburgh Acad, Wellington, Wadham Coll Oxford; *m* 1, 1961 (m dis 1970), Catherine Shuckburgh; 2 s; m 2, 1973, Martha Bates; 2 da; *Career* served Army Gold Coast 1955-56; novelist and historian; Henry Fell Harvard Univ 1960-61, fell All Souls' Oxford 1959-65, visiting prof NY and Colombia Univs 1966-67, reader in social and political theory Brunel Univ 1967-70, Regent's lectr Univ of California 1974, visiting prof Univ of Bristol 1985; literary ed New Statesman 1979-80, co-chm Writers' Guild 1981-82; *Books* At Fever Pitch (1959, winner of Authors' Club Award and John Llewelyn Rhys Prize), Comrade Jacob (1961), The Decline of the West (1966), The Occupation (1971), The K-Factor(1983), News From Nowhere (1986), Veronica or the Two, Nations (1988); *plays* The Demonstration (1969), The Fourth World (1973); *radio plays* The Zimbabwe Tapes (1983), Henry and the Dogs (1986), Sanctions (1988); *non-fiction* Communism and the French Intellectuals 1914-1960 (1964), The Left in Europe Since 1789 (1966), Essential Writings of Karl Marx (ed, 1967), Fanon (1970), The Illusion (1971), The Fellow-Travellers (1973, revised ed 1988), Cuba, Yes ? (1974), Collisions: Essays and Reviews (1974), The Great Fear: the anti-communist campaign under Truman and Eisenhower (1978), Under the Skin: the Death of White Rhodesia (1983), The Espionage of the Saints (1986), Sixty-Eight: the Year of the Barricades (1988); *Style—* David Caute, Esq; 41 Westcroft Sq, London W6

CAUTLEY, (Edward) Paul Ronald; s of Lt Cdr Ronald Lockwood Cautley, KSG, RNVR (d 1981), of 9 North End Rd, London, and Ena Lily, *née* Medwin (d 1966); *b* 1 March 1940; *Educ* Downside, Harvard Business Sch (AMP); *m* 3 Sept 1966, Sandra Elizabeth (Liz), da of Capt Frederick David Baker; 2 da (Victoria Louise b 20 April 1968, Emma Jane b 20 Dec 1972); *Career* trained soldier 4 Inf Bn HAC 1958-60, cmmnd 2 Lt City of London Unit RM Res 1960-62, Lt-Actg Capt (SCC) CO Sherbourne House Marine Cadet Unit London 1962-68; sales rep Central Press Feature 1958-60, retail sales mangr ICI Paints 1960-62, fin mangr Goode Durrant & Murray 1962-64, gen mangr Marling Industries Ltd 1964-66, account dir S H Benson Ltd 1966-70, dir new prod devpt Bd BR 1970-73, chm Strategy International Ltd 1974-; dep chm: Heritage Projects Ltd 1989-, Settle and Carlisle Railway Development Co 1990-; dir inward int business devpt Urban Transportation Development Corporation Ltd Canada 1979-87, mktg dir Economist Intelligence Unit 1981-82, dir Inward Investmt Programme London Docklands Devpt Corp 1982-88, mktg dir British Urban Development Ltd 1988-89; memb Ctee and Cncl: Downside Settlement London 1958-, Centre Charles Peguy London 1960-63, Sherborne House London 1962-70, Licensing Exec Soc; govr S of England Agric Soc; *Books* The Cautley Chronicle (1986); *Recreations* veteran hockey, photography, watercolour painting, philately, fell walking; *Clubs* Army and Navy; *Style—* Paul Cautley, Esq; 13 The Ivory House, St Katherine Docks, London E1 9AT (☎ 071 488 9644); Strategy International Ltd, World Trade Centre, London E1 9AA (☎ 071 480 5562, fax 071 488 9643)

CAVALIER, David John; s of John Richard Cavalier, of Bloxwich, Birmingham, and Jackie Ormma, *née* Wheatley; *b* 12 Feb 1962; *Educ* Mandeville County Secdy Sch, Aylesbury Coll of Further Educn (City and Guilds Certs, Cert of Royal Inst of Health and Hygiene), Ealing Coll of Higher Educn (City and Guilds Cert); *m* 2 Feb 1985, Susan Caroline, da of Ronald Dorsett; 1 da (Jennifer b 22 Oct 1988); *Career* commis chef Royal Garden Hotel 1979-81, first commis chef Grosvenor House Hotel 1981-82, chef de partie Dorchester Hotel 1982-84, sous chef Auberge du Mail France 1984, first sous chef Berkeley Hotel 1984-85; chef and proprietor: Pebbles Restaurant 1985-87, Cavalier's Restaurant 1987-; winner: Gold medal (potato work) Hotel Olympia, Gold medal for best exhibit in jr class, finalist Young Chef of the Year competition 1987; awarded: 1 rosette AA Guide, 1 star Michelin Guide, black clover Ackerman Guide, 1 star Egon Ronay; memb Restaurant Assoc GB 1985; *Recreations* classic cars; *Style—* David Cavalier, Esq; MCN Restaurants Ltd, Cavaliers Restaurant, 129 Queenstown Rd, London SW8 3RH (☎ 071 720 6960)

CAVALIER, Steve Ronald; s of Ronald Ernest Cavalier, of Romford, Essex, and Jean, *née* Chinery; *b* 25 June 1952; *Educ* Harold Hill GS Essex, Colchester Sch of Art; *m* 1 Sept 1979, Christine, da of William Alfred Guerrier; 1 s (James William b 11 Feb 1985), 1 da (Clare Jean b 31 Aug 1982); *Career* photographer; asst with advertising photographers London 1971-77, fndr Steve Cavalier Studios 1977- (Central London then moving to St John's Wood); Gold and Silver awards Design and Art Directors Assoc, Gold and Silver Campaign Press awards, Gold award The One Show NY, commendation Benson & Hedges Gold award 1990; memb Assoc of Fashion, Advertising and Editorial Photographers; *Style—* Steve Cavalier, Esq; Steve Cavalier Studios, 25 Woronzow Rd, St John's Wood, London NW8 6AY (☎ 071 586 7418, fax 071 586 7419)

CAVALIERO, Roderick; s of Eric Cavaliero (d 1961), and Valerie de Vesci, *née* Logan (d 1975); *b* 21 March 1928; *Educ* Tonbridge, Hertford Coll Oxford (BA); *m* 31 Aug 1957, Mary, da of John McDonnell (d 1981); 1 s (Rohan b 1963), 4 da (Louisa b 1958, Annamaria b 1960, Rosalind b 1967, Juliana b 1969); *Career* Br Cncl offr 1958-88: rep Brazil 1967-70, controller personnel and staff recruitment 1970-75, rep Italy 1975-77, asst DG 1977-82, dep DG 1982-88; chm Educn and Trg Export Ctee 1979-88, pres Br Educnl Equipment Assoc 1988-; tstee: Charles Wallace India Tst 1982-, St George's Eng Sch Rome 1982-; memb Cncl: Br Sch at Rome, Centre for Br Teachers, Keats-Shelley Meml Assoc, Christian Orgns Res and Advsy Tst; *Books* Olympia and the Angel (1958), The Last of the Crusaders (1960); *Recreations* gardening, reading, writing; *Style—* Roderick Cavaliero, Esq; 10 Lansdowne Rd, Tunbridge Wells, Kent TN1 2NJ (☎ 0892 33452)

CAVAN, 13 Earl of (I 1647); Roger Cavan Lambart; also Viscount Kilcoursie (I 1647) and Lord Lambart, Baron of Cavan (I 1617); o s of Frederick Cavan Lambart (d 1963; o s of Maj Charles Edward Kilcoursie Lambart, 4 s of Maj Frederick Richard Henry Lambart, 2 s of Cdr Hon Oliver Matthew Lambart, RN, 2 s of 7 Earl of Cavan), and Audrey May, *née* Dunham; s kinsman, 12 Earl of Cavan, TD 1988; *b* 1 Sept 1944; *Educ* Wilson's Sch Wallington Surrey; *Heir* kinsman, Arthur Oliver Reid b 28 Jan 1909; *Style—* The Rt Hon the Earl of Cavan; 34 Woodleigh Gdns, London SW16

CAVANAGH, Ann; *née* Fairbairn; da of Kenneth Huntsman Fairbairn, of Labourne Fell

Farm, Chopwell, Newcastle upon Tyne, and Aileen, *née* Thompson; *b* 7 May 1954; *Educ* Newcastle upon Tyne (BSc); *m* 20 Sept 1975 (m dis 1989), George Cavanagh, s of George Cavanagh; 2 s (Neal George b 22 Aug 1980, Ross b 2 Jan 1984); *Career* asst accountant Assoc Br Foods 1978-84, co sec Romag Hldgs plc 1988-; fin dir: Romag Glass Products Ltd and Romag Security Laminators 1987-, Romag Electro-Optics Ltd 1988; treas Romag Inc 1988-, relinquished positions held at Romag, currently fin dir Mari Advanced Microelectronics Ltd Gateshead; ACMA 1983, FCMA 1990; *Recreations* riding; *Style*— Mrs Ann Cavanagh; Broomfield House, Derwent View, Chopwell, Newcastle upon Tyne NE17 7AN (☎ 0207 561 001); Mari Advanced Microelectronics Ltd, Gateshead, Tyne and Wear (☎ 091 490 1515, fax 091 490 0013)

CAVANAGH, Rev Charles Terrence Stephen; s of Arthur Lawrence Cavanagh (d 1963), of USA, and Coleen, *née* Ludrick; *b* 29 July 1949; *Educ* Univ of Oklahoma (BLitt), Univ of Cambridge (BA, MA), Univ of Oxford (Cert in Theol); *Career* Hedderwick Stirling Grumbar & Co 1978-81; SG Warburg & Co 1981-91, Mercury Asset Mgmnt plc 1981-91 (dir 1984-91), dir Kleinwort Benson Investment Management Ltd 1991-; ordained priest 1980; hon curate: St Peter's Clapham 1980-84, St Peter's Streatham 1985-; dir and treas Extemporary Dance Theatre Ltd 1985- (actg chm 1989-90); *Recreations* modern dance, cooking, wine; *Clubs* Athenaeum; *Style*— The Rev Charles Cavanagh; 34 Tasman Rd, London SW9 9LU (☎ 071 737 2269); Kleinwort Benson Investment Management Ltd, 10 Fenchurch St, London EC3M 3LB (☎ 071 956 6600)

CAVANAGH, John Bryan; s of Cyril Cavanagh (d 1941), and Annie Frances, *née* Murphy (d 1966); *b* 28 Sept 1914; *Educ* St Paul's, trained with Capt Edward Molyneux in London and Paris 1932-40; *Career* Intelligence Corps 1940, Capt GS Camouflage 1944; on demobilization travelled throughout USA studying fashion promotion, PA to Pierre Balmain Paris 1947-51, opened: own business 1952, John Cavanagh Boutique 1959; elected to Incorporated Soc of London Fashion Designers 1952 (vice-chm 1956-59); took own complete collection to Paris 1953, designed clothes for late Princess Marina and wedding dresses for the Duchess of Kent and Princess Alexandra; former chm and md John Cavanagh Ltd; Gold Medal Munich 1954; *Recreations* theatre, swimming, travelling; *Style*— John Cavanagh, Esq; 10 Birchlands Ave, London SW12 8ND (☎ 081 673 1504)

CAVAZZA, Lady Charlotte Sarah Alexandra; *née* Chetwynd-Talbot; da of 21 Earl of Shrewsbury and Waterford (d 1980), and his 1 w, Nadine Muriel, yr da of late Brig-Gen Cyril Randell Crofton, CBE; *b* 18 Nov 1938; *m* 1965, Camillo Cavazza dei Conti Cavazza (d 1981); 4 s, 3 da; *Style*— The Lady Charlotte Cavazza; S Felice del Benaco, Brescia, Italy

CAVE; *see*: Haddon-Cave

CAVE, Sir Charles Edward Coleridge; 4 Bt (UK 1896), JP (Devon 1972), DL (1977); only s of Sir Edward Cave, 3 Bt (d 1946), by his w Betty Christabel, da of Maj Rennell Coleridge, ggn of S T Coleridge, the poet, and 3 cous of 2 Baron Coleridge; *b* 28 Feb 1927; *Educ* Eton; *m* 1957, Mary Elizabeth, da of John Francis Gore, CVO, TD (d 1983, 3 s of Sir Francis Gore, KCB, who was nephew of 4 Earl of Arran), and Lady Janet Campbell, er da of 4 Earl Cawdor; 4 s (John b 1958, Nicholas b 1961, Thomas b 1964, Richard b 1967); *Heir* s, John Cave; *Career* formerly Lt Devonshire Regt; ADC to Govr Punjab 1947; High Sheriff of Devon 1969; FRICS; *Style*— Sir Charles Cave, Bt, JP, DL; Sidbury Manor, Sidmouth, Devon (☎ 039 57 207)

CAVE, Francis Joseph (Frank); ERD (1968); s of Joseph Cave (d 1950), of Leicester, and Emily, *née* Potter (d 1938); *b* 11 June 1912; *Educ* Mill Hill Boys' Sch Leicester, Leicester Coll of Art and Technol, Northampton Poly London, Univ of Liverpool, Univ of London (BSc); *m* 14 Nov 1939, (Sophia) Joan, da of Tom Herrick (d 1947), of Leicester; 1 s (Anthony b 13 Oct 1946), 1 da (Frances b 9 Sept 1942); *Career* Res Cmmn RE 1936, 105 Corps FD Park Co Liverpool 1937-39, WWII active serv, FD Co RE Dunkirk 1940, Maj 62 FD Co RE, Maj 58 Mech Equipment Co RE (serv India, Assam, Burma) returned from Rangoon 1945; trainee and articled civil engr 1928-33, asst engr (Willesden, Birkenhead, Oxford) 1933-39, chief asst engr Willesden 1946-48, dep borough engr West Ham 1948-52, borough engr Northampton 1952-58, borough surveyor Hendon Middx 1958-65, city engr Westminster 1965-74, md Halcrow Caribean Ltd WI 1975-78, conslt engr and surveyor 1978-; memb and chm Tech and Advsy Ctees: RICS, Inst Municipal Engrs, Method of Measurement (Inst Civil Engrs); Br Standards Inst: memb Cncl Codes of Practise for Bldg and Codes of Practice for Mechanical Engrs, memb Drafting Ctees; memb: Examination Panel London Dist Surveyors, Bd Govrs Westminster Tech Coll; chm Cncl Royal Soc of Health 1969, pres Rotary Club Westminster West 1973; hon memb: American Public Health Assoc 1969, Inst Public Health 1971; Freeman City of London, Liveryman Worshipful Co of Paviors 1966; FRSH 1948 (memb 1935), FIMunE 1952 (memb 1936), FICE 1955 (memb 1938), FRICS 1955 (memb 1948), FRTPI 1958 (memb 1949), FRSA 1972; *Recreations* travelling, art, DIY; *Clubs* RAC; *Style*— Frank Cave, Esq, ERD; 8 Borodale, Kirkwick Ave, Harpenden, Herts AL5 2QW (☎ 0582 712666)

CAVE, Hugh Walford Melville; s of Alexander Melville Cave (d 1964), and Mary Elizabeth, *née* Bennett (d 1987); *b* 10 July 1932; *Educ* Shrewsbury; *m* 14 Oct 1961, Diana Patricia, da of Brig Edward Antrobus James, OBE, TD, DL (d 1976); 2 s (Timothy b 1962, Andrew b 1964), 1 da (Victoria b 1966); *Career* Nat Serv RA, Lt TA; chartered surveyor; sr ptnr Chesshire Gibson Chartered Surveyors of Birmingham, London and LA 1982-88 (ptnr 1961-88); dir Debenham Tewson and Chinnocks plc 1988-, chm Debenham Tewson Chesshire 1988-; chm: Rhodes Almshouse Tst, Old Salopian Club 1978-79; surveyor to Sutton Coldfield Municipal Charities; Freeman City of London, memb Worshipful Co of Chartered Surveyors; *Recreations* golf; *Clubs* Army and Navy (Birmingham), Little Aston Golf; *Style*— Hugh W M Cave, Esq; 2 Heather Court Gardens, Four Oaks, Sutton Coldfield, W Midlands (☎ 021 308 2004); 10 Colmore Row, Birmingham (☎ 021 200 2050)

CAVE, John Arthur; s of Ernest and Eva Mary Cave; *b* 30 Jan 1915; *Educ* Loughborough GS; *m* 1937, Peggy Pauline, yst da of Frederick Charles Matthews Browne; 2 s, 2 da; *Career* Capt Royal Tank Regt (UK and India); dir Midland Bank 1975-80; chm: Forward Tst Ltd, Midland Bank Fin Corp Ltd, Midland Montagu Leasing Ltd 1975-80; memb Cncl Chartered Inst Bankers 1967-75 (dep chm 1973-75); FCIB; *Style*— John Cave, Esq; Dolphin House, Centre Cliff, Southwold, Suffolk IP18 6EN (☎ 0502 722232)

CAVE, John Charles; s and h of Sir Charles Cave, 4 Bt; *b* 8 Sept 1958; *Educ* Eton; *m* 1984, Carey Diana, er da of John Lloyd, of Combeland, Cadeleigh, Tiverton, Devon; 1 s (George b 1987), 1 da (Alice b 1989); *Style*— John Cave, Esq; Buckley, Sidbury, Sidmouth, Devon (☎ 039 57 212)

CAVE, Hon Mrs (Julia Claire Denholm); da of Baron Barnetson (Life Peer, d 1981), and Joan Fairley, *née* Davidson; *b* 23 Oct 1963; *Educ* Benenden, Queen's Secretarial Coll London, Pru Leith's Sch of Wine & Cookery; *m* 22 Sept 1990, Dr Timothy Richard Cave; *Career* theatrical agent; *Style*— The Hon Mrs T R Cave; c/o Broom, Chillies Lane, Crowborough, E Sussex TN6 3TB

CAVE, Prof Terence Christopher; s of Alfred Cyril Cave (d 1979), and Sylvia Norah, *née* Norman (d 1989); *b* 1 Dec 1938; *Educ* Winchester, Gonville and Caius Coll Cambridge (BA, MA, DPhil); *m* 31 July 1965 (m dis 1990), Helen Elizabeth; 1 s (Christopher b 1969), 1 da (Hilary b 1970); *Career* lectr Univ of St Andrews 1963-65 (asst lectr 1962-63), sr lectr Univ of Warwick 1970-72 (lectr 1965-70), prof of French literature Univ of Oxford 1989- (fell and tutor St John's Coll 1972-); visiting posts: Cornell Univ 1967-68, Univ of California Santa Barbara 1976, Univ of Virginia 1979, Princeton Univ 1984; visiting fell All Souls Coll Oxford 1971; *Books* Devotional Poetry in France (1969), The Cornucopian Text (1979), Recognitions (1988); *Style*— Prof Terence Cave; St John's Coll, Oxford OX1 3JP (☎ 0865 277 345)

CAVE-WOOD, Geoffrey Peter; s of John Frederick Cave-Wood (d 1986), and Norah Margaret Brisley, *née* Veal; *b* 25 June 1938; *Educ* Dover Coll; *m* 8 June 1968, Rosalind Mary, da of Richard Clippingdale (d 1977); 2 da (Philippa b 21 Aug 1969, Anna b 28 Oct 1972); *Career* chm and co fndr Cave Wood Transport Ltd 1962-; govr Brenchwood Sch High Wycombe, chm Festival of Languages, UK del EEC Liaison Ctee CLECAT Brussels, chm Int Gp of Road Haulage Assoc; MCIT; *Recreations* sport, gardening, travel, European history; *Style*— Geoffrey Cave-Wood, Esq; Chevin, Hervines Road, Amersham, Bucks HP6 5HS; Cave Wood Transport Ltd, PO Box 92, Coronation Rd, Cressex Industrial Estate, High Wycombe, Bucks HP12 3TW (☎ 0494 446541, telex 837766, fax 0494 447329, car 0836 536653)

CAVE-BROWNE-CAVE, John Robert Charles; s and h of Sir Robert Cave-Brown-Cave, 16 Bt; *b* 22 June 1957; *Style*— John Cave-Brown-Cave Esq

CAVE-BROWNE-CAVE, Myles; s of Bryan Cave-Browne-Cave, OBE (d 1980), of Birket Houses, Winster, Windermere, and Margaret, *née* Cooke, MBE (d 1978); *b* 26 Aug 1949; *Educ* Rugby, St Edmund Hall Oxford (MA); *m* 24 Oct 1986, Sally Jayne, da of Geoffrey Lilley, of 15 Kings Ave, Higham Ferrers, Northants; *Career* admitted slr 1974; ptnr Denton Hall Burgin & Warrens; *Style*— Myles Cave-Browne-Cave, Esq; Denton Hall Burgin & Warrens, Five Chancery Lane, Clifford's Inn, London EC4 (☎ 071 242 1212)

CAVE-BROWNE-CAVE, Sir Robert; 16 Bt (1641 E); s of Sir Clement Cave-Browne-Cave, 15 Bt (d 1945); *b* 8 June 1929; *Educ* St George's Sch Vancouver, Univ Sch Victoria, British Columbia Univ; *m* 1, 1954 (m dis 1975), Lois Shirley, da of John Chalmers Huggard, of Winnipeg; 1 s, 1 da; m 2, 1977, Joan Shirley, da of Dr Kenneth Ashe Peacock, of W Vancouver, BC; *Heir* s, John Cave-Brown-Cave; *Career* pres Cave and Co Ltd, Seabord Chemicals Ltd; *Style*— Sir Robert Cave-Browne-Cave, Bt; 6087 Wiltshire St, Vancouver, British Columbia, Canada

CAVELL, Rt Rev John Kingsmill; o s of William H G Cavell, of Deal, Kent, and Edith May, *née* Warner; *b* 4 Nov 1916; *Educ* Sir Roger Manwood's GS Kent, Queens' Coll Cambridge (MA), Wycliffe Hall Oxford; *m* 1942, Mary Grossett, da of Christopher Penman, of Devizes, Wilts; 1 da (Margaret); *Career* ordained 1940; vicar Christ Church Cheltenham 1952-62, St Andrew's Plymouth 1962-72 (formerly prebendary of Exeter Cathedral and rural dean of Plymouth); bishop: Southampton 1972-84, HM Prisons 1975-85; asst bishop of Salisbury and hon canon of Salisbury Cathedral 1988-; vice pres Soc of Genealogists; *Recreations* genealogy, local history; *Style*— The Right Rev John Cavell; 5 Constable Way, West Harnham, Salisbury SP2 8LN (☎ 0722 334782)

CAVENAGH, Winifred Elizabeth; OBE, JP; da of Arthur Speakman (d 1960), and Ethel Speakman (d 1969); *Educ* Broughton & Crumpsall HS, UCL, LSE (BSc Econ), Univ of Birmingham (PhD); *m* 5 Nov 1938, Hugh Cavenagh (d 1967), s of Edward Cavenagh (d 1931); *Career* with Miny of Labour 1941-45; Univ of Birmingham 1946-76 (prof emeritus 1976); visiting prof Ghana Univ 1971, Moir/Cullis lecture fellowship USA 1977 and Canada 1980, chm (pt/t) Indust Tbnl 1974-77; memb: United Birmingham Hosps Bd 1958-64, Home Office Probation Recruitment & Trg Ctee 1958-67, Advsy Ctee on Juvenile Delinquency 1964-65; memb Lord Chllr Ctee on: Legal Aid 1960-71, Trg of Magistrates 1965-73; nat chm Assoc of Social Workers 1955-57; memb: Magistrates Assoc Cncl 1965-78, Birmingham Educn Ctee 1946-66, W Midlands Econ Planning Cncl 1967-71; *Style*— Prof W E Cavenagh, OBE, JP; 25 High Point, Richmond Hill Rd, Edgbaston, Birmingham B15 3RU (☎ 021 454 0109)

CAVENAGH-MAINWARING, Charles Rafe Gordon; s of Capt Maurice Kildare Cavenagh-Mainwaring, DSO, RN, and Iris Mary, *née* Denaro; *Educ* Downside; *m* 20 Oct 1973, Rosemary Lee, da of Capt Thomas Lee Reay Hardy (d 1982), of London; 1 s (Rupert William b 1976); *Career* Lt RM Reserve 1964-67, Lt HAC (RHA) 1967-73, transferred to RARO 1974; dir Hinton Hill Underwriting Agents Ltd 1987-89, conslt Allied Dunbar 1990-; govr Salesian Coll; underwriting memb Lloyd's; Knight of Honour and Devotion Sovereign Mil Order of Malta, Knight of Justice of the Sacred Mil Order of Constantine of St George; *Recreations* shooting, skiing, watching rugby union football, tennis; *Clubs* Hurlingham; *Style*— Charles Cavenagh-Mainwaring, Esq; 3 Bridge Lane, London SW11 3AD; 47 Cadogan Gardens, London SW3 (☎ 071 223 2237); (☎ 071 799 3830 ext 275, fax 071 222 7385)

CAVENAGH-MAINWARING, Guy; s of Rafe Gordon Dutton Cavenagh-Mainwaring, *qv*, of Whitmore Hall, Staffs (High Sheriff of Staffs 1954), by his w Rosemary Mainwaring, da of Sir Arthur Murray Cudmore, CMG, MB; *b* 22 Feb 1934; *Educ* privately; *m* 1961, Margery Christine Rachel, da of Eric Rowland James Robbins; 1 s (Edward Rowland b 1962), 3 da (Tara Rose b 1964, Fleur Amicia b 1970, Rosanna Rachel b 1972 (decd)); *Career* landowner and farmer; High Sheriff of Staffs 1977-78; *Style*— Guy Cavenagh-Mainwaring, Esq; Hillside Farm, Whitmore, Staffs (☎ 0782 680478); 22 Lakeman St, N Adelaide, S Australia (☎ 010 61 8 267 4294)

CAVENAGH-MAINWARING, Capt Maurice Kildare; DSO (1940); s of Maj James Gordon Cavenagh-Mainwaring (d 1938), of Whitmore Hall, Staffords; *b* 13 April 1908; *Educ* Dartmouth; *m* 1933, Iris Mary, da of Col Charles Albert Denaro, OBE, of Valletta, Malta; 1 s; *Career* Capt RN 1951, Naval Attaché Paris 1957-60, ADC to HM the Queen 1960, Cdr Legion d'Honneur 1960, ret 1960; joined Simpson (Piccadilly) Ltd 1961; *Clubs* Naval and Military, Union (Malta); *Style*— Capt Maurice Cavenagh-Mainwaring, DSO, RN; 47 Cadogan Gdns, London SW3 (☎ 071 584 7870)

CAVENAGH-MAINWARING, Rafe Gordon Dutton; er s of Maj James Gordon Cavenagh-Mainwaring (d 1938), of Whitmore Hall, and Evelyn Dutton, *née* Green (d 1963); *b* 20 July 1906; *Educ* Cheltenham; *m* 1931, Rosemary, er da of Sir Arthur Murray Cudmore, CMG (d 1951), of Adelaide, S Australia; 1 s (Guy, *qv*); *Career* landowner; JP Staffs 1932-55, High Sheriff 1954-55, Patron of the Living of Whitmore, 33rd Hereditary Lord of the Manors of Whitmore and Biddulph; *Style*— Rafe Cavenagh-Mainwaring Esq; Whitmore Hall, Whitmore, Newcastle-under-Lyme, Staffs ST5 5HW (☎ 0782 680235); 22 Lakeman St, N Adelaide, S Australia 5006 (☎ 010 61 8 267 4294)

CAVENDISH, Anthony John; s of George Henry Frederick Cavendish (d 1932); *b* 20 July 1927; *Educ* Lyceum Alpinum, Univ of London (BA); *m* 1980, Elspeth Gail, da of Montagu Frank Macdonald, of Poole; 1 s (Julius b 1981), 1 da (Charlotte b 1984); *Career* Maj Army 1945-48; HM Foreign and Dip Serv 1948-53; foreign corr UPI 1953-60 (France, Poland, Hungary, ME), banker; dir: Brandts 1972-1975, Hong Kong Shanghai Bank 1975-78, Overland Trust Bank 1986-, Overland Trust Ltd, Overland Trust International plc; chm: Contship (UK) Ltd 1987-, Lonham Insurance Group Ltd, Arrow Freight Ltd 1989-, The Fountainhead Gp SA, Anglo Romanian Corporation, Policy Network Ltd, Euro-Rand Securities plc; Parly candidate (Cons) Harlow 1973; Freeman City of London; *Books* Inside Intelligence; *Recreations* cooking, music, winter sports, power boating; *Clubs* Carlton, Cavalry and Guards', Special Forces, Royal

Southern Yacht, Travellers' (Paris), St Moritz Tobogganing; *Style*— Anthony Cavendish, Esq; Lowfields, Hartley Wintney, Hants (☎ 025 126 4158)

CAVENDISH, Lady Elizabeth Georgiana Alice; LVO (1976), JP (London 1961); da of late 10 Duke of Devonshire, KG, MBE, TD; *b* 24 April 1926; *Career* appointed an extra lady-in-waiting to HRH The Princess Margaret 1954; chm: of N Westminster PSD 1980-83, Inner London Juvenile Court 1983-86, Bd of Visitors Wandsworth Prison 1970-73; memb Bd of Advertising Standards Authy 1981-; lay memb: the Senate of the Inns of Court Professional Conduct Ctee 1983, Cncl of Mgmnt St Christophers' Hospice 1990; chm Cancer Research Campaign 1981-; memb: Marre Ctee on the Future of Legal Profession 1986-, pres Cncl; *Style*— The Lady Elizabeth Cavendish, LVO, JP; 19 Radnor Walk, SW3 (☎ 071 352 0774); Moor View, Edensor, Bakewell, Derbyshire (☎ 024 688 2204)

CAVENDISH, Hon John Charles Gregory; yr s of 5 Baron Chesham, PC, TD (d 1989); *b* 23 Nov 1952; *Educ* Eton, Jesus Coll Cambridge; *m* 3 July 1976, Lucinda Mary, da of Richard Hugh Corbett (d 1974); *Career* shipbroker; with Tradax England Ltd (grain shippers) 1974-81, E D and F Man Ltd (sugar shippers) 1981-85, Braemar Chartering Ltd 1985-88; shooting instr, princ Cavendish Sporting 1988-; *Recreations* motor sports, country life and sports; *Style*— The Hon John Cavendish; Hall Farm, Farringdon, Alton, Hants (☎ 042 058 275)

CAVENDISH, Michael Edward; s of Morton Edward Cavendish (d 1940), and Agnes Emily, *née* Pattison (d 1976); *b* 5 Aug 1936; *Educ* St Clement Dane's GS, Univ of London Guy's Hosp Med Sch (BSc, MB BS) Univ of Liverpool (MCh Orth); *m* 6 July 1963, Jean Ann, da of Edward Willis (d 1987); 5 s (Andrew Morton b 1954, Paul b 1965, Michael James b 1968, John Richard b 1972, b James Edward b 1980), 1 da (Fiona Jane b 1966); *Career* orthopaedic house surgn Guy's Hosp 1961-68, orthopaedic registrar and sr registrar United Liverpool Hosps 1968-72, conslt orthopaedic surgn St Helens and Knowsley Health Authy 1972-, papers on joint replacement and related basic res in particular joint replacement of elbow; chm Fund Raising Ctee St Helens YMCA 1989, pres St Helens Med Soc 1985 (sec), past pres Liverpool Orthopaedic Circle; memb: St Helens Rotary Club, Liverpool Med Inst, SECEC 1987, Br Elbow and Shoulder Soc 1989; FRCS 1967, FBr Orthopaedic Assoc 1969; *Recreations* sailing; *Style*— Michael Cavendish, Esq; 88 Rodney Street, Liverpool L1 9AR (☎ 051 708 6070)

CAVENDISH, Maj-Gen Peter Boucher; CB (1981), OBE (1969), DL (1989); s of Brig Ronald Valentine Cecil Cavendish, OBE, MC (ka 1943, gs of Lt-Col William Cavendish, Groom-in-Waiting to Queen Victoria, and Lady Emily Lambton, da of 1 Earl of Durham. William was gs of 1 Earl of Burlington of the 1831 creation and 1 cous of 7 Duke of Devonshire), and Helen, *née* Boucher; *b* 26 Aug 1925; *Educ* Abberley Hall Worcester, Winchester, New Coll Oxford; *m* 1952, Marion Loudon, 2 da of Robert Constantine, TD, JP, and Marie, *née* van Haaren (descended from William the Silent, Prince of Orange); 3 s (Ronald b 1954, Mark b 1955, Rupert b 1962); *Career* enlisted 1943, cmmnd Royal Dragoons 1945, 3 King's Own Hussars 1946 and Queens Own Hussars 1958, 14/20 Hussars 1965 (CO 1966-69 and Hon Col 1976-81), Cmdt RAC Centre 1971-74, sec to Mil Ctee Int Mil Staff HQ NATO 1975-78, dir Armaments Standardisation and Interoperability Div 1978-81, chm Mil Agency for Standardisation NATO HQ 1978-81; Hon Col Queen's Own Mercian Yeo TAVR 1982-87, Col Cmdt the Yeomanry 1986-90, High Sheriff of Derbyshire 1986; Peak Park Planning Bd 1982-91 (vice chm 1987-91); *Style*— Maj-Gen Peter Cavendish, CB, OBE, DL; The Rock Cottage, Middleton-by-Youlgrave, Bakewell, Derby DE4 1LS (☎ 0629 636 225)

CAVENDISH, Hon Roderick Alexander; s and h of 7 Baron Waterpark; *b* 10 Oct 1959; *m* 2 Sept 1989, Anne, da of Hon Luke Asquith, *qv*; 1 s (Luke Frederick b 17 Sept 1990); *Style*— The Hon Roderick Cavendish

CAVENDISH-TRIBE, Hon Mrs (Winifred); *née* Cavendish; 3 and yst da of 6 Baron Waterpark (d 1948), and his 2 w, May (d 1969), da of William Ernest Burbidge; *b* 1 June 1909; *Educ* St Monica's Priory Dorset; *m* 13 Dec 1929, Capt Albert Frank Tribe, who later assumed additional surname of Cavendish (d 1962), 4 s of late Lt Cdr Arthur Ernest Tribe, RNR; 1 s; *Style*— The Hon Mrs Cavendish-Tribe; Saxons Beech Hill, Bridge, nr Canterbury, Kent

CAWDOR, 6 Earl (1827 UK); Hugh John Vaughan Campbell; also Baron Cawdor of Castlemartin (GB 1796) and Viscount Emlyn (UK 1827); The full designation of the Earldom in its patent of 1827 was Earl Cawdor of Castlemartin; s of 5 Earl Cawdor (d 1970), by his 1 w Wilma Mairi (d 1982), da of Vincent Cartwright Vickers, of Aldenham; *b* 6 Sept 1932; *Educ* Eton, Magdalen Coll Oxford, RAC Cirencester; *m* 1, 1957 (m dis 1979), Cathryn, da of Maj-Gen Sir Robert Hinde, KBE, CB, DSO, by his w Evelyn, 3 da of Henry Fitzherbert, JP, of Yeldersley Hall, Derbys; 2 s, 3 da; m 2, 1979, Countess Angelika Ilona Lazansky von Bukowa; *Heir* s, Viscount Emlyn; *Career* High Sheriff of Carmarthenshire 1964; FSA, FRICS; *Style*— The Rt Hon the Earl Cawdor, FSA; Cawdor Castle, Nairn; Cawdor Estate Office, Nairn (☎ 06677 666, telex 75225)

CAWLEY, Sir Charles Mills; KB (1965), CBE (1957, OBE 1946); s of John Cawley (d 1938), of Gillingham, Kent, and Emily Cawley; *b* 17 May 1907; *Educ* Sir Joseph Williamson's Mathematical Sch Rochester, Imperial Coll of Sci and Technol (DIC, MSc, PhD, DSc); *m* 1934, Florence Mary Ellaline, da of James Shepherd (d 1925), of York; 1 da; *Career* Capt Army (Special Serv) 1945; temporarily employed with the rank of Col by the Control Cmmn for Germany 1946-47, IDC 1949; employed Fuel Res Station DSIR 1929-53 (seconded to the Petroleum Warfare Dept 1939-45), dir DSIR HQ 1953-59, chief scientist Miny of Power 1959-67, cmmr Civil Serv 1967-69, ret; fell Imperial Coll of Sci and Technol; ARCS, FRSC, FInstE, FRSA; *Style*— Sir Charles Cawley, KB, CBE; 8 Glen Gardens, Ferring-by-Sea, Worthing, West Sussex BN12 5HG (☎ 0903 501850)

CAWLEY, 3 Baron (1918 UK); Sir Frederick Lee Cawley; 3 Bt (UK 1906); s of 2 Baron Cawley (d 1954), and Vivienne (d 1978, aged 100), da of Harold Lee, of Manchester and sis of Sir Kenneth Lee, 1 and last Bt; *b* 27 July 1913; *Educ* Eton, New Coll Oxford (BA, MA); *m* 1944, Rosemary Joan, da of Reginald Edward Marsden, former bursar of Eton, and Hon Vere Dillon (sis of 18 and 19 Viscounts Dillon), and whose twin sis Iris m Lord Cawley's yr bro, Hon Stephen Cawley, *qv* ; 6 s, 1 da; *Heir* s, Hon John Francis Cawley; *Career* served WWII Capt RA Leics Yeo (wounded) NW Europe; called to the Bar Lincoln's Inn 1938, practised 1946-73; dep chm Ctees House of Lords 1958-67, and chm of many private bill select ctees; *Style*— The Rt Hon Lord Cawley; Bircher Hall, Leominster, Herefordshire HR6 0AX (☎ 056 885 218)

CAWLEY, Hon John Francis; s and h of 3 Baron Cawley, *qv*; *b* 28 Sept 1946; *Educ* Eton; *m* 1979, Regina Sarabia, da of late Marqués de Hazas (cr of 1873 by King Amadeus I), of Juan Bravo 10, Madrid 6; 3 s (William Robert Harold b 2 July 1981, Thomas Frederick José-Luis b 1982, Andrew David b 1988), 1 da (Susan Mary b 1980); *Style*— The Hon John Cawley; Castle Grounds, Ashton, Leominster, Herefordshire HR6 0DN (☎ 058 472 209)

CAWLEY, Dr Michael Ian David; s of late William Miller Seddon Cawley, CBE, of Bexhill, E Sussex, and Edith Mary, *née* Setchell; *b* 14 Oct 1935; *Educ* Caterham Sch Surrey, Bart's Med Coll Univ of London (MB BS, MD, MRCP); *Career* Nat Serv Lt and Capt RAMC 1960-62, surgn Lt Cdr RNR 1970-; house offr 1959-60: Norwich, Bournemouth, Bart's; med registrar 1962-68: Bart's, Lewisham Hosp London; Aylwen res fell Bart's 1965-66, sr registrar in med Bristol Royal Hosp 1968-70, ARC visiting res fell Univ of Texas at Dallas 1971-72, lectr in rheumatology Univ of Manchester 1970-73; conslt physician rheumatology: Wrigtington Hosp Lancs 1973-74, Univ of Southampton Hosps 1974- (hon sr lectr 1990-), civilian conslt to RN 1989-, author of papers and chapters on rheumatic diseases; memb: Ctee on Rheumatology RCP 1983-89 (dist tutor 1987-), Cncl Br Soc of Rheumatology 1986-88, Central Conslts and Specialists Ctee BMA 1986-; pres S Wales S West and Wessex Rheumatology Club 1986-89; memb: American Coll of Rheumatology, Br Soc for Rheumatology; Freeman Worshipful Soc of Apothecaries 1982; FRCP 1979; *Recreations* classical music, sailing, skiing; *Clubs* Royal Lymington Yacht, Royal Navy Sailing Association, Ski Club of Great Britain; *Style*— Dr Michael Cawley; 4 Pond Cottages, Braishfield, Romsey, Hants SO51 0PR (☎ 0794 68584); Southampton General Hospital, Shirley, Southampton S09 4XY (☎ 0703 796770)

CAWLEY, Hon Stephen Robert; 2 s of 2 Baron Cawley, JP, by his w Vivienne, da of Harold Lee; *b* 22 Oct 1915; *Educ* Eton, New Coll Oxford (MA, BSc); *m* 1952, Iris Edrica, da of Reginald Marsden and Hon Vere, aunt of late 20 Viscount Dillon; 3 s (Alec b 1954, James b 1956, Martin b 1959); 1 da (Yoland b 1957); *Career* served WWII with Royal Signals; JP: Lancashire 1951-53, Surrey 1955-74, Hereford and Worcester 1978-83; Parly candidate (Lib): Stretford (Gen Election) 1950, High Peak 1951 1955 and 1959, Esher 1964 and 1966; dir bleaching dyeing and printing of calico piece goods and manufacture of plastic chemical plant, ret; prime warden Dyers' Co 1970-71; *Style*— The Hon Stephen Cawley; Woodhay, Tilford Rd, Hindhead, Surrey GU26 6QY (☎ 042 860 6856)

CAWLEY, Hon William Frederick; 2 s of 3 Baron Cawley, *qv*; *b* 7 Dec 1947; *Educ* Eton, New Coll Oxford (MA); *m* 1979 (m dis 1988), Philippa J, er da of Philip Hoare, DFC, of The Playle, Weycombe Rd, Haslemere, Surrey; 1 s (Edward Frederick b 1980), 1 da (Elizabeth Lena b 1982); *Style*— The Hon William Cawley

CAWS, Richard Byron; CBE (1984); s of Maxwell Caws, of London (d 1976), and Edith Caws (d 1979); *b* 9 March 1927; *m* 28 May 1948, Fiona Muriel Ruth Elton, da of Lt Col Edwin Darling, MC, RA (d 1949); 2 s (Eian b 1950, Andrew b 1952, decd), 2 da (Genevra b 1949, Alexandra b 1953); *Career* chm Caws & Morris Chartered Surveyors London 1987-, sr conslt (Real Estate) Goldman Sachs Int Corp London 1987-; ptnr: Nightingale Page and Bennett Chartered Surveyors Kingston upon Thames 1944-60, Debenham Tewson and Chinnocks Chartered Surveyors London 1961-87; chm: Jr Orgn RICS 1959-60, Property Ctee Cmmn for the New Towns 1978- (memb 1976-); Crown Estates Cmmr 1971-, Dobry Ctee on Review of the Devpt Control System 1973-75, DOE Advsy Gp on Commercial Property Devpt 1973-77; dep chm DoE Property Advsy Gp 1978-88, govr RAC 1985-88; Master Worshipful Co of Chartered Surveyors 1982-83; *Recreations* sailing, travel; *Clubs* Boodle's, Royal Thames Yacht, Little Ship; *Style*— Richard Caws, Esq, CBE; 36 Mount Park Rd, Ealing, London W5 2RS (☎ 081 997 7739); Caws & Morris Assoc Ltd, Chancery House, 53/64 Chancery Lane, London WC2A 1QU (☎ 071 404 4303, fax : 071 831 0390)

CAWTHRA, David Wilkinson; s of Jack Cawthra (d 1974), and Dorothy, *née* Wilkinson; *b* 5 March 1943; *Educ* Heath GS Halifax , Univ of Birmingham (BSc); *m* Maureen Mabel, da of late Eric Arthur Williamson; 1 s (Richard Giles b 18 Oct 1969), 1 da (Caroline Eleanor b 30 Jan 1974); *Career* Mitchell Construction Co Ltd: jt engr 1964, site agent 1967, contracts mangr 1970; divnl dir Tarmac Construction Ltd 1976-79 (contracts mangr 1973-76), gen mangr Balfour Beatty Ltd 1981 (divnl dir 1979); md: Balfour Beatty Construction Ltd 1985, Balfour Beatty Ltd 1988; chief exec Balfour Beatty Ltd 1990; Freeman City of London, memb Worshipful Co of Engineers; FICE 1980, FIHT 1980, CBIM 1989, FEng 1990; *Recreations* hillwalking, golf, American history; *Clubs* RAC, Pall Mall; *Style*— David Cawthra, Esq; Balfour Beatty Ltd, 7 Mayday Rd, Thornton Heath, Surrey CR7 7XA (☎ 081 683 6042, fax 081 689 5867)

CAYFORD, Dame Florence Evelyn; DBE (1965), JP (Co of London 1941); da of late George William Bunch, and Mary S A Bunch; *b* 14 June 1897; *Educ* County Secondary Sch St Pancras, Paddington Tech Inst; *m* 1923, John Cayford, s of Alfred Cayford; 2 s; *Career* chm London CC 1960-61, memb GLC 1964-67, Mayor of London Borough of Camden 1969; Freeman of Hampstead; chm Metropolitan Water Bd 1966-67; *Style*— Dame Florence Cayford, DBE, JP; 26 Hemstal Rd, Hampstead, London NW6 (☎ 071 624 6181)

CAYLEY, Dr (Arthur) Charles Digby; s of Dr Forde Everard de Wend Cayley, MBE, of 67 Wish Rd, Hove, Sussex BN3 4LN, and Eileen Lillian, *née* Dalton; *b* 8 Nov 1946; *Educ* Middx Hosp Med Sch Univ of London (MB BS); *m* 1 Nov 1969, Jeanette Ann, da of George Richard Avery (d 1968), of Plymouth; 3 s (George b 1971, Adam b 1975, Seth b 1980); *Career* sr registrar in geriatric medicine and hon lectr Middx Hosp 1974-76, conslt physician in medicine of the elderly Brent Health Authy (now Parkside Health Authy) 1976-, recognised teacher of the Univ of London, hon clinical sr lectr St Mary's Hosp Med Sch Univ of London; contrib: Lancet, Br Med Jl, Res and Clinical Forums, Post Grad Med Jl, Br Jl of Hosp Med, Care of the Elderly; memb: Br Geriatric Soc (currently chm of NW Thames region), BMA; memb Ctee of the Brent Triangle; FRCP 1989 (memb 1973); *Books* Hospital Geriatric Medicine (1987); *Recreations* walking, listening to classical music; *Style*— Dr Charles Cayley; Dept of Medicine for the Elderly, Central Middlesex Hospital, Acton Lane, London NW10 7NS (☎ 081 453 2184)

CAYLEY, Sir Digby William David; 11 Bt (UK 1661); o s of William Arthur Seton Cayley (d 1964), ggs of 7 Bt; suc his kinsman Maj Sir Kenelm Henry Ernest Cayley, 10 Bt 1967; *b* 3 June 1944; *Educ* Malvern, Downing Coll Cambridge; *m* 19 July 1969, Christine Mary, o da of late Derek Francis Gaunt, of Ilkley; 2 da; *Heir* kinsman, George Paul Cayley b 23 May 1940; *Career* asst classics master Stonyhurst Coll 1973-; *Style*— Sir Digby Cayley, Bt; 12 Lensfield Rd, Cambridge

CAYLEY, George Paul; s of late Capt Charles Cayley, ggs of 7 Bt; hp of kinsman, Sir Digby Cayley, 11 Bt; *b* 23 May 1940; *Educ* Felsted; *m* 1967, Shirley Southwell, da of Frank Woodward Petford, of Kirby Cane, Norfolk; 2 s; *Style*— George Cayley, Esq; Applegarth, Brewers Green, Roydon, Diss, Norfolk

CAYZER, Hon Avon Arthur; s of 2 Baron Rotherwick; *b* 13 Sept 1968; *Style*— The Hon Avon Cayzer

CAYZER, Hon Charles William; s of 2 Baron Rotherwick; *b* 26 April 1957; *m* 1985, Amanda C S, 2 da of John Squire, of Marbella, Spain; *Style*— The Hon Charles Cayzer

CAYZER, Hon Elizabeth; yr da of Baron Cayzer; *b* 16 Jan 1946; *Style*— The Hon Elizabeth Cayzer

CAYZER, Sir James Arthur; 5 Bt (UK 1904), of Gartmore, Co Perth; s of Sir Charles William Cayzer, 3 Bt, MP (d 1940), and Eileen, OBE (d 1981), da of James Meakin (d 1912), and Emma Beatrice (d 1935), later wife of 3 Earl Sondes; suc his bro, Sir Nigel John Cayzer, 4 Bt, 1943; *b* 15 Nov 1931; *Educ* Eton; *Heir* kinsman, Lord Cayzer; *Career* dir Caledonia Investments 1958-88, Cayzer Trust Co 1988-; *Clubs* Carlton; *Style*— Sir James Cayzer, Bt; Kinpurnie Castle, Newtyle, Angus PH12 8TW (☎ 082 85 207)

CAYZER, Baron (Life Peer UK 1981), of St Mary Axe in the City of London; Sir (William) Nicholas Cayzer; 2nd Bt (UK 1921), of Roffey Park, Horsham, Co Sussex; er s of Sir August Cayzer, 1 Bt, JP (d 1943, himself 3 s of Sir Charles Cayzer, 1s Bt, of Gartmore), and Ina, da of William Stancomb, JP; hp of 1 cous once removed, Sir James Cayzer, 5th Bt, of Gartmore; *b* 21 Jan 1910; *Educ* Eton, CCC Cambridge; *m* 1935, Elizabeth Catherine, da of late Owain Williams; 2 da (Hon Nichola (Hon Mrs Colvin) b 1937, Hon Elizabeth b 1946); *Heir* (to Btcy only) none; *Career* chm: Caledonia Investment, Clan Line Steamers 1928-87, Cayzer Irvine & Co Ltd 1929-87, Union Castle Mail Steamship Co Ltd 1955-87; *Style*— The Rt Hon the Lord Cayzer; 95 Eaton Square, London SW1 (☎ 071 235 5551); The Grove, Walsham-le-Willows, Suffolk (☎ 0359 259 263)

CAYZER, Nigel Kenneth; s of Anthony Galliers-Pratt, of Mawley Hall, Worcs, and Angela, da of Sir Charles Cayzer, 3 Bt (decd); *b* 30 April 1954; *Educ* Eton; *m* 1986, Henrietta, da of Sir Richard Sykes 7 Bt (d 1978); 1 s (b 24 March 1988), 1 da (b 17 Jan 1990); *Career* chm Allied Insur Brokers Gp plc; *Clubs* Turf, White's; *Style*— Nigel Cayzer, Esq; Thriepley House, Lundie, Dundee DD2 5PA (☎ 0382 581268); 15 West Halkin Street, London SW1 (☎ 071 235 1478)

CAYZER, Hon (Herbert) Robin; eld s and h of 2nd Baron Rotherwick; *b* 12 March 1954; *Educ* Harrow; *m* 1982, Sara J M, da of R J McAlpine, of Swettenham Hall, Swettenham, Cheshire, and Mrs J McAlpine, of Lower Carden Hall, Malpas, Cheshire; 1 da (Harriette b 1986); *Style*— The Hon Herbert Cayzer

CAZALET, Hon Lady (Camilla Jane); *née* Gage; da of 6 Viscount Gage, KCVO, by his 1 w, Hon Imogen Grenfell; *b* 12 July 1937; *Educ* Benenden; *m* 24 April 1965, Hon Sir Edward Stephen Cazalet (Hon Mr Justice Cazalet), *qv*; 2 s, 1 da; *Career* dir Lumley Cazalet 1967-; tstee Glyndebourne Arts Tst 1978-; *Recreations* tennis, music; *Clubs* Queen's; *Style*— The Hon Lady Cazalet; Shaw Farm, Plumpton Green, Lewes, Sussex BN7 3DG (☎ 0273 890 207); 58 Seymour Walk, London SW10 9NF (☎ 071 352 0401)

CAZALET, Hon Mr Justice; Sir Edward Stephen; DL (E Sussex 1989); s of Peter Victor Ferdinand Cazalet, JP, DL (d 1973), the race horse trainer, and his 1 w, Leonora, *née* Rowley, step da of Sir P G Wodehouse; *b* 26 April 1936; *Educ* Eton, ChCh Oxford; *m* 24 April 1965, Hon Camilla Jane, da of Viscount Gage, KCVO; 2 s (David b 1967, Hal b 1969), 1 da (Lara b 1973); *Career* subaltern Welsh Guards 1954-56; barr; chm Horse Race Betting Levy Appeal Tbnl 1979-88, QC 1980-88; bencher Inner Temple 1985, rec of Crown Court 1985-88, judge of the High Court of Justice 1988-; fell Eton Coll 1989; kt 1988; *Recreations* riding, ball games, chess; *Clubs* Garrick, White's; *Style*— The Hon Mr Justice Cazalet, DL; Royal Courts of Justice, Strand, London WC2A 2LL

CAZALET, Lady; Elise; da of James Percival Winterbotham, of Cheltenham; *m* 1928, Vice Adm Sir Peter Grenville Lyon Cazalet, KBE, CB, DSO and bar, DSC (d 1982); 4 s; *Style*— Lady Cazalet; 16 High Hurst Close, Newick, Lewes, E Sussex

CAZALET, (Charles) Julian; s of Vice Adm Sir Peter Grenville Lyon Cazalet, KBE, CB, DSO, DSC (d 1982), of Newick, E Sussex, and Lady Beatrice Elise, *née* Winterbotham; *b* 29 Nov 1947; *Educ* Uppingham, Magdalene Coll Cambridge (MA); *m* 29 Nov 1986, Jennifer Clare, da of Maurice Nelson Little (d 1985), of Laverton, Gloucs; 1 s (Charles b 1987), 1 da (Fleur b 1989); *Career* ptnr Cazenove and Co Stockbrokers 1978-; FCA 1977; *Recreations* sailing, skiing; *Clubs* City Univ; *Style*— Julian Cazalet, Esq; 38 Norland Sq, London W11 4PZ (☎ 071 727 1756); Cazenove and Co, 12 Tokenhouse Yard, London EC2R 7AN (☎ 071 588 2828, fax 071 606 9205)

CAZALET, Sir Peter Grenville; s of Vice Adm Sir Peter Grenville Lyon Cazalet, KBE, CB, DSO, DSC (d 1982), and Beatrice Elise, *née* Winterbotham, *qv*; *b* 26 Feb 1929; *Educ* Uppingham, Magdalene Coll Cambridge (MA); *m* 1957, Jane Jennifer, yr da of Charles Harry Rew (d 1972), of Guernsey; 3 s; *Career* dep chm BP Petroleum Co plc 1986-89 (md 1981-); dir: P and O Steam Navigation Co Ltd 1980-, Thomas De la Rue Co plc 1983-; chm APV plc 1989-, dep chm GKN plc 1989-; tstee The Wellcome Tst 1989-; kt 1989; *Recreations* theatre, travel; *Clubs* Brooks's, Royal Wimbledon Golf, MCC; *Style*— Sir Peter Cazalet; APV plc, 2 Lygon Place, London SW1W 0JR (☎ 071 730 7244, fax 071 730 2660, telex 92546

CAZALET, Raymond Percival Saint George; s of Vice Adm Sir Peter Genville Lyon Cazalet, KBE, CB, DSO, DSC; *b* 23 April 1931; *Educ* Uppingham Sch; *m* 1962, Deborah Caroline, *née* Fuggles-Couchman; 3 s; *Career* chief accountant Marshall-Andrew and Co Ltd 1959-61, chm Henderson Administration Ltd 1961-; FCA; *Recreations* tennis; *Clubs* City of London; *Style*— Raymond Cazalet, Esq; 4 Kelso Pla, London W8 (☎ 071 937 6446)

CAZALY, Peter Bernard; s of Bernard Philip Cazaly (d 1978), of Ripley, Surrey, and Clarice, *née* Neale; *b* 19 Sept 1934; *Educ* Kingstone GS; *m* 30 March 1957, Valerie Joy, da of Philip Hutton (d 1968), of Stoneleigh, Surrey; 1 s (Howard b 1958), 1 da (Belinda Jane b 1960); *Career* RAF 1951-54; TV sound operator BBC 1955-58, tech supervisor ABC TV 1958-68, dir of prodn London Weekend TV Ltd 1968-89, md London Weekend TV Prodn Facilities Ltd 1989-; memb: RTS, BAFTA; *Style*— Peter Cazaly, Esq; Claremont, Bunch Lane, Haslemere, Surrey GU27 1ET (☎ 0428 61317); SE1 9LT (☎ 071 261 3114, fax 071 261 3111, car 0860 268765)

CAZENOVE, Bernard Michael de Lerisson; TD; s of late David Michael de Lerisson Cazenove, and Euphemia, *née* MacLean; *b* 14 June 1947; *Educ* Radley, RMA Sandhurst; *m* 19 Dec 1971, Caroline June, da of Richard Moore (d 1963), of Wellington, NZ; 2 s (Richard b 1974, George b 1977), 1 da (Edwina b 1984); *Career* cmmnd Coldstream Guard 1967, ADC to HE Governor General of New Zealand 1970, transferred Parachute Regt (TA) 1973; ptnr Cazenove and Co (Stock Brokers) 1982- (joined 1973); memb Int Stock Exchange; *Clubs* Whites, Pratts; *Style*— Bernard Cazenove, Esq, TD; 20 Edenhurst Ave, London SW6 3PB; Cazenove & Co, 12 Tokenhouse Yard, London EC2 7AN (☎ 071 588 2828)

CAZENOVE, Christopher Lerisson; s of Brig Arnold de Lerisson Cazenove, CBE, DSO, MVO (d 1969; descended from Arnaud de Cazenove, Seigneur de Lerisson, of Guienne, France who m 1, 1578, Anne de Bruil, and m 2, 1596, Marie de Laumond), and Elizabeth Laura, 3 da of late Sir Eustace Gurney, JP, of Walsingham Abbey, Norfolk; *b* 17 Dec 1943; *Educ* Eton, Bristol Old Vic Theatre Sch; *m* 8 Sept 1973, Angharad Mary Rees, the actress, da of Prof Linford Rees, CBE, FRCP, FRCPsych; 2 s (Linford b 20 July 1974, Rhys William b 12 Dec 1976); *Career* actor; West End: The Lionel Touch 1969, My Darling Daisy 1970, The Winslow Boy 1970, Joking Apart 1979; Broadway: Goodbye Fidel 1980; TV incl: The Regiment 1971-72, The British Hero, The Pathfinders, K is for Killer 1973, Duchess of Duke Street 1976-77, Jenny's War, Lace II, Dynasty 1986-87, Ticket to Ride 1988-89, To Be the Best 1990; Films incl: Royal Flash 1975, East of Elephant Rock 1976, Zulu Dawn 1979, Eye of the Needle 1980, From A Far Country 1980, Heat and Dust 1982, Until September 1984, The Fantasist 1985, Souvenir 1987, Hold my Hand I'm Dying 1988, Three Men And a Little Lady 1990, Aces 1991; *Style*— Christopher Cazenove, Esq; c/o Michael Whitehall, 124 Gloucester Rd, London SW1

CAZENOVE, Henry de Lerisson; s of Maj Philip Henry de Lerisson Cazenove, TD, of Cottesbrooke Cottage, Northampton (d 1978), and Aurea Ethelwyn Allix; *b* 13 Jan 1943; *Educ* Eton; *Career* Lt Northamptonshire Yeo TA (now disbanded) 1963-69; ptnr Cazenove and Co 1972- (joined 1963); memb Stock Exchange; govr and tstee St Andrews Hosp, Northampton; Freeman City of London 1980; *Books* A Short History of The Northamptonshire Yeomanry (1966); *Recreations* shooting, travel, gardening; *Clubs* White's, Pratt's, City of London, MCC; *Style*— Henry Cazenove, Esq; Cottesbrooke Cottage, Northampton; Milner St, London, SW3; Cazenove and Co, 12 Tokenhouse Yard, London, EC2 (☎ 071 588 2828)

CECIL, Hon Anthony Henry Amherst; yr s of 3 Baron Amherst of Hackney, CBE (d 1980); *b* 1 April 1947; *Educ* Eton; *m* 1, 1969 (m dis 1974), Fenella Jane, da of David George Crichton, MVO; m 2, 1974, Jane Elizabeth, da of Philip Norman Elston Holbrook; 2 s (Henry Edward Amherst b 1976, Thomas Anthony Amherst b 1981), 1 da (Georgiana Helen Amherst b 1979); *Style*— The Hon Anthony Cecil; Bucks Farm, Shorwell, Isle of Wight

CECIL, Hon Anthony Robert; s and h of 3 Baron Rockley, and Lady Sarah Primrose Beatrix, da of 7 Earl Cadogan, MC; *b* 29 July 1961; *Educ* Eton, Cambridge; *m* 9 Jan 1988, Katherine Jane, da of G A Whalley, of Chipperfield, Herts; *Recreations* rugby, squash, tennis; *Style*— The Hon Anthony Cecil; Lytchett Heath, Poole, Dorset (☎ 0202 622228)

CECIL, Hon Camilla Sarah; da of 3 Baron Rockley; *b* 8 Feb 1965; *Educ* North Foreland Lodge, Cambridge Coll of Arts; *Career* magazine journalist; *Style*— The Hon Camilla Cecil

CECIL, Lord Charles Edward Vere (Gascoyne-); s of 6 Marquess of Salisbury; *b* 13 July 1949; *Educ* Eton, Ch Ch Oxford; *Career* md Berkeley Govett (UK) Ltd; pres Herts Assoc Youth Clubs, vice chm Rambert Dance Co; *Clubs* Turf, Beefsteak, Pratt's; *Style*— The Lord Charles Cecil; 21 Hollywood Rd, London SW10 (☎ 071 352 1169)

CECIL, Hon Charles Evelyn; 2 s of 2 Baron Rockley; *b* 15 Nov 1936; *Educ* Eton; *m* 1965, Jennifer, da of Duncan Mackinnon and Pamela, da of Capt Robert Brassey, JP, DL (nephew of 1 Earl Brassey, JP, DL, and 1 cous of 1 Baron Brassey of Apethorpe, JP, DL; Pamela's mother was the Capt's 1 w, Violet Lowry-Corry, great niece of 3 Earl Belmore; the Capt's mother was Hon Matilda Bingham, OBE, da of 4 Baron Clanmorris) and 2 cous of the writer Charlotte Bingham; 1 s, 2 da; *Style*— The Hon Charles Cecil; Wilcote House, Charlbury, Oxon (☎ 099 386 355)

CECIL, Henry Richard Amherst; 4 s (twin) of Hon Henry Kerr Auchmuty Cecil (ka 1942), and Elizabeth Rohays Mary, *née* Burnett of Leys (later Lady Boyd-Rochfort); *b* 11 Jan 1943; *Educ* Canford, RAC Cirencester; *m* 18 Oct 1966 (m dis), Julia, da of Sir (Charles Francis) Noel Murless (d 1987); 1 s (Noel b 3 Feb 1973), 1 da (Katrina b 17 June 1971); *Career* leading racehorse trainer on the flat; trained 2 Derby winners, 2 Oaks winners, 2 2000 Guineas winners, 3 1000 Guineas winners, and 4 St Leger winners; *Books* On The Level; *Recreations* gardening; Warren Place, Newmarket, (Suffolk CB8 8QQ (☎ 0638 662387); office ☎ 0638 662192; fax, 0638 669005; telex , 817759 CECIL G)

CECIL, Jonathan Hugh; s of Lord Edward Christian David Gascoyne Cecil, CH (d 1986), of Red Lion House, Cranborne, and Rachel Mary Veronica, *née* MacCarthy (d 1982); *b* 22 Feb 1939; *Educ* Eton, New Coll Oxford (BA), LAMDA; *m* 1, 1963, Vivien Sarah Frances, da of David G Heilbron, of Glasgow; m 2, 3 Nov 1976, Anna Sharkey; *Career* actor and writer; theatre incl: A Heritage and its History 1965, Halfway Up the Tree 1967, The Ruling Class 1969, Lulu 1971, Cowardy Custard 1972, The Bed Before Yesterday 1976, The Orchestra 1981, Good Morning Bill 1987, Uncle Vanya 1988, Poor Nanny 1989, The Dressmaker 1990; films incl: The Great St Trinians Train Robbery 1965, Otley 1968, Catch Me a Spy 1971, Barry Lyndon 1973, Joseph Andrews 1976, History of the World Part 1 1980, E la Nave Va (Fellini) 1983, The Fool 1990, Tchin Tchin 1990; tv incl: Maggie 1964, Loves Labours Lost 1975, Gulliver in Lilliput 1981, The Puppet Man 1984, 13 at Dinner 1985, Murder in 3 Acts 1987, The Sign of Command 1989; has also starred in numerous comedy series; contrib to: The Independent, The Spectator, The Evening Standard; *Recreations* writing, reading, history of theatre and music hall; *Clubs* Garrick; *Style*— Jonathan Cecil, Esq; c/o Kate Feast Management, 43A Princess Rd, London NW1 (☎ 071 586 5502)

CECIL, Lord Michael Hugh (Gascoyne-); s of 6 Marquess of Salisbury; *b* 1960; *m* 1986, Camilla, da of late Maj Richard Scott; 1 da (b 23 Oct 1989); *Career* cmmnd Grenadier Gds 1980; *Style*— The Lord Michael Cecil

CECIL, Rear Adm Sir (Oswald) Nigel Amherst; KBE (1979), CB (1978); s of Cdr the Hon Henry Cecil, OBE, RN (d 1962; himself 4 s of Baroness Amherst of Hackney by her husb Lord William Cecil, CVO, 3 s of 3 Marquess of Exeter) and Hon Yvonne Cornwallis (d 1983), 3 da of 1 Baron Cornwallis; *b* 11 Nov 1925; *Educ* Ludgrove, RNC Dartmouth; *m* 1961, Annette (CStJ 1980), er da of Maj Robert Barclay, TD, of Bury Hill, Dorking, Surrey; 1 s (Robert b 1965); *Career* joined Navy 1939, Flag Lt to Adm Br Jt Services Mission Washington DC 1948-50, Cdr 1959, Chief Staff Officer London Division RNR 1959-61; cmd: HMS Corunna 1961-63, HMS Royal Arthur 1963-66, Capt 1966; Central Defence Staff 1966-69; Capt (D) Dartmouth Trg Sqdn and in cmd HM Ships Tenby and Scarborough 1969-71, Cdre Sr Br Naval Offr S Africa, naval attaché Cape Town and in cmd HMS Afrikander 1971-73, dir Naval Operational Requirements 1974-75, Naval ADC to HM The Queen 1975, Rear Adm 1975, Cdr Br Forces Malta and flag offr Malta 1975-79, Cdr NATO S Eastern Mediterranean 1975-77, ret 1979; Lt-Govr IOM 1980-85; dir Asheville Construction Co 1987-; KStJ 1980 (OStJ 1971); FBIM 1980; *Clubs* White's, MCC; *Style*— Rear Adm Sir Nigel Cecil, KBE, CB; c/o C Hoare and Co, 37 Fleet St, London EC4P 4DQ

CECIL, Robert; CMG (1959); s of Charles Cecil (d 1916), of Southbourne, Bournemouth, and Marjorie, *née* Porteous (d 1965); *b* 25 March 1913; *Educ* Wellington Coll, Cambridge (MA); *m* 17 Sept 1938, Kathleen Mary, da of Col Cecil Colvile Marindin, CBE, DSO (d 1932); 1 s (Robert Eden b 1945), 2 da (Veronica b 1941, Brigid b 1944); *Career* head of American Dept FO 1951, consul gen Hanover 1955, DG Br Info Servs NY 1959, head of cultural rels FO 1962, reader in German history Univ of Reading 1968, chm Grad Sch of Euro Studies Reading 1976; chm Inst for Cultural Res 1966-90; *Books* Life in Edwardian England (1969), Myth of the Master Race (1972), Hitler's Decision to Invade Russia (1975), A Divided Life, Biography of Donald Maclean (1988); *Recreations* writing poetry; *Style*— Robert Cecil, Esq, CMG

CECIL, Lady Rose Alice Elizabeth (Gascoyne-); has retained her maiden name; da of 6 Marquess of Salisbury, *qv*; *b* 11 Sept 1956; *Educ* privately; *m* 9 Feb 1985, Mark Flawn Thomas, yst s of Peter Flawn Thomas, of Shortbridge Hill, Sussex; *Career* artist; *Recreations* travelling, motorbikes, opera, films; *Style*— The Lady Rose Cecil

CECIL, Lord Valentine William (Gascoyne-); s of 6 Marquess of Salisbury; *b* 13 May 1952; *Educ* Eton; *Career* a page of honour to HM Queen Elizabeth The Queen Mother 1966-67, Major Gren Gds; *Recreations* shooting, flying; *Clubs* Turf, Pratt's, Special Forces, Beefsteak; *Style*— The Lord Valentine Cecil; c/o Hatfield House, Hatfield, Herts; 11 Shalcomb Street, London SW10

CELESTIN, (Louis) Roger; s of Louis Abel Celestin CBE, MC (d 1955), of Mauritius, and Marie Marcelle, *née* Legris (d 1962); *b* 19 Oct 1925; *Educ* Royal Coll of Mauritius, UCL (MB BS); *m* 1, 6 Aug 1954 (m dis 1967), Patricia Irene, da of Herbert Bernard Thomas; 2 da (Claire b 1957, Michele b 1958); m 2, 4 July 1968, Shirley June, da of Harry Gledhill; *Career* surgn and gastroenterologist; registrar Royal Postgrad Med Sch

Hammersmith Hosp, sr registrar Bristol Royal Infirmary, conslt surgn Frenchay Hosp 1968-, clinical lectr Univ of Bristol 1968-; author of chapters in numerous maj textbooks, inventor of oesophageal prosthesis and oesophageal dilators; pres: Anglo-French Med Soc 1985-, Cossham Med Soc 1989-90; past pres Ileostomy Assoc, ARRIS and Gale lectr RCS 1973; FRCS, FRCSEd, Br Soc of Endoscopy, Br Soc of Gastroenterology; *Books* Disorders of the Oesophagus (with Watson, 1984), The Surgery and Management of Intestinal Stomas (1987); *Recreations* travelling, numismatics, opera; *Style—* Roger Celestin, Esq; Sutton House, Clifton Down, The Promenade, Clifton, Bristol BS8 3HT (☎ 0272 737360); Departments of Surgery and of Gastroenterology, Frenchay Hospital, Bristol BS16 ILE (☎ 0272 701212)

CELLAN-JONES, (Alan) James Gwynne; s of Cecil John Cellan-Jones, OBE (d 1968, Lt-Col RAMC), of Swansea, and Lavinia Alicia Sophia, *née* Johnson-Dailey, MBE (d 1963); *b* 13 July 1931; *Educ* Dragon Sch, Lycée Jaccard Lausanne, Charterhouse, St John's Coll Cambridge (BA, MA); *m* 2 April 1959, Margaret Shirley, da of Ernest William Eavis (d 1972), of Burnham on Sea; 3 s (Rory b 1960, Simon b 1962, Deiniol b 1965), 1 da (Lavinia b 1967); *Career* Nat Serv cmmnd RE 1953, Troop Cdr Korea later Airborne; dir BBC 1963 (joined as callboy 1950); freelance dir: Forsyte Saga, Portrait of a Lady, Jennie (with Lee Remick), Caesar and Cleopatra (with Alec Guinness); dir: The Kingfisher (with Rex Harrison), Bequest to the Nation (with Peter Finch and Glenda Jackson), Much Ado About Nothing (Royal Lyceum Edinburgh), The Adams Chronicles NY 1976-; head of plays BBC TV 1976-79; dir: School Play, The Day Christ Died, A Fine Romance, Oxbridge Blues, Comedy of Errors, Fortunes of War, A Perfect Hero; writer; DGA award 1976, Cable award 1985; memb: Cncl DGGB (vice pres 1989), BAFTA (chm 1983-85); *Recreations* scuba diving, wine making; *Clubs* Garrick; *Style—* James Cellan-Jones, Esq; 19 Cumberland Ave, Kew, Surrey (☎ 081 940 8742); Worthy Cottage, Pilton, nr Shepton Mallet, Somerset ; c/o Jane Annakin, Wm Morris (UK) Ltd, 20th Century House, Soho Square, London W1 (☎ 071 434 2192)

CELLAN-JONES, (Nicholas) Rory; s of James Cellan-Jones, of Kew, Surrey, and Sylvia, *née* Parish; *b* 17 Jan 1958; *Educ* Dulwich, Jesus Coll Cambridge (BA); *m* 7 April 1990, Diane Coyle; 1 s (Adam Joseph b 13 Sept 1990); *Career* BBC TV: researcher Look North BBC Leeds 1981-83, 1983-85 (sub ed TV News London, asst prod Newsnight, prodr TV News Special Projects), reporter BBC Wales Cardiff, reporter Breakfast Time 1988, business reporter TV News 1989-90, reporter Money Programme 1990-; *Style—* Rory Cellan-Jones, Esq; BBC TV, Lime Grove, London W12 7RU (☎ 081 576 1122)

CELY TREVILIAN, Maj Richard Edwin Fearing; TD, DL (Somerset 1982); Lord of the Manors of Midelney and Drayton; eld s of Maj Maurice Fearing Cely Trevilian, JP, DL (d 1932), and Mary, *née* Athill; *b* 25 Dec 1912; *Educ* Radley; *m* 26 Sept 1936, Daphne Olive, o da of Sir Digby Lawson, 2 Bt, TD, JP; 1 s, 3 da; *Career* served WW II as Maj in N Somerset Yeo in M East, Mediterranean, NW Europe (despatches); High Sheriff Somerset 1961; hon fellow Woodard Corpn; *Recreations* country pursuits; *Clubs* Army and Navy, MCC; *Style—* Major Richard Cely Trevilian, TD, DL; Midelney Manor, Drayton, Langport, Somerset (☎ 0458 251229)

CENTNER, Hon Mrs (Anne Catherine); da of 2 Viscount Leathers; *b* 1 Jan 1944; *Educ* Benenden; *m* 1977, Arthur Sydney Centner; 1 da (Lucy Emma b 1977); *Style—* The Hon Mrs Centner; 11 Orchard Road, Orchards, Johannesburg 2192, South Africa

CHACKSFIELD, Air Vice-Marshal Sir Bernard Albert; KBE (1968, OBE 1945), CB (1961); s of Edgar Chacksfield (d 1919), of Ilford, Essex; *b* 13 April 1913; *Educ* County HS, RAF Halton, RAF Cranwell; *m* 1, 1937, Myrtle Elsa Alexena (d 1984), da of Walter Matthews (d 1947), of Rickmansworth, Herts; 2 s, 2 da; m 2, 1985, Elizabeth Beatrice, da of James Meek (d 1969), and wid of Frederick Ody (d 1982); *Career* joined RAF 1928, Gp Capt 1951, Air Cdre 1956 (Fighter Cmd), Actg Air Vice-Marshal SASO Tech Trg Cmd 1960, AOC No 22 Group 1960-62, Cmdt-Gen RAF Regt and Inspr Ground Defence 1963-68, ret 1968; chief cmmr Scouts for England 1968-80, pres Soc Aeronautical Engrs (now Br Model Flying Assoc) 1969-; chm: Burma Star Assoc 1979-, Bd Royal Masonic Hosp 1988-; CEng, FRAeS; *Recreations* travelling, youth work, flying, sailing, music, drama; *Clubs* RAF; *Style—* Air Vice-Marshal Sir Bernard Chacksfield, KBE, CB; No 8 Rowan House, Bourne End, Bucks SL8 5TG (☎ 062 85 20829)

CHADD, David Francis Lanfear; s of Joseph Chadd (d 1976), and Hilda Birica Lanfear (d 1983); *b* 10 Sept 1943; *Educ* Keble Coll Oxford (MA); *m* 23 Sept 1983, Julia Mary Martin, da of Dr Alan John Rowe, OBE, of Haughley Grange, Stowmarket, Suffolk; 2 s (Alexander b 1984, Tobias b 1988), 1 da (Helena b 1986); *Career* asst lectr Univ of Durham 1966-67; UEA: lectr 1967-79, sr lectr 1979, dean Sch of Art History and Music 1987-90; sec Henry Bradshaw Soc 1985-, memb Int Advsy Ed Bd Plain Song and Medieval Music 1989-; numerous articles in learned jnls and collections; *Recreations* gardening, mountaineering, visual arts, repairing old houses; *Style—* David Chadd, Esq; Thornage Old Rectory, Holt, North Norfolk (☎ 0263 861096); University of East Anglia, Norwich (☎ 0603 592454, fax 0603 58553)

CHADD, Col George Victor Nudd; OBE (1973), TD (1974), JP (1950), DL (1972); s of George Bertie Chadd (d 1940), of Four Stones, Corton, Lowestoft , Suffolk, and Ellen Edith, *née* Nudd (d 1966); *b* 19 Sept 1907; *Educ* Bishop's Stortford Coll, Sorbonne Paris; *m* 10 June 1950, Margaret Ruth, da of Sir Henry Seymour Collett, 2 Bt (d 1972), of The Knoll, Stone Rd, Bromley Kent: 4 s (Christopher George Andrew b 1951 d 1974, (Richard) Jonathon b 1953, Timothy Charles b 1955 d 1976, Nicholas Martyn Philip b 1958); *Career* Inf Bn HAC 1926-30, Capt 103 Suffolk Field Bde RA (TA) 1930, Maj Batty Cmd 107 HAA Regt RA 1940, Lt-Col CO 100 HAA Regt RA 1941, serv in UK ME N Africa Sicily Italy (dispatches), Mil Cmdt No 2 Internment Camp Italy 1945-46, CO 660 HAA Regt RA (TA) 1947-50, TARO 1950-58, Col dep Cmdt Suffolk ACF 1958-60, Cmdt Suffolk ACF 1961-68, chm Suffolk TAVR and Cadets 1967-76, Hon Col Suffolk ACF 1975-82; dir GB Chadd Ltd 1929, chm and md GB Chadd (Hldgs) Ltd and assoc cos 1948-; former chm Suffolk TAVR Assoc, vice chm Lowestoft Borough Bench, chm Broads One Design Club 1972-; High Steward of Southwold Suffolk 1967; *Recreations* skiing, sailing, tennis, swimming, hunting; *Clubs* Naval and Military, Royal Norfolk and Suffolk Yacht, Broads One Design (Yacht BOD 'Harlequin'), Br Ski; *Style—* Col George Chadd, OBE, TD, JP, DL; Mardle House, Wangford, Beccles, Suffolk NR34 8AU (☎ 0502 78 334); GB Chadd Hldgs Ltd, 66/76 London Rd North, Lowestoft, Suffolk NR32 1ES (☎ 0502 572391, fax 0502 501483)

CHADD, Mrs Margaret Ruth; MBE (1991), JP (Suffolk 1968); da of Sir Henry Collett, 2 Bt, of The Knoll, Stone Rd, Bromley, Kent, and Ruth Mildred, *née* Hatch; *b* 7 June 1922; *Educ* Kinnaird Park Sch Bromley, LSE, Inst of Hosp Almoners (AIMSW); *m* 10 June 1950, Col George V N Chadd, OBE, TD, JP, DL, s of George Bertie Chadd (d 1940), of Four Stones, Corton, nr Lowestoft, Suffolk; 4 s (Christopher George Andrew b 1951, d 1974, Richard Jonathan b 1953, Timothy Charles b 1955 d 1976, Nicholas Martin Philip b 1958); *Career* hosp almoner Queen Victoria Hosp E Grinstead Sussex 1941-45, co almoner E Sussex CC Lewes Sussex 1948-50, dir GB Chadd (Holdings) Ltd Lowestoft Suffolk; joined BRCS 1941 (now welfare offr and hon vice pres Suffolk Branch); hon organising sec Waveney & N Suffolk CRUSE (bereavement care) 1978-, fndr tstee PACT Suffolk (parents conciliation tst) 1987; BASW; *Books* The Collett Saga (1988), Senescali Sudwoldienses being Lives of the High Stewards of Southwold (with Alan Bottomley, 1989); *Recreations* skiing, sailing, tennis, gardening, genealogy, swimming; *Clubs* VAD, Women of the Year Assoc; *Style—* Mrs Margaret Chadd, MBE, JP; Mardle House, Wangford, nr Beccles, Suffolk NR34 8AU (☎ 0502 78334); G B Chadd (Holdings) Ltd, London Rd, North Lowestoft, Suffolk (☎ 0502 588 085)

CHADWICK, Dr David William; s of Harold Chadwick (d 1979), of Rochdale, and Elsie, *née* Mills (d 1983); *b* 14 Dec 1946; *Educ* Bolton Sch, St Catherine's Coll Oxford (MA, DM); *m* 30 July 1969, Vivienne Ruth, da of Richard Jones (d 1979), of St Helens; 1 s (Benjamin b 1975), 1 da (Ellen b 1977); *Career* lectr neurology Univ Dept Neurology Inst Psychiatry London 1974-76, first asst neurology Univ of Newcastle-upon-Tyne 1978-79, conslt neurologist Mersey RHA 1979-; sec Br branch Int League Against Epilepsy 1984-88; FRCP 1984; *Books* Living With Epilepsy (1987), Medical Neurology (1989); *Style—* Dr David Chadwick; Dept of Med and Surgical Neurology, Walton Hosp, Rice Lane, Liverpool L9 1AE (☎ 051 525 3611 ext 4348)

CHADWICK, Derek James; s of Dennis Edmund Chadwick (d 1955), and Ida Chadwick (d 1979); *b* 9 Feb 1948; *Educ* St Joseph's Coll Blackpool, Keble Coll Oxford (Pfizer Industl scholar, Open scholar, sr scholar, BA, BSc, MA, DPhil); *m* 20 Dec 1980, Susan, da of Dr (Hugh) Alastair Reid, OBE (d 1983); 2 s (Andrew John b 1984, (Frederick) Mark b 1986); *Career* ICI fell Univ of Cambridge 1972-73, Prize fell Magdalen Coll Oxford 1973-77, Royal Soc Euro Exchange fell ETH-Zürich (Switzerland) 1975-77; Univ of Liverpool 1977-88: lectr, sr lectr, reader; Emilio Noelting visiting prof Ecole Nationale Supérieur Mulhouse France 1988; dir The Ciba Fndn London 1988-; memb Worshipful Soc of Apothecaries of London 1990; FRSC 1982; *Books* contrib to: Aromatic & Heteroaromatic Chemistry (1979), Comprehensive Heterocyclic Chemistry (1984), The Research and Academic Users' Guide to the IBMPC (1988), Physical and Theoretical Aspects of 1H-Pyrroles (1990); *Recreations* gardening, music, skiing; *Style—* Dr Derek Chadwick; 4 Bromley Ave, Bromley, Kent BR1 4BQ (☎ 081 460 3332); The Ciba Foundation, 41 Portland Place, London W1N 4BN (☎ 071 636 9456, fax 071 436 2840)

CHADWICK, Donald; s of Rennie Chadwick (d 1944); *b* 12 March 1934; *Educ* Bury GS; *m* 1955, Sheila Mary, da of Norman Jackson, of Lilliesleaf; 3 children; *Career* accountant; fin dir Carrington Viyella Ltd 1962-80, md Claridge Mills Ltd 1980-86 (weavers of wool, silk, cashmere; Queen's Award for Export 1982 and 1987); md Ledatec Ltd (mfrs of Non-Woven Textiles); FCMA; *Recreations* golf; *Clubs* Selkirk Rotary; *Style—* Donald Chadwick, Esq; Ruberslaw, Midlem, Selkirk (☎ 083 57 469); Ledatec Ltd, Blackburn, Lancs (☎ 0254 56 413)

CHADWICK, Fiona Jane; da of William Max Darrowclough Chadwick (d 1989), and Anne, *née* Whithead; *b* 13 May 1960; *Educ* Royal Ballet Sch; *Career* ballerina; Royal Ballet Co: joined 1978, soloist 1981, princ 1984; danced leading roles incl: Swan Lake, Sleeping Beauty, Giselle, The Nutcracker Suite, Romeo and Juliet, La Fille Mac Gardee, Cinderella, Ride of Spring, Apollo, Prince of the Pagodas, Bayadere, Scenes of Ballet, Firebird, Daiser de la Fee, Gloria, Galanteries Pursuit; *Style—* Miss Fiona Chadwick; Royal Opera House, Covent Garden, London WC2 (☎ 071 240 1200)

CHADWICK, Lady Georgia Mary Caroline; *née* Byng; er da of 8 Earl of Strafford, *qv*, and Mrs Christopher Bland; *b* 6 Sept 1965; *m* 11 Oct 1990, Daniel S Chadwick, yr s of Lynn Chadwick, of Lypiatt, Glos; *Style—* The Lady Georgia Chadwick

CHADWICK, Helen; da of William Clare Chadwick, of Surrey, and Angelina Polynikis Bardopoulou; *b* 18 May 1953; *Educ* Croydon HS, Brighton Poly (BA), Chelsea Sch of Art (MA); *Career* artist 1977-; solo exhibitions: In the Kitchen (Art Nat London) 1978, Train of Thought (Acme Gallery London, Spectre Gallery Newcastle) 1978-79, Fine Art/Fine Ale (Sheffield Poly) 1982, Ego Geometria Sum (Art and Res Exchange Belfast, Aspex Gallery Portsmouth, Riverside Studios London) 1983-85, Of Mutability (ICA London, Ikon Gallery Birmingham, Harris Museum Preston, Kunstvereun Freiburg, Third Eye Centre Glasgow) 1986-87, Blood Hyphen (Clerkenwell Med Mission London for Edge '88) 1988, Viral Landscapes (Museum of Modern Art Oxford) 1989 and (121 Art Gallery Antwerp, Friedman Guinness Gallery Frankfurt) 1990, Meat Lamps (Ehlers Caudhill Gallery Chicago, Burden Gallery Aperture Fndn NY) 1990; gp exhibitions incl: New Contemporaries (Film Co-op London) 1977, Some Sculpture Now (Brighton Poly Gallery) 1983, Performance Art (film prog Tate Gallery London) 1985, Staging the Self (Nat Portrait Gallery London and touring) 1986, The Turner Prize (Tate Gallery London) 1987, Towards a Bigger Picture II (USA Museum, Tate Gallery, Liverpool) 1988, Photography Now (USA Museum London) 1989, Images of Women (Leeds City Museum & Art Gallery) 1989, In Her Image (Barlowe Toll Fine Arts NY) 1990, Withdrawal: Objects, Signs, Commodities (forum Stadtpark Graz) 1990; author and contrib numerous catalogues and other pubns incl: New Perspectives on the Nude (ffotogallery Cardiff, 1983), Staging the Self (Nat Portrait Gallery London) 1986, The Nude 1989, Images of Women (Leeds City Art Galleries) 1989, Enfleshings 1989, British Art Now: A Subjective View 1990; work in several pub collections; *Awards* Arts Cncl film distribution award 1980, Artist in Indust fellowship (Yorkshire Arts & John Smith's Brewery) 1981, Gtr London Arts Assoc visual arts maj award 1981, Artist in Schs award (Northern Arts & Newcastle City Schs) 1983, artist in residence (Birmingham City Museum and Art Gallery and W Midlands Arts) 1986, shortlisted for Turner prize 1987, artist in nat parks (DOE, USA Museum, Pembrokeshire Nat Park 1988, Bill Brandt award 1990; *Style—* Ms Helen Chadwick; Interim Art, 20 Dering St, London W1R 9AA (☎ 071 495 4580, fax 495 3552)

CHADWICK, Prof Henry; KBE (1989); s of John Chadwick (d 1931), of Bromley, Kent, and Edith, *née* Horrocks; bro of late Sir John and Prof Owen Chadwick, *qv*, and of Lady McNicoll (w of Vice Adm Sir Alan McNicol, former Australian ambass to Turkey); *b* 23 June 1920; *Educ* Eton, Magdalene Coll Cambridge (DD); *m* 1945, Margaret Elizabeth, da of late W Pemell Brownrigg, of Moorhill, Co Kildare; *Career* former regius prof of divinity and canon of Ch Ch Oxford (dean 1969-79), hon canon of Ely 1979-, regius prof of divinity Univ of Cambridge 1979-82, master of Peterhouse Cambridge 1987-; fell Magdalene Coll Cambridge 1979-86; *Recreations* music; *Clubs* Royal Commonwealth, Cambridge Univ Wanderers (hockey), Oxford and Cambridge; *Style—* Prof Henry Chadwick, KBE; Peterhouse, Cambridge (☎ 0223 338211)

CHADWICK, Dr John; s of late Fred Chadwick, ISO, and late Margaret Pamela, *née* Bray; *b* 21 May 1920; *Educ* St Paul's, Corpus Christi Coll Cambridge (MA, LittD); *m* 10 July 1947, Joan Isobel, da of Thomas Edgar Hill, MBE (d 1963); 1 s (Anthony b 1954); *Career* WWII, Lt RNVSR 1940-45; ed asst Oxford Latin Dictionary 1946-52, P M Laurence reader in classics Univ of Cambridge 1966-84 (asst lectr 1952-54, lectr 1954-66), hon fell Downing Coll Cambridge 1984- (Collins fell 1960-84); hon degrees: Univ of Athens 1958, Université Libre de Bruxelles 1969, Trinity Coll Dublin 1971, Univ of the Basque Country 1985, Univ of Salzburg 1990; corr memb: Deutsches Archäologisches Institut zu Berlin 1957, Oesterreichische Akademie der Wissenschaften 1974, Académie des Inscriptions et Belles Lettres Institut de France 1975 (Associé étranger 1985); hon fell Athens Archaeological Soc 1974 (hon cncllr 1987), pres Swedenberg Soc London 1987; Cdr Order of the Phoenix Repub of Greece 1984; FBA; *Books* The Medical Works of Hippocrates (with W N Mann, 1950), Documents in Mycenaean Greek (with M Ventris, 1956), The Decipherment of Linear B (1958), The Mycenaean World (1976), Corpus of Mycenaean Inscriptions from Knossos Vol 1 (ed-in-chief, 1986), Linear B and Related Scripts (1987), E Swedenborg - The True Christian Religion (translator, 1988); *Recreations* travel; *Style*— Dr John Chadwick; 75 Gough Way, Cambridge CB3 9LN (☎ 0223 356864)

CHADWICK, (Gerald William St) John; CMG (1961); s of John Frederick Chadwick; *b* 28 May 1915; *Educ* Lancing, St Catharine's Coll Cambridge; *m* 1938, Madeleine, da of René Boucheron; 2 s; *Career* Colonial Office 1938, Dominions Office 1940; Commonwealth Relations Office asst under-sec of state 1960-66 (formerly asst sec); govr Commonwealth Inst 1967-; first dir Commonwealth Fndn 1966-; author; *Style*— John Chadwick Esq, CMG; 11 Cumberland House, Kensington Rd, London W8

CHADWICK, John Murray; ED (1979), QC (1980); s of Capt Hector George Chadwick, (ka 1942), and Margaret Corry, *née* Laing (d 1977); *b* 20 Jan 1941; *Educ* Rugby, Magdalene Coll Cambridge (MA); *m* 5 Dec 1975, Diana Mary, da of Charles Marshall Blunt, DL (d 1986), of March, Cambs; 2 da (Jane b 1976, Elizabeth b 1978); *Career* Maj (TAVR) 4 Bn Royal Green Jackets 1973-76; called to the Bar Inner Temple 1966, bencher 1986, rec Crown Ct; jr counsel Dept of Trade 1974-80, judge of the Cts of Appeal of Guernsey and Jersey 1986; memb Wine Standards Bd of Vintners' Co 1983-90, memb Gen Cncl of the Bar 1989-; *Recreations* sailing; *Clubs* Cavalry and Guards', Royal Yacht Squadron; *Style*— John Chadwick Esq, QC; Essex Court, Temple, London EC4Y 9AR (☎ 071 583 2000, fax 071 583 0118)

CHADWICK, Sir Joshua Kenneth Burton; 3 Bt (UK 1935), of Bidston, Co Palatine of Chester; s of Sir Robert Burton-Chadwick, 2 Bt (d 1983), and his 2 w (Beryl) Joan, *née* Brailsford; *b* 1 Feb 1954; *Style*— Sir Joshua Burton-Chadwick, Bt; 3/1933 Gold Coast, Highway, Burleigh Heads, Queensland 4220, Australia

CHADWICK, Julian William Mark; s of Douglas Herbert Chadwick, of Beaconsfield, Bucks, and Elizabeth Mary, *née* Evans; *b* 3 Jan 1957; *Educ* RGS High Wycombe, ChCh Oxford (MA); *Career* admitted slr 1982; ptnr: Gamlens 1985-90, Penningtons 1990-; sr master Christ Church and Farley Hill Beagles; memb: Law Soc, Assoc Masters of Beagles and Harriers; *Recreations* field sports; *Clubs* Oxford & Cambridge; *Style*— Julian Chadwick, Esq; 105 Station Rd, Beaconsfield, Bucks (☎ 0494 674319); Penningtons, Clements House, 99 Aldwych, London WC2B 4LJ (☎ 071 242 4422); Bryntawel, Drefach, Llanbydder, Dyfed (☎ 0570 480 267)

CHADWICK, Lynn Russell; CBE (1964); s of Verner Russell Chadwick (d 1957), and Margery Brown, *née* Lynn (d 1936); *b* 24 Nov 1914; *Educ* Merchant Taylors'; *m* 1, (m dis), Charlotte Ann Secord; 1 s (Simon David b 8 May 1942); m 2, Frances Mary Jamieson (d 1964); 2 da (Sarah Russell b 25 Nov 1958, Sophie Russell b 20 May 1960); m 3, 4 June 1965, Eva Yvonne, da of Gabriel Etien Reiner (d 1942), of Hungary; 1 s (Daniel Sebastian b 25 May 1965); *Career* Lt (A) Fleet Air Arm RNVR 1941-44; sculptor; numerous exhibitions UK and abroad; work in public collections: Tate, Br Cncl, Arts Cncl of GB, V&A, Pembroke Coll Oxford, City Art Gallery (Bristol), Art Gallery (Brighton), Whitworth Art Gallery (Univ of Manchester), Musée National D'Art Moderne (Paris), Boymans van Beuningen Museum (Rotterdam), Staaliche Graphische Sammlung (Munich), Art Gallery (Gothenburg), Musées Royaut des Beaux-Arts de Belgique (Brussels), Galleria D'Arte Moderna (Rome), Museo Civico (Turin), Nat Gallery of SA (Adelaide), Nat Gallery of Canada (Ottawa), Museum of Fine Arts (Montreal), Museum of Modern Art (NY), Carnegie Inst (Pittsburgh), Albright Art Gallery (Buffalo), Art Inst (Chicago), Inst de Artes Contemporáneas (Lima); Officier Ordre des Arts et Lettres (France) 1986, Order of Andres Bello First Class (Venezuela); *Style*— Lynn Chadwick, Esq, CBE; Lypiatt Park, Stroud, Gloucestershire GL6 7LL (☎ 0452 770 210)

CHADWICK, Prof (William) Owen; OM (1983), KBE (1982); s of John Chadwick (d 1931), of Bromley, Kent; er bro of Very Rev Prof Henry Chadwick, *qv*, yr bro of Sir John Chadwick (d 1987), and also bro of Lady McNicoll (w of Vice Adm Sir Alan McNicoll (d 1987), former Australian ambass to Turkey); *b* 20 May 1916; *Educ* Tonbridge, St John's Coll Cambridge; *m* 1949, Ruth Romaine, eldest da of Bertrand Leslie Hallward, formerly Vice-Chllr of Univ of Nottingham; 2 s, 2 da; *Career* former dean and fellow of Trinity Hall Cambridge, sometime chm tstees Univ Coll later Wolfson Coll Cambridge, hon fell 1977, regius prof of mod history Univ of Cambridge 1968-83, vice chllr 1969-71, master of Selwyn Coll 1956-83; memb Royal Cmmn on Historical Manuscripts 1984-, chllr Univ of East Anglia 1985-, chm Nat Portrait Gallery 1988- (tstee 1978); Hon DD: St Andrews, Oxford; Hon DLitt: Kent, Bristol, London, E Anglia, Cambridge; Hon DLett Columbia USA, Hon LLD Aberdeen, DD 1955, FBA (pres 1981-85); *Books* Newman (1983), Hensley Henson (1983), Britain and the Vatican during the Second World War (1987), Michael Ramsey (1989); *Style*— Prof Owen Chadwick, OM, KBE; 67 Grantchester St, Cambridge (☎ 0223 314000)

CHADWICK, Peter; s of Kenneth Fred Chadwick (d 1985), and Grace Jean, *née* Holden; *b* 19 Aug 1946; *Educ* St Paul's, Churchill Coll Cambridge (BA, MA); *m* 27 Oct 1971, Diana Kathryn Lillian, da of Frank Richard Stanford Kellett; 1 da (Lindsey Nicola b 1974); *Career* princ Dept of Indust 1977-79; Peat Marwick Mitchell and Co (now Peat Marwick McLintock): ptnr 1982 currently managing ptnr Kent; ACA 1970, FCA 1979; *Recreations* art, travel; *Style*— Peter Chadwick, Esq; The Old Rectory, Little Chart, Ashford, Kent TN27 0QH; Peat Marwick McLintock, Barnham Court, Teston, Maidstone, Kent ME18 5BZ (☎ 0622 814 814, fax 0622 814 888); 16-17 Lower Bridge St, Canterbury, Kent CT1 2LG (☎ 0227 762 800, fax 0227 762 810)

CHADWICK, Prof Peter; s of Jack Chadwick, Huddersfield, and Marjorie, *née* Castle (d 1982); *b* 23 March 1931; *Educ* Huddersfield Coll, Univ of Manchester (BSc), Univ of Cambridge (PhD, ScD); *m* 2 April 1956, Sheila (Gladys), da of Clarence Frederick Slater (d 1939), of Colchester; 2 da (Janice b 1958, Susan b 1970); *Career* sr scientific offr AWRE Aldermaston 1957-59 (scientific offr 1955-57), sr lectr in applied mathematics Univ of Sheffield 1964-65 (lectr 1959-64), dean Sch of Maths and Physics UEA Norwich 1979-82 (prof of mathematics 1965-); visiting prof Univ of Queensland 1972; FRS; *Books* Continuum Mechanics Concise Theory and Problems (1976); *Recreations* walking, music; *Style*— Prof Peter Chadwick, FRS; 8 Stratford Crescent, Cringleford, Norwich NR4 7SF (☎ 0603 51655); School of Mathematics, University of East Anglia, University Plain, Norwich NR4 7TJ (☎ 0603 56161, ext 2848)

CHADWICK, Peter Douglas; s of Douglas Herbert Chadwick, of Beaconsfield, Bucks and Bryntawel, Llanwenog, Dyfed, and Elizabeth Mary (Nan), *née* Evans; *b* 27 Jan 1947; *Educ* Royal GS High Wycombe, UCL (BA); *Career* memb staff Church Cmmrs for England 1970-87 (seconded to Gen Synod C of E 1978-82), sec Church Urban Fund 1987-; *Recreations* East European and Oriental studies, cycling; *Style*— Peter Chadwick, Esq; 60 Sutherland Sq, Walworth, London SE17 3EL (☎ 071 703 8314); Church Urban Fund, 2 Gt Peter St, London SW1P 3LX (☎ 071 222 7010, fax 071 222 5490, telex 916450 CHCOMM G)

CHADWICK, Robert; s of Jack Chadwick, of Inchkeith Court, Cadham, Glenrothes, Fife, and Margaret, *née* Lyons; *b* 18 Aug 1949; *Educ* Montrose Acad; *m* 9 May 1988, Eileen Joan, da of Flying Offr Leo Hubert Skelton (d 1938); *Career* RA 22 Battery Sch of Artillery Larkhill 1966-70; Meterological Office: joined 1970, Prestwick Airport 1970-83, forecaster 1984, Glasgow Weather Centre 1984-88, higher forecaster 1988, RAF Honington 1988-; Flt Lt RAFVR 1990-; memb: Trollope Soc, Br Field Sports Soc, BASC, Game Conservancy, CGA, Inst of Mathematics and its Applications 1989, Inst of Physics 1990; FRMetS 1987; FRGS 1990; *Recreations* shooting, fishing, reading, following the hunt; *Clubs* Sloane, Commonwealth; RAF; *Style*— Robert Chadwick, Esq; Officers Mess, RAF Honington, Bury St Edmunds, Suffolk

CHADWICK, Terry; s of Parker Chadwick (d 1966), and Helen Elizabeth, *née* Hooler (d 1956); *b* 21 Jan 1933; *Educ* Clitheroe Royal GS, Univ of Leeds (BSc), King George VI Memorial Fell (1956), Univ of California Berkeley (MS); *m* 22 April 1957, Marguerite Elizabeth, da of Arthur Ashworth, of Penrhyn Bay, Llandudno; 4 s (Iven b 1960, Stephen b 1962, Martin b 1963, Aran b 1966), 1 da (Lynn b 1958); *Career* conslt civil and structural engr, fndr Deleuw Chadwick Oheocha 1959, estab related practice in Nigeria 1960 (responsible for bridges, bldgs and highways); in UK designed: underground railway proposed for Manchester, precint centre Univ of Manchester, new HQ Barclays Bank Knutsford; chm Parkside Scout and Guides 1979-82; MConsE, FICE, MICEI; *Recreations* fell walking, skiing, golf, classical music; *Clubs* Bramall Park Golf; *Style*— Terry Chadwick, Esq; 5 Ladybrook Road, Bramhall, Stockport (☎ 061 485 2868), Clemence House, Mellor Road, Cheadle Hulme, Stockport (☎ 061 486 0011)

CHADWICK, Timothy John Mackenzie; s of Arthur John MacKenzie Chadwick, of Gstaad, Switzerland, and Patricia Cambell, *née* Hiller; *b* 19 Aug 1946; *Educ* Le Rosey Sch Switzerland, Amherst Coll USA, Trinity Coll Oxford; *m* 26 June 1980, Jacqueline Brewster, *née* Johnson; 1 s (William Hiller MacKennzie b 26 Oct 1982); *Career* md: Assoc Business Progs Ltd 1975-78, Aurum Press Ltd 1978-, Noyden Properties Ltd 1979-; dir: Benecia Industs Inc California USA 1987-, Hamleys of Regent St Ltd 1989-, Tunsure Ltd 1990-; *Recreations* skiing, tennis, reading, leaning on fences; *Clubs* Knickerbocker (USA), Queen's, Vincent's, Brook's; *Style*— Timothy Chadwick, Esq; 3 Eaton Terrace, London SW1; Aurum Press Ltd, 33 Museum St, London WC1 (☎ 071 631 4596, fax 071 580 2496, car 0836 266 977, telex 299557)

CHADWYCK-HEALEY, Sir Charles Edward; 5 Bt (UK 1919); s of Sir Charles Chadwyck-Healey, 4 Bt, OBE, TD, (d 1986), and Viola, *née* Lubbock; *b* 13 May 1940; *Educ* Eton, Trinity Coll Oxford (MA); *m* 16 Sept 1967, Angela Mary, eldest da of late John Metson of Little Dunmow, Essex; 1 s, 2 da; *Heir* s, Edward Alexander b 2 June 1972; *Career* publisher; chm and md Chadwyck-Healey Ltd 1973-; pres Chadwyck-Healey Inc 1981-, dir Chadwyck-Healey France SARL 1985-; *Clubs* Brooks's; *Style*— Sir Charles Chadwyck-Healey, Bt; Manor Farm, Bassingbourn, Cambs (☎ 0763 242 447)

CHAITOW, Christopher John Adam; s of Boris Reuben Chaitow, of Stellenbosch, Cape Province, SA, and of Elizabeth, *née* Rice (d 1980); *b* 19 Jan 1943; *Educ* Worthing HS; *m* 18 May 1974, Susan Patricia, da of George Joseph Foley, of Keystone Rd, Cardiff; 1 s (Daniel b 1984), 1 da (Ella b 1983); *Career* trainee Northcote & Co 1964-68, res/institutional sales 1968-70, ptnr Beamish & Co 1970-75, institutional sales Northcote & Co 1975-79; tech analysis: Simon & Coates 1979-86, Chase Manhattan Securities 1986, Morgan Grenfell Securities 1986-88; dir Value and Momentum Research and Chartroom UK 1989-; publisher (jtly with Laing and Cruickshank): Value and Momentum, Markets Perspective; *Recreations* music, golf; *Style*— Christopher Chaitow, Esq; Caroline House, 29/30 Alwyne Rd, London N1 (☎ 071 226 4471); Value and Momentum Research, 19th Floor, 77 London Wall, London EC2M 1BU (☎ 071 638 6450, fax 071 256 9263)

CHAKRABORTI, Dr Debabrata; s of Nagendra Nath Chakraborti (d 1966), of Bally, Howrah, India, and Suniti Majumder; *b* 1 Jan 1937; *Educ* Univ of Calcutta (MB BS, DPM), Conjoint Bd Eng (DPM), MRCPsych; *m* 10 July 1966, Monika, da of Kumud Ranjan Chowdhury (d 1987); 1 s (Saptarshi b 14 June 1968), 1 da (Debika b 11 Dec 1973); *Career* consIt psychiatrist in mental handicap W Norfolk and Wisbech Health Authy 1976-, speciality tutor in mental handicap Little Plumstead Hosp Norwich; Br Med Jl: book reviews, TV reviews, contraception and the mentally handicapped (jtly, 1984), sterilisation and the mentally handicapped; asst devpt NHS facilities for mentally handicapped W Norfolk; memb BMA; *Recreations* writing, listening to Indian music, reading biographies; *Style*— Dr Debabrata Chakraborti; 4 Binham Rd, Priory Park, South Wootton, King's Lynn, Norfolk PE30 3TB (☎ 0553 671869); Park View Resource Centre, Birch Tree Close, London Rd, King's Lynn, Norfolk PE30 5QD (☎ 0553 766266 ext 5512)

CHAKRABORTY, Dr Sucharu Kumar; s of Madhu Sudan Chakraborty (d 1970), of Azimganj, W Bengal, India, and Santi, *née* Choudhury; *b* 1 June 1932; *Educ* Jiaganj EC Inst, Calcutta Univ (MB BS); *m* 14 Dec 1966, Pratima, da of Bimal Kumar Mookerjee, of Darjeeling, India; 2 da (Radha Rupa b 1969, Devika Mimi b 1970); *Career* Gen Infirmary Pontefract: registrar anaesthetist 1967-70, sr registrar anaesthetist 1970-71, consIt anaesthetist 1971-; dir Ropergate Properties Ltd Pontefract W Yorks; memb: Yorks Soc of Anaesthetists, Intractable Pain Soc GB, Obstetric Anaesthetists Assoc; memb BMA, FFARCS 1969; *Recreations* swimming, photography; *Style*— Dr Sucharu Chakraborty; Santi, Went Edge Road, Kirk-Smeaton, Pontefract, W Yorkshire WF8 3JS (☎ 0977 621326); Consultant Anaesthetist, General Infirmary, Pontefract, W Yorkshire (☎ 0977 600600)

CHALDECOTT, Axel James; s of John James Chaldecott, of 13 The Paddocks, Beltinge, Kent, and Alix Mathilde, *née* Von Kauffmann; *b* 11 Dec 1954; *Educ* Charterhouse, Canterbury Coll of Art (BA); *m* 14 Feb 1987, Claire, da of Kenneth Evans; *Career* art dir: Ogilvy & Mather 1977-80, Crawfords 1980-81, Gold Greenlees Trott 1981-85; creative gp head Wight Collins Rutherford Scott 1985-87, creative ptnr Howell Henry Chaldecott Lury 1987-; *Style*— Axel Chaldecott, Esq; Howell Henry Chaldecott Lury, Kent House, 14-17 Markets Place, Great Titchfield St, London W1N 7AJ (☎ 071 436 3333, fax 071 436 2677)

CHALDECOTT, (Oswald) Harry; s of Lt-Col Oswald Arthur Chaldecott (d 1964), of Kirby Lonsdale, and Margaret Ursula (d 1959), da of Sir Henry Worsley-Taylor, Bt (1924), was MP for Blackpool 1901-13; *b* 29 June 1928; *Educ* Wellington, Peterhouse Univ of Cambridge (BA); *m* 1 July 1960, Grizel Mary Virginia, da of Rear Adm John Grant, of London SW6; 2 da (Perilla b 1961, Alexandra b 1964); *Career* stockbroker; investmt advsr J A Scrimegour 1953-67; ptnr: J A Scrimgeour 1968-75, Stock and Co 1976-85; assoc dir Stock Beech and Co 1985-89, James Capel & Co 1990-91; *Recreations* travel, walking, gardening; *Clubs* City Univ Hurlingham; *Style*— Harry Chaldecott, Esq; c/o Aitken Hume Ltd, 30 City Road, London EC1Y 2AY

CHALFONT, Baron (Life Peer UK 1964); Alun Arthur Gwynne Jones; OBE (1961), MC (1957), PC (1964); s of Arthur Gwynne Jones (d 1982), and Eliza Alice, *née* Hardman (d 1975); *b* 5 Dec 1919; *Educ* West Monmouth Sch, Sch of Slavonic Studies Univ of London; *m* 1948, Mona, da of late Harry Douglas Mitchell, of Grimsby; 1 c decd; *Career* sits as Independent in House of Lords, chm Lords All-Party Defence Gp; Brevet Lt-Col (ret) S Wales Borderers (Reg Army Offr 1940-61), served Burma, Ethiopia, Malaya, Cyprus, Egypt; former defence and mil correspondent The Times; min of state FO 1964-70, Br perm rep to WEU 1969-70; foreign ed New Statesman 1970-71; dir IBM UK Hldgs Ltd, IBM UK Ltd 1973-90; non-exec dir Lazard Bros 1981-90, pres Nottingham Building Soc 1983-90; chm: Euro Atlantic Gp, Exec Ctee Pilgrims Soc; pres Royal Nat Inst for Deaf; *Books* The Sword and the Spirit (1963), The Great Commanders (1973), Montgomery of Alamein (1976), Waterloo: Story of Three Armies (1979), Star Wars: Suicide or Survival (1985); *Recreations* music, theatre; *Clubs* Garrick, MCC; *Style*— The Rt Hon the Lord Chalfont, OBE, MC, PC; 65 Ashley Gdns, London SW1; Radio Authority, 70 Brompton Rd, London SW3 IEY (☎ 071 824 7800)

CHALK, Clive Andrew; s of Herbert Chalk (d 1981), of Chelsfield, Kent, and Gertrude Edith, *née* Taylor; *b* 2 Nov 1946; *Educ* St Dunstan's Coll, Univ of Exeter (LLB), Harvard Business Sch (AMP); *m* 1, 3 Oct 1970 (m dis), Judith Rosamond, da of Dr Samuel Dudley Sawyer; 2 da (Harriet Rosamond Louise b 17 Oct 1975, Olivia Emma Jane b 8 March 1977); m 2, 20 Dec 1985, Iris Marita, da of Lars Hjelt; 2 s (Nicholas Gyles Edward b 24 Sept 1986, Jonathan Clive Alexander b 20 Jan 1989); *Career* CA; Coopers & Lybrand 1968-73, Williams & Glyn's Bank 1973-77, dir Samuel Montagu & Co Ltd 1982- (joined 1977); FCA 1972; *Recreations* sailing, skiing, golf, cricket, rugby, bridge, opera, ballet; *Clubs* Royal Thames Yacht, Little Ship, Harvard Business Sch of London; *Style—* Clive Chalk, Esq; Samuel Montagu and Co Ltd, 10 Lower Thames St, London EC3R 6AE (☎ 071 260 9270, fax 071 623 5512, car 0836 564801)

CHALK, Gilbert John; s of Ronald Arthur Chalk, of Herts, and Elizabeth, *née* Talbot; *b* 21 Sept 1947; *Educ* Lancing, Univ of Southampton (BSc), Univ of Lancaster (MA), Univ of Columbia New York; *m* 9 June 1975, Gillian Frances Audrey, da of Sir Gervase Blois, 10 Bt (d 1967); 2 s (Alexander John Gervase b 1976, Christopher Harry Gilbert b 1985), 1 da (Nicola Elizabeth b 1978); *Career* dir: Centaur Communications Ltd 1981-, Hambros Bank Ltd 1984-, Hambro Group Investments 1988-; md Hambro European Ventures Ltd 1987-; MBA; *Recreations* tennis, riding, skiing; *Clubs* Queen's, Berkshire Golf; *Style—* Gilbert Chalk, Esq; 103 Elgin Crescent, London W11 2JF (☎ 071 727 1981); Foxcote Grange, Andoversford, Glos (☎ 0242 820322); Hambros Bank Ltd, 41 Tower Hill, London EC3N 4HA (☎ 071 480 5000)

CHALK, Kenneth Stephen; s of Montague Frederick Chalk, and Jean Patricia, *née* Craig (d 1983); *b* 27 Dec 1947; *Educ* St Nicholas GS Northwood Middx; *m* 1970, Susan Margaret; 1 s (James b 4 April 1975), 2 da (Zoe b 6 Dec 1972, Naomi b 26 Sept 1979); *Career* CA; articled Mann Judd & Co London 1966-71, Hendry Rae & Court Perth WA 1971-73, ptnr Tansley Witt & Co Bristol 1975 (joined London office 1973, merger with Arthur Andersen 1979), ptnr Arthur Andersen Bristol 1979-87, ptnr in charge of Corp Special Servs Div Touche Ross Manchester 1990- (merger with Spicer & Oppenheim 1990, formerly ptnr with that firm); memb: Soc of Practitioners in Insolvency, Inst of Credit Mgmnt; licensed insolvency practitioner, FCA 1970 (ACA 1970); *Recreations* travel, music, theatre, walking; *Style—* Kenneth Chalk, Esq; Touche Ross & Co, 12 Booth St, Manchester M60 2ED (☎ 061 236 9721, fax 061 228 2681)

CHALK, Philip Alexander Forbes; s of Charles Philip Chalk, of Much Hadham, Herts (d 1954), and Ann, *née* Forbes (d 1974); *b* 1 May 1930; *Educ* Selwyn Coll Univ of Cambridge, The London Hosp Med Coll (MA, MB BChir); *m* 17 May 1958, Jean Graham, da of Bertram Doughty (d 1978), of Gt Dunmow, Essex; 1 s (David b 1959), 2 da (Alison b 1961, Hilary b 1963); *Career* consult obstetrician and gynaecologist The Royal Free Hosp London 1969-; formerly resident accoucheur The London Hosp 1958, registrar and sr registrar The Middlesex Hosp 1964-69; govr Queen Mary Coll London; memb Ct Asst Worshipful Co of Drapers; FRCS, FRCOG; *Recreations* fishing, campanology, Suffolk sheep; *Clubs* Royal Soc of Med; *Style—* Philip Chalk, Esq; 5 Devonshire Mews North, London W1; The Old Rectory, Whepstead, Bury St Edmunds; 114 Harley St, London W1N 1AG (☎ 071 486 2445)

CHALKER, Rt Hon Lynda; MP (C) Wallasey 1974-; PC (1987); da of late Sidney Henry James Bates, and late Marjorie Kathleen Randell; *b* 29 April 1942; *Educ* Roedean, Univ of Heidelberg, Westfield Coll London, Central London Poly; *m* 1, 1967 (m dis 1973), Eric Robert Chalker (chm Greater London Young Conservatives 1966-67, also fndr memb Set the Party Free one-memb one-vote selection procedure for party and local cncl candidates); m 2, 1981, Clive Landa (chm Tory Reform Gp 1979-82 and chm Young Cons 1972-74); *Career* former statistician Unilever subsid, market researcher Shell Mex and BP, chief exec Int Div Louis Harris International; chm Gtr London Young Cons 1969-70 (nat vice chm 1970-71), memb BBC Gen Advsy Ctee 1975-79, oppn spokesman Social Servs 1976-79; Parly under sec of state: DHSS 1979-82, Tport 1982-83; min of state: Tport 1983-86, FCO 1986-; min for Overseas Devpt 1989-; *Recreations* theatre, driving; *Style—* The Rt Hon Lynda Chalker, MP; House of Commons, London SW1A 0AA (☎ 071 219 5098)

CHALLACOMBE, Dr David Nicholas; s of Harold Bruce Challacombe (d 1985), of Lulworth, Dorset, and Nancy Llinos, *née* Williams; *b* 22 June 1936; *Educ* Truro Sch Cornwall, Harrisons Coll Barbados, KCH (MD), Univ of London; *m* 19 Jan 1963, Janice Stewart, da of Alfred Henry Siemon (d 1986), of Perth, W Australia; 1 s (Andrew Nicholas b 1965), 1 da (Emma Jane b 1967); *Career* house offr KCH 1960-61, sr house offr Hosp for Sick Children Gt Ormond St 1963, registrar St Mary's Hosp London 1965-68, sr registrar Bristol Royal Hosp for Sick Children 1968-70, lectr Univ of Birmingham 1970-73, conslt paediatrician Somerset Health Authy 1973-; hon med offr Somerset CCC 1974-85; chm: SW Regnl Paediatric Advsy Ctee, W Somerset Ethical Ctee; memb: Euro Soc for Paediatric Gastroenterology and Nutrition, British Paediatric Assoc, Br Soc of Gastroenterology; MRCS, FRCP; *Books* Food Allergy (1985); *Publications* author of numerous publications on paediatric and adult gastroenterological res topics; *publications* author of numerous publications on paediatric res topics; *Recreations* watching and playing cricket, eighteenth century English porcelain; *Style—* Dr David Challacombe; The Somerset Children's Research Unit, Musgrove Park Hospital, Taunton, Somerset TA1 5DA (☎ 0823 333444); 2 Mount Terrace, Mount St, Taunton, Somerset TA1 3QG (☎ 0823 337164)

CHALLIS, Dr Christopher Edgar; s of Edgar Challis (d 1957) of Leeds, and Hilda May, *née* Elsworth (d 1989); *b* 5 Feb 1939; *Educ* Cockburn HS Leeds, Univ of Bristol (BA, Cert Ed, PhD); *m* 4 Jan 1967, Christine Joyce, da of Bernard Arthur Black, of Nottingham; *Career* Univ of Leeds: asst lectr 1964-67, lectr 1967-78, sr lectr 1978-82, reader 1982-, chm of the sch 1988-; ed British Numismatic Journal 1980-89; pres Br Numismatic Soc 1988-, tstee UK Numismatic Tst 1988; FRHistS 1970, FSA 1987; *Books* The Tudor Coinage (1978); *Recreations* walking, horse-riding; *Style—* Dr Christopher Challis; Wychwood, West End, Ampleforth, N Yorks YO6 4DU; School of History, University of Leeds, Leeds LS2 9JT (☎ 0532 431751)

CHALLIS, George Hubert; CBE (1991); s of Hubert William Challis (d 1969); *b* 26 May 1921; *Educ* King Edward VI Sch Stourbridge; *m* 1946, Margaret Beatrice, da of Reginald Percy Bonner (d 1965); 1 s, 1 da; *Career* served 1940-46 1/9 Gurkha Rifles (despatches twice); banker and co dir; with Lloyds Bank plc 1938-81 (head of Premises Div 1974-81); dir: Lloyds Bank Property Co 1974-81, Towco Group Ltd 1982-84, Westminster Property Group plc 1983-84; memb: Ct of Common Cncl (City of London) 1978-, Cncl London Chamber of Commerce and Indust 1979-89, Thames Water Authy 1982-83; dep govr The Hon Irish Soc 1983-84; chm: City Lands and Bridge House Estates Ctee 1990, Port and City Health and Social Servs Ctee 1988-90; Renter Warden Worshipful Co of Tobacco Pipe Makers and Tobacco Blenders 1990-91, Hon Clerk Worshipful Co of Chartered Secretaries and Administrators 1984-; Cdr of the Order of Merit (Federal Republic of Germany) 1986, Commendatore Order of Merit (Republic of Italy) 1990; *Recreations* travel, reading, music; *Clubs* RAC, MCC, Guildhall, City Livery; *Style—* George Challis, Esq, CBE; 77 West Hill Ave, Epsom, Surrey KT19 8JX (☎ 0372 721705)

CHALLIS, Susan Carol; da of Lt Cdr Derek Gordon Shotton, of Southleigh Rd, Havant, Hants, and Jacqueline Mary, *née* Brisker; *b* 11 Aug 1965; *Educ* Great Salterns Sch Portsmouth, Loughborough Univ of Technol (BSc); *m* 27 Feb 1988, John Henry Challis, s of John Albert Challis, of Furzefield, Slindon Bottom Rd, Slindon, W Sussex; *Career* trampolinist; Br ladies champion: 1980, 1981, 1982, 1984, 1985, 1987, 1990; Euro youth champion 1982 (runner up 1980), Euro champion 1983 (runner up 1981 and 1989), World champion 1984, World synchronized champion (with Kyrstyan McDonald) 1984, placed third World Championships 1990; *Style—* Mrs Susan Challis; 25 Gallico Close, Loughborough, Leicestershire (☎ 0509 262867)

CHALMERS, Dr Alastair Hugh; s of Sqdn Ldr Hugh Alexander Cuthill Chalmers (d 1980), and Celia Marion Chalmers; *b* 21 April 1944; *Educ* Lancing, Queens' Coll Cambridge (MA), Guy's Hosp; *m* 11 Sept 1971, Helen Anne, da of John Robinson (d 1986); 1 s (Nicholas b 1973), 1 da (Suzanne b 1977); *Career* conslt radiologist Wessex RHA 1978-; FRCR, FRCP; *Books* chapters in: Recent Advances in Radiology (1979), Clinical Endocrinology (1984), Radiology of the Liver, Gallbladder and Biliary Tract (1989); *Recreations* photography, walking, music, gardening; *Style—* Dr Alastair Chalmers; 2 Springfield Place, Lansdown, Bath BA1 5RA; Dept of Radiology, Royal United Hosp, Combe Park, Bath BA1 3NG (☎ 0225 823241)

CHALMERS, Craig Minto; s of Robert Brian Chalmers, and Georgina Byers, *née* Minto; *b* 15 Oct 1968; *Educ* Melrose GS, Earlston HS; *Career* Rugby Union fly-half Melrose RFC and Scotland (13 caps); clubs: Melrose RFC, Barbarians RFC; rep: Scotland U15, Scotland U18, Scotland U19, Scotland U21, Scotland B (debut 1988, youngest rep player); Scotland: debut v Wales 1989, Grand Slam winners 1990, tour NZ (2 tests) 1990; British Lions tour Aust (1 test) 1989, Barbarians (5 games); scorer of 77 points for Scotland (3 tries, 3 drop goals, 4 conversions, 16 penalties); mktg rep Scottish Power Bd; *Recreations* golf, snooker, tennis, football; *Clubs* Melrose Golf; *Style—* Craig Chalmers, Esq; Abbey Vale, Gattonside, Melrose, Roxburghshire, Scotland TD6 9NB (☎ 089682 2752); c/o Melrose RFC, The Greenyards, Melrose, Roxburghshire TD6 9SA (☎ 089 682 2993)

CHALMERS, Capt David McKenzie; s of Dr R M Chalmers (d 1954), of London, and Jane Mildred, *née* Findlay; *b* 14 Sept 1936; *Educ* Cranleigh Sch, De Havilland Aeronautical Tech Sch; *m* 5 Sept 1964, Hon Lydia Elizabeth Palmer, da of late Lord Macdermott, MC; 2 s (Douglas McKenzie b 1966, John McDermott b 1969); *Career* RAF 1958-66, pilot, Flt Lt; aeronautical engr 1954-58, airline pilot 1966- (command 1973); *Recreations* gliding; *Style—* Capt David Chalmers; The Old School House, Beech Hill, Reading, Berk RG7 2BE (☎ 0734 882186); British Airways, PO Box 10, Heathrow Airport, Middx

CHALMERS, Harvey Paxton; s of William Harvey Chalmers (d 1985), and Elizabeth, *née* Davidson; *b* 18 Feb 1947; *Educ* Univ of Glasgow (LLB), Magdalene Coll Cambridge (PhD); *Career* admitted slr 1978; articled clerk Shepherd & Wedderburn WS 1972-74, slr Linklaters & Paines 1974-85, ptnr Simmons & Simmons 1986- (slr 1985-86); memb: Law Soc, Law Soc of Scotland; *Style—* H P Chalmers, Esq; 14 Dominion St, London EC2M 2RJ (☎ 071 628 2020, fax 071 588 4129)

CHALMERS, Judith; da of David Norman Chalmers (d 1953), and Millie Locke, *née* Broadhurst; *Educ* Withington Girls' Sch Manchester, LAMDA; *m* 3 Jan 1964, Neil Durden-Smith, s of Anthony James Durden-Smith, FRCS (d 1963); 1 s (Mark b 1 Oct 1968), 1 da (Emma b 4 March 1967); *Career* began broadcasting in Manchester BBC Children's Hour at age of 13 (while still at school); interviewer/presenter many radio and TV programmes in north and then London from 1960 with BBC; joined Thames TV with own afternoon programme 1972; first series of travel programme Wish You Were Here 1973 (current series is seventeenth); developed own idea for home interest programme Hot Property since 1987; joined Radio 2 to host own daily programme 1990; commentator for many royal and state occasions; travel ed Woman's Realm; past memb Nat Consumer Cncl; memb Peacock Ctee on Broadcasting; Freeman City of London; memb: British Guild of Travel Writers, British Assoc of Travel Editors; *Books* Wish You Were Here ...?: 50 of the Best Holidays (1987); *Recreations* walking, bird watching, photography; *Clubs* Wig and Pen, Mossiman's Rugby; *Style—* Miss Judith Chalmers; International Management Gp, 23 Eyot Gardens, London W6 9TN (☎ 081 846 8070)

CHALMERS, Hon Mrs (Lydia Elizabeth Palmer); *née* MacDermott; da of Baron MacDermott, MC, PC (Life Peer, d 1979); *b* 6 June 1939; *Educ* Wycombe Abbey Sch, Belfast Coll of Art; *m* 1964, Capt David McKenzie Chalmers, *qv*, yr s of Dr Robert Miller Chalmers (d 1954), of Wandsworth; 2 s (Douglas b 1966, John b 1969); *Career* artist; *Style—* The Hon Mrs Chalmers; Old School House, Beech Hill, Reading, Berks RG7 2BE

CHALMERS, Dr Neil Robert; s of William King Chalmers, and Irene Margaret, *née* Pemberton; *b* 19 June 1942; *Educ* King's Coll Sch Wimbledon, Magdalen Coll Oxford (BA), St John's Coll Cambridge (PhD); *m* 28 Feb 1970, Monica Elizabeth, *née* Byanjeru; 2 da (Emily Anne Nsemere b 5 Dec 1970, Louise Jane Kobuyenje b 11 Oct 1978); *Career* lectr in zoology Makerere Univ Coll Kampala Uganda 1966-69, scientific dir Nat Primate Res Centre Nairobi Kenya 1969-70, dean of sci Open Univ 1985-88 (lectr, sr lectr then reader in biology 1970-85), dir Natural History Museum 1988-; pres Assoc for the Study of Animal Behaviour 1989-; FZS, FLS, FIBiol, FRSA 1988; *Books* Social Behaviour in Primates (1979), contrib numerous papers on animal behaviour to various jls; *Recreations* music, squash; *Style—* Dr Neil Chalmers; Natural History British Museum, Cromwell Road, London SW7 5BD (☎ 071 938 9123, fax 071 938 8799)

CHALMERS, Norman Ashley; s of Reginald Chalmers (d 1984), of Berkhamsted, and Francis, *née* Flynn (d 1980); *b* 19 June 1933; *Educ* Berkhamsted Sch, RMA Sandhurst; *m* 12 July 1958, Susan, da of Leslie Bradford Harvey (d 1984), of Nantwich, Cheshire; 2 da (Caroline b 3 March 1964, Sarah b 23 Oct 1966); *Career* The Black Watch Royal Highland Regt 1951-58, cmmnd 1953; sr ptnr Arthur Andersen & Co CAs, dep chm Nat Mutual Life Assur Soc 1980-; chm: London & Clydeside Hldgs plc 1974-, Silver Estates Gp 1980-, Corporate Comms plc 1988-; chm Families at Risk 1987-, dir World Family of Foster Parents Plan 1983-, memb Ct of Assts Worshipful Co of Gardeners, Freeman City of London; FCA; *Recreations* golf, shooting, fishing; *Clubs* Wentworth, Stoke Poges, City Livery United Wards; *Style—* Norman Chalmers, Esq; Brook House, Templewood Lane, Farnham Common, Bucks SL2 3HW; 1 Surrey St, London WC2R 2PS (☎ 071 438 3743)

CHALMERS, Dr Robert James Guille; s of James Alexander Chalmers, of Oxford, and Lois Guille, *née* Taudevin (d 1980); *b* 18 Nov 1950; *Educ* St Edwards Sch Oxford, Middx Hosp Med Sch (MB BS); *m* 1 Oct 1988, Elizabeth Joyce, da of Leonard Cater (d 1980), of Bal West, Penzance; *Career* conslt dermatologist 1983-; The Skin Hosp Salford, Manchester Royal Infirmary, Bolton and Bury Health Authys; MRCP; *Recreations* travelling, playing the bassoon; *Clubs* Royal Society of Medicine; *Style—* Dr Robert Chalmers; 16 Oaker Avenue, West Didsbury, Manchester M20 8XH; The Skin Hospital, Chapel Street, Salford, Manchester M60 9EP (☎ 061 789 7373)

CHALMERS, William Gordon; CB (1980), MC (1944); s of Robert Wilson Chalmers, and Mary Robertson, *née* Clark; *b* 4 June 1922; *Educ* Robert Gordon's Coll Aberdeen, Univ of Aberdeen; *m* 1948, Margaret Helen McLeod; 1 s, 1 da; *Career* admitted slr; asst Crown Office 1963-67, dep crown agent 1967-74, crown agent for Scot 1974-84; *Recreations* bridge, golf; *Clubs* Royal Over-Seas League; *Style—* William Chalmers, Esq, CB, MC; 3/4 Rocheid Park, East Fettes Ave, Edinburgh EH4 1RP

CHALONER, John Seymour; s of Ernest Joseph Chaloner (d 1954), and Lenore Maud, MBE, *née* Barling (d 1974); *b* 5 Nov 1924; *Educ* Beltane Sch Wimbledon, Carleton Coll Ottawa Canada; *m* 1, 1952; 2 s (Nicholas b 1956, Ben b 1960); m 2, 1978, Patricia Ann; *Career* served as Maj Westminster Dragoons in NW Europe 1944-45; founded Post War German Newspapers inc Der Spiegel 1946; fndr and chm Seymour Press Group London 1948-76, awarded Officers Cross of the Order of Mint of the Federal Republic of Germany (1990); memb Wandsworth Borough Cncl 1961-68; govr St George's Hosp London 1961-68; author: Three for The Road, To Europe with Love, To The Manor Born, Bottom Line, 9 illustrated childrens titles; chm Publishing Div Inst of Dirs 1984-; *Recreations* shooting, hunting, sailing, skiing; *Style—* John Chaloner, Esq; 4 Warwick Square, London SW1 (☎ 071 834 9871); Sandfold Farm, Selmeston, Sussex (☎ 0323 870391)

CHALONER, Hon Thomas Peregrine Long (Perry); s and h of 3 Baron Gisborough; *b* 17 Jan 1961; *Educ* Univ of Buckingham (LLB), Barrister at Law (Inner Temple); *Career* pilot; *Recreations* diving, windsurfing, aerobatics; *Style—* The Hon Perry Chaloner; 114 Lupus St, London SW1

CHALSTREY, Leonard John; s of Leonard Chalstrey, of Tipton, Staffordshire, and Frances Mary, *née* Lakin; *b* 17 March 1931; *Educ* Dudley Sch, Queens' Coll Cambridge, St Bartholomew's Hosp Med Coll (MA, MD, BChir, FRCS); *m* 6 Sept 1958, Aileen Beatrice, da of Harold Bayes (d 1984); 1 s (Jonathan b 1962), 1 da (Susan b 1959); *Career* conslt surgn St Bart's and Homerton Hosps 1969-, sr lectr in surgery St Bart's Med Coll 1969-; examiner in surgery: Univ of London 1976-, Univ of Cambridge 1988-; hon cnslt surgn St Luke's Hosp for the Clergy; Alderman (Ward of Vintry) Corpn City of London 1984- (memb Common Cncl 1981-), memb Ct of City Univ; memb Ct of Assts: Worshipful Soc of Apothecaries of London, Worshipful Co of Barbers 1987; memb Guild of Freemen City of London; fell Hunterian Soc, memb Br Soc of Gastroenterology, memb Assoc of Surgns of GB and Ireland; FRSM; *Books* Gastro-Intestinal Disorders (1986); contributor: numerous papers on surgical subjects to medical press GB and USA, Maingot's Abdominal Operations (7th edn 1980, 8th edn 1985), Cancer in the Elderly (1990); *Recreations* painting in oils; *Clubs* United Oxford and Cambridge Univ, The City Livery Guildhall; *Style—* L J Chalstrey, Esq; Danebury, The Chine, London N21 2EG (☎ 081 360 8921); 116 Harley Street, London W1N 1AG (☎ 071 935 7413)

CHALTON, Simon Nicholas Charlton; s of Thomas Ley Chalton (d 1978), of Leeds, and Constance Mary, *née* Whittle (d 1946); *b* 7 June 1932; *Educ* Stowe; *m* 2 May 1959, Linda Mary, da of Donald Frank Chowan; 1 s (Giles Edward Ley b 12 Nov 1960), 2 da (Nicola Jane b 23 Sept 1963, Cardine Mary b 5 April 1966); *Career* admitted slr 1958; ptnr Dibb Lupton & Co, ret 1990, currently independent conslt; current directorships incl: Yorkshire Post Newspapers Ltd, The West of England Trust Ltd, dep chm London Group Limited; memb: Disciplinary Appeal Ctee ICEAW, Intellectual Property Ctee BCS; chm Ctee Int Bar Assoc; memb: Law Soc, BSC, CIArb; *Books* Data Protection Law (with Shelagh Gaskill, 1988), Encyclopaedia of Data Protection (with Shelagh Gaskill, 1988); *Recreations* gardening, theatre, music, walking; *Clubs* The Leeds; *Style—* Simon Chalton, Esq

CHAMBERLAIN, Alec Francis Roy; s of Peter Desmond Chamberlain, of 32 Hollow Lane, Ramsey, Huntingdon, Cambs, and Edith Kate, *née* Chatfield; *b* 20 June 1964; *Educ* Rjamsey Ailwyn Sch, Ramsey Abbey Sch; *m* 27 June 1987, Jane Elizabeth, da of Colin Andrew Osborne; *Career* professional footballer; Ipswich Town 1981-82 (no appearances), Colchester Utd 1982-87 (217 appearences), Everton FC 1987-88 (no appearances), on loan to Tramere Rovers 1987 (16 appearances), Luton Town 1988- (debut 1989, over 80 appearances); *Recreations* golf, cricket; *Style—* Alec Chamberlain, Esq; Luton Town FC, Kenilworth Stadium, 1 Maple Rd, Luton, Beds LU4 8AW (☎ 0582 411622, fax 0582 405070)

CHAMBERLAIN, Arthur; s of Lt-Col Arthur Chamberlain, MC, TD (d 1986), of Edgbaston, Birmingham, and Elizabeth Susan, *née* Edwards (d 1986); *b* 20 Feb 1952; *Educ* Milton Abbey Sch, Oxford Poly; *m* 18 June 1988, Dominique Jane Patricia, da of Robert Rossborough, of Geneva; *Career* Bank of London and S America Ecuador 1975-76, Bank of London and Montreal Guatemala 1976-77, Lloyds Bank International London 1977-79, dir Banco La Guaira International Venezuela 1979-82, md Lloyds Bank Nigeria Ltd 1982-84, sr corporate mgr Lloyds Bank plc London 1984-; *Recreations* shooting, fishing, travel, photography; *Clubs* East India; *Style—* Arthur Chamberlain, Esq; Lloyds Bank plc, Corporate Banking Division, 6-8 Eastcheap, London EC3 (☎ 071 418 3621)

CHAMBERLAIN, Lady Catherine Laura; *née* Chetwynd-Talbot; 3 da (by 1 m) of late 21 Earl of Shrewsbury and Waterford; *b* 4 Aug 1945; *m* 1966, Richard Sebastian Endicott Chamberlain, eldest s of Lawrence Endicott Chamberlain, of The Dairy House, Tonerspuddle, Dorset; 1 s, 2 da; *Style—* The Lady Catherine Chamberlain; Stocks Farm, Burley Street, Ringwood, Hants

CHAMBERLAIN, Prof Geoffrey Victor Price; RD (1974); s of Albert Victor Chamberlain, MBE (d 1978), of Penylan, Cardiff, and Irene May, *née* Price, MBE, of Westgate St, Cardiff; *b* 21 April 1930; *Educ* Llandaff Cathedral Sch, Cowbridge GS, UCL, University Coll Hosp Med Sch (MB BS, MD); *m* 23 June 1956, Prof Jocelyn Olivia Peter Chamberlain, da of Sir Peter Kerley, KCVO (d 1979), of Putney, London; 3 s (Christopher b 1957, Mark b 1959, Patrick b 1962), 2 da (Hilary b 1961, Virginia b 1966); *Career* RNVR 1955-57, RNR 1957-74, Surgn Lt 1955-61, Surgn Lt Cmdr 1961-, Surgn Cdr 1970-74, ret 1974; demonstrator in anatomy Royal Univ of Malta 1956-57; researcher: Royal Postgraduate Med Sch, Hosp for Sick Children Great Ormond Street (and others) 1958-62, sr registrar King's Coll Hosp 1962-69 (registrar); visiting res fell George Washington Univ USA 1966-67, conslt obstetrician & gynaecologist Queen Charlotte's Hosp for Women 1970-82, head Dept of Obstetrics & Gynaecology St George's Hosp Med Sch 1982- (also prof); visiting prof: USA 1984, Hong Kong 1985, Brisbane 1987, SA 1988; med examiner: Univ of London 1972-, Univ of Liverpool 1973-75 and 1991, Univ of Manchester 1979-83, Univ of Birmingham 1979-82, Univ of Cambridge 1981-86, Univ of Glasgow 1985-87, Univ of Kuala Lumpur 1986-87, Univ of Nottingham 1987-90, Univ of Wales 1988-90, Univ of Malta 1988-; examiner RCOG 1972-, chm Medical Ctee Nat Birthday Tst, chm Assoc of Profs in Obstetrics and Gynaecology, former chm Blair Bell Res Soc, hon gynaecologist Br Airways, fell UCL, former vice pres RCOG, treas RSM, inspr of Nullity; Freeman of the City of London 1982; FRCS 1960, MRCOG 1963, FRCOG 1978; *Books* Lecture Notes in Obstetrics (1984), Practice of Obstetrics and Gynaecology (1985), Pregnancy Survival Manual (1986), Birthplace (1987), Lecture Notes in Gynaecology (1988, 1989), Manual of Obstetrics (1988), Obstetrics (1989), Ten Teachers in Obstetrics and Gynaecology (1990), Contemporary Reviews in Obstetrics and Gynaecology (ed); *Recreations* opera, gardening, writing, travel; *Clubs* Perinatal, Blair Bell Soc, McDonald; *Style—* Prof Geoffrey Chamberlain; Department of Obstetrics & Gynaecology, St George's Hospital Medical Sch, Cranmer Terrace, London SW17 ORE (☎ 081 672 9944 ext 55956, fax 081 767 9585, telex 945291 SAGEMS G)

CHAMBERLAIN, Air Vice-Marshal George Philip; CB (1946), OBE (1941); s of George Arthur Raddon Chamberlain (d 1953), of Enville, Stourbridge, Worcs; *b* 18 Aug 1905; *Educ* Denstone Coll, RAF Cranwell; *m* 1930, Alfreda Rosamond, da of F M Kedward, of Swingfield, Kent; 1 s, 1 da; *Career* cmmnd RAF 1925, AOA Fighter Cmd 1954-57, Air Vice-Marshal 1955, dep controller of electronics Miny of Supply 1957, Miny of Aviation 1959-60, ret 1960; md Collins Radio Co of England Ltd 1962-66, (non-exec dir 1966-75), aviation and electronics conslt; *Recreations* gardening; *Style—* Air Vice-Marshal Philip Chamberlain, CB, OBE; Little Orchard, 12 Adelaide Close, Stanmore, Middx (☎ 081 954 0710)

CHAMBERLAIN, Kevin John; s of Arthur James Chamberlain, of Purley, Surrey, and Gladys Mary, *née* Harris; *b* 31 Jan 1942; *Educ* Wimbledon Coll, Kings Coll London (LLB); *m* 23 Sept 1967, Pia Rosita, da of Jean Frauenlob, of Geneva, Switzerland; 1 da (Georgina b 26 Aug 1975); *Career* called to the Bar Inner Temple 1965; FCO: asst legal advsr 1965-73, legal advsr Br Mil Govt Berlin 1973-76, first sec (legal advsr) HM Embassy Bonn 1976-78, legal cnsllr 1979-83, cnsllr (legal advsr) Office of the UK Perm Rep to the EC 1983-87 (legal cnsllr 1987-90, dep legal advsr 1990-); *Recreations* opera, riding, tennis, skiing; *Style—* Kevin Chamberlain, Esq; Foreign and Commonwealth Office, London SW1 2AH (☎ 071 270 3084)

CHAMBERLAIN, (Leslie) Neville; CBE (1990); s of Leslie Chamberlain (d 1970), and Doris Anne, *née* Thompson; *b* 3 Oct 1939; *Educ* King James GS Bishop Auckland, King's Coll Univ of Durham; *m* 13 April 1971, Joy Rachel, da of Capt William Wellings (d 1979); 1 s (Andrew b 1984), 3 da (Louise b 1972, Elizabeth b 1974, Christina b 1981); *Career* UKAEA: mgmnt trainee 1962-64, health physicist Springfields 1964-67, res scientist Capenhurst 1967-71; mangr URENCO 1971-77; BNFL: works mangr Springfields 1977-81, enrichment business mangr Risley 1981-84, dir Enrichment Div Risley 1984-86; chief exec British Nuclear Fuels plc Risley 1986-; FInstM, CBIM, MInstPh; *Recreations* racing, swimming, music; *Style—* Neville Chamberlain, Esq, CBE; Spring House, 56 Brimstage Rd, Heswall, Wirrall L60 1XG (☎ 051 342 5981); British Nuclear Fuels plc, Risley, Warrington, Cheshire (☎ 0925 835 006, fax 0925 817625, telex 627581, car 0860 388846)

CHAMBERLAIN, Peter Edwin; s of Dr Eric Alfred Charles Chamberlain, OBE, and Susan Winifred Louise, *née* Bone; *b* 25 July 1939; *Educ* Royal HS, Univ of Edinburgh (BSc), RNC Manadon, RNC Greenwich, RCDS; *m* 27 July 1963, Irene May, *née* Frew; 2 s (Mark b 1964, Paul b 1965), 1 da (Louise b 1970); *Career* asst constructor ship and submarine design ME and Bath 1963-68, constructor 1968-69, submarine construction Birkenhead 1969-72, ship structures R&D Dunfermline 1972-74, mgmnt of postgrad progs of Naval Architecture UCL 1974-77, Ship Design Bath 1977-78, chief constructor and head of Secretariat to DG Ships 1978-80, Surface Ship Forward Design Bath 1980-82, asst sec head of Secretariat to MGO London 1984-85, under sec dir gen Future Material Programmes 1985-87, dep controller Warship Equipment 1987-88, chief Underwater Systems Exec 1988-89, head Def Res Agency Implementation Team 1989-; RCNC 1960, FRINA 1986, FEng 1988; *Recreations* jogging, music, visual arts, poetry, computing; *Style—* Peter Chamberlain, Esq; Ministry of Defence, St George's Court, 14 New Oxford St, London WC1A 1EJ

CHAMBERLAIN, (Richard) Sebastian Endicott; s of Lawrence Endicott Chamberlain, of The Dairy House, Tonerspuddle, Dorchester, and Anne Zacyntha, *née* Eastwood (d 1969); *b* 13 April 1942; *Educ* Radley; *m* 1 Oct 1966, Lady Catherine Laura Chetwynd-Talbot, da of late 21 Earl of Shrewsbury and Waterford; 1 s (Tom b 1973), 2 da (Sophie b 1968, Amy b 1971); *Career* London div RNR 1961-70, demobbed as Lt; Maguire Roy Marshall (formerly Maguire Kingsmill): joined 1960, ptnr 1974; W Greenwell & Co 1986, dir Greenwell Montagu Stockbrokers; memb New Forest Dist Cncl 1973-79; Freeman: City of London 1963, Worshipful Co of Cordwainers 1963; memb Int Stock Exchange 1964; *Recreations* sailing; *Clubs* Royal Lymington Yacht; *Style—* Sebastian Chamberlain, Esq; Stocks Farm, Burley St, Ringwood, Hampshire (☎ 042 53 3313); 98 High St, Lymington, Hampshire (☎ 0590 674288)

CHAMBERLAIN, William Richard Frank; s of Lt Cdr Richard Chamberlain (d 1967), and Elizabeth, *née* Robson (d 1965); *b* 13 April 1925; *Educ* Uppingham; *m* 1960, Gillian Diarmid, da of Laurence Malcolm Trevor Castle; 1 s, 1 da; *Career* dir Kingsgrange plc; pres Northants CCC, chm Test and County Cricket Bd, High Sheriff of Northamptonshire 1990-91; *Recreations* shooting, cricket; *Clubs* Naval and Military, MCC; *Style—* William Chamberlain Esq; Manor House, Swineshead, Bedford MK44 2AF (☎ 0234 708283)

CHAMBERLAYNE, Lt-Col John Edward Stanes; DL (1967); s of Col Edward Tankerville Chamberlayne, DSO, DL, JP (d 1963), of Chipping Norton, Oxon, and Susan Katherine Scott MacKirdy; *b* 26 Nov 1910; *Educ* Eton, ChCh Oxford (MA); *m* 29 Oct 1936, Daphne Helena, da of Col George Henry Barnett, CMG, DSO (d 1942), of Glympton Park, Woodstock, Oxon; 2 s (Simon John b 1940, Mark Edward b 1942); *Career* 16/5 Lancers 1931, Res of Offrs 1948; Mayor of Chipping Norton 1953-55, JP (Oxon) 1953-80, High Sheriff Oxon 1966; hon sec MFHA 1956-76; *Recreations* hunting, racing; *Clubs* Jockey, Cavalry and Guards'; *Style—* Lt-Col John Chamberlayne, DL; Old Rectory, Churchill, Oxford (☎ 060 8658 601)

CHAMBERLAYNE-MACDONALD, Major Nigel Donald Peter; LVO (1960), OBE (1980), DL (1975); s of Sir Geoffrey Bosville Macdonald of the Isles, 15 Bt, MBE (d 1951), and Hon Rachael Audrey, *née* Campbell (d 1978); *b* 10 June 1927; *Educ* Radley; *m* 15 April 1958, Penelope Mary Alexandra, da of Tankerville Chamberlayne; 2 s (Alexander Nigel Bosville b 1959, Thomas Somerled b 1969), 2 da (Diana Mary (Countess of Lindsay) b 1961, Frances Penelope b 1965, d 1985); *Career* cmmnd Scots Gds 1946, served Italy 1946-47 and Malaya 1950-51, Canal Zone 1952-53; equerry to HRH The Duke of Gloucester 1954-55, and asst private sec 1958-60; High Sheriff Hampshire 1974-75; a Gentleman Usher to HM The Queen 1979; memb The Queen's Body Guard for Scotland (Royal Co of Archers); chm Hants Assoc of Boys' Clubs 1967-82, a vice chm Nat Assoc of Boys' Clubs 1969-90; pres: The Coaching Club 1982-90, Eastleigh and Chandlers Ford Boy Scouts Assoc; OStJ 1958; *Recreations* coaching, shooting, stalking; *Clubs* White's, Brooks's, Pratt's, Royal Yacht Squadron; *Style—* Major Nigel Chamberlayne-MacDonald, LVO, OBE, DL; Cranbury Park, Winchester, Hants SO21 2HL (☎ 0703 252617); Glaschoille House, Knoydart, Mallaig (☎ 0687 2244); 17 William Mews, London SW1 (☎ 071 235 5867)

CHAMBERLEN, Capt Christopher John Tankerville; LVO (1972); s of Leonard Saunders Chamberlen (d 1987), and Lillian Margaret, *née* Webley; *b* 3 Sept 1933; *Educ* RNC Dartmouth; *m* 6 Aug 1967, Eila Margaret, da of Maj George Danielsen, MBE (d 1943); 3 da (Venetia b 1968, Annabel b 1969, Jessica b 1972); *Career* RN Capt; QHM Portsmouth 1984-87; ret 1988; *Recreations* painting, shooting, riding, racing; *Clubs* RYS, Boodles, Farmers; *Style—* Capt Christopher Chamberlen, LVO, RN; West Hall, Upham, Hants SO3 1JD (☎ 04896 674)

CHAMBERLEN, Nicholas Hugh; s of Rev Leonard Saunders Chamberlen, MC (d 1987), of Heathfield, Sussex, and Lillian Margaret, *née* Webley; *b* 18 April 1939; *Educ* Sherborne, Lincoln Coll Oxford (BA); *m* 18 Sept 1962, Jane Mary, da of Paul Lindo (d 1970); 3 s (Julian b 1964, Mark b 1965, Alexander b 1970), 1 da (Camilla b 1967); *Career* Nat Serv RN 1957-59, Lt RNR, with NCR 1962-67; Clive Discount Co Ltd 1967- (dir 1969, chm 1977-); chm: London Discount Market Assoc 1985-87, European Corporate Finance Prudential-Bache Securities (UK) Inc 1990-; *Recreations* shooting, golf, cricket; *Clubs* Portland, Turf, R & A; *Style—* Nicholas Chamberlen, Esq; 9 Devonshire Square, London EC2M 4HP (☎ 081 548 4042, fax 081 548 5384, telex 895 8901)

CHAMBERLIN, Peter Guy; s of Guy Ronald Chamberlin (d 1991), and his 1 w, Geraldine Mary, *née* Payne Cook (d 1963); *b* 23 June 1942; *Educ* Eton, Aix-en-Provence Univ, RMA Sandhurst; *m* 30 Nov 1968, Marion Jacqueline, da of Lt-Col John Alan Burns (d 1987); 1 s (Edward b 1974), 2 da (Lucinda b 1970, Vanessa b 1977); *Career* Army Offr; cmmnd Green Jackets 1963; served Far East, Berlin, W Germany, NI, Canada, Hong Kong, Lt-Col CO Light Div Depot Winchester, SHAPE MA D/Saceur, UKLO Heeresamt, Cologne, ret 1989; Christies Fine Arts Auctioneers 1989-; *Recreations* cricket, golf, tennis and racquets, military history; *Clubs* MCC, I Zingari; *Style—* Peter G Chamberlin, Esq; Coldharbour House, St Mary Bourne, Andover, Hants (☎ 0264 738283)

CHAMBERLIN, Richard Alexander; s of John Alexander Chamberlin, MC, of Lenham, Kent, and Kathleen Mary, *née* Fraser (d 1990); *b* 1 July 1951; *Educ* The King's Sch Canterbury, Jesus Coll Cambridge (BA); *m* 1977, Mary-Angela, da of Norman William Stoakes Franks, of Folkestone, Kent; 2 da (Zoe b 1977, Naomi b 1979); *Career* articled Clerk Wedlake Bell 1973-75, admitted slr 1975, ptnr Freshfields 1981 (joined 1976); memb Worshipful Co of Solicitors; memb Law Soc; *Recreations* archaeology, sailing; *Clubs* Leander, Kent Archaeological Soc, Cambridge Soc (Kent Branch); *Style—* Richard Chamberlin, Esq; Whitefriars, 65 Fleet St, London EC4Y 1HT (☎ 071 936 4000)

CHAMBERS, Prof Andrew David; s of (Lewis) Harold Chambers (d 1963), of Brundle, Norfolk, and Florence Lilian, *née* Barton (d 1979); *b* 7 April 1943; *Educ* St Albans Sch, Hatfield Coll Durham (BA); *m* 1, 1969 (m dis 1984), Mary Elizabeth Ann Kilbey; 2 s (Gregory b 1976, Thomas b 1979); m 2, 2 Oct 1987, Celia Barrington, da of Rev Hugh Pruen, of Ashleigh, Old Bolingbroke, Lincs; 1 s (Theo b 1990), 1 da (Chloë b 1988), 1 step s (Henry b 1985); *Career* audit sr Arthur Anderson & Co 1965-69, admin exec Barker & Dobson 1969-70, systems gp mangr fin United Biscuits 1970-71; City University Business School: lectr Computer Applications in Accountancy 1971-74, Leverhulme sr res fell Internal Auditing 1974-78, sr lectr Audit and Mgmnt Control 1978-83, prof Internal Auditing 1983-, admin sub-dean 1983-86, dean 1986- (acting dean 1985-86); visiting prof Computer Auditing Univ of Leuven Belgium 1980-81; warden Northampton Hall City Univ 1983-86 (dep warden 1972-76); memb: Cncl BCS 1979-82, Educn Training & Technol Transfer Ctee Br Malaysian Soc 1987-; govr Islington Green Sch; FBCS, FCCA, FCA (memb IT Ctee 1986-), FIIA (chm Res Ctee 1985-86); *Books* Keeping Computers Under Control (with O J Hanson, 1975), Internal Auditing (1981), Computer Auditing (1981); *Recreations* family, conservation; *Clubs* Reform, Travellers'; *Style—* Prof Andrew Chambers; City University Business School, Frobisher Crescent, Barbican Centre, London EC2Y 8HB (☎ 071 920 0111, fax 071 588 2756)

CHAMBERS, Antony Craven; s of Brig Samuel Craven Chambers, CBE, of 45 Hillhead Rd, Fareham, and Mary Agnes, *née* McAllister; *b* 8 Dec 1943; *Educ* Ampleforth, St Catherine's Coll Oxford (MA), Manchester Business Sch (MBA); *m* 24 July 1965, Rosemary Isabel, da of Wing Cdr Gerald Constable Maxwell, DFC, AFC, AEM (d 1959), of Alresford House, Alresford, Hants; 3 s (Dominic b 1966, Sebastian b 1967, Mungo b 1977), 2 da (Antonia b 1974, Alexandra b 1979); *Career* joined Gren Gds 1966, platoon cdr Cyprus and UK, signals offr 1 Bn serv Muscat and Trucial States 1968, 2 i/c Rifle Co NI 1969-70; asst investmt mangr Hill Samuei & Co Ltd 1970-71; First Chicago 1972: N Sea project fin 1972-74, business devpt UK Branch Network 1975-77, mangr Mktg Divs 1978-81, gp head banking and mktg 1982-83, head strategic planning Euro 1984; dir Robert Fleming & Co Ltd (responsible for commercial banking) 1984-; memb: Exec Ctee and Control Bd Army Benevolent Fndn 1979, Offrs Assoc 1985; tstee Help the Aged 1987; *Recreations* sailing; *Style—* Antony Chambers, Esq; Lake House, Alresford, Hampshire (☎ 0962 733148); Robert Fleming & Co Ltd, 25 Copthall Ave, London EC2R 7DR (☎ 071 638 5858, fax 071 256 5036, telex 297451)

CHAMBERS, David John; s of George Alfred Chambers, of Middx, and Marie Louise, *née* Ackerman; *b* 19 April 1930; *Educ* Lower Sch of John Lyon Harrow; *m* 1956, Preto Hermione, da of George Chick Aggett (d 1971), of Kenya; 1 s (Peter b 1958), 2 da (Clare b 1960, Susan b 1964); *Career* non marine underwriter Lloyds 1966-1987, dir Bain Dawes underwriting agency 1980-86, md Gilliat Scotford and Hayworth Ltd 1987 (jt md 1966-86); *Books* Cock-A-Hoop, A Bibliography of the Golden Cockerel Press 1949-61 (with Christopher Sandford, 1976), Joan Hassall engravings and drawings (1985), Private Press Books, An Annual Bibliography (ed 1963-79), The Private Library, Quarterly Jl of the Private Libraries Assoc (ed 1979-); *Recreations* book collecting, printing; *Clubs* Double Crown, Private Libraries Assoc, Bibliographical Soc, Assoc Internationale de Bibliophilie; *Style—* David John Chambers, Esq; Ravelston, South View Rd, Pinner, Middx HA5 3YD

CHAMBERS, David Phillip; s of Joseph Christopher Chambers, 7 Perth Close, Huntley Way, Kingston, and Bernadette Mary, *née* Costello (d 1978); *b* 2 Aug 1953; *Educ* Beaufoy Sch Lambeth, Slough Coll of Further Educn (City and Guilds basic cookery), Ealing Coll of Further Educn (City and Guilds Chefs Dip), Westminster Coll of Further Educn; *m* 7 March 1987, Helena, da of Branko Nikola Jovicich; 2 da (Zoe Anne B 17 April 1975, Amy Louise b 21 Aug 1978); *Career* apprentice chef: Piccadilly Hotel 1969-70, St Ermins Hotel 1970-71; chef tournant St Ermins Hotel 1971-72, chef saucier East Indian Sports and Public Schools Club 1972, Claridges Hotel 1973-74 (commis poissonier, commis saucier), chef gardemanger St Ermins Hotel 1974; sous chef: Mullard House 1974-75, Army and Navy Club 1975-76, Carlton Tower Hotel 1976-78; executive chef Portman Intercontinental 1980-81 (sous chef rising to first sous chef 1978-80), exec chef Le Restaurant Dolphin Square 1981, first sous chef Hyatt Carlton Tower 1981-82, chef de cuisine Dukes Hotel 1982-85, exec head chef Le Meridien Picadilly 1985-; various tv appearances; awards for the Oak Room Restaurant: one Michelin Star, one AA rosette, one Star Egon Ronay, 4/5 Good Food Guide; memb Academie de Culinare de France; *Recreations* cooking, reading; *Style—* David Chambers, Esq; Le Meridien London, 21 Piccadilly, London W1V OBA (☎ 071 734 8000, fax 071 437 3574)

CHAMBERS, Dr Douglas Robert (Bob); s of Douglas Henry Chambers, of East Sheen (d 1979), and Elizabeth Chambers, *née* Paterson, of Richmond (d 1987); *b* 2 Nov 1929; *Educ* Sheen GS, Kings Coll London (AKC, MB BS), Univ of London (external LLB), Univ Coll Swansea (MA); *m* 8 Jan 1955, Barbara (June) *née* Rowe; 1 s (Robert Mark b 1958), 2 da (Barbara Lynn b 1955, Judith Elizabeth b 1961); *Career* Flt Lt RAF med branch 1955-58 (served Jordan 1956-57); called to the Bar Lincoln's Inn 1965; med dir Hoechst Pharmaceuticals 1965-70, HM Coroner Inner N London 1970-; hon lectr in legal med: City Univ, Univ Coll and Royal Free Hosps; awarded Baron C ver Heyden de Lancey Law/Medicine prize by RSM 1990; *Recreations* history of coroners, scouting; *Clubs* Auriol-Kensington Rowing, Wig and Pen; *Style—* Dr Bob Chambers; 4 Ormond Ave, Richmond, Surrey TW10 6TN (☎ 081 940 7745); Coroners Ct, St Pancras, London NW1 (☎ 071 387 4882)

CHAMBERS, Graham Leonard; s of Leonard Chambers, of Ipswich, Suffolk, and Agnes, *née* Thorpe; *b* 16 June 1946; *Educ* Tower Ramparts State Sch Ipswich, Ipswich Civic Centre; *m* 12 Sept 1970, Judith Joan, da of John McArthur; 1 s (Thomas McArthur b 18 April 1985), 2 da (Olivia Judith b 10 June 1982, Camilla Iona b 15 Aug 1988); *Career* articled clerk Scrutton & Goodchild Ipswich 1964-69, ptnr Dixon Wilson 1969-; FCA, ATII; *Recreations* sport, popular music; *Clubs* Bellhouse Leisure (Gerrards Cross), Chalfont St Peter Squash; *Style—* Graham Chambers, Esq; Dixon Wilson, PO Box 900, Rotherwick House, 3 Thomas Moore St, London E1 9YX (☎ 071 628 6321, fax 071 702 9769)

CHAMBERS, Lucinda Anne; da of Michael and Anne Chambers; *b* 17 Dec 1959; *Educ* Convent of the Sacred Heart Woldingham; 1 s (Toby Knott b 23 Feb 1988); *Career* sr fashion ed Elle Magazine UK 1986-88, exec fashion ed Vogue Magazine 1988- (former asst ed); *Style—* Miss Lucinda Chambers; 29 Oaklands Grove, London W12 0JA; Vogue, Vogue House, Hannover Square, London W1 (☎ 071 499 9080)

CHAMBERS, Nicholas Mordaunt; QC (1985); s of Marcus Mordaunt Bertrand Chambers, and Lona Margit, *née* Gross (d 1987); *b* 25 Feb 1944; *Educ* King's Sch Worcester, Hertford Coll Oxford; *m* 1966, Sarah Elizabeth, da of Thomas Herbert Fothergill Banks; 2 s 1 da; *Career* called to the Bar Gray's Inn 1966; rec 1987; *Recreations* sketching; *Clubs* Garrick, Lansdowne; *Style—* Nicholas Chambers, Esq, QC; Brick Court Chambers, 15-19 Devereux Court, London WC2R 3JJ (☎ 071 583 0777)

CHAMBERS, Prof Richard Dickinson; *b* 16 March 1935; *Educ* Stanley GS, Univ of Durham (PhD, DSc); *m* 17 Aug 1959, Anne, *née* Boyd; 1 s (Mark b 1963), 1 da (Louise b 1965); *Career* res fell Univ of BC Canada 1959-60, visiting lectr Fulbright Fell Case Western Reserve Univ Cleveland Ohio 1966-67, fndn fell Univ of Durham 1988-89 (lectr 1960, reader 1968, prof 1976, head of dept 1983-86); memb: Royal Soc Chem, American Chem Soc; *Books* Fluorine in Organic Chemistry (1973); *Recreations* opera, soccer, jogging; *Style—* Prof Richard Chambers; 5 Aykley Green, Whitesmocks, Durham DH1 4LN (☎ 091 3865791); Department of Chemistry, University Science Laboratories, South Rd, Durham DH1 3LE (☎ 091 3743120, fax 091 374 3741, telex 537351 DURLIB G)

CHAMBERS, Robert George; s of Peter Bertram Chambers, of Rushford Hall, Rushford, Thetford, Norfolk, and Wendy, *née* Randall; *b* 30 May 1954; *Educ* Dundle, Univ of Hull (BSc); *m* 16 May 1987, (Christine) Belinda, da of Roy Johnson, of Holmcroft, Littlington, Hertfordshire; 1 s (Nicholas b 6 Dec 1989), 1 da (Serena b 13 Dec 1990); *Career* ptnr Wedd Durlacher Mordaunt and Co 1985; dir: Barclays de Zoete Wedd 1986, Hoare Govett Securities 1989; memb London Stock Exchange 1980; *Recreations* shooting, fishing, cricket, golf; *Clubs* MCC, Royal Worlington Golf; *Style—* Robert Chambers, Esq; 106 Oakley St, London SW3 5NR (☎ 071 352 4100) Security Pacific House, 4 Broad Gate, London EC2 (☎ 071 601 0101)

CHAMBERS, Sidney Hamilton Beadnall; CBE (1972); Sidney Harry Chambers (d 1971), and Marjorie Kathleen Chambers (d 1985); *b* 9 Jan 1935; *Educ* Chatsworth HS Wahroonga; *m* 1955, Marguerite Sinclair, da of John Keith Shirley (d 1952); 3 s (Sidney b 1961, John b 1966, William b 1971); *Career* fndr Whale Three Minute Car Wash Pty Ltd; chm: Kruger Mining Co Pty Ltd, Rand Mining Co Pty Ltd, Foundation Constructions Pty Ltd; *Recreations* cricket, tennis, running; *Clubs* Australian American, Tattersalls (Sydney), Sydney Cricket Ground, Royal Agriculture Soc; *Style—* Sidney Chambers, Esq, CBE; Ellerslie, 3 Cross Street, Mosman, NSW 2088, Australia

CHAMBERS, Timothy Lachlan (Tim); adopted s of Victor Lachlan Chambers (d 1970), of Purley, Surrey, and Elsie Ruth, *née* Reynolds; *b* 11 Feb 1946; *Educ* Wallington Co GS, King's Coll London and King's Coll Hosp Univ of London (MB BS); *m* 9 Oct 1971, (Elizabeth) Joanna, da of John Carrington Ward (d 1989), of Barnstone, Notts; 1 s (Oliver b 1978), 2 da (Catherine b 1973, Rachel b 1976); *Career* conslt physician: Derbyshire Children's Hosp and Children's Depts of Nottingham Hosps 1976-79, Royal Hosp for Sick Children Bristol, Paediatric Dept Southmead Hosp 1979-; lectr in child health Univ of Bristol 1979- (clinical dean 1983-90); pres Union of Nat Euro Paediatric Socs and Assocs 1990; memb: Cncl RCP 1990, Cncl Bristol Medico-Legal Soc 1990-, med advsr Br Agencies for Adoption and Fostering (SW and Wales) 1983-; patron Lifeline charity, tstee St John's Mother and Baby Home, former hon sec Br Paediatric Assoc; Liveryman Worshipful Soc of Apothecaries 1982, Freeman City of London 1983; FRCP 1983, FRCPE 1985, MFPaed, RCPI 1989; *Books* Fluid Therapy in Childhood (1987), author of numerous contribs to scientific and lay literature; *Recreations* sundry spiritual, sensual and visceral; *Clubs* Athenaeum; *Style—* Dr T L Chambers; 4 Clyde Park, Bristol, Avon BS6 6RR (☎ 0272 742814); 2 Clifton Park, Bristol BS8 3BS (☎ 0272 730622)

CHAMPION, Dr Audrey Elizabeth; da of Robert George Champion, of Alveston N Avon, and Muriel Madge, *née* Matthews; *b* 13 July 1951; *Educ* Thornbury GS, Univ of Sheffield (MB ChB); *m* 8 Oct 1977, John Robert Glover Rogerson, s of Benjamin Rogerson, of Morley Leeds (d 1955); 1 s (Alstair b 1989), 1 da (Kathryn b 1987); *Career* conslt in radiotherapy and oncology Sheffield Health Authy and visiting conslt Doncaster Health Authy 1984-; memb BMA; MRCP 1977, FRCR 1981; *Style—* Dr Audrey Champion; Weston Park Hospital, Sheffield S10 2SJ (☎ 0742 670222)

CHAMPION, John Stuart; CMG (1977), OBE (1963); s of Rev Sir Reginald Stuart Champion, KCMG, OBE (d 1982), of Tunbridge Wells, Kent, and Margaret (d 1989), da of late Very Rev W Macgregor; *b* 17 May 1921; *Educ* Shrewsbury, Balliol Coll Oxford (BA); *m* 1944, Olive Lawrencina, da of Lawrence Durning Holt (d 1961), of Liverpool (Lord Mayor 1930); 5 s, 2 da; *Career* cmmnd Lt 11 Hussars (PAO) 1941-46, served Western Desert, Italy, and NW Europe; Colonial Serv (later HMOCS) Uganda 1946-63: dist cmmr 1954, asst fin sec 1956, actg perm sec Min of Health 1959, perm sec Min of Internal Affrs 1960, ret 1963; princ CRO 1963, 1 sec FCO 1965, head of chancery Tehran 1968, cncllr Amman 1971 (chargé d'affaires 1972), FCO 1973, Br resident cmmr Anglo/French Condominium of the New Hebrides 1975-78, ret 1978; memb W Midlands RHA 1980-81, chm Herefordshire Health Authy 1982-86, govr Royal Nat Coll for the Blind 1980- (vice chm 1985-); chm: St John Cncl for Hereford and Worcester 1987-, Cncl of Friends of Hereford Cathedral 1988-; OStJ (1987); *Recreations* hill walking, golf, music; *Style—* J S Champion, Esq, CMG, OBE; Farmore, Callow, Hereford HR2 8DB (☎ 0432 274875)

CHAMPION, Baroness; Mary Emma; *née* Williams; da of David Williams, of Pwllgwaun, Pontypridd, Glam; *m* 1930, Baron Champion (Life Peer; d 1985); 1 da (Hon Mrs Chubb, *qv*); *Style—* The Rt Hon Lady Champion; 22 Lanelay Terrace, Pontypridd, Mid Glam CF37 1ER (☎ 0443 402349)

CHAMPION, Robert (Bob); MBE; s of Bob Champion (d 1987), and Phyllis Doreen Champion, of Newmarket, Suffolk; *b* 4 June 1948; *Educ* Earl Haig Sch Guisborough Yorks; *m* 1, Oct 1982 (m dis 1985), Jo Champion; 1 s (Michael Robert b 1983); m 2, Oct 1987, Denise Frances (Dee), da of Frank Leonard Taylor (d 1972), of Hatfield Heath, Bishops Stortford; 1 da (Henrietta Camilla b 1988); *Career* jockey and trainer; one of the four top jockeys of the 1970s, recovered from cancer to win 1981 Grand National on Aldaniti (portrayed by John Hurt in film Champions premiered 1984); fndr Bob Champion Cancer Tst; *Books* Champions; *Recreations* riding; *Style—* Bob Champion, Esq, MBE; 'Beechers', Hamilton Rd, Newmarket, Suffolk (☎ 0636 666546)

CHAMPION, Dr Robert Harold; s of Harold George Champion (d 1965), of Ivy Hatch, Sevenoaks Kent, and Elsie Kate, *née* Burgess; *b* 21 March 1929; *Educ* Blundells, Gonville and Caius Coll Cambridge (MA, MB BChir); *m* 21 April 1965, Phylis Laura, da of Sir John Henry Gaddum, KBE (d 1965), of Cambridge; 2 s (David

Russell b 1970 d 1983, Richard John b 1973, d 1990), 1 da (Clare Diana b 1968); *Career* Nat Serv RAMC 1954-56; conslt dermatologist Addenbrooke's Hosp Cambridge 1961-90; pres Br Assoc of Dermatologists 1988-89 (ed 1974-81); FRCP 1974 (MRCP 1957); *Books* Urticaria (with R P Warin, 1974), The Urticarias (with M W Greaves, A Kobza Black and R J Pye, 1985), Textbook of Dermatology (ed A J Rook, D J Wilkinson, F J Ebling, J L 4 edn, 1986), Recent advances in Dermatology (edn 7, 1986 edn 8, 1990); *Recreations* postal history, music, bird watching walking; *Style—* Dr Robert Champion; Addenbrooke's Hospital, Hills Road, Cambridge CB2 2QQ (☎ 0223 216501, fax 0223 336709)

CHAMPNESS, John Ashley; *b* 17 April 1938; *m* Sandra; 2 da (Joanna Louise, Charlotte Helen); *Career* dir Lowndes Lambert Group Ltd, chm & md Lowndes Lambert Marine Ltd; dir: Wallem Lambert (Hong Kong) Ltd, Lowndes Lambert Marine Holdings Ltd, Jeffreys Coates and Associates Ltd; *Style—* John Champness, Esq; Stoneraise, Plummers Plain, Horsham, Sussex; 53 Eastcheap, London EC3P 3HL (☎ 071 283 2000)

CHANCE, Alan Derek; s of Derek Arthur Chance, of The Grange, Funtington, Chichester, and Kay, *née* Renshaw (d 1988); *b* 12 April 1951; *Educ* Eton, Merton Coll Oxford (BA); *m* 30 May 1981, Sarah Elizabeth, da of (William) Dennis Delany, of Chelwood, West Broyle Dr, nr Chichester; 2 s (Benjamin b 1984, Thomas b 1987); *Career* dir Streets Financial Ltd 1979-83, chm Chance Plastics Ltd 1978-87, dir Money Marketing Ltd 1983-86, md The Moorgate Group plc 1988-89 (dir 1986), chm %g Ltd 1990-, ptnr Chance Jarosz 1990-; *Recreations* skiing, backgammon, croquet; *Clubs* Hurlingham; *Style—* Alan Chance, Esq; Chance Jarosz, 2 Leathermarket Street, London SE1 3HN (☎ 071 357 7263)

CHANCE, Lady (Hilda) Ava Fiona Nancy; *née* Baird; 3 and yst da of 1 Viscount Stonehaven, GCMG, DSO, PC (d 1941), and Countess of Kintore (d 1974); *b* 20 April 1919; *m* 12 June 1945, Lt-Col Ronald Fulton Lucas Chance, MC, er s of Walter Lucas Chance, JP (d 1962), of Mill Green House, Wargrave, Berks; 1 s, 1 da; *Style—* The Lady Ava Chance; 2 Abbot's Garden, Malmesbury, Wilts SN16 9HY (☎ 0666 822185)

CHANCE, Sir (George) Jeremy (ffolliott); 4 Bt (UK 1900), of Grand Avenue, Hove, Co Sussex; s of Sir Roger James Ferguson Chance, 3 Bt, MC (d 1987), and Mary Georgina, *née* Rowney (d 1984); *b* 24 Feb 1926; *Educ* Gordonstoun, Ch Ch Oxford (MA); *m* 4 March 1950, his cousin, Cecilia Mary Elizabeth, 2 da of Sir Hugh Chance, CBE; 2 s, 2 da; *Heir* s, John Sebastian Chance b 2 Oct 1954; *Career* late Lt RNVR, former dir Massey-Ferguson Ltd Coventry; *Recreations* making lakes, planting trees, choral singing, painting; *Style—* Sir Jeremy Chance, Bt; Rhosgyll Fawr, Chwilog, Pwllheli, Gwynedd (☎ 0766 810584)

CHANCE, Michael Edward Ferguson; s of John Wybergh Chance (d 1984), of 59 Lyall Mews, London, and Wendy Muriel Chance (d 1970); *b* 7 March 1955; *Educ* Eton, King's Coll Cambridge (MA); *Career* opera and concert singer; BBC Promenade Concerts 1985-, Lincoln Centre NY 1985, La Scala Milan 1985, Lyon Opera 1985, Paris Opera 1988, princ singer Kent Opera 1984-88, debut Glyndebourne Festival 1989; *Style—* Michael Chance, Esq; c/o Lies Askonas Ltd, 186 Drury Lane, London WC2B 5RY (☎ 071 405 1808)

CHANCE, Michael Spencer; s of Ernest Horace Chance (d 1980), of Church Stretton, Shropshire, and Florence, *née* Kitson; *b* 14 May 1938; *Educ* Rossall; *m* 9 June 1962, Enid Mabel, da of Harry Carter (d 1958), of West Hagley, Worcs; 3 da (Karen b 1963, Helen b 1965, Susan b 1965); *Career* slr; Asst Dir Pub Prosecutions 1981-85, chief crown prosecutor for N London 1986-87, dep dir Serious Fraud Office 1987-90; *Style—* Michael Chance, Esq; 16 Frithsden, Hemel Hempstead, Herts HP1 3DD (☎ 0442 875687)

CHANCELLOR, Alexander Surtees; s of Sir Christopher Chancellor, CMG, and Sylvia, eld da of Sir Richard Paget, 2 Bt, and his 1 w, Lady Muriel Finch-Hatton, CBE, only da of 12 Earl of Winchilsea and Nottingham; *b* 4 Jan 1940; *Educ* Eton, Trinity Hall Cambridge; *m* 1964, Susanna, da of Martin Debenham, JP (3 s of Sir Ernest Debenham, 1 Bt, JP, and Cecily, niece of Rt Hon Joseph Chamberlain); 2 da; *Career* Reuters News Agency 1964-74, ed The Spectator 1975-84, asst ed Sunday Telegraph 1984-86; dep ed Sunday Telegraph 1986, US ed The Independent 1986-88, ed The Independent Magazine 1988-; *Style—* Alexander Chancellor, Esq; The Independent Magazine, 40 City Rd, London EC1

CHANCELLOR, Antony Charles Beresford; s of Francis Beresford Chancellor (d 1972), and Esther Georgina Mary, *née* Holland (d 1961); *b* 26 March 1929; *Educ* Stowe; *m* 5 Oct 1957, Honor Rosemary, da of John Fabian Boucher; 3 s (James Henry Beresford b 28 Feb 1960, Andrew William Beresford b 5 March 1963, David Charles Beresford b 8 Feb 1967), 1 da (Sarah Frances b 16 Oct 1958 d 1966); *Career* stockbroker de Zeoke & Gordon 1951-57, asst investment mangr Friend's Provident 1957-62; investment dir: Henry Ansbacher & Co 1962-68, Dawnay Day & Co Ltd 1968-80; dir Tring Hall Securities 1980-81, assoc Universal Medical & General 1981-83; dir: IFICO Investment Services 1983-85, Thornton Management Ltd 1985-; assoc memb Soc of Investmt Analysis 1961; memb: Counsel and Care for the Elderly 1979, Fin Ctee Relate Marriage Guidance Cncl 1986, IOD; *Recreations* gardening, reading, music; *Style—* Antony Chancellor, Esq; Thornton Management Ltd, 33 Cavendish Square, London W1M 0DH (☎ 071 493 7262, fax 071 409 0590)

CHANDLER, Charles Henry; s of late Charles Chandler; *b* 6 March 1940; *Educ* Highgate; *m* 1965, Christine Elizabeth, *née* Dunn; 1 s (Stephen), 1 da (Dani); *Career* chm Walthamstow Stadium Ltd 1976-; md: Greyhound Racing Assoc Ltd 1972-, GRA Ltd 1983-; *Style—* Charles Chandler, Esq; Mymfield, Kentish Lane, Brookmans Park, Herts AL9 6NQ (☎ office 081 902 8833, home 0707 52478)

CHANDLER, Sir Geoffrey; CBE (1976); s of Dr Frederick George Chandler (d 1942), and Marjorie, *née* Raimes, of Newdigate, Surrey (d 1988); *b* 15 Nov 1922; *Educ* Sherborne, Trinity Coll Cambridge (MA); *m* 1955, Lucy Bertha, da of Prof Patrick Buxton, CMG (d 1956); 4 da; *Career* Financial Times 1951-56; Royal Dutch/Shell Group 1956-78 (chm and md Shell Trinidad Ltd 1964-69; dir: Shell International, Shell Petroleum, Shell Petroleum NV); dir gen NEDO 1978-83, dir Indust Year 1986 1984-86, ldr Indust Matters 1987-89, indust advsr to Royal Soc of Arts 1987-, chm Nat Cncl for Voluntary Orgns 1989-; kt 1983; *Recreations* gardening, music; *Clubs* Athenaeum; *Style—* Sir Geoffrey Chandler, CBE; 46 Hyde Vale, Greenwich, London SE10 8HP (☎ 081 692 5304)

CHANDLER, Godfrey John; *b* 4 July 1925; *Educ* Clarks Coll London; *m* 1948, Audrey Haydee; 3 s (Timothy b 1952, Graham b 1953, Henry b 1960), 1 da (Susan b 1949); *Career* ptnr Cazenove & Co 1957-85; dir: Globe Investment Trust plc 1980-90, Strata Investment Trust plc 1985-90, Stratton Investment Trust plc 1986-90, Lloyds Development Capital Ltd 1986-90, Halifax Building Soc (London Bd 1981-87); dep chm W H Smith Group 1982-88; hon fell Darwin Coll Cambridge, visiting fell Henley Coll of Mgmnt; *Recreations* gardening, chess; *Clubs* City of London; *Style—* Godfrey Chandler, Esq; Stormont Court, Godden Green, Sevenoaks, Kent TN15 OJS (☎ 0732 61505)

CHANDLER, (William) John; s of Harold Grant Chandler (d 1985); *b* 31 May 1932; *Educ* Welwyn Garden City GS, Jesus Coll Cambridge (MA), Brunel Univ (PhD); *m* 1956, Margaret Rosa, da of Herbert B Thomas (d 1977); 3 c; *Career* called to the Bar Middle Temple; International Publishing Corp: co sec 1963, admin dir 1970; exec and planning dir Reed Int 1975, strategic mgmnt conslt 1988; chm: Chandlers, James Wilk Assoc Ltd, KC Publishing Ltd; prof Dept of Cybernetics Brunel Univ; ASCA, FCybS; *Books* Techniques of Scenario Planning (with Reed economist Paul Cockle, 19 Science of History (1984), Practical Business Planning (1987); *Recreations* yachting, music, history; *Clubs* Royal Thames Yacht; *Style—* John Chandler, Esq; 3 Willow Grove, Welwyn Garden City, Herts (☎ 0707 324600)

CHANDLER, Laurence George; JP (1985); s of Frederick Arthur Chandler (d 1986), of 24 Wingrave Rd, London W6, and Daisy Annie Chandler, *née* Hollingbery (d 1990); *b* 19 Sept 1937; *Educ* Balham and Tooting Coll of Commerce; *m* 25 May 1963, Beryl Celia, da of Cecil Charles Richards, of 8 Hayling Ave, Feltham, Middx; 2 s (Barry Laurence b 1967, Robert Alun b 1970), 1 da (Anne-Marie b 1965); *Career* CA; dir: Beryl Properties (Kingston) Ltd 1976, Adastral Aircraft Ltd 1976, Indent Aviation (UK) Ltd 1977, Kerry Tree Ltd 1982, Stoic Insur Servs Ltd 1986, Stoic Fin Servs Ltd 1986; hon auditor: Kingston Onward Tst, Peterborough Benevolent Soc, South Lodge Housing Assoc; *Recreations* cricket umpire, duplicate bridge, gardening; *Clubs* Kingston YMCA (chm), Duplicate Bridge, Hurlingham Oddfellows Cricket (pres); *Style—* Laurence Chandler, Esq, JP; 25 Church Meadow, Long Ditton, Surbiton, Surrey KT6 5EP (☎ 081 398 1295); Parman House, 30-36 Fife Rd, Kingston upon Thames, Surrey KT1 1SU

CHANDLER, Robert William; s of Robert Samuel (d 1970), of Tylers Green, Bucks, and Amy Lilian, *née* Glascoe (d 1989); *b* 19 March 1920; *Educ* NW Poly; *m* 29 Jan 1944, Elizabeth, da of William Greenham (d 1966), of Hants; 1 s (Dennis b 1946); *Career* war serv: Royal Signals; business conslt, freelance journalist; dir: Brax Ltd, Palmer Brackenbury Ltd 1965-, NSS Newsagents 1965-, Good News 1973-, RS McColl Ltd 1975-; addresses business seminars for gps of retailers; memb Inst of Journalists; *Books* Just Imagine (1986), Story of W Lavington Church (1988); *Recreations* writing; *Clubs* IOD; *Style—* Robert W Chandler, Esq; Woodpeckers, Pinewood Way, Midhurst, W Sussex GU29 9LN (☎ 0730 815187)

CHANDLER, Susan Patricia (Sue); da of Roy Chandler, and Margaret, *née* Baker; *b* 20 April 1967; *Educ* Tonbridge GS for Girls, West London Inst of Higher Educn (BSc); *Career* hockey player; England appearances: under 18 1983-85 (vice capt 1984-85), under 21 1985-89 (capt 1988-89), 6 full caps 1989-91, 11 full indoor caps 1989-91; physiology and biomechanics technician West London Inst of Higher Educn 1989-90, teacher Alleyn's Sch Dulwich 1990-; *Recreations* all sports, reading, music, theatre; *Style—* Miss Sue Chandler; 100 Evelyn Rd, Otford, Sevenoaks, Kent TN14 5PU (☎ 09592 3620); 2 Deronda Rd, Herne Hill, London SE24 9BG (☎ 081 671 2665)

CHANDLER, Prof Tony John; s of Harold William Chandler (d 1975), and Florence Ellen, *née* Moore (d 1970); *b* 7 Nov 1928; *Educ* Alderman Newton GS Leicester, King's Coll London (BSc, DipEd, MSc, PhD, MA); *m* 4 Sept 1954, Margaret Joyce; 1 s (Adrian Mark b 1960), 1 da (Kathryn Anne (Mrs Peneycad) b 1957); *Career* Nat Serv 1 Lt RAF 1950-52; prof: UCL 1969-73 (lectr 1956-65, reader 1965-69), Univ of Manchester 1973-77; master of Birkbeck Coll London 1977-79 (lectr 1952-56); author numerous articles in meteorological and geographical jls; vice pres RMS 1973-75 (sec 1969-73); memb: NERC, Ctee of Experts on Major Hazards Health and Safety Exec, Royal Cmmn on Environmental Pollution 1973-77, Royal Soc Study Gp on Pollution in the Atmosphere 1974-77, Standing Ctee on Energy and the Environment 1978; *Books* The Climate of London (1965), Modern Meteorology and Climatology (1972 and 1981); *Recreations* clockmaking and collecting, reading, travel, music; *Style—* Prof Tony Chandler; Charnwood, 44 Knoll Rise, Orpington, Kent BR6 0EL (☎ 0689 832880); Department of Geography, University College London, 26 Bedford Way, London WC1H 0AP (☎ 071 387 7050, fax 071 380 7565)

CHANDLEY, (Charles William) Duncan; s of Samuel Chandley (d 1978), of Stockport, Cheshire, and Annie, *née* Kemp (d 1965); *b* 23 June 1940; *Educ* Stockport Sch; *m* 3 Aug 1963, Anne, da of George Robert Forster (d 1957), of Macclesfield, Cheshire; 2 da (Victoria b 1965, Elizabeth b 1967); *Career* CA 1962; certified accountant 1972; ptnr Thomas Silvey Campbell and Bowden 1964-68, divnl internal auditor Organics and Pharmaceuticals Divs ICI 1968-70, sr ptnr Proud Goulbourn and Co 1985- (ptnr 1972-); dir: Leafstan Ltd 1972-, Clevebrook Ltd 1979-, Bribow Ltd 1982-, Northwest Management Servs Ltd 1984-90; sec Blackstock (Financiers) Ltd 1974-; *Recreations* chess, swimming; *Clubs* Bramhall chess; *Style—* Duncan Chandley, Esq; 14 Avondale Ave, Hazel Grove, Stockport, Cheshire (☎ 061 483 7626); 103 Castle St, Edgeley, Stockport SK3 9AR (☎ 061 480 1928)

CHANDOS, 3 Viscount (1954 UK); Thomas Orlando Lyttelton; s of 2 Viscount Chandos (d 1980, himself ggs of 4 Baron Cobham) and Caroline (da of Sir Alan Lascelles, who was in his turn gs of 4 Earl of Harewood); *b* 12 Feb 1953; *Educ* Eton, Worcester Coll Oxford; *m* 19 Oct 1985, Arabella Sarah Lucy, da of Adrian Bailey, by his 1 wife Mary Katherine (now Lady Mary Russell), o da of 12 Earl of Haddington, KT; 2 s (Hon Oliver, Hon Benedict b 30 April 1988), 1 da (b 19 March 1990); *Heir* s, Hon Oliver Antony Lyttelton b 21 Feb 1986; *Career* assist dir Kleinwort Benson Jan 1982-; sat in Lords as Cross Bencher to Nov 1981 when joined SDP; *Style—* The Rt Hon the Viscount Chandos; The Vyne, Sherborne St John, Basingstoke, Hants (☎ 0256 881227)

CHANDOS-POLE, Maj (John) Walkelyne; JP (Derbyshire 1951), DL (1961); s of Col Reginald Walkelyne Chandos-Pole, TD, JP (d 1930), and his 2 wife, Inez Blanche Marie Clotilde Eva, *née* Arent (d 1941); *b* 4 Nov 1913; *Educ* Eton, RMC; *m* 1947, Ilsa Jill Barstz, er da of late Emil Ernst Barstz, of Zürich; 1 da (and 1 s decd); *Career* Maj late Grenadier Gds; ADC to Viceroy of India 1938-39; High Sheriff of Derbyshire 1959; *Recreations* shooting; *Clubs* Army and Navy, Lansdowne, Derby County, MCC; *Style—* Maj Walkelyne Chandos-Pole, JP, DL; Radburne Hall, Kirk Langley, Derby DE6 4LZ (☎ 033 124 246)

CHANIN, Christopher John Munday; *Educ* East Ham GS, Polytechnic of the South Bank (BA, RIBA Graduate Dip Part 1), Polytechnic of North London, Open Univ; *Career* engrg asst Haden Young (H & V Consultants) 1963-65; architectural asst: GMW Partnership (Architects) 1965-67, Charringtons Architects Dept 1967-68; John Lewis Partnership Architects Dept 1968-69, estates mangr and architectural asst Caters Estate Department 1969-74, project controller Fitch & Co 1974-79, sr designer Stewart McColl Design Associates 1979, project architect GMW Partnership 1979-80, sr designer and assoc AID (AIDCOM PLC) Design Consultants 1980-82; assoc dir: Conran Associates 1982-83, Fitch & Co 1983-87 (and divnl dir); McColl Ltd: divnl dir 1987-,gp dir of interiors 1988-, md of interiors (London) 1988-, dir S & P McColl 1989-, dir Walker Group McColl 1990-; memb Westminster C of C, assoc Chartered Inst of Building; MCSD, FBIM, FRSA; *Recreations* flying, clay pigeon and target shooting, walking, theatre, mountain biking, philosophy, classic cars, material arts, art and architecture - particularly historic buildings; *Clubs* RAC, Stapleford Flying; *Style—* Christopher Chanin, Esq

CHANNING, Leslie Thomas; s of Richard Channing (d 1958), of 30 Pembridge Avenue, Twickenham, and Salome Charlotte, *née* Munns (d 1956); *b* 24 April 1916; *Educ* Wandsworth Co Sch, Regent St Poly Sch of Architecture; *m* 1, 30 March 1940, Florence Helen (d 1986), da of Thomas Cole, of 30 Hounslow Gardens, Hounslow; 1 s (Richard Arthur b 1946), 1 da (Elaine Margaret b 1941); m 2, 5 June 1987, Audrey Joan, *née* Glanvill; *Career* served WWII Flying Offr RAF Vol Res (BEF camouflage and intelligence) 1940-44, SEAC 1944-46; asst architect: London CC 1946-48, Middx CC 1948-55, Official Architects Dept Church Cmmrs 1955-77; work incl: bishops houses, churches, parsonages, Bishop's House Manchester 1964, new Church of St Richard's Hanworth 1963; artist; exhibited regularly in: Art Soc's Exhibitions, Mall Galleries, United Soc, Nat Soc; one man exhibition of landscapes and watercolours Fairfield Hall Croydon 1980; memb: Thames Valley Arts Club, United Soc of Artists; assoc memb Nat Soc of Painters Sculptors and Printmakers; ARIBA; *Recreations* landscape water colour painting, rambling; *Clubs* United Artist, Thames Valley Arts; *Style*— Leslie Channing, Esq; 4 Raleigh Way, Hanworth, Middlesex TW13 7NX (☎ 081 890 3110)

CHANNON, Derek French; s of John French Channon; *b* 4 March 1939; *Educ* Eastbourne GS, Univ Coll London (BSc), Univ of Manchester (MBA), Harvard Grad Sch of Business Admin (DBA); *m* 1963, Ann Lesley (m dis 1987); 1 s, 1 da; *Career* formerly with Royal Dutch Shell Gp, md Evode Hldgs 1976-77, prof of marketing Manchester Business Sch 1978-90; prof of strategic mgmnt and mktg Imperial Coll London 1990-; assoc dir Manchester Business Sch 1986-87; dir Royal Bank of Scotland 1988; pres Strategic Mgmnt Soc 1986-88; *Books* Strategy and Structure of British Enterprise (1973), The Service Industries (1976), British Banking Strategy (1977), Multinational Strategic Planning (1979), Bank Strategic Management and Marketing (1986), Global Banking Strategy (1988); *Style*— Prof Derek Channon

CHANNON, Gordon Anthony; s of Walter Henry Channon (d 1953), of St Thomas, Exeter, and Rose, *née* Kelly (d 1968); *b* 2 July 1926; *Educ* The John Stocker Sch Exeter, Univ of Exeter (MA); *m* 3 Sept 1966, Christine, da of Willie Doughty; 2 c (Helen Louise b 30 June 1967, Alistair John b 14 Feb 1969, d 26 Jan 1975); *Career* Yeo & Co: articled clerk 1952-57, qualified chartered accountant 1957, ptnr 1959-69; tax ptnr Simpkins Edwards 1969-; p/t lectr Dept of Economics Univ of Exeter 1975-; chm: S W Soc of CAs Tax Ctee 1980-, Exeter & Dist Soc of CAs 1985-86; pres: S W Branch Inst of Taxation 1984-87, S W Eng Branch Chartered Assoc of Certified Accountants 1985-86, S W Soc of CAs 1990-91 (EC rep 1989-); FCA 1967 (ACA 1957), FTII 1980, FCCA 1980, MBIM 1975; *Books* Inheritance Tax (with J Coombes 1988), Economics of Taxation Work Book (jtly, 1978-); *Recreations* hiking; *Style*— Gordon Channon, Esq; 12 Cricket Field Court, Cricket Field Lane, Budleigh Salterton, Devon EX9 6JB (☎ 03954 2927); Simpkins Edwards, Chartered Accountants, Michael House, Castle St, Exeter, Devon EX4 3LQ (☎ 0392 211233, fax 0392 413173)

CHANNON, Michael Ronald (Charles); s of Ronald Arthur Channon (d 1970), and Kathleen, *née* Gamblin; *b* 7 June 1936; *Educ* Battersea GS, Jesus Coll Camb (MA); *Career* assoc dir British Market Research Bureau 1961-70, creative mangr and sr assoc dir J Walter Thompson 1972-74 (accountant dir 1970-72), vice chm Ayer Barker Ltd 1977-85 (dir 1974-85), special advsr Charles Barker Gp 1985-88, dir of studies Inst of Practitioners in Advertising 1985-; author of numerous papers on res, account planning and advertising; memb: Market Res Soc, Advertising Assoc Info Ctee, London Diocesan Synod; guardian of the Shrine of Our Lady of Walsingham; FIPA, FRSA; *Books* Advertising Works 3 (ed, 1975), Advertising Works 4 (ed 1987); *Recreations* decorative arts, architecture, gardens; *Clubs* Reform; *Style*— Charles Channon, Esq; Lower Ground Floor Flat, 21 Edith Rd, London W14 0SU (☎ 071 602 8009); Institute of Practitioners in Advertising, 44 Belgrave Square, London SW1X 9QS (☎ 071 235 7020)

CHANNON, Rt Hon (Henry) Paul Guinness; PC (1980), MP Southend W 1959-; s of late Sir Henry ('Chips') Channon, MP (d 1958), of Kelvedon Hall, Brentwood, Essex, and Lady Honor Svejdar, *née* Guinness, da of 2 Earl of Iveagh; *b* 9 Oct 1935; *Educ* Eton, Ch Ch Oxford; *m* 1963, Ingrid, formerly w of Hon Jonathan Guinness, *qv*, and da of Maj Guy Wyndham, MC (gs of Hon Percy Wyndham, 2 s of 1 Baron Leconfield), by his 2 w Grethe, da of G Wulfsberg, of Bergen, Norway; 1 s (Henry b 1970), 2 da (Olivia d 1986, Georgia b 1966); *Career* served RHG 1954-56; Min of Power 1959-60, PPS to: Home Sec 1960-62, Foreign Sec 1963-64; oppn spokesman Arts and Amenities 1967-70, Parly sec Miny Housing and Local Govt 1970, Parly under-sec Environment 1970-72, min of state N Ireland 1972, min Housing and Construction Environment Dept 1972-74, oppn spokesman Prices and Consumer Protection 1974, oppn spokesman Environmental Affairs 1974-75, min of state CSD 1979-81, min for the Arts 1981-83, min for Trade 1983-86, sec of state for Trade and Indust 1986-87, sec of state for Tport 1987-July 1989; *Style*— The Rt Hon Paul Channon, MP; House of Commons, London

CHANON, Charles; s of Ben Shimon Shimon (d 1974), and Behar Zelda (d 1989); *b* 16 May 1934; *Educ* Ecole Alliance Française Baghdad, Shamash Sch Baghdad, Technion Israel Inst of Tech Haifa (BSc); *m* 22 July 1964 (m dis 1986), Nepomiachty Marina, da of Leonid (d 1962) 1 s (Robert b 7 Oct 1965), 2 da (Sophie b 23 May 1967, Nathalie b 6 May 1975); *Career* design engr Schwartz Hautmont Paris 1957-60 (chief engr Paris 1960-6 chief engr London 1964-69, assoc ptnr Lowe Rodin and OTH 1969-71), md OTH UK London 1971-73 pres Charles Chanon and ptnrs London 1973-, main bd dir Finotel plc London 1984-; contrib num articles to professional jls; MInstM 1972, FBIM (MBIM 1973), CEng 1975, MICE 1975; *Books* Construction in the Common Market (1974); *Recreations* swimming, shooting, music; *Style*— Charles Chanon, Esq; 12 Admiral Court, Chelsea Harbour, London SW10 0XD (☎ 071 823 3159); Charles Chanon & Partners, 9 Belgrave Rd, London SW1V 1QB (☎ 071 828 7570/5470, fax 071 233 6024)

CHANT, Anthony; s of Percival James Chant, and Ethel Eleanor, *née* Quick (d 1987); *b* 21 Feb 1938; *Educ* Hitchin GS, Univ of London (BSc, MB BS, MS); *m* 21 March 1959, Ann Nadia, da of Edwin Venning (d 1940); 3 s (Ben b 1963, Harvey b 1964, Thomas b 1966); *Career* conslt vascular surgn Wessex Med Sch; Southampton Univ Hosps; author of works on vascular physiology, vascular and gen surgery, med mgmnt and ethics; FRCS; *Recreations* fishing; *Style*— Anthony Chant, Esq; Royal South Hants Hospital, Southampton (☎ 0703 634288 ext 2405/2654)

CHANT, (Leonard Ernest) John; CBE (1986); s of Leonard Joseph Chant (d 1949), of Chard, Somerset, and Dorothy Frances Chant (d 1938); *b* 23 April 1938; *Educ* Huish Episcopi, Yeovil Tech Coll, Bristol Poly, Univ of Edinburgh (Cert PSW, CSW); *m* 31 Aug 1963, Catherine Joyce, da of John Orr (d 1977), of Moffat, Scotland; 1 s (Eric John), 2 da (Kitty, Laura); *Career* dir social servs Somerset CC 1975-88 (supt mental welfare offr 1970-72, asst dir 1972-74), dir social work Lothian Regnl Cncl 1988, social servs assessor Cleveland Child Abuse Enquiry 1988; vice pres Somerset Alcoholism Cncl, SRN, RMN; *Recreations* fly fishing, collecting vintage pens, English watercolours; *Style*— John Chant, Esq, CBE; c/o Lothian Regional Council, Edinburgh

CHANT-SEMPILL, Hon Ian David Whitemore; s (by 2 m) of Lady Sempill, *qv*; *b* 2 April 1951; *Educ* Oratory Sch; *m* 1980, Amanda, yr da of Anthony Dallas, of Blackmoor, Burghfield, Berks; 1 s (Hamish b 1987), 1 da (Clementine b 1985); *Career* Maj Gordon Highlanders; ADC to GOC Scotland 1975-76, Adjt 1 Bn The Gordon Highlanders 1976-78, SO3 G3 HQ33 Armd Bde 1983-84, SO2 DS JDSC 1987-; *Recreations* shooting, fishing, cooking, country pursuits; *Style*— The Hon Ian Chant-Sempill

CHANTER, Rev Canon Anthony R; s of Charles Harry Chanter (d 1989), of Jersey, CI, and Eva Marjorie, *née* Le Cornu (d 1966); *b* 24 Oct 1937; *Educ* Hautlieu Sch Jersey, Salisbury Theol Coll, Open Univ (BA), Univ of London (MA); *m* 10 Sept 1966, Yvonne, da of Flt Lt William Reid (ka 1944); 2 da (Fiona b 31 May 1968, Alison b 15 May 1975); *Career* priest vicar Lincoln Cathedral 1970-73; headmaster: Bishop King Sch Lincoln 1970-73, Grey Court Sch Ham Richmond upon Thames 1973-77, Bishop Reindorp Sch Guildford 1977-84; dir of educn Diocese of Guildford 1984-, hon canon Guildford Cathedral 1984-; memb Educn Ctee Surrey CC 1984-, dir Guildford Diocesan Bd of Fin; memb Nat Assoc of Headteachers; *Books* Student Profiling (co-author 1980); *Recreations* golf, cricket, squash, windsurfing, music, opera; *Clubs* Sion Coll, Worplesdon Golf; *Style*— The Rev Canon Anthony Chanter; Grasshoppers, Woodland Ave, Cranleigh, Surrey GU6 7HU (☎ 0483 273833); Diocesan House, Quarry St, Guildford, Surrey (☎ 0483 571836)

CHANTLER, Prof Cyril; s of Fred Chantler (d 1957), of Blackpool, Lancashire, and Marjorie, *née* Clark; *b* 12 May 1939; *Educ* Wrekin Coll Shropshire, St Catharines Coll Cambridge (BA), Guys Hosp Med Sch (MB BChir), Univ of Cambridge (MD); *m* 1963, Shireen M Saleh; 2 s (Paul Frederick b 29 July 1965, Jonathan Mark b 22 June 1967), 1 da (Nariane Emma b 24 May 1970); *Career* house physician and registrar London Chest Hosp 1965; sr house offr: Whittington Hosp London 1966, Hosp for Sick Children Great Ormond St 1968; sr house offr in paediatrics RPMS 1967, registrar Queen Elizabeth Hosp for Children London 1968; Guy's Hosp: house offr 1963-64, sr registrar 1970, sr lectr in paediatrics and conslt paediatrician 1971, chm Paediatrics Div 1977-80, chm Mgmnt Bd and unit gen mangr 1985-88; prof of paediatric nephrology Guy's Hosp Med Sch 1980, clinical dean United Med and Dental Schs of Guy's and St Thomas' Hosp 1989-; MRC: memb external staff 1967, clinical research fell 1967, Inst of Child Health 1969, travelling fell Univ of Calif 1971; memb: Registration Ctee Euro Dialysis and Transplant Assoc 1975-80, Euro Soc for Paediatric Nephrology 1978-81 (memb Cncl 1978-81), Br Paediatric Assoc 1983-86 (memb Academic Bd 1983-86), NHS Policy Bd 1989-, Cncl Renal Assoc 1981, Grants Cncl Br Kidney Patients Assoc 1985-; med advsr Children Nationwide Med Res Fund 1986-; examiner in paediatrics: Univ of Hong Kong 1985, Univ of Birmingham 1985-87, Conjoint Bd 1979-85, RCP 1985-, Univ of Kebangsaan 1988, Royal Coll of Surgery of Ireland 1990; RCP: lectr 1987, pro-censor 1989, censor 1990; *publications* Jt author of reports for Br Assoc of Paediatric Nephrology: Future Care of Children with Renal Failure (1975), Siting of Units to Care for Children with Chronic Renel Failure (1980); Contrib to scientific literature on paediatrics, kidney disease and managment in the NHS; *Recreations* squash, golf, walking, reading, opera; *Style*— Prof C Chantler; 60 Herne Hill, London SE24 9QP (☎ 071 274 6061); Dean's Office, United Medical and Dental Schools, Guy's Hospital, London SE1 9RT (☎ 071 955 4222, fax 071 407 0082)

CHANTRY, Dr George William; s of George William Chantry (d 1979), of Wallasey, Merseyside, and Sophia Veronica, *née* Johnson (d 1973); *b* 13 April 1933; *Educ* St Francis Xavier's Coll Liverpool, ChCh Oxford (MA, DPhil); *m* Diana Margaret Rhodes, da of William Rhodes Martin, (d 1969), of Little Hampton, Sussex; 2 s (Richard b 1959, Paul b 1967), 1 da (Catherine b 1961); *Career* res assoc Cornell Univ 1958-60; NPL Teddington: sr res fell 1960-62, sr sci offr 1962-67, princ sci offr 1967-73, sr princ sci offr 1973-82; cnsllr (sci and technol) HM Embassy Bonn 1982-85, asst dir (indust) SDIPO/MOD 1985-90, dir Euro Ops Carnham & Assocs and conslt on SDI Technology Transfer to the MOD 1990-; FInstP 1973, FIEE 1976, CEng 1976, CPhys 1985; *Books* incl Long-Wave Optics (1982); *Recreations* music, philately, bridge, gardening; *Style*— Dr George Chantry; 42 Cranwell Grove, Shepperton, Middx TW17 0JR (☎ 0932 560524, business ☎ 0932 569951, fax 071 2184081)

CHAPLIN, Hon Mrs Niall; Angela Marjory; only da of Hon Claud Lambton (d 1945, 7 s of 2nd Earl of Durham) by his w Lettice (herself 2 da of Edward Wormald); *b* 12 Oct 1902; *m* 1961, as his 2 w, Hon Niall Greville Chaplin (d 1963, yr s of 2nd Viscount Chaplin); *Style*— The Hon Mrs Niall Chaplin; Flat 4, 34 Ennismore Gdns, London SW7 (☎ 071 589 7997)

CHAPLIN, Bob; s of Dennis Robert Chaplin, of Battle, E Sussex, and Barbara Annie, *née* Crouch; *b* 22 May 1947; *Educ* Ravensbourne Coll of Art and Design (Dip AD), Brighton Coll of Art (ATC); *m* 1, 27 Jan 1972 (m dis 1984), Susannah, *née* Porter; 1 s (William Robert George b 1975), 1 da (Elizabeth b 1972); m 2, 2 Nov 1986, Prudence Mary, da of Jerome Sloane; *Career* artist and specialist in painted and photographic techniques; works in collections at: Tate Gallery, Victoria and Albert, Arts Cncl of GB, Br Cncl, Stedelijk Amsterdam, Museum of Modern Art NY; memb: Trout Unlimited, Theodore Gordon Flyfishers NY; *Books* North Norway-Nord Norge (1985), Postcards to the Undercliff (with Keith Please, 1986); *Recreations* flyfishing, gardening; *Style*— Bob Chaplin, Esq; 245 Main St, PO Box 41, Route 97, Hampton, CT 06247, USA (☎ 010 1 203 455 0596)

CHAPLIN, John Cyril; CBE (1988); s of Ernest Stanley Chaplin, of Beckthorns, Keswick, Cumbria (d 1966), and Isobel, *née* Mackereth (d 1944); *b* 13 Aug 1926; *Educ* Keswick Sch Cumbria; *m* 17 Sept 1949, Ruth Marianne, da of Raymond Livingstone (d 1961), of Village Farm, Owslebury, Winchester, Hants; 2 s (Peter b 1951, Alistair b 1965), 2 da (Rosalind b 1954, Sarah b 1958); *Career* aeronautical engr; CAA: DG Airworthiness 1979-83, gp dir Safety Regulation 1983-88, memb Bd 1983-88, chm Ops Advsy Ctee 1984-; FEng; *Recreations* sailing, photography; *Clubs* Cruising Assoc; *Style*— John Chaplin, Esq, CBE; Norman Croft, Vicarage Lane, Mattingley, Basingstoke, Hampshire RG27 8LF (☎ 0734 326 207)

CHAPLIN, (Sybil) Judith; da of Theodore Thomas Schofield (d 1981), of The Grove, Harpenden, Herts, and Sybil, *née* Saunders (d 1988); *b* 19 Aug 1939; *Educ* Wycombe Abbey Sch, Girton Coll Cambridge (MA), UEA (Dip Econ); *m* 1, 30 June 1962 (m dis 1979), Hon Robert Horatio Walpole (now 10 Baron Walpole, *qv*); m 2, 21 Sept 1984, (Frederick John) Michael Chaplin, CBE, JP; *Career* headmistress ind pre-preparatory sch 1967-75, Martin & Acock accountants Norwich 1977-82, Cons Res Dept Central Office 1983-86, head of policy unit IOD 1987-88; special advsr to Chancellor of the Exchequer 1988-90, political sec to PM 1990-; vice chm Educn Ctee Assoc of Co Cncls; memb: Burnham Ctee, Secdy Exam Cncl, Interim Advsy Ctee on Teachers' Pay, Nat Fndn for Educnl Res, BTEC; *Recreations* opera, long distance walking, riding; *Style*— Mrs Judith Chaplin; 10 Downing St, London SW1

CHAPLIN, Lady; Oona; da of Eugene Gladstone O'Neill (d 1953), the American Playwright, and his 3 wife Agnes Boulton (d 1968); *m* 1943, as his 4 wife, Sir Charles Spencer Chaplin, KBE (Charlie Chaplin, d 1977, actor and producer); 3 s (Michael b 1946, Eugene b 1953, Christopher b 1962), 5 da (Geraldine b 1944, Josephine b 1949, Victoria b 1951, Jane b 1957, Annette b 1959); *Style*— Lady Chaplin; c/o United Artists Ltd, 142 Wardour St, London W1

CHAPLIN, Viscountess; Hon Rosemary; *née* Lyttelton; only da of 1 Viscount Chandos, DSO, MC (d 1972), by his w Lady Moira Osborne (herself 4 da of 10 Duke of Leeds) (d 1972); *b* 30 May 1922; *m* 1951, as his 2 w, 3 and last Viscount Chaplin (d 1981); 2 da (Hon Miranda and Hon Christina Chaplin, *qqv*); *Style*— The Rt Hon the Viscountess Chaplin; Wadstray House, Blackawton, Totnes, S Devon (☎ 080 421 232); 61 Ladbroke Rd, London, W11 3PN

CHAPLIN, William John Montague; s of late Rev Canon William Robert Moffett Chaplin; *b* 28 Feb 1932; *Educ* Shrewsbury, St Edmund Hall Oxford; *m* 1957, Claire Mary, *née* Pedder; 3 s, 1 da; *Career* farmer and co dir; chm Titus Wilson and Sons Ltd 1975-90; dir: Hawker Marris Ltd 1966-79, Thomas Reed Ltd 1969-, S Cumbria and N Lancs Management Ltd 1984-; High Sheriff of Cumbria 1982-83; memb: Lake District

Special Planning Bd 1982-85, National Tst Regnl Ctee 1985-89; chm Exec Ctee Abott Hall Art Gallery 1986-89; *Style—* W J M Chaplin, Esq; Finsthwaite House, nr Ulverston, Cumbria (☎ 05395 31339)

CHAPMAN; *see*: Dugan-Chapman

CHAPMAN, Angela Mary; da of Frank Dyson Rowe, of Cleveland, and Mary, *née* Almond; *b* 2 Jan 1940; *Educ* Queen Victoria HS Stockton-on-Tees, Sorbonne (Diplôme de Civilisation Française), Univ of Bristol (scholarship, BA); *m* 20 June 1959, Ian Michael Chapman, s of Oswald Percy Chapman (d 1973); 2 s (Jonathan Ashley b 23 July 1960, Callum Michael b 23 Oct 1963); *Career* teacher of French Bede Sch Sunderland 1970-80, dep head Newcastle-upon-Tyne Church HS 1980-84 headteacher Central Newcastle HS GPDST 1984-; FRSA; *Recreations* walking, tennis, Western Front; *Style—* Mrs Angela Chapman, FRSA; 14 Alpine Way, Humbledon Hill, Sunderland, Tyne & Wear SR3 1TN (☎ office 091 2811768)

CHAPMAN, Prof Antony John; s of Arthur Charles Chapman, of Canterbury, and Joan Muriel Chapman; *b* 21 April 1947; *Educ* Bexley GS, Univ of Leicester (BSc, PhD); *m* 1 June 1985, Siriol Sophia Jones, da of Cledan David, of Llanddowror, Dyfed; 2 s (David Charles Luke b 1987, Luke Christopher David b 1989); *Career* sr lectr UWIST Cardiff 1978-83 (lectr 1971-78), dir Centre for Applied Psychological Studies Univ of Leeds 1987- (pres 1983-), author 12 books 1976-, ed British Journal of Psychology 1989-; pres Br Psychological Soc 1988-89; FBPsS; *Style—* Prof Antony Chapman; Dept of Psychology, University of Leeds, Leeds LS2 9JT (☎ 0532 335717, fax 0532 335749, telex 556473)

CHAPMAN, Barbara, Lady; Barbara May; *née* Tonks; da of Hubert Tonks, of Delmar, Halgranoya, Ceylon, and Harvington, nr Evesham, Worcs; *m* 18 Jan 1941, Sir Robin (Robert Macgowan) Chapman, 2 Bt, CBE, TD, JP, DL (d 1987); 2 s, 1 da; *Career* Pres: Jarrow Cons Assoc, St Clare's Hospice South Shields, South Shields Ladies Lifeboat Guild; vice pres: YWCA North East Area, Tyne & Wear SSAFA; vice chm S Tyneside NSPCC; patron: 3 c's S Tyneside Archbishop's Inner City project, S Tyneside Vol Project; *Style—* Barbara, Lady Chapman; Pinfold House, Cleadon, Sunderland (☎ 091 536 7451)

CHAPMAN, Christine M; OBE (1984); da of Richard D F Chapman (d 1978), and Doris M, *née* Hulbert; *b* 15 Oct 1927; *Educ* Kings Norton GS, Goldsmith Coll Univ of London (BSc, MPhil); *Career* tutor Gen Hosp Birmingham 1951-52 (registered nurse and staff nurse 1949-50, night sister 1950-51); nurse tutor: Royal Salop Infirmary Shrewsbury 1957-59 (ward sister 1952-55), The Middx Hosp London 1959-60; lectr in health serv mgmnt Univ of York, dean of nursing studies Univ of Wales Coll of Med 1987- (dir 1972, prof 1984, retd 1989, emeritus prof 1989-); chm: RCN Bd of Educn 1976-89, Welsh Nat Bd for Nursing Midwifery Health Visiting 1986-90; lay memb GMC 1987-; FRCN (1977 MRCN 1949), FRSM 1988; *Books* Sociology for Nurses (3 edn, 1986), Theory of Nursing (1987), Professional and Ethical Issues in Nursing (with P Burnard, 1988), Nursing Education; The Way Ahead (with P Burnard, 1989); *Recreations* music, gardening, embroidery; *Style—* Prof Christine Chapman, OBE; Pedlars, Pound Lane, Woodbury, Devon

CHAPMAN, Christopher Henry George (Kit); MBE (1989); s of Peter Francis Chapman, of Taunton, and Georgette (Etty), *née* Rosi; *b* 10 March 1947; *Educ* Taunton Sch, Univ of Surrey (BSc, pres Food and Wine Soc); *m* 1971, (Marie) Louise Anne, da of Peter Edward Guiver; 2 s (Dominic Alexander Pierre b 1973, Nicholas Mark Christopher b 1975); *Career* advertising exec 1969-76 (ultimately with Benton and Bowles Ltd), md The Castle Hotel Taunton 1980- (mktg dir 1976-80), columnist Caterer and Hotelkeeper 1983-88; W Country Tourist Bd: memb Exec Ctee 1977-, chm Commercial Memb's Gp 1980-86, vice pres 1986-; ministerial appointee Exmoor Nat Park Ctee 1979-81, chm Prestige Hotels 1985-87; memb: Leisure Industs Econ Devpt Ctee NEDC 1987-89, Nat Advsy Catering Cncl 1987-, Bd Somerset Training and Enterprise Cncl (TEC) 1989-; *Awards* Caterer and Hotelkeeper awards (CATEYS) Tourism Award 1987, Ward Cavendish Trophy for the Small Business Award 1980 and 1981, British Airways and BTA award for Overseas Mktg 1981, Good Hotel Guide César award for Best Town Hotel 1987, RAC Blue Ribbon award 1987, 1988, 1989 and 1990, Caterer and Hotelkeeper awards (CATEYS) Function Menu of the Year award 1989; Freeman City of London 1984; Master Innholder 1984, FTS, FHCIMA; *Publications* Tourism...Asset for all Seasons (1982), Local Authorities and the Private Sector: Towards a Business Partnership (1983), A Guide to Business Entertaining in the West Country (1986), Great British Chefs (1989); shortlisted for the 1990 André Simon Book Award; *Recreations* good food and wine, walking the Quantocks with the dogs, reading, keeping a journal; *Clubs* Garrick, One Ninety Queensgate; *Style—* Kit Chapman, Esq, MBE; The Castle Hotel, Taunton, Somerset TA1 1NF (☎ 0823 272671, fax 0823 336066)

CHAPMAN, Prof Christopher Hugh; s of John Harold Chapman, of Vicarage Field, Church Road, Milton under Wychwood, Oxford, and Margaret Joan, *née* Weeks; *b* 5 May 1945; *Educ* Latymer Upper Sch, Christ's Coll Cambridge (BA, MA, PhD); *m* 1 June 1974, Lillian, da of Michael Tarapaski, of Redwater, Alberta, Canada; 1 s (Timothy b 26 May 1978), 1 da (Heather b 24 June 1981); *Career* asst prof Dept of Geology and Geophysics Univ California Berkley 1972-73, assoc prof Dept of Physics Univ of Alberta Canada 1973-74 (asst prof 1969-72), Green scholar Univ of California San Diego 1978-79, prof Dept of Physics Univ of Toronto Canada 1980-84 and 1988-90 (assoc prof 1974-80), prof of geophysics Dept of Earth Sciences Cambridge 1984-88, scientific advsr Schlumberger Cambridge Research 1991-; memb: SEG, SSA, FRAS, FAGU; *Recreations* sailing, photography; *Style—* Prof Christopher Chapman; 7 Spinney Drive, Great Shelford, Cambridge CB2 5LY (☎ 0223 845007); Schlumberger Cambridge Research, PO Box 153, Cambridge CB3 0HG (☎ 0223 325576)

CHAPMAN, Colin; s of Charles Stocker Chapman (d 1974), and Norah Veronica, *née* Onions (d 1983); *b* 3 April 1935; *Educ* Malet Lambert HS Kingston Upon Hull, Univ of Keele (BA), UEA (MA), Cambridge Inst of Educn (Adv Dip Ed); *m* 1962, Shelagh Margaret, da of Walter McCann; 1 s (Michael b 1963); *Career* prospecting offr NCB Opencast Exec 1957-60; teacher: Kingston HS and Elizabethan Hall Kingston upon Hull, Silver Jubilee and County Upper Schs Bury St Edmunds, Thurleston HS Ipswich; educnl conslt; asst chief examiner E Anglian Bd 1967-70, examiner London and E Anglian Gp (1971-88), sci advsr Suffolk CC 1976-86 (Home Office, Home Def Coll 1978); contrib to quarterly journal ILS, fndr Pan Meadow International Lilac Collection; trumpet player Blackshaw Jazz band 1960-68; *Recreations* cricket, rugby, collecting trees and books, growing antique fruit, trout fishing, music; *Clubs* MCC, Int Lilac Soc, Arboricultural Assoc, RHS, Suffolk Soil Assoc; *Style—* Colin Chapman, Esq; Norman's Farm, Wyverstone, Stowmarket, Suffolk IP14 4SF (☎ 0449 781 081)

CHAPMAN, His Hon Cyril Donald; QC (1965); s of Cyril Chapman and Frances Elizabeth, *née* Braithwaite; *b* 17 Sept 1920; *Educ* Roundhay Sch Leeds, BNC Oxford; *m* 1, 1950 (m dis 1959), Audrey Margaret Fraser, *née* Gough; 1 s; m 2, 1960, Muriel Falconer Bristow; 1 s; *Career* RNVR 1940-45; barr 1947, contested (C): E Leeds 1955, Goole 1964, Brighouse and Spenborough 1966; recorder of: Huddersfield 1965-69, Bradford 1969-71; circuit judge 1972-86, ret 1986; *Style—* His Hon Donald Chapman, QC; Hill Top, Collingham, Wetherby, W Yorks (☎ 0937 572813)

CHAPMAN, Sir David Robert Macgowan; 3 Bt (UK 1958), of Cleadon, Tyne & Wear; s of Sir Robin Chapman, 2 Bt, CBE, TD, JP, DL (d 1987), and Barbara May, *née* Tonks; *b* 16 Dec 1941; *Educ* Marlborough, McGill Univ Montreal (B Com); *m* 19 June 1965, Maria Elizabeth de Gosztonyi-Zsolnay, da of Dr N de Mattyasovszky-Zsolnay, of Montreal, Canada; 1 s (Michael b 1969), 1 da (Christina b 1970); *Heir* s, Michael Nicholas Chapman, b 21 May 1969; *Career* stockbroker; dir: Wise Speke Ltd, North of England Bldg Soc; chm northern unit of the Stock Exchange; *Recreations* travel, tennis, reading; *Clubs* Lansdowne, Northern Counties (Newcastle); *Style—* Sir David Chapman, Bt; Westmount, 14 West Park Rd, Cleadon, Sunderland SR6 7RR (☎ 091 536 7887); Wise Speke Ltd, Commercial Union House; 39 Pilgrim St, Newcastle upon Tyne NE1 6RQ (☎ 091 261 1266)

CHAPMAN, Denis Henry Clarke; s of Alderman R F Chapman, JP (d 1963), of Scarborough, and Henrietta, *née* Stothard (d 1985); *b* 26 May 1934; *Educ* Scarborough Coll; *m* 4 April 1959, Mavis Lee, da of Robert Duncanson (d 1961); 1 s (Robert b 1971), 2 da (Fiona b 1966, Lisa b 1968); *Career* RAF 1952-54; chartered surveyor; chief exec H C Chapman & Son; memb: Gen Cncl RICS 1984-, Lloyd's 1979-; FRICS, FSVA, FRVA; *Recreations* farming, shooting, gardening, walking; *Clubs* Farmers; *Style—* Denis H C Chapman, Esq; Stoneway House, Scalby, Scarborough YO13 0RU (☎ 0723 372 428) H C Chapman & Son, The Auction Mart, North St, Scarborough YO11 1DL (☎ 0723 372 424, fax 0723 500 697)

CHAPMAN, Dennis; s of George Henry Chapman, da of Katherine Hannah Beckwith *née* Magnus; *b* 6 May 1927; *Educ* Univ of London (BSc), Univ of Liverpool (PhD), Univ of London (DSc); *m* 1948, Elsie Margaret, da of Capt William Stephenson; 2 s (Michael, Paul), 1 da (Alison); *Career* Comyns Berkeley fell Caius Coll Cambridge 1960-63, head Gen Res Div Unilever Ltd 1963-69, assoc prof Univ of Sheffield 1968-76, sr Wellcome Tst fell 1976-77; Royal Free Hosp Sch of Med: prof biophysical chem, head dept of protein and molecular biol 1977-, head div of basic med sciences 1980-89, vice dean 1990, chm Educn Ctee 1990; fndr and dir Biocompatibles Ltd; visiting prof Univ of: California, Catania, Bologna Meml, Penn State USA, Royal Free Hosp Sch of Med medal 1987; author of over 400 scientific pubns; Hon DSc: Utrecht Univ, Memorial Univ; hon MRCP, FRS, FRSC; *Books* Biological Membranes Volume I-V; *Recreations* golf, spanish; *Clubs* Athenaeum; *Style—* Prof Dennis Chapman, FRS; 103 Gregories Rd, Beaconsfield, Bucks, HP9 1HZ (☎ 0494 672 051); Royal Free Hospital School of Medicine, Dept of Protein & Molecular Biology, Rowland Hill Street, London, NW3 2PF (☎ 071 794 0500 ext 3246)

CHAPMAN, Derek James; s of Eric James Chapman (d 1980), of Southampton, and Phyllis Edith, *née* Cook; *b* 1 Oct 1940; *Educ* King Edward VI Sch Southampton; *m* ; 2 s (Adam Geoffrey b 19 Aug 1972, Stephen Alistair b 4 Oct 1973); *Career* CA 1968 (Taxation prize ICAEW); Touche Ross & Co: joined 1967, tax ptnr 1972-83, ptnr i/c Southern Region Tax Function 1983-; FCA (ACA 1968), ATII 1968; *Recreations* golf; *Clubs* Hindhead Golf; *Style—* Derek Chapman, Esq; Touche Ross, Hill House, 1 Little New St, London EC4A 3TR (☎ 071 936 3000, fax 071 583 8517)

CHAPMAN, Derek Reginald; s of Reginald Chapman (d 1986), of Romney, Lee Grove, Chigwell, Essex, and Ethel Maud, *née* March (d 1982); *b* 17 May 1932; *Educ* Buckhurst Hill GS, Univ Coll Oxford (BA), Univ of London (LLB); *m* 21 June 1958, Joan Marjorie, da of Thomas Bartram (d 1976), of Grange Farm, Stillingfleet, Yorks; 2 s (Peter b 1961, Michael b 1965), 1 da (Helen b 1959); *Career* E Edwards Son & Noice: articled clerk 1954-57, asst slr 1957-59, ptnr 1959-; gen cmmr for taxes 1982-, pres Mid Essex Law Soc 1972 (sec 1967-69); chm: Billericay Round Table, Billericay Chamber of Trade, Mayflower 70 (to commemorate the 350 anniversary of the Mayflower sailing to the New World), Eastern Area Ctee Legal Aid 1989 (memb 1981-); vice chm Carnival Ctee, sec and chm Basildon and Billericay Lib Assocs (agent Gen Election Oct 1974), former memb Nat Freedom of Info Ctee; Freeman City of London 1982, Liveryman Worshipful Co of Painter Stainers 1982; memb Law Soc 1958; *Recreations* tennis, bridge, music; *Style—* Derek Chapman, Esq; Hill House, 39 Stock Rd, Billericay, Essex CM12 0AR (☎ 0277 652 443); Three Horseshoes House, 139 High St, Billericay, Essex CM12 9AF (☎ 0277 658 551, fax 0277 630 024)

CHAPMAN, Ernest; s of Arthur Leslie Chapman (d 1983), of 7 Gainford Road, Moorends, Doncaster, S Yorkshire, and Alice, *née* Lucas (d 1978); *b* 2 Dec 1933; *Educ* Thorne GS Nr Doncaster, St John's Coll Oxford (BA); *m* 4 Aug 1956, Dorothy, da of Alfred Sutton (d 1978), of 3 Hollingthorpe Court, Hall Green, Wakefield; 3 s (Michael b 1958, Neil b 1960, Alexander b 1963), 1 da (Sarah b 1966); *Career* Nat Serv; Sgt RAEC 1952-54; admitted slr 1961; in private practice; sr ptnr Dixon, Coles and Gill, Wakefield 1979-; Registrar Wakefield Dio 1979- (dep registrar 1969-79), dep coroner 1990- (dep asst coroner 1984-90), dep co and high ct registrar 1989-; memb Wakefield Festival Chorus; pres: Wakefield Amateur Operatic Soc, Stanley Falcon Cricket Club, Yorks Cricket Cncl 1982-84; Law Soc; *Recreations* cricket, singing, languages, sport in general; *Style—* Ernest Chapman, Esq; 1 Pennine View, Darton, Barnsley, S Yorkshire S75 5AT (☎ 0226 382 796); Bank House, Burton Street, Wakefield, W Yorkshire WF1 2DA (☎ 0924 373 467, fax 0924 366 234)

CHAPMAN, Hon Mrs ((Catherine) Fiona); *née* Robertson; da of 1 Baron Robertson of Oakridge, GCB, GBE, KCMG, KCVO, DSO, MC; *b* 13 Aug 1939; *m* 1965, Allan Claude Chapman, er s of Claude Frederick Chapman, of Accrington, Lancs; 2 da (twins); *Career* dist cncllr Mid Bedfordshsire DC; *Style—* The Hon Mrs Chapman; 23 Church End, Milton Bryan, Milton Keynes MK17 9HR

CHAPMAN, Frank Watson; s of Thomas Chapman (d 1965), of Bournemouth, and Beatrice, *née* Padgett (d 1976); *b* 7 Nov 1929; *Educ* Swindon Coll, Marine Sch of South Shields; *m* 18 March 1955, Wendy Joanna, da of Roger Philip Holly (d 1972), of Switzerland; 1 s (Thomas b 1963), 1 da (Susie b 1956); *Career* cadet MN 1946; deck offr: Union Steamship Co NZ 1951-54, Royal Mail Lines 1954-58, Cunard Steamship Co 1958-62; salesman Telephone Rentals 1962; fndr and md 1964: Bahamas Properties Ltd, Sovereign Travel Ltd; purchased Lord Rannoch and Forest Hills Hotels Scotland 1974, fndr Multi-Ownership & Hotels Ltd 1975 (thereby becoming fndr of Timeshare in UK), 2 devpt in Wales 1978, 3 devpt Forest Hills Hotel 1980, sold co to Barratt Developments plc 1982 (md until 1988), fndr and chm Sovereign Travel & Leisure Group plc 1988-, dir Biocure Holdings plc 1989-; memb Lloyd's; *Recreations* travel, gardening, reading, swimming; *Style—* Frank Chapman, Esq; Norbury Park, Mickleham, Surrey RH5 6DN (☎ 0372 372 633); Sovereign Travel & Leisure Group plc, 2 Chertsey St, Guildford, Surrey GU1 4HD (fax 0483 726 217, telex 858 623)

CHAPMAN, Frederick John; s of Reginald John Chapman (d 1981), and Elizabeth, *née* Hughes (d 1946); *b* 24 June 1939; *Educ* Sutton GS; *m* 4 Nov 1964, Paula Brenda, da of Victor Lewis Waller, of Capdepera, Majorca, Spain; 1 s (Daniel b 1979), 2 da (Emma b 1966, Melissa b 1968); *Career* 2 Lt Queens Royal Surrey Regt 1960-62; Export Credits Guarantee Dept: joined 1958, princ 1969, asst sec 1977, princ estab and fin offr (under sec) 1982; treas Europe Varity Corp 1988, vice pres and treas Varity Corp 1989; *Recreations* reading, music; *Style—* Frederick Chapman, Esq; Varity House, 35 Davies St, London W1Y 2EA (☎ 071 491 7000, fax 071 491 5271, telex 28 346)

CHAPMAN, Dr Hugh Patrick Attwood; s of Prof Garth Chapman, of Grove House, Callis St, Clare, Suffolk, and Margaret Hilda, *née* Wigley; *b* 22 Dec 1945; *Educ* Brentwood Sch Essex, UCL (BA), Inst of Archaeology Univ of London (PhD); *m* 24 May 1969, Jacqueline, da of Dr Alvan Watson Hagger, of Brentwood, Essex; 3 da (Sarah b 11 May 1973, Julia b 8 Sept 1975, Annabel b 6 April 1980); *Career* dep dir

Museum of London 1980-88 (keeper Dept of Prehistoric and Roman Antiquities 1978-88), gen sec Society of Antiquaries of London 1988-; author of articles and archaeological reports in learned journals; former memb Cncl: Br Archaeological Assoc, Royal Archaeological Inst, Soc for the Promotion of Roman Studies, Musuems Assoc, Soc of Museum Archaeologists, London and Middlesex Archaeological Soc; FSA 1977, FMA 1988; *Recreations* cycling, squash, theatre, models; *Style*— Dr Hugh Chapman, FSA; 39 Mundania Rd, London SE22 0NH (☎ 081 693 4012); Society of Antiquaries of London, Burlington House, Picadilly, London W1V 0HS (☎ 071 734 0193, fax 071 287 6967)

CHAPMAN, (Francis) Ian; CBE (1988); s of Rev Peter Chapman (d 1962), of Glasgow, and Frances Maud, *née* Burdett; *b* 26 Oct 1925; *Educ* Shawlands Acad Glasgow, Ommer Sch of Music Glasgow, Scot Royal Acad of Music; *m* 1953, Marjory Stewart, *née* Swinton; 1 s, 1 da; *Career* Air Crew Cadet RAF 1943-44, Nat Serv Coal Mines 1945-47; William Collins Sons & Co Ltd: joined as mgmnt trainee 1947, trainee sales rep NY branch 1950-51, gen sales mangr London 1955, gp sales dir 1959; jt md William Collins (Holdings) Ltd 1967 (dep chm 1976); dir: Hatchards Ltd 1961, Pan Books Ltd 1962-84, Ancient House Bookshop (Ipswich) Ltd 1972-89, Scottish Opera Theatre Royal Ltd 1974-79, Book Tokens Ltd 1981-, IRN Ltd 1983-85, Stanley Botes Ltd 1985-89; chm: Radio Clyde Ltd 1972-, Hatchards Ltd 1976-89, Harvill Press Ltd 1976-89, William Collins Publishers Ltd 1979, The Listener 1988-; chm and gp chief exec William Collins plc 1981-89, non-exec dir Guinness plc 1986-, jt chm Harper and Row NY 1987-89, chm and md Chapmans Publishers 1989-; Publishers Assoc: memb Cncl 1962-77, vice pres 1978 and 1981, pres 1979; memb Bd Book Devpt Cncl 1967, tstee Book Trade Benevolent Soc 1982-, memb Governing Cncl SCOTBIC 1983, chm Advsy Bd Univ of Strathclyde Business School 1985-88, Scot Free Enterprise Award 1985; Hon DLitt Univ of Strathclyde 1990; CBIM 1982, FRSA 1985; *Recreations* music, golf, reading, skiing; *Clubs* Garrick, Royal Wimbledon Golf, MCC, Prestwick; *Style*— Ian Chapman, Esq, CBE; Chapmans Publishers, 141-143 Drury Lane, London WC2 B5TB (☎ 071 497 1199, fax 071 497 2728)

CHAPMAN, (Marcus) James Franklin; s of James John Chapman (d 1976), of Heswall, Wirral, and Jean *née* Franklin-Hindle; *b* 12 May 1944; *Educ* Stowe; *m* 1967, Marion Jeannette, da of Albert Cassir; 1 s (Michael James Cassir b 3 May 1973), 1 da (Sally Jean b 7 Jan 1971); *Career* articled clerk Wt Beavan & Co Liverpool 1962-65: R H Jones & Chapman (Jones Chapman Harland 1968): trainee 1965-67, ptnr 1967-78, sr ptnr 1978-86, md 1986-88; md Royal Life Estates (NW) Ltd 1988-, dir Royal Life Estates Ltd 1988-; fell Nat Assoc Estate Agents 1974; *Recreations* vintage cars; *Style*— Marcus Chapman, Esq; Wicksted Old Hall, Wirswall, Whitchurch, Shropshire SY13 4LE; Royal Life Estates (North West) Ltd, Warrington House, Rossmore Rd East, Ellesmere Port, South Wirral L65 3AJ (☎ 051 355 6318, fax 051 357 2801)

CHAPMAN, James Keith (Ben); s of John Hartley Chapman (d 1983), of Kirkby Stephen, Cumbria, and Elsie Vera, *née* Bousfield (d 1978); *b* 8 July 1940; *Educ* Appleby GS Cumbria; *m* 1970 (m dis 1984), Jane Deirdre, da of Norman Roffe, of Morecambe, Lancs; 3 da (Bridget b 1971, Charlotte b 1973, Clare b 1975); *Career* PO RAFVR (T) 1959-61; Miny of Pensions and Nat Insur 1958-62, Miny of Aviation BAA 1962-67, Rochdale Ctee of Inquiry into Shipping 1967-70, BOT 1970-74, first sec (commercial) Dar es Salaam 1974-78, first sec (econ) Accra 1978-81, asst sec DTI 1981-87, commercial cnsllr Bt Embassy Beijing 1987-90; memb: chemicals EDC, Tyre EDC, Plastics Processing EDC; chm Forward Assessment Gp; Int Natural Rubber Agreement: chm UNCTAD Econ ctee, chm buffer stook, DG Int Wool Study Gp; FBIM; *Recreations* opera, theatre, music, walking; *Style*— Ben Chapman, Esq; Department of Trade and Industry, 1 Victoria St, London SW1

CHAPMAN, John Clifford; Dr; s of James Clifford Crossley Chapman (d 1983), and Marion, *née* Harrison; *b* 21 Feb 1923; *Educ* Ilford HS, Imperial Coll London (BSc, PhD); *m* 18 Oct 1947, Roberta Blanche, da of Robert Broughton Gingell; 1 s (Andrew b 1958), 1 da (Sarah b 1953); *Career* Capt RE 1942-46; res fell and reader in Structural Engrg Imperial Coll 1950-71, dir Constructional Steel R and D Orgn 1971-73, gp tech dir George Wimpey plc 1973-81, dir Chapman Dowling Assoc Ltd Consulting Engrs; FEng 1979, FCGI 1988, FICE, FRINA, FIStructE, MConsE; *Books* many papers on structural engrg in professional jls; *Recreations* tennis, squash, mountain walking, music; *Clubs* Athenaeum; *Style*— Dr John C Chapman; Chapman & Dowling Assocs, 41 Oathall Rd, Haywards Heath, West Sussex RH16 3EG

CHAPMAN, Kenneth James; s of Kenneth Roland Chapman, of Lincoln, and Marie Louise, *née* Robinson; *b* 14 Sept 1950; *Educ* Hornchurch GS, The Sweyne Sch Rayleigh, Essex, Univ of Wales (BSc, DipTP); *m* 31 Aug 1970, Pamela Margaret, da of Alan Henry Sertin, of Midsomer Norton, Bath, Avon; 2 s (Mark b 1974, Daniel b 1979), 1 da (Kelly b and d 1977); *Career* Glamorgan CC 1972-73, Mid Glamorgan CC 1974-75, Monmouth Borough Cncl 1975-79, Edwin H Bradley & Sons Ltd 1979-81, managing ptnr Chapman Warren 1981-; chm Swindon Town FC; memb Cncl Swindon Chamber of Commerce and Indust; MRTPI 1978, MBIM 1979; *Recreations* hockey, power boats, junior soccer; *Style*— Kenneth Chapman, Esq; Brynards Hill Farm, Wootton Bassett, Wiltshire SN4 7ER (☎ 0793 850015); Chapman Warren, Town Planning & Development Consultants, Fairwater House, 1 High Street, Wroughton, Swindon, Wiltshire (☎ 0793 814800, fax 0793 814818, car 0836 251321); Swindon Town Football Club, The County Ground, Swindon, Wiltshire (☎ 0793 430430)

CHAPMAN, Leslie Charles; eldest s of Charles Richard Chapman (d 1977), and Lilian Elizabeth Chapman (d 1934); *b* 14 Sept 1919; *Educ* Bishopshalt Sch Hillingdon; *m* 1947, Beryl Edith, da of Bertram George England, of Leighton Buzzard; 1 s (Robin); *Career* army 1939-45; civil servant; regnl dir Southern Region DOE, memb Exec London Tport; memb: Nat Cncl of Freedom Assoc, Freedom of Info Assoc Nat Cncl; chm Campaign Against Waste in Public Expenditure; *Books* Your Disobedient Servant (1979), Waste Away (1982); *Recreations* music, gardening; *Style*— Leslie Chapman, Esq; Caradog, Ffarmers, Llanwrda, Dyfed

CHAPMAN, Mark Fenger; CVO (1979); s of late Geoffrey Walter Chapman, of Dyfed, and Esther Maria Hauch, *née* Fenger; *b* 12 Sept 1934; *Educ* Cranbrook Sch, St Catharine's Coll Cambridge (BA), SOAS; *m* 28 July 1959, Patricia Mary, da of late Henry Nelson Long, of Norfolk; 4 s (Giles b 1960, Jeremy b 1962 (d 1983), Julian b 1965, Adrian b 1971); *Career* Nat Serv 1953-55 Royal Sussex Regt, Nigeria Regt, Lt 1955; HM Dip Serv 1958-89: third (later second) sec Bangkok 1959-63, second (later first) sec FO 1963-67, head Chancery Maseru 1967-71, asst head dept FCO 1971-74, head Chancery Vienna 1975-76, dep high cmmr Lusaka 1976-79, Dip Serv inspr 1979-82, cnsllr The Hague 1982-86, ambass Reykjavik 1986-89; *Clubs* Royal Cwlth Soc; *Style*— Mark Chapman, Esq, CVO; Half Moon House, Briston, Melton Constable, Norfolk NR24 2LG

CHAPMAN, Michael Christopher; s of George Thomas Lisle Chapman, and Kathleen, *née* Pallister; *b* 12 June 1950; *Educ* Friend's Sch Cumberland; *m* 18 Sept 1976, Sheena Mary, da of Alan Christopher Craig, of Wark, Northumberland; 1 da (Helen b 1980); *Career* Deloitte Haskins & Sells 1968-78, gp fin controller and co sec Barratt Developments plc 1978-85, fin dir Bryant Group plc 1985-; govr Sharmans Cross Jr Sch Solihull W Midlands; FCA; *Recreations* mountaineering, hill walking; *Clubs* Wanneys Climbing; *Style*— Michael Chapman, Esq; Bryant Group plc, Cranmore House, Cranmore Boulevard, Shirley, Solihull, West Midlands B90 4SD (☎ 021 711 1212, fax 021 711 2610)

CHAPMAN, Nigel Peter; s of Lt Col Sidney Rex Chapman, MC, of Lincolnshire, and Joan Mary, *née* Bates; *b* 31 Jan 1950; *Educ* Kimbolton Sch; *m* 26 Sept 1981, Heather Elizabeth, da of James Lindsay, of London; 2 s (Nicolas b 1982, Daniel b 1984), 1 da (Jennifer b 1987); *Career* CA; sr ptnr Chapman Wong CA (joined firm 1975); *Recreations* tennis, cricket; *Clubs* RAC, Lansdowne; *Style*— Nigel P Chapman, Esq; 10 Ripple Vale Grove, London N1 (☎ 01 607 1353); Chapman Wong, Chartered Accountants, New Concordia Wharf, Mill Street, London SE1 2BA (☎ 01 231 8761, fax 01 237 5946)

CHAPMAN, Peter Richard; s of Lt Ernest Richard Chapman RNVR (d 1974) and Edith Winifred, *née* Softly; *b* 1 April 1942; *Educ* St Paul's Cathedral Choir Sch, St John's Sch Leatherhead; *m* 1 June 1974, Stephanie Daynel, da of Kenneth Paul Alexander Watson; s (Richard b 1975, Philip b 1978); *Career* CA 1964; Ogden Parsons & Co: joined 1959, ptnr 1970-71; ptnr: Harmood Banner & Co 1972-73, Deloitte Haskins & Sells 1974-90, Coopers & Lybrand Deloitte 1990- (chm Banking Indust Gp); chm: DH&S Banking Indust Gp 1983-89, CCAB Banking Sub Ctee; memb: ICAEW Parly and Business Law Ctee, Sch Cncl St Paul's Cathedral Choir Sch, Church Urban Fund, Ct of Advsrs St Paul's Cathedral, Surrey Hockey Assoc, Tadworth Church Choir; Ctee memb: Gresham Club, Info Technol Skills Agency 1985-88; FCA, CMI; *Recreations* golf, music, hockey; *Style*— Peter Chapman, Esq; Coopers & Lybrand Deloitte, 128 Queen Victoria St, London EC4P 4JX, (☎ 071 248 3913, fax 071 248 3623)

CHAPMAN, Prof Reginald Alfred; s of Reginald William Chapman (d 1986), and Hilda Georgina, *née* Pendergast; *b* 14 June 1937; *Educ* The Roan Sch, Kings Coll London (BSc), St Salvators Coll Univ of St Andrews (PhD, DSc); *m* 21 April 1964, Veronique Peach, da of Arthur Peach Taylor (d 1974); 2 s (Matthew b 23 Aug 1965, Sebastian b 18 Aug 1969), 1 da (Cressida b 16 Dec 1971); *Career* Nat Serv RAF; res fell DSIR 1964-67, reader in physiology Univ of Leicester 1974-85 (lectr 1967-74), prof Univ of Bristol 1985-; hon sec The Physiological Soc 1985- (memb Ctee 1982-), convenor Heads of Univ Depts of Physiology 1988-; *Books* A Practical Course in Physiology (1978), A Course in Practical Physiology (1979), author of numerous articles in scientific jls; *Recreations* walking, restoring furniture and clocks; *Style*— Prof Reginald Chapman; The Physiological Society, Dept of Physiology, School of Veterinary Science, Park Row, Bristol BS1 5LS (☎ 0272 260360, fax 0272 303211)

CHAPMAN, Hon Mrs (Rhiannon Elisabeth); *née* Philipps; da (by 1 m) of 2 Viscount St Davids; *b* 21 Sept 1946; *Educ* Tormead Sch, King's Coll London Univ (LLB); *m* 1974, Donald Hudson Chapman, s of late Francis Robert Chapman; 2 step s; *Career* dir personnel Int Stock Exchange 1980-; memb Universities Funding Cncl; ptnr Pennyloaf Wines; FIPM; *Recreations* golf, good food and wine, handcrafts; *Clubs* New Cavendish, St Enedoc Golf; *Style*— The Hon Mrs Chapman; Pennyloaf, Odsey, Ashwell, Herts (☎ 046 274 2725); The International Stock Exchange, London EC2N 1HP (☎ 071 588 2355)

CHAPMAN, Roger Michael; s of Trevor Chapman, of Merlewood, Throwley Forstal, Faversham, Kent, and Janet Anne, *née* Trippett; *b* 1 May 1959; *Educ* Borden GS; *m* 30 Nov 1985, Catherine Helen, da of David Hamilton McCree; 2 s (Christopher James Hamilton b 6 Aug 1987, Thomas William Harry b 1 Dec 1990); *Career* golfer; Eng amateur champion 1979, Eng boys youths and sr level and GB and Ireland youths and sr level Walker Cup 1981, professional 1981-; second place: Spanish Open 1982, Zambia Open 1984, Kenya Open 1987, Jersey Open 1989, Dutch Open 1989 and 1990; low round 61 Ebel Swiss Masters, Zimbabwe champion 1988; *Recreations* fishing, tennis, most sports; *Style*— Roger Chapman, Esq; Jeremy Ward, Management & Marketing International, 2-6 Rickett St, Fulham, London (☎ 071 385 9289, fax 071 385 0876)

CHAPMAN, Dr Roger William Gibson; s of Lt-Col Roy Chapman, OBE, of 75 Danygraig, Pantmawr, Whitchurch, S Wales, and Margaret Gibson, *née* Abraham; *b* 16 Feb 1949; *Educ* Whitchurch GS Cardiff, St Bartholomew's Hosp Med Sch (BSc, MD, MB BS); *m* 24 Apr 1972, Gillian Patricia, da of Dr James C Prestwich (d 1969), of Portsmouth; 3 s (James b 1977, Andrew b 1979, George b 1983), 1 da (Emily b 1987); *Career* house physician St Bartholomew's Hosp 1974, med registrar Southampton 1976-78, med lectr Liver Unit Royal Free Hosp 1978-81; conslt physician John Radcliff Hosp Oxford 1987- (sr registrar 1981-87); sec Br Assoc for the Study of the Liver 1990; MRCP 1976; *Books* Topics in Gastroenterology (edited and written with Dr D P Sewell, 1985); *Recreations* tennis, golf, skiing, cinema; *Style*— Dr Roger Chapman; Dept of Gastroenterology, John Radcliffe Hospital, Headington, Oxford OX3 9DU ☎ (0865 817770)

CHAPMAN, Ronald Arthur; s of Samuel Arthur Chapman (d 1963), and Lily Hester, *née* Biggs (d 1963); *b* 14 Jan 1924; *Educ* Leyton Co HS Edmonton Latymer Sch; *m* 30 March 1950, Joan, da of Robert Underwood Brewer (d 1970); 2 s (Paul Roger b 7 Feb 1953, David Christopher b 20 Nov 1955), 1 da (Janet Elizabeth b 2 Jan 1959); *Career* War Service 1942-46, served France, Belguim and Germany; printer and photographer at Photographs for Industry 1946-51, fndr own photographic orgn 1951; memb: Enfield Round Table 1950 (chm 1961), Enfield Chamber of Trade 1951, Enfield Rotary Club 1964 (pres 1971, awarded Paul Harris Fellowship 1988); sec (from inception) Enfield Civic Soc (until merged with Enfield Preservation Soc); assoc Inst of Br Photographers 1954, FRPS 1960 (ARPS 1948), FBIPP 1973, fell Master Photographers Assoc 1989; *Recreations* swimming, travel, music; *Clubs* Professional Photographers of America, Royal Photographic Soc, Inst of Br Photography. Master Photographers Assoc; *Style*— Ronald Chapman, Esq; Studio 3, 832 Green Lanes, Winchmore Hill, London N21 2RT (☎ 081 360 9433/9434)

CHAPMAN, Roy de Courcy; s of (Edward Frederic) Gilbert Chapman and Aline de Courcy Ireland; *b* 1 Oct 1936; *Educ* Univ of St Andrews, Moray House Coll of Educn Edinburgh; *m* 1959, Valerie Rosemary Small; 2 s, 1 da; *Career* former head of modern languages Marlborough, rector Glasgow Acad 1975, headmaster Malvern 1983-; chm Common Entrance Bd 1988-; *Books* Le Français Contemporain (1972), Le Français Contemporain: Passages for Comprehension and Translation (with D Whiting, 1975); *Style*— Roy de Courcy Chapman, Esq; Malvern College, Malvern, Worcs (☎ 0684 892333)

CHAPMAN, Roy John; s of William George Chapman (d 1978), of Kettering, and Frances Harriet, *née* Yeomans (d 1981); *b* 30 Nov 1936; *Educ* Kettering GS, St Catharine's Coll Cambridge (MA); *m* 23 Sept 1961, Janet Gibbeson, da of Roy Gibbeson Taylor (d 1955), of Worthing, Sussex, and Vera Constance Taylor; 2 s (William b 1962, Henry b 1972), 1 da (Lucy b 1964); *Career* CA; Arthur Andersen & Co 1958-: ptnr 1970-, managing ptnr London 1984-, managing ptnr UK 1989-; memb: Advsy Cncl London Enterprise Agency 1985-88, Governing Body of SOAS (Univ of London) 1990-; FCA, FIMC, CBIM, FBPICS; *Recreations* cricket, walking, opera, literature, idling; *Clubs* United Oxford and Cambridge Univ, Hawks, MCC; *Style*— Roy Chapman, Esq; Arthur Andersen & Co, 1 Surrey Street, London WC2 (☎ 071 836 1200, fax 071 831 1133, telex 8812 711)

CHAPMAN, Sir Stephen; s of late Sir Sydney John Chapman, KCB, CBE (d 1951), and Mabel Gwendoline Chapman, JP, *née* Mordey (d 1958); *b* 5 June 1907; *Educ* Westminster, Trinity Coll Cambridge; *m* 1963, Pauline, da of Lt-Col Allcard (d 1970), and wid of Dimitri de Lobel Niewiarowski; *Career* called to the Bar 1931; former rec: Rochester, Cambridge, Liverpool; judge of the Crown Ct Liverpool 1963-66, judge of the High Ct of Justice (Queen's Bench Div) 1966-81, ret; kt 1966; Atkins Encyclopedia of Court Forms (contrib 1938), Halsbury's Laws of England (contrib 1958), Statutes on the Law of Torts (contrib 1962); *Clubs* United Oxford and Cambridge Univ; *Style—* Sir Stephen Chapman; 72 Thomas More Hse, Barbican, London EC2Y 8BT (☎ 071 628 9251)

CHAPMAN, Sydney Brookes; MP (Cons) Chipping Barnet 1979-; s of W Dobson Chapman (d 1965), of Prestbury, Cheshire, and Edith Laura, *née* Wadge (d 1978); *b* 17 Oct 1935; *Educ* Rugby, Univ of Manchester; *m* 1976 (m dis 1987), Claire Lesley, *née* Davies; 2 s, 1 da; *Career* memb Exec Ctee Nat Union of Cons and Unionist Assocs 1961-70, nat chm Young Cons 1964-66 contested Stalybridge and Hyde 1964, MP Birmingham Handsworth 1970-74; pps: Sec State Tport 1979-81, Sec State Social Servs 1981-83; memb Select Ctee: Environment 1983-87, House of Commons Service 1983-87; appointed govt whip 1988, Lord Cmmr of HM Treasy 1990- non practising chartered architect and chartered town and country planner; vice pres Cncl RIBA 1974-76 (memb 1972-76); former initiator Nat Tree Planting Year 1973; pres: Arboricultural Assoc 1983-89, London Green Belt Cncl 1986-89; patron Tree Cncl; Queen's Silver Jubilee medal 1977; FRTPI, Hon FIAAS, Hon FFB, FRSA; *Clubs* United and Cecil (vice chm); *Style—* Sydney Chapman Esq, MP; House of Commons, London SW1A 0AA

CHAPPEL, Lt-Col William Arthur Brian; s of Maj-Gen Brian Herbert Chappel, DSO (d 1964), and Irene Mabel, *née* Maltby (d 1978); *b* 30 June 1925; *Educ* Marlborough, Jesus Coll Cambridge; *m* 3 Nov 1951, Sheila Margaret, da of George Foster Ibbotson (d 1969), of Ainsdale, Southport, Lancs; 2 s (Christopher b 1952, Nicholas b 1957); *Career* served RE 1943-77, ret as Lt-Col; sr exec Sir William Halcrow and Partners Ltd 1977-89, ret; *Recreations* golf, reading, gardening; *Style—* Lt-Col William Chappel; The Old Manor, Chirton, Devizes, Wilts SN10 3QS (☎ 038084 777)

CHAPPELL, Edwin Brian Horst; s of Edwin Barnard Henry Chappell (d 1957), of London, and Vera Vita Muriel, *née* Karr de Karroff (d 1975); *b* 11 Feb 1929; *Educ* Royal Masonic Sch; *m* 3 Oct 1953, Yvonne Audrey, da of Wilfrid John Nolan (d 1968), of Twickenham; 1 s (Edwin b 1962); *Career* property registrar Royal Dutch/Shell Group; hon steward Westminster Abbey, clerk of the Guild of St Bride, memb Exec Ctee London Soc, sec Omnibus Soc; Freeman City of London 1950, Liveryman Worshipful Co of Makers of Playing Cards 1984 (elected to 1990); FRSA 1950; *Recreations* transport especially road transport, London especially City of London; *Clubs* City Livery; *Style—* E B H Chappell, Esq; The Spinney, Meadow Rd, Ashtead, Surrey KT21 1QR (☎ 0372 272 631)

CHAPPELL, Helen Diane; da of George Chappell, and Olivia Patricia, *née* Spellman; *b* 5 March 1955; *Educ* Pasir Panjang Sch Singapore, The Downer Sch Middx, New Hall Cambridge (BA, MA); *Career* journalist; feature writer New Society magazine 1981-84, winner Catherine Pakenham Award 1980-81, Co columnist 1984-87, Third Person columnist Guardian 1987-89; current contrib to: Observer, New Statesman and Society magazine, Independent on Sunday; memb New Hall Soc; *Books* The Other Britain (contrib, 1982), The Bedside Guardian (contrib 1990); *Style—* Ms Helen Chappell; c/o Independent On Sunday, 40 City Road, London EC1Y 2DB (☎ 071 415 1369)

CHAPPELL, (Edwin) Philip; CBE (1976); s of Rev Claude Roland Chappell (d 1972), of Oakwood Lodge, Lambourn, Berks, and Laura Harland, *née* Hudson (d 1980); *b* 12 June 1929; *Educ* Marlborough, ChCh Oxford (MA 1953); *m* 10 Feb 1962, Julia Clavering, da of (Harry) Wilfred House, DSO, MC (d 1987), of The Old Rectory, Stutton, Suffolk; 1 s (Luke b 1968), 3 da (Miranda b 1963, Lucy b 1969, Jessica b 1973); *Career* Nat Serv 1947-48; vice chm Morgan Grenfell 1979-85 (joined 1954, dir 1964-85); non-exec dir: Bank of New Zealand (London Bd) 1967-89, Fisons plc 1969-; chm Nat Ports Cncl 1971-77, non-exec dir GKN plc 1974-89, advsr Assoc of Investment Tsts 1986-, memb Fin Ctee Int Chamber of Commerce 1986-; non-exec dir: Forestry Investment Management Ltd 1986-, Br Rail Property Bd 1986-, Interallianz (London) Ltd 1987-; govr BBC 1976-81, chm EDC Food and Drink Mfrg 1976-80, memb Barbican Centre Ctee 1977-, dir City Arts Tst 1977-; treas: RSA 1982-87 (dir exams 1987-89), City Univ 1988-, Georgian Gp 1988-; Freeman City of London 1981; FCIB 1968, FCIT 1972, CBIM 1974; *Books* Pensions and Privilege (1988); *Recreations* music, sailing, tax reform; *Clubs* Athenaeum, Garrick; *Style—* Philip Chappell, Esq, CBE; 22 Frognal Lane, London NW3 7DT (☎ 071 435 8627); Association of Investment Trust Companies, Park House (6th floor), 16 Finsbury Circus, London EC2M 7JJ (☎ 071 588 5347, fax 071 638 1803)

CHAPPELL, Robert William; s of Norman William Chappell, OBE, of 95 Hainault Rd, Chigwell, Essex, and Mary, *née* Caola; *b* 31 May 1942; *Educ* St Bonaventure's Sch Forest Gate, The City Univ (MPhil, DipOphthalmic Optics); *m* 11 May 1968, Carole Patricia, da of Cyril John Horwood (d 1979); 1 s (Simon b 1973), 2 da (Sarah b 1970, Emma b 1974); *Career* md Pell Optical Ltd 1974- (sales mangr 1967, dir 1970); admin offr Br Optical Students Assoc 1967-70, cncl memb Br Optical Assoc 1978-80, treas Br Assoc of Young Optometrists 1979-81, govr Faculty of Dispensing Opticians 1980-84, treas Br College of Optometrists 1982- (cncl memb 1980-); memb: Gen Optical Cncl 1983-, Mgmnt Ctee London Refraction Hosp 1987-; nat cncllr Round Table 1978-83 (chm Ongar 1975-76, chm Area 33 1977-83); Freeman City of London 1966, Liveryman Worshipful Co of Spectacle Makers 1985; FBCO, FInstD; *Recreations* antique collecting, photography, tennis, skiing; *Style—* Robert Chappell, Esq; The Weft House, Cornells Lane, Widdington, Saffron Walden, Essex CB11 3SP (☎ 0799 40301); Pell Optical Company Ltd, Supra House, Woodford Bridge, Essex IG8 8EG (☎ 081 504 8888, fax 081 506 0169)

CHAPPELL, Lt-Col Robin Henville; OBE (1973); s of Lt-Col Hereward Chappell, OBE (d 1970), and Aileen, *née* Davis; *b* 19 Jan 1931; *Educ* Wellington, RMA Sandhurst, Staff Coll Camberley; *m* 1 April 1959, Joanell Vera, da of Bernard Studd (d 1967); 2 s (Bruce b 1961 (d 1976), Gavin b 1963), 1 da (Kathryn b 1966); *Career* Army Offr: Queen's regt, Co 2 (Co Armagh) Bn UDR 1971, Co 11 (Craigavon) Bn UDR 1972, Def Attaché Sofia 1974-76, ret 1988; *Recreations* cricket, squash, tennis, golf, shooting; *Clubs* MCC, Army and Navy; *Style—* Lt-Col Robin Chappell, OBE; c/o Lloyds Bank Ltd, 37 Market Place, Warminster, Wilts

CHAPPELL, William Evelyn; s of Archibald Walter Chappell, and Edith Eva Clara Blair-Staples (d 1952); *b* 22 Sept 1907; *Educ* Chelsea Sch of Art, studied dancing under Marie Rambert; *Career* Nat Serv 1940-45 (two years overseas), Capt RA; dancer, designer, theatre dir, painter, illustrator, writer; first appearance on stage 1929, joined Sadlers Wells Co 1934, (designed scenery and costumes 1934-); designed costumes and scenery Covent Garden 1947-; work incl: Les Rendezvous, Les Patineurs, Coppelia, Giselle, Handel's Samson, Frederick Ashton's Walk to the Paradise Garden, Ashton's Rhapsody (costumes); prodr: Lyric Revue 1951, Globe Revue 1952, High Spirits (Hippodrome) 1953, At the Lyric 1953, Going to Town (St Martin's) 1954, asst dir Moby Dick (with Orson Welles) (Duke of York Theatre), The Buccaneer (Lyric Hammersmith and The Apollo Theatre) 1955, The Rivals (Saville), Beaux Stratagem (Chichester), Violins of St Jacques (Sadler's Wells), English Eccentrics, Love and a Bottle, Passion Flower Hotel (Prince of Wales Theatre), Travelling Light (Prince of Wales), Espresso Bongo (Saville), Living For Pleasure (Garrick), Where's Charley? (Palace Theatre); appeared in and assisted Orson Welles with film The Trial; dir: The Chalk Garden starring Gladys Cooper-her last appearance in the theatre (Haymarket) 1971, Offenbach's Robinson Crusoe (Sadlers Wells) 1973, Cockie (Vaudeville) 1973, Oh Kay! (Westminster) 1974, nat tour In Praise of Love 1974, Fallen Angels (Dublin Festival) 1975, Marriage of Figaro (Sadlers Wells) 1977, The Master's Voice (Dublin Theatre Festival) 1977, Memoir 1978, Gianni Schicci 1978, Nijinsky (film) 1979, Same Time Next Year (Dublin Festival) 1980, A Little Bit on the Side (revue with Beryl Reid) 1983, Speak of the Devil, Arsenic and Old Lace (Dublin Theatre Festival) 1985; designs for Giselle including two prodns for Anton Dolin; choreographed: Travesties 1974, Bloomsbury 1974; directed, designed costumes and choreographed: Purcells Fairy Queen 1974, Donizetti's Torquato Tasso 1975, Lully's Alceste 1975, The Rivals 1976; teacher and advsr for: L'Apres Midi D'Un Faune Nureyev season 1979, Joffrey Ballet NY 1979; TV shows with Beryl Reid; illustrator of several books; *Books* Studies in Ballet (ed and jt author), Edward Burra: a painter remembered by his friends (1982), Well Dearie: the letters of Edward Burra; *Style—* William Chappell, Esq

CHAPPIN, Andrew Darryl; s of Dennis John Chappin, and Margaret Violet, *née* Howell; *b* 9 July 1954; *Educ* St Albans Sch, Brighton Poly Faculty of Art & Design (BA); *m* 22 Aug 1987, Sonia Dawn, da of Alan McCririck; *Career* designer Granada Publishing 1977-78, asst art ed New Scientist 1978-79, sr designer Now! magazine 1979-81, art ed Eagle Moss Publications April-Nov 1981, designer The Times 1981-82, art ed Sunday Express Magazine 1982-86, art dir London Daily News 1986-87, art ed Financial Times 1987-; Soc of Newspaper Design USA: award of excellence 1988 and 1990, Silver award 1990; NDA/Linotype Awards (with David Case): Best Designed Newspaper 1990, Best News Pages 1990; memb: D & ADA 1988, Soc of Newspaper Design USA 1987; jt fndr Euro Soc for News Design; *Recreations* playing rugby, skiing, watching football, cinema, reading newspapers & magazines, modern music; *Clubs* Old Albanian Rugby; *Style—* Andrew Chappin, Esq; Financial Times, Number One, Southwark Bridge, London SE1 9HL (☎ 071 873 3328, fax 071 407 5700)

CHAPPLE, Hon Barry Joseph; yr s of Baron Chapple (Life Peer), *qv*; *b* 1951; *Educ* Hawes Down Comprehensive Sch; *m* 1980, Angela Christina, da of Kenneth R Medgett; 1 s (James Robert b 1985), 1 da (Kate Helen b 1983); *Style—* The Hon Barry Chapple; c/o The Rt Hon Lord Chapple, EETPU, Hayes Court, West Common Road, Bromley BR2 7AU

CHAPPLE, Brian Bedford; s of Richard Chapple, of The Cottage, Heatherhurst Grange, Deepcut, Surrey, and Violet Elizabeth, *née* Groves (d 1973); *b* 6 Feb 1939; *Educ* St Clement Danes GS; *m* 30 Sept 1961, Wendy Ann, da of Kenneth Andrew Cole; 1 da (Amanda b 27 March 1967); *Career* CA Clark Whitehill (formerly Clark Battams) 1963; ptnr Arthur Young & Co (formerly Angus Campbell & Co, previously Josolyne Layton Bennett); dep chm Minet Holdings plc 1983; FCA 1973, FICT 1983; *Recreations* golf, motor boats, horses; *Clubs* RAC, Crockford, Army Golf; *Style—* Brian Chapple, Esq; Minet Holdings plc, 100 Leman St, London E1 8HG (☎ 071 481 0707, fax 071 488 9786, telex 8813901)

CHAPPLE, Brian John; s of Capt John Ernest Chapple (d 1977), and Mildred, *née* Fairbrother (d 1988); *b* 24 March 1945; *Educ* Highgate Sch, RAM (GRSM, LRAM); *m* 20 Dec 1973, Janet Mary, *née* Whittaker-Coldron; 1 da (Rosalind Bailey); *Career* composer; compositions incl: Trees Revisited 1970, Hallelujahs 1971, Scherzos 1970 (premiered Proms Royal Albert Hall 1976), 5 Blake Songs, Praeludiana (premiered Royal Festival Hall) 1973, Green and Pleasant (won BBC Monarchy 1000 Prize) 1973, Veni Sancte Spiritus 1974, In Ecclesiis 1976, Piano Concerto 1977, Cantica 1978, Venus Fly Trap (cmmnd London Sinfonietta) 1979, Little Symphony (cmmnd Haydn Society) 1982, Lamentations of Jeremiah 1984, Piano Sonata 1986, Magnificat 1987, Confitebor 1989, In Memoriam 1989, Tribute 1989, Anthems and Canticles for New Coll Oxford and Canterbury Cathedral, childrens songs and piano music: PRS, MCPS; *Style—* Brian Chapple, Esq; 31 Warwick Rd, New Barnet, Herts EN5 5EQ; c/o Chester Music, 8/9 Frith St, London W1V 5TZ

CHAPPLE, Baron (Life Peer UK 1985), of Hoxton, Greater London; Francis Joseph Chapple (Frank); s of Frank Chapple, of Shoreditch, and his w, Emily, da of Joseph Rook, of Hoxton; *b* 1921,Aug; *Educ* Elementary Sch; *m* 1944, Joan Jeanette, da of James Nicholls; 2 s (Hon Roger Francis b 1947, Hon Barry Joseph b 1951); *Career* electrician; memb TUC Gen Council 1971, gen sec Electrical, Electronic, Telecommunication and Plumbing Union 1966-84; dir: National Nuclear Corpn 1980-, Southern Water Authority 1983-, Inner City Enterprises 1983-; chm TUC 1982-83; memb NEDC; *Style—* The Rt Hon Lord Chapple; EETPU, Hayes Court, West Common Rd, Bromley, Kent

CHAPPLE, General Sir John Lyon; GCB, CBE; s of Charles Chapple, (d 1970), and Dr Elsie Chapple, *née* Lyon (d 1989); *b* 27 May 1931; *Educ* Haileybury, Imperial Serv Coll, Trinity Coll Cambridge (MA); *m* 31 March 1959, Annabel, da of John Hill; 1 s (David b 1962), 3 da (Lady John Townshend b 5 Dec 1960, Kate b 29 April 1963, Mrs John Holt b 15 Oct 1964); *Career* Nat Serv joined KRRC 1949, cmmnd RA 1950; joined 2 KEO Goorkhas 1954; served: Malaya, Borneo Hong Kong; Staff Coll 1962, jssc 1969, cmd 1 Bn 2 Goorkhas 1970-72, DS Staff Coll 1972-73, Bde Cdr 48 Goorkha Inf Bde 1976, Goorkha Field Force 1977-78, PSO to CDS 1978-79, Cdr Br Forces Hong Kong and Maj-Gen Bde of Goorkhas 1980-82, Dir Mil Ops 1982-84, Dep CDS (progs and personnel) 1985-87, Col 2 Goorkhas 1986-, C in C UKLF 1987-88, ADC Gen to HM The Queen 1987-, CGS 1988-; tstee WWF UK 1985-, King Mahendra UK Tst for Nature Conservation 1986-; memb: Conservation Fdn RSPB, ICBP, Norfolk Naturalist Tst; Flora and Fauna Preservation Soc; pres Army Ornithological Soc; Freeman City of London 1990; memb Mil Hist Soc, chm Soc for Army Hist Res 1984; dep chm Cncl Nat Army Museum 1987-; FZS 1954, FRGS 1954, FLS 1988; *Clubs* Beefsteak; *Style—* Gen Sir John Chapple, GCB, CBE

CHAPPLE, Prof (Alfred) John Victor; s of Alfred Edward Chapple (d 1942), and Frances Lilian, *née* Taylor (d 1972); *b* 25 April 1928; *Educ* St Boniface's Coll Plymouth, UCL (BA, MA); *m* 6 Aug 1955, Kathleen, da of James Sheridan Bolton (d 1979); 4 s (Andrew b 1958, John b 1960, James b 1964, Christopher b 1967), 1 da (Clare b 1962); *Career* Nat Serv RA 1946-49: 2 Lt 1947, short serv cmmn as Lt; res asst Yale Univ 1955-58, asst Univ of Aberdeen 1958-59, lectr then sr lectr Univ of Manchester 1959-71, prof of English (currently pt/t) Univ of Hull 1971- (dean of Arts 1980-82, pro vice chllr 1985-88); memb Int Assoc of Profs of English 1986-, chm Gaskell Soc 1990-; *Books* Documentary and Imaginative Literature 1880-1920 (1970), Elizabeth Gaskell: A Portrait In Letters (1980), Science and Literature in the Nineteenth Century (1986); *Recreations* music, wine, gardening, calligraphy; *Style—* Prof John Chapple

CHAPPLE, Hon Roger Francis; er s of Baron Chapple (Life Peer), *qv*; *b* 1947; *Educ* Brooke House Comprehensive Sch; *m* 1969, Susan Audrey, da of Charles F W Brown; 2 s (David b 1974, Robin b 1981), 1 da (Rachel b 1972); *Style—* Hon Roger Chapple; c/o The Rt Hon Lord Chapple, EETPU, Hayes Court, West Common Road, Bromley BR2 7AU

CHAPRONIERE, Kenneth Roger; s of Arthur James Chaproniere (d 1978), and Joyce

Marion, *née* Cook; *b* 25 July 1948; *Educ* Peckham Manor Sch, Guild Hall Sch of Music and Drama; *m* 1, 29 July 1967 (m dis 1972), Sally Carlsson; m 2, 3 Feb 1989, Josephine Mary, *née* Robbie, wid of Patrick Hutber; *Career* BBC Radio 3 1971-75 and 1978-79, English Bach Festival 1975-77, Liszt Festival of London 1977, Victor Hochausor Ltd 1978, The Stables Wavendon 1979-88, London Bach Orch 1988-; *Recreations* swimming, food and wine, antiques; *Clubs* Royal Overseas League; *Style—* Kenneth R Chaproniere, Esq; 3 The Clock House, Little Brickhill, Buckinghamshire MK17 9NR; 80A Fentiman Rd, London SW8 1LA

CHAPUT DE SAINTONGE, Dr (David) Mark; s of Lt-Col Rolland Alfred Aime, CMG (d 1989), and Barbara, *née* Watts; *b* 1 Oct 1942; *Educ* Whitgift Sch Croydon, London Hosp Med Coll (BSc, PhD, MB BS); *m* 15 Dec 1973, Gail Nicola, da of Norman Mason (d 1985); 3 s (Luke b 1976, Daniel b 1978, Edward b 1980); *Career* sr house offr Med Unit Nottingham Gen Hosp 1968-69, sr lectr in clinical pharmacology and therapeutics London Hosp Med Coll 1973- (lectr 1969); conslt physician in gen med: Bethnal Green Hosp 1976-79, London Hosp 1976-; sr lectr in clinical pharmacology Bart's 1981-; assoc Center Res on Judgement Policy at Inst Cognitive Sci Univ of Colorado 1984-, memb Ed Bd Br Jl Clinical Pharmacology 1983-89, dep ed Drug and Therapeutics Bulletin 1986-90; FRCP 1986; *Books* Current Problems in Clinical Trials (with Prof D W Vere, 1984), numerous scientific papers on clinical trials and med judgement; *Recreations* pottery, shooting; *Style—* Dr Mark Chaput de Saintonge

CHARAP, Prof John Michael; s of Samuel Lewis Charap, of Stanmore, Middx, and Irene, *née* Shaw (d 1984); *b* 1 Jan 1935; *Educ* City of London Sch, Trinity Coll Cambridge (MA, PhD); *m* 11 June 1961, Ellen Elfrieda, da of Eric Kuhn (d 1986); 1 s (David b 1965); *Career* res assoc: Univ of Chicago 1959-60, Univ of California (Berkeley) 1960-62; memb Inst for Advanced Study Princeton NJ, lectr in physics Imperial Coll London 1964-65 (sr scientific offr 1963-64); Queen Mary Coll (since 1989 Queen Mary and Westfield Coll) London: reader in theoretical physics 1965-78, prof of theoretical physics 1978-, head of Dept of Physics 1980-85, dean of Faculty of Sci 1982-85, pro princ 1987-89, vice princ 1989-90; Univ of London: chm Bd of Studies in Physics 1976-80, memb Senate 1981-, memb Ct 1989-; memb: American Physical Soc 1960-, European Physical Soc 1980-; FInstP 1979; *Recreations* walking, talking; *Style—* Prof John Charap; 67 South Hill Park, London NW3 2SS (☎ 071 975 5039, fax 081 981 7517, telex 893750)

CHARD, Prof Tim; s of Dr Henry Francis Chard (d 1983), of London, and Dorothea Elaine, *née* Marsh; *b* 4 June 1937; *Educ* Merchant Taylors, St Thomas's Hosp Med Sch Univ of London (MB, MD); *m* 1, 1965 (m dis 1978), Marty Jane, *née* Batten; 2 s (Declan Tarn b 1970, Jiri Alexander b 1972); m 2, 1978, Linda Kay, *née* Elmore; *Career* jr hosp posts 1960-65, fell MRC 1965-68, prof of Obstetrics, gynaecology and reproductive physiology St Bartholomew's Hosp (sr lectr 1968-73 formerly lectr); author of numerous scientific papers; memb various public and private sector ctees; FRCOG 1975; medal of the Univ of Helsinki; *Books* Radioimmunoassay (1986), Computing for Clinicians (1988), Basic Sciences for Obstetrics (1990); *Recreations* fine arts; *Style—* Prof Tim Chard; 509 Mountjoy House, Barbican, London EC2Y 8BP (☎ 071 628 4570); Reproductive Physiology, St Bartholomew's Hosp, London EC1A 7BE (☎ 071 601 8250, 071 601 8251, 071 600 1439)

CHARITY, William Brian; s of Arthur William Charity (d 1977), of Merseyside, and Gertrude, *née* Hopley (d 1983); *b* 10 Oct 1934; *Educ* Kirkham GS; *m* 1961, Jean Mary, da of Thomas Rennison (d 1969); 2 da (Claire Michelle (Mrs Venn) b 1964, Mandy Jane b 1965); *Career* ptnr Parker Edwards and Co 1961-64; chief exec: of overseas ops Norcros plc 1977-79, Edward Le Bas Ltd 1979-89, Tex Holdings plc 1985-; chm: Woolaway Homes Ltd 1979-, BSP International Foundation Ltd 1979-, Tex Steel Tubes Ltd 1979-, AK Precision Mouldings Ltd 1986-, Quinton-Kaines Ltd 1987, Tex Plastic Products Ltd 1990; memb Deanery Synod of Ipswich and St Edmundsbury C of E; FCA; *Recreations* philately, sports; *Clubs* Eastern Counties Rugby Union, Essex County Cricket, Norfolk County Cricket, Oriental; *Style—* William B Charity, Esq; The Deans, Newton Green, Sudbury, Suffolk CO10 0QS (☎ 0787 79992); c/o Tex Holdings plc, Claydon, Ipswich, Suffolk (☎ 0473 830144, fax 0473 832545)

CHARKHAM, Jonathan Philip; s of Louis Charkham (d 1962), of London, and Phoebe Beatrice, *née* Miller; *b* 17 Oct 1930; *Educ* St Paul's, Jesus Coll Cambridge (MA); *m* 3 Nov 1954, Moira Elizabeth Frances, da of Barnett Alfred Salmon (d 1965), of London; 2 s (Graham b 1959, Rupert (twin) b 1959), 1 da (Fiona (Mrs Shackleton) b 1956); *Career* called to the Bar Inner Temple 1953; md Morris Charkham Ltd 1953-63, divnl dir Rest Assured 1963-68; Civil Serv 1969-82, on secondment from Bank of England as dir PRO NED 1982-85, chief advsr Bank of England 1985-88, advsr to the Govrs 1988-; memb Ctee Knightsbridge Assoc; Freeman City of London, Master Worshipful Co of Upholders 1979-80 and 1980-81; CBIM 1988, FRSA; *Books* Effective Boards (1985), Non Executive Directors: A Practical Guide (1987), Corporate Governance and the Market for Control of Companies (1989), Corporate Governance and the Market for Companies: Aspects of the Shareholders Role (1989); *Recreations* golf, music, shooting, wine; *Clubs* Athenaeum, City Livery, MCC; *Style—* Jonathan Charkham Esq; The Yellow House, 22 Montpelier Place, Knightsbridge, London SW7 1HL (☎ 071 589 9879); Bank of England, Threadneedle Street, London EC2 (☎ 071 601 4497)

CHARLEMONT, Dorothy, Viscountess; Dorothy Jessie Caulfeild; da of Albert A Johnston (d 1936), of Ottawa, Canada; *m* 1930, 13 Viscount Charlemont (d 1985); *Style—* The Rt Hon Dorothy, Viscountess Charlemont; Apt 915, 2055 Carling Avenue, Ottawa, Ontario, Canada K2A 1G6

CHARLEMONT, 14 Viscount (I 1665); John Day Caulfeild; also Lord Caulfeild, Baron of Charlemont (I 1620); s of Eric St George Caulfeild (d 1975), and Edith Evelyn, da of Frederick William Day, of Ottawa; suc unc, 13 Viscount (d 1985); *b* 19 March 1934; *m* 1, 1964, Judith Ann (d 1971), da of James Dodd, of Ontario; 1 s, 1 da (Hon Janis Ann b 1968); m 2, 1972, Janet Evelyn, da of Orville Nancekivell, of Ontario; *Heir* s, Hon John Dodd Caulfeild b 15 May 1966; *Style—* The Rt Hon the Viscount Charlemont; 39 Rossburn Drive, Etobicoke, Ontario M9C 2P9, Canada

CHARLES, Arthur William Hessin; s of Arthur Attwood Sinclair Charles, of The Round Oak, Tenbury Well, Worcs, and Dr May Davis Charles, *née* Westerman; *b* 25 March 1948; *Educ* Malvern Coll, Christ's Coll Cambridge (MA); *m* 22 June 1974, Lydia Margaret, da of John Barlow Ainscow, of Rock Garth, Gale Rigg, Ambleside, Cumbria; 1 s (Simon b 1980), 1 da (Florence b 1983); *Career* called to the Bar Lincoln's Inn 1971, jr counsel to the Crown Chancery 1986-89, first jr counsel to the Treasy in chancery matters 1989; *Recreations* golf and tennis; *Clubs* Hawks, Denham Golf; *Style—* William Charles, Esq; 13 Old Sq, Lincoln's Inn, London WC2A 3UA (☎ 071 404 4800, fax 071 405 4267, telex 22487 INNLAW G)

CHARLES, His Hon Judge Bernard Leopold (Leo); QC (1980); s of Chaskiel Charles (d 1960), of 48 Grosvenor Square, London W1, and Mary, *née* Harris (d 1980); *b* 16 May 1929; *Educ* Kings' Coll Taunton; *m* 13 Aug 1958, Margaret Daphne, da of Arthur Lawrence Abel (d 1978), of 48 Harley St, London W1; 1 s Edward Duncan b 1963), 2 da (Margaret Lucy b 1966, Katriona Mary Katy b 1968); *Career* Nat Serv 1948-50, Capt RAEC 1949; called to the Bar Gray's Inn 1955, judge SE Circuit 1990- (rec 1985-90); *Recreations* music, gardening; *Style—* His Hon Judge Charles, QC; 8 Henniker Mews, London SW3; Eaton Lodge, 2 Crossbush Rd, Felpham, West Sussex; Lamb Building, Temple, London EC4 (☎ 071 353 6701, fax 071 353 4686, telex 261511 JURIST G)

CHARLES, Caroline (Mrs Malcolm Valentine); *b* 18 May 1942; *Educ* Sacred Heart Convent Woldingham Surrey, Swindon Coll of Art Wilts; *m* 8 Jan 1966, Malcolm Valentine; 2 c (Kate, Alex); *Career* fashion designer, apprentice to Michael Sherard British Couture Curzon St London 1960, worked for Mary Quant London 1961, estab Caroline Charles London 1963; *Awards*: Yardley Young Designer award NY 1964, Evening Standard Design award 1978; exhibitor V & A Museum Summer Exhibition 1989; *Books* Weekend Wardrobe; *Recreations* travel, theatre, tennis; *Clubs* British Colour Textile Group; *Style—* Ms Caroline Charles; 56-57 Beauchamp Place, London SW3 1NY (☎ 071 225 3197, fax 071 584 2521)

CHARLES, Lady; Gipsy Joan; da of late Sir Walter Lawrence (d 1939), of Hyde Hall, Sawbridgeworth, Herts, and Mabel, *née* Woollard; *m* 1957, as his 2 w, Sir Noel Hughes Havelock Charles, 3 Bt, KCMG, MC (d 1975, when title became extinct); *Style—* Lady Charles; 36 Sloane Court West, London SW3

CHARLES, Jacqueline Fay; JP (Barnet, 1968); da of Henry Burton, QC (d 1952), and Hilda, *née* Shaffer (d 1986); *b* 26 Aug 1934; *Educ* Roedean, Kings Coll Univ of London (LLB, JELF medal 1955); *m* 14 July 1957, Eric Charles, s of Joseph John Charles (d 1951); 2 s (John b 1959, Henry b 1961), 1 da (Susan b 1964); *Career* called to the Bar Gray's Inn 1956; asst to town clerk Southwark Borough Cncl 1956, law reporter 1964-78; chm: Rent Assessment Ctee 1978-, Social Security Tbnl 1985-; memb CAB 1966-70; *Recreations* reading, travel, music; *Style—* Mrs Jacqueline Charles, JP; 38 Chester Close North, Regents Park, London NW1 4JE (☎ 071 935 6968)

CHARLES, Peter Dominic; s of Kenneth Charles (d 1970), of Liverpool, and Julia, *née* Norton (d 1975); *b* 18 Jan 1960; *Career* professional show jumper; winner individual Grand Prix Royal Int Horse Show 1986, memb World Cup winning team Brussels 1986, winner Individual Grand Prix World Cup Meeting Holland 1987, memb Winning Nations Cup Team: Belgium Ireland and Canada 1988, Switzerland Germany and Canada 1989; *Style—* Peter Charles, Esq; Ellis Farm, Wildmoor, Sherfield-on-Loddon, Basingstoke, Hampshire RG27 0HF (☎ 0256 882255)

CHARLES, Lady; Winifred Marie; *née* Heath; *m* 1959, as his 2 w, Sir John Pendrill Charles, KCVO, MC (d 1984), partner Allen and Overy 1947-78; 3 da; *Recreations* travel, walking, theatre, studying people, psychology, politics; *Style—* Lady Charles; 42 Belgrave Mews South, London SW1X 8BT (☎ 071 235 5792)

CHARLESTON, Robert Jesse; s of Sydney James Charleston (d 1961), Lektor, Stockholms Högskola, and Katherine Sarah, *née* Jesse (d 1980); *b* 3 April 1916; *Educ* Berkhamsted Sch Herts, New Coll Oxford (MA); *m* 17 Dec 1941, (Elfrida Violet) Joan, da of Herbert Niel Randle, CIE (d 1972), of Richmond, Surrey; 1 s (Robin b 13 April 1948), 1 da (Jenny (Mrs Stringer) b 21 July 1943); *Career* V A Museum: asst keeper 1948, dep keeper 1959, keeper 1963-76; vice pres English Ceramic Circle 1974, pres Glass Circle 1975, memb Reviewing Ctee on Export of Works of Art 1979-84, pres of Fells of Corning Museum of Glass 1982, fell Soc of Glass Technol; FSA; *Books* incl: Roman Pottery (1955), ? English Ceramics, 1580-1830 (with D Towner, 1977), Islamic Pottery (1979), Masterpieces of Glass (1980), Maioliche e Porcellane: Inghilterra, Paesi Scandinavi, Russia (1982), English Glass and the Glass Used in England, c400 - 1940 (1984); *Recreations* reading, walking, music; *Style—* Robert Charleston, Esq, FSA; Whittington Court, Whittington, Cheltenham, Glos GL54 4HF (☎ 0242 820 218)

CHARLESWORTH, David Anthony; s of David Harold Charlesworth, MBE (d 1970), and Jessie Vilma, *née* Waldron (d 1970); *b* 19 July 1936; *Educ* Haileybury, ISC; *m* 1970 (m dis 1975), Carol Ann, *née* Green; *Career* Capt RAPC; dir and sec: Sika Contracts Group of Cos 1965-76, Surban Trading Co Ltd 1968-; dir: SGB Group 1973-76, Johnson and Avon Ltd 1977-82, Michael Ashby Fine Art Ltd 1978-84, NHM Agency Holdings Ltd 1982-, Michael Watson (Management) Ltd 1983-87, P J Dewey (Agencies) Co 1983-, Shaftesbury Mews Co Ltd 1984-, Nelson Hurst & Marsh Agencies Ltd 1985-90, Jardine (Lloyd's Agencies) 1990-, Rimmer Properties Limited 1990-; underwriting memb of Lloyd's 1975-; *Recreations* bridge, listening to Mozart, motorcycling, reading biographies; *Clubs* IOD; *Style—* David Charlesworth, Esq; 1 Shaftesbury Mews, Stratford Rd, London W8 6QR (☎ 071 937 3550); 41 Seawest Boulevard De La Plage, Le Touquet, 62520, France (☎ 010 33 21 05 68 44)

CHARLESWORTH, His Hon Judge Peter James; s of Joseph William Charlesworth (d 1969), of East Yorkshire, and Florence Mary, *née* Fisher; *b* 24 Aug 1944; *Educ* Hull GS, Univ of Leeds (LLB, LLM); *m* 12 Aug 1967, Elizabeth Mary, da of Ronald Herbert Postill (d 1945), of East Yorkshire; 1 s (Robin b 1972), 1 da (Caroline b 1975); *Career* called to the Bar Inner Temple 1966, rec 1982-89, circuit judge 1989-; *Recreations* tennis, rugby league (spectating), walking in the Yorkshire dales; *Clubs* Hull Rugby League FC (vice pres), Leeds YMCA (tennis); *Style—* His Hon Judge Charlesworth; Daleswood, Creskeld Gardens, Bramhope, Leeds LS16 9EN (☎ 0532 674377); 53 Piecefields, Threshfield, nr Skipton BD23 5MR (☎ 0532 752046)

CHARLTON, Clive Arthur Cyril; s of Harold Arthur Charlton (d 1965), of Bexhill, Sussex, and Hilda Gertrude, *née* White (d 1968); *b* 30 Sept 1932; *Educ* King's Coll Taunton, Univ of London, Bart's (MB BS, MS); *m* 9 July 1960, Sheelagh Jennifer, da of Gordon Edward Price (d 1986), of London; 3 s (Simon b 1961, Jason b 1968, Harry b 1970), 1 da (Clare b 1963); *Career* res fell Dept of Surgery Univ of Kentucky Med Sch USA 1965-66, sr registrar St Paul's Hosp and Inst of Urology London 1967-68; conslt urological surgn: Bart's 1968-72, Royal Utd Hosp Bath 1972-; memb Cncl: Section of Urology RSM 1973-76, Br Assoc of Urological Surgns 1979-82 and 1984-87; memb Editorial Ctee Br Jl of Surgery 1979-86, asst ed Br Jl of Urology 1981-90, hon sr clinical lectr Inst of Urology 1984-, memb Bd of Examiners RCS 1988-, memb Bath DHA 1982-84; Freeman City of London 1973, Yeoman Worshipful Soc of Apothecaries 1971; FRSM 1968, FRCS 1963; *Books* The Urological System (2 edn, 1984); (contrib): Calculus Disease (1988), New Trends in Urinary Tract Infections (1988), Operative Surgery and Management (1987), Textbook Of Genito-Urinary Surgery (1986); *Recreations* golf, theatre, biographies, medical history; *Style—* Clive Charlton, Esq; Radford Villa, Timsbury, nr Bath (☎ 0761 70658); Department Of Urology, Royal United Hospital, Bath BA1 3NG; The Bath Clinic, Claverton Down Rd, Bath BA2 7BR (☎ 0225 835555)

CHARLTON, David; s of Robert Charlton (d 1968), of Kenilworth, and Alice Jane Stephenson, *née* Pescod; *b* 17 Oct 1936; *Educ* Dame Allan's Sch Newcastle upon Tyne, Univ of Durham Law Sch; *m* 4 Aug 1975, Doreen, da of Joseph Woodward, of Kenilworth; 1 s (Angus b 1964); *Career* admitted slr 1959; arbitrator; sr ptnr Angel and Co Coventry and Kenilworth 1966-90; chm of Tbnls and memb Panel of Arbitrators Chartered Inst of Arbitrators, arbitrations lawyer to Law Soc; chm Talisman Theatre Kenilworth, co slr to Euro Ferries plc 1962-66, memb Kenilworth UDC 1970-74; Liveryman Worshipful Co of Arbitrators; FCIArb; *Recreations* performing arts, golf; *Clubs* Royal Over-Seas League; *Style—* David Charlton, Esq; Charnwood, 59 Queens Road, Kenilworth, Warwickshire CV8 1JS (☎ 0926 54453)

CHARLTON, Prof Donald Geoffrey; s of Harry Charlton (d 1984), of Bispham, Lancashire, and Hilda, *née* Whittle; *b* 8 April 1925; *Educ* Bolton Sch, St Edmund Hall

Oxford, Emmanuel Coll Cambridge (MA), Univ of London (PhD); *m* 26 June 1952, Thelma Doreen, da of Albert Wilfred Masters (d 1983), of Warwick; 1 s (Nicholas b 1957), 2 da (Katharine b 1955, Jane b 1961); *Career* RN 1943-46; visiting prof of French Univ of Toronto 1961-62, sr lectr in French Univ of Hull 1962-64 (lectr 1949-62), prof Univ of Warwick 1964-89, visiting prof Univ of California Berkeley 1966, Gifford lectr Univ of St Andrews 1981-82; memb Assoc of Univ Profs of French, pres Soc for French Studies 1988-90; *Books* Positivist Thought in France 1852-1870 (1959), Secular Religions in France 1815-1870 (1963), France A Companion to French Studies (2 edn, 1979), The French Romantics (1984), New Images of the Natural In France 1750-1800 (1984); *Recreations* travel, reading, work; *Style*— Prof Donald Charlton; 1 St James's Park, Portland Place, Bath BA1 2SS; c/o Department of French Studies, University of Warwick, Coventry CV4 7AL

CHARLTON, (Richard Wingate) Edward; s of Col Wingate Charlton, OBE, DL, of Great Canfield Park, Takeley, Essex, and Angela Margot, *née* Windle; *b* 3 May 1948; *Educ* Eton, Univ of Neuchatel; *m* 1 Feb 1979, Claudine Marie Germaine, da of Maître Hubert Maringe (d 1988), of Champlin, Premery, Nievre, France; 1 s (Andrew b 9 Nov 1981), 2 da (Emma b 29 Sept 1985, Jessica b 28 April 1989); *Career* Frere Cholmeley & Co slrs 1968-73, Swales & Co 1974-76, Hambros Bank 1977-81, exec dir Banque Paribas London 1981-88, chief exec Banque Internationale À Luxembourg London 1988, Slr of the Supreme Ct 1976; Freeman City of London, Liveryman Worshipful Co of Merchant Taylors; *Recreations* theatre, cinema, tennis, football, travel; *Clubs* Whites, Turf; *Style*— Edward Charlton, Esq; Banque Internationale À Luxembourg, Priory House, 1 Mitre Sq London EC3A 5BS (☎ 071 623 3110, telex 884 032)

CHARLTON, Prof Graham; s of Simpson Rutherford Charlton (d 1981), of Newbiggin by Sea, Northumberland, and Georgina, *née* Graham; *b* 15 Oct 1928; *Educ* Bedlington GS Northumberland, St John's Coll York, Univ of Durham (BDS), Univ of Bristol (MDS), RCS Edinburgh; *m* 14 July 1956, Stella, da of George W Dobson; 2 s (Bruce b 1959, Fraser b 1967), 1 da (Penelope b 1960); *Career* Nat Serv; gen dental practice Torquay 1958-64, clinical dean Univ of Bristol 1975-78 (lectr 1964-72, conslt sr lectr 1972-78), dean of dental studies Univ of Edinburgh 1978-83 (prof of cons dentistry 1978-); memb Gen Dental Cncl 1978-84; memb FDS, MRCSEd; *Style*— Prof Graham Charlton; Carnethy, Bog Rd, Penicuik, Edinburgh EH26 9BT (☎ 0968 73639), Dental School, Chambers St, Edinburgh EH1 1JA (☎ 031 225 9511)

CHARLTON, (Thomas Alfred) Graham; CB (1970); 3 s of Frederick William Charlton (d 1973), of Purley, Surrey, and Marian, *née* Butterworth (d 1974), bro of F Noel Charlton, *qv*; *b* 29 Aug 1913; *Educ* Rugby, CCC Cambridge (BA); *m* 1940, Margaret Ethel, yr da of Albert E Furst, of Chesham Bois, Bucks; 3 da; *Career* WO 1936, asst private sec to Sec of State 1937-39, Cabinet Office 1947-49, loaned to NATO 1950-52, cmd sec BAOR 1952-55, asst under sec of state WO 1960, Air Miny 1963, Navy Dept 1968; sec Trade Marks Patents and Designs Fedn 1973-84; *Recreations* golf, gardening; *Clubs* Beaconsfield Golf; *Style*— Graham Charlton, Esq, CB; Victoria House, Elm Rd, Penn, Bucks

CHARLTON, (William Wingate) Hugo; s of Lt Col D R W G Collins-Charlton, MBE, DL, and Angela Margot, *née* Windle; *b* 23 Sept 1951; *Educ* Eton, Univ of York (BA); *m* 21 Oct 1978 (m dis 1984), Caroline Olivia, da of Geoffrey Victor Leigh Holbech, of Farnborough Hall, Farnborough, Warwickshire; *Career* called to the Bar Gray's Inn 1978; Distillers Company 1977-84, in practice as barr 1986-; Inns of Court and City Yeomanry 1987-; Freeman: City of London, Worshipful Co of Merchant Taylors; *Recreations* riding, skiing, scuba; *Clubs* Bucks; *Style*— Hugo Charlton, Esq; 5 Pump Court, Temple, London EC4 (☎ 071 5837133)

CHARLTON, John Fraser; s of late Dr Paul Henry Charlton, of Cardigan, Dyfed, and Margaret, *née* Smith; *b* 23 April 1940; *Educ* Winchester, Magdalene Coll Cambridge (BA); *m* 1966, Susan Ann, da of Walter Herbert Allan, of Esher, Surrey; 1 s (David b 1969), 2 da (Anna b 1967, Lisa b 1971); *Career* publisher; dir: Chatto and Windus 1967-, The Hogarth Press 1970-, Chatto Bodley Head and Jonathan Cape Ltd 1977-89 (co name changed to Random House UK Ltd 1988); chm: Great Gardens of England Investmts Ltd, Chatto and Windus Ltd 1985; *Recreations* sport; *Clubs* Garrick, Groucho's, Hurlingham; *Style*— John Charlton Esq; 4 Selwood Place, London SW7 3QQ (☎ 071 370 1711); Chatto and Windus Ltd, 20 Vauxhall Bridge Rd, London SW1V 2SA (☎ 071 973 9740)

CHARLTON, Maj (Frederick) John; JP (1957); s of Maj George Charlton Anne, OBE (d 1960), of Burghwallis Hall, Doncaster, Yorks (gf assumed name of Anne on inheriting Burghwallis Hall; reverted to Charlton by deed poll 1951), and Amy Violet, *née* Montagu (d 1935); *b* 9 Nov 1914; *Educ* Ampleforth, RMC Sandhurst; *m* 4 Mar 1944, Mary Ellen (Mamie), da of William Henry Charlton (d 1950), of Hesleyside, Bellingham, Northumberland; 5 da (Jenny b 1946, d 1976, Kate b 1948, d 1976, Henrietta b 1951, Teresa b 1953, Josephine b 1961); *Career* cmmnd 2 Lt KOYLI 1934, serv Burma 1936-42 (despatches), Staff Coll Quetta 1942-43, HQ Combined Ops India 1943, served France, Holland, Germany 1944-45, DAQMG 1 Airborne Div 1945, Inst Sch of Land/Air Warfare 1946-48, Hong Kong 1948-49, ret 1949; pres N Tyne and Redesdale Agric Soc 1950-; memb Bellingham RDC 1951-79; High Sheriff Northumberland 1957; *Style*— Maj John Charlton, JP; Hesleyside, Bellingham, Hexham, Northumberland (☎ 0660 202 12)

CHARLTON, Prof Kenneth; s of late George Charlton, and Lottie, *née* Little (d 1976); *b* 11 July 1925; *Educ* Chester GS, Univ of Glasgow (MA, MEd), Jordanhill Coll of Educn Glasgow; *m* 2 April 1953, Maud Tulloch, da of Peter Renwick Brown, MBE (d 1955); 1 s (Peter b 3 Feb 1957), 1 da (Shelagh b 3 June 1955); *Career* Sub Lt RNVR 1943-46; history master Dalziel HS Motherwell 1950, sr history master Uddingston GS Lanarkshire 1950-54, sr lectr in educn Univ of Keele 1964-66 (lectr 1954-64), prof of history and philosophy of educn Univ of Birmingham 1966-72, prof of history of educn and dean Faculty of Educn King's Coll London 1972-83, emeritus prof of history of educn Univ of London 1983-, Leverhulme Tst emeritus res fellowship 1984-86, visiting scholar Rockefeller Fndn Centre Bellagio Italy Feb-March 1989; Br Cncl distinguished visiting fell Japan 1990; *Books* Education in Renaissance England (1955); *Recreations* gardening, listening to music; *Style*— Prof Kenneth Charlton; 128 Ridge Langley, Sanderstead, Croydon, Surrey CR2 OAS (☎ 081 651 1488)

CHARLTON, Louise; da of John Charlton, and Patricia Mary Crawford, *née* Hulme; *b* 25 May 1960; *m* 1985, Andrew, s of David Durant; *Career* Broadstreet Assocs 1984-87, dir Brunswick Public Relations 1987-; *Recreations* ornthology, swimming; *Style*— Ms Louise Charlton; Brunswick Public Relations Ltd, 17 Lincoln's Inn Fields, London WC2A 3ED (☎ 071 404 5959, fax 071 831 2823)

CHARLTON, Prof (Thomas) Malcolm; s of William Charlton (d 1974), of Great Wyrley, Staffs, and Emily May, *née* Wallbank (d 1950); *b* 1 Sept 1923; *Educ* Doncaster GS, Univ Coll Nottingham (BSc), Univ of Cambridge (MA); *m* 18 Sept 1950, Valerie, da of Dr Colin McCulloch (d 1947), of Hexham; 3 s (Richard b 1951, William b and d 1956, Edward b 1958); *Career* jr sci offr Miny of Aircraft Prodn TRE Malvern 1943-46, asst engr Merz and McLellan 1946-54, lectr in engrg Univ of Cambridge 1954-63 (fell and tutor Sidney Sussex Coll 1959-63), prof of civil engrg Queen's Univ Belfast 1963-70 (dean Faculty of Applied Sci 1967-70), Jackson prof of engrg Univ of Aberdeen 1970-79 (professor emeritus 1979-), historian of engrg sci 1979-, memb: Advsy Cncl UDR 1969-71, Bd of Fin Diocese of Hereford 1980; hon foreign memb Finnish Acad of Tech Sciences 1967, FRSE 1973, Personal Symposium Turin Politecnico 1989; *Books* Model Analysis of Structures (1954, 1966), Energy Principles in Applied Statics (1959), Analysis of Statically-Indeterminate Frameworks (1961), Principles of Structural Analysis (1969, 1977, Arabic translation 1984), Energy Principles in Theory of Structures (1973), A History of Theory of Structures in the Nineteenth Century (1982); *Recreations* walking, ecclesiastical history; *Clubs* Bath & County; *Style*— Prof Malcolm Charlton; The Old School House, 72 North St, Burwell, Cambridge CB5 OBB (☎ 0638-741351)

CHARLTON, Mervyn; s of Rowland Charlton (d 1986), of Warwick, and Madge Louise, *née* Eaton; *b* 2 July 1945; *Educ* Nottingham Art Coll; *m* 1982, Ann, da of John James Hewitson; 1 s (Conrad Alexander b 1 March 1986); *Career* artist-in-residence Guildford House 1983; solo exhibitions: Moira Kelly Fine Art 1981 and 1982, Festival Gallery Bath 1983, Sally Hunter/Patrick Seale Fine Art 1985, Anne Berthoud Gallery 1988, Sally Hunter Fine Art 1989; gp exhibitions incl: Metro Show (Docklands Art Gallery) 1980, Eastern Arts Third and Fourth Nat Exhibition Tours (Tolly Cobbald) 1981 and 1983, Subjective Eye Midland Gp (Nottingham and tour) 1981-82, Whitechapel Open (Whitechapel Gallery) 1982-84, The London Gp (Camden Arts Centre and tour) 1982, Eight in the Eighties (NY) 1983, Art for Schs (Gainsborough's House 1983 and Sackhouse Gallery Norwich 1984), Summer Exhibition (Royal Acad) 1984, Bath Festival Show 1984 and 1987, Curwen Gallery 1984, Side By Side (Nat Art Gallery Kuala Lumpur and Br Cncl tour) 1985, Vorpal Gallery (NY) 1987, Mixed Summer Show (Thumb Gallery) 1990, CAS Art Market (Smith's Gallery) 1990; collections incl: Br Petroleum, Unilever, Euro Parly Luxembourg, Leics Schs, Blond Fine Art, Guildford House, Nat Art Gallery Kuala Lumpur, South Eastern Arts, Lady Antonia Fraser, Lady Patricia Gibberd; Gulbenkian Printmaker Award 1983; *Style*— Mervyn Charlton, Esq; 2 Herbert Cottages, Elm Grove Rd, Cobham, Surrey KT11 3HE (☎ 0932 862379)

CHARLTON, (Frederick) Noel; CB (1961), CBE (1946); s of Frederick William Charlton (d 1973), of Purley, Surrey, and Marian, *née* Butterworth (d 1974); bro of T A Graham Charlton, *qv*; *b* 4 Dec 1906; *Educ* Rugby, Hertford Coll Oxford (MA); *m* 1932, Maud Helen, da of Charles Walter Rudgard, of Davington, Faversham, Kent; *Career* admitted slr 1932, Slr's Dept Treasy 1946-71, princ asst slr Litigation 1956-71, sec Lord Chllr's Ctee on Defamation 1971-74, Dept of Energy (Legal Branch) 1975-81; *Recreations* golf, travel; *Clubs* Army and Navy; *Style*— Noel Charlton, Esq, CB, CBE; 4 Newton Rd, Purley, Surrey (☎ 081 660 2802)

CHARLTON, Philip; OBE (1987); s of late George Charlton, of Chester, and Lottie, *née* Little (d 1976); *b* 31 July 1930; *Educ* City GS Chester; *m* 27 June 1953, Jessie, da of Joseph Boulton (d 1966), of Chester; 1 s (Philip John b 1962), 1 da (Margaret b 1959); *Career* Nat Serv RN 1947-49; gen mangr: Chester Savings Bank 1966-75, TSB Wales and Border Counties 1975-81; memb and dep chief gen mangr Tstee Savings Banks Central Bd 1981-82 (chief gen mangr 1982-); dir: TSB Computer Servs (Wythenshawe) Ltd 1976-81, TSB Tst Co Ltd 1979-82, TSB Hldgs Ltd 1982-, TSB Gp Computer Servs Ltd 1981-84, Central Tstee Savings Bank 1982-; chief gen mangr TSB England and Wales 1983-85, dir TSB England and Wales 1985-87, gp chief exec TSB Group plc 1986-89 (non-exec dep chm 1990-); memb Cncl The Inst of Bankers 1982- (dep chm 1988-89); memb Bd of Admin of the Int Savings Banks Inst Geneva 1985- (vice pres 1985-90, pres 1990-); FCIB, CBIM, FRSA, memb Bd of Admin Euro Savings Banks Gp Brussels 1989-; *Clubs* Chester City, RAC; *Style*— Philip Charlton, Esq, OBE; 62 Quinta Drive, Arkley, Herts EN5 3BE (☎ 081 440 4477); TSB Gp plc, 25 Milk St, London EC2V 8LU (☎ 071 606 7070, fax 071 606 0510, telex 8812487)

CHARLTON, (Robert Joseph) Robin; s of James Charlton, MM (d 1978), of Tyldesley, Manchester, and Mary Elizabeth, *née* Crompton (d 1977); *b* 27 May 1933; *Educ* Manchester GS, Univ of Manchester (BA); *m* 31 March 1962, Joan, da of George Sydney Firth, of 26 Schofield Lane, Atherton, Manchester; 1 da (Helen b 1964); *Career* admitted chartered accountant 1957; ptnr: Mellor Snape & Co 1970-76, Josolyne Layton-Bennett & Co 1976-81, Arthur Young 1981-87, Alexander Layton 1987-; fndr pres of S Cheshire Jr Chamber 1969-70, pres Crewe Dist Chamber of Trade 1975-76; treas: Crewe Constituency Cons Assoc 1974-83, Crewe & Nantwich Cons Assoc 1983-88; memb Crewe Rotary Club 1979-, nat treas Br Jr Chamber 1973, senator Jr Chamber Int 1974-, treas Abbeyfield Crewe & Nantwich Soc Ltd 1981-, tstee Crewe & Nantwich Talking Newspaper for the Visually Handicapped 1989, govr Ruskin Co HS 1990-; FCA; *Recreations* watching cricket, lecturing on the peerage; *Clubs* Lancashire Co Cricket; *Style*— Robin Charlton, Esq; Roldal, 43 Pit Lane, Hough, Crewe, Cheshire CW2 5JH (☎ 0270 841 759); 130-132 Nantwich Road, Crewe, Cheshire CW2 6AZ (☎ 0270 213 475)

CHARLTON, Lt-Col (Richard) Wingate Collins; OBE (1975, MBE 1961), DL (Essex, 1971); s of Brig-Gen Claud Edward Charles Graham Charlton, CB, CMG, DSO, DL (d 1961), and Gwendoline Sylvia, *née* Whitaker (d 1964); ggs of Col Richard Edward Charlton; *b* 30 July 1913; *Educ* Eton, RMC Sandhurst; *m* 26 May 1945, Angela Margot, da of late Norman Whitmore Windle; 2 s (Richard Wingate Edward b 3 May 1948, William Wingate Hugo b 23 Sept 1951); *Career* 2 Lt 8 Hussars 1933, served Palestinian campaign 1936, WWII TJFF Syria (wounded, despatches), Cdr 2 Bedouin Mechanised Regt Arab Legion, ME Staff Coll 1943, serv Para Regt, SOE NW Euro 8 Hussars 1946, 2 i/c 8 Hussars, GSI II trg directorate WO 1947, RASC Offrs' Sch, 2 i/c Northants Yeo, mil and air attaché Br Embassy Damascus 1958-61, HQ Allied Land Forces Central Euro; dep chm Royal Humane Soc 1962-77 ; memb: Chelmsford and Deanery Synods, Court and Cncl Univ of Essex; pres: SSAFA, Essex Co Playing Fields; chm Essex Army Benevolent Fund, dep cmmr St John Ambulance Essex, High Sheriff of Essex 1976-77; Freeman City of London; FRSA 1947, OStJ 1979; DSC (US Army), 3 cl Order of the Istiqlal (Jordan) 1943; *Books* Verses (1937), More Verses (1938); *Recreations* fox and hare hunting (in England), stag hunting (in France); *Clubs* Cavalry and Guards'; *Style*— Lt-Col Wingate Charlton, OBE, DL; Great Canfield Park, Takeley, nr Bishop's Stortford, Herts CM22 6SS (☎ 0279 870256)

CHARMAN, Michael; s of Edwin Henry Charman (d 1969), and Doris Ada, *née* Whitehead (d 1985); *b* 28 May 1920; *Educ* St Paul's; *m* 13 April 1946, Florence Joyce (Joy), da of The Rev Prebendary Thomas Harry Philips Hyatt (d 1941), Prebendary of Lichfield Cathedral; 1 s (David Michael b 1948), 1 da (Philippa Joyce b 1951); *Career* TA 1938, War Serv 44 Leicesters 1939-43, invalided out; admitted slr 1945, HM coroner City of Leicester and S Leics 1969-90; hon lay canon Leicester Cathedral 1963-; chm The Royal Leicesters Rutland and Wycliffe Soc for the Blind 1975-, hon slr The Samaritans 1975-88; chm Glebe Ctee Leicester Diocesan Bd of Fin 1980-; *Recreations* books, bridge, golf; *Clubs* Leicestershire Book Soc, The Leicestershire, The Leicestershire Golf, The Far and Near; *Style*— Michael Charman, Esq; 40 Bankart Ave, Leicester LE2 2DB (☎ 0533 707789); Freer Bouskell Solicitors, 10 New St, Leicester LE1 5ND (☎ 0533 516624)

CHARNLEY, Lady; Jill Margaret; *née* Heaver; *m* 1957, Sir John Charnley, CBE, FRCS, FRS (d 1982), sometime prof orthopaedic surgery Manchester Univ; 1 s, 1 da; *Style*— Lady Charnley; Copse Cottage, 13 Sandy Lane, nr Chippenham, Wilts (☎ 0380 850 606)

CHARNLEY, Sir (William) John; CB (1973); s of George Edward Charnley (d 1983), and Catherine Charnley; *b* 4 Sept 1922; *Educ* Oulton HS Liverpool, Univ of Liverpool (MEng); *m* 1945, Mary, da of Richard Paden (d 1933); 1 s, 1 da; *Career* aeronautical engr; chief scientist RAF 1973-77, controller R & D Estabs and Res MOD 1977-82 (controller guided weapons and electronics 1972-73), tech conslt 1982-; conslt: Short Bros plc, CAA, Graviner Ltd; pres Royal Inst of Navigation 1987-90, tstee Richard Ormonde Shuttleworth Remembrance Tst; FRAeS 1966 (Silver medal 1973, Gold medal 1980), FRIN 1963 (Bronze medal 1960), FEng 1982, Cumberbatch Trophy (Guild of Air Pilots, Air Navigators) 1964; Hon DEng Univ of Liverpool 1988; kt 1981; *Recreations* all sport, hill walking, chess; *Clubs* RAF; *Style—* Sir John Charnley, CB; Kirkstones, 29 Brackendale Close, Camberley, Surrey GU15 1HP (☎ 0276 22547)

CHARNOCK, (Frederick) Mark Luckhoff; s of Frederick Niven Charnock, of Cape Town, SA, and Alta Anna, *née* Luckhoff; *b* 20 June 1945; *Educ* Diocesan Coll Cape Town SA, Univ of Cape Town (MB ChB) FRCS (Eng), FRCSEd, FRCOG; *m* 8 April 1970, Margaret Isobel, da of Frances Neale Murray, of Cape Town, South Africa; 1 s (Alasdair b 1984), 1 da (Annabel b 1982); *Career* house offr: Queen Charlotte's Hosp 1971, Samaritan Hosp 1975-76; registrar and sr registrar Bart's 1977-80, conslt obstetrician and gynaecologist Radcliffe and Churchill Hosp Oxford, hon sr lectr Univ of Oxford, examiner for Univs of Oxford, Cambridge, and London; memb and cncllr: RCOG 1983-89, RCS; sec RSM 1989-90; Liveryman of Worshipful Soc of Apothecaries (1989), Freeman City of London (1985); *Recreations* tennis, skiing, reading, opera, art; *Style—* Mark Charnock, Esq; Manor Farm House, Bletchingdon, Oxon OX6 3DP (☎ 0869 50149); 23 Banbury Road, Oxford OX2 6NN (☎ 0865 512729)

CHARRINGTON, Gerald Anthony; JP (Essex 1982), DL (Essex 1977); o s of Brig Harold Vincent Spencer Charrington, DSO, MC, of Winchfield House, Hants, and Eleanor Sophia Campbell, *née* Jeffreys; *b* 14 July 1926; *Educ* Eton, RMA Sandhurst, Staff Coll; *m* 28 Sept 1957, Susannah Elizabeth, da of late Brig Ord Henderson Tidbury, MC, of The Greate House, Layer de la Haye, Essex; 3 s, 1 da; *Career* 9/12 Royal Lancers 1946-67, ret as Maj; farmer 1969-90; memb Gen Synod 1970-90, lay chm Chelmsford Diocesan Synod 1976-90, memb Redundant Churches Fund 1977-90, church cmmr 1978-88, High Sheriff of Essex 1981-82; Master Worshipful Co of Broderers 1988; *Recreations* shooting, beagling, Tudor brickwork, church architecture; *Clubs* Athenaeum; *Style—* Gerald Charrington, Esq, JP, DL; Griffins, Kelvedon, Essex CO5 9AH (☎ 0376 72197)

CHARRINGTON, Timothy Somerset; s of Maj Edward Craven Charrington (d 1971), of Alton, and Betty, *née* Bowles (d 1987); *b* 18 March 1938; *Educ* Malvern, Harper Adams Agric Coll, Oxford Air Trg Sch; *m* 16 Nov 1974, Elisabeth Anne Fiennes, da of Dr John Ley Greaves, of E Worldham Manor, Alton (d 1987); 2 s (Oliver b 1980, Hugh b 1983), 1 da (Sarah b 1977); *Career* airline pilot, capt with BA; *Recreations* fishing, tennis, windsurfing; *Style—* Timothy Charrington, Esq; The Croft, Farringdon, Alton, Hants GU34 3DT (☎ 042 058 200)

CHARTERIS, Hon Andrew Martin; er s of Baron Charteris of Amisfield, GCB, GCVO, QSO, OBE, PC (Life Peer), *qv*; *b* 19 Aug 1947; *Educ* Milton Abbey; *Style—* The Hon Andrew Charteris

CHARTERIS, Hon Harold Francis; yr s of Baron Charteris of Amisfield, GCB, GCVO, QSO, OBE, PC, *qv*; *b* 11 Jan 1950; *Educ* Eton, Pembroke Coll Oxford; *m* 1984, Blandine Marie, elder da of Roger Desmons, of 14 rue Wilhelm, Paris, 16; 2 da (Zoe France b 1984, Julia Marie b 29 Nov 1985); *Style—* The Hon Harold Charteris

CHARTERIS, Lt-Col John Anthony; MC (1972); s of Lt-Col John Douglas Archibald Charteris (d 1977), of Cullivait, Locharbriggs, Dumfries, and Joan Winifred, *née* Hobson; *b* 4 Sept 1940; *Educ* Wellington, RMA Sandhurst; *m* 5 Aug 1967, Antoinette Daphne Margaret, da of late Lt-Col Reginald Higginson Lowe, of Southview, Bradninch, Devon; 1 s (John Nicholas Robert Dunbar b 21 Oct 1977), 2 da (Camilla Antoinette 10 Sept 1968, Annabel Claire b 27 July 1970); *Career* cmmnd Royal Scots 1961; served: Libya, Aden, Borneo, Hong Kong, Malaysia, NI, Falkland Islands; cdr Recruiting and Liaison Staff Scotland 1987-89; *Recreations* hunting, shooting, fishing, stalking, skiing; *Clubs* Army & Navy, New (Edinburgh), Royal Scots, Whistle; *Style—* Lt-Col John Charteris, MC; Cullivait, Locharbriggs, Dumfries, Scotland 0387 710352)

CHARTERIS, Leslie; *b* 12 May 1907; *m* 1 (m dis 1937), Pauline Schishkan; 1 da; m 2, (m dis 1941), Barbara Meyer; m 3 (m dis 1951), Elizabeth Bryant Borst; m 4, Audrey Long; *Career* author; entertainer for many years, traveller and adventurer, creator of The Saint (trans into 15 languages, character appeared in films, on radio, TV and comic strip); pubns incl: Meet the Tiger (1928), Enter the Saint, The Last Hero, Knight Templar, Featuring the Saint, Alies the Saint, She Was a Lady (filmed 1938 as The Saint Strikes Back), The Holy Terror (filmed 1939 as The Saint in London), Getaways, Once More the Saint, The Brighter Buccaneer, The Misfortunes of Mr Teal, Boodle, The Saint Goes On, The Saint in New York (filmed 1938), Saint Overboard (1936), The Ace of Knaves (1937), Thieves Picinic (1937), Juan Belmonte, Killer of Bulls: The Autobiography of a Matador (1937), Prelude for War (1938), Follow The Saints (1938), The Happy Highwayman (1939), The First Saint Omnibus (1939), The Saint in Miami (1941), The Saint Goes West (1942), The Saint Steps In (1944), The Saint on Guard (1945), The Saint Sees it Through (1946), Call for the Saint (1948), Saint Errant (1948), The Second Saint Onmibus (1952), The Saint on the Spanish Main (1955), The Saint Around the World (1957), Thanks to the Saint (1958), Senor Saint (1959), The Saint to the Rescue (1961), Trust the Saint (1962), The Saint in the Sun (1964), Vendetta for the Saint (1965, filmed 1968), The Saint on TV (1968), The Saint Returns (1969), The Saint and the Fiction Makers (1969), The Saint Abroad (1970), The Saint in Pursuit (1971), The Saint and the People Importers (1971), Paleneo (1972), Saints Alive (1974), Catch the Saint (1975), The Saint and the Hapsburg Necklace (1976), Send for the Saint (1977), The Saint in Trouble (1978), The Saint and the Templar Treasure (1979), Count on the Saint (1980), The Fantastic Saint (1982), Salvage for the Saint (1983); supervising ed Saint Magazine 1953-67, editorial conslt (new) Saint Magazine 1984-85, columnist Gourmet Magazine 1966-68, special corr and Hollywood scenarist, contrib to leading Eng and American magazines and newspapers; *Recreations* eating, drinking, horseracing, sailing, fishing, loafing; *Clubs* Mensa, Yacht Club de Cannes; *Style—* Leslie Charteris, Esq; Thompson Levett & Co, 3 Great Marlborough St, London W1V 2AR

CHARTERIS, Hon Mrs Guy; Violet; da of Alfred Charles Masterton Porter, of Dundee; *m* 5 Oct 1945, as his 2 w, Capt Hon Guy Laurence Charteris (d 21 Sept 1967), 2 s of 11 Earl of Wemyss and (7 of) March; *Style—* The Hon Mrs Guy Charteris; The Old House, Didbrook, Nr Cheltenham, Glos (☎ 0242 621 236)

CHARTERIS OF AMISFIELD, Baroness; Hon (Mary) Gay Hobart; da of 1 Visc Margesson (d 1965); *b* 3 May 1919; *m* 16 Dec 1944, Baron Charteris of Amisfield, GCB, GCVO, QSO, OBE, PC *qv*; 2 s, 1 da; *Style—* The Lady Charteris of Amisfield; Provost's Lodge, Eton College, Windsor, Berks (☎ 0753 866304/865689); Wood Stanway Hse, Winchcombe, Cheltenham, Glos GL54 5PG (☎ 038 673 480)

CHARTERIS OF AMISFIELD, Baron (Life Peer UK 1977), of Amisfield, E Lothian; Hon Martin Michael Charles Charteris; GCB (1977, KCB 1972, CB 1958), GCVO (1976, KCVO 1962, MVO 1953), QSO (1978), OBE (1946), PC (1972); s of late Capt (Hugo Francis Charteris) Lord Elcho (d 1916), and bro of 12 Earl of Wemyss and March; *b* 7 Sept 1913; *Educ* Eton, Sandhurst; *m* 16 Dec 1944, Hon (Mary) Gay Hobart Margesson, da of 1 Viscount Margesson; 2 s (Hon Andrew Martin b 1947, Hon Harold Francis b 1950), 1 da (Hon Francesca Mary (Hon Mrs Pearson) b 1945); *Career* Lt KRRC 1936, serv WWII Middle E, Palestine, Lt-Col 1944; private sec to HRH The Princess Elizabeth 1950-52, asst private sec to HM The Queen 1952-72, private sec to HM The Queen and keeper of HM's Archives 1972-77, a permanent lord in waiting to HM The Queen 1978-; dir: De La Rue Co 1978-85, Rio Tinto Zinc Corpn 1978-84, Claridge's and Connaught Hotels; provost of Eton 1978-91; tstee Br Museum 1979-89, chm tstees Nat Heritage Meml Fund 1980; Hon DCL (Oxon) 1978, Hon LLD (London) 1981; *Style—* The Rt Hon the Lord Charteris of Amisfield, GCB, GCVO, QSO, OBE, PC; Provost's Lodge, Eton College, Windsor, Berks (☎ 0753 866304); Wood Stanway Hse, Wood Stanway, Cheltenham, Glos (☎ 038 673 480)

CHARVET, Richard Christopher Larkins; RD (1972), JP; s of Patrice Edouard Charvet, and Eleanor Margaret Charvet; *b* 12 Dec 1936; *Educ* Rugby; *m* 1, 30 Sept 1961 (m dis 1988), Elizabeth Joan, da of Hubert Johnson; 2 s (Charles Richard de Merle b 1963, Edward Bryan Nugent b 1972), 1 da (Alexandra Mary Dashwood b 1965); m 2, Marilyn Jean, da of Derek Bal; *Career* clerk Union Castle Line 1956-58; dir: Killick Martin and Co Ltd 1958-81 (clerk 1958-67), Vogt and Maguire Ltd 1981-88, assoc dir Anglo Soviet Shipping Ltd 1988-; Common Councilman City of London 1973-78, Alderman Aldgate Ward 1978-85, Queen's Sheriff 1984; chm: Royalist Appeal 1985, St John's Ambulance Centenary City Appeal 1987-, RNLI City of London Branch 1988; Freeman City of London 1962, Prime Warden Worshipful Co of Shipwrights 1985, Master Guild of World Traders 1990; FRSA, FBIM, MITT, ACIArb, FICS; JSM 1979, OStJ 1984, CStJ 1989; *Books* Peter and Tom in the Lord Mayor's Show (1981); *Recreations* sailing, gardening, people; *Style—* Richard Charvet, Esq, RD, JP; Anglo Soviet Shipping Ltd, 10 Lloyds Ave, London EC3 (☎ 071 488 1399)

CHASSELS, (James) David Simpson; s of Robert Brown Chassels, and Frances Amelia, *née* Simpson; *b* 2 April 1947; *Educ* Rannoch Sch; *m* 21 May 1976, Angela Elizabeth, da of James Nicol Martin Bulloch; 2 s (Ross b 30 Nov 1977, Scott b 29 March 1980), 1 da (Nicola b 28 Feb 1983); *Career* CA: French & Cowan Glasgow 1965-70, Arthur Young Edinburgh 1970-74, 3i Investmt Exec Glasgow & Edinburgh (formerly ICFC) 1974-81 (dir 3i Corporate Fin 1981-); govr Rannoch Sch 1972-, memb Polmont Borstal Visiting Ctee 1978-83; former Deacon Incorporaton of Barbers Trades House of Glasgow 1985-86; MICAS 1973; *Recreations* sailing, skiing; *Clubs* RSAC, CCC; *Style—* David Chassels, Esq; 10 Duart Drive, Newton Mearns, Glasgow G77 5DS (☎ 041 639 3914); 3i Corporate Finance Ltd, 20 Blythswood Sq, Glasgow, G2 4AR (☎ 041 248 4456, fax 041 248 3245, car 0836 706604, telex 917844)

CHASTNEY, John Garner; s of Alec Richardson Chastney (d 1981), and Constance Mary, *née* Edwards; *b* 5 Jan 1947; *Educ* Henry Mellish GS Nottingham, Univ of Lancaster (MA); *m* 4 Aug 1973, Susan Thirza, da of Norman Dunkerley; 2 s (Martin Richard b 1980, David Paul b 1982), 1 da (Catherine Jane b 1978); *Career* CA; princ lectr Sheffield City Poly 1974-79, Neville Russell 1990- (sr nat trg mangr 1979-83, devpt ptnr 1983-88); on secondment: under sec DTI, dir Indust Devpt Unit 1988-90; prize essayist; FCA 1973; *Books* True and Fair View (1974), European Financial Reporting: The Netherlands (with J H Beeny, 1976); *Clubs* Square Mile; *Style—* John Chastney, Esq; 246 Bishopsgate, London EC2M 4PB (☎ 071 377 1000, fax 071 377 8931)

CHATAWAY, Rt Hon Christopher John; PC (1970); s of James Denys Percival Chataway, OBE (d 1953), of 46 De Vere Gdns, W8; *b* 31 Jan 1931; *Educ* Sherborne, Magdalen Coll Oxford; *m* 1, 1959 (m dis 1975), Anna Maria, da of H Lett; 2 s, 1 da; m 2, 1976, Carola Cecil Walker, da of Maj Charles Ashton, DSO; 2 s; *Career* Olympic runner 1952 and 1956 (world record holder 5,000 metres 1954); TV News reporter 1955-59; MP (C) Lewisham N 1959-66, Chichester 1969-74; Parly under sec Dept of Educn and Sci 1962-64; min: Posts and Telecommunications 1970-72, Industrial Devpt 1972-74; md Orion Royal Bank 1974-88; dir: British Electric Traction Co 1974-, Crown Communications plc 1987-; chm: Action Aid 1985- (hon treas 1975-85), Groundwork 1985-89; *Style—* The Rt Hon Christopher Chataway; 27 Randolph Crescent, London W9

CHATAWAY, Michael Denys; s of James Denys Percival Chataway, OBE (d 1953), and Margaret Pritchard, *née* Smith (d 1988); *b* 23 July 1934; *Educ* Sherborne, Magdalen Coll Oxford (BA); *m* 1 Aug 1970, Caroline Mary, da of Lt-Col E H Colville, DSO, RA (d 1980); 1 s (James b 1973), 1 da (Charlotte b 1976); *Career* Nat Serv 2 Lt 1 Bn KRRC 1953; chm C Czarnikow Ltd 1985- (dir 1971-), dir London Futures and Options Exchange 1987; *Style—* Michael Chataway, Esq; The Old Rectory, Tichborne, nr Alresford, Hants; C Czarnikow Ltd, 66 Mark Lane, London, EC3P 3EA (☎ 071 480 9300)

CHATER, Geoffrey (aka Geoffrey Chater Robinson); s of Lawrence Chater Robinson (d 1978), of Morval, Kingsgate, Broadstairs, and Gwendoline Dorcas, *née* Gwynn; *b* 23 March 1921; *Educ* Marlborough, Chillon Coll Glion-sur-Montreux Switzerland; *m* 22 June 1949, Jennifer Robin Fergus, da of Francis James Hill, of Fiveacres, Wormley, Surrey; 2 s (Simon, Piers), 1 da (Annabel); *Career* WWII serv 1940-45, cmmnd Royal Fus 1941, serv UK and N Ireland 1942, Leics Regt Karachi 1943, N Staffs Regt Arakan Burma and Dinapore India 1943-44, Capt 1944, reinforced Royal Worcs Regt Burma 1945; actor, devised and performed revue for battalion in Pyinmana 1945; early theatre work incl: Theatre Royal Windsor 1946-47, Alexandra Theatre Birmingham 1948-49, Shakespeare Season Old Vic Theatre 1954-55; London theatre work incl: Duke of Florence in Women Beware Women (RSC, 1962), Yslaev in A Month in the Country (with Ingrid Bergman and Michael Redgrave, Cambridge Theatre 1965), Henry Craxton in Cousin Vladimir (RSC, 1978), Polonius in Hamlet (Royal Court Theatre, 1980), The Doctor in Three Sisters (Albery Theatre, 1987), films incl: If, 10 Rillington Place, Barry Lyndon, Ghandi; numerous tv appearances incl: Dusty Miller in The Last Reunion (1956), Stanly Leibowitz in The Scotsboro Case (1972), Control in The Specialist (1979), Guy Lidell in Blunt (1987), Rafe Hollingsworth in Chelworth (1988), Fabian in Rumpole of the Bailey (1990); *Recreations* golf, swimming, crocquet, watching cricket; *Clubs* MCC, Rye Golf; *Style—* Geoffrey Chater, Esq

CHATER, Stephen Paul; s of John Charles Chater, of Hartlepool, Cleveland, and Patricia Norby, *née* Oakes; *b* 2 March 1956; *Educ* Hartlepool GS, ChCh Oxford (MA); *m* 10 Sept 1988, Susan Frances Margaret, da of Charles Harborne Stuart, of Combe, Oxford; *Career* slr; ptnr Allen & Overy 1989- (articled 1979-81, asst slr 1981-88); Freeman Worshipful Co of Slrs 1989; memb Law Soc; *Recreations* music (London Philharmonic Choir), genealogy, political biographies; *Style—* Stephen Chater, Esq; 79 Merton Hall Rd, Wimbledon, London SW19 3PX (☎ 081 540 7487); Allen & Overy, 9 Cheapside, London EC2V 6AD (☎ 071 248 9898, fax 071 236 2192, telex 8812801)

CHATFIELD, 2 Baron (1937 UK); Ernle David Lewis Chatfield; s of 1 Baron Chatfield, GCB, OM, KCMG, CVO, PC (Admiral of the Fleet, d 1967); *b* 2 Jan 1917; *Educ* Dartmouth, Trinity Coll Cambridge; *m* 16 May 1969, (Felicia Mary) Elizabeth, da of late Dr John R Bulman, of Hereford; *Career* ADC to Govr-Gen of Canada 1940-44; *Style—* The Rt Hon the Lord Chatfield; 535 Island Road, Victoria, BC V8S 2T7, Canada

CHATFIELD, John Freeman; CBE (1982), DL (E Sussex 1986); s of Cecil Freeman

Chatfield (d 1974), of The Lodge, Blackwater Rd, Eastbourne, and Florence Dorothy, *née* Greed (d 1985); *b* 28 Oct 1929; *Educ* Southdown Coll Eastbourne, Roborough Sch Eastbourne, Lawrence Sheriff Sch Rugby, Lewes GS, Sch of Law London; *m* 18 Sept 1954, Barbara Elizabeth, da of Frank Hubert Trickett (d 1969), of Montford, nr Shrewsbury, Shropshire; *Career* conslt slr; ldr East Sussex CC 1981-85 (chm 1985-87, vice chm 1987-89); chm: Sussex Police Authy, Police Ctee ACC, Official Side Police Negotiating Bd UK 1982-85; pres Eastbourne Cons Assoc 1975-, vice chm Exec Cncl ACC (ldr Cons Gp) 1986-89, chm Exec Cncl ACC 1989-; chm: UK Local Govt Int Bureau 1989-, Consultative Cncl of Local and Regnl Authys in Europe with the Euro Cmmn 1990-, Int Cncl for Local Environment Initiatives 1990-; memb: Ct of Cncl Univ of Sussex 1981-85, Police Advsy Bd England and Wales 1980-85, Cons Nat Local Govt Advsy Ctee 1982- (vice chm 1989-), Nat Union of Cons and Assocs Nat Exec Ctee, Cncl Pestalozzi Tst; *Recreations* music, theatre; *Style*— John F Chatfield, Esq, CBE, DL; Underhill House, Went Way, East Dean, Eastbourne, E Sussex BN20 0DB (☎ 0323 423 397); 306 Nell Gwynne House, Sloane Ave, London SW3 (☎ 071 589 1627)

CHATMAN, William C; s of Edgar T Chatman (d 1939), and Gertrude, *née* Hewett (d 1977); *b* 20 Nov 1930; *Educ* Drexel Univ (BSc ChemEng) 1952; *m* 6 Sept 1952, Helen S, da of August Siefert (d 1981); 3 da (Linda (Mrs Thomsen) b 1954, Sandra (Mrs Loether) b 1957, Susan (Mrs Webb) b 1960); *Career* engr; dir of ops Société Foster Wheeler Francaise 1983-86, chm and chief exec Foster Wheeler Ltd 1986-; dir American C of C (UK); CEng, FICHE, CBIM; *Recreations* singing (London Philharmonic Choir), skiing; *Style*— William C Chatman, Esq; 12A Hornton Street, London W8 4NR; c/o Foster Wheeler Ltd, Foster Wheeler House, Station Road, Reading, Berks RG1 1LX

CHATT, Prof Joseph; CBE (1978); s of Joseph Chatt (d 1929), of Caldbeck, Cumbria, and M Elsie, *née* Parker (d 1972); *b* 6 Nov 1914; *Educ* Nelson Sch Wigton Cumbria, Emmanuel Coll Cambridge (BA, PhD, MA, ScD); *m* 31 May 1947, Ethel, *née* Williams; 1 s (Joseph b 16 May 1951), 1 da (Elizabeth b 12 March 1948); *Career* res chemist Woowich Arsenal 1941-42, res later chief chemist Peter Spence Sons Ltd Widnes 1942-46, ICI res fell Imperial Coll London 1946-47, head Inorganic Chemistry Dept Butterwick (later Akers) Res Laboratories ICI Ltd Welwyn 1947-60, gp mangr Akers Gp Res Dept Heavy Organic Chemicals Div ICI Ltd 1961-62, prof inorganic chemistry QMC London 1964, prof of chemistry Univ of Sussex 1964-80 (emeritus prof 1980-), dir Unit of Nitrogen Fixation Agric Res Cncl 1963-80; active in int and nat bodies concerned with chemistry especially Int Union of Pure and Applied Chemistry 1950-; hon memb: Nat Acad of Portugal 1978, Indian Nat Sci Acad 1980, NY Acad of Sciences 1978, Royal Physiological Soc of Lund 1984, American Acad of Arts and Sciences 1985; Hon DSc: Univ of E Anglia 1974, Sussex Univ 1982; Hon Dr Pierre et Marie Curie Paris 1981, Filasofie Dr Lund Sweden 1986, Wolf Fndn Prize Chemistry 1981; FRSC (formerly CS) 1937: memb Cncl 1952-65 and 1972-76, hon sec 1956-62, vice pres 1962-65 and 1972-74, pres Dalton Div 1972-74; FRS 1961: memb Cncl, Davy Medal Chemistry, Parly and Sci Ctee 1961-62), fell American Chemical Soc 1961, IUPAC 1984; *Recreations* numismatics, art, history; *Clubs* Civil Service; *Style*— Prof Joseph Chatt, CBE, FRS; 16 Tongdean Road, Hove, E Sussex BN3 6QE (☎ 0273 554 377); School of Chemistry & Molecular Sciences, Univ of Sussex, Falmer, Brighton BN1 9QJ (☎ 0273 606 755)

CHATTERJEE, Mira; da of Dr Haradlan Chatterjee (Capt IMS/IAMC SEAC, Burma Star), of Maya Cottage, Chase Lane, Lambourne Rd, Chigwell, Essex, and Kamala, *née* Banerjee; *b* 19 April 1948; *Educ* City of London Sch for Girls; *m* 19 April 1980, Dr Gautam Chaudhuri, s of Dr Punendu Chandhuri, of Calcutta; 1 da (Sandra b 28 Jan 1981); *Career* called to the Bar Middle Temple 1973, in practice SE circuit; *Recreations* reading, philosophy; *Clubs* Wig and Pen; *Style*— Miss Mira Chatterjee; 4 Brick Court, Middle Temple, London EC4 (☎ 071 353 1492/3/4, fax 071 583 8645)

CHATTERJEE, Dr Satya Saran; OBE (1971); s of Basanta Kumar Chatterjee (d 1956), of Patna India, and Sabani Chatterjee (d 1924); *b* 16 July 1922; *Educ* Patna Univ; *m* 1948, Enid May, da of Joseph Adlington (d 1965), of Birmingham; 1 s (Nigel), 2 da (Camille, Petula); *Career* Capt Indian Army 1944; conslt chest physician i/c Dept of Respiratory Physiology Wythenshawe Hosp Manchester 1959-87; pres Overseas Doctors' Assoc; memb North Western RHA 1976-86; memb: Standing Advsy Cncl on Race Relations 1977-86, GMC 1979-; res papers on various projects related to cardio/pulmonary disorders; *Recreations* gardening, bridge; *Clubs* Manchester Bridge, Rotary (Wythenshawe); *Style*— Dr Satya Chatterjee, OBE; March, 20 Macclesfield Rd, Wilmslow, Cheshire SK9 2AF (☎ 0625 522559)

CHATTERTON, (Charles) Robert; s of Charles Chatterton (d 1952), of Penarth, Glamorgan, and Lilian, *née* Saunders (d 1972); *b* 30 Sept 1913; *Educ* Cardiff GS, Cardiff Tech Coll, Bloggs Coll Cardiff; *m* 21 Aug 1937, Lilian May (d 1990), da of Howard Henry Sladen (d 1959), of Cardiff; 1 s (Peter b 1939), 1 da (Susan b 1947); *Career* TA 1937-45, Welsh Regt 1939, cmmnd Queen's Own Royal West Kents 1940, A/Maj, served overseas (despatches twice); chm: Reardon Smith Group of Cos 1970-85 (jr accountant 1929, asst co sec 1961, dir and co sec 1963), Cardiff Ship Management & Services Ltd 1985- (and dir); dir Bank of Wales plc 1974-88; chm: Horton and Port Eynon Lifeboat Ctee, The Missions to Seamen (Cardiff Station); Liveryman Worshipful Co of Shipwrights; Queens Silver Jubilee medal; FInstD; *Recreations* ornithology, walking, fishing; *Clubs* Cardiff Business; *Style*— Robert Chatterton, Esq; Green Meadow, Ger y Llan, St Nicholas, Cardiff CF5 6SY (☎ 0446 760723); Dominions House South, Queen St, Cardiff

CHATTINGTON, Barry John; s of John William Chattington (d 1967), of Kent, and Rose Amelia, *née* Darlington; *b* 24 April 1947; *Educ* Dartford Tech High Sch; *Career* asst film ed 1963-66, film ed 1966-, film dir 1972-; md Goldcrest Facilities Ltd 1988, currently md Brent Walker Facilities Ltd (parent co of Elstree Studios, Roger Cherrill Ltd and Cherry Video Ltd); works incl: numerous long and short films for Paul McCartney Pink Floyd and others, drama series US TV, major documentary Kuwait TV, charity films with the Prince of Wales and the Princess Royal; awards: 4 Golden Halos from S Calif Motion Picture Cncl, Silver award NY Int Film and TV Festival 1982, numerous D & ADA award commendations; memb Br Kinematograph Sound & TV Soc 1963; chm: Directors Guild of GB 1985-86, Producers and Directors Section ACTT 1985-86; Br delegate on Federation Europeene des Industries Techniques de l'Image et du Son; *Clubs* Groucho, Variety, Reform, Chelsea Arts; *Style*— Barry Chattington, Esq; Roger Cherrill Ltd, 65-66 Dean St, London W1V 6PL (☎ 071 437 7972, fax 071 437 6411)

CHATTO, Beth; da of late William George Little, and late Bessie Beatrice, *née* Styles; *b* 27 June 1923; *m* Andrew Edward Chatto, s of Andrew Chatto; 2 da (Diana Peacock b 17 March 1946, Mary Elizabeth Marshall 7 Sept 1948); *Career* proprietor Unusual Plants 1967-89, formed Limited co The Beth Chatto Gardens 1989-; lectr various venues professionally and for charity 1967-; memb RHS: Victoria medal of Honour 1988, Lawrence Memorial medal 1988; Hon DUniv Essex 1988; *Books* The Dry Garden (1978), The Damp Garden (1982), Plant Portraits (1985), Beth Chatto's Garden Notebook (1988), The Green Tapestry (1989); *Recreations* gardening, music, reading, cooking, my family; *Style*— Mrs Beth Chatto; The Beth Chatto Gardens, Elmstead Market, Cholchester, Essex CO7 7DB (☎ 0206 82 2007, fax 0206 825933)

CHATWOOD, Albert Rawsthorne; s of Albert Chatwood (d 1972), of Devon, and Jessie Dunbar, *née* Wilson (d 1979); *b* 9 July 1931; *Educ* Holloway Sch St John's Newfoundland, Prince of Wales Coll St John's; *Career* statistician Iron Ore Co of Canada Labrador City 1962-79, treas and chm Labrador City Library Bd 1964-78, hon treas Anglican Charitable Fndn for Children 1980-; *Recreations* walking, music, reading, gardening; *Clubs* Royal Overseas League; *Style*— Albert R Chatwood, Esq; 8 Prince William Place, St John's, Newfoundland, Canada A1B 1A5 (☎ 709 722 8261); Chesterblade, Chamberlains, CBS, Newfoundland, Canada, A0A 2YO (☎ 709 834 2815)

CHAVASSE, Christopher Patrick Grant; s of Alban Ludovick Grant Chavasse (d 1953), of Colne House, Rickmansworth, and Maureen Shingler, *née* Whalley; *b* 14 March 1928; *Educ* Bedford, Clare Coll Cambridge (MA); *m* 1955, Audrey Mary, da of the late Hugh Robert Leonard, of Ladywalk, Heronsgate; 2 s (Nicholas Robert Grant b 1956, Timothy James Grant b 1960), 1 da (Kathryn Margaret Grant b 1957); *Career* cmmnd RB 1947, served Palestine (despatches) 1948, RAFVR 1949; admitted slr 1955; ptnr: Jacobs and Greenwood 1960, Woodham Smith 1970; pres Holborn Law Soc 1977-78, trustee Nat Assoc of Decorative and Fine Art Socs 1986-, chm NADFAS Tours Ltd 1986-; hon steward Westminster Abbey 1950-, treas St Mary le Bow Church 1981-88, sec Governing Body of Oundle and Laxton Schs 1981-88; Clerk Worshipful Co of Grocers 1981-88, memb Ct Corp of Sons of the Clergy 1985; *Publications* Conveyancing Costs (1971), Non Contentious Costs (1975), The Discretionary Items in Contentious Costs (1980); articles in: Law Soc Gazette, New Law Journal, and Slrs Journal; *Recreations* sailing; *Style*— Christopher Chavasse, Esq; Duncannon House, Stoke Gabriel, nr Totnes, S Devon TQ9 6QY (☎ 080428 291)

CHAVASSE, Patrick Alban Grant; s of Alban Ludovic Grant Chavasse (d 1954), of Colne House, Rickmansworth, Herts, and Maureen Lilian Abbott, *née* Whalley; *b* 6 Aug 1935; *Educ* Bedford Sch, Clare Coll Cambridge (BA, MA); *m* 7 Sept 1963, Ann Muriel, da of Wing Cdr John Coverdale (d 1943); 2 s (Richard b 1966, Peter b 1972), 1 da (Clare b 1964); *Career* admitted slr 1962; asst slr Slaughter & May London 1962-64 (articled clerk 1959-62), ptnr Wansbroughs Willey Hargrave (formerly Wansbroughs) Bristol 1967- (asst slr 1964-67); memb Cncl Bristol C of C and Indust 1978-, hon legal advsr 1980-; memb: Bristol Law Soc, Progressive Businesses Club, Lions Club of Portishead (pres 1978-79); memb Law Soc; *Recreations* golf, bridge, motoring; *Clubs* Clevedon Golf; *Style*— Patrick Chavasse, Esq; 103 Temple St, Bristol, Avon (☎ 0272 268981, fax 0272 291582)

CHAWLA, Dr Shanti Lal; s of Puran Chand Chawla, of Delhi, and Indra Wati Chawla; *b* 26 Oct 1936; *Educ* Univ of Delhi (BSc), Punjab Univ India (LSMF, MB BS), London (DMRT), Dublin (FFR, RCSI); *m* 12 May 1967, Mrs Kamlesh, da of Chuni Lal Monga, of New Delhi; 2 da (Sangita b 21 Feb 1971, Rita b 26 May 1972); *Career* house surgn Dayanand Med Coll India 1963-64, asst surgn Govt Dispensary Gurgoan India 1964, res MO in med and surgery Tirath Ram Hosp Delhi 1966-67, asst surgn Govt Dispensary Delhi 1967-69, registrar in radiotherapy Cookridge Hosp Leeds 1971-72 (sr house offr 1969-71), sr registrar Catterbridge Hosp Cheshire 1974-80 (registrar in radiotherapy 1972-74), conslt and head of dept S Cleveland Hosp 1980- (conslt in radiotherapy and oncology 1980), hon clinical lectr in radiotherapy Univ of Newcastle upon Tyne 1980-, winner Gold award Northern Regnl Health Authy Newcastle 1990; numerous pubns in jls, vice pres Indian Assoc of Cleveland 1990 (pres 1987-89), treas Hindu Cultural Soc 1990- (sec 1985-89), treas Indian Doctors of Cleveland, memb various orgns of Middlesbrough Cncl; memb BMA, MRCR, FFR, RCSI; *Style*— Dr Shanti Chawla; 1 West Moor Close, Yarm TS15 9RG; South Cleveland Hospital, Marton Rd, Middlesbrough, Cleveland (☎ 0642 850850)

CHAWORTH-MUSTERS, Hon Mrs (Mary Victoria); *née* Monckton; eldest da of 8 Viscount Galway, PC, GCMG, DSO, OBE (d 1943); *b* 5 Jan 1924; *m* 1, 20 Aug 1947 (m dis 1972), David Henry Fetherstonhaugh, Coldstream Gds, of late Lt-Col Timothy Fetherstonhaugh, DSO, of Kirkoswald, Penrith; 2 s (Hugh Simon b 1949, m 1971 Louise, adopted da of Hon Hanning Phillips, m s of 1 Baron Milford; Henry George b 1954, m 1978 Nicola Payne-Gallwey), 1 da (Victoria Bronwen b 1951); m 2, 1974, Maj Robert Patricius Chaworth-Musters, yr s of Lt-Col John Neville Chaworth-Musters, DSO, OBE, TD, of Annesley Park, Notts; *Style*— The Hon Mrs Chaworth-Musters; Felley Priory, Jacksdale, Notts

CHAWORTH-MUSTERS, Maj Robert Patricius; s of Col John Nevile Chaworth-Musters, DSO, OBE (d 1970), of Annesley Park, Nottinghamshire, and Daphne, *née* Wilberforce Bell, OBE (d 1973); *b* 7 May 1923; *Educ* Eton, RMC Sandhurst; *m* 1, 22 Feb 1951, Diana Margaret (d 1973), da of Col Edward Robert Clayton, of Northmoor, Dulverton, Somerset; 2 da (Venetia b 6 June 1954, Sophia b 28 Oct 1957 d 1972); m 2, 30 March 1974, Mary Victoria Fetherstonhaugh, da of Viscount George Vere Arundel Monckton Arundel, of Galway; *Career* Coldstream Gds 1942-60, served N Africa and Italy 1943-45, ADC to GOC Malta 1948, Malaya 1949; farmer; *Recreations* fishing, shooting; *Clubs* Bucks, Pratts; *Style*— Maj Robert Chaworth-Musters; Felley Priory, Jacksdale, Notts NG16 5FL (☎ 0773 810 230)

CHAYTOR, Sir George Reginald; 8 Bt (UK 1831), of Croft, Yorkshire, and Witton Castle, Durham; s of William Richard Carter Chaytor (d 1973), gs of 2 Bt, and Anna Laura, *née* Fawcett (d 1947); suc kinsman, Sir William Chaytor, 7 Bt, 1976; *b* 28 Oct 1912; *m* 1970, Mrs Elsie Magdeline Rogers; *Heir* cousin, (Herbert) Gordon Chaytor; *Career* patron (alternatively) of Witton-le-Wear Vicarage; *Style*— Sir George Chaytor, Bt; c/o Mrs E J Dauncey, 7596 Lougheed Highway, N Burnaby, BC, Canada

CHAYTOR, (Herbert) Gordon; s of Herbert Archibald Chaytor (d 1979); hp of cous, Sir George Chaytor, 8 Bt; *b* 1922; *m* 1947, Mary Alice, da of Thomas Craven; 3 s (Bruce Gordon b 1949, Kenneth Reginald b 1952, Robert David b 1958); *Style*— Gordon Chaytor, Esq; Honeymoon Bay, British Columbia, Canada

CHAYTOR, Patricia, Lady; Patricia Nora; da of Loftus Joseph McCaffry and former w of George Walkley Alderman; *m* 28 July 1947, Sir William Henry Clervaux Chaytor, 7 Bt (d 1976); 1 da; *Style*— Patricia, Lady Chaytor

CHAZAL; *see*: de Chazal

CHAZAN, Dr Bernard Issac; s of Rev Philip Chazan (d 1961), of Glasgow, and Millicent, *née* Levine (d 1980); *b* 1 June 1931; *Educ* Queen's Park Secdy Sch Glasgow, Univ of Glasgow (MB ChB, MD); *m* 1, 29 Dec 1959 (m dis 1975), Valerie, da of S C Levy, of Mill Hill, London; 2 s (Yigal b 20 Nov 1961, Guy b 20 Sept 1965), 1 da (Sharon b 12 May 1963, d 12 Oct 1987); m 2, 23 Oct 1977, Irene Anne, da of Max Silberg, of Leeds; *Career* Nat Serv RAMC: Lt 1956-57, Capt 1957-58; asst physician Hadassah Med Sch Jerusalem 1961-65, sr asst physician Meir Hosp Kfar Saba Israel 1965-67, res assoc med Joslin Res Lab Boston 1967-69, sr resident Joslin Clinic 1969, conslt physician Sunderland Dist Gen 1969- (physician i/c Endocrine Unit 1976-, physician i/c Diabetic Section 1973-); memb: BMA, Br Diabetic Assoc, AJEX, IMA; MRCP 1958, FRCP 1976; *Books* Treatment of Diabetic Retinopathy (1969), Systematic Endocrine Investigation (1986); *Recreations* walking, piano playing, Hebrew literature; *Style*— Dr Bernard Chazan; Department of Medicine, District General Hospital, Sunderland SR4 7TP (☎ 091 565 6256)

CHEADLE, Sir Eric Wallers; CBE (1973), DL (1985); s of late Edgar Cheadle and Nellie, *née* Pimley; *b* 14 May 1908; *Educ* Farnworth GS; *m* 1938, Pamela, da of Alfred Hulme; 2 s; *Career* served RAFVR 1941-46, Sqdn Ldr; joined Evening Chronicle and Daily Dispatch 1924, dep md Thomson Orgn 1959-74 (dir 1949-74, ret 1974), dir

Thomson Int Press Consultancy Ltd; pres: Assoc of Lancastrians in London 1959 and 1973, Newspaper Soc 1970-71 (memb Cncl 1959-78), Manchester Publicity Assoc 1972-74 (Gold medal 1973); memb: Newspaper Publishers' Assoc Cncl 1947-74, Cncl Imperial Soc of Knights Bachelor 1979-, St Brides' Fleet St Restoration Appeal Ctee; Printers' Charitable Corpn: pres 1974, chm 1975-81, tstee 1981-; chm: Advsy Ctee Chest Heart and Stroke Assoc Appeal 1982-, Nat Stroke Campaign 1986-89, St Albans Cathedral Tst and Appeal 1982-, vice chm Shrine of St Albans Restoration Appeal, dir Herts Groundwork Tst; hon Life Memb Friends of St Albans City Hosp, lay canon St Albans Cathedral 1989, pres Herts branch English Speaking Union 1989-; kt 1978; *Books* The Roll of Knights Bachelor (1981); Chivalry (ed, Knights Bachelor Newsletter); *Recreations* watching cricket, travel, reading and talking about newspapers; *Clubs* MCC, Wig and Pen, Press, Variety; *Style—* Sir Eric Cheadle, CBE, DL; The Old Church House, 172 Fishpool St, St Albans, Herts AL3 4SB (☎ 0727 59 639)

CHEADLE, (Eric) Neville; s of Sir Eric W Cheadle, CBE, DL, of St Albans, Herts, and Lady Pamela Cheadle; *b* 10 May 1940; *Educ* Mill Hill Sch, London Poly (Dip Comm Eng/Admin), NATO Res fell at Stanford Graduate Sch of Business; *m* 1 Sept 1964, Hilary Ann; 3 s (Timothy b 1968, Jeremy b 1969, Duncan b 1971); m 2, 29 July 1989, Jean Patricia (Trish); *Career* graduate apprentice Standard Telephones & Cables Ltd 1959-64, sales and admin mangr Elliot Automation Ltd 1965-68; Price Waterhouse: joined 1968, mangr 1973, ptnr 1977, exchange visit to Kuwait 1977, ptnr London Mgmnt Consultancy Servs 1981-88 (nat dir 1985-88, Euro sr ptnr 1988-); FIMC 1985; *Recreations* sailing, cricket, amateur radio; *Clubs* MCC; *Style—* Neville Cheadle, Esq; Price Waterhouse Management Consultants, Milton Gate, 1 Moor Lane, London EC2Y 9PB (☎ 071 939 3000, fax 071 638 1358)

CHEALES, Maxwell Bellingham; s of late Lt-Col Ralph Cheales; *b* 4 Nov 1929; *Educ* Michaelhouse SA, Pembroke Coll Cambridge; *m* 1960, Hermione Ann, *née* Hogarth; 1 s, 2 da; *Career* dir Hill Samuel and Co Ltd 1965-77, Hogarth Shipping Co Ltd Glasgow: md 1971-84, chm 1978-84, fin conslt 1984-; FCA; *Style—* Maxwell Cheales, Esq; Blewburton Hall, Aston Upthorpe, Didcot, Oxon OX11 9EE (☎ 0235 850772)

CHECKETTS, Sir David John; KCVO (1979, CVO 1969, MVO 1966); 3 s of late Reginald Ernest George Checketts, and late Frances Mary Checketts; *b* 23 Aug 1930; *m* 1958, Rachel Leila Warren Herrick; 1 s, 3 da; *Career* RATG Rhodesia 1948-49, 14 Sqdn Germany 1950-54, FWS Leconfield 1954-57, Air ADC AFMED Malta 1957-59, 3 Sqdn Germany 1960-61, ret Sqdn-Ldr 1967; equerry to HRH The Duke of Edinburgh 1961-66, equerry to HRH The Prince of Wales 1967-70 and extra equerry 1979-, private sec 1970-78; dir: Global Aviation Printing Ltd, Brieftag Ltd, Seatic Co Ltd, Global Money Placement Ltd, Penselworth Ltd; chm: Rainbow Boats Tst, The Wilderness Foundation UK; FInstD, memb IISS; *Style—* Sir David Checketts, KCVO; Church Cottage, Winkfield, Windsor, Berks

CHECKETTS, Ronald Harry George; MBE (1981); s of Reginald Ernest George Checketts (Fl Lt RAF, d 1948), and Francis Mary, *née* Hagger (d 1965); *b* 30 May 1921; *Educ* Salters Hill Rd Sch West Norwood London, Gipsy Rd Sch West Norwood London; *m* 16 Aug 1947, Joan Rose, da of Henry Castle (d 1966); 1 s (Adrian Michel b 7 Sept 1958); *Career* RN 1936-53 Ships: HMS Ganges, Ramillies, Glorious, Arethusa, Capetown, Liverpool, Manxman, Sheffield, Rnella W/T Station Malta, HMS Loch Shin, Mercury, Phoebe, Manxman; Reuters News Agency 1953-56, HM Dip Serv 1956-81; auxiliary coastguard Lands End Cornwall 1981-86, town clerk Marazion Cornwall 1985; memb: RSGB 1983, RNARS 1983; *Recreations* sailing, amateur radio; *Clubs* Special Forces, The White Elephant, Mounts Bay Sailing Cornwall; *Style—* Ronald Checketts, Esq, MBE; Bromly's Farm, Pool St, Hinton, Woodford Halse, Nr Daventry, Northants NN11 6TS (☎ 0327 620159)

CHECKLAND, Michael; s of Leslie Checkland (d 1980), and Ivy Florence, *née* Bemand; *b* 13 March 1936; *Educ* King Edward's GS Fiveways Birmingham, Wadham Coll Oxford; *m* 1, 25 March 1960 (m dis 1983), Shirley Frances Corbett; 2 s (Philip Michael b 1962, Richard Bruce b 1965), 1 da (Helen Julia b 1968); m 2, 23 Oct 1987, Susan, da of Ernest Harold Walker, ISO; *Career* auditor Parkinson Cowan Ltd 1959-62, accountant Thorn Electronics 1962-64; BBC: sr cost accountant 1964-67, head of Central Finance Unit 1969-71, chief accountant Central Finance Services 1969, chief accountant Television 1971, fin controller 1976, controller planning and resource mgmnt Television 1977, dir of resources Television 1982, chm BBC Enterprises 1986-87 (dir 1979-), dep dir gen 1985, dir gen 1987-, dir Visnews 1980-85; fell and vice pres Royal Television Soc, pres Cwlth Broadcasting Assoc 1987-88; hon fell Wadham Coll Oxford 1989; FCMA; *Recreations* music, theatre, travel; *Style—* Michael Checkland, Esq; Director-General, BBC, Broadcasting House, London W1A 1AA (☎ 071 580 4468, telex 265781)

CHECKLAND, Prof Peter Bernard; s of Norman Checkland (d 1983), and Doris, *née* Hiscox (d 1976); *b* 18 Dec 1930; *Educ* George Dixons GS Birmingham, St John's Coll Oxford (BSc); *m* 29 July 1955, Glenys Margaret, da of Leonard George Partridge (d 1936); 2 da (Kristina b 13 May 1959, Katherine b 22 July 1961); *Career* Nat Serv RAF Sgt-instr 1948-49; tech offr, section ldr, assoc res mangr ICI Fibres Ltd 1955-69, prof of systems Univ of Lancaster 1969-, hon consit prof Northwestern Poly Univ Xi'an China 1987-, visiting prof Univ of New England Aust 1990-; former memb: UK Nat Ctee for Int Inst for Applied Systems Analysis, DTI Ctee for Terotechnol; memb: Operational Res Soc, Int Soc for the Systems Sciences (pres 1986-87); *Books* Systems Thinking, Systems Practice (1981), Soft Systems Methodology in Action (with J Scholes, 1990); *Recreations* rock climbing, studying the evolution of the jazz idiom; *Style—* Prof Peter Checkland; Department of Systems and Information Management, University of Lancaster, Bailrigg, Lancaster LA1 4YX (☎ 0524 65201, 65111 Lancul G, 0524 63806)

CHECKLAND, Sarah Jane; da of Prof Sydney George Checkland (d 1986), of Cambridge, and Edith Olive, *née* Anthony; *b* 14 June 1954; *Educ* The Mount York, UEA (BA); *Career* former tour guide, singer Zanzibar Club, dep ed Homes and Jobs magazine 1979, press offr Nat Gallery 1979-83, sub ed arts and focus page Sunday Times 1983-85, art critic Sunday Today March-Nov 1986, freelance galleries corr The Times 1984-86, freelance art sales writer The Sunday Times 1984-86, art critic and corr London Daily News 1986-87, art market corr The Times 1987-; *Recreations* making music; *Clubs* Groucho; *Style—* Ms Sarah Jane Checkland; Fine Arts Writer, The Times, 1 Pennington St, London E1 9XN (☎ 071 782 5971)

CHECKLEY, Jonathan Richard Parknell; s of Stephen Henry Cooper Checkley (d 1984), and Beryl, *née* Parnell; *b* 4 Dec 1951; *Educ* Warwick Sch, St Peter's Coll Oxford (BSc); *m* 20 May 1978, Amanda Ellen, da of Frank Reuben Rubens (d 1985); 2 s (Edward b 1984, Timothy b 1987), 1 da (Laura b 1981); *Career* ptnr Clay and Ptnrs, consulting actuaries 1977-; FIA; *Recreations* reading, walking, music, water colour painting, gardening; *Style—* Jonathan Checkley, Esq; Clay & Partners, 61 Brook Street, London W1Y 2HN (☎ 071 408 1600, fax 071 499 0711, telex 27167 CLAYCO G)

CHECKLEY, Dr Stuart Arthur; s of Arthur William George Checkley, of Eastbridge, Suffolk, and Hilda Dorothy, *née* Chapman; *b* 15 Dec 1945; *Educ* St Albans Sch, Brasenose Coll Oxford (BA, BMBCh); *m* 1 Aug 1970, Marilyn Jane, da of Dr Percy Cyril Connick Evans, of Hampton, Middx; 1 s (Andrew John b 15 March 1977), 1 da (Anna Mary b 2 July 1974); *Career* consit psychiatrist Maudsley Hosp, dean Inst of Psychiatry; numerous articles in jls; FRCPsych, MRCP; *Recreations* bird watching; *Style—* Dr Stuart Checkley; Institute of Psychiatry, De Crespigny Park, London SE5 8AF (☎ 071 703 5411, fax 071 703 5796)

CHEDLOW, Barry William; QC (1969); *b* 8 Oct 1921; *Educ* Burnage HS, Univ of Manchester; *m* 1944, Anne Sheldon; 1 s, 1 da; *Career* Flt Lt RAF 1943; barr 1947, rec of the Crown Ct 1974-; memb Criminal Injuries Compensation Bd 1976; *Style—* Barry Chedlow, Esq, QC; 12 King's Bench Walk, Temple, London EC4 (☎ 071 583 0811); Little Kimblewick Farm, Finch Lane, Amersham, Bucks (☎ 0494 762156)

CHEESBROUGH, John Wright; AEA (1958); s of George Cheesbrough, of Thorne, Yorks (d 1971), and Edith, *née* Wright (d 1935); *b* 26 May 1914; *Educ* Thorne GS, Univ of Sheffield; *m* 3 Nov 1946, Muriel Mary, da of Richard Finney Wain (d 1953); 1 s (John Stephen b 31 Dec 1952), 1 da (Mary Ruth (Mrs Peck) b 3 Nov 1948); *Career* WWII RAF 1939-45, RA TA 1947-52, Royal Auxiliary Air Force 1952-61; admitted slr 1936, sr ptnr Coles & James 1959-84 (consit 1984-89); clerk to gen cmmrs of income tax: Upper Pevensey and Pevensey Liberty 1957-72, Pevensey Div 1972-89; dep dist registrar High Ct 1967-87, notary public 1948; dir: Hydro Hotel (Eastbourne) plc 1957-(chm 1974-), Abbeyfield (Eastbourne) Soc Ltd 1962-87; Liveryman City of London Slrs' Co 1979; memb Law Soc, FIOD 1981; *Clubs* City Livery, Devonshire (Eastbourne, chm 1983-86); *Style—* John Cheesbrough, Esq, AEA; 47 Osborne Rd, Eastbourne, East Sussex (☎ 0323 29002)

CHEESEMAN, Prof Ian Clifford; s of Richard Charles Cheeseman (d 1962), and Emily Ethel, *née* Clifford (d 1962); *b* 12 June 1926; *Educ* Andover GS, Imperial Coll Sci and Tech (BSc, PhD); *m* 27 July 1957, Margaret Edith, da of Christopher Allen Pither (d 1970); 1 s (Richard Iain b 16 July 1960), 2 da (Angela Rachel (Mrs Degallaix) b 8 July 1958, Jeannette Sarah (Mrs Sax) b 17 March 1962); *Career* aeroelastician Vickers Supermarine 1951-53, head of helicopter res A&AEE Boscomebe Down 1953-56, theoretical physicist on weapon effects AWRE 1956-58, head of Powered Lift and Noise Div Nat Gas Turbine Establishment Pyestock 1958-70; Univ of Southampton: Westland prof of helicopter engrg 1970-83, head Dept of Aeronautics and Astronautics 1978-83, visiting and emeritus prof 1983-; res dir Stewart Hughes Ltd 1983-88, ind consit 1988-; memb and pres Airship Assoc; ARCS, FRAS 1966, CEng 1966; *Books* 40 Years of the Spitfire (with R A East); *Recreations* gardening, dog breeding, concert going; *Style—* Prof Ian Cheeseman; Abbey View, Tarrant Keynston, Blandford Forum, Dorset DT11 9JE (☎ 0258 456877); Dept of Aeronautics of Astronautics, Univ of Southampton, Southampton SO9 5NH (☎ 0703 595000 ext 2597)

CHEESMAN, Dr (Anthony David) Tony; s of Leslie Charles Cheesman, of Shoreham-by-Sea (d 1968), and Eileen, *née* Griggs; *b* 14 Nov 1939; *Educ* Steyning GS, Charing Cross Hosp Medical Sch, Univ of London (BSc, MB BS); *m* 26 Sept 1966, Janet, da of Eric James Bristow, of Haywards Heath, Sussex; 2 s (David b 1969, James b 1972), 1 da (Katherine b 1974); *Career* consit surgn; ENT surgn Univ Hosp of W Indies Jamaica 1972-74, otolaryngologist head and neck surgn Charing Cross Hosp, Royal Nat Throat Nose and and Ear Hosp; memb Ct of Examiners RCS; FRCS; *Books* numerous papers and chapters on otolaryngology; *Recreations* yachting, skiing, flying, avoiding correspondence; *Clubs* Royal Soc of Medicine, Sussex Yacht, Politzer Soc; *Style—* Dr Tony Cheesman, Esq; 6 Thornhill Bridge Wharf, Islington, London N1 0RU (☎ 071 837 0709); 128 Harley St, London W1N 1AH (☎ 071 486 9400)

CHEETHAM, Anthony John Valerian; s of Sir Nicolas John Alexander Cheetham, KCMG, *qv*, of 50 Cadogan Square, London, and Jean Evison, *née* Corfe; *b* 12 April 1943; *Educ* Eton, Balliol Coll Oxford (BA); *m* 1, 1969 (m dis), Julia Rollason; 2 s (Nicolas b 1971, Oliver b 1973), 1 da (Flavia b 1976); m 2, 1979, Rosemary de Courcy; 2 da (Emma b 1981, Rebecca b 1983); *Career* editorial dir Shere Books 1968-; md: Futura Publications 1973-, Macdonalds Futura 1979-, Century Hutchinson 1985-; chm Century Publishing 1982-85, chm and chief exec Random Century Group 1989-; *Books* Richard III (1972); *Recreations* walking, tennis, gardening; *Style—* Anthony Cheetham, Esq; 20 Grove Park, Camberwell, London SE5 8LH; Paxford Manor, Paxford, nr Chipping Campden, Glos GL55 6XP; Random Century House, 20 Vauxhall Bridge Rd, London SW1V 2SA (☎ 071 973 9000, fax 071 233 6115, telex 299080 RANDOM G)

CHEETHAM, Francis William; OBE (1979); s of Francis Cheetham (d 1966),and Doris Elizabeth Cheetham (d 1939); *b* 5 Feb 1928; *Educ* King Edward VII Sch Sheffield, Univ of Sheffield (MA); *m* 19 April 1954, Monica, da of Arthur Fairhurst (d 1963); 3 s (Paul b 1958, Dominic b 1960, Mark b 1964), 1 da (Claire b 1968); *Career* dep art dir and curator Castle Museum Nottingham 1960-63, dir: City of Norwich Museums 1963-74, Norfolk Museums Serv 1974-90; museums advsr to ACC 1976-84; pres Museums Assoc 1978-79, pres Norfolk Contemporary Crafts Soc 1985- (chm 1972-85), chm Norfolk and Norwich Film Theatre 1968-70; memb: Mgmnt Ctee Norfolk and Norwich Triennial Festival 1966-89, Bd of Norwich Puppet Theatre 1981-87, Mgmnt Ctee of Eastern Arts Assoc 1987-89, Exec Bd ICOM UK 1981-85, Bd of Radio Broadland 1983-; chm Melton Arts Trust 1990-; Winston Churchill Fell 1967; FMA 1966, FRSA 1986; *Books* Medieval English Alabaster Carvings in the Castle Museum, Nottingham (1962), English Medieval Alabasters: catalogue of the collection in the Victoria and Albert Museum (1984); *Recreations* hill walking, listening to music especially early and baroque; *Style—* Francis Cheetham, Esq, OBE; 25 St Andrews Ave, Thorpe St Andrew, Norwich, Norfolk (☎ 0603 340 91)

CHEETHAM, John Frederick Thomas; CB (1978); s of James Oldham Cheetham (d 1965), and Gwendoline, *née* Hambly (d 1968); *b* 27 March 1919; *Educ* Penarth GS, Univ of Wales; *m* 1943, Yvonne Marie, da of James Alexander Smith (d 1968); 1 s (David), 1 da (Jane); *Career* former dep sec Exchequer and Audit Dept (sec 1975-79); *Recreations* gardening, family genealogy; *Clubs* MCC; *Style—* John Cheetham, Esq, CB; 70 Chatsworth Rd, Croydon, Surrey (☎ 081 688 3740)

CHEETHAM, Prof Juliet; da of Col Harold Neville Blair, of London, and Isabel, *née* Sanders (d 1988); *b* 12 Oct 1939; *Educ* Univ of St Andrews (MA), Univ of Oxford; *m* 26 April 1965, (Christopher) Paul Cheetam, s of Robert Cheetham, of Wallasey; 1 s (Matthew b 1969), 2 da (Rebecca b 1972, Sophie b 1983); *Career* probation offr 1959-65, lectr in applied social studies and fell Green Coll Oxford 1965-85; memb: Ctee of Enquiry into the Working of the Abortion Act 1971-74, Cmmn for Racial Equality 1977-84, Social Security Advsy Ctee 1983-84; currently prof and dir Social Work Res Centre Univ of Stirling; BASW; *Books* Social Work with Immigrants (1972), Unwanted Pregnancy and Counselling (1977), Social Work and Ethnicity (1982), Social Work with Black Children and their Families (1986); *Recreations* canal boats; *Style—* Prof Juliet Cheetham; 101 Woodstock Rd, Oxford; 34 Danube St, Edinburgh EN4 1NT (☎ 031 343 1108); Social Work Research Centre, Stirling University (☎ 0786 677221, fax 0786 63060)

CHEETHAM, Sir Nicolas John Alexander; KCMG (1964, CMG 1953); s of late Sir Milne Cheetham, KCMG (d 1938) and his 1 wife (m dis 1923) Anastasia Cheetham CBE, DStJ (later Mrs Nigel Law) (d 1976), *née* Mouravieff; *b* 8 Oct 1910; *Educ* Eton, Ch Ch Oxford; *m* 1, 1937 (m dis 1960), Jean Evison, da of Col Arthur Cecil Corfe, DSO (d 1949); 2 s; m 2, 1960, Lady Mabel Kathleen (d 1985), da of 8 Earl of Roden and formerly w of Richard Neville Brooke; *Career* joined HM Dip Serv 1934, min to Hungary 1959-61, asst under sec FO 1961-64, ambass to Mexico 1964-68; *Books* A History of Mexico, New Spain, Mediaeval Greece, Keepers of the Keys; *Style—* Sir Nicolas Cheetham, KCMG; 50 Cadogan Square, London SW1

CHEEVERS, Anthony William; s of Thomas Joseph Cheevers (d 1984), and Jessie, *née* Strahan; *b* 1 May 1956; *Educ* Finchley GS, Royal Holloway Coll, Univ of London (BMus); *Career* joined BBC 1978, radio prodr BBC Radio 3 Music Dept 1984-90; *Style—* Anthony Cheevers, Esq; BBC Radio 3, 16 Langham St, London W1A 1AA (☎ 071 927 5875, fax 071 637 3009)

CHEKE, Dudley John; CMG (1961); s of Thomas William Cheke (d 1960), and Bertha Elizabeth, *née* Boyten (d 1964); *b* 14 June 1912; *Educ* St Christopher Sch Herts, Emmanuel Coll Cambridge (MA); *m* Yvonne Carmen (d 1991), da of Rear Adm Martin John Coucher de Méric, MVO (d 1943); 2 s (Anthony, Robert); *Career* HM Dip Serv: min HM Embassy Tokyo 1963-67, ambass to the Ivory Coast Niger and Upper Volta 1967-70; chm Japan Soc of London 1979-82; *Recreations* gardening, bird-watching, theatre, opera; *Clubs* United Oxford and Cambridge Univ, Union Soc Cambridge; *Style—* Dudley Cheke, Esq, CMG

CHELMER, Baron (Life Peer UK 1963), of Margaretting, Co Essex; Eric Cyril Boyd Edwards; MC (1944), TD, JP (Essex 1950), DL (1971); s of Col Cyril Ernest Edwards, DSO, MC, TD, JP, DL (d 1953), of Bullwood Hall, Hockley, Essex, and Jessie, *née* Boyd; *b* 9 Oct 1914; *Educ* Felsted, Univ of London (LLB); *m* 2 June 1939, Enid, da of Frank W Harvey, of Leigh-on-Sea, Essex; 1 s (Hon Robin Ernest b 1940); *Career* served WWII Lt-Col Essex Yeo; admitted slr 1937; former chm National Union of Conservative Assocs 1957-64, treas Conservative Party 1965-77; chm Provident Financial Group 1977-83, dir NEM Group of Cos 1977-; chm Greycoats Estates Ltd; kt 1954; *Recreations* improving; *Clubs* Carlton, Buck's, Royal Ocean Racing; *Style—* The Rt Hon the Lord Chelmer, MC, TD, JP, DL; Peacocks, Margaretting, Ingatestone, Essex CM4 9HY (☎ 0277 35/3181)

CHELMSFORD, 3 Viscount (UK 1921); Frederic Jan Thesiger; also Baron Chelmsford (UK 1858); s of 2 Viscount (d 1970), and Gilian Lubbock (great niece of 1 Baron Avebury); 1 cous once removed of Wilfrid Thesiger, the Arabist and traveller; *b* 7 March 1931; *m* 16 Aug 1958, Clare Rendle, da of Dr George Rendle Rolston, of Haslemere, Surrey; 1 s, 1 da (Hon Tiffany b 23 April 1968); *Heir* Hon Frederic Thesiger, *qv*; *Career* late Lt Inns of Ct Regt; Lloyd's insur broker; *Style—* The Rt Hon the Viscount Chelmsford; 26 Ormonde Gate, London SW3 (☎ 071 352 5636)

CHELMSFORD, 7 Bishop of (cr 1914) 1986-; Rt Rev John Waine; s of late William Waine; *b* 20 June 1930; *Educ* Prescot GS, Manchester Univ (BA), Ridley Hall Cambridge; *m* 1957, Patricia Zena, da of late Bertram Stephenson Haikney; 3 s; *Career* Pilot Offr RAF; ordained: deacon 1955, priest 1956; vicar: Ditton 1960-64, Holy Trinity Southport 1964-69; rector Kirkby 1969-75, bishop suffragan of Stafford 1975-78, bishop of St Edmundsbury and Ipswich 1978-86; Clerk of the Closet to HM The Queen 1989-; Chaplain OStJ; *Clubs* RAF; *Style—* The Rt Rev the Bishop of Chelmsford; Bishopscourt, Margaretting, Ingatestone, Essex CM4 0HD; (☎ 0277 352001)

CHELSEA, Viscount; Charles Gerald John Cadogan; s and h of 7 Earl Cadogan; *b* 24 March 1937; *Educ* Eton; *m* 1, 6 June 1963, Lady Philippa Dorothy Bluett Wallop (d 31 Aug 1984), 2 da of 9 Earl of Portsmouth (d 1984); 2 s (Hon Edward b 1966, Hon William b 1973), 1 da (Hon Anna-Karina b 1964); m 2, 1989, Jennifer Jane Greig, da of J E K Rae, and Mrs S Z de Ferranti; *Heir* s, Hon Edward Charles Cadogan b 10 May 1966; *Career* dir Cadogan Estates and Group Cos; *Style—* Viscount Chelsea; 7 Smith St, London SW3 (☎ 071 730 2465); Marndhill, Ardington, Wantage, Oxon (☎ 0235 833 273)

CHELSOM, Peter Anthony; s of Maj Reginald James Chelsom (d 1970), and Catherine, *née* Rodan (d 1977); *b* 20 April 1956; *Educ* Wrekin Coll, Central Sch of Speech & Drama; *Career* actor; leading roles: Royal Shakespeare Co, Nat Theatre, Royal Ct; TV incl: Sorrell and Son, Woman of Substance, Christmas Present; writer and dir films: Treacle (BAFTA nomination), Funny Bones (cmmnd Working Title), Hear My Song (in production for Limelight); dir commercials; memb: Equity, ACTT; *Clubs* RAC, Pall Mall; *Style—* Peter Chelsom, Esq; John Swannell Films, 5 Charlotte Mews, London W1

CHELTENHAM, Archdeacon of; *see*: Lewis, Ven John Arthur

CHELTON, Capt Lewis William Leonard; s of Lewis Walter Chelton (d 1959), and Doris May, *née* Gamblin (d 1961); *b* 19 Dec 1934; *Educ* RNC Dartmouth; *m* 11 May 1957, Daphne Joan, da of Lt-Col R P Landon, MC, RA (d 1936); 3 s (Simon Roger Lewis b 1958, Roderick Charles Dominic b 1960, Hugo Rupert Philip b 1966); *Career* RN: Naval Cadet 1951, Midshipman 1953, Sub Lt 1955, Lt 1956, staff of Flag Offr Flying Trg 1956-57; serv in: HMS Torquay, HMS Scarborough (5 Frigate Sqdn) 1958-59; staff of C in C Med 1960-61, HMS Caprice (8 Destroyer Sqdn) 1962-64, Lt Cdr 1964, legal trg 1964-66, called to the Bar Inner Temple 1966, sec to Cdr Naval Forces Gulf (Sr Naval Offr Persian Gulf) 1967-69, asst sec to Flag Offr Scotland and NI 1970-71, serv HMS Hampshire 1972, Cdr 1972, sec to Flag Offr Carriers and Amphibious Ships 1973-74, NDC Latimer 1975, HMS Fearless 1976-77, naval admin plans MOD 1978-79, Fleet Supply Offr 1979-81, Capt 1981, Chief Naval Judge Advocate 1982-84, dep dir Naval Serv Conditions, ret 1987; sec Engrg Cncl; *Recreations* shooting, gardening, country pursuits; *Clubs* Farmers; *Style—* Capt Lewis Chelton, RN; Palmers Green House, Hatch Beauchamp, Nr Taunton, Somerset (☎ 0823 480 221); 51 Badminton Rd, London SW12; The Secretary of the Engrg Cncl, 10 Maltravers St, London WC2 (☎ 071 240 7891, fax 071 240 7517, telex 279177)

CHEMPIN, Beryl Margaret; da of Authur Harold Jordan Perry, MM, of Birmingham, and Ada Dora, *née* Banner; *Educ* King Edward's HS, Birmingham Secretarial Sch, Birmingham Conservatoir (formerly Birmingham Sch of Music); *m* 1, late Arnold Chempin; 2 da (Jenny Margaret (Mrs Renowden), Judith Ursula (Mrs Wallis)); m 2, late Bernard While; m 3, Prof Denis Matthews, CBE; *Career* freelance sec and translator, pianist, music lectr, adjudicator (home and abroad); piano teacher: Birmingham Conservatoir Birmingham Jr Sch of Music; private music teacher, memb lecturing panel Int Piano Teachers Consits; contrib: Musical Times, Music Teacher, Music Jnl; Midland Woman of the Year 1977, Nat Award for Piano Teaching 1983; ISM Birmingham Centre: sec 1964-74, memb cncl 1969-71 and 1982-84, warden and chm private teachers section 1969, chm 1975-85; lectr Euro Piano Teachers Assoc; memb: City of Birmingham Symphony Orch Soc, Br Fedn of Music Festivals, King Edwards HS Old Edwardians; FTCL, LRAM, ARCM, LTCL, ABSM; *Recreations* reading, languages, art, cooking; *Style—* Ms Beryl Chempin; 10 Russell Rd, Moseley, Birmingham B13 8RD (☎ 021 449 3055)

CHEN, Shwing Chong; s of Ping Liem Chen (d 1963), of Sri Lanka, and Chu Lan Chen (d 1977); *b* 1 Sept 1934; *Educ* Wesley Coll Colombo (Hill medal for best scholar 1954), Univ of Ceylon (BA, MB BS); *m* 24 Nov 1957, Ai Bow, da of Chang Yung Yoe, of India (d 1975); 3 s (Terng Fong b 1960, Terng Weng b 1962, Terng Bhing b 1965), 1 da (Hui Fong b 1958); *Career* conslt orthopaedic surgn Enfield Gp of Hosps 1972-; sr orthopaedic registrar: St Bart's Hosp, Royal Nat Orthopaedic Hosp Norfolk and Norwich Hosp 1968-72 (Benjamin Gooch prize 1969-70); orthopaedic registrar Hammersmith Hosp 1967-68; designer of: Chen Tennis Elbow Strap, Enfield Total Knee Prosthesis; pres: Br Orthopaedic Soc for Surgery of the Foot 1979, Rheumatoid Arthritis Surgical Soc 1989; FRCS; *Recreations* skiing, sailing, swimming; *Clubs* RSM; *Style—* S C Chen, Esq; 66 Mymms Drive, Brookmans Park, Herts AL9 7AD (☎ 0707 58538); 152 Harley St, London W1N 1HH (☎ 071 935 3834)

CHENEVIÈRE, Lady Selina Clare; *née* Shirley; yst da of 13 Earl Ferrers, PC, DL, *qv*; *b* 1958; *m* 11 March 1989, Antoine R B Chenevière, yr s of Bertrand Chenevière, of Geneva, and Madame Harritina Panitza-Yablansky, of Florence; 1 da (Francesca Mary b 15 Oct 1990); *Style—* The Lady Selina Chenevière; c/o The Rt Hon the Earl Ferrers, PC, DL, Ditchingham Hall, Bungay, Suffolk

CHENEVIX-TRENCH, Timothy Christopher John; s of Christopher John Chenevix-Trench, MBE, and Mary Elizabeth Catherine, *née* Allen (d 1990); *b* 5 Oct 1938; *Educ* King's Sch Canterbury, CCC Oxford (MA); *m* 1, 3 Sept 1961 (m dis 1972), Penelope Mary, *née* Travers; 3 da (Katherine Rae (Mrs Slater) b 8 June 1964, Alison Mary (Mrs Hill) b 20 Aug 1965, Phillida b 26 May 1967); m 2, 1974, Stella Maris, *née* Henderson; *Career* ICI 1961-67, Mgmnt Dynamics 1967-69, Scicon 1969-72, dir Miles Roman Ltd 1972-73, advsr HM Treasy 1973-76, Shell International Petroleum Co 1976-82, Heidrick & Struggles 1982-85, md Richdata Ltd 1985-; Liveryman Worshipful Co of Mercers; *Recreations* family, head hunting; *Clubs* Naval & Military; *Style—* Timothy Chenevix-Trench, Esq; Richdata Ltd, 13 Camden Passage, London N1 8EA (☎ 071 359 1200)

CHENEY, Donald Harvey; s of Arthur Stanley Cheney (d 1975), and Jessie Cheney (d 1986); *b* 16 Jan 1931; *Educ* Eggars GS Alton Hants, Harrow Weald Co GS Middx, Regent St Poly Sch of Architecture (Dip Arch); *m* 13 Feb 1956, Gillian Evelyn Florence Frances Cheney, JP, da of Guy Holman Tatum (d 1969); 3 da (Frances b 1956, Fiona (Mrs Ford) b 1960, Claire b 1968); *Career* qualified as architect 1955; in practice: NZ 1956-62, S Coast of England 1963-(ptnr 1970-); cncl memb RIBA 1983, external examiner Canterbury Sch of Architecture 1982-87, memb Franco-Br Union of Architects 1977-; chm Hythe Venetian Fete 1978-86, Hythe town cncllr 1981-86; Freeman City of London 1983; memb: Worshipful Co of Arbitrators 1983, Worshipful Co of Architects 1985; MRIBA 1956, assoc memb NZ Inst of Architects 1956, CIArb 1976; *Recreations* sailing, photography; *Clubs* Royal Cinque Ports YC, St John House; *Style—* Donald Cheney, Esq; Crosstrees, North Rd, Hythe, Kent (☎ 0303 68720); La Lande Du Burgos, Guehenno 56, France; The Tramway Stables, Rampart Rd, Hythe, Kent CT21 5BG (☎ 0303 260 515, fax 0303 68214, car 0860 729 904)

CHEONG, Lee; s of Ah Tay Cheong (d 1973), of London, and Bessie Amelia, *née* Simmonds; *b* 21 April 1945; *Educ* St Pauls Way Secdy Sch, Hornsey Coll of Art (Dip in Interior Design), London Coll of Furniture (Dip in Furniture Design); *Career* freelance designer 1969-72 (clients incl BBC and major brewery), specialist furniture designer Coventry City Architects 1973-78, interior designer Wessex RHA 1978-90, assoc in charge of interior design Medical Design Practice 1990-; FCSD 1986-; *Recreations* badminton, skiing, music, theatre; *Style—* Lee Cheong, Esq; 2 The Terrace, Easton, Hampshire SO21 1EG (☎ 0962 78 713); Medical Design Practice, Highcroft, Romsey Rd, Winchester, Hampshire SO22 5DH (☎ 0962 854477, fax 0962 869565)

CHERNIAVSKY, Andrew Scott; s of David Blythe Cherniavsky (d 1954), and Peggy Claire, *née* Scott; *b* 27 April 1949; *Educ* Lycee Francais London, Univ of Edinburgh (MA); *m* 1 July 1977, Caroline Maria Aviva, da of Josef Schuck, of London; 1 s (Paul Alexander b 1982), 1 da (Kate Isabella b 1980); *Career* dir: Prolific Group plc 1988-89, Prolific Financial Management 1986-89; chm Prolific Unit Trust Managers 1988-; *Recreations* music, squash, tennis, fishing, sailing; *Clubs* Hampstead Cricket; *Style—* Andrew Cherniavsky, Esq; Walbrook House, 23 Walbrook, London EC4N 3LD (☎ 071 280 3700, telex 8814349)

CHERNS, Penelope Ann (Penny); da of Albert Bernard Cherns (d 1987), of Sussex, and Barbara Simone, *née* Brotman; *b* 21 May 1948; *Educ* North London Collegiate Sch, Univ of Kent (BA), Drama Centre London (Dip in Directing); *Career* director; *Theatre* Northcott Theatre Exeter: Hallo and Goodbye Pal Joey 1974, Stop The World 1975, My Fair Lady 1975, West Side Story 1976; Avon Touring Co (Learning The Game 1976), ICA and Sheffield Crucible Studio (Smile for Jesus 1976, Wreckers 1977), Gateway Theatre Chester (A Winter's Tale 1977, Guys and Dolls 1977, Cabaret 1977), Royal Shakespeare Co (Queen Christina 1977), Haymarket Leicester (School for Clowns 1977), Bristol Old Vic (Dusa, Fish, Stas and Vi 1977), Soho Poly (Prodigal Father 1978), Nottingham Playhouse (Kiss Me Kate 1978, Beaux Stratagem 1978, Alice 1978), Palace Theatre Watford (You Never Can Tell 1978), Palace Theatre Watford (Side By Side By Sondheim 1979), Nottingham Playhouse (Julius Caesar 1979, Teeth 'n' Smiles 1979), Bristol Old Vic (Statements 1979, Trees in the Wind 1979), Royal Ct (Trees in the Wind 1980), New End (Herdes 1979, Letters Home 1980, Strangers 1981), Newcastle Playhouse (Chicago 1981, Pinocchio 1981), Churchill Theatre Bromley (The Boyfriend 1982), Br Cncl India Tour (Duet for One 1983), Haymarket Theatre Leicester (Day In The Life of Joe Egg 1984), Asian Co-op Theatre (Vigilantes 1985), Monstrous Regiment (Mourning Pictures 1981, Alarms 1986), Riverside Studios (Alarms 1987), The King's Head (Panorama 1988), Greenwich Theatre (The Millionairess 1988), Royal Ct Theatre (Iranian Nights 1989); tv and film incl: Letters Home (Channel 4 1982), Prisoners of Incest (BBC Horizon 1983), Battered Baby (BBC Horizon 1985), Home Front (BBC 1988), Iranian Nights (Channel 4 1989), Bite the Ballot (Channel 4 1989), Mixing It (Channel 4 1990), And The Cow Jumped Over The Moon (BBC 1990), Clients and Professionals and Managing Change (Melrose Film Productions 1990); asst prodr The Inner Eye (Channel 4 1986); script conslt: Channel 4 1987, Warner Sisters (Hothouse Warner Sisters 1989); numerous teaching appts incl: LAMDA, RADA Drama Centre, RCM, Trent Poly, Univ of Loughborough, Oslo, Univ of Iowa, Juillard Sch NY, Guildhall Sch of Drama, Cultura Inglesa Sao Paolo Brazil, Anglo Inst Montevideo Uruguay, Amsterdam Int Theatre Workshop; *Recreations* travel, languages, swimming; *Style—* Ms Penny Cherns

CHERRY, Alan Herbert; MBE (1985); *Career* chm and gp md Countryside Properties plc 1981; pres Housebuilders Fedn 1988; memb: Inquiry into Br Housing 1984-85, Inner City Cmmn; bd memb Teesside Devpt Corp, advsy bd memb Nat Westminster Bank plc, govr Anglia Higher Educn Coll; Freeman City of London, memb Worshipful Co of Blacksmiths; FRICS, FSVA; *Style—* Alan Cherry, Esq, MBE; Countryside House, The Warley Hill Business Park, Brentwood, Essex CM13 3AT (☎ 0277 260000, fax 0277 260175)

CHERRY, (George) Anthony; s of Capt Harold Edward Cherry (d 1930), of Rolleston, Burton-on-Trent, and Agnes Irene, *née* Bairstow (d 1963); *b* 20 May 1918; *Educ* Elms Sch Colwall, Denstone Coll Staffordshire; *m* 10 July 1946, Ellan Angus, da of David George Thompson (d 1985), of Rosyth, Fife; 2 s (Christopher b 1947, Iain b 1956), 1 da (Elizabeth b 1950); *Career* served in army Sherwood Foresters 1940-47: Maj ME 1941-42, POW 1942-45, War Office Mil Intelligence 1945-46; CA Price Waterhouse 1946-81 (nat dir 1974-79), dep chm Price Waterhouse Int 1979-81; Liveryman Worshipful Co of Gardeners of London; *Recreations* gardening, flintstone walling, golf; *Style—* Anthony Cherry, Esq; Forge House, Nyton Rd, Eastergate, Chichester, W Sussex PO20 6UP (☎ 0243 543086)

CHERRY, Colin; s of Reginald Cherry (d 1970), of Hull, and Dorothy, *née* Brooks (d 1939); *b* 20 Nov 1931; *Educ* Hymers Coll; *m* 2 Aug 1958, Marjorie Rose, da of

Thomas Harman, of Holderness; 2 da (Nicola (Mrs Gatt) b 1962, Jacqueline b 1965); *Career* Nat Serv RAEC 1950-52, Lt TA E Yorks Regt 1952-58; Inland Revenue 1952, HM Inspr of Taxes 1958-85, under sec Dir of Operations Inland Revenue 1985-90; *Clubs* Reform; *Style—* Colin Cherry, Esq; 13 Wathen Rd, Dorking, Surrey RH4 1JZ (☎ 0306 885921)

CHERRY, Prof Gordon Emanuel; s of Emanuel Cherry, and Nora, *née* Goddard; *b* 6 Feb 1931; *Educ* Holgate and Dist GS Barnsley, QMC London; *m* 8 June 1957, Margaret Mary Loudon, da of Thomas Loudon Cox; 1 s (Iain b 1969), 2 da (Shona b 1959, Shelagh b 1962); *Career* local govt 1956-68 (res offr Newcastle City Planning Dept 1963-68); Univ of Birmingham: sr lectr 1968, prof of urban and regnl planning 1976-81, dean Faculty of Commerce and Social Sci 1981-86, head Sch of Geography 1987-; pres RTPI 1978-79, tstee Bournville Village; Hon DSc Heriot Watt 1984; FRTPI 1961, FRICS 1961, FRGS 1989; *Books* Town Planning in its Social Context (1970), Urban Change and Planning (1974), Environmental Planning Vol II - National Parks and Recreation in the Countryside (1975), The Politics of Town Planning (1982), Cities and Plans (1988); *Recreations* enjoying convivial company; *Style—* Prof Gordon Cherry; Quaker Ridge, 66 Meriden Rd, Hampton in Arden, Solihull, West Midlands B92 0BT (☎ 06755 3200); School of Geography, University of Birmingham, Edgbaston, Birmingham B15 2TT (☎ 021 414 5537)

CHERRY, John Mitchell; QC (1988); s of John William (Jack) Cherry (d 1967), of Cheshunt, Herts, and Dorothy Mary, *née* Maybury (d 1975); *b* 10 Sept 1937; *Educ* Cheshunt GS; *m* 7 Nov 1972, Eunice Ann; 2 s (Troy Alexander b 10 July 1968, Matthew John b 13 April 1971), 2 da (Suzanne Marie b 3 Jan 1970, Katherine Ann (twin) b 3 Jan 1970); *Career* called to the Bar 1961, asst recorder 1984, recorder 1987; govr; *Recreations* cricket, rugby, food, wine; *Style—* John Cherry, Esq, QC; Winterton, Turkey St, Enfield, Middlesex EN1 4RJ (☎ 0992 719018); 1 Temple Gardens, Temple, London EC4Y 9BB (☎ 071 353 0407, fax 071 353 3969)

CHERRY, Richard John; s of John Cherry, and Rosina Florence, *née* Walker; *b* 3 Feb 1944; *Educ* Enfield GS, London Hosp Med Coll (MB BS); *m* 18 May 1968, Pamela Joan, da of Roy Percival Stanley Bevin; 1 s (David b 1971), 1 da (Elizabeth b 1972); *Career* conslt orthopaedic surgn E Birmingham Hosp 1977; memb: Christian Med Fellowship, BMA; FRCS 1972, FBIM 1980; *Recreations* music, photography, sailing, skiing; *Clubs* Naughton Dunn, Olton Mere; *Style—* Richard Cherry, Esq; 95 Kineton Green Road, Olton, Solihull B92 7DT (☎ 021 706 8842); East Birmingham Hospital, Bordesley Green East, Birmingham (☎ 021 766 6611)

CHERRY, Prof Richard John; s of Leslie George Cherry (d 1970), and Dorothy Emily, *née* Tasker (d 1969); *b* 3 Jan 1939; *Educ* Hitchin Boys GS, St John's Coll Oxford (BA), Univ of Sheffield (PhD); *m* 23 June 1962, Georgine Mary, da of George Walter Ansell; 2 s (Simon Richard b 1965, Matthew James b 1972); *Career* scientific offr SERL 1960-64, scientist Unilever Res 1964-70, res fell Dept of Chemistry Univ of Sheffield 1970-73, privat dozent Dept of Biochemistry ETH Zürich 1973-82, prof of biological chemistry Univ of Essex 1982-; memb Editorial Bd: Biochemical Journal 1984-, European Journal of Biophysics 1984-; Ruzicka prize for chem Switzerland 1981; memb: Biochemical Soc 1971, Biophysical Soc 1973; *Books* Techniques for the Analysis of Membrane Proteins (with C I Ragan, 1986); *Recreations* photography, gardening, music; *Style—* Prof Richard Cherry; Dept of Chemistry and Biological Chemistry, University of Essex, Colchester CO4 3SQ (☎ 0206 872244, fax 0206 873598)

CHESHAM, Dowager Baroness; Mary Edmunds; *née* Marshall; 4 da of late David Gregory Marshall, MBE, of White Hill, Fen Ditton, Cambs; *m* 28 Sept 1937, 5 Baron Chesham, PC, TD (d 1989); 2 s (6 Baron, Hon John Charles Gregory Cavendish, *qqv*), 2 da (Hon Mrs Price, Hon Mrs Tufnell, *qqv*); *Style—* The Rt Hon the Dowager Lady Chesham; Manor Farm, Preston Candover, nr Basingstoke, Hants RG25 2EN (☎ 025 687 230)

CHESHAM, 6 Baron (UK 1858); Nicholas Charles Cavendish; er s of 5 Baron Chesham, PC, TD (d 1989); *b* 7 Nov 1941; *Educ* Eton; *m* 1, 4 Nov 1965 (m dis 1969), Susan Donne, eldest da of Frederick Guy Beauchamp, MB, ChB, of 119 Harley St; m 2, 1973, Suzanne Adrienne, eldest da of late Alan Gray Byrne, of Sydney; 2 s (Hon Charles Gray Compton, Hon William George b 13 April 1980); *Heir* s, Hon Charles Gray Compton Cavendish b 11 Nov 1974; *Career* chartered accountant; investment advsr; *Recreations* tennis, skiing, shooting; *Clubs* Pratt's, Australian (Sydney), Royal Sydney Golf; *Style—* The Rt Hon the Lord Chesham; 54B Wentworth Rd, Vaucluse, NSW 2030, Australia

CHESHIRE, Lt-Col Colin Charles Chance; s of ACM Sir Walter Graeme Cheshire, GBE, KCB, ADC (d 1978), and Mary Cheshire, DL, of 106 Christchurch Rd, Winchester; *b* 23 Aug 1941; *Educ* Worksop; *m* 1, 8 Aug 1968, Cherida Evelyn, da of ACM Sir Wallace Kyle, GCB, KCVO, CBE, DSO, DFC, *qv*; 1 s (Christopher b 1971), 1 da (Philippa b 1969); m 2, 2 Oct 1976, Angela Mary, da of D Fulcher, of Bury St Edmunds, Suffolk; 2 step da (Sarah McMillen b 1968, Emma McMillen b 1970); *Career* Lt-Col RTR (ret 1981), served: Aden, Borneo, Singapore, Malaysia, BAOR, NI, UK, Armour Sch Bovington Camp 1968 (tt), RMC of Sci 1972-73 and Staff Coll Camberley 1974- (psc); sales and marketing mangr: def equipment Vickers Instruments Ltd York 1981-83, army systems Ferranti Computer Systems Ltd Cwmbran 1983-85; gp sales and mktg dir Wallop Gp Andover (md Walloptronics Ltd) 1985-87; bursar Oundle Sch; rifle shooting (internat full bore); rep: England 1970-, GB 1970- (vice capt 1982-89, adj 1988), Army 1967-81, Yorks, Hereford Worcs and Hants (capt 1987-89); cmdt Br Cadet Athelings Rifle Team 1990, vice chm NRA Exec Ctee 1990-, memb NRA Cncl 1990-; FBIM, MBIM; *Recreations* shooting, squash, golf; *Clubs* Army and Navy, HAC; *Style—* Lt-Col Colin Cheshire; Bear Lodge, Glapthorn Rd, Oundle, Peterborough PE8 4JA (☎ 0832 273537); Bursar's Office: Church St, Oundle, Peterborough PE8 4EE (☎ 0832 273434)

CHESHIRE, David Frederick; s of Frederick Thomas Cheshire, and Doris Emily, *née* Johns; *b* 23 July 1935; *Educ* Northampton GS, Univ of Nottingham (BA); *m* 26 Sept 1964, Joy Diana, da of Louis Roy Ashley; 1 s (Henry b 22 Dec 1976), 1 da (Ellen b 9 May 1970); *Career* Nat Serv, RN leading coder (educnl) Gibraltar 1958-59; music and drama librarian Staffs Co Library 1962-64, dep librarian Birmingham Sch of Arts and Crafts 1964-67; librarian: Hornsey Coll of Art 1968-72, faculty of art and design Middx Poly 1972-86; res and info offr Theatre Tst 1986-; ALA (1962); *Books* Theatre: A Readers Guide (1964), Music Hall in Britain (1972), British Music Hall: a bibliography (1981), The Old Vic (1984), Portrait of Ellen Terry (1989); *Recreations* watching cricket; *Clubs* MCC; *Style—* David Cheshire, Esq; 27 Lauradale Rd, Fortis Green, London N2 9LT (☎ 081 883 1940); Theatres Trust, 10 St Martin's Court, London WC2N 4ASJ (☎ 071 836 8591)

CHESHIRE, Group Capt (Geoffrey) Leonard; VC (1944), OM (1981), DSO (1940, and Bar 1942, 1943), DFC (1941); s of late Geoffrey Chevalier Cheshire (d 1978), and his 1 wife Primrose, *née* Barstow (d 1962); *b* 7 Sept 1917; *Educ* Stowe, Merton Coll Oxford; *m* 2, 1959, Susan Ryder (Baroness Ryder of Warsaw, *qv*); 1 s, 1 da; *Career* joined Univ of Oxford Sqdn 1936, RAFR 1937, Pilot Offr RAF 1939, Wing Cdr 1944, Gp Capt 1944, ret 1946; fndr Leonard Cheshire Fndn; co-fndr: Ryder-Cheshire Mission for the Relief of Suffering, Meml Fund for Disaster Relief; Hon Master of Bench Gray's Inn 1983; Hon DCL Univ of Oxford; Hon LLD: Univ of Liverpool 1973; Manchester Poly 1979, Univ of Nottingham 1981, Univ of Bristol 1985, Univ of Kent 1986; *Books* Bomber Pilot (1943), Pilgrimage to the Shroud (1956), The Face of Victory (1961), The Hidden World (1981), The Light of Many Suns (1985); *Style—* Group Capt Leonard Cheshire, VC, OM, DSO, DFC; Cavendish, Suffolk; The Leonard Cheshire Foundation, 26-29 Maunsel St, London SW1P 2QN (☎ 071 828 1822)

CHESHIRE, Dr Mary Elisabeth; da of Rev John Whitehead Cheshire (d 1964), and Janet Galloway Angus, *née* Morrison; *b* 23 Sept 1936; *Educ* Northampton HS for Girls, Newcastle Church HS, King's Coll Med Sch, Newcastle upon Tyne Med Sch (MB BS); *Career* pre registration and jr anaesthetic trg at Middlesbrough Gen Hosp 1959-63, registrar in anaesthetics United Cardiff Hosp 1963-64; Teeside Hosp Gp: sr registrar 1964-66, conslt anaesthetist 1966-; memb: NFWI, World Wide Fund for Nature, RSPCA, Nat Tst, Donkey Sanctuary, NSPCC, Ex Servs Mental Welfare Assoc, BMA Assoc of Anaesthetists; fell RSPB, FFARCS, DA; *Recreations* gardening, dressmaking and ladies tailoring; *Style—* Dr Mary Cheshire; Dept of Anaesthesia, South Cleveland Hospital, Marton Rd, Middlesbrough, Cleveland TS3 4BW (☎ 0642 829631)

CHESHIRE, Dr (Christopher) Michael; s of Gordon Sydney (d 1983), of Birmingham, and Vera, *née* Hepburn; *b* 18 July 1946; *Educ* West Bromwich GS, Univ of Manchester (BSc, MB ChB); *m* 1 Aug 1970, Jane Mary, da of Claude Cordle, of Norwich; 1 s (Jonathan Christopher b 5 Nov 1980), 1 da (Amy Tamsin b 1 April 1977); *Career* house offr Manchester Royal Infirmary and Hope Hosp Salford 1976-77 (pharmacist 1969-71), SHO Central and S Manchester Hosps 1976-79, lectr in geriatric med Univ of Manchester 1979-83, conslt physician in geriatric med Manchester Royal Infirmary and Barnes Hosp 1983; memb Br Geriatrics Soc; MRCP 1979; *Recreations* gardening, squash, running; *Style—* Dr Michael Cheshire; 38 The Crescent, Davenport, Stockport, Cheshire SK3 8SN (☎ 061 483 2972); Barnes Hospital, Cheadle, Cheshire; The Royal Infirmary, Oxford Rd, Manchester (☎ 061 491 2300, 061 276 1234)

CHESSHYRE, (David) Hubert Boothby; LVO (1988); s of Col Hubert Layard Chesshyre, of Whatmer Hall, Sturry, Canterbury (d 1981), and Katharine Anne, *née* Boothby; *b* 22 June 1940; *Educ* King's Sch Canterbury, Trinity Coll Cambridge (MA), ChCh Oxford (DipEd); *Career* former vintner and language teacher; green staff offr at Investiture of Prince of Wales 1969, Rouge Croix Pursuivant 1970-78, on staff of Sir Anthony Wagner as Garter King of Arms 1971-78, Chester Herald of Arms 1978-; memb: Hon Artillery Co 1964-65, Bach Choir, Madrigal Soc, Soc of Genealogists; fell Heraldry Soc 1990 (memb Cncl 1973-85), lay clerk Southwark Cathedral, lectr for NADFAS and Foyles; hon genealogist Royal Victorian Order 1987, sec of the Order of the Garter 1988; Freeman City of London; FSA; *Books* Heraldry of the World (ed, 1973), The Identification of Coats of Arms on British Silver (1978), The Green, A History of the Heart of Bethnal Green (with A J Robinson, 1978), Heralds of Today (with Adrian Ailes, 1985); *Recreations* singing, gardening, motorcycling; *Style—* Hubert Chesshyre, Esq, LVO, FSA, Chester Herald of Arms; Hawthorn Cottage, 1 Flamborough Walk, London E14 7LS; College of Arms, Queen Victoria St, London EC4V 4BT (☎ 071 248 1137)

CHESTER, Charlie, né Cecil Victor Manser; MBE (1990); s of George Henry Manser (d 1952), of Clapham, London, and Ethel May, *née* Henty (d 1968); *b* 26 April 1914; *Educ* MEADS Eastbourne, Stonhouse St Sch Clapham London; *m* Dorita, da of Capt Arthur Langley; 1 s (Peter Charles b 1941); *Career* served WWII 1940-46; messenger and traveller for embroidery co 1928-31; former: memb band, guitar playing yodeller (winner of over 80 talent shows); later stand up comic; professional by 1933, first bdcast 1937, toured music halls as Cheerful Charlie Chester, numerous pantomimes incl 7 years with Jack and Jill (for Emile Littler); conscripted 1940, Sgt 6 Bn RIF, transferred Field Security and Intelligence, later formed The Central Pool of Artists (new regt of front line solider entertainers, with Col Basil Brown and Capt George Black, later known as Stars in Battledress); served: Normandy, Belgium, Holland, Germany; formed Crazy Gang for Merry Go Round (radio show representing Army) until demob 1946; bdcaster Stand Easy (The Charlie Chester Crazy Gang; first show to beat ITMA in listening figures) 1946-48, then toured under George and Alfred Black until 1953; solo artiste since 1953; songwriter of many hits; TV shows/ appearances incl: Charlie Chester Show, Educated Evans, Take Pot Luck, Red Peppers, The Two Charlies; stage appearances incl: A Midsummer Night's Dream, Done in Oils (farce), Big Bad Mouse, Boeing Boeing, Just the Ticket; long serving memb Lord's Taverners and Variety Club of GB; patron: Young Farmer's Club Devon, S Wales Contingent Normandy Veterans' Assoc; pres sixth Whistable Scouts; winner 4 certificates Lions Int Award; memb Grand Order of Water Rats 1948- (king rat 1952, poet laureate 1953); OStJ 1990; *Books* incl: My Lords Ladies and Gentleman (1972), Bouquet of Verse (1972), The World is Full of Charlies (autobiography, 1974), Grains of Greatness (1975), Overture to Anthem (1977), Cry Simba (1977), Legend of Laughter-Grand Order of Water Rats (1984); *Recreations* painting (for charity), composing songs and military marches; *Style—* Charlie Chester, Esq, MBE; Charlie Chester Productions, The Glen, Chestfield, Whitstable, Kent CT5 3JH

CHESTER, 39 Bishop of, 1982-; Rt Rev Michael Alfred Baughen; patron of 114 livings, Canonries of his Cathedral, the Archdeaconries of Chester and Macclesfield, and the Chancellorship of the Diocese; The See, anciently part of the diocese of Lichfield, was erected into a distinct Bishopric by Henry VIII in 1541, and the abbey-church of St Werburgh became its Cathedral; s of Alfred Henry Baughen (d 1956), and Clarice Adelaide Baughen (d 1986); *b* 7 June 1930; *Educ* Bromley Co GS, Univ of London, Oak Hill Theol Coll (BD); *m* 1956, Myrtle Newcomb Phillips; 2 s, 1 da; *Career* served in Royal Signals 1948-50; with Martins Bank 1946-48 and 1950-51; ordained: deacon 1956, priest 1957; curate in Nottingham and Reigate, candidates sec Church Pastoral Aid Soc 1961-64, rector Holy Trinity Rusholme 1964-70, vicar All Souls Langham Place 1970-75 (next to Broadcasting House and whence BBC transmitted daily services), rector 1975-82, area dean St Marylebone 1978-82, prebendary St Paul's 1979-82; memb Gen Synod 1975-; *Style—* The Rt Rev the Lord Bishop of Chester; Bishop's House, Abbey Square, Chester CH1 2JD (☎ 0244 350864)

CHESTER, Richard Waugh; s of Cyril Waugh Chester, of Great Broughton, Yorkshire, and Margaret, *née* Dally; *b* 19 April 1943; *Educ* Friends' Sch Great Ayton, Royal Acad of Music (ARCM, GRSM); *m* 12 Dec 1970, Sarah, da of Thomas Arthur Leopold Chapman-Mortimer (d 1979); 1 s (Matthew b 1973), 2 da (Lucy b 1976, Emily b 1979); *Career* flautist; fndr memb Nash Ensemble 1965; BBC NI 1965-67; princ flautist and soloist with performances of works by: Mozart, Nielson, Chaminade, Martin; Scottish Nat Orchestra 1967-87; fndr memb and solo flautist Cantilena 1971, admin Nat Youth Orchestra of Scotland 1987; memb: Music Ctee Scottish Arts Cncl, exec Nat Assoc of Youth Orchestras; former memb Bd Scottish Nat Orchestra, chm Glasgow Festival Strings; govr St Mary's Music Sch, conductor and examiner; *Recreations* squash, walking, tennis, reading; *Style—* Richard Chester, Esq; Milton of Cardross, Port of Menteith, Stirling, Scotland (☎ 087 75 634); 3 La Belle Place, Glasgow (☎ 041 332 8311, fax 041 332 3915)

CHESTER, Prof Theodore Edward; CBE (1967); *b* 28 June 1908; *Educ* Univ of Manchester (MA, Dip Commerce); *m* 1940, Mimi; 1 s; *Career* teaching and res in law and admin 1931-39, asst mangr London city firm 1946-48, dir Acton Soc Tst 1952-55

(sr res worker 1948-52); Univ of Manchester: prof of social admin 1955-75, dean Faculty of Econ and Social Studies 1962-63, sr res fell and emeritus prof 1976-78, dir mgmnt prog for clinicians 1979-; memb Cncl Fin and Gen Purposes Ctee Manchester Business Sch 1964-86; Kenneth Pray visiting prof Univ of Pa 1968, first Kellogg visiting prof Washington Univ St Louis 1969 and 1970, memb Summer Faculty Sloan Inst of Health Servs Admin Cornell Univ 1972-87, Ford Fndn travelling fellowships 1960 and 1967, WMO staff trg programme 1963-, UN Res Inst for Econ and Social Studies 1968; memb: Nat Selection Ctee for the Recruitment of Sr Hosp Admin Staff 1956-66, Advsy Ctee on Mgmnt Efficiency in the Health Serv 1959-65, Trg and Social Workers and Health Visitors 1963-65, Ctee on Tech Coll Resources 1964-69, Inter Agency Inst of Fed Health Execs (USA) 1980-84; pres Corpn of Secs 1955-66; advsr: social affairs div OECD 1965-66, Turkish State Planning Orgn on Health and Welfare Problems 1964; Golden Needle of Honour Austrian Hosp Dirs Assoc 1970, The Grand Gold Komturcross for Servs to the Health Serv Austria 1980; numerous pubns incl: Patterns of Organisation (1952), Management under Nationalisation (1953), The Central Control of the Service (1958), Post War Growth of Management in Western Europe (1961), The British NHS (1970), The Swedish NHS (1970), Management for Clinicians (1982), Alternative Systems in Organising and Controlling Health Services: public health systems in a democratic society (1985), The Prospects for Rationing - an international view (1986); *Recreations* travel, music, swimming, detective stories; *Style*— Prof Theodore Chester, CBE; 189 Grove Lane, Hale, Attrincham, Cheshire (☎ 061 980 2828)

CHESTERFIELD, The Ven Archdeacon of; see: Phizackerley, The Ven Gerald Robert Phizackerley

CHESTERMAN, (Henry) David; s of Sir Clement Chesterman (d 1983), and Winifred, *née* Spear (d 1981); *b* 17 April 1920; *Educ* Monkton Combe Sch Bath; *m* 5 Sept 1945, Jean, da of Sir Harold Kenward (d 1947); 2 s (Andrew b 1946, Daniel b 1954), 1 da (Clare b 1949); *Career* served army 1940-45; Dunlop Rubber Co Ltd 1945-66, PA to Sir Robert Mayer chm of Youth and Music; mangr Ernest Read Music Assoc 1971-76, dir Br Cncl for Prevention of Blindness 1976-; *Recreations* music, tennis, walking, theatre, getting to know 6 grandchildren; *Style*— David Chesterman, Esq; 15 Shire Lane, Chorleywood, Herts WD3 5NQ; 12 Harcourt Street, London W1H 1DS (☎ 071 724 3716)

CHESTERMAN, Sir Ross; s of Dudley Edmund Chesterman (d 1950), of Bexhill, Sussex, and Ettie Esther, *née* Thorington; *b* 27 April 1909; *Educ* Hastings GS, Imperial Coll London (BSc, MSc, PhD, Acland Eng Essay Prizeman); *m* 1, 1938, Audrey Mary (d 1982), da of Rev Arthur Herbert Horlick (d 1950), of Portishead; 1 s (John), 1 da (Jane); m 2, 1985, Patricia, da of Frederic Burns Bell; *Career* sci master in various grammar schs, former headmaster Meols Cop Secdy Sch Southport, chemistry lectr Woolwich Poly, sch inspr and chief county schs inspr Worcs 1948-53, warden Goldsmiths' Coll Univ of London 1953-74 (hon fell 1980), dean Coll of Craft Educn 1958-60 (hon fell 1958), Ford Foundation Travel Award to American Univ 1966, educnl conslt to numerous overseas countries 1966-73, master Coll of Craft Design and Technol 1982-; author of scientific papers in chemical jls and jls of natural history and articles in educnl periodicals; chm: Nat Cncl for Supply and Trg of Teachers Overseas 1971, Advsy Ctee for Teacher Trg Overseas FCO (ODA) 1972-74; Freeman and Liveryman Worshipful Co of Goldsmiths; kt 1970; *Books* Teacher Training in Some American Universities (1967); *Recreations* music, painting, natural history, travel; *Style*— Sir Ross Chesterman; The Garden House, 6 High St, Lancaster LA1 1LA (☎ 0524 65687)

CHESTERS, Prof Graham; s of Thomas Leslie Chesters (d 1972), and Nellie, *née* Tortington; *b* 10 Oct 1944; *Educ* Crewe Co GS, Univ Coll of Swansea (BA, MA); *m* 26 Oct 1968, Veronica Anne; 1 s (Tim b 1976), 1 da (Anna b 1982); *Career* lectr in French Queen's Univ Belfast 1970-72; Univ of Hull: lectr in French 1972-80, sr lectr 1980-88, prof 1988; dean of Sch of Euro Languages and Cultures 1988-; dir Computers in Teaching Initiative Centre for Modern Languages 1989; *Books* Some Functions of Sound-Repetition (1975), Anthology of Modern French Poetry (1976), The Appreciation of Modern French Poetry (1976), Baudelaire and the Poetics of Craft (1988); *Recreations* chess; *Style*— Prof Chesters; School of European Languages and Cultures, University of Hull, Hull (☎ 0482 465625, fax 0482 465991)

CHESTERTON, Fiona Mary; da of Clarence Herbert Chesterton (d 1977), of Leicester, and Mary Biddulph; *b* 19 May 1952; *Educ* Wyggeston Girl's GS Leicester, Lady Margaret Hall Oxford (BA); *m* 1 Jan 1980, Howard Anderson, s of late John Anderson; 2 da (Sarah Elizabeth b 26 June 1984, Rachel Clare b 22 April 1987); *Career* ed Newsroom South East BBC TV 1987- (news trainee 1975-77, TV news scriptwriter 1977-79), prodr TV current affairs esp Nationwide 1979-87 (former asst prodr and prodr), ed London Plus 1987-89; *Recreations* swimming, gardening, tennis (when time); *Style*— Ms Fiona Chesterton; Islington, London N1 (office ☎ 081 207 8785)

CHESTERTON, (John Sydney) Keith; s of Maj Hugh Chesteron, MBE (d 1962), of Sussex, and Phyllis Mary, *née* Harries (d 1986); *b* 26 April 1927; *Educ* Sherborne, Corpus Christi Coll Cambridge; *m* 1, 29 March 1953 (m dis), Penelope Ann; 1 s (Christopher b 1957), 1 da (Venetia b 1955); m 2, 19 Aug 1964, Diana Margaret; *Career* Lt RN 1945-56; admitted slr 1961; HM Coroner IOW 1980-; *Recreations* sailing, gardening; *Clubs* Royal Naval Sailing Assoc, Royal Victoria Yacht, Seaview Yacht; *Style*— Keith Chesterton, Esq; Shirleys Yard, Yafford, Shorwell, Isle of Wight; 36 Union St, Ryde, Isle of Wight (☎ 0983 63305)

CHESTERTON, Sir Oliver Sidney; MC (1943); s of Frank Sidney Chesterton, and Nora Chesterton; *b* 28 Jan 1913; *Educ* Rugby; *m* 1944, Violet Ethel, yst da of Henry Robert Jameson, of Dublin; 2 s (Michael, Sam), 1 da (Jane); *Career* served WWII Irish Gds; Crown Estate Cmmr 1969-83; qualified as chartered surveyor 1934, sr ptnr Chesterton and Sons, chm Woolwich Equitable Building Society 1976-84 (formerly vice-chm); dir: Property Growth Assurance 1972-85, London Life Association 1975-84, Estates Property Investment Company 1979-88; govr Rugby Sch 1972-89; FRICS (hon sec 1972-74, formerly pres); kt 1969; *Clubs* White's; *Style*— Sir Oliver Chesterton, MC; Hookfield House, Abinger Common, Dorking, Surrey

CHESWORTH, Donald Piers; OBE (1987); s of Frederick Gladstone Chesworth (d 1975), and Daisy, *née* Radmore (d 1987); *b* 30 Jan 1923; *Educ* King Edward VI Sch Camp Hill Birmingham, LSE; *Career* WWII NFS, RAF 1940-45; lab advsr Tanganyika Govt (and chm Territorial Minimum Wages Bd) 1961-62; Mauritius Govt: lab advsr (and chm Sugar Wages Cncls) 1962-65, pt/t chm Salaries Cmmn 1973-77, chm enquiry into position of families without wage earners 1981, govt salaries cmmr 1987-89; memb Econs Branch ILO Geneva 1967, dir Notting Hill Social Cncl 1968-77, warden Toynbee Hall (univs settlement in East London) 1977-87, conslt social affrs Kumagai Gumi UK 1987-, dir Citicare St Clements plc 1988-; Parly candidate (Lab): Warwick and Leamington 1945, Bromsgrove 1950 and 1951; memb (Lab) LCC Kensington North Div 1952-65 (whip and memb Policy Ctee), co-opted memb Educnl Ctee ILEA 1970-77, memb Cncl War on Want 1965-76 (chm 1967-1968 and 1970-74), alderman Royal Borough Kensington and Chelsea 1971-77; memb Ct of Govrs LSE 1973-78; tstee: Mutual Aid Centre London 1977-, Hilden Charitable Fund 1978-, Aldgate Freedom Fndn 1978-, Ctee for Restoration of Tower of London Children's Beach 1990-; govr City and East London Coll 1978-, memb Cncl for the Furtherance of Tower Hamlets Adult Educn 1991-, dir Attlee Meml Fndn 1979-81 (tstee 1977-); chm: govrs Tower Hamlets Adult Educn Inst 1987-91, Spitalfields Heritage Centre 1988-; *Books* contribs: Statutory Wage Fixing in Developing Countries (ILO Geneva 1968), International Labour Review (ILO); *Recreations* travel; *Clubs* Reform; *Style*— Donald Chesworth, Esq, OBE; 16 Evershed House, Old Castle St, London E1 7NU (☎ 071 247 4580)

CHESWORTH, John; s of Frank Chesworth (d 1970), and Florence Lilian, *née* Battye; *b* 8 June 1937; *Educ* Burnage GS; *m* 1, 24 June 1961 (m dis 1972), Wendy Ann Smith; 3 da (Debra b 1 May 1962, Sandra b 8 June 1967, Diane b 1 March 1969); m 2, 17 March 1973, (Elizabeth) Ann, da of Frank Noel Martin, of Stockport, Cheshire; 2 s (James b 21 Oct 1974, Robert b 28 June 1977); *Career* articled clerk Burne Phillips & Co 1958-63, chartered accountant Deloitte & Co 1964-67, fin accountant Kellogg Co of GB Ltd 1967-68, gp accountant Nemo Heat Treatments Ltd 1968-71, chief exec Blandburgh Nemo Group 1972-, jt md Bodycote International plc 1980-, non-exec chm Zinc Alloy Ltd 1980-, chm Capital and Counties Developments Ltd 1989-; memb ICAEW; *Books* The Economics of Heat Treatment (Iron & Steel, 1971), Heat Treatment 50 Years On (Metallurgia, 1985), The Changing Role of Sub Contract Heat Treatment (Foundry trade jl, 1987), Leading With Quality (Quality in Action, 1988); *Recreations* sailing, golf, swimming, soccer; *Clubs* Tytherington, Royal Yacht; *Style*— John Chesworth, Esq; Oulton Farm, Rushton Spencer, Macclesfield, Cheshire (☎ 0260 226 314); Bodycote International plc, 140 Kingsway, Manchester 19 (☎ 061 257 2345)

CHETWODE, Hon Christopher Roger; s of late Capt Roger Charles George Chetwode and bro of 2 Baron Chetwode; raised to rank of Baron's son 1951; *b* 24 March 1940; *Educ* Eton; *m* 25 July 1961, Hon Philippa Mary Imogen, *née* Brand, yr da of 5 Visc Hampden; 5 s; *Style*— The Hon Christopher Chetwode; Hill House, Cheriton, Alresford, Hants

CHETWODE, 2 Baron (UK 1945); Sir Philip Chetwode; 8 Bt (E 1700); s (by 1 m) of Capt Hon Roger Chetwode (d 1940, s of 1 Baron), and Hon Molly, *née* Berry, da of 1 Visc Camrose; suc grandfather 1950; *b* 26 March 1937; *Educ* Eton; *m* 1, 10 Aug 1967 (m dis 1979), Susan Janet, da of Capt Voltelin James Howard Van der Byl, DSC, RN (ret), and formerly wife of Alwyn Richard Dudley Smith; 2 s (Hon Roger b 1968, Hon Alexander b 1969), 1 da (Hon Miranda b 1974); m 2, 12 July 1990, Mrs Fiona Holt; *Heir* s, Hon Roger Chetwode b 29 May 1968; *Career* Capt (ret) Royal Horse Guards; *Clubs* White's; *Style*— The Rt Hon the Lord Chetwode; The Mill House, Chilton Foliat, Hungerford, Berks

CHETWODE, Hon Mrs (Philippa Mary Imogen); *née* Brand; yr da of 5 Viscount Hampden; *b* 7 April 1942; *m* 25 July 1961, Hon Christopher Roger Chetwode, yr bro of 2 Baron Chetwode; 5 s; *Style*— The Hon Mrs Chetwode; Hill House, Cheriton, Alresford, Hants

CHETWODE, Lady Willa; *née* Elliot; yst da of 5 Earl of Minto (d 1975); *b* 21 March 1924; *m* 9 Oct 1946, Maj (George) David Chetwode, MBE, 2 s of Adm Sir George Knightley Chetwode, KCB, CBE (d 1957), who was bro of 1 Baron Chetwode; 1 s, 5 da; *Style*— The Lady Willa Chetwode; Swiss Farm House, Upper Slaughter, Cheltenham, Glos GL54 2JP

CHETWOOD, Sir Clifford Jack; s of Stanley Jack Chetwood, and Doris May Palmer; *b* 2 Nov 1928; *m* 1953, Pamela Phyllis Sherlock; 1 s, 3 da; *Career* chm George Wimpey 1984- (md and chief exec 1982); tstee Victoria and Albert Museum; chm Devpt Tst ICE 1989, pres Building Employers Confedn 1989; memb cncl Imperial Soc of Knights Bachelor 1988, pres The Royal Ct Club Hampton Ct Palace 1989; Hon FICE; FCIOB, FRSA, FRSH; Prince Philip Medal for Exceptional Service to Industry 1987 (City and Guilds Inst); kt 1987; *Style*— Sir Clifford Chetwood; c/o George Wimpey Plc, 27 Hammersmith Grove, London W6 7EN (☎ 081 748 2000)

CHETWYN, Robert; s of Frederick Reuben Suckling (d 1963), and Eleanor Lavinia, *née* Boffee; *b* 7 Sept 1933; *Educ* Rutlish Sch Merton, Central Sch of Drama; *Career* actor with Dundee Repertory Co 1952; in repertory at: Hull, Alexandra Theatre Birmingham 1954, Birmingham Rep Theatre 1954-56; various tv plays 1956-59, first prodn Five Finger Exercise (Salisbury Playhouse) 1960, dir of prodns Opera House Harrogate 1961-62, artistic dir Ipswich Arts 1962-64, assoc dir Mermaid 1966; *plays* The Beaver Coat-3 one-act plays by Shaw, There's A Girl in my Soup (Globe) 1966, Music Box (NY) 1967, A Present For The Past (Edinburgh Festival) 1966, The Flip Side (Apollo) 1967, The Importance of Being Earnest (Haymarket) 1968, What the Butler Saw (Queens) 1968, The Country Wife (Chichester Festival) 1968, The Band-Waggon (Mermaid 1968 and Sydney 1970), Cannibal Crackers (Hampstead) 1969, When We Are Married (Strand) 1970, Hamlet (in Rome, Zurich, Vienna, Antwerp, Cologne, Cambridge) 1971, The Sandboy (Greenwich), Parents Day (Globe) 1972, Restez Donc Jusq'au Petit Dejeuner (Belgium) 1973, Who's Who (Fortune) 1973, At The End Of The Day (Savoy) 1973, Chez Nous (Globe) 1974, Qui Est Qui (Belgium) 1974, The Doctors Dilemma (Mermaid) 1976, Getting Away with Murder (Comedy) 1976, A Murder is Announced (Vaudeville) 1977, Arms and the Man (Greenwich) 1978, Bent (Royal Ct and transferred to Criterion) 1979, Pygmalion (Nat Theatre of Belgium), Moving (Queens) 1981, Beethoven's Tenth (Vaudeville, Los Angeles and NY) 1983, Number One (Queens) 1984, Why Me? (Strand) 1985, Selling the Sizzle (Hampstead); major TV work: Private Shultz 1980-81, The Irish RM 1982, Tropical Moon Over Dorking 1984, That Uncertain Feeling 1985, Born in the Gardens 1985-86, Small World 1987-88, The Case of the Late Pig 1989; *Recreations* sport, gardening; *Style*— Robert Chetwyn, Esq; 1 Wilton Court, Eccleston Square, London SW1V 1PH (☎ 071 834 6485)

CHETWYND, 10 Viscount (I 1717); Adam Richard John Casson; also Baron Rathdown (I 1717); s of 9 Viscount (d 1965); *b* 2 Feb 1935; *Educ* Eton; *m* 1, 19 Feb 1966 (m dis 1974), Celia Grace, er da of Cdr Alexander Robert Ramsay, DSC, RNVR; 2 s (Hon Adam, Hon Robert Duncan (twin) b 26 Feb 1969), 1 da (Hon Emma Grace b 5 May 1967); m 2, 1975, Angela May, da of Jack Payne McCarthy (d 1982), of Nottingham; *Heir* s, Hon Adam Douglas Chetwynd b 26 Feb 1969; *Career* Lt Queen's Own Cameron Highlanders; life assurance agent Prudential Assurance Co of SA Ltd 1978-; fellow Inst of Life and Pension Advsrs; Freeman Guild of Air Pilots and Air Navigators; *Recreations* squash, travel, flying; *Clubs* Rand; *Style*— The Rt Hon the Viscount Chetwynd; c/o J G Ouvry, Lee Bolton and Lee, 1 The Sanctuary, Westminster, London SW1; Prudential Assurance Co of SA Ltd, Sandton Branch, Johannesburg, South Africa (☎ 011 783 7125)

CHETWYND, Sir Arthur Ralph Talbot; 8 Bt (GB 1795), of Brocton Hall, Staffordshire; s of Hon (William) Ralph Chetwynd, MLA, MC (d 1957), bro of 7 Bt; and Frances Mary Jupe (d 1986); suc unc 1972; *b* 28 Oct 1913; *Educ* Provincial Normal Sch, UBC; *m* 26 Aug 1940, Marjory May MacDonald, da of Robert Bruce Lang (d 1940), of Vancouver; 2 s (Robin, William Richard); *Heir* s, Robin John Talbot Chetwynd, b 21 Aug 1941; *Career* served RCAF 1943-45; rancher in BC 1928-35; teacher 1935-38; physical rehabilitation 1939-42; chief instructor in medical reconditioning RCAF, assoc in physical and health educn Univ of Toronto 1946-52, pres and gen mangr Chetwynd Productions Ltd (Toronto) 1950-78, chm bd Chetwynd Publications Inc 1985; pres Brocton Hall Communications (Toronto) 1978-; Order of

Barbados (Silver Crown of Merit) 1984, Queen's Jubilee Medal 1977, Voluntary Serv and Victory Medals 1945; pres Brocton Hall Communications Ltd 1978-, has served in Red Cross Soc and many other organizations; memb: Nat Cncl Royal Cwlth Soc, Churchill Soc, Monarchist League, Heraldry Soc; *Recreations* swimming, golf, travel; *Clubs* The Toronto Hunt, Albany (Toronto), Empire (Canada), Royal Cwlth Soc (Toronto (chm 1982-87), and London); *Style*— Sir Arthur Chetwynd, Bt; 117 King St East, Cobourg, Ontario K9A 1LZ

CHETWYND, Hon (Mary Diana) Eve; da of 8 Viscount Chetwynd (d 1936); *b* 19 July 1908; *Educ* privately and in Paris, St Thomas's Hosp; *Career* SRN, SCM, MTD, HVCert; nurse, midwife, health visitor, now ret; pres East Herts Branch Royal Coll of Midwives; *Recreations* travelling, meeting people, gardening; *Style*— The Hon Eve Chetwynd; 6 Hulton Drive, Emberton, nr Olney, Bucks MK46 5BY (☎ 0234 711457)

CHETWYND, Lady; Laura Ellen; da of John Mallaby, JP; granted rank and precedence of a knight's widow; *m* 1968, as his 2 wife, George Roland Chetwynd, CBE (kt 1982, d 2 Sept 1982); *Style*— Lady Chetwynd

CHETWYND, Hon Mrs John; Margaret Agnes; da of Maj-Gen Hugh Clement Sutton, CB, CMG (d 1928), and his 2 wife, Hon Alexandra Mary Elizabeth, *née* Wood (d 1965), eldest da of 2 Viscount Halifax ; *m* 6 April 1937, Hon John Julian Chetwynd (s of late 8 Viscount Chetwynd and who d 22 April 1966); 2 s; *Style*— The Hon Mrs John Chetwynd; 3 Cadogan Sq, London SW1 (☎ 071 235 7612)

CHETWYND-TALBOT, Capt (Edward) Hugh Frederick; MBE (1945); yr s of Gilbert Edward Chetwynd-Talbot (d 1950), and Geraldine Mary, *née* Murray (d 1953); *b* 19 Jan 1909; *Educ* Haileybury, RMA Woolwich; *m* 27 July 1935, Cynthia Phoebe, da of Noel McGrigor Phillips (d 1942), of Stoke d'Abernon Manor, Surrey; 1 s (Mark b 1941), 2 da (Anthea b 1939, Meriel b 1944); *Career* cmmnd RA 1929, served India and WWII (disabled 1939); asst sec Irish Turf Club 1947-55, bursar Worksop Coll 1955-63, chm Kiplin Estate (Charitable) Tst 1970-89; Anglican lay reader; author; *Books* The English Achilles: Life of John Talbot, First Earl of Shrewsbury 1383-1453 (1981); *Recreations* travel, genealogy, historical research (medieval); *Style*— Capt Hugh Chetwynd-Talbot, MBE; Mead Acre, Milton Lilbourne, Pewsey, Wilts SN9 5LQ (☎ 0672 62229)

CHETWYND-TALBOT, Hon Paul Alexander Anthony Bueno; yr s (by 1 m) of late 21 Earl of Shrewsbury and Waterford, and Nadine Muriel, *née* Crofton-Atkins; *b* 25 Nov 1957; *Educ* Eton, ChCh Oxford; *m* 1982, Sarah Elizabeth, da of Simon Hildebrand Melville Bradley, of 34 Ballingdon Rd, London SW11; 2 s (Harry b 1985, Jack b 1987); *Career* insurance broker; *Style*— The Hon Paul Chetwynd-Talbot; The Bowring Building, Tower Place, London EC3P 3BE

CHETWYND-TALBOT, His Hon Richard Michael Arthur; s of late Rev Arthur Talbot (s of Rev Hon Arthur Chetwynd-Talbot, 3 s of 2 Earl Talbot); 2 cous twice removed of 21 Earl of Shrewsbury and Waterford, the Premier Earl (on the Roll) of England and Ireland; *b* 28 Sept 1911; *Educ* Harrow, Magdalene Coll Cambridge; *Career* called to the Bar Middle Temple 1936; bencher 1962, chm Salop QS 1967-71 (dep chm 1950-67), former rec Banbury (hon rec 1972), circuit judge 1972-83; *Style*— His Hon Richard Chetwynd-Talbot; 7 St Leonard's Close, Bridgnorth, Salop (☎ 074 6276 3619)

CHEUNG, Prof Yau-Kai; s of Cheung Tze-Shiu, of Hong Kong, and Yip Lai King (d 1937); *b* 18 Sept 1934; *Educ* S China Inst of Technol (BSc), Univ of Wales (PhD, DSC, Higher Doctorate), Univ of Adelaide (DEng, Higher Doctorate); *m* 28 Sept 1961, Chu Yuk Baw, da of Chu Tak Cheong; 3 c (Ngai Wah b 2 May 1963, Ngai Tseung b 25 Dec 1964, Ngai Fung b 4 April 1966); *Career* structural engr Chengchow Honan China 1958-61; Univ of Wales: res asst 1961-64, sr res fell 1964-65, lectr in civil engrg 1965-67; prof of civil engrg Univ of Calgary Canada 1970-74 (assoc prof 1967-70), prof of civil engrg and chm of Dept Univ of Adelaide Aust 1974-77; Univ of Hong Kong: prof and head of civil and structural engrg 1977-, dir High Building Res Centre 1977-81, dean of engrg and architecture 1978-, dean of engrg 1978-87, pro vice chancellor 1988-; Telford Premium from ICE, Nat Natural Sci award China 1989, Guangdong Provincial Natural Sci award 1988; hon fellowship Univ Coll Swansea, Hon DUniv Shanghai Univ of Technol; FEng, CEng, FICE, FIStructE; *Books* Finite Strip in Structural Analysis; author of numerous papers and publications on engrg; *Style*— Prof Yau-Kai Cheung; Dept of Civil and Structural Engineering, University of Hong Kong, Hong Kong (☎ 852 859 2666, fax 852 559 5337)

CHEVALLIER GUILD, John Marjoribanks; s of Cyril Harrower Guild (d 1978), and Perronelle Mary, *née* Chevallier; *b* 23 Aug 1933; *Educ* RN Coll Dartmouth; *m* 18 Dec 1965, Jennifer Isobel, da of Col Brian Sherlock Gooch, DSO, TD, DL, JP; 2 s (John Barrington b 1967, Henry b 1968); *Career* Lt Cdr RN serv at sea 1951-63, HM Yacht Britannia 1959, Staff Coll Camberley 1964, cmd HM Ships Badminton, Upton, Bronington 1965-67, served BRNC Dartmouth 1967-69; ret RN to take over family owned cyder, apple juice and cyder vinegar business Aspall Cyder (estab 1728); *Recreations* country pursuits; *Style*— John Chevallier Guild, Esq; Aspall Hall, Stowmarket, Suffolk IP14 6PD (☎ 0728 860492); Aspall Cyder, Aspall Hall, Stowmarket, Suffolk IP14 6PD (☎ 0728 860510, fax 0728 861031)

CHEVILLARD, Pierre Marie; s of Etienne Chevillard, of Regny, France, and Thérese, *née* Becouze; *b* 15 Aug 1958; *Educ* local schs Regny France; *m* 5 June 1982, Alison Jane, da of Leonard Simpson Beamish; 1 s (Jacques Leonard b 5 July 1986), 1 da (Lauren Marie b 11 Dec 1984); *Career* head chef; apprentice Les Favieres L'hopital sur Rhins 1973-76, commis Troisgros Roanne 1976-79; Chewton Glen Ho☎ chef garde mangr 1980, sous chef 1981, head chef 1982-; memb Academie Culinaire de France UK, awarded Michelin rosette; *Recreations* jogging, tennis; *Style*— Pierre Chevillard, Esq; Chewton Glen Hotel, New Milton, Hants BH25 6QS (☎ 0425 275 341)

CHEVSKA, Maria Elizabeth; da of Klemens Skwarczewski (d 1985), and Susan Tovell; *b* 30 Oct 1948; *Educ* Our Lady's Convent Abingdon Oxon, Oxford Poly, Byam Shaw Sch of Art London; *Career* artist; head of painting Ruskin Sch of Fine Art Univ of Oxford (fell BNC); solo exhibitions incl: Battersea Art Centre London 1979, Air Gallery London 1982, Midland Group Nottingham 1985, Mario Flecha Gallery London 1986, Chapter Gallery Cardiff 1986, Bernard Jacobson Gallery London 1987, Anderson O'Day Gallery London 1989, 1990, Brasenose Coll Oxford 1990; gp exhibitions incl: Art and the Sea (John Hansard Gallery Univ of Southampton, ICA London) 1981, British Drawing (Hayward Annual London) 1982, Whitechapel Open (Whitechapel Gallery London) 1983-1989, Gulbenkian Fndn Award Winners Prints (touring GB and Ireland) 1983, New Blood on Paper (MOMA Oxford) 1983, New Images in Printmaking (Blond Fine Art London) 1984, Landscape Memory and Desire (Serpentine Gallery London) 1984, Air Gallery Retrospective (London) 1985, Four Selected Painters (City of London Festival Guildhall London) 1986, Sea (Laing Gallery Newcastle upon Tyne) 1986, 8x8 (Curwen Gallery London) 1987, Advent Calendar (Gallery North Kirby Lonsdale) 1989, XXII Int Festival of Painting (Chateau Musee Music Grimaldi France) 1990; work in pub collections: Arts Cncl of GB, Bolton City Art Gallery, Gulbenkian Fndn, Br Cncl, World Bank, Contemporary Art Soc; *Awards* Arts Cncl of GB award 1977, Gtr London Arts Assoc award 1979, 1984, Gulbenkian Fndn Printmakers award 1982; *Style*— Ms Maria Chevska; Anderson O'Day Gallery, 255 Portobello Rd, London W11 1LR

CHEWTON, Viscount; James Sherbrooke; s and h of 12 Earl Waldegrave, KG, GCVO, TD; *b* 8 Dec 1940; *Educ* Eton, Trinity Coll Cambridge; *m* 12 April 1986, Mary Alison Anthea, da of Sir Robert Allason Furness, KBE, CMG (d 1954), of South Lodge, Little Shelford, Cambs; 2 s (Edward Robert b 1986, Robert Arthur Riversdale b 1989); *Clubs* Beefsteak, Leander; *Style*— Viscount Chewton; Priory Farm, Chewton Mendip, Bath (☎ 076 121 666)

CHEYNE, David Watson; s of Brig William Watson Cheyne, DSO, OBE (d 1970), and Laurel Audrey, *née* Hutchison; *b* 30 Dec 1948; *Educ* Stowe, Trinity Coll Cambridge (BA); *m* 22 April 1978, (Judith) Gay McAuslane, da of David Anstruther Passey, of 3 Gregory Place, London W8; 3 s (Alexander William David b 25 Nov 1980, Rory Alistair Watson b 22 Aug 1984, Rupert Valentine Hutchison b 20 Feb 1989); *Career* ptnr Linklaters and Paines 1980- (articled clerk 1972-74, asst slr 1974-80); memb City of London Solicitors Co 1980; memb Law Soc; *Recreations* shooting, fishing, collecting antiques; *Style*— David Cheyne, Esq; 19 Ladbroke Gardens, London W11 2PT (☎ 071 229 0096); Linklaters & Paines, 59-67 Gresham St, London EC2V 7JA (☎ 071 606 7080, fax 071 606 5113, telex 884349,888167)

CHEYNE, (William) Gerald; s of Brig William Watson Cheyne, DSO, OBE (d 1970), and Laurel Audrey, *née* Hutchison; *b* 13 April 1950; *Educ* Stowe, Trinity Coll Cambridge (BA); *m* 29 July 1978 (m dis 1984), Clare Rosdew, *née* Vanderstegen-Drake; 1 da (Katie b 1980); *Career* Capt 1 Bn Queens Own Highlanders 1972-77; Peat Marwick Mitchell & Co CAs 1977-82, Larpent Newton & Co Ltd 1982-84; dir: Henderson Crosthwaite & Co 1987 (joined 1985), Guinness Mahon & Co Ltd, Henderson Crosthwaite Corporate Finance Ltd 1988-90; ACA 1981; *Recreations* golf, tennis, sailing, piano; *Style*— W G Cheyne, Esq; 32 Ringmer Ave, London SW6 5LW (☎ 071 731 1806); Guinness Mahon & Co Ltd, 32 St Mary At Hill, London EC3 3AJ (☎ 071 623 9333, fax 071 929 3398)

CHEYNE, Major Sir Joseph Lister Watson; 3 Bt (UK 1908), OBE (1976); s of Col Sir Joseph Cheyne, 2 Bt, MC (d 1957); *b* 10 Oct 1914; *Educ* Stowe, CCC Cambridge; *m* 1, 14 Jan 1938 (m dis 1955), Mary Mort (d 29 Oct 1959), er da of Vice Adm John Derwent Allen, CB (d 1958); 1 s, 1 da; m 2, 6 Aug 1955, Cicely, da of Thomas Metcalfe, of Padiham, Lancs; 2 s, 1 da; *Heir* s, Patrick John Lister Cheyne, *qv*; *Career* served WWII North Africa and Italy, Maj; former first sec Br Embassy Rome; curator Keats Shelley Meml House Rome 1976-90; *Clubs* Boodle's, Circolo della Caccia (Rome); *Style*— Major Sir Joseph Cheyne, Bt, OBE; Po di Serse, Via Po del Vento 19 A, Paciano (PG) 06060, Italy (☎ 010 39 75 83 01 29); Leagarth, Fetlar, Shetland

CHEYNE, Patrick John Lister; s (by 1 m) and h of Sir Joseph Cheyne, 3 Bt, OBE; *b* 2 July 1941; *Educ* Lancing; *m* 8 June 1968, Helen Louise Trevor, yr da of Louis Smith, of Marine Lodge, 25 Driftwood Gardens, Southsea; 1 s, 3 da; *Career* short serv cmmn Lt RN; fine art valuer and auctioneer; FSVA; *Recreations* squash, photography, gardening; *Style*— Patrick Cheyne, Esq; 37 Chapel Lane, Hale Barns, Cheshire WA15 0AG (☎ 061 980 3094, 061 941 4879)

CHIANDETTI, Gian Battista (Tito); s of Giovanni Battista Chiandetti (d 1942), and Pauline, *née* Caron (d 1980); *b* 17 March 1935; *Educ* Douai Sch Woolhampton Berks, Harvard Business Sch; *m* 18 March 1968, Maria-Elisa, da of Mario Bulferi-Bulferetti, of Lugano, Switzerland; 1 s (Marco Paolo Angelo b 25 Aug 1973), 1 da (Corinna Elena Paola b 13 Nov 1970); *Career* Trusthouse Forte: md Prods 1973-75, dir Trusthouse Forte Ltd 1975-, with Trusthouse Forte Catering Ltd 1977-84 (md 1979-84), dep chief exec 1984-; memb Cncl Food from Britain 1989-; FHCIMA; *Recreations* mountain walking, swimming, rock collecting; *Style*— Tito Chiandetti, Esq; Daneswood, Monks Walk, South Ascot, Berks SL5 9AZ (☎ 0344 26036); Trusthouse Forte plc, 166 High Holborn, London WC1V 6TT (☎ 071 836 7744, fax 071 240 9993, telex 264678 THFPLC)

CHIBBETT, Geoffrey John; s of Ernest James Chibbett (d 1955), barrister, of Hoylake, Cheshire; *b* 2 Sept 1928; *Educ* Stowe, Liverpool Univ (BCom); *m* 1977, Diana Leslie, da of Frederick Green (d 1963), of London; 1 s, 1 da; *Career* chm: Kango Wolf Power Tools Ltd, Ralliwolf Ltd (Bombay), Dobson Park Industries plc (engrg div), Klynton Davis Group Ltd; former pres Cheshire LTA; former warrant holder to HM The Queen; FCA; *Recreations* lawn tennis, golf; *Clubs* Royal Liverpool Golf; *Style*— Geoffrey Chibbett, Esq; Withamside, Church Street, Long Bennington, nr Newark, Notts (☎ 0400 81249); Klynton Davis Group Ltd, Forest Rd, Leicester

CHICHESTER, Hon Lady (Anne Rachel Pearl); *née* Douglas-Scott-Montagu; da of 2 Baron Montagu of Beaulieu, KCIE, CSI (d 1929), and his 2 w, Alice Pearl, er da of late Major Edward Barrington Crake; *b* 4 Oct 1921; *m* 1, 2 March 1946, Maj Howel Joseph Moore-Gwyn, Welsh Guards (d 20 Sept 1947), only s of late Major Joseph Gwyn Moore-Gwyn, of Duffryn, Glamorgan, and Abercrave, Brecknock; 1 s; m 2, 23 Sept 1950, Sir (Edward) John Chichester, 11 Bt; 2 s, 2 da (and 1 da decd); *Career* served with Red Cross WWII; JP Hampshire 1968-80; fndr/proprietor Rachel Scott Designs 1979; chm New Forest and W Hants area Br Heart Fndn 1968-; *Style*— The Hon Lady Chichester; Battramsley Lodge, Boldre, Nr Lymington, Hants SO41 8PT

CHICHESTER, Archdeacon of; *see*: Hobbs, Ven Keith

CHICHESTER, Dermot Michael Claud; s of Lord Desmond Chichester, MC, of Preston Hills, Preston, Hitchin, Herts, and Felicity Stella, *née* Harrison; *b* 22 Nov 1953; *Educ* Harrow; *m* 1, 26 April 1975 (m dis 1979), Frances Jane Berners, da of Michael Edward Ranulph Allsopp, of Little Coxwell Grove, Farringdon, Oxon; m 2, 14 July 1982, Shan, da of Alastair Ros McIndoe (d 1984); 1 s (Rory b 1985), 2 da (Ottilie b 1988, Sapphira b 1990); *Career* joined Christie's Fine Art Auctioneers 1974; md: Christie's Scotland Ltd 1982, Christie's S Kensington Ltd 1987, Christie Manson and Woods Ltd 1990; *Recreations* cricket, golf, shooting, tennis, skiing; *Clubs* Whites; *Style*— Dermot Chichester, Esq; Lowick House, Lowick, Kettering, Northamptonshire NN14 3BL (☎ 08012 4993); 8 King St, London SW1Y 6QT (☎ 071 839 9060, fax 071 839 1611, tlx 91642, car 0860 615534)

CHICHESTER, Major Lord Desmond Clive; MC (1944); s of 4 Baron Templemore (d 1953), and bro of 7 Marquess of Donegall; raised to the rank of a Marquess's son 1977; *b* 27 Jan 1920; *Educ* Harrow, Ch Ch Oxford (MA); *m* 1, 7 March 1946, Lorna Althea Chichester, MBE (d 9 April 1948), da of Capt Montagu Hamer Ravenhill, and wid of Capt Richard Cecil Twining, Welsh Guards, and previously of P/O Geoffrey Christopher Appleby Holt, RAF; 1 s; m 2, 12 April 1951, Felicity Stella, 6 da of Maj John Fenwick Harrison, JP, DL, of King's Walden, Bury, Herts; 1 s; *Career* served WWII (despatches 1943), Maj Coldstream Gds (ret); ADC to Govr-Gen of Canada 1948-50; memb Stock Exchange 1952-75; chm Colne Valley Water Co 1983-88 (dir 1956-); *Recreations* shooting, racing; *Clubs* Whites; *Style*— Major Lord Desmond Chichester, MC; Preston Hill, Preston, Hitchin, Herts (☎ 0462 456965); Colne Valley Water Co, Blackwell House, Aldenham Road, Watford, Herts (☎ 0923 223333)

CHICHESTER, 99 Bishop of 1974-; Rt Rev Eric Waldram Kemp; Bishopric founded in Isle of Selsey by Wilfrid, 2 Archbishop of York, removed to Chichester by Stigand after 1075; patron of 96 livings and 9 alternately, the Archdeaconries of Chichester, Lewes and Hastings, and Horsham, and the Prebends (including the three residentiaries) in the Cathedral; s of Tom Kemp, and Florence Lilian, *née* Waldram, of Grove House, Waltham, Grimsby, Lincs; *b* 27 April 1915; *Educ* Brigg GS Lincs, Exeter Coll Oxford, St Stephen's House Oxford; *m* 1953, Leslie Patricia, 3 da of late Rt Rev Kenneth Escott Kirk, former Bishop of Oxford (d 1954); 1 s, 4 da; *Career* deacon 1939, fell and chaplain Exeter Coll Oxford 1946-69, dean of Worcester 1969-74; author; Hon DD Berne Univ 1987, Hon DLitt Univ of Sussex, DD Oxon; *Style*— The Rt Rev the Lord Bishop of Chichester; The Palace, Chichester, Sussex (☎ 0243 782161)

CHICHESTER, James Henry Edward; s and h of Sir Edward John Chichester, 11 Bt, *qv*; *b* 15 Oct 1951; *Educ* Eton; *m* 10 Feb 1990, (Margaret) Anne, o da of Maj John Wakelyne Chandos- Pole, JP, DL, of Radburne Hall, Derbyshire; *Career* fndr of Chichester Trees and Shrubs Ltd; *Recreations* shooting, fishing, big game hunting and dendrology; *Style*— James Chichester, Esq; The Mill House, Beaulieu, Brockenhurst, Hants SO42 7YG (☎ 0590 612198, fax 0590 612194)

CHICHESTER, Sir (Edward) John; 11 Bt (E 1641), of Raleigh, Devonshire; s of Cdr Sir Edward Chichester, 10 Bt, RN (ret, d 1940); *b* 14 April 1916; *Educ* Radley, Sandhurst; *m* 23 Sept 1950, Hon Anne Rachel Pearl Douglas-Scott-Montagu, da of 2 Baron Montagu of Beaulieu; 2 s, 2 da (1 da decd); *Heir* s, James Chichester, *qv*; *Career* serv WWII former Capt Royal Scots Fusiliers, Lt RNVR, King's Foreign Serv Messenger 1947-50, ICI Ltd 1950-60; patron of one living; *Style*— Sir John Chichester, Bt; Battramsley Lodge, Boldre, Lymington, Hants

CHICHESTER, 9 Earl of (UK 1801); Sir John Nicholas Pelham; 14 Bt (E 1611); also Baron Pelham of Stanmer (GB 1762); s of 8 Earl of Chichester (ka 1944), and Ursula (d 1989), da of Walter de Pannwitz, of Benebroek, Holland; *b* 14 April 1944,(posthumously); *Educ* Stanbridge Earls Sch, Mozarteum Salzburg; *m* 1975, Mrs June Marijke Hall, da of Gp-Capt E D Wells, DSO, DFC, of Marbella; 1 da (Lady Eliza b 12 May 1983); *Heir* kinsman, Richard Pelham; *Career* farmer; *Recreations* music, theatre, tennis, riding; *Style*— The Rt Hon the Earl of Chichester; 53 Shawfield St, London SW3 (☎ 01 352 1516); Little Durnford Manor, Salisbury, Wilts

CHICHESTER, Julian Edward; *b* 16 Oct 1949; *Educ* Bedales, Univ of Sussex; *Career* called to the Bar Inner Temple 1977; *Recreations* photography, modelmaking, skiing, scuba, diving, travel; *Style*— Julian Chichester, Esq; 4/5 Gray's Inn Square, Gray's Inn, London WC1R 5AY (☎ 071 404 5252, fax 071 242 7803, telex 8953743 GALAW)

CHICHESTER-CLARK, Hon Fiona; da of Baron Moyola (Life Peer), *qv*; *b* 1960; *Educ* Knighton House Blandford, Cranborne Chase Wilts; *Career* antique furniture restorer and cabinet maker; *Recreations* shooting, fishing, tennis; *Style*— The Hon Fiona Chichester-Clark

CHICHESTER-CLARK, Sir Robert (Robin); s of Capt James Jackson Lenox-Conyngham Chichester-Clark, DSO, DL, MP, and Marion Caroline Dehra, *née* Chichester (later Mrs Charles Edward Brackenbury); bro of Rt Hon Lord Moyola, PC, DL, *qv*; *b* 10 Jan 1928; *Educ* Magdalene Coll Cambridge (BA); *m* 1, 6 Nov 1953 (m dis 1972), Jane Helen, o child of Air Marshal Sir (Robert) Victor Goddard, KCB; 1 s, 2 da; m 2, 1974, Caroline, o da of Col Anthony Bull, CBE, RE, of 35 Clareville Grove, London SW7; 2 s; *Career* MP (UU) for Londonderry City and Co 1955-74, Lord Cmmr of the Treasy 1960-61, comptroller of HM Household 1961-64; chief oppn spokesman on: NI 1964-70, Public Bldg and Works and The Arts 1965-70; min of state Dept of Employment 1972-74; mgmnt conslt; dir: Alfred Booth and Co 1975-86, Welbeck Gp Ltd; Hon FIWM; kt 1974; *Clubs* Brooks's; *Style*— Sir Robin Chichester-Clark

CHICK, Jonathan Dale; s of Cdr William E Chick, DSC, of Darlington, and Vonda Hope, *née* Dale; *b* 23 April 1945; *Educ* Queen Elizabeth GS Darlington, Corpus Christi Coll Cambridge (MA), Univ of Edinburgh (MB ChB, MPhil); *m* 8 March 1969, Josephine Anna; 2 s (Gregory b 8 Sept 1976, Aylwin b 24 Nov 1978); *Career* med posts Edinburgh teaching hosps 1971-76, memb scientific staff MRC 1976-79, conslt psychiatrist and pt/t sr lectr in psychiatry Univ of Edinburgh 1979-, over 50 contribs to scientific books and jls; advsr WHO, hon memb Minister of Tport Med Advsy Ctee On Driving and Alcohol and Substance Abuse; MRCP 1973, FRCPsych 1988, FRCP (Edin) 1990; *Books* Drinking Problems (1984); *Style*— Dr Jonathan Chick; Royal Edinburgh Hospital, Edinburgh EH10 5DF (☎ 031 447 2011, fax 031 447 6860, telex 7274 UNIVED G)

CHIENE, John; *b* 27 Jan 1937; *Educ* Rugby, Queens' Coll Cambridge; *m* ; 1 s, 1 da; *Career* memb Stock Exchange 1964; sr ptnr Wood, Mackenzie and Co (stockbrokers); *Recreations* golf, music; *Clubs* Cavalry and Guards, City, New (Edinburgh); *Style*— John Chiene Esq; Stone House, Snowdenham Links Rd, Bramley, Guildford, Surrey; Wood, Mackenzie and Co, 62-63 Threadneedle St, London EC2R 8HP (☎ 01 600 3600; telex 883369)

CHIGNALL, John Horsley; s of Horace Victor Chignall, (d 1952), of Uckfield Sussex, and Ethel Kate, *née* Godwin (d 1972); *b* 26 July 1926; *Educ* Poly Regent St London; *m* 26 Aug 1948, Esme Elizabeth, da of Sidney James Michel (d 1962); 1 da (Linda Susan b 20 July 1949); *Career* civilian attached to Special Serv Divn US Army 1944-46; dir: AE Medway & Co Ltd 1947-54, JH Chignall & Co Ltd 1954-82; chm: Pleasure Heating Ltd, Pleasure Heating Fin & Dept Ltd, Pleasure Investmts Ltd; FBIM; *Recreations* shooting, golf, tennis, sailing; *Clubs* Stoke Poges Golf, Pinner Hill Golf (Capt 1966); *Style*— J Horsley Chignall, Esq; Cedar House, Camp Road, Gerrards Cross, Bucks; Vallee du Fournel, Roquebrune sur Argens, Cote D'Azur France

CHIGNELL, Anthony Hugh; s of Thomas Hugh Chignell (d 1965), and Phyllis Una, *née* Green; *b* 14 April 1939; *Educ* Downside, St Thomas Hosp London (MB BS, DO); *m* 16 June 1962, Phillippa Price, da of Rear Adm F B P Brayne-Nicholls, CB, DSC, RN, of 3 Tedworth Sq, London; 1 s (Christopher Damien b 1965), 2 da (Caroline Paula b 1963, Georgina Natalie b 1966); *Career* conslt ophthalmic surgn St Thomas' Hosp 1973-, civilian conslt in ophthalmology to Army 1983-, conslt surgn King Edward VII Hosp for Offrs 1985-, advsr in ophthalmology to Met Police 1987-; author of numerous papers on retinal detachment surgery; govr Royal Nat Coll for the Blind 1987-, memb Cncl Guide Dogs for the Blind 1989-; memb: Oxford Ophthalmology, Club Jules Gonin; OstJ; memb Ct Worshipful Co Spectacle Makers 1987; FRCS 1968; *Books* Retinal Detachment Surgery (2 edns); *Recreations* fly fishing, golf, the country; *Clubs* Fly Fishers, Anglo Belgian; *Style*— Anthony Chignell Esq; 44 Wimpole St, London W1M 7DG, (☎ 071 935 7022, fax 071 224 3722)

CHILCOTT, Gareth James; s of Dai Chilcott, 3 Thanet Rd, Bedminster, Bristol, and Doreen Chilcott; *b* 20 Nov 1956; *Educ* Park Comprehensive; *m* Ann, 1 da of Idris Walters; *Career* Rugby Union prop forward Bath RFC and England; clubs: Old Redcliffians RFC, Bath RFC 1976- (over 300 appearances, incl 6 cup final victories); rep: Somerset Colts, Somerset RFU, South and Southwest Counties RFU; England: debut v Aust 1984, Five Nations debut v Ireland 1985, memb World Cup squad Aust 1987, tour Aust and Fiji 1988; Br Lions tour Aust 1989; french polisher, lumberjack, mangr Security company, md Chauffeur Co; *Books* Cooch Mr Chilcott to You (1990); *Recreations* golf, boxing, any sports, spending time with wife and friends; *Style*— Gareth Chilcott, Esq; Pollingers Ltd, Locksbrook Trading Estate, Bath BA1 3DZ (☎ 0225 446936, fax 0225 482650)

CHILD, Alan Arthur; MBE (1989); s of Walter Henry Child (d 1954); *b* 7 July 1912; *Educ* Alleyns Sch; *m* 1941, Olive Ella, da of Archibald Wood (d 1981); 1 s, 1 da; *Career* Capt RA UK Belgium and Germany; insur and pension fund conslt, former chief exec dir C T Bowring and Layborn Ltd (chm 1974-78), pres Soc of Pension Consultants 1970-72, chm Hosp Saving Assoc 1975-, memb Occupational Pensions Bd 1973-84; pres Croydon N E Cons Assoc 1986-; *Clubs* Inst of Dirs, Croydon Cons; *Style*— Alan Child, Esq, MBE; 35 Campion Close, Coombe Road, Croydon, Surrey CR0 5SN (☎ 081 688 4126)

CHILD, (John) Christopher; s of Ernest Henry Child (d 1962), of Southwold, and Barbara Christobel, *née* Hebbert (d 1962); *b* 5 March 1927; *Educ* Orley Farm Sch Harrow, Aldenham, de Havilland Aeronautical Sch Hatfield; *m* 26 Feb 1949, Elisabeth Anne, da of Frank Wilkinson Fish, MC; 1 s (Andrew b 1950), 1 da (Sarah b 1953); *Career* aeronautical engr 1948, specialist in design of film cameras for harsh environments, student of Irish Folk Life, antique restorer and dealer 1970-; *Recreations* photography, wood turning, collecting artifacts; *Style*— Christopher Child, Esq; Meadowbank, Morchard Bishop, Crediton, Devon (☎ 036 37 456)

CHILD, Dr David Francis; s of Canon William Thomas Child (d 1978), and Mary Minwel, *née* Price (d 1990); *b* 4 Feb 1944; *Educ* Abersychan GS, Univ of Birmingham (MB ChB); *m* 6 Dec 1975, Sheila Margaret, da of Rev Robert Edwards McLean (d 1972); 1 s (John Robert b 8 July 1984); *Career* RMO Hammersmith Hosp 1972-75, lectr in med Univ of Manchester 1975-79, conslt physician Wrexham Maelor Hosp 1979-; res papers on endocrinology and diabetes; dir Wales Diabetes Res Tst; FRCP 1988; *Recreations* photography, model railways; *Style*— Dr David Child; 63 Wynnstay Lane, Marford, Wrexham, Clwyd LL12 8LH; Wrexham Maelor Hospital, Wrexham, Clwyd LL13 7TD (☎ 0978 291100, fax 0978 290951)

CHILD, Denis Marsden; CBE (1987); s of Percival Snowden (d 1964), and Alice Snowden (d 1963); *b* 1 Nov 1926; *Educ* Woodhouse Grove Sch; *m* 1973, Patricia, da of Arthur Charlton (d 1979); 2 s (Nicholas b 1958, Richard b 1961), 1 da (Elizabeth b 1956); *Career* dir: Coutts and Co 1983-, Nat Westminster Bank 1986- (ret as dep gp ch exec 1986); bd memb: IBM UK Pensions Tst Ltd 1984-, Eurotunnel Gp; memb: Accounting Standards Ctee 1985-90, Securities and Investmts Bd 1986; chm: Br Bankers Assoc Exec Ctee 1986-87, Investors Compensation Scheme 1990-; FIB, FCT, FBIM; *Recreations* golf, gardening; *Clubs* Stoke Poges Golf; *Style*— Denis Child, Esq, CBE; Hill House, Ascott, Shipston-on-Stour, Warwickshire CV36 5PP

CHILD, Dennis; s of Ronald Wren Child (d 1986), of Longridge, Preston, Lancs, and Elsie Mais, *née* Dennis; *b* 10 July 1932; *Educ* Blackburn Technical HS and Coll, Univ of London (BSc), Univ of Leeds (MEd), Univ of Bradford (PhD); *m* 10 July 1954, Eveline, da of Thomas Barton (d 1979); 1 s (Paul b 1962), 1 da (Louise (Mrs Greaves) b 1964); *Career* navigator and pilot offr RAF 1951-54; asst teacher in gen sci Easingwold Comprehensive Sch York 1957-59, asst teacher in physics and chemistry Bootham Sch York 1959-62, sr lectr in educn City of Leeds Coll of Educn 1962-67, sr lectr in psychology of educn Univ of Bradford 1973-76 (lectr 1967-73), visiting res prof Psychology Dept Univ of Illinois 1972-73 (visiting prof to Educnl Psychology Dept 1973), prof and head of educn Univ of Newcastle upon Tyne 1976-81, head Sch of Educn Univ of Leeds 1984-87 (prof educnl psychology 1981-); examining posts incl: educnl examiner for Hull, Nottingham, Exeter, Leeds, educnl psychology examiner Sheffield 1974-77, chief external examiner in educnl psychology Univ of Bristol 1975-80, external examiner in educn Leeds 1976-80, chief external examiner in education psychology Sunderland Poly 1978-82, examiner in physiotherapy London 1982-86, chief external examiner in educnl psychology Cambridge 1983-86, examiner for MEd Cambridge 1988-, Hong Kong 1988- and Hull 1988-; advsr: Canadian Jl of Behavioural Science, Jl of Multivariate Experimental Personality and Clinical Psychology, Durham and Newcastle Res Review; ed Br Jl of Educational Psychology 1976-84; memb: Educn Ctee CNAA, Educnl Res Bd SSRC, sub ctees for allocation to insts and for microcomputers in schs, Exec Ctee UCET Bd of Studies Coll of Radiographers, Advsy Panel Univ of London, Br Psychological Soc Pubns Ctee, Electors Panel for Profs of Educn Univ of Cambridge, Educn Advsy Panel Yorkshire Arts, Bd of Govrs Northern Contemporary Sch of Dance; chm: Academic and Registration Bd Coll of Speech Therapists (memb Ethics Ctee), Educn Advsy Panel London Festival Ballet (memb Bd of Govrs), Cncl for the Advancement of Communication with the Deaf; advsr Br Cncl; FBPsS, FCST, CPsychol; *Books* incl:The Essentials of Factor Analysis (1970, 2 edn 1990), Initiating Research in Colleges of Education (jtly, 1968), Motivation and Dynamic Structure (with Prof R B Cattell, 1975), Psychology and the Teacher (1986), Applications of Psychology for the Teacher (1986), Nurse Selection - Helping Applicants and Selectors Make Decisions (1988), Theory and Practice of Education (gen ed); contrib incl: British Journal of Educational Psychology, Education (1965), British Journal of Social and Clincial Psychology (1966), Educational Research (1970), Physiotherapy (1974), British Journal of Guidance and Counselling (1976), Vocational Aspect (1979), Personality, Cognition and Values (1985), The Analysis of Personality in Research and Assessment: A Tribute to Raymond B Cattell (1988); *Recreations* walking, travel, member of Bradford Festival Choral Society, watching ballet, north of England artists; *Style*— Prof Dennis Child; School of Education, University of Leeds, Leeds LS2 9JT (☎ 0532 334544)

CHILD, Graham Derek; s of Albert Edward Child, of Broadstone, Dorset, and Phyllis, *née* Wooldridge (d 1973); *b* 24 June 1943; *Educ* Bedford Sch, Worcester Coll Oxford (MA); *Career* Slaughter and May: asst slr 1968-75, ptnr 1976-; memb Law Soc; *Books* Common Market Law of Competition (with CW Bellamy QC, 1987); *Recreations* outdoor activities, European languages; *Style*— Graham Child, Esq; 35 Basinghall St, London EC2V 5DB (☎ 071 600 1200, fax 071 726 0038)

CHILD, Sir (Coles John) Jeremy; 3 Bt (UK 1919), of Bromley Palace, Bromley, Kent; s of Sir Coles John Child, 2 Bt (d 1971), and Sheila, *née* Mathewson (d 1964); *b* 20 Sept 1944; *Educ* Eton, Poitiers Univ (Dip); *m* 1, 1971 (m dis 1976), Deborah Jane, da of Henry Percival Snelling; 1 da ((Honor) Melissa b 1973); m 2, 1978 (m dis 1987), Jan, actress, yst da of Bernard Todd, of Kingston-upon-Thames; 1 s ((Coles John) Alexander b 10 May 1982), 1 da (Leonora b 25 July 1980); m 3, 1987, Elizabeth, yst da of Rev Grenville Morgan, of Canterbury, Kent; 1 s (Patrick Grenville b 3 Jan 1991), 1 da (Eliza Caroline b 29 Jan 1989); *Heir* s, Coles John Alexander; *Career* actor; *TV*: Father dear Father, Wings, Glittering Prizes, Edward and Mrs Simpson, The Jewel in the Crown, Fairly Secret Army, First Among Equals, Game Set and Match; *Films*: High Road to China (1982), Give My Regards to Broad St (1982/83), A Fish Called Wanda (1987), Taffin (1987); *Recreations* flying, squash, travel, photography, cooking, gardening; *Clubs* Garrick, Roehampton; *Style*— Sir Jeremy Child, Bt; The Old Mill House, Mill Lane, Benson, Oxon

CHILD, John Frederick; s of Frederick George Child (d 1980), and Doris Frances, *née* Henley; *b* 18 April 1942; *Educ* King Edward's Sch Bath, Univ of Southampton (BA), Sidney Sussex Coll Cambridge (scholar, LLB), Univ of Columbia, Leiden (Dip American Law); *m* 2 Sept 1972, Dr Jean Alexander, da of Dr Albert Alexander Cunningham, of Glenone, Haymeads Drive, Esher; 2 s (Andrew b 25 May 1974, Jeremy b 11 May 1977); *Career* Chancery Barr; Droop Scholar and Tancred Common Law Student, Hon Soc of Lincoln's Inn, supervisor in law Sidney Sussex Coll Cambridge 1966-1978; memb: Lincoln's Inn, Chancery Bar Assoc, Revenue Bar Assoc; *Books* Main Contrib Vol 19 (Sale of Land) Encyclopaedia of Forms and Precedents (4 edn), Accumulation and Maintenance Settlements, Encyclopedia of Forms and Precedent (4 edn); *Recreations* tennis, badminton; *Style*— John Child, Esq; 17 Olds Buildings, Lincolns Inn, London, WC2A 3UP (☎ 071 405 9653/071 831 1621, fax 071 405 5032)

CHILD-VILLIERS, Hon Charles Victor; s of 9 Earl of Jersey; *b* 10 Jan 1952; *m*

1975 (m dis 1989), Brigitte Elisabeth Germaine, da of Rolland Marchand; 2 da (Eleanor b 1979, Béatrice b 1981); *Style*— The Hon Charles Child-Villiers; 2 La Hougue Grange, Grouville, Jersey, CI (fax 0534 53731)

CHILD-VILLIERS, (Edward) John Mansel; s of Sqdn Ldr The Hon Edward Mansel Child-Villiers (d 1980), and Mary Barbara Emma Torrens, *née* Frampton; *b* 29 April 1935; *Educ* Harrow; *m* 2 June 1958, Celia Elinor Vadyn, da of Cyril Hall Green (d 1973) (see Debrett's Peerage, Blake Bt); 2 s (Alexander b 1961, Roderick b 1963); *Career* memb Lloyd's 1962-; literary executor 18 Baron Dunsany 1966-; *Recreations* Bordeaux wines; *Style*— John Child-Villiers, Esq; Stable House, Mystole, Canterbury, Kent CT4 7DB (☎ 0227 738729)

CHILDERLEY, Stuart Michael; s of Michael Childerley, of Steep Holme, South Clifton, Newark, Notts NG23 7AA, and Ann, *née* Baker; *b* 17 Feb 1966; *Educ* Burleigh Community Coll; *Career* yachtsman; World Youth champion 1984, Finn Dinghy Class Euro champion 1987, fourth place Finn class Olympic Games 1988; Br Team: won the Admirals Cup on Indulgence 1989; coach The Royal Yachting Assoc Youth Prog; *Recreations* golf, squash, swimming; *Clubs* Royal Southern Yacht, Staunton Harold Sailing; *Style*— Stuart Childerley, Esq

CHILDS, John Henry; s of Sydney Alfred Childs (d 1983), and Barbara Elaine, *née* Westlake (d 1985); *b* 15 Aug 1951; *Educ* Audley Park Secdy Sch Torquay; *m* 11 Nov 1978, Jane Anne, da of John Evans; 2 s (Lee Robert b 28 Nov 1980, Scott Alexander b 21 Aug 1984); *Career* professional cricketer; represented Devon Minor co team (also under 15 and under 19 level); Gloucestershire CCC 1975-84: debut 1975, awarded county cap 1977, 203 appearances; Essex CCC 1985-: debut 1985, awarded county cap 1986, 115 appearances; 2 Test matches England v W Indies (Old Trafford and Oval) 1988; advanced cricket coach, qualified signwriter; *Recreations* golf and most ball sports, theatre, enjoying family time; *Style*— John Childs, Esq; Essex CCC, County Ground, New Writtle St, Chelmsford CM2 OPE (☎ 0245 252420, fax 0245 491607)

CHILDS, Norman; s of Rev Leonard Arthur Childs, of Melton Mowbray, Leicestershire and Dorothy May, *née* Taylor; *b* 14 Nov 1944; *Educ* The Winifred Portland Sch, Nottingham Coll of Art, Central London Poly, Harrow Coll of Technol; *m* 16 April 1966, Judith, da of Alfred Lidster; 1 s (Nigel Christopher b 9 Feb 1974), 1 da (Helen Ruth b 10 July 1971); *Career* asst med photographer Inst of Obstetrics and Gynaecology Chelsea Hosp for Women 1963-64, photographer Chester Beatty Res Inst, Inst of Cancer Res 1964-67, head Photographic Unit Colt International Ltd Havant Hants 1967-77, M T Walters & Assocs Mexborough S Yorks 1977-81 (assignments ME and Sudan), set up Norman Childs Photography 1981; Br Inst of Professional Photography: memb Industl Ctee 1977-82, memb Cncl 1979-82; memb Admissions and Qualifications Bd 1986-; CSD assessor of external examinations in photography Blackpool Coll of Technol 1983-86, memb Industl Liaison Ctee Wednesbury Coll of Technol 1984; *awards* best black and white photograph Financial Times 1972, BIPP Wessex and Yorkshire Region award 1975 and 1978, 3M Professional Photographic Products award 1980, BIPP Central Region awards 1984, 1985 and 1987, Silver award World Cncl of Professional Photographers 1988-89 ; FBIPP 1977, FCSD 1980; *Recreations* land yachting; *Clubs* Anglia Land Yacht (memb ctee); *Style*— Norman Childs, Esq; Norman Childs Photography, 10 Midland Road, Hemel Hempstead, Herts HP2 5BH (☎ 0442 259265)

CHILLINGWORTH, John Henry; *b* 18 Jan 1928; *Career* trainee Hulton Press Ltd 1944-46; served RE as field engr instr and photographer 1944-46; photo journalist Picture Post 1949-56, freelance photo journalist 1956-68, ptnr Harvey Chillingworth & Walklin (advertising and marketing agency) 1968-74, exec dir Hilary Green & Ptnrs Ltd (advertising agency) 1974-75, dir Chillingworth Advertising Management Ltd 1975-79, mangr gp publicity Celcon Gp 1979-85, ptnr JHC Communication (mktg advertising and creative consultancy) 1985-; BIPP Presidential Award 1988; former FBIPP, former FCSD, MCIM; *Style*— John Chillingworth, Esq; 17 The Greencroft, Salisbury, Wiltshire SP1 1JD (☎ 0722 328255, fax 0722 328956)

CHILSTON, 4 Viscount (UK 1911); Alastair George Akers-Douglas; s of late Capt Ian Stanley Akers-Douglas (gs of 1 Viscount Chilston), by his 2 w, Phyllis Rosemary; suc kinsman, 3 Viscount Chilston, 1982; *b* 5 Sept 1946; *Educ* Ashdown House, Eton; *m* 1971, Juliet Anne, da of late Lt-Col Nigel Lovett, of The Old Rectory, Inwardleigh, Okehampton, Devon; 3 s (Hon Oliver, Hon Alexander Hugh b 1975, Hon Dominic b 1979); *Heir* s, Hon Oliver Ian Akers-Douglas b 17 Oct 1973; *Career* film producer; *Style*— The Rt Hon the Viscount Chilston; The Old Rectory, Twyford, nr Winchester, Hants (☎ 0962 712300)

CHILTON, Air Marshal Sir (Charles) Edward; KBE (1959, CBE 1945), CB (1951); o s of Joseph Charles Chilton (d 1966), of Southsea, Hants, and Olive Minette, *née* Dowling; *b* 1 Nov 1906; *m* 1, 21 Sept 1929, Betty Ursula (d 1963), 2 da of late Bernard Temple Wrinch, of Grove House, Denham, Suffolk; 1 s; m 2, 14 Sept 1964, (Margaret Elizabeth) Joyce, wid of A W Cornforth, *née* Fenwick; *Career* Air Cdre 1950, Air Marshal 1959, AOC-in-C Coastal Cmd and Maritime Air Cdr E Atlantic Area and Cdr Maritime Air Channel and S North Sea 1959-62; air historian and lectr on mil subjects; former conslt and dir IBM, int conslt def systems and data processing; int conslt; fndr fell Royal Inst of Navigation; air master navigator (1937), specialist navigator RAF 1931; Grand Cross of Prince Henry the Navigator (Portugal) 1960, Order of Polonia Restituta (Poland) 1945; *Books* biographies: Air Chief Marshal Sir Philip Jollbert, Air Chief Marshal the Hon Sir Ralph Cochrane, Rear Adm Sir Murray Sueter, Wing Cdr J C Porte; author of numerous published articles on navigation and maritime subjects; *Recreations* sailing, fishing, walking; *Clubs* RAFSA (Vice Adm), RGYC (Vice Patron), RAF, Phyllis Court (Henley); *Style*— Air Marshal Sir Edward Chilton, KBE, CB; 11 Charles House, Phyllis Court Drive, Henley-on-Thames, Oxon (☎ 049 157 3836)

CHILTON, James Richard; s of Col Richard Chilton; *b* 2 Jan 1941; *Educ* Winchester; *m* 1964, Margaret Ann, *née* McKay; 1 s, 3 da; *Career* served 1 The Royal Dragoons, Arabian Peninsular 1960, Malaysia 1961-62; dir McKay Securities plc 1973-; *Recreations* skiing, plantsmanship, vinousness; *Clubs* Cavalry and Guards'; *Style*— James Chilton, Esq; Hyde House, Great Missenden, Bucks; Maufant Manor, Jersey, CI

CHILTON, (Frederick) Paul; s of Charles Frederick Chilton, of 167 Birling Rd, Erith, Kent, and Elizabeth, *née* Docherty; *b* 28 July 1946; *Educ* St Stephens Roman Catholic Sch, NW Kent Coll of Technol; *Career* dep chm Alexander Howden Ltd; memb The UK Int Insur Brokers Ctee; *Recreations* equestrian sports; *Clubs* Les Ambassadeurs; *Style*— Paul Chilton, Esq; Alexander Howden Ltd, 8 Devonshire Sq, London EC2M 4PL (☎ 01 623 5500, fax 01 621 1511, telex 882171)

CHILVER, Brian Outram; s of Flt Lt Bertram Montagu Chilver (d 1990), and Edith Gwendoline, *née* Adams (d 1984); *b* 17 June 1933; *Educ* Univ Coll Sch; *m* 23 June 1956, Erica Mary, da of Lawrence Trewhella Howell, of 23 Bury Drive, Goring on Sea, Sussex; 2 s (Andrew b 1961, David b 1963), 2 da (Hazel b 1957, Heather b 1959); *Career* Flying Offr RAF 1955-57; trainee CA Temple Gothard and Co 1949-55 (qualified 1954), Barton Mayhew 1957-59, sr ptnr Temple Gothard 1974-85 (re-joined 1959, ptnr 1960), conslt Touche Ross and Co 1985-87; exec chm: Laing Properties plc 1987-90 (non-exec dir 1982, dep chm 1986), Seafield plc 1990-; non-exec dir John Laing plc 1988-, non-exec chm Eskmuir Properties Ltd 1990-; dir: Regions Beyond Missionary Union 1960, Yeovil Livestock Auctioners Ltd 1965, Hildenborough Evangelistic Tst Ltd 1982, Eskmuir Ltd 1987; chm TEAR Fund 1990; FCA, ACWA; *Recreations* walking, swimming, reading, travel, involved in christian charitable activity in UK and overseas; *Style*— Brian Chilver, Esq; Bretaye, Limbourne Lane, Fittleworth, W Sussex RH20 1HR (☎ 079 882 366); Seafield plc, 9 Chesterfield St, London W1X 7HF (☎ 071 493 2627, fax 071 493 7387)

CHILVER, Baron (Life Peer UK 1987), of Cranfield, Beds; Sir (Amos) Henry Chilver; FRS (1982); e s of Amos Henry Chilver, of Southend-on-Sea, and A E Chilver, *née* Mack; *b* 30 Oct 1926; *Educ* Southend HS, Univ of Bristol; *m* 1959, Claudia Mary Beverley, o da of Sir Wilfrid Vernon Grigson, CSI (d 1948), of Pelynt, Cornwall; 3 s (Hon John b 1964, Hon Mark b 1965, Hon Paul b 1967), 2 da (Hon Helen (Hon Mrs Prentice) b 1960, Hon Sarah b 1962); *Career* prof of civil engrg London Univ 1961-69, vice chllr Cranfield Inst of Technol 1970-89; chm: ECC Group plc 1989-, Milton Keynes Development Corporation 1983-; dir: ICI plc 1990-, Porton International plc 1989-, Ling Dynamic Systems Ltd 1989-, BASE International Holdings 1988-; pres: Inst of Mgmnt Servs 1982-, Inst of Materials Mgmnt 1986-; Hon DSc: Leeds 1982, Bristol 1983, Salford 1983, Strathclyde 1986, Bath 1986, Cranfield 1989, Buckingham 1990, Compiegne (France) 1990; hon fell CCC Cambridge 1981; FRS 1982, FEng, CBIM; kt 1978; *Clubs* Athenaeum, United Oxford and Cambridge; *Style*— The Rt Hon Lord Chilver, FRS; Lanlawren House, Trenewen, Looe, Cornwall PL13 2PZ; ECC Group plc, 125 Wood St, London EC2V 7AQ (☎ 071 696 9229, fax 071 696 9079)

CHILVERS, Brian; s of Gordon Edward Chilvers, of Limpsfield, Surrey (d 1988), and Caroline, *née* Nendick; *b* 15 Jan 1931; *Educ* Brentwood Sch, Queen Mary Coll London, London Hosp Med Coll (LDS, RCS, BDS), Forsyth Dental Infirmary Harvard Med Centre Boston Mass (Fulbright scholar); *m* 1972, Annabel Hiscocks, da of Dr Henry F Hiscocks, OBE; 1 s (Benjamin James Nendick b 24 Jan 1972), 1 da (Sarah Annabel Hilary b 17 Oct 1979); *Career* capt RADC East Africa 1956-58; res house surgn London Hosp 1954, dental intern Forsyth Infirmary Harvard Med Centre Boston 1954-55, registrar in oral surgery London Hosp 1968-60, sr registrar Royal Dental Hosp London 1960-61, full time practice 1961-; East Africa Service medal 1957; memb: BDA 1954, Federation Dentaire International 1957; FRSM 1962; *Recreations* sailing, gardening; *Style*— Brian Chilvers, Esq; The Orchard, Heronsgate, Rickmansworth, Herts WD3 5DB (☎ 0923 282147); 67 Wimpole St, London W1M 7DE (☎ 071 935 9373)

CHILVERS, Donald Richard; s of Gordon Edward Chilvers (d 1988), of Limpsfield, and Caroline, *née* Nendick; *b* 1 Feb 1929; *Educ* Bancrofts Sch; *m* 25 Nov 1961, Rosemary, da of Archibald Watson (d 1979), of Edinburgh; 1 s (Angus b 1965), 3 da (Penelope b 1962, Felicity b 1967, Camilla b 1969); *Career* Nat Serv cmmnd 1951-53; ptnr Coopers and Lybrand 1961-, dir Jackson Stops & Co; memb: Sandilands Ctee of Inflation 1977-78, Industl Advsy Bd 1979-82; vice pres Invalid Children's Aid Nationwide; seconded to Miny of Energy 1961; FCA 1951, FCMA 1952; *Books* Receivership Manual (1971), Litigation Support (1988); *Recreations* golf, gardening; *Style*— Donald Chilvers, Esq; The Old Rectory, Brightwell Baldwin, Oxon; 17 Callcott St, London WC8 (☎ 0491 61 2432)

CHIN, Dr Lincoln Li-Jen; s of Pun-Jian Chin, and Grace Chin, *née* Sun; *b* 2 Nov 1942; *Educ* Christ's Coll Cambridge (BA, MA), MIT USA (ScD); *m* 21 Jan 1971, Lillian Chen Ming, da of Wen Hsiung Chu; 1 s (Nicholas b 1973), 1 da (Tamara b 1975); *Career* dep chm Chindwell Co Ltd; *Recreations* walking, swimming, travelling, music; *Clubs* Utd Oxford and Cambridge; *Style*— Dr Lincoln Chin; Chindwell Co Ltd, Hyde House, The Hyde, London NW9 6JT (☎ 081 205 6171, telex 923441, fax 081 205 8800)

CHINN, Sir Trevor Edwin; CVO; s of Rosser Chinn, and Sarah, *née* Feitelson; *b* 24 July 1935; *Educ* Clifton, King's Coll Cambridge; *m* 1965, Susan Avril, da of Louis Speelman; 2 s (David b 1966, Simon b 1969); *Career* Lex Service plc: joined 1955, joined bd 1959, md 1968, chm and md 1973, chm and chief exec 1987; memb Governing Cncl Business in the Community 1983; memb Cncl: Royal Shakespeare Theatre, Prince's Youth Business Tst; tstee: Friends of Duke of Edinburgh's Award Scheme 1978-88 (chm), Royal Acad Tst, Hamstead Theatre Tst; chief barker Variety Club of GB 1978 and 1977 (memb exec bd), vice chm Great Ormond St Hosp Redevpt Appeal, pres Jt Israel Appeal of GB, chm Br/Israel Public Affrs Centre; Freeman: City of London, Worshipful Co of Painter-Stainers; kt 1990; *Recreations* fishing, scuba diving; *Clubs* RAC, Harvard (New York); *Style*— Sir Trevor Chinn, CVO; Lex Service plc, Lex House, 17 Connaught Place, London W2 2EL (☎ 071 723 1212, telex 23668 LEXGRP G, fax 071 723 5732)

CHIPPERFIELD, David Alan; s of Alan John Chipperfield, and Peggy *née* Singleton; *b* 18 Dec 1953; *Educ* Wellington, Architectural Association (AA Dip); 3 s (Chester, Gabriel, Raphael); *Career* architect, princ David Chipperfield Architects, visiting lectr Harvard Univ 1986-87; shops for: Issey Miyake London and Japan 1986-87, Arnolfini Gallery Bristol 1987, private museum Tokyo 1987-; fndr and dir 9H Gallery London; RIBA; *Style*— David Chipperfield, Esq; 28 Cleveland Square, London W2 6DD (☎ 071 262 5238); David Chipperfield Architects, 1a Cobham Mews, Agar Grove, London NW1 9SB (☎ 071 267 9422, fax 071 267 9347)

CHIPPINDALE, Christopher Ralph; s of Keith Chippindale, and Ruth Chippindale; *b* 13 Oct 1951; *Educ* Sedbergh, St John's Coll Cambridge (BA), Girton Coll Cambridge (PhD); *m* 1976, Anne, *née* Lowe; 2 s, 2 da; *Career* ed: Penguin Books, Hutchinson Publishing Gp 1974-82, Antiquity 1987-; res fell in archaeology Girton Coll Cambridge 1985-87, asst curator Cambridge Univ Museum of Archaeology and Anthropology 1987-; *Books* Stonehenge Complete (1983), Who Owns Stonehenge? (1990); *Recreations* archaeology, worrying; *Style*— Christopher Chippindale, Esq; 85 Hills Rd, Cambridge

CHIPPINDALE, Hon Mrs (Margaret Ruth); *née* Ritchie; da of 2 Baron Ritchie of Dundee (d 1948), and sis of 3, 4 and 5 Barons; *b* 13 Nov 1913; *m* 10 Sept 1943, Maj (William Arthur) Martin Chippindale, o child of Edgar John Chippindale (d 1937), of Flackley Ash, Peasmarsh, Sussex, and Hon Mary Cassandra, *née* Hill (d 1968, having been granted the title, rank and precedence of a baron's da which would have been hers had her father survived to succeed to the barony of Sandys); 1 s, 1 da; *Style*— The Hon Mrs Chippindale; 5 Fair Meadow, Playden, Rye, Sussex TN31 7NL

CHISHOLM, Prof Alexander William John (Alec); s of Thomas Alexander Chisholm (d 1948), of Bryn yr Efail Cwm y Glo Gwynedd, and Maude Mary, *née* Robinson (d 1972); *b* 18 April 1922; *Educ* Brentwood Sch Essex, Northampton Poly, Manchester Coll of Sci and Technol, Royal Tech Coll Salford, Univ of London (BSc); *m* 29 March 1945, Aline Mary, da of Roy Eastwood; 1 s (Roger b 21 Oct 1951), 1 da (Diana b 4 June 1955); *Career* Nat Fire Serv WWII; gp head Res Dept Metropolitan Vickers Electrical Co Ltd 1944-49, sr scientific offr (later princ scientific offr) Nat Engrg Laborator 1949-57, UK scientific mission Br Embassy USA 1952-54, head Dept of Mechanical Engrg (later prof) Royal Coll of Advanced Technol Salford 1957-67, prof of mechanical engrg Univ of Salford 1967-82, res prof (later professorial fell) Univ of Salford 1982-, visitor Engrg Dept Univ of Cambridge, visiting fell Wolfson Coll Cambridge 1973-74, chm Univ of Salford Industrial Centre Ltd 1976-82; chm: Indust Admin Gp IMechE 1960-62, Prodn Engrg Ctee Nat Cncl for Technol Awards (vice chm Bd of Studies Engrg, govr 1960-65), Engrg Profs Conf 1976-80; pres CIRP 1983-84 (hon life memb 1987); memb Technol Ctee UGC 1969-74, memb Ct Cranfield Inst of Technol 1974-; author of numerous papers in tech and professional literature; FIMechE 1959, FIProdE 1963; *Recreations* hill walking, sailing, tree planting; *Clubs* Athenaeum; *Style—* Prof Alec Chisholm; 12 Legh Rd, Prestbury, Macclesfield, Cheshire SK10 4HX (☎ 0625 829 412); University of Salford, The Crescent, Salford M5 4WT (☎ 061 745 5000 ext 3772, fax 061 745 5999, telex SULIB)

CHISHOLM, Hon Mrs (Annabel Jane); *née* Hennessy; da of 2 Baron Windlesham (d 1962); *b* 20 Dec 1937; *m* 4 May 1963, (Ian) Duncan Chisholm, MA, MB, MRCP, MRCPsych, DPM, o son of John Michael Chisholm (d 1946), of Westminster Gdns, SW1, and Nutley, Sussex; 4 s; *Style—* The Hon Mrs Chisholm; Bourton House, Flax Bourton, Somerset (☎ 027 583 2250)

CHISHOLM, Hon Mrs (Caroline Elizabeth); *née* Wyndham; da of 6 Baron Leconfield and (1) Egremont (d 1972), and Pamela Wyndham-Quin, gda of 5 Earl of Dunraven and Mountearl; *b* 23 Dec 1951; *m* 1976, Colin Chisholm, s of Archibald Hugh Tennent Chisholm, CBE, of 107 Hamilton Terrace, NW8; 2 s, 1 da; *Style—* The Hon Mrs Chisholm

CHISHOLM, Lady; Margaret Grace; *née* Brantom; da of J H Brantom; *m* 1, -- Crofton-Atkins; m 2, 1956, as his 3 wife, Sir Henry Chisholm, CBE, FCA, first chm Corby Devpt Corpn (d 20 July 1981); *Style—* Lady Chisholm; Scott's Grove House, Chobham, Woking, Surrey (☎ 0276 858660)

CHISHOLM, Prof Michael Donald Inglis; s of Samuel Martin Chisholm (d 1985), of London, and Alice Winifred, *née* Lee; *b* 10 June 1931; *Educ* St Christopher Sch Letchworth Herts, St Catharine's Coll Cambridge (MA); *m* 1, 12 Sept 1959 (m dis 1981), Edith Gretchen Emma, da of Adolf Hoof (d 1984); 1 s (Andrew b 1966), 2 da (Annabel b 1960, Julia b 1962); m 2, 13 Dec 1987, Judith Carola, da of Henry Murray (d 1960); *Career* Nat Serv 1950-51, cmmnd 2 Lt 1950; dept demonstrator Inst for Agric Econ (formerly Inst for Res in Agric Econs) 1954-59, lectr in geography Bedford Coll London 1962-64 (asst lectr 1960-62), visiting sr lectr in geography Univ of Ibadan Nigeria 1964-65, prof of econ and social geography Univ of Bristol 1972-76 (lectr in geography 1965-67, reader in econ geography 1967-72), prof of geography Univ of Cambridge 1976-, head Dept of Geography Univ of Cambridge 1976-84; memb: SSRC 1967-72, Local Govt Boundary Cmmn for Eng 1971-78, Rural Devpt Cmmn 1981-90, Eng Advsy Ctee on Telecommunication 1990-; conservator for the River Cam 1979-; memb Inst Br Geographers 1954-, FRGS 1954-; *Books* Rural Settlement and Land Use (1962), Modern World Development (1982), Freight Flows and Spatial Aspects of the British Economy (jtly, 1973), The Changing Pattern of Employment (jtly, 1973), Inner City Waste Land (jtly, 1987), Regional Forecasting (jt ed, 1971), Spatial Policy Problems of the British Economy (jt ed, 1971); *Style—* Prof Michael Chisholm; University of Cambridge, Department of Geography, Downing Place, Cambridge CB2 3EN (☎ 333396, 333399, fax 0223 333392)

CHISHOLM, Dr (Diana) Morag; da of Prof Erik Chisholm (d 1965), and Diana Brodie Chisholm (d 1984); *b* 11 June 1933; *Educ* Univ of Capetown (MB ChB, MD); *m* 12 Dec 1952, Professor Ralph Wright (d 1990); 5 da (Dr Teresa Lyn Wright b 9 Feb 1954, Dr Deirdre Jane Wright b 4 Jan 1957, Jennifer Gail b 3 Feb 1959, Dr Fiona Alison Wright b 4 March 1963, Erika Morag b 15 Dec 1965); *Career* res asst Dep of Haematology and Med Radcliffe Infirmary Oxford 1962-71, res fell Dept of Haematology Yale Univ Med Sch 1968-69, lectr in haematology Univ of Southampton 1974-75, conslt haematologist and sr lectr in haematology Univ of Southampton Gp of Hosps; memb: BMA, Br Soc for Haematology; FRCPath 1986; *Style—* Dr Morag Chisholm; St Cross Lodge, St Cross Road, Winchester SO23 9RX (☎ 0962 866499); Department of Haematology, Southampton General Hospital, Tremona Rd, Southampton SO9 4VY (☎ 0703 796267)

CHISM, Nigel William Michael Goddard; s of His Hon Judge Michael William McGladdery Chism, of Hong Kong, and May Elizabeth Collins, *née* Goddard; *b* 2 July 1954; *Educ* The John Lyon Sch Harrow, Poly of Central London; *m* Christine Pamela, da of Eric Leonard Brown, of Berks; 1 s (William b 23 July 1982); *Career* TA 4 V Bn Royal Green Jackets 1972-75; CA; Arthur Young (formerly Josolyne Layton Bennett and Co) 1974-82, asst govt auditor Bermuda 1982-83, jt md Kingsway Rowland Ltd 1988-90 (chief accountant 1983-85, fin dir 1985-88), md Crescent Africa plc 1990-; ACA 1979; *Recreations* motoring and car restoration, travel, shooting, reading; *Style—* Nigel Chism, Esq; 98 Wakehurst Rd, London SW11 6BT (☎ 071 228 0226); Crescent Africa plc, 48 Grays Inn Rd, London WC1X 8LT (☎ 071 404 0550, fax 071 430 2907, telex 928442)

CHITNIS, Baron (Life Peer UK 1977), of Ryedale, Co N Yorks; Pratap Chidamber Chitnis; s of late Chidamber N Chitnis, and Lucia Mallik; *b* 1 May 1936; *Educ* Penryn Sch, Stonyhurst, Univ of Birmingham, Univ of Kansas; *m* 1964, Anne, da of Frank Mansell Brand; 1 s (decd); *Career* sits as ind peer in House of Lords, head of Liberal Pty Orgn 1966-69; chief exec Rowntree Soc Serv Tst 1974 (dir 1975-88); memb Community Relations Cmmn 1970-77; chm Br Refugee Cncl 1986-; author of ind reports on the elections in Zimbabwe 1979 and 1980, Guyana 1980, El Salvador 1982, 1984 and 1988 and Nicaragua 1984; *Style—* The Lord Chitnis; House of Lords, London SW1A 0PW

CHITTENDEN, Keith Alan; s of Norman Jack Chittenden, of Uppingham, Rutland; *b* 26 March 1934; *Educ* Nottingham HS, Imp Coll London (BSc); *m* 1959, Sylvia June, da of Frederick Henry Wearing, of Dunmow; 1 s, 1 da; *Career* gen mangr Marconi Space and Defence Systems (Frimley) 1981-82; md Marconi Radar Systems (Chelmsford) 1982-; CEng; *Recreations* riding, golf, theatre; *Clubs* Royal Commonwealth Soc; *Style—* Keith Chittenden Esq; The Old Red Lion, Stebbing, Dunmow, Essex (☎ 037 186 272)

CHITTLEBURGH, Cdr Edward Hayden; MBE (1960); s of James Edward Chittleburgh, of Walton-on-Thames, Surrey, and Elsie Elizabeth (d 1981); *b* 25 July 1921; *Educ* Bedford Sch, Imp Coll (BSc Eng, DIC); *m* 3 July 1946, Winifred Margaret (d 1990), da of Malcolm Myers (d 1950); 1 da (Julia b 1950); *Career* Cdr RN 1949-66; UNESCO chief technical advsr Kenya Poly Nairobi 1966-73, trg advsr Chief Training Unit World Bank 1973-80, conslt 1980-; CEng, FIEE; *Recreations* golf, watching cricket; *Clubs* Army and Navy, MCC; *Style—* Cdr Edward Chittleburgh, RN (ret); The Mill House, Howsham, York (☎ 0653 81643); 35 Cranley Gdns, London SW7 (☎ 01 373 2941)

CHITTOCK, John Dudley; OBE (1982); s of James Hiram Chittock (d 1973), of Leytonstone, and Phyllis Lucy Milner (d 1985); *b* 29 May 1928; *Educ* Oxford and Elson House, Forestdene, SW Essex Tech Coll; *m* 1947, Joyce Kate, da of Roy Ayrton Winter (d 1969), of Kent; *Career* writer, film prodr, publisher; exec ed Focal Press 1954-58, sr ptnr Films of Indust 1958-61, video and film columnist The Financial Times 1963-87, chm Screen Digest 1974 (fndr chm 1971), conslt ed Royal TV Soc Journal 1978-82, dir Nat Video Corporation Ltd 1981-86, non-exec chm NVC Cable Ltd 1983-86, dep chm Br Screen Advsy Cncl 1986-, prodr and dir over 30 documentary films; author of numerous articles, books and papers about films, TV and video; various chairmanships of film and TV indust ctees; chm The Grierson Tst 1989 (fndr 1974); Queens Silver Jubilee Medal 1977; Hood Medal Royal Photographic Soc 1973; FRPS, FRTS, FBKS; *Recreations* period home and antiques, cooking, gardening, work, the arts; *Style—* John Chittock, Esq, OBE; The Old Vicarage, Wickhambrook, Suffolk (☎ 0440 820314); 37 Gower St, London WC1E 6HH (☎ 071 580 2842)

CHITTOCK, Ronald Ernest; s of Reginald Ernest Chittock (d 1974), of London, and Clara Beatrice, *née* Jenkins; *b* 8 Feb 1931; *Educ* Borough Poly, Nat Coll; *m* 1, 1 Aug 1953 (m dis 1972), Betty, da of Erwin Short; 1 s (Barrie b 1956), 1 da (Diane b 1960); m 2, 16 Aug 1982, Irene Winifred, *née* Jackman; *Career* Nat Serv RN 1949-51; draughtsman Utilities London Ltd 1947-52, engr Troughton and Young (Heating) Ltd 1952-58, sr ptnr J E Greatorex and Ptnrs 1977-87 (ptnr 1958-76), freelance computer software mktg 1987-; author of various articles and papers on technical subjects; CEng, FIMechE, FCIBSE, MConsE, FRSA 1976; *Recreations* American automobiles, hi-fi, video, photography; *Style—* Ronald Chittock, Esq; St Martins, 68 Shelvers Way, Tadworth, Surrey KT20 5QF (☎ 0737 357086)

CHITTY, Andrew Edward Willes; s and h of Sir Thomas Chitty, 3 Bt; *b* 20 Nov 1953; *Style—* Andrew Chitty Esq

CHITTY, Dr Anthony; s of Ashley George Chitty (d 1980), of Surrey, and Doris Ellen Mary Buck; *b* 29 May 1931; *Educ* The Glyn GS Epsom, Imperial Coll London (BSc, PhD, DIC, CEng); *m* 1956, Audrey, da Edward Charles Munro (d 1965); 2 s (Martin b 1958, David b 1962), 1 da (Claire b 1960); *Career* GEC Res Labs 1953-55; head Creep of Steels Lab ERA 1959-63, GEC Power Gp 1963-66, chief metallurgist CA Parsons 1966-73; dir: Advanced Technol Div, Clarke Chapman-John Thompson 1973-78, Int Res and Devpt Co 1978-79; gen mangr engrg prods NEI Parsons 1979-84; regnl industl advsr DTI NE Reg 1984-88, dir Corporate Engrg Northern Engrg Industs 1989-; dep chm Bd Newcastle Technol Centre 1985-88 (chm 1988-); visiting prof Univ of Aston 1977-84; *Style—* Dr Anthony Chitty; 1 Willow Way, Darras Hall, Ponteland, Newcastle Upon Tyne

CHITTY, Bernard Anthony; s of Edward Chitty (d 1970), of Broadstairs, Kent, and Anne Josephine *née* Lowe; *b* 9 Aug 1951; *Educ* Chatham House County GS Ramsgate, Univ of Reading (BA); *m* 20 Nov 1981, Vivienne Mandy, da of Mervyn Grant (d 1960), of Cardiff 1 s (Jack b 1987), 1 da (Leanne b 1985); *Career* Coopers and Lybrand London 1974-77; Unilever: London 1978, Lagos Nigeria 1979, London 1980; fin controller PA Consulting Services Ltd 1980-86; dir: McAvoy Wreford Bayley Ltd 1986-, HR and H Consensus Res Int Ltd 1988-, Falcon Designs Ltd 1988-; gp co sec and asst gp fin dir The VPI Gp plc; memb of Eng Schoolboys Hockey XI 1969 (Capt 1970), memb Eng under 22 Hockey XI 1971 and 1972; FCA 1983; *Recreations* most sports, DIY, current affairs; *Clubs* Dulwich Hockey; *Style—* Bernard A Chitty, Esq; 36 Southwood Gardens, Hinchley Wood, Esher, Surrey, KT10 0DE (☎ 081 398 2292); 32 Grosvenor Gardens, London, SW1W 0DH (☎ 071 730 3456, fax 071 730 6663, telex 296 846 BIZOM G)

CHITTY, Sir Thomas Willes; 3 Bt (UK 1924), of The Temple; s of Sir (Thomas) Henry Willes Chitty, 2 Bt (d 1955); *b* 2 March 1926; *Educ* Winchester, Univ Coll Oxford; *m* 23 Aug 1951, Susan Elspeth Russell (author), da of Rudolph Glossop; 1 s, 3 da; *Heir* s, Andrew Edward Willes Chitty b 20 Nov 1953; *Career* served RN 1944-47, Granada Arts fell Univ of York 1964-65, visiting prof Boston Univ 1969-70; novelist, biographer (pen name: Thomas Hinde); *Style—* Sir Thomas Chitty, Bt; Bow Cottage, West Hoathly, Sussex

CHOAT, Jonathan Martin Cameron; *b* 8 Jan 1940; *Career* mktg: Lever Bros, Texaco, J Lyons, Burmah Oil; co fndr and md Cameron Choat and Partners (PR consultancy); *Style—* Jonathan Choat Esq; The Rookery, Walsham, Le Willows, Bury St Edmunds, Suffolk IP31 3BD; Cameron Choat & Partners, Bury House, 126-128 Cromwell Rd, London SW7 4ET (☎ 071 373 4537)

CHOLERTON, (Frederick) Arthur; CBE (1978); s of Frederick Arthur Cholerton (d 1968), of Stoke-on-Trent, and Charlotte, *née* Wagstaff (d 1968); *b* 15 April 1917; *Educ* Penkhull Sr Sch Stoke-on-Trent; *m* 25 Feb 1939, Ethel, da of late Albert Jackson, of Stoke-on-Trent; 1 s (Frederick Arthur b 1939, d 1940); *Career* footplate London Midland and Scot Railway 1934, ret as engine driver from BR 1977; memb North Staffs Postal Users Advsy Ctee; dir: Univ of Keele Sci Park Ltd, Staffordshire Cable Ltd; chm: N Staffs Hosp Bldg Tst, The Bldg Blocks Appeal, N Staffs Bereavement Centre, Staffs E Euro Constituency Lab Pty, Stoke-on-Trent S Constituency Lab Pty; Staffs CC: memb 1973-89, vice chm 1973-77, oppn ldr 1977-81, chm 1981-89; vice pres: Staffs Community Cncl, Staffs Forum of Vol Orgns; Lord Mayor Stoke-on-Trent 1971-72 (cncl memb 1951-87); Freeman City of Stoke-on-Trent 1989, Hon M Univ of Keele 1988, Freedom of Accra (Ghana) 1988; *Recreations* gardening, serv with voluntary charitable organisations; *Style—* Arthur Cholerton, Esq, CBE; 12 Werburgh Drive, Trentham, Stoke-on-Trent, Staffs ST4 8JP (☎ 0782 657457)

CHOLMELEY, Cecilia, Lady; Cecilia; da of William Henry Ellice, of Ewhurst Manor, Shermanbury, Horsham, Sussex; *m* 23 July 1931, Lt-Col Sir Hugh John Francis Sibthorp Cholmeley, 5 Bt, CB, DSO (d 1 Feb 1964); 1 s; *Style—* Cecilia, Lady Cholmeley; The Dower House, Easton, Grantham, Lincs

CHOLMELEY, Sir Montague John; 6 Bt (UK 1806), of Easton, Lincolnshire; s of Lt-Col Sir Hugh Cholmeley, 5 Bt, CB, DSO (d 1964); *b* 27 March 1935; *Educ* Eton; *m* 18 Oct 1960, Juliet Auriol Sally, yr da of Maj-Gen Sir (Eustace) John Bloss Nelson, KCVO, CB, DSO, OBE, MC, *qv*; 1 s, 2 da (Camilla b 1962, Davina b 1964); *Heir* s, Hugh John Frederick Sebastian Cholmeley b 3 Jan 1968; *Career* Grenadier Gds 1954-64; *Style—* Sir Montague Cholmeley, Bt; Church Farm, Burton le Coggles, Grantham, Lincs (☎ 047 684 329); Easton Hall, Grantham

CHOLMONDELEY, 7 Marquess of (UK 1815); David George Philip Cholmondeley; also Viscount Cholmondeley of Kells (I 1661), Baron Cholmondeley of Namptwich (E 1689), Viscount Malpas and Earl of Cholmondeley (GB 1706), Baron Newborough (I 1715), Baron Newburgh (GB 1716), and Earl of Rocksavage (UK 1815); o s of 6 Marquess of Cholmondeley, GCVO, MC (d 1990); *b* 27 June 1960; *Educ* Eton, La Sorbonne Paris; *Heir* cousin, Charles George Cholmondeley b 1959; *Career* a page of honour to HM The Queen 1974-76; jt Hereditary Lord Great Chamberlain of England 1990-; *Style—* The Most Hon the Marquess of Cholmondeley; Cholmondeley Castle, Malpas, Cheshire (☎ 082 922 202); Houghton Hall, King's Lynn, Norfolk

CHOLMONDELEY, Marchioness of; Lavinia Margaret; *née* Leslie; o da of late Lt-Col John Leslie, DSO, MC, of Appletree Cottage, Brancaster, Norfolk, and Margaret Nanette Helen, *née* Gilliat; *b* 9 Sept 1921; *m* 14 June 1947, 6 Marquess of Cholmondeley, GCVO, MC (d 1990); 1 s, 3 da; *Style—* The Most Hon the Marchioness of Cholmondeley; Cholmondeley Castle, Malpas, Cheshire

CHOLMONDELEY CLARKE, Marshal Butler; s of Maj Cecil Cholmondeley Clarke (d 1924), of Holycross, Co Tipperary, and late Fanny Ethel Carter; *b* 14 July 1919; *Educ* Aldenham; *m* 1947, Joan Roberta, da of late John Kyle Stephens, JP, of Holywood, Co Down; 2 s (Edward, Robert); *Career* slr 1943, ptnr Burton Yeates and Hart slrs 1946-72; pres City of Westminster Law Soc 1971-72, memb Cncl of Law Soc 1966-72; chm: Family Law Ctee 1970-72, Legal Aid Ctee 1972, Chancery Procedure Ctee 1968-72; master of the Supreme Ct of Judicature (Chancery Div) 1973-, ecclesiastical examiner Dio of London, tstee Utd Law Clerks' Soc, ed of The Supreme Ct Practice; *Recreations* reading; *Clubs* Turf; *Style—* Marshal Cholmondeley Clarke, Esq; 16 Cheyne Ct, Flood St, London SW3 5TP; Royal Cts of Justice, Strand, London

CHOMÉ WILSON, Prof Maryse Ingrid; da of Eric Edouard Percy Chomé (d 1979), of Bergerac, France, and Winsome, *née* Coe; *Educ* Ecole de Jeunes Filles Bergerac, Bournemouth Sch for Girls, Royal Acad of Music, Conservatoire de Musique Paris; *m* 23 Aug 1958, Frank Ernest Wilson, s of Frank Harvey Wilson (d 1984), of 22 St Dionis Rd, Fulham, London; 2 s (Douglas Eric Frank b 1959, Nicholas Clyde b 1960); *Career* violoncellist, performer and teacher; princ cello: Walter Gore Ballet Co Orch 1954, Alexandra Chamber Orch (and soloist) 1955, Festival Ballet Orch 1955-57, Royal Ballet Orch 1957-58, Jose Limon American Dance Co Orch 1958; memb: BBC Concert Orch 1958-59, Grissell Piano Quartet 1963, prof of jr exhibitors RAM 1964, prof and examiner of violoncello Trinity Coll of Music 1965, lectr TCM, dep govr American Biographical Inst Res Assoc 1990-; regular performer with ENO until 1980s; hon fell Trinity Coll of Music London; LRAM, ARCM; *Recreations* genealogy, gardening, art; *Clubs* RAM; *Style—* Prof Maryse Chomé Wilson; 61 Twyford Ave, Acton, London W3 9PZ (☎ 081 992 1430); Trinity College of Music, 11-13 Mandeville Place, London W1M 6AW (☎ 071 935 5773)

CHONG, Monica; da of Philip Chong (d 1981), and Margaret, *née* Lau; *b* 16 Jan 1958; *Educ* Maryknoll Sisters Sch Hong Kong, St Catherines Sch Sydney, Chelsea Sch of Art (BA); *Career* PA to Bridget Jacquetty 1977-78, first collection under own label 1978-79, exhibited London Designers Collections 1980-, Tricouille 1983-86; design conslt: Br Caledonian Airways 1985, BUPA 1986, Nat Hosp Nervous Diseases 1988; A Barbie Retrospective Exhibition Paris 1986; judged fashion design competition Portugal on invitation of Portuguese Govt 1987; collections exhibited: City of London presents Br Fashion in Aid of Action Res for Crippled Children 1988, The Clothes Show (BBC 1) 1988; career featured on Orient Express (Channel 4) 1986; *Recreations* collecting antique jewellery and art; *Style—* Ms Monica Chong; 49 Brompton Rd, 2rd Floor, London SW3 (☎ 071 581 9952, fax 071 581 3529, telex 8951859)

CHONG, Dr Sonny Kwang Fook; s of Eugene Ngiap Lye Chong, of Malacca, Malaysia, and Anna Kim Neo, *née* Choo; *b* 18 Oct 1949; *Educ* St Francis Institution and HS Melacca, Faculty of Med Univ Malaya (MMed, MSc, MD); *m* 20 April 1974, Valerie Yee May, da of Yang Seong Teck (d 1964); 2 s (Christopher b 12 April 1985, Mervyn b 15 Nov 1988), 2 da (Natalie b 27 July 1978, Natasha b 5 July 1983); *Career* paediatric registrar Westminster Childrens Hosp London 1980, CIRCA fell in paedatric gastroenterology St Barts Hosp and hon sr registrar Queen Elizabeth Hosp for Children London 1981, lectr in child health Kings Coll Hosp and Med Sch 1984, conslt paediatrician Gravesend and N Kent Hosp 1988-; visiting prof: Children's Hosp Pittsburgh 1988, Riley Children's Hosp Indianapolis 1989; conslt paediatrician to the Royal Brunei Family; asst hon gen sec: Int Acad of Paediatrics and Trans-disciplinary Educn, Int Coll of Paediatrics 1985-86; memb: Br Paediatric Gastroenterology Soc 1985, Br Soc Immunology 1988-, Br Paediatric Assoc 1982-; Malaysian Br Cwlth fencing team memb 1970-; MRCP 1977; *Recreations* fencing, badminton, classical guitar; *Style—* Dr Sonny Chong; Gravesend & North Kent Hospital, Bath St, Gravesend, Kent DA11 0DG (☎ 0474 564333)

CHOO, Jimmy; s of Kee-Yin Choo, of Penang, Malaysia, and Ah-Yin Moo Choo; *b* 15 Nov 1952; *Educ* Cordwainer Coll; *Career* shoe designer; started own label 1988; conslt and featured on The Clothes Show (BBC), coutouriers worked with incl: Marc Bolan, Bruce Oldfield, Anouska Hempel, Tomas Starzewski; fashion designers worked with incl: Jasper conran, Edina Ronay, Alistar Blair; MSIAD, Royal Chartered Designer; *Style—* Jimmy Choo, Esq; Studio 50, The Metropolitan Workshop, Enfield Rd, London N1 5AZ (☎ 071 249 2082)

CHOPE, Christopher Robert; OBE (1983), MP (Cons) Southampton Itchen 1983-; s of His Hon Judge Robert Charles Chope (d 1988), and Pamela, *née* Durell; *b* 19 May 1947; *Educ* Marlborough, Univ of St Andrews (LLB); *m* Christine, *née* Hutchinson; 1 da; *Career* called to the Bar 1972; ldr Wandsworth Borough Cncl 1979-83 (memb 1974-83); Parly under-sec of state: DOE 1986-90, Dept of Transport 1990-; *Style—* Christopher Chope, Esq, OBE, MP; House of Commons, London SW1

CHORARIA, (Bhim) Raj; s of Shri Panna Lal Choraria (d 1956), of Panna Estate, Nagaur, and Shrimati Naini Devi, *née* Sancheti (d 1975); *b* 16 Nov 1936; *Educ* Presidency Coll Calcutta, The Med Coll Calcutta (MB BS), Gujrat Univ (MD), Univ of Aberdeen (DMRD); *m* 1 July 1963, Vimala, da of Shri KM Jain (d 1960), of Jodhpur, India; 1 s (Sumeet b 1972), 2 da (Roopali b 1966, Sonali b 1971); *Career* NCC India 1955-60; personal physician to Mr JK Birla Delhi 1964-66, chief radiologist SDM Hosp cum Med Res Inst Jaipur 1972-76, sr registrar Glasgow Royal Infirmary 1981-85, conslt radiologist Tameside Gen Hosp 1985-; memb: ODA, BMA; MRCS; *Recreations* yoga, ballroom dancing; *Clubs* Forum Ballroom Dancing; *Style—* Raj Choraria, Esq; Tameside General Hospital, Fountain St, Ashton-under-Lyne, Lancs (☎ 061 330 8373 ext 6556)

CHORLEY, Francis Kenneth (Frank); CBE (1982); s of Francis Henry Chorley (d 1981), and Eva Ellen, *née* Veale; *b* 29 July 1926; *Educ* Rutlish Sch Merton; *m* 1954, Lorna Stella Brooks; 2 s (Julian Francis b 2 Aug 1957, Marcus Jeremy b 10 April 1961); *Career* Plessey Co 1951-60, tech dir Epsylon Industries 1960-63, div mangr GEC Electronics Ltd 1963-64, dir and gen mangr then md GEC-AEI Electronic Ltd 1964-67, dir and gen mangr GEC-AEI Telecommunications Ltd 1967-74; md Plessey Avionics & Communications Ltd 1974-78, md and dep chm Plessey Electronic Systems Ltd 1979-83, exec chm Plessey Telecommunications and Office Systems Ltd 1983-86, dep chief exec The Plessey Co plc 1983-86 (memb Bd 1978-86) non-exec dir Pirelli Focum Ltd 1987-; chm: 3 Net Ltd 1987-, Waycom Holdings Ltd 1989-; pt/t memb Bd CAA 1987; memb: Cncl CGLI 1983-, Engrg Cncl 1986-; pres IERE 1987-88, former pres IEE, vice pres TEMA 1986-87; winner Princ Philip medal CGLI 1983; Freeman City of London; Liveryman: Worshipful Co of Scientific Instrument Makers, Worshipful Co of Engrs; FInstD, FEng, FIEE, FRSA, CBIM; *Recreations* photography, music, sailing; *Clubs* East India, Royal Air Force Yacht; *Style—* Frank Chorley, Esq, CBE; 15 Crown Reach, Grosvenor Rd, London SW1V 3JY (☎ 071 828 5824); The Stabling, London Rd, Headbourne Worthy, Winchester, Hants SO23 7JJ (☎ 0962 882349)

CHORLEY, Richard Abdiel; VRD (1964); s of William Samuel Chorley (d 1971), of Bowdon, Cheshire, and Grace Caroline Emma, *née* Moss (d 1982); *b* 4 Jan 1923; *Educ* Altrincham GS, Univ of Manchester (BScTech); *m* 26 July 1948, (Kathleen) Joanna, da of Gp Capt Alfred Hugh Stradling, DSO, of Willingdon, Sussex; 1 s (Simon b 1953), 2 da (Susan b 1951, Alison b 1955); *Career* RNVR: Electrical Sub Lt 1944-46, Lt 1949-57, Lt Cdr 1957-58; Lt Cdr RNR 1958-64; res engr Metro Vickers Electrical Co 1947-51, asst chief electrical engr British Messier Ltd 1951-55, res gp mangr Smiths Industries Aerospace & Defence Systems Ltd 1955-84, memb Alvey Directorate DTI 1984-86; chm: Tewkesbury and Dist Choral Soc, Music Vera Cheltenham; hon asst organist Tewkesbury Abbey; MIEE 1951; *Recreations* music, walking, swimming; *Style—* Richard Chorley, Esq; Monastery Cottage, Abbey Precinct, Tewkesbury, Gloucs GL20 5SR (☎ 0684 293 063)

CHORLEY, Prof Richard John; s of Walter Joseph Chorley (d 1952) of Bridgwater, Somerset, and Ellen Mary, *née* Ketnor (d 1965); *b* 4 Sept 1927; *Educ* Minehead GS, Univ of Oxford (MA), Univ of Cambridge (ScD); *m* 11 Sept 1965, Rosemary Joan Macdonald, da of David George More (d 1986), of Cambridge; 1 s (Richard b 1966), 1 da (Eleanor b 1968); *Career* Nat Serv Lt RE 1946-48; instr: in geography Columbia Univ NY 1952-54, in geology Brown Univ USA 1954-57; Univ of Cambridge: demonstrator in geography 1958, lectr 1963, reader in geography, hominen chair in geography, head Dept of Geography 1984-89, vice master Sidney Sussex Coll Cambridge 1990-; memb Cncl RGS, pres Cambridge branch Geographical Assoc, corresponding memb Italian Geographical Soc; *Books* incl: The History of the Study of Landforms (jtly, 1964), Atmosphere, Weather and Climate (jtly, 1968), Spatial Analysis in Geography (ed jtly, 1971), Directions in Geography (ed jtly, 1973), Environmental Systems, Philosophy, Analysis and Control (Jtly, 1978), Geomorphology (jtly, 1984); *Recreations* gardening, genealogy; *Style—* Prof Richard Chorley; 76 Grantchester Meadows, Cambridge CB3 9JL; Dept of Geography, University of Cambridge, Downing Place, Cambridge CB2 3EN (☎ 0223 333399)

CHORLEY, 2 Baron (UK 1945); Roger Richard Edward Chorley; s of 1 Baron Chorley, QC (d 1978); *b* 14 Aug 1930; *Educ* Stowe, Gonville and Caius Coll Cambridge (BA); *m* 31 Oct 1964, Ann Elizabeth, yr da of late Archibald Scott Debenham, of Ingatestone, Essex; 2 s (Hon Nicholas Rupert, Hon Christopher Robert Hopkinson b 1968); *Heir* s, Hon Nicholas Rupert Chorley b 15 July 1966; *Career* memb: Royal Cmmn on the Press 1975-78, Ordnance Survey Advsy Bd 1982-85, Bd British Cncl 1981- (vice chm 1991-); ptnr Coopers & Lybrand (CA) 1967-89; pres Royal Geographical Soc 1987-90, chm Nat Tst 1991-; FCA; *Style—* The Rt Hon the Lord Chorley; House of Lords, London SW1

CHOULARTON, Elizabeth Michèle; da of Bernard Taylor, and Pauline Elizabeth, *née* Stephenson; *b* 4 Feb 1955; *Educ* Cransley Sch, Altrincham GS; *m* 20 Oct 1982, Stephen Derek Choularton, s of Cyril Powell Choularton (d 1984); 2 s (Michael Alexander b 1984, Matthew Taylor); *Career* dir: Girl of Mann Ltd, Choulartons plc; *Style—* Mrs Elizabeth Choularton; Choulartons plc, 1 Pudding Lane, London EC3R 8AB (☎ 071 283 7671, fax 071 283 4869)

CHOULARTON, Stephen Derek; s of Cyril Choularton; *b* 29 March 1949; *Educ* Monte Rosa Montreux; *m* 1982, Elizabeth, *née* Taylor; 1 s; *Career* banker; William Deacons Bank Ltd 1965, Henry Cooke and Son 1968, md C P Choularton Sons and Ptnrs Ltd (dir 1970-83), chm Choularton plc; *Style—* Stephen Choularton, Esq; 24 Clavendon Gardens, London W9 1AZ (☎ 071 283 7671)

CHOVIL, (Edward) Roger Clive; s of Clive Newey Chovil (d 1978), and Marjorie Mary, *née* Coffey; *b* 29 Sept 1945; *Educ* Shrewsbury; *m* Elizabeth Alison Mary, da of Roger Petitpierre; 3 c (Lucy Elizabeth Patricia b 1976, Tania Kate Marie b 1978, Charles Roger Michael b 1980); *Career* ptnr Cooper & Lybrand Deloitte 1978 (joined 1965); Freeman City of London; FCA; *Clubs* RAC; *Style—* Roger Chovil, Esq; Coopers & Lybrand Deloitte, PO Box 207, 128 Queen Victoria St, London EC4P 4JX (☎ 071 454 4595, fax 071 489 1651)

CHOWN, Christopher Richard; s of Dr Charles Stanley Malcolm Chown, of Bets-y-Coed, Gwynedd, and Elisabeth Annan, *née* Dickson (d 1978); *b* 29 June 1957; *m* 26 June 1988, Gunna, da of Heine Á Troǿdni (d 1987), of Groǿnlandsfekagid, Faroe Islands; 1 step s (Peder b 7 June 1970) 1 step da (Tania b 29 May 1966); *Career* audit jr Peat Marwick Mitchell 1980-81, rebuilt and converted derelict house in Clapham 1982-83, kitchen asst teacher La Petite Cuisine Sch of Cookery Richmond 1983-84, commis chef Terrace Restaurant Dorchester 1984, sous chef Restaurant Riesbächli Zürich Switzerland 1984-85; converted and opended Plas Bodegroes 1986; *awards* Good Food Guide Gwynedd Newcomer of the Year 1988, Michelin Red M 1989, Taste of Wales Restaurant of the Year 1990, Good Food Guide Highest Rated Restaurant in Wales 1990 and 1991, AA Guide Rosette for Cooking 1991, Michelin Star 1991 (the only one in Wales); memb NE Wales Tourism Mktg Bureau 1986-, treas Llyn Peninsula Tourist Assoc 1986-88, memb Taste of Wales 1989-; *Recreations* photography, architecture, gardening, music and opera; *Style—* Christopher Chown, Esq; Plas Bodegroes Ltd, Pwllheli, Gwynedd LL53 5TH (☎ 0758 612363, fax 0758 612363)

CHOYCE, Prof (David) Peter; s of Prof Charles Coley Choyce, CMG, CBE (d 1937), and Gwendolen Alice, *née* Dobbing (d 1957); *b* 1 March 1919; *Educ* Stowe, UCL (BSc, MB BS), UCH (MS), Moorfields Eye Hosp and Inst of Ophthalmology London; *m* 3 Sept 1949, Diana, da of Thomas Nadin (d 1978), of Leigh on Sea; 3 s (Jonathan b 1951, David Gregory b 1955, Matthew Quentin b 1963); *Career* med offr HM Tports 1942-46; served N and S Atlantic, Caribbean, Med, Indian Ocean; world authority on: intraocular lenses and implants, refractive surgery, tropical ophthalmology; Hunterian prof RCS, overseas conslt Dept of Ophthalmology Henry Ford Hosp Detroit; hon memb: Int Intraocular Implant Club, American UK Japanese and Yugoslav Implant Socs; conslt in ophthalmology: Southend on Sea Gp Hosps 1953-84, Hosp Tropical Diseases 1953-88; Palealogus Award Kerato Refractive Soc 1986; Liveryman Worshipful Soc of Apothecaries; FRSM 1942, FRCS 1947, FCOphth 1988; *Books* Intra-Ocular Lenses and Implants (1964); *Recreations* golf, history, food and wine, the opposite sex; *Clubs* Rochford Hundred Golf, Moor Park Golf; *Style—* Prof Peter Choyce; 9 Drake Road, Westcliff on Sea, Essex SS0 8LR (☎ 0702 343 810, fax 0702 342 611); 45 Wimpole St, London WIM 7DG (☎ 071 935 3411); Vila Colunata, Praia da Luz, Algarve, Portugal

CHRISFIELD, Lawrence John (Larry); s of Sydney George Chrisfield (d 1977), and Minnie, *née* Underwood; *b* 31 March 1938; *Educ* St Saviors GS; *m* Patricia Maureen, *née* Scoble; 4 c (Cindy Jane b 1961, Susan Melinda b 1962, Carol Ann b 1964, David Alexander b 1967); *Career* Merrett Son and Street 1955-63 (articled clerk, accountant), Arthur Young McClelland Moores & Co 1963-72 (tax sr, mangr), UK tax mangr Unilever plc 1972-74, ptnr Arthur Young (now Ernst & Young) 1975- (mangr 1974-75); FCA 1963, ATII 1963; *Recreations* amateur dramatics, photography; *Style—* Larry Chrisfield, Esq; 121 King George St, Greenwich, London SE10 8PX (☎ 081 858 5147); Ernst & Young, Becket House, 1 Lambeth Palace Rd, London SE1 7EU (☎ 071 928 2000, fax 071 401 2136)

CHRISTIAN, Hon Mrs (Margaret Anne); *née* Mackay; da of 13 Lord Reay; *b* 13 March 1941; *m* 1976, Allen Leslie Christian, of Chicago and Florida; *Style—* The Hon Mrs Christian; Buttonwood Bay AA8, Key Largo, Florida, USA; Upper Huntlywood, Earlston, Berwickshire

CHRISTIAN, Nigel Robin Gladwyn; s of Geoffrey Gladwyn Christian (d 1960), of 9 Cadogan Square, London, and Patricia Wynne Cavendish, *née* Shelly (d 1988); *b* 4 Aug 1942; *Educ* Harcourt Sch, Cranleigh; *m* 22 July 1972, Susan Anne Leila, da of Col Robert de Lisle King, CBE, of Berries Maple Cottage, Smarden, nr Ashford Kent; 2 s (Alexander b 1974, Edward b 1981), 1 da (Annabel b 1977); *Career* Price Forbes 1960-61, Lambert Bros 1962-64; dir: Leslie & Godwin Ltd 1987- (joined 1964, asst dir 1972), Leslie & Godwin Aviation Ltd 1980, dep chm Leslie and Godwin Aviation Holdings Ltd 1989-, dir Leslie & Godwin International Ltd 1990-; *Recreations* gardening, golf, tennis, sailing, skiing; *Clubs* Rye Golf; *Style—* N R G Christian, Esq; Leslie and Godwin, PO Box 219, 6 Braham St, London E1 8ED (☎ 071 480 7200, fax 071 480 7450, telex 8950221 CORPO G)

CHRISTIAN, Reginald Frank; of Herbert Alexander Christian (d 1965), of Liverpool, and Jessie Gower, *née* Scott (d 1969); *b* 9 Aug 1924; *Educ* Liverpool Inst, Queen's Coll Oxford (MA); *m* 29 March 1952, Rosalind Iris, da of Capt Malcolm Napier (d 1973), of Brockenhurst, Hants; 1 s (Giles Nicholas b 1955), 1 da (Jessica Ilott b 1953); *Career* WWII Flying Offr 231 Sqdn and Atlantic Ferry Unit RAF 1943-46; FO Br Embassy Moscow 1949-50, lectr in Russian Univ of Liverpool 1951-55, prof of Russian and head of dept Univ of Birmingham 1955-56 (former sr lectr), assoc dir Centre for

Russian and E European Studies 1963-66, visiting prof McGill Univ Montreal 1961-62, visiting prof Moscow 1964-65, prof of Russian and head of dept Univ of St Andrews 1966- (dean faculty of arts), memb Int Ctee of Slavists; vice pres Assoc of Teachers of Russian 1959-, pres Br Univs Assoc of Slavists 1975-78; *Books* Korolenko's Siberia (1954), Russian Syntax (1957), Tolstoy's War and Peace (1961), Russian Prose Composition (1962), Tolstoy - A Critical Introduction (1969), Tolstoy's Letters (ed and trans, 1978), Tolstoy's Diaries (ed and trans, 1985); *Recreations* violin, hill-walking; *Style*— Prof Reginald Christian; University of St Andrews, St Andrews, Fife (☎ 0334 76161)

CHRISTIANS, Sharon Jane; da of John Hlywka (d 1982), and Rose Theresa, *née* Yastremski (d 1990); *b* 6 Oct 1951; *Educ* Notre Dame Coll Sch Canada, Carleton Univ of Ottawa Canada (BA); *m* 28 Aug 1988, Ian Douglas Christians, s of Douglas Tamplin Christians, of Swansea, Wales; *Career* researcher and speech writer House of Commons Ottawa Canada 1972-75, dir Ontario Youth Secretariat 1975-76, fed affrs analyst Canadian Inst of CA 1976-78; dir public affrs: Northern Pipeline Agency Alaska Highway Gas Pipeline Project Canada 1978-80, Ontario Energy Corporation 1980-82; mangr International Communications General Electric USA 1982-88; dir corporate affrs: Thorn EMI plc 1988-90, Stanhope Properties plc 1990-; assoc memb IOD 1988, FRSA 1990; *Recreations* Russian studies, Georgian period furniture, 18th century Dutch painters, tennis, gardening, languages; *Style*— Mrs Sharon Christians; Director, Stanhope Properties plc, Lansdowne House, Berkeley Square, London W1X 6BP (☎ 071 495 7575, fax 071 495 3330, car 0831 582321)

CHRISTIE, (Forrest) Brian; s of Lt-Col George Hewitt Christie (d 1951), of Eastbourne, and Audrey Maude, *née* Forrest (d 1959); *b* 10 Jan 1934; *Educ* Tonbridge, Univ of London (BDS, DOrth); *m* 28 July 1962, Jennifer Anne, da of Gp Capt John Gilbert Wigley (d 1979), of Epsom, Surrey; 1 s (Rawdon b 1967), 1 da (Nicola b 1966); *Career* conslt orthodontist 1972-75: Glasgow Dental Hosp, Royal Hosp for Sick Children Glasgow, Plastic Surgery Unit Canniesburn Glasgow; conslt orthordontist Stoke Mandeville Hosp and Wycombe Gen Hosp 1975-, chm Paisley and Aylesbury Sections BDA; memb; ctee several amateur operatic societies, Craniofacial Soc; memb: FDS, FRcsED, FRCS; *Books* contrib: Surgery in Infancy and Childhood (ed W H Dennison, 1971), Plastic Surgery in Infancy and Childhood (ed J C Mustarde and I T Jackson); *Recreations* music, fell walking, golf; *Clubs* 250, Chesterton Golf; *Style*— Brian Christie, Esq; Dept of Oral Surgery and Orthodontics, Stoke Mandeville Hospital, Aylesbury, Bucks (☎ 0296 84111)

CHRISTIE, Campbell; s of Thomas Christie (d 1944), and Johnina, *née* Rolling (d 1965); *b* 23 Aug 1937; *Educ* Albert Senior Secdy Sch Glasgow, Langside Coll Glasgow, Woolwich Poly London; *m* 2 Feb 1963, Elizabeth Brown, da of Alexander Cameron (d 1968); 2 s (Andrew Cameron b 1963, Douglas Campbell b 1965); *Career* RN 1956-58; Civil Serv: Admiralty 1954-59, DHSS 1959- 72; Soc of Civil and Public Servants 1972-85 (dep gen sec 1975-85), gen sec Scottish TUC 1986-, visiting prof Glasgow Coll of Techol; memb Bd: Wildcat Theatre Co, Scottish Nat Orchestra, Theatre Royal Opera, Lothian Enterprise Bd; memb: EEC Economic and Social Ctee, Scottish Economic Cncl, NEDC EDC for Electronic Industs; *Recreations* golf; *Clubs* Glenbenvie Golf; *Style*— Campbell Christie, Esq; 31 Dumyat Drive, Falkirk FK1 5PA (☎ 0324 24555); 16 Woodlands Terrace, Glasgow G5 (☎ 041 332 4946)

CHRISTIE, David Henderson; s of Lt-Col Frederick Crawford Christie (d 1986), and Audrey, *née* Henderson (d 1986); *b* 25 March 1949; *Educ* Oundle, Univ of Liverpool (BCom); *m* 16 Sept 1978, Catherine Mary Scott (Kate), da of Sir John Cobb (d 1977); 2 da (Emma b 26 Jan 1981, Celia b 5 Aug 1983); *Career* called to the Bar Inner Temple 1973, in practice SE Circuit; specialities: civil and criminal fraud, commercial, matrimonial fin; *Recreations* sailing, golf, reading; *Style*— David Christie, Esq; 1 Essex Court, Temple, London EC4Y 9AR (☎ 071 936 3030, fax 071 583 1606)

CHRISTIE, Sir George William Langham; DL (E Sussex 1983); s of John Christie, CH, MC (d 1962), and Audrey, *née* Mildmay (d 1953); *b* 31 Dec 1934; *Educ* Eton, Trinity Coll Cambridge; *m* 8 Aug 1958, (Patricia) Mary, da of late Ivor Percy Nicholson, and step da of Cdr Alan McGaw; 3 s (Hector b 1961, Augustus b 1963, Ptolemy (Tolly) b 1971), 1 da (Louise b 1966); *Career* exec chm Glyndebourne Productions Ltd 1956-, fndr chm London Sinfonietta 1968-88; Cavaliere al Merito della Repubblica Italiana 1977, hon doctorate in music Univ of Sussex 1990; hon FRCM 1986, hon FRNCM 1986; kt 1984; *Style*— Sir George Christie, DL; Glyndebourne, Lewes, E Sussex BN8 5U8 (☎ 0273 812321, fax 0273 812783, telex 877862 GLYOP G)

CHRISTIE, Prof Ian Ralph; s of John Reid Christie (d 1948), and Gladys Lillian, *née* Whatley (d 1987); *b* 11 May 1919; *Educ* Royal GS Worcester, Magdalen Coll Oxford (BA, MA); *Career* RAF Equipment Branch 1940-46, cmmnd 1942; Foreign Serv: W Africa 1943-44, India 1945-46; univ teacher; UCL: asst lectr history 1948, lectr 1951, reader 1960, prof modern Br history 1966, dean of arts 1971-73, chm History Dept 1975-79, Astor prof of Br history 1979-84; memb Ed Bd of The History of Parl Tst 1973-; FRHistS: literary dir 1964-70, cncl memb 1970-74; FBA 1977; *Books* The End of North's Ministry 1780-82 (1958), Wilkes, Wyvill and Reform (1962), Crisis of Empire (1966), Myth and Reality in Late Eighteenth Century British Politics (1970), The Correspondence of Jeremy Bentham Vol 3 (ed, 1971), Empire or Independence (with B W Labaree, 1976), Bibliography of British History 1789-1851 (with Lucy M Brown, 1977), Wars and Revolutions, Britain 1760-1815 (1982), Stress and Stability in Late Eighteenth-Century Britain (1984); *Style*— Prof Ian R Christie; 10 Green Lane, Croxley Green, Herts WD3 3HR (☎ 0923 773008)

CHRISTIE, Lady Jean Agatha; *née* Dundas; yst da of 2 Marquess of Zetland; *b* 4 May 1916; *m* 2 Sept 1939, Capt Hector Lorenzo Christie, MBE (d 1969), o s of William Lorenzo Christie, JP, of Jervaulx Abbey; 1 s, 1 da; *Style*— The Lady Jean Christie; Seven Springs, Upper Lambourn, Berks

CHRISTIE, John Belford Wilson; CBE (1981); s of John Aitken Christie (d 1928), and Mary, *née* Belford (d 1932); *b* 4 May 1914; *Educ* Merchiston Castle Sch, St John's Coll Cambridge (BA), Univ of Edinburgh (LLB); *m* 14 Sept 1939, Christine Isobel Syme, da of Rev John Thomas Arnott (d 1920); 4 da (Jennifer b 1940, Catrine (Mrs Waller) b 1942, Ann (Mrs Henry) b 1943, Francesca (Mrs Dawson) b 1955); *Career* WWII RNVR, Active Serv 1939-46, asst sec to Flag Offr Levant and E Med 1945; admitted Faculty of Advocates 1939, Sheriff Subst Western Div Dumfries and Galloway 1948-55, Sheriff Tayside Central and Fife (formerly Perth and Angus of Dundee 1955-83; hon lectr Dept of Private Law Univ of Dundee; memb: Queens Coll Cncl Univ of St Andrews 1960-67, Univ Ct Univ of Dundee 1967-75, Parole Bd for Scot 1967-73; Hon LLD Univ of Dundee 1977; Knight of the Order of the Holy Sepulchre of Jerusalem 1987; *Recreations* golf; *Clubs* New (Edinburgh), Royal and Ancient (St Andrews); *Style*— John Christie, Esq, CBE; Annsmuir Farm, Ladybank, Fife (☎ 0337 304 80)

CHRISTIE, John Ireland; s of John Ireland Christie, of Tanadice Court, Clepington St, Dundee, and Catherine Duke, *née* McDonald; *b* 8 May 1962; *Educ* Menziehill HS, Kingsway Tech Coll; *m* 24 June 1989, Angela, da of William McGoldrick, of 33a Inver Terrace, Muirhead, By Dundee; 2 s (Barry John Ireland b 16 Jan 1983, Jordan James Doyle b 18 May 1990), 1 da (Lisa Victoria b 24 Sept); *Career* hockey player; 52 int hockey caps for Scotland; Silver Medal Under 21 Euro Championships, top goalscorer indoor hockey in Scotland 1985-89, most goals scored in one game indoor (21), most goals scored in season (265 in 63 games); plays for NMP Menzieshill: Midlands League winners 1978-89, Glenfiddich winners 1985 and 1988, League and Cup winners 1988; *Style*— John Christie, Esq; 231 Dochart Terrace, Dundee, Scotland (☎ 0382 68195); 353 Clepington Rd, Dundee (☎ 0382 23141 ext 4793)

CHRISTIE, Linford; MBE (1990); *b* 2 April 1960; *Career* athlete; full UK int 1980-; achievements at 100m: UK champion 1985, 1987,1990, AAA champion 1986, 1988, 1989, Gold medal Euro Championships 1986 and 1990, Gold medal Cwlth Games 1990 (Silver medal 1986), Gold medal Euro Cup 1987 and 1989, Silver medal Olympic Games 1988, Gold medal World Cup 1989; achievments at 200m: AAA indoor champion 1981, 1982, 1987, 1988, 1989, UK champion 1985 and 1988, AAA champion 1988, Gold medal Euro Indoor Championships 1986 (Bronze 1988), Gold medal Euro Cup 1987, Bronze medal Euro Championships 1990; achievments at 60m: Gold medal Euro Indoor Championships 1986, AAA indoor champion 1989 and 1990; also winner various 4 x 100m relay medals; UK records: 600m, 100m, 200m, 4 x 100m relay (also Cwlth record); Male Athlete of the Year Br Athletics Writers' Assoc 1988; involved with various charities incl: Westminster Drugs Project, Nat Assoc of Boy's Clubs, Nat Assoc of Youth Clubs; Freeman Borough of Hammersmith and Fulham 1988; contrib monthly column Athletics Today; *Books* Linford Christie: An Autobiography (1989); *Style*— Linford Christie, MBE; Amateur Athletic Association, Edgbaston House, 3 Duchess Place, off Hagley Road, Edgbaston, Birmingham B16 8NM (☎ 021 456 4050)

CHRISTIE, Nigel Bryan; s of Wing Cdr George Edward Bryan Christie (d 1961), and Hilda Nevyth Sheila, *née* Warr; *b* 30 Dec 1948; *Educ* Trinity Coll Glenalmond, Univ of St Andrews (MA), program for mgmnt devpt Harvard Sch of Business Admin; *m* 1974, Catriona Rowena Beveridge, da of Capt Robert Ronald Beveridge Mackenzie; 2 s (Roderick b 1977, Gavin b 1979); *Career* md Kidder Peabody International Ltd; FCA; *Recreations* golf, tennis, skiing; *Clubs* Royal and Ancient Golf, Hurlingham, Racquet (New York), Stanwich (Greenwich, Connecticut, USA); *Style*— Nigel Christie, Esq; 115 Abbotsbury Rd, London W14 8EP; Kidder Peabody International Ltd 107 Cheapside, London EC2V 6DD (☎ 071 480 8409)

CHRISTIE, Mrs M J G; Philippa; *see*: Pearce, Miss Philippa

CHRISTIE, Dr Socrates Panteles; s of Pantelis Christodou Lides Christe of Pantele Christie, and Olga *née* Hellenas; *b* 26 Jan 1920; *Educ* Univ of Athens (Dip), Univ of London (BSc, PhD); *m* 1950, Erasmia-Emma, da of Sir R Stakis; 1 s (John Alexander), 4 da (Katrina Olga, Daphne Anastasia, Pandora Elisa, Latona Flora Anna); *Career* civil engr Errochty Hydroelectric Scheme 1948-49, sr civil/structural engr Br London Midland Region 1950-51, Richard Costain 1950-55, fndr SP Christie and Partners (princ ptnr) 1950-, UCL lectr in engrg 1955-80; fndr Worshipful Co of Constructors (former master), memb Worshipful Co of Paviors; FICE, FISTtructE, MConsE, FFB, FIArb, MINSTHE, MSocCE, FRSA; Freeman City of London; St Andrews Cross of the Greek Orthodox Patriarch in Constantinople; *Recreations* fishing, gardening; *Clubs* St Stephens and Constitutional, RAG, IOD; *Style*— Dr Socrates Christie; 23 Bloomsbury Square, London WC1A 2PJ (☎ 071 636 3867, fax 071 631 0309, car 214799/371810)

CHRISTIE, Stuart; s of Samuel Albert Christie (d 1977), and Alice Duncan, *née* Fellows; *b* 26 Nov 1934; *Educ* Liverpool Inst HS, Univ of Liverpool (LLB); *m* 1972, Elizabeth Mary, da of late His Hon Edward Steel; 2 c (Elspeth Victoria b 19 Nov 1976, Iain Duncan b 17 Feb 1978); *Career* Nat Serv RA 1959-61; Alsop Stevens & Co (now Alsop Wilkinson): articled clerk 1954-58, asst slr 1958-59 and 1961-63, ptnr 1963-; memb City of London Slrs' Co, Freeman City of London (by purchase); memb: The Law Soc, The Notaries Soc; *Recreations* choral singing (Royal Liverpool Philharmonic Choir); *Clubs* Athenaeum (Liverpool); *Style*— Stuart Christie, Esq; 70 Knowsley Rd, Cressington Park, Liverpool L19 OPG (☎ 051 427 3760); Alsop Wilkinson, India Buildings, Water St, Liverpool L2 ONH (☎ 051 227 3060)

CHRISTIE, Terry; s of Peter Christie (d 1968), of Edinburgh, and Bridget, *née* McGreevy; *b* 16 Dec 1942; *Educ* Holy Cross Acad, Univ of Edinburgh (BSc); *m* 1, 1965, Margaret Elizabeth, da of John Ferguson; 2 s (Kevan John b 18 Sept 1968, Martin Peter b 7 Nov 1971); m 2, 1988, Susan Dorothy, da of Charles Forbes; 1 da (Carol b 20 March 1987); *Career* football manager and school teacher; player: Dundee 1960-65, Raith Rovers 1965-66, Hawick Royal Albert 1966-68, Stirling Albion 1968-74, Newtongrange 1974-78 (player-mangr); Meadowbank Thistle: asst mangr 1978-80, mangr 1980-, dir 1983-; full time teacher 1966-; head teacher: Ainslie Park HS 1982-87, Musselburgh GS 1987-; *Recreations* golf, reading, social drink, good company; *Style*— Terry Christie, Esq; 76 Meadow Field Terrace, Edinburgh EH8 7NU (☎ 031 661 1486)

CHRISTIE, Timothy John Alexander; s of Michael Alexander Hunter Christie, and Pamela Mary, *née* Du Sautoy (d 1987); *b* 2 June 1943; *Educ* Radley, London Business Sch; *m* 27 Jan 1966, Annabelle Bronson, da of Sir Donald Albery (d 1988); 3 s (Oliver b 1971, Nicholas b 1973, William b 1977); *Career* mktg exec London Press Exchange Ltd 1963-64, mktg res exec Honda (UK) Ltd 1964-65, account exec London Press Exchange Ltd 1966-67, account rep J Walter Thompson Co Ltd 1968-71; Alexander Engineering Co Ltd: mktg mangr 1971-75, mktg dir 1976-81, md 1981-; Freeman City of London 1968, Liveryman Worshipful Co of Coach Makers and Coach Harness Makers 1968; *Recreations* sailing, tennis, skiing; *Clubs* Seaview Yacht; *Style*— Timothy Christie, Esq; Alexander Engneering Co Ltd, Haddenham, Bucks HP17 8BZ (☎ 0844 291 345, fax 0844 291 320, telex 83504)

CHRISTIE, Sir William; MBE (1970), JP (Belfast 1951), DL (Belfast 1977); s of Richard and Ellen Christie, of Belfast; *b* 1 June 1913; *Educ* Ward Sch Bangor N Ireland; *m* 1935, Selina, *née* Pattison; 1 s (and 1 s decd), 2 da; *Career* High Sheriff Belfast 1964-65, Lord Mayor 1972-75 (Dep Mayor 1969), Alderman 1973-77; co dir; kt 1975; *Style*— Sir William Christie, MBE, JP, DL

CHRISTIE, (Eric) William Hunter; s of Harold Alfred Hunter Christie, QC, TD, treas Lincoln's Inn (d 1960), and Norah Agnes Veronica, *née* Brooks (d 1965); gs of Sir William Christie, FRS, Astronomer Royal (by his w Violette, 3 da of Sir Alfred Hickman, 1 Bt, MP), ggs of Prof Samuel Hunter Christie, FRS, and gggs of James Christie (b 1739), of Leicester Sq (collateral of Christie of Durie); *b* 18 Aug 1922; *Educ* Marlborough, RMA Sandhurst; *m* 20 May 1950, Dorothy Ursula Merle, da of Roderick Macleod, of Pippins Toft, Angmering, Sussex (d 1947); 2 s (Robert b 1951, Nial b 1960), 2 da (Fiona b 1956, Catriona b 1968); *Career* Lt Coldstream Gds 1941-43 (wounded); FO: S American Dept 1944-46, 3 sec Br Embassy Buenos Aires 1946-48; Scott Polar Res Inst Cambridge 1948-50; called to the Bar Lincoln's Inn 1952; bencher 1989; memb: Cncl Inland Waterways Assoc 1950-52 (hon life memb 1968), Chelsea Met Borough Cncl 1956-65 (chm Ctees of Cncl); hon sec UK Falkland Island Ctee 1968-76, chm Falkland Island Res and Devpt Assoc Ltd (Falkland Island Off) 1976-83; chm: S Atlantic Fisheries Ctee 1977-82, Falkland Island Assoc 1983-85; memb Ct Worshipful Co of Clockmakers 1968 (Master 1979), pres Br Horological Inst 1979, pres Nat Clock and Watchmakers Benevolent Soc 1979; FBHI; *Books* The Antarctic Problem: An Historical and Political Study (1950), Portrait of Trent in Collection Portraits of Rivers (1953); contributor to legal and specialist publications; *Recreations* country life; *Clubs* Flyfishers'; *Style*— William Christie, Esq; 13 Old Square, Lincoln's Inn, London WC2A 3UA (☎ 071 404 4800, fax Gps 2 and 3 071 405 4267, telex

22487 INNLAW G)

CHRISTIE-BROWN, Jeremy Robin Warrington; s of Robson Christie-Brown (d 1971), and Mildred, *née* Warrington (d 1970); *b* 15 July 1936; *Educ* Harrow, Univ of Oxford (MA), Univ Coll Hosp Med Sch (BM BCh, DPM); *m* 3 Nov 1962, Margaret Elizabeth, da of Frederick Stafford (d 1979); 2 s (Dominic b 9 Oct 1963, Jonathan b 15 Nov 1964), 1 da (Sarah b 3 May 1968); *Career* conslt psychiatrist UCU and Friern Hosp 1971-76, conslt psychiatrist The Maudsley Hosp 1976-; *Style—* Jeremy Christie-Brown, Esq; 11 Sydenham Hill, London SE26 6SH

CHRISTIE-MILLER, Andrew William Michael; o s of Maj Samuel Vandeleur Christie-Miller, CBE (d 1968), of Clarendon Park, Salisbury, and Esmée Antoinette Fraser, *née* Hutcheson; *see* Burke's Landed Gentry, 18 edn, vol II, 1969; *b* 22 Sept 1950; *Educ* Eton, RAC Cirencester (Dip Rural Estate Mgmnt, Dip Advanced Farm Mgmnt); *m* 6 Feb 1976, Barbara, da of Maj Charles Alexander Neil (d 1959), of 18 Lansdowne Road, London W11; 1 s (Alexander William Henry b 1982), 2 da (Rebecca Claire b 1976, Victoria Phoebe b 1978); *Career* Spicer & Pegler 1970-73, Savills 1978-82; memb CLA exec, chm Timber Growers United Kingdom (TGUK); memb Wilts CC 1985-; ARICS 1979; *Recreations* shooting, travel, bicycling, conservation; *Clubs* White's, New (Edinburgh); *Style—* Andrew Christie-Miller, Esq; Clarendon Park, Salisbury, Wilts SP5 3EP (☎ 0722 710217); Estate Office, Clarendon Park, Salisbury, Wilts SP5 3EW (☎ 0722 710233, car 0836 740220)

CHRISTIE-MILLER, Lt-Col John Aylmer; CBE (1960, OBE 1944), TD (1946), DL (Cheshire 1963); s of Sir Geoffry Christie-Miller (d 1969), of Cheshire, and Kathleen Olive, *née* Thorpe (d 1965); *b* 12 Aug 1911; *Educ* Eton; *m* 28 Oct 1939, Bridget Wilbraham, da of Cdr Noel Wilbraham Dixon, OBE, RN (d 1960), of Cheshire; 3 da (Caroline (Mrs Cannon-Brookes) b 1942, Lydia (Mrs McClure) b 1947, Charlotte (Mrs Beatson) b 1949); *Career* WWII Lt-Col Cheshire Regt served: W Desert, N Africa, Sicily, Italy, Germany 1939-45; dir: Christy & Co Ltd 1935-80, Swain & Co Ltd 1946-79; JP 1949-74, High Sheriff 1974-75; pres: Br Felt Hat Manufacturers Fedn 1950-51, Euro Assoc of Hat Manufacturers 1957-64, Stockport and Dist TSB 1969-75; chm Cheshire T and A F A 1965-68; Master Worshipful Co of Feltmakers 1956-57; *Recreations* travel, gardening; *Clubs* Army and Navy; *Style—* Lt-Col John Christie-Miller, CBE, TD, DL; Manor House, Bourton-on-the-Hill, Moreton-in-Marsh, Glos GL56 9AQ (☎ 0386 700642)

CHRISTISON, Gen Sir (Alexander Frank) Philip; 4 Bt (UK 1871), of Moray Place, Edinburgh, GBE (1948, KBE 1944), CB (1943), DSO (1945), MC and Bar (1915, 1917), DL (Roxburghshire 1956); s of Surgn-Gen Sir Alexander Christison, 2 Bt (d 1918); suc half-bro, 3 Bt 1945; *b* 17 Nov 1893; *Educ* Edinburgh Acad, Univ Coll Oxford (BA); *m* 1, 29 Feb 1916, Lizzie Isobel (d 1974), da of Rt Rev Anthony Mitchell, Bishop of Aberdeen and Orkney (d 1917); 1 s (ka Burma 1942), 2 da (and 1 decd); m 2, 1974, Jessie Vida Wallace Smith, MBE; *Career* 2 Lt Cameron Highlanders 1914, cmd to Seaforth Highlanders 1918-19, Lt-Col Duke of Wellington's Regt 1937 (Col 1947-57), cmd Gurkha Bde 1938, Cmdt Staff Coll 1940, Brig Gen Staff 1941, cmd 15 (Scottish) Div 1941-43, Burma Campaign 1943-45, cmd 15 Corps, 14 Army and Allied Land Forces S E Asia, cmd Netherland E Indies Campaign 1945-46, Gen 1947, Col 10 (Princess Mary's Own) Gurkha Rifles 1947-57, ADC Gen to HM The King 1947-49, GOC-in-C Northern Command 1946-47, GOC-in-C Scot Cmd and Govr Edinburgh Castle 1947-49; Hon Col Coast Regt RA 1950-57; dir Cochran and Co Ltd 1950-70, chm Alban Timber Ltd 1953-79; memb Nat Cncl BBC 1965-69; fruit farmer and ornithologist; hon fell Univ Coll Oxford; *Books* Birds of Baluchistan; *Recreations* field sports, ornithology; *Clubs* New (Edinburgh); *Style—* General Sir Philip Christison, Bt, GBE, CB, DSO, MC, DL; The Croft, Melrose, Roxburghshire (☎ 089 682 2456)

CHRISTMAS, Colin Adrian; s of R F Christmas, and M Haskey; *b* 11 Dec 1938; *Educ* Forest Sch, architectural Colls Essex and London; *m* 31 March 1962, Elisa Curling, da of H H Curling Hope; 1 s (Paul b 7 Feb 1968), 1 da (Laura b 14 Oct 1966); *Career* with Sir Giles Gilbert Scott Son and Partner 1959-63; work on: Liverpool Cathedral, Bankside Power Station, Bromsgrove Sch Chapel; Fitzroy Robinson Partnership: designer/planner 1963, ptnr 1987; designs for: shopping, office, residential, industl, leisure and sporting complexes in UK and abroad; designing and implementing extension and refurbishment of Royal Exchange London 1983-91; *Books* The Caliphs Design, edited by Paul Edwards (conslt, 1986); *Recreations* east coast sailing from Queens Head to Ramsholt Arms, music, travel, art; *Style—* Colin Christmas, Esq; 67 Paramount Court, University St, London WC1 6JP (☎ 071 388 2185); The Fitzroy Robinson Partnership, 77 Portland Place, London W1 (☎ 071 636 8033)

CHRISTMAS, Dr David; s of Henry Christmas, Pulley Hall, Lower Pulley Lane, Bayston Hill, Shrewsbury, Shropshire, and Irene Elsie, *née* Teece; *b* 27 April 1953; *Educ* Priory Sch for Boys Shrewsbury, Univ of Birmingham (MB ChB); *m* 12 April 1980, Amanda Victoria Anne, da of Roy Griffiths, of 49 King St, Shrewsbury, Shropshire; 1 s (Matthew b 1982), 1 da (Kate b 1985); *Career* house offr: gen surgery 1976, gen med 1977; conslt in anaesthetics and intensive care Telford Gen Hosp 1989- (sr offr 1977-79, registrar 1979-81, sr registrar 1981-83, conslt in anaesthetics 1984-89); memb: Royal Soc for Nature Conservation, Wildfowl Tst, fell RSPB; fell Coll of Anaesthetists 1980, memb Intensive Care Soc 1983; *Recreations* ornithology; *Style—* Dr David Christmas; The Lodge, Uffington, Shrewsbury, Shropshire SY4 4SQ (☎ 0743 77479); Dept of Anaesthetics, Princess Royal Hospital, Apley Castle, Telford, Shropshire TF6 6TF (☎ 0952 641222)

CHRISTMAS, Elizabeth Mary; MBE (1989); da of Frederick Galway Christmas (d 1938), of Kensington, and Sybil Mary, *née* Christmas (d 1940); *b* 4 May 1926; *Educ* Our Lady of Sion London, Holy Cross Convent Chalfont St Peter Bucks; *Career* WWII FANY 1944-45; private sec to Baroness Pat Hornsby-Smith 1951-55, buyer for Schweppes 1956-65; mayor of RBK & C 1969-70 (cncllr 1952-); vice chm Royal Marsden Hosp 1980-90 (memb Bd 1971-90), memb Bd Brompton Heart and Chest Hosp 1972-90, chm and vice chm of two sch bds 1973-; depot organiser for Royal Br Legion Poppy Appeal Earls Ct Area; *Recreations* tennis, riding; *Clubs* Special Forces, Knightsbridge; *Style—* Miss Elizabeth Christmas, MBE

CHRISTODOULOU, Helen Joan; da of Constantine Christodoulou, MBE (d 1987), of London, and Catherine, *née* Hadjipandeli; *b* 5 Oct 1949; *Educ* Townmead Sch, QMC (LLB); *m* 24 Jan 1981, Demetre Emmanuel Sotiropoulos, s of Emmanuel Sotiropoulos (d 1961), of Lafkos, Greece; 2 s (Nicholas b 6 Dec 1985, Anastasis b 6 June 1989), 1 da (Katherine b 15 May 1983); *Career* called to the Bar Middle temple 1972; memb: Gray's Inn, senate Bar Cncl; *Recreations* travel, theatre, opera, dining out; *Style—* Miss Helen Christodoulou; 17 Delamere Road, Ealing, London W5 3JL (☎ 081 840 1382); 5 Pump Court, Temple, London EC4 (☎ 071 583 7133, fax 071 353 4910)

CHRISTOFAS, Sir Kenneth Cavendish; KCMG (1982, CMG 1969), MBE (1944); o s of late Edward Julius Goodwin (d 1921), and Lillian Christofas, step s of late Alexander Christofas; *b* 18 Aug 1917; *Educ* Merchant Taylors', UCL; *m* 1948, Jessica Laura, da of Thomas Sparshott (d 1953); 2 da; *Career* War Serv 1939-46 (Lt-Col); joined Foreign Serv 1948, min and dep head UK Delegation to the Euro Communities 1969-72; *Recreations* railways, music; *Clubs* East India, Devonshire, Sports and Public Schools; *Style—* Sir Kenneth Christofas, KCMG, MBE; 3 The Ridge, Bolsover Rd, Eastbourne, Sussex BN20 7JE (☎ 0323 22384)

CHRISTOPHER, (Phyllis) Ann; da of William Christopher (d 1986), of Rickmansworth, Herts, and Phyllis, *née* Vennal; *b* 4 Dec 1947; *Educ* Watford Girls GS, Harrow Sch of Art, W of Eng Coll of Art (Dip AD); *m* 19 July 1969, Kenneth Harold Cook, s of Harold Gilbert Cook, of Oldland Common, nr Bristol; *Career* sculptor; numerous gp and solo exhibitions 1969-; works in public collections incl: Bristol City Art Gallery, Univ of Bristol, Glynn Vivienne Art Gallery Swansea, Royal W of Eng Acad, Chantrey Bequest Royal Acad, Harrison Weir Collection London; RWA 1983 (assoc 1972), RA 1989 (assoc 1980); *Recreations* cinema, travel, architecture, gardens; *Style—* Miss Ann Christopher

CHRISTOPHER, Anthony Martin Grosvenor; CBE (1984); s of George Russell Christopher (d 1951), and Helen Kathleen Milford, *née* Rowley (d 1971); *b* 25 April 1925; *Educ* Cheltenham GS, Westminster Coll of Commerce; *m* 1962, Adela Joy Thompson; *Career* IRSF: asst sec 1957-60, asst gen sec 1960-74, jt gen sec 1975, gen sec 1976-88; dir Civil Serv Bldg Soc 1958-87, pres TUC Gen Cncl 1988-89 (memb 1976-89); memb: Bd Civil Serv Housing Assoc 1958 (vice chm 1988), Cncl of Nat Assoc for Care and Resettlement of Offenders 1956 (chm 1973), Home Sec's Advsy Cncl for Probation and After-Care Ctee 1966-79, Home Sec's Working Party on Treatment of Habitual Drunken Offenders 1969-71, Cncl of Policy Studies Inst, Cncl Inst of Manpower Studies, Econ Social Res Cncl 1985-88, TUC Gen Cncl 1976-89, TUC Econ Ctee 1977-89, TUC Educn Ctee 1977-85, TUC Employment Policy and Orgn Ctee 1979-89, TUC Int Ctee 1982-89, TUC Media Working Gp 1979-89 (chm 1985-89), TUC Fin Gen Purposes Ctee 1984-89, TUC Educn and Trg Ctee 1985-86, Tax Consultative Ctee 1974-88, Royal Cmmn on Distribution of Income and Wealth 1979-80, IBA 1978-83, Bdcasting Complaints Cmmn 1989, Audit Cmmn 1989, Gen Med Cncl 1989, Ind Inquiry into Rover Cowley Works Closure Proposals 1990; tstee Inst for Public Policy Res; chm: Trades Union Unit Trust Mangrs Ltd 1983, NEDO Tyre Ind Econ Devpt Ctee 1983-84, Alcoholics Recovery Project 1970-76; *Books* Policy for Poverty (1970), The Wealth Report (jtly, 1979); *Recreations* gardening, reading, music; *Clubs* Wig and Pen; *Style—* Anthony Christopher, Esq, CBE; c/o Lloyds Bank, 130 High St, Cheltenham, Glos GL50 1EW

CHRISTOPHER, John (*né* Sam Youd); s of Sam Youd (d 1966), and Harriet, *née* Hawkins (d 1949); *b* 16 April 1922; *Educ* Peter Symonds Sch; *m* 1, 1946 (m dis 1978), Joyce, *née* Fairbairn; 1 s (Nicholas b 20 June 1951), 4 da (Rose b 1 July 1953, Elizabeth b 14 Sept 1955, Sheila b 27 July 1957, Margret b 11 April 1959); m 2, 24 Dec 1980, Jessica, *née* Ball; *Career* writer; fiction for adults: The Death of Grass (1956), The World in Winter (1962), The Possessors (1965), A Wrinkle in the Skin (1965), The Little People (1966), Pendulum (1968); fiction for young people: The Tripods trilogy (1967-68), The Lotus Caves (1969), The Guardians (1970), The Sword trilogy (1970-72), Dom and Va (1973), Wild Jack (1974), Empty World (1977), The Fireball trilogy (1981-86), When The Tripods Came (1988); Atlantic award in lit 1947, Guardian award 1971, Christopher award 1971, Jugendbuchpreis 1976, George Stone children's books award 1977; memb Soc of Authors 1948-, chm Soc of Authors Children's Writers Gp 1983-85 (memb 1977-); *Recreations* dogless dog walking and counting blessings; *Clubs* United (Guernsey), Royal Channel Islands Yacht (Guernsey), Academy; *Style—* John Christopher, Esq; 1 Whitefriars, Conduit Hill, Rye, East Sussex TN31 7LE (☎ 0797 224557)

CHRISTOPHER, John Anthony; CB (1983); s of John William Christopher (d 1974), and Dorothy, *née* Southwell (d 1983); *b* 19 June 1924; *Educ* Sir George Monoux GS, Univ of London (BSc); *m* 1947, Pamela Evelyn, da of Charles Hardy (d 1971); 1 s (Geoffrey), 1 da (Sheila), and 1 s dec'd; *Career* RAF Flt Lt 1943-47; chartered surveyor; dist valuer Lincoln 1965-72, chief valuer valuation office Inland Revenue and memb Bd of Inland Revenue 1981-84, memb Bd Surveyors Books 1984-; cncl memb RICS 1981-85; FRICS; *Recreations* golf, sailing, music; *Clubs* BSc (Estate Mgmnt (pres 1980-81); *Style—* John Christopher Esq, CB; 40 Svenskaby, Orton Wistow, Peterborough, Cambs PE2 0YZ (☎ 0733 238199)

CHRISTOPHERSEN, (Gunnar) Rolf; DFC (1943); s of Oscar Christophersen (d 1940), of Bromley, Kent, and Sigrid, *née* Myhre (d 1971); *b* 20 Nov 1921; *Educ* Cranleigh Sch, CCC Oxford (MA); *m* 4 Feb 1966, Angela Gwen, da of James Ernest Hadfield (d 1968), of Southport, Lancs; 2 da ((Astrid) Miranda b 1969, Olivia Kirsten b 1971); *Career* Flt Lt RAF 1941-46; chm J John Masters Hldgs Ltd 1973-83; dir: British Match Corporation 1966-74, Wilkinson Match Ltd 1974-81; chm Pipesmokers' Cncl 1982-, vice chm Anglo-Norse Soc 1956-; Master Worshipful Co of Tobacco Pipe Makers and Tobacco Blenders 1980-81; FIOD; *Recreations* sailing, travel, squash, music; *Clubs* RAF Yacht; *Style—* Rolf Christophersen, Esq, DFC; 25 St Ann's Villas, London W11 4RT (☎ 071 603 9089)

CHRISTOPHERSON, Hon Mrs (Griselda Etheldreda Clodagh); *née* O'Brien; 2 da of 15 Baron Inchiquin (d 1929); *b* 19 Oct 1906; *m* 14 March 1953, as his 2 wife, David Clifford Christopherson, DSC, yr s of Henry Clifford Christopherson (d 1973); 2 step-da; *Style—* The Hon Mrs Christopherson; The Dower House, 53 Firs Chase, West Mersea, Colchester, Essex CO5 8NN (☎ 0206 382868)

CHRISTOPHERSON, Romola Carol Andrea; da of Albert Edward Christopherson, and Kathleen, *née* Marfitt; *b* 10 Jan 1939; *Educ* Collegiate Sch for Girls Leicester, St Hugh's Coll Oxford (BA); *Career* DSIR Miny of Technol 1962-70, Dept of Environment 1970-78, MAFF 1978-81, N Ireland Office 1981-83, dep press sec to PM 1983-84, head of info Dept of Energy 1984-86, dir of info Dept of Health (formerly DHSS) 1986-; *Recreations* amateur dramatics, antiques; *Style—* Ms Romola Christopherson; Department of Health, Richmond House, Whitehall, London SW1A 2NS

CHRYSTAL, Prof (Kenneth) Alexander; s of Kenneth Hugh Chrystal (d 1945), and Dorothy Belle, *née* Anderson; *b* 21 Jan 1946; *Educ* Oldershaw GS Wallasey, Univ of Exeter (BA, MA, PhD); *m* 4 April 1972 (m dis 1978); 1 s (Mark Kenneth James b 1972); *Career* lectr: Univ of Manchester 1971-72, civil Serv Coll 1972-75; econ advsr HM Treasy 1975-76, lectr Univ of Essex 1976-84, visiting prof Univ of California at Davis 1979-80, visiting scholar Federal Reserve Bank of St Louis 1983-84, prof economics Univ of Sheffield 1984-88, Nat West Bank prof City Univ Business Sch 1988-; FSS 1967; *Books* Controversies in Macroeconomics (1979), Political economics (with J Alt, 1983), Exchange Rates and the Open Economy (ed with R Sedgwick, 1987); *Recreations* squash, tennis, economics; *Clubs* Hallamshire; *Style—* Prof Alexander Chrystal; 5 Park Ave, Sheffield S10 3EY (☎ 0742 663867); 1 Bunhill Row, London EC2 (☎ 071 628 2953); Department of Banking and Finance, City Univ Business School, Barbican Centre, London EC2Y 8HB (☎ 071 920 0111 ext 2250, fax 071 588 2756)

CHU, Dr Anthony Christopher; s of Yu-Chang Chu, of 11 North Gray Rd, Bexley, Kent, and Frances Nelly Chu; *b* 13 May 1951; *Educ* Alleyn's Sch Dulwich, Guy's Hosp Med Sch (BSc, MB BS); *m* 11 March 1978 (m dis 1987), Sian Meryl, da of John Daniel Griffths, of Hailey Manor, Hailey, Oxon; 2 da (Jessica Louise b 1979, Alexandra Mary b 1980); m 2, 30 Dec 1989, Jenny Frances, da of Robert Morris, of Shrub Farm, Haughley Green, Suffolk; *Career* various posts NHS 1975-80, sr staff assoc coll of physicians and surgns Columbia Presbyterian Hosp New York 1980-81, sr registrar St John's Hosp for Skin Diseases 1981-82; sr lectr (also conslt dermatologist and Wellcome sr res fell): Royal Post Grad Med Sch Hammersmith Hosp, St John's Hosp for Skin Diseases 1982-89; sr lectr and conslt dermatologist: Royal Postgrad Med Sch

Hammersmith Hosp, Ealing Hosp 1989-; memb and sec: Int Histiocyte Soc, Br Assoc of Univ Teachers of Dermatology; Liveryman Worshipful Soc of Apothecaries 1989; MRCP 1978; *Recreations* horticulture, painting; *Style—* Dr Anthony Chu; Unit of Dermatology, Royal Postgraduate Medical School, Hammersmith Hospital, Du Cane Rd, London W12 0NN (☎ 081 740 3264)

CHUBB, Hon Mrs (Barbara); *née* Champion; da of Baron Champion (Life Peer) (d 1985); *b* 14 Dec 1931; *Educ* Pontypridd Girls' GS, Rachel McMillan Training Coll; *m* 10 Aug 1957, Trevor Chubb, s of Robert Rees Chubb (d 1962), of Pontypridd; 3 da (Alison b 1960, Judith b 1963, Claire b 1968); *Recreations* painting; *Style—* The Hon Mrs Chubb; 160 Redland Road, Redland, Bristol, BS6 6YG

CHUBB, Hon Charles Henry Thomas; s of 3 Baron Hayter, KCVO, CBE; *b* 1949; *Educ* Marlborough, King's Coll Cambridge (BA, MA), St Bartholomew's Hosp London (MB BS); *m* 13 Jan 1979, (Ann) Nicola, da of Charles William Stewart French Manning (d 1982); 2 s (Mark Henry b 1980, Jack Charles b 1985), 2 da (Josephine Anne b 1983, Alice Christine b 1989); *Career* principal in gen med practice; memb BMA 1978, MRCGP 1982; *Style—* The Hon Charles Chubb; c/o Kidlington Health Centre, Oxford Road, Kidlington, Oxon OX5 1AP (☎ 08675 5211)

CHUBB, Cdr The Hon David William Early; RN (ret); yr s of 2 Baron Hayter (d 1967); *b* 31 May 1914; *Educ* RNC Dartmouth; *m* 2 Dec 1939, Veronica, da of William Clifton, of Shanghai; 1 s; *Career* Cdr RN (ret), Far E 1939-45 (despatches, POW); *Style—* Cdr the Hon David Chubb, RN

CHUBB, Hon John Andrew; s of 3 Baron Hayter, KCVO, CBE; *b* 20 April 1946; *Educ* Marlborough, Southampton Univ (BSc, MA); *m* 1975, Sandy, da of late Alfred E Brereton; 1 s, 1 da; *Career* dep chief accountant Oxford Univ; Liveryman of Worshipful Co of Weavers; FCA; *Recreations* windsurfing; *Style—* The Hon John Chubb; Manor Farm House, Warborough, Oxon

CHUBB, Hon (George) William Michael; s and h of 3 Baron Hayter, KCVO, CBE; *b* 9 Oct 1943; *Educ* Marlborough, Nottingham Univ (BSc); *m* 8 Jan 1983, Waltraud, yr da of J Flackl, of Sydney, Aust; 1 s (Thomas Frederik b 1986); *Style—* The Hon William Chubb; Mapledurwell House, Mapledurwell, nr Basingstoke, Hants RG25 2LT

CHUCK, Peter John; s of Albert Edward Chuck (d 1955), of London, and Ada Florence, *née* Heming (d 1947); *b* 23 Oct 1930; *m* 2 Feb 1957, Winnifred Kathleen, da of Capt Robert Michie (d 1983), of Cupar, Fife; 1 s (Robert Alistair b 9 Nov 1959), 1 da (Fiona Anne b 9 Nov 1957); *Career* RN 1959; surveyor; Bernard Thorpe 1958-86: ptnr Edinburgh 1959, Paris 1973, Westminster 1975, City of London 1979; Freeman City of London, Liveryman Worshipful Co of Gold & Silver Wyre Drawers 1983; FRICS 1953; *Recreations* golf, philately, foreign travel; *Style—* Peter Chuck, Esq; 3 Broadhurst Close, Richmond, Surrey, TW10 6HU (☎ 081 948 4062)

CHUNN, Louise; da of Jeremiah Alfred Chunn, of 469 Parnell Rd, Auckland 1, New Zealand, and Yvonne Chunn; *b* 24 July 1956; *Educ* St Joseph's Convent Otahuhu NZ, Baradene Coll Remuera NZ, Univ of Aukland NZ (BA); *m* 15 Aug 1981 (sep), Dominic Anthony Free; 1 s (Charlie b 11 March 1986), 1 da (Alice b 23 June 1988); *Career* ed Just Seventeen 1985-86, dep ed Elle 1986-89, ed Guardian Women's Page 1989-; *Style—* Ms Louise Chunn; The Guardian, 119 Farringdon Road, London EC1R 3ER (☎ 071 239 9597)

CHURCH, Ian Berkeley; s of late Leslie Humphreys Church, DSO, TD, of Church Brampton, Northants, and Leila Grace, *née* Berkeley; *b* 23 Jan 1927; *Educ* Stowe; *m* 14 Feb 1956, Elizabeth Anne Linley, da of Lt-Col Linley Francis Messel, TD (d 1980); 1 s, 1 da; *Career* chm Church and Co plc (mfrs and retailers of shoes), dir Faber Prest plc; *Clubs* Bucks; *Style—* Ian Church, Esq; 12 Cranley Mews, London SW7 (☎ 071 373 8278)

CHURCH, Ian D; s of John Jasper (d 1980), of London, and Violet Kathleen, *née* Treacher; *Educ* Roan Sch; *m* 3 Oct 1964, Christine Mabel, da of Arthur Frank Stevenson, of Newick, East Sussex; 1 da (Nicola b 1970); *Career* journalist: Press Assoc 1964-66, The Scotsman 1966-68, The Times 1968-72; Official Report (Hansard): reporter 1972-88, dep ed 1988, ed 1989-; *Recreations* photography, writing fiction; *Style—* Ian Church, Esq; Official Report (Hansard), House of Commons, London SW1A 0AA (☎ 071 219 3388, fax 071 219 3049)

CHURCH, James Victor; s of James Haslem Church, BEM (d 1970), and Elsie Dorothy Church; *b* 22 Oct 1930; *Educ* Alleyn's Sch Dulwich, Rossall Sch Fleetwood; *m* 30 Mar 1957, Janice Violet, da of William Linton, of Hayes, Kent; 2 s (Andrew James b 1959, Jonathan Charles Linton b 1962); *Career* Nat Serv cmmnd RCS 1949-50, TA (Lt) 1950-55; James Capel & Co (incorporating Nathan & Rosselli) 1947-89 (dir 1973-1987); dir James Capel Moneybroking Ltd 1986-89; dir & chm: NHL Second Funding plc, NHL Third Funding plc, NHL First Funding plc, dir Blue Chip Mortgage Passthrough Ltd (No 1); chm: Community Advsy Bd AMI- Sloane Hosp Beckenham, Ravensbourne Light Operatic Soc; ACIS (1953); *Recreations* skiing, bridge, golf; *Clubs* City of London; *Style—* James V Church, Esq

CHURCH, Richard Edmund; s of Cdr William John Patrick Church, DSO, DSC (d 1963), of Weybridge, Surrey, and Rosemary Mary Church (d 1963); *b* 23 June 1950; *Educ* Downside, Trinity Coll Dublin (BA, LLB); *m* 11 Dec 1976, Susan Primrose, da of Maurice Hall, of Farnham, Surrey; 3 s (Andrew b 1977, Francis b 1979, Philip b 1984); *Career* admitted slr 1976; ptnr: Richards Butler 1981-88, More Fisher Brown 1988-; memb Law Soc; *Recreations* cricket (county cricketer Co Kildare), squash; *Style—* Richard Church, Esq; The Firs, Pangbourne Rd, Upper Basildon, Berkshire (☎ 0491 671 428); 1 Norton Folegate, London EC1 (☎ 071 247 0438, fax 071 247 0639)

CHURCH, Prof Roy Anthony; s of William Alfred Church (d 1973), of Kettering, and Lillian Gertrude Church (d 1990); *b* 21 Feb 1935; *Educ* Kettering GS, Univ of Nottingham (BA, PhD); *m* 10 Oct 1959, Gwenllian Elizabeth, da of James Whyte Martin (d 1984), of Kettering; 3 s (Benjamin b 1964, Joseph b 1969, Thomas b 1970), 1 da (Naomi b 1980); *Career* econ historian; BBC 1958-60, Purdue Univ Indiana USA 1960-61, Univ of Washington Seattle USA 1961-62, Univ of Br Columbia Vancouver Canada 1962-63, Univ of Birmingham 1963-72, UEA 1972-; memb: Cncl of Econ History Soc, Social Sci Res Cncl Business Archives Cncl, Econ and Social Res Cncl; FRHistS 1972; *Books* Economic and Social Change in a Midland Town 1815-1900: Victorian Nottingham (1966), Kenricks in Hardware: A Family Business, 1790-1965 (1969), The Great Victorian Boom (1975), Herbert Austin: The British Motor Car Industry to 1941 (1979), The Dynamics of Victorian Business (ed, 1980), The History of the British Coal Industry, Volume 3: 1830-1913, Victorian Pre-eminence (1986); *Recreations* tennis, badminton, fell walking, theatre; *Style—* Prof Roy Church; School of Economic and Social Studies, University of East Anglia, Norwich (☎ 0603 56161)

CHURCH, William Henry; s of Henry Albion Church (d 1981), and Iris Edith, *née* Duddy (d 1986); *b* 23 July 1946; *Educ* St Joseph's Coll Ipswich, King's Coll, Univ of London (MB BS); *m* 6 Jan 1973, Jane Ann, da of Hugh Parry, of Bryn Mawr, Anelog, Aberdaron, Gwynedd; 3 s (Edward b 1974, James b 1976, Martin b 1977), 1 da (Sarah b 1981); *Career* sr registrar in ophthalmology Royal Victoria Infirmary Newcastle upon Tyne 1984-88, conslt Ophthalmologist Aberdeen Royal Infirmary 1988-; mountaineering achievements: first solo ascent N Face Mount Kenya 1969, first ascent N face Koh-i-Mondi Afghanistan with P Boardman M Wragg C Fitzhugh 1972; MRCP 1975, FRCS 1983; *Recreations* mountaineering, rock climbing, skiing; *Clubs* Alpine; *Style—* William Church, Esq; Glenseaton Lodge, Balgownie, Aberdeen AB2 8LS (☎ 0224 702381); Aberdeen Royal Infirmary, Foresthill, Aberdeen AB9 22B (☎ 0224 681818)

CHURCHHOUSE, Prof Robert Francis; CBE (1982); s of Robert Francis Churchhouse, of Manchester, and Agnes, *née* Howard (d 1985); *b* 30 Dec 1927; *Educ* St Bede's Coll Manchester, Univ of Manchester (BSc), Univ of Cambridge (PhD); *m* 7 Aug 1954, Julia Gertrude, da of John McCarthy (d 1929), of Irlam, Lancs; 3 s (Gerard b 1955, Robert b 1956, John b 1960); *Career* sci serv RN 1952-63; head of programming Atlas Computer Laboratory 1963-71, prof of computing maths Univ Coll Cardiff 1971-; chm Computer Bd 1979-83, pres Inst of Maths and its Applications 1986-88, memb Univs Funding Cncl 1989; FRAS 1962, FIMA 1964, FBCS 1967; KSG 1988; *Books* Computers in Mathematical Research (with JC Herz, 1968), The Computer in Literary and Linguistic Studies (with A Jones, 1976), Numerical Analysis (1978), Handbook of Applicable Mathematics Vol III (1981); *Recreations* cricket, astronomy; *Clubs* Challenor; *Style—* Prof Robert Churchhouse, CBE; 15 Holly Grove, Lisvane, Cardiff CF4 5UJ (☎ 0222 750 250); Department of Computing Mathematics, University of Wales College of Cardiff, Mathematics Institute, Senghennydd Rd, Cardiff CF2 4YN (☎ 0222 874 812, fax 0222 371 921, telex 498635)

CHURCHILL, John George Spencer; s of Maj John Strange Spencer Churchill (d 1947, gson of 7 Duke of Marlborough), and Lady Gwendoline Bertie (d 1941), da of 7 Earl of Abingdon; *b* 31 May 1909; *Educ* Harrow, Oxford, Central Sch of Arts and Crafts, Ruskin Sch Oxford (privately); *m* 1, 13 May 1934 (m dis 1938), Angela Mary, da of late Capt George Culme Seymour, KRRC; 1 da (Sarah); m 2, 20 May 1941 (m dis 1953), Mary, o da of late Kenneth Cookson, of Wynberg, Cape Province, S Africa; m 3, 5 March 1953, Mrs Kathlyn Maude Muriel Hall Tandy (d 1957), o da of Maj-Gen Watter Samuel Hall Beddall, CB, OBE; m 4, 27 Aug 1958 (m dis 1972), Anna Gunvor Maria, da of Johan Janson, of Kristianstad, Sweden, and wid of Granger Boston; *Career* artist, author; murals: incised relief carving on slate and cement cast busts Marlborough Pavilion, Chartwell Westerham Kent (Nat Tst) 1949, London from the South Bank (Simpsons Piccadilly) 1957; painting Save the Forests World Wildlife Fund 1985-; *Books* Crowded Canvas (1960), A Churchill Canvas (USA) (1961), Vanishing Day (1989); *Recreations* music, travel; *Clubs* Chelsea Arts, Press, Cincinnati (Washington DC); *Style—* John G Spencer Churchill Esq; 40 Elsham Rd, Kensington, London W14 8HB (☎ 071 602 4666)

CHURCHILL, 3 Viscount (UK 1902); Victor George Spencer; also Baron Churchill (UK 1815); s of 1 Viscount Churchill, GCVO (d 1934), by his 2 w Christine Sinclair (Lady Oliphant); suc half-bro 1973; *b* 31 July 1934; *Educ* Eton, New Coll Oxford; *Heir* (to Barony only) kinsman, Richard Spencer; *Career* Lt Scots Gds 1953-55; Morgan Grenfell and Co Ltd 1958-74, investmt mangr The Central Bd of the Church of England and the Charities Official Investmt Fund 1974; dir: Local Authorities' Mutual Investmt Tst 1978, Church Charity and Local Authority Fund Managers Ltd; *Style—* The Rt Hon the Viscount Churchill; 6 Cumberland Mansions, George St, London W1H 5TE (☎ 071 262 6223)

CHURCHILL, Winston Spencer; MP (C) Davyhulme (Manchester) 1983-; s of late Randolph Frederick Edward Spencer Churchill, MBE (s of Sir Winston Churchill) by his 1 w, Hon Pamela Digby (now Hon Mrs Averell Harriman), da of 11 Baron Digby, KG, DSO, MC, TD; *b* 10 Oct 1940; *Educ* Eton, ChCh Oxford; *m* 15 July 1964, Mary Caroline, da of late Sir Gerard d'Erlanger, CBE; 2 s, 2 da; *Career* author, journalist and war corr 1964-, The Times 1969-70; contested (C) Manchester (Gorton Div) 1967, MP (C) Stretford Lancs 1970-83; PPS: to Min of Housing and Construction 1970-72, to Min of State FCO 1972-72; Cons spokesman on Def 1976-78, vice chm Cons Pty Def Ctee 1979-83, memb Exec 1922 Ctee 1979-83, treas 1987-88, Cons Party coordinator for Def and Disarmament and chm of Campaign and Multilateral Disarmament 1982-84; *Books* First Journey (1964), The Six Day War (1967), Defending the West (1980), Memoirs and Adventures (1989); *Clubs* Buck's, White's, Press; *Style—* Winston S Churchill, Esq, MP; House of Commons, London SW1A 0AA (☎ 071 219 3405)

CHURCHILL-DAVIDSON, Dudley; RD and Clasp; s of Dr Frederick Churchill-Davidson (d 1961), and Marie Peacock, *née* Jacques (d 1976); *b* 11 May 1927; *Educ* Charterhouse, Trinity Coll Cambridge, St Thomas' Hosp Med Sch, (MA, MB BCHIR); *Career* Nat Service RN, Surgn Lt RNVR 1953-55; ret Surgn Capt RNR (Hon Col RMR for life); conslt orthopaedic surgeon; NHS 1985 (ret); registrar and sr in orthopaedic surgery at St Peter's Hosp Chertsey and the Rowly Bristow Orthopaedic Hosp in Surrey 1958-61, first asst to Orthopaedic Dept St Georges Hosp London 1961-66; conslt orthopaedic surgeon to: Royal London Homoeopathic Hosp 1966, The Kensington and Chelsea Gp of Hosps 1967-72; FRCS; *Recreations* gardening, travel; *Clubs* Bucks; *Style—* Dudley Churchill-Davidson, Esq, RD; 1 Montagu Mews South, London W1H 1TE (☎ 071 724 0482)

CHURCHMAN, Michael Anthony; s of Richard John Churchman (d 1978), of Islington, London, and Mary, *née* Bradley; *b* 6 Feb 1952; *Educ* St Ignatius Coll London, Worcester Coll Oxford (MA); *m* 1974, Christine Elizabeth, da of Bryan Bernard George Dyer, of Cotmer Rd, Lowestoft, Suffolk; 3 s (Anthony Laurence b 4 Aug 1979, Christopher Michael b 28 July 1981, Alexander Richard b 19 Nov 1986); *Career* account exec Young and Rubicam 1973-75, account mangr Benton and Bowles 1975-77, account supervisor Lintas 1977-79, account dir Wasey Campbell Ewald 1979-83; bd dir: AAP Ketchum 1983-87, Grey Ltd 1987-89; md PML Creative Strategy 1990-; IPA: vice chm Advertising Controls Gp, memb Euro Mgmnt Gp, memb Public Attitudes to Advertising Gp; memb: Advertising Advsy Ctee ITC, Advertising Assoc Exec Ctee, Ctee of Advertising Practice, Cncl of Nat Advertising Benevolent Soc 1975-, IOD (dip in co mgmnt 1988); FIPA 1989 (MIPA 1982); *Recreations* family activities, running, reading, classical music (esp Mozart), theatre going; *Clubs* United Oxford and Cambridge Univ, IOD; *Style—* Michael Churchman, Esq; 20 Rutland Place, Maidenhead, Berkshire SL6 4JA (☎ 0628 39404); PML Creative Strategy plc, Brettenham House South, Lancaster Place, London WC2E 7EN (☎ 071 379 5952, fax 071 831 1557, mobile phone 086 047 4435)

CHURCHWARD, (Peter) Robert Shordiche; s of Capt Paul Rycaut de Shordiche Shordiche-Churchward, Coldstream Gds (d 1981), explorer and writer, and Claire Isabel, *née* Whitaker (d 1981); *b* 3 Feb 1950; *Educ* Tabley House Knutsford Cheshire; *m* 22 May 1976, Ida Catherine Morwenna, da of Gp Capt Desmond Spencer, CBE (ret), *qv*, of Cornwall; 1 s (Matthew b 1977), 2 da (Victoria b 1981, Thomasina b 1984); *Career* wine specialist, auctioneer Phillips Gp Int 1985- (formerly Phillips wine conslt), contributor Law Soc Jl and numerous wine periodicals; head Bonhams Wine Dept 1974-83; *Recreations* riding, tennis, amateur mountaineering, most outdoor pursuits; *Style—* Robert Churchward, Esq; Phillips, 39 Park End St, Oxford OX1 1JD (☎ 0865 723524)

CHURSTON, 4 Baron (UK 1858); Sir Richard Francis Roger Yarde-Buller; 6 Bt (GB 1790), VRD; s of 3 Baron (d 1930); bro of Viscountess Camrose, Denise Lady Ebury, Lydia, Duchess of Bedford and late Primrose, Countess Cadogan; *b* 12 Feb 1910; *Educ* Eton; *m* 1, 5 Jan 1933 (m dis 1943), Elizabeth Mary (d 23 Sept 1951), da of Lt-Col William Baring Du Pre, JP, DL; 1 s, 1 da; m 2, 31 March 1949, Sandra (d 1979), da of Percy Needham, and former w of Jack Dunfee, and previously of Claud

Harold Bertram (Arthur) Griffiths; m 3, Mrs Olga Alice Muriel Blair; *Heir* s, Hon John Yarde-Buller; *Career* Lt-Cdr RNVR, ret; patron of two livings; bore one of the Golden Spurs at Coronations of King George VI and Queen Elizabeth II; *Clubs* RYS; *Style—* The Rt Hon the Lord Churston, VRD; Pendragon, Fort George, Guernsey, Channel Islands (☎ 28550)

CHURTON, Hon Mrs (Katherine); *née* Tyrell-Kenyon; only da of 5 Baron Kenyon; *b* 21 April 1959; *m* 1985, David Nigel Vardon Churton, MBE, elder s of Col G V Churton, MBE, MC, TD, of Manley Cottage, Manley, nr Warrington, Cheshire; 2 s (Oscar Vardon b 1987, Rollo Crispin b 1989); *Style—* The Hon Mrs Churton

CHUTE, Robin Vere; Lord of the Manor of Sherborne St John; s of Anthony Vere Chute (d 1987), of Suffolk, and Daphne Gore, *née* Darley; family descends from Alexander Chute, living 1268; Philip Chute was standard bearer to Henry VIII, and Chaloner Chute (1595-1659) speaker of the House of Commons, and first Chute of The Vyne, Basingstoke (*see* Burke's Landed Gentry, 1937 edn); *b* 24 May 1947; *Educ* Winchester, RAC Cirencester; *m* 30 Sept 1978, Julia Mary Susan, da of Maj John Sylvester Perkins, of Chippenham, Wilts; 1 s (Charles John Vere b 1981), 1 da (Arabella Julia Handasyd b 1984); *Career* estates bursar of Winchester Coll 1981; farmer 1987; FRICS 1982; *Recreations* shooting, fishing, cricket, rackets; *Clubs* MCC, T & R Assoc; *Style—* R V Chute, Esq; 15 Kingsgate Street, Winchester, Hants; Winchester College, Winchester, Hants (☎ 0962 64242)

CHUTE, Terence Michael; s of George James Chute (d 1972), and Minnie Margaret Chute (d 1974); *b* 14 March 1936; *Educ* Clapham Xavarien Coll; *m* 28 June 1958, Pauline Gloria, *née* Prentice; 1 s (Julian b 1968), 1 da (Nicola b 1963); *Career* Photo-Me Int plc 1966-: appointed co sec, dir 1977, jt md 1984, sole md and memb Bd Exec Ctee 1985, chm 1988; FICA 1964; *Recreations* golf, reading, music, gardening; *Style—* Terence M Chute, Esq; Redwoods, off Blacksmith Lane, Chilworth, Surrey GU4 8NU (☎ 0483 35781)

CHYNOWETH, David Boyd; s of Ernest Chynoweth (d 1982), and Blodwen, *née* Griffiths; *b* 26 Dec 1944; *Educ* Simon Langton Sch Canterbury, Univ of Nottingham (BA); *m* 15 June 1968, Margaret, da of Thomas Slater, of Park House, Edensor, Derbyshire; 1 s (Richard b 1981), 2 da (Susan b 1971, Claire b 1974); *Career* dep co treas W Suffolk CC 1969-73, co treas S Yorks CC 1973-85; dir of fin Lothian Regnl Cncl 1985; *Recreations* sailing, photography; *Clubs* Royal Over-Seas League; *Style—* David Chynoweth, Esq; Ardvulin, 37 Clifford Rd, N Berwick, E Lothian (☎ 0620 3652)

CIECHANOWIECKI, Count Andrew Stanislaus; s of Count George Ciechanowiecki (d 1930), Polish diplomat and landowner, and Matilda, *née* Countess Osiecimska-Hutten-Czapska, Dame of Hon and Dev SMOM, Dame Gd Cross of Justice, Constantinian Order of St George; *b* 28 Sept 1924,Warsaw; *Educ* Lycée S Batory Warsaw, Higher Sch Ec Studies Kraków (BA), Jagiellonian Univ Kraków (MA), Karl Eberhard Univ Tübingen (PhD); *Career* anti Nazi resistance in Poland 1942-45 (Polish war decorations); cnsllr Polish FO in govt of National Unity and chef de protocole Min Foreign Trade 1945-46; political prisoner 1950-56; former lectr Jagiellonian Univ Kraków; former museum curator in Poland; md Mallett at Bourdon House (London) 1961-65, md: Heim Gallery (London) Ltd 1965-86, Old Masters Gallery (London) Ltd 1986-; fndr Ciechanowiecki Art Fndn Royal Castle Warsaw; tstee various Polish charities abroad; memb numerous learned bodies; FSA; Hon PhD Univ of Warsaw, various other academic awards; Kt Cdr Polonia Restituta, (Govt in Exile), Kt Grand Cross Order of St Gregory the Great (Holy See), Kt Cdr Order of Merit (Italy), Cdr Grosses Silbernes Ehrenzeichen (Austria), Cdr Order of Merit (Senegal), Bundesverdienstkreuz first Class, (Germany), Chevalier Légion d'Honneur (France), Kt Grand Cross of Hon and Dev and Kt Grand Cross of Merit SMOM, first vice pres Polish Assoc of SMOM, Kt Order of St Januarius, Bailiff Grand Cross of Justice Constantinian Order of St George (decorated with the Collar), Royal House of Naples, Kt Cdr Order SS Mauritius and Lazarus (Royal House of Savoy); medal "Merentibus" Jagiellonian Univ Kraków; *Books* author of several books and numerous articles in the field of art and history of culture; *Recreations* reading, travelling; *Clubs* Brooks, Polish Hearth; *Style—* Count Andrew Ciechanowiecki; 44 Sydney St, London SW3 6PX (☎ 071 352 1395; 071 930 1145)

CIERACH, Lindka Rosalind Wanda; da of Edek Cierach, MBE, of Starydom, St Just-in-Roseland, Truro, Cornwall, and Diana Rosemary, *née* Wilson; f mapped large tracts of Africa, decorated for Battle of Monte Cassino with highest Order of Virtuti Military, Kirzyz Walecznych, Star medal 1939-44, Star Italian Campaign, Star of Monte Cassino, Star Defense MBE; *b* 8 June 1952; *Educ* Uganda, Convent of the Holy Child Jesus Sussex; *Career* fashion designer, designed wedding dress for Duchess of York's marriage on 23 July 1986, winner Designer of the Year Award 1987; *Recreations* travelling, photography, swimming, cooking, music, opera; *Style—* Miss Lindka R W Cierach; 54 Hartismere Rd, London SW6 7UD (☎ 071 381 4436)

CINA, Colin; s of Louis Cina of Glasgow, and Ettie, *née* Barkofsky; *b* 24 April 1943; *Educ* Glasgow Sch of Art, Central Sch of Art (Dip AD); *m* 1962, Gill, *née* Nicholas; 2 da (Jane b 1972, Chloe b 1976); *Career* visiting fell in fine art Univ of Newcastle upon Tyne 1971-72; pt/t teaching: Manchester Sch of Art (fine art) 1967-71, Central Sch of Art 1968-75; princ lectr in charge of painting Wimbledon Sch of Art 1975-80 (acting head of fine art 1975-76), head of fine art Chelsea Sch of Art 1988 (head of Painting Dept 1980), dean Sch of Art Chelsea Coll of Art and Design 1989; fine art and fndn external examiner for various colls and polys; artist; recent solo exhibitions incl: Serpentine Gallery 1980, Library Gallery Univ of Surrey 1983, Angela Flowers London 1984; recent gp exhibitions incl: Redhill Street Open Studios London 1987, 21st Anniversary Exhibition of Richard Demarco Gallery (Smiths Gallery) London 1988, Scottish Art Since 1900 (Gallery of Modern Art Edinburgh Festival 1989-90), Barbican Art Gallery Londonn 1989/90, Master Class (London Inst Gallery) 1991; works in public collections incl: Arts Cncl of GB, City Art Gallery Bristol, Contemporary Arts Soc, CNAA, Scot Arts Cncl, Scot Nat Gallery of Modern Art Edinburgh, Nat Gallery of Iceland, V & A; author of various articles and catalogues; govr London Inst 1986-89 (memb of various Ctees); coll govr: Canterbury Coll of Art 1982-86, Duncan of Jordanstone Sch of Art univ of Dundee 1989; CNAA Fine Art Panel: specialist advsr 1982-, memb of Panel 1985-87, specialist registrar 1987-; memb Architects and Artists Action Gp 1983-84, co-opted memb NATFHE London Inst Coordinating Ctee 1986-88, London region memb Steering Ctee Nat Assoc for Fine Art Educn (vice chm 1988-89, chm 1989-90); conslt for various insts incl: BBC, Dept of Tport, Kent Inst of Art and Design, RNIB; *Style—* Colin Cina, Esq; 37 Delaney St, London NW1 7RX (☎ 071 387 8607); Flowers East Gallery, 199/205 Richmond Rd, London E8 (☎ 081 985 3333)

CINNAMOND, Prof Michael James; s of James Herbert Cinnamond (d 1977), and Mary Elizabeth, *née* Stewart; *b* 16 Sept 1943; *Educ* The Methodist Coll Belfast, The Queen's Univ Belfast (MB BCh, BAO); *m* 18 Dec 1965, Judith Patricia, da of William Edmund Guthrie, of 3 Seacliffe Close, Newcastle, Co Down; 2 s (Michael b 8 Nov 1966, Neill b 31 March 1971), 1 da (Adrienne b 7 Nov 1972); *Career* conslt otolaryngologist 1976-79: Royal Belfast Hosp for Sick Children, Royal Victoria Hosp, Belfast City Hosp; sr lectr otorhinolaryngology Queen's Univ Belfast 1979-81; conslt paediatric otolaryngologist 1979-81 and 1981-: Royal Belfast Hosp for Sick Children, Belfast City Hosp; prof of otorhinolaryngology Queen's Univ Belfast 1981-; memb: Industl Injuries Advsy Cncl, Speciality Advsy Ctee in Otolaryngology to Jt Ctee Higher Surgical Trg; FRCS Ed 1974, FRCSI ad eundem 1987; *Books* Scott-Brown's Otolaryngology 5 edn (contrib, 1987), Accident and Emergency Medicine 2 edn (contrib, 1989); *Style—* Prof Michael Cinnamond; 10 Governor's Ridge Park, Carnreagh, Hillsborough, Co Down, Northern Ireland BT26 6LD (☎ 0846 683090); Department of Otorhinolaryngology, University Floor, Tower Block, Belfast City Hospital, Belfast BT9 7AB (☎ 0232 329241 ext 2356)

CIPOLLA, Joseph Angelo; s of Anthony Joseph Cipolla, of Buffalo, New York, USA, and Joanna, *née* D'anna; *b* 16 Nov 1959; *Educ* Saint Joseph's Collegiate Inst, American Acad of Ballet, Buffalo State Coll; *m* 30 July 1983, Julie Patrica, da of Patrick Felix; 2 da (Joanna Leanne b 22 May 1987, Natalie Rose b 2 Sept 1990); *Career* ballet dancer; with Dance Theatre of Harlem 1979-86; performances incl: Swan Lake, Giselle, The Four Temperments, Square Dance, Agon, Serenade, Voluntaries, Fete Noir, Equus, Fall River Legend, A Streetcar Named Desire, Firebird, Paquita, Graduation Ball, Mirage, Troy Game; princ dancer Sadler's Wells Royal Ballet 1986-; performances incl: Prince Siegfried in Swan Lake, Franz in Coppelia, Colas in La Fille Mal Gardee, Albrecht in Giselle, Prince Florimund in The Sleeping Beauty, Captain Belaye in Pineapple Poll, Fred Beenstock in Hobson's Choice; other appearances: A Street Car Named Desire for PBS TV shown on C4, the White House 1980, closing ceremony Olympic Games in LA 1984, opening of The Fonteyn Centre 1990, Margot Fonteyn's Magic of Dance; *Recreations* movies (cinema), wine; *Style—* Joseph Cipolla, Esq; Birmingham Royal Ballet, Roseberry Ave, London EC1R 4TN

CITRINE, 2 Baron (UK 1946), of Wembley, Co Middlesex; Norman Arthur Citrine; s of 1 Baron Citrine, GBE, PC (d 1983, former chm Central Electricity Authority, pres World Fedn of Trade Unions, chm World Anti-Nazi Cncl, gen sec TUC), and Doris Helen (d 1973), da of Edgar Slade; *b* 27 Sept 1914; *Educ* Univ Coll Sch, LLB London; *m* 4 Jan 1939, Kathleen Alice, da of late George Thomas Chilvers, of Saxmundham, Suffolk; 1 da; *Heir* bro, Dr the Hon Ronald Eric Citrine; *Career* Lt RNVR 1940-46; slr and advocate 1937-84, author of legal and technical works, lectr, legal adviser to TUC 1946-51; pres Devon and Exeter Law Soc 1971-72; *Recreations* yachting, camping, hiking, painting, rambling, music, literature, art, numerous constructional crafts; *Style—* The Rt Hon the Lord Citrine; Casa Katrina, The Mount, Opua, Bay of Islands, New Zealand

CITRINE, Hon Ronald Eric; s of 1 Baron Citrine; hp to bro, 2 Baron Citrine; *b* 19 May 1919; *Educ* Univ Coll Sch, UCL; *m* 27 July 1945, Mary, da of Reginald Williams, of Wembley; *Career* MRCS, LRCP; *Style—* The Hon Ronald Citrine; Paihia, Bay of Islands, North Island, New Zealand

CLAGUE, Andrew Charlesworth; s of John Charlesworth Clague, of Canterbury, and Margaret Elsie, *née* Musgrave; *b* 15 May 1951; *Educ* St Edmunds Sch Canterbury, Kent Inst of Design (Dip Arch); *m* 23 June 1973, Alison Francesca, da of Dennis Arthur Land, of 6 Eversley Crescent, London; 2 s (James Charlesworth, Nicholas Charlesworth), 2 da (Anna Genevieve, Isabel Lucy); *Career* sr ptnr Clague (Architects, Town Planners and Landscape Architects): Canterbury (HQ), Ashford Kent, Midhurst W Sussex; fndr and dir Countryman Properties Ltd 1986; sec St Edmunds Soc (of St Edmunds Sch Old Boys); memb: RIBA Practice Ctee (HQ), Rotary Club (Canterbury), Canterbury Conservation Advsy Ctee Canterbury Soc; chm: Round Table (Canterbury and Dist), RIBA (Canterbury and Dist), SE Region Practice Ctee RIBA; *Recreations* windsurfing, music; *Clubs* Kent and Canterbury, Inst of Dirs; *Style—* Andrew Clague, Esq; The Old Rectory Cottage, Ickham, Canterbury CT3 1QN (☎ 0227 721400); Clague, 62 Burgate, Canterbury, Kent CT1 2HJ (☎ 0227 762 060, fax 0227 762 149, car 0860 301 449)

CLAGUE, (Albert) Clive Taylor; s of Albert Taylor Clague (d 1955), of Sale, Cheshire, and Ella, *née* Jones; *b* 22 Jan 1928; *m* 1, 20 Aug 1957 (m dis 1979), Valerie Ruth; 2 s (Nicholas b 1958, Stephen b 1960); m 2, 30 Dec 1982, Frances Mary, da of Keith William Robinson, OBE, of Harrogate; *Career* mktg dir: Imperial Group plc 1961-67, Granada Group plc 1967-69; gen mangr Gallaher Group plc 1969-71, chm and chief exec R & G Cuthbert plc 1971-80, chief exec E J Arnold & Sons Ltd 1980-82, chm Stadium Limited 1982-; dir: Electra Investment Trust plc 1984-, Electra Kingsway Ltd (and numerous subsid cos), Electra Risk Capital plc 1984-; non-exec chm: Wardle Storeys plc 1982-, Bowes Darby Design Associates Limited 1986-, Prospect Group Limited 1988-; non-exec dir: RFD Group plc 1985-, CDB Meats Limited 1985-, Unipart Group of Companies Limited 1986-, Unipart Group of Companies (Trustees) Limited 1987-, Beaujersey Holdings Limited 1988-, Healthcall Group plc 1990-, Jarvis Hotels Limited 1990-; *Recreations* walking, fishing, theatre, ballet, family; *Style—* Clive Clague, Esq; Swindon Hill, Kirkby Overblow, Harrogate, North Yorkshire HG3 1HJ (☎ 0423 871662); 29 Lancaster Drive, Prestons Rd, London E14 9PT (☎ 071 987 4482); Electra Investment Trust plc, 65 Kingsway, London WC2B 6QT (☎ 071 831 6464, fax 071 404 5388, telex 265525, car 0836 233156)

CLAGUE, Dr Roy Bridson; s of William Alan Clague, of Douglas, IOM, and Doris, *née* Bridson; *b* 16 Jan 1948; *Educ* Douglas HS for Boys IOM, Univ of Newcastle upon Tyne (MB BS, MD); *m* 16 Jan 1971, Helen da of John de Legh, of Manchester; 3 da (Bethany b 1971, Emma b 1973, Joanna b 1978); *Career* registrar in gen med 1973-76, sr registrar in rheumatology 1976-80, trg fell MRC 1976-79, conslt rheumatologist Withington Hosp Manchester and Devonshire Royal Hosp Derbyshire 1980-; memb Rheumatology Cmmn RP, pres local branches of Arthritic and Rheumatism Cncl in IOM and Buxton; MRCP 1974, FRCP 1989; *Recreations* golf, previously dinghy sailing; *Style—* Dr Roy Clague; Withington Hospital, W Didsbury, Manchester (☎ 061 445 8111); Devonshire Royal Hospital, Buxton, Derbyshire

CLAMP, Prof John Richard; s of William Stephen Clamp (d 1966), of London, and Florence Ivy, *née* Larcombe (d 1981); *b* 7 May 1927; *Educ* Wallington Co Sch, Univ of Bristol (MB ChB, BSc, PhD, MD); *m* June 1962, Anita Betty, da of Frederick Davies (d 1966), of London; 2 s (John b 1965, Nicholas b 1967), 1 da (Janita Ronny b 1963); *Career* Capt E Surrey Regt 1945-48; res fell UCH London 1961-62, res fell Dept of Biochemistry Univ of Florida 1962-63, Univ of Bristol 1963-; numerous articles in jls; FRCP, FRSC; *Recreations* archaeology; *Style—* Prof John Clamp; 26 Victoria Square, Clifton, Bristol BS8 4EW (☎ 0272 736222); Dept of Medicine, University of Bristol, Bristol Royal Infirmary, Bristol BS2 8HW (☎ 0272 276388)

CLANCARTY, 8 Earl of (I 1803); (William Francis) Brinsley Le Poer Trench; also (sits as) Viscount Clancarty (UK 1823), Baron Kilconnel (I 1793), Viscount Dunlo (I 1801), Baron Trench (UK 1815), Marquess of Heusden in the Netherlands (1818); s of late 5 Earl of Clancarty; suc his half-bro 1975; *b* 18 Sept 1911; *Educ* Nautical Coll Pangbourne; *m* 1, 6 June 1940 (m dis 1947), Diana Joan, da of Sir William Younger, 2 Bt; m 2, 16 June 1961 (m dis 1969), Wilma Dorothy Millen, da of S R Vermilyea, of USA, and former w of William Burke Belknap, Jr; m 3, 1974, Mrs Mildred Alleyn Spong (d 1975); m 4, 1976, May, o da of late E Radonicich, and widow of Cdr Frank M Beasley, RN; *Heir* nephew, Nicholas Le Poer Trench; *Career* chm House of Lords UFO Study Gp; author (as Brinsley Le Poer Trench); *Books* The Sky People, Men Among Mankind, Forgotten Heritage, The Flying Saucer Story, Operation Earth, The Eternal Subject, Secret of the Ages; *Style—* The Rt Hon the Earl of Clancarty; 51 Eaton Place, London SW1

CLANCARTY, Cora, Countess of; Cora Maria Edith; *née* Spooner; er da of H H Spooner, of Thornton Hall, Surrey; *m* 12 March 1919, as his 2 w, 6 Earl of Clancarty (d 1971); 1 s (decd), 3 da; *Style—* The Rt Hon Cora, Countess of Clancarty; Old Vicarage, Moulsford, nr Wallingford, Oxon

CLANDERMOND, Count of (Kingdom of Munster ca 1250 by King Donal II; confirmed Kingdom of France 1756 by King Louis XV); John Andrew Brodie-Davison; o s of John Spence Gibson Davison, Count of Clandermond (head of the family of Davison of Broughshane and cousin of Baron Broughshane), and Iris Elizabeth Andrew Brodie (descended from the ancient Scottish Chiefly House of Brodie of Brodie); suc 1979; *b* 1954; *Educ* privately; *Career* memb several foreign orders including Kt Sacred Military Order of Constantine St George of Naples; Fell: Royal Cwlth Soc, Winston Churchill Memorial Tst, Royal Soc of Antiquaries of Ireland; memb Royal Celtic Soc of Edinburgh; *Clubs* Royal Commonwealth Soc; *Style—* The Count of Clandermond; 16 rue al Kortobi, Marshan, Tangier, Morocco

CLANFIELD, Viscount; Ashton Robert Gerard Peel; s and h of 3 Earl Peel; *b* 16 Sept 1976; *Style—* Viscount Clanfield; Gunnerside Lodge, Gunnerside, Richmond, N Yorks

CLANMORRIS, 8 Baron (I 1800) Simon John Ward Bingham; s of 7 Baron Clanmorris (d 1988), and Madeleine Mary, da of Clement Ebel; *b* 25 Oct 1937; *Educ* Downside, Queens' Coll Cambridge (BA, MA); *m* 1971, Gizella Maria, da of Sandor Zverko, of Budapest (d 1979); 1 da (Lucy Katherine Gizella); *Heir* kinsman, John Temple Bingham b 22 Feb 1923; *Career* 13/18 Royal Hussars (QMO) 1956-58; CA, ACA 1965, FCA 1975; *Recreations* skiing, sailing; *Style—* Lord Clanmorris; 22 Falkland House, Marloes Rd, London W8 5LF

CLANRANALD, The Capt of (c 1380); Ranald Alexander Macdonald of Clanranald; 24 Chief of Clanranald; s of Capt Kenneth Macdonald, DSO (d 1938), of Inchkenneth and Gribune; suc kinsman Angus Macdonald, Capt of Clanranald 1944; *b* 27 March 1934; *Educ* Christ's Hosp; *m* 1961, Jane, da of Ivar Campbell-Davys, of Llandovery; 2 s (Ranald b 1963, Andrew b 1966), 1 da (Catriona b 1972); *Heir* s, Ranald (Og Angus) Macdonald, yr of Clanranald, b 17 Sept 1963; *Career* fndr, chm and md Tektura Wallcoverings, chm Br Contract Furnishing Assoc 1975-76; memb Standing Cncl Scot Chiefs 1957-, pres Highland Soc London 1988-91 (dir 1959-80), vice pres Caledonian Catholic Assoc London, exec chm Clan Donald Lands Tst 1978-80, chm Museum of Isles 1980-89; Kt of Justice Constantinian Order of St George 1982; *Recreations* off-shore sailing, fishing; *Clubs* Turf, White's, Pratts, Beefsteak, Puffin's, New (Edinburgh); *Style—* The Captain of Clanranald; Wester Lix House, Killin, Perthshire (☎ 056 72 651); 70B Pavillion Rd, London SW1X 0ES (☎ 071 581 5967); Tektura Ltd, 4-10 Rodney St, London N1 9JH (☎ 071 837 8787, telex 269931)

CLANWILLIAM, Catherine, Countess of; Catherine; *née* Loyd; yst da of Arthur Thomas Loyd, OBE, of Lockinge, Wantage, Berks (d 1944), and Dorothy, *née* Willert (d 1966); *b* 1 June 1923; *m* 1 Dec 1948, 6 Earl of Clanwilliam (d 1989); 6 da (Lady Selina Timpson, Countess of Belmore, Lady Julia Hiscox, Lady Laura Reid, Lady Katharine Wills, Lady Sophia Heywood); *Style—* The Rt Hon Catherine, Countess of Clanwilliam; Maizley Cottage, Oare, Marlborough, Wilts (☎ 0672 63491)

CLANWILLIAM, 7 Earl of (I 1776); Sir John Herbert Meade; 9 Bt (I 1703); also (sits as) Baron Clanwilliam (UK 1828), Viscount Clanwilliam and Baron Gillford (I 1766); yr of Adm the Hon Sir Herbert Meade-Fetherstonhaugh, GCVO, CB, DSO s of 4 Earl of Clanwilliam); suc his cousin, 6 Earl of Clanwilliam, 1989; *b* 27 Sept 1919; *Educ* RNC Dartmouth; *m* 1956, Maxine, o da of late James Adrian Hayden Scott, and former w of Michael John Willson Levien; 1 s (Lord Gillford), 2 da (Lady Rowena Katherine b 1957, Lady Tania Frances (Lady Tania Compton) b 1963); *Heir* s, Lord Gillford, *qv*; *Clubs* Turf; *Style—* The Rt Hon the Earl of Clanwilliam; House of Lords, London SW1

CLAPHAM, Adam John; s of Sir Michael Clapham, of 26 Hill St, London W1, and The Hon Lady Elisabeth, *née* The Hon Elisabeth Russell Rea; *b* 8 April 1940; *Educ* Bryanston, Univ of Grenoble; *Career* Anglia TV 1960-63, scriptwriter ABC TV 1963; BBC TV: prodr Man Alive 1965-69 (ed 1972-75), prodr Braden's Week 1969-71, exec prodr documentary features 1975-82; chief exec Griffin Prodns 1982-; Leverhulme fell Sri Lanka 1981; Freeman City of London 1976, Liveryman Worshipful Co of Bowyers 1976; *Books* As Nature Intended (1982); *Clubs* Oriental; *Style—* Adam Clapham, Esq; 254 Alexandra Park Rd, London N22 4BG (☎ 081 889 9035); Griffin Prodns, Balfour House, 46-54 Great Titchfield St, London W1P 7AE (☎ 071 636 5066, fax 071 436 3232, telex 261799)

CLAPHAM, His Hon Brian Ralph; s of late Isaac Bleazard Clapham, and Laura Alice, *née* Meech; *b* 1 July 1913; *Educ* Tonbridge, Wadham Coll Oxford, UCL, Open Univ; *m* 1961, Margaret, da of Dr Rudolph Pius Warburg; 2 s; *Career* called to the Bar 1936; Parly candidate (Lab): Tonbridge 1950, Billericay 1951 and 1955, Chelmsford 1959; circuit judge 1974-85; govr West Kent Coll, memb Tonbridge and later Southborough Urban DCs 1947-74 (chm Tonbridge Urban DC 1959-60); Freeman City of London; FCIArb; *Recreations* walking and talking; *Style—* His Hon Brian Clapham; Crown Court, Maidstone, Kent

CLAPHAM, Prof Christopher S; s of Anthony Clapham (d 1973), and Veronica Mary, *née* Lake; *b* 3 March 1941; *Educ* Bryanston, Keble Coll Oxford (MA, DPhil); *m* 1 Nov 1975, Caroline Margaret, da of Brig John J S Tutton, CBE, of Awre, Glos; 1 s (Thomas b 1979), 1 da (Phoebe b 1977); *Career* lectr in law Univ of Addis Ababa 1966-67, res fell Univ of Manchester 1968-71, prof of politics and int rels Univ of Lancaster 1989- (lectr 1971-74, sr lectr 1974-89); memb Cncl: Br Tst for Ornithology 1976-79, African Studies Assoc of the UK 1981-84 and 1989-; Liveryman Worshipful Co of Ironmongers 1968; *Books* Haile-Selassie's Government (1969), Liberia and Sierra Leone (1976), Third World Politics (1985), Transformation and Continuity in Revolutionary Ethiopia (1988); *Recreations* ornithology; *Style—* Prof Christopher Clapham; Dept of Politics & International Relations, Univ of Lancaster, Lancaster LA1 4YL (☎ 0529 65201 ext 4264, telex 65111 LANCUL G)

CLAPHAM, Diana Mary (Tiny); da of Col D C Clapham, of Blue House Farm, Mattingley, Basingstoke, Hants, and Jennifer Audrey, *née* Vaughan; *b* 8 June 1957; *Educ* Daneshill, Hurst Lodge, St Mary's Guildford; *Career* three day eventer; achievements incl: memb Br team Dutch Three Day Event Championship winners 1975, 1978, 1983 (runners up 1979), memb Br team Jr Euro Championship winners 1975, seventh place Euro Championships 1981, tenth place World Championships 1982, memb Silver medal winning team Euro Championships 1983, winner Daily Telegraph Cup Sherborne 1983, team Silver medal Olympic Games LA 1984, memb team Int Three Day Event Championship winners Sweden 1985, winner Weston Park Subaru Championships 1987 (runner up 1986), third place Burghley 1987, runner up Windsor 1987, winner Locko Part Intermediate Championships 1987, winner Osbertn 1987, winner Rothefield Intermediate Event 1989, placed Badminton 4 times; merit award BHS 1985, winner 2 Armarda Dishes (for completing Badminton 10 times), awarded various medals Fédération Equestre Internationale; *Recreations* skiing, fashion, travelling when possible; *Style—* Miss Tiny Clapham; Point Farm, Stathern, Milton Mowbray, Leicestershire LE14 4HW (☎ 0949 60637)

CLAPHAM, Hon Lady (Elisabeth Russell); *née* Rea; JP (1956 supp 1981-); yr da of 1 Baron Rea of Eskdale PC (d 1948); *b* 2 May 1911; *Educ* Priorsfield Sch, Newnham Coll Cambridge (MA); *m* 18 May 1935, Sir Michael Clapham, KBE, *qv*; 3 s, 1 da; *Career* welfare offr Miny of Labour 1940-42; chm Birmingham Settlement 1955-61, JP Birmingham 1957-61, Juvenile Magistrate 1958-61, London 1963-81, JP SW Magistrates Court 1963-81 (chm 1972-75); *Style—* The Hon Lady Clapham, JP; 26 Hill St, W1X 7FU

CLAPHAM, Sir Michael John Sinclair; KBE (1973); s of Prof Sir John Clapham, CBE, LittD, FBA (d 1946), of Storey's End, Cambridge, and Mary Margaret, *née* Green (d 1965); *b* 17 Jan 1912; *Educ* Marlborough, King's Coll Cambridge (BA, MA); *m* 18 May 1935, Hon Elisabeth Russell Rea, *qv*, da of 1st Baron Rea of Eskdale; 3 s (Adam, Charles, Giles), 1 da (Antonia); *Career* dep chm: ICI plc 1968-71 (dir 1961-74), Lloyds Bank plc 1974-81 (dir 1971-82); pres CBI 1972-74; chm: IMI plc 1974-81, BPM Holdings plc 1974-81; non-exec dir: Grindleys Bank Ltd 1975-84, Heylesbury (UK) Ltd 1988-90, Stoll Moss Theatres Ltd 1986-90; Hon DSc Aston (1973), Hon LLD CNAA (1978), Hon LLD London (1984); *Recreations* sailing, cooking; *Clubs* Royal Yacht Sqdn; *Style—* Sir Michael Clapham, KBE; 26 Hill St, London W1X 7FU (☎ 071 499 1240)

CLAPPERTON, (Alexander) Wallace Ford; s of Alexander Clapperton (d 1943), of Edinburgh, and Kathleen Nora, *née* Ford; *b* 22 July 1934; *Educ* Charterhouse; *m* 27 March 1965, Catherine Anne, da of Sir Henry Horsman, MC (d 1966), of Bermuda; 1 s (Graeme Alexander Ford b 1969), 1 da (Alison Nicola b 1967); *Career* Nat Serv RCS 1957-59; ptnr de Zoete and Bevan stockbrokers (formerly de Zoete and Gorton) 1963-86, dir Barclays de Zoete Wedd Securities Ltd 1986-; MICAS; *Recreations* golf, skiing; *Clubs* Hon Co of Edinburgh Golfers, Denham Golf, Woburn Golf, City of London; *Style—* Wallace Clapperton, Esq; Broomfield House, Broomfield Hill, Great Missenden, Bucks HP16 9HT (☎ 02406 2559); Ebbgate House, 2 Swan Lane, London EC4R 3TS (☎ 071 623 2323, fax 071 626 1879, telex 9413230)

CLARE, Prof Anthony Ward; *née* Blackwood; s of Bernard J Clare, of 29 Albany Rd, Ranelagh, Dublin 6, and Mary Agnes, *née* Dunne; *b* 24 Dec 1942; *Educ* Gonzaga Coll Dublin, Univ Coll Dublin (MB BCh, BAO, MD), London Univ (MPhil); *m* 4 Oct 1966, Jane Carmel, da of Gabriel Sarsfield Hogan (d 1989), of Shelbourne Rd, Dublin 4; 3 s (Simon John b 1970, Peter Tobias b 1975, Sebastian Patrick b 1985), 4 da (Rachel Judith b 1967, Eleanor Ruth b 1971, Sophie Carolyn b 1978, Justine Chiara b 1982); *Career* intern St Joseph Hosp Syracuse NY 1966-67; registrar: St Patrick's Hosp Dublin 1967-69, Bethlem Royal and Maudsley Hosps London 1970-72; dep dir Gen Practice Res Unit Inst of Psychiatry 1979-82 (sr registrar and res worker 1973-78), prof and head Dept of Psychological Med St Bart's Hosp Med Coll 1982-88, med dir St Patrick's Hosp Dublin and prof of clinical psychiatry Trin Coll Dublin 1989-; memb Health Educn Authy, chm Centre Ctee King Edward's Hosp Fund for London; numerous broadcasts incl: Let's Talk About Me, In The Psychiatrist's Chair (BBC 1982), Stop The Week; FRCPI 1983, FRCPsych 1986; *Books* Psychiatry in Dissent (1976, 2 edn 1980), Let's Talk About Me (1981), In the Psychiatrist's Chair (1984), Lovelaw (1986); *Recreations* tennis, opera, family life; *Style—* Prof Anthony W Clare; 87 Coper's Cope Road, Beckenham, Kent BR3 1NR (☎ 081 650 1784); Delville, Lucan, Co Dublin, Republic of Ireland (☎ 0001 264782); St Patrick's Hospital, James's St, Dublin 8, Republic of Ireland (☎ 0001 775423)

CLARE, George; s of Ernst Klaar (d 1942, Auschwitz), and Stella Klaar, *née* Schapira (d 1942, Auschwitz); *b* 21 Dec 1920; *Educ* Univ of London; *m* 1, Lisel, *née* Beck; 1 s (Andrew b 1951), 2 da (Sylvia b 1945, Jacqueline b 1954); m 2, Christel, *née* Vorbringer; 1 da (Anna-Juliana b 1965); *Career* served HM Forces 1941-46; control offr Grade 1 (Lt-Col) Control Cmmn for Germany (Br Element) 1949-54; dir and chief UK rep Axel Springer 1963-83 (joined Hamburg 1954); writer; Books: Last Waltz in Vienna (1981, W H Smith Lit award 1982), Berlin Days 1946-1947 (1989); pres UK Chapter Int Advertising Assoc 1981-83, memb Bd German C of C London until 1983; *Recreations* writing, painting, being with family and friends; *Style—* George Clare, Esq

CLARE, (Adrian) George Howe; s of Ernest Vivian Clare, and Betty Kennedy, *née* Hester; *b* 27 Sept 1937; *Educ* Bickley Park Sch, Radley; *m* Helen Aline, da of late Edgar Frederick Shannon, of New Malden, Surrey; 3 da (Rosamund b 1964, Alison b 1966, Belinda b 1967); *Career* Nat Serv Royal Ulster Rifles 1957-58, TA London Irish Rifles 1958-63; gen sec Euro Actuarial Consultancy Servs, princ Watsons Europe; sec Effingham Housing Assoc, Horsley Choral Soc, King George Fifth Playing Fields Ctee; memb Worshipful Co of Master Joiners & Ceilers 1987-88; FPMI, ACII, MBIM; *Recreations* singing, travel, politics; *Clubs* RAC; *Style—* George Clare, Esq; Old Vicarage, Church St, Effingham, Leatherhead, Surrey KT24 2LX (☎ 0372 458435); Watsons Europe, London Rd, Reigate

CLARE, Hon Mrs (Pauline Rosemary); *née* Addington; 4 da of 7 Viscount Sidmouth; *b* 18 Feb 1951; *m* 1973, Paul Christopher Clare; *Style—* The Hon Mrs Clare; Glenarth, Abernarth, Aberaeron, Dyfed

CLARENDON, 7 Earl of (GB 1776); George Frederick Laurence Hyde Villiers; also Baron Hyde (GB 1756); s of late Lord Hyde and late Hon Marion, *née* Glyn, da of 4 Baron Wolverton; suc gf 1955; *b* 2 Feb 1933; *Educ* Eton, Univ of Madrid; *m* 1974, Jane Diana, da of Edward William Dawson (d 1979), of Idmiston, Salisbury, Wilts; 1 s (George Edward Laurence, Lord Hyde b 12 Feb 1976), 1 da (Lady Sarah Katherine Jane Villiers b 1977); *Heir* s, Lord Hyde; *Career* page of honour to HM King George VI 1948-49; Lt RHG 1951-53; Glyn Mills and Co 1955-60, Seccombe Marshall and Campion 1960- (md 1962, chm 1985); *Style—* The Rt Hon the Earl of Clarendon; 5 Astell St, London SW3 3RT (☎ 071 352 9131); Soberton Mill, Swanmore, Hants SO3 2QF (☎ 0329 833118)

CLARFELT, Hon Mrs (Christina Marjorie); o da of Baron Campbell of Croy, MC, PC (Life Peer), *qv*; *b* 24 Nov 1953; *Educ* West Heath; *m* 23 April 1980, Mark Michael Clarfelt, s of Jack Gerald Clarfelt, *qv*; 1 s (Max b 1986), 3 da (Alice b 1982, Tessa b 1984, Harriet b 1990); *Style—* Mrs Clarfelt; 8 Vicarage Gardens, London W8

CLARFELT, Jack Gerald; s of Barnet Clarfelt (d 1976), and Rene, *née* Frankel (d 1970); *b* 7 Feb 1914; *Educ* Grocers' Co Sch, Sorbonne; *m* 29 Sept 1948, Rebecca Esther (Baba), da of David Fredman (d 1975); 1 s (Mark Michael b 1952), 1 da (Georgina Caroline b 1949); *Career* cmmnd Queen's 1943-45, Royal Regt West Surrey 1944; admitted slr 1937; md: Home Killed Meat Assoc 1940-43 and 1945-54, Fatstock Mktg Corp 1954-60; chm and chief exec Smithfield & Zwanenberg Group Ltd 1960-73, dir S & W Berisford International, dep exec and chm Fatstock Mktg Corp 1975-79; farmer and dir of family private property cos; Freeman City of London; memb: Worshipful Co of Butchers, Slrs' Livery Co, Law Soc; *Recreations* shooting, fishing, golf, walking; *Clubs* City of London Livery; *Style—* Jack Clarfelt, Esq; Flat 1, 76 Hamilton Terrace, London NW8 9UL; Linhay Meads, Timsbury, Romsey, Hants SO51 OLA; 4 Castle Row, Horticultural Place, London W4 4JQ (☎ 081 747 1725, fax 081 994 9796)

CLARIDGE, Prof Michael Frederick; s of Frederick William Claridge (d 1965), of Rugby, Warwickshire, and Eva Alice, *née* Jeffery (d 1969); *b* 2 June 1934; *Educ* Lawrence Sheriff Sch Rugby, Keble Coll Oxford (MA, DPhil); *m* 30 Sept 1967, (Lindsey) Clare, da of Gilbert Hellings (d 1973), of Shipton under Wychwood, Oxon; 2 s (John, Robert), 1 da (Elin); *Career* Univ Coll Cardiff: lectr in zoology 1959-76, reader in entomology 1977-83, personal chair of entomology 1983-, acting head of zoology 1987-88; head of Sch Pure and Applied Biology Univ of Wales Cardiff 1989-; pres

Linnean Soc of London 1988-91 (memb Cncl 1984-); memb: Cncl Royal Entomological Soc 1971-74, British Ecological Soc (memb Cncl 1976-79), Systematics Assoc (memb Cncl 1984-87); FLS, FRES, FIBiol; *Books* The Leafhoppers and Planthoppers (contrib, 1985), The Organization of Communities, Past and Present (contrib, 1987), Prospects in Systematics (contrib, 1988); *Recreations* cricket, music, natural history; *Style—* Prof Michael Claridge; 84 The Hollies, Quakers Yard, Treharris, Mid Glamorgan CF46 5PP (☎ 0443 410734); School of Pure & Applied Biology, University of Wales, Cardiff CF1 3TL (☎ 0222 874147)

CLARK *see also*: Chichester-Clark, Stewart Clark

CLARK, Rt Hon Alan Kenneth McKenzie; PC (1991), MP (C) Plymouth Sutton Feb 1974-; s of Baron Clark, OM, CH, KCB (Life Peer, d 1983) and his 1 w Elizabeth, *née* Martin (d 1976); *b* 13 April 1928; *Educ* Eton, ChCh Oxford; *m* 1958, Caroline Jane, da of Col Leslie Brindley Bream Beuttler (and ggda of Hon George Ogilvie-Grant, 6 s of 6 Earl of Seafield); 2 s (James, Andrew); *Career* served in Household Cavalry Trg Regt 1946 and RAuxAF 1952-54; barr Inner Temple; mil historian, memb Inst Strategic Studies and Royal United Services Inst for Def Studies; vice chm Parly Def Ctee, memb Parly Home Affrs Ctee; under sec of state Employment (responsibilities incl legislation on trade union's political levy) 1983-86, min for Trade 1986-89, min for Defence Procurement 1989-; *Clubs* Brooks's, Pratt's; *Style—* The Rt Hon Alan Clark, MP; Saltwood Castle, Kent CT21 4QU (☎ 0303 267190)

CLARK, His Honour Judge Albert William; s of William Clark (d 1927), and Cissy, *née* Annis (d 1983); *b* 23 Sept 1922; *Educ* Christ's Coll Finchley; *m* 1951, Frances Philippa, da of Dr Samuel Lavington-Hart, of Cambridge and Tientsin China; 1 s (Adrian), 1 da (Susan); *Career* served WWII Patrol Serv N Atlantic 1941-45; called to the Bar 1949, met magistrate 1970, acting dep chm London Sessions 1971 dep circuit judge 1972, circuit judge Inner London Crown Court (SE) 1981-; *Recreations* fishing, walking, boating (MY Pelham); *Style—* His Honour Judge Albert Clark; 31 Hill Court, Wimbledon Hill Rd, Wimbledon, London SW19 7PD (☎ 081 947 8041); Pelham, 45 West Parade, Worthing, Sussex BN11 5ES (☎ 0903 47472)

CLARK, Alistair Campbell; s of Peter Campbell Clark (d 1960, Argyll & Sutherland Highlanders), of Barnhill, Dundee, Angus, and Janet Mtichell, *née* Scott; *b* 4 March 1933; *Educ* Grove Acad Broughty Ferry, Univ of St Andrews (MA, LLB, pres Law Soc); *m* 30 Nov 1960, Evelyn Macdonald, da of John Bell Johnston (d 1954), of Osborne House, Turriff, Aberdeenshire; 3 s (Johnston Peter b 29 Oct 1962, Alistair Struan b 11 Oct 1964, Campbell John Scott b 2 Nov 1971); *Career* admitted slr 1957, Blackadder Reid Johnston (formerly Reid Johnston Bell & Henderson) Solicitors Dundee 1961- (ptnr, jt sr ptnr); Hon Sheriff Tayside Central and Fife 1986-, memb and latterly chm Angus Legal Aid Ctee 1968-82, memb Tayside Children's Panel Advsy Ctee 1980-82, dean Faculty of Procurators & Slrs Dundee 1979-81, fndr chm Broughty Ferry & Dist Round Table, fndr pres Claverhouse Rotary Club Dundee, pres Law Soc of Scotland 1989-90 (memb Cncl 1982-); *Recreations* golf, travel and family life; *Clubs* New (Edinburgh), Royal and Ancient St Andrews, Angus Golf; *Style—* Alistair C Clark, Esq; Blythehill, 16 Balmyle Rd, West Ferry, Dundee (☎ 0382 77989); 30/34 Reform St, Dundee (☎ 0382 29222, fax 0382 201132, telex 76343 BRJSOL G)

CLARK, (Wilfred) Allan; s of John Wilfred Clark (d 1969), and Lavinia Clark, *née* Light (d 1940); *b* 18 Nov 1927; *Educ* Shipley Central Sch, Manchester Sch of Art, Aston Univ; *m* 20 March 1954, Emmie Catherine, da of Albert Edward Hillman; 2 da (Catherine Joy b 1955, Lindsay Gail b 1958); *Career* Mil Serv RE, served Malaya, Singapore, UK; architect, ptnr Percy Thomas Partnership 1975-; FRIBA, DipLA, FFB; *Recreations* golf, walking, painting; *Clubs* Nottingham, Notts Utd Servs, Royal Over-Seas League; *Style—* Allan Clark, Esq; Woodlands, Bunny Hill, Bunny, Nottingham NG11 6QQ; Percy Thomas Partnership Architects, Imperial Buildings, 20 Victoria Street, Nottingham NG1 2JS (☎ 0602 587095, fax 0602 414256, telex 449966)

CLARK, Andrew William; s of Lawrence George Stanley Clark, of Hayling Island, Hampshire, and Hilary Ann, *née* Rowe; *b* 25 Aug 1957; *Educ* Haberdashers' Aske's, Univ of Southampton (BSc); *m* 15 Aug 1981, Vanessa Fay, da of Prof Ronald Duncan Bradley; 1 s (George William b 12 Feb 1988), 2 da (Sarah Hilary b 3 Nov 1985, Philippa Mary b 29 July 1989); *Career* Vosper Thornycroft (UK) Ltd Southampton: graduate trainee 1978-80, design engr 1980-82, princ engr 1982-84; tech mangr Nautech Ltd 1984- (project mangr April 1984-Nov 1984); coordinator design team (winner 3 Br Design awards); MRINA 1988, CEng 1988; *Recreations* sailing, classic cars, running; *Clubs* Jaguar Enthusiasts; *Style—* Andrew Clark, Esq; c/o Nautech Ltd, Anchorage Park, Portsmouth, Hampshire PO3 5TD (☎ 0705 693611, fax 0705 694642)

CLARK, (Charles) Anthony; s of Stephen Clark (d 1965), and Winifred Clark (d 1971); *b* 13 June 1940; *Educ* King's Coll Sch Wimbledon, Pembroke Coll Oxford (MA); *m* 1968, Penelope Margaret, da of A John Brett (d 1979); 1 s (Jonathan b 1977), 2 da (Philippa b 1969, Joanna b 1971); *Career* head of Higher Educn Branch and under sec Dept of Educn and Sci; *Recreations* running, golf, sailing, reading; *Style—* Anthony Clark, Esq; The Paddock, Guildford Rd, Effingham, Surrey (☎ 0372 452337); Dept of Education and Science, London SE1 7PH (☎ 071 934 9912)

CLARK, Dr Charles Shirer; s of Charles Clark (d 1974), of Kemnay, Aberdeenshire, and Mary Ann, *née* Shirer; *b* 12 April 1918; *Educ* Monymusk Sch Aberdeenshire, Robert Gordon's Tech Coll (MPS), Univ of Aberdeen (MB ChB); *m* 5 Feb 1946, Marcelle Pamela Jacqueline, da of Henry Thomas Marrable (d 1974), of Shoreham, Kent; 1 s (Dingle), 3 da (Vivien Ogston, Alison Yardley, Kirsty Summers); *Career* various med posts London 1943-48; RAF Flt Lt; called to the Bar Middle Temple 1958, dep coroner St Pancras 1958-62, asst dep coroner W Middx 1958-62; HM coroner Essex 1962; author of various med articles; pres Soc of Coroners of Eng and Wales 1989-90; FRSM; *Recreations* football, golf; *Clubs* Royal Blackheath Golf, Frinton Golf; *Style—* Dr Charles Clark; 9 Kings Orchard, Eltham, London SE9 5TJ (☎ 081 850 8422)

CLARK, Dr Charles Victor; s of Dennis Clark, and Margaret, *née* Slowther; *b* 11 Aug 1956; *Educ* George Heriot's Sch Edinburgh, Univ of Edinburgh (BSc, MB ChB, MD, ChM, DSc); *m* 15 Dec 1983, Maureen, da of James Corr (d 1978); *Career* sr surgical registrar Moorfields Eye Hosp London 1986-88, conslt ophthalmic surgn Royal Infirmary of Edinburgh and sr lectr in ophthalmology Univ of Edinburgh 1988-; specialist in Glaucoma and Diabetic Eye Disease; author of over 40 scientific papers; memb: Medical and Scientific Section Br Diabetic Assoc, Assoc for Eye Res, Oxford Ophthalmological Congress, Clinical Autonomic Res Soc; fell RMS; FRCSEd 1985, FCOphth 1988; *Recreations* photography, music, theatre, rugby football; *Style—* Dr Charles Clark; 30 McLaren Rd, Edinburgh EH9 2BN; Princess Alexandra Eye Pavilion, Chalmers St, Edinburgh EH3 9HA (☎ 031 229 2477 ext 4075)

CLARK, Christopher Harvey; QC (1989); s of Maj Harvey Frederick Beckford Clark, of The Hill, Loperwood Lane, Calmore, Southampton, and Winifred Julia, *née* Caesar; *b* 20 Dec 1946; *Educ* Taunton's Sch Southampton, The Queen's Coll Oxford (MA); *m* 25 March 1972, Gillian Elizabeth Ann, da of Anthony Mullen, of The Long House, Ramridge Park, Weyhill, Andover, Hants; 1 s (Patrick Harvey b 1974), 2 da (Melanie Julia b 1976, Lucy Elizabeth b 1980); *Career* called to the Bar 1969; memb Western Circuit 1970-, asst rec 1982-86, rec of the Crown Ct 1986-; chm Western Circuit Fees and Legal Aid Ctee 1989; memb Wine Ctee of the Western Circuit 1985-90, chm Stockbridge Dramatic Soc 1977-, memb Longstock Parish Cncl 1979-, youth club organiser (The Longstock Tadpoles) 1981-; *Recreations* amateur dramatics, golf, cricket, gardening, skiing, reading; *Clubs* Hampshire (Winchester); *Style—* C H Clark, Esq, QC; 3 Pump Court, Temple, London EC4Y 7AJ (☎ 071 353 0711, fax 071 353 3319); 31 Southgate St, Winchester, Hampshire (☎ 0962 68161, fax 0962 67645)

CLARK, Clive Henry; s of Henry Stephen Clark, and Helena Cissie, *née* Hosegood; *b* 24 Aug 1941; *Educ* King Edward VI GS Chelmsford; *m* 6 July 1968, Gillian Moira, da of Oswald John Casey (d 1977); 3 da (Sharon, Melissa, Nicole); *Career* CA; ptnr Allfields 1973, dep managing ptnr Finnie Ross Allfields, exec ptnr Finnie & Co 1983; non-exec dir Assoc of Practising Accountants; FCA 1963; *Recreations* gardening, travel; *Style—* Clive Clark, Esq; Highport, 424 Baddow Rd, Great Baddow, Chelmsford (☎ 0245 72100); Kreston House, 8 Gate St, London WC2A 3HJ (☎ 071 831 9100, fax 071 831 2666, car 0836 723976, telex 897205)

CLARK, Sir Colin Douglas; 4 Bt (UK 1917), of Dunlambert, City of Belfast; MC; s of Sir George Ernest Clark, 2 Bt, DL (d 1950); suc bro, Sir George Anthony Clark, 3 Bt 1991; *b* 20 July 1918; *Educ* Eton, Trinity Coll Cambridge (BA, MA); *m* 19 Dec 1946, Margaret Coleman, yst da of late Maj-Gen Sir Charlton Watson Spinks, KBE, DSO, and widow of Maj Guy William Going Threlfall, MC, 8 Hus; 1 s (Jonathan George b 1947), 2 da (Sarah Louise (Mrs Kohler) b 1949, Gillian Margaret Anne (Mrs Spain) b 1957); *Heir* s, Jonathan George Clark b 9 Oct 1947; *Career* served WWII 1939-45 as Maj RE (despatches); *Style—* Sir Colin Clark, Bt, MC; Flaxpool House, Crowcombe, Taunton, Somerset

CLARK, Hon Colin MacArthur; s of Baron Clark, OM, CH, KCB (Life Peer, d 1983) and (1 w) Elizabeth, *née* Martin (d 1976); *b* 1932; *Educ* Eton, Ch Ch Oxford; *m* 1, 1961 (m dis 1969), Violette Verdy; m 2, 1971 (m dis), Faith Beatrice, formerly w of Julian Shuckburgh, and da of Sir Paul Hervé Giraud Wright, *qv*; m 3, Helena Sin, da of Cheung Wan Li (d 1969), of Hong Kong; *Style—* The Hon Colin Clark

CLARK, Daphne Diana; MBE (1983); da of William David Hooper (d 1949), and Muriel Rose, *née* Chell; *b* 18 Jan 1931; *Educ* Godolphin and Latymer Sch Hammersmith; *m* 28 June 1958, Ian Lawreston Clark (d 1981), s of Leonard Lawreston Clark (d 1983); 1 s (Jonathan David b 25 May 1959), 1 da (Diana Elizabeth b 20 Aug 1960, d 1973); *Career* dir and sec Richmond upon Thames Churches Housing Tst Gp 1971-; tstee: Sutton Housing Tst, Housing Assoc Charitable Tst; ctee memb: Network Housing Assoc Gp, Shaftesbury Housing Assoc; fell Inst of Housing; *Recreations* home and family related; *Style—* Mrs Daphne Clark, MBE; Centre House, 68 Sheen Lane, London SW14 8LP (☎ 081 878 9522, fax 081 878 6482)

CLARK, Dr David Findlay; OBE (1990); s of Rev Dr David Findlay Clark (d 1966), and Annie, *née* McKenzie (d 1963); *b* 30 May 1930; *Educ* Banff Acad, Univ of Aberdeen (MA, PhD); *m* 9 Oct 1954, Janet Anne, da of Gavin M Stephen, of Brechin, Angus; 2 da (Morag Anne (Mrs Baptie) b 1955, Linda Jane (Mrs Wimble) b 1958); *Career* Flying Offr RAF 1951-53, RAFVR 1953-57; psychologist Leicester Industl Rehabilitation Unit 1953-56, princ clinical psychologist Leicester Area Clinical Psychology Serv 1960-66 (sr clinical psychologist 1956-60), dir and top grade clinical psychologist Grampian Health Bd 1966-90, clinical sr lectr Dept of Mental Health Univ of Aberdeen 1966-; former: chm Div of Clinical Psychology Br Psychological Soc (memb Cncl), memb Health Serv Planning Cncl, town and co cncllr Banff and Banffshire; Hon Sheriff Grampian and Highlands and Island at Banff, safeguarder (in terms of SWK Scotland Act); Fell Br Psychological Soc 1969; *Books* Help, Hospitals and the Handicapped (1984), contrib to major textbooks; *Recreations* sailing, golf, photography, painting, squash, guitar, piano, travel, writing; *Clubs* Duff House Royal Golf, Banff Rotary (past pres); *Style—* Dr David Clark, OBE; Glendeveron, 8 Deveron Terrace, Banff AB45 1BB Scotland (☎ 02612 2624)

CLARK, Dr David George; MP (Lab) South Shields 1979-; s of George Clark, and Janet, of Askham, Cumbria; *b* 19 Oct 1939; *Educ* Windermere GS, Univ of Manchester (BA, MSc), Univ of Sheffield (PhD); *m* 1970, Christine, da of Ronald Kirkby, of Grasmere; 1 da; *Career* former forester, laboratory asst, student teacher, univ lectr; contested (Lab) Manchester Withington 1966, MP Colne Valley 1970-74 (contested again Oct 1974), oppn spokesman (Agric and Food) 1973-74, oppn spokesman Defence 1980-81, front bench oppn spokesman Environment 1981-87, princ oppn spokesman on Agric and Rural Affairs 1987-; *Books* Industrial Manager (1966), Radicalism to Socialism (1981), Victor Grayson (1985); *Style—* Dr David Clark, MP; House of Commons, London SW1A 0AA

CLARK, David Wincott; s of Jack Wincott Clark, of Halnackar, W Sussex, and Winifred Mary, *née* Watling (d 1988); *b* 21 June 1947; *Educ* Archbishop Tenison's GS, Queen Mary Coll Univ of London (BSc); *m* 20 July 1974, Susan Margaret, da of Maj Kenneth McCrae Cowan, RA; 2 s (Matthew b 1980, Daniel b 1981), 2 da (Sarah b 1985, Elinor b 1989); *Career* Bankers' Tst Int 1969-76, dep gen mangr Commerzbank AG 1976-90, gp treas Midland Bank 1990-; chm Forex Assoc London 1987-88 (memb Ctee 1982), sec gen Assoc Cambiste Internationale 1988-, memb Euro Advsy Ctee Chicago Mercantile Exchange; memb Ctee Rotherfield Cons Assoc; FRSA; *Recreations* rugby, angling, sailing; *Style—* David Clark, Esq; Readings Farm, Rotherfield, E Sussex (☎ 089 285 2360); 10-11 Austin Friars, London EC2N 2HE (☎ 071 638 5895)

CLARK, Derek; s of Kenneth Clark (d 1989), of Clacton-on-Sea, and Daphne, *née* Davies; *b* 12 June 1951; *Educ* Imperial Coll London (BSc, Sailing purple); *m* 27 Dec 1985, Grace; *Career* yachtsman; achievements incl: 470 class Olympic Games 1976, Americas Cup challenger Victory '83 1982-83, Americas Cup defender Kookabura III 1987, Admirals' Cup winners 1989, Enterprise world champions 1974; records: 470 class World Cup 1976, 3 Two Ton worlds Poole 1981, 2 One Ton worlds Naples 1989; engr and professional driver: Holehaven Creek 1975, Sullon Voe Oil Terminal 1976, Tilbury Dock Flood Prevention 1977; film set designer and builder Pirates (dir Polanski) 1984; Churchill fell 1983; *Books* New America's Cup Rule (co-author), Whitbread Rule (co-author); *Recreations* windsurfing, cycling, walking, reading; *Style—* Derek Clark, Esq

CLARK, Derek John; s of Robert Clark (d 1970), of Eastbourne, and Florence Mary, *née* Wise (d 1960); *b* 17 June 1929; *Educ* Selhurst GS, SE London Tech Coll; *m* 21 March 1949, Edna Doris, da of Alfred Coome (d 1966), of Croydon; 1 s (Paul Wesley b 1949), 1 da (Laura Alison b 1955); *Career* Nat Serv RAF 1948-49; asst sec (later comptroller) RICS 1966-70, dir of admin Inst of Cost Mgmnt Accountants 1970-82, sec Inst of Structural Engrs 1982-; FCIS 1982; *Recreations* squash, athletics; *Style—* Derek Clark, Esq; 7 Elvington Green, Hayesford Park, Bromley, Kent BR2 9DE (☎ 081 460 9055); The Inst of Structural Engineers, 11 Upper Belgrave St, London SW1X 8BH (☎ 071 235 4535)

CLARK, Dingle Charles; s of Dr Charles Clark, *qv*, of London, and Marcelle Pamela, *née* Marrable; *b* 7 June 1959; *Educ* Eltham Coll London, Univ of Southampton (BSc); *m* 15 April 1989, Caroline, da of John Patrick Hough, of Blackheath; 1 da (Charlotte Annabel Felicity b 18 Jan 1991); *Career* called to the Bar Middle Temple 1981, pt/t lectr Cncl of Legal Educn 1987-; memb London Borough of Greenwich 1982-, chief whip Cons Pty 1985-90; govr Woolwich Coll 1990-; *Recreations* golf, football; *Clubs* Royal Blackheath Golf, Frinton Golf; *Style—* Dingle Clark, Esq; 24 Corner Green,

Blackheath, London (☎ 071 852 8212); 9 Kings Bench Walk, Temple, London EC4 (☎ 071 353 7202, fax 071 583 2030)

CLARK, Dr Douglas Henderson; s of William Robb Clark (d 1932), of Cummock, Ayrshire, and Jane Henderson Clark (d 1979); *b* 20 Jan 1917; *Educ* Ayr Acad, Glasgow Univ (MD, ChM, DSc), John Hopkins Hosp Baltimore USA; *m* 5 April 1950, Morag (d 1972), da of Capt Donald Kennedy, of Glasgow (d 1930); 3 s (William Robb Kennedy b 1951, Donald Kennedy b 1955, Alan Douglas b 1957); *Career* Capt RAMC 1941-46; served: India, Burma, Malaya; surgn Western Infimary, ret 1982; pres RCP Glasgow 1980-82, memb Ct Glasgow Univ 1982-90; Hon DSc Glasgow Univ; fell Acad of Med Singapore 1982, Hon FRCS 1983, Hon FRCS Ireland, fell Coll of Surgns SA 1980; *Style—* Dr Douglas Clark; 36 Southbrae Drive, Glasgow G13 1PZ (☎ 041 959 3556)

CLARK, Eric; s of Horace Ernest Clark (d 1978), of Weston-super-Mare, Somerset, and Hilda Dorothy, *née* Mitchley; *b* 29 July 1937; *Educ* Handsworth GS; *m* 12 April 1972, Marcelle, da of Jacob Bernstein (d 1956), of Manchester; 1 s (Daniel b 1980), 2 da (Rachael b 1975, Charlotte b 1978); *Career* staff reporter The Daily Mail 1962-64, staff writer The Guardian 1964-66, various appts The Observer 1966-72, articles published in foreign newspapers incl Melbourne Age and Wash Post, writer of fiction and non fiction 1972-; *Books* Corps Diplomatique (1973), Black Gambit (1978), The Sleeper (1979), Send in The Lions (1981), Chinese Burn (1984), The Want Makers: The World of Advertising, How They Make You Buy (1988); Fell Eng Centre Int PEN; memb: Soc of Authors, Crime Writers Assoc; *Clubs* Savile; *Style—* Eric Clark, Esq; c/o Jonathan Clowes Ltd, Iron Bridge House, Bridge Approach, London NW1 8BD (☎ 071 722 7674)

CLARK, Sir Francis Drake; 5 Bt (UK 1886), of Melville Crescent, Edinburgh; s of Sir Thomas Clark, 3 Bt (d 1977); suc bro, Sir John Douglas Clark, 4 Bt 1991; *b* 16 July 1924; *Educ* Edinburgh Acad; *m* 14 Aug 1958, Mary, yr da of late John Alban Andrews, MC, FRCS; 1 s (Edward Drake b 27 April 1966); *Heir* s, Edward Drake Clark b 1966; *Career* RN 1943-46; *Style—* Sir Francis Clark, Bt; Woodend Cottages, Burgh-next-Aylsham, Norfolk

CLARK, Geoffrey Mossop; TD (1962); s of Maj James John Clark (d 1947), and Muriel Rose, *née* Mossop (d 1976); *b* 23 Oct 1928; *Educ* Quarry Bank Sch Liverpool; *m* 1, 10 Aug 1956 (m dis 1979), Ruth, da of Llewellyn Merrick-Jones (d 1974); 3 da (Deborah b 17 March 1958 d 1970, Philippa b 30 June 1960, Rebecca b 19 June 1968); m 2, 25 April 1981, Diana Celia, da of Ronald George Murphy (d 1971); *Career* cmmnd Royal Signals 1948; TA 1949-68: cmd 307 Signal Sqdn 1963-66, 1 Sqdn 59 Signal Regt 1966-68; Royal Insurance 1950-81 (mangr Leeds Life Branch 1973-81), md Stylo Insurance and Management Ltd 1981-90; Insur Inst of Leeds: sec 1973-80, pres 1982-83, currently vice pres; independent chartered insurance practitioner; FCII 1958; *Recreations* golf, gardening; *Clubs* Pannal Golf; *Style—* Geoffrey Clark, Esq, TD; Mill Cottage, Pannal, Harrogate, N Yorks GH3 1JY (☎ 0423 879 387)

CLARK, George Thomas; s of George Clark (d 1938), of 33 Sedley Taylor Rd, Cambridge, and the late Daisy Elizabeth, *née* Jaques; *b* 24 May 1919; *Educ* Perse Sch Cambridge, Jesus Coll Cambridge (MA, LLB); *m* 10 Nov 1941, Barbara Elizabeth (Betty) (d 1986), da of the late Charles Frederick Morley, of 36 Barrow Rd, Cambridge; 1 s (Timothy Glanvil Clark), 1 da (Patricia Mary (Mrs Barnes)); *Career* cmmnd 1939, Arborfield 1939-40, Staff Lt 1940-41; posted: REMBR via Liverpool 1943 (ended up in Beolali), 1 Indian Regt Muslim Hindu mix, 8 Sikh Regt, 9 Raj (demobbed Maj 1946); WWII Victory Medal; articled clerk Landons 1946-48, admitted slr 1948; Freshfields: mangr 1949, ptnr 1952, ret 1982; chm Cowden Villiage Hall Ctee; pres: Cowden & Dist Hort Soc, Cowden & Dist Sports Assoc; charitable work; Freeman City of London, Master City of London Slrs Co 1976-77; memb Law Soc, FRSA, Kentucky Colonel USA; *Recreations* gardening, walking, reading, writing letters, music; *Clubs* Oriental; *Style—* George Clark, Esq

CLARK, Gillian Margaret; da of John Francis Foulger Clark, of The Moorings, Chart Sutton, Maidstone, Kent ME17 3SB, and Patricia Moira, *née* Rodger; *b* 2 Sept 1961; *Educ* Ashford Sch for Girls; *Career* sportswoman (badminton); Euro Jr Champion Ladies Doubles 1979; Cwlth Games 1982: Team Gold, Ladies Doubles Silver, Singles Bronze; World Championships Ladies Doubles Bronze 1983, Euro Champion Ladies Doubles 1982, 1984 and 1986; Cwlth Games 1986: Team Gold, Ladies Doubles Gold, Singles Bronze; Cwlth Games 1990: Team Gold, Ladies Doubles Silver, Mixed Doubles Bronze; Euro Champion Mixed Doubles and Ladies Doubles Silver 1988; memb England Badminton Team with 104 caps; chm: Int Badminton Players Fedn, English Badminton Players Assoc; *Clubs* All England Badminton, Wimbledon Squash & Badminton; *Style—* Miss Gillian Clark

CLARK, Gillian Margaret Rose; da of Cyril Geoffrey Gunning Lockwood (d 1981), and Vera Irene Lockwood, *née* Marchant, of Kimber Close, Lancing, Sussex; *b* 15 Jan 1949; *Educ* Varndean GS for Girls; *m* 16 Oct 1982, Philip Stephen Clark; 1 da (Juliette Annabelle b 11 March 1984); *Career* Eagle Star: joined as accident underwriting clerk 1968, head clerk Chatham branch 1972-74, accident underwriting superintendent Maidstone 1974-81, underwriting superintendent UK 1981-82, asst planning mangr 1982-83, asst mktg mangr 1983-86, mktg servs mangr 1986-88, mktg mangr UK Gen Div 1988-90, business devpt mangr 1990-; FCII 1974, AIPM 1979, DipMktg, MinstM, MCIM 1986, memb Soc of Fellows London 1987, chartered insurer 1989; *Recreations* golf and squash; *Style—* Mrs Gillian Clark; Keswick House, 16 Keswick Road, Orpington, Kent BR6 OEU (☎ 0689 870300); Eagle Star Insurance Co Ltd, 60 St Mary Axe, London EC3A 8JQ (☎ 071 929 1111 x 33800, fax 071 895 0497)

CLARK, Rev (Charles) Gordon Froggatt; s of Rev Charles Clark (d 1940), and Amy, *née* Froggatt; *b* 21 April 1907; *Educ* Oakham Sch, Emmanuel Coll Cambridge (MA), Wycliffe Hall Oxford; *m* 10 Feb 1934, Joan, da of Capt Raleigh Hills (d 1938), of Wood End, Cromford, Derbys; 2 da (Ruth b 21 April 1935, Susan b 28 Aug 1938); *Career* ordained: deacon 1931, priest 1932; asst curate: St John Ealing 1931-33, St Matthew Bayswater 1933-35; rector Ilmington Diocese of Coventry 1935-40; perpetual curate Somercotes Diocese of Derby 1940-43, rector Barton Seagrave Diocese of Peterborough 1943-48, vicar All Saints Crowborough Diocese of Chichester 1948-67, chaplain Kent Sussex Hosp Tunbridge Wells Diocese of Rochester 1968-80, commissary to Bishop of Ekiti (Nigeria) 1967-, hon curate Tunbridge Wells Holy Trinity with Christ Church Rochester 1967-80 (licence to officiate 1967-85); permission to officiate: Chichester 1967-89, Canterbury 1967-87; hon curate Penshurst and Fordcombe Rochester 1980-84 (permission to officiate 1985-89), permission to officiate Diocese of Peterborough 1989-, vice pres Church Missionary Soc; dir: Reformation Church Tst, Bowles Outdoor Pursuits Centre 1964-88, Corp of the Sons of the Clergy 1958-88; life memb Crowborough C of C, govr Wadhurst Coll 1949-89, memb Stamford Rotary Club (Lincs); Liveryman Worshipful Co of Grocers 1933; *Recreations* bowls; *Clubs* National, City Livery; *Style—* The Rev Gordon Clark; 4 Village Farm Close, Castor, nr Peterborough, Cambs PE5 7BX (☎ 0733 380527)

CLARK, Graham Ronald; s of Ronald Edward Clark, of 17 Lea Rd, Lea, Preston, Lancs, and Annie, *née* Eckersley (d 1984); *b* 10 Nov 1941; *Educ* Kirkham GS Lancs, Loughborough Coll of Educn (DLC), Univ of Loughborough (MSc); *m* 1, 9 April 1966 (m dis 1975), Susan, da of late Walter George Fenn, of Oxford; m 2, 31 March 1979, Joan Barbara, da of Albert Frederick Lawrence (d 1956), of Dunstable, Beds; 1 step da (Sarah Elisabeth b 8 Oct 1965); *Career* opera singer, character tenor; teacher 1964-69, sr regnl offr The Sports Cncl 1971-75; princ Scottish Opera 1975-77, debut London Bomarzo (Ginastera) 1976, princ ENO 1978-85; roles incl: Alexey in The Gambler (Prokofiev), Mephistopheles in Doktor Faustus (Busoni); freelance 1985-, guest artist at: Bayreuther Festspiele Germany (incl David in Die Meistersinger, Mime and Loge in Ring) 1981-90, Met Opera NY 1985-90, Vienna Staatsoper, Munich, Zurich, Paris, Barcelona, Amsterdam, Turin, Rome, Toronto, WNO; Laurence Olivier award 1986; *Recreations* sports; *Clubs* Lansdowne; *Style—* Graham Clark, Esq; c/o Ingpen & Williams Ltd, 14 Kensington Court, London W8

CLARK, Guy Wyndham Niall Hamilton; JP (1981), DL (Renfrewshire 1987); s of Capt George Hubert Wyndham Clark (d 1978), and Lavinia Maraguita Smith, *née* Shaw Stewart (d 1971); *b* 28 March 1944; *Educ* Eton, Mons OCS; *m* 28 Jan 1968, Brighid Lovell, da of Maj Lovell Greene, of SA; 2 s (Charles Guy Lovell Wyndham, Thomas Houston Marcus Wyndham), 1 da (Nicola); *Career* cmmnd Coldstream Gds 1962-67; investmt mangr Murray Johnstone Ltd Glasgow 1973-77, ptnr RC Greig & Co (stockbrokers) Glasgow 1977-86, dir Greig Middleton & Co Ltd (stockbrokers) 1986-; memb Exec Ctee Erskine Hosp for Disabled Servicemen Renfrewshire; memb Int Stock Exchange 1983; *Recreations* shooting, hunting, racing, fishing; *Clubs* Turf, Western; *Style—* Guy Clark, Esq; Braeton House, Inverkip, Renfrewshire, PA16 ODU (☎ 0475 520619); Greig, Middleton & Co Ltd, Pacific House, 70 Wellington St, Glasgow G2 6UD (fax 041 221 5286, telex 776695)

CLARK, Henry Percival Bolton; *b* 4 Oct 1944; *Educ* The Dragon Sch Oxford, Harrow; *m* 2 Dec 1978, Gill; 1 s (Austen b 1980), 1 da (Celia b 1982); *Career* managing ptnr Nottingham office Ernst & Young; dir: Bridge Housing Soc Ltd, Notts Business Venture; treas Harby PCC; CA; *Recreations* avoiding all sport; *Style—* Henry Clark, Esq; 10/12 The Ropewalk, Nottingham NG1 5DT (☎ 0602 411861, fax 0602 483 369)

CLARK, Howard Keith; s of James Keith Clark, of Leeds, and Doris Clark (d 1964); *b* 26 Aug 1954; *Educ* Rothwell Secdy Modern Sch; *m* 1 (m dis 1981), Christine; 1 da (Angela b 8 April 1975); m 2, 12 Nov 1983, Beverley Jane, da of Frank Lawson; 1 s (Benjamin Edward b 19 Dec 1990); *Career* professional golfer 1973-; amateur record: boys champion 1971, Yorks champion 1973, youth int 1973, English Walker Cup team Home Ints 1973; professional wins: Tournament Player's under 25 champion 1976, Madrid Open 1978, 1984 and 1986, Portuguese Open 1978, PGA champion Wentworth 1984, Jersey Open 1985, Glasgow Open 1985, Spanish Open 1986, Moroccan Open 1987, PLM Open 1987, English Open 1988; England appearances: World Cup 3 times, Hennessey Cup 1984 (winners), Dunhill Cup 1987 (winners); memb Ryder Cup team 1977, 1981, 1985 (winners), 1987 (winners) and 1989; wholesale fruit market porter 1970, clerical offr Electoral Registration Office Leeds 1971 and 1972 (winters only); *Books* What's Your Sport? (with Mitchell Platts); *Recreations* snooker, sports cars (trying to keep them on the road), rugby league (Leeds); *Style—* Howard Clark, Esq; c/o PGA European Tour, Wentworth Club, Virginia Water, Surrey (☎ 0344 842881)

CLARK, Hugh Victor; s of Lt Cdr Philip Neville Clark, VRD, RNR, of Gorsley, Hereford, and Worcestershire and Winifred Betty, *née* Kiddle; *b* 18 May 1948; *Educ* Brewood GS Staffs; *m* 5 Dec 1970, Rosemary Anne, da of Kenneth Walter Solloway, of Wolverhampton; 1 s (Richard Ian b 1974), 1 da (Michelle Emma b 1977); *Career* Westminster Bank Ltd 1965-67, Canadian Imperial Bank of Commerce 1967-70, Nat Westminster Bank Ltd 1970-77; Tarmac plc: treas accountant 1978-83, asst gp treas 1983-87, gp treas 1987-; ACIB 1975, FCT 1982; *Recreations* photography, motor racing; *Style—* Hugh Clark, Esq; Tarmac plc, Hilton Hall, Essington, Wolverhampton WV11 2BQ (☎ 0902 307407, fax 0902 307408, telex 338544)

CLARK, Ian Robertson; CBE (1979); s of Alexander Clark, and Annie Dundas, *née* Watson; *b* 18 Jan 1939; *Educ* Dalziel HS Motherwell; *m* 1961, Jean Scott Waddell, *née* Lang; 1 s, 1 da; *Career* chm: Ventures Div Costain Group, Sigma Resources plc 1986-88, Br Nat Oil Corpn 1976-82, BNOC Ventures; jt md Britoil 1982-85; former co treas Zetland CC; chief exec Shetlands Islands Cncl 1974-76; *Books* Resevoir of Power (1979); *Recreations* reading, writing, walking; *Style—* Ian Clark, Esq, CBE; 16 Pan's Gardens, Camberley, Surrey GU15 1HY

CLARK, Sir John Allen; eld s of Sir Allen Clark (d 1962), and Jocelyn, *née* Culverhouse; bro of Michael William Clark, *qv*; *b* 14 Feb 1926; *Educ* Harrow, Trinity Coll Cambridge; *m* 1, 1952 (m dis 1962), Deirdre Kathleen, da of Samuel Herbert Waterhouse; 1 s, 1 da; m 2, 1970, Olivia, da of H Pratt; 2 s (twins), 1 da; *Career* served WWII RNVR (Sub-Lt); received early industl trg with Met Vickers and Ford Motor co; spent year in USA studying electronics indust; asst to gen mangr Plessey International Ltd 1949, dir and gen mangr Plessey (Ireland) and Wireless Telephone Co 1950; The Plessey Co Ltd: dir 1953, md 1962-70, dep chm 1967-70, chm and chief exec 1970-89; dir: International Computers Ltd 1968-79, Banque Nationale de Paris Ltd 1976-89; pres Telecommunications Engrg and Mfrg Assoc 1964-66 and 1971-73; chm Wavertree Technol Park 1983-88; vice pres: Inst of Works Mangrs, Engrg Employers' Fedn; memb: Nat Defence Industs Cncl, Engrg Industs Cncl 1975-89; govr Harrow Sch 1982-; Order of Henry the Navigator (Portugal) 1973; kt 1971; *Recreations* shooting, riding; *Clubs* Boodles; *Style—* Sir John Clark; Redenham Park, Redenham, Nr Andover, Hants

CLARK, John Edward; s of Albert Edward Clark (d 1973), of Kent, and Edith, *née* Brown (d 1984); *b* 18 Oct 1932; *Educ* Clitheroe Royal GS, Keble Coll Oxford (MA, BCL); *m* 1969, Judith Rosemary, da of Dr Arnold Marklew Lester; 1 s (Roy), 2 da (Katherine, decd, Claire); *Career* called to the Bar; dep sec Nat Assoc of Parish Cncls 1961-78, sec Nat Assoc of Local Cncls 1978-; *Recreations* board games, collecting detective fiction, walking; *Style—* John Clark Esq; 113 Turney Rd, London SE21 7JB (☎ 071 274 1381); 108 Great Russell St, London WC1B 3LD (☎ 071 637 1865)

CLARK, Keith; s of Douglas William Clark (d 1967), of Chichester, Sussex, and Evelyn Lucy, *née* Longlands; *b* 25 Oct 1944; *Educ* Chichester HS for Boys, St Catherine's Coll Oxford (MA, BA); *m* 2 Nov 1976, Linda Sue, da of Eric Woodler, Ringwood, Hants; 1 s (Nicholas Howard Douglas b 1980), 1 da (Katherine Sara Amy b 1984); *Career* slr; ptnr (joined 1971, specialising in fin law and debt restructuring, various mgmnt appts) Clifford Chance 1977-; memb: Law Soc 1971, Slrs Benevolent Soc, Int Bar Assoc; *Recreations* hiking, family, drama; *Style—* Keith Clark, Esq; Royex House, Aldermanbury Sq, London EC2V 7LD (☎ 071 600 0808, fax 071 726 8561, telex 8959991)

CLARK, Ven Kenneth James; DSC (1944); s of Francis James Clark, OBE, of 15 Elizabeth Ct, Hempstead Rd, Watford, Herts, and Winifred Adelaide, *née* Martin (d 1984); *b* 31 May 1922; *Educ* Watford GS, St Catherine's Coll Oxford (MA), Cuddesdon Theol Coll Oxford; *m* 24 July 1948, Elisabeth Mary Monica Helen, da of Arthur St George Joseph McCarthy Huggett (d 1968); 3 s (Simon b 1954, Alistair b 1954, Jonathan b 1958), 3 da (Marguerite b 1949, Christine b 1951, Rachel b 1964); *Career* cadet RN 1939, midshipman 1940, Lt 1942, served in submarines 1942-46; baptist min Forest Row Sussex 1950-52; ordained (C of E): deacon 1952, priest 1953; curate: Brinkworth 1952-53, Cricklade and Latton 1953-56; vicar: Holy Cross Inns Court Bristol 1956-61, Westbury-on-Trym Bristol 1961-72, St Mary Redcliffe Bristol 1972-82; rural dean Bedminster 1973-79, hon canon Bristol 1974-, archdeacon of Swindon 1982-; *Recreations* music, travel; *Style—* The Ven the Archdeacon of Swindon; 70 Bath Rd, Swindon, Wilts SN1 4AY (☎ 0793 695 059)

CLARK, His Hon Judge (Francis) Leo; QC (1972); s of Sydney John Clark (d 1969), of Oxford, and Florence Lilian, *née* Huxtable; *b* 15 Dec 1920; *Educ* Bablake Sch, St Peter's Coll Oxford; *m* 1, 1957, Denise Jacqueline, da of Raymond Rambaud, of Paris; 1 s; m 2, 1967, Dr Daphne Margaret Clark, da of David Humphreys, of Hitchin; *Career* called to the Bar 1947, rec Crown Ct 1972-76, circuit judge 1976-; hon rec of Oxford 1979-; *Style*— His Hon Judge Leo Clark, QC; c/o The Combined Court Centre, Saint Aldates, Oxford

CLARK, Martin Paul; s of Keith Samuel Clark, and Rose Ann Clark; *b* 27 Oct 1968; *Educ* Dormston Secdy Modern Sch Sedgley; *Career* professional snooker player 1987-; amateur: Sedgley Ex-Serviceman's Club, Whitemore Cons Club, Wednesbury Cons Club, winner 28 tournaments, top ranked player before turning professional; England: 4 jr appearances Home Int Championships 1985, 5 sr appearances Home Int Championships 1986 (amateur world record break of 141 v Wales); *Recreations* supporting Wolves FC; *Style*— Martin Clark, Esq; 46 Gibbons Hill Rd, Sedgley, West Midlands DY3 1QA (☎ 0902 675014)

CLARK, Dr Michael; MP (Cons) Rochford 1983-; s of late Mervyn Clark and Sybilla Norma, *née* Winscott; *b* 8 Aug 1935; *Educ* King Edward VI GS Retford, King's Coll London, St John's Coll Cambridge, Univ of Minnesota; *m* 1958, Valerie Ethel, da of C S Harbord; 1 s, 1 da; *Career* mgmnt conslt and industl chemist; ICI 1960-66, Smiths Industs 1966-69, PA Consulting Gp 1969-; chm Cambridge Cons Assoc 1980-83 (treas 1975-78, vice chm 1978-80); contested (C) Ilkeston 1979; hon sec Parly and Scientific Ctee 1985-, Anglo-Nepalese All Pty Gp 1985-, All Pty Gp for the Chem Indust 1985-; hon treas: Br-Malawi All Pty Gp 1987-, Exec Ctee Inter Pty Union 1987, All Pty Space Ctee 1988-; memb House of Commons Select Ctee for Energy 1983- (chm 1989-) fell King's Coll London 1987; FRSC 1988; *Recreations* golf, gardening, DIY; *Clubs* Carlton, Rochford Cons; *Style*— Dr Michael Clark, MP; House of Commons, London SW1A 0AA

CLARK, Michael William; CBE (1977), DL (1988); s of Sir Allen Clark (d 1962), of Braxted Park, Witham, Essex, and Jocelyn Anina Marie Louise, *née* Culverhouse (d 1964); *b* 7 May 1927; *Educ* Harrow; *m* 1, 1955, Shirley, *née* Macphadzen (d 1974); 1 s (Duncan), 2 da (Marion b 1957 d 1988, Miranda (Mrs Carew-Jones)), 1 step s (Matthew Harragin b 1953); m 2, 6 April 1985, Virginia Ann, Marchioness Camden, da of Francis Harry Hume Finlaison (d 1968); *Career* Subaltern Grenadier Guards 1945-48; Plessey Co: joined 1950, fndr chm Plessey Electronic Systems, former dep chm and dep chief exec, ret 1987; memb: Electronics EDC 1975-80, Cncl IOD, Nat Electronics Cncl, Ct Univ of Essex; pres Essex Branch: SSAFA, Grenadier Gds Assoc; CIEE, CompIERE; *Recreations* shooting, fishing, forestry; *Clubs* Boodle's, Pratt's; *Style*— Michael Clark, Esq, CBE, DL; 16 Ranelagh House, Chelsea, London SW3 3EL; Braxted Park, Witham, Essex CM8 3EN

CLARK, Hon Mrs (Moira Muriel); o da of Baron Sorensen (Life Peer, d 1971); *b* 6 Oct 1917; *m* 13 Oct 1951, Derek Gerald Clark, JP, s of Wilfred Charles Clark (d 1971), of 12 Smeaton Rd, Woodford Bridge, Essex; 2 da; *Style*— The Hon Mrs Clark; 15 Crossing Rd, Epping, Essex

CLARK, Oswald William Hugh; CBE (1978); s of Rev Hugh Miller Allison Clark (d 1962), of Raynes Park, London SW20, and Mabel Bessie Clark (d 1969); *b* 26 Nov 1917; *Educ* Rutlish Sch Merton, Univ of London (BA, BD); *m* 23 July 1966, Diana Mary, da of William Alfred Hine, of New Milton, Hants; 1 da (Alison Mary Cynthia b 1967); *Career* WWII Maj 2 Derbyshire Yeomanry 8 Army ME NW Europe; asst dir gen GLC 1973-79 (formerly London Co Cncl, joined 1937); C of E: memb Gen Synod (formerly Church Assembly) 1948-90, memb Standing and Legislative Ctees 1950-90, memb Standing Orders Ctee 1950-90, church cmmr 1958-88, chm House of Laity 1979-85 (vice chm 1970-79), vice pres Corp of Church House 1981-, memb Crown Appts Cmmn 1987-90; life fell Guild of Guide Lectrs 1982-, princ Soc of the Faith 1987-; memb Worshipful Co of Parish Clerks; *Recreations* history of London, Goss china, heraldry; *Clubs* Cavalry and Guards, Pratt's; *Style*— O W H Clark, Esq, CBE; 8 Courtlands Ave, Hampton, Middx TW12 3NT (☎ 081 979 1081)

CLARK, His Hon Judge Paul Nicholas Rowntree; s of Henry Rowntree Clark (d 1975), and Gwendoline Victoria Clark; *b* 17 Aug 1940; *Educ* Bristol GS, New Coll Oxford (MA); *m* 9 Sept 1967, Diana Barbara, da of Maurice Stapenhill Bishop, of Lyme Regis, Dorset; 2 s (Oliver b 1972, Edward b 1977), 1 da (Harriet b 1970); *Career* called to the Bar Middle Temple (Harmsworth scholar) 1966, bencher 1982, barr practising on Oxford Circuit, later Midland and Oxford Circuit 1966-85, recorder 1981, circuit judge 1985-; *Style*— His Hon Judge Paul Clark; 2 Harcourt Buildings, Temple, London EC4Y 9DB

CLARK, Raymond Vincent; s of Peter Clark, of Broxbourne, Herts, and Eileen, *née* Rothery; *b* 26 Feb 1946; *Educ* Tottenham Boys Sch, NE London Poly (Dip Arch); *m* 16 Aug 1969, Gillian Elizabeth, da of Henry Cook, of Frinton, Essex; 2 s (Simon b 15 May 1978, Iain b 22 July 1982); *Career* ptnr Clark Hatt Quirke Partnership 1982- (co-fndr); memb: RIBA 1976, ARCUK 1976; *Style*— Raymond Clark, Esq; Knot's Foss, 73 Hall Lane, Gt Chishill, Royston, Herts (0763 838 785); Clark Hatt Quirke Partnership, The Maltings, 44 Whitehorse St, Baldock, Hertfordshire (☎ 0462 895 110, fax 0462 895 099)

CLARK, Sir Robert Anthony; DSC (1944); yr s of John Clark and Gladys, *née* Dyer; *b* 6 Jan 1924; *Educ* Highgate, King's Coll Cambridge; *m* 1949, Andolyn Marjorie Beynon Lewis; 2 s, 1 da; *Career* ptnr Slaughter and May Slrs 1953; Hill Samuel Bank Ltd 1974-, TSB Hill Samuel Bank Hldg Co plc 1981-89 (joined 1961, later Philip Hill, Higginson, Erlangers Ltd), IMI 1981-89, Alfred McAlpine plc 1958-, Marley plc 1985-89, dir Shell Tport and Trading 1982-, Racal Telecom plc 1988-, vice chm SmithKline Beecham plc 1986-; chm: Doctors and Dentist Review Body 1979-86, Charing Cross Hosp Med Sch 1981-; Hon DSc Cranfield 1982; kt 1976; *Clubs* Pratt's; *Style*— Sir Robert Clark, DSC; Deputy Chairman, TSB Gp plc, 100 Wood St, London EC2P 2AJ (☎ 071 628 8011); Munstead Wood, Godalming, Surrey (☎ 048 68 7867)

CLARK, Prof Robert Bernard; s of Joseph Laurence Clark (d 1980), of London and Burrowbridge, Somerset, and Dorothy, *née* Halden (d 1988); *b* 13 Oct 1923; *Educ* St Marylebone GS, Univ of London (BSc), Univ of Exeter (BSc), Univ of Glasgow (PhD), Univ of London (DSc); *m* 1, 19 July 1956 (m dis 1969), Mary Eleanor, da of Walter Lawrence (d 1969), of San Francisco, USA; m 2, 30 Dec 1970, Susan Diana, da of Lt-Col Leonard Smith (d 1971), of Haslemere, Surrey; 1 s (Stephen Robert Leonard b 1975), 1 da (Juliet Louise b 1972); *Career* asst in zoology Univ of Glasgow 1950-53, asst prof of zoology Univ of Calif at Berkeley USA 1953-55, lectr in zoology Univ of Bristol 1956-65, prof of zoology and dir The Dove Marine Laboratory Univ of Newcastle upon Tyne 1965-89; memb: NERC 1971-77 and 1982-85, Royal Cmmn on Environmental Pollution 1978-82, Advsy Cmmn on Pesticides 1985-90; FIBiol 1966, FLS 1969, FRSE 1970; *Books* Dynamics in Metazoan Evolution (1964), Invertebrate Panorama (1971), Marine Pollution (1986), Marine Pollution Bulletin (ed); *Style*— Prof Robert Clark, FRSE; Highbury House, Highbury, Newcastle upon Tyne NE2 3LN (☎ 091 281 4672); Department of Biology, The University, Newcastle upon Tyne NE1 7RU (☎ 091 222 6656)

CLARK, Robert John Whitten; s of Robert Joseph Clark, MBE (d 1963), of Edinburgh, and Patricia Lewis, *née* Whitten (d 1976); *b* 29 Sept 1932; *Educ* George Heriot's Sch Edinburgh; *m* 22 June 1957, Christine Margaret, da of Robert Reid (d 1977), of West Calder, Midlothian; 1 s (Colin Michael b 9 Jan 1960), 1 da (Alison Ishbel (Mrs Hendry) b 14 Dec 1963); *Career* Scottish Educn Dept: joined 1949, various appts rising to private sec to Sec of Dept 1960-61, head teacher Training Branch 1967-69, head Schs Branch 1969-73; head Children's Hearings Branch Social Work Services Gp 1973-75, head Children's Div Social Work Services Gp 1975-76, head List D (Approved) Schs Div Social Work Services Gp 1976-79; head: Home Def and Emergency Servs Co-ordination Div Scottish Home and Health Dept 1979-85, Fisheries Regimes Fishstock Mgmnt Mktg and Trade Div Dept of Agric and Fisheries for Scotland 1985-87; former capt and former pres Edinburgh and Dist Civil Service Golfing Soc, former vice capt Scottish Civil Service Golfing Soc; *Recreations* travel, golf, reading, gardening; *Clubs* Royal Burgess Golfing Soc of Edinburgh, Scottish Educn Dept Golf (capt 1984-85); *Style*— Robert J W Clark, Esq; 39 Gordon Rd, Edinburgh EH12 6LZ (☎ 031 334 4312)

CLARK, Prof Robin Jon Hawes; s of Reginald Hawes Clark, of Christchurch, NZ, and Marjorie Alice, *née* Thomas; *b* 16 Feb 1935; *Educ* Christ's Coll Christchurch NZ, Canterbury Univ Coll Univ of NZ (BSc, MSc), UCL (PhD, DSc); *m* 30 May 1964, Beatrice Rawdin, da of Ellis Rawdin Brown (d 1978); 1 s (Matthew b 14 Dec 1971), 1 da (Victoria b 23 June 1967); *Career* UCL: asst lectr 1962, lectr 1963-71, reader 1972-81, prof 1982-88, dean of sci 1988-89, Sir William Ramsay prof and head Dept of Chem 1989-; senator Univ of London 1988-; visiting prof: Columbia Univ 1965, Padua 1967, Western Ontario 1968, Texas A and M 1978, Bern 1979, Fribourg 1979, Amsterdam 1979, Auckland 1981, Odense 1982, Sydney 1985, Bordeaux 1988; Royal Soc of Chemistry lectr: Tilden 1983-84, Nyholm 1989-90, Thomas Graham; hon memb RSNZ 1989, FRCS 1969, FRS 1990, memb Academia Europaea 1990; *Books* The Chemistry of Titanium and Vanadium (1968), The Chemistry of Titanium Zirconium and Hafnium (1973), The Chemistry of Vanadium Niobium and Titanium (1973), Advances in Spectroscopy Vols 1-18 (co ed, 1975-89), Raman Spectroscopy (co ed, 1988), author of over 300 scientific papers; *Recreations* golf, tennis, swimming, skiing, bridge, music, theatre; *Clubs* Athenaeum, Porters Park; *Style*— Prof Robin Clark, FRS; 3A Loom Lane, Radlett, Herts WD7 8AA (☎ 0923 85 7899); Christopher Ingold Laboratories, University College London, 20 Gordon St, London WC1H 0AJ (☎ 071 387 7050, fax 071 380 7457)

CLARK, Dr (Francis) Ronald; s of Frank Clark (d 1964), and Effie Gray, *née* Wilson (d 1989); *b* 7 May 1929; *Educ* Alloa Acad, Univ of Edinburgh (MB ChB); *m* 28 Dec 1960, Dr Margaret Aitken, da of Thomas Archibald Aitken (d 1932); 1 s (Colin b 1963), 2 da (Jane b 1962, Sarah b 1965); *Career* Capt RAMC, med offr 5 Dragoon Gds 1953-54, currently conslt obstetrician and gynaecologist Lothian Health Bd, hon sr lectr Univ of Edinburgh 1966-; FRCSE, FRCOG, fell Edinburgh Obstetrical Soc, memb Edinburgh Medico-Chirugical Soc; *Style*— Dr Ronald Clark; 10 Lomond Road, Edinburgh EH5 3JR (☎ 031 552 2867); Western General Hospital, Edinburgh EH4 2XU (☎ 031 332 2525)

CLARK, Prof Ronald George; s of George Clark (d 1968), of Loanhead, Cairnie, Aberdeenshire, and Gladys, *née* Taylor (d 1987); *b* 9 Aug 1928; *Educ* Aberdeen Acad, Univ of Aberdeen (MB ChB); *m* 10 Sept 1960, Tamar Welsh, da of Walter Erskine Harvie (d 1961), of Duntocher, Dumbartonshire; 2 da (Tamar Taylor b 1962, Deborah Harvie b 1964); *Career* lectr Univ of Glasgow 1961-65, surgical res fell Harvard Univ 1960-61; Univ of Sheffield: sr lectr in surgery 1966-71, prof of surgery 1971-, dean Faculty of Med and Dentistry 1982-85, pro vice chllr 1988-; memb: Gen Med Cncl 1982-, Gen Dental Cncl 1989-; sci govr Br Nutrition Fndn 1983-, memb Cncl Nutrition Soc 1981-84, exec chm Euro Soc of Parental and Enteral Nutrition 1982-87; FRCS, FRCS (Edinburgh); memb: Assoc of Surgns 1969, RSM 1979; *Recreations* golf, walking; *Clubs* RSM, Cwlth Soc; *Style*— Prof Ronald Clark; 2 Chesterwood Drive, Sheffield S10 5DU (☎ 0742 663601); Clinical Sciences Centre, Northern General Hosp, Sheffield S5 7AU (☎ 0742 434343 ext 4191)

CLARK, Prof Stephen Richard Lyster; s of David Allen Richard Clark (d 1986), and Mary Kathleen, *née* Finney; *b* 30 Oct 1945; *Educ* Nottingham HS, Balliol and All Souls Colls Oxford (MA, DPhil); *m* 1 July 1972 (Edith) Gillian, da of Prof John Callan James Metford, of 2 Parrys Close, Bristol; 1 s (Samuel b 1974), 2 da (Dorothea b 1976, Verity b 1985); *Career* fell All Souls Coll Oxford 1968-74, lectr in moral philosophy Univ of Glasgow 1974-83 (Gifford lectr 1982), prof of philosophy Univ of Liverpool 1984-, ed Jl of Applied Philosophy, Stanton lectr Univ of Cambridge 1987-89, Wilde lectr Univ of Oxford 1990, memb Cncl Royal Inst of Philosophy; *Books* Aristotle's Man (1975), The Moral Status of Animals (1977), The Nature of the Beast (1982), From Athens to Jerusalem (1984), The Mysteries of Religion (1986), La Naturaleza De La Bestia (1987), Money, Obedience and Affection (ed, 1989), Civil Peace and Sacred Order (1989), A Parliament of Souls (1990); *Recreations* science fiction, computers; *Style*— Prof Stephen Clark; 1 Arnside Road, Oxton, Birkenhead, Merseyside L43 2JU (☎ 051 6534908); Dept of Philosophy, University of Liverpool, PO Box 147 Liverpool L69 3BX (☎ 051 794 2788)

CLARK, Terence George; OBE (1980); s of George Cyril Clark (d 1960); *b* 6 March 1922; *Educ* Southampton Poly, Regent Poly; *m* 1946, Patricia Eve, da of George Alfred Careford (d 1968), horticulturist; 2 s (Nigel, Graeme); *Career* military and civil airfield construction 1940-45; fndr memb Soil Mechanics Ltd 1944-61; md and chm ELE Ltd 1961-82; pres Soil-Test Inc Chicago 1980-82; dep chm and md Mowlem Engrg Prods Div 1980-82; ret from Mowlem Gp 1982; dir: Terry Turner Ltd (mktg consltS) 1980-, sr ptnr Terry Clark Assocs 1980-, chm Herts and Beds EEC Business Cncl 1980-83; dep chm C Stevens and Son (Weighing Machines) Ltd 1985-; chm: Unimetrics Ltd 1985-, AWT Ltd 1985-, Dunwich Museum Charity 1985-; *Recreations* numismatics, horticulture, music, piano; *Style*— Terence Clark, Esq, OBE; St James House, Park Rd, Toddington, Beds (☎ 052 55 2060), Heathfield House, Westleton Rd, Dunwich, Suffolk (☎ 0728 73578)

CLARK, Sir Terence Joseph; KBE (1990), CMG (1985), CVO (1978); s of Joseph Henry Clark (d 1971), of London, and Mary Ann Matilda Clark; *b* 19 June 1934; *Educ* Parmiter's Foundation Sch London, Univ of Grenoble, Univ of Cambridge, Univ of London, Univ of Freiburg; *m* 1960, Lieselotte Rosa Marie, da of Lt Cdr Erich Ernst Müller, of Kiel; 2 s (Adrian, Martin), 1 da (Sonja); *Career* Pilot Offr RAF VR 1955, entered HM Foreign Serv 1955, ME Centre of Arab Studies Lebanon 1956-57; third sec Political Residency, Bahrain 1957-58, Br Embassy Amman Jordan 1958-60, vice consul Br Consulate Gen Casablanca 1960-62, FO 1962-65, asst political agent Dubai Trucial States 1965-68, first sec (Info) Belgrade 1969-71, head of Chancery and Consul Muscat Oman 1972-73, asst head ME Dept FCO 1974-75, cncllr (Info) Bonn 1976-79, cncllr Belgrade 1979-82, dep ldr of UK Delgn to Conf on Security and Cooperation in Europe (Madrid) 1982-83, head of Info Dept FCO 1983-85, ambass Rep of Iraq 1985-89, ambass Sultanate of Oman 1990-; hon vice pres Br Archaeological Expedition to Iraq 1985-89; *Recreations* salukis, tennis, walking; *Clubs* Hurlingham, Royal Cwlth Soc; *Style*— Sir Terence Clark, KBE, CMG, CVO; c/o FCO, King Charles St, London SW1A 2AH

CLARK, (Alastair) Trevor; CBE (1976), LVO (1974); s of Dr William George Clark, CBE, KHP (d 1957), and Gladys Catherine, *née* Harrison (d 1969); *b* 10 June 1923; *Educ* Glasgow and Edinburgh Acads, Magdalen Coll Oxford (MA); *m* 1 May 1965, Hilary Agnes, da of Dr John Binnie Mackenzie Anderson (d 1944); *Career* WWII, cmmnd Queen's Own Cameron Highlanders second RWAFF (temp Maj), served Nigeria, India, Burma 1942-46; served Admin Branch HM Colonial Serv (later HMOCS): Nigeria (sec to Cncl, sr dist offr) 1949-59, Hong Kong (clerk of Cncls, princ asst Colonial Sec, dir social welfare, dep and actg dir Urban Servs, acting chm Urban Cncl) 1960-72, W Pacific (chief sec High Cmmn, dep and acting govr Solomon Islands) 1972-77, ret 1977; called to the Bar Middle Temple 1963; USA State Dept Country Ldr Fellowship 1972, UN Conf on Human Environment Stockholm 1972; memb: Scot Museums Cncl 1980-90 (chm 1981-84 and 1987-90), Museums Assoc Cncl 1982-86 and 1990- (memb Inst Conslt Ctee 1989-), Sec of State's Ctee for Scotland's Museum Advsy Bd 1983-85, Ctee Area Museum Cncls (vice chm) 1983-84, Nat Museums of Scotland Charitable Tst 1987-; tstee Bd of Nat Museum of Scotland 1985-87, jt fndr Hong Kong Outward Bound Sch 1966, chm Edinburgh Heritage Tst 1984-; memb: Cons Advsy Ctee on Arts and Heritage 1988-, Edinburgh Int Festival Cncl 1980-86; govr Edinburgh Filmhouse 1980-84 and 1987-, dir Edinburgh Acad 1979-84, cncllr Nat Tst for Scotland 1981-84 and 1987-90; Leverhulme Tst Grant 1979-81 (biographer of Sir Abubakar Tafawa Balewa, late PM of Nigeria); memb: City of Edinburgh DC 1980-88, Lothian Health Bd 1981-89, Race Relations Panel (Scot Sheriff Cts) 1983-; *Recreations* listening to music and opera, books, theatre, netsuke, cartophily; *Clubs* Athenaeum, New (Edinburgh); *Style*— Trevor Clark, Esq, CBE, LVO; 11 Ramsay Garden, Edinburgh, EH1 2NA (☎ 031 225 8070)

CLARK, Cdr Victor Cecil Froggatt; DSC (1940 and bar 1942); s of Rev Charles Clark (d 1940), of The Valley Hse, Glassmill Lane, Bromley, Kent, and Amy, *née* Froggatt (d 1966); *b* 24 May 1908; *Educ* Haileybury; *m* 10 May 1975, Danae Heather, da of Frederick James Stileman (d 1982), of Broadwood Farm, Dunster, Somerset; 2 da (Jessica b 1976, Rosalind b 1980); *Career* RN: cadet 1926, Midshipman Med Fleet (HMS Valiant, HMS Wren, HMS Warspite, HMS Courageous) 1927-29, Sub Lt courses Portsmouth and Greenwich 1930, Med Fleet HMS Anthony 1931-32, Home Fleet HMS Watchman 1932-34, Boys Trg Estab HMS Ganges 1935-37, HMS Wild Swan Jubilee Review 1937, Med Fleet HMS Warspite 1937-38, Home Fleet HMS Punjabi active serv Battle Narvik 1938-40, i/c HMS Anthony 1940-41, HMS Repulse (sunk in action off Singapore) organised commando raids (W Coast Raiders) during Malayan Campaign 1941-42, carried out secret evaluation of 2000 troops from behind Japanese lines (sunk in action with superior Japanese forces, wounded one and a half days in water with broken arm, 6 weeks in Sumatran jungle, betrayed to Japanese 1942, POW Sumatra and Singapore 1942-45), i/c HMS Loch Tralaig and HMS Loch Dunvegan 1946-47, Trg Offr Sea Cadet HQ London 1947-53, ret as Cdr 1953; circumnavigation (48000 miles) yacht Solace 1953-59, lecture tours 1960-61, sail trg i/c schooners Prince Louis and Capt Scott 1962-74; Freeman City of London 1930, Liveryman Worshipful Co of Grocers 1935; *Books* On The Wind of a Dream (1960); *Recreations* walking, riding, tennis, sailing; *Clubs* Royal Cwlth Soc, Ocean Cruising, RN; *Style*— Cdr Victor Clark, DSC, RN

CLARK, Maj (Henry) Wallace Stuart; MBE (1970), DL (1963); s of Maj Harry Francis Clark, MBE, JP, RA (d 1977), of Rockwood, Upperlands, and Sybil Emily, *née* Stuart; dir of family business (linen mfrs in Upperlands since 1736, celebrated 250th anniversary in 1986); *b* 20 Nov 1926; *Educ* Shrewsbury; *m* 1956, June Elisabeth Lester, da of James Lester Deane, of Belfast; 2 s; *Career* Maj Ulster Def Regt (NI), Lt RNVR Bomb and Mine Disposal UK, Dist Cmdt Ulster Special Constabulary; dir William Clark and Sons Ltd (est 1736) Linen Mfrs 1972-; *Books* North and East Coasts of Ireland (1957), Guns in Ulster (1963), Rathlin Island (1970), Sailing Round Ireland (1975), Linen on the Green (1982); *Recreations* sailing (yacht Wild Goose of Moyle); *Clubs* Royal Cruising, Irish Cruising; *Style*— Maj Wallace Clark, MBE, DL; Gorteade Cottage, Upperlands, Maghera, Co Londonderry (☎ 0648 42737)

CLARK, Rt Hon Sir William Gibson; MP (C) S Croydon 1974-, PC (1990); s of Hugh Clark, of 17 Cautley Ave, London; *b* 18 Oct 1917; *m* 1944, Irene Dorothy Dawson, da of E F Rands, of Grimsby, Lincs; 3 s, 1 da; *Career* served WWII UK and India; contested (C) Northampton 1955; MP (C): Nottingham S 1959-66, E Surrey 1970-74; oppn front bench spokesman Econs 1964-66, jt dep chm Cons Pty Orgn 1975-77 (jt treas 1974-75), chm Cons Fin Ctee 1979-; chm Anglo Austrian Soc 1983; Freeman City of London; ACA; Austrian Grand Gold Cross Austria 1989; kt 1979; *Clubs* Buck's, Carlton; *Style*— The Rt Hon Sir William Clark, MP; 3 Barton St, London SW1 (☎ 071 222 5759); The Clock House, Box End, Bedford (☎ 0234 852361)

CLARK, William James; s of William Clark, of Glencarse, Scot, and Elizabeth Shanks Clark; *b* 3 May 1950; *Educ* Dundee HS, Univ of Edinburgh (BSc), Univ of W Ontario Canada (MBA); *m* 28 Aug 1981, Karen Neergaard, da of HE Jorgen Holm, of the Danish Embassy, Kuala Lumpur; 2 da; *Career* Chem Bank: mktg offr 1974-79, regnl mktg mangr Singapore 1979-80, gen mangr Singapore 1980-83, regnl mangr (energy and minerals) London 1984-87, regnl mangr (origination and corp fin) London 1987-; represented GB in athletics 1973-75, UK triple jump champion 1974, Scot triple jump champion 1975 and 1977-78; *Recreations* sport, farming; *Clubs* RAC, Annabel's; *Style*— William J Clark, Esq; Chemical Bank, 180 Strand, London WC2R 1EX (☎ 071 380 5151)

CLARKE; *see*: Osmond-Clarke

CLARKE, Andrew Bertram; s of Arthur Bertram Clarke, and Violet Doris, *née* Lewis; *b* 23 Aug 1956; *Educ* Crewe Co GS, King's Coll London (LLB, AKC), Lincoln Coll Oxford (BCL); *m* 1 Aug 1981, Victoria Clare, da of Kelsey Thomas; 1 s (Christopher Harding b 1985), 2 da (Judith Ellen b 1987, Alexandra Clare b 1990); *Career* called to the Bar Middle Temple 1981; *Recreations* watching cricket, collecting modern prints; *Clubs* Gloucestershire CCC; *Style*— Andrew Clarke, Esq; 38 Albury Ride, Cheshunt, Herts (☎ 0992 31269); 2 Crown Office Row, Temple, London EC4Y 7HJ (☎ 071 583 2681, fax 071 583 2850)

CLARKE, Anthony Peter; QC (1979); s of Harry Alston Clarke (d 1979), and Isobel, *née* Kay; *b* 13 May 1943; *Educ* Oakham Sch, King's Coll Cambridge; *m* 7 Sept 1968, Rosemary, da of K W Adam, of Barnham, Sussex; 2 s (Ben b 7 Jan 1972, Thomas b 20 June 1973), 1 da (Sally b 3 June 1977); *Career* called to the Bar Middle Temple 1965, rec 1985-, bencher 1987-; arbitrator: Lloyds, ICC; wreck cmmr; memb de la Chambre Arbitrale Maritime; *Recreations* tennis, golf, holidays; *Style*— Anthony Clarke, Esq, QC; Lewes Heath, Horsmonden, Kent TN12 8EE (☎ 0892 723783); 2 Essex Court, Temple, London EC4Y 9AP (☎ 071 583 8381, fax 071 353 0998, telex 8812528 ADROIT)

CLARKE, Arthur C(harles); CBE (1989); s of Charles Wright Clarke and Nora Mary, *née* Willis; *b* 16 Dec 1917; *Educ* Huish's GS Taunton, King's Coll London (BSc); *m* 1953 (m dis 1964), Marilyn Mayfield; *Career* serv WWII, Flt Lt RAF 1941-46; author and scientist; auditor HM Exchequer and Audit Dept 1936-41, asst ed Physics Abstracts IEE 1949-50, underwater explorer Great Barrier Reef 1954-63; lectr covering Apollo Missions CBS TV USA 1957-70; chllr: Univ of Moratuwa Sri Lanka 1969-, Int Space Univ 1989; Vikram Sarabhal prof PRL Ahmedabad India 1980, Marconi Int fell 1982; dir: Rocket Publishing Co (UK), Underwater Safaris (Sri Lanka); chm: Br Interplanetary Soc 1947-50 and 1953, hon chm Soc of Satellite Professionals, pres Br Sci Fiction Assoc, hon vice pres H G Wells Soc; patron Arthur Clarke Centre for Modern Technol; memb: Cncl Soc of Authors, Advsy Cncl Int Sci Policy Fndn; numerous awards and honours incl: Frankin Inst Stuart Ballentine Gold medal 1963, Hon DSc Beaver Coll Pennsylvania 1971, Bradford Washburn award Boston Museum of Sci 1977, Hon DSc Univ of Moratuwa 1979, IEEE Centennial medal (pres Sci Award) 1986, Charles A Lindbergh award 1987, DLitt Univ of Bath 1988, RA Heinlein Meml award Nat Space Soc 1990, hon life pres UN Assoc of Sri Lanka 1990, Oscar nominee for 2001 screamplay, Grand Master Sci Fiction Writers of American 1983; memb: Br Astronomical Soc, Sci Fiction Writers of America; MRAS, FRAS, FRSA; author of over 70 books; *Books incl* Arthur C Clarke's Mysterious World (1980; with Simon Welfare and John Fairley, also YTV Series), Arthur C Clarke's World of Strange Powers (with Simon Welfare and John Fairley, 1984), Ascent to Orbit (1984), *fiction* Childhoods End (1953), 2001: A Space Odyssey (1968), The Sentinel (1984), The Songs of Distant Earth (1986), 2061: Odyssey Three; *Recreations* table tennis, computers, observing Equatorial skies through telescope; *Style*— Arthur C Clarke, Esq, CBE; Leslie's House, 25 Barnes Place, Colombo 7, Sri Lanka (☎ Colombo 694255, 699757); Rocket Publishing Co, Dene Court, Bishop's Lydeard TA4 3LT (☎ 0823 432671); c/o David Higham Associates, 5-8 Lower John St, Golden Sq, London W1R 4HA

CLARKE, Sir (Henry) Ashley; GCMG (1962, KCMG 1952, CMG 1946), GCVO 1961; s of Henry Hugh Rose Clarke (d 1962), of Rottingdean, Sussex, and Rachel Hill, *née* Duncan; *b* 26 June 1903; *Educ* Repton, Pembroke Coll Cambridge (MA, hon fellow 1962); *m* 1, 15 June 1937 (m dis 1960), Virginia Bell, of New York; m 2, Aug 1962, Frances Pickett, OBE (1984), da of John Molyneux, of Stourbridge, Worcs; *Career* joined Dip Serv 1925; served: Budapest, Warsaw, Constantinople, FO, League of Nations, Tokyo; min: Lisbon 1944-46, Paris 1946-49; dep under sec of state FO 1949-53, ambass to Italy 1953-62, ret; memb Nat Theatre Bd 1962-66; govr BBC 1962-67; chm: Royal Acad of Dancing 1964-69, Italian Art and Archives Rescue Fund 1966-70; vice chm Venice in Peril Fund 1970-84 (pres 1984-); dir Royal Acad of Music 1973-84 (hon fellow), vice pres Ancient Monuments Soc; Pietro Torta prize (Venice) 1976, Kt of St Mark (Venice) 1979; Kt Grand Cross Order of Merit (Italy) 1961, Kt Grand Cross Order of St Gregory the Great 1976; Freeman City of Venice 1985; FSA; *Recreations* music; *Clubs* Athenaeum, Garrick; *Style*— Sir Ashley Clarke, GCMG, GCVO, FSA; Bushy Cottage, The Green, Hampton Court, Surrey KT8 9BS (☎ 081 943-2709); Fondamenta Bonlini 1113, Dorsoduro, 30123 Venice, Italy (☎ Venice 5206530)

CLARKE, Barry Michael; s of Ronald Leslie Clarke (d 1981), and Violet Ann, *née* Johnson, of Shoeburyness, Essex; *b* 18 April 1941; *Educ* Southend HS for Boys, Coll of Estate Mgmnt; *m* 1964, Valerie Brenda, da of Norman Henry Staines; 2 s (Jeremy Ian b 30 Nov 1967, Benjamin David b 3 Dec 1969); *Career* articled pupil to Chief Estates Offr Basildon Devpt Corp 1957-61, tech offr Office of the Receiver Metropolitan Police District 1961-63, dep real estate mangr FW Woolworth & Co Ltd 1963-67, dep estates offr South Eastern Gas 1967-77; dir of property resources British Shipbuilders 1977-86, dir Stewart Newiss (London) Ltd and Stewart Newiss (Newcastle) Ltd 1986-, seconded as gp property controller to Rover Group plc 1987-89, gp md Colliers Stewart Newiss 1990-; FRICS 1975 (ARICS 1964), MInstD; *Recreations* golf, skiing, snooker; *Clubs* Wellington, Holtye Golf (pres, former capt); *Style*— Barry Clarke, Esq; Stream Cottage, Stream Park, Felbridge, East Grinstead, West Sussex RH19 7QN (☎ 0342 322954); Colliers Stewart Newiss, 20 Conduit St, London W1R 9TD (☎ 071 493 6010, fax 071 495 4343, car 0860 599729)

CLARKE, Lady Betty Jocelyne; *née* Bourke; da of 8 Earl of Mayo (d 1939), and his 2 wife Margaret Anah, *née* Harvey Scott (d 1964); *b* 18 Aug 1917; *Educ* Queen Anne's Caversham Berks; *m* 1, 21 May 1943, Capt Ronald Banon, late 60 Rifles (d 1943), o s of Brig-Gen Lionel Banon, CB; m 2, 27 April 1953, Samuel Clarke; 2 da (Elizabeth b 1955, Jocelyne b 1957); *Style*— The Lady Betty Clarke; 361 Woodstock Rd, Oxford OX2 8AA

CLARKE, Brian; s of Edward Ord Clarke, (d 1979), and Lilian, *née* Whitehead; *b* 2 July 1953; *Educ* Clarksfield Sch Oldham, Oldham Sch of Arts and Crafts (jr scholarship), Burnley Sch of Art, The North Devon Coll of Art and Design (dip in art and design); *m* Elizabeth Cecila, da of Rev John Finch; 1 s (Daniel John Finch b 11 Feb 1989); *Career* artist; major exhibitions: Glass/Light Exhibition (Festival of the City of London with John Piper and Marc Chagall) 1979, Der Architektur der Synagogue (Deutsches Architekturmuseum Frankfurt) 1988; self titled exhibitions: New Paintings Constructions and Prints (RIBA) 1981, Paintings (Robert Fraser Gallery Cork St) 1983, 1976-86 Seibu Museum of Art Tokyo 1987, Malerei und Farbfenster 1977-88 (Hessisches Landesmuseum) 1988, Imitations of Mortality (Galerie Karsten Greve Koln Germany), Paintings (Indar Pasrich Gallery New Delhi) 1989, Into and Out of Architecture (Mayor Gallery London) 1990, Architecture and Stained Glass (Sezon Museum of Art Tokyo) 1990; major works: St Gabriel's Church Blackburn 1976, All Saints Church Habergham 1976, Queens Med Centre Nottingham 1978, Laver's & Barraud Building London 1981, Olympus Optical Europa Gmb Headquarters Building Hamburg 1981, King Kahled Int Airport Riyadh Saudi Arabia 1982, The Buxton Thermal Baths Derbyshire 1987, The Lake Sagami Country Club Yamanishi Japan 1988, The New Synagogue Darmstadt Germany 1988, Victoria Quarter Leeds 1989, Cibreo Restaurant Tokyo 1990, Stansted Airport Essex 1991, The Spindles Shopping Centre Oldham 1991, Espana Telefonica Barcelona 1991; Churchill fellowship in architectural art 1974, Art and Work award-special commendation 1989, Europa Nostra award 1990; memb Cncl Winston Churchill Meml Tst 1985-, tstee and memb Ctee Robert Fraser Fndn 1990-; subject of six books; judge: The BBC Design Awards 1990, Royal Fine Art Cmmn and Sunday Times Architecture Award 1991; FRSA 1988; *Recreations* reading; *Clubs* The Toucan; *Style*— Brian Clarke, Esq; Peel Cottage, 80 Peel St, London W8 7PF; The Mayor Gallery, 22A Cork St, London W1X 1HB (☎ 071 734 3558, fax 071 494 1377)

CLARKE, Bruce Robert Duncan; s of Robert Duncan Clarke (d 1936), of Elbury, Worcs, and Beatrice Gertrude, *née* Rose (d 1978); *b* 3 Oct 1924; *Educ* Clifton, Trinity Coll Cambridge (MA, LLM); *m* 24 July 1965, Margaret, da of Thomas Alfred Matthews (d 1947), of Canford Cliffs, Poole; *Career* WWII Royal Corps of Signals and Intelligence 1943-46; served: UK 1943-45, Egypt and India 1945-46; slr Elvy Robb & Co 1948-54; Br Oxygen Co Ltd 1954-62: asst sec 1956, sec 1958, admin offr Tech Div 1961-62; Slrs Office Inland Revenue 1962-90: legal asst 1962-67, sr legal asst 1967-80, asst slr 1980-88, princ legal offr 1988-90 (rating valuation); dir RN Ltd 1981-88; memb Fin Ctee RIIA 1958-70; memb: Law Soc, Mensa, Inst Hist Res; MInstD; *Recreations* reading, wine, good talk; *Clubs* Athenaeum; *Style*— Bruce Clarke, Esq; 7 Warwick Square, London SW1V 2AA (☎ 071 834 2635)

CLARKE, Prof Bryan Campbell; s of Robert Campbell Clarke (d 1941), of Sywell Hall, Sywell, Northants, and Gladys Mary, *née* Carter (d 1987); *b* 24 June 1932; *Educ* Fay Sch Southborough Mass, Magdalen Coll Sch Oxford, Magdalen Coll Oxford (MA, DPhil); *m* 20 Aug 1960, Dr Ann Gillian, da of Prof John Jewkes, CBE (d 1988), of Boar's Hill, Oxford; 1 s (Peter b 1971), 1 da (Alexandra b 1975); *Career* PO RAF 1951-52; Univ of Edinburgh: asst in zoology 1959-63, lectr in zoology, reader in zoology 1969-71; prof of genetics Univ of Nottingham 1971- (vice dean of sci 1986-89); SERC sr res fell 1976-81; vice pres: Genetical Soc 1981, Linnean Soc 1983-85, Soc for the Study of Evolution (USA) 1990; scientific expeditions: to Morocco 1955,

Polynesia 1962, 1967, 1968, 1980 and 1982; chm Terrestrial Life Sciences Ctee NERC 1983-86, memb Biological Sciences Sub Ctee UGC 1987-89 (memb Advsy Panel UFC 1990-); ed: Heredity 1977-84, Proceedings of the Royal Soc, Series B 1989-; FRS 1982; *Books* Berber Village (1959), The Evolution of DNA Sequences (ed, 1986), Frequency-Dependent Selection (ed, 1988); *Recreations* painting, archaeology; *Clubs* RAF; *Style—* Prof Bryan Clarke, FRS; Linden Cottage, School Lane, Colston Bassett, Nottingham NG12 3FD (☎ 0949 81243); Dept of Genetics, Queen's Medical Centre, Clifton Boulevard, Nottingham NG7 2UH (☎ 0602 420639)

CLARKE, Charles Nigel; CBE (1987); s of Charles Cyril Clarke (d 1968), of Gatcombe Court, Flax Bourton, and Olga Helena, *née* Robinson (d 1971); *b* 3 Aug 1926; *Educ* Radley; *m* 21 Jun 1952, Stella Rosemary, da of John Herbert King, of Somerlea, Langford, Somerset; 4 s (Giles b 1953, Nigel b 1957, Henry b 1959, Matthew b 1963), 1 da (Bridget b 1955); *Career* Lt Welsh Gds 1944-48, served Germany; admitted slr 1951, Notary Public 1953, sr ptnr Osborne Clarke slrs Bristol, London, Brussels, Copenhagen 1985- (ptnr 1952); memb and chm various Health Bds and Authys 1952-86; memb Cncl Nat Assoc of Health Authys 1982-86, tstee Bristol Municipal Charities 1962-87 (chm 1976-87), special tstee United Bristol Hosp 1974- (chm 1974-82 and 1986-); memb Cncl Univ of Bristol 1969-86; maitre commanderie de Bordeaux Bristol 1980-, Lord of the Manor of Gatcombe and patron of the living of Wanstrow and Cloford; memb Soc of Merchant Venturers (master 1967); Hon DLitt Univ of Bristol; *Recreations* wine, military history, roses, travel; *Clubs* Army and Navy; *Style—* Charles Clarke, Esq, CBE; Gatcombe Court, Flax Bourton, Bristol BS19 1PX (☎ 0275 393141); 30 Queen Charlotte St, Bristol BS99 7QQ (☎ 0272 230220, fax 0272 279209, car 0860 661 322, telex 44734G)

CLARKE, Dr Charles Richard Astley; s of Sir Cyril Clarke, KBE, FRS, and Frieda Margaret Mary, *née* Hart; *b* 12 Feb 1944; *Educ* Rugby, Gonville and Caius Coll Cambridge (BA); *m* 23 March 1971, Dr Ruth Seifert, da of Sigmund Seifert (d 1978), of London; 2 da (Rebecca Astley b 1973, Naomi Astley b 1976); *Career* conslt neurologist: Bart's 1979-, Whipps Cross Hosp London 1983-; chm Dept of Neurology and Neurosurgery London Bridge Hosp 1989-, clinical dir Dept of Clinical Neurosciences Bart's 1990-; hon med offr Br Mountaineering Cncl 1981-89, chm Mount Everest Fndn 1990, vice pres Alpine Club 1990-; Freeman: Worshipful Soc of Apothecaries, City of London 1984; FRCP; *Books* Everest the Unclimbed Ridge (with C J S Bonington, 1983); *Recreations* mountaineering, model flying, sailing; *Clubs* Alpine, Royal Geographical Soc; *Style—* Dr Charles Clarke; 152 Harley Street, London W1 1HH (☎ 071 935 0444/3834, fax 071 224 2574, telex 927026 LBHOSP G)

CLARKE, Charles St George Stephenson; s of John Philip Stephenson Clarke, of Broadhurst Manor, Sussex (d 1969), and Kathleen Adeline Jane Loftus St George Clarke (d 1979); *b* 19 April 1924; *Educ* Eton; *m* 1, 20 Jan 1959, Therese Emilie Edwige Elvire, da of Gen Husson, of Toulon, France; 2 s (Edmund John b 1959, Richard Louis b 1961); m 2, Susanna Elizabeth, *née* Harrison; *Career* Powell Duffryn Gp 1942, ret 1989; dir: Ramteazle, Clothworkers Foundation; chm for 15 years Shires Investment Co plc (now dep chm); chm: Golden Rain Ltd, Edric Property and Investment Co; Fndr Master Worshipful Co of Fuellers, Past Master Worshipful Co of Clothworkers; *Recreations* shooting, fishing, gardening; *Clubs* Boodles, Pratts; *Style—* Charles Clarke, Esq; Mill House, Letcombe Regis, Oxon OX12 9JD

CLARKE, Christopher David (Chris); s of Frank Clarke, of 77 Mellor Lane, Mellor, nr Blackburn, and Barbara, *née* Holgate; *b* 4 July 1971; *Educ* Queen Elisabeth's GS Blackburn, Univ of Essex; *Career* croquet player; Southport 1988-89, capt Colchester 1990-, represented GB 1988 and 1990 (Sonoma-Cutrer World Invitational Championships); achievements incl: runner up Northern Championships 1987, nat jr champion 1988, Eastern champion 1988 and 1990, winner Presidents Cup 1988, runner up Western Championships 1988, semi-finalist Br Open Championship 1988, runner up World Doubles Championship 1989 (with R Fulford), winner Nat Inter-Club Competition 1990, winner Br Open Doubles Championship 1990 (with R Rulford, runner up 1988 and 1989); youngest winner Presidents Cup Hurlingham aged 17, voted best under 21 player in the world 1988; *Recreations* ten-pin bowling, bridge, most sports; *Style—* Chris Clarke, Esq; 77 Mellor Lane, Mellor, nr Blackburn, Lancs BB2 7EW (☎ 0254 812412); Colchester Croquet Club, Elianore Rd, Colchester (☎ 0206 42973)

CLARKE, Christopher George; s of Philip George Clarke, and Jose Margaret Clarke (d 1979); *b* 18 Sept 1944; *Educ* Radley; *m* 1 June 1968, Jane, *née* Ellis; 2 da (Natasha Jane b 12 June 1970, Vanessa Clare b 5 April 1973); *Career* articled clerk Hodgson Morris & Co Chartered Accountants 1963-67 (qualified 1967), investmt mangr JH Vavasseur London 1972- (Wm Brandts 1968-72); Henderson Admin Ltd: joined 1974, dir 1976-, head of investment 1983-; dir Electric and Gen Investment Co plc, dir English Nat Investment Co plc; memb Investmt Advsy Ctee of Charities Aid Fndn, tstee and treas Sir Robert Menzies Meml Tst, memb Cncl Radley Coll, govr Tudor Hall Sch Banbury; *Style—* Christopher Clarke, Esq; Henderson Administration Group plc, 3 Finsbury Ave, London EC2M 2PA (☎ 071 638 5757, fax 071 377 5742, telex 88461 gfriarg, car 0836 293619)

CLARKE, Christopher John David; s of Maj John Herbert Thomson Clarke (d 1983), and Hazel, *née* Chapman (d 1988); *b* 21 March 1950; *Educ* Fettes; *Career* admitted slr England 1974 and Hong Kong 1974; ptnr Denton Hall Burgin & Warrens 1979, memb: Int Bar Assoc, Law Assoc; *Recreations* travel, food; *Clubs* Oriental; *Style—* Christopher Clarke, Esq; Denton Hall Burgin and Warrens, 5 Chancery Lane, Clifford's Inn, London EC4A 1BU (☎ 071 242 1212, fax 071 404 0087)

CLARKE, Christopher Simon Courtenay Stephenson; QC (1984); yr s of Rev John Stephenson Clarke (d 1982), and Enid Courtenay, *née* Manico; *b* 14 March 1947; *Educ* Marlborough, Gonville and Caius Coll Cambridge (MA); *m* 14 Sept 1974, Caroline Anne, da of Prof Charles Montague Fletcher, CBE, *qv*; 1 s (Edward b 31 May 1981), 2 da (Henrietta b 16 Aug 1977, Louisa b 21 June 1979); *Career* called to the Bar Middle Temple 1969; advocate of the Supreme Ct of the Turks and Caicos Is 1975, chm Ctee of Inquiry of States of Guernsey into Barnett Christie (Fin) Ltd 1985-87, cncllr Int Bar Assoc 1987-, rec 1990; *Clubs* Brooks's, Hurlingham; *Style—* Christopher Clarke Esq, QC; 42 The Chase, London SW4 0NH (☎ 071 622 0765); 1 Brick Court, Temple, London EC4 (☎ 071 583 0777, telex 892687)

CLARKE, Prof Sir Cyril Astley; KBE (1974, CBE 1969); s of Astley Vavasour Clarke, MD, JP, DL, and Ethel Mary, *née* Gee (d 1965); *b* 22 Aug 1907; *Educ* Oundle, Gonville and Caius Coll Cambridge, Guy's Hosp London; *m* 1935, Frieda (Féo) Margaret Mary, da of Alexander John Campbell Hart; 3 s; *Career* dir Res Unit RCP 1983-88; FRS 1970, hon fell Royal Soc of Med 1982, MD, ScD; prof of med Liverpool Univ, dir Nuffield Unit of Med Genetics 1965-72 (now emeritus prof and hon fell), pres Royal Coll of Physicians 1972-77, chm Cncl Br Heart Fndn 1982-87; hon conslt physician: Royal Infirmary, Broadgreen Hosp, Utd Liverpool Hosps; chm Br Soc for Res on Ageing 1987-; Buchanan medal Royal Society 1990; pres elect (June 1991) Royal Entomological Soc of London; Hon DSc Univs of: Edinburgh, Leicester, E Anglia, Birmingham, Liverpool, Sussex, Hull, Wales, London; *Books* Genetics for the Clinician, Selected Topics in Medical Genetics, Rhesus Haemolytic Disease, selected papers and extracts, Human Genetics and Medicine (1970, 1972, 1987); *Recreations* sailing (yacht Hobby IV), butterfly genetics; *Clubs* Athenaeum, Oxford and Cambridge Sailing Soc, Explorers (New York); *Style—* Prof Sir Cyril Clarke, KBE, FRS; 43 Caldy Rd, W Kirby, Wirral, Merseyside L48 2HF (☎ 051 625 8811); Royal Coll of Physicians, Regent's Park, London NW1 (☎ 071 935 1174); Department of Genetics & Microbiology, University of Liverpool, PO Box 147, Liverpool L69 3BX

CLARKE, David Barry; s of Dr Leslie Thomas Clarke, TD (d 1963), of Birmingham, and Norah, *née* Chapman; *b* 11 June 1930; *Educ* St Philip's GS, Univ of Birmingham (MB, ChB, LRCP); *m* 26 Oct 1957, June, da of Percy Hall Romney (d 1981), of Birmingham; 1 s (Jocelyn b 1958) 2 da (Hilary b 1960, Vivienne b 1964); *Career* Nat Serv: Capt RAMC 1955-57;sr lectr thoracic surgery Univ of Birmingham 1969-71, consIt cardiothoracic surgn Queen Elizabeth Hosp Birmingham 1971-90 (sr registrar thoracic surgery 1964-69), sr lectr thoracic surgery Univ of Birmingham 1969-71, Hunterian prof RCS; memb: Soc of Cardiothoracic Surgns, Cardiac Soc, Br Thoracic Soc, Birmingham Watercolour Soc, Ct of Examiners RCS (formally chm); FRCS 1959; *Books* contrib: Intrathoracic Crises (1968), A Practise of Cardiothoracic Surgery (1971), Intensive Care for Nurses (1971); *Recreations* water colour painting, music, period model ships; *Clubs* Army and Navy; *Style—* David Clarke, Esq; Cardiac Surgery Unit, Queen Elizabeth Hospital, Edgbaston, Birmingham 15 (☎ 021 472 1311)

CLARKE, David Clive; QC; s of Philip George Clarke, of Kilconquhar, Fife, and José Margaret, *née* Fletcher (d 1979); *b* 16 July 1942; *Educ* Winchester, Magdalene Coll Cambridge (BA, MA); *m* 2 Aug 1969, Alison Claire, da of Rt Rev (Percy) James Brazier (d 1989); 3 s (Andrew b 1970, Jonathan b 1972, Edward b 1975); *Career* called to the Bar Inner Temple 1965, Northern Circuit (treas 1988), rec 1981; *Recreations* canals, sailing, swimming; *Style—* David Clarke, Esq, QC; 5 Essex Ct, Temple, London EC4Y 9AH (☎ 071 353 4363, fax 071 583 1491); 25 Byrom St, Manchester M3 4PF (☎ 061 834 5238, fax 061 834 0394)

CLARKE, David Hilton; s of Hilton Swift Clarke, CBE, of 4 Coverdale Ave, Cooden, nr Bexhill, Sussex, and Sibyl Muriel, *née* Salter (d 1975); *b* 9 Jan 1938; *Educ* Hurstpierpoint Coll Sussex; *m* 27 Feb 1965, Leonora Virginia, da of Capt Campbell Marshall (d 1970); 2 s (Edward Hilton b 23 Feb 1966, Campbell David Hilton b 10 Aug 1967); *Career* Nat Serv RN 1956-58, Leading Seaman RNR 1967-72; asst and trainee Anthony Gibbs and Sons Ltd 1958-67, dir Gerrard and National Holdings plc 1974- (joined 1967); chm Fin Ctee Middx Hosp Med Sch, memb Fin Ctee UCL; sec Coaching Club, memb Roehampton Boys Club; Freeman City of London 1984; *Recreations* sailing, skiing; *Clubs* Royal Ocean Racing, Royal Cornwall Yacht; *Style—* David Clarke, Esq; 8 Parthenia Rd, Fulham, London SW6 4BD; Gerrard and National Holdings plc, 33 Lombard St, London EC3 (☎ 071 628 9981)

CLARKE, Douglas Hewitt; s of Reginald Douglas Clarke (d 1979), of Liverpool, and Mabel Hewitt, *née* Drew (d 1958); *b* 17 July 1934; *Educ* Liverpool Inst HS for boys, Birkenhead Tech Coll, Univ of Durham Kings Coll; *m* 1, 24 April 1963 (m dis 1968), Eileen Elizabeth Hilton; m 2, 21 May 1977, Christine Mary Jacobs; 1 s (Alexander Douglas b 19 March 1987), 1 da (Karen Mary b 11 April 1978); *Career* asst naval architect Cammell Laird & Co Ltd 1968-71, ship surveyor Lloyds Register of Shipping 1971-78, dir Bestgrange Ltd 1978-, Ship System Engrg Gp (SSEG) 1986-87; pres UK Assoc of Professional Engrs 1974-76; memb: Nautical Inst Computers and Communications Working Gp, Info Technol Working Gp; Inst Mechanical and Gen Technician Engrs: chm 1976-78, pres 1978-80, hon treas 1985-88; advsr to HM Princ Sec of State for Trade & Indust (Efficient Ship Programme) 1987-, memb IEC TC80 Working Gp on Digital Interfaces for Navigation Equipment 1987; memb and hon treas London Branch Royal Inst of Naval Architects, memb Surrey ECRO and Engrg Cncl Assembly; author of numerous articles in journals and magazines and for nat institutions (Institution Gold Medal 'Powering of Ships' 1963, Institution Silver Medal 'Some Notes on Escalators and their Use in Ships' 1959); Freeman City of London 1983, Liveryman Worshipful Co of Shipwrights 1983; CEng, FRINA 1983, FIMarE 1987, CNI 1988, FIMechIE; *Recreations* water colour painting; *Style—* Douglas Clarke, Esq; 10 Treadwell Rd, Epsom, Surrey KT18 5JW (☎ 0372 729 910); Bestgrage Ltd, c/o 10 Treadwell Rd

CLARKE, Dr Edwin Sisterson; s of J H Clarke, and Nellie, *née* Sisterson; *b* 18 June 1919; *Educ* Jarrow Central Sch, Univ of Durham Med Sch at Newcastle (MB BS, MD), Univ of Chicago Med Sch (MD); *m* 1, Dec 1949 (m dis), Margaret Elsie Morrison; 2 s (Andrew b 1951, William b 1952); m 2, Dec 1958 (m dis), Beryl Eilleen Brock; 1 da (Sarah b 1963); m 3, March 1982, Gaynor Crawford; *Career* graded specialist in neurology RAMC 1946-48, conslt neurologist Royal Postgrad Med Sch 1954-58, asst prof of history of med The Johns Hopkins Univ 1961-62, visiting assoc prof of history of med Yale Univ 1962-63, sr lectr then reader in history of med UCL 1966-73; dir The Wellcome Inst for the History of Med 1973-79; FRSM 1950, FRCP 1970; *Books* The Human Brain and Spinal Cord (jtly, 1968), Modern Methods in the History of Medicine (ed, 1970), An Illustrated History of Brain Localization (jtly, 1971), 19th Century Origins of Neuroscientific Concepts (jtly, 1987); *Recreations* book collecting, local history; *Style—* Dr Edwin Clarke; The Old Rectory, Donington-on-Bain, Lincolnshire LN11 9QZ; University Laboratory of Physiology, Parks Rd, Oxford OX1 3PT (☎ 0865 272543)

CLARKE, Hon Mrs (Eleanor Geraldine); *née* de Courcy; 4 da of 29 Baron Kingsale, DSO (d 1969); *b* 1919; *m* 10 April 1940 (m dis 1947), John Campbell Clarke (d 17 June 1966), s of late Dr Hugh Campbell Wilson Clarke, of Ashton-upon-Mersey, Cheshire; 1 s (Peter b 1945); *Style—* The Hon Mrs Clarke; 48 Fore St, North Tawton, Devon

CLARKE, Sir Ellis Emmanuel Innocent; TC (1969), GCMG (1972, CMG 1960); o s of late Cecil El and Elma Clarke; *b* 28 Dec 1917; *Educ* St Mary's Coll Trinidad, London Univ; *m* 1952, Eyrmyntrude, eldest da of William Hurford Hagley, OBE, of St George's, Grenada; 2 s, 1 da; *Career* barr 1940, in private practice to 1954; former perm rep to UN for Trinidad and Tobago, ambass to US 1962-73, to Mexico 1966-73, govr gen and C-in-C Repub of Trinidad and Tobago 1973-76, president 1976-; hon fell University Coll London 1983; KStJ 1973; kt 1963; *Style—* Sir Ellis Clarke, TC, GCMG; President's House, Port of Spain, Trinidad

CLARKE, Geoffrey; s of John Moulding Clarke, and Janet, *née* Petts; *b* 28 Nov 1924; *Educ* RCA; *m* ; 2 s; *Career* artist and sculptor; Exhibitions: Gimpel Fils Gallery 1952 and 1955, Redfern Gallery 1965, Tranman Gallery 1975, 1976 and 1982; cmmnd work incl: iron sculpture Time Life Building New Bond Street London, cast aluminium relief sculpture Castrol House Marylebone Road London, mosaics Univ of Liverpool Physics Block and Basildon New Town, stained glass windows Treasury Lincoln Cathedral, bronze sculpture Thorn Electric Building Upper St Martin's Lane London, relief sculpture on Canberra and Oriana, three stained glass windows, high altar, cross and candlesticks and the flying cross and crown of thorns Coventry Cathedral; ARCA; *Style—* Geoffrey Clarke, Esq; Stowe Hill, Hartest, Bury St Edmunds, Suffolk IP29 4EQ (☎ 0284 830 319)

CLARKE, Gordon Oscar Burland; OBE (1980), TD (1957); s of Douglas Burland Clarke (d 1955), and Elsie Mary, *née* Wrigley (d 1972); *b* 23 March 1922; *Educ* Altrincham HS, Univ of Manchester (CEng); *m* 1950, Marion, da of Osmond Rutherford, of Norwich; 1 s (Jeremy), 1 da (Victoria); *Career* RE 1942-47, served in France, Germany and India, Capt; divnl mangr BR: Edinburgh 1968-70, Norwich 1970-83; regnl chm CBI 1978-80, memb CBI Cncl 1974-83, consulting engr 1983-; *Recreations* sailing, Times crossword; *Style—* Gordon Clarke, Esq, OBE, TD; 86

Charles Close, Wroxham, Norwich, Norfolk NR12 8TT (☎ 0603 782610)

CLARKE, Graham Neil; s of Henry Charles Owen Clarke, MVO, and Doris May, *née* Morgan; *b* 23 July 1956; *Educ* Rutherford Sch London, Sch of Horticulture Wisley; *m* 2 Feb 1980, Denise Carole, da of Robert Fraser Anderson; 1 da (Rebecca Sarah b 1990); *Career* gardener: Buckingham Palace 1975-76, Royal Parks Nursery 1976; Amateur Gardening: sub-ed 1976-79, chief sub-ed 1979-81, dep ed 1981-86; ed: Home Plus Magazine 1985, Amateur Gardening 1986-; memb Exec Ctee RHS Garden Club 1975-82, prodr and presenter Hosp Radio London and Bournemouth 1976-89; FLS; *Books* Step-By-Step Pruning (1984), A-Z of Garden Plants (1985), Autumn/Winter Colour in the Garden (1986), Your Gardening Questions Answered (1987), The Complete Book of Plant Propagation (1990); *Recreations* gardening, radio, philately; *Style*— Graham Clarke, Esq; Amateur Gardening, Westover House, West Quam Rd, Poole, Dorset BH15 1JG (☎ 0202 680586, fax 0202 674335)

CLARKE, Graham Staward; TD (1971); s of Douglas Staward Clarke (d 1949), and Beatrice, *née* Auld (d 1988); *b* 16 March 1937; *Educ* St Bees Sch Cumberland, Emmanuel Coll Cambridge (MA); *m* 1964, Rita Elisabeth Karoline, da of Oskar Becker (d 1961); 1 s (Douglas b 1968), 1 da (Tessa b 1965); *Career* Maj RA, euro theatre; gp fin dir: Telex Computers Ltd 1972-75, Coles Cranes Ltd 1976-81, Fairey Holdings Ltd 1981-84; md Energy and Military Engrg Div Fairey Holdings Ltd 1984-86; chm: Fairey Engineering Ltd 1984-86, Elequip Ltd 1984-86; dir: Fairey Holdings Ltd 1981-86, Fairey Construction Ltd 1984-86, Mathews and Yates Ltd 1984-86, Fairey Nuclear Ltd 1984-86, Fairey Developments Ltd 1981-86; chm Bourn Management Consits Ltd 1985-, chm and md Bourn Developments 1986-, proprietor Bourn Estates 1980-; FCA, FRSA; *Recreations* bridge, travel, business management; *Clubs* RAC, IOD; *Style*— Graham Clarke Esq, TD; Bourn Reach, Montrose Gdns, Oxshott, Surrey, KT22 0UU (☎ 0372 843655); Bourn Management Consultants Ltd, Bourn Reach, Montrose Gdns, Oxshott, Surrey KT22 OUU (☎ 0372 843445, fax 0372 842216)

CLARKE, James Dudley Henderson; BEM (1988); s of James Dudley Clarke (d 1945), of Shepperton, Middx, and Ethel Eliza Hambly, *née* Johnson; *b* 14 May 1923; *Educ* Reay Sch London; *m* 15 May 1942, (Muriel) Jean, da of Clarence Carthew Quick (d 1966); 1 s (James), 2 da ('Tricia, Lynne); *Career* WWII Intelligence Corps 1941-46; md Zetters Gp plc 1965; vice chm: Zetters Int Pools Ltd, Metagraph Ltd, Zetters Mktg Ltd; govr The London Marathon, memb Sports Aid Fndn; churchwarden Frinton-on-Sea; Freeman City of London 1982, Liveryman Worshipful Co of Govrs 1982; *Recreations* cricket, golf, reading; *Clubs* MCC; *Style*— James Clarke, Esq, BEM; 86/88 Clerkenwell Rd, London EC1 (☎ 071 253 5376, fax 071 253 1584)

CLARKE, James Henry; s of Edward Clarke (d 1959), of Tynemouth, and Jane Elizabeth, *née* Turnbull (d 1921); *b* 27 June 1913; *Educ* Rutherford Tech Coll Newcastle, Marine Sch of South Shields; *m* 19 Oct 1938, Florence (d 1987), da of George Bell (d 1921), of Wylam, Northumberland; *Career* chief engr offr (formerly J-s 2 engr offr) Merchant Navy 1935-46; lines: Hopemount Shipping Co Ltd, Blue Funnel Line, C T Bowring & Co Ltd; WWII S Atlantic, France and N Atlantic convoys, seconded Royal Fleet Auxiliary (oiling RN ships at sea); British Tanker Co: served UK, Egypt, Persian Gulf, Indian Ocean, India, Burma, Singapore, Iraq, Iran; sr asst J G Harrison (naval architect-consulting engr) 1946-50, chief marine supt engr and tech consultant Chandris England Ltd and Chandris (London) Services Ltd 1950-84; memb: Langbourn Ward Club, Lime St Ward Club, Bishopsgate Ward Club; Freeman City of London 1963, Liveryman Worshipful Co of Shipwrights 1964; CEng 1968, FRINA 1960, FIMarE 1942, FCMS 1950; *Recreations* maritime history, famous passenger ships, DIY, Greece; *Clubs* City Livery, City Livery Yacht, City Livery Music; *Style*— James H Clarke, Esq; Greenacres, 8 Shalford Rd, Guildford, Surrey GU4 8BL, (☎ 0483 576384)

CLARKE, James Samuel; MC (1943, and bar 1944); s of James Henry Clarke (d 1951), of Horley, Surrey, and Deborah Florence, *née* Moliver (d 1984); *b* 19 Jan 1921; *Educ* Reigate GS, St Catharine's Coll Cambridge (MA); *m* 1949, Ilse, da of Herman-Max Cohen, of Germany; 2 da (Jane, Susan); *Career* cmmnd Royal Irish Fus 1941-45, served 1 Bn N Africa and Italy, demob Maj 1945; called to the Bar Middle Temple 1946, entered legal serv 1953, under sec and princ asst slr Inland Revenue 1970-81; ret; md Bishop and Clark Ltd 1981-; *Recreations* gardening, sailing; *Clubs* Nat Lib, RAC; *Style*— James Clarke, Esq, MC; Dormers, The Downs, Givons, Grove, Leatherhead, Surrey (☎ 0372 378254); Bishop and Clarke Ltd, Hereford House, Massetts Rd, Horley, Surrey (☎ 0293 782 288)

CLARKE, Prof John; s of Victor Patrick Clarke, of Cambridge, and Ethel May, *née* Blowers (d 1978); *b* 10 Feb 1942; *Educ* Perse Sch for Boys Cambridge, Univ of Cambridge (BA, MA, PhD); *m* 15 Sept 1979, Grethe, da of Hartwig Fog Pedersen (d 1990), of Copenhagen; 1 da (Elizabeth Jane b 1980); *Career* postdoctoral fell Univ of California 1968-69, princ investigator Materials and Chemical Sciences Div Lawrence Berkeley Laboratory 1969-, asst prof Univ of California Berkeley 1969-71 (assoc prof 1971-73, prof of physics 1973-); visiting appts: Cavendish Laboratory Cambridge 1972 and 1979, HC Orsted Inst Copenhagen 1972, 1979 and 1985, Univ of Karlsruhe Germany 1978, CEN Saclay France 1986, visiting fell Clare Hall Cambridge 1989; Alfred P Sloan Fndn fellowship 1970-72, Adolph C and Mary Sprague Miller res professorship 1975-76, John Simon Guggenheim fellowship 1977-78; Charles Vernon Boys prize Br Inst Physics 1977, Soc of Exploration Geophysics award for best paper in Geophysics (with T D Gamble and W M Goubau) 1979, Technology Magazine Technology 100 award (with Gamble and Goubau) 1981, Distinguished Teaching award Univ of California Berkeley 1983, award for sustained outstanding res in Solid State Physics in Dept of Energy's 1986 Materials Sciences Res Competition, California Scientist of the Year 1987, Fritz London meml award for Low Temperture Physics 1987; fell: AAAS 1982, American Physical Society 1985; FRS 1986; *Style*— Prof John Clarke, FRS; Department of Physics, University of California, Berkeley, Calif 94720, USA (☎ 0101 415 642 3069, fax 0101 415 643 8497)

CLARKE, Prof John Frederick; s of Frederick William Clarke (d 1974), and Clara Auguste Antonie, *née* Nauen (d 1975); *b* 1 May 1927; *Educ* Warwick Sch, QMC (BSc, PhD); *m* 19 Dec 1953, Jean Ruth, da of Joseph Alfred Hector Roberts Gentle (d 1960), 2 da (Jenny b 1956, Julie b 1957); *Career* pupil pilot Naval Aviation RN 1946-48; aerodynamist English Electric Co Ltd 1956-57, lectr Coll of Aeronautics Cranfield 1958-65, Fulbright scholar and visiting assoc prof of Stanford Univ Calif 1961-62, reader Cranfield Inst of Technol 1965-72 (prof theoretical gas dynamics 1972-), visiting prof at various UK, Euro, Aust and US Univs, memb various ctees for sci, author of various contribs to learned jls; FIMA 1965, FRAeS 1969, FRSA 1986, FRS 1987; *Books* The Dynamics of Real Gases (with M McChesney, 1964), Dynamics of Relaxing Gases (with M McChesney, 1976); *Recreations* Sunday painter; *Style*— Prof John F Clarke, FRS; Field House, Green Lane, Aspley Guise MK17 8EN (☎ 0908 582234); Aerodynamics, Coll of Aeronautics, Cranfield Inst of Technology, Cranfield, Bedford MK43 0AL (☎ 0234 750 111, ext 2123, telex 825072 CITECH G)

CLARKE, Prof John Innes; DL (Co Durham 1990); s of Bernard Griffith Clarke, of 53 West Way, Bournemouth, and Edith Louie, *née* Mott; *b* 7 Jan 1929; *Educ* Bournemouth Sch, Univ of Aberdeen (MA, PhD), Univ of Paris; *m* 2 April 1955, Dorothy Anne, da of George May Watkinson (decd), of Ashbourne, Derbyshire; 3 da (Gemma b 1956, Anna b 1959, Lucy b 1969); *Career* Nat Serv FO RAF 1952-54; asst lectr in geography Univ of Aberdeen 1954-55, lectr in geography Univ of Durham 1955-63; prof of geography: Univ Coll of Sierra Leone 1963-65, Univ of Durham 1968-90 (reader 1965-68); pro vice chllr and sub warden Univ of Durham 1984-90; chm: Exec Ctee HESIN 1987-89, Durham Health Authy 1990-; FRSA, FRGS; *Books* Population Geography (1965), Population Geography and Developing Countries (1971); ed: An Advanced Geography of Africa (1975), Geography and Population (1984); co-ed: Population & Development Projects in Africa (1985), Population & Disaster (1989), Mountain Population Pressure (1990); *Recreations* hill walking, family history, travel; *Style*— Prof John Clarke, DL; Tower Cottage, The Avenue, Durham DH1 4EB (☎ 091 384 8350); Durham Health Authy, Appleton House, Lancaster Rd, Durham DH1 5XZ (☎ 091 386 4911, fax 091 384 9444)

CLARKE, John Neil; s of George Philip Clarke (d 1969); *b* 7 Aug 1934; *Educ* Rugby, King's Coll London (LLB); *m* 1958, Sonia Heather, *née* Beckett; 3 s; *Career* dep chm Charter Consolidated plc 1982-88 (chief exec 1980-88); chm: Johnson Matthey plc 1984-89, Molins plc 1989-, Genchem Holdings Ltd 1989-; dir Travis Perkins plc 1990-; FCA; *Clubs* MCC, Royal W Norfolk Golf, Addington Golf; *Style*— J Neil Clarke Esq; High Willows, 18 Park Ave, Farnborough Park, Kent BR6 8LL (☎ 0689 851651); The Cottage, Hall Lane, Thornham, Norfolk; 35 Ely Place, London EC1N 6TD (☎ 071 831 8889)

CLARKE, John Spencer; VRD (1965); s of Col John Turner Parker Clarke (d 1957), and Olive Maude Marie, *née* Keeshan (d 1959); *b* 20 Aug 1923; *Educ* St Edward's Sch Oxford, St Edmund Hall Oxford (MA); *m* 17 May 1958, Joan Margaret, da of Capt Richard Edwardes (d 1967); 2 s (Charles b 1960, James b 1964), 2 da (Sally b 1959, Fiona b 1963); *Career* RN 1941, RNR 1946; Solent Div RNR, cmmnd 1967-71; admitted slr 1955, sr ptnr Clarke and Son 1958, supt registrar Basingstoke 1960-76, Hants coroner 1962-89; pres: Hampshire Law Soc 1973, Coroners Soc of England and Wales 1981, chm Royal Nat Mission to Deep Sea Fishermen; *Recreations* sailing; *Clubs* The Naval, RNSA, Island Sailing, OGA, Lloyds Yacht; *Style*— Capt John Clarke, VRD; The Roos, Whitchurch, Hants (☎ 0256 892396); Manor House, Winchester Rd, Basingstoke, Hants (☎ 0256 20555)

CLARKE, His Hon Judge Sir Jonathan Dennis; eldest s of Dennis Robert Clarke (Master of the Supreme Court, d 1967) and Caroline Alice, *née* Hill; *b* 19 Jan 1930; *Educ* Kidstones Sch, Univ Coll London; *m* 1956, Susan Margaret Elizabeth Ashworth; 1 s, 3 da; *Career* rec Crown Court 1972-82, circuit judge (Western) 1982-; ptnr Townsends 1959-82; pres Law Soc; kt 1981; *Style*— His Hon Judge Sir Jonathan Clarke; c/o Midland Bank, 1 Wood St, Swindon, Wilts

CLARKE, Rt Hon Kenneth Harry; PC (1984), QC (1980), MP (C) Rushcliffe Notts 1970-; s of Kenneth Clarke, of Nottingham; *b* 2 July 1940; *Educ* Nottingham HS, Gonville and Caius Coll Cambridge (pres Union); *m* 1964, Gillian Mary, da of Bruce Edwards, of Sidcup, Kent; 1 s, 1 da; *Career* called to the Bar Gray's Inn 1963, bencher 1989, former oppn spokesman on Social Servs and Indust, Parly under sec Dept of Tport 1979-82, Min of State (Health) DHSS 1982-85, memb Health Servs Supervisory Bd 1983-85, HM Paymaster Gen and Min for Employment 1985-87, chllr of the Duchy of Lancaster and Min for Trade and Indust 1987-88; Sec of State for Health July 1988- Nov 1990; Sec of State for Education and Science Nov 1990-; *Recreations* modern jazz, bird watching, watching football and cricket; *Style*— The Rt Hon Kenneth Clarke, QC, MP; House of Commons, London SW1A 0AA

CLARKE, (Samuel) Lawrence Harrison; CBE (1988); s of Samuel Harrison Clarke, CBE, of Stevenage, and Frances Mary, *née* Blowers (d 1976); *b* 16 Dec 1929; *Educ* Westminster, Trinity Coll Cambridge (BA); *m* 10 June 1952, Ruth Joan, da of Oscar William Godwin, OBE, of Old Colwyn (d 1958); 1 s (Christopher b 1958), 3 da (Susan b 1953, Mary b 1956, Janet b 1960); *Career* asst tech dir GEC plc 1981-91, dir Alvey Programme 1987 (dep dir 1983-87), chm Zebra Parallel Ltd 1988-89, Image Stare Holdings plc 1989-; visiting prof UCL 1983-; FIEE, FBCS; *Recreations* skiing, Scottish dancing; *Clubs* SCGB; *Style*— Laurence Clarke, Esq, CBE; 31 Craigweil Ave, Radlett, Herts WD7 7ET (☎ 092 385 2418)

CLARKE, Col (Henry) Leslie; TD (1949, 3 Clasps 1950, 1956, 1961), DL (Gtr London 1977); s of Harry Stanley Clarke, OBE, JP (d 1969), of 10 Cranbourne Court, Hermon Hill, London, and Lilian Margaret, *née* Wells (d 1925); *b* 15 June 1920; *Educ* Brentwood Sch, Inst of Exports (Dip M); *m* 1, 11 Nov 1950, Kathleen Doris (d 1973), da of George Forest Hoyles (d 1951), of Newton Hall, Wisbech, Cambs; m 2, 19 Jan 1974, Coral Norah, da of Frank Hollis Anthony (d 1975), of London; *Career* WWII cmmnd 2 Lt Essex Regt TA 1939, transferred RA 1940, served Africa and ME, demobbed as Maj 1947; TA: Maj 599 Essex HAA Regt, Lt-Col 1958, Col GS Dep Cdr RA 1962, transferred on ret RARO 1965; ADC to HM The Queen 1966-71; ret from pharmaceutical industry; JP West Ham 1950; DL Essex 1961-77, rep DL Borough of Ealing 1983; pres: Ealing Branch Royal Br Legion 1988-, Ealing and Hanwell Dist Scouts 1988-; Liveryman of the Worshipful Co of Barbers 1974; MIM; *Recreations* walking; *Style*— Col Leslie Clarke, TD, DL; 11 Dalling Rd, Ravenscourt Park, London W6 0JD (☎ 081 747 0837)

CLARKE, (Victor) Lindsay; s of Victor Metcalfe Clarke (d 1972), of Halifax , W Yorkshire, and Clara, *née* Bell; *b* 14 Aug 1939; *Educ* Heath GS Halifax , King's Coll Cambridge (BA); *m* 1, 1961 (m dis 1972), Carolyn Pattinson; 1 da (Madeleine Sara b 1966); m 2, 1980, Phoebe Clare Mackmin, *née* Harris; *Career* novelist; sr master ODA Secdy Sch Ghana 1962-65, lectr Gt Yarmouth Coll of Further Educn 1965-67, coordinator of Liberal Studies Norwich City Coll 1967-70, co-dir Euro Centre Friend's World Coll 1970-79; memb PEN Int 1989; *Books* Sunday Whiteman (1987), The Chymical Wedding (Whitbread award for fiction, 1989); *Recreations* life drawing, divination, shooting pool; *Style*— Lindsay Clarke, Esq; Peters Fraser & Dunlop, The Chambers, Chelsea Harbour, London SW10 0XF (☎ 071 376 7676, fax 071 352 7356)

CLARKE, Martin Courtenay; s of Douglas Archibald Clarke, of London, and Marjorie, *née* Blinkhorn (d 1987); *b* 7 Jan 1941; *Educ* Winchester, Trinity Coll Cambridge (MA); *m* 5 Sept 1974, Esmee Frances, da of Col J F Cottrell, OBE, MC (d 1972), of Exmouth; *Career* Touche Ross and Co Chartered Accountants: ptnr 1973, nat dir Res Devpt 1982-87, nat dir of mktg 1987-90, ptnr i/c Corp Fin Gp 1988-; dir Haymills Holdings Ltd; memb Auditing Practices Ctee Consultative Ctee of Accounting Bodies 1982-88; Liveryman: Worshipful Co of Merchant Taylors 1970, Worshipful Co of Loriners 1983; FCA 1973; *Recreations* sailing, diving, skiing, opera, reading; *Clubs* City of London, Lansdowne; *Style*— Martin Clarke, Esq; 91 Bedford Gardens, Kensington, London W8 7EQ; Hill House, 1 Little New St, London EC4A 3TR (☎ 071 936 3000, fax 071 583 8517, telex 884739 TRLDNG)

CLARKE, Mary; da of late Frederick Clarke, and Ethel Kate, *née* Reynolds (d 1984); *b* 23 Aug 1923; *Educ* Mary Datchelor Girls Sch; *Career* ed The Dancing Times London 1963-, ballet critic The Guardian 1977-; author; memb Grand Cncl The Royal Acad of Dancing; Queen Elizabeth II Coronation award RAD 1990; *Books* The Sadler's Wells Ballet: A History and an Appreciation (1955), Dancers of Mercury: the Story of Ballet Rambert (1962), Design for Ballet (with Clement Crisp, 1978), The History of Dance (1981); Encyclopedia Britannica (contrib, 1974); *Recreations* watching dancing, travel, reading; *Clubs* Gautier; *Style*— Miss Mary Clarke; 54 Ripplevale Grove, Islington, London N1 1HT; The Dancing Times, 45-47 Clerkenwell Green, London EC1R OBE (☎ 071 250 3006, fax 071 253 6679)

CLARKE, (Christopher) Michael; s of Patrick Reginald Rudland Clarke, of Helmsley, N Yorks, and Margaret Catherine, *née* Waugh; *b* 29 Aug 1952; *Educ* Felsted, Univ of Manchester (BA); *m* 1 July 1978, Deborah Clare, da of Paul Wilfred Cowling; 2 s (Oliver Paul b 29 June 1984, Alexander Patrick b 19 April 1986); *Career* art asst York Art Gallery 1973-76, res asst Br Museum 1976-77, asst keeper i/c prints Whitworth Art Gallery Univ of Manchester 1978-84, keeper Nat Gallery of Scotland 1987- (asst keeper 1984-87); visiting fell Paul Mellon Centre for Studies in Br Art Yale Univ 1984; *Books* The Tempting Prospect: A Social History of English Watercolours (1981), The Arrogant Connoisseur: Richard Payne Knight (co ed with Nicolas Penny, 1982), The Draughtsman's Art: Master Drawings in the Whitworth Art Gallery (1982), Lighting Up The Landscape: French Impressionism And Its Origins (1986), Corot And The Art Of Landscape (1991); *Recreations* golf, badminton, music; *Style*— Michael Clarke, Esq; 9A Summerside St, Trinity, Edinburgh, Scotland EH6 4NT (☎ 031 554 7167); National Gallery of Scotland, The Mound, Edinburgh, Scotland EH2 2EL (☎ 031 556 8921, fax 031 220 0917)

CLARKE, (John) Michael; s of Harold Vivian Clarke (d 1983), and Orpah Clarke (d 1976); *b* 24 Feb 1932; *Educ* Scarborough Coll; *m* 1982, Dr Susan Margaret, da of Herbert Wrigley (d 1973); 1 s (Jeremy b 1985), 1 da (Emily b 1984); *Career* fin investor; Cons memb: Rotherham Cncl 1966-74, S Yorks CC 1974-82; Rotary pres 1978-79, chm Rotherham Cons Assoc 1979-82 and 1989-; Hon FRGS; *Recreations* sailing, French tradition hunting with the Sologne, skiing; *Clubs* Rotherham, Sheffield Corinthian Sailing (cdre 1983-84); *Style*— Michael Clarke, Esq; Weetwood, 187 Moorgate Rd, Rotherham, S Yorks S60 3AX (☎ 0709 382852); The White House, Belvedere Close, Bridlington, North Humberside YO15 3LZ (☎ 0262 679000)

CLARKE, Michael John Marshal; s of Adm Sir Marshal Llewelyn Clarke, KBE, CB, DSC (d 1959), and Ina Leonora, *née* Edwards; *b* 3 Feb 1927; *Educ* St Edward's Sch Oxford, Trinity Coll Oxford; *m* 1954, Flavia Dorothea, da of Air Chief Marshal Sir (William) Alec Coryton, KCB, KBE, MVO, DFC, *qv*; 1 s, 1 da; *Career* Capt (TA) Rifle Bde; dir personnel servs Br Steel corp; personnel conslt; memb: Central Arbitration Ctee, Police Arbitration Tbnl, Arts Cncl of Great Britain, Welsh Arts Cncl, Cncl of Nat Museum of Wales; High Sheriff of Gwent 1985-86, chm govrs Haberdashers' Aske's and Monmouth Schs; *Recreations* shooting, landscape painting, growing vines; *Style*— Michael Clarke, Esq; Osbaston House, Monmouth, Gwent NP5 4BB (☎ 0600 3596)

CLARKE, Olive; MBE (1978), JP (1960); da of George Teasdale (d 1984), of Audlands, Preston Patrick, Milnthorpe, Cumbria, and Sarah, *née* Fawcett (d 1981); *b* 19 May 1922; *Educ* Kendal HS; *m* 10 April 1947, Arthur, s of James Anthony Clarke (d 1968), of Capewray Old Hall, Carnforth, Lancs; 2 da (Gwendaline Olive (Mrs Cleverly) b 20 Oct 1949, Alison Sarah (Mrs Boxford) b 10 Oct 1951); *Career* in farming partnership 1947-, chm Transport Users Consultative Ctee for N Western England (by appt DTI) 1979-90; chm Womens' Insts 1968-78, memb Bd of Visitors to Durham Prison (Home Office appt) 1971-, life vice pres fedn of Young Farmers Clubs 1974, chm S Cumbria Magistrates Assoc 1981-88, chm then pres Westmoreland and Furness Country Landowners Assoc 1984-88, tstee Frieda Scott Tst; *Recreations* gardening, travel, use of the English language; *Clubs* Farmers; *Style*— Mrs Olive Clarke, MBE, JP; Kaker Mill, Preston Patrick, Milnthorpe, Cumbria LA7 7NZ (☎ 04487 239); Chairman, Transport Users Consultative Committee for N Western England, Boulton House, 17-21 Chorlton St, Manchester M1 3HY (☎ 061 228 6247)

CLARKE, Maj Peter Cecil; CVO (1969, MVO 1964); s of late Capt Edward Denman Clarke, CBE, MC (d 1966), of Crossways, Binstead, Isle of Wight, and Audrey, *née* Rant; *b* 9 Aug 1927; *Educ* Eton, RMC Sandhurst; *m* 1950, Rosemary Virginia Margaret Harmsworth, da of late T C Durham, of Appomattox, Virginia, USA; 1 s, 2 da; *Career* Maj (ret) 3 The King's Own Hussars and 14/20 King's Hussars 1945-64; asst priv sec then comptroller to HRH Princess Marina, Duchess of Kent 1961-68, comptroller and extra equerry to HRH Princess Alexandra, the Hon Mrs Angus Ogilvy 1964-69, chief clerk Duchy of Lancaster 1969-, JP Hants 1971-81; *Style*— Major Peter Clarke, CVO; 6 Gordon Place, W8 (☎ home 071 937 0356, office 071 836 8277)

CLARKE, Dr Peter Frederick; s of John William Clarke (d 1987), and Winifred, *née* Hadfield; *b* 21 July 1942; *Educ* Eastbourne GS, St John's Coll Cambridge (BA, MA, PhD, LittD); *m* 29 March 1969 (m dis 1990), Dillon, *née* Cheetham; 2 da (Emily Jane b 4 July 1974, Liberty Lucy (twin) b 4 July 1974); *Career* reader in modern history UCL 1978-80 (asst lectr then lectr in history 1966-78), reader in modern history and fell St John's Coll Cambridge 1987- (lectr in history, fell and tutor 1980-87); chm: Cambs Area Pty of SDP 1981-82, Editorial Bd Twentieth Century British History; FBA 1989; *Books* Lancashire and the New Liberalism (1971), Liberals and Social Democrats (1978), The Keynesian Revolution in the Making (1988), A Question of Leadership: from Gladstone to Thatcher (1991); *Style*— Dr Peter Clarke; St John's College, Cambridge CB2 1TP (☎ 0223 338726)

CLARKE, Peter Lovat; JP (1970); s of Harold Clarke (d 1945), of Warrington, and Alice Taylor; *b* 25 July 1934; *Educ* Ellesmere; *m* 1956, Audrey Christine, da of Walter Jonathan Elston, of Cheshire; 3 s (John b 1956, Simon and Timothy b 1964 (twins), 1 da (Denise b 1959); *Career* dir: Greenall Whitley plc; chm: Gilbert and John Greenall Ltd, Cellar 5 Ltd, Stretton Leisure Ltd, Cellar 5, Harvey Prince and Co Ltd, G & J Drinks Direct, Greenall Export Ltd, Corry's Soft Drinks Ltd, Bombay Spirits Co Ltd, Wilderspool Commercial Hldgs Ltd, Clansouth Ltd, Stretton Automatics Ltd, Warrington Festival Tst Ltd, Warrington Industrial Training Tst Ltd, Greenall Whitley Take-Home (sales) Ltd, Greenall Whitley Exports Ltd, Cambrian Soft Drinks Ltd; memb Worshipful Co of Distillers 1979; *Recreations* golf, music, reading, swimming; *Clubs* Warrington Golf, Wine and Spirit over 40 Club, Majority, Walton Investment; *Style*— Peter Clarke, Esq, JP; Brook House, Cann Lane, Appleton, nr Warrington, Cheshire (☎ 0925 61660); Gilbert and John Greenhall Ltd, PO Box No 3, Causeway Distillery, Warrington, Cheshire (☎ 0925 50111)

CLARKE, Philip Michael; s of Gerald Michael Richard Clarke (d 1988), of Hagley, W Mids, and Phyllis Mary, *née* Adams; *b* 31 May 1954; *Educ* Oundle, Univ of Birmingham (BSc, B Comm); *m* 21 July 1986, Rachel Barbara Lucia, da of Bernard Laurence O'Hare (d 1988), of Burton-On-Trent, Derbys; 1 s (George b 1988); *Career* Clamason Ind Ltd 1977- (commercial dir 1981-86, md 1986); chm Providence Gp Trg Scheme Ltd; CEngMIProdE; *Recreations* golf; *Clubs* Stourbridge GC; *Style*— Philip Clarke, Esq; 25 Station Rd, Hagley, W Mids DY9 0NU (☎ 0562 886 062); Clamason Industries Ltd, Gibbons Industrial Park, Kingswinford, W Mids DY6 8XG (☎ 0384 400 000, fax 0384 279 222, telex 334 580)

CLARKE, Richard Allen; s of Allen Lee Clarke, of London, and Anne Clarke; *b* 19 Aug 1942; *Educ* Aldenham, The Architectural Assoc Sch (AA Dipl); *m* 11 May 1968, Mary Mildred Irene, da of Dr James Francis Hanratty, OBE, of London; 2 s (Jason b 1970, Dominic b 1979), 2 da (Antonia b 1973, Louisa b 1976); *Career* sr ptnr Clifford Tee & Gale 1977-; Freeman City of London 1964; memb RIBA; *Recreations* shooting, gardening; *Style*— Richard Clarke, Esq; Carnleigh, Mount Pleasant, Sparrows Green, Wadhurst, E Sussex TN5 6UH (☎ 0892 883263); Clifford Tee & Gale, 5 Eccleston St, London SW1W 9LY (☎ 071 730 9633, fax 071 730 0965, car 0860 222632)

CLARKE, Robert Charles; s of John Edward Kenyon Clarke (d 1980), and Elsie Mary, *née* Rand; *b* 15 April 1943; *Educ* John Lyon Sch, Harrow; *m* 11 April 1970, Christine Marjorie, da of Ronald Charles Gardner, of Knowle West Midlands; 2 s (Jonathan b 1970, Laurence b 1972), 2 da (Eleanor b 1974, Georgina b 1977); *Career* CA; Barton Mayhew 1962-70, Peat Marwick Mitchell 1970-72, Viney Merretts 1972-80, BDO Binder Hamlyn 1980-; Freeman: City of London 1976, Chartered Accountants Livery Co 1976; FCA 1971; *Recreations* golf; *Clubs* MCC; *Style*— Robert Clarke, Esq; Hudnall Farm, Little Gaddesden, Berkhamstead, Herts HP4 1QN (☎ 044 284 3214); BDO Binder Hamyln, 8 St Bride St, London EC4A 4DA (☎ 071 353 3020, fax 071 583 0031)

CLARKE, Robert Cyril; s of Robert Henry Clarke (d 1964), and Rose, *née* Bratton (d 1952); *b* 28 March 1929; *Educ* Dulwich, Pembroke Coll Oxford (MA); *m* 12 July 1952, Evelyn Mary (Lynne), da of Cyrus Harper (d 1959); 3 s (Tristan b 26 May 1956, Jonathan b (twin) 26 May 1956, Ben b 13 July 1966), 1 da (Anna b 19 May 1969); *Career* Royal West Kent Regt 1947-49; trainee Cadbury Bros Ltd 1952-54, gen mangr John Forrest Ltd 1954-57, marketing dir Cadbury Confectionary 1957-62, md Cadbury Cakes Ltd 1962-69, chm Cadbury Cakes and dir Cadbury Schweppes Foods Ltd 1969-71, md McVitie & Cadbury Cakes Ltd 1971-74; United Biscuits (UK) Ltd: joined Bd 1974, md 1977; chm and md United Biscuits (UK) Ltd and dir United Biscuits (Hldgs) plc 1984, gp chief exec United Biscuits (Hldgs) plc 1986-; memb Cncl: Cake & Biscuit Alliance 1965-83, ISBA 1977-84; memb Resources Ctee Food & Drink Fedn 1984; memb EDC for Food and Drink Indust 1984, non-exec memb Thames Water plc 1988; *Recreations* reading, walking, renovating old buildings, planting trees; *Style*— Robert C Clarke, Esq; United Biscuits (Holdings) plc, Grant House, Syon Lane, Isleworth, Middlesex TW7 5NN (☎ 081 560 3131, fax 081 895 4657, telex 8954657)

CLARKE, Robert MacDonald; s of Samuel Frank Clarke, of Bournemouth, and Anne *née* Franklin; *b* 16 Dec 1944; *Educ* High Storrs GS Sheffield; *m* 10 Sept 1967, Sandra Lynne, da of Leo Edwards Morgan, of Great Missenden; 1 s (Adam Edward b 1970), 1 da (Sarah Lyn b 1972); *Career* accountant Yorks Electricity Bd, mgmnt conslt Spicer & Pegler, chm and md Royco plc; FCCA 1968; *Style*— Robert Clarke, Esq; Royco Plc, Royco House, Liston Rd, Marlow (☎ 06284 6922, 0836 716666, 06284 3880)

CLARKE, Robert Sandifer; s of Robert Arthur Clarke (d 1988), of Abinger Manor, Abinger Common, Surrey, and Agnes Joyce, *née* Coventry (d 1987); *b* 9 May 1934; *Educ* Westminster, ChCh Oxford (MA), College of Law; *m* 14 Sept 1964, Cherry June Leslie, da of William Attwood Waudby, of Mombasa, Kenya; 1 s (Damian Rupert b 4 Jan 1967), 2 da (Vanessa-Jane b 4 Sept 1965, Georgina Ann b 16 Sept 1975); *Career* Nat Serv RN 1952; cmmnd RNVR: Midshipman 1952, Sub Lt 1953, Lt 1955, ret 1960; slr 1962, sr ptnr Wood Nash (formerly ptnr), UK ed Droit Et Affaires France 1968-75; chm: Fedn Field Sports Assocs (UK) of EEC 1978-83, Br Delgn to Int Cncl of Hunting and Conservation of Game UK 1983-90; vice pres and fell Game Conservancy Fordingbridge; Freeman City of London 1975, Liveryman Worshipful Co of Gunmakers 1975; memb Law Soc 1962; *Recreations* sailing, shooting, skiing, tennis, travel; *Clubs* Turf, Oxford & Cambridge, Shikar; *Style*— Robert Clarke, Esq; Abinger Manor, Abinger Common, Surrey; 2 Cheyne Mews, Cheyne Walk, Chelsea, London SW3 (☎ 071 242 7322); 6 Raymond Buildings, Gray's Inn, London (☎ 071 242 7322, fax 071 831 9041, telex 21143 WNANDW G)

CLARKE, Rev Robert Sydney; s of George Sydney Clarke (d 1968), and Elizabeth, *née* Rowe (d 1985); *b* 31 Oct 1935; *Educ* St Dunstan's Coll, King's Coll London (AKC); *Career* The Buffs Royal E Kent Regt Mau Mau Campaign Kenya 1954-56; curate Hendon Parish Church 1965; chaplain: New Cross Hosp Wolverhampton 1970, Herrison and West Dorset Hosps 1974, Westminster Hosp and Westminster Med Sch Univ of London 1979, Winchester Health Authy 1985; chaplain to HM The Queen 1987; memb Gen Synod Church of England's Cncl for Hosp Chaplaincy 1976; *Recreations* music, travel, dog showing, dog breeding; *Clubs* Kennel; *Style*— The Rev Robert Clarke; 22 The Harrage, Romsey, Hampshire SO51 8AE; Chaplains Office, Royal Hants County Hospital, Winchester, Hants

CLARKE, Roger Eric; s of Frederick Cuérel Clarke, of Petts Wood, Kent, and Hilda Josephine, *née* Holbrook (d 1980); *b* 13 June 1939; *Educ* UCS Hampstead, CCC Cambridge (MA); *m* 8 Oct 1983, Elizabeth Jane, da of Gordon William Pingstone, of Beckenham, Kent; 1 da (Rebecca b 1986); *Career* positions held: Civil Aviation Divs of Miny of Aviation, BOT and Dept of Trade and Tport 1961-72 and 1980-85; air traffic rights advsr to Govt Fiji 1972-74, asst sec Insur and Overseas Trade Divs Dept of Trade 1975-80, under sec Dept of Tport (Civil Aviation Policy Directorate 1985, Public Tport Directorate 1989); *Recreations* family, friends, church, garden, walking, theatre, music, languages, travel; *Clubs* Reform; *Style*— Roger Clarke, Esq; Dept of Tport, 2 Marsham St, London SW1P 3EB (☎ 071 276 5020/5026, fax 071 276 0818, telex 22

CLARKE, Dr Roger Howard; *b* 22 Aug 1943; *Educ* King Edward VI Sch Stourbridge, Univ of Birmingham (BSc, MSc), Poly of Central London (PhD); *m* 15 Oct 1966, Sandra Ann; 1 s, 1 da; *Career* res offr CEGB 1965-77; NRPB: head of Nuclear Power Assessments 1978-82, Bd Sec 1983-87, dir 1987-; memb: Int Cmmn on Radiological Protection, CEC Gp of Experts in Basic Safety Standards for Radiation Protection; chm OECD Nuclear Energy Agency Ctee on Radiation Protection and Public Health, alternate UK delegate to UN Sci Ctee on Effects of Atomic Radiation; fell Inst of Radiation Protection; *publications:* Carcinogenesis and Radiation Risk: A Biomathematical Reconnaissance (with W V Mayneord, 1977), author of numerous papers in the scientific literature; *Recreations* theatre, gardening, travel; *Style*— Dr Roger Clarke; Corner Cottage, Woolton Hill, Newbury, Berks RG15 9XJ (☎ 0635 253957); Nat Radiological Protection Bd, Chilton, Didcot, Oxon OX11 0RQ (☎ 0235 831600, fax 0235 833891, telex 837124 RADPRO G)

CLARKE, Roy; *b* 28 Jan 1930; *m* 1953, Enid, *née* Kitching; 1 s (Stephen b 1955), 1 da (Julia b 1958); *Career* writer; formerly: soldier, salesman, policeman, teacher; full time writer 1965-; TV series: The Misfits 1970, Last of The Summer Wine 1972-, Open All Hours 1975-, Keeping Up Appearances 1990; Writer's Guild award best series 1970, Pye Television award 1982; Hon DLitt Bradford; *Recreations* reading, watching nature; *Style*— Roy Clarke, Esq; c/o Sheila Lemon (Lemon, Unna & Durbridge), 24 Pottery Lane, Holland Park, London W11 4LZ (☎ 071 727 1346, fax 071 727 9037)

CLARKE, Roy H; s of Henry Clarke (d 1975), and Florence Ruth, *née* Bavage; *b* 14 July 1935; *Educ* Strodes Sch; *m* 3 Sept 1960, Sylvia Maud, da of Fred Snell (d 1985); 2 s (Martin b 1965, Simon b 1970); *Career* dir: Systems Ltd 1984-, Basic Ltd 1984-; govr BUPA 1984, md BUPA Insur 1987; *Recreations* sailing, fly fishing; *Clubs* RNSA; *Style*— R H Clarke, Esq; BUPA Ltd, Rowell House, Essex St, London WC2

CLARKE, Rupert Grant Alexander; s and h of Maj Sir Rupert Clarke, 3 Bt, MBE; *b* 12 Dec 1947; *m* 1978, Susannah, da of Sir (Richard) Robert Law-Smith; 1 s, 2 da; *Style*— Rupert Clarke, Esq

CLARKE, Maj Sir Rupert William John; 3 Bt (UK 1882), of Rupertswood, Colony of Victoria; MBE (1943); s of Sir Rupert Turner Havelock Clarke, 2 Bt (d 1926); *b* 5 Nov 1919; *Educ* Eton, Magdalen Coll Oxford (MA), FAIM; *m* 21 Jan 1947, Kathleen Grant, da of Peter Grant Hay (d 1961), of Melbourne; 2 s (and 1 s decd), 1 da; *Heir* s, Rupert Clarke; *Career* served WWII, Maj Irish Gds (despatches); chm: Cadbury Schweppes Australia Ltd, P and O Australia Ltd, Nat Australia Bank Ltd; dir: Morganite Australia Pty Ltd, Custom Credit Hldgs Ltd; hon fell Trinity Coll Melbourne; Order of Grimaldis 1975, Légion d'Honneur (France) 1979; *Recreations* racing, swimming; *Clubs* Melbourne, Australian, Athenaeum (Melbourne), Union (Sydney), Queensland, Victoria Amateur Turf, Cavalry and Gds (London); *Style*— Maj

Sir Rupert Clarke, Bt, MBE; Bolinda Vale, Clarkefield, Vic 3430, Australia (☎ 010 61 05 428 5111); Richmond House, 56 Avoca St, Melbourne, Vic 3141, Australia (☎ 010 61 03 266 1045); office: Nat Bank House, 500 Bourke St, Melbourne, Vic 3000, Australia (☎ 010 61 03 602 3088, telefax 010 61 03 670 2629)

CLARKE, Sally Vanessa; da of Brian Trent Clarke, of Surrey, and Sheila Margaret, *née* Coomber; *b* 6 Jan 1954; *Educ* Guildford HS, Croydon Tech Coll (Dip in Hotel and Catering Ops); *Career* studied and worked in Paris (Cordon Bleu Advanced Cert) 1974-75, asst cook Leiths Good Food Catering Co 1976-77, head teacher and demonstrator Leiths Sch of Food and Wine 1977-79, moved to Los Angeles to work with Michael McCarty and helped set up Michaels Santa Monica 1979, asst cook and asst night mangr Michaels Santa Monica Calif and West Beach Cafe Venice Calif 1980-83; opened: Clarke's in London 1984, & Clarke's 1988, Clarke's Bread 1989; *Recreations* cooking, eating, drinking good wine, opera; *Style—* Miss Sally Clarke; Clarke's, 124 Kensington Church St, London W8 4BH (☎ 071 221 9225)

CLARKE, Stella Rosemary; JP, DL (Avon 1982); da of John Herbert King (d 1973), of Somerlea, Langford, Somerset, and Mollie Isobel Bruce, *née* Riches (d 1983); *b* 16 Feb 1932; *Educ* Cheltenham Ladies Coll, Trinity Coll Dublin; *m* 21 June 1952, Charles Nigel Clarke, s of Charles Cyril Clarke (d 1953); 4 s (Giles b 1953, Nigel b 1957, Henry b 1959, Matthew b 1963), 1 da (Bridget b 1955); *Career* chm Long Ashton RDC 1972-74 (memb 1955-74), memb Woodspring DC 1974-77; magistrate Bristol City Bench 1968- (chm 1991-), formed Zenzele self-build housing gp in St Paul's Bristol 1981, involved with other housing projects; govr BBC 1974-81, vice chm Knightstone Housing Assoc 1985- (memb 1980), chm of Cncl Univ of Bristol 1987- (memb 1982-); memb: Bristol Urban Devpt Corp 1988-, Housing Corp 1988-; *Recreations* family, diversity of life, poetry, jigsaw puzzles, needlepoint; *Style—* Mrs Stella Clarke, JP, DL; Gatcombe Court, Flax Bourton, Bristol BS19 1PX (☎ 0255 393141)

CLARKE, Stephen Patrick; s of Leslie Clarke, of 30 Church St, Weaverham, Northwich, Cheshire, and Anne Mary, *née* Jones (d 1981); *b* 23 March 1948; *Educ* Rostrevor Coll Adelaide S Australia, Univ of Hull (LLB); *m* 6 July 1974, Margaret Roberta, da of Robert Millar, of Buckna, Co Antrim, N Ireland; 2 s (Christopher James b 1975, Andrew Paul b 1977); *Career* called to the Bar Inner Temple 1971; memb Wales and Chester Circuit (jr 1988-89), asst rec Crown Ct, vice chm Shropshire Cricket Assoc; *Recreations* golf, cricket, theatre; *Clubs* Church Stretton Golf; *Style—* Stephen Clarke, Esq; 18 Crescent Place, Townwalls, Shrewsbury SY1 1TQ (☎ 0743 62615); 21 White Friars Chester CH1 1N2 (☎ 0244 323070)

CLARKE, Stewart William; s of Albert Edward Clarke (d 1975), and Elsie Jane, *née* Parker; *b* 12 March 1936; *Educ* Nottingham HS, Univ of Birmingham (MB ChB, MD); *m* 9 June 1962, Gillian Mary, da of Harry Douglas Acres, of The White Cottage, Sandy Lane, Kingswood, Surrey; 2 s (Jonathon b 29 Nov 1968, Andrew b 15 Dec 1971); *Career* asst prof of med Univ of California San Francisco 1969-70, lectr in med Queen Elizabeth Hosp Birmingham 1970-71, conslt physician in gen and thoracic med The Royal Free and Brompton 1971-, conslt physician The King Edward VII Hosp for Officers 1976-; author of numerous papers and chapters on lung disease; sec of The Thoracic Soc 1975-81, chm Med Advsy Ctee of King Edward VII Hosp Midhurst, fell American Coll of Chest Physicians 1984-, censor of the RCP 1987-89, pres Euro Resp Soc 1990; FRCP 1974, Assoc of Physicians of GB and Ireland, memb RSM; *Books* Aerosols and the Lung (1984), Fibreoptic Bronchoscopy (1987); *Recreations* sports fanatic, rugby, squash, golf; *Clubs* Saracens Football, Hampstead Cricket, Salcombe Yacht, Hadley Wood Golf; *Style—* Dr Stewart Clarke; Oak House, 13 Hadley Grove, Hadley Green, Barnet, Herts EN5 4PH (☎ 081 449 2416); 148 Harley Street, London W1N 1AH (☎ 071 487 5020)

CLARKE, Thomas; CBE (1980), JP Lanark (1972), MP (Lab) Monklands West 1983-; s of James Clarke, and Mary, *née* Gordon; *b* 10 Jan 1941; *Educ* Columba HS, Coatbridge and Scottish Coll of Commerce; *Career* former asst dir Scottish Film Cncl; MP (Lab) Coatbridge and Airdire 1982-83; memb Coatbridge Cncl 1964-74, provost Monklands DC 1974-82; pres Convention of Scottish Local Authorities 1978-80 (vice pres 1976-78), sponsor Disabled Persons' Act 1986, govr BFI; *Books* Managing Third World Debt (co-author); *Style—* Thomas Clarke, Esq, CBE, JP, MP; House of Commons, SW1

CLARKE, Thomas Sydney (Tom); s of Thomas William Clarke, of Stubbington, Hants, and Evelyn Elizabeth, *née* Hodge (d 1962); *b* 29 April 1939; *Educ* Isleworth GS; *m* 12 Sept 1961, Margaret Jean, da of Archibald Morgan (d 1953); 1 s (Morgan b 1968), 2 da (Heather b 1964, Donna b 1966); *Career* journalist: Hayes Chronicle, Herts Advertiser St Albans, The Chronicle Bulawayo Southern Rhodesia, Daily and Sunday Nation Nairobi Kenya, Daily Express London, Queen Magazine, Evening Standard; Sports ed: Evening Standard 1972-74, Daily Mail 1975-86, The Times 1986-; former capt Press Golfing Soc; *Recreations* watching sport, playing golf; *Clubs* Thorndon Park Golf, Lord's Taverners, Sloane; *Style—* Tom Clarke, Esq; 11 Thorndon Hall, Ingrave, Brentwood, Essex CM13 3RJ (☎ 0277 811 835); The Times, 1 Pennington St, London E1 9XN (☎ 071 782 5944, fax 071 782 5046, telex 262141)

CLARKE, (George) Timothy Horace De Courquetaine; s of Denis Horace Hilary Clarke, of Old Timbers, Little Witley, Worcs, and Louise Marie, *née* Schlincker; *b* 20 April 1949; *Educ* Oundle, St John's Coll Cambridge (MA); *m* 2 Sept 1989, Henrietta Barbara, da of Alexander Neilson Strachan Walker, CMG (d 1980); *Career* admitted slr 1974; ptnr Linklaters & Paines 1982-; *Recreations* gardening, reading, France; *Style—* Timothy Clarke, Esq; Linklaters & Paines, Barrington House, 59-67 Gresham St, London EC2V 7JA (☎ 071 606 7080, fax 071 606 5113)

CLARKE, Sir (Charles Mansfield) Tobias; 6 Bt (UK 1831), of Dunham Lodge, Norfolk; adopted name Tobias 1962; s of Sir Humphrey Orme Clarke, 5 Bt (d 1973); *b* 8 Sept 1939; *Educ* Eton, Ch Ch Oxford, The Sorbonne, New York Univ; *m* 1, 1971 (m dis 1979), Charlotte, da of Roderick Walter; m 2, 1984, Teresa Lorraine Aphrodite, da of Somerset Struben de Chair, of St Osyth's Priory, Essex; 1 da (Theodora b 1985); *Heir* half-bro, Orme Clarke; *Career* vice pres London Branch of Bankers' Tst Co New York; hon treas Standing Cncl of the Baronetage 1980-; *Style—* Sir Tobias Clarke, Bt; 80a Campden Hill Rd, London W8 (☎ 071 937 6213); The Church House, Bibury, Glos (☎ 028 574 225)

CLARKE, William Malpas; CBE (1976); s of Ernest Clarke (d 1963), and Florence, *née* Wright (d 1973); *b* 5 June 1922; *Educ* Audenshaw GS, Univ of Manchester (BA); *m* 1, 1946, Margaret Braithwaite; 2 da (Deborah, Pamela); m 2, 1973, Faith Elizabeth, da of Lionel Dawson, of Bucks; *Career* journalist; Manchester Guardian: ed staff 1948-56, asst fin ed 1955-56; The Times: ed staff 1956-66, dep city ed 1956-57, city ed 1957-62, fin and indust ed 1962-66; conslt The Banker 1967-76 (ed 1966), dir of Studies Ctee on Invisible Exports 1966-67, dir Perm Ctee on Invisible Exports 1968 (Ctee became Br Invisible Exports Cncl 1983), fndr dir Euromoney 1969-84, chm City Telecommunications Ctee 1972-87, dir gen and dep chm Br Invisible Exports Cncl 1976-87, dep chm City Communications Centre 1976-87; dir: Grindlays Bank 1966-85 and 1987-89, ANZ Hldgs 1985-87, ANZ Grindlays Bank 1989-, Swiss Re-Insur (UK); chm: Grindlays Bank (Jersey) 1976-, ANZ Merchant Bank 1987-; govr: Gt Ormond St Hosp for Sick Children 1982-90, Greenwich Theatre 1984-87; chm Appeal Tstees Gt Ormond St Hosp 1984-; cncl memb RIIA 1970-83; tstee Harold Wincott Fndn 1970-, chm Harold Wincott Financial Journalist of the Year Award Panel 1971-; *Books* The City's Invisible Earnings (1958), Private Enterprise in Developing Countries (1966), The City in the World Economy (1965, 1967), Britains Invisible Earnings (for the Ctee on Invisible Exports, 1967), The World's Money (1970, US edition 1972), Money Markets of the World (1971), Inside the City (1979, paperback 1983), How the City of London Works (1986, 1988), The Secret Life of Wilkie Collins (1988), Planning for Europe: 1992 (1989); *Recreations* books, theatre; *Clubs* Reform; *Style—* William Clarke, Esq, CBE; 37 Park Vista, Greenwich, London SE10 (☎ 081 858 0979); ANZ Merchant Bank, Palace House, 3 Cathedral St, London SE1 (☎ 071 378 2904)

CLARKSON, Ven Alan Geoffrey; s of Geoffrey Archibald Clarkson, OBE (d 1980), of Lyndhurst, and Essie Isabel Bruce, *née* Bruce-Porter (d 1981); *b* 14 Feb 1934; *Educ* Sherborne, Christ's Coll Cambridge (MA), Wycliffe Hall Oxford; *m* 10 Sept 1959, Monica Ruth, da of Rev Harcourt Robert Henry Lightburne (d 1949), of Upchurch, Kent; 2 s (John b 1961, Michael b 1964), 1 da (Anne b 1960); *Career* Nat Serv 1952-54, cmmnd Lt; ordained deacon 1959, priest 1960; curate: Penn Wolverhampton 1959-60, St Oswald's Oswestry 1960-63, Wrington with Redhill 1963-65; incumbent vicar Chewton Mendip with Emborough 1965-74; vicar: St John's Glastonbury with Godney 1974-84, W Pennard 1981-84, Meare 1981-84, St Benedict Glastonbury 1982-84, Burley 1984-; archdeacon of Winchester and hon canon Winchester Cathedral 1984-; proctor in convocation 1970-75 and 1990-, diocesan ecumenical offr 1965-75; *Recreations* gardening, photography, DIY, wood turning, singing; *Style—* The Ven the Archdeacon of Winchester; The Vicarage, Church Corner, Burley, Ringwood, Hants BH24 4AP (☎ 04253 2303)

CLARKSON, Alan Malcolm; *b* 12 Sept 1936; *Educ* Nunthorpe GS York; *m* Pauline Rita, *née* Musgrove; 1 s (Kevin Mark b 10 Feb 1964), 1 da (Karen Dawn b 26 April 1967); *Career* swimming administrator; former int swimmer, competed in Cwlth Games 1958, represented GB 1959-62; hon treas: Amateur Swimming Assoc 1986-, Amateur Swimming Fedn of GB 1986-; pres: Yorkshire Amateur Swimming Assoc, N Eastern Counties Amateur Swimming Assoc; memb: Tech Swimming Ctee Fèdèration Internationale de Natation Amateur, Swimming Ctee LEN, BOA; qualified CA; sr ptnr Plummer Clarkson & Lester; FCA; *Clubs* York City Baths; *Style—* Alan Clarkson, Esq; Amateur Swimming Association, Finance Office, 37 Monkgate, York (☎ 0904 647199, fax 0904 622195)

CLARKSON, Prof Brian Leonard; s of Leonard Coleman Clarkson, of Driffield, E Yorks, and Gertrude Irene, *née* Shouler; *b* 28 July 1930; *Educ* Beverley GS E Yorks, Univ of Leeds (BSc, PhD); *m* 5 Sept 1953, Margaret Elaine, da of Frank Bancroft Wilby (d 1976), of Hedge End, Southampton; 3 s (Stephen Anthony b 1955, John Michael b 1957, Paul Richard b 1965), 1 da (Carol Margaret b 1960); *Career* structural engr de Havilland Aircraft Co 1953-57, Sir Alan Cobham res fell Univ of Southampton 1957-58, lectr Dept of Aeronautics Univ of Southampton 1958-63, lectr and sr lectr Inst of Sound and Vibration Res 1963-66; Univ of Southampton: prof vibration studies 1966-82, dir Inst of Sound Vibration Res 1967-78, dean of engrg 1978-80, dep vice chllr 1980-82; sr res assoc NASA USA 1970-71, princ Univ Coll Swansea 1982-, vice chllr Univ of Wales 1987-89; memb Wintech Advsy Bd, sec Int Cmmn on Acoustics 1975-81, pres Inst of Acoustics 1980-82, pres Fedn of Acoustical Socs of Europe 1982-84, memb SERC 1984-88; Hon DSc: Univ of Leeds 1984, Univ of Southampton 1987, Univ of Sains Malaysia 1990; FEng 1986, FInst of Acoustics, FSoc of Environmental Engrgs, FRAeS; *Recreations* walking, gardening; *Clubs* Athenaeum; *Style—* Prof Brian Clarkson; Danver House, 236 Gower Rd, Sketty, Swansea SA2 9JJ (☎ 0792 202 329); The Univ Coll of Swansea, Singleton Pk, Swansea SA2 8PP (☎ 0792 295154, fax 0792 295 655, telex 48358 UL

CLARKSON, Hon Judge; Derek Joshua; QC (1969); s of Albert Clarkson (d 1955), of Pudsey, Yorks, and Winifred Charlotte, *née* James; *b* 10 Dec 1929; *Educ* Pudsey GS, King's Coll London, (LLB); *m* 1960, Peternella Marie-Luise Ilse, da of R Canenbley, of Leer, Germany; 1 s, 1 da; *Career* Nat Serv RAF 1952-54; barr 1951; rec: Rotherham 1967-72, Huddersfield 1972, Crown Ct 1972-77; circuit judge (SE) 1977-, Middx liaison judge 1985-; *Recreations* walking, theatre, book collecting; *Style—* His Hon Judge Clarkson, QC; 24 John Islip St, London SW1; 72A Cornwall Rd, Harrogate, N Yorks

CLARKSON, Euan Neilson Kerr; s of Dr Alexander Clarkson (d 1946), of Newcastle upon Tyne, and Helen, *née* Griffin (d 1977); *b* 9 May 1937; *Educ* Shrewsbury, Univ of Cambridge (MA, PhD), Univ of Edinburgh (DSc); *m* 31 Aug 1962, Cynthia Margaret, da of Eric Cowie (d 1979), of Kirby Moorside, Yorks; 4 s (John Alexander Joseph b 21 Nov 1965, Peter Bruce Mark b 21 Jan 1967, Thomas Hamish Martin b 29 Jan 1971, Matthew Dougal Charles b 10 March 1973); *Career* Nat Serv 1955-57; Univ of Edinburgh: asst lectr 1963-65, lectr 1965-78, dir of studies 1967-73, assoc dean Sci Faculty 1978-81, sr lectr 1978-81, reader in geology and geophysics 1981-; 61 sci articles in learned jls; memb Edinburgh Geological Soc (pres 1985-87), tstee Natural History Museum 1987-; FRSE; *Books* Invertebrate Palaeontology and Evolution (1979, 2 edn, 1986); *Recreations* classical music, fell-walking, story-writing, history; *Style—* Dr Euan Clarkson, FRSE; 4 Cluny Place, Edinburgh, Scotland EH10 4RL (☎ 031 447 2248); Dept of Geology and Geophysics, University of Edinburgh, King's Buildings, West Mains Rd, Edinburgh, Scotland EH9 3JW (☎ 031 667 1081 ext 8514)

CLARKSON, Gerald Dawson; CBE (1990), QFSM (1983); s of Alexander Dickie Clarkson (d 1986), of St Mary Cray, Kent, and Agnes Tierney, *née* Price; *b* 4 June 1939; *Educ* Westminster Tech Coll, Poly of Central London (BA); *m* 21 March 1959, Rose Lilian, da of Thomas Montague Hodgson (d 1971), of Clapham; 1 s (Nicholas b 1963), 1 da (Penelope b 1965); *Career* Nat Serv RE 1959-61; London Fire Brigade: joined 1961, station offr 1969, asst divnl offr 1972, divnl offr 1974, dep asst chief offr 1979, asst chief offr 1980, awarded Fire Serv Long Serv and Good Conduct Medal 1981, dep chief offr 1983, chief exec 1987; Good Conduct Medal 1981, offr brother O St J 1989; memb Central Fire Brigades Advsy Cncl 1980, advsr to Assoc of Met Authys 1987, vice pres Cwlth and Overseas Fire Serv Assoc 1989 (pres 1990), and memb Fedn Br Fire Orgns 1989 (chm 1990), dir NFPA USA 1990; Freeman City of London 1983, fndr Master of the Guild of Firefighters; FBIM 1978, FIMS 1979, FRSH 1987, hon fell IFE 1989-; *Recreations* music, sailing, fishing; *Clubs* The East India; *Style—* Gerald Clarkson, Esq, QFSM; London Fire & Civil Defence Authority, London Fire Brigade Headquarters, 8 Albert Embankment, London SE1 7SD (☎ 071 587 4000, fax 071 587 4169, telex 918200)

CLARKSON WEBB, Hon Mrs (Ruth Isabel); *née* Wakefield; da of 1 Baron Wakefield of Kendal (d 1983), and Rowena Doris (d 1981), da of late Dr Llewellyn Lewis, OBE, JP; *b* 12 Oct 1932; *m* 1 June 1955, Maj Nigel James Clarkson Webb (d 1987), yst s of William Thomas Clarkson Webb (d 1966), of Shortlands, Shortheath, Farnham, Surrey, and 25 Weymouth St, London W1; 1 s (Edward b 1966), 2 da (Georgina b 1957, Carolyn b 1958); *Style—* The Hon Mrs Clarkson Webb; Buckstone House, Carnforth, Lancs (☎ 0524 781 585)

CLARRICOATS, Prof Peter John Bell; s of John Clarricoats OBE (d 1969), of London, and Alice Cecilia, *née* Bell (d 1982); *b* 6 April 1932; *Educ* Minchenden GS, Imperial Coll London (BSc, PhD, DSc); *m* 1, 6 Aug 1955 (m dis 1963), (Mary) Gillian Stephenson, da of George Gerald Hall (d 1971), of Leeds; 1 s (Michael b 1960), 1 da (Alison b 1962); m 2, 19 Oct 1968, Phyllis Joan, da of Reginald Blackburn Lloyd (d

1989), of Newton Abbot; 2 da (Angela b 1969, Caroline b 1969); *Career* scientific staff GEC 1953-59; lectr: Queens Univ of Belfast 1959-62, Univ of Sheffield 1962-63; prof Univ of Leeds 1963-67; QMC London 1968-: dean of engrg 1977-80, head of electronic engrg 1979-, govr 1976-79 and 1987-90; Coopers Hill Meml Prize (IEE) 1964, Measurement Prize (IEE) 1989, JJ Thomson Medal (IEE) 1989, Euro Microwave Prize 1989; chm: IEE Electronics Div 1979, Br Nat Ctee for Radio Sci 1985-89, and numerous conferences on microwaves and antennae; appt Distinguished lectr IEEE Antennae and Propagation 1986-88, vice pres IEE 1989; FInstP 1964, FIEE 1968, FIEEE 1968, FCGI 1980, FEng 1983, FRS 1990; *Books* Microwave Ferrites (1960), Corrugated Horns for Microwave Antennas (1984); *Recreations* formerly mountaineering and squash, classical music and photography; *Style*— Prof Peter Clarricoats, FRS; 7 Falcon Close, Sawbridgeworth, Herts CM21 OAX (☎ 0279 723 561); Department of Electronic Engineering, Queen Mary and Westerfield College, University of London, Mile End Road, London E1 4NS (☎ 081 975 5330, fax 081 981 0259)

CLARY, Julian Peter McDonald; s of Peter John Clary, and Brenda, *née* McDonald; *b* 25 May 1959; *Educ* St Benedicts Sch Ealing, Goldsmiths Coll London (BA); *Career* comedian and entertainer; tv appearances: Saturday Night Live (LWT), Friday Live (LWT), Aspel & Company (LWT), Wogan (BBC1), Last Resort (C4), Clive Anderson Talks Back (C4), Cilla Says Goodbye to 88 (LWT), Trick or Treat (LWT), Open Air (BBC 1), Sticky Moments with Julian Clary (C4), One Hour with Jonathan Ross (C4), Not The Royal Variety (LWT), Paramount City (BBC 1), Sunday Sunday (LWT), Tonight Live with Steve Vizard Australia TV; radio appearances: Steve Wright in the Afternoon (BBC Radio 1), Hey Radio (BBC Radio 1), Big Fun Show (BBC Radio 4), Brian Hayes Show (LBC), John Sachs Show (Capital Radio), Janice Long Show (GLR); records released: Leader of the Pack (10 Records/Virgin) 1988, Wandrin' Star (Wonderdog Records Ltd) 1990; video: Julian Clary aka The Joan Collins Fan Club - The Mincing Machine 1989; *Books* My Life with Fanny the Wonder Dog; *Recreations* housework; *Style*— Julian Clary, Esq; Wonder-Dog Productions, 26 Noel St, London W1 (☎ 071 287 3303)

CLATWORTHY, Robert Ernest; s of Ernest William Clatworthy (d 1985), of Bridgwater, Som, and Gladys, *née* Tugela; *b* 31 Jan 1928; *Educ* Dr Morgan's GS Bridgwater, W of England Coll of Art, Chelsea Sch of Art, Slade Sch of Fine Art; *m* 1954 (m dis 1966), Pamela, *née* Gordon; 2 s (Benn b 1955, Thomas b 1959), 1 da (Sarah Alexandra b 1957); *Career* Nat Serv head of fine art wing E Formation Coll 1949; lectr W of Eng Coll of Art 1967-71, visiting tutor RCA 1960-72, memb Fine Art Panel Nat Cncl for Dips in Art and Design 1961-72, govr St Martin's Sch of Art 1970-71, head of Dept of Fine Art Central Sch of Art and Design 1971-75; exhibitions: Hanover Gallery, Waddington Galleries, Holland Park Open Air Sculpture, Battersea Park Open Air Sculpture, Br Sculpture in the Sixties Tate Gallery, Br Sculptors Burlington House 1972, Basil Jacobs Fine Art Ltd, Diploma Galleries Burlington House, Photographer's Gallery, Quinton Green Gallery, Chapman Gallery, Keith Chapman 1990; works in the collections of: Arts Cncl, Contemporary Art Soc, Tate Gallery V & A, GLC, Nat Portrait Gallery, Monumental Horse and Rider; ARA 1968, RA 1973; *Recreations* music; *Clubs* Chelsea Arts; *Style*— Robert Clatworthy, Esq; Moelfre, Cynghordy, Llandovery, Dyfed SA20 0UW (☎ 0550 20 201)

CLAUSON, Oliver Drake Husey; s of Sir Gerard Leslie Makins Clauson, KCMG, OBE (d 1974), and Honor Emily Mary, *née* Husey (d 1978); *b* 23 April 1927; *Educ* Eton, CCC Oxford (MA); *m* 14 Jan 1955, Barbara Susan, da of Major De Symons Harry Lewis-Barned (d 1964), of Maidstone; 3 s (Richard b 1956, Julian b 1960, Francis b 1964), 1 da (Antonia b 1958); *Career* insur clerk Lloyd's 1952-56, underwriting memb of Lloyd's 1956-, claims adjudicator leading Personal Accident and Travel Syndicate 1965-90, dir CCGH Agency Ltd; Liveryman Worshipful Co of Merchant Taylors 1950; *Recreations* amateur acting, producing, stage hand; *Clubs* Army and Navy, Lansdowne; *Style*— Oliver D H Clauson, Esq; Applegarth, Ogbourne St George, Marlborough, Wilts SN8 1SU (☎ 067284 219)

CLAVERING, Col John Muir; OBE (1973), MC (1972); s of Alan Douglas Clavering (d 1982), of Tullochard Lairg, and Agnes Evelyn Muir, *née* Stewart (d 1985); *b* 20 March 1938; *Educ* Fettes; *m* 31 March 1965, Jennifer Mary, da of Patrick Wood Sim (d 1952); 3 da (Philippa b 1967, Rosanna b 1968, Henrietta b 1970); *Career* Lt-Col cmdg Scots Gds 1985-87 (cmmnd 1960, CO 2 Bn 1979-81); vice pres Reg Cmmns Bd 1987-88, Army Univ Liaison Offr Scotland 1988-; memb: Queen's Bodyguard for Scotland (Royal Co of Archers), Highland Soc of London; *Recreations* fishing, stalking, shooting, gardening; *Clubs* Perth, Shikar; *Style*— Col John Clavering, OBE, MC

CLAXTON, Lt-Col David John; LVO (1985), TD (1973); s of Rt Rev Charles Robert Claxton, former Bishop of Blackburn, and Jane, *née* Stevenson; *b* 15 July 1933; *Educ* Haileybury, Queens' Coll Cambridge (BA, MA); *m* 1, 30 Sept 1967 (m dis 1985), Elizabeth Anne, da of Maj Thomas Henry Baker Cresswell, DL, UL, of Preston Tower, Chathill, Northumberland; 3 s (Charles b 1968, Piers b 1970, Christopher b 1971), 1 da (Tassagrie b 1975); m 2, 27 Sept 1986, Pamela, da of Charles Mycock (d 1989), of Harpur Hill, Buxton, Derbys; 1 step da (Sharon b 1967); *Career* Duke of Lancaster's Own Yeo 1960-78: Offr Cadet 1960-61, cmmnd 2 Lt 1961, Co Lt-Col 1974-78; asst farm mangr 1952-54, ptnr Joshua Bury Earle & Co Manchester (chartered surveyors and land agents) 1957-73, surveyor of lands Crewe Survey of the Duchy of Lancaster 1973-89; currently chartered valuation surveyor and land agent Ford House Pre Cheshire; formerly: hon sec Bow Gp (NW), chm Lancs Cheshire and IOM Branch (land agency and agric div) RICS, pres Cheshire Agric Valuers Assoc, churchwarden Barthomley; Cheshire Co rep Marie Curie Meml Fndn 1989-; FRICS 1963, FAAV 1971; *Recreations* skiing, sailing, mountaineering; *Style*— Lt-Col David Claxton, LVO, TD; Ford House, Prestbury, Cheshire SK10 4DG (☎ 0625 827572/ 829348)

CLAXTON, Geoffrey Dudley; s of George Philip Claxton (d 1975), and May, *née* Tyrell (d 1981); *b* 29 Nov 1937; *Educ* N Walsham Secdy Mod, Norwich Tech Coll, Lowestoft Tech, Llandaff Tech; *m* 20 April 1963, Edna Christine, da of Cecil Kittle (d 1983); *Career* apprentice engr 1954-60, engr 1960-62, sr engr 1962-63; BBC: laboratory technician Design Dept 1963-64, broadcast engr 1964-66, supt Electronic Workshop 1966-; memb Inst of Radio Electronic Engrg, CEng, MIERE, MIEE; *Recreations* private pilot, builder of a 2 seat aircraft; *Clubs* Glamorgan Flying; *Style*— Geoffrey Claxton, Esq; 23 Talbot Close, Talbot Green, Pontyclun, Glam CF7 8AS (☎ 0443 225360); British Broadcasting Corporation, Broadcasting House, Llantrisant Rd, Llandaff, Cardiff (☎ 0222 572302)

CLAXTON, Maj-Gen Patrick Fisher; CB (1972), OBE (1946); s of late Rear Adm Ernest William Claxton, and Kathleen O'Callaghan, *née* Fisher; *b* 13 March 1915; *Educ* Sutton Valence Sch, St John's Coll Cambridge; *m* 1941, Jóna Gudrún Gunnarsdóttir (d 1980), da of Gunnar Gunnarsson, of Reykjavik, Iceland; 2 da; *Career* Cdt Sch of Transport and ADC to HM the Queen 1966-68, Transport Offr-in-Chief (Army) 1969-71, ret; gen mangr Regular Forces Employment Assoc 1971-81; *Style*— Maj-Gen Patrick Claxton, CB, OBE; The Lodge, Beacon Hill Park, Hindhead, Surrey (☎ 0428 604437)

CLAY, David Nicholas; s of John Clay, and Edith Mary Clay; *b* 18 Jan 1944; *Educ* Ellesmere Coll Shropshire, King's Coll London (LLB); *Career* slr; sr ptnr Dodds Ashcroft Liverpool 1986 (articled clerk 1966), merged with Davies Wallis Foyster 1988; *Style*— David Clay, Esq; Davies Wallis Foyster, 5 Castle Street, Liverpool, L2 4XE (☎ 051 236 6226, fax 051 236 3088)

CLAY, Jeremy Arden; s of Henry Arthur Clay (d 1971), of Castle Hill, Lower Fulbrook, Warwick, and Daphne Sybil Pauline, *née* Atkinson; *b* 30 June 1938; *Educ* Eton, RAC Cirencester; *m* 12 June 1971, Susan Caroline, da of Frank Tate Chapman (d 1978); 1 s (Richard Henry Arden b 4 Feb 1977), 1 da (Nicola Olivia b 12 July 1974); *Career* RN 1957-59; farmer; dir Bencraft Ltd; MRAC 1961; *Recreations* shooting, sailing, gardening; *Clubs* MCC, RASE; *Style*— Jeremy Clay, Esq; Castle Farm, Lower Fulbrook, Warwick

CLAY, Jeremy Peter Foster; s of Gerard Leigh Clay, of Brockhampton Cottage, nr Hereford, and Drucilla Madelaine, *née* Foster (d 1960); *b* 26 July 1932; *Educ* Eton, Cirencester Agric Coll; *m* 1, 20 Oct 1956 (m dis), Ann Julie, da of Dr Basil Rathburn Fuller, MC (d 1962), of St Micheal's Lodge, St Cross Rd, Winchester; 1 s (Peter Robert b 1958); m 2, 1962, Mary Elizabeth Anne, *née* Pryce Jenkins; 1 da (Luccilla b 1964); *Career* farmer; memb Ctee: CLA, NFU; *Recreations* fishing, shooting; *Style*— Jeremy Clay, Esq; Fawley Court, nr Hereford HR1 4SP (☎ 0432 840247); 94 Eaton Place, London SW1

CLAY, His Honour John Lionel; TD (1961); s of Capt Lionel Pilleau Clay (ka 1918), of Rastrick House, Yorks and Mary Winifred Muriel, da of Ralph Walker; *b* 31 Jan 1918; *Educ* Harrow, CCC Oxford (MA); *m* 30 Aug 1952, Elizabeth, 2 da of Rev Canon Maurice George Jesser Ponsonby, MC gs of 2 Baron de Mauley (d 1943), and the Lady Phyllis Sydney, OBE (d 1942), eld da of 1 Earl Buxton; 1 s (Andrew b 1962), 3 da (Fiona b 1954, Catriona b 1955, Joanna b 1958); *Career* served WWII 8 Army (despatches), Rifle Bde, served TA London Rifle Bde Rangers and SAS; barr 1947, rec 1975-77, Circuit Judge 1977-88; Freeman City of London 1980, Liveryman Worshipful Co of Gardeners; *Recreations* gardening, fishing; *Style*— His Honour John Clay, TD; Newtimber Place, Hassocks, Sussex (☎ 0273 833104)

CLAY, John Martin; s of Sir Henry Clay (d 1954), and his 1 wife Gladys, *née* Priestman; *b* 20 Aug 1927; *Educ* Eton, Magdalen Coll Oxford; *m* 1952, Susan Jennifer, da of Lt-Gen Sir Euan Miller, KCB, KBE, DSO, MC (d 1985); 4 s; *Career* chm Johnson and Firth Brown Ltd; former dir Bank of England, dir Hambros plc; *Recreations* sailing; *Clubs* Medway Yacht; *Style*— John Clay, Esq; 41 Tower Hill, London EC3

CLAY, John Peter; s of Harold Peter Clay (d 1970), and Mary Dansie Clay (d 1974); *b* 26 June 1934; *Educ* St Paul's, Queen's Coll Oxford (MA); *m* 1972, Jennifer Mary Ellen, (*qv*), da of Dr William Ernest Coutts, of Wiltshire; 3 da (Teresa, Lalage, Xanthe); *Career* investmt mangr; Vickers da Costa Ltd: joined 1957, dep chm 1976-81; chm Globe International Ltd 1981-; memb Cncl Stock Exchange 1974-77; *Recreations* real tennis, flying; *Clubs* City, Queen's, Tuxedo, Sky (New York); *Style*— John Clay, Esq; 54 Ebury Mews, London SW1W 9NY (☎ 071 730 5368); Maison de la Voûte, Place de l'Amour, La Garde-Freinet, 83680 Var (☎ 94 436 871); 123 East 30th Street, New York, NY 10016

CLAY, Dowager Lady; Phyllis Mary; *née* Paramore; yr da of Richard Horace Paramore, MD, FRCS; *b* 19 April 1907; *m* 1933, Sir Henry Felix Clay, 6 Bt (d 1985); 1 s (Richard Henry) , 2 da (Jenny Elizabeth Murray, Sarah Richenda Wise); *Recreations* sailing, gardening, chatting; *Clubs* Aldeburgh Yacht, New Cavendish; *Style*— Dowager Lady Clay; Wheelwrights, Cocking, Midhurst, Sussex

CLAY, Sir Richard Henry; 7 Bt (UK 1841), of Fulwell Lodge, Middlesex; s of Sir Henry Felix Clay, 6 Bt (d 1985), and Phyllis Mary, *née* Paramore (*see* Clay, Dowager Lady); *b* 2 June 1940; *Educ* Eton; *m* 14 Sept 1963, Alison Mary, da of Dr James Gordon Fife, of Summerhill, Aldeburgh, Suffolk; 3 s (Charles Richard, Thomas Henry b 28 July 1967, James Felix b 13 April 1969), 2 da (Virginia Rachel 7 July 1964, Catherine b 9 June 1971); *Heir* s, Charles Richard Clay b 18 Dec 1965; *Career* FCA 1966; *Recreations* sailing; *Clubs* Aldeburgh Yacht; *Style*— Sir Richard Clay, Bt; The Copse, Shiplate Rd, Bleadon, Avon BS24 ONX (☎ 0934 815 203)

CLAY, Robert Alan; MP (Lab) Sunderland North 1983-; *b* 2 Oct 1946; *Educ* Bedford Sch, Gonville and Caius Coll Cambridge; *m* 1980, Uta Christa; *Style*— Bob Clay, Esq, MP; House of Commons, London SW1

CLAY, Trevor; CBE (1990); s of Joseph Reginald George Clay (d 1970), and Florence Emma Steptoe; *b* 10 May 1936; *Educ* Nuneaton, Bethlem Royal and Maudsley Hosps, Brunel Univ; *Career* gen sec Royal Coll of Nursing of the UK 1982-89; MPhil, RGN, RMN, FRCN; *Books* Nurses: Power and Politics (1987); *Recreations* music, good friends, theatre; *Style*— Trevor Clay, Esq, CBE; c/o Royal Coll of Nursing of the UK, 20 Cavendish Sq, London W1M 0AB (☎ 071 409 3333)

CLAYDEN, Dr Graham Stuart; s of Colin Stewart Clayden (d 1985), of Bournemouth, and Amy Joyce, *née* Burrough; *b* 8 Jan 1947; *Educ* Bournemouth Sch, Univ of London (MD); *m* 25 Aug 1970, Christine, da of Reginald Thomas Steele (d 1980); 1 s (Jonathan Stuart b 1972), 1 da (Anna Francesca b 1974); *Career* sr registrar in paediatrics Hosp for Sick Children Gt Ormond St 1977, sr lectr and hon conslt in paediatrics St Thomas' Hosp 1977-89, reader in paediatric's and hon conslt UMDS 1989-; memb Bd Dartmouth House Centre, memb Academic Bd Br Paediatric Assoc, founding govr Br Paediatric Computer and Info Gp; MRCP 1972, FRCP 1984; *Books* Treatment and Prognosis in Paediatrics (1988), Catechism in Paediatrics (1987); *Recreations* choral singing, bassoon; *Style*— Dr Graham Clayden; Paediatric Unit, United Medical and Dental Schools of Guy's and St Thomas's Hospitals, Lambeth Palace Rd, London SE1 7EH (☎ 071 928 9292, ext 3046)

CLAYDON, David Anthony; s of Victor Edwin Claydon (d 1975), of Southampton, and Muriel Mary, *née* Davis; *b* 13 Sept 1935; *Educ* King Edward VI Sch Southampton, St John's Coll Cambridge (BA); *m* 4 April 1959, Gaynor, da of Harold Herbert Childs; 1 s (David Christopher b 20 April 1973), 3 da (Joanna Jane b 4 Nov 1962, Amanda Mary b 9 Oct 1964, Katharine Sarah b 29 Jan 1969); *Career* section leader Res Dept Distillers Co 1963-64 (joined as process engr 1957); BP: project mangr BP Chemicals Ltd Salt End Works Hull 1964-69 (works mangr 1969-73), div mangr Supply Dept BP International London 1973-76, commercial vice pres BP N America NY USA 1976-79, gen mangr Engrg Dept BP Chemicals Ltd London 1979-81 (dir 1981-82), gen mangr BP Engrg Dept London 1982, chief exec BP Engr and Tech Centre London 1983-85, chief exec BP Gas London 1985-88, pres and chief exec BP Canada Inc Calgary Alberta 1988-; FICE, FEng; *Recreations* woodwork and joinery, tennis, DIY, fundraising for Calgary charitable instns incl Glenbow Museum Calgary; *Clubs* Calgary Petroleum, Ranchmen's; *Style*— David Claydon, Esq; 1327 Frontenac Ave SW, Calgary, Alberta, T2T 1C1, Canada (☎ 010 1 403 244 0699); BP Canada Inc, 2100, 855 Second Ave Second St SW, Cagary, Alberta T2P 3B6, Canada (☎ 010 1 403 237 1123)

CLAYDON, Geoffrey Bernard; CB (1990); s of Bernard Claydon (d 1978), and Edith Mary, *née* Lucas; *b* 14 Sept 1930; *Educ* Leeds Modern, King Edward's Birmingham, Univ of Birmingham (LLB); *Career* articled clerk Pinsent & Co Birmingham 1950, slr of The Supreme Court 1954, sr legal asst Treasy Slrs Dept 1965 (legal asst 1959), asst slr DTI 1973, asst Treasy slr 1974, princ asst Treasy slr and legal advsr DEn 1980-90, review of private legislative procedures DTP 1990-, vice chm Nat Tramway Museum 1969- (sec 1958-84), vice pres Light Rail Transit Assoc 1968- (chm 1963-68);

chm: Tramway & Light Railway Soc 1967-, Consultative Panel for the Preservation of Br Tport Relics 1982-, memb Inst of Tport Admin 1972-; memb Ed Bd Jl of Energy and Natural Resources Law 1983-1990; *Recreations* rail transport, travel; *Clubs* Royal Automobile; *Style—* Geoffrey Claydon, Esq, CB; 23 Baron's Keep, London W14 9AT (☎ 071 603 6400); Department of Transport, 2 Marsham Street Westminster, London SW1P 3EB (☎ 071 276 0591, fax 071 276 0818)

CLAYDON, Russell; s of Brian Claydon, of Cambridge, and Daphne, *née* Cross; *b* 19 Nov 1965; *Educ* Netherhall Sch; *m* Jackie Williamson; *Career* golfer; tournament victories incl: Cambridgeshire amateur champion 1987 and 1988, Eng amateur champion 1988, winner Silver Medal Br Open 1989, Henry Cotton Rookie of the Year 1990; runner up: Australian Masters 1989, Volvo Open 1990; played for Eng v: Wales 1988, Scotland 1988, Ireland 1988, Spain 1989; played for GB and Ireland v USA in Walker Cup 1989; course records incl: Gog Magog (amateur), Camberley Heath (amateur), Huntingdale (amateur), Ugolino (professional); *Recreations* football, bridge, horseracing and the arts; *Style—* Russell Claydon, Esq; Robert Arnold, Corner House, Carlyle Rd, Cambridge (☎ 0223 312465, fax 0223 312460)

CLAYMAN, Stanley Joseph; s of Norman Clayman (d 1983), and Sophie, *née* Chisell (d 1964); *b* 24 Nov 1935; *Educ* St Paul's, Univ of London (LLB); *m* 6 Oct 1964, Joy Lilian Sally, da of Angel Dell (d 1970); 2 da (Linda b 1966, Helen b 1969); *Career* slr in private practice 1958-65; dir First Nat Fin Corp 1985- (joined 1965); gen cmmr of taxes; Freeman City of London Slr's Co; memb Law Soc 1958; *Recreations* music, theatre, cricket, horticulture; *Clubs* MCC, IOD; *Style—* Stanley Clayman, Esq; 127 The Reddings, Mill Hill, London NW7 4JP (☎ 081 959 7888); First Nat Fin Corpn plc, PO Box 505, St Alphage Hse, Fore St, London EC2P 2NJ (☎ 071 638 2855, fax 071 628 9963)

CLAYSON, Peter John; s of Francis Henry Clayson (d 1988), of Crewe, and Sarah Anne *née* Wyatt (d 1952); *b* 29 May 1933; *Educ* Crewe GS, Liverpool Univ (B Eng); *m* 29 Mar 1960, (m dis) 1981, Barbara, da of Hubert Coyne (d 1983); 1 s (Jonathan Mark b 1962), 3 da (Amanda Jane b 1961, Katherine Anne and Jacqueline Nancy b 1964 (twins)); m 2, 1986, Rita Kotchinsky; *Career* electrical offr MN 1956-59, commissioning engr 1960-63, power station engr 1963-65, res engr 1915-68, chief engr 1968-74, ptnr Heap & Digby Consultants 1974-81; gp dir Molt Macdonald 1986- (dir 1981-86) and chm Molt Macdonald (M & E, Midlands, Southern, NI); chm Haggie Patterson; FIEE, FIMechE, FCIBSE, FRSA; *Recreations* golf, squash; *Clubs* Lingfield Squash; *Style—* Peter Clayson, Esq

CLAYTON, Adam; s of Brian and Josephine (Joe) Clayton; *b* 13 March 1960; *Educ* Castle Park Sch Dalkey, St Columba's Coll Rathfarnham; *Career* bass player and fndr memb U2 1978-; U2 formed in Dublin with Bono, *qv* (vocals, guitar), The Edge, *qv* (guitors, piano, vocals), and Larry Mullen, *qv* (drums); U2 played first London dates and released U23 (EP 1979, CBS Ireland) 1979, band signed to Island Records and released Boy (LP 1980) and three singles 1980, toured UK, US, Belguim and Holland 1980, released October (LP 1981, Silver disc) which entered UK charts at No 11 and three singles Fire, Gloria and A Celebration giving the band their first UK charts entries 1981-82, band toured extensively in UK, US, Ireland and Europe 1981-83, New Year's Day (single 1983) gave band their first UK Top Ten hit, War (LP 1983, US Gold disc) entered UK charts at No 1 and US Top Ten, band toured US and UK 1983, Under A Blood Red Sky (live album 1983, UK Platinum disc) entered UK charts at No 2, voted Band of the Year Rolling Stone Writers Poll 1984, Pride (In the Name of Love) single produced by Brian Eno and Daniel Lanois reached No 3 in UK charts gaining Silver disc 1984, band toured Aust, NZ and Europe, The Unforgettable Fire (LP 1984) entered UK charts at No 1, Unforgettable Fire (single 1985) entered UK charts at No 8; played: Madison Square Garden NY, Longest Day Festival Milton Keynes Bowl, Croke Park Dublin, Live Aid Wembley (Best Live Aid Performance Rolling Stone Readers Poll 1986) 1985; voted Best Band Rolling Stone Readers Poll 1986 (joint No 1 Critics Poll); played: Self Aid Dublin, A Conspiracy of Hope (Amnesty Int Tour) 1986; The Joshua Tree (LP 1987, Grammy award Album of the Year, 12 million worldwide sales) entered UK charts at No 1 as fastest selling album in Br music history and reached No 1 in US charts; With Or Without You (single 1987), I Still Haven't Found What I'm Looking For (single 1987), Where The Streets Have No Name (single 1987) released and entered UK charts; first three singles from The Joshua Tree reached No 1 in US charts; world tour opens Arizona 1987; 100 shows in US and Europe incl: Wembley Stadium, Madison Square Gardens NY, Sun Devil Stadium Arizona and Croke Park Dublin (winners Grammy award Best Rock Performance 1987-88); Desire (single 1988) gives U2 their first No 1 single, Rattle & Hum (LP 1988) entered UK charts at No 1, U2 play Smile Jamaica (Dominion Theatre) in aid of hurricane disaster relief 1988, world premiere U2 Rattle & Hum (film 1988) Dublin, Angel of Harlem (single 1988) entered UK charts at No 10; Grammy awards: Best Rock Performance (Desire) 1989, Best Video (Where The Streets Have No Name) 1989; When Love Comes to Town (single 1989), All I Want Is You (single 1989) released, band toured Aust 1989, New Year's Eve 1989 concert at Point Depot Dublin (broadcast live to Europe and USSR, 500 million estimated audience), recorded Night & Day for Aids benefit LP (Red, Hot & Blue) 1990; *Style—* Adam Clayton, Esq; c/o Prinicple Management, 30-32 Sir John Rogerson's Quay, Dublin 2, Ireland (☎ 01 777 330, fax 777 276)

CLAYTON, Sir David Robert; 12 Bt (GB 1732), of Marden Park, Surrey; s of Sir Arthur Harold Clayton, 11 Bt, DSC (d 1985), and his 2 w, Alexandra, *née* Andreevsky; *b* 12 Dec 1936; *Educ* HMS Conway, Sir John Cass Coll London; *m* 1971, Julia Louise, da of Charles Henry Redfearn (d 1969); 2 s (Robert, John Richard b 1978); *Heir* s, Robert Philip, b 8 July 1975; *Career* Capt Merchant Navy; *Recreations* shooting, sailing; *Clubs* Royal Dart Yacht, Penarth Yacht (hon memb); *Style—* Sir David Clayton, Bt; Rock House, Kingswear, Dartmouth, Devon

CLAYTON, Diana, Lady; Diana Katherine Mary; o da of Capt Charles Alverey Grazebrook, 60 Rifles (ka Givenchy 1915); *b* 19 May 1913; *m* 1, 1934, Peter Neve; 2 da; m 2, - Bircham; m 3, 1965, as his 4 w, Sir Arthur Harold Clayton, 11 Bt, DSC (d 1985); *Style—* Diana, Lady Clayton; Colonsay, Kingswear, Dartmouth, Devon

CLAYTON, Francis Howard; s of Rev Arthur Clayton (d 1960), of Lichfield, and Frances Ella, *née* Warren (d 1974); *b* 20 May 1918; *Educ* St John's Sch Leatherhead, Univ of Birmingham (BCom); *m* 29 July 1942, Helen Margaret (d 1988), da of Dr Henry Doig, of Lennoxtown, Stirlingshire; 1 s (John b 1950), 2 da (Elizabeth b 1943, Margaret b 1948); *Career* WWII 1939-46: commnd RA 1942, S Staffs Regt 1944 (wounded in action Holland 1944, leg amputated); asst sec Manor Hosp Walsall 1949-56; lectr: Wednesbury Coll of Commerce 1957-61, Tamworth Coll of Further Educn 1961-67; freelance writer 1967-, dir Lichfield Cathedral Arts Ltd 1980-1991; memb Lichfield DC 1976-87 (chm 1983-84); Lichfield: Sheriff 1978-79, Mayor 1987-88; *Books* The Atmospheric Railways (1966), The Duffield Bank and Eaton Railways (1967), Atlantic Bridgehead (1968), Coaching City (1970), Cathedral City (1976), The Great Swinfen Case (1980), Loyal and Ancient City (1986); *Recreations* historic res, music, reading; *Style—* Francis Clayton, Esq; 2a Brownsfield Rd, Lichfield, Staffs

CLAYTON, Air Marshal Sir Gareth Thomas Butler; KCB (1970, CB 1962), DFC (1940, and Bar 1944); s of Thomas Clayton, and Katherine, of The Beacon, Torquay, Devon; *b* 13 Nov 1914; *Educ* Rossall; *m* 1938, Elisabeth Marian, da of Thomas Keates, of Barons Court; 3 da; *Career* entered RAF 1936, DG RAF Personal Servs 1966-69, COS HQ RAF Strike Cmd 1969-70, Air Sec MOD 1970-72, ret; chm RAFA 1978-81, pres NW Area RAFA 1983-88; *Clubs* RAF; *Style—* Air Marshal Sir Gareth Clayton, KCB, DFC

CLAYTON, John Robert; CBE (1987); s of late John Clayton; *b* 29 March 1922; *Educ* Highgate, LSE; *m* 1, 1943 (m dis 1956), Doris Louise, *née* Usherwood; m 2, 1958, Aileen Bowen, *née* Morris (d 1981); m 3, 1984, Dr Jean Olive Boyton, da of Ernest Marks (d 1978); 1 s; *Career* serv WWII, Capt RCS; industl advsr Fed Govt of Nigeria 1951-61; ptnr John Tyzack and Ptnrs Ltd 1961-69, gp md Pauls and Whites plc (maltsters and animal feed gp) 1970-82; dir: Nat West Bank (SE Regnl Bd) 1974-89, Richard Clay and Co plc 1977-86, Dewe Rogerson Gp Ltd 1981-; IPSENTA Ltd 1982-89 (chm 1982-85); chm: Agric Trg Bd 1983-89, Thurlow Nunn Hldgs Ltd 1983-89; memb Suffolk CC 1982-89 (vice chm Educn Ctee 1985-89); gen cmmr of Income Tax 1976-; memb Ct: Univ of Essex 1987-90, Cranfield Inst of Technol 1981-; memb IOD; CBIM; *Clubs* Oriental; *Style—* John R Clayton, Esq, CBE; Erie House, Hadleigh, Suffolk IP7 5AG (☎ 0473 823316)

CLAYTON, Prof Keith Martin; s of Edgar Francis Clayton (d 1978), and Constance Annie, *née* Clark (d 1985); *b* 25 Sept 1928; *Educ* Bedales Sch, Univ of Sheffield (BSc, MSc), Univ of London (PhD); *m* 1, 1950 (m dis 1976); m 2, 29 Dec 1976, Jennifer Nan; 3 s, 1 da; *Career* Nat Serv 2 Lt RE 1951-53; LSE 1953-67: asst lectr, lectr, reader; UEA Norwich: prof of environmental sciences 1967-, dean 1967-71, pro vice chllr 1971-73, dean 1987-; memb: Cncl NERC 1971-74, Univ Grants Ctee 1974-84, Defence Environment Ctee 1990-; *Style—* Prof Keith Clayton, CBE; Well Close, Pound Lane, Norwich NR7 OUA (☎ 0603 33780); School of Environmental Sciences, University of East Anglia, Norwich NR4 7TJ (☎ 0603 592533)

CLAYTON, Margaret Ann; da of Percy Clayton (d 1970), and Kathleen, *née* Payne; *b* 7 May 1941; *Educ* Christs Hosp Hertford, Birkbeck Coll London (MA, MSc); *Career* civil servant Home Office 1960-: resident chm Civil Service Selection Bd 1983, establishment offr 1984-86, dir of servs Prison Dept 1986-90, asst under sec of state 1986-90; *Recreations* reading, gardening, theatre, equitation; *Clubs* Reform; *Style—* Miss Margaret Clayton; Home Office, 50 Queen Anne's Gate, London SW1H 9AT (☎ 071 273 2435)

CLAYTON, Michael Aylwin; s of Aylwin Goff Clayton, of Bournemouth, Dorset, and Norah Kathleen Joan, *née* Banfield (d 1978); *b* 20 Nov 1934; *Educ* Bournemouth GS; *m* 1, Mary; 1 s (Marcus b 1967), 1 da (Maxine (Mrs Butler-Gallie) b 1965); m 2, 1979, Barbara J Ryman; m 3, 28 Oct 1988, Marilyn Crowhurst, da of Ernest George John Orrin; *Career* journalist, author, broadcaster; news corr BBC radio and TV 1965-73, ed Horse and Hound 1973-; *Recreations* foxhunting; *Style—* Michael Clayton, Esq

CLAYTON, Michael Denzil Grierson; s of Derrick Grierson Clayton (d 1973), and Audrey Evelyn, *née* Villiers (d 1981); *b* 27 May 1931; *Educ* Rugby; *m* 16 April 1966, Georgina Mary Gabrielle, da of Maj Sir Charles Buchanan (d 1984); 1 s (Roger Lancelot b 1969), 1 da (Harriet Beatrix Evelyn b 1971); *Career* Cheshire (Earl of Chesters) Yeomanry 1954, Kent and Co of London Yeomanry 1959, ret as Maj 1965; Christies: joined 1959, opened Geneva office 1967, dir London 1970, dir Scot 1978; memb: Dance Ctee Arts Cncl 1983-90, Curatorial Ctee Nat Tst for Scotland 1983-, Arts Cncl for Scotland 1984-87; Freeman Worshipful Co of Goldsmiths; memb Incorporation of Goldsmiths of Edinburgh; *Books* Collectors Dictionary of Silver and Gold of Great Britain and North America (1969), Christie's Pictorial History of English and American Silver (1985); *Recreations* hill walking, archaeology; *Clubs* New (Edinburgh); *Style—* Michael Clayton, Esq; 6 Cobden Crescent, Edinburgh EH9 2BG; Christies, 5 Wemyss Place, Edinburgh (☎ 031 225 4756)

CLAYTON, Richard Anthony; s of Dennis Lloyd Clayton (d 1969), of London, and Patricia Estelle, *née* Morris; *b* 25 May 1954; *Educ* Westminster, Univ of Oxford; *m* (m dis 1987); 1 s (Benjamin Daniel); *Career* called to the Bar Middle Temple 1977; S Islington Law Centre 1980-82, Osler Hoskin & Harcourt Toronto Canada 1983; memb Ctee Legal Action Gp 1985-; *Books* Practise and Procedure at Industrial Tribunals (1986), Civil Actions Against the Police (1988), Suing the Police (1989); *Recreations* reading, theatre, cinema, travel; *Style—* Richard Clayton, Esq; New Court, Temple, London EC4 (☎ 071 583 6166, fax 071 583 2827)

CLAYTON-WELCH, Anthony Roy; s of Flt Lt Roy Hector Welch, AFC, AE, of Flamstead, Herts, and Barbara Joan, *née* Clayton; *b* 5 Sept 1942; *Educ* St Albans Abbey Sch, Poly of Central London (Dip Arch), Carp Sch (scholarship); *m* 4 Feb 1967, Kathleen Margaret, da of Henry Samuel Norman, of Wembley Park, Middx; 1 s (Bruno b 20 Oct 1975), 1 da (Sophie b 27 Sept 1977); *Career* TA Offr Trg Corps 1962-64; architectural conslt to Camus (GB) Ltd 1967-70, London ptnr Melich & Welch Florida USA 1970-74, fndn ptnr Renton Welch Partnership 1974-; adjudicator and ctee memb Royal Jubilee Tst and Princes Tst; awards incl: Carpenters Award 1965, Civic Design Award 1987, Educational Award 1988; educnl advsr: DES, DOW; vice chm Local Bd Sch Govrs St John's Sch Stanmore; memb RIBA 1966-, ARIBA; *Books* 3-D Structural Model Analysis of Space Frames (1967), Rationalised Constructions (1970), Herts CC Educational Building: An Appraisal 1942-70 (1986); *Recreations* tennis, squash, swimming, water skiing, modelling, voice-overs; *Clubs* The Arts, Morton's, RAF, St Stephens; *Style—* Anthony Clayton-Welch, Esq; Brousings, The Grove, Stanmore Common, Middlesex HA7 4LD (☎ 081 954 4625); Renton Welch Partnership, 12 Stucley Place, Camden Town, London NW1 8NS (☎ 071 482 1418, fax 071 482 1071)

CLEALL, Charles; s of Sydney Cleal (d 1973), and Dorothy Bound (d 1978); *b* 1 June 1927; *Educ* Hampton Sch Middlesex, Univ of London (BMus), Univ of Wales (MA); *m* 1953, Mary, da of George Lee Turner (d 1979), of Archery Lodge, Ashford, Middlesex; 2 da (Anne, Alisoun); *Career* cmmnd music advsr RN 1946-48; prof of solo singing, voice prodn and choral repertoire Trinity Coll Music London 1949-52, conductor Morley Coll Orchestra 1949-51, organist and choirmaster Wesley's Chapel London 1950-52, conductor Glasgow Choral Union 1952-54, BBC music asst Midland Region 1954-55, music master Glyn County Sch Ewell 1955-66, conductor Aldeburgh Festival Choir 1957-60; organist and choirmaster: St Paul's Portman Sq London 1957-61, Holy Trinity Guildford 1961-65; lectr in music Froebel Inst 1967-68, advsr in music London Borough of Harrow 1968-72, music specialist for the Northern Div of Her Majesty's Inspectorate in Scotland 1972-87, ed jl of The Ernest George White Soc 1983-88, registered teacher The Sch of Sinus Tone 1985-; Warden Educn Section Incorporated Soc of Musicians 1971-72; *Books* Voice Production in Choral Technique (1955, revised and enlarged edn, 1970), The Selection and Training of Mixed Choirs in Churches (1960), Sixty Songs from Sankey (1960), John Merbecke's Music for the Congregation at Holy Communion (ed, 1963), Music and Holiness (1964), Authentic Chanting (1969), Plainsong for Pleasure (1969), A Guide to 'Vanity Fair' (1982); *Recreations* reading, writing, genealogy; *Style—* Charles Cleall, Esq; 10 Carronhall, Stonehaven, Kincardineshire AB3 2HF

CLEAR, Michael Charles; MBE (1943), TD; s of Charles Arnold Clear (d 1945), and Ruth, *née* Wilkinson (d 1966); *b* 12 Oct 1913; *Educ* Trent, Imperial Coll London (BSc); *m* 1945, Kathleen, da of Charles Mieville Chevalier (d 1951); 1 s (Jeremy b 1951), 1 da (Derryn b 1946); *Career* WW11 Lt-Col REME 1939-45 (despatches 1942); Royal Cmmn Inventors Award for the Scorpian Flail Tank 1947; md Brush Electric

Engr Co Ltd (Hawker Siddeley Gp) 1945-64, gp md Tillotson & Sons Ltd 1964-71, md MK Electric Ltd 1971-75; dir Parkington Co Ltd 1977-; non-exec dir Metal Box (overseas) Ltd 1958-61, Dubilier plc 1976-87; ACGI, CEng, FIMechE, FIEE; *Recreations* gardening, bridge, golf; *Style—* Michael Clear, Esq, MBE, TD; 8 Paterson Drive, Woodhouse Eaves, Leicestershire LE12 8RL; Parkington Co Ltd, 44 Green St, London W1Y 3FJ (☎ 071 629 8916, fax 071 493 3800, telex 9401 6116 GRST)

CLEARY, (Owen) Alistair; s of Bernard Cleary (d 1968), and Mary Weir, *née* Hamilton (d 1985); *b* 20 June 1931; *Educ* Leith Acad, Royal HS of Edinburgh, Univ of Edinburgh (MA, LLB); *m* 6 Aug 1960, (Elsie) Dylena, da of Adriaan Hendricus Stander Fourie (d 1960), and Susan Jessie, *née* Oosthuizen; 1 step s Adrian James Cook b 1953), 1 step da (Mrs Arlene Dawn Shuttleworth b 1951), 1 da (Susan-Mary Hamilton b 1966); *Career* slr and Notary Public; former dean of Faculty of Procurators of Caithness (sr memb Caithness Bar), former depute-procurator fiscal of Caithness; currently clerk to Gen Cmmnrs of Income Tax; memb: Scot Congregational Church, Aid to the Persecuted, Christian Aid, Christian Mission to the Communist World; ran marathons 1981-86: Dublin, Boston, Paris, Wild Coast (Natal SA) and The Flying Fox (England); Silver medal (200 m) Scot Veteran Track and Field Championships 1986; first Caithness Sportsman of the Year 1983; *Recreations* rugby, baseball, athletics, Australian rules football, photography, writing, poetry, gardening, astronomy, Scottish, Southern African and American history and politics, travel; *Clubs* Royal HS, RHSAC, Scottish Veteran Harriers, WAGAC; *Style—* Alistair Cleary, Esq; Elangeni, 5 Upper Dunbar Street, Wick, Caithness (☎ 0955 2447)

CLEARY, Sir Joseph Jackson; JP (Liverpool 1936); s of Joseph Cleary, JP, of Liverpool; *b* 26 Oct 1902; *Educ* Holy Trinity C of E Sch Anfield, Skerry's Coll Liverpool; *m* 1945, Ethel McColl; *Career* contested (Lab): E Toxteth Div Liverpool 1929, W Derby 1931; MP (Lab) Wavertree Div of Liverpool Feb-Oct 1935; Lord Mayor of Liverpool 1949-50: Hon Freeman City of Liverpool 1970; kt 1965; *Style—* Sir Joseph Cleary, JP; 115 Riverview Heights, Liverpool L19 OLQ (☎ 051 427 2133)

CLEASBY, John Victor; s of Thomas Victor Cleasby (d 1957), of Leeds, Yorkshire, and Grace, *née* Buckle (d 1974); *b* 4 Oct 1932; *Educ* Ludlow GS, Royal Sch of Mines, Univ of London (BSc, ARSM); *m* Sheila Ann, da of John Spencer Williams; 2 da (Tanya Deirdre (Mrs Brand) b 22 Jan 1963), Julia Vikki b 9 Dec 1969); *Career* Nat Serv cmmnd RE 1955-57; gen underground experience Roan Antelope Copper Mines Ltd 1953-57, graduate trainee rising to underground mangr Vaal Reefs Gold Mining Co SA 1959-64, underground mangr rising to asst mangr Western Deep Levels Gold Mining Co S Africa 1964-68, project mangr for design and construction of Cleveland Potash Mine UK 1969-73, gen mangr De Beers Consolidated Mines Ltd S Africa 1973-76; 1976-89: consltg engr Anglo American Corp, consltg engr and head of Tech Dept and alternate dir Charter Conslidated plc, consltg engr Sierra Leone diamond mining ops De Beers, dir several mining and industl cos; private conslt 1989- (work for DTI, Cleveland Potash Ltd and Several cos in the Far East); memb Cncl Inst of Mining and Metallurgy, chm Scholarships Ctee , tstee Mining Assoc, govr Camborne Sch of Mines; Consolidated Goldfields Gold Medal Inst of Mining and Metallurgy 1974, Metallurgy Silver Medal for best paper 1975; Freeman City of London 1990, Liveryman Worshipful Co of Engrs 1991; fell Fellowship of Engineering, FIMM; *Publications* papers: Shaft Sinking at Boulby Mine, Environmental Aspects of Boulby Mine, Availability of Strategic Minerals, Mining Practice in the Kimberley Division of De Beers Consolidated Mines Ltd; *Recreations* jogging; *Style—* John Cleasby, Esq; 10 Coombe Neville, Warren Rd, Kingston-upon-Thames, Surrey KT2 7HW (☎ 081 949 4791)

CLEAVER, Anthony Brian; s of William Brian Cleaver (d 1969), and Dorothea Early Cleaver (d 1989); *b* 10 April 1938; *Educ* Berkhamsted Sch, Trinity Coll Oxford (MA); *m* 1962, Mary Teresa, *née* Cotter; 1 s (Paul Anthony b 31 Aug 1972); *Career* IBM (United Kingdom) Ltd: trainee instr 1962, conslt systems engr 1968, branch mangr 1979, dist mangr 1974-76, sales dir 1976-77, div dir 1977-80; asst to Vice Pres (Devpt) World Trade Corporation USA; IBM Europe: gp dir 1980, vice pres Mktg & Servs 1981-82; IBM UK: gen mangr 1982-86, chief exec 1986-, chm 1990, currently chm chief exec IBM (United Kingdom) Holdings Ltd; non-exec dir General Accident Fire and Life Assurance Corporation plc 1988-; dir Nat Computing Centre 1977-80; memb Cncl: Templeton Coll Oxford 1982-, Policy Studies Inst 1985-89, RIPA 1986-89; memb Bd: Centre for Econ & Environmental Devpt 1985- (dep chm 1989-), Assoc for Business Sponsorship of the Arts 1986-, ENO 1988-, American C of C 1987-90; memb: Presidents' Ctee Business In The Community 1986- (chm Business In The Environment 1989-), Presidents' Ctee CBI 1988-, BOTB 1988-91, Nat Trg Task Force 1989-; chm of Govrs Birkbeck Coll Univ of London 1989-; hon fell Trinity Coll Oxford 1989, UN Environment Prog Global 500; FBCS 1976; *Recreations* music, opera, cricket, golf, skiing, tennis, reading; *Clubs* Reform, MCC, Lords Taverners; *Style—* Anthony Cleaver, Esq; IBM (United Kingdom) Ltd, PO Box 41, North Harbour, Portsmouth, Hants PO6 3AV (☎ 07053 21212)

CLEAVER, Air Vice-Marshal Peter Charles; CB (1971), OBE (1945); s of William Henry Cleaver (d 1966), of Warwick; *b* 6 July 1919; *Educ* Warwick Sch, Coll of Aeronautics (MSc), Staff Coll Haifa, IDC; *m* 1948, Jean, da of John Edward Birkett Fairclough (d 1948), of Ledbury; 2 s; *Career* Offr cmdg RAF Swanson Morley 1962-63, AOEng: Flying Trg Cmd 1963-65, HQ FEAF 1967-69, Air Support Cmd 1969-72, ret; sec Cranfield Inst of Technol 1973-78; *Recreations* gardening, walking; *Clubs* RAF; *Style—* Air Vice-Marshal Peter Cleaver, CB, OBE; Willow House, Watling St, Little Brickhill, Milton Keynes, Bucks MK17 9LS

CLEAVER, William Benjamin; s of David John Cleaver (d 1963), of Rhondda, and Blodwen, *née* Miles (d 1948); *b* 15 Sept 1921; *Educ* Pentre GS Rhondda, Univ of Wales (BSc); *m* 1943, Mary Watkin, da of Watkin James (d 1951), of Dyfed; 1 s (John), 2 da (Pamela, Patricia); *Career* mining engr; NCB: area gen mangr 1958-67, dep dir (mining) 1967-83, ret 1983; Welsh Rugby Int 1947-50 14 caps, Br Lion NZ and Aust 1950, fndr chm Welsh Youth Rugby Union 1949-57; vice-chm Welsh Arts Cncl 1977-83; memb Arts Cncl GB 1980-83; sec Contemporary Art Soc for Wales 1973-; memb Cncl Nat Museum Wales 1977-, chm Cncl Museums in Wales 1986-; FIMinE; OStJ; *Recreations* rugby football, fine arts, wine appreciation; *Clubs* Cardiff and County, Saville; *Style—* William Cleaver, Esq; 29 Lon-y-Deri, Rhiwbina, Cardiff CF4 6JN (☎ 0222 693242)

CLEDWYN OF PENRHOS, Baron (Life Peer UK 1979), of Holyhead in the Isle of Anglesey; Cledwyn Hughes; CH (1977), PC (1966); s of late Rev Henry David Hughes, of Frondeg, Holyhead, and Emily Hughes; *b* 14 Sept 1916; *Educ* Holyhead GS, Univ Coll of Wales Aberystwyth; *m* 1949, Jean Beatrice, JP, da of Capt Jesse Hughes, of Holyhead; 1 s (Hon Harri Cledwyn b 1955), 1 da (Hon Emily Ann (Hon Mrs Wright) b 1950); *Career* served RAFVR WWII; memb Anglesey CC 1946-52; slr 1940; MP (L) Anglesey 1951-79 (also candidate 1945 and 1950), min of Agric, Fish and Food 1968-70, oppn spokesman on Agric, Fish and Food 1970-72, cmmr of House of Commons 1979, chm House of Lords Select Ctee on Agric and Food 1980-83, dep ldr oppn in Lords 1979-82 (ldr 1982-), oppn spokesman (Lords) on Civil Serv, Foreign Affrs and Welsh Affrs 1983-; former chm Welsh Parly Pty and Parly Labour Pty 1974-79; dir: Shell UK Ltd 1980-, Anglesey Aluminium Ltd 1980-, Holyhead Towing Ltd 1980-; regnl advsr Midland Bank (with responsibilities for Wales) 1979-; memb Co Cncls Assoc 1980-; pres: Housing and Town Planning Cncl 1980-, Age Concern Wales 1980-, Soc of Welsh People Overseas 1980-, UCW Aberystwyth 1976-; Hon Freedom Beaumaris 1972, Freeman Borough of Anglesey 1976, Hon LLD Wales 1970, Alderman Anglesey CC 1973; min of state for the Cwlth 1964-66, sec of state for Wales 1966-68, pres Univ Coll of Wales 1975-85, pro chllr Univ of Wales 1985-; *Style—* The Rt Hon the Lord Cledwyn of Penrhos, CH, PC; Penmorfa, Trearddur, Holyhead, Gwynedd (☎ 0407 860544)

CLEERE, Dr Henry Forester; s of Christopher Henry John Cleere (d 1981), of London, and Frances Eleanor, *née* King (d 1970); *b* 2 Dec 1926; *Educ* Beckenham GS, UCL (BA), Univ of London Inst of Archaeology (PhD); *m* 1, 1950 (m dis), Dorothy Percy; 1 s (Christopher), 1 da (Elizabeth); m 2, 1974, Pamela Joan, da of Stanley Vertue (d 1979), of Tadley, Hants; 2 da (Josephine, Catherine); *Career* dep sec Iron and Steel Inst London 1952-71, industl devpt offr UN Industl Devpt Orgn Vienna 1972-73; archaeologist; dir Cncl Br Archaeology 1974-; memb Exec Ctee Int Cncl on Monuments and Sites; pres Sussex Archaeological Soc 1987-; hon visiting fell Univ of York 1988-, res fell Univ of Paris (Sorbonne) 1989-; FSA, FBIM; *Clubs* Athenaeum; *Style—* Dr Henry Cleere, FSA; Acres Rise, Lower Platts, Ticehurst, Wadhurst, E Sussex TN5 7DD (☎ 0580 200752); 112 Kennington Rd, London SE11 6RE (☎ 071 582 0494)

CLEGG, (William Gavin) Anthony; s of GH Clegg, of Poole Hall, Nantwich, Cheshire, and Francis May Angela, *née* Joynson (d 1987); *b* 15 Jan 1940; *Educ* Heatherdown Sch, Eton, Grenoble Univ France; *m* 3 Feb 1985, Caroline Janet, da of J Doniger; *Career* ptnr Grieveson Grant and Co 1972-86, former dir Kleinwort Benson Gilts Ltd; *Style—* A Clegg, Esq

CLEGG, Prof Arthur Bradbury; s of Frederick Bradbury Clegg (d 1970), and Beatrice, *née* Andrew (d 1980); *b* 15 March 1929; *Educ* Birkenhead Sch, King's Coll Cambridge (BA, PhD, MA); *m* 23 Oct 1956, Marguerite, da of Arthur G Davis (d 1958); 1 s (Peter David b 30 March 1962), 1 da (Karen Marguerite (Mrs Coumbe) b 21 April 1960); *Career* res fell California Inst of Technol 1955-58, sr res offr Dept of Nuclear Physics Univ of Oxford 1958-66, sr res fell Jesus Coll Oxford 1964-66, prof of nuclear physics Univ of Lancaster 1966-; writer numerous res papers; memb: Sci Res Cncl Nuclear Physics Bd 1969-73, Particle Physics Ctee Sci and Engrg Res Cncl 1986-89; FInstP 1966-; *Books* High Energy Nuclear Reactions (1964); *Recreations* fell walking; *Style—* Prof Arthur Clegg; Strawberry Bank, Westbourne Rd, Lancaster, Lancs LA1 5EF (☎ 0524 69797); Univ of Lancaster, Dept of Physics, Lancaster, Lancs LA1 4YB (☎ 0524 65201 ext 3238, fax 0524 63806, telex 65111 LANCUL G)

CLEGG, Christopher; s of William Henry Clegg (d 1945), and Elinor Mary Constance Clement, *née* Bowen (d 1954); *b* 5 Jan 1926; *Educ* Eton, Guys Hosp London (BDS); *m* 21 May 1955, Diana, da of John Brant Butland (d 1960), of West Byfleet, Surrey; 3 da (Fiona b 1956, Jane Louise b 1957 d 1959, Sophia Philippa b 1960); *Career* Inf in Ranks 1943-45, cmmnd RASC Serv Egypt and Palestine 1945, military mission Greece 1946-47, Flt Lt RAF Regt 1948, Aden Levies 1949, RAF Levies Iraq 1950, serv UK 1950-56, Capt RADC (TA) 1970-75; dental surgn: Farnham 1967-76, City of Liverpool Field Ambulance (TA) 1970-74, Hants 1976-; memb Local Ctee Cons Party; memb Br Dental Assoc 1963-; *Recreations* archaeology, sailing, skiing, riding, gardening, sheep; *Clubs* Key Haven Yacht, Winchester Med and Dental Soc; *Style—* Christopher Clegg, Esq; Ryedown Farmhouse, Ryedown Lane, E Wellow, Romsey (☎ 0794 23393)

CLEGG, Jeremy Paul Jermyn; s of Maj Benjamin Beattie Clegg, MC, of The Lawn, Ridgeway, nr Sheffield, and Rosemary Anne, *née* Coles (d 1955); *b* 11 July 1948; *Educ* St Anselms Bakewell, Fettes, Univ of Sussex (BSc); *m* 24 March 1973, Marilyn Anne, da of Edward Towndrow, of Barnet, Herts; 1 s (Oliver b 14 Feb 1980), 1 da (Anna-Louise b 6 March 1978); *Career* Commercial Union 1970, Leslie & Godwin 1974, MPA Ltd 1982; dir: Baring Investmt Mgmnt (Baring Brothers & Co) 1986, Henderson Pension Fund Management (Henderson Administration plc) 1990; *Recreations* golf, tennis, photography; *Style—* Jeremy Clegg, Esq; The Moorings, Bowling Alley, Crondall, Farnham, Surrey (☎ 0252 850229); Henderson Pension Fund Management Ltd, 3 Finsbury Ave, London EC2M 2PA (☎ 071 638 5757, fax 071 377 5742, telex 884616 A/BG FRIARG)

CLEGG, John Fawcett; s of Lt Henry Fawcett Clegg (d 1960), and Vera Mary, *née* Fricker; *b* 24 May 1939; *Educ* Rugby, St Johns Coll Cambridge (MA, MB BChir); *m* 18 Oct 1969, Hilary Mary, da of Philip Crabtree; 3 da (Alison Margaret b 9 July 1970, Fiona Louise b 26 April 1973, Charlotte Elizabeth b 15 March 1975); *Career* William Clarke meml fell Hammersmith Hosp London 1965-67, registrar in surgery Davyhulme Park Hosp Manchester 1968, sr registrar Manchester Royal Infirmary 1969-72, conslt surgn Leighton Hosp 1973-, examiner in surgery RCSE; memb: Cncl Assoc Surgns GB and Ireland, Manchester Med Soc, Liverpool and NW Surgical Soc; pres Vascular Soc; memb Manchester Med Soc; memb RSM, FRCS, FRCSEd, memb Société Int de Chirurgie; *Recreations* golf, historical literature; *Clubs* Sandway Golf; *Style—* John Clegg, Esq; Whitethorne, 8 The Crescent, Hartford, Northwich, Cheshire (☎ 0606 76400); Leighton Hospital, Crewe, Cheshire (☎ 0270 255141, car 0860 269031)

CLEGG, (William Edwin) Morris; s of Norman Clegg (d 1962), and Ada Nina, *née* Fisher (d 1988); *b* 6 May 1930; *Educ* Cowley Sch, HMS Conway (trg ship); *m* 1958, Judith Anne, da of George Wardle (d 1983), of Liverpool; 2 s (Mark William Norman b 1959, Richard Henry Morris b 1962), 2 da (Rosemary Anne b 1960, Jane Amanda Judith b 1967); *Career* reader Anglican Church 1957-; chm: Cleggs of Prescot Ltd 1962-85 (dir 1957-62), Pioneer Replacement Services Ltd 1970-83, Lancaster Court (Chorley) Ltd 1970-83; dir: Knowsley Sports Club Ltd 1980-87, Charles Baynes plc 1984-, Job Ownership Ltd 1985-; chm G M Building Systems Ltd 1985-89; dir: Astra Ind Holdings plc 1985-87, The Guy Pilkington Memorial Hospital Ltd 1986-; chm Gawsworth Finance Ltd 1986-, dir Holroyd and Meek Ltd 1987-, chm Royal Stafford China Ltd 1987-88; memb St Helens Community Trust Investment Mgmnt Ctee 1984-89 (chm 1989-), memb Clergy Selection Panel Chester Diocese 1987-89, underwriting name at Lloyds 1985; *Recreations* reading, walking, gardening, piano; *Style—* Morris Clegg, Esq; The Old Rectory, Gawsworth, Cheshire SK11 9RJ (☎ 0260 223 372)

CLEGG, Nicholas Peter; s of Dr Hugh Anthony Clegg, CBE (d 1983); *b* 24 May 1936; *Educ* Bryanston, Trinity Coll Cambridge (BA); *m* 1959, Eulalie, da of Herman van den Wall Bake; 3 s, 1 da; *Career* banker; with Royal Netherlands Blast Furnaces and Steelworks 1960-62, Proctor and Gamble Brussels 1962-64; dir Hill Samuel and Co Ltd 1970-; *Recreations* gardening, skiing, listening to music; *Style—* Nicholas Clegg Esq; The Leather Bottle, Wainhill, Chinnor, Oxford OX9 4AB; Hill Samuel and Co, 100 Wood St, London EC2P 2AJ (☎ 071 628 8011, telex 888822)

CLEGG, Richard Ninian Barwick; QC (1979); o s of Sir Cuthbert Barwick Clegg, TD, JP (d 1986), and Helen Margaret, *née* Jefferson (d 1987); *b* 28 June 1938; *Educ* Charterhouse, Trinity Coll Oxford (MA); *m* 3 Aug 1963, Katherine Veronica, da of Andrew Archibald Henry Douglas, of Ashley, Shalbourne, Wilts; 2 s (Aidan b 1966, Sebastian b 1969), 1 da (Flavia b 1968); *Career* called to the Bar Inner Temple 1960; bencher 1985, recorder of Crown Court 1978-; chm NW Section Bow Gp 1964-66, vice chm Bow Gp 1965-66, chm Winston Circle 1965-66, pres Heywood and Royton Cons Assoc 1965-68; capt Oxford Pentathlon Team 1959; *Recreations* hunting, shooting, fishing, skiing, travel, music, books; *Clubs* Lansdowne; *Style—* Richard

Clegg, Esq, QC; The Old Rectory, Brereton, via Sandbach, Cheshire (☎ 0477 32358); 5 Essex Court, Temple, London EC4 (☎ 071 353 4365, fax 071 583 1491)

CLEGG, Ronald Anthony (Tony); s of Stanley Clegg, and Cicely, *née* Bentley; *b* 8 April 1937; *Educ* Bickerton House of Southport Lancs; *m* 9 March 1963, Dorothy Eve; 3 da (Virginia b 1965, Fiona b 1966, Victoria b 1970); *Career* mangr Mountain Mills Co Ltd 1961 (dir 1963), jt md Leigh Mills Co Ltd 1972 (merged with above to form Mountleigh Group Ltd 1979), chm and chief exec Mountleigh Group plc 1983-89, dir Wembley plc 1987-90; chm Leeds Gen Purposes The Prince's Youth Business Tst, memb Cncl Yorkshire Agricultural Soc; chm: Br Soc for Clinical Cytology Appeal, Leeds Special Appeal Cancer Res Macmillan Fund; patron Leeds Riding for the Disabled Yorkshire; Liveryman Worshipful Co of Turners; CBIM, FInstD; *Recreations* riding, breeding highland cattle, racehorses, music; *Style*— Tony Clegg, Esq; The Old Hall, Bramham, Wetherby, W Yorks LS23 6QR; E & F Securities 22 Gilbert St, London W1Y 1RJ

CLEGG, Hon Mrs (Sally Mary); *née* Atkins; 3 and yst da of Baron Colnbrook, KCMG, PC (Life Peer), *qv*; *b* 18 Feb 1948; *m* 1970, William Field Clegg; 1 s (William Humphrey b 1975), 1 da (Islay Mary b 1973); *Style*— The Hon Mrs Clegg; Homer House, Ipsden, Oxon

CLEGG, Sir Walter; s of Edwin Clegg, of Blackpool; *b* 18 April 1920; *Educ* Bury GS, Arnold Sch Blackpool, Manchester Univ Law Sch; *m* 1951, Elise Margaret, da of J Hargreaves, of Blackpool; *Career* solicitor 1947, practising to 1961; MP (C) N Fylde 1966-83, MP(C) Wyre 1983-87; a lord cmmr HM Treasury 1970-72, vice chamberlain HM Household 1972-73, comptroller 1973-74, Opposition Whip 1967-69 and 1974, kt 1980; *Style*— Sir Walter Clegg; Beech House, Raikes Rd, Little Thornton, nr Blackpool (☎ 0253 826131)

CLEGG-HILL, Hon Mrs Frederic; Alice Dorothy; yr da of Rear Adm Cuthbert Godfrey Chapman, MVO (d 1931), and Hon Dorothy Beatrix Wynn, da of 3 Baron Newborough; *b* 21 Sept 1910; *m* 18 Nov 1938, Maj Hon Frederic Raymond Clegg-Hill (ka 1945), yr s of 6 Viscount Hill (d 1957); 1 s (Peter David Raymond Charles, *qv*); *Style*— The Hon Mrs Frederic Clegg-Hill; The Old Forge, Stone in Oxney, nr Tenterden, Kent

CLEGG-HILL, Peter David Raymond Charles; s of Maj Hon Frederic Raymond Clegg-Hill (ka 1945), 2 s of 6 Viscount Hill, and Hon Mrs Frederic Clegg-Hill, *qv*; hp to Viscountcy of cous, 8 Viscount Hill; *b* 17 Oct 1945, (posthumous); *Educ* Tabley House Sch; *m* 1973, Sharon Ruth Deane, of NZ; 2 s (Paul b 1979, Michael Charles David b 1988), 5 da (Catherine b 1974, Jennifer b 1976, Susan b 1980, Rachel b 1984, Mellisa b 1986); *Career* farmer; *Style*— Peter Clegg-Hill, Esq; The Old Forge, Stone-in-Oxney, Tenterden, Kent

CLELAND, William Paton; s of Sir John Burton Cleland (d 1971), of Adelaide, S Aust, and Dora Isabel, *née* Paton (d 1955); *b* 30 May 1912; *Educ* Scotch Coll Adelaide, Univ of Adelaide; *m* 18 May 1940, Norah, da of George Elijah Goodhart (d 1957), of Hampstead, London; 2 s (John Goodhart b 1942, Peter George b 1948), 1 da (Janet Elizabeth (Mrs Scurr) b 1944); *Career* WWII EMS 1939-45; conslt thoracic surgn: KCH, Brompton Chest Hosp, Hammersmith Hosp, RN (civilian conslt); sr lectr Royal Postgrad Med Sch, dir Dept Surgery Inst Diseases of Chest, advsr in thoracic surgery Dept of Health; Freeman City of London, Liveryman Worshipful Soc of Apothecaries; FRCS 1945, FRCP 1967, FACS 1969; Cdr: Order of Falcon Iceland, Order of Lion Finland; *Books* Medical Surgical Cardiology (jtly), Short Practice Surgery (contrib); *Recreations* fishing, gardening, apiarist; *Style*— William Cleland, Esq; Green Meadows, Goodworth Clatford, Andover, Hampshire SP11 7HH (☎ 0264 24327)

CLELLAND, David Gordon; MP Tynebridge 1985; s of Archibald (Clem) Clelland, of 157 Avenue Rd, Gateshead, and Ellen, *née* Butchart; *b* 27 June 1943; *Educ* Kelvin Grove Boys Sch Gateshead, Gateshead and Hebburn Tech Coll; *m* 31 March 1965, Maureen, da of William Potts; 2 da (Jillian, Vicki); *Career* apprentice electrical fitter 1959-64, electrical tester 1964-81; shop steward AEU 1965-79, memb Works Ctee, sec Combine Ctee, sec Health and Safety Ctee; memb Lab Party 1970-, prospective Parly candidate Gateshead West 1981-83; memb Gateshead Cncl 1972-86 (chm Parks and Recreation 1976-84, leade 1984-86); nat sec Assoc of Cncllrs 1981-86; *Recreations* golf, music, reading; *Style*— David Clelland, Esq; House of Commons, Westminster, London SW1A NAA

CLEMENCE, (John) Alistair; TD (1972); s of L A Clemence (d 1978), of Bexhill on Sea, and Helen, *née* Gillies (d 1982); *b* 17 May 1937; *Educ* Tonbridge; *m* 8 April 1967, Heather May Kerr, da of Canon C J Offer (d 1964), of Ightham, Kent; 3 s (William b 1969, James b 1970, Jonathan b 1973); *Career* Nat Serv Seaforth Highlanders 1956-58, 2 Lt 1957; London Scottish Regt TA 1959-72, Lt 1959, Capt 1963, Maj 1970-; Regtl Col 1989, Dep Hon Col 1/51 Highland Vols 1989; CA; ptnr Finnie & Co (formerly L A Clemence & Co) 1966-; Liveryman Worshipful Co of Skinners 1969; FCA, FInstD, FBIM; *Recreations* gardening; *Clubs* Army and Navy; *Style*— J A Clemence, Esq, TD; Bassetts, Mill Lane, Hildenborough, Kent TN11 9LX; 46 Church Ave, Beckenham, Kent BR3 1DT (☎ 081 658 7911)

CLEMENS, Brian Horace; s of Albert George Clemens (d 1987), of 5 Arthur St, Ampthill, Beds, and Susannah, *née* O'Grady; *b* 30 July 1931; *m* 1, (m dis 1964), Brenda, *née* Prior; m 2, 23 Nov 1979, Janet Elizabeth, da of Filory Loveday East (d 1985), of 12 The Comyns, Bushey Heath, Herts; 2 s (Samuel Joshua Twain b 16 Aug 1980, George Barnaby Langhorne b 14 Dec 1982); *Career* Nat Serv RAOC 1949-51; TV series: prodr and writer The Avengers 1964-70, prodr and writer The New Avengers 1976-78, creator My Wife Next Door 1975 (BAFTA Award), creator prodr and writer The Professionals 1978-82, creator and writer Blueblood 1988-89; feature films: writer Blind Terror/See No Evil 1973 (Edgar Alan Poe Award), prodr and writer Dr Jekyll and Sister Hyde 1973 (Cinema Fantastique Award), writer prodr and dir Captain Kronos 1973, writer Golden Voyage of Sinbad 1974 (Fantasy Film Award); writer teleplay Scene of the Crime 1968 (Edgar Alan Poe Award; writer stage plays: Shock 1969, Edge of Darkness 1974, Sting in the Tale 1984, Inside Job 1988; co-prodr The Wicked Stage (amateur prodns to aid nominated charities); memb Writers Guilds of GB and America; *Books* Rabbit Pie (1990); *Recreations* writing, walking, wine, Ferrari cars; *Style*— Brian Clemens, Esq; Park Farm Cottage, Ampthill, Beds (☎ 0525 402215, fax 0525 402954); Flat 6, 5 Talbot Square, London W2; El Cortijo Viejo, Jesus Pobre, Denia, Alicante, Spain

CLEMENT, Hon Mrs (Diana Brenda); *née* Richards; da of 1 Baron Milverton, GCMG (d 1978); *b* 9 Aug 1928; *Educ* Havergal Coll Toronto, Cheltenham Ladies' Coll, Univ of London (BA), Sorbonne; *m* 1 Sept 1960 (m dis), Sqdn-Ldr Glyn John Clement, RAF (ret); 1 s (Paul Nicholas Arthur), 1 da (Caroline Brenda); *Style*— The Hon Mrs Clement; The Bell House, Kewstoke Rd, Worle, Weston-super-Mare

CLEMENT, Dr Michele Ingrid; da of Maj Joseph Cyril Clement (d 1984), and Joyce Mona Clement; *b* 18 Sept 1951; *Educ* Queenswood Sch, UCL (BSc), UCH (MB BS); *m* 30 May 1981, Timothy Henry Corn, s of Harold Henry Corn (d 1985); 2 s (Edward Harry b 1983, Charles Joseph b 1985); *Career* med qualifications and house post UCH; jr med posts: King's Coll Hosp 1977-78, UCH 1978-79; dermatology trg: St John's Hosp 1980, King's Coll Hosp 1980-87; appointed conslt dermatologist Bromley Health Authy 1987; MRCP 1978; *Books* Topical Steroids for Skin Disorders (1987); *Style*— Dr Michele Clement; Dermatology Department, Farnborough Hospital, Farnborough Common, Orpington, Kent BR6 8ND (☎ 0689 85 63333 ext 295)

CLEMENT-JONES, Timothy Francis; CBE (1988); s of Maurice Llewelyn Clement-Jones (d 1988), of Haywards Heath, Sussex, and Margaret Jean, *née* Hudson; *b* 26 Oct 1949; *Educ* Haileybury, Trinity Coll Cambridge (MA); *m* 14 June 1973, Dr Vicky Veronica Clement-Jones (d 1987), fndr of Br Assoc of Cancer Utd Patients, da of Teddy Yip, of Hong Kong; *Career* slr; articled clerk Coward Chance 1972-74, assoc Joynson-Hicks & Co 1974-76, corp lawyer Letraset Int Ltd 1976-80, asst head (later head) Legal Servs LWT Ltd 1980-83, legal dir retailing div Grand Met plc 1984-86, gp co sec and legal advsr Kingfisher plc (formerly Woolworth Hldgs plc) 1986-; chm: Assoc of Lib Lawyers 1982-86, Lib Pty 1986-88; dep chm Fed Exec SLD 1989-; tstee Br Assoc of Cancer Utd Patients, memb Crime Concern Advsy Bd; memb Law Soc; *Recreations* walking, travelling, reading, eating, talking; *Clubs* National Liberal; *Style*— Timothy Clement-Jones, Esq, CBE; 10 Northbourne Rd, London SW4 7DJ (☎ 071 627 0556); c/o Woolworth Hldgs plc 119, Marylebone Rd, London NW1 (☎ 071 724 7749)

CLEMENTI, David Cecil; s of Air Vice-Marshal Cresswell Montagu Clementi, CB, CBE, and Susan, da of late Sir (Edward) Henry Pelham, KCB; gs of Sir Cecil Clementi, GCMG (d 1947); *b* 25 Feb 1949; *Educ* Winchester, Univ of Oxford (MA), Harvard Business Sch (MBA); *m* 23 Sept 1972, Sarah Louise (Sally), da of Dr Anthony Beach Cowley; 1 s (Tom b 17 April 1979), 1 da (Anna b 26 Nov 1976); *Career* with Arthur Andersen & Co 1970-73; qualified as CA 1973; joined Kleinwort Benson Ltd 1975 (dir 1981-); memb Worshipful Co of Mercers; FCA; *Style*— David C Clementi, Esq; c/o Kleinwort Benson Ltd, 20 Fenchurch St, London EC3 3DB (☎ 071 623 8000)

CLEMENTS, David Blakeley; s of Arnold Clements, of 36 Birch Barn Way, Northampton, and Winifred Clements (d 1987); *b* 28 April 1935; *Educ* Northampton GS; *m* 26 March 1960, Jean Gardner, da of Ernest Stanley (d 1944); 1 s (Richard b 15 Jan 1965), 1 da (Suzanne b 23 Sept 1963); *Career* house surgn: Manchester Royal Eye Hosp 1960, Withington Hosp 1961; registrar St pauls Eye Hosp Liverpool (house surgn 1962-66); conslt ophthaalmic surgn: Alder Hey Hosp, St Helens Hosp; memb Cheshire Family Practitioners Ctee 1983-89; fell Coll of Ophthalmologists; *Recreations* golf; *Style*— David Clements, Esq; 3 Thornhill Close, Aughton, Ormskirk, W Lancs (☎ 0695 423841); 27 Rodney St, Liverpool, Merseyside (☎ 051 709 0353)

CLEMENTS, (Gilbert) Edward Isaac; s of Gilbert Edward Clements, of 26 Abbotsford Rd, Redland, Bristol, and Violet Victoria, *née* Dean; *b* 23 Feb 1915; *Educ* Bristol GS, UCL (LLB); *m* 1950 (m dis 1961), Maureen Elizabeth Charlotte (Valerie), *née* Stitson; 1 da (Lady Anne Clements Eyre w of Sir Reginald Eyre); *Career* RAF 1940-47: pilot, sector controller, ops offr (Normandy invasion) special liaison offr 1 Allied Airborne Army SHAEF 3 American Army and SACSEA; called to the Bar Middle Temple 1946; fire mangr Bedford General Insurance Co 1957-73, vice chm Bedford Building Soc 1965-86 (dir 1962-65), fire mangr Zurich Insurance Co 1973-76 (fire and accident mangr 1970-72), sec Vectis Property Gp 1978-; Farringdon Without City Ward: common councilman 1960-, dep 1965; memb MENSA 1959-, London branch chm Chartered Inst of Secs 1966; Freeman: City of London 1953; Upper Warden Worshipful Co of: Scriveners, Chartered Secs and Administrators (Memb Ct of Assts); FCIS 1948, FCII 1940; *Recreations* walking and reading; *Clubs* Reform, Guildhall, City Livery; *Style*— Edward Clements, Esq; 2 Plowden Buildings, Temple, London EC4Y 9AS (☎ 071 353 0035)

CLEMENTS, Leslie Craig; s of Leslie Sidney Harold Clements (d 1960), and Annie Boomer, *née* Rae; *b* 31 Dec 1940; *Educ* Selborne Sch, Ealing Tech Coll, Univ of Bristol (BA); *m* 30 May 1970, Carole, da of Frederick Allen (d 1970); 1 s (Adam Craig b 4 May 1975); *Career* sr ptnr Merchant and Co; FICA; *Recreations* sch govr, badminton, bowls, aquatics; *Clubs* Saints Bowls, Perivale Bowls; *Style*— L Craig Clements, Esq; Matlock House, 229 High St, Acton, London W3 9BY (☎ 081 992 7811, fax 081 993 7109)

CLEMENTS, Paul Michael; s of Stanley Clements, and Edna, *née* Garber; *b* 29 April 1953; *Educ* Haberdashers' Aske's, Univ of Birmingham (LLB); *m* 4 June 1983, Pamela Anne, da of Robert David Poulton Hughes; 1 s (Simon Lewis b 11 June 1985); *Career* admitted slr 1977; litigation asst Bird & Bird 1977-79; Crossman Block & Keith: litigation asst 1979-80, salaried ptnr 1980-84, equity ptnr 1985-87; equity ptnr and head Litigation Dept Withers Crossman Block 1988-89, equity ptnr and managing ptnr Crossman Block 1989-; memb Ctee: City of Westminster Law Soc, London Solicitor's Litigation Assoc; memb Law Soc; *Recreations* amateur drama participant, rugby, opera, classical music; *Clubs* RAC; *Style*— Paul Clements, Esq; Crossman Block Solicitors, 199 Strand, London WC2R 1DR (☎ 071 836 2000, fax 071 240 2648, telex 21457 CBLDN G)

CLEMENTS, Philip Alexander; s of Ronald Alexander Clements, of Canterbury, Kent, and Phyllis Clements; *b* 27 July 1958; *Educ* Simon Langton GS Canterbury, Canterbury Coll of Art (BA); *m* Maria Anne, da of Derek Herring; 1 s (Thomas Alexander b 2 Oct 1988); *Career* jr designer J Sainsbury plc 1980-82, packaging designer Allied International Designers 1982-88, assoc creative dir The Design Bridge (UK) Ltd 1988-; design projects incl: Sharwoods Indian Foods, Brooke Bond, Oxo, Terrys, Reed International; *Style*— Philip Clements, Esq; The Design Bridge (UK) Ltd, 8-16 Cromer St, London WC1 9LX (☎ 071 833 1311, 071 837 3084)

CLEMENTS, Roger Varley; s of Harold William Clements, of 19-21 High St, Harpole, Northampton, and Rose Maud, *née* Smith (d 1978); *b* 26 Feb 1936; *Educ* St Lawrence Coll Ramsgate, CCC Oxford (BA, MA, BM BCh), UCH London; *m* 1, 10 Sept 1959 (m dis 1967), Clemency Mary Holme, da of Thomas Fox; m 2, 1971, Charlotte Susan, da of Maj Charles Robins, of 4 Ross Ave, Leasowe, Wirral; 1 s (Charles Maxwell b 29 March 1974), 1 da ((Esther) Lucy b 27 Feb 1976); *Career* conslt obstetrician and gynaecologist N Middx Hosp London 1973-, hon gynaecologist Hammersmith Hosp London, asst prof UK Faculty St George's Med Sch Grenada W Indies; papers on: central venous pressure monitoring in obstetrics, infertility, high risk pregnancy, osteomalacia in pregnancy, medical negligence; examiner: Central Midwives Bd, Conjoint Bd, RCOG, Univ of Ibadan Nigeria, W African Coll of Surgns, Post Grad Coll of Nigeria; chm Dist Med Advsy Ctee Haringey Health Authy 1988-91, dir Clinical Strategy North Middx NHS Tst 1991-; Freeman City of London 1984; Liveryman: Worshipful Soc of Apothecaries London 1983, Worshipful Co of Barbers London 1986; memb BMA, fell RSM; *Books* First Baby After 30 (1985); *Recreations* cricket, opera; *Clubs* MCC, Savile; *Style*— Roger Clements, Esq; 111 Harley St, London W1N 1DG (☎ 071 486 1781, 071 637 0701, fax 071 224 3852, 0860 252 376)

CLEMENTS, Prof Ronald Ernest; s of Cyril George Clements (d 1976), and Elizabeth, *née* Cook; *b* 27 May 1929; *Educ* Buckhurst Hill Co HS, Spurgeon's Coll, Christ's Coll Cambridge; *m* Valerie Winifred, da of Sidney Matthew John Suffield (d 1989); 2 da (Gillian b 1962, Marian b 1964); *Career* lectr: Univ of Edinburgh 1960-67, Univ of Cambridge 1967-83; prof theology King's Coll London 1983-; baptist min 1956-; DLitt Univ of Acadia NS Canada 1982; memb Soc Old Testament Study (pres 1985); *Books* God And Temple (1965), A Century of Old Testament Study (1975), Old Testament Theology (1979), Isaiah 1-39 (1980), The World of Ancient Israel (ed, 1989); *Recreations* walking, photography; *Style*— Prof Ronald Clements; 8 Brookfield Rd, Coton, Cambridge CB3 7PT (☎ 0954 210593); Faculty of Theology, King's Coll,

Strand, London WC2R 3LS (☎ 071 836 5454)

CLEMENTS, Col William Holliwell; s of Henry Clements, of 10 Tor Grange, Holywood, Co Down, and Gladys Nellie, *née* Atkinson; *b* 9 March 1937; *Educ* Cambell Coll Belfast, The Queen's Univ of Belfast (LLB); *m* 16 Dec 1961, Elizabeth, da of Cochrane Morrison, of 8 Seaview Drive, Portstewart, Co Londonderry, NI; 2 s (Nicholas William Simon b 13 Aug 1963, Andrew Timothy Michael b 27 March 1968), 1 da (Jessica Jane b 28 April 1966); *Career* cmmnd Royal Ulster Rifles 1960, Aust Staff Coll 1969, instr RMC Duntroon Aust 1974-76, Co 1 Bn Royal Irish Rangers 1976-78, asst mil sec MOD 1978-81, instr Nigerian Armed Forces Staff Coll 1981-83; def mil and air attaché Br Embassy: Peking 1985-88, Rangoon 1990; memb RSAA; *Recreations* travel, history, shooting, chinese snuff bottles; *Clubs* Army and Navy; *Style—* Col William Clements; Ministry of Defence, Main Building, Whitehall, London SW1A 2HB

CLEMINSON, Sir James Arnold Stacey; KBE (1990), MC (1945), DL (Norfolk 1983); s of late Arnold Russel Cleminson, JP, himself sometime chm Reckitt and Colman, and Florence, da of James Stacey, of New Zealand; *b* 31 Aug 1921; *Educ* Rugby; *m* 1950, Helen Juliet Measor; 1 s, 2 da; *Career* served WWII Para Regt; chm Reckitt and Colman Ltd 1977-86 (chief exec 1973-80, joined 1946, dir overseas co 1957, chief exec 1973-80); dir: Norwich Union 1979- (vice chm 1983-), non-exec United Biscuits (Holdings) 1982-89, Fenners plc 1989-; memb CBI Cncl 1978 (pres 1984-86), pres Food Mfrs Fedn 1980-82, chm Food and Drink Industs Cncl 1983-84, pres Endeavour Trg 1984-; chm: BOTB 1986-90, AP Bank 1986-, Jeyes Hygiene 1985-89; chm Nurses Pay Bd 1986-90; Hon Fell RCGP Hon Doctor of Law Univ of Hull (1985); kt 1982; *Recreations* field sports, golf; *Clubs* Boodles; *Style—* Sir James Cleminson, KBE, MC, DL; Loddon Hall, Hales, Norfolk (☎ 0508 20717); 135 Cranmer Court, Whiteheads Grove, Chelsea, London

CLEMITS, John Henry; s of Cyril Thomas Clemits (d 1955), and Minnie Alberta Clemits (d 1968); *b* 16 Feb 1934; *Educ* Sutton HS for Boys Plymouth, Plymouth Coll of Art; *m* 14 June 1958, (Elizabeth) Angela, da of Frederick John Moon; 1 s (Roger b 1965), 1 da (Elizabeth b 1962); *Career* Capt RE (TA) 43 Wessex Div and Royal Monmouthshire RE (Militia) 1964-69; chartered architect; civil servant: New Works planning offr, Property Servs Agency Germany 1975-79; dir of works (Army) PSA Chessington 1979-85; dir for Wales PSA Cardiff 1985-90, md PSA Projects Cardiff 1990-; FRSA, memb ARIBA (distinction in thesis); *Recreations* golf, choral singing, music, DIY; *Clubs* The Naval, Civil Serv; *Style—* John Clemits, Esq; The Lodge, Hendrescythan Creigiau, Nr Cardiff CF4 8NN (☎ 0222 891786); Managing Director PSA Projects CArdiff, St Agnes Rd, Gabalfa, Cardiff (☎ 0222 586760, fax 0222 614288)

CLEMMENCE, John William; s of Bertie Leonard Clemmence (d 1964), and Dorothy Margaret, *née* Tune, of London; *b* 11 Aug 1948; *Educ* Roan GS Greenwich London; *m* 1975, Glynis Irene, da of Ernest Jackson; 1 s (Ian John b 9 Nov 1979), 1 da (Sarah Louise b 7 July 1982); *Career* CA; Geoffrey Schofield & Co 1964-70, Binder Hamlyn 1970-75, Finnie & Co (and predecessor firms) 1975-; memb Inst Taxation 1969, MICA 1970; *Recreations* sports (played for Leeds CC for 5 years); *Style—* John Clemmence, Esq; Finnie & Co, Bridge House, Westgate, Leeds LS1 4ND (☎ 0532 442331, fax 0532 422116)

CLEMPSON, Vincent Richard; *b* 2 Oct 1953; *Educ* Churchill Coll Cambridge (BA, Dip Crim); *Career* admitted slr 1979, ptnr Freshfields 1986-; memb: Intellectual Property Sub Ctee City of London Slrs Co, London Young Slrs Gp; memb Law Soc; *Style—* Vincent Clempson, Esq; Freshfields, Grindall House, 25 Newgate St, London EC1A 7L (☎ 071 606 6677)

CLEOBURY, Nicholas Randall; s of Dr John Frank Cleobury, of Croft House, Street End, Lower Hardes, Canterbury, Kent, and Brenda Julie, *née* Randall; *b* 23 June 1950; *Educ* King's Sch Worcester, Worcester Coll Oxford (MA); *m* 4 Nov 1978, Heather Noelle, da of Noel Kay (d 1981), of 8 Station Rd, Upper Poppleton, York; 1 s (Simon Randall b 23 Oct 1979), 1 da (Sophie Noelle b 12 Dec 1981); *Career* asst organist: Chichester Cathedral 1971-72, Christ Church Oxford 1972-76; chorus master Glyndebourne Opera 1977-79, asst dir BBC Singers 1978-80, princ conductor of opera RAM 1981-87, dir Aquarius 1983-, music dir Broomhill 1990-; 1980-: int conductor working throughout UK, Europe and Scandinavia, regular TV and BBC Radio and Prom appearances, numerous commercial recordings; princ guest conductor Gävle Orch (Sweden) 1989-, princ conductor city of East Anglian Orchestral Assoc 1990-; FRCO 1968; hon RAM 1985; *Recreations* cricket, reading, walking, food, wine; *Clubs* Savage; *Style—* Nicholas Cleobury, Esq; China Cottage, Church Lane, Petham, Canterbury, Kent CT4 5RD (☎ 0227 70 584, fax 0227 70 827)

CLEOBURY, Stephen John; s of Dr John Frank Cleobury, of Croft House, Canterbury, and Brenda Julie, *née* Randall; *b* 31 Dec 1948; *Educ* King's Sch Worcester, St John's Coll Cambridge (MA, MusB); *m* 3 July 1971, Penelope Jane, da of William Francis Holloway (d 1984); 2 da (Suzannah b 1973, Laura b 1976); *Career* organist St Matthew's Church Northampton, dir of Music Northampton GS 1971-74, sub-organist Westminster Abbey 1974-78, master of music Westminster Cathedral 1979-82, fell organist and dir of music King's Coll Cambridge 1982-, Conductor CUMS 1983-; hon sec Royal Coll of Organists 1981-90 (pres 1990-); pres: Inc Assoc of Organists 1985-87, Cathedral Organist's Assoc 1988-90; memb Cncl Royal Sch of Church Music 1981-; FRCO, ISM; *Style—* Stephen Cleobury, Esq; 85 Gough Way, Newnham, Cambridge CB3 9LN (☎ 0223 359461); King's College, Cambridge CB2 1ST (☎ 0223 350411 ext 224)

CLEPHAN, Derek Peter; s of George Keith Clephan (d 1982), and Bertha Mary, *née* Speakman; *b* 27 June 1938; *Educ* Dudley GS Worcs, Univ of Birmingham (LLM); *m* 21 Dec 1971, Joy, da of Sidney William Fryer, of Sheffield; 2 s (Mark b 20 Nov 1973, John b 25 Feb 1975), 1 da (Trudie b 14 July 1976); *Career* admitted slr 1963, asst town clerk Sheffield 1971-74; dir: admin Barnsley 1974-89, legal servs Kent CC; pres Assoc of Dist Secs 1983-84; *Style—* Derek Clephan, Esq; 21 Dewar Drive, Sheffield, S Yorks S7 2GQ (☎ 0742 369192); County Hall, Maidstone, Kent ME14 1XQ (☎ 0622 694302, fax 0622 694402)

CLERK, Robert Maxwell; s and h of Sir John Clerk, 10 Bt; *b* 3 April 1945; *Educ* Winchester, Univ of London (BSc); *m* 1970, Felicity Faye, *née* Collins; 2 s, 1 da; *Career* ptnr Smiths Gore chartered surveyors; chm Assoc of Scottish Dist Salmon Fishery Bds, memb Salmon Advsy Ctee; FRICS; *Recreations* fishing, stalking, skiing, gardening; *Clubs* New (Edinburgh); *Style—* Robert Clerk Esq; Lachlanwells, Forres, Morayshire

CLERK OF PENICUIK, Sir John Dutton; 10 Bt (NS 1679), of Penicuik, Edinburgh, CBE (1966), VRD, JP; s of Sir George Clerk, 9 Bt (d 1943); *b* 30 Jan 1917; *Educ* Stowe; *m* 10 June 1944, Evelyn Elizabeth, er da of late William Robertson; 2 s, 2 da; *Heir* s, Robert Maxwell Clerk, *qv*; *Career* Cdre RNR ret; Ensign Queen's Body Guard for Scotland (Royal Co of Archers); Lord-Lt Midlothian 1972- (formerly Vice-Lt, DL 1956); FRSE 1977; *Style—* Sir John Clerk, Bt, CBE, VRD, JP, FRSE; Penicuik House, Penicuik, Midlothian EH26 9LA (☎ 0968 74318)

CLERKE, Francis Ludlow Longueville; s and h of Sir John Edward Longueville Clerke, 12 Bt, *qv*; *b* 25 Jan 1953; *Educ* Diocesan Coll Cape Town, Stellenbosch Univ (BA), Witwatersrand Univ (LLB); *m* 1982, Vanessa Anne, only da of Charles Cosman Citron (d 1974), of Mouille Point, Cape Town, S Africa; *Career* solicitor (South Africa); *Recreations* windsurfing, squash; *Clubs* Western Province Sports (Cape Town); *Style—* Francis Clerke, Esq

CLERKE, Sir John Edward Longueville; 12 Bt (E 1660), of Hitcham, Buckinghamshire; s of Francis William Talbot Clerke (ka 1916), s of 11 Bt; suc gf 1930; *b* 29 Oct 1913; *Educ* Eton, Magdalene Coll Cambridge (MA); *m* 1948, Mary, da of Lt-Col Ivor Reginald Beviss Bond, OBE, MC (d 1967); 1 s, 2 da; *Heir* s, Francis Clerke, *qv*; *Career* Capt Royal Wilts Yeo (TA); FCA 1948, ret; *Recreations* lawn tennis, shooting, fishing; *Clubs* Lansdowne; *Style—* Sir John Clerke, Bt; Holly Tree House, Pound Pill, Corsham, Wilts SN13 9HT (☎ 0249 713760)

CLERKE BROWN, Col Arthur; OBE (1944); s of John Clerke Brown (d 1964), and Gwen Clerke Brown, *née* Bros (d 1969); family have owned Kingston Blount Estate since 1810; *b* 8 Aug 1912; *Educ* Eton, RMC Sandhurst; *m* 12 Feb 1944, Anne Carlotta *née* Rawle, da of late Capt William Rawle; 1 da (Angela b 1949); *Career* Army Offr and landowner; cmmnd Oxford and Bucks LI 1933-64; served: France 1940, France and Germany 1944-46, HQ Far East Land Forces 1946-48, HQ Rhine Army 1959-62; jt master Colchester Garrison Beagles 1936-39, master Catterick Garrison Beagles 1951-55, jt MFH S Oxfordshire Hounds 1967-70, chm Oxon Branch CLA 1976-79, memb Point-to-Point Secs Ctee 1971- (chm 1976-79); *Recreations* hunting, racing, cricket, shooting; *Clubs* Army and Navy, MCC; *Style—* Col Arthur Clerke Brown, OBE; Kingston Grove, Kingston Blount, Oxford (☎ 0844 51356)

CLEVERDON, Julia Charity; (Mrs John Garnett); da of Douglas Cleverdon (d 1987), of London, and Elinor Nest Lewis; *b* 19 April 1950; *Educ* Camden Sch for Girls, Newnham Coll Cambridge (BA); *m* 1, 30 June 1973 (m dis), Martin Ollard; m 2, 3 April 1985, William John Poulton Maxwell Garnett, CBE, s of Maxwell Garnett, of Horestone Point (d 1960); 2 da (Victoria b 1985, Charity b 1982); *Career* dir of Educn: The Industl Soc 1981-87, md devpt Business in the Community 1988-; memb Sch Curriculum Devpt Ctee 1984; chm: Economic Awareness Ctee, Nat Curriculum Cncl; tstee 300 Gp, fndn govr Camden Sch for Girls, govr Queen Margaret's Sch York, vice pres Newnham Coll Roll; *Recreations* gardening, cooking, junk shops; *Clubs* Reform; *Style—* Ms Julia C Cleverdon; 8 Alwyne Rd, London N1 2HH; 227A City Rd, London

CLEVERLEY FORD, Rev Preb Douglas William; yr s of Arthur James Ford (d 1918), and Mildred, *née* Cleverley (d 1969); *b* 4 March 1914; *Educ* Great Yarmouth GS, Univ of London (BD, MTh); *m* 1939, Olga Mary, er da of Dr Thomas Bewley Gilbart-Smith (d 1955), and Elizabeth Girdler, *née* Eddison (d 1965); *Career* deacon 1937, priest 1938, vicar Holy Trinity South Kensington 1955-74, rural dean of Westminster 1965-74, preb St Paul's Cathedral 1968-74 (emeritus 1974-), provincial canon York 1969-, chaplain to HM The Queen 1973-84, sr chaplain to the Archbishop of Canterbury 1975-80, 6 preacher of Canterbury Cathedral 1982-; *Recreations* gardening; *Clubs* Athenaeum; *Style—* The Rev Prebendary Douglas Cleverley Ford; Rostrevor, Lingfield, Surrey RH7 6BZ (☎ 0342 832461)

CLEWS, Michael Graham; s of Reginald Alan Frederick Clews, of Bristol, and Alwine Annie, *née* Adams; *b* 11 Oct 1944; *Educ* Kingswood GS, Oxford Sch of Architecture (DipArch); *m* 24 July 1971, Heather Jane, da of Douglas Charles Sharratt, of Coventry; 2 s (Charles b 1978, Jonathan b 1983, d 1984), 2 da (Camilla b 1976, Helena b 1985); *Career* architect; fndr ptnr Clews Architectural Partnership 1972-; works incl historic buildings: Compton Verney, Croome Court, Boscobel House; conslt to PSA on historic buildings 1984-87 (historic buildings survey Oxfordshire, Warwickshire and Northamptonshire for DOE); pilot project for computerisation of historic building records for E Heritage; Surveyor Oxford diocesian; ARIBA; *Recreations* sailing, golf, squash; *Clubs* Tadmarton Heath Golf, Beauchamp Squash; *Style—* Michael Clews, Esq; The Old Vicarage, Great Bourton, Banbury, Oxon (☎ 0295 75621); Clews Architects Partnership, The Coach House, Great Bourton, Banbury, Oxon (☎ 0295 758101)

CLIFF HODGES, Hon Mrs (Linnéa Nilsson); *née* Birkett; da of 1 Baron Birkett, PC (d 1962); *b* 27 June 1923; *m* 25 June 1949, Gavin Cliff Hodges (b 25 Nov 1916), eldest s of late William Cliff Hodges, MD, of Perrydene, Hascombe, Godalming, Surrey; 1 s, 3 da; *Recreations* music, gardening, books; *Style—* The Hon Mrs Cliff Hodges; Briar Cottage, Packers Hill, Holwell, Sherborne, Dorset DT9 5LN (☎ 0963 23285)

CLIFFORD, Brian David; s of Lt W D Clifford (d 1978), and Doris Septima, *née* Magnay; *b* 15 July 1942; *Educ* Downhills Central Sch London; *m* 1, 5 Nov 1965 (m dis), Jenny Margaret, da of Morgan Goronwy Rees (d 1980); 2 s (Samuel William b 29 May 1966, Benjamin Luke b 24 Oct 1968); m 2, 22 Oct 1977, Linda Mary, *née* Stearns; *Career* picture ed Womans Mirror Magazine 1961-62, dep picture ed Sunday Mirror 1962-65, exec picture ed Sun Newspaper 1965-66, night picture ed Daily Mail 1966-67, prodr Yorkshire TV 1968; BBC TV: script writer TV News 1969, stills mangr 1969-73, sales mangr Photographs 1973-79, ed Picture Publicity 1979-86, chief asst Info Div 1986-87, dep head Info Div 1987-88, head of Info Servs 1988-; Tottenham Schoolboys footballer 1956-57, head chorister St Philip's Church 1955-57; rugby coach Cranbrook RFC 1979-, memb Mgmnt Ctee Biddenden CC 1980; memb NUJ; *Recreations* horse breeding, photography, watching Tottenham Hotspur; *Style—* Brian Clifford, Esq; Mount House, Sissinghurst Castle, Cranbrook, Kent TN17 2AB (☎ 0580 713668)

CLIFFORD, Charles Joseph; s of Sir Roger Charles Joseph Gerrard Clifford, 6 Bt (d 1982); twin br and hp of Sir Roger Joseph Gerrard Clifford, 7 Bt; *b* 5 June 1936; *m* 1983, Sally Madeline, da of William Hartgill Pennefather Green; *Style—* Charles Clifford, Esq; c/o 135 Totara St, Christchurch, New Zealand

CLIFFORD, David; s of late Robert Clifford; *b* 20 July 1940; *Educ* Friends' Sch Great Ayton, Sunderland Tech Coll, Newcastle Coll of Further Education; *m* 1963, Margaret; 2 s; *Career* gen mangr Econofreight Transport Ltd 1976-78, dir and gen mangr Seaham Harbour Dock Co 1978-, md Seaham Harbour Dock Co 1983-; dir Co Durham Trg and Enterprise Cncl 1989-, chm Durham Ground Work Trust; memb of the Inst of Mgmnt Servs MMS, MCIT; *Clubs* Rotary of Seaham; *Style—* David Clifford, Esq; Rosedale, Dene House Road, Seaham, Co Durham (☎ 091 581 2230)

CLIFFORD, David Robert; s of Harold Robert Clifford, of Aylesbury, Bucks, and Marjorie Clare, *née* Elliott; *b* 20 Dec 1943; *Educ* William Ellis Sch, Univ of Leeds (BA); *m* Jennifer Anne, da of Dr Cyril Frank Cosin; 1 s (Nicholas Robert b 23 Sept 1973); *Career* campaign planning exec London Press Exchange 1965-68, mktg exec Foote Cone & Belding 1968-69; Collett Dickenson Pearce & Partners: sr mktg and res exec 1969, assoc dir 1972, fndr Account Planning Dept 1972, dir 1973, dir KVH (subsid, Holland) 1976-78, new business dir 1982, vice chm 1986-; MIPA 1974; *Recreations* arduous walking (preferably abroad), incessant reading, listening to Radio 4; *Clubs* MCC, Rusi; *Style—* David Clifford, Esq; Collett Dickenson Pearce & Ptnrs, 110 Euston Rd, London NW1 2DQ (☎ 071 388 2424, fax 071 380 1217)

CLIFFORD, Dr Kevin Martin Andrew; s of Joseph William Clifford, of Bridge Farm, Darley Bridge, nr Matlock, Derbys, and Rona Joyce, *née* Watkinson; *b* 4 May 1948; *Educ* Ernest Bailey GS Matlock, Guys Hosp Med Sch (MB BS, LRCP); *m* 27 Nov 1976, Anne; 1 s (Martin b 1983), 2 da (Rebecca b 1980, Lucy b 1985); *Career* conslt radiologist S Tees Health Authy 1983-; memb Br Soc of Interventional Radiologists 1987; MRCS, FRCR 1982; *Style—* Dr Kevin Clifford; Dept of Radiology, South Cleveland Hospital, Marton Rd, Middlesborough, Cleveland (☎ 0642 850850, car 0860

319482)

CLIFFORD, Peter; *b* 30 March 1926; *Career* products mangr Johnson & Johnson GB Ltd 1948-55; mktg mangr: William Pearson Ltd 1955-63, Holt Products Ltd 1964-67; gp market res mangr Westminster Press Ltd 1967-86, md Mktg & Media Research Ltd 1986-; memb Newspaper Soc Regnl Newspaper Res Forum; MCIM 1956, MIAMA 1968, memb MRS; *Books* Test Marketing; *Recreations* church organist; *Clubs* The Organ; *Style—* Peter Clifford, Esq; 3 Grove Road, Thornton Heath, Surrey CR7 6HN (☎ 081 684 2965); Marketing & Media Research Ltd, 3 Grove Road, Thornton Heath, Surrey CR7 6HN (☎ 081 684 2965)

CLIFFORD, Sir Roger Joseph Gerrard; 7 Bt (UK 1887), of Flaxbourne, Marlborough, New Zealand; s (twin, by 1 m) of Sir Roger Clifford, 6 Bt (d 1982); *b* 5 June 1936; *m* 12 April 1968, Joanna Theresa, da of Cyril James Ward, of Christchurch, New Zealand, and gda of Sir Cyril Rupert Joseph Ward, 2 Bt; 2 da (Angela b 1971, Annabel b 1973); *Heir* bro, Charles Joseph Clifford, *qv*; *Style—* Sir Roger Clifford, Bt; 135 Totara Street, Christchurch 4, New Zealand

CLIFFORD, Hon Rollo Hugh; yr s of 13 Baron Clifford of Chudleigh, *qv*; *b* 15 March 1954; *Educ* Downside; *m* 1, 1977, Fiona Margaret, da of Richard Todd, actor; 2 s (Christopher Rollo, Alasdair Rollo), 1 da (Elizabeth Alice); m 2, 9 Nov 1989, Mrs Caroline Peta Versen, da of Peter Marshall Roberts, of Sydney, Australia; 1 da (Sophie Katharine Rose b 5 March 1991); *Career* md Rollo Clifford Associates Ltd, chm The Clifford Consultancy, md Respublica Ltd, dir Fixed Asset Finance Ltd; *Recreations* sailing, gardening, fishing, shooting; *Clubs* Bucks, RYS, Royal Ocean Racing, Royal Thames Yacht; *Style—* The Hon Rollo Clifford; Worthy Manor, Porlock Weir, Minehead, Somerset TA24 8PG

CLIFFORD, Timothy Peter Plint; s of Derek Plint Clifford, of Hartlip Place, Sittingbourne, Kent, and Ann, *née* Pierson (d 1984); cadet branch of Marcher family seated in Gloucestershire since 11th Century; *b* 26 Jan 1946; *Educ* Sherborne Dorset, Courtauld Inst, Univ of London (BA), Dip Fine Art Museums Assoc; *m* 1968, Jane Olivia, yr da of Sir George Paterson, QC, OBE, of Sherborne, Dorset; 1 da (Pandora b 1973); *Career* asst keeper: Dept of Paintings City Art Galleries 1968-72 (acting keeper 1972), Dept of Ceramics Victoria and Albert Museum London 1972, Dept of Prints and Drawings British Museum London 1976-78; dir: Manchester City Arts Gallery 1978-84, Nat Galleries of Scotland 1984-; memb Bd Br Cncl; tstee Abbot Hall Art Gallery; Freeman Worshipful Co of Goldsmiths; AMA, FRSA; Cavaliere al Ordine nel Merito della Repubblica Italiana; *Recreations* shooting, birdwatching; *Clubs* Turf, Beefsteak, New (Edinburgh); *Style—* Timothy Clifford, Esq; National Gallery of Scotland, The Mound, Edinburgh EH2 2EL (☎ 031 556 8921)

CLIFFORD OF CHUDLEIGH, Baroness; Hon Katharine Vavasseur; *née* Fisher; 2 da of 2 Baron Fisher (d 1955), and Jane, *née* Morgan (d 1955); *b* 3 Nov 1919; *m* 29 Jan 1945, 13 Baron Clifford of Chudleigh (d 1988); *Style—* Katharine, Lady Clifford of Chudleigh; La Colline, St Jacques, St Peter Port, Guernsey, CI (☎ 0481 25047)

CLIFFORD OF CHUDLEIGH, 14 Baron (E 1672) Thomas Hugh Clifford; Count of the Holy Roman Empire; s of 13 Baron Clifford of Chudleigh (d 1988), and Katharine, Lady Clifford of Chudleigh, *qv*; *b* 17 March 1948; *Educ* Downside; *m* 15 Dec 1980, (Muriel) Suzanne, yr da of Maj Campbell Austin; 2 s (Hon Alexander Thomas Hugh b 24 Sept 1985, Hon Edward George Hugh b 1988), 1 da (Hon Georgina Apollonia b 1983); *Heir* s, Hon Alexander Thomas Hugh Clifford b 24 Sept 1985; *Career* late Capt Coldstream Gds, served Norway, Turkey, Berlin, Ireland, British Honduras (Belize); mangr: The Clifford Estate Co, Ugbrooke Enterprises, Ugbrooke Reception Enterprise; KSOM; *Style—* Capt the Rt Hon the Lord Clifford of Chudleigh; Ugbrooke Park, Chudleigh, S Devon TQ13 OAD (☎ 0626 852179)

CLIFT, Richard Dennis; CMG (1984); s of late Dennis Victor Clift, and Helen Wilmot, *née* Evans; *b* 18 May 1933; *Educ* St Edward's Sch Oxford, Pembroke Coll Cambridge (BA); *m* 1, 1957 (m dis 1982), Barbara Mary Travis; 3 da; m 2, 1982, Jane Rosamund Barker, *née* Homfray; *Career* FO 1956-57, office of Br Chargé D'Affaires Peking 1958-60, Br Embassy Berne 1961-62, UK delgn to NATO Paris 1962-64, FO 1964-68, head of chancery Br High Cmmn Kuala Lumpur 1969-71, FCO 1971-73, cnsllr (commercial) Peking 1974-76, Canadian Nat Def Coll 1976-77, seconded to NI Office 1977-79, head of Hong Kong and Gen Dept FCO 1979-1984, Br high cmmr Freetown 1984-1986, political advsr Hong Kong 1987-89, ret 1989; student London Coll of Furniture 1989; *Recreations* sailing, walking, woodwork; *Style—* Richard Clift, Esq, CMG; 18 Langwood Chase, Teddington, Middx

CLIFT, Robert John; s of Alfred Whittier Clift, of Balsall Common, Coventry, and Edna Joyce, *née* Guest; *b* 1 Aug 1962; *Educ* Bablake Sch Coventry, Univ of Nottingham (BA); *m* 26 Sept 1987, Helen Claire, da of William Henry Beck, of Sidcup, Kent; *Career* hockey player; Champions' Trophy: Bronze medallist Karachi 1984, Silver medallist Perth 1985; World Cup Silver medallist London 1986, Euro Cup Silver medallist Moscow 1987, Olympic Games Gold medallist Seoul 1988; 118 caps England and GB; ACIB; *Recreations* golf, hockey; *Clubs* East Grinstead; *Style—* Robert Clift, Esq; Midland Bank plc, 3rd Floor, 117 Great Portland St, London W1A 4UY (☎ 071 323 4008, fax 580 6754)

CLIFT, Prof Roland; s of Leslie William Clift, of Wallington, Surrey, and Ivy Florence Gertrude, *née* Wheeler; *b* 19 Nov 1942; *Educ* Trinity Sch of John Whitgift Croydon, Trinity Coll Cambridge (scholar, BA, MA, TRC Fox prize for chemical engrg), McGill Univ Montreal (PhD); *m* 1, 14 Sept 1968, Rosena Valory, da of Robert Bruce Davison; 1 da (Vanessa b 14 July 1972); m 2, 3 March 1979, Diana Helen, da of William Reginald Dermot Manning; 2 s (Julian William Dermot b 2 Oct 1979, Adrian Manning b 3 July 1982); *Career* tech offr and chem engr Imperial Chemical Industries Ltd 1964-67; McGill Univ Montreal: lectr 1967-70, asst prof 1970-72, assoc prof 1972-75; visiting prof Universitá di Napoli 1973-74, lectr in chem engrg Imperial Coll London 1975-76; Univ of Cambridge: lectr in chem engrg 1976-81, fell of Trinity Coll 1978-81, praelector 1980-81; prof of chem engrg and head of Dept of Chem and Process Engrg Univ of Surrey 1981-, ed in chief Powder Technology 1987-; dir: Clifmar Associates Ltd 1986-, Particle Consultants Ltd 1988; Henry Marion Howe medal of American Soc for Metals 1976, Moulton medal of Inst of Chem Engrs 1979; hon citizen of Augusta Georgia 1987; FIChemE 1984 (MIChem 1979) FEng 1986; *Books* Bubbles, Drops and Particles (with J R Grace & M E Weber, 1978), Fluidization (ed with J F Davidson & D Harrison, 1985); *Recreations* music; *Style—* Prof Roland Clift; 93 Peperharow Rd, Godalming, Surrey GU7 2PN (☎ 0483 417922); Department of Chemical and Process Engineering, University of Surrey, Guildford, Surrey GU2 2XH (☎ 0483 509239, fax 0483 303807)

CLIFTON, Gerald Michael; s of Frederick Maurice Clifton (d 1988), of Rainford, Lancs, and Jane, *née* Hayes (d 1986); *b* 3 July 1947; *Educ* Liverpool Coll, Brasenose Coll Oxford (open classical scholar, MA); *m* 21 July 1973, Rosemary Anne Vera, da of Reginald Edward Jackson, of Birkdale, Southport; 2 s (Gerald Rupert Edward b 1977, Giles Michael Charles b 1980); *Career* called to the Bar Middle Temple 1970; asst rec of the Crown Ct 1982-88, rec Northern Circuit 1988-; *Recreations* sailing, tennis, walking, philately; *Clubs* West Kirby Sailing; *Style—* G M Clifton, Esq; Norton, 298 Telegraph Rd, Heswall, Wirral, Cheshire; Peel House, 5/7 Harrington St, Liverpool L2 9QA (☎ 051 236 4321)

CLIFTON, (John) Ian Ernest; s of John Clifton (d 1973), of Edinburgh, and Daisy, *née* Deacon; *b* 26 Aug 1932; *Educ* Boroughmuir HS Edinburgh, Skerry's Coll Edinburgh, Open Univ (BA); *m* 1957, Margaret Govenlock Hepburn; 1 s (Neil Ian b 5 Feb 1959), 1 da (Fiona Anne b 2 March 1965); *Career* athletics administrator; competitive career: Edinburgh Southern Harriers 1949-50 and 1957-65, Lincoln Wellington 1950-57; achievements: Edinburgh Southern Harriers youth champion 1950, Scot Boys' Brigade cross country champion 1950, E Counties cross country champion 1954-55, Lincs Co mile winner 1954-55, Manchester-Blackpool relay medal 1955; athletics admin 1966-; Edinburgh Southern Harriers: memb Ctee 1966-85, vice pres 1968-70 and 1977-78, pres 1970-71 and 1979-80; Scot Cross Country Union: memb Ctee 1974-, chm Organising Ctee World Cross Country Championships 1976-78, vice pres 1977-78, pres 1978-79, gen sec 1982-; sec UK Cross Country Cmmn 1989- (sr UK team mangr World Cross Country Championships 1990); Scot Amateur Athletics Assoc: memb Ctee 1979-88, vice pres 1985, pres 1986, immediate past pres 1987-88; memb: Scot Cwlth Games Cncl 1982-88, UK Civil Serv Athletic Assoc 1971-85, Ctee Scot Civil Serv Athletic Assoc 1972-85 (fndr sec 1972), Scot Civil Serv Sports Cncl 1971-85; Edinburgh Area Civil Serv Sports Assoc: memb 1971-85, chm 1982-85, life memb 1985; Civil Serv: clerical offr BT 1950-55, offr then higher exec offr Customs & Excise 1955-85, sr exec offr Customs & Excise 1985-; *Recreations* reading, hill walking, athletics and cross country; *Style—* Ian Clifton, Esq; 8 Craigshannoch Rd, Wormit, Fife DD6 8ND (☎ 0382 541815)

CLIFTON, Nigel John; s of Henry Clifton, of Helonsburgh, Dunbartonshire, and Pamela, *née* Damment; *b* 19 Nov 1951; *Educ* Wellinborough Sch, Univ of St Andrews (MA); *m* 1974, Elizabeth, *née* Dacre; 1 s (Andrew James b 1977); *Career* dep hosp admin Northern General Hosp Sheffield 1976-81, sr admin W Fife Hosp 1981-83; gen mangr: Community and Acute Servs Chesterfield Royal Hosp 1983-87, Univ Hosp Queens Med Centre Nottingham 1987-99; dist gen mangr Salisbury Health Authy 1990-; memb Inst Health Servs Mgmnt 1979; *Recreations* watching cricket, archery, cooking; *Style—* Nigel Clifton, Esq; Salisbury Health Authourity, Odstock Hospital, Salisbury, Wiltshire SP2 8BJ (☎ 0722 336262, car 0831 554924)

CLIFTON, Hon Mrs (Patricia Mairead Janet); *née* Anderson; da of 2 Viscount Waverley (d 1990), and Lorna Myrtle Ann, *née* Ledgerwood; *b* 2 March 1955; *m* 1, 1 June 1979 (m dis 1983); m 2, 6 May 1989, Leon Clifton, of Colorado, USA; 1 s (b 8 Sept 1990); *Recreations* 3 day eventing, dressage; *Clubs* Lansdowne; *Style—* The Hon Mrs Clifton; Chanders, Aldworth, Berks RG8 9RU

CLIFTON, Lt-Col Peter Thomas; CVO (1979), DSO (1945), DL (1954); s of Lt-Col Percy Clifton, CMG, DSO, TD (d 1945), of Clifton Hall, Nottingham, who was twin brother of Sir Hervey Ronald Bruce, 5 Bt (he assumed the surname Clifton by Royal Licence 1919), and his 2 wife Evelyn Mary Amelia (d 1969), da of Maj Thomas Leith, DL (nephew of Baron Burgh); *b* 24 Jan 1911; *Educ* Eton, RMC Sandhurst; *m* 1, 2 June 1934 (m dis 1936), Ursula Sybil, da of Sir Edward Hussey Packe, KBE, of Prestwold Hall, Leics; m 2, 1948, Patricia Mary Adela, yr da of late Maj James Miller Gibson-Watt, and wid of Maj Robert Nevill Cobbold, Welsh Guards; 2 da (*see* Seddon-Brown, Georgina Anne); *Career* 2 Lt Grenadier Gds 1931, Lt-Col 1944; memb HM Body Guard of Hon Corps of Gentlemen at Arms 1960-, Clerk of the Cheque and Adjutant 1973-79, Standard Bearer 1979-81, ret; JP: Notts 1952-59, Hants 1964-81; *Clubs* Royal Yacht Squadron, Cavalry and Guards, Whites; *Style—* Lt-Col Peter Clifton, CVO, DSO, DL; Dummer House, Basingstoke, Hants RG25 2AG (☎ 025 675 397306)

CLIFTON OF RATHMORE, Lord; Ivo Donald Stuart Bligh; s and h of 11 Earl of Darnley; *b* 17 April 1968; *Style—* Lord Clifton of Rathmore

CLIFTON-SAMUEL, Anthony David; s of David Clifton-Samuel (d 1960), of London, and Sarah Vera, *née* Cohen; *b* 25 June 1932; *Educ* Emscote Lawns Sch Warwickshire, Merchant Taylors, Univ Tutorial Coll The Royal Dental Hosp of London, Sch of Dental Surgery (BDS, LDS MRCS, The Parris prize, Robert Woodhouse prize); *m* 26 March 1961, Andrée Josephine, da of Alfred Falcke Fredericks; 1 s (Jason Ian b 1 April 1967), 1 da (Ruth Charlotte b 27 March 1965); *Career* Nat Serv Royal Army Dental Corps 1956-58 (Lt 1956, Capt 1957); OC Army Dental Centre Limassol 1956-57, Derna Cyrennaica 1957-58; in private practice 1958-60, own practice Kensington 1960-81 (Harley St 1965-); memb Kensington Chelsea & Westminster Local Dental Ctee 1964-, rep London Local Dental Ctee (later Fedn) 1966-88, dental rep St Charles Hosp Med Soc; Gen Dental Practitioners Assoc: joined 1962, chm Southern Branch 1970-85, vice chm Assoc 1978-79 and 1981-82, pres 1979-81, vice pres 1987-; memb BDA until 1970 (served on Rep Bd); *Recreations* motor boating, mechanical engineering, electronics, photography, DIY reading; *Clubs* Kensington Rotary, Royal Yachting Assoc; *Style—* Mr Anthony D Clifton-Samuel; 42 Harley St, London W1N 1AB (☎ 071 636 9789)

CLINCH, David John (Joe); s of Thomas Charles Clinch, of Surrey, and Madge Isobel, *née* Saker (d 1984); ancestors were brewers bankers and blanket Weavers of Witney; *b* 14 Feb 1937; *Educ* Nautical Coll Pangbourne, Univ of Durham (BA), Indiana Univ USA (MBA); *m* 1963, Hilary, da of John Herbert Jacques (d 1984), of Claxby, Lincs; 1 s (John), 1 da (Helen); *Career* Nat Serv 1955-57, RN Acting Sub-Lt; admin Univ of Sussex 1963-69, sec Open Univ 1981- (dep sec and registrar 1969-80); *Recreations* music, walking, bird watching; *Style—* Joe Clinch, Esq; 39 Tudor Gardens, Stony Stratford, Milton Keynes MK11 1HX (☎ 0908 562 475); The Open University, Walton Hall, Milton Keynes MK7 6AA (☎ 0908 653 213)

CLINCH, Brig John Charles (Johnny); CBE (1974); s of William Norman Charles Clinch, OBE (d 1964), of Brighton, and Alice Maude, *née* Whittington (d 1985); *b* 15 Aug 1921; *Educ* Brighton Coll; *m* 4 Jan 1947, Nan Rennie, da of Capt Norman Harold Zimmern, MC (d 1980), of Hampstead; 1 s (David b 15 May 1951), 1 da (Angela b 21 March 1948); *Career* Army Security Vetting Unit 1976-86, enlisted 1939, cmmnd Royal Signals 1941, Gds Armd Div 1941-45; serv: UK, NW, Europe, ME, Palestine 1945-47; instr RMA Sandhurst 1952-55, special emp Mil Forces Malaya 1955-58, cmd Queens Gurkha Signals 1962-65, CSO London Dist 1965-66, CAFSO RAF Germany 1966-69, cmd 4 Signal Gp 1969-70, Cmdt AAC Harrogate 1970-71, cmd 2 Signal Bde 1971-74, vice pres Regular Cmmn Bd 1974-76; chm The Radio Amateur Invalid and Blind Club; memb: Royal Br Legion, Radio Soc of GB; MBIM 1966; *Recreations* shooting, fly fishing, sailing, amateur radio (call sign G3MJK), gardening; *Clubs* former memb Army & Navy; *Style—* Brig Johnny Clinch, CBE; The Pippins, Dummer Road, Axford, Basingstoke, Hants RG25 2ED (☎ 0256 389439)

CLINTON, (Robert) Alan; s of John (d 1972), of Birmingham, and Leah Millington (d 1986); *b* 12 July 1931; *Educ* George Dixon GS Birmingham, Manchester Business Sch; *m* 1956, Valerie Joy, da of Herbert Allan Falconer (d 1981), of Birmingham; *Career* joined PO 1948, asst dir (personnel) PO HQ 1975, asst dir (operations) 1976, regional dir Eastern Postal Region 1978, dir Postal Operations 1979, memb PO Bd London 1981-85, resigned 1985; gp md Picton House Ltd 1986; dir: Picton House (Leicester) Ltd, Picton House Properties Ltd, Picton Homes Ltd, Picton Homes (Wales) Ltd 1986, Picton Homes (Gwent) Ltd, Picton House (W London) Ltd, Picton House Investments Ltd, Picton House Ltd, Picton House (East Anglia) Ltd, Pembroke Services Ltd 1988; Freeman City of London 1979, Liveryman Worshipful Co of Carmen 1981; FCIT 1982; *Recreations* music, walking, sailing; *Clubs* City of London, City Livery; Colne Yacht (Brightlinsea); *Style—* Alan Clinton, Esq; Summer Cottage,

The Quay, St Osyth, Clacton-on-Sea, Essex CO16 8EW (☎ 0255 820 360); Flat 19, No 4 Crane Court, Fleet St, London EC4A 2EJ (☎ 071 353 7509); Picton House Ltd, 108 Fenchurch St, London EC3M 5JJ (☎ 071 480 5740, fax 071 480 5745)

CLINTON-DAVIS, Baron (Life Peer UK 1990), of Hackney in the London Borough of Hackney; Stanley Clinton Clinton-Davis; s of Sidney Davis; assumed the surname of Clinton-Davis by Deed Poll 1990; *b* 6 Dec 1928; *Educ* Hackney Downs Sch, Mercers Sch, King's Coll London; *m* 1954, Frances Jane, *née* Lucas; 1 s, 3 da; *Career* MP (Lab) Hackney Central 1970-83, parly under sec Trade 1974-79, oppn front bench spokesman Trade 1979-81, Foreign and Cwlth Affrs 1981-83; Parly candidate: Portsmouth Langstone 1955, Yarmouth 1959 & 1964; memb APEX, pres Br Multiple Sclerosis Soc (Hackney Branch), cnclir (Hackney) 1959-71, Mayor Hackney 1968-69; slr 1953-; memb: Cmmn of Euro Communities (responsible for tport, environmental and nuclear safety) 1985-89, Cncl Zoological Soc; vice pres: Soc of Lab Lawyers 1987-, Inst of Environmental Health Officers; tstee: Int Shakespeare Globe Centre, Bernt Carlsson Tst; hon memb Exec Cncl of Justice, memb UN Selection Ctee Sasakawa Enviroment Project 1989-, dir Jewish Chronicle 1989-, conslt on euro law and affrs with S J Berwin & Co slrs 1989-; pres: Euro Cockpit Assoc 1990-, Huddleston Centre, Soc of Lab Lawyers 1990-; chm Refugee Cncl 1989-; Grand Cross Order of Leopold II (Belgium) for servs to the EC (1990); *Books* Report of a British Parliamentary Delegation (jtly, 1982); *Recreations* reading political biographies, golf, watching assoc football; *Style*— The Rt Hon Lord Clinton-Davis; 22 Bracknell Gate, Hampstead, London NW3

CLITHEROE, 2 Baron (UK 1955), also 3 Bt (UK 1945) Ralph John Assheton; DL (Lancs); Lord of the Honour of Clitheroe and Hundred of Blackburn; s of 1 Baron Clitheroe, KCVO, PC (d 1984), and Hon Sylvia Benita Frances, *née* Hotham (d 1991), er da of 6 Baron Hotham; *b* 3 Nov 1929; *Educ* Eton, ChCh Oxford (MA); *m* 2 May 1961, Juliet, o da of Lt-Col Christopher Lionel Hanbury, MBE, TD; 2 s (Ralph, John), 1 da (Elizabeth); *Heir* s, Hon Ralph Christopher Assheton, *qv*; *Career* late Life Guards; former dir: RTZ Corporation plc, First Interstate Bank of California, American Mining Congress; former chm RTZ Borax, currently chm The Yorkshire Bank PLC and dir Halliburton Company; Liveryman Worshipful Co of Skinners'; *Clubs* Boodle's, Pratt's, RAC; *Style*— The Rt Hon Lord Clitheroe; Downham Hall, Clitheroe, Lancs BB7 4DN

CLIVE, Eric McCredie; s of Robert M Clive (d 1971), and Mary, *née* McCredie (d 1976); *b* 24 July 1938; *Educ* Stranraer Acad, Stranraer HS, Univ of Edinburgh (MA LLB), Univ of Michigan (LLM), Univ of Virginia (SJD); *m* 6 Sept 1962, Kay, da of Rev Alastair McLeman (d 1940); 4 c (Gael b 6 Sept 1963, Alastair M M b 19 March 1965, Sally b 22 March 1968, Rachel b 9 Sept 1969); *Career* slr; Univ of Edinburgh: lectr 1962-69, sr lectr 1969-75, reader 1975-77, prof of Scots law 1977-81; memb Scottish Law Commission 1981-; *Books* Law of Husband and Wife in Scotland (1974, 2 edn 1982), Scots Law for Journalists (jtly 1965, 5 edn 1988); *Recreations* hill walking, chess; *Style*— Eric Clive, Esq; Scottish Law Commission, 140 Causewayside, Edinburgh (☎ 031 668 2131)

CLIVE, Viscount; John George Herbert; eldest s and h of 7 Earl of Powis, *qv*; *b* 19 May 1952; *Educ* Wellington Coll, McMaster Univ Ontario (MA); *m* 1977, Marijke, eldest da of Maarten N Guther, of Hamilton, Ontario, Canada; 1 son (Hon Jonathan Nicholas William), 2 da (Hon Stephanie Moira Christina b 1982, Hon Samantha Julie Esther b 1988); *Heir* s, Hon Jonathan Nicholas William Herbert b 5 Dec 1979; 284 Wilson Street West, Ancaster, Ontario, Canada; 284 Wilson Street West, Ancaster, Ontario, Canada

CLIVE, Lady Mary Katharine; *née* Pakenham; 2 da of 5 Earl of Longford, KP, MVO (ka 1915); *b* 23 Aug 1907; *m* 30 Dec 1939, Maj Meysey George Dallas Clive, Grenadier Gds (ka 1 May 1943), er s of late Lt-Col Percy Archer Clive, MP, JP, DL, of Whitfield, Hereford; 1 s, 1 da; *Books* Christmas with the Savages (1955), The Day of Reckoning (1964), This Son of York (1973); *Style*— The Lady Mary Clive; Whitfield, Allensmore, Herefordshire

CLIVE-PONSONBY-FANE, Charles Edward Brabazon; JP (1979); s of late Nicholas Brabazon Clive-Ponsonby-Fane, 2 s of Edward Clive (1 cous four times removed of (Robert) Clive of India) by Edward's w Violet, ggda of 4 Earl of Bessborough by Lady Maria Fane (da of 10 Earl of Westmorland); Nicholas m, Petronilla Dunsterville, whose mother was Eveline, da of Sir Frederick Goldney, 3 and penultimate Bt, JP; *b* 10 Aug 1941; *Educ* Harrow, L'Institut de Touraine France, RAC Cirencester; *m* 1974, Judy Barbara, *née* Bushby; 1 s, 2 da; *Career* viticulturalist, distiller; High Sheriff of Somerset 1984; *Books* We Started a Stately Home (1980); *Recreations* cricket; *Clubs* I Zingari; *Style*— Charles Clive-Ponsonby-Fane, Esq, JP; Brympton d'Evercy, Yeovil, Somerset BA22 8TD

CLOAKE, Graham Arthur; s of late Wilfred Cloake; *b* 1 Jan 1934; *Educ* Badingham Coll; *m* 1961, Jennifer Noel, da of late Frank Sidney Smith, of New Malden, Surrey; 2 s, 1 da; *Career* dir: Greenwell Montagu Stockbrokers, Effess Farms Ltd; *Recreations* gardening, swimming; *Clubs* City of London; *Style*— Graham Cloake, Esq; 13 Preston Rd, Wimbledon, London SW20 (☎ 081 947 2962); Greenwell Montagu Stockbrokers, 114 Old Broad St, London EC2 (☎ 071 588 8817)

CLOAKE, John Cecil; CMG (1977); s of late Dr Cecil Stedman Cloake, of Wimbledon, and Maude Osborne *née* Newling; *b* 2 Dec 1924; *Educ* KCS Wimbledon, Peterhouse Cambridge; *m* 1956, Margaret Thomure Morris, of Washington, DC, USA; 1 s; *Career* Army 1943-46; Dip Serv 1948-81; cnsllr (commercial) Tehran 1968-72, head Trade Relations and Exports Dept FCO 1973-76, ambass to Bulgaria 1976-80; hon treas Br Inst of Persian Studies 1982-90; chm: Richmond Local History Soc 1985-90 (pres 1990-), Museum of Richmond 1986-; *Books* Templer, Tiger of Malaya (1985); *Style*— John Cloake Esq, CMG; 4 The Terrace, 140 Richmond Hill, Richmond, Surrey TW10 6RN

CLODE, Dame (Emma) Frances Heather; *née* Marc; DBE (1974, CBE 1969, OBE 1955, MBE 1951); da of Alexander Marc, and Florence Marc; *b* 12 Aug 1903; *Educ* privately; *m* 1927, Col Charles Mathew Clode, MC (d 1948), s of Sir Walker Baker Clode, KC; 1 s (Walter); *Career* WRVS: joined 1939, serv Cambridge 1940-45, HQ 1945, chm 1971-74 (vice chm 1967); CStJ 1973; *Style*— Dame Frances Clode, DBE; 19 Rushers Close, Pershore, Worcs, WR10 1HF

CLODE, Michael Leslie Hailey; s of Capt Roger Leslie Clode, RN, of Kynance, 22 Cheltenham Crescent, Lee-on-Solent, Hants, and Patricia Mary, *née* Kyd; *b* 5 Oct 1943; *Educ* St Edward Sch Oxford; *m* 4 April 1970, Isobel McLeod, da of Henry Watson Carrick (d 1976); 4 da (Fiona b 1972, Alison b 1974, Jennifer b 1977, Camilla b 1982); *Career* slr; ptnr Freshfields 1974-, memb Cncl St Leonards Sch St Andrews Fife; Freeman: City of London, Worshipful Co of Solicitors; memb Law Soc; *Recreations* skiing, breeding Aberdeen Angus Cattle; *Style*— Michael Clode, Esq; 56 Brompton Square, London SW3 2AG; Chesters, Orchard Way, Esher, Surrey KT10 9DY; Little Kilry, By Blairgowrie, Perthshire PH11 8HY; Freshfields, Whitefriars, 65 Fleet St, London EC4Y 1HT (☎ 071 936 4000, fax 071 248 3487, telex 889292)

CLOGHER, Bishop of 1986-; Rt Rev Brian Desmond Anthony Hannon; s of the Ven (Arthur) Gordon Hannon (d 1978), and Hilda Catherine Stewart-Moore, *née* Denny; *b* 5 Oct 1936; *Educ* St Columbia's Coll Dublin, Trinity Coll Dublin (BA, MA); *m* 10 Sept 1964, Maeve Geraldine Audley, *née* Butler, da of Capt Edward Walter Charles Butler (d 1988); 3 s (Desmond b 1965, Brendan b 1968, Neil b 1970); *Career* ordained C of I: deacon 1961, priest 1962; Diocese of Derry: curate All Saints Clooney 1961-64, rector Desertmartin 1964-69, rector Christ Church Londonderry 1969-82, rural dean Londonderry 1977-82; Diocese of Clogher: rector St Macartin's Cath Enniskillen 1982-86, canon Clogher Cath 1982, dean 1985, bishop 1986; memb Central Ctee World Cncl of Churches 1983-91, chm Western Educn and Library Bd NI 1985-87 and 1989-91; Athletics: capt Dublin Univ 1958, All Ireland 440 Hurdles Champion 1959, Trinity Pink; memb House of Bishops (C of I); *Recreations* walking, travel, photography, music; *Clubs* Friendly Brothers of St Patrick (Dublin), Knights of Campanile (Dublin); *Style*— The Rt Rev Brian D A Hannon; The See House, Fivemiletown, Co Tyrone, N Ireland BT75 0QP, NI (☎ 03655 21265)

CLOGHER, Bishop (RC) of 1979-; Most Rev Joseph Augustine; s of Edward Duffy (d 1956), and Brigid MacEntee (d 1963); *b* 3 Feb 1934; *Educ* Maynooth (BD), Nat Univ of Ireland (MA, HDipEd); *Books* Patrick In His Own Words (1985), Lough Derg Guide (1978); *Recreations* history, travel; *Style*— The Most Rev the Bishop of Clogher; Bishop's House, Monaghan, Ireland (☎ 047 81019)

CLOKE, Anthony John (Tony); s of Maj John Nicholas Cloke (d 1985), of Walsall, and May Eddy, *née* Craghill; *b* 10 Jan 1943; *Educ* Queen Mary's GS Walsall, Clare Coll Cambridge (MA); *m* 7 June 1969, Ann Gwendoline, da of Bertie Cordy (d 1981), of Usk; 2 s (John b 1970, Richard b 1972), 1 da (Caroline b 1974); *Career* admitted slr 1970; ptnr Peter Peter and Wright (and its predecessors) 1973-; slr of the Supreme Ct 1970; widespread involvement in local orgns and activities; *Recreations* farming, golf; *Style*— Tony Cloke, Esq; Peter, Peter and Wright, 1 West Street, Okehampton, Devon (☎ 0837 2379, fax 0837 3604)

CLOKE, Richard Owen; s of late Owen William Cloke, MBE, of 25 Priests Lane, Brentwood, Essex, and Barbara Ethel Beatrice *née* Abbott; *b* 3 May 1944; *Educ* Reading Sch; *m* 26 June 1969, Carol Ann, da of Frank Wadsworth; 2 s (Ian, Andrew), 1 da (Jackie); *Career* branch mangr Barclays Bank plc 1979-83 (joined 1960, asst district mangr 1976-79), asst dir Barclays Merchant Bank Ltd 1983-85, dir Barclays de Zoete Wedd Ltd 1986-; *Recreations* tennis, badminton, golf; *Style*— Richard Cloke, Esq; Barclays De Zoete Wedd Ltd, Ebbgate House, 2 Swan Lane, London, EC4R 3TS, (☎ 071 956 3132, fax 071 956 4296)

CLORE, Melanie Sarah Jane; da of Martin Clore, of London, and Cynthia Clore; *b* 28 Jan 1960; *Educ* Channing Sch Highgate, Univ of Manchester (BA); *Career* Sotheby's: graduate trainee 1981, jr cataloguer in Impressionist and Modern Art Dept 1982, auctioneer 1985-, departmental dir of Impressionist and Modern Art Dept 1986, dir 1988-; fndn tstee Whitechapel Art Gallery 1988-; *Recreations* travel, cinema; *Clubs* Groucho; *Style*— Ms Melanie Clore; Director, Impressionist and Modern Art Dept, Sotheby's, 34-35 New Bond St, London W1A 2AA (☎ 071 408 5394)

CLOSE, David John; s of John Edward Close (d 1969); *b* 10 May 1929; *Educ* Queen Elizabeth's GS Mansfield, King's Coll London; *m* 1971, Jan, *née* Wileman; 2 da; *Career* personnel offr NCB 1956-63, gp personnel mangr Sangamo Weston 1963-64, personnel mangr Pirelli 1965-69; personnel and admin dir: Davy and Utd Engr 1969-71, Kearney and Trecker 1971-73; gen personnel mangr Reliant Motor Co 1973-74; personnel dir Simon Engrg (contracting gp) 1974-83, gp human resources dir Simon Engrg plc 1983-; FIPM, FBIM, FIIM; *Recreations* walking, gardening, DIY, music; *Style*— David Close, Esq

CLOSE, Richard Charles; s of Lt-Col Richard Alwen Close, and Marjorie Anne, *née* Bartlett; *b* 3 Sept 1949; *Educ* Canford, Sidney Sussex Coll Cambridge (MA); *m* 4 Aug 1973, (Elizabeth) Janet Beatrice, da of Gavin Leggat Brown; 1 s (Thomas b 20 Jan 1986), 1 da (Lisa b 16 May 1982); *Career* audit mangr Arthur Young Milan 1974-81, euro treas Sperry Corpn 1984-86 (regnl dir Internal Audit 1981-84), fin dir Unisys Ltd 1986-87, memb Bd Corp Fin and Planning The PO 1989- (dir Corp Fin 1987-89); memb ICA 1974; ACT 1985, FCA 1979; *Recreations* tennis, fishing, walking; *Style*— Richard Close, Esq; Post Office Headquarters, 30 St James's Sq, London SW17 4PY (☎ 071 389 8050, fax 071 389 8074, car 0831 513215)

CLOSE-BROOKS, Jonathan Roger; s of Roger Close-Brooks, DSO (d 1980), and Marian, *née* Beesly; *b* 26 Dec 1943; *Educ* Radley, Oriel Coll Oxford (MA); *m* 24 July 1971, Carolyn Elizabeth Rosemary, da of Brig Gilbert Coghlan Wells, CBE, MC; 2 s (Oliver Charles Roger b 14 May 1978, Henry Roland Gilbert b 13 May 1984), 1 da (Camilla Margaret Jane b 12 July 1985); *Career* articled clerk Jackson Pixley (accountants) 1966-69; ptnr: S R Scott Stratten & Co (stockbrokers) 1971-74 (trainee clerk 1969-71), Seymour Pierce and Co (incorporating SR Scott Stratten and Co) 1976-87 (assoc 1974-76); dir: Seymour Pierce & Co Ltd 1987, Seymour Pierce Butterfield Ltd 1987-; memb Int Stock Exchange 1971; *Recreations* skiing, boating, bicycling; *Clubs* Leander, Oriel Tortoise Boat; *Style*— Jonathan Close-Brooks, Esq; 71 Blenheim Crescent, London W11 2EG (☎ 071 229 0545); Seymour Pierce Butterfield Ltd, 10 Old Jewry, London EC2R 8EA (☎ 071 628 4981, fax 071 606 2405)

CLOTHIER, Sir Cecil Montacute; KCB (1982), QC (1965); s of Hugh Montacute Clothier (d 1961), of Blundellsands, Liverpool; *b* 28 Aug 1919; *Educ* Stonyhurst, Lincoln Coll Oxford (BCL, MA); *m* 1943, Mary Elizabeth (d 1984), da of Ernest Glover Bush (d 1962), of Aughton, Lancs; 1 s, 2 da; *Career* served WWII 51 Highland Div, Army Staff Washington DC, Hon Lt-Col Royal Signals; called to the Bar Inner Temple 1950, bencher 1972, rec Blackpool 1965-72, judge Ct of Appeal IOM 1972-78, legal assessor to Gen Medical and Gen Dental Cncls 1972-78; memb Royal Cmmn on NHS 1976-78, Parly cmmr Administration and Health Service of England Wales and Scotland 1979-84; chm: Police Complaints Authy 1985-89, Cncl on Tbnls 1989-; Rock Carling fell 1988; Hon LLD Univ of Hull 1983; hon fell Lincoln Coll Oxford 1984, hon memb Assoc of Anaesthetists, hon FRPharmS 1990-; *Clubs* Athenaeum; *Style*— Sir Cecil Clothier, KCB, QC; 2 King's Bench Walk, Temple, London EC4Y 7DE

CLOUDSLEY-THOMPSON, Prof John Leonard; s of Dr Ashley George Gyton Thompson (d 1983), and Muriel Elaine, *née* Griffiths; *b* 23 May 1921; *Educ* Marlborough, Pembroke Coll Cambridge (BA, MA, PhD), Univ of London (DSc); *m* May 1944, (Jessie) Anne, da of Capt John Leslie Cloudsley (d 1968); 3 s (Hugh b 1944, Timothy b 1948, Peter b 1952); *Career* cmmnd 4 QOH 1941, transferred 4 Co London Yeo (Sharpshooters), served N Africa (Opn Crusader) 1941-42, Knightsbridge tank battle (severely wounded), instr Sandhurst (Capt) 1943, rejoined Regt for D Day (escaped from Villers Bocage), served Caen offensive (Operation Goodwood) 1944, Hon Rank of Capt on resignation; lectr in zoology King's Coll London 1950-60 (awarded PhD), prof of zoology Univ of Khartoum and keeper Sudan Natural History Museum 1960-71, prof of zoology (now emeritus prof) Birkbeck Coll Univ of London 1972-86 (Leverhulme emeritus fell 1987-89), memb Sci Fndn, sr res fell Univ of Mexico Albuquerque 1969; visiting prof: Univ of Kuwait 1978 and 1983, Univ of Nigeria 1981, Univ of Qatar 1986, Sultan Qaboos Univ Muscat 1988; visiting res fell ANU 1987; Namib Desert Ecological Res Unit 1989, chm Br Naturalists Assoc 1974-83 (vice pres 1985-), Biological Cncl 1977-82 (medal 1985); pres: Br Arachnological Soc 1982-85 (vice pres 1985-86), Br Soc for Chronobiology 1985-87; vice pres: Linnean Soc 1975-76 and 1977-78, first World Congress of Herpetology 1989; hon memb: Royal African Soc 1969- (medal 1969), Br Herpetological Soc 1983-; KSS Charter award Inst of Biology 1981, JH Grundy medal RAMC 1987; ed Journal of Arid Environments 1978-; Freeman City of London 1945, Liveryman Worshipful Co of Skinners 1952; Hon DSc and gold medal Univ of Khartoum 1981; FIBiol 1962, FWA

1962, FRES, FLS, FZS; *Books* 50 books incl: Spiders, Scorpions, Centipedes and Mites (1958), Zoology of Tropical Africa (1969), The Temperature and Water Relations of Reptiles (1971), Insects and History (1976), Why the Dinosaurs Became Extinct (1978), Tooth and Claw (1980), Evolution and Adaptation of Terrestial Arthropods (1988), Ecophysiology of Desert Arthropods and Reptiles (1991), Nile Quest (novel, 1991); *Recreations* music (especially opera), photography, travel; *Style—* Prof Cloudsley-Thompson; Flat 9, 4 Craven Hill, London W2 3DS (☎ 071 723 5214); Department of Biology (Medawar Building), UCL, Univ of London, Gower St, London WC1E 6BT (☎ 071 387 7050, ext 3587)

CLOUGH, (John) Alan; CBE (1972), MC (1945); s of John Clough (d 1982), and Yvonne, *née* Dollfus; *b* 20 March 1924; *Educ* Marlborough, Univ of Leeds; *m* 1, 1949 (m dis 1961), Margaret Joy, da of A Catton, of Kirkby Overblow; 1 s, 2 da; m 2, 1961, Mary Cowan, da of Harold Mathew Stuart Catherwood; 1 s, 1 da; *Career* Capt, serv N Africa and Italy 1943-47, Maj TA Yorks Hussars 1947-53; chm: Wool Industs Res Assoc 1967-69, Wool Textile Delgn 1969-72; pres: Br Textile Confedn 1974-77, Comitextil-Brussels (co-ordinating Ctee for Textile Industries in EEC) 1975-77, Textile Inst 1979-81, Confedn of Br Wool Textiles 1982-84; chm: Br Mohair Spinners Ltd to 1984, Textile Res Cncl 1984-89, Instant Muscle 1989-; Past Mayor Co of Merchants of the Staple of England; *Recreations* travelling, gardening, fishing; *Clubs* Boodle's; *Style—* Alan Clough, Esq, CBE, MC; The Hays, Monks Eleigh, Suffolk

CLOUGH, (Arthur) Gordon; s of James Stanley Gordon Clough (d 1965), and Annie, *née* Pickston; *b* 26 Aug 1934; *Educ* Bolton Sch, Magdalen Coll Oxford (BA, William Doncaster scholar); *m* June 1959, Carolyn Stafford; 1 s (Jonathan b 1960), 3 da (Penelope b 1963, Elizabeth b 1966, Eleanor b 1970); *Career* Nat Serv Lt Cdr (S) RN 1953-55; BBC: studio mangr 1958-60, Russian prog organiser 1960-68, duty ed Radio News Features 1968-73; freelance presenter: World at One, PM, World This Weekend 1973-; co-chm: Round Britain Quiz, Round Europe Quiz, Transatlantic Quiz 1976-; documentary feature writer and reporter Radio 4: Let There Be No More War, Revolution without Shots, The Indissoluble Union, Whose Shall Be The Land, Death of a Superpower; awards: Sony Radio awards (for World this Weekend 1986, Indissoluble Union 1990); *Publications* trans from Russian: Years off my Life by Gen A V Gorbatov (with Tony Cash, 1964), The Ordeal by V Bykov (1972), Hostages by G Svirsky (1976), The Yawning Heights by A Zinoviev (1979), The Radiant Future by A Zinoviev (1981); trans from French: The Elusive Revolution by Raymond Aron (1971), The Art of the Surrealists by A Alexandrian (1972), Octobriana: Progressive Political Pornography (1972); author of occasional articles in The Listener etc; *Recreations* cooking, crossword puzzles, coarse chess; *Style—* Gordon Clough, Esq

CLOUGH, Prunella; da of Eric Clough Taylor, and Thora Clough Taylor; *Educ* Chelsea Sch of Art; *Career* painter; clerical and draughtsman's wartime jobs 1940-45, former teacher Chelsea Sch of Art, teacher Wimbledon Sch of Art; solo exhibitions: Leger Gallery 1947, Roland Browse and Delblanco 1949, Leicester Galleries London 1953, Whitechapel Gallery 1960, Grosvenor Gallery 1964 and 1967, Graves Art Gallery Sheffield 1972, New Art Centre 1973, 1975, 1976, 1979, 1982, Serpentine Gallery 1976, Nat Gallery of Modern Art Edinburgh 1976, Artspace Galleries Aberdeen 1981, Fitzwilliam Museum Cambridge 1982, Warwick Arts Trust 1982, Annely Juda Fine Art 1989; gp exhibitions incl: Pittsburgh Int (Carnegie Inst) 1950, Vision and Reality (Wakefield City Art Gallery) 1956, Museum of Modern Art Oxford 1966, Desborough Gallery (Perth Aust) 1974, Br Art 1952-1977 (Royal Acad) 1977, Studio ODD Hiroshima 1984, Albermarle Gallery 1988; collections incl: Clare Coll Cambridge, Art Gallery of NSW, Tate Gallery, V & A, Nuffield Fndn, DES; City of London Midsummer prize 1977; *Style—* Ms Prunella Clough

CLOVER, Charles Robert Harold; s of Harold Percy Clover (d 1973), and Diana Patricia Hutchinson, *née* Smith (d 1975); *b* 22 Aug 1958; *Educ* Westminster, Univ of York (BA); *m* Pamela Anne, da of Leonard C Roberts; *Career* asst ed The Spectator 1979; Daily Telegraph: features sub ed 1981, reporter Peterborough Column 1982, rock critic 1983-86, TV critic and feature writer 1986-87, environment corr 1987-89, environment ed 1989-; nat jounalist Media Natura's Br environment and media awards 1989; *Recreations* fly fishing, American black music, exploring the countryside; *Style—* Charles Clover, Esq; Daily Telegraph, 181 Marsh Wall, London E14 (☎ 071 538 6409, fax 071 538 7842)

CLOVER, His Hon (Robert) Gordon; TD (1951), QC (1958); s of Lt-Col Henry Edward Clover (d 1964), and Catherine Clifford Clover (d 1965); *b* 14 Nov 1911; *Educ* Lancing, Exeter Coll Oxford (MA, BCL); *m* 1947, Elizabeth Suzanne, da of Archibald McCorquodale (d 1920); 2 s (Thomas, Stephen); *Career* served in RA 1939-45, N Africa and Italy (despatches 1944); called to the Bar 1935, practised on Northern Circuit 1936-61, rec Blackpool 1960-61, dep cmmr for purposes of Nat Insur Acts 1961-65, dep chm QS Bucks 1969-71, former Co Ct judge, circuit judge 1965-82; *Style—* His Hon Gordon Clover, TD, QC; 10 Westcliff, Sheringham, Norfolk NR26 8JT

CLOW, Robert Christopher; s of Ronald Robert Clow, of 16 Hudson Close, Dovercourt, Essex, and Esme Joan, *née* Street; *b* 27 March 1948; *Educ* Aloysius Coll Highgate; *m* 1, 2 Feb 1969 (m dis 1978), Monica Mary, *née* Stratta; 2 da (Sandra Monica b 1969, Sarah Jennifer b 1971); m 2, 21 July 1981, Philippa, da of Capt Edward Atkinson (d 1970); *Career* CA 1973, ptnr Gordon Kanter & Co 1975-81, sole practitioner 1981-; FCA 1978; *Recreations* squash, sub-aqua, sailing, bridge, theatre, gardening; *Clubs* RAC; *Style—* Robert Clow, Esq; Netherfield, 10 Batchworth Lane, Northwood, Middx (☎ 092 74 25715); 18a Northampton Square, London EC1 (☎ 081 428 4038)

CLOWES, Alfred William; s of Alfred Clowes (d 1973), of Stoke on Trent, and Mary Ann, *née* Cain (d 1974); *b* 17 Dec 1931; *Educ* Hanley County GS Stoke on Trent; *m* 31 March 1956, Joan, da of Thomas Colclough (d 1978), of Cheddleton, nr Leek, Staffs; 2 da (Angela b 1957, Julie b 1960); *Career* gen sec Ceramic and Allied Trades Union 1980- (asst gen sec 1975-80); *Recreations* golf; *Clubs* Westwood Golf (Staffs); Ceramic and Allied Trades Union, Hillcrest House, Garth Street, Hanley, Stoke-on-Trent, Staffs ST1 2AB (☎ 0782 272755, fax 0782 284902)

CLOWES, Col Sir Henry Nelson; KCVO (1981, CVO 1977), DSO (1945), OBE (1953); yr s of Maj Ernest William Clowes, DSO (d 1951), of Bradley Hall, Ashbourne, Derbys, by his w Blanche, da of Rear Adm Hon Algernon Littleton, who was 2 s of 2 Baron Hatherton; the Admiral's w was Lady Margaret Needham, sis of 2 Earl of Kilmorey; *b* 21 Oct 1911; *Educ* Eton, Sandhurst; *m* 1941, Diana Katharine, MBE, da of Maj Basil Kerr, DSC (d 1957; himself ggs of 6 Marquess of Lothian by his 2 w, who was Lady Harriet Scott, da of 3 Duke of Buccleuch); 1 s (Capt Andrew Henry Clowes, Scots Gds (ret 1967), sometime Equerry to HRH The (1) Duke of Gloucester, m 1967, Georgiana, da of Richard Cavendish, of Holker Hall, Cumbria); *Career* served Scots Gds 1931-57 (cmd 2 Bn then 1 Bn, Lt-Col cmdg 1954-57, ret 1957); Lt Hon Corps Gentlemen at Arms 1976-81 (joined 1961, Clerk of the Cheque and Adj 1966, Standard Bearer 1973-76); *Recreations* gardening, shooting, fishing, travel; *Clubs* Cavalry and Guards, Shikar, Pratt's; *Style—* Colonel Sir Henry Clowes, KCVO, DSO, OBE; 57 Perrymead St, London SW6 3SN (☎ 071 736 7901)

CLOWES, Lady Rose; *née* Nevill; 3 and yst da of 5 Marquess of Abergavenny; *b* 15 July 1950; *m* 8 March 1990, George Mark Somerset Clowes, er s of Archibald Somerset Clowes, of Ashlands, Billesdon, Leics; 1 s (Toby Harry Somerset b 24 Nov 1990); *Style—* The Lady Rose Clowes; c/o The Most Hon the Marquess of Abergavenny, KG, OBE, Eridge Park, Tunbridge Wells, Kent, TN3 9JT

CLUBB, Dr Alexander William; s of Alexander Geddes Clubb (d 1982), and Isabella, *née* Shivas; *b* 7 May 1931; *Educ* Banchory Acad, Univ of Aberdeen (MB ChB); *m* 1 Aug 1958, Hylda Mary (Hylary), da of Edward Foster (d 1980); 2 s (Angus Stanley, Donald William), 1 da (Elspeth Mary); *Career* Capt and Sr Surgn RAMC; registrar City Gen Hosp Sheffield, sr registrar Birmingham RHA, conslt N Staffs AHA, vice pres Stoke City FC 1987- (dir 1973-87); dir: Mail Order Med Supplies Ltd, Pathtec Laboratory Servs Ltd; GSM Cyprus 1961; memb: BMA, ARM 1966-68; FInstD 1987; *Recreations* squash; *Clubs* Trentham Golf; *Style—* Dr Alexander Clubb; The Woodlands, Granville Terrace, Stone, Staffs ST15 8DF (☎ 0785 812663); Keele Univ, Pathtec Lab Servs Ltd, Old Chemistry Block, Keele, Staffs ST5 5JX (☎ 0782 620062, fax 0782 620250, car 0860 388245)

CLUCAS, Sir Kenneth Henry; KCB (1976, CB 1969); o s of Rev J H Clucas (d 1963); *b* 18 Nov 1921; *Educ* Kingswood Sch, Emmanuel Coll Cambridge; *m* 1960, Barbara, da of Rear Adm R P Hunter, USN (ret), of Washington, DC, USA; 2 da; *Career* served WWII RCS; civil serv: second sec lab HM Embassy Cairo 1950, under sec Miny of Lab 1966-68, sec Nat Bd Prices and Incomes 1968-71, dep sec CSD and first CS Cmmr 1971-73, dep sec DTI 1974; perm sec: Dept of Prices and Consumer Protection 1974-79, Dept of Trade 1979-82 (ret); memb Cncl on Tbnls 1983-89, chm: Nat Assoc of Citizens' Advice Bureaux 1984-89, Nuffield Fndn Ctee of Inquiry into Pharmacy 1983-86; memb Cncl Fin Intermediaries Mangrs and Brokers Regulatory Assoc 1986, member's Ombudsman Lloyds of London 1988-; Hon FRPharmS 1989; *Style—* Sir Kenneth Clucas, KCB; Cariad, Knoll Rd, Godalming, Surrey (☎ 0483 416430)

CLUETT, Shelagh; da of Edwin Geoffrey Cluett (d 1986), and Majorie Mary, *née* Gatehouse (d 1978); *b* 17 Dec 1947; *Educ* Brockenhurst St Martins Sch of Art, Hornsey Coll of Art (BA), Chelsea Sch of Art (higher postgrad dip); *Career* Chelsea Sch of Art (princ lectr in MA Sculpture 1980-), visiting artist: Central Sch of Art, Wolverhampton Poly, Sheffield Poly, NE London Poly, Bath Acad, Canterbury Coll of Art, Univ of Syracuse, RCA, Royal Acad of Art, Slade Sch, Edinburgh Coll of Art, Univ of Ulster, Duncan of Jordanstown, S Glamorgan Inst, Manchester Poly, N Staffordshire Poly, Newcastle Poly, Brighton Poly, Portsmouth Poly, Winchester Sch of Art, Gloucestershire Coll of the Arts, Ecole des Beaux Arts Macon (Erasmus project in collaboration with Brera Acad Milan); external examiner CNAA for Bahons, MA, MPhil progs at various insts incl: Middlesex Poly, Glasgow Sch of Art, Newcastle Poly; exhibitions incl: 7+4 (Richard Demarco Gallery Edinburgh) 1974, Cleveland Int Drawing Biennale 1977, 12 sculptors (WSCAD Gallery) 1978, The First Exhibition (Nicola Jacobs Gallery) 1979, New Sculpture (Ikon Gallery Birmingham) 1979, 55 Wapping Artists (London) 1979, Kunst Idag 1 (Ordropgaard Copenhagen) 1980, Eight Women Artists (Acme Gallery) 1980, 30 ex-ILEA (Whitechapel Art Gallery) 1981, One Person Show (Nicola Jacobs Gallery, Paris Biennale) 1982, Musee des Beaux Arts (Tourcoing France) 1982, Dienst Beelende Kunst (Kruithuis Den Bosch Holland) 1983, Nocturn (Siegal Contemporary Art NY), One Person Show (Nicola Jacobs Gallery) 1984, One Person Show (Herbert Art Gallery Coventry) 1985, The Last Wapping Show 1985, The National Garden Festival (Stoke on Trent) 1986, Nicola Jacobs Gallery 1986, Metal and Motion (Brighton Museum and touring) 1987, Recent Acquisitions of C A S (Mayor Gallery) 1988, Royal Academy Summer Exhibition 1989; study visits: Burma, Thailand, Malaysia and Sumatra 1988, Laos and Vietnam 1990; memb: Fine Art Bd Panel CNAA 1983-88, Ctee Art Accord, Sculpture Panel Br Sch at Rome; exhibition selector: New Contempories (ICA), Midland View (Midland Gp Nottingham), Camden Open (Camden Inst); *Recreations* travel; *Clubs* Chelsea Arts; *Style—* Ms Shelagh Cluett; Chelsea College of Art & Design, Manresa Rd, London SW3 6LS (☎ 071 351 3844, fax 071 352 8721)

CLUFF, John Gordon (Algy); s of Harold Cluff (d 1989), and Freda Cluff; *b* 19 April 1940; *Educ* Stowe; *Career* Mil Serv: Lt Gren Gds 1959-62, Capt Gds Parachute Co 1962-64, serv W Africa, Cyprus, Malaysia; chm and chief exec Cluff Resources, chm The Spectator; dir: Apollo Magazine, Henry Sotheran & Sons; Parly candidate (C) Ardwick Manchester 1966; tstee Anglo-Hong Kong Tst; *Clubs* White's, Beefsteak, Boodle's, Royal Northern (Aberdeen); *Style—* Algy Cluff, Esq; 58 St James's St, London SW1 (☎ 071 493 8272)

CLUGSTON, John Westland Antony; s of Leonard Gordon Clugston, OBE, DL (d 1984), and Sybil Mary Bacon (d 1981); *b* 16 May 1938; *Educ* Sandroyd, Gordonstoun; *m* 1, 6 June 1969, Patricia, da of Gordon Columba Harvey, of Chance Wood, Manby Louth, Lincs; 2 s (Alistair b 1970, David b 1972), 2 da (Linda b 1973, Christina b 1976); m 2, Jane Elizabeth Ann, da of Charles Burtt Marfleet (d 1967), of Wykeham Hall, Ludford, Lincs; *Career* Lt Sherwood Rangers Yeo (TA); apprentice: at Huttenwerk Rheinhausen A G Iron and Steel Works 1958-60, Lorraine Escaut Iron and Steel Works at Mont-St-Martin and Senelle (France) 1960-61; dir: Clugston Holdings Ltd 1964, Rhoadstone Div Activities 1965-68 (dir for all subsidiary co's 1970; chm: Roadstone Div 1969, Reclamation Div and St Vincent Plant Ltd 1980; gp vice chm and md: Colvilles Clugston Shanks (Holdings) Ltd, Colvilles Clugston Shanks Ltd 1984, Clydesdale Excavating and Construction Co Ltd 1987-; chm and md: Clugston Hldgs Ltd 1984 (gp vice chm and md 1978), Clugston Group Ltd 1991-; past pres Humbeside Branch of the Br Inst of Mgmnt; govr Brigg Prep Sch, chm E Glanford Scouts; memb Cncl BACMI, pres Lincolnshire Iron and Steel Inst 1989-90; assoc Inst of Quarrying; Freeman City of London, Liveryman Worshipful Co of Paviors 1965 (elected to the Ct 1986); FIHT 1984; *Recreations* shooting, fishing, tennis, music; *Style—* J W A Clugston, Esq; The Old Vicarage, Scawby, Brigg, Lincs DN20 9LX (☎ 0652 57100); Clugston Ltd, St Vincent Hse, Normanby Rd, Scunthorpe, S Humberside DN15 8QT (☎ 0724 843491, telex 527345, fax 0724 281

CLUNIES-ROSS, Prof Anthony Ian; s of Sir Ian Clunies-Ross, CMG (d 1959), and Janet Leslie, *née* Carter (d 1986); *b* 9 March 1932; *Educ* Knox GS Sydney, Scotch Coll Melbourne, Univ of Melbourne (BA), Pembroke Coll Cambridge (MA); *m* 1 July 1961, Morag Fraser, da of James Faulds McVey (d 1975); 2 s (James b 1962 d 1985, David b 1964), 2 da (Sarah b 1965, Brigit b 1972); *Career* lectr then sr lectr in economics Monash Univ 1961-67, sr lectr then prof in economics Univ of Papua New Guinea 1967-74, lectr, sr lectr then prof in economics Univ of Strathclyde 1975-; *Books* One Per Cent: The Case for Greater Australian Foreign Aid (jtly, 1963), Australia and Nuclear Weapons (jtly, 1966) Alternative Strategies for Papua New Guinea (jtly, 1973), Taxation of Mineral Rent (jtly, 1983), Migrants From Fifty Villages (1984); *Recreations* swimming, gardening; *Style—* Prof Anthony Clunies-Ross; Railway Cottage, Kinbuck, Dunblane, Perthshire, Scotland FK15 0NL (☎ 0786 822684); Dept of Economics, Univ of Strathclyde, Glasgow G4 OLN (☎ 041 552 4400)

CLUTTERBUCK, Vice Adm Sir David Granville; KBE (1968), CB (1965); s of Charles Granville Clutterbuck (d 1958); *b* 25 Jan 1913; *Educ* HMS Conway; *m* 1937, Rose Mere, da of Hubert Earle Vaile, of Auckland, NZ; 2 da; *Career* joined RN 1929, Rear Adm 1963, Vice Adm 1966, Dep Supreme Allied Cdr Atlantic 1966-68, (now ret); admin dir Business Graduates Assoc Ltd 1969-83; *Style—* Vice Adm Sir David Clutterbuck, KBE, CB; Burrard Cottage, Walhampton, Lymington, Hampshire SO41 5SA

CLUTTERBUCK, Jasper Meadows; s of late Hugh Meadows Clutterbuck; *b* 5 Feb 1935; *Educ* Eton; *m* 1958, Marguerite Susan, *née* Birnie; 1 s, 1 da; *Career* Lt Coldstream Gds 1953-56; dir Whitbread & Co 1975-88, chief exec Morland & Co plc; *Style—* Jasper Clutterbuck, Esq; Mottisfont House, Mottisfont, nr Romsey, Hants SO5 0LN

CLUTTERBUCK, Maj-Gen Richard Lewis; CB (1971), OBE (1958); s of Col Lewis St John Rawlinson Clutterbuck, OBE, late RA (d 1965), and Isabella Jessie, *née* Jocelyn (d 1968), ggda of 2 Earl of Roden; *b* 22 Nov 1917; *Educ* Radley, Pembroke Coll Cambridge (MA), Univ of London (PhD); *m* 1948, Angela Muriel, da of Col Bernard Cole Barford, RA, of Bishop's Waltham; 3 s (Peter, Robin, Julian); *Career* 2 Lt RE 1937, Maj-Gen 1968, chief instr (Army) Royal Coll of Def Studies 1971-72, Col Cmdt RE 1972-77; reader in political conflict Univ of Exeter 1972-83, non exec dir Control Risks Ltd 1977-87; author; BBC Gen Advsy Cncl 1975-81; *Books* The Media and Political Violence (1983), Industrial Conflict and Democracy (1984), Conflict and Violence in Singapore and Malaysia (1985), The Future of Political Violence (1986), Kidnap, Hijack and Extortion (1987), Terrorism and Guerrilla Warfare (1990), Terrorism Drugs and Crime in Europe after 1992 (1990); *Clubs* Army and Navy, Royal Cwlth Soc; *Style—* Maj-Gen Richard Clutterbuck, CB, OBE; Dept of Politics, Univ of Exeter EX4 4RJ

CLUTTON, (Bernard Geoffrey) Owen; s of Maj Arthur Henry Clutton, MC (d 1979), and Joyce, *née* Worthington; *b* 3 March 1951; *Educ* St Aidans Coll Grahamstown, Univ of Witwatersrand (BA, LLB), Univ of Oxford (BCL); *m* 12 Oct 1979, Rosemary Elizabeth, da of Geoffrey Thomas Skett; 1 s (William Edward Henry b 28 March 1988), 1 da (Alice Elizabeth Katherine b 5 Aug 1990); *Career* admitted slr 1980; ptnr Macfarlanes 1984-; President's Certificate Nat Playing Fields Assoc; Liveryman Worshipful Co of Slrs; memb Law Soc, ATII; *Style—* Owen Clutton, Esq; Macfarlanes, 10 Norwich St, London EC4A 1BD (☎ 071 831 9222, telex 296381, fax 071 831 9607)

CLUTTON, Rafe Henry; s of Robin John Clutton (d 1978), and Rosalie Muriel, *née* Birch (d 1978); *b* 13 June 1929; *Educ* Tonbridge; *m* 1954, Jill Olwyn, da of John Albert Evans, of Haywards Heath, Sussex; 4 s (Owen b 1958, Gareth b 1960, Jonathan b 1962, Niall b 1964), 1 da (Helen b 1968); *Career* chartered surveyor; ptnr Cluttons 1955-; dir: Legal and Gen Gp Ltd 1972-, Haslemere Estates 1990; memb Nat Theatre Bd 1976-, chm Royal Fndn of Greycoat Hosp, Salvation Army Housing Assoc 1987-; FRICS; *Recreations* reading, hill walking; *Clubs* Royal Thames Yacht, City of London; *Style—* Rafe Clutton, Esq; Fairfield, North Chailey, Sussex (☎ 082 572 2431), 45 Berkeley Square, London W1X 5DB (☎ 071 408 1010, telex 23620)

CLUTTON, Lady Sarah Margaret; *née* Fitzalan-Howard; da of 16 Duke of Norfolk, KG, GCVO, GBE, TD, PC (d 1975); *b* 28 Sept 1941; *m* 25 March 1988, Nigel Clutton, s of Robin John Clutton (d 1978), and bro of Rafe Henry Clutton, *qv*; *Career* awarded Pro Ecclesia et Pontifice (highest papal award for ladies) 1983; *Style—* The Lady Sarah Clutton; The Dover House, Poling, Arundel, West Sussex BN18 9PX

CLWYD, Ann (Ann Clwyd Roberts); MP (Lab) Cynon Valley 1984-; da of Gwilym Henri Lewis, and Elizabeth Ann Lewis; *b* 21 March 1937; *Educ* Holywell GS, The Queen's Sch Chester, Univ Coll Bangor; *m* 1963, Owen Dryhurst Roberts; *Career* contested (Lab) Denbigh 1970 and Gloucester Oct 1974, MEP (Lab) Mid and W Wales 1979-84; shadow educn jr min 1987-88, shadow women's affairs min 1987-88, shadow sec of state for overseas devpt 1989-; journalist The Guardian and The Observer; broadcaster; vice chm Welsh Arts Cncl 1975-79, memb Lab NEC 1983-84; *Style—* Ms Ann Clwyd, MP; 70 St Michael's Rd, Llandaff, Cardiff; House of Commons, London SW1 (☎ 071 219 3000)

CLWYD, 3 Baron (UK 1919); Sir (John) Anthony Roberts; 3 Bt (UK 1908); o s of 2 Baron Clwyd (d 1987), and Joan de Bois, *née* Murray (d 1985); *b* 2 Jan 1935; *Educ* Harrow, Trinity Coll Cambridge; *m* 1969, (Linda) Geraldine, yr da of Charles Eugene Cannons, of Sanderstead, Surrey; 3 s (Hon (John) Murray, Hon Jeremy Trevor b 1973, Hon Hugh Gerald Arthur b 1977); *Heir* s, Hon (John) Murray Roberts b 27 Aug 1971; *Career* called to the Bar Gray's Inn 1970; civil servant; *Recreations* music, literature; *Style—* The Rt Hon Lord Clwyd; 24 Salisbury Avenue, Cheam, Sutton, Surrey (☎ 081 642 2527)

CLYDE, Lady Elizabeth; *née* Wellesley; da of 7 Duke of Wellington, KG; *b* 26 Dec 1918; *m* 18 Nov 1939 (m dis 1959), Maj Thomas Clyde, RHG, s of William Pancoast Clyde, of New York; 2 s (of whom the er is Jeremy Clyde, the actor) (and 1 s decd); *Style—* The Lady Elizabeth Clyde; Oliver's Farm, Bramley, Basingstoke, Hants

CLYDE, The Hon Lord; James John Clyde; QC (1971); s of Rt Hon Lord Clyde (d 1975), and Margaret Letitia Dubuisson (d 1974); *b* 29 Jan 1932; *Educ* The Edinburgh Acad, Univ of Oxford (BA), Univ of Edinburgh (LLB); *m* 1963, Ann Clunie, da of Donald Robert Armstrong Hoblyn (d 1975); 2 s (James b 1969, Timothy b 1973); *Career* advocate Scotland 1959, advocate dep 1973-74, chllr to Bishop of Argyll and the Isles 1972-85, memb Scottish Valuation Advsy Cncl 1972- (vice-chm 1980-87, chm 1987-), ldr UK Delgn to the CCBE 1981-84, chm Medical Appeal Tribunals 1974-85, judge in the Cts of Appeal for Jersey and Guernsey 1979-85, senator Coll of Justice 1985-; tstee St Mary's Music Sch 1978-, dir Edinburgh Acad 1979-88, vice pres The Royal Blind Asylum and Sch 1987-, pres Scottish Young Lawyers Assoc 1988-, chm Cncl St George's Sch for Girls 1989-, govr Napier Poly 1989-, assessor to Chllr of Univ of Edinburgh 1989-; tstee Nat Library of Scotland 1977-; *Recreations* music, gardening; *Clubs* New (Edinburgh); *Style—* The Hon Lord Clyde; 9 Heriot Row, Edinburgh EH3 6HU (☎ 031 556 7114)

CLYDESMUIR, 2 Baron (UK 1948); Ronald John Bilsland Colville; KT (1972), CB (1965), MBE (1944), TD; s of 1 Baron Clydesmuir, PC, GCIE, TD (d 1954); *b* 21 May 1917; *Educ* Charterhouse, Trinity Cambridge; *m* 10 April 1946, Joan Marguerita, er da of Lt-Col Ernest Brabazon Booth, DSO, MD; 2 s, 2 da; *Heir* s, Hon David Colville; *Career* Lord-Lt Lanarkshire 1963 (formerly Vice-Lt, DL 1955), Capt Gen Royal Co of Archers (Queen's Body Guard for Scotland), dep govr The British Linen Bank 1966-71, dir Bank of Scotland 1971-87 (govr 1972-81), Scottish Provident Instn, Barclays Bank 1972-82; chm North Sea Assets Ltd; *Style—* The Rt Hon the Lord Clydesmuir, KT, CB, MBE, TD; Langlees House, Biggar, Lanarkshire (☎ 0899 20057)

COAD, Jonathan George; *b* 2 Feb 1945; *Educ* Lancing, Keble Coll Oxford (BA); *m* 16 April 1976, Vivienne Jaques; 2 da (Jennifer b 1982, Felicity b 1986); *Career* historian, archaeologist; inspr of ancient monuments with Historic Bldgs and Monuments Cmmn; hon sec Royal Archaeological Inst; vice pres: Soc for Nautical Res, Navy Records Soc; FSA; *Books* Historic Architecture of The Royal Navy (1983), The Royal Dockyards 1690-1850, Architecture and Engineering Works of the Sailing Navy (1989); *Recreations* reading, travel, woodworking; *Clubs* Eclectic; *Style—* Jonathan G Coad, Esq, FSA; Baileys Reed, Salehurst, Sussex TN32 5JP

COAKHAM, Hugh Beresford; s of William Coakham (d 1973), and Evelyn Grace, *née* Cale; *b* 17 Sept 1944; *Educ* Windsor GS, UCL (BSc), UCH (MB BS, MRCP); *m* 15 May 1972, Elspeth Margaret, da of Harold Macfarlane; 2 s (Alexander b 22 Dec 1978, Jonathan b 24 April 1982), 1 da (Simone b 29 May 1977); *Career* conslt neurosurgn Frenchay Hosp and Bristol Royal Infirmary 1980-, dir Brain Tumour Res Laboratory 1980-, clinical dir Imperial Cancer Res Fund Paediatric and Neuro-Oncology Group 1990-; memb: Soc of Br Neurological Surgns, Br Neuropathalogical Assoc, Br Neuro-Oncology Gp, Euro Assoc of Neurosurgical Soc; Heart of Gold Award BBC TV 1988 (for NHS fundraising); FRCS 1974; *Books* Recent Advances in Neuropathology (contrib, 1985), Tumours of the Brain (contrib, 1986), Biology of Brain Tumours (contrib, 1986), Medulloblastoma: Clinical and Biological Aspects (contrib, 1986), Progress in Surgery - Vol 2 (contrib, 1987), Progress in Paediatric Surgery - Vol 22 (contrib, 1989); *Recreations* jazz saxaphone, walking, swimming; *Style—* Hugh Coakham, Esq; Mansion House Stables, Litfield Rd, Clifton, Bristol BS8 3LL (☎ 0272 734963); Dept of Neurological Surgery, Frenchay Hospital, Bristol BS16 1LE (☎ 0272 701212, fax 0272 701508)

COALES, Prof John Flavell; CBE (1974, OBE 1945); s of John Dennis Coales, DSc (d 1942), of Cobham, and Marion Beatrix, *née* Flavell, ARCM (d 1962); *b* 14 Sept 1907; *Educ* Berkhamsted Sch, Sidney Sussex Coll Cambridge (BA, MA, ScD); *m* 1 Aug 1936, (Mary) Dorothea Violet, da of Rev Henry Lewis Guthrie Alison (d 1958), vicar of Kintbury, Berks; 2 s (Edward b 16 May 1939, Martin b 16 March 1943), 2 da (Susan b 17 May 1937, Alison b 7 Jan 1942); *Career* Admiralty Dept of Sci Res and Experiment: jr sci offr 1929-32, sci offr 1933-39, sr sci offr 1940-43, princ 1944-46 (temp Cdr RNVR); res dir Elliott Bros (London) 1946-52; prof emeritus of engrg Univ of Cambridge 1974- (asst dir res 1952-55, lectr 1956-57, reader 1958-64, prof 1965-74); chm UK Automation Cncl 1963-66, Cncl of Engrg Insts 1975-76; pres Int Fedn of Automatic Control 1963-66; Freeman City of London, Liveryman Worshipful Co of Engineers; Hon DSc City Univ (1971), Hon DTech Univ of Loughborough (1977), Hon DEng Univ of Sheffield (1978), hon fell Hatfield Poly (1971); FIEE 1943, FInstP 1946, FICE 1973, FIEEE 1968, FRS 1970, Hon FIEE 1985, Hon FInstMC 1971, FIAgrE 1975, FEng 1976; foreign memb Serbian Acadamy of Sciences; *Books* Automatic and Remote Control (ed, 1967); many papers in tech jnls on elec engrg, systems engrg and educn; *Style—* Prof John Coales, CBE, FRS; Cambridge University Engineering Dept, Trumpington St, Cambridge CB2 1PZ

COATES; *see*: Milnes-Coates

COATES, Anne Voase (Mrs Anne Hickox); da of Maj Laurence Calvert Coates (d 1968), and Kathleen Voase, *née* Rank (d 1977); *b* 12 Dec 1925; *Educ* High Trees Sch Horley; *m* 24 April 1958 (m dis), Douglas Arthur Hickox (d 1988), s of Horace Robert Hickox (d 1987); 2 s (Anthony Laurence Vose b 30 Jan 1959, James Douglas Rank b 20 June 1965), 1 da (Emma Elizabeth b 11 April 1964); *Career* film ed; work incl: Lawrence of Arabia 1961-62, Becket 1963, Tunes of Glory 1960, Murder on the Orient Express 1975, The Elephant Man 1980, Greystoke Lord of the Apes 1983, Ragtime 1984; prodr The Medusa Touch 1977; two BAFTA nominations 1975 and 1981, Acad award USA 1962 (nominations 1964 and 1981), two ACE nominations USA 1962 and 1964; memb: Acad of Motion Picture Arts and Scis, BAFTA; *Style—* Ms Anne Coates; 64 Chelsea Park Gardens, London SW3 6AE (☎ 071 352 6716); 8455 Fountain Ave (Apt 621), Los Angeles, California 90069, USA (☎ 213 654 7282)

COATES, Caroline Mary; da of Clifford Coates, of Haworth, W Yorks, and Brenda Mary Coates; *b* 28 March 1954; *Educ* Keighley Girls GS, Wall Hall Coll (Cambridge Inst) Alderham W Herts; *m* 1 May 1987, Seamus Deane Potter, s of Maj John Deane Potter, (d 1982); *Career* fndr Amalgamated Talent (promotional gp for fashion designers), exec i/c Hyper Hyper (High St Ken London) 1986-87, opened Boyd Storey (Newburgh St London) 1987 (now md Boyd Storey design ptnrship); dir Fashion Acts, exec on Mgmnt Bd Br Knitting and Clothing Export Cncl, memb: Designers Gp Br Fashion Cncl, BIC, CEC; *Style—* Ms Caroline Coates; Battersea, London; Jimena, Spain; 12 Newburgh St, London W1V 1LG (☎ 071 494 3188)

COATES, David Charlton Frederick; s and h of Brig Sir Frederick Coates, 2 Bt; *b* 16 Feb 1948; *Educ* Millfield; *m* 1973, Christine Helen, da of Lewis F Marshall, of Ely, Cambs; 2 s (James Gregory David b 12 March 1977, Robert Lewis Edward b 22 July 1980); *Style—* David Coates, Esq; 30 Hauxton Rd, Little Shelford, Cambridge

COATES, Brig Sir Frederick Gregory Lindsay; 2 Bt (UK 1921), of Haypark, City of Belfast; s of Sir William Frederick Coates, 1 Bt (d 1932); *b* 19 May 1916; *Educ* Eton, Sandhurst; *m* 1940, Joan Nugent, da of Maj-Gen Sir Charlton Spinks, KBE, DSO (d 1959); 1 s, 2 da; *Heir* s, David Coates; *Career* Royal Tank Regt 1936, served WW II Middle East and NW Europe (wounded 2), War Office and Miny of Supply 1950-66, asst military attaché Stockholm 1953-56, Brig Br Defence Staff Washington DC 1966-69, mil advsr Defence Sales MOD 1969-71, ret; *Recreations* yachting; *Clubs* Royal Yacht Sqdn, Royal Ocean Racing, Royal Motor Yacht, RAC Yacht, Royal Lymington Yacht; *Style—* Brig Sir Frederick Coates, Bt; Launchfield, Briantspuddle, Dorchester, Dorset DT2 7HN (☎ 0929 471229)

COATES, Prof John Henry; s of James Henry Coates (d 1970), of Australia, and Beryl Lilian, *née* Lee (d 1952); *b* 26 Jan 1945; *Educ* Australian Nat Univ (BSc), Ecole Normale Superieure Paris, Univ of Cambridge; *m* 8 Jan 1966, Julie Mildred, da of Henry Basil Turner (d 1988); 1 s (David b 3 Jan 1970, Stephen b 7 Nov 1971, Philip b 22 June 1973); *Career* asst prof Harvard Univ 1969-72, assoc prof Stanford Univ 1972-75, lectr Univ of Cambridge 1975-77; prof: Australian Nat Univ 1977-78, Université de Paris XI (Orsay) 1978-85, and dir of mathematics Ecolé Normale Superieure Paris 1985-86; fell Emmanuel Coll Cambridge 1975-77 and 1986-, Sadleirian prof of mathematics Univ of Cambridge 1986-; pres London Mathematical Soc 1988-90, vice pres Int Mathematical Union 1991-95; FRS 1985; *Style—* Prof John Coates, FRS; 104 Mawson Rd, Cambridge CB1 2EA (☎ 0223 60884); Department of Pure Mathematics and Mathematical Statistics, University of Cambridge, 16 Mill Lane, Cambridge CB2 1SB (☎ 0223 337978, fax 0223 337920)

COATES, Prof Kenneth Sydney; MEP (Lab) Nottingham 1989; s of Eric Arthur Coates, and Mary Coates; *b* 16 Sept 1930; *Educ* Univ of Nottingham (BA); *m* 1969, Tamara Tura; 3 s, 3 da, (1 da decd); *Career* miner Notts Coalfield 1948-56 (various underground jobs, ripper at coal face 1950-56), Adult Education Univ of Nottingham 1960-89 (asst tutor, tutor, sr tutor, reader 1980-89); chm Human Rights Sub-Ctee Euro Parliament; jt fndr Movement for Euro Nuclear Disarmament 1980 (jt sec Liaison Ctee 1981-89), memb Bertrand Russell Peace Fndn 1965-, ed Spokesman pubns, launched European Lab Forum journal 1990; special prof Reader Adult Education Univ of Nottingham 1989-; *Books* Poverty: the Forgotten Englishmen (with Bill Silburn, 1970, 4 edn 1983), Industrial Democracy in Great Britian (with Tony Topham, 1967, 3 edn 1976), The New Unionism (with Tony Topham, 1972, 2 edn 1974), Trade Unions in Britain (with Tony Topham, 1980, 3 edn 1988); *Recreations* walking, reading; *Style—* Prof Kenneth Coates, MEP; Bertrand Russell House, Gamble Street, Nottingham NG7 4ET (☎ 0602 424285)

COATES, Marten Frank; s of Frank Herbert Coates, of Trentham Staffordshire, and Violet, *née* Livermore; *b* 26 March 1947; *Educ* Pockington Sch Yorks, Univ of Durham (BA); *m* 17 Feb 1973, Susan, da of Dr Derek Hugh Anton-Stephens, of Leighton Powys; 3 da (Laura Jane b 17 March 1977, Anna Louise b 10 Oct 1978, Mary Elizabeth (twin) b 10 Oct 1978); *Career* called to the Bar Inner Temple 1972, practising barr, asst rec of the Crown Ct 1989; *Recreations* genealogy, gardening, walking, wine, cooking; *Style—* Martin Coates, Esq; 3 Fountain Ct, Steelhouse Lane, Birmingham B4 6DR (☎ 021 236 5854, fax 021 236 7008)

COATES, Michael Arthur; s of Joseph Michael Smith Coates, OBE (d 1984), of Elmfield, Wylam, Northumberland, and Lilian Warren, *née* Murray (d 1973); *b* 12 May 1924; *Educ* Uppingham; *m* 1, 1952 (m dis 1970), Audrey Hampton, da of Arthur

William Thorne, of St Nicholas Close, Wimborne, Dorset; 1 s (Simon Michael b 1 July 1959), 2 da (Amanda b 23 March 1954, Catherine Lilian Mary b 28 March 1962); m 2, 1971 (m dis 1980), Mrs Hazel Ruth (Sally) Rogers, *née* Thorne; *Career* served WWII Med 1942-47; Price Waterhouse: Newcastle 1947-54, London 1954-59, ptnr 1959-88, sr ptnr UK 1975-82; chm Price Waterhouse World Firm 1982-88; memb Tbnl under Banking Act 1979; Freeman City of London, Liveryman Worshipful Co of Chartered Accountants; *Recreations* horticulture, antiques, reading, railways, photography; *Style*— Michael Coates, Esq; 20 Wilton Crescent, London SW1X 8SA (☎ 071 235 4423); Cantray House, Croy, Inverness-shire (☎ 066 78 204); Price Waterhouse World Firm Ltd, Southwark Towers, 32 London Bridge Street, London SE1 9SY (☎ 071 939 3000, fax 071 378 0647, telex 884657)

COATES, Michael Odiarne; s of Gordon Lionel Coates (d 1990), of Oxted, Surrey, and Dorothy Madeleine, *née* Nelson; *b* 4 July 1938; *Educ* Haileybury & ISC; *m* 20 April 1963, Frances Ann, da of Harold P S Paish; 2 da (Annabel Frances b 29 March 1965, Rebecca Jane b 21 April 1967); *Career* qualified charterd quantity surveyor 1962, jt sr ptnr Gardiner of Theobald 1979- (ptnr 1966-); memb Cncl Benenden Sch 1982-; Court Asst Worshipful Co of Surveyors, memb Worshipful Co of Masons; FRICS 1971; *Recreations* wife and family, farming and viticulture, sports; *Clubs* Boodles; *Style*— Michael Coates, Esq; Great Shoesmiths Farm, White Gates Lane, Wadhurst, East Sussex TN5 6QG (☎ 089 288 2156); Gardiner & Theobald, 49 Bedford Square, London WC1B 3EB (☎ 071 637 2468, fax 071 323 3851)

COATES, Roger Frederick; s of Harry Coates, DCM (d 1962), and Grace, *née* Milnes (d 1963); *b* 12 Sept 1937; *Educ* St Peters Sch York, Univ of Sheffield (LLB); *m* 11 June 1960, (Patricia) Anne, da of Aubrey Beresford; 2 da (Joanna Louise b 1965, Caroline Amanda b 1969); *Career* slr; sr ptnr Buller Jeffries 1973- (joined 1965), dep coroner Birmingham 1971-80; memb Law Soc 1961; *Recreations* antiques, fine art, photography; *Clubs* The Birmingham; *Style*— Roger Coates, Esq; Buller Jeffries, 48 Temple Street, Birmingham B2 5NL (☎ 021 643 8201)

COATES, William Muir Nelson; s of Victor Airth Coates, of Belfast, and Margaret Winifred, *née* Stewart (d 1975); *b* 18 June 1934; *Educ* Fettes, Univ of Edinburgh (BSc); *m* 26 March 1959, Christine, da of Keneth McLeod; 1 s (Iain Roderick b 1968), 1 da (Audrey Diana b 1960); *Career* Flt Lt RAF 1960-63; md Currall Lewis & Martin Ltd 1979; chm Fedn of Civil Engrg Contractors (Midlands) 1989; CEng, MICE; *Style*— William Coates, Esq; Boxmoor, Meer End, Kenilworth, Warwickshire CV8 1PW (☎ 0676 32038); Currall, Lewis & Martin Ltd, 11 Booth St, Birmingham B21 0BL (☎ 021 554 6531, fax 021 554 2423)

COATESWORTH, Lt-Col David; MBE (1943); s of David Coatesworth (d 1971), and Sarah Ann, *née* Beevers (d 1986); *b* 3 Feb 1920; *Educ* Manchester GS, Univ of Manchester (BSc, MSc), Graduate Army Staff Coll; *m* 2 June 1945, Constance Ellen Mary, da of George Newson (d 1968); 1 s (David Philip Richard b 1949), 1 da (Sarah Ann b 1953); *Career* war serv RS and Gen Staff, Signal Offr to Gen Montgomery at El Alamein, then Chief Wireless Offr 8 Army HQ, instr ME Staff Sch 1944, regular army until 1962, sr Br offr NATO HQ SE Europe, Brevet Lt-Col 1959; princ Norfolk Coll of Arts and Technol 1965-73, dir of Educn Norfolk 1973-80, chm Cncl for BBC Radio Norfolk 1980-84; memb: Cncl Nat Academic Awards 1970-73, Technician Educn Cncl 1971-74, City and Guilds of London Examinations Bd 1974-77, Construction Indust Trg Bd 1974-88, Nat Advsy Bd Duke of Edinburgh Award Scheme; vice pres: Norfolk Scout Assoc 1974-85, Royal Norfolk Agric Assoc 1985-; chm Broadland Housing Assoc 1989-, former pres Rotary Club of Thorpe St Andrew Norwich; *Recreations* golf, trout fishing; *Style*— Lt-Col David Coatesworth, MBE; 3 Camberley Rd, Norwich, Norfolk NR4 6SJ (☎ 0603 52391)

COATS, Sir Alastair Francis Stuart; 4 Bt (UK 1905), of Auchendrane, Maybole, Co Ayr; s of Lt-Col Sir James Coats, 3 Bt, MC (d 1966); *b* 18 Nov 1921; *Educ* Eton; *m* 6 Feb 1947, Lukyn, da of Capt Charles Gordon; 1 s, 1 da; *Heir* s, Alexander Coats; *Career* Capt Coldstream Gds 1939-45; *Style*— Sir Alastair Coats, Bt; Birchwood House, Durford Wood, Petersfield, Hants GU31 5AW (☎ 0780 892254)

COATS, Alexander James; s and h of Sir Alastair Coats, 4 Bt, *qv*; *b* 6 July 1951; *Educ* Eton; *Style*— Alexander Coats, Esq

COATS, Dr David Jervis; CBE (1984); s of The Rev William Holms Coats, DD (d 1954), of Glasgow, and Murie Gwendoline, *née* Fowler (d 1984); *b* 25 Jan 1924; *Educ* HS of Glasgow, Univ of Glasgow (BSc); *m* 24 March 1955, Hazel Bell, da of John Livingstone (d 1979), of Glasgow: 1 s (Michael b 1960), 2 da (Gillian b 1956, Pamela b 1958); *Career* REME 1943-47, Major cmdg Mobile Workshop Company in India 1947; Babtie Shaw and Morton: ptnr 1962-79, sr ptnr 1979-87, sr conslt 1988-; chm Assoc Consulting Engrs 1979-80; vice pres Br Section Int Cmmn Large Dams 1983-86 (chm 1980-83), convenor Glasgow Univ Business Ctee of General Cncl 1982-85; chm: Glasgow Univ Tst 1985-, Scot Construction Indust Gp 1986-; vice pres Inst Civil Engrs 1987-89; Hon DSc Univ of Glasgow 1984; FICE, FEng, FRSE; *Recreations* walking, swimming; *Clubs* Caledonian, RSAC (Glasgow); *Style*— Dr David Coats, CBE; 7 Kilmardinny Cres, Bearsden, Glasgow G61 3NP (☎ 041 942 2593); Babtie Shaw and Morton, 95 Bothwell St, Glasgow G2 7HX (☎ 041 204 2511, fax 041 226 3109, telex 77202 BA

COATS, Hon Lady (Elizabeth Lilian Graham); *née* MacAndrew; da of 1 Baron MacAndrew, TD, PC (d 1979), by his 1 wife Lilian Cathleen, *née* Curran; *b* 23 Aug 1929; *m* 8 Feb 1950, Sir William David Coats, *qv* 2 s, 1 da; *Style*— The Hon Lady Coats; The Cottage, Symington, Ayrshire

COATS, Lt Cdr James Alexander Pountney; s of Ian P Coats, DL (d 1980), of Carse, Tarbert, Argyll, and Hilda May, *née* Latta; *b* 31 Dec 1927; *Educ* Lockers Park, W Downs, Britannia Naval Coll Dartmouth, RNC Greenwich; *m* 26 Aug 1961, Sarah Margaret, da of Adm Sir Mark Pizey, GBE, CB, DSO, DL, of Burnham on Sea, Somerset; 3 da (Amanda b 1964, Fiona b 1966, Annie b 1969); *Career* Lt Cdr RN, torpedo and anti submarine specialist 1967; ret; hill farmer; *Recreations* trout fishing, pheasant shooting; *Clubs* Royal Naval Argyll; *Style*— Lt Cdr James A P Coats; Gorten, Carse, Tarbert, Argyll PA29 6YB

COATS, Percy Murray; s of Percy Murray Coats (d 1968), and Lizzie Burroughs Blance (d 1980); *b* 8 Jan 1941; *Educ* Highgate, Bishop Vesey's GS Warwicks ,Univ of London, St George's Hosp (MB BS, DCH); *m* 20 Sept 1975, Margaret Elisabeth Joan, da of Donald Clarence Ashley; 1 s (Edward b 1980), 3 da (Louise b 1976, Caroline b 1978, Maria b 1981); *Career* Surgn Lt RN 1966-72; Queen Charlotte's and Chelsea Hosp for Women 1973-74, King's Coll Hosp 1974-80, conslt obstetrician and gynaecologist SW Surrey Health Dist 1980-, dist tutor in obstetrics and gynaecology SW Surrey, special professional interest ultrasound subfertility; author of specialist medical papers; Liveryman Worshipful Soc of Apothecaries; memb: BMA, Euro Assoc of Gynaecologists and Obstetricians, London Obstetrics and Gynaecological Soc; MRCP, FRCS 1974, FRCOG 1988; *publications*: specialist medical papers; *Recreations* fly fishing; *Clubs* Royal Soc of Med Carlton; *Style*— Percy M Coats, Esq; Fairacre, Horsham Rd, Bramley, Surrey GU5 0AW; Private Consulting Rooms, 8 Waterden Rd, Guildford, Surrey (☎ 0483 68286)

COATS, Sir William David; s of Thomas Heywood Coats (d 1958), of Nitshall, Glasgow (nephew of 1 Baron Glentamar), and Olivia Violet, *née* Pitman; *b* 25 July 1924; *Educ* Eton; *m* 8 Feb 1950, Hon Elizabeth Lilian Graham, da of 1 Baron MacAndrew, PC, TD; 2 s, 1 da; *Career* former chm Coats Paton plc; dir: Clydesdale Bank, South of Scotland Electricity Bd, Murray Caledonian Investmt Tst, Weir Gp; LLD; kt 1985; *Style*— Sir William Coats; c/o Coats Paton plc, 155 Vincent St, Glasgow, G2 5PA (☎ 041 221 8711)

COBB, Henry Stephen (Harry); yst s of Ernest Cobb (d 1945), of Wallasey, and Violet Kate, *née* Sleath (d 1975); *b* 17 Nov 1926; *Educ* Birkenhead Sch, LSE (BA, MA), Univ of Liverpool (Archive Dip); *m* 5 April 1969, Eileen Margaret, da of Alfred John Downer (d 1964), of London; *Career* archivist Church Missionary Soc 1951-53, asst archivist House of Lords 1953-59, asst Clerk of the Records House of Lords 1959-73, dep Clerk 1973-81, Clerk of the Records 1981-; chm Soc of Archivists 1982-84; FSA 1967, FRHistS 1970; *Books* The Local Port Book of Southampton 1439-40 (1961), The Overseas Trade of London 1480-81: Exchequer Customs Accounts (1990); *Recreations* music, historical res; *Style*— Harry Cobb, Esq, FSA; 1 Childs Way, Hampstead Garden Suburb, London NW11 6XU (☎ 081 458 3688); Record Office, House of Lords, London SW1A 0PW (☎ 071 219 3073)

COBB, John Martin; RN; s of Richard Martin Cobb (d 1966), of Rochester, Kent, and Ursula Joan, *née* Abell (d 1990); *b* 28 Sept 1931; *Educ* Canford; *m* 25 July 1959, Susan Mary Cochrane, yst da of Roderick Watson (d 1975), of London; 1 s (James b 1964), 2 da (Mary b 1960, Philippa b 1962); *Career* seaman offr RN 1949-69; served Far East, Aust, Med, W Indies and the Persian Gulf, cmd landing ship and anti-submarine frigate; def policy staff MOD 1966-69, ret as Cdr (RN) 1969; Private Clients Dept Sheppards Stockbrokers 1969-91 (ptnr and dir i/c 1982-88); dir: Thoraton Asian Emerging Markets Investment Trust, South of England Centre; chm Private Client Investment Managers and Stockbrokers (APCIMS) 1990-; vice chm Temple Grove Prep Sch Uckfield Sussex; memb Stock Exchange; *Recreations* skiing, sailing, gardening,music; *Clubs* Itchenor Sailing; *Style*— J M Cobb, Esq; No 1 London Bridge, London SE1 9QU (☎ 071 378 7000, fax 071 378 7585)

COBB, Prof Richard Charles; CBE (1978); s of Francis Hills Cobb, Sudan CS, and Dora, *née* Swindale; *b* 20 May 1917; *Educ* Shrewsbury, Merton Coll Oxford; *m* 1963, Margaret Tennant; 4 s, 1 da; *Career* prof of modern history Oxford Univ 1973-84; sr research fell Worcester Coll Oxford 1984-; author; FBA 1967; *Books* Still Life: Sketches from a Tunbridge Wells Childhood (1983); *Style*— Prof Richard Cobb, CBE; Worcester College, Oxford

COBB, Russell Alan; s of Alan Walter Cobb, of Leicester, and Betty Margaret, *née* Black; *b* 18 May 1961; *Educ* Woodbank Sch Leicester, Trent Coll Nottingham; *m* Sharon Ann, da of John Anthony Spiers; 1 s (Joshua James b 17 Aug 1990); *Career* professional cricketer; Leicestershire CCC 1978-: first class debut 1980, awarded county cap 1986, 118 first class appearances; represented Young England on tour Aust 1979 and W Indies 1980; off-seasons: player and coach SA various winters, advtg sales Leics CCC, Bridgeport Machines Ltd; advanced coaching award NCA; *Recreations* gardening, spending time with my family, flying; *Style*— Russell Cobb, Esq; Leicestershire CCC, Grace Rd, Leicester LE2 8AD (☎ 0533 832128, fax 0533 440363)

COBB, Timothy Humphry (Tim); s of Humphry Henry Cobb (d 1949), of Harrow Weald, Middx, and Edith Muriel, *née* Stogdon (d 1948); *b* 4 July 1909; *Educ* Harrow, Magdalene Coll Cambridge (BA, MA); *m* 23 April 1952, Cecilia Mary Josephine (Celia), da of Walter George Chapman (d 1974), of Dorset House, London; 2 s (Kenneth b 1954, Martin b 1959), 1 da (Josephine b 1955); *Career* asst master Middx Sch Concord Mass USA 1931-32, asst master Bryanston Sch 1932-47; headmaster: King's Coll Budo Kampala Uganda 1947-58, Dover Coll Kent 1958-73; sec Uganda Headmasters Assoc, memb Headmasters Conf 1958-73; *Recreations* music, railways; *Clubs* MCC; *Style*— T H Cobb, Esq; Parkgate Farm, Framlingham, Woodbridge, Suffolk IP13 9JH (☎ 072 875 672)

COBBAN, Sir James (Macdonald); CBE (1971), TD (1950), JP (Berks 1950, Oxon 1974), DL (Berks 1966, Oxon 1974); s of Alexander Macdonald Cobban (d 1956), of Scunthorpe; *b* 14 Sept 1910; *Educ* Pocklington Sch, Jesus Coll Cambridge (MA), Univ of Vienna, Pembroke Coll Oxford (MA); *m* 1942, Lorna Mary (d 1961), da of George Stanley Withers Marlow, of Sydenham; 4 da (and 1 s decd); *Career* asst master King Edward VI Sch Southampton 1933-36, classical sixth form master Dulwich Coll 1936-40 and 1946-47; 2 Lt TA (Gen List) 1937, Intelligence Corps 1941, GSO3 Directorate of Mil Intelligence 1941, DAQMG Combined Ops HQ 1943, Staff Offr CCG 1944, Lt-Col 1945; headmaster Abingdon Sch 1947-70; former chm Abingdon Co Bench, dep chm Governing Bodies Assoc 1976-82 (hon life memb 1981); former govr: Stowe, Wellington, Campion Sch (Athens), St Helen's Sch, St Stephen's House; former memb Gen Synod Church of England; kt 1982; *Recreations* walking; *Clubs* East India, Public Schools; *Style*— Sir James Cobban, CBE, TD, DL; 10 Coverdale Court, Preston Road, Yeovil BA21 3AQ (☎ 0935 77835)

COBBE, Stuart Malcolm; s of Brian Morton Cobbe, OBE, of 7 Kew St, Brighton, and Catherine Mary, *née* Caddy (d 1985); *b* 2 May 1948; *Educ* Royal GS Guildford, Univ of Cambridge (MA, MD), St Thomas's Hosp Med Sch (MB BChir); *m* 11 Dec 1970, Patricia Frances, da of George Bertram Barrett, of 10 Town Court Path, Woodberry Down, London; 3 da (Lindsay Ann b 21 Aug 1974, Heather Jane (twin) b 21 Aug 1974, Sarah Caroline b 9 May 1977); *Career* gen med trg in Nottingham, Birmingham, Worthing and St Thomas's Hosp London 1972-76, registrar in cardiology Nat Heart Hosp London 1976-77, res fell in cardiology Cardiothoracic Inst London 1977-79, sr registrar in cardiology John Radcliffe Hosp London 1979-81, res fell Univ of Heidelberg W Germany 1981-82, clinical reader John Radcliffe Hosp Oxford 1982-85, Walton prof of med cardiology Univ of Glasgow 1985-; author of over fifty scientific papers on cardiac metabolism and cardiac arrhythmias; memb: Br Cardiac Soc, Assoc of Physicians of GB and I; FRCP, FRCPG; *Recreations* walking; *Style*— Prof Stuart Cobbe; Dept of Medical Cardiology, Royal Infirmary, 10 Alexandra Parade, Glasgow G31 2ER (☎ 041 552 3535 ext 5388, fax 041 552 4683)

COBBING, Richard Geoffrey; s of Geoffrey Henry Cobbing, and Valerie, *née* Adams; *b* 15 Oct 1967; *Educ* Hookergate Sch Rowlands Gill; *Career* trampolinist; ranked GB number one 1987-91; winner of: Polish World Cup 1985, Czechoslovakia World Cup 1986-87, Four Nations Cup 1987 and 1988, Br Hermesetas World Cup 1987, trampoline competition at 1989 World Games; professional high diver 1988; world record holder: most somersaults in a minute (75) 1989, most consecutive somersaults (2609) 1989; Br freestyle skiing aerials champion 1990, memb English freestyle skiing team; chm FLIP (Fedn Linking Inverted Performers); memb: Br Ski Fedn, Superschs Fundraising Orgn, Br Trampoline Fedn; *Recreations* high diver, tumbler, listening to rythm and blues music, freestyle (aerobatic) skiing; *Clubs* Metro Trampoline; *Style*— Richard Cobbing, Esq; 27 Glamis Crescent, Lockhaugh, Rowlands Gill, Tyne & Wear (☎ 0207 542948); 49 Ivy Drive, Lightwater, Surrey (☎ 0276 79562, car 0836 632364)

COBBOLD, Anthony Alan Russell; s of Rowland Hope Cobbold, of Bristol (d 1986), and Mary Selby, *née* Parkin; descended from Robert Cobbold, of Tostock, Suffolk (d 1603), founder of the brewing family; ggs of Sir Harry Parkes, GCMG, KCB (d 1885), envoy extraordinaire and min plen in Japan and China; n of Vice-Adm Sir Charles Hughes Hallett, KCB, CBE (d 1985); *b* 15 March 1935; *Educ* Marlborough, Gonville and Caius Coll Cambridge (BA); *m* 1, 15 Aug 1959, Margaret Elizabeth, da of Prof J W Cecil Turner (d 1968), of Cambridge; 3 s (Timothy b 1962, Humphrey b 1964, Jeremy b 1969); m 2, 25 April 1974, Jillianne Bridget, formerly wife of Capt Martin J Minter-Kemp, and da of Lt-Col Denis Lucius Alban Gibbs, DSO (d 1984), of Tavistock, Devon; 1 step s (Robin b 1963), 2 step da (Emma b 1960, Claire (twin) b 1963); *Career* Lt Duke of Edinburgh's Royal Regt 1953-55; W & T Avery Ltd 1958-66, W D and H O Wills 1966-71, Evode Gp plc 1971-87 and 1990-, chief exec Regnl Building Centres Ltd 1988-89; dir: Evode Roofing Ltd 1973-87, Evode Jt Sealing 1973-87, Evode Gp plc 1980-87, Tekurat Insulations Ltd 1980-87, Building Centre Gp Ltd 1985-88, British Roof Mart Ltd 1986-87; *Recreations* genealogy, woodland mgmnt; *Clubs* IOD; *Style*— Anthony Cobbold, Esq; The Vineyard, Weston under Redcastle, Shrewsbury SY4 5JY (☎ 063084 344)

COBBOLD, 2 Baron (UK 1960), of Knebworth, Co Hertford; David Antony Fromanteel Lytton Cobbold; er s of 1 Baron Cobbold, KG, GCVO, PC (d 1987); assumed by Deed Poll 1960 the additional surname of Lytton before his patronymic; *b* 14 July 1937; *Educ* Eton, Trinity Coll Cambridge (BA); *m* 7 Jan 1961, Christine Elizabeth, 3 da of Maj Sir Dennis Frederick Bankes Stucley, 5 Bt (d 1983); 3 s (Hon Henry Fromanteel, Hon Peter Guy Fromanteel b 1964, Hon Richard Stucley Fromanteel b 1968, a Page of Honour to HM The Queen 1980-82), 1 da (Hon Rosina Kim b 1971); *Heir* s, Hon Henry Fromanteel Lytton Cobbold, b 12 May 1962; *Career* served in RAF 1955-57; Bank of London and S America 1962-72, Finance for Industry 1974-79, BP 1979-87, TSB England and Wales plc 1987-88; dir: Hill Samuel Bank Ltd 1988-89, 39 Production Co Ltd 1987-, Gaiacorp UK Ltd 1989-; chm: Lytton Enterprises Ltd 1970-, Stevenage Community Tst; fell ACT 1983-, hon treas Historic Houses Assoc 1988-; *Style*— The Lord Cobbold; Knebworth House, Knebworth, Herts

COBBOLD, (Michael) David Nevill; CBE (1983), DL (Gtr London); s of Geoffrey Wyndham Nevill Cobbold (d 1980), and Cicely Helen, *née* Middleton (d 1969); *b* 21 Oct 1919; *Educ* Charterhouse, Univ of Oxford (MA); *m* 1949, Ann Rosemary, da of John Christopher Trevor (d 1960); 3 s (Charles (decd), Richard, Christopher), 1 da (Gillian); *Career* Maj The Buffs; slr; ptnr Stileman Neate and Topping 1949-83, conslt Messrs Beachcrofts 1983-; memb Westminster City Cncl 1949-86 (ldr 1964-65 and 1977-83), Mayor 1958-59, Lord Mayor 1973-74; chm Soc Responsibility Ctee for the London Episcopal Area 1988-; *Recreations* gardening, architecture; *Style*— David Cobbold, Esq, CBE, DL; 31 Ashley Court, Morpeth Terrace, London SW1P 1EN (☎ 071 834 5020); Beachcrofts Stanleys, 20 Furnival St, London EC4A 1BN (☎ 071 242 1011, telex 264607 BEALAW G)

COBBOLD, Dowager Baroness; Lady (Margaret) Hermione Millicent; *née* Lytton; da of 2 Earl of Lytton, KG, GCSI, GCIE, PC (d 1947); *b* 31 Aug 1905; *m* 3 April 1930, 1 Baron Cobbold, KG, GCVO, PC (d 1987); 2 s, 1 da (and 1 da decd); *Style*— The Rt Hon the Dowager Lady Cobbold; Lake House, Knebworth, Herts (☎ 0438 812310)

COBBOLD, Patrick Mark; s of Ivan Murray Cobbold (d 1944), of Glemham Hall, Woodbridge, Suffolk, and Lady Blanche Katharine, *née* Cavendish (d 1987), da of 9 Duke of Devonshire; *b* 20 June 1934; *Educ* Eton; *Career* short serv cmmn Scots Gds 1952-55; ADC Govr of the Bahamas 1957-60; chm Ipswich Town FC; *Recreations* fishing, shooting; *Clubs* Whites, Pratts; *Style*— Patrick Cobbold, Esq; Glemham Hall, Woodbridge, Suffolk (☎ 0728 746219)

COBBOLD, Hon Rowland John Fromanteel; yr s of 1 Baron Cobbold, KG, GCVO, PC; *b* 20 June 1944; *Educ* Eton, Trinity Coll Cambridge (MA); *m* 3 June 1969, Sophia Augusta, da of the late B N White-Spunner, 1 s, 1 da; *Career* Lt Kent and Co of London Yeo (TA); with BOAC/Br Airways: joined 1980, gen mangr Euro 1981-85, gen mangr Mktg 1985-86, dir Bd and Mktg 1987; *Clubs* Brooks's, RAC, Hong Kong, Shek-O; *Style*— The Hon Rowland Cobbold; Cathay Pacific Airways Ltd, Swire House, Hong Kong (☎ 584 25100); 6 Deep Water Bay Rd, Hong Kong; Lower Town Farmhouse, Clifton Hampden, Oxon

COBDEN, Dr Irving; s of Manuel Cobden, of Newcastle upon Tyne, and Fay, *née* Alexander; *b* 18 May 1950; *Educ* Royal GS Newcastle, Univ of Newcastle Med Sch (MB BS, MD); *m* Jennifer Deborah, da of Mark Gilbert; 3 da (Sarah b 1975, Gemma b 1977, Laura b 1982); *Career* conslt physician N Tyneside Health Authy 1985-, conslt gastroenterologist Freeman Hosp 1985-, clinical tutor in postgrad med 1986-, Wyeth USA Travelling fell 1988; contrib many pubns on gastroenterology; pres Tyne and Wear branch of Cogliac Soc, hon fell Société Royale Belgede de Gastro Enterologie; MRCP 1976, MBSG; *Recreations* bridge, angling, travel, golf; *Style*— Dr Irving Cobden; Preston Hosp, N Shields, Tyne & Wear NE29 OLR; Freeman Hosp, Freeman Rd, Newcastle-Upon-Tyne NE7 7DN (☎ 091 259 6660)

COBHAM, 11 Viscount (GB 1718); Sir John William Leonard Lyttelton; 14 Bt (E 1618); also Baron Cobham (GB 1718), Lord Lyttelton, Baron of Frankley (1756, renewed 1794), and Baron Westcote of Ballymore (I 1776); s of 10 Viscount, KG, PC, GCMG, GCVO, TD (d 1977); *b* 5 June 1943; *Educ* Eton, Christ's Coll New Zealand, RAC Cirencester; *m* 1974, Penelope Ann, eldest da of late Roy Cooper, of Moss Farm, Ollerton, nr Knutsford, Cheshire; *Heir* bro, Hon Christopher Lyttelton; *Career* ptnr Hagley Hall Farms 1976-; *Style*— The Rt Hon the Viscount Cobham; Hagley Hall, Stourbridge, W Midlands DY9 9LG (☎ 0562 885823); 20 Kylestrome House, Cundy St, Ebury St, London SW1 (☎ 071 730 5756)

COBHAM, Michael John; CBE (1981); s of Sir Alan John Cobham, KBE, AFC (d 1973), and Gladys Marie, *née* Lloyd (d 1961); *b* 22 Feb 1927; *Educ* Malvern, Trinity Coll Camb (BA, MA); *m* 1, 1954 (m dis 1972), June Oakes; m 2, 1973, Nadine Felicity, da of William Abbott, of Wimborne, Dorset; 1 da; *Career* chm and chief exec FR Group plc; chm: Flight Refuelling Ltd, Alan Cobham Engrg Ltd, Stanley Aviation Corp (Denver USA), Hymatic Engrg Co Ltd, FR Aviation Ltd, WES Plastics Ltd, Carleton Technols Inc (Buffalo NY USA), Chelton (Electrostatics) Ltd; FRAeS, CBIM; *Recreations* sailing and skiing; *Clubs* Royal Thames Yacht, Royal Southern Yacht, Naval and Military; *Style*— Michael Cobham Esq, CBE; c/o FR Group plc, Wimborne, Dorset (☎ 0202 882121)

COBLEY, Kenneth John; s of John Cowan Cobley (d 1959), of Heath House, Crockham Hill, Edenbridge, and Minnie May Kitts (d 1982); *b* 31 Jan 1917; *Educ* Marlborough, Imp Coll of Sci London; *m* 1, 21 June 1958, Elizabeth Sally Jane Robertshaw; 3 s (Peter David b 1959, Charles Seymour b 1961, Ian Blake b 1965); m 2, 22 Dec 1990, (Jane) Charlotte Leslie, *née* Sande; *Career* joined Richard Seymour Cobley Ltd Bideford Devon as trainee (later md 9P bulbfarms Eng and Scot); served WWII: joined army 1939, Range Offr RA Sch of Gunnery Larkhill, joined 53 Medium Regt RA 1943 (served Normandy), promoted Capt 1945; fndr: Photo Plastics, Int Sch of Colour Photography 1951, Colour Processing Laboratories Edenbridge (now CPL Group) 1952, Standeasy Display Systems 1970, CPL Exhibitions 1970, Electric Icon Computer Graphics Bristol 1986, Electric Icon Birmingham 1988; chm and md CPL Group; FBIPP 1970; *Recreations* skiing and all watersports; *Style*— Kenneth Cobley, Esq; Maple Cottage, Holtye Road, Cowden, Nr Edenbridge, Kent (☎ 0342 850292); Colour Processing Laboratories, Fircroft Way, Edenbridge, Kent TN8 6ET (☎ 0732 862555)

COBURN, Alfred Henry (Mick); CBE (1979); s of Alfred George Coburn (d 1977); *b* 12 Feb 1922; *Educ* Sidcup GS; *m* 1, 1944, Betty Winifred (d 1981), da of Flt Lt Percy Robinson (d 1960); 2 da; m 2, 1984, Mary Vera, da of Harold Thomas Read; *Career* chm: Britfish 1959-69, Findus UK Ltd (Holding Co) to 1983; md: Findul Ltd 1965-83, Chambourcy Food Products Ltd 1973-83; dir: The Nestle Co (UK) Ltd (Holding Co) to 1983, B G Foods Ltd 1984-; past pres UK Assoc Frozen Food Prodrs; FRSA, FIGD; *Recreations* golf, horse racing, travel; *Clubs* Wellington, RAC; *Style*— Mick Coburn, Esq, CBE; Goodwood, Burnhams Rd, Bookham, Surrey KT23 3BB (☎ 0372 452970)

COCHAND, Charles Maclean; s of Louis Emile Cochand, DFC, Croix De Guerre, and Morna Aldous, *née* Maclean; *b* 2 May 1951; *Educ* Aiglon Coll Chesieres Villars, Univ of Western Ontario (BA); *m* 6 July 1982, Judith Ann, da of John David Harrison, MBE; 3 s (Nicholas John b 1984, Matthew Charles b 1986, Alexander Maclean b 1989); *Career* called to the Bar Middle Temple 1978; dist cmmr Kensington Chelsea and Westminster Scout Assoc (medal of merit 1985); *Recreations* sailing, skiing, scouting; *Clubs* Eagle Ski (Gstaad), Annabel's; *Style*— Charles Cochand, Esq; 60 Wandle Rd, Wandsworth Common, London SW17 7DW (☎ 081 767 1651); De Grassi Pt, RR1 Lefroy, Ontario, Canada LOL 1WO; 17 Carlton Crescent, Southampton SO9 5AL

COCHRANE, (Alexander John) Cameron; MBE (1987); s of late Dr Alexander Younger Cochrane (d 1988), of Edinburgh, and Jenny Johnstone, *née* Morris; *b* 19 July 1933; *Educ* Edinburgh Acad, Univ Coll Oxford (MA); *m* 14 Aug 1958, Rosemary Aline, da of Robert Alexander Ogg (d 1974), of Glasgow; 1 s (David Alexander Cameron b 1968), 2 da (Fiona b 1961, Sandra (Mrs Gamba) b 1964); *Career* Nat Serv 2 Lt RA 1952-54; Maj CCF St Edwards Sch 1957-66, Maj ACF Cumberland and Westmorland 1966-69; asst master St Edwards Sch Oxford 1957-66, warden Brathay Hall Ambleside Cumbria 1966-70, asst dir of educn City of Edinburgh 1970-74; headmaster: Arnold Sch Blackpool 1974-79, Fettes Coll Edinburgh 1979-88; princ Prince Willem-Alexander Coll The Netherlands 1988-; hon fell Dept of Educational Studies Univ of Edinburgh 1973-74, co-opted memb Lancs Educn Ctee 1976-79; chm of govrs: Ullswater Outward Bound Sch 1979-84, Loch Eil Outward Bound Sch 1984-88; vice pres Lothian Fedn of Boys' Clubs 1987 (chm 1981-84), chm HMC servs Sub Ctee Inter-Service Ctee 1982-88; cmdt XIII Cwlth Games Athletes' Village Edinburgh 1986; memb: Outward Bound Tst Cncl 1979-88, Advsy Ctee Duke of Edinburgh's award 1982-87; elder Church of Scotland 1972-; MBIM 1987; *Recreations* games, high lands, beaches, music, people; *Clubs* Public Schools, New (Edinburgh), MCC, Vincent's (Oxford); *Style*— Cameron Cochrane, Esq, MBE; Gravenallee 22, 7591 PE DENEKAMP, The Netherlands (☎ home 05413 4485, office 05413 3485)

COCHRANE, David; s of James Douglas Cochrane, of Edinburgh, and Margaret, *née* Milne (d 1943); *b* 18 July 1943; *Educ* Edinburgh Acad, Edinburgh Coll of Art; *m* 29 June 1970, Jacqueline, da of George Edward Buller (d 1980); 2 s (John b 1 Nov 1971, Peter b 3 March 1973); *Career* assoc Reiach and Hall Architects Edinburgh 1975; ptnr: Reiach, Hall Blyth Iran 1977, Reiach & Hall and Reiach Hall Blyth Edinburgh 1980, Cochrane McGregor Architects and Planners Edinburgh 1982; exec dir Cochrane McGregor Ltd Edinburgh, London and Glasgow 1987-; Edinburgh Coll of Art: Dip Arch 1968, Dip TP 1970; RIBA 1972, ARIAS 1974, MRTPI 1980; *Recreations* golf, gardening; *Clubs* North Berwick Golf; *Style*— David Cochrane, Esq; c/o Cochrane McGregor Ltd, Architecture Planning Design Management, 3 St Andrew Square, Edinburgh EH2 2BD (☎ 031 557 4022, fax 031 556 7559, car 0860 326332)

COCHRANE, Dr Gordon McLellan (Mac); s of Robert Brown Cochrane, of 8 Tommy Taylors Lane, Cheltenham, and Ivy, *née* Elvidge; *b* 24 Feb 1945; *Educ* Tudor Grange GS Solihull, Univ of London (BSc, MB BS); *m* 3 Sept 1966, Jill Lesley, da of Lt Sidney Herbert Castleton, of 11 Yew Tree Lane, Solihull; 1 s (James b 15 April 1974), 1 da (Katie b 12 March 1979); *Career* sr house offr and registrar Brompton Hosp 1971-73, conslt physician Guy's 1977- (houseman 1969-70, lectr and registrar 1973-79), hon sr lectr in physicology UMDS, chm of confidential inquiry into the death of Ms S Bull for Greenwich Health Authy, SE Thames RHA and DHSS 1985-86; educnl film Understanding Asthma won BMA film competition Gold Award 1984, BLAT trophy 1985; Univ of London rep to Greenwich Health Authy 1983-, ed bd Thorax 1984-, cncl memb and chm of Manpower ctee Br Thoracic Soc 1989, Int Bd of Soc of Euro Pneumologists; FRCP 1985 (MRCP 1972), FRSM 1986; *Books* Bronchodilator Therapy (ed, 1984), Colour Atlas of Asthma (jtly, 1989); articles: Asthma Mortality (jtly Thorax, 1975), Management of Asthma in Genral Practice (jtly Respiratory Medicine, 1989); *Recreations* skiing, badminton, wine tasting, photography; *Style*— Dr Mac Cochrane; Dept of Thoracic Medicine, Guy's Hospital, London Bridge, London SE1 9RT (☎ 071 955 4148)

COCHRANE, Ian Andrew; s of Lt-Col W A Cochrane (d 1989), of Haxby, York, and Rebecca, *née* Segal (d 1989); *b* 8 Feb 1951; *Educ* Archbishop Holgates GS York, Univ of Manchester (BSc); *m* 3 Aug 1974, Jennifer Wilna, da of Donald Edward Crisp (d 1983); 3 s (Mark b 1980, James b 1982, Adam b 1984); *Career* CA Arthur Andersen 1973-78; chief exec Fitch-RS plc 1979-90; FCA 1976; *Recreations* classic cars, tennis, gardening; *Clubs* Groucho's; *Style*— Ian Cochrane, Esq; Woolton House, Oval Way, Gerrards Cross, Bucks

COCHRANE, John Patrick Stuart; s of Herbert Lees Cochrane, of Hythe, Kent, and Sheila, *née* Haslop; *b* 5 July 1944; *Educ* St Paul's, Middx Hosp Med Sch (MB BS, MS); *m* 22 June 1968, Caroline Louisa, da of Capt Charles Henry Potten (d 1962); 1 s (Richard b 1974), 1 da (Joanna b 1975); *Career* conslt surgn; training posts 1967-81, Whittington Hosp and Royal Northern Hospitals 1981-, undergraduate subdean Univ Coll Middlesex Sch of Med 1982-86, hon conslt surgn Hosp of St John and St Elisabeth NW8; hon sr clinical lectr: Univ Coll, Middlesex Sch of Med; Penrose May tutor RCS 1990-, Univ of London external examiner MB BS, recognised teacher, postgrad dean Whittington Hosp, dir of Academic Centre 1987-90; FRSM, FRCS, Fell Assoc of Surgns of GB and Ireland; *Books* The Breast Book (1989), Complete Guide to Breast Health, author of contribs to various med pubns; *Style*— John Cochrane, Esq; 22 Woodside Avenue, Highgate, London N6 4SS (☎ 081 444 9180); 19 Wimpole St, London W1M 7AD (☎ 071 637 9755)

COCHRANE, Hon (John Douglas) Julian; 3 s of late 2 Baron Cochrane; *b* 12 June 1929; *Educ* Eton; *m* 25 Nov 1965, Vaila Rose, yr da of Cdr Robert Dalby, RN (ret), of Castle Donington, Leics; 1 s (John Colin b 1969), 2 da (Julietta Anne b 1966, Alice Georgina b 1974); *Style*— The Hon Julian Cochrane; Townend House, Hopton, Derbys

COCHRANE, Sir (Henry) Marc Sursock; 4 Bt (UK 1903); s of Sir Desmond Oriel Alastair George Weston Cochrane, 3 Bt (d 1979); *b* 23 Oct 1946; *Educ* Eton, Trinity Coll Dublin (BBS, MA); *m* 28 June 1969, Hala, 2 da of Fuad Mahmoud Bey es-Said, of Beirut; 2 s, 1 da; *Heir* s, Alexander Desmond Sursock Cochrane b 7 May 1973; *Career* hon consul gen for Ireland in Lebanon 1979-84; dir: Hambros Bank Ltd 1979-85, GT Management plc 1985-; tstee Chester Beatty Library and Gallery of Oriental Art Dublin; *Recreations* electronics, skiing, shooting; *Clubs* Annabel's, Ham & Petersham Rifle and pistol; *Style*— Sir Marc Cochrane, Bt; Woodbrook, Bray, Co Wicklow, Eire (☎ 821421); Palais Sursock, Beirut, Lebanon (☎ 331607 334663)

COCHRANE, Lady Tanya Jean Farquhar; da (by 1 m) of 14 Earl of Dundonald; *b* 9 July 1964; *Educ* Benenden; *Career* memb Anglo-Chilean Soc; *Recreations* music, theatre, sport; *Style*— The Lady Tanya Cochrane; 7 Campana Road, London SW6 4AS

COCHRANE OF CULTS, 4 Baron (UK 1919); (Ralph Henry) Vere Cochrane; DL (Fife); s of 2 Baron Cochrane of Cults, DSO (d 1968), and his 1 w, Hon Elin, *née* Douglas-Pennant (d 1934), da of 2 Baron Penrhyn; suc bro, 3 Baron 1990; *b* 20 Sept

1926; *Educ* Eton, King's Coll Cambridge (MA); *m* 18 Dec 1956, Janet Mary Watson, da of Dr William Hunter Watson Cheyne MB, MRCS, LRCP (d 1957); 2 s (Hon Thomas Hunter Vere b 1957, Hon Michael Charles Nicholas b 1959); *Heir* Hon Thomas Hunter Vere Cochrane b 7 Sept 1957; *Career* Lt RE Germany; farmer; gen cmmr of Income Tax; chm Craigtoun Meadows Ltd; underwriting memb Lloyd's 1965; memb Queen's Body Guard for Scotland (Royal Co of Archers); *Recreations* skiing; *Clubs* New (Edinburgh); *Style—* The Rt Hon Lord Cochrane of Cults; Cults House, Cupar, Fife KY15 5RD

COCKBURN, (John) Alasdair Murray; s of James Ronald Murray Cockburn, of Westcroft, Knockbuckle Rd, Kilmacolm, and Evelyn Marguerite, *née* Mathieson; *b* 10 July 1946; *Educ* Glenalmond Coll, Univ of Aberdeen (LLB); *m* 19 April 1976, Carole Agnes, da of Karl Godfrey Mohr (d 1972), of Bramhall, Cheshire; 1 s (Iain b 1980), 1 da (Gail b 1977); *Career* CA; ptnr Coopers & Lybrand Deloitte; *Recreations* golf, sailing; *Clubs* Caledonian; *Style—* Alasdair Cockburn, Esq; Catherston, 5 Pine Ridge Dr, Lower Bourne, Farnham, Surrey (☎ 0252 715529); Coopers & Lybrand Deloitte, Plumtree Ct, London (☎ 071 583 5000)

COCKBURN, Charles Christopher; s and h of Sir John Eliot Cockburn, 12 Bt, of 48 Frewin Rd, Wandsworth Common, London, and Glory Patricia, *née* Mullings; *b* 19 Nov 1950; *Educ* Emanuel Sch, City of London Poly (BA), Garnett Coll; *m* 1, 1978, Beverly, o da of B Stangroom, of Richmond, Surrey; m 2, 1985, Margaret Ruth, da of Samuel Esmond Bell, of 18 Portland Drive, Bury Green, Cheshunt, Herts; 1 s (Christopher Samuel Alexander b 24 March 1986), 1 da (Charlotte Elspeth Catherine (twin) b 24 March 1986); *Career* lectr; conslt in govt relations, ed Financial Regulation Review, chief exec Portcullis Research (govt relations conslts); *Recreations* rowing, cycling, song writing, travelling; *Clubs* Twickenham Rowing; *Style—* Charles Cockburn, Esq; 4 Connaught Rd, Teddington, Middlesex TW11 0PS; Portcullis Research, 3/19 Holmbush Rd, Putney, London SW15 3LE (☎ 081 789 2798)

COCKBURN, Prof Forrester; s of Forrester Cockburn, and Violet Elizabeth, *née* Bunce; *b* 13 Oct 1934; *Educ* Leith Acad, Univ of Edinburgh (MB ChB, MD); *m* 15 Jan 1960, Alison Fisher, da of Roger Allison Grieve; 2 s (David, John); *Career* Huntington - Hartford res fell Univ of Boston USA 1963-65, Nuffield sr res fell Univ of Oxford 1965-66, Wellcome sr res fell Univ of Edinburgh 1966-71, sr lectr Dept of Child Life and Health Univ of Edinburgh 1971-77, Samson Gemmell prof of child health Royal Hosp for Sick Children Glasgow 1977-; *Books* Neonatal Medicine (with Drillien, 1974), Practical Paediatric Problems (with Hutchinson, 6 edn, 1986), Craig's Care of the Newly Born Infant (with Turner and Douglas, 1988 Fetal and Neonatal Growth (1988); *Recreations* sailing; *Style—* Prof Forrester Cockburn; 53 Hamilton Drive, Glasgow G12 8DP (☎ 041 339 2973); Dept of Child Health, Royal Hosp for Sick Children, Yorkhill, Glasgow G3 8SJ (☎ 041 339 8888, ext 4235)

COCKBURN, James Angus; s of Carleton Varty Cockburn, of 11 Craigmillar Ave, Milngavie, Glasgow, and Margaret, *née* Robertson; *b* 6 Dec 1939; *Educ* George Heriots Hosp, Edinburgh Univ Sch of Arch; *m* 1 Aug 1964, Shirley Elizabeth, da of Walter Ronald Brotherstone (d 1967); 4 s (Christopher Dean b 1966, Jonathan James b 1968, Nicholas Carl b 1970, Jason Angus b 1972); *Career* chartered architect; Mowlem (Scotland) Ltd 1966-68, Lyon Gp (Scotland) Ltd 1968-71, ptnr Robin Claton Ptnrship 1971-74, princ Cockburn Assocs 1974-, md Berkeley Estates (Scotland) Ltd; has taken part in major city centre devpts Scotland, urban renewal projects; *Recreations* travel, sailing, skiing, fishing, swimming, golf, bridge, theatre; *Clubs* Merchants House, W of Scotland Rugby Football, Bearsden Ski, Chamber of Commerce, Douglas Park Golf; *Style—* James Cockburn, Esq; Craigallander, 35 Craigmillar Ave, Milngavie, Glasgow (☎ 041 956 5167); Trinity House, Lynedoch St, Glasgow G3 6AB (☎ 041 332 3667, car ☎ 0836 664353)

COCKBURN, Sir John Elliot; 12 Bt of that Ilk (NS 1671); s of Lt-Col Sir John Cockburn, 11 Bt, DSO (d 1949), and Isabel Hunter, *née* McQueen (d 1978); *b* 7 Dec 1925; *Educ* RNC Dartmouth, RAC Cirencester; *m* 7 Sept 1949, Glory Patricia, er da of late Nigel Tudway Mullings, of Dollar Street, Cirencester, Glos; 3 s, 2 da; *Heir* s, Charles Cockburn; *Career* served RAFVR 1944-48; wine broker; *Style—* Sir John Cockburn, Bt; 48 Frewin Rd, London SW18 3LP

COCKBURN, Sir Robert; KBE (1960, OBE 1946), CB (1953); 2 s of late Rev Robert Tough Cockburn (d 1990), of Columba Manse, Belford, Northumberland; *b* 31 March 1909; *Educ* Southern Secdy Sch, Municipal Coll Portsmouth, Univ of London (MSc Eng, PhD), Univ of Cambridge (MA); *m* 1935, Phyllis, da of late Frederick Hoyland; 2 da; *Career* scientific advsr to Air Miny 1948-53, chief scientist Miny of Aviation 1959-64, dir RAE Farnborough 1964-69, chm Nat Computing Centre 1970-77, sr res fell Churchill Cambridge 1970-77; chm: TV Advsy Ctee for Posts and Telecommunications 1971-73, BBC Engrg Advsy Cncl 1973-81; US Medal for Merit; FEng, Hon FRAeS, FIEE, FInst; *Style—* Sir Robert Cockburn, KBE, CB; 1 Firethorn Close, Longmead, Fleet, Hants GU13 9TR (☎ 0252 615518)

COCKBURN, William; CBE (1990), TD (1980); s of Edward Cockburn (d 1986), of Edinburgh, and Alice, *née* Brennan (d 1983); *b* 28 Feb 1943; *Educ* Holy Cross Acad Edinburgh (Dip); *m* 25 Jul 1970, Susan Elisabeth, da of Maj William Phillpots, MBE; 2 da (Rachel b 1974, Rebecca b 1977); *Career* TA RE Postal and Courier Serv 1968, appt Col 1986; PO: Glasgow 1961, PA to Chm 1971-73, asst dir of fin and planning 1973-77, dir of Central Planning 1977-78, dir postal fin 1978-79, dir London Postal Regn 1979-82, memb PO Bd 1981, memb for Fin Counter Servs and Planning 1982-84, memb for Royal Mail Ops 1984-86; md Royal Mail 1986-; non exec dir: VAT Watkins Hldgs Ltd 1985-, Business in the Community Bd 1990-; Freedom City of London 1980; *Style—* William Cockburn, Esq, CBE, TD; Royal Mail House, 148-166 Old St, London EC1V 9HQ

COCKBURN-CAMPBELL, Alexander Thomas; s and h of Sir Thomas Cockburn-Campbell, 6 Bt; *b* 16 March 1945; *m* 1969, Kerry Anne, eldest da of Sgt K Johnson; 1 s (Thomas Justin b 10 Feb 1974), 1 da (Felicity Anne b 9 June 1981); *Style—* Alexander Cockburn-Campbell, Esq; 29 Champlin Way, Ferndale 6155, W Australia

COCKBURN-CAMPBELL, Sir Thomas; 6 Bt (UK 1821), of Gartsford, Ross-shire; s of Sir Alexander Thomas Cockburn-Campbell, 5 Bt (d 1935), and Maude Frances Lorenzo, *née* Giles (d 1926); *b* 8 Dec 1918; *Educ* Church of England GS Melbourne Aust; *m* 1, 24 June 1944 (m dis 1981), (Josephine) Zoi, eldest da of Harold Douglas Forward, of Cunjardine, W Australia; 1 s (Alexander); m 2, 19 June 1982 (m dis 1990), Janice Laraine, da of William John Pascoe of 2 Sutton Court, Bundoora 3038 Victoria, Australia; *Heir* s, Alexander Thomas Cockburn-Campbell; *Career* pastoralist, publican, nursery owner, now ret; *Recreations* antique collecting, reading, writing (Autobiography); *Style—* Sir Thomas Cockburn-Campbell, Bt; Gartsford Cottage, 14 Lincoln St, York 6302, Western Australia

COCKCROFT, Maj (Jon) Barnaby Briggs; s of Maj Eric Briggs Cockcroft (d 1977), of Bryn Dinarth, Colwyn Bay, and Olive Mary, *née* Brown; *b* 27 Aug 1936; *Educ* Sherborne, RMA Sandhurst, Staff Coll Camberley; *m* 4 Oct 1960, Audrey Mary, da of Lt-Col Robert Charles Henry Kidd, OBE (d 1970), of Moat House, Fincham, Norfolk; 1 s (Capt Rupert b 1963), 1 da (Laura b 1967); *Career* Maj Welsh Gds: represented Army at Rugby Football, served Aden 1965-66, NI 1973, Hong Kong 1979-81, ret 1983; HM Body Guard Hon Corps of Gentlemen-At-Arms 1987-; sec City of London TAVRA 1985-; Freeman City of London; *Recreations* gardening, shooting; *Clubs* Lansdowne; *Style—* Maj Barnaby Cockcroft; Holt End House, Ashford Hill, Newbury, Berks (☎ 0734 813727); Duke of Yorks HQ, Chelsea, London SW3 4RY (☎ 071 730 8131)

COCKCROFT, Dr John Anthony Eric; s of Eric William Cockcroft, OBE (d 1979), of Todmorden, Yorks, and Haidee Greenlees, *née* Sutcliffe (d 1980); *b* 9 Aug 1934; *Educ* Todmorden GS, Univ of Cambridge (tech state scholarship, BA, MA), Univ of Aberdeen (MLitt), Univ of Manchester (PhD); *m* 5 Sept 1965, Victoria Mary, da of Frank Lawrence Hartley, of Castleford, W Yorks; 2 s (John b 1972, Alexander b 1974), 1 da (Vicki b 1967); *Career* Nat Serv cmmn RTR Germany 1955-56 (Sword of Honour), TA cmmn Duke of Lancasters Own Yeomanry Manchester 1959-65; Ford Motor Co 1959, UK private indust 1960-64, OECD Paris sci and devpt fell Miny of Economic Coordination Athens 1965-67, UK private industry 1968-69, FCO and ODA advsr Inter Ministerial Investment Advsy Ctee Kabul 1970-72, UN expert Miny of Nat Economy Amman 1973, md Anglo W German Manufacturing Co 1974-78, fell NATO Brussels 1979-80, UN conslt Dar es Salaam 1980, fell Centre for Def Studies Univ of Aberdeen 1980, prof of economics and mgmnt Nigeria 1982, Killam fell centre for foreign policy studies Dalhousie Univ Canada 1982-84, leader Int Mgmnt Consultancy Team World Bank and Price Waterhouse Dhaka 1985, md Manchester UK 1986-89; author of private papers for govts and int orgns incl: Science and Development, The Pilot Teams Greece (OECD, jtly), Alliance Economic Co-operation & Military Assistance in South-East Flank (NATO), Contemporary Soviet Strategy & Space Weapons (thesis, Univ of Manchester); FInstD 1975, MSIAD 1975, CText 1978; memb: RUSI 1979, IISS 1980, RIIA 1980; FTI 1986; *Recreations* music, pictures and prints, tennis, swimming, supporting Leeds & Manchester United and Kippax Welfare AFC U-15's; *Clubs* Cavalry & Guards; *Style—* Dr John Cockcroft; The Old Vicarage, Ledsham, Milford, Leeds LS25 5LT (☎ 0977 683326); Allied Textiles Companies plc, Highburton, Huddersfield, W Yorkshire HD8 0QJ (☎ 0535 273221)

COCKCROFT, John Hoyle; s of Lionel Fielden Cockcroft, of Todmordern, Yorks, and Jenny, *née* Hoyle; nephew of Sir John Cockcroft (d 1967), who was winner of Nobel prize for physics 1951 and first master of Churchill Coll Cambridge; *b* 6 July 1934; *Educ* Oundle, St John's Coll Cambridge (MA); *m* 1971, Tessa Fay, da of Dr William Shepley (d 1968); 3 da (Lucia b 1972, Gemma b 1974, Eloise b 1978); *Career* electronics economist; feature writer and investmt analyst The Financial Times 1959-61, economist and analyst (acquisitions) GKN 1962-67, seconded to Treasy Public Enterprise Div 1965-66, econ leader writer Daily Telegraph 1967-74; MP(C) Nantwich 1974-79, memb Select Ctee on Nationalised Industs (tport) 1975-79, Co Secretaries Bill (private memb) 1978-79; Parly conslt: Br Field Sports Soc 1975-76, ICS 1977-79; dir: RSJ Aviation (aircraft brokers) 1979-, Spalding Securities (investmt advsrs) 1982-, Communications Educnl Servs 1983- (chm 1989-), BR (eastern region bd) 1984-89, Innovare (electronics) 1986-90 J England Group plc 1991-; conslt and historian Guest Keen and Nettlefolds 1971-76; conslt: Datsun (Nissan) UK 1980-81, Cray Electronics 1982-84, Wedgwood 1983-84, Crystalate Holdings 1984-87, Camden Assocs (political PR) 1984-88 Charles Barker City 1991-; electronics economist and conslt stockbroking CCF Laurence Prust Corporation Fin 1986-90; columnist and contrib to: Microscope 1982-85, Banking World 1984-87, Electronics Times 1985-89; *Publications* Reforming the Constitution (jtly, 1968), Self-Help Reborn (jtly, 1969), Why England Sleeps (1971), Internal History of Guest Keen and Nettlefolds (jtly, 1976), Microelectronics (2 edn, 1983), Microtechnology in Banking (1984); *Recreations* reading, writing, walking, entertaining; *Style—* John Cockcroft, Esq; Mitchell's Farmhouse, Stapleford Tawney, Essex RM4 1SS (☎ 04028 254)

COCKCROFT, Sir Wilfred Halliday; s of Wilfred Cockcroft (d 1958), of Keighley, Yorks, and Bessie, *née* Halliday (d 1967); *b* 7 June 1923; *Educ* Keighley Boys' GS, Balliol Coll Oxford (MA, DPhil); *m* 1, 1949, Barbara Rhona Huggan (d 1982); 2 s; m 2, 1982, Vivien, da of David Lloyd, of Warmington; *Career* prof of pure mathematics Univ of Hull 1961-73, vice chllr New Univ of Ulster 1976-82, chm Secdy Examination Cncl 1983-89, chm Educn Project Resources; FIMA; kt 1982; *Clubs* Athenaeum; *Style—* Sir Wilfred Cockcroft; The Old Rectory, Warmington OX17 1BU

COCKELL, Michael Henry; s of Charles Seaton (d 1966), and Elise Seaton Mandeville (d 1973); *b* 30 Aug 1933; *m* 15 July 1961, (Elizabeth) Janet, da of Dr Gilbert Jamieson Meikle (d 1975); 1 s (Charles Seaton b 21 May 1967), 3 da (Nicola Ann b 13 July 1963, Susan Louise b 28 Dec 1964, Lucinda Jane (twin) b 21 May 1967); *Career* Nat Serv 1952-54, HAC 1954-60; underwriter GN Rouse & others (Syndicate 570) 1968-89, dir Willis Faber & Dumas (UA) Ltd 1969-85; chm: MH Cockell & Co Ltd 1978-87, Harris & Dixon (UA) Ltd 1982-86; chm Lloyds's Non-Marine Assoc 1983 (dep chm 1982), dep chm Lloyd's 1986 (memb Cncl 1984-87 and 1990-93), sr ptnr MH Cockell & Partners 1986-; *Recreations* sport (especially cricket), music, ornithology gardening, fishing and the countryside; *Clubs* MCC, HAC, City of London; *Style—* Michael Cockell, Esq

COCKERAM, Eric Paul; s of John Winter Cockeram (d 1976), of Birkenhead, Cheshire, and Mildred Edith, *née* O'Neill (d 1977); *b* 4 July 1924; *Educ* The Leys Sch Cambridge; *m* 2 July 1949, Frances Gertrude, da of Herbert Irving (d 1979), of Birkenhead; 2 s (Howard b 1950, James b 1955), 2 da (Susan b 1952, Julia (twin) b 1955); *Career* Capt Gloucestershire Regt 1942-46, D-Day landings (wounded twice); MP (C): Bebington 1970-Feb 1974, Ludlow 1979-87; former PPS to: Chllr of the Exchequer, Min for Industry, Min for Posts and Telecommunications; chm: Watson Prickard Ltd, Northern Property Two Ltd; dir: TSB (NW) Ltd, Midshires Bldg Soc, Muller Gp (UK) Ltd; memb Lloyds; Liveryman (and memb Ct) Worshipful Co of Glovers; Freeman: City of London, City of Springfield Illinois USA; JP Liverpool 1960; *Recreations* shooting, golf, bridge; *Clubs* Carlton; *Style—* Eric Cockeram, Esq; Fairway Lodge, Caldy, Wirral L48 1NB (☎ 051 625 1100); Watson Prickard Ltd, North John Street, Liverpool L2 4SH (☎ 051 236 8841)

COCKERELL, Sir Christopher Sydney; CBE (1966); s of Sir Sydney Cockerell (d 1962), and Florence Kate, *née* Kingsford (d 1949); *b* 4 June 1910; *Educ* Gresham's, Peterhouse Cambridge (MA); *m* 1937, Margaret Elinor, da of John Horace Belsham (d 1947); 2 da; *Career* inventor of the hovercraft; pupil W H Allen's 1931-33, in charge of aircraft navigational and communications equipment Marc 1935-51 (filed 36 patents); started boat-bldg business on the Broads 1950 (chm Ripplecraft Co Lt 1950-79), commenced work on hovercraft 1953, experimental craft operated crossing Channel 1959 (filed 56 patents), former dir and consIt Hovercraft Development Ltd; commenced work on extraction of power from sea waves 1972 (filed 3 patents), formed Wavepower Ltd 1974 (chm 1974-82); Albert medal RSA 1966, Royal medal Royal Soc 1966, Inst of Mech Engrs James Watt Int Gold medal 1983; Hon Doctorate RCA 1968; Hon DSc: Univ of Leicester 1967, Heriot-Watt Univ 1971, Univ of London 1975; FRS 1967, RDI 1987; kt 1969; *Recreations* fishing, gardening, the visual arts; *Style—* Sir Christopher Cockerell, CBE, FRS; 16 Prospect Place, Hythe, Hants SO4 6AU (☎ 0703 842931)

COCKERILL, Glenn; s of Ron Cockerill, of Cleethorpes, S Humberside, and Thelma, *née* Burtoft; *b* 25 Aug 1959; *Educ* North Clee Secdy Sch, Lyndsay HS; *m* 12 June 1982, Sharon Elizabeth Eleanor, da of Dennis Wilfred Turner; 3 s (Liam Ben b 2 June 1984, Sam Joseph b 9 Aug 1986, Joss Adam b 19 April 1989); *Career* professional footballer; Lincoln City 1976-79: debut 1977, 74 appearances, 10 goals; Swindon Town

1979-81: joined for a fee of £110,000, 29 appearances, 1 goal; Lincoln City 1981-84: rejoined for a fee of £40,000, 139 appearances, 26 goals; Sheffield Utd 1984-85: joined for a fee of £125,000, 69 appearances, 11 goals; Southampton 1985-: joined for a fee of £225,000, over 200 appearances, over 30 goals; *Recreations* music, driving, gardening; *Style—* Glenn Cockerill, Esq; Southampton FC, The Dell, Milton Rd, Southampton SO9 4XX (☎ 0703 220505)

COCKERTON, Rev John Clifford Penn; s of William Penn Cockerton (d 1944), and Eleanor, *née* Culshaw (d 1945); *b* 27 June 1927; *Educ* Wirral GS, Univ of Liverpool (BA, DipEd), Univ of Oxford (MA), Wycliffe Hall Oxford; *m* 21 Aug 1974, Diana Margaret (d 1987), da of Walter Smith (d 1987); *Career* ordained deacon 1954, priest 1955, curate St Helens Liverpool 1954-58, tutor Cranmer Hall Durham 1958-60 (chaplain 1960-63), vice princ St John's Coll Durham 1963-70, warden Cranmer Hall Durham 1968-70, princ St John's Coll Durham 1970-78; rector Wheldrake York 1978- (with Thorganby 1985-), canon and prebendary York Minster 1987-; *Recreations* music; *Style—* The Rev Canon John Cockerton; The Rectory, 3 Church Lane, Wheldrake, York YO4 6AW (☎ 090 489 230)

COCKETT, Frank Bernard; s of Rev Dr Charles Bernard Cockett (d 1965), of Melbourne, Aust, and Florence, *née* Champion (d 1951); *b* 22 April 1916; *Educ* Bedford Sch, St Thomas's Hosp London (BSc, MB BS, MS); *m* 1, Felicity Ann (d 1958), da of Col James Thackeray Fisher, DSO; 1 s (James Robin Bernard b 4 May 1951), 2 da (Judith Sophia b 12 Aug 1947, Sally Ann b 15 Aug 1949); m 2, 17 Nov 1960, Dorothea Ann, *née* Newman; 2 s (Richard Bernard b 22 April 1962, Peter Bernard (twin) b 22 April 1962); *Career* Sqdn Ldr and surgical specialist RAFVR 1942-46; conslt surgn: St Thomas' Hosp 1954-81 (resident asst surgn 1948-50, sr lectr surgical unit 1950-54), King Edward VII Hosp for Offrs 1970-86; Rovsing Medal Danish Surgical Soc 1977, Ratschow Medal German Angiology Soc 1989; pres Vascular Surgical Soc of GB and Ireland 1980 (fndr memb), chm Venous Forum RSM 1985-87 (fndr memb), fell Assoc of Surgns of GB and Ireland, memb Euro Soc of Cardiovascular Surgery; FRCS; *Books* The Pathology and Surgery of the Veins of the Lower Limb (2 edn, 197 The Maltese Penguin (1990); *Recreations* sailing, collecting marine pictures, writing; *Clubs* Little Ship, Island Sailing, Lansdowne; *Style—* Frank Cockett, Esq; 14 Essex Villas, Kensington, London W8 7BN (☎ 071 937 9883); 38 Devonshire Place W1N 1PE (☎ 071 580 3612)

COCKETT, Geoffrey Howard; s of William Cockett (d 1970), of Southampton, and Edith Gertrude, *née* Dinham (d 1957); *b* 18 March 1926; *Educ* King Edward VI Sch Southampton, Univ of Southampton (BSc); *m* 1951, Elizabeth Mary Florence, da of Stanley Frederick Bagshaw (d 1970), of Orpington; 2 da (Juliet, Jenny-Sarah); *Career* chartered physicist; res scientist: Royal Aircraft Establishment 1948-52, Armament Res Establishment 1952-67, Henley Mgmnt Coll 1968; supt Physics Res Chem Def Establishment 1968-71, supt Optics and Surveillance System RARDE 1971-76, head Applied Physics Gp 1976-83; dep dir (systems) and chief scientific offr RARDE 1983-86, conslt scientist MOD Whitehall 1987-; memb Orpington Sports Club, vice pres Old Edwardians Assoc 1990; FInstP; *Recreations* opera, photography, under gardening; *Style—* Geoffrey Cockett, Esq; RARDE, Fort Halstead, Sevenoaks, Kent TN14 7BP

COCKFIELD, Baron (Life Peer UK 1978), of Dover, Co Kent; (Francis) Arthur Cockfield; PC (1982); 2 s of Lt C F Cockfield (ka 1916), and Louisa, *née* James; *b* 28 Sept 1916; *Educ* Dover GS, LSE; *m* Aileen Monica Mudie, choreographer; *Career* called to the Bar Inner Temple 1942, former fin dir and chief exec Boots Pure Drug Co Ltd, dir of statistics and intelligence Bd of Inland Revenue 1944; Cmmn of Inland Revenue 1951; pres Royal Statistical Soc 1968; advisor on Fiscal Policy to Chllr of Exchequer 1970-73; chm Price Cmmn 1973-77; min of state Treasy 1979-82, sec state Trade 1982-83, pres BOT; chllr Duchy of Lancaster 1983-; vice-pres Cmmn of European Communities of 1985-88; Grand Cross of the Order of Leopold II (Belgium); Hon LLD: Fordham Univ NY, Univ of Sheffield; Hon DUniv Univ of Surrey; kt 1973; *Style—* The Rt Hon the Lord Cockfield, PC; House of Lords, Westminster, London SW1

COCKING, Prof Edward Charles Daniel; s of Charles Edward Cocking (d 1965), and Mary, *née* Murray; *b* 26 Sept 1931; *Educ* Buckhurst Hill County HS Essex, Univ of Bristol (BSc, PhD, DSc); *m* 6 Aug 1960, Bernadette, da of Frank Keane (d 1948); 1 s (Sean Daniel b 1961), 1 da (Sarah Anne b 1966); *Career* civil serv cmmn res fell 1956-59; Univ of Nottingham: lectr in plant physiology 1959-66, reader in botany 1966-68, prof of botany and head of Dept of Botany 1969; memb: Bd of Tstees Royal Botanical Gardens Kew 1983-, Cncl Royal Society 1986-88, Lawes Agric Tst Ctee Rothamsted Experimental Station 1987-; Royal Soc assessor AFRC 1988-90, memb Cncl AFRC 1990- (chm Plants & Environment Res Ctee); FRS 1983; *Books* Introduction to the Principles of Plant Physiology (with W Stiles, 1969); *Recreations* walking, travelling by train, occassional chess; *Style—* Prof Edward Cocking, FRS; 30 Patterdale Rd, Woodthorpe, Nottingham NG5 4LQ (☎ 0602 262452); Plant Genetic Manipulation Group, University of Nottingham NG7 2RD (☎ 0602 484848 ext 2201, fax 0602 424270, telex 37346 UNINOT G)

COCKING, Maurice Douglas; s of Cecil Maurice Cocking (d 1967) of Hastings and Amelia *née* Shorter (d 1972); *b* 28 Oct 1930; *Educ* Beckenham GS, Univ of Exeter (BA), Univ of London (BSc); *m* 11 Sept 1954, Patricia da of James Charles Fowler (d 1966) of Sevenoaks, 2 s (Crispian b 1961, Kester b 1962); *Career* Nat Serv BAOR 1949-51; fin journalist 1955; city ed: Empire News 1958, Daily Sketch 1964; fndr and chm FABUS Fin and Business PR Ltd 1967, fin journalist Sunday Times and Daily Express; Liveryman Worshipful Co: of Basketmakers (steward), of Tallow Chandlers; *Recreations* verse, oenology, equestrianism; *Clubs* City Livery, IOD, Farringdon Ward and Utd Wards, City, Pickwick; *Style—* Maurice D Cocking, Esq; Pantiles Chambers, High Street, Tunbridge Wells (☎ 0892 548933)

COCKMAN, Derrick Harry; s of Walter John Cockman (d 1972), and Minnie Mabel, *née* Street (d 1980); *b* 15 Feb 1927; *Educ* Hertford GS; *m* 1, 4 June 1949 (m dis 1972), Joyce Iris, da of David Roberts (d 1966); 3 s (Michael b 1954, Peter b 1955, Philip b 1962); m 2, 24 Feb 1973, Sandrina Antonietta, *née* Gallina; 1 s (Alessandro b 1966), 1 da (Vanessas b 1968); *Career* RAMC 1945-48; md H H Robertson Germany and Belgium 1966-68, pres Managment Control Systems Italy 1968-71; fin dir: ITT Europe 1971-75, Graco Europe 1975-78, FIAT Argentina 1978-81, Campbell Soups Argentina and UK 1981-88; ind mgmnt conslt 1988-; ASAA 1952, FCA 1964; *Recreations* tennis, skiing; *Style—* Derrick Cockman, Esq; Tower House, 1 Temple Gardens, Brighton, E Sussex BN1 3AE (☎ 0273 29510, fax 0273 747774); 2 Villagio Monacò, Capo San Vito (Trapani), Sicily

COCKRAM, Sir John; s of Alfred John Cockram (d 1956), of Highgate, and Beatrice Elizabeth Cockram; *b* 10 July 1908; *Educ* St Aloysius Coll Highgate; *m* 1937, Phyllis Eleanor, o da of Albert Henning, of Loughton, Essex; 1 s, 2 da; *Career* former gen mangr and dir Colne Valley Water Co, former dir and chm Rickmansworth Water Co; memb Thames Conservancy 1954-74, pres Exec Ctee Br Waterworks Ctee 1957-58 (memb 1948-74, memb Centra Ctee 1955-74), memb Hertfordshire CC 1949-74 (chm 1961-65), life govr Haileybury; FCA; kt 1964; *Style—* Sir John Cockram; Rebels' Corner, The Common, Chorleywood, Rickmansworth, Herts WD3 5LT

COCKRILL, Maurice Edwin; s of William Edwin Cockrill (d 1970), of Wrexham, Clwyd, and Edith, *née* Godfrey (d 1966); *b* 8 Oct 1936; *Educ* Grove Park GS Wrexham, Wrexham Sch of Art, Univ of Reading; 2 s (Steven Paul b 1958, Joel b 1964); ptnr Helen Moslin; 1 s (William Alexander b 1989); *Career* artist; lectr Faculty of Art Liverpool Poly 1967-80; visiting tutor: Winchester Sch of Art 1984-85, Central Sch of Art 1985-88, RCA 1988, Slade Sch of Art 1990, St Martin's Sch of Art 1984-90; solo exhibitions incl: Peterloo Gallery Manchester 1971, Serpentine Gallery London 1971, Bluecoat Gallery Liverpool 1974, 1979, 1980 and 1982, Liverpool Acad Gallery 1976, Municipal Art Gallery Bootle Liverpool 1978, St Paul's Gallery Leeds 1979, Seven in Two (Lime Street Station Liverpool) 1979-80, February Festival Cmmn Milton Keynes 1981, Univ of Nottingham 1983, Edward Totah Gallery London 1984 and 1985, Kunstmuseum Düsseldorf 1985, Udo Bugdahn Gallery Düsseldorf 1986, Bernard Jacobson Gallery London 1987 and 1990 (NY 1988); gp exhibitions incl: Art in a City (ICA London) 1967, Spectrum North (Arts Cncl Tour) 1971, John Moores Liverpool Exhibition 9 (prizewinner) 1974, The Face of Merseyside (Walker Art Gallery Liverpool) 1976, Arts Cncl Collection 1976-77 (Hayward Gallery London) 1977, Cleveland Int Drawing Biennale 1981, British Drawing (Hayward Annual London) 1982, Royal Acad Summer Exhibition London 1984, Hommage aux Femmes (ICC Berlin, Leverkusen Cologne) 1985, Athena Art Awards Barbican 1987, John Moores Exhibition 14 1987, Mother and Child (Lefevre Gallery London) 1988, Recent Paintings (Bernard Jacobson Gallery) 1989; work in several public and private collections: *Awards* prizewinner Arts Cncl Flags and other Projects Royal Festival Hall 1977, maj award Arts Cncl of GB 1977-78, project at Lime St Station Liverpool, Arts Cncl Work of Art in Public Spaces 1978-79; *Clubs* Chelsea Arts; *Style—* Maurice Cockrill, Esq; Bernard Jacobson Gallery, 14A Clifford St, London W1X 1RF (☎ 071 495 8575, fax 071 495 6210)

COCKROFT, Richard Robert; s of Albert Hainsworth Cockroft, of Devon, and Jocelyn Courtney Cockcroft, OBE, *née* Dart; *b* 7 March 1939; *Educ* Exeter Sch, Trinity Coll Cambridge (MA); *m* 1962, Judith Prunella, da of Cecil Victor Alexander Wearn (d 1964); 1 s (Timothy b 1967), 1 da (Georgina b 1965); *Career* dir Towry Law and Co Ltd 1966-84, md Towry Law (Hldgs) Ltd 1971-84, dir M & G Group plc 1984-88, md M & G Assurance Group Ltd 1984-88, chm Independent Market Assistance Group Ltd 1987-88; dir (Membership and Practice) FIMBRA 1988-; FCII, FRSA; *Recreations* golf, real tennis; *Clubs* MCC, East Berks Golf; *Style—* Richard R Cockroft, Esq; Arborfield House, Arborfield, nr Reading, Berkshire RG2 9JB

COCKS, Freda Mary; *née* Wood; OBE (1972), JP (1968); da of Frank Wood (d 1985), and Mary, *née* Turner (d 1968); *b* 30 July 1915; *Educ* St Peters Sch Birmingham, Queen's Coll Birmingham; *m* 20 Oct 1942, Donald Francis Melvin (d 1979), s of Melvin Francis (d 1968); 2 da (Janet Mary b 2 July 1943, Christine Ann b 11 June 1944 d 1946); *Career* nurse 1938-41, hotelier 1949-79; chm: Housing Birmingham 1968-72, gen purposes 1980-82; memb Area West Health Authy; vice pres Carers Assoc, pres League of Friends: Dudley Rd Hosp, Womens Hosp, Birmingham Eye Hosp; memb: Elfrida Rathbone Assoc, Hestia Housing Assoc; pres Mission to Seamen Birmingham Branch, fndr Birmingham Hosp Broadcasting Assoc, pres Edgbaston Cons Assoc; memb City Cncl of 1957-90 (dep chm 1982-86), Lord Mayor of Birmingham 1976-77; Freeman City of Birmingham 1986, Hon Alderman 1990-; Freedom of Du Panne Belgium 1978; *Recreations* hospitals, social services, walking; *Clubs* Soroptomist (Birmingham); *Style—* Mrs Freda Cocks, OBE, JP; 332 Hagley Rd, Edgbaston, Birmingham B16 8BH (☎ 021 420 1140); The Council House, Birmingham (☎ 021 235 2130)

COCKS, Dr Leonard Robert Morrison (Robin); TD (1979); s of Ralph Morrison Cocks (d 1970), and Lucille Mary, *née* Blackler; *b* 17 June 1938; *Educ* Felsted, Hertford Coll Oxford (BA, MA, DPhil, DSc); *m* 31 Aug 1962, Elaine Margaret, da of Canon J B Sturdy; 1 s (Mark b 1964), 2 da (Zoe b 1967, Julia b 1970); *Career* 2 Lt RA 1957-59, active serv Malaya; scientist Nat History Museum 1965, keeper of palaeontology, cmmr Int Cmmn on Zoological Nomenclature 1980-; sec Geological Soc 1985-89, pres Palaeontological Assoc 1986-88; FGS; *Books* The Evolving Earth (1981), contrib to over 80 articles in sci jls on geology and palaeontology; *Style—* Dr Robin Cocks, TD; 12 Winchester Park, Bromley BR2 0PY; Natural History Museum, Cromwell Rd, London SW7 5BD (☎ 071 938 8845)

COCKS OF HARTCLIFFE, Baron (Life Peer UK 1987), of Chinnor, Co Oxfordshire; Michael Francis Lovell Cocks; PC (1976); s of late Rev Harry F Lovell Cocks, of Amersham; *b* 19 Aug 1929; *Educ* Univ of Bristol; *m* 1, 1954, Janet Macfarlane; 2 s, 2 da; m 2, 1979, Valerie Davis; *Career* MP (Lab) Bristol South 1970-87; asst govt whip 1974-76; Parly sec to Treasury and govt chief whip 1976-79; opposition chief whip 1979-85; *Style—* The Rt Hon Lord Cocks of Hartcliffe, PC; c/o House of Lords, London SW1

COCKSHAW, Alan; s of John Cockshaw (d 1986), and Maud, *née* Simpson; *b* 14 July 1937; *Educ* Farnworth GS; *m* 17 Dec 1960, Brenda, da of Fred Payne; 1 s (John Nigel b 1964); 3 da (Elizabeth Ann b 1967, Sally Louise b 1970, Catherine Helen b 1979); *Career* formerly chief exec: Fairclough Civil Engr Ltd 1978-85, Fairclough-Parkinson Mining Ltd 1982-85, Fairclough Engr Ltd 1983-84; exec chm AMEC plc 1988- (gp chief exec 1984-88); hon degree in civil engrg Univ of Leeds; *Recreations* rugby (both codes), cricket, walking, gardening; *Style—* Alan Cockshaw, Esq; Red Hill House, 4 Waterbridge, The Green, Worsley, Manchester M28 4NL (☎ 061 794 5972); AMEC plc, Sandiway House, Northwich, Cheshire CW8 2YA (☎ 0606 883885, telex 669708, fax 0606 883996)

CODARIN, Judith; da of William Ernest Walker (d 1971), of Thornham, N Norfolk, and Mary Eileen Jacob; *b* 8 July 1946; *Educ* Kings Lynn HS for Girls, Norwich Sch of Art, Birmingham Coll of Art; *m* Armando Codarin, s of Venceslao Codarin; 1 s (Pierre Daniel b 28 April 1980), 1 da (Melanie Maria b 8 Dec 1973); *Career* design conslt; architectural asst Casson Conder & Partners 1968-72, with Conran Design Group (now Fitch & Co) 1972-73, freelance res and commercial illustrating designing and tech drawing for cos incl: McColl, Ryman, Rottenberg Associates 1973-76; working with: Franco Nadali Ltd 1973-84, Baker Sayer 1984-88; running Judith Codarin Interior Designers & Management 1988-; author of numerous published articles, developed and ran own restaurant 1978-86; parent govr St Bernards Convent HS; CSD: memb Cncl 1988, memb Interiors Gp; memb Assoc of Facilities Mangrs; *Recreations* walking, swimming, driving through Europe to Italy every year looking at buildings; *Style—* Mrs Judith Codarin; Judith Codarin Interior Designers & Design Management, 14 Rivera Drive, Southend on Sea, Essex SS1 2RB (☎ 0702 469140, fax 0702 463343)

CODD, (Ronald) Geoffrey; s of Thomas Reuben Codd (d 1976), and Betty Leyster Justice, *née* Sturt; *b* 20 Aug 1932; *Educ* Cathedral Sch Llandaff, The College Llandovery, Presentation Coll Cobh Co Cork; *m* 2 April 1960, Christine Ellen Leone, da of Flt Lt Reginald Arthur John Robertson, of Endways, The Tye, Barking, Needham Market, Suffolk; 1 s (Justin b 27 Oct 1968), 2 da (Louise b 11 May 1962, Emma b 19 July 1966); *Career* RAF Tport Command 1952-57; Rolls-Royce 1957-58, International Computers 1958-61, Marconi Co 1961-70, J Bibby and Sons 1970-74, Weir Group 1974-80, Brooke Bond Group 1981-86, dir Info and Risk Management ECGD 1986-89, managing ptnr Interchange Associates 1989-, involved with Info Technol Policy Gp; Freeman Worshipful Co of Info Technologists; FBCS, FBIM, MIOD; *Books* contrib to business publications; *Recreations* sailing, theatre, practical pastimes; *Clubs* Royal Northern and Clyde Yacht; *Style—* Geoffrey Codd, Esq;

Chesterton, Three Gates Lane, Haslemere, Surrey GU27 2LD (☎ 0428 642163)

CODD, (Robin Hugh Ian Anthony) Patrick; TD (1978, 2 Bars); s of Lionel Hugh Codd (d 1979), of Oakford, N Devon, and Isabel Elma, *née* Berry (d 1985); *b* 11 Nov 1937; *Educ* Belmont Coll; *m* 1, Patricia, *née* Grant; 1 da (Antoinette Elizabeth Gallies b May 1964); m 2, Susan Ann, *née* Turner; 1 da (Devina Holly Chelsea Elma b 16 Jan 1987); *Career* journalist/reporter: North Devon Journal Herald, Western Evening Herald, The Sun, Daily Mail, Daily Express; Daily Star: helped launch as feature writer Oct 1978, show business and news ed 1981, show business ed 1987-; *Recreations* TA, cinema, Camra recommended pubs, Golden Age American comics; *Style—* Patrick Codd, Esq, TD; 2 Fairlawn Close, Kingston Hill, Kingston upon Thames, Surrey KT2 7JW (☎ 081 549 5760); Daily Star, Express Newspaper plc, Ludgate House, 245 Blackfriars Rd, London SE1 9UX (☎ 071 922 7446, fax 071 922 7962)

CODRINGTON, Christopher George Wayne; s (by 2 m) and h of Sir Simon Codrington, 3 Bt; *b* 20 Feb 1960; *Educ* Hawtreys, Millfield Coll, Royal Agric Coll Cirencester; *Career* pres Codrington Oil & Gas Inc; dir: Codrington Corporation, Conservatives Abroad (Texas); *Style—* Christopher G W Codrington, Esq; 13405 North-West Freeway, Suite 310, Houston, Texas 77040, USA

CODRINGTON, Giles Peter; s of late Lt-Cdr Sir William Codrington, 7 Bt and hp of bro, 8 Bt; *b* 28 Oct 1943; *Recreations* sailing; *Clubs* Antique Yacht; *Style—* Giles Codrington, Esq

CODRINGTON, Ian Charles; s of Charles Leonard Winterforde Codrington (d 1972), of Bedford, and Enid Mary, *née* Harley (d 1988); *b* 11 Feb 1938; *Educ* Bedford Sch, Fitzwilliam Coll Cambridge (MA); *m* 1962 (m dis 1988), Alice Jennifer Katharine, *née* Laborde; 1 s (Charles b 1967), 2 da (Alice b 1963, Sarah b 1965); *Career* admitted slr 1962; currently sr ptnr Sharman & Trethewy, NP; memb ctee Billy Goat Soc, dep pres Bedford Rowing Club, memb ctee Leander Club Henley-on-Thames, sec Bedford Regatta and Bedford Head of River, former pres Bedford Castle Rotary Club, involved with Paines Plough Ltd (theatre Co); FBIM, memb Law Soc; *Recreations* rowing; *Clubs* Bedford, The 1900; *Style—* Ian Codrington, Esq, Sharman & Trethewy, 1 Harpur St, Bedford MK40 1PF (☎ 0234 41171 fax 0234 52114); Sharman & Trethewy, 1 Harpur St, Bedford MK40 IPF (☎ 0234 341171 fax 0234 352114)

CODRINGTON, Sir Simon Francis Bethell; 3 Bt (UK 1876), of Dodington, Gloucestershire; s of Sir Christopher Codrington, 2 Bt (d 1979), and his 1 wife Joan Mary, *née* Hague-Cook (d 1961); *b* 14 Aug 1923; *Educ* Eton; *m* 1, 3 May 1947 (m dis 1959) Joanne, da of John William Molineaux, of Rock Castle, Kilmacsimon, Co Cork, and widow of William Humphrey Austin Thompson; m 2, 1959 (m dis 1979), Pamela Joy Halliday, da of Maj George Walter Bentley Wise, MBE; 3 s; m 3, 1980 (m dis 1988), Mrs Sarah (Sally) Gwynne Gaze, *née* Pennell; m 4, 1989, Shirley Ann, da of Percival Lionel Davis; *Heir* s, Christopher Codrington; *Career* formerly Maj Coldstream Gds, served WW II Italy; *Style—* Sir Simon Codrington, Bt; Dodington, Chipping Sodbury, Avon

CODRINGTON, Sir William Alexander; 8 Bt (GB 1721), of Dodington, Gloucestershire; s of Lt-Cdr Sir William Codrington, 5 Bt (d 1961); *b* 5 July 1934; *Educ* St Andrew Coll S Africa, S African Naval Coll; *Heir* bro, Giles Codrington; *Career* Merchant Navy 1952; Worldwide Shipping 1976, memb Hon Co of Master Mariners, FNI; *Style—* Sir William Codrington, Bt; 99 St James Drive, Wandsworth Common, London SW17

CODRON, Michael Victor; CBE (1989); s of I A Codron (d 1981), and Lily, *née* Morgenstern (d 1981); *b* 8 June 1930; *Educ* St Paul's, Worcester Coll Oxford (BA); *Career* theatrical prodr and mangr, owner Vaudeville Theatre; dir: Royal National Theatre, Hampstead Theatre, Aldwych Theatre, Adelphi Theatre, Theatre Mutual Insurance Co; prodns: Share My Lettuce, Breath of Spring 1957, The Caretaker 1960, Loot 1965, The Killing of Sister George 1968, The Boyfriend (revival) 1967, Absurd Person Singular 1973, Funny Peculiar 1976, The Unvarnished Truth 1978, The Dresser 1980, Noises Off 1982, A View from A Bridge 1987, Uncle Vanya 1988, Henceforward 1988; film: Clockwise 1986; *Recreations* collecting Carolinia (of Brunswick) memorabilia; *Clubs* Garrick; *Style—* Michael Codron, Esq, CBE; Aldwych Theatre Offices, Aldwych, London WC2 (☎ 071 240 8291, fax 071 240 8467)

CODY, Sebastian; s of Stephen Cody (d 1990), and Maria Schenker-Angerer; *b* 6 Oct 1956; *Educ* King Alfred Sch Hampstead, Univ of Vienna, Univ of York (BA), Nat Film Sch (trained as dir); *Career* researcher BBC TV 1979; prodr and dir: Why Do I Believe You...1983, Before His Very Eyes 1984; staff prodr Royal Opera House Covent Garden 1985, tv prodr Abracadabra 1986, ed After Dark (Channel 4 TV) 1987-91; freelance writer and journalist 1979-; exec prodr for Open Media 1987- (The Secret Cabaret (1990), James Randi Investigates (1991)); *Clubs* The London Library; *Style—* Sebastian Cody, Esq; 9 Leamington Road Villas, London W11 1HS (☎ 071 221 3658)

COE, (Albert) Harry; *b* 28 May 1944; *m* ; 2 children; *Career* fin dir: Granada Television 1981-88, Airtours plc 1988-; *Recreations* cricket, tennis, golf, skiing; *Style—* Harry Coe Esq; 48 Broad Walk, Wilmslow, Cheshire SK9 5PL (☎ 0625 522 315); Granada TV, Manchester M60 9EA (☎ 061 832 7211)

COË, Peter John Tudor; s of John Robert Tudor Coë (d 1983), and Kathleen Eleanor, *née* Grant; *b* 19 May 1959; *Educ* Clifton, Univ of York; *Career* financial and economic correspondent TV AM 1987-; presenter: Money Matters (TV am) 1987-89, European Business Today (NHK/FNN) 1990-; newsreader (TV am) 1990-; memb NUJ; *Recreations* swimming, skiing, films, theatre; *Clubs* Savile; *Style—* Peter Coë, Esq; TV-AM, Hawley Crescent, Camden Lock, London NW1 8EF (☎ 071 267 8389, fax 071 267 6513); Savile Club, 69 Brook St, London W1

COE, Sebastian Newbold; OBE (1990, MBE 1981); s of Peter Coe, and Angela, *née* Lall; *b* 29 Sept 1956; *Educ* Tapton Sch Sheffield, Univ of Loughborough (BSc); *m* 23 Aug 1990, Nicola McIrvine; *Career* athlete; broken 12 world records incl 800m (current holder) 1500m and 1 mile, Olympic gold 1500m, silver 800m at Moscow Olympics in 1980 and Los Angeles Olympics 1984, World Cup gold 800m 1981, gold Euro 800m 1986; vice chm Sport Cncl of GB 1986 (memb 1983-), chm Sports Cncls Olympic Review 1985-86; memb: Health Educn Authy (formerly Health Educn Cncl) 1986-, Athletes Cmmn, med cmmn Int Olympic Ctee; assoc memb Academie Des Sports France 1982-; Kiphuth Fellowship Univ of Yale 1982, Hon DTech Univ of Loughborough; *Books* Running Free, Running for Fitness with Peter Coe (1983), The Olympians (1984); *Clubs* East India and Sportsmans; *Style—* Sebastian Coe, Esq; The Levitt Group, Devonshire House, 1 Devonshire Street, London W1N 1FX

COFFIN, Dr Brian John; s of John Francis Charles Coffin (d 1975), of Bournemouth, Dorset, and Marjorie Gwendoline, *née* Henson; *b* 24 Aug 1937; *Educ* Canford, King's Coll (BSc, PhD); *m* 22 Oct 1960, Paula Patricia, JP, da of Robert Thomas Ingham, of Normandy, nr Guildford, Surrey; 1 da (Linda-Jane b 24 Oct 1961); *Career* sr lectr in chemistry South Bank Poly 1968-; govr: Royal GS 1977-, Charterhouse 1981-, Tomlinscote Sch Frimley 1988; cncllr Heatherside and Parkside Div Surrey CC 1970-, memb exec cncl Assoc of CCs 1981-; chm: London and SE Region Library Cncl 1975-, Surrey Educn Ctee 1981-85, Surrey Fire Bde Ctee 1985-89; memb NW Surrey Cons Assoc; *Books* Chemistry of Organic Compounds (contrib 1976 and 1983); *Recreations* travel, gardening; *Style—* Dr Brian Coffin; 37 High Beeches, Frimley, Camberley, Surrey GU16 5UG (☎ 0276 243 90); South Bank Poly, Borough Rd, London SE1 (☎ 071 928 8989, ext 2226)

COFFIN, Cyril Edwin; CBE (1984); s of Percy Edwin Coffin (d 1962), of Timsbury, Romsey, Hants, and Helena Constance, *née* Carter; *b* 29 June 1919; *Educ* KCS Wimbledon, King's Coll Cambridge (BA, MA); *m* 29 March 1947, Joyce Mary, da of Cyril Richmond Tobitt, MBE (d 1983), of Castle Hedingham, Essex; 1 s (Christopher b 1948), 2 da (Margaret b 1950, Philippa b 1952 d 1953); *Career* Gunner RA 1939, Royal Scots 1940, cmmnd RIASC 1941, Capt 1941, cmd Field Supply Depots at Imphal and Palel 1942-44, Stocks Offr Advanced Base Supply Depot Chittagong 1945, DADST HQ Allied Land Forces SE Asia 1945; princ Miny of Food 1948 (asst princ 1947), asst sec MAFF 1957, Office of Min for Sci 1963, under sec Miny of Technol 1966 (later Dept of Prices & Consumer Protection), DG Food Mfrs' Fedn 1977-84; area co-ordinator local neighbourhood watch scheme; FRSA 1978; *Books* Working with Whitehall (1987); *Recreations* genealogy, music, learning languages; *Style—* Cyril Coffin, Esq, CBE; 54 Cambridge Ave, New Malden, Surrey KT3 4LE (☎ 081 942 0763)

COGGAN, Baron (Life Peer UK 1980), of Canterbury and Sissinghurst, Co Kent; Rt Rev the Rt Hon (Frederick) Donald Coggan; PC (1961); s of late Cornish Arthur Coggan, of London, and Fannie Sarah Coggan; *b* 9 Oct 1909; *Educ* Merchant Taylors', St John's Coll Cambridge (MA), Wycliffe Hall Oxford, DD Lambeth 1957; *m* 1935, Jean Braithwaite, da of Dr William Loudon Strain, of Wimbledon; 2 da; *Career* asst lectr in Semitic languages and literatures Manchester Univ 1931-34, ordained 1934, curate St Mary Islington 1934-37, prof of new testament Wycliffe Coll Toronto 1937-44 (BD, DD hc), princ London Coll of Divinity 1944-56; bishop of Bradford 1956-61; archbishop of York 1961-74 and Canterbury 1974-80; prelate of the Ven Order of St John of Jerusalem 1967-90; chm Liturgical Cmmn 1960-64; pro-chllr: York Univ 1962-74, Hull Univ 1968-74; pres Soc for Old Testament Studies 1967-68, hon pres Int Cncl of Christians and Jews; Hon Freeman City of Canterbury 1976; Hon DD: Cambridge, Leeds, Aberdeen, Tokyo, Saskatoon, Huron, Hull, Manchester, Moravian Theol Seminary, Virginia Theol Seminary; Hon LLD Liverpool, HHD Westminster Choir Coll Princeton, Hon DLitt Lancaster, STD (hc) Gen Theol Seminary NY, Hon DCL Kent, DUniv York; FKC; *Books Incl:* The Heart of the Christian Faith (1978), The Name above all Names (1981), Sure Foundation (1981), Mission to the World (1982), Paul: Portrait of a Revolutionary (1984), The Sacrament of the Word (1987), Cuthbert Bardsley: Bishop, Evangelist, Pastor (1989); *Recreations* gardening, motoring, music; *Clubs* Athenaeum; *Style—* The Rt Rev the Rt Hon Lord Coggan, PC; 28 Lions Hall, St Swithun St, Winchester SO23 9HW (☎ 0962 864289)

COGGAN, Hon Ruth Evelyn; OBE (1984); da of Rt Rev and Rt Hon Lord Coggan of Sissinghurst and Canterbury, PC, DD, and Jean Braithwaite, *née* Strain; *b* 8 July 1940; *Educ* St Helen's Sch, Northwood, Univ of Leeds (MB ChB); *Career* gynaecologist Pennell Meml Hosp Bannu N W Frontier Province Pakistan 1970-; FRCOG; Sitara-i-Qaid-i-Azam (Pakistan) 1985; *Style—* The Hon Ruth Coggan; 15 Plough Way, Badger Farm, Winchester, SO22 4PX

COGHILL, Sir Egerton James Nevill Tobias (Toby); 8 Bt (GB 1778), of Coghill, Yorkshire; s of Sir Joscelyn Ambrose Cramer Coghill, 7 Bt (d 1983) and his 1 w Elizabeth Gwendoline, *née* Atkins (d 1980); *b* 26 March 1930; *Educ* Gordonstoun, Pembroke Coll Cambridge (MA); *m* 12 April 1958, Gabrielle Nancy, da of Maj Douglas Claud Dudley Ryder, of Rempstone, Corfe Castle, Dorset; 1 s, 1 da (Elizabeth b 1962); *Heir* s, Patrick Kendal Farley Coghill; *Career* architect 1952-56, indust devpt 1956-59, mgmnt consultancy 1959-61, teacher 1961-64, headmaster Aberlour House 1964-89, investmt cnsllr Valu-Trac 1990; chm: Scot Schs Ski Assoc 1974-77, Inc Assoc of Prep Schs (Scot) 1984-87, Ind Schs Info Serv (Scot) 1982-89; *Recreations* country pursuits; *Clubs* Royal Ocean Racing; *Style—* Sir Toby Coghill, Bt

COGHILL, Hon Mrs (Patricia Mary); *née* St Clair; o da of 16 Lord Sinclair, MVO (d 1957); *b* 17 March 1912; *m* 15 March 1940, Lt-Col Charles Archibald Richard Coghill, OBE, Scots Gds (d 1975), s of Norman Coghill, of Almington Hall, Market Drayton; 1 s (Hugh b 1950, m 1973 Edwina Wells, 3 s), 2 da (Sarah b 1948, m 1972 Peter Hopkins; Jane b 1949, m 1970 Graham Merrison); *Style—* The Hon Mrs Coghill; Three Ways, Yelverton Rd, Framingham Earl, Norwich NR14 7SD

COGHILL, Patrick Kendal Farley; s and h of Sir Toby Coghill, 8 Bt; *b* 3 Nov 1960; *Career* dir Front Page Publications Ltd; *Recreations* skiing, windsurfing, offshore sailing; *Style—* Patrick Coghill, Esq; 26 Gowrie Road, London SW11 5NR (☎ 071 350 1355)

COGHLAN, Gerard Anthony Dillon; OBE (1982); s of Herbert George Coghlan (d 1943), and Norah Elizabeth, *née* Dillon (d 1976); *b* 6 Nov 1920; *Educ* St Philips GS Birmingham, Univ of Birmingham (BSc); *m* 13 Sept 1947, Mary Theresa, da of Ernest Arthur Eden (d 1956), of Birmingham; 2 s (Michael b 5 Nov 1951, Simon b 30 Oct 1959), 1 da (Louise b 21 July 1949); *Career* 2 Lt RAOC, 2 Lt and Lt REME 1942, Capt (EME 3 Class) 1943, EME (RA) Gds Div until 1946; asst chief engr Kenrick & Jefferson 1947-48, head of work study (head of corp planning, chief engr, works mangr) Haworth & Co Ltd Manchester 1948-56, mgmnt conslt Tube Investmt Gp Servs 1956-58, exec Wrights Ropes 1958-60, mgmnt conslt Neville Industl Consults Ltd 1960-63, dir and gen mangr Midland Industl Issues Ltd 1963-67; Duport Ltd 1967-71: head of gp mgmnt servs, dir of personnel and industl rels, dep chm Duport Computer Servs, dir Duport Servs Ltd; memb Industl Tbnls 1979-89, chm W Birmingham Health Authy 1981-, memb Police Complaints Bd 1983-85; treas Knutsford Cons Assoc 1956, pres Harborne Ward Cons Assoc 1971- (chm 1960-71), guardian The Birm Proof House 1973-90, Cncl memb Univ of Birmingham 1975- (life govr 1978-), chm of Cncl for School/Work Links 1979-89, gen cmmr of taxes, JP Birmingham 1961-90; Freeman City of London, Liveryman Worshipful Co of Glovers 1978; CEng, FIProdE, MIMechE, MIEE; KSG Knight of the Most Noble and Equestrian Order of St Gregory (Pap Award) 1980; *Recreations* golf; *Clubs* Naval & Military, The Birmingham, Edgbaston Golf; *Style—* Gerard Coghlan, Esq, OBE; 10 Hamilton Ave, Harborne, Birmingham B17 8AJ (☎ 021 429 1613); District Office, West Birmingham Health Authy, Dudley Rd Hosp, Dudley Rd, Birmingham B18 7QH (☎ 021 554 3801, fax 021 551 5562)

COGHLAN, Terence Augustine; s of Austin Coghlan (d 1981), of Horsted Keynes, Sussex, and Ruby, *née* Comrie; *b* 17 Aug 1945; *Educ* Downside, Univ of Perugia, Univ of Oxford (MA); *m* 11 Aug 1973, Angela, da of Rev F E Westmacott (d 1987), of Barsham, Suffolk; 1 s (Thomas Alexander b 1975), 2 da (Candida Mary b 1978, Anna Frances b 1988); *Career* RAFVR (Oxford Univ Air Sqdn) 1964-67; called to the Bar Inner Temple 1968; in practice 1968-, asst rec of the Crown Ct 1985-89, rec 1989-; dir City of London Sinfonia; memb Inner Temple; *Recreations* music, cricket, windsurfing, cooking, skiing, wines (drinking & making); *Style—* T A Coghlan, Esq; 1 Crown Office Row, Temple, London EC4Y 7HH (☎ 071 353 3150, fax 071 583 1700)

COGHLAN, Timothy Boyle Lake; *b* 29 March 1939; *Educ* Rugby, Pembroke Coll Cambridge; *m* 1966, Elizabeth, da of Fredrick, and Mary af Petersens; 1 s (Henry), 1 da (Melindy); *Career* partner de Zoete and Bevan, dir Barclays de Zoete Wedd Holdings Ltd; *Style—* Timothy Coghlan, Esq; Barclays de Zoete Wedd, Ebbgate House, 2 Swan Lane, London ECHR 3TS (☎ 071 623 2323, telex 888221)

COGILL, Julie Antoinette; da of Arthur Harold Berry (d 1971), of Blackburn, and

Mary Margaret, *née* Driscoll; *b* 25 Aug 1945; *Educ* Notre Dame GS Blackburn, Univ of Liverpool (BSc), King's Coll London (MA); *m* 1967, Stephen Richard Cogill, s of Joseph Cogill (d 1981), of Scarborough; 3 children (Adelene Mary b 1968, Eleanor Ruth b 1969, Geoffrey Owen b 1971); *Career* sr teacher and head of mathematics Tolworth Girl's Sch 1980-87, sr educn offr BBC 1988 (educn offr 1987-88); memb: Mathematical Assoc, Assoc of Teachers of Mathematics, Royal Television Soc; *Recreations* walking, sailing, skiing; *Style*— Mrs Julie Cogill; 60 Ranelagh Road, Ealing, London W5 5RP; BBC Education, 407 Villiers House, Ealing, London W5 2PA (☎ 081 991 8041)

COGSWELL, Dr Jeremy John; s of Dr Alan Philip Lloyd Cogswell (d 1973), and Audrey Sylvia, *née* Jackson; *b* 10 Sept 1937; *Educ* Radley Coll, St John's Coll Cambridge (MA, MB BChir, MD); *m* 22 April 1972, Saranna Leigh, da of Bryan Leigh Heseltine, of Bath; 1 s (Oliver b 1974), 1 da (Katherine b 1975); *Career* paediatrician; formerly Paediatric res fell Univ of Colorado Med Center, respiratory research fell Hosp for Sick Children Gt Ormond Street, sr registrar Dept of Paediatrics Guys Hosp, cnslt paediatrician E Dorset Health Dist; author of papers on paediatric respiratory medicine; FRCP; *Recreations* skiing, viticulture; *Style*— Dr Jeremy J Cogswell; Warmwell Farm, Flowers Drove, Lytchett Matravers, Poole, Dorset BH16 6BX (☎ 0258 857115); Poole General Hospital (☎ 0202 675100)

COHAN, Robert P; Hon CBE (1988); s of Walter and Billie Cohan; *b* 27 March 1925; *Educ* Martha Graham Sch NY; *Career* joined Martha Graham Co 1946 (ptnr 1950, co-dir 1966); artistic dir Contemporary Dance Trust Ltd 1967, fndr artistic dir and prime choreographer London Contemporary Dance 1969-, artistic advsr Batsheva Co Israel 1980; dir: Univ of York, Toronto Choreographic Summer Sch 1977, Gulbenkian Choreographic Summer Sch Univ of Surrey 1978, 1979 and 1982; Banff Sch of Fine Arts Choregraphic Seminar Canada 1980; choreographic seminar: NZ 1982, Vancouver 1985; with London Contemporary Dance Theatre (LCDT) has toured over 50 countries throughout: Europe, E Europe, S America, N America, USA; works incl: Cell 1969 (BBC TV 1982), Stages 1971, Waterless Method of Swimming Instruction 1974 (BBC TV), Class 1975, Stabat Mater 1975 (BBC TV), Masque of Separation 1975, Khamsin 1976, Nympheas 1976 (BBC TV 1983), Forest 1977 (BBC TV), Eos 1978, Songs Lamentations and Praises 1979, Dances of Love and Death 1981, Agora 1984 (with music by Geoffrey Burgon), A Mass for Man broadcast Nov 1985, Ceremony 1986, Interrogations 1986, Video Life 1986; LCDT was only Br dance co invited to Olympic Arts Festival Los Angel 1984 and Seoul 1988, performed at Karmiel Dance Festival Israel 1988; won Evening Standard award for Most Outstanding Achievement in Ballet award from Soc of West End Theatres 1978; *Books* Contemporary Dance Workshop (1986), ed Chores and Dance International Journal, ed-in-chief Choreography and Dance Journal; *Style*— Robert Cohan, Esq; The Place, 17 Dukes Road, London, WC1H 9AB, (☎ 071 387 0324)

COHEN; *see*: Waley-Cohen

COHEN, Alan Abraham; s of Tobias Cohen (d 1947), of London, and Rose Cohen, *née* Posner (d 1987); *b* 17 Nov 1935; *Educ* Elmhurst Sch, Hendon Technical Coll; *m* 14 June 1959, Karen Frances, da of Alfred Bernard Cold, of 7 York Ct, Alermans Hill, London; 1 s (Philip b 1962), 1 da (Susan b 1964); *Career* chartered accountant, sr ptnr Wilson Green Gibbs Chartered Accountants 1969-; *Recreations* squash, gardening, music; *Style*— Alan Cohen, Esq; 31 Camlet Way, Hadley Wood, Herts EN4 0LJ (☎ 081 441 9079); 5 Southampton Place, London WC1A 20A (☎ 071 404 4949, fax 071 405 3322)

COHEN, Dr (Stanley) Bernard; s of Dr A Cohen, of 168 Queens Drive, Liverpool, and Sophia, *née* Newman; *b* 8 Nov 1938; *Educ* Liverpool Coll, Univ of Liverpool (MB ChB, MD); *m* 9 April 1972, Alison Margot, da of Maj Alan Glass, of Flat 6, Westwood Lodge, Leicester Rd, Hale, Cheshire; 3 s (Graeme, Stuart, Richard); *Career* conslt physician 1975-, sr res fell John S Hopkins Baltimore 1974-75; FRCP 1980 (MRCP 1967); *Recreations* music, bridge, theatre; *Style*— Dr Bernard Cohen; Walton and Fazakerley Hospitals, Liverpool 9 (☎ 051 525 3611)

COHEN, Christopher David Arthur; s of His Hon Nathaniel Arthur Jim Cohen, of Crockham Hill, Edenbridge, Kent, and Judith Alexandra Grace Luard (d 1974); *b* 23 June 1928; *Educ* Rugby; *m* 18 Sept 1954, Judith Mary Pyne; 2 s (Peter b 1961, Michael b 1961), 1 da (Virginia b 1959); *Career* Nat Serv 1946-48; articled clerk 1948, admitted slr 1954; ptnr Holman Fenwick and Willan 1961-89, slr Staff Pension Fund; memb Law Soc; Freeman City of London, Liveryman Worshipful Co of Slrs; *Style*— Christopher Cohen, Esq; The Farmhouse, Winkhurst Green, Ide Hill, Kent (☎ 073 275 257)

COHEN, Dr (Johnson) David; s of John Solomon Cohen (d 1974), and Golda, *née* Brenner (d 1968); *b* 6 Jan 1930; *Educ* Christ's Coll Finchley, Lincoln Coll Oxford (MA), Brandeis Univ USA, King's Coll London, Westminster Hosp Med Sch (MB BS); *m* 28 Aug 1962, Veronica Jane Addison, da of Felix Addison Salmon (d 1969), of London; 2 da (Imogen b 1964, Olivia b 1966); *Career* gen practitioner; memb: Camden and Islington AHA 1973-78, Hampstead DHA 1983-87; govr Hosps for Sick Children Great Ormond St 1974-79, special tstee Royal Free Hosp 1984-88; chm: Camden and Islington Family Practioner Ctee 1982-87, Camden and Islington Local Medical Ctee 1983-86, Hampstead District Medical Ctee 1983-84, chm John S Cohen Fndn 1974- (tstee 1965-), David Cohen Family Charitable Tst 1981-; govr Royal Ballet Schs 1978-; memb: Int Bd of Govrs Hebrew Univ of Jerusalem 1975-, Exec Ctee Prison Reform Tst 1985-88, Bd Opera Factory 1986-, Ballet Bd Royal Opera House Covent Garden 1987-, Bd ENO 1988-, Cncl London Sinfonietta 1989; vice pres London Int String Quartet Competition 1989; chm Opera 80 1987; memb: Cncl of Friends ENO 1990-, Bd Shared Experience Theatre Co 1990-, Cncl of Friends Courtauld Inst 1990-; tstee ENO and Sandler's Wells Benevolent Fund 1990-; hon fell Lincolns Coll Oxford; Freeman City of London 1982; FRCGP, MRCS, LRCP; *Recreations* music, theatre, the arts; *Clubs* Savile; *Style*— Dr David Cohen; 33a Elsworthy Rd, London NW3 3BT (☎ 071 722 0746)

COHEN, Edmund George; s of Henry Cohen; *b* 16 Sept 1926; *Educ* Harrow, Jesus Coll Cambridge (MA); *m* 1951, Daphne, *née* Froomberg; 2 s; *Career* chm Courts (Furnishers) Ltd 1976-86; *Style*— Edmund Cohen, Esq; 15 Somerset Rd, Wimbledon, London SW19 (☎ 081 947 0975)

COHEN, George Reginald; *b* 22 Oct 1939; *Educ* St Johns Church Sch Fulham, Henry Compton Sch Fulham; *m* Daphne; 2 s (Andrew b 31 Dec 1964, Antony b 12 Aug 1967); *Career* former professional footballer; 408 appearances Fulham 1956-69; England caps: 3 inter-league, 8 under 23, 37 full; memb England World Cup winning team v W Germany 1966; jr player: W London Schs, London Boys Premier team, Middlesex Youth; md George R Cohen Property Partnership Ltd, dir Redmire Ltd; *Recreations* golf, walking, reading; *Style*— George Cohen, Esq

COHEN, Prof Gerald Allan; s of Morrie Cohen (d 1985), of Montreal, and Bella, *née* Lipkin (d 1972); *b* 14 April 1941; *Educ* Strathcona Acad Montreal, McGill Univ (BA), Oxford Univ (BPhil); *m* 24 July 1965, Margaret Florence, da of Henry Aubrey Pearce, of Whitstable, Kent; 1 s (Gideon Patrick Edward b 22 Oct 1966), 2 da (Miriam Florence Laura b 20 Dec 1970, Sarah Judith Tamara b 6 Aug 1975); *Career* reader in philosophy UCL 1978-85 (lectr 1963-78), visiting asst prof McGill Univ 1965, visiting assoc prof Princetown Univ 1975, currently Chichele prof of social and political theory and fell All Souls Coll Oxford; FBA; *Books* Karl Marx's Theory of History (1978), History Labour and Freedom (1988); *Recreations* Guardian crossword puzzles, reading about art and architecture; *Style*— Prof Gerald Cohen; All Souls Coll, Oxford OX1 4AL (☎ 0865 279339, fax 0865 279299)

COHEN, Harry Michael; MP (Lab) Leyton 1983-; *b* 10 Dec 1949; *Style*— Harry Cohen Esq, MP; House of Commons, London SW1

COHEN, Hon Hugh Lionel; yr s of Baron Cohen (Life Peer, d 1973); *b* 14 Jan 1925; *Educ* Eton, New Coll Oxford; *m* 7 Oct 1953, Jane, da of Rt Hon Sir Seymour Edward Karminski; 3 s; *Career* RNVR 1939-68; *Style*— The Hon Hugh Cohen; Overbrook House, Devil's Highway, Crowthorne, Berks RG11 6BJ

COHEN, Ivor Harold; CBE (1985), TD (1968); s of Jack Cohen (d 1987), of 1 St Luke's Close, London, and Anne, *née* Victor (d 1980); *b* 28 April 1931; *Educ* Central Fndn Sch London, UCL (BA); *m* 4 Jan 1963, Betty Edith, da of Reginald George Appleby (d 1974); 1 da (Elisabeth b 1966); *Career* Nat Serv Royal Signals 1952-54, 2/Lt 1953, TA 1954-69, Maj 1964; Arthur Lyon & Co (Engrs) Ltd 1954-55, Sturtevant Engrg Co Ltd 1955-57, md Mullard Ltd 1979-87 (joined 1957, divnl dir 1973-77); dir: Philips Lighting 1977-79, Philips Electronics Ltd 1984-87; chm Remploy Ltd 1987-; advsr: Alan Patricof Assocs Ltd 1987-, Comet Group plc 1987-90; dir: AB Electronic Products Group plc 1987-, Oce (UK) Ltd 1988-, Redifon Holdings Ltd 1989-, Redifon Ltd 1989-, PA Holdings Ltd 1989-; memb Steering Bd Radiocommunication Agency 1990-; dir Radio Industs Cncl (RIC) 1980-87; memb: Teletext & Viewdata Steering Gp 1980-84, Cncl Electronic Components Indust Fedn (ECIF) 1980-87, Info Technol Advsy Panel (ITAP) 1981-86, Cncl of Mgmnt Br Schs Technol 1984-87 (tstee dir 1987-89), Computer Software and Communications Requirements Bd DTI 1984-88, Cncl Euro Electronic Components Assoc 1985-87, DTI Steering Gp on Telecommunications Infrastructure 1987-88, Schs Examination & Assessment Cncl 1988-90; NEDO: memb Electronic Components EDC 1980-87, chm Electronic Industs EDC 1990 (memb 1982-86 and 1988-), chm Electronic Applications Sector Group 1988-90; memb: Mgmnt Advsy Gp IT Res Inst Brighton Poly 1987-, Editorial Bd Nat Electronics Review 1988-90; hon memb CGLI 1989; Freeman City of London, Liveryman Worshipful Co of Scientific Instrument Makers; fell UCL 1987; FRSA 1981, CIEE 1988, FIOD 1988; *Recreations* reading, opera, sculpting (occasionally), walking in towns; *Clubs* Army & Navy, East India; *Style*— Ivor Cohen, Esq, CBE, TD; 24 Selborne Rd, Croydon, Surrey CR0 5JQ

COHEN, Janet; da of George Edric Neel (d 1952), of 1 Oakhill Ave, London, and Mary Isabel, *née* Budge; *b* 4 July 1940; *Educ* South Hampstead HS, Newnham Coll Cambridge (BA); *m* 1, 10 June 1964 (m dis 1968), Michael Rodney Newton Moore, s of Gen Sir (James) Rodney Newton Moore (d 1980); *m* 2, 18 Dec 1971, James Lionel Cohen, s of Dr Richard Henry Lionel Cohen, CB, of The End House South, Lady Margaret Rd, Cambridge; 2 s (Henry b 1973, Richard b 1975), 1 da (Isobel b 1979); *Career* articled clerk Frere Cholmeley 1963-65, admitted slr 1965, ABT Assoc Cambridge Mass USA 1965-67, John Laing Construction 1967-69, princ (later asst sec) DTI 1969-82; dir: Cafe Pelican Ltd 1983-90, F Charterhouse Bank Ltd 1987- (joined 1982); assoc fell Newnham Coll Cambridge 1988-; *Books* Deaths Bright Angel (as Janet Neel 1988, John Creesy award for best first crime novel), Death on Site (1989); *Recreations* writing, theatre, restaurants; *Style*— Mrs Janet Cohen; 50 Blenheim Terrace, London NW8 0EG (☎ 071 625 5809); 1 Paternoster Row, St Pauls, London EC4M 7DH (☎ 071 248 4000, fax 071 248 1998)

COHEN, Jennifer Ann; *née* Page; da of Surgn Lt-Cdr John Percy Page (d 1972), and Katharine Isobel, *née* Maskey; *b* 13 April 1959; *Educ* Maidstone GS for Girls; *m* 10 Sept 1988, Peter Arthur David Cohen, s of Christopher David Arthur Cohen, of The Farmhouse, Winkhurst Green, Ide Hill, Kent; *Career* trainee buyer Harrods Ltd Knightsbridge 1976-78; advertising mangr: Kent Messenger Newspaper 1978-81, C Cheney & Assocs Hong Kong 1981-84, sr sales exec Financial Times Magazines London 1986-; advertisement sale mangr Euromoney Publications plc Hong Kong; *Recreations* scuba diving, tennis, windsurfing; *Style*— Mrs Peter Cohen; 1 Town Centre Crescent, Hong Lok Yuen, Tai Po, New Territories, Hong Kong (☎ 651 9419); Euromoney Publications plc, 20/F Trust Tower, 68 Johnstone Rd, Hong Kong (☎ 529 5009)

COHEN, Jeremy Sandford; s of His Hon Judge N A J Cohen, of Kent, and Judith A G Luard (d 1974); *b* 14 June 1930; *Educ* Rugby, Trinity Coll Cambridge (BA); *m* 1962, Susan Kirsteen, da of William Le B Egerton (d 1947); 1 s (Thomas b 1965), 1 da (Lucy b 1968); *Career* insurance broker; dir Willis Faber plc 1984; *Recreations* music, farming; *Clubs* United Oxford and Cambridge Univ; *Style*— Jeremy Cohen, Esq; Wiston Mill, Nayland, Suffolk (☎ 0206 262219)

COHEN, Hon John Christopher Coleman; s of Baron Cohen of Brighton (Life Peer, d 1966); *b* 13 July 1940; *Educ* Stowe, McGill Univ; *m* 20 Feb 1965, Anne-Marie, da of Eugene Krauss, of Paris; 1 s; *Style*— The Hon John Cohen; 47 Quickswood, Chalcots Park, NW3

COHEN, John Louis (Brunel); OBE (1989); yr s of Maj Sir (Jack Ben) Brunel Cohen, KBE (d 1965), and Vera Evelyn, er da of Sir Stuart Montague Samuel, 1 Bt (d 1926); *b* 13 June 1922; *Educ* Cheltenham; *m* 1, 4 March 1951, Simone Delores Everitt (d 1969), da of late Robert L de Vergriette, of Paris; 2 s (Richard Stuart b 17 Aug 1952); m 2, 1972, Christine Bowman Blaney, da of late John Rothwell Dixon; *Career* Cunard Steamship Co 1946-59, C T Bowring (insur) 1959-87 (ret); underwriting memb Lloyd's 1960; chm Not Forgotten Assoc 1979- (memb 1965-), memb Benevolent Ctee Royal Br Legion 1983-88; Master Worshipful Co of Gardeners 1977-78; *Recreations* sailing, travel, horse racing; *Clubs* Carlton, Royal Southern Yacht; *Style*— John Cohen, Esq, OBE; Flat 5, 17 Cheyne Gardens, London SW3 5QT (☎ 071 351 6505); Aymer View, Ringmore, Kingsbridge, South Devon TQ7 4JH (☎ 0548 810 245)

COHEN, Dr Jonathan; s of Dr Norman A Cohen, of London, and Ruth N, *née* Kimche; *b* 11 Oct 1949; *Educ* William Ellis GS, Univ of London (BSc, MB BS, MSc); *m* 6 Jan 1974, Dr Neomi Cohen, da of Richard Weingarten (d 1968), of India; 1 s (Richard b 1981), 1 da (Joanna b 1979); *Career* Hammersmith Hosp Royal Postgrad Med Sch London: reader in infectious diseases, hon conslt physician, head of Infectious Diseases Unit; author scientific papers and contrib to books on infection and infectious disease; *Recreations* skiing, photography; *Style*— Dr Jonathan Cohen; Infectious Diseases Unit, Dept of Bacteriology, Hammersmith Hosital, Royal Postgraduate Medical School, Du Cane Rd, London W12 0NN (☎ 081 740 3222, fax 081 749 2281)

COHEN, Dr (Laurence) Jonathan; s of Israel Cohen (d 1961), of London, and Theresa Cohen (d 1983); *b* 7 May 1923; *Educ* St Pauls, Balliol Coll Oxford (BA, MA, DLitt); *m* 1 July 1953, Gillian Mary, da of Albert Slee (d 1975), of Guildford; 3 s (Stephen Benedict b 4 July 1956, Daniel Charles b 26 October 1957, Robin John b 16 March 1959), 1 da (Juliet Rose b 8 April 1960); *Career* Lt sp RNVR 1945 (Naval Intelligence 1942-45); asst Dept of Logic and Metaphysics Univ of Edinburgh 1947-50, lectr in philosophy Univ of St Andrews at Dundee 1950-57, visiting lectr Hebrew Univ of Jerusalem 1952, fell and praelector in philosophy The Queens Coll Oxford 1957-90 (emeritus fell 1990-); visiting prof: Univ of Columbia USA 1967-68, Yale Univ USA 1972-73; visiting fell Res Sch of Social Sci Aust Nat Univ 1980, hon prof NW Univ Xian China 1987, visiting prof NW Univ USA 1988, pres Br Soc for Philosophy of Sci 1977-79, chm Br Nat Ctee for Logic Methodology and Philosophy of Sci 1986-90, co-pres Int Union for History and Philosophy of Sci 1987-91, vice pres Oxfordshire Branch Cncl for Protection of Rural Eng 1988-, FBA 1973; *Books* The Principles of World Citizenship (1954), The Diversity of Meaning (1962), The Implications of Induction (1970), The Probable and the Provable (1977), The Dialogue of Reason (1986), An Introduction to the Philosophy of Induction and Probability (1989); *Recreations* gardening, walking; *Style*— Dr Jonathan Cohen; Sturt House, East End, North Leigh, Oxon OX8 6QA; The Queen's College, Oxford OX1 4AW (☎ 0865 276931, fax 0865 790819)

COHEN, Lawrence Francis Richard; s of Harris Cohen of Willesden, and Sarah *née* Rich; *b* 4 Nov 1951; *Educ* Preston manor Sch, Birmingham Univ (LLB), Inns of Court Sch of Law; *m* 24 May 1986, Alison Jane, da of Dr Rowland Patrick Bradshaw of Cobham, Surrey; 1 da (Sophie 1987); *Career* Barrister at Law 1974-; ACIA 1986; *Recreations* reading, walking; *Style*— Lawrence F R Cohen, Esq; 24 Old Buildings, Lincoln's Inn, London, WC2A 3UJ (☎ 01 4040946)

COHEN, Hon Leonard Harold Lionel; er s of Baron Cohen (Life Peer, d 1973); *b* 1 Jan 1922; *Educ* Eton, New Coll Oxford (BA, MA); *m* 14 July 1949, Eleanor Lucy, da of late Philip Quixano Henriques; 2 s, 1 da; *Career* Rifle Bde 1939-45; barr 1948, bencher Lincoln's Inn 1989; former dir Hill Samuel and Co; former md S Hoffnung and Co Ltd; chm United Service Trustees 1976-81; DG Accepting Houses Ctee 1976-82; chm: Ariel UK Ltd 1982-88, Secure Retirement plc 1987-, Royal Free Hosp Med Sch Cncl, Community Tst for Berkshire 1988-; memb governing body The Judd Sch Tonbridge; Liveryman Worshipful Co of Skinners' (Master 1971-72); High Sheriff of Berkshire 1987-88; *Recreations* gardening, reading, shooting; *Clubs* White's, Swinley Forest Golf; *Style*— The Hon Leonard Cohen; Dovecote House, Swallowfield Park, Reading, Berks RG7 1TG (☎ 0734 884775)

COHEN, Leslie Samuel; s of Harold Leopold Cohen, JP (d 1936), of 5 Palace Green, London, and Barwythe, Studham, Beds, and Clara, *née* Stern (d 1963); *b* 24 Aug 1910; *Educ* Charterhouse, Christs' Coll Cambridge (BA); *m* 1, 16 March 1935 (m dis 1942), Joan Lucy Eggar, da of John Kyrke Smith; 1 da (Penelope Clare (Mrs Roy Gluckstein) b 17 Oct 1938); m 2, Dorothy Victoria Mary (d 1987), da of John De La Mare; *Career* WWII Capt 5 Kings Regt, motor contact offr HQ Br Troops NI 1940, jr staff Coll Course Oxford 1942, GSO3 area HQ Sleaford Lincs 1942, GSO3 WO 1943; trainee Macy's Dept Store NYC 1932; Lewis's Ltd 1933-: various mgmnt appts 1933-39, bd memb 1949, bd memb Lewis's Investmt Tst 1964-, dep chm Lewis Ltd 1964-; chm: bd of govrs David Lewis Orgn Liverpool, bd of mgmnt Textile Benevolent Assoc 1968-86; pres Liverpool Jewish Youth and Community Centre; Freeman City of London 1964, memb Worshipful Co of Furniture Makers 1964; *Recreations* shooting, horse racing; *Clubs* Carlton; *Style*— Leslie Cohen, Esq

COHEN, Michael Alan; s of Harris Cohen, of London, and Cissie, *née* Rich; *b* 30 July 1933; *Educ* Ilford Co HS, UCL (LLB); *m* 3 July 1955, Ann Cohen; 1 s (Julian Andrew b 1967), 1 da (Nicola Amanda b 1970); *Career* Flt Lt RAF 1955-58; md Avery Rich Assocs Ltd; called to the Bar; ptnr: Michael Cohen Assocs, Ara Financial Servs; dir: ARA Life Assur Servs, ARA Conf Servs; practising arbitrator; vice pres Br Insur Law Assoc, chm Br Acad of Experts; memb: Disciplinary Tbnl Inst of Actuaries, Cncl Friends of UCL, various ctees Chartered Inst of Arbitrators; mediator, registered insur broker, ind fin advsr; Freeman City of London; Liveryman Worshipful Cos: Spectacle Makers, Insurers and Arbitrators; FCIArb, FBSC, FBAE, FRSA, memb Hon Soc of Gray's Inn; *Recreations* sailing, swimming, driving, collecting, yoga; *Clubs* Naval and Military, Royal Southern Yacht, City Livery; *Style*— Michael Cohen, Esq; 90 Bedford Ct Mansions, Bedford Ave, London WC1B 3AE (☎ 071 637 0333, fax 071 637 1893, telex 23873 ARA G)

COHEN, Lt-Col Mordaunt; TD (1954), DL (Tyne and Wear 1986); s of Israel Ellis Cohen (d 1946), and Sophie, *née* Cohen; *b* 6 Aug 1916; *m* 1953, Judge Myrella Cohen, QC, *qv*, da of Samuel Cohen (d 1948); 1 s (Jeffrey), 1 da (Sheila); *Career* RA 1940-46, seconded RWAFF (despatches), served TA 1947-55, CO 463 (M) HAA Regt, RA (TA) 1954-55; admitted slr 1938; ldr Sunderland CBC 1971-72 (Alderman 1967-74); chm: Sunderland Educn Ctee 1970-72, NE Cncl of Educn Ctees 1971, cncllr Tyne and Wear CC 1973-74; dep chm Northern Traffic Cmmrs 1973-74, chm Mental Health Review Tbnl 1967-76, regnl chm of Industl Tbnls 1976-89 (chm 1974-76); memb Ct Univ of Newcastle upon Tyne 1968-72; pres Sunderland Law Soc 1970; hon life pres Sunderland Hebrew Congregation; memb Bd of Deputies of Br Jews (chm Provincial Ctee and dir Central Enquiry Desk), former memb Chief Rabbinate Cncl; tstee Ajex Charitable Tst, memb Ajex Nat Exec Cncl, chm Sunderland Poly 1969-72; *Recreations* watching sport, playing bowls, communal service, promoting inter-faith understanding; *Style*— Lt-Col Mordaunt Cohen, TD, DL; Flat 1 Peters Lodge, 2 Stonegrove, Edgware, Middlesex HA8 7TY

COHEN, Her Hon Judge Myrella; QC (1970); da of Samuel Cohen (d 1948), of Manchester, and Sarah Cohen (d 1978); *b* 16 Dec 1927; *Educ* Manchester HS for Girls, Colwyn Bay GS, Univ of Manchester (LLB); *m* 1953, Lt-Col Mordaunt Cohen, TD, DL, *qv*; 1 s, 1 da; *Career* called to the Bar Grays Inn 1950, rec Kingston upon Hull 1971-72, circuit judge 1972- (also sits as judge of Family Div), memb parole Bd 1983-86; *Clubs* Soroptimist International; *Style*— Her Hon Judge Myrella Cohen, QC; c/o Crown Court, St Albans, Herts

COHEN, His Hon Judge Nathaniel Arthur (Jim); JP (Surrey 1958); 2 s of Sir Benjamin Arthur Cohen, KC (d 1942), and Margaret Abigail, *née* Cohen; *b* 19 Jan 1898; *Educ* Rugby, CCC Oxford; *m* 1, 1927 (m dis), Judith Alexandra Grace, da of Capt Sandford William Luard; 2 s (Christopher, Jeremy); m 2, 1936, Joyce, da of Harvey Collingridge, of Woking, Surrey; *Career* called to the Bar 1923, circuit judge 1955-70; *Style*— His Hon Judge Cohen, JP; Bay Tree Cottage, Crockham Hill, Edenbridge, Kent

COHEN, (George) Nigel; s of Anthony Van den Burgh Cohen (d 1985), and Judy, *née* Tack; *b* 26 Dec 1959; *Educ* St Paul's Sch, City of London Poly (OND); *Career* CA; supervisor Ernst & Young 1978-82, mangr Nyman Libson Paul 1984-86, ptnr Vandenburghs 1986; ACA 1983; *Recreations* photography, electronics; *Style*— G Nigel Cohen, Esq; Vandenburgh House, Latimer Rd, London W10 6QZ (☎ 081 968 0123, fax 081 968 0124)

COHEN, Prof Philip; s of Jacob D Cohen, of London, and Fanny *née* Bragman; *b* 22 July 1945; *Educ* Hendon Co GS, UCL (BSc, PhD); *m* 17 Feb 1969, Patricia Townsend, da of Charles H T Wade, of Greenmount, Lancs; 1 s (Simon Daniel b 1977), 1 da (Suzanne (Emma) b 1974); *Career* SRC/NATO fell Univ of Washington Seattle 1969-71; Royal Soc Res Prof Univ of Dundee 1984-, (lectr in biochemistry 1971-78, reader in biochemistry 1978-81, prof of enzymology 1981-84); author of over 250 articles in learned jls; Colworth medal Br Biochemical Soc 1977, Anniversary prize Fedn of Euro Biochemical Socs 1977; FRS (1984), FRSE (1984); *Books* Control of Enzyme Activity (1976, 2 edn 1983, trans into German, Italian, Russian and Malay), Molecular Aspects of Cellular Regulation (series ed); *Style*— Prof Philip Cohen; Inverbay II, Invergowrie, Dundee, DD2 5DQ (☎ 0382 562 328); Department of Biochemistry, University of Dundee, Dundee, Scotland (☎ 0382 307238, fax 0382 23778)

COHEN, Robert; s of Raymond Cohen, and Anthya, *née* Rael; *b* 15 June 1959; *Educ* Purcell Sch, Guildhall Sch (Cert of Advanced Solo Studies); *m* 1 Aug 1987, Rachel, *née* Smith; *Career* concert cellist; concerto debut Royal Festival Hall 1971; recital debuts: Wigmore Hall 1976, NY 1979, LA 1979, Washington DC 1979; major concerto tours since 1980: USA, Europe, Eastern Europe, Scandinavia, UK, NZ, Aust; orchs: all major Br orchs, Detroit Symphony, Swiss Romande, Rotterdam Philharmonic, Helsinki Philharmonic, Leipzig Gewandhaus, Netherlands Philharmonic, Oslo Philharmonic, ECYO, Sydney Symphony; chamber ptnrs: Amadeus Quartet, Peter Donohoe, Alan Gravill, Cohen Trio; many TV and radio appearances incl documentary about him (Thames TV 1979); recordings: Elgar Cello Concerto (silver disc), Dvorak Cello Concerto,Tchaikovsky Rococo Variations, Grieg Sonata/Franck Sonata, Rodrigo Concierto En Modo Galante; virtuoso cello music: Locatelli Sonata, Chopin Intro and Polonaise Brillante, Dvorak Rondo, Popper 3 pieces, Beethoven Triple Concerto (with F P Zimmerman and W Manz), Dvorak Complete Piano Trios (with Cohen Trio), Schubert String Quintet (with Amadeus Quartet), Bach 6 Solo Suites, Howard Blake Diversions; gives master classes in: USA, Finland, France, Turkey, Czechoslavakia, UK, Germany, NZ; winner: Suggia prize 1967-71, Martin Tst award 1973-75, Young Concert Artists Int Competition NY 1978, Piatigorsky prize USA-Czechoslovakia 1978, UNESCO Int Competition 1980; patron Beauchamp Music Club, dir Charleston Manor Festival E Sussex 1989-, fell Purcell Sch for Young Musicians; memb Inc Soc of Musicians; *Recreations* photography, squash, cars and driving, computers; *Clubs* Inst of Advanced Motorists; *Style*— Robert Cohen, Esq; Intermusica Artists Management, 16 Duncan Terrace, London N1 8BZ (☎ 071 278 5455, fax 071 278 8434, telex 9312102058)

COHEN, Prof Robert Donald; *b* 11 Oct 1933; *Educ* Clifton, Trinity Coll Cambridge (MA, MD); *m* 14 Feb 1961, Barbara Joan, *née* Boucher; 1 s (Martin b 1966), 1 da (Susan b 1963); *Career* The London Hosp Med Coll Univ of London: prof of metabolic med 1974-82, prof of med 1982-; chm: DHSS Computer R & D Ctee 1976-80, Special Advsy Ctee in Gen Internal Med 1985-90, Jt Ctee on Higher Med Trg 1985-90; memb: GMC 1988-, Cncl Imperial Cancer Res Fund 1989-, Physiological Systems Bd MRC 1990-; FRCP 1971; *Books* Clinical and Biochemical Aspects of Lactic Acidosis (with H F Woods, 1976), The Metabolic and Molecular Basis of Aquired Disease (ed with B Lewis and K G M M Albesti, and A M Denman); *Recreations* water colour painting, sailing; *Style*— Prof Robert Cohen; Medical Unit, The Royal London Hospital, Whitechapel Rd, London E1 1BB (☎ 071 377 77110, fax 071 377 7677)

COHEN, Ronald Mourad; s of Michael Mourad Cohen, of Cadogan Gardens, London SW1, and Sonia Sophie, *née* Douek; *b* 1 Aug 1945; *Educ* Orange Hill GS London, Exeter Coll Oxford (BA), Harvard Business Sch (MBA); *m* 1, Dec 1972 (m dis 1975), Carol Marylene, da of Gérard Belmont, of Geneva; m 2, Dec 1983 (m dis 1986), Claire Whitmore, da of Thomas Enders, of New York; m 3, 5 March 1987, Sharon Ruth, da of Joseph Harel, of NY and Tel Aviv; 1 da (Tamara b 7 Oct 1987); *Career* conslt McKinsey & Co (UK and Italy) 1969-71, chargé de mission Institut de Développement Industriel France 1971-72, fndr chm The MMG Patricof Gp plc 1972-; chm: The Sterling Publishing Gp plc, James Neill Holdings plc; fndr dir: Br Venture Capital Assoc (former chm), Euro Venture Capital Assoc; dir My Kinda Town Gp; advsr Inter-Action Gp (charity); former pres Oxford Union Soc; Lib candidate Kensington North Gen Election 1974 and London West for Euro Parl 1979; memb Young Presidents' Orgn; *Recreations* music, art, tennis, travel; *Clubs* RAC, RIIA; *Style*— Ronald Cohen, Esq; 23 Chester Terrace, Regent's Park, London NW1 4ND; The MMG Patricof Gp plc, 24 Upper Brook St, London W1Y 1PD (☎ 071 872 6300, fax 071 629 9035)

COHEN, Prof Samuel Isaac; s of Gershon Cohen (d 1963), of Cardiff, and Ada, *née* Samuel; *b* 22 Nov 1925; *Educ* Cardiff HS, Univ of Wales (BSc, MB ChB), Univ of London (MD); *m* 24 May 1955, Vivienne, da of Samuel William Wolfson (d 1974), of London; 1 s (Michael Ben-Gershon b 1960), 1 da (Elizabeth Hacohen b 1962); *Career* conslt psychiatrist The London Hosp 1963-83, hon conslt psychiatrist The Brompton Hosp 1971-83, prof of psychiatry The London Hosp Med Coll Univ of London 1983-, chm Med Cncl of The London Hosp 1985-88; Royal Coll of Psychiatrists: memb Cncl 1974-79, Ct of Electors 1975- 78, chm East Anglian Div 1981-86; regnl advsr NE Thames RHA 1982-88, med examiner Gen Med Cncl 1982-; FRCP, FRCPsych; *Books* contributed to Asthma (1977 and 1983), Medicine and Psychiatry (1982 and 1984), papers on Asthma, Cushing's Syndrome and Physical Symptoms in Psychiatric Disorders; *Style*— Prof Samuel I Cohen; 8 Linnell Drive, London NW11 7LT (☎ 081 455 4781); The London Hosp Med Coll, Turner St, Whitechapel, London E1 2AD (☎ 071 377 7344)

COHEN, Veronica Jane Addison; da of Maj Felix Addison Salmon (d 1969), and Rosemary Estelle, *née* Lever (d 1989); *b* 4 April 1939; *Educ* Bedales; *m* 28 Aug 1962, Dr (Johnson) David Cohen, s of John S Cohen (d 1974); 2 da (Imogen b 1964, Olivia b 1966); *Career* tstee: David Cohen Family Charitable Tst, Koestler Award Tst; memb: WRVS, Cncl MOMA Oxford, London Contemporary Dance Trust; voluntary prison work; *Recreations* art, history, playing the flute, writing poetry, dog lover; *Style*— Ms Veronica Cohen; 33 Elsworthy Road, London NW3 3BT

COHN, Prof Paul Moritz; s of late James Cohn and late Julia Mathilde, *née* Cohen; *b* 8 Jan 1924; *Educ* Trinity Coll Cambridge (BA, MA, PhD); *m* 27 March 1958, Deirdre Sonia Sharon, da of Arthur David Finkle (d 1968), of London; 2 da (Juliet, Ursula); *Career* Chargé de Recherches (CNRS) Univ of Nancy France 1951-52, lectr Univ of Manchester 1952-62, reader QMC London 1962-67, prof and head Dept of Maths Bedford Coll London 1967-84, prof UCL 1984-86 (Astor prof 1986-, prof emeritus 1989); visiting prof: Yale Univ, Univ of California at Berkeley, Univ of Chicago, SUNY Stonybrook, Rutgers Univ, Univ of Paris, Tulane Univ, Indian Inst of Technol Delhi, Univ of Alberta, Carleton Univ, Haifa Technion, Univ of Iowa, Univ of Bielefeld, Univ of Frankfurt, Bar Ilan Univ, Univ d'Etat Mons; author and editor; ctee memb SRC Maths 1977-79, chm Nat Ctee for Maths 1988-89, pres London Math Soc 1982-84 (memb 1957); FRS 1980 (cncl memb 1985-87); *Books* Lie Groups (1957), Linear Equations (1958), Solid Geometry (1961), Universal Algebra (1965, 1981), Free Rings and Their Relations (1971, 1985), Skew Field Constructions (1977), Algebra I (1974, 1982), Algebra II (1977, 1989), Algebra III (1990) translations into Spanish, Italian, Russian, Chinese; *Recreations* language in all its forms; *Style*— Prof P M Cohn; Dept of Mathematics, University College London, Gower St, London WC1E 6BT (☎ 071 387 7050)

COIA, Ferdinando; s of Ernesto Coia (d 1938), of Glasgow, and Filomena, *née* Cocozza (d 1974); *b* 19 Aug 1928; *Educ* Camphill Sr Secdy Sch Paisley, Univ of Glasgow (BSc); *m* 12 May 1954, Jane, da of James Lockhart (d 1961), of Glasgow; 3 s (Paul b 1955, Gerard b 1955, Martin b 1958), 1 da (Denise b 1958); *Career* Nat Serv Army RHA BAOR; former dir of facilties Scottish TV; dir: Theatrical Enterprises Ltd, William Mutrie and Son; chm The Scot Centre, The Royal TV Soc 1976; ret 1988; *Recreations* curling, golf; *Style*— Ferdinando Coia, Esq

COKAYNE, Hon Edmund Willoughby Marsham; 2 s of late 1 Baron Cullen of Ashbourne, KBE (d 1932), and Grace Margaret (d 1971), da of Rev Hon John Marsham (s of 3 Earl of Romney); hp of bro, 2 Baron; *b* 18 May 1916; *Educ* Eton, Royal Sch of Mines; *m* 18 May 1943, Janet Manson, da of William Douglas Watson (d 1916), of Canterbury; 1 da; *Career* late Fl Lt RAF; mining engr (ret); *Style*— The Hon Edmund Cokayne; PRI Site 52 Comp, 5, Merritt, BC VOK2BO, Canada (☎ 604 378

9462, 836 3155 office 836 2141)

COKAYNE, (Hon) John O'Brien Marsham; does not use courtesy style; s of late 1 Baron Cullen of Ashbourne, KBE (d 1932), and Grace Margaret (d 1973), da of Rev the Hon the John Marsham (s of 3 Earl of Romney); *b* 11 Oct 1920; *Educ* Eton; *m* 1 May 1948, Anne Frances (d 1973), er da of late Bertram Clayton, of Clayton, of Wakefield, Yorks; 1 s (Michael John b 28 Nov 1950); *Style—* John Cokayne; 14 St Omer Rd, Cowley, Oxford OX3 4HB (☎ 0865 774 867)

COKE, Cyril Edward Rigby; s of Edward Rigby Coke (d 1951), and Phyllis Muriel, *née* Austin (d 1979); *b* 29 July 1914; *Educ* Haileybury; *m* 1, 5 may 1934, Suzanne Grasett; 1 s (Michael b 1938), 1 da (Judith b 1936); m 2, 1954, Muriel, da of Wilfred Young (d 1964); *Career* WWII 1941-45 Royal Canadian Artillery (Maj), served Italy; worked on feature films as PA, prodn mangr and casting dir with Frank Launder and Sidney Gilliat 1946-55, TV drama dir Assoc Rediffusion from 1955-65, freelance thereafter; notable prodns incl: Crime and Punishment (best dir award), The Rat Catchers, Darkness at Noon, Malice Aforethought, Pride and Prejudice; *Recreations* golf; *Style—* Cyril E R Coke, Esq; Stanhope Castle, Stanhope, Co Durham DL13 2LY (☎ 0388 528809)

COKE, Viscount; Edward Douglas Coke; s and h of 6 Earl of Leicester, *qv*; *b* 6 May 1936; *Educ* St Andrew's Coll Grahamstown S Africa; *m* 1, 28 April 1962 (m dis 1985), Valeria, eld da of Leonard A Potter, of Berkhamstead, Herts; 2 s (Hon Thomas, Hon Rupert Henry John b 1975), 1 da (Hon Laura-Jane Elizabeth b 1968); m 2, 1986, Mrs Sarah de Chair; *Heir* s, Hon Thomas Coke; *Style—* Viscount Coke; Holkham Hall, Wells, Norfolk (☎ 0328 710227)

COKE, Edward Peter; s of Lt Cdr John Hodson Coke, RN, of Tone Lodge, Birtley, Hexham, Northumberland, and Kathleen Mary, *née* Pennington; *b* 12 Oct 1948; *Educ* St John's Coll Southsea, Univ of Warwick (LLB); *m* 6 July 1968, Josephine Linette, da of Frederick Francis Kennard (d 1987); 1 s (Dominic Francis), 2 da (Sarah Marie, Jessica Mary); *Career* trainee mangr W Woolworth 1966-69, postman PO 1969-71, sr advsy offr Consumer Protection Dept W Midlands CC; called to the Bar 1976, tenant St Ives Chambers 1977- (head of Chambers 1990-), ctee memb Legal Aid Ctee Legal Aid Bd Area No6; memb: Inner Temple, Midland & Oxford Circuit, Birmingham Medico Legal Soc, Assoc Lawyers for Defence of the Unborn; memb Cncl for the Protection of Rural England; *Recreations* dry fly fishing, walking, theatre, collecting Royal Navy Memorabilla; *Style—* Edward Coke, Esq; St Ive's Chambers, 9 Fountain Court, Steelhouse Lane, Birmingham B4 6DR (☎ 021 236 0863/0929/8952, fax 021 236 6961)

COKE, Hon Thomas Edward (Tom); er s, and h, of Viscount Coke, and gs of 6 Earl of Leicester; *b* 6 July 1965; *Educ* Eton, Univ of Manchester (BA); *Career* page of honour to HM The Queen to 1981; *Style—* The Hon Tom Coke

COKE, Hon Wenman John; s of 6 Earl of Leicester; *b* 24 May 1940; *Educ* St Andrew's Coll Grahamstown; *m* 1969, Carolyn May, er da of late D D Steuart Redler, of Cape Town , S Africa; 2 s, 1 da; *Style—* The Hon Wenman Coke; 106 Park St, Vryheid, Natal

COKE-STEEL, David; s of Ronald Coke-Steel (d 1963), of Trusley Old Hall, Derbyshire, and Frances H, *née* Coke; *b* 24 Jan 1944; *Educ* Wellington, Univ of London, Coll of Estate Mgmnt (BSc); *m* 14 April 1979, Jane Elizabeth, da of Hon Dean J Eyre, of 517 Wilbrod St, Ottawa, Ontario, Canada; 1 s (Edward b 1983), 2 da (Celia b 1979, Sophie b 1982); *Career* land and estate agent John D Wood & Co 1971-76, landowner and farmer 1977-; memb: Derbyshire Historic Bldgs Tst, Nat Tst, Cncl for Preservation of Rural England; *Recreations* music (esp opera), trout fishing, travelling (esp Third World), Eng art and architecture, early Eng porcelain; *Style—* David Coke-Steel, Esq; Trusley Old Hall, Derbyshire

COKER, Bryan Sydney; s of Sydney Orlando Coker (d 1954), of Grays, Essex, and Lilian Rose, *née* Harford-Roberts (d 1971); *b* 25 Dec 1924; *Educ* Palmer's Endowed Sch Essex; *m* 20 Aug 1949, Doreen Edith, da of Francis James Caton (d 1970), of Grays, Essex; 3 da (Jane b 1950, Gillian b 1955, Alison b 1964); *Career* CA; ptnr Rowland Hall & Co 1955-88, sec Thurrock District Assoc of Industries 1966-88; gen sec World Cncl of Young Men's Service Clubs 1973-79; former fin dir Grays AFC, pres Rotary Club of Grays Thurrock 1981-82; memb Essex CC Educn Ctee 1970-77; chm: Tstees of William Palmer's Charity, Govrs of Palmer's VI Form Coll, Thurrock Tech Coll; pres Nat Assoc of Round Tables 1963-64; memb Cncl Assoc Examining Bd; FCA; *Recreations* association football, rotary, canasta; *Clubs* Grays Athletic Football, Rotary (Grays Thurrock), Grays 41; *Style—* Bryan Coker, Esq; Alfriston, 14 College Avenue, Grays, Essex (☎ 0375 374949)

COKER, Frank Percival Charles; s of Frank Percival Coker (d 1972), of Broadclyst, Devon, and Winifred Clara, *née* Pearse (d 1972); *b* 2 Nov 1927; *Educ* King Edward VI GS Totnes, Imperial Coll London (BSc, DIC); *m* 7 Aug 1953, Mary, da of John Gerrard (d 1963), of Stoak, Cheshire; 3 s (John b 1955, Timothy b 1960, Richard (twin) b 1960), 1 da (Jane b 1954); *Career* engr Shell Petroleum Ltd 1948-50, section engr ICI Ltd 1951-60, dir Simon Engineering Group of Cos 1961-74, chief exec Wormald Int (UK) Ltd 1974-77, dir Scientific Design Co Ltd 1977-80, mktg mangr Worley Engrg Ltd 1981-82, fndr and chm Tylatron Ltd 1982-; conslt Costain Gp 1984-88, chm Nobel Systems Ltd 1984-; arbitrator, sch govr; Freeman City of London; ACGI, CEng, FIMechE 1957, FIChemE 1957, FCIArb 1977; *Clubs* Dartmouth Yacht; *Style—* Frank Coker, Esq

COKER, Michael Alexander O'Neil; s of Alexander Albert Coker, MBE (d 1986), of Oxford, and May Lucy, *née* Riley; *b* 13 Jan 1933; *Educ* Prince Henry's Sch Evesham, The Royal Liberty Sch Romford, RAM, Univ of Birmingham (Advanced Supplementary Certificate for Teachers of Handicapped Children), Univ of Sussex; *Career* Bishop Otter Coll Chichester 1971-82: sr lectr in educn studies (special and remedial educn), course tutor (advanced dip for teachers of children with special needs); dir of computer servs Marlborough Coll 1982-; contributor to books on computing; memb: Natural History Ctee Wilts Archaeological and Natural History Soc, Old Marlburian Club; LRAM, ARCM; *Recreations* gardening, music, astrology, early science, natural history; *Style—* Michael Coker, Esq; Rose-bush Cottage, Brunton, Collingbourne Kingston, Marlborough, Wilts; Marlborough College, Marlborough, Wilts (☎ 0672 515511 ext 249)

COKER, Peter Godfrey; *b* 27 July 1926; *Educ* St Martin's Sch of Art, RCA; *m* 1951, Vera Joyce Crook; 1 s (decd); *Career* Arm 1943-46; one-man exhibitions: Zwemmer Gallery 1956, 1957, 1959, 1964, 1967, Magdalane Street Gallery Cambridge 1968, Stone Gallery Newcastle 1969, Thackeray Gallery London 1970, 1972, 1974, 1975, 1976, 1978, Gallery 10 London 1980, 1982, 1984, 1986, 1988, 1989; retrospective exhibitions: Colchester, Bath, London, Sheffield 1972-73, Chelmsford and Essex Museum 1978, RA 1979, Fitzwilliam Museum Cambridge 1989; Gp Exhibitions include: Young Contemporaries 1950 and 1957, Contemporary Art Soc, Tate Gallery 1958, 1958, English Artists (Jorden Galleries Toronto) 1958, Recent Acquisitions Contemporary Art Soc 1959, Towards Art (RCA) 1952-62, Bicenterary exhibition (1768-1968) RA 1968, Painting 1950-57 (Scot Arts Cncl Glasgow) 1969, New 20th Century Acquisitions (Nat Portrait Gallery) 1986, This Land is Our Land (Aspects of Agriculture in English Art) 1989; seclected public collections: Birmingham City Museums and Art Gallery, Br Museum, Nat Portrait Gallery, RA, RCA, Tate Gallery, V&A Museum, City Art Gallery Manchester, Stedelijk Museum Ostend, Salford Museum & Art Gallery, Abbot Hall Art Gallery Kendal; RA 1972 (ARA 1965), ARCA 1953; *Books* Etching Techniques (1976); *Style—* Peter Coker, Esq; The Red House, Mistley, Manningtree, Essex

COLBECK-WELCH, Air Vice-Marshal Edward Lawrence; CB (1960), OBE (1948), DFC (1941); s of Major G S M Colbeck-Welch, MC, (d 1943), of Collingham, Yorks; *b* 29 Jan 1914; *Educ* Leeds GS; *m* 1938, Doreen (d 1988), da of T G Jenkin, LDS RCS, of Sliema, Malta; 1 s, 2 da; *Career* RAF 1933, No 22 Sqdn 1934-37, asst adj No 603 (City of Edinburgh) Sqdn AAF 1938, adj No 600 (City of London) Sqdn AAF 1939, CO No 29 (NF) Sqdn 1941-42, student RAF Staff Coll 1942, Ops Staff HQ No 10 Gp 1943-44, HQ 2 TAF and CO No 139 Wing 1944-45, dep dir of Ops Air Defence, Air Miny 1945-47, student US Armed Forces Staff Coll 1947, BJSM Washington 1948-49, OC RAF Coltishall 1950, OC RAF Horsham St Faith 1951-53, Gp Capt 1952, AMP's Dept Air Miny 1954-55, student IDC 1956, Cmdt Central Fighter Estab 1957-58, Air Cdre 1958, SASO HQ No 13 (F) Gp 1959, Air Vice-Marshal 1961, SASO HQ Fighter Command 1960-63, ret; *Recreations* sailing; *Clubs* Royal Channel Islands Yacht, St Helier Yacht; *Style—* Air Vice-Marshal Edward Colbeck-Welch, CB, OBE, DFC; La Côte au Palier, St Martin, Jersey, CI (☎ 0534 52962)

COLBORNE-MALPAS, Hon Mrs (Venetia Jane); *née* Manners; er da of 5 Baron Manners; *b* 30 July 1950; *m* 1972, Alasdair John Colborne-Malpas; *Style—* The Hon Mrs Colborne-Malpas; Keeper's Cottage, Ramsdell, Hants

COLCHESTER, Dr Alan Charles Francis; s of John Sparrow Colchester (d 1981), of East Chiltington, Sussex, and Norah Diana Taylor, *née* Pengelley; *b* 4 Oct 1947; *Educ* Haileybury, BNC Oxford (BA), UCH London (BM BCh), Univ of London (PhD); *m* 17 Aug 1974, Nicola Jane, da of Edward Rocksborough Smith (d 1989), of Briantspuddle, Dorset; 1 s (Rupert b 1984), 2 da (Nancy b 1979, Emily b 1981); *Career* research MO RAF Inst of Aviation Med Farnborough 1978-81, registrar in neurology The London Hosp 1982-83, sr registrar in neurology Atkinson Morley's and St George's Hosps 1983-87, conslt neurologist and sr lectr Guy's Hosp London 1987-; researcher into cerebral circulation, computer vision and med image analysis; MRCP 1977, FRSM 1983; *Recreations* music, natural history, inventing; *Style—* Dr Alan Colchester; The Old Rectory, Stowting, nr Ashford, Kent TN25 6BE (☎ 0303 862474); Dept of Neurology, Guy's Hospital, St Thomas Street, London SE1 9RT (☎ 071 955 4162)

COLCHESTER, Archdeacon of; *see*: Stroud, The Ven Ernest Charles Frederick

COLCHESTER, Charles Meredith Hastings; s of Rev Halsey Sparrowe Colchester, CMG, OBE, of The Vicarage, Gt Tew, Oxon, and Rozanne Felicity Hastings, *née* Medhurst; *b* 12 Jan 1950; *Educ* The Dragon Sch, Radley, Magdalen Coll Oxford (BA); *m* 3 July 1976, Serena Laura Peabody, da of Hon John M W North (d 1987), of Wickhambreaux, Kent; 3 s (Alexander North Peabody b 1981, Benjamin Medhurst Pawson b 1983, Zachary Wheatland Maynard b 1988), 2 da (Tamara Sarah Sparrowe b 1985, Chloë b 1991); *Career* dir: The Well Tst 1978, The Initiative Project Tst 1980; Christian Action Res and Educn: chm of campaigns 1982, gen dir 1987-; dir Tear Fund 1989-, chm of tstees Dolphin Sch Tst 1988-, church warden Holy Trinity Church Brompton 1978-, dir Well Marine Reinsurance Advisors Ltd 1986-; *Recreations* wife and children, water colouring, travel, reading; *Clubs* Travellers; *Style—* Charles Colchester, Esq; 53 Romney St, London SW1P 3RF (☎ 071 233 0455, fax 071 233 0983)

COLCHESTER, Dr Marcus Edward Medhurst; s of Rev Capt Halsey Sparrowe Colchester, CMG, OBE, and Rozanne Felicity Hastings, *née* Medhurst; *b* 15 May 1953; *Educ* Dragon Sch Oxford, Radley, Magdalen Coll Oxford (MA, Dip Ethnology, DPhil); *m* 25 Feb 1984, Jillian Rowena, da of Arthur David Miles, of Nova Scotia, Canada; 2 s (Kito b 1985, Meredith b 1988); *Career* conslt anthropologist Venezuela 1982, regnl coordinator idigenous census Venezuela 1983, Survival Int 1983-89, World Rainforest Movement 1990; *Books* The Health and Survival of the Venezuelan Yanoama (1985), Pirates, Squatters and Poachers: The Dispossession of the Native Peoples of Sarawak (1989), Rainforest: Land Use Options in Amazonia (1989), The Tropical Forestry Action Plan: What Progress? (1990); *Style—* Dr Marcus Colchester; Cob Cottage, Chadlington, nr Charlbury, Oxen OX7 3NA (☎ 060 876 691); 8 Chapel Row, Chadlington OX7 3NA (☎ 060 876 691, fax 060 876 743)

COLCHESTER, Nicholas Benedick Sparrowe; s of Rev Halsey Sparrowe Colchester, CMG, OBE, and Rozanne Felicity Hastings *née* Medhurst; *b* 20 Dec 1946; *Educ* Radley, Magdalen Coll Oxford; *m* 28 May 1976, Laurence Lucie Antoinette, da of Jean Louis Armand Schloesing; 2 s (Max b 1983, Felix b 1985); *Career* Financial Times: joined 1968, NY corr 1970-73, Bonn corr 1973-77, foreign ed 1980-86; The Economist: joined 1986, business ed 1988, currently dep ed; Chevalier de L'ordre National du Merite 1988; *Books* Europe Relaunched (jtly, 1990); *Recreations* travel, music, theatre; *Clubs* Garrick; *Style—* Nicholas B S Colchester, Esq; 37 Arundel Gardens, London W11 (☎ 071 221 2829); Soulages, Lasalle, Gard, France; The Economist, 25 St James' Street, London, SW1 (☎ 071 839 7000)

COLCLOUGH, Christopher Gordon; s of George Dudley Colclough (d 1958), of 44 Manor House, Marylebone Rd, London, and Helen Scott, *née* Jenkins (d 1979); *b* 22 April 1914; *Educ* Charterhouse, Trinity Coll Cambridge (MA); *m* 25 April 1942, Enid Coral, da of late James Stewart; 1 s (Christopher Angus b 1945), 1 da (Carol Ila b 1943); *Career* TA serv 3 Bn London Scottish 1939, OCTU Filey 1940, 2 Lt-Capt 151 Regt RA (Ayreshire Yeo) 1941-43, Maj 2 Corps Staff and 21 Army Gp Staff 1944-45; admitted slr 1938; Linklaters & Paines 1939, ptnr Johnson Jecks & Landons 1946-63, md Bombay Burmah Trading Corporation Ltd Bombay 1964-68, chm Wallace Bros Trading & Industrial Ltd 1968-72, conslt slr 1972-; sec Wentworth Estate Rds Ctee (former chm); Freeman City of London, Liveryman Worshipful Co of Slrs; memb Law Soc 1938; *Recreations* rowing, golf; *Clubs* Leander, Wentworth, Oriental; *Style—* Christopher Colclough, Esq; 8 Virginia Beeches, Virginia Water, Surrey GU25 4LT (☎ 0344 842120); Wentworth Club, Virginia Water, Surrey GU25 4LS (☎ 0344 842819)

COLDSTREAM, Sir George Phillips; KCB (1955, CB 1949), KCVO (1968), QC (1960); s of Francis Menzies Coldstream (d 1958), of East Blatchington, Seaford, E Sussex, and Carlotta Mary, *née* Young (d 1940); *b* 20 Dec 1907; *Educ* Bilton Grange, Rugby, Oriel Coll Oxford (MA); *m* 1, 29 Sept 1934 (m dis 1948), (Mary) Morna, da of Maj Alistair Drummond Carmichael (d 1967), of Balendoch, Meigle, Perthshire; 2 da (Grizelda Morna b 1938 d 1945, Rosamund Charlotte b 1939); m 2, 1949, Sheila Hope, da of Lt-Col George Patrick Grant, DSO (d 1955), of Grove House, Woodbridge, Suffolk, and widow of Lt-Col John Henry Whitty, DSO, MC; *Career* Called to the Bar Lincoln's Inn 1930; practised at Chancery Bar 1931-34, asst to Parly Counsel HM Treasury 1934-39, legal asst Lord Chancellor's Office House of Lords 1939-44, memb British War Crimes Executive 1942-46, Dep Clerk of the Crown in Chancery 1944-54, Clerk of the Crown in Chancery and Perm Sec Lord Chancellor's Office House of Lords 1954-68; memb Royal Cmmn on Assizes and Quarter Sessions 1967-70, special conslt American Inst of Judicial Admin 1968-72, chm Cncl of Legal Educn 1970-73, memb Top Salaries Review Body 1971-83; Hon LLD Columbia Univ USA 1966; Hon Memb American Bar Assoc, Hon Memb American Coll of Trial Lawyers; *Recreations* sailing, golf; *Clubs* Athenaeum, Royal Cruising, Vincents (Oxford); *Style—* Sir George Coldstream, KCB, KCVO, QC; The Gate House, East Blatchington, Seaford, E Sussex BN25 2AH (☎ 0323 892801)

COLDWELL, Pattie Ann; da of Gordon Elison Coldwell, and Eunice Mary, *née* Salter; *b* 14 May 1952; *Educ* Clitheroe Royal GS for Girls, High Wycombe Coll of Technol and Art; *Career* Granada Reports 1973-76, BBC Nationwide and Watchdog 1976-80; presenter: You and Yours BBC Radio 4 1980-84, Open Air BBC 1 1985-88, On The House BBC 2 1984-, Out of Order ITV 1984-89; prodr and presenter Remember Terry BBC documentary; memb: NUJ, Equity; *Recreations* horse riding, writing, films, music, sport, gardening, DIY; *Style—* Miss Pattie Coldwell; Flat 1, 40 Ainger Road, London NW3 3AT

COLDWELLS, Rev Canon Alan Alfred; s of Alfred Carpenter Coldwells (d 1962), and Leila Philis Eugenie, *née* Livings; *b* 15 Jan 1930; *Educ* Haileybury and ISC, Univ Coll Oxford (BA, MA), Wells Theol Coll; *m* 5 Jan 1963, (Mary) Patricia, da of Arthur Leonard Hemsley, of Rugby; 1 s (Adam b 1969), 2 da (Katie b 1963, Lotti b 1966); *Career* Nat Serv 2 Lt RASC 1948-50; deacon 1955, priest 1956, curate Rugby St Andrew Dio of Coventry 1955-62, curate i/c St George Rugby 1956-62, perpetual curate Sprowston Norwich 1962-73, rector Beeston St Andrew Norwich 1962-73; rural dean: Norwich North 1970-72, Rugby 1973-78; rector Rugby St Andrew 1973-87, hon canon Coventry Cathedral 1983-, canon of Windsor 1987-; dir Norwich Samaritans 1970-72; Freeman City of London 1954, Liveryman Worshipful Co of Vintners' Co 1954; *Books* The Story of St Andrew's Rugby (1979); *Recreations* art, painting, local history; *Style—* The Rev Canon Alan Coldwells; 6 The Cloisters, Windsor Castle, Berks SL4 1NJ (☎ 0753 866 313)

COLE, Barry M; s of Theodore Cole (d 1975), and Marjorie Ray, *née* Leewarden; *b* 24 Oct 1944; *Educ* Rugby, Hotel Sch Lausanne Switzerland; *m* 6 April 1971, Jill Valerie, *née* Minton; 1 da (Sara-Louise), 1 s (Benjamin); *Career* Grand Metropolitan Hotels 1967-73 (reception Washington Hotel, cashier Mayfair Hotel; asst mangr: Rubens, Rembrandt; area mangr County Div George Hotel Edinburgh); worked 1970-73: International Basle, Chateau Louis XIII Cannes, Savoy, Claridges, Sacher Hotel Vienna; 1973-79: dir The Fernley Bath and The Grange Keynsham, dir and ptnr The Cathedral Salisbury; proprietor 1979-85: The Three Cocks Hotel nr Hay-on-Wye, The Old Barn Inn, The Wellington Brecon; md The Osborne Hotel and Luxury Timeshare Torquay 1985-; Freeman City of London 1983; Master Innholder 1983, FTS 1980, FHCIMA, FInstSMM 1987; *Recreations* hunting, watersports; *Style—* Barry Cole, Esq; 8 Hesketh Crescent, Torquay, Devon TQ1 2LL (☎ 0803 213311); The Osborne Hotel Torquay Ltd, Hesketh Crescent, Torquay, Devon TQ1 2LL (☎ 0803 213311, fax 0803 296788)

COLE, Hon Mrs (Cecilia Anne); *née* Ridley; da of 4 Viscount Ridley, TD, JP, DL; *b* 1 Dec 1953; *m* 1978, Berkeley Arthur Cole, s of Arthur Cole, bro of 6 Earl of Enniskillen, MBE, JP, DL; 1 s (b 1986); *Style—* The Hon Mrs Cole; 151 Battersea Rise, London SW11 1HP

COLE, Cherry Elizabeth (Mrs Fawkes); da of Brian William Cole (d 1978), of Solihull, and Patricia Anne, *née* Smith; *b* 14 Oct 1949; *Educ* Newport HS, Solihull HS; *m* 17 April 1971, Richard Brian Fawkes, s of Stanley Victor Fawkes (d 1949), of Camberley; 2 s (Harry b 20 March 1984, Leo b 5 June 1986); *Career* BBC TV 1967-82: PA then researcher then asst prodr Outside Broadcasts, prodr Presentation; head of Presentation Channel 4 TV 1988- (presentation ed 1982-88); memb BAFTA; *Recreations* sleeping, swimming, skiing; *Style—* Ms Cherry Cole; 66 Castlebar Park, Ealing, London W5 1BU; Channel Four Television, 60 Charlotte St, London W1P 2AX (☎ 071 927 8626, fax 071 323 4677)

COLE, Col Sir (Alexander) Colin; KCVO (1983, CVO 1979, MVO 1977), TD (1972); s of Capt Edward Harold Cole (d 1963), of Croham Hurst, Surrey, and Blanche Ruby Lavinia, *née* Wallis (d 1984); *b* 16 May 1922; *Educ* Dulwich, Brasenose Coll Oxford (MA, BCL); *m* 5 June 1944, Valerie, o da of late Capt Stanley Walter Card; 4 s (Giles b 1949, Nicholas b 1951, Alexander b 1953, Christopher b 1955), 3 da (Frances b 1956, Mary b 1960, Jane b 1965); *Career* served WWII Capt Coldstream Gds; Maj Inf Bn HAC 1963, Maj 1967, Bt Lt-Col (later Hon Col) 6/7 Volunteer Bn The Queen's Regt 1981-86, Col RARO 1986-; called to the Bar Inner Temple 1949, hon bencher 1988; Fitzalan Pursuivant of Arms Extraordinary 1953, Portcullis Pursuivant of Arms 1957, Windsor Herald of Arms 1966, Garter Principal King of Arms 1978- (registrar and librarian Coll of Arms 1967-74); govr and chm of Bd of Govrs Alleyn's Coll of God's Gift Dulwich 1987-; pres Royal Soc of St George 1982-; fell Heraldry Soc; kt princ Imperial Soc of Knights Bachelor 1983-; Sheriff City of London 1976-77; memb Ct of Common Cncl City of London Ward of Castle Baynard 1964-; OStJ; memb Court of Assts HAC 1962-89; Freeman, Liveryman and memb Ct Worshipful Cos of: Basketmakers, Scriveners, Painter Stainers; FSA, FRSA; Cruz Distinguida San Raimundo de Penafort; *Clubs* Cavalry and Guards', City Livery; *Style—* Col Sir Colin Cole, KCVO, TD, Garter Principal King of Arms; College of Arms, Queen Victoria St, London EC4 (☎ 071 248 1188); Holly House, Burstow, Surrey

COLE, Sir David Lee; KCMG (1975, CMG 1965), MC (1944); s of late Brig David Henry Cole, CBE (d 1957), and Charlotte Louisa Ryles, *née* Wedgwood; *b* 31 Aug 1920; *Educ* Cheltenham, Sidney Sussex Coll Cambridge; *m* 1945, Dorothy, *née* Patton; 1 s (David b 1950); *Career* Royal Inniskilling Fusiliers 1940-45 (serv in Sicily and Italy); Dominions Office 1947; Dip Serv: private sec to Rt Hon the Earl of Home 1957-60, high cmmr Malawi 1964-67, min (political) New Delhi 1967-70, asst under-sec of state FCO 1970-73, ambass to Thailand 1973-78, ret; *Books* Rough Road to Rome (1983); *Recreations* watercolour painting; *Style—* Sir David Cole, KCMG, MC; 19 Burghley House, Somerset Rd, Wimbledon, London SW19 5JB

COLE, Frank George Francis; *b* 3 Nov 1918; *Educ* Manchester GS; *m* 1, 1940, Gwendoline Mary Laver (decd); 2 s, 1 da; m 2, Barbara Mary Booth, *née* Gornall; *Career* chm Nat Exhibition Centre Ltd 1970-75, former dep chm Armstrong Equipment plc; currently dir: Rical Ltd, William Mitchell (Sinkers) Ltd, Mitchell Grieve Ltd, Alexander Stenhouse UK Ltd, Frank Cole (Consultancy) Ltd; past pres Birmingham Chamber of Indust and Commerce, life govr Univ of Birmingham; competed in 1990 Wimbledon Nat Veterans Championships of GB; CBIM; *Style—* Frank Cole, Esq; Northcot, 128 Station Rd, Balsall Common, Coventry, W Midlands CV7 7FF (☎ 0676 32105)

COLE, Geoffrey Christopher; s of Roy Cole, of Essex, and Rose, *née* Blanking (d 1981); *b* 4 Oct 1947; *Educ* Mayfield Sch for Boys; *m* 1971, Jennifer Mary, da of John Bertram Symonds (d 1965); 2 s (Martin b 1973, Stuart b 1974), 1 da (Victoria b 1977); *Career* chm Geof Cole Associates; prev advtg commercial dir Saatchi and Saatchi (formerly dep media dir); chm Pinnacle Posters Ltd, chm and md Acme Media Ltd; *Recreations* game fishing, chess, keen sportsman; *Clubs* Three Rivers Golf, Cold Norton, Badminton, Sportsman, Tudor; *Style—* Geoffrey Cole, Esq; Watkins Lodge, Green Lane, Burnham On Crouch, Essex CMO 6PU; 64 Charlotte Sreet, London W1 (☎ 071 323 9119)

COLE, Graham; *b* 26 Aug 1946; *Educ* Univ of Exeter (BA); *Career* CA; ptnr corporate fin Coopers & Lybrand Deloitte (formerly Deloitte Haskins & Sells); Freeman City of London; FCA, assoc memb BR Assoc Hotel Accountants; *Recreations* shooting, collecting antiquarian maps; *Clubs* Les Ambassadeurs; *Style—* Graham Cole, Esq; Coopers & Lybrand Deloitte, Plumtree Court, London EC4A 4HT (☎ 071 583 5000, fax 071 822 8500, telex 887470)

COLE, John Morrison; s of George Cole, and Alice Jane Cole; *b* 23 Nov 1927; *Educ* Belfast Royal Acad, Univ of London (BA); *m* 1956, Margaret Isobel, da of John S Williamson, of Belfast; 4 s; *Career* Belfast Telegraph 1945-56 (reporter, industl corr, municipal corr, political corr); The Guardian: reporter 1956-57, labour corr 1957-63, news ed 1963-69, dep ed 1969-75; dep ed The Observer 1976-81 (asst ed 1975), political ed BBC 1981-; *Books* The Poor of the Earth (1976), The Thatcher Years: a decade of revolution in British politics (1987), contrib to various books on British and Irish politics; *Recreations* reading, travel; *Clubs* Athenaeum; *Style—* John Cole; BBC Office, House of Commons, Westminster, London SW1A 0AA (☎ 071 219 4765)

COLE, Maggie; da of Robert Lawrence Cole, of NY, and Cyrella, *née* Golden (d 1972); *b* 30 March 1952; *Educ* Nyack HS NY, Juilliard Sch, Lawrence Univ, Geneva Conservatory of Music; *m* 21 March 1982, Richard Paul Macphail, s of Maj David Lamont Macphail, of Chichester; *Career* harpsicordist; recordings made of Bach, Scarlatti and other Seventeenth and Eighteenth century composers for: Hyperion, Amon Ra, Virgin; performed at a series of Bach concerts at the Wigmore Hall 1985, numerous recordings for BBC Radio 3 and concerts throughout: Europe, USA, Poland, and Russia; active in organising music in local primary schs in Notting Hill, fund raiser through charity concerts for London Lighthouse (the first hospice for AIDS sufferers in the UK); *Recreations* swimming, walking, reading, looking at paintings; *Style—* Miss Maggie Cole; c/o Robert White Artist Management, 182 Moselle Ave, London N22 6EX (☎ 071 221 4681)

COLE, Nicholas Stephen Edward; s of Col Sir Colin Cole, KCVO, TD, BCL, MA, FSA, Garter Principal King of Arms, *qv*, of Holly House, Church Rd, Burstow, Horley, Surrey, and Valerie, *née* Card; *b* 23 Aug 1951; *Educ* Hurstpierpoint Coll, Central Sch of Art & Design London (BA); *m* 30 Oct 1976, Suzanne Maryanne, da of John Duncan Rae; 2 s (Edward b 7 Sept 1979, Frederick b 14 Oct 1981), 1 da (Stephanie b 13 Aug 1977); *Career* assoc Jack Howe & Assoc 1975-76, art dir PD Design Co Ltd 1979-82; fndr and sr ptnr Cole Design Assocs (graphics, displays and interiors); Freeman City of London, Liveryman Worshipful Co of Scriveners 1975; MCSD 1974; *Style—* Nicholas Cole, Esq; Kemps House, E Chiltington, Lewes, E Sussex BN7 3QT (☎ 0273 890520); Cole Design Associates, Cambridge Grove, Hove, E Sussex BN3 3ED (☎ 0273 890590, 0273 822929, fax 0273 822939, car 0860 225969)

COLE, Robert Henry; s of Henry George (d 1960), and Anne Elizabeth, *née* Simmonds; *b* 5 May 1934; *Educ* Wilson's London, Ruskin Coll Oxford; *m* 26 April 1958, Pamela Jean, da of Stanley Arthur Figg (d 1960), of London; *Career* gp trg offr Kelihers London 1967-72 (corrector of the press 1955-66), servs mangr Br Printing and Communication Corpn London 1973-86, press servs mangr Maxwell Communication Corp London 1987-; memb Governing Cncl Printers Charitable Corp; Freeman City of London 1957, life memb Guild of Freemen of the City of London 1957; Liveryman: Worshipful Co of Stationers 1971, Worshipful Co of Makers of Playing Cards 1979; MBIM 1969, MITD 1969, FRSA 1970, MIOP 1971, MIIM 1979; *Recreations* walking, reading; *Style—* Robert H Cole, Esq; 11 Sheridan Crescent, Chislehurst, Kent BR7 5RZ (☎ 081 467 9939); Maxwell Communication Corporation plc, Holborn Circus, London EC1P 1DQ, (☎ 071 377 4731, fax 071 353 0360, telex 888804)

COLE, Stephanie; *Educ* Bristol Old Vic Theatre Sch; *m* ; 1 da (Emma); *Career* actress; debut Bristol Old Vic regnl theatre incl: Manchester Royal Exchange, Birmingham Repertory, Liverpool Everyman, Salisbury, Richmond Orange Tree; West End theatre: The Relapse (Old Vic), The Tinker (Comedy), Rose (Duke of York), Noises Off (Savoy), Steel Magnolias (Lyric); tv incl: Tenko, Open All Hours, A Bit of a Do, Soldiering On (BBC Talking Heads monologue), Return of the Antelope, Going Gently, Amy, Tears in the Rain, Waiting for God; teacher Actors Centre; *Recreations* playing the guitar, ukelele, recorder; *Style—* Ms Stephanie Cole; Michael Ladkin Personal Management, 11 Southwick Mews, London W12 (☎ 071 402 6644, fax 071 402 1559)

COLE, William Charles; s of Albert William Cole (d 1989), of West Wickham, Kent, and Rosina, *née* Garratt; *b* 13 Jan 1946; *Educ* St Joseph's Coll; *m* 9 Sept 1972, Sally Freda, da of Frederick James Still (d 1988), of Croydon, Surrey; 2 da (Emma b 6 Dec 1974, Hannah b 27 Dec 1977); *Career* CA 1970-73, stockjobber Stocken and Lazarus 1973-87, merged with Akroyd and Smithers Plc 1977 and Warburg Securities 1987, fin and admin dir Olliff & Ptnrs Plc 1987-; memb: The Stock Exchange 1981, The Securities Assoc 1988; FCA 1970; *Recreations* golf, tennis, swimming; *Clubs* RAC, Cherry Lodge Golf; *Style—* William C Cole, Esq; The White House, 15 Park Ave, Farnborough Park, Orpington, Kent BR6 8LJ (☎ 0689 851833); Olliff & Ptnrs Plc, Saddlers House, Gutter Lane, Cheapside, London EC2V 6BR (☎ 071 374 0191, telex 919325, fax 071 374 2063, car 0860 211876)

COLE, Dr William Charles; LVO (1966); s of Frederick George Cole and Maria, *née* Fry; *b* 9 Oct 1909; *Educ* St Olave's GS, RAM; *m* 1, Elizabeth Brown Caw (d 1942); 3 da; m 2, Winifred Grace Mitchell; 1 s; *Career* former prof and lectr RAM and former lectr Royal Acad of Dancing, Master of the Music HM The Queen's Chapel of the Savoy 1954-, hon sec Royal Philharmonic Soc 1969-81, past pres and hon treas Cncl Royal Coll of Organists (memb 1960-), chm Central Music Library 1972-; FRAM, FRCM, FRCO, FSA; *Books* The Form of Music (1969); articles on stained glass in learned jls; *Recreations* stained glass; *Clubs* Garrick; *Style—* Dr William Cole, LVO; Barnacre, Wood Rd, Hindhead, Surrey (☎ 042 873 4917)

COLE-ADAMS, David John; s of Bernard Randall Cole-Adams (d 1945), step s of Brig Charles Frederick Cunningham Macaskie, CMG (d 1969), of Stanthorpe, Aust, and Doris, *née* Legg; *b* 21 May 1942; *Educ* The Southport Sch Southport Aust, Queensland Univ Aust (B Arch); *m* 30 Nov 1968, Mary Theresa, da of Archibald Desmond Freeman, of Inverell, Aust; 2 s (Thomas b 1970, Oliver b 1972), 2 da (Elizabeth b 1968, Agnes b 1974); *Career* architect; Kenzie Lovell Ptnrship (formally Ronald Fielding Ptnrship) 1968-87: assoc 1972, sr assoc 1976, ptnr 1984; md Kenzie Lovell Architects Ltd 1987-; pres Cities of London & Westminster Soc of Architects 1982-84 (hon sec 1974-80); chm: London region RIBA 1986-88 (vice chm 1984-86), London Devpt Control Forum 1986-; Freeman: City of London 1980, Worshipful Co of Tylers and Bricklayers (1984), Worshipful Co of Chartered Architects 1984 (Ct of Asst 1987); ARAIA 1967, RIBA 1968, FRSA 1990; *Recreations* cooking, philately, walking; *Style—* David Cole-Adams, Esq; 134 Muswell Hill Rd, London N10 3JD (☎ 081 883 3665); Kenzie Lovell Architects, 113 Southwark St, London SE1 OJF (☎ 071 928 8201, fax 071 928 1828, telex 267592)

COLE-FONTAYN, Hon Mrs (Barbara Wendy Maia); *née* Latham; da of 1 Baron Latham (d 1970); *b* 7 Jan 1920; *Educ* Hendon Coll; *m* 1, 17 April 1941 (m dis 1945), Capt Denis Charles Wildish, RASC, s of Charles Albert Wildish; m 2, 26 Oct 1946 (m diss 1951), Peter Anthony Charles Kurt Bruckmann, er s of Kurt Bruckmann, of Linakers, Cookham Dean, Berks; 1 da; m 3, 1966, Malcolm Blundell Cole-Fontayn; *Career* 1942-44 war as 1 class Aircraft woman WAAF; *Style—* The Hon Mrs Cole-Fontayn

COLE-HAMILTON, (Arthur) Richard; s of John Cole-Hamilton, CBE, DL, of Kilwinning, Ayrshire, and Gladys, *née* Cowie; *b* 8 May 1935; *Educ* Ardrossan Acad,

Loretto, Univ of Cambridge (BA); *m* 16 Feb 1963, Prudence Ann, da of Dr Lindsay Lamb, of Edinburgh; 1 s (John Liston b 11 March 1971), 2 da (Patricia Joy b 17 Feb 1964, Sara Louise b 21 June 1967); *Career* Nat Serv, 2 Lt Argyll & Sutherland Highlanders; CA; ptnr Brechin Cole-Hamilton CA's 1962-67; Clydesdale Bank plc: asst mangr 1967, head office mangr 1976, chief gen mangr 1982, dir and chief exec 1987; memb: Cncl Inst of CA's (Scot) 1981-85, Bd of Tstees Nat Galleries of Scot 1986-, Exec Ctee Erskine Hosp; dep chm Ctee Scot Clearing Bankers 1989-91 (chm 1985-87), pres Inst of Bankers (Scot) 1988-90, dep chm Scot Cncl Devpt and Indust 1989, dir Glasgow C of C, hon pres Ayrshire Chamber of Indust and Commerce; patron Dyslexia Inst (Scot) Bursary Fund FTIS (Scot); *Recreations* golf; *Clubs* Royal & Ancient (memb Fin Ctee), Prestwick Golf (capt 1987-88), Western Highland Bde; *Style—* Richard Cole-Hamilton, Esq; Troon, Ayrshire; 30 St Vincent Pl, Glasgow G1 2HL (☎ 041 248 7070, fax 041 204 1527)

COLE-HAMILTON, Richard Arthur; s of the Ven Richard Meryn Cole-Hamilton (d 1959), formerly Archdeacon of Brecon, and Margaret, *née* Bennett (d 1954); *b* 24 Oct 1912; *Educ* Marlborough, Worcester Coll Oxford (BA, MA, Dip Ed); *m* 9 Aug 1947, (Ruth Kathleen) Betty, da of Sir William Lorenzo Parker, 3 Bt, OBE (d 1971), of Llangattock Ct, Crickhowell, Breconshire; 3 s (Robin b 1948, (Richard) Simon b 1951, (William Mervyn) John b 1954); *Career* TA Gen Serv Sch's OTC 1936-40, serv WWII, The Royal Scots Regt 1940-42, Maj 1 Bn The Cameronians (Scots Rifles) 1942-46, Adj, detached for course in Japanese language SIMLA 1944-45, Wilton Park German POW Rehabilitation Centre 1945-46; asst master St Albans Sch 1936-38; Fettes Coll Edinburgh: asst master 1938-55, housemaster 1955-69, second master 1969-77, acting headmaster 1978-79, keeper of the register 1978-; memb Bd of Dirs Royal Blind Asylum and Sch Edinburgh 1978-88; *Style—* Richard Cole-Hamilton, Esq; Hawthorn Villa, 386 Ferry Rd, Edbinburgh EH5 3QG (☎ 031 552 4423); Fettes College, Edinburgh (☎ 031 332 2281)

COLEBROOK, Miles William Merrill; s of Peter Merrill Colebrook, Mc, JP, of Hawthorne Hill, Maidenhead, Berks, and Joyce Hay, *née* Ruthven (d 1969); *b* 14 Jan 1948; *Educ* Shrewsbury, Ann Arbor Univ Michigan; *m* 1 Sept 1973, Jane Margaret, da of John Scott Findlay, of Widford, Herts; 2 s (Thomas b 1978, George b 1987) 1 da (Lucy b 1977); *Career* J Walter Thompson: media exec 1966-70, account exec 1970-78, bd dir 1978-85, md 1985-88, pres and COO Europe 1988-; FIPA 1990; *Recreations* shooting, skiing, cooking; *Style—* Miles Colebrook, Esq; 6 Whittingstall Rd, London, SW6; South Farm, Sparsholt, Wantage, Oxon; J Walter Thompson, 40 Berkeley Square, London W1X 6AD (☎ 071 4994040, fax 071 499 1254, telex 22871)

COLEBY, Anthony Laurie; s of Dr Leslie James Moger Coleby (d 1971), and Laurie, *née* Shuttleworth; *b* 27 April 1935; *Educ* Winchester, CCC Cambridge; *m* 1966, Rosemary Melian Elisabeth, da of Sir (Isham) Peter Garran KCMG, *qv*; 1 s, 2 da; *Career* PA to md IMF 1964-67; Bank of England: dep chief cashier 1973-80, asst dir 1980-86, chief monetary advsr to Govr 1986-90, exec dir 1990; *Recreations* choral singing, railways, transport; *Clubs* Overseas Bankers; *Style—* Anthony Coleby, Esq; Bank of England, London EC2 (☎ 071 601 4444)

COLEGATE, Raymond; CBE (1982); s of Ernest William Colegate, of 19 Arnold Rd, Gravesend, Kent, and Violet Mary Dubettier Annett Colegate; *b* 31 Aug 1927; *Educ* Co Sch for Boys Gravesend, LSE (BA); *m* 6 April 1961, Cecilia Mary (Sally), da of James Healy (d 1970); 1 s (John b 1965), 1 da (Joanne b 1968); *Career* BOT 1949, Central Stat Office 1952-53, asst private sec to pres BOT 1955-56 (treasy 1957-59), EFTA Secretariat Geneva Brussels 1960-64, CRE Dept BOT 1964-67, Aviation Dept BOT and DTI 1967-72; CAA: head Econ Policy and Licensing Dept 1972-75, head Econ Dept 1975-77, gp dir econ regulation 1977-89, non-exec dir 1989-90, air tport conslt 1990-; md Global Aviation Consultants Ltd 1991-; FCIT; *Recreations* travel, music, reflection; *Style—* Raymond Colegate, Esq, CBE; 40 Lebanon Park, Twickenham, Middx TW1 3DG

COLEMAN, Professor Alice Mary; da of Bertie Coleman, DCM (d 1970), and Elizabeth Mary, *née* White (d 1959); *b* 8 June 1923; *Educ* Clarendon House Sch Ramsgate, Furzedown Coll (teacher's cert), Birkbeck Coll London (BA), King's Coll London (MA); *Career* teacher i/c geography Northfleet Central Sch Kent 1943-48; Kings Coll London 1948-: memb academic staff 1948, asst lectr, sr lectr, reader, prof, fell 1980, emeritus prof 1988-; sabbaticals: John Hopkins Univ Baltimore USA 1957-58, Canadian Federal Dept of Energy Mines and Resources 1965, Univ of Western Ontario (first holder of visiting professorship for Distinguished Women Social Scientists) 1976,Hokkaido Univ of Educn Asahikawa Japan 1985; dir: Second Land Utilisation Survey of Britain 1960s, DICE; res contract DOE DICE Project for Design Improvement of Problem Estates 1988; Gill Meml award RGS 1963, Times/Veuve Clicquot award 1974, Busk Gold medal RGS 1987; pres Isle of Thanet Geographical Assoc; memb RGS 1948; *Books* The Planning Challenge of the Ottawa Area (1969), Canadian Settlement and Enviromental Planning (1976), Utopia on Trial (1985); *Recreations* reading, graphology; *Style—* Prof Alice Coleman; King's College, Strand, London WC2R 2LS (☎ 071 873 2610)

COLEMAN, Francis Arthur; s of Bernard James Coleman (d 1939), of Montreal, and Blanche Marie, *née* Preneloup (d 1952); *b* 12 Jan 1924; *Educ* McGill Univ Montreal, Conservatorium of Music, Conservatorie de Musique et d'Art Dramatique de la Province de Quebec (diploma), Rochester Univ NY, Eastman Sch of Music; *m* 1, 1956 (m dis 1963) Christian McDonald; m 2, 30 July 1966, Ann, da of Claude Ripley Beach (d 1968), of Eastbourne; 2 da (Charlotte b 3 April 1968, Lisa b 10 July 1970); *Career* RCAF Sqdn 406 Westmount Montreal; TV prodr and dir, then prog controller CBMT Montreal, CBC radio Canada 1952-58; prodr and dir: Granada TV 1958-59, ATV 1959-64; exec prodr: LWT 1971-76, Thames TV 1977-83; exec prodr i/c prodn CTVC Churchs TV Bushey Course dir London Int Film Sch 1985-; visiting lectr City Univ The Barbican 1987; awards: Best Canadian Variety 1957, Coronation Medal CBC London TV prodn of The Coronation 1952, Leonard Brett Award best TV prodn 'On the Braden Beat' and 'ci La France' 1965, Gafan prize, first Br Award London Weekend Adult Series 'On Reflection' 1974, Golden Prague BBC TV first Br Award as writer of new version of Mozart's The Impresario 1975, Prix Italia (first Br Music Prize) Britten's cantata St Nicolas 1982; chm Liberal Working Party on the Media, fndr memb Liberal Arts Panel, fndr ITV Arts Panel, fndr memb Euro Bdcasting Union Music Experts Gp, memb ACTT 1958; fell IBA; chevalier Ordre des Arts French Miny of Culture; *Books* Exploring TV (1970), Great Britain (McDonalds Countries series, 1971), Building a Record Library (1971), Bluffer's Guide to Opera (1973), Bluff Your Way in Ballet (1974); *Recreations* music, food, drink; *Clubs* Seven Dials Fox House; *Style—* Francis Coleman, Esq; 24 Shelton St, Covent Garden, London WC2H 9HP (☎ 081 883 6111)

COLEMAN, Gordon Barton; s of Walter Robert Granville Coleman, of Eastbourne, Sussex, and Olive May, *née* Buckenham; *b* 10 July 1924; *Educ* Brentwood Sch; *m* 14 April 1956, Marie Jessie Thérèse (Moira), da of William Vogt; 2 da (Sylvia b 10 Dec 1957, Brenda b 28 Sept 1959); *Career* Army 1942-47, cmmnd Royal Welch Fusiliers 1943, Platoon Cdr Duke of Wellingtons Regt in Normandy 1944 (wounded Aug 1944), Capt 1945; gen mangr for Brazil FS Hampshire & Co Ltd 1960-61, fndr International Licensing (jl acknowledged as world ldr in field technol trans and licensing of patents) 1964-; currently chm and md Projects for Indust Ltd (a company aiding industrialisation in the developing world); *Recreations* equestrian sports, golf, gardening, antiques restoration; *Clubs* Northwood GC, Royal Eastbourne GC; *Style—* Gordon Coleman, Esq; 17 Farm Ave, Harrow, Middx HA2 7LP (☎ 081 868 9951); 92 Cannon Lane, Pinner, Middx HA5 1HT (☎ 081 866 2812, fax : 081 429 2030)

COLEMAN, John Ennis; CB (1990); s of Donald Stafford Coleman (d 1968), of 8 Carlisle Rd, Eastbourne, Sussex, and Dorothy Jean Balieff, *née* Ennis (d 1980); *b* 12 Nov 1930; *Educ* Dean Close Sch Cheltenham, Dulwich, Univ of Oxford (MA); *m* 29 March 1958, Doreen Gwendoline, da of Percy Hellinger (d 1970), of Wimbledon; 1 s (David b 1968), 1 da (Kathryn b 1964); *Career* admitted slr 1957; Treasy Slrs Dept: legal asst 1958-64, sr legal asst 1964-71, asst slr 1971-80; legal under sec Depts of Indust and Trade 1980-83, conslt Dept of Educn and Sci 1990- (legal advsr 1983-90); *Style—* John Coleman, Esq, CB; Department of Education and Science, Elizabeth House, York Rd, London SE1 7PH (☎ 071 934 9223)

COLEMAN, John Raymond; s of James Alexander Coleman (d 1967), and Cathleen Kelly, *née* Lucas; *b* 23 Jan 1948; *Educ* Univ of Strathclyde (BA, MSc); *m* 25 Nov 1972, Rose Ann, da of James William Johnson (d 1985); 3 s (Iain James b 1973, James Edward b 1975, Alan Stephen b 1981); *Career* sr ptnr: Coleman Ballantine Partnership 1977, Coleman Ballantine of Gibraltar 1986; dir Mainhead Properties 1984, ptnr Property Marketing Conslts 1987; cncl memb of RIAS; FRIAS; *Style—* John R Coleman, Esq; Waltry, Milton of Campsie, Glasgow G65 8AA; 9/10 Woodside Crescent, Glasgow G3 7UL (☎ 041 332 1818, fax 041 332 6433)

COLEMAN, Malcolm Jerry; s of Colin Coleman (d 1975), and Esta, *née* Joel; *b* 9 Dec 1938; *Educ* Whittinghame Coll Brighton, City of London Sch; *m* 17 June 1962, Deanne Elaine Bernice, da of Hilary Louis Clive, of London and Portugal; 2 s (Jeremy Andrew b 1963, Daniel Clive b 1964), 1 da (Sara Melanie b 1966); *Career* sr ptnr Jeffreys Henry, dir Managed Growth Investments Ltd, FCA; *Recreations* Golf, Bridge; *Clubs* Potters Bar Golf (Capt 1974-75, chm 1980-87); *Style—* Malcolm J Coleman, Esq; 37 Springfield Rd, London NW8; Fansgate, 5-7 Cranwood St, London EC1 V9EE (telex 892907, fax 071 608 1983)

COLEMAN, (Elizabeth) Maryla Helen; da of Zygmunt Karol Lambert Chojecki (d 1983), of Bannisters, Exlade St, Woodcote, Oxon, and Caroline Elizabeth Chojecka, *née* Rowett, MBE; *b* 28 March 1954; *Educ* St Josephs Convent Reading Berks, Univ of London (BA); *m* 1 Dec 1973 (m dis 1981), Antony Gerard Coleman, s of Michael Coleman (d 1974), of Dalkey, Co Dublin, Ireland; *Career* md Chiampesan Bros (UK) Ltd 1979, dir Far East Pearls Ltd 1983, fndr Maryla Coleman Assocs; *Style—* Mrs Maryla Coleman; 1 Coach and Horses Yd, Savile Row, London W1

COLEMAN, Monica; da of George Henry Coleman (d 1956), of Christchurch, Hants, and Lilian Marie, *née* Murray (d 1960); *b* 25 Oct 1934; *Educ* Kings Thorpe Sch; *Career* artist specialising in oil paintings of the New Forest, TV appearances incl BBC TV's New Foresters 1981; patron New Forest Deer Protection Cncl; fndr memb Friends of the New Forest; memb: Forestry Cmmn New Forest Badger Gp, Society of Women Writers and Journalists; *Books* Monica Coleman's New Forest (1987); *Recreations* walking and observing the wildlife in the New Forest; *Style—* Miss Monica Coleman; Allward, 5 Parsonage Barn Lane, Ringwood, Hampshire BH24 1PS (☎ 0425 475948)

COLEMAN, Nick; s of Ivan Mark Coleman, of West Hampstead, London NW6, and Loretta, *née* Franks; *b* 2 Dec 1961; *Educ* West HS for boys Essex, Southend Tech Coll, Kingston Poly, St Martin's Sch of Art (BA); *Career* fashion designer; menswear designer Burberrys July-Dec 1984, estab own label Nick Coleman 1985, first collection Dustbowl '86 shown London 1985; subsequent collections incl: Shadow of the Spirit 1986-87, Legion of the Lost 1987, Teeth of the Hydra 1987-88, V 1988, Deus ex Machina 1989, Mondo Nuovo Man/Woman 1989-90; menswear designer and conslt Corneliani 1989-90, jt fndr (with Katherine Hamnett) Nick Coleman Ltd 1989-, first collection Kimota Returns 1990-91, first major catwalk show London 1990; subsequent collections: X 1991 (accompanied by catwalk show, appearances on BBC Clothes Show), Modern European Explorers 1991-92; fndr: Solaris (house music club) 1989-90, Kimota Nightclub 1989-90; memb London Fashion Cncl 1989; *Recreations* music, collecting African art, reading, work; *Style—* Nick Coleman, Esq; Nick Coleman Ltd, 202 New North Road, London N1 7BJ (☎ 071 359 5702, fax 071 354 5246)

COLEMAN, Prof Robert George Gilbert; s of George Gilbert Coleman (d 1953), of Wellington, NZ, and Rosina Emily, *née* Warner (d 1964); *b* 2 Oct 1929; *Educ* St Mark's Sch, Rongotai Coll, Wellington Coll, Victoria Univ of Wellington (MA), Emmanuel Coll Cambridge (BA, MA); *m* 28 June 1958, Dorothy, da of Rufus Gabe (d 1956), of Ystalyfera; 1 s (Ian Gilbert b 1965); *Career* lectr in humanity Kings Coll Aberdeen 1955-60; Emmanuel Coll Cambridge: fell 1960, lectr in classics 1960-85, tutor 1963-71, librarian 1980-85, prof of comparative philology 1985-; *Books* The Eclogues of Vergil (ed with intro 1977); *Recreations* music, conversation, exploring strange towns; *Style—* Prof Robert Coleman; 7 Linton Rd, Balsham, Cambridge CB4 3PE; Emmanuel College Cambridge CB2 3A (☎ 0223 334 200)

COLEMAN, Robert John; s of Lt Cdr Frederick Coleman, RN; *b* 8 Sept 1943; *Educ* Devonport HS for Boys Plymouth, Jesus Coll Oxford (BA), Univ of Chicago Law Sch (JD); *m* 23 Sept 1966, Malinda Tigay, da of Preston Skidmore Cutler; 2 da (Emily Ann b 1975, Laura Elizabeth b 1979); *Career* lectr in law Univ of Birmingham 1967-70, fndr memb Legal Aid and Advice Centre Birmingham Settlement 1968-70, called to the Bar 1969, barr at law in civil practice London 1970-73, memb Home Office Legal Advsrs Branch 1973; Euro Cmmn: admin later princ admin 1974-82, dep head of Div (Safeguard Measures and Removal of Non-Tariff Barriers) 1983, head of Div (Intellectual Property and Unfair Competition) 1984-87, dir (Pub Procurement) 1987-90, dir (Approximation of Laws, Freedom of Establishment and Freedom to Provide Services, the Professions) 1990-; *Publications* Forcible Entry: Substance and Procedure (jtly with I R Scott, 1970), Problèmes Actuels de la Consolidation des Comptes: Les Aspects Européens (1977), The European Commission and the Multinational Enterprise 1977 to 1980 (1982), Accounting and Auditing Research and the European Community (1983), European Community Initiatives Concerning Copywright (1987), Opening Up of Public Procurement (1990); *Recreations* cycling, music; *Style—* Robert Coleman, Esq; 114 rue des Deux Tours, 1030 Brussels, Belgium (☎ 010 32 218 38 65); Comission of the European Communities, 200 Rue La Loi (Nerviens 9/21A), 1049 Bruxelles, Belgium (☎ 010 32 235 5025, fax 010 32 235 9331, telex 21877 COMEU B)

COLEMAN, Rodney Bernard; s of Jacob Henry Coleman (d 1990), of 3 Osterley Road, London, and Rosina, *née* Kelly; *b* 16 Nov 1945; *Educ* Joseph Priestley Secdy Tech Sch, Brooke House Sch, Poly of Central London (LLB); *m* 1 Nov 1986, Marijana, da of Jovo Skorupan of Vuceticev Prilaz No 3, 41000 Zagreb, Yugoslavia; *Career* with civil serv: Dept of Employment and Productivity 1967-68, Office of Population Censuses and Surveys 1969-71f, MOD 1971-79; called to the Bar Gray's Inn 1978; memb Cons Pty Hackney 1973-; Hackney Cncl (C) Candidate: 1974, 1982, 1986, 1990; former govr: Princess May Primary Sch, Sir Thomas Abney Primary Sch; *Recreations* music, bridge; *Style—* Rodney Coleman, Esq; 3 Osterley Rd, London N16 8SN; 1 Stone Bldgs, Lower Ground Floor, Lincoln's Inn, London WC2A 3XB (☎ 071 405 1673)

COLEMAN, Sylvia May; da of Capt Gordon Barton Coleman, of Harrow, Middx, and Marie Jessie Therese, *née* Vogt; *b* 10 Dec 1957; *Educ* Harrow Co GS for Girls, Univ of Birmingham (LLB), Coll of Law Lancaster Gate; *Career* admitted slr 1982; Stephenson Harwood 1980-85, co lawyer Gallaher Ltd 1985-86, co lawyer and co sec Sony Music Ent (UK) Ltd (formerly CBS Records) 1987-, md The Entertainment Zone 1989-; jt UK promoter Ceroc Dance 1983-, co-organiser Annual Ceroc Charity Ball, memb Action Aid; memb Law Soc 1980; *Recreations* dance, music, entertaining; *Clubs* The Kensington Close; *Style*— Miss Sylvia Coleman; 20 Courtfield Gardens, London SW5 OPD (☎ 071 370 5161); 17/19 Soho Sq, London W1V 6HE (☎ 071 734 8181, ext 305, fax 071 734 4321, telex 24203 CBSREC G)

COLEMAN, Talbot Pascoe Hilbut; s of Jack Talbot Coleman (d 1966), of Bristol, and Amelia Marjorie *née* Butt; *b* 10 Oct 1934; *Educ* Cardiff HS; *m* 9 Aug 1958, (Kathryn) Ann Louise, da of Flt-Lt Hugh David McDougall, of Godalming, Surrey; 1 s (Nial Talbot b 1961), 1 da (Charlotte Ann Louise b 1962); *Career* Flt offr RAF 1952-54, RAFVR 1959-65; Thames Bd Mills Ltd 1956-66, md Assi Pulp and Paper Sales UK Ltd 1966-; pres UK Paper Agents Assoc 1984-86, chm Croydon Central Cons Assoc 1985-88; memb: Worshipful Co of Gold and Silver Wyre Drawers 1979, Worshipful Co of Stationers and Newspaper Makers 1984; *Recreations* golf, cricket, reading; *Clubs* Carlton, MCC; *Style*— Talbot Coleman, Esq; 1 Upfield, Croydon

COLEMAN, Terence Francis Frank (Terry); s of Jack Coleman (d 1978), of Poole, Dorset, and Doreen, *née* Grose; *b* 13 Feb 1931; *Educ* Univ of London (LLB); *Career* journalist: Poole Herald, Savoir Faire (ed), Sunday Mercury, Birmingham Post; The Guardian: reporter, arts corr, chief feature writer 1961-74; special writer Daily Mail 1974-76; The Guardian: chief feature writer 1976-78, New York corr 1981, special corr 1982-89; assoc ed The Independent 1989-; *awards* Feature Writer of the Year Br Press Awards 1983, Journalist of the Year Granada Awards 1987; *Books* The Railway Navvies (Yorkshire Post Prize for the Best Book of the Year, 1965), A Girl for the Afternoons (1965), Providence and Mr Hardy with Lois Deacon, 1966), The Only True History (collected journalism, 1969), Passage to America (1972), The Liners (1976), An Indiscretion in the Life of an Heiress (ed 1976), The Scented Brawl (collected journalism, 1978), Southern Cross (1979), Thanksgiving (1981), Movers and Shakers (collected interviews, 1987), Thatcher's Britain (1987); *Recreations* cricket, opera, circumnavigation; *Clubs* MCC; *Style*— Terry Coleman, Esq; 18 North Side, London SW4

COLEMAN-SMITH, Brian Francis; s of Derek Gordon Coleman-Smith of Putney, London SW15 and Patricia Edwina Cronin (d 1972); *b* 26 Oct 1944; *Educ* Emanuel Sch; *m* 19 Oct 1984, Frances Mary, da of John Alexander Gladstone; 2 step s (Douglas Croxford b 22 Jan 1973, Bruce Croxford b 21 Sept 1979), 1 step da (Alison Croxford b 13 June 1970); *Career* northern fin advertisement mangr the Guardian 1976-79, advertisement dir Financial Weekly 1979-81, fin sales dir The Guardian 1981-85; dir: Burson-Marsteller Financial 1985-89, Burson-Marsteller Ltd 1989-; *Recreations* sport, theatre, cinema, classical music; *Clubs* Wimbledon Squash & Badminton; *Style*— Brian Coleman-Smith, Esq

COLERAINE, 2 Baron (UK 1954); (James) Martin Bonar Law; s of 1 Baron, PC (d 1980, himself s of Andrew Bonar Law, Prime Minister 1922-23); *b* 8 Aug 1931; *Educ* Eton, Trinity Coll Oxford; *m* 1, 30 April 1958 (m dis 1966), Emma Elizabeth, o da of late Nigel Richards; 2 da; *m* 2, 21 Aug 1966, (Anne) Patricia, yr da of Maj-Gen Ralph Henry Farrant, CB, of King's Acre, Wareham, Dorset; 1 s (Hon James b 1975), 2 da (Hon Henrietta b 1968, Hon Juliana b 1971); *Heir* s, Hon James Law; *Career* sits as Conservative in House of Lords; *Style*— The Rt Hon the Lord Coleraine; 3/5 Kensington Pk Gdns, W11 (☎ 071 221 4148)

COLERIDGE, David Ean; s of late Guy Cecil Richard Coleridge, MC, and Katherine Cicely Stewart Smith; *b* 7 June 1932; *Educ* Eton; *m* 1955, Susan, *née* Senior; 3 s; *Career* Lloyd's underwriter; chm Sturge Group of Cos 1978-, dep chm Lloyd's 1985, 1988, 1989 (chm 1991); *Recreations* shooting, golf, early Eng watercolours, family; *Style*— David Coleridge, Esq; 37 Egerton Terrace, London SW3 2BU; Spring Pond, Wispers, nr Midhurst, W Sussex; Sturge Holdings plc, 9 Devonshire Square, London EC2M 4YL (☎ 071 623 8822, fax 623 3386, telex 894156 STUR)

COLERIDGE, Lady (Marguerite) Georgina Christine; *née* Hay; 2 da of 11 Marquess of Tweeddale (d 1967), and his 1 wife Marguerite Christine, *née* Ralli (d 1944); *b* 19 March 1916; *m* 20 Sept 1941, Capt Arthur Nicholas Coleridge, late Irish Gds (d 1987), s of John Duke Coleridge, FRIBA (d 1934), of Darby Green House, Blackwater, Hants; 1 da (Mrs Neil Sonita Sida); *Career* National Magazine Co Ltd 1937-39, with Country Life 1945, ed Homes and Gardens 1949-63; dir: Country Life Ltd 1962-74, George Newnes Ltd 1963-69; publisher: Homes and Gardens, Woman's Journal 1969-71, Ideal Home 1970-71; dir special projects IPC Women's Magazines 1971-74, conslt IPC Women's Magazines 1974-82; dir Public Relations Cncl Ltd 1974-82; chm: Inst of Journalists (London Dist) 1954 (fell 1970), Women's Press Club 1959 (pres 1965-67); memb Int Assoc of Women and Home Page Journalists 1968-74, assoc Women in Public Relations 1972-, assoc memb Ladies Jockey Assoc of GB, fndr memb Media Soc Ltd (Inst of Journalists Fndn) 1973-76, fndr and vice pres Woman of the Year Lunches; vice pres Greater London Fund for the Blind 1981, pres Friends of Moorfields 1981; Freeman Worshipful Co of Stationers and Newspapermakers 1973; *Publications* Grand Smashional Pointers (cartoons, 1934), I Know What I Like (1959), That's Racing (1978), and many articles; *Recreations* racing, writing, cooking, nothing highbrow; *Style*— The Lady Georgina Coleridge; 33 Peel St, London W8 (☎ 071 727 7732)

COLERIDGE, Nicholas David; s of David Ean Coleridge, and Susan, *née* Senior; *b* 4 March 1957; *Educ* Eton, Trinity Coll Cambridge; *Career* assoc ed Tatler 1980-82, columnist Evening Standard 1982-84, assoc ed Harpers and Queen 1984-86 (ed 1986-89), ed dir Conde Nast Publications; Young Journalist of the Year 1984; *Books* Tunnel Vision (collected journalism, 1982), Shooting Stars (1984), Around the World in 78 Days (1984), The Fashion Conspiracy (1988), How I met My Wife and Other Stories (1991); *Recreations* travel, shuttlecock; *Clubs* Harry's Bar; *Style*— Nicholas Coleridge, Esq; 24 Chepstow Crescent, London W11 (☎ 071 221 4293); 1 Hanover Square, London W1 (☎ 071 499 9080)

COLERIDGE, Dowager Baroness; (Cecilia) Rosamund; *née* Fisher; er da of Adm Sir William Wordsworth Fisher, GCB, GCVO (d 1937), and Cecilia, *née* Warre-Cornish; *m* 28 Aug 1936, 4 Baron Coleridge, KBE, DL (d 1984); 2 s (5 Baron and Hon Samuel, *qqv*); *Clubs* Army and Navy; *Style*— The Rt Hon the Dowager Lady Coleridge; The Manor House, Ottery St Mary, S Devon (☎ (040 481) 4201)

COLERIDGE, Lt-Col Hon Samuel John Taylor; yr s of 4 Baron Coleridge, KBE, DL (d 1984), and Dowager Baroness Coleridge, *qv*; *b* 5 Feb 1942; *Educ* Winchester, Trinity Coll Oxford; *m* 1973, Patricia Susan, yr da of John Basil Edwards, CBE, of Cradley, nr Malvern, Worcs; 2 da (Jessica Alice Seymour b 1974, Clara Emily Taylor b 1976); *Career* Lt-Col Grenadier Gds; attached Army Air Corps 1964-68; Mil Attaché Algiers and Tunis 1985-88, sr liaison offr to French Forces in Germany 1988-91; *Style*— Lt-Col The Hon Samuel Coleridge; 43 Vogesenstrasse, 7570 Baden-Baden, W Germany

COLERIDGE, 5 Baron (UK 1873); William Duke Coleridge; er s of 4 Baron Coleridge, KBE, DL (d 1984; ggs of 1 Baron who was gn Samuel Taylor Coleridge, the poet), and Rosamund, Baroness Coleridge, *qv*; *b* 18 June 1937; *Educ* Eton, RMA Sandhurst; *m* 1, 17 Feb 1962 (m dis 1977), Everild Tania, da of Lt-Col Beauchamp Hambrough, OBE; 1 s, 2 da (Hon Tania Rosamund b 1966, Hon Sophia Tamsin b 1970); m 2, 1977, Pamela, da of George William Baker, CBE, VRD; 2 da (Hon Vanessa Layla b 1978, Hon Katharine Suzannah b 1981); *Heir* s, Hon James Duke Coleridge b 5 June 1967; *Career* served Kings African Rifles (pre Kenyan Independence) and Kenyan Army; Maj Coldstream Gds (ret), commanded Guards Independent Parachute Co 1970-72; govr Royal West of England Sch for Deaf, patron Colway Theatre Tst; *Recreations* golf, tennis, water-skiing; *Style*— The Rt Hon the Lord Coleridge; The Chanter's House, Ottery St Mary, S Devon (☎ 040 481 2417)

COLES, Adrian Michael; s of Kenneth Ernest Coles, and Constance Mary, *née* Sykes; *b* 19 April 1954; *Educ* Holly Lodge Smethwick, Univ of Nottingham (BA), Univ of Sheffield (MA); *m* 23 May 1981, Marion Alma, da of Joseph Henry Hoare; 1 s (David), 1 da (Verity); *Career* economist Electricity Cncl 1976-79, head of External Relations Dept Bldg Socs Assoc 1986- (economist 1979-81, head of Econs and Statistics Dept 1981-86); examiner econ affrs CBSI 1984-87; sch govr, memb Ctee housing assoc (chm 1990-), dir Housing centre Trust; regular contrib: CBSI Jl, Bldg Soc Gazette, Housing Fin Int, Bldg Soc Yearbook; *Recreations* family, swimming; *Style*— Adrian Coles, Esq; 3 Savile Row, London, WIX 1AF (☎ 071 437 0655, fax 071 734 6416, telex 2438 BSAG)

COLES, Hon Mrs (Bridget Mary); *née* Hope; 1 da of 2 Baron Rankeillour, GCIE, MC (d 1958), by Grizel, da of Brig-Gen Sir Robert Gilmour, 1 Bt, CB, CVO, DSO; *b* 17 Oct 1920; *m* 25 Jan 1942, Lt-Col George Henry Hugh Coles, The East Yorks Regt, s of late Lt-Col James Hugh Coles, DSO, The East Yorks Regt; 3 da; *Style*— The Hon Mrs Coles; 25 Kings Court North, Kings Rd, London SW3 (☎ 071 352 8570)

COLES, Prof Bryan Randell; s of Charles Frederick Coles (d 1974), of Cardiff, Wales and Olive Irene, *née* Randell (d 1975); *b* 9 June 1926; *Educ* Canton HS Cardiff, Univ of Wales Cardiff (BSc), Jesus Coll Oxford (DPhil); *m* 27 July 1955, Merivan, da of W Ace Robinson (d 1935), of Minneapolis USA; 2 s (Matthew b 1965, Jonathan b 1967); *Career* Physics Dept Imperial Coll London: lectr 1950-60, reader 1960-65, prof 1965-, pro rector 1986-; dean RCS 1984-86, visiting prof Univ of California 1969 (Univ of Minnesota 1983), bd chm Taylor & Francis Scientific publishers 1976-; chm: Physics Ctee SRC 1973-77, Neutron Beam Ctee SERC 1984-88; FInstP 1968; *Books* Atomic Theory for Students of Metallurgy (with W Hume-Rothery 1969), Electronic Structures of Solids (with A D Caplin, 1976); *Recreations* music, theatre, natural history; *Style*— Prof Bryan Coles; 61 Courtfield Gdns, London SW5 (☎ 071 373 3539); Shoe Cottage, Vines Cross, Horam, E Sussex; Imperial Coll, London SW7; Taylor & Francis Ltd, 4 John St, London WC1

COLES, His Hon Judge Gerald James Kay; QC (1976); s of James William Coles (d 1977), of Redcar, Yorkshire, and Jane Elizabeth Kay (d 1981); *b* 6 May 1933; *Educ* Coatham Sch, Sir William Turner's Sch Redcar, BNC Oxford (BA, BCL), Harvard Law Sch USA (LLM); *m* 22 Feb 1958, Kathleen Yolande, da of Alfred John Hobson (d 1970); 3 s (Andrew James b 1961, Christopher John Kay b 1963, Matthew Henry b 1970); *Career* called to the Bar Middle Temple 1957, practised London and NE Circuit 1957-85, prosecuting counsel to the Inland Revenue 1971-76, rec 1972-85, circuit judge 1985; memb Mental Health Review Tbnl 1985; *Recreations* music, theatre, photography, opera; *Clubs* Yorkshire; *Style*— His Hon Judge Coles, QC; Redwood, Dean Lane, Hawksworth, Guiseley, Leeds LS20 8NY (☎ 0943 72688)

COLES, Ian Ronald; s of Ronald Frederick Coles, of 18 Park Ave, Mexborough, South Yorks, and Rosena, *née* Haigh; *b* 12 Sept 1956; *Educ* Mexborough GS, Univ of Cambridge (BA), Univ of Harvard (LLM); *m* 27 March 1988, Bethann, da of Bernard Firestone (d 1989); 1 da (Katharine Emma Mary b 15 Aug 1990); *Career* called to the Bar Lincoln's Inn 1979; attorney NY State Bar 1983, lectr in law City of London Poly 1978-80, assoc Mayer Brown and Platt NY and London 1981-86 (ptnr London 1986-); memb: Bar Assoc for Commerce Fin and Indust 1979, NY State Bar Assoc 1983, Int Bar Assoc 1988, Assoc des Jeunes Avocats 1989; *Recreations* music, photography, books, skiing; *Clubs* Raffles; *Style*— Ian Coles, Esq; Mayer Brown & Platt, 162 Queen Victoria St, London EC4V 4BS (☎ 071 248 1465, telex 8811095, fax 071 329 4465)

COLES, Joanna Louise; da of Michael Edward Coles, and Margaret Coles; *b* 20 April 1962; *Educ* Prince Henry's Comprehensive Sch Otley W Yorks, UEA (BA); *Career* graduate trainee The Spectator (contrib The Guardian) 1984-86, dep literary ed The Spectator 1986-89; news/feature writer: Daily Telegraph 1989-, The Guardian; reviewer for Kaleidoscope BBC Radio 4; *Recreations* riding, theatre; *Clubs* Westminster Dining, Women's Press; *Style*— Miss Joanna Coles; The Guardian, 119 Farringdon Rd, London EC1 2ER (☎ 071 278 2332)

COLES, HE Sir (Arthur) John; KCMG (1989, CMG 1984); s of Arthur Strixton Coles, and Doris Gwendoline Coles; *b* 13 Nov 1937; *Educ* Magdalen Coll Sch Brackley, Magdalen Coll Oxford (BA); *m* 1965, Anne Mary Sutherland (MA, PhD), da of Christopher Graham, of Farthings, Pilley Hill, Pilley, Lymington, Hants; 2 s, 1 da; *Career* served HM Forces 1955-57; HM Dip Serv 1960-: Middle Eastern Centre for Arabic Studies Lebanon 1960-62, third sec Khartoum 1962-64, FO 1964-68, asst political agent Trucial States (Dubai) 1968-71, FCO 1971-75, head of chancery Cairo 1975-77, cnsllr (Developing Countries) UK Perm Mission to EEC 1977-80, head of S Asian Dept FCO 1980-81, private sec to the PM 1981-84, ambass to Jordan 1984-88, high cmmr Aust 1988-; *Style*— HE Sir John Coles, KCMG; British High Commission, Commonwealth Ave, Canberra, Australia

COLES, Dame Mabel Irene; DBE (1971, CBE 1965); da of late Edward Johnston; *m* 1927, Sir Edgar Barton Coles (d 1981); 1 s, 2 da; *Career* pres Australian Women's Liberal Club 1965-, dir Asthma Foundation of Victoria 1965, pres Royal Women's Hosp Melbourne 1968-72; *Style*— Dame Mabel Coles, DBE; Hendra, Williams Rd, Mount Eliza, Vic 3930, Australia

COLES, Ronald John; s of Reginald Herbert Coles, and Mary McAlpine McLeish, *née* Leslie; *b* 18 July 1944; *Educ* Wellingborough GS, Sunderland Coll of Educn, Univ of Leeds; *m* 22 Nov 1969, Stefanie, da of late Richard Ewart Smith; 1 s (Toby b 4 Aug 1975), 1 da (Melanie b 11 June 1973); *Career* BBC Radio: prodr local and network radio 1969-75, trg instr radio prodn techniques 1975-76, prog organiser Nottingham 1976-78, mangr Sheffield 1978-80; md: Radio Trent Ltd 1980-89, Midlands Radio plc 1989-; Assoc Ind Radio Contractors: chm Labour Relations Ctee 1984-82, 1983 and 1986, elected to Cncl 1984-82 (chm 1986-87), chm of finance 1988-; memb: Cncl of Radio Academy 1989-, IOD, Rare Breeds Survival Tst, Notts Beekeepers Assoc; *Recreations* beekeeping, goats, bearded collie dogs, winemaking, photography; *Style*— Ronald Coles, Esq; Manor Farm, Main Street, Upton, Nr Newark, Notts NG23 5ST (☎ 0636 812289); Midlands Radio plc, 29/31 Castle Gate, Nottingham NG1 7AP (☎ 0602 503020, fax 0602 582606, telex 37463, car 0831 553395)

COLFOX, Lady; Frederica Loveday; da of Adm Sir Victor Crutchley, VC, KCB, DSC (d 1986), and Joan Elizabeth Loveday, *née* Coryton (d 1982); *b* 28 Dec 1934; *Educ* Heathfield, Ascot; *m* 13 Jan 1962, Sir John, s of S W Philip Colfox, Bt, MC (d 1966); 2 s (Philip b 27 Dec 1962, Edward b 14 Jan 1969), 3 da (Victoria b 14 Jan 1964, Charlotte b 28 Jan 1966, Connie b 20 July 1971); *Career* The Witt Library, Courtauld Inst of Art until 1961; chm The Environmental Med Fndn (acting chm 1987); *Recreations* childish pursuits; *Style*— Lady Colfox; Symondsbury House, Bridport, Dorset DT6 6HB, (☎ 0308 22956)

COLFOX, Sir (William) John; 2 Bt (UK 1939), of Symondsbury, Co Dorset, JP (Dorset 1962); s of Sir Philip Colfox, 1 Bt, MC, DL (d 1966), and Mary Frances, *née* Symes-Bullen (d 1973); *b* 25 April 1924; *Educ* Eton; *m* 13 Jan 1962, Frederica Loveday, da of Adm Sir Victor Crutchley, VC, KCB, DSC, DL, of Mappercombe Manor, Bridport, Dorset, *qv*; 2 s, 3 da; *Heir* s, Philip Colfox, *qv*; *Career* Lt RNVR 1939-45; land agent 1950, chm land Settlement Assoc 1979-81, dir TV SW 1981-; High Sheriff of Dorset 1969; *Style*— Sir John Colfox, Bt, JP, DL; Symondsbury Hse, Bridport, Dorset (☎ 0308 22956)

COLFOX, Philip John; s and h of Sir William John Colfox, 2 Bt; *b* 27 Dec 1962; *Educ* Eton; *Career* businessman; trained with Jardine Thompson Graham Ltd 1982-85; md: Symondsbsury House Ltd 1987, Philip Colfox Ltd (Building Contractors) 1989; *Recreations* fox hunting, shooting; *Style*— Philip Colfox Esq; 284 Wandsworth Bridge Rd, London SW6 2UA (☎ 071 736 9293)

COLGRAIN, 3 Baron (UK 1946); David Colin Campbell; s of 2 Baron Colgrain, MC (d 1973), and Margaret Emily (Madge), *née* Carver (d 1989); *b* 24 April 1920; *Educ* Eton, Trinity Coll Cambridge; *m* 1, 20 June 1945 (m dis 1964), Veronica Margaret, da of late Lt-Col William Leckie Webster, RAMC; 1 s, 1 da; m 2, 1973, Mrs Sheila McLeod Hudson; *Heir* s, Hon Alastair Campbell; *Career* served WWII, Lt 9 Lancers, UK and ME (wounded Alamein 1942); exec Grindlays Bank: India and Pakistan 1945-48, London 1949; Antony Gibbs & Sons Ltd and successive cos 1949-83 (dir 1954-83, ret 1983); chm Alexander & Berendt Ltd 1967-; *Recreations* music, farming, forestry; *Clubs* Cavalry and Guards'; *Style*— The Rt Hon the Lord Colgrain; Bushes Farm, Weald, Sevenoaks, Kent (☎ 0732 463279)

COLHOUN, Prof John; s of James Colhoun (d 1935), of Castlederg, Co Tyrone, and Rebecca, *née* Lecky (d 1963); *b* 15 May 1913; *Educ* Edwards Sch Castlederg Co Tyrone, The Queen's Univ Belfast (BSc, BAgr, MAgr), Imperial Coll of Sci London (DIC), Univ of London (PhD, DSc); *m* 29 July 1949, Margaret Waterhouse, da of Prof Gilbert Waterhouse, of Belfast; 3 da (Lucy (Mrs Loerzer) b 1950, Georgiana (Mrs Golub) b 1956, Jacqueline (Mrs Chaddock) b 1959); *Career* Miny of Agric for NI: res asst 1939-46, sr sci offr 1946-50, princ sec offr 1951-60; Queen's Univ of Belfast:asst lectr in agric botany 1940-42, asst lectr 1942-45, jr lectr 1945-46, lectr 1946-54, reader in mycology and plant pathology 1954-60; Univ of Manchester: Barker prof of cryptogamic botany 1960-80, dean Faculty of Sci 1974 and 1975, pro vice chllr 1977-80, prof emeritus 1980; jt ed-in-chief Jl of Phytopathology (Phytopathologische Zeitschrift) 1973-91; pres: The Queen's Univ Assoc 1960-61, Br Mycological Soc 1963, The Queen's Univ Club London 1983-85; chm: Fedn of Br Plant Pathologists 1968, Int Ctee of Fusarium Workers 1968-73, Ctee of Euro Discussion Gps in Plant Pathology 1968-75, Sub Ctee on Res on Cereals ARC 1973-78; memb: governing body Glasshouse Crops Res Inst Littlehampton 1967-77, Plants and Soils Ctee ARC 1968-78, Univ of Manchester Cncl and Ct 1973-76 and 1977-80; visiting prof State Univ of Washington USA 1969; govr: Hulme Hall Tst Fndn 1964-, Manchester HS for Girls 1961-85, City of Manchester Coll of Higher Educn 1978-83; chm: Bd for Awards in Affiliated Colls Univ of Manchester 1977-80; Ctee Ashburne Hall Manchester 1970-80, Ctee The Manchester Museum 1974-80 (memb 1960-); président d'honneur Third Euro Congress of Mycology 1963, hon memb Br Soc for Plant Pathology 1989; FLS 1955, FIBiol 1963; Univ of Manchester (MSc, ex-officio degree 1964); *Books* Diseases of The Flax Plant (1947), Clubroot Disease of Crucifers Caused by *Plasmodiophora brassicae* Woron (1958); authors of numerous papers in: Annals of Applied Biology, Annals of Botany, Trans British Mycological Soc, Nature, Phytopathologische Zeitschrift, Annales Academie Scientiarum Feenicae, Annales Agriculturae Fennaie, Seed Scienicer and Technology, Annual Review of Phytopathology; *Clubs* Athenaeum; *Style*— Prof John Colhoun; 12 Southdown Cres, Cheadle Hulme, Cheshire SK8 6EQ (☎ 061 485 2084)

COLIN, John Fitzmaurice; s of Bishop Gerald Fitzmaurice Colin, of Orchard Close, Louth, Lincs, and Iris Susan Stuart, *née* Weir; *b* 8 March 1942; *Educ* King's Coll London (MB BS), Westminster Med Sch Univ of London (MS); *m* 20 July 1974, Christel Elizabeth, da of Franciskus Kern (d 1981), of Ziegenhain, W Germany; 3 da (Katharine b 1976, Alexandra b 1979, Anna b 1981); *Career* tutor RCS 1975-79; Westminster Hosp: house physician 1965-66, sr registrar 1975-79; conslt surgn United Norwich Hosp 1979-; memb: Assoc of Surgns of GB and I, Vascular Surgical Soc; FRSM, MRCS, LRCP, FRCS; *Recreations* fishing, tennis; *Clubs* Strangers (Elm Hill Norwich); *Style*— John Colin, Esq; 419 Unthank Road, Norwich, Norfolk NR4 7QB (☎ 0603 259925), Norfolk & Norwich Hospital, West Norwich Hospital, BUPA Hospital, Norwich

COLIN-JONES, Duncan Gadsby; s of Dr Colin Edgar Colin-Jones, of 14 Woodruff Dr, Hove, Sussex, and Beatrice, *née* Gadsby; *b* 13 April 1939; *Educ* Brighton Coll, Bart's (MB BS, MD); *m* 25 May 1963, Carol, *née* Ditchburn; 1 s (David Duncan b 1966), 1 da (Susan Mary b 1964); *Career* conslt physician and gastroenterologist Queen Alexandra Hosp Portsmouth 1975-, hon sr lectr Univ of Southampton; memb Advsy Ctee on Drugs Dept of Health 1985-, vice-pres endoscopy and memb Bd Govrs Euro Endoscopy Assoc, treas Br Soc Gastroenterology 1987- (former chm Endoscopy Ctee and vice pres endoscopy 1984-85), regnl advsr RCP 1982-84; FRCP 1977; *Style*— Duncan Colin-Jones, Esq; 21 Evelegh Road, Farlington PO6 1DJ, Queen Alexandra Hospital, Portsmouth PO6 3LY (☎ 0705 379451)

COLKER, Richard Frank; s of Frank Colker (d 1986), of St Clair Shores, Michigan, USA, and Marjorie, *née* Humphry; *b* 5 Oct 1945; *Educ* Univ of Michigan State, E Lansing USA (BA); *m* 24 Nov 1979, Marie-Claude, da of Jean-Louis Fouché, of Carquefou, France; 3 da (Emilie b 1980, Jennifer b 1982, Stephanie b 1985); *Career* served US Army until 1968; Wells Fargo Bank San Francisco US 1969-72 (London 1973-75), vice pres corp fin Banque de la Société Financière Europèenne Paris 1976-83, md investmt banking Kidder Peabody Int London 1983-90, chm R F Colker & Co London 1990-; *Recreations* golf, classical music, European history; *Clubs* Royal St George's Golf (Kent), Union (New York); *Style*— Richard Colker, Esq; 6 Pelham Place, London SW7 (☎ 071 581 5631); 39 South St, Mayfair, London W1Y 5PD (☎ 071 409 2324)

COLLACOTT, Peter Barrie; s of Dr Ralph Albert Collacott, of 1 Fordview Close, Great Glen, Leicester, and Ruby Hilda, *née* Nash; *b* 19 June 1944; *Educ* King's Sch Rochester; *m* 4 Sept 1971, Frances Rosamond, da of Lt Cdr Hibbard (d 1983), of 585 Maidstone Road, Blue Bell Hill, Rochester, Kent; 2 s (Nicholas b 1973, Piers b 1978), 2 da (Esther b 1976, Hannah b 1985); *Career* CA; articled clerk Jackson Pixley 1963-68, audit sr Price Waterhouse 1968-71; accountant: Keyser Ullman Ltd 1971-75, NM Rothschild & Sons Ltd 1976-79; accountant/sec MOD 1977-79, auditor gen Govt of Tonga 1979-80, fin controller 1980-85; fin dir: NM Rothschild Asset Mgmnt Ltd, NM Rothschild Fund Mgmnt Ltd; non exec dir NM Rothschild Asset Mgmnt (CI) Ltd; FICA; *Recreations* cricket, squash, tennis; *Style*— Peter B Collacott, Esq; Chart Cottage, Seal Chart, Sevenoaks, Kent; NM Rothschild Asset Management Ltd, Five Arrows House, St Swithins Lane, London, EC4N 8NR (☎ 071 280 5000, fax 071 929 1643, telex 888031)

COLLCUTT, Michael Francis; s of Edgar Hugh Collcutt, OBE (d 1967), of Robartes, Falmouth Rd, Truro, Cornwall, and Dorothy Marie, *née* Smith (d 1978); *b* 28 July 1928; *Educ* Truro Cathedral Sch, Pembroke Coll Cambridge (BA); *m* 6 March 1954, Iris Audrey, da of George Sowry, of Eastbourne; 1 s (Christopher b 1961), 1 da (Catherine b 1958); *Career* Mil Serv 2 Lt RA 1947-49; admitted slr 1955, sr ptnr Toller Hales and Collcutt; dir numerous private cos, underwriting memb of Lloyds; HM Coroner of Northamptonshire; *Recreations* golf, fishing, shooting; *Clubs* IOD, Northampton County Golf, Luffenham Heath Golf, Kettering Golf (pres), Northampton and County, Hawks; *Style*— Michael F Collcutt, Esq; Isebrook Cottage, Finedon, Wellingborough, Northants; Toller Hales and Collcutt, 55 Headlands, Kettering, Northants NN15 7EY (☎ 0536 83671, telex 341861, fax 0536 410068)

COLLEE, Prof (John) Gerald; CBE (1991); s of John Gerald Collee, JP (d 1983), of Blenheim, Bo'ness, and Mary Hay Wilson Kirsopp, *née* Cassels; *b* 10 May 1929; *Educ* Bo'ness Acad, Edinburgh Acad, Univ of Edinburgh (MB ChB, MD); *m* 1 April 1952, Isobel McNay, da of George Beaumont Galbraith, of Upper Kinneil, Bo'ness; 2 s (John b 1956, George b 1959), 1 da (Carol b 1953); *Career* Nat Serv Capt RAMC 1952-54: RMO 5 Royal Northumberland Fusiliers, OC Medical Reception Station Newcastle-upon-Tyne; house physician Roodlands Hosp Haddington 1951, asst Gp Shifnal 1954-55; Univ of Edinburgh Med Sch: lectr in bacteriology 1955-64, sr lectr and hon conslt 1964-70, reader 1970-74, personal prof 1974-79; prof of bacteriology, head of Dept and chief bacteriologist Edinburgh Royal Infirmary 1979 conslt advsr in microbiology Scottish Home and Health Dept; MRCPath 1964, FRCPath 1975, MRCP (Edin) 1977, FRCP (Edin 1979); *Books* Practical Medical Microbiology (author and ed), author, contrib, ed numerous textbooks, numerous papers in learned jls; *Recreations* woodwork, light mechanics, music, painting, poetry, fishing; *Clubs* Scottish Arts, RAMC (Millbank); *Style*— Prof Gerald Collee, CBE; 45 Grange Road, Edinburgh, Scotland EH9 1UF; Department of Bacteriology, University Medical School, Teviot Place, Edinburgh EH8 9AG (☎ 031 667 1011, fax 031 662 4135, telex 72744 UNIVED G)

COLLER, Mervyn Tarrant; s of Maj Raymond Geoffrey Coller, RA (d 1940), and Beryl Mary Lempriere, *née* Back (d 1950); *b* 7 Nov 1929; *Educ* Eton; *m* 22 Sept 1955, Cecilia Mary, da of Capt Stuart Cozens-Hardy, Boardman (ka 1943); 2 s (Richard Stuart b 1959, Nicholas Lempriere b 1962); *Career* chm and md Pertwee and Back Ltd 1962-; pres Great Yarmouth Chamber of Commerce 1982-85; *Recreations* trout fishing, gardening; *Style*— Mervyn Coller, Esq; Loke House, Sutton, Stalham, Norwich, Norfolk (☎ (0692) 80527); Pertwee and Back Ltd, Southgates Road, Great Yarmouth (☎ (0493) 844922)

COLLESTATTE; *see*: Manassei di Collestatte

COLLET, Harald Johan Holger; s of Harald P O Collet (d 1972), Estate Owner, of Chamberlain, Denmark, and Else Collet, *née* Collett; *b* 13 Oct 1947; *Educ* St Gall Business Sch, Switzerland (BA), Wharton Sch of Fin, Univ of Penns, USA; *m* 30 Aug 1975, Marianne, da of Lars Erick Sundberg (d 1968), chief exec, Overums Bruk, Sweden; 1 s (Johan b 1986); 3 da (Michaela b 1980, Stephanie b 1982, Alexandra b 1985); *Career* Lt Danish Royal Guards; investmt banker Salomon Bro 1986; dir: Hambros Bank 1984-86, Nordic Bank 1982-84, V UK Hldgs Ltd; vice pres and dir Hanover Tst 1974-82; *Recreations* tennis, golf, shooting; *Clubs* Hurlingham, Royal Wimbldeon Golf; *Style*— Harald Collet, Esq; Salomon Brothers International Ltd, 111 Buckingham Palace Rd, London SW1W 0SB (☎ 071 721 3829)

COLLET, Robert Thomson (Robin); s of Robert Alan Collet (d 1979), of Epsom, and Jean Edith Isobel, *née* Thomson; *b* 26 Nov 1939; *Educ* Malvern, Pembroke Coll Cambridge (MA); *m* 6 May 1972, Olivia Diana Mary, da of Leonard Clough-Taylor; 1 s (Henry b 1977), 1 da (Eloise b 1974); *Career* CA; dir Tilhill Forestry Ltd 1979-; Freeman City of London 1964, memb Worshipful Co of Coopers 1964; FCA 1966; *Recreations* golf, skiing, walking; *Style*— Robin Collet, Esq; The School House, Wimble Hill, Crondall, Farnham, Surrey GU10 5KL (☎ 0252 850 824); Tilhill Forestry Ltd, Greenhills, Tilford, Farnham, Surrey (☎ 025 125 4771, fax 025 125 4758)

COLLETT, Sir Christopher; GBE (1988), JP (City of London 1979); 2 s of Sir Henry Seymour Collett, 2 Bt (d 1971); *b* 10 June 1931; *Educ* Harrow, Emmanuel Cambridge (MA); *m* 1959, Christine Anne, da of Oswald Hardy Griffiths, of Nunthorpe, Yorks; 2 s, 1 da; *Career* Capt RA (TA); ptnr Ernst & Young Chartered Accountants London; memb Court of Common Cncl Broad Street Ward City of London 1973-79, Alderman 1979-, Sheriff City of London 1985-86, Lord Mayor 1988-89; Master Worshipful Co of Glovers 1981; memb: Guild of Freemen Worshipful Co of Chartered Accountants in England and Wales, City of London TAVR Ctee; govr: Bridewell Royal Hosp 1982-, Haberdashers' Aske's Schools Elstree 1982-; govr King Edwards Sch, Witley 1987-, memb Cncl Action Research for the Crippled Child 1984-, pres Broad Street Ward Club 1979-; Hon DSc City Univ 1988; KStJ 1988; Cdr Order of Merit Federal Republic of Germany 1986, Order of Merit (Class II) State of Qatar 1985, Order of Civil Merit (Class II) Spain 1986, Cdr Order of the Niger (Class I) Nigeria 1989, Order of Independence (Class II) UAE; *Recreations* gardening, fishing; *Clubs* City of London, City Livery; *Style*— Sir Christopher Collett, GBE; 121 Home Park Rd, Wimbledon, SW19

COLLETT, Sir Ian Seymour; 3 Bt (UK 1934), of Bridge Ward in the City of London; s of David Seymour Collett (d 1962), by his w, now Lady Miskin (w of His Honour Judge Sir James Miskin, QC); suc gf 1971; *b* 5 Oct 1953; *Educ* Lancing Coll; *m* 18 Sept 1982, Philippa, da of James R I Hawkins, of Preston St Mary, Suffolk; 1 s (Anthony b 1984), 1 da (Georgina b 1986); *Heir* s, Anthony Collett, b 1984; *Recreations* fishing, shooting, cricket; *Clubs* MCC; *Style*— Sir Ian Collett, Bt; Pound Farm, Great Glemham, Suffolk

COLLETT, Michael Frederick; s of Victor Valentine Collett (d 1986), of 24 Arleston Drive, Wollaton, Nottingham, and Jennie, *née* Truswell (d 1937); *b* 7 July 1933; *Educ* Whitgift Sch Croydon, Queens' Coll Cambridge (MA); *m* 1, 17 Aug 1957 (m dis 1973), Elizabeth Anne, da of Gerald Leon, of Toorak, Aust; m 2, 25 Feb 1978, Cynthia Barbara, da of Albert Henry Lee James (d 1973), of Erdington, Birmingham; 1 s (Christopher Andrew), 2 step s (Stuart James Hands, Michael Charles Hands), 1 step da (Claire Elizabeth Hands); *Career* Nat Serv RA 1951-53, 2 Lt; TA 1953-74: Lt 460 HAA Regt RA 1953-55, Capt 265 Light Air Def Regt 1955-69, Maj London and Kent Artillery (CADRE Regt, Cdr), Maj 6 (Vol) Bn The Queens Regt 1971-74 (Co Cdr); Equity and Law Life Assoc Soc: joined 1956, staff mangr 1969-77, policy serv mangr 1977-88; dir Chamber Devpt Assoc Br Chambers of Commerce 1988-90; pres: Birmingham Actuarial Soc 1980, Warwick Avon Rotary Club 1980-81; vice pres Coventry C of C (pres 1986-88), Bd Coventry Poly; Freeman City of London 1974; FIA 1962; *Recreations* philately; *Clubs* Army and Navy; *Style*— Michael F Collett, Esq; Stable Hollow, 50A Kenilworth Rd, Leamington Spa, Warwicks; (☎ 0926 423641); Trevan, Station Rd, Deganwy, nr Conwy, N Wales

COLLETT, Ruth, Lady; Ruth Mildred; *née* Hatch; er da of late William Thomas Hatch, of Bromley, Kent; *m* 22 Nov 1920, Sir Henry Seymour Collett, 2 Bt (d 1971); 2 s, 1 da (1 s decd); *Style*— Ruth, Lady Collett; Flat 1, Sunset House, Godyll Road, Southwold, Suffolk

COLLEY, Maj Gen David Bryan Hall; CB, CBE (OBE 1977, MBE 1968); s of Lawson Colley (d 1970), of Sutton Coldfield, and Alice, *née* Hall (d 1989); *b* 5 June 1934; *Educ* King Edward's Sch Birmingham, RMA Sandhurst; *m* 30 Sept 1957, Marie Therese, da of Louis Auguste Prefontaine (d 1966), of Edmonton, Alberta, Canada; 1 s (John b 1961), 1 da (Michele b 1959); *Career* cmmnd: RASC 1954, RCT 1965; regtl appts in Germany, Belgium, UK, Hong Kong and Singapore; Student Staff Coll Camberley 1964, JSSC Latimer 1970, CO Gurkha Tport Regt & 31 Regt RCT 1971-74, Staff HQ 1 (Br) Corps 1974-77, Cmd Logistic Support Gp 1977-80, Col AQ (Ops and Plans) and dir Admin Planning MOD (Army) 1980-82, Cmd Tport 1 (Br) Corps 1983-86, dir gen Tport and Movements (Army) 1986-88, Col Cmdt RCT 1988-; dir gen Road Haulage Assoc 1988-; Freeman City of London 1986, Hon Liveryman Worshipful Co of Carmen 1986; FCIT; *Recreations* travel, walking; *Clubs* Army & Navy; *Style—* Maj Gen D B H Colley, CB, CBE; c/o Midland Bank Plc, Church Green West, Redditch, Worcs, B97 4EA

COLLEY, Surgn Rear Adm Ian Harris; OBE (1963); s of Aubrey James Colley, and Violet Fulford Colley; *b* 14 Oct 1922; *Educ* Hanley Castle GS, King's Coll London, King's Coll Hosp (MB BS); *m* 1952, Joy Kathleen, *née* Goodacre; *Career* RN Med Serv 1948-80; MO HMS Cardigan Bay and HMS Consort 1949-52, serv with Fleet Air Arm 1955-78, PMO HMS Centaur, MO i/c Air Med Sch, pres Central Air Med Bd, cmd MO to Flag Offr Naval Air Cmd, Surgn Rear Adm (ships and establishments) 1978-80, ret; QHP 1978-80, conslt in aviation med, former examiner to Conjoint Bd RCS and RCP for dip aviation med, vice pres RNLI 1989 (former hon conslt in occupational med, chm Med Survival Ctee); author of papers on aviation med; CStJ 1980; *Style—* Surgn Rear Adm I H Colley, OBE; c/o Royal Bank of Scotland, Inveraray, Argyll PA32 8TY

COLLIE, George Francis; CBE (1964, MBE 1943), JP (Aberdeen); s of late George Duncan Collie (d 1946), of Morkeu, Cults, Aberdeenshire; *b* 1 April 1909; *Educ* Aberdeen GS, Univ of Aberdeen (BL); *m* 1949, Margery Constance Fullarton, OBE, da of Rev James Wishart, of Irvine, Ayrshire; 2 s; *Career* advocate Aberdeen; sr ptnr James and George Collie Solicitors Aberdeen, ret; dir Aberdeen Univ Press (chm 1959-79); Hon Col 51 Highland Div RASC and RTC 1964-72; Hon Sheriff of Grampian Highland and Islands at Aberdeen; *Clubs* Army and Navy, Royal Northern (Aberdeen); *Style—* George F Collie, Esq, CBE, JP; Morkeu, Cults, Aberdeen AB1 9PT (☎ 0224 867636); A33 Le Surcouf, Cannes Marina, 06210 Mandelieu, France (☎ 93 49 36 24)

COLLIER, Andrew John; s of Francis George Collier (d 1976), and Margaret Nancy, *née* Nockles; *b* 29 Oct 1939; *Educ* Univ Coll Sch, St Johns Coll Cambridge (MA); *m* 25 July 1964, Gillian Ann, da of George Thomas Ernest Churchill (ka 1945); 2 da (Susan b 1965, Sarah b 1968); *Career* asst master Winchester Coll 1962-68, Hants CC Educn Dept 1968-71, sr asst educn offr Bucks 1971-77, chief educn offr Lancs 1980 (dep chief offr 1977-79); memb: Cncl Univ of Lancaster 1981-86 and 1988-, Visiting Ctee Open Univ 1982-88, Cncl for Accreditation of Teacher Educn 1984-89, Nat Trg Task Force 1989-; advsr: Assoc of CC's, Cncl of LEA's; pres: Lancs Young Farmers Clubs 1985-88, Soc of Educn Offrs 1990; Liveryman Worshipful Co of Wheelwrights 1972; FRSA; *Recreations* opera, walking, the greenhouse; *Clubs* Athenaeum, Leander; *Style—* Andrew Collier, Esq; Education Dept, PO Box 61, County Hall, Preston PR1 8RJ (☎ 0772 263646, fax 0772 263630)

COLLIER, Anthony; s of Anthony Collier (d 1983); *b* 4 Jan 1947; *Educ* St Mary's GS, Middlesbrough, Leics Poly (Dip Arch); *m* 23 Sept 1973, Judith Ann, da of Henry Reginald Page, of Yorks; 1 s (Stephen Benedict b 1977), 1 da (Louise Helen b 1979); *Career* architect and interior designer; DoE medal Good Design in Housing Awards 1979, Civic Tst Commended 1978; has designed and supervised many projects for new buildings and refurbishment of existing or derelict buildings, especially in areas to be revitalised; RIBA; *Recreations* travel, golf, tennis, art, music; *Style—* Anthony Collier, Esq; Wadcrag, Wythop Mill, Embleton, Cockermouth, Cumbria (☎ Bassenthwaite Lake 634); work: South Quay Studios, 2-3 South Quay, Maryport, Cumbria CA15 8AB (☎ 0900 814271, fax 0900 818506)

COLLIER, (Andrew) James; CB (1976); s of Joseph Veasy Collier (d 1963), of London, and Dorothy Murray (d 1981); *b* 12 July 1923; *Educ* Harrow, Ch Ch Oxford (MA); *m* 1950, Bridget, da of George Eberstadt (d 1963), of London; 2 da (Caroline b 1952, Lucy-Anne b 1955); *Career* served RHA Capt 1942-46; HM Treas 1948-70, private sec to Chancellors of the Exchequer: Rt Hon Harold Macmillan, Rt Hon Peter Thorneycroft, Rt Hon Derek Heathcoat Amory; dep sec Dept of Health; now conslt and co dir; memb Special Hosps Service Authy; *Clubs* Athenaeum; *Style—* James Collier, Esq, CB; 10 Lambourne Avenue, Wimbledon SW19 7DW (☎ 081 879 3560)

COLLIER, Hon Mrs (Muriel Joan Lowry); *née* Lamb; yst da of 1 Baron Rochester, CMG (d 1955); *b* 1921; *Educ* LMH Oxford; *m* 29 Aug 1947 (m dis 1957), William Oswald Collier, o s of Sir Laurence Collier, KCMG (sometime Ambass Oslo and s of Hon John Collier, OBE, 2 s of 1 Baron Monkswell, by John's 2 w Ethel, sis of his 1 w and 5 da of Rt Hon Thomas Huxley, PC, FRS, and 1 cous once removed of Aldous Huxley, the novelist, and Sir Julian Huxley, the biologist); 1 s, 1 da; *Career* sr lectr educn Loughborough Coll Educn; late 3 sec Br Embassy Oslo; *Style—* The Hon Mrs Collier; 26 George St, Cambridge

COLLIER, Neil Adrian José; s of William Adrian Larry Collier (disclaimed Barony of Monkswell for life 1964) (d 1984), and his 2 w, Helen, *née* Dunbar; *b* 20 Aug 1948; *Educ* George Heriot's Sch Edinburgh, Univ of E Anglia (BSc), Univ of Leicester; *m* 1, 2 Aug 1975 (m dis 1985), Frances Myra Chapman; m 2, 11 June 1987, Judith Brandes, da of Rico G Bosca (d 1966); *Career* school teacher 1976-88; foreman landscape construction 1988-90 (Rare Earth Landscape); owner landscape construction co Live Oak Landscape 1990-; *Recreations* folk dancing, hiking; *Clubs* Berkeley Folk Dance; *Style—* Neil Collier, Esq; 1335 Peralta Ave, Berkeley, Cal 94702, USA (☎ 0101 415 524 2671); Live Oak Landscape, 1335 Peralta Ave, Berkeley, Cal 94702, USA (☎ 0101 415 527 9445)

COLLIER, Roy Sefton; s of Samuel Collier (d 1962), of Manchester, and Margaret Cordelia, *née* Bellis (d 1964); *b* 8 May 1931; *Educ* Whitworth St High Sch Manchester; *m* 1, 1 June 1957, Enid Mavis, s of Alderman A T Barratt (d 1965); 1 s (Christopher b 1954, d 1978), 1 da (Helen b 1962); m 2, 2 April 1977, Margaret Ann, s of T S Rodger (d 1947); *Career* Nat Serv Pay Corps Germany; CA; treas N Counties Archery Soc 1972-, dir Grand Nat Archery Soc Cncl; treas Soc of Archers and Antiquaries 1979-; FCA, ATII; *Recreations* golf; *Clubs* Heaton Moor Golf, Archery North Cheshire Bowman; *Style—* Roy S Collier, Esq; 488 Parrs Wood Road, East Didsbury, Manchester M20 0QQ (☎ 061 445 6508); 15 Edge Lane, Stretford, Manchester M32 8HN (☎ 061 865 8915)

COLLIN, Lady Clarissa; *née* Duncombe; JP; da of 3 Earl of Feversham (d 1963, when the Earldom became extinct, but the Barony of Feversham passed to a kinsman); *b* 11 Oct 1938; *Educ* Heathfield, Paris France; *m* 14 Dec 1966, Nicholas Spencer Compton Collin, s of late Maj Francis Spencer Collin, of 42 Eaton Place, SW1 and Fullers Farm, West Grinstead, Horsham, Sussex; 1 s, 1 da; *Career* farming; *Recreations* gardening, country activities; *Style—* The Lady Clarissa Collin, JP; Wytherstone House, Pockley, York (☎ 0439 70398)

COLLIN, Maj-Gen Geoffrey de Egglesfield; CB (1975), MC (1944), DL (N Yorks 1977); s of late Charles de Egglesfield Collin (d 1960), of Ripon, and Catherine Mary, *née* Smith; *b* 18 July 1921; *Educ* Wellington; *m* 1949, Angela Stella, da of Lt-Col Noel Charles Secombe Young (d 1966), of Roecliffe, York; 1 s, 3 da; *Career* 2 Lt RA 1941, Maj-Gen RA HQ BAOR 1971-73, GOC NE Dist York 1973-76, ret, Col Cmdt RA 1976-83; hon dir Gt Yorks Show 1976-87, pt/t chm Civil Serv Selection Panel 1978-, pres Yorks Agric Soc 1988; *Recreations* fishing, ornithology, photography; *Clubs* Army and Navy; *Style—* Maj-Gen Geoffrey Collin, CB, MC, DL

COLLIN, Jack; s of John Collin, and Amy Maud *née* Burton; *b* 23 April 1945; *Educ* Consett GS, Univ of Newcastle (MB BS, MD), Mayo Clinic USA, Univ of Oxford (MA); *m* 17 July 1971, Christine Frances, da of Albert Proud (d 1973), of Durham; 3 s (Neil b 1976, Graham b 1980, Ivan b 1985), 1 da (Beth b 1974); *Career* registrar in surgery Newcastle 1971-80, res fell Mayo Clinic USA 1977, Arris and Gale lectr RCS 1976, euro fell Surgical Res Soc 1979, Moynihan travelling fell Assoc of Surgeons 1980, reader in surgery Oxon 1980-, conslt surgn John Radcliffe Hosp, professorial fell Trinity Coll Oxford, Hunterian Prof RCS 1988-89; Jacksonian Prizwinner RCS 1979, Jobst Prize Vascular Surgical Soc 1990; memb: Dist Res Ctee, Regnl Med Advsy Ctee, Bd of Faculty Clinical Medicine; examiner: in surgery Univ of Oxford, in anatomy RCS; memb: Governing Body and Bursarial Ctee Trinity Coll, Gen Purposes Ctee Faculty of Clinical Med; memb: Vascular Surgical Soc 1982, Euro Vascular Surgical Soc 1988; FRCS 1972; *Recreations* food, family, gardening; *Style—* Jack Collin, Esq; Nuffield Department of Surgery, John Radcliffe Hospital, Oxford, OX3 9DU (☎ 0865 221 284, 221 286, fax 0865 726 753, telex 83147 VIAORGATT : NDS)

COLLIN, John Richard Olaf; s of Dr John Olaf Collin, MB, BChir, of Broom Cottage, Ashdown Rd, Forest Row, E Sussex, and Ellen Vera, *née* Knudsen; *b* 1 May 1943; *Educ* Charterhouse, Univ of Cambridge (MA, MB); *Career* ophthalmic surgeon with conslt appts to Moorfields Eye Hosp and Hosp for Sick Children, Great Ormond Street 1981 (special interest in eyelid surgery); FRCS, DO; *Books* publications on ophthalmic plastic surgery incl: A Manual of Systematic Eyelid Surgery (1983, 2 edn 1989); *Recreations* sailing, shooting, tennis, hunting, opera; *Clubs* Royal Ocean Racing, Hurlingham; *Style—* J R O Collin, Esq; 67 Harley Street, London W1N 1DE (☎ 071 486 2699)

COLLIN, Sandy; *b* 30 March 1930; *m* 19 Dec 1953, Margaret Elizabeth; 1 s (Gordon Iain Alexander b 12 Aug 1960), 2 da ((Linday) Fiona b 17 Feb 1959, Sally Anne b 29 Jan 1963); *Career* dir Frazer and Glass Ltd 1965, chm Thurger Bardex plc 1985 (dir 1975, md 1978); CBIM; *Recreations* golf, gardening; *Style—* Sandy Collin, Esq; Thurgar Bardex plc, Telford Way, Kettering, Northants NN16 8UY (☎ 0536 410 111, telex 34435, fax 0536 410 174)

COLLING, Ronald Norris; s of Archibald Robert Colling (d 1958), and Lily, *née* Norris; *b* 11 July 1936; *Educ* William Hulme's GS Manchester; *m* 22 Sept 1978, Lynne Patricia, da of Keith Martin Belcher, of Cheshire; 2 s (John b 1983, Peter b 1986); *Career* chm and fndr: Norkem Holdings plc gp of cos; *Style—* Ronald N Colling, Esq; Meadow Lodge, School Lane, Ollerton, Knutsford, Cheshire WA16 8SJ; 15 Ruskin Court, Knutsford, Cheshire WA16 6HN (☎ 0565 755550, telex 669629, fax 0565 755496)

COLLINGE, (Richard) Paul; s of Graham Collinge (d 1965), and Winifred Mary, *née* Farley (d 1969); *b* 26 June 1946; *Educ* (Architectural) Thames Poly (ATP); *m* 23 March 1968, Jean Mary, da of George Robert Dewey, of 235 Desborough Avenue, High Wycombe, Bucks; 2 s (Jake b 2 May 1974, Luke b 14 Sept 1976), 1 da (Emma b 23 Oct 1972); *Career* princ Aldington Craig & Collinge 1986- (ptnr from 1979); external examiner N London Poly Sch of Architecture 1986-89, assessor RIBA awards 1988; selected in 1985 as one of the 40 under 40 young architects; design awards received: RIBA 1978 (commendation) and 1987, DoE Good Housing award 1978, Civic Tst awards 1978, 1987 and 1988, Brick Devpt Assoc Biennial award 1979; RIBA 1972, MCSD 1984; *Recreations* cricket, golf; *Clubs* Thame Cricket; *Style—* Paul Collinge, Esq; Aldington Craig & Collinge, 6 High St, Haddenham, Bucks HP17 6ER (☎ 0844 291228, fax 0844 292448)

COLLINGHAM, Christopher Eric; s of Harold Eric Collingham, of Carlton-in-Lindrick, Notts, and Olive, *née* Radcliffe; *b* 4 Aug 1952; *Educ* Henry Harland Sch Workshop, Granville Coll Sheffield; *m* 5 July 1975, Michele Kathleen, da of Eric Keep, of Carlton in Lindrick, Notts; *Career* BBC: communications engr 1971-78, mangr special projects 1978-82; TV-am plc 1982-89: chief engr 1983-89; md Broadcast Projects Ltd 1989-; memb RTS; *Recreations* gliding, power flying; *Style—* Christopher Collingham, Esq; 2 Longdean Park, Hemel Hempstead, Herts HP3 8BS

COLLINGS, Peter Glydon; s of Alfred James Collings, of 3 Kenilworth Ct, Poole, Dorset, and Margot Lavinia, *née* Harper; *b* 4 Nov 1942; *Educ* Worksop Coll; *m* 1 Sept 1967, Rosemary Anne, da of Henry William Wesley-Harkcom (d 1966); 2 da (Sarah Jane b 1968, Emma Louise b 1970); *Career* asst regnl mangr Old Broad St Securities Ltd Birmingham 1970-75, regnl mangr Grindlays Industl Fin Ltd Birmingham 1976-82, jt chief exec W Midlands Enterprise Bd Ltd 1982-; dir: Aston Manor Brewery Co Ltd 1986-, Tangye Ltd 1986-87, Raydyot Ltd 1987-; FCA 1966-; *Recreations* rugby football, cricket; *Clubs* Sutton Coldfield RFC (vice pres), Warwickshire CCC; *Style—* Peter Collings, Esq; Squirrels Leap, 15 Oaklands Rd, Four Oaks, Sutton Coldfield, W Midlands B74 2TB (☎ 021 308 5434); Wellington House, 31/34 Waterloo St, Birmingham B2 5TJ (☎ 021 236 8855, fax 021 233 3942)

COLLINS, Adrian John Reginald; s of John Reginald Maulden Collins MBE, and Jennifer Anne *née* Wasey; *b* 29 May 1954; *Educ* Leys Sch Cambridge; *m* 6 Aug 1984, (m dis), Ailie Ford; 1 s (Mark John Ford), 1 da (Seil Charlotte); *Career* chief exec: Gartmore Investmt 1974-84, Royal Tst Asset Mgmnt Ltd 1985-90, Fincorp Int Ltd 1984; *Style—* Adrian Collins, Esq; 4 Campden Hill Sq, London W8 7LB (☎ 071 229 5100, fax 071 221 7157)

COLLINS, Alan John Charles; s of Charles Albert Collins (d 1987), of Rayleigh, Essex, and Lilian Maud, *née* Williamson (d 1960); *b* 23 Nov 1942; *Educ* Royal Liberty Sch Essex; *m* 7 March 1970, Cleusa, da of Pedro Luiz Calgaro (d 1984), of Sao Paulo, Brazil; 1 s (Robert b 1972), 1 da (Lisa b 1976); *Career* elected memb Lloyds 1976; chm and chief exec: PSM Holdings Ltd 1986-, PS Mosse and Partners Ltd (Lloyd's Brokers) 1988- (dir 1971, md 1979); *Recreations* tennis, skiing, golf; *Clubs* Connaught (London), Slim Jim's; *Style—* Alan Collins, Esq; 69 Downs Hill, Beckenham, Kent BR3 2HD (☎ 081 6589868)

COLLINS, Aletta Rachel; da of Michael John Collins, of Lower Street, Cavendish, Suffolk, and Sonja Anne, *née* O'Hanlon; *b* 12 April 1967; *Educ* LCDT; *Career* choreographer; memb 4D Performance Group 1987-88, cmmnd Place Portfolio choreographer 1988, choreographer Phoenix Dance Co Leeds (Digital Dance award) 1988, res choreographer Place Theatre 1988-89, dancer LCDT 1990-; freelance choreography incl: Stand By Your Man (LCDT), Samson and Dalila (Bregenz Festival) 1988 and 1989, Carmen (Earls Court, Tokyo, Aust), The Aletta Collins Collection (Place Theatre), Beatrice and Benedict (ENO), Sunday in the Park with George (NT), It's Gonna Rain (LDCT), Gang of Five (Bonnie Bird award, Phoenix Dance Co) 1990; prizes incl: first prize 2 Concorso Internazionale Di Citta Cagliari Italy 1987, major prize for Dance Theatre Twentieth Int Choreographic Meeting Bagnolet France 1990; *Style—* Ms Aletta Collins; Harriet Cruickshank, Cruickshank-Cazenove Limited, 97 Old South Lambeth Rd, London SW8 (☎ 071 735 2933, fax 071 820 1081)

COLLINS, (John) Alford Kingswell; MC, TD; s of John Preedy Collins (d 1964), of IOW, and Marion Martha, *née* Kingswell (d 1951); *b* 19 June 1920; *Educ* Denstone Coll; *m* 3 April 1952, June, da of Stanley H Matthews (d 1985), of IOW; 1 s (David b 1956), 2 da (Diana b 1954, Angela b 1958); *Career* chm: Upward and Rich plc 1952-74, Vectis Stone Group plc 1965-85, Medens Trust Ltd 1973-85, Southern Vectis plc 1986-; dir: Brown Shipley and Co 1981-85, Bardon Hill Group plc 1985-86, Blackgang

Hotels Ltd, Celtic Oil Supplies Ltd, Channel Oil Ltd, Cheek Bros Ltd, Island oils Ltd, Wall Bros (Piling) Ltd; FCA; *Recreations* travel, sailing, walking; *Clubs* Island Sailing, Royal Solent Yacht, IOD; *Style—* Alford Collins, Esq, MC, TD; 34 Wilver Rd, Newport, Isle of Wight PO30 5DT (☎ 0983 523096); Lugley House, Lugley St, Newport, Isle of Wight PO30 5EX (☎ 0983 521236)

COLLINS, Andrew Seymour; TD (1977); s of Seymour John Collins, JP (d 1970), and Nancye Westray, *née* Yarwood; *b* 2 Nov 1944; *Educ* Radley, Coll of Law; *m* 1, 17 July 1971 (m dis 1985), Susan Lucretia, da of Cdr John Weston Chase, RN (d 1989); 3 s (Charles b 1972, James b 1975, Giles b 1977) 1 da (Amelia b 1974); m 2, 26 Nov 1986, Virginia Mary Crisp, da of John Richard Craik-White, MC (d 1988); *Career* HAC 1964, cmmnd 1969, transferred 68 Signals Sqdn (Inns of Ct & City yeo) 1970 (cmd 1977-80), SO 2 Directorate of Army Reserves and Cadets 1983-88, transferred RARO 1988, serv as selected mil memb City of London TA & VRA 1978- (Gtr London 1985-); slr of the Supreme Ct 1969, ptnr Walker Martineau 1986-, co dir in fields of investmt and hotels; Gen Cmmr of Taxes 1983; Liveryman Worshipful Co of Fanmakers 1970 (asst 1985), Liveryman Worshipful Co of Slrs; memb: Law Soc, Holborn Law Soc, City of London Law Soc; *Recreations* sailing, hunting, shooting, tennis; *Clubs* Royal Thames Yacht, HAC; *Style—* Andrew Collins, Esq, TD; The Old Rectory, Eydon, Daventry, Northants NN11 6QE (☎ 0327 60745); 38 Belleville Rd, London SW11 6QT (☎ 071 350 1452); 64 Queen St, London EC4R 1AD (☎ 071 236 4232, fax 071 236 2525, telex 28843, car 0836 738 273)

COLLINS, Sir Arthur James Robert; KCVO (1980, CVO 1963), ERD; s of Col William Fellowes Collins, DSO, JP, DL, of Cundall Manor, York, Lord of the Manor of Cundall and Patron of the livings of Cundall and Farnham, and Lady Evelyn Innes-Ker, OBE (4 da of 7 Duke of Roxburghe); *b* 10 July 1911; *Educ* Eton, Ch Ch Oxford (MA); *m* 1965, Elizabeth, da of Rear Adm Sir Arthur Bromley, 8 Bt, KCMG, KCVO, and widow of 6 Baron Sudeley killed on active serv (1941); *Career* WWII, Maj RHG, Adj 2 Household Cavalry Regt (despatches); slr, ptnr Withers and Co 1937, sr ptnr 1962-82; conslt 1982; *Clubs* Turf, White's; *Style—* Sir Arthur Collins, KCVO, ERD; Kirkman Bank, Knaresborough, N Yorks (☎ 0423 863136); 38 Clarence Terrace, London NW1 (☎ 071 723 4198)

COLLINS, Arthur John; OBE (1973); s of Reginald Collins, and Margery Collins; *b* 17 May 1931; *Educ* Purley GS; *m* 1952, Enid Stableford; 1 s, 1 da; *Career* served RAF 1949-51; joined FCO 1968 from Miny of Health (where private sec to perm sec and sec), asst head Latin America and Caribbean Depts FCO 1974-77, cnsllr and head of chancery UK Delgn to OECD Paris 1978-81, UK high cmmr PNG 1982-85, cnsllr and advsr on mgmnt FCO 1986-88, ret; appointed protocol rep of Foreign and Cwlth Sec of State; *Style—* Arthur Collins, OBE; Foreign and Commonwealth Office, King Charles St, London SW1

COLLINS, Audrey Towl; da of Lt-Col C B Collins, CMG, DSO (d 1917), and Florence, *née* Towl (d 1957); *b* 14 April 1915; *Educ* Royal Sch Bath, Bedford Coll London (Hockey and Cricket blues); *Career* pres Women's Cricket Assoc 1982-; hockey player: Lancs, Herts; cricket player: Lancs, East, North, England v Aust 1937, selected for England tour to Aust 1939 (cancelled due to WWII); chemistry teacher: Liverpool Coll Huyton 1937-45, St Albans Girls' GS 1945-47 and 1950-75 (head of sci and dep head), Presbyterian Ladies' Coll Melbourne 1948-49; *Recreations* music, soroptimism, sport and its administration; *Style—* Miss Audrey Collins; Women's Cricket Association, 41 St Michael's Lane, Headingley, Leeds LS6 3BR (☎ 0532 742398)

COLLINS, Basil Eugene Sinclair; CBE (1983); s of Albert Collins (d 1971), and Pauline Alicia, *née* Wright; *b* 21 Dec 1923; *Educ* Great Yarmouth GS; *m* 1942, Doris, da of Harry Meyer Slott (d 1944); 2 da; *Career* dep chm and chief exec Cadbury Schweppes plc 1980-83 (md 1974-80), chm Nabisco Group Ltd 1984-89; dir: Thomas Cook Group 1980-85, British Airways 1982-88, Royal Mint 1984-88; life vice pres Royal Coll of Nursing (hon treas, chm of Fin Ctee 1970-86), memb Cncl UEA 1987, tstee and dir Inst of Econ Affrs 1987; FZS, FRSA; *Recreations* music, languages, English countryside; *Clubs* Carlton; *Style—* Basil Collins Esq, CBE; Wyddial Parva, Buntingford, Herts SG9 0EL

COLLINS, Bryan; s of Leslie George Thomas Collins (d 1981), and Ivy Clara, *née* Biggs; *b* 21 April 1936; *Educ* Cambridge Central GS; *m* 1 March 1958, Mary Josephine, da of Walter George Cole (d 1970), of Cambridge; 1 s (Timothy Howard b 1961), 1 da (Louise Mary b 1963); *Career* md and chief exec Bristow Helicopter Group Ltd 1979-; chm Bromley Family Health Serv Authy Practitioner Ctee 1985-; FSCA, FRAeS; *Recreations* cricket, badminton, tennis, squash, shooting; *Clubs* IOD, Royal Soc of Medicine; *Style—* Bryan Collins, Esq; Wymondley, Hookwood Park, Limpsfield, Surrey RH8 0SG (☎ 0883 723281); Bristow Helicopter Group Ltd, Redhill Aerodrome, Surrey RH1 5JZ (☎ 0737 822353, telex 21913, fax 0737 822694)

COLLINS, Charles Douglas; s of Prof Douglas Henry Collins, OBE (d 1964), of Sheffield, and Jean, *née* Wright; *b* 19 March 1939; *Educ* St Edward's Sch Oxford, Queens' Coll Cambridge (MA, MB BChir), Univ of Sheffield (MB, ChM); *m* 5 June 1965, Johanna Temlett, da of Jack Marke (d 1977), of Huish Champflower, Somerset; 2 s (James b 8 Dec 1969, William b 15 July 1974), 1 da (Victoria b 11 Feb 1971); *Career* conslt surgn in Taunton 1973-; regnl advsr RCS 1990-; memb: BMA 1963-, RSM 1984; FRCS 1967; *Style—* Charles Collins, Esq; Crowcombe House, Crowcombe, Taunton, Somerset (☎ 09848 266); Taunton and Somerset Hosp, Musgrove Park, Taunton, Somerset (☎ 0823 333444)

COLLINS, David Stuart; s of James Henry Collins, of Dalkeith, Midlothian, Scotland, and Hilda, *née* Oldfield (d 1977); *b* 24 Feb 1945; *Educ* Fazakerley Comprehensive Liverpool, Liverpool Coll of Commerce; *m* 14 Oct 1967, Penelope Noël, da of Herbert Lancelot Charters, of 36 Avondale Avenue, Maghull, Liverpool; 1 s (Mark Stuart b 1977), 1 da (Nicola Caroline b 1980); *Career* Granada Publishing Ltd: mangr S Africa 1974-77, area sales mangr N Africa, M East, India and Pakistan 1977-81, trade mangr 1981-83; export sales mangr Harrap Ltd 1983-84 (sales dir 1984-); Columbus Books Ltd 1986-; *Recreations* travel, walking, reading, swimming, good conversation; *Style—* David Stuart Collins, Esq; 152A Park Street Lane, Park St, St Albans AL2 2AU (☎ 0727 73866); Harrap Ltd, 19-23 Ludgate Hill, London EC4M 7PD (☎ 071 248 6444, telex 28673, fax 071 248 3357)

COLLINS, Edward Geoffrey Lissant; OBE (1983); s of George Geoffrey Collins (d 1978), of Rochdale, and Lucy May Capstick, *née* Squires (d 1980); *b* 1 May 1936; *Educ* Rossall and William Hulme's GS Manchester; *m* 16 April 1966, Hilary Elizabeth, da of William Dryland, of Rochdale; 3 s (William b 1967, David b 1968, Francis b 1972); *Career* admitted slr 1959, sr ptnr Jackson Stoney & Co Rochdale 1976-; memb Rochdale: CC 1965-71, Met Borough Cncl 1973-86 (ldr of Cncl 1976-80 and 1982-86); pres Rochdale and Dist Blind Welfare Soc; chm: Rochdale Music Soc, Tstees Rochdale Curtain Theatre; memb Rochdale Parish Church PCC; *Recreations* reading, music, theatre, gardening, walking; *Style—* Edward Collins, Esq, OBE; Rose Villa, Edenfield Rd, Rochdale, Lancs (☎ 0706 42172); The Old Parsonage, 2 St Mary's Gate, Rochdale, Lancs (☎ 0706 44187)

COLLINS, Mrs Michael; (Lesley) Elizabeth; *see*: Appleby, (Lesley) Elizabeth

COLLINS, (John) Grenville; s of John Aloysius Collins (d 1969), of London, and Joan Leigh, *née* Price; *b* 24 Jan 1943; *Educ* St Edward's Sch Oxford; *m* 22 Aug 1966, Susan Elizabeth Carr, da of Lt-Col Arthur Henry Carr Sutherland, OBE, MC, DL, (d 1962), of Cringletie, Peebles, Scotland; 1 da (Ika b 23 Nov 1974); *Career* head of Islamic studies at Beshara Sch of Intensive Esoteric Educn Sherborne Gloucs 1975-78; G & A Kelly Ltd 1984-, Beshara Design Co Ltd 1990-, Breyberry Ltd 1987-; charity tstee: Beshara Tst 1971-90, Chisholme Inst 1985-89; chm Muhyiddin Ibn Arabi Soc (Oxford, Istanbul, San Francisco, Sydney); author of papers on esoteric subjects; *Recreations* travelling, publishing; *Style—* Grenville Collins, Esq; Kingham House, Kingham, Oxford OX7 6YA; 82 St George's Square, London SW1 (☎ 060871 520)

COLLINS, Hannah; da of Clifford Collins, of Horsham, Sussex, and Christine Collins; *b* 10 Aug 1956; *Educ* Lady Eleanor Holles Sch, Slade Sch of Fine Art UCL (Dip in Fine Art) Fulbright-Hays scholar to USA; partner, John Egan; 1 s (Echo Collins Egan b 29 Feb 1988); *Career* artist and photographer; lectr in fine art Chelsea Sch of Fine Art London; solo exhibitions: Films Stills (Matt's Gallery, London) 1986, New Works (ICA) 1988, Viewpoints (Walker Art Centre, Minneapolis) 1989, Xavier Hufbens Gallery Brussels 1989, Galerie Tanit Cologne Germany 1990; gp exhibitions: Antidotes to Madness (Riverside Studios, London) 1986, The British Edge (ICA Boston USA) 1987, The Big Picture-The New Photography (John and Mable Ringling Museum, Florida) 1987, Australian Biennale Sydney and Melbourne 1988, Aperto '88 (Venice Biennale Italy) 1988, A British View (Museum für Gestaltung Zürich) 1988, Another Objectivity (ICA) 1988, Matter of Facts (Musée des Beaux Arts, Nantes) 1988, Une Autre Objectivité (Centre Nationale Des Arts Plastiques, Paris) 1989, Portraits (Contemporary Art Fndn) 1989, Shifting Focus (Arnolfini Gallery, Bristol) 1989, Polaroid Works (V & A Museum) 1989, Stuart Regen Gallery LA 1990, British Artists in Russia (Kiev and Moscow) 1990, Art and Photography (Modern Art Museum Kyoto and Museum of Modern Art Tokyo) 1990; work in public collections of: Eastern Arts Assoc England, Polaroid Int, Arts Cncl of GB, Br Cncl, Walker Art Center Minneapolis, V & A Museum London, FRAC Rhone Alpes France, FRAC Lyon France, FRAC Bretagne France, FNAC France; *Style—* Ms Hannah Collins; 5 Beck Rd, London E8 (☎ 081 310 4183); Baixada de Viladecols 2TER 08002 Barcelona, Spain; Matt's Gallery, 10 Martello St, London E8 (☎ 071 249 3799)

COLLINS, Henry Ernest (Harry); s of Edwin Collins (d 1955), of 28 Hardinge Rd, London, and Florence Louise, *née* Scarbrow (d 1969); *b* 19 Jan 1920; *Educ* Kilburn GS; *Career* cmmnd pilot RAF 1941, serv with 264 Sqdn Night Fighters (Boulton - Paul Defiants), test pilot attached to 1 CRU Aston Down, demob 1946; CA; Morton Moller Sheen & Co 1936, Sir William Garthwaite & Co Ltd (Insur Brokers), Co-operative Permanent Bldg Soc (now Nationwide) 1938, A C Eaves Ltd 1946-55, F J Parsons Ltd 1955-62, Journal of Park Admin Ltd 1972, conslt Adam Publishing Ltd 1988- (fndr 1973, sold firm to Inst of Groundsmanship 1987); hon life memb: Constitutional Brondesbury, Cricklewood and Willesdon Green Conservative Club Kensal Rise; memb Old Creightonians Assoc, vice pres The Lighthouse Club (former chm Cncl); Freeman: City of London 1976, Worshipful Co of Paviors; *Recreations* cricket, golf, cooking; *Clubs* RAF, Rugby, The Lighthouse, South Hampstead Cricket, Sudbury Golf; *Style—* Harry Collins, Esq; 82 Hawes Close, Northwood, Middx HA6 1EW (☎ 092 74 29570); Adam Publishing Ltd, 21 Northwick Ave, Harrow Middx HA3 0AA (☎ 081 907 8052)

COLLINS, Jeffrey Hamilton; *b* 22 April 1930; *Educ* Univ of London (BSc, MSc, DSc); *Career* laboratory technician Physics Dept Guy's Hosp Med Sch 1946-48, scientific staff memb GEC Hirst Res Centre 1951-56, pt/t lectr Mathematics Dept Sir John Cass Coll London 1955-56, sr staff engr Ferranti Ltd Edinburgh 1956-57, lectr then sr lectr Dept of Electrical Engineering Univ of Glasgow 1959-66, res engr Stanford Univ 1966-68, dir physical sci Dept Electronics Div Rockwell International and res dir autonetics Rockwell International Science Center, prof of Industl Electronics Dept of Electrical Engrg Univ of Edinburgh 1973-77 (res prof 1970-73), visiting prof of electrical engrg The Univ of Texas at Arlington 1976-77; dir: Scottish Engineering Training Scheme Ltd 1981-83, Integrated Microapplications Ltd 1981-84, Racal Group Services Ltd 1981, Racal-MESL Ltd 1970-81 (formerly MESL Ltd), Filtronic Components Ltd 1981-85, Advent Technology 1981-86, Scottish Electronics Technology Group 1983-86, Burr-Brown Ltd 1984-86, Lattice-Logic Ltd 1986; Univ of Edinburgh: prof of electical engrg and head Dept of Electrical Engrg 1977-84, emeritus prof of electrical engrg and fell The Centre for Speech Technol Res 1984-87, currently chm of Edinburgh Parallel Computing Centre; dir Automation and Robotics Res Inst The Univ of Texas at Arlington 1987-90, currently sr tech specialist Lothian Regnl Cncl Edinburgh; 192 pubns in sci and engrg jls; IEE 1985-86 (chm Electronics Div UK, memb Cncl, memb Learned Soc Bd); memb: Information Engrg Ctee SERC 1983-86, computer Bd for Univs and Res Cncls Dept of Educn and Sci 1984-86, Advanced Devices and Materials Ctee DTI 1984-86, Cncl Fellowship of Engrg 1984-86; hon fell Univ of Edinburgh, CPhys, FEng (CEng), FIEE, FInstP, FIEEE, FRSE; *Style—* Prof Jeffrey Collins, Esq, FRSE; 3-4 Teresa Place, Edinburgh, Lothian, Scotland EH10 5UB (☎ 031 228 4395)

COLLINS, Joan; da of Joseph William Collins (d 1988), and his 1 w, Elsa, *née* Bessant (d 1962); *b* 23 May 1933; *Educ* Francis Holland Sch St Margaret's Middx, RADA; *m* 1, 23 May 1954 (m dis 1957), Maxwell Reed, actor (d 1974); m 2, May 1963 (m dis), Anthony Newley, actor; 1 s (Alexander b 8 Sept 1965), 1 da (Tara b 12 Oct 1963); m 3, Feb 1972 (m dis 1983), Ron Kass, film prodr; 1 da (Katyana b 20 June 1972); m 4, 6 Nov 1985 (m dis 1987), Peter Holm; *Career* film and TV actress since 1951, GB films incl: The Road to Hong Kong (1962), Can Hieronymus Merkin Ever Forget Mercy Humppe and Find True Happiness (1969), Tales From the Crypt (1972), The Big Sleep (1977), The Stud (1978), The Bitch (1979); US films incl: Land of the Pharaohs (1954), The Virgin Queen (1955), The Opposite Sex (1956), Rally Round the Flag, Boys (1958), Esther and the King (1960); Br TV incl: Tales of the Unexpected, The Persuaders; US TV incl: Star Trek (1975), Batman (1975), The Moneychangers (1976), Mission Impossible (1976), Police Woman (1976), Starsky and Hutch (1978), Space 1999 (1979), Fantasy Island (1981), The Making of a Male Model (1983), My Life as a Man (1984), Dynasty (1981-), Sins (1985), Monte Carlo (1986); awards: Hollywood Women's Press Club Golden Apple award (1982), Golden Globe award 'Best Actress in a TV Drama' (Alexis in Dynasty) (1983), People's Choice award 'Most Popular Actress' (1983, 1984); theatre Private Lives (Aldwych Theatre) 1990; *Books* Past Imperfect (1978), Joan Collins' Beauty Book (1982), Katy: A Fight for Life (1983), Prime Time (1988), Love and Desire and Hate (1990); *Recreations* travelling, collecting 18 Century antiques, writing; *Style—* Joan Collins; 15363 Mulholland Drive, Los Angeles, California 90077; c/o Rogers and Cowan, 27 Albemarle St, W1X 3FA (☎ 071 499 0691, fax 071 495 1275)

COLLINS, John Alexander; s of Maj John Constantine Collins of Bodmin Cornwall, and Nancy Isobel, *née* Mitchell; *b* 10 Dec 1941; *Educ* Campbell Coll Belfast, Univ of Reading (BSc); *m* 24 April 1965, Susan Mary, da of Robert Reid Hooper, of Wimbourne, Dorset; 1 s (Robert b 18 May 1970), 1 da (Helen b 18 June 1968); *Career* md Shell Chemicals UK and md Shell UK 1984-89, supply and mktg coordinator 1989-90, dir Shell International 1989-, chm and chief exec Shell UK 1990-; *Recreations* opera, theatre, sailing, riding, golf, tennis, a love of the New Forest; *Style—* John Collins, Esq; Shell UK Limited, Shell-Mex House, Strand, London WC2R 0DX (☎ 071 257 3000, fax 071 257 1382, telex 22585 SHELLG)

COLLINS, John Frederick Norman; OBE; s of Harry Norman Collins (d 1973) of

Chester, and Doris Emily Collins (d 1972); *b* 15 Sept 1924; *Educ* King Edward's Sch Birmingham, Birmingham Sch of Architecture (Dip Arch), Sch of Planning and Res for Regnl Devpt London (SP Dip); *m* 1, 27 July 1955, Angela Mary (Jill) (d 1973), da of Donald Hutton Cox (1973); 3 s (Timothy John b 12 Feb 1959, Dr Matthew James b 12 May 1960, Richard Studholme b 26 April 1971), 3 da (Emma Louise (Mrs M Hawkins) b 26 April 1962, Katharine Lucy b 8 June 1965, Joanna Mary b 11 Aug 1968); m 2, 14 May 1976, Mary Muriel; *Career* RAF 1944-47, leading aircraftsman, served Africa and Aden project architect local authy housing Birmingham 1953-55, architect and town planner gp ldr Coventry 1955-59, project architect works abroad (Cyprus) then sr architect R & D WO Works Directorate 1959-63, sr assoc Graeme Shankland Assocs Liverpool 1963-67, co planner Cheshire CC 1969-88 (2 dep co planning offr 1967-69), ptnr Long Collins Partnership Chester 1988-; pres Chester Soc of Architects 1983-85, chm NW regnl Cncl RIBA; memb RIBA 1951, FRTPI 1955 (Cncl 1970-, pres 1980-82); *Recreations* theatre, sailing, travel; *Style*— John Collins, Esq, OBE; Greenlooms, Hargrave, Chester, Ches CH3 7RX; Glan Yr Aig, Borth, Ceredigion, Dyfed (☎ 0829 41070); Long Collins Partnership, Richmond Place, 125 Boughton, Chester, Ches CH3 5BJ (☎ 0244 312 387, fax 0244 320 072)

COLLINS, John Hardie; OBE (1966); s of William Smithson Collins (d 1949), of Rhiwbina, Cardiff, and Hannah Jane, *née* Wilson; *b* 26 Feb 1923; *Educ* Cowbridge GS, Univ Coll Cardiff (BSc); *m* 20 Dec 1947, Dorothy (d 1980), da of Jack Archibald (d 1953), of Bristol; 1 s (Anthony, decd), 1 da (Jean); m 2, 21 Feb 1981, Rona, da of Abraham Mottershead; *Career* industl chemist 1943-81; ldr Cheshire CC, former ldr Widnes and Halton Borough Cncls, Hon Freeman City of Widnes 1973; *Recreations* golf, music; *Style*— John Collins, Esq, OBE; 5 Shelley Rd, Widnes, Lancs; County Hall, Chester

COLLINS, John Joseph; s of Patrick Collins (d 1982), of Killiney, Dublin, Ireland, and Mary Josephine, *née* O'Brien (d 1954); *b* 23 May 1944; *m* 25 Jan 1970, (Eline) Mary, da of James Cullen (d 1978); 2 s (Patrick James b 1971, Paul Ivor b 1976), 1 da (Aisling Mary b 1972); *Career* called to the Bar King's Inns Ireland 1967, in practice 1967-71, called to the Bar Middle Temple 1971-, fndr chambers at 11 South Square Gray's Inn 1980, fndr and head of chambers in Lewes 1987-; memb Supreme Ct of NSW; *Recreations* reading, walking, swimming; *Style*— John Collins, Esq; Hazeldene, 703 Pinner Road, Pinner, Middlesex (☎ 081 868 4106), Westgate Chambers, 144 High Street, Lewes (☎ 0273 480510, fax 0273 483179)

COLLINS, John Morris; s of Emmanuel Cohen, MBE (d 1980), of 1 Primley Park View, Leeds, and Ruby Cohen (d 1988); *b* 25 June 1931; *Educ* Leeds GS, Queen's Coll Oxford (MA); *m* 19 March 1968, Sheila, da of David Brummer, of 14 Raleigh Close, Hendon, London NW4; 1 da (Simone Natalie b 1974); *Career* called to the Bar Middle Temple 1956, dep co ct judge 1970-71, asst rec 1971, dep circuit judge 1972-80, Crown Ct rec 1980-; *Recreations* walking; *Style*— John M Collins, Esq; 14 Sandhill Oval, Leeds LS17 8EA (☎ 0532 686 008); Pearl Chambers Leeds LS1 5BZ (☎ 0532 451 986)

COLLINS, Dr John Vincent; s of Thomas Ernest Collins, of Denham, Bucks (d 1987), and Zillah Phoebe, *née* Jessop; *b* 16 July 1938; *Educ* Univ of London (BDS, MB BS, MD, MRCP); *m* 1963, Helen Eluned, da of William Alan Cash; 1 s (Jonathan James b March 1972), 1 da (Philippa Helen b Sept 1977); *Career* house physician 1966-67, house surgn 1966-67, sr house offr neurology St Mary's Hosp 1967, med registrar 1968-70, sr med registrar Westminster and Brompton Hosp 1970-72, sr lectr in med and conslt physician Bart's Med Coll 1973-76; conslt physician: Royal Brompton Heart and National Hosp 1976-, Riverside Health Authy 1979-, Westminster Hosp; dir: Chest Dept Westminster Hosp, Fibreoptic Bronchoscopy Unit Royal Brompton Hosp; hon sr lectr Cardiothoracic Inst; FRCP 1981; memb: Br Thoracic Soc, BMA, American Thoracic Soc; fell Int Acad of Chest Physicians and Surgns; *Books* Synopsis of Chest Medicine (1979), Practical Bronchoscopy (co-author, 1986); *Recreations* squash, tennis, painting and drawing; *Style*— Dr John Collins; Royal Brompton and National Heart Hospital, Sydney St, London SW3 6NP; Westminster Hospital, Dean Ryle St, London SW1P 2AP; Westminster Hospital, London SW1; 28 Weymouth St, London W1N 3FA (☎ 071 351 8030)

COLLINS, Julian Peter; s of Edward Arthur Burnette Collins, and Dorothy, *née* Wragg (d 1989); *b* 15 Nov 1942; *Educ* Nottingham HS, Gonville and Caius Coll Cambridge (MA, LLM); *Career* admitted slr 1967, head of Industl Branch Legal Dept NCB 1973, legal advsr and slr Br Coal Corpn 1988; memb: Law Soc, Int Bar Assoc; *Recreations* theatre, travel; *Style*— Julian Collins, Esq; 59 Gilpin Avenue, E Sheen, London SW14 8QX (☎ 081 876 6347); Hobart House, Grosvenor Place, London SW1X 7AE (☎ 071 235 2020, fax 071 235 2020 ext 34309, telex 882161 CBHOB 9)

COLLINS, Kenneth Darlingston; MEP (Lab) Strathclyde E 1979-; s of late Nicholas Collins and Ellen Williamson; *b* 12 Aug 1939; *Educ* St John's GS, Hamilton Acad, Univ of Glasgow (BSc), Univ of Strathclyde (MSc); *m* 1966, Georgina Frances, *née* Pollard; 1 s, 1 da; *Career* former tutor-organiser WEA; social geographer; lectr Glasgow Coll of Bldg 1967-69, lectr Paisley Coll of Technol 1969-79; dep ldr Labour Gp Euro Parl 1979-84, chm Environment Ctee 1979-84 and 1989- (vice chm 1984-87); Euro Parl socialist spokesman on environment, public health, and consumer protection 1984-89; memb: E Kilbride Town and DC 1973-79, Lanark CC 1973-75, E Kilbride Devpt Corpn 1976-79, Socialist Int Environment Ctee, Fabian Soc, Socialist Environment and Resources Assoc, Amnesty Int, Labour Movement in Europe, World Disarmament Movement, Scot Educn and Action for Devpt, Friends of the Earth (Scotland); hon vice pres: Royal Environmental Health Inst of Scot, Int Fedn on Environmental Health, Inst of Trading Standards Admin; Euro advsr: ACTT, EETPU, NALGO; *Style*— Kenneth Collins Esq, MEP; 11 Stuarton Park, East Kilbride, Lanarkshire G74 4UA (☎ 03552 37282, fax 03552 49670)

COLLINS, Lewis; *b* 27 May 1946; *Educ* LAMDA; *Career* actor; theatre incl: full repertory season Chesterfield Theatre 1970, major classical roles (The Citizen's Theatre Glasgow, Edinburgh Festival) 1971-73, The Farm (dir Lyndsey Anderson, Royal Court, transferred Mayfair W End) 1973-74, Dialogue Between Friends (Open Space) 1974, Blues White and Reds 1974, City Sugar (UK tour Prospect Theatre Co) 1976, Christmas pantomimes (His Majesty's Theatre, Theatre Royal, Hanley Trent Theatre Stockport) 1981-85, Death Trap (Aust tour) 1986; tv incl: The Real Inspector Hound 1973, The Cuckoo Waltz 1974-76, The New Avengers 1977, The Professionals 1977-81, A Night on the Town 1983, Jack the Ripper 1988, The Man Who Knew Too Little 1988, A Ghost in Monte Carlo 1989; films: Who Dares Wins 1982, Codename Wildgeese 1984, Commando Leopard 1985, The Commander 1987; dir: Double Double (Actors Maximus Arena, co-author with James Saunders) 1973, The Real Inspector Hound (Actors Maximus Arena) 1973, Rita Joe (Univ of Vancouver) 1973; lectr and conducted workshops UCLA; memb Actors' Equity; *Style*— Lewis Collins, Esq; International Creative Management, 388/396 Oxford Street, London W1N 9HE

COLLINS, (John) Martin; QC (1972); s of John Lissant Collins (d 1962), of Grange-over-Sands, Lancs, and Marjorie Mary, *née* Jefferson (d 1982); *b* 24 Jan 1929; *Educ* Uppingham, Univ of Manchester (Dauntsey prize int law); *m* Daphne Mary, da of George Swindells (d 1960), of Prestbury; 2 s (Benedict George, Toby Francis), 1 da (Arabella Jane); *Career* called to the Bar Grays Inn 1952 (Gibraltar 1990); dep chm Cumberland Quarter Sessions 1964-72, rec Crown Court 1972-88, bencher of Grays Inn 1981, judge of appeal Jersey and Guernsey 1984-; memb: Senate of Inns of Court and Bar 1981-84, Gen Cncl of the Bar 1991; Liveryman Worshipful Co of Makers of Playing Cards 1982; *Clubs* Athenaeum, Carlton; *Style*— Martin Collins, Esq, QC; 15 Ranelagh Grove, London SW1 (☎ 071 730 6200); 10 Essex St, Outer Temple, London WC2 (☎ 071 240 6981, fax 071 240 7722)

COLLINS, Michael Brendan; OBE (1983, MBE 1969); s of Daniel James Collins, GM, (d 1962), of Cardiff, and Mary Bridget, *née* Kennedy; *Educ* St Illtyd's Coll Cardiff, UCL; *m* 2 April 1959, Elena, da of Dr Mario Lozar (d 1963), of Milan; *Career* HM Forces 1953-55; entered FO 1956, Santiago Chile 1959-61, consul Cuba 1962-63, FCO 1964-66, consul (previously second then first sec) Prague 1967-69, dep High cmmr The Gambia 1970-72, head of Chancery Algiers 1972-75, first sec FCO 1975-78, consul commercial Montreal 1979-80, consul Atlantic Provinces of Canada 1981-83, econ and commercial cnsllr Brussels 1984-87, HM consul-gen Istanbul 1988-; *Recreations* fishing, shooting, golf, walking, music, reading; *Clubs* Army and Navy; *Style*— Michael Collins, Esq, OBE; c/o Foreign and Commonwealth Office, King Charles Street London, SW1 2AH

COLLINS, Michael Geoffrey; QC (1988); s of (Francis) Geoffrey Collins (d 1982), of Scottburgh, Natal, SA, and Margaret Isabelle, *née* Harper-Gow (d 1989); *b* 4 March 1948; *Educ* Peterhouse Marandellas Rhodesia, Univ of Exeter (LLB); *m* 13 April 1985, Bonnie Gayle Bird (has retained her maiden name), da of John Wilbur Bird (d 1988), of New Albany, Indiana, USA; *Career* called to the Bar Gray's Inn 1971; *Books* Private International Litigation (contrib, 1988); *Recreations* golf, tennis, watercolour painting, amateur dramatics; *Clubs* Woking Golf; *Style*— Michael Collins, Esq, QC; Coonamessett, Bramshott Chase, Hindhead, Surrey GU26 6DG; 9809 E Bexhill Drive, Kensington, Maryland 20895, USA; 4 Essex Court, Temple, London EC4Y 9AJ (☎ 071 583 9191, telex Comcas London 888465, fax 071 353 3421)

COLLINS, Michael John; s of Frederick Allenby Collins, and Gwendoline Violet, *née* Hersey-Walker; *b* 27 Jan 1962; *Educ* RCM (ARCM Hons); *Career* musician; Nash Ensemble 1982-88; principal clarinet: London Sinfonietta 1982-, Philharmonia Orch 1988-; prof RCM 1985-; winner: BBC TV Young Musician of the Year 1978, Leeds Nat Competition for Musicians 1980, Int Rostrum of Young Performers UNESCO 1985, Worshipful Co of Musicians Medal 1980, Tagore Gold Medal RCM; *Recreations* record collecting; *Style*— Michael Collins, Esq; 59 Harlington Road West, Feltham, Middlesex TW14 0JG (☎ 081 890 9326; Clarion Concert Agency, 64 Whitehall Park, London N19 3TN (☎ 071 272 4413, fax 071 272 5125, telex 9312100406 CL)

COLLINS, Dr Michael Lawrence; s of Sidney Collins, of 4 Birkdale Walk, Leeds 17, and Essie, *née* Gross; *b* 26 May 1943; *Educ* Roundhay Sch Leeds, Univ of Leeds Sch of Med (MB ChB); *m* 27 June 1971, Jackie, da of Theodore Hall, of 3 Garmont Rd, Leeds 7; 1 s (Spencer b 1974), 1 da (Antonia b 1977); *Career* house surgn and sr house offr United Leeds Hosps 1969-72, teaching fell Univ of BC 1972-73, registrar Leeds Maternity Hosp and Hosp for Women 1973-76 (house surgn, sr house offr 1969-72), specialist in gynaecological endocrinology and infertility McMaster Univ Med Centre Ontario Canada 1977-79, princ gen practice Middx 1980-84, specialist practise in gynaecological endocrinology 1980-, med advsr Well Woman Clinics 1980-; memb: Hillingolon FPC 1980-84, Hillingdon Local Med Ctee, Hillingdon Brunel Univ Liaison Ctee; MDU; memb: BMA, RSM; *Recreations* art, photography, writing, antiquarian books, croquet; *Clubs* Phyllis Court, Henley; *Style*— Dr Michael Collins; 144 Harley St, London W1N 1AH (☎ 071 935 0023)

COLLINS, Neil Adam; s of Clive Dinant Collins, and Joan Jarret, *née* Phillips; *b* 20 Jan 1947; *Educ* Uppingham, Selwyn Coll Cambridge; *m* 1981, Vivien Goldsmith; 1 da (Alice Laura b 30 July 1982); *Career* journalist: Accountancy Age and Investors' Guardian 1970-74, Daily Mail 1974-79; city ed: Evening Standard 1979-84, The Sunday Times 1984-86, The Daily Telegraph 1986-; *Style*— Neil Collins, Esq; 26 Lloyd Square, London WC1X 9AD; The Daily Telegraph, 4 Fore St, London EC2Y 5DT (☎ 071 538 6900)

COLLINS, Air Vice-Marshal Peter Spencer; CB (1985), AFC (1961); s of Sqdn-Ldr Frederick Wildbore Collins, OBE (d 1962), of Essex, and Mary, *née* Spencer (d 1939); *b* 19 March 1930; *Educ* Royal GS High Wycombe, Univ of Birmingham (BA); *m* 25 June 1953, Sheila Mary, da of Sidney John Perks (d 1985), of Wolverhampton; 3 s (Timothy b 1955, Paul b 1960, Christopher b 1963), 1 da (Fiona b 1957); *Career* RAF 1951-85; cmd: No 111 Sqdn 1970-72, RAF Gutersloh 1974-76; dir of forward policy (RAF) 1978-81; Sr Air Staff Offrs No 11 Gp 1981-83; dir gen of Communications, Info Systems and Orgn 1983-85; non exec dir Marconi Radar Systems 1985-; conslt GEC-Marconi Research Centre 1989-; FBIM; *Recreations* golf, music; *Clubs* RAF; *Style*— Air Vice-Marshal Peter Collins, CB, AFC; MRSL, Writtle Road, Chelmsford, Essex (☎ 0245 267111)

COLLINS, Dr Peter Victor; s of Canon Lewis John Collins (d 1982), and Diana Clavering, *née* Elliot; *b* 27 June 1948; *Educ* Eton, Trinity Coll Cambridge, (BA, PhD); *m* 29 Oct 1983, Dawn Elisabeth, *née* Grimshaw; 2 s (Tolomey John b 1986, Oscar Barnaby b 1988); *Career* divnl mangr GEC Hirst Res Centre 1974-85, tech mangr Marconi Maritime Applied Res Laboratory 1985-88, mangr Future Technol Marconi Underwater Systems Ltd 1988-; *Recreations* bridge; *Style*— Dr Peter Collins; 75 Christchurch Road, St Cross, Winchester, Hants SO23 9TG (☎ 0962 862361) Marconi Underwater Systems, Croxley Mill, Blackmoor Lane, Watford, Herts WD1 8YR (☎ 0932 57719, fax 09235 7777, telex 893327)

COLLINS, Prof Philip Arthur William; s of Arthur Henry Collins (d 1963), of Little Burstead, Essex, and Winifred Nellie, *née* Bowmaker (d 1968); *b* 28 May 1923; *Educ* Brentwood Sch, Emmanuel Coll Cambridge (BA, MA); *m* 1, 1952 (m dis 1963) Mildred, *née* Lowe; m 2, 18 Aug 1965, Joyce, da of James Wilfred Dickens; 2 s (Simon Charles Oliver, Marcus James Arthur), 1 da (Rosamund Patricia); *Career* Sgt RAOC 1942-44, Lt Royal Norfolk Regt 1944-45; Univ of Leicester 1947-: warden of Vaughan Coll 1954-62, prof of Eng 1964-82, public orator 1976-78 and 1980-82; visiting prof: Univ of California 1967, Univ of Columbia 1969, Univ of Victoria NZ 1974; scripted and appeared on BBC TV and Radio progs, co author The Canker and the Rose (Mermaid Theatre London) 1964; sec Leicester Theatre Tst 1962 87; memb: Arts Cncl Drama Panel 1970-75, Nat Theatre Bd of Dirs 1976-82; govr Br American Drama Acad 1983-, chm Tennyson Soc 1983-, pres Dickens Fellowship 1984-86; *Books* Dickens and Crime (1962), Dickens; the Critical Heritage (1971), Thackeray: Interviews and Recollections (1983); *Recreations* theatre, music; *Style*— Prof Philip Collins; 26 Knighton Drive, Leicester LE2 3HB (☎ 0533 706026)

COLLINS, Roy William; s of Charles Albert Collins (d 1987), and Lilian Maud, *née* Williamson (d 1960); *b* 17 July 1948; *Educ* South East Essex County Tech HS; *m* 1, 1971 (m dis 1975), Barbara Anne, *née* Askew; m 2, 1987, Sheila Anne Love, step da of Leslie Arthur Love; 1 da (Lucy Elizabeth b 3 Jan 1987); *Career* general reporter Barking Advertiser 1967, sports ed Express & Independent Walthamstow 1967-68, sports writer Essex & East London Newspapers 1968-69, sports columnist Evening Echo Southend 1969-74, freelance sports and news features journalist Fleet Street 1974-79, gen sports writer then columnist Sunday People 1979-83, freelance sports and gen journalist 1983-86, chief sports writer and columnist Today 1986-; memb: SWA, Football Writers' Assoc; *Recreations* tennis, running, chess, pubs, horse racing; *Clubs* Nothing Writers' Overseas Dining (treas), Coolhurst Tennis; *Style*— Roy

Collins, Esq; 48 Rosebery Rd, Muswell Hill, London N10 2LJ (☎ 081 883 6706); Today Newspaper, 70 Vauxhall Bridge Rd, Pimlico, London SW1V 2RP (☎ 071 630 1300, fax 071 630 6839)

COLLINS, Lady Sara Elena; *née* Hely-Hutchinson; o da of 7 Earl of Donoughmore; *b* 22 Aug 1930; *m* 2 Aug 1951, William Janson Collins (6 6 Oct 1929), er s of Sir William Alexander Roy Collins, CBE (d 1983); 1 s, 3 da; *Style*— The Lady Sara Collins; House of Craigie, by Kilmarnock, Ayrshire

COLLINS, Terence Bernard; s of late George Bernard Collins and Helen Teresa, *née* Goodfellow; *b* 3 March 1927; *Educ* Marist Coll Hull, Univ of St Andrews (MA); *m* 1956, Barbara, *née* Lowday; 2 s, 2 da; *Career* dir: Hoechst UK 1979-86, A G Stanley 1979-86, Hoechst Aust Investmts Pty 1980-86, Mayborn Group plc 1986-, Cranfield Precision Engineering Ltd 1990-; chm: Berger Jenson Nicholson 1984-86 (md 1975-86), Phoenix Developments 1987-, Cranfield Conference Services 1988 (dir 1986-), Mgmnt Ctee Kingline Consultancy Ltd 1989-90; dir CIT Holdings 1989-, chm Cranfield Ventures 1989; memb Int Fellowship Ctee Duke of Edinburgh's Award 1987-89 (memb Int 1978-86), memb Cncl Cranfield Inst of Technol 1977-, tstee Atlas Fndn 1986-, vice chm Cncl Buckingham Univ 1987- (chm Fin and Gen Purposes Ctee 1987-); *Recreations* music, golf, gardening; *Clubs* Directors', Aldeburgh Golf, Cook Society; *Style*— Terence Collins, Esq; Aldehurst, Church Walk, Aldeburgh, Suffolk IP15 5DX

COLLINS, Lt-Col William John Neilson; s of William John Collins (d 1986), of Dunfermline, Fife, and Ann French Moncur, *née* Neilson (d 1980); *b* 25 March 1940; *Educ* Univ of St Andrews (BDS, FDS), Univ of London (MSc); *m* 16 Oct 1963, Vanda, da of Guido Corrieri (d 1987), of Dunfermline, Fife; 1 s (Simon b 27 June 1969), 2 da (Lesley b 11 Aug 1964, Anneli b 19 May 1968); *Career* Army 1962-79 serv in Hong Kong, Borneo, Germany, UK, ret Lt-Col, conslt Dental surgn TA 205 Gen Hosp RAMC (V); dir sch of dental hygiene Glasgow Dental Hosp 1979-90, hon lectr Univ of Glasgow 1979-90,chief dental offr for NI 1990-; examiner: Nat Exam Bd for Dental Surgery Assts, Royal Soc of Health, RCPS Glasgow, Gen Dental Cncl; author of numerous lectureships; numerous papers in jls; chm W Lothian Children's Panel Advsy Ctee, sec W Lothian Branch of Soldier's Sailor's Airmen's Families Assoc; RCPSGlas; *Books* Handbook for Dental Hygienists (with J Forrest and T Walsh, 1978), Guide to Periodontics (with W Jenkins and C Allan, 1984), Dental Hygienist Self-Assessment Book (1984); *Recreations* Rotary club, music; *Clubs* Bathgate Golf; *Style*— Lt-Col William Collins; Brucefield, Marjoribanks St, Bathgate, West Lothian EH48 1AH (☎ 0506 632658); Chief Dental Officer, DHSS, Dundonald House, Upper Newtonards Rd, Belfast BT3

COLLINSON, Alicia Hester; da of His Hon Judge Richard Jeffreys Hampton Collinson, (d 1983), and Gwendolen Hester, *née* Ward; *b* 12 Aug 1956; *Educ* Birkenhead HS, St Hugh's Coll Oxford (MA, MPhil); *m* 23 April 1988, Damian Howard Green, s of Howard Green, KSG; 1 da; *Career* barrister; memb Bar Cncl; *Clubs* Oxford Union, The Coningsby; *Style*— Miss Alicia Collinson; 2 Harcourt Buildings, Temple, London EC4 9DB (☎ 071 353 6961, fax 071 353 6968); Harcourt Chambers, Churchill House, St Aldates Courtyard, 38 St Aldates, Oxford OX1 1BN (☎ 0865 791559, fax 0865 791585)

COLLINSON, Anthony Raymond; s of Jack Collinson, of Ballacatier Farm, Bradden, IOM, and Irene Collinson; *b* 9 April 1949; *Educ* Lancaster Royal GS; *m* 1 March 1975, Carol Ann, da of (Patrick) David Horsfall, of Poole House, Arkholme, Carnforth (s of Sir Donald Horsfall, 2 Bt); 1 s (Jack b 4 Aug 1980), 1 da (Poppy b 9 Aug 1983); *Career* slr, sr ptnr Whiteside & Knowles, Morecambe 1983- (ptnr 1975-); hon sec Lancaster and Morecambe Law Soc 1978, dir Slrs' Benevolent Assoc, hon sec PCC St Mary's Borwick; tstee St John's Hospice Lancaster; underwriting memb Lloyd's; *Recreations* country pursuits, reading, local history; *Style*— Anthony Collinson, Esq; The Coach House, Capernwray, Carnforth, Lancashire LA6 1AL (☎ 0524 734333); 5/7 Skipton St, Morecambe, Lancashire LA4 4AW (☎ 0524 416315, fax 0524 831008)

COLLINSON, Leonard; s of Sidney Lupton Collinson (d 1987), and Jane, *née* Crooks, of Immingham; *b* 30 March 1934; *Educ* Humberstone Fndn Sch Cleethorpes, Univ of Nottingham (Dip); *m* 17 Sept 1955, Shirley Grace, da of Ernest Frederick Funnell (d 1962); 2 s (Christopher b 1956, Andrew b 1962); *Career* Nat Serv RAF 1952-54; dep nat mangr Co-operative Wholesale Soc Baking Gp 1958-66, dir of Manpower Plessey Telecommunications and Office Systems 1966-71, exec chm CGA Gp Ltd 1971-; Liverpool Industl Mission 1966-; CBI: Smaller Firms Cncl 1980-86, regnl cncllr 1987-; dir: United Gas Industs 1975-82, Wormald Int Holdings 1979-83, Euro Info Centre North West 1989-, Manchester TEC 1989-, Universities Superannuation Scheme 1989-; FIPM 1970, FIMC 1980, CBIM 1985, FITD 1967, MCIM 1967; *Books* Employment Law Keynotes (with CM Hodkinson, 1985), Manual for Small Business (1983), The Line Manager's Employment Law (6 ed since 1978); *Recreations* canals, stamps, the business; *Clubs* RAC, Portico; *Style*— Leonard Collinson, Esq; Whimbrel, Kirklake Rd, Formby, Merseyside L37 2DA (☎ 07048 76928); CGA Group Ltd, Colgran Hse, 20 Worsley Rd, Swinton, Manchester M27 1WW (☎ 061 793 9028, fax 061 794 0012)

COLLINSON, Capt Peter Robert Holt; s of Herbert Collinson (d 1951), of Manchester, and Elsie, *née* Holt (d 1978); *b* 25 Oct 1929; *Educ* Manchester GS, RNC Dartmouth, Jesus Coll Cambridge (MA); *m* 16 Aug 1952, Elaine Dora, da of Ernest Shawcross (d 1990), of Cheshire; 1 da (Janet b 1956); *Career* RN 1947-82, Advanced Guided Weapon Course RMCS 1957-58, dir Weapon Systems (Polaris) 1976-79, Capt HMS Collingwood 1979-81, ADC 1982; gen mangr Marconi Underwater Systems Ltd 1982-85, dist gen mangr West Cumbria Health Authy 1985-; pres: Whitehaven Sea Cadet Corps 1985-, Whitehaven RN Assoc 1985-; CEng, FIEE; *Recreations* fly fishing; *Style*— Capt Peter Collinson; Skald How, Applethwaite, Keswick, Cumbria (☎ 07687 72245); West Cumberland Hospital, Whitehaven, Cumbria (☎ 0946 3181, telex and fax 0946 63931)

COLLIS, Richard John; *b* 11 Nov 1904; *Educ* Newport GS Essex; *m* 1, 12 July 1930, Kathleen, *née* Hallett (d 1951), 1 s (John Richard b 1937), 1 da (Patricia Anne (Mrs F S Brazier) b 1939); m 2, 8 June 1957, Marjorie, da of late Sir Henry Ridpath; *Career* chm and dir Ridpath Bros Ltd (London) 1950-; pres: Imported Meat Trade Assoc 1968-69, Butchers & Drovers Charitable Inst 1959; Freeman Worshipful Co of Butchers 1951; Order of Merit (Poland) 1984; *Clubs* City Livery, Canada, Royal Smithfield; *Style*— Richard Collis, Esq; Great Notts, Bovinger, Ongar, Essex CM5 0LU (☎ 0277 890227); Ridpath Bros Ltd, 228 Central Markets, Smithfield, London EC1A 9LH (☎ 071 248 8471)

COLLISCHON, (Robert) David; s of Robert Frederick Collischon (d 1969), and Vera May, *née* Pilbeam; *Educ* Chigwell Sch; *m* 3 April 1965, Lesley Elizabeth, *née* Chard; 1 s (Adrian Robert b 1975), 2 da (Lois Anne b 1970, Hayley Claire b 1971); *Career* mktg mangr Fontana Books 1962-64, sales dir Studio Vista Ltd 1964-69, Crowell Collier MacMillian 1969-72, md Gower Press Ltd 1976 (Mktg Div 1972-73), chm Bowker Publishing Co Ltd 1982-85 (md 1977-81), chm and md Norman & Hill Ltd 1980-87, chm Filofax 1987- (chief exec 1987-90); chm Fin Ctee and govr and tstee Davenant Fndn Sch 1988-; *Books* Furniture Making (1967); *Recreations* sailing, golf, badminton, bridge, music, gardening; *Clubs* IOD; *Style*— David Collischon, Esq; Filofax plc, Filofax House, Forest Rd, Ilford, Essex IG6 3HP (☎ 081 501 3911, fax 081 500 7265, telex 268658)

COLLISON, Baron (Life Peer UK 1964), of Cheshunt, Co Hertford; Harold Francis Collison; CBE (1961); *b* 10 May 1909; *Educ* Hay Currie LCC Sch, Crypt Sch Gloucester; *m* 1, 15 May 1940, Mary (d 9 Sept 1945), da of Frederick Smith, of The Hollies, Shepshed, Leics; m 2, 31 Jan 1946, Ivy Kate, da of Walter Frederick Hanks (d 1949), of Burleigh, nr Stroud, Glos; *Career* farm worker 1934-44; gen sec Nat Union of Agric Workers 1953-69 (official 1944-46, chm Supplementary Benefits Cmmn 1969-75); pres Int Fedn of Agric and Allied Workers 1960-76; chm TUC 1964-65 (memb Gen Cncl 1953-69); chm Agric Apprenticeship Cncl 1968-74; pres Assoc of Agric 1976-84; chm Land Settlement Assoc 1977-79 (vice-chm 1964-77); memb: Governing Body Int Labour Orgn 1960-69, Pilkington Ctee on Broadcasting 1960-62, Royal Cmmn on Trade Unions and Employers Assoc 1965-68; *Recreations* gardening, chess; *Style*— The Rt Hon the Lord Collison, CBE; Honeywood, 163 Old Nazeing Rd, Broxbourne, Herts EN10 6QT (☎ 0992 463597)

COLLIVER, Douglas John; s of Douglas John Colliver (d 1983), of Farnborough, Hants and Alice Emily, *née* White; *b* 22 March 1947; *Educ* The GS Farnborough, Univ of Bristol (LLB); *m* 27 Feb 1971, Lulu, da of Henry William Hayes (d 1983), of Camberley, Surrey; 3 s (Toby b 1972, Jasper b 1979, Giles b 1981), 1 da (Sophy b 1974); *Career* articled clerk Durrant Cooper and Hambling 1969-71, ptnr Norton Rose Botterell and Roche 1978- (joined 1973); memb: Int Bar Assoc, Law Soc; *Recreations* reading, music, tennis, walking; *Clubs* St George's Hill Lawn Tennis; *Style*— Douglas Colliver, Esq; Kempson House, Camomile St, London EC3A 7AN (☎ 071 283 2434, fax 071 588 1181, telex 883652)

COLLS, Alan Howard Crawfurd; s of Maj Derek Archibald Colls, MBE, of 4 Carlton Lodge, 37-39 Lowndes St, SW1, and Amy, *née* Christie-Crawfurd (d 1982); *b* 15 Dec 1941; *Educ* Harrow; *m* 20 March 1969, Janet Mary, da of Maj Michael Gillespie (d 1986); 1 s (Toby b 19 Dec 1970), 1 da (Nina b 15 Jan 1970); *Career* dir Stewart Wrightson Holdings plc 1981-87; chm: Stewart Wrightson Aviation Ltd 1975-86, Stewart Wrightson Int Gp 1981-85, Stewart Wrightson Ltd 1986-87, Nicholson Chamberlain Colls Ltd 1988-; dep chm Lloyd's Insurance Brokers' Ctee 1986-87 and 1989-90; *Recreations* tennis, golf, travel; *Clubs* Annabel's; *Style*— Alan Colls, Esq; 17 Ansdell Terrace, London W8 5BY (☎ 071 937 7226); Nicholson Chamberlain Colls Ltd, PO Box 615, Beaufort House, 15 St Botolph St, London EC3A 7QQ (☎ 071 247 4466, ext 2001, fax 071 375 1760, telex 929464)

COLLUM, Hugh Robert; s of Robert Archibald Hugh (d 1976), and Marie Vivien, *née* Skinner (d 1978); *b* 29 June 1940; *Educ* Eton; *m* 24 July 1965, Elizabeth Noel, da of Gordon Stewart, of Pontefract, Yorks; 2 da (Lucinda Elizabeth b 1967, Melissa Jane b 1969); *Career* Coopers and Lybrand 1959-64, dir Plymouth Breweries Ltd, Courage Western Ltd 1965-72; fin dir: Courage Ltd 1973-81, Cadbury Schweppes plc 1981-86, Beecham Gp plc 1987-89, SmithKline Beecham plc 1989-; non-exec dir: Imperial Tobacco Ltd 1978-81, Ladbroke Courage Holidays Ltd 1976-81, Cncl of Brewers Soc 1978-81, Sedgwick Gp plc 1987-; chm The Hundred Group of Fin Dirs 1990-; FCA; *Recreations* sport, opera, shooting, travel; *Clubs* Boodle's, MCC; *Style*— Hugh R Collum, Esq; Clinton Lodge, Fletching, E Sussex TN22 3ST (☎ 082 572 2952); SmithKline Beecham plc, SB House, Brentford, Middx TW8 9BD (☎ 081 975 3721, fax 081 847 6225)

COLLYEAR, Sir John Gowen; s of John Robert Collyear (d 1968), and Amy Elizabeth, *née* Gowen; *b* 19 Feb 1927; *Educ* Watford GS, Univ of Manchester, Univ of Leeds (BSc); *m* 1953, Catherine Barbara, da of William James Newman; 1 s (John), 2 da (Elizabeth, Kathryn); *Career* Lt RE; engr; chm: Glacier Metal Co Ltd 1972-76, AE plc (formerly Assoc Engrg) 1981-86 (gp md 1975-81), M K Electric Group plc 1987-88, United Machinery Group Ltd; FEng, FIMechE, FIProdE, FRSA, CBIM; kt 1986; *Books* Management Precepts (1975), The Practice of First Level Management (1976); *Recreations* golf, bridge, music; *Clubs* Athenaeum; *Style*— Sir John Collyear; Walnut Tree House, Nether Westcote, Oxon OX7 6SD (☎ 0993 831247)

COLLYMORE, Peter Keith; s of Eric Claude Collymore (d 1965), and Evelyn Marjorie, *née* Keith (d 1987); *b* 20 April 1929; *Educ* Marlborough, Univ of Cambridge (MA), Architectural Assoc Sch (Dip); *Career* Nat Serv 2 Lt 1947-49, architect; Skidmore Owings and Merrill NY 1956, asst architect Robert Mathew and Johnson Marshall London 1957-59, fndr memb an Association of Architects 1964; some 300 projects incl: library and rehearsal room for Benjamin Britten Aldeburgh, studies and house at Lancing Coll Sussex, many private houses and small shops nationally assessor for Civic Tst, memb Library Ctee RBA; conservation RIBA 1955; *Books* House Conservation and Renewal (1974), The Architecture of Ralph Erskine (1982); *Recreations* cricket, painting; *Clubs* MCC; *Style*— Peter Collymore, Esq; Barrington Cottage, Byworth, Petworth, W Sussex GU28 0HJ, Peter Collymore & Associates Architects, 80 Lamble St, London NW5 4AB (☎ 071 267 7567)

COLMAN, Anthony David; QC (1977); s of Solomon Colman (d 1991), of Larchfield Manor, Harrogate, and Helen, *née* Weiss (d 1987); *b* 27 May 1938; *Educ* Harrogate GS, Trinity Hall Cambridge (BA, MA); *m* 23 Aug 1964, Angela Barbara, da of Hyman Glynn (d 1984), of London; 2 da (Deborah b 1967, Rosalind b 1971); *Career* Nat Serv Instr RAEC 1957-59; called to the Bar Gray's Inn 1962; in commercial practice 1963 (specialising in shipping, int trade and insur), chm ctees of enquiry and disciplinary ctees at Lloyds 1982-84, rec Crown Ct 1985, bencher Gray's Inn 1986, dep High Ct judge 1987, memb Bar Cncl 1989-, treas Commercial Bar Assoc 1989-; FCIArb 1978; *Books* Mathew's Practice of the Commercial Court (2 edn 1965), The Practice and Procedure of the Commercial Court (1983, 2 edn 1986, 3 edn 1990); *Recreations* cricket, tennis, gardening; *Style*— Anthony Colman, QC; 4 Essex Court, Temple, London EC4Y 9AJ (☎ 071 583 9191, fax 071 353 3421)

COLMAN, Hon Mrs (Cynthia); 2 da (twin) of 1 Baron Sherfield, GCB, GCMG; *b* 11 July 1935; *m* 4 March 1967, Oliver James Colman, yr s of Sir Jeremiah Colman, 2 Bt (d 1961), and bro of 3 Bt; 1 s, 1 da; *Style*— The Hon Mrs Colman; 35 Greville Rd, London NW6

COLMAN, Prof David Robert; s of Colin Robert Colman, of London, and Jessica Ada, *née* Gregson (d 1972); *b* 14 May 1940; *Educ* Bury GS, Latymer Upper Sch, Wye Coll Univ of London (BSc), Univ of Illinois (MS), Univ of Manchester (PhD); *m* 9 Aug 1969, Susan, da of William Blundell (d 1952); 2 da (Lucy b 1974, Sophie b 1976); *Career* res asst Univ of Illinois 1963-65, tech advsr Govt of Malawi 1972-73, visiting prof Cornell Univ 1978-79, prof Univ of Manchester 1979- (lectr 1965-74, sr lectr 1974-79); chm Exec Agric Economics Soc 1980-83 and 1989-91; AES 1965-, IAEA 1974 (AAEA 1968); *Books* The United Kingdom Cereals Market (1972), Economics of Change in Less-Developed Countries (2 edn, 1986), Principles of Agricultural Economics (1989); *Recreations* squash, fishing, philately, theatre, food and drink; *Style*— Prof David Colman; 11 Brooklyn Crescent, Cheadle, Cheshire SK8 1DX, Department of Agricultural Economics, University of Manchester, Manchester M13 9PL (☎ 061 2754793, fax 061 2754751)

COLMAN, Jeremiah Michael Powlett (Jamie); s and h of Sir Michael Colman, 3 Bt; *b* 23 Jan 1958; *Educ* Eton, Univ of Leicester (LLB); *m* 10 Oct 1981, Susan Elizabeth, da of John Henry Britland, of York; 2 s (Joseph Jeremiah b 31 Nov 1988, Nathaniel James b 19 July 1990), 1 da (Eleanor b 1985); *Career* slr, trg conslt; *Style*— Jamie Colman, Esq; 12 Eland Rd, London SW11

COLMAN, Jeremy Gye; s of Philip Colman, and Georgina Maude, *née* Gye; *b* 9 April

1948; *Educ* John Lyon Sch Harrow, Peterhouse Cambridge (MA), Imperial Coll London (MSc, DIC); *m* 20 Oct 1978, Patricia Ann, da of Willliam Walter Stewart; *Career* CS offr 1971-75, princ HM Treasy 1975-78, CS Dept 1978-81, private sec to Head of Home Civil Service 1980-81, princ HM Treasy 1981-84, private sec to Permanent Sec and Jt Head of Home Civil Service 1981-82, asst sec HM Treasy 1984-87; dir County NatWest Ltd 1988-90, ptnr Price Waterhouse 1991-; *Recreations* cookery, opera, wine; *Clubs* United Oxford and Cambridge Univ, Ski Club of Great Britain; *Style*— J G Colman, Esq; 283 Shakespeare Tower, Barbican, London EC24 8DR (☎ 071 638 1748); Price Waterhouse, Southwark Towers, London SE1 (☎ 071 939 3000)

COLMAN, Keith Thomas; s of Thomas Arthur Colman, of Melton Constable, Norfolk, and Lorna Margaret, *née* Warnes; *b* 30 Aug 1952; *Educ* Fakenham GS, Univ of London (BSc); *m* 27 July 1974, Denise Jane, da of Jack Donald Matsell (d 1977); 2 s (Adam b 1978, Alistair b 1983), 2 da (Rebecca b 1980, Eleanor b 1987); *Career* CA; trainee 1974-78, Ernst & Whinney 1978-81; ptnr: Neville Russell 1982-86, The Colman Dring Partnership 1987-; md The Fin Advice Centre 1988-; winner fin advsr Unit Tst Assoc Mktg Awards 1989; chm of govrs Avenue First and govr Middle Sch Norwich, tstee Dove Tst Norwich, a ldr of Norwich Community Church, advsr to Life for the World Drug Rehabilitation Centre Norwich, Matthew Project (young people's advice serv) Norwich; FCA 1982; *Recreations* squash, DIY, soccer, family; *Style*— Keith Colman, Esq; The Colman Dring Partnership, 2 Dove St, Norwich NR2 1DE (☎ 0603 617 009, fax 0603 620 213)

COLMAN, Lady Mary Cecilia; *née* Bowes-Lyon; da (twin) of Hon Michael Claude Hamilton Bowes-Lyon (d 1953), 5 s of 14 Earl of Strathmore; sis of 17 Earl; raised to the rank of an Earl's da 1974; *b* 30 Jan 1932; *m* 10 Nov 1951, Timothy James Alan Colman, *qv*; 2 s, 3 da; *Career* an extra lady-in-waiting to HRH Princess Alexandra, the Hon Mrs Angus Ogilvy 1970-; *Style*— Lady Mary Colman; Bixley Manor, Norwich, Norfolk NR14 8SJ

COLMAN, Sir Michael Jeremiah; 3 Bt (UK 1907), of Gatton Park, Surrey; s of Sir Jeremiah Colman, 2 Bt (d 1961); *b* 7 July 1928; *Educ* Eton; *m* 29 Oct 1955, Judith Jean Wallop, da of Vice Adm Sir Peveril William-Powlett, KCB, CBE, DSO; 2 s, 3 da; *Heir* s, Jeremiah Colman; *Career* chm Reckitt and Colman plc; memb Cncl: Royal Warrant Holders 1977- (pres 1984); memb Cncl Chemical Industries Assoc 1983-84; asst dir of Trinity House - memb Lighthouse Bd; memb Court of the Skinners' Co; memb Cncl of the Scouts Assoc; memb Gen Cncl and Finance Ctee of King Edward's Hosp Fund for London; dir The UK Centre for Economic and Environmental Development; special tstee for St Mary's Hosp, tstee The Royal Fndn Grey Coat Hosp, dir Foreign & Colonial Ventures Advsrs Ltd; FRSA; *Recreations* farming, forestry, golf, shooting; *Clubs* Cavalry and Guards'; *Style*— Sir Michael Colman, Bt; Malshanger, Basingstoke, Hants (☎ 0256 780241); Tarvie, Bridge of Cally, Blairgowrie, Perthshire (☎ 025 081 264); Reckitt and Colman plc, One Burlington Lane, London W4 2RW (☎ 081 994 6464, telex 21268)

COLMAN, Timothy James Alan; s of Capt Geoffrey Russell Rees Colman, (d 1935), of Framingham Chase, Norwich; *b* 19 Sept 1929; *Educ* RNC Dartmouth and Greenwich; *m* 1951, Lady Mary Cecilia Bowes-Lyon (*see* Lady Mary Cecilia Colman); 2 s, 3 da; *Career* RN 1943-53, Lt 1950; chm Eastern Counties Newspapers Gp Ltd 1969-, dir Anglia Television Gp Ltd 1987-; former dir: Reckitt & Colman plc 1978-89, Whitbread & Co plc 1980-86; JP Norfolk 1958, Lord Lieut Norfolk 1978 (DL Norfolk 1968), High Sheriff Norfolk 1970, pro-chllr Univ of East Anglia 1974- (chm Cncl 1974-85), tstee Carnegie UK Tst (chm 1982-87), chm Royal Norfolk Agric Assoc 1984- (pres 1982), chm of Tstees Norfolk and Norwich Festival; memb: Countryside Cmmn 1971-76, Advsy Ctee England Nature Conservancy Cncl 1974-80, Water Space Amenity Cmmn 1973-76; chm Norfolk Naturalists Tst 1962-74; Hon DCL (E Anglia) 1973; KStJ 1979; *Clubs* Turf, Pratt's, Norfolk, Royal Yacht Squadron; *Style*— Timothy Colman, Esq; Bixley Manor, Norwich, Norfolk NR14 8SJ (☎ 0603 625298)

COLNBROOK, Baron (Life Peer UK 1987), of Waltham St Lawrence, Co Berks; Sir Humphrey Edward Gregory Atkins; KCMG (1983), PC (1973); o s of Capt Edward Davis Atkins (d 1925), of Nyeri, Kenya, and Mary Violet, *née* Preston (d 1975); *b* 12 Aug 1922; *Educ* Wellington; *m* 21 Jan 1944, (Adela) Margaret Atkins, JP, yst da of Sir Robert Spencer-Nairn, 1 Bt, TD, JP, DL (d 1960); 1 s (Hon Charles Edward Spencer, *qv*), 3 da (Hon Mrs Schroeder, Hon Mrs Keay, Hon Mrs Clegg, *qqqv*); *Career* served WW II Lt RN Atlantic and Mediterranean; MP (C): Merton and Morden Surrey 1955-70, Spelthorne Surrey 1970-87; Parly sec to Treasury and Govt chief whip 1973-74, oppn chief whip 1974-79, sec of state for NI 1979-81, Lord Privy Seal and princ FCO spokesman in Commons 1981-82; chm Airey Neave Tst 1983-90; pres Nat Union of Conservative and Unio Assocs 1985-86, chm Assoc of Cons Peers 1990-; *Recreations* shooting, sailing, golf; *Clubs* Brooks's; *Style*— The Rt Hon Lord Colnbrook, KCMG, PC; Tuckenhams, Waltham St Lawrence, Berks RG10 0JH

COLONNA-CZOSNOWSKI, Karol Anthony; s of Eustace Colonna-Czosnowski (descended from Roscislaw, whose designation of Comes (which he appears to have born c 1250) was essentially a feudal one, in some ways comparable with W Euro seigneuries or lordships; a sr branch of the family was granted the title of Count by King Umberto I of Italy 24 Oct 1887 and by Pope Leo XIII 8 April 1897; *b* 24 Feb 1921; *Educ* St Joseph's Coll, Chyrow, Poland; *m* 1948, Maria, da of late Baron Stanislas Heydel of Siechow, Poland; *Career* cmmd 1 Polish Lancers Regt Italy 1944, chm Bishopsgate Steels Ltd and associated companies; *Recreations* foxhunting; *Clubs* Brooks's; *Style*— Karol Colonna-Czosnowski, Esq; Saddlecombe Stud, Hurst Lane, Headley, Surrey KT18 6DY (☎ 0372 379 443)

COLOVER, Robert Mark; s of Sqdn Ldr Jack Colover, and Sarina Frances, *née* Politi; *b* 23 May 1953; *Educ* St Dunstan's Coll; *m* 9 Sept 1979, Hanna, da of Paul Kudelka (d 1982), of Streatham Hill, London; 2 s (Daniel b 24 Aug 1983, Joel b 16 Nov 1989), 1 da (Sarah b 20 July 1985); *Career* called to the Bar Middle Temple 1975; Certificate in Criminology (Distinction); govr Woodmansterne Sch, memb Panel Lay Visitors Lambeth Police Stations; memb: NACRO, Howard League for Penal Reform, Br Soc of Criminology, ISTD; *Recreations* cycling, kites, opera, family; *Style*— Robert Colover, Esq; 10 Heybridge Ave, Streatham Common, London SW16 3DT (☎ 081 764 9655), 4 Brick Court, Temple, London EC4 (☎ 071 3531492, fax 071 5838645)

COLQUHOUN, Maj-Gen Sir Cyril Harry; KCVO (1968, CVO 1965), CB (1955), OBE (1945); s of late Capt Harry Colquhoun; *b* 16 Aug 1903; *Educ* RMA Woolwich; *m* 1930, Stella Irene, yr da of late W C Rose, of Kotagiri, India, and Cheam, Surrey; 1 s; *Career* cmmnd Royal Field Artillery 1923, served WW II, France 1939-40 (despatches), Europe 1944-45 (despatches), Palestine 1946-48 (despatches), cmd 1 and 6 Field Regts RA and 76 Field Regt, CRA 6 Airborne Div 1946-48, CRA 61 Div 1945, CRA 1 Div 1948-50, Cmdt School of Artillery 1951-53, GOC 50 (Northumbria) Inf Div (TA) and Northumbrian Dist 1953-56, GOC troops Malta 1956-59, ret 1960; Col Cmdt: RA 1962-69, Royal Malta Artillery 1962-70; sec Central Chancery of the Orders of Knighthood 1960-68; extra gentleman usher to HM The Queen 1968-; *Recreations* shooting, gardening; *Clubs* Army and Navy; *Style*— Maj-Gen Sir Cyril Colquhoun, KCVO, CB, OBE; Longwalls, Shenington, Banbury, Oxon OX15 6NQ (☎ (029 587) 246)

COLQUHOUN, (Ernest) Patrick; s of Wing-Cdr Edgar Edmund Colquhoun, MBE (d 1953), of Staffs, and Elizabeth, *née* Makin (d 1986); *b* 5 Jan 1937; *Educ* Shrewsbury; *m* 16 Jan 1964, Patricia Susan Alexandra, da of Flt Lt Frederick Versen (d 1953); 3 s (James b 1966, Henry b 1969, Frederick b 1980); *Career* Lt Scots Gds 1955-57; banker; vice pres Swiss Bank Corp 1983-88; md Henderson Administration Ltd 1969-76, dir Electra Group Services Ltd 1978-79; memb: Advsy Cncl Brazilian Investmts SA 1975-, Trading Ctee Royal Sch of Needlework 1988-89; *Recreations* shooting, cricket, music, antique collecting; *Clubs* Boodle's, Pratt's; *Style*— Patrick Colquhoun, Esq; 40 Markham St, London SW3 3NR (☎ 071 352 2737)

COLQUHOUN-DENVERS, Nicholas John Arthur; s of H E John Dalrymple Colquhoun-Denvers, Australian Consul-Gen, of Bombay, India, and Winifred May, *née* Mitchell; *b* 5 Jan 1949; *Educ* Christ Church Coll, Perth; *m* 20 May 1978, Anne Patricia, da of Maj Charles Walter Douglas Wellesley Alexander, late of 3 Carabiniers and Royal Scots Dragoon Gds (d 1983); *Career* offr RA served BAOR, Hong Kong, N Ireland Capt 1969-77, ret; sec to Chm Australian Public Service Bd Canberra 1966-69, with Adnan Khashoggi's Triad Corpn 1977-85; md: CLC 1985-87, Hurlingham (Mgmnt) Ltd 1987-; dir Fal Energy (UK) Ltd; Gen Service Medal 1971; *Recreations* polo, shooting, skiing; *Clubs* Carlton, Gds Polo, Ham Polo; *Style*— Nicholas Colquhoun-Denvers, Esq; 10 Catherine Place, London SW1E 6HF (☎ 071 834 1666/6646); Grosvenor Gardens House, Grosvenor Gardens, London SW1W 0BS (☎ 071 233 5733, car 0836 796100, 0836 796114)

COLQUHOUN OF LUSS, Capt Sir Ivar Iain; 8 Bt (GB 1786), JP (Dunbartonshire 1951), DL (1952); Chief of the Clan Colquhoun; s of Lt-Col Sir Iain Colquhoun, 7 Bt, KT, DSO, LLD (d 1948); *b* 4 Jan 1916; *Educ* Eton; *m* 17 April 1943, Kathleen, 2 da of late Walter Atholl Duncan, of 53 Cadogan Square, SW1; 1 s (and 1 s decd), 1 da; *Heir* s, Malcolm Colquhoun; *Career* Capt Grenadier Gds; Hon Sheriff (former Hon Sheriff substitute); *Clubs* White's, Puffin's, Royal Ocean Racing; *Style*— Capt Sir Ivar Colquhoun of Luss, Bt, JP, DL; 37 Radnor Walk, London SW3 (☎ 071 352 9510); Eilean da Mheinn, Crinan, Argyllshire; Camstraddan, Luss, Dunbartonshire (☎ 043 686 245)

COLQUHOUN, YR OF LUSS, Malcolm Rory; s and h of Capt Sir Ivar Colquhoun of Luss, 8 Bt; *b* 20 Dec 1947; *Educ* Eton; *m* 1, 1978, Susan, da of Stewart W Timmerman, of Harrisburg, Penn, USA; m 2, 6 Oct 1989, Katharine A H, eldest da of A C Mears, of Canberra, Australia; *Style*— Malcolm Colquhoun, yr of Luss

COLSON, Jeremy Richard; s of Cecil K W Colson, of London, and Hilda, *née* Richards; *b* 7 Nov 1947; *Educ* Oundle; *m* 17 Oct 1970 (m dis 1980), Geraldine Louise, da of Philip Stevens, of Crediton, Devon; 1 da (Zoe Victoria b 1976); *Career* CA; gp fin dir Donald Macpherson Group plc 1982-85, Bestwood plc 1985-89, fin dir Vickring Ltd 1990-; FCA 1970, FACT 1985; *Recreations* sailing; *Style*— Jeremy R Colson, Esq; Rowhorne Farm, Nadderwater, Exeter, Devon EX4 2LQ (☎ 039 281277)

COLSON, Maurice John; s of Louis-Philippe Colson (d 1984), and Kathleen, *née* Burke (d 1959); *b* 25 June 1942; *Educ* Loyola Montreal (BA 1963), McGill Univ (MBA), Oxford Univ; *m* Sept 1969 (m dis 1974); 1 s (Christopher Sean b 10 Feb 1974), 1 da (Kathryn b 22 April 1972); *Career* dir gen financing Montreal Olympics Organising Ctee 1974-77, vice pres McLeod Young Weir 1977-80, vice pres and dir First Marathon Securities 1980-86, md Richardson Greenshields of Canada 1986-, dir Northair Mines Ltd; Freeman City of London 1987; *Clubs* Annabel's, United Oxford and Cambridge, Toronto Lawn Tennis; *Style*— Maurice Colson, Esq; 48 Cadogan Sq, London SW1 (☎ 071 584 7599); 1/9 City Rd, Lowndes House, London EC1Y 1BH (☎ 071 638 8831, fax 071 628 2114, telex 887439)

COLSTON, His Hon Judge; Colin Charles; QC; yr s of Eric Lawrence Colston, JP (d 1975), of Buckinghamshire, and Catherine Colston; *b* 2 Oct 1937; *Educ* Rugby, Trinity Hall Cambridge (MA); *m* 23 March 1963, Edith Helga, da of Dr Wilhelm Hille, of Austria; 2 s (Martin b 1965, Dominic b 1968), 1 da (Helen-Jane b 1970); *Career* Nat Serv 1956-58, cmmnd RNR 1957-64, Lt RNR; called to the Bar Gray's Inn 1962; Midland and Oxford Circuit (formerly Midland Circuit) (rec Midland C 1968-69); memb of the Senate of the Inns of Court and Bar 1977-80, rec Crown Court 1978-83, circuit judge 1983-, res judge of Crown Court at St Albans 1989-; chm St Albans Diocesan Bd of Patronage; *Recreations* shooting, fishing; *Style*— His Hon Judge Colston, QC; The Crown Court, St Albans, Herts

COLSTON, Michael; s of Sir Charles Blampied Colston, CBE, MC, DCM (d 1969), and Eliza Foster, MBE (d 1964), da of W A Shaw; *b* 24 July 1932; *Educ* Ridley Coll Canada, Stowe, Gonville and Caius Coll Cambridge; *m* 1, 1956 (m dis), Jane Olivia, da of Denys Kilham Roberts (d 1970); 3 da (Katrina b 1957, Quita b 1959, Melissa b 1961); m 2, 1977, Judith Angela, da of Group Capt Nelson Briggs, CBE, AFC; *Career* served Korea, Lt 17/21 Lancers, seconded 1 RTR; fndr dir Charles Colston Gp Ltd (formerly Colston Appliances Ltd) 1955-89; chm: Colston Consultants Ltd 1989-, Tallent Engineering Ltd 1969-90; chm and md Colston Domestic Appliances Ltd 1969-79; memb: Thames Valley Branch IOD 1977- (currently pres), Southern Regnl Cncl CBI 1986-88 (chm), Cncl IOD 1978-, Cncl CBI 1984-, Soc of Motor Manufacturers and Traders Cncl 1987-90; *Recreations* fishing, shooting, tennis; *Style*— Michael Colston, Esq; C6 Albany, Piccadilly, London W1V 9RF (☎ 071 734 2452); Colston Consultants Ltd, PO Box 15, Henley-on-Thames, Oxon RG9 6HT (☎ 0491 641668, fax 0491 641938)

COLT, Sir Edward William Dutton; 10 Bt (E 1694), of St James's-in-the-Fields Liberty of Westminster, Middlesex; s of Major John Rochfort Colt, N Staffs Regt (d 1944), half-bro of 9 Bt; suc unc Sir Henry Archer Colt, 9 Bt, DSO, MC (d 1951); *b* 22 Sept 1936; *Educ* Stoke House Seaford, Douai Sch, Univ Coll London; *m* 1, 20 Aug 1966 (m dis 1972), Jane Caroline, da of James Histed Lewis; m 2, 1979, Suzanne Nelson, *née* Knickerbocker; 1 s (Tristan b 1983), 1 da (Angela Cecily b 1979); *Heir* s, Tristan Charles Edward, b 27 June 1983; *Career* asst attending physician St Luke's Hosp New York; MB, MRCP, FACP; *Style*— Sir Edward Colt, Bt; 12 East 88 St, New York, NY 10028, USA

COLTART, Col George John Letham; TD; s of George James Letham Coltart, MC (d 1974), and Augustine, *née* Claireaux (d 1973); *b* 2 Feb 1929; *Educ* George Watson Coll Edinburgh, RMA Sandhurst, King's Coll Cambridge (MA), Cornell Univ NY USA (MSc, King George VI Memorial fell); *m* 17 Feb 1958, Inger Christina, da of Ivar-Ragnar Larsson (d 1974), of Gothenburg Sweden; 1 s (Neil b 1962), 1 da (Karin b 1963); *Career* cmmnd RE 1949, Staff Coll Camberly 1962, DAA and QMG 5 Infantry Bde 1963-65, OC 51 Field Sqdn RE 1965-66, CO Edinburgh and Heriot Watt UOTC 1972-74, TA Col Lowlands 1975-79, ret 1982; presently sr lectr civil engrg Heriot-Watt Univ Edinburgh (joined academic staff 1966); chm Lowland TA and VRA 1986; MICE 1961; *Recreations* walking, res forces, restoring buildings; *Clubs* Royal Cwlth Soc; *Style*— Col George Coltart, TD; Napier House, 8 Colinton Rd, Edinburgh, EH10 5DS (☎ 031 447 6314); Polskeoch, Thornhill, Dumfriesshire DG3 4NN; Heriot-Watt Univ, Riccarton, Edinburgh EH14 4AS (☎ 031 449 5111, fax 031 451 3170)

COLTART, Dr (Douglas) John; s of Frank Joseph John Coltart (d 1974), of Blandford, Dorset, and Hilda Kate, *née* Moore; *b* 7 Oct 1943; *Educ* Hardye's Sch Dorchester, Bart's Med Sch, Univ of London (MD); *m* 7 May 1977, Linda Maitland, da of Stuart Douglas Luxon, of Maidensgrove, Riversdale, Bourne End, Bucks; 1 s (Rupert b 4 July 1978), 2 da (Cordelia b 7 Feb 1980, Clementine b 23 Sept 1982); *Career* conslt physician and cardiologist Royal Masonic Hosp London 1974, conslt physician to St

Luke's Hosp for The Clergy 1975 and St Dunstan's Hops for the Blind 1980, currently conslt physician and cardiologist St Thomas' Hosp London; visiting prof: univs in Middle East and Far East, Stanford Univ USA, author of chapters in textbooks of med and over 200 scientific pubns sec Br Cardiac Soc, vice pres Postgrad Fedn, memb Exec Bds Br Heart Fndn Coronary Prevention Gp; memb: Br Cardiac Soc, Med Defence Union; Buckston Browne Prize of the Harveian Soc; Freeman Worshipful Soc of Apothecaries; FRCP, FACC, FESC; *Books* Cardio-vascular Pharmacology (textbook); *Recreations* athletics, tennis, keep fit; *Style—* Dr John Coltart; 47 Weymouth Street, London W1N 3LD (☎ 071 4865787, fax 071 486 5470, car 0860 735242

COLTHURST, Caroline Romaine; *née* Combe; da of late Cdr Anthony Boyce Combe (d 1990), of Grove Cottage, South Creake, nr Fakenham, Norfolk, and late Sybil Barbara Grant, *née* Farquhar; *b* 29 Jan 1935; *Educ* Sydenham House; *m* 22 May 1968, George Silver Oliver Annesley Colthurst, yr s of Sir Richard St John Jeffreyes Colthurst, 8 Bt, of Blarney Castle, Co Cork, Eire; 2 da (Romaine b 9 April 1969, Rowena b 15 Sept 1971); *Career* fashion ed 1958-67: Vogue, Sunday Times, Daily Mail, Harpers Bazaar; patron living of St Michael's & All Angels' Pitchford, Acton Burnell, Rodesley and Condover; *Recreations* chess, bridge, fauna and flora conservation, ballet, classical music, computer adventure games, cats, logic problems, historic houses; *Style—* Mrs Caroline Colthurst; Pitchford Hall, nr Condover, Shropshire (☎ 06944 205)

COLTHURST, Charles St John; s and h of Sir Richard Colthurst, 9 Bt; *b* 21 May 1955; *Educ* Eton, Magdalene Coll Cambridge, Univ Coll Dublin; *m* 31 Oct 1987, Nora Mary, da of Mortimer Kelleher, of Dooniskey, Lissarda, Co Cork; 1 s (John Conway La Touche b 13 Oct 1988), 1 da (Charlotte Louisa Margaret b 31 May 1990); *Career* slr (Law Soc of Ireland); farmer; *Recreations* tennis, watersports, golf, skiing, reading; *Clubs* MCC, City Univ, Royal Irish Automobile, Royal Dublin Soc; *Style—* Charles Colthurst, Esq

COLTHURST, (George Silver) Oliver Annesley; s of Sir Richard St John Jefferyes Colthurst, 8 Bt (d 1955), of Blarney Castle, Co Cork, and Denys Maida Hanmer, *née* West (d 1965); *b* 1 March 1931; *Educ* Harrow, Trinity Coll Cambridge (MA); *m* 1, 10 Oct 1959 (m dis 1966), Hon Elizabeth Sophia Sidney, eld da of 1 Viscount De L'Isle, VC, KG, GCMG, GCVO, PC; 1 da (Shaunagh Anne Henrietta (Mrs Thomas Heneage) b 1961); m 2, 22 May 1968, Caroline Romaine, 2 da of Cdr Anthony Boyce Combe, RN (d 1990), of South Creake, Fakenham, Norfolk; 2 da (Romaine Louisa b 1969, Rowena Barbara b 1971); *Career* Nat Serv 2 Lt LG; memb London Stock Exchange; ptnr: de Zoete & Gorton 1961-76, de Zoete-Bevan 1976-81; underwriting memb of Lloyd's; memb Ct of Common Cncl (Broad Street Ward) 1976-80; Liveryman Goldsmith's Co; *Recreations* tennis, shooting, dendrology; *Clubs* Turf, Pratt's, MCC; *Style—* Oliver Colthurst, Esq; Pitchford Hall, Shrewsbury, Shropshire (☎ 06944 205); Charterhouse Tilney, 15 Pride Hill, Shrewsbsury, Shropshire (☎ 0743 51374)

COLTHURST, Sir Richard La Touche; 9 Bt (I 1744), of Ardrum, Inniscarra, Co Cork; s of Sir Richard St John Jefferyes Colthurst, 8 Bt (d 1955), and Denis Maida Hanmer, *née* West (d 1965); *b* 14 Aug 1928; *Educ* Harrow, Peterhouse Cambridge; *m* 24 Oct 1953, Janet Georgina, da of Leonard Almroth Wilson-Wright (d 1971), of Coolcarrigan, Co Kildare; 3 s (Charles b 21 May 1955, James b 1957, Henry b 1959), 1 da (Georgina b 1961); *Heir* s, Charles St John Colthurst; *Career* underwriting memb of Lloyd's; Freeman of City of London, Liveryman Worshipful Co of Grocers; *Recreations* cricket, gardening, forestry; *Clubs* City University, MCC; *Style—* Sir Richard Colthurst, Bt; Blarney Castle, Co Cork, Irish Republic

COLTMAN, David Alexander; s of Col Thomas Alexander Hamilton Coltman, OBE, DL, RA, of Ayrshire, and Susan Stella Tufton; *b* 5 Aug 1942; *Educ* Eton, Edinburgh Univ; *m* 1972, Mary Cecilia, 3 da of 1 Viscount Whitelaw; 1 da (Susannah Lucy b 1987); *Career* md British Caledonian Airways 1984; *Recreations* shooting; *Clubs* Caledonian; *Style—* David A Coltman, Esq; Haystoun, Peebles; Caledonian House, Crawley, Sussex (☎ 0293 27890, telex 87161 BCAL G)

COLTMAN, (Arthur) Leycester Scott; s of Arthur Cranfield Coltman (d 1982), and Vera, *née* Vaid (d 1971); *b* 24 May 1938; *Educ* Rugby, Magdalene Coll Cambridge; *m* 21 March 1969, (Maria) Piedad Josefina, *née* Cantos Aberasturi, da of Excmo Sr Antonio Cantos Guerrero, of Gen Moscardo 20, Madrid 20, Spain; 2 s (Roland b 1974, Stephen b 1978), 1 da (Beatrice b 1971); *Career* FCO: joined 1961, third sec Copenhagen 1963-64; second sec: Cairo 1964-66, Madrid 1966-69; Manchester Business Sch 1969-70 (sabbatical year), FCO 1970-74, first sec Brasilia 1974-77, FCO 1977-79; cnsllr and head of chancery: Mexico City 1979-83, Brussels 1983-87; head Mexico and Central American Dept FCO 1987-90, head Latin America Dept FCO 1990-91, HM Ambass Cuba 1991-; *Recreations* squash, chess, books, music; *Style—* Leycester Coltman, Esq; c/o Foreign & Commonwealth Office (Havana), King Charles St, London SW1A 2AH

COLTMAN, Hon Mrs (Mary Cecilia); da of 1 Viscount Whitelaw; *b* 1947; *m* 1972, David Alexander Coltman, s of Col Thomas Alexander Hamilton Coltman, OBE, RA, DL, and Susan Stella, da of late Hon Charles Henry Tufton, CMG; 1 da (b 1987); *Style—* The Hon Mrs Coltman; Haystoun House, Peebles

COLTON, Christopher Lewis; s of Lewis Henry Colton (d 1983), of Northfield, Nottingham, and Florence Clarke, *née* Haynes; *b* 9 Sept 1937; *Educ* Worksop Coll, St Thomas's Hosp Med Sch (MB BS); *m* 1, 16 Feb 1960 (m dis 1980), Verena Hilary, da of Anthony David Hunt (d 1980), of Chichester; 3 s (Mark Anthony b 1 Aug 1960, Carl Andrew b 5 July 1962, Douglas John b 14 Sept 1963), 1 da (Samantha Mary b 15 Dec 1964); m 2, 2 Dec 1980, Josephine Mary, da of Joseph Peacock, of Barnsley, S Yorks; *Career* Hon Lt-Col Nigerian armed forces med servs 1968; lectr in orthopaedic surgery Inst of Orthopaedics Univ of London 1970-73, sr surgical offr Royal Nat Orthopaedic Hosp London 1970-73, conslt trauma and orthopaedic surgn Nottingham Univ Hosp 1973-; hon treas Br Orthopaedic Assoc; FRCS 1963, LRCP, fell Br orthopaedic assoc 1973, FRCSEd 1979; *Books* Orthopaedics (with Hughes and Benson, 1987), Frontiers in Fracture Management (with Bunker and Webb, 1988); *Recreations* running, skiing, computer graphics, public speaking; *Style—* Christopher Colton, Esq; The Laurels, 588 Derby Rd, Adams Hill, Nottingham NG7 2GZ (☎ 0602 785907, fax 0602 423606); Nottingham University Hospital, Queen's Medical Centre, Nottingham NG7 2UH (☎ 0601 421421, fax 0602 423656, car 0836 671 670)

COLTON, Mary Winifred; da of James Colton (d 1952), and Winifred Alice, *née* Smith; *b* 2 Jan 1933; *Educ* Kingsbury Co Sch, Univ of London (LLB); *Career* called to the Bar Middle Temple 1955, SE Circuit, rec 1989; *Style—* Miss Mary Colton; 4 Brick Court, The Temple, London EC4Y 9AD (☎ 071 583 8455)

COLTRANE, Robbie (formerly McMillan); s of Dr Ian Bayler McMillan (d 1969), of Rutherglen, Glasgow, and Jean Ross, *née* Howie; *b* 31 March 1950; *Educ* Trinity Coll Glenalmond, Glasgow Sch of Art (Dip Drawing and Painting); *Career* actor; theatre: toured univs with the San Quentin Theatre Workshop 1974-75, Snobs and Yobs Edinburgh Festival 1980, Your Obedient Servant (one man show on Dr Samuel Johnson) Lyric Hammersmith 1987, Mistero Buffo 1990; TV appearances incl: Jasper Carrot Live, Alfresco (2 series), Kick Up the Eighties, The Lenny Henry Show, The Comic Strip Presents (various programmes), Laugh I Neary Paid My Licence Fee, The Young Ones (several guest roles), Saturday Night Live, Girls on Top, The Tube (guest spots), Hooray for Holyrood (documentary about Edinburgh Film Festival), Tutti Frutti (lead role), Blackadder III (guest role) and Blackadder Xmas Special, Emma Thompson Show, Arena, Robbie Coltrane Special, GLC and S Atlantic Raiders (Comic Strip Presents), Mistero Buffo 1990; Films incl: Scrubbers 1982, The Supergrass (Comic Strip Feature Film) 1984, Defence of the Realm 1985, Revolution 1985, Caravaggio 1985, Absolute Beginners 1985, Mona Lisa 1985, Eat the Rich 1987, The Fruit Machine 1987, Slipstream 1988, Danny Champion of the World 1988, Henry V (Falstaff) 1988, Let It Ride 1988, Nuns on the Run 1989, Perfectly Normal 1989, Pope Must Die 1990; involved with: Lab Pty, Amnesty, Greenpeace, Friends of the Earth, CND, Freeze; hon pres Herriot-Watt Univ; *Recreations* vintage cars, painting, sailing, clubs, playing piano; *Clubs* Groucho's, Colony Room, Moscow, Glasgow Arts, Zanzibar; *Style—* Robbie Coltrane, Esq; c/o CDA, 47 Courtfield Rd, London SW3 (☎ 071 370 0708, fax 071 835 1403)

COLVILLE, Hon Andrew John; 2 s of 2 Baron Clydesmuir, KT, CB, MBE, TD; *b* 30 May 1953; *m* 1978, Elaine Genevieve, *née* Davy; 1 s (Patrick b 1988), 1 da (Emily b 1986); *Style—* The Hon Andrew Colville

COLVILLE, Hon Angus Richmond; yst s of Cdr 3 Visc Colville of Culross, RN (k on active service 1945); *b* 29 April 1939; *Educ* Rugby; *Career* Lt Grenadier Gds (Reserve); chartered surveyor; ptnr Colville Tavistock; FRICS; *Style—* The Hon Angus Colville; 1 Bedford Place, Tavistock, Devon PL19 8AZ (☎ 0822 614206, office 0822 614507)

COLVILLE, Hon (Charles) Anthony; 2 s of 3 Viscount Colville of Culross (ka 1945), of Kinneff, Kincardineshire, Scotland, and Kathleen Myrtle Colville, OBE, *née* Gale (d 1986); *b* 5 Aug 1935; *Educ* Rugby, Magdalen Coll Oxford (BA); *m* 2 Oct 1965, Katherine, da of Humphrey John Sankey (d 1945), of Kinangop, Kenya; 2 s (Robert Quintin Oxnam b 1971, Charles Alexander b 1974); *Career* Sub Lt RNVR; HM Overseas Civil Serv Kenya 1958-64; articled clerk Clifford-Turner and Co 1966-69, ptnr The Buss Murton Partnership 1972-; memb Slrs Benevolent Assoc, chm Tunbridge Wells Branch Br Diabetic Assoc; memb Law Soc; *Recreations* history, music; *Style—* The Hon C A Colville; Rydes, Nevill Court, Tunbridge Wells, Kent TN4 8NL (☎ 0892 542514); The Buss Murton Partnership, The Priory, Tunbridge Wells, Kent TN1 1JJ (☎ 0892 510222, fax 0892 510333)

COLVILLE, Master of; Hon Charles Mark Townshend Colville; s and h of 4 Visc Colville of Culross; *b* 5 Sept 1959; *Educ* Rugby, Durham Univ; *Style—* The Master of Colville

COLVILLE, Hon David Ronald; s and h of 2 Baron Clydesmuir, KT, CB, MBE, TD, *qv*; *b* 8 April 1949; *Educ* Charterhouse; *m* 1978, Aline Frances, da of Peter Merriam, of Holton Lodge, Holton St Mary, Suffolk; 2 s, 2 da; *Style—* The Hon David Colville

COLVILLE, Lady Joan; *née* Child-Villiers; er da of 8 Earl of Jersey (d 1923); *b* 26 Sept 1911; *m* 21 Jan 1933, Lt David Richard Colville, RNVR, (d 1986), s of late Hon George Charles Colville, MBE (3 s of 1 Viscount Colville of Culross); 2 s, 3 da; *Style—* The Lady Joan Colville; Old Vicarage, Dorton, nr Aylesbury, Bucks

COLVILLE, John; s of James Colville, and Mary Jane, *née* Orr; *b* 28 June 1930; *Educ* Royal Belfast Acad Inst, Queen's Univ Belfast; *m* 11 October 1956, Edith Naomi, da of T J Johnston; 2 s (James Jay b 1958, John Colin b 1960); *Career* conslt plastic surgn, pres Br Soc for Surgery of the Hand 1988, pres Br Assoc of Plastic Surgns 1990; FRCSEd, FRCSI; *Recreations* sailing, model engrg; *Style—* John Colville, Esq; Belmore, Ballylesson, Belfast BT8, 7 Derryvolgie Ave, Belfast BT9 (☎ 0232 381530)

COLVILLE, Lady Margaret; *née* Egerton; da of 4 Earl of Ellesmere; *b* 20 July 1918; *m* 20 Oct 1948, Sir John Colville, *qv*; 2 s, 1 da; *Career* ATS (Jr Subaltern) 1939-45; lady-in-waiting to HRH Princess Elizabeth 1946-49, extra lady-in-waiting to HM Queen Elizabeth The Queen Mother; pres: Cecil Houses Inc, Friendly Almshouses; *Style—* The Lady Margaret Colville; The Close, Broughton, nr Stockbridge, Hants (☎ 0794 301331)

COLVILLE, Dr Robert Lawson Kellock; s of William Innes Colville (d 1974), of Glasgow, and Lille, *née* Lawson (d 1955); *b* 13 Feb 1928; *Educ* Hutchesons' Boys GS, Univ of Glasgow (MB ChB); *m* 12 Aug 1954, Jean Murray, da of William Angus McKenzie (d 1981), of Glasgow; 2 s (Douglas (Dr) b 1956, Graeme b 1959); *Career* Nat Serv Lt RA 1946-48; assoc adviser in gen practice Univ of Glasgow 1975; RCGP: chm W of Scot Faculty 1981-85, vice chm UK Cncl 1985-86, chm Educn Div 1986-89; chm Open Learning Unit Scot Cncl for Postgrad Med Educn; DRCOG 1954, FRCGP 1978, AFOM 1981; *Recreations* golf; *Clubs* Prestwick Golf, Western Games Golf, Pollock Golf Royal Scot Automobile; *Style—* Dr Robert Colville; Tulach Ard, Braehead, Thorntonhall, Glasgow G74 5AQ (☎ 041 6441664); 43 Los Altos de Marbella, Marbella, Costa del Sol, Spain; Health Centre, Victoria St, Blantyre, Glasgow G72 OBS (☎ 0698 826331 4)

COLVILLE OF CULROSS, 4 Viscount (UK 1902); John Mark Alexander Colville; QC (1978); also 14 Lord Colville of Culross (S precedency 1609) and 4 Baron Colville of Culross (UK 1885); s of 3 Viscount (k on active service 1945); 1 cous of Lord Carrington and 1 cous once removed of Sir John Colville, *qv*; *b* 19 July 1933; *Educ* Rugby, New Coll Oxford; *m* 1, 4 Oct 1958 (m dis 1973), Mary Elizabeth, da of Col Mostyn Hird Wheeler Webb-Bowen, RM; 4 s; m 2, 1974, Margaret Birgitta Colville, LLB, JP (Inner London), barr 1985, da of Maj-Gen Cyril Henry Norton, CB, CBE, DSO, and former w of 2 Viscount Davidson; 1 s (Hon Edmund Carleton b 1978); *Heir* s, Master of Colville; *Career* sits as Conservative Peer in Lords; Lt Gren Gds (Reserve); called to the Bar Lincoln's Inn 1960, bencher Lincoln's Inn 1986, rec 1990-; min of state Home Office 1972-74, UK rep UN Human Rights Cmmn 1980-83, special rapporteur on Guatemala 1983-87; exec dir Br Electric Traction Co 1981-84, and cos in gp 1968-84, dir Securities and Future Association; chm: Mental Health Act Cmmn 1983-1987, Alcohol Educn and Res Cncl 1984-90, Parole Bd for England and Wales 1988-; memb Royal Co of Archers (Queen's Body Gd for Scotland); *Style—* The Rt Hon the Viscount Colville of Culross, QC; Worlingham Hall, Beccles, Suffolk (☎ 0502 713191); 2 Mitre Court Buildings, Temple, London EC4Y 7BX (☎ 071 583 1355)

COLVIN, Dr Brian Trevor; s of Clifford James Leslie Colvin (d 1990), of Sevenoaks, and Ivy Emmeline, *née* Goodchild; *b* 17 Jan 1946; *Educ* Sevenoaks Sch, Clare Coll Cambridge (BA, BChir, MA, MB), London Hosp Med Coll (MRCP); *m* 21 Aug 1971, Kathryn Frances, da of Ernest Osborne (d 1966); *Career* sr lectr haematology and conslt haematologist: Royal London Hosp and Med Coll 1977-, St Peter's Hosp Gp and Inst of Urology 1977-86; med postgrad sub dean London Hosp Med Coll 1987- (sr clinical tutor 1985-87), conslt advsr of Acute Unit Royal London Hosp 1988-; memb Standing Ctee of Membs RCP 1973-77, chm NE Thames Regnl Assoc of Haematologists 1981-84; memb: Med Advsy Gp The Haemophilia Soc 1982-, Ctee Br Soc for Haematology 1983-86; sec Haemostasis and Thrombosis Sub Ctee 1986-, examiner RCPath 1984, memb Cncl Pathology Section of RSM 1989-; memb BMA, FRCPath 1988 (MRCPath 1976), FRCP 1990, FRSM 1989; author of various papers, articles and contrib to books incl Haematology Pocket Consultant (with A C Newland, 1988); *Recreations* foreign travel, opera, cricket; *Clubs* Marylebone CC; *Style—* Dr Brian Colvin; Department of Haematology, Royal London Hospital, Whitechapel Rd, London E1 1BB (☎ 071 377 7455)

COLVIN, David Hugh; s of Maj Leslie Hubert Boyd Colvin, MC, of Great Baddow, Essex, and Edna Mary, *née* Parrott; *b* 23 Jan 1941; *Educ* Lincoln Sch, Trinity Coll

Oxford (MA); *m* 15 May 1971, Diana Caroline Carew, da of Gordon MacPherson Lang Smith, of London W1; 1 s (Thomas b 1983), 1 da (Charlotte b 1991); *Career* asst princ Bd of Trade 1966; HM Foreign Serv 1967: Central Dept FO 1967, second sec Bangkok 1968-71, Euro Integration Dept FCO 1971-75, first sec Paris 1975-77, first sec (press and info) UK Perm Representation to the Euro Community Brussels, 1977-82, cnsllr on loan to the Cabinet office 1982-85, cnsllr and head of Chancery Budapest 1985-88, head SE Asian Dept FCO 1988-; *Recreations* squash, tennis, shooting; *Clubs* The Travellers'; *Style—* David Colvin, Esq; c/o FCO, King Charles St, London, SW1 (☎ 071 270 2438)

COLVIN, John Horace Ragnar; CMG (1967); s of Adm Sir Ragnar Musgrave Colvin, KBE, CB (d 1953), and Frances Sibyl, *née* Kays (d 1985); *b* 18 June 1922; *Educ* RNC Dartmouth, Univ of London; *m* 1, Nov 1948 (m dis 1961), (Elizabeth) Anne, da of Walford Manifold, MC (d 1960), of Mortlake, Victoria, Aust; 1 s (Mark b 1953), 1 da (Zoe b 1955); m 2, 11 Nov 1967, Moranna Sibyle de Lerisson, da of David de Lerisson Cazenove (d 1989), of Woodham Mortimer Lodge, Essex; 1 s (David b 1970), 1 da (Joanna b 1968); *Career* HM Dip Serv 1951-80; Oslo, Vienna, Kuala Lumpur, Hanoi (HM consul-general), Ulan Bator (HM ambass), Washington; vice pres and dir int rels Chase Manhattan Bank 1980-86, dir Robert Fraser & Ptnrs; *Clubs* Beefsteak, Brooks's; *Style—* John Colvin, Esq, CMG; 12A Evelyn Mansions, Carlisle Place, London SW1 (☎ 071 834 6514)

COLVIN, Michael Keith Beale; MP (C) Romsey and Waterside 1983-; s of Capt Ivan Beale Colvin, RN, and Joy Frances, OBE, *née* Arbuthnot (*see* Burke's Landed Gentry, 18 edn, Vol I, 1965); *b* 27 Sept 1932; *Educ* Eton, RMA Sandhurst, RAC Cirencester; *m* 1956, Hon Nichola, da of Baron Cayzer (Life Peer), *qv*; 1 s (James b 1965), 2 da (Amanda b 1957, Arabella b 1960); *Career* served Grenadier Guards 1950-57: Queen's Co 1954-55, BAOR Berlin 1954, Suez Campaign, Cyprus 1956-57; J Walter Thompson Co Ltd 1958-63, Andover RDC 1965-72; landowner, farmer; vice chm Test Valley Borough Cncl 1972-74, dep chm Winchester Cons Assoc 1973-76; MP Bristol NW 1979-83; PPS: to Baroness Young Dep Foreign Sec 1983-85, to Rt Hon Richard Luce FCO and Min of the Arts and Civil Serv 1983-87; memb Employment Select Ctee 1981-83, sec Cons Foreign Affrs Ctee 1987-91 (vice chm 1991-); chm: Cons Aviation Ctee 1982-83 and 1987-, West Country MPs 1982-83, Br Gibraltar Gp, Cncl for Country Sports 1987-; vice chm: Cons Smaller Business Ctee 1980-83, Br Bophuthatswana Gp, Br Field Sports Soc 1987-; pres Hampshire Young Farmers' Clubs 1973-75, govr Enham Village Centre 1965-; Parly advsr Nat Licenced Victuallers Assoc 1983-88; memb Lloyd's; *Books* Britain, a View from Westminster (jtly); *Recreations* painting, field sports; *Clubs* Turf, Pratt's; *Style—* Michael Colvin, Esq, MP; Tangley House, Andover, Hants SP11 0SH (☎ 026 470 215); c/o The House of Commons, London SW1 (☎ 071 219 4208)

COLVIN, Hon Mrs (Nichola); *née* Cayzer; er da of Baron Cayzer (Life Peer); *b* 27 May 1937; *m* 15 Sept 1956, Michael Keith Beale Colvin, MP, *qv*; 1 s, 2 da; *Style—* The Hon Mrs Colvin; Tangley House, Andover, Hampshire

COLVIN-SMITH, (Harry) Alexander; s of Maj Peter Molison Colvin-Smith, DL, of Ashkirk House, Ashkirk, Selkirk and Daphne Alexine, *née* Cochran; *b* 22 July 1953; *Educ* Oundle, Heriot Watt Univ; *m* 10 Jan 1981, Inese, da of Andreis Jurevics, of 23 Myrtle St, W Heidelberg, Victoria 3081, Aust; *Career* joined family owned gp of cos 1975; currently dir: N Eastern Motors Ltd, N Eastern Motors (Scotland) Ltd, Colvin Smith (Construction) Ltd, Letterbox Marketing Ltd, Colvinaire Ltd, Ponteland Hldgs Ltd; *Recreations* gardening, music, overseas travel; *Style—* Alexander Colvin-Smith, Esq; Priestbridge House, Morpeth, Northumberland NE61 3DG (☎ 0670 787381), 1A High Row, Lemington, Newcastle upon Tyne NE15 8SE (☎ 091 2676271, fax 091 2290155)

COLWYN, 3 Baron (UK 1917); Sir (Ian) Anthony Hamilton-Smith; 3 Bt (UK 1912), CBE (1989); s of 2 Baron Colwyn (d 1966); *b* 1 Jan 1942; *Educ* Cheltenham Coll, Univ of London; *m* 1, 30 May 1964 (m dis 1977), Sonia Jane, er da of Peter Henry Geoffrey Morgan; 1 s, 1 da (Hon Jacqueline b 5 March 1967); m 2, 1977, Nicola Jeanne, da of Arthur Tyers; 2 da (Hon Kirsten b 17 Jan 1981, Hon Tanya b 14 Jan 1983); *Heir* s, Hon Craig Peter Hamilton-Smith b 13 Oct 1969; *Career* sits as Conservative in House of Lords; BDS, LDS, RCS, dental surgeon 1966-; musician, leader of own dance band and orchestra; dir Jazz FM; pres: jtly Parly All Pty Gp on Alternative and Complimentary Medicine 1989, Natural Medicines Soc 1988; *Style—* The Rt Hon the Lord Colwyn, CBE; 53 Wimpole St, London W1M 7DF (☎ 071 935 6809)

COLWYN, Miriam, Lady; Miriam Gwendoline; o da of late Victor Bruce Ferguson, of Abbotsdene, Charlton Kings, Cheltenham; *m* 21 Dec 1940 (m dis 1951), as his 1 wife, m 2 Baron Colwyn (d 1966); 2 s (3 Baron and Hon Timothy Smith); *Style—* Miriam, Lady Colwyn; Cantley, 32 Bafford Lane, Charlton Kings, Cheltenham, Glos GL53 8DL

COLYER, John Stuart; QC (1976); s of Stanley Herbert Colyer, MBE (d 1986), of Worthing, Sussex and Sevenoaks, Kent, and Louisa, *née* Randle (d 1976); *b* 25 April 1935; *Educ* Dudley GS, Shrewsbury, Worcester Coll Oxford (open scholar); *m* 24 June 1961, Emily Warner, da of the late Stanley Leyland Dutrow, of blue Ridge Summit, Pa, USA; 2 da (Elizabeth Emily b 13 April 1964, Mary Susan b 2 July 1969); *Career* Nat Serv 1953-55, 2 Lt RA, serv BAOR with T Battery (Shah Sujah's Troop) RA at Celle; called to the Bar 1959; instr Univ of Pennsylvania Law Sch Philadelphia USA 1959-60 (asst prof 1960-61), practised at Eng Bar Oxford Midland and Oxford Circuits 1962-, bencher Middle Temple 1983; Inns of Court Sch of Law: lectr in Law of Landlord and Tenant 1983-, hon reader 1982; memb Cncl of Legal Educn 1983-, chm Lawyers' Christian Fellowship 1981-89; rec Crown Court 1985; *Books* Modern View Law of Torts (1966), Encyclopaedia Forms and Precedents (Landlord and Tenant) (ed jtly, 4 edn, vols 11 and 12), Megarry's Rent Acts (gen ed, 11 edn, 1988); *Recreations* travel, gardening (especially collecting & growing Lithops & cacti), opera; *Style—* John Stuart Colyer, Esq, QC; Falcon Chambers, Falcon Court London EC4Y 1AA (☎ 071 353 2484, fax 071 353 1261)

COLYER-FERGUSSON, Sir James Herbert Hamilton; 4 Bt (UK 1866), of Spitalhaugh, Peeblesshire; s of Max Colyer-Fergusson, Capt RASC, s of 3 Bt, (ka 1940); suc gf 1951; *b* 10 Jan 1917; *Educ* Harrow, Balliol Coll Oxford (BA, MA); *Heir* none; *Career* formerly Capt The Buffs; offr British Railways, ret; *Style—* Sir James Colyer-Fergusson, Bt; 61 Onslow Sq, London SW7 3LS

COLYTON, 1 Baron (UK 1956), of Farway, Co Devon and Taunton, Co Somerset; Henry Lennox d'Aubigné Hopkinson; CMG (1944), PC (1952); s of Sir Henry Hopkinson, KCVO (d 1936), of Duntisbourne Manor House, Cirencester, Glos, and 2 Hans St, SW1, by his w, Marie Ruan (d 1949), da of Francis Blake DuBois, of St Croix, Virgin Is, and Montclair, NJ, USA; *b* 3 Jan 1902; *Educ* Eton, Trinity Coll Cambridge; *m* 1, 10 Nov 1927, Alice Labouisse (d 30 April 1953), da of Henry Lane Eno (d 1928) of Maine, USA; 1 s (Hon Nicholas), 1 da (twins, da decd in infancy); m 2, 11 Dec 1956, Barbara Estella, da of Stephen Barb (d 1920) of New York, and formerly w of Charles Samuel Addams; *Heir* s, Hon Nicholas Hopkinson; *Career* HM Diplomatic Service 1924-1946, asst sec War Cabinet Office 1939-40, political advsr to Min of State M East 1941-43, HM min Lisbon 1943, dep high cmmr and vice-pres Allied Control Commn in Italy 1944-46; dir Cons Parly Secretariat 1946-49; MP (C) Taunton Somerset 1950-56, sec for Overseas Trade 1951-52, min of state for Colonial Affairs 1952-55, delegate Gen Assembly UN 1952-55; chm: Anglo-Egyptian Resettlement Bd 1957-60, Joint East and Central Africa Bd 1960-65, Tanganyika Concessions Ltd 1966-72; awarded Royal Humane Soc's Award for Saving Life from Drowning 1919; Grand Cross Order of Prince Henry the Navigator (Portugal), Grand Cordon of Order of Stia Negara (Brunei), Cdr Order of Zaire; OStJ 1959; *Recreations* hunting, polo, shooting; *Clubs* White's, Buck's, Beefsteak; *Style—* The Rt Hon The Lord Colyton, CMG, PC; Le Formentor, Av Princesse Grace, Monte Carlo, Monaco (☎ 33 93 30 92 96)

COMBE, Lady Mary Esther Constance; *née* Needham; da of late Maj the Hon Francis Edward Needham, MVO (d 1955, 2 s of 3 Earl of Kilmorey); sis of 5 Earl of Kilmorey; *b* 2 Dec 1918; *m* 14 July 1949, Cdr Anthony Boyce Combe, RN (ret) (d 1990), eldest s of late Maj Boyce Combe, of Great Holt, Farnham, Surrey; 3 s, 1 da; *Style—* The Lady Mary Combe; Grove Cottage, South Creake, Fakenham, Norfolk

COMBE, Lady Silvia Beatrice; *née* Coke; da of 4 Earl of Leicester (d 1949); *b* 1909; *m* 1932, Capt Simon Harvey Combe, MC (d 1965); 1 s, 1 da; *Career* JP; *Style—* The Lady Silvia Combe, JP; The Manor House, Burnham Thorpe, Kings Lynn

COMBER, Ven Anthony James; s of Prof Norman Mederson Comber (d 1953), and Nellie, *née* Finch (d 1983); *b* 20 April 1927; *Educ* Leeds GS, Univ of Leeds (MSc), Univ of Durham (Dip Theol), Univ of Munich; *Career* colliery dep Rossington 1952-53; vicar: Oulton 1960-69, Hunslet 1969-77; rural dean of Armley 1972-75 and 1979-82, rector of Farnley 1977-82, archdeacon of Leeds 1982-; *Recreations* walking in Bavaria, politics; *Clubs* Leeds; *Style—* Ven the Archdeacon of Leeds; 712 Foundry Lane, Leeds LS14 6BL (☎ 0532 602069)

COMBERMERE, 5 Viscount (UK 1826); Sir Michael Wellington Stapleton-Cotton; 10 Bt (E 1677); Baron Combermere (UK 1814); s of 4 Viscount Combermere (d 1969); *b* 8 Aug 1929; *Educ* Eton, King's Coll London (BD, MTh); *m* 4 Feb 1961, Pamela Elizabeth, da of Rev Robert Gustavus Coulson, of The Old Vicarage, Moulsford, nr Wallingford, Oxon 1 s, 2 da; *Heir* s, Hon Thomas Robert Wellington Stapleton-Cotton b 30 Aug 1969; *Career* short serv cmmn pilot RAF 1950-58, ret as Flt-Lt; lectr in biblical and religious studies Birkbeck Coll Centre for Extra Mural Studies Univ of London 1972- (sr lectr 1988-); chm World Congress of Faiths 1983-88; *Clubs* RAC; *Style—* The Rt Hon the Viscount Combermere; 46 Smith St, London SW3 (☎ 071 352 1319)

COMBIE, Prof Alistair Cameron; s of William David (d 1949), of Maranthona, Longreach, Queensland, Australia, and Janet Wilmina, *née* Macdonald (d 1975); *b* 4 Nov 1915; *Educ* Geelong GS Victoria Australia, Trinity Coll Univ of Melbourne (BSc), Jesus Coll Cambridge (PhD), Univ of Oxford (MA); *m* 3 Dec 1943, Nancy, da of Col Donald Hey, MC (d 1953), of Bramhope Manor, nr Leeds; 3 s (Charles b 1947, James b 1951, Nicholas b 1954), 1 da (Sophie b 1946); *Career* res offr Zoology Laboratory Univ of Cambridge 1941-46; lectr: history and philosophy of sci UCL 1946-53 (nominated reader), history of sci Univ of Oxford 1953-83 (fell Trinity Coll 1969-83); prof history of sci and medicine Smith Coll Mass 1983-85 (Kennedy Prof in the Renaissance 1982); visiting prof: Univ of Washington 1953-54, Princeton 1959-60, Tokyo 1976, Sorbonne Paris 1982-83, Williams Coll Mass 1984, Ecole des Hautes Etudes Paris 1989; memb: Cncl Sci Museum 1962-66, Br Nat Ctee History of Sci 1963-69; pres Br Soc History of Sci 1964-66 (memb 1946); Hon DLitt Univ of Durham 1979; FRHistS 1970; Académie Internationale d'Histoire des Sciences 1957 (pres 1968-71), Academia Leopoldina 1972; *Books* Augustine to Galileo (1952 4 ed 1979), Robert Grosseteste (1953 3 ed 1971), Scientific Change (1963), Science Optics and Music in Medieval and Early Modern Thought (1990), Styles of Scientific Thinking in the European Tradition (1990); *Recreations* literature, travel, landscape gardening; *Clubs* Brooks's; *Style—* Prof Alistair Combie; Orchardlea, Boars Hill, Oxford OX1 5DF (☎ 0865 735 692)

COMBS, Sir Willis Ide; KCVO (1974), CMG (1962); s of Willis Ide Combs of Napier, NZ; *b* 6 May 1916; *Educ* Dannevirke HS, Victoria Coll NZ, St John's Coll Cambridge; *m* 1942, Grace Willis; 2 da (*see* Viscount Raynham); *Career* Foreign, later Diplomatic, Serv 1947-75; Paris, Rio de Janiero, Peking, counsellor Baghdad, Rangoon, asst under-sec of state FCO 1968, ambass to Indonesia 1970-75, ret; *Style—* Sir Willis Combs, KCVO, CMG; Sunset, Wadhurst Park, Wadhurst, E Sussex

COMER, Michael Edward Cowpland; s of Rev Ernest Comer (d 1948), and Agnes Millicent Enid Comer (d 1989); *b* 2 May 1928; *Educ* St John's Sch Leatherhead, Balliol Coll Oxford (MA); *m* 6 April 1974, Shirley Patricia Long-Innes, da of Caryl Thain (d 1969); *Career* master Blundell's Sch 1951-64, rec St John's Sch Leatherhead 1984- (master 1964, house master 1975-83); pres Assoc Reps of Old Pupils Socs 1974- (fndr chm and sec 1970-74), pres Old Johnian Soc 1985 (hon sec 1964-); *Recreations* cricket, gardening, golf; *Clubs* MCC, Incogniti Cricket, Reigate Heath Golf, St Enodoc Golf; *Style—* Michael Comer, Esq; Barn Cottage, Church Rd, Leigh, Reigate, Surrey RH2 8RF (☎ 030 678 347); St John's School, Leatherhead (☎ 0372 376 077)

COMFORT, Alexander; s of late Alexander Charles Comfort, and Daisy Elizabeth Comfort; *b* 10 Feb 1920; *Educ* Highgate Sch, Trinity Coll Cambridge (Robert Styring Scholar, sr scholar, MB BCh, MA), London Hosp (scholar, DCH, PhD, DSc); *m* 1, 1943 (m dis 1973), Ruth Muriel Harris; 1 s; m 2, 1973, Jane Tristram Henderson; *Career* physician, poet, novelist; lectr physiology London Hosp Med Coll 1948-51, hon res assoc Dept of Zoology UCL 1951-73, dir res gerontology UCL 1966-73, clinical lectr Dept of Psychiatry Stanford Univ 1979-83, prof Dept of Pathology Univ of California Sch of Med 1976-78, conslt psychiatrist Brentwood VA Hosp LA 1978-81, adjunct prof Neuropsychiatric Inst Univ of California 1980-, conslt Ventura Co Hosp (Medical Educn) 1981-; pres Br Soc for Res on Ageing 1967, memb RSM; *publications* The Silver River (1973), No Such Liberty (novel, 1941), Into Egypt (play, 1942), A Wreath for the Living (poems, 1943), The Almond Tree (novel, 1943), The Powerhouse (novel, 1944), Letters From an Outpost (Stories, 1947), Art & Social Responsibility (essays, 1974), The Signal to Engage (poems, 1974), On This Side Nothing (novel, 1948), Barbarism and Sexual Freedom (essays, 1948), Authority and Delinquency in the Modern State (social psychology, 1950), Come Out to Play (novel, 1961), The Koka Shastra (tranlation, 1964), The Process of Ageing (science, 1965), The Joy of Sex (counselling, 1973), More Joy of Sex (counselling, 1974), The Facts of Love (1979), A Practice of Geriatric Psychiatry (1979), Tetrarch (trilogy of novels, 1980), Reality and Empathy (1983), What about Alcohol? (with Jane T Comfort, textbook, 1983), The Patient (novel, 1987), The Philosophers (novel, 1989); *Style—* Dr Alexander Comfort; The Windmill House, Cranbrook, Kent TN17 3AH

COMINS, Peter Crawford Melhuish; s of late Capt Dennis Comins, MC; *b* 25 Nov 1930; *Educ* Ampleforth, Lincoln Coll Oxford; *m* 1963, Dinah, *née* Collins; 3 s; *Career* dir: Borax Consolidated Ltd, Borax Hldgs Ltd 1969-, Lowestoft Enterprise Tst 1987-; *Recreations* shooting, skiing, swimming; *Style—* Peter Comins, Esq; Hornlie House, Wiveton, Holt, Norfolk (☎ 0263 740311)

COMLEY, Brett Nicholas; s of Ernest Phillip Comley, and Eve Annesley, *née* Brand; *b* 8 Dec 1958; *Educ* BCom SA; *Career* SAAF 1976-77; mangr Deloitte Haskins and Sells SA 1981-84 (London 1984-86), dir SBCI Savory Milln 1988- (chief fin offr 1986, bd dir 1986-87, memb Exec Ctee 1987-88); memb: Natal Soc of CAs 1983, SA Inst of CAs 1983; Civil Award for Bravery from the High Sheriff of London 1987; *Style—*

Brett Comley, Esq; SBCI Savory Milln, 3 London Wall Buildings, London EC2

COMNINOS, Michael; s of John Michael Comninos (d 1976), of Holland Park, London, and Elsie Rose, *née* Turner (d 1990); *b* 25 July 1931; *Educ* Malvern; *m* 14 Jan 1956, Ann, da of Stanley Graves (d 1985); 1 s (Charles b 1956), 1 da (Sarah Helen b 1962); *Career* Lt RTR 1950-52; ptnr N M Rothschild & Sons 1965-70 (clerk and mangr 1954-65), dir N M Rothschild & Sons Ltd 1970-; FCIB, FCIS, FCT, AMSIA; *Recreations* collecting antiquities, skiing; *Clubs* Brooks's; *Style—* Michael Comninos, Esq; Staithe House, Chiswick Mall, London W4 2PR (☎ 081 995 8026); New Court, St Swithin's Lane, London EC4P 4DU (☎ 071 280 5704, fax 071 929 1643, telex 888031)

COMPIGNÉ-ROGERS, Robin Christopher; s of Maj Leslie Robert Sidney Rogers, CPM (mangr rubber plantation in Malaya 1927-64), and Patricia Dorothy Madeleine, *née* Compigné-Stone; *b* 12 March 1941; *Educ* Taunton Sch Somerset, Royal Tunbridge Wells Coll of Art; *m* 1, 18 March 1967 (m dis); 1 s (Julian Simon Compigné b 1969), 1 da (Samantha Compigné b 1968); m 2, Sara Phillips, *née* Dawson-Walker; 1 da (Katherine Sheila Compigné b 1981); *Career* trainee rubber planter 1960-61, mgmnt trainee P & O Lines London 1961-1962, mercantile asst Mackinnon Mackenzie Hong Kong and Singapore 1962-1969, dep shipping mangr P & O Agents Durban SA 1969-1970, admin mangr SA and Namibia Western Bank Johannesburg 1970-1971, special projects mangr Freemans Mail Order Co 1971-1973, md Robinstudio 1979-1983; heraldic artist and calligrapher 1979-; fndr memb Most Honourable Company of Armigers 1987 (armorist and Kent representative 1987, registrar 1988); fell Huguenot Soc of GB and Ireland; memb: Heraldry Soc, Royal Tunbridge Wells Chamber of Commerce; *Recreations* music, oil painting, family history and genealogy, rugby fanatic; *Style—* Robin Compigné-Rogers, Esq; 17 Westwell Ct, Tenterden, Kent TN30 6TS (☎ 05806 2203)

COMPSTON, His Hon Judge Christopher Dean; s of Vice Adm Sir Peter Maxwell Compston, KCB, *qv* and Valerie Marjorie, *née* Bocquet; *b* 5 May 1940; *Educ* Epsom Coll, Magdalen Coll Oxford (MA); *m* 1, Bronwen, da of Martin Henniker Gotley, of Derwenlas, Machynlleth, Wales; m 2, Caroline Philippa, da of Paul Odgers, of Haddenham, Bucks; 3 s (Harry b 1969 (decd), Joshua b 1970, Rupert b 1987), 2 da (Emily b 1972, Harriet b 1985); *Recreations* the arts; *Style—* His Honour Judge Christopher Compston; c/o 6 King's Bench Walk, Temple, London EC4

COMPSTON, Vice Adm Sir Peter Maxwell; KCB (1970, CB 1967); s of Dr George Dean Compston, of Halton, Yorks; *b* 12 Sept 1915; *Educ* Epsom Coll; *m* 1, 1939 (m dis), Valerie M Bocquet; 1 s, 1 da; m 2, 1954, Angela, da of late Harry Brickwood, of Bembridge, IOW; *Career* RN 1937, Rear Adm 1965, Chief of Br Naval Staff and NA Washington 1965-67, flag offr Flotillas W Fleet 1967-68, Dep SACLANT (Vice Adm) 1968-70, ret; *Style—* Vice Admiral Sir Peter Compston, KCB; Holmwood, Stroud, nr Petersfield, Hants

COMPTON, Earl; Daniel Bingham Compton; s and h of 7 Marquess of Northampton; *b* 16 Jan 1973; *Style—* Earl Compton; Compton Wynyates, Tysoe, Warwicks CV35 0UD

COMPTON, Sir Edmund Gerald; GCB (1971, KCB 1965, CB 1948), KBE (1955); er s of late Edmund Spencer Compton, MC, of Pailton House, Rugby; *b* 30 July 1906; *Educ* Rugby, New Coll Oxford; *m* 1934, Betty Tresyllian (d 1987), 2 da of Hakewill Tresyllian Williams, JP, DL (d 1929), of Churchill Court, Kidderminster, Worcs; 1 s, 4 da; *Career* Civil Service 1929, Colonial Office 1930, Treasury 1931-57, Comptroller and Auditor General Exchequer and Audit Dept 1958-66, Parly Cmmr for Admin 1967-71 (and in Northern Ireland 1969-71); *Style—* Sir Edmund Compton, GCB, KBE; 1/80 Elm Park Gardens, London SW10 9PD (☎ 071 351 3790)

COMPTON, Hon Mrs (Gillian Sarah); *née* Blease; o da of Baron Blease, JP (Life Peer), *qv* b 1948; *b* 1948; *m* 1972, John Compton; issue; *Style—* The Hon Mrs Compton; 17 Station Road, Craigavad, Co Down BT18 OBP, Northern Ireland

COMPTON, Ivor; s of Samuel Harry Cohen (d 1940), and Jane Anne, *née* Kanovich (d 1964); *b* 12 Aug 1933; *Educ* Hackney Down GS; *m* 3 July 1955, Lorna Frances, da of Lewis Greene (d 1984); 1 s (Stanford Harvey b 1957), 1 da (Michèle Alison b 1959); *Career* RAF 1951-53; chm and md Hall of Cards Ltd 1968-; chm: Lorimist Ltd, City Cards Ltd 1981-; *Recreations* golf, theatre, family and charitable works; *Clubs* Potters Bar Golf, MCC, IOD; *Style—* Ivor Compton, Esq; Letchmore Lodge, Aldenham Rd, Elstree, Herts WD6 3AB (☎ 081 953 1986); Hall of Cards Ltd, Stanford House, Oldfield Lane North, Greenford, Middx UB6 0AL (☎ 081 578 0293)

COMPTON, John Cole; MBE (1989); s of John Compton (d 1964), of Belmont, Corsham, Wilts, and Ada, *née* Keable (d 1953); *b* 1 Jan 1923; *Educ* Blundell's, Univ of Edinburgh (BSc); *m* 30 Dec 1948, Elizabeth Beatrice, da of Maj Geoffrey Cox (d 1934), of Stramartine, Angus; 2 da (Margaret (Maggie) b 11 Feb 1950, Alison (Mrs Bell) b 4 Feb 1952); *Career* cmmnd RE 1941-45; farmer and landowner; former memb: Scottish Agric Res and Devpt Advsy Cncl, Ctee for Scotland NCC; memb: Exec Ctee Nat Tst for Scotland, Exec Ctee Scottish Wildlife Tst; former chm Land Use Ctee Scottish Landowners Fedn (memb Cncl), vice chm Tay River Purification Bd, former memb Angus CC, fndr memb Childrens Panel Advsy Ctee for Angus; Freeman: City of London 1946, Worshipful Co of Goldsmiths 1946; Hon Feuar Letham Angus 1975; *Recreations* riding, gardening, land use and nature conservation studies at home and abroad, sailing, foreign travel; *Style—* John Compton, Esq, MBE; Ward of Turin, Forfar, Angus DD8 2TF (☎ 030 783 253)

COMPTON, Peter John; s of John Matthew Bowring Compton (d 1967), of Leigh-on-Sea, Essex, and Amy Gwendoline Lucas (d 1968); *b* 26 June 1938; *Educ* Belfairs HS Leigh-on-Sea Essex; *m* 25 May 1968 (m dis 1987), Mary Elisabeth, da of late Hubert William Jones, of Rayleigh, Essex; 3 da (Nicola b 1969, Stephanie b 1971, Andrea b 1973); *Career* film and sound ed and prodr; asst Br Movietone News 1955, currently chm and md Filmtel Prodns Ltd, co author screenplay and co prodr Goldie 1990, prodr and dir documentaries 1990, ed TV drama series Gateway for Cannes Prodns Finland 1991; tv work incl The Sweeney; films incl : The Killing Fields, Brazil, White City, A Room with a View; memb BAFTA 1975, MBKS 1985; *Recreations* athletics, photography, theatre; *Style—* Peter Compton, Esq; 23 Little Wheatley Chase, Rayleigh, Essex SS6 9EH (☎ 0268 780787); 3 Upper Waun St, Blachavon, Gwent NP4 9QF (☎ 0495 792896)

COMPTON, Robert Edward John; DL (N Yorks 1981); s of Maj Edward Robert Francis Compton, JP, DL (d 1977; s of Lord Alwyne Compton, DSO, DL, 3 s of 4 Marquess of Northampton), and his 1 w, Sylvia, *née* Farquharson (d 1950); *b* 11 July 1922; *Educ* Eton, Magdalen Coll Oxford; *m* 5 July 1951, (Ursula) Jane, 2 da of Maj Rodolph Kenyon-Slaney, JP, DL, and formerly w of (i) Lt-Col Peter Lindsay, DSO (d 1971), (ii) Sir Max Aitken, 2 Bt, DSO, DFC (d 1985), by whom she had 2 das; 2 s (James Alwyne b 30 May 1953, Richard Clephane b 16 April 1957); *Career* served WW II with Coldstream Guards 1941-46 (wounded), military asst to British Ambass Vienna 1945-46 with rank of Maj; sr account exec W S Crawford Ltd advertising agency 1951-54; Time Life Int 1954; advertsing dir Time UK 1958-62; dir Time Life Int Ltd 1958-90; (chm 1979-90, md 1985-87); public affairs dir Time Life Int Europe 1965-70; chm: Newby Hall Estate Co Ltd 1965-69, CXL UK Ltd 1971-73; bd dir Extel Corp Chicago 1973-80; dir Transtel Communications Ltd 1974-83; pres Highline Fin Services 1985; vice chm Nat Tst Yorkshire Ctee 1970-85; pres Ripon Tourist Assoc, former pres Dales Centre Nat Tst; memb Gardens Panel Nat Tst (former memb Properties Ctee); pres: N of England Horticultural Soc 1984-86, Northern Horticultural Soc 1986-; chm Nat Cncl for Conservation of Plants and Gardens 1988-; High Sheriff North Yorkshire 1977; FIOD 1951; *Recreations* gardening, music, golf, shooting; *Clubs* White's, Buck's, Swinley Forest Golf; *Style—* Robin Compton Esq, DL; 17 Brompton Square, London SW3 2AD; Newby Hall, Ripon, N Yorkshire (☎ 042332 3315); Time Life International Ltd, Time Life Building, New Bond St, London W1Y 0AA (☎ 071 499 4080, fax 071 499 9377, telex 22557)

COMPTON, Lord William James Bingham; s of 6 Marquess of Northampton, DSO (d 1978); *b* 26 Nov 1947; *Educ* Bryanston; *m* 1973, Marlene, da of late Francis Hosie; 1 s, 1 da; *Style—* The Lord William Compton; 50 Bedford Gardens, London W8

COMRIE, Rear Adm Alexander Peter; CB (1982); s of late Robert Duncan Comrie (d 1957), and Phyllis Dorothy, *née* Jubb; *b* 27 March 1924; *Educ* Sutton Valence, RCDS; *m* 1945, Madeleine Irene (d 1983), da of Leslie Bullock (d 1956); 1 s, 1 da; *Career* RN 1945, Capt HMS Daedalus 1974-75, dir Weapons Co ordination and Acceptance (Naval) 1975-77, dep controller Aircraft MOD (PE) 1978-81, dir gen Aircraft (Naval) 1981-83, ret; co dir and chm 1983-, def conslt 1984-, chm Exec Gp Ctee 3 of the Engrg Cncl 1986-, vice pres Instn Electrical Engrs 1988- (memb Cncl 1981-84); CEng, FIEE, FRAeS, Eur Ing; *Recreations* sailing, gardening; *Clubs* Royal Cwlth Soc, Hayling Is Sailing; *Style—* Rear Adm Alexander Comrie, CB; c/o National Westminster Bank plc, 23 West St, Havant, Hants PO9 1EU

COMYN, Andrew John (Andy); s of John Spencer Comyn, of 29 Rowan Drive, Cheadle Hulme, Stockport, and Evelyn Belle, *née* Williams; *b* 2 Aug 1968; *Educ* Cheadle Hulme HS, Univ of Birmingham (BSc); *Career* professional football player; schoolboy player Blackburn Rovers and Manchester Utd (no appearances), amateur Alvechurch 1988-89 (55 appearances); Aston Villa: joined 1989-, debut v Liverpool Aug 1989, 13 appearances; *Recreations* golf, swimming, relaxing with my fiancée; *Style—* Andy Comyn, Esq; Aston Villa FC, Villa Park, Trinity Rd, Witton, Birmingham (☎ 021 327 6604)

COMYN, The Hon Sir James Peter; o s of late James Comyn, QC, of Dublin, and late Mary Comyn; *b* 8 March 1921; *Educ* The Oratory, New Coll Oxford (MA); *m* 1967, Anne, da of late Philip Chaundler, MC, of Biggleswade, Beds; 1 s, 1 da; *Career* former pres Oxford Union; called to the Bar Ireland 1947, rec Crown Court 1972-77; judge: High Court Family Div 1978-79, Queen's Bench Div 1979-85; chm Bar Council 1973-74, vice chm Parole Board 1980-85; kt 1978; *Style—* The Hon Sir James Comyn; Belvin, Tara, Co Meath, Ireland

COMYNS, Jacqueline Roberta; da of Jack Fisher (d 1979), and Belle, *née* Offenbach; *b* 27 April 1943; *Educ* Hendon Co GS, LSE (LLB); *m* 29 Aug 1963, Dr Malcolm John Comyns, s of Louis Comyns (d 1962); 1 s (David b 13 Aug 1975); *Career* called to the Bar Inner Temple 1969, SE Circuit, Met Stipendiary Magistrate 1982-; *Recreations* travel, theatre, bridge; *Style—* Mrs Jacqueline Comyns; Tower Bridge Magistrates Ct, Tooley St, London SE1 2JY (☎ 071 407 4232)

CONAN DOYLE, Air Cmdt Dame Jean Lena Annette (Lady Bromet); DBE (1963, OBE 1948), AE; da of late Sir Arthur Conan Doyle; *b* 21 Dec 1912; *m* 1965, Air Vice-Marshal Sir Geoffrey Bromet (d 1983, lieut-govr Isle of Man 1945-52); *Career* No 46 (Co of Sussex) ATS RAF Co 1938, dep dir WRAF 1952-54 and 1960-62, Air Cmdt 1963, dir WRAF 1963-66, Hon ADC to HM The Queen 1963-66, ret 1966; pres Not Forgotten Assoc; holder of father's USA copyright; *Style—* Air Cmdt Dame Jean Conan Doyle, DBE, AE; Flat 6, 72 Cadogan Sq, London SW1

CONANT, (Simon) Edward Christopher; s and h of Sir John Conant, 2 Bt, *qv*, and Periwinkle Elizabeth, *née* Thorp (d 1985); *b* 13 Oct 1958; *Educ* Eton, RAC Cirencester; *Career* chartered surveyor; underwriting memb Lloyd's 1984; ARICS 1986; *Style—* Edward Conant, Esq; The Estate Office, Lyndon Hall, Oakham, Rutland LE15 8TU (☎ 057 285 786)

CONANT, Guy Timothy Geoffrey; DL (Northants 1972), JP (Northants 1960); s of Sir Roger Conant, 1 Bt (d 1973), and Daphne Lorraine, *née* Learoyd (d 1979); *b* 7 Oct 1924; *Educ* Stowe; *m* 1, 27 June 1953 (m dis), Elizabeth, da of Alfred Trevor Handley, of IOW; 1 s (Rupert b 1964), 3 da (Sheena b 1954, Jane b 1955, Diana b 1960); m 2, 31 Jan 1981, Davina Huntley, da of Sir Guy Holland, 3 Bt; 1 da (Melissa b 1984); *Career* Flt Lt RAF; High Sheriff of Northants 1969; landowner and farmer; *Recreations* shooting, fishing; *Clubs* Boodle's; *Style—* Guy T G Conant, Esq, DL; Bulwick Park, Corby, Northants (☎ 078 085 245)

CONANT, Sir John Ernest Michael; 2 Bt (UK 1954), of Lyndon, Co Rutland; s of Sir Roger Conant, 1 Bt, CVO (d 1973); *b* 24 April 1923; *Educ* Eton, Corpus Christi Coll Cambridge; *m* 16 Sept 1950, Periwinkle Elizabeth (d 1985), da of late Dudley Thorp, of Brothers House, Kimbolton, Hunts; 2 s (and 1 decd), 2 da; *Heir* s, (Simon) Edward Conant, *qv*; *Career* farmer, High Sheriff Rutland 1960; *Style—* Sir John Conant, Bt; Lyndon Hall, Oakham, Rutland (☎ 057285 275)

CONCANNON, Rt Hon John Dennis (Don); PC (1978); s of James Concannon, formerly of Rossington, Doncaster, subsequently of Somercotes, Derby; *b* 16 May 1930; *Educ* Rossington Secdy Sch, WEA; *m* 1953, Iris May, da of Charles Wilson, of Mansfield; 2 s, 2 da; *Career* served Coldstream Gds 1947-53; memb NUM 1953-66, memb Mansfield Borough Cncl 1963-, MP (Lab) Mansfield 1966-87, asst govt whip 1968-70, oppn whip 1970-74, vice chamberlain HM Household 1974, min of state NI Off 1976-79 (Parly under sec of state 1974-76); oppn spokesman: Def 1979-81, NI 1981-83; memb: Select Ctee for Energy 1983-87, Cwlth War Graves Cmmn 1986-; *Style—* The Rt Hon Don Concannon; 69 Skegby Lane, Mansfield, Notts (☎ 0623 27235)

CONCANNON, Undine Mary; da of Maj John Noel Concannon (d 1940), and Ursula Mary, *née* Fountaine; *b* 5 June 1940; *Educ* Wimbledon HS, Trinity Coll Dublin (BA); *Career* Ibbs and Tillett concert and artist management 1964-74, freelance orchestral mangr 1973-78, admin London Planetarium 1974-, archivist Mme Tussaud's 1978-; vice pres assoc for astronomy educn; *Recreations* music, theatre, opera, travel, gardening; *Style—* Miss Undine Concannon; London Planetarium, Marylebone Rd, London NW1 5LR (☎ 071 486 1121, fax 071 935 8906)

CONCANON, (Brian) Anthony Ross; s of Austin Brian Concanon (d 1965), of Plymouth, and Joyce Ruth, *née* Chadderton; *b* 2 March 1943; *Educ* Downside; *m* 1 (m dis); 2 s (Lee b 1966, Jonathan b 1977), 3 da (Tracey b 1961, Nina b 1964, Juliet b 1974); m 2, 31 May 1986, Annabell; *Career* Deloitte Haskins & Sells 1961-71, Norton Rose 1971-76; admitted slr 1976; UK tax attorney Texaco (UK) Ltd 1976-78; corporate tax ptnr McKenna & Co 1981- (joined 1978); ICEAW 1967, memb Law Soc 1976; CA 1967; *Recreations* english cartography; *Clubs* Royal Automobile; *Style—* Anthony Concanon, Esq; Mitre House, 160 Aldersgate St, London EC1A 4DD (☎ 071 606 9000)

CONDLIFFE, Gregor Stuart; s of Wilfred Condliffe (d 1984), of Exmouth, Devon, and Marion Condliffe (d 1983); *b* 28 May 1943; *Educ* Kingsmoor Sch Glossop, Hulme GS for Boys Oldham, Univ of Nottingham (DipArch); *m* 24 July 1971, Frances Gillian, da of Charles Edward Berry, of Titchfield, Hants; 2 s (Otto b 1973, Ivan b 1978), 1 da (Emma b 1974); *Career* Corby New Town Corp 1969-72, architect Salisbury Dist Cncl 1974-81, ed Assoc of Official Architects public authorities handbook 1981-84; started private practice in own name 1981; elected co cncllr (Lib) Salisbury-Harnham 1985, memb Lib Democrats/Lab Co Cncl; chm: Tport and Waste Disposal Ctee, Property Ctee; RIBA; *Recreations* politics, community project work, gardening; *Clubs* Salisbury Liberal (fndr life memb); *Style—* Gregor S Condliffe, Esq; 14 Sussex Rd, Harnham, Salisbury, Wilts (☎ 0722 23833); Carter House, 6-10 Salt Lane, Salisbury (☎ 0722 331877)

CONEY, Christopher Ronald Ramsden; s of Alfred Coney, and Margaret, *née* Ramsden; *b* 29 May 1956; *Educ* Univ of Southampton (LLB); *Career* called to the Bar Inner Temple 1979; *Style—* Christopher Coney, Esq; 1 Temple Gardens, London EC4 (☎ 071 353 3737)

CONGLETON, 8 Baron (UK 1841); Sir Christopher Patrick Parnell; 11 Bt (I 1766); s of 6 Baron Congleton (d 1932), and Hon Edith Mary Palmer Howard, MBE, da of late Baroness Strathcona and Mount Royal (in her own right) and R J B Howard; suc bro 1967; *b* 11 March 1930; *Educ* Eton, New Coll Oxford (MA); *m* 19 Nov 1955, Anna Hedvig, er da of Gustav Adolf Sommerelt, of Oslo, Norway; 2 s, 3 da; *Heir* s, Hon John Parnell; *Career* Salisbury and Wilton RDC 1964-74 (chm 1971), chm Salisbury and S Wilts Museum 1972-77, pres Br Ski Fedn 1976-81, chm Sandroyd Sch Tst 1980-84, memb Advsy Bd for Redundant Churches 1981-87; tstee: Sandroyd Sch Tst 1972- (chm 1980-84), Wessex Med Sch Tst 1984-90, Southampton Univ Devpt Tst 1986-; Hon LLD Univ of Southampton 1990; *Recreations* music, fishing, skiing; *Style—* The Rt Hon the Lord Congleton; West End Farm, Ebbesbourne Wake, Salisbury, Wilts

CONGREVE, Ambrose Christian; CBE (1965); o child of Maj John Congreve, JP, DL (d 1957), whose mother was Hon Alice Dillon, da of 3rd Baron Clonbrock), by his w Lady Irène, *née* Ponsonby (d 1962), da of 8th Earl of Bessborough, KP, CB, CVO; *b* 4 April 1907; *Educ* Eton, Trinity Coll Cambridge; *m* 1935, Margaret, da of Dr Arthur Graham Glasgow, of Richmond, Va, USA; *Career* served WWII Air Miny Intelligence and Miny of Supply; with Unilever 1929-36 in UK and China; chm Humphreys and Glasgow Ltd 1955-84; Veitch Meml Gold medal; FIChemE 1967; *Clubs* Beefsteak; *Style—* Ambrose Congreve, Esq, CBE; Warwick House, Stable Yard, St James', London (☎ 071 839 3301), Mount Congreve, Waterford, Eire (☎ 010 353 51 84103)

CONGREVE, Andrew Christopher; s of Percy Douglas Congreve, of Luton, Beds, and Constance, *née* Farmer (d 1933); *b* 23 May 1931; *Educ* St George's Sch Harpenden, Univ of London (LLB); *m* 27 April 1968, Pauline Ann, da of Aneurin David Owen; 2 da (Lucy Pauline Alexandra b 17 June 1970, Katharine Andrea Mary b 22 March 1973); *Career* slr; Herbert Smith: joined 1959, ptnr 1963, head of Property Dept 1985-88, managing ptnr 1987-; memb: Law Soc 1959-, City of London Slrs Co 1963-; *Recreations* theatre, travel, music; *Clubs* Hurlingham; *Style—* Andrew Congreve, Esq; Herbert Smith, Exchange House, Primose St, London EC2A 2HS (☎ 071 374 8000, fax 071 496 0043)

CONI, Nicholas Keith; *b* 29 May 1935

CONI, Peter Richard Carstairs; OBE (1987), QC (1980); s of Eric Charles Coni (d 1942) of Wellington, NZ, and Leslie Sybil Carstairs, *née* Pearson (d 1973); *b* 20 Nov 1935; *Educ* Uppingham, St Catharine's Coll, Cambridge (MA); *Career* called to the Bar Inner Temple 1960, rec 1985, master of the bench Inner Temple 1986; memb: Cncl Amateur Rowing Assoc 1962- (memb Exec Ctee 1968-, chm 1970-77), London Rowing Club 1961- (pres 1988-), Ctee Leander Club 1983-89; steward Henley Royal Regatta 1974 (chm 1978-), chm 1986 World Rowing Championships; memb: Thames Water Authy 1978-83, Nat Olympic Ctee 1990-; treas FISA 1990-; FISA medal of honour 1986; memb of Court Worshipful Co of Needlemakers, Freeman City of London; *Recreations* sports admin, good food, modern art, English literature; *Clubs* Athenaeum, Garrick, London Rowing, Leander; *Style—* Peter Coni, Esq, OBE, QC; 3 Churton Place, London SW1V 2LN (☎ 071 828 2135); 44 Vicarage Rd, Henley-on-Thames, Oxon RG9 1HW (☎ 0491 577930); 1 Gray's Inn Square, Gray's Inn, London WC1R 5AG (☎ 071 404 5416, fax 071 405 9942)

CONINGSBY, Thomas Arthur Charles; QC (1986); s of Francis Charles Coningsby, of Banstead, Surrey, and Eilleen Rowena, *née* Monson; *b* 21 April 1933; *Educ* Epsom Coll, Queens' Coll Cambridge (MA); *m* 8 Aug 1959, Elaine Mary, da of Edwin Stanley Treacher (d 1983), of Sussex; 2 s (Andrew b 1960, James b 1964), 3 da (Sara b 1962, Elizabeth b 1963, Katharine (twin) b 1963); *Career* Nat Serv Cmmn, RA 1951-53, TA, City of London Field Regt and Aerial Photographic Interpretation (Intelligence Corps) Capt 1953-67; called to the Bar Gray's Inn 1957, rec of the Crown Ct 1986-; chllr Diocese of York 1977, vicar gen Province of York 1980-, chllr Diocese of Peterborough 1989-; memb: Gen Synod of C of E 1970-, Legal Advsy Cmmn of Gen Synod 1976-; chm Chipstead Village Preservation Soc 1983-88, memb Matrimonial Causes Rule Ctee 1985-89, chm Family Law Assoc 1988-90 (sec 1986-88); memb: Gen Cncl of the Bar 1988-90, Supreme Ct Procedure Ctee 1988-; *Recreations* lawn tennis; *Style—* Thomas Coningsby, Esq, QC; Leyfields, Elmore Rd, Chipstead, Surrey (☎ 0737 553304); 3 Dr Johnson's Buildings, Temple, London EC4 (☎ 071 353 4854, fax 071 583 8784)

CONLAN, John Oliver; s of Eugene J Conlan, of Dublin, Ireland, and Bridgid, *née* Hayes; *b* 13 July 1942; *Educ* Thurles CBS, Ireland; *m* 19 March 1968, Carolyn Sylvia, da of Raymond Ingram, of Luton, Beds; 3 da (Tara Louise b 1972, Amanda Carolyn b 1973, Alison Theresa b 1980); *Career* md: EMI Leisure 1980-81, Trust House Forte Leisure 1981-83, First Leisure Corp plc 1983-88 (chief exec 1988-); gen cmmr for taxes London 1986-; *Recreations* golf; *Style—* John Conlan, Esq; First Leisure Corp, 7 Soho St, London W1V 5FA (☎ 071 437 9727, car 0836 231396)

CONLEY, Sandra (Mrs Grater); da of Ronald Conley (d 1960), of Hatfield, Herts, and Sophia Emily, *née* Ward (d 1980); *b* 24 Oct 1943; *Educ* Royal Ballet Upper Sch; *m* 28 Dec 1968, Adrian Michael Grater, s of Montague Lewis Grater (d 1980), of Crawley Down, Sussex; 1 da (Abigail b Dec 1974); *Career* ballerina: Sadler's Wells Royal Ballet 1962-70 (soloist 1968), Royal Ballet 1970- (princ 1978, princ character artist 1989); appearances: Swan Lake, Giselle, A Month in the Country, Mayerling, Isadora, Sleeping Beauty; *Recreations* reading, theatre; *Style—* Miss Sandra Conley; 21 Trent Avenue, Ealing, London W5 4TL

CONLIN, Geoffrey David; s of Geoffrey Charles Conlin (d 1943), and Mary Agnes Conlin; *b* 17 Dec 1938; *Educ* RMA Sandhurst; *m* 23 Sept 1972, Caroline Margaret, da of Capt Melville Stuart Jameson (d 1971), of Easter Logie, Blairgowrie, Perthshire; 3 s (Nicholas b 1974, Geoffrey b 1976, James b 1984), 1 da (Elizabeth b 1975); *Career* joined Army 1956, cmmnd Royal Irish Fusiliers 1958, resigned 1970; called to the Bar Inner Temple 1973; asst rec 1987; chm Res Ctee Soc of Cons Lawyers 1980-83; *Recreations* shooting; *Clubs* Boodle's, Pratt's; *Style—* Geoffrey Conlin, Esq; 3 Sergeant's Inn, London EC4Y 1BQ (☎ 071 353 5537, fax 071 353 0425, telex 264093)

CONNAL, William Thayne; s of Robert Connal, of Slamannan, and Sarah, *née* Macallister (d 1984); *b* 17 July 1940; *Educ* Falkirk HS, Edinburgh Coll of Art, Heriot-Watt Univ (DA, BArch); *m* 16 Dec 1962, Rudra, da of D N Shroff (d 1989), of Bombay; 3 da (Criana b 1964, Sulina b 1968, Athena b 1969); *Career* architect; in practice until 1981 (India, ME, N Africa); APP Overseas Ltd 1981-87 (maj conservation projects in Iraq, Saudi Arabia, Oman), APP Horsham and Edinburgh 1987-; work documented in various jnls and on film; AIIA 1971, MAPM 1982; *Recreations* hill walking, climbing, music; *Clubs* Oriental, Bombay Gymkhana, Baghdad Al Wiyah; *Style—* William Connal, Esq; 2 Regent Terrace, Edinburgh RH13 5EU (☎ 031 556 7164); Apna Cottage, Juhu Tara, Bombay; APP, APP House, 100 Station Rd, Horsham RH13 5EU (☎ 0403 210612, fax 0403 210617)

CONNAUGHTON, Col Richard Michael; s of Thomas Connaughton (d 1981), of Huntingdon, and Joan Florence, *née* Lisher (d 1979); *b* 20 Jan 1942; *Educ* Duke of York's Royal Military Sch Dover, MPhil (Cantab); *m* 12 June 1971, (Annis Rosemary) Georgina, da of Capt George Frederik Matthew Best, OBE, of Dorset; 1 s (Michael b 1972), 1 da (Emma b 1974); *Career* RMA Sandhurst 1960-61, III Co RASC (Guided Weapons) W Germany 1962-64, 28 Co Gurkha Army Serv Corps Hong Kong 1965-67, Jr Ldrs' RCT Taunton 1967-69, 28 Sqdn Gurkha Tport Regt Hong Kong 1969-71 (Adj 1971-73), student Army Staff Coll Camberley 1974, GS0 2 Co-ord MVEE Chertsey 1975-76, cmd 2 Sqdn RCT W Germany 1977-79, 2 i/c Logistic Supprt Gp Regt Aldershot 1979-81, cmd 1 Armd Div Tport Regt RCT W Germany 1982-84, memb Directing Staff Army Staff Coll Camberley and Australian Army Cmd and Staff Coll Fort Queenscliff Victoria 1984-86, Col Tport HQ BAOR W Germany 1987-89; def fellowship St John's Coll Cambridge 1989-90, Colonel defence studies 1990-; FBIM 1981, FCIT 1989; *Books* The War of The Rising Sun and Tumbling Bear (1989), The Republic of the Ushakovka (1990), Military Intervention and the Logic of War (1991); *Recreations* writing, family, tennis; *Clubs* Army and Navy; *Style—* Col Richard Connaughton

CONNELL, Lady Alexandra Victoria Caroline Anne; *née* Hay; da of Countess of Erroll (who retained her maiden name Hay under Scots Law and d 1978), and her 1 husband, Sir (Rupert) Iain Kay Moncreiffe of that Ilk, 11 Bt (d 1985); *b* 30 July 1955; *m* 22 Feb 1989, Jolyon C N Connell, eldest s of Christopher Connell, of Pitlochry, Perthshire; 1 s (Ivar Francis Grey de Miremont Wigan b 1979), 1 da (Flora Diana Katharine Cecilia b 24 Feb 1990); *Style—* The Lady Alexandra Connell

CONNELL, David Allan Maclean; s of late John Maclean Connell; *b* 18 Jan 1930; *Educ* Stowe, Ch Ch Oxford; *m* 1954, Bridget Willink, *née* Fletcher; 3 children; *Career* md White Horse Distillers Ltd, md and vice chm John Walker and Sons Ltd; dir: Distillers Co plc, United Distillers plc; chm Scotch Whisky Assoc; *Clubs* Vincents (Oxford), MCC; *Style—* David Connell, Esq; Windy Ridge, Effingham Common Rd, Effingham, Surrey; United Distillers Plc, Landmark House, Hammersmith Bridge Rd, London W6 9DP (☎ 081 846 8040)

CONNELL, Edward Arthur; s of Edward Connell (d 1950), of London, and Mary Ann, *née* Gadsby; *b* 26 Oct 1919; *Educ* Camberwell Sch of Arts and Crafts, London Coll of Printing; *m* 21 Aug 1949, May, da of Percy Godfrey Sims (d 1952), of London; 1 da (Janet May (Mrs Blackledge) b 1956); *Career* RAC 1940, W/Cpl 1944, demob 1946, discharged from Army Res on med grounds 1952; lectr Camberwell Sch of Arts and Crafts 1946-60; Colour Printing Co: mangr 1948-53, dir 1953-70, md 1970-75, chm 1975-84, ret; memb: Beckenham Cons Assoc, Bromley Art Soc, RSPB; City & Guilds of London Silver medal 1946; Freeman: City of London 1967, Worshipful Co of Feltmakers 1975; memb Inst of Printing 1950-85; *Recreations* oil painting, gardening, motoring; *Clubs* United Wards, Guild of Freemen; *Style—* Edward Connell, Esq; 41 Kenwood Drive, Beckenham, Kent BR3 2QY (☎ 01 650 9324)

CONNELL, (Frances) Elizabeth; da of (Gordon) Raymond Connell (d 1968), and (Maud) Elizabeth, *née* Scott; *b* 22 Oct 1946; *Educ* Springs Convent S Africa, Univ of Witwatersrand, Johannesburg Coll of Educn, London Opera Centre; *Career* opera singer; debut: Wexford Festival 1972, Aust Opera 1973-75, ENO 1975-80, Covent Garden 1976, Bayreuth 1980, La Scala 1981, Salzburg 1983, Glyndebourne 1985, Metropolitan Opera 1985, Paris 1987; has sung with maj orchs, opera houses, festivals and maestri throughout the world; recordings incl: duets with Sutherland and Pavarotti, I Due Foscari, Suor Angelica, Guglielmo Tell, Poliuto, Mahler No 8, Mendelssohn No 2, Schubert Lieder recital, Vaughan Williams Serenade to Music, Schoenberg Gurrelieder, Lohengrin; awarded Maggie Teyte prize 1972; *Style—* Ms Elizabeth Connell; S A Gorlinsky, 34 Dover St, London W1X 4NJ (☎ 071 493 9158, fax 071 629 0017)

CONNELL, John MacFarlane; s of late John Maclean Connell, and Mollie Isobel MacFarlane; *b* 29 Dec 1924; *Educ* Stowe, Ch Ch Oxford; *m* 1949, Jean Matheson, da of late Maj George Sutherland Mackay; 2 s; *Career* joined Tanqueray Gordon 1946, md to 1971; dir Distillers Co 1965, DCL Management Ctee 1971, chm Distillers Co 1983-; *Style—* John Connell Esq; The Distillers Co plc, Distillers House, 20 St James's Sq, London SW1Y 4JF (☎ 071 930 1040)

CONNELL, John William; s of William J Connell (d 1947), and Maud Emily Edge (d 1983); *b* 4 Feb 1933; *Educ* St Edward's Coll Liverpool; *m* 28 Sept 1957, Joan, da of Walter Bromley (d 1978); 3 da (Gillian b 1962, Janet b 1964, Elizabeth b 1965); *Career* chm Liverpool and London Steamship Protection and Indemnity Assoc Ltd, md Bibby Financial Servs Ltd; dir of numerous cos incl: Bibby Line Ltd, Liverpool and London P & I Mgmnt Ltd, Grayhill Ins Co (Bermuda) Ltd, Grayhill Insur (Cayman) Ltd; *Style—* John Connell, Esq; 401 Norwich House, Water St, Liverpool L2 8UW (☎ 051 236 0492)

CONNELL, Michael Bryan; QC (1981); s of L Connell, and J Connell (d 1969); *b* 6 Aug 1939; *Educ* Harrow, Brasenose Coll Oxford (MA); *m* 17 Dec 1965, Anne Joan, da of late E P Pulham; 3 s (Sean James b 7 Sept 1967, Jonathan Edward b 26 Aug 1968, Simon Michael b 16 Aug 1979), 1 da (Lisa Anne b 16 Nov 1970); *Career* called to the Bar Inner Temple 1962, recorder 1980, bencher 1988; govr Harrow Sch; memb Worshipful Co of Farriers; *Recreations* steeplechasing, fox hunting; *Clubs* Buck's, Jockey; *Style—* Michael Connell, Esq, QC; Queen Elizabeth Buildings, Temple, London EC4 (☎ 071 583 7837, fax 071 353 5422)

CONNELL, Dr Philip Henry; CBE (1986); s of George Henry Connell (d 1928), of Selby, Yorks, and Evelyn Hilda Sykes (d 1969); *b* 6 July 1921; *Educ* St Pauls, Bart's Hosp London (MB BS, MRCS, LRCP, DPM, MD); *m* 1, April 1948 (m dis 1973), (Marjorie) Helen, da of John Gilham, of Ashford, Kent; 2 s (Michael Charles b 25 Jan 1953, David Nicholas b 19 Aug 1955); m 2, Cecily Mary (Celia), da of Edward Russell Harper, MC (d 1959); *Career* house physician St Stephens Hosp London 1951-53, registrar and sr registrar Inst of Psychiatry Bethlem Royal Hosp and Maudsley Hosp 1953-58, conslt psychiatrist and physician i/c Child Psychiatry Unit Newcastle Gen Hosp in assoc with Kings Coll Univ of Durham 1957-63, physician Bethlem Royal Hosp and Maudsley Hosp 1963-86; numerous contrib to professional jls and pubns; extensive nat and int work on drug addiction and dependence for: WHO, Cncl of Europe, CENTO and on maladjusted and psychiatrically ill children and adolescents; memb: Standing Mental Health Advsy Ctee DHSS 1966-72 (vice chm 1967-72), Standing Advsy Ctee on Drug Dependence (Wayne Ctee 1966- and Sub Ctees), Wootton Ctees on cannabis and LSD amphetamines and barbiturates; conslt advsr (addiction) DHSS 1966-71 and 1981-86, pres Soc for Study of Addiction 1973-78, vice pres Int Cncl on Alcohol and Addictions 1982 (chm Scientific and Prof Advsy Bd 1971-79); chm: Inst for Study of Drug Dependence 1975-, Advsy Cncl on Misuse of Drugs 1982-88 (statutory body set up under the Misuse of Drugs Act 1977), Sec of State for Tport's Advsy Panel on Alcohol Abuse 1988-; memb: Cncl Royal Medico-Psychological Assoc 1962-67, Royal Coll of Psychiatrists 1971-81 (vice pres 1979-81), Mgmnt Ctee Inst of Psychiatry 1968-74; chm Med Ctee Bethlem Royal Hosp and Maudsley Hosp 1969-72 (memb Bd of Govrs 1966-73); memb: Trethowan Ctee DHSS (the role of psychologists in Health Serv) 1968-72, Gen Med Cncl 1979-91; preliminary screener for health 1982-91, Dent Meml lectr Kings Coll and Soc for Study of Addiction 1983, memb ed bds of med jls, emeritus physician Bethlem Royal Hosp and Maudsley Hosp 1986-; memb Bd of Govrs Mowden Hall Sch Northumberland and 1976-82; FRCP 1971, FRCPsych 1971; *Books* Amphetamine Psychosis (1958), Cannabis and Man (jt ed, 1975); *Recreations* bridge, music; *Clubs* Athenaeum; *Style—* Dr P H Connell, CBE; 25 Oxford Rd, Putney, London SW15 2LG; Consulting Rooms, 21 Wimpole St, London W1M 7AD (☎ 071 636 2220)

CONNELL, Stephanie Lee; da of George Saul (d 1982), of Yorks, and Tena, *née* Wheater (d 1987); *b* 21 Aug 1945; *Educ* Univ of London (Dip Ed), Univ of Leeds (Dip EFL), Bristol Univ (Med), NE London Poly (MA); *m* 30 Oct 1971 (m dis 1980); *Career* sr lectr NE London Poly 1972-, educn advsr and conslt writer Thames TV plc 1975-, literary conslt and contributor Anabas Productions 1986-, freelance writer; *Recreations* learning and appreciating Louis Roederer Cristal; *Style—* Miss Stephanie Connell; Thorndon Hall, Apt 46, Ingrave, Brentwood, Essex; Polytechnic of East London, Livingstone House, Stratford, London E15 (☎ 081 590 7722)

CONNELL, Lady Susan Jean; *née* Carnegie; yr da of 12 Earl of Northesk (d 1975), and Dorothy Mary, *née* Campion (d 1969); *b* 20 Aug 1930; *Educ* Moreton Hall Sch, Courtauld Inst of Art London Univ; *m* 21 May 1955, David Blackall Connell, MB BS, er son of Dr Arthur Blackall Connell; 2 s (Timothy b 1956, Alistair b 1960), 1 da (Caroline b 1958); *Career* picture restorer, memb UK Inst for Conservation; *Recreations* sailing; *Clubs* Royal Dart Yacht, Inst of Advanced Motorists; *Style—* The Lady Susan Connell; Lower Wreyland, Lustleigh, Newton Abbot, Devon TQ13 9TS (☎ 064 77 262)

CONNER, Angela Mary (Mrs Conner Bulmer); da of Judge Cyril Conner, of Midhurst, Sussex, and Mary Stephanie, *née* Douglass; *Educ* spent much of childhood travelling, attended approx 14 schs; *m* John Frederick Bulmer; 1 da (Sophia Georgia McCullough Bulmer); *Career* sculptor; painted pub signs and drew cartoons for music publisher while still at school, solo exhibition Walker Gallery aged 21, documents offr Special Ctee UN NY, designer Design Dept UN, illustrator Columbia Univ Press, acting art dir Reporter Magazine; worked for Barbara Hepworth UK then full-time painter and sculptor, work incl 350 paintings of East River from one window of the UN Building; exhibitions incl solo: Browse & Darby, Istanbul Biennale, Lincoln Centre NY, UN, Jewish Art Museum NY; mixed: Chicago Arts Fair, Gimpel Fils NY, Carnegie Museum Pittsburgh, Nat Portrait Gallery London, Washington Museum, RA; researched and developed use of water for sculpture in contemporary art and contrib to field of environmental art; important public works incl: Victims of Yalta Meml (Brompton Rd London), Quartet, Water Sculpture and Plaza (Heinz Hall Pittsburgh USA), large scale water sculptures for King Fahid and Aston Univ, steel sculpture for St Andrews Cuffley St Albans, sculptured arch for Warwickshire Educn Ctee, numerous cmmns for Duke of Devonshire Collection, three works for Lincoln Center NY; portraits of: Harold MacMillan (Earl of Stockton), Sir John Betjeman, Lord Goodman, Lucien Freud, Rab Butler; *Awards* Honor award of American Inst of Architects, winner Lexington Airport Int Competition, Best Br Equestrian Sculpture award of Br Sporting Art Tst; winner: Hereford City Nat Competition, W Midlands Arts Nat Competition for Aston Univ (18 foot Centre Piece); fell Soc of Equestrian Artists, fell Royal Soc of Br Sculptors; *Recreations* breeding and using Morgan horses and co-founding the breed in Europe; *Style—* Ms Angela Conner; George and Dragon Hall, Mary Place, London W11 4PL; Monnington Court, Monnington on Wye, Hereford HR4 7NL

CONNER, Rev David John; s of William Ernest Conner (d 1989), and Joan Millington, *née* Cheek; *b* 6 April 1947; *Educ* Erith GS, Exeter Coll Oxford (Symes exhibitioner, MA), St Stephen's House Oxford; *m* 10 July 1969, Jayne Maria, da of Lt-Col George E Evans, OBE; 2 s (Andrew David b 1970, Jonathan Paul b 1972); *Career* chaplain St Edward's Sch Oxford 1973-80 (asst chaplain 1971-73), team vicar Wolvercote with Summertown Oxford 1976-80, sr chaplain Winchester Coll 1980-86, vicar St Mary the Great with St Michaels Cambridge 1987-, rural dean of Cambridge 1989-; *Recreations* reading and friends; *Style—* The Rev David Conner; Great St Mary's Vicarage, 39 Madingley Rd, Cambridge CB3 0EL (☎ 0223 355285); Great St Mary's, The University Church, Cambridge CB2 3PQ (☎ 0223 350914)

CONNERADE, Prof Jean-Patrick; s of George Auguste Joseph Louis Connerade, and Marguerite Marie, *née* David; *b* 6 May 1943; *Educ* Lycée Français Charles De Gaulle, Imperial Coll London (BSc, PhD, DIC, DSc); *m* 19 Dec 1970, Jocelyne Charlette, da of Eugene Dubois, of 30 Rue Des Graviers, Mareil-Marly, France (d 1988); 1 s (Florent b 1971), 1 da (Laetita b 1973); *Career* ESRO fell 1968-70, scientist Euro Space Res Inst Italy 1970-73, visiting prof Ecole Normale Supérieure Paris 1979-80, prof of atomic and molecular physics Imperial Coll London 1985- (lectr 1973-79, reader 1980-85); guest researcher Physikalisches Institut Univ of Bonn 1969-; hon ed of jl Physics B, hon treas Save Br Sci Soc, memb Ampboard of Euro Physical Soc; MInstP; *Books* Atomic and Molecular Physics in High Field (co-ed, 1982), Giant Resonances in Atoms Molecules and Solids (1986); *Recreations* painting; *Style—* Prof Jean-Patrick Connerade; 76 Granville Rd, London SW18 5SG; Blackett Laboratory, Imperial College of Science Technology and Medicine, Prince Consort Rd, London SW7 2BZ (☎ 071 225 8860, fax 071 589 9463, telex 929484 IMPCOLG)

CONNERY, Sean (Thomas); s of Joseph Connery, and Euphamia; *b* 25 Aug 1930; *m* 1, 29 Nov 1962 (m dis 1974), Diane (who m 2, 1985, Anthony Shaffer, playwright), da of Sir Raphael West Cilento (d 1985), and former w of Andrea Volpt; 1 s (Jason b 1963 (actor)); m 2, Jan 1975, Micheline Roquebrune; *Career* actor; incl: Tarzan's Greatest Adventure (1959), The Longest Day (1962), Dr No (1963), From Russia With Love (1964), Goldfinger (1965), Thunderball (1965), A Fine Madness (1966), You Only Live Twice (1967), Shalako (1968), Diamonds are Forever (1971), Murder on the Orient Express (1974), The Man Who Would be King (1975), Outland (1981), The Name of the Rose (1986), The Untouchables (1987), etc; fell Royal Scottish Academy of Music and Drama; Hon DLitt Heriot-Watt Univ 1981; *Style—* Sean Connery Esq; Michael S Ovitz, Creative Artists Agency Inc, Suite 1400, 1888 Century Pk E, Los Angeles, Calif 90067, USA

CONNICK, Harold Ivor; s of Aaron Connick, of London (d 1963), and Raie, *née* Winner (d 1972); *b* 25 Jan 1927; *Educ* Ealing GS, LSE (LLB); *m* 16 Oct 1955, Claire Grace, da of John William Benson, of 9 Roehampton Close, London; 2 s (David b 1956, Jeremy b 1963), 1 da (Lesley b 1956); *Career* admitted slr 1952; sr ptnr Thornton Lynne and Lawson; attached Army War Crimes Singapore 1946-48; dir: UDS Group plc 1975-83 (dep chm 1983), Land Securities plc 1987-; vice pres Br ORT 1989- (chm 1984-89); *Recreations* golf, theatre, cricket; *Clubs* MCC, Roehampton, IOD; *Style—* H I Connick, Esq; 54 Fairacres, Roehampton Lane, London SW15 5LX (☎ 081 876 7188); 56 Portland Place, London W1N 4BD (☎ 071 580 6688, fax 071 637 1558, telex 263200 TLLAWS)

CONNOCK, Stephen Leslie; s of Leslie Thomas Connock, of Peterborough, Cambs, and Gladys Edna, *née* Chappell; *b* 16 Nov 1949; *Educ* Sheffield Univ (BA), LSE (MPhil); *m* 18 Aug 1973, Margaret Anne, da of Richard Bolger, of Palmers Green, London; 2 s (Adrian b 1981, Mark b 1985); *Career* mgmnt devpt manager Philips Electronics 1985-87 (industl relations mangr 1979-85), gen mangr human resources Pearl Assur 1987-; MIPM 1973; *Books* Industrial Relations Training for Managers, Cost Effective Strategies in Industral Relations (1985); *Recreations* music, writing; *Style—* Stephen Connock, Esq; Pearl Assurance, High Holborn, London WC1V 7EB (☎ 071 405 8441)

CONNOLLY, Dr John Henry; s of John Henry Connolly (d 1953), of 8 Roslyn Ave, Bangor, Co Down, and Catherine Anne, *née* Campbell (d 1973); *b* 4 Sept 1930; *Educ* Bangor GS, the Queen's Univ of Belfast (MB BCh, MD); *m* 11 April 1963, Patricia Wilhelmina Robinson, da of Thomas Dennison Corbett (d 1982), of 103 Victoria Rd, Bangor, Co Down; 1 s (Paul b 1964); *Career* res fell Nat Fund for Poliomyelitis Res 1956-57, visiting asst prof Johns Hopkins Univ Baltimore USA 1959-60, hon lectr in microbiology Queen's Univ Belfast 1960-, conslt virologist Royal Victoria Hosp Belfast 1968-; memb Jt Advsy Ctee on Dangerous Pathogens of Health and Agric Mins and Health and Safety Cmmn London 1983-87, govr Bangor GS; MRCPI 1964, FRCPI 1975, MRCPath 1966, FRCPath 1978; *Publications* numerous papers on polio vaccines, Q fever and measles virus in subacute sclerosing panencephalitis; *Recreations* golf, sailing; *Clubs* Bangor Golf (Co Down); *Style—* Dr John Connolly; 50 Broadway, Bangor, Co Down BT20 4RG (☎ 0247 460020), Regional Virus Laboratory, Royal Victoria Hospital, Belfast BT12 6BN (☎ 0232 240503 ext 2662, fax 0232 240899)

CONNOLLY, Joseph Edward; s of Patrick Joseph Connolly (d 1985), and Kathryn Mary, *née* Mcnaney; *b* 15 June 1950; *Educ* Cornell Univ (AB), Harvard Univ (MBA); *Career* second vice pres Continental Bank London 1975-81, gp head Bank of Boston London 1981-83, sr analyst Moody's Investors NY 1984-86, dir Euro Ratings Ltd London 1986-88, vice pres and gp head Citibank London 1988-; memb Irish Club of Eaton Square London; *Books* The International Data Communications Market; *Recreations* racing, looking at pictures, squash; *Style—* Joseph Connolly, Esq; 52A Eaton Place, London SW1 (☎ 071 245 1223); 83 Montvale Ave, Woburn, Massachuetts; Citibank NA, 335 Strand, London WC1 (☎ 071 438 0437)

CONNOLLY, Dr (Charles) Kevin; TD (1981); s of Dr Charles Vincent Connolly (d 1961), of Rothwell, Kettering, Northamptonshire, and Frances Elliott, *née* Turner; *b* 26 Sept 1936; *Educ* Ampleforth, Gonville and Caius Coll Cambridge, Middx Hosp Med Sch (MA, MB BChir); *m* 24 Oct 1970, Rachel Bronwen, da of Lewis Philip Jameson Evans (d 1972), of Bromsgrove, Worcs; 3 da (Kate b 1971, Celia b 1973, Clare b 1975); *Career* house physician Middx Hosp 1961, resident med offr Brompton Hosp 1963, sr med registrar St Georges Hosp 1967, conslt physician Darlington and Northallerton Hosp 1970-, clinical tutor Northallerton Health Dist 1974-82, examiner Temporary Registration and Provisional Licence Assessment Bd 1975-, hon clinical lectr Dept of medicine Univ of Newcastle upon Tyne 1988-; vice pres Nat Assoc of Clinical Tutors 1981-83, past and present memb various ctees RCP and Br Thoracic Soc; pres: Northallerton Div Br Med Assoc 1974-76, Yorks Thoracic Soc 1982-84, Northern Thoracic Soc; memb: Darlington Health Authy 1981, Thoracic Soc, Med Res Soc, Exec and Med Ctees Breathe North Appeal; Liveryman Worshipful Co of Apothecaries 1964; MRCP 1964, FRCP 1977; *Recreations* tennis, skiing; *Style—* Dr C K Connolly, TD; Aldbrough House, Aldbrough St John, Richmond, N Yorks DL11 7TP (☎ 0325 374 244); 39 Stanhope Rd, Darlington, Co Durham (☎ 0325 462 593)

CONNOLLY, Patrick; s of Eugene Connolly, and Teresa, *née* Brogan; *b* 25 June 1970; *Educ* St John Bosco Secdy Sch; *Career* professional footballer Dundee Utd, debut 1988, over 25 appearances; Scotland: 4 youth caps, 3 under 21 caps in Euro Championships; *Recreations* listening to music, watching films; *Style—* Patrick Connolly, Esq; Dundee Utd FC, Tannadice Park, Tannadice St, Dundee

CONNOLLY, Rainier Campbell; s of George Augustus Victor Connolly (d 1952), of Brighton, and Margaret Winifred, *née* Edgell (d 1981); *b* 15 July 1919; *Educ* Bedford Sch, St Bartholomew's Med Coll; *m* 20 Nov 1948, Elizabeth Fowler, da of Prof Charles Gilbert Cullis (d 1944); 1 s (Richard b 1955), 2 da (Susan b 1949, Janet b 1952); *Career* 2 Lt Royal Sussex Regt TA 1937-39; Maj RAMC 1943-47, Italy 1943-45 (despatches), India 1945-46; neurosurgeon St Bartholomew's Hosp 1959-84; conslt neurosurgeon: King Edward VII Hosp for Offrs, Royal Victoria Hosp 1948-52, Midland Centre for Neurosurgery 1952-59, Royal Nat Orthopaedic Hosp 1959-84; civilian conslt in neurosurgery to RN 1971-84, Hunterian Prof RCS 1961; pres Neurological Section RSM 1981; Freeman City of London, Liveryman Worshipful Soc of Apothecaries; FRCS 1947; *Recreations* foreign travelling; *Style—* Rainier Campbell Connolly, Esq; 149 Harley St, London W1N 2DH (☎ 071 935 4444); Manor Lodge, Rickmansworth Rd, Northwood, Middx HA6 2QT

CONNOLLY, Terence Ralph; s of Ralph Dennis Connolly, of Esher, Surrey, and Doreen Mabel Connolly; *b* 28 Sept 1943; *Educ* Surbiton GS; *m* 16 July 1966, Kathryn Mary; 2 da (Emma Claire b 1970, Sarah Louise b 1976); *Career* gp md Chrysalis Gp plc 1973, FICA 1966; *Recreations* sailing; *Clubs* Reform; *Style—* Terence R Connolly, Esq; High Trees, Hydon Heath, Godalming, Surrey (☎ 04868 212261); 12 Stratford Place, London W1 (☎ 071 408 2355)

CONNOR, Howard Arthur; s of Arthur Albert William Connor (d 1969, Sgt RAF), of 10 Mansfield Hill, Chingford, London, and Winifred Edith, *née* Rugg (d 1983); *b* 31 Jan 1938; *Educ* Richmond House Sch Chingford, Chingford Co HS; *m* 23 July 1960, Dorothy Myrtle, da of Frederick Hobbs (d 1981), of 34 Elmfield Rd, Chingford, London; 2 da (Alison b 1964, Melinda b 1966); *Career* CA; princ G H Attenborough and Co, md The Business and Financial Advisory Co Ltd; life vice pres Hoddesdon and Broxbourne C of C, chm Broxbourne Parliamentary Gp, memb Cons Assoc Business Gp; FCA, ATII; *Recreations* horse riding, skiing, badminton; *Clubs* Burford, Rotary of Hoddesdon (former pres); *Style—* Howard Connor, Esq; Spinney House, The Spinney, Broxbourne, Hertfordshire (☎ 0992 468071); 34 Fawkon Walk, Hoddesdon, Herts (☎ 0992 460016)

CONNOR, Prof James Michael; s of James Connor (d 1981), of Grappenhall, Cheshire, and Mona, *née* Hall; *b* 18 June 1951; *Educ* Lymm GS, Univ of Liverpool (BSc, MB ChB, MD); *m* 6 Jan 1979, Rachel Alyson Clare, da of Donald Brooks, of Woodbridge, Suffolk; 2 da (Emily b 1986, Katherine b 1987); *Career* res fell Univ of Liverpool 1977-79, resident in internal med and instr in med genetics Johns Hopkins Univ Baltimore USA 1979-82, Wellcome Tst Sr Lectr Univ of Glasgow 1984-87, prof of med genetics, dir of the W of Scotland Regnl Genetics Serv and hon conslt Univ of Glasgow 1987-; memb: Jt Ctee on Higher Med Trg, RCP Standing Ctee on Clinical Genetics; FRCP Glasgow; *Books* Essential Medical Genetics (3 edn, 1990), Prenatal Diagnosis in Obstetric Practice (1989); *Recreations* fly fishing, windsurfing; *Style—* Prof James Connor; Westbank Cottage, 84 Montgomery Street, Eaglesham, Strathclyde G76 0AU (☎ 035 53 2626); University of Medical Genetics, Duncan Guthrie Institute, Yorkhill, Glasgow G3 8SJ (☎ 041 339 6996, fax 041 357 4277)

CONNOR, Jeremy George; s of Joseph Connor (d 1975), and Mabel Emmeline, *née* Adams (d 1985); *b* 14 Dec 1938; *Educ* Beaumont, UCL (LLB, DRS); *Career* called to the Bar Middle Temple 1961; rec SE Circuit, appointed to Treasy List Central Criminal Ct 1973, Met Stipendiary Magistrate 1979-, chm Inner London Juvenile Courts 1980-, memb Central Cncl of Probation Exec Ctee 1981, chm Inner London Probation Ctee 1989-, Br Acad of Forensic Sciences 1989 (chem Exec Cncl 1983); Freeman City of London 1980, memb Livery Ctee Worshipful Co of Fanmakers 1987-; underwriting memb of Lloyds; *Publications* chapter (Jury) in Archbold, Criminal Pleading, Evidence and Practice (38 and 39 edns); *Recreations* travel, theatre, occasional broadcasting; *Clubs* Garrick, RSM; *Style—* Jeremy Connor, Esq; Bow Street Court, London WC2

CONNOR, Leslie John; s of William John Connor (d 1980), of Lancs, and Doris Eliza, *née* Neild; *b* 23 April 1932; *Educ* St Mary's Coll Crosby, Univ of Liverpool (BA), California Univ of Advanced Studies (MBA); *m* 1951, Jean Margaret, da of Roger Pendleton, of Lancashire; 2 da (Christine Lesley b 1964, Hilary Elaine b 1968); *Career* exec trainee C and A Modes 1956-58, Gt Universal Stores 1958-63, Connor Fin Corp 1963-, md Leisure and Gen Hldgs Ltd 1970-73, fndr and chm First Castle Electronics plc 1973-86; dir: Connor Fin Advsy Servs Ltd, Connor Fin Corp, L J Connor Conslts Ltd, W J Connor Properties (and Publishing) Ltd, Southern Litho Supplies Ltd, Manordale Developments Ltd, Manordale (Southern) Ltd, Midview Ltd; Br Show Pony Soc (BSPS): cncl memb 1978-83, treas 1979-83, tstee 1979-, vice pres 1983-; tstee Monks Ferry Trg Tst 1988-; *Books* The Managed Growth of a Quoted British Public Company, The Working Hunter Pony (jtly); *Recreations* showing horses, farming, antiques, porcelain and painting, walking, writing, golf; *Clubs* Farmers; *Style—* Leslie Connor, Esq; Greenbank, Prescot Rd, Aughton, Lancashire L39 5AG (☎ 0695 423573, fax 0695 423395); Connor Finance Corp Ltd, Bowker's Green Court, Bowker's Green Aughton, Lancashire L39 6TA (☎ 0695 424200, fax 0695 424109)

CONNOR, (Patrick) Rearden; MBE (1967); s of John Connor, and Bridget Riordan; *b* 19 Feb 1907; *Educ* Presentation Coll Cork; *m* 1942, Malinka Marie, da of Benjamin West Smith (d 1927), of Folkingham, Lincs; *Career* Res and Devpt Dept of MOD; critic of fiction The Fortnightly 1935-37, reader of fiction for Cassell 1948-56; work has been included in: Best Short Stories anthology twice, Pick of Today's Short Stories, Whit Burnett anthology (USA); author; *Books* Shake Hands with the Devil (filmed 1958), Rude Earth, Salute to Aphrodite (USA), I am Death, Time to Kill (USA), Men Must Live, The Sword of Love, Wife to Colum, The Devil Among the Tailors, My Love to the Gallows, Hunger of the Heart, The Singing Stone, The House of Cain; under the pen name Peter Malin: To Kill Is My Vocation, River, Sing me a Song, Kobo the Brave; *Clubs* Soc of Authors; *Style—* Rearden Connor, Esq, MBE; 79 Balsdean Rd, Woodingdean, Brighton BN2 6PG (☎ 0273 34032)

CONNOR, Roger David; s of Thomas Bernard Connor, of Aisby, Lincolns (d 1962), and Susie Violet, *née* Spittlehouse (d 1964); *b* 8 June 1939; *Educ* Merchant Taylors', Brunel Coll of Advanced Sci and Technol; *m* 25 March 1967, Sandra, da of Eldred Rolef Holmes, of Bicester, Oxon; 2 s (Hugh b 1969, Rupert b 1970); *Career* admitted slr 1968; ptnr Messrs Hodders 1970-83, met stipendiary magistrate 1983-, rec of Crown Ct 1987; memb Ctee of Magistrates 1986; *Recreations* music, gardening, golf, bee keeping; *Style—* Roger Connor, Esq; Bourn's Meadow, Little Missenden, Amersham, Bucks HP7 0RF (☎ 02406 2760); Marylebone Magistrates' Court, London NW1 5QJ (☎ 071 703 0909)

CONNOR, Bishop of, 1987-; Rt Rev Samuel Greenfield Poyntz; s of Rev James Poyntz (d 1968), and Katharine Jane Poyntz; *b* 4 March 1926; *Educ* Portora Royal Sch Enniskillen, Univ of Dublin (MA, BD, PhD); *m* 1952, Noreen Henrietta Armstrong; 1 s, 2 da; *Career* deacon 1950, priest 1951, archdeacon of Dublin and examining chaplain to Archbishop of Dublin 1974-78, Bishop of Cork Cloyne and Ross 1978-87; chm Irish Cncl of Churches 1986-88, vice pres Br Cncl of Churches 1987-90; *Style—* The Rt Rev the Lord Bishop of Connor; Bishop's House, 22 Deramore Park, Belfast, Northern Ireland BT9 5JU

CONOLEY, Mary Patricia; da of Sir Jack Rampton, of Tonbridge, Kent, and Lady Eileen, *née* Hart; *b* 7 Sept 1951; *Educ* Walthamstow Hall Kent, Univ of Birmingham (BA); *m* 1972, (m dis 1980), Christopher Conoley; *Career* PR offr (UK) The Dredging & Construction Co Ltd 1973-77, PR consultant UK and Aust 1977-81, sr public affairs offr Woodside Offshore Petroleum PTY Ltd 1981-84, gp PR exec The Littlewoods Organisation 1985-88, dir Shandwick Communications Ltd 1989-, jt md Shandwick PR 1991-; FRGS 1984; *Recreations* skiing, diving, horse riding; *Style—* Mrs Mary Conoley; Shandwick Communications Ltd, 114 Cromwell Rd, London SW7 (☎ 071 835 1001, fax 071 373 4311)

CONOLLY-CAREW, Capt Hon Patrick Thomas; s and h of 6 Baron Carew, CBE; *b* 6 March 1938; *Educ* Harrow, RMA Sandhurst; *m* 30 April 1962, Celia Mary, da of Col Hon (Charles) Guy Cubitt, CBE, DSO, TD; 1 s, 3 da; *Career* late Capt RHG, former int show jumping rider; memb Irish Olympic Three Day Event team: Mexico 1968, Munich 1972, Montreal 1976; pres Equestrian Fedn of Ireland 1979-84, chm Three Day Event Ctee Federatian Equestre Internatienale (memb Bureau) 1989; *Recreations* all equestrian sports, shooting, cricket, bridge; *Clubs* Cavalry and Guards', Kildare St and Univ (Dublin); *Style—* Capt the Hon Patrick Conolly-Carew; Donadea House, Naas, Co Kildare, Ireland

CONQUEST, (George) Robert Acworth; OBE (1955); s of Robert Folger Westcott Conquest (d 1959), of Vence, Alpes Maritimes, and Rosamund Alys, *née* Acworth (d 1973); *b* 15 July 1917; *Educ* Winchester, Univ of Grenoble, Magdalen Coll Oxford (MA, DLitt); *m* 1, 1942 (m dis 1948), Joan, *née* Watkins; 2 s (John b 1943, Richard b 1945); m 2, 1948 (m dis 1962), Tatiana, *née* Mikhailova; m 3, 1964 (m dis 1978), Caroleen, *née* Macfarlane; m 4, 1979, Elizabeth, da of late Col Richard D Neece, USAF; *Career* Capt Oxfordshire and Bucks LI 1939-46; HM Foreign Serv 1946-56: 2 sec Sofia, 1 Sec UK Delgn to the UN, princ FO; fell LSE 1956-58, visiting poet Univ of Buffalo 1959-60, lit ed The Spectator 1962-63, sr fell Columbia Univ 1964-65, fell The Woodrow Wilson Int Center 1976-77, sr res fell The Hoover Inst Stanford Univ 1977-79 and 1981-, visiting scholar The Heritage Fndn 1980-81, res assoc Harvard Univ 1983-; memb Soc for the Promotion of Roman Studies; FRSL 1972, FBIS 1968; *Books* incl: Poems (1955), Power and Policy in the USSR (1961), Between Mar and Venus (1963), The Great Terror (1968), Lenin (1972), The Abomination of Moab (1979), Present Danger (1979), Forays (1979), The Harvest of Sorrow (1986), New and Collected Poems (1988); *Clubs* Traveller's; *Style—* Robert Conquest, Esq, OBE; 52 Peter Coutts Circle, Stanford, California 94305, USA; Hoover Institution, Stanford, California 94305, USA (☎ 415 723 1647)

CONRAD, Conrad John; s of Marc Scheinberg (d 1981), of London, and Martha, *née* Greenberg; *b* 25 May 1919; *Educ* Tollington GS Muswell Hill; *m* 25 July 1942, Florence Louisa Ellen (Flon), da of late George Webb; 1 s (Gary Kelvyn b 17 Aug 1945), 1 da (Lois Karyl b 10 April 1949); *Career* WWII section ldr NCC 1939-46; Merit Toys plc (formerly J & L Randall Ltd): joined 1946, chief buyer 1949, exec dir 1957, bd dir 1963, chief exec 1978, ret 1988; joined parent co Bluebird Toys plc 1988, resigned 1989; ind conslt to toy indust 1989-; qualified Samaritans; *Recreations* philately, photography, swimming; *Style—* Conrad Conrad, Esq; Ashmount, 81 Hatfield Rd, Potters Bar, Herts EN6 1NZ (☎ 0707 55992, fax 0707 47323)

CONRAN, Elizabeth Margaret; *née* Johnston; da of James Johnston (d 1954), and Elizabeth Russell, *née* Wilson (d 1987); *b* 5 May 1939; *Educ* Falkirk HS, Univ of Glasgow (MA); *m* 26 Nov 1970, (George) Loraine Conran (d 1986), s of Col George Hay Montgomery Conran (d 1940); 1 da (Violet b 1972); *Career* res asst Univ of Glasgow 1959-60, asst curator The Iveagh Bequest Kenwood London 1960-63, keeper of paintings City Art Gallery Manchester 1963-74, arts advsr Greater Manchester Cncl 1974-79, curator The Bowes Museum Barnard Castle Co Durham 1979-; tstee Teesdale Preservation Tst; FMA 1969, FRSA 1987; *Recreations* dance, gardens; *Style—* Mrs Elizabeth Conran; 31 Thorngate, Barnard Castle, Co Durham DL12 8QB (☎ 0833 31055); The Bowes Museum, Barnard Castle, Co Durham DL12 8NP (☎ 0833 690 606)

CONRAN, Jasper Alexander; s of Sir Terence Conran, *qv*, and Shirley Ida, *née* Pearce; *b* 12 Dec 1959; *Educ* Bryanston, Parsons Sch of Design NY; *Career* md and designer Jasper Conran Ltd; Fil d'Or (Int Linen award) 1982 and 1983, British Fashion Cncl Designer of the Year award 1986-87, Fashion Gp of America award 1987; costumes for Almeida Theatre prodn of Anouilh's The Rehearsal Sept 1990, transferred to Garrick Theatre Nov 1990; *Style—* Jasper Conran Esq; 49-50 Gt Marlborough St, London W1V 1DB (☎ 071 437 0386 and 071 439 8572, fax 071 734 7761, telex 24517 JASPER G)

CONRAN, Shirley Ida; da of W Thirlby Pearce, and Ida Pearce; *b* 21 Sept 1932; *Educ* St Paul's Girls' Sch; *m* 1955 (m dis 1962), as his 2 w, Terence Orby Conran (now Sir Terence), *qv*; 2 s; *Career* designer; co fndr Conran Fabrics Ltd 1957; memb Selection Ctee Design Centre 1961; journalist, first woman's ed Observer Colour Magazine 1964, with Observer to 1969, woman ed Daily Mail 1969-70; *Books* Superwoman (1975), Superwoman Year Book (1976), Actionwomen (1977), Futurewomen (with E Sidney), Lace (1982), The Magic Garden (1983), Lace 2 (1985), Savages (1987); *Style—* Ms Shirley Conran; 39 Avenue Princesse Grace, Monaco

CONRAN, Sir Terence Orby; *b* 4 Oct 1931; *Educ* Bryanston; *m* 1, 1955 (m dis 1962), Shirley Ida Pearce (*see* Shirley Conran); 2 s; m 2, 1963, Caroline Herbert (the cookery writer Caroline Conran); 2 s, 1 da; *Career* chm Conran Holdings Ltd 1965-68; jt chm Ryman Conran Ltd 1968-71; dir: Conran Ink Ltd 1969, Conran Design Gp 1971; chm Habitat Gp Ltd 1971; dir The Neal Street Restaurant 1972; chm Habitat France SA 1973; dir: Conran Stores Inc 1977-, Electra Risk Capital Gp plc 1981-84; chm J Hepworth and Son Ltd 1981-83 (dir 1979-83); dir Conran Roche Ltd 1982; chm Habitat Mothercare plc 1982; dir Conran Octopus 1983; chm Richard Shops 1983-87; dir Heal and Son Ltd 1983-87; chm Butlers Wharf Ltd 1984; dir Michelin House Development 1985; vice pres FNAC 1985; dir: BHS 1986, Bibendum Restaurant Ltd 1986; chm and chief exec Storehouse plc (following merger of Habitat/Mothercare and BHS) 1986-90; FSIAD; presented with SIAD medal 1980; RSA Bicentenary Medal 1984; Hon FRIBA 1984; memb: Cncl RCA, V and A Advsy Cncl 1979-83, Tstee V and A 1984-; established Conran Foundation for design educ and research 1981; kt 1982; *Books* The House Book (1974), The Kitchen Book (1977), The Bedroom and Bathroom Book (1978), The Cook Book (with Caroline Conran, 1980), The New House Book (1985), Conran Director of Design (1985), Plants at Home (1986), The Soft Furnishings Book (1986), Terence Conran's France (1987); *Recreations* gardening, cooking; *Style—* Sir Terence Conran; Storehouse plc, The Heal's Building, 196 Tottenham Court Rd, London W1P 9LD (☎ 071 631 0101)

CONROY, Harry; *b* 6 April 1943; *m* Margaret; 3 children; *Career* trainee laboratory technician Southern Gen Hosp 1961-62, night messenger (copy boy) Scottish Daily Express 1962-63; reporter Scottish Daily Mail 1966-67, fin corr Daily Record 1969- (reporter 1964-66 and 1967-69); dep father of chapel Daily Record and Sunday Mail Chapel 1968-69, father of chapel Daily Record and Sunday Mail NUJ Chapel 1975-77, Nat Exec Cncl memb for nat newspapers and agencies outside London 1982- (vice pres 1980-81, pres 1981-82), chm Scotland W Area Cncl 1980-81; ADM delegate: 1970, 1971, 1972, 1973, 1975; TUC delegate: 1981, 1982, 1983; STUC delegate: 1981, 1982, 1983, 1984, 1985; FOC Daily Record and Sunday Mail 1984-; memb ASTMS 1961-62, assoc memb Gen and Municipal Boilermakers Union 1984-85, gen sec NUJ 1986- (memb 1963-); *Style—* Harry Conroy, Esq; NUJ, Acorn Ho, 314-320 Gray's Inn Rd, London WC1X 8DP

CONROY, Stephen Alexander; s of Stephen James Conroy, of Renton, Dunbartonshire, and Elizabeth Ann, *née* Walker; *b* 2 March 1964; *Educ* St Patricks HS Dunbarton, Glasgow Sch of Art (BA, Harry McLean Bequest, Jock McFie award, postgrad award); *Career* artist; solo exhibitions: Marlborough Fine Art London and tour 1989, Glasgow Art Gallery & Museum 1989, Whitworth Art Gallery Manchester 1989; gp exhibitions incl: The Vigorous Imagination - New Scottish Art (Scottish Nat Gallery of Modern Art, Edinburgh) 1987, The New British Painting tour USA 1988, Scottish Art Since 1990 (Scottish Nat Gallery of Modern Art Edinburgh and The Barbican London) 1989, Glasgows Great British Art Exhibition 1990; work in the collections of: Aberdeen Art Gallery, The British Cncl, Birmingham Art Gallery, Contemporary Art Soc, Metropolitan Museum of Art NY, RCS, Robert Fleming Holdings Ltd, Scottish Nat Gallery of Modern Art, Scottish Nat Portrait Gallery; *Style—* Stephen Conroy, Esq; Marlborough Fine Art, 6 Albemarle St, London W1X 4BY (☎ 071 629 5161, fax 071 629 6338)

CONROY HAWKS, Lady Kara Virginia Louisa; *née* King-Tenison; da of 10 Earl of Kingston (d 1948); *b* 1938; *m* 1964 (m dis 1974), Anthony John Conroy Hawks, MB BS, DCH; 1 da; *Style—* The Lady Kara Conroy Hawks; White Gates, Old Romsey Rd, Cadnam, Southampton SO4 2NP

CONSTABLE, Prof (Charles) John; s of Charles Constable, of Bedford, and Gladys May, *née* Morris; *b* 20 Jan 1936; *Educ* Durham Sch, Univ of Cambridge (MA), Univ of London (BSc), Harvard (DBA); *m* 9 April 1960, Elisabeth Mary, da of Ronald Light (d 1981); 3 s (Charles b 1962, Giles b 1965, Piers b 1971), 1 da (Harriet b 1961); *Career* mgmnt educator and consit; visiting prof Cranfield Sch of Mgmnt and Manchester Business Sch; prof of mgmnt Cranfield Sch of Mgmnt 1971-82 (dir 1982-85); dir gen Br Inst of Mgmnt 1985-86; non-exec dir: Lodge Ceramics Ltd and SIMAC Ltd 1982-90, International Military Services Ltd 1984-, Lloyds-Abbey-Life Plc 1987-; govr and dep chm Harpur Tst 1979-; memb: NEDO Heavy Electrical Machinery EDC 1977-87, N Beds DHA 1987-90; chm Bright Technical Developments Ltd 1989-; *Books* Group Assessment Programmes (with D A Smith, 1966), Text and Cases in Operations Management (with C C New, 1976), Cases in Strategic Management (with J Stopford and D Channon, 1980), The Making of British Managers (with R McCormick, 1987); *Recreations* family, golf; *Clubs* Bedfordshire Golf, Minehead and W Somerset Golf; *Style—* Professor John Constable; 20 Kimbolton Rd, Bedford MK40 2NR (☎ 0234 212576); Gore Point, Porlock Weir, Minehead, Somerset

CONSTABLE, Group Captain John Hurn; s of Prof F H Constable (d 1975), and Sance Helena Catherock, *née* Robson (d 1981); *b* 19 Aug 1934; *Educ* Hitchin GS, RAF Coll, RAF Staff Coll, Nat Def Coll, Open Univ, Univ of London (BA); *m* 12 Aug 1961, Karin, da of Karsten Emmanuel Amundsen, of Oslo, Norway; 1 s (Harald John Catherock b 6 June 1962), 1 da (Helen Katrine (Dr Lindley) b 19 Nov 1964); *Career* cmmnd RAF (Sec Branch) 1956; various appts incl: MOD, Norway, Germany then RAF Wyton 1976-78, Directing Staff Nat Def Coll 1978-80, dep dir RAF Ground Trg MOD 1980-83, cmd accountant RAF Support Cmd 1983-87, ret 1987; ed jls: RAF Coll, RAF Staff Coll, Nat Def Coll; hon sec St Boniface PCC 1970-73, hon treas St Mary's PCC 1983-85; Freeman City of London 1982, memb Ct of Assts Worshipful Co Chartered Secs and Admins 1987-; hon sec City of London Sheriffs' Soc 1987-, secondary of London and Under Sheriff and High Bailiff of Southwark 1987-; FRGS 1975, FRSA 1977, FCIS 1977 (2 prizes), FInstAM 1977, FBIM 1980; *Recreations* fell walking, travel, classical music and art, history; *Clubs* RAF; *Style—* Group Captain John Constable; Central Criminal Ct, Old Bailey, London EC4M 7BS (☎ 071 248 3277)

CONSTABLE, Dr (Frank) Leonard; TD (1965), DL (1988), QHP (1975); s of Francis

Albert Constable (d 1974), and Mary, *née* Nichol (d 1979); *b* 28 May 1920; *Educ* Dame Allan's Sch, Univ of Durham (BSc, MB BS, MD); *m* 7 July 1951, Jean Margaret, da of Cdr Ivor McIvor, RN (d 1956); 3 s (John b 1957, Christopher b 1959, Timothy b 1962); *Career* Lt REME 1942-46, Maj RAMC 1951-73 (latterly Lt-Col), Col cmmd 201 Gen Hosp 1973, Dep Cdr NE Dist TA 1973-79, cmdt Tyne & Wear Army Cadet force 1979-81, Hon Col 251 Field Ambulance 1978-84; house physician Royal Victoria Infirmary Newcastle upon Tyne 1951-53, lectr Univ of Edinburgh 1953-61, conslt microbiologist Royal Victoria Infirmary 1961-85; cdr Northumbria St John's Ambulance; FRCPath 1963; KStJ; *Recreations* fly fishing; *Style*— Dr Leonard Constable, TD, DL, QHP; 17 Roseworth Ave, Gosforth, Newcastle upon Tyne NE3 1NB (☎ 091 285 1223)

CONSTANT, p Richard Ashley Mayricke; MBE (1983); s of Maj Ashley Henry Constant (d 1985), and Mabel Catherine (Kate), *née* Meyricke (d 1972); *b* 25 Nov 1954; *Educ* King's Sch Canterbury, Univ of Durham (BA), RMAS; *m* 1984, Melinda Jane, da of late H J Davies; 2 s (Llewelyn Ashley Meyricke b 1985, Tristam Ashley Meyricke b 1987), 2 da (Sophia b 1989, Rosanna (twin) b 1989); *Career* cmmnd Royal Green Jackets 1973, ret with the rank of maj; merchant banker Robert Fleming & Co Limited 1985-89; md: Valin Pollen plc 1990 (asst md Investor Relations 1989), Gavin Anderson & Company UK Limited 1991; *Recreations* shooting, fishing; *Clubs* Royal Green Jackets, Wig and Pen; *Style*— Richard Constant, Esq, MBE; Park Lodge, Aislaby, nr Whitby, North Yorkshire (☎ 0947 810250); Gavin Anderson & Co Ltd, 18 Grosvenor Gardens, London SW1W 8DH (☎ 071 730 3456)

CONSTANTINE, David John; s of William Bernard Constantine, of Deganwy, North Wales, and Bertha, *née* Gleave; *b* 4 March 1944; *Educ* Manchester GS, Wadham Coll Oxford (BA, DPhil); *m* 9 July 1966, Helen Frances, da of Richard Stanley Best; 1 s (Simon Martin b 1 Oct 1972), 1 da (Mary Ann b 27 Nov 1968); *Career* sr lectr in German Univ of Durham 1979-80 (lectr 1969-79), fell in German Queen's Coll Oxford 1980-; poetry: A Brightness to Cast Shadows (1980), Watching for Dolphins (1983, Alice Hunt Barlett award), Madder (1987, Southern Arts Literature prize); fiction: Davies (1985); Selected Poems of Friedrich Hölderlin (trans, 1990); academic works: Early Greek Travellers and the Hellenic Ideal (1984, Runciman prize), Hölderlin (1988); fndr memb Durham Cyrenians (a charity for the homeless, sec 1972-80); *Recreations* walking; *Style*— David Constantine, Esq

CONSTANTINE, Air Chief Marshal Sir Hugh Alex; KBE (1958, CBE 1944), CB (1946), DSO (1942); s of Cdr Henry Constantine, RN, of Southsea, Hants, and Alice Louise Squire; *b* 23 May 1908; *Educ* Christ's Hosp, RAF Coll Cranwell; *m* 1937, Helen, da of J W Bourke, of Sydney, Aust; 1 da; *Career* cmmnd RAF 1927, 56(F) Sqdn CFS instr, RAF Armour Cars (Iraq, despatches) 1934-36, dep Chief of Staff SHAPE 1957-58, bomber cmd 1939-45, Cmd 5 Bomber Gp 1945 (despatches), Air Marshal 1958, AOC-in-C Flying Trg Cmd 1959-61, Cmdt IDC 1961-64, Air Chief Marshal 1961, ret 1964; coordinator Anglo-American Community Relns MOD (Air) 1964-77; Hon LLD Univ of Warwick 1978; *Style*— Air Chief Marshal Sir Hugh Constantine, KBE, CB, DSO; 14 Cadogan Court, Draycott Ave, London SW3 3BX (☎ 071 581 8821)

CONSTANTINE, Joseph; s of Maj Robert Alfred Constantine, TD, JP (d 1968), and Marie Leonie Françoise Van Haaren, eleventh in descent through female line from William the Silent, Count of Nassau in the Netherlands and Prince of Orange; *b* 12 Feb 1928; *Educ* Eton; *m* 1954, Mary Rose, da of late Harwood Lawrence Cotter, and Rosemary, Lady Ley (d 1977), yr da of late Capt Duncan Macpherson, RN, and sister of late Francis Cameron Macpherson of Cluny, 26 Chief of Clan Macpherson; 2 da (Annette (Hon Mrs Jonathan Boyd) b 1956, Susannah b 1962); *Career* Lt Coldstream Gds 1946-48; chm Constantine Hldgs Ltd 1964-; FRICS 1955; *Recreations* painting; *Clubs* Brooks's, Turf; *Style*— Joseph Constantine Esq; 9 Canning Place, London W8 (☎ 071 584 7640); The Priory, Knipton, Grantham, Lincs (☎ 047 6870 238)

CONSTANTINE OF STANMORE, Baron (Life Peer UK 1981), of Stanmore in Greater London; Theodore Constantine; CBE (1956), AE (1945), DL (Greater London 1967); s of Leonard Constantine, of London, and Fanny Louise Constantine; *b* 15 March 1910; *Educ* Acton Coll; *m* 1935, Sylvia Mary (d 1990), yr da of Wallace Henry Legge-Pointing, of London; 1 s (Hon Roy b 1936), 1 da (Hon Jill (Hon Mrs Murray) b 1938); *Career* sits as Conservative Peer in the House of Lords; served WWII RAuxAF; dir of industrial hldg co 1956-59, chm of public companies 1959-85; chm Anscon Ltd; pres National Union Cons and Unionist Assocs 1980- (chm 1967-68); High Sheriff Greater London 1967; Master Worshipful Co of Coachmakers 1975, Freeman City of London; kt 1964; *Recreations* reading, walking, watching motor racing; *Clubs* Carlton, Buck's; *Style*— The Rt Hon Lord Constantine of Stanmore, CBE, AE, DL; Hunters Beck, Uxbridge Rd, Stanmore, Middx

CONSTANTINIDES, Prof Anthony George; s of George Anthony Constantinides, and Paraskeve Constantinides Skaliondas; *b* 1 Jan 1943; *Educ* The Pancyprian Gymnasium, Univ of London (BSc, PhD); *m* 21 Dec 1968, Pamela Maureen, da of Anthony Robert Bowman (ka 1940); 1 s (George Anthony b 23 Oct 1975); *Career* sr res fell the PO Res Dept 1968-70, prof in signal processing Imperial Coll of Sci and Technol 1983- (lectr then reader 1970-83); MIEEE 1978, FIEE 1985, FRSA 1986; Chevalier Palmers Academiques France; *Recreations* reading; *Style*— Prof Anthony Constantinides; 17 Leinster Rd, London N10 3AN; Imperial College of Science Technology and Medicine, Dept of Electrical Engineering, Exhibition Rd, London SW7 2BT (☎ 071 589 5111)

CONSTANTINOU, Achilleas; s of Nicos Constatinou (d 1971), of London, and Efthymia, *née* Cleanthous; *b* 21 April 1948; *Educ* Arnos Secdy Modern Sch Southgate London, Waltham Forest Tech Coll, King's Coll London (LLB); *m* Androulla, da of George Georgallides; 3 s (Alexander Nicholas b 21 June 1981, Nicholas George b 3 May 1982, Marcus Aristos b 18 July 1990), 1 da (Lana Marie b 4 Aug 1984); *Career* opened first shop Aristos (first floor, 45 Carnaby St) 1966, opened first ground floor shop Blooshp 1968, joined family co full-time 1971, by 1973 owned 6 retail outlets in Carnaby St and Oxford St, a wholesale showroom in Great Portland St and Headquarters in Marylebone, chm and md Ariella Fashions Ltd & Group of Cos 1985-, (in 1985 won two Woman Fashion awards for Best Cocktail Dress and Best Evening Dress); fndr Br Fashion Design Protection Assoc 1974 (in 1980 FDPA succeeded in persuading judges of the High Ct to enforce copyright protection for garment designs), advsr to Govt on amendments to Design Copyright and Patents Act 1988, UK rep EEC meeting of Assoc Européene des Industries de L'Habillement; fndr memb Fashion Indust Action Gp (responsible for formation of Br Fashion Cncl), fndr memb and dir Br Fashion Cncl (memb Exhibitor's Ctee), memb: Advsy Bd London Fashion Exhibition, former chm Women's Wear Exec Ctee Br Knitting Clothing and Export Cncl; memb Gray's Inn; *Books* Design Protection (contrib); *Style*— Achilleas Constantinou, Esq; Ariella Fashions Ltd, Aristos House, 25 Watsons Road, Wood Green, London N22 4TE (☎ 081 888 1213, fax 081 889 8736)

CONTEH, John Anthony; s of Amadu Frank Conteh, and Rachel Hannah; *b* 27 May 1951; *Educ* Sacred Heart Jr Sch, St Kevins Comprehensive Kirkby Liverpool; *m* Veronica Anne, da of Stanley Smith; 1 s (James Alexander b 1977), 1 da (Joanna Louise b 1978); *Career* boxer; ABA Champion: Middleweight 1970, Light Heavyweight 1971; Cwlth Games Middleweight Champion Edinburgh 1970; Light Heavyweight Champion: Br, Euro, Cwlth 1973; WBC World Light Heavyweight Champion 1974, Br Superstars Champion 1974; *Books* I Conteh (autobiography, 1982); *Recreations* golf, piano; *Clubs* Moor Park GC; *Style*— John Conteh, Esq; 13 Downalong, Bushey Heath, Herts WD2 1HZ (☎ 081 950 0106)

CONTI, Rt Rev Mario; *see*: Aberdeen, Bishop of (RC)

CONTI, Thomas A (Tom); s of Alfonso Conti (d 1961), of Paisley, Renfrewshire, and Mary McGoldrick (d 1979); *b* 22 Nov 1941; *Educ* Royal Scottish Acad of Music; *m* 1967, Katherine Drummond, da of Wilson George Drummond Tait, of Edinburgh; 1 da (Nina b 1973); *Career* actor 1960-, dir; London appearances incl: Savages (Royal Court and Comedy 1973), The Devil's Disciple (RSC Aldwych 1976), Whose Life is it Anyway? (Mermaid and Savoy 1978 and NY 1979, SWET Award for Best Actor in a new play, Variety Club of GB Award for Best Stage Actor 1978, Tony Award for Best Actor 1979), They're Playing Our Song (Shaftesbury 1980), Romantic Comedy (Apollo 1983); directed: Last Licks (Broadway 1979), Before the Party (Oxford Playhouse and Queen's 1980), The Housekeeper (Apollo 1982); films incl: Galileo (1974), Flame (1974), Eclipse (1975), Full Circle (1977), The Duelists (1977), The Wall (1980), Merry Christmas, Mr Lawrence (1983), Reuben, Reuben (1983), Miracles, Heavenly Pursuits, Beyond Therapy, Saving Grace, American Dreamer, Two Brothers Running, White Roses, Shirley Valentine; tv appearances incl: Madame Bovary, The Norman Conquests, Glittering Prizes 1984-87; tv films incl: The Quick and the Dead, The Beate Klarsfeld Story (tv mini series) etc; *Clubs* Garrick; *Style*— Tom Conti Esq; c/o Chatto & Linnit, Prince of Wales Theatre, Coventry St, London W1

CONVILLE, David Henry; OBE (1983); s of Lt-Col Leopold Henry George Conville, CBE (d 1979), of Convillepur Farm, Sahiwal, Pakistan, and Katherine Mary, *née* Gispert (d 1973); *b* 4 June 1929; *Educ* Marlborough, St John's Coll Oxford, RADA; *m* 1, Jean Margaret Bury (d 1967); 1 da (Clare b 14 Oct 1959); m 2, 2 Jan 1970, Philippa Juliet Antonia, da of Alfred John Gordge (d 1959); 1 s (Leo b 23 Jan 1979); *Career* Nat Serv 1947-49, cmmnd Royal Welch Fus, 2 Lt 4 Bn Nigeria Regt Royal WAFF; Ipswich Rep Theatre 1952, Stratford Meml Theatre Co 1955 and 1957, fndr David Conville Prodns (toured 1959), first London prodns 1960, Toad of Toad Hall West End Christmas 1960-84, fndr New Shakespeare Co 1962, dir New Shakespeare Co at open air theatre Regent's Park 1962-86, pres Soc of West End Theatre 1975, 1976 and 1983; plays written incl: The Wind in the Willows 1984, Look Here Old Son 1986, Obituaries 1988; awarded Coronation medal 1953; chm: Drama Centre 1982-89, The New Shakespeare Co; memb: Arts Cncl Drama Panel 1988-91, Soc of West End Theatres, Theatre Managers' Assoc; *Recreations* walking, reading, tennis, wine; *Clubs* Garrick, Roehampton; *Style*— David Conville, Esq, OBE; 17 Gwendolen Ave, London SW15 6ET

CONWAY, Dr David Ian; *b* 21 April 1948; *Educ* Manchester GS, Univ of Manchester (MB ChB, MD); *m* 23 Oct 1975, Pauline; 3 s (Johnathan b 1978, Benjamin b 1984, Duncan b 1988), 4 da (Rachel b 1979, Heather b 1981, Felicity b 1982, Rebecca b 1986); *Career* lectr obstetrics and gynaecology (specialising in infertility) Univ of Bristol 1980-84; conslt; Monklands Dist Gen Hosp Airdrie, Bellshill Maternity Hosp Bellshill Lanarkshire 1984-; MRCOG 1977; *Recreations* my family; *Style*— Dr David Conway; 53 Kirkintilloch Road, Lenzie, Glasgow, Scotland G66 4LB (☎ 041 7761463), Monklands District General Hospital, Monkscourt Ave, Airdrie, Lanarkshire, Scotland (☎ 0236 69344), Glasgow Nuffield Hospital, Beaconsfield Road, Glasgow (☎ 041 3349441)

CONWAY, Derek Leslie; (C) Shrewsbury at Atchan 1983-; s of Leslie Conway, and Florence Gwendoline, *née* Bailes; *b* 15 Feb 1953; *Educ* Beacon Hill Boys' Sch; *m* 1980, Colette Elizabeth Mary, da of Charles Lamb; 2 s (Henry b 1982, Fredrick b 1985), 1 da (Claudia b 6 March 1989); *Career* PPS to Min of State for Wales 1988-; memb Cons Pty Nat Exec 1972-81, nat vice chm Young Cons 1973-75; Parly candidate: (C) Durham Oct 1974, Newcastle upon Tyne East 1979; borough cncllr 1974-78, ldr Tyne and Wear Met CC 1979-82 (memb 1977-83); memb: Bd Washington Devpt Corpn 1979-83, Bd Newcastle Airport 1979-82, Select Ctee on Agric, Select Ctee on Tport, Select Ctee on Armed Forces Discipline 199-91; Maj 5 Bn The LI TA; *Clubs* Beaconsfield, Shrewsbury; *Style*— Derek Conway Esq, MP; House of Commons, London SW1A 0AA

CONWAY, Prof Gordon Richard; s of Cyril Gordon Conway (d 1977), of Kingston, Surrey, and Thelma, *née* Goodwin; *b* 6 July 1938; *Educ* Kingston GS, Kingston Tech Coll, UCNW Bangor (BSc), Univ of Cambridge (Dip Ag Sc), Univ of West Indies Trinidad (DTA), Univ of California Davis (PhD); *m* 20 March 1966, Susan Mary, da of Harold Mumford, of Winchester, Hants; 1 s (Simon Goodwin b 10 Feb 1967), 2 da (Katherine Ellen b 2 March 1973, Zoe Martha (twin)); *Career* entomologist State of Sabah Malaysia 1961-66, lectr (later reader, prof and visiting prof), Imperial Coll 1970-; representative The Ford Foundation New Delhi 1989-; memb Royal Cmmn Environmental Pollution 1984-88; FIBiol; *Books* Pest and Pathogen Control (1980), After The Green Revolution (jtly, 1989); *Recreations* travel; *Style*— Prof Gordon Conway

CONWAY, (David) Martin; s of Lt-Col Geoffrey Seymour Conway, MC (d 1984), of Portpatrick, Galloway, and Elsie, *née* Phillips; *b* 22 Aug 1935; *Educ* Sedbergh, Gonville and Caius Coll Cambridge (BA, MA); *m* 10 March 1962, Ruth Fairey, da of Rev Richard Daniel (d 1983), of Audlem, Cheshire; 1 s (John b 1967), 2 da (Ann, Moira (Mrs Zheng)); *Career* int sec Student Christian Movement GB and Ireland 1958-61, study sec World Student Christian Fedn Geneva 1961-67, C of E's sec for Chaplaincies in Higher Educn London 1967-70, ed and pubns sec World Cncl of Churches Geneva 1970-74, asst gen sec Br Cncl of Churches London 1974-83, tutor in church and soc Ripon Coll Cuddesdon Oxford and dir Oxford Inst for Church and Soc 1983-86, pres Selly Oak Colls Birmingham 1986-; ed: Oxford Papers on Contemporary Soc 1984-86, Christians Together newsletter; chm Birmingham Diocesan Cncl for Mission and Unity, vice chm Friends of the Church in China; *Books* The Undivided Vision (1966), Seeing Education Whole (1970), The Christian Enterprise in Higher Education (1971), Look Listen Care (1983); *Recreations* friends, travel, music; *Style*— Martin Conway, Esq; President's House, Selly Oak Colleges, Birmingham B29 6LQ (☎ 021 472 2462); President's Office, Selly Oak Colleges, Birmingham B29 6LQ (☎ 021 472 4231, fax 021 472 8882, telex 334349 SELLYO G)

CONWAY, Robert David; s of Walter Conway, of Guildford; *b* 11 Dec 1949; *Educ* Univ of London (LLB); *m* 17 Jan 1976, Patricia Lock; 2 da (Anna b 6 Oct 1978, Laura b 20 Sept 1980); *Career* tax offr 1969, DPP 1973, barr Inner Temple 1974, SE circuit, lectr in law and legal conslt to Legal Protection Insur Co; writer and performer (as Walter Zerlin Jr); winner Edinburgh Festival Scotsman Award 1975 and 1980, own tv show on Granada, six plays published and performed worldwide; dir: Entertainment Machine Theatre Co, Coups De Theatre Ltd, Conway McGillivray Publishing House; legal advsr to A Fish Called Wanda, and Marlon Brando's A Dry White Season; *Books* Miss You've Dropped Your Briefs (cartoonist), The British Alternative Theatre Directory (ed yearly); *Recreations* art, music, swimming; *Style*— Robert Conway, Esq; 92 South Lane, New Malden, Surrey (☎ 081 949 1689); 7 Stone Buildings, Lincoln's Inn, London WC2A 3SZ (☎ 071 242 0961)

CONWAY, Robert John; s of Ernest Conway, and Jean Patricia; *b* 10 June 1951; *Educ* Univ of Salford (Bsc); *m* 1 July 1972, Susan Mary; 1 s (Matthew James b 1975), 3 da

(Claire Louise b 1977, Charlotte Elizabeth b 1979, Caroline Michele b 1980); *Career* CA; ptnr Price Waterhouse; FCA; *Style—* Robert Conway, Esq; Primavera, Goodworth Clatford, nr Andover, Hampshire (☎ 0264 323454); Price Waterhouse, The Quay, 30 Channel Way, Ocean Village, Southampton, Hants (☎ 0703 330077)

CONYERS, Nicholas Charles; s of Edwin Keith Conyers, and Elizabeth, *née* Manning; *b* 31 Aug 1955; *Educ* Ellesmere Coll Shropshire; *m* 29 March 1980, Shirley Anne, da of Thomas Leslie Barrowby; 1 s (John b 3 July 1987), 1 da (Alison b 28 June 1983); *Career* Mercantile Credit 1977-80 asst dir Towry Law Group 1980-85, dir Pearson Jones & Co Ltd 1985-; memb FIMBRA; *Recreations* walking, cycling, classic cars; *Style—* Nicholas Conyers, Esq; Pearson Jones and Co Ltd, Clayton Wood Close, West Park Ring Rd, Leeds LS16 6QE (☎ 0532 304804, fax 0532 744365, car 0836 630381)

CONYNGHAM, 7 Marquess (I 1816); Frederick William Henry Francis Conyngham; also (sits as) Baron Minster (UK 1821), Earl Conyngham (I 1781), Baron Conyngham (I 1781), Viscount Conyngham (I 1789), Viscount Mount Charles (I 1797), Earl of Mount Charles and Viscount Slane (I 1816); patron of one living; s of 6 Marquess Conyngham (d 1974), by his 2 wife Antoinette Winifred, *née* Thompson (d 1966); *b* 13 March 1924; *Educ* Eton; *m* 1, 29 April 1950 (m dis 1970), Eileen Wren, o da of Capt Clement Wren Newsam; 3 s; m 2, 1971, Elizabeth Ann, yr da of late Frederick Molyneux Hughes, of Fareham, Hants, and formerly w of David Sutherland Rudd; m 3, 1980, Daphne Georgina Adelaide (d 24 Nov 1986), eldest da of R C Armour, and formerly w of C P V Walker; m 4, 29 May 1987, (Emma Christianne) Annabelle, o da of (Denys) Martin Agnew, of Grosvener Court, Grove Road, East Cliffe, Bournemouth; *Heir* s, Earl of Mount Charles; *Career* late Capt Irish Gds; *Style—* The Most Hon the Marquess Conyngham; Bifrons, nr Canterbury, Kent; Myrtle Hill, Ramsey, Isle of Man

CONYNGHAM, Lord (Frederick William) Patrick; 3 s of 7th Marquess Conyngham by his 1 w, Eileen; *b* 23 March 1959; *m* 1 Dec 1990, Charlotte M T G, er da of Donald Black, of Edenwood, Cupar, Fife; *Style—* The Lord Patrick Conyngham

CONYNGHAM, Lord Simon Charles Eveleigh Wren; 2 s of 7th Marquess Conyngham by his 1 w, Eileen; *b* 20 Nov 1953; *Educ* Harrow; *m* 1978 (m dis), Emma S, da of Wing Cdr F W Breeze; 1 da (Chloe Wren b 1980); *Career* caterer, runs Staveley's (former fish and chip shop); *Style—* The Lord Simon Conyngham

COODE-ADAMS, (John) Giles Selby; s of Geoffrey Coode-Adams (d 1986), and Cynthia Mildred, *née* Selby-Bigge; *b* 30 Aug 1938; *Educ* Eton; *m* 30 April 1960, Sonia Elisabeth, da of Laurence Frederick York (d 1965); 1 s (Ben b 19 Aug 1965), 1 da (Henrietta Guest b 5 Feb 1962); *Career* 2 Lt 16/5 Queen's Royal Lancers 1956-58; ptnr L Messel 1967- (joined 1959, taken over by Shearson Lehman Hutton 1984), md Lehman Brothers 1985-; former memb Cncl Univ of Essex; Freeman: City of London, Worshipful Co of Merchant Taylors; *Recreations* fishing, music, gardening; *Clubs* Boodle's; *Style—* Giles Coode-Adams, Esq; Lehman Brothers International, 1 Broadgate, London EC2 (☎ 071 260 2122)

COOGAN, Ven Robert Arthur William; s of Ronald Dudley Coogan (d 1965), and Joyce Elizabeth, *née* Roberts (d 1971); *b* 11 July 1929; *Educ* Launceston HS, Univ of Tasmania (BA), Univ of Durham (DipTheol); *Career* asst curate St Andrew Plaistow 1953-56, rector Bothwell Tasmania 1956-62; vicar: St John N Woolwich 1962-73, St Stephen Hampstead 1973-77, St Stephen with All Hallows Hampstead 1977-85; priest i/c All Hallows Gospel Oak 1974-77; area dean: S Camden 1975-81, N Camden 1978-83; prebendary St Pauls Cathedral 1982-85, commissary for Bishop of Tasmania 1968-88, examining chaplain Bishop of Edmonton 1985-, archdeacon of Hampstead 1985-; *Recreations* reading, gardening, travel; *Clubs* The Oriental; *Style—* The Ven the Archdeacon of Hampstead; 27 Thurlow Rd, Hampstead, London NW3 5PP (☎ 071 435 5890, fax 071 435 6049)

COOK, Prof Alan Hugh; s of late Reginald Thomas Cook, OBE, and Ethel Cook; *b* 2 Dec 1922; *Educ* Westcliff HS for Boys, Corpus Christ Coll Cambridge (MA, PhD, ScD); *m* 1948, Isabell Weir Adamson, 1 s, 1 da; *Career* Univ of Cambridge: Jackson prof of natural philosophy 1972-, head of Dept of Physics 1979-84, master of Selwyn Coll 1983-; memb Science and Engrg Res Cncl FRSE 1984-; FRS 1969, FRSE 1970, memb Soc Straniero Accad Naz dei Lincei (Rome); kt 1988; *Books* Gravity and the Earth, Global Geophysics, Interference of Electromagnetic Waves, Physics of the Earth and Planets, Celestial Masers, Interiors of the Planets, The Motion of the Moon; *Recreations* travel, amateur theatre, painting, gardening; *Clubs* explorers (NY), United Oxford and Cambridge; *Style—* Prof Sir Alan Cook, FRS, FRSE; Selwyn College, Cambridge CB3 9DQ

COOK, Allan Vincent Cannon; s of Cyril Percy Cannon Cook (d 1957), and Jocelyne Marie Anne, *née* Cockell; *b* 28 Feb 1940; *Educ* Wimbledon Coll, LSE (BSc Econ); *Career* audit sr Knox Cropper & Co Chartered Accountants 1964-65 (articled clerk 1961-64); Unilever: accounting mangr then system analyst MacFisheries 1966-71, accountant Central Pensions Dept 1971-75, memb fin gp 1975-78, asst accounting principles offr 1978-79, seconded as sec IASC 1979-81; head of accounting res Shell International Petroleum Co 1982-90; chm Working Gp on Accounting Standards BIAC OECD; memb: Consultative Gp IASC, Accounting Standards Ctee 1987-90; tech dir Accounting Standards Bd 1990-; numerous contribs to learned jls; FCA 1974 (ACA 1964); *Recreations* theatre, music, walking; *Clubs* LSE; *Style—* Allan Cook, Esq; Accounting Standards Board, Holborn Hall, 100 Gray's Inn Rd, London WC1X 8AL (☎ 071 404 8818, fax 071 404 4497)

COOK, Andrew Charles (Andy); s of Benjamin Cook, of Romsey, Hants, and Patricia, *née* Gladish; *b* 10 Aug 1969; *Educ* Mountbatten Secdy Sch, Southampton Tech Coll; *Career* professional footballer Southampton, debut 1987 v Manchester Utd, 19 appearances; schoolboy rep: Eastleigh & Winchester Dist, Hants, S England; most promising athlete Southampton aged 14; *Recreations* badminton, snooker, fishing; *Style—* Andy Cook, Esq; Southampton FC, The Dell, Milton Rd, Southampton SO9 4XX (☎ 0703 220505)

COOK, Andrew Donald Douglas; s of Donald George Cook, JP (d 1988), of 15 Pointers Hill, Westcott, Dorking, Surrey, and Jean, *née* Douglas; *b* 25 Jan 1939; *Educ* Harrow; *m* 1, 4 July 1964 (m dis 1985), Venice Ann, da of Dane Henry Donaldson (d 1987), of 46 Barnmeadow Lane, Great Bookham, Surrey; 1 da (Isobel Christiane b 1 Nov 1969); m 2, 11 Dec 1985, Vivien Hamilton, da of Eric Sutcliffe Aspinall, of 4 Dixs Close, Heacham, Norfolk; *Career* Nat Serv E Surrey Regt (later Queens Surreys) 1958-60; C E Heath & Co Ltd 1957-63; James Walker & Co Ltd 1964-: tech trainee 1964-67, tech sales rep 1967-69, asst London sales mangr 1969-72, London sales mangr 1972-79, asst to Bd of Dir 1980-81, commercial off mangr 1981-83, dir 1984-; dir James Walker Group Ltd 1990-; chm Leatherhead Round Table 1978-79; *Recreations* golf, motoring; *Clubs* RAC, Oil Industs, Effingham Golf; *Style—* Andrew Cook, Esq; Pooks Hollow, Glendene Avenue, East Horsley, Leatherhead, Surrey KT24 5AY (☎ 048 652 707); James Walker & Co Ltd, Lion Works, Woking, Surrey GU22 8AP (☎ 0483 757 575, fax 0483 755 711, telex 859221 LIONWK G)

COOK, Beryl Francis; da of Adrian Stephen Barton Lansley, and Ella, *née* Farmer-Francis; *b* 10 Sept 1926; *Educ* Kendrick Girls' Sch Reading; *m* 2 Oct 1948, John Victor Cook, s of Victor Harry Cook (d 1980); 1 s (John Lansley b 24 May 1950); *Career* artist; exhibitions: Plymouth Art Centre 1975, Whitechapel Gallery London 1976, The Craft of Art Walker Gallery Liverpool 1979, Musée de Cahors 1981, Chelmsford Gallery Museum 1982, Portal Gallery London 1985; retrospective exhibition (travelling): Plymouth Museum, Stoke-on-Trent, Preston, Nottingham and Edinburgh 1988-89; *Books* The Works (1978), Private View (1980), One Man Show (1981), Beryl Cook's New York (1985), Beryl Cook's London (1988); illustrated: Seven Years and a Day (1980), Bertie and the Big Red Ball (1982), My Granny (1983), Mr Norris Changes Trains (1990); *Recreations* reading, travel; *Clubs* Lansdowne; *Style—* Mrs Beryl Cook; 3 Athenaeum St, The Hoe, Plymouth PL1 2RQ; Rogers Coleridge & White, 20 Powis Mews, London W11

COOK, Bob; *Career* writer; novels incl: Disorderly Elements 1985, Question of Identity 1987, Faceless Mortals 1988, Paper Chase 1989, Fire and Forget 1990; *Style—* Bob Cook, Esq; c/o Richard Scott Simon Ltd, 43 Doughty Street, London WC1

COOK, Brian Francis; s of Harry Cook (d 1959), and Renia Maria, *née* Conlon (d 1962); *b* 13 Feb 1933; *Educ* St Bede's GS Bradford, Univ of Manchester (BA), Downing Coll and St Edmund's House Cambridge (BA, MA), Br Sch at Athens; *m* 18 Aug 1962, Veronica Mary Teresa, da of Bernard Dewhirst (d 1974); *Career* Nat Serv 1956-58, 16/15 The Queen's Royal Lancers; Dept of Greek and Roman Art Metropolitan Museum of Art NY: curatorial asst 1960, asst curator 1961, assoc curator 1965-69; keeper of greek and roman antiquities Br Museum 1976- (asst keeper 1969-76); corres memb German Archaeological Inst 1977, FSA 1971; *Books* Inscribed Hadra Vases in The Metropolitan Museum of Art (1966), Greek and Roman Art in the British Museum (1976), The Elgin Marbles (1984), The Townley Marbles (1985), Greek Inscriptions (1987), The Rogozen Treasure (ed, 1989); *Recreations* reading, gardening; *Clubs* Challoner; *Style—* B F Cook, Esq; 4 Belmont Ave, Barnet, Herts EN4 9LJ (☎ 081 440 6590); British Museum, London WC1B 3DG (☎ 071 636 1555 ext 8411, 071 323 8411)

COOK, (John) Brian; OBE (1988); s of John Wesley Cook (d 1967), of Leeds, Yorks, and Violet Mary Cook (d 1984); *b* 17 April 1931; *Educ* Leeds GS, BNC Oxford (BA, MA); *m* 1960, Barbara Avis, da of William Hugh Russell (d 1976); 1 da (Barbara Ann b 1962); *Career* Nat Serv 2 Lt REME 1953-55; Royal Dutch Shell: joined Netherlands 1955, later engr Brunei and Sarawak, Indonesia 1961, Venezuela 1964, Italy 1970, transferred Nigeria 1972 (engrg mangr 1975); engrg mangr Shell Expro UK 1981-88 (formerly mangr Design and Tech Servs); memb Bd Marine Technol Directorate Ltd; chm Process Industs Div Inst of Mechanical Engrs, hon pres Assoc of Br Offshore Indust; Liveryman Worshipful Co of Engrs 1988; FEng 1988, FIMechE 1975; *Recreations* sailing, vintage cars; *Style—* Brian Cook, Esq, OBE; 21 King George Square, Richmond, Surrey TW10 6LF (☎ 081 332 1874)

COOK, Charles Alfred George; MC (1944), GM (1944); s of Charles Frederick Cook (d 1939), of London, and Beatrice Alice Grist (d 1935); *b* 20 Aug 1913; *Educ* St Edward's Sch Oxford, Univ of London, Univ of Aston (DSc); *m* 1939, Edna Constance, da of Herbert Dobson (d 1917), of London; 1 s (John), 1 da (Jill); *Career* served WWII Capt and Maj RAMC 1939-45; conslt ophthalmic surgn emeritus Guys Hosp 1954, Moorfields Eye Hosp 1956-, Moorfields res fell Inst of Ophthalmology 1951-55; memb Ct of Examiners RCS 1964-70, vice dean Inst of Ophthalmology 1959-62 (memb Ctee of Mgmnt); govr: Moorfields Eye Hosp 1962-65, Royal Nat Coll for the Blind 1965-; *Recreations* reading, exploring countryside; *Clubs* Garrick, Athenaeum; *Style—* Charles Cook, Esq, MC, GM; 13 Clarence Terrace, Regents Park, London NW1 4RD

COOK, Charles Stuart; s of Norman Charles Cook, of 6 St Thomas Terrace, St Thomas St, Wells, Somerset, and Dorothy Ida, *née* Waters; *b* 19 Dec 1936; *Educ* King Edward VI Sch Southampton, Alleyn's Sch Dulwich, St Catherine's Coll Oxford (MA); *m* 28 July 1962 (m dis 1986), Jennifer, da of George Henry Baugh (d 1988), of Sweetings, Aberthin near Cowbridge, S Glamorgan; 2 s (Adam b 1966, Edward b 1969); *Career* Nat Serv 2 Lt The Buffs, The Royal East Kent Regt 1956-58, Capt TA List B 1961-74; asst master St Dunstans Coll London 1961-67, called to the Bar Lincolns Inn 1966; Hardwicke scholar 1963, Sir Thomas More bursary 1966, in practice 1967-, chm Med Appeals Tbnl 1979-90, asst rec 1981-86, rec 1986-, jr of the Wales and Chester Circuit 1987-88; Llandaff PCC 1978-82; Criminal Bar Assoc 1988; *Recreations* fine wines, photography, travel; *Style—* Charles Cook, Esq; Eaton House, 183 Cathedral Road, Cardiff, South Glamorgan CF1 9PN (☎ 0222 390743), 33 Park Place, Cardiff CF1 3BA (☎ 0222 233313, fax 0222 228294)

COOK, Christopher Paul; s of Edward Peter Cook, of Gt Broughton, N Yorks, and Joyce, *née* Layland; *b* 24 Jan 1959; *Educ* Barnard Castle Sch, Univ of Exeter/Exeter Coll of Art (BA, Combined Arts prize, Gladys Hunkin Poetry prize), Royal Coll of Art (MA, J Andrew Lloyd scholar, Anstruther award, John Minton Travel award), Accademia de Belle Arti Bologna (Italian Govt scholar); *m* Jennifer Jane, da of Edward John Mellings; 2 s (Matthew b 13 Jan 1983, Samuel b 3 Nov 1988); *Career* artist, poet; New Nerves (Rougemont Press, 1983), The Choosing and other Poems (Peca Books, 1984), A Mythic Cycle (Ernst Press, 1989), fell in painting Exeter Coll of Art 1989, assoc lectr Poly SW 1990-; visiting lectr: Birmingham Poly 1990-, St Martins 1990-, Kingston Poly 1990-, Royal Coll of Art 1990-, Wimbledon Coll of Art 1990-, Stadelschule, Frankfurt-am-Main; *one man exhibitions*: Camden Arts Centre 1985, British Council Centre Amsterdam 1985, Spacex Gallery Exeter 1986, Galleria Maggiore Bologna 1987, Benjamin Rhodes Gallery 1988 and 1990, The Cleveland Gallery Middlesbrough 1989, Plymouth Arts Centre 1989; *group exhibitions incl*: The Sheffield Open (Mappin Gallery) 1985, The Camden Annual 1984 prizewinner, 1985 1986, Royal Over-Seas League Annual 1985 prizwinner, 1986, 1987, IBM South Bank, Athena Int Art Awards (Mall Galleries) 1985, Young Contemporaries (Whitworth Gallery Manchester) 1985, Tradition and Innovation in Printmaking Today (Milton Keynes and tour) 1986, The Human Touch (Fischer Fine Art) 1986, Due Pittori Inglesi (Associazone Italo-Brittanica Bologna) 1987, Artists who studied with Peter de Francia (Camden Arts Centre) 1987, Romantic Visions (Camden Arts Centre) 1988, Bound Image Nigel Greenwood Gallery 1988, Figure 2: A Personal Mythology (Welsh Arts Cncl tour) 1988, Six Benjamin Rhodes Gallery Artists (Richard Demarco Gallery Edinburgh) 1989, Metropolitan Museum of Art New York, Real Life Stories (Cleveland Gallery, Middlesbrough) 1989, Eros in Albion (Casa Masaccio, San Giovanni Valdarno, Italy) 1989, 3 Ways (Br Cncl/RCA tour to Hungary and Poland 1990, A Tribute to Peter Fuller (Beaux Arts, Bath) 1990, Los Angeles ICAF (Benjamin Rhodes Gallery) 1990; Brewhouse Open prize 1989, Lucy Morrison Meml prize (Royal Over-Seas League Annual) 1990 e; *Style—* Christopher Cook, Esq; c/o Benjamin Rhodes Gallery, 4 New Burlington Place, London W1X 1SB (☎ 071 434 1768)

COOK, Christopher William Batstone; s of Cecil Batstone Cook (d 1965), and Penelope, *née* Mayall; *b* 21 Jan 1951; *Educ* Eton; *m* 15 July 1978, Margaret Anne, da of Maj John Christopher Blackett Ord, of Whitfield Hall, Hexham, Northumberland; 2 s (Edward b 1982, Benjamin b 1983), 1 da (Emma b 1980); *Career* Lloyds broker; dir: Bowring Space Projects 1979-, C T Bowring & Co (Insurance) Ltd 1980-; exec dir Bowring Aviation Ltd 1985, Marsh & McLennan Worldwide 1988; *Recreations* shooting, stalking, fishing; *Style—* Christopher W B Cook, Esq; 24 Granard Rd, London SW12 8UL (☎ 081 675 0239); The Bowring Building, Tower Place, London EC3P 3BE (☎ 071 357 5380, fax 071 621 1627, car ☎ 0860 331 075)

COOK, Sir Christopher Wymondham Rayner Herbert; 5 Bt (UK 1886) of Doughty House, Richmond, Surrey; s of Sir Francis Cook, 4 Bt (d 1978); *b* 24 March 1938;

Educ King's Sch Canterbury; *m* 1, 1958 (m dis 1975), Mrs Malina Gunasekera; 1 s (Richard b 1959), 1 da (Priscilla b 1968); m 2, 1975, Mrs Margaret Miller, da of late John Murray; 1 s (Alexander b 1980), 1 da (Caroline b 1978); *Heir* s, Richard Cook; *Career* dir Diamond Guarantees Ltd 1980-; *Style—* Sir Christopher Cook, Bt; La Fontenelle, Ville au Roi, St Peter Port, Guernsey, CI

COOK, (Jeremy) David; s of Thomas Brian Cook (d 1989), and Pauline Isable Cook; *b* 18 May 1958; *Educ* Laurence Jackson Sch Guisborough, Prior Pursglove Coll, Univ of Keele (BA); *Career* called to the Bar Grays Inn 1982; *Recreations* travel, literature; *Style—* David Cook, Esq; Lamb Building, Temple, London EC4 7AS (☎ 01 353 0744, fax 01 353 0535)

COOK, David Ronald; JP (1989); s of Charles Henry Cook, of Bristol, and Myrtle Ovington, *née* Harwood (d 1989); *b* 9 Nov 1943; *Educ* Thornbury GS; *m* 1, Frances Ann, *née* Leigh (d 1972); 2 da (Vicky Frances Leigh (Mrs Moss) b 24 April 1965, Jennifer Elaine Leigh b 9 Sept 1966); m 2, 21 June 1974, Angela Susan, da of Cecil Robert Cogdell (d 1988); 1 s (Charles David b 14 Aug 1978); *Career* articled clerk Parker Leader and Co Bristol 1960-65, audit sr Ricketts Cooper and Co 1965-69; ptnr: Burkett James and Co 1969-81, Pannell Kerr Forster (Bristol) 1981- (chm and managing ptnr 1985-); treas Bristol Referees Soc (RFU); FCA 1972 (ACA 1966), MInstD 1990; *Recreations* rugby football, squash, boating; *Clubs* Clifton, Redwood Lodge; *Style—* David Cook, Esq; Harwood House, Ham Lane, Dundry, Bristol BS18 8JA (☎ 0272 643 763); Pannell Kerr Forster, Pannell House, The Promenade, Clifton, Bristol BS8 3LX (☎ 0272 736 841, fax 0272 741 238, car 0860 393 735)

COOK, Francis; MP (Lab) Stockton North 1983-; s of James and Elizabeth May Cook; *b* 3 Nov 1935; *Educ* Corby Sch Sunderland, De La Salle Manchester, Instit of Educn Leeds; *m* 1959, Patricia, da of Thomas Lundrigan; 1 s, 3 da; *Career* sponsored by MSF; memb Select Ctee for Employment 1983-87, oppn Whip 1987-, memb: Select Ctee on Procedure of the House 1988-, N Atlantic Assembley 1988-; *Style—* Frank Cook, MP; House of Commons, London SW1

COOK, Commodore Henry Home; s of George Home Cook (d 1920), of Westfield, Bowden, Cheshire, and Lilian Elena Anna Stewart, *née* Byng-Hall (d 1951); *b* 24 Jan 1918; *Educ* Pangbourne Coll; *m* 26 June 1943, Theffania (Fania), da of Arthur Percival Saunders (d 1956), of Latchmore Cottage, Gerrards Cross, Bucks and Highlands, Bolney, Sussex; 2 s (Martin b 1944, Charles b 1958), 2 da (Sarah b 1948, Alice b 1955); *Career* RN: Cadet 1936, Cdre 1973, head Br Def Staff Canada 1970-72, ADC to HM The Queen 1971-72, dir PR RN 1966-70; HM Naval Attaché 1963-66: Ankara, Teheran, Bagdad, Damascus, Amman; Cdr RNC Greenwich 1960-63; dir of admin Ellerman Gp Shipping Div 1973-80, dir Christopher Gold Assocs Ltd 1974-87, assoc advsr Industl Soc 1980-81, vice pres Cncl Inst Admin Mgmnt 1982- (chm 1981), gen cmmr of Income Tax 1982-, dir PR Operation Raleigh 1984-87, PR conslt 1987-; chm The Chiltern Soc 1988-, hon sec Missions to Seamen Chalfont St Peter 1988-; memb Worshipful Co of Shipwrights 1968-, Freeman City of London 1967-; Dip Communication Advtg Mktg Fndn, FInstAM, FBIM, MIPR; *Recreations* fishing; *Clubs* Army & Navy, Wig & Pen; *Style—* Cdre Henry Home Cook; Ramblers Cottage, Layters Green, Chalfort St Peter, Bucks SL9 8TH (☎ 0753 883 724)

COOK, Dr John Barry; s of Albert Edward Cook, of Gloucester, and Beatrice Irene, *née* Blake (d 1978); *b* 9 May 1940; *Educ* Sir Thomas Rich's Sch Gloucester, King's Coll London (BSc, AKC), Guy's Hosp Med Sch Univ of London (PhD); *m* 1964, Vivien Margaret Roxana, da of Capt Victor Lamb, CBE, RN, of St Albans, Hertfordshire; 2 s (David b 1967, Richard b 1972), 1 da (Susan b 1969); *Career* lectr in physics Guy's Hosp Med Sch 1964-65, sr sci master and head of Physics Dept Haileybury Coll 1965-72; headmaster: Christ Coll Brecon 1973-82, Epsom Coll 1982-; *Books* Multiple Choice Questions in A-level Physics, Multiple Choice Questions in O-level Physics, Solid State Biophysics; *Recreations* most sports, philately, photography; *Clubs* East India, Devonshire, Sports and Public Schools; *Style—* Dr John Cook; Headmaster's House, Epsom College, Surrey KT17 4JQ (☎ 0372 722118); Epsom Coll, Surrey KT17 4JQ (☎ 0372 723621)

COOK, Kandis; *b* 10 May 1950; *Educ* Nova Scotia Coll of Art and Design, Halifax Nova Scotia Canada (BA), ENO (design course); *m* ; 1 s (Turner Moyse b 10 Oct 1987), 1 da (Kate Moyse b 29 May 1980); *Career* set and costume designer: Dr Faustus (Lyric Hammersmith and Fortune), Berenice (Lyric), Britannicus (Lyric), Faith Healer (Royal Court), Women beware Women (Royal Court), Grace of Mary Traverse (Royal Court), Bite of the Night (RSC), Epicoene (RSC Swan), The Last Days of Don Juan (RSC), Orlando (Wexford Opera Festival), Arden of Faversham (RSC), Hamlet (Donmar Warehouse and Piccadilly); costume designer The Relapse (Lyric Hammersmith); *Style—* Ms Kandis Cook

COOK, Kathryn Jane; *née* Smallwood; MBE (1986); s of George Henry Smallwood, of Tadley, Hampshire, and Sylvia Phyllis, *née* Briggs; *b* 3 May 1960; *Educ* The Hurst Secondary Sch Baughurst, Queen Mary's VI Form Coll Basingstoke, West London Inst of Higher Educn, Birmingham Poly; *m* 1982, Garry Peter Cook, s of Eric Cook, of Walsall, W Midlands; *Career* Cwlth Games Gold Medallist 4 x 100m relay 1978 (WAAAs Champion 100 and 200m), Euro Championships Silver Medallist 4 x 100m 1978, Olympic Games Bronze Medallist 4 x 100m relay 1980 (WAAAs Champion 100 and 200m), World Cup Silver Medallist 100m 1981, Euro Championships Silver Medallist 200m and 4 x 100m relay 1982, Cwlth Games Silver Medallist 200 and (Gold Medal 4 x 100m relay) 1982; World Championships Bronze Medallist 200m, Silver Medallist 4 x 100m relay 1983; WAAAs Champion 100m and 200m 1984, Olympic Games Bronze Medallist 400m and 4 x 100m relay 1984; Cwlth Games 1986: Gold Medallist 4 x 100m relay (Silver Medallist 4 x 400m, Silver Medallist 200m, Bronze Medallist 400m; UK records in: 100m, 200m, 300m, 400m and 4 x 100m relay; Cwlth record holder in the 400m; voted Female Athlete of the Year by Br Athletic Writers in 1980, 1981 and 1982; ret from competition 1987; *Style—* Mrs Kathryn Cook, MBE; 85 Mellish Rd, Walsall, W Midlands WS4 2DF

COOK, Kenneth Anthony; s of Walter Cook (d 1953), and Marion Grace Berry, *née* Lovell (d 1988); *b* 11 March 1933; *Educ* Haberdashers' Aske's; *m* 5 July 1952, (Jeanne) Sylvia, da of Thomas Harris; 4 s (Martin b 1960, Ian b 1961, Simon b 1964, Brian b 1967); *Career* Pannell Kerr Forster 1954-63, ptnr Judkins CA's 1963-; FCA, FCIS, ATII, FBIM; *Recreations* swimming; *Clubs* Farmers, Castle (Rochester); *Style—* Kenneth Cook, Esq; Newnham Court, Detling, Maidstone, Kent ME14 3ER (☎ 0622 37948); 16 Star Hill, Rochester, Kent ME1 1UU (☎ 0634 830321, fax 0634 830969, telex 9401 6714 JUDKE, car 0836 213163)

COOK, Lindsay Mary; da of Francis John Cook (d 1972), and Elsie Mary, *née* Gilliatt; *b* 24 July 1951; *Educ* Havelock Comp Sch Grimsby, The Open Univ (BA); *m* 1 May 1987, Tony Wilkinson, s of Ernest Wilkinson; 2 s (Rory b 14 Aug 1988, Gray b 27 Jan 1991); *Career* trainee journalist Grimsby Evening Telegraph 1969-74, reporter and consumer writer Morning Telegraph Sheffield 1974-76, freelance writer Sunday Times 1976-77, freelance contrib Money Mail (pt of Daily Mail) 1977-79, United Newspapers London 1977-86 (number 3 on newsdesk, features dept, dep London ed 1984), personal fin ed The Daily Telegraph 1986-89, money ed The Times 1990-; Personal Finance Journalist of the Year 1987; *Books* The Money Diet, Three Months To Financial Fitness (1986); *Recreations* food, theatre; *Style—* Miss Lindsay Cook; The Times, 1 Pennington St, London E1 9XN (☎ 071 782 5083, fax 071 782 5112)

COOK, His Hon Judge Michael John; s of George Henry Cook (d 1947), and Nora Wilson, *née* Mackman; *b* 20 June 1930; *Educ* Leeds Grammar Sch, Worksop Coll, Leeds Univ; *m* 1, 1958, Anne Margaret Vaughan; 3 s, 1 da; m 2, 1974, Patricia Anne Sturdy; 1 da; *Career* Lt RA (Nat Serv Canal Zone); slr; sr ptnr Ward Bowie 1968-86, rec Crown Ct 1980-86; circuit judge SE Circuit 1986-; author and broadcaster; past pres London Slrs Litigation Assoc; *Recreations* gardening, reading, theatre; *Clubs* The Law Soc; *Style—* His Hon Judge Michael Cook

COOK, Nicholas Grant Billson; s of Peter Billson Cook, of Leicestershire, and Cynthia Margaret, *née* Grant; *b* 17 June 1956; *Educ* Lutterworth High GS; *Career* cricketer; Leicestershire CCC 1975-85 (first XI debut 1978), Northamptonshire CCC 1986-, represented Young England v Young West Indies 1974, England debut v NZ at Lords 1983, 15 Caps 1983-87, 3 One Day Internationals; overseas England tours: NZ and Pakistan 1984, Pakistan 1987, Nehru Trophy 1989; *Recreations* soccer, horse racing; *Style—* Nicholas Cook, Esq; Northamptonshire CCC, County Ground, Wantage Rd, Northampton NN1 4TV (☎ 0604 32917)

COOK, Noelin Catherine; da of James J Fehily (d 1980), of Ireland, and Bridget M, *née* Crookes (d 1975); *b* 20 Dec 1934; *Educ* St Louis Convent Monaghan Ireland, Univ Coll Dublin (MB BCh, BAO, MCh Otolaryngology); *m* 2 Aug 1972, Daniel Cook, s of Frederick Cook (d 1989), of Upton on Severn; 1 da (Emily Jane b 17 Sept 1973); *Career* Mater Hosp Dublin 1963-64, Royal Infirmary Leicester 1965-66, Victoria Hosp Blackpool 1967-68, Throat and Ear Hosp Brighton 1969, Univ Coll Hosp London 1969-72, sr registrar ENT rotation post Queen Elizabeth Med Centre Birmingham 1972-78, conslt ENT surgn Worcester Royal Infimrary 1979-; FRCS 1969; *Recreations* walking, skiing, cycling; *Style—* Mrs Noelin Cook; The Chantry, Woodsheads Road, Malvern WR14 3DD, Worcester Royal Infirmary, Castle St, Worcester (☎ 0905 763333)

COOK, Patrick Donald; s of Donald George Herbert Cook, of 1 Kings Walk, Henley on Thames, Oxon, and Doreen Elizabeth, *née* Simpson; *b* 11 July 1956; *Educ* Abingdon Sch, Pembroke Coll Oxford (MA); *m* 10 Oct 1981, Caroline Elizabeth, da of John Graves, of Kings Cottage, Bishops Tawton, Barnstaple, Devon; 2 da (Megan Elizabeth b 25 April 1986, Florence Emma b 4 Oct 1989); *Career* admited slr 1981; ptnr Osborne Clarke 1986, licensed insolvency practitioner 1989; memb: Law Society 1981, Insolvency Lawyers Assoc 1989; *Recreations* sports (various), theatre, reading, gardening; *Style—* Patrick Cook, Esq; Withy Tree House, Stone Allerton, Axbridge, Somerset, Osborne Clark 30 Queen Charlotte St, Bristol BS99 7QQ (☎ 0272 230220)

COOK, Peter Charles Henry; s of Leslie Cook; *b* 13 June 1935; *Educ* Manchester GS; *m* 1957, Olive, *née* Poulton; 2 s, 1 da; *Career* former div fin dir Tube Investments Ltd, dir Simon Engineering plc (fin dir to 1981, md Industl Servs Div); FCA, ACMA; *Style—* Peter Cook Esq; Simon Engineering, Bird Hall Lane, Cheadle Heath, Stockport

COOK, Peter Robert; s of Fredrick Cook (d 1988), and Mabel Florence Cook; *b* 19 June 1939; *Educ* Elmbridge Sch Cranleigh Surrey, Colchester Inst (HND); *m* 25 March 1967, Dorothy Anne, da of Walter Green (d 1986), of Hoyland Common, Yorks; 1 s (Stephen Robert b 12 Dec 1970), 1 da (Louise Anne b 7 Jan 1972); *Career* jt md Wilkin & Sons Tiptree 1986 (sales mangr 1969, sales dir 1980); memb UKPMA Ctee FDF; memb Chartered Inst of Mktg; *Recreations* golf; *Clubs* Quietwaters Golf, Farmers; *Style—* Peter Cook, Esq; Gate House, Cherry Chase, Tiptree, Essex CO5 0AE (☎ 0621 815562); Messrs Wilkin & Sons Ltd, Tiptree, Essex CO5 0RF (☎ 0621 815407, fax 0621 819468, telex 995577)

COOK, Richard Herbert Aster Maurice; s (by 1 m) and h of Sir Christopher Cook, 5 Bt; *b* 30 June 1959; *Style—* Richard Cook, Esq

COOK, Robert Finlayson (Robin); MP (Lab) Livingston 1983-; s of Peter Cook and Christina, *née* Lynch; *b* 28 Feb 1946; *Educ* Aberdeen GS, Edinburgh Univ; *m* 1969, Margaret K Whitmore; 2 s; *Career* formerly: chm Edinburgh Corpn Housing Ctee, Scottish Assoc Labour Student Organisations, tutor-organiser with WEA; memb Tribune Gp; MP (Lab) Edinburgh Central 1974-1983, oppn front bench spokesman Treasury and Econ Affrs 1980-Nov 1983, Lab leadership campaign mangr for Rt Hon Neil Kinnock 1983, elected to shadow cabinet and front bench spokesman European and Community Affrs Nov 1983-84; PLP campaign coordinator 1984-86; front bench spokesperson for Trade and the City 1986-87, shadow sec of state for Health and Social Security 1987-; *Style—* Robin Cook, Esq, MP; House of Commons, London SW1 (☎ 071 219 5120)

COOK, Roy Edward; s of Herbert Edward Cook (d 1972), of Horsforth, W Yorks; *b* 25 April 1927; *Educ* Dauntsey's Sch Devizes; *m* 1973, Shevaun Mary, da of John Knock of Howsham Hall, York; 3 s (and 1 s, 2 da by previous m); *Career* dir Derwent Valley Hldgs plc; *Recreations* sailing (yachts: 'Dicer'), country life; *Clubs* Royal Cruising, Royal Yorks YC (Cdre 1979-80); *Style—* Roy Cook, Esq; Kyreham House, Crambe, York (☎ 065 381 268)

COOK, Hon Mrs (Sarah Isobel); da of Baron Murray of Epping Forest (Life Peer); *b* 1959; *m* 1983, Ian Cook; *Style—* The Hon Mrs Cook; c/o 29 The Crescent, Laughton, Essex

COOK, Susan Lorraine (Sue); da of William Arthur Thomas, of Ickenham, Middx, and Kathleen May, *née* Prow; *b* 30 March 1949; *Educ* Vyner's GS Hillingdon, Univ of Leicester (BA); *m* 20 May 1981 (m dis 1987), John Christopher Williams, s of Leonard Williams (d 1988), of The Monkey Sanctuary, Looe, Cornwall; 1 s (Alexander Charles (Charlie) b 12 Oct 1982); ptnr since 1985, William James Macqueen; 1 da (Megan Jane Emily b 30 March 1988); *Career* radio prodr and broadcaster Capital Radio 1974-76, radio presenter of documentaries and topical features for BBC Radio Four and World Service, reporter and presenter for BBC TV's Nationwide 1979-83, presenter BBC TV: Pebble Mill at One, Breakfast Time, Out of Court, Crimewatch UK, Daytime Live, Having a Baby, Children in Need Appeal, That's the Way the Money Goes, Omnibus at the Proms , The Story of the London Sinfonietta, The Children's Royal Variety Performance; involved in work with charities helping children, animals and the elderly; patron of Zoo Check, memb Advsy Cncl Citizenship Fndn; *Books* Accident Action (jtly, 1978), Crimewatch UK (jtly, 1987), The Crimewatch Guide to Home Security and Personal Safety (1988); *Recreations* tennis, singing, spending time at home with the family; *Style—* Miss Sue Cook; c/o Ms S Freathy, Curtis Brown, 162 Regent Street, London W1R 5TB (☎ 071 872 0331, fax 071 284 0667)

COOK, Thomas Roger Edward; o s of Lt-Col Sir Thomas Cook, JP (d 1970), of Sennowe Park, and Gweneth , o da of Spencer Evan Jones; gggs of Thomas Cook (d 1884), fndr of the famous travel agency; *b* 21 Aug 1936; *Educ* Eton, RAC Cirencester; *m* 1, 14 Sept 1960, Virginia (d 1978), yr da of Leslie Aked (d 1964), of Forest Manor, Knaresborough, Yorkshire; m 2, Carola, da of Capt Roger Harvey, (d 1976), of Parliament Piece, Ramsbury, Wilts; *Career* Lt Gren Guards 1954-56; farmer, forester and landowner; chm: Royal Forestry Soc (E Anglia) 1970-73, CLA (Norfolk) 1979-81; memb: Rural Development Cmmn 1983-, Regional Advsry Ctee Forestry Cmmn 1988-; High Sheriff Norfolk 1991-; *Recreations* country pursuits, flying; *Clubs* The Air Sqdn, White's, Pratt's, Norfolk, Allsorts (Norfolk); *Style—* Thomas R E Cook, Esq; Sennowe Park, Guist, Norfolk (☎ 032878 202)

COOKE; *see*: Fletcher-Cooke

COOKE, Alan; s of Colin Cooke, and Shelia, *née* Harris; *b* 23 March 1966; *Educ* Tupton Hall Comp Sch; *Career* table tennis player; team Gold medallist Cwlth

Championships 1985, champion Nat Top 12 1987-90, team Silver medallist Euro Championships 1988, Eng Nat Champion 1988 and 1989, team Gold medallist and mens singles Gold Medallist Cwlth Championships 1989, currently Cwlth champion; currently world counter hitting record holder with Desmond Douglas (170 hits in one minute); *Style—* Alan Cooke, Esq; 23 Elvaston Rd, North Wingfield, Chesterfield, Derbyshire S42 5HH, 28 Parwich Rd, North Wingfield, Chesterfield, Derbyshire S42 5JU (☎ 0246 852332)

COOKE, Rear Adm Anthony John; CB (1980); s of Rear Adm John Ernest Cooke, CB (d 1980), and Kathleen Mary, *née* Haward (d 1976); *b* 21 Sept 1927; *Educ* St Edward's Sch Oxford; *m* 1951, Margaret Anne, da of Frederick Charles Hynard; 2 s, 3 da; *Career* RN 1945, Cdre in Cmd Clyde Submarine Base 1973-75, Rear Adm 1976, sr naval memb directing staff RCDS 1975-78, Adm Pres RNC Greenwich 1978-80; Freeman City of London, memb Ct of Assts Shipwrights' Co; private sec to Lord Mayor of London 1981-; OStJ (1990); *Recreations* philately; *Clubs* City Livery; *Style—* Rear Admiral Anthony Cooke, CB; Chalkhurst, Eynsford, Kent (☎ 0332 862789)

COOKE, Anthony Roderick Chichester Bancroft; yr twin s of Maj-Gen Ronald Basil Bowen Bancroft Cooke, CB, CBE, DSO (d 1971), and Joan (d 1989), da of late Maj Claude Chichester, of Tunworth Down House, Basingstoke; *b* 24 July 1941; *Educ* Ampleforth, London Business Sch (MSc); *m* 1972, Daryll, *née* Aird-Ross; 2 s, 1 da; *Career* CA 1964; chm and chief exec Ellerman Lines plc 1985-87 (dir 1976), chm and md Cunard Ellerman Ltd 1987-; FCA 1964; *Style—* Anthony Cooke, Esq; Poland Court, Odiham, Hants RG25 1JL (☎ 0256 702060); 16 Ennismore Mews, London SW7 1AN (☎ 071 589 0901); Cunard Ellerman Ltd, Ellerman House, 12-20 Camomile St, London EC3A 7EX (☎ 071 283 4311, fax 071 626 5025, telex 884771/2)

COOKE, Christopher Edward Cobden; s of Reginald Garforth Cooke, of Marlow, Bucks, and Phylis Mary Blackburn, *née* Wilde; *b* 18 April 1944; *Educ* King Williams Coll IOM, Univ of Southampton (LLB); *m* 26 July 1969, (Greta) Yvonne, da of Raymond Vere Alberto (d 1979); 3 da (Lisa b 25 May 1971, Lucy b 11 March 1973, Lindy b 19 Jan 1977); *Career* slr; ptnr Rooks Rider (formerly Rooks & Co) Lincoln's Inn London 1970-; memb: Law Soc 1969, Holborn Law Soc 1988; Freeman: City of London 1966, City of Monroe Louisiana 1986; Liveryman Worshipful Co of Makers of Playing Cards 1966; *Recreations* skiing; *Style—* Christopher Cooke, Esq; Chubbers, Sterlings Field, Cookham Dean, Berks (☎ 0628 473642); Rooks Rider, 8/9 New Square, Lincoln's Inn, London WC2A 3QJ (☎ 071 831 7767, fax 071 242 7149, mobile tel 0860 729 920/0836 284 560, telex 261302)

COOKE, David Charles; s of Frederick John Edward Cooke (d 1969), of Clitheroe, Lancs, and Hilda, *née* Hughes; *b* 22 March 1938; *Educ* Accrington GS Lancs, Univ of Manchester (LLB); *Career* admitted slr 1961; asst slr: Hall Brydon & Co Manchester 1961-64, King & Partridge Madras India 1964-67; sr ptnr Pinsent & Co Birmingham 1987- (asst slr 1967-69, ptnr 1969-87); sec W Midlands Devpt Agency; memb: Law Soc 1961-, Birmingham Law Soc 1967-; *Recreations* classical music, fell walking, fine arts, rugby union (watching), sheep; *Style—* David Cooke, Esq; Pinsent & Co, Post & Mail House, 26 Colmore Circus, Birmingham B4 6BH (☎ 021 200 1050, fax 021 200 1040, telex 335101 PINCO G)

COOKE, David John; s of Matthew Peterson Cooke, of Rugby, and Margaret Rose; *b* 23 Aug 1956; *Educ* Lawrence Sheriff Sch Rugby, Trinity Coll Cambridge (MA); *m* 31 March 1979, Susan Margaret, da of Albert Arthur George, of Rugby; 1 s (Stephen b 1984), 1 da (Helen b 1986); *Career* ptnr Pinsent & Co slrs 1982-, licensed insolvency practitioner; memb Law Soc; *Recreations* sailing; *Style—* D J Cooke, Esq; Pinsent & Co, Post & Mail House, 26 Colmore Circus, Birmingham B4 6BH (☎ 021 200 1050, fax 021 200 1040, telex 335101 PINCO G)

COOKE, Col Sir David William Perceval; 12 Bt (E 1661), of Wheatley Hall, Yorks; s of Sir Charles Arthur John Cooke, 11 Bt, of Fowey, Cornwall (d 1978), and Diana, *née* Perceval; *b* 28 April 1935; *Educ* Wellington, RMA Sandhurst, Open Univ (BA); *m* 30 March 1959, Margaret Frances, da of Herbert Skinner (d 1984), of Knutsford; 3 da (Sara b 1960, Louise b 1962, Catherine b 1968); *Heir* kinsman, Edmund Cooke-Yarborough; *Career* 4/7 RDG 1955, RASC 1958, RCT 1965, ret 1990; dir Finance & Resources Bradford City Technology Coll 1990-; *Recreations* bird-watching, walking, social and local history, fishing; *Style—* Col Sir David Cooke, Bt; c/o Midland Bank, 19 Princess St, Knutsford, Cheshire WA16 6BZ

COOKE, Diana, Lady; Diana; o da of Maj-Gen Sir Edward Maxwell Perceval, KCB, DSO, JP (d 1955), of The Grange, Farnham, Surrey, and his 2 wife Norah, *née* Mayne; *m* 12 July 1932, Maj Sir Charles Arthur John Cooke, 11 Bt (d 1978); 1 s, 1 da; *Style—* Diana, Lady Cooke; 15 The Esplanade, Fowey, Cornwall

COOKE, George Venables; CBE (1978); s of William Geoffrey Cooke (d 1967), of Sandbach, Cheshire, and Constance Eva, *née* Venables (d 1976); *b* 8 Sept 1918; *Educ* Sandbach Sch Cheshire, Lincoln Coll Oxford (MA, Dip Ed); *m* 11 Oct 1941, Doreen, da of Harold Cooke (d 1984), of Sandbach, Cheshire; 1 s (Robin b 1946), 2 da (Susan (Mrs Wilson) b 1951, Prudence (Mrs James) b 1954); *Career* WWII 1939-46, 7 Cheshire Regt TA, RMC Sandhurst, 10 Lancashire Fusiliers, HQ XIV Army, Maj; teacher Manchester GS 1947-51, prof asst (educn) W Riding of Yorks CC 1951-53, asst dir of educn Liverpool 1953-58, dep dir of educn Sheffield 1958-64, dir of educn Lindsey (Lincs) CC 1965-74, co educn offr Lincs CC 1974-78, gen sec Soc of Educn Offrs 1978-84 (pres 1975-76); chm Sec of States Advsy Ctee on Handicapped Children 1973-74, vice chm Nat Ctee of Enquiry into Special Educn (Warnock Ctee) 1974-78, memb Parole Bd 1984-87, chm Lincs and Humberside Arts 1987-; *Books* Education Committees (with P Gosden, 1986); *Recreations* golf, gardening; *Clubs* Royal Overseas League; *Style—* George Cooke, Esq, CBE; White House, Grange Lane, Riseholme, Lincoln LN2 2LQ (☎ 0522 522667)

COOKE, Gilbert Andrew; s of Gilbert N Cooke, and Laurie Cooke; *b* 7 March 1923; *Educ* Bournemouth Sch; *m* 1949, Katherine Margaret Mary McGovern; 1 s, 1 da; *Career* CA; md C T Bowring and Co Ltd 1976 (dir 1969-88), chm and chief exec 1982-88; FCA; *Style—* Gilbert Cooke Esq; Kilmarth, 66 Onslow Rd, Burwood Park, Walton-on-Thames, Surrey (☎ 0932 240451)

COOKE, (John) Howard; s of Capt Jack Cooke, MC, of Exeter, Devon, and Ellen Jean, *née* Passmore; *b* 7 Jan 1952; *Educ* Exeter Sch, QMC London (LLB); *m* 1, 22 July 1972 (m dis 1983), Sally-Anne, da of Sydney Evans; m 2, 25 March 1983, Dr (Jayne) Elizabeth Mann; 2 da (Elena b 1983, Lauren b 1986); *Career* admitted slr 1976; ptnr Frere Cholmeley 1980; memb Law Soc; *Recreations* country pursuits; *Style—* Howard Cooke, Esq; 28 Lincoln's Inn Fields, London WC2A 3HH (☎ 071 405 7878, fax 071 405 9056, telex 27623)

COOKE, Jean Esme Oregon; da of Arthur Oregon Cooke, and Dorothy Emily, *née* Cranefield (d 1981); *b* 18 Feb 1927; *Educ* Blackheath HS, Central Sch of Art and Crafts, Goldsmiths Coll Sch of Art (Dip Art & Design), Camberwell Sch of Art, City and Guilds Coll of Arts, RCA (DipArt and Design); *m* 2 April 1953, John Randal Bratby; 3 s (David Johnathon Fernando b 1955, Jason Sovereign b 1959, Dan Edvardo Joachim Jesse b 1968), 1 d (Wendy Dolores Carmen Hirondell b 1970); *Career* artist; lectr: Oxford Sch of Art, Royal Coll of Art 1964-74; Chantry Bequest Purchases 1969 and 1972; portraits: Dr Egon Wellesz, Dr Walter Oakshott for Lincoln Coll Oxford, Mrs Mary Bennett for St Hildas 1976, John Bratby for Royal Coll of Art Collection; self portrait: Tate, Royal Acad Collection; pres Friends of Woodlands Art Gallery; RA 1972; *Recreations* Tai Chi, finding stones on the beach, riding a bike, swimming; *Clubs* Arts; *Style—* Miss Jean Cooke; 7 Hardy Road, Blackheath, London SE3 7NS (☎ 081 858 6288)

COOKE, Jeremy Lionel; QC (1990); s of Eric Edwin Cooke, of Warlingham, Surrey, and Margaret Lilian, *née* Taylor; *b* 28 April 1949; *Educ* Whitgift Sch Croydon, St Edmund Hall Oxford (open exhibition, MA, Rugby blues 1968 and 1969); *m* 24 June 1972, Barbara Helen, da of Geoffrey Curtis Willey, of Wallington, Surrey; 1 s (Samuel b 29 June 1984), 2 da (Emily b 3 June 1978, Josie b 28 March 1980); *Career* slr; Coward Chance 1973-76; called to the Bar 1976; *Recreations* youth work; *Style—* Jeremy Cooke, Esq, QC; 7 Kings Bench Walk, Temple, London EC4Y 7DS (☎ 071 583 0404, fax 071 583 0950)

COOKE, John Arthur; s of Arthur Hafford Cooke MBE (d 1987), Warden New Coll Oxford, and Ilse Cooke, *née* Sachs (d 1973); *b* 13 April 1943; *Educ* Dragon Sch Oxford, Magdalen Coll Sch Oxford, Univ of Heidelberg, King's Coll Univ of Cambridge (BA, MA), LSE; *m* 21 Feb 1970, Tania Frances, da of Alexander Cochrane Crichton; 1 s (Alexander b 1975), 2 da (Olga b 1972, Beatrice b 1977); *Career* Civil Serv 1966: asst princ Bd of Trade 1966, second sec (later first sec) UK delgn to Euro Communities 1969-73, Dept of Trade 1973-76, office of the UK perm rep to Euro Communities 1976-77, Dept of Trade 1977-80 (institut int d'admin publique Paris 1979), asst sec Dept of Trade 1980-84, seconded asst dir Morgan Grenfell & Co 1984-85, Dept of Trade 1985-87, under sec Dept of Trade 1987-; bd memb St Luke's Community Tst, non-exec dir RTZ Pillar Ltd 1990-; *Recreations* reading, travelling, looking at buildings; *Clubs* Utd Oxford and Cambridge, Cambridge Union; *Style—* John Cooke, Esq; Department of Trade and Industry, 1 Victoria St, London SW1H OET (☎ 071 215 7877, fax 071 222 2629, telex 8811074/5 DTHQ G)

COOKE, Air Vice-Marshal John Nigel Carlyle; CB (1984), OBE (1954); s of Air Marshal Sir Cyril Bertram Cooke, KCB, CBE (d 1972), and Elizabeth Amelia Phyllis, *née* Davies; *b* 16 Jan 1922; *Educ* Felsted, St Mary's Hosp Paddington (MD); *m* 1958, Elizabeth Helena Murray Johnstone; 2 s, 1 da; *Career* prof of aviation med 1974-79, dean of Air Force Med 1979-83, sr conslt RAF 1983-85, ret 1985; conslt CAA, conslt advsr to Sultan of Oman's Air Force 1985-90; conslt physician King Edward VII Hosp Midhurst 1988-; FRCP, FRCP (Edinburgh), MFOM; *Recreations* fly fishing, gliding; *Clubs* RAF; *Style—* Air Vice-Marshal John Cooke, CB, OBE; 4 Lincoln Close, Stoke Mandeville, Bucks (☎ 029 61 3852)

COOKE, John Patrick; s of Patrick Cooke (d 1967), of Kilkenny (d 1967), and Winifred Cooke; *b* 18 June 1933; *Educ* Good Cnsl Coll New Ross Co Wexford; *m* 26 Sept 1959, Avril, da of Alfred Palmer, of Croxley Green, Herts; 3 s (Andrew b 1962, Kevin b 1963, Jonathan b 1970); *Career* banking, vice-pres Citibank NA 1977-; exec dir Citicorp Investmt Bank Ltd 1979-; *Recreations* golf; *Clubs* Burhill GC, Weybridge Surrey, Portmarnock Dublin, Aloha GC, Marbella; *Style—* John P Cooke, Esq; Spinney Lodge, Firlands, Weybridge, Surrey (☎ (0932) 847105); Citicorp Investment Bank Ltd, 335 Strand, London WC2; 71 St Stephens Green, Dublin, Ireland

COOKE, Capt Jonathan Gervaise Fitzpatrick; OBE (1983); s of Rear Adm John Gervaise Beresford Cooke, CB (d 1976), and Helen Beatrice, *née* Cameron; *b* 26 March 1943; *Educ* Summerfields Oxford, Marlborough, RNC Dartmouth; *m* 9 April 1983, Henrietta Lorraine Deschamps, da of the late Lt-Col Saunders Edward Chamier, MC, of Green Hedges, Wadhurst, E Sussex; 1 s (Hugo b 1987), 2 da (Arabella b 1984, Serena b 1985); *Career* RN 1961-89; cmd three submarines (HMS Rorqual 1974-76, HMS Churcill 1981-82, HMS Warspite 1980-84), Cdr submarine sea trg 1984-86, Capt 3 Submarine Sqdn 1986-89; Br Naval Attache Paris; *Recreations* tennis, reading, skiing, country sports; *Clubs* Naval and Military, Queens, Cercle Interalliee Paris; *Style—* Capt Jonathan Cooke, OBE; 10 Boulevard Flandrin, Paris 75016, France; Downstead House, Morestead, Winchester, Hants SO21 1LF (☎ 096 274209)

COOKE, (Patrick) Joseph Dominic; s of Patrick Cooke, of Galway, and Mary, *née* Naughton of Galway; *b* 9 Aug 1931; *Educ* St Joseph's Coll, Univ Coll Galway (BEng); *m* 31 Dec 1960, Margaret Mary, da of Dr Valentine Vincent Brown (d 1968); 2 s (Patrick Vincent b 11 Dec 1961, Robert Joseph b 11 Oct 1989), 4 da (Elizabeth Mary b 22 April 1963, Catherine Louise b 25 Aug 1964, Barbara Mair b 8 Jan 1966, Johanna Mair (twin) b 8 Jan 1966); *Career* graduate trainee United Steel Companies Ltd 1952-54, Workington Iron and Steel Co (Branch of United Steel Co) 1954-60, princ ptnr Urwick Orr 1970-73 (sr ptnr 1967-70), princ Cooke Management Consultants 1973-87, non-exec dir EMAP plc 1984-, md The Daily Telegraph plc 1987-; MICE, MIMechE, FIMC (Strand Smith award 1967); *Recreations* golf, gardening; *Style—* Joseph Cooke, Esq; The Daily Telegraph, 181 Marsh Wall, London E14 9SR (☎ 071 538 5000)

COOKE, His Honour Judge; (Richard) Kenneth; OBE (1945); s of Richard Cooke, and Beatrice Mary; *b* 17 March 1917; *Educ* Sebright Sch Wolverley, Univ of Birmingham; *m* 1945, Gwendoline Mary Black; *Career* slr 1939, practising 1945-52, clerk to Justices 1952-70, metropolitan stipendiary magistrate 1970, recorder of the Crown Court 1972-1980, a Circuit judge (SE) 1980-; memb Lord Chllr's Advsy Ctee on Trg of Magistrates 1979-; hon dep chm Magistrates Assoc 1981-82 (chm Legal Ctee 1980-); licensed reader Rochester Diocese 1970-; pres South West London Branch Magistrates Assoc 1984-; *Style—* His Honour Judge Cooke, OBE; 8 St Paul's Sq, Church Rd, Bromley, Kent (☎ 081 464 6761)

COOKE, Martin James Paul; s of Lt-Col Cedric Paul Cooke (d 1974), and Katharine Norah Blanche *née* Lowick; *b* 25 Jan 1947; *Educ* Haileybury, Imperial Serv Coll; *m* 1, 19 Oct 1974 (m dis 1983), Janet Elizabeth, da of Alan Byrne, of Llanderffel, N Wales; 1 s (Nicholas b 1978), 1 da (Anna b 1976); m 2, 4 Jan 1985, Frances Mary, da of John Peter Jackson (d 1985), of Croydon; 3 s (Jonathon b 1986, Charles b 1988, Benedict b 1990); *Career* CA; Touche Ross & Co 1969-72, ptnr Rensburg Stockbrokers 1976 (joined 1972), non-exec dir Radio City plc 1987, chm Northern Stock Exchange Conference 1988, dir BWD Rensburg Ltd 1988; chm Chester Summer Music Festival 1979-81 (fin dir 1978-87), St Endellion Summer Festival 1990-91; vice pres Liverpool Soc of CAs 1990-91; memb Stock Exchange 1973; FCA 1969, AMSIA 1973; *Recreations* sailing, music; *Clubs* Grosvenor (Chester), Racquets (Liverpool); *Style—* Martin Cooke, Esq; Holywell Farm, Clutton, Tattenhall, Chester, Cheshire; B W D Rensburg Ltd, Silkhouse Court, Tithebarn St, Liverpool L2 2NH (☎ 051 227 2030)

COOKE, Michael Edmond; s of Michael Joseph Cooke, (d 1960), of Thornton Kingston Hill, Kingston-on-Thames, Surrey, and late Mary Margaret, *née* Donaghy; *b* 21 Aug 1929; *Educ* Beaumont Coll Old Windsor Berks, Lincoln Coll Oxford (MA); *m* 11 March 1961, Jennifer Gwendoline, s of Earnest J Jack (d 1981), of Crossbush, Summerley, Middleton-on-Sea, Sussex; 1 s (Tristan b 19 Jan 1966), 2 da (Olivia b 12 March 1964, Anastasia b 9 Jan 1968); *Career* 2 Lt RA 1948-49, serv ME; called to the Bar Middle Temple 1954; Nat Bank Ltd 1961-69: chief account, sec, asst gen mangr; jt md Banque Paribas London 1969-79; chm: Paribas Guernsey Ltd, PIL Petroleum & Energy Ltd, Triton Petroleum Ltd 1972-88; dir: High Park Securities Inc (USA) 1981-85, Cordal Corp Devpt Ltd 1980-, Chiers HFC Int Ltd, Copadrex N Sea Petroleum Ltd, EC (Hldgs) Ltd, R & W Hawthorne Leslie & Co Ltd, Heurty Ltd, Heurty Furnaces Ltd, Nuclear Tport Ltd, Paribas Fin Ltd, Torhurst Ltd; md Third Triton Petroleum Ltd 1980-86; memb: Lloyds, Middle Temple; *Recreations* tennis, golf, cricket; *Clubs* City Univ, City of London, Hurlingham, Royal Wimbledon Golf, MCC; *Style—* Michael Cooke, Esq; 14 Highbury Rd, Wimbledon, London SW19 7PR; (☎ 081

946 1533, 081 946 5821)

COOKE, Michael John; s of John Cooke (d 1981), and Reneê Elizabeth, *née* Holmes; *b* 18 Nov 1945; *Educ* Riland, Bedford; *m* 31 Aug 1968, Janet Margaret, da of William Mason Fullerton; 3 s (James b 1970, Matthew b 1972, Alexander b 1985), 2 da (Melissa b 1976, Louise b 1978); *Career* CA; dir Baltic Anglo Technol Ltd 1983; Lord of the Manor of Edingale; specialist in Soviet Trade; *Recreations* cricket, football, golf; *Style*— Michael Cooke, Esq; Whinrigg House, Borrowcop Lane, Lichfield, Staffs WS14 9DF; Baltic Anglo Technology Ltd, 2 Duke St, Sutton Coldfield, West Midlands B72 1RJ (☎ 021 355 0762, telex 334264, fax 021 335 8216)

COOKE, Nicholas Huxley; s of Geoffrey Whithall Cooke, of Worthing, Sussex, and Anne Heathorn, *née* Huxley (d 1989); *b* 6 May 1944; *Educ* Charterhouse, Worcester Coll Oxford (MA); *m* 27 June 1970, Anne, da of James Whittington Landon, DFC, of West Chiltington, Sussex; 2 s (James b 1983, Toby b 1986), 3 da (Fenella b 1973, Sophie b 1976, Caroline b 1978); *Career* dir: British Trust for Conservation Volunteers Scotland 1978-84, Scottish Conservation Projects Trust 1984-; memb: Scottish Ctee for Euro Year of the Enviroment 1987-88, UK 2000 Scotland 1987-, Assoc of Chief Offrs of Scot Voluntary Orgns 1989; memb Bd: Scot Cncl for Voluntary Orgns, Tst for Urban Ecology; pres Amateur Entomologists Soc 1975 (treas 1972-78); *Recreations* outdoor conservation work, walking, photography, fly fishing; *Style*— Nicholas Cooke, Esq; Easter Stonefield, Port of Menteith, Stirling FK8 3RD (☎ 08772411); Scottish Conservation Projects Trust, Balallan House, 24 Allan Park, Stirling FK8 2QG (☎ 0786 79697, fax 0786 65359)

COOKE, Nigel Frank; s of Nigel Cuthbert Cooke (d 1951), of Kassa House, Kassa, Plateau Province, N Nigeria, and Catherine Cooke, *née* Woodhams (d 1964); *b* 25 April 1916; *Educ* Ipswich Sch, Gonville and Caius Coll Cambridge (MA); *m* 16 Nov 1957, Heather Elizabeth Seymour (d 1989), da of Arthur Henry Seymour Vivian (d 1985), of 24 Sandy Lodge Rd, Moor Park, Rickmansworth, Herts; 2 s (Richard b 1958, Timothy b 1960), 1 da (Catherine b 1964); *Career* Lt Nigeria Regt 1939-43, Admin Serv N Nigeria 1938-62, sr resident 1959-62, i/c Kano Province 1961-62, head of mgmnt recruitment Courtaulds 1964-80, chm Moor Park (1958) Ltd 1985; figured in Tales From the Dark Continent by Charles Allen; *Recreations* reading, bridge, golf; *Clubs* United Oxford and Cambridge Univ, Moor Park Golf; *Style*— Nigel Cooke, Esq; 25 Russell Rd, Moor Park, Northwood, Middlesex HA6 2LP (☎ 092 74 21900)

COOKE, Peter Stephen; s of Henry Peter Cooke (d 1988), and Patricia Jean Cooke, *née* Wearing; *b* 13 April 1948; *Educ* Guildford Royal GS, Univ of Southampton (BSc); *m* 1, 24 July 1971 (m dis 1989), Patricia Ann, da of Robert Frederick Meredith; 2 da (Alexander b 1978, Amy b 1979); m 2, 15 July 1989, Elizabeth Margaret, da of Glyndwr Thomas; *Career* slr; legal advsr to Engrg Employers' Fedn 1978-83, ptnr Theodore Goddard 1984-; memb Worshipful Co of Slrs 1989; memb Law Soc; *Books* Croners Employment Law (1980), Croners Industrial Relations Law (contrib 1989); *Recreations* music, cycling and sailing; *Style*— Peter Cooke, Esq; 302 Cromwell Tower, Barbican, London EC2Y 8DD; Theodore Goddard, 150 Aldersgate St, London EC1A 4EJ (☎ 071 6068855, telex 884678, fax 071 6064390)

COOKE, (William) Peter; s of Douglas Edgar Cooke, MC (Lt Durham LI, d 1964), of Gerrards Cross, Bucks, and Florence May, *née* Mills (d 1986); *b* 1 Feb 1932; *Educ* Kingswood Sch Bath, Merton Coll Oxford (MA); *m* 22 April 1957, Maureen Elizabeth, da of Dr E A Haslam-Fox (d 1975) of Holmes Chapel, Cheshire; 2 s (Nicholas b 1959, Andrew b 1964), 2 da (Caroline b 1960, Stephanie b 1970); *Career* Nat Serv RA 1951; joined Bank of England 1955; seconded: to Bank for International Settlements Basle Switzerland 1958-59, as pa to Md IMF Washington DC 1961-65, as sec City Takeover Panel 1968-69; Bank of England: first dep chief cashier 1970-73, advsr to Govrs 1973-76, head Banking Supervision 1976-85, assoc dir 1982-88; chm: City EEC Ctee 1973-80, Ctee on Banking Regulations and Supervisory Practices Bank for International Settlements Basle Switzerland 1977-88, Price Waterhouse World Regulatory Advsy Serv 1989-; dir Safra Republic Holdings SA 1989-; chm Merton Soc 1979-; govr Pangbourne Coll 1982-, memb Bd The Housing Corpn 1988-, memb Mgmnt Ctee Church Housing Assoc 1977-; *Recreations* music, golf, travel; *Clubs* Reform, Overseas Bankers, Denham Golf; *Style*— Peter Cooke, Esq; Price Waterhouse, Southwark Towers, 32 London Bridge St, London SE1 9SY (☎ 071 939 3000, fax 071 378 0647, telex 884657/8)

COOKE, Maj Randle Henry; LVO; s of Col HRV Cooke Dalicote Hall (d 1971), of Bridgenorth, Shropshire, and EFK (d 1978); *b* 26 April 1930; *Educ* Eton; *m* 19 Dec 1960, Clare, da of CJM Bennett, CBE, The Penthouse, 15 St Olave's Court St, Petersburgh Place, London; 1 s (David b 27 May 1986), 1 da (Priscilla b 7 Nov 1961); *Career* 2 Lt 8 KRI Hussars 1949, served Korea with Regt and USAF (POW) 1950-53, ADC to GOC 7 Armoured Div 1955, regl adj 1957, instr RMA Sandhurst 1960, Sqdn Cdr QRIH Malaya, Borneo and Germany 1963, GSO3 (SD) HQ 1 Div 1965, equerry to Duke to Edinburgh 1968-71, private sec to Lord Mayor of London 1972-74, dir personnel and admin Alginate Industs plc 1974-78; md: ARA Int Ltd 1984-86, Mervyn Hughes International Ltd 1986-87, Randle Cooke and Associates recruitment constls 1987-; Freeman City of London 1971; *Recreations* most things to do with water; *Clubs* Cavalry and Guards, Caterpillar; *Style*— Maj Randle Cooke, LVO; Coney Hill House, Gt Missenden, Bucks HP16 9PE (☎ 02406 2147); Randle Cooke and Associates, International Recruitment Consultants, London House, 53-54 Haymarket London SW1Y 4RP (☎ 071 925 0177, fax 071 930 4261)

COOKE, Raymond Edgar; OBE; s of late Edgar Jonathan Cooke; *b* 14 Feb 1925; *Educ* Univ of London; *m* 1948 (m dis 1968), Marjorie Evelyn; 1 s, 1 da; m 2 1987, Jennifer, da of Léon J Goossens CBE (d 1988); *Career* former designs engineer BBC; tech dir Wharfedale Wireless Works Ltd 1955-61; fndr and md KEF Electronics Ltd 1961-88 (now life pres); FRSA, FBKSTS, FAES; *Style*— Raymond Cooke Esq, OBE; Kingswood Lodge, Nevill Park, Tunbridge Wells, Kent (☎ 0892 31843, office 0622 672261, fax 0662 50653, telex Kefel G 96140)

COOKE, Rt Hon Mr Justice; Rt Hon Sir Robin Brunskill; KBE (1986), PC (1977); s of Hon Mr Justice (Philip Brunskill) Cooke, MC (d 1956), and Valmai Digby Gore; *b* 9 May 1926; *Educ* Wanganui Collegiate Sch, Victoria Univ Coll Wellington NZ (LLM), Gonville and Caius Cambridge (MA, PhD, hon fellow); *m* 1952, Phyllis Annette, da of Malcolm Balgownie Miller (d 1968); 3 s; *Career* called to the Bar NZ 1950, Inner Temple 1954 (hon bencher 1985), practised NZ 1955-72, QC 1964, judge of Court of Appeal of New Zealand 1976- (pres 1986-); Hon LLD Victoria Univ Coll 1989; kt 1977; *Clubs* United Oxford and Cambridge University (London), Wellington (NZ); *Style*— The Rt Hon Sir Robin Cooke; 4 Homewood Cres, Karori, Wellington, New Zealand (☎ 010 64 4 768 059); President's Chambers, Court of Appeal (☎ 010 64 4 726 398)

COOKE, His Honour Judge Roger Arnold; s of Stanley Gordon Cooke, of Nether Alderley, Cheshire, and Frances Mabel, *née* Reading; *b* 30 Nov 1939; *Educ* Repton, Magdalen Coll Oxford (BA, MA); *m* 16 May 1970, Hilary, da of Eric Robertson, of Shorwell, IOW; 2 s (James b 1972, Thomas b 1975), 2 da (Elizabeth b 1973, Mary b 1979); *Career* called to Bar Middle Temple 1962 (Astbury scholar), ad eundem Lincoln's Inn 1967; practice at the Chancery Bar 1963-89, head of Chambers 1985-88, jt head of Chambers 1988-89, rec 1987-89 (asst rec 1982-87), circuit judge 1989; pt/t students offr Lincoln's Inn 1976-80, hon sec Chancery Bar Assoc 1979-89, memb Disciplinary Tbnls Bar 1988-89; Churchwarden Little Berkhamstead 1979-, memb Fin and Gen Purpose Ctee Broxbourne (C) Assoc 1986-89; Freeman (by purchase) City of London 1986; *Recreations* gardening, photography, history, old buildings, food; *Clubs* Royal Inst of GB; *Style*— His Honour Judge Roger Cooke; Law Courts, Woodall House, Lordship Lane, London N22

COOKE, Roger Malcolm; s of Sidney Cooke, and Elsie Cooke; *b* 12 March 1945; *Educ* Thames Valley GS; *m* 7 Sept 1968, Antoinette Mary; 1 s (Gregory b 22 Sept 1973), 1 da (Amanda b 4 June 1971); *Career* CA 1968; articled clerk Garner & Co Chartered Accountants 1962-68; Arthur Andersen & Co: joined 1968, ptnr 1976-, head of London Tax Div 1979-89, area co-ordinator tax for Europe ME Africa and India 1989-, head of UK tax practice and dep managing ptnr UK 1989-; FCA 1968, FTII 1969; *Recreations* cricket, tennis, football, skiing, squash; *Style*— Roger Cooke, Esq; Arthur Andersen & Co, 1 Surrey St, London WC2R 2PS (☎ 071 438 3207, fax 071 438 3630)

COOKE, Prof Ronald Urwick; s of Ernest Oswald Cooke (d 1948), of Maidstone, Kent, and Lilian, *née* Mount (d 1949); *b* 1 Sept 1941; *Educ* Ashford GS, UCL (BSc, MSc, PhD, DSc); *m* 4 Jan 1968, Barbara Anne, da of Albert Henry Baldwin (d 1969), of Petts Wood, Kent; 1 s (Graham Stephen b 1971), 1 da (Emma Louise b 1974); *Career* Dept of Geography UCL: lectr 1961-75, reader 1975, prof and head 1981-, dean of arts 1991, vice provost 1991; Bedford Coll London: prof 1975-81, dean of Sci 1978-80, vice princ 1979-80; govr: Watford Boys GS, Watford Girls GS; memb: RGS, Inst Br Geographers (pres 1991), Geological Soc of London; *Books* incl: Geomorphology in Deserts (with A Warren, 1973), Geomorphology in Environmental Management (with J C Doornkamp, 1974, 2 edn 1990), Arroyos and Environmental Change in the American Southwest (with R W Reeves, 1976), Environmental Hazards in Los Angeles (1984), Urban Geomorphology in Dry Lands (with D Brunsden, J C Dornkamp and DKC Jones, 1982); *Clubs* Athenaeum; *Style*— Prof Ronald Cooke; Dept of Geography, University Coll London, 26 Bedford Way, London WC1N OAP (☎ 071 380 7562)

COOKE, Roy; JP (Gravesend 1972, W Midlands 1976); s of Reginald Herbert Cooke, of Sale, Cheshire, and Alice, *née* Brown; *b* 6 May 1930; *Educ* Manchester GS (Scholar), Trinity Coll Oxford (MA); *m* 1957, Claire Marion Medlicott, da of Lt-Col Clifford Stanley Woodward, CBE, JP, DL (d 1974), of Bridgend, Glam; 3 s (Richard, Jeremy, Michael); *Career* Mil Serv 1951-54, short serv cmmn RAEC, Actg-Maj Staff Offr, HQ N Army Gp, NATO; schoolmaster: Gillingham GS Kent 1955-56, Woking GS Surrey 1956-58, Manchester GS 1958-64; head of foreign languages Stockport Sch 1964-68; headmaster: Gravesend GS 1968-74, King Henry VIII Sch Coventry 1974-77, Coventry Sch; dir Coventry Sch Fndn; memb Headmasters' Conf; *Recreations* reading, music, travel, gardening, photography, fell walking; *Clubs* East India and Public Schs; *Style*— Roy Cooke Esq, JP; 10 Stivichall Croft, Coventry; Coventry Sch, King Henry VIII, Warwick Rd, Coventry CV3 6AQ (☎ 0203 675050)

COOKE, Hon Mrs (Sarah Myfida Mary); *née* Tyrell-Kenyon; MBE (1952); da of 4 Baron Kenyon (d 1927); *b* 13 Sept 1917; *m* 10 Oct 1966, Col Desmond Aubrey Robert Bancroft Cooke (d 1987), late 13/18 Hussars, yst s of late Lt-Col Sydney Fitzwyman Cooke, of Orwell Lodge, Horsham, Sussex; *Career* formerly in VAD; former vice-chm Victoria League for Cwlth Friendship (prev gen Hospitality sec); *Style*— The Hon Mrs Cooke; 10 Guthrie St, London SW3 6NU

COOKE, Simon Henry; s of George Bristow Cooke, DFC (d 1989), of Gestingthorpe Hall, Halstead, Essex, and Frances Evelina, *née* Hopkinson; *b* 16 April 1932; *Educ* Marlborough, Gonville and Caius Coll Cambridge (MA); *m* 9 June 1956, Anne Gillian De Horne, da of Brig John Theodore De Horne Vaizey, of Attwoods, Halstead, Essex (1982); 3 s (Jonathan b 1959, Adam b 1960, Matthew b 1964); *Career* admitted slr 1957, ptnr Bristows Cooke & Carpmael 1960-, chm Critchley Ltd 1978; non-exec dir: Trico Folberth Ltd, Bausch & Lomb UK Ltd; chm Govrs Newport Free GS Essex; memb Law Soc; *Recreations* bird watching, skiing, shooting, travel, gardening; *Style*— Simon Cooke, Esq; Deers, Clavering, Saffron Walden, Essex (☎ 0799 778342); 10 Lincolns Inn Fields, London WC2A 3BP (☎ 071 242 0462, fax 071 242 1232, 071 831 3537, telex 27487)

COOKE, Stephen Giles; s of Basil Cooke, of Codicote, Herts, and Dora Cynthia, *née* Richards; *b* 30 July 1946; *Educ* Stamford Sch; *m* Jane Lesley, da of Cowper Fredrick Ide; 2 s (Henry Stephen b 1975, James Cowper b 1979); *Career* admited slr 1971; articled clerk Clay Allison & Clark Worksop Notts, ptnr Withers 1973- (joined 1971); memb Gen Ctee The Ockenden Venture (refugee charity); *Books* Inheritance Tax and Lifetime Gifts (1987); *Recreations* gardening, tennis; *Style*— Stephen Cooke, Esq; Amersham House, 25 Compton Way, Farnham, Surrey GU10 1QT; Withers, 20 Essex St, London WC2R 3AL (☎ 071 836 8400, fax 071 240 2278)

COOKE, Stephen Paul; s of James Armitage Cooke, of Junipers, Dunsfold, and Beryl Margaret, *née* Jarvis; *b* 8 April 1950; *Educ* Cranleigh Sch, Imperial Coll London (BSc, ARCS); *m* 23 Sept 1972, Penelope Anne, da of John Reginald Franklin, of Cranleigh, Surrey; 2 s (Alistair b 1976, Thomas b 1977), 1 da (Polly b 1986); *Career* ptnr Montagu Loebl Stanley & Co 1976, md Montagu Loebl Stanley Fin Servs 1984, chief exec Gerrard Vivian Gray Ltd 1987-; dir: Gerrard Vivian Gray Ltd, Gerrard Vivian Gp Fin Servs Ltd, Gerrard Vivian Gp Nominees Ltd; AMSIA, memb Cncl Stock Exchange; dir: Trade Markets Managing Bd, Settlement Services Bd (memb Membership Sub-Ctee); *Recreations* tennis, horse racing; *Clubs* City of London; *Style*— Stepehn Cooke, Esq; Gerrard Vivian Gray Ltd, Burne House, 88 High Holborn, London WC1V 7EB (☎ 071 831 8883, fax 071 831 9938, telex 887080)

COOKE-PRIEST, Rear Adm Colin Herbert Dickinson; s of Dr William Hereward Dickinson Priest (d 1988), of Jersey, and Harriet Lesley Josephine, *née* Cooke; *b* 17 March 1939; *Educ* Marlborough, Britannia RNC Dartmouth; *m* 20 March 1965, Susan Mary Diana (Sue), da of Air Vice-Marshal John Forde Hobler, CB, CBE, of Queensland, Australia; 2 s (Nicholas b 1969, James b 1971), 2 da (Diana b 1966, Marina b 1974); *Career* Cdr RN 1973, CO HMS Plymouth 1975, Capt 1980, CO HMS Boxer 1983, dir Martime Tactical Sch 1985, CO HMS Brilliant and Capt (F) Second Frigate Sqdn 1987, Cdr RN Task Force Gulf 1988, Rear Adm RN 1989, Dep Asst Chief of Staff (OPS) SHAPE Belgium 1989, Flag Offr Naval Aviation; Freeman City of London 1986, Liveryman Worshipful Cos of Coachmakers and Coach Harness Makers 1986; *Recreations* hockey, cricket, DIY; *Style*— Rear Adm Colin Cooke-Priest

COOKE-YARBOROUGH, Edmund Harry; s of George Eustace Cooke-Yarborough (d 1938); kinsman and hp of Sir David Cooke, 12 Bt; *b* 25 Dec 1918; *Educ* Canford, Ch Ch Oxford (MA); *m* 1952, Anthea Katharine, da of John Alexander Dixon (d 1976), of Market Harborough; 1 s, 1 da; *Career* chief head Instrumentation and Applied Physics Div UK Atomic Energy Authy 1957-80, chief res scientist 1980-82; dir E H Cooke-Yarborough Ltd 1986-; FEng 1980, FInstP, FIEE; *Books* An Introduction to Transistor Circuits (1957, second edn 1960); *Recreations* tracing archaeological alignments, digital computing, Stirling engines, motor cars; *Style*— Edmund Cooke-Yarborough Esq; Lincoln Lodge, Longworth, nr Abingdon, Oxon

COOKSEY, David James Scott; s of late Dr Frank Sebastian Cooksey, CBE, of Suffolk, and Muriel Mary, *née* Scott; *b* 14 May 1940; *Educ* Westminster, St Edmund Hall Oxford (MA); *m* 1973, Janet Clouston Bewley, da of Dr Ian Aysgarth Bewley Cathie, of Glocs; 1 s (Alexander b 1976), 1 da (Leanda b 1974), 1 step da (Atlanta

Wardell-Yerburgh); *Career* chm Advent Ltd 1987- (md 1981-87); dir: Agricultural Genetics Co 1983-, British Venture Capital Association 1983-89 (chm 1983-84); European Silicon Structures 1985-, Advent Int Corp 1985-90; chm Audit Cmmn for Local Govt in England and Wales 1986-, memb Innovation Advsy Bd DTI 1988-; *Recreations* sailing, property restoration, performing and visual arts; *Clubs* Royal Thames Yacht, New (Edinburgh); *Style—* David Cooksey, Esq; Advent Ltd, 25 Buckingham Gate, London SW1E 6LD (☎ 071 630 9811)

COOKSON, Hon Mrs (Angela Mary Martyn); *née* Martyn-Hemphill; er da of 5 Baron Hemphill; *b* 26 Jan 1953; *m* 2 Oct 1982, Robert Edwin Cookson, s of Capt Peter Henry Cookson, MC, of Lower Slaughter, Glos; 1 s (Edward Peter b 1 May 1988), 1 da (Serena Louise b 16 Nov 1986); *Style—* The Hon Mrs Cookson; Manor Farm, Upper Slaughter, Cheltenham, Glos GL54 2JJ

COOKSON, Anthony John (Tony); s of John Cookson (d 1971), of Ipswich, and Joyce Creaser, *née* Hutchison; *b* 3 June 1940; *Educ* Northgate GS Ipswich; *m* 8 Oct 1967, Janet, da of Kenneth Noble, of Ipswich; 1 s (John Alexander b 1978), 2 da (Samantha Jo b 1970, Tara Danielle b 1971); *Career* Hadleigh Industries Group plc: joined 1961, md 1971, gp chief exec 1987; hon treas The Energy Industs Cncl; Freeman: City of London, Worshipful Co of Founders; FBIM 1986; *Recreations* golf, squash, travel, reading; *Clubs* Woodbridge Golf, Annabels; *Style—* Tony Cookson, Esq; Hadleigh Industries Group plc, Cromwell Court, No 5 Greyfriars Road, Ipswich, Suffolk IP1 1XG (☎ 0473 231031, fax 0473 232126)

COOKSON, Catherine Ann; OBE (1985); da of Catherine Fawcett; *b* 20 June 1906; *m* 1940, Thomas Henry Cookson; *Career* novelist, 68 novels published in English and 17 Foreign languages; *Publications include* Kate Hannigan (1950), Maggie Rowan (1954), A Grand Man (1954) (filmed as Jacqueline 1956), The Lord and Mary Ann (1956), Rooney (1957) (filmed 1958), The Menagerie (1958), The Devil and Mary Ann (1958), Fenwick Houses (1960), Love and Mary Ann (1961), Life and Mary Ann (1962), Marriage and Mary Ann (1964), Mary Ann's Angels (1965), Matty Doolin (1965), Katie Mullholland (1967), Mary Ann and Bill (1967), Our Kate (autobiog 1969), The Nice Bloke (1969), The Glass Virgin (1970), The Mallen Streak (1973), The Mallen Girl (1974), The Mallen Litter (1974), Our John Willie (1974), The Invisible Cord (1975), Go Tell It to Mrs Golightly (1977), The Cinder Path (1978), Tilly Trotter (1980), Tilly Trotty Wed (1981), Tilly Trotter Widowed (1982), A Dinner of Herbs (1985), Harold (1985), The Moth (1986), Catherine Cookson Country (memoirs, 1986), The Parson's Daughter (1987), The Cultured Handmaiden (1988), Let Me Make Myself Plain (A personal anthology, 1988), The Harrogate Secret (1989), The Black Candle (1989), The Wingless Bird (1990), The Gillyvons (1991); Hon MA Univ of Newcastle upon Tyne 1983; *Recreations* painting; *Style—* Mrs Catherine Cookson; Bristol Lodge, Langley on Tyne, Hexham, Northumberland

COOKSON, Clive Michael; s of Richard Clive Cookson, and Ellen, *née* Fawwaz; *b* 13 Feb 1952; *Educ* Winchester, BNC Oxford (BA); *m* 8 April 1978, Caroline Davidson; 1 s (Robert b 9 Oct 1984), 1 da (Emma b 10 July 1986); *Career* journalist; trainee journalist Luton Evening Post Thomson Regional Newspapers 1974-76, American ed (in Washington) Times Higher Education Supplement 1977-81 (science corr 1976-77), technol corr The Times 1981-83, sci and med corr BBC Radio 1983-87, chem and pharmaceutical corr Financial Times 1990- (technol ed 1987-90); Feature Writer of the Year (UK Technol Press Awards) 1988 and 1989; *Style—* Clive Cookson, Esq; The Financial Times, 1 Southwark Bridge, London SE1 9HL

COOKSON, Lt-Col Michael John Blencowe; OBE (1986), TD (1969), DL (Northumberland 1983); s of Col John Charles Blencowe Cookson, DSO, TD, DL (d 1987), and Mary Marjorie Banks (now Fanshawe), *née* Askew; *b* 13 Oct 1927; *Educ* Eton, RAC Cirencester; *m* 26 Sept 1957, Rosemary Elizabeth, da of David Aubry Haggie (d 1958), of Red Hall, Haughton-le-Skerne, Darlington; 1 s (James b 1965), 3 da (Jane b 1958, Sarah b 1960, Rosie-Anne b 1963); *Career* Army 1945, posted to E African Forces 1947, demob 1948; joined Northumberland Hussars TA 1952, cmd Cadre N Hussars 1969-71, Cadre enlarged to form part of Queens Own Yeomanry became 2 i/c, ret 1972; Hon Col Northumberland Hussar Sqdns Queens Own Yeomanry 1988; memb Exec Ctee Northumberland Assoc of Boys' Clubs 1964-86 (chm 1974-86); joint master: Haydon Foxhounds 1955-58, Morpeth Foxhounds 1960 and 1970-; contested (Cons) NW Durham Constituency 1977, memb Morpeth RDC 1965-74, High Sheriff of Northumberland 1976, Vice-Lieut for Northumberland 1987; chm: Northumberland Hussar Regtl Assoc 1977-87, Queen's Silver Jubilee Appeal 1978; *Recreations* gardening, foxhunting; *Clubs* Northern Counties (Newcastle); *Style—* Lt-Col Michael Cookson, OBE, TD, DL; Meldon Park, Morpeth, Northumberland NE61 3SW (☎ 067 072 661)

COOKSON, Prof Richard Clive; s of Clive Cookson (d 1971), of Nether Warden, Hexham, Northumberland, and Marion Amy, *née* James (d 1961); *b* 27 Aug 1922; *Educ* Harrow, Trinity Coll Cambridge (BA, MA, PhD); *m* 4 Nov 1948, Ellen, da of Dr Amin Fawaz, of Lebanon; 2 s (Clive b 1952, Hugh b 1954); *Career* res fell Harvard Univ 1948, res chemist Glaxo Labs 1949-51, lectr Birkbeck Coll London 1951-57, prof chemistry Univ of Southampton 1957-85, visiting prof Univ of California 1960; Freeman City of Newcastle upon Tyne; FRSC 1959, FRS 1968; *Style—* Prof R C Cookson, FRS; Manor House, Stratford Tony, Salisbury SP5 4AT

COOLING, Cyril Ivor; s of Frank Cooling (d 1970), and Lilian, *née* Waygood (d 1970); *b* 9 June 1923; *Educ* Chislehurst and Sidcup GS, Univ Coll London (Bucknill scholar), Univ Coll Hosp (MB BS); *m* 21 July 1946, Phyllis Mary Clapson; 3 s (David Ivor b 3 May 1951, Trevor James (twin) b 3 May 1951, Richard Andrew b 25 March 1955), 1 da (Vanessa Mary b 9 March 1988); *Career* conslt surgeon: Royal Marsden Hosp London and Sutton 1963-77, Post Office and Civil Service Sanatorium Soc 1977; med Superintendent Benenden Chest Hosp 1977-85, ret 1990; hon conslt surgeon Manor House Hosp London 1963-77, hon lectr Chester Beatty Cancer Res Unit 1963-77; FRSM, FRCS; *Recreations* handcraft, dancing; *Style—* Cyril Cooling, Esq

COOLING, John Michael; OBE, JP (1966); s of John William Cooling (d 1980), and Nellie, *née* Jones (d 1986); *b* 27 April 1920; *Educ* King's Coll Sch Wimbledon, Imperial Coll of Sci Technol & Med (BSc Eng); *m* 14 Feb 1952, Theresa Frances, da of John MacSharry; 2 s (John Breffni Marius b 17 Dec 1953, Michael Turlough Spencer b 5 Nov 1957), 1 da (Aoife Marie-Thérèse b 20 Sept 1960); *Career* Lieut (E) RN HMS Victorious HMS Fencer HMS Cleveland 1940-46; J Jeffreys and Co: design engr 1946-49, mangr McCann Ltd Dublin (subsid co) 1949-54, dir 1954-60, jt md 1960-73, chm 1968-73; chief engr & commercial dir of Belfour Kilpatrick 1973-79, chm and md of Heduco Ltd 1979-, dir Beaumont (UK) Ltd 1987-, md of Ind Operation & Maintenance Ltd 1983-; pres: Heating and Ventilating Contractors Assoc 1969-70, CIBSE 1975-76 (gold medal 1987); hon fell American Soc of Heating Refrigeration and Air Conditioning Engrs 1984; memb Worshipful Co of Fanmakers 1965, Worshipful Co of Plumbers 1975; FIMechE 1947, FCIBSE 1949, FIEE 1973, FEng 1985, FCGI 1986; *Recreations* golf, video film making; *Clubs* Royal Wimbledon Golf; *Style—* Michael Cooling, Esq, OBE; Valldemosa, 26 Conway Rd, Wimbledon, London SW20 8PA (☎ 081 946 3432); Heduco ltd, St Georges House, 195/203 Waterloo Rd, London SE1 8XJ (☎ 071 633 2380, fax 071 261 9551)

COOLS-LARTIGUE, Sir Louis; OBE (1955); s of Theodore Cools-Lartigue, of Roseau, Dominica, and Emily, *née* Giraud; *b* 18 Jan 1905; *Educ* Convents of St Lucia and Dominica, Dominica GS; *m* 1932, Eugene, da of Robert W Royer; 2 s, 4 da; *Career* Dominica Civil Service 1924, chief sec Windward Islands 1951, ret 1960, govr of Dominica 1967-78, KStJ 1975; kt 1968; *Style—* Sir Louis Cools-Lartigue, OBE; 7 Virgin Lane, Roseau, Commonwealth of Dominica, West Indies

COOMBE, Anthony Joseph; s of Edwin Harry Coombe (d Burma 1944), of Thorverton, Devon, and Kathleen Joyce Wellington, *née* Garland-Wells; *b* 23 May 1942; *Educ* Sherborne Sch, Sidney Sussex Coll Cambridge (BA, MA); *m* 3 Feb 1968, Helen Elizabeth, da of Hugh Campbell Crawford, of St Johns Wood; 4 da (Hannah b 1970, Tabitha b 1971, Thomasina b 1976, Tessa b 1978); *Career* mktg dir Sturtevant Welbeck Ltd 1973-78; Sturtevant Engineering Co Ltd: dep md 1978-83, md 1983-91; memb Westminster North Cons Assoc; FInstD 1974, MInstM 1974; *Style—* Anthony Coombe, Esq; 1 Woronzow Rd, St Johns Wood, London NW8 6QB (☎ 071 722 0234); 88 Les Oliviers, 1 Avenue Des Hellenes, Beaulieu Sur Mer, France AM; Sturtevant Engineering Co Ltd, Westergate Rd, Moulsecoomb Way, Brighton BN2 4QB (☎ 0273 601 666, fax 0273 570 549, telex 87658)

COOMBE, Denys Baynham; s of Arthur Edward (d 1936), and Phyllis Mina, *née* Baynham (d 1964); *b* 21 Nov 1918; *Educ* Blundell's Sch, Architectural Assoc Sch of Architecture London (AADip); *m* 30 Aug 1952, June Swinford, da of John Lindsay Lee-Jones (d 1974); 1 s (Nicholas b 1957), 1 da (Rosemary b 1953); *Career* architect; served Royal Bombay Sappers and Miners WW II; princ DB and JS Coombe Chartered Architects 1964; MRIBA; *Recreations* music, gardening, walking; *Clubs* Architectural Assoc; *Style—* Denys B Coombe, Esq; 21 Petworth Rd, Haslemere, Surrey (☎ 0428 643572)

COOMBE, Donald Howard; JP (1973); er s of Howard James Coombe (d 1988); *b* 21 Oct 1927; *Educ* Northbrook C of E Sch Lee, Roan Sch Greenwich, Univ of The World (MA); *m* 5 June 1948, Betty Joyce, da of George William Adie (d 1938); 2 s (Richard Howard b 25 April 1953, David b 8 Oct 1958); *Career* RN 1942-47, hon cmmn to adm Texas Navy 1976; chm: RTC Ltd Lloyds Brokers 1971-, Portcullis Insurance Services Ltd 1985-; memb Lloyds 1974; fndr chm: Coombe Tst Fund, Coombe Holiday Tst Fund; chm Victoria Wellesley Tst (all registered charities for Needy Children), govr Baring Primary Sch, dep pres Thanet Red Cross, former cmmr Scouts Assoc; hon attorney-gen N Carolina, chm of bench 1982, cmmr Income Tax 1978-85; Freeman: City of London 1970, City of Dallas Texas 1976; Liveryman Worshipful Co of Poulters 1978; Order of St George Sweden 1974; *Recreations* charity fund raising, social work, boxing; *Clubs* National Sporting, Wig & Pen; *Style—* Donald H Coombe, Esq, JP; Sunarise, Beckenham Place Park, Kent BR3 2BN (☎ 081 658 2714, fax 081 663 3932); 7 Lovat Lane, London EC3R 8DT (☎ 071 283 7367, fax 071 283 3593)

COOMBE, His Hon Judge Gerald Hugh; s of Capt William Stafford Coombe (d 1962), and Mabel Florence, *née* Bullas (d 1983); *b* 16 Dec 1925; *Educ* Alleyn's Sch Dulwich, Hele's Sch Exeter, Univ of Oxford (MA); *m* 17 Aug 1957, Zoe Margaret, da of Sidney Ivor Richards, of Penarth, S Wales; 1 s (Robert b 1960), 1 da (Fiona b 1963); *Career* RAF Navigator 1944-48; slr Whitehead Monckton and Co Maidstone 1953-86, HM coroner Maidstone Kent Dist 1962-86, circuit judge 1986-; *Clubs* RAF; *Style—* His Hon Judge Gerald Coombe

COOMBE, John David; s of Sidney Coombe; *b* 17 March 1945; *Educ* Haberdashers' Aske's, Univ of London (BSc); *m* 1970, Gail Alicia, *née* Brazier; 3 da; *Career* CA; gp treas The Charterhouse Gp plc 1976-84, mangr fin and treasy Charter Consolidated plc 1984-86, fin controller Glaxo Hldgs 1986-; *Style—* John Coombe, Esq; Up Yonder, 76 Valley Rd, Rickmansworth, Herts (☎ 0923 776817)

COOMBE, (John) Kinred; s of G A Coombe, MC (d 1968), and Louise Marie, *née* Hockley (d 1984); *b* 15 Dec 1925; *Educ* Mill Hill Sch; *m* 7 June 1956, (Dorothy) Moira, da of Stanley Lockwood (d 1958), of Harrogate; *Career* Capt TA 1944-47; chm and md Leaf & Carver Ltd; gen cmmnr for Income Tax; Freeman: City of London, Worshipful Co of Painter-Stainers 1955; *Recreations* rugby football admin, yachting, shooting, fishing; *Clubs* Royal Thames Yacht, Old Millhillian's; *Style—* Kinred Coombe, Esq; Etna House, 350 Kennington Rd, London SE11 4LH (☎ 071 735 8434, fax 071 793 0462, telex 919349)

COOMBE, His Hon Judge Michael Rew; s of John Rew Coombe (d 1985), of Hunton Bridge, King's Langley, Herts, and Phyllis Mary (d 1980); *b* 17 June 1930; *Educ* Berkhamsted, New Coll Oxford (MA); *m* 7 Jan 1961, (Elizabeth) Anne, da of Tom Hull (d 1957); 3 s (Nicholas b Dec 1961, Jonathan b and d 1966, Peter b 1970), 1 da (Juliet b 1967); *Career* Nat Serv RAF; called to the Bar Middle Temple 1957, second prosecuting counsel to the Inland Revenue Central Criminal Ct and 5 Cts of London Sessions 1971, second counsel to the Crown Inner London Sessions 1971-74, first counsel to the Crown Inner London Crown Ct 1974, second jr prosecuting counsel to the Crown Central Criminal Ct 1975-77 (fourth jr 1974-75), rec of the Crown Ct 1976-85, first jr prosecuting counsel to the Crown Central Criminal Ct 1977-78, a sr prosecuting counsel to the Crown at the Central Criminal Ct 1978-85, master of the Bench Middle Temple 1984-, circuit judge 1985, judge Central Criminal Ct 1986-; Freeman City of London 1986; *Recreations* theatre, antiquity, art and architecture, printing; *Style—* His Hon Judge Coombe; Central Criminal Court, Old Bailey, City of London

COOMBE-TENNANT, Alexander John Serocold; s of Charles Coombe Tennant, JP (d 1928), of Cadoxton Lodge, Vale of Neath, S Wales, and Winifred Margaret, *née* Serocold, JP, (d 1956); *b* 20 Nov 1909; *Educ* Sherborne, Trinity Coll Cambridge (BA); *m* 10 Sept 1954, Jenifer Margaret, da of Frederic Luttman-Johnson, JP; 3 s (Charles b 1955, John b 1957, Mark b 1958), 2 da (Rosalie b 1960, Susanna b 1964); *Career* min of Econ Warfare 1940-45, Army Gen List 2/Lt A/Major 1944; stockbroker, memb LSE; ptnr Cazenove & Co 1952-79; dir: Société Générale Merchant Bank plc 1979-, GT Japan Investment plc 1979-89, Monterey Tst SA Luxembourg; chm Port Tennant Co Ltd; Freeman City of London, Liveryman Worshipful Co of Clothworkers (1955); *Clubs* Naval and Military; *Style—* A J S Coombe-Tennant, Esq; Gostrode Farm, Chiddingfold, Godalming, Surrey GU8 4SR (☎ 0428 4598); c/o G T Management plc, 8 Devonshire Square, London EC2

COOMBES, Lt-Col Brian John Nevill; s of Reginald Ernest Coombes (d 1965), of Ruislip, and Margaret Theodora, *née* Nevill (d 1980); *b* 1 March 1937; *Educ* The King's Sch Harrow; *m* 31 March 1973, Alana Stephannie, da of Maj Kenneth Clifford Dudley, of Chalfont St Peter, Bucks; 1 s (Dominic b 2 Oct 1975), 1 da (Kirsty b 6 Sept 1979); *Career* cmmnd Royal Tank Regt 1956, GSO 3 Ops HQ 7 Armd Bde 1969-71, 2 i/c 4 Royal Tank Regt 1976-77, Exec Offr and Mil Asst to Sr Br Staff Offr HQ Allied Forces Central Europe 1978-81, Lt-Col 1980, COS HQ Aldershot Garrison 1981-83, ret 1983; dep registrar Corp of the Sons of the Clergy 1983-; memb Fleet Parochial Parish Cncl, govr All Saint's C of E Sch Fleet, govr Yateley Manor Prep Sch, parish clerk St John's Westminster; memb Worshipful Co of Parish Clerks; *Recreations* fly fishing, wine making, occasional shooting; *Style—* Lt-Col Brian Coombes; Brook End, 8 Albany Road, Fleet, Hampshire, GU13 9PJ (☎ 0252 622745); Corporation of the Sons of the Clergy, 1 Dean Trench St, Westminster SW1P 3HB (☎ 071 222 1138)

COOMBES, Prof (Raoul) Charles Dalmedo Stuart; s of Col R C Coombes, MC, of The Old Priest House, Aldbourne, nr Marlborough, Wiltshire, and Doreen Mary, *née* Ellis; *b* 20 April 1949; *Educ* Douai Sch, St George's Hosp Med Sch (MB BS), UCL

(PhD, MD); *m* 27 July 1984, Caroline Sarah, da of David Oakes, of Sunnyside, Cowley Hill Lane, St Helens, Merseyside; 1 s (Jack Raoul b 1985), 2 da (Sophie Flora b 1987, Matilda Rose, b 1989); *Career* med res fell MRC 1974-76; Royal Marsden Hosp: sr registrar 1976-78, sr lectr 1979-84, hon conslt 1979-; sr clinical scientist and hon sr lectr Ludwig Inst for Cancer Res 1979-88, head Clinical Oncology Unit St George's Hosp 1988-90, conslt med oncologist and hon sr lectr St George's Hosp Med Sch 1988-90; prof of med oncology and dir Cancer Res Campaign Laboratories, co-ordinator of nat and int trials for Int Collaborative Cancer Gp; memb: SW Thames Regnl Cancer Gp, Br Breast Gp 1988, Br Assoc Cancer Res 1988, American Assoc Cancer Res 1988; FRCP 1988 (MRCP 1973); *Books* Breast Cancer Management (ed, 1984), New Endocrinology of Cancer (1987); *Recreations* painting; *Style—* Prof Charles Coombes; Charing Cross and Westminster Medical School, St Dunstan's Rd, London W6 (☎ 081 846 1418, fax 081 741 0731)

COOMBS, Anthony Michael Vincent; MP (C) Wyre Forest 1987-; s of Clifford Keith Coombs, of Stripes Hill House, Knowle, nr Solihull, W Midlands, and Celia Mary Gostling, *née* Vincent; *b* 18 Nov 1952; *Educ* Charterhouse, Worcester Coll Oxford (MA); *m* 21 Sept 1984, Andrea Caroline, da of Daniel Pritchard, of 11 Exeter Rd, Netherton Dudley, W Midlands; 1 s (Alexander Graham David); *Career* founder and md Grevayne Properties Ltd; dir: Tweedies (Wolverhampton) Ltd 1976, Sartorial Shops Ltd 1976; sec: Back Bench Educn Ctee, All Party Human Rights Gp; Parly private sec to David Mellor, QC, MP (Min of State Home Office) 1989-; *Recreations* tennis, golf, skiing, football, music; *Style—* Anthony M V Coombs, Esq, MP; 47 Clarence St, Kidderminster (☎ 0562 752 439); Grevayne Properties Ltd, 51/53 Edgbaston St, Birmingham B5 4QH (☎ 021 622 4881, car ☎ 0860 516400)

COOMBS, Brian William James; s of Ernest William Coombs (d 1982), of Weston-super-Mare, Avon, and Grace Lilian, *née* Horrell; *b* 2 July 1932; *Educ* Lewisham Sch; *m* 23 June 1956, Joyce Margaret, da of William Henry Higgs (d 1987), of Wednesbury, West Midlands; 2 s (James b 1960, Peter b 1963), 1 da (Ruth b 1966); *Career* RAF Statistics Branch 1954-56; Price Waterhouse & Co chartered accountants 1957-58, Aluminium Bronze Co Ltd 1958-60, co sec Halladay's Ltd 1960-66, mgmnt accountant Tubes Ltd (TI Gp) 1966-69, sec and fin accountant TI Steel Tube Division Ltd 1970-73, fin dir TI Accles & Pollock Ltd 1973-84, fin dir Lewis Woolf Griptight Ltd 1985-90, chief fin offr L W G Holdings Ltd 1985-90, international business consultant 1991-; covenant sec St Matthew's Parish Church Walsall; memb: Walsall Family Health Servs Authy, London Business Sch Alumni Assoc; FCA 1954, FCMA 1969; *Recreations* sculpture, genealogy, walking, classic cars; *Style—* Brian Coombs, Esq; 12 Gorway Rd, Walsall, West Midlands WS1 3BB (☎ 0922 21530); 161-165 Churchill Parade, Birchfield Rd, Perry Barr, Birmingham B19 1LL (☎ 021 523 6363, fax 021 544 1434)

COOMBS, Derek Michael; s of Clifford Coombs (d 1975), and Elizabeth Mary, *née* Evans (d 1974); *b* 12 Aug 1937; *Educ* Bromsgrove Sch; *m* 1, 28 Jan 1959 (m dis 1985), Patricia Teresa, *née* O'Toole; 1 s (Fiann b 27 Sept 1968), 1 da (Siân b 1 Feb 1967); m 2, 14 June 1986, Jennifer Sheila, da of Lt Cdr Edward Lonsdale, DSO, RN, of Langness, Woodgaston Lane, Hayling Island, Hants; 1 s (Jack Edward Clifford b 21 Sept 1987); *Career* chm Hardanger Props plc 1972-, dir Metalrax Gp plc 1975-, chm and md S & U Stores plc 1976-; named as one of the top 100 in The British Entrepreneur 1988; journalist; MP (C) Yardley 1970-74; govr Royal Hosp & Home Putney; *Recreations* friends, tennis, skiing; *Style—* Derek Coombs, Esq; Cheyne Row, London SW3

COOMBS, Prof Robert Royston Amos (Robin); s of late Charles Royston Amos Coombs, and Edris Owen Coombs (d 1972); *b* 9 Jan 1921; *Educ* Diocesan Coll Cape Town SA, Univ of Edinburgh (BSc), Univ of Cambridge (PhD, ScD); *m* 13 Sept 1952, Anne Marion, da of Charles Geoffrey Blomfield; 1 s (Robert Christopher b 30 Aug 1954), 1 da (Rosalind Edris Lucy b 13 Jan 1956); *Career* WWII vol Royal Scots 1939, reserved occupation; Univ of Cambridge: Stringer fell King's Coll 1947-56, asst dir res Dept of Pathology 1948, reader in immunology 1962, fell Corpus Christi Coll 1962-, Quick prof of biology Immunology Div Dept of Pathology 1965, emeritus prof 1988; foreign corr Royal Belgium Acad Medicine 1979; Hon MD Linköping Sweden 1973, Hon Dr Med Vet Copenhagen 1979, Hon DSc Guelph Canada 1981, Hon DSc Edinburgh 1984; FRS 1965, FRCPath 1968, MRCVS 1943, Hon FRCP 1973; *Books* Serology of Conglutination (with A M Coombs and D G Ingram, 1961), Clinical Aspects of Immunology (co-ed with PGH Gell 1963, 1968, 1975); *Style—* Prof Robin Coombs, FRS; 6 Selwyn Gdns, Cambridge CB3 9AX (☎ 0223 352681)

COOMBS, Simon Christopher; MP (C) Swindon 1983-; s of Ian Peter Coombs (d 1981), of Weston-super-Mare, and Rachel Margaret Anne, *née* Robins; *b* 21 Feb 1947; *Educ* Wycliffe Coll, Univ of Reading (BA, MPhil); *m* 1983, Kathryn Lee Coe Royce; *Career* memb: Reading CBC 1969-72, Reading Borough Cncl 1973-84 (Transportation Ctee 1976-83); chm Wessex Young Cons 1973-76, dep Cons ldr 1976-81 (chief whip 1983); mktg exec Br Telecom and PO Telecommunications 1970-81, mktg mangr Telex Networks Br Telecom 1981-83; chm Cons Party Wessex Area 1980-83, memb Nat Exec Cons Pty 1980-83, PPS to Min for Info Technol 1984, PPS to Min for the Environment 1984-85, chm All Pty Cable and Satellite TV Gp, treas Parly Information Technol Ctee, chm All Pty Food and Health Forum, memb Employment Select Ctee 1987-, vice chm Conservative Back Bench Tourism Ctee, chm Anglo-Malawi Parly Gp; *Recreations* cricket, philately, music; *Clubs* Swindon Conservative; *Style—* Simon Coombs, Esq, MP; House of Commons, London SW1

COONEY, Raymond George Alfred (Ray); s of Gerard Joseph (d 1987), of London, and Olive Harriet, *née* Clarke (d 1975); *b* 30 May 1932; *Educ* Alleyn's Coll Dulwich; *m* 8 Dec 1962, Linda Ann, da of Leonard Spencer Dixon (d 1985), of Epping; 2 s (Danny b 1964, Michael b 1966); *Career* Nat Serv RASC 1950-52; actor, writer, prodr, dir; acting debut Sons of Norway Palace Theatre 1946; playwright: One For The Pot (1961), Chase Me Comrade (1964), Charlie Girl (1965), Not Now Darling (1967), Move Over Mrs Markham (1969), Why Not Stay for Breakfast? (1970), There Goes the Bride (1974), Run for your Wife (1983), Two into One (1984), Wife Begins at Forty (1985), It Runs In the Family (1989); dir of most of the above; prodr: Lloyd George knew My Father (1972), Say Goodnight to Grandma (1973), At the End of the Day (1973), The Dame of Sark (1974), A Ghost on Tiptoe (1974), Bodies (1980), Whose Life Is It Anyway? (1980), They're Playing Our Song (1980), Elvis (1981), Duet for One (1981), Children of a Lesser God (1982); fndr The Theatre of Comedy Co 1983 (artistic dir 1983-88); memb Actors' Equity; *Recreations* tennis, swimming; *Style—* Ray Cooney, Esq; 1-3 Spring Gdns, London SW1 (☎ 071 839 5098)

COOP, Geoffrey Brian; s of Roy Coop, of Raymonds Hill, Axminster, Devon (d 1989), and Doris, *née* Hall (d 1970); *b* 30 March 1933; *Educ* Cheltenham, Clare Coll Cambridge (MA); *m* 20 July 1962, (Margaret) Valerie, da of Fredrick George Tanton; 1 s (Andrew Christopher b 1970), 1 da (Joanna Kate b 1968); *Career* ptnr Rowley Pemberton and Co (later Rowley Pemberton Roberts and Co) 1960-81, ptnr of fin and admin Pannell Kerr Forster (on merger with Rowley Pemberton Roberts and Co) 1981; FCA; *Recreations* cdre Hayling Island Sailing club, theatre, yacht racing; *Clubs* Royal Thames Yacht, Lloyd's Yacht, Hayling Island Sailing (cdre); *Style—* Geoffrey Coop, Esq; The Old Barn, 45 Bath Rd, Emsworth, Hants PO10 7ER (☎ 0243 374 376); Pannell Kerr Forster, Pannell House, Park St, Guildford, Surrey GU1 4HN (☎ 048 364 646)

COOP, Sir Maurice Fletcher; s of George Harry Coop (d 1922), and Ada, *née* Fletcher; *b* 11 Sept 1907; *Educ* Epworth Coll Rhyl, Emmanuel Coll Cambridge; *m* 18 March 1948, Elsie Hilda, da of Harry Robert Brazier; *Career* slr 1932; dir Dunlop Rubber Co Ltd 1966-70; chm Standing Ctee to Govt on Patents; kt 1973; *Recreations* association football, cricket; *Clubs* Utd Oxford and Cambridge Univ; *Style—* Sir Maurice Coop; 39 Hill St, Berkeley Sq, London W1 (☎ 071 491 4549); Brendon Cottage, Punchbowl Lane, Dorking, Surrey (☎ 0306 882835)

COOPER *see also*: Ashley-Cooper, Astley Cooper, Mansfield Cooper

COOPER, Hon Artemis (Alice Clare Antonia Opportune); only da of 2 Viscount Norwich; *b* 22 April 1953; *m* 1 Feb 1986, Antony James Beevor, s of John Grosvenor Beevor, OBE (d 1987), of 161 Fulham Rd, London SW3; 1 da (b 19 Jan 1990); *Career* writer; *Style—* The Hon Artemis Cooper; 54 St Maur Rd, London SW6

COOPER, Dr Barrington Spencer; s of Maurice Lionel Cooper (d 1950), and Dena, *née* Orman (d 1959); *b* 15 Jan 1923; *Educ* Grocers' Co Sch, Queens' Coll Cambridge (BA), Bart's Med Sch London (MB BS), Cancer Meml Hosp NY Univ; *m* 1, Fay Helena, *née* Harman; 1 da (Victoria Ann b 18 Feb 1957); m 2, 16 Dec 1988, Jane Eva Livermore Wallace, da of Edward Charles Livermore (d 1976), of Knight's Hill Farm, Westhill, Buntingford, Herts; *Career* Capt RAMC 1947-49; formerly: house physician Whittington Hosp and Ashford Co Hosp, med registrar Oster House Hosp, clinical asst in psychiatry Bart's, London Jewish Hosp and Nat Hosp for Nervous Diseases, visiting physician Fndn for Manic Depression NYC, corr assoc WHO Psychosocial Centre Stockholm, psychosomatic investigator for WHO, med advsr for various hosp projects and private cos; currently: dir Allied Med Diagnostic Clinic, visitor Boston Univ Med Sch, consulting physician The Clinic of Psychotherapy and Bowden House Clinic, visiting physician The Strang Inst of Preventive Med NYC; med advsr: West One Prodns Inc, Fabyan Films Ltd, World Film Servs, New Media Med Univ; author of various specialist papers; dir Fabyan Ltd and Fabyan Films Ltd; independent film prodr: The One-Eyed Soldiers, The Doctor and the Devils; memb: Assoc of Independent Prodns, BAFTA; fndr Salerno Int Youth Orchestra Festival; fell Psychosomatic Res Soc; memb: RSM, Med Section Br Psychological Soc, Soc of Clinical Psychiatrists, Br Assoc of Counselling, Assoc of Family Therapy, London Jewish Hosp Soc; affiliate RCPsych; MRCGP, FRSH; *Books* Helix (script, 1982), Travel Sickness (1982), Cockpits (1987), Consumer Guide to Prescription Medicines (1989); *Recreations* film, music, theatre, fine arts, swimming, sailing, rowing; *Clubs* RSM, Regency; *Style—* Dr Barrington Cooper; Flat F 21 Devonshire Place, London W1N 1PD (☎ 071 935 0113, fax 071 486 0505)

COOPER, Beryl Phyllis; QC (1977); o da of Charles Augustus Cooper (d 1981), and Phyllis Lillie, *née* Burrows; *b* 24 Nov 1927; *Educ* Surbiton HS, Univ of Birmingham (BCom); *Career* recorder of the Crown Court 1977-; memb: Criminal Injuries Compensation Bd 1978, Nurses and Professions Allied to Medicine Pay Review Bd 1984, Bench Gray's Inn (1988); *Recreations* golf, swimming, theatre; *Clubs* English Speaking Union, Caledonian (Edinburgh); *Style—* Miss Beryl Cooper, QC; 31 Alleyn Park, Dulwich, London SE21 (☎ 081 670 7012); 8d South Cliff Tower, Eastbourne, Sussex; 2 Dr Johnson's Buildings, Temple, London EC4 (☎ 071 353 5371)

COOPER, Brian; s of Frederick Hubert Cooper, and Florence Mabel, *née* Field; *b* 1 Jan 1936; *Educ* St Albans Sch, De Havilland Aeronautical Tech Sch, Hatfield Poly, London Business Sch; *m* 21 Nov 1959, Marjorie Anne (Sue), da of Ronald John More (d 1973); 2 da (Jenny b 1962, Charlotte b 1967); *Career* Flying Offr RAF 1959-62; subsidiary co dir: Firth Cleveland GKN Gps (Germany, UK) 1962-74, Bowater Corpn Ltd (UK, France, Belgium, Holland, Germany) 1974-84; asst md Hargreaves Gp plc 1984-87, dir Coalite Gp plc 1987-; hon fell Brighton Poly 1987; CEng, MRAeS, FIMechE; *Recreations* squash, sailing, skiing; *Clubs* RAF; *Style—* Brian Cooper, Esq; Marton Cum Grafton, N Yorks; Coalite Gp plc, PO Box 21, Chesterfield, Derbys S44 6AB (☎ 0246 822281, fax 0246 240265)

COOPER, Dr Brian Thomas; s of Dr Andrew Matthew Cooper (d 1979), of West Wellow, Romsey, Hampshire, and Irene Elizabeth, *née* Roulsten; *b* 20 May 1947; *Educ* Monkton Combe Sch Bath, Univ of Birmingham (BSc, MB ChB, MD); *m* 31 Aug 1973, Dr Griselda Mary Cooper, da of Dr Charles James Constantine Davey, of Box, Chippenham, Wiltshire; 1 da (Charlotte b 4 Aug 1987); *Career* lectr in med Univ of Bristol 1978-85, conslt physician Dunedin Hosp Dunedin NZ 1985-86, conslt physician Dudley Rd Hosp and Edgebaston Nuffield Hosp Birmingham, sr clinical lectr in med Univ of Birmingham 1987-; MRCP 1974, MBSG 1979; *Books* Manual of Gastroenterology (1987); *Recreations* military history, classical music and opera, skiing; *Style—* Dr Brian Cooper; 36 Anstruther Rd, Edgebaston, Birmingham B15 3NW (☎ 021 456 2174); Dudley Rd Hosp, Gastroenterology Unit, Birmingham B18 7QH (☎ 021 554 3801 ext 4590)

COOPER, Caroline Amanda; da of Kenneth Charles Cooper, of Bury St Edmunds, and Elizabeth Taylor; *b* 9 March 1961; *Educ* Culford Sch Bury St Edmunds, Univ of Reading (BA), London Coll of Printing; *Career* copywriter Conran Design July-Oct 1984, sr copywriter Watson Ward Albert Varndell 1984-88 (jr copywriter 1983-84), copy chief Option One Direct 1988-90, creative dir Rapier Stead and Bowden 1990-; winner various Br and Euro Direct Mktg awards and Echo awards, Copywriter of the Year award BDMA 1987; *Recreations* painting, travelling; *Style—* Miss Caroline Cooper; Rapier, Stead and Bowden, 8-9 Carlisle St, London W1 (☎ 071 494 4415)

COOPER, Prof Cary Lynn; s of Harry Cooper, of Los Angeles, California, USA, and Caroline Lillian, *née* Greenberg; *b* 28 April 1940; *Educ* Fairfax Sch Los Angeles, Univ of California (BS, MBA), Univ of Leeds (PhD); *m* 1, 1970 (m dis 1984), (Edna) June Taylor; 1 s (Hamish Scott b 1972), 1 da (Natasha Beth b 1974); m 2, 1984, Rachel Faith Davies; 2 da (Laura Anne b 1982, Sarah Kate b 1984); *Career* prof of mgmnt educn methods UMIST 1975-79, prof of organisational psychology UMIST, ed-in-chief Jl for Organizational Behavior 1980-, past advsr WHO and ILO 1982-84, memb Bd of Tstees American Inst of Stress, recipient BPS Myers lecture 1986, hon prof of psychology Univ of Manchester 1986-, pres Br Acad of Mgmnt 1986-, chm Professional Affrs Ctee (OPD) Int Assoc of Applied Psychology 1987-, past advsr Home Office on Police Stress 1982-84; Hon MSC Univ of Manchester 1979; memb American Physics Soc, PS, FBPsS, pres BAM, IAAP; *Books incl*: T-Groups (1971), Theories of Group Processes (1976), Developing Social Skills in Managers (1976), Stress at Work (jtly, 1978), Executives Under Pressure (1978), Behavioural Problems in Organisations (1979), Learning From Others in Groups (1979), The Executive Gypsy (1979), Current Concerns in Occupational Stress (1980), The Stress Check (1980), Improving Interpersonal Relations (1981), Psychology and Management (1982), Management Education (jtly, 1982), Stress Research (1983), Public Faces, Private Lives (jtly, 1984), Working Women (jtly, 1984), Psychology for Managers (jtly, 1984), Change Makers (jtly, 1985), Man and Accidents Offshore (jtly, 1986), Pilots Under Stress (jtly, 1986), Women and Information Technology (jtly, 1987), Pressure Sensitive (jtly, 1988), High Flyers (jtly, 1988), Living with Stress (1988), Early Retirement (jtly, 1989), Career Couples (jtly, 1989), Managing People at Work (jtly, 1989), International Review of Industrial and Organisational Psychology (jtly, 1990), Understanding Stress in Health Care Professionals (jtly, 1990); *Recreations* swimming, reading, squash, writing children's books, following politics; *Clubs* St James'; *Style—* Prof C L Cooper; 25 Lostock Hall Rd, Poynton, Cheshire (☎ 0625 871 450);

Manchester Sch of Management, Univ of Manchester Inst of Science & Tech, PO Box 88, Manchester M60 1QD (☎ 061 200 3440, fax 061 228 7040)

COOPER, David Jackson; s of late Charles Cooper; *b* 3 Feb 1929; *Educ* Churchers' Coll Petersfield, Univ Coll Southampton, Univ Coll of N Wales; *m* 1954, Patricia Mary; 3 s, 2 da; *Career* md Forest Thinnings Ltd 1962-, dir Economic Forestry (Holdings) Ltd 1977-, dir Furniture and Timber Industry Training Bd 1979-, sr vice pres British Timber Merchants' Assoc 1980-; *Style—* David Cooper, Esq; Candovers, Hartley Mauditt, Alton, Hants (☎ 042 050 293; office: 0420 83504)

COOPER, David John; s of John Alec Cooper, of London, and Norma May, *née* Kennard; *b* 4 July 1951; *Educ* Green Sch, Univ of London (BEd); *m* 20 Jan 1979, Dr Winifred Dorothy Jane Cooper, da of William Harvey Cantrell (d 1974); 1 da (Laura Kirsten Jacqueline b 23 June 1982); *Career* analyst Unilever plc 1967-71, chemistry teacher Barking Abbey 1974-75, business devpt and mktg exec Baxter Inc 1975-79, mktg exec Smith and Nephew Ltd 1979-82, businesss devpt and mktg exec LIG Int Ltd, dir Pfizer Inc 1984-87, corporate financier Robert Flemings 1987-88, fndr and jt md Boston Capital Europe 1988-, md Protean Enterprises International Ltd; Freeman City of London 1985, Liveryman Worshipful Co of Marketers 1985; FBIM 1984, FInstD 1984, FCInstM 1984, MCInstB 1987, memb Soc Chem Indust; *Clubs* Savage, City Livery, City Livery Yacht; *Style—* David Cooper, Esq; 3 Fairlawn Drive, Woodford Green, Essex IG8 9AW (☎ 081 504 1272, 0831 455011, fax 081 504 4509); Lou Cantou, CEPS, Roqueburn, 34390 France; Protean Enterprises International Ltd, 3 Fairlawn Drive, Woodford Green, Essex 1G8 9AW (☎ 081 504 1272, fax 081 504 4509), Boston Capital Europe Ltd, 19 Buckingham St, London WC2N 6EF (☎ 071 839 9800, fax 071 839 1871)

COOPER, Dennis Henry; OBE (1985); s of Frank Toogood Cooper (d 1963), and Germaine Eugenie Victorine, *née* Flant, of Birchington-on-Sea, Kent; *b* 16 Oct 1934; *Educ* Surbiton Co GS; *m* 21 April 1958, Rosemary Wendy Sands, da of Robert Sands Springett (d 1990), of Birchington-on-Sea, Kent; 2 s (Michael b 1963, Christopher b 1967), 3 da (Caroline b 1959, Gillian b 1961, Susan b 1970); *Career* Nat Serv Intelligence Corps Russian language trg Univ of Cambridge; joined HM Foreign Serv 1951; overseas postings: Jedda 1956, Budapest 1956-58, The Hague 1960-62, Miami 1963-67, Dallas 1973-77, Moscow 1980-83 (1958-59 and 1970-72), Chicago 1983-86, Paris 1986-90; *Recreations* golf, music, walking; *Clubs* Dulwich and Sydenham Golf; *Style—* Dennis Cooper, Esq, OBE; Foreign & Commonwealth Office, King Charles Street, London SW1A 2AH

COOPER, Derek Macdonald; s of Stephen George Cooper (d 1958), and late Jessie Margaret Macdonald; *b* 25 May 1925; *Educ* Raynes Park Co Sch, Portree HS, Wadham Coll Oxford (MA); *m* 17 Oct 1953, Janet Marian, da of Robert Feaster; 1 s (Nicholas b 1957), 1 da (Penelope Jane b 1954); *Career* Leading Seaman RNVR 1943-47; broadcaster, journalist and author; prodr Radio Malaya 1950 (ret controller of progs 1960), prodr Roving Report ITN 1960-61; radio progs incl: Today, Ten O'Clock Newstime, PM, Town and Country, A La Carte, Home This Afternoon, Frankly Speaking, Two of a Kind, You and Yours, Northbeat, New Worlds, Asian Club, Speaking for Myself, Conversations with Cooper, Friday Call, It's Your Line, The Food Programme, Offshore Britons, Person to Person, Meridien Book Programme; TV progs incl: World in Action, Tomorrow's World, Breathing Space, A Taste of Britain, The Caterers, World About Us, I Am An Engineer, Men and Materials, Apart from Oil, Money Wise, One in a Hundred, The Living Body, From the Face of the Earth, Scotland's Larder, This Food Business, Distilling Whisky Galore; columnist: The Listener, The Guardian, Observer magazine, World Medicine, Scottish Field, Sunday Standard, Homes and Gardens, Good Food Saga magazine, Scotland on Sunday; contrib: Taste, A La Carte, The West Highland Free Press; Glenfiddich Trophy as wine and food writer 1973 and 1980, Broadcaster of the Year 1984; fndr memb and first chm Guild of Food Writers 1985-88 (pres 1988); *Books* The Bad Food Guide (1967), The Beverage Report (1970), The Gullibility Gap (1974), Hebridean Connection (1977, revised edn 1991), Skye (second edn 1977, third edn 1989), Guide to the Whiskies of Scotland (1978), Road to the Isles (1979, Scottish Arts Cncl award 1980, second edn 1990), Enjoying Scotch (with Diane Pattullo, 1980), Wine with Food (1980, second edn 1986), The Whisky Roads of Scotland (1982), The Century Companion to Whiskies (1983), Skye Remembered (1983), The World of Cooking (1983), The Road to Mingulay (1985, second edn 1988) The Gunge File (1986), A Taste of Scotch (1989); *Style—* Derek Cooper, Esq; 4 St Helena Terrace, Richmond, Surrey TW9 1NR (☎ 071 940 7051); Seafield House, Portree, Isle of Skye (☎ 0478 2380)

COOPER, Wing Cdr Donald Arthur; CBE (1990), AFC (1961); s of Albert Arthur Cooper (d 1965), and Elizabeth Barbara, *née* Edmonds; *b* 27 Sept 1930; *Educ* Queen's Coll Br Guiana, RAF Coll Cranwell, Open Univ (BA); *m* 5 April 1958, (Ann) Belinda, da of Adm Sir Charles Woodhouse, KCB (d 1978); 3 s (Andrew b 1959, Duncan b 1961, Angus b 1964); *Career* pilot on day fighter and trg sqdns RAF 1952-56, Empire Test Pilots Sch 1957, pilot Experimental Flying Dept RAE Farnborough 1958-60, RAF Staff Coll 1961 (airline tport pilot's licence: helicopters 1961, aeroplanes 1972), Sqdn Cdr CFS Helicopter Wing 1962-64, HQ Flying Trg Cmd 1964-66, Def Ops Requirements Staff MOD 1966-70, ret 1970; chief inspr Air Accidents Investigations Branch Dept of Transport (formerly Accidents Investigation Branch Bd of Trade) 1986-90; FRAeS 1984; *Recreations* amateur dramatics, walking, dancing; *Style—* Wing Cdr Donald Cooper, CBE, AFC; 7 Lynch Rd, Farnham, Surrey GU9 8BZ (☎ 0252 715 519)

COOPER, Donald Frederick; OBE (1978); s of Henry John Neiles Cooper (d 1978), and Mabel, *née* Bartlett (d 1973); *b* 10 Nov 1920; *Educ* Itchen GS Southampton; *m* 7 March 1945, Robertha Margaret (Bobbie), da of James Peterson (d 1921); 1 s (John Neils b 1949), 1 da (Jacqueline Margaret b 1946); *Career* WWII RE: 4 Inf Div (wounded Dunkirk) 1939-41, 1 Airborne Div 1941-46, demobbed Warrant Offr Class 1; purchasing mangr: Trussed Concrete Steel Co Ltd 1946-56 (formerly purchasing offr), NCB E Mids Area 7 1956-63, Southern Gas 1963-67; dir purchasing Br Gas Corp 1967-80, fndr Coopers (Little Marlow) Ltd, advsr to govr and statutory authys Thailand, Hong Kong, Singapore and Ireland 1980-88; author of various papers on energy 1970-80; Liveryman Worshipful Co of Basketmakers; FInstPS 1965 (memb 1947, pres 1972-73), memb Int Fedn Purchasing 1972 (pres 1979-81); Cdr Most Noble Order of Crown of Thailand 1983; *Recreations* spectator of cricket and music; *Clubs* MCC, RAC; *Style—* Donald F Cooper, Esq, OBE; Westridge, Elm Lane, Well End, Bourne End, Bucks SL8 5PG

COOPER, Dowager Lady; Dorothy Frances Hendrika; *née* Deen; da of late Emile Deen; *m* 1933, Sir Francis Ashmole Cooper, 4 Bt (d 1987); 1 s (Sir Richard Cooper, 5 Bt), 3 da (Elizabeth Sally Ann b 1936, d 1978, Jacqueline Margaret b 1939, Dione Frances b 1944); *Style—* Dowager Lady Cooper; Mas Folie, 06490 Tourrettes sur Loup, France

COOPER, Prof Edward Holmes; s of Alfred Harold Cooper (d 1978), and Edith, *née* Larkin (d 1974); *b* 6 April 1927; *Educ* Berkhamstead Sch, St Mary's Hosp Med Sch, Worcester Coll Oxford (MD, DSc, DPhil); *m* 21 Aug 1956, Patricia Janet, da of Hubert George Gower (d 1979); 2 s (Andrew b 1961, Simon b 1963), 3 da (Jane b 1956, Sarah b 1958, Joanna b 1966); *Career* Nat Serv Capt RAMC 1951-53, Maj RAMC AER 1954-66; res posts RAMC 1950-59, med res fell St Mary's Hosp London 1959-65, sr lectr Inst of Cancer Res London 1965-67, prof cancer res Univ of Leeds 1967-88, emeritus prof; FRCP; *Recreations* walking; *Style—* Prof Edward Cooper; 29 Shadwell Lane, Leeds LS17 6DP (☎ 0532 686250), Diagnostic Development Unit, University of Leeds LS2 9NL

COOPER, Eileen; *b* 1953; *Educ* Goldsmiths' Coll London, Royal Coll of Art; *Career* artist; lectr St Martins; solo exhibitions: AIR Gallery 1979, House Gallery 1981, Blond Fine Art 1982, 1983 and 1985, Artspace Aberdeen 1985, Castlefield Gallery Manchester 1986, Artsite Gallery Bath 1987, Benjamin Rhodes Gallery 1988, 1989 and 1990; group exhibitions incl: New Contemporaries 1974 and 1976, Royal Acad Summer Show 1977, 1982, 1984, Whitechapel Open 1982, 1983 and 1987, The Image as Catalyst (Ashindean Museum Oxford) 1984, Ten Years at Air 1985, The Int Festival of Painting Cagnes France 1985, Ljubljana (Int Biennial of Graphic Art Yugoslavia) 1985 and 1987, Proud and Prejudiced (Twining Gallery NY) 1985, The Flower Show (Stoke on Trent Museum, touring) 1986, John Moores (Walker Art Gallery Liverpool) 1986, The Self Portrait - A Modern View (Artsite Bath, touring) 1987, Royal Over-Seas League Annual 1987 and 1988, Painters at the Royal Coll of Art (150 Annual Exhibition) 1988, Ikon Gallery Birmingham (touring) 1988, Athena Art Awards (Barbican) 1988, Figuring Out The 80's (Laing Gallery Newcastle) 1988, The New British Painting (Contemporary Arts Centre Cincinnati, touring) 1988, Figure 2: A Private Mythology (Aberystwyth Arts Centre, touring) 1988, Freedom (launch of illustrated book for Amnesty Int, Flowers East) 1988, Survival Int Auction (Harewood House Leeds) 1989, Picturing People (Br Cncl tour Kuala Lumpur, Hong Kong and Singapore) 1989, 3 Ways (Royal Coll of Art/Br Cncl tour E Europe) 1990; work in the collections of: Open Univ, Imp Coll London, Br Cncl, Kunsthalle Nuremberg, Arts Cncl of GB, Contemporary Arts Soc, Unilever PLC, Cleveland Gallery, Arthur Andersen & Co, Coopers & Lybrand Deloitte; *Style—* Ms Eileen Cooper; c/o Benjamin Rhodes Gallery, 4 New Burlington Place, London W1X 1SB (☎ 071 434 1768/9, fax 071 287 8841)

COOPER, Rt Hon Sir Frank; GCB (1979, KCB 1974, CB 1970), CMG (1961), PC (1983); s of late Valentine H Cooper, of 37 The Square, Fairfield, Manchester; *b* 2 Dec 1922; *Educ* Manchester GS, Pembroke Coll Oxford (hon fell 1976); *m* 1948, Peggie, da of F J Claxton; 2 s, 1 da; *Career* pilot RAF 1941-46; joined Civil Serv 1948, dep under sec of state MOD 1968-70, dep sec CSD 1970-73, perm under sec of state NI Office 1973-76, perm under sec of state MOD 1976-82, ret 1982; dir: Babcock 1983-89, Morgan Crucible 1983-, N M Rothschild and Sons 1983-; chm High Integrity Systems 1986-; memb Cncl King's Coll London 1983-89 (govr 1982, fell 1987); chm: King's Coll Med and Dental Sch 1984-89, Imperial Coll 1988- (fell 1988); visitor Univ of Loughborough 1988-; chm: Cranbrook Sch 1984 (govr 1982), Liddell Hart Tstees 1986-, Inst of Contemprary Br History 1986-; vice pres Army Records Soc 1989- (vice chm 1986-88), memb Advsy Cncl on Public Records 1989-; pres Assoc of Lancastrians in London 1991; *Clubs* Athenaeum, Naval and Military, RAF; *Style—* The Rt Hon Sir Frank Cooper, GCB, CMG; Delafield, 34 Camden Park Rd, Chislehurst, Kent BR7 5HG

COOPER, George John; s of Maj Sir Charles Eric Cooper, 5 Bt (d 1984), and his 2 wife, Mary Elisabeth, *née* Graham-Clarke; hp of bro, Sir William Daniel Charles Cooper, 6 Bt, *qv*; *b* 28 June 1956; *Educ* Harrow; *Career* vice chm IDDA; *Recreations* hunting, eventing, gardening; *Style—* George Cooper, Esq; 19 Norfolk Mansions, Prince of Wales Drive, London SW11 4HL (☎ 071 720 5927); Hinton House, Ablington, Bibury, Cirencester, Glos; Chelsea Green Designs Ltd, 26 Cale Street, London SW3 3QU (☎ 071 581 9119, fax 071 584 7225, car 0860 261364)

COOPER, Gen Sir George Leslie Conroy; GCB (1984, KCB 1979), MC (1953), DL (1990); s of Lt-Col G C Cooper (d 1978), of Bulmer Tye House, Sudbury, Suffolk, and Yvonne Victoria, *née* Hughes (d 1978); *b* 10 Aug 1925; *Educ* Downside, Trinity Coll Cambridge; *m* 1957, Cynthia Mary, da of Capt Trevor Hume, of Old Harlow, Essex; 1 s (Timothy b 1958), 1 da (Clare b 1961); *Career* Lt-Col RE 4 Div 1966-68 (Bengal Sappers and Miners 1945-48, Korea 1952-53); instr: Sandhurst, Staff Coll Camberley; Cmd 19 Airportable Inf Bde 1969-71, dir Army Staff Duties 1976-79, GOC SE Dist 1979-81 (SW Dist 1974-75), Gen 1981, Adj-Gen MOD 1981-84; Col Cmdt: RE 1980-, RPC 1981-85; Col The Queen's Gurkha Engrs 1981-91; ADC Gen to HM The Queen 1982-84; Chief Royal Engr 1987-; memb Bd of Mgmnt GEC UK, dir Mgmnt Devpt GEC 1985-86, chm HGP Managing Agency Ltd 1990-; chm Infantile Hypercalcaemia Fndn 1981-, memb Cncl Action Res 1983-; *Recreations* shooting, gardening; *Clubs* Army and Navy, MCC; *Style—* Sir George Cooper, GCB, MC, DL; c/o Barclays Bank Ltd, 3-5 King St, Reading, Berks RG1 2HD

COOPER, Sir Gilbert Alexander; CBE (1964), ED (1943); s of Alexander Samuel, and Laura Ann Cooper; *b* 31 July 1903; *Educ* Saltus GS Bermuda, McGill Univ Canada; *Career* memb House of Assembly Bermuda 1948-68, memb Legislative Assembly 1968-72, kt 1972; *Style—* Sir Gilbert Cooper, CBE, ED; Shoreland, Pembroke, Bermuda HM05 (☎ 5 4189)

COOPER, Dr Griselda Mary; da of Dr Charles James Constantine Davey, of Ashley Croft, Box Corsham, Wilts, and Dr Gwyneth June, *née* Pearson; *b* 8 April 1949; *Educ* Bath HS, Univ of Birmingham (MB ChB); *m* 31 Aug 1973, Dr Brian Thomas Cooper, s of Dr Andrew Matthew Cooper (d 1979); 1 da (Charlotte b 1987); *Career* sr lectr in anaesthesia Univ of Bristol 1981-87, conslt anaesthetist Dunedin Public Hosp NZ 1985-86, sr lectr in anaesthesia Univ of Birmingham 1988-; Fell Coll of Anaesthetists; *Recreations* walking, skiing, embroidery; *Style—* Dr Griselda Cooper; 36 Anstruther Road, Edgbaston, Birmingham B15 3NW (☎ 021 456 2174), Birmingham Maternity Hospital, QE Medical Centre, Edgbaston, Birmingham B15 2TG (☎ 021 472 1377)

COOPER, Gyles Penry; s of Penry Lowick Cooper, of London; *b* 8 Nov 1942; *Educ* Felsted, St John's Coll Oxford (MA); *Career* CA 1968; Samuel Montagu & Co Ltd 1968-79, Société Générale Bank Ltd 1979-82; dir: Aitken Hume Ltd 1982-84, Chemical Bank Interntional Ltd 1984-85; non-exec dir Stagescreen Prodns Ltd 1984-89, md First Austrian International Ltd 1988-; chm Highgate Cemetery Ltd 1986-87, tstee The Highgate Cemetery Charity 1988-; Freeman City of London 1979; *Style—* Gyles Cooper, Esq; First Austrian International Ltd, Eldon House, 2 Eldon Street, London EC2M 7BX

COOPER, Hon Jason Charles Duff Bede; s and h of 2 Viscount Norwich; *b* 27 Oct 1959; *Educ* Eton, New Coll Oxford (BA), Oxford Poly (BA, Dip Arch); *Career* architect, designer, journalist; *Recreations* piano, travel, skiing; *Style—* Jason Cooper; 24 Blomfield Rd, London W9

COOPER, Jilly; da of Brig W B Sallitt, OBE (d 1982), and Mary Elain, *née* Whincup; *b* 21 Feb 1937; *Educ* Godolphin Sch Salisbury; *m* 7 Oct 1961, Leo Cooper, s of Leonard Cooper, of Norfolk; 1 s (Matthew Felix b 5 Sept 1969), 1 da (Emily b 13 June 1971); *Career* writer; former cub reporter Middlesex Independent Brentford 1955-57, followed by several jobs incl info offr, puppy fat model and switch board wrecker; newspaper columnist: Sunday Times 1969-82, Mail on Sunday 1982-87; memb Cncl Nat Canine Def League; *Books* author of 33 books incl: Class (1979), The Common Years (1984), Riders (1985), Rivals (1988); *Recreations* wild flowers, reading, mongrels, merry making and music; *Style—* Mrs Jilly Cooper; c/o Desmond Elliott Ltd, 15-17 King Street, St James's, London SW1 (☎ 071 930 0097)

COOPER, Joan Davies; CB 1972; da of Valentine Holland Cooper (d 1941), of Manchester, and Louisa Wynnefred Cooper (d 1977); *b* 12 Aug 1914; *Educ* Fairfield HS nr Manchester, Univ of Manchester (BA), Nat Inst for Social Work; *Career* Teaching and Probation Serv 1937-41, asst dir of educn Derbyshire 1941-48, children's offr E Sussex 1948-65, chief inspr Children's Dept Home Office 1965-71, dir social work serv Dept of Health and Social Security 1971-76; vice pres Nat Children's Bureau 1963-, memb Social Sci Res Cncl 1972-76; chm: Nat Assoc for Care and Resettlement of Offender Ctee on Juvenile Crime 1977-85, Int Expert Ctee on Access To Records 1977, Central Cncl for Education and Trg of Social Workers 1984-87, Ind Representation for Children in Trouble 1984-; pres Housing Assoc Lewers Sussex 1984-88, chm Care for the Carers E Sussex 1986-, tstee Homestart Consultancy, chm Child Abuse Review Ctee E Sussex 1984-87; hon visiting res fell Univ of Sussex 1978-; Freedom City of Narvik (Norway) 1963; FRAnthropl 1972; *Books* Patterns of Family Placement (1978), Social Groupwork with Elderly People In Hospital (1980), The Creation of the British Personal Social Services (1983); *Recreations* walking and travel; *Clubs* University Women's; *Style—* Miss Joan Cooper, CB; 44 Greyfriars, Court Road, Lewes, Sussex BN7 1RF (☎ 0273 472604)

COOPER, John; s of Kenneth Cooper, of Manchester, and Irene, *née* Wright; *b* 29 April 1955; *Educ* Manchester GS, Royal Coll of Music (ARCM), King's Coll Cambridge (MA); *m* 5 Oct 1983, Jane Mary, da of Alan Arthur Kingshotte, of Strawberry Hill; 1 s (Benedict b 26 April 1988), 1 da (Charlotte b 28 Aug 1984); *Career* admitted slr 1979, ptnr Lovell White & King 1985-88 (articled clerk 1977), ptnr Lovell White Durrant 1988-; Freeman Worshipful Co of Slrs 1981; memb Law Soc; *Recreations* golf, horse racing, wine; *Style—* John Cooper, Esq; 65 Holborn Viaduct, London EC1 (☎ 071 236 0066, fax 071 236 0084); 37 Ave Pierre 1er de Serbie, 75008 Paris (☎ 49 52 04 26, fax 47 23 96 12)

COOPER, John David Timothy; s of Donald James Cooper, of Taunton, and Enid Anne, *née* Hawker; *b* 30 Jan 1950; *Educ* Taunton Sch; *m* 23 March 1974, Jean Craig Churchill, da of James Galloway Forsyth (d 1983); 1 s (David b 1978), 1 da (Ann b 1975); *Career* admitted slr 1973; ptnr Clarke Willmott and Clarke 1980-; chm Somerset Young Slrs 1982, dep dist judge of the High Ct and Co Ct 1988; 2 XI player Somerset CCC 1969-74; memb Cncl Taunton Sch; memb: Law Soc 1974, Somerset Law Soc 1974; *Recreations* cricket; *Style—* John Cooper, Esq; Andes, 15 Batts Park, Taunton, Somerset TA1 4RE (☎ 0823 333235); Clarke Willmott and Clarke, 50-54 Fore St, Chard, Somerset TA20 1QA (☎ 0460 62777, fax 0460 67750, telex 46208)

COOPER, John Edwyn; s of Reginald Vincent Cooper, MBE, and Mildred Anne, *née* Clayton; *b* 18 Sept 1949; *Educ* Kingsbury Co GS, Univ of Hull (BSc); *m* 1, 1972 (m dis 1988), Patricia Anne, da of Wing Cdr Gordon F Turner, of Watford, Herts; m 2, 19 May 1988, Penelope Freda, da of Douglas Keith Walters (d 1968); 1 s (James Alexander b 10 March 1988); *Career* asst master in mathematics Hymers Coll Hull 1971-72, UK trg mangr Wang UK 1981-86, dir of educn NCR 1986-88, mgmnt info servs dir Wang UK 1988-; memb Bd of Govrs Richmond-upon-Thames Coll; Freeman City of London 1982, memb Worshipful Co of Plumbers 1982; *Recreations* golf, food and wine; *Style—* John Cooper, Esq; Appletree Cottage, 20B Langley Avenue, Surbiton, Surrey; Wang, Unit 4, Great West Plaza, Great West Road, Brentford (☎ 081 862 2610)

COOPER, Ven John Leslie; s of Leslie Cooper (d 1974), of East Molesey, Surrey, and Iris May, *née* Johnston (d 1989); *b* 16 Dec 1933; *Educ* Tiffin Sch Kingston Surrey, Kings Coll Univ of London (BD, MPhil); *m* 19 Dec 1959, Gillian Mary, da of Eric Dodds (d 1986), of Esher, Surrey; 2 s (Jonathan Mark Eric b 1962, Philip Justin Michael b 1964), 1 da (Penelope Sue b 1963); *Career* Nat Serv 2 Lt, RA Germany 1952-54; Gen Electric Co 1954-59; asst curate All Saints King's Heath Birmingham 1962-65, chaplain HM Prison Serv 1965-72, res fell Queen's Coll Birmingham 1972-73, incumbent St Paul Balsall Heath Birmingham 1973-82, archdeacon of Aston and canon residentiary St Philip's Cathedral 1982-90, archdeacon of Coleshill 1990-; *Recreations* photography, reading, music, carpentry, walking, swimming, travel; *Style—* The Ven the Archdeacon of Coleshill; 93 Coleshill Rd, Marston Green, Birmingham B37 7HT (☎ 021 779 4959, fax 027 779 6665)

COOPER, Rear Adm John Spencer; OBE (1974); s of Harold Spencer Cooper, of Hong Kong (d 1972), and Barbara, *née* Highet (d 1974); *b* 5 April 1933; *Educ* St Edward's Sch Oxford, Clare Coll Cambridge (MA); *m* 13 Aug 1966, Jacqueline Street, *née* Taylor; 2 da (Philippa b 1967, Lucy b 1970); *Career* chief strategic systems exec 1985-88; dir gen strategic weapon systems 1981-85, sr UK Polaris rep Washington 1978-80, dir Trials (Polaris) 1976-78, with Ferranti Int 1988-; *Recreations* sailing; *Style—* Rear Adm J S Cooper, OBE; 3 Burlington Ave, Kew Gdns, Richmond, Surrey TW9 4DF (☎ 081 876 3675)

COOPER, Joseph Elliott Needham; OBE (1982); s of Wilfred Needham Cooper (d 1949), of Westbury-on-Trym, and Elsie Goodacre, *née* Elliott (d 1963); *b* 7 Oct 1912; *Educ* Clifton, Keble Coll Oxford (MA); *m* 1, 15 Nov 1947, (Marjorie) Jean (d 1973), da of Gp Capt Sir Louis Greig, KBE, CVO, DL (d 1953), of Thatched House Lodge, Richmond Park; m 2, 4 July 1975, Carol Vivien Nelson, da of Charles John Nelson Borg (d 1986), of Brighton; *Career* WWII: 66 Searchlight Regt RA, cmmnd 2 Lt 1941, Capt 1943, WO Sch Aircraft Recognition 1944, served GHQ AA Troops (21 Army Gp Rear) Normandy 1944, demobbed 1946; composer and arranger GPO Film Unit 1936-37, trained as concert pianist under Egon Petri, arrangement of Vaughan Williams Piano Concerto for 2 pianos (with co 1946, debut Wigmore Hall 1947, concerto debut Philharmonia Orch 1950, debut BBC Promenade Concerts Royal Albert Hall 1953); various piano recordings incl The World of Joseph Cooper; tours: India 1953, extensively Br Isles and continent; chm Face the Music BBC TV 1966-84, pres Dorking Halls Concertgoers Soc 1985-90; vice pres: 2 Care (formerly SOS Soc Old People's Homes) 1970-, Music Cncl English Speaking Union 1985-; former pres: Surrey Philharmonic Soc, Box Hill Musical Festival, Reigate Music Soc; memb: Music Panel Arts Cncl (chm Piano Sub Ctee) 1966-71, Jury Anglo-French Music Scholarships 1985-, Ctee for an Organ St John's Smith Square 1986-, Cncl Musicians Benevolent Fund 1987-; tstee Countess of Munster Musical Tst 1975-80, govr Clifton Coll, patron St George's Music Tst Bristol 1982-; Freeman City of London, Liveryman Worshipful Co of Musicians 1963; ARCM; *Books* Hidden Melodies (1975), More Hidden Melodies (1976), Still More Hidden Melodies (1978), Facing the Music (autobiography, 1979); *Recreations* countryside, animals, church architecture; *Clubs* Garrick; *Style—* Joseph Cooper, Esq, OBE; Octagon Lodge, Ranmore, nr Dorking, Surrey RH5 6SX (☎ 04865 2658)

COOPER, Kenneth Reginald; s of Reginald Frederick Cooper, of Old Park Rd, Palmers Green, London, and Louisa May, *née* Turner (d 1962); *b* 28 June 1931; *Educ* Queen Elizabeth's GS Barnet, New Coll Oxford (MA); *m* 21 Dec 1955, Olga Ruth, da of Ernest Charles Harvey, MBE (d 1955); 2 s (Richard b 1960, Nicholas b 1961), 2 da (Sharon b 1959, Caroline b 1968); *Career* Nat Serv 2 Lt Royal Warwicks Regt 1949-51, Lt TA 1951-54; Miny of Labour 1954-61, HM Treasy 1961-65, princ private sec to Min of Labour 1966-67, asst sec Industl Trg 1967-70; chief exec: Employment Serv Agency 1970-74, Trg Servs Agency 1974-79; dir gen Building Employers' Confedn 1979-84, chief exec Br Library 1984-; CBIM 1988, FIPM 1975, FITD 1980, Hon FIIS 1988, FRSA 1988; *Style—* Kenneth Cooper, Esq; 2 Sheraton St, London W1V 4BH (☎ 071 323 7273, fax 071 323 7268, car 0860 822 458)

COOPER, Kevin Edwin; s of Gerald Edwin Cooper, at 22 Broomhill Rd, Hucknall, Nottingham, and Margaret, *née* Burton; *b* 27 Dec 1957; *Educ* Hucknall Nat Secdy Sch; *m* Linda Carol, da of Grenvill Spencer; 2 da (Kelly Louise b 9 April 1982, Tara Amy b 22 Nov 1984); *Career* cricketer; debut Notts CCC 1976 (269 first class appearances), toured with Derek Robbins under 23 XI on Australasian tour 1979-80; played for Nedlands CC Perth WA 1978-79; 10 wickets for 6 runs in one innings playing for Hucknall Ramblers CC against Sutton Colliery Mansfield and Dist League, best bowling performance Notts CCC 8 for 44 Notts v Middx Lords 1984, 101 first class wickets 1988, total number of first class wickets 704; *Recreations* golf, clay pigeon shooting; *Style—* Kevin Cooper, Esq; Notts County Cricket Club, Tent Bridge, Nottingham NG2 6AG (☎ 0602 821525)

COOPER, Lt-Col (Leonard) Malcolm; TD (1945); s of Ernest Leonard Cooper (d 1940), of Great Brake, Ottery, St Mary, Devon, and Elspeth, *née* Kellie MacAllum (d 1966); *b* 11 Aug 1913; *Educ* Sherborne; *m* 7 Oct 1960, (Eleanora) Joan, da of Francis William Elcock Massey (d 1964), of Bembridge, IOW; *Career* cmmnd 4 Bn Devonshire Regt (TA) 1932, Staff Coll Camberley 1941, served N Africa and Italy, Lt-Col 1943 (despatches); slr 1936, ptnr Knapp-fishers until 1980, conslt Richards Butler; memb Law Soc 1936; *Recreations* foxhunting, deer stalking, horse racing; *Clubs* Boodle's, Pratt's, Jockey; *Style—* Lt-Col Malcolm Cooper, TD; Mount Pleasant, Church St, Ropley, Hants SO24 0DR (☎ 0962 77 3361); 61 St Mary Axe, London EC3

COOPER, Elisabeth, Lady; Mary Elisabeth; da of Capt John Eagles Henry Graham-Clarke, of Frocester Manor, Stonehouse, Glos, and Margaret, *née* Rouse; *b* 31 Oct 1917; *m* 1 (m dis), Robert Erland Nicholai d'Abo; 1 s (Robin); m 2, 17 Dec 1953, as his 2 wife, Sir Charles Eric Daniel Cooper, 5 Bt (d 1984); 2 s (William Daniel Charles, George John); *Style—* Elisabeth, Lady Cooper; Pudley Cottage, Castle St, Aldbourne, Wiltshire SN8 2DA (☎ 0672 40274)

COOPER, Lady Maureen Isabel; *née* Le Poer Trench; eldest da of late 6 Earl of Clancarty; *b* 20 Dec 1923; *m* 16 March 1949, Christopher Colin Cooper, o son of late Maj Colin Cooper, of Barnwell Castle, Northants; 1 s (Simon b 1956), 1 da (Claudia b 1952); *Style—* The Lady Maureen Cooper; 542 Guadalmina Alta, San Pedro de Alcantara, Malaga, Spain

COOPER, Natasha; *see*: Wright, (Idonea) Daphne

COOPER, Patrick Ernest; s of Stuart Ranson Cooper (d 1966), and Lila Flemmich Cooper (d 1954); *b* 27 March 1935; *Educ* Wellesley House Broadstairs, Rugby; *m* 1963, Katrina Farnham, da of Frederick Windisch (d 1979), of Connecticut, USA; 2 da (Alexandra b 1967, Lila b 1970); *Career* Coldstream Guards 1953-55, cmmnd W Yorkshire Regt, served Malaysia and NI, TA 1955-61, ret Capt, CA; Cooper Bros audit mangr Lybrand Ross Bros and Montgomery 1961-62, dir Clive Discount and Co Ltd 1967, chief exec Clive Hldgs Gp 1971-72 (chm 1972), dir of fin servs Sime Darby Hldgs Ltd 1973, md Steel Bros and Co Ltd 1977 (dep chief exec and dep chm 1978), dep chm and chief exec Spinneys 1948 Ltd Jan 1980 (chm May 1980), chief exec Steel Bros Hldgs plc 1984; dir: Steel Bros Hldgs plc 1977-87, Steel Bros and Co Ltd 1977-87, Spinneys 1948 Ltd 1977-87, Goode Durrant PLC 1988-; non-exec dir MK Electric Gp 1983-88; Liveryman Worshipful Co of Vintners; *Recreations* golf, tennis, skiing, shooting, bridge, backgammon; *Clubs* Boodle's, Royal Ashdown Forest Golf, Royal St George's Golf; *Style—* Patrick Cooper, Esq; Glebe Ho, Fletching, Sussex (☎ 082 572 2104)

COOPER, Paul Michael; s of Robert Arthur Horne Cooper (d 1977), of Marderby Grange, Felixkirk, Thirsk, N Yorks, and Felicity Anne, *née* Preston; *b* 28 Sept 1958; *Educ* Stowe, Institut De Brittanique Sorbonne Paris; *Career* asst to Ed Statistical Record Sires 1977-80; owner of race horses in England, Italy and USA 1980-; fndr: Fonaview Ltd (suppliers of horse racing info) 1987, Paul Cooper Ltd 1989; memb ROA; *Recreations* shooting, tennis, golf, horse-racing; *Clubs* Ritz, Crockfords, David Lloyd; *Style—* Paul Cooper, Esq; 39 Kenilworth Court, Lower Richmond Road, London SW15 1EN (☎ 081 789 5385, 081 788 9621), Fonaview Ltd, St Nicholas House, The Mount, Guildford, Surrey GU2 5HN (☎ 0483 301152, 0483 301159, fax 0483 301148, car 505340)

COOPER, Prof Philip Anthony Robert; s of Stanley Ernest Cooper, and Amy May, *née* Coleman; *b* 13 Jan 1950; *Educ* Felsted, Univ of Leeds (BSc), Univ of Cambridge (MA); *m* 17 July 1976, (Elizabeth) Jane, da of Dr Harold Leslie Keer Whitehouse; 1 s (Oliver Edward Keer b 1986), 2 da (Harriet Amy Jane b 1980, Emily Sarah Rose b 1982); *Career* lectr Univ of Cambridge Sch of Architecture 1974-78, engr Harris and Sutherland (London and Cambridge) 1978-, assoc and currently dir Harris and Sutherland Consultant Civil and Structural Engineers, prof structural design (first in UK) 1986-; memb Univ of Cambridge Graduate Centre; MIStructE; *Recreations* tennis, music, windsurfing; *Style—* Prof Philip Cooper; 2 Pound Hill, Cambridge, Cambridgeshire CB3 0AE (☎ 0223 312055); Harris & Sutherland, 15 Sturton St, Cambridge CB1 2QG (☎ 0223 65731, fax 0223 61332)

COOPER, Philip John; CB (1989); s of Charles Cooper (d 1980), and Mildred Annie, *née* Marlow (d 1981); *b* 15 Sept 1929; *Educ* Deacons Sch Peterborough, Univ of Leicester (BSc); *m* 1, 1 Aug 1953, Dorothy Joan Chapman (d 1982), da of James Chapman (d 1970), of Rhos on Sea, N Wales; 2 da (Vivien Anne b 1954, Valerie Joan b 1957); m 2, 8 Aug 1986, Pamela Mary Coad (d 1988), da of Henry John Pysden (d 1979), of Durban, South Africa; *Career* Nat Serv 2 Lt Royal Signals 1953-55; govt chemist 1952, Dept of Sci and Industl Res 1956-67, princ Miny of Technol 1967, PPS to Min for Industl Devpt 1972-73, under sec DOI and DTI 1979-89 (asst sec 1973-79), dir Warren Spring Lab DTI 1984-85; comptroller-gen The Patent Office DTI 1986-89; author of various papers on analytical and chemical matters; *Style—* Philip Cooper, Esq, CB; Abbottsmead, Sandy Lane, Kingswood, Surrey KT20 6ND (☎ 0737 833039)

COOPER, Richard Devereux Burcombe; s of Alexander Burcombe Cooper, of Downleaze, Bristol, and Alma Gwendoline, *née* Harris; *b* 10 April 1943; *Educ* Clifton, The Taft Sch Watertown Connecticut USA, Trinity Coll Cambridge (MA); *m* 19 July 1975, Janet, da of Lt-Col Archibald Michael Lyle, DL, of Riemore Lodge, Dunkeld, Perthshire; 3 da (Daisy b 17 Sept 1983, Hester b 21 Dec 1985, Tilly b 18 July 1988); *Career* ptnr Slaughter and May 1975-, (slr 1965-); Eng int real tennis player: versus France 1967 and 1984, versus Australia 1969 and 1984; Cambridge blue: squash 1964, real tennis 1965; vice pres PHAB, former chm Tennis & Rackets Assoc Devpt and Young Professionals Prog; Freeman Worshipful Co of Goldsmiths 1986-; memb: Law Soc 1968, Hong Kong Law Soc 1986; *Recreations* music, tennis, shooting, travel, Chinese paintings, languages; *Clubs* Boodle's, MCC, Queen's, Hawks, Jesters', Hong Kong; *Style—* Richard Cooper, Esq; 29 Lansdowne Gardens, London SW8 2EQ, 35 Basinghall St, London EC2V 5BD (☎ 071 600 1200, telex 883486, fax 071 726 0038)

COOPER, Richard John; s of William George Cooper (d 1979); *Educ* Slough GS; *m* 1950, Margaret Pauline, *née* Gould; 1 s, 1 da; *Career* former regional pres (Berks, Bucks and Oxon Region) Construction Surveyors Inst, dir Farrow Construction Ltd; *Recreations* deep sea fishing, golf, youth work; *Clubs* Eccentric; *Style—* Richard Cooper, Esq; Brantwood, 39 Littleton Rd, Harrow, Middlesex

COOPER, Dr Richard Michael; s of Harry Cecil Cohen, of 24 Barrydene, London, and Sadie, *née* Speier; *b* 25 Nov 1940; *Educ* Belmont, Mill Hill Sch, Charing Cross Hosp (Gynaecology prize, Forensic Med prize); *m* Dawne Cooper, JP, da of Alfred

Matlow; 1 s (Adam b 31 July 1968), 2 da (Louise b 8 May 1972, Gabrielle b 22 Nov 1972); *Career* house appts at Charing Cross Hosp and Mount Vernon Hosp; princ in gen practice: 74 Brooksby's Walk London 1966-70, 71 Amhurst Park London 1970-76; in private practice 17 Harley St 1976-; med conslt: Bank of America, Gambia High Cmmn; med examiner numerous insurance cos, chief med offr Jewish Agency; FRSM 1969; fell: Assurance Med Soc, Hunterian Soc; *Recreations* family, broadcasting, fund raising, and other communal activities, writing med articles; *Clubs* Old Millhillians, Knightsbridge Speakers'; *Style—* Dr Richard Cooper; Wildbrook, 34 Uxbridge Rd, Stanmore, Middx HA7 3LQ (☎ 081 954 8445/9291); The Richard Cooper Practice, 17 Harley St, London W1N 1DA (☎ 071 580 3324, 071 636 3126, fax 071 436 0661, car 0836 617894)

COOPER, Sir Richard Powell; 5 Bt (UK 1905), of Shenstone Court, Shenstone, Co Stafford; s of Sir Francis Ashmole (Frank) Cooper, 4 Bt (d 1987), and Dorothy Francis Hendrika, *née* Deen; *b* 13 April 1934; *Educ* Marlborough; *m* 2 Oct 1957, Angela Marjorie, er da of late Eric Wilson, of Stockton-on-Tees; 1 s (Richard Adrian b 1960), 2 da (Jane Alice b 1958, Belinda Gay b 1963); *Heir* s, Richard Adrian b 21 Aug 1960; *Career* memb RAS 1976, chm Rare Breeds Survival Trust 1990; *Recreations* foxhunting; *Clubs* Carlton, Buck's; *Style—* Sir Richard Cooper, Bt; Lower Farm, Chedington, Beaminster, Dorset DT8 3HY

COOPER, Robert; s of Alfred Cooper, of The Manor, Ogbourne Maisey, Marlborough, Wilts, and Marguerite Mary, *née* Bailey; *b* 18 Feb 1932; *Educ* Radley; *m* 1957 (m dis); 2 s (Alexander b 1960, Charles b 1961), 1 da (Carina b 1961); *Career* TA Capt RWY; chm and chief exec: Coopers Holdings Ltd, Coopers (Metals) Ltd (Queen's Award for Export 1982), Coopers (Swindon) Ltd; pres Br Scrap Fedn 1984-1985; Queen's Award for Export 1986; memb Worshipful Co of Butchers; *Recreations* country pursuits; *Clubs* Cavalry and Guards'; *Style—* Robert Cooper, Esq; Ablington Manor, Bibury, Cirencester, Glos (☎ 028 574 363); Coopers Holdings Ltd, Bridge House, Gipsy Lane, Swindon, Wilts SN2 6DZ (☎ 0793 532111, fax 0793 614214, telex 44251)

COOPER, Robert Douglas; s of Peter Cooper (d 1962), and Marguerite, *née* Slater; *b* 16 March 1939; *Educ* Daniel Stewart's Coll Edinburgh, Heriot Watt Univ; *Career* Bass plc 1960, md Charringtons Inns and Taverns Ltd; *Recreations* golf; *Clubs* Royal and Ancient, Royal Mid-Surrey; *Style—* Robert Cooper, Esq; 1 Wildcroft Manor, Putney Heath, London SW15 3TS; Charrington & Co Ltd, North Woolwich Rd, London E16 2AD

COOPER, Robert Francis; MVO (1975); s of Norman Cooper (d 1966), and Frances Cooper; *b* 28 Aug 1947; *Educ* Delamere School Nairobi, Worcester Coll Oxford (BA), Univ of Pensylvania (MA); *Career* HM Diplomatic Serv 1970, FCO 1970-71, Language Study 1971-73, Br Embassy Tokyo 1973-77, FCO 1979-82, seconded to Bank of England 1982-84, UK rep to EC Brussels 1984-87, head Far Eastern Dept FCO 1987-89, head of Policy Planning Staff 1989-; Order of the Sacred Treasure (4 Class) Japan (1973); *Recreations* bicycles, bridge and the Bard; *Style—* Robert Cooper, Esq, MVO; c/o Foreign & Commonwealth Office, King Charles Street, London SW1A 2AH (☎ 071 270 2911, 071 270 3510)

COOPER, Robert George; CBE (1987); s of William Hugh Cooper, of Castlefinn, Co Donegal (d 1975), and Annie Cooper; *b* 24 June 1936; *Educ* Foyle Coll Londonderry, Queen's Univ Belfast (LLB); *m* 2 Nov 1974, Patricia Frances, da of Gerald Nichol, of Belfast; 1 s (William Gerald b 1975), 1 da (Anne Cecilia b 1977); *Career* industl rels offr ICT 1958-64, sec NI Engrg Employers' Assoc 1964-72, jt political chm Alliance Pty of NI 1970-73 (fndr memb 1970, gen sec 1972-74), elected W Belfast memb NI Assembly 1973-75 (participant in Darlington and Sunningdale Constitutional Confs), min of Manpower NI Powersharing Govt 1974, elected W Belfast memb NI Constitutional Convention 1975-76; chm and chief exec Fair Employment Agency 1976-89, chm Fair Employment Cmmn 1990-; memb: Standing Advsy Cmmn on Human Rights 1976-, Equal Opportunities Cmmn for NI 1976-83; *Style—* Robert Cooper, Esq, CBE; Lynwood, 104 Bangor Road, Holywood, Co Down, N Ireland (☎ 023 17 2071); Andras House, 60 Gt Victoria St, Belfast (☎ 0232 240020, fax 331544)

COOPER, (Hulbert) Rodney; s of Hulbert Francis Cooper (d 1959), of Bromley, Kent, and Dorothy Amy Burtt (d 1966); *b* 11 April 1933; *Educ* Bromley GS, Univ of London (BSc), Ravensbourne Coll of Art & Design, Central Sch of Art, Royal Naval Coll Greenwich; *m* 7 Oct 1961, (Mary) Anne, da of Aubrey George Eames (d 1962), of Bromley, Kent; 1 s (Matthew b 1963), 1 da (Nancy b 1967); *Career* Lt RN 1957-60 served HMS Ocean, Port Educn Offr Chatham; sci advsr Br Pavilion Brussels World Fair 1956, res chemist A Wander Ltd 1960-63, designer Sir Basil Spence and Ptnrs 1963-70; Bldg Design Ptnrship 1970-: assoc 1973-80, ptnr 1980-84, sr ptnr 1984- (responsible for interior, graphic and product design); external examiner: Univ of Wales Architectural Sch, Middx Poly; lectr Ravensbourne Coll of Design; FCSD 1975; *Books* The Trade Report (1988), Specification (3 edn, 1989), contrib to architectural and design jnls; *Recreations* cine photography, clarinet, tennis, driving fast cars, making people laugh; *Style—* Rodney Cooper, Esq; Building Design Partnership, PO Box 4WD, 16 Gresse St, London W1A 4WD (☎ 071 631 4733, fax 071 631 0393, telex 25322)

COOPER, Dr Rosemary Anne; da of Dr William Francis Cooper (d 1950), and Eileen Beryl, *née* Hall (d 1976); *b* 6 April 1925; *Educ* Westonbirt Sch, Cheltenham, Girton Coll Cambridge, KCH Med Sch (MA, MB BChir, MRCP); *m* 14 Jan 1956, Walter van't Hoff, s of Robert van't Hoff (d 1979); 3 s (William b 1958, Hugh b 1960, Graham b 1961); *Career* med registrar: Westminster Hosp 1955-56, London Hosp 1959-62; Fulbright scholar 1956-57, res fell paediatrics Harvard Univ USA at Children's Med Centre Boston 1956-57, conslt clinical neurophysiologist North Staffordshire Hosp Centre 1958-1989, sr res fell clinical neurophysiology Univ of Keele 1980-1989; memb: Jt Ctee on Higher Med Trg 1976-84, Hon Advsy Neurology Panel Dept of Tport 1988; pres: The Electroencephalographic Soc 1982-84, Assoc of Br Clinical Neurophysiologists 1984-87, Electrophysiological Technologists' Assoc 1987-; FRCP 1977, FRSM; *Recreations* music, travel, sailing; *Clubs* Hardway Sailing, Trollope Soc, English Speaking Union, Cruising Assoc; *Style—* Dr Rosemary Cooper; Granida, 9 East Street, Hambledon, Hampshire PO7 6RX (☎ 0705 632382)

COOPER, Maj-Gen Simon Christie; s of Maj-Gen Kenneth Christie Cooper, CB, DSO, OBE (d 1981), of Dorset, and Barbara Mary, *née* Harding-Newman (d 1988); *b* 5 Feb 1936; *Educ* Winchester, Hamburg Univ; *m* 1967, Juliet Elizabeth, da of Cdr Geoffrey Inderwick Palmer, of Somerset; 1 s (Jonathan Francis Christie b 1969), 1 da (Venetia Elizabeth Somerset b 1971); *Career* cmmnd Life Gds 1956; served 1957-63: Aden, London, BAOR; Capt Adj Household Cavalry Regt 1963-65, ADC to CDS Earl Mountbatten of Burma 1965-66, Borneo Malaya 1966-67, Staff Coll 1968, BAOR 1969-75, CO Life Gds 1974-76, GSOI Staff Coll 1976-78, OC Household Cavalry and Silver Stick in Waiting 1978-81, cmdt RAC Centre 1981-82, RCDS 1983, dir RAC 1984-87, cmdt RMA Sandhurst 1987-89, Maj-Gen cmdg Household Div GOC and London Dist 1989-; Hon Col Westminster Dragoons and Hon Col Royal Yeo 1987-; *Recreations* tennis, cricket, sailing, shooting, skiing; *Clubs* MCC; *Style—* Maj-Gen Simon Cooper; c/o Royal Bank of Scotland, Holts, Lawrie House, Farnborough, Hants GU14 7PQ

COOPER, Thomas Joshua; s of Duahne William Cooper, of Yuma, Arizona, USA, and Nancy, *née* Roseman (d 1964); *b* 19 Dec 1946; *Educ* Humboldt State Univ Calif (BA, Secdy Teaching Credential, Community Teaching Credential), Univ of New Mexico Alberquerque (MA); partner, Catherine Alice, da of James Patrick Mooney, of Den Hague, Netherlands; *Career* visual artist 1969-; teacher of photography Arcata HS Calif 1969, instr in photography Coll of the Redwoods Community Coll Eureka Calif 1970, teacher Dana Elementary Sch Nipomo Calif 1971, visiting lectr in photography Inst of American Indian Art Santa Fe New Mexico 1973, course dir for photographic studies and sr lectr in photography and history of photography Trent Poly Nottingham 1973-76, visiting asst prof of art Humboldt State Univ 1978-80, visiting artist Univ of Tasmania Sch of Art 1982; giver of annual workshops: The Photographers Place Bradbourne 1982-, Salzburg Coll Salzburg Austria 1986-; founding head Dept of Photography Sch of Fine Art Glasgow Sch of Art 1982-; memb: Photography Advsy Panel Scottish Arts Cncl 1986, Photography Bd CNAA 1986-87, Art Ctee Scottish Arts Cncl 1989-; major exhibitions incl: Images of our Mortality (Robert Self Gallery) 1977, A Quality of Dancing (Humboldt State Univ) 1984, American Photography: 1945-1980 (Barbican Art Gallery) 1985-86, The Hayward Annual (Hayward Gallery) 1985; John Weber Gallery 1988 and 1990, The Swelling of the Sea (Art Gallery and Museum Kelvingrove Glasgow) 1990; *Publications incl* Dialogue with Photography (1979), Between Dark and Dark (1985), Dreaming the Gokstadt (1988); works in public collections throughout the world; awards: John D Phelan award in Art & Literature 1970, maj photography bursary Arts Cncl of GB 1976, Photography fell Nat Endowment of the Arts USA 1978; memb Soc for Photographic Educn 1969, fndr memb Scottish Soc for the History of Photography 1983, professional memb SSA 1984; *Recreations* cinema, reading, music (Renaissance, choral, country & western, operatic), athletics, barbeques, walking, wine; *Style—* Thomas Joshua Cooper, Esq; c/o Graeme Murray, Graeme Murray Gallery, 15 Scotland St, Edinburgh EH3 (☎ 031 556 6020, fax 031 557 3214), John Weber, John Weber Gallery, 142 Greene St, New York City, NY 10012, (☎ 010 212 966 6115, fax 010 212 941 8727)

COOPER, William; s of Ernest Hoff (d 1960), of Crewe, and Edith Annie, *née* Summerfield (d 1979); *b* 4 Aug 1910; *Educ* Crewe Co Secdy Sch, Christ's Coll Cambridge (MA); *m* 3 Jan 1951, Joyce Barbara (d 1988), da of Rev William Frederick Harr of Bristol; 2 da (Louisa b 1953, Catherine b 1955); *Career* Sqdn Ldr RAFVR 1940-46; asst cmmr Civil Serv Cmmn 1945-58; personnel consIt: UKAEA 1958-72, CEGB 1958-72, Cmmn of Euro Communities 1972-73; asst dir Civil Serv Selection Bd 1973-75, memb Bd of Crown Agents 1975-77, personnel advsr Millbank Tech Serv 1955-77; writer; adjunct prof of Eng lit Syracuse Univ London Centre 1977-90; FRSL, memb Int PEN; *Books* (as H S Hoff): Trina (1934), Rhea (1935), Lisa (1937), Three Marriages (1946); (as William Cooper): Scenes From Provincial Life (1950), The Struggles of Albert Woods (1952), The Ever-Interesting Topic (1953), Disquiet and Peace (1956), Young People (1958), C P Snow (Br Cncl Bibliographic Series, Writers and Their Work no 11, 1959), Prince Genji (a play, 1960), Scenes from Married Life (1961), Memoirs of a New Man (1966), You Want The Right Frame of Reference (1971), Shall We Ever Know (1971), Love on The Coast (1973), You're Not Alone (1976), Scenes From Metropolitan Life (1982), Scenes From Later Life (1983), Scenes From Early Life (1990); *Recreations* swimming; *Clubs* Savile; *Style—* William Cooper, Esq; 22 Kenilworth Ct, Lower Richmond Rd, London SW15 1EW (☎ 081 788 8326)

COOPER, Sir William Daniel Charles; 6 Bt (UK 1863) of Woollahra, New South Wales; s of Sir Charles Eric Daniel Cooper, 5 Bt (d 1984) by 2 wife - *see* Cooper, Lady (Mary Elisabeth); *b* 5 March 1955; *m* 22 Aug 1988, Julia Nicholson; *Heir* bro, George John Cooper, *qv*; *Career* dir: The Gdn Maintenance Serv, GMS Vehicles; *Style—* Sir William D C Cooper, Bt; 1 Victoria Cottages, Andover Road, Micheldever Station, Winchester SO21 3AX

COOPER, Maj-Gen William Frank; CBE (1972), MC (1945); s of Allan Cooper (d 1959), of Hazards, Shawford, Hants, and late Margaret Martha, *née* Pothelary; *b* 30 May 1921; *Educ* Sherborne; *m* 10 Aug 1945, Elizabeth Mary, da of George Finch (d 1918); 1 s (Allan George b 1950), 1 da (Gillian (Mrs Hewitt) b 1947); *Career* WWII cmmnd RE 1940, served N Africa and Italy, Staff Coll 1951, Co Field Sqdn RE Malayan Emergency, instr Staff Coll 1958-60, CRE 3 Div 1961-63, Lt-Col Staff HQ ME 1963-65, Brig Chief Engr 1968-70, Maj-Gen 1973-76; Mil advsr GKN Gp 1976-83, dir gen Rectifiers' and Distillers' Assoc and Vodka Trade Assoc 1976-90; *Recreations* fly fishing, bird watching, reading; *Clubs* Army and Navy; *Style—* Maj-Gen William Cooper, CBE, MC; Neals, Aldbourne, Marlborough, Wilts SN8 2DW (☎ 0672 407 16); 110 Kensington Park Rd, London W11 2PJ (☎ 071 229 9222)

COOPER-HEYMAN, Hon Mrs (Isobel); *née* Pargiter; da of Baron Pargiter, CBE (Life Peer); *b* 8 Sept 1931; *m* 26 June 1964, Ernest Cooper-Heyman, s of Harry Cooper-Heyman; *Career* pharmaceutical chemist; *Recreations* opera, theatre, travel; *Style—* The Hon Mrs Cooper-Heyman; 34 Van Dyke Close, Redhill, Surrey RH1 2DS

COOPER-KEY, Hon Lady (Lorna Peggy Vyvyan); *née* Harmsworth; da of 2 Viscount Rothermere (d 1979), by his 1 w Margaret; *b* 24 Oct 1920; *m* 11 Jan 1941, Sir Neill Cooper-Key (d 1981), er s of late Capt Edmund Moore Cooper-Key, CB, MVO, RN; 1 da (Emma Charlotte b 1958) and 1 da decd), 2 s decd; *Style—* The Hon Lady Cooper-Key; 1 Ave de Grande Bretagne, Monte Carlo

COOTE, Rev Bernard Albert Ernest; s of Albert Coote (d 1988, age 100), of Steyning, Sussex, and Emma Jane, *née* Tye (d 1957); *b* 11 Aug 1928; *Educ* Steyning GS, Univ of London (BD); *m* 17 Aug 1957, Ann, da of Donovan Hopper; 2 s (John b 1958, Michael b 1960); *Career* RAF 1946-49; vicar Sutton Valence and E Sutton 1963-76, dir Royal Sch for the Blind Leatherhead 1976-; chm Ctee on the Multihandcapped Blind 1984; *Recreations* cricket, walking, travel, music; *Style—* The Rev Bernard Coote; 2 Reigate Rd, Leatherhead, Surrey (☎ 0372 376 395); 6 Coxham Lane, Steyning, W Sussex; Royal School for the Blind, Leatherhead, Surrey (☎ 0372 373 733)

COOTE, Sir Christopher John; 15 Bt (I 1621), of Castle Cuffe, Queen's County, Ireland; s of Rear-Adm Sir John Coote, 14 Bt, CB, CBE, DSC (d 1978); *b* 22 Sept 1928; *Educ* Winchester, Christ Church Oxford (MA); *m* 23 Aug 1952, Anne Georgiana, yr da of Lt-Col Donald James Handford, RA (d 1980), of Guyers, Corsham, Wilts; 1 s, 1 da; *Heir* s, Nicholas Coote; *Career* late Lt 17/21 Lancers; coffee and tea merchant 1952-; *Style—* Sir Christopher Coote, Bt

COOTE, Prof John Haven; s of Albert Ernest Coote (d 1967), of Enfield, and Gladys Mary Elizabeth, *née* Noble; *b* 5 Jan 1937; *Educ* Enfield GS, Chelsea Coll, Royal Free Hosp Sch of Med, Univ of London (BSc, PhD), Univ of Birmingham (DSc); *m* 28 Dec 1974, Susan Mary, da of Lt Dr William Hawkins Hylton (d 1989), of Clevedon; 1 s (Edward John b 1976), 2 da (Rachel Elizabeth b 1978, Naomi Caroline b 1981); *Career* Univ of Birmingham: lectr 1967, sr lectr 1970, reader 1977, prof of physiology and head of Dept 1984, Bowman prof of physiology 1985, head Sch of Basic Med WSi 1988; hon lectr Royal Free Hosp Sch of Med 1966, visiting prof Tokyo 1974, visiting prof Shanghai 1989; memb: Ctee Physiological Soc 1976-80, Soc for Experimental Biology 1976-; FBiol 1988, CBiol 1988; *Recreations* running, mountaineering (Birmingham Med Res Expeditionary Soc); *Clubs* Univ of London Graduate Mountaineering; *Style—* Prof John Coote; Department of Physiology, The Medical School, University of Birmingham, Birmingham B15 2TJ (☎ 021 414 6915/6, fax 021 414 6924, telex 338938 SPAHY G)

COOTE, Nicholas Patrick; s and h of Sir Christopher Coote, 15 Bt; *b* 28 July 1953;

Educ Winchester; *m* 1980, Mona, da of late Moushegh Bedelian; 1 s (Rory Alasdair 3 April 1987), 1 da (Eleanor Marianne b 1984); *Career* British Airways; *Style*— Nicholas Coote, Esq

COOTE, Rt Rev Roderic Norman Coote; s of Cdr Bernard T Coote (d 1955), of Woodham Park Way, W Byfleet, Surrey, and Grace Harriet, *née* Robinson; *b* 13 April 1915; *Educ* Woking Co Sch, Trinity Coll Dublin (DD); *m* 1964, Erica Lynette, da of late Rev Eric G Shrubbs, MBE, Rector of Lawshall, Suffolk; 1 s, 2 da; *Career* curate 1938-41, SPG missionary 1942-51, bishop of Gambia and the Rio Pongas 1951-57, suffragan bishop of Fulham 1957-66, archdeacon of Colchester 1969-72, suffragan bishop of Colchester 1966-87, asst bishop in Dio of London 1987-; *Style*— The Rt Rev Roderic Coote; 58 Broom Park, Teddington TW11 9RS (☎ 081 943 3648)

COPCUTT, Ronald William James; s of William Norton Copcutt (d 1948), of 18 Cecil Rd, Southgate, London N14, and Hilda, *née* Hayward (d 1977); *b* 2 Feb 1916; *Educ* Coopers' Co Sch; *m* 1, Margaret (d 1966), da of Harold de la Mare (d 1949), of Greenwich, London; m 2, 3 Sept 1966, Vappu Hely, da of Väinö Nikolai Kunnas (d 1988), of Finland; 1 s (Nicholas William Väinö b 1971); *Career* WWII Civil Def Serv; sales rep Glovers Dyers & Cleaners Ltd 1932-44; dir: Copcutt Dobinson Ltd 1944-66, Frearsonia Ltd 1959-66, Keystone Cleaners Ltd 1948-68, BB&H Carpets Ltd 1960-66, Carpet Installations Ltd 1963-66; exec offr GLC 1967-81; chm: Miny Nat Insur and Pensions Local Advsy Ctee for NW Essex 1958- (memb 1949-), Miny of Health and Soc Security Redbridge and Waltham Forest Local A Ctee 1967-72, Dyehards Club 1950, Eltham Southend Res Assoc 1976-79, Eltham Assocs Ctee 1976-78; vice chm Crown Woods Sch Assoc 1984-86; memb: Dept of Health & Soc Security Local Appeals Tbnl 1950-88, Indust Injury Tbnl 1950-67, Miny of Lab & Nat Serv Mil Hardships & Reinstatement Ctee 1950-65, Coborn Estates Ctee 1959-71, Managing Ctee Nat Lib Club 1960-72, Lib Indust & Commercial Cncl 1961, Cncl of London & Southern Dyers & Cleaners 1948-53, pres GLC Branch NALGO 1973-74, Exec Ctee of Assoc of Voluntary Aided Secondary Schs 1981-88; govr Stepney & Bow Educnl Fndn 1959-, pres Old Coopers' Assoc 1967-68, tstee Gladstone Library 1964-78, specialist advsr to CAB on Tbnl Appeals 1988-; Freeman City of London 1952, Liveryman Worshipful Co of Coopers; *Clubs* Surrey CC, National Liberal; *Style*— Ronald Copcutt, Esq; 4 Enslin Rd, Eltham, London SE9 5BP (☎ 081 850 6401)

COPE, David Robert; s of Dr Cuthbert Leslie Cope (d 1975), and Eileen Gertrude, *née* Putt (d 1987); *b* 24 Oct 1944; *Educ* Winchester, Clare Coll Cambridge (BA, MA); *m* 2 April 1966, Gillian Margaret, da of Richard Eyton Peck, of Wenhaston, Suffolk; 1 s (Damian b 1967), 2 da (Claire b 1968, Genevieve b 1974); *Career* asst master Eton 1965-67, asst Br Cncl rep cultural attaché Mexico City 1968-70, asst master Bryanston Sch 1970-73; headmaster: Dover Coll 1973-81, Br Sch of Paris 1981-86; master Marlborough 1986-; FRSA 1978; *Recreations* music, travel; *Clubs* Athenaeum; *Style*— David Cope, Esq; The Master's Lodge, Marlborough College, Wiltshire SN8 1PA (☎ 0672 512140)

COPE, David Robert; s of Lawrence William Cope (d 1990), and Ethel Anne, *née* Harris (d 1980); *Educ* KCS Wimbledon, Univ of Cambridge (BA, MA), LSE (MSc); *m* 1 Sept 1973, Sharon Marie, da of J Edmund Kelly Jr, of Kenmore, NY, USA; *Career* res offr UCL 1968-70, lectr Univ of Nottingham 1970-81, environmental team ldr Int Energy Agency Coal Res 1981-86, dir UK Centre for Econ and Environmental Devpt 1986-; memb Inst of Energy; *Books* Energy Policy and Land-Use Planning - an International Perspective (with P Hills and P James, 1984); *Recreations* hill walking, woodworking, classical music; *Clubs* Europe House; *Style*— David R Cope, Esq; The UK Centre for Economic and Environmental Development, Suite E, 3 King's Parade, Cambridge CB2 1SJ (☎ 0223 67799)

COPE, Lady; Eveline; da of late Alfred Eaton Bishop, of Gloucester; *m* 18 April 1936, as his 2 w, Sir Mordaunt Leckonby Cope, 16 Bt, MC (d 1972, when title became extinct); *Style*— Lady Cope; 5 Headbourne Worthy House, Winchester, Hants

COPE, Rt Hon John Ambrose; PC (1988); MP (C) Northavon 1983-; s of late George Arnold Cope, MC, FRIBA, of Leicester; *b* 13 May 1937; *Educ* Oakham Sch Rutland; *m* 1969, Djemila, da of Col P V Lovell Payne, of Martinstown, Dorset; 2 da; *Career* chartered accountant; personal asst to Chm Cons Party 1967-70, Parly candidate (C) Woolwich E 1970, special asst to Sec of State for Trade and Industry 1972-74; MP (C) South Glos 1974-83, govt whip 1979-87, a lord cmmnr of the Treasury 1981-83, dep chief whip and treas HM's Household 1983-87; former minister of state Dept of Employment and minister for Small Firms 1987-89; dep chm Conservative Party 1990-; FCA; *Style*— Rt Hon John Cope, MP; House of Commons, London SW1A 0AA

COPE, Samantha Mary; da of John Martin Brentnall Cope, and of Davina Rosemary Enid Nutting (resumed maiden name upon divorce 1969, and was *k* in a motor accident with her only son, Jonathan Edric 1976), only child of Edric Nutting (*ka* 1943, 2 s of Sir Harold Nutting, 2 Bt) by his w, Lady Rosemary Eliot (d 1963), elder da of 6 Earl of St Germans by his w, Lady Blanche Somerset, da of 9 Duke of Beaufort; co-heiress to baronies of Botetourt and Herbert which fell into abeyance upon the death of 10 Duke of Beaufort 1984; *b* 23 Sept 1963; *Style*— Miss Samantha Cope

COPE, Wendy Mary; da of Fred Stanley Cope (d 1971), of Kent, and Alice Mary, *née* Hand; *b* 21 July 1945; *Educ* Farringtons Sch Chislehurst Kent, St Hilda's Coll Oxford (MA), Westminster Coll Oxford (DipEd); *Career* primary sch teacher: London Borough of Newham 1967-69, ILEA 1969-86 (seconded to Contact Newspaper as Arts and Reviews ed 1982-84, pt/t teacher 1984-86); freelance writer 1986-; Cholmondeley award for Poetry 1987; *Books* Making Cocoa for Kingsley Amis (1986), Twiddling Your Thumbs (1988), The River Girl (1991), Is That The New Moon? Poems by Women Poets (ed, 1988); *Recreations* playing the piano; *Style*— Ms Wendy Cope; c/o Faber & Faber, 3 Queen Square, London WC1N 3AU (☎ 071 465 0045)

COPE-STRACHAN, Lady; Joan Penelope; *née* Cope; da of Sir Denzil Cope, 14 Bt (Cope of Hanwell, Oxfordshire); assumed surname Cope-Strachan by deed poll 1969; *b* 1 Jan 1926; *Educ* at home; *m* 1949, Sir Duncan Alexander Grant, 13 Bt (d 1961); 3 s, 2 da; *Heir* er s, Sir Patrick Alexander Benedict Grant, 14 Bt, of Tomintool House, Flichity, Strathnairn, Inverness-shire; *Career* nurse during WWII; writer; former co dir and rep in Ireland of Société d'Etudes Techniques et Scientifiques of Avignon; *Books* Arabian Andalusian Casidas; *Recreations* piano, genealogy, conversation; *Style*— Lady Cope-Strachan; 34 Morehampton Rd, Ballsbridge, Dublin 4, Eire

COPELAND, Col Christopher John Blanchard; s of Dr Francis John Copeland, of Rustington, West Sussex, and Betty, *née* Walker; *b* 12 July 1943; *Educ* Sherborne, RMA Sandhurst; *m* 9 Nov 1968, Penelope, da of Cdr M L Woollcombe OBE, of Glebe Cottage, Fochabers, Scotland; 1 s (Nicholas b 26 April 1974), 1 da (Melanie b 25 August 1971); *Career* Adjutant 7 Para RHA 1973-75, staff coll 1976 Bty Cmd 1978-80, staff Coll Instr Nigeria 1980-83, CO 1983-85, Chief of Staff 1987-; memb Ctee Br Ski Fedn; FBIM 1989; *Recreations* golf, skiing, sailing; *Clubs* Royal Ocean Racing; *Style*— Col Christopher Copeland; 2 Liskeard Gardens, Blackheath, London SE3 0PN; Headquarters, Director Royal Artillery, Woolwich, SE18 3BH (☎ 081 854 2242, fax 081 854 3059)

COPELAND, (Richard) Spencer Charles; s of Richard Ronald John Copeland CBE, JP, DL (d 1958), of Kibblestone Hall, Stone, Staffs, and Ida, *née* Fenzi (d 1964); *b* 18 Dec 1918; *Educ* St Peter's Ct Broadstairs Kent, Harrow, Alpine Coll Switzerland, Trinity Coll Cambridge (MA); *m* 1, 1940 (m dis), Sonia, da of late W J B Chambers, of Hoylake; 1 s (David b 1943); m 2, 1966, Jean, da of William Turner (d 1985), of Stoke-on-Trent; 1 s (William John Taylor b 1966), 1 adopted da (Elizabeth b 1956); *Career* Lt RA LAA 1940-45; W T Copeland and Sons Ltd 1947 (later Spode Ltd): dir 1947, md 1955-66, chm 1966-71; dir Caverswall China Co Ltd 1975-81; fndr and fell Inst of Ceramics 1955, pres Br Ceramic Soc 1959-60, vice pres Assoc Euro de Ceramique 1960-62, pres Staffordshire Soc 1969-71, gen cmmr of Income Tax 1970-, memb Cncl of Univ Coll North Staffordshire (now Univ of Keele) 1953-; Hon MA Univ of Keele 1987; Freeman City of London, Liveryman Worshipful Co of Goldsmiths; *Books* The Transactions of the British Ceramic Society (contrib, 1952 and 1955); *Recreations* skiing, sailing; *Clubs* Royal Over-seas League, Ski Club of GB, Royal Cwlth Yacht; *Style*— R Spencer C Copeland, Esq; Trelissick, Feock, Truro, Cornwall TR3 6QL (☎ 0872 862248)

COPELAND, Stephen Andrew; s of Derek Copeland, of Moss Cottage, Edleston, Cheshire, and Peggy, *née* Strangward; *b* 7 May 1946; *Educ* Nantwich GS, St Bartholomew's Hosp Med Sch London (MB BS); *m* 3 April 1972, Jennifer Ann, da of Dr John Almeyda, KSG (d 1986); 1 s (Matthew b 17 March 1976), 1 da (Sara Clare b 26 Feb 1973); *Career* sr registrar Bart's 1975-79, clinical lectr Royal Nat Orthopaedic Hosp 1978, conslt orthopaedic surgn Royal Berkshire Hosp Reading 1979, memb Editorial Bd JBJS, hon memb American Shoulder Surgery Soc, ABC travelling fell, fndr memb Br Shoulder and Elbow Soc, developed own design of shoulder replacement; author of papers on shoulder surgery; *Books* Fractures and Dislocations, Shoulder Surgery (contrib), Rheumatoid Surgery; *Recreations* tennis, windsurfing; *Style*— Stephen Copeland, Esq; Woodlands, Woodlands Rd, Harpsden, Henley-on-Thames, Oxfordshire RG9 4AA (☎ 073 52240 2144); Whitley Glebe, 11 Glebe Rd, Reading, Berks (☎ 0734 752097)

COPEMAN, Dr Peter William Monckton; s of William Sydney Charles Copeman, CBE, TD, JP, MA, MD, FRCP (d 1970), and Helen, *née* Bourne (d 1980); head of the Copeman family formerly of Sparham, Norfolk (*see* Burke's Landed Gentry, 18 edn, Vol III, 1972); *b* 9 April 1932; *Educ* Eton, CCC Cambridge (MA, MD), St Thomas's Hosp; *m* 19 May 1973, Lindsey Bridget, da of David Vaughan Brims, Heddon Hall, Heddon-on-the-Wall, Northumberland; 1 s (Andrew b 1980), 3 da (Mary b 1975, Louisa b 1977, Caroline b 1980); *Career* conslt physician i/c Dept of Dermatology Westminster and Westminster Children's Hosp, clinician and res; cncllr The Game Conservancy; patron Living of St James the Less Hadleigh Essex, patron, tstee and churchwarden St Mary's Bourne St London; Liveryman Worshipful Soc of Apothecaries; OStJ; FRCP 1975; *Clubs* Athenaeum; *Style*— Dr Peter Copeman; 20 Spencer Park, London SW18 2SZ (☎ 081 874 7549); 82 Sloane St, London SW1X 9PA (☎ 071 245 9333); Abshiel Farm, Morpeth, Northumberland NE65 8QN (☎ 067 072 268)

COPISAROW, Sir Alcon Charles; o s of late Dr Maurice Copisarow, of Manchester, and Eda Copisarow; *b* 25 June 1920; *Educ* Univ of Manchester, Imperial Coll London, Sorbonne (DSc); *m* 1953, Diana Elissa, yr da of Maj Ellis James Castello, MC, TD (d 1983); 2 s, 2 da; *Career* serv WWII Lt RN; HM cnsllr (scientific) Br Embassy Paris 1954-60, dir Dept of Scientific and Industl Res 1960-62, chief tech offr NEDC 1962-64, chief scientific offr Miny of Technol 1964-66, sr ptnr McKinsey and Co Inc 1966-76, former dir Br Leyland; memb: Br Nat Oil Corp, Touche Remnant Holdings, Press Cncl; dep chm of Govrs ESU, tstee Duke of Edinburgh's Award, govr Benenden Sch; chm: Trinity Coll of Music London, Youth Business Initiative, The Prince's Youth Business Tst; memb Admin Cncl Royal Jubilee Tsts, currently chm Gen Cmmrs for Income Tax, external memb Cncl of Lloyd's, dep chm Lloyd's Tercentenary Fndn (former chm); dir: Windsor Festival, chm APA Venture Capital Funds; Hon Freeman City of London; Kt 1988; *Clubs* Athenaeum (chm), Beefsteak; *Style*— Sir Alcon Copisarow; 25 Launceston Place, London W8 5RN

COPLAND-GRIFFITHS, Dr Michael Charles; s of Lt Cdr (Frederick) Charles Brandling Copland-Griffiths, MBE, of Bramley Cottage, Trowle House, Wingfield, Trowbridge, Wiltshire, and Mary Esmah Elizabeth, *née* Fry; *b* 7 Nov 1946; *Educ* Bradfield Coll, Anglo-Euro Coll of Chiropractic (Dr of Chiropractic); *m* 1, 28 Aug 1976 (m dis 1980), (Lorna) Penelope, da of John Napthine, of Spondon, Derbyshire; m 2, 6 Dec 1980, Noelle Mary (Penny), da of Herbert Bexon Spencer (d 1989), of Horton, nr Wimborne, Dorset; *Career* memb Faculty Anglo-Euro Coll of Chiropractic 1977-81 (memb Cncl 1978-80); Br Chiropractic Assoc: memb Cncl 1979-, asst sec 1979-85, pres 1985-87, memb Fin & Gen Purposes Ctee 1986-88 (chm 1986-87), chm Parly Ctee 1987-90 (memb 1987-); memb Advsy Ctee & Educn Ctee Inst of Complementary Med 1982-85, vice pres Anglo Euro Coll of Chiropractic Alumni Assoc 1982-; Cncl for Complementary & Alternative Med: memb Ctee 1984-89, vice chm 1986-89; memb Bd of Advsrs Jl of Alternative and Complementary Med 1986-; Br rep Euro Chiropractors' Union; *Books* Dynamic Chiropractic Today - The Mechanics of Health (1990); *Recreations* archaeology, post-medieval country pottery, history, natural history, British heritage, organic gardening, contemporary ceramics; *Style*— Dr Michael Copland-Griffiths; Trowle House, Wingfield, Trowbridge, Wiltshire BA14 9LE (☎ 0225 752199); Wingfield Chiropractic Clinic, Trowle House, Wingfield, Trowbridge, Wiltshire BA14 9LE (☎ 0225 752199); Blandford Chiropractic Clinic, 11 Damory Court St, Blandford Forum, Dorset DT11 7QU (☎ 0258 455214)

COPLESTON, Michael Vernon Gordon; s of Edward Arthur Vernon Gordon Copleston (d 1968), of Wimbledon, and Rose, *née* Hunter (d 1974); *b* 11 Nov 1942; *Educ* Rutlish Sch Merton London; *m* 29 Sept 1971, Jill Irene, *née* Pinney, of Yeovil; 2 s (Simon b 4 May 1973, Eddie b 25 Aug 1977), 1 da (Philippa b 5 Dec 1974); *Career* Corp of Lloyd's 1960-64, broker Stewart Smith & Co 1964-68; currently jt owner with Mrs Jill Copleston of Johnson Fry (Insurance Brokers) Ltd (joined 1969, princ, chm, md); treas: local Cons assoc, Area Guide Dogs for the Blind; memb: Surrey Assoc of Cricket Coaches; ABIBA 1975; memb: Insur Brokers' Registration Cncl 1981, RHS; *Recreations* cricket, tennis, coaching cricket and rugger; *Clubs* MCC, Surrey CCC; *Style*— Michael Copleston, Esq; Aldermoor Cottage, Holmbury St Mary, Surrey RH5 6NR (☎ 0306 730 439); Johnson Fry (Insurance Brokers) Ltd, Barrington House, Westcott, Surrey RH4 3NW (☎ 0306 887 941, fax 0306 740 360)

COPLESTONE-BOUGHEY, His Honour Judge; John Fenton; s of late Cdr A F Coplestone-Boughey, RN; *b* 5 Feb 1912; *Educ* Shrewsbury, BNC Oxford; *m* 1944, Gilian Beatrice, *née* Counsell; 1 s, 1 da; *Career* barr 1935, former dir Chester Chronicle and Associated Newspapers, circuit judge 1969-85; *Clubs* Athenaeum; *Style*— His Honour Judge Coplestone-Boughey; 82 Oakley St, London SW3 5NP (☎ 071 352 6287)

COPLEY, Paul MacKriell; s of Harold Copley (d 1971), of Denby Dale, W Yorks, and Rene, *née* Hudson; *b* 25 Nov 1944; *Educ* Penistone GS, Northern Counties Coll of Educn (Acsr Drama Bd Teachers Cert); *m* 7 July 1972, (Primula) Natasha Mary Menzies, da of Lt-Col John Menzies Pyne (d 1965); *Career* actor and writer; theatre incl: For King and Country 1976 (Actor of the Year in a New Play, Most Promising Actor), Sisters 1978, Whose Life is it Anyway 1979, Rita Sue And Bob Too 1982, Other Worlds 1983, King Lear 1987 (part of the Fool with Anthony Quayle as Lear), Twelfth Night 1987, Prin 1989, The Awakening 1990; TV incl: Days of Hope 1974, Chester Mystery Plays 1976, Treasure Island 1977, Travellers 1978, Cries from Watchtower 1979, Death of a Princess 1980, A Room for the Winter 1981, The

Gathering Seed 1983, The Bird Fancier 1984, Dangerous Journey 1985, Oedipus at Colonus 1986, Gruey 1987, Young Charlie Chaplin 1988, Testimony of a Child 1989, Landmarks - Christopher Columbus 1990; films include: Alfie Darling 1974, A Bridge Too Far 1976, Zulu Dawn 1979, Doll's Eye 1982, Ends and Means 1984, War and Remembrance 1987, The Pile Rats 1988; radio incl: The Marshalling Yard 1986, King St Junior (series), The Pilgrim's Progess 1988, Jesus (1990); writing credits incl: Hitch 1976, Pillion 1977, Viaduct 1979, Tapster 1981, Fire Eaters 1984, Calling 1986, Magellan 1987; *Recreations* swimming, motorcycling, travel, photography; *Style*— Paul Copley, Esq; Kate Feast Management, 43A Princess Rd, London NW1 8JS (☎ 071 586 5502); Margaret Ramsay Ltd, 14A Goodwins Ct, St Martin's Lane, London WC2N 4LL (☎ 071 240 0691)

COPPEL, Laurence Adrian; s of Henry Coppel, of Belfast (d 1979), and Anne Coppel (d 1964); *b* 15 May 1939; *Educ* Belfast Royal Acad, Queen's Univ Belfast (BSc); *m* 28 Oct 1964, Geraldine Ann, da of David Morrison, of Natanya; 2 s (Kenton Andrew b 1968, Mark Hugo b 1972); *Career* exec dir: Singer & Friedlander Ltd 1971-, Singer & Friedlander Group plc 1987-; dir: Nottingham Bldg Soc 1985-, British Polythene plc 1989-, Singer Whitaker Ltd 1989-; FCA; *Recreations* sailing, wines; *Clubs* Nautico Oliva; *Style*— Laurence Coppel, Esq; 206 Derby Rd, Nottingham (☎ 0602 419 721, fax 0602 417 992)

COPPELL, Stephen James (Steve); s of James Coppell, and Christina Mary, *née* Howell; *b* 9 July 1955; *Educ* Quarry Bank Comp Liverpool, Univ of Liverpool; *m* 22 June 1981, Jane Eileen, *née* Humphreys; 1 s (Mark Stephen b 14 March 1986); *Career* professional football manager; player: Tranmere Rovers 1973-75, Manchester Utd (over 400 appearances) 1975-84; England: 1 under 23 cap, 42 full caps 1978-83, played in World Cup Spain 1982; honours as player Manchester Utd: FA Cup 1977 (runners up 1976 and 1979), runners up League Cup 1983; Crystal Palace: mangr 1984-, promotion to Div 1 1989, runners up FA Cup 1990; chm Professional Footballers' Assoc 1982-84; *Recreations* all sports, family; *Style*— Steve Coppell, Esq; Crystal Palace FC, Selhurst Park, London SE25 (☎ 081 653 4462)

COPPEN, Dr Alec James; s of Herbert John Wardle Coppen (d 1974), of London, and Marguerite Mary Annie, *née* Henshaw (d 1971); *b* 29 Jan 1923; *Educ* Dulwich, Univ of Bristol (MB ChB, MD, DSc), Maudsley Hosp, London Univ (DPM); *m* 9 Aug 1952, Gunhild Margareta, da of Albert Andersson, of Bastad, Sweden; 1 s (Michael Coppen b 1953); *Career* Br Army 1942-46; registrar then sr registrar Maudsley Hosp 1954-59, MRC Neuropsychiatry Res Unit 1957-74, MRC External Staff 1974-; conslt psychiatrist: St Ebba's Hosp 1959-64, West Park Hosp 1964-; hon conslt St George's Hosp 1965-70, head WHO designated Centre Biological Psychiatry UK 1974-, conslt WHO 1977-, examiner Royal Coll Psychiatry 1973-77, Andrew Woods visiting prof Iowa Univ 1981; lectr in: Europe, N and S America, Asia, Africa; memb Cncl and chm Res and Clinical Section RMPA 1965-70, chm Biology Psychiatry Section World Psychiatric Assoc 1972, pres Br Assoc Psychopharmacology 1975; memb: Collegium Internationale Neuropsychopharmacologicum 1960- (memb Cncl 1979, pres 1990), RSM 1960-, Br Pharmocological Soc 1977-; memb Special Health Authy Bethlem Royal and Maudsley Hosp 1982-, hon memb Mexican Inst Culture; author numerous scientific papers on mental health; Freeman City of London 1980, Liveryman Worshipful Soc of Apothecaries 1985 (memb 1980); hon memb Swedish Psychiatric Assoc 1977, corr memb American Coll Neuropsychopharmacology 1977, distinguished fell APA 1981, MRCP 1975, FRCP 1980, FRCPsych 1971; *Books* Recent Developments in Schizophrenia (1967), Recent Developments in Affective Disorders (1968), Biological Psychiatry (1968), Psychopharmacology of Affective Disorders (1979), Depressive Illness: Biological and Psychopharmacological Issues (1981); *Recreations* golf, opera, photography; *Clubs* Athenaeum, The Harveian Soc, RAC; *Style*— Dr Alec Coppen; 5 Walnut Close, Epsom, Surrey KT18 5JL (☎ 03727 20 800); MRC Neuropsychiatry Research Laboratory, West Park Hospital, Epsom, Surrey KT19 8PB (☎ 03727 26 459, fax 03727 42 602)

COPPEN, Dr Michael James; s of Dr Alec James Coppen, of 5 Walnut Close, Epsom, Surrey, and Gunhild Margaretta, *née* Andersson; *b* 3 Dec 1953; *Educ* Epsom Coll, Royal Free Hosp Univ of London (MB BS); *m* 3 Sep 1983, Regina, Poh Gek, da of Goh Choe Jim (d 1987); *Career* sr house offr (later registrar) Guy's Hosp 1979-82, sr registrar UCH and Whittington Hosp 1982-87, conslt histopathologist Mayday Univ Hosp 1987-; MRCPath 1985, memb Assoc Clinical Pathologists; *Books* pubns incl Evaluation of Buffy Coat Microscopy for the Early Diagnosis of Bacteraemia (1981); *Recreations* golf, reading, music; *Clubs* Royal Automobile, Hole in One; *Style*— Dr Michael Coppen; Sentosa Chalet, 53 Larkspur Way, West Ewell, Epsom, Surrey KT19 9LS (☎ 081 397 9510); Dept of Histopathology, Mayday Hospital, Mayday Rd, Thornton Heath, Surrey (☎ 081 684 6999 ext 4076)

COPPER, Robert James; s of James Dale Copper (d 1954), and Daisy Louise, *née* Clark (d 1971); *b* 6 Jan 1915; *Educ* Rottingdean C of E Sch; *m* 10 May 1941, Marian Joan (d 1983), da of Albert Deal (d 1960), of Sussex; 1 s (John b 1949), 1 da (Jill b 1944); *Career* Trooper Life Gds 1933-35; detective constable W Sussex Constabulary 1937-46; writer, broadcaster, traditional singer, author as Bob Copper; *Books* A Song for Every Season (Robert Pitman prize, 1971), Songs and Southern Breezes (1973), Early to Rise (1976); *Recreations* country walking, painting; *Style*— Robert J Copper, Esq; Broom Cottage, 73 Telscombe Rd, Peacehaven, E Sussex BN10 7UB (☎ 0273 583 549)

COPPLESTONE, Frank Henry; 2 s of late Rev Frank T Copplestone; *b* 26 Feb 1925; *Educ* Truro Sch, Nottingham Univ; *m* 1, 1950, Margaret Mary (d 1973), da of late Edward Walker; 3 s; m 2, 1977 (m dis 1988), Mrs Penelope Ann Labovitch, da of Ben Perrick; 1 step s, 1 step da; m 3, Fenella Mary Salgado; 1 step s, 1 step da; *Career* dir: prog planning ITV Network 1968-75, ITV News Ltd 1977-81, ITV Publications Ltd 1976-81; md Southern TV 1976-88, media conslt 1988; *Style*— Frank Copplestone, Esq; Pen An Mor, 39 Esplanade, Fowey, Cornwall PL23 1HY

COPPOCK, David Arthur; CB (1990); s of Oswald John Coppock of Fordingbridge (d 1979), and Ada Katherine, *née* Beaven (d 1979); *b* 19 April 1931; *Educ* Bishop Wordsworth Sch, Guys Hosp (BDS), George Washington Univ (MSc); *m* 1, 31 May 1956, Maria Averil, *née* Ferreira (d 1985); 2 da (Phillipa (Mrs McIntyre) b 1957, Nicola (Mrs Tims) b 1959); m 2, 1 M 1990, Sally Annette Neville, *née* Cook; *Career* entered RN 1955; HM Ships: Eagle 1956, Tamar Hong Kong 1959, Hermes 1963, Rooke Gibraltar 1965; US Navy Exchange Bethesda MD 1972, Naval Dental Serv 1980, Cmd dental surgn to C in C Naval Home Cmd 1983, dir Naval Dental Serv 1985, dir Def Dental Servs 1988-, ret 1990; QHDS 1985-90; *Recreations* fly fishing, tennis, golf; *Clubs* RSM; *Style*— Surgn Rear Adm David Coppock, CB; First Avenue House, High Holborn WC1 (☎ 071 430 5993)

COPPOCK, Lawrence Patrick; s of Eric Francis Coppock, of Harrogate, and Betty Winifred, *née* Wilson; *b* 27 Jan 1952; *Educ* Royal GS, King George V GS; *m* 1 May 1982, Gillian Mary, da of Richard Charles Darby, of Stratford-on-Avon; 2 da (Katherine b 1984, Victoria b 1987); *Career* CA; Coopers & Lybrand 1971-75, sr analyst BL International 1976-78, fin controller Lex Service plc 1978-83, gp fin dir Heron Motor Group 1983-84, gp fin controller Heron Corporation plc 1985, fin and ops dir HP Bulmer Drinks Ltd 1986-88, fin dir B and Q plc 1988-; memb local Cons Party, former treas Kyre Church Restoration; FCA 1980; *Recreations* skiing, walking; *Style*— Lawrence Coppock, Esq; The Close, Church Lane, Braishfield, nr Romsey, Hants SO51 OQH (☎ 0794 68284); B & Q plc, Portswood House, 1 Hampshire Corporate Park, Chandlers Ford, Eastleigh, Hants SO5 3YX (☎ 0703 256256, fax 0703 256030, car 0836 708957, telex 47233)

COPPOCK, Prof (John) Terence; s of Capt Arthur Leslie Coppock (d 1962), and Valerie Margaret, *née* Phillips (d 1981); *b* 2 June 1921; *Educ* Penarth County Sch, Queens' Coll Cambridge (BA, MA), Univ of London (PhD); *m* 6 Aug 1953, Sheila Mary (d 1990), da of Dr Gerard Burnett (d 1985); 1 s (John b 1960), 1 da (Helena b 1955); *Career* cmmnd Welch Regt 1941, serv ME 1942-46, Lt RA 1942; clerical offr Lord Chllr Dept 1938-46, exec offr Miny of Works 1946-47, offr Customs and Excise 1947; UCL Dept of Geography: asst lectr 1950, lectr 1952, reader 1964; prof of geography Univ of Edinburgh 1965 (emeritus 1986); sec and treas Carnegie Tst for Univs for Scot, visiting prof of geography Birkbeck Coll, fell UCL; vice pres: Scot Recreational Land Assoc, Scot Inland Waterways Assoc, RGS of Scot; memb Scot Sport Cncl 1976-87, chm Exec Ctee Scot Field Studies Assoc 1977-80; MIBG 1948- (pres 1973-74), FRGS 1950, FBA 1975, FRSE 1976, FTS 1980, FRSA 1981, FRSGS 1988; *Books* The Changing Use of Land in Britain (with R H Best, 1962), An Agricultural Atlas of England and Wales (1964); *Recreations* badminton, walking, listening to music; *Style*— Prof J T Coppock; 57 Braid Ave, Edinburgh EH10 6EB (☎ 031 447 3443); Carnegie Trust for the Universities of Scotland, 22 Hanover St, Edinburgh EH2 2EN (☎ 031 220 1217)

CORAL, Bernard; s of Joseph Coral, of 84 Dorset House, Gloucester Place, London NW1, and Dorothy Helen, *née* Precha; *b* 10 Jan 1929; *Educ* Dame Alice Owens; *m* 11 March 1953, Diane Jean, da of William Charles Cameron (d 1956); 1 s (Anthony Paul b 1955), 2 da (Joanna Marie b 1956, Michele Alexandra b 1965); *Career* Nat Serv 1947-49; dir Joe Coral Ltd (later Coral Leisure plc) 1944 -80; chm: Coral & Co 1981, Wig and Pen Club 1981-, Bud Flanagan Leukaemia Fund; *Recreations* golf; *Clubs* Porters Park Golf; *Style*— Bernard Coral, Esq; 19E Grove End Rd, St Johns Wood, London NW8 9SD (☎ 071 289 9125); 229-230 Strand, London WC2 (☎ 071 583 7255, car 0860 370 037)

CORAM JAMES, John; s of Peter Maunde Coram James, of The Pump House, Bishopton, Stratford-on-Avon, and Denise Mary, *née* Bond; *Educ* The Oratory Sch Woodcote Berks; *m* 27 Nov 1973, Caroline Jane, da of Geoffrey Jack Marks, of Remenham Ct, Henley-on-Thames; 2 s (Henry b 1981, Edward b 1988), 1 da (Clementine b 1987); *Career* admitted slr 1975; sr ptnr Needham & James Stratford-on-Avon 1987- (joined as salaried ptnr 1975, equity ptnr 1979); memb Law Soc 1975-; *Recreations* hunting, photography; *Style*— John Coram James, Esq; The Chantry, Bourton-on-the-Hill, Moreton-in-Marsh, Gloucestershire GL56 9AG (☎ 0386 700876); 25 Meer St, Stratford-on-Avon, Warwickshire (☎ 0789 414444, fax 0789 296608, telex 0789 312258)

CORBALLY STOURTON, Hon Mrs Edward; Beatrice Cicely; da of late Harold Ethelbert Page, of Wragby, Lincs and Titchwell, Norfolk; *m* 1934, Hon Edward Plantagenet Joseph Corbally Stourton, DSO (d 6 March 1966, having assumed in 1927, the additional name of Corbally), yst s of 23 Baron Mowbray, 24 Baron Segrave, and 20 Baron Stourton (d 1893); 1 s, 1 da; *Style*— The Hon Mrs Edward P J Corbally Stourton; Arlonstown Cottage, Dunsany, Co Meath, Eire (☎ 046 25290)

CORBEN, David Edward; s of Cyril Edward Corben, of Mayfield Cottage, Manor Rd South, Elmbridge, Surrey, and Florence Ethel Jessie, *née* Lewthwaite; *b* 5 March 1945; *Educ* St Paul's; *m* 1, 4 Jan 1969 (m dis), Fiona Elizabeth Macleod, da of Prof David Stern, of Teddington, Middx; 1 s (Mark b 1971), 1 da (Victoria b 1973); m 2, 7 May 1988, Miranda Davies, da of David McCormick, of Salisbury, Wilts; *Career* Lloyd's broker; Jardine Thompson Graham: dir 1971-, md 1976, chm 1986; dir: Jardine Insur Brokers plc 1981-, Lloyd-Roberts Gilkes 1976-, Jardine Reinsurance Hldg 1983-; chm Matheson and Co 1984-; memb Lloyd's; *Recreations* skiing, golf, tennis, motor racing, riding, rugby football; *Clubs* Gresham, Roehampton; *Style*— David Corben, Esq; 42 Roedean Crescent, Roehampton, London SW15 (☎ 081 876 1969); 6 Crutched Friars, London EC3N 2HT (☎ 071 528 4444)

CORBET, Lt-Col Sir John Vincent; 7 Bt (UK 1808) of Moreton Corbet, Shrops, MBE (1946), JP (Salop 1957), DL (1961); s of Archer Henry Corbet (d 1950, ggs of 1 Bt), and Anne Maria (Anita), *née* Buxton (d 1951); suc kinsman Sir Gerald Vincent Corbet, 6 Bt 1955; *b* 27 Feb 1911; *Educ* Shrewsbury, RMA Woolwich, Magdalene Coll Cambridge (MA); *m* 1, 1 Feb 1937 (m dis 1948), Elfrida Isobel, eldest da of A G Francis; m 2, 18 Oct 1948, Doreen Elizabeth Stewart (d 6 April 1964), da of Arthur William Gibbon Ritchie, and formerly w of Richard Gray; m 3, 4 Jan 1965, Annie Elizabeth, MBE, da of James Lorimer, of Christchurch, NZ; *Career* War Serv RE India, Burma, Malaya 1942-46 (despatches), ret 1955; High Sheriff of Shropshire 1966, co cncllr 1973-87; OStJ; *Recreations* sailing; *Clubs* Royal Thames Yacht; *Style*— Lt-Col Sir John Corbet, Bt, MBE, JP, DL; Acton Reynald, nr Shrewsbury, Shropshire SY4 4DS (☎ 093 928 259)

CORBET, Prof Philip Steven; s of Alexander Steven Corbet (d 1948), of Tilehurst, Reading, Berks, and Irene Trewavas (d 1989), of Newlyn, Cornwall; *b* 21 May 1929; *Educ* Nelson Boys' Coll NZ, Dauntseys Sch W Lavington Wilts, Univ of Reading (BSc, DSc), Univ of Cambridge (PhD, ScD); *m* 1, 9 Feb 1957 (m dis 1979), Hildegard Gertrud, da of Otto Keller (d 1959), of Tübingen, W Germany; m 2, 15 Oct 1980 (m dis 1987), Laila Kristin Kjellström; 1 da (Katarina); m 3, 31 Dec 1987, Mary Elizabeth Canvin; *Career* zoologist E African Freshwater Fisheries Res Orgn Jinja Uganda 1954-57, entomologist E African Virus Res Orgn Entebbe Uganda 1957-62, res scientist Entomology Res Inst Canada Dept of Agric Ottawa Canada 1962-67, dir Res Inst Canada Dept of Agric Belleville Ontario Canada 1967-71, prof and chm Dept of Biology Univ of Waterloo Ontario Canada 1971-74, prof and dir Jt Centre for Environmental Scis Univ of Canterbury and Lincoln Coll Canterbury NZ 1974-78, prof Dept of Zoology Univ of Canterbury Christchurch NZ 1978-80, head Dept of Biological Scis Univ of Dundee 1983-86 (prof of zoology 1980-90, prof emeritus 1990-); visiting cwlth prof Dept of Applied Biology Univ of Cambridge 1979-80; memb NZ Environmental Cncl 1976-79, pres Br Dragonfly Soc 1983-; memb: Hon Int Odonatological Soc 1985, Ctee for Scot Nature Conservancy Cncl 1986-; fell Royal Entomological Soc of London 1950-, Entomological Soc of Canada 1974 (pres 1971-72, Gold medal 1974); FInstBiol 1967, FRSTM & H 1985, FRSE 1987; *Books* Dragonflies (with C Longfield and N W Moore, 1960), A Biology of Dragonflies (1962), The Odonata of Canada and Alaska (with E M Walker, 1975); *Recreations* natural history, music; *Clubs* Arctic; *Style*— Prof Philip S Corbet; The Old Manse, 45 Lanark Rd, Edinburgh EH14 1TL (☎ 031 443 4685); Dept of Zoology, University of Edinburgh, West Mains Rd, Edinburgh EH9 3JT (☎ 031 667 1081 ext 5457)

CORBETT, Hon Mrs (Catherine); *née* Lyon-Dalberg-Acton; 3 da of 3 Baron Acton, CMG, MBE, TD (d 1989); *b* 30 Sept 1939; *m* 20 Feb 1960, Hon Joseph Mervyn Corbett, 4 s (but 2 surviving) of 2 Baron Rowallan, KT, KBE, MC, TD; 1 s, 1 da; *Style*— The Hon Mrs Corbett; Chittlegrove, Rendcomb, nr Cirencester, Glos

CORBETT, Gerald Michael Nolan; s of John Michael Nolan Corbett (d 1982), of Old Horsmans, Sedlescombe, Sussex, and Pamela Muriel *née* Gay; *b* 7 Sept 1951; *Educ* Tonbridge, Pembroke Coll Cambridge (foundation scholar, MA), London Business Sch (MSc), Harvard Business Sch (exchange scholarship); *m* 19 April 1976, Virginia

Moore, da of Neill Newsum, of The Old Rectory, Hindolueston, Norfolk; 1 s (John b 20 Jan 1981), 3 da (Sarah b 4 June 1979, Olivia b 13 Nov 1982, Josephine b 4 Oct 1984); *Career* conslt and case leader Boston Consulting Gp 1976-82; Dixons Gp plc: gp fin controller 1982-85, corporate fin dir 1985-87; fin dir Redland plc 1987-; Freeman: City of London, Worshipful Co of Glaziers 1988; *Recreations* country pursuits; *Style—* Gerald Corbett, Esq; Holtsmere End Farmhouse, Redbourn, Herts (☎ 058 285 2336); Redland plc, Redland House, Reigate, Surrey (☎ 07373 42488, car tel 0836 253136)

CORBETT, Hon John Polson Cameron; s and h of 3 Baron Rowallan and his 1 w Eleanor; *b* 8 March 1947; *Educ* Eton, RAC Cirencester; *m* 1, 1971 (m dis 1983), (Susan) Jane Diane, da of James Green, of S Linden, Northumberland; 1 s (Jason b 1972), 1 da (Joanna b 1974); m 2, 17 April 1984, Sandrew Filomena, da of William Bryson, of Holland Green, Kilmaurs, Ayrshire; 1 s (Cameron b 1985), 1 da (Soay b 1988); *Career* estate agent; chm Heritage Circle 1980-; organiser: 2 horse trials at Rowallan (affiliated to BHS), show jumping festival at Rowallan (affiliated to BSJA); ARICS; landowner (1000 acres); *Recreations* skiing, riding, commentator; *Style—* The Hon John Corbett; Meikle Mosside, Fenwick, Ayrshire (☎ 05606 769)

CORBETT, Hon Joseph Mervyn; 4 s (but 2 surviving) of 2 Baron Rowallan, KT, KBE, MC, TD, DL (d 1977); *b* 22 April 1929; *Educ* Eton, Corpus Christi Coll Cambridge; *m* 20 Feb 1960 Hon Catherine Lyon-Dalberg-Acton, da of 3 Baron Acton, CMG, MBE, TD; 1 s (Sebastian b 1963), 1 da (Victoria (Mrs Merrill) b 1961); *Style—* The Hon Joseph Corbett; Chittlegrove, Rendcomb, nr Cirencester, Glos

CORBETT, Hon Mrs (Melanie June); *née* Moynihan; da of 2 Baron Moynihan (d 1965), and his 2 w June Elizabeth, *née* Hopkins; *b* 19 Aug 1957; *m* 30 July 1983, Peter-John Stuart Corbett, s of late John M N Corbett, of Sedlescombe, Sussex; 2 da (Poppy Ann b 18 Aug 1986, Daisy Angelica Jak b 10 Dec 1988), 1 s (Edward John Patrick b 5 Sept 1990); *Style—* The Hon Mrs Corbett

CORBETT, Nigel Stephen; s of Gerald Maurice Stephen Corbett, of 34 Chester Row, London SW1, and Elizabeth Mary Barber, *née* Lindsell; *b* 4 April 1942; *Educ* St Georges Sch Windsor, Wellington; *m* 7 April 1966, Margaret, da of Douglas Theodore Freebody; 2 da (Charlotte-Anne b 8 Aug 1968, Tara Margaret b 7 Oct 1969); *Career* hotelier, restauranteur, night club owner; Rehearsal Room Night Club Royal Court Theatre 1964-66, Angelique Restaurant Discotheque King's Road Chelsea 1967-72, Françoise Club King's Road Chelsea 1969-79, Summer Lodge Country House Hotel 1979-; Cezar award Good Hotel Guide 1985, runner up Egon Ronay Hotel of the Year 1987, Holiday Which? Countryhouse Weekend Hotel of the Year 1987; memb Yeovil Coll Catering Liaison Ctee; *Recreations* travel; *Style—* Nigel Corbett, Esq; Summer Lodge Country House Hotel, Evershot, Dorset DT2 0JR (☎ 0935 83424)

CORBETT, (Richard) Panton; s of Richard William Corbett, TD (d 1987), and Doris Vaughan, *née* Kimber; *b* 17 Feb 1938; *Educ* Eton, Aix en Provence Univ; *m* 1, 28 April 1962 (m dis 1973), Leila Francis, *née* Wolsten-Croft; 1 s (Oliver b 1965); m 2, 11 July 1974, Antoinette Sibley, CBE, *qv*, da of E G Sibley, of Birchington on Sea; 1 s (Isambard b 1980), 1 da (Eloise b 1975); *Career* 2 Lt Welsh Gds 1957; md Singer and Friedlander Holdings plc 1973-; dir: Saxon Oil plc 1980-86, First British American Corporation Ltd 1976, Interfinance and Investment Corporation 1974-80, Tex Holdings 1987; tstee Royal Ballet Benevolent Fund, memb Exec and Fin Ctee Royal Acad of Dancing, dir Royal Opera House Tst; Freeman City of Shrewsbury 1979; *Recreations* tennis, shooting, opera, skiing, fishing; *Clubs* Boodle's, Queen's; *Style—* Panton Corbett, Esq; 24 Chapel St, London SW1X 7BY (☎ 071 235 4506); 2 Grove Farm, Longnor, nr Shrewsbury; 21 New Street, Bishopsgate, London EC2M 4HR (☎ 071 623 3000, fax 071 623 2122, telex 886977)

CORBETT, Peter George; s of Dr John Hotchkins Corbett, and Patricia Kathleen, *née* Hope; *b* 13 April 1952; *Educ* Liverpool Coll, Liverpool Coll of Art and Design (fndn), Manchester Regnl Coll of Art and Design (BA); *Career* artist, oil on canvas; memb: Creative Minds Arts Gp Ctee 1978-81, New Age Festival Organising Ctee 1983 and 1984; lead singer and fndr memb rock band Aquarian 1983-85, composer Dr F and The TV Kids (Unity Theatre Liverpool) 1985, fndr memb Merseyside Contemporary Artists Mgmnt Ctee (formerly Liverpool Acad of Arts) 1988, chm and fndr memb Merseyside Visual Arts Festival 1989-90; exhibitions incl: Centre Gallery Liverpool 1979, Liverpool Playhouse 1982, Acorn Gallery Liverpool 1985, Major Merseyside Artists Exhibition (Port of Liverpool Building) 1988, Merseyside Contemporary Artists Exhibition (Albert Dock Liverpool) 1988, Surreal Objects Exhibition (Tate Gallery Liverpool) 1989, Unity Theatre Liverpool 1990; memb: Nat Artists Assoc (chm Merseyside Branch), Design and Artists Copywright Soc; friend Acorn Gallery Liverpool, fndr memb Order of St Francis Liberal Catholic Church; *Publications* contrib to numerous creative jls; *Recreations* musical composition, playing the piano, meditation, yoga, contemporary dance; *Style—* Peter Corbett, Esq; Flat 4, 7 Gambier Terrace, Hope St, Liverpool 1

CORBETT, Peter Richard; s of John Lionel Garton Corbett, of Hampshire and Isle of Mull, and Susan Irene Sibil, *née* Wykeham; *b* 25 Feb 1968; *Educ* Radley; *m* 23 March 1968, Margaret Catherine, da of Richard Holiday Pott, OBE (d 1968); 2 s (Richard b 1972, Charles b 1976), 1 da (Catherine b 1969); *Career* ptnr Pearsons 1974-86, dir John D Wood and Co; FRICS; *Recreations* shooting, Dorset Horn sheep; *Style—* Peter R Corbett, Esq, FRICS; Dene House, Binley, St Mary Bourne, Hampshire

CORBETT, Hon Robert Cameron; s of 2 Baron Rowallan, KT, KBE, MC, TD, DL; *b* 29 Nov 1940; *Educ* Eton, ChCh Oxford; *Career* MFH Eglinton Foxhounds 1975-; memb Ctee Nat Tst for Scotland 1982-; *Clubs* White's, Beefsteak, Turf, Pratt's, Puffin's (Edinburgh); *Style—* The Hon Robert Corbett; Cankerton, Stewarton, Kilmarnock, Ayrshire (☎ 0560 82963)

CORBETT, Maj-Gen Robert John Swan; CB (1991); s of Robert Hugh Swan Corbett (d 1988), of Boughton Monchelsea, and Yalding Hill, Kent, and Patricia Elizabeth Cavan-Lambart (d 1988); *b* 16 May 1940; *Educ* Shrewsbury; *m* 23 Sept 1966, Susan Margaret Anne, da of Brig Michael James Palmer O'Cock, CBE, MC, of Kington Langley, Wilts; 3 s (Tom b 6 Dec 1967, Jonathan b 30 May 1969, Michael b 7 June 1973); *Career* cmmnd 1959, Staff Coll Camberley 1972-73, Cdr Gds' Independent Parachute Co 1973-75, Adj Sandhurst 1975-78, 2 i/c 1 Bn Ir Gds 1978-79, US Armed Forces Staff Coll 1979-80, Bde Maj (Lt Col) Household Div 1980-81, Co 1 Bn Ir Gds 1981-84, chief of Staff Br Forces Falkland Islands 1984-85, cdr 5 Airborne bde 1985-87, Royal Coll of Def Studies 1987, dir def prog MOD 1987-88, GOC and cmdt Br Sector Berlin until German Unification 1990; Regtl Lt Col Ir Gds 1988; Freeman City of London 1961, Liveryman Worshipful Co of Vintners 1975; MBIM; *Recreations* reading, travel, English parish church architecture; *Clubs* Army and Navy, Pratts; *Style—* Maj-Gen Robert Corbett, CB; c/o 1st British Corps, BFPO 39

CORBETT, Robin; MP (Lab) Birmingham Erdington 1983-; s of Thomas Corbett, of West Bromwich, Staffs, and Margaret Adele Mainwaring; *b* 22 Dec 1933; *Educ* Holly Lodge GS Smethwick; *m* 1970, Val Hudson; 1 da; *Career* sr Lab advsr IPC Magazines Ltd 1969-74; contested (Lab): Hemel Hempstead 1966, Feb 1974, West Derby (by-election) 1967; MP (Lab) Hemel Hempstead Oct 1974-1979; communications consIt 1979-83; chm PLP Home Affairs Gp 1983-85, jt sec Aust and NZ Parly Gp 1983, W Midlands Lab Whip 1984-85, memb Select Ctee on Home Affrs 1983-85, front bench spokesman Home Affrs 1985-; vice chm: All-party Motor Industry Gp 1987-, Friends of Cyprus 1987-; memb Cncl: RCVS 1989-, Save The Children 1987-90; *Recreations* walking, collecting bric-à-brac; *Style—* Robin Corbett, Esq, MP; House of Commons, London SW1A 0AA

CORBETT, Timothy William Edward; er s of Richard William Corbett, TD (d 1987), of Grove Farm House, Longnor, nr Shrewsbury, and Doris Vaughan, *née* Kimber; descended from the Ven Joseph Plymley, archdeacon of Shropshire (d 1830), who assumed the surname and arms of Corbett by Royal Licence 1804 o s to the Longnor estates which had been in possession of a cadet branch of the Corbets of Caus Castle since early in the 17th cent (*see* Burke's Landed Gentry, 18 edn, vol II, 1969); *b* 6 Nov 1935; *Educ* Eton, Univ of Aix-en-Provence, RAC Cirencester; *m* 27 Feb 1965, (Iza) Priscilla, 2 da of Lt-Col Stephen S Murcott, of The Old Rectory, Neenton, Bridgnorth, Shropshire; 2 s (James Edward Isham b 14 Aug 1971, Thomas Alexander Caradoc b 23 July 1983), 2 da (Sophie Louisa b 10 June 1966, Isabelle Sarah b 1 Feb 1968); *Career* farmer; chm Shropshire Branch Nat Farmers' Union 1979; memb Shropshire CC 1981-85; *Recreations* skiing, shooting, windsurfing, bridge, humorous conversation; *Style—* Timothy Corbett, Esq; Dower House, Longnor, nr Shrewsbury, Shropshire (☎ 074373 628)

CORBETT, William Jesse (Bill); s of William Jesse Corbett (d 1960), of Birmingham, and Dora, *née* Ruffles; *b* 21 Feb 1938; *Educ* Billesley Secdy Modern Sch; *Career* children's writer; formerly employed as: factory worker, merchant navy galley-boy, army physical trg instr, furniture remover, building worker; book incl: The Song of Pentecost (1982), Pentecost and the Chosen One (1984), The End of the Tale (1985), Pentecost of Lickey Top (1987), The Bear Who Stood on His Head (1988), Dear Grumble (1989), Toby's Iceberg (1990); Whitbread award 1982; *Recreations* reading, music (loud symphonies), solitude; *Style—* Bill Corbett, Esq; Murray Pollinger Literary Agent, 222 Old Brompton Rd, London SW5 0BZ (☎ 071 373 4711)

CORBY, Sir (Frederick) Brian; s of Charles Walter Corby (d 1984), of Raunds, Northants, and Millicent, *née* Pentelow; *b* 10 May 1929; *Educ* Kimbolton Sch, St John's Coll Cambridge (MA); *m* 1 Aug 1952, Elizabeth Mairi, da of Dr Archibald McInnes (d 1973); 1 s (Nicholas b 1960), 2 da (Fiona b 1955, Jane b 1957); *Career* chm: Prudential Corp plc 1990- (gp chief exec 1982-90), Prudential Assurance Co Ltd 1982-90, Mercantile and General Reinsurance Co plc 1985-90; dir Bank of England 1985-, pres CBI 1990-; chm South Bank Bd 1990-; Hon DSc City Univ London 1989; FIA 1955; kt 1989; *Recreations* golf, gardening, reading; *Style—* Sir Brian Corby; Prudential Corporation plc, 1 Stephen St, London W1P 2AP (☎ 071 405 9222)

CORBY, Peter John Siddons; s of John Siddons Corby (d 1955), and Helen Anna, *née* Ratray (d 1974); *b* 8 July 1924; *Educ* Taplow GS; *m* 1, 16 Dec 1950 (m dis 1959), Gail Susan Clifford-Marshall; 1 s (Michael b 1951), 1 adopted s (Mark b 1950); m 2, 2 April 1960, Ines Rosemary, da of Dr George Anderson Mandow, of The Sloop, 89 High St, Cowes, IOW; 1 s (John b 1962); *Career* RAFVR 1942-48, War Serv Aircrew 4 Gp Bomber Cmd, transferred Class E Reserve RAFVRT 1948, resigned 1951; regained original family business Corbys Ltd and John Corby Ltd Windsor, created manufactured and marketed many products incl The Corby Electric Trouser Press (1961); dir numerous cos 1950-89 incl: Thomas Jourdan plc, Colour Centre Ltd, Savetower Ltd; non exec dir various cos; port offr (Cowes) Ocean Cruising Club; Freeman City of London 1977, Liveryman Worshipful Co of Marketors 1978 (guild memb); FIOD 1955, memb Lloyds 1974; *Recreations* sailing, bridge; *Clubs* Royal London Yacht, Oriental, Ocean Cruising; *Style—* Peter Corby, Esq; The Sloop, 89 High St, Cowes, Isle of Wight PO31 7AW (☎ 0983 292188)

CORBYN, Jeremy Bernard; MP (Lab) Islington North 1983-; s of David Benjamin Corbyn; *b* 26 May 1949; *Educ* Adams GS Newport Shropshire; *m* issue; *Career* memb Haringey Borough Cncl 1974-83, NUPE area offr until 1983; *Recreations* running, gardening, keeps chickens; *Style—* Jeremy Corbyn, Esq, MP; House of Commons, London SW1A 0AA

CORCUERA, Lady Mary Virginia Shirley; *née* Acheson; 3 and yst da of Lt-Col 5 Earl of Gosford, DL, MC (d 1954), by his 1 w; *b* 1919; *m* 12 Dec 1941, Fernando Corcuera (d 1978), s of Pedro L Corcuera y Palomar, of Mexico City; 2 s, 3 da; *Style—* The Lady Mary Corcuera; Hidalgo 14, San Angel, Mexico City 01000, Mexico (☎ 5 48 95 33/34)

CORDIAL, Ian Fergusson; s of late John Cordial; *b* 14 Nov 1926; *Educ* Kilmarnock Acad, Univ of Edinburgh (MA); *m* 1953, Anna Hall Scobbie, *née* Hood; 1 s, 2 da; *Career* dir Patons and Baldwins Ltd, chm British Hand Knitting Assoc; rugby internationalist; memb and vice chm Yorks RHA 1982-86; memb and vice chm Darlington DHA 1990; *Style—* Ian Cordial, Esq; The Ashes, Barton, Richmond, N Yorks (☎ 0325 377232)

CORDINGLEY, Lady Emma Geraldine Anne; *née* Wallop; da of Viscount Lymington (d 1984), and sis of 10 Earl of Portsmouth; *b* 1958; *m* 1981, Gerald Thomas Cordingley, s of late Thomas Cordingley of Bridlington, Yorks; 2 da (Katie Madelaine b 1983, Venetia Ruth b 1985); *Style—* The Lady Emma Cordingley; Cheesecombe Farm, Hawkley, Liss

CORDINGLEY, Maj-Gen John Edward; OBE (1959); s of Air Vice Marshal Sir John Walter Cordingley, KCB, KCVO, CBE (d 1977), and Elizabeth Ruth, *née* Carpenter (d 1938); *b* 1 Sept 1916; *Educ* Sherborne, RMA Woolwich; *m* 1, 8 Feb 1940 (m dis 1961), Ruth Pamela, yr da of Maj Sydney Alexander Boddam-Whetham, DSO, MC, RA (d 1925); 2 s (Michael, Patrick); m 2, 1961, Audrey Helen Anne, da of Maj-Gen Frederick George Beaumont-Nesbitt, CVO, CBE, MC (d 1971), and formerly w of Maj Gordon Rennie (d 1984); 2 step da; *Career* cmmnd 2 Lt RA 1936, served WWII Europe and Far East, Bde Cdr 1961-62, IDC 1963, Dir Work Study MOD 1964-66, Dep Dir RA 1967-68, Maj-Gen RA BAOR 1968-71, ret; bursar Sherborne 1971-73; Col Cmdt RA 1973-81, regtl comptroller RA 1975-82 and 1984-85; dir J W Carpenter 1977-89 (chm 1984-87); MBIM, FInstD; *Recreations* golf, gardening; *Clubs* Army and Navy, Senior Golfers; *Style—* Maj-Gen John Cordingley, OBE; Church Farm House, Rotherwick, Nr Basingstoke, Hants RG27 9BG (☎ 025 676 2734)

CORDINGLY, Dr David Michael Bradley; s of Rt Rev Eric William Bradley Cordingly, MBE (d 1976), and Mary Eileen, *née* Mathews; *b* 5 Dec 1938; *Educ* Christ's Hosp, Oriel Coll Oxford (MA), Univ of Sussex (DPhil); *m* 8 May 1971, Shirley Elizabeth, da of Ian Gibson Robin; 1 s (Matthew), 1 da (Rebecca); *Career* graphic designer with various design gps and publishers 1960-68, exhibition designer Br Museum 1968-71, keeper of Art Gallery and Museum The Royal Pavilion and Museums Brighton 1971-78, asst dir The Museum of London 1978-80, head of exhibitions Nat Maritime Museum 1989- (asst keeper 1980-86, keeper of pictures 1986-89); contrib articles: Burlington Magazine, The Connoisseur, Apollo Magazine; FRSA 1974; Order of the White Rose (Finland) 1986; *Books* Marine Painting in England (1974), Painters of the Sea (1979), The Art of the Van de Veldes (1982), Nicholas Pocock (1986), Captain James Cook, Navigator (ed 1988); *Style—* Dr David Cordingly; 2 Vine Place, Brighton, Sussex BN1 3HE; The National Maritime Museum, Greenwich, London SE10 9NF (☎ 081 858 4422)

CORDLE, John Howard; s of Earnest William Cordle (d 1967); *b* 11 Oct 1912; *Educ* City of London Sch; *m* 1, 9 Aug 1938 (m dis 1956), Grace Lucy, da of Air Cdre the Rev James Rowland Walkey, CBE; 3 s (Anthony John b 29 July 1939, Paul Howard b 29 Jan 1941, Charles Henry b 1 Sept 1945), 1 da (Rosanne b 6 April 1948 d 1970); m

2, 1957 (m dis 1966) Venetia, da of Col Alistair Maynard, OBE; 1 s (Rupert b 14 May 1959), 3 da (Sophie b 9 Feb 1958, Marina (Hon Mrs Michael Pearson) b 6 May 1960, Rachel b 3 Aug 1963); m 3, 7 Feb 1976, Terttu Maija, da of Herra Mikko Ilmari Heikura (d 1951), of Nurmes, Finland; 2 s (John-William b 17 Feb 1981, Howard b 29 June 1983); *Career* RAF (cmmnd) 1940-45; chm EW Cordle & Son Ltd 1957 (dir 1946, md 1954), owner C of E Newspaper 1959-64; dir: Church Soc 1951, Amalgamated Developers 1970; memb Lloyds 1952; chm Wessex Aid to Drug Addicts 1986-, princ Cordle Tst (for speech impaired children); MP (Bournemouth and Christchurch 1959-77); life govr and fell St Paul's and St Mary's Coll Cheltenham; Freeman: City of London, Worshipful Co of Founders 1957 (under warden 1988-89, upper warden 1989-90, 625 Master 1990-91); memb: UK Delegation to Cncl of Europe 1974-77, Western Euro Union Paris 1974-77, Nat Church Assembly 1946-53; chm Oxford Tst of Churches Patronage Bd 1955-; Grand Band Order of the Star of Africa (Liberia); *Recreations* shooting, golf, tennis, gardening; *Clubs* Carlton, National, Royal Cwlth, ESU; *Style*— John Cordle, Esq; Malmesbury House, The Close, Salisbury, Wilts (☎ 0722 27027)

CORDREY, Peter Graham; s of Wing-Cdr Percival William George Cordrey, and Marjorie Joan, *née* Strickland; *b* 1 June 1947; *Educ* Wellingborough Sch, City Univ (MSc); *m* 1972, Carol Anne, da of Peter Lawrence Ashworth; 2 da (Joanne b 1979, Rowena b 1982); *Career* merchant banker and chartered accountant; head of banking Singer & Friedlander Ltd (dir Bank 1982); dir: First British American Corporation Ltd, Singer and Friedlander Leasing Ltd, City & Provincial Home Loans Ltd; *Recreations* tennis, golf, swimming; *Clubs* St George's Hill Tennis; *Style*— Peter Cordrey, Esq; Ockham End, Old Lane, Cobham, Surrey KT11 1NF (☎ 0932 67997); Singer & Friedlander Ltd, 21 New St, Bishopsgate, London EC2 (☎ 071 623 3000)

CORDY, Timothy Soames (Tim); s of John Knutt Cordy, and Margaret Winifred, *née* Sheward; *b* 17 May 1949; *Educ* Dragon Sch Oxford, Sherborne, Univ of Durham (BA), Univ of Glasgow (MPhil); *m* 1974, Dr Jill Margaret Tattersall; 2 c; *Career* asst city planning offr Leicester City Cncl 1980-85 (joined 1974), Communaute Urbaine de Strasbourg 1978-79, asst chief exec Bolton Municipal Borough Cncl 1985-87; chief exec RSNC 1987-; author of articles on housing renewal, local econ devpt and Asian retailing; memb bd: UK 2000, Volunteer Centre UK; MRTPI 1976; *Recreations* music, food, France; *Style*— Tim Cordy, Esq; RSNC, The Green, Witham Park, Waterside South, Lincoln LN5 7JR (☎ 0522 544400, fax 0522 511616)

CORDY-SIMPSON, Brig Roderick Alexander; OBE (1984); s of Col John Roger Cordy-Simpson, CBE, MC (d 1979), of Overblow House, Shrone, Kent, and Ursula Margaret, *née* West; *b* 29 Feb 1944; *Educ* Radley; *m* 21 Dec 1974, Virginia Rosemary, da of Col Peter Jarrat Lewis (d 1983), of Thedwastre White House, Thurston, Suffolk; 1 s (Angus b 1978), 1 da (Zoë b 1976); *Career* cmd 13/18 Royal Hussars 1983-86 (cmmnd 1963), cmd 4 Armoured Brigade 1988-90; *Recreations* skiing, shooting, squash; *Clubs* Cavalry and Guards; *Style*— Brig Roderick Cordy-Simpson, OBE; Headquarters Northern Army Gp, British Forces Post Office 40; c/o Coutts & Co, 440 The Strand, London WC2 R0QS

COREN, Alan; s of Samuel and Martha Coren; *b* 27 June 1938; *Educ* East Barnet GS, Wadham Oxford, Yale, Univ of California at Berkeley; *m* 14 Oct 1963, Anne, da of Michael Kasriel (d 1981), of London; 1 s (Giles b 1969), 1 da (Victoria b 1972); *Career* joined Punch 1963, asst ed 1963-66, literary ed 1966-68, dep ed 1968-78, ed 1978-87; ed The Listener 1988-; TV critic The Times 1971-78; columnist: Daily Mail 1972-76, and Mail on Sunday 1984-, The Times 1971-; contribs incl: Sunday Times, TLS, rector St Andrew's Univ 1973-76; *Books* The Dog It Was That Died (1965), All Except the Bastard (1969), The Sanity Inspector (1974), The Bulletins of Idi Amin (1974), Golfing for Cats (1974), The Further Bulletins of Idi Amin (1975), The Lady From Stalingrad Mansions (1977), The Peanut Papers (1977), The Rhinestone as Big as the Ritz (1979), Tissues for Men (1980), The Best of Alan Coren (1980), The Cricklewood Diet (1982), Present Laughter (1982), The Penguin Book of Modern Humour (ed 1983), Bumf (1984), Something for the Weekend (1986), Bin Ends (1987), The Pick of Punch (ed annual) 1979-, The Punch Book of Short Stories, Book 1 (ed 1979), Book 2 (1980), Book 3 (1981), etc; TV series The Losers (1978); *Recreations* broadcasting, riding, bridge; *Style*— Alan Coren, Esq; Wit's End, Godshill Wood, Fordingbridge, Hants; The Listener, 199 Old Marylebone Road, London NW1 (☎ 071 258 3581)

COREN, Anne; da of Michael Maximilian Kasriel (d 1981), and Isabel, *née* Koss; *b* 8 July 1940; *Educ* North London Collegiate Sch, Royal Free Hosp Sch of Med Univ of London (MB BS); *m* 14 Oct 1963, Alan Coren, *qv*, s of Sam Coren (d 1989); 1 s (Giles b 1969), 1 da (Victoria b 1972); *Career* Nat Heart Hosp, Charing Cross Hosp, sr registrar Middx Hosp, currently conslt anaesthetist Moorfields Eye Hosp; fell Coll of Anaesthetists; memb: Assoc of Anaesthetists, RSM; FFARCS; *Recreations* family life, travel, bridge; *Style*— Mrs Anne Coren; c/o Miss A Gooch, Stables Cottage, 173 Stanmore Hill, Stanmore, Middx HA7 3EW (☎ 081 954 5641, fax 081 435 8938)

CORFE, Harold Martin; s of Ernest William Corfe, LDS, RCS (d 1964), and Ethel, *née* Smith (d 1951); serv S Africa 1900-01 as one of first 4 dental surgns attached Br Army; *b* 13 July 1922; *Educ* Highgate Sch; *m* 17 June 1960, Elizabeth Rosaleen Mary, step-da of Lt-Col Stanley Middleton, OBE (d 1986); 3 s (Nicholas b 1962, Patrick b 1964, Crispin b 1966); *Career* Sgt Royal Tank Regt 1942-46, serv: N Africa, Italy; sr ptnr Greene and Co 1973-86, chm Discretionary Unit Fund Mangrs Ltd, dir Rights and Issues Investmt Tst plc; memb Int Stock Exchange; *Recreations* golf, tennis, gardening, swimming; *Clubs* IOD; *Style*— H M Corfe, Esq; Faircrouch, Wadhurst, E Sussex TN5 6PS (☎ 089 288 2358); 66 Wilson St, London EC2A 2BL (☎ 071 247 0007)

CORFIELD, Rt Hon Sir Frederick Vernon; PC (1970), QC (1972); o s of late Brig Frederick Alleyne Corfield, DSO, OBE, IA (d 1939), of Chatwall Hall, Leebotwood, Shrops, and Mary Graham, *née* Vernon (d 1968); *b* 1 June 1915; *Educ* Cheltenham, RMA Woolwich; *m* 1945, Elizabeth Mary Ruth, yr da of Edmund Coston Taylor, JP, of Arden, Church Stretton, Shrops; *Career* WWII served RA (despatches, POW); called to the Bar Middle Temple 1945; bencher of the Middle Temple; MP (C) S Glos 1955-74, min Aerospace DTI 1971-72, min Aviation Supply 1970-71, min state BOT June-Oct 1970, jt Parly sec Miny Housing and Local Govt 1962-64, rec Crown Ct 1979-87; vice chm Br Waterways Bd 1980-83 (memb 1974-83); dir: Mid-Kent Water Co, Mid Kent Hldgs plc; chm LAPDA 1975-89; kt 1972; *Books* Compensation & The Town & Country Planning Act (1959), The Community Law Act (1975), Compensation & The Compulsary Acquisition of Land (with R Carnwath, 1976); *Clubs* Army and Navy; *Style*— The Rt Hon Sir Frederick Corfield, QC; Wordings Orchard, Sheepscombe, nr Stroud, Glos

CORFIELD, Sir Kenneth George; s of Stanley Corfield, and Dorothy Elizabeth, *née* Mason; *b* 27 Jan 1924; *Educ* Wolverhampton Poly; *m* 1960; 1 da; *Career* formerly with ICI Metals, md K G Corfield Ltd 1950-60; formerly: exec dir Parkinson Cowan, dep chm STC; dir Midland Bank 1979-, tstee Sci Museum 1975-, pres Telecommunications Engrg Mfrs' Assoc 1974-80, vice pres Engrg Employers' Fedn 1979-85; former memb Cncl: CBI, IOD; vice pres BIM 1978, 1 chm Br Engrg Cncl 1982-84, chm Standard Telephones and Cables plc 1979-85 (dir 1969-85), vice pres ITT Europe Inc 1967-85, sr offr International Telephone and Telegraph Corporation (UK) 1974-85, memb Advsy Cncl for Applied R&D 1981-84; dir: Britoil Ltd 1982-88; Octagon Group 1987-, Distributed Information Processing Ltd 1987-; chm Tanks Consolidated Investments PLC, memb Bd Companhia Do Caminho de Ferro de Benquela 1990-; memb Mgmnt Cncl Templeton Coll (Oxford Centre for Mgmnt Studies); Freeman City of London; Liveryman: Worshipful Co of Engrs, Worshipful Co of Scientific Instrument Makers; Hon DUniv Surrey 1976; Hon DSc: City Univ 1981, Univ of Bath 1982, Univ of London 1982, Aston Univ 1985; Hon Degree Univ of Strathclyde 1982, Hon DEng Univ of Bradford 1983, Hon Degree Open Univ 1985, Hon DSc Technology Loughborough Univ of Technol 1983; past pres IOD; CEng, FEng, FIMechE, CBIM, CompIEE; kt 1980; *Recreations* photography, music; *Clubs* Carlton; *Style*— Sir Kenneth Corfield; 6 John St, London WC1N 2ES

CORK, Sir Kenneth Russell; GBE (1978); s of late William Henry Cork, of Hatch End, Middx, and Maud Alice, *née* Nunn; *b* 21 Aug 1913; *Educ* Berkhamsted Sch; *m* 1937, Nina, da of late Ernest Alfred Lippold; 1 s, 1 da; *Career* serv WWII Lt-Col Italy and ME; common councilman Ward of Billingsgate 1950-70, alderman Tower Ward 1970-83, alderman sheriff City of London 1975-76, Lord Mayor of London 1978-79, one of HM Lts for City of London 1980; sr ptnr W H Cork Gully and Co 1946-83; Liveryman: Worshipful Co of Horners, Worshipful Co of CAs in England and Wales; Hon Freeman Inst of Chartered Secs and Admin; pres: city branch IOD, city branch BIM; Hon DLitt; FCA, FRSA, FCIS, FBIM; Cdr de l'Ordre du Mérite (France), Order of Rio Branco (Brazil) 1976, Grand Oficiàl da Ordem Militaire de Cristo (Portugal), Order of Diplomatic Service Merit Gwanghwa Medal (Korea) 1979; KStJ 1979; *Books* Cork on Cork (1988); *Recreations* sailing, photography, painting; *Clubs* Royal Thames Yacht, City Livery, Little Ship; *Style*— Sir Kenneth Cork, GBE; Cherry Trees, Grimms Hill, Great Missenden, Bucks (☎ 02406 2628)

CORK, Lt-Col Norman Barrington; s of William Henry Cork (d 1940), of Hatch End, Middx, and Maud Alice, *née* Nunn (d 1964); *b* 8 Nov 1910; *Educ* Berhamsted Sch; *m* 1, 15 June 1935, Beryl May (d 1966), da of Herbert Ancell (d 1959), of Moor Park, Herts; 1 s (Michael b 26 Oct 1938), 1 da (Patricia b 28 Aug 1942); m 2, 22 March 1967, Pauline May, da of Charles Chamont (d 1971); *Career* serv Queen's Own Oxfordshire Hussars, WO section RA 2B and MI (L), later i/c Op Snowflake, seconded to Swedish Army on liaison upon cessation of hostilities, then to Swiss Army on liaison, ret 1946; rejoined family firm of CAs in City of London 1946-; former dir and chm of various companies (now ret); memb Exec Ctee of Cncl of Mgmnt White Ensign Assoc HMS Belfast (London, SE1), former gen cmmr of income tax (hon) in City of London; former chm Cons Assoc of Latimer and Ley Hill; Ordre Souverain De Saint-Jean De Jerusalem, Hon Maj Swiss Army 1946; *Recreations* shooting, golf; *Clubs* Royal Cinque Ports Golf (Kent), Denham (Bucks); *Style*— Lt-Col N Barrington Cork; The Home Farm, Latimer, Bucks HP5 1TZ (☎ 0494 76 2475); 10 Lowndes St, London SW1X 9EU (☎ 071 235 4516, car 0836 220 505)

CORK, Richard Graham; s of Hubert Henry Cork, of 44 Vellore Lane, Bath, Avon, and Beatrice Hester, *née* Smale; *b* 25 March 1947; *Educ* Kingswood Sch Bath, Trinity Hall Cambridge (BA, MA, PhD); *m* 1970, Vena, da of James Jackson; 2 s (Adam James b 1974, Joe John b 1980), 2 da (Polly Beatrice b 1975, Katy Anna b 1978); *Career* author, critic and broadcaster; art critic: Evening Standard 1969-77 and 1980-83, The Listener 1984-90; ed Studio International 1975-79, Slade prof of fine art Univ of Cambridge 1989-90; books: Vorticism and Abstract Art in the First Machine Age (vol 1 1975, vol 2 1976), The Social Role of Art Essays in Criticism for a Newspaper Public (1979), Art Beyond the Gallery in Early Twentieth- Century England (1985), David Bomberg (1987); organiser of various exhibitions incl: Vorticism and Its Allies (Hayward Gallery) 1974, David Bomberg Retrospective (Tate Gallery) 1988; numerous broadcasts; Durning-Lawrence lectures UCL 1987, John Llewelyn Rhys Meml prize 1976, Sir Banister Fletcher award 1985; memb: British Cncl Fine Arts Advsy Ctee, Art Advsy Gp South Bank Bd; tstee Public Art Devpt Tst; *Recreations* looking at art; *Style*— Richard Cork, Esq; 24 Milman Rd, London NW6 6EG

CORK, Roger William; s of Sir Kenneth Russell Cork, GBE, of Great Missenden, *qv*, and Lady Nina, *née* Lippold; *b* 31 March 1947; *Educ* St Martins Sch Northwood, Uppingham; *m* 9 May 1970, Barbara Anita Pauline, da of Reginald Harper, of Herne Bay; 1 s (Christopher b 1971), 2 da (Melissa b 1973, Georgina b 1974); *Career* CA; articled Moore Stephens & Co 1965-69; ptnr W H Cork Gully 1970- (joined 1969, W H Cork Gully changed to Cork Gully 1980 and associated with Coopers & Lybrand 1980 which changed name to Coopers & Lybrand Deloitte 1990); ptnr: Cork Gully 1980-, Coopers & Lybrand 1980-, Coopers & Lybrand Deloitte 1990-; memb: Exec Ctee Bucks Assoc of Youth Clubs, PCC St Mary at Hill, PCC and churchwarden St Olaves; churchwarden St Andrew Hubbard, chm tstees All Hallows Devpt Tst, govr St Dunstan's Coll Educnl Fndn (chm 1991-), tstee Tower Hill Tst, hon memb Ct HAC, memb City of London Archaeological Tst, magistrate, alderman Ward of Tower City of London 1983- (common councilman 1978-83), fndr memb Tower Ward Club (pres 1984-), master Billingsgate Ward Club 1980-81; Freeman: City of London, Worshipful Co of Bowyers (Master 1990-), Worshipful Co of Butchers, Worshipful Co of CAs; memb Guild of World Traders, fndr pres Fedn of Euro Credit Mgmnt Assocs, memb IOD (chm City of London branch); vice pres ICM 1989- (former chm); jt chm Br Red Cross City of London 1990-; offr (bro) OStJ; FCA, FIPA, FICM; *Recreations* sailing, photography, DIY; *Clubs* Livery, Hardway Sailing, RYA; *Style*— Roger Cork, Esq; Rabbs, The Lee, Great Missenden, Bucks HP16 9NX (☎ 024 020 296); Cork Gully, Shelley House, 3 Noble St, London EC2V 7DQ (☎ 071 606 7700, fax 071 606 9887, car 0860 311610, telex 884 730 CORKY G)

CORK AND ORRERY, 13th Earl of (I 1620); Patrick Reginald Boyle; also (sits as) Baron Boyle of Marston (GB 1711), Baron Boyle of Youghal (I 1616), Viscount Dungarvan (I 1620), Viscount Boyle of Kinalmeaky, Baron of Bandon Bridge and Baron Boyle of Broghill (I 1628), Earl of Orrery (I 1660); s of Major the Hon Reginald Courtenay Boyle, MBE, MC (d 1946); suc unc, 12 Earl 1967 (whose ancestor, 5 Earl, gave his name to the astronomical instrument known as an Orrery); *b* 7 Feb 1910; *Educ* Harrow, Sandhurst; *m* 1, 1952, Dorothy Kate (d 1978), da of Robert Ramsden and formerly w of (1) Marchese Demetrio Imperiali di Francavilla and (2) G F Scelsi; m 2, 1978, Mary Gabrielle, da of late Louis Ginnett and widow of Kenneth McFarlane Walker; *Heir* bro, Hon John Boyle, DSC; *Career* serv Burma Rifles SE Asia 1941-45, Maj Cameronians Scottish Rifles (severely wounded), Parachute Regt; sits as Cons in House of Lords; dep speaker and dep chm of ctees House of Lords 1973-78, memb of Cncl Cancer Res Campaign, hereditary life govr and exec-chm Christian Faith Soc, vice pres St Christophers Hospice Sydenham; FRSA; *Style*— The Rt Hon the Earl of Cork and Orrery; Flint House, Heyshott, Midhurst, W Sussex

CORKE, Martin Dewe; JP, DL; s of Lt-Col Francis St Clair Corke (d 1971), and Aileen Joyce, *née* Lake (d 1989); *b* 8 June 1923; *Educ* Radley; *m* 1, 1948, Jean Violet Burton Denholm, da of George Denholm Armour (d 1949); 2 s (Piers, Nicholas), 2 da (Penelope, Juliet); m 2, 1984, Frances Margrete, da of Harold Marks, of London; *Career* WWII Capt India 1942-45; chm: Theatre Royal Bury St Edmunds 1980, West Suffolk Health Authy 1982; brewery dir; md: Suffolk Group Radio 1981, Greene King and Sons plc 1983; Capt Suffolk CCC 1946-65; played hockey for Berks and Cambs; *Recreations* foxhunting; *Clubs* MCC; *Style*— Martin Corke, Esq, JP, DL; Old Rectory, Great Whelnetham, Bury St Edmunds (☎ 028 486 233)

CORKE, Hon Mrs (Shirley Frances); *née* Bridges; da of 1 Baron Bridges, KG, GCB,

GCVO, MC, FRS (d 1969), and Hon Katharine, da of 2 Baron Farrer; *b* 23 Oct 1924; *m* 15 June 1957, Hilary Topham Corke, s of Alfred Topham Corke (d 1935), of Malvern, Worcs; 1 s, 3 da; *Style—* The Hon Mrs Corke; Eversheds, Abinger Hammer, Surrey

CORKE, Trafford Willoughby; s of Dr Antony Trafford Kernot Corke, of Lymington, Hampshire, and Marjorie, *née* Bassett; *b* 9 Feb 1948; *Educ* Clifton Coll Bristol; *m* 26 July 1976, Avril Bevan, da of William Davies, of Milford-on-Sea, Hampshire; 1 s (Peter Trafford Michael b 22 March 1978), 1 da (Helen Charlotte Avril b 4 April 1980), 1 step s (Mathew Mansell Walker b 28 March 1972); *Career* press and agency appts 1966-78, chm Willoughby Stewart Assocs Ltd 1978-, dir Sadler Int Ltd 1988-; MInstM 1977-; *Recreations* skiing, yachting, croquet, lawn mowing; *Clubs* Empress Garden, Berkeley Street; *Style—* Trafford W Corke, Esq; 50 Christchurch Rd, Ringwood, Hampshire BH24 1DW (☎ 0425 478 001, fax 0425 479 988, car 0836 291 262, telex 418428 WSAWSA G)

CORKERY, Michael; QC (1981); s of Charles Timothy Corkery (d 1968), of London, and Nellie Marie, *née* Royal; *b* 20 May 1926; *Educ* Kings Sch Canterbury; *m* 29 July 1967, Juliet Shore, da of Harold Glyn Foulkes (d 1966), of Shrewsbury; 1 s (Nicholas b 8 June 1968), 1 da (Charlotte b 29 May 1970); *Career* Lt Welsh Gds 1944-48; called to the Bar Lincoln's Inn 1949; Jr Treasury Counsel 1959-70, Sr Treasury Counsel 1970, 1 Sr Treasury Counsel Central Criminal Ct 1979-81; bencher Lincoln's Inn 1973; *Recreations* fishing, shooting, sailing, music, gardening; *Clubs* Cavalry and Guards', Hurlingham, Itchenor Sailing, Guards' Polo, Friends of Arundel Cricket; *Style—* Michael Corkery, Esq, QC; 5 Paper Buildings, Temple, London EC4 (☎ 071 583 6117)

CORKILL, David Samuel; s of David Corkill, and Elizabeth Corkill; *b* 15 Feb 1960; *Educ* Dundonald Boys HS; *Career* professional bowler; winner: Br Isles fours 1978, 1979, 1982, Irish Nat 1978, 1980, 1982, 1983, 1987, 1988, Br Isles singles 1981 and 1988, Superbowl 1986 and 1988; represented Ireland in: Cwlth Games 1982 and 1990, World Championships 1984; runner up UK singles 1987 and 1989; author of articles on coaching; Irish staff bowls coach and umpire; *Recreations* music, antiques, sports, cars, most sports; *Clubs* Belfast Indoor Bowling, Knock Bowling; *Style—* David Corkill, Esq; 98 Sandown Road, Belfast, County Down, Northern Ireland BT5 6GW; Central Training Unit, EH & SSB, 216 Belmont Rd, Belfast (☎ 0232 652713)

CORLETT, Clive William; s of Frederick William Corlett (d 1973), of Bebington, Wirral, and Hanna Corlett; *b* 14 June 1938; *Educ* Birkenhead Sch, BNC Coll Oxford (BA); *m* 15 Feb 1964, Margaret Catherine, da of John Mathew Jones (d 1977), of Moelfre, Anglesey; 1 s (Stephen b 1975); *Career* joined Inland Revenue 1960; seconded to: Civil Serv Selection Bd 1970, HM Treasy 1972-74 (as private sec to Chllr of the Exchequer) and 1979-81; under sec Bd of Inland Revenue 1985-; *Recreations* walking; *Style—* Clive W Corlett, Esq; Somerset House, Strand, London, WC2

CORLETT, Dr Ewan Christian Brew; OBE; s of Malcolm James John Corlett (d 1956), and Catherine Ann, *née* Brew (d 1964); *b* 11 Feb 1923; *Educ* King William's Coll IOM, Univ of Oxford (MA), Univ of Durham (Phd); *m* 1945, Edna Lilian, da of Arthur James Buggs, of Bromley, Kent; 3 s (Nigel, Brian, Malcolm); *Career* naval architect; chm and md Burness Corlett and Partners 1952-88 (naval architects and marine conslts); vice pres and naval architect to GB Project; tstee Nat Maritime Museum Greenwich; Prime Warden Worshipful Co of Shipwrights; hon vice pres Royal Inst of Naval Architects, FEng 1974; *Recreations* yachting (yacht 'Stronnag'), model shipbuilding, astronomy; *Clubs* Manx Sailing and Cruising; *Style—* Dr Ewan Corlett, OBE; Cottimans, Port-e-Vullen, Ramsey IOM (☎ 0624 814009); Burness, Corlett and Ptnrs, Shipdesine House, Ramsey, IOM (☎ 0624 813210)

CORLETT, Gerald Lingham; s of late Alfred Lingham Corlett; *b* 8 May 1925; *Educ* Rossall, Univ of Aberdeen; *m* 1957, Helen, *née* Williamson; 3 s, 1 da; *Career* Lt Royal Indian Artillery; chm: Higsons Brewery plc 1982-88 (dir 1955-88), Radio City (Sound of Merseyside) plc 1985-88; dir Westminster (Liverpool) Trust; tstee: AC Morrell Settlement, Bluecoat Sch Liverpool, Bluecoat Soc Liverpool, Lasers for Life Trust; cncl memb Rossall Sch; *Style—* Gerald Corlett, Esq; Kirk House, 4 Abbey Rd, W Kirby, Merseyside L48 7EW (☎ 051 625 5425)

CORLEY, Sir Kenneth Sholl Ferrand; s of late Sidney Walter Corley, of London, and late A L Corley; *b* 3 Nov 1908; *Educ* St Bees Cumberland; *m* 1937, Olwen Mary, da of Maurice Hart Yeoman, of London; 1 s, 1 da; *Career* chm and chief exec Joseph Lucas (Industries) Ltd 1969-73 (joined 1927); Chevalier de la Legion D'Honneur; kt 1972; *Clubs* Royal Automobile; *Style—* Sir Kenneth Corley; 34 Dingle Lane, Solihull, W Midlands (☎ (021 705 1597); Yewtree, Wasdale, Cumbria (☎ 09406 285)

CORLEY, His Honour; Michael Early Ferrand; s of Ferrand Edward Corley, and Elsie Maria Corley; *b* 11 Oct 1909; *Educ* Marlborough, Oriel Coll Oxford; *Career* called to the Bar 1934, circuit judge 1967-82 (ret); *Style—* His Honour Michael Corley; The Old Rectory, Rectory Road, Broome, Norfolk NR35 2HU

CORLEY, Peter Maurice Sinclair; s of James Maurice Corley (d 1975), and Barbara Shearer, *née* Sinclair; *b* 15 June 1933; *Educ* Marlborough, Kings Coll Cambridge (MA); *m* 11 March 1961, Dr Marjorie Constance Corley, da of William John Doddridge (d 1982); 2 da (Carolyn b 1963, Rosalind b 1968); *Career* entered civil serv 1957, commercial sec Brussels 1969-71, dir gen Econ Cooperation Office Riyadh 1976-78, under sec DTI 1981-; *Recreations* bookbinding; *Clubs* Oxford and Cambridge; *Style—* Peter Corley, Esq; c/o Dept of Trade and Industry, 1 Victoria St, London SW1H 0ET

CORLEY, Roger David; s of Thomas Arthur Corley (d 1989), and Erica, *née* Trent; *b* 13 April 1933; *Educ* Hymers Coll Kingston upon Hull, Univ of Manchester (BSc); *m* 14 May 1964, Brigitte, da of Leo Hubert Anton Roeder (d 1977); 3 s (Martin b 1966, Kevin b 1969, Steffan b 1971); *Career* Nat Serv Sub Lt RNVR 1954-56; Clerical Med and Gen Life Assur Soc 1956-: investmt mangr 1961-72, actuary 1972-80, dir 1975, dep gen mangr 1980-82, gen mangr 1982; Inst of Actuaries: fell 1960, memb Cncl 1976-, hon sec 1980-82, vice pres 1985-88, pres 1988-90; memb Cncl Int Actuarial Assoc 1983- (vice pres 1990-); Freeman City of London 1979, memb Court Worshipful Co of Actuaries 1985- (Liveryman 1979); FIA 1960, ASA 1970, DGVM 1975; ASIA 1985, FRSA 1990; *Recreations* music, theatre, opera, visual arts, books, travel; *Clubs* Army and Navy, IOD, Gallio, Actuaries; *Style—* Roger Corley, Esq; Clerical, Medical and General Life Assurance Society, 15 St James's Square, London SW1Y 4LQ (☎ 081 930 5474, telex 97432)

CORMACK, Ian Donald; s of Andrew Gray Cormack, of Falmouth, Cornwall, and Eliza Cormack; *b* 12 Nov 1947; *Educ* Falmouth GS, Pembroke Coll Oxford (BA); *m* 14 Sept 1968, (Elizabeth) Susan, da of Mark Tallack (d 1976), of Penryn, Cornwall; 1 s (James Mark Ian (Jamie) b 1975), 1 da (Sally Elizabeth b 1979); *Career* joined Citibank (part of Citicorp) 1969-; dir: SCAM 1976-78, Euro Trg Centre 1979, personnel dir N Europe 1980-84, head Fin Insts Gp UK 1984-88; chm: Citicorp UK Pension Fund 1980-89, Citicorp Tstee Co 1987-, Infocast Ltd 1988-; head Fin Insts gp Euro 1989-; memb: Cncl of Assoc of Payment Clearing Systems, Clearing House Formation Ctee (ISE), TAURUS Audit Ctee Advsy Gp Pembroke Coll Oxford, Bd Securities Settlement Bd of Int Stock Exchange, Bd Cedel SA Luxembourg; chm APACS Cncl Risk Steering gp; chm Woolnoth Soc City of London; *Recreations* skiing, golf, fly-fishing, theatre; *Clubs* Overseas Bankers, RAC; *Style—* Ian Cormack, Esq; Holly Lodge, Lammas Lane, Esher, Surrey KT10 8PA (☎ 0372 467730); Citibank NA, 336 Strand, London (☎ 071 234 5333, fax 071 234 5277)

CORMACK, Hon Mrs ((Gwendoline Rita) Jean); *née* Davies; yr da of 1 Baron Davies of Plas Dinam, Llandinam, Montgomeryshire (d 1944), and Henrietta Margaret, *née* Fergusson (d 1948); *b* 1929,May; *Educ* Havergal Coll Toronto Canada, Downe House, House of Citizenship; *m* 1950 (m dis 1979), John McRae Cormack, AFC, s of Lt-Col H S Cormack of Mossgiel, Culver Road, Felpham, Sussex (d 1952); 1 s (Michael d 1980), 3 da (Shara, Amanda, Teresa); *Career* memb: General Cncl and Ctee of Mgmnt Atlantic Salmon Tst, Exec Ctee of the David Davies Meml Tst of Int Affrs; *Recreations* fishing; *Style—* The Hon Mrs Cormack

CORMACK, Lady Miranda Maxwell; *née* Fyfe; da of 1 and last Earl of Kilmuir, PC, GCVO (d 1967); *b* 13 Dec 1938; *m* 2 April 1960, Michael Ormiston Cormack, er s of late H M Cormack, of Bookham, Newton Valence, Hants; 2 s, 1 da; *Career* teacher; *Style—* The Lady Miranda Cormack; 31 White Hart Wood, Sevenoaks, Kent TN13 1RS (☎ 0732 457230)

CORMACK, Patrick Thomas; MP (C) S Staffs 1983-; s of Thomas Charles Cormack, of Grimsby, and Kathleen Mary Cormack; *b* 18 May 1939; *Educ* St James's Choir Sch Grimsby, Havelock Sch Grimsby, Univ of Hull; *m* 1967, Kathleen Mary, da of William Eric McDonald, of Aberdeen; 2 s; *Career* second master St James's Choir Sch Grimsby 1961-66, former English master and asst housemaster Wrekin Coll, head of History Dept Brewood GS Stafford; MP (C): Cannock 1970-74, Staffs SW 1974-83; PPS to jt Parly Secs DHSS 1970-73; chm: All-Party Ctee Widows and One Parent Families 1974, Cons Pry Arts and Heritage Ctee 1979-83, All-Party Heritage Ctee 1979-; memb: Select Ctee Educn Science and Arts 1979-83, Speaker's Panel of Chairmen in the House of Commons 1983-, chm House of Commons Works of Art Ctee 1987-, recitation warden St Margaret's Westminster 1978-90, Parly warden 1990-; memb: Faculty Jurisdiction Cmmn, Royal Cmmn on Historical Manuscripts 1981-, Historic Buildings Cncl 1979-85, Cncl for Br Archaeology; tstee Historic Churches Preservation Tst, vice chm Heritage in Danger, memb Cncl of Winston Churchill Memorial Trust 1983-; Honorary Citizen of Texas; FSA; *Books* Heritage in Danger (1976), Right Turn (1978), Westminster Palace and Parliament (1981), Castles of Britain (1982), Wilberforce the Nation's Conscience (1983), English Cathedrals (1984); *Recreations* visiting old churches, fighting philistines, not sitting on fences; *Clubs* Athenaeum, Brooks's; *Style—* Patrick Cormack, Esq, MP; House of Commons, London SW1A 0AA (☎ 071 219 5019/5514)

CORMACK, Prof Richard Melville; s of Dr William Sloan Cormack (d 1973), and Jean Wilson, *née* Niven (d 1982); *b* 12 March 1935; *Educ* Glasgow Acad, Univ of Cambridge (MA, Dip Math Stat), Univ of London (BSc), Univ of Aberdeen (PhD); *m* 1 Sept 1960, Edith, da of James Edward Whittaker, OBE, (d 1973); 1 s (Andrew b 1963), 1 da (Anne b 1966); *Career* lectr in statistics Univ of Aberdeen 1956-66, sr lectr in statistics Univ of Edinburgh 1966-72, prof of statistics Univ of St Andrews 1972-, visiting prof Univ of Washington 1986 (1964-65); memb NERC 1983-89; Biometric Soc: Br sec 1970-77, int pres 1980-81; memb Cncl: RSS 1980-84, S Univs Cncl on entrance 1982-89, Cncl Freshwater Biological Assoc 1978-83 and 1987-; FRSE 1974, memb ISI 1972; *Books* The Statistical Argument (1971), vols 5 and 8 of ISEP Statistical Ecology Series (ed 1979); *Recreations* photography, music, hill walking; *Style—* Prof Richard Cormack; Eldon, 58 Buchanan Gardens, St Andrews, Fife KY16 9LX; Dept of Mathematical and Computational Sciences, Univ of St Andrews, North Haugh, St Andrews, Fife KY16 9SS (☎ 0334 76161 ext 8118, fax 0334 74487, telex 9312110846 SAG)

CORMAN, Charles; *b* 23 Oct 1934; *Educ* St Paul's Sch, UCL (LLB), Univ of California (scholar, fell, LLM); *Career* assoc Goldstein Judd & Gurfein NY (attorneys) 1960; Titmuss Sainer & Webb: articles 1955-58, asst slr 1959 and 1960-61, ptnr 1963-; *Style—* Charles Corman, Esq; Titmuss Sainer & Webb, 2 Serjeants' Inn, London EC4Y 1LT (☎ 071 583 5353, fax 071 353 3683)

CORMICK, Michael James; s of Colin Cormick, of Melbourne, Victoria, Australia, and Shirley, *née* Saffron; *b* 2 Sept 1963; *Educ* St Johns Coll Melbourne, Aust Soc of Entertainers; *Career* actor; TV work in Aust 1977-87, toured Aust casino circuit; understudy Time 1987, Phantom of the Opera (Her Majesty's) 1988-; *Style—* Michael Cormick, Esq; The Phantom of the Opera, Her Majesty's Theatre, Haymarket, London SW1

CORNEJO, Maria Soledad (Mrs Borthwick); da of Jorge Cornejo, of Portugal, and Maria Amelia Fernandez (d 1977); *b* 4 Oct 1962; *Educ* Stockport Coll Graphics (HND), Ravensbourne Coll of Arts (BA); *m* 14 Oct 1988, Mark George Alexander, s of Sir John Borthwick, of Bermuda; *Career* fndr Richmond/Cornejo 1985-88, license Japan 26 shops 1986, license Japan shoes 1986, fndr Maria Cornejo Paris 1989-; *Recreations* books, travel; *Style—* Miss Maria Cornejo; 80 Rue Saint Denis, Paris 75001, France (☎ 42 33 92 11); Chelsea Manor Studios, No 1 Flood St, London SW1 (☎ 071 351 7411, fax 071 351 9541, telex 918 259)

CORNELIUS, David Frederick; s of Frederick Marcus Nightingale Cornelius (d 1958), and Florence Kate, *née* Allen (d 1982); *b* 7 May 1932; *Educ* Teignmouth GS, Univ of Exeter (scholar, BSc); *m* 3 Nov 1956, Susan, da of Edward William Auston (d 1980); 2 s (Philip David Muir b 1962, Darrell John b 1964), 2 da (Elizabeth Susan b 1968, Victoria Ruth b 1971); *Career* res sci Royal Naval Scientific Service 1953-58, section head (res) UKAEA 1958-65, divnl head (res) Transport & Road Research Laboratory 1970-72 (section head (res) 1965-70), asst dir Building Research Establishment 1973-78, head Sci Policy & Progs Dept of Tport 1978-82; Transport & Road Research Laboratory: asst dir 1982-84, dep dir 1984-88, dir 1988-; memb Cncl: CIRIA, Inst of Highways & Transportation; memb Ct Univ of Surrey; FInstP 1978, FIHT 1988, FRSA 1990; author of scientific papers to professional institutions and int conferences; *Recreations* antiques, carvanning in Europe, swimming, cycling; *Clubs* Civil Service; *Style—* David Cornelius, Esq; Transport and Road Research Laboratory, Old Wokingham Rd, Crowthorne, Berkshire RG11 6AU (☎ 0344 770001, fax 0344 770761, telex 848272)

CORNELIUS, Debbie Alison; da of Donald Stewart Cornelius, of Harlow, Essex, and Brenda, *née* Woollett; *b* 25 July 1966; *Educ* Mark Hall Comp Sch Harlow; *Career* croquet player; debut 1985, played for Ipswich Croquet Club in Nat Interclub Competition 1987-89, played Sonoma Cutrer Championship Calif (finished 5 equal); nat titles held: Br Mixed Doubles champion (with GN Aspinall) 1987, Br Women's champion 1988, New Zealand Women's champion 1990, New Zealand Mixed Doubles champion (with J Hogan) 1990, US Open Doubles champion (with R Fleming) 1990; 18 in Br rankings 1990, 33 in World rankings 1990; trainee accountant; *Style—* Miss Debbie Cornelius; Pear Tree Cottage, Hobbs Cross, Harlow, Essex CM17 ONN (☎ 0279 429316)

CORNER, (John) Michael; OBE (1990); s of Thomas Matthias Corner, of Bishop Auckland, Co Durham, and Winifred, *née* Bell; *b* 2 Oct 1939; *Educ* King James I GS Bishop Auckland, Univ of Manchester; *m* 3 Sept 1963, Gwendoline, da of Robert William Cook, of Bishop Auckland, Co Durham; 1 s (Adam b 1966); *Career* news ed Northern Echo Darlington 1966-68 (reporter 1960-64, chief reporter 1964-66); asst ed: Morning Telegraph Sheffield 1973-78 (night news ed 1968-73), The Star Sheffield 1978-82; ed: Sheffield Weekly Gazette 1982-83, The Star Sheffield 1983-; dir Sheffield

Newspapers 1983, Sheffield Partnerships 1990; memb: Br Section of Int Press Inst 1984-90, Cncl of Cwlth Press Union, BBC NE Advsy Cncl 1987-90, Cncl of Sheffield C of C, Sheffield Indust Year Ctee and Indust Matters Ctee, Sheffield Image Ctee, Univ of Sheffield Chllrs Ctee on Br Assoc, Guild of Br Newspaper Eds 1982; tstee: Northern Radio, Five Wiers Walk, The Star Old Folk's Fund; winner Cwlth Press scholarship 1975; vice chm Parly and Legal Ctee Guild of Br Newspaper Eds 1989-90 (chm 1986-89); *Recreations* gardening, snooker; *Style*— Michael Corner, Esq, OBE; 11 Winchester Crescent, Sheffield S10 4ED; The Star, York St, Sheffield S1 1PU (☎ 0742 767676, fax 0742 725978, telex 265863)

CORNER, Timothy Frank; s of Frank Herbert Corner (d 1983), of Bolton, Lancs, and June, *née* Benson; *b* 25 July 1958; *Educ* Bolton Sch, Magdalen Coll Oxford (Demy (Open Scholar) MA, BCL); *Career* called to the Bar Gray's Inn 1981; *Recreations* reading, gardening and book reviewing; *Style*— Timothy Corner, Esq; 2 Mitre Ct Bldgs, Temple, London EC4Y 7BX (☎ 071 583 1355, fax 071 583 1672)

CORNES, David Langford; s of Alan Howard Cornes (d 1974), of Endon, Staffs, and Joyce, *née* Phillipson; *b* 31 Aug 1944; *Educ* Rydal Sch, King's Coll London (BSc); *m* 27 July 1978, Katrina Penelope Darking; 2 s (Oliver William b 1972, Edward Fergus b 1982), 1 da (Charlotte Lucy b 1970); *Career* slr, sr ptnr Winward Fearon & Co; MICE, CEng, AKC; *Recreations* gardening, walking; *Clubs* National Liberal; *Style*— David Cornes, Esq; Manor Cottage, The Manor House, Little Gaddesden, Berkhamsted, Herts HP4 1PL (☎ 044 284 3336); Winward Fearon & Co, 35 Bow St, London WC2E 7AU (☎ 071 836 9081, fax 071 836 8382, telex 267651 WEWIN)

CORNES, John Addis; s of John Frederick Cornes; *b* 16 Aug 1944; *Educ* Eton, Univ of Oxford; *m* 1971, Veronica Mary Alicia; 2 c; *Career* dir: W Downs Sch Ltd, Langton Investment Services, Brown Shipley Unit Trust Management, Brown Shipley Asset Management; *Recreations* walking, watching sport; *Style*— John Cornes, Esq; Woodgates Farm, East Bergholt, Colchester, Essex

CORNESS, Sir Colin Ross; s of late Thomas Corness and Mary Evlyne, *née* Lovelace; *b* 9 Oct 1931; *Educ* Uppingham, Magdalene Cambridge (BA, MA), Harvard; *Career* Lt 3 Carabiniers (Prince of Wales) Dragoons Gds; barr 1956; chm Redland plc 1977- (md 1967-82); dir: W H Smith and Son plc 1980-87, Chubb and Son plc 1974-84, Nat West Bank (SE Regnl Bd) 1982-86, Courtaulds plc 1986-, Bank of England 1987-, Gordon Russell plc 1985-89, S G Warburg Group plc 1987-, Unitech plc 1987-; memb: Nat Econ Devpt Ctee for Bldg 1980-84, Indust Devpt Advsy Bd 1982-84 Advsy Bd Br-American C of C 1987-; pres Nat Cncl of Bldg Materials Prods 1985-87; kt 1986; *Recreations* tennis, music, travel; *Clubs* White's, Cavalry and Guards, Australian (Sydney); *Style*— Sir Colin Corness; Redland plc, Redland House, Reigate, Surrey RH2 0SJ (☎ 0737 242488, telex 28626)

CORNFORD, Sir (Edward) Clifford; KCB (1977, CB 1966); s of John Herbert Cornford, of E Grinstead; *b* 6 Feb 1918; *Educ* Kimbolton Sch, Jesus Coll Cambridge; *m* 1945, Catherine, da of Frank Muir; 3 s, 3 da; *Career* Royal Aircraft Establishment 1938; chief exec and perm under-sec of state MOD (Procurement Exec) 1975-77, chief of Defence Procurement 1977-80; FRAeS, FEng; *Style*— Sir Clifford Cornford, KCB; Beechurst, Shaftesbury Rd, Woking, Surrey (☎ 0483 768919)

CORNFORD, Geoffrey Arthur; TD (1945); s of the late Arthur Cornford, and Alice Camfield; *b* 25 April 1920; *Educ* Lewes Co Sch; *m* 25 Jan 1947, Lois Louise, da of Gerald Owen Quekett; 1 s (Simon Geoffrey), 2 da (Anstice Louise, Gillian Lois); *Career* WWII 1939-45; joined as Sapper RE 1939, evacuated Dunkirk, cmmnd 1942, served Greece (acting Lt-Col), N Africa, Sicily, Italy and Austria with 13 Corps and Popskis Private Army; articled T Burdett, engr Uckfield RDC, asst engr Godstone RDC, town planning offr Uckfield RDC and Hailsham RDC, mangr (E Sussex) A C Draycott, ptnr Cornford Scott Robins Tunbridge Wells; past chm and md: White Chalk Investments, Chalk Blue Estates, Gustaways Properties, Beaufield Homes; chm: Ultramark Ltd, Mistywell Ltd; memb: Crowborough CC (past hon sec, chm and Capt), Eastbourne CC (past Capt), Sussex RFU (past pres and 53 years on Ctee), Sussex CCC (vice chm 1966-68); exec chm Sussex Playing Fields Assoc; Freeman City of London 1966, Liveryman Gold and Silver Wyre Drawers Co 1966; *Clubs* MCC; *Style*— G A Cornford, Esq, TD; Little Swaines, 173 Turkey Rd, Bexhill (☎ 04243 6139); Enterprise Centre, Station Parade, Eastbourne (☎ 0323 639 504)

CORNICK, Col Anthony Emlyn; s of late Alfred George Cornick, and late Tydvil, *née* Evans; *b* 19 Jan 1938; *Educ* Berkhamsted Sch, RMA Sandhurst; *m* 6 Aug 1966, Judith Cornick; 1 s (Simon Charles b 9 Aug 1969), 1 da (Clare Louise b 26 Oct 1967); *Career* Army 1956-: Bn Cdr 1979-81, plans policy staff SHAPE 1981-85, defence commitments staff MOD 1985-86, DA, NA, MA in Amman Jordan 1986-90, MLRS Int Corp 1990-; *Recreations* ornithology, music, travel, golf; *Style*— Col Anthony Cornick

CORNICK, Roger Courtenay; s of William Charles Cornick (d 1968) , of Singapore, and Cynthia Avisa Louise, *née* Courtenay; *b* 13 Feb 1944; *Educ* various army schs in Egypt, Queen Elizabeth's Sch Crediton Devon; *m* Celia Elizabeth, da of Mrs Irene Wilson; 2 da (Kate Elizabeth b April 1979, Victoria Rose b Feb 1981); *Career* trainee Royal Insurance Group 1963-68, rep Abbey Life Assurance Co 1968-70, asst dir Hambro Life Assurance Ltd 1970-77, dir Crown Financial Management Ltd 1977-80, ptnr Courtenay Manning Partners 1980-83, dep chm and gp mktg dir Perpetual plc 1982-; memb Exec Ctee Unit Tst Assoc; *Recreations* golf, tennis, skiing, theatre; *Clubs* Riverside, Royal Mid-Surrey Golf; *Style*— Roger Cornick, Esq; Perpetual plc, 48 Hart Street, Henley-on-Thames, Oxon RG9 2AZ (☎ 0491 576868, fax 0491 578926, car 0831 212458)

CORNISH, Alan Stewart; s of Alfred Stewart Cornish (d 1980), of Orpington, Kent, and Ann Selina, *née* Westgate; *b* 27 April 1944; *Educ* Beckenham and Penge Coll; *m* 8 March 1969, Daphne Elisabeth, da of Charles Gordon Saunders; 3 s (Nigel b 1972, Graham b 1975, Iain b 1982); *Career* gp fin controller Assoc Communications Corpn plc 1975-82, vice pres Euro regnl office RCA records 1982-84, gp chief exec Good Relations Group plc 1984-86, gp md Lowe Bell Communications Ltd 1986-89; chm and chief exec Deal Holdings Ltd 1989-90, chm Cornish Ltd 1989-; fndr memb Orpington Dist Guide Dogs for the Blind Assoc; London Borough of Bromley: cnclIr 1974-80, dep ldr 1976-78, dep mayor 1978-79; FCMA 1976 (assoc 1971), FBIM 1978, FInstD 1986; *Recreations* sport; *Clubs* local CC, local golf, local badminton; *Style*— Alan Cornish, Esq; Aspens, 42 Oxenden Wood Road, Chelsfield Park, Orpington, Kent BR6 6HP (☎ 0689 860092, fax 0689 86091, car 0836 279308)

CORNISH, Anthony; s of Alfred Cornish, of Chingford, Essex; *b* 7 April 1935; *m* Linda Polan; 1 s (Simon); *Career* announcer and disc jockey Forces Bdcasting Serv Austria 1953-55, actor and stage mangr various repertory theatres 1955-58, artistic dir Civic Theatre Chesterfield 1959-62, radio drama prodr BBC Midland Region 1964-74, deviser and prodr weekly serial United, freelance dir Crescent Alexandra & Repertory Theatres Birmingham, artist in residence Tufts Univ Medford USA 1969-70, dir Tufts Univ Jr Year Abroad Programme London 1971-77, literary and prodn mangr and assoc dir Haymarket Theatre Leicester 1974-76, freelance dir Shaw Theatre London and Bristol Old Vic 1977-80, drama supervisor Capital Radio London and visiting lectr Univ of Hull 1980-84, freelance dir and teacher 1984-; prodns incl: Two Gentlemen of Verona, Tonight We Improvise, Tribeckett (all at Cornell Univ), House of Bernarda Alba (Webber Douglas Acad) 1988, 6 premieres by Andrew Davies and Vaclav Havel, Twelfth Night (Perishable Theatre) 1989, Take Back What's Yours (Warehouse Theatre) 1989, Importance of Being Earnest (Pearl Theatre, NY) 1990, The Taming of the Shrew (Tomar, Portugal) 1990; Major Barbara (Pearl Theatre) 1990; co prodr The Forsythe Chronicles (BBC Radio 4) 1990; princ tutor Young Professional Directors Course British Theatre Assoc 1989-90; memb: Dirs' Guild of GB, Guild of Drama Adjudicators, Radio Acad, Accreditation Panel Nat Cncl for Drama Training; *Style*— Anthony Cornish, Esq; Elspeth Cochrane Agency, 11/13 Orlando Rd, London SW4 OLE (☎ 071 622 0314)

CORNISH, (Robert) Francis; LVO (1978); s of C D Cornish; *b* 18 May 1942; *Educ* Charterhouse, RMA Sandhurst; *m* 1964, Alison Jane Dundas; 3 da; *Career* cmmnd 14/20 King's Hussars 1962; entered FCO 1968, Kuala Lumpur 1970, Jakarta 1971, first sec FCO 1973, Bonn 1976-80, asst private sec to HRH The Prince of Wales 1980-83, high cmmr Brunei 1983-1986, cnsllr (info) Washington and head of Br Info Servs NY 1986-90; *Clubs* Cavalry and Guards; *Style*— Francis Cornish, Esq, LVO; c/o Foreign and Cwlth Office, King Charles St, London SW1

CORNISH, Prof Frederick Hector John; s of Robert Hector Cornish (d 1977), of Crediton, Devon, and Margaret Elizabeth, *née* Helmore (d 1975); *b* 29 June 1930; *Educ* Queen Elizabeth's GS, Crediton, Wadham Coll Oxford (MA, DPhil); *m* 4 Jan 1958, Monica Rosalie Hope; 2 s (John b 1961, Richard b 1965), 1 da (Rachel b 1959); *Career* Nat Serv instr Lt RN 1956-59; jr lectr in mathematics Univ of Oxford 1953-54, res fell Univ of BC Vancouver 1954-56, sr lectr Univ of Leeds 1965 (lectr 1959); Univ of York: prof of mathematics 1967-79, acting vice chllr 1978, dep vice chllr 1979-81 (1975-78); memb York Civic Tst; *Recreations* music, gardening, hill walking, DIY; *Style*— Prof Frederick Cornish; Lime Tree House, 99 Front St, Acomb, York (☎ 0904 798022); Department of Mathematics, University of York, Heslington, York YO1 5DD (☎ 0904 433074)

CORNISH, James Easton; s of Eric Easton Cornish, of Scotland, and Ivie Hedworth, *née* McCulloch; *b* 5 Aug 1939; *Educ* Eton, Wadham Coll Oxford; *m* 1968, Ursula, da of Prof H R Pink, of German Fed Rep; 1 s (Toby b 1972); *Career* HM Dip Serv 1961-85: HM Embassy Bonn, BMG Berlin, HM Embassy Washington, Central Policy Review Staff; asst dir Phillips and Drew 1985-87, Co Nat West Securities 1987, euro market strategist 1988; *Recreations* reading; *Style*— James Cornish, Esq; c/o County Nat West Securities, 135 Bishopsgate, London EC2M 3XT

CORNISH, Prof William Rodolph; s of Jack Rodolph Cornish (d 1978) and Elizabeth Ellen, *née* Reid; *b* 9 Aug 1937; *Educ* St Peter's Coll Adelaide, Univ of Adelaide (LLB), Univ of Oxford (BCL); *m* 25 July 1964, Lovedy Elizabeth, da of Edward Christopher Moule (d 1942); 1 s (Peter b 1968), 2 da (Anna b 1970, Cecilia b 1972); *Career* lectr in law LSE 1962-68, reader QMC London 1969-70, prof of English law LSE 1970-90, prof of law Univ of Cambridge 1990-; external academic memb Max Planck Inst for Patent Law Munich 1989-; *Books* The Jury (2 edn, 1970), Intellectual Property: Patents, Copyright, Trade Marks and Allied Rights (2 edn, 1989), Law and Society in England 1750-1950 (1989); *Style*— Prof William Cornish; Magdalene College, Cambridge

CORNOCK, Maj-Gen Charles Gordon; CB (1988), MBE (1974); s of Gordon Wallace Cornock (d 1978), of Warwicks, and Edith Mary, *née* Keeley; *b* 25 April 1935; *Educ* King Alfred Sch, RMA Sandhurst; *m* 1962, Kay, da of Cyril John Sidney Smith (d 1987), of Jersey; 2 s (Ian b 1963, James b 1966); *Career* cmmnd RA 1956, CO 7 Para RHA 1974-76 (despatches 1975), Cdr RA 3 Armd Div 1979-81, student Royal Coll of Def Studies 1982, Dep Cmdt Army Staff Coll Camberley, dir RA 1984-86, Chief of Staff Live Oak 1986-; mangr England Jrs Hockey Team 1978-79; bursar Cranleigh Sch 1990-; FBIM; *Recreations* hockey, tennis, golf, skiing, water skiing; *Clubs* La Moye Golf, West Hill Golf, Special Forces; *Style*— Maj-Gen Charles Cornock, CB, MBE; Cranmore Horseshoe Lane, Cranleigh, Surrey

CORNTHWAITE, Dr Derek; s of Harold Cornthwaite, of 51 Crimicar Lane, Sheffield, and Florence, *née* Jubb; *b* 5 Dec 1938; *Educ* The Leys Sch Cambridge, Univ of Sheffield (BSc, PhD), Columbia Univ NY; *m* 28 Jan 1965, Pamela Mary, da of Rev Canon James Brown (Canon of Sheffield Cathedral, d 1983); 1 s (Mark b 1968), 1 da (Sarah b 1974); *Career* chm: ICI (China) Ltd Hong Kong 1976-79, ICI Zeltia SA Spain 1980-88, Sopra SA France 1979-86, Solplant Spa Italy 1979-85, Br Agrochemicals Assoc 1983-84, Sincair McGill Ltd UK 1980-88, Société European de Semance SA Belgium 1987; dir: Plant Protection Div ICI plc UK 1979-90, Garst Co USA 1985-90; pres Agric Products Gp ICI Americas Inc 1987-90; vice-pres ICI Americas Inc USA 1987-90, exec vice pres Diversey Corporation Canada 1990- co-winner of MacRobert award 1978; *Recreations* sailing, squash, music, opera; *Clubs* Farmers; *Style*— Dr Derek Cornthwaite; Diversey Corporation, 201 City Centre Drive, Mississanga, Ontario, LSB 279, Canada

CORNWALL, Archdeacon of; *see*: Ravenscroft, Ven Raymond Lockwood

CORNWALL-JONES, Mark Ralph; s of Brig Arthur Thomas Cornwall-Jones, CMG, CBE (d 1980), and Marie Joan Evelyn, *née* Hammersley-Smith; *b* 14 Feb 1933; *Educ* Glenalmond Coll, Jesus Coll Cambridge (MA); *m* 1959, Priscilla, da of Col Harold E Yeo (d 1957); 3 s (Adam b 1964, Matthew b 1967, Jason b 1969), 1 da (Kate b 1961); *Career* investmt mangr: The Debenture Corporation 1959-67, John Govett and Co Ltd 1967-90 (investmt dir 1983-88); dir: Halifax Building Society, Ecclesiastical Insurance Group, Century Oils Group, Govett Oriental Investment Trust, Updown Investment Co, Trades Union Unit Trust; *Recreations* books, stalking, gardening, sailing, carpentry; *Clubs* Boodles; *Style*— Mark Cornwall-Jones, Esq; Erin House, 3 Albert Bridge Rd, Battersea SW11 4PX; The Counting House, 53 Tooley St, London SE1

CORNWALL-LEGH, Hon Richard Henry; o s and h of 5 Baron Grey of Codnor, CBE, AE, DL, *qv*; *b* 14 May 1936; *Educ* Stowe; *m* 1974, Joanna Storm, 7 and yst da of Sir Kenelm Henry Ernest Cayley, 10 Bt (d 1976); 3 s (Richard Stephen Cayley b 1976, Kenelm Michael b 1978, George Henry b 1982), 1 da (Caroline Philadelphia b 1983); *Career* late RN (Gen Serv Medal, Suez); landowner, farmer and dir of private cos; memb British Ski Team 1959-61 (Capt 1960-61); *Style*— The Hon Richard Cornwall-Legh; Dairy Farm, High Legh, Knutsford, Cheshire WA16 0QS

CORNWALLIS, Hon (Patrick Wykeham) David; 2 s (but only s by 2 w) of 3 Baron Cornwallis, OBE, DL; *b* 28 May 1952; *Educ* Lancing, Aiglon Coll Switzerland; *m* 1977, Susannah, da of William Edward Guest, of Rufford Abbey, Notts, and widow of Stephen Thursfield; 3 s (Patrick Wykeham James b 1977, Thomas Wykeham Charles b 1980, William Wykeham George b 1982); *Style*— The Hon David Cornwallis; Hamnish Court, Hamnish, Leominster, Herefordshire

CORNWALLIS, 3 Baron (UK 1927); Fiennes Neil Wykeham Cornwallis; OBE (1963), DL (Kent 1976); only s of 2 Baron Cornwallis, KBE, KCVO, MC, JP, DL (d 1982), by his 1 w, Cecily (d 1943), da of Sir James Heron Walker, 3 Bt; *b* 29 June 1921; *Educ* Eton; *m* 1, 17 Oct 1942 (m dis 1948), Judith, o da of Lt-Col Geoffrey Lacy Scott, TD; 1 s, 1 da (decd); m 2, 1 June 1951, Agnes Jean, yr da of Capt Henderson Russell Landale; 1 s, 3 da; *Heir* s (by 1 w), Hon Jeremy Cornwallis, *qv*; *Career* served WWII Lt Coldstream Gds (1941-44, then invalided); pres: Br Agric Contractors' Assoc 1952-54, Nat Assoc Agric Contractors 1957-63 and 1986-; dir Planet Building Society 1968- (chm 1971-75); chm: Magnet and Planet Building Society 1975-79, Town and Country Building Society 1979-81 (dir 1979-), CBI Smaller Firms Cncl 1974-82 (chm 1979-82), English Apples and Pears Ltd 1989-; memb Bd of Tstees Chevening Estate 1979-; rep of Horticultural Co-operatives in EEC 1975-86; vice pres Fedn of Agric

Co-operatives 1984-86; chm: FAC Fruit Forum 1972-89, Kingdom Quality Assur Scheme 1986-89; Pro Grand Master (Freemasons) United Grand Lodge 1982- (previously Dep Grand Master); FIHort; *Recreations* fishing; *Clubs* Brooks's, Farmers', Pratt's; *Style*— The Rt Hon the Lord Cornwallis, OBE, DL; Ruck Farm, Horsmonden, Tonbridge, Kent TN12 8DT (☎ 089 272 2267); Dundurn House, St Fillans, Crieff, Perthshire (☎ 076 485 252); 25B Queens' Gate Mews, London SW7 5QL (☎ 071 589 1167)

CORNWALLIS, Hon (Fiennes Wykeham) Jeremy; er s (but sole surviving child by 1 w) of 3 Baron Cornwallis, OBE, DL; *b* 25 May 1946; *Educ* Eton, RAC Cirencester; *m* 29 March 1969, Sara Gray de Neufville, da of Lt-Col Nigel Stockwell, of Benenden, Kent; 1 s (Fiennes Alexander Wykeham-Martin b 1987), 2 da (Anna Julia Gray b 1971, Charlotte Louise b 1972); *Style*— The Hon Jeremy Cornwallis; 15 Mablethorpe Road, London SW6 6AQ (☎ 071 381 5307)

CORNWELL, Judy Valerie; JP (1985); da of Darcy Nigel Barry Cornwell (d 1967), of Aust, and Irene, *née* McCullen; *b* 22 Feb 1940; *Educ* Convent of Mercy Aust, Lewes GS Sussex; *m* 18 Dec 1960, John Kelsall Parry, s of Edward Parry (d 1983), of Loughborough; 1 s (Edward Dylan b 20 June 1965); *Career* actress; TV: Younger Generation plays 1961, nominated Tommorrow's Star Actress Daily Mirror 1961, Call Me Daddy (winner Emmy award) 1967, Moody and Pegg 1974, nominated Best Actress SFTA for Cakes and Ale 1974, Good Companions 1980, Keeping Up Appearances (BBC) 1990-91; radio series Navy Lark 1962; theatre: Oh! What A Lovely War 1963, RSC season at Stratford upon Avon 1972, Bed Before Yesterday (Lyric) 1976, Rose (NZ tour) 1981, The Government Inspector 1988; film: Wuthering Heights 1971, Santa Claus The Movie 1985; pres: Relate (Brighton), Nat Assoc of Deaf Children (E Sussex); memb: Bd Inst of Alcohol Studies 1983-91, Bd West Pier Tst 1974-89, Cncl Equity 1982-85; memb: Equity 1955, Soc of Authors 1986, PEN 1989; *Books* Cow and Cowparsley (1985), Fishcakes at the Ritz (1989); *Recreations* travel, philosophy, reading; *Style*— Ms Judy Cornwell, JP; c/o Ken McReddie Ltd, 91 Regent St, London W1R 7TB (☎ 071 439 1456)

CORNWELL, Rupert Howard; s of Ronald Cornwell (d 1975), of Maidenhead, and Jean Margaret Cornwell; *b* 22 Feb 1946; *Educ* Winchester, Magdalen Coll Oxford (BA); *m* 1, April 1972, Angela Doria; 1 s (Simon b Oct 1974); m 2, March 1988, Susan Jean, da of Samuel Smith, of Edwardsville, Illinois; *Career* journalist; Reuters: joined 1968, London 1968, Paris 1969, Brussels 1969-70, Paris 1970-72; Financial Times: joined 1972, Foreign Desk 1972, Paris Bureau 1973-76, lobby corr Westminster 1976-78, Rome corr 1978-83, Bonn corr 1983-86; The Independent: joined 1986, Moscow corr 1987-91, Washington corr 1991-; Foreign Correspondent of the Year (Granada) 1988 and 1989, David Holden prize 1989; *Books* God's Banker, The Life of Roberto Calvi (1983); *Recreations* foreign languages, cricket, travel; *Style*— Rupert Cornwell, Esq; The Independent, 40 City Road, London EC1Y 2DB (☎ 071 253 1222)

CORNWELL, (Stanley) Vyvyan Parry; MC (1946); s of Stanley William Cornwell (d 1958), and Catherine Nellie Dora, *née* Parry (descended from Harry Court, sometime High Sheriff of Worcs and cdr of Royalist Forces 1640s and 1650s); *b* 13 Oct 1914; *Educ* Clifton, Univ of Oxford (MA); *m* 12 Dec 1942, Doreen Mabel, da of Andrew Grieve (d 1970); 3 da (Joanne b 1944, Carolyn b 1947, Felicity b 1952); *Career* WWII Lt-Col RA NW Europe 1939-45; formerly ptnr Coopers Lybrand; dir: Bristol Utd Press 1961-, Bristol Evening Post 1978-; occasional broadcaster on agric accounting topics; former pres Bristol C of C and Indust; *Books* Management Accounting for Agriculture; *Recreations* walking, bridge; *Style*— Vyvyan Cornwell, Esq, MC; 9 Marklands, Julian Rd, Sneyd Park, Bristol (☎ 0272 687 248)

CORRALL, Dr Roger James Martin; s of Alfred James Corrall (d 1985), of Sutton Coldfield, and Amy Adeline, *née* Martin; *b* 4 Aug 1944; *Educ* Univ of Edinburgh (BSc, MB ChB, MD); *m* 19 Feb 1972, Rhona Lockyer, da of Maxwell Cameron McIntosh; 1 s (Euan James b 4 April 1974), 1 da (Fiona Helen b 1 Jan 1976); *Career* registrar gen med diabetes and metabolic disorders Royal Infirmary Edinburgh 1970-71, clinical res fell endocrinology Case Western Reserve Univ Cleveland Ohio 1971-73, sr registrar Edinburgh Northern Gp of Hosps 1975, hon clinical tutor dept med Univ of Edinburgh 1975, conslt physician specialising in diabetes and endocrinology Bristol Royal Infirmary 1979-; author of in excess of 140 scientific pubns on diabetes, clinical endocrinology and hypoglycaemia; memb: Br Diabetic Assoc, Autonomic Research Soc, Euro Assoc for the Study of Diabetes, Euro Soc for Clinical Investigation; MRS, memb RSM, MRCP 1970, FRCPE 1984, FRCP 1985; *Recreations* music, theatre, the arts, wine, history, British countryside, dogs; *Style*— Dr Roger Corrall; 64 Pembroke Road, Clifton, Bristol, Avon BS8 3DX; Department of Medicine, Bristol Royal Infirmary, Bristol BS2 8HW (☎ 0272 230000)

CORRAN, Hon Mrs (Miranda Amadea); *née* Chaplin; er da of 3 and last Viscount Chaplin (d 1981), by his 2 w, Hon Rosemary Lyttelton, da of 1 Viscount Chandos; *b* 3 Jan 1956; *m* 1980, Brian Corran; 1 s (Hereward b 1981); *Style*— Hon Mrs Corran; Wadstray House, Blackawton, Totnes, S Devon

CORRE, John Howard Abraham; s of Eric Albert Abraham Corre, of London, and Rosalind Freda, *née* Brookman; *b* 29 Aug 1944; *Educ* Marylebone GS; *m* 25 May 1969, Tabby, da of Maurice Silas, of London; 1 s (David Abraham b 14 Jan 1974), 2 da (Lisa Danielle b 22 June 1970, Joanne Deborah b 14 Feb 1972); *Career* ptnr Auerbach Hope CA 1971-; non exec dir: Intereuropean Property Hldgs Ltd 1976-79, Frank Usher Hldgs plc 1986-; memb Rhodes Boyson Parly Club, govr JFS Sch; FCA; *Recreations* soccer, tennis, theatre, jogging; *Style*— John Corre, Esq; Auerbach Hope, 58-60 Berners St, London WIP 4JS (☎ 071 637 4121, fax 071 636 5330, telex AUERBA 25894, car 0836 597 242)

CORRIE, John Alexander; s of John Corrie (d 1965), of Kirkcudbright, and Helen Brown; *b* 29 July 1935; *Educ* Kirkcudbright Acad, George Watson's Coll, Lincoln Agric Coll NZ; *m* 1965, (Jean) Sandra Hardie; 1 s, 2 da; *Career* farmer Scotland (also NZ), national sheepshearing champion 1959; lectr: Br Wool Mktg Bd 1967-74, Agric Trg Bd 1969-74; Parly candidate (Cons): N Lanark 1964, Central Ayr 1966; MP (Cons): Bute and N Ayr 1974-83, Cunninghame North 1983-87; oppn whip 1975-76 (resigned over devolution), PPS to George Younger as Sec of State for Scotland 1979-81, sec All-Pty Br-Turkish Ctee 1979-87, memb Select Ctee Scottish Affrs 1981-83, chm Scottish Cons Backbench Ctee 1981-83, ldr Cons Gp on Scottish Affrs 1982-87, sec Cons Backbench Fish-farming Ctee 1982-87, sec Cons Backbench Forestry Ctee 1982-85; MEP 1975-76 and 1977-79; memb: Cncl of Europe and W Euro Union 1983-87, Cncl Nat Cattle Breeders Assoc, Central Tport Consultative Ctee (London) 1989-; chm Tport Users Consultative Ctee (Scotland) 1989-; Wilberforce award for humane work on abortion reform 1981; *Books* Forestry in Europe, The Importance of Forestry in the World Economy, Fish Farming in Europe; *Recreations* shooting, fishing, tennis, car racing, hang gliding; *Style*— John Corrie, Esq; Park of Tongland, Kirkcudbright DG6 4NE (☎ 055 722 232)

CORRIGAN, Thomas Stephen; s of Thomas Corrigan, and Renée Victorine, *née* Chaborel; *b* 2 July 1932; *Educ* Beulah Hill; *m* 1963, Sally Margaret, da of George Ernest Everitt (d 1980); 2 da; *Career* CA; chm: Inveresk Gp Ltd 1974-83 (md 1971-83), Havelock Europa plc 1983-89, PO Users' Nat Cncl 1984-, Rex Stewart Group Ltd 1987-90; dir McNicholas Construction (Holdings) Ltd; pres Br Paper and Bd Indust Fedn 1975-77; Master Worshipful Co of: Makers of Playing Cards 1978-79, Stationers and Newspaper Makers 1990-91; *Recreations* golf, tennis, bridge; *Clubs* MCC; *Style*— Thomas Corrigan, Esq; Woodend, The Chase, Kingswood, Surrey KT20 6HZ (☎ 0737 832709); 57 Marsham Court, Marsham St, London SW1P 4JZ

CORRIN, His Hon Deemster; John William; s of Evan Cain Corrin (d 1967), of IOM, and Dorothy Mildred, *née* Teare (d 1990); *b* 6 Jan 1932; *Educ* King William's Coll; *m* 1961, Dorothy Patricia, da of John Stanley Lace (d 1964), of IOM; 1 da (Jane b 1965); *Career* HM first deemster, clerk of the Rolls 1988-, HM attorney gen for IOM 1974-80, HM second deemster 1980-88, dep govr IOM 1988-; *Recreations* music, bridge, gardening; *Clubs* Ellan Vannin (IOM); *Style*— His Hon Deemster Corrin; 28 Devonshire Rd, Douglas, Isle of Man (☎ 0624 621806); Rolls Office, Douglas, Isle of Man (☎ 0624 673358)

CORRY, Cynthia, Lady; Cynthia Marjorie Patricia; da of late Capt Frederick Henry Mahony; *m* 1, Capt David Polson (decd); m 2, 29 Jan 1946, as his 2 w, Sir James Corry, 3 Bt (d 1987); 1 da (Amanda Jane); *Style*— Lady Cynthia Corry; Dunraven, Fauvic, Jersey, CI

CORRY, James Michael; s and h of Lt Cdr Sir William Corry, 4 Bt; *b* 3 Oct 1946; *Educ* Downside; *m* 1973, Sheridan Lorraine, da of Arthur Peter Ashbourne, of Crowland, Peterborough; 3 s (William James Alexander b 1981, Robert Philip John b 1984, Christopher Myles Anthony b 1987); *Career* various appts Shell-Mex and BP 1966-75 and BP 1975-; currently in International Trading Div BP Oil Int (London); *Style*— James Corry, Esq; 24 Ligo Ave, Stoke Mandeville, Aylesbury, Bucks HP22 5TX

CORRY, Viscount; John Armar Galbraith Lowry-Corry; s and h of 8 Earl of Belmore; *b* 2 Nov 1985; *Style*— Viscount Corry

CORRY, (Thornton) Roger; s of Wing Cdr Brian George Corry, OBE, DFC, AE (d 1973), of Ardvara, Cultra, Holywood, Co Down, and Nora St Clair, *née* Boyd (d 1988); *b* 22 Feb 1943; *Educ* Campbell Coll Belfast; *m* 24 March 1972, Carol Elizabeth, da of Howard Kent Finlay (d 1973), of Church Rd, Helen's Bay, Co Down; 2 s (Simon b 16 Feb 1973, James b 28 Jan 1976), 1 da (Victoria b 26 May 1980); *Career* chm: James P Corry & Co Ltd 1985- (dir 1974-), James P Corry Holdings Ltd 1985-; memb: Dept of Manpower Servs Mgmnt Advsy Ctee 1975-78, Belfast Harbour Cmmn 1985-, Bd Business in the Community; FBIM, FInstD; *Recreations* flying, tennis, squash, golf, boating, vintage cars; *Clubs* Royal Belfast Golf, MG Car, Ulster Vintage Car, Royal North of Ireland Yacht, Ulster Flying, Ulster Reform; *Style*— T Roger Corry, Esq; Ardvara, Cultra, Holywood, Co Down BT18 0AX (☎ 023 17 2020); Springfield Rd, Belfast BT12 7EH (☎ 0232 243 661, fax 0232 232 123)

CORRY, Lt Cdr Sir William James; 4 Bt (UK 1885), of Dunraven, Co Antrim; s (by 1 m) of Sir James Corry, 3 Bt (d 1987); *b* 1 Aug 1924; *m* 8 Dec 1945, Diana Pamela Mary, da of Lt-Col James Burne Lapsley, MC, IMS; 4 s, 2 da; *Heir* s, James Michael Corry b 1946; *Career* Lt Cdr RN (ret); *Style*— Lt Cdr Sir William Corry, Bt; East Hillerton House, Hillerton Cross, Bow, Crediton, Devon EX17 5AD (☎ 03633 82407)

CORSAR, Col Charles Herbert Kenneth; LVO (1989), OBE (1981), TD 1960, DL (Midlothian 1975); s of Capt Kenneth Charles Corsar (d 1967), of Midlothian, and Winifred Paton, *née* Herdman (d 1989); *b* 13 May 1926; *Educ* Merchiston Castle Sch, King's Coll Cambridge (MA); *m* 25 April 1953, Mary Drummond Buchanan-Smith, da of Rt Hon Lord Balerno of Currie (see Peerage and Baronetage); 2 s (George b 1954, David b 1957), 3 da (Kathleen b 1960 d 1960, Katharine b 1961, Mary b 1965); *Career* TA Col 1972-75, Hon ADC to HM The Queen 1977-81, Hon Col 1/52 Lowland Volunteers 1975-87, chm Lowland TA & VRA 1984-87; DL Midlothian 1975, cncllr for Midlothian 1958-67, JP 1965, zone cmmr Home Def E Scotland 1972-75, pres Edinburgh Bn Boys' Bde 1969-87 (vice-pres UK 1970), chm Scottish Standing Conf of Voluntary Youth Orgns 1973-78, memb Scottish Sports Cncl 1972-75, chm Earl Haig Fund Scotland 1984-90; govr: Merchiston Castle Sch 1975-89, Clifton Hall Sch 1965; sec Royal Jubilee and Prince's Tsts (Lothians and Borders) 1977; sec for Scot Duke of Edinburgh's Award 1966-87; *Recreations* shooting, gardening, beekeeping; *Clubs* New (Edinburgh); *Style*— Col Charles H K Corsar, LVO, OBE, TD, DL; Burg, Torloisk, Ulva Ferry, Isle of Mull (☎ 068 85 289); 11 Ainslie Place, Edinburgh EN3 6AS (☎ 031 225 6318)

CORSAR, Hon Mrs (Mary Drummond); *née* Buchanan-Smith; o da of Brig Baron Balerno, CBE, TD (Life Peer, d 1984), and Mary Kathleen, *née* Smith, of Pittodrie (d 1947); *b* 8 July 1927; *Educ* Westbourne, St Denis, Univ of Edinburgh (MA); *m* 25 April 1953, Col Charles Herbert Kenneth Corsar, LVO, OBE, TD, JP, DL, The Royal Scots, s of Kenneth Charles Corsar (d 1967), of Cairniehill; 2 s (George b 1954, David b 1957), 2 da (Katharine b 1961, Mary b 1965), and 1 da d in infancy (1960); *Career* dep chief cmmr Girl Guides Scotland 1972-77, chm WRVS Scotland 1982-88, chm WRVS 1988- (vice chm 1984-88); govr Fettes Coll 1982-, hon pres Scottish Women's Amateur Athletic Assoc 1973-, memb Visiting Ctee Glenochil Young Offenders Inst 1972-; memb: Convocation Heriot Watt Univ 1986-, Parole Bd for Scotland 1982-89; *Recreations* hill walking, embroidery, the family; *Clubs* New (Edinburgh), Lansdowne, Scottish Ladies Climbing; *Style*— The Hon Mrs Corsar; Burg, Torloisk, Ulva Ferry, Isle of Mull (☎ 068 85 289)

CORSIE, Richard; s of Ronnie Corsie, of 7 Marionville, Medway, Edinburgh, and Joyce, *née* Brown; *b* 27 Nov 1966; *m* 24 June 1988, Suzanne Joyce, da of William Gillies Scott; *Career* bowls player; Scot indoor caps 1984-89, bronze medal Cwlth Games Edinburgh 1986, Hong Kong singles and pairs champion 1987, 1988, Br Is singles champion 1988, Austn World Classic pairs champion 1988, World indoor bowls champion 1989; *Style*— Richard Corsie, Esq; 14 Waverley Park, Edinburgh EH8

CORTAZZI, Sir (Henry Arthur) Hugh; GCMG (1984, KCMG 1980, CMG 1969); s of Frederick Edward Mervyn Cortazzi (d 1966), of Sedbergh, Yorks, and Madge, *née* Miller (d 1945); *b* 2 May 1924; *Educ* Sedbergh, Univ of St Andrews, Univ of London; *m* 3 April 1956, Elizabeth Esther, da of George Henry Simon Montagu (d 1976), of London; 1 s (William b 1961), 2 da (Rosemary b 1964, Charlotte b 1967); *Career* served RAF 1943-47; joined FO 1949, former cnsllr (Commercial) Tokyo, RCDS 1971-72, min (Commercial) Washington 1972-75, dep under sec of state FCO 1975-80, ambass to Japan 1980-84; dir: Hill Samuel Bank Ltd 1984-, F & C Pacific Investment Trust 1984-, G T Japan Investment Trust 1984-, Thornton Pacific Investment Trust SA 1986-; memb ESRC 1984-90, pres Asiatic Soc of Japan 1982 and 1983, chm Cncl Japan Soc London 1985-, memb Ct Univ of Sussex 1985-; Hon DUniv Stirling 1988, hon fell Robinson Coll Cambridge 1988; *Books* translations from Japanese: Genji Keita: The Ogre and other stories of Japanese Salarymen (1972), The Guardian God of Golf and other humorous stories (1972), both reprinted as The Lucky One (1980); edited: Mary Crawford Fraser: A Diplomat's Wife in Japan; Sketches at the turn of the Century (1982), Isles of Gold: Antique maps of Japan (1983), Higashi no Shimaguni, Nishi no Shimaguni (1984), Zoku Higashi no Shimaguni Nishi no Shimaguni (collections of articles and speeches in Japanese, 1987), Thoughts from a Sussex Garden (1984), Second Thoughts (1985), Japanese Encounter (1987, essays for Japanese students of English), Dr Willis in Japan: British medical pioneer 1862-1877 (1985), Japanese translation: Aru Eijin Ishi no Bakumatsu Ishin (1986), Mitford's Japan: The Memoirs and Recollections of the First Lord Redesdale (ed); Japanese translation: Aru Eikoku Gaikokan no Meiji Ishin (1985), Victorians in Japan: In and around the Treaty Ports

(1987), Ishin No Minato No Eijintachi; ed with George Webb: Kipling's Japan (1988), The Japanese Achievement (1990); author of articles on Japanese themes in English and Japanese publications; *Recreations* music, opera, gardening; *Clubs* RAF; *Style*— Sir Hugh Cortazzi, GCMG; c/o Hill Samuel Bank Ltd, 100 Wood St, London EC2P 2AJ (☎ 071 628 8011, fax 071 726 4671, telex 888822)

CORVEDALE, Viscount; Benedict Alexander Stanley Baldwin; eldest s and h of 4 Earl Baldwin of Bewdley; *b* 28 Dec 1973; *Educ* Bryanston; *Style*— Viscount Corvedale; Manor Farm House, Godstow Road, Upper Wolvercote, Oxon OX2 8AJ (☎ 0865 52683)

CORY, Charles Raymond; CBE (1982); s of Charles Kingsley Cory (d 1967), and Ethel Muriel, *née* Cottam (d 1975); *b* 20 Oct 1922; *Educ* Harrow, ChCh Oxford; *m* 1, 19 Oct 1946, Vivienne Mary (d 1988), da of Maj John Fenn Roberts, MC (d 1971), of Kelowna, BC; 3 da (Elizabeth b 1948, Rosemary b 1950, Charlotte b 1953); m 2, 2 Sept 1989, Mrs Betty Horley; *Career* served WWII Lt RNVR N Atlantic, Channel, N Sea, C-in-C's commendation 1944; chm: John Cory and Sons Ltd 1965-, Mountstuart Dry Docks 1962-66, vice chm: Br Tport Docks Bd 1970-80 (memb 1966), AB Electrical Products GR Ltd 1978-; chm: S Glamorgan Health Authy 1974-84, Milford Haven Conservancy Bd 1982-; memb Mgmnt Ctee RNLI 1954- (vice pres 1969, dep chm 1985-), Church in Wales: chm Fin Ctee 1975-88, dep chm Rep Body 1985 (hon treas 1988); chm: Welsh Cncl Mission to Seamen 1984-, Cncl Univ of Wales Coll of Med 1988-; *Recreations* skiing, countryside; *Clubs* Cardiff and County; *Style*— Raymond Cory, Esq, CBE; The Coach House, Llanblethian, Cowbridge, South Glamorgan, (☎ 044 677 2251; The Ridge, Wotton-Under-Edge, Glos; office: Mount Stuart House, Cardiff (☎ 0222 488321, telex 498350)

CORY, Sir Clinton James Donald; 4 Bt (UK 1919), of Coryton, Whitchurch, Glamorgan; 2 s of Sir Donald Cory, 2 Bt (d 1935); suc bro 1941; *b* 1 March 1909; *Educ* Brighton Coll and abroad; *m* 14 Sept 1935, Mary, da of Arthur Douglas Hunt, MD, ChB; 1 s; *Heir* s, Clinton Charles Donald Cory; *Career* Sqdn Ldr RAFVR; *Style*— Sir Clinton Cory, Bt; 18 Cloisters Rd, Letchworth Garden City, Herts (☎ 0462 677 206)

CORY, (Clinton Charles) Donald; s and h of Sir Clinton Cory, 4 Bt; *b* 13 Sept 1937; *Educ* Brighton Coll and abroad; *Recreations* collecting Greek and Roman antiquities, student of classical studies; *Style*— Donald Cory, Esq; (☎ 0462 677 206)

CORY, Harold Frederick Wensley; JP; s of Herbert Cory (d 1946), of Little Missenden, Bucks, and Edith Mercy, *née* Wensley (d 1978); *b* 18 April 1927; *Educ* The Grocer's Sch London, Goldsmith's Coll London; *m* 1, 1951 (m dis 1976), Yvonne Margaret, *née* Hales; 2 s (Hugh b 29 Oct 1954, Matthew b 24 July 1957), 2 da (Catherine (Mrs Henderson) b 19 April 1952, Emma (Mrs Robinson) b 19 Aug 1953); m 2, 23 March 1976, Olga Mavis Brocklehurst, *née* Wain; *Career* instr Educn Corps 1945-48; trainee sub ed Reuters News Agency Fleet St 1944-45, mangr Putmans book publishers 1949-53, chm and md Santype Ltd 1953-61, chm Cory Adams MacKay Ltd 1963-67, sole proprietor W Wilts Trading Estate 1963-; magistrate 1970- (currently dep chm Salisbury Bench); chm: Community Cncl for Wilts 1973-77, W Wilts Enterprise Agency 1986-, Salisbury Museum Costume Gallery Appeal (tstee coordinator 1989-90), Cncl and chm of tstees Salisbury and S Wilts Museum 1973-77 (chm of mgmnt 1963-67, vice pres and tstee); past vice chm and franchise winner IBA Local Radio Station Swindon and W Wilts (now GWR), co-ordinator of the five Parlimentary Assocs in Wilts in the Lib interest 1975-85; regnl dir Govt Agency Co-SIRA Wilts, Dorset and Avon prior to merger with Devpt Cmmn (now Rural Devpt Cmmn); memb: Cncl Wilts Folk Life Soc (fndr chm), Wilts Archaeological and Natural History Soc, Hants and Wilts Local Valuation Panel; tstee Salisbury Hosps Tst Scanner Appeal; memb: Howard League for Penal Reforms, Nat Cncl CBI, Nat Art Collections Fund (Wilts rep 1977-), Zoological Soc; Friend of Wexford Festival, memb Cncl of Mgmnt and Friend of Salisbury Festival, tstee The Water Meadows Tst Salisbury; name at Lloyds 1977-; Hornby Award 1989; *Recreations* the pictorial arts, music, gardens, cricket; *Style*— Harold Cory, Esq, JP; The North Canonry, The Close, Salisbury, Wiltshire SP1 2EN (☎ 0722 335682); High Street Close Gate, Salisbury, Wilts SP1 2EL (☎ 0722 335908)

CORY, John; JP (Glam 1961), DL (Glam 1968); er s of John Herbert Cory (d 1939), of The Grange, St Brides-super-Ely, S Glam; *b* 30 June 1928; *Educ* Eton, Trinity Coll Cambridge; *m* 1965, Sarah Christine, er da of John Meade, JP, DL, of Maran Hassa, Itton, Gwent; 2 da; *Career* dir John Cory and Sons Ltd, former chm Cardiff RDC; jt MFH Glamorgan 1962-67; High Sheriff Glamorgan 1959-60, vice Lord Lt S Glam 1990-; KStJ; *Clubs* Cardiff and Country; *Style*— John Cory, Esq, JP, DL; The Grange, St Brides-super-Ely, Cardiff (☎ 0446 760211)

CORY-WRIGHT, Elizabeth; OBE, DL (Herts 1982); yr da of James Archibald Morrison, DSO (unc of 1 Baron Margadale) by his 1 w Hon Mary Hill-Trevor (6 da of 1 Baron Trevor); *b* 5 July 1909; *m* 1, 1930 (m dis 1940), Nigel Gunnis, yst s of Francis Gunnis, of Hamsell Manor, Eridge, Sussex; 2 da (Lady Farnham, Gillian); m 2, 1940, as his 2 w, Eric Martin-Smith, sometime MP Grantham; 2 da (Joanna b 1942, Lucinda b 1948); m 3, Michael Cory-Wright, 2 s of Sir Geoffrey Cory-Wright, 3 Bt, by his w Felicity, da of Sir Herbert Beerbohm-Tree, the actor-manager; *Style*— Mrs Michael Cory-Wright, OBE, DL; Codicote Lodge, Hitchin, Herts

CORY-WRIGHT, Francis Newman; s of Ronald Cory-Wright, MC (d 1932), of Wicken Bonhunt, Essex, and Geraldine Mary, *née* Villiers-Stuart (d 1976); *b* 21 July 1925; *Educ* Eton, Merton Coll Oxford (MA); *Career* WWII offr 15/19 Kings Royal Hussars (wounded in action in Germany); memb: Exec Ctee United Dominions Trust Ltd 1959-63, Lloyds 1964-; conslt Gt Bernera Industries Ltd Western Isles Scotland; dir Herts Archaeological Tst, hon sec Luton and Dist Assoc for the Control of Aircraft Noise, memb Herts Co Assoc of Change-Ringers; Queen's Foreign Serv Messenger 1964-82; FZS; *Recreations* shooting, stalking, angling; *Clubs* City Univ; *Style*— Francis Cory-Wright, Esq; Oakridge, Little Gaddesden, Herts (☎ 044284 3485); 36 Highdown Road, Hove, Sussex

CORY-WRIGHT, Lady Jane Katherine; *née* Douglas; da of 11 Marquess of Queensberry (d 1954), and his 2 w Cathleen Sabine, *née* Mann (d 1959); *b* 18 Dec 1926; *m* 25 Aug 1949 (m dis 1983), David Arthur Cory-Wright, 3 s of Maj Sir Geoffrey Cory-Wright, 3 Bt (d 1969); 3 s; *Style*— Lady Jane Cory-Wright; 11 Stowe Rd, London W12 8BQ

CORY-WRIGHT, Sir Richard Michael; 4 Bt (UK 1903), of Caen Wood Towers, Highgate, St Pancras, Co London and Hornsey, Middx; s of Capt (Anthony John) Julian Cory-Wright (ka 1944), and gs of Capt Sir Geoffrey Cory-Wright, 3 Bt (d 1969); *b* 17 Jan 1944; *Educ* Eton, Birmingham Univ; *m* 1976, Veronica Mary, o da of James Harold Lucas Bolton; 3 s; *Heir* s, Roland Anthony Cory-Wright b 11 March 1979; *Career* patron of one living; *Style*— Sir Richard Cory-Wright, Bt; Cox's Farm, Winterbrook Lane, Wallingford, Oxon OX10 9RE

COSEDGE, Andrew John; s of David Ernest Cosedge, of Bexleyheath, Kent, and Edna Amy Mary, *née* Cull; *b* 13 Jan 1949; *Educ* Christ's Hosp, Univ of Exeter (LLB); *m* 14 June 1986, Denise Hazel, da of Anthony Raymond Teasdale, of Sutton Coldfield; 1 da (Elizabeth Alexandra b 4 May 1989); *Career* called to the Bar Inner Temple 1972; chm Old Blues RFC; *Recreations* rugby; *Clubs* Old Blues RFC; *Style*— Andrew Cosedge, Esq; 17 Sevenoaks Rd, Borough Green, Kent TN15 8AX (☎ 0732 884456); 3 Stone Buildings, Lincoln's Inn, London WC2A 3XL (☎ 071 242 4937, fax 071 405 3896)

COSGRAVE, Lady Louisa; er da of 6 Earl Cathcart, CB, DSO, MC, *qv*; *b* 27 April 1948; *m* 1975, Norman Kirkpatrick Cosgrave; *Style*— Lady Louisa Cosgrave; Totterdown Lodge, Inkpen, nr Hungerford, Berks

COSGRAVE, Dr Patrick John Francis; s of Patrick John Cosgrave (d 1952), of Dublin, and Margaret Anne, *née* Fitzgerald (d 1977); *b* 28 Sept 1941; *Educ* St Vincent's Sch Dublin, Univ Coll Dublin (BA, MA), Peterhouse Cambridge (PhD); *m* 1, 1965 (m dis), Ruth, da of Prof Robin Dudley Edwards (d 1988), of Dublin; m 2 (m dis 1980), Norma Alicia Green, da of Douglas Cooper; m 3, Shirley, da of Gp Capt Ralph Ward; 1 da (Rebecca Jane b 10 Oct 1974); *Career* media writer; fndr and first ed London Office RTE 1968-69, desk offr CRD Home Office affrs 1969-71, political and dep ed Spectator 1971-75 (leader and feature writer 1975-79), features ed Telegraph Magazine 1974-76 , special advsr to Rt Hon Margaret Thatcher 1975-79, managing ed Quartet Crime 1979-81, freelance writer and journalist 1982-; presenter: What the Papers Say (Channel 4), The Week In Westminster (Radio 4); Sacks lectr Oxford Centre for Postgraduate Hebrew Studies; memb: Cons Pty, Bruges Gp, Friends of the Union, TE Lawrence Soc; *Books* The Public Poetry of Robert Lowell (1969), Churchill at War (1975), Cheyney's Law (1976), Margaret Thatcher: A Tory and her Party (1978, updated and reprinted as Margaret Thatcher: Prime Minister, 1979), The Three Colonels (1979), RA Butler: An English Life (1981), Adventure of State (1984), Thatcher: The First Term (1985), Carrington: A Life and a Policy (1985), The Lives of Enoch Powell (1989); contrib: The Spectator, The Times, Daily Telegraph, The Independent, Sunday Telegraph, Telegraph Magazine, Daily Express, Wall Street Journal, Literary Review, American Spectator, Encounter, National Review, New Law Journal, Le Point; *Recreations* dogs, cricket, roses, thrillers; *Style*— Dr Patrick Cosgrave; 21 Thornton Rd, London SW12 0JX (☎ 081 671 0637)

COSH, (Ethel Eleanor) Mary; da of Arthur Lionel Strode Cosh (d 1952), of Bristol, and Ellen, *née* Janisch (d 1931); *Educ* Clifton HS Bristol, St Anne's Coll Oxford (BA, MA); *Career* freelance writer, historian, architectural historian and lectr; contrib to: The Times, TLS, Glasgow Herald, Country Life, Spectator; memb all Nat Conservation Orgns, former ctee memb Soc of Architectural Historians of GB, vice chm Islington Soc, ctee memb and former chm Islington Archaeology and History Soc; FSA 1987; *Books* The Real World (1961), Inveraray and the Dukes of Argyll (with late Ian Lindsay, 1973, paperback edn, 1988), A Historical Walk through Clerkenwell (2 edn, 1987), With Gurdjieff in St Petersburg and Paris (with late Anna Butkovsky, 1980), A Historical Walk through Barnsbury (1981), The New River (2 edn, 1988), The Squares of Islington (1990); *Recreations* opera, reading, historical research; *Style*— Ms Mary Cosh, FSA; 10 Albion Mews, London N1 1JX (☎ 071 607 9305)

COSH, Nicholas John; s of John Henry Cosh; *b* 6 Aug 1946; *Educ* Dulwich Coll, Queens' Coll Cambridge; *m* 1973, Anne Rosemary, da of Lewis Nickolls, CBE (d 1970); 2 s; *Career* professional cricketer Surrey CCC 1968-70, CA, merchant banker, dir Charterhouse Japhet Ltd 1978 (joined 1972); FCA; *Recreations* cricket (blue 1966-68), golf, bridge, opera, rugby (blue 1966); *Clubs* MCC (ctee memb), Hawks; *Style*— Nicholas Cosh, Esq; 1 Paternoster Row, St Paul's, London EC4 (☎ 071 248 3999)

COSSENS, Richard John; s of Col John Bisp Cossens, MBE (d 1975), and Margaret, *née* Hunt (d 1989); *b* 15 Oct 1938; *Educ* Taunton Sch, RAF Coll Cranwell; *m* 23 May 1964, Geraldine Ann, da of Bryan Lewis (d 1969); 1 s (Benjamin Mathew John), 1 da (Philippa Sarah Jean); *Career* md Forenede Papir (UK) Ltd 1971-90 (merged with Papyrus Ltd 1990), md Papyrus Ltd 1990-; Freeman City of London, Liveryman Worshipful Co of Stationers and Newspapermakers; *Recreations* golf, cricket, claret; *Clubs* MCC, Royal Ashdown Forest GC; *Style*— Richard Cossens, Esq; The Old House, Funnells Farm, Nutley, Sussex (☎ 082 571 2509); Papyrus Ltd, Elm Park Court, Brighton Road, Crawley RH11 9BP (☎ 0293 616565, fax 0293 616088, telex 87216 PAPUK G, car 0860 611935)

COSSEY, Errol Paul; s of Frederick John Cossey, and Patricia Alexander, *née* McCormack; *b* 18 May 1943; *Educ* Wentworth HS; *m* 10 Sept 1966, Sandra Marjorie Rose, da of Leonard William Francis Tatton-Bennett; 1 s (Adam b 6 July 1972), 1 da (Fiona b 4 Sept 1974); *Career* commercial dir Dan Air Services 1973-78, founding dir and md Air Europe Ltd 1979-85, founding dir and chief exec Air 2000 Ltd 1986-, chm Aerospace Management 1985-; *Style*— Errol Paul Cossey, Esq; Oakdale, Broadfield Park, Crawley, W Sussex (☎ 0293 518 966, fax 0293 22927)

COSSHAM, (Christopher) Hugh; CB (1989); s of William Lorimer Cossham (d 1954), of Bristol, and Gwendolin Ebba, *née* Ramsden (d 1972); *b* 12 April 1929; *Educ* Monkton Coombe Sch Bristol; *m* 1 Feb 1958, Joanna, da of Capt Maurice Henry Howard-Smith (d 1967), of Houghton Regis, Beds; 1 s (Nigel b 1962), 1 da (Jenny b 1963); *Career* called to the Bar Gray's Inn 1958, legal asst BOT 1958, sr legal asst dir of Public Prosecutions 1964, sr asst dir of Public Prosecutions (NI) 1972-89; former dep Met Stipendiary Magistrate; *Recreations* cycling, listening to Wagner; *Clubs* Civil Service; *Style*— Hugh Cossham, Esq, CB; Valhalla, 1 The Grange, High St, Portishead, Avon BS20 9QL (☎ 0272 8450237)

COSSINS, John Brown; s of Albert Joseph Cossins, of Fairway, North Rd, Havering-atte-Bower, Romford, Essex, and Elizabeth Henrietta, *née* Brown; *b* 15 Nov 1939; *Educ* Clark's Sch for Boys Ilford Essex, NE London Poly; *m* 9 March 1968, Christine Millicent, da of Henry George Avis, of Romford, Essex; 2 s (Alexander b 1969, Jonathan b 1971); *Career* Thomas Saunders Ptnrship 1962-: assoc 1968-74, ptnr 1974-88, jt managing ptnr 1988-; ARIBA 1966, FCSD 1985; *Recreations* golf, gardening, shooting; *Style*— John B Cossins, Esq; 168 High St, Ingatestone, Essex CM4 9ET (☎ 0277 353263); The Thomas Saunders Partnership, 15 Old Ford Rd, London E2 9PJ (☎ 081 980 4400, fax 081 981 6417, telex 897590)

COSSONS, Neil; OBE (1982); s of Arthur Cossons (d 1963), of Beeston, Notts, and Evelyn Edith, *née* Bettle (d 1986); *b* 15 Jan 1939; *Educ* Henry Mellish GS Nottingham, Univ of Liverpool (BA, MA); *m* 7 Aug 1965, Veronica, da of Henry Edwards (d 1986), of Liverpool; 2 s (Nigel b 1966, Malcolm b 1972), 1 da (Elisabeth b 1967); *Career* dep dir City of Liverpool Museums 1969-71; dir: Ironbridge Gorge Museum Tst 1971-83, Nat Maritime Museum 1983-86, Sci Museum 1986-; pres: Museums Assoc 1981-82, Assoc of Ind Museums 1983-(chm 1977-83); cmmr Historic Bldgs and Monuments Cmmn for England (English Heritage) 1989- (memb Ancient Monuments Advsy Ctee 1984-) memb: BBC Gen Advsy Cncl 1987-90, Design Cncl 1990-; govr: RCA, Imperial Coll of Sci Technol and Med 1989-; tstee: Mary Rose Tst 1983-, Ironbridge Gorge Museum Tst 1987-, HMS Warrior Tst 1988-; Freeman City of London 1983; Hon: DSocSci Univ of Birmingham 1979, DUniv Open Univ 1984, DLitt Univ of Liverpool 1989; hon fell RCA; FSA 1968, FMA 1970, FRSA 1988; *Books* Industrial Archaeology of the Bristol Region (with R A Buchanan, 1968), Industrial Archaeology (1975 and 1987), Ironbridge: Landscape of Industry (with H Sowden, 1977), The Iron Bridge: Symbol of the Industrial Revolution (with B S Trinder, 1979 and 1989); *Clubs* Athenaeum; *Style*— Neil Cossons, Esq, OBE; Church Hill, Ironbridge, Shropshire TF8 7PW (☎ 0952 43270); Science Museum, London SW7 2DD (☎ 071 938 8003, fax 071 938 8002, telex 21200 SCMLIB G)

COSTA SANSEVERINO DI BISIGNANO, Hon Mrs (Julia Collbran); *née* Cokayne; da (by 1 m) of 2 Baron Cullen of Ashbourne, MBE; *b* 1943; *m* 1968 (m dis 1989), Don

Francesco Costa Sanseverino di Bisignano; 2 s (Edoardo b 1969, Alessandro b 1971), 1 da (Sveva); *Style*— The Hon Mrs Costa Sanseverino di Bisignano; 75 Cadogan Gardens, London SW3

COSTALAS, Mohyin; *Career* architectural asst Singapore Associate Architects 1972-76, full and pt/t asst designer Co-Existence London 1977-80; designer: Architects 61 Singapore 1980-82, Interplan Design Association Singapore 1982-83; sr designer DP Architects Singapore 1983-85, assoc and design mangr A + DP PTE Ltd Hong Kong (DP Architects' Hong Kong Office) 1985-86, freelance designer (working on Legal & General Insurance) Arup Associates London 1986, sr designer Wolff Olins/Hamilton London 1986- (projects incl: Horner Collis & Kirvan (advertising agency), Heidrick & Struggles Ltd (head hunters), Herbert Johnson (hatters), Church and General (insurers), The Wellcome Foundation, Allied Irish Bank in Ireland and the UK); *Style*— Ms Mohyin Costalas; Wolff Olins Ltd, 22 Dukes Rd, London WC1

COSTAR, Sir Norman Edgar; KCMG (1963, CMG 1953); *b* 18 May 1909; *Educ* Battersea GS, Jesus Coll Cambridge; *Career* Colonial Office 1932, Dominions Office 1935; UK High Cmmr's Office: Canberra 1937-39, Wellington NZ 1945-47; dep UK high cmmr: Ceylon 1953-57, Australia 1960-62; British high cmmr: Trinidad and Tobago 1962-66, Cyprus 1967-69; Immigration Appeals adjudicator 1970-81; *Clubs* United Oxford and Cambridge; *Style*— Sir Norman Costar, KCMG

COSTELLO, Dr John Francis; *b* 22 Sept 1944; *Educ* Belvedere Coll Dublin, Univ Coll Dublin, Mater Hosp Dublin (MB BCh, BAO, MD); *Career* house physician Mater Hosp Dublin 1969 (house surgn 1968), post registration house physician St Stephen's Hosp 1969-70, sr house offr Royal Northern Hosp 1970-71, sr house offr Royal Post Grad Med Sch Hammersmith Hosp London 1971, registrar Brompton Hosp 1972-74 (sr house offr 1972), lectr Dept of Med Univ of Edinburgh and Royal Infirmary 1974-75, asst prof of med and attending physician and dir Pulmonary Function Laboratory San Francisco Gen Hosp and Univ of Calif 1975-77; Kings Coll Hosp London: conslt physician in gen med with a special interest in respiratory disease 1978-, dir Dept of Thoracic Med 1982-, sr lectr in med Kings Coll Sch of Med and Dentistry 1982-, clinical dir of acute servs (Camberwell Health Authy) 1989-, chm of conslts 1989-; author of numerous papers, reviews and chapters on thoracic med; exec memb Camberwell Health Authy; memb: Ethics Ctee, Jt Res Ctee; FRCP; *Style*— Dr John Costello; 262 Worple Road, Wimbledon, London SW20 8RG (☎ 081 879 1309); Department of Thoracic Medicine, King's College School of Medicine and Dentistry, Denmark Hill, London SE5 8RX (☎ 071 326 3165); Cromwell Hospital, Cromwell Rd, London SW5 0TU (☎ 071 370 4233); Lister Hospital, Chelsea Bridge Rd, London SW1W 8RH (☎ 071 730 3417)

COSTER, Peter Lloyd; JP (Middx 1978-); s of Charles Edward Coster, and Maude, *née* Wearing; *b* 19 Jan 1934; *Educ* East Barnet GS; *m* 8 May 1955, Sylvia Iris, da of Frederick Gordon Hills, of Enfield, Middx; 3 da (Tracey Susan (Mrs Perkins) b 22 July 1957, Sharon Elizabeth (Mrs Crofton-Diggens) b 18 April 1960, Sarah Jane (Mrs Dowling) b 23 July 1963); *Career* Midland Bank 1952, The Scottish Life Assurance Co 1955-89, md C & G Guardian; dir: Cheltenham & Gloucester Building Society 1990-, Guardian Building Society 1983-90, Team Agencies plc 1986-87; Freeman City of London 1982, Liveryman Worshipful Co of Insurers 1983; memb Magistrates Assoc, MInstM 1978; *Recreations* golf, painting, gardening; *Clubs* Caledonian, Wig and Pen; *Style*— Peter L Coster, Esq, JP; Clarendon, 53 Old Park View, Enfield, Middx EN2 7EQ; Coastguard Cottage, Bacton, Norfolk; 120 High Holborn, London WC1V 6RH (☎ 071 242 3142)

COTES, Dr John Everard; s of Everard Charles Cotes (d 1943), of Oxshott, Surrey, and Phoebe Violet, *née* Delaforce; *b* 24 Feb 1924; *Educ* Leighton Park Sch Reading, New Coll Oxford (DM, DSc); *m* 1, 27 Aug 1949, Patricia (d 1975), da of John Beckingham (d 1941), of Salisbury, Rhodesia; 2 s (Peter b 1950, Simon b 1963), 1 da (Lucy b 1954); m 2, 15 July 1978, Dr Sarah Jane Pearce, da of Alexander Pearce, of Saffron Walden, Essex; 1 s (Roger b 1984); *Career* MO RAF Inst of Aviation Med 1950-52; memb scientific staff MRC Pneumoconosis Unit 1952-89, Rockefeller fell John Hopkins Hosp Baltimore 1955-56, hon res fell (formerly reader) dept of occupational health Univ of Newcastle upon Tyne; sec Thoracic Soc 1972-78, vice pres Euro Soc for Clinical Respiratory Physiology 1972-75; Freeman: City of London 1946, Grocer's Co 1946, City of New Orleans 1972; memb RSM, FRCP 1969; *Books* Lung Function Assessment and Application in Medicine (1979), Work Related Lung Disorders (with J Steel, 1987); *Recreations* outdoor pursuits; *Style*— Dr John Cotes; 9 Almoner's Barn, Durham DH1 3TZ; Respiration and Exercise Laboratory, Division of Environmental and Occupational Medicine, Medical School, Framlington Place, Newcastle upon Tyne (☎ 091 222 6000, fax 091 222 6706)

COTES, Peter; s of Walter Arthur Boulting, impressario and entrepreneur (d 1957), and Rose, *née* Bennett (d 1981); *b* 19 March 1912; *Educ* Latymer, privately educated, Italia Conti; *m* 1, 1937, Myfanwy, da of Taliasin Jones; m 2, 19 May 1948, Joan, da of Wallace Miller; *Career* mil serv Queens Westminster, RAF, ENSA, Army Kinematograph Serv, Home Guard; theatrical and film prodr and dir; made theatrical debut in Arms of Vesta Tilley (Portsmouth Hippodrome) and at age of 10 as page to Robert Loraine's Henry V at Theatre Royal Drury Lane (King George's Fund for Actors 1924); West End prodns incl: Pick Up Girl 1946, The Master Builder 1948, Miss Julie 1949, Come Back Little Sheba 1951, The Man 1952, The Father 1952, The Mousetrap 1952, A Pin to See the Peepshow 1953 (Broadway), Happy Holiday 1954, The Cardinal 1957, The Rope Dancers 1959, Hidden Stranger 1962 (Broadway), Paint Myself Black 1965, The Impossible Years 1966, Look, No Hands! 1971; films: The Right Person, Jane Clegg, Waterfront; sr drama dir AR-TV 1955-58, supervising prodr Drama Channel 7 Melbourne 1961, play prodr Anglia TV 1964; TV incl: Woman in a Dressing Gown, The Haven, Look in a Window, What the Public Wants, Candida, The Infinite Shoeblack, Wild Justice, Shadow of the Vine; prodr and writer numerous radio prodns; co dir: Live Theatre, Peter Cotes Productions Ltd, Cotes Logan Productions, Brompton Theatre Co; memb: Medico-Legal Soc, Our Soc, TMA, Equity, ACTT; FRSA, Knight of Mark Twain; *Books* No Star Nonsense (1949), The Little Fellow (1951), George Robey (1972), Circus (1976), The Barbirollis (A Musical Marriage) (1983); contrib to : The Guardian, The Times, The Daily Telegraph, The Independent; *Clubs* Savage; *Style*— Peter Cotes, Esq; 7 Hill Lawn Ct, Chipping Norton, Oxon OX7 5NF (☎ 0608 641208)

COTIER, James Charles; s of James Charles Cotier, of 81 Walsingham Rd, Southend-on-Sea, Essex, and Edna Roberts (d 1984); *b* 8 March 1949; *Educ* Wentworth Secdy Modern, Southend Art Coll; *m* 27 May 1987, Louise Roxane, da of David Hugh Jenkins; 2 da (Francesca Alice b 28 Dec 1987, Isabella Fleur 23 Nov 1990); *Career* apprentice photographer to Terence Donovan 1971-74, advertising photographer with top agencies 1974-; winner of: numerous D & ADA awards, campaign press and poster awards, Creative Circle awards; exhibitor Hamilton's Gallery 1983; *Books* Nudes in Budapest (1991); *Recreations* photography, painting, cooking; *Style*— James Cotier, Esq; James Cotier Ltd, 11 St Lukes Mews, London W11 (☎ 071 229 9833)

COTMAN, (Harold) Peter; s of Dr Harold Herbert Cotman (d 1930), of Chatham, and Mary, *née* Knowles (d 1976); *b* 5 Nov 1929; *Educ* Epsom Coll; *m* 20 Sept 1956 (m dis 1988), Merrill Doris Eleda, da of Charles William Akerman (d 1976); 1 s (John b 1959), 3 da (Rebecca (Mrs Ward)b 1960, Helen b 1962, Hilary b 1965); *Career* slr; Freeman Worshipful Co of Vintners; *Recreations* snorkelling, history, genealogy; *Style*— Peter Cotman, Esq; 3 Bull Farm Mews, Bull Lane, Matlock, Derbyshire DE4 5NB (☎ 0629 55466)

COTON, Tony; s of William Thomas Coton, of Tamworth, Staffs, and Gladys Joan, *née* Hitchcock (d 1982); *b* 19 May 1961; *Educ* Mercian Boys Sch Tamworth; 2 da (Natalie Elizabeth b 1 March 1986, Emily Susan b 7 July 1988); *Career* professional footballer; 95 appearances Birmingham City 1980-84, 300 appearances Watford 1984-90, transferred to Manchester City for a fee of £1m July 1990-; saved a penalty with first touch in league football on debut for Birmingham City; 2 Player of the Year awards Birmingham City, 3 Player of the Year awards Watford, twice voted Best Goalkeeper Div 2; *Style*— Tony Coton, Esq; Manchester City FC, Maine Rd, Moss Side, Manchester (☎ 061 226 1191)

COTRAN, Dr Eugene; s of Michael Cotran (d 1985), Chief Justice Cameroon, and Hassiba, *née* Khouri; *b* 6 Aug 1938; *Educ* Victoria Coll Alexandria Egypt, Univ of Leeds (LLM), Trinity Hall Cambridge (Dip Int Law, LLD); *m* 6 Oct 1963, Christiane, da of Homer Avierino (d 1972); 3 s (Marc b 1964, Patrick b 1966, Paul b 1972), 1 da (Layla b 1980); *Career* called to Bar Lincoln's Inn 1959; lectr SOAS Univ of London 1962-77, judge High Ct Kenya 1977-82, practice in African Cwlth and int law; visiting prof in law (with ref to Africa and ME) and chm Centre for Islamic and ME Law SOAS Univ of London; rec of the Crown Ct, Int Arbitrator; FCIArb; *Books* Re-statement of African Law (Kenya 1963), Case Book on Kenya Customary Laws (1987); *Recreations* racing, swimming, bridge; *Clubs* Garrick; *Style*— Dr Eugene Cotran; 16 Hart Grove, London W5 3NB (☎ 081 992 0432); 2 Paper Buildings, Temple, London EC4Y 7ET (☎ 071 936 2611, fax 071 583 3423)

COTRUBAS, Ileana; da of Vasile Cotrubas, and Maria Cotrubas; *b* 9 June 1939, in Romania; *Educ* Scuola Speciala de Musica, Bucharest Conservatory, Vienna Acad; *m* 1972, Manfred Ramin; *Career* opera singer; debut at Opera Romana as Ynoild 1964; Frankfurt Opera 1967-70; has performed: Salzburg Festival, Glyndebourne Festival, Florence Festival, Royal Opera House Covent Garden, Wiener Staatsoper, La Scala Milan, Metropolitan Opera New York; main repertoire incl; Mimi, Susanna, Pamina, Amina, Norina, Adina, Gilda, Violetta, Micaela, Antonia, Tatyana, Melisande; recordings incl: Bach cantatas, Mozart masses, Brahms requiem, and complete opera performances of Rinaldo, Cosi fan Tutte, Le Nozze di Figaro, Die Zauberflöte, La Traviata, Rigoletto, Carmen, Manon and L'Elisir d'Amore; Austrian Kammersängerin 1981, Great Offr of the Order Sant'Iiago da Espada Portugal 1990; *Style*— Miss Ileana Cotrubas

COTTAM, Graeme Robin; s of Desmond Augustine Herbert Cottam, and Rosella Fothergill, *née* Smith; *b* 6 June 1955; *Educ* Reed's Sch Cobham Surrey, Univ of Bristol (LLB); *Career* called to the Bar Middle Temple 1978, Price Waterhouse 1979-, ptnr E European Servs; assoc ICAEW 1983; *Recreations* theatre, local history, travel; *Style*— Graeme Cottam, Esq; 5 Trinity Church Square, London SE1 4HU (☎ 071 403 4630); No 1 London Bridge, London SE1 9QL (☎ 071 939 3000, fax 071 403 5265, telex 886029)

COTTAM, Harold; s of Rev Canon Frank Cottam (d 1974), and Elizabeth, *née* Wilson (d 1982); *b* 12 Oct 1938; *Educ* Bedford Sch; *m* 1962, Lyn, *née* Minton; 2 da (Hilary Anne b 21 Jan 1965, Rachel Marjorie b 25 May 1966); *Career* head of corp planning SmithKline Beecham UK 1964-66, commercial dir for Spain Simon Engineering Group 1966-68, currently managing ptnr for UK Ernst & Young (ptnr 1968-); FCA (ACA 1960); *Recreations* music, tennis, farming; *Style*— Harold Cottam, Esq; Ernst & Young, 1 Lambeth Palace Rd, London SE1 7EU (☎ 071 931 3002, fax 071 928 1345)

COTTAM, James Barrie; s of James Cottam, of Maryland, 59 The Common, W Wratting, Cambridge, and Agnes, *née* Stokes; *b* 3 June 1947; *Educ* North Kesteven GS, Leicester Poly (Dip); *m* 20 May 1972, Angela Helen, da of Alistair Charles Mirren Scott, of Dunsdale Lodge, Westerham, Kent; 1 da (Sophie Clare Louise b 1980); *Career* ptnr John Leonard Partnership 1974-87, formed James Cottam & Co Ltd 1987; memb: PCC St Mary with St Peter London, Ctee Earls Ct Gardens Residents' Ctee; Freeman City of London, memb Worshipful Co of Farriers 1979; assoc RICS; *Clubs* Carlton; *Style*— James Cottam, Esq; 2 Earls Ct Gdns, London SW5 OTD (☎ 071 373 7530); 38 Thurloe Place, London SW7 2HP (☎ 071 823 9883, car 0860 390634)

COTTAM, Robert Gwynne; s of Maj-Gen The Rev A E Cottam, CB, CBE, MC (d 1964), of Bodiam Rectory, Robertsbridge, Sussex, and Margaret Eileen, *née* Haselden; *b* 5 June 1934; *Educ* Marlborough; *m* 7 Oct 1967, Morella Cumberland, da of Lt-Col Anthony Gerald Bartholmew Walker, of Chattis Hill House, Stoorbridge, Hants; 2 s (Charles b 1969, Henry b 1973), 1 da (Rosemary b 1971); *Career* Nat Serv 2 Lt E Surrey Regt 1953-54; mgmnt trg Watney Combe Reid Brewers 1955-59; with Grieveson Grant & Co Stockbrokers 1959-64; ptnr: W I Carr Sons & Co 1965-82, Grieveson Grant & Co 1982-86; dir Kleinwort Benson Securities 1987-; *Recreations* golf, tennis, opera; *Clubs* MCC, City of London, Gresham; *Style*— Robert Cottam, Esq; 7 Stanford Rd, London W8 5PP; Kleinwort Benson Securities Ltd, 20 Fenchurch St, London EC3P 3DB (☎ 071 937 2308)

COTTEE, David; s of William Victor Cottee, of Essex, and Eileen May, *née* Bray; *b* 9 April 1948; *Educ* Maldon GS, Kingston-upon-Thames Sch of Architecture (DArch, Architect RIBA); *m* 1985, Sylvia Mary, da of Dr Peter Ambrose Walford, of Essex; 1 s (Julian b 1985), 1 step da (Louise b 1976); *Career* architect; fndr ptnr The Architects Group Partnership 1983-; *Recreations* skiing, watersports; *Style*— David Cottee, Esq; 3 Geoffrey Bishop Ave, Fulbourn, Cambridge (☎ 0223 880616); Maris Lane, Trumpington, Cambridge (☎ 0223 843511)

COTTELL, Michael Norman Tizard; OBE (1988); s of Norman James Cottell (d 1973), of Southampton, and Eileen Claire Cottell; *b* 25 July 1931; *Educ* Peter Symonds Sch Winchester, Univ Coll Southampton, Univ of Birmingham; *m* 1 June 1957, Joan Florence, da of Edward Clarence Dolton (d 1973), of Winchester; 2 s (Paul b 24 Feb 1959, Robert b 24 April b 1961); *Career* Nat Serv RE 1951-53, Suez Crisis 1956; highway engr 1948-67: Hants, Glos, Berks, Northants; asst to co surveyor Suffolk CC 1967-73, dep co surveyor E Sussex CC 1973-76; co surveyor: Northants 1976-84, Kent 1984-; FEng 1990, FICE 1958 (MICE), FIHT 1954, MBIM 1971; *Recreations* swimming, sailing, music, travel, theatre; *Clubs* RAC; *Style*— Michael Cottell, Esq, OBE; Kent County Council, Springfield, Maidstone, Kent ME14 2LQ (☎ 0622 671411); Salcey Lawn, Harrow Court, Stockbury, Sittingbourne, Kent ME9 7VQ

COTTENHAM, 8 Earl of (UK 1850); Sir Kenelm Charles Everard Digby Pepys; 11 and 10 Bt (GB 1784 and UK 1801); also Baron Cottenham (UK 1836) and Viscount Crowhurst (UK 1850); s of 7 Earl (d 1968, 2 cous 7 times removed of Samuel Pepys, the diarist); *b* 27 Nov 1948; *Educ* Eton; *m* 1975, Sarah, yr da of Capt Samuel Richard Le Hunte Lombard-Hobson, CVO, OBE, RN; 2 s (Viscount Crowhurst, Hon Sam Richard b 26 April 1986), 1 da (Lady Georgina Marye b 9 Oct 1981); *Heir* s, Mark John Henry, Viscount Crowhurst b 11 Oct 1983; *Style*— The Rt Hon the Earl of Cottenham; Priory Manor, Kington St Michael, Chippenham, Wilts SN14 6JR (☎ 024 975 262)

COTTER, Sir Delaval James Alfred; 6 Bt (I 1763) of Rockforest, Cork, DSO (1944); s of Sir James Cotter, 5 Bt (d 1924); *b* 29 April 1911; *Educ* Malvern, RMC Sandhurst; *m* 1, 29 Sept 1943 (m dis 1949), Roma, o da of Adrian Rome, of

Dalswinton Lodge, Salisbury, S Rhodesia, and wid of Sqdn Ldr Kenneth A Kerr MacEwen; 2 da; m 2, 9 Dec 1952, Eveline Mary (d 1991), eld da of late Evelyn John Mardon, and wid of Lt-Col John Frederick Paterson, OBE; *Heir* n, Patrick Cotter; *Career* late 13/18 Royal Hussars, NW Europe 1944-45; JP Wilts 1962-63; *Clubs* Army and Navy; *Style—* Sir Delaval Cotter, Bt, DSO; Green Lines, Iwerne Courtney, Blandford Forum, Dorset

COTTER, Patrick Laurence Delaval; s of Laurence Stopford Llewelyn Cotter (ka 1943), yr s of 5 Bt, and Grace Mary, *née* Downing; hp of unc, Sir Delaval Cotter, 6 Bt; *b* 21 Nov 1941; *Educ* Blundell's, RAC Cirencester; *m* 1967, Janet, da of George Potter, of Goldthorne, Barnstaple, N Devon; 1 s, 2 da; *Career* antique dealer; *Style—* Patrick Cotter, Esq; Lower Winsham Farm, Knowle, Braunton, Devon

COTTERELL, Christopher Sturge; s of Richard Archbold Cotterell; *b* 1 Oct 1932; *Educ* Beaumont Coll; *m* 1960, Angela Mary, da of late Leslie Cheshire, OBE; 2 s; *Career* 2 Lt King's Shropshire LI Korea, Capt 4 Bn (TA); co dir 1961-82; chm Fibre Bldg Board Fedn 1972-75, jt md Machin and Kingsley Ltd 1979-82, pres Timber Trade Fedn 1981-82, princ Chris Cotterell and Assocs 1982-; appeal dir and charity conslt; *Recreations* cricket, genealogy particularly in NZ, horology; *Style—* Christopher Cotterell, Esq; 166 Cambridge St, London SW1V 4QE (☎ 071 821 7828)

COTTERELL, (Alan) Geoffrey; s of Graham Cotterell (d 1967), and Millicent Louise Crews (d 1982); *b* 24 Nov 1919; *Educ* Bishop's Stortford Coll; *Career* serv WWII RA 1940-46; author; *Books* Then a Soldier (1944), This is the Way (1947), Randle in Springtime (1949), Strait and Narrow (1950), Westward the Sun (1952), The Strange Enchantment (1956), Tea at Shadow Creek (1958), Tiara Tahiti (1960), Go Said the Bird (1966), Bowers of Innocence (1970), Amsterdam the Life of a City (1972); *Recreations* golf; *Clubs* RAC, Cooden Beach Golf; *Style—* Geoffrey Cotterell, Esq; 2 Fulbourne Hse, Blackwater Rd, Eastbourne BN20 7DN (☎ 0323 29477)

COTTERELL, Hon Mrs (Harriet Pauline Sophia); *née* Stonor; yst da of 6 Baron Camoys (d 1976); *b* 6 Jan 1943; *m* 24 July 1965, Jonathan Julian Cotterell, o son of Maj Leonard Evelyn Cotterell; 2 s, 1 da; *Style—* The Hon Mrs Cotterell; Steeple Manor, Steeple, nr Wareham, Dorset

COTTERELL, Henry Richard Geers (Harry); s and h of Sir John Cotterell, 6 Bt; *b* 22 Aug 1961; *m* 5 July 1986, Carolyn Suzanne, elder da of John Moore Beckwith-Smith, of Maybanks Manor, Rudgwick, Sussex; *Career* cmmnd Blues and Royals 1981; *Style—* Harry Cotterell, Esq

COTTERELL, Sir John Henry Geers; 6 Bt (UK 1805) of Garnons, Herefordshire; DL (Hereford and Worcester); s of Lt-Col Sir Richard Cotterell, 5 Bt, CBE (d 1978), and 1 w, Lady Lettice, *née* Lygon (d 1973, da of 7 Earl Beauchamp, KG, KCMG, TD, PC, and Lady Lettice Grosvenor, da of late Earl Grosvenor, s of 1 Duke of Westminster); *b* 8 May 1935; *Educ* Eton, RMC Sandhurst; *m* 7 Oct 1959, Vanda Alexandra Clare, da of Maj Philip Alexander Clement Bridgewater; 3 s, 1 da; *Heir* s, Henry Cotterell, *qv*; *Career* offr Royal Horse Gds 1955-61; chm Hereford and Worcs CC 1977-81; chm: Radio Wyvern, Hereford Mappa Mundi Trust, Rural Voice; memb The Jockey Club; pres Nat Fedn of Young Farmers Clubs; *Style—* Sir John Cotterell, Bt, DL; Garnons, nr Hereford HR4 7JU (☎ 098 122 232)

COTTERELL, Hon Lady (Molly Patricia); *née* Berry; da of late 1 Viscount Camrose; *b* 1915; *m* 1, 19 May 1936, Capt Roger Charles George Chetwode (d 14 Aug 1940), o s of Field Marshal 1 Baron Chetwode, GCB, OM, GCSI, KCMG, DSO; 2 s; m 2, 23 March 1942 (m dis 1948), 1 Baron Sherwood; m 3, 21 July 1958, as his 2 w, Sir Richard Charles Geers Cotterell, 5 Bt, CBE, TD (d 1978); *Style—* The Hon Lady Cotterell; Flat 1, 4 Eaton Place, London SW1

COTTERILL, John Anthony; s of Herbert Cotterill, and Vera Cotterill (d 1985); *b* 22 June 1940; *Educ* Univ of Durham (MB BS, BSc), Univ of Newcastle upon Tyne (MD); *m* 26 Sept 1964, Sarah Cotterill; 3 da (Susan b 1964, Judith b 1967, Lindsay Claire b 1969); *Career* conslt dermatologist Leeds Gen Infirmary; *Books* The Acnes (with WJ Cunliffe, 1972); *Recreations* golf; *Style—* John Cotterill, Esq; 56 Broomfield, Adel, Leeds 16; Dermatology Dept, Leeds General Infirmary, Great George St, Leeds, W Yorks LS1 3EX (☎ 0532 432799)

COTTERILL, Stephen John (Steve); s of Patricia Ann Cotterill, *née* Thornley; *b* 20 July 1964; *Educ* Arle Comp Sch Cheltenham; *m* 30 July 1988, Teresa Jane, da of Anthony Victor Irwin; 1 da (Rebecca Joanne b 28 July 1990); *Career* professional footballer 1989-; amateur: Cheltenham Town 1980-87, Alvechurch 1987, transferred for a fee of £4,000 to Burton Albion 1987-89; Wimbledon: joined for a fee of £120,000 1989-, 9 appearances, 3 goals; formerly worked: Post Office Cheltenham, Sharpe & Fisher Building Supplies; *Recreations* all sporting activities; *Style—* Steve Cotterill, Esq; Wimbledon FC, 49 Durnsford Rd, Wimbledon, London SW19 (☎ 081 946 6311)

COTTESLOE, 4 Baron (UK 1874); Sir John Walgrave Halford Fremantle; 4 Bt (UK 1821), GBE (1960), TD; Baron of the Austrian Empire (1816); s of 3 Baron Cottesloe, CB, VD, TD (d 1956), and Florence (d 1956), da of Thomas Tapling; *b* 2 March 1900; *Educ* Eton, Trinity Coll Cambridge; *m* 1, 16 Feb 1926 (m dis 1945), Lady Elizabeth Harris, da of 5 Earl of Malmesbury, and Hon Dorothy, CBE, da of 6 Baron Calthorpe; 1 s, 1 da; m 2, 26 March 1959, Gloria Jean Irene Dunn, da of W E Hill, of Barnstaple, N Devon; 1 s, 2 da; *Heir* s, Cdr the Hon John Fremantle (RN ret), *qv*; *Career* sits as Conservative in House of Lords; former chm: Br Postgrad Med Fedn, Royal Postgrad Med Sch, Hammersmith Hosp; chm: NW Met Regnl Hosp Bd 1953-60, Tate Gallery 1959-60, South Bank Theatre Bd 1962-77, Arts Cncl 1960-65, Heritage in Danger 1973-; former vice-chm Port of London Authy; chm Thomas Tapling and Co Ltd; former chm The Dogs' Home Battersea 1970-82; dep pres Nat Rifle Assoc (and former chm); pres The Royal Russell Sch, former pres Leander Club, govr King Edward VII's Hosp Fund 1973-83; former hon sec Amateur Rowing Assoc, steward Henley Royal Regatta; former memb: Hampstead Borough Cncl, London Co Cncl; former DL Co London; fell Royal Postgrad Med Sch, hon fell Westfield Coll London Univ; *Recreations* rowed in winning Cambridge crew 1921 and 1922 Boat Races; several times Match Rifle Champion at Bisley and memb English Eight in long range match for Elcho Shield on 54 occasions; *Clubs* Travellers'; *Style—* The Rt Hon the Lord Cottesloe, GBE, TD

COTTIER, Timothy Robin; s of Maj Gordon Cottier, of Conway, Wales, and Alice, *née* Moffat (d 1989); *b* 27 Dec 1953; *Educ* Merchant Taylors Sch; *m* 1980, Helen Adele, da of late Douglas Constantine, of St Clements, Jersey; 2 da (Sophia b 1983, Claudia b 1985); *Career* CA 1977; Price Waterhouse and Co Bahamas 1978-80, estab Corporate Finance Leeds Trust plc and others 1981-; chm: Lakeview Bank of the Bahamas 1979-82, Rini Tea Co plc 1980-90, Leeds Trust plc 1982- (chief exec), Nuwara Eliya Tea Plantations plc 1982-, Sunwest Airlines Inc 1982-89, Swan Valley Minerals Pty 1983-, Transmeridian Offshore Oil plc 1984-, Amanda Hall Fashions Ltd 1984-, Highlands Rubber and Coffee Ltd 1984-, Charles Graham Textiles Ltd 1984-, Western Reef Gold Mining Pty 1985-, Antonia and Charlotte Interior Designs plc 1985-, Larchfield Corpn Plc, Larchfield Racing Syndicate Ltd, Yacht Holidays plc, Audiotext plc 1987-89, Olicana Securities plc, Leeds Securities Ltd, Westpennant Ltd 1989-, Portland Exec Recruitment Ltd 1989-; FCA 1982; *Recreations* shooting, sailing, gardening, golf, tennis, travel; *Clubs* Leeds, RAC, Public Schs, Nassau Yacht, Cayman Yacht, Golf Del Sur Golf, Loftus Hill Golf; *Style—* Timothy Cottier, Esq; Larchfield, Harrogate, N Yorks HG1 2NH (☎ 0423 524655); 29 Sunningdale Village, Golf Del Sur, Tenerife, Canary Islands; Leeds Trust plc (☎ 0532 442060, fax 0532 440506)

COTTINGHAM, Barrie; s of John Cottingham, of Sheffield, and Eleanor, *née* Price; *b* 5 Oct 1933; *Educ* Carfield Sch Sheffield; *m* 5 Oct 1957, Kathleen, da of John Ernest Morton (d 1945), of Sheffield; 1 s (Nigel David b 13 Dec 1964), 1 da (Michelle Jayne b 5 Aug 1962); *Career* RAF 1955-57, cmmnd PO 1956; Coopers & Lybrand (became Coopers & Lybrand Deloitte 1990): ptnr 1964, memb UK Bd, exec ptnr i/c of the regions; pres Sheffield and Dist Soc of CAs 1964, memb Liaison Ctee on Mgmnt and Econ Studies Univ of Sheffield, hon auditor Sheffield C of C; FCA 1955, ATII 1965; *Recreations* squash, golf, watching rugby and cricket, oil painting, opera; *Clubs* Naval and Military, Sheffield; *Style—* Barrie Cottingham, Esq; Coopers & Lybrand Deloitte, Albion Ct, 5 Albion Place, Leeds LS1 6JP (☎ 0532 431343, fax GPS 2/3 Auto 0532 424009, telex 5562 Answerback 556230 COLYLD G)

COTTLE, Gerry; s of Reginald Brookes Cottle (d 1975), of Highbury, London, and Joan Miriam, *née* Ward, of Streatham, London; *b* 7 April 1945; *Educ* Rutlish Sch Wimbledon; *m* 7 Dec 1968, Betty, da of James Fossett (d 1972), of Henley-in-Arden; 1 s (Gerry b 1981), 3 da (Sarah b 1970, April b 1973, Juliette b 1976); *Career* ran away from school and joined a small circus becoming juggler and equestrian 1961, formed Gerry Cottle's Circus 1974, flew complete circus to Oman for Sultan's birthday 1976; subsequent overseas tours 1981-84: Bahrain, Iran, Shajah, Iceland, Hong Kong, Macau, Singapore, Malaysia; currently world's most travelled circus touring two units 46 weeks a year (one currently undertaking first tour of Europe by a British circus), presents London's Christmans Circus each year at Wembley; memb: Variety Club of GB, Circus Proprietors' Assoc 1973-; *Recreations* horse riding, collecting show business memorabilia; *Style—* Gerry Cottle, Esq; Woburn Park Farm, Addlestone Moor, Weybridge, Surrey KT15 2QE (☎ 0932 857 779); Gerry Cottle's Circus Ltd, Addlestone Moor, Weybridge, Surrey KT15 2QE (☎ 0932 857 779, fax 0932 859 902, car 0836 691 111)

COTTON, Dr Bernard Edward; CBE (1976); s of Hugh Harry Cotton (d 1963), and Alice Cotton; *b* 8 Oct 1920; *Educ* Sheffield City GS, Univ of Sheffield; *m* 1944, Stephanie Anne, da of Rev Arthur Evelyn Furnival (d 1960); 3 s; *Career* served WWII, Lt Worcs Yeo 6 Airborne Div France and Normandy, Ardennes Rhine Airborne Landing; pres Samuel Osborn and Co Ltd 1978-79 (chm and chief exec 1969-78), dir Renold plc 1979-84; dep chm: Baker Perkins plc 1982-86, John Mountford Co Ltd Manchester 1984-87; chm Yorks and Humberside Econ Planning Cncl 1970-79, pres Yorks and Humberside Devpt Assoc 1973-84, memb BR Rail (Eastern Region) 1976-85; chm: Health Serv Supply Cncl 1980-85, South Yorkshire Residuary Body 1985-89; pro-chllr Univ of Sheffield 1983-87; Master Co of Cutlers in Hallamshire 1979; hon fell Sheffield City Poly 1980, Hon LLD (Sheffield); *Recreations* gardening, quiet pursuits; *Style—* Dr Bernard Cotton, CBE; Stubbin House, Carsick Hill, Sheffield S10 3LU (☎ 0742 303082)

COTTON, Bernard James; s of Raymond Cotton, and Helen Stuart, *née* Watt; *b* 30 June 1948; *Educ* Hitchin GS, Northampton GS, Univ of Cambridge (BA); *m* 21 Oct 1972, Jane Mary, da of James Kenneth Tee; 2 s (James Matthew b 6 Aug 1976, Alastair Charles b 13 Dec 1978); *Career* hockey player; clubs: Bluehearts 1961-63, Northampton Saints 1963-67, Cambridge Univ 1967-71, Southgate 1971-79, Bedford 1979-86; County: Northamptonshire 1965-71, Hertfordshire 1971-76; England U19 1966-67; 72 England caps 1970-78, 55 GB caps 1971-80; int championships: 6 place Munich Olympic Games 1972, 6 place World Cup Amsterdam 1973, 6 place World Cup Kuala Lumpur 1975, 7 place Buenos Aires World Cup 1978, 6 place Euro Cup Brussels 1970, 4 place Euro Cup Madrid 1974, 3 place Euro Cup Hannover 1978, 3 place Champions Trophy Lahore 1979, 6 place Champions Trophy Karachi 1980; mangr England 1986- (Euro Silver medallists), asst mangr GB 1984-88 (Olympic Gold medallists Seoul 1988), mangr GB Hockey 1988-, nat teams admin Hockey Assoc 1987-; asst master Bishops Stortford Coll 1971-77, head of geography Bedford Sch 1977-87; *Style—* Bernard Cotton, Esq; The Hockey Association, 16 Northdown St, London N1 9BG (☎ 071 837 8878, fax 071 837 8163)

COTTON, Diana Rosemary; QC (1983); da of Arthur Frank Edward Cotton, of Herts, and Muriel, *née* John; *b* 30 Nov 1941; *Educ* Berkhamsted Sch for Girls, Lady Margaret Hall Oxford (exhibitioner, MA); *m* 1966, Richard Bellerby Allan, s of John Bellerby Allan (d 1985), of Oxon; 2 s (Jonathan b 1972, Jeremy b 1974), 1 da (Joanna b 1977); *Career* barr, rec 1982; *Recreations* my family, sport; *Style—* Miss Diana Cotton, QC; Devereux Chambers, Devereux Court, Temple, London WC2 (☎ 071 353 7534)

COTTON, Prof Henry Charles; s of James Campbell Cotton, of Westcliffe on Sea, Essex, and Dorothy Frances, *née* Welch; *b* 27 April 1920; *Educ* W Kensington Central Sch, Wandsworth Tech Inst, Battersea Poly, Scottish Coll of Commerce; *m* 27 Dec 1955, Constance Ethel, da of John Urquhart; 1 s (Henry James Urquhart b 22 Sept 1959), 1 da (Laura Jane Urquhart b 13 Jan 1961); *Career* staff sgt REME 1941-46; indentured apprentice welding engr ARC Manufacturing Co Ltd 1936-41, welding inspection and testing engr 1941, sr res engr Welding Consumables 1950-52 (res engr 1946-49), tech mangr ARC Manufacting Co Ltd Glasgow 1956-59 (works mangr 1953-56); British Petroleum Co Ltd: welding supt 1959-64, chief welding engr 1965-76, engrg assoc 1977-80; sr conslt CAPCIS-UMIST 1980-, conslt The Welding Inst 1980-; Harry Brooker Platinum medal The Welding Inst, gave John Player Lecture IMechE; FEng, FIM, FIProdE, MIMechE; hon fell: Soc of Engrs, The Welding Inst; memb Br Inst of Non Destructive Testing; *Style—* Prof Henry Cotton; 12 Avondale Road, South Benfleet, Essex SS7 1EJ; CAPCIS-UMIST, University of Manchester Institute of Science and Technology, Bainbridge House, Granby Row, Manchester M1 2PW (☎ 061 236 6573, fax 061 228 7846, telex 668810 CAPCIS G)

COTTON, His Hon Judge; John Anthony; s of Frederick Thomas Hooley Cotton, of Harrogate, and Catherine Mary Cotton; *b* 6 March 1926; *Educ* Stonyhurst, Lincoln Coll Oxford; *m* 1960, Johanna Aritia, da of Johan Adriaan van Lookeren Campagne, of Holland; 3 s, 2 da; *Career* called to the Bar 1949, dep chm W Riding of Yorks Quarter Sessions 1967-71,rec of Halifax 1971, rec of Crown Ct 1972, circuit judge 1973-; *Style—* His Hon Judge Cotton; 81 Lyndhurst Rd, Sheffield

COTTON, Sir John Richard; KCMG (1969, CMG 1959), OBE (1947, MBE 1944); s of Julian James Cotton, ICS (d 1927), and Sophia Raffaela, *née* Ricciardi-Arlotta (d 1958); *b* 22 Jan 1909; *Educ* Wellington, RMC Sandhurst; *m* 1937, Mary Bridget, da of Nicholas Connors, of Stradbally, Co Waterford; 3 s (David, John, Brian); *Career* 8 Light Cavalry IA 1929-37, Maj; Indian Political Serv 1934-47: Aden 1934-35, HM Legation Addis Ababa 1935, Persian Gulf 1937-38, Rajputana 1939-41, Hyderabad 1941-44, Kathiawar 1944-46, Political Dept Delhi 1946-47; HM Foreign Serv 1947-69: Foreign Office 1948-51, consul-gen Madrid 1951-54, consul-gen Leopoldville 1954-57, consllr Brussels 1957-62, consul-gen Sao Paolo 1962-65, ambass Kinshasa 1965-69; adjudicator Immigration Tbnls 1970-81; *Recreations* golf, photography; *Clubs* Army and Navy; *Style—* Sir John Cotton, KCMG, OBE; Lansing House, Hartley Wintney, Hants (☎ 0251 26 2681)

COTTON, Lt Cdr (George) Lennox; DSC (1942), DL; s of Thomas Dawson Cotton (d 1970), and May, *née* Lennox (d 1976); *b* 25 Oct 1915; *Educ* Castle Park Dublin, Wrekin Coll Shropshire; *m* 1939, Eileen Geraldine, da of Maj Gerald William Ewart; 3 da (Caroline, Elizabeth, Kathleen); *Career* Ulster Div RNVR 1936; HMS Hermes 1939-40, Motor Torpedo Boats including CO 50 MTB Flotilla 1940-44, HMS Mull of

Galloway 1945; slr; dir Caledon Estate Co; *Recreations* shooting, golf, riding, racing; *Clubs* Ulster Reform (Belfast), Royal Co Down Golf; *Style—* Lt Cdr Lennox Cotton, DSC, DL; Clontagh Lodge, Crossgar, Co Down, N Ireland (☎ 0396 831077); 7-11 Linenhall St, Belfast (☎ 0232 322204)

COTTON, Leonard Thomas; s of Edward George Cotton (d 1973), and Elizabeth Minnie Cotton; *b* 5 Dec 1922; *Educ* King's Coll Sch Wimbledon, Oriel Coll Oxford, King's Coll Hosp (MA, MCh, BM BCh); *m* 20 Aug 1946, Frances Joan, *née* Bryan; 1 s(Thomas Edward Guy b 3 Aug 1950), 2 da (Ruth Frances b 16 Feb 1955, Elizabeth Mary b 30 Sept 1960); *Career* Nat Serv Maj RAMC (Surgical Div Tidworth Mil Hosp 1949-51); conslt surgn KCH 1957-88, dir Dept of Med Engrg and Physics KCS of Med 1967-88, dean and vice dean KCH Med Sch 1976-83, dean KCS of Med and Dentistry 1983-88; MRCS, FRCS (Eng), LRCP; *Books* Short Textbook of Surgery (with Selwyn Taylor, 1967), Surgical Catechism (1986); *Recreations* walking, travelling; *Clubs* Garrick; *Style—* Leonard Cotton, Esq; 3 Dome Hill Park, London SE26 6SP (☎ 081 778 8047); KCH Private Patients Wing (☎ 071 274 8570)

COTTON, Prof Roger Ernest; s of Frederick Stanley Cotton (d 1981), and Lillie, *née* Slater (d 1981); *b* 15 Sept 1926; *Educ* Derby Sch, Univ of London, Middx Hosp Med Sch (MB BS, MD); *m* 1, 12 May 1956 (m dis), Sheila Elizabeth Campbell (d 1986), da of Donald Logan (d 1968); 2 s (Andrew Robin b 1958, Richard John b 1961); m 2, 20 Oct 1989, Susan Veronica, *née* Towse; *Career* RAF med serv 1950-52; visiting prof of pathology N Western Univ Chicago USA 1959-60, sr lectr in pathology Middx Hosp 1960-63 (lectr 1952-59), emeritus pathologist City Hosp Nottingham 1990- (formerly pathologist 1963-90), special prof of diagnostic oncology Univ of Nottingham 1974-90, ed (fndn) Histopathology 1975-84, vice chm Nottinghamshire Health Authy 1977-81, int pres Int Acad of Pathology 1982-84; chm Crest Appeal and Nottingham ctee Cancer Res Campaign; FRCPath 1973 (MRCPath 1963); *Books* Lecture Notes on Pathology (3 edn, 1983); *Recreations* golf, gardening, music; *Style—* Prof Roger Cotton; Northfield Farmhouse, Wysall, Nottingham NG12 5QW (☎ 0509 881252)

COTTON, Thomas; s of Lt-Col B H C Cotton, OBE, RE (d 1970), of Blackheath, London, and Susanna, *née* Corner (d 1981); *b* 6 Jan 1936; *Educ* Cheltenham, Pembroke Coll Cambridge, Cranfield Coll of Aeronautics (DipOR); *m* 3 April 1964, Amanda Mary, da of Dr H P Hutchinson; 3 s (Benjamin b 1964, Christopher b 1966, Daniel b 1968); *Career* Nat Serv, Field Troop Cdr RE BAOR 1954-56, PO RAFVR 1956-58; Rootes Group Ltd 1958-68, gen mangr Lancer Boss Group 1968, sr exec Indust Reorganisation Corp 1968-70, exec dir Colour and IC Gas 1970-85, mgmnt conslt 1985-86, dir Fin and Support Servs IMRO 1986-; involved in local voluntary work and charities; memb IOD; *Recreations* family; *Clubs* IOD; *Style—* T Cotton, Esq; IMRO Ltd, Broadwalk House, 5 Appold St, London EC2A 2LL

COTTON, William Frederick (Bill); OBE (1976), JP (Richmond 1976); s of William Edward (Billy) Cotton, and Mabel Hope; *b* 23 April 1928; *Educ* Ardingly; *m* 1, 1950, Bernadine Maud Sinclair; 3 da; m 2, 1965, Ann Corfield, *née* Bucknall; 1 step da; *Career* former jt md Michael Reine Music Co; head of variety BBC TV 1967-70, head of light entertainment 1970-77 (prodr 1956-62, asst head 1962-67), controller BBC 1 1977-81, dep md BBC TV 1981-82, chm BBC Enterprises, memb Bd of Mgmnt and first dir of Devpt and Progs BBC TV 1982-, md BBC DBS 1982-; *Style—* Bill Cotton, Esq, OBE, JP; BBC TV, Television Centre, London W12 7RJ (☎ 081 743 8000)

COTTRELL, Sir Alan Howard; s of Albert Cottrell, and Elizabeth Cottrell, of Birmingham; *b* 17 July 1919; *Educ* Moseley GS, Univ of Birmingham; *m* 1944, Jean Elizabeth, da of Ernest William Harber; 1 s; *Career* former lectr and prof of physical metallurgy Univ of Birmingham, chief scientific advsr HM Govt 1971-74 (formerly dep chief); former vice pres Royal Soc, master Jesus Coll Cambridge 1974-86, vice chllr Univ of Cambridge 1977-79; memb Security Cmmn 1981-; Hon DSc: Oxford 1979, Birmingham 1983; FRS; kt 1971; *Style—* Sir Alan Cottrell, FRS; 40 Maids Causeway, Cambridge CB5 8DD (☎ 0223 63806)

COTTRELL, Bryce Arthur Murray; s of Brig Arthur Foulkes Baglietto Cottrell, DSO, OBE (d 1962), of Boughton Lees, Ashford, Kent, and Mary Barbara, *née* Nicoll (d 1986); *b* 16 Sept 1931; *Educ* Charterhouse, CCC Oxford (MA); *m* 1955, Jeane Dolores, da of R P Monk (d 1942), of Coventry; 2 s, 2 da; *Career* memb Stock Exchange 1958, chm Phillips and Drew Stockbrokers 1985-88 (ptnr 1963-85); funding dir CCC Oxford 1990-, govr St Leonards Mayfield Sch; CBIM; *Recreations* railways, spectator sports, paintings; *Clubs* City of London; *Style—* Bryce Cottrell, Esq; Boscobel House, Bourne Lane, Tonbridge, Kent TN9 1LG (☎ 0732 353 959)

COTTRELL, David Vernon Swynfen; s of George Swinfen Cottrell (d 1960), of the Manor House, Bredon, Hereford & Worcester, and Dorothy Mary Catherine, *née* Liddell (d 1957); *b* 15 Nov 1923; *Educ* Eton, Windsor, Trinity Coll Cambridge; *m* 6 June 1950, Leontine Mariette (Marylena), da of Capt James Allan Dyson Perrins, MC (d 1974), of Waresley House, Hartlebury, Worcs; 1 s (Mark b 1955), 1 da (Sarah (Mrs Macinnes) b 1953), 1 step s (Rupert b 1945), 1 step da (Rozanna (Mrs Hammond) b 1946); *Career* RNVR 1942-46; admitted slr 1951, conslt practising Birmingham, ret 1990; chm and dir: S J Bishop & Son Ltd IOW 1955-63, Waterloo House (Birmingham) Ltd 1957-, Temple St (Birmingham) Ltd 1957-88; dir Dares Brewery Ltd Birmingham 1960-63, fndr and life dir Newater Investments Ltd Birmingham 1963-, chm Tewkesbury Marina Ltd 1969- (md 1969-90); memb Cncl Assoc Brokers & Yacht Agents 1970-89, vice chm Nat Yacht Harbour Assoc 1984-90 (memb Cncl 1972-, vice pres 1974-76, pres and chm 1979-82), chm Midlands Region Br Marine Indust Fedn 1988-90; High Sheriff Hereford and Worcs 1976; memb Cncl Lower Avon Navigation Tst 1951-, pres Gloucs Branch Inland Waterways Assoc 1976- (chm 1974-76), memb Yacht Brokers Designers and Surveyors Assoc 1975; memb Law Soc 1951-90; *Recreations* yachting, shooting, landscape painting; *Clubs* Royal Yacht Sqdn (Cowes IOW), Royal Solent Yacht; *Style—* David Cottrell, Esq; The Tewkesbury Marina Ltd, Bredon Rd, Tewkesbury, Gloucestershire (☎ 0684 293 737)

COTTRELL, Hon Mrs (Fiona Caroline Mary); *née* Watson; 2 da of 3 Baron Manton; *b* 26 Sept 1953; *m* 1978, Mark Swinfen Cottrell, s of D V S Cottrell; 1 da (Laura Marina b 30 June 1988); *Style—* The Hon Mrs Cottrell; Molehill, Paris, Ashton-under-Hill, Evesham, Worcs

COTTRELL, Henry Claude; s of Henry Cottrell (d 1953); *b* 13 June 1921; *Educ* Lawrence Sheriff Sch Rugby; *m* 1949, Audrey, da of Thomas Hannah (d 1936); 1 s; *Career* served WWII, RAF; actuary; sr ptnr Phillips and Drew stockbrokers 1972-78; dir: AMEV Ltd, Caffyns plc; chm Watts Blake Bearne and Co plc; Liveryman: Worshipful Co of Glass Sellers (Master 1977-78), Worshipful Co of Actuaries (Master 1981-82); receiver gen Order of St John 1981-86, OStJ 1979, KStJ 1981; *Recreations* fly-fishing; *Clubs* City Livery; *Style—* Henry Cottrell, Esq; Whitecraigs, Parkfield, Sevenoaks, Kent TN15 0HX (☎ 0732 61228)

COTTRELL, James Swinfen; s of Cdr Vincent Swinfen Cottrell (d 1956); *b* 10 Sept 1932; *Educ* Pangbourne Coll; *Career* shipbroker; dir Howe Robinson (Holdings) Ltd; MICS; *Recreations* sailing; *Clubs* Royal Solent Yacht, Brooks's, City of London; *Style—* James Cottrell, Esq; 41 Queensdale Rd, London W11 (☎ 071 488 3444)

COTTRELL, Richard John; MEP (EDG) Bristol 1979-; s of John Charles Cottrell and Winifred, *née* Barter; *b* 11 July 1943; *Educ* Court Fields Sch Wellington Somerset; *m* 1965, Dinah Louise, da of Leonard David; 2 da; *Career* journalist; formerly with Bristol Evening Post and Harlech TV; *Recreations* travel; *Style—* Richard Cottrell, Esq, MEP; Dean House, Bower Ashton, Bristol

COTTRELL, (Patrick) Rupert; s of Patrick Nelson Hickman, of Hale Park, Fordingbridge, Hants, and Leontine Mariette, *née* Dyson-Perrins; gs of Sir Alfred Hickman, 2 Bt (see Peerage and Baronetage); assumed by Deed Poll 1953 the surname of Cottrell in lieu of that of Hickman; *b* 14 June 1945; *Educ* Gordonstoun; *m* 1, 19 Oct 1968 (m dis 1989), Claire, da of Lt-Col James Grey Round, OBE, JP, DL, of Bailey Meadow House, Birch, Colchester, Essex; 1 s (Nicholas Rupert b 21 Aug 1970), 1 da (Jessica Victoria b 19 April 1974); m 2, 17 July 1989, Anne, o da of late Arthur Holbrook, of Leics; *Career* Macnicol & Co 1964-65, Montagu Loebl Stanley 1965-68, Cazenove & Co 1968-80, ptnr Birch Farms 1975-89, dir Maronhart Ltd 1978, chm and md Salamander Restorations 1980-; exec dir: Buzzacott Investment Management Ltd, Buzzacott Nominees Ltd 1984-90, Project 84 (Chelmsford) Ltd 1986-90, Bell Lawrie White 1990-, Hill Samuel Private Unit Management Ltd 1990- (joined Hill Samuel 1990); memb Cncl: FIMBRA 1986-90 (memb of Membership Sub Ctee 1987), Nat Assoc of Boys' Clubs 1985; chm Essex Assoc of Boys' Clubs 1985 (vice chm 1983); memb: Lloyd's, IMRO; *Recreations* reading, sailing, fishing, hunting, shooting; *Clubs* Royal Yacht Sqdn, Boodle's, Beefsteak, Royal London Yacht, Jockey Club Rooms; *Style—* Rupert Cottrell, Esq; Home Farm, Pakenham, Bury St Edmunds, Suffolk IP31 2LW; 4 Wood St, London EC2V 7JB (☎ 071 600 0336, fax 071 606 3408, telex 268483 BUZZ G, car 0860 352899)

COTTRILL, Major (Geoffrey) Michael Cameron; MBE (1977); s of Charles Rashleigh Stanhope Cottrill (d 1949), and Elsie, *née* Wright (d 1976); *b* 11 June 1929; *Educ* Repton, Sandhurst; *Career* soldier; Hong Kong 1950-52, Korea 1954, ADC GOC Singapore 1955-56, instr Eaton Hall OCS 1958-59, Staff Coll 1962, Sultan's Armed Forces Muscat and Oman 1963, HQ FARELF Singapore 1964-66 and 1968-70, Asst mil attaché Australia and N Zealand 1970-72, Abu Dhabi Def Force 1973-74, MS CBF Hong Kong 1974-77, Sec Allied Staff Berlin 1977-79, Co-ordinator Royal Sch of Artillery 1979-81, ret; *Recreations* polo, shooting, chorister, travel; *Clubs* Army and Navy, Victoria (Jersey); *Style—* Major Michael Cottrill, MBE; 52 High St, Codford St Mary, Warminster, Wilts BA12 0NB (☎ 0985 50507); HQ Director Army Air Corps, Middle Wallop, Stockbridge, Hants

COTTS, Richard Crichton Mitchell; s and h of Sir (Robert) Crichton Mitchell Cotts, 3 Bt; *b* 26 July 1946; *Educ* Oratory Sch; *Style—* Richard Cotts, Esq

COUCHMAN, Ernest Henry; s of Henry Ernest Couchman, of Grays, Essex, and Eliza Gladys, *née* Glasson (d 1974); *b* 6 March 1939; *Educ* William Palmer Endowed Sch for Boys; *m* 14 Sept 1963, Patricia, da of Keith Robinson (d 1978); 1 s (James b 1968), 2 da (Caroline b 1972, Judith b 1978); *Career* CA; chief accountant Baird & Tatlock London Ltd 1965-68, head of business and professional studies Redditch Coll 1980-86, head of professional accounting studies SW London Coll 1986-88, Chart Foulks Lynch plc 1989-90, Matthew Boulton Coll 1990-; lay pastor Studley Baptist Church 1978-84; FCA; *Recreations* music; *Style—* Ernest H Couchman, Esq; 4 Stapleton Rd, Studley, Warwickshire (☎ 0527 85 2101); Hope St, Birmingham (☎ 021 446 4545)

COUCHMAN, James Randall; MP (Cons) Gillingham 1983-; s of Stanley Randall Couchman, and Alison Margaret Couchman; *b* 11 Feb 1942; *Educ* Cranleigh Sch, King's Coll Newcastle upon Tyne; *m* 1967, Barbara Jean, da of Max Heilbrun (d 1956); 1 s, 1 da; *Career* memb Bexley Borough Cncl 1974-82, chm Bexley Social Servs 1975-78 and 1980-82, Parly candidate (Cons) Chester le Street 1979, dir Chiswick Caterers Ltd 1980-, chm Bexley Health Authy 1981-83, PPS to Sec of State for Social Security 1984-90; *Style—* James Couchman, Esq, MP; House of Commons, London SW1

COUCHMAN, Martin; s of Frederick Alfred James Couchman (d 1970), of Halstead, Kent, and Pamela Mary, *née* Argent; *b* 28 Sept 1947; *Educ* Sutton Valence, Exeter Coll Oxford (BA); *m* 29 Oct 1983, Carolyn Mary Constance, da of Victor Frow Roberts (d 1987), of Childer Thornton, Cheshire; 2 s (Edmund b 1985, William b 1987), 1 da (Annie b 1989); *Career* bldg indust 1970-77; Nat Econ Devpt Office: indust advsr 1977-84, head of admin 1984-87, on secondment as UK dir of Euro Year of the Environment 1987-88, sec to Nat Econ Devpt Cncl 1988-; *Recreations* amateur dramatics, Anglo-Saxon history, armchair archaeology; *Style—* Martin Couchman, Esq

COULL, Prof Alexander (Alex); s of William Coull (d 1964), of Peterhead, and Jane Ritchie, *née* Reid (d 1969); *b* 20 June 1931; *Educ* Peterhead Acad, Univ of Aberdeen (BSc Eng, PhD, DSc), Cranfield Inst of Technol (MSc); *m* 27 Dec 1962, Frances Bruce, da of Francis T C Moir (d 1988), of Aberdeen; 1 s (Gavin b 1967), 2 da (Alison b 1964, Moyra b 1969); *Career* res asst MIT (USA) 1955, structural engr Eng Electric Co Ltd 1955-57; lectr in: engrg Univ of Aberdeen 1957-57, civil engrg Univ of Southampton 1962-66; prof of structural engrg Univ of Strathclyde 1967-76 (dean 1969-72), Regius prof of civil engrg Univ of Glasgow 1977- (dean of engrg 1981-84); chm Clyde Estuary Amenity Cncl 1981-86, govr Glasgow Coll 1987-, past memb Ctee Inst of Structural Engrs (Scottish Branch); chm: Ctee on Tall Concrete and Masonry Bldgs, Cncl on Tall Bldgs and Urban Habitat 1984-; FICE 1973, FIStructE 1973, FRSE 1971; *Books* ed: Tall Buildings (1967), Fundamentals of Structural Theory (1972); *Recreations* golf, skiing, hill-walking; *Clubs* Buchanan Castle Golf; *Style—* Prof Alex Coull; 11 Blackwood Rd, Milngavie, Glasgow G62 7LB (☎ 041 956 1655); Department of Civil Engineering, University of Glasgow, Glasgow G12 8QQ (☎ 041 339 8855 ext 5200, fax 041 330 4808, telex 777 070)

COULL, Maj-Gen John Taylor; s of John Sandeman Coull (d 1970), of Aberdeen, and Ethel Marjory, *née* Taylor; *b* 4 March 1934; *Educ* Robert Gordon's Coll Aberdeen, Univ of Aberdeen (MB, ChB); *m* 27 Dec 1958, Mildred, da of Francis Thomson Macfarlane, of Bickley, Bromley; 3 s (Stephen John b 1960, Gordon David b 1962, Andrew Thomson b 1965); *Career* cmmnd RAMC 1960; conslt: gen surgery 1969, orthopaedic surgery 1972; advsr on orthopaedic surgery MOD 1977-86, conslt surgn BAOR 1986-88, dir of surgery and conslt surgn to the Army 1988-, conslt surgn Royal Hosp Chelsea; author of articles on hip dislocation amputation and fracture fixation; contrib: Field Surgery Pocket Book, Rob Smith Surgery; FRCS, FBOA (Cncl 1985-87), FRSM; *Recreations* house maintenance, woodwork, gardening; *Clubs* RSM; *Style—* Maj-Gen John Coull; Ministry of Defence, First Avenue House, High Holborn, London WC1V 6HE (☎ 071 430 5825)

COULMAN, Michael Raymond; s of Col Edward Raymond Coulman, OBE, TD (d 1956), of Bracken Cottage, Newtown, Newbury, Berks, and Margaret Annie, *née* Stow (d 1984); *b* 28 Oct 1932; *Educ* Winchester, Trinity Coll Oxford (BA, MA); *m* 1, 23 July 1969, Jacqueline (d 1980), da of Anthony Cuthbert Morris Marsham (d 1975), of West Malling, Kent; 1 s (Robert b 1973), 1 da (Camilla b 1977); m 2, 9 April 1981, Patricia Margaret, da of The Hon Edward Carson (d 1987), of Hastings, Sussex; 3 step da (Lucy Fyfe-Jamieson b 1972, Georgina b 1976, Sophie b 1976); *Career* 2 Lt KRRC 1951-53; with Anglo American Corp SA 1957-62; stockbroker; ptnr Sheppards 1968-85 (then taken over by BAII), dir Personal Financial Management Tunbridge Wells Kent 1989-; *Recreations* golf; *Clubs* MCC, I Zingari, Tennis and Racquets Assoc, Rye Golf; *Style—* Michael Coulman, Esq; Bainden Farmhouse, Horsmonden, Tonbridge, Kent (☎ 089 272 2528); Personal Financial Management, Tunbridge Wells, Kent (☎ 0892 510 510)

COULSFIELD, Hon Lord; John Taylor Cameron; QC (Scot, 1973); s of John Reid

Cameron, MA (d 1958), former Dir of Education, Dundee, and Annie Duncan, *née* Taylor (d 1982); *b* 24 April 1934; *Educ* Fettes Coll, CCC Oxford (MA), Edinburgh Univ (LLB); *m* 4 Sept 1964, Bridget Deirdre, da of Ian Caldwell Purston Sloan, The Black Watch (d 1940); *Career* admitted Faculty of Advocates 1960; lectr in public law Edinburgh Univ 1960-64; QC 1973; advocate-depute 1977-79; keeper of Advocates' Library 1977-87; judge Courts of Appeal of Jersey and Guernsey 1986-87; chm Medical Appeals Tribunals 1985-87; Senator of Coll of Justice with title of Lord Coulsfield 1987-; *Style*— The Hon Lord Coulsfield; 17 Moray Place, Edinburgh EH3 6DT (☎ 031 225 7695)

COULSHED, Brig Dame (Mary) Frances; DBE (1953, CBE 1949), TD (1951); da of Wilfred Coulshed and Maud, *née* Mullin; *b* 10 Nov 1904; *Educ* Parkfields Cedars Derby, Convent of the Sacred Heart Kensington; *Career* ATS 1938-49, subsequently WRAC 1949-54; served WWII, NW Europe Campaign (despatches), Dep Dir Anti-Aircraft Cmd 1946-50, Dep Dir War Office 1950, Dir WRAC 1951-54, Brig, ret; ADC to HM The King 1951, ADC to HM The Queen 1952-54; Order of Leopold I of Belgium with Palm, Croix de Guerre with Palm 1946; *Style*— Brig Dame Frances Coulshed, DBE, TD; 815 Endsleigh Court, Upper Woburn Place, London WC1

COULSON, Ann Margaret; da of Sidney Herbert Wood (d 1972), and Ada, *née* Mills (d 1969); *b* 11 March 1935; *Educ* Chippenham GS, UCL (BSc), Univ of Manchester (Dip Soc Admin); *m* 19 Aug 1958, Peter James Coulson, s of Leslie Gerald Bell Coulson (d 1970) of Albury, Surrey; 2 s (Jeremy Richard b 12 April 1964, Michael Hugh b 5 May 1966), 1 da (Nancy Margaret b 19 Dec 1962); *Career* lectr then sr lectr Bromsgrove Coll 1968-76, asst dir N Worcs Coll 1976-80, dir of planning W Midlands RHA 1988-91 (serv/capital planning 1980-88); gen mangr Age Concern Solihull 1991-; memb: Bd of Dirs BRMB (local radio stn) 1982-89, IBA 1976-80, Birmingham Vol Serv Cncl 1975-81, cnllr City of Birmingham 1973-79; *Recreations* sailing, cooking; *Style*— Mrs Ann Coulson; Rowans, Leamington Hastings, nr Rugby, Warwickshire CV23 8DY (☎ 0926 633 264); Age Concern Metropolitan Borough of Solihull, 9 Herbert Rd, Solihull B91 3QE (tel 021 705 9128)

COULSON, Sir John Eltringham; KCMG (1957, CMG 1946); er s of Henry John Coulson (d 1959), of Bickley, Kent; *b* 13 Sept 1909; *Educ* Rugby, CCC Cambridge; *m* 1944, Mavis Ninette, da of late Edwin Beazley, of Coleman's Hatch, Sussex; 2 s; *Career* Dip Serv: dep UK rep to UN NY 1950-52, asst under sec of state FO 1952-55, min Washington 1955-57, seconded to Paymaster Gen's Office 1957, ambass to Sweden 1960-63, dep under sec of state FO 1963-65, chief Dip Serv Admin 1965, sec gen EFTA 1965-72; pres Hants BRCS 1972-79; *Style*— Sir John Coulson, KCMG; The Old Mill, Selborne, Hants (☎ 042 050 288)

COULSON, His Honour Judge; (James) Michael; s of William Coulson (d 1979), of Wold Newton Hall, nr Driffield, E Yorks, and Kathleen, *née* Abbott (d 1984); *b* 23 Nov 1927; *Educ* Fulneck Sch Yorkshire, Merton Coll Oxford, RAC Cirencester; *m* 1, 1 May 1955, Dilys, da of David Adair Jones of Knapton Hall, Merton, Yorkshire; 1 s (David James Ivo b 1963); m 2, Jan 1976, Barbara Elizabeth Islay, da of Dr Roland Moncrieff Chambers, of 37 Beaconsfield Rd, London SE3, 1 s (Timothy James Edward b 1978), 1 da (Sarah Elizabeth Rosamond b 1984); *Career* Major East Riding Yeomanry, ret; barr Middle Temple 1951, dep chm North Riding Quarter Sessions, asst recorder to Sheffield; MP (C) Kingston upon Hull North 1959-64, PPS to Slr Gen 1962-64; circuit judge Midlands and Oxford 1983, dep chm Northern Agricultural Land Tribunal 1967-72; regional chm of Indust Tribunals 1972-83; *Recreations* hunting, reading, gardening, country life; *Clubs* Cavalry and Guards until 1980 when resigned on increase of subscriptions; *Style*— His Hon Judge Coulson; The Tithe Barn, Wymondham, Melton Mowbray, Leicestershire

COULSON, (Bevis) Michael Leigh; s of Capt Thomas William Bevis Coulson (d 1944), of Coulsdon, Surrey, and Vera, *née* Leigh; *b* 18 May 1945; *Educ* Charterhouse, Univ of Liverpool, City of London Coll (BSc), Drew Univ Madison New Jersey USA, American Univ Washington DC USA; *m* 2 Oct 1971, Hilary Ann, da of Dr William Henry Cotton Croft; 3 da (Alice b 1978, Mary b 1981, Lisa b 1981); *Career* stockbroking investmt analysis 1970-; head mining res Phillips & Drew 1982-86, dir and head Mining Dept Kitcat & Aitken; Freeman City of London 1985, memb Worshipful Co of Weavers 1985; memb Soc of Investmt Analysts 1975; *Recreations* cricket, football, horticulture; *Style*— Michael Coulson, Esq; 9 Brodrick Rd, London SW17 7DZ (☎ 081 767 1608)

COULTASS, (George Thomas) Clive; *b* 5 July 1931; *Educ* Tadcaster GS Yorkshire, Univ of Sheffield (BA), King's Coll London (Educn Cert); *m* 17 Sept 1962, Norma Morris; *Career* teacher various schools in London 1956-62, lectr and sr lectr in history James Graham Coll Leeds 1962-69; Imp War Museum 1969-: keeper of film programming 1969-70, keeper Dept of Film 1970-84, keeper AV records 1984-91; author of several articles in historical jls and organiser of various film historical confs; vice pres Int Assoc for AV Media in Historical Res and Educn 1978-85; *Books* Images for Battle (1989); *Recreations* music, travel, reading; *Style*— Clive Coultass, Esq; 39 Fairfield Grove, London SE7 8UA

COULTER, Michael Daley; s of Thomas Coulter (d 1976), and Elizabeth, *née* Daley; *b* 29 Aug 1952; *Educ* Holy Cross HS Hamilton; *m* 1 March 1976, Louise, da of William Brogan, of Glasgow; 2 s (Luke b 1981, Eliot b 1987), 2 da (Ruth b 1983, Sophie b 1985); *Career* dir of photography; films incl: No Surrender, Heavenly Pursuits, The Good Father, Housekeeping, The Dressmaker, Breaking In, Diamond Skulls, Bearskin; memb BSC; *Recreations* music (playing and listening); *Clubs* Leander; *Style*— Michael Coulter, Esq; 4 Turnberry Ave, Glasgow G11 5AG (☎ 041 339 0378)

COULTER, Roger Frederick; s of Thomas Coulter, of Thurgarton, and Freda Lucy, *née* Shaw; *b* 1 Oct 1946; *Educ* King's Sch Worcester; *m* 12 June 1971, Caroline Rosemary, da of James Whitehead, MC (d 1982); 2 da (Victoria b 1974, Diana b 1977); *Career* chm Shaw & Lyddon Ltd Nottingham, chm Ernest Clark Ltd Nottingham (formerly non-exec dir); *Recreations* shooting, motoring in France; *Style*— Roger F Coulter, Esq; Elmcote, Whatton, Nottinghamshire (☎ 0949 50265, 0602 475130); 20-22 Broad St, Nottingham NG1 3AL; Les Plages de Cavaliere, 83980 Le Lavads, VAR, France

COUNSELL, Her Honour Judge Hazel Rosemary; da of Arthur Henry Counsell, and Elsie Winifred Counsell; *b* 7 Jan 1931; *Educ* Clifton HS, La Châtellanie Switzerland, Bristol Univ; *m* 1980, Judge Peter Fallon, QC, *qv*; *Career* called to the Bar 1956, legal dept Min of Labour 1959-62, recorder Crown Court 1976-77, circuit judge 1978-; memb Matrimonial Causes Ctee 1983-87; *Style*— Her Hon Judge Hazel Counsell; Crown Court, Guildhall, Bristol

COUNSELL, His Honour Judge; Paul Hayward; s of Frederick Charles and Edna Counsell; *b* 13 Nov 1926; *Educ* Colston Sch Bristol, Queen's Coll Oxford; *m* 1959, Joan Agnes Strachan; 1 s, 2 da; *Career* slr 1951, barr 1962, slr-gen Rhodesia 1963-64, Zambia 1964, a circuit judge 1973-; *Style*— His Hon Judge Counsell; c/o Hitchin County Court, Station House, Nightingale Rd, Hitchin, Herts (☎ (0462) 50011)

COUPE, Barry Desmond; s of Harold Desmond Coupe of Dorincourt, 2 Rothesay Rd, Talbot Woods, Bournemouth and Alice *née* Roberts; *b* 4 June 1951; *Educ* Canford Sch, Leeds Sch of Architecture (BA, Dip Arch); *m* 6 May 1978, Shan Patricia da of James Ninian Reid Wilson, of Friston Cottage, Northbourne, Bournemouth; 2 s (Matthew b 6 Sept 1981, Benjamin b 11 Feb 1985); *Career* architect; Fitzroy Robinson & Ptnrs 1977-80, fndr ptnr Forum Architects 1980-; works incl: Nobelight Bldg 1983, leisure complex Whittaker House 1984, offrs club RAF Milden Hall 1986, Beehive Shopping Centre Cambridge 1987, Bow Housing 1989; HQ bldg Domino plc Cambridge 1987; Usafe Design award 1986/87/88/89; Usafe World Wide Award 1986, Civic Tst award, commendation 1987 ; memb Cambridge Granta Round Table, tstee Cambridge Children's Hospice, RIBA 1979; *Recreations* classic cars, motor sport, photography, round table; *Style*— Barry Coupe, Esq; The Old Rectory, Ashley, Newmarket, Suffolk CB8 9DU, (☎ 0638 730751); Forum Architects, Elmhurst, Brooklands Ave, Cambridge, (☎ 0223 66616, fax 0223 66714, car 0831 252504)

COUPER, Dudley William Malcolm; s of Leslie Claude Couper (d 1962), of Farnham, Surrey, and Beatrice Ena, *née* Greengrass; *b* 9 April 1935; *Educ* Cranleigh Sch, Keble Coll Oxford (MA); *m* 3 June 1961, Jill, da of William Ronald Trumper (d 1965), of Devizes, Wilts; 1 s (Duncan b 1968), 2 da (Sarah b 1962, Joanna b 1963); *Career* slr with Rowe and Maw: ptnr 1965-, head of Property Dept 1968-, fin ptnr 1969-90, chm Exec Ctee 1987-90; govr Cranleigh Sch 1983-; memb Law Soc 1960; memb MCC; *Recreations* golf and sport of all kinds, travel; *Style*— Dudley Couper, Esq; Five Ways House, Tennyson's Lane, Haslemere, Surrey; Rowe & Maw, 20 Black Friars Lane, London EC4V 6HD (☎ 071 248 4282, telex 262787, fax 071 248 2009)

COUPER, Heather Anita; da of George Couper Elder Couper, of Bexhill on Sea, E Sussex, and Anita, *née* Taylor (d 1984); *b* 2 June 1949; *Educ* St Mary's GS, Univ of Leicester (BSc), Univ of Oxford; *Career* mgmnt trainee Peter Robinson Ltd 1967-69, res asst Cambridge Observatories 1969-70, lectr Greenwich Planetarium 1977-83, broadcaster and writer on astronomy and sci 1983-; tv presenter Channel 4: The Planets 1985, The Stars 4 1988; dir Pioneer Film and TV Productions 1988-, The Neptune Encounter ITV 1989; astronomy columnist The Independent, presenter and contrib for many radio programmes incl seeing stars BBC World Serv; pres: Br Astronomical Assoc 1984-86, Jr Astronomical Soc 1987-89; FRAS 1970; *Books* twenty pubns incl: The Space Scientist series, The Universe, The Restless Universe, The Stars, The Planets; *Recreations* travel, the English countryside, wine, food, music; *Style*— Miss Heather Couper

COUPER, Sir (Robert) Nicholas Oliver; 6 Bt (UK 1841); s of Maj Sir George Rupert Cecil Couper, 5 Bt (d 1975), and Margaret Grace, *née* Thomas (d 1984); *b* 9 Oct 1945; *Educ* Eton, RMA Sandhurst; *m* 1972 (m dis), Curzon Henrietta, da of Maj George Burrell MacKean, JP, DL (d 1983); 1 s, 1 da (Caroline b 1979); *Heir* s, James George Couper b 27 Oct 1977; *Career* Acting Maj Blues and Royals (ret); estate agent; ptnr Savills; dir: Aylesfords & Co, Lane Fox; *Style*— Sir Nicholas Couper, Bt; 79 Devonshire Rd, London W4 2HU (☎ 081 995 5603); Lane Fox, 38 Bampton St, Tiverton, Devon EX16 6AH (☎ 0884 242468)

COUPLAND, (William) James; s of William Arthur Coupland, and Patricia Anne, *née* Martin; *b* 25 May 1957; *Educ* Kings Coll Sch Wimbledon; *m* 13 Sept 1980, Helen Jane, da of Charles Alfred Everett; 3 s (Christopher Everett, Benjamin Jake b 1981, Joshua James b 1987); *Career* dir Shearson American Express Ltd 1982, md Shearson Lehman Metals Ltd 1985, dir Shearson Lehman Hutton Commodities Tokyo Ltd, sr vice pres Shearson Lehman Hutton 1986, chm Shearson Lehman Hutton Commodities 1987; FRSA; *Recreations* tennis, painting; *Style*— James Coupland, Esq; 5 Durrington Park, Wimbledon, London SW20 8NU; Lehman Brothers Commodities Ltd, One Broadgate, London EC2M 7HA (☎ 071 601 0011, telex 917273, fax 071 260 2516, car 0836 519 040)

COUPLAND, Prof Rex Ernest; s of Ernest Coupland (d 1978), of Mirfield, Yorks, and Doris, *née* Threadgold; *b* 30 Jan 1924; *m* 14 July 1947, (Lucy) Eileen, da of William Sargent (d 1950), of Smallrice, Sandon, Staffs; 1 s (Michael Adam b 22 July 1953), 1 da (Lesley Diana Eileen b 11 Feb 1950); *Career* Nat Serv MD RAF 1948-50; house surgn Leeds Gen Infirmary 1947, lectr Univ of Leeds 1950-58, asst prof Univ of Minnesota 1955-56, Cox prof of anatomy Univ of St Andrews 1958-68, dean Faculty of Med Univ of Nottingham 1981-87 (Fndn prof of human morphology 1968-89); memb MRC Biological Res Bd 1964-70; chm: MRC Non-Ionizing Radiation Ctee 1970-89, Med Advsy Bd Crippling Diseases 1971-75; pres: Anatomical Soc GBI 1976-78, Br Assoc of Clinical Anatomists 1977-82; memb: Derby AHA 1978-81, Trent RHA 1981-88, Central Notts DHA 1988- (GMC 1981-88); FRS (E) 1970; *Books* The Natural History of the Chromaffin Cell (1965), Enterochromaffin and Related Cells (co ed with T Fujita, 1976), Peripheral Neuroendocrine Interaction (ed with WG Forssman, 1978), contrib numerous articles in learned jls; *Recreations* gardening, watercolour painting, shooting; *Clubs* RSM; *Style*— Prof Rex Coupland, FRSE; Foxhollow, Quaker Lane, Farnsfield, Notts NG22 8EE (☎ 0623 882 028); The Medical School, Queens Medical Centre, Nottingham NG22 8EE (☎ 0602 421 421)

COURAGE, Maj-Gen Walter James; MBE (1979); s of Walter Henry Phipps (d 1983), and Nancy Mary Gardner, *née* Reeves, and step s of Lt-Col Nigel Anthony Courage, MC (d 1964); *b* 25 Sept 1940; *Educ* Abingdon Sch, RMA Sandhurst; *m* 10 Oct 1964, Lavinia Patricia, da of John Emerson Crawhall Wood (d 1981); 1 s (Sebastian b 1 June 1971), 1 da (Camilla b 25 May 1969); *Career* cmmnd 5 Royal Inniskilling Dragoon Guards 1961, cmdg regt 1982-84, divnl Col Staff Coll 1984, cdr 4 Armoured Brig 1984-88, chief of staff UN Force in Cyprus 1988-; *Recreations* shooting, cricket, polo, fishing, golf; *Clubs* Marylebone Cricket, Cavalry and Guards, I Zingari; *Style*— Maj-Gen Walter Courage, MBE; Headquarters United Nations Forces in Cyprus, BFPO 567 (☎ 010 357 02 359020)

COURT, Dr Glyn; s of William George Court (d 1953), of Roadwater, and Ada, *née* Palser (d 1967); *b* 13 May 1924; *Educ* Taunton Sch, Univ Coll Exeter, Univ of London (BA, PhD), Univ of Paris (Br Inst), Univ of Grenoble; *m* 23 Sept 1950, Clare Ann, da of Maj G E Carpenter, MC, of Budleigh Salterton, Devon; 1 s (Mark), 3 da (Alison, Joy, Philippa); *Career* Queen's Royal Regt (TA Res) 1942, incorporated 1944, Fourteenth Army 1944-45; head of modern languages depts 1959-74; Lib Pty: chm Branch, Area and Div Torrington N Devon and Bridgwater 1958-71, Parly candidate Westbury 1974 (twice) and N Dorset 1979, Euro Parly candidate W Midlands 1979; winner Brain of Britain 1973; memb: Ilfracombe UDC 1964-67, Old Cleeve PC 1968-, Somerset CC 1973-77 and 1985-, (vice chm 1987-89); chm: libraries and museums, highways, Dillington Coll Adult Educn, Quantock Hills Jt Liaison Gp, Rural Development Area; memb ACC Nat Parks Ctee, vice chm Exmoor Soc 1985-88, Methodist local preacher 1958-, fndr memb and sec Burma Star Assoc W Somerset 1985-; *Books* West Somerset in Times Past (1981), Somerset Carols (1983), Exmoor National Park (1987); *Recreations* travel, exploring the countryside, local history (chm soc), European languages, genealogy, music; *Clubs* Blake Lib (Bridgwater, pres); *Style*— Dr Glyn Court; Sunbeam House, Roadwater, W Somerset; County Hall, Taunton TA1 4DY (☎ 0823 333451)

COURT, Michael Edward; s of Edward George Bertram Court, of Sheperdswell, Kent, and Patricia Margaret, *née* Shipley; *b* 24 Jan 1956; *Educ* Dover GS, Univ Coll Oxford (MA); partner, A J Connell; *Career* with various advertising agencies 1977-: intially with Leo Burnett, Wasey Campbell-Ewald (account handler rising to copywriter) 1977-79, Foote Cone & Belding 1979-81, Carter Hedger Mitchell (now Hedger Mitchell Stark); six months at TBWA; fndr ptnr Still Price Court Twivy D'Souza until 1989 (when sold to Interpublic), creative dir Young & Rubicam Aug

1990- (joined Feb); winner awards for: BA, London Transport, Iru Bru, Olivetti, Gatwick Express, Krups, Mates Condoms, Red Mountain, Warburtons, Virgin Atlantic, RCN; memb D&ADA 1980; *Recreations* ships, ocean liners and cruises; *Style—* Michael Court, Esq; 33 Warrington Crescent, Maida Vale, London W9 1EJ (☎ 071 289 6668); Young and Rubicam, Greater London House, Hampstead Road, London NW1 (☎ 071 380 6659)

COURT, Dr Stephen Alistair; s of Arthur Geoffrey Court, and Jean Isobel; *b* 16 June 1951; *Educ* Pinner GS, Univ of Bristol Med Sch (BSc, MB ChB, MRCP); *m* 28 April 1990, Naomi, da of Ronald Slopes; *Career* medical and surgical house jobs Bristol Royal Infirmary, conslt physician Royal Oman Police Hosp Muscat 1980-85, in private practice Harley Street 1985-; memb BMA 1975, MRCP 1977; *Recreations* golf, squash; *Clubs* RAC; *Style—* Dr Stephen Court; 18 The Woodlands, Chesham Bois, Amersham, Bucks HP6 5JP (☎ 0444 724011); 16 Harmont House, 20 Harley St, London W1N 1AL (☎ 071 580 5411, fax 071 323 3418)

COURT-BROWN, Charles Michael; s of William Michael Court-Brown, OBE (d 1968), and Caroline Gordon Stephen, *née* Thom; *b* 3 Feb 1948; *Educ* George Watson's Coll Edinburgh, Univ of Aberdeen (BSc), Univ of Edinburgh (MD, MB ChB); *m* 6 July 1974, Jacqueline Yek Quen, da of To Leong Mok; 1 s (Michael b 1988), 1 da (Johanna b 1979); *Career* conslt orthopaedic surgn 1985-, sr lectr Dept of Orthopaedic Surgery Univ of Edinburgh 1985; fndr memb Br Trauma Soc; fell BOA, FRCS 1979, BORS 1983, FRCS (Ed orth) 1984; *Books* External Skeletal Fixation (1984), Atlas of Intramedullary Nailing of the Tibia and Femur (1991); *Recreations* house building, cooking; *Style—* Charles Court-Brown, Esq; Craigesk House, Lothian Bridge, Dalkeith, Scotland EH22 4TP; Princess Margaret Rose Orthopaedic Hospital, Fairmilehead, Edinburgh EH10 7ED (☎ 031 455 4123, fax 031 445 3440)

COURTAULD, Samuel; s of Major George Courtauld (d 1980), of Essex, and Claudine Suzanne, *née* Booth (d 1983); The Courtaulds were a Huguenot family from Ile d'Oleron near La Rochelle, came to England in 1680's, 3 generations were practicing goldsmiths in London and subsequent predecessors became involved in weaving business and foun Courtaulds Ltd; *b* 14 March 1940; *Educ* Gordonstoun, McGill Univ Canada, Sorbonne; *m* 2 April 1963, Annette Susan, da of Major Chandos Ormsby Jodrell Godwin-Williams (d 1985), of Kent; 1 s (Samuel b 1969), 3 da (Serena b 1964, Melissa (Mrs Jones) b 1965, Lucinda b and d 1968); *Career* late 2 Lt Grenadier Gds; investmt advsr; memb Int Stock Exchange, Freeman City of London, Liveryman Worhshipful Co of Goldsmiths; *Recreations* shooting, fencing, gardening, campanology; *Clubs* First Guards, Special Forces; *Style—* Samuel Courtauld, Esq; Don Johns Farm, Earls Colne, Colchester, Essex (☎ 0787 222627); 55N Hans Road, London SW3 (☎ 071 589 6042); Greenwell Montague, 114 Old Broad Street, London (☎ 071 588 8817)

COURTENAY, Lady (Camilla) Gabrielle; da of late 16 Earl of Devon; *b* 8 April 1913; *Educ* The Maynard Exeter; *Style—* Lady Gabrielle Courtenay; The Briary, Exton, Exeter, Devon

COURTENAY, Lord; Hugh Rupert Courtenay; s and h of 17 Earl of Devon; *b* 5 May 1942; *Educ* Winchester, Magdalene Coll Cambridge; *m* 9 Sept 1967, Dianna Frances, elder da of late Jack Watherston, of Menslaws, Jedburgh, Roxburghshire; 1 s, 3 da (Hon Rebecca Eildon b 1969, Hon Eleonora Venetia b 1971, Hon Camilla Mary b 1974); *Heir* s, Hon Charles Peregrine Courtenay b 14 Aug 1975; *Career* chartered surveyor, farmer and landowner; *Style—* Lord Courtenay; Powderham Castle, nr Exeter, Devon EX6 8JQ (☎ 0626 890252)

COURTENAY, Lady Mary Elizabeth; 2 da of 16 Earl of Devon (d 1935); *b* 15 Jan 1910; *Career* SRN, State Cert Midwife, Badge of Honour (Red Cross); *Recreations* gardening; *Style—* Lady Mary Courtenay; The Briary, Exton, Exeter, Devon EX3 0PN

COURTIS, John; s of Fl Lt Thomas Courtis (d 1976), of Stock, Ingatestone, Essex, and Marjorie May, *née* Dodson (m 2 Massey); *b* 14 July 1937; *Educ* Westminster; *m* 15 Jan 1966, da of William McCall-Smith (d 1970), of Weavers, Stradishall, Suffolk; 1 s (Neil Thomas b 1970), 1 da (Claudia Janet b 1969); *Career* RAF 1960-63, Pilot Offr 1960-61 served Saxa Vord, Shetland; Flying Offr 1961-63; fin analyst Ford Motor Co 1963-67; dir: Reed Executive 1967-71, Executive Appointments Ltd 1971-74; chm: John Courtis & Ptnrs Ltd 1974-, DEEKO plc 1981-88, FRES 1985-88; dir Recruitment Soc 1986-; memb Ctee Friends of New Shakespeare Co 1988-; FCA 1959; *Books* Communicating for Results (1974), Money Matters for Managers (1976), Cost Effective Recruitment (1985), Selling Yourself in the Management Market (1986), Managing by Mistake (1987), Marketing Services (1987), Interviews: Skills and Strategy (1988), Bluffers Guide to Management 1986 (Accountancy 1987, Photography 1988); *Recreations* writing, cooking; *Clubs* Savile, RAF; *Style—* John Courtis, Esq; 31 Longmoore St, London SW1V 1JQ (☎ 071 834 5592); 104 Marylebone Lane, London W1M 5FU (☎ 071 486 6849, fax 071 487 4600)

COURTNEY, Diana Jean; da of Albert John Courtney, of 18 Corney Rd, Chiswick, London, and Sophia, *née* Fogg; *b* 20 March 1939; *Educ* Lourdes Mount Convent; *m* 1966 (m dis 1985), Edward John Charles, s of Edward George; 2 da (Nicola Diana b 9 Aug 1971, Antonia Jean b 17 April 1975); *Career* articled clerk Rexworthy Bonsor & Simons 1955-60; ptnr: Herbert Openheimer Nathan & Vandyk 1966-88 (slr 1961-66), Denton Hall Burgin & Warresn 1988- (after merger with Herbert Openheimer Nathan & Vandyk); memb: Law Soc 1960, Anglo American Real Property Inst; MInstD; *Recreations* horse racing, gardening, squash, riding; *Style—* Ms Diana Courtney; Denton Hall Burgin & Warrens, Five Chancery Lane, Cliffords Inn, London EC4A 1BU (☎ 071 242 1212, fax 071 404 0087)

COURTNEY, Nicholas Piers; s of Capt Frederick Harold Demming Courtney (d 1980), and Sybil, *née* Leigh-Pemberton (d 1972); *b* 20 Dec 1944; *Educ* The Nautical Coll Pangbourne, RAC Cirencester (Estate Mgmnt); *m* 30 Oct 1980, Vanessa Sylvia, da of John Bishop Hardwicke; *Career* land agent Greville Haggate & Co 1966-69; gen mangr The Mustique Co Mustique St Vincent W Indies 1970-74; ARICS 1967; *Books* The Tiger (1980), Royal Children (1982), Sporting Royals (1983), The Very Best of British (1986), In Society (1987), Sisters-in-Law (1988), Windsor Castle (1989), The Mall (1989), Shakespeare's Stratford (1990); *Recreations* shooting, gardening; *Clubs* Brooks's, Hurlingham; *Style—* Nicholas P Courtney, Esq; 9 Kempson Road, London SW6 4PX

COURTNEY, Rohan Richard; s of Arthur Richard Courtney, of Chingford, London, and Cecelia, *née* Harrington; *b* 28 Jan 1948; *Educ* William Morris GS London; *m* 12 Jan 1974, Marilyn, da of Ernest Arthur Charles Goward (d 1972), of Waltham Cross, Herts; 1 s (Liam b 1975), 1 da (Siân b 1977); *Career* former banker, business conslt; National Provincial Bank London 1965-68; mangr: Rothschild Intercontinental Bank Ltd London 1968-75, Amex Bank Ltd London 1975-76; asst dir Amex Bancom Ltd Hong Kong 1976-78, md Euro Asian Fin (HK) Ltd Hong Kong 1978-80, sr mangr Creditanstalt Bankverein London 1980-82, gen mangr State Bank of New S Wales London 1982-90, md Rohan Courtney Ltd; Freeman of the City of London, Liveryman The Worshipful Co of Wool Men; *Recreations* country pursuits; *Clubs* Royal Overseas League, Royal Cwlth Soc, City Livery, Hong Kong CC; *Style—* Rohan Courtney, Esq; Old Hill, Radwinter, Saffron Walden, Essex CB10 2TL (☎ 079 987 674, fax 079 987 829); Rohan Courtney Ltd, 1st Floor, Salters Hall, 4 Fore St, London EC2Y 5DA (☎ 071 334 9650, fax 071 334 9651)

COURTOWN, 9 Earl of (I 1762); James Patrick Montagu Burgoyne Winthrop Stopford; also (sits as) Baron Saltersford (GB 1796), Baron Courtown (I 1758), Viscount Stopford (I 1762); s of 8 Earl of Courtown, OBE, TD, DL (d 1975); *b* 19 March 1954; *Educ* Eton, Berkshire Agric Coll, RAC Cirencester; *m* 6 July 1985, Elisabeth Dorothy, yr da of Ian Rodger Dunnett, of Pinders, Broad Campden, Glos; 1 s, 1 da (Lady Rosanna Elisabeth Alice b 13 Sept 1986); *Heir* s, James Richard Ian Montagu, Viscount Stopford b 30 March 1988; *Career* land agent; *Style—* The Rt Hon the Earl of Courtown; Pear Tree House, Broadway, Worcs

COURTOWN, Patricia, Countess of; Patricia; 3 da of late Capt Harry Stephen Winthrop of Auckland, New Zealand; *b* 25 Feb 1917; *m* 23 Feb 1951, as his 2 w, 8 Earl of Courtown (d 1975); 2 s, 1 da; *Style—* Rt Hon Patricia, Countess of Courtown; Threeways, Seer Green Lane, Jordans, Bucks

COUSE, Philip Edward; s of Oliver Couse (d 1969), of Birmingham, and Marion Couse (d 1968); *b* 24 March 1936; *Educ* Uppingham, Hackey Sch USA; *m* 1, May 1962 (m dis 1973), Jane Diana, da of Vernon Nicholson (d 1968); 2 s (James b 1963, Anthony b 1965), 1 da (Amanda b 1969); m 2, 13 April 1978, Carol Ann Pruitt, da of Ralph Johannessen (d 1985); 1 step da (Delaine Pruitt b 1969); *Career* CA; ptnr Coopers & Lybrand 1966-90; pres ICAEW 1989-90 (memb Cncl 1978-, vice pres 1987-88, dep pres 1988-89); pres: Birmingham CAs' Students Soc 1977-78, Birmingham and West Midlands Soc of CAs 1982-83, dir Hillstone Sch Tst Ltd Malvern 1971-86, pres Birmingham and Edgbaston Debating Soc 1977-78, chm Edgbaston C of E Coll for Girls Ltd 1982-88; treas: Bishop of Worcester's Miny Fund 1970-90, CAs' Dining Club (pres 1989-), Birmingham Eye Fndn (tstee); memb: Arthritis and Rheumatism Cncl W Midlands, Queen Elizabeth Hosp Birmingham Jubilee Appeal Ctee, Birmingham Diocesan Bd of Fin 1990-; dir Birmingham Repertory Theatre Ltd 1990-; Liveryman Worshipful Co of CAs in England and Wales 1987; FCA 1961; *Recreations* music, woodwork, watching rugby football; *Clubs* RAC; *Style—* Philip Couse, Esq; 15 Chad Road, Edgbaston, Birmingham B15 3ER; Coopers & Lybrand, 43 Temple Row, Birmingham B2 5JT (☎ 021 233 1100, fax 021 200 4040, telex 337892)

COUSINS, Capt Jack; s of Herbert Sidney Cousins (d 1954), of Leigh on Sea, Essex, and Mabel Irene Hilda, *née* Andrews (d 1968); *b* 2 Feb 1920; *Educ* Storrington Coll, Alleyn Ct Sch, Highfield Coll, Chalkwell Hall Sch, Westcliff HS, TS Mercury, Sir John Cass Coll Univ of London (Master Mariner Foreign Going); *m* 26 June 1948, Joyce Patricia (d 1969), da of Stanley Hennessy (d 1965), of Broomfield, Essex; 4 s (David b 1950, Roger b 1954, Simon b 1955, Andrew b 1958); *Career* Merchant Aircraft Carrier Amastra: 4 offr 1940, 3 offr 1941, 2 offr 1942, 1 offr 1943; Marine Offr/Master Basra Port Directorate Iraq 1948, with Marine Supts Dept Shaw Savill Line 1950; Royal Docks 1951-: harbour inspr, asst dockmaster, sr asst dockmaster, dep dockmaster; traffic co-ordinator/asst harbour master Port of London Authy, marine conslt 1981; int sports corr 1981; Port of London rep to Perm Int Assoc of Navigation Congresses 1957- (individual memb 1980-); memb Tech Ctee Hon Co of Master Mariners 1965-; London Maritime Assoc: hon sec 1956-69, vice chm 1969, vice chm and hon treas 1980; memb Nat Union of Marine Aviation and Shipping Tport Offrs 1956 (liaison offr 1956), former pres 1987 and P/R offr Essex Co Amateur Swimming Assoc, hon facilities sec Southern Cos Amateur Swimming Assoc 1976 (memb 1976), vice pres and life memb Southend-on-Sea Swimming Club (chm Multi Nat Ctee), patron Little Theatre Club; life memb: Old Westcliffians Assoc RFC, Southend Airport Club, LSO Club, Les Amis d'Edith Piaf Paris, Nat Film Theatre Club, Br Film Inst, The Folio Soc; publicity offr TS Mercury Old Boys Assoc; memb: Nat Swimming Pool Strategy Working Pty Sports Cncl 1976, Swimming Liaison Gp Eastern Sports Cncl 1976, Br Swimming Coaches Assoc 1980; memb Hon Co of Master Mariners 1959; Freeman City of London 1969, Liveryman Honourable Co of Master Mariners; *Recreations* swimming, skiing, theatre (shareholder: Really Useful Gp Ltd), philately, music, travel; *Style—* Capt Jack Cousins; Villa Valeta, 208 Carlton Ave, Westcliff-on-Sea, Essex SS0 0QD, (☎ 0702 343779); Piz D'Err, Dischmastrasse 20, 7260 Davos Dorf, Switzerland

COUSINS, John Peter; s of The Rt Hon Frank Cousins (1986), and Annie Elizabeth (Nance), *née* Judd; *b* 31 Oct 1931; *Educ* Doncaster Central Sch, Pelham County Sch; *m* 1, April 1959 (m dis 1975), Joan, *née* Hollingdale, da of Arthur Hubbard (d 1970); 3 da (Jill b 1959, Jane b 1961, Judith b 1965); m 2, 28 Feb 1976, Pauline Ellen; *Career* engine fitter RAF 1953-56; nat sec TGWU 1966-75 (dist offr 1963-66), dir Manpower and Industl Relations Nat Econ Devpt Office 1975-79, personnel dir Plessy Telecommunications and Office Systems Ltd 1979-81, dir Personnel and Industl Relations John Brown plc 1981-83, gen sec Claering Bank Union 1983-86, personnel dir Maxwell-Pergamon Publishing Corp 1986-88; chm: Nat Economics Devpt Office Drop Forgings Sector Working Pty 1976-78, Br Cncl of Productivity Assocs 1979-82, Nat Econ Devpt Office Rubber Tyre Sector Working Pty 1978-82; cmmr The Country Cmmn 1972-84, travelling fell Kingston Regnl Mgmnt Centre 1977-86; memb: Sandford Ctee 1971-72, bd The New Towns Cmmn 1974-79, cncl Royal Soc for the Protection of Birds 1982-86 (and Fin and Gen Purpose Ctee), bd the Royal Botanic Gdns Kew 1983-88, cncl UK WWF 1984-90, Educn 2000 1983-90 (fndr and tstee); FBIM 1987; lectr, broadcaster and writer on industl and labour relations; *Books* Managing for Profit (1980); *Recreations* music, walking, golf; *Style—* John Cousins, Esq; 1 White House, Vicarage Crescent, Battersea, London SW11 3LJ (☎ 071 924 2075); Marina de Cesares, CN 340, KM146, Cesares, Malaga, Spain; Albany Life Assurance, Vistec House, 185 London Rd, Croydon CR9 1AU (☎ 081 680 9357, fax 081 681 7849); Cousins Financial Services, 3 Library Ramp, Gibraltar (☎ 010 350 73437)

COUSINS, John Stewart; s of Leslie Raymond Cousins (d 1976), of Ferndown, Dorset, and Margaret Betty Kate, *née* Fry; *b* 31 July 1940; *Educ* Brentwood Sch, Britannia RNC Dartmouth, Jesus Coll Cambridge (MA); *m* 1, 26 Oct 1970 (m dis 1979), Anne Elizabeth, da of Patrick O'Leary (d 1976), of Llanishen, Glamorgan; 1 da (Charlotte b 1973); m 2, 28 Dec 1979, Geraldine Anne, da of Col Thomas Ivan Bowers, CBE, DSO, MC (d 1980), of Yateley, Hants; *Career* RN 1958-62, cmmnd Sub Lt 1960, served Far East in HMS Belfast and HMS Maryton; Kleinwort Benson Ltd: joined 1966, Far East rep Tokyo 1970-73, md Hong Kong Branch 1973-78; fin advsr to chm Porodisa Gp Indonesia 1979-80, ptnr de Zoete and Bevan 1980-85, dir Barclays de Zoete Wedd Securities 1985-, currently md Barclays de Zoete Wedd Equities Ltd; memb Panel on Takeovers and Mergers Hong Kong 1976-78; AMSIA 1968, memb Stock Exchange 1982; *Recreations* racing, rugby, cricket, field sports; *Clubs* Brooks's, Caledonian; *Style—* John Cousins, Esq; 73 Redcliffe Gardens, London SW10 (☎ 071 373 1919); Barclays de Zoete Wedd, Ebbgate House, 2 Swan Lane, London EC4 (☎ 071 623 2323, fax 071 956 4725, telex 081 881 2124

COUSINS, Raymond John Randal; s of Henry George Cousins (d 1983), and Freda Isabella *née* Roberts; *b* 14 July 1938; *Educ* Alleyn's Sch, King's Coll London (BSc); *m* 28 Dec 1963, Ruth Imogen, da of William Charles Vigurs (d 1982); 2 da (Fiona Mary b 4 Oct 1967, Kirstie Ann b 6 Oct 1969); *Career* ptnr Cyril Blumfield and Ptnrs 1973-; govr: Alleyn's Sch Ctee, Alleyn's Estates; treas ACE South East, church warden St Stephen's S Dulwich, chm BSI Ctee; Liveryman: Worshipful Co of Woolmen 1973 (clerk 1975-87, court 1986-), Worshipful Co of Engrs 1983 (court, asst clerk 1983-);

EUR Ing, CEng, FICE, FIStructE, MConsE; *Recreations* golf, squash, hill walking; *Clubs* Athenaeum, City Livery, Dulwich and Sydenham Hill Golf; *Style—* Eurling Raymond J R Cousins; 33 Hitherwood Drive, London SE19 1XA (☎ 081 670 4673); Cyril Blumfield & Partners, 192-198 Vauxhall Bridge Rd, London SW1V 1DX (☎ 071 834 3631, fax 071 630 9632)

COUSINS, Robin John; s of Frederick Charles Cousins, of Baridon House, Knole Park, Almondsbury, and Edna Valerie Higgs; *b* 17 Aug 1957; *Educ* Henbury Comp Sch; *Career* ice skater; Bristol Ice Dance and Figure Skating Club 1968-80, nat primary champion 1969, nat jr champion 1972, nat sr champion 1976-79, int team memb 1973-80, Olympic team memb Insbruck 1976, Olympic team memb Lake Placid 1980; Euro Championships: Bronze medal 1977, Silver medal 1979, Gold medal 1980; World Championships: Bronze medal 1978, Silver medal 1979, Silver medal 1980; Gold medal Olympic Games 1980, World freeskating champion 1978, 1979 and 1980, BBC Sports personality of the year 1980, peoples choice award sports 1980; world record for highest Axel jump (5.81 m) and back flip (5. 48 m) at Richmond Ice Rink 1983; appearances incl: Holiday on Ice 1980-83, Skateaway (own series HIV) 1984, Robin Cousins Electric Ice (world tour) 1984, Robin Cousins Ice Majesty (world tour) 1986, various tv shows (incl Royal Command Performance); 11 Gold medals World Pro Skate Championships 1983-86, World professional Champion 1983, 1984 and 1986; currently: vice pres and artistic dir Ice Castle International Training Center Calif, memb Bd of Dirs Foundation for International Ice Skating Advancement; *Style—* Robin Cousins, Esq; Lee S Mimms & Assoc, 12031 Ventura Blvd, Suite 1, Studio City, Calif 91604 USA (☎ 0101 818 985 0567)

COUTANCHE, Jurat the Hon John Alexander Gore; s of Baron Coutanche (Life Peer, d 1973); *b* 25 May 1925; *Educ* Sherborne; *m* 1, 1 Sept 1949, Jean Veronica (d 1977), da of late Alexander Thomson Dawson, of Portelet House, Jersey; 1 s, 2 da; m 2, 1978, Gillian Margaret, da of late Brig John Douglas Fellowes Fisher, CBE; *Career* Lt-Cdr RNR; Jurat of Royal Court of Jersey and Lt Bailiff; *Clubs* Royal Channel Islands Yacht; *Style—* Jurat the Hon John Coutanche; Clos des Tours, St Aubin, Jersey, CI

COUTINHO, Graça (Mrs Manuel Castilho); *b* 26 Feb 1949; *Educ* Lisbon Fine Art Sch, St Martin's Sch of Art (ILEA scholarship, Gulbenkian scholarship); *m* Manuel Castilho, s of His Excellency Guilhere Castilho; 2 da (Branca b 15 March 1974, Sara b 12 Sept 1980); *Career* artist; solo exhibitions: Modern Art Gallery Lisbon 1975 and 1983, Galeria Modulo (Oporto 1978, Lisbon 1980), Riverside Studios London 1979, Quadrum Gallery Lisbon 1986, Bertramd Gallery 1986, The Showroom Gallery London 1987, Todd Gallery London 1988 1989 and 1990, Calouste Gulbenkian Museum Lisbon 1989, Graça Fonseca Gallery Lisbon 1990 and 1991; gp exhibitions incl: Portuguese Contemporary Art (Lisbon 1975, San Paulo and Rio de Janeiro 1976), Lunds Kuntshall Lunds Sweden 1976, Beograd Belgrade 1977, Sao Paulo Biennale Brazil 1979, Paris Biennale 1980, Drawings (German Inst) Lisbon 1984, painting and a sculpture for Gaby Agis performance (Almeida Theatre) 1985, ARCO (Quadram Gallery) Madrid 1986, John Moores Exhibition Liverpool 1987 and 1989, Art Fair (Air Gallery) London 1988, Works on Paper (Todd Gallery) London 1990, Large Works/Gallery Artists (Art 91 Business Design Centre London) 1991; *Style—* Ms Graca Coutinho; Todd Gallery, 326 Portobello Rd, London W10 5RU (☎ 081 960 6209)

COUTTS, Alan; s of Stanley Coutts, of 4 Rossdale Road, Putney, London SW15 and Eva Betty, *née* Gregory; *b* 6 Oct 1947; *Educ* Wandsworth Sch; *m* 8 Oct 1976, Philomena Margaret, da of Thomas Joseph Walsh, of 3 Collingwood Place, Walton on Thames, Surrey; 4 s (Mark b 1977, Stuart b 1978, Daniel b 1981, Thomas b 1983); *Career* dir Robert Fraser and Ptnrs Ltd 1979-88, Regentcrest plc 1987-; memb Inst of Taxation; *Recreations* tennis, watersports, theatre; *Style—* Alan Coutts, Esq; 7 Conduit Street, London W1R 9TG (☎ 071 408 1485)

COUTTS, (Thomas) Gordon; QC (1973); s of Thomas Coutts (d 1976), and Evelyn Gordon Coutts; *b* 5 July 1933; *Educ* Aberdeen GS, Univ of Aberdeen (MA, LLB); *m* 1 Aug 1959, Winifred Katherine, da of William Alexander Scott (d 1982); 1 s (Julian b 1962), 1 da (Charlotte b 1964); *Career* passed Advocate 1959, standing junior counsel to Dept of Agric and Fisheries (Scot) 1965-7 chm: Industl Tbnls 1972, Med Appeal Tbnls 1984, VAT Tbnls 1990; *Recreations* golf, stamp collecting; *Clubs* New (Edinburgh), Bruntsfield Links Golf (Edinburgh); *Style—* T Gordon Coutts, Esq, QC; 6 Heriot Row, Edinburgh, EH3 6HU (☎ 031 556 3042)

COUTTS, Herbert; s of the late Herbert Coutts, and the late Agnes, *née* Boyle; *b* 9 March 1944; *Educ* Morgan Acad Dundee; *m* 24 Dec 1970, Angela Elizabeth Mason, da of late Henry Smith; 1 s (Christopher b 10 Feb 1976), 3 da (Antonia b 17 Nov 1971, Naomi b 12 April 1977, Lydia b 31 Dec 1980); *Career* keeper of Antiquities and Bygones Dundee Museum 1968-71 (asst keeper 1965-68), supt of Edinburgh City Museum 1971-73, city curator Edinburgh City Museums and Galleries 1973-; princ pubns: Ancient Monuments of Tayside (1970), Tayside Before History (1971), Edinburgh: An Illustrated History (1975), Huntly House (1980), Lady Stair's House (1980); exhibition catalogues incl Edinburgh Crafts (with R A Hill, 1973), Aince a Bailie Aye a Bailie (1974), Gold of The Pharaohs (ed, 1988), Dinosaurs Alive (ed, 1990), Sweat of the Sun - Gold of Peru; maj projects: City of Edinburgh Art Centre (1980), Museum of Childhood Extension (1986), The Peoples Story Museum (1989); vice pres Museum Assts Gp 1967-70; memb: Govt Ctee on Future of Scotland's Museums and Galleries 1978-80 (report published 1981), Cncl of Museums Assoc 1977-78 and 1986-88, Bd of Scottish Museums Cncl 1971-74 and 1986-88; museums advsr to Convention of Scottish Local Authys 1986-90, tstee Paxton House 1988-, tstee E Lothian Community Devpt Tst 1989-; contested S Angus (Lab) 1970; SBStJ 1977, AMA 1970, FSAScot 1965, FMA 1976; *Recreations* gardening, swimming, music, family; *Style—* Herbert Coutts, Esq; Kirkhill House, Queen's Rd, Dunbar, East Lothian, EH42 1LN (☎ 0368 63113); Huntly House Museum, 142 Canongate, Edinburgh, EH1 8DD (☎ 031 225 2424 ext 6607)

COUTTS DONALD, William Frederick James; s of late William Coutts Donald; *b* 27 Sept 1940; *Educ* Westminster Sch, Edinburgh Univ; *m* 1980, Priscilla Mary, *née* Aldington; 1 da; *Career* CA; dir Horne Bros Ltd 1974-; *Style—* William Coutts Donald, Esq; 47 Rosebank, 47 Holyport Rd, SW6 (☎ 071 381 3616)

COUVE DE MURVILLE, Most Rev Maurice Noël Léon; *see*: Birmingham, Archbishop of (RC)

COUZENS, Sir Kenneth Edward; KCB (1979, CB 1976); s of Albert Edward Couzens (d 1968), and May Phoebe, *née* Biddlecombe (d 1973); *b* 29 May 1925; *Educ* Portsmouth GS, Caius Coll Cambridge (BA), Univ of London (BA); *m* 1947, Muriel Eileen, da of Albert Fey (d 1943); 1 s, 1 da; *Career* dep sec HM Treasy (joined 1951) Incomes Policy and Pub Fin 1973-77, second perm sec Overseas Fin 1977-82, perm sec Dept of Energy 1982-85; dep chm British Coal Corporation 1985-88, chm Coal Products Ltd 1988-, dir Credit Lyonnais Capital Markets plc 1989-; memb Advsy Bd Nat Econ Res Assocs 1987-; *Recreations* gardening, reading, travelling; *Clubs* Reform; *Style—* Sir Kenneth Couzens, KCB; Coverts Edge, Woodsway, Oxshott, Surrey (☎ 0372 843207)

COVE-SMITH, Dr (John) Rodney; s of Dr R Cove-Smith (d 1988), and Florence Margaret, *née* Harris (d 1989); *b* 26 Jan 1943; *Educ* Rugby, Gonville and Caius Coll Cambridge (MA, MB BChir, MD); *m* 26 April 1969, Jacqueline Mary (Jackie), da of D K G Morgan, of 8 Foxgrove Ave, Beckenham, Kent; 3 da (Julia Elizabeth b 1972, Andrea Lesley b 1975, Laura Suzanne b 1980); *Career* house surgn Peace Memorial Hosp Watford Herts 1967-68, house physician St Thomas's Hosp 1968-69; registrar: Dorset Co Hosp 1969-71, Nottingham City Hosp 1971-72; sr registrar in gen med and nephrology City Hosp Nottingham 1972-78, hon sr registrar in nephrology Guy's 1976-77, conslt physician and nephrologist S Tees Health Authy 1978-, clinical tutor Univ of Newcastle 1986-; author various chapters and papers on renal med, particularly use of drugs in renal disease; memb: Br Diabetic Assoc, Euro Dialysis and Transplant Assoc, Br Transplant Soc; memb BMA, FRCP; *Recreations* sport (hockey, squash), music; *Style—* Dr Rodney Cove-Smith; Kirby House, Kirby-in-Cleveland, Middlesborough, Cleveland TS9 7AN (☎ 0642 712618); Dept of Nephrology, South Cleveland Hospital, Middlesbrough, Cleveland (☎ 0642 850850)

COVEN, Edwina Olwyn; CBE (1988), DL (1987); da of Sir Samuel Instone, DL, and Lady Alice Instone; *b* 23 Oct 1921; *Educ* St Winifred's Ramsgate, Queen's Coll London, Lycée Victor Duruy Paris, Marlborough Gate Secretarial Coll London; *m* 1951, Frank Coven; *Career* Private ATS (later Maj WRAC); army interpreter (French) serv UK and overseas incl: staff appts, Plans and Policy Div, Western Union Def Orgn (subsequently NATO), directorate manpower WO 1942-56; children's writer Fleetway Pubns 1959-84; gen features writer: She, Harper's, BBC Woman's Hour; performer and advsr children's and teenage ITV; memb Advsy Cncl BBC Radio London 1978-81, dir TV-am 1985- (vice chm, 1990-); stores conslt on promotion and fashion 1960-77, memb Advsy Ctee (Clothing and Footwear Sub Ctee) BSI 1971-73; chm Davbro Chemists 1967-71; JP Inner London N Westminster 1965-72 (dep chm 71-72), JP City of London 1969-88 (dep chm 1971-88), HM Lieut City of London 1981-, rep DL Greater London 1988-, chm City of London Police Ctee 1984-87 (dep chm 1983-84), memb Police Ctee AMA 1984-, memb Jt Ctee of Mgmnt London Ct of Int Arbitration 1983-89; Dowgate Ward City of London: memb Ct of Common Cncl 1972-, elected alderman 1973 and 1974, dep 1975-; chief commoner City of London 1987-88; chm WRAC Assoc 1989-90 (memb Cncl 1973-90 vice pres 1984-88, vice chm 1985-89); memb: TAVRA City of London 1979-86, Assoc Speakers 1975-, London Home Safety Cncl 1980-84; vice chm Cities of London and Westminster Home Safety Cncl 1984-89, vice pres Nat Orgn for Women's Mgmnt Educn 1983-, chm Ctee for 860th Anniversary Mayoralty of Corpn of London 1988-90, memb Bd of Govrs City of London Sch 1972-77, chm Bd of Govrs City of London Sch for Girls 1978-81; Liveryman Worshipful Co of Spectacle Makers 1972-, Hon Liveryman Worshipful Co of Lightmongers 1989-, memb Royal Soc of St George 1972-, chm Vintry and Dowgate Wards Club 1977, Hon Capt of Police Salt Lake City 1986-; vice pres: Operation Raleigh 1989-, FANY 1989-; Order of Wissam Alouite Class 111 (Morocco) 1987, OStJ 1987; *Books* Tales of Oaktree Kitchen (2 edn, 1960); *Recreations* homemaking generally, lawn tennis, watching a variety of spectator sports; *Clubs* Queen's, Hurlingham, Devonshire (Eastbourne); *Style—* Mrs Edwina Coven, CBE, DL; 22 Cadogan Ct, Draycott Ave, London SW3 3BX (☎ 071 589 8286)

COVENEY, Gerald Boore; s of Major Ronald Leslie Coveney, RE (d 1980), of Deepcut, Camberley, Surrey, and Hilary Elsie Boore; *b* 7 July 1938; *Educ* Farnham GS; *m* 1 Nov 1969, Shirley Rosemary Ann, da of Ronald Edmund Messenger, of Sussex; 2 s (Scott b 1971, Laurence b 1973); *Career* Lt-Sgt Platoon Instr Coldsteam Gds; chm and md Gerry Coveney and Assoc (Ad Agency) 1984-, asst dir JWT 1969-74; md: BMDC 1972-74, Lansdowne Marketing 1974-81, Lansdowne Euro 1981-84; memb Cncl IGD (Inst of Grocery Distribution); assoc memb: FDF (Food and Drink Fedn), CIES (Int Chain Stores Assoc); former chm Strangers Gallery; memb Marketing Ctee Lord's Taverners, Ctee Local C Assoc (former chm, former cllr (C)); *Recreations* home and family, swimming; *Clubs* Strangers Gallery; *Style—* Gerald B Coveney, Esq; Minden Lodge, Deepcut, Camberley, Surrey; Cavendish House, 51-55 Mortimer Street, London W1 (☎ 071 631 0016, fax 071 255 2003, car ☎ 0836 219096)

COVENEY, John Michael; s of Dr William Finbarr Coveney (d 1976), of Northampton, and Angela Elizabeth, *née* Godber; *b* 20 Sept 1951; *Educ* Franciscan Coll Buckingham, Northampton GS, King's Coll London (LLB); *m* 6 July 1974, Sarah Ann Mary, da of Dr Robert Arthur Sladden; 2 s (James Robert Finbarr b 1983, Nicholas Michael Julius b 1986); *Career* called to the Bar Middle Temple 1974-; memb: Hon Soc of Middle Temple, Criminal Bar Assoc, Br Horse Soc, Br Showjumping Assoc; *Recreations* riding, music, reading, travel; *Style—* John Coveney, Esq; Rothwell, Northamptonshire; 3 Temple Gardens, London EC4 (☎ 071 583 1155)

COVENEY, Michael William; s of William Coveney, and Violet Amy Perry; *b* 24 July 1948; *Educ* St Ignatius Coll, Worcester Coll Oxford; *m* Susan Monica Hyman; 1 s (Thomas Geoffrey Coveney b 16 Dec 1977); *Career* ed Plays and Players 1975-78 (asst ed 1973-75), theatre critic and dep arts ed Financial Times 1981-89 (contrib 1972-80), theatre critic The Observer 1990-; *Books* The Citz (1990); *Recreations* music, tennis, travel; *Style—* Michael Coveney, Esq; The Observer, Chelsea Bridge House, Queenstown Road, London SW8 4NN (☎ 071 627 0700)

COVENTRY, 11 Earl of (E 1697); George William Coventry; Viscount Deerhurst (I 1697); s of 10 Earl (ka 1940), and Hon Nesta Donne Philipps (who m 2, 1953, Maj Terence Fisher-Hoch), da of 1 and last Baron Kylsant; *b* 25 Jan 1934; *Educ* Eton, RMA Sandhurst; *m* 1, 22 March 1955 (m dis 1963), Marie Farquhar-Médard, da of William S Médard, of St Louis, USA; 1 s; m 2, 1969 (m dis 1975), Ann, da of Frederick William James Cripps; m 3, 1980, Valerie Birch; *Heir* s, Viscount Deerhurst, *qv*; *Career* late 2 Lt Gren Gds; *Style—* The Rt Hon The Earl of Coventry; Earls Croome Court, Earls Croome, Worcester

COVENTRY, Lady Maria Alice; resumed maiden name Coventry 1968; yst da of 10 Earl of Coventry (d 1940), and Hon Nesta Donne Philipps, da of 1 Baron Kylsant; *b* 2 Oct 1931; *m* 6 May 1954 (m dis 1968), John Richard Lewes, er s of late Capt John Hugh Lewes, CBE, DSC, RN (ret), of White Willows, Yelverton, Devon; *Style—* The Lady Maria Coventry; Levant Lodge, Earls Croome, Worcester

COVENTRY, Bishop of 1985-; Rt Rev Simon Barrington-Ward; s of Robert McGowan Barrington-Ward, DSO, MC (d 1948), of London, and Margaret Adele Barrington-Ward (d 1975); *b* 27 May 1930; *Educ* Eton, Magdalene Coll Cambridge (BA, MA), Westcott House Cambridge; *m* 13 Sept 1963, Jean Caverhill, da of Dr Hugh William Young Taylor, of Edinburgh; 2 s (Mary Caverhill b 1969, Helen McGowan b 1971); *Career* Nat Serv RAF 1949-50, PO 1949; lektor Free Univ Berlin 1953-54, chaplain Magdalene Coll Cambridge 1956; ordained: deacon 1956, priest 1957; lectr Univ of Ibadan Nigeria 1960-63, fell and dean Magdalene Coll Cambridge 1963-70, princ Crowther Hall Coll and Selly Oak Coll 1970-75, gen sec Church Missionary Soc 1975-85; chm Partnership for World Mission Int Affairs and Devpt Ctee; Chaplain to HM the Queen 1984-85; Prelate Order of St Michael and St George 1989-; Hon DD Wycliffe Hall Toronto 1983; FRAI; *Books* Love Will Out (1988); *Recreations* walking, bicycling; *Style—* The Rt Rev the Bishop of Coventry; Bishop's House, Davenport Rd, Coventry CV5 6PW (☎ 0203 672244)

COVERDALE, Stephen Peter; s of John Peter Coverdale, of Strensall, N Yorkshire, and Margaret Anne, *née* Cordukes; *b* 20 Nov 1954; *Educ* St Peter's Sch York, Emmanuel Coll Cambridge (Cricket blue); *m* 2 July 1977, Mary Jane, da of Michael Riddelsdell; 2 s (Paul Stephen b 24 July 1983, Duncan Philip b 14 Feb 1986), 1 da (Ruth Margaret b 12 Oct 1988); *Career* cricket administrator; former player: Yorkshire

CCC 1973-82, first class debut v Notts 1973, Young England v Young West Indies 1974; sec and mangr then chief exec Northamptonshire CCC 1985-; admitted slr, sports ed BBC Radio Leeds 1982-85; *Recreations* all sport, biographies, reading newspapers; *Style*— Stephen Coverdale, Esq; Northamptonshire CCC, County Ground, Wantage Road, Northampton NN1 4TJ (☎ 0604 32917, fax 0604 232855)

COVILL, Richard Vernon; s of Frederick Charles Covill and Gladys Bertha Covill; *b* 23 July 1934; *Educ* Shrewsbury Sch, Pembroke Coll Oxford; *m* 1958, Sian Mary, da of David Thomas Prichard (d 1943); 1 s (Charles b 1969), 2 da (Sarah b 1965, Harriet b 1971); *Career* barr at law; md The Head Wrightson Machine Co Ltd (part of Davy Corpn, mfr of equipment for the metal industries) 1975-82; Queen's Award for Export 1982, dir Davy McKee (Poole) Ltd; *Clubs* Cavalry and Guards; *Style*— Richard Covill, Esq; 51 Elgin Rd, Talbot Woods, Bournemouth (☎ 0202 529301); Davy McKee (Poole) Ltd, Wallisdown Road, Poole, Dorset (☎ 0202 537000)

COWAN, Brig (James) Alan Comrie; MBE (1956); s of Alexander Comrie Cowan, MC (d 1937), and Helen May Isobel, *née* Finlayson (d 1988); *b* 20 Sept 1923; *Educ* Rugby; *m* 2 Dec 1948, Jennifer Evelyn, da of Roland Evelyn Bland (d 1974), of Cornwell Glebe, Kingham, Oxon; 2 s (Anthony b 28 March 1953, Adrian b 16 Jan 1955), 1 da (Varian b 18 Oct 1950); *Career* cmmnd Rifle Bde 1942, served UK, Egypt and Italy 1942-45, regtl and staff appts in Egypt, Univ of Oxford, BAOR, Army Staff Coll, WO, Kenya, Malaya 1945-60, DS Army Staff Coll Camberley 1961-63, CO 1 Royal Leicesters (later 4 Royal Anglian) in UK, Aden and Malta 1964-66, GSO 1 17 Div Malaysia 1966-67, Col GS MOD London 1967-69, Cmd 8 Inf Bde NI 1970-71, DAG HQ UK Land Forces Wiltshire 1972-75; NI Office London 1975-80: princ for Industl Econ and Social Affrs 1975-78, asst sec 1978; sec Govt Hospitality Fund 1980-; Freeman City of London 1985; *Recreations* current affairs, music, theatre, countryside; *Clubs* Army and Navy, MCC; *Style*— Brig Alan Cowan, MBE; c/o Hoare & Co, 37 Fleet Street, London EC4P 4DQ; Government Hospitality Fund, 8 Cleveland Row, St James's London SW1A 1DH (☎ 071 210 4280, fax 071 930 1148)

COWAN, Brig Colin Hunter; CBE (1984); s of Lt Col Samuel Hunter Cowan, DSO (d 1953), and Jean Mildred, *née* Hore (d 1967); *b* 16 Oct 1920; *Educ* Wellington, RMA Woolwich, Trinity Coll Cambridge (MA); *m* 1, 17 Sept 1949, Elizabeth (d 1985), da of Stephen Williamson, MC (d 1986); 2 s (Michael b 1951, Simon b 1954), 1 da (Elizabeth b 1956); m 2, 16 July 1988, Janet, wid of A H Burnett (d 1979), da of Capt John Mackay (d 1975); *Career* cmmnd RE 1940, Royal Bombay Sappers and Miners 1942-46, WO (AG's Dept) 1952-54, cmd Malta Forces Sqdn RE 1954-56, WO (MO Directorate) 1957-60, cmd Engr Regt BAOR 1960-63, def advsr UK Mission to UN NY 1964-66, MOD (Army SD Directorate) 1966-68 (Brig Engr Plans 1969-70); chief exec Cumbernauld Devpt Corpn 1970-85; DL Dunbartonshire 1974-88; MICE 1967, FRSA 1984; *Recreations* walking, music, photography; *Clubs* New (Edinburgh); *Style*— Brig Colin Cowan, CBE; 12B Greenhill Gardens, Edinburgh EH10 4BW (☎ 031 447 9768)

COWAN, Dr David Lockhart; s of Dr James Lockhart Cowan, JP, TD (d 1970), and Meryl Lockhart, *née* Cook; *b* 30 June 1941; *Educ* George Watson Coll Edinburgh, Trinity Coll of Glenalmond Perthshire, Univ of Edinburgh (MB ChB); *m* 16 Sept 1966, Eileen May, da of Rev John William Gordon Masterton, of 19 Braid Ave, Edinburgh; 3 s (Christopher b 26 July 1967, Richard b 19 Oct 1969, Douglas b 31 May 1973), 1 da (Lindsey b 7 Jan 1971); *Career* chief resident prof Bryce Gen Hosp Toronto 1968-69; consIt otolaryngologist 1972-: City Hosp, Western Gen Hosp, Royal Hosp for Sick Children Edinburgh; hon sr lectr Univ of Edinburgh; hon sec laryngology section RSM, FRCSEd 1968; *Books* Paediatric Otolaryngology (1982), Logan Turner's Diseases of the Ears Nose Throat (jtly, 1980), Coping with Ear Problems (1985); *Recreations* golf, sailing, all sports; *Clubs* Honourable Co of Edinburgh Golfers (Muirfield), Bruntsfield Links Golfing Soc (Edinburgh), Elie Golf House; *Style*— Dr David Cowan; 28 Braid Hills Rd, Edinburgh EH10 6HY (☎ 031 447 3424); 14 Moray Pl, Edinburgh EH3 6DT (☎ 031 225 4843)

COWAN, David Neville; s of Roy Neville Cowan (d 1987), of Heyshott, W Sussex, and Dorne Margaret, *née* Burgoyne-Johnson; *b* 21 May 1950; *Educ* Marlborough, Univ of Bath (BSc, BArch); *m* 23 Aug 1975, Gillian Judith, da of David Hay Davidson, OBE (d 1983), of Lymington, Hants; 2 s (Jonathan b 1979, Christopher b 1988); *Career* architect 1975; formed David Cowan Associates 1983; dir: David Cowan Associates 1989, Charterfield Gp of Cos 1985; RIBA 1976; *Recreations* skiing, badminton, riding; *Style*— David N Cowan, Esq; Oak Tree Cottage, Nursery Lane, Maresfield, E Sussex (☎ 0825 2751); David Cowan Associates Ltd, Greenstede House, Station Rd, East Grinstead, W Sussex (☎ 0342 410 242)

COWAN, (Harold) Derrick; s of Samuel David Cowan (d 1979); *b* 19 June 1923; *Educ* University Coll Sch; *m* 1948, June Beryl; 2 c; *Career* served RAF in M East; chm Cowan de Groot plc 1978-88; *Recreations* golf, bridge, walking; *Clubs* Casanova; *Style*— Derrick Cowan, Esq; 47 Springfield Rd, London NW8 0QJ (☎ 071 624 6244)

COWAN, Eric Cecil; s of Cecil Cowan, of Bangor Road, Holywood, Co Down, NI, and Mrs Cowan, *née* Cosgrove; *b* 10 May 1929; *Educ* Sullivan Upper Sch Holywood, Queen's Univ Belfast (MB BCh, BAO, MCh, PhD); *m* 14 July 1955, Cynthia Joan, JP; 3 s (Keith b 28 Sept 1957, Nicholas b 17 Dec 1959, Peter b 7 Feb 1962); *Career* currently sr ophthalmic surgn Royal Victoria Hosp and City Hosp Belfast; external examiner in surgery: RCS, RCSI, Queens Univ Belfast; FRCS, FRCSI, FACS, FCOpth; *Recreations* surgery, designing and making surgical instruments, yachting; *Style*— Eric Cowan, Esq; Glenmakieran, 141 Bangor Rd, Holywood, Co Down, N Ireland (☎ 023 17 3311); Shore Cottage, Castleport, Burtonport, Dungloe, Co Donegal, Republic of Ireland; 115 Eglantine Ave, Belfast, NI BT9 6EX (☎ 0232 665795); Eye and Ear Clinic, Royal Victoria Hospital, Belfast; Eye Unit, City Hospital, Belfast

COWAN, Henry (Harry); s of Thomas Cowan, of Coatbridge, Lanarkshire, Scotland, and Annie Divens McKenzie, *née* Gregor; *b* 23 Sept 1947; *Educ* St Patricks Sch Coatbridge, Strathclyde Univ of Glasgow (BSc); *m* 12 April 1971, Alice, da of Patrick Smith (1969); 1 s (Martin b 16 Aug 1973), 1 da (Debbie b 15 April 1976); *Career* mangr regnl customer support Sperry Univac 1977-74, commercial mangr WM Press Group 1979-84, mangr corpn info systems Amersham Int 1984, ops dir Aetna Int 1984-88; dir: Pugh Carmichael Consits 1988-89, Apollo Gp of Co's 1988-; md Group Alpha Ltd 1989-; *Books* State of the Art Report (1986); *Recreations* rugby referee (London Soc), photography, squash; *Style*— Harry Cowan, Esq; 14 Lytton Rd, Hatch End, Middlesex, HA5 4RH; Group Alpha Ltd, Judd House, Ripper Road, Barking, Essex IGU OTU (☎ 081 428 0302, fax 081 595 2981, car 0860 581268)

COWAN, Prof (William) Maxwell; s of Adam Cowan (d 1981), and Jessie Sloan, *née* Maxwell (d 1986); *b* 27 Sept 1931; *Educ* Selbourne Coll London, Univ of Witwatersrand SA (BSc), Univ of Oxford (BM BCh, MA, DPhil); *m* 31 March 1956, Margaret, *née* Sherlock; 2 s (Stephen Maxwell b 1959, David Maxwell b 1962), 1 da (Ruth Margaret b 1957); *Career* univ lectr Univ of Oxford 1958-66, assoc prof Univ of Wisconsin 1966-68, prof and dept head Washington Univ Sch of Medicine St Louis Missouri 1968-80, prof Salk Inst La Jolla Calif 1980-86, vice chllr Washington Univ 1986-87, vice pres and chief scientific offr Howard Hughes Medical Inst Bethesda Maryland 1988-; hon fell Pembroke Coll Oxford 1987 (fell 1960-66); fell American Acad of Arts and Scis 1976; memb: Inst of Medicine 1978, American Philosophical Soc 1987, Soc for Neuroscience (pres 1978); foreign memb Norwegian Acad of Scis; foreign assoc: Royal Soc of SA, US Nat Acad of Scis 1981; FRS 1982; *Books* ed numerous vols on Neuroscience and Related Areas (1974); *Recreations* photography; *Style*— Prof Maxwell Cowan, FRS; 6337 Windermere Circle, North Bethesda, Maryland 20852, USA (☎ 301 493 9097); Howard Hughes Medical Inst, 6701 Rockledge, Bethesda, Maryland 20817, USA (☎ 301 571 0320, fax 301 571 0596)

COWAN, Michael John Julian; s of Kenneth Christopher Armstrong Cowan (d 1955), and Flora Muriel, *née* Stewart; *b* 24 June 1952; *Educ* Midhurst GS Sussex, Churchill Coll Cambridge (MA); *m* 26 Sept 1981, Hilary Jane, da of Albert Edward Slade (d 1987); 2 da (Eleanor Josephine, Philippa Rose); *Career* investmt advsr NM Rothschild & Sons Ltd 1973-78, investmt dir Lazard Bros & Co Ltd 1979-87, princ Morgan Stanley International 1987-; *Recreations* golf, tennis, DIY; *Style*— Michael Cowan, Esq; Ranmoor, 5 Fairmile Ave, Cobham, Surrey KT11 2JA (☎ 0932 865400); 1 Undershaft, London EC3P 3HP (☎ 071 709 3516, fax 071 283 4455, telex 917141)

COWAN, Sir Robert; s of Dr John McQueen Cowan and May Cowan; *b* 27 July 1932; *Educ* Edinburgh Acad, Univ of Edinburgh (MA); *m* 1959, Margaret Morton, *née* Dewar; 2 da (Frances, Katherine); *Career* RAF educn branch 1955-58; Fisons Ltd 1958-62, asst to sales dir Wolsey Ltd 1962-64, mktg conslt PA Management Consultants Ltd, overseas assignments in Iran and Yugoslavia, dir of consulting servs PA Hong Kong 1975-52 (incl assignments in USA, Japan, Thailand, Singapore, The Philippines and Indonesia); chm Highlands and Islands Devpt Bd 1982-, memb Bd Scottish Devpt Agency 1982-; memb: Ct Univ of Aberdeen 1989-, Gen Advsy Cncl BBC 1989-; govr Napier Coll Edinburgh 1989; Hon LLD Univ of Aberdeen 1987, Hon D Univ Univ of Stirling 1990; kt 1988; *Clubs* New (Edinburgh), Hong Kong; *Style*— Sir Robert Cowan Esq; The Old Manse, Farr Inverness-shire 1V1 2XA (☎ 08083 209); Highlands and Islands Development Board, Bridge House, Bank Street, Inverness (☎ 0463 234171, telex 75267)

COWAN, Robert Christopher; s of Philip Leslie Cowan (d 1987), of Rustington, Sussex, and Anne Marie-Louise, *née* Cammiade; *b* 27 Aug 1949; *Educ* St Bonaventure's Sch, LSE; *m* 1975 (m dis 1981), Susan Ann Greenway; partner Carole Anne, da of Reginald Fowler; 1 s (Thomas Richard Faure b 1986), 2 da (Charlotte Ellen b 1985, Alana Marie-Louise b 1989); *Career* reporter Leamington Spa Courier 1970-74, prodn ed Melody Maker 1974-76, features sub ed rising to chief features sub ed London Evening Standard 1976-86, chief features sub ed London Daily News 1986-87, The Times 1987-88, features ed The Scotsman 1988-90, oped ed The Daily Telegraph 1990-; newspaper design award 1989 and 1990 for feature pages and regnl daily papers; *Recreations* tennis, music, garden demolition; *Style*— Robert Cowan, Esq; Daily Telegraph, Peterborough Court At South Quay, 181 Marsh Wall, London E14 9SR (☎ 071 538 6415, fax 071 538 3810)

COWARD, Clive Alan; s of Charles Richard Coward, and Catherine Ellen Elizabeth, *née* Summersbee; *b* 30 Aug 1945; *Educ* King's Coll Sch Wimbledon, Pembroke Coll Cambridge (MA); *m* 6 July 1968, (Mary) Frances, da of Edward Vernon Geden (d 1981); 2 s (James b 1971, Giles b 1974), 1 da (Tammy b 1973); *Career* S G Whitaker Ltd: non exec dir 1968, exec dir 1970, md 1973, chm 1990-; jt md London Shop plc 1986-89; pres Capel and Dist Horticulture Soc, vice pres Capel CC; memb Govt Ctee of Inquiry into Mgmnt of Flats (NUGEE Ctee); Freeman: City of London, Worshipful Co of Fletchers (Master 1988-89), Worshipful Co of Chartered Surveyors; FRICS (pres planning and Devpt Div 1990-91); *Recreations* skiing, tennis, windsurfing, running; *Clubs* City Livery; *Style*— Clive Coward, Esq; Hope Hse, Great Peter St, London SW1P 3LT (☎ 071 222 2837)

COWARD, David John; CMG (1965), OBE (1962); s of Robert James Coward (d 1962), of Exmouth, and Beatrice, *née* Masters (d 1961); *b* 21 March 1917; *Educ* Exmouth GS, Sch of Law; *m* 25 Sept 1954, Joan Margaret, da of Reginald Frank (d 1959), of Doncaster, Yorks; 3 da (Susan Fischel b 1957, Ruth Coward b 1960, Vivienne Coward b 1967); *Career* WWII RN 1939-47, served HMS King George V 1941-43, HMS Benbow sec to SBNO Trinidad 1943-46, ADC to Govr to Trinidad 1947, demob Lt Cdr RNVR; admitted slr 1938; Colonial Legal Serv Kenya: asst registrar general 1948, dep registrar general 1952, registrar general public tstee and official receiver 1955-82 (permanent sec Miny of Justice and Constitutional Affrs Kenya 1963-64); Kenya Police Reserve 1949-63 (latterly as sr supt i/c Nairobi Area); chm Working Pty on the Future of the Company Secretarial Profession Kenya 1979-80, memb Accountants Registration Bd 1978-82, tstee Nat Museums of Kenya 1979-82; awarded Silver medal of the Int Olympic Ctee 1981 (for servs to the Olympic Movement); Freeman City of London 1984, memb Worshipful Co of Chartered Secretaries and Administrators 1985; FCIS 1961, ACIArb 1984; *Recreations* golf, genealogy; *Clubs* Nairobi and Limuru (Kenya), West Sussex Golf; *Style*— David Coward, Esq, CMG, OBE; North Perretts, Spinney Lane, West Chiltington, West Sussex RH20 2NX (☎ 0903 742521)

COWARD, Robert Alan; *b* 9 Dec 1951; *Educ* Univ of Nottingham (BMedSci, BM BS, DM); *m* Dr Stephanie A Coward, *née* Gomm; 1 s (Thomas b 19 May 1988); *Career* house physician City Hospital Nottingham, sr house offr in haematology (former house surgn) Gen Hosp Nottingham, sr house offr in med Hope Hosp Salford, res fell (former registrar) Manchester Royal Infirmary, sr registrar in renal med Royal Hallamshire Hosp Sheffield, conslt physician and nephrologist Royal Preston 1985-; author of papers on: multiple myeloma and renal diseases, vasculitis and the kidney; memb: Renal Assoc, Euro Dialysis Transplant Assoc, Int Soc of Nephrology, Manchester Med Soc; MRCP; *Books* Case Presentation in Renal Medicine (1984); *Recreations* photography, gardening; *Style*— Robert Coward, Esq; 18 Briksdal Way, Lostock, Bolton BL6 4PG; Dept Renal Medicine, Royal Preston Hospital, Sharoe Green Lane, Fulwood, Preston PR2 4HT (☎ 0772 710 744)

COWARD, (John) Stephen; QC (1984); s of Frank Coward (d 1980), of Huddersfield, and Kathleen, *née* Bell; *b* 15 Nov 1937; *Educ* King James's GS Huddersfield, Univ Coll London (LLB); *m* 4 March 1967, Ann Lesley, da of Frederick Leslie Pye, of 17 Ashburnham Crescent, Leighton Buzzard, Beds; 4 da (Victoria b 1969, Sarah b 1971, Laura b 1974, Sophie b 1976); *Career* served RAF 1957-59; lectr in law and constitutional history UCL and Police Coll Bramshill 1962-64; barr Inner Temple 1964; recorder of Crown Ct 1980; chm Scaldwell Educnl Charity, memb Scaldwell Chamber Choir; *Recreations* wine, gardening, singing; *Clubs* Northampton and County, Scaldwell; *Style*— Stephen Coward, Esq, QC; The Grange, Scaldwell, Northampton NN6 9JP (☎ 0604 880255); 2 Crown Office Row, Temple, London EC4Y 7HJ (☎ 071 353 1365, car tel 0860 489443)

COWDEROY, Norman Derrick; s of Frank Cecil Cowderoy (d 1957), of Esher, Surrey, and Celia Winifred Cowderoy (d 1988); *b* 11 June 1928; *Educ* Kingston GS, Balliol Coll Oxford (BA); *m* 20 Aug 1955, Jennifer Margaret Veryan, da of Cyril Hadlow Colton, CBE (d 1988), of Cobham, Surrey; 3 s (Adrian, James, David); *Career* Army 1946-48, 2 Lt 1947, RHA Palestine 1947-48; shipbroker; sr exec dir H Clarkson and Co Ltd 1974-86 (joined 1949, dir 1966-74); shipping conslt 1987; viticulturalist, started Rock Lodge Vineyard Sussex 1965, fndr memb English Vineyards Assoc, fndr Weald and Downlands Vineyard Assoc (chm 1989); Freeman of City of London 1952, Liveryman Worshipful Co of Shipwrights 1974; *Recreations* listening to music; *Style*— Norman Cowderoy, Esq; Rock Lodge, Scaynes Hill, West Sussex (☎ 0444 831224);

Rock Lodge Vineyard, Scaynes Hill, West Sussex (☎ 0444 831567, fax 0444 831 541)

COWDRAY, Lady Anne Pamela; *née* Bridgeman; da of 5 Earl of Bradford (d 1957); *b* 12 June 1913; *m* 19 July 1939 (m dis 1950), 3 Viscount Cowdray, TD, DL; 1 s, 2 da; *Style*— The Lady Anne Cowdray; Broadleas, Devizes, Wilts

COWDRAY, 3 Viscount (UK 1917); Sir Weetman John Churchill Pearson; 3 Bt (UK 1894), TD; also Baron Cowdray (UK 1910); s (twin) of 2 Viscount (d 1933), and late Agnes Beryl (d 1948), da of Lord Edward Spencer-Churchill (5 s of 6 Duke of Marlborough); bro of late Hon Mrs Campbell-Preston, late Lady McCorquodale, of Newton, and Nancy, Viscountess Blakenham, Hon Mrs Hugh Carter and Hon Mrs John Lakin; *b* 27 Feb 1910; *Educ* Eton, ChCh Oxford; *m* 1, 19 July 1939 (m dis 1950), Lady Anne Bridgeman, da of 5 Earl of Bradford; 1 s, 2 da; m 2, 4 March 1953, Elizabeth Georgiana Mather, da of late Sir Anthony Mather-Jackson, 6 Bt; 1 s, 2 da; *Heir* s, Hon Michael Pearson; *Career* Capt Sussex Yeomanry; PPS to Under Sec of State for Air 1941-42; chm S Pearson and Son Ltd 1954-77, pres Pearson plc; *Clubs* White's, Cavalry and Guards; *Style*— The Rt Hon Viscount Cowdray, TD; Cowdray Park, Midhurst, W Sussex (☎ 0730 812461); Dunecht, Skene, Aberdeenshire (☎ 033 06 244); 17th Floor, Millbank Tower, Millbank, London SW1P 4QZ

COWDREY, Christopher Stuart; *b* 20 Oct 1957; *Educ* Tonbridge Sch; *m* 1 Jan 1989, Christel Magareta, da of Carl-Johan Arne Holst-Sande; *Career* Kent CCC: joined 1976, co cap 1979, capt 1985-90, played in over 300 matches; Int career: played for Eng under 19 team versus' W Indies 1974, capt Young Eng to W Indies 1976, Eng debut in Bombay 1984, played in all 5 test matches in victorious Eng tour to India 1984-85, capt of Eng versus W Indies at Headingley 1988; played: 6 Internationals, 3 one day Internationals; took a wicket on fourth ball in test match cricket bowling Kapil Dev, scored a century in first innings in the Benson & Hedges competition; *Books* Good Enough (with Jonathan Smith, 1986), Whats Your Sport (with David Lemmon, 1988); *Recreations* golf, soccer, writing, backgammon and all sports; *Style*— Christopher Cowdrey, Esq; Kent County Cricket Club, St Lawrence Ground, Old Dover Rd, Canterbury, Kent (☎ 0227 456886)

COWDREY, (Michael) Colin; CBE (1972); s of late Ernest Arthur Cowdrey, of Bangalore, India, and Kathleen Mary, *née* Taylor; *b* 24 Dec 1932; *Educ* Tonbridge, BNC Oxford; *m* 1, 1956 (m dis), Penelope Susan, da of late Stuart Chiesman, of Chislehurst, Kent; 3 s, 1 da; m 2, 1985, Lady Herries of Terregles, *qv*; *Career* cricketer, capt Kent CCC 1957-71, 112 appearances for England, capt 23 times; conslt Barclays Bank plc S E Region; pres MCC 1987, chm Int Cricket Cncl 1989; master Worshipful Co of Skinners' 1986; *Recreations* golf; *Clubs* Boodle's, MCC; *Style*— Colin Cowdrey, Esq, CBE; c/o Barclays Bank plc, 10-12 Church Rd, Haywards Heath, W Sussex RH16 3Y

COWDRY, Quentin Francis; s of Brig Denzil Adrian Cowdry, of Woodbridge, Suffolk, and Fay Mary, *née* Willcocks; *b* 27 Feb 1956; *Educ* Woodbridge Sch Suffolk, Univ of Leicester (BA); *m* 27 Feb 1988, Zoë Laine, da of William McIntyre; *Career* graduate trainee reporter Nottingham Evening Post 1978-81, shipping reporter Southern Evening Echo 1981-84, reporter Sunday Telegraph 1984-86, reporter and lobby corr Daily Telegraph 1986-89, home affairs corr The Times 1989-; *Recreations* shooting, fly fishing, skiing, keeping fit; *Style*— Quentin Cowdry, Esq; The Times, 1 Pennington St, London E1 9XN (☎ 071 782 5928)

COWDY, Hon Mrs (Haidee Marylyn Antonina); *née* Rawlinson; da of Baron Rawlinson of Ewell, PC, QC (Life Peer), *qv*, by his 1 w Mrs Haidee Turner; *b* 9 May 1948; *m* 1968, (William) Richard Annesley; 1 s, 1 da; m 2, 1985, Maj Ralph Edward Cope Cowdy, DL, elder s of Robert McKean Cowdy; *Recreations* riding; *Style*— The Hon Mrs Cowdy; Summer Island, Loughgall, Co Armagh, N Ireland

COWDY, Susan; MBE (1981); da of Capt Ivor Stewart-Liberty (d 1953), of Bucks, and Evelyn Katherine, *née* Phipps (d 1966); *b* 6 Aug 1914; *Educ* Common Lane House Sch Letchmore Heath Herts, Bishops Tatchbrook Finishing Sch Warwicks; *m* 31 Aug 1935, late John Bernard Cowdy, s of Edward Cowdy, DL (d 1934), of N Ireland; 1 s (Michael b 1936), 2 da (Fenella b 1936, Evelyn b 1938); *Career* amateur natural historian and wildlife conservationist; pres: Bucks Bird Club, Chesham and Dist Natural History Soc; vice pres: Bardsey Island Tst, Bucks Archaeological Soc, The Berks Buckinghamshire and Oxfordshire Naturalists' Tst; pres The Lee Old Church Tst; formerly cncl memb CPRE (Bucks); Formerly; cncl memb RSPB, hon sec and vice pres Br Tst for Ornithology; *Recreations* study of flora and fauna in British Isles; *Style*— Mrs Susan Cowdy, MBE; Rushmere, The Lee, Great Missenden, Bucks (☎ 024 020 341)

COWELL, Alan Christopher; MC (1944); s of Edmund Frederick Cowell (d 1928); *b* 4 Feb 1920; *Educ* St Christopher Sch Letchworth; *m* 1949, Muriel Dorothy, da of Ben Marsden (d 1953), of Ahmedabad, India; 2 s, 1 da; *Career* Maj Indian Army, Assam and Burma; dir: Electronic Rentals Group and subsidiary cos 1947-85, Byrne Davy (UK) Ltd; *Recreations* racing, rowing, rugby, wrestling; *Clubs* Army and Navy; *Style*— Alan Cowell, Esq, MC; Old Park, Rusper, Horsham, Sussex RH12 4QT (☎ 0293 871452, fax 0293 871696)

COWELL, Peter Reginald; s of Reginald Ernest Cowell, CBE (d 1982) of Lowmoor, Craddock, Cullompton, Devon, and Philippa Eleanor Frances Anne *née* Prettejohn; *b* 9 March 1942; *Educ* Bedford Sch, Gonville and Caius Coll Cambridge (MA); *m* 4 Aug 1975, Penelope Jane, da of Andrew John Presgrave Bowring (d 1987), of New Romney, Kent; 2 s (Nicholas b 1976, William b 1980), 1 da (Sarah b 1980); *Career* called to the Bar Middle Temple 1964; asst Recorder 1985-, memb Senate Inns of Ct 1975-78; occasional memb Ctee: Thames Hare and Hounds Club, The Old Stagers; *Books* Cowell, A Genealogy (1986); *Recreations* running, acting, genealogy; *Style*— Peter R Cowell, Esq; 141 Palewell Park, East Sheen, London, SW14 (☎ 081 878 2434); 3 New Square, Lincoln's Inn, London, WC2A 3RS (☎ 071 405 5577)

COWELL, Prof Raymond; s of Cecil Cowell (d 1970), and Susan, *née* Green; *b* 3 Sept 1937; *Educ* St Aidan's GS Sunderland, Univ of Bristol (scholarship, studentship, BA, PhD), Univ of Cambridge (post grad Cert Ed, annual essay prize Educn Dept); *m* 14 Aug 1963, Sheila, da of George Bolton (d 1970); 1 s (Simon Jonathan b 1965), 1 da (Emma Victoria b 1968); *Career* asst engrg master Royal GS Newcastle upon Tyne 1962-66, sr lectr Trinity and All Saints Coll Leeds 1966-70, head of Engrg Dept Nottingham Coll of Educn 1970-73, dep rector Sunderland Poly 1981-87 (dean 1974-80), dir and chief exec Nottingham Poly 1988-; memb: CNAA 1974-77 1981-85, Unit for Devpt of Adult and Continuing Educn 1986-90, Mgmnt Ctee of Dirs of Polys 1989-, Br Cncl Ctee for Int Cooperation in Higher Educn 1990; memb Bd Greater Nottingham Trg and Enterprise Cncl 1990; *Books* Twelve Modern Dramatists (1967), W B Yeats (1969), Edition of Richard II (1969), Critics on Yeats (1971), Critics on Wordsworth (1973), The Critical Enterprise (1975); *Recreations* music, theatre, golf; *Clubs* Liberal; *Style*— Prof Raymond Cowell; Nottingham Polytechnic, Burton St, Nottingham NG1 4BU (☎ 0602 418418, fax 0602 473523, telex 377534)

COWELL, Robert Douglas; s of Douglas Walter Cowell, of Newport, Gwent, and Gladys, *née* Williams; *b* 9 Feb 1947; *Educ* Newport GS Gwent, Balliol Coll Oxford (BA, MA, PhD); *m* 1, 18 Oct 1969 (m dis 1984), Janice Carol; 2 da (Elizabeth Sarah b 1978, Julia Mary b 1980); m 2, 24 July 1986, Elizabeth Henrietta, da of Timothy Patrick Neligan, of Esher, Surrey; *Career* night shift foreman Turner & Newall Ltd 1972, investmt analyst Hoare Govett Ltd 1972-77, UK corporate devpt mangr Hanson Trust plc 1977-80, md Hoare Govett Securities (Hoare Govett) 1980-89, chm Quoted UK Ltd 1982-89, ptnr Makinson Cowell 1989-; *Recreations* horse racing, golf; *Style*— Robert Cowell, Esq; Makinson Cowell, 16-18 St John's Lane, London, EC1M 4BS (☎ 071 490 4977, fax 071 490 5712)

COWELL, Roger Housden; s of Ernest Frederick Cowell; *b* 3 Sept 1939; *Educ* King's Sch Rochester; *m* 1963, Margaret Anne, *née* Hillier; 1 s, 1 da; *Career* md Ace Filtration Ltd, dir Climavent SA Paris; CEng; *Recreations* squash, gardening, horology; *Clubs* Rumford; *Style*— Roger Cowell, Esq; Rooks Drift, Southfleet, Kent (☎ 047 483 2660); Airflow Works, Seymour Rd, Northfleet, Kent DA11 7BW (☎ 0474 325666, fax 0474 333132)

COWEN, Alan Geoffrey Yale (Geoff); s of Alan Cowen (d 1975), and Agnes, *née* Yale (d 1960); *b* 24 Sept 1937; *Educ* St Edward's Coll Liverpool; *m* 22 Sept 1962, Eileen Frances, da of Reginald Altoft Johnston, of 35 Hillview, Henleaze, Bristol; 2 da (Sian b 18 March 1965, Sara b 17 May 1966); *Career* Nat Serv Sgt RAEC 1959-61; various appts in publishing 1962-, appointed md Phaidon Press 1987; *Recreations* rugby; *Clubs* Maidenhead Rugby (fixture sec); *Style*— Geoff Cowen, Esq; Egerton Cottage, 31 Furze Platt Rd, Maidenhead, Berks SL6 7NE (☎ 0628 29237), Phaidon Press Ltd, Jordan Hill, Oxford OX2 8DP (☎ 0865 310664, fax 0865 310662, telex 38802)

COWEN, John Rutland; s of late John William Cowen; *b* 18 Oct 1931; *Educ* Aldenham; *m* 1, 1955 (m dis 1979), Jennifer Alice; m 2, 1980 (m dis 1987), Marie Victoria Gwendolyn; m 3, 1988, Suzanne Frances; 2 da; *Career* chm: March Group plc, J Day Group Ltd, Norman Hay plc, Materic Managements Services Ltd; CBIM, FInstD, FCIM; *Clubs* City Livery; *Style*— John Cowen, Esq; 36 Iverna Gardens, London W8 6TW (☎ 071 937 7625)

COWEN, Maurice Clifford; s of Bartley Cowen (d 1972), of London, and Joan Evelyn, *née* Homewood; *b* 29 Jan 1946; *Educ* Haverstock Sch, Univ of Sheffield (LLB, Edward Bramley Law prize); *m* 10 Aug 1968, Anne Margaret; 2 s (Matthew Duncan b 22 Jan 1974, Robert James b 30 Sept 1976); *Career* asst slr Slaughter and May 1970-72 (articled clerk 1968-70); Booth & Co: joined 1973, ptnr 1974-, head Co Law Dept 1989, memb Mgmnt Bd 1990; memb Law Soc 1970; *Recreations* literature, opera, music, golf, sailing, fellwalking; *Style*— Maurice Cowen, Esq; Booth & Co, Sovereign House, South Parade, Leeds LS1 1HQ (☎ 0532 832000, fax 0532 832060)

COWEN, Hon Mrs (Shelagh Mary); yr da of 1 and last Baron Rank, JP (d 1972), and Hon Laura Ellen Marshall (er da of 1 and last Baron Marshall of Chipstead); *b* 14 March 1923; *m* 1, 22 Aug 1945 (m dis 1955), Fred Morris Packard, s of late Morris Packard, of Los Angeles; 1 s, 1 da; m 2, 23 Jan 1957, Major Rosslyn Fairfax Huxley Cowen, MBE, s of Edward George Huxley Cowen, MRCP (d 1962), of 42 Upper Brook St, W1; 2 s; *Style*— The Hon Mrs Cowen; Shawdon, Glanton, Northumberland

COWEN, Rt Hon Sir Zelman; AK (1977), GCMG (1977, CMG 1968), GCVO (1980), PC (1981), QC (1972); s of Bernard Cowen (d 1975), and Sara, *née* Granat; *b* 7 Oct 1919; *Educ* Scotch Coll Melbourne, Melbourne Univ, New and Oriel Colls Oxford (BCL, MA, DCL); *m* 1945, Anna, da of Hyman Joseph Wittner, (d 1974), of Melbourne; 3 s, 1 da; *Career* called to the Bar Gray's Inn 1947 (hon bencher 1978), barr Victoria 1951, QC Queensland (Aust) 1971; prof of public law and dean of Faculty of Law Melbourne Univ 1951-66, vice chllr Univ of New England NSW 1967-70, Univ of Queensland 1970-77; govr gen of Australia 1977-82, chm Press Cncl (UK) 1983-88; provost Oriel Coll Oxford 1982-90, pro vice chllr Univ of Oxford 1988-90, KStJ 1977; Knight Grand Cross of the Order of Merit of the Italian Republic 1990; kt 1976; *for further details see Debrett's Handbook of Australia and New Zealand*; *Style*— The Rt Hon Sir Zelman Cowen, AK, GCMG, GCVO, QC; Commonwealth Offices, 4 Treasury Place, East Melbourne, Victoria 3002, Australia

COWGILL, Brig Anthony Wilson; MBE (1945); s of Harold Wilson Cowgill (d 1965), and Hilda, *née* Garrett (d 1933); *b* 7 Nov 1915; *Educ* Manchester GS, Univ of Birmingham (BSc), RCMS; *m* 2 April 1949, Joan Noel Mary, da of Peter James Stewart (d 1960); 1 s (Andrew Anthony b 1957), 1 da (Patricia Anne b 1951); *Career* cmmnd 1939, Def HQ Ottawa 1943-44, NW Europe 1944-45, GHQ India 1947, AHQ Pakistan 1948, Cwlth Div Korea 1953-54, MOD 1962-65 and 1966-69, ret as Brig 1969; chief indust engr Rolls Royce Ltd 1969-77, dir Br Mgmnt Data Fndn 1981-, headed Br Mgmnt Advanced Tech study teams to US, Japan and Eur 1980-88; chm Klagenfurt Conspiracy inquiry which cleared Harold Macmillan (late Lord Stockton) of War crimes charges 1986-90; FIMechE, FIEE, FMS, int fell American Soc for Advancement of Engrg, Int Technol Transfer award 1987; *Books* Energy Management (1980), Management of Automation (1982), The Repatriations from Austria in 1945 (with Lord Brimelow and Christopher Booker, 1990); *Recreations* golf; *Clubs* Army and Navy, RAC; *Style*— Brig Anthony Cowgill, MBE; Highfield, Longridge, Sheepscombe, Stroud, Glos GL6 7QU (☎ 0452 813211)

COWGILL, Bryan; *b* 27 May 1927; *Educ* Clitheroe GS; *m* 1966, Jennifer E Baker, 2 s; *Career* Lt 3 Royal Marine Commando Bde 1943-47; former head of BBC Sport and BBC TV Outside Broadcasts Gp, later controller BBC 1, md Thames TV 1977-85, dir ITV, chm UPITN 1983-85; *Style*— Bryan Cowgill, Esq; 68 Chiswick Staithe, London W4 3TP

COWHAM, David Francis; s of Francis Ronald Cowham, of Gt Rossington, Glos, and Patricia, *née* Warwick; *b* 10 June 1940; *Educ* Owens Sch; *m* 2 June 1962, Kay Miriam, da of Charles Ward, of Histon, Cambs; 1 s (David b 1967), 1 da (Alison b 1965); *Career* banker, dir First Nat Fin Corpn plc 1985-, asst md First Nat Securities Ltd 1972-; *Recreations* theatre, literature, horseracing; *Clubs* Newmarket Race; *Style*— David F Cowham, Esq; Temple Close, Watford, Herts (☎ 0923 228161); First National House, Harrow, Middx (☎ 01 861 1313, car 0836 295 834)

COWIE, Alfred George Adam; s of Dr Alfred Cowie, DSO, TD (d 1987), of Aberdeen, and Edith Aileen Meldrum; *b* 22 Aug 1937; *Educ* Aberdeen GS, Leeds GS, Gonville and Caius Coll Cambridge (BA, MA), UCH (MB BChir); *m* 1 Aug 1959, Barbara Jean, da of Victor Henry Kelly (d 1979), of 9 Islington Place, Brighton 7, Sussex; 2 da (Fiona b 30 March 1963, Alison (Mrs Marshall) b 13 Feb 1965); *Career* conslt surgn Hosp for Tropical Diseases London 1974, conslt urologist UCH 1982 (sr lectr Dept of Surgery 1974, conslt sur 1974, teacher in surgery 1975), sr lectr Inst of Urology London 1982, conslt urologist Middx Hosp 1984, hon conslt surgn St Luke's Hosp for the Clergy 1984; chm Regnl Trg Ctee NE Thames RHA, memb Ctee Bloomsbury Health Authy London; memb: BMA 1962, RSM 1984; FRCS 1984; *Recreations* hill walking, vintage cars, DIY; *Style*— Alfred Cowie, Esq; 9 Burcote Road, Wandsworth, London SW18; University College Hospital, Gower St, London WC1 (☎ 071 387 8323)

COWIE, (Thomas) Andrew; s of Thomas Cowie of Broadwood Hall, Lanchester, Co Durham, *qv*; *b* 17 Feb 1950; *Educ* Rugby, Magdalene Coll Cambridge; *Recreations* golf, squash; *Clubs* Hawks, Jesters; *Style*— Andrew Cowie, Esq; Ruffside Hall, Ruffside, Co Durham DH8 9TY

COWIE, Billy; s of James Reid Cowie, of Scotland, and Mary Thomson, *née* Lauchlan; *b* 21 Aug 1954; *Educ* Portobello Comp Secdy Sch, Univ of Edinburgh (BMus); *Career* artistic dir, choreographer and composer (with Liz Aggiss) for: The Wild Wigglers (formed 1982, performed ICA, Wembley Arena, Le Zenith Paris), Divas Dance Company (formed 1985; performances incl: Torei en Veran Veta Arnold 1986-87,

Eleven Executions 1988, Dorothy and Klaus 1989-91, Drool and Drivel They Care 1990 (Zap cmmn), French Songs 1991; cmmnd by: Extemporary Dance Theatre for Dead Steps 1988-89, Carousel for Banda Banda 1989 and La Soupe 1990; music for TV incl: Love Affair with Nature (Channel 4), Putting on the South (TVS), POV (ITV), ICA 40 Year Retrospective (BBC 2); musical recordings incl: Youth in Asia (LP), Beethoven in Love (EP), Eleven Executions (CD), Banda Banda (CD); awards incl: Special award (Brighton Festival, 1989), ZAP award for Dance (Brighton Festival, 1989), BBC Radio award (Brighton Festival, 1990), Alliance & Leicester award (Brighton Festival, 1990), Time Out/Dance Umbrella award 1990; *Recreations* cinema; *Style—* Billy Cowie, Esq; 10-11 Pavilion Parade, Brighton BN2 1RA (☎ 0273 604141)

COWIE, Rev Dr Leonard Wallace; s of Rev Reginald George Cowie (d 1952), of Lincs, and Ella Constance, *née* Peerless; *b* 10 May 1919; *Educ* Royal GS Newcastle upon Tyne, Univ of Oxford (MA), Univ of London (MA, PhD); *m* 9 Aug 1949, Evelyn Elizabeth, da of Robert Trafford (d 1948), of Peterborough; 1 s (Alan b 1955); *Career* clerk in Holy Orders; lectr: St Mark and St John's Coll Chelsea 1945-68, Roehampton Inst of Higher Educn 1969-82; *Books* Henry Newman 1708-43 (1956), The March of the Cross (1962), Eighteenth-Century Europe (1963), Martin Luther (1969), The Reformation (1974), The French Revolution (1987), Lord Nelson, A Bibliography (1990); *Recreations* gardening, town walking; *Clubs* Athenaeum; *Style—* Rev Dr Leonard W Cowie; 38 Stratton Road, Merton Park, London SW11 3JG

COWIE, (John) Michael; s of Stanley Reader Cowie, and Janetta Brand, *née* Ramsay; *b* 2 Dec 1948; *Educ* Dundee HS; *m* 26 March 1976, Helen Boswell (Eilidh), da of James John MacAskill, of Drynoch, Carbost, Isle of Skye; 2 s (Stephen Alasdair b 1978, James Alexander b 1981), 1 da (Susan Victoria b 1983); *Career* CA; admitted Scot Inst 1973; Thomson McLintock (Dundee then Edinburgh) 1967-76, Ben Line (Edinburgh) 1977-79, Seaforth Maritime Ltd (Aberdeen) 1980-87, Belhaven plc (Perth) 1987-89; dir: Seaforth Maritime Ltd and subsidiaries 1986-87, The National Hyperbaric Centre Ltd 1986-87, Belhaven plc 1987-89, Shield Diagnostics Ltd (Dundee) 1989-; *Recreations* rugby (ret), squash, water skiing, music, reading (railways), wine; *Style—* Michael Cowie, Esq; 123 Glasgow Road, Perth PH2 0LU (☎ 0738 22039); Shield Diagnostics Ltd, The Technology Park, Dundee DD2 1SW (☎ 0382 561000, fax 0382 561056)

COWIE, Thomas; OBE (1982); s of Thomas Stephenson Knowles Cowie (d 1960), and Florence, *née* Russell (d 1984); *b* 9 Sept 1922; *Educ* Bede GS Sunderland; *m* 1, 1948, Lillas Roberts, *née* Hunnam; 1 s (Thomas Andrew b 1950, *qv*), 4 da (Elizabeth b 1951, Susan b 1953, Sarah b 1959, Emma b 1962); m 2, 1975, Mrs Diana Carole Wentworth Evans; 3 da (Alexandra b 1975, Charlotte b 1978, Victoria b 1982), 1 step s (Steven b 1964), 1 step da (Catherine b 1965); *Career* chm and chief exec T Cowie plc; landowner (1620 acres); *Recreations* shooting, walking; *Style—* Thomas Cowie, Esq, OBE; Broadwood Hall, Lanchester, Co Durham (☎ 0207 520 464); T Cowie plc, Millfield House, Hylton Rd, Sunderland SR4 7BA (☎ 091 514 4122 telex 537065)

COWIE, Hon Lord; William Lorn Kerr Cowie; QC (Scot 1967); s of late Charles Rennie Cowie, MBE, and Norah Slimmon Kerr; *b* 1 June 1926; *Educ* Fettes Coll, Clare Coll Cambridge, Glasgow Univ; *m* 1958, Camilla Henrietta Grizel, da of Randall Colvin Hoyle; 2 s, 2 da; *Career* Sub Lt RNVR 1944-47, advocate Scotland 1952, appointed a senator of the Coll of Justice in Scotland with title of Lord Cowie 1977; *Clubs* New (Edinburgh), RSAC Glasgow; *Style—* The Hon Lord Cowie, QC; 20 Blacket Place, Edinburgh 9 (☎ 031 667 8238)

COWLEY, Elsie, Countess; (Mary) Elsie; *née* May; *m* 1, Joseph Torbet Himes (decd); 1 s (George Hadley Himes); m 2, 1933, as his 2 w, 4 Earl Cowley (d 1962); 2 s (7 Earl, Hon Brian Timothy Wellesley); *Style—* The Rt Hon Elsie, Countess Cowley; 4900 Plumas St, Reno, Nevada 89509, USA

COWLEY, 7 Earl (UK 1857); Garret Graham Wellesley; also Baron Cowley of Wellesley (UK 1828), Viscount Dangan (UK 1857); s of 4 Earl Cowley (d 1962), by his 2 w, Mary Elsie May; suc half n, 6 Earl, 1975; *b* 30 July 1934; *Educ* Univ of S California (BS), Harvard Univ (MBA); *m* 1, 1961 (m dis 1966), Elizabeth Susanne, da of late Hayes Lennon; 1 s, 1 da; m 2, 1968, Isabelle O'Bready; m 3, 1981, Paige Deming; *Heir* s, Viscount Dangan, *qv*; *Career* gp vice pres Bank of America NT and SA London; Int Investment Management Service 1980-85; dir Bank of America Int (London) 1978-85, dir various Bank of America Tst Cos; chm Cowley & Co financial and business conslts 1985-90; investmt ptnr Thomas R Miller & Son (Bermuda) 1990-; *Style—* The Rt Hon the Earl Cowley; PO Box 221, Douglas, Isle of Man

COWLEY, Dr James; CBE (1984); *b* 18 Aug 1924; *Educ* UK Class 1 Combined Cert of Competency (Steam and Motor), Extra First Class Cert of Competency (Steam and Motor). 1MechEng final exam in Workshop Mgmnt and Indsutl Admn, Univ of London (BSc), Univ Coll Univ of London (PhD); *m* 1957, Jean Straughan; 2 s (John James b 1960, Martin Straughan b 1968); *Career* mechanical engrg apprentice Thomas Dryden and Sons Ltd Preston 1939-44; marine engr 1944-52: Bibby Bros Liverpool, Hopemount Shipping Co, Lyle Shipping Co Glasgow, Shell Tankers; Dept of Transport Marine Survey Orgn: engr and ship surveyor 1952-61, print engr and ship surveyor 1961-70, chief examiner of engrs 1970-73, chief surveyor 1973-76, engr surveyor-in-chief 1976-81, surveyor gen of ships 1981-88, ret 1988; hon exec chm The Maersk Co (IOM) Ltd 1988-, perm rep Republic of Vanuatu Int Maritime Orgn UN 1989-, marine cnslt 1990-; Int Maritime Prize Int Maritime Orgn UN 1987, Denry Gold medal Inst of Marine Engrs 1982; FEng 1983, FIMarE 1961, FIMechE 1963, hon fell Noutical Inst, Euro Engr Award 1980; *Recreations* ballroom dancing; *Style—* Dr James Cowley, CBE; 21 Stanstead Road, Caterham, Surrey CR3 6AD (☎ 0883 345774, fax 0883 341093); The Maersk Company (IOM) Ltd, Portland House, Station Road, Ballasalla, Isle of Man (☎ 0624 822667, fax 0624 822618)

COWLEY, Lt-Gen Sir John Guise; GC (AM 1935), KBE (1958, CBE 1946, OBE 1943), CB (1954); s of Rev Henry Guise Beatson Cowley (d 1938), of Fourgates, Dorchester, Dorset; *b* 20 Aug 1905; *Educ* Wellington, RMA Woolwich; *m* 1941, Irene Sybil, da of Percy Dreuille Millen, of Berkhamsted, Herts; 1 s, 3 da; *Career* 2 Lt RE 1925, Lt-Gen 1957, controller of munitions Min of Supply 1957-60, Master-Gen of the Ordnance and memb Army Cncl WO 1960-62, ret; chm: Bowmaker Ltd 1962-71, Keith and Henderson Ltd 1973-76, Polamco Engrg 1976; former dir: C T Bowring and Co Ltd, Alastair Watson Ltd, British Oxygen Ltd; chm of govrs and vice pres: Wellington Coll 1969-76, Brockenhurst Coll 1977-83; Kt Cdr of the Order of Orange Nassau (Netherlands) 1946; FRSA; *Style—* Lt-Gen Sir John Cowley, GC, KBE, CB; Whitemoor, Sandy Down, Boldre, Lymington, Hants (☎ 0590 23369)

COWLEY, John Henry Stewart; s of Kenneth Cyril Cowley (d 1983), of Douglas, IOM, and Daphne, *née* Leake; *b* 20 Feb 1947; *Educ* King Wiliam's Coll; *m* 1, 12 May 1971, Mary, da of late Geoffrey Whitehead, of Manchester; 1 s (George Edward Douglas b 1976), 1 da (Joanne Jane Caroline b 1973); m 2, 20 March 1986, Carolyn, da of Barry Walter Golding Thompson, of Tunbridge Wells; 1 s (Daniel Kenneth Gordon b 1986); *Career* brewer, dir: Heron and Brearley Ltd (now Isle of Man Breweries Ltd) 1972, Okell and Son Ltd (brewers) 1972, Warburg Investmt Management (IOM) Ltd 1980, Bowring Tyson (IOM) Ltd 1984, Castletown Brewery Ltd 1986; chm and md IOM Breweries Ltd 1983; cncl memb IOM Chamber of Commerce 1985 (chm 1981-83, pres 1983-85); *Recreations* game shooting, sailing; *Clubs* Manx Automobile, Ellan Vannin; *Style—* John Cowley, Esq; Rock Villa, Strathallan Road, Onchan, IOM (☎ 0624 75478); Isle of Man Breweries Ltd, 25 Drumgold Street, Douglas, IOM (☎ 0624 74611, telex , 629781 BREWMN G)

COWLEY, Patrick Martin; s of Denis Martin Cowley, QC (d 1985), and Margaret Hazel, *née* Teare, of Ellan Vannin, The Quay, Castletown, IOM; *b* 18 Aug 1941; *Educ* Radley; *m* 1 Oct 1966, Alison Mary, da of Archibald Robert Alexander Marshall (d 1963); 1 s (Philip b 1970), 2 da (Penelope b 1967, Alexandra b 1980); *Career* conslt Cowley Groves Co Ltd 1986; dir: Mercury Fund Mangrs (IOM) Ltd 1980, Douglas Gas Light Co 1985; vice chm IOM Childrens Home; *Recreations* motor racing, reading, shooting; *Clubs* Ellan Vannin, Executive; *Style—* Patrick Cowley, Esq; Sherdley, Princes Road, Douglas, IOM (☎ 0624 620060); Cowley Groves Co Ltd, 43 Athol St, Douglas, IOM

COWLEY, Prof Roger Arthur; s of Cecil Arthur Cowley (d 1964), of Romford, Essex, and Mildred Sarah, *née* Nash; *b* 24 Feb 1939; *Educ* Brentwood Sch, Univ of Cambridge (BA, PhD); *m* 4 April 1964, Sheila Joyce, da of Charles Wells (d 1970), of Romford, Essex; 1 s (Kevin David b 1969), 1 da (Sandra Elizabeth b 1966); *Career* res fell Trinity Hall Cambridge 1963-64, res offr Atomic Energy Canada Ltd 1964-70, prof of physics Univ of Edinburgh 1970-88, prof of experimental philosophy Univ of Oxford 1988-; FRSE 1971, FRS 1978; *Books* Structural Phase Transitions (1981); *Style—* Prof Roger Cowley, FRS, FRSE; Tredinnock, Harcourt Hill, Oxford OX2 9AS (☎ 0865 247 570); Clarendon Laboratory, Parks Rd, Oxford OX1 3P4 (☎ 0865 272 224)

COWLEY, Simon Charles; s of Charles Woods Cowley (d 1987) Sussex, and Ruth Heloise, *née* Portch; *b* 30 Aug 1949; *Educ* Malvern; *m* Annette Maria, da of Frank George Bevis (d 1986); 2 da (Georgina b 1984, Samantha b 1988); *Career* dir: Streets Fin Ltd 1979-86, AIM Technology Ltd 1987, AIM Cambridge Ltd 1987, Prime Management Ltd 1988-, Image Store Holdings plc 1989-, Data and Image Processing (UK) Ltd 1990-, Cellular Telecom Ltd 1990-; FCA; *Books* Practice Development, A Guide to Marketing Techniques for Accountants; *Recreations* squash, cooking; *Style—* Simon Cowley, Esq; 9 Studdridge St, London SW6

COWLEY, William; s of Ralph Smith Cowley (d 1949), and Dora, *née* Munns (d 1982); *b* 27 July 1925; *Educ* John Clare Sch Northampton, Northampton Coll of Technol; *m* 6 Sept 1945, Marjorie Barbara, da of Walter James Humphries, MBE (d 1974); 1 s (Martyn Barry Cowley b 1948); *Career* md Airflow Steamlines plc; chm: Pegasus Phosprime Ltd, S Whiteley & Sons Ltd; *Recreations* golf, gardening; *Clubs* Northants County GC, IOD; *Style—* William Cowley, Esq; 67 Abington Park Crescent, Northampton (☎ 0604 406994); Airflow Streamlines plc, Main Road, Far Cotton, Northampton (☎ 0604 762261, fax 0604 701405)

COWLING, (Thomas) Gareth; s of Clifford Cowling (d 1987), and Beryl Elizabeth, *née* Thomas; *b* 12 Nov 1944; *Educ* Eastbourne Coll; *m* 6 June 1970, Jill Ann, da of late Francis Neville Stephens; 1 s (Rupert b 13 Dec 1973), 1 da (Camilla b 16 March 1976); *Career* admitted slr 1969; asst slrs Dept New Scotland Yard 1969-72, called to the Bar Middle Temple 1972, ad eundem Western Circuit 1972; stipendiary magistrate: Metropolitan Area 1988-89, Hants 1989; *Clubs* Hampshire; *Style—* Gareth Cowling, Esq; The Law Courts, Winston Churchill Ave, Portsmouth, Hants (☎ 0705 819421)

COWLING, Maurice John; s of Reginald Frederick Cowling (d 1962), of London, and May, *née* Roberts (d 1963); *b* 6 Sept 1926; *Educ* Battersea GS, Jesus Coll Cambridge (BA); *Career* Capt Queen's Royal Regt British and Indian Armies; Univ of Cambridge: fell Jesus Coll 1950-53 and 1961-63, lectr in history 1961-76, fell and dir of studies in history Peterhouse 1963-, reader in history 1976-88; literary ed The Spectator 1970-71, prof of religion Columbia Univ NY 1989; Parly candidate (Cons) Notts 1958-59, memb Cambridgeshire and Isle of Ely CC 1966-70; *Books* Midland Liberalism (1963), Disraeli Gladstone and Revolution (1967), The Impact of Labour (1971), The Impact of Hitler (1975), Conservative Essays (ed, 1979), Religion and Public Doctrine in Modern England (vol I 1980, vol II 1985); *Style—* Maurice Cowling, Esq; Peterhouse, Cambridge CB2 1RD (☎ 0223 338200)

COWPER, Barry William Meadows; s of William Coburn Cowper (d 1986), of Angmering on Sea, Sussex, and Gertrude Botterill, *née* Rolls; *b* 13 July 1933; *Educ* Aldenham, Trinity Hall Cambridge (MA); *m* 9 March 1968, Brenda Mary, da of William Wallace Pelham, of Auckland, NZ; 2 s (Andrew b 1973, Timothy b 1974), 1 da (Philippa b 1970); *Career* ptnr George Henderson & Co Stockbrokers (later Henderson Crosthwaite & Co 1974) 1970-86, dir Henderson Crosthwaite Ltd 1987-; *Clubs* Leander, Hawks, City Univ; *Style—* Barry W M Cowper, Esq; PO Box 442, 32 St Mary At Hill, London, EC3P 3AJ (☎ 071 283 8577, fax 071 623 1997, telex 884035)

COWPER, John Clive; s of Harold Ernest Cowper (d 1987), of Southend, and Elizabeth Cowper; *b* 27 Nov 1945; *Educ* Sir William Collins Tech Coll; *m* 24 May 1969, Joan Grace Margaret, da of David Evans (d 1982), of London; 2 s (John Christopher b 1970, David James b 1976), 1 da (Natalie Julia b 1972); *Career* quantity surveyor David Esdales 1969-72, project executive Kenny and Reynold Ltd 1972-75, md Apeils Gp Holding Ltd 1979-89 (dir 1975-79); FIOS; *Recreations* triathlons, marathons; *Style—* John Cowper, Esq; 52 Grove Avenue, London N10 2AN (☎ 01 444 7162); Apeils Group, Unit F, Dalroard Industrial Estate, Dallow Rd, Luton, Beds (☎ 0582 456633, fax 0582 33043)

COWPERTHWAITE, Sir John James; KBE (1968), CMG (1964), OBE (1960); s of late John James Cowperthwaite of Edinburgh, and Jessie Wemyss Barron, *née* Jarvis; *b* 25 April 1915; *Educ* Merchiston Castle Sch, Univ of St Andrews, Christ's Coll Cambridge; *m* 1941, Sheila Mary, da of Alexander Thomson, of Aberdeen; 1 s; *Career* colonial admin service Hong Kong 1941, Sierra Leone 1942-45, fin sec Hong Kong 1961-71, int advr Jardine Fleming and Co Ltd 1972-82; *Clubs* Royal Hong Kong Jockey, Royal Hong Kong Golf, Royal and Ancient Golf; *Style—* Sir John Cowperthwaite, KBE, CMG; 25 South St, St Andrews, Fife (☎ 0334 74759)

COX, His Honour Judge Anthony; (James) Anthony; s of Herbert Sidney Cox (d 1972), and Gwendolin Margaret Cox (d 1973); *b* 21 April 1924; *Educ* Cotham Sch Bristol, Univ of Bristol (LLB); *m* 1950, Doris Margaret, da of Vincent Percy Fretwell (d 1933); 3 s, 1 da; *Career* War Serv RM 1943-46; barr 1949, rec of the Crown Court 1972-76, circuit judge 1976; *Recreations* cricket, golf, sailing, the arts; *Clubs* MCC, Royal Western Yacht, Yealm Yacht, Bigbury Golf; *Style—* His Hon Judge Anthony Cox; c/o The Courts Administrator, The Castle, Exeter, Devon

COX, Sir Anthony Wakefield; CBE (1972); s of William Edward Cox, CBE (d 1960), of Teddington, and Elsie Gertrude, *née* Wakefield (d 1967); bro of Oliver Cox, *qv*; *b* 18 July 1915; *Educ* Mill Hill, Architectural Assoc Sch of Architecture; *m* 1943, Susan Babington, da of Sir Henry Babington Smith, GBE (d 1923); 2 da; *Career* served WWII, Capt RE; ptnr Architects' Co-Partnership 1939-80; pres Architectural Assoc 1962-63, memb Royal Fine Art Cmmn 1970-85; FRIBA, FRSA; kt 1983; *Style—* Sir Anthony Cox, CBE; 5 Bacon's Lane, Highgate, London N6 (☎ 081 340 2543)

COX, Prof Antony Dawson; s of William Ronald Cox (d 1970), and Dorothy, *née* Gerrard (d 1961); *b* 2 Dec 1935; *Educ* Bryanston, Gonville and Caius Coll Cambridge (MA, MB BCh), St Thomas's Hosp London (M Phil); *m* 1 July 1961, (Pamela) Teresa, da of Capt Egerton Gervase Edward Harcourt-Vernon, MC (d 1976); 3 s (Simon b 1962, Nicholas b 1964, Hugo Francis b 1967); *Career* Nat Serv 2 Lt RA 1954-56; conslt in child and adolescent psychiatry Bethlem Royal and Maudsley Hosps London 1976-85, hon conslt in child and adolescent psychiatry to Br Army 1984-, sr lectr Inst of Psychiatry London 1985-87, Mersey RHA prof of child and adolescent psychiatry at Univ of Liverpool (fndn chair) 1987-89, prof of child and adolescent psychiatry UMDS of Guy's and St Thomas's Hosps Univ of London 1990-; tstee Assoc for Child Psychology and Psychiatry; memb BMA, FRSM, FRCPsych 1979, FRCP 1987; *Recreations* local and family history, music; *Style*— Prof Antony Cox; Flat 11, 92-94 Great Titchfield St, London W18 7AG; Wensley Hall, Wensley, Matlock, Derbyshire

COX, Arthur; *Career* professional football manager; player then youth coach Coventry City; coach: Walsall, Aston Villa, Preston North End, Halifax Town; asst mangr Sunderland then Blackpool; mangr: Chesterfield 1976-80, Newcastle Utd 1980-84, Derby County 1984-; achievements: Preston North End Div 3 Champions (coach), Sunderland FA cup winners 1973 (asst mangr), Newcastle promoted to Div 1 1984, Derby promoted to Div 2 1986 and Div 2 Championship 1987 (mangr); *Style*— Arthur Cox, Esq; Manager, Derby County FC, Baseball Ground, Shaftesbury Crescent, Derby DE3 8NB (☎ 0332 40105)

COX, Dr (Christopher) Barry; s of Herbert Ernest Cox (d 1983), and May, *née* Bell; *b* 29 July 1931; *Educ* St Paul's, Balliol Coll Oxford (BA, MA), St John's Coll Cambridge (PhD), Univ of London (DSc); *m* 6 April 1961, Sheila, da of William Edward Morgan (d 1978); 2 s (Timothy b 1962, Justin b 1970), 1 da (Sally b 1964); *Career* King's Coll London: asst lectr Zoology 1956-59, lectr 1959-66, sr lectr 1966-69, reader 1969-76, prof 1976-82, head Dept of Zoology 1982-85, head Dept of Biology 1985-88, prof Div Biosphere Sciences 1988-89, asst princ 1989-; Harkness Fell Cwlth Fund Harvard 1959, sr Fulbright fell Stanford 1989; former chm: Woodcote Residents Assoc, Action Ctee for Epsom, Epsom Protection Soc; Freeman City of London 1983; memb Palaeontological Assoc 1960 (vice pres 1980-81); *Books* Prehistoric World (1975), Biogeography an Ecological & Historical Approach (fourth edn 1985), Macmillans Illustrated Encyclopaedia of Dinosaurs and Prehistoric Animals 1988, Atlas of the Living World 1989; *Recreations* theatre, tennis, gardening; *Style*— Dr Barry Cox; Conifers, Grange Rd, Leatherhead, Surrey KT22 7JS (☎ 0372 273 167); Div of Biosphere Sciences, King's Coll, Campden Hill Rd, London W8 7AH (☎ 071 333 4316)

COX, Barry Geoffrey; *b* 25 May 1942; *Educ* Tiffin Sch Kingston Surrey, Magdalen Coll Oxford (BA); *m* 2, 1984, Katie Kay; 2 s, 2 da; *Career* journalist with: The Scotsman 1965-67, Sunday Telegraph 1967-70; reporter and prodr Granada TV 1970-74; London Weekend TV: ed 1974-77, head of current affrs 1977-81, controller of features and current affrs 1981-87, dir of corp affrs 1987-; currently dir LWT (Holdings) plc; sec Br Exec Int Press Inst; *Books* Civil Liberties In Britain (1975), The Fall of Scotland Yard (jtly, 1977); *Style*— Barry Cox, Esq; LWT, South Bank Television Centre, Upper Ground, London SE1 9LT

COX, Bradley Richard; s of Leslie Charles Cox (d 1978); *b* 12 Dec 1936; *Educ* Greenmore Coll; *m* Patricia; 1 da; *Career* Nat Serv RAF; dir: TFL Group Holdings Ltd, Dean & Bowes Gp plc, Queen's Award for Export 1979; memb Lloyds, FInstD; *Recreations* sailing, tennis, shooting; *Clubs* Sporting, Diners; *Style*— Bradley Cox, Esq

COX, (Charles) Brian; s of Hedley Ernest Cox, (d 1988), and Rose, *née* Thompson (d 1938); *b* 5 Sept 1928; *Educ* Wintringham Secdy Sch, Pembroke Coll Cambridge (MA, MLitt); *m* 7 Aug 1954, Jean, da of Harold Willmer (d 1968); 1 s (Richard Hedley b 1955), 2 da (Sally Jean b 1958, Celia Willmer b 1960); *Career* Mil Serv 1947-49: RAEC, WOII 1948; lectr Univ of Hull 1954-66, prof of Eng lit Univ of Manchester 1966-76 (dean Faculty of Arts 1984-86), visiting assoc prof Univ of Calif Berkeley 1964-65, John Edward Taylor prof of Eng lit 1976-, Brown fell Univ of the South Sewanee Tennessee 1980, pres Nat Cncl for Educnl Standards 1984-89 (chm 1979-84), pro-vice chllr Univ of Manchester 1987-; memb Kingman Ctee 1987-88, chm Nat Curriculum Eng Working Gp 1988-89; co-ed: Critical Quarterly 1959-, Black Papers on Educn 1969-77; *Books* The Free Spirit (1963), Modern Poetry (ed with A E Dyson, 1963), Practical Criticism of Poetry (ed with A E Dyson, 1965), Joseph Conrad: The Modern Imagination (1974), Every Common Sight (1981), Two-Headed Monster (1985); *Recreations* Manchester Utd, walking; *Clubs* Lansdowne; *Style*— Prof Brian Cox, CBE; 20 Park Gates Drive, Cheadle Hulme, Cheshire SK8 7DF (☎ 061 485 2162); Department of English, The University, Manchester M13 9PL (☎ 061 275 2000)

COX, Brian Robert Escott; QC (1974); s of George Robert Escott Cox, of Solihull; *b* 30 Sept 1932; *Educ* Rugby, Oriel Coll Oxford (BA); *m* 9 Aug 1969, Noelle, da of Dominique Gilormini, of Patrimonio, Corsica; 1 s (Richard b 10 Feb 1971), 1 da (Caroline b 8 Jan 1976); *Career* called to the Bar Lincoln's Inn 1954; practised: Jr Bar 1954-74, Midland and Oxford Circuit 1954-; rec Crown Ct 1972, Lord Chllrs' list of Dep High Ct Judges 1979, master of bench Lincoln's Inn 1985; *Style*— Brian Cox, Esq, QC, 1 King's Bench Walk, Temple, London EC4Y 7DR (☎ 071 353 8436)

COX, Baroness (Life Peer UK 1982), of Queensbury in Greater London; Caroline Anne Cox; Cdr Cross Order of Merit Republic of Poland 1990; da of Robert John McNeill Love, MS, FRCS (d 1974), of Brickendon, Herts, and Dorothy Ida, *née* Borland; *b* 7 July 1937; *Educ* Channing Sch Highgate, London Univ (BSc, MSc Econ); *m* 1959, Murray Newell Cox, FRCPsych, s of Rev Roland Lee Cox, of London; 2 s (Hon Robin Michael b 1959, Hon Jonathan Murray b 1962), 1 da (Hon Philippa Ruth Dorothy b 1965); *Career* sits as Cons Peer in House of Lords (deputy speaker); head Dept of Sociology N London Poly 1974-77; dir Nursing Education Research Unit, Chelsea Coll London Univ 1977-83; baroness-in-waiting and govt whip 1985; *Books* The Right to Learn (co-author with Dr John Marks); Sociology: An Introduction for Nurses, Midwives and Health Visitors; *Recreations* squash, campanology, hill walking; *Clubs* Royal Cwlth Soc; *Style*— The Rt Hon Lady Cox; 1 Arnellan House, 144-146 Slough Lane, Kingsbury, London NW9 8XJ (☎ 081 204 2321); The White House, Wyke Hall, Gillingham, Dorset SP8 4WS (☎ 0747 3436)

COX, Charles; s of Harry Cox, of London, and Myra Emily, *née* Brooking; *b* 25 Sept 1949; *Educ* Stratford GS London; *m* 12 April 1975, Sandra Carol, da of Victor Anthony Willis Taylor (d 1974); 1 s (Peter b 1978), 1 da (Helen b 1976); *Career* CA; Turquands Barton Mayhew 1968-79, ptnr Pannell Kerr Forster 1984- (joined 1979); memb PCC St Andrew's Church Hornchurch; FCA 1972; *Recreations* jogging, reading, Scout ldr, running a youth club; *Clubs* RAC; *Style*— Charles Cox, Esq; Pannell Kerr Forster, New Garden House, 78 Hatton Garden, London EC1N 8JA (☎ 071 831 7393, fax 071 405 6736, telex 295 928)

COX, Brig Charles Francis; OBE (1945); s of Maj William Stanley Ramsay Cox (d 1954), of Ashe Leigh, Ross, Herefords, and Margaret Emma, *née* Whinfield (d 1968); *see Burkes's Landed Gentry 1952, Kennedy-Cox*; *b* 28 April 1907; *Educ* Wellington, RMC Sandhurst; *m* 22 Nov 1955, Susan, da of Lt-Col J F Colvin, OBE, MC, JP, DL (d 1984), of Woldringfold, Horsham, Sussex; *see Burkes Landed Gentry, 18 edn Vol I 1965, Colvin of Monkhams Hall*; 1 s (Christopher b 13 March 1957), 2 da (Camilla Rosemary b 20 Oct 1958, Serena Mary (Mrs Merton) b 1 May 1962); *Career* 1 Bn S Wales Borderers 1926, served: UK, Egypt, Palestine, Hong Kong; Gold Coast Regt RWAFF 1932-38 (Adj and QM), Staff Capt HQ Br Forces Palestine and TransJordan 1938-39, 2 Bn SW Borderers Norway 1940, 2 Bn Gold Coast Regt RWAFF Gambia 1940-42; OC 5 Bn Gold Coast Regt: Gold Coast, Nigeria, India 1942-43, Burma 1943-44; OC 2 Bn E Surrey Regt 1945, OC 1 Bn S Wales Borderers Palestine and Cyprus 1945-48, dep pres Regular Cmmns Bd 1948-50, OC 1 Bn S Wales Borderers Eritrea and BAOR 1951-53, cmdt All Arms Trg Centre Sennelager BAOR 1953-54, cmd 133 Inf Bde UK 1954-57; asst cmmr-in-chief St John Ambulance Bde 1960-66; OStJ 1960; *Clubs* Naval & Military; *Style*— Brig Charles Cox, OBE; Broadwell House, Broadwell, Lechlade, Glos GL7 3QS (☎ 036 786 230)

COX, Christopher Charles Arthur; s of Col Harold Bernard Cox, of Farnham, Surrey (d 1990), and Ivie Vera, *née* Warren (d 1981); *b* 21 July 1944; *Educ* St Edwards Sch Oxford, Hertford Coll Oxford (BCL, MA); *m* 5 May 1984, Kathleen Susan Anne May, da of James Buist Mackenzie (d 1976), of Madrid, Spain; 2 da (Andrea b 1986, Georgina b 1987); *Career* admitted slr 1970; Coward Chance 1968-77, Spicer & Oppenheim 1981-84, ptnr Nabarro Nathanson 1986- (slr 1984-86); memb Tax Ctee ICC; Freeman City of London 1986; memb Law Soc 1970; *Books* Partnership Taxation (jtly, 1979), Capital Gains Tax on Businesses (jtly, 1986); *Recreations* mountain walking, music, theatre; *Style*— Christopher Cox, Esq; Nabarro Nathanson, 50 Stratton St, London W1X 5FL (☎ 071 493 9933, fax 071 629 7900, telex 8813144 G)

COX, His Hon (Albert) Edward; s of Frederick Stringer Cox; *b* 26 Sept 1916; *m* 1962, Alwyne Winifred Cox, JP; *Career* slr 1938, princ ptnr Claude Hornby and Cox 1946-76, rec 1972-77, circuit judge 1977, ret 1989; memb Parole Bd 1970-74, chm The London (Metropolis) Licensing Planning Ctee 1979; pres Br Acad of Forensic Sci 1978; *Style*— His Hon Edward Cox; 38 Carlton Hill, London NW8; Petit Bois, Teilhet, Arriége, France

COX, Rev Canon Eric William; s of Sydney Eric Cox (d 1979), of Beeston, Nottingham, and Maude Marie Cox; *b* 17 July 1930; *Educ* Henry Mellish GS Bulwell Notts, Bede Coll Durham (BA), Wells Theol Coll; *m* 7 Jan 1959, Jennifer Anne, da of Lt-Col The Rev Maurice James Fraser Wilson (d 1985), of Baschurch, Shropshire; 4 s (Peter b 1959, Timothy b 1960, Paul b 1963, Andrew b 1968), 1 da (Joanna b 1966); *Career* RAF 1949-51; ordained: deacon 1956, priest 1957; asst curate St Mary Magdalene Sutton-in-Ashfield 1956-59, asst chaplain Utd Anglican Church Brussels Belgium 1959-62; vicar: St Lukes Winnington Northwich Cheshire 1962-71, St Michael and All Angels Middlewich Cheshire 1971-; rector St John Evangelist Byley-cum-Leese Cheshire 1973-, rural dean Middlewich 1980-, hon canon Chester Cathedral 1984-; chm: govrs Sir John Deane's Coll Northwich, Middlewich and Dist Community Assoc; govr Middlewich HS, memb Rotary Club Northwich (past pres); *Style*— The Rev Canon Eric Cox; The Vicarage, 37 Queen St, Middlewich, Cheshire CW10 9AR (☎ 060 684 3124)

COX, Sir Geoffrey Sandford; CBE (1959, MBE 1945); s of (Charles William) Sandford Cox, of Wellington, NZ, and Mary, *née* MacGregor; *b* 7 April 1910; *Educ* Southland HS NZ, Otago Univ NZ, Oriel Coll Oxford; *m* 1935, Cecily Barbara Talbot, da of Alexander Turner, of Fernhurst, Sussex; 2 s, 2 da; *Career* WWII serv NZ Army in Med; journalist; formerly reporter with News Chronicle, Daily Express); ed and chief exec ITN, 1956-68 (fndr News at Ten), dep chm Yorkshire TV 1968-71, chm Tyne Tees TV 1972-74, chm UPITN Inc (USA) 1975-81, London Broadcasting Co 1977-81, ind dir The Observer 1981-89; kt 1966; *Books* Defence of Madrid (1937), The Red Army Moves (1941), Road to Trieste (1947), Race for Trieste (1978), See It Happen (1983), A Tale of Two Battles (1987), Countdown to War (1989); *Recreations* fishing, tracing Roman roads; *Clubs* Garrick; *Style*— Sir Geoffrey Cox, CBE

COX, Gilbert Henry; s of Cecil Henry Cox, of Manston Drive, Bishop's Stortford; *b* 12 April 1936; *Educ* Newport GS Essex; *m* 1, 7 Sept (m dis), Pamela Edith, da of Ernest Walter Arthur Firman; 1 s (Timothy Henry b 29 Dec 1960); m 2, 11 Oct 1969 (m dis), Valerie Iris, da of Jack Henry Gilder; *Career* Associated Press Fleet Street 1952-55, Freelance press photographer 1955-59, proprietor Cox Photography 1959-; Hon Professional Fame Photographer (Norway) 1986; memb Professional Photographers of America 1975, FBIPP 1975 (assoc 1970), FRPS 1976 (ARPS 1973); *Recreations* scuba-diving; *Style*— Gilbert Cox, Esq; Cox Photography, 3 Northgate End, Bishop's Stortford, Herts (☎ 0279 652024, fax 0279 505046)

COX, Sir (Ernest) Gordon; KBE (1964), TD; s of Ernest Henry Cox (d 1987), of Bath, and Rosina, *née* Ring (d 1931); *b* 24 April 1906; *Educ* City of Bath Boys' Sch, Univ of Bristol (DSc); *m* 1, 1929, Lucie Grace (d 1962), da of Charles Baker (d 1949); 1 s (Keith), 1 da (Patricia); m 2, 1968, Prof Mary Rosaleen Truter, da of Dr Douglas Norman Jackman (d 1976), of Battersea; *Career* served WWII Lt-Col NW Europe; reader in Chem Crystallography Univ of Birmingham 1940, prof of Inorganic and Structural Chemistry Univ of Leeds 1945-60, sec ARC 1960-71; Hon LLD Bristol, Hon DSc: Birmingham, Newcastle, E Anglia, Bath; FInstP, FI Biol, C Chem, Hon assoc, RCVS, FRS; *Clubs* Athenaeum, Lansdowne, English-Speaking Union; *Style*— Sir Gordon Cox, KBE, TD; 117 Hampstead Way, London NW11 7JN (☎ 081 455 2618)

COX, Graham Clive; s of Harry Albert Cox, MBE, of Purley, and Lydia Louisa, *née* Willcocks (d 1986); *b* 16 May 1933; *Educ* Whitgift Sch, Imperial Coll London (BSc, MSc, DIC); *m* 28 April 1962, Sarah Helen, da of Gerald Spencer Beesly (d 1977); 1 s (John b 1964), 1 da (Emma b 1967); *Career* Capt RE: 131 Parachute Engr Regt 1955-56, 42 Survey Engr Regt 1956-59, 135 Survey Engr Regt 1959-62; Cleveland Bridge and Engrg Co Ltd 1954-63, Rees Gp 1963-65, sr res engr LB of Croydon 1965-70, design team leader GLC 1970-74, mangr devpt Thames Water Authy 1974-84, conslt McDowells Ltd 1991- (dir 1985-90); Lewis Angel Medal Inst of Municipal Engrs 1982, Frederick Palmer Prize Inst of Civil Engrs 1983, Frederick Vick Award Inst of Pub Health Engrs 1983; nat chm Assoc of Closed Circuit TV Surveyors 1985-, memb Cncl Inst of Pub Health Engrs 1984-87 (chm Met Dist 1981-83); Freeman: City of London 1985, Worshipful Co of Paviors 1987; FIPHE 1970, FIMunE 1982, FICE 1984, FIWEM 1987, MConsE 1988; *Books* 43 pubns incl: The Sewers of the Thames Water Authority (1976), Underground Heritage (1981), Renewal of Urban Water and Sewerage Systems (1982), Problems of the Nations Sewers (1984); *Recreations* sailing, gardening, flint wall building; *Style*— Graham Cox, Esq; White Lodge, Sandy Lane, Kingswood, Surrey KT20 6NE (☎ 0737 832 784); McDowells Ltd, Bailey House, 215 Barnett Wood Lane, Ashtead, Surrey KT21 2DH (☎ 0372 277771, fax 0372 276668)

COX, Hilary Jane; da of Arthur T Cox, of Bath, and Edith, *née* O' Leary; *b* 25 Jan 1957; *Educ* La Sante Union Convent Bath, Univ of Manchester (BSc, MPS), Thames Business Sch (MBA); *Career* pharmacist St Thomas' Hosp 1979, sr pharmacist Guys Hosp 1984; Greenwich Dist Hosp: dist pharmacist 1986, dep unit gen mangr 1987, unit gen mangr 1990-; memb Br Judo Squad 1980; MRPharms 1979; *Recreations* squash, golf, swimming, skiing; *Style*— Ms Hilary Cox; Greenwich District Hospital, Vanbrugh Hill, London SE10 9HE

COX, James Henry; OBE (1971); s of Henry Walter Cox (d 1922), and Harriet Eliza, *née* Tucker (d 1931); *b* 24 April 1912; *Educ* Hoe GS, Sutton HS, HM Dockyard Sch, Univ of London; *m* 3 Jan 1937, (Gladys) Frances, da of Percival Thomas Davis (d 1941); *Career* served on staff of HM Dockyard Simonstown 1939-47; Admty Whitehall 1937-39, HM Dockyard Devonport 1947, dep chief surveyor Marine Dept Bd of Trade 1971-76 (joined 1947), dir and conslt advsr Sir J H Biles & Co Ltd; FRINA 1953, FI Mar E1957, C Eng 1969, FCI Arb 1976; papers incl: Design for Welding 1946 (Harvey Shacklock Gold Medal) Ship Design Aspects Of The Safe Containment of Dangerous Chemicals 1971, Fishing Vessel Safety 1976 (Samuel Baxter prize), The Evolution of Safety Requirements for Dynamically Supported Craft; *Recreations* watching rugby and golf; *Style—* James Cox, Esq, OBE; 31 Hurstleigh Drive, Redhill, Surrey RH1 2AA; Sir J H Biles & Co Ltd, Blackhall House, Blackhall Lane, Paisley PA1 1AT (☎ 041 848 1771, telex 778995 SEADRECG, fax 041 889 5479)

COX, John; s of Frank Beddoe Cox; *b* 26 Nov 1946; *Educ* Queen Mary's GS Walsall; *m* 1971, Rosemary Anne, *née* Chisholm; 2 da (Deborah b 1974, Sarah b 1976); *Career* dir: E Walters (Ludlow) Ltd 1979, Heaps of Nantwich Ltd 1977, Tillies-Paveley Ltd 1978, E Walters (Brownhills) Ltd 1988; FCA; *Clubs* Ludlow Golf; *Style—* John Cox Esq; The Forge, Orleton, nr Ludlow, Shropshire SY8 4HR (☎ 056 885 373); E Walters (Ludlow) Ltd, Old Street, Ludlow, Shropshire SY8 1NR (☎ 0584 3221)

COX, John; s of Leonard John Cox (d 1984), of Bristol, and Ethel Minnie May, *née* McGill (d 1980); *b* 12 March 1935; *Educ* Queen Elizabeth's Hosp Bristol, St Edmund Hall Oxford (BA); *Career* Nat Serv RN 1953-55; freelance dir theatre, TV, opera 1959-, dir of prodns Glyndebourne Festival Opera 1971-81, gen admin and artistic dir Scot Opera 1982-86, prodn dir Royal Opera 1988-; prodns for: La Scala Milan, Met NY, Munich, Frankfurt, Cologne, Stockholm, Brussels, Amsterdam, San Francisco, Sydney, ENO, Florence, Salzburg, Santa Fe, etc; maj interpreter: R Strauss, Stravinsky, Mozart; fndr dir of Music Theatre Ensemble; world premiers of: Goehr, Birtwistle; UK premiers: Ravel, L'Enfant Et Les Sortileges, Stravinsky, Oedipus Rex; memb Bd Greenwich Theatre; *Recreations* horticulture, fine art; *Clubs* Garrick; *Style—* John Cox, Esq; Royal Opera House, Covent Garden

COX, John Edward; s of Edward Ralph Cox, of Sutton-on-Sea, Lincolnshire, and Evelyn Lavinia Mary, *née* Pawley; *b* 18 Oct 1946; *Educ* The GS Brigg Lincs, Brasenose Coll Oxford (BA); *m* 17 Jan 1974, Diane, da of Bernard Sutcliffe (d 1985), of Hemingford Grey, Cambs; 1 da (Laura b 29 Jan 1976); *Career* called to the Bar Middle Temple; sales mangr: Int Book Info Services Ltd 1968-71, Sales Mangr The Open Univ 1971-76, md Open Univ Educnl Enterprises Ltd 1976-81, mktg dir telepublishing Butterworth and Co Ltd 1981-83, md Scholastic Publications Ltd 1983-90, periodicals dir B H Blackwell Ltd 1990; memb Air Travel Trust Ctee, chm Air Tport Users Ctee; memb BIM 1977, M Inst D 1990; *Recreations* philately, conversation; *Style—* John Cox, Esq; The Pippins, 6 Lees Close, Whittlebury, Towcester, Northants NN12 8XF (☎ 0327 857908), B H Blackwell Ltd, PO Box 40, Hythe Bridge Street, Oxford OX1 2EU (☎ 0865 792792, fax 0865 791438)

COX, (Wilfred) John Joseph; *b* 17 July 1927; *Educ* Moseley GS; *m* 6 June 1951, Joan Rose Cox; 1 da (Elaine b 4 April 1954); *Career* Fleet Air Arm 1944-47; chm John Bradley (Hldgs) Ltd; chm and dir: Aston Screw & Rivet Ltd, Fam Dise Ltd; dir John Bradley Ltd; former pres Rotary Club Halesowen, mason; FInstD; *Recreations* golf, rugby football; *Clubs* Moseley RFC, Truro RFC, Gay Hill Golf; *Style—* John Cox, Esq; 1-3 Duddleston Mill Trading Estate, Duddleston Mill Rd, Saltley, Birmingham B8 1BD (☎ 021 359 8721, telex 334241 G, fax 021 359 6302)

COX, (Edward) John Machell; s of Sqdn Ldr Edward Machell Cox, and Joan Edith, *née* Hewlett; *b* 18 Sept 1934; *Educ* Charterhouse, St Peters Hall Oxford (MA); *m* 29 May 1965, Elizabeth Jean, da of Maj Anthony Frederick Halliday Godfrey (ka France 1939); 1 s (Charles Mark), 1 da (Victoria); *Career* Nat Serv Lt RASC 1953-55; CA, ptnr: Brown Peet & Tilly 1969-71, Howard Tilly 1971-88, Baker Tilly 1988-; mayor Royal Borough of Kensington and Chelsea 1986-87 (cncllr 1974); memb: Mgmnt Ctee Octavia Hill & Rowe Housing Assoc, Br Museum (Nat Hist) Devpt Tst, Ctee Brighter Kensington & Chelsea Soc; judge London in Bloom competitions; Freeman City of London, memb Worshipful Co of Fruiterers; FCA; *Clubs* Hurlingham; *Style—* E J M Cox, Esq; 13 St Ann's Villas, Royal Crescent, London W11 4RT (☎ 071 603 9828); Baker Tilly, Commonwealth House, 1 New Oxford St, London WC1A 1PF (☎ 071 404 5541, fax 071 405 2836, telex 21595)

COX, Vice Adm Sir John Michael Holland; KCB (1982); s of late Thomas Cox, MBE, and Daisy Anne Cox; *b* 27 Oct 1928,Peking; *Educ* Hilton Coll Natal SA, RNC Dartmouth; *m* 1962, Anne Garden Farquharson, da of Donald Farquharson Seth Smith, MC, and formerly wife of Jacob, Viscount Folkestone (now 8 Earl of Radnor); 1 s, 1 da; *Career* HMS Britannia RNC 1946, ADC to Gen Sir Robert Mansergh C-in-C Allied Forces N Europe 1952 and to Govr of Victoria 1955, Cdr 1962, Capt 1968, naval attache Bonn 1969, Cdr guided missile destroyer HMS Norfolk 1972, dir Naval Ops and Trade 1973-75, Cdre NATO Standing Naval Force Atlantic 1976-77, Rear Adm 1977, COS to C-in-C Naval Home Cmd 1977-79, Cdr Anti-Submarine Gp 2 and Flag Offr Third Flotilla 1979-82, Vice Adm 1981, Flag Offr Naval Air Cmd 1982-83, ret; dir: Spastics Soc 1984-88, Soundalive 1988-; *Recreations* gardening, all sport; *Style—* Vice Adm Sir John Cox, KCB; Rake, Liss, Hants; c/o MOD Personnel Records, Whitehall, SW1

COX, Dr Maria Louise; da of Michael P Ahuja (d 1977), and Melanie, *née* Braganza (d 1984); *b* 10 May 1951; *Educ* Our Lady's Convent London, UCL, Univ Coll Hosp Med Sch (MB BS); *m* 11 Jan 1975, Steven Alan Lissant Cox, s of Alan Henry Cox, of The Shires, Beechwood Rd, Beaconsfield, Bucks; 2 s (Andrew b 1976, David b 1981), 1 da (Stephanie b 1979); *Career* conslt physician in med for the elderly SW Hertfordshire DHA; memb Br Geriatric Soc; memb BMA, MRCP; *Style—* Dr Maria Cox; The Shires, 14 Beechwood Rd, Beaconsfield, Buckinghamshire (☎ 0494 672953); Watford General Hospital, Vicarage Rd, Watford, Hertfordshire WD1 8HB (☎ 0923 244366)

COX, Neil Derek; s of Clifford Walter Earnest, and Meryl Rita, *née* Holland; *b* 1 Aug 1955; *Educ* King Edward VI GS Stafford, Glasgow Dept of Optometry (BSc); *m* 23 March 1981, Averin Moira, da of Philip Anthony Donovan; 1 s (Andrew b 1986), 2 da (Katy b 1984, Jocelyn b 1990); *Career* sr optometrist Moorfields and KCH London, private contact lens practice London; memb Cncl Int Glaucoma Assoc, lectured widely and published papers on clinical applications of contact lenses; Liveryman Worshipful Co of Spetaclemakers; FBCO 1978; *Recreations* wine, food, photography; *Style—* Neil D Cox, Esq; 28 Weymouth St, London W1N 3FA (☎ 071 631 1046)

COX, Nicholas Anthony David; s of David Cox, artist (d 1979), and Margaret Eva, *née* Maclean; *b* 9 Aug 1942; *Educ* Nautical Coll, Pangbourne (RNSchol); *m* 1, 21 March 1964 (m dis 1972), (Barbara) Jennifer Downing-Smith; 1 s (James b 13 April 1970); m 2, 4 Oct 1972, (Angela) Wendy Robinson, da of Dr Robert Mason Bolam, of Ferndown, Dorset; 3 step s (Simon Robinson b 24 June 1963, Timothy Robinson b 8 Dec 1964, Matthew Robinson b 8 April 1967); *Career* navigation offr P & O 1958-61, broker and underwriter Lloyds 1961-68; yacht designer and boatbuilder: dir Impact Boats Ltd 1970-; ACII; *Recreations* shooting, sailing, golf, gardening; *Style—* N A D Cox, Esq; Top Hall, Lyndon, Rutland; Impact Boats Ltd, Edithweston, Rutland (☎ 0780 721 556)

COX, Norman Arthur; s of John Charles Cox (d 1966), and Florence *née* Walton (d 1966); *b* 19 Oct 1927; *Educ* Ilford HS, Coll of Law; *m* 26 July 1952, Pamela Mary, da of Arthur Cook (d 1930), of Barking, Essex; 2 s (Nigel Paul b 1953, Nicholas John b 1968), 1 da (Glenda Mary b 1957); *Career* slr, sr ptnr Kenwright-Cox 1971-, pres W Essex Law Soc 1973-74, treas London Slr's Litigation Assoc 1987-; memb Law Soc; *Recreations* walking, gardening, concert-going; *Style—* Norman Cox, Esq; Elizabeth House, 4-7 Fulwood Place, Gray's Inn, London WC1V 6HG (☎ 071 242 0672, fax 071 831 9477)

COX, Oliver Jasper; CBE (1981); s of William Edward Cox, CBE (d 1960), of Teddington, and Elsie Gertrude Wakefield (d 1967); bro of Sir Anthony Wakefield Cox, *qv*; *b* 20 April 1920; *Educ* Mill Hill Sch, Architectural Assoc Sch of Architecture (AA Dip); *m* 1953, Jeanne Denise, da of Denis Cooper (d 1964), of Cambridge; 1 s (Paul), 2 da (Lucy, Jane); *Career* architect, painter, draughtsman, New Schs Div Herts CC Architects Dept 1948-49; Architects Dept Housing Div LCC 1950-59, dep chief architect and ldr R and D Gp MOHLG 1960-64, sr ptnr Shankland Cox, Architects and Planners 1965-85; *Recreations* painting, drawing, print making; *Style—* Oliver Cox Esq, CBE; 22 Grove Terrace, London NW5 1PL (☎ 071 485 6929)

COX, Patrick Lathbridge; s of Terry Brian Cox, of Victoria, BC, Canada, and Maureen Patricia, *née* Clarke; *b* 19 March 1963; *Educ* Cordwainer's Coll Hackney (DATech 1985); *Career* footwear designer; work included in collections of: Vivienne Westwood, John Galliano, Richard James, Alistair Blair, Lanvin, John Flett London and Paris 1985-90; exhibited in: Aust Nat Gallery, V & A; *Style—* Patrick Cox, Esq

COX, Peter Donald; s of Edward Donald Cox (d 1980); *b* 19 Aug 1928; *Educ* RNC Dartmouth; *m* 1953, Philippa Belle, da of Philip Brandon, of Wellington NZ; 1 s, 2 da; *Career* Lt Cdr RN, ret 1958; exec dir James Pearsall & Co Ltd 1961-78; dir: Bridport-Gundry plc 1964, Crewkerne Textiles 1983; md: Crewkerne Textiles Ltd 1978-83, all subsids of Bridport-Gundry Holdings, Redport Net Co Ltd 1983-; *Recreations* golf, tennis, bridge, philately; *Clubs* Naval; *Style—* Peter Cox, Esq; Mayfield, West Monkton, Taunton, Somerset (☎ 0823 412382); Redport Net Co Ltd, 94 East St, Bridport, Dorset

COX, Dr Robin Anthony Frederick; s of Ronald Frederick Cox (d 1986), of 6 Upcher Ct, The Esplanade, Sheringham, Norfolk, and Hilda Mary, *née* Johnson (d 1990); *b* 29 Nov 1935; *Educ* Ashby-de-la-Zouch GS, Gonville and Caius Coll Cambridge (MA, MB BChir), Guy's Hosp; *m* 8 Sept 1962, Maureen Jennifer, da of William Jackson Moore (d 1969), of N Walsham, Norfolk; 1 s (Andrew b 1967), 1 da (Fiona b 1964); *Career* princ med practice Gorleston on Sea Norfolk 1964-76, dir North Sea Med Centre 1972-76, med dir Phillips Petroleum Co Europe and Africa 1976-86; chief med offr; CEGB 1986-90, National Power; former: pres Gorleston Rotary Club, chm Diving Med Advsy Ctee, chm Cambridge Bird Club; sec Int Assoc Physicians for Overseas Serv, asst registrar Faculty Occupational Med, Liveryman Worshipful Soc of Apothecaries, Freeman City of London 1978; FRCP, FFOM, Bronze medallist Royal Humane Soc 1974; *Books* Offshore Medicine (1982); *Recreations* ornithology, fly fishing, gardening, photography, walking; *Clubs* Athenaeum, British Ornithologists; *Style—* Dr Robin Cox; Linden House, Long Lane, Fowlmere, Royston, Herts SG8 7TG (☎ 0763 208636); National Power Company, Sudbury House, 15 Newgate St, London EC1A 7AU (☎ 071 634 6244, fax 071 634 7020)

COX, Hon Robin Michael; er s of Baroness Cox (Life Peer) and Dr Murray Newell Cox; *b* 1959; *Educ* Kingsbury HS, The Royal Free Hosp Sch of Med London Univ (MB BS 1984); *m* 1985, Penelope Jane, da of Dr Richard Michael Griffin, of 64 Warwick Road, Bishop's Stortford, Herts; *Career* Surg Sub Lt RN; *Style—* The Hon Robin Cox; The Royal Naval Hospital, Plymouth PL1 3JY

COX, Dr (John) Rodgers; s of John Cox, of 80 Slayleigh Lane, Sheffield S10 3RH, and Alice, *née* Rodgers (d 1984); *b* 6 May 1927; *Educ* Nottingham HS, Univ of Sheffield Med Sch (MB ChB, MD); *m* 22 Dec 1952, Shelagh Marjorie, da of William James Bains (d 1969), of Sunningdale, Chapel Street, Kirkby-in-Ashfield Notts; 1 s (James Alan John b 1964), 2 da (Susan James Lewis b 1960, Lyn Joanne Smith b 1961); *Career* GP Sheffield 1956-66; conslt physician 1966-: St Georges Hosp Sheffield, Nether Edge Hosp, Royal Hallamshire Hosp; pubns incl: Sodium Content and Urinary Aldersterone Excretion in Patients with Congestive Cardiac Failure in Comparison with Normal Patients, Potassium and Sodium Distribution in Cardiac Failure, Effect of Enzyme Therapy on Plasma Lipid Levels in the Elderly, Lithium in Depression, Potassium Supplements and Total Body Potassium in Elderly Subjects; Capt Hallam CC Sheffield 1967-74; chm Sheffield Div BMS 1980, memb Exec Ctee Age Concern 1982-88, pres Br Assoc Servs To The Elderly 1989 (chm 1982-88); MRCPsych 1971, MRCGP, FRCP 1973, memb: Br Geriatric Soc, Soc of Endocrinology; *Books* Principles And Practise of Geriatric Medicine (contrib 1985); *Recreations* golf; *Style—* Dr Rodgers Cox; 80 Slayleigh Lane, Sheffield S10 3RH (☎ 0742 305443); Dept Medicine & Rehabilitation, Nether Edge Hospital, Osbourne Rd, Sheffield S11 1EL (☎ 0742 500222)

COX, Simon Foster Trenchard; s of Foster Trenchard Cox, of Stone House, Godalming, Surrey, and Madeleine Winifred Needham, *née* Cooper (d 1989); *b* 17 Jan 1956; *Educ* Eton, Trinity Coll Oxford (MA); *Career* HAC 1980-88, cmmnd 1985; admitted slr 1980; Norton Rose: articled clerk 1978-80, slr 1980-88, ptnr 1988-; Freeman City of London Slrs Co; memb Law Soc 1980; *Recreations* water sports, country sports; *Clubs* HAC; *Style—* Simon Cox, Esq; Norton Rose, Kempson House, Camomile St, London EC3A 7AN (☎ 071 283 2434, fax 071 588 1181, telex 883652)

COX, Stephen Joseph; s of Leonard John Cox (d 1984), of Bristol, and Ethel Mini May McGill (d 1980); *Educ* St Mary Redcliffe Sch Bristol, Central Sch of Art and Design; *m* 1 June 1970, Judith, da of John Douglas Atkins, of Well Court Farm, Tyler Hill, nr Canterbury, Kent; 1 s (Pelé Delaney), 1 da (Georgia); *Career* sculptor; pt/t lectr at several colls of art, assoc lectr Brighton Poly 1968-81; one man exhibitions incl: Tate Gallery London, Nigel Greenwood Gallery London, Oxford Museum of Modern Art, Midland Group Gallery Nottingham, Amsterdam, Milan, Rome, Florence, Geneva, Basle, Paris, New Delhi (Br rep Indian Triennale 1986); gp exhibitions incl: Paris Biennale 1977, British Sculpture in the Twentieth Century (Whitechapel Art Gallery 1981), Venice Biennale 1982, New Art (Tate Gallery London 1983), Int Garden Festival Liverpool 1984, International Survey of Painting and Sculpture 1984 (New York Museum of Modern Art), 40 Years of Modern Art 1945-85 (Tate Gallery London), British Art in the 1980's (Brussels Museum of Modern Art); works in collections incl: Tate Gallery, Br Cncl, Walker Art Gallery Liverpool, Henry Moore Centre for Sculpture, Groningen Museum Netherlands, Peter Ludwig Collection FRG, Fogg Museum USA; FCO cmmn for Cairo Opera House 1988-89; installations: granite sculpture Ganapathi & Davi (Broadgate London 1989), granite sculpture (new Br Cncl building New Delhi 1991); recent sculpture subject of film by Henry Moore Fndn 1991; joined Waddington Gallery London 1990; Arts Cncl major awards 1978 and 1980, Br Cncl bursaries 1978 and 1979; Hakene Open Air Museum prize Japan 1985, Indian Triennale Gold medal 1986; Goldhill Sculpture prize Royal Acad 1988; *Recreations* cricket, golf; *Clubs* Groucho, Chelsea Arts; *Style—* Stephen Cox, Esq; 154 Barnsbury Rd, London N1 OER

COX, Thomas Michael; MP (Lab) Tooting 1983; *b* 1930; *Educ* LSE; *Career* MP (Lab): Wandsworth Central 1970-74, Wandsworth Tooting 1974-1983; former Asst Gov Whip, Lord Cmmr of the Treasury 1977-79; *Style—* Thomas Cox Esq, MP; House of Commons, SW1

COX, Timothy John Lomas; TD (1971); s of Arthur Cox (d 1979), of Lower Willingdon, Sussex, and Winifred Mabel, *née* Lomas-Smith (d 1975); *b* 9 March 1939; *Educ* King's Sch Rochester; *m* 5 Sept 1970, Julia Rosemary, da of Henry Francis Workman (d 1988), of Grantown on Spey, Morayshire; 1 s (Adrian b 1974), 1 da (Rosemary b 1976); *Career* cmmnd 2 Lt RA TA 1959, (actg Maj 1970-), Central Vol HQ RA 1973-89 (Maj 1975-89); admitted slr 1962; ptnr Oswald Hickson Collier & Co 1966-; memb various professional and mil assocs; Freeman City of London 1983, Freeman and Liveryman Worshipful Co of Painter Stainers; *Recreations* photography, scuba diving, country pursuits; *Style—* Timothy Cox, Esq, TD; Messrs Oswald

Hickson Collier & Co, Essex House, Essex St, Strand, London, WC2R 3AQ (☎ 071 836 8333, fax 071 240 2236)

COX, Prof Timothy Martin; s of William Neville Cox, of Leics, and Joan Desirée, *née* Ward; *b* 10 May 1948; *Educ* The London Hosp Med Coll Univ of London (MSc, MD), Univ of Cambridge (MA); *m* 18 Jan 1975, Susan Ruth, da of Harry Philips Mason, of Builth Wells, Powys; 3 s (Andrew Martin b 1978, Stephen Edward b 1981, Christopher James b 1988), 1 da (Elizabeth 1986); *Career* house physician and surgn Professorial Units The London Hosp 1971-72, jr lectr in morbid anatomy Bernard Baron Inst 1972-74, jr clinical posts United Oxford Hosp 1974-75, Wellcome Tst sr clinical fell 1979-85; Royal Post Grad Med Sch: jr clinical posts 1974, registrar, hon sr registrar and MRC res fell 1975-79, sr lectr 1985-87, sr lectr in haemotology and conslt Dept of Med 1987-89; visiting scientist Dept of Biology, MIT 1983-84; memb Assoc of Physicians of GB and Ireland 1984; FRCP 1984; *Recreations* music, melanic moths; *Style—* Prof Timothy Cox; 29 High St, Cottenham, Cambridge; Department of Medicine, University of Cambridge School of Clinical Medicine, Addenbrooke's Hospital, Hills Rd, Cambridge CB2 2QQ (☎ 0223 336866)

COX, Sir Trenchard; CBE (1954); s of late William Pallett Cox, of London, and Marion Beverley; *b* 31 July 1905; *Educ* Eton, King's Coll Cambridge; *m* 1935, Mary Désirée (d 1973), da of Sir Hugh Anderson (d 1928), Master of Gonville and Caius Coll Cambridge; *Career* former vice pres RSA, dir Birmingham Museum and Art Gallery, dir and sec V and A Museum 1956-66; author of gallery guides and books on art; Chev of the Légion d'Honneur; FRSA, FSA, FMA; kt 1961; *Style—* Sir Trenchard Cox, CBE; 33 Queen's Gate Gdns, London SW7 (☎ 071 584 0231)

COXALL, David Oxford; s of William Oxford Coxall (d 1981), of Benson, Oxon, and Mary Grace Newton, *née* Gould (d 1988); *b* 19 July 1943; *m* ; 1 s (Lindsay Oxford b 11 April 1973), 3 da (Emily Oxford b 4 April 1971, Alexandra May Oxford b 29 March 1988, Grace Helen Oxford b 11 Jan 1990); *Career* admitted slr 1968; sr ptnr Alfred Truman & Son; memb Law Soc; *Recreations* ball sports, fishing, motor-cycling, reading; *Style—* David Coxall, Esq; The Old Court House, 5 Sheep St, Bicester, Oxon OX6 7JB (☎ 0869 252761, fax 0869 246619)

COXEN, Lady; Kathleen Alice; da of late Edward Doncaster, of Snettisham, Norfolk and Sleaford, Lincs; *m* 1912, Maj Sir William George Coxen, 1 Bt (Lord Mayor of London 1939-40, d 1946 when title became extinct); *Style—* Lady Coxen; 8a Wellswood Park, Torquay, Devon

COXON, Dr Ann Yvonne; da of James Stanley Coxon (d 1979), of Sussex, and Elizabeth Anne, *née* Traute (d 1985); *Educ* Farnborough Hill Coll, Guy's Hosp (MB BS, DCH, MRCP); *Career* initial training: Guy's Hosp, Whittington Hosp, Hammersmith Hosp, Gt Ormond St Hosp; Gp Reading 1969-74; hosp training in neurology: Hammersmith Hosp, Nat Hosp Queen Square 1975-82; in independent practice 1982-, conslt physician Portmen Clinic 1982-, med dir Howard Foundation Res 1985-; memb: Med Soc of London, Harvcian Soc, RSM; *Recreations* sculpture, comparative religion, physical fitness; *Style—* Dr Ann Coxon; 97 Harley St, London W1 (☎ 071 486 2534, fax 071 224 1705, car 0836 747900)

COXWELL-ROGERS, Col Richard Annesley; s of Maj-Gen Norman Annesley Coxwell-Rogers, CB, CBE, DSO (d 1985), of Cheltenham, and Diana Mary, *née* Coston; *b* 26 April 1932; *Educ* Eton, Sandhurst; *m* 21 Sept 1965, Martha Felicity, da of Col G T Hurrell, OBE (d 1989); 2 s (James b 1969, Edward b 1973); *Career* serv 15/19 The Kings Royal Hussars 1952-82 (CO Regt 1973-75): Malaya, Germany, UK; appointed Col 15/19 Hussars 1988; area appeals organiser Avon, Glos and Wilts Cancer Research Campaign; *Recreations* hunting, shooting; *Clubs* Cavalry and Guards; *Style—* Col Richard A Coxwell-Rogers; c/o Cavalry and Guards Club, 127 Piccadilly, London W1V 0PX

COYLE, John Stephen; s of John James Coyle (d 1968), of Buckhurst Hill, Essex, and Barbara, *née* Higham; *b* 27 Dec 1944; *Educ* St Ignatius Coll; *m* 17 March 1990, Laura Frances, da of Charles Patrick Hart; 2 s (Daniel John Alan b 1981, Adam Stephen James b 1983), 2 da (Justine Danielle b 1969, Stephanie Jane b 1971); *Career* staff writer and analyst Stock Exchange Gazette (Investors Chronicle) 1962-65, staff writer Sunday Telegraph 1965-68, asst city ed The Evening News 1968-69; sr conslt: Streets Public Relations 1969-70, Shareholder Relations 1970-71; md Corporate Public Relations 1971-73, city reporter Evening Standard 1973-76, freelance journalist 1976-78, managing ed Accountancy Age 1978-79, dir of pub affrs Myson Group PLC 1979-81, md Broad Street Associates 1981-88, chm and chief exec Square Mile Communications LTD 1988-; *Recreations* cricket, riding, reading; *Clubs* Tramp, Rags, White City All Stars, Room 74; *Style—* John Coyle, Esq; 524 Willoughby House, The Barbican, London EC2 (☎ 071 638 3745); Sudbury Ley, Little Sampford, Saffron Walden, Essex (☎ 0799 86 316); Square Mile Communications Ltd, Glade House, Carter Lane, London EC4 (☎ 071 329 4496, fax 071 329 0310, car 0836 762 807)

COYLE, Michael Thomas Patrick; s of Michael Coyle (d 1985), and Mary Elizabeth, *née* Skelly; *b* 21 Jan 1955; *Educ* Finchley Catholic GS, UEA (BA), Lancaster Gate Coll of Law; *Career* advertising exec; trainee rising to account mangr Young & Rubicam 1979-83, account mangr rising to account dir Saatchi & Saatchi 1983-88, Ogilvy & Mather 1988-89 (dir (Australia), client service dir, dep md), dir BSB Dorland 1989-; *Recreations* reading, music, travelling, cricket, football, bobsleigh; *Clubs* Albanian Assoc; *Style—* Michael Coyle, Esq; 5 Maryon Mews, Hampstead Heath, London NW3 2PU (☎ 071 262 5077, fax 071 258 3757)

COYTE, Kenneth Anthony; s of Stanley Edward Coyte (d 1953), of Leeds, and Amy Vera, *née* Pote (d 1953); *b* 6 Feb 1932; *Educ* Blundell's, Sidney Sussex Coll Cambridge (MA); *m* 7 Jan 1956, Patricia Claire, da of William Macke (d 1979), of Cincinnati, Ohio, USA; 3 s (Anthony b 1958, Benjamin b 1963, Matthew b 1966), 3 da (Nerissa b 1956, Rebecca b 1961, Amy b 1962); *Career* 2 Lt RE 1950; film critic; Saturday Review NY 1955, TV reporter UP Movietone 1955-56, vice pres UP ITN 1968-80; World Wide TV News: pres 1980-, dir UK Ltd 1980-, dir TV-AM News Ltd 1981-; memb RTS; *Style—* Kenneth Coyte, Esq; Worldwide Television News, 31 Foley St, London W1P 7LB (☎ 071 3233255, fax 071 5801437, telex 23915)

COZENS-HARDY, Hon Beryl Gladys; OBE (1971), JP (Norfolk); da of 3 Baron Cozens-Hardy (d 1956); *b* 30 Nov 1911; *Career* chm World Ctee World Assoc of Girl Guides and Girl Scouts 1972-75; *Style—* The Hon Beryl Cozens-Hardy, OBE, JP; The Glebe, Letheringsett, Holt, Norfolk

CRABTREE, Maj-Gen Derek Thomas; CB (1983); s of late William Edward Crabtree, and Winifred Hilda Burton, *née* Wood; *b* 21 Jan 1930; *Educ* St Brendan's Coll Bristol; *m* 1960, Daphne Christine, *née* Mason, 1 s, 1 da; *Career* dir gen of Weapons (Army) MOD 1980-84; Col Duke of Edinburgh's Royal Regt (Berks and Wilts) 1982-87; 1988-89 gen mangr Regular Forces Employment Assoc 1987-; *Clubs* Army and Navy; *Style—* Maj-Gen Derek Crabtree, CB; c/o Army and Navy Club, 36 Pall Mall, London SW1

CRABTREE, His Hon Judge; Jonathan; s of Charles Harold Crabtree (d 1981), of Stansfield Hall, Todmorden, Lancs, and Elsie Marion, *née* Gaukroger; *b* 17 April 1934; *Educ* Bootham Sch, St John's Coll Camb (MA, LLM); *m* 1, 27 Aug 1957 (m dis 1974), Caroline Ruth Keigwin, da of Alan Edward Oliver (d 1983), of Lewes, Sussex; 2 s (Abraham John b 5 Aug 1963, Daniel Edward b 5 Dec 1965, d 1983), 3 da (Harriet Mary b 25 Nov 1958, Rose Charity b 10 Dec 1961, (Alice) Ann b 15 July 1964); m 2, 13 June 1980, Wendy Elizabeth, da of Douglas Robert Ward (d 1956); *Career* Seaman RN 1952-54; HM inspr of factories 1958-60, called to the Bar Gray's Inn 1960, rec 1974-86, circuit judge 1986-; *Recreations* history and archaeology, cooking; *Style—* His Hon Judge Crabtree; Courts Administrator, 10 Floor, Pennine House, 20/2 Hawley St, Sheffield S1 2EA (☎ 0742 755866)

CRABTREE, (John) Raymond; s of late Harold Crabtree; *b* 1 May 1925; *Educ* Emanuel Sch, Christ's Coll Cambridge; *m* 1959, Evelyn Mary, da of Capt Charles Benstead, MC (d 1980); 1 s, 2 da; *Career* chartered civil engr; dir PA Management Consultants Ltd 1973-84 (joined 1955), chm Pyrok Holdings Ltd 1984-85, dir LAST (Metals) Ltd 1987-; *Clubs* Naval; *Style—* Raymond Crabtree, Esq; Bank House, Tanworth-in-Arden, Solihull, W Mids (☎ 056 44 2291)

CRABTREE TAYLOR, Neil Barry; s of Barry Joseph Crabtree Taylor, of 54 Bute Gardens, London, and Mary Ellesmore, *née* Millbourn; *b* 19 Feb 1961; *Educ* Seaford Coll; *Career* md: Crabtree Taylor Int 1983- (dir 1981-), Formech Ltd 1984-; pres Formech Inc USA 1987, chm Formech Int 1988; *Recreations* boating, water skiing; *Style—* Neil Crabtree Taylor, Esq; Formech, 72 West End Rd, High Wycombe, Bucks HP11 2QQ (☎ 0494 471137)

CRACE, Andrew Laurence Spencer; s of Harold Clarence Crace (d 1971), of Much Hadham, Herts, and Gladys Caroline, *née* Wise (d 1977); descendant of Edward Crace, coach designer and appointed keeper of pictures to the Royal Palaces 1790; John and Frederick Crace furniture/wallpaper designers and manufacturers concerned with the interior decoration of the Royal Opera House, Carlton House, The Royal Pavilion Brighton, the Palace of Westminster; *b* 28 May 1953; *Educ* Coll of Estate Mgmnt, Univ of Reading; *Career* designer and retailer predominantly of furniture, garden products and buildings; proprietor: Alitag Plant Labels 1980, Andrew Crace Designs 1983; ARICS 1980; *Recreations* travel, photography, sculpture, opera, music, gardening, bricklaying; *Style—* Andrew L S Crace, Esq; Harefield House, Much Hadham, Herts SG10 6ER; (☎ 027 984 2685, fax 027 984 3646)

CRACKNELL, Prof Arthur Philip; s of Christopher Theodore Cracknell (d 1969), of Ilford, and Phyllis Mary, *née* Staines (d 1985); *b* 18 May 1940; *Educ* Chigwell Sch Essex, Pembroke Coll Cambridge (MA), The Queen's Coll Oxford (DPhil), Univ of Singapore (MSc); *m* 13 April 1966, Margaret Florence, da of James Grant (d 1972), of Gateshead; 1 s (Christopher Paul b 15 April 1967), 2 da (Anne Patricia b 3 March 1972, Andrée Jacqueline b 30 Nov 1975); *Career* lectr in physics: Univ of Singapore 1964-67, Univ of Essex 1967-70; prof of theoretical physics Univ of Dundee 1978- (sr lectr 1970-74, 1974-78); ed International Journal of Remote Sensing 1983; former chm Remote Sensing Soc, memb various ctees RSE; FInstP 1970, FRSE 1976; *Books* Applied Group Theory (1968), The Fermi Surfaces of Metals (jtly, 1971), Ultrasonics (1980), Computer Programs for Image Processing of Remote Sensing Data (ed, 1982), Magnetism in Solids: Some Current Topics (ed jtly, 1982), Remote Sensing Applications in Marine Science and Technology (ed, 1983); author of numerous scientific res papers in scientific journals; *Recreations* reading, hill-walking, gardening; *Style—* Prof Arthur Cracknell; 54 Hamilton Street, Barnhill, Broughty Ferry, Dundee DD5 2RE; Dept of Applied Physics and Electronic and Manufacturing Engineering University of Dundee, Dundee DD1 4HN Scotland UK (☎ 0382 23181 ext 4549, fax 0382 2028 telex 931211 0826 DU G)

CRACKNELL, (William) Martin; s of John Sidney Cracknell (d 1975), of Exeter, and Sybil Marian, *née* Wood (d 1976); *b* 24 June 1929; *Educ* St Edward's Sch Oxford, RMA Sandhurst; *m* 1962, Gillian, da of Gp Capt Claude Frederick Goatcher (d 1981), of Gt Missenden, Bucks; 2 s (Charles b 1963, James b 1968), 2 da (Katherine b 1964, Emma b 1966); *Career* Royal Green Jackets 1947-69, Major; active serv: Cyprus, Egypt, Borneo; Br Printing Industries Fedn 1969-76; chief exec Glenrothes Development Corporation 1976; chm: Scot Ctee, German Chamber of Indust and Commerce in the UK; FInstD; *Recreations* gardening, shooting, walking; *Clubs* Royal Green Jackets; *Style—* Martin Cracknell, Esq; Alburne Knowe, Orchard Drive, Glenrothes, Fife KY7 5RG (☎ 0592 752413); Glenrothes Development Corporation, Unicorn House, Glenrothes, Fife KY7 5PD (☎ 0592 754343)

CRACKNELL, His Hon Judge (Malcolm) Thomas; s of Percy Thomas Cracknell (d 1988), and Doris Louise Cracknell; *b* 12 Dec 1943; *Educ* Royal Liberty Sch Romford Univ of Hull (LLB), Kings Coll London (LLM); *m* 1, 1968 (m dis 1980) Ann; 1 s (Simon Anthony b 1970), 1 da (Rebecca Judith b 1972); m 2, 30 July 1988, Felicity Anne, da of Prof David M Davies, of Shotley Bridge; 1 da (Alexandra Flora Louise b 1990); *Career* lectr in law Univ of Hull 1968-74, barr 1970-89, asst rec 1984, rec Crown Ct 1988, judge 1989-; *Recreations* golf, gardening, walking, reading; *Style—* His Hon Judge Cracknell

CRACROFT-ELEY, (Robert) Robin Peel Charles; er s of (Charles Ryves) Maxwell Eley, OBE (d 1983), of East Bergholt Place, Suffolk, and his 1 w, Violet Eva, yr da of Col Herbert Haworth Peel, CBE, of Highlands, East Bergholt; assumed the additional surname of Cracroft by Deed Poll 1988; *b* 23 Jan 1931; *Educ* Eton; *m* 31 Oct 1959, Bridget Katharine, 3 da of Lt-Col Sir Weston Cracroft- Amcotts, MC, JP, DL (d 1975), of Hackthorn Hall, Lincoln; 1 s ((Charles) William Amcotts b 8 March 1963), 1 da (Annabel Louise Cracroft b 15 Jan 1961); *Career* Nat Serv cmmn 8 Royal Tank Regt 1950; farmer, ptnr R P C & B K Eley, Hackthorn Hall, Lincoln; chm: East Bergholt Estate Co Ltd, Bromhead Nursing Home Tst Ltd; memb: Cncl Lincs Agric Soc, Lincs CC 1984- (chm Property Mgmnt Ctee 1986-); govr William Farr (C of E) Comprehensive Sch 1987-; Freeman City of London, memb Worshipful Co of Farmers 1988; *Recreations* country sports, tennis, sailing, travel; *Style—* Robin Cracroft-Eley, Esq; Hackthorn Hall, Lincoln LN2 3PQ (☎ 0673 60212; Estate Office ☎ 0673 60423)

CRADDOCK, (William) Aleck; LVO (1981); *b* 1924,Nov; *Educ* City of London Sch; *m* 1947, Olive Mary Brown; 1 s, 1 da; *Career* joined Druce and Craddock, Craddock and Tomkins Ltd (family firm) 1946; Harrods Ltd: joined as asst to Food Mangr 1954, dir 1964, dir and gen mangr 1970, asst md 1975, md 1980-84, chm 1981-86, dep chm 1987-88; dir: House of Fraser Ltd 1980, Cartier Ltd 1986-; dep chm Drapers Drapers Cottage Homes 1987- (pres Appeal 1985-86); pres Twenty Club 1988; Liveryman Worshipful Co of Cooks 1972; Cavaliere Ufficiale (Fourth Class) Order Al Merito Della Repubblica Italiana 1980; *Recreations* fell walking, golf, water colour painting; *Clubs* Guards' Polo (life memb); *Style—* Aleck Craddock, Esq, LVO; c/o Harrods Ltd, 87-135 Brompton Road, Knightsbridge, London SW1X 7XL (☎ 071 730 1234)

CRADDOCK, Malcolm Gordon; s of Gilbert Craddock, and Evelyn Marion, *née* Gordon; *b* 2 Aug 1938; *Educ* St Albans Sch, Queens' Coll Cambridge (MA); *m* 29 May 1965, Jenni, da of David Maclay; 2 s (Sam, Ben), 1 da (Emily); *Career* entered film industry 1962; asst dir to Joseph Losey 1964-66: Accident, Modesty Blaise; dir: Mr Lewis 1965, The Beach 1967; film dir of TV commercials (Sunday Times awards) 1966-, founding ptnr and dir Picture Palace Prodns 1970; prodr TV drama 1984-: Tandoori Nights (Channel Four) 1985-87, Ping Pong (Venice Int Film Festival) 1986, twenty one short films, 4 Minutes (winner Gold Award for Drama NY 1986), Firing the Bullets, Hunting the Squirrel and Pushed (Channel Four and ECA) 1989-90; contrib: Eurocops series When Love Dies (4 Play series) 1990, The Orchid House (series for Channel 4) 1991; *Recreations* tennis, watching Tottenham Hotspur; *Clubs* The Groucho; *Style—* Malcolm Craddock, Esq; Randolph House, 13 Randolph Rd, London W9 1AN (☎ 071 286 2812); Picture Palace Productions Limited, 6-10

Lexington St, London W1R 3HS (☎ 071 439 9882, fax 071 734 8574)

CRADDOCK, Nigel Christopher; s of William Alfred Craddock (d 1976), of 20 St Ronans Rd, Harrogate, N Yorks, and Louisa Maud, *née* Edmanson (d 1974); *b* 30 Aug 1937; *Educ* Harrogate GS; *m* 24 Sept 1966, Penelope Jane, da of Laurence Sydney Stevens (d 1987), of Landamere, Ampney Crucis, Cirencester, Glos; 3 s (Alexander, James, Daniel); *Career* Nat Serv RAF 1956-58; dir: Hogg Robinson (UK) Ltd 1965-77, Barclays Insurance Services Co Ltd 1977-, Spread Eagle Insurance Co Ltd 1986-; sales dir Barclays Unit Trusts and Insurance 1985-86, md Barclays Insurance Brokers Int Ltd 1986-; memb: Berkhamsted Cons Party, Worshipful Co of Insurers; FCII 1969, memb Soc of Fellows; *Recreations* golf, rugby, cricket, reading, walking; *Style—* Nigel Craddock, Esq; Barclays Insurance Brokers Int Ltd, Capital House, 42 Weston St, London SE1 3QA (☎ 071 378 6410)

CRADICK, (Christopher) Roger; s of Henry Cyril Cradick (d 1986), and Rita, *née* Perkin; *b* 6 Nov 1932; *Educ* Penarth GS, Llandovery Coll; *m* 1, 15 June 1957, Mary Elizabeth, da of late Frederick John Stephenson; 2 s (Simon b 18 Jan 1960, Neil b 14 Jan 1965), 1 da (Sian Elizabeth b 7 July 1962); m 2, 2 Sept 1968, Gillian Susan, da of Ernest Whetter (d 1982); 1 s (Richard b 21 May 1970); *Career* admitted slr 1954; dep dist registrar High Ct and dep Co Ct registrar High Ct and dep Co Ct registrar 1976-; chm: Social Security Appeals Tbnl 1979-85, Med Appeals Tbnl 1985-; pres Cardiff and Dist Law Soc 1985-86, memb Bye Laws Revision Sub Ctee Law Soc; memb Law Soc 1956; *Recreations* rugby football (former referee), gardening; *Clubs* Old Penarthians RFC (vice pres); *Style—* Roger Cradick, Esq; St Andrews Rd, Dinas Powis, South Glamorgan CF6 4HB; Morgan Bruce, Bradley Court, Park Place, Cardiff CF1 3DP (☎ 0222 233677, fax 0222 399288)

CRADOCK, Sir Percy; GCMG (1983, KCMG 1980, CMG 1968); *b* 26 Oct 1923; *Educ* St John's Coll Camb; *m* 1953, Birthe Marie Dyrlund; *Career* HM Dip Serv: joined FO 1954, first sec Kuala Lumpur 1957-61, Hong Kong 1961, first sec Peking 1962, FO 1963-66, cnsllr and head of chancery Peking 1966-68, Chargé d'Affaires Peking 1968-69, head of planning staff FCO 1969-71, under-sec Cabinet Office 1971-75, leader UK Delegn Geneva Test Ban Discussions 1977-78, ambass E Germany 1976-78, ambass People's Republic of China 1978-83, continuing responsibility for negotiations over future of Hong Kong 1983-84; foreign policy advsr to the Prime Minister 1984-; hon fell St John's Coll Cambridge 1982; *Style—* Sir Percy Cradock, GCMG; c/o 10 Downing St, London SW1

CRADOCK-HARTOPP, Sir John Edmund; 9 Bt (GB 1796), of Freathby, Leics, TD; s of Francis Gerald Cradock-Hartopp (d 1946, s of late Col Edmund Charles Cradock-Hartopp, 2 s of 3 Bt); suc kinsman, Sir George Francis Fleetwood Cradock-Hartopp, 8 Bt, 1949; *b* 8 April 1912; *Educ* Uppingham; *m* 29 April 1953, Prudence, 2 da of Sir Frederick William Leith-Ross, GCMG, KCB; 3 da; *Heir* cous, Lt Cdr Kenneth Alston Cradock-Hartopp, MBE, DSC, RN; *Career* served WWII as Major RE (despatches twice); dir Firth Brown Tools Ltd 1961-76; *Recreations* golf (semi-finalist English Golf Championships 1935, first reserve Eng v France 1935), cricket, tennis, motoring; *Clubs* East India, Devonshire, Sports and Public Schools, MCC, Royal and Ancient (St Andrews); *Style—* Sir John Cradock-Hartopp, Bt, TD; The Cottage, 27 Wool Rd, Wimbledon Common, SW20

CRADOCK-HARTOPP, Lt Cdr Kenneth Alston; MBE (1946), DSC (1952); s of Maj Louis Montague Cradock-Hartopp (d 1957), and Marjorie Somerville, *née* Watson (d 1971); hp of cous, Sir John Edmund Cradock-Hartopp, 9 Bt; *b* 26 Feb 1918; *m* 18 June 1942, Gwendolyn Amy Lilian, da of late Capt Victor Crowther Upton; 1 da; *Career* Lt Cdr (ret) RN; served WWII and Korea (cmd HMNZ frigate Taupo 1951-52); chm Royal Naval Amateur Radio Soc 1984-87; FRGS 1949; Legion of Merit (USA) 1953; *Style—* Lt Cdr Kenneth Cradock-Hartopp, MBE, DSC; Keepers, Yeovilton, Yeovil, Somerset BA22 8EX (☎ 0935 840240)

CRAFT, Prof Ian Logan; s of Reginald Thomas Craft, St John's, Thorrington Rd, Great Bentley, Essex, and Mary Lois, *née* Logan; *b* 11 July 1937; *Educ* Owen Sch London, Univ of London, Westminster Hosp Med Sch (MB BS); *m* 19 Dec 1959, Jacqueline Rivers, s of John James Symmons (d 1985), of 9 Merricks Ct, Temple Sheen, London; 2 s (Simon b 4 Sept 1964, Adrian b 1 Sept 1968); *Career* house offr Radiotherapy Dept and Dept of Obstetrics and Gynaecology Westminster Hosp 1961-62, sr house offr (later house surgn and house physician) St James Hosp Balham 1962-63, house surgn Hammersmith Hosp 1965, sr house offr (later surgical registrar) Professional Unit Westminster Hosp 1965-66, resident med offr Queen Charlotte's Hosp London 1967, gynaecological registrar (later resident registrar) Inst of Obstetrics and Gynaecology Chelsea Hosp for Women 1968-69, resident med offr Gen Lying-In Hosp London 1969, registrar Queen Mary's Hosp Roehampton 1970, sr registrar Westminster Hosp London 1970, rotational sr registrar Kingston Hosp Surrey 1971-72, sr lectr and hon conslt Queen Charlotte's Hosp and Chelsea Hosp for Women 1972-76, prof of obstetrics and gynaecology Royal Free Hosp Sch of Med 1976-82 dir of gynaecology Cromwell Hosp London 1982-85, dir of fertility and obstetrics studies Humana Hosp Wellington London 1985, dir London Fetility Centre 1990; visiting prof UCL; frequent lectr and prolific contrib to med literature; life memb: Zoological Soc, Nat Tst, RNLI, Friends of St Paul's Cathedral, Friends of Durham Cathedral, Turner Soc, Walpole Soc; FRCS 1966, MRCOG 1970, FRCOG 1986; memb: RSM, Br Fertility Soc, Harveian Soc (London); *Recreations* art, ceramics, sculpture, music, opera, theatre, most sports, antiquities; *Clubs* Heritage, Natural Pursuits, Ornithology; *Style—* Prof Ian Craft; 17 Park St James, Prince Albert Road, London NW8 (☎ 081 586 6001); Cozens House, 112A Harley St, London W1 (☎ 071 224 0707, Fax 071 224 3120)

CRAFT, Prof Maurice; s of Jack Craft (d 1952), of London, and Polly, *née* Lewis (d 1973); *b* 4 May 1932; *Educ* Colfe's GS, LSE (BSc), Sch of Educn Univ of Dublin (HDipEd), Inst of Educn Univ of London (AcadDipEd), Univ of Liverpool (PhD), Univ of Nottingham (DLitt); *m* 19 May 1957, Alma, da of Ellis Sampson (d 1975), of Dublin; 2 da (Anna b 1961, Naomi b 1964); *Career* Nat Serv 1953-55, cmmnd 2 Lt RAOC served Suez Canal Zone, appointed acting Capt; head Dept of Sociology Edge Hill Coll of Educn 1960-67, sr lectr Univ of Exeter 1967-74, prof of educn La Trobe Univ Melbourne 1974-76, Goldsmith's prof of educn Univ of London 1976-80, prof of educn Univ of Nottingham 1980-89 (pro vice chllr 1983-87, former Dean of Faculty and chm of Sch of Educn), fndn dean of humanities and social science Hong Kong Univ of Sci and Tech 1989-; author of numerous learned books, monographs and papers; UK del to UNESCO, Cncl of Europe and EEC Confs; vice chm CVU; memb: Exec Ctee UCET, CNAA; *Books* Family, Class and Education (1970), Teaching in a multicultral Society (1981), Change in Teacher Education (1984), Education and Cultural Pluralism (1984); *Recreations* music, walking; *Style—* Prof Maurice Craft; Hong Kong University of Science and Technology, 13/F World Shipping Centre, 7 Canton Rd, Hong Kong

CRAIG, Dr Brian George; s of Very Rev Dr Williams Magee Craig, of Moira Co Down, and Maud, *née* Macrory; *b* 6 Sept 1953; *Educ* Portadown Coll, Queen's Univ Belfast (MD, BCh, BAO); *m* Jennifer, da of Albert Mawhinney, of 46 Princess Way, Portadown; 2 s (Adam b 1984, Matthew b 1986); *Career* sr registrar: cardiology Royal Victoria Hosp 1982-83, Hosp for Sick Children Toronto Canada (clinical fell in paediatric cardiology) 1983-85, paediatrics Royal Belfast Hosp for Sick Children 1985-86; conslt in paediatric cardiology Royal Belfast Hosp for Sick Children 1986-; memb: Ulster Paediatric Soc 1979-, Br Paediatric Cardiology Gp 1987-, Br Paediatric Assoc 1988-, Irish Cardiac Soc 1988-, Br Cardiac Soc 1990, ctee Presbyterian Church, Boys Bde; Hon MD Queen's Univ Belfast; MRCP (UK) 1980; numerous publications in learned jnls; *Recreations* gardening, family; *Style—* Dr Brian Craig; 10 Plantation Ave, Lisburn, Co Antrim, N Ireland BT27 5BL (☎ 0846 671587); Royal Belfast Hospital for Sick Children, 180-184 Falls Rd, Belfast, N Ireland BT12 6BE (☎ 0232 240503 ext 239)

CRAIG, (Hildreth) Charles; *b* 4 Oct 1923; *Educ* Pimms Acad; *m* 20 June 1945, Audrey Doris, *née* Wells; 2 s (Michael b 20 July 1946, Nigel b 6 June 1948), 1 da (Alison b 15 Dec 1958); *Career* Civil Def 1940-42, RCS 1942, 52 Lowland Div UK & BLA, cmmnd Highland LI 1945, seconded to the Royal West African Frontier Force, demobbed 1948; Adams & Son (Printers) Rye 1937-40, Sweet & Maxwell Law Publishers 1937-40, mangr Wine and Spirit Dept Woodheads Brewery 1947-52, Taplow & Co 1952-67, prodn dir Bass Charrington Vintners 1962-67, chm Invergordon Distillers (Hldgs) 1983- (md 1967-83); The Scotch Whisky Assoc: lectr 1958-75, memb Pub Affrs Ctee 1975-77, memb Cncl 1977-89, hon treas 1978-89; *Books* Glenpatrick The Story of an Unsuccessful Distillery (1982); *Clubs* Caledonian; *Style—* Charles Craig, Esq; The Cummins, Aldham, Colchester CO6 3PN (☎ 0206 242230); 9-21 Salamander Place, Leith, Edinburgh EH6 7JL (☎ 031 554 4404, fax 031 554 1531, telex 72624)

CRAIG, Charles James; s of James Craig (d 1928), and Anna Rosina Craig (d 1921); *b* 3 Dec 1919; *m* 1946, Dorothy, da of Victor Wilson (d 1953); 1 s (Stephen), 1 da (Gilda); *Career* operatic tenor; has performed in all major opera houses of the world, specializing in the role of Othello, and all other dramatic tenor roles (esp those of Verdi, Puccini, Wagner); *Recreations* motoring, gardening, cooking; *Style—* Charles Craig Esq; Whitfield Stone Haze House, Nr Brackley, Northants (☎ 02805 268)

CRAIG, Colin Fetherston; s of Rev Cuthbert Leslie Craig (d 1982), of Weardale, and Muriel, *née* Cole; *b* 29 Aug 1947; *Educ* Kent Coll Canterbury, Kingston Coll of Art; *m* 4 July 1989, Linda Jayne, da of Edward Howard; *Career* creative dir: Cogent Elliott Ltd 1975-78, Doyle Dane Bernbach Ltd 1978-79, Grierson Cockman Craig & Druiff Ltd 1979-86, Grey Ltd 1986-87, Holmes Knight Ritchie Ltd 1987-; writer of music for TV and radio 1968-, lectr in TV technique, writer of screenplays for TV and cinema, winner of over 50 nat and int TV awards, multi-instrumentalist, singer, conductor; memb: D & AD 1969, Songwriters Guild 1978, PRS 1977; *Recreations* yoga, horticulture, cinema, church, dalmatians; *Clubs* Lansdowne; *Style—* Colin Craig, Esq; TBWA Holmes Knight Ritchie Ltd; 8 Crinan St, Battle Bridge Basin, London N1 9UF (☎ 071 833 5544, fax 071 833 8751, telex 264002)

CRAIG, Marshal of the RAF David Brownrigg; GCB (1984, KCB 1980, CB 1978), OBE (1967); s of Maj Francis Brownrigg Craig (d 1943), and Olive Craig (d 1958); *b* 17 Sept 1929; *Educ* Radley, Lincoln Coll Oxford; *m* 1955, Elisabeth June, da of Charles James Derenburg (d 1976); 1 s, 1 da; *Career* cmmnd RAF 1951, AOC No 1 Gp RAF Strike Cmd 1978-80, vice-chief of Air Staff 1980-82, AOC-in-C Strike Cmd and C-in-C UKAF 1982-85, Chief of Air Staff 1985-88, Chief of Def Staff 1988-, Marshal of the RAF 1988-; *Clubs* RAF; *Style—* Marshal of the RAF Sir David Craig, GCB, OBE; c/o Royal Bank of Scotland, 9 Pall Mall, London SW1Y 5LX

CRAIG, Dr Donald Gwynvor; s of Donald Craig (d 1964), of Sheffield, Yorks, and Elizabeth May, *née* Williams (d 1980); *b* 19 Aug 1929; *Educ* King Edward VII Sch Sheffield, Balliol Coll Oxford (MA, BM BCh), St Thomas' Hosp London (DRCOG, DMJ, DVSA); *m* 3 July 1954, (Dorothy) Jill, da of Rt Hon EL Burgin (d 1945), of Harpenden; 4 da (Meredith Ann b 1955, Corinna b 1956, Lucinda Mary b 1959, Annabel Clare b 1962); *Career* Capt RAMC (regtl MO 1 Bn WG) 1955-57; sr lectr Dept Gen Practice Guy's Hosp Med Sch, sr ptnr Thamesmead Med Assocs 1975-89, sr forensic med examiner Met Police 1980-89, clinical asst: colposcopy and genito urinary med Freedom Fields Hosp Plymouth 1989-, dir Workwell; Freeman City of London 1970, Liveryman Worshipful Soc Apothecaries 1974 (memb Livery Ctee 1982-86); memb: Assoc Police Surgns, Soc Occupational Med, Assur Med Soc, Med Soc Study of Venereal Diseases; FRCGP, memb RSM; *Recreations* sailing, big projects, geology; *Clubs* Litte Ship; *Style—* Dr D G Craig; Pentecost, Veryan, Truro, Cornwall TR2 5QA (☎ 0872 501450)

CRAIG, Capt Ian Wallace; s of Dr Daniel MacKinnon Craig, DSO (d 1982), and Phyllis Clifton, *née* Garrett; *b* 7 Aug 1943; *Educ* Framlingham Coll Suffolk, RNEC Manadon Plymouth (DipMech Engrg); *m* 16 Nov 1968, Jacqueline Wendy, da of Dr E J Grierson, of Saltash, Cornwall; 1 s (Andrew b 4 Jan 1970), 1 da (Juliet b 20 May 1972); *Career* HMS Albion 1967-69, HMS Ganges 1971-74, HMS Tiger 1974, RN Staff Coll 1975-78, marine engr offr HMS Ardent 1975-78, Cdr 1979, directorate of naval offrs appts (engrg) MOD(N) 1979-81, sqdn marine engr Offr to 4 Frigate Sqdn HMS Avenger 1981-83, Trg Cdr HMS Sultan 1983-85, exec offr BRNC Dartmouth 1985-85, Capt 1986, HM Naval Base Rosyth 1986-87, dep dir of naval manpower planning MOD(N) 1987-89, RCDS 1990 fleet marine engr offr Fleet Engrg Staff 1991; Rear Cdre (dinghies) RNSA, chm Bosun Dinghy Class Assoc; CEng, FIMechE, FIMarE; *Recreations* tennis, walking, sailing; *Clubs* RNSA; *Style—* Capt Ian Craig, RN; Ministry of Defence, London

CRAIG, Sir (Albert) James Macqueen; GCMG (1984, KCMG 1981, CMG 1975); s of James Craig (d 1954), of Scone by Perth, and Florence, *née* Morris; *b* 13 July 1924; *Educ* Liverpool Inst HS, Queen's Coll Oxford, Magdalen Coll Oxford, Univ of Cairo; *m* 1952, Margaret Hutchinson; 3 s, 1 da; *Career* former lectr in Arabic Univ of Durham; Foreign Serv 1956; ambass: Syria 1976-79, Saudi Arabia 1979-84; visiting prof in Arabic Univ of Oxford 1985-, lectr Pembroke Coll, sr asst memb St Anthony's Coll Oxford 1988 (fell 1970-71); DG ME Assoc 1985-; dir: Saudi-Br Bank 1985-, Hong Kong Egyptian Bank 1987; advsr Hong Kong and Shanghai Bank 1985-; chm Roxby Engineering International Ltd; hon fell Centre for Middle Eastern and Islamic Studies Univ of Durham 1986; pres British Soc for Middle East Studies 1987; OStJ 1984 (memb Cncl 1984-90); *Clubs* Travellers'; *Style—* Sir James Craig, GCMG; 33 Bury St, London SW1

CRAIG, John Egwin; OBE (1990); s of Thomas Joseph Alexander Craig, CIE (d 1969), and Mabel Frances, *née* Quinnell (d 1979); *b* 16 Aug 1932; *Educ* Charterhouse; *m* 27 June, 1959, Patricia, da of Exmo Senor Joao Costa Lopes (d 1980), of Sintra, Portugal; 3 s (Colin b 5 Dec 1960, Andrew b 15 June 1962, James b 12 Oct 1968); *Career* cmmnd Royal Irish Fusilliers 1950; Cooper Bros 1958-61, The Stock Exchange 1961-64; md N M Rothschild & SM Ltd 1981-88 (joined 1964, dir 1970); chm: Jupiter European Investment Trust plc, Greyfriars Investment Company plc, Powerscreen Int plc; dir: Standard Chartered plc, Jupiter Tarbutt Ltd, United Dutch Holdings NV; dir Int Fund for Ireland (UK govt appt); govr Abingdon Sch; FCA, FRSA; *Clubs* Brooks's; *Style—* John Craig, Esq, OBE; Saxonbury House, Frant, nr Tunbridge Wells, Kent TN3 9HJ (☎ 0892 75 644); New Court, St Swithin's Lane, London EC4P 4DU (☎ 071 280 5000, fax 071 929 1643)

CRAIG, Col John Mirrlees; TD (1970), DL (Gtr London 1970); s of Col Hugh Craig, OBE, TD, DL, Woodlands, Tudor Close, Woodford Green, Essex, and Elsie Evelyn, *née* Mallender; *b* 28 May 1936; *Educ* Chigwell Sch; *m* 5 Sept 1960, Susan, da of Maurice Carter (d 1988), of Romsey, Hants; 2 s (Stephen George b 1 March 1964, Giles Hugh Mirrlees b 1 May 1967); *Career* Nat Serv cmmnd 10 Royal Hussars 1956-

58; TA: Lt troop ldr City of London Yeo 1958-60, Capt Inns of Ct & City Yeo 1960-67, Capt 2 i/c HQ Sqdn Royal Yeo 1967-69, Lt-Col (formerly Maj) cmdg offr 71 Yeo Regt 1969-78, Col dep cdr 2 Gp 1978-79, TA Col (North) HQ London Dist 1979-81, Col TA project team ldr MOD-DARC 1982-88; memb Lloyds 1986, dir Caird Group plc 1987-88; chm and md: Scrolapoint Ltd, Scrolapoint Development Co Ltd, JMC Investments Ltd, George M Craig & Sons Ltd, Aldwych Investments Ltd, Market Investments Ltd, IJB Partners Ltd, Town Houses Woodbridge Ltd, WCA (Sudbury) Investments Ltd, JMC Overseas Ltd, Hinton Marine Ltd, L'Immobiliere Franco-Britannique SA; ADC to HM The Queen 1980-84, rep DL for Islington, memb HM Cmmn of Lieutenancy for the City of London; memb: Cncl Union Jack Club, HAC, Cncl Reserve Forces Assoc; chm Yeo Benevolent Fund: vice chm Gtr London TA & VRA, life managing govr Royal Scottish Corp; Freeman City of London, Liveryman Worshipful Co of Fanmakers; memb: Guild of Freemen, Castle Baynard Ward Club; FInstD; *Recreations* sailing, skiing; *Clubs* Cavalry & Guards, Royal Thames Yacht, City Livery; *Style*— Col John Craig, TD, DL; 15 Union Square, London N1 7DH (☎ 071 704 9555); Scrolapoint Ltd, 10 Benezet St, Ipswich, Suffolk (☎ 0473 211918/9, 0473 254 630, fax 0473 250 052, car 0860 629 633)

CRAIG, Rev Maxwell Davidson; *b* 25 Dec 1931; *m* 1957, Janet; 1 s, 3 da; *Career* Nat Serv Argytt & Sutherland Highlanders 1954-56; graduate apprentice United Steel Co Ltd 1956-57, asst princ Miny of Labour 1957-61, student asst St Cuthbert's Edinburgh 1962-64, asst St John's Oxgangs 1965-66, ordained minister Grahamston Parish Church Falkirk 1966-73, minister Wellington Parish Church Glasgow 1973-89, ecumenical charge St Columba's Bridge of Don Aberdeen 1989-90, appointed chaplain to The Queen in Scotland 1986, gen sec Action of Churches Together in Scotland 1991; convener: Sectional Ctee on Auxiliary Miny (vice convener Educn for the Miny Ctee) 1980-84, Church and Nation Ctee 1984-88, memb Multilateral Church Conversation; chm: Hillhead Housing Assoc 1977-88, Scottish TV Religious Advsy Ctee 1987-89, Children's Panel; telephone samaritan; *Recreations* hill walking, squash; *Style*— The Rev Maxwell Craig; 9 Kilbryde Crescent, Dunblane, Perthshire FK15 9BA

CRAIG, Dr (James) Oscar Max Clark; s of James Oscar Max Clark Craig, and Olivia Craig; *b* 7 May 1927; *Educ* St Andrews Coll Dublin; *m* 18 Oct 1950, Louise, da of Henry Burleigh; 4 da (Siobhan b 12 June 1958, Louise b 31 March 1960, Finella b 15 Oct 1960, Sheena b 21 June 1968); *Career* surgn RAF 1954-56; asst in general practice 1950-51, house surgn St Helier Hosp Carshalton 1951-52, GP Sutton 1952-54, sr house surgn Hammersmith Hosp 1956-57; St Mary's Hosp London: registrar and sr registrar in radiology 1957-63, conslt radiologist 1963-, dir clinical studies St Mary's Hosp Med Sch 1969-75, dir postgrad studies 1979-81; pres Royal Coll of Radiologists 1989; Freeman City of London; hon memb RCSI 1985 ; memb Cncl Medical Protection Soc; memb BIR, fell Assoc of Clinical Anatomy, FRCSI 1956, FFR 1961, FRCR 1975, Hon FFR RCSI 1985, MRCP 1989; *Books* author of numerous papers on radiology and med; *Recreations* country walking; *Clubs* Garrick, Marylebone Cricket; *Style*— Dr Oscar Craig; The White House, 18 Sandy Lane, Cheam, Surrey (☎ 081 642 2696); 36 Haterley Court, Hatherley Grove, Bayswater, London W2 (☎ 081 221 3454); Dept of Diagnostic Radiology, St Mary's Hospital, London W2 (☎ 071 725 6666)

CRAIG, Very Rev Prof Robert; CBE (1981); s of John Craig (stone mason, d 1972), and Anne Peggie Craig (linen weaver, d 1924); *b* 22 March 1917; *Educ* Fife CC Schs, St Andrews Univ (MA, BD, PhD), Union Theological Seminary NY USA (STM); *m* 1950, Olga Wanda, da of Michael Strzelec (d 1941); 1 s (John Michael Robert b 1961), 1 da (Anna Helena b 1956); *Career* Chaplain (4 class) Br Army: UK, NW Europe, Egypt, Palestine 1942-47, mentioned in despatches Normandy 1944; moderator of the General Assembly of the Church of Scotland 1986-87, min of St Andrew's Scots Memorial Church Jerusalem 1980-85; Univ of Zimbabwe: prof of theology 1963-80, princ and vice chllr 1969-80, now prof emeritus; prof of religion Smith Coll Northampton Mass USA 1957-63, prof of divinity Univ of Natal SA 1950-57; Hon CF 1947, Hon DD St Andrews Univ 1967; Hon LLD: Univ of Witwatersrand 1979, Univ of Birmingham 1980, Univ of Natal 1981; Hon DLitt Univ of Zimbabwe 1981; hon fell Zimbabwe Inst of Engrs 1976; City of Jerusalem medal 1985, memb Jerusalem Fndn 1989-, Golden Jubilee medal Witwatersrand Univ 1977; *Books* Social Concern in the Thought of William Temple (1963); *Recreations* listening and talking to people, contemporary and recent history, light classical music; *Clubs* Kate Kennedy, University Staff, Students' Union (St Andrews), YMCA (Jerusalem); *Style*— The Very Rev Prof Robert Craig, CBE; West Port, Falkland, Fife KY7 7BL (☎ 0337 57238)

CRAIG, Stuart Bowen; s of Alexander Craig, and Maureen Lydia Frances, *née* Frost; *b* 15 Aug 1943; *Educ* Kingston GS, Univ of Southampton (LLB); *m* 1967, Lynnard Graham, da of Geoffrey Clay Whitehurst (d 1944); 1 s (Nolan b 1969), 1 da (Natasha b 1971); *Career* dir: Kleinwort Benson Investmt Mgmnt Ltd 1978-86, Kleinwort Grieveson Investmt Mgmnt Ltd 1986-87, Fraser Green Ltd 1987-88, Nikko Fraser Green Ltd 1988-; govr Kingston GS 1978-; tstee Charinco/Charishare 1978-, assoc memb Soc of Investment Analysts; memb: Int Stock Exchange London 1987-, Pensions Res Accountants Gp 1988-, Investment Ctee Soc of Pension Conslts 1988-; FCA; *Recreations* rowing, cycling, driving, sailing, swimming, food and wine; *Clubs* Weybridge Rowing (vice pres), All Wheel Drive, Weybridge Cricket, Curry Leander, S Caernarvonshire Yacht, Abersoch Powerboat, Tramp; *Style*— Stuart Craig, Esq; Little Spinney, Caenshill Rd, Weybridge, Surrey KT13 0SW (☎ 0932 848539); Fraser Green, 2 Friars Lane, Richmond, Surrey TW9 1NL (☎ 081 948 0164, fax 081 948 4275, telex 9413827)

CRAIG, (Anne Gwendoline) Wendy; da of George Dixon Craig (d 1968) and Anne Lindsay; *b* 20 June 1934; *Educ* Durham HS for Girls, Darlington HS, Yarm GS, Central Sch of Speech Training and Dramatic Art; *m* 30 Sept 1955, John Alexander (Jack), s of John Bentley (d 1944); 2 s (Alastair b 5 April 1957, Ross b 10 Nov 1961); *Career* actress; Ipswich Repertory Theatre 1953, Epitaph For George Dillon Royal Court 1957 and Broadway, The Wrong Side of the Park 1960, The Gingerman, Ride A Cock Horse, I Love You Mrs Patterson, Finishing Touches, Peter Pan 1968, Breezeblock Park 1975, Beyond Reasonable Doubt Queen's Theatre 1987; TV series: Not In Front Of The Children, And Mother Makes Three, And Mother Makes Five, Nanny, Butterflies, Laura and Disorder; Films: The Mindbenders, The Servant (British Academy nomination), The Nanny 1966, Just Like A Woman, I'll Never Forget What's-Is-Name, Joseph Andrews; LP recordings: Tales of Beatrix Potter (Gold disc), Show Me The Way 1988, I'm Growing 1990; BAFTA award Best Actress 1968, BBC Personality of the Year 1969 (ITV 1973); *Books* Happy Endings (1972), The Busy Mums Cook Book (1983), Busy Mums Baking Book (1986), Kid's Stuff (1988); *Recreations* walking, gardening; *Style*— Miss Wendy Craig; c/o Richard Hatton, 29 Roehampton Gate, London SW15 5JR

CRAIG, Rt Hon William; PC (NI 1963); s of late John Craig, of Milecross, Newtownards, Co Down, and Mary Kathleen, *née* Lamont; *b* 2 Dec 1924; *Educ* Dungannon Royal Sch, Larne GS, Queen's Univ Belfast; *m* 1960, Doris, da of Ewald Hilgendorff, of Hamburg; 2 s; *Career* slr 1952, MP (U) Larne Div Antrim NI Parly 1960-73, MP (UU) Belfast E 1974-79, min of Devpt 1965-66, fndr and former ldr Ulster Vanguard and Vanguard Unionist Parties; *Style*— The Rt Hon William Craig; c/o N Ireland Privy Council Office, Whitehall SW1 1AT

CRAIG-COOPER, Sir (Frederick Howard) Michael; CBE (1982), TD (3 bars), DL (Gtr London 1986-); s of Frederick William Valentine Craig-Cooper (d 1975), and Elizabeth Oliver-Thompson, *née* Macdonald; *b* 28 Jan 1936; *Educ* Horris Hill, Stowe, Coll of Law London; *m* 8 March 1968, Elizabeth Snagge, MVO, da of Leonard William Snagge (d 1971); 1 s (Peter b 3 March 1972); *Career* Nat Serv RA served combined ops UK Malta and Cyprus 1954-56; TA 1956-88; cmd NGLO Unit 29 Commando Regt RA 1972-75; articled slr (to Sir Arthur Driver) Jaques & Co 1956-61, slr Allen & Overy 1962-64; Inco Ltd 1964-85: dir of cos in UK, Europe, Africa, ME and India 1972-84, conslt and non-exec dir UK and ME 1984-85; Parly candidate (C) Houghton-Le-Spring 1966 and 1970; dir: Craig Lloyd Ltd 1968-, Paul Ray Int 1984-, Carré Orban & Ptnrs Ltd 1989-; Rep Lt Kensington and Chelsea 1987-; Royal Borough of Kensington & Chelsea: cncllr 1968-74, memb Cncl 1968-78, chief whip 1971-74, chm Fin Ctee 1972-74, memb Investmt Panel 1973-, Alderman 1974-78; chm: Chelsea Cons Assoc 1974-77 (pres 1983-), Cons Nat Property Advsy Ctee 1986-, Employers Support Ctee TAVRA Gtr London 1987-90, Order of St John for London 1990-; tstee Copper Devpt Tst Fund 1974-85, treas Gtr London Area Nat Union of Cons and Unionist Assocs 1975-84 (memb 1975-); memb Cncl Mining Assoc of UK 1977-82; Freeman City of London 1964, Liveryman Worshipful Co of Drapers 1970 (jr warden 1987-88, Court of Assts 1987-); memb: Law Soc 1962, Inst of Arbitrators; Offr Order of Merit with Swords of Sovereign Mil Order of Malta (1986), OStJ 1978; KStJ 1990; *Recreations* admiring wife's gardening; *Clubs* Pratts, Whites; *Style*— Sir Michael Craig-Cooper, CBE, TD, DL; Carré Orban and Paul Ray Int, 44 St James's Place, London SW1A 1NS (☎ 071 491 1266, fax 071 491 4609)

CRAIG HARVEY, Lady Julia Helen; *née* Percy; 3 da of 10 Duke of Northumberland, KG, GCVO, TD, PC (d 1988); *b* 12 Nov 1950; *m* 11 June 1983, Nicholas Robert Craig Harvey, er s of Andrew John Craig Harvey, of Lainston House, Sparshott, Hants; 1 s (Christopher Hugh b 4 Oct 1988), 1 da (Georgina Elizabeth b 29 May 1986); *Career* res; *Style*— Lady Julia Craig Harvey; 7 Sibella Road, London SW4

CRAIG-McFEELY, Lt Cdr Gerald Martin; s of Lt Col Cecil Michael Craig-McFeely, DSO, MBE, MC (d 1948), and Nancy Elton, *née* Mann (d 1981); *b* 5 April 1932; *Educ* Downside; *m* 12 April 1958, Joanna Mary Moubray, da of Douglas Jenkins; 2 s (Simon b 1959, Peter b 1971), 2 da (Julia b 1962, Mary b 1967); *Career* RN 1950-69, long TAs HMS Vernon 1957, HMS Defender 1958-61, 1 Submarine Sqdn 1961-63, staff offr ops 26 Escort Sqdn Far East 1963-65, HMS Vernon 1965-66, Naval Intelligence 1967-69, ret Lt Cdr 1969; Lazard Brothers and Co Ltd 1974- (personnel dir 1987-); ACIS 1970; *Recreations* fly-fishing, shooting, painting; *Style*— Lt Cdr Gerald Craig-McFeely; Tintern, Hill Brow, Liss, Hants GU33 7QA (☎ 0730 892138); Lazard Brothers and Co Ltd, 21 Moorfields, London EC2P 2HT (☎ 071 588 2721)

CRAIGAVON, Viscountess; (Angela) Fiona; *née* Tatchell; yr da of late Percy Tatchell, MRCS, LRCP (d 1948), of 29 Barkston Gdns, London SW; *m* 22 Nov 1939, 2 Viscount Craigavon (d 1974); 1 s (3 Viscount), 2 da (Hon Mrs MacInnes, Hon Mrs MacDonald); *Style*— The Rt Hon the Viscountess Craigavon; 27 Launceston Place, W8

CRAIGAVON, 3 Viscount (UK 1927); Sir Janric Fraser Craig; 3 Bt (UK 1918); s of 2 Viscount Craigavon (d 1974); *b* 9 June 1944; *Educ* Eton, London Univ (BA, BSc); *Heir* none; *Career* FCA; *Style*— The Rt Hon The Viscount Craigavon; 17 Launceston Place, London W8

CRAIGEN, Desmond Seaward; s of John Craigen, of London (d 1934), and Anne Amelia (d 1958); *b* 31 July 1916; *Educ* Holloway Sch, Kings Coll London (BA); *m* 24 Feb 1961, Elena Ines, da of Norman de Launay Oldham (d 1975); 1 s (Jeremy John b 1963), 1 da (Barbara Claire b 1957); *Career* served as Maj 53 Reconnaissance Regt NW Europe 1944-46 (despatches); Prudential Assurance Co 1934-81: India 1950-57, dep gen mngr 1968, gen mngr 1969-78, chief gen mngr 1979-81; dir Prudential Corp 1982-89, chm Vanburgh Life Assur Co 1982-87, dir Pioneer Concrete (Hldgs) Co 1982-89; *Recreations* music, reading; *Style*— Desmond Craigen, Esq; 44 Crondace Rd, London SW6 4BT

CRAIGEN, James Mark (Jim); JP; eldest s of late James Craigen, of Glasgow, and late Isabel Craigen; *b* 2 Aug 1938; *Educ* Shawlands Acad Glasgow, Univ of Strathclyde, Heriot-Watt Univ (M Litt); *m* 20 March 1971, Sheena, da of late James Millar, of Linlithgow; *Career* compositor 1954-61, industl rels asst Scot Gas 1963-64, asst sec Scot TUC 1964-68, asst sec Scot Business Educn Cncl 1968-74; MP (Lab and Co-op) Glasgow Maryhill 1974-87); PPS to sec of state Scot 1974-76, memb UK Delgn Cncl of Europe 1976-80, chm Select Ctee Employment 1982-83 (memb 1979-83), oppn front bench spokesman Scot 1983-85; dir and sec Scot Fedn of Housing Assocs 1988-; tstee Nat Museums of Scot 1985-; CBIM; *Style*— Jim Craigen, Esq, JP; SFHA, 40 Castle St North, Edinburgh EH2 3BN

CRAIGIE, Colin; s of James Patrick Craigie, of Glasgow (d 1924), and Isabella Baird *née* Weir, of Glasgow (d 1952); *b* 28 Sept 1923; *Educ* Univ of London (BSc Econ); *m* 23 March 1956, Catherine Boyd, da of Daniel Alexander Mackay (d 1951); 1 s (Colin Russell b 1958), 1 da (Gail Roger b 1960); *Career* fin controller Consolidated Gold Fields plc 1966-70; fin dir: Lines Bros Ltd 1971, STC (SA) Ltd 1971-73, Meyer Int plc 1982-88, Int Timber Corporation plc 1973-82; ACMA, MCT; *Recreations* cricket, marriage, philosophy; *Clubs* MCC; *Style*— Colin Craigie, Esq; 23A Barkston Gardens, London SW5 0ER (☎ 071 373 3781)

CRAIGMYLE, 3 Baron (UK 1929); Thomas Donald Mackay Shaw; s of 2 Baron Craigmyle (d 1944), and Lady Margaret Cargill Mackay (d 1958), da of 1 Earl of Inchcape; *b* 17 Nov 1923; *Educ* Eton, Trinity Coll Oxford (MA); *m* 22 Sept 1955, Anthea Esther Christine Theresa, da of late Edward Charles Rich, of 31 Yeomans Row, London SW3; 3 s (Thomas, Justin, Joseph), 3 da (Alison, Catriona, Madeleine); *Heir* s, Hon Thomas Columba Shaw, *qv*; *Career* chm: Craigmyle and Co Ltd, Claridge Mills Ltd (Queen's award for Export 1982 and 1987); pres Br Assoc SMO Malta; vice pres Catholic Union of GB; FRSA; KStJ; *Clubs* Royal Thames Yacht, Caledonian; *Style*— The Rt Hon the Lord Craigmyle; 18 The Boltons, London SW10 9SY (☎ 071 373 3533/5157); Scottas, Knoydart, Inverness-shire PH41 4PL

CRAIGTON, Baron (Life Peer UK 1959), of Renfield, Co of City of Glasgow; (Jack) Nixon Browne; CBE (1944), PC (1961); s of Edwin Gilbert Izod, of Rugby and Johannesburg, and Kathleen Roie, *née* Duke; assumed stepfather's surname of Browne in lieu of patronymic 1920; *b* 3 Sept 1904; *Educ* Cheltenham; *m* 1, 1936 (m dis 1949), Helen Anne, da of late G J Inglis, of Glasgow; 1 s (Hon John Nixon, decd); m 2, 11 Feb 1950, Eileen Humphrey, da of Henry Whitford Nolan, of London; *Career* sits as (C) Peer in House of Lords; serv WWII Actg Gp Capt RAF Balloon Cmd 1939-45; contested (C) Govan Glasgow 1945, MP (C) Govan 1950-55, MP Craigton Glasgow 1955-Sept 1959, PPS to sec of state for Scotland 1952-55, Parly under sec Scottish Office 1955-59, min of state 1959-64; chm All Pty Conservation Gp of Both Houses 1972-; chm Utd Biscuits (Hldgs) Ltd 1967-72; pres Westminster C of C 1966-83 (chm 1954); chm: Cncl for Environmental Conservation 1972-83, Fedn of Zoological Gdns 1975-81; vice pres World Wildlife Fund 1979 (memb Cncl 1962-); pres Fauna and Flora Preservation Soc 1989 (memb Cncl 1960-, chm 1983); memb Cncl RSA 1975-80; *Recreations* gardening, small boats; *Clubs* Buck's; *Style*— The Rt Hon The Lord Craigton, CBE, PC; Friary House, Friary Island, Wraysbury, nr Staines, Middx TW19 5JR (☎ 0784 482213/2357)

CRAIK, Capt (Joseph) Ian; s of John Norman Craik (d 1961), late and Susan Beatrice Craik, *née* Bainbridge; *b* 21 April 1927; *Educ* Luton Modern Sch, Dept of Navigation

Univ of Southampton; *m* 29 Dec 1953, Yvonne Barbara, da of Thomas Isaac Heeks, of Southampton; 2 s (Joseph Douglas b 1957, Norman Andrew b 1961); *Career* Deck Offr (late Capt) Shell Tankers 1945-56; Gulf Oil: joined 1957, tport mangr for Far East (Tokyo) 1962, Marine Co Orindator (Pittsburgh Head Office) 1967; chm and md Stewart and Craik Technology Co (Scots) 1984-86; master mariner, MRIN; *Recreations* yachting (cruising); *Clubs* Tollesbury Cruising; *Style—* Capt Ian Craik; Marlside, Boreland, Lockerbie, Dumfries DG11 2LU (☎ 054 16 298)

CRAIK, Col Robert Rainey; OBE, TD, JP, DL (Lancs 1983); s of G B Craik of Tannadice, Angus; *b* 25 March 1925; *Educ* Forfar Acad; *m* 1957, Sybil M Carr; 1 s (Timothy), 1 da (Susannah (Mrs Rupert Chenevix-Trench)); *Career* WWII served NW Europe and India, TA 1958-81; land surveyor and co dir; chm: Westhoughton Cons Assoc 1977-83, NW of England and IOM TAVRA 1987-90; Hon Col Cheshire ACF 1989-; *Recreations* shooting, skiing, poetry, people; *Clubs* Army and Navy; *Style—* Robert Craik, Esq, OBE, TD, JP, DL; The Old Rectory, Mawdesley, Ormskirk, Lancs L40 3TD (☎ 0704 822787)

CRAIK, Prof Thomas Wallace; s of Thomas Craik (d 1969), of Warrington and Ada, *née* Atherton (d 1974); *b* 17 April 1927; *Educ* Boteler GS Warrington, Christ's Coll Cambridge (MA, PhD); *m* 25 Aug 1955 (m dis 1975), Wendy Ann, da of James Garfield Sowter (d 1979), of Kingston upon Thames; 1 s (Roger b 1956); *Career* lectr in English Univ of Leicester 1953-65, lectr then sr lectr Univ of Aberdeen 1965-72, prof Univ of Dundee 1973-77, prof Univ of Durham 1977-89; *Books* The Tudor Interlude (1958), The Comic Tales of Chaucer (1964); ed: Massinger, The City Madam (1964), Massinger, A New Way to Pay Old Debts (1964), Sidney, Poetry and Prose (1965), Marlowe, The Jew of Malta (1966), Minor Elizabethan Tragedies (1974), Shakespeare, Twelfth Night (1975), Donne, Poetry and Prose (1986), Beaumont and Fletcher, The Maid's Tragedy (1988), Shakespeare, The Merry Wives of Windsor (1989); gen ed and contrib to The "Revels" History of Drama in English (1975-83); *Recreations* acting and directing, music, painting; *Style—* Prof Thomas Craik; 58 Albert St, Durham DH1 4RJ (☎ 091 384 4528); School of English, University of Durham, Elvet Riverside, New Elvet, Durham DH1 3JT (☎ 091 374 2000)

CRAINER, George Scott; s of George William Crainer; *b* 29 April 1936; *Educ* Greenock HS; *m* 1959, Isobel, da of David Webster (d 1967); 2 c; *Career* CA; md Bury and Masco (Holdings) Ltd 1975-79, dir and div chief exec Scapa Group plc 1978-87, chm (and major shareholder) Seamark Systems Ltd 1987-; FCMA; *Recreations* golf, music; *Style—* George Crainer, Esq; 6 Johnsburn Park, Balerno, Midlothian EH14 7NA

CRAM, Prof (William) John; s of Rev Frederick Charles Cram, of Harby, Leics, and Laura Mary, *née* Redhead; *b* 6 Sept 1940; *Educ* Kingswood Sch, St John's Coll Cambridge (MA, Phd); *m* 25 July 1965, Patricia Jean, da of Reginald Middleditch (d 1987); 2 s (Nicholas b 1973, Roderick b 1976); *Career* sr res asst UEA 1967-68; Univ of Sydney Aust: lectr in biology 1969, sr lectr 1975, reader 1979-84; Univ of Newcastle upon Tyne: prof of plant biology 1984-, head Dept of Plant Biology 1984-88, head Dept of Biology 1988; author of numerous scientific papers; memb Plant Biology Ctee Soc for Experimental Biology 1984-87; *Recreations* violin, running, gardening; *Style—* Prof John Cram; 62 Willow Way, Darras Hall, Ponteland, Northumberland; Dept of Biology, Ridley Building, The University, Newcastle upon Tyne (☎ 091 2226661, telex 53654 UNINEW G, fax 091 266 1182)

CRAM, Stephen (Steve); MBE (1986); s of William Frank Cram, and Maria Helene, *née* Korte; *b* 14 Oct 1960; *Educ* Jarrow GS, Newcastle Poly (BA); *m* 17 Dec 1983, Karen Anne, da of John Andrew Waters; 1 da (Josephine); *Career* middle distance runner; Cwlth Games: Gold medallist 1500m 1982 and 1986, Gold medallist 800m 1986; World Championship Gold medallist 1500m 1983; Euro Championship: Gold medallist 1500m 1982 and 1986, Bronze medallist 800m 1986; Olympic Games Silver medallist 1984, memb Br Olympic Squad 1988; world record holder of the mile; former world record holder: 1500 m, and 2000 m; pres London and Southern England Branch Sunderland AFC Supporters Assoc; Hon Fell Sunderland Poly; *Recreations* golf, snooker; *Clubs* Jarrow and Hebburn AC, Sunderland AFC; *Style—* Steve Cram, Esq, MBE; c/o John Hockey Associates, 170 King's Road, London SW3 4UP (☎ 071 352 1251)

CRAMMOND, Ian Ashley; s of Ronald Charles Crammond (d 1980), and Rosemary Joan Victoria, *née* Ashley; *b* 26 March 1951; *Educ* Magdalen Coll Sch Oxford, Pembroke Coll Cambridge (MA); *m* 1982, Wendy Ann, da of Huw Pritchard (d 1980); *Career* graduate trainee then account exec Leo Burnett Ltd 1972-74, account exec then account mangr Benton & Bowles 1974-76, account mangr then account dir Davidson Pearce Ltd 1976-82 (associate dir 1980-82), bd account dir Allen Brady & Marsh 1984-85, bd account dir Ogilvy & Mather London 1986-87 (account dir 1985-86); business devpt dir: Brunning Advertising (also client services dir) 1987-88, GGK London Ltd 1989-; 2nd IPA Advtg Effectiveness awards 1982 (commendation new prods and services); memb: IPA 1982, Mktg Soc 1986; *Books* Advertising Works 2 (contrib, 1982); *Recreations* photography, mountain walking, motor sports; *Clubs* Alfa Romeo Owners; *Style—* Ian Crammond, Esq; GGK London Ltd, 76 Dean St, London W1V 5AH (☎ 071 734 0511, fax 071 287 9788)

CRAMOND, Ronald Duncan; CBE (1987); s of Adam Cramond, of Edinburgh (d 1974), and Margaret Weir, *née* McAulay (d 1978); late wife Connie MacGregor direct descendant of John MacGregor, personal attendant and piper to Prince Charles Edward Stuart; *b* 22 March 1927; *Educ* George Heriot's Sch, Univ of Edinburgh (MA); *m* 18 March 1954, Constance Margaret (d 1985), da of John MacGregor, of Auchterarder (d 1964); 1 s (Kenneth b 1959), 1 da (Fiona b 1957); *Career* Royal Scots, Europe 1949-51; private sec to Parly Under Sec Scottish Office 1956-7; post graduate fell applied econs Univ of Glasgow 1963; Haldane Medallist Royal Inst of Pub Admin 1964; Under Sec Scottish Office 1971-83, dep chm Highlands and Islands Devpt Bd 1983-88; memb Scottish Tourist Bd 1985-88; Commr Countryside Commn for Scotland 1988-, tstee Royal Museum of Scotland 1985-, chm Scottish Museums Cncl 1990-; FBIM; FSA(S) cncl memb; *Books* Housing Policy in Scotland; *Recreations* golf, hill walking; *Clubs* Scottish Arts (Edinburgh); *Style—* Ronald D Cramond, Esq, CBE; c/o Countryside Commission for Scotland, Battleby, Redgorton, Perth

CRAMP, Prof Rosemary Jean; CBE; da of Robert Raymond Kingston Cramp, Hallaton, Leics, and Vera Grace, *née* Ractliffe (d 1965); *b* 6 May 1929; *Educ* Market Harborough GS, St Anne's Coll Univ of Oxford (MA, B Litt); *Career* lectr St Anne's Coll Oxford 1950-55; Univ of Durham: lectr 1955-60, sr lectr 1966-71, prof 1971-90, prof emeritus 1990-; archaeological advsr Durham Cathedral, tstee Br Museum, pres Cncl Br Achaeology, cmmr Royal Cmmn of Ancient and Historical Monuments for Scotland, former pres Cumberland and Westmorland Antiquarian and Archaeological Soc, memb Redundant Churches Advsy Bd; FSA; *Books* Corpus of Anglo Saxon Stone Sculpture (vol 1 1984, vol 2 with RN Bailey 1988); *Recreations* cooking, walking, reading; *Clubs* United Oxford & Cambridge Univ; *Style—* Prof Rosemary Cramp, CBE; 5 Leazes Place, Durham DH1 1RE (☎ 091 3861843)

CRAMPTON, Peter Duncan; MEP (Lab) Humberside 1989-; s of Edmund Crampton (d 1954), and Louisa, *née* Thurman (d 1967); *b* 10 June 1932; *Educ* Blackpool GS, Univ of Nottingham (BA), Univ of Birmingham (MA), Univ of Hull (Dip in W Euro Studies), Univ of London (PGCE); *m* Margaret Eva, da of George William McMillan (d 1955); 2 s (David b 1962, Robert b 1964); *Career* statistician Plessey Co 1955-56, geography teacher Coventry 1957-61, educn offr Uganda 1961-64; geography lectr: Tech Coll Birmingham 1964-70; Hull Coll of Educn 1970-85, pt/t lectr writer and Parly asst 1985-89; chm: Euro Nuclear Disarmament 1984-86, CND Int Ctee 1988-; *Books* Voices for One World (contrib 1988); *Style—* Peter Crampton, Esq, MEP; 135 Westbourne Avenue, Hull HU5 3HU (☎ 0482 449337, fax 0482 449403)

CRAMPTON, (Arthur Edward) Seán; MC (1943), GM (1944), TD (1946); eldest s of Joshua Crampton (d 1979), and Ethel Mary, *née* Dyas (d 1979); *b* 15 March 1918; *Educ* Vittoria Jr Sch of Art, Birmingham Central Coll of Art; *m* 1959, Patricia Elizabeth Cardew, eldest da of Col Leslie John Cardew Wood; 1 s (Daniel), 4 da (Bridget, Katinka, Nicolette, Harriet); *Career* Nat Serv WWII; Capt London Irish Rifles: Western Desert, Sicily (MC), Italy (GM), wounded; sculptor FRBS (pres 1965-70); memb Art Workers Guild (master 1979); chair of Govrs Camberwell Sch of Art 1983-88; govr London Inst 1986-89; author of innumerable works throughout UK and USA; *Books* Humans, Beasts, Birds; *Clubs* Athenaeum, Chelsea Arts; *Style—* Seán Crampton Esq, MC, GM, TD; Rookery Farmhouse, Calne, Wilts SN11 0LH (☎ 0249 814068)

CRAMSIE, Lt-Col Alexander James; DL; s of Col Alexander James Henry Cramsie, OBE, DL, JP (d 1987), of O'Harabrook, Ballymoney, Co Antrim, NI, and Gabrielle Patricia, *née* Hornby; *b* 31 May 1941; *Educ* Wellington, RMA Sandhurst; *m* 11 Sept 1965, Bridget, da of Lt-Col Walter Derek Hamilton Duke, MC (Gordon Highlanders), of Langford Cottage, Fivehead, Somerset; 2 s (Rupert b 1966, Alexander b 1969); *Career* Lt Col (ret) Queen's Royal Irish Hussars 1961-81, cmd Queen's Own Yeomanry 1981-84, served Aden, Malaya, Borneo and NI; landowner, steward INHS Ctee, regnl organiser Army Benevolent Fund NI; won Grand Mil Gold Cup 1976 and 1983; *Recreations* hunting, racing, shooting, tennis; *Style—* Lt-Col A J Cramsie, DL; O'Harabrook, Ballymoney, Co Antrim, N Ireland (☎ 02656 66273)

CRAMSIE, Marcus James Lendrum; s of Arthur Vacquerie Cramsie, of Co Tyrone, NI, and Susan Doreen, *née* Lendrum; *b* 24 April 1950; *Educ* Charterhouse, Trinity Hall Cambridge (MA); *m* 19 March 1983, Carol Lesley, *née* Slow; 1 s (Rory b 1990), 2 da (Camilla b 1984, Louise b 1986); *Career* Price Waterhouse 1972-76, dir Kleinwort Benson Ltd 1986- (joined 1976); FCA; *Recreations* golf, shooting, tennis; *Style—* Marcus Cramsie, Esq; 20 Lyford Rd, London SW18; Kleinwort Benson Ltd, 20 Fenchurch St, London EC3 (☎ 071 623 8000)

CRAN, James Douglas; MP (C) Beverley 1987-; s of James Cran, of Aberdeen, and Jane McDonald Cran (d 1986); *b* 28 Jan 1944; *Educ* Ruthrieston Sch Aberdeen, Aberdeen Coll of Commerce, Kings Coll Univ of Aberdeen (MA); *m* 1973, Penelope Barbara, da of Richard Thomas Parker Wilson, of Bristol; 1 da (Alexandra Penelope b 1981); *Career* reseacher Cons Res Dept 1970-71, sec and chief exec Nat Assoc of Pension Funds 1971-79, W Midlands dir CBI 1984-87 (Northern dir 1979-84), memb House of Commons Select Ctee on Trade and Indust 1987-; *Recreations* travelling, reading biographies and autobiographies; *Style—* James Cran, Esq, MP; House of Commons, London SW1A 0AA (☎ 071 219 4445)

CRAN, Mark Dyson Gordon; QC (1988); s of Gordon Cran (d 1972), and Diana, *née* Mallinson; *b* 18 May 1948; *Educ* Gordonstoun, Millfield, Univ of Bristol (LLB); *m* 29 July 1983 (m dis 1986), Prudence Elizabeth, *née* Hayles; *Career* called to the Bar Gray's Inn 1973; practices London; *Recreations* country sports, convivial disputation, wine and food, books and theatre; *Style—* Mark Cran, Esq, QC; 1 Brick Court Chambers, 15-19 Devereux Court, London WC2R 3JJ (☎ 071 583 0777, fax 071 583 9401, telex 892687 IBRICK G)

CRANBORNE, Viscount; Robert Michael James (Gascoyne) Cecil; DL (Dorset 1988), MP (C) Dorset S 1979-; s and h of 6 Marquess of Salisbury; *b* 30 Sept 1946; *Educ* Eton, Oxford; *m* 1970, Hannah Ann, da of Lt-Col William Joseph Stirling of Keir, gs of Sir William Stirling-Maxwell, 9 Bt, (a Baronetcy dormant since 1956); 2 s (Hon Robert b 1970, Hon James Richard b 1973), 3 da (Hon Elizabeth Ann b 1972, Hon Georgiana b 1977, Hon Katherine b (twin) 1977); *Career* chm Afghanistan Support Ctee; PPS to Cranley Onslow as Min State FCO April-May 1982 when resigned to be free to criticise Govt's Ulster devolution plans; fndr memb Blue Chip Tory dining club; *Style—* Viscount Cranborne, DL, MP; The Lodge House, Hatfield Park, Herts; Tregonwell Lodge, Cranborne, Wimborne, Dorset

CRANBROOK, Dowager Countess of; Fidelity; OBE, JP; o da of Hugh Exton Seebohm, JP (d 1946), of Poynder's End, Hitchin, and his 1 wife Leslie, *née* Gribble (d 1913); sister of Baron Seebohm (Life Peer); *b* 1912; *m* 26 July 1932, as his 2 w, 4 Earl of Cranbrook, CBE (d 1978); 2 s, 3 da; *Career* JP; *Style—* The Rt Hon The Dowager Countess of Cranbrook, OBE, JP; Red House Farm, Great Glemham, Saxmundham, Suffolk

CRANBROOK, 5 Earl of (UK 1892); Gathorne Gathorne-Hardy; also Viscount Cranbrook (UK 1878), Baron Medway (UK 1892); s of 4 Earl, CBE (d 1978) by his 2 w, Dowager Countess Cranbrook, OBE, JP, *qv*; *b* 20 June 1933; *Educ* Eton, Corpus Christi Coll Cambridge (MA), Univ of Birmingham (PhD); *m* 9 May 1967, Caroline, o da of Col Ralph George Edward Jarvis, of Doddington Hall, Lincoln, by his w Antonia Meade (*see* Peerage Earl of Clanwilliam); 2 s (John Jason Lord Medway b 1968, Hon Argus Edward b 1973), 1 da (Lady Flora b 1971); *Career* Univ of Malaya 1961-70, ed Ibis 1973-80; memb Sub Ctee F (Environment) Select Ctee on Euro Communities House of Lords 1979-90, chm Nat Conservancy Cncl for Eng 1990-; memb: Royal Cmmn on Environmental Pollution 1981-, Natural Environment Res Cncl 1982-88, Broads Authy 1988-, Nat Conservancy Cncl 1990; non-exec dir: Anglian Water 1987-, Harwich Haven Authy 1989-; Skinner and Freeman of City of London; CBiol, Hon DSc Univ of Aberdeen, FLS, FZS, FRGS; OStJ, DL; *Books* Mammals of Malaya, Mammals of Borneo, Mammals of SE Asia; *Style—* The Rt Hon the Earl of Cranbrook; c/o Nature Conservancy Council for England, Northminster House, Peterborough PE1 2UA (☎ 0733 898290, fax 072 878339)

CRANCH, (Arthur) Graeme; s of Arthur Lakeman Cranch (d 1942), of 119 Cambridge Rd, Wimbledon, and Jessie Cowie, *née* Murdoch (d 1952); *Educ* King's Coll Sch; *m* 10 Aug 1940, Molly Pernelle, da of Alfred Heath Pryce (d 1978); 2 da (Carol b 1942, Alison b 1947); *Career* TA 1938, cmmnd RA 1940, Capt 1942, Adj 1942, served Air Def of GB; mgmnt trainee (later mktg exec) Rowntree & Co York 1929, res exec London Pres Exchange Ltd 1936; Mather & Crowther Ltd (later Ogilvy & Mather Ltd): res dir 1946, appointed to bd and dir of subsid cos 1954; fndr memb and former pres: Market Res Soc, ESOMAR; former chm Int Mktg Fedn, chm Ctee Int C of C Paris, memb Incorporated Practitioners in Advtg, mktg conslt UN/FAO Rome; govr King's Coll Sch; Liveryman Worshipful Co of Carmen 1956; FIPA; *Recreations* antiques, watching cricket, gardening, foreign travel; *Clubs* East India, MCC; *Style—* Graeme Cranch, Esq; Summerlea, Beverley Lane, Coombe Hill, Kingston upon Thames, Surrey KT2 7EE

CRANE, Edwin Arthur; s of Charles Edmund Crane (d 1966), of Thorpe House, Moira Rd, Ashby-de-la-Zouch, Leics, and Lilian Elizabeth, *née* Bartlett (d 1956); *b* 11 June 1918; *Educ* Repton, Clare Coll Cambridge (BA); *m* 1 Sept 1943, Joan Ellen, da of Harold Langrish (d 1969), of 76 Chichester Rd, Bognor Regis, Sussex; 2 s (David b 1950, John b 1953), 2 da (Mary b 1944, Frances b 1947); *Career* Maj RASC UK and W Europe 1941-46; slr conslt Crane and Walton Ashby-de-la-Zouch Coalville and

Leicester, dir and vice chm Coalville Permanent Building Society 1957-76, chm Breedon plc 1987- (dir 1970-); Tstee Savings Bank 1957-74, Tstee Savings Bank of Leicester and Nottingham 1978-80; pres Leicester Law Soc 1972, memb Leics CC 1977-85; *Recreations* local history, walking; *Style—* E A Crane, Esq; 11 Church St, Swepstone, Leics LE6 1SA (☎ 0530 70639); South St, Ashby-de-la-Zouch, Leics Le6 5BT (☎ 0530 414111)

CRANE, Geoffrey David; s of Frederick David Crane (d 1982), and Marion Doris, *née* Gorman (d 1973); *b* 13 Oct 1934; *Educ* City of London Sch, Trinity Hall Cambridge (MA); *m* 1962, Gillian Margaret, da of Harry Thomas Austin (d 1979); 1 da (Jessica b 1968); *Career* RAF Flying Offr 1956-58; asst private sec to Min of Works 1961-62; sec: Historic Bldgs Cncl for Scot, Ancient Monuments Bd for Scot 1962-66; private sec to Min of Public Bldg and Works 1968-69, head of machinery of Govt Div CS Dept 1970-72, dep dir Central Unit on Environment Pollution DOE 1972-75; DOE and Tport: dir of Res Ops 1978-80, dir of Personnel Mgmnt and Trg 1981-85, regl dir Eastern Region 1985-89; head Freight Directorate Dept of Tport 1989-90; *Recreations* classical music, industrial archaeology, mathematics; *Clubs* RAF, Civil Service; *Style—* Geoffrey Crane Esq; 6 The Paddock, Datchet, Berkshire SL3 9DL (☎ 0753 43644)

CRANE, Sir James William Donald; CBE (1977); s of William James Crane, and Ivy Winifred Crane; *b* 1 Jan 1921; *m* 1942, Patricia Elizabeth Hodge; 1 s, 1 da; *Career* joined Metropolitan Police 1946, chief inspector of constabulary 1979-82 (formerly inspector); memb Parole Bd 1983-; kt 1980; *Style—* Sir James Crane, CBE; Home Office, 50 Queen Anne's Gate, London SW1

CRANE, His Hon Judge; Peter Francis; s of Francis Roger Crane, of Northants, and Jean Berenice, *née* Hadfield (d 1987); *b* 14 Jan 1940; *Educ* Nottingham HS, Highgate Sch, Gonville and Caius Coll Cambridge (MA, LLM), Tulane Univ USA (LLM); *m* 1967, Elizabeth Mary, da of Noel Bawtry Pittman, of Northants; 4 da (Anna b 1968, Kate b 1969, Rebecca b 1972, Lucy b 1974); *Career* barr MO Circuit 1964-87, rec 1982-87, circuit judge 1987-; memb: Senate of the Inns of Court and the Bar 1983-86, Professional Conduct Ctee 1984-86, Bar Ctee 1985-86; *Recreations* reading, walking, gardening, wine; *Clubs* Northampton and County; *Style—* His Hon Judge Crane; The Glebe House, Pytchley, Kettering, Northants NN14 1EW

CRANE, Robert Coutts; s of William Crane (d 1980), of Stirlingshire, and Mary Shearer, *née* Coutts; *b* 16 May 1935; *Educ* Denny HS, Inst of Chartered Accountants of Scotland (1957); *m* 1960, Anna Katerin, Jephson, da of Capt John Arthur Jephson-Jones (d 1964), of Fife; 1 s (John b 1961), 1 da (Sheenagh b 1963); *Career* RN Sub Lt 1958-59, Capt UDR 1971-73; dep accountant BP Refinery Grangemouth 1960-63; chief accountant, dep gen mangr Highland Printers Ltd 1963-67, md Belfast Telegraph Newspapers Ltd 1979- (accountant 1967, dep production mangr 1970, production mangr 1971, gen mangr Weekly Newspapers 1971 (asst md 1973); md Chester Charonicle & Associate Newspapers Ltd 1976-78; *Recreations* trout fishing, photography; *Style—* Robert C Crane, Esq; Logwood Mill, 22 Logwood Rd, Ballyclare, Co Antrim BT39 9LR; Belfast Telegraph Newapapers Ltd, Royal Avenue, Belfast BT1 1EB (☎ 0232 221242, fax 0232 246560)

CRANE, (Thomas Peter) Robin; s of Thomas Tavershm Crane (d 1987), and Lilian Crane; *b* 8 Nov 1931; *Educ* Christ's Hosp; *m* 15 Aug 1955, Wendy Elisabeth, da of Lt-Col Frederick Skipwith (d 1960); 2 da (Jenni b 1958, Caroline b 1969); *Career* reg cmmn RASC 1950-57, resigned as Capt; maltster: Arthur Guinness & Co 1957-59, Sandars & Co 1959-67; film dir and prodr World About Us BBC (Mirror Observed, The Other Iceland, Rabbits - Wanted Dead or Alive?, Butterflies); Br Sponsored Film Festivals Gold Awards for: Event Horse 1975, The Colourmen 1984, Heritage of the Forest 1984; NY Film & TV Festival Silver Award for Mirror to the Fun 1984; chm Sussex Wildlife Tst (memb Cncl 1969-); FRES 1979; *Recreations* nature conservation, music, tennis, golf; *Clubs* British Acad of Film and TV Arts; *Style—* Robin Crane, Esq; Bridge Cottage, Well Lane, Midhurst, West Sussex GU29 9QQ

CRANE, Teresa; da of Jack Goodsell (d 1964), of Hornchurch, and Teresa, *née* Overson; *b* 10 June 1938; *Educ* Hornchurch GS; *m* 10 Oct 1960, Anthony Charles Crane; 1 s (Andrew Anthony b 1962), 1 da (Michele Jacqueline (Mrs Smith) b 1964); *Career* writer; books: Molly (1980), A Fragile Peace (1981), The Rose Stone (1984), Sweet Songbird (1987), Hawthorne Heritage (1988), Tomorrow Jerusalem (1990); vice pres of Essex Red Cross; *Recreations* reading, music, cooking, walking, travelling, although not necessary always in that order; *Style—* Mrs Teresa Crane; Blake Friedmann Literary Agency, 37-41 Gower St, London WC1E 6HH (☎ 071 631 4331, fax 071 323 1274)

CRANFIELD, Richard William Lionel; s of Lionel Sydney William Cranfield (d 1965), of Tewin, Herts, and Audrey Cecil Martin, *née* Pank; *b* 19 Jan 1956; *Educ* Winchester, Fitzwilliam Coll Cambridge (MA); *m* 26 Sept 1981, Gillian Isabel, da of Archibald Spence Fleming (d 1979), of Graden, Kelso, Roxburghshire; 1 s (Edward), 2 da (Sophie, Henrietta); *Career* Lt HAC 1979-86; admitted slr 1980; ptnr Allen & Overy; Freeman City of London 1985, memb Worshipful Co of Merchant Taylors; memb Law Soc; *Recreations* golf, field sports; *Style—* Richard Cranfield, Esq; 9 Cheapside, London EC2V 6AD (☎ 071 248 9898, fax 071 236 2192)

CRANLEY, Viscount; Rupert Charles William Bullard Onslow; s and h of 7 Earl of Onslow; *b* 16 June 1967; *Educ* Eton; *Recreations* country sports; *Style—* Viscount Cranley; Temple Court, Clandon Park, Guildford, Surrey

CRANMER-BYNG, John Launcelot; MC (1944); s of Capt Launcelot Alfred Cranmer-Byng (d 1945), and his 2 wife Daisy Elaine, *née* Beach (d 1981); hp of kinsman, 11 Viscount Torrington; *b* 18 March 1919; *Educ* Haileybury, King's Coll Cambridge (MA); *m* 19 Jan 1955, Margaret Ellen, o da of Reginald Herbert Hardy, of Sevenoaks, Kent; 1 s, 2 da; *Career* served WWII as Maj Airborne Forces; lectr in history Univ of Hong Kong 1956-64, prof of history Univ of Toronto 1964-84; *Recreations* ornithology; *Style—* John Cranmer-Byng, Esq, MC; 27 Idleswift Drive, Thornhill, Ontario, Canada

CRANSTON, Prof Maurice William; s of William Cranston (d 1944), of Edinburgh, and Catherine, *née* Harris (d 1932); *b* 8 May 1920; *Educ* St Catherine's Coll Oxford (MA, BLitt); *m* 11 Nov 1958, Baroness Maximiliana, da of Baron Theodor von und zu Fraunberg (d 1948), of Florence, Italy; 2 s (Nicholas b 1960, Stephen b 1962); *Career* Civil Def London 1939-45; Univ of London: social philosophy 1950-59, lectr in political sci 1959-64, reader 1964-69; prof of political sci LSE 1969-85; literary advsr Methuen & Co 1959-69; visiting prof: Univ of Harvard 1965-66, Dartmouth Coll USA 1970-71, Univ of Br Columbia 1973, Ecole des Hautes Etudes Paris 1977, Fndn Thiers Paris 1982, Univ of California at San Diego 1986-91; vice pres Alliance Francaise en Angleterre 1964-, registrar Royal Literary Fund 1973-79, pres Inst International de Philosophie Politique 1978-81; hon fell St Catherine's Coll Oxford; FRSL 1958; Commandeur de l'Ordre des Palmes Academiques France 1987; *Books* Freedom (1953), John Locke (1957), Sartre (1964), What are Human Rights (1963), Political Dialogues (1968), Language and Philosophy (1969), The Mask of Politics (1973), Jean-Jacques; The Early Life of J J Rousseau (1983), Philosophers and Pamphleteers (1984), The Noble Savage (1991); *Recreations* walking; *Clubs* Garrick; *Style—* Prof Maurice Cranston; 1A Kent Terrace, Regents Park, London NW1 4RP (☎ 071 262 2698); London School of Economics, London WC2A 2AE (☎ 071 405 7686, fax 071 242 0392)

CRANSTON, Prof Ross Frederick; s of Frederick Hugh Cranston, of Brisbane, Aust, and Edna Elizabeth, *née* Davies; *b* 23 July 1948; *Educ* Nundah State Sch, Wavell HS Brisbane, Univ of Queensland (BA, LLB), Harvard Univ (LLM), Univ of Oxford (DPhil); *m* 1, 5 March 1976 (m dis 1985), Dr (Barbara) Jane Stapleton, da of Colin Arthur Stapleton, of Sydney; m 2, 25 Aug 1988, Elizabeth Anna, da of Leslie Victor Whyatt, of Kent; *Career* lectr in law Univ of Warwick 1975-77, called to the Bar Gray's Inn 1976; Aust Nat Univ 1978-86, Sir John Lubbock prof of banking law Univ of London 1986-, dir Centre for Commercial Law Studies Queen Mary and Westfield Coll 1989- (dean Faculty of Laws 1988-); conslt Ctee of Inquiry concerning Public Duty and Private Interest 1979, memb Legal Advsy Panel Nat Consumer Cncl 1987- (1976-77); conslt: Sri Lankan Govt and World Bank 1988, Hungarian Govt and World Bank 1990; *Books* Regulating Business (1979), Law and Economics (jt ed, 1981), Consumers and the Law (2 edn, 1984), Delays and Efficiency in Civil Litigation (jtly, 1984), Legal Foundations of the Welfare State (1985), Law, Government and Public Policy (1987), Legal Issues of Cross-Border Banking (ed, 1989), 1992: The Legal Implications for Banking and Finance (ed, 1989), Banks, Liability and Risk (ed, 1990); *Clubs* Reform; *Style—* Prof Ross Cranston; 117 Dacre Park, London SE13 5BZ; Faculty of Laws, Queen Mary & Westfield College, University of London, 339 Mile End Rd, London E1 4NS (☎ 071 975 5117, fax 081 980 1079); 3 Gray's Inn Place, London WC1R 5EA (☎ 071 831 8441, fax 071 831 8479)

CRANWORTH, 3 Baron (UK 1899); Philip Bertram Gurdon; s of Hon Robin Gurdon (ka 1942, s of late 2 Baron, KG, MC, who d 1964) and late Hon Yoskyl Pearson, da of 2 Viscount Cowdray (who m 2, Lt-Col Alistair Gibb, and m 3, 1 Baron McCorquodale of Newton, KCVO, PC); *b* 24 May 1940; *Educ* Eton, Magdalene Coll Cambridge; *m* 18 Jan 1968, Frances Henrietta, da of late Lord William Walter Montagu Douglas Scott, MC (s of 7 Duke of Buccleuch), and Lady Rachel Douglas-Home (da of 13 Earl of Home); 2 s (Hon Sacha William Robin b 1970, Hon Brampton Charles b 1975) 1 da (Hon Louisa-Jane b 1969); *Career* late Lt Royal Wilts Yeo; *Style—* The Rt Hon The Lord Cranworth; Grundisburgh Hall, Woodbridge, Suffolk

CRAPP, Leslie Rufus; s of Edward Crapp of Jersey, and Lilian Annie, *née* Horn; *b* 20 May 1935; *Educ* Victoria Coll Jersey; *m* 16 Aug 1962, Annette Desirée, da of Albert Charles Le Cuirot (d 1976); 2 s (Nicholas b 1963, Jonathan b 1973), 1 da (Vanessa b 1967); *Career* chartered accountant; former sr ptnr Coopers and Lybrand (CI), dir TSB Channel Islands Ltd; hon chm Jersey Family Nursing Servs, hon treas Jersey Branch Save the Children; *Recreations* gardening, walking, french cuisine, art and antique collecting; *Style—* Leslie R Crapp, Esq; La Botellerie, Rue de la Botellerie, St Ouens, Jersey JE3 2HL (☎ 0534 83855)

CRASTON, Rev Canon (Richard) Colin; s of Albert Edward Craston (d 1977), and Ethel Craston (d 1962); *b* 31 Dec 1922; *Educ* Preston GS, Univ of Bristol (BA), Univ of London (BD); *m* 10 July 1948, Ruth; 1 s (Andrew b 4 Dec 1951), 1 da (Carolyn Edmonds b 17 Sept 1954); *Career* RN 1941-46; curate of Nicholas Durham 1951-54, team rector of St Paul with Emmanuel Bolton 1954-, area dean Bolton 1972-, chaplain to HM The Queen 1985-, chm House of Clergy Diocese of Manchester 1982-; memb: Standing Ctee Gen Synod 1976-, Crown Appointments Cmmn 1982-; vice chm Anglican Consultative Cncl 1986-90 (chm 1990-); *Books* Biblical Headship and the Ordination of Women (1986), Authority in the Anglican Communion (contrib, 1987), Open to the Spirit (ed, 1987), Anglicanism and the Universal Church (contrib, 1990), Robert Runcie - A Portrait By His Friends (contrib, 1990); *Style—* The Rev Canon Colin Craston; St Paul's Vicarage, 174 Chorley New Rd, Bolton, Lancashire BL1 4PF (☎ 0204 42303)

CRATES, (Cecil) Ralph Stuart; s of Cecil James Gildroy Crates, of Kingswood, nr Bristol, and Hilda Clara Diana, *née* Randall (d 1958); *b* 4 Sept 1927; *Educ* Cannings Coll Bristol, Kingswood GS, W of Eng Coll of Art, Loughborough Coll of Technol; *m* 26 July 1952, Rosemary Maud, da of Rev George Killingback Spurgeon Edgley, of Bristol; *Career* teacher of handicrafts and music Filton and Wellington Schs 1947-57, appt by Colonial Office as educn offr, posted to N region Nigeria 1957-87, served in craft schs Mashi and Idah; princ of Teacher Trg Colls: Mubi, Gombe, Toro, Borno; state planning offr and dir of tech educn Min of Educn Govt of Borno State, currently teaching and ind conslt in design technology communication and further educn; memb: W Country Scribes, Inst Data Processing Mgmnt; *Recreations* music, calligraphy, gliding; *Clubs* New Cavendish; *Style—* Ralph Crates, Esq; 35 Buckwell Rd, Wellington, Somerset (☎ 0823 662770)

CRATHORNE, 2 Baron (UK 1959); Sir Charles James Dugdale; 2 Bt (UK 1945), DL (Cleveland 1983); s of 1 Baron, TD, PC (d 1977), and Nancy, OBE (d 1969), da of Sir Charles Tennant, 1 Bt; *b* 12 Sept 1939; *Educ* Eton, Trinity Coll Cambridge; *m* 1970, Sylvia Mary, da of Brig Arthur Montgomery, OBE, TD; 1 s (Hon Thomas Arthur John Dugdale b 1977), 2 da (Hon Charlotte b 1972, Hon Katharine b 1980); *Heir* s, Hon Thomas Dugdale; *Career* with Sotheby and Co 1963-66, asst to pres Parke-Bernet NY 1966-69, James Dugdale and Assocs London (Ind Fine Art Consultancy Serv) 1969-; fine art lectr; dir: Cliveden Hotel, Woodhouse Securities Ltd 1989; tstee Captain Cook Tst; chm the Georgian Gp 1990; contribs to Apollo and The Connisseur; memb: Ct of the Univ of Leeds 1985, Yarm Civic Soc 1987 (pres), Ctee Pevsner Meml Tst (1986), Works of Art Sub Ctee Westminster 1983, Ed Bd House Magazine 1983, Cons Advsy Gp on the Arts and Heritage 1988-, Yorks Regnl Ctee Nat Tst 1974-84 and 1988-; vice chm All Pty Photography Gp 1988; hon sec: All Party Parliamentary Arts and Heritage Gp 1981; pres: Cleveland Family History Sec 1988, Cleveland Sea Cadets 1988, Hambledon Dist CPRE 1988, Cleveland Assoc of Nat Tst 1982; govr Queen Margaret's Sch York 1986-; memb Design Panel of Sheffield Devpt Corpn 1989-; patron: Attingham Tst for the Study of the Br Country House 1990-, Cleveland Community Fndn 1990-; FRSA (memb Cncl RSA 1983-88); *Books* Edouard Vuillard (jtly 1967), Tennants Stalk (jtly 1973), A Present from Crathorne (jtly, 1989); *Recreations* photography, travel, country life; *Style—* The Rt Hon the Lord Crathorne, DL; 52 Lower Sloane St, London SW1W 8BS (☎ 071 730 9131); Crathorne House, Yarm, Cleveland TS15 0AT (☎ 0642 700431); House of Lords, London SW1

CRATON, David Malcolm; s of George Edgar Maurice Craton (d 1946), and Edith, *née* Izzard (d 1973); *b* 9 May 1934; *Educ* Royal Wanstead Sch, Phillips Acad Andover Mass, LSE (Leverhulme scholar, BSc Econ); *m* 19 July 1958, Sheila Ann, *née* Ollis; 3 s (Jonathan Peter Michael b 15 June 1965, Paul Anthony Maurice b 14 Jan 1970, Timothy Charles Matthew (twin) b 1970), 2 da (Caroline Beverley b 1 May 1962, Sarah Elizabeth b 20 April 1967); *Career* Nat Serv RE 1953-55; prod mangr Morphy-Richards Ltd 1959-60, mktg exec Foote Cone & Belding 1960-61; General Electric Co: advtg mangr 1961-62, mktg mangr 1962-64, divisional mangr domestic appliances 1964-66; sales dir Remington Electric 1966-67, Bd dir (and md of subsids) Erwin Wasey (Inter Public) 1967-71, chm and chief exec CLK Group plc 1972-90 (estab as Craton Lodge & Knight Ltd 1972, public USM Co 1984); MInstM 1971, MIMC 1986; *Recreations* riding, sailing, sheep farming, history; *Style—* David Craton, Esq; Harford Farm, Mount Scippett, Forest Green Rd, Holyport, Berkshire SL6 2NN (☎ 0628 20555); Innovation Management International, Lyric House, 149 Hammersmith Rd, London W14 0QL (☎ 071 371 4771)

CRAUFORD, Peter Lane; s of William Harold Lane Crauford (d 1954), and Phyllis Maud Crauford; *b* 3 June 1917; *Educ* Highgate Sch, Peterhouse Cambridge (MA,

LLM); *m* 14 Aug 1954, Aileen Veronica, da of Thomas McCabe (d 1983); 2 da (Patricia Lane b 1956, Nicola Lane b 1957); *Career* Maj Royal Signals 1939-46, served: M East, Ceylon, India, Burma; slr 1948-, sr ptnr Chambers Rutland Crauford; *Recreations* golf, theatre, gardening; *Clubs* MCC, Hawks (Cambridge); *Style—* Peter L Crauford, Esq; Greenfields, Waggon Rd, Hadley Wood, Herts; 351 Regents Park Rd, London N3 1DJ (☎ 081 346 8333)

CRAUFURD; *see*: Houison Craufurd

CRAUFURD, Sir Robert James; 9 Bt (GB 1781), of Kilbirney, N Britain; s of Sir James Craufurd, 8 Bt (d 1970); *b* 18 March 1937; *Educ* Harrow, Univ Coll Oxford (MA); *m* 1, 1964 (m dis 1987), Catherine Penelope, yr da of late Capt Horatio Westmacott, RN, of Torquay, Devon; 3 da (Caroline b 1965, Penelope b 1967, Veronica b 1969); m 2, 1987, Georgina Anne, da of late John Russell, of Lymington, Hants; *Career* memb London Stock Exchange 1969; *Style—* Sir Robert Craufurd, Bt; 7 Waldemar Ave, London SW6 5LB

CRAUFURD, Ruth, Lady; Ruth Marjorie; da of Frederic Corder, linen draper, of Ipswich; *b* 9 Oct 1899; *Educ* Ipswich Girls' HS, Girton Coll Cambridge (BA); *m* 11 April 1931, Sir James Gregan Craufurd, 8 Bt (d 1970); 1 s, 2 da; *Career* formerly private sec to: Charles Williams, MP for Torquay, Dartmouth and Paignton, Maj-Gen Sir Reginald Hoskins, CB, CMG, DSO; tstee of Aldbury Memorial Almshouses; *Recreations* writing poems, operettas and stories, some of which have been published; *Clubs* United Oxford and Cambridge; *Style—* Ruth, Lady Craufurd; Brightwood, Aldbury, Tring, Herts HP23 5SF (☎ 044 285 262)

CRAVEN, 9 Earl of (GB 1801); Benjamin Robert Joseph Craven; also Baron Craven (E 1665), Viscount Uffington (GB 1801); o s of 8 Earl of Craven (d following a motor accident 1990), and Theresa Maria Bernadette, da of Arthur John Downes, of Blackhall, Clane, Co Kildare; *b* 13 June 1989; *Style—* The Rt Hon the Earl of Craven; Peelings Manor, nr Pevensey, E Sussex

CRAVEN, Gemma; da of Gabriel Bernard Craven, of Leigh-on-Sea, Essex (formerly of Dublin), and Lillian Elizabeth Josephine, *née* Byrne; *b* 1 June 1950; *Educ* Loretto, St Bernard's Convent Westcliff-on-Sea, Bush Davies Sch; *m* 10 June 1988, David Beamish, s of Phillip Beamish of Greasby, Wirral; *Career* actress; stage debut Let's Get a Divorce Palace Theatre Westcliff 1968, West End debut Anya in Fiddler on the Roof 1970, Audrey! 1971, Trelawney 1972; Chichester Festival Theatre 1974: R Loves J, Dandy Dick, The Confederacy, A Month in the Country; Bristol Old Vic: The Threepenny Opera 1975; West End performances incl: Songbook 1979, They're Playing Our Song 1980-81 (SWET award Best Actress in a Musical), Song and Dance 1982, Loot 1984 (City Limits' Best Comedy Actress); NT 1985-87: A Chorus of Disapproval, Jacobowsky and the Colonel,The Magistrate, Three Men on a Horse; Nellie Forbush in South Pacific 1988-89 (Prince of Wales Theatre London); Films incl: The Slipper and the Rose 1976 (Variety Club's Film Actress of the Year), Why Not Stay For Breakfast?, Wagner; TV incl: Pennies from Heaven 1977, Emily, East Lynne, She Loves me; *Recreations* cooking; *Style—* Miss Gemma Craven; c/o Stella Richards Mgmnt, 42 Hazlebury Rd, London SW6 2ND (☎ 071 736 7786, fax 071 731 5082)

CRAVEN, John Raymond; s of Bill Craven (d 1990), of Harrogate, N Yorkshire, and Marie, *née* Noble (d 1989); *b* 16 Aug 1940; *Educ* Leeds Modern GS, Leeds Coll of Commerce; *m* 27 March 1971, Jean Marilyn, da of Alfred (Blackie) Howe, CBE (d 1974); 2 da (Emma Katherine b 30 Nov 1972, Victoria Jane b 12 April 1975); *Career* journalist and presenter; commercial apprenticeship Yorkshire Imperial Metals Leeds; jr reporter The Harrogate Advertiser (later reporter The Yorkshire Post and freelance reporter for nat press); BBC: news writer 1965, TV reporter Points West (BBC Bristol) 1970, presenter Search (current affairs magazine for children) 1971, presenter and later ed John Craven's Newsround 1972-89; other tv credits: Swap Shop, Saturday Superstore, Breakthrough, Story Behind The Story; radio credits incl: Start the Week (deputising for Jimmy Young & Gloria Hunniford); columnist Radio Times 1980-88; currently: presenter Country File (weekley rural and environmental magazine BBC TV), weekly columnist Woman's Realm; winner: Bafta award for best children's tv documentary 1975, Pye TV award for distinguished services to tv 1983, TV Times award for top children's personality 1983; vice pres Wildlife Hosp Tst, memb Cncl Worldwide Fund for Nature; pres: Young People's Tst for the Environment, Uphill Ski Club, Young Archaelogists Club, Chesham Light Opera Co; *Books* John Craven's Newsworld (1980), John Craven's Wildlife Report (1981), Breakthrough (with Molly Cox, 1981), Charles & Diana (1982), Young Photographer (with John Wasley, 1982), And Finally (1984), Wildlife in the News (with Mark Carwardine, 1990); *Recreations* golf, swimming, walking in the countryside, aviation; *Style—* John Craven, Esq; c/o Noel Gay Artists, 24 Denmark Street, London WC2 8NJ (☎ 071 836 3941, fax 071 379 7027)

CRAVEN, Lady; Marjorie Kathleen Wallis; da of late Alfred Henry Hopkins; *m* 1945, as his 2 w, Sir Derek Worthington Clunes Craven, 2 Bt (d 1946, when title became extinct); *Style—* Lady Craven; Aberfeldie, Peckon's Hill, Ludwell, Shaftesbury, Dorset

CRAVEN, Air Marshal Sir Robert Edward; KBE (1970, OBE 1954), CB (1966), DFC (1940); s of Gerald Craven, of Port Elizabeth, SA, and Edith Craven; *b* 16 Jan 1916; *Educ* Scarborough Coll; *m* 1940, Joan, da of Capt E S Peters; 1 s, 1 da; *Career* MN 1932-37, joined RAF 1937, cmd RAF Eastleigh and RAF Lyneham, Air Vice-Marshal 1965, SASO Flying Trg Cmd 1967, SASO Trg Cmd 1968-69, Cdr Maritime Air Forces (AOC 18 Gp) 1969-72, Air Marshal 1970, ret 1972; Order of Menelik (Ethiopia) 1955; *Clubs* RAF; *Style—* Air Marshal Sir Robert Craven, KBE, CB, DFC; Letcombe House, Letcombe Regis, Oxon

CRAVEN, Rupert José Evelyn; s of Maj Hon Rupert Cecil Craven, OBE (d 1959, 2 s of 3 Earl of Craven) by 2 w, Josephine Marguerite (d 1971), da of José Reixach; *b* 22 March 1926; *m* 22 Oct 1955, Margaret Campbell (d 1985), da of Alexander Smith, MBE, of Glasgow and Alness; *Career* Lt Cdr RN; *Style—* Rupert Craven, Esq; Swordly, Bettyhill, by Thurso, Caithness KW14 7TA

CRAVEN-SMITH-MILNES, Richard Assheton; s of Ralph Assheton Craven-Smith-Milnes, and Elizabeth Josephine Anne, *née* Topham; *b* 27 July 1935; *Educ* Eton, Trinity Coll Cambridge (MA); *m* 25 May 1963, Jane Alexandra, da of The Hon Alexander Valentine Rutherford Abbott (d 1978), of Perth, WA; 1 s (Charles b 1968), 2 da (Anna b 1964, Clare b 1967); *Career* Nat Serv 2 Lt 17-21 Lancers 1953-55, Sherwood Rangers Yeo 1955-64; Lloyds insur broker 1962-72, chm and md Red Griffin Ltd 1973-; High Sherriff of Notts 1989-90; *Clubs* Whites; *Style—* Richard Craven-Smith-Milnes, Esq; Winkburn Hall, nr Newark, Notts; Middleham House, Middleham, Leyburn, N Yorks (☎ 0636 86465)

CRAWFORD, Alexander Hamilton; s of James Allison Crawford (d 1978), and Betsy, *née* Hughes (d 1950); *b* 15 Jan 1944; *Educ* Queen Mary's Sch Basingstoke Hants, Imp Coll London (BSc), Open Univ Business Sch (Dip in Management); *m* 1, 6 Jan 1968 (m dis 1982), Lesley Sandra Jane; 1 s (Stephen Nicholas b 8 July 1981), 2 da (Alison Mary b 6 Jan 1971, Sarah Louis b 30 May 1973); m 2, 1 June 1982, Jennifer Mary Evans, *née* Stuart; *Career* managing ed IPC Sci & Technol Press 1967-72, sci ed Euro Physical Soc 1972-73, mathematics teacher Aldershot Manor Sch 1974-77, engr ed Electrical Review 1977-80, euro ed Energy Developments 1981; ed: Health & Safety at Work 1982-87, Laboratory News 1987-; memb: Rushmoor Borough Cncl 1976-85, Nat Consumer Cncl 1977-82, Hampshire CC 1981-82; MInstP 1970, MBIM 1990, FRMS 1990; *Recreations* swimming; *Style—* Alexander Crawford, Esq; 17 Cargate Avenue, Aldershot, Hampshire GU11 3EP (☎ 0252 314708); Laboratory News, PO Box 109, Scarbrook Rd, Croydon CR9 1OH (☎ 081 688 7788, fax 081 688 9300, telex 946665)

CRAWFORD, Lady Béatrice Madeleine Jacqueline; da of Roger Hutter, of Paris, and Elisabeth, *née* Métin; *b* 21 Oct 1936; *Educ* Sorbonne (Lèsl), Stanford Univ (MA, PhD); *m* 21 Oct 1963, Sir Frederick Crawford, s of William Crawford (d 1955); 1 s (Eric b 1968), 1 da (Isabelle b 1965); *Career* Stanford Univ: teaching asst 1967-72, lectr 1972-78, lectr in undergraduate studies 1974-76; tutor in extramural studies Univ of Birmingham 1985-87; govr: Schs of King Edward VI Fndn Birmingham, Edgbaston HS for Girls; *Recreations* literary criticism, writing, tennis, walking; *Clubs* Edgbaston Priory; *Style—* Lady Crawford; Aston House, 1 Arthur Rd, Edgbaston, Birmingham B15 2UW (☎ 021 454 7545)

CRAWFORD, Daniel Frank; s of Frank Lewis Crawford, and Edna, *née* Partington; *b* 11 Dec 1945; *m* 19 May 1985, Stephany, da of Lt Cdr, Howard Wrigg USM (ret) Chicago, USA; 1 step da (Katey); *Career* mangr and artistic dir King's Head Theatre; West End prod/co-prod: Kennedy's Children (Arts Theatre 1975), Spokesong (Vaudeville Theatre, 1977), Fearless Frank (Princess Theatre NYC, 1980), Mr Cinders (Fortune Theatre, 1983), Wonderful Town (Queen's Theatre, 1986), Easy Virtue (Garrick Theatre, 1988), Artist Descending a Staircase (1988), panel memb Vivian Ellis prize for New Musical Writing, memb Islington Theatre Assoc; *Recreations* survival courses; *Clubs* Savage, Grouchos; *Style—* Daniel Crawford, Esq; King's Head, 115 Upper St, Islington, London N1 (☎ 071 226 8561, 071 226 1916, 071 226 0364)

CRAWFORD, Dennis Bryon; OBE (1984); s of Albert Edward Crawford (d 1964), of Hull, Yorks, and Lily, *née* Jubb (d 1968); *b* 8 Nov 1923; *Educ* Benmore Forest Sch, Hull Coll of Commerce; *m* 2 April 1955, Stella Fraser, da of William Thomson (d 1978), of Dumfries; 1 s (Mark b 1957), 1 da (Carol); *Career* Forestry Cmmn: 1945-54, Regnl Tech Offr Co-op Forestry Soc 1954-57, Regnl Man Scottish Woodland Owners Assoc 1957-67, md Scottish Woodland Owners Assoc Commercial Ltd 1967-83, chartered forestry conslt (pt/t); chm Timber Growers UK Tech Ctee; memb: Govt Cncl, Forestry Cmmn S Scotland Regnl Advsy Bd, HGTAC Supply and Demand Ctee, Forestry Cmmn Gt Spruce Bark Beetle Control Gp; FICFor, FArborA, FBIM, FRSA; *Recreations* botany, photography, scottish pottery, music; *Clubs* Caledonian Edinburgh; *Style—* Dennis B Crawford, OBE; Craiglatch, Clovenfords, Border, Scotland; 17 Leyden Grove, Clovenfords, Galashiels TD1 3NF (☎ 089 685624)

CRAWFORD, Prof Sir Frederick William; s of Wiliam Crawford (d 1955), and Victoria Maud, *née* Careless (d 1988); *b* 28 July 1931; *Educ* George Dixon GS Birmingham, Univ of London (BSc, MSc, DSc), Univ of Liverpool (PhD, DipEd, DEng); *m* 21 Oct 1963, Béatrice Madeleine Jacqueline, da of Roger Hutter, of Paris; 1 s (Eric b 1968), 1 da (Isabelle b 1965); *Career* scientist NCB Mining Res Estab Middx 1956-57, sr lectr in electrical engrg Coll of Advanced Technol Birmingham 1958-59; Stanford Univ California 1959-82: prof of electrical engrg 1969-82, chm Inst for Plasma Res 1973-80; vice-chllr Univ of Aston 1980-; non-exec dir: Legal & General Group 1988-, Bowater 1989-, Power Gen 1990-; Freeman City of London 1986, Liveryman Worshipful Co of Engrs 1987; FEng 1985, FIEE 1965, FIEEE 1972, FInstP 1964, FAPS 1965, FIMA 1978, CBIM 1986; kt 1986; *Clubs* Athenaeum; *Style—* Prof Sir Frederick Crawford; Aston House, 1 Arthur Rd, Edgbaston, Birmingham B15 2UW (☎ 021 454 7545); Aston University, Aston Triangle, Birmingham B4 7ET (☎ 021 359 3611, fax 021 359 2792, telex 336997 UNIAST G)

CRAWFORD, Lt-Col Henry George Walker; s of Maj Henry Gerald Crawford, MC (d 1972), of Arigna, Dunmurry, Co Antrim, NI, and Ella, *née* Ferguson (d 1989); *b* 16 May 1928; *Educ* Portora Royal Sch Enniskillen NI, RMA Sandhurst; *m* 1 (m dis), 4 July 1953, Pamella Mary, *née* Key; 2 da (Caroline Elizabeth b 30 Oct 1959, Sarah Ann b 14 Jan 1967); m 2, 24 June 1976, Susan, da of Alan Robert Calder-Smith (d 1986); *Career* cmmd RE 1948, ret as Lt-Col 1975; parish cncllr (currently clerk to Cncl) 1982-87, memb Wiltshire CC 1985-89 (vice chm 1988-89), chm Wiltshire Branch Transport 2000; *Recreations* painting, reading, walking; *Style—* Lt-Col Henry Crawford; Pennybourne, 99 Sunton, Collingbourne Ducis, Marlborough Ducis, Marlborough SN8 3DZ (☎ 0264 850293)

CRAWFORD, Iain Padraig; s of Peter Crawford (d 1953), of Glasgow, and Joan, *née* Macdonald (d 1931); *b* 21 Jan 1922; *Educ* Inverness Acad, Jordanhill Coll Sch Glasgow; *m* 1, 4 Oct 1945 (m dis), Maja Margherita Angela Querini, da of Attillo Zennaro, of Venice, Italy; 1 s (Michael Iain Peter b 31 Dec 1948), 1 da (Francesca b 3 Nov 1950); m 2, 1959, Neil b 1 Oct 1960); m 3, 23 Dec 1985, Kathy Isobel Miller, *née* Hay; *Career* Cadet Clan Line MN 1939-41, L RN 1941-45 (dispatches); journalist Edinburgh Evening Dispatch Bulletin 1946-50, publicity offr BBC 1950-54; journalist 1958-63: Daily Record, Daily Express, Evening Standard; publicity dir: Edinburgh Festival 1973-80, Scottish Opera 1980-81; currently author TV scriptwriter and broadcaster journalist; books incl: 3 biographies, The Burning Sea, Scare the Gentle Citizen, The Profumo Affair, The Havana Cigar, The Open Guide to the Old Course and St Andrews, Held in Trust, The Alexander Score; work for stage and TV inc: Broomstick Over Badenoch, Under the Light, The Cruel Dead-line, Travel with Iain Crawford; Lib candidate: Edinburgh N 1951, Stroud 1963; *Recreations* music, golf, watching rugby, travel, French and Italian; *Clubs* Scottish Arts, North Berwick Golf, New Golf, St Andrews; *Style—* Iain Crawford, Esq; 42 Braid Crescent, Edinburgh EH10 6AU (☎ 031 4471497)

CRAWFORD, Maj-Gen Ian Campbell; CBE (1982); *b* 17 June 1932; *Educ* Dumfries Acad, Univ of Edinburgh (MB ChB); *m* 4 April 1959, Phyllis Mary; 1 s (Niall b 1967), 1 da (Fiona b 1960); *Career* conslt physician (Cardiology) Queen Elizabeth Mil Hosp Woolwich 1977-83 and 1985-90; dir Army Med and consltg physician to the Army; FRCPE 1972, FRCP 1986; *Style—* Maj-Gen Ian C Crawford, CBE; The Arbour, Bobbing, Kent (☎ 0795 842292); Queen Elizabeth Mil Hosp, Woolwich SE18 (☎ 081 856 5533)

CRAWFORD, Major John Middleton; MC (1941); s of Maj-Gen John Scott Crawford, CB, CBE (d 1979), and Amy Middleton, *née* Andrews; *b* 26 Jan 1921; *Educ* Liverpool Coll, Royal Mil Coll; *m* 30 March 1946, Suzanne Euphrosine, da of Cyril Banner (d 1964); *Career* enlisted Inns of Ct Regt, cmmnd RASC 1939, serv Western Desert 1941-42, captured Tobruk 1942, escaped Bolzano 1943 on fall of Italy, recaptured 1944, released 1945, asst Mil attache Washington, served Malaya 1947-51, ret; Samuel Banner & Co Ltd 1953-57, fndr own laundry and dry cleaning business 1957-80; memb: Surrey CC 1969-70, Surrey Heath Borough Cncl 1987-91; various posts local Cons branch 1967-84; Freeman City of London, memb Worshipful Co of Carmen; *Books* Peter Beigel's Racing Pictures by Michael Joseph (ed, photographer and commentator, 1984); *Recreations* water colour painting, walking, horses and dogs; *Style—* Maj John Crawford, MC; Forge Cottage, School Rd, Windlesham, Surrey (☎ 0276 72101)

CRAWFORD, Kenneth Neville; s of Frank Westwood Crawford (d 1985), of Salford, Lancs, and Edith Wrigley (d 1986); *b* 19 April 1932; *Educ* Salford GS; *m* 2 April 1955, Jean Mary, da of Frank Walker (d 1983), of Timperley, Cheshire; 2 s (Duncan b 1958,

Graham b 1963); *Career* law clerk: Salford City Cncl 1949-60, Stevenage Devpt Corp 1960-64; sr conveyancing exec Bowcock and Pursaill Leek 1965-75, chief legal exec Borough Cncl of Newcastle-under-Lyme 1975-; hon sec Brindley Mill Preservation Tst 1970- (Brindley Mill and James Brindley Museum); Inst of Legal Execs: memb Cncl 1977-, chm Law Reform, pres 1979-80; fell Inst of Legal Execs 1963, MBIM 1978; *Books* History of the McVannel Clan (1981); *Recreations* cycling, photography, theatre; *Style*— Kenneth Crawford, Esq; 5 Daintry St, Leek, Staffs ST13 5PG (☎ 0538 384195); Central Services Dept, Civic Offices, Merrial St, Newcastle-under-Lyme, Staffs ST5 2AG (☎ 0782 717717)

CRAWFORD, Lincoln; s of Norman Crawford (d 1983), and Ena Crawford (d 1972); *b* 1 Nov 1946; *Educ* Univ Tutorial Coll London, Brunel Univ (LLB); *m* 26 July 1976, Janet, da of John Clegg (d 1987); 3 s (Douglas Luke b 4 Dec 1978, Paul David b 26 Aug 1981, Jack Justin b 7 Sept 1988); *Career* called to the Bar 1977; dir Lloyd Crawford Ltd; advsr to Lord Scarman during Brixton disorders 1981, exec memb Prison Reform Tst; memb: Cmmn for Racial Equality 1984, Parole Bd 1985-88; memb: Business and Mgmnt Ctee Polys and Colls Funding Cncl (PCFC), Bd for Social Responsibility C of E, W Indian Standing Conf, Mgmnt Ctee Tooting Youth Project; memb Ed Bd New Community; chm: Princes Tst Sports Ctee 1989, Ind Adoption Serv; participant Duke of Edinburgh Study Conf 1989, govr Hampstead Comprehensive Sch, delivers bi-monthly lecture to Police Coll Bramshill; ombudsperson Community Radio Assoc, head patron of Rapport; *Recreations* squash, swimming; *Clubs* Commonwealth; *Style*— Lincoln Crawford, Esq; 32 Kylemore Rd, West Hampstead, London NW6 2PT (☎ 071 624 0206); 12 Kings Beach Walk, Temple, London EC4 (☎ 071 583 0811, fax 071 583 7228)

CRAWFORD, Lyle David; JP (1986-); s of Robert Lyle Crawford (d 1971), of Bute, and Nanny Hutchison, *née* Duncan; *b* 26 May 1946; *Educ* N Berwick HS; *m* 1 July 1971, Margaret Ann, da of Robert Sinclair Anderson (d 1979); 2 da (Catriona b 1973, Mairi b 1975); *Career* CA 1969; princ Lyle Crawford and Co, dir D C Watson and Sons (Fenton Barns) Ltd and subsids 1971-; ATII 1968; *Recreations* North Berwick Pipe Band; *Clubs* N Berwick Burns; *Style*— Lyle D Crawford, Esq, JP; Glenorchy, 15 Glenorchy Rd, N Berwick, E Lothian (☎ 0620 3484)

CRAWFORD, Prof Michael Hewson; s of Brian Hewson Crawford, and Margarethe Bettina, *née* Nagel; *b* 7 Dec 1939; *Educ* St Paul's Sch, Oriel Coll Oxford (BA, MA), Br Sch at Rome (scholar); *Career* Jane Eliza Procter visiting fell Princeton Univ 1964-65; Christ's Coll Univ of Cambridge: res fell 1964-69, fell 1969-86, lectr 1969-86; visiting prof: Univ of Pavia 1983, Ecole Normale Supérieure Paris 1984, Univ of Padua 1986, Sorbonne Paris 1988-89, Univ of San Marino 1989, Univ of Statale Milan 1990, Univ of L'Aquila 1990, Univ of Pavia 1991; jt dir: Excavations of Fregellae 1980-86, Valpolcevera Project 1987-; chm Jt Assoc of Classical Teachers Ancient History Ctee 1978-84, vice pres Roman Soc 1981-; ed: Papers of the Br Sch at Rome 1975-79, Jl of Roman Studies 1980-84; prof of ancient history UCL 1986-; FBA 1980; *Books* Roman Republican Coin Hoards (1969), Roman Republican Coinage (1974), Archaic and Classical Greece (with D Whitehead, 1982), Coinage and Money under the Roman Republic (1985), L'impero romana e la struttura economica e sociale delle province (1986), The Coinage of the Roman World in the Late Republic (with A Burnett, 1987); contribs to Annales, Economic History Review, Jl of Roman Studies; *Style*— Prof Michael Crawford; Department of History, University College, Gower Street, London WC1E 6BT (☎ 071 380 7396)

CRAWFORD, (George) Michael Warren Brown; s of Surgn Capt Thomas George Brown Crawford, RN (d 1988), and Eleanor Mary, *née* Warren; *b* 11 Jan 1942; *Educ* Rugby; *m* 8 Jan 1972, Jane Elizabeth, da of Capt Alastair James Petrie-Hay, RN; 2 s (Freddy b 8 Aug 1973, Thomas b 7 Nov 1975), 1 da (Victoria b 22 Oct 1979); *Career* Bank of England 1960-63, Buckmaster & Moore 1963-65 and 1970-86 (ptnr 1984-86), IBM Aust Ltd 1966-70; memb Int Stock Exchange 1983; dir: Citymax Integrated Info Systems Ltd 1984, Credit Suisse Buckmaster & Moore Ltd 1986-90, SJ Berwin & Co 1990-; *Recreations* shooting, sailing; *Clubs* Little Ship; *Style*— Michael Crawford, Esq; Mount Cross, The Quag, Minsted, Midhurst, Sussex (☎ 073 081 4284); S J Berwin & Co, 236 Grays Inn Rd, London WC1X 5HB (☎ 071 278 0444, fax 071 833 2860)

CRAWFORD, (Robert) Norman; CBE (1973); s of William Crawford (d 1944), of Londonderry, and Annie Catherine, *née* Rexter (d 1942); *b* 14 June 1923; *Educ* Foyle Coll Londonderry, The Queen's Univ of Belfast (BComSc); *m* 1948, Jean Marie Patricia, da of Hugh Carson (d 1954), of Portrush; 1 s (David), 5 da (Jennifer, Catherine, Mary, Zelda, Emma); *Career* CA; md The McNeill Gp (NI) Ltd 1960-68; chm: Nature Reserves Ctee 1966-85, NI Tport Hldg Co 1968-75; dir and chief exec William Clark and Sons Ltd 1983-87; pres: NI Outward Bound Assoc 1975-, NI C of C and Indust 1967-, Belfast Branch BIM 1972-; vice pres S Belfast Scout Cncl 1984-; chm: R N Crawford and Co Business Advisory 1968-, Regnl Cncl BIM 1968-, NI Wildlife Campaign; memb Senate of Queen's Univ Belfast; *Clubs* Ulster Reform; *Style*— R Norman Crawford, Esq, CBE; 4 Fort Rd, Helens Bay, Bangor, Co Down

CRAWFORD, Robert Caldwell; s of William Caldwell Crawford (d 1960), of Earraid, Biggar Rd, Edinburgh, and Janet Margaret, *née* Benson (d 1961); *b* 18 April 1925; *Educ* Melville Coll Edinburgh, Keswick GS, Guildhall Sch of Music London; *m* 1, 9 July 1949, Stephanie, *née* Frankel (d 1974); 1 s (Elliot Caldwell b 16 May 1952), 1 da (Judith Margaret b 6 March 1956); m 2, 17 July 1978, Alison, da of Prof Robin Kemsley Orr, CBE, of 16 Cranmer Rd, Cambridge; *Career* music prodr BBC 1970-85, chm Caird Music Advsy Ctee 1978-; composer; works incl: 1 sonata, 6 bagatelles, 2 string quartets, 1 octet 1986; chm Scottish Branch Composers Guild of GB 1967-70; *Recreations* hill walking, bee keeping, woodwork; *Style*— Robert Crawford, Esq; 12 Inverleith Terrace, Edinburgh EH3 5NS (☎ 031 556 3600)

CRAWFORD, Robert Gammie; CBE (1990); s of William Crawford (d 1980), of Aberdeen, and Janet Beveridge, *née* Gammie (d 1974); *b* 20 March 1924; *Educ* Robert Gordon's Coll Aberdeen; *m* 4 Sept 1947, Rita, da of August Daniel Veiss (d 1975), of Latvia; 1 da (Fiona b 1959); *Career* Flt Lt navigator RAF 1942-47; admitted slr 1950; ptnr Ince and Co (int shipping lawyers) 1950-73; chm: Silver Line Ltd and subsids 1974-, Silver Navigation Ltd; dir AVDEL plc 1983-, Sterling Underwriting Agencies Ltd 1988-; chm UK War Risk Club 1982-, memb Bd Lloyd's Register of Shipping 1982-, dir UK Protection and Indemnity Club 1983-, memb Bd Civil Aviation Authy 1984-, vice chm Port of London Authy 1985-, dir UK Freight Demurrage Club 1987-, chm Highlands and Islands Airports Ltd 1986-, govr Robert Gordon's Coll Aberdeen; memb Lloyds's 1975-; *Recreations* shooting, golf, reading, conversation; *Clubs* Carlton; *Style*— Robert G Crawford, Esq, CBE; 9 London House, Avenue Rd, London NW8 7PX (☎ 071 483 2754); West Mains of Auchenhove, Lumphanan, Aberdeenshire (☎ 03398 83208/667); CAA, Rm T 1410, CAA House, Kemble St, London WC2B 6TE (☎ 071 832 5754)

CRAWFORD, Prof Robert MacGregor Martyn; s of Dr Crawford, Robert Mac Gregor Cleland (d 1981), and Bethic Rankyn, *née* Martyn (d 1976); *b* 30 May 1934; *Educ* Glasgow Acad, Univ of Glasgow (BSc), Liége (Docteur en Sciences Naturelles); *m* 20 June 1964, Barbara Elizabeth, da of Percy Hall (d 1979); 1 s (Magnus b 29 Oct 1971); *Career* prof of plant ecology Univ of St Andrews 1977- (lectr in botany 1962-72, reader 1972-77); FRSE, FIBiol; *Books* Studies in Plant Survival (1989); *Recreations* photography, music; *Style*— Prof Robert Crawford, FRSE; Kincaple Cottage, St Andrews, Fife KY16 9SH (☎ 033485 214); Sir Harold Mitchell Building, The University, St Andrews, Fife KY16 9AL (☎ 0334 76161, fax 0334 78399)

CRAWFORD, Robert William Kenneth; s of Hugh Merrall Crawford (d 1982), of West Bergholt, Colchester, Essex, and Mary, *née* Percival; *b* 3 July 1945; *Educ* Culford Sch, Pembroke Coll Oxford (BA); *m* 9 Dec 1975, Vivienne Sylvia, da of Boghdan Andre Polakowski; 1 s (Alistair b 1987), 1 da (Helen b 1984); *Career* Imperial War Museum: head res and info office 1971-89, keeper Dept of Photographs 1975-83, asst dir 1979-82, dep dir gen 1982-; *Style*— R W K Crawford, Esq; Imperial War Museum, Lambeth Rd, London SE1 6HZ (☎ 071 416 5206)

CRAWFORD, Stephany Light Smith; da of Lt Cdr Howard Allen Weiss, of Chicago, Illinois, and Joan, *née* Light Smith; *b* 28 Feb 1954; *Educ* Univ of Milwaukee Wisconsin, Institut de Allende San Miguel De Allende Mexico, Chicago Art Inst, California Coll of Art; *m* 1, 11 July 1980 (m dis 1984), Matthew Eliot Kastin; 1 da (Katherine); m 2, 10 May 1985, Daniel Frank Crawford; *Career* artist and poet; exhibitions New York, San Francisco, London; artist in residence New York Experimental Glass Workshop 1980, fndr Archangel Exhibitions 1988; curator and co-organises: The London Influence Slaughterhouse Gallery 1988, Americans Abroad Smiths Gallery and King's Head Theatre 1989; memb Bd Dir King's Head Theatre 1986-, originator Islington Theatre Assoc 1986; *Books* Stonehouse I, Stonehouse II; *Recreations* dreaming, dining, museums, galleries, film, theatres, being with husband and child; *Clubs* Groucho; *Style*— Ms Stephany Crawford; The Kings Head Theatre, 115 Upper St, London N1; 22 Crooked Well, Kington, Hereford

CRAWFORD, Sir (Robert) Stewart; GCMG (1973, KCMG 1966, CMG 1951), CVO (1955); s of Sir William Crawford, KBE (d 1950), and Marion Stewart, *née* Whitelaw; *b* 27 Aug 1913; *Educ* Gresham's, Oriel Coll Oxford; *m* 1938, Mary Katharine, da of late Eric Corbett, of Gorse Hill, Witley, Surrey; 3 s (1 s decd), 1 da; *Career* Air Miny 1936; FO 1947, political resident Persian Gulf 1966-70, dep under sec FCO 1970-73, chm Ctee of Broadcasting Coverage 1973-74, BBC Gen Advsy Cncl 1975-84, Broadcasters Audience Res Bd 1980-88; *Clubs* United Oxford & Cambridge, Phyllis Court; *Style*— Sir Stewart Crawford, GCMG, CVO; 19 Adam Court, Bell St, Henley-on-Thames, Oxon (☎ 0491 574 702)

CRAWFORD, Susan Louise (Mrs Jeremy Phipps); da of Lt Cdr Wilfrid Hornby Crawford, RN, and late Patricia Mary, *née* McCosh; *b* 11 May 1941; *Educ* St Denis Sch Edinbugh, Prior's Field Godalming, Studio Simi Florence Italy; *m* 12 Oct 1974, Jeremy Joseph Julian Phipps, s of Lt Alan Phipps (ka 1942); 1 s (Jake shimi Alan b 29 Aug 1975), 1 da (Jemma Louise Rose b 21 July 1977); *Career* artist and equestrian portrait painter; portrait cmmns incl: HM The Queen (mounted), HRH The Prince of Wales (mounted), HM Queen Elizabeth the Queen Mother (for the Black Watch Regt), HRH The Princess Margaret, Countess of Snowdon (for The Royal Highland Fusilliers), HH The Sultan of Brunei, HRH THe Pricess Royal (mounted), sixteen Epsom Derby winners and steeplechasers incl Red Rum, Arkle and Desert Orchid; collections worldwide and expos at: The Royal Scot Acad, The Nat Portrait Gallery, The Royal Acad of Arts, The Royal Soc of Portrait Painters; *Style*— Ms Susan Crawford; c/o Tryon Gallery, Cork St, London W1

CRAWFORD, Lady Susanna; *née* Montgomerie; eld da of late 17 Earl of Eglinton and Winton and Ursula, da of Hon Ronald Watson (s of late Baron Watson, Life Peer); *b* 19 Oct 1941; *m* 25 May 1963, Capt David Dundas Euing Crawford, late Royal Scots Greys, o son of Brig Alastair Wardrop Euing Crawford, JP, VL, of Auchentroig, Buchlyvie, Stirlingshire; 2 s (twins); 1 da; *Style*— Lady Susanna Crawford

CRAWFORD, Sir Theodore (Theo); s of Theodore Crawford (d 1925), and Sarah, *née* Mansfield (d 1958); *b* 23 Dec 1911; *Educ* St Peter's Sch York, Glasgow Acad, Univ of Glasgow (BSc, MB ChB, MD); *m* 1, 1938, Margaret Donald (d 1973), da of Dr George Green, DSC; 2 s, 3 da; m 2, 1974, Priscilla Leathley, da of Guy Leathley Chater (d 1974); *Career* served RAMC 1941-45, UK, France, Belgium and Germany, Maj; dir of pathological services St George's Hosp and Med Sch 1946-77, prof of pathology Univ of London 1948-77, now emeritus; hon sec Cancer Res Campaign 1967-70 (chm sci ctee 1955-67); pres Royal Coll of Pathologists 1969-72, cnslt advsr in pathology Dept of Health 1969-78; Hon LLD Univ of Glasgow 1979; FRCP (Glasgow 1962), FRCPath 1963, FRCP (London) 1964; kt 1973; *Books* Modern Trends in Pathology (ed, 1967), The Pathology of Ischaemic Heart Disease (1977); *Recreations* gardening, music, walking; *Clubs* Sloane; *Style*— Sir Theo Crawford; 9 Asher Reeds, Langton Green, Tunbridge Wells, Kent TN3 0AL (☎ 089 286 3341)

CRAWFORD, Vice Adm Sir William Godfrey; KBE (1961), CB (1958), DSC (1941); s of Henry Edward Venner Crawford, JP (d 1937), of Wyld Court, Axminster, Devon; *b* 14 Sept 1907; *Educ* RNC Dartmouth; *m* 29 April 1939, Mary Felicity Rosa, 2 da of Sir Philip Williams, 2 Bt (d 1958); 3 s, 1 da; *Career* Lt RN 1929, Rear Adm 1956, Imperial Def Coll 1956-58, flag offr Sea Training 1958-60, Vice Adm 1959, cdr Br Navy Staff and naval attaché Washington 1960-62, ret 1963; dir Overseas Offices BTA 1964-72; *Clubs* Naval and Military, Royal Cruising; *Style*— Vice Adm Sir William Crawford, KBE, CB, DSC; Broadlands, Whitchurch Canonicorum, Bridport, Dorset DT6 6RJ (☎ 0297 89591)

CRAWFORD, His Hon Judge William Hamilton Raymund; QC (1980); s of Col Mervyn Crawford, DSO, JP, DL (d 1977), of Dunscore, Dumfriesshire, and Martha Hamilton, *née* Walker; *b* 10 Nov 1936; *Educ* Winchester, Emmanuel Coll Cambridge; *m* 1965, Marilyn Jean, da of John Millar Colville; 1 s, 2 da; *Heir* Alexander Mervyn Colville Crawford; *Career* barr 1964, dep chm Agric Land Tbnl 1978, rec Crown Ct 1979-, circuit judge 1986; *Recreations* fishing, shooting, hill farming; *Clubs* Naval and Military, Northern Counties; *Style*— His Hon Judge William Crawford, QC; c/o The Crown Court, Newcastle upon Tyne

CRAWFORD AND BALCARRES, Mary, Countess of; Mary Katherine; *née* Cavendish; da of late Col the Rt Hon Lord Richard Cavendish, CB, CMG, PC (gs of 7 Duke of Devonshire), and Lady Moyra de Vere Beauclerk (da of 10 Duke of St Albans); *b* 20 July 1903; *m* 9 Dec 1925, 28 (and 11) Earl (d 1975); 3 s (29 Earl, Hon Patrick Lindsay, Hon Thomas Lindsay); *Style*— The Rt Hon Mary, Countess of Crawford and Balcarres; Garden Flat, Balcarres, Colinsburgh, Fife (☎ 033 334 520)

CRAWFORD AND BALCARRES, 29 (and 12) Earl of (S 1398, 1651 respectively); Robert Alexander Lindsay; DL (Fife), PC (1972); also Lord Lindsay (of Crawford; *ante* 1143), Lord Lindsay of Balcarres (S 1633), Lord Lindsay and Balniel (S 1651), Baron Wigan of Haigh Hall (UK 1826), Baron Balniel (Life Peer UK 1974); Premier Earl of Scotland in precedence; maintains private officer-of-arms (Endure Pursuivant); s of 28 Earl, KT, GBE, FSA (d 1975), and Mary, da of late Col the Rt Hon Lord Richard Cavendish, CB, CMG, PC (gs of 7 Duke of Devonshire); *b* 5 March 1927; *Educ* Eton, Trinity Coll Cambridge; *m* 27 Dec 1949, Ruth Beatrice, da of Leo Meyer-Bechtler, of Zürich; 2 s, 2 da; *Heir* s, Lord Balniel; *Career* Grenadier Gds 1945-49; MP (C): Hertford 1955-74, Welwyn and Hatfield Feb-Sept 1974; PPS to Fin Sec of Treasy 1955-57, min Housing and Local Govt 1957-60; memb Shadow Cabinet (Health and Social Security) 1967-70, min of state Def 1970-72, min of state Foreign and Cwlth Affrs 1972-74, chm Lombard N Central Bank 1976-80; vice-chm Sun Alliance Insur Gp 1975-; dir: Nat Westminster Bank 1975-88, Scottish American Investmt Tst 1978-88; first Crown Estate cmmr and chm 1980-1985; pres RDCs Assoc 1959-65; chm: Nat Assoc for Mental Health 1963-70, Historic Buildings Cncl for

Scotland 1976-83, Royal Cmmn on the Ancient and Historical Monuments for Scotland 1985-; Crown tstee and chm Bd of Nat Library of Scotland 1990-; *Style*— The Rt Hon the Earl of Crawford and Balcarres, DL, PC; House of Lords, London SW1

CRAWFORD-SMITH, (Robert) Ian; s of Capt Brodie Crawford-Smith (d 1956), of Guildford, Surrey, and Catherine Galen Cowie, *née* Burns (d 1974); *b* 14 Dec 1931; *Educ* HS Harrow Middx; *m* 13 Aug 1955, Ann Sheila, da of Edmund Thomas Hudson (d 1984), of Holton Heath, Dorset; 1 s (Philip Duncan b 1960), 1 da (Joanna Louise b 1962); *Career* Royal Tank Regt 1950-52; underwriter Northern Assoc Co Ltd 1952-65, dir H Clarkson Insur Hldgs Ltd (later Clarkson Puckle Ltd) 1965-86, vice chm Birchgrey Ltd (promoters of Euro Open golf tournament and gen sports promoters) 1981-, dir Berkeley (Insur) Ltd, and insur conslt Hambros Bank 1986-; memb: Family Practitioners Ctee 1960-73, Bucks Exec Ctee 1965-69, Round Table 1964-72; chm local hosps 1965-71; Freeman City of London, Liveryman Worshipful Co of Insurers; Chartered Insurance Practitioners, ACII 1956, FInstD 1980, FBII BA; *Recreations* golf, wine, watching sport generally; *Clubs* IOD, MCC, Sportsman (Palm Beach); *Style*— Ian Crawford-Smith, Esq; Cranford Chiltern Road, Chesham Bois, Amersham, Bucks HP6 5PH; 41 Tower Hill, London EC3N 4HA (☎ 071 480 5000, fax 071 702 4424, telex 883851, car 0836 283904)

CRAWFURD, Dr (Anthony) Raymond; s of Kenneth Crawfurd, of Rogers Lane, Stoke Poges, Bucks, and Mary Isabel, *née* Jarrett; *b* 14 Jan 1942; *Educ* Winchester, Magdalen Coll Oxford (MA, BM BCh), King's Coll Hosp Med Sch (MRCP); *m* 4 Oct 1969, Dr Dorothy Mair Crawfurd, da of Rev David Charles Elijah Rowlands (d 1975), of Treorchy; 1 s (James b 1974), 1 da (Kate b 1971); *Career* jr hosp posts 1967-70: King's Coll Hosp, Royal Liverpool Childrens' Hosp, Alder Hey Hosp, Kent and Canterbury Hosp; princ in gen practice 1971-, sr ptnr Dr Crawfurd and Ptnrs 1989; memb: Med Sub Ctee Br Olympic Assoc, Med Cmmn Fedn Internationale D'Escrime; chm: Tenterden Day Centre, Kent Co Amateur Fencing Assoc; govr Tenterden Infants Sch, hon med offr Amateur Fencing Assoc; Freeman City of London 1967, Liveryman Worshipful Soc of Apothecaries 1967; LMSSA 1966; *Recreations* fencing, heraldry, skiing; *Style*— Dr Raymond Crawfurd; Seymour House, Shoreham Lane, St Michaels, Tenterden, Kent (☎ 05806 2967); Ivy Court, Tenterden, Kent TN30 6RB (☎ 05806 3666)

CRAWLEY, Alan Edward; s of Albert Edward Crawley (d 1977), and Hilda, *née* Browning (d 1934); *b* 12 May 1930; *Educ* Battersea GS, Hertford GS; *m* 1, 21 March 1965 (m dis 1990), Margaret Jean , da of Herbert Ernest Hayne (d 1980); 2 s (Andrew b 1967, Mark b 1970); m 2, 1990, Vanessa Peterson; *Career* fndr and dir Crawley Warren Gp 1973-90, memb Lloyds Insur Brokers 1976-90, chm VW Broad Underwriting Agency Ltd 1990-; *Recreations* golf, philately, reading; *Clubs* Les Ambassadeurs, RAC; *Style*— Alan Crawley, Esq; The Crescent, 5 Sextant Avenue, Compass Point, London E14 9DX

CRAWLEY, Charles Aidan Stafford; s of Maj Kenneth Arnold Gibbs Crawley (d 1988), of The Livery, West Winterslow, Salisbury, Wiltshire, and Pamela Mary, *née* Vickers (d 1962); *b* 26 Dec 1945; *Educ* Harrow; *m* 8 July 1971, Nicola d'Anyers, da of Guy Russell d'Anyers Willis; 1 s Thomas Antony Kenneth b 17 Oct 1974), 1 da (Rosanna Clare Pamela b 19 May 1977); *Career* short service cmmn Coldstream Guards 1965-68; Coutts and Co 1968-77, dir Stenhouse Reed Shaw (MA) Ltd 1979; dir 1981: Harman Hedley Agencies Ltd, Hedley and Redgrove Agenices Ltd, Redgrove and Everington Ltd, Harman Gardner Roberts Ltd; dir 1982: Stenhouse Harman (MA) Ltd, Stenhouse Epps (MA) Ltd, Stenhouse Patrick (MA) Ltd; dir 1985: Bankside Membs Agency, Bankside Syndicates Ltd; *Recreations* golf, skiing, gardening; *Clubs* Whites, Pratts, City, Vanderbilt Raquet; *Style*— Charles Crawley, Esq; 15 Albert Square, London SW8 1BS (☎ 071 582 9377); Bankside Members Agency Ltd, c/o Lloyd's (☎ 071 481 0888, fax 071 702 1920, telex 8814440)

CRAWLEY, Christine; MEP (Lab) Birmingham E 1989-; *b* 1950; *Career* former teacher, town and dist cncllr in Oxon, candidate for SE Staffs in gen election 1983; Euro Parl: chair Womens Rights Ctee, memb Econ Monetary and Indust Ctee, memb Budgets Ctee; memb: Fabian Soc, Co-operative Party, CND, Mfrg Sci and Fin Union; *Recreations* Latin American lit, amateur dramatics, attending local football matches in Birmingham; *Style*— Mrs Christine Crawley, MEP; c/o Birmingham District Labour Party, 16 Bristol Street, Birmingham B5 7AA (☎ 021 622 2270, fax 021 666 7322)

CRAWLEY, Frederick William; s of William Clement Crawley (d 1962), and Elsie Florence, *née* Valentine (d 1984); *b* 10 June 1926; *m* 1951, Ruth Eva, da of Dr Hans Jungmann (d 1970); 2 da (Nicola, Fiona); *Career* Lloyds Bank plc: jt gen mangr 1975, asst chief gen mangr 1977-78, dep chief gen mangr 1978-84, chief gen mangr 1985, dep chief exec 1985-87, dir 1985-88; exec dir Lloyds Bank Int 1975-76, vice chm and chief exec offr Lloyds Bank California 1983-84; dir: Lloyds Devpt Capital Ltd, Alliance & Leicester Building Soc (dep chm), Barratt Devpt plc; dep chm Girobank plc, chm Betta Stores plc; hon treas RAF Benevolent Fund; FCIB, CBIM; *Recreations* aviation, shooting, photography; *Clubs* Overseas Bankers; *Style*— Frederick Crawley, Esq; 4 The Hexagon, Fitzroy Park, London N6 6HR (☎ 081 341 2279)

CRAWLEY, John Maurice; s of Charles William Crawley, and Kathleen Elizabeth, *née* Leahy (d 1982); *b* 27 Sept 1933; *Educ* Rugby, New Coll Oxford (MA); *m* 22 April 1978, Jane, da of Alexander Meadows Rendel, CBE; 3 s (Richard b 1980, Edmund b 1982, Ben b 1985); *Career* Inland Revenue: joined 1959, princ 1963-69, asst sec 1969-79 (seconded to Cabinet Office CPRS 1973-76), appointed under sec 1979, Cabinet Office CPRS 1979-81, dir Oil and Interest Policy Div 1981-85, princ fin offr and dir of manpower and support servs 1985-; *Recreations* music, walking; *Style*— John Crawley, Esq; Inland Revenue, Somerset House, London WC2R 1LB

CRAWLEY, Peter Stanbridge; s of William John Crawley (d 1965), and Grace Loelia, *née* Pegg; *b* 4 Dec 1923; *Educ* Univ Coll Sch Hampstead London; *m* 20 May 1950, Joan Elizabeth Spicer, da of Dr Percy Peter James Stewa OBE (d 1924); 2 s (Richard b 1951, Patrick b 1952), 1 da (Jane b 1957); *Career* WWII RAC RASC Capt 1942-47; princ dir Faber & Faber Ltd 1964-73 (dir 1961-64), dir Faber Music Ltd 1965-73; ind publisher in assoc with Victor Gollancz Ltd 1973-; publisher: Master Bridge Series, architectural history books; illustrated (photographs) many architectural history books; *Recreations* golf, reading, photography, music, bird-watching; *Clubs* Savile; *Style*— Peter Crawley, Esq; Garth House, Hertingfordbury, Hertford SG14 2LG (☎ 0992 582963); Victor Gollancz Ltd, 14 Henrietta Street, London WC2E 8QJ (☎ 071 836 2006, fax 071 379 09340)

CRAWLEY, Thomas Henry Raymond; s of Charles William Crawley, of Cambridge, and Kathleen Elizabeth, *née* Leahy (d 1982); *b* 17 May 1936; *Educ* Rugby, Trinity Coll Cambridge (MA); *m* 22 April 1961, Felicity Merville, da of Gerald Ashworth Bateman (ret RN Cdr); 1 s (Charles b 1965), 2 da (Alice b 1967, Tessa b 1969); *Career* Martin's Bank Ltd 1959-61; admitted slr 1965, ptnr Turner Kenneth Brown 1967-, slr Hong Kong 1986, sr res ptnr Turner Kenneth Brown Hong Kong 1988-90; City of London Solicitors Prize and Charles Steele prize 1964; Freeman City of London 1985, Liveryman Worshipful Co of Solicitors 1987; memb: Law Soc, Law Soc Hong Kong; *Clubs* Travellers', Hong Kong; *Style*— Thomas Crawley, Esq; 36 Wilmington Ave, London W4 3HA; Plas Hendy, Bryngwyn, nr Raglan, Gwent; 100 Fetter Lane, London EC4A 1DD

CRAWLEY-BOEVEY, Thomas Hyde Crawley-Boevey; s and h of Sir Thomas Crawley-Boevey, 8 Bt; *b* 26 June 1958; *Style*— Thomas Crawley-Boevey Esq

CRAWLEY-BOEVEY, Sir Thomas Michael Blake; 8 Bt (GB 1784) of Highgrove, Glos; s of Sir Launcelot Valentine Hyde Crawley-Boevey, 7 Bt (d 1968), and Elizabeth Goodeth, da of Herbert d'Auvergne Innes; *b* 29 Sept 1928; *Educ* Wellington, St John's Coll Cambridge; *m* 16 Feb 1957, Laura (d 1979), da of late Jan Pouwels Coelingh, of Wassenaar, Netherlands; 2 s; *Heir* s, Thomas Crawley-Boevey; *Career* former shipping agent; ed Money Which? 1968-76, ed Which? 1976-80, ed-in-chief 1980-82; memb Cncl Insurance Ombudsman Bureau 1985-; *Books* Buying, Selling and Owning Shares (1987), Finance Your Future (1989); *Clubs* Gower and Swansea Bay Windsurfing, Grafham Water Sailing; *Style*— Sir Thomas Crawley-Boevey, Bt; Trebanau, Cilycwm, Llandovery, Dyfed SA20 OHP (☎ 0550 20496)

CRAWSHAW, Sir Edward Weston (Daniel); QC (Aden 1949); s of Godfrey Edward Crawshaw (d 1938), of Yorks; *b* 10 Sept 1903; *Educ* St Bees Sch, Selwyn Coll Cambridge; *m* 1942, Rosemary, da of Roger Carpenter Treffry, of Cornwall; 1 s (and 1 decd), 2 da; *Career* admitted slr 1929; called to the Bar 1946; attorney-gen Aden 1947-52, Puisne judge Tanganyika 1952-60, justice of appeal Ct of Appeal for E Africa 1960-65, cmmr Foreign Compensation Cmmn 1965-75; kt 1964; *Style*— Sir Daniel Crawshaw, QC; 1 Fort Rd, Guildford, Surrey (☎ 0483 576883)

CRAWSHAW, Gillian Anne (Jill); da of William Sumner Crawshaw (d 1983), and Trudy, *née* Riding; *b* 13 Oct 1943; *Educ* West Kirby GS for Girls, St Anne's Coll Oxford (MA); *m* 1973, Stephen Rudolf Danos, s of Sir Laszlo Danos (d 1935); 2 s (Toby William Laszlo b 1974, Dominic Stephen Robert b 1977); *Career* freelance travel writer for numerous publications (incl 19, Petticoat) 1966-71; travel ed: Daily Mail 1971-82, Evening Standard 1982-87, Sunday Express and Sunday Express Magazine 1987-; currently regular contrib to various magazines radio and TV programmes incl LBC, sole travel contrib The Doomsday Book project; awarded Travel Writer of the Year three times commended Br Press Awards, twice awarded French Govt Writers Awards; *Books* Holidays with Children at Home & Abroad (1982); *Recreations* oriental carpets, Georgian architecture, skiing, obsessional travel, food, deserts; *Style*— Mrs Jill Crawshaw; Pond House, 54 Highgate West Hill, London N6 6DA (☎ 081 340 0307, fax 081 348 3782); Sunday Express, Ludgate House, 245 Blackfriars Rd, London SE1 9UX (☎ 071 928 8000, fax 071 633 0244)

CRAWSHAW, 4 Baron (UK 1892); Sir William Michael Clifton Brooks; 4 Bt (UK 1891); s of 3 Baron (d 1946), and Sheila, da of late Lt-Col P R Clifton, CMG, DSO; *b* 25 March 1933; *Educ* Eton, Ch Ch Oxford; *Heir* bro, Hon David Brooks; *Career* sits as (C) in House of Lords; lord of the manor of Long Whatton, patron of the Living of Shepshed; treas Loughborough Conservative Assoc 1954-58; co cmmr Leics Boy Scouts 1958-; *Style*— The Rt Hon The Lord Crawshaw; Whatton, Loughborough, Leics (☎ 026 475 225)

CRAWSHAY, Capt Martin Richard Charles; s of Capt Walter Stanley Cubitt Crawshay (d 1955), of The Old Rectory, Carleton Forehoe, Norwich, Norfolk, and Elaine Grace (Betty), *née* Osborne (d 1972); *b* 16 Jan 1928; *Educ* Eton, RMA Sandhurst; *m* 24 Oct 1967, Joanna Deborah Grania, da of Maj Thomas Henry Bevan, MC (d 1964), of Milltown Grange, Castlebellingham, Co Louth; 1 s (Charles Martin b 1969); *Career* Adj: 16/5 The Queens Royal Lancers 1956-57 (cmmnd 1949), Univ of Oxford OTC 1959-61; racing liaison exec Horserace Betting Levy Bd 1963-; sec Veterinary Advsy Ctee and Horserace Scientific Advsy Ctee; hon memb Br Equine Veterinary Assoc; underwriting memb of Lloyds; *Recreations* racing, shooting, croquet, wildlife; *Clubs* Cavalry and Guards; *Style*— Capt Martin Crawshay; The Old Vicarage, Leavenheath, Colchester, Essex CO6 4PT (☎ 0787 210384); Horserace Betting Levy Board, 52 Grosvener Gardens, London SW1 (☎ 071 730 4540)

CRAWSHAY, Walter Brian Julian; s of Capt Walter Stanley Cubitt Crawshay (d 1955), of The Old Rectory, Carlton Forehoe, nr Norwich, and Elaine Grace (Betty), *née* Osborne (d 1972); *b* 28 Dec 1922; *Educ* Eton; *m* 6 Aug 1954, Ann Euphane, da of Arthur Woodman Blair, of Clint Stenton, by Dunbar, East Lothian; 1 s (William b 1960), 2 da (Emma b 1955, Louisa (Mrs Barrie) b 1958); *Career* WWII Cyrencacia, Tunisia, Italy, XII Royal Lancers 1941 (despatches 1944), Staff Coll Camberley 1952, HQ1 Br Corps 1953, retired Maj 1955; dir: Youngs Crawshay & Youngs Ltd 1955, Bullard & Sons Ltd 1956, Watney Combe Reid Ltd London 1966, Watney Mann Ltd and subsids 1970, assoc cos 1978; treas Tasburgh PCC, memb Depwade Rural Dist Cncl 1960-63; *Recreations* fishing, shooting, gardening, ballet; *Clubs* New (Edinburgh); *Style*— Julian Crawshay, Esq; Tasburgh Grange, Norwich NR15 1AR (☎ 0508 470 634)

CRAWSHAY, Col Sir William Robert; DSO (1945), ERD, TD, DL (Glam 1964, Monmouthshire 1970, Gwent 1974); s of Capt Jack William Leslie Crawshay, MC (d 1950; whose mother Mary was da of Sir John Leslie, 1 Bt), sometime of Caversham Park, Oxon, by his w Claire, *née* Stickelbaut (who m subsequently Hon George Egerton, 2 s of 5 Earl of Wilton); *b* 27 May 1920; *Educ* Eton; *m* 1950, Elisabeth Mary Boyd Reynolds, da of Lt-Col Guy Franklin Reynolds, MC (d 1950); *Career* cmmnd (SR) 1 Royal Welch Fusiliers 1939, SOE France 1944-45, served WWII (despatches twice); Parachute Regt (TA) 1947-60, ADC to HM The Queen 1966-71, Hon Col 3 Royal Regt of Wales (Volunteer) Bn 1970-82; Vice-Lord Lt of Gwent 1979- (DL Glam 1964, Monmouthshire 1970, Gwent 1974); served Arts Cncl of GB 1962-74, chm Welsh Arts Cncl 1968-74, pres: National Museum of Wales 1977-82, Royal Br Legion Wales Area 1974-88; chm Univ Coll Cardiff Cncl 1966-87; Chev Légion d'Honneur 1945, Croix de Guerre 1945; KStJ 1969; kt 1972; *Clubs* White's, Cardiff and County; *Style*— Col Sir William Crawshay, DSO, ERD, TD, DL, HM Vice Lord-Lt for Gwent; Llanfair Court, Abergavenny, Gwent (☎ 087 384 0215)

CREAGH, Giles Peter Vandeleur; TD (1967); s of Lt Cdr Giles Desmond Vandeleur Creagh, RNVR (d 1963), of Blo' Norton, Norfolk, and Olga, *née* Beckwith (d 1983); *b* 21 Nov 1927; *Educ* Marlborough, Clare Coll Cambridge (MA); *m* 1 Sept 1962, Jean Margaret Heather, da of Godfrey George Hoole (d 1980), of Krugersdorp, SA; 2 s (Desmond Giles Vandeleur b 1963, Henry Giles Vandeleur b 1965); *Career* Maj (TA) Suffolk Regt, JRRU, 23 SAS, Int Corps; slr; dir Bury St Edmund's Building Society 1969-88, local dir Cheltenham & Gloucester Building Society 1988-89; registrar and legal sec Diocese of St Edmundsbury and Ipswich 1956-75, pres Suffolk and North Essex Law Soc 1984-85, chm Social Security Appeal Tbnls 1984-; *Clubs* United Oxford and Cambridge, Special Forces; *Style*— Giles Creagh, Esq, TD; The Old Rectory, Market Weston, Diss, Norfolk IP22 2PE; Greene and Greene, 80 Guildhall Street, Bury St Edmunds, Suffolk IP33 1QB (☎ 0284 762211, fax 0284 705739)

CREAN, Dr Gerard Patrick; s of Patrick Joseph Crean (d 1953), of Courtown Harbour, Co Wexford, Eire, and Katherine Frances, *née* Dunn (d 1960); *b* 1 May 1927; *Educ* Rockwell Coll Co Tipperary, Univ Coll Dublin (MB BCh, BAO), Univ of Edinburgh (PhD); *m* 16 Aug 1960, Janice Dodds, da of Thomas McKean Mathieson (d 1985), of Luanshya, Zambia; 1 s (Justin b 30 March 1964), 2 da (Kate b 16 Aug 1961, Stephanie b 10 Oct 1962); *Career* house offr Mater Misericordia Hosp Dublin 1953-54, clinical asst Dept of Med Royal Infirmary Edinburgh 1954-56; Western Gen Hosp Edinburgh: house offr 1954-56, registrar, sr registrar 1956-59, memb staff Clinical Endocrinology Res Unit MRC, hon conslt physician 1959-67; hon lectr Dept of Therapeutics Univ of Edinburgh 1964-67, conslt physician Southern Gen Hosp Glasgow 1967-; hon lectr Univ of Glasgow 1967-; visiting prof in physiology Univ of Pa USA

1972, dir Diagnostic Methodology Res Unit Southern Gen Hosp 1974-; pres Br Soc of Gastroenterology 1986; memb: Soc of Gastroenterology, Scot Assoc of Physicians, Scot Soc of Experimental Med, Assoc of Physicians of of GB and Ireland, Caledonian Soc of Gastroenterology, Prout Club, Liver Club, Glasgow Gastroenterology Club; fndr memb and pres Scot Fiddle Orchestra; FRCP (Edinburgh 1965, Glasgow 1978, Ireland 1988); *Books* The Physiology of Gastric Secretion (contrib, 1967), Davidson's Principles and Practice of Medicine (contrib, 1971), An intergrated Textbook of Gastroenterology (contrib, 1971,) Peptic Ulcer; Problem Areas in Diagnosis (contrib, 1983), Peptic Ulcer Disease (contrib, 1985); *Recreations* traditional fiddle playing, golf, history of Antartic exploration; *Style—* Dr Gerard Crean; St Ronan's, Duchal Rd, Kilmacolm, Renfrewshire PA13 4AY (☎ 0505 87 2504); Gastrointestinal Centre, Southern General Hospital, Glasgow G51 4TF (☎ 041 445 2466)

CREASE, David Plaistow; s of Gilbert Crease, of Beckenham, Kent (d 1971), and Margaret Frances Plaistow (d 1981); *b* 22 July 1928; *Educ* Christ's Hosp, Gonville and Caius Coll Cambridge (MA) Edinburgh Coll of Art (Diploma); *m* 15 Aug 1969, Jane Rosemary, da of Harold Leonard Goodey, of Reading; 1 da (Hermione b 1970); *Career* architect Public Works Dept Hong Kong 1955-59, practised in Brasilia Brazil 1960-63, chief architect Design Unit Univ of York 1966-81: (works incl housing at Heslington, York and elsewhere in Yorks; ptnr own practice 1981; princ current work Bishops Wharf York); ARIBA; *Recreations* hunting the clean boot (human scent) with bloodhounds; *Style—* David P Crease, Esq; Old Carlton Farm, Warthill, York YO3 9XS (☎ 0904 400315); Crease, Edmonds, Strickland, Architects, Bishopgate Hse, Skeldergate Bridge, York YO2 1JH (☎ 0904 641289)

CREASEY, Prof David John; s of Roy William Creasey (d 1985), of Alcester, Warwickshire, and Olga Ada Mary Creasey; *b* 20 April 1938; *Educ* Raynes Park Co GS for Boys, Univ of Southampton (BSc), Univ of Birmingham (PhD); *m* 25 Aug 1961, Glenys Irene, da of Reginald Date, of Charlton, Pershore, Worcs; 1 s (Mark b 2 Nov 1971), 1 da (Ruth b 12 Feb 1968); *Career* devpt engr GEC Telecommunications Coventry 1962-63 (apprentice 1957-62); Univ of Birmingham: Hirst res fell 1963-65, lectr, sr lectr 1965-87, prof of electronic engrg 1987-, head sch of electronic and electrical engrg 1990-; memb: Soc for Underwater Technol, Nat Tst; MIEE 1980; *Books* Advanced Signal Processing (1985); *Recreations* gardening, photography; *Clubs* Nat Trust, Caravan; *Style—* Prof David Creasey; The Old Mill, Penn Lane, Tanworth in Arden, Solihull, Birmingham B15 2TT (☎ 056 44 2417), School of Electronic & Electrical Engineering, University of Birmingham, Edgbaston, Birmingham B15 2TT (☎ 021 414 4283, telex 338938 SPAPHY G, fax 021 141 4291)

CREASEY, David Somersall; s of David Edward Creasey (d 1954), of Leeds, and Margaret Agnes, *née* Eve (d 1960); *b* 28 Feb 1924; *Educ* Leeds GS, Univ of Leeds (LLB Hons); *m* 6 Jan 1951, Lois Barbara, da of William Morris Morden Dorset (d 1953); 2 s (Andrew b 1956, Julian b 1952), 2 da (Caroline b 1960, Philippa b 1953); *Career* war serv RAF bomber, cmd navigator; admitted slr; dir and sec Leeds Abbeyfield Soc; *Recreations* golf, bridge; *Clubs* Leeds, Skrack Lions (past pres); *Style—* David S Creasey, Esq; The Spinney, 142 Adel Lane, Leeds (☎ 679288)

CREASEY, Richard John; s of John Creasey, MBE (d 1973), and (Evelyn) Jean, *née* Fudge; *b* 28 Aug 1944; *Educ* Malvern; *m* 5 Jan 1968, Wendy; 2 s (Simon b 19 July 1972, Guy b 1 May 1974), 1 da (Sarah b 19 Jan 1980); *Career* Granada TV: researcher 1965-72, prodr 1972-74; ATV Network: prodr 1974-77, exec prodr 1977-78, head of documentaries 1978-81; controller of Features Central TV 1981-90; dir Special Projects Central TV 1990-; chm Soviet Br Creative Assoc 1989- (dep chm 1989), tstee and co fndr: TV Tst for the Environment, TVE; vice chm Wildscreen Tst; *Recreations* family, reading; *Clubs* BAFTA, RTS; *Style—* Richard Creasey, Esq; Manor House, Wolverton, Stratford-on-Avon, Warwickshire CV37 0HH (☎ 0789 731373), 40A Elmbank Mansions, Elmbank Gardens, Barnes, London SW13 ONS (☎ 01 878 2380), Central Independent Television, Hesketh House, 43/45 Portman Square, London W1H 9FG (☎ 071 486 6688, fax 071 224 3849)

CREBER, Frank Paul; s of Dr Geoffrey Tremain Creber, of Applecroft, Brooklane, Wood Green, Fordingbridge, Hants, and Hilda, *née* Lewey; *b* 12 Jan 1959; *Educ* Dr Challoner's GS Amersham Bucks, Univ of Newcastle-upon-Tyne (BA), Chelsea Sch of Art (MA); *m* 1982, Marguerite Honor Blake, da of The Rev Canon Peter Douglas Stuart Blake; 2 s (Theodore Sebastion Peter b 1983, Nicholas Tremaine b 1986); *Career* artist; most important works: White Light/Yellow Light (1987), Within One Flame go Two As One (1987), Open State (1988), Colonial Comedy (1988), Spent (1989), Man with Bird (1989), Sun and Cloud (1990), Cliff Dance (1990); exhibitions incl: Barclays Bank Young Painters Competition (Henry Moore Gallery, RCA London) 1987, Sue Williams (Portobello Rd London) 1988, Picker Fellowship Show (Kingston Poly) 1988, two man show (Diorama Gallery London) 1988, solo Show (Sue Williams Gallery Portobello Rd London) 1989, Picker Fellows At Kingston (Watermans Art Centre Brentford) 1989, Artist of The Day (Flowers East London) 1989, The New Generation (Auction at Bonhams Knightsbridge London) 1990, two persons show (Paton Gallery) 1990, gp show (ROI at Lloyds London) 1990, works in collections: Unilever plc, Arthur Anderson & Co, Art for Hosps, Stanhope Construction Ltd; awards, prizewinner Avon Open (Artiste Gallery Bath) 1984, prize winner Brewhouse Open (Taunton) 1985, Herbert Read fellowship Chelsea Sch of Art 1986, jt winner Barclays Bank Young Painters award 1987, Picker fellowship Kingston Poly 1987-88; *Style—* Frank Creber, Esq; 43 Jennings Rd, East Dulwich, London SE22 9JU (☎ 081 693 5944); Studio 12, 165 Childers St, Deptford, London SE8 5JR (☎ 081 692 1612)

CREDITON, Bishop of 1984-; Rt Rev Peter Everard Coleman; s of Geoffrey Everard Coleman (d 1942), of Ware Herts, and Lilian Bessie, *née* Cook (d 1982); *b* 28 Aug 1928; *Educ* Haileybury, Univ of London (LLB), Univ of Bristol (MLitt); *m* 14 May 1960, HSH Princess Elisabeth Donata Regina Emma Clementine, yst da of HSH Prince Heinrich XXXIX Reuss (d 1946); 2 s (Basil b 1963, Benedict b 1965), 2 da (Antonia b 1961, Elena b 1969); *Career* Mil Serv RHG and RA, 2nd Lt 1947-49; called to the Bar Middle Temple 1965; ordained Bristol 1955, chaplain and lectr King's Coll London 1960-66, vicar St Paul's Clifton, chaplain Univ of Bristol 1966-71, canon residentiary and dir of trg Bristol 1971-81, archdeacon of Worcester 1981-84; clerical memb Ct of Archers 1980-, memb Gen Synod (House of Bishops) 1990-, jt ed Theology 1982-; *Books* Experiments with Prayer (1961), A Christian Approach to Television (1968), Christian Attitudes to Homosexuality (1980), Gay Christians - A Moral Dilemma (1989), Ordination of Women (1990); *Recreations* film making, fishing; *Style—* The Rt Rev the Bishop of Crediton; 10 The Close, Exeter EX1 1EZ

CREED, Peter Howard; s of Sidney Howard Creed (d 1971), of Wolverhampton, and Gladys Marguerite, *née* Shaw (d 1977); *b* 27 June 1931; *Educ* Tettenhall Coll Wolverhampton; *m* 1956, Joan, da of Henry Francis (d 1986), of Wolverhampton; 2 s (Michael b 1958, Charles b 1962); *Career* SAC RAF 1954-56; joined Express and Star; advertisement rep 1957; advertisement mangr: Shropshire Star 1964 (dir 1968-73), Express and Star 1973; gp advertisement dir The Midlands News Assoc Ltd 1980- (incl Express and Star, Shropshire Star and Shropshire Weekly Newspapers); dir Precision Colour Printing Ltd Telford 1981-84; chm Newspaper Advertising Conference Ctee 1977-83 (memb Advertising Ctee 1975-); Newspaper Soc rep on Code of Advertising Practice Ctee for Advertising Standards Authy 1985-; govr Tettenhall Coll 1978-; *Recreations* cricket, golf, ardent Wolves Football Club supporter; *Clubs* Penn Cricket (Wolverhampton), Wrekin Golf; *Style—* Peter Creed, Esq; 218 Henwood Rd, Tettenhall, Wolverhampton, West Midlands WV6 8NZ (☎ 0902 752653); The Midland News Association Ltd, Queen St, Wolverhampton, West Midlands WV1 3BU (☎ 0902 313131, fax 0902 772415)

CREEK, Malcolm Lars; LVO (1980), OBE (1985); s of Edgar Creek (d 1977), of Edmonton, Alberta, Canada, and Lily, *née* Robertshaw (d 1950); *b* 2 April 1931; *Educ* Belle Vue Sch Bradford, London Univ (BA); *m* 1, (m dis 1970), Moira; 1 s (Jeremy b 1960), 1 da (Helen b 1955); m 2, 17 July 1970, Gillian Mary, da of Arthur Ridley Bell (d 1989), of Bertram Drive North, Meols, Wirral; 1 s (Richard b 1975), 2 da (Alison b 1973, Sarah b 1974); *Career* Nat Serv 1950-52; FO 1950 and 1952-56, vice consul Mogadishiu and Harare 1956-58, FO 1958-59, 2 sec Mexico City 1959-62 (Abidjan 1962-64, Santiago 1964-68), 1 sec and head of Chancery San Jose 1968-71 (Havana 1972-74), FO 1974-77, 1 sec Tunis 1978-81 (Lima 1981-85), high cmmr Vila Vanuatu 1985-88, consul-gen Auckland 1988-; *Recreations* cricket, tennis; *Clubs* Northern, Auckland; *Style—* Malcolm Creek, Esq, LVO, OBE; 17 Bertram Drive North, Meols, Wirral, Ches L47 OLN (☎ 051 632 5820)

CREER, Kenneth Ernest; s of Ernest Lyons Creer (d 1989), of Isle of Man, and Robina, *née* Kelly (d 1975); *b* 29 Aug 1937; *Educ* Douglas HS Isle of Man, Salisbury Sch of Art Wiltshire, Central London Poly, Br Inst of Professional Photography; *m* 5 Dec 1964, Pauline Winifred, da of Leslie James Artis: 3 s (Colin Leslie b 12 Dec 1965, Peter b 21 May 1968, Paul Robin b 18 March 1976); *Career* apprentice photographer S R Kreig Ltd Isle of Man 1954-57, photographer 16 Ind Parachute Bde 1957-60, photographic printer Speedy Photographic London 1960-61, sr photographer Metropolitan Police New Scotland Yard 1963-68 (photographer 1961-63); Metropolitan Police Forensic Sci Lab: head Photographic Section 1968-69, princ photographer 1969-83, chief photographer 1983-; responsible for the introduction of specialist criminalogical photographic techniques; lectr and author of numerous papers on criminological photographic matters; Richard Farrant Meml trophy for distinction in applied photography 1983; FBIPP 1983 (memb 1964), FRPS 1986; *Recreations* sailing, golf; *Style—* Kenneth Creer, Esq; Head of Photo Section, Metropolitan Police, Forensic Science Laboratory, 109 Lambeth Rd, London SE1 7LP (☎ 071 230 6279)

CREER, (Dahlis) Virginia; da of Cdre Bruce Loxton, RAN (ret), of Sydney, Aust, and Dahlis Ailsa, *née* Robertson; *b* 4 Feb 1948; *Educ* Ascham Sch Sydney Aust, Univ of Sydney (BA); *m* 1971, David Victor Charles Creer, s of Victor Charles Hamish Creer; 1 s (Benjamin Fulke Matthew b 7 Sept 1976), 1 da (Camilla Dahlis Elizabeth b 12 July 1979); *Career* Mktg Div Unilever Ltd 1969-72, asst brand mangr then brand mangr Schweppes Ltd 1972-77 (mktg mangr 1976), account dir Grey Advertising Ltd 1978-80; Davidson Pearce Ltd: sr planner 1980, Bd dir 1982, agency devpt dir 1985-87, exec planning and devpt dir 1987-88; asst md BMP Davidson Pearce Ltd 1988-89, managing ptnr BMP DDB Needham Ltd 1989 (md BMP 4 1991); memb: Mktg Soc 1976, MRS 1980, IPA 1982, WACL 1990; *Recreations* running, riding, sailing; *Style—* Mrs Virginia Creer; BMP DDB Needham, 12 Bishops Bridge Rd, London W2 6AA (☎ 071 258 3979, fax 071 258 4455, mobile 0831 441667)

CREESE, Prof Richard; TD (1965); s of Leonard Creese (d 1947), of Clifton, Bristol, and Nellie Hawkesford, *née* James (d 1983); *b* 4 Dec 1919; *Educ* Clifton, King's Coll London, Westminster Med Sch, Univ of London (MB BS, PhD); *m* 8 May 1943, Louise May, da of Leon Jean Doumeyrou (d 1956), of Paris; 2 s (Anthony b 1949, Martin b 1950), 1 da (Claire b 1958); *Career* RMO The Queen's Bays 1946-47, RAMC (TA) 1948-81, Col L/RAMC (V) 1976; London Hosp Med Coll 1950-60, visiting asst prof Univ of California Los Angeles 1955-56, St Marys Hosp Med Sch 1961-82 (prof of physiology 1968-); govr Henry Compton Sch Fulham 1972-75; Mickle fell Univ of London 1959; Freeman City of London 1968, Liveryman Worshipful Soc of Apothecaries 1966; FRSM 1952, memb Physiological Soc 1953; *Books* Recent Advances in Physiology (ed, 1963); *Recreations* travel, history, drama, running; *Clubs* Garrick, Thames Hare and Hounds; *Style—* Prof Richard Creese, TD; 93 Lonsdale Rd, London SW13 9DA (☎ 081 748 7002)

CREGGY, Stuart; JP (Westminster 1979); s of Leslie Creggy (d 1972), and Fay, *née* Schneider; *b* 27 May 1939; *Educ* Western Univ USA (MA), Law Soc Sch of Law; *Career* slr 1963, cmmr for oaths 1969, currently sr ptnr Talbot Creggy & Co; chm: Juvenile Diabetes Fndn, Sussex Co Freeholds plc; memb Variety Club of GB; memb Law Soc, fell Royal Philatelic Soc, FBIM, FFA, ACIArb; *Recreations* swimming, philately; *Clubs* RAC; *Style—* Stuart Creggy, Esq, JP; 58 Viceroy Ct, Prince Albert Rd, St Johns Wood, London NW8 7PS (☎ 071 586 4465); 38 Queen Anne St, London W1M 9LB (☎ 071 637 8865, fax 071 637 2630, car 0836 234 008, 0836 234 009, telex 8954619)

CREIGHTON, Alan Joseph; s of Joseph Kenneth Creighton (d 1975), and Iris Mary, *née* McShea (d 1978); *b* 21 Nov 1936; *Educ* Gillingham Co GS, Royal Naval Engrg Coll Manadon Plymouth, RNC Greenwich; *m* 25 July 1959, Judith, da of Jack Bayford, of West Littleton; 2 da (Helen b 4 June 1962, Hannah b 13 April 1965); *Career* chief constructor MOD (N) 1974-80 (asst constructor 1961-65, constructor 1965-74), RCDS 1980-81, seconded as tech dir to Yarrow Shipbuilders 1981-84, DG MOD (PE) 1986-89 (dir 1984-86), Chief Underwater Systems Exec 1989-; FRINA 1981; *Recreations* music, cabinet making, sailing, swimming, DIY; *Style—* Alan Creighton, Esq; Home Farm Cottage, West Littleton, Marshfield, Chippenham SN 14 8JE (☎ 0225 891 021); Ministry of Defence (PE), Foxhill, Bath (☎ 0225 883634)

CRESSMAN, Harry Gordon; s of Harry Edwin Cressman (d 1965); *b* 10 Jan 1927; *Educ* Eversfield Prep Sch, Black-Foxe Mil Inst Los Angeles California; *m* 1948, Barbara Ann, *née* Brodine, 2 s, 1 da; *Career* Tech Sgt US Army Coast Artillery; joined Bristol St Motors Ltd 1948 (dir 1949, md 1951), md chm and chief exec BSC Int 1967-80, dir: Heron Motor Gp Ltd 1980 (md 1981), Heron Corpn Ltd 1981-; DG American Chamber of Commerce (UK) 1982; *Recreations* travel, racing, football, boats; *Clubs* American, Carlton, Lyford Cay (Nassau), Port La Galère (France), Ends of the Earth; *Style—* Harry Cressman Esq; 34 Petersham Place, S Kensington, London SW7 (☎ 071 584 2731); Eastcote Paddocks, Hampton-in-Arden, Solihull, W Midlands (☎ 067 55 2168); 1 Ave de l'Astrolabe, Port La Galère, Theoule, Alpes Maritimes, France (☎ 010 33 93 90 32 26)

CRESSWELL; *see*: Baker-Cresswell

CRESSWELL, Amos Samuel; s of Amos Cresswell (d 1978), of Walsall Wood, Staffs, and Jane, *née* Marriott (d 1972); *b* 21 April 1926; *Educ* Queen Mary's GS Walsall, Univ Coll Durham (BA), Wesley House and Fitzwilliam Coll Cambridge (BA, MA), Theological Seminary Bethel bei Bielefield Westphalia Germany; *m* 11 Feb 1956, Evelyn Rosemary, da of Walter Marchbanks (d 1980), of Barnes, London; 2 s (Stephen Amos, Martin James), 1 da (Rosemary Jane); *Career* teacher of English and Latin HS for Boys Colchester 1947-49; methodist minister Clitheroe 1949-50, asst tutor in New Testament Richmond Methodist Coll Univ of London 1953-56, Methodist minister Darlaston 1956-61, New Testament tutor Cliff Coll Calver Derbyshire 1961-66, ed Advance (a weekly jl) 1961-63, minister Bramhall Circuit Cheadle Hulme 1966-73, supt minister Welwyn Herts 1973-76, chm Plymouth and Exeter Methodist Dist 1976-; pres Methodist Conf of UK and Ireland 1983-84; memb Rotary Club: Darlaston 1957-61, Cheadle Cheshire 1968-73, Welwyn Garden City 1973-76; fndr Darlaston Fellowship for the Disabled 1960, pres Devonshire Assoc (for the Advancement of Sci

Literature and Art) 1985-86; *Books* The Story of Cliff - History of Cliff Coll (2 edn, 1983), The Story They Told - a Study of the Passion and Resurrection (1966), Life Power and Hope - a Study of the Holy Spirit (1971), Lord I've Had Enough (book of sermons and adresses, 1991); *Style—* The Rev Amos Cresswell; 18 Velwell Rd, Exeter, Devon EC4 4LE (☎ 0392 72541)

CRESSWELL, Helen (Mrs Brian Rowe); da of Joseph Edward Cresswell, and Annie Edna, *née* Clarke; *b* 1934,July; *Educ* Nottingham Girls HS, King's Coll London (BA); *m* 1962, Brian Rowe; 2 da; *Career* freelance author and TV scriptwriter; TV series: Lizzie Dripping 1973-75, Jumbo Spencer 1976, The Bagthorpe Saga 1980, The Secret World of Polly Flint 1986, Moondial 1988, Five Children and It (adaptation) 1991; author numerous plays; *Publications* Sonya-by-the-Shire (1961), Jumbo Spencer (1963), The White Sea Horse (1964), Pietro and the Mule (1965), Jumbo Back to Nature (1965), Where The Wind Blows (1966), Jumbo Afloat (1966), The Piemakers (1967), A Tide for the Captain (1967), The Signposters (1968), The Sea Piper (1968), The Barge Children (1968), The Night-Watchmen (1969), A Game of Catch (1969), A Gift from Winklesea (1969), The Outlanders (1970), The Wilkeses (1970), The Bird Fancier (1971), At the Stroke of Midnight (1971), Lizzie Dripping (1972), The Bongleweed (1972), Lizzie Dripping Again (1974), Butterfly Chase (1975), The Winter of the Birds (1975), My Aunt Polly (1979), My Aunt Polly by the Sea (1980), Dear Shrink (1982), The Secret World of Polly Flint (1982), Ellie and the Hagwitch (1984), Ordinary Jack (1977), Absolute Zero (1978), Bagthorpes Unlimited (1978), Bagthorpes v The World (1979), Bagthorpes Abroad (1984), Bagthorpes Haunted (1985), Moondial (1987), Time Out (1987), Bagthorpes Liberated (1988), The Story of Grace Darling (1998), Two Hoots (1988), Whatever Happened in Winklesea ? (1989), Rosie and the Boredom Eater (1989), Almost Goodbye Guzzler (1990), Hokey Pokey Did It! (1990), Meet Posy Bates (1990), Posy Bates Again (1991), Lizzie Dripping and The Witch (1991); *Recreations* watercolour painting, collecting books, antiques and coincidences, sundial watching; *Style—* Ms Helen Cresswell; Old Church Farm, Eakring, Newark, Notts NG22 0DA (☎ 0623 870 401)

CRESSWELL, Dr Lyell Richard; s of Jack Cecil Cresswell (d 1986), and Muriel Minnie, *née* Sharp (d 1982); *b* 13 Oct 1944; *Educ* Victoria Univ of Wellington NZ (BMus), Univ of Toronto (MusM), Univ of Aberdeen (PhD); *m* 4 Jan 1972, Catherine Isabel, da of Keith James Mawson, of Otaki, NZ; *Career* composer; works incl: Concerto for Violin and Orchestra (1970), Salm (1977), Prayer for the Cure of a Sprained Back (1979), The Silver Pipes of Ur (1981), Le Sucre du Printemps (1982), O! (1982), Concerto for Cello and Orchestra (1984), The Fallen Dog (1984), Our Day Begins at Midninght (1985), To Aspro Pano Sto Aspro (1985), Speak For Us Great Sea (1985), A Modern Ecstasy (1986), The Pumpkin Massacre (1987), Sextet (1988), Passacagli (1988), Ixion (1988), Voices of Ocean Winds (1989); memb: The Composers Guild of GB, The Assoc of Professional Composers, The Scottish Soc of Composers, The Composers Assoc of NZ; *Recreations* illustrating the book of Ezekiel; *Style—* Dr Lyell Cresswell; 4 Leslie Place, Edinburgh, Scotland EH4 1NQ (☎ 031 332 9181)

CRESSWELL, Hon Mr Justice; Sir Peter John; s of Rev Canon JJ Cresswell, of 12 Eastleach, Glos, and Madeleine, *née* Foley; *b* 24 April 1944; *Educ* St John's Sch Leatherhead, Queen's Coll Cambridge (MA, LLM); *m* 29 April 1972, Caroline, da of Maj Gen Sir Philip Ward, KCVO, CBE, DL, of The Old Rectory, Patching, Sussex; 2 s (Oliver b 11 Nov 1973 d 1988, Mark b 25 Sept 1975); *Career* called to the Bar Gray's Inn 1966, QC 1983, rec 1986, Judge of the High Court 1991; chm London Common Law and Commercial Bar Assoc 1985-87; memb Senate of Inns of Ct and Bar 1981-86, bencher of Gray's Inn 1989; chm: Gen Cncl of the Bar 1990 (memb 1987-90, vice chm 1989), Cncl Cystic Fibrosis Res Tst (Exec Ctee); hon memb Canadian Bar Assoc 1990; kt 1991; *Books* Encyclopaedia of Banking Law (1982-91); *Recreations* fly-fishing, river management, the Outer Hebrides; *Clubs* Flyfisher's; *Style—* The Hon Mr Justice Cresswell; Royal Courts of Justice, Strand, London WC2A 2LL

CRESSWELL, Brig David Hector Craig; s of Lt-Col John Hector Creswell, OBE, of Colchester, Essex, and Laurette Maxwell, *née* Craig; *b* 12 May 1942; *Educ* Wellington, RMA Sandhurst; *m* 30 Sept 1967, Pamela Mary Scott, da of Dr Denis Dearman Matthews (d 1986), of Winchester; 2 s (Edward b 1969, Nicholas b 1972); *Career* reg cmmn RA 1962, asst def attaché Copenhagen 1979-81, co 40 Field Regt RA 1981-84, directing staff Royal Mil Coll of Sci 1984-85, superintendent Proof and Experimental Estab Shoeburyness 1985-87, dir Rapier 1988-; FBIM 1986; *Recreations* sailing, golf, skiing, walking, reading; *Style—* Brig David Creswell; Fleetbank House, 2-6 Salisbury Square, London EC4Y 8AT (☎ 071 632 4108)

CRESWELL, Simon Hawkshaw; s of Capt John Creswell (d 1973), of Ellerslie, Cattistock, Dorset, and Crystal Mary Olivia, *née* Hawkshaw; *b* 19 Jan 1932; *Educ* RNC Dartmouth, Magdalene Coll Cambridge (BA, MA); *m* 7 May 1962, Sarah, da of Col Frederick Arthur Stanley, OBE (d 1979), of Bramshott Lodge, Liphook, Hants; 1 s (Alexander b 1965), 2 da (Miranda b 1963, Sophia b 1969); *Career* Naval Cadet 1945-50; CA 1961, Coopers and Lybrand Paris 1962-67, Price Waterhouse Paris 1967-72, Price Waterhouse London 1972-73, Commercial Union Assurance Soc plc 1973-83, gen sec Nat Soc for Cancer Relief 1983-86, fundraising admin Scout Assoc 1986-; treas Carr Comm Soc 1978-88; FICA; *Recreations* field sports, history, cooking; *Clubs* Traveller's; *Style—* Simon Creswell, Esq; The Scout Association Baden-Powell House, London SW7 5JS (☎ 071 584 7030, fax 071 581 9953)

CRETNEY, Prof Stephen Michael; s of Fred Cretney (d 1980), and Winifred Mary Valentine, *née* Rowlands (d 1982); *Educ* The Manchester Warehousemen and Clerks Orphan Schs Cheadle Hulme, Magdalen Coll Oxford (DCL, MA); *m* 7 July 1973, Antonia Lois, da of Cdr Anthony George Glanusk Vanrenen, RN, of Fordingbridge, Hants; 2 s (Matthew b 1975, Edward b 1979); *Career* Nat Serv 1954-56; admitted slr 1962, ptnr Macfarlanes 1964-65, Kenya Sch of Law Nairobi 1966-67, Univ of Southampton 1967-68, fell Exeter Coll Oxford 1968-78, law cmmr 1978-83, prof of law Univ of Bristol 1983- (dean of Faculty 1984-88); pt/t chm Social Security and Med Appeals Tbnls 1984-; memb: Ctee on Prison Disciplinary System, Judicial Studies Bd Civil and Family Ctee 1985-90; chm Ctee of Heads Univ Law Schs 1986-88; FBA 1985; *Books* Principles of Family Law (5 edn 1990), author of other legal texts and articles in learned jls; *Recreations* scholarship; *Clubs* Utd Oxford and Cambridge; *Style—* Prof Stephen Cretney; 15 Canynge Sq, Clifton, Bristol BS8 3LA (☎ 0272 732983, 0272 303371)

CRETTON, Hon Mrs (Catherine Anne); *née* Vesey; 2 da of 6 Viscount de Vesci (d 1983), and Susan Anne, *née* Armstrong-Jones (d 1986), sis of 1 Earl of Snowden, *qv*; *b* 19 May 1953; *m* June 1984, Bruno Cretton; 2 s (Matthew, Alexis), 1 da (Cecily); *Style—* The Hon Mrs Cretton; 121 Chemin de La Moraine, 74400 Argentière, France

CREWDSON, Hon Mrs (Aurelia Margaret Amherst); *née* Cecil; da of 4 Baron Amherst of Hackney; *b* 19 July 1966; *Educ* Prior's Field, Queensgate; *m* 20 Dec 1990, Giles Wilson Mervyn Crewdson, o s of (Wilson) Peregrine Nicholas Crewdson and Hon Lucy Clara, *née* Beckett, o da of 3 Baron Grimthorpe; *Career* md Aurelia Public Relations; *Style—* The Hon Mrs Crewdson; 1a Cornwall Mews South, London SW7

CREWDSON, John Francis; s of Maj Eric Crewdson, MC, DL (d 1969), and Mary Stuart, *née* Fyers (d 1961); *b* 27 Nov 1923; *Educ* Dragon Sch Oxford, Shrewsbury, Jesus Coll Cambridge (BA, MB BChir); *m* 1, 1946, Gillian Dallas, da of Arthur Dallas Lawton Harington (d 1980); 2 da (Jacqueline b 1948, Ingrid Gillian b 1952); m 2, 1959, Patricia Marie, da of Dr William King Carew (d 1956); 1 s (Charles Willian Nepean b 1964); *Career* WWII Lt RNVR served motor torpedo boats N Sea; opthalmologist St Thomas's Hosp 1950-81 (conslt 1974-81), conslt French Hosp 1973-81, chief clinic asst Moorfields Eye Hosp 1958-81; vice chm NW Sea Cadet Corps 1987-; *Clubs* Naval; *Style—* John F Crewdson, Esq; Winster House, Winster, Windermere, Cumbria LA23 3NU (☎ 096 62 2680)

CREWDSON, Hon Mrs (Lucy Clare); *née* Beckett; only da of Lt-Col 3 Baron Grimthorpe, DL (d 1963), by his 1 w; *b* 5 Sept 1926; *m* 12 July 1957, Wilson Peregrine Nicholas Crewdson, s of Brig Wilson Theodore Oliver Crewdson, CBE; 1 s, 3 da (1 da decd); *Style—* The Hon Mrs Crewdson; Oak House, Otley, nr Ipswich, Suffolk

CREWE, Candida Annabel; da of Quentin Hugh Crewe, of Le Grand Banc, Oppedette, 04110, France and Angela Maureen, *née* Huth; *b* 6 June 1964; *Educ* The Manor Sch Great Durnford Wilts, St Mary's Sch Calne Wilts, Headington Sch Oxford; *Career* bookshop asst 1983-86, jr ed Quartet Books Ltd London 1986-, journalist weekly column London Evening Standard 1985-86; freelance journalist 1986-91: The Spectator, The Independent, The Times, The Daily Telegraph, The Sunday Telegraph, The Observer, The Sunday Times, Tatler, Harpers & Queen, Marie-Claire, You Magazine, The Evening Standard; pubns incl: Focus (1985), Romantic Hero (1986), Accommodating Molly (1989), Mad About Bees (1991); *awards* runner-up for Catherine Pakenham meml award for journalism 1987; memb PEN Int; *Recreations* photography; *Clubs* Groucho; *Style—* Miss Candida Crewe; Imogen Parker, A P Watt Ltd, 20 John St, London WC1N 2DR (☎ 071 405 6774, fax 071 831 2154)

CREWE, Prof Ivor Martin; s of Francis Crewe, of 10 Spath Rd, West Didsbury, Manchester, and Lilly Edith, *née* Neustadtl; *b* 15 Oct 1945; *Educ* Manchester GS, Exeter Coll Oxford (MA), LSE (MSc); *m* 3 July 1968, Jill Barbara, da of Dr Theo Gadian, of 1 Park Lodge, 30 Park St, Salford; 2 s (Ben b 1974, Daniel b 1977), 1 da (Deborah b 1972); *Career* asst lectr Dept of Politics Univ of Lancaster 1967-69, jr res fell Nuffield Coll Oxford 1969-71; Univ of Essex: lectr 1971, sr lectr 1974, dir ESRC data archive 1974-82, prof 1982-; co-dir British Election Study 1977-82, ed British Journal of Political Sci 1977-82 and 1984-88; commentator on elections and public opinion BBC TV and the Times; memb: Political Studies Assoc, American Political Studies Assoc; *Books* A Social Survey of Higher Civil Service (1969), Decade of Dealignment (1983), British Parliamentary Constituencies (1984); *Recreations* opera; *Style—* Prof I M Crewe; Dept of Government, Univ of Essex, Colchester, Essex CO4 3SQ (☎ 0206 872129, fax 0206 873598)

CREWE, Quentin Hugh; s of Maj Hugh Dodds Crewe, CMG, TD, of HM Consular Serv (*née* Dodds but changed name by deed poll 1945) and Lady Annabel, da of 1 and last Marquess of Crewe, KG, PC, JP; *b* 14 Nov 1926; *Educ* Eton, Trinity Coll Cambridge; *m* 1, 1956, Martha Sharp; 1 s (Sebastian b 1958), 1 da (Sabrina b 1959); m 2, 1961, Angela Huth; 1 da (Candida b 1964) (and 1 s decd); 1970 (m dis 1983), Susan, da of Capt Richard Cavendish, JP, DL (s of Col Rt Hon Lord Richard Cavendish, CB, CMG, yr bro of 9 Duke of Devonshire); 1 s (Nathaniel b 1971), 1 da (Charity b 1972); *Career* journalist (articles particularly on food) and author; has written for Queen, Vogue, Daily Mail, Sunday Times, Sunday Mirror, Sunday Telegraph, Spectator; *Books* A Curse of Blossom 1960, Frontiers of Privilege 1961, Great Chefs of France 1979, International Pocket Food Book 1980, In Search of the Sahara 1983, The Last Maharaja 1985, Touch the Happy Isles 1987, In the Realms of Gold 1989; *Recreations* travel; *Clubs* Tarporley Hunt; *Style—* Quentin Crewe, Esq; Le Grand Banc, 04110 Oppedette, France; 1 Arundel Gardens, London W11 2LN

CREWE, Rosemary Anne (Romy); da of John Eric Crewe (d 1990), of Orton House, Lower Penn, Wolverhampton, and Rachael, *née* Kemp; *b* 18 May 1951; *Educ* Headington Sch Oxford, Wolverhampton Business Coll (Dip Business Studies), Welsh Sch of Occupational Therapy (Dip of Coll of Occupational Therapists), Univ of Southampton (Chest Heart & Stroke Assoc scholar, Postgrad Dip); *Career* basic grade occupational therapist New Cross Hosp Wolverhampton 1972-73, sr II occupational therapist Rivermead Rehabilitation Centre Oxford 1975-76 (basic grade 1973-75), project worker Equipment for the Disabled Oxford RHA Feb-May 1976, head IV occupational therapist Mary Marlborough Lodge Oxford 1978-80 (sr II 1976-78), research fell Univ of Southampton 1980-81, freelance seating conslt 1981-83; sr I occupational therapist: Westerlea Sch for Spastics Edinburgh Jan-Sept 1982, St Columba's Hospice Edinburgh 1982-83; head III occupational therapist City Hosp Edinburgh 1984-86 (locum sr I occupational therapist 1983-84), head II occupational therapist Stoke Mandeville Hosp Aylesbury 1986-90, freelance rehabilitation conslt and personal injury claims cost assessor 1990-, lectr on various topics related to disablement; Soc for Tissue Viability 1981- (fndr memb, memb Cncl, memb Educn Ctee, former memb Conferences Ctee); former memb: DHSS Wheelchair Review Ctee, Coll of Occupational Therapists Specialisation Ctee; former treas Oxford Regnl Gp of Occupational Therapist; former chm: Oxford Area Gp of Occupational Therapist, Scottish Res Special Interest Gp; former advsr West German Govt Wheelchair Technol Gp; clinical reviewer: Br Jl Occupational Therapy, Gerontology Jl; professional advsr McColl Ctee, memb HCC/40 (Wheelchairs) BSI; memb: Biological Engineering Soc 1982, (Dip of Univ of Southampton), Coll of Occupational Therapist (DipCOT) 1972, State Registered Occupational Therapist 1972; pioneer & developer methods and equipment to improve comfort of the wheelchair bound and to prevent sitting induced pressure sores; *Books* The Hospital Wheelchair (1981), Pressure Sores: Prevention and Treatment (contrib 1983), Wheelchairs - A Guide to Clinical Prescripton (with E Williams, H Hill & G Cochrane, 1982), author of numerous articles in various learned jls; *Style—* Miss Romy Crewe; Church Barn, Oving, nr Aylesbury, Bucks HP22 4HN (☎ 0296 641189); 27A Montgomery St, Edinburgh EH7 5JU (☎ 031 557 6100); Tyneholm House Nursing Home, Pencaitland, East Lothian EH34 5DJ (☎ 0875 340708, car 0836 318415)

CREWE, Thomas Cavey; s of Henry Alexander Crewe (d 1959), of Christchurch, NZ, and Ethel Ina, *née* Gillman (d 1945); *b* 5 Oct 1925; *Educ* Christchurch Boys HS, Univ of Otago (BDS); *m* 5 April 1952, Gweneth Jessie (d 1986), da of Francis Frederickk Jolly (d 1957), of Auckland, NZ; 1 s (Simon b 1958), 1 da (Rachel (Mrs Fairhead) b 1960); *Career* RNZAF 1945; conslt oral and maxillofacial surgn 1959-90, civil conslt to RN 1970-90; memb: Forensic Sci Soc, Br As soc of Forensic Odontologists, Cncl IAOMS 1982-88; pres Oral Surgery Club GB 1989-90; memb: RCS (FDS 1960-), BDA, BAOMS (pres 1984-85), IAOMS, RN Med Club; FRSM; *Recreations* photography, travel, walking; *Clubs* RSM; *Style—* Thomas Crewe, Esq; 2 Torland Road, Hartley, Plymouth, Devon PL3 5TS (☎ 0752 772422)

CREWE-READ, Hon Mrs (Diana Mary Wroughton); *née* Robins; da of 1 and last Baron Robins, KBE, DSO, ED (d 1962); *b* 11 Nov 1920; *Educ* St Mary's Wantage; *m* 22 June 1940, Col John Offley Crewe-Read, OBE, 3 s of Col Randolph Offley Crewe-Read, DSO, JP (d 1933); 2 s (David Offley b 1944, Christopher Thomas Malcolm b 1951), 1 da (Joanna Christina (Mrs Morton) b 1941); *Style—* The Hon Mrs Crewe-Read; Croft House, Aston Tirrold, Didcot, Oxon (☎ 0235 850318)

CREWS, Hon Mrs (Anne Pauline); *née* Irby; da of 9 Baron Boston (d 1978), by his 1 w; *b* 28 Feb 1927; *Educ* Seaford Ladies Coll, Central and Camberwell Schs of Art and Craft; *m* 1951, Prof Sydney James Crews, s of Sydney Kirby Crews (d 1977); 1 s

(Francis b 1953), 2 da (Emma b 1956, Bridget b 1963); *Career* artist, ceramic sculpture, water colours, print maker; art teacher and lectr for 20 years in Birmingham; *Books* (illustrator) Solid Citizens - a study of sculpture in Birmingham; *Recreations* swimming, architectural walks; *Style—* The Hon Mrs Crews; 77 Wellington Rd, Edgbaston, Birmingham B15 2ET (☎ 021 440 3459)

CRIBB, Evelyn Francis Theodore; s of Canon Charles Theodore Cribb (d 1976); descended from John Evelyn (b 1620), the diarist, one of the original fellows of the Royal Soc; *b* 24 June 1929; *Educ* Marlborough, Christs Coll Camb; *m* 1956 (m dis), Jane Howard, da of Ronald Le Grice Eyre (d 1940); 1 s, 2 da; m 2, Annabelle Southon; *Career* called to the Bar Middle Temple 1954; appointments General Motors, GEC, BOC; dir: Freemans plc 1977-89 (co sec 1971-89), Brixton Info Technol Centre, Direct Mail Servs Standards Bd 1983-; chm: Peckham Settlement, Cncl BASSAC 1983-85; memb Fulham Cncl (Cons ldr) 1959-62, CBI Cncl; dir Commercial Union Local Bd 1983-88; Business in the Community Cncl; dep chm S London Business Initiative 1989-, chm Mailing Preference Serv 1987-89; memb: European Cmmn's Advsy Ctee on Commerce and Distribution (rapporteur gen for consumer affrs) 1986-, Copyright Trib 1990-; tstee Freemans Tst 1979-, assoc memb Hockey Assoc; *Style—* Evelyn Cribb, Esq; The Squirrels, Fox Corner, Worplesdon, Guildford, Surrey GU3 3PP (☎ 0483 236278)

CRIBB, Graham Thame Stanley; OBE (1985); s of John Stanley Cribb (d 1970), of St Margarets, E Twickenham, and Florence Winifred Constance, *née* Thame (d 1969); *b* 7 Nov 1924; *Educ* Isleworth County GS, Downing Coll Cambridge (BA, MA) Imperial Coll of Sci and Technol (DIC), Princeton Univ NJ; *m* 29 July 1950, Stella Rosemary, da of Joseph Charles Templeman (d 1958), of Hounslow; 2 s (Christopher Joseph Stanley b 5 Jan 1956, Richard Graham Stanley b 26 June 1959); *Career* RE 1943-46, cmmnd 2 Lt 1944, Lt 1945, Capt 1945, serv NW Euro 1945, India, Malaysia and Singapore 1945-46; Br Gas plc: res chemist Fulham Res Lab N Thames Gas 1949, section ldr Chemical Engrg Gp 1955, tech offr Devpt and Planning Section Gas Cncl 1961, devpt engr Prodn and Supply Div 1966, dir London Res Station Br Gas Corpn 1975, ret 1988; hon sec Inst of Gas Engrs 1987- (pres 1985-86); corr sch govrs Goring C of E Primary Sch; memb: Goring and Streatley Probus, Guild of Servers Church of St Thomas of Canterbury Goring on Thames; Freeman City of London 1984, memb Worshipful Co of Engrs 1984; CEng, FIGasE 1969, FIChemE 1984, FRSA 1988, FCGI 1989; *Recreations* DIY, gardening, rowing, swimming, narrowboat owner; *Clubs* Leander, Twickenham Rowing, Wallingford Rowing; *Style—* Graham Cribb, Esq; 11 Holmlea Rd, Goring on Thames, Reading, Berks RG8 9EX (☎ 0491 872202)

CRIBBINS, Bernard; s of John Edward Cribbins (d 1964), and Ethel, *née* Clarkson (d 1989); *b* 29 Dec 1928; *Educ* St Annes Elementary Sch Oldham Lancs; *m* 27 Aug 1955, Gillian Isabella, da of Maj Donald Victor Charles McBarnet (ka 1943); *Career* Nat Serv 1947-49: Parachute Regt, serv 3 Bn (later 2/3 Bn) Palestine 1947-48, 16 Div HQ Germany; asst stage mangr student Oldham Repertory Theatre (aged 14); Repertory: Hornchurch, Liverpool, Manchester, Weston-Super-Mare; first West End appearance Comedy of Errors Arts Theatre 1956; London theatre incl: Harmony Close, Lady at the Wheel, New Cranks, And Another Thing, The Big Tickle, Hook Line and Sinker, Not Now Darling, There Goes The Bride, Run for Your Wife, Guys and Dolls, Anything Goes; own TV series: Cribbins, Cuffy, Langley Bottom; TV: title role in Dangerous Davies, Good Old Days, Shillingbury Tales, High and Dry, Fawlty Towers, Call My Bluff; voices for The Wombles and Buzby; films incl: The Railway Children 1971, Casino Royale, Two Way Stretch, Wrong Arm of the Law, She, Carry On Jack, Carry On Spying, The Water Babies; recorded hit records incl: Right Said Fred, Hole in the Ground, Gossip Calypso; memb Cncl Action Res for the Crippled Child, vice pres SPARKS; *Recreations* fishing, shooting, golf; *Style—* Bernard Cribbins, Esq; c/o James Sharkey Assoc Ltd, 15 Golden Square, London W1R 3AG

CRICHTON, Sir Andrew Maitland-Makgill; s of Lt-Col David Edward Maitland-Makgill-Crichton, Cameron Highlanders (d 1952), and Phyllis, *née* Cuthbert (d 1982); *b* 28 Dec 1910; *Educ* Wellington Coll; *m* 1948, Isabel, da of Andrew McGill, of Sydney, NSW, Australia, and widow of John Eric Bain; *Career* co dir; former vice chm Port of London Authority; kt 1963; *Style—* Sir Andrew Maitland-Makgill-Crichton; 55 Hans Place, Knightsbridge, London SW1 (☎ 071 584 1209)

CRICHTON, Charles Ainslie; s of John Douglas Crichton (d 1963), of Wallasey, and Hester Wingate *née* Ainslie (d 1959); *b* 6 Aug 1910; *Educ* Oundle, New Coll Oxford (BA); *m* 1, Dec 1936 (m dis), Pearl Allan; 2 s (David b 1938, Nicholas b 1943); m 2, Nadine Charlotte Haze; *Career* film writer and dir; co-directed Dead of Night 1947; directed: Hue and Cry 1947, Against the Wind, Another Shore, Dance Hall, The Lavender Hill Mob 1951, The Titfield Thunderbolt 1953, The Love Lottery, The Divided Heart, Law and Disorder, Floods of Fear, Battle of the Sexes 1959, Boy Who Stole a Million 1960, The Third Secret 1963, He Who Rides a Tiger 1965, A Fish Called Wanda 1987; numerous TV credits incl: Danger Man, The Avengers, Black Beauty, Space 1999, Smuggler, Adventurer; *Recreations* fishing, photography; *Style—* Charles Crichton, Esq; 1 Southwell Gardens, London (☎ 071 373 6546)

CRICHTON, Viscount; John Henry Michael Ninian Crichton; s and h of 6 Earl of Erne; *b* 19 June 1971; *Educ* Sunningdale Sch, Shiplake Coll, L'Institut de Touraine Tours France; *Recreations* theatre, arts, tennis, shooting, fishing; *Clubs* 151 Club, Lough Erne Yacht; *Style—* Viscount Crichton; Flat 4, 40 Harcourt Terrace, London SW10 (☎ 071 370 5969); Crom Castle, Newtown Butler, Co Fermanagh, Northern Ireland (☎ 036 573 208); Perkins & Partners, 1/2 Charlotte Mews, Tottenham Street, London W1P 1LN (☎ 071 636 3456, fax 071 631 1548)

CRICHTON, Lady (Margaret Vanderlip); JP; da of Col Livingston Watrous, of Washington, DC and Nantucket, Mass, USA; *m* 1944, Sir (John) Robertson (Dunn) Crichton (Judge of Crown Court and Judge of High Court Queen's Bench Div; d 1985); 2 s, 1 da; *Style—* Lady Crichton, JP; Bell House, 22 Albert Square, Bowdon, Altrincham, Cheshire WA14 2ND

CRICHTON, Maurice; s of Maurice Crichton (d 1957), of Glasgow, and Jenny Shirra, *née* Ferguson (d 1964); *b* 4 June 1928; *Educ* Cargilfield Sch, Sedbergh; *m* 30 April 1959, Diana Russell, da of John Russell Lang, CBE, of Tetbury, Glos; 3 s (Russell Lang b 1960, Maurice Peter b 1964, David Ferguson b 1968), 1 da (Caroline Anne b 1962); *Career* Nat Serv Royal tank Regt 1947-49; CA 1954; ptnr Wilson Stirling & Co Glasgow 1956, subsequently ptnr Touche Ross & Co, ret from practice 1986; dir: Woolwich Equitable Bldg Soc 1977-, Macphie of Glenbervie Ltd; vice chm Bd of Irvine Devpt Corp; Deacon Convener of Trades of Glasgow 1988-89; *Recreations* golf, shooting, music; *Clubs* Caledonian, Western (Glasgow); *Style—* Maurice Crichton, Esq; Hall of Caldwell, Uplawmoor, Glasgow G78 4BW (☎ 050585 248); The Marne, Grange Rd, Earlsferry, Leven, Fife (☎ 0333 330 222)

CRICHTON, Nicholas; s of Charles Ainslie Crichton, and Vera Pearl McCallum, *née* Harman-Mills; *b* 23 Oct 1943; *Educ* Haileybury, Queens Univ Belfast (LLB); *m* 29 March 1973, Ann Valerie, da of Col John Eliot Jackson, of Lopcombe Corner, nr Salisbury, Wilts; 2 s (Simon b 25 Feb 1975, Ian b 12 Jan 1977); *Career* admitted slr 1970; asst slr Currey & Co 1970-71 (articled 1968-70), ptnr Nicholls Christie & Crocker 1974-86 (asst slr 1972-74); met stipendiary magistrate 1987- (asst recorder 1991-); *Recreations* cricket, golf, watching rugby, gardening, birdwatching, walking; *Style—* Nicholas Crichton, Esq; c/o Thames Magistrates Court, 58 Bow Rd, London E3 4DJ

CRICHTON, Patrick Henry Douglas; TD (1946); s of Col Hon Sir George Arthur Charles Crichton, GCVO (d 1952 s of 4 Earl of Erne), of Queen's Acre, Windsor, Berks, and Lady Mary Augusta, *née* Dawson (d 1961 da of 2 Earl of Dartrey (extinct 1933)); *b* 16 Aug 1919; *Educ* Eton, Univ of Oxford; *m* 1 Oct 1948, Gillian Moyra, da of Rt Hon Sir Alexander George Montagu Cadogan OM, GCMG, KCB (d 1968); 2 s (Hugh b (twin) 1949, Desmond b 1953); 1 da (Jane b (twin) 1949); *Career* WWII 1939-46, served in Europe (despatches), Malaya, Indonesia; Gilmour & Co Ltd Brewers (Sheffield) 1946-51, ptnr Buckmaster & Moore (stockbrokers) 1951-60, dep chm Foreign and Colonial Investment Tst and other Tsts; chm Queen Elizabeth's Fndn for the Disabled; *Clubs* Boodle's, MCC; *Style—* Patrick Crichton, Esq, TD; West Field Cottage, Upton Grey, Basingstoke, Hants (☎ 0256 862 230); Exchange House, Primrose St, London EC2R 2NY (☎ 071 628 8000)

CRICHTON-STUART, Lady James; Anna Rose; da of late Maj Henry McClintock Bunbury Bramwell, 2 Baron Rathdonnell, sometime master Duhallow Hunt, of The White House, Mallow, Co Cork, and Philippa (yst da of Thomas Joseph Carroll-Leahy, JP, sometime master The Woodfort Harriers); *b* 30 May 1940; *Educ* Newhall Sch Chelmsford; *m* 1970, as his 2 w, Lord James Charles Crichton-Stuart (d 1982), 3 but yr surviving s of 5 Marquess of Bute; 3 s (William b 1971, Hugh b 1973, Alexander b 1982); *Style—* The Lady James Crichton-Stuart; Upton Grey House, Upton Grey, Basingstoke, Hants RG25 2RE

CRICHTON-STUART, Lord Anthony; 2 s of 6 Marquess of Bute, JP; *b* 14 May 1961; *Educ* Ampleforth, Univ of Durham; *m* 8 Sept 1990, Alison J, yr da of Keith Bruce, of Highgate, London; *Career* art expert; Old Master Paintings Dept Christie's; *Style—* The Lord Anthony Crichton-Stuart; 15 Fabian Road, London SW6

CRICHTON-STUART, Lady David; Helen; da of William Kerr McColl; *m* 1972, Lord David Ogden Crichton-Stuart (d 1977), s of 5 Marquess of Bute; 1 s, 1 da; *Style—* The Lady David Crichton-Stuart; Kames Court, Cronkbourne, Braddan, Isle of Man

CRICHTON-STUART, Lady Janet Egidia; *née* Montgomerie; 2 da of late 16 Earl of Eglinton and Winton by 1 w, Lady Beatrice Dalrymple, da of 11 Earl of Stair; *b* 3 May 1911; *m* 18 April 1934, Capt Lord Robert Crichton-Stuart, Scots Gds (d 1976), s of 4 Marquess of Bute; 2 s; *Style—* The Lady Janet Crichton-Stuart; Wards Cottage, Gartocharn, Dunbarton (☎ 038 983 461)

CRICK, Prof Bernard Rowland; s of Harry Edgar Crick (d 1968), of Natal, SA, and Florence Clara, *née* Cook (d 1987); *b* 16 Dec 1929; *Educ* Whitgift Sch, UCL (BSc), LSE (PhD), Harvard Univ; *m* 18 Sept 1953 (m dis 1980), Joyce Pumpfrey Morgan; 2 s (Oliver, Tom); *Career* lectr LSE 1957-59; prof of politics: Univ of Sheffield 1965-71, Birkbeck Coll London 1971-84; hon fell Univ of Edinburgh 1984-; jt ed The Political Quarterly 1966-80, winner Yorks Post Book of the Year Award 1980; memb Cncl of the Hansard Soc 1962-, hon pres of Politics Assoc 1970-76; chm: The Political Quarterly Publishing Co 1980, Orwell Memorial Tst 1981; Hon DSSC Queen's Univ Belfast 1987, Hon Dr of Arts Univ of Sheffield 1990, Hon Dr of Letters E London Poly 1990; *Books* The American Science of Politics (1958), In Defence of Politics (1962), The Reform of Parliament (1964), Crime, Rape and Gin (1975), George Orwell, A Life (1980), Socialism (1987), Essays on Politics and Literature (1989), Political Thoughts and Polemics (1990); *Recreations* polemicising, book and theatre reviewing, hill walking, bee-keeping; *Clubs* Savile, Scottish Arts, Univ of Edinburgh; *Style—* Prof Bernard Crick; 8 Bellevue Terrace, Edinburgh EH7 4DT (☎ 034 557 2517)

CRICK, Charles Anthony; s of Maurice Arthur Crick, TD (d 1979), of 42 Westwood Park Road, Peterborough, and Margaret Matilda, *née* Edney; *b* 7 May 1949; *Educ* Oundle Sch, UCL (LLB); *Career* admitted slr 1974, articled clerk and asst slr Allen and Overy 1972-80, asst slr Middleton Potts and Co 1980-81, ptnr D J Freeman and Co 1981-; Freeman City of London Slrs Co 1986; memb Law Soc; *Recreations* golf, music, painting; *Clubs* Hunstanton GC; *Style—* Charles Crick, Esq; 31 Ulundi Rd, London SE3 7UQ

CRICK, Richard William; s of Cyril Albert Edden Crick (d 1988), of Jhansi, Rectory Rd, Easton-in-Gordano, Avon, and Blanche Helen, *née* Prewett; *b* 7 June 1946; *Educ* Clifton Coll, Brasenose Coll Oxford (MA); *m* 17 July 1971 (sep), Judith Margaret, da of Huw Jackson (d 1982), of Gateshead; 1 s (James b 1974), 1 da (Sally b 1977); *Career* CA Deloitte Haskins and Sells 1967-71; banker: Hill Samuel and Co Ltd 1972-87 (dir 1981-87), md Hill Samuel Merchant Bank (SA) Ltd 1981-85, dir Barclays de Zoete Wedd Ltd 1988-; *Recreations* golf, skiing, sailing, travel, wine; *Clubs* St Enodoc Golf; *Style—* Richard W Crick, Esq; 2 Craven Hill Mews, London W2 (☎ 071 402 8096); The Granary, Alton Priors, nr Marlborough, Wiltshire (☎ 0672 851663); Barclays de Zoete Wedd Ltd, Ebbgate House, 2 Swan Lane, London EC4 (☎ 071 623 2323, fax 071 956 2407)

CRICK, Ronald Pitts; s of Owen John Pitts Crick (d 1972), of Minehead, Somerset, and Margaret, *née* Daw (d 1970); *b* 5 Feb 1917; *Educ* Latymer Upper Sch London, King's Coll Hosp Med Sch; *m* 22 March 1941, Jocelyn Mary Grenfell, da of Leonard Adolph Charles Robins (d 1968), of Hendon; 4 s (Martin b 1942, Jonathan b 1948, Adrian b 1950, Humphrey b 1957), 1 da (Gillian b 1944); *Career* surgn South America route MN 1939-40, surgn Lt RNVR Fleet Air Arm Atlantic, Indian Ocean, Pacific theatres 1940-46; Kings Coll Hosp: ophthalmic registrar 1946-50, conslt ophthalmic surgn 1950-82, hon conslt ophthalmic surgn 1982-; Royal Eye Hosp: ophthalmic registrar 1946-50, conslt surgn 1950-69; conslt ophthalmic surgn Belgrave Hosp for Children 1950-66, examiner RCS 1961-68; King's Coll Med Sch: teacher of ophthalmology 1960-82, lectr emeritus in ophthalmology 1982-; memb Ophthalmic Speciality Ctee SE Thames Regnl Hosp Bd 1970-82; chm: Ophthalmic Trg Ctee SE Thames RHA 1973-82, Int Glaucoma Assoc 1974-; Duke-Elder Glaucoma Award American Soc of Contemporary Ophthalmology 1985; MRCS, LRCP 1939, memb Oxford Ophthalmology Congress 1943, DOMS (RCS) 1946, FRCS 1950, FRSM 1950, charter memb Int Congress American Soc Contemporary Ophthalmology 19 FCOpth 1988; *Books* contributed chapter: The Computerised Monitoring of Glaucoma in Glaucoma-Contemporary International Concepts (J Bellows, 1979), The Diagnosis of Chronic Simple Glaucoma in Glaucoma (J Cairns, 1985), All About Glaucoma (1981), A Textbook of Clinical Ophthalmology (1987); *Recreations* motoring, sailing, swimming; *Clubs* RAC, Royal Motor Yacht; *Style—* Ronald Pitts Crick, Esq; Sandbanks House, Panorama Rd, Sandbanks, Poole, Dorset, BH13 7RD (☎ 0202 707 560); Kings Coll Hosp, Denmark Hill, London, SE5 9RS (☎ 071 274 6222)

CRICKHOWELL, Baron (Life Peer UK 1987), of Pont Esgob in the Black Mountains and Co of Powys; (Roger) Nicholas Edwards; PC (1979); s of (Herbert Cecil) Ralph Edwards, CBE, FSA (d 1977), and Marjorie Ingham Brooke; *b* 25 Feb 1934; *Educ* Westminster, Trinity Coll Cambridge (BA, MA); *m* 1963, Ankaret, da of William James Healing, of Kinsham House, nr Tewkesbury, Glos; 1 s (Hon Rupert Timothy Guy b 1954), 2 da (Hon Sophie Elizabeth Ankaret b 1966, Hon Olivia Caroline b 1970); *Career* 2 Lt Royal Welch Fusiliers 1952-54; employed at Lloyd's by Wm Brandt's 1957-76 (memb Lloyd's 1968-), chief exec Insur Gp; dir: Wm Brandt's Ltd 1974-76, R W Sturge (Holdings) Ltd 1970-76, PA International and Sturge Underwriting Agency Ltd 1977-79, Globtik Tankers Ltd 1976-79, Ryan International plc and subsids 1987-89, Association of British Ports Holdings plc 1987, HTV Group plc 1987-; dep chm Anglesey Mining plc 1988-; MP (Cons) for Pembroke 1970-87 (ret), memb Shadow Cabinet and Cons Front Bench spokesman on Welsh Affairs 1974-79, sec of State of Wales 1979-87; chm: Nat Rivers Authority Advsy Ctee 1988-89, Nat Rivers Authority 1989-; memb Ctee The Automobile Assoc; pres: Univ of Wales Coll of Cardiff 1988-, Contemporary Art Soc for Wales 1988-, South East Wales Arts Assoc 1987-; memb Cncl Welsh Nat Opera; *Recreations* fishing, gardening, collecting drawings & watercolours; *Clubs* Carlton, Cardiff and County; *Style*— The Rt Hon Lord Crickhowell, PC; Pont Esgob Mill, Forest Coal Pit, nr Abergavenny, Gwent N57 7LS; 4 Henning St, London SW11 3DR

CRICKMAY, Anthony John Edward; *b* 20 May 1937; *Educ* Belmont Westcott Surrey; *Career* asst to Loite Meitner Graf (portrait photographer) 1955-58, freelance photographer 1958-; works incl: The Stone Flower (Kirov Ballet) 1961, Cavalteria Rusticana (Royal Opera House) 1961; photographs of: HM Queen Elizabeth The Queen Mother, Princess Margaret Countess of Snowdon, Princess Michael of Kent, Prince Michael of Kent, Princess Alexandra; exhibition Dance Images V & A Theatre Museum Jan-Sept 1991; *Books* photographs for: Principles of Classical Dance (1979), Lynn Seymour (1980), Dancers (1982), Massage (1987), Portrait of The Royal Ballet (1988); *Recreations* multifarious; *Style*— Anthony Crickmay, Esq; 74 Farm Lane, London SW6 1QA (☎ 071 736 0296)

CRICKMAY, John Rackstrow; s of John Edward Crickmay (d 1931), of Weybridge, and Constance May, *née* Bowyer (d 1968); *b* 16 May 1914; *Educ* Brighton Coll; *m* 31 Oct 1939, Peggy Margaret Hilda, *née* Rainer; 1 s (Michael b 1947); *Career* Artists Rifles 1936, Royal Regt of Artillery 1939-46, served in Far East (POW 1942-45); Legal and Gen Assur Soc: surveyor 1936-46, chief estates surveyor 1946-74, conslt to property interests 1974-; pres: Br Chapter Real Estate Property Fedn 1966, Chartered Auctioneers and Estate Agents Inst 1968; hon treas RICS 1980-85 (memb cncl 1972-85), dir Ecclesiastical Insur Off 1980-84, chm Percy Bilton plc 1984-89 (dir 1980-89); govr Royal Star & Garter Richmond 1975-, almoner Christ's Hosp 1977 (dep chm 1984); Freeman City of London 1956, Master Worshipful Co of Ironmongers 1976 (Yeoman 1956), hon fell Coll of Estate Mgmnt 1988; FRICS; Medal of Int Real Estate Fedn 1974; *Recreations* cricket, golf; *Clubs* Oriental, MCC, W Sussex GC; *Style*— John Crickmay, Esq; Old Walls, Rectory Lane, Philborough, W Sussex RH20 2AF (☎ 079 82 2336)

CRIGHTON, Prof David George; s of George Wolfe Johnston Crighton (d 1976), and Violet Grace, *née* Garrison; *b* 15 Nov 1942; *Educ* Watford Boys GS, St John's Coll Cambridge (BA, MA), Imperial Coll London (PhD); *m* 1, 2 March 1969 (m dis 1986), Mary Christine, da of Stanley James West, of Tamworth; 1 s (Benjamin b 23 April 1970), 1 da (Beth b 3 Oct 1971); m 2, 6 Sept 1986, Johanna Veronica, *née* Hol; *Career* prof of applied mathematics Univ of Leeds 1974-85; Univ of Cambridge: prof of applied mathematics 1986-, professorial fell St John's Coll 1986-; author of various scientific papers in jls and conf proceedings on fluid mechanics, acoustics, wave theory and applied mathematics; chm: Jt Mathematical Cncl of UK, Euro Mechanics Cncl; FRAeS 1982, FIMA 1986, FIOA 1988; *Recreations* music, opera; *Style*— Prof David G Crighton; The Laurels, 58 Girton Rd, Cambridge CB3 0LN (☎ 0223 277 100); Univ of Cambridge, DAMTP, Silver St, Cambridge CB3 9EW (☎ 0223 337 860, fax 0223 337 918, telex 81240 G)

CRIGMAN, David Ian; QC (1989); s of Jack Crigman (d 1987), and Sylvia, *née* Rich; *b* 16 Aug 1945; *Educ* King Edward's Sch Birmingham, Univ of Leeds (LLB); *m* 20 Aug 1980, Judith Ann, da of Mark Penny; 1 s (Sam Mark b 7 April 1982); *Career* called to the Bar Gray's Inn 1969, rec Crown Court 1985; *Recreations* writing, tennis, skiing; *Style*— David Crigman, Esq, QC; 1 Fountain Court, Steelhouse Lane, Birmingham B4 6DR (☎ 021 236 5721, fax 021 236 3639)

CRILL, Sir Peter Leslie; CBE (1980); s of Sydney George Crill (d 1959), of Jersey, Connetable of St Clement 1916-58, and Olive, *née* Le Gros (d 1978); family were boatbuilders who came to Jersey from Mannheim in 1785; *b* 1 Feb 1925; *Educ* Victoria Coll Jersey, Exeter Coll Oxford (MA); *m* 1953, Abigail Florence Rosaline (MB), da of Albert Ernest Dodd, JP (d 1949), of Dromara, NI; 3 da (Joanna b 1954, Anthea b 1956, Helena b 1958); *Career* barr Middle Temple 1949, Jersey Bar 1949, States of Jersey Dep for St Clement 1951-58, States of Jersey Senator 1960-62, slr gen Jersey 1962-69, attorney gen Jersey 1969-75, dep bailiff 1975-86, bailiff 1986-; kt 1987; *Recreations* riding, sailing; *Clubs* United Oxford and Cambridge, Royal Yacht Sqdn; *Style*— Sir Peter Crill, CBE; Beechfield House, Trinity, Jersey; Bailiff's Chambers, Royal Court House, Jersey (0534 77111)

CRIPP, Robin Douglas; s of Reginald Henry John Cripp (d 1988), of 10 Leonards Rd, Frimley, Surrey, and Edith May, *née* Tilby; *b* 8 Aug 1944; *Educ* Wandsworth Comp Sch; *m* 1 June 1968, Cheryl Francis, da of Alfred Lawrence Du Preez, of Southampton; 1 s (Peter Howard b 25 Aug 1969), 1 da (Katie Helen b 25 June 1975); *Career* Redfearn and Redfearn Estate Agents (office boy to mangr) 1960-71, conslt and dir various property cos 1972-74, negotiator with Willmotts of London 1974-79, formed Barnard Marcus & Co (estate agents) 1979; *Recreations* golf, travel; *Clubs* Coombe Hill Golf, RAC, Annabels, The Clermont; *Style*— Robin Cripp, Esq; Commercial Hse, 64-66 Glenthorne Rd, London W6 0LR (☎ 081 741 8088, car 0860 223 793, fax 081 741 2188, telex 269595 BARMAR G)

CRIPPIN, Harry Trevor; s of Harry Crippin and Mary Elizabeth, *née* Settle; *b* 14 May 1929; *Educ* Leigh GS Lancashire; *m* 19 Sept 1959, Hilda Green, JP; 1 s (Paul b 1966), 1 da (Hilary b 1960); *Career* LAC RAF 1947-49, asst town clerk Manchester 1970-74, dep dir admin Manchester 1974, city sec Cardiff City Cncl 1974-79, chief exec and town clerk Cardiff City Cncl 1979-88; OStJ; FCIS, FBIM, DMA; *Style*— Harry Crippin, Esq; 37 Ely Rd, Llandaff, Cardiff CF5 2JF (☎ 0222 564103)

CRIPPS, (Matthew) Anthony Leonard; CBE (1971), DSO (1943), TD (1947), QC (1958); s of Maj Hon Leonard Harrison Cripps, CBE (d 1959, 3 s of 1 Baron Parmoor), and Miriam Barbara, *née* Joyce (d 1960); hp of cousin, 4 Baron Parmoor; *b* 30 Dec 1913; *Educ* Eton, ChCh Oxford (MA); *m* 21 June 1941, (Dorothea) Margaret, da of George Johnson-Scott (d 1964), of Hill House, Ashby-de-la-Zouch; 3 s (Seddon b 1942, Jeremy b 1943, James b 1956); *Career* 2 Lt to Lt-Col Royal Leics Regt TA 1933-45; called to the Bar Middle Temple 1938 (bencher 1965, dep treas 1982, treas 1983), Inner Temple 1961, Hong Kong 1974, Singapore 1987; rec: Nottingham 1961-71, Crown Ct 1972-77; judge Ct of Arches 1969-80, dep sr judge Br Sovereign Bases Area Cyprus 1978-90; memb: Senate Four Inns of Ct 1967-71 and 1982-83, Bar Cncl 1967-69 and 1970-74; chm: Disciplinary Ctee Milk Mktg Bd 1956-90, IOM Agric Mktg Cmmn 1961-62, Home Sec's Advsy Ctee on Serv Candidates 1966-, Nat Panel Approved Coal Merchants Scheme 1972-90, Legal Advsy Ctee RSPCA 1977-90; memb Agric Wages Bd 1964-73; memb Miny of Agric Ctees of Inquiry: foot and mouth disease 1968-69, export of live animals for slaughter 1973-74; chm: Reigate Cons Assoc 1961-64, Res Ctee Soc of Cons Lawyers 1963-67, Cons Pty Res Ctee of Inquiry into discrimination against women in law and admin 1968-69; memb Exec Ctee Nat Union of Cons Assocs 1964-72, cmmr local govt election petitions 1978-82; pres Coal Trade Benevolent Assoc 1983; Worshipful Co of Fuellers': Jr Warden 1988, Sr Warden 1989, Master 1990-91; *Books* Agriculture Act (1947), Agricultural Holdings Act (1948), Cripps on Compensation (9 edn); *Recreations* travel, forestry, family life; *Clubs* Brooks's, Lansdowne, Phyllis Court; *Style*— Anthony Cripps, Esq, CBE, DSO, TD, QC; Woodhurst, McCrae's Walk, Wargrave, Berks RG10 8LN (☎ 073440 3449); chambers: 1 Harcourt Buildings, Temple, London EC4Y 9DA (☎ 071 353 9421/9151, fax 071 353 4170, telex 8956718 CRIPPS G)

CRIPPS, Brian Edward; s of Henry George Cripps (d 1961), and Winifred Ena, *née* Perkins; *b* 19 Aug 1932; *Educ* Belmont Newbury; *m* 1, 3 June 1961 (m dis 1969), Jean Patricia Harvey; 1 s (Anthony b 1966), 2 da (Victoria b 1962, Rebecca b 1965); m 2, 23 May 1969, Caroline Ann Hardman, da of Sir Richard Ian Samuel Bayliss, KCVO, of London SW7; 1 step s (Peter b 1965), 1 da (Charlotte b 1970); *Career* CA; ptnr Cripps Weston; FCA; *Recreations* golf, foreign travel; *Clubs* Roehampton; *Style*— Brian Cripps, Esq; 2 Burdenshott Ave, Richmond, Surrey TW10 5ED; 206 Upper Richmond Rd, West London SW14 8AH

CRIPPS, Edward James Spencer; s of Sir (Cyril) Humphrey Cripps, DL, *qv*, and Lady Dorothea Casson Cripps, *née* Cook; *b* 20 Oct 1951; *Educ* Oundle, St John's Coll Cambridge; *m* 21 June 1975, Patricia Ellen, da of Cyril Eric Francis; *Career* memb Cncl of Mgmnt Cripps Fndn 1978; dir: Pianoforte Supples Ltd 1978-, Velcro Industries NV 1986-; govr Northampton HS for Girls 1985-, tstee Northampton HS for Girls and Peterborough Cathedral Tsts 1988-; *Recreations* golf, snooker, walking; *Style*— Edward Cripps, Esq; Oakdene Cottage, 23 Water Lane, Sherington, Newport Pagnell, Bucks MK16 9NP (☎ 0908 611108); Simplex Works, Roade, Northampton NN7 2LG (☎ 0604 862441, fax 0604 862919)

CRIPPS, Sir (Cyril) Humphrey; DL (Northants 1985); s of Sir Cyril Thomas Cripps, MBE (d 1979), and Amy Elizabeth, *née* Humphrey (d 1984); *b* 2 Oct 1915; *Educ* Northampton GS, St John's Coll Cambridge (MA); *m* 1942, Dorothea Casson, da of Reginald Percy Cook (d 1968); 3 s (Robert, John (d 1989), Edward), 1 da (Eleanor); *Career* md Pianoforte Supplies Ltd 1960- (chm 1979-); chm: Air BVI 1971-86, Velcro Indust NV 1973-, Cripps Fndn 1979-; memb: Northants CC 1963-74 (ldr Independents), New CC 1973-81; bd memb Northampton Devpt Corp 1968-85, life memb of ct Nottingham Univ 1953-, fndn govr Bilton Grange Prep Sch 1957-80; govr: Northampton GS 1963-74, Northampton Sch for Boys 1977-81 (vice chm fndn tst 1970-81 and 1986-88, chm 1988-), Northampton HS for Girls 1966- (chm 1972-84); tstee: Cripps Postgrad Med Centre at Northampton Gen Hosp 1969-, Univ of Nottingham Devpt Tst 1990-; memb Tsts for Fabric of Peterborough Cathedral 1975-, pres Johnian Soc 1966; hon fell: Cripps Hall Univ of Nottingham 1959, St John's Coll Cambridge 1966, Magdalene Coll Cambridge 1971, Selwyn Coll Cambridge 1971, Queens' Coll Cambridge 1979; Hon DSc Nottingham 1975, Hon LLD Cantab 1976; Liveryman: Worshipful Co of Wheelwrights 1957 (memb ct 1970, Master 1982), Worshipful Co of Tallow Chandlers 1983; Freeman City of London 1957, High Sheriff Northamptonshire 1985-86; FCS, FRIC, CChem, FRSC; kt 1989; *Recreations* travel, photography, natural history (entomology-rhopalocera), philately; *Style*— Sir Humphrey Cripps, DL; Bull's Head Farm, Eakley Lanes, Stoke Goldington, Newport Pagnell, Bucks MK16 8LP (☎ 0908 55223); Simplex Works, Roade, Northampton NN7 2LG (☎ 0604 862441)

CRIPPS, Sir John Stafford; CBE (1968); s of Rt Hon Sir Stafford Cripps, CH, FRS, QC, sometime Chllr Exchequer (himself yst s of 1 Baron Parmoor), and Dame Isobel Cripps, GBE, *née* Swithinbank; *b* 10 May 1912; *Educ* Winchester, Balliol Coll Oxford; *m* 1, 29 Dec 1936 (m dis 1971), Ursula, da of Arthur Cedric Davy, of Whirlow Court, Sheffield; 4 s, 2 da; m 2, 1971, Ann Elizabeth, da of Edwin G K Farwell, of Swanage; *Career* ed The Countryman 1947-71; chm: RDCs Assoc 1967-70 (memb Witney RDC 1946-74), Countryside Cmmn 1970-77, Rural Ctee Nat Cncl Soc Serv; memb: Exec Ctee CPRE 1963-69, South East Economic Planning Cncl 1966-73, Nature Conservancy 1970-73, Defence Lands Ctee 1971-73, Water Space Amenity Cmmn 1977-80, Devpt Cmmn 1978-82; pres Camping and Caravanning Club of GB and Ireland 1981-91; kt 1978; *Recreations* walking, gardening, photography; *Clubs* Farmers'; *Style*— Sir John Cripps, CBE; Fox House, Filkins, Lechlade, Glos GL7 3JQ (☎ 036 786 209)

CRIPPS, Michael Frederick; s of Maj Charles Philip Cripps, TD, of Sussex, and Betty Christine, *née* Flinn; *b* 22 Oct 1947; *Educ* Felsted, Medway Coll (HNC); *m* 23 April 1982, Carolyn Louise, da of Elie Gabriel Farah; 2 s (Nicholas Frederick b 1985, Christopher Philip b 1988), 1 step s (Alexander Timothy James b 1974); *Career* dist mangr Johnson Gp 1969-72, branch mangr Drake Conslts 1972-73; Cripps Sears & Ptnrs Ltd (formerly Cripps Sears & Assocs): ptnr 1973-78, chm and md 1982-; memb Ctee Japan Assoc; MIPM, FInstD 1985; *Recreations* sport generally - active rugby football player & supporter, people, travel, contemporary & classical live music; *Clubs* City of London, MCC; *Style*— Michael Cripps, Esq; Cripps, Sears & Partners, International Buildings, 71 Kingsway, London, WC2B 6ST (☎ 071 404 5701, fax 01 242 0515, 081 893 155)

CRIPPS, Philip Charles; s of Alan Derek Cripps (d 1958), and Winifred Mary Cripps (d 1958); *b* 29 Dec 1945; *Educ* Royal Pinner Sch Harrow, Aston Univ (BA); *m* 24 June 1967, Jayne, da of Stanley Roney; 2 da (Michelle b 21 Jan 1971, Cara b 7 Jan 1975); *Career* md Thameside Ltd Int Mgmnt Conslts 1977-; non-exec dir various companies 1979-; pop single The Joker charted 1983; lectr UK, USA, Europe; *Recreations* squash, water skiing; *Clubs* Lingfield Health, Maidenhead, Westhorpe Water Ski Marlow; *Style*— Philip C Cripps, Esq; Thameside Ltd, International Management Consultants, Thameside House, Lower Rd, Chinnor, Oxon (☎ 0844 53678, car 0836 581744)

CRIPWELL, Peter; s of Felix John Cripwell, and Barbara Bamford, *née* Mayall; *b* 3 Aug 1932; *Educ* The Old Hall Shropshire, Repton, RWA Sch of Architecture Bristol; *m* Elizabeth Marcia, da of Marcus Reginald Cholmondeley Overton (d 1940); 4 s (Andrew b 1962, Charles b 1963, Angus b 1965, Crispin b 1966), 1 da (Charlotte b 1970); *Career* chartered architect in private practice in Hereford 1961-; *Recreations* watercolour painting, walking, sailing, skiing, shooting; *Style*— Peter Cripwell, Esq; Lower Upcott, Almeley, Herefordshire HR3 6LA; 3 St Nicholas Street, Hereford, HR4 0BG (☎ 0432 266578)

CRISFORD, John Northcote; s of George Northcote Crisford, CBE, and Effie Mary, *née* Saul; *b* 27 Sept 1915; *Educ* Brighton Coll; *m* 28 June 1947, Prunella Beatrice Evelyn, da of John Ridout-Evans (d 1971); 1 s (Timothy b 1951), 2 da (Mary b 1949, Felicity b 1959); *Career* WWII served RASC, 1939-45 Lancs Fusiliers, Intelligence Corps (India), Capt; advertising; Unilever Ltd, Lintas Ltd 1932-39; dep chief regnl offr Central Office of Info Cambridge 1947-48, UK info offr Sydney 1949-51, dep publicity mangr The Metal Box Co Ltd 1957-62, assoc dir Planned PR (subsidiary of Young and Rubicam Ltd) 1963-66; head of PR Br Tport Docks Bd 1966-77; chm Winsford Parish Cncl 1980-87, LEA govr Winsford Sch 1989-; ed Four Parishes magazine 1989-, established Nether Halse Books 1981 (publishing own poetry, local guide and history books); memb: Cncl Inst of PR 1959-61, 1963-65 and 1966-72 (pres 1970-71), IPR Examinations Bd 1962-67; govr of Communication, Advertising and Mkting Educn Fndn 1969-72 (CAM Dip PR), memb PR Inst of Aust 1950-53, visiting lectr Br Tport Docks Bd Staff Coll 1968-77, lectrs on poetry to clubs, schools, etc 1984 to date; FRSA 1954, FIPR 1969 (pres 1970-71); *Publications* incl: Public Relations Advances (1973), Management Guide to Corporate Identity (contrib, 1971), The Role of PR in Management (contrib, 1972); A Poet's Gift (1981), Were I a Giant (1983), Lot 201

(1984), A Gloria for Special Occasions (1988), William Dicker - a great Exmoor Schoolmaster (1991); *Recreations* writing, reading, walking, amateur dramatics; *Style—* John Crisford, Esq; Nether Halse, Winsford, Minehead, Somerset TA24 7JE (☎ 064 385 314); Nether Halse Books, Winsford, Minehead, Somerset TA24 7JE (☎ 064 385 314)

CRISP, Dr Adrian James; s of Bertram William Crisp, of Harrow Weald, Middx, and Mary Louise, *née* Butland; *b* 21 Nov 1948; *Educ* Univ Coll Sch London, Magdalene Coll Camb (MA, MB BChir, MD, MRCP), UCH London; *m* 6 July 1974, Lesley Roberta, da of Archibald Shaw (d 1981), of Harrow, Middx; 1 s (Alasdair James Gavin b 1977, d 1990), 1 da (Alison Victoria b 1979); *Career* house offr and sr house offr UCH and Northwick Park Hosp Harrow 1974-78, med registrar UCH 1978-80, sr registrar Guy's Hosp 1980-85, res fell Massachusetts Gen Hosp and Harvard Univ 1982-83, conslt rheumatologist Newmarket Gen Hosp 1985-; Addenbrookes Hosp Cambridge: conslt rheumatologist 1985-, dir Bone Density Unit 1989-, postgrad clinical tutor 1990-; memb Editorial Bd Rheumatology Review; memb: Br Soc for Rheumatology, Bone and Tooth Soc; contrib to Oxford Textbook of Diabetes Mellitus; DRCOG 1977; *Recreations* military history, cricket, pre 1960 British films; *Style—* Dr Adrian Crisp; Arran House, 19 Cambridge Rd, Little Abington, Cambridgeshire CB1 6BL (☎ 0223 891141); Addenbrooke's Hospital, Cambridge CB2 2QQ (☎ 0223 216254)

CRISP, Bernard David James; s of Bertie Bela Crisp (d 1968); *b* 11 June 1926; *Educ* Whitgift, Univ of Liverpool; *m* 1947, Lorna Jean, da of Sydney James Clarke (d 1971); 1 s, 1 da; *Career* Lt RNVR; ret md Cunard Travel; dir: Cunard Line, Cunard Hotels; chm SSAFA (Central London); OStJ; FCIM; *Recreations* writing, gardening; *Style—* Bernard Crisp, Esq; 2 Norfolk Ave, Sanderstead, Surrey

CRISP, John Charles; s and h of Sir (John) Peter Crisp, 4 Bt; *b* 10 Dec 1955; *Style—* John Crisp Esq

CRISP, John William Maxwell; s of John Francis Crisp (d 1949), of Berkshire, and Lady Dora Scott , *née* Fox; *b* 10 Nov 1929; *Educ* Eton; *m* 1956, Elizabeth Frances Mary, da of Capt H B Barclay, OBE, MC, of Kenya; 2 s (Hugh b 1958, William b 1960); *Career* 2 Lt Kings Royal Rifle Corps 1949-50, Capt (TA) Queen's Westminster Rifles; chm: London Section Inst of Brewing 1964-66, Allied Brewing Trades Assoc 1970, Maltsters Assoc of GB 1973-74, Crisp Malting Ltd 1962-, Anglia Maltings Holdings Ltd 1982-; hon sec Hurlingham Polo Assoc; fell Inst of Brewing, FRSA; *Recreations* shooting, sailing, walking, tennis; *Clubs* Lansdowne, Green Jackets; *Style—* John Crisp, Esq; Winterlake, Kirtlington, Oxford OX5 3HG (☎ 0869 50384)

CRISP, (Edmund) Nigel Ramsay; s of Edmund Theodore Crisp, of Leamington Spa, and Dorothy Shephard, *née* Ramsay; *b* 14 Jan 1952; *Educ* Uppingham, St Johns Coll Cambridge (MA); *m* 1 May 1976, Siân Elaine, da of David Edward Jenkins; 1 s (Edmund Alastair David b 4 Sept 1984), 1 da (Charlotte Madeleine Duffryn b 4 March 1982); *Career* dep community devpt offr Halewood Community Cncl 1973-76, prodn mangr Trebor Ltd 1977-81, dir Cambridgeshire Community Cncl 1981-86; gen mangr: Mental Handicap Unit East Berks Health Authy 1986-88, Wexham Park Hosp 1988-90, Heatherwood and Wexham Park Hosps Unit East Berkshire Health Authy 1990-; licentiate Inst of Health Serv Mgmnt; *Recreations* countryside, travel, reading; *Style—* Nigel Crisp, Esq; Heatherwood and Wexham Park Hospitals, Wexham Park Hospital, Wexham, Slough, Berkshire SL2 4HL (☎ 0753 34567)

CRISP, Sir (John) Peter; 4 Bt (UK 1913) of Bungay, Suffolk; s of Sir John Wilson Crisp, 3 Bt (d 1950), and Marjorie, *née* Shriver (d 1977); *b* 19 May 1925; *Educ* Westminster; *m* 5 June 1954, Judith Mary, yst da of Herbert Edward Gillett (d 1954), of Marlborough, Wilts, and niece of Sir Harold Gillett, Bt; 3 s, 1 da; *Heir* s, John Crisp; *Career* slr (ret) Ashurst Morris Crisp and Co; *Style—* Sir Peter Crisp, Bt; Crabtree Cottage, Drungewick Lane, Loxwood, W Sussex (☎ 752374)

CRISP, Major (John) Simon; s of Major R J S Crisp (d 1966), of Kirby Cane Hall, Bungay, Suffolk, and Barbara Alexandra, *née* Gooch (d 1986); *b* 19 Jan 1937; *Educ* Eton, RMA Sandhurst; *m* 7 Nov 1975, Christine, da of Count Freidrich-Franz Grote (d 1942), of Schloss Varchentin, Mecklenburg, Germany; 1 s (Edward b 12 Aug 1976); *Career* cmmnd RHG (The Blues) 1956, ret 1976; memb: St John Ambulance (Norfolk), Diocesan Synod; jt master Waveney Harriers 1978-81; Order of Storr (N Class) Afghanistan 1971; *Recreations* hunting, shooting, racing; *Clubs* Whites, Pratts; *Style—* Maj Simon Crisp; Kirby Cane Hall, Bungay, Suffolk (☎ 050 845 232)

CRISPE, Robert Nicholas; s of Leslie Herbert Crispe (d 1972), and Marion Horner, *née* Redwood (d 1984); *b* 17 Oct 1931; *Educ* Uppingham, Worcester Coll Oxford (MA); *m* 18 April 1964 (m dis 1973), Margaret Gillian Duffield; 1 s (James b 1968), 1 da (Louisa b 1966); m 2, 18 June 1977, Mrs Diana Betty Boyle, da of Capt Aldridge (Bill) Evelegh, OBE, RN (d 1973); *Career* Nat Serv; RA (HAA) 1950-55, 1 Regt HAC (RHA) 1955-64; md Butler and Crispe Ltd 1967-69 (co sec 1959-69), chief accountant Multitone Electric Co Ltd 1969-71; co sec: Ventas Distribution Ltd 1971-73, Curtis Brown Ltd 1973-75; fin dir Glass's Guide Service Ltd 1987- (co sec 1975-); memb Co of Pikemen and Musketeers HAC 1972-; FCA 1959; *Recreations* choral singing, gardening, travel, maps; *Clubs* HAC; *Style—* Robert Crispe, Esq; Hook Farm House, Hook, Basingstoke, Hants RG27 9EQ (☎ 0256 762471); Glass's Guide Service Ltd, Elgin House, St Georges Ave, Weybridge, Surrey KTB 0BX (☎ 0932 853211, fax 0932 849299, telex 8955347)

CRISPIN, Nicholas Geoffrey; JP; s of Geoffrey Hollis Crispin, QC (d 1976), of Chipperfield, Herts, and Winifred, *née* Baldwin; *b* 20 Feb 1944; *Educ* Shrewsbury, Pembroke Coll Oxford; *Career* broker at Lloyd's 1966-69, schoolmaster in Uganda, Ascension Island and UK 1970-; memb Lloyd's 1982-; Freeman City of London, Liveryman Co of Fan Makers (1968); *Recreations* walking, African affairs; *Style—* Nicholas Crispin, Esq, JP; 36 Little Gaddesden, Berkhamsted, Herts; Longdean School, Hemel Hempstead, Herts

CRITCHELL, Martin Thomas; s of Lionel James Critchell (d 1971), and Irene Florence, *née* Thomas; *b* 24 Sept 1942; *Educ* Betteshanger Sch Kent, Felsted, Oxford Sch of Architecture; *m* 26 Sept 1970, Jillian Ann, da of Francis Edward Coombe, of Cornwall; 2 s (Andrew b 14 June 1971, Alistair b 14 June 1971), 1 da (Kate b 26 Oct 1975); *Career* CA; co fndr and dir Critchell Harrington & Ptnrs Ltd (architects and town planners); ARIBA, FIAA; *Recreations* rifle shooting, skiing; *Clubs* National Rifle Assoc (life memb); *Style—* Martin Critchell, Esq; Cowdry Barn, Birdham, Chichester, W Sussex PO20 7BX (☎ 0245 511031); 44A North Street, Chichester, W Sussex PO19 1NF (☎ 0243 780351, fax 0243 782917)

CRITCHETT, Sir Ian George Lorraine; 3 Bt (UK 1908), of Harley St, Boro' of St Marylebone; s of Sir Montague Critchett, 2 Bt (d 1941), and Innes, *née* Wiehe (d 1982); *b* 9 Dec 1920; *Educ* Harrow, Clare Coll Cambridge (BA); *m* 1, 9 Oct 1948, Paulette Mary Lorraine (d 4 May 1962), eld da of late Col Henry Brabazon Humfrey; m 2, 10 Feb 1964, Jocelyn Daphne Margret, eldest da of Cdr Christopher Mildmay Hall, of Higher Boswarva, Penzance, Cornwall; 1 s, 1 da; *Heir* s, Charles George Montague Critchett; *Career* RAFVR 1942-1946; FO 1948, 3 sec Vienna 1950, 2 sec Bucharest 1951, 2 sec Cairo 1956, 1 sec and later cnsllr FCO 1962, ret 1980; *Clubs* Travellers', MCC; *Style—* Sir Ian Critchett, Bt; Uplands Lodge, Pains Hill, Limpsfield, Oxted, Surrey (☎ 0883 72 2371)

CRITCHLEY, Dr Edmund Michael Rhys; s of Prof A Michael Critchley, and Dr Doris Critchley, *née* Rees; *b* 25 Dec 1931; *Educ* Stowe, Lincoln Coll Oxford (DM), KCH Med Sch; *m* 1964, Dr Mair, da of Ivor Bowen; 2 s (Giles b 1965, Hugo b 1967), 1 da (Helen b 1968); *Career* Capt RAMC; sr registrar UCH 1964-66, instr in neurology Univ of Lexington Med Centre 1966-68, conslt neurologist Preston and N Lancs 1968; memb Cncl Assoc Br Neurologists 1985-88; FRCP (memb Cncl 1988-), FRCPE; *Books* Hallucinations and Their Impact on Art (1987), Speech and Language Disorders (1987), Neurological Emergencies (1988); *Style—* Dr Edmund Critchley; 18 Merlin Rd, Blackburn, Lancs BB2 7BA (☎ 0254 60342); Dept of Neurology, Royal Preston Hospital, Preston, Lancs (☎ 0772 710556)

CRITCHLEY, Julian Michael Gordon; MP (C) Aldershot 1970-; s of Dr Macdonald Critchley, CBE and his 1 w Edna Auldeth, *née* Morris (d 1974); *b* 8 Dec 1930; *Educ* Shrewsbury, Sorbonne, Pembroke Coll Oxford (MA); *m* 1, 15 Oct 1955 (m dis 1965), Paula Joan, da of Paul Baron; 2 da (Julie b 20 Nov 1957, Susannah b 26 Sept 1961); m 2, April 1965, Mrs Heather Anne Goodrick, da of Charlie Moores (d 1949); 1 s (Joshua b 7 Sept 1970), 1 da (Melissa b 19 Jan 1967); *Career* writer, journalist; MP (C) Rochester and Chatham 1959-64; chm Bow Gp 1966-67; dir Br Bd of Boxing Control; *Books* The Conservative Opportunity (ed, 1965), Collective Security (with O Pick, 1975), Warning and Response (1978), NATO and the Soviet Union in the 80s (1980), Westminster Blues (1985), Heseltine (1987), A View from Westminster (ed, 1987), Palace of Varieties (1989); *Recreations* collecting early Staffordshire and Shropshire Pottery; *Style—* Julian Critchley, Esq, MP; The Brewer's House, 18 Bridge Sq, Farnham, Surrey (☎ 0252 722075); House of Commons, London SW1 (☎ 071 219 5170)

CRITCHLEY, Philip; CB (1990); s of Henry Stephen Critchley (d 1980), of Cumbria, and Edith Adela, *née* Currie (d 1980); *b* 31 Jan 1931; *Educ* Manchester GS, Balliol Coll Oxford (MA); *m* 1962, Stella Ann, da of Frederick John Barnes, of Kent; 2 s (Conrad b 1965, Brian b 1966), 1 da (Rachel b 1971); *Career* Nat Serv Intelligence Corps 1953-55, Corp BAOR; civil servant; under sec DOE, dir of network mgmnt and maintenance (highways) Dept of Tport; supporter: Ashford Youth Theatre, Local Philosophy Group; FRSA; *Recreations* tree conservation, writing poetry; *Clubs* Blackheath Harriers, Oxford Union; *Style—* Philip Critchley, Esq, CB; Redstone House, Maidstone Road, Ashford, Kent TN25 4NP (☎ 0233 621037; US/DMNAM, Department of Transport, Monck St, London SW1P 3EB (☎ 071 276 2830)

CRITCHLEY, Tom; s of Leonard Critchley (d 1986), and Jessie, *née* Turner (d 1988); *b* 17 Aug 1928; *Educ* Sheffield Coll of Technol; *m* 15 Dec 1951, Margaret, da of Frederick Bland (d 1934); 1 s (Andrew b 1959); *Career* Davy-Ashmore Group 1951-66, Cammell Laird and Upper Clyde Groups 1966-69, JCB Group 1969-70, EMI Group 1970-80, head Investmt Casting Misson to Canada; UN advsr: Tanzanian Govt, High Cmmn for Refugees; memb Bd Nat Inst of Govt Purchasing USA 1977-78, UK del Int Fedn of Purchasing and Materials Mgmnt 1978-82, sr ptnr Int Consultancy Practice 1980-85, faculty memb Mgmnt Centre Europe 1980-86, dir Int Mgmnt Inst 1984-88, under sec Dept of Health 1986-; Inst of Purchasing and Supply: fell 1967, chm of Cncl 1974-75, pres 1977-78, chm External Affrs 1978-82, chm Int Cncl 1979-82; memb NHS Mgmnt Bd for Procurement and Distribution 1987-; *Recreations* competitive sports, live theatre, North American history; *Style—* Tom Critchley, Esq; 3 Lincoln Close, Stoke Mandeville, nr Aylesbury, Bucks HP22 5YS

CRITCHLOW, Howard Arthur; s of Arthur Critchlow, of Nottingham, and Edith Ellen, *née* Evans (d 1972); *b* 22 April 1943; *Educ* Nottingham HS, Univ of Sheffield (BDS); *m* 5 Dec 1970, Avril, da of George Pyne, of Sheffield; 1 s (Edward b 1972), 1 da (Bridget b 1974); *Career* conslt oral surgn 1976-: Glasgow Dental Hosp, Stobhill Gen Hosp, Royal Hosp for Sick Children Glasgow; res work in: cryosurgery, laser surgery, dental implants; memb BDA 1965, FBAOMS 1976, FDSRCS (Eng), FDSRCP (Glas); *Recreations* hill walking, running, gardening, DIY, keep fit; *Clubs* 41 Club; *Style—* Howard Critchlow, Esq; Glasgow Dental Hospital, 378 Sauchiehall St, Glasgow G2 3JZ (☎ 041 332 7020)

CRITCHLOW, Keith Barry; s of Michael Bernard Critchlow (d 1972), of London, and Rozalind Ruby, *née* Weston-Mann (d 1983); *b* 16 March 1933; *Educ* Summerhill Sch, St Martins Sch of Art London (Inter NDD), RCA (ARCA); *m* Gail Susan, da of Geoffrey W Henebery; 1 s (Matthew Alexander), 4 da (Louise Penelope, Amanda Jane, Amelia Poppy, Dawn Kathy); *Career* Nat Serv RAF 1951-53; lectr at most Art & Architecture Schools in the UK; teaching appts at: Harrow, Sir John Cass, Hornsey, Watford, Wimbledon, The Slade, The Royal Coll; appts abroad incl: Ghana, Kuwait, Sweden, Aust, India, USA, Canada, Jordan, Iran, Saudi Arabia; former: tutor and res dir The Architectural Assoc, tutor in painting Sch of the Royal Coll of Art, tutor Slade Sch, dir Visual Islamic Arts Unit Royal Coll of Art; fndr own architectural design office; buildings designed in: USA, Kuwait, Saudi Arabia, Iran, Krishnamurti Study Centre in UK; FRCA 1986 (Dr 1989), FDIH (USA) 1987; *Books* Order in Space (1969), Chartres Maze; a model of the Universe?, Islamic Pattern; a cosmological approach, The Sphere, Soul & Androgyne, Into the Hidden Environment, Time Stands Still; *Recreations* painting, writing, geometry, walking, photography, meditation; *Style—* Dr Keith Critchlow; VIA Royal Coll of Art, Exhibition Rd, London SW7 2EU (☎ 071 584 5020 ext 294, 071 627 4326)

CROCK, Henry Vernon; s of Vernon John Crock (d 1963), of Perth, WA, and Annie, *née* Doyle (d 1973); *b* 14 Sept 1929; *Educ* St Louis Sch Perth WA, Univ of WA, Univ of Melbourne (MB, BS, MD, MS, Gold medallist Anatomy Dept); *m* 15 March 1958, Dr (Mary) Carmel Crock, da of Sylvester Michael Shorten (d 1966), of Melbourne, Victoria Aust; 2 s (Vernon Michael b 1963, Damian Luke b 1965), 3 da (Catherine Mary b 1958, Elizabeth Anne b 1960, Carmel Therese b 1962); *Career* St Vincents Hosp Melbourne: jr res MO 1954, sr res MO 1955, sr surgical registrar 1957; sr demonstrator Anatomy Dept Univ of Melbourne 1956 (res tutor Newman Coll), Nuffield Dominions' clinical asst in Orthopaedic Surgery Nuffield Orthopaedic Centre Univ of Oxford 1957-60 (lectr in Orthopaedic surgery 1959-60), sr hon orthopaedic surgn St Vincents Hosp Univ of Melbourne 1961-86, assoc prof Dept of Surgery Univ of Melbourne 1978-86 (special lectr in orthopaedic surgery 1961-86); memb Aust Rheumatism Assoc 1966-86; Aust Orthopaedic Assoc: memb Victorian Bd of Studies 1968-80, memb Fed Exec Bd 1972-73, memb Fed Prog Ctee 1972-75, memb Fed Ctee for Continuing Educn 1974-75, sec for Registrar Training Prog Victorian Branch 1976-80; corresponding memb Scoliosis Res Soc 1974-90, rep (Aust) Ed Bd Br Jl of Bone and Joint Surgery 1976-80; pres: Facet Club of Aust (Spinal Surgery) 1977-79, Int Soc for the Study of Lumbar Spine 1984-85; fndr memb Euro Spine Soc 1990; hon sr lectr in orthopaedic surgery Royal Postgrad Med Sch Hammersmith 1986, hon res fell Anatomy Dept RCS 1986; LO Betts meml Gold medal Orthopaedic Assoc 1976, Sir Alan Newton prize Royal Australasian Coll of Surgeons 1977, Wood-Jones Medal RCS 1983; FRCS 1957, FRACS 1961, FBOA 1989; *Books* The Blood Supply of the Lower Limb Bones in Man (1967), The Blood supply of the Vertebral Column and Spinal Cord in Man (with Dr H Yoshizawa, 1977), Practice of Spinal Surgery (1984), The Conus Medullaris and Cauda Equina in Man (with Dr M Yamagishi and Dr M C Crock 1986), many contribs to learned medical journals; *Recreations* collecting fine art, technical photography; *Clubs* The Melbourne, Associated; *Style—* Henry Crock, Esq; Cromwell Hospital, Cromwell Rd, London SW5 0TU (☎ 071 373 2591, fax 071 373 9525)

CROCKATT, Lt Cdr (Douglas) Allan; OBE (1981, MBE 1971), RD (1978), JP (WR

Yorks 1956), DL (1971); s of Douglas Crockatt JP, (d 1980), of Wetherby, W Yorks, and Ella, *née* Lethem (d 1981); *b* 31 Jan 1923; *Educ* Bootham Sch York, Trinity Hall Cambridge, Univ of Southampton; *m* 10 Aug 1946, Helen Townley (d 1985), da of Capt Thomas Arthur Tatton, MC (d 1968), of Cuerden Hall, Lancs; 1 da; *Career* WWII RNVR, Western Approaches and N Russia 1942-46; RNVSR 1946-64, RNR active list 1964-82; dep chm Johnson Group Cleaners 1976-84 (dir 1961-84), dir Johnson Group Inc (USA) until 1984; memb: CC W Riding Yorks 1953-58, Lord Chllr's Advsy Ctee for Trg of Magistrates 1964-79; local dir Martins and Barclays Banks W Yorks Bd 1964-84, memb Multiple Shops Fedn Cncl 1972-77, chm Trg Ctee Magistrates Assoc Cncl 1974-80 (memb 1959-80), memb Lord Chllr's Magistrates Cts Rule Ctee 1979-81, life vice pres W Yorks Branch Magistrates Assoc 1980 (hon sec 1958-72, chm 1975-77, pres 1977-79); Freeman City of London 1958-, memb Worshipful Co of Dyers; Vice Lord-Lieut of West Yorks 1985-; Hon LLD Univ of Leeds 1990; *Recreations* cricket, sailing (yacht 'Union Jack'), fishing; *Clubs* Army and Navy, RNSA, Driffield Anglers; *Style—* Lt Cdr Allan Crockatt, OBE, RD, DL; Paddock House, Sicklinghall, Wetherby, W Yorks LS22 4BJ (☎ 0937 582844)

CROCKATT, John Lethem; JP; s of Douglas Crockatt, JP, LLD (d 1980), of Wetherby, W Yorks, and Ella, *née* Lethem (d 1981); *b* 7 June 1920; *Educ* Bootham Sch York, Trinity Hall Cambridge (educ interrupted by WWII), Univ of London (LLB); *m* 1941, Josephine Rose, *née* Dickenson; 5 s, 1 da; *Career* Nat Serv WWII Merchant Navy 1939-45 (inc 1 year seamanship instr at first Outward Bound Sch); chm: Johnson Group Cleaners 1975-85, (trainee 1946), American Cos 1985-87; pres Merseyside Pre-Retirement Assoc, vice pres Merseyside and Deeside Outward Bound Assoc; memb Ct Worshipful Co of Dyers (formerly Prime Warden); FRSA; *Recreations* sailing, reading, music, heraldry; *Clubs* Army and Navy, Royal Overseas, Holyhead Sailing, Cruising Assoc; *Style—* John L Crockatt Esq; Rosemount, 112 Victoria Road, Formby, Liverpool L37 1LP, Merseyside

CROCKATT, Maj Richard Meredith; s of Brig Norman Richard Crockatt, CBE, DSO, MC (d 1956), of Ulverscroft, Virginia Water, Surrey, and Sidney Alice Rose, *née* Tweedy (d 1962); *b* 27 Nov 1921; *Educ* Rugby; *m* 6 Dec 1947, Elizabeth, da of André Falck (d 1958), of Southampton; *Career* regular offr The Royal Scots 1941-56, India and Burma (despatches) 1942-45, Capt 1944, Malaya 1946, Maj 1951, Staff Coll 1951 (psc), Korea, Egypt, Cyprus 1954-56; memb London Stock Exchange 1956; ptnr: Earnshaw Haes and Sons 1956-76, James Capel and Co 1976-87; chm: James Capel and Co (CI) 1985-87, CI Portfolio Mangrs 1988-90 dir Quilter Gordison Channel Islands 1990-; *Recreations* golf; *Clubs* White's, Swinley Forest Golf, Victoria (Jersey); *Style—* Maj Richard M Crockatt; La Petite Lande, Corbière, Jersey, Channel Islands (☎ 0534 42864)

CROCKER, Prof Alan Godfrey; s of Percival Thomas Crocker (d 1951), of Pontypridd, Mid Glamorgan, and (Alice) Maud, *née* Chown (d 1988); *b* 6 Oct 1935; *Educ* Pontypridd Boys' GS, Imp Coll London (BSc, DSc), Univ of Sheffield (PhD); *m* 29 Dec 1959, Glenys Mary, da of Bernard Oddie, of Clitheroe, Lancs; 1 s (Gareth Richard b 1967); *Career* Univ of Surrey Dept of Physics: lectr 1959-65, reader 1965-81, prof 1981-, head of dept 1991-; author of many sci papers in sci jls on defects in crystals and their influence on mechanical properties; chm Guildford Inst, chm Univ ctee validating degrees of Assoc Insts, past chm Wind and Watermill Section, Soc for the Protection of Ancient Buildings; chm: Gunpowder Mills Study Gp, Surrey Ind History Gp; vice chm Br Assoc of Paper Historians; ARCS, FInstP 1967, FIM 1970-88, FSA 1989, CEng 1978; *Books* Catteshall Mill (with G M Crocker, 1981), Paper Mills of the Tillingbourne Valley (1988), The Diaries of James Simmons (with M Kane 1990); *Recreations* industrial archaeology, hill walking; *Clubs* Soc of Antiquaries; *Style—* Prof Alan Crocker, FSA; 6 Burwood Close, Guildford, Surrey GU1 2SB (☎ 0483 65821); Department of Physics, University of Surrey, Guildford, Surrey GU2 5XH (☎ 0483 571281 ext 2690, telex 859331, fax 0438 304212)

CROCKER, James William Tailby; s of Sir William Charles Crocker (d 1973), and Mary Madeline, *née* Tailby (d 1953); *b* 10 July 1925; *Educ* Marlborough, Clare Coll Cambridge (MA); *m* 26 July 1948, Barbara, da of Harold Riversdale Morgan (d 1950); 1 s (Simon b 1948); *Career* Lt RNVR 1944-46; admitted slr 1952, dir United Services Auto Association Ltd 1952-, conslt Messrs William Charles Crocker; *Recreations* vintage cars and motor cycles, music; *Clubs* Arts; *Style—* James W T Crocker, Esq; 15 Graham Terrace, London SW1; Messrs William Charles Crocker, New Mercury House, 81-82 Farringdon St, London EC4A 4BT (☎ 071 353 0311, fax 071 583 1417, telex 93121 33171 CBG)

CROCKER, Dr John; s of Norman Kenneth Thornton Crocker, of Bexhill-on-Sea, E Sussex, and Olga Elspeth Crocker, *née* Robertson; *b* 18 June 1951; *Educ* Sevenoaks Sch Kent, Univ of Cambridge (MA, MD); *m* 29 Jan 1972, Catherine Barbara, da of Lord Tombs, of Honington Lodge, Honington nr Shipston-on-Stour, Warwicks; 1 s (Stephen John b 16 Jan 1980); *Career* lectr in pathology Univ of Birmingham 1976-83, conslt histopathologist and sr clinical lectr E Birminham Hosp 1983-; author of numerous papers, editorials, reviews and chapters on the pathology of malignant lymphomas, leukaemia and Hodgkin's disease; sec of W Midlands Oncology Assoc, memb Br Lymphoma Gp; memb: Pathological Soc of GB and Ireland, Assoc of Clinical Pathologists; fell Royal Microscopical Soc; MRCPath 1981; *Recreations* classical music, literature, computing; *Style—* Dr John Crocker; Chiltern, 226 Blossomfield Rd, Solihull, West Midlands B91 1NT; Histopathology Dept, E Birmingham Hospital, Birmingham B9 5ST (☎ 021 766 6611)

CROCKER, Trevor James Codrington; s of Henry Ernest Crocker (d 1966), and Lily Lavinia, *née* Davis (d 1969); *b* 14 March 1925; *Educ* Reigate GS, Univ of London (BSc), City Univ (MPhil), RCM; *m* 20 March 1954, Sylvia, da of Frederick George Hill (d 1975), of Epsom, Surrey; 3 da (Diana, b 1955, Pamela b 1958, Susan b 1961); *Career* co-fndr and chm Engineering Surveys Ltd 1960-70, fndr conslt Trevor Crocker & Partners International Consulting Engineers 1988- (fndr and chm 1960-88), fndr Crocker Group of conslts, non-exec dir Allied Partnership Group plc 1986-89; arbitrator numerous engrg disputes; City Univ: memb Ct 1972-91, chm convocation 1982-86 (dep chm 1980-82); memb London Ctee Glastonbury Abbey Devpt Tst; Freeman City of London, Master Worshipful Co of Glaziers and Painters of glass 1987-88, co-fndr Worshipful Co of Engrs (jr and sr warden), Liveryman Worshipful Co of Fan Makers; FICE 1965, FIMechE 1968, FIE (Aust) 1968, ARCM 1970, FCIArb 1972; *Recreations* offshore sailing, music-making; *Clubs* East India, City Livery; *Style—* Trevor Crocker, Esq; Freshwinds, Spinney Lane, Itchenor, Chichester, West Sussex; 4 Ormsby, Grange Rd, Sutton, Surrey SM2 6TH (☎ 081 643 3056)

CROCKETT, Clifden Robert; s of Leonard Marshall Crockett, OBE (d 1951), of Northampton, and Eleanor Carol Crockett, *née* Baker (d 1989); gf Sir James H Clifden Crockett (d 1931), of Northampton; *b* 27 May 1922; *Educ* Charterhouse, Trinity Hall Cambridge, Open Univ (BA); *m* 3 April 1948, Winifred Muriel, da of Norman Henry Mohun, (d 1977), of Kettering; 2 s (John b 1951, Nigel b 1954); *Career* Lt Royal Signals 1941-46, Italy, Palestine; slr: to Duchy of Lancaster 1966-73, with Treasy Slr 1974-85 (ed of Statutory Publications 1982-85); *Recreations* photography, music; *Style—* Clifden R Crockett, Esq; 19 The Avenue, Dallington, Northampton (☎ 0604 751813)

CROCKETT, Pippa Beryl; da of Philip Henry Crockett, MBE, and Beryl, *née* Wright (d 1969); *b* 23 July 1955; *Educ* Abbotsholme Sch; *Career* dir: County Leatherwear 1976, Hustwick Ltd 1979; md: County Leatherwear (Tinter Ltd) 1987, County Chamois Co Ltd 1987 (dir 1980, md 1987); ptnr Heart of England Antiques 1987; assoc memb Int Export Assoc 1978; *Recreations* water skiing, sailing, skiing, golf; *Style—* Miss Pippa Crockett; Chestnut House, Chestnut Lane, Clifton Campville, Tamworth, Staffs B79 0BW; County Chamois Co Ltd, John St Leatherworks, Glascote, Tamworth, Staffs B77 3EA (☎ 0827 63672, fax 0827 62365, telex 335623 CADGE, car 0860 434003)

CROCKFORD, Philip David Vyvyan; s of Philip Theodore Clive Crockford (d 1950), and Muriel Mary, *née* Moorhouse (d 1988); *b* 21 Nov 1930; *Educ* Merchant Taylors', RMA Sandhurst; *m* 11 July 1953, Margaret Kathleen, da of Maj Charles Deane Cowper; 1 s (Adrian Robert Vyvyan b 27 April 1956), 2 da (Sarah Claire d'Ambrumenil b 25 Aug 1954, Charlotte Kathleen Winifred Joy b 2 March 1962); *Career* cmmnd RA 1951-55; formerly: sales and mktg IBM (UK) Ltd, PA to mgmnt conslts; dir: Willis Faber & Dumas Ltd, Alexander Howden Underwriting Ltd; md Crockford Devitt Underwriting Agencies Ltd; memb Lloyd's; *Recreations* foxhunting, collecting antiquarian books; *Clubs* City Univ; *Style—* David Crockford, Esq; Maroon House, Mark Lane, London EC3

CROFT, Col (Noel) Andrew Cotton; DSO (1945), OBE (1970); s of Rev Canon Robert William Croft (d 1947), of Kelvedon Vicarage, Essex, and Lottie Alice Bland, *née* Clayton (d 1962); *b* 30 Nov 1906; *Educ* Lancing, Stowe, ChCh Oxford (MA), Sch of Technol Manchester; *m* 24 July 1952, Rosalind, da of Cdr A H de Kantzow, DSO, RN (d 1928); 3 da (Clare b 1953, Corinna b 1955, Julia b 1957); *Career* under mangr cotton trade Carlisle 1929-32; memb Br Trans-Greenland expdn (Guinness Book of Records longest self-supporting dog-sledge journey) 1933-34; ADC to Maharajah of Cooch Behar India 1934-35; 2 i/c Oxford Univ Arctic expdn to North East Land 1935-36, Ethnological Expdn to Swedish Lapland 1937-38; res Cambridge Univ 1938-39; WWII: serv Capt 1939, cmd WO mission to Russo-Finnish War 1939-40, Bde Intellingence Offr Ind Companies Norwegian Campaign 1940, advsr Admty Combined Ops 1940-41, Maj 1941, asst mil attaché Stockholm 1941-42, OC sea or parachute ops (Norway, Corsica, Italy, France, Denmark), Lt-Col 1945; asst dir of sci res WO 1945-48, WO rep Canadian Arctic Exercise Musk-Ox 1945-46, sr observer NW Frontier Trials India 1946-47, attached Canadian Army 1947-48, GSOI WO 1948-51, Br Jt Servs Mission USA 1952-54, sr liaison offr HQ Continental Armies, OC Inf Jr Ldrs Bn Plymouth 1954-57; cmdt: Army Apprentices Sch Harrogate 1957-60, Met Police Cadet Corps 1960-71; fell RGS (BACK award 1945 and 46, hon sec 1951, memb Cncl 1949-51), corresponding fell Arctic Inst of N America, life memb RIIA; Polar medal 1942 (Clasp Arctic 1935-36); *Books* Polar Exploration (1939, 2 edn 1947), Under The Pole Star (with AR Glen, 1937); *Recreations* sailing, skiing, mountaineering, photography; *Clubs* Alpine, Special Forces (tstee), Arctic (memb and former sec); *Style—* Col Andrew Croft, DSO, OBE; The River House, 52 Strand-on-the-Green, London W4 3PD (☎ 081 994 6359)

CROFT, Hon Bernard William Henry Page; s and h of 2 Baron Croft by his w, Lady Antoinette Fredericka Hersey Cecilia Conyngham (d 1959), da of 6 Marquess Conyngham; *b* 28 Aug 1949; *Educ* Stowe, Wales Univ (BSc); *Style—* The Hon Bernard Croft

CROFT, Charles Beresford; s of Arthur James Croft (d 1979), and Margaret Bays Conyers, *née* Wright; *b* 14 Jan 1943; *Educ* Worksop Coll, Leeds Univ Medical Sch (MB, ChB Hon); *m* 23 March 1968, Hilary Louise Whitaker, da of Ronald Whitaker (d 1968); 1 da (Emma Louise b 1972); *Career* conslt surgn and assoc prof Albert Einstein Sch of Med NY 1974-79; conslt surgn: The Royal Nat Throat Nose and Ear Hosp London, The Nat Heart and Chest Hosp London 1979-; civil conslt Laryngology RAF 1983-; FRCS Eng (1970), FRCS Ed (1972); *Recreations* golf, tennis, sailing; *Clubs* Moor Park Golf, RSM; *Style—* Charles B Croft, Esq; Rye Lodge, 91 Copsewood Way, Northwood, Middx (☎ 0923 23793); 55 Harley St, London W1N 1DD (☎ 071 580 2426)

CROFT, David; OBE; s of Reginald Sharland (d 1944), of Hollywood, and Anne, *née* Croft (d 1960); *b* 7 Sept 1922; *Educ* Rugby; *m* 2 June 1952, Ann Callender, da of Reginald Coupland (d 1983), 4 s (Nicholas b 26 March 1953, John b 11 May 1964, Richard b 18 Nov 1969, Tim b 10 Sept 1973); 3 da (Penelope b 10 April 1954, Jane b 16 July 1960, Rebecca b 23 Jan 1962); *Career* WWII RA 1942, Dorset Regt 1944; served: N Africa, India, Malaya, WO; final rank Maj; actor 1946, BBC writer 1951-, script ed Rediffusion 1955; writer dir: Tyne Tees 1960-61, BBC 1962; co-writer, prod and dir: Dad's Army, It Ain't 'Alf Hot Mum, Are You Being Served, Hi De Hi, Allo Allo; You Rang Milord; memb BAFTA; *Style—* David Croft, Esq, OBE; BBC TV, Television Centre, Shepherds Bush, London

CROFT, His Hon Judge David Legh; QC (1982); s of Alan Croft (d 1965), of Dore, Sheffield, and Doreen Mary, *née* Mitchell; *b* 14 Aug 1937; *Educ* Haileybury, Univ of Nottingham (LLB); *m* 27 July 1963, Susan Mary, da of George Richard Winnington Bagnall (d 1982), of Wickham, nr Newbury, Berks; 2 s (Rupert Legh b 1966, Jocelyn Harry b 1968); *Career* called to the Bar Middle Temple 1960, rec 1985, Circuit Judge 1987; *Recreations* cooking; *Style—* His Hon Judge Croft, QC

CROFT, Dr Desmond Nicholas; s of Dr Charles Richard Croft, TD (d 1981), of Plymouth, Devon and Phyllis Mary, *née* Lee (d 1985); *b* 14 June 1931; *Educ* St John's Winnipeg, Westminster, Trinity Coll Oxford (BM BCh, MA, DM); *m* 1960, Dr (Hilary) Diana Russel Rendle, da of Hilary Cameron Russel Rendle (d 1944), of Singapore; 2 s (Charles b 1960, Nicholas b 1963), 1 da (Hilary b 1966); *Career* Nat Serv Capt RAMC, jr med specialist Br Mil Hosp Tripoli 1959-61; Nuffield Foundation fell Boston USA 1961-65, MRC fell 1963-64, conslt physician St Thomas' Hosp 1969-; pres: Nuclear Med Section Union of Euro Med Specialists, Br Nuclear Med Soc (1976-78); examiner MD and MS Univ of London, fndr memb Euro Nuclear Med Soc and memb Int Sci Ctee 1980-86, chm Medical and Surgical Offrs Ctee St Thomas' Hosp 1986-89; FRCP 1975, FRCR 1986; FRSM; *Books* 112 contributions to scientific literature in British Medical Journal, Gut, Clinical Science, Nuclear Medicine Communications, European Journal of Nuclear Medicine and other learned jls; *Recreations* rowing, golf, fishing; *Style—* Dr Desmond Croft; Bourne House, Hurstbourne Priors, Whitchurch, Hampshire RG28 7SB (☎ 0256 89 2665); St Thomas' Hospital, London SE1 7EH (☎ 071 928 9292 ext 2163)

CROFT, Giles Laurance; s of John Croft, of The Cloisters, Perrymead, Avon; *b* 20 June 1957; *Educ* Combe Sch, City of Bath Tech Coll; *Career* dir Bath Young Peoples Theatre Co 1978-80, regnl ed Bananas magazine 1979-80, admin Le Metro Theatre Co Bath 1980-82, artistic dir Gate Theatre 1985-89, series ed Absolute Classics 1988-90, literary mangr Royal Nat Theatre 1989-; many prodns as dir incl: Conversations with a Cupboard Man (Lyric Hammersmith) 1983, Written in Sickness (Upstream London) 1984, Orphee (Upstream) 1984, Elmer Gantry (Gate Theatre) 1986, The Boxer (Edinburgh Festival) 1986, Naomi (Gate Theatre) 1987, The Infant (Gate Theatre) 1989; author of many short stories and articles (published and bdcast); memb Dirs Guild of GB; *Style—* Giles Croft, Esq; 110b Sandmere Rd, London SW4; Royal National Theatre, South Bank, London SE1 9PX (☎ 071 928 2033)

CROFT, Maj The Rev John Armentières; MC (1944); s of late Brig Gen WD Croft, CB, CMG, DSO (d 1968), of The Anchorage, Mawnan, Falmouth, and Esme Sutton (d

1977); *b* 1 Jan 1915; *Educ* Stowe, RMC Sandhurst, Staff Coll Ouetta, Salisbury Theological Coll; *m* 19 July 1948, Sheila Kathleen, da of James Arthur Ford (Maj TA, d 1951), of Pengreep, Ponsanooth, nr Truro, Cornwall; 1 s (Hugh b 1954), 1 da (Patricia Lucy (Mrs Rowe) b 1951); *Career* cmmnd 1934, attached Duke of Wellington Regt serv NW Frontier 1935 (despatches), serv 20 Lancers Royal Deccan Horse 1935-43, transferred 1/16 Punjab Regt in Imphal 1943, wounded 1944, staff coll transferred RA, staff appts HG 4 AA Gp and W Africa, ret 1953; asst curate of Madron The Old Parish Church of Penzance, vicar of Gwinear Cornwall 1960-70, help as ret vicar: Cornwall, S Devon, Dorset/Wilts, Camelot (Bath and Wells); hon chaplain Penzance Sea Cadets 1961-70; *Recreations* riding, rambling; *Clubs* Army & Navy; *Style—* Maj The Rev John Croft, MC; Vine House, The Common, Wincanton, Somerset (☎ 0963 32253)

CROFT, (Ivor) John; CBE (1982); s of Oswald Hamilton Croft (d 1980), and Augusta Doris, *née* Phillips (d 1985); *b* 6 Jan 1923; *Educ* Westminster, ChCh Oxford (Hinchcliffe scholar in modern history, MA), Inst of Educn Univ of London, LSE (MA); *Career* temp jr admin offr FO 1942-45, asst teacher London CC 1949-51; Home Office: inspr Childrens' Dept 1952-66, sr res offr 1966-72, head of Res Unit 1972-81, head of Res and Planning Unit 1981-83; chm Criminological Scientific Cncl Euro Ctee on Crime Problems Cncl of Europe 1981-83 (memb 1978-83); various one-man shows as a painter 1958-; memb Exec Ctee Eng Assoc, chm Pembridge Assoc, memb ctee Peel Heritage Tst; memb Tbnl Interception of Communications Act 1988; author of various publications on crime published by the Home Office and Cons Study Gp on Crime; *Clubs* Reform; *Style—* John Croft, Esq, CBE; 30 Stanley Rd, Peel, Isle of Man (☎ 0624 84 3707)

CROFT, (Herbert) Kemble; s of (Herbert) William Croft (d 1964), and Marjory Kemble Howden (d 1951); *b* 20 July 1930; *Educ* Downside, Royal West of England Acad, Sch of Architecture; *m* 9 May 1964, Juliet Sara, da of late Dr Robin Williamson; 2 s (John b 1965, Thomas b 1970), 1 da (Kate b 1966); *Career* Nat Serv cmmnd 2 Lt RA; regnl architect NW Thames RHA, chm First Hosp Architecture 1986-; *Recreations* theatre, history of art, sport; *Style—* Kemble Croft, Esq; 2 Hillyard Barns, Sutton Courtenay, Oxon OX14 4BJ (☎ 0235 847439); First Hosp Architecture, 12-18 Grosvenor Gardens, London SW1 W0DH (☎ 071 824 8215, fax 071 730 4816)

CROFT, 2 Baron (UK 1940); Sir Michael Henry Glendower Page Croft; 2 Bt (UK 1924); s of 1 Baron, CMG, TD, PC (d 1947), and Hon Nancy Beatrice Borwick, da of 1 Baron Borwick; *b* 20 Aug 1916; *Educ* Eton, Trinity Hall Cambridge; *m* 1948, Lady Antoinette Conyngham (d 1959), da of 6 Marquess Conyngham; 1 s, 1 da; *Heir* s, Hon Bernard Croft; *Career* barr 1952; former dir Henry Page and Co and Ware Properties Ltd; underwriting memb Lloyd's 1971-; FRSA; OStJ; *Style—* The Rt Hon the Lord Croft; Croft Castle, nr Leominster, Herefordshire

CROFT, Oliver Albert (Olly); s of Oliver Walter John Croft (d 1976), and May Gladys, *née* Robertson (d 1937); *b* 17 Nov 1929; *m* 20 Dec 1952, Lorna Mae, da of late John Aubrey Cannon; 3 s (Roy George b 26 Dec 1953, Paul John b 20 nov 1959, Oliver John b 20 Oct 1963), 2 da (Lesly Joan b 21 April 1955, Elaine Corrine b 14 Sept 1956); *Career* darts administrator; fndr: British Darts Organisation 1973, World Darts Federation 1976, numerous world darts events, England darts team; current positions: md Br Darts Orgn Enterprises Ltd, gen sec Br Darts Orgn, hon gen sec England Darts Orgn, sec gen World Darts Fedn, mangr England darts team 1973-; also fndr tiling co Croft Bros (London) Ltd 1954-; *Style—* Olly Croft, Esq; 47 Creighton Avenue, Muswell Hill, London N10 1NR (☎ 081 883 5055)

CROFT, Sir Owen Glendower; 14 Bt (E 1671), of Croft Castle, Herefordshire; s of Sir Bernard Croft, 13 Bt (d 1984), and Helen Margaret, *née* Weaver; *b* 26 April 1932; *m* 1959, Sally, da of Dr Thomas Montagu Mansfield, of Brisbane, Australia; 1 s (Thomas), 2 da (Patricia b 1960, Georgiana b 1964); *Heir* s, Thomas Jasper, *qv*; *Style—* Sir Owen Croft, Bt; Salisbury Court, Uralla, NSW 2358, Australia

CROFT, Thomas Jasper; s and h of Sir Owen Glendower Croft, 14 Bt, *qv*, and Sally Patricia, da of Dr Thomas Montagu Mansfield; *b* 3 Nov 1962; *Educ* The Armidale Sch, Darling Downs Inst (Assoc Dip Mech Eng); *m* 29 Jan 1989, Catherine Fiona, da of Graham William White; *Career* owner/mangr contract tree planting business; *Recreations* ornithology, bush walking, photography; *Style—* Thomas Croft, Esq; 51 Park Street, Uralla, NSW 2358, Australia (☎ 010 61 067 784730)

CROFT, Sir Thomas Stephen Hutton; 6 Bt (UK 1818), of Cowling Hall, Yorks; s of Maj Sir John Archibald Radcliffe Croft, 5 Bt (d 1990), and Lucy Elizabeth, *née* Jupp; *b* 12 June 1959; *Educ* King's Sch Canterbury, UCL (BSc), RCA (MA); *Heir* u, Cyril Bernard Croft b 1918; *Career* architect; *Style—* Sir Thomas Croft, Bt; 53 Leinster Sq, London W2 4PV (☎ 071 229 6547)

CROFT BAKER, Michael Anthony; s of Alec Croft Baker (d 1989), and Violet Maryon, *née* Clark; *b* 27 April 1936; *Educ* City of London Sch, King's Coll Univ of London (LLB); *m* 25 May 1968, Yvonne Beryl Mabel, da of Capt Kenneth George Hall, of Grouville, Jersey, CI; 2 s (James, Edward); *Career* admitted slr 1960; ptnr Theodore Goddard 1965-; Freeman Worshipful Co of Solicitors 1967; memb Law Soc 1957; *Recreations* gardening, sport, music; *Style—* Michael Croft Baker, Esq; Byways, Gregories Farm Lane, Beaconsfield, Bucks HP9 1HJ; 150 Aldersgate St, London EC1A 4EJ (☎ 071 606 8855, fax 071 606 4390, telex 884678)

CROFT-SMITH, Graham; s of Thomas John Winter Smith (d 1975); *b* 3 Oct 1951; *Educ* Highgate Wood Comprehensive Haringey London; *m* 29 Sept 1973, Josephine, da of Francois Mangion; 1 s (Steven b 22 March 1984), 1 da (Jane b 17 March 1980); *Career* dir Alexanders Rouse Ltd; *Recreations* golf, light music (not classical); *Style—* Graham Croft-Smith, Esq; Alexanders Rouse Ltd, 1 St Katherines Way, London E1 9UN (☎ 071 481 0283, car 0034 217897)

CROFTON, Derek Fergus Regan; s of late William Crofton; *b* 15 Feb 1934; *Educ* Rockwell Coll, Univ Coll Dublin; *m* 1959, Marian Emily, *née* Lindsay; 2 s, 1 da; *Career* chartered accountant 1958, finance dir and co sec Shell Chemicals UK Ltd 1974-, chm Vencel Resil Ltd 1974-, dir Ward Blenkinsop Ltd; *Style—* Derek Crofton Esq; The Red Lodge, North Rd, Hale, Cheshire (☎ 061 980 8280)

CROFTON, Hon Georgiana Ann; has resumed maiden name; da of 5 Baron Crofton (d 1974); *b* 29 July 1955; *m* 1980 (m dis 1986), Brent Hutchinson, s of Ivan Hutchinson; 1 s (Blaise b 1982), 1 da (Louisa b 1981); *Career* film producer; *Style—* The Hon Georgiana Crofton; c/o The Red House, Inistioge, Co Kilkenny, Republic of Ireland

CROFTON, 7 Baron (I 1797); Guy Patrick Gilbert Crofton; 10 Bt (I 1758); s of 5 Baron Crofton (d 1974); suc bro, 6 Baron 1989; *b* 17 June 1951; *Educ* Theresianistische Akademie Vienna, Midhurst GS; *m* 1985, Gillian Susan Burroughs, o da of Harry Godfrey Mitchell Bass, CMG, of Reepham, Norfolk; 2 s (Hon (Edward) Harry Piers, Hon (Charles) Marcus George (twin) b 23 Jan 1988); *Heir* s, Hon (Edward) Harry Piers Crofton b 23 Jan 1988; *Career* Maj 9/12 R Lancers (POW); *Clubs* Cavalry and Guards'; *Style—* The Rt Hon the Lord Crofton; c/o Royal Bank of Scotland, Holts Branch, 22 Whitehall, London SW1

CROFTON, Sir John Wenman; er s of Dr William Mervyn Crofton; *b* 1912; *Educ* Tonbridge, Sidney Sussex Coll Cambridge (BA, MA, MD), St Thomas' Hosp (MB BCh); *m* 1945, Eileen Chris Mercer, MBE (1984); *Career* sr lectr in med Postgrad Med Sch of London 1947-51, prof of respiratory diseases and tuberculosis Univ of Edinburgh 1952-77, dean Faculty of Med 1963-66, vice princ 1970-71; pres Royal Coll of Physicians Edinburgh 1973-76; FRCP, FRCPE, FACP, FRACP, FRCPI, FFCM, Hon FRACP; kt 1977; *Style—* Sir John Crofton; 13 Spylaw Bank Rd, Edinburgh EH13 0JW (☎ 031 441 3730)

CROFTON, Sir Malby Sturges; 5 Bt (UK 1838), of Longford House, Sligo (but name does not, at time of going to press, appear on the Official Roll of Baronets); s of Sir Malby Richard Henry Crofton, 4 Bt, DSO and Bar (d 1962); *b* 11 Jan 1923; *Educ* Eton, Trinity Coll Cambridge; *m* 14 Jan 1961 (m dis 1966), Elizabeth Madeline Nina, da of late Maj Rhys Clavell Mansel, of Ropley Manor, Alresford, Hants; *Heir* kinsman, (Henry Edward) Melville Crofton; *Career* Mayor Kensington and Chelsea 1978- (Leader Kensington Boro Cncl 1968-77), ptnr Messrs Fenn and Crosthwaite, memb London Stock Exchange 1957-75, memb GLC 1970-73 and (N Ealing) 1977; *Style—* Sir Malby Crofton, Bt; Longford House, Co Sligo, Eire; 17 Launceston Place, W8

CROFTON, Margaret, Lady; Margaret Amelia; *née* Dallett; da of Judge Morris Dallett (d 1917), of Philadelphia, USA; *b* 1 April 1907; *m* 20 June 1933, as his 3 w, Lt-Col Sir Morgan George Crofton, 6 Bt, DSO (d 8 Dec 1958); 2 s (Hugh Denis b 1937, Edward Morgan b 1945); *Style—* Margaret, Lady Crofton; Robin Cottage, Sway Rd, Brockenhurst, Hants (☎ 0590 22139)

CROFTON, Mary, Baroness; Mary Irvine; *née* Friend; eldest da of Maj James Irvine Hatfield Friend, OBE, MC, DL (d 1955), and Louie Gertrude, *née* Cowley (d 1963); *b* 24 Sept 1920; *m* 1, 1951 (m dis 1963), Robert Thomas Francis Flach; 2 s; m 2, 19 Dec 1964, as his 2 w, 5 Baron Crofton (d 1974); *Style—* The Rt Hon Mary, Lady Crofton; Flat 1, 123 Gloucester Terrace, London W2 (☎ 071 402 5015)

CROFTON, Maureen, Baroness; Maureen Jacqueline; da of Stanley James Bray, of Taunton, Som; *m* 1976, 6 Baron Crofton (d 1989); 1 da (Hon Freya Charlotte b 1983); *Style—* The Rt Hon Maureen, Lady Crofton; Briscoe Cottage, Ford Street, nr Wellington, Somerset

CROFTON, (Henry Edward) Melville; MBE (1970); s of Brig Roger Crofton, CIE, MC (d 1972), by 2 w Dorothy Frances (d 1953), da of Col Henry Melville Hatchell, DSO; hp of kinsman, Sir Malby Crofton, 5 Bt; *b* 15 Aug 1931; *Educ* Hilton Coll Natal, Trinity Coll Cambridge; *m* 10 Dec 1955, Mary Brigid, twin da of late Gerald K Riddle, of Buttercombe, Ogwell, Newton Abbot, Devon; 2 s (Julian b 1958, Nigel b 1964), 1 da (Nicola b 1961); *Career* former princ admin offr HMOCS; conslt in industl devpt trg 1978-; *Style—* Melville Crofton Esq, MBE; Haldon, St Giles Hill, Winchester, Hants

CROFTON, Dr Richard Wenman; s of Prof Sir John Wenman Crofton, qv, and Eileen Chris Crofton, MBE; *b* 2 Oct 1947; *Educ* The Edinburgh Acad, Sidney Sussex Coll Cambridge, Univ of Edinburgh (MA, MB ChB); *m* 25 April 1975, Susan Anne, da of William Henry James (d 1979), of Beverley, Yorks; 1 s (David b 8 Aug 1978), 1 da (Eilidh b 17 Nov 1984); *Career* MRC res fell Dept of Therapeutics Univ of Edinburgh 1973-77, res fell Dept of Infectious Diseases Leiden Univ The Netherlands 1974-76, registrar Aberdeen Teaching Hosps 1977-79, lectr Dept of Med Univ of Aberdeen 1979-83, conslt physician Law Hosp Carluke 1983-; FRCPE 1986, memb Br Soc of Gastroenterology; *Recreations* family life, the outdoors, bird watching; *Style—* Dr Richard Crofton; 22 Silverdale Crescent, Lanark, Lanarkshire ML11 9HW (☎ 0555 61394); Law Hospital, Carluke, Lanarkshire ML8 5ER (☎ 0698 351100)

CROFTS-GREENE, Dr Basil Wilson Harvey; o s of William Granville Greene (d 1919), of Fitzwilliam Sq, Dublin, and Charlotte Elizabeth Wilson, *née* Harvey (d 1972), g niece of Prof W Nesbitt, of Queen's Univ, and sis of Canon W Nesbitt Harvey (d 1981); assumed by deed poll 1948 additional name of Crofts; *b* 27 March 1918; *Educ* St Andrew's Coll, Univ of Dublin, King's Inns Dublin, Univ de la Romande Switzerland (MA, PhD); *m* 1946, Rosamund Patricia Nason, of Ballyhoura Lodge, Co Cork, o child of Christopher Nason Crofts (d 1947); tenth in descent from Thomas Croftes who d 1612, of West Stow and Sexham Parva, Suffolk, by his w Susan, maternal gda of 1 Baron Wentworth); 1 s (Nigel Harvey Nason b 1948, *qv*); *Career* landowner, dir Pet Fair Ltd Cork City; *Recreations* german shepherd dog judge and breeder, study of alternative medicine, genealogy; *Clubs* Royal Irish Automobile; *Style—* Dr Basil Crofts-Greene; Strancally Castle, Knockanore, Co Waterford, Eire (☎ 024 97164)

CROFTS-GREENE, Nigel Harvey Nason; s of Basil Crofts-Greene, *qv*, and Rosamund Patricia Nason, *née* Crofts; *b* 9 Feb 1948; *Educ* Kingstown Sch, RAC Cirencester; *Career* farmer, md Pet Fair Ltd Cork City; *Recreations* militaria, water skiing, wind surfing; *Style—* N H N Crofts-Greene, Esq; Strancally Castle, Knockanore, Co Waterford, Ireland (☎ 024 97164)

CROHAM, Baron (Life Peer UK 1977), of London Borough of Croydon; Sir Douglas Albert Vivian Allen; GCB (1973, KCB 1967, CB 1963); s of Albert John Allen (ka 1918), of Croydon, Surrey; *b* 15 Dec 1917; *Educ* Wallington GS, LSE (BSc); *m* 1941, Sybil Eileen, da of John Marco Allegro (d 1964), of Carshalton, Surrey; 2 s (Hon John Douglas b 1945, Hon Richard Anthony b 1950), 1 da (Hon Rosamund Sybil (Hon Mrs Sulyák) b 1942); *Career* former civil serv; perm sec: Treasy 1968-74, CSD 1974-77; chm British National Oil Corporation 1982-86 (dep chm 1978-82); dir: Pilkington Bros Ltd 1978-, Guinness Mahon & Co Ltd 1989-; chm: Guinness Peat Group 1983-87, Trinity Insurance Ltd 1988-; industl advsr to Govr of Bank of England 1978-83; chm: Anglo-German Fndn 1981-, Review of Univ Grants Ctee 1985-87; *Recreations* woodwork; *Clubs* Reform, Civil Service; *Style—* The Rt Hon the Lord Croham, GCB; 9 Manor Way, South Croydon, Surrey (☎ 081 688 0496); Guinness Mahon Holdings Group plc, 32 St Mary at Hill, London EC3P 3AJ (☎ 071 623 6222, telex 893065)

CROISDALE-APPLEBY, Dr David; s of Mark Appleby (d 1980), of Belford, Northumberland, and Florence Isabel, *née* White; *b* 6 Feb 1946; *Educ* Royal GS Newcastle upon Tyne, Univ of London (MA), Univ of Newcastle (BSc), Brunel Univ (MSc Tech), Univ of Lancaster (PhD); *m* 3 Aug 1968, Carolynn Elizabeth, da of Maj Alan Cuthbert Croisdale, MBE (d 1974); 3 s (Mycroft b 1971, Lindsay b 1973, Merton b 1976), 1 da (Catriona b 1984); *Career* chief exec Allen Brady & Marsh Ltd 1979-82, worldwide ops dir SSC & B Lintas Ltd 1982-84; chm: Creative Synergy Ltd 1984-, The DCA Co Ltd 1985-, Retail Trading Developments Ltd 1986-, Marylebone Railway World Ltd 1986-, Salmon Ventures Ltd 1987-; churchwarden St Michael's & All The Angels Amersham Bucks; FRSA 1988; *Recreations* motor racing, Lutyens, Aston Martins; *Style—* Dr David Croisdale-Appleby; Abbotsholme, Amersham, Bucks (☎ 0494 725 194); The Old Coach House, Bamburgh, Northumberland; 29 Daventry St, London NW1 (☎ 071 402 4225)

CROKER, Arthur Raymond; s of Edward Croker (d 1951), and Phylis Helen Savage (d 1978); ggs of Frederick James Savage, personal detective to Queen Victoria 1885-93; *b* 16 Aug 1939; *Educ* Bristol Pro Cathedral Sch; *m* 29 Sept 1962, Mary Elizabeth Clarke, da of Capt John Patrick (d 1987), of Dublin, Eire; 3 s (Damian b 1963, Mark b 1964, John b 1978); *Career* fin accountant in private practice; ptnr Yewtree Int; dist cncllr 1968-72; memb Soc of Cons Accountants; ACEA, AIIA; *Recreations* squash, golf; *Clubs* Cadbury Country, Lions Club of Nailsea; *Style—* Arthur R Croker, Esq; Yew Trees, Beckets Lane, Nailsea, Avon BS19 2LY (☎ 0272 856 376); Croker Robb & Co, The Old Post Office, Station Rd, Congresbury, Avon (☎ 0934 835 485); Arthur Croker & Co, 10a Church St, Tetbury, Glos Gl8 8JG (☎ 0666 503484)

CROKER, Edgar Alfred (Ted); CBE (1989); s of Harry Croker (d 1954), and Winifred, *née* Coton (d 1950); *b* 13 Feb 1924; *Educ* Kingston Tech Coll; *m* 1952, Kathleen Grace, da of Cornelius Mullins (d 1950); 1 s (Andrew), 2 da (Alison, Louise);

Career served WWII Flt Lt RAF 1942-46, Flt Lt RAFVR 1947-55; professional footballer: Charlton Athletic 1947-51, Headington Utd 1951-56; sales dir Douglas Equipment 1956-61, chm and md Liner-Croker Ltd 1961-73; chm Liner Concrete Machinery Co Ltd 1971-73, gen sec and chief exec The Football Assoc 1973-89; chm: Harrington Kilbride Ltd 1989-, PEL Stadium Seating PLC; dir Sports Aid Enterprise Ltd, chm Torch Trophy Tst; hon vice pres The Football Assoc; King's Commendation for Brave Conduct; *Books* The Next Voice You Hear Will Be (autobiography); *Recreations* golf, tennis, bridge; *Clubs* Sportsman, RAF, New (Cheltenham); *Style—* Ted Croker, Esq, CBE; South Court, 45 The Park, Cheltenham, Glos (☎ 0242 224 970)

CROLL, Prof James George Arthur; s of Keith Waghorn Croll (d 1976), and Jean, *née* Campbell; *b* 16 Oct 1943; *Educ* Palmerston North Boy's HS NZ, Univ of Canterbury Christchurch NZ (BE, Phd); *m* 16 Dec 1966, Elisabeth Joan, da of Robert Colston Sprackett, of Auckland, NZ; 1 s (Nicholas James b 1974), 1 da (Katherine Elisabeth b 1978); *Career* asst engr NZ Miny of Works 1961-67, prof of structural engrg UCL 1985- (res fell 1967-70, lectr 1970-82, reader in structural engrg 1982-85); former: sec and chm Br Soc for Social Responsibility in Sci, sec Jt Br Ctee For Stress Analysis; FIStructE, FIMA, FEng; *Books* Elements of Structural Stability (1973), Force Systems & Equilibrium (1975); *Recreations* music, sailing, skiing, painting; *Clubs* Hayling Island Sailing; *Style—* Prof James Croll; 92 Highgate Hill, Highgate, London N6 5HE (☎ 081 348 7731); Dept of Civil Engineering, University College London, London WC1E 6BT (☎ 071 387 7050 ext 2721, telex 296273 UCLENG G, fax 071 380 0986)

CROMARTIE, 5 Earl of (UK 1861); John Ruaridh Grant MacKenzie; also Viscount Tarbat (UK 1861), Baron Castlehaven (1861), Baron MacLeod of Castle Leod (UK 1861); chief of the Clan Mackenzie; s of 4 Earl of Cromartie, MC, TD (d 1989), and his 2 w, Olga, *née* Laurance; *b* 12 June 1948; *Educ* Rannoch Sch Perthshire, Univ of Strathclyde; *m* 1, 1973 (m dis 1983), Helen, da of John Murray; 1 s (decd); m 2, 1985, Janet Clare, da of Christopher James Harley, of Strathpeffer; 2 s (Colin Ruaridh, Viscount Tarbat b 7 Sept 1987, Hon Alasdair Kenelm Stuart b 6 Dec 1989); *Heir* s, Viscount Tarbat b 7 Sept 1987; *Career* memb Inst Explosive Engrs 1982-, explosives conslt, editor Explosives Engineering; *Books* Rock and Ice Climbs in Skye (SMT); part author: Cold Climbs, Classic Rock, Wild Walks and many magazine articles both in the climbing and explosives press; *Recreations* mountaineering, geology, art; *Clubs* Scottish Mountaineering, Army and Navy, Pratt's; *Style—* The Rt Hon the Earl of Cromartie; Castle Leod, Strathpeffer, Ross-shire IV14 9AA

CROMARTIE, Lilias, Countess of; Lilias Janet Garvie; da of Prof (James) Walter McLeod, OBE, FRS, FRSE (d 1978), of Edinburgh, and his 1 w, Jane Christina, *née* Garvie (d 1953); *Educ* Univ of Leeds (MB ChB); *m* 1, 1940 (m dis), Lt-Col D S Richard, MBE; 2 s; m 2, 1 Dec 1962, as his 3 w, 4 Earl of Cromartie, MC, TD, JP, DL (d 1989); *Style—* Lilias, Countess of Cromartie

CROMBIE, Alastair Charles MacDonald; s of Alistair Cameron Crombie, of Oxford, and Nancy, *née* Hey; *b* 14 July 1947; *Educ* Downside Sch, St Andrews Univ (MA); *Career* journalist: Investors Chronicle 1977-79, Investors in Industry 1979-81; Corp Fin Dept Guinness Mahon & Co Ltd 1982-85; ptnr Robson Rhodes 1985-; *Recreations* music, tennis, skiing, travel; *Style—* Charles Crombie, Esq; 186, City Rd, London, EC1V 2NY, (☎ 071 251 1644, fax 071 250 0801)

CROMBIE, Prof Alexander Leaster; s of Richard Crombie (d 1987), and Annie Drummond (d 1983); *b* 7 Aug 1935; *Educ* Cork GS, Galashiels Acad, Univ of Edinburgh (MB ChB); *m* 26 Aug 1961, Margaret Ann, da of David Alexander Adamson (d 1981); 2 s (Richard David, David Alexander), 2 da (Pauline Ann, Louise Margaret); *Career* clinical tutor in ophthalmology Univ of Edinburgh 1964-67, MRC fell John Hopkins Univ Baltimore USA 1965-66, conslt ophthalmologist Royal Victoria Infirmary Newcastle upon Tyne 1967-; Univ of Newcastle upon Tyne: prof of ophthalmology 1976-, assoc dean Med Sch 1981-89, dean of med 1989-; author of chapters in books on ophthalmology, medical ethics and medical education; vice pres Coll of Ophthalmologists, pres Age Concern Newcastle, tstee Northumbria Calvert Tst, memb Univ Devpt Tst; FRCSEd 1964, FCOphth 1989; *Recreations* golf, reading, music, art, walking; *Style—* Prof Alexander Crombie; 19 Graham Park Road, Gosforth, Newcastle upon Tyne (☎ 091 285 2378); 6 The Granary, Dunbar, East Lothian, Scotland; The Medical School, University of Newcastle upon Tyne, Framlington Place, Newcastle upon Tyne NE2 4HH (☎ 091 222 6000)

CROMBIE, Alexander Llewellyn Wallace; s of James Wallace Crombie (d 1947), and Sarah Emily, *née* Morris; *b* 19 July 1943; *Educ* Ellesmere Coll, Worcester Coll For The Blind, Nottingham Univ (LLB); *m* 8 April 1972, Caroline Cawood, da of David John Laurance; 2 s (Duncan b 1975, Hamish b 1978), 1 da (Sarah b 1973); *Career* admitted slr 1955, sr ptnr Crombie Collins & Haddon-Grant 1971-88; ptnr Ironsides Ray & Vials 1988-; chm: Consumer Cncl for Visually Handicapped Leics 1982-89, Nat Library for the Blind 1982-87, Braille Chess Assoc 1987-89; memb Law Soc; *Style—* Alexander Crombie, Esq; Elwyn House, Market Place, Uppingham, Leics (fax 0572 821502)

CROME, David Robert; s of Robert Crome (d 1962), and Margaret, *née* Williamson; *b* 23 Nov 1937; *Educ* William Hulme's GS Manchester; *m* 28 Sept 1963, Sandra Joan, da of Albert Storrs, of Lowestoft; 3 da (Ruth Margaret b 1964, Helen Jayne (Mrs Hardy) b 1965, Wendy May b 1970); *Career* admitted slr 1960; snr ptnr Dunne & Crome 1964, princ magistrate (later chief magistrate and acting chief justice) Solomon Islands 1980-82, asst rec SE Circuit 1989; chm of Industl Tbnls 1990; Parly candidate (Lib) Lowestoft (now Waveney) Div 1966 and 1970; Liveryman Worshipful Co of Arbitrators; FCIArb 1973; *Recreations* sailing, singing (tenor), cycling; *Clubs* Royal Norfolk and Suffolk Yacht, Norfolk, Wig and Pen; *Style—* David Robert Crome, Esq; Underhill, Poughfer's Pightle, Puddingmoor, Beccles, Suffolk NR34 9PJ (☎ 0502 716949)

CROMER, 3 Earl of (UK 1901); George Rowland Stanley Baring; KG (1977), GCMG (1974, KCMG 1971), MBE (mil 1945), PC (1966); also Baron Cromer (UK 1892), Viscount Cromer (UK 1899), Viscount Errington (UK 1901); s of 2 Earl, GCB, GCIE, GCVO, PC (d 1953), and Lady Ruby Elliot, 2 da of 4 Earl of Minto, KG, GCSI, GCMG; *b* 28 July 1918,HM King George V stood sponsor; *Educ* Eton, Trinity Coll Cambridge; *m* 10 Jan 1942, Hon Esmé Mary Gabrielle Harmsworth, CVO, da of 2 Viscount Rothermere; 2 s, 1 da (decd); *Heir* s, Viscount Errington; *Career* served WWII, NW Europe (despatches) Lt-Col Gren Gds; page of honour to HM King George V 1933-35 and to Queen Mary at Coronation 1937; econ min HM Embassy Washington, head of Treasury Delgn (and UK exec dir IMF, IBRD, IFC) 1959-61, govr Bank of England 1961-66, govr IBRD and dir Bank of Int Settlements Basle 1961-66, dir Compagnie Financière de Suez 1967-82; chm: London Multinational Bank Ltd 1967-70, IBM (UK) Ltd 1967-70 and 1974-79; dir: Daily Mail and General Tst Co Ltd 1974- (and 1949-61, 1966-70), Imperial Gp Ltd 1974-80, P & O 1974-80, Shell Tport and Trading Co Ltd 1974-89, Robeco Gp of Investmt Tsts Rotterdam 1977-88, IBM World Trade Corpn NY 1977-83, Barfield Tst Co Ltd Guernsey 1979-89, Baring Henderson Gilt Fund 1979-; memb Advsy Cncl IBM Corpn NY 1967-88; advsr Baring Bros and Co Ltd 1974- (md 1948-61, sr ptnr and md 1966-70); chm Int Advsy Cncl Morgan Guaranty Tst Co of NY 1977-88; int advsr Marsh and McLennan Cos NY; HM ambass Washington 1971-74; HM Lieut City of London 1961-; DL Kent 1968-79; chm Churchill Meml Tst 1979; Hon LLD New York 1966; *Clubs* Brooks's, Beefsteak, White's; *Style—* The Rt Hon The Earl of Cromer, KG, GCMG, MBE, PC; Beaufield House, St Saviour, Jersey, Channel Islands (☎ 0534 61671); Morgan Guaranty Tst Co of New York, Queensway House, Queen St, St Helier, Jersey, Channel Islands (☎ 0534 71566, telex 4192358)

CROMIE, Stephen John Henry; s of Dr Brian William Cromie, of 14 Park St, Kings Cliffe, Northants, and Heather Anne Howie, *née* Wood; *b* 13 Jan 1957; *Educ* Abingdon Sch, Downing Coll Cambridge (MA); *m* 28 Aug 1982, Marianne Frances, da of John Edward Burton, East Ewell, Surrey; 1 s (Jonathan b 1989); *Career* admitted slr 1981; ptnr Linklaters & Paines 1987- (joined 1979); memb: Law Soc, City of London Slr's Co; *Books* International Commercial Litigation (jtly, 1990); *Recreations* wine, cooking, cycling; *Style—* S J H Cromie, Esq; 4 Huntingdon St, London N1 1BU; Barrington House, 59/67 Gresham St, London EC2V 7JA (☎ 071 606 7080, fax 071 606 5113, telex 884349)

CROMPTON, Prof David William Thomasson; s of Arthur Thomasson Crompton, of Bolton, Lancashire, and Gladys, *née* Mather; *b* 5 Dec 1937; *Educ* Bolton Sch, Univ of Cambridge (BA, MA, PhD, ScD); *m* 14 April 1962, Effie Mary, da of Robert Marshall (d 1989), of Stowmarket, Suffolk; 1 s (John b 1963), 2 da (Tessa b 1964, Virginia b 1967); *Career* Nat Serv 2 Lt Kings Own Royal Regt 1956-58; lectr Univ of Cambridge 1968-85 (asst in res 1963-68), vice master Sidney Sussex Coll 1981-83 (res fell 1964-65, fell 1965- 1965-85), adjunct prof Div of Nutritional Sciences Cornell Univ NY 1981, John Graham Kerr prof of zoology Univ of Glasgow 1985; Scientific medal The Zoological Soc of London 1977; fndr memb Br Soc for Parasitology 1962, memb American Inst of Nutrition 1981, co ed Parasitology 1972-82; memb: Aquatic Life Sciences Ctee NERC 1981-84, WHO Expert Ctee for Parasitic Diseases 1985-; dir Co of Biologists Ltd 1985-, head of WHO Collaborating Centre for Ascariasis at Univ of Glasgow 1989, memb American Soc of Parasitology 1989; fell Royal Soc of Tropical Med and Hygiene 1986, FIBiol 1979, FZS 1980, FRSE 1989; *Books* An Ecological Approach to Acanthocephalan Physiology (1970), Parasitic Worms (with S M Joyner, 1980), Parasites and People (1984), Biology of the Acanthocephala (ed with B B Nickol), Ascariasis and its Public Health Significance (ed with M C Nesheim and Z S Pawlowski, 1985), Ascariasis and its Prevention and Control (ed with M C Nesheim and Z S Pawlowski, 1989); *Recreations* hill walking, fishing, books, terriers, especially bull terriers; *Style—* Prof David Crompton, FRSE; 7 Kirklee Terrace, Glasgow, Scotland G12 0TQ (☎ 041 357 2631); Department of Zoology, School of Biological Sciences, University of Glasgow, Glasgow G12 8QQ (☎ 041 330 5395, fax 041 330 5971, telex 777070)

CROMPTON, Prof Gareth; s of Edward Crompton (d 1986), of Drefach-Felindre, Dyfed, and Annie Jane, *née* Jones; *b* 9 Jan 1937; *Educ* Llandysul GS, Univ of Wales Coll of Med (MB BCh); *m* 12 June 1965, Valmai Gloria, da of Reginald Thomas Lalande (d 1969), of Barry, S Glamorgan; 1 da (Elspeth b 1974); *Career* prof of public health med Univ of Wales Coll of Med, chief admin med offr and dir public health med S Glam Health Authy 1989-, chief med offr Welsh Office 1978-89, area med offr Gwynedd Area Health Authy 1974-77, Anglesey CC 1966-73 (co med offr, co welfare offr, princ schs med offr), specialty advsr Health Serv cmmr for England and Wales 1974-77, advsr in Wales of Faculty of Community Med of RCP 1974-77, chm Anglesey Disablement Advsy Ctee 1969-77, sec Fluoridation Study Gp of Soc Med Offrs of Health 1969-73; memb: Gen Med Cncl 1981-83 and 1987-89, Med Advsy Ctee to Registrar Gen 1988-90; QHP 1984-87; DPH 1964, DRCOG 1962, FFCM 1976, FRCP 1986, FFPHM 1989; *Recreations* bowls, gardening, golf, watching rugby football; *Clubs* Cardiff Athletic; *Style—* Prof Gareth Crompton; Temple of Peace and Health, Cathays Park, Cardiff, CF1 3NW (☎ 0222 231021, fax 0222 238606)

CROMPTON, (Michael) Robin; s of James Dale Crompton (d 1971), of Leyland, and Elsie, *née* Harrison; *b* 19 March 1938; *Educ* Manchester GS, Jesus Coll Cambridge (BA, MA); *Career* lectr Inst of Applied Linguistics Univ of Heidelberg W Germany 1964-71; HM Dip Serv 1971; Br High Cmmn: Lagos 1973-76, Nairobi 1978-83; dep head of mission Br Embassy Kinshasa 1983-87, FCO 1987- (London 1971-73, 1976-78); memb: Nat Trust, Nat Cncl of Civil Liberties, Anti-Apartheid Movement, Friends of the Earth, World Expeditionary Assoc, Literacy Guild, Signatory Charter, Old Mancunians Assoc, Jesus Coll Cambridge Soc; *Books* Britain's Relations with SW Germany (with Dr W Engelmann, trans 1965), The History of Heidelberg University (trans 1966), Goethe: Visits to Heidelberg (1966), Fontane: Wanderings Through Berlin (1968); *Recreations* music, travel, motoring, walking, reading; *Clubs* Cwlth Soc; *Style—* Robin Crompton, Esq; c/o Foreign & Commonwealth Office, King Charles St, London SW1 (☎ 071 270 2889)

CROMPTON, Air Cdre Roy Hartley; OBE (1962); s of Francis John Crompton (d 1970), of Bedford, and Harriet Ann, *née* Hartley (d 1973); *b* 24 April 1921; *Educ* Bedford Sch, UCL (BA); *m* 1 (m dis 1961); m 2, 1961, Rita Mabel, da of late Robert Leslie of Dumfries, Scotland; 1 da (Sheena Patricia b 1963); *Career* Nat Serv WWII and immediate post-war flying and staff appts 1942-59, OC Flying RAF Oakington 1959-62, Chiefs of Staff Secretariat 1962-64, Station Cdr RAF Linton-on-Ouse 1965-67, Def Policy Staff MOD London 1968-69, Gp Dir RAF Staff Coll Bracknell 1970, project offr for establishing Nat Def Coll Latimer 1970-71, AOC and Cmdt Central Flying Sch Little Rissington 1972-74, Gp Dir HO CD Coll Easingwold 1974-85, re-employed to head a Nat CD project 1987-88; played cricket: Derbyshire II 1938, Beds 1946-47; Capt Easingwold GC 1985-86, co helper RAF Benevolent Fund, vice pres York Branch RAF Assoc, fndr and life memb The Spitfire Soc, chm Newton & Dist Branch Royal Br Legion, memb Assoc of Voluntary Guides City of York, dep pres Soc of Indust Emergency Servs Offrs; FBIM; *Books* Guide to Emergency Planning (jtly, 1986); *Recreations* golf, horticulture, music; *Clubs* RAF; *Style—* Air Cdre Roy Crompton, OBE; Sharnford Lodge, Huby, York YO6 1HT

CROMPTON, Dr (Michael) Rufus; s of Clifford Crompton (d 1972), of Worthing, and Sarah Aston, *née* Winterburn (d 1988); *b* 9 Sept 1931; *Educ* Shrewsbury, UCH London (MB BS, MD, PhD, DMJ); *m* 3 May 1972, (Yvonne) Anne, da of Bertram Pulford, of Epsom; 2 da (Yvette Selina Ashton b 10 Feb 1973, Danielle Dorothea Clare b 4 Jan 1977); *Career* sr registrar Nat Hosp Queens Square London 1957; Dept of Neurosurgery St George's Hosp London: sr registrar 1959, conslt neuropathologist 1963, conslt forensic pathologist 1970; providing forensic serv to Her Majesty's Coroner and the Met Police; memb: Br Assoc of Forensic Med 1963, Medico Legal Soc 1963; MRCS, LRCP, FRCPath; *Books* Closed Head Injury, Its Pathology and Legal Medicine (1985); *Recreations* supporting family riding activities; *Clubs* Hurlingham; *Style—* Dr Rufus Crompton; 3 Lansdowne Crescent, London W11 2NH (☎ 071 727 3325); Department of Forensic Medicine, St George's Hospital Medical School, London SW17 0RE (☎ 081 672 9944 ext 55240-1)

CROMPTON, Hon Mrs (Virginia Mary Clementine); da of 2 Baron Keyes; *b* 20 March 1950; *m* 1972, Rev (Roger) Martyn Francis Crompton; 4 da (Heather b 1976, Bryony b 1978, Rowan b 1981, Holly b 1983); *Style—* Mrs Crompton; The Vicarage, Church St, Golcar, Huddersfield HD7 4PX

CROMWELL, 7 Baron (E 1375); Godfrey John Bewicke-Copley; s of 6 Baron Cromwell (d 1982; Barony abeyant 1497 to 1923, when abeyance terminated in favour of present Baron's gf, 5 Baron); *b* 4 March 1960; *m* 23 June 1990, Elizabeth A, da of

John Hawksley; *Heir* yr bro, Hon Thomas Bewicke-Copley; *Style—* The Rt Hon the Lord Cromwell; c/o House of Lords, London SW1

CROMWELL, Baroness; The Rt Hon The Lady (Doris) Vivian; yst da of Hugh de Lisle Penfold, of IOM; *m* 16 Jan 1954, 6 Baron Cromwell (d 1982); 2 s (7 Baron, Hon Thomas Bewicke-Copley), 2 da (Hon Anne Bewicke-Copley, Hon Davina Bewicke-Copley); *Style—* The Rt Hon Vivian, Lady Cromwell

CRONIN, Damian Francis; *Career* Rugby Union lock forward Bath RFC and Scotland; clubs: Bath RFC, Ilford Wanderers, Barbarians RFC, Penguins RFC, Anglo-Scots; Scotland: debut v Ireland 1988, Grand Slam winners 1990, tour Zimbabwe 1988, tour Japan 1989, tour NZ 1990; *Recreations* antiques and restoration, squash; *Style—* Damian Cronin, Esq; Bath Rugby Club, Recreation Ground, Bath, Avon

CRONIN, Hon Mrs (Jane); *née* Elton; 2 da of 2 Baron Elton; *b* 15 Jan 1962; *m* 29 April 1989, James A J Cronin, s of Vincent Cronin, of Hyde Park Square, London W2; *Style—* The Hon Mrs Cronin

CRONIN, Tacey Marguerite (Mrs David Bain); da of Flt Lt Anthony Arthur Cronin (d 1972), and Margaret Elizabeth, *née* Roberts; *b* 28 June 1959; *Educ* Stamford HS, Bristol Univ (LLB); *m* 3 Jan 1987, David Ian Bain, s of Capt David Walter Bain (d 1975); 1 da (Athene Margaret b 1990); *Career* called to the Bar Middle Temple 1982; memb: Bar Cncl 1985-86, Gen Cncl of the Bar 1987; *Recreations* theatre, golf, motor racing, travel; *Style—* Ms Tacey Cronin; Albion Chambers East, Broad St, Bristol BS1 1DR (☎ 0272 272144, fax 0272 262569)

CRONIN, Vincent Archibald Patrick; s of Archibald Joseph Cronin (d 1981), of Vevey, Switzerland, and Agnes Mary, *née* Gibson (d 1981); *b* 24 May 1924; *Educ* Ampleforth, Trinity Coll Oxford (BA); *m* 25 Aug 1949, Chantal, da of Comte Jean De Rolland (d 1985), of Manoir De Brion, Dragey Par, Sartilly 50530, France; 2 s (James b 1956, Luan b 1959), 3 da (Sulvilie b 1951, Dauphine b 1962, Natalie b 1967); *Career* author; memb Cncl RSL 1976-86; *Books* incl: The Golden Honeycombe (1954), The Wire Man From the West (1955), A Pearl to India (1959), Louis XIV (1964), Napoleon (1964), The Florentine Renaissance (1967), The View From Planet Earth (1981); *Recreations* swimming, tennis; *Style—* Vincent Cronin, Esq; Manoir De Brion, Dragey Par, Sartilly 50530, France; c/o Collins, 8 Grafton St, London W1X 3LA

CRONK, Anthony; s of Capt William Douglas Cronk (d 1947), and Evelyn Joyce, *née* Hanson-Dodwell; *b* 24 July 1917; *Educ* Tonbridge, Wye Coll London; *m* 26 Feb 1949, Margaret, da of Capt E C J Spencer (d 1975); 2 s (Paul Ricard b 1951, Quentin Charles Bargrave b 1959), 1 da (Felicity Mary b 1949); *Career* served WWII Maj RA; Lloyd's underwriter 1960-84; farmer, now ret; vice pres Kent Co Agric Soc 1968- (fin chm 1964-74), memb Hops Marketing Bd 1955-65, tstee Marshall's Charity 1975-; author of books on local history and vernacular buildings; FSA 1978, FRSA 1973; *Clubs* Farmers', Castle (Rochester); *Style—* Anthony Cronk, Esq, FSA; c/o The Royal Bank of Scotland, 67 Lombard Street, London EC3P 3DL

CROOK, Anthony Donald (Tony); s of Thomas Roland (d 1926), of Woodland Grange, Hoghton, nr Preston, Lancs, and Emily, *née* Allsup; *b* 16 Feb 1923; *Educ* Clifton, Sidney Sussex Coll Cambridge; *m* 28 June 1943, Dianne Ada, da of William Smith (d 1958), of Lincoln; 1 da (Carole Anne); *Career* RAF 1939-46 (despatches twice), Flt Lt 1945; formed racing car partnership with Raymond Mays 1945, won first post-war motor race to be held in Britain 1946, raced and distributed Bristol Cars made by Bristol Aeroplane Co; over 400 races incl: formula one and two, Grand Prix and speed hill climbs 1946-55; bought (with the late Sir George White) Bristol Cars 1960 (by 1973 sole owner, md and chm); *Clubs* Br Racing Drivers; *Style—* Tony Crook, Esq; Bristol Cars Ltd, Head Office, 368-370 Kensington High St, London W14 8NL (☎ 071 603 0366)

CROOK, Clive Walter Levers; s of Frank Harefield Crook, and May, *née* Williams; *b* 29 July 1936; *Educ* Southall Tech Coll Southall Middx; *m* 10 Sept 1960, Jill Marion, da of J R Metson; 1 da (Helen Alison b 17 April 1965); *Career* dir: Banque Kleinwort Benson SA of Geneva 1978 (ret 1990), Wotherspoon Holdings Ltd; *Recreations* golf, music, piano; *Clubs* Wasps RFC, Harrow RFC, Eastcote Cricket, Moor Park Golf; *Style—* Clive W L Crook, Esq; 43 Highview, Pinner, Middx HA5 3PE (☎ 081 868 7610)

CROOK, Colin; s of Richard Crook (d 1970), and Ruth Crook (d 1971); *b* 1 June 1942; *Educ* Harris Coll Preston, Liverpool Poly; *m* 1965, Dorothy Jean, da of Alfred Edward Taylor, of Wallasey; 2 da; *Career* Motorola (USA) 1969-79, dir advanced systems gp ops MGR Microcomputers 1975-78; md: Zynar Holdings BV, Rank Precision Industries 1978-80, Br Telecom Enterprises; chm: HBS Ltd (UK) 1980-83, Nestar Systems (USA) 1980-83; memb Main Bd BT 1983-1984, sr vice pres Data General Corpn 1984-89, chm Corp Technol Ctee Citicorp NY USA 1990-; FEng, MIEE, MIERE, MIEEE, MACM (USA); *Recreations* photography, sailing, reading, travel; *Style—* Colin Crook, Esq; The Old School House, Harvest Hill, Hedsor, Bourne End, Bucks SL8 5JJ (☎ 062 8527479); Citibank, 399 Park Ave, NY, NY 10043, USA

CROOK, 2 Baron (UK 1947), of Carshalton, Co Surrey; Douglas Edwin Crook; o s of 1 Baron Crook (d 1989), and Ida Gertrude Catherine, *née* Haddon (d 1985); *b* 19 Nov 1926; *Educ* Whitgift Middle Sch Croydon, Imperial Coll London (ACGI, BSc, DIC); *m* 15 Feb 1954, Ellenor, da of Robert Rouse (d 1962), of Sunderland; 1 s (Hon Robert Douglas Edwin b 29 May 1955), 1 da (Hon Catherine Hilary (Hon Mrs (Christopher John) Ramsdale) b 22 May 1960); *Heir* s, Hon Robert Douglas Edwin Crook b 1955; *Career* CEng, MICE; *Style—* The Rt Hon Lord Crook; Ridgehill Barn, Etchinghill, Folkestone, Kent CT18 8BP (☎ 0303 863 353)

CROOK, Frances Rachel; da of Maurice Crook (d 1977), of London, and Sheila Sibson-Turnbull; *b* 18 Dec 1952; *Educ* Camden Sch London, Univ of Liverpool (BA), Univ of Lancaster (PGCE); 1 da (Sarah Rose Eleanor b 27 May 1988); *Career* campaign organiser Amnesty Int 1980-85, dir Howard League for Penal Reform 1985-; councillor Barnet Borough 1982-90, memb: Lab Party, CND, TGWU; *Style—* Ms Frances Crook; The Howard League, 708 Holloway Road, London N19 3NL (☎ 071 281 7722)

CROOK, Prof (Joseph) Mordaunt; s of Austin Mordaunt Crook (d 1967), and Florence Irene, *née* Woolfendon (d 1986); *b* 27 Feb 1937; *Educ* Wimbledon Coll, BNC Oxford (MA, DPhil); *m* 1, 4 Jul 1964, Margaret Constance, da of James Mulholland (d 1974); m 2, 9 July 1975, Susan, da of Frederick Hoyland Mayor (d 1972); *Career* lectr Bedford Coll London 1965-75, res fell Warburg Inst 1970-71, reader in architectural hist Univ of London 1975-81, Slade prof of fine art Univ of Oxford 1979-80, visiting fell BNC Oxford 1979-80, prof of architectural history Univ of London 1981-, visiting fell and Waynflete lectr Magdalen Coll Oxford 1985, visiting fell Gonville and Caius Coll Cambridge 1986, public orator Univ of London 1988-91; memb Historic Bldgs Cncl for Eng 1974-84, pres Soc of Architectural Historians (GB); Freeman Goldsmiths Co 1978 (Liveryman 1984); FSA, FBA; *Books* The British Museum (1972), The Greek Revival (1972), The History of The King's Works (1973-76), William Burges and the High Victorian Dream (1981), The Dilemma of Style: Architectural Ideas from the Picturesque to the Post-Modern (1987); *Recreations* strolling; *Clubs* Athenaeum, Brooks's; *Style—* Prof J M Crook, FSA; 55 Gloucester Ave, London NW1 7BA (☎ 071 485 8280); Royal Holloway and Bedford New Coll, Egham, Surrey (☎ 0784 34455)

CROOK, Paul; s of William Giles Crook, of Poole, Dorset, and Helen Margaret, *née* Swales; *b* 6 March 1952; *Educ* Ruzawi Sch Zimbabwe, Peterhouse Sch Zimbabwe, Jesus Coll Cambridge (MA, LLB); *m* 11 Sept 1976, Dr Susan Jill, da of Dr Andrew Ernest Dossetor, of Newmarket, Suffolk; 2 s (John b 1988, Peter b 1990), 1 da (Anne b 1986); *Career* admitted slr 1978, ptnr Allen & Overy 1984-; Freeman City of London Slrs Co 1984; memb Law Soc; *Recreations* golf, hockey, skiing, squash, tennis; *Style—* Paul Crook, Esq; Allen & Overy, 9 Cheapside, London EC2V 6AD (☎ 071 248 9898, fax 071 236 2192, telex 881 2801)

CROOKALL, Prof John Roland; s of Dr Robert Crookall (d 1981), and Gladys Kate, *née* Stoneham (d 1969); *b* 5 May 1935; *Educ* Willesden Coll of Technol (HNC), Imperial Coll (DIC), Univ of Nottingham (PhD); *m* 19 June 1965, Gretta Mary, da of Basil Blaxley Inger; 2 s (Barry Nicholas b 5 Oct 1966, Andrew Spencer b 1 Oct 1967), 1 da (Sheila Elizabeth Anne b 8 May 1972); *Career* performance and design engr aero-engines de Havilland Engine Co Ltd 1957-61 (engrg apprentice 1952-57), visiting lectr Willesden Coll of Technol 1958-62, PhD res Univ of Nottingham 1962-65, lectr and course mangr MSc course in prodn technol Imperial Coll London 1965-74; Cranfield Inst of Technol: prof of mfrg systems 1974-90, head Dept for Design of Machine Systems 1982-84, prof of mfrg 1990-; conslt Cranfield Unit for Precision Engrg 1980-90, fndr and chm Computer Intergrated Manufacturing Inst Cranfield 1985-90, fndr and head Coll of Manufacturing Cranfield 1985-90, memb Bd CIM Technology Ltd 1985-90, currently chm CIRP (UK) Ltd; memb numerous ctees and professional bodies incl: memb and chm UK Bd Int Inst for Prodn Engrg Res (CIRP), memb and UK rep Int Fedn of Info Processing (IFIP); external examiner 5 undergraduate prodn and mechanical engrg courses within UK, author numerous learned papers and publications; *awards* Inst of Mechanical Engrs: James Clayton fell 1962, James Clayton prize 1965, E Midlands Branch prize 1965; meritorious commendation 1986, Indust Year Awards DTI 1986; sr memb American Soc of Mfrg Engrs, FEng, CEng, FIMechE, FIProdE, MBIM, MBAE, memb Royal Coll of Organists; *Style—* Prof John R Crookall; J R Crookall and Associates, 12 Hall Close, Harrold, Bedford MK43 7DU (☎ 0234 720475, fax 0234 720675)

CROOKE, Dr John Walter; s of William Grosvenor Crooke (d 1985), of Lincs, and Esmé Beatrice, *née* Greene (d 1989); *b* 7 July 1933; *Educ* Scunthorpe GS, UCH London (BSc, MB BS, DA); *m* 28 Oct 1961, Mary Lynn, da of Angus Ernest Gibson (d 1980), of Lincoln; 1 s (James), 1 da (Heather); *Career* Nat Serv Capt RAMC, anaesthetist Br Mily Hosp Benghazi N Africa; conslt anaesthetist Royal Liverpool Hosp Liverpool Health Authy 1968-, pt/t demonstrator Dept of Anaesthesia Univ of Liverpool 1978 (pt/t lectr Dept of Dental Surgery); med rep Mersey Regnl Supplies Ctee, memb Assoc of Anaesthetists, fell Coll of Anaesthetists; memb: HCSA, BMA; *Recreations* flying (PPL), car restoration, fishing, cycling; *Clubs* Aston Martin Owners, Lotus, RSPB; *Style—* Dr John W Crooke; The Pingles, 12 Park Avenue, Crosby, Liverpool L23 2SP (☎ 051 924 5758); Dept of Anaesthesia, 12th Floor, Royal Liverpool Hospital, Prescot St, Liverpool (☎ 051 706 2000)

CROOKENDEN, Lt-Gen Sir Napier; KCB (1970, CB 1966), DSO (1945), OBE (1954), DL (Kent 1979); 2 s of Col Arthur Crookenden, CBE, DSO (d 1962), and Dorothy, *née* Rowlandson; *b* 31 Aug 1915; *Educ* Wellington, RMC Sandhurst; *m* 3 Aug 1948, Hon Patricia Nassau, da of 2 Baron Kindersley, CBE, MC; 2 s, 2 da; *Career* Cheshire Regt 1935, CO 9 Para Br 1944-46 and 16 Para Bde 1960-61, dir Land/Air Warfare 1964-66, Comdt Royal Mil Coll of Science 1958-59, Col The Cheshire Regt 1969-71, GOC-in-C Western Cmd 1969-72, Col Cmdt Prince of Wales Div 1971-74; dir: SE Regnl Bd Lloyds Bank Ltd 1973-86, Flextech Ltd 1973-86; tstee Imperial War Museum 1973-83, chm SSAFA 1974-85, Lt HM Tower of London 1975-81; *Books* Drop Zone Normandy (1976), Airborne at War (1978), Battle of the Bulge 1944 (1980); *Clubs* Army and Navy; *Style—* Lt-Gen Sir Napier Crookenden, KCB, DSO, OBE, DL; Twin Firs, Four Elms, Edenbridge, Kent TN8 6PL (☎ 073 270 229)

CROOKENDEN, Hon Lady (Patricia Nassau); *née* Kindersley; er da of 2 Baron Kindersley, CBE, MC (d 1976); *b* 5 Aug 1922; *m* 3 Aug 1948, Lt-Gen Sir Napier Crookenden, KCB, DSO, OBE, *qv*; 2 s, 2 da; *Style—* The Hon Lady Crookenden; Twin Firs, Four Elms, Edenbridge, Kent TN8 6PL

CROOKENDEN, Simon Robert; s of Maj Spencer Crookenden, CBE, MC, of Reston Hall, Staveley, Kendal, Cumbria, and late Jean, *née* Dewing; *b* 27 Sept 1946; *Educ* Winchester, Corpus Christi Coll Cambridge (MA); *m* 20 Aug 1983, Sarah Anne Georgina Margaret, da of George Leonard Pragnell, of 2 Paragon Terrace, Bath Rd, Cheltenham; 1 s (Thomas Henry b 19 Sept 1987), 1 da (Rebecca Jean b 9 Nov 1985); *Career* called to the Bar Gray's Inn 1974; *Recreations* rowing; *Clubs* London Rowing; *Style—* Simon Crookenden, Esq; 4 Essex Court, Temple, London EC4 (☎ 071 583 9191)

CROOKS, John Leslie; s of Henry Leslie Crooks (d 1976), of Scarborough, and Elizabeth Ellen, *née* Johnson (d 1987); *b* 5 May 1928; *Educ* Uppingham, Univ of London (MRCVS); *m* 10 May 1952, Dorothy Heather, da of Thomas Reginald Broumpton (d 1967), of Driffield; 1 s (James b 1956), 2 da (Annette b 1954, Elizabeth b 1960); *Career* vet surgn; dir Veterinary Drug Co plc 1958 (chm 1982); pres Br Vet Assoc 1983-84; Liveryman Worshipful Co of Farriers; *Recreations* shooting, fishing, gardening, cooking; *Clubs* Royal Soc of Medicine; *Style—* John L Crooks, Esq; Westwood Mill, Beverley HU17 8RG (☎ 0482 881296); Veterinary Drug Co plc, Common Rd, Dunnington, York YO1 5RU (☎ 0904 48844, telex 57588 VETDRUG)

CROOKS, Stanley George; s of Wallace George Crooks (d 1978), and Alice Mary, *née* Clancy (d 1989); *b* 3 March 1925; *Educ* St Marylebone GS London, Univ of London (BSc, BSc Econ); *m* 22 July 1950, Gwendoline May, da of Arthur George Hatch; 1 s (Andrew b 1959), 1 da (Julia b 1961); *Career* Royal Artillery 1943-47 (service Burma 1944-45, Indochina 1945, Mala 1946, Hong Kong 1947); Pirelli Group of Companies 1950-; Pirelli General Ltd Southampton 1950-71 (md 1967-71), Societe Internationale Pirelli Basle 1971-82 (dep gen mangr 1971-74, gen mangr 1974-82), dir and gen mangr Pirelli Societe Generale Basle (1982-87); chm: Pirelli General plc 1987-, Pirelli Ltd 1987-, Pirelli Construction Co Ltd 1982-, Pirelli Focom Ltd 1987-; vice chm Pirelli UK plc 1989-; vice chm of Cncl Univ of Southampton 1987-; chm: Univ of Southampton Univ Mgmnt Sch 1990-, govrs Southampton Inst of Higher Educ 1988-90, pres Southern Sci and Technol Forum 1977-; Hon DSc Southampton 1977; FIEE 1965, CBIM 1970; *Recreations* gardening, music, reading; *Style—* Stanley Crooks, Esq; Bournewood House, Bourne Lane, Twyford, Winchester, Hampshire SO21 1NX; Pirelli UK plc, 40 Chancery Lane, London WC2A 1JH (☎ 071 242 8881, fax 071 430 1096, telex 22520)

CROOKSHANK, John Kennedy; s of Lt-Col C K Crookshank; *b* 15 Aug 1932; *Educ* Repton, Sandhurst; *m* 1974, Diana Lesley, da of Cdr Brookes; 1 s, 1 da, 4 step children; *Career* Capt 5 Royal Inniskilling Dragoon Gds; ADC to govr of Gibraltar 1958-60; publishing dir Reed Business Publishing 1972-; *Recreations* sailing, skiing, ornithology, archaeology, travel, book collecting; *Clubs* Royal London Yacht, RAC, Emsworth Sailing; *Style—* John Kennedy Crookshank, Esq; Ivy House, Westbourne, Emsworth, Hants

CROOKSTON, Peter Christian; s of Robert Crookston (d 1969), and Nancy Hedley; *b* 30 Dec 1936; *Educ* Clegwell Sch Hebburn on Tyne, Newcastle upon Tyne Coll of Commerce; *m* 1, Julia Hampton (m dis 1974); 1 s (James b 21 Feb 1970); m 2, 31 March 1988, Zoe Zenghelis, da of John Tsakiris (d 1985), of Herodotou 12, Athens,

Greece; *Career* ed Nova magazine 1969-71; features ed: Sunday Times 1971-73, The Observer 1973-77; ed: The Observer Magazine 1977-82, Geo International 1988-90; dep ed Departures 1990-; *Books* Villain (1967), Village England (1979), Island Britain (1981), The Ages of Britain (1982); *Clubs* Chelsea Arts, The Groucho; *Style—* Peter Crookston, Esq; 84 Portland Road, London W11 4LQ; 3 Tottenham St, London W1P 9PB (☎ 071 631 3484, fax 071 323 4672)

CROOM, David Halliday; s of Sir John Croom (d 1986), of Edinburgh, and Valerie Enid, *née* Samuel; *b* 26 June 1946; *Educ* Trinity Coll Glenalmond, Magdalen Coll Oxford; *m* 30 June 1979, Laura, da of Edward Koffenberger, of Newark, Delaware, USA; 2 s (James b 1983, Patrick b 1985), 1 da (Zoe b 1988); *Career* co-fndr and jt md Croom Helm Ltd 1972-86, md Academic Div Associated Book Publishers 1986-87, md Routledge Ltd 1988; *Recreations* collecting contemporary art; *Clubs* Savile; *Style—* David Croom, Esq; Routledge Ltd, 11 New Fetter Lane, London EC4P 4EE (☎ 071 583 9855, telex 263398 Routledge, fax 071 583 0701)

CROOM, Lady; Endi Valerie; *née* Samuel; da of Dr David Samuel, JP; *m* 1940, Sir John Halliday Croom, TD (d 1986); 1 s, 1 da; *Career* actress known as Valerie Tudor; *Style—* Lady Croom; 27 Learmonth Terrace, Edinburgh EH4 1NZ (☎ 031 332 5933)

CROOM-JOHNSON, Rt Hon Sir David Powell; PC (1984), DSC (1944), VRD (1953); 3 s of late Hon Sir Reginald Powell Croom-Johnson (d 1957), sometime a Judge of the High Court, and Lady Ruby Ernestine, *née* Hobbs (d 1961); *b* 28 Nov 1914; *Educ* Stowe, Trinity Hall Cambridge (hon fell 1985); *m* 1940, Barbara Douglas, da of Erskine Douglas Warren, of Toronto, Canada; 1 da; *Career* barr 1938, QC 1958, rec Winchester 1962-71, judge of Courts of Appeal Jersey and Guernsey 1966-71, high court judge (Queen's Bench Div) 1971-84, Lord Justice of Appeal 1984-89; kt 1971; *Clubs* Garrick; *Style—* The Rt Hon Sir David Croom-Johnson, DSC, VRD; Royal Courts of Justice, Strand, London WC2

CROPPER, Hilary Mary; da of Arnold Trueman, of Cheshire, and Madeline Emily, *née* Sutton; *b* 9 Jan 1941; *Educ* Univ of Salford (BSc); *m* 16 Sept 1963, Peter John Cropper, s of Samuel Cropper; 1 s (Carl St John b 1971), 2 da (Elizabeth b 1969, Charlotte b 1973); *Career* various sr mgmnt positions ICL 1970-85, chief exec FI Group plc 1985-, non-exec dir TSB Bank plc 1987-90, non-exec memb Post Office Board 1990; Freeman: City of London 1987, Worshipful Co of Information Technologists 1987; CBIM 1988; *Style—* Mrs Hilary Cropper; Woodlands, Pink Rd, Parslows Hillock, Lacey Green, nr Aylesbury, Bucks (☎ 0494 488227); FI Gp plc, Campus 300, Maylands Ave, Hemel Hempstead, Herts HP2 7EZ (☎ 0442 233339, fax 0442 238400)

CROPPER, James Anthony; DL (1986 Cumbria); s of Anthony Charles Cropper (d 1967), of Tolson Hall, Kendal, and Philippa Mary Gloria, *née* Clutterbuck; *b* 22 Dec 1938; *Educ* Eton, Magdalene Coll Cambridge (BA); *m* 30 June 1967, Susan Rosemary, da of Col F J N Davis (d 1988), of Northwood, Middx; 2 s (Charles Michael Anthony b 1969, d 1974, Mark b 1974), 1 da (Sarah b 1972); *Career* dir: James Cropper PLC (papermakers) 1966- (chm 1971-), East Lancs Paper Group PLC 1982-84, NW Water Group PLC 1989-90; pres Br Paper and Bd Indust Fedn 1987-89; dir Cumbria Rural Enterprise Agency 1987-, chm govrs of Abbot Hall Art Gallery and Museum 1983-88; memb: S Westmorland RDC 1967-74, Lancs River Authy 1968-74, NW Water Authy 1973-80 and 1987-89, S Lakeland Dist Cncl 1974-77; High Sheriff of Westmorland 1971; FCA; *Recreations* shooting, skiing, windsurfing; *Clubs* Brooks's; *Style—* James Cropper, Esq, DL; Tolson Hall, Kendal, Cumbria (☎ 0539 722011); James Cropper PLC, Burneside Mills, Kendal, Cumbria (☎ 0539 722002)

CROPPER, Peter John; s of Samuel Duncan Cropper (d 1961), and Anna Southwell, *née* Parkinson (d 1990); *b* 7 Feb 1940; *Educ* Salford GS, Univ of Manchester; *m* 16 Sept 1963, Hilary Mary, da of Arnold Trueman, of Bollington, Cheshire; 1 s (Carl b Oct 1971), 2 da (Elizabeth b Dec 1969, Charlotte b Feb 1973); *Career* various tech and mgmnt appts AEI and English Electric 1960-68, software devpt mangr ICL 1968-75, gen mangr Computer Gp CWS Ltd 1975-80; md: STC IDEC Ltd 1980-85, STC Technology Ltd 1985-87; dir corporate info systems STC plc 1987-, non-exec dir Imagedisplay Ltd; Freeman City of London 1988, Liveryman Worshipful Co of Scientific Instrument Makers, memb Ct of Assts Co of Information Technologists; FBCS, FBIM, MIDPM; *Recreations* squash, bridge, theatre; *Style—* Peter Cropper, Esq; Woodlands, Pink Road, Lacey Green, Aylesbury, Bucks HP17 0RJ (☎ 0494 488227); STC PLC, Corporate Information Systems, Oakleigh Rd South, New Southgate, London N11 1HB (☎ 081 945 2062, fax 081 945 2050, car 0836 230191)

CROPPER, Ralph; s of Charles William Cropper, and Florence, *née* Betts; *b* 6 June 1913; *Educ* LSE (BA, MSc); *m* 25 May 1935, Irene Amy; 4 c; *Career* sr exec offr Road Haulage Assoc until 1949, ind tport conslt 1949-; md: Conquers Transport Ltd 1952-82, Transport Counsellors Ltd 1956-80; former vice pres Deptford Cons Assoc; chm: Movement for London 1982-, Copers Cope Res Assoc; memb: SE Gas Consultative Ctee for 25 years (chm numerous ctees), industl tbnls for 15 years; Freeman City of London, Liveryman Worshipful Co of Carmen; FCIT, FREconS; *Clubs* City Livery; *Style—* Ralph Cropper, Esq; Dunbar, Beckenham Place Park, Beckenham, Kent BR3 2BP (☎ 081 650 1546)

CROPPER, Hon Mrs (Rosalind Evelyn); *née* Younger; da of 3 Viscount Younger of Leckie, OBE, TD; *b* 12 Oct 1937; *m* 14 May 1960, Thomas Ross Charles Cropper, s of Cecil Howe Cropper, DSO, MC, of Sydney; 2 s, 2 da; *Style—* The Hon Mrs Cropper; Greenhills, Willow Tree, NSW, Australia

CROQUET, Jean-Louis; s of Marcel Croquet (d 1988), and Marguerite Guillou; *b* 28 June 1943; *Educ* DESS (Sciences Economiques); *m* Ingrid Farasek; 2 s (David b 1968, Thomas b 1986), 1 da (Anne b 1988); *Career* mktg mangr Pernod Ricard Group 1969-72, fndr chm Motivation 1973-85; fndr: Telemetric cie 1986, Croquet cie 1988, Virtus Group 1989; exec dir: Addison plc France, Infus Germany, BVA France, Motivac Italy, Motivaction France, Telemetric Europe; memb Versailles C of C; Decoration Merite Agricole (Chevalier); *Books* Paroles Aux Agriculteurs; *Recreations* rugby; *Clubs* Versailles Rugby; *Style—* Jean-Louis Croquet, Esq; 9 Boulevard de la Reine, 78000 Versailles F (☎ 30240808); Virtus Group, 191 av gal Leclerc, 78220 Viro flay (☎ 30240808)

CROSBIE, William; s of Archibald Shearer Crosbie (d 1961), of Faucheong, Hankow, Huphe, China, and Mary Nicol, *née* Edgar (d 1948); *b* 31 Jan 1915; *Educ* Glasgow Acad, Glasgow Sch of Art/Univ (BA), Studio of Fernand Leger Paris, Academy de la Grande Chaumiere Paris; *m* 1, 2 Oct 1944, (Mary) Grace McPhail (d 1973); 2 da ((Mary) Pauline Elizabeth b 7 July 1947, Michelle Louise b 6 April 1951 d 24 April 1951); m 2, 6 June 1975, (Margaret) Anne, da of Sydney Roger (d 1976), of Persia; *Career* conscript MN 1942-45; artist studies in schs and studios in Paris, Brussels, Athens, Istanbul, Cairo, Rome, Florence; has exhibited on average every 2 years 1946-; principally one man exhibitions: Glasgow, Edinburgh, London, USA, Brussels, Hamburg; has works in: Kelvingrove Galleries Glasgow, Arts Cncl, Scottish provincial galleries, Edinburgh City Arts Centre (mural) 1980, Scottish Gallery of Modern Art 1980, Sydney State Gallery Aust, Wellington NZ, Royal Collection UK, Refectory Fruit Market Gallery Edinburgh 1980, Nat Library of Scotland 1986; works in many private collections; govr: Edinburgh Coll of Art 1972-75, Glasgow Sch of Art 1975-81; keeper RSA 1977-85; RGI 1975, RSA 1967 (hon prof); *Recreations* sailing, history (art & medieval); *Clubs* RNC Yacht, LSC, GAC; *Style—* William Crosbie, Esq; Rushes House, 10 Winchester Rd, Petersfield, Hants, GU32 3BY (☎ 0730 66899)

CROSBY, John Rutherford; s of John Charles Crosby (d 1938), of Colchester, and Florence Nightingale, *née* Rutherford (d 1982); *b* 1 May 1933; *Educ* Univ of Durham (BA), Univ of London (MA), Univ Coll Cardiff (Dip in Personnel Mgmnt); *m* 10 March 1962, Rosalind Elizabeth, da of Gilbert Baynon Williams (d 1968); 2 s (Neil b 1966, David b 1968), 1 da (Sarah (Mrs Perrin) b 1963); *Career* personnel mgmnt appts with EMI and Costain Group 1958-68, sr conslt Hay MSL 1968-76, personnel dir British American Tobacco Co Ltd 1983-88 (head of personnel servs 1976-83), dir of gp personnel BAT Industries 1988-; Inst of Personnel Mgmnt: vice pres 1979-81, pres 1985-87, chm IPM Services 1985-87, chm IPM Advsy Ctee on Nominations 1987-89; memb Cncl Voluntary Serv Overseas 1983-; memb: Civil Serv Final Selection Bd 1984-, Business Liaison Ctee London Business Sch 1984-90, NEDO Steering Gp on Human Resource Devpt 1986-87, Ind Assessment and Research Centre 1988- (dir 1989-); govr: Farnham Castle Centre for Int Briefing 1983-, Croydon Coll 1987- (vice chm govrs 1989-); tstee Overseas Students Tst 1988-; Freeman of Colchester 1971; CIPM 1980, CBIM 1983, FInstD 1984; *Books* Handbook of Management Development (contrib 1986 and 1991); *Recreations* music (particularly opera), theatre, avoiding all gardening; *Clubs* Oriental, IOD; *Style—* John Crosby, Esq; 70 Woodcote Valley Rd, Purley, Surrey CR8 3BD (☎ 081 660 2717); BAT Industries plc, Windsor House, 50 Victoria St, London SW1H 0NL (☎ 071 222 7979)

CROSET, Paul John Francis; OBE (1967); s of Louis Paul Croset (d 1982), and May Eveline, *née* Garrett (d 1989); *b* 15 March 1919; *Educ* Rishworth Sch, Stamford Sch; *m* 26 Aug 1944 (m dis 1985), (Margaret) Vivien, da of William Suckling, of Radlett, Herts; 3 da (Jacqueline b 1946, Jane b 1948, Louise b 1956); *Career* served WWII Maj RE with BEF, BNAF, CMF; engr; chm and fndr Holset Engineering Co Ltd 1952-, md BHD Engineers 1959-73, underwriting memb Lloyd's 1968-, dep chm Readicut International plc 1984-89 (dir 1969-89, chm 1977-84), local dir Barclay Bank plc Leeds 1977-84; dir: Cummins Engine Co Ltd 1981-84, Hepworth plc 1985-89; conslt to Dept of Engrg Univ of Warwick 1989; Freeman City of London 1972, Liveryman Worshipful Co of Founders 1973; FRSA 1973, CBIM 1980; *Recreations* fishing, shooting, horology; *Clubs* Army and Navy, RAC; *Style—* Paul Croset Esq, OBE; Summer Court, 1a Otley Road, Harrogate, N Yorkshire HG2 ODJ (☎ 0423 568216)

CROSLAND, John David; s of Harold Leslie Crosland (d 1942), and Margaret Jarratt; *b* 17 Oct 1936; *Educ* Silcoates Sch, St Catharine's Coll Cambridge (MA); *m* 31 March 1967, Susan Jane Frances, da of Wilfrid Francis Anthony Meynell; 1 s (Timothy John Edward b 1970), 1 da (Jane Ellen Lucy b 1972); *Career* merchant banker; dir Robert Fleming Hldgs Ltd 1973-90; conslt Robert Fleming & Co Ltd 1990-; non exec dir: Bankers Investmt Tst plc, Bryant Gp plc, Concentric plc, Fleming Japanese Investmt Tst plc; *Style—* John D Crosland, Esq; 17 Gerard Rd, Barnes SW13 9RQ (☎ 081 748 1663); Stone Cottage, Marehill, Pulborough, W Sussex; Robert Fleming Holdings Ltd, 25 Copthall Ave, London EC2

CROSLAND, Prof Maurice Pierre; s of David Crosland, and Berthe, *née* Mispoulet; *b* 19 March 1931; *Educ* Stationers Sch, Univ of London (BSc, MSc, PhD); *m* 22 April 1957, Joan Mary, da of William Cooley; 3 s (Peter b 1959, Michael b 1962, Paul b 1966), 1 da (Margaret b 1964); *Career* visiting prof: Univ of California Berkeley 1967, Cornell Univ NY 1967-68; reader in history of sci Univ of Leeds 1969-74 (lectr 1963), visiting prof Univ of Pennsylvania 1971, prof of history of sci and dir of Unit for the History Philosophy and Social Rels of Sci Univ of Kent Canterbury 1974-; hon ed Br Jl for History of Sci 1965-71, pres Br Soc for the History of Sci 1974-76, memb Int Acad of History of Sci 1976-; Dexter award American Chem Soc 1984; *Books* The Society of Arcueil: A View of French Science at the Time of Napoleon I (1967), Historical Studies in the Language of Chemistry (2 edn, 1978), Science in France in the Revolutionary Era Described by Thomas Bugge (1969), The Science of Matter: A Historical Survey (1971), The Emergence of Science in Western Europe (1975), Gay-Lussac, Scientist and Bourgeois (1978), Science under Control: The French Academy of Sciences 1795-1914 (1991); *Recreations* walking, listening to classical music, continental travel, cycling; *Style—* Prof Maurice Crosland; Unit for History of Science, Physics Building, University of Kent, Canterbury, Kent CT2 7NR (☎ 0227 764000)

CROSS, Prof Anthony Glenn; s of Walter Sidney Cross (d 1941), and Ada, *née* Lawson; *b* 21 Oct 1936; *Educ* High Pavement Sch Nottingham, Trinity Hall Cambridge (Wootan Isaacs scholar, MA, PhD) Univ of Harvard (AM), UEA (D Litt); *m* 11 Aug 1960, Margaret, da of Eric Arthur Elson (d 1986); 2 da (Jane b 1964, Serena b 1967); *Career* Nat Serv 1955-57; Frank Knox Meml fell Univ of Harvard 1960-61, reader UEA 1972-81 (lectr 1964-69, sr lectr 1969-72); visiting fell: Centre for Advanced Study Univ of Illinois 1968-69, All Souls Coll Oxford 1977-78; Roberts prof of Russian Univ of Leeds 1981-85, prof of slavonic studies Univ of Cambridge 1985-; memb Br Univs Assoc of Slavists (pres 1982-84); fell Br Acad 1989; *Books* N M Karamzin (1971), Russia Under Western Eyes (1971), Anglo-Russian Relations in the Eighteenth Century (1977), By the Banks of The Thames: Russians in Eighteenth Century Britain (1980), The Russian Theme in English Literature (1985); *Recreations* collecting books, watching cricket; *Style—* Prof Anthony Cross; Dept of Slavonic Studies, Univ of Cambridge, Sidgwick Avenue, Cambridge, CB2 9DA (☎ 0223 335007)

CROSS, 3 Viscount (UK 1886); Assheton Henry Cross; s of 2 Viscount (d 1932), and Maud, da of late Maj-Gen Inigo Richmond Jones, CVO, CB (Maud's maternal gf was Hon Richard Charteris, 2 s of 9 Earl of Wemyss and March); *b* 7 May 1920; *Educ* Shrewsbury, Magdalene Coll Cambridge; *m* 1, 12 Jan 1952 (m dis 1957), Patricia Mary, da of Edward Pearson Hewetson, of Windermere; 2 da (Hon Venetia Clare b 1953, Hon Nicola b 1954); m 2, 1972 (m dis 1977), Mrs Victoria Webb; m 3, 1983, (m dis 1987), Mrs Patricia J Rossiter; *Heir* none; *Career* sits as Conservative Peer in House of Lords; formerly Capt Scots Gds; *Clubs* Cavalry and Guards; *Style—* The Rt Hon The Viscount Cross; Delph Cottage, Itchenor, Sussex

CROSS, Beverley; s of George Cross, theatrical mangr, and Eileen Williams, actress; *b* 13 April 1931; *Educ* Pangbourne, Balliol Coll Oxford; *m* 1975, Dame Maggie Smith, DBE, the actress, *qv*; *Career* playwright, screenwriter and librettist; work incl: One More River, Strip The Willow, Boeing Boeing, Half a Sixpence, The Mines of Sulphur, Hans Anderson, The Great Society, Jorrocks, The Scarlet Pimpernel, The Rising of the Moon, Catherine Howard, Miranda; *Clubs* Garrick; *Style—* Beverley Cross, Esq; Curtis Brown Ltd, 162 Regent St, London W1R 5TA (☎ 071 437 9700)

CROSS, Prof (Margaret) Claire; da of Frederick Leonard Cross (d 1964), of Leicester, and Rebecca *née* Newton (d 1984), of Leicester; *b* 25 Oct 1932; *Educ* Wyggeston GS Leicester, Girton Coll Cambridge (BA, PhD); *Career* co archivist for Cambridgeshire 1958-61, Int fell American Assoc of Univ Women 1961-62, res fell Univ of Reading, currently prof Dept of History Univ of York (formerly lectr, sr lectr, reader); numerous pubns in jls; memb: Royal Historical Soc, Ecclesiastical History Soc, Historical Assoc; FRHistS; *Books* The Free Grammar School of Leicester (1953), The Puritan Earl: The Life of Henry Hastings (1966), The Royal Supremacy in the Elizabethan Church (1969), Church and People 1450-1660: The Triumph of the Laity in the English Church (1976), York Clergy Wills 1520-1600: I the Minister Clergy (1984), Urban Magistrates and Ministers: Religion in Hull and Leeds from the Reformation to the Civil War (1985), Law and Government under the Tudors: Essays Presented to Sir Geoffrey Elton on his Retirement (1988), York Clergy Wills 1520-1600: 2 The City

Clergy (1989); *Recreations* gardening; *Style*— Prof Claire Cross; 17 Pear Tree Court, York YO1 2DF (☎ 0904 654221); Dept of History, University of York, Heslington, York YO1 5DD (☎ 0904 430000 ext 2959)

CROSS, Denis Charles; s of late Lt Charles Cross, RN; *b* 13 May 1938; *Educ* Downside, Balliol Oxford; *m* 1963, Margaret McAdam, *née* Black; 2 s, 3 da; *Career* dir Hambros Bank Ltd 1971-; *Style*— Denis Cross Esq; 18 Bolingbroke Grove, London SW11 (☎ 081 673 8187)

CROSS, (John) Dennis; s of Colin Cross (d 1978), and Edith, *née* Griffiths (d 1938); *b* 16 June 1935; *Educ* Clacton-on-Sea Co HS; *m* 19 July 1958, Shirley Phyllis da of late Henry Charles Paynter; 1 s (Jason Andrew b 9 April 1967), 1 da (Caroline Nicola b 22 July 1969); *Career* Nat Serv RAF 1958-60; articled clerk: Bewsusaw Butt Eves Colchester 1951-54, Moller Morton & Co London 1951-58; ptnr then sr ptnr Chater & Myhill 1962-67 (joined 1960), sr ptnr KPMG Peat Marwick McLintock Cambridge 1987-90; treas RNLI Cambridge (Silver badge 1988), vice pres Cambridge United FC; ACA 1958, memb Insolvency Practitioners Assoc 1978; *Recreations* sailing, golf; *Clubs* Walton and Frinton Yacht, Cambridge Rutherford Rotary, Cambridge Business and Professional Mens; *Style*— Dennis Cross, Esq; KPMG Peat Marwick McLintock, Chater House, 37 Hills Rd, Cambridge CB2 1XL (☎ 0223 66692, fax 0223 460701)

CROSS, Hon Mrs ((Rosamond Stella) Frances); *née* Byng; 4 da of 10 Viscount Torrington (d 1961); *b* 23 Jan 1937; *m* 10 Sept 1960 (m dis 1985), Antony Brockington Cobb, eldest s of Basil Brockington Cobb, of Merridale, East Wellow, nr Romsey, Hants; 1 s (Dorian Byng b 1965), 1 da (Michelle Pandora b 1961); assumed surname of Cross by Deed Poll; *Style*— The Hon Mrs Cross; 2 St Boniface Rd, Ventnor, Isle of Wight

CROSS, Rev Hugh Geoffrey; s of Rev Arthur James Cross (d 1945), and Frieda Annie, *née* Stern (d 1981); *b* 1 June 1930; *Educ* Bulawayo Tech Sch, Bristol Baptist Coll; *m* 10 July 1954, Doreen Barbara, da of Oliver Cecil Lay (d 1979); 2 s (Allan b 1959, Graham b 1957), 2 da (Janet b 1955, Kathleen b 1962); *Career* Baptist min: Swallownest and Treeton 1954-61, Morice Baptist Church Plymouth 1961-65; missionary bookseller 1965-68, min Grove Hill Ecumenical Project Hemel Hempstead 1969-79, ecumenical offr Br Cncl of Churches 1979-90, ecumenical moderator Milton Keynes Christian Cncl 1991-; *Recreations* dinghy sailing; *Style*— The Rev Hugh G Cross; The Cross and Stable, Downs Barn, Milton Keynes MK14 7RZ (☎ 0908 692945)

CROSS, Dr James Raison; TD; s of George Cross (d 1952), of Nuneaton, and Vera Estelle Cross, *née* Raison; *b* 28 Sept 1926; *Educ* Repton, Univ of Birmingham (MB ChB); *m* 14 Sept 1957, Ann Christian, da of Lt-Col Hugh Young (d 1961), of Liverpool; 2 s (Andrew b 1960, Michael b 1962), 1 da (Hilary b 1964); *Career* TA 1949-; commanding offr 208 Gen Hosp 1974, apptd Hon Col 1982; appointed hon physician to HM The Queen 1977; conslt anaesthetist S Cheshire 1960-; pres Liverpool Soc of Anaesthists 1984-86, FFARCS 1957; *Recreations* gardening, walking; *Style*— Dr James Cross, TD; Cliffe Cottage, Wrinehill Road, Wybunbury, Nantwich, Cheshire CW5 7NV (☎ 0270 841252); Leighton Hospital, Crewe

CROSS, (William Richard) Jason Blount; s of Richard Blount Cross, of Chichester, and Margaret Marmion, *née* Crocker; *b* 15 Nov 1945; *Educ* Downside; *m* 13 Sept 1969, Frances Catherine Dawes, da of Dr John Fletcher Ramsden (d 1955); 2 s (Mark b 1973, Ivan b 1973), 1 da (Tanya b 1971); *Career* ptnr Josolyne Layton-Bennet & Co 1972-77, ICFC Bristol 1977-80, local dir 3i London 1980-86, ptnr and head UK of corp fin, Grant Thornton 1987-; ACA 1970, FCA 1977; *Recreations* history, wine, sailing, armchair sport; *Clubs* Army and Navy, Chichester Yacht; *Style*— Jason Cross, Esq; Grant Thornton, Grant Thornton House, Melton St, Euston Square, London NW1 2EP (☎ 071 383 5100, fax 071 383 4715, telex 28984)

CROSS, Joan; CBE; *b* 7 Sept 1900; *Educ* St Pauls; *Career* joined Old Vic 1924, progressed from small singing roles to princ roles; dir Sadlers Wells Opera Co 1940-45, fndr memb English Opera Gp 1945, created Ellen Orford (Peter Grimes), Female Chorus (Rape of Lucretia), Lady Billows (Albert Herring), Queen Elizabeth (Gloriana), Mrs Grose (The Turn of the Screw); *Recreations* collector of books and pictures; *Style*— Miss Joan Cross, CBE; Garrett House, Park Rd, Aldeburgh, Suffolk

CROSS, Air Chief Marshal Sir Kenneth Bryan Boyd; KCB (1959, CB 1954), CBE (1945), DSO (1943), DFC (1940); s of Pembroke H C Cross, of Eastoke Lodge, Hayling Island, and Jean, *née* Boyd; *b* 4 Oct 1911; *Educ* Kingswood Sch Bath; *m* 15 Jan 1945, Brenda Megan, da of Wing-Cdr Frank James Bickley Powell, of Hinton Cottage, Hinton, nr Melkesham, Wilts; 2 s, 1 da; *Career* RAF 1930, AOCIC Bomber Cmd 1959-63, Air Chief Marshal 1965, AOCIC Tport Cmd 1963-66, ret 1967; dir Red Cross London Branch, ret 1981; *Clubs* RAF; *Style*— Air Chief Marshal Sir Kenneth Cross, KCB, CBE, DSO, DFC; 12 Callow St, London SW3

CROSS, Robert Kingsley; s of Dr John Cross, of Bingley, W Yorks; *b* 19 Aug 1942; *Educ* Bradford GS; *m* 1967, Angela Mary, da of Sydney Seymour, of Bradford; 2 da; *Career* dir and sec Heydemann Shaw Ltd (subsid of Coats Viyella plc) 1974-; FCA, MIEx; *Recreations* travel, sailing, gardening; *Style*— Robert Cross, Esq; Little Oaks, Ridgeway, Tranmere Park, Guiseley, W Yorks LS20 8JA (☎ 0943 77152, office: 0274 874361)

CROSS, (Harold) William; s of John Edward Cross (d 1953), of Doncaster, Yorks, and Bertha Lillian, *née* Lake (d 1965); *b* 17 April 1922; *Educ* Doncaster GS; *m* 26 April 1947, Olive Mary (d 1988), da of Eric Hubert Swinstead (d 1956), of Buckhurst Hill, Essex; 2 s (David Andrew b 1951, Stephen John b 1953); m 2, 3 June 1989, Pamela Marion, da of Philip Dilkes (d 1987), of Warrington, Lancs; *Career* pilot Fleet Air Arm RNVR 1941-46; Colonial Serv E Africa 1947-53; fin controller Tunnel Portland Cement Co Ltd 1954-60, exec vice pres Diversey Corpn USA 1960-70, chm and chief exec Brent Chemicals Int plc 1970-85, chm Elswick plc 1985-; chm: Mission Aviation Fellowship, UK Evangilisation Tst; former chm Covenanters Youth Movement, churchwarden and lay reader C of E; FICA 1953; *Recreations* sailing, windsurfing, fell walking, music, reading, theology; *Clubs* RAC, Phyllis Court (Henley); *Style*— William Cross, Esq; Field House, Church Lane, Mickleton, Chipping Campden, Glos (☎ 0386 438485); Elswick plc, Alcester, Warwicks (☎ 0789 400333, fax 0789 400794, car 0836 286848)

CROSS BROWN, Tom; s of Christopher James Cross Brown, and Georgina, *née* Forrester; *b* 22 Dec 1947; *Educ* Uppingham, BNC Oxford (MA), INSEAD (MBA); *m* 1972, Susan Rosemary, da of Col Mansel Halkett Jackson (d 1967); 1 s (Nicol b 1975), 3 da (Gemma b 1977, Amelia b 1982, Claire (twin) b 1982); *Career* dir Lazard Bros and Co Ltd 1985-, non exec dir Whitegate Leisure plc; *Style*— Tom Cross Brown, Esq; Shipton Old Farm, Winslow, Buckingham MK18 3JL; 21 Moorfields, London EC2P 2HT

CROSS OF CHELSEA, Baroness Mildred Joan Cross; *née* Eardley-Wilmot; o da of Lt-Col Theodore Eardley-Wilmot, DSO (ka 1918; gn of Sir John Eardley-Wilmot, 2 Bt), and Mildred Clare, *née* Reynolds (d 1956); *b* 12 Jan 1912; *m* 1, 28 June 1939, Thomas Walton Davies (d 1948), o s of David Davies, MB, MRCS, LRCP, of Hurst View, Tunbridge Wells, Kent; 1 s (Charles b 1943), 2 da (Caroline b 1941, Sophia (Mrs Henning Rasmussen) b 1946); m 2, 23 Feb 1952, Baron Cross of Chelsea, PC (Life Peer; d 1989); 1 da (Julia (Hon Mrs Openshaw), *qv*); *Style*— The Rt Hon Lady Cross of Chelsea; The Bridge House, Leintwardine, Craven Arms, Shropshire (☎ 054 73 205)

CROSSE, John Ernest; s of Ernest Crosse (d 1972); *b* 11 Jan 1926; *Educ* Sebright Sch nr Kidderminster; *m* 1, 1952, Evelyn; m 2, 1981, Janet; 2 s, 2 da; *Career* SEAC 1945-47; md: Solartron Engrg Ltd 1952-58, Solartron (Farnborough) Ltd 1958-63; chm Plasmec plc 1963-; CBIM; *Style*— John Crosse, Esq; The Mill House, Frensham, Farnham, Surrey (☎ 0251 25 2979); Plasmec plc, Weydon Lane, Farnham, Surrey (☎ 0252 721 236)

CROSSETT, Robert Nelson (Tom); *b* 27 May 1938; *Educ* Campbell Coll Belfast, Queen's Univ Belfast (BSc, BAS), Lincoln Coll Oxford (DPhil), Univ of Capetown, UEA; *m* ; 2c; *Career* cmmnd pilot Gen Duties Branch RAFVR; gp ldr Environmental Studies Aust Atomic Energy Cmmn Res Establishment Sydney 1966-69, sr sci offr ARC Letcombe Laboratory 1969-72, crop devpt offr Scot Agric Devpt Cncl 1972-75 (sec Crops Ctee), agric res advsr Sci Advsrs Unit Dept of Agric and Fisheries Scot 1975-78; MAFF: sci liaison offr Horticulture and Soils 1978-84, head Food Sci Div 1984-85, chief scientist Fisheries and Food 1985-89; environment dir National Power 1989-; chm: Steering Gp on Food Surveillance 1985-89, AFRC 1985-89, CMO's Ctee on Med Aspects of Food Policy 1985-89, Supervisory Bd of the laboratory of the Govt chemist 1985-89; FIFST 1986; *Publications* papers on plant physiology, marine biology and food science; *Recreations* walking, gardening, orienteering, boats; *Style*— Robert Crossett, Esq; Bray, Co Wicklow, Republic of Ireland; National Power, Sudbury House, 15 Newgate St, London EC1A 7AU

CROSSLAND, Anthony; s of Ernest Thomas Crossland (d 1968), and Frances Edith Crossland (d 1969); *b* 4 Aug 1931; *Educ* High Pavement Sch Nottingham, ChCh Oxford (BMus, MA); *m* 3 Dec 1960, Barbara Helen, da of Herbert Pullar-Strecker (d 1976); 1 s (Nicholas Anthony James b 1962), 2 da (Caroline Sarah b 1964, Victoria Jane b 1967); *Career* asst organist: Christ Church Cathedral Oxford 1957-61, Wells Cathedral 1961-70; organist and master of the choristers Wells Cathedral 1971- ; pres Cathedral Organists' Assoc 1983-85; FRCO 1957, ARCM; *Recreations* photography, reading; *Style*— Anthony Crossland, Esq; 15 Vicars' Close, Wells, Somerset BA5 2UJ (☎ 0749 73526); The Cathedral Office, West Cloister, Wells Cathedral, Wells, Somerset (☎ 0749 74483)

CROSSLAND, Prof Sir Bernard; CBE (1980); s of Reginald Francis Crossland (d 1976), and Kathleen Mary, *née* Rudduck (d 1950); *b* 20 Oct 1923; *Educ* Simon Langton GS Canterbury, Derby Regnl Tech Coll, Univ Coll of Nottingham, (BSc, MSc, PhD, DSc); *m* 25 July 1946, Audrey, da of Frank Elliott Birks (d 1961), 2 da (Jennifer b 1948, Mary Anne b 1952); *Career* tech asst Rolls Royce Ltd 1943-45 (apprentice 1940-44), lectr Luton Tech Coll 1945-46, sr lectr in mechanical engrg (formerly asst lectr and lectr) Univ of Bristol 1946-59; Queen's Univ of Belfast: prof and head of Dept of Mechanical and Industl Engrg 1959-84, dean of Engrg Faculty, pro vice chllr 1978-82; assessor King's Cross Underground Fire Investigation 1988; chm: Youth Careers Guidance Cmmn 1975-81, NI Manpower Cncl 1981-86; memb: NI Trg Cncl 1964-81, NI Econ Cncl 1981-85, AFRC 1981-87, NI Ind Devpt Bd 1982-87, Engrg Cncl 1983-88; Freeman City of London 1987, memb Worshipful Co of Engrs 1988; Hon DSc: Univ of Ireland 1984, Univ of Dublin 1985, Univ of Edinburgh 1987, The Queens Univ Belfast 1988, Univ of Aston 1988, Cranfield Inst of Technol 1989; FIMechE (pres 1986-87), Hon FIW, Hon MASME, MRIA, FEng, FRS (vice pres 1984-86); kt 1990; *Recreations* walking, music, travel; *Clubs* Athenaeum; *Style*— Prof Sir Bernard Crossland, CBE, FRS; 16 Malone Ct, Belfast BT9 6PA (☎ 0232 67 495); The Queen's University, Belfast BT7 1NN (☎ 0232 247 303, fax 0232 247 895, telex 74487)

CROSSLAND, Sir Leonard; s of Joseph William Crossland (d 1962), of Stocksbridge, Sheffield, and Frances Crossland; *b* 2 March 1914; *m* 1964, Joan, da of Stanley Percival Brewer, of Bath; *Career* served WWII Europe; chm and dir Ford Motor Co Ltd 1968-72; chm: Eaton Ltd 1974-, Energy Research and Development Ltd 1974-; farmer (700 acres); kt 1969; *Recreations* shooting, fishing, golf; *Clubs* RAC, American, City Livery, BRDC; *Style*— Sir Leonard Crossland; Abbotts Hall, Gt Wigborough, Colchester, Essex CO5 7RZ (☎ 020 635 456/301)

CROSSLAND, Prof Ronald Arthur; s of Ralph Crossland (d 1972), of Nottingham, and Ethel, *née* Scattergood (d 1974); *b* 31 Aug 1920; *Educ* Nottingham HS, King's Coll Cambridge; *Career* served RA 1941-45, Lt 19 Field Regt RA (1st Div); serv in GB, Tunisia and Italy; Henry fell Yale Univ 1946-48; sr Student Ctee for Studentships in Oriental Languages and Literatures (Hittite philology) 1948-51, hon asst lectr in ancient history Univ of Birmingham 1950-51, lectr in Ancient History King's Coll, Univ of Durham and Newcastle upon Tyne 1951-58, Harris fell King's Coll Cambridge 1952-56, prof of Greek Univ of Sheffield 1958-82; British Cncl visiting lectr in Czechoslovakia 1961, visiting prof of Linguistics Texas Univ (Austin) 1962, Collitz visiting prof of Linguistics Michigan Univ 1967; dean of the Faculty of Arts Univ of Sheffield 1973-75; visiting fell in classics Victoria Univ of Wellington 1979; emeritus prof of Greek Univ of Sheffield 1982-; FSA; *Publications* Immigrants from the North (Cambridge Ancient History, revised edn, 1/2, Chapter XXVII 1971), Linguistic Problems of the Balkan Area (Cambridge Ancient History, revised edn, Chapter 20c 1982), Bronze Age Migrations in the Aegean (with Ann Birchall, 1973), Early Greek Migrations (in M Grant, editor), Civilization of the Ancient Mediterranean (1987); *Recreations* travel, music; *Style*— Prof Ronald Crossland, FSA; 59 Sherlock Close, Cambridge CB3 0HP (☎ 0223 358 085); University of Sheffield, Sheffield S10 2TN (☎ 0742 768 555, ext 4603)

CROSSLEY, Elizabeth, Lady; Elizabeth Joyce; da of late Enoch Shenton, of Boxmoor, Herts; *m* 16 Dec 1954, as his 2 w, Sir Kenneth Irwin Crossley, 2 Bt (d 1957); *Style*— Elizabeth, Lady Crossley; The Old Bakery, Milton Lilbourne, Pewsey, Wilts SN9 5LQ

CROSSLEY, Sir Nicholas John; 4 Bt (UK 1909), of Glenfield, Dunham Massey, Co Chester; er s of Sir Christopher John Crossley, 3 Bt (d 1989), and his 1 w, Carolyne Louise, da of late L Grey Sykes; *b* 10 Dec 1962; *Heir* bro, Julian Charles Crossley b 1964; *Style*— Sir Nicholas Crossley, Bt; c/o 6B Laverton Mews, London SW5

CROSSLEY, Hon (Richard) Nicholas; TD (1974), DL (N Yorks 1988); s of 2 Baron Somerleyton, MC (d 1959), and Bridget, *née* Hoare (d 1990); *b* 24 Dec 1932; *Educ* Eton, RMA Sandhurst; *m* 30 April 1958, Alexandra Ann Maitland (d 1990), da of Wing Cdr Charles Donald Graham Welch, of Perrot Farm, Graffham, Sussex; 1 s, 2 da; *Career* farmer 1963-89, MFH 1969; Capt 9 Queen's Royal Lancers (ret), Maj Queen's Own Yeo (TA), CO Queen's Own Yeo 1973-76, Bt-Col 1977, Col TA NE Dist 1978-81, ADC (TAVR) to HM The Queen 1980-84; memb HM Body Guard of Hon Corps of Gentlemen at Arms 1982-; High Sheriff N Yorks 1989-90; area gov Ocean Youth Club 1985-, tstee for Stable Lads Welfare Tst 1984-; *Recreations* hunting, shooting, stalking, sailing; *Clubs* Cavalry and Guards', Pratt's; *Style*— Col the Hon Nicholas Crossley, TD, DL; Westfield Farm, Norton, Malton, N Yorks YO17 9PL

CROSSLEY, Paul Christopher Richard; s of Frank Crossley (d 1948), and Myra, *née* Barrowcliffe (d 1979); *b* 17 May 1944; *Educ* Silcoates Sch Wakefield, Mansfield Coll Oxford; *Career* int concert career with world's leading orchs, ensembles, and conductors; solo recitalist and regular broadcaster; works specially written for him by leading composers incl: Adams, Berio, Gorecki, Henze, Takemitsu, Tippett; artistic dir London Sinfonietta 1988; sixteen TV progs on prominent composers; recordings incl:

Liszt: A Recital 1983, Ravel: Complete Piano Music 1983, Fauré: Complete Piano Music 1983-87, Tippett: Sonatas 1-4 1985, Messiaen: Turangalila-Symphonie 1986, Messiaen Des Canyons aux Etoiles Oiseaux Exotiques, Couleurs de la Cité Celeste 1988, Poulenc: Complete Piano Music 1989, Stravinsky: Complete Music for Piano and Orchestra 1990, Adams: Eros Piano 1991, Takemitsu: Riverrun 1991; *Recreations* mah-jongg, reading; *Style*— Paul Crossley, Esq; Van Walsum Management, 26 Wadham Road, London SW15

CROSSLEY, Maj-Gen Ralph John; CB (1987), CBE (1981); s of Edward Crossley (d 1978), of Sussex, and Eva Mary, *née* Farnworth (d 1965); *b* 11 Oct 1933; *Educ* Felsted; *m* 1957, Marion Hilary, da of Herbert Wilfred Bacon (d 1975), of Salisbury; 1 s (Robin), 1 da (Amanda); *Career* Army Offr; Dep Cmdt RMC of Science 1982, Dir Gen Weapons (Army 1984), ret 1986; dir def policy Avon Rubber plc 1987; chm Salisbury Health Authy; *Recreations* golf, reading, gardening, walking; *Clubs* Nat Tst; *Style*— Maj-Gen Ralph Crossley, CB, CBE; c/o Midland Bank, Salisbury, Wilts

CROSSLEY-HOLLAND, Kevin John William; s of Peter Charles Crossley-Holland of Llangeler, Llandysul, Dyfed, and Joan Mary Crossley-Holland, *née* Cowper, MBE; *b* 7 Feb 1941; *Educ* Bryanston, St Edmund Hall Oxford (BA); *m* 1, 6 July 1963 (m dis 1972), Caroline Fendall, da of Prof Leonard M Thompson, of Connecticut, USA; 2 s (Kieran b 1963, Dominic b 1967); m 2, 23 Sept 1972 (m dis 1978), Ruth, da of John Marris, of Swanage; m 3, 26 March 1982, Gillian Paula, da of the late Peter Cook, of Eaton Bank, Derbyshire; 2 da (Oenone b 1982, Eleanor b 1986); *Career* ed Macmillan & Co 1962-69, Gregory fell in poetry Univ of Leeds 1969-71, talks prodr BBC 1972, ed dir Victor Gollancz 1972-77, lectr in English, Tufts in London program 1969-78, lektor Regensburg Univ 1979-80, Arts Cncl fellow in writing Winchester Sch of Art 1983 and 1984, visiting prof St Olaf Coll Minnesota 1987 1988 1989; ed conslt Boydell and Brewer 1987-89; chm E Arts Assoc Literature Panel 1986-89; vice chm tstees and chm Friends of Wingfield Coll; *poetry*: 5 vols inc Waterslain (1986), The Painting-Room (1988), New and Selected Poems 1965-1990 (1991); *for Children*: The Green Children (1966, Arts Cncl award), Storm (1985, Carnegie medal), British Folk Tales (1987), Sleeping Nanna (1989); *translations from Old English*: Beowulf (jtly, 1968); The Norse Myths (1981), Pieces of Land (1972), The Stones Remain (1989);*edited*: The Anglo-Saxon World (1982), Folk-Tales of The British Isles (1985), The Oxford Book of Travel Verse (1986); *Opera* The Green Children (with Nicola LeFanu, 1990); *Recreations* music, tennis, archaeology, travel; *Style*— Kevin Crossley-Holland, Esq; The Old Vicarage, Walsham-le-Willows, Bury St Edmunds, Suffolk (☎ 0359 259 267)

CROSSMAN, David; s of Henry William Crossman (d 1966), and Gertrude Edith Mary, *née* Glasscock; *b* 12 Jan 1947; *Educ* Belmont Sch Tottenham, City Coll for Further Educn London; *m* 1 s (Tom Dow-Smith b 1972); *Career* professional TV prodr and dir 1974-; credits incl: The London Programme 1977, A Question of Sex 1978, The Cannon and Ball Show 1979-81, Metal Mickey 1980-81, A Week in Politics 1982, Chips Comic 1983, The Pocket Money Programme 1984-85, The Editors 1990; individual memb IPPA, memb Dirs Guild of GB; *Recreations* photography, motoring, fatherhood; *Style*— David Crossman, Esq; Flat One, 58 Wickham Rd, Beckenham, Kent BR3 2RQ (☎ 081 658 2012); Dareks Production House (fax 081 658 2012)

CROSSMAN, Lady Rose Maureen; *née* Alexander; o da of Field Marshal 1 Earl Alexander of Tunis, KG, OM, GCB, GCMG, CSI, DSO, MC, PC (d 1969); *b* 28 Oct 1932; *m* 20 Jan 1956, Lt-Col Humphrey Crossman, JP, DL, s of Maj-Gen Francis Lindisfarne Morley Crossman, CB, DSO, MC (d 1947), of Cheswick Hse, Berwick-upon-Tweed; 1 s, 1 da; *Style*— Lady Rose Crossman; Cheswick House, Berwick upon Tweed, Northumberland TD15 2RL

CROSSWELL, Michael Stephen; s of Charles Henry Crosswell (d 1976), and Cecilia Margaret, *née* Jones; *b* 23 Jan 1943; *Educ* Stawley GS S London; *m* 14 June 1980, da of George Marvin of Milton Keynes, Bucks; *Career* dir Blue Arrow plc (chief exec MAIN division, employment group); vice chm Federation of Recruitment and Employment Services (FRES) (chm 1988-); *Recreations* golf; *Clubs* Woburn Golf; *Style*— Michael S Crosswell, Esq; Plovers, Hatching Green, Harpenden, Hertfordshire (☎ (05827) 64269); Iviercury House, Triton Cdourt, Finsbury Square, London EC2 (☎ 071 256 5011)

CROSTHWAITE, Andrew Donald; s of Donald Rothery Crosthwaite, of Lytham, Lancashire, and Jean Mary, *née* Cavill; *b* 16 March 1957; *Educ* Manchester GS, Worcester Coll Oxford (BA); *m* Eleanor Patricia, da of Paddy Morahan; 2 s (Matthew Andrew b 10 May 1990, Sam Neil (twin)); *Career* advtg exec; Ogilvy & Mather 1978-81, McCormick Publicis 1981-82, Doyle Dane Bernbach 1982-85; FCO Ltd: joined 1985, dir 1986, currently planning ptnr; *Recreations* jigsaws of all descriptions; *Style*— Andrew Crosthwaite, Esq; FCO Ltd, Eldon House, 1 Dorset St, London W1H 4BD (☎ 071 935 0334, fax 071 486 7092)

CROSTHWAITE, Peregrine Kenneth Oughton; s of Kenneth Alan Crosthwaite, and Nora Elsie, *née* Oughton; *b* 24 March 1949; *Educ* St Paul's, Trinity Coll Oxford (MA); *m* 29 Oct 1982, Valerie Janet, da of Sir Albert Cahn; 2 s (Nicholas Anthony b 22 Jan 1985, Thomas William b 23 Oct 1986), 1 da (Sally-Anne Claire b 8 May 1989); *Career* joined Fenn & Crosthwaite 1972 (merged with George Henderson to become Henderson Crosthwaite 1975), ptnr Henderson Crosthwaite 1979-89, currently md Henderson Crosthwaite Institutional Brokers Ltd; memb: Worshipful Co of Merchant taylors, Freeman City of London; memb London Stock Exchange 1975; *Recreations* cricket, squash, tennis, golf, skiing, music, books, theatre; *Style*— Peregrine Crosthwaite, Esq; 30 Larpent Ave, London SW15 6UU (☎ 081 788 2073); Henderson Crosthwaite Institutional Brokers Ltd, 32 St Mary at Hill, London EC3P 3AJ (☎ 071 623 9992, fax 071 528 0884)

CROUCH, Dr Colin John; s of Charles John Crouch (d 1990), of Charlbury, Oxon, and Doris Beatrice, *née* Baker (d 1990); *b* 1 March 1944; *Educ* Latymer Upper Sch Hammersmith, LSE (BA), Univ of Oxford (DPhil); *m* 10 June 1970, Joan Ann, da of David Freedman (d 1972), of London E1; 2 s (Daniel b 1974, Ben b 1978); *Career* lectr in sociology: LSE 1969-70, Univ of Bath 1972-73; reader LSE 1980-85 (lectr 1973-79, sr lectr 1979-80), fell and tutor in politics Trinity Coll and faculty lectr in sociology Univ of Oxford 1985- (chm Sub-Faculty of Sociology 1987-89, proctor 1990-91), res interests the comparative study of industl relations systems in Western Europe; ed: Stress and Contradiction in Modern Capitalism (with Lindberg et al, 1975), Br Political Sociology Yearbook Vol III Participation in Politics (1977), The Resurgence of Class Conflict in Western Europe since 1968 vol I Nat Studies vol II comparative Analyses (with A Pizzorno, 1978), State and Economics in Contemporary Capitalism (1979), Int Yearbook of Organizations Democracy vol I Organizational Democracy and Political Processes (with F Heller, 1983), The New Centralism (with D Marguand, 1989), Corporatism and Accountability Organised Interests in Br Public Life (with R P Dore, 1990), European Industrial Relations: the Challenge of Flexibility (with G Baglioni, 1990), The Politics of 1992 (with D Marquand, 1990); memb Oxford West and Abingdon Lab Pty, referee class 3 Oxfordshire Football Assoc; memb Standing Ctee of Ct of Govrs LSE 1980-84, jt ed The Political Quarterly 1985-, chm Fabian Soc 1976 (memb Exec Ctee 1969-78); *Books* The Student Revolt (1970), Class Conflict and the Industrial Relations Crisis (1977), The Politics of Industrial Relations (2 edn 1982), Trade Unions the Logic of Collective Action (1982); *Recreations* playing violin, listening to music, gardening; *Style*— Dr Colin Crouch; 109 Southmoor Rd, Oxford OX2 6RE (☎ 0865 54688); Trinity Coll, Oxford OX1 3BH (☎ 0865 279 879, 279 900)

CROUCH, Sir David Lance; s of Charles Littler Stanley Crouch (d 1966), of Northwood, Middx, and Rosalie Kate, *née* Croom (d 1972); *b* 23 June 1919; *Educ* Univ Coll Sch; *m* 5 July 1947, Margaret Maplesden, da of Maj Sydney Maplesden Noakes, DSO, of Shorne, Kent; 1 s (Patrick b 19 May 1954), 1 da (Vanessa b 11 Oct 1951); *Career* served RA 1939-46, Maj, attached RAF 1944-45, service in N Africa, Europe, Burma; dir Westminster Communications Group Ltd; Parly Candidate (Cons) W Leeds 1959, MP (Cons) Canterbury 1966-87; memb: SE Thames RHA 1970-84, Cncl Univ of Kent at Canterbury 1971, MRC 1984-87; chm: The Kent Soc 1987-, The Theatres Tst 1987-; govr Kent Inst of Art and Design 1988-, tstee Crisis at Christmas; Hon DCL Univ of Kent at Canterbury 1987; FRSA; kt 1987; *Books* A Canterbury Tale (1987); *Recreations* golf, painting; *Clubs* Athenaeum, MCC; *Style*— Sir David Crouch; The Oast House, Fisher St, Badlesmere, Faversham, Kent (☎ 0227 730528)

CROUCHER, Norman Colville; s of Wilfred Gladston Croucher, MBE, and Mary Kate, *née* Bennett; *b* 17 May 1915; *Educ* Bristol GS, Monkton Coomb Sch; *m* 1, 18 Nov 1939, Mary Millicent (d 1987), da of late C M Lane, of Bristol; 2 s (Richard Colville b 1944, Brian Robert b 1946); m 2, Oct 1988, Jane Cleverley; *Career* tech/liaison engr Harland Engineering Co Ltd Alloa 1937-46, chief M & E asst engr J Taylor & Sons London 1958-61, tech/works dir KSB Manufacturing Co Ltd 1961-75, conslt engr 1975-83; life vice pres Br Pump Mfrs Assoc 1983- (memb 1964-83, chm Tech Ctee 1971-83); chm: BSI ME/29 Ctee 1972-83, ISO TC/115 Ctee 1972-83; chief scrutineer Motor Sport Div RAC 1957-85, former Cncl memb BARC; Freeman City of London, Liveryman Worshipful Co of Blacksmiths 1964; *Recreations* motor sport; *Clubs* RAC; *Style*— Norman Croucher, Esq; 7 Vavasour House, North Embankment, Dartmouth, Devon TQ6 9PW (☎ 08043 4053)

CROW, Jonathan Rupert; s of Michael Frederick Crow, and Edith Mae, *née* Quayle; *b* 25 June 1958; *Educ* St Pauls, Univ of Oxford (BA); *Career* called to the Bar Lincoln's Inn 1981; *Style*— Jonathan Crow, Esq; 23 Holland Park Mews, London W1 3SX; 4 Stone Buildings, Lincoln's Inn, London WC2A 3XT (☎ 071 242 5524, fax 071 831 7907, telex 892300 ADVICE G)

CROW, Dr Julie Carol; da of Dr Eric George Hemphill Carter, and Phyllis Elsie, *née* Crump; *b* 26 Feb 1942; *Educ* Chislehurst and Sidcup Girls GS, London Hosp Med Coll Univ of London; *m* 22 Jan 1966, Dr Timothy John Crow, s of Percy Arthur Crow; 1 s (Oliver b 10 April 1971), 1 da (Louise b 21 Feb 1974); *Career* house physician and surgn Aberdeen 1966; Univ of Aberdeen: lectr in pathology 1968-71, pt/t lectr 1971-73; Northwick Park Hosp: pt/t registrar 1975-76, pt/t sr registrar 1976-82, locum conslt histopathology 1983-85; sr lectr in histopathology Royal Free Hosp of Med 1985- (hon conslt); NE Thames regnl advsr to Royal Coll of Pathologists; memb: BMA, MWF, ACP, IAP; FRCPath 1989; *Recreations* chinese brush painting, calligraphy, juggling, reading, watching TV; *Style*— Dr Julie Crow; 16 Northwick Circle, Kenton, Harrow, Middlesex HA3 0EJ; Department of Histopathology, Royal Free Hospital and School of Medicine, Pond St, London NW3 2QG (☎ 071 794 0500 ext 3169, fax 071 435 5342)

CROW, (Hilary) Stephen; s of Aubrey Everard Crow, of Crowborough, Sussex, and Ivy Marion, *née* Warltier (d 1990); *b* 2 Sept 1934; *Educ* Leek HS, William Ellis Sch, St Catharine's Coll Cambridge; *m* 8 April 1958, Margaret, da of Frederick Anderson (d 1961); 2 s (Andrew b 1962, Matthew b 1965), 1 da (Anne b 1958); *Career* Nat Serv RA Intelligence Corps 1952-54; various appts in Lancashire CC and Southport CBC 1957-72, divnl planning offr and princ asst co planning offr Hertfordshire CC 1972-76 (planning inspector 1976-); FRTPI (M) 1963, FRGS 1965; *Style*— Stephen Crow, Esq; Tollgate House, Houlton St, Bristol BS2 9DJ (☎ 0272 218963, telex 449321, fax 0272 218769)

CROWDEN, James Gee Pascoe; JP (Wisbech 1969), DL (Cambridgeshire 1971); yr s of Lt-Col R J C Crowden, MC, of Peterborough; *b* 14 Nov 1927; *Educ* Bedford Sch, Pembroke Coll Cambridge (MA); *m* 1955, Kathleen Mary (d 1989), wid of Capt F A Grounds, and da of late J W Loughlin, of Upwell; 1 s (decd); *Career* cmmnd Royal Lincs Regt 1947; chartered surveyor; rowed in Oxford and Cambridge Boat Race 1951 and 1952 (pres 1952), Capt GB VIII Euro Championships Macon 1951 (Gold medallists), rowed 1950 Euro Championships and 1952 Olympics, coached 20 Cambridge crews 1953-75, steward and memb Ctee of Mgmnt Henley Royal Regatta, memb Cncl Amateur Rowing Assoc 1957-77, sr ptnr Grounds & Co 1974-88; chm: Appeals Exec Ctee Peterborough Cathedral 1979, Cambs Olympic Appeals 1984 and 1988; vice pres Br Olympic Assoc 1988-; govr: King's Sch Peterborough, St Hugh's Sch Woodhall Spa; memb Ely Diocesan Pastoral Ctee 1969-89; former pres Agric Valuers' Assocs of: Herts Beds and Bucks, Lincs, Norfolk, Cambs, Wisbech; high sheriff Cambs and Isle of Ely 1970, vice ld-lt Cambs 1985; sr warden Co of Watermen and Lightermen of the River Thames; FRSA 1990; *Recreations* rowing, shooting; *Clubs* East India, Devonshire, Sports and Public Schs, Hawks', Univ Pitt, Cambridge County, Leander, Sette of Odd Volumes; *Style*— J G P Crowden, Esq, JP, DL; 19 North Brink, Wisbech, Cambs PE13 1JR (☎ 0945 583320)

CROWDER, Frederick Petre; QC (1964); s of Sir John Ellenborough Crowder (d 1961), and Florence Gertrude Petre (d 1981); *b* 18 July 1919; *Educ* Eton, ChCh Oxford; *m* 12 July 1948, Hon Patricia Winifred Mary, da of 25 Baron Mowbray, MC (d 1965) (also 26 Baron Segrave and 22 Baron Stourton); 2 s (Richard b 1950, John b 1954); *Career* served 1939-45 War as Maj Coldm Gds (N Africa, Italy, and Burma); barr Inner Temple 1948, master of the Bench 1971; SE Circuit, recorder of Gravesend 1960-67; Herts QS, chm 1963-71; contested (C) N Tottenham 1945; MP (C): Ruislip-Northwood 1950-74, Hillingdon, Ruislip-Northwood 1974-79; PPS to: Slr-Gen 1952-54, attorney-gen 1954-62; recorder (formerly of Colchester) 1967-; treas of Inner Temple 1991 (reader 1990); *Clubs* Pratt's; *Style*— Frederick P Crowder, Esq, QC; 8 Quarrendon St, SW6 3SU (☎ 071 731 6342); 2 Harcourt Bldgs, Temple EC4 (☎ 071 353 2112)

CROWDER, Ven Norman Harry; s of Laurence Smethurst Crowder (d 1977), and Frances Annie, *née* Hicks; *b* 20 Oct 1926; *Educ* Nottingham HS, St John's Coll Cambridge (MA), Westcott House Theol Coll Cambridge; *m* 16 Dec 1971, Pauleen Florence Alison, *née* Styles; 1 s (Richard b 1973); *Career* curate St Mary's Radcliffe-on-Trent 1952-55, residential chaplain to Bishop of Portsmouth 1955-59; chaplain Canford Sch 1964-72 (asst chaplain 1959-64), vicar of St John's Oakfield Ryde IOW 1972-75, dir of religious educn Portsmouth Dio and residentiary canon of Portsmouth Cathedral 1972-85, archdeacon of Portsmouth 1985-; *Recreations* water colour, travel; *Clubs* MCC; *Style*— The Ven the Archdeacon of Portsmouth; Victoria Lodge, 36 Osborn Road, Fareham, Hants PO16 7DS (☎ 0329 280101)

CROWDER, Hon Mrs (Patricia Winifred Mary); *née* Stourton; da of 25 Baron Mowbray, 26 Segrave and 22 Stourton, MC (d 1965); *b* 2 Nov 1924; *m* 12 July 1948, Frederick Petre Crowder, QC, MP, *qv*; 2 s (Richard John b 1950; John George b 1954); *Career* Foreign Office; *Style*— The Hon Mrs Crowder; 8 Quarrendon St, London SW6 3SU (☎ 071 731 6342)

CROWDY, Edmund Porter; VRD; s of Lt-Col Charles R Crowdy (d 1938), and Kate, *née* Porter; bro of Maj-Gen Joseph Crowdy, *qv*; *b* 13 March 1925; *Educ* Gresham's Sch, Sidney Sussex Coll Cambridge; *m* 1958, Sheila Mary, *née* Davison; 2 s (Nicholas, Charles), 2 da (Sarah b 1962, Philippa b 1967); *Career* Cmdr RNVR; engineer; md:

Hawthorn Leslie (Engineers) Ltd 1972-78, Clark-Hawthorn Ltd 1978-80, Doxford Engines Ltd 1980-, Br Shipbuilders (Engrg and Tech Services) Ltd 1981-1984, ret; FEng; *Recreations* campanology, golf; *Style—* Edmund Crowdy Esq, VRD; 18 Manor Rd, Benton, Newcastle upon Tyne (☎ (091) 2666418)

CROWDY, Maj-Gen Joseph Porter; CB (1984), QHP (1981); s of Lt-Col Charles R Crowdy (d 1938), and Kate, *née* Porter; bro Edmund Crowdy, *qv*; *b* 19 Nov 1923; *Educ* Gresham's Sch, Edinburgh Univ (MB ChB, DTM and H); *m* 1948, Beryl Elisabeth Sapsford; 4 da; *Career* house surgeon Norfolk and Norwich Hosp 1947-48, joined RAMC 1949, former Commandant and postgraduate dean RAMC; FFCM, MFOM; *Style—* Maj-Gen Joseph Crowdy, CB, QHP; 5 Atterbury St, London SW1P 4RQ (☎ 071 821 7086)

CROWE, Brian Lee; CMG (1985); s of Eric Eyre Crowe (d 1952) and Virginia Bolling *née* , Teusler (d 1981); *b* 5 Jan 1938; *Educ* Sherbourne Sch, Magdalen Coll Oxford; *m* 19 Jan 1969, Virginia da of Col George Willis, MC, OBE (d 1980); 2 s (Alexander b 1972, Charles b 1975); *Career* FO 1961, Br Embassy Moscow 1962-64, FCO London 1965-68; Br Embassy: Washington 1968-73, Bonn 1973-76; head policy planning staff FCO London 1976-78, head of Chancery UK Perm Rep to EEc Brussels 1979-81, head of Euro Community Dept FCO London 1982-84, min commercial Br Embassy Washington 1985-; *Recreations* tennis, squash, winter sports; *Style—* Brian Crowe, Esq, CMG; c/o FCO, King Charles Street, London, SW1

CROWE, David Edward Aubrey; s of Norman Ronald Aubrey Crowe (d 1983), and Barbara Lythgoe, *née* Jones; *b* 31 Aug 1939; *Educ* Cranleigh Sch Surrey, Christ Church Oxford (MA); *m* 8 June 1963, Helen Margaret, da of George Denis Dale (d 1983); 2 da (Sarah b 1967, Lucy b 1971); *Career* slr 1964; ptnr: HA Crowe and Co 1964-68, Gouldens 1968-89 (conslt 1989-); dir Braithwaite plc; Parly candidate (Lib): Bromley 1970, Ravensbourne 1974; ldr Lib Gp Bromley Cncl 1974-78, vice chm London Lib Pty 1975, chm Bromley Consumer Gp 1978-79; hon sec Beckenham and Bromley Nat Tst 1979-88 (chm 1975-79), memb Advsy Bd Acad of Ancient Music; memb Law Soc F; *Recreations* opera going, gardening; *Clubs* Oxford and Cambridge, National Liberal; *Style—* David Crowe, Esq; 22 Tudor Street, London EC4Y OJJ (☎ 071 583 7777, fax 071 583 3051)

CROWE, Dame Sylvia; DBE (1973, CBE 1967); da of Eyre Crowe; *b* 1901; *Educ* Berkhamsted, Swanley Hort Coll; *Career* served FANY and ATS 1939-45; designed gardens 1927-39, landscape architect in private practice 1945-; work as conslt incl: Harlow and Basildon New Town Corporations, CEGB for Trawsfynydd and Wylfa Nuclear Power Stations, Forestry Cmmn, reclamation of land after 1952 floods, gardens for Univ of Oxford and Cwlth Inst London; reservoirs: Bewl Bridge Wimbleball and Rutland Water; pres Inst Landscape Architects 1957-59, vice pres Int Fedn of Landscape Architecture 1964 (sec 1948-59), hon Inst of Landscape Architects, chm Tree Cncl 1974-76; Hon DLitt Univ of Newcastle 1975, Hon LLD Univ of Sussex 1978, Hon DLitt Heriott Watt Univ Edinburgh; hon fell Inst of Foresters, hon FRIBA 1969; *Books Incl:* Tomorrow's Landscape (1956), Garden Design (1958, 2 edn 1981), Landscape Power, Landscape Roads, Pattern of Landscape; *Recreations* gardening, walking, countryside; *Style—* Dame Sylvia Crowe, DBE; 59 Ladbroke Grove, London W11 3AT (☎ 071 727 7794)

CROWLEY-BAINTON, Dr Theresa; da of Joseph Crowley, of Bucks, and Margaret Mary, *née* Heaton; *b* 4 Nov 1953; *Educ* Notre Dame London, Bedford Coll Univ of London (BSc), UCL (PhD); *m* 18 Aug 1979, Christopher Stephen Bainton, s of David Bainton, of Dorset; *Career* chartered psychologist; Austin Knight Ltd 1974-75, Department of Employment 1975-77 and 1983-85, Kiernan & Co (UK) Ltd 1978-83, Cabinet Office 1985-86, HM Treasy 1986-88, Policy Studies Inst 1988-, Industl Soc 1988-, hon sec Div of Occupational Psychology Br Pyschological Soc; author of several reports on empoyment and unemployment; *Books* Redundancy (1985), many papers on employment and unemployment; *Recreations* riding, archaeology, the Western Mystery tradition; *Clubs* National Liberal; *Style—* Dr Theresa Crowley-Bainton; Raven Cottage, 2 Ravensbourne Gdns, Ealing, London W13 8EW; The Industrial Soc, 48 Bryanston Square, London W1

CROWLEY-MILLING, Air Marshal Sir Denis; KCB (1973), CBE (1963), DSO (1943), DFC (1941, and Bar 1942); s of Thomas William Crowley-Milling (d 1954), of Colwyn Bay, N Wales, and Gillian May, *née* Chinnery (d 1941); *b* 22 March 1919; *Educ* Malvern; *m* 1943, Lorna Jean Jeboult, da of H J Stuttard, of Park Lodge, Deganwy, N Wales; 1 s decd, 2 da; *Career* Rolls Royce apprentice and RAFVR 1937-39, Sqdns 615, 242, 610 and 181 1939-44, AOC No 38 Gp RAF Odiham 1970-72, AOC 46 Gp RAF Upavon 1973, UK rep Perm Mil Deputies Gp CENTO 1974-75; controller RAF Benevolent Fund 1975-81; Gentleman Usher of the Scarlet Rod to the Order of the Bath 1979-85 (registrar and sec 1985-90); *Style—* Air Marshal Sir Denis Crowley-Milling, KCB, CBE, DSO, DFC; c/o Barclays Bank plc, 46 Park Lane, London W1A 4EE

CROWLEY-MILLING, Michael Crowley; CMG (1982); s of Thomas William Crowley-Milling (d 1954), of Colwyn Bay, N Wales and Gillian May, *née* Chinnery (d 1942); *b* 7 May 1917; *Educ* Radley Coll, St John's Coll Cambridge (MA); *m* 1957, Gee, da of William Gray Dickson (d 1983), of West Ferry, Dundee; *Career* electrical engr Metropolitan-Vickers Electric Co Ltd 1938-63: devpt of radar 1938-46, design and devpt of electron linear accelerators for physics med and irradiation purposes 1946-63; Daresbury Nuclear Physics Lab 1963-71; Euro Orgn for Nuclear Res (CERN) Geneva 1971-83: responsible for control system for Super Proton Synchrotron (SPS) 19 div leader 1977-78, dir Acceleration Program 1979-80, conslt 1981-85; SLAC Stanford Univ (USA) 1983-85, conslt Los Alamos Nat Lab USA 1985-, dir Crowley Conslts 1984-; CEng, FIEE; *Books* Accelerator Control Systems (ed, 1986), Accelerator and Large Experimental Physics Control Systems (ed, 1990), various articles in tech press on accelerators and control systems; *Recreations* vintage cars, sailing (yacht 'SPS'); *Clubs* VSCC, LPYC; *Style—* Michael Crowley-Milling, Esq, CMG; c/o Barclays Bank plc, 40 Conway Rd, Colwyn Bay, Clwyd LL29 7HU

CROWN, Dr Sidney; s of Saul Crown (d 1983), and Lily, *née* Levin (d 1969); *b* 11 Sept 1924; *Educ* King Alfred Sch London, Univ of London (PhD), Middx Hosp; *m* 21 March 1964, June Madge, da of Edward Downes (d 1979); 2 s (David Eliot b 1967, Giles Humphry b 1969), 1 da (Anna Louise b 1966); *Career* houseman and registrar Middx Hosp, sr registrar Nat Hosp, conslt psychiatrist London Hosp (ret 1989); author of numerous scientific pubns; asst ed British Journal of Psychiatry 1979-, ed British Journal of Medical Psychology 1981-89; FRCP, FRCPsych; *Books* Essential Principles of Psychiatry (1969), Psychosexual Problems (1976), Contemporary Psychiatry (1980); *Recreations* music, opera, theatre, running, squash; *Style—* Dr Sidney Crown; 118 Whitfield St, London W1P 5RZ (☎ 071 387 6787); 14 Devonshire Place, London W1N 1PB (☎ 071 935 0646)

CROWSON, Richard Borman; CMG (1986); s of Clarence Borman Crowson (d 1980), of Gainsborough, and Cecilia May, *née* Ramsden (d 1973); *b* 23 July 1929; *Educ* Queen Elizabeth's GS Gainsborough, Downing Coll Cambridge (MA); *m* 1, 29 Feb 1960 (m dis 1974), Sylvia, *née* Cavalier; 1 s (Anthony b 26 Feb 1961), 1 da (Hilary b 3 March 1964); m 2, 21 May 1983, Judith Elaine, da of Marion Earl Clark, of Lincoln, Nebraska, USA; 1 step s (David b 5 Aug 1967); *Career* HM Colonial Serv Uganda 1955-62, FO 1962-63, 1 Sec (Commercial) Br Embassy Tokoyo 1963-68, dep high cmmr Barbados 1968-70, FCO 1970-74, cnsllr (Commercial & Aid) Br Embassy Jakarta 1975-77, cnsllr (Hong Kong Affairs) Br Embassy Washington (also accredited in Ottawa) 1977-82, cnsllr Br Embassy Berne 1983-85, Br high cmmr Mauritius and concurrently HM Ambass Fed Islamic Repub of the Comoros 1985-89; FCIS 1962; *Recreations* music, theatre; *Clubs* Royal Cwlth Soc; *Style—* Richard Crowson, Esq, CMG; 67 Crofton Rd, Orpington, Kent (☎ 0689 891320)

CROWTHER, Anthony Herbert; s of Herbert Crowther, of London, and May Ingldew, *née* Kirby; *b* 3 Sept 1940; *Educ* St Peter's Sch York, St Catharine's Coll Cambridge (MA), Architectural Assoc Sch of Architecture London (AA Dip); *m* 18 Mar 1967, Valerie, da of Montague Brown, of York; 1 s (Simon b 4 Aug 1971), 1 da (Emma b 10 Nov 1968); *Career* architect 1968; worked in various offices in GB, Germany and USA until 1972, ptnr Greenway Ptnrs 1975-; memb RIBA 1969; *Recreations* reading and looking, antiques, wine, gardening, penguins, squash; *Style—* Anthony Crowther, Esq; 77 The Chase, London SW4 0NR (☎ 071 622 2081); Greenway and Partners, Branch Hill Mews, London NW3 7LT (☎ 071 435 6091)

CROWTHER, Hon Charles Worth; s of Baron Crowther (Life Peer, d 1972); *b* 31 Jan 1939; *Educ* Winchester, Harvard (AB 1960), Corpus Christi Coll Camb (BA 1962); *m* 20 July 1963, Barbara Sylvia, yr da of Prof Norman Merrett Hancox, MD, of Moorside House, Neston, Cheshire; 1 s, 1 da; *Style—* The Hon Charles Crowther; Bourne Bank, Bourne End, Bucks

CROWTHER, Hon David Richard Geoffrey; 2 s of Baron Crowther (Life Peer, d 1972); *b* 19 Aug 1943; *Educ* Eton, King's Coll Camb (BA 1965); *m* 1974, Martina, *née* Menn-Fink; *Style—* The Hon David Crowther

CROWTHER, Eric John Ronald; OBE (1977); s of Stephen Charles Crowther (d 1943), and Olive Beatrix, *née* Selby (d 1951); *b* 4 Aug 1924; *m* 1959, Elke Auguste Ottilie, da of Ludwig Winkelmann (d 1976), of Germany; 1 s (Edward b 1963), 1 da (Evelyn b 1961); *Career* WWII RN Med 1943-47; winner Inns of Court Contest in Advocacy 1951; called to the Bar Lincoln's Inn 1951-68; metropolitan stipendary magistrate 1968-89; rec Inner London Crown Courts 1983-; lectr: English Br Cncl 1951-81, evidence to RN 1968-89, elocution and advocacy Cncl of Legal Educn 1955-; chm Training Sub Ctee Inner London Magistrates 1981-89; ed Commonwealth Judicial Journal 1973-77; hon offr Int Students House 1981-; *Books* Advocacy for the Advocate (1984), Last in the List (1988), Look What's on the Bench! (1991); *Style—* Eric J R Crowther, Esq, OBE; 21 Old Buildings, Lincoln's Inn WC2

CROWTHER, Leslie Douglas Sargent; s of Leslie Frederick Crowther (d 1955), of Twickenham, Middx, and Ethel Maraquita, *née* Goulder (d 1951); *b* 6 Feb 1933; *Educ* Nottingham HS, Thames Valley GS, Cone Ripman Sch, RAM; *m* 1954, Jean Elizabeth, da of Walter James Osborne Stone; 1 s (Nicholas James b 10 June 1965), 4 da (Lindsay Jane b 9 Dec 1954, Elizabeth Ann (twin) b 9 Dec 1954, Caroline Susan b 29 Dec 1958, Charlotte Louise b 29 Nov 1962); *Career* entertainer; Ovaltiney's Concert Party of the Air (Radio Luxembourg) 1949, various schs broadcasts for BBC 1948-50, Open Air Theatre Regent's Park 1949, early radio work incl Accent on Youth; theatre work incl: High Spirits (London Hippodrome Theatre) and six seasons with the Fol de Rols, Let Sleeping Wives Lie (Garrick Theatre) 1967-69, Aladdin (London Palladium) 1970-71, Royal Variety Show 1970, cabaret at London's Savoy Hotel 1970, panto season Richmond Theatre 1977, summer season New Arts Theatre Poole 1978, panto Alexandra Theatre Birmingham 1978-79, summer season Opera House Jersey 1979; panto: Theatre Royal Bath 1979-80, Ashcroft Theatre Croydon 1981, Sparrows Nest Lowestoft 1981, New Theatre Cardiff 1982-83, Kings Theatre Southsea 1982-83, His Majesty's Theatre Aberdeen 1983-84; recent theatre work incl: Bud 'n' Ches and Underneath the Arches (Prince of Wales Theatre London), Robinson Crusoe (Theatre Royal Bath) 1988-89, Ashcroft Theatre Croydon 1989- 90; tv work: first tv series was High Summer, followed by The Black and White Minstrel Show, Crackerjack (for eight years), Saturday Crowd, Crowther's in Town and the Leslie Crowther Show (London Weekend TV), My Good Women (ATV) 1970-73, Who's Baby 1983-84, The Price is Right 1984-, Stars In Their Eyes (Granada TV) 1990; chm Stars Orgn for Spastics, pres Lord's Taverners 1991-92 (memb 1965-); Memb Grand Order of the Water Rat 1970-; *Recreations* walking, watching cricket, collecting antiques and British postage stamps, theatre, concerts; *Style—* Leslie Crowther, Esq; Leslie Crowther Ltd, 30 Lord's View, St John's Wood Rd, London NW8 7HL (☎ 071 289 3226)

CROWTHER, Peter Hayden; s of Charles William Crowther (d 1970), of S Glam, and Gwendoline Gladys, *née* Matthews (d 1965); *b* 1 June 1926; *Educ* Barry Boys' Sch, Manchester Coll of Technol; *m* 12 March 1955, Anne Marie, da of Sir Richard Rylandes Costain, CBE (d 1966), of Surrey; 1 s (Hugh b 1958), 1 da (Penelope b 1960); *Career* Lt RE 1945-48 BAOR; chartered engr, joined Babcock and Wilcox Ltd 1948, md Bailey Meters and Controls Ltd 1963-74, dir Babcock and Wilcox (UK Investmts) Ltd 1968-72, chm Digimatics Ltd 1971-74, dir Babcock and Wilcox (Mgmnt) Ltd 1972-74; joined Vickers plc 1975, chm local bd Vickers Engrg Gp Newcastle 1975-80, dir Vickers Engrg Gp 1975-80, chm and md B A J Vickers Ltd 1984-85, chm and md B A J Ltd 1985-86, dep chm B A J Hldgs 1985-87 (non-exec dir 1987); memb: Northern Industl Devpt Bd 1978-80, Herefordshire DHA 1988-; ret; CEng, MInstE, FBIM, FRSA; *Recreations* reading; *Clubs* Army and Navy; *Style—* Peter Crowther, Esq; Highbridge Farm, Ledbury, Herefordshire HR8 2HT (☎ 0531 2798)

CROWTHER, (Joseph) Stanley; MP (Lab) Rotherham 1976-; s of Cyril Joseph Crowther (d 1970), of Rotherham and Florence Mildred, *née* Beckett; *b* 30 May 1925; *Educ* Rotherham GS, Rotherham Coll of Technol; *m* 1948, Margaret, da of Llewellyn Royston (d 1956), of Huddersfield; 2 s; *Career* journalist formerly with Yorkshire Evening Post; Mayor of Rotherham 1971-72 and 1975-76; *Style—* Stanley Crowther Esq, MP; 15 Clifton Cres South, Rotherham (☎ (0709) 64559)

CROWTHER, Thomas Rowland; QC (1981); s of Dr Kenneth Vincent Crowther, of Gwent, and Winifred Anita, *née* Rowland; *b* 11 Sept 1937; *Educ* Newport HS, Keble Coll Oxford (MA); *m* 1969, Gillian Jane, da of William Leslie Prince (d 1978); 1 s (Thomas b 1970), 1 da (Lucy b 1971); *Career* barr 1960, in practice Oxford Circuit 1960-69, in practice Wales and Chester Circuit 1970-84, jr of Wales and Chester Circuit 1974, rec Crown Ct 1980-84, Crown Ct judge 1985; dir Gwent Area Broadcasting Ltd 1982-84; *Recreations* garden, trout fishing, golf; *Clubs* Cardiff and County, Newport Golf; *Style—* His Hon Judge Crowther, QC; Lansor, nr Caerleon, Gwent NP6 1LS (☎ 063 349 224)

CROWTHER-ALWYN, Peter; s of Rev Vivian Crowther-Alwyn (d 1967), of Ipswich, Suffolk, and Jessie, *née* Hough; *b* 14 April 1944; *Educ* Rossall Sch Fleetwood Lancs; *m* 5 Nov 1977, Irene Elizabeth, da of James Stewart Young; 2 da (Victoria Louise b 13 Feb 1979, Alexandra b 15 April 1981); *Career* articled clerk Clark Son & Moyle Ipswich 1962-66, audit clerk Paterson & Thompson 1966-67, audit sr Coopers & Lybrand Birmingham 1967-68; Pannell Fitzpatrick & Co: audit sr Port of Spain Trinidad 1968-70, resident ptnr Grenada 1972-75 (resident mangr 1970-71), seconded to Monrovia Liberia 1976-77; Pannell Kerr Forster: ptnr and dir Monrovia Liberia 1977-79, ptnr Banjul The Gambia 1987- (resident ptnr 1978-87), fin and admin ptnr Central Admin UK 1988-; memb Exec Ctee Gambia C of C & Indust 1978-87, Royal Danish Consul Banjul The Gambia 1985-87; chm Fajara Club The Gambia 1986-87 (treas 1984-86, chm Admissions Ctee 1978-79), chm Royal Soc of St George Banjul

(The Gambia) Branch 1984-87; FCA 1979 (ACA 1968), FBIM 1990 (MBIM 1972), MInstD 1988; *Recreations* golf, model car collecting, watching television, reading, DIY; *Clubs* Royal Over-Seas League, Fajara Club (The Gambia); *Style—* Peter Crowther-Alwyn, Esq; Lings Farm, 47 Main St, Keyworth, Notts NG12 5AA (☎ 06077 6646); Pannell Kerr Forster, Harby Lodge, 13 Pelham Rd, Notts NG5 1AP (☎ 0602 606260, fax 0602 622229, car 0860 743733)

CROWTHER-HUNT, Hon Mrs Elizabeth Anne; *née* Crowther-Hunt; eldest da of Baron Crowther-Hunt (Life Peer); *b* 1947; *m* 1976, Peter John Coulson; 2 c; *Style—* The Hon Elizabeth Crowther-Hunt; 37 Deodar Rd, Putney, London SW15 2NP

CROWTHER-HUNT, Baroness; Joyce; *née* Stackhouse; DL (Oxfordshire) 1978; da of late Rev Joseph Stackhouse, of Walsall Wood, Staffs; *m* 1944, Baron Crowther-Hunt (Life Peer d 1987); 3 da; *Career* pres Oxfordshire Girl Guides 1990; awarded Lazo de Dama de Isabel la Católica 1991; *Style—* The Rt Hon the Lady Crowther-Hunt, DL; 14 Apsley Road, Oxford (☎ 0865 58342)

CROXFORD, David; s of Frederick William Gordon Croxford (ka 1944), and Lucy May, *née* Williams; *b* 3 Oct 1937; *Educ* Hinchley Wood Co Sch Esher Surrey; *m* 5 July 1975, Victoria Wendy, da of Robert Francis Fort; *Career* CA 1962; trained and qualified with Hagley Knight & Co 1955-62, Tansley Witt & Co (now pt of MacIntyre Hudson) 1962-64, Ogden Parsons & Co (now pt of Coopers & Lybrand Deloitte) 1964-67, mangr Bird & Partners 1968-71; Moore Stephens: sr and managerial positions Bermuda 1972-77, tranferred to Jersey 1977, accounts controller 1977, special servs mangr 1979, ptnr 1980-; memb: ICAEW 1962, Jersey Soc of Chartered and Certified Accountants 1977, Jersey Assoc of Practising Chartered and Certified Accountants 1981, Jersey Taxation Soc 1986, IOD 1988; Licenced Insolvency Practitioner 1989; *Recreations* singing (choral and sacred), golf, music, gardening; *Clubs* La Moye Golf (Jersey), Jersey Gilbert and Sullivan Soc, Jersey Amateur Dramatic; *Style—* David Croxford, Esq; Moore Stephens, PO Box 236, Equity & Law House, La Motte St, St Helier, Jersey, Channel Islands (☎ 0534 75391, 0534 79970)

CROXON, Derrick Gwynn; s of Charles William Croxon (d 1968) of Maidstone, Kent; *b* 10 Jan 1923; *Educ* King's Sch Rochester, UCL; *m* 1947, Rachel Ann, da of late William Griffith Thomas; 2 da; *Career* Capt RE, Major RASC Italy; chem engineer/gen mgmnt trainee Reed Int 1949; md Kimberly-Clark Ltd 1961-83 (works dir 1954), ret as conslt; *Recreations* tennis, sailing, beekeeping; *Clubs* Medway Yacht; *Style—* Derrick Croxon, Esq; Somerfield Rd, Maidstone, Kent (☎ 0622 758161)

CROYDON, David John; s of John Farley Croydon, of Stourbridge, West Midlands, and Patricia Ethel, *née* Lloyd; *b* 26 Feb 1949; *Educ* King Edward VI GS Stourbridge, Univ of London (BA); *m* 29 July 1972, Catherine Mary, da of James Goddard, of Birmingham; 1 s (Luke James b 20 Jan 1981), 1 da (Madeleine Lucy b 26 June 1986); *Career* advertising exec 3M Corpn 1977-80, account mangr MSW Promotions 1980-81, account dir Counter Products Mktg 1981-86, fndr and md Marketing Principles Ltd Sales Promotion Consultancy 1986-; memb: Sales Promotion Conslts Assoc, Inst of Sales Promotion; *Recreations* rugby football; *Clubs* Chinnor, Saracens, Middx; *Style—* David Croydon, Esq; Monks Hill, South Hills, Brill, Aylesbury, Bucks; Marketing Principles Ltd, Frewin Chambers, Frewin Court, Cornmarket, Oxford (☎ 0865 791854, fax 0865 791852, car 0836 334150)

CROZIER, Brian Rossiter; s of Robert Henry Crozier (d 1939), and Elsa, *née* McGillivray (d 1957); *b* 4 Aug 1918; *Educ* Lycée Montpellier France, Peterborough Coll Harrow, Trinity Coll of Music London; *m* 7 Sept 1940, Mary Lillian (Lila), da of Charles Augustus Samuel (d 1965); 1 s (Michael b 1948), 3 da (Kathryn-Anne (Mrs Choguill) b 1941, Isobel (Mrs Colbourn) b 1944, Caroline (Mrs Wyeth) b 1953); *Career* WWII aeronautical inspection 1941-43; music and art critic London 1936-39; reporter and sub-ed: Stoke-on-Trent, Stockport, London 1940-41, News Chronicle 1944-48; sub-ed and writer Sydney Morning Herald Aust 1948-51, correspondent Reuters 1951-52 (sub-ed 1943-44), features ed Straits Times Singapore 1952-53, leader writer and corr, ed of Foreign Report The Economist 1954-64, commentator for the BBC Overseas Servs 1954-66, chm Forum World features 1965-74, Inst for the Study of Conflct 1979- (co-fndr and dir 1970-79); columnist: National Review NY 1978-, Now! London 1980-81, The Times 1982-84; conslt 1979-; named in The Guinness Book of Records as the writer who has interviewed most heads of state and govt in the world (64) 1948-89; *Books* The Rebels (1960), The Morning After (1963), Neo-Colonialism (1964), South-East Asia in Turmoil (1965), The Struggle for the Third World (1966), Franco (1967), The Masters of Power (1969), The Future of Communist Power (1970), DeGaulle (1973), A Theory of Conflict (1974), The Man Who Lost China (Chiang Kai-Shek) (1977), Strategy of Survival (1978), The Minimum State (1979), Franco: Crepúsculo de un hombre (1980), The Price of Peace (1980), Socialism Explained (jtly, 1984), This War Called Peace (jtly, 1984), The Andropov Deception (under pseudonym John Rossiter, 1984), The Grenada Documents (ed 1987), Socialism: Dream and Reality (1987), The Gorbachev Phenomenon (1990); *Recreations* piano, taping stereo; *Clubs* RAC; *Style—* Brian Crozier, Esq; 303 Linen Hall, 162-168 Regent St, London W1R 5TB (☎ 071 437 8172, fax 071 494 0511); Kulm House, Dollis Ave, Finchley London N3 1DA

CROZIER, John; *b* 28 June 1946; *Educ* Tiffin Sch, Univ of Bristol (BA), Kingston Poly (Dip in mgmnt studies); *m* (m dis); 2 c; *Career* Avon Cosmetics UK Ltd 1968-71 (job evaluation offr and personnel offr, sr personnel offr), personnel mangr Human Resources and Sales and Distribution Lyons Bakery Ltd 1971-73; Rank Xerox International Ltd: personnel mangr Midland and West 1973-75, personnel mangr UK Operations 1975-82, Euro personnel mangr 1978-82; Grand Metropolitan plc: personnel and comunications dir Chef & Brewer 1982-84, personnel PR and Communications dir Grand Metropolitan Retailing Ltd 1984-86; Heidrick & Struggles International Inc 1986-88 (ptnr Euro Practice, exec search conslt); Lopex plc 1988- (chm and chief exec Riley Advertising Ltd, chm LSR (International) Ltd (Human Resources Group), exec dir Lopex plc; MInstD 1985, memb Inst of Practitioners in Advertising; *Style—* John Crozier, Esq; 32 Staveley Rd, Chiswick, London W4 (☎ 081 995 7482, office 081 846 9933)

CROZIER, William Frederick Grenfell; s of Frederick Crozier (d 1973), and Millicent, *née* Grenfell; *b* 25 July 1917; *Educ* Stockport GS, Univ of Manchester (BSc, MSc); *m* 4 Oct 1941, Esme Augusta, da of Frederick Stokes (d 1951), of Blankney, Lincoln; 1 s (Peter Michael Anthony b 4 Nov 1943), 1 da (Rosemary b 31 Oct 1947); *Career* Public Works jr engr 1939-40; War Serv RE 1940-46, 612 Field Sqdn (ret Actg Maj); chief structural engr George Wimpey & Co 1946-58, chief engr GKN Reinforcements (London) 1958-61; ptnr: Frederick J Brand & Ptnrs 1961-64, Brill & Crozier 1964-71; sr ptnr Crozier, Haskell-Thomas & Ptnrs 1971-83; tech sec and pubns offr Fédération Internationale de la Précontrainte 1967 (hon memb 1986); Liveryman Worshipful Co of Plaisterers 1977; MICE 1948, FICE 1956; *Recreations* bridge; *Clubs* Hillingdon AC (Hon life memb), Northwood Golf (former Capt); *Style—* William Crozier, Esq; 85 Hoylake Crescent, Ickenham, Middlesex UB10 8JG (☎ 0895 633626)

CRUICKSHANK, Alexander Andrew Campbell; s of Alexander Cruickshank, MA, MB, CHB, FRCS (d 1980), and Eileen Bertha, *née* Coleman; *b* 30 Nov 1945; *Educ* Haileybury and ISC, Peterhouse Camb (MA); *m* 19 May 1973, Susan Mary, da of Alan Pearce Greenaway, Esq, JP; 2 s (David b 1976, Benjamin b 1982), 1 da (Sarah b 1974); *Career* Esso Petroleum Co Refinery and Distribution Planning 1967-72, Automated Real-Time Investmts Exch Ltd 1973-78, Orion Royal Bank Ltd 1979 (dir 1985-88), sr dir Continental Bank NA 1988-90, exec dir Sumitomo Fin Int 1990-; Liveryman Worshipful Co of Gardeners; *Recreations* golf, reading, gardening; *Clubs* St George's Hill Golf, City Livery, United Wards, City Pickwick (hon sec); *Style—* A A C Cruickshank, Esq; The Doone, Byfleet Rd, Cobham, Surrey KT11 1EA (☎ 0932 64714); 107 Cheapside, London EC2V 6DT (☎ 071 606 3001)

CRUICKSHANK, Alistair Ronald; s of Francis John Cruickshank (d 1969), of Aberdeen, and Kate Cameron, *née* Brittain; *b* 2 Oct 1944; *Educ* Aberdeen GS, Univ of Aberdeen (MA); *m* 29 March 1967, Sandra, da of John Noble, of Aberdeen; 3 da (Jennifer b 1970, Caroline b 1973, Diana b 1975); *Career* MAFF: asst princ 1966, asst private sec to min 1969-70, princ 1970, head Eggs and Poultry Branch 1970-74, head Milk Branch 1974-78, asst sec 1978, head Mktg Policy and Potatoes Div 1978-81, head Meat Hygiene Div 1982-84, head Milk Div 1984-86, under sec 1986, head Animal Health Gp 1986-89, princ fin offr 1989-; *Recreations* visiting old buildings, growing vegetables; *Style—* Alistair Cruickshank, Esq; Ministry of Agriculture, Fisheries and Food, 3-8 Whitehall Place, London SW1A 2HH

CRUICKSHANK, Donald Gordon; s of Donald Campbell Cruickshank, of Ingleholm, Fochabers, Moray, Scotland, and Margaret Buchan *née* Morrison; *b* 17 Sept 1942; *Educ* Fordyce Acad, Univ of Aberdeen (MA), Manchester Business Sch (MBA); *m* 17 Oct 1964, Elizabeth Buchan, da of Alexander Watt Taylor, of Fraserburgh, Aberdeenshire, Scotland; 1 s (Stewart b 1965), 1 da (Karen b 1969); *Career* CA; McKingsey and Co Inc 1972-77; dir and gen mangr Sunday Times, Times Newspapers Ltd 1977-80; dir Pearson Longman Ltd 1980-84; md Virgin Gp plc 1984-; chm Wandsworth District Health Authority 1986-; CA; *Recreations* opera, theatre, golf, sport; *Style—* Donald G Cruickshank, Esq; 95-99 Ladbroke Grove, London W11 1PG (☎ 071 229 1282, fax 071 727 8200)

CRUICKSHANK, George; s of George Cruickshank; *b* 13 July 1936; *Educ* Melville Coll, Heriot Watt Univ Edinburgh; *m* Catherine, *née* Macdonald; 1 s, 1 da; *Career* dir: Scottish Discount Co Ltd, Lloyds Bowmaker Gp of Cos; chm RIGP Fin; *Recreations* golf, curling, rugby, skiing, bridge; *Clubs* Royal Burgess Golf (Edinburgh), Curling, Caermount Golf; *Style—* George Cruickshank, Esq; 28 Inveralmond Drive, Edinburgh EH4 6J (☎ 031 336 4481); Lloyds Bowmaker Fin Gp, Fin House, Orchard Brae, Edinburgh EH4 1PF (☎ 031 332 2451)

CRUICKSHANK, Prof John; s of Arthur Cruickshank (d 1957), of Belfast, and Eva, *née* Shummacher (d 1974); *b* 18 July 1924; *Educ* Royal Belfast Academical Inst, Trinity Coll Dublin (BA, MA, PhD, LittD), École Normale Supérieure Paris; *m* 1, 3 May 1949 (m dis 1972), Kathleen Mary, da of late Arthur Gutteridge; 1 s (Michael John b 4 Nov 1957); m 2, 1 Sept 1972, Maguerite Doreen Penny, da of Harold Whaley (d 1982); *Career* WWII cryptographer Mil Intelligence 1943-45; lectr (later sr lectr) in French Univ of Southampton 1949-62, prof of French Univ of Sussex 1962-89, ret; chm Arts Sub Ctee UGC 1970-77 (memb 1970-77), pres Soc for French Studies 1980-82, memb Modern Humanities Res Assoc; *Books* Albert Camus and the Literature of Revolt (1959), Montherlant (1964), French Literature and its Background (ed 6 vols, 1968-70), Benjamin Constant (1974), Variations on Catastrophe: Some French Responses to the Great War (1982), Pascal: Pensées (1983); *Recreations* walking, birdwatching; *Style—* Prof John Cruickshank; Woodpeckers, East Hoathly, Lewes, E Sussex BN8 6QL (☎ 082584 364)

CRUICKSHANK, Dr John Gladstone (Ian); s of Prof John Cecil Cruickshank, MD (d 1956), of London, and Mabel Elizabeth, *née* Harvey; *b* 17 Oct 1930; *Educ* Highgate Sch, UCL (MB BS, MRCS, LRCP), Univ of Cambridge (MA), Univ of Birmingham (MD, MRCPath); *m* 27 Dec 1958, Margaret Montague, da of Lt-Col Charles Philip Heath, DSO (d 1988), of Cullompton, Devon; 1 s (John b 1967), 3 da (Isobel 1960, Catriona b 1961, Morag b 1963); *Career* RAF pilot offr 1948-50; lectr in pathology Univ of Cambridge 1957-64, lectr in microbiology Univ of Birmingham 1964-68, dean of Faculty of Med Univ of Rhodesia 1973-75 (prof of med microbiology 1968-76), dir Public Health Laboratory Exeter 1988- (dep dir 1976-88); memb Cncl Univ of Rhodesia 1970-75, regnl rep RCPath 1986-88, visiting conslt WHO 1987; FRCPath 1978; *Recreations* reading, tennis, music, the countryside; *Style—* Dr Ian Cruickshank; Coombe Farm, Knowle, Cullompton, Devon EX15 1PT (☎ 0884 33533); Public Health Laboratory, Church Lane, Exeter, Devon EX2 5AD (☎ 0392 402972, fax 0392 412835)

CRUICKSHANK, Dr Roger John; s of Dr (John) Norman Cruickshank, DSC, MC (d 1986), of Brill, Bucks, and (Helen) May Elizabeth, *née* Slimmon; *b* 8 Feb 1926; *Educ* Gresham's Sch Holt, Univ of Glasgow (MB ChB); *m* 1, 23 Feb 1952, Jane Eluned; 3 s (Matthew b 1953, Adam b 1956, Benjamin b 1957), 1 da (Emma b 1955); m 2, 17 July 1986, Mary Glenallan Kathleen, da of Lester Dan Bray, of Salisbury, Wilts; 2 step s (Julian b 1961, Matthew b 1967), 1 step da (Caroline b 1962); *Career* Admiralty Ferry Service 1944-46; Surgn Lt RNVR 1949-51; general practitioner 1952-73, clinical asst (psychiatry) St Bernard's Hosp 1977-80, med offr HM Prison Grendon 1980-; *Recreations* trout fishing, travel, ornithology; *Style—* Dr Roger Cruickshank, Esq; Corner House, The Green, Brill, Aylesbury, Bucks (☎ 0844 237811); HMP Grendon, Grendon Underwood Aylesbury, Bucks (☎ 029 677 301)

CRUICKSHANK, Hon Mrs (Victoria Elizabeth); *née* Mills; el da of 4 Baron Hillingdon (d 1978); *b* 23 July 1948; *m* 1, 1971 (m dis 1979), Anthony Roff; 2 da; m 2, 1981, D G R Cruickshank; 1 da; *Style—* The Hon Mrs Cruickshank; Elder St, Spitalfields, London E1

CRUICKSHANK OF AUCHREOCH, Martin Melvin; s of Brig Martin Melvin Cruickshank, CIE (d 1964), and Florence Watson Cruickshank (d 1976); *b* 17 Sept 1933; *Educ* Rugby, Eaton Hall, Corpus Christi Coll Cambridge; *m* 1 March 1958, Rona, da of Mary Fenella Paton of Grandhome (d 1949), of Grandhome House, Aberdeen; 3 s (Martin b 1960, Nicholas b 1961 d 1973, Paul b 1963), 1 da (Fenella b 1959); *Career* cmmnd Gordon Highlanders 1952, serv Malaya 1952-53 (despatches), Cyprus 1955-56, Germany 1960-61, Congo 1962 (Co cmd), Nigeria 1962-64 (chief instr Offr Cadet Sch, Bde Maj and Dep Cmdt Nigerian Military Coll), ret 1967; landowner; dir Blairmore Society Ltd (chm 1979-85); sec and past pres Strathfillan Golf Club; Order of St John in Scotland: memb Cncl 1970-75, memb Chapter 1970-91; KStJ (1982); FRGS; *Recreations* travel (particularly deserts), bird watching, golf, music, oenology; *Clubs* Army and Navy; *Style—* M M Cruickshank of Auchreoch; Auchreoch, Crianlarich, Perthshire (☎ 08384 218)

CRUM EWING, Humphry John Frederick; s of Humphry William Erskine Crum Ewing (d 1985) (and gggs of Humphry Ewing Crum Ewing, of Strathleven, Dunbartonshire, MP for Paisley 1857-74), and Winifred Mary, *née* Kyle (d 1988); *b* 11 May 1934; *Educ* Marlborough, Ch Ch Oxford (MA); *m* 1, 30 April 1964, Carolyn Joan Maule (d 1975), da of Lt-Col Ian Burn-Murdoch, OBE, IA (d 1963), and formerly w of 3 Baron Wrenbury; 1 s (Alexander b 1966), 2 da (Arabella b 1967, Nicola b and d 1969); m 2, 14 Feb 1980, Mrs Janet Angela Tomlinson, da of Leonard Bates (d 1965), of Leicester; *Career* public and int affrs conslt, pres Oxford Univ Cons Assoc 1956, contested (C) Swansea East Constituency 1959, chm Ingersoll Gp 1966-69, Rajawella Cos 1976-79; advsr to: Shadow Foreign Sec 1977-79, Min for Consumer Affrs 1981-83, Min for Higher Educn and Sci 1987-90, Min for Trg and Tourism 1990-; treas

Secretaries - Arts Cncl House of Commons 1990-; *Recreations* bridge, cooking, travelling, collecting; *Style—* Humphry Crum Ewing, Esq; 63 Baker St, Reading RG1 7XY (☎ 0734 585096)

CRUMMEY, (John) Andrew; s of John G Crummey, of Craiglockhart Park, Edinburgh, and Erica, *née* Summers; *b* 16 Dec 1955; *Educ* St Bees Sch Cumbria; *Career* advertisement exec Scotsman Publications Ltd 1978-80, sales mangr What's On? pubn 1980-82, scottish mangr Oracle Teletext 1984-85; Scottish TV: sales and mktg exec 1982-84, sales mangr 1985-88, sales controller 1988; *Recreations* golf; *Clubs* Gullane Golf, Royal Blackheath Golf; *Style—* Andrew Crummey, Esq; 6 Dean Park Mews, Edinburgh EH4 1EF (☎ 031 332 5016), Scottish Television plc, Cowcaddens, Glasgow (☎ 041 332 9999)

CRUMPLIN, Michael Kenneth Hugh; s of Col WCD Crumplin, of Trewythen Hall, Gresford, and Muriel Elizabeth Kerr Barley (d 1970); *b* 12 Aug 1942; *Educ* Wellington, Middx Hosp Med Sch (MB BS); *m* 29 May 1965, Elizabeth Ann, da of Maj Guy William Walker Bunting; 2 s (Ian Douglas b 22 Sep 1970, Patrick Gordon b 17 June 1972), 1 da (Fiona Jane Kerr b 1 July 1977); *Career* house surgn and house physician: Middx Hosp 1965, Central Middx Hosp 1966; sr house offr Middx Hosp 1966, registrar in surgery Princess Margaret Hosp Swindon and Middx Hosp 1970-72, sr registrar United Birmingham Hosps 1973-77 (res fell and hon sr registrar 1972-73), conslt gen surgn Clwyd S Dist 1977-; memb Standing Ctee Wales; RCS regnl advsr surgery N Wales; memb: Court Examiners RCS, Hosp Specialists and Conslts' Assoc, Ed Bd British Journal of Surgery; former memb Cncl Assoc Surgns GB and; LRCP, MRCS, FRCS; *Books* numerous articles for medical journals; *Recreations* Scottish country dancing, military history (Battle of Waterloo); *Clubs* East India; *Style—* Michael Crumplin, Esq; Greenridges, Wynnstay Lane, Marford, Nr Wrexham, Clwyd LL12 8LH (☎ 097 854071); Maelor General Hospital, Watery Rd, Wrexham, Clwyd (☎ 097 8291100)

CRUMPTON, Michael Joseph; s of Charles Crumpton, and Edith Crumpton; *b* 7 June 1929; *Educ* Poole GS, Univ Coll Southampton, London Inst of Preventive Med (BSc, PhD); *m* 1960, Janet Elizabeth, *née* Dean; 1 s (Andrew), 2 da (Jenny, Caroline); *Career* Nat Serv RAMC 1953-55; memb Scientific Staff Microbiological Res Estab Porton 1955-60, visiting fell Nat Inst of Health Bethesda Maryland 1959-60, res fell Dept of Immunology St Mary's Hosp Med Sch London 1960-66, memb Scientific Staff Nat Inst for Med Res Mill Hill 1966-79 (head of Biochemistry Div 1976-79), dep dir Imperial Cancer Res Fund 1979-; visiting fell John Curtin Sch for Med Res Aust Nat Univ Canberra 1973-74; chm: Sci Advsy Bd Biomed Res Centre Univ of Br Columbia Vancouver 1987-, WHO Steering Ctee for Encapsulated Bacteria 1988- (memb 1984-); memb: Cell Bd MRC 1979-83, Sci Cncl Celltech Ltd 1980, EMBO 1982-, Scientific Advsy Ctee Lister Inst 1986-, Cncl Royal Inst 1986- (Davy Faraday Laboratory Ctee 1985- (chm of Ctee 1988), Sloan Ctee General Motors Res Fndn 1986-88, MRC AIDS Directed Steering Ctee Programme 1987-, Scientific Ctee Swiss Inst for Experimental Cancer Res 1989-, Governing Body BPMF 1987-; memb Ed Bd: Biochemical Journal 1966-73 (dep chm 1969-72), Euro Journal of Immunology 1972-86, Immunochemistry 1975-79, Immunogenetics 1979-85, Biochemistry Int 1980-86, Molecular Biology and Medicine 1983-86, Human Immunology; regnl ed Molecular Immunology 1982-86; Biochemistry Soc visiting lectr Aust 1983; FRS 1979; *Recreations* gardening, reading; *Style—* Michael Crumpton, Esq, FRS; 33 Homefield Road, Radlett, Herts WD7 8PX (☎ 09276 4675)

CRUSH, Harvey Michael; s of George Stanley Crush (d 1970), of Chislehurst, Kent, and Alison Isabel, *née* Lang; *b* 12 April 1939; *Educ* Chigwell Sch Essex; *m* 1, 21 Aug 1965 (m dis 1982), Diana, da of Frederick Joseph Bassett (d 1965), of Coulsdon, Surrey; 1 s (Nicholas b 1 Dec 1967), 1 da (Emily b 21 May 1971); m 2, 9 Dec 1982, Margaret (Maggie) Rose, da of Nicholas Dixson (d 1986); *Career* admitted slr 1963; ptnr Norton Rose 1968-, dir TOSG Trust Fund Ltd 1970-; memb Supreme Court Rule Ctee 1984-88; vice pres City of London Law Soc 1989-, hon slr Assoc of Br Aviation Conslts; hon life memb Sevenoaks and Dist Motor Club (chm 1968-71); Liveryman: Worshipful Co of Slrs 1982 (memb Court of Assistants 1987-), Worshipful Co of Farriers 1984; MRAeS 1980; memb Law Soc; *Recreations* travel, flying, motor sport; *Style—* Harvey Crush, Esq; Kempson House, Camomile St, London EC3A 7AN (☎ 071 283 2434, fax 071 588 1181)

CRUTCH, Frank Peter Garth; s of Frank Crutch, of 14 Highway Road, Thurmaston, Leicester, and Mary Annie Voce; gf Albert Crutch (decd), Master of Hounds Quorn Hunt; *b* 22 March 1940; *Educ* Woodbank Preparatory Sch, Humphrey Perkins Sch, Leicester Coll of Art (Nat Dip design), RCA (Dip Des RCA); *m* 28 March 1964, Mo Ashley; 2 da (Sarah Louise b 1970, Emma Lucy Jane b 1972); *Career* designer; worked with: Sir Basil Spence on the New Sussex Univ 1962-65, Sir Terence Conran, major project The Establishment of Habitat and its products 1965-70; founder memb and bd dir Fitch and Co Design Consultants plc 1970-87 (major project design of all public spaces at Terminal 4 Heathrow); freelance consultnt 1987; built collection of 50s, 60s, 70s historic Italian sports racing cars, established own consultancy 'Peter C' Design and established own racing team 'Scuderia Britalia' 1987; *Recreations* classic motor racing; *Clubs* 96, Ferrari Owners, Scuderia Del Portello; *Style—* F P G Crutch, Esq; 182 London Rd, Twickenham, Middlesex TW1 1EX (☎ 081 892 8234); Flanders House, Crackington, Haven, Cornwall

CRUTHERS, Sir James Winter; s of James William Cruthers and Kate Cruthers (d 1950); *b* 20 Dec 1924; *Educ* Perth Tech Coll; *m* 1950, Alwyn Sheila, da of late Jack Della; 1 s, 1 da; *Career* magazines ed W Aust Newspapers Ltd 1953, chm and md TVW Enterprises Ltd 1975-81, chm Aust Film Cmmn 1981, dir News Corpn Ltd 1981-, News America Holdings Inc 1985-, Sky TV plc 1984-, chm West pre Ltd; Queen's Jubilee Medal 1977, W Aust Citizen of the Year 1980; kt 1980; *see Debrett's Handbook of Australia and New Zealand for further details*; *Style—* Sir James Cruthers; c/o Westpre Ltd, 34 Stirling Street, Perth 6001, Western Aust

CRUTTWELL, Christopher George; s of Reginald Quentin Cruttwell (d 1968), and Joan, *née* McCausland (d 1969); *b* 25 July 1932; *Educ* King's Sch Bruton, St John's Coll Oxford (BA); *m* 14 April 1971, Patricia Valerie, da of Albert George Long (d 1984); 1 s (Stephen John b 1972), 1 da (Elizabeth Ann b 1974); *Career* admitted slr 1959; ptnr Gouldens 1963; hon slr to Nat Philately Soc; memb Law Soc; *Recreations* philately, hockey; *Style—* Christopher Cruttwell, Esq; 35 Old Lodge Lane, Purley, Surrey CR2 4DL (☎ 081 668 3035); Gouldens, 22 Tudor St, London EC4Y 0JJ (☎ 071 583 7777, telex 21520, fax 071 583 3051)

CRWYS-WILLIAMS, Air Vice-Marshal David Owen; CB (1990); s of late Gareth Crwys-Williams, OBE, of Llangollen, Clwyd, and Frances Ellen, *née* Strange; *b* 24 Dec 1940; *Educ* Oakham Sch, RAF Coll Cranwell; *m* 1, 1963 (m dis 1972), Jennifer Jean, *née* Pearce; m 2, 31 March 1973, Irene (Suzie), da of late D J T Whan, of Kendal, Cumbria; 1 s (Huw David b 20 Nov 1975), 2 da (Kirsty Jane b 20 Feb 1977, Claire Elizabeth b 4 Nov 1981); *Career* RAF Coll Cranwell 1958-61, commissioned as pilot 1961, 30 Sqdn Kenya 1961-63, 47 Sqdn RAF Abingdon 1964-66, ADC to C-in-C RAF Trg Cmd 1966-68, Sqdn Ldr 1969, OC 46 Sqdn RAF Abingdon 1969-71, OC Ops RAF Masirah Oman 1972, Army Staff Coll 1973, Personal Staff Offr to C-in-C Near East Air Force 1974-75, Wing Cdr 1975, OC 230 Sqdn RAF Odiham 1975-77, Personnel Offr MOD 1977-79, Gp Capt 1979, Dep Dir Air Plans MOD 1979-81, station Cdr RAF Shawbury 1982-84, RCDS 1985, Air Cdre 1985, Dir of Air Support (later Dir of Air Staff Duties) 1986-88, Air Vice-Marshal 1988, Cdr Br Forces Falkland Islands 1988-89, Dir Gen RAF Personnel Services MOD; *Recreations* furniture restoration, fishing, walking; *Clubs* RAF; *Style—* Air Vice-Marshal David Crwys-Williams, CB; Ministry of Defence, Adastral House, Theobalds Rd, London WC1 (☎ 071 430 7239)

CRYER, Amanda; da of Joseph William Clark (d 1981), of 11 Grove Vale, Chislehurst, Kent, and Cecily May, *née* Whittall; *b* 1 April 1957; *Educ* Bullers Wood Sch for Girls, City of London Poly, Univ of Neuchâtel Switzerland, Coll for Distributive Trades (Cert in Communications, Advtg and Mktg); *m* 13 June 1987, Andrew Michael Cryer, s of Arthur Cryer; 1 s (Thomas Joseph Arthur b 6 March 1990); *Career* account exec Burson-Marsteller Ltd 1981-84 (trainee 1978-81); Cameron Choat & Partners: sr account exec 1984-85, account dir 1985-87, Bd dir 1987-; MInstM, MIPR; *Recreations* swimming, theatre; *Style—* Mrs Amanda Cryer; Cameron, Choat & Partners, 126-128 Cromwell Rd, London SW7 4ET (☎ 071 373 4537, fax 071 373 3926)

CRYER, (George) Bob; MP (L) Bradford South 1987-; *b* 3 Dec 1934; *Educ* Salt HS Shipley, Univ of Hull; *m* 1963, Ann, *née* Place; 1 s, 1 da; *Career* convener Campaign Gp of Labour MPs 1982-83; contested Darwen Lancs 1964, memb Keighley Boro Cncl 1971-74, MP (L) Keighley Feb 1974-83, parly under sec of state Dept of Indust 1976-78, chm jt and commons select ctees statutory instruments 1979-83 and 1987-; chair Parliamentary Labour Party Employment Ctee 1987-; *Style—* Robert Cryer Esq, MP; 6 Ashfield Avenue, Shipley, W.Yorks BD18 3AL (☎ Bradford 584701)

CRYMBLE, Bernard; s of Clarence Frederick Crymble (d 1950), of Newcastle Upon Tyne, and Martha, *née* Gell (d 1976); *b* 6 May 1928; *Educ* Univ of Durham (MBBS); *m* 1, 4 July 1951, Elizabeth Anne (d 1967), da of John Robert Barnett (d 1965), of Middlesborough; 1 s (Gavin Vaughan b 1958), 1 da (Jane b 1954); m 2, 12 Nov 1967, Patricia (d 1984), da of John Riddel (d 1980), of Gosforth, Northumberland; m 3, 31 Aug 1984, Elaine, da of Robert Duncan of Helensborough, Scot; *Career* Nat Serv Maj RAMC 1952-54; sr lectr neurosurgery Univ of London 1967-69; conslt neurosurgeon: E and W Sussex 1969-88, emeritus 1988-; dep coroner E Sussex 1988-, memb Coroners Soc 1989, pres Brighton and Sussex Med-Chi Soc 1985; Freeman City of London 1976, Liveryman Worshipful Co of Apothecaries 1976; FRCS 1959, SBNS 1965, FRSM 1970; *Books* Intensive Care (contrib second edn, 1984); *Recreations* Romano-British archaeology, walking, golf; *Clubs* Athenaeum, Army and Navy; *Style—* Bernard Crymble, Esq; Westwood, North Common Rd, Wivelsfield Green, Haywards Heath, W Sussex RH17 7RJ (☎ 0444 84 607); 25 Westbourne Villas, Hove, E Sussex BN3 4GF (☎ 0273 720 217)

CRYSTAL, Alan Maurice; s of Leo Crystal, and Marion Crystal; *b* 2 Sept 1954; *Educ* Latymer Upper Sch London, King's Coll London, Westminster Med Sch London (MB BS); *m* 7 Sept 1980, Gillian Elizabeth, da of John Williams, MBE, of Canford Cliffs, Poole; 2 da (Charlotte Jayne b 16 May 1983, Stephanie Nicole b 18 March 1985); *Career* conslt gynaecologist and obstetrician Royal Berkshire Hosp Reading: FRCS Ed 1983, MRCOG 1983; *Recreations* golf, tennis; *Style—* Alan Crystal, Esq; Creek Cottage, Lashbrook Road, Lower Shiplake, Henley-on-Thames RG9 3NX; 72 Berkeley Ave, Reading (☎ 0734 584711)

CRYSTAL, Prof David; s of Samuel Cyril Crystal, of London, and Mary Agnes, *née* Morris; *b* 6 July 1941; *Educ* St Mary's Coll Liverpool, UCL (BA), Univ of London (PhD); *m* 1, 1 April 1964, Molly Irene (d 1976), da of Capt Robert Stack (d 1965); 2 s (Steven David b 1964, Timothy Joseph b 1969, d 1972), 2 da (Susan Mary b 1966, Lucy Alexandra b 1973); m 2, Hilary Frances, da of Capt Kenneth Norman (d 1990), of Cuffley, Herts; 1 s (Benjamin Peter b 1977); *Career* res asst Survey of English Usage UCL 1962-63, asst lectr linguistics Univ Coll of North Wales 1965-69; Univ of Reading: lectr 1965-69, reader 1969-75, prof of linguistics 1975-85; hon prof of linguistics Univ of North Wales (Bangor) 1985-; ed: Journal of Child Language 1974-85, The Language Library 1978-, Applied Language Studies 1980-84, Child Language Teaching and Therapy 1985-, Linguistics Abstracts 1985-; assoc ed Journal of Linguistics 1970-73, co-ed Studies in Language Disability 1974-, consulting ed English Today 1984-, usage ed Great Illustrated Dictionary (Readers Digest, 1984); author of numerous pubns connected with the English language and linguistics; fell Coll of Speech Therapists 1983, FRSA 1983; *Books incl*: The Cambridge Encyclopedia of Language (ed, 1987), Cambridge Encyclopedia (ed, 1990); *Recreations* cinema, music, bibliophily; *Style—* Prof David Crystal; Akaroa, Gors Avenue, Holyhead, Gwynedd LL65 1PB (☎ 0407 762764); PO Box 5, Holyhead, Gwynedd LL65 1RG (fax 0407 7659728)

CRYSTAL, Jonathan; s of Samuel Cyril Crystal, OBE, of London, and Rachel Ethel, *née* Trewish; *b* 20 Dec 1949; *Educ* Leeds GS, QMC (LLB); *m* 13 Jul 1987, Ashley Drew, da of Harry Copeland; *Career* called to the Bar Middle Temple 1972; memb Hon Soc of Middle Temple; *Recreations* sports, travel; *Style—* J Crystal, Esq; 2 Harcourt Bldgs, Temple, London EC4 (☎ 071 353 2622, fax 071 353 5405)

CRYSTAL, Peter Maurice; s of Boris Leonard Crystal, of Leeds, and Pauline Mary, *née* Fox; *b* 7 Jan 1948; *Educ* Leeds GS, St Edmund Hall Oxford (MA), McGill Univ (LLM); *m* 2 July 1978, Lena Elisabeth, da of Bror Olsson (d 1972), of Karlstad, Sweden; 2 da (Emma, Anna); *Career* sr ptnr Memery Crystal slrs; Parlimentary candidate for Leeds NE (SDP) 1983 and 1987; memb Law Soc; *Recreations* tennis and all sports, travel; *Clubs* Reform, Athenaeum, Hurlingham; *Style—* Peter Crystal, Esq; 31 Southampton Row, London WC1B 5HT (☎ 071 242 5905, fax 071 242 2058, telex 298957)

CSÁKY, John Bernard; *b* 31 Aug 1945; *Style—* John Csáky, Esq; 57 Waterloo Road, Bedford MK40 3PG (☎ 0234 54095)

CUBBON, Sir Brian Crossland; GCB (1984, KCB 1977, CB 1974); *b* 9 April 1928; *Educ* Bury GS, Trinity Coll Cambridge; *m* 1956, Elizabeth Lorin Richardson; 3 s, 1 da; *Career* Home Office 1951; perm under sec of state N I Office 1976-79, perm under sec of state Home Office 1979-88; *Style—* Sir Brian Cubbon, GCB; Home Office, Queen Anne's Gate, London SW1H 9AT

CUBEY, Dr (Robert) Bevis; s of Dr Donald Robert Cubey, of Whitley Bay, Northumberland, and Nita Margaret Howard, *née* Allen (d 1986); *b* 5 April 1938; *Educ* Rossall and St Catharine's Coll Cambridge (MA, MB BChir); *m* 22 Sept 1962, Ann Marples, da of Oscar Slack, of Burton-on-Trent; 1 s (Mark b 1966), 3 da (Fritha b 1965, Janet b 1973, Tanya b 1979); *Career* surgical specialist Masasi Dist Hosp Tanzania 1967-71; conslt ophthalmic surgn: Ipswich Suffolk 1976-84, W Cumbria 1984-; scientific papers on surgical and ophthalmological topics: FRCSEd, FRCS, FRCSI, FCOphth; *Recreations* fell walking, singing, farming, gardening; *Style—* Dr Bevis Cubey; Hopebeck, Vale of Lorton, Cockermouth, Cumbria CA13 9UD (☎ 0900 85667); Cumbrian Independent Hospital, Branthwaite Rd, Workington, Cumbria (☎ 0900 67111)

CUBITT, Sir Hugh Guy; CBE (1977), JP (Surrey 1964), DL (Gtr London 1978); s of Col Hon (Charles) Guy Cubitt, CBE, DSO, TD, DL (d 1979), 6 s of 2 Baron Ashcombe, and Rosamond Mary Edith *née* Cholmeley (d 1984); *b* 2 July 1928; *Educ* RNC Dartmouth; *m* 26 June 1958, Linda Ishbel, da of Hon Angus Campbell, CBE, JP (d 1966), yr s of 1 Baron Colgrain; 1 s (Jonathan Guy b 1962), 2 da (Joanna Mary (Mrs Smyth-Osbourne) b 1960, Victoria Jane (Mrs Harding-Rolls) b 1964); *Career* Lt RN Korea 1949-50; memb Westminster City Cncl 1963-78 (alderman 1974, ldr 1972-77),

Lord Mayor Westminster 1977-78; Cubitt and West 1962-79; dir: Property Security Investment Trust 1962-, National Westminster Bank 1977-90 (memb UK Advsy Bd 1990); chm: Housing Corp 1980-90, Lombard North Central 1980-; cmmr English Heritage 1988-, High Sheriff of Surrey 1983; Freeman City of London 1975, Liveryman Worshipful Co of Needlemakers 1975-87; Hon FRAM 1985; FRICS 1970, FRSA; kt 1983; *Recreations* travel, photography, country sports; *Clubs* Boodle's; *Style*— Sir Hugh Cubitt, CBE, JP, DL; Chapel House, West Humble, Dorking, Surrey RH5 6AY (☎ 0306 882 994)

CUBITT, (Mark) Robin; s of late Maj the Hon Archibald Edward Cubitt (5 s of 2 Baron Ashcombe), by 2 w, Sibell, da of Ronald Collet Norman; bro of Countess of Harrington (*see* Harrington, Earl of); hp of 4 Baron Ashcombe, *qv*; *b* 13 June 1936; *Educ* Gordonstoun; *m* 21 July 1962, Juliet Perpetua, da of late Edward Corbet Woodall, OBE, of The Red House, Clifton Hampden, Abingdon, Berks; 3 s (Mark b 1964, David b 1966, Hugo b 1967); *Style*— Robin Cubitt, Esq; Annagh, Coolbawn, Nenagh, Co Tipperary, Ireland

CUCCIO, John; *b* 31 May 1947; *Educ* Liverpool Coll, Univ of Liverpool, Univ of South Florida; *Career* dental surgn Harley St 1977- (specialist in advanced restorative and cosmetic dentistry incl implants and guided tissue regeneration); cmmnd RADC(V) TA 1984; memb: BDA, Br Soc of Peridontology, Br Dental Implant Soc; *Recreations* hill walking, shooting, deer stalking; *Clubs* Naval and Military; *Style*— John Cuccio, Esq; 78 Harley St, London W1N 1AE (☎ 071 436 2750)

CUCKNEY, Sir John Graham; s of Air Vice-Marshal Ernest John Cuckney, CB, CBE, DSC (d 1965), and Lilian, *née* Williams; *b* 12 July 1925; *Educ* Shrewsbury, Univ of St Andrews; *m* 1960, Muriel, da of late Walter Scott Boyd; *Career* chm: Royal Insurance Holdings plc 1985- (dir 1979-, dep chm 1983-85), 3i Gp plc 1987-; dep chm TI Group plc 1985-90; dir: Brixton Estate plc 1985-, Lazard Bros & Co Ltd 1988-90, Glaxo Holdings plc 1990-; former chm: Westland Group plc, The Thomas Cook Group Ltd, John Brown plc, Brooke Bond Group plc, International Military Services Ltd, PLA, Standard Industrial Trust; *Style*— Sir John Cuckney; 3i Group plc, 91 Waterloo Rd, London SE1 8XP

CUDDEFORD, Norman Allan; s of Charles Leonard Allan Cuddeford (d 1986), of Leigh-on-Sea, and Gwendoline May, *née* Hockley (d 1985); *b* 8 Jan 1933; *Educ* Felsted; *m* 1, 1963 (m dis 1975), Penelope Alexandra Cuddeford; 1 s (Alastair b 1964); m 2, 12 April 1975, Maria Concepcion del Carmen, da of Dr Erasmo Hoyo Hernandez, of Mexico City; 1 da (Vanessa b 1980), and 1 step da (Ana Gabriela b 1971); *Career* Nat Serv RAF 1952-54, cmmnd 1953, later CO RAF Sennen (at that time the youngest CO in RAF); associated with Lloyds of London since 1955; freelance sports commentator (covering athletics, cricket, tennis) BBC radio 1965-; dir S B J Devitt Ltd 1988-; memb of Rottingdean Preservation Soc; Freeman City of London 1956, Liveryman Worshipful Co of Glass Sellers; *Recreations* travel, good company and convivial conversation, cricket; *Clubs* RAF, MCC, Lloyds Motor, Rugby Club of London; *Style*— Norman Cuddeford, Esq; Point Clear, Lustrells Rd, Rottingdean, Sussex (☎ 0273 304 943); 6 Kinburn St, London SE16; S B J Devitt Ltd, 100 Whitechapel Rd, London E1 (☎ 071 247 8888)

CUDLIPP, Baron (Life Peer UK 1974), of Aldingbourne, Co W Sussex; Hugh Kinsman Cudlipp; OBE (1945); s of William Cudlipp, of Cardiff; *b* 28 Aug 1913; *Educ* Howard Gdns Sch Cardiff; *m* 1; m 2, 1945, Eileen Ascroft (d 1962); m 3, 1963, Jodi, da of late John L Hyland, of Palm Beach, Florida, USA; *Career* Lab Whip House of Lords until Nov 1981 when resigned to join SDP (now Liberal Democrats); journalist; chm IPC Ltd 1968-73 (formerly dep chm), dep chm Reed International Board 1970-73, former dir Associated TV Ltd, chm IPC Newspaper Div 1970-73, Mirror Newspapers Ltd 1963-68; kt 1973; *Books* Publish and Be Damned! (1955), At Your Peril (1962), Walking on the Water (1976), The Prerogative of the Harlot (1980); *Style*— The Rt Hon the Lord Cudlipp, OBE

CUDMORE, Harold; s of Harold Cudmore, and Sheila, *née* Coleman (d 1948); *b* 21 April 1944; *Career* sailor; skipper White Crusader Br Americas Cup challenger 1986-87, mangr successful Br Admirals Cup team 1989, winner over 20 major regattas and world championships; *Clubs* Royal Cork Yacht, Royal Thames Yacht, Royal Ocean Racing, Fort Worth Boat; *Style*— Harold Cudmore, Esq; 9 Queen's Road, Cowes, Isle of Wight PO31 8BQ (☎ 0983 291376, fax 0983 291771)

CUENE-GRANDIDIER, Richard John Davis; s of Jean Alphonse Cuene-Grandidier, of Les Alluets-le-Roi, 78580 Maule, France, and Paula Susan, *née* Davis, of Orvault, Nantes, France; *b* 13 Sept 1955; *Educ* Holmewood House, Downside; *m* 1, 13 June 1982 (m dis); 1 da (Sophie b 1985); m 2, 1 July 1989, Sara Anne, *née* Chell; *Career* various appts Nat West Bank plc 1976-86, account mangr London branch Société Générale 1989- (deputy 1987-89); *Recreations* officiating at motor sport events, riding, shooting; *Clubs* Br Racing and Sport Car; *Style*— Richard Cuene-Grandidier, Esq; 10 Ingham Rd, London NW6 1DE (☎ 071 435 5893); Société Générale, 60 Gracechurch St, PO Box 513, London EC3V 0HD (☎ 071 626 5400, fax 071 623 7761, telex 886611)

CUEVAS-CANCINO, HE Señor Francisco; s of José Luis Cuevas, architect (d 1952), and Sofia Cancino; *b* 7 May 1921; *Educ* Free Faculty of Law Mexico City, McGill Univ Montreal (MCL); *m* 1, 1946, Ana Hilditch, 2 s, 1 da; m 2, 1968, Esmeralda, da of Fernando Arboleda (d 1954); *Career* joined Mexican Foreign Service 1946, ambassador 1965-, Mexican ambassador to UK and to Republic of Ireland 1983-; Foreign Service Decoration (Mexico) 1972; Order of the Liberator 1970 and Order of Andrés Bello (Venezuela) 1973; *Recreations* icons; *Clubs* Travellers', Garrick; *Style*— HE Señor Francisco Cuevas-Cancino; Mexican Embassy, 48 Belgrave Sq, London SW1 8QY

CUFFLIN, Michael John; OBE (1984); s of Harry Bradshaw Cufflin (d 1963), of 70 Shanklin Drive, Leicester, and Annie Elizabeth, *née* Palmer (d 1985); *b* 21 Aug 1932; *Educ* Wyggeston Boys' GS Leicester, Worcester Coll Oxford (MA); *m* 23 April 1960, Susan Jenifer, da of William Pollard (d 1949), of Four Oaks, Sutton Coldfield; 2 s (Oliver b 3 March 1962, Edward b 1 Dec 1967), 2 da (Joanna b 27 Jan 1961, Lucy b 26 June 1963); *Career* stockbroker; P N Kemp-Gee and Co 1954-59, chm Wilshere Baldwin and Co 1986- (joined 1959); chm: Leicester GS Tst since fndn of sch in 1981, Br Aust Soc (Leics Branch), Leicester Cons Fed; dir Leicester Action for Youth Tst Leicester YMCA, hon treas Leics Co Nursing Assoc, vice chm Leicester Twinning Assoc, pres Leicester Cons Euro Cncl, memb Leicester CC 1967-89, Lord Mayor of Leicester 1984-85; memb TSA; *Recreations* gardening; *Clubs* The Leicestershire, Leicester Rotary; *Style*— Michael Cufflin, Esq, OBE; 10 Southernhay Rd, Leicester LE2 3TJ (☎ 0533 703063); Wilshere Baldwin and Co, 19 The Crescent, King St, Leicester LE1 6RX (☎ 0533 541344, fax 0533 550969)

CULE, Dr John Hedley; s of Walter Edwards Cule (d 1942), of Glamorgan, and Annie, *née* Russ (d 1940); *b* 7 Feb 1920; *Educ* Porth Co Sch, Kingswood Sch Bath, Trinity Hall Cambridge (MA, MD, LRCP), King's Coll Hosp; *m* 23 March 1944, Joyce Leslie, da of Henry Phillips Bonser (d 1962); 2 s (Simon b 1949, Peter b 1951), 1 da (Myfanwy b 1955); *Career* WWII Capt RAMC served Italy (despatches) 1943-46; surgical registrar Addenbrooke's Hosp 1947, med registrar KCH 1948, princ NHS partnership Camberley 1948-71, psychiatrist St Davids Hosp Carmarthen and Psychiatric Unit W Wales Gen Hosp 1972-86; lectr in history of med Univ of Wales Coll of Med 1972-; pres: Osler Club London 1972-, History of Med Soc of Wales 1978-80, Br Soc for History of Med 1985-87 (vice pres 1984, treas 1972-82); vice pres Int Soc for History of Med 1989-; memb Cncl Harveian Soc 1964; vice chm Sanders Watney Tst (Driving for the Disabled) 1986-; High Sheriff Co of Dyfed 1985-86; chm Welsh Branch Br Driving Soc; Freeman City of London, Liveryman Worshipful Soc of Apothecaries; MRCS, FRCGP; *Books* Wreath on the Crown (1967), A Doctor for the People (1980), Child Care through the Centuries (jt ed, 1986); *Recreations* horse carriage driving trials, fly fishing; *Clubs* Royal Society of Medicine; *Style*— Dr John H Cule; Abereinon, Capel Dewi, Llandysul, Dyfed, SA44 4PP (☎ (055 936) 2229)

CULHANE, Prof (John) Leonard; s of late John Thomas Culhane, and late Mary Agnes, *née* Durkin; *b* 14 Oct 1937; *Educ* Clongowes Wood Coll, Univ Coll Dublin (BSc, MSc), Univ Coll London (PhD); *m* 7 Sept 1961, Mary Brigid, da of late James Smith; 2 s (Simon b 22 Sept 1963, Laurence b 18 Feb 1966); *Career* prof Physics Dept Univ Coll London 1981 (res asst 1963, lectr 1967, reader 1976), sr scientist Lockleed Palo Alto Laboratory 1969-70, dir Mullard Space Sci Laboratory 1983-, author of more than 200 scientific papers on solar and cosmic astronomy x-ray instrumentation and spectroscopy; memb: Cncl Univ of Surrey 1985-88, Sci Bd Astronomy SERC 1989-; chm: Space Sci Prog Bd 1989-, British Nat Ctee Space Res 1989-; UK delegate and vice chm ESA SPC 1990-; FRS 1985; memb: IAU, American Astronomical Soc, RAS; *Books* X-Ray Astronomy (with P Sanford, 1981); *Recreations* music, racing cars; *Style*— Prof Leonard Culhane, FRS; Ariel Hse, Holmbury St Mary, Dorking, Surrey RH5 6NS (☎ 0483 277051); Mullard Space Sci Laboratory, Univ Coll London, Holmbury St Mary, Dorking, Surrey RH5 6NT (☎ 0483 274111, fax 0483 278312, telex 859185 UCMSSL G)

CULLEARN, David Beverley; s of Jack Cullearn (d 1944), of Bradford, and Gladys Irene, *née* Earnshaw; *b* 22 April 1941; *Educ* Grange GS Bradford, Leeds Sch of Archictecture (Dip Arch); *m* 12 June 1962, Suzanne Mary, da of Arthur Joseph Sherry; 2 s (Dominic b 1 Feb 1964, Patrick b 10 March 1968), 1 da (Odette b 1 Feb 1963); *Career* architect and painter in watercolours; sr ptnr Cullearn & Phillips Manchester and London; awards: Structural Steel Design award 1987, Malcolm Dean Design award 1987, Off of the Year award Volvo HQ 1987-88, Civic Tst awards; exhibitions: Phillips Gallery, Manchester Art Gallery, Royal Acad; exhibition sec Soc of Architect Artists; memb RIBA; *Recreations* mountain walking, horse racing, architecture, painting; *Style*— David Cullearn, Esq; High Royd, Northgate, Honley, Huddersfield HD7 2QL (☎ 0484 663 633); 8 King St, Manchester M2 6AQ (☎ 061 832 3667, fax 061 832 3795); 50 Lisson St, London (☎ 071 724 4430, fax 071 724 9844)

CULLEN, Prof Alexander Lamb; OBE (1960); s of Richard Henry Cullen, of Lincoln, and Jessie, *née* Lamb; *b* 30 April 1920; *Educ* Lincoln Sch, Imperial Coll London (BSc, PhD, DSc); *m* 24 Aug 1920, Margaret da of Andrew Lamb, OBE, of Southgate, N London; 2 s (Michael b 1941, David b 1942) 1 da (Isobel b 1946); *Career* scientist Royal Aircraft Estab 1940-46; lectr and reader Univ Coll London 1946-55, prof and head Dept of Elec Engrg Univ of Sheffield, Pender prof elec engrg and head of dept 1967-80, sr fell SERC at UCL 1980-83, hon res associate 1983; hon prof NW Poly Univ Xian China; Hon DSc Chinese Univ of Hong Kong 1983, Hon DEng Sheffield Univ 1985, Hon DSc Univ of Kent at Canterbury 1986; FIEE, FCGI 1964, FIEEE (1967), F Eng 1977, FRS 1977, Hon FIERE 1987, Hon FIEE 1989; *Books* Microwave Measurement (with H M Barlow, 1950); *Recreations* music; *Clubs* English Speaking Union; *Style*— Prof Alexander Cullen, OBE, FRS; Univ Coll London, Torrington Place, London WC1E 7JE (☎ 071 387 7050)

CULLEN, Alma Valerie; da of Frank Fitzpatrick, and Elsie, *née* Harrison; *Educ* Childwall Valley High Sch Liverpool, Univ of Liverpool (MA); *m* James Cullen; 1 s, 1 da; *Career* radio and TV playwright 1970-; twelve plays for BBC radio; TV works incl: The Caledonian Cascade (Granada) 1979, Northern Lights (STV) 1984, Winter Sunlight (Limehouse for Channel 4), Intimate Contact (Central) 1987, episodes of Inspector Morse (Central) 1989 and 90; *Clubs* Univ (Edinburgh); *Style*— Ms Alma Cullen; c/o Lemon and Durbridge Ltd, 24 Pottery Lane, London W11 4LZ (☎ 071 229 9216)

CULLEN, Prof Christopher Noel (Chris); s of Patricia, *née* Cody; *b* 25 Dec 1949; *Educ* N Manchester GS, Univ Coll of N Wales Bangor (BA, PhD); *Career* dir of clinical psychology servs to people with mental handicaps Salford HA 1983-86, SSMH chair of learning difficulties Univ of St Andrews 1986-; former chm Prof Affrs Bd Br Psychological Soc; fell Br Psychological Soc 1983; *Books* Human Operant Conditioning and Behaviour Modification (ed with G Davey, 1988); *Recreations* climbing, fell running; *Clubs* Mynydd Climbing; *Style*— Prof Chris Cullen; Psychological Laboratory, University of St Andrews, St Andrews, Fife KY16 9JU (☎ 0334 76161, fax 0334 75851)

CULLEN, Hon Lord Cullen (William) Douglas; s of Sheriff Kenneth Douglas Cullen (d 1956), and Gladys Margaret, *née* Douglas-Wilson; *b* 18 Nov 1935; *Educ* Dundee HS, Univ of St Andrews (MA), Univ of Edinburgh (LLB); *m* 1961, Rosamond Mary, da of William Henry Nassau Downer, OBE, of NI; 2 s, (Christopher, Adrian), 2 da (Sophia, Felicity); *Career* advocate 1960, standing jr counsel to HM Customs and Excise 1970-73, advocate-deputy 1978-81; chm: Med Appeal Tbnl 1977-86, Cncl The Cockburn Assoc (Edinburgh Civic Tst) 1984-86, Ct of Inquiry into Piper Aplha Disaster 1988-; senator Coll of Justice in Scot 1986; memb Royal Cmmn on Ancient and Historical Monuments of Scot 1987-; QC 1973-90; *Recreations* gardening, natural history; *Clubs* New (Edinburgh); *Style*— The Hon Lord Cullen; Court of Sessions, Parliament House, Edinburgh EH1 1RQ (☎ 031 225 2595)

CULLEN, Hon Mrs (Harriet Mary Margaret); *née* Berry; da of Baron Hartwell, MBE, TD (Life Peer); *b* 8 Nov 1944; *m* 1981, Don Martín Cullen, er s of Don Martín Cullen and Doña Mercedes Artayeta Uriburu, of Buenos Aires; 2 s (Miguel b 1982, Domingo b 1983); *Style*— The Hon Mrs Cullen; 117 Cheyne Walk, London SW10

CULLEN, Dr (Edward) John; s of William Henry Pearson Cullen, and Ellen Emma Cullen; *b* 19 Oct 1926; *Educ* Univ of Cambridge (MA, PhD), Univ of Texas (MS); *m* 1954, Betty Davall Hopkins; 2 s, 2 da; *Career* dep chm Rohm and Haas (UK) Ltd until 1983; chm Health and Safety Cmmn 1983-, pres Inst of Chemical Engrs 1988-89; memb: Engrg Cncl 1990, HRH Duke of Edinburgh's Cwlth Study Conf Cncl 1990; FRSA 1988; *Recreations* gardening, swimming, reading, walking; *Clubs* IOD; *Style*— Dr John Cullen; Health and Safety Commission, Baynards House, 1 Chepstow Place, London W2 4TF (☎ 071 243 6610, fax 071 727 1202)

CULLEN, John Gavin; s of Gavin Hunter Cullen (d 1964), and Alice Mary, *née* Grieve (d 1966); *b* 30 April 1936; *Educ* Robert Gordon's Coll Aberdeen, RCM, Christ's Coll Cambridge (organ scholar, MA); *m* 9 April 1966, Mary Elaine, da of The Ven Thomas Berkeley Randolph (Archdeacon of Hereford and Canon of Hereford Cathedral, d 1987); 2 s (Christopher b 1967, Jonathan b 1974), 1 da (Alison b 1969); *Career* organist and master of choristers St Andrew's Cathedral Aberdeen 1961-63, dir of music Abingdon Sch Oxford 1964-67, dir of music and organist Tonbridge Sch Kent 1967-, conductor and musical dir Tonbridge Philharmonic Soc 1967-; composer of several compositions for choir and organ; chm: Educn Section ISM 1979-80, Public and Prep Schs Music Ctee 1980-85; examiner The Assoc Bd of Royal Schools of Music, vice pres The Curwen Inst; FRCO, ARCM, memb Incorp Soc of Musicians; *Recreations* family and friends, smallholding, golf; *Style*— John Cullen, Esq; The Old

Farm House, Golden Green, Tonbridge, Kent (☎ 0732 850 739); Tonbridge Sch, Kent (☎ 0732 365555)

CULLEN, Dr Michael Henry; s of Charles Gavin Cullen, and Olive, *née* Walker; *b* 29 March 1947; *Educ* Queen Elizabeth's Sch Barnet, Univ of Bristol (BSc, MB ChB, MD); *m* 1, 2 July 1972 (m dis 1988), Rosemary Elizabeth; 3 s (Matthew Jacob b 13 March 1974, Alexander James b 11 Dec 1976, Thomas Oliver b 7 July 1980); m 2, 20 Aug 1989, Alison Helen, da of David Machin; *Career* conslt med oncologist Queen Elizabeth Hosp and sr clinical lectr in oncology Univ of Birmingham 1982-, clinical dir Dept of Radiotherapy and Oncology Queen Elizabeth Hosp 1990-; author of pubns on: lung cancer, testicular cancer, lymphoma; memb: Int Assoc for the Study of Lung Cancer, Euro Assoc of Med Oncologists, Br Assoc for Cancer Res, MRC Working Pty on Testicular Tumours; asst sec Assoc of Cancer Physicians; FRCP 1988; *Recreations* tennis, skiing, wine tasting, classical guitar playing, fine art collecting; *Clubs* Friend of the Royal Birmingham Soc of Artists; *Style—* Dr Michael Cullen; 55 Elmfield Crescent, Moseley, Birmingham B13 9TL (☎ 021 449 1438); Queen Elizabeth Hospital, Edgbaston, Birmingham B15 2TH (☎ 021 472 1311, fax 021 414 3800)

CULLEN, (Charles) Nigel; OBE (1987), TD (1976, and 2 Bars 1982 and 1990); s of Peter Carver Cullen (d 1990), of Mapperley Park, Nottingham, and Dorothy, *née* Woodward; *b* 26 Sept 1944; *Educ* Trent Coll; *m* 15 April 1981, Brenda Suzanne, da of Flt Offr Franklin Paul Bowen, US Army, of Oklahoma, USA; 1 s (Stephen James b 1971), 1 da (Emily Josephine b 1979); *Career* TA: cmmnd 1964, platoon cdr 5/8 Bn Sherwood Foresters 1964-67, platoon cdr Mercian Vol 1967-72, co cdr 3 WFR 1972-78, GSO 2 V Notts 1978-81, 2 i/c 3 WFR 1981-83, SO 2 G3 V 54 Inf Bde 1984, CO 3 WFR 1984-87, SO 1 G3 V E Dist 1987-88, dep cdr 54 Inf Bde 1988-; admitted slr 1970, ptnr Dowson Wadsworth and Sellers, NP; dep pres Notts C of C and Indust, pres Notts City Business Club 1989-90, hon slr City of Notts Scouts; memb: Notts Law Soc, The Notaries' Soc; memb Law Soc; *Recreations* jogging, bridge, theatre, photography; *Clubs* Notts Athletic; *Style—* Nigel Cullen, Esq, OBE, TD; 10 Sefton Drive, Mapperley Pk, Notts NG3 5ER (☎ 0602 606906); Dowson Wadsworth and Sellers, 13 Weekday Cross, Notts NG1 2GG (☎ 0602 501087, fax 0602 588379, car 0860 385115)

CULLEN, Peter; DSC (1944); s of late Walter Cullen; *b* 22 Aug 1920; *Educ* Rugby, Univ of Oxford; *m* 1941, Jane Primrose, *née* Greener; 4 s, 2 da; *Career* Lt RN; chm Cullens Stores plc 1980-85 (md 1978-85); *Recreations* hunting, stalking, walking; *Style—* Peter Cullen Esq, DSC; The Old Rectory, Winkfield, Windsor, Berks (☎ 0344 882623)

CULLEN, Sarah; da of late Edward Cullen, and Martha Bradley; *b* 6 Oct 1949; *Educ* Notre Dame HS Leeds and Southport, UCL (BA); *m* 1 Feb 1986, Thomas Kieran Davenay, s of Capt Thomas Joseph Devaney (Tom), of Liverpool; *Career* reporter ITN 1987 (writer 1972-78, reporter 1978-83, home affairs corr 1983-87; *Books* In Praise of Panic (1982); *Recreations* messing about in boats, cooking, talking to my husband; *Clubs* Sligo Yacht; *Style—* Miss Sarah Cullen; Independent Televison News, 48 Wells St, London W1P 4DE (☎ 071 637 2424)

CULLEN, Timothy William Brian (Tim); s of James Brian Cullen, CBE (d 1972), and Sybil Kathleen, *née* Jones; *b* 23 March 1944; *Educ* King William's Coll Isle of Man, Trinity Coll Dublin Ireland (MA); *m* 19 July 1980, Nora Denise, da of Vytautas Meskauskas, of Pompano Beach, Florida, USA; 1 s (Brian b 1986), 1 da (Jura b 1982); *Career* English teacher St Edward's Sch Florida USA 1967-69, press spokesman Ford Motor Co Ltd Warley England 1969-73, int press spokesman Ford Motor Co Dearborn Michigan USA 1973-75, int pub affairs admin Continental Bank Chicago USA 1975-78, various external affairs posts World Bank Washington DC USA 1978-84, chief of external affairs Euro Office World Bank Paris France 1984-90, chief of Info and Public Affrs World Bank Washington DC; pres Bd of Dirs Int Sch of Paris France 1988-89; *Books* Yugoslavia and The World Book (1979); *Recreations* cooking, photography, fishing; *Clubs* East India; *Style—* Tim Cullen, Esq; 7012 River Road, Bethesda MD 20817, USA (☎ 010 301 320 0024); 1818 H Street, NW Washington DC 20433, USA (☎ 0101 202 473 1782, fax 010 1 202 676 0578, telex Will 64145 WORLDBANK)

CULLEN OF ASHBOURNE, 2 Baron (UK 1920); Charles Borlase Marsham Cokayne; MBE (1945); s of 1 Baron Cullen of Ashbourne, KBE (d 1932, whose f was the celebrated G(eorge) E(dward) C(okayne), Clarenceux King of Arms and ed of The Complete Peerage); *b* 6 Oct 1912; *Educ* Eton; *m* 1, 2 July 1942 (m dis 1947), Valerie Catherine Mary, da of late William Henry Collbran; 1 da (Hon Mrs Costa Sanseverino, *qv*); m 2, 21 June 1948, Patricia Mary, er da of Col S Clulow-Gray; *Heir* bro, Hon Edmund Cokayne; *Career* Maj RCS (TA), served WWII; one of HM Lts City of London 1976, a lord in waiting to HM (govt whip) 1979-82; amateur tennis champion 1947 and 1952; *Clubs* MCC, Swinley Forest Golf; *Style—* The Rt Hon the Lord Cullen of Ashbourne, MBE; 75 Cadogan Gardens, London SW3 2RB (☎ 071 589 1981)

CULLIMORE, Colin Stuart; CBE (1978); s of Reginald Victor Cullimore (d 1960), and May Maria, *née* Jay; *b* 13 July 1931; *Educ* Westminster, Nat Coll of Food Technol; *m* 1952, Kathleen Anyta, da of Edgar Lamming (d 1951); 1 s (Jeremy Stuart b 1953); *Career* cmmnd Royal Scots Fus, seconded Parachute Regt 1951, serv Cyprus, Egypt, Maj 1956, 10 Bn Parachute Regt (TA) 1960; gen mangr: Payne & Son Ltd 1960-65, J H Dewhurst Ltd 1969; md J H Dewhurst Ltd 1976-90; dir: Albion Insurance Co Ltd, External Affrs Vestey Group Cos 1991-; chm: Retail Consortium Food Ctee 1973-74, Multiple Shops Fedn 1977-79; dep chm: Meat Promotion Exec 1975-78, Inst of Meat 1982-83; pres Br Retailers Assoc 1984-89 (vice pres 1979-84), dir NAAFI 1984-; vice chm: Retail Consortium 1985-88, Coll Distributive Trades 1976-79; vice pres Confedn of Euro Retailers 1982-88; memb: Advsy Bd Food From Br, Ctee for Commerce and Distribution of EEC 1984-; govr London Inst 1988-90, tstee Airborne Assault Normandy Tst; Freeman of City of London 1972, Liveryman of Worshipful Co of Butchers; Gold medal of Inst of Meat 1956, Butchers' Co Gold medal 1956; CBIM 1984, FInstD 1973, MRSH 1956, MInstM 1956, FRSA 1988; *Clubs* Naval and Military, IOD, Farmers'; *Style—* Colin Cullimore, Esq, CBE; 143 Whitehall Court, Westminster SW1A 2EP (☎ 071 839 3761); Palazzo Gianbatista, Zurrieq, Malta; 14 West Smithfield, London WC1A 9JL (☎ 071 248 1212, fax 071 236 5220, car 0836 788444)

CULLIMORE, William Rae; s of William Cullimore (d 1949), of Christleton House, Chester; *b* 28 Nov 1918; *Educ* Shrewsbury, Gonville and Caius Coll Cambridge (MA); *m* 1948, Stella Mabel Florence, da of James Douglas Russell, CBE (d 1964), of Hinderton Croft, Neston, Wirral; 1 s, 1 da; *Career* admitted slr 1949; clerk Dean and Chapter Chester Cathedral; dir Chester Waterworks Co; *Recreations* gardening; *Clubs* Farmers'; *Style—* William Rae Cullimore, Esq; Faulkners Lodge, Christleton, Chester; Manor Farm, Morton, Thornbury, Avon

CULLINAN, Hon Mrs (Dorothea Joy); da of 1 Baron Horder, GCVO, MD (d 1955); *b* 1905; *m* 17 Sept 1930, Edward Revill Cullinan, CBE, MD, FRCP (d 16 March 1965), s of late Dr Edward Cullinan; 3 s, 1 da; *Style—* The Hon Mrs Cullinan; 10 Camden Mews, London NW1

CULLINAN, Edward Horder; CBE; s of Dr Edward Revill Cullinan, CBE (d 1965), and Dorothea Joy, *née* Horder; *b* 17 July 1931; *Educ* Ampleforth, Cambridge Univ (BA), Architectural Assoc (AA Dip), Univ of California at Berkeley; *m* Rosalind Sylvia, *née* Yeates; 1 s (Thomas Edward b 1965), 2 da (Emma Louise b 1962, Kate b 1963); *Career* Nat Serv Lt RE 1949-51; architect; in practice London 1959, fndr Edward Cullinan Architects 1968-; second year master Univ of Cambridge Dept of Architecture 1968-73, Bannister Fletcher prof Univ of London 1978-79; visiting critic 1973-85: Toronto, Cincinatti, MIT; Graham Willis prof Univ of Sheffield 1985-87, George Simpson prof Univ of Edinburgh 1987-89; sponsor: Architects for Peace, UK Architects Against Apartheid, Freeze; architect memb Duchy of Cornwall Wildlife and Environment Gp; FRSA 1981, ARA 1989; *Books* Edward Cullinan Architects (1984); *Recreations* building, horticulture, silviculture, skiing, surfing; *Style—* Edward Cullinan, Esq, CBE; Gib Tor, Quarnford, Buxton, Derbyshire; 57D Jamestown Rd, London NW1 (☎ 071 485 2267, fax 071 267 2385)

CULLINGFORD, Eric Coome Maynard; CMG (1963); s of Francis James Cullingford (d 1944), and Lilian Mabel, *née* Dunstan (d 1942); *b* 15 March 1910; *Educ* City of London Sch, St Catharine's Coll Cambridge (MA); *m* 1936, Friedel, da of Karl Fuchs; 2 s (Martin, Cedric), 1 da (Christine); *Career* Manpower Div of Control Cmmn for Germany 1951, lab attache Br Embassy Bonn 1961-65 and 1968-72, asst sec Min of Labour, ret 1972; *Books* Trade Unions in West Germany; The Pirates of Shearwater Island; *Style—* Eric Cullingford Esq, CMG; Flat 1, 25 Avenue Road, Malvern, Worcs

CULLIS, Prof Charles Fowler; s of Prof Charles Gilbert Cullis (d 1941), of Wimbledon, London SW19, and Winifred Jefford, *née* Fowler (d 1976); *b* 31 Aug 1922; *Educ* Stowe, Trinity Coll Oxford (BA, BSc, DPhil, MA, DSc); *m* 3 Sept 1958, (Marjorie) Elizabeth, da of Sir Austin Innes Anderson (d 1973), of Clandon Surrey; 2 s (Jonathan b 1961, Philip b 1967), 2 da (Jane b 1963, Eleanor b 1965); *Career* ICI res fell Univ of Oxford 1947-50, lectr in physical chemistry Imperial Coll London 1950-59 (sr lectr in chemical engrg 1959-64), reader in combustion chemistry Univ of London 1964-66, prof of physical chemistry City Univ 1967-84 (head Chemistry Dept 1973-84, pro vice chllr 1980-84, Saddlers res prof 1984-87, Leverhulme emeritus res fell 1987-89, emeritus prof), visiting prof Univ of California Berkeley 1966, visiting scientist CSIRO Sydney 1970, academic visitor NSW Institute of Technology Ltd 1974; cncllr Mid Sussex 1986-; dir City Technology Ltd (Queen's Award for Technol 1982 and 1985, and for Export 1988) 1977-; chm Safety in Mines Res Advsy Bd 1980-88; govr: City of London Poly 1982-84, Haywards Heath Coll 1986-, Oathall Community Coll 1986-; Liveryman Worshipful Co of Bakers 1983-; FRSC 1958, FRSA 1983; *Books* The Combustion of Organic Polymers (1981), The Detection and Measurement of Hazardous Gases (1981), author of numerous original scientific papers; *Recreations* music, theatre, travel, golf; *Clubs* Athenaeum; *Style—* Prof Charles Cullis; City Univ, Northampton Square, London EC1V OHB (☎ 071 253 4399 ext 3510, fax 071 250 0837)

CULLIS, Jeffrey; s of Donald Oscar Cullis (d 1974), of Nottingham, and Ada Elizabeth, *née* Fleet; *b* 9 Aug 1934; *Educ* The Becket Sch Nottingham; *m* 29 May 1965, Petrina Joan (d 1982), da of Alan Barker, of Nottingham; 2 s (James b 1967, Mark b 1972), 1 da (Sarah b 1969); *Career* Mil Serv 1952-54; RAMC 1952-53, Corporal 1 Bn N Staffs Korea 1953-54; sales dir Pressac Holdings plc 1976-; dir: Pressac Ltd 1971-, Pressaco SRL (Milan), Pressac Inc (Detroit USA); MCIM; *Recreations* hill walking, golf, sailing; *Clubs* Rushcliffe Golf (Notts), Rutland Sailing; *Style—* Jeffrey Cullis, Esq; 18 Groveside Crescent, Clifton Village, Nottingham NG11 8NT (☎ 0602 216317); Pressac Holdings plc, Park House, 104 Derby Rd, Long Eaton, Nottingham NG10 4LS (☎ 0602 462525, fax 462481)

CULLIS, Michael Fowler; CVO (1955); s of Emeritus Prof Charles Gilbert Cullis (d 1941), of London, and Winifred Jefford Fowler (d 1976); *b* 22 Oct 1914; *Educ* Wellington, Brasenose Coll Oxford (scholar) MA; *m* 1968, Catherine Cameron, da of Alexander Cook Robertson, of Arbroath, Scotland; *Career* mil intelligence Gibraltar 1939-40, min of Econ Warfare London, Spain and Portugal 1940-44, dip serv 1945-58, FO responsible for Austria 1945-50; regnl information cnsllr Oslo and Copenhagen 1951-58, advsr to Govr of Malta 1959-61; sr res fell Atlantic Inst Paris 1962-65; dip serv, dir: of Arms Control and Disarmament 1967-74, conslt Non-Governmental Bodies 1975-79; dir European Cultural Fndn Amsterdam; writer and broadcaster; *Clubs* Athenaeum (London); *Style—* Michael Cullis, Esq, CVO; County End, Bushey Heath, Herts WD2 1NY (☎ 081 950 1057)

CULLUM, Simon Edward; s of Denis John Cullum (d 1976), and Phylis Ethel, *née* Hoare; *b* 11 Jan 1943; *Educ* Brighton Hove and E Sussex GS; *m* 1, 8 Aug 1963 (m dis 1978), Janet Claire, da of Thomas Watkins (d 1977); 2 s (Benedict Simon b 1964, Damian Sebastian b 1969), 1 da (Rebecca Jane b 1966); m 2, Sept 1982, Carolyn Margaret, da of David Gover, of Long Ashton, Avon; 2 s (Barnaby David Owain b 1983, Joshua John b 1985), 1 da (Kimberley Nastasha (twin) b 1985); *Career* Chartered Bank 1961-64, Charles Barker City Ltd 1964-79, Response Advertising Ltd 1979-83, St James Alliance Ltd 1983-89, mgmnt conslt 1990-; MIPA 1973; *Recreations* swimming, reading, gardening; *Style—* Simon Cullum, Esq; Holly House, Horse Shoe Lane, Chipping Sodbury, Bristol BS17 6ET (☎ 0454 320 972)

CULME-SEYMOUR, Cdr Sir Michael; 5 Bt (UK 1809), of Highmount, Co Limerick, and Friery Park, Devonshire; s of Vice Adm Sir Michael Culme-Seymour, 4 Bt, KCB, MVO (d 1925), and Florence Agnes Louisa (d 1956); *b* 26 April 1909; *m* 18 March 1948, Lady (Mary) Faith (d 1983), da of 9 Earl of Sandwich, and formerly wife of late Philip Booth Nesbitt; 2 s (decd), 1 step da ((Caroline) Gemma (Mrs Best) b 1939); *Heir* kinsman, Michael Patrick Culme-Seymour b 1962; *Career* joined RN 1926, ADC to Govr Gen of Canada 1933-35, served WWII (despatches), served IDC 1946-47, ret 1947; succeeded Rev Wentworth Watson to the Rockingham Castle Estates 1925, passed them to nephew Cdr L M M Saunders Watson 1969; farmer and landowner; memb Northants CC 1948-55, JP Northants 1949, DL Northants 1958-71, High Sheriff Northants 1966; Bledisloe Gold medal for Landowners 1972; memb Contemporary Art Soc, Historic Houses Assoc, Country Landowner Assoc; *Clubs* Brooks's; *Style—* Cdr Sir Michael Culme-Seymour, Bt, RN; Wytherston, Powerstock, Bridport, Dorset (☎ 030 885 211)

CULSHAW, Robert Nicholas; MVO (1979); s of Ivan Culshaw, and Edith Marjorie Jose, *née* Barnard; *b* 22 Dec 1952; *Educ* Univ Coll Sch Hampstead, King's Coll Cambridge (BA, MA); *m* 19 March 1977, Elaine Ritchie, da of Alan Clegg; *Career* HM Diplomatic Serv; FCO 1974-75, MECAS 1975-76, Muscat 1977-79, Khartoum 1979-80, Rome 1980-84, FCO London 1984-88, Athens 1989-; *Recreations* singing, skiing; *Style—* Robert Culshaw, Esq, MVO

CULVERHOUSE, Barbara Mary; da of Cyril Russell Dashwood, CBE (d 1962), and Laura Louise, *née* Steward (d 1959); *b* 16 April 1921; *Educ* Roedean; *m* 8 Feb 1947, Percival Emerson Culverhouse (d 1968), s of Percival Emerson Culverhouse (d 1953); 2 s (Ian b 1950, Hugh b 1951), 1 da (Lynette b 1948); *Career* CA in sole practice 1966-89; dir: Harthall Securities Ltd, Ian Culverhouse & Co Ltd; memb ICAEW 1944-(memb of Cncl 1981-87), tstee Old Roedeanian Assoc, memb Ct of Assts Worshipful Co of CAs; FCA; *Recreations* music, walking, travelling; *Style—* Mrs Barbara M Culverhouse; Wayside, Penn, High Wycombe, Bucks HP10 8LY (☎ 049481 2120)

CULVERHOUSE, Lt-Col (Arthur) Graham Hewitt; MBE, TD; s of Herbert Sydney Culverhouse, and Lillian Augusta *née* Hewitt; *b* 30 Dec 1907; *Educ* Victoria Coll Jersey; *m* 15 April 1931, Joyce, da of Clifton C Crowther (d 1946), of Oxshott, Surrey; 2 da (Elizabeth Ann Hewitt, Sally Rosina Hewitt); *Career* pre-war audit clerk and accounts student Standard Telephone and Cable Sgt Hon Artillery Co, War Serv Army Offr E Surrey Regt; Lt-Col: served Dunkirk, Italy, Greece; post-war: Aldershot (Mons OCTU), Nigeria, Southern Cmd Germany; dir Dawcul Ltd 1960-; *Recreations* hockey, squash; *Style—* Lt-Col Graham Culverhouse, MBE, TD; White Gates, Snowhill, Dinton, Salisbury; Dawcul House, 42 West Street, Marlow

CULYER, Prof Anthony John; s of Thomas Reginald Culyer (d 1979), and Betty Ely, *née* Headland; *b* 1 July 1942; *Educ* Sir William Borlase's Sch Marlow, King's Sch Worcester, Univ of Exeter (BA), UCLA; *m* 26 Aug 1966, Sieglinde Birgit, da of Kurt Kraut (d 1947); 1 s, 1 da; *Career* Univ of York 1969-: lectr, sr lectr, reader, prof of econs and head Dept of Econs and Related Studies 1986-; visiting prof: Queens Univ Canada 1976, Trent Univ Canada 1985-86, Medis Inst Munich 1990, Toronto Univ Canada 1991-; William Evans visiting prof Otago Univ NZ 1979, co-ed Journal of Health Economics 1982-; non-exec memb N Allerton Health Authy; professional conslt to: UK Dept of Health, OECD, EEC, WHO, Govt of Canada, Govt of NZ; memb Office of Health Econs: Ed Policy Ctee, Ed Bd; memb Coll Ctee King's Fund Coll London; memb Ed Bd Econ Review, Soc Scis and Med; memb Conf of Heads of Univ Depts of Econs 1987-; memb and founding chm Health Economists Study Gp; church organist and choirmaster; chm York Dist of Royal Sch of Church Music; *Publications incl* Health Economics (1973), Economics of Social Policy (1973), Benham's Economics (1973), Economic Policies and Social Goals (1974), Need and the National Health Service (1976), Annotated Bibliography of Health Economics (1977), Human Resources and Public Finance (1977), Economic Aspects of Health Services (1978), Measuring Health (1978), Political Economy of Social Policy (1980), Economic and Medical Evaluation of Health Care Technologies (1983), Health Indicators (1983), Economics (1985), Public Finance and Social Policy (1985), International Bibliography of Health Economics (1986), Public and Private Health Services (1986), Health Care Expenditures in Canada (1988) Perspectives on the Future of Health Care in Europe (1989), Standards for Socioeconomic Evaluation of Health Care Products and Services (1990), Competition in Health Care (1990); also over 100 articles and pamphlets; *Recreations* music; *Style—* Prof Anthony Culyer; The Laurels, Barmby Moor, York, YO4 5EJ (☎ 0759 302639); Dept of Economics and Related Studies, University of York, Heslington, York, YO1 5DD (☎ 0904 433762/433789, fax 0904 433433, telex 57933 YORKUL)

CUMANI, Luca Matteo; s of Sergio Cumani (d 1980), and Elena, *née* Cardini; *b* 7 April 1949; *Educ* Milan; *m* 1979, Sara Doon, da of Simon Patrick Conyngham Plunket; 1 s (Matthew Sergio Simon b 1981), 1 da (Francesca Deepsea b 1983); *Career* trainer; rider of 85 winners in Italy France and UK, won Moet and Chandon on Meissen and Prix Paul Noel de la Houtre on Harland 1972, Champion amateur (Italy) 1972; asst trainer: to S Cumani, to H R A Cecil 1974-75; first held trainer's licence 1976; horses trained incl: Kahyasi, Three Legs, Freeze The Secret, Spring in Deepsea, Alma Aga, Old Country, Triple Tipple, Tolomeo, Commanche Run, Free Guest, Bairn, Embla, Then Again, Celestial Storm, Half a Year, Casey, Infamy, Markofdistinction; races won incl: Ever Ready Derby, Irish Derby, St Leger, Italian Derby, Premio Roma (twice), Arlington Million Rothmans International, E P Taylor Stakes Juddmonte International Stakes, Phoenix Champion Stakes, St James's Palace Stakes (twice), Cheveley Park Stakes, Prix Royal Oak; *Style—* Luca Cumani, Esq

CUMBER, Sir John Alfred; CMG (1966), MBE (1953), TD (1946); s of Alfred Joseph Cumber (d 1964), and Alexandra Irene, *née* Elliot (d 1956); *b* 30 Sept 1920; *Educ* Richmond (Surrey) Co Sch, Richmond Art Sch, LSE; *m* 1945, Margaret Anne, da of Martin Tripp (d 1960); 2 s (Mervyn, Nigel); *Career* WWII 1939-46 with Royal Fus and 2 Punjab Regt in New Guinea and Burma, ret as Maj; HM Colonial Serv Kenya 1947-63, ret as sr dist cmmr; admin Cayman Islands, HM cmmr Anguilla 1964-69; dir gen Save the Children Fund 1971-85; kt 1985; *Recreations* art, music, gardening, travel; *Clubs* Royal Cwlth Soc; *Style—* Sir John Cumber, CMG, MBE, TD; Barton cottage, Throwleigh, Devon EX20 2HS (☎ 064 723 519)

CUMBERLAND, Dr David Charles; s of Frank Charles Cumberland, of Pleasington, nr Blackburn, Lancs, and Edna Constance, *née* Hodson; *b* 17 Aug 1944; *Educ* Queen Elizabeth GS Blackburn, Univ of Edinburgh Med Sch (MB ChB); *m* 26 Dec 1970, Marilyn Susan, da of Colin Rowley (d 1974); 2 da (Louise Helen b 21 Aug 1973, Melanie Claire b 9 April 1976); *Career* conslt cardiovascular radiologist Sheffield Health Authy specializing in treatment of arterial disease by balloon dilatation, lasers and ultrasound 1975-, conslt in cardiovascular studies San Francisco Heart Inst; author of numerous articles in jls; memb: BMA, Br Cardiac Soc, Cncl of Br Cardiovascular Intervention Soc; fndr chm Br Coronary Angioplasty Gp; FRCR 1973, FRCPEd 1986; *Books* Recent Advances in Radiology and Medical Imaging (jtly, 1986), Endovascular Surgery (jtly, 1989), Laser Angioplasty (jtly, 1989); *Recreations* jiu jitsu, sailing, country walking; *Style—* Dr David Cumberland; 21 Blacka Moor Crescent, Dore, Sheffield, South Yorkshire S17 3GL (☎ 0742 362612); Northern General Hospital, Department of Radiology, Sheffield S5 7AU (☎ 0742 434343, fax 0742 560472)

CUMBERLEGE, Baroness (Life Peer UK 1990), of Newick, Co E Sussex; Julia Frances Cumberlege; CBE (1985), DL (East Sussex 1986); da of Dr Lambert Ulrich Camm, of Appleton, Newick, Sussex, and Mary Geraldine Gertrude, *née* Russell (d 1962); *b* 27 Jan 1943; *Educ* Convent of the Sacred Heart Kent; *m* 14 Jan 1961, Patrick Francis Howard Cumberlege, s of Geoffrey Fenwick Jocelyn Cumberlege DSO, MC (d 1979); 3 s (Hon Mark b 1961, Hon Justin b 1964, Hon Oliver b 1968); *Career* memb: Lewes Dist Cncl 1966-79 (ldr 1977-78), E Sussex CC 1974-85 (chm Social Servs Ctee 1979-82); JP 1973-85; memb E Sussex AHA 1977-81; chm: Brighton Health Authy 1981-88, Nat Assoc of Health Authorities 1987-88, SW Thames RHA 1988-; memb: NHS Policy Bd 1989-, Cncl St George's Med Sch, Press Cncl 1977-83, Appts Cmmn 1984-; chm Review of Community Nursing for Eng 1985, vice pres Royal Coll of Nursing 1988, govr several schs, memb Cncl Brighton Poly 1987-89 (memb Formation Ctee 1988-89); *Clubs* RSM, New Cavendish; *Style—* The Rt Hon Baroness Cumberlege, CBE, DL; Vuggles Farm, Newick, Lewes, Sussex BN8 4RU (☎ 0273 400 453, fax 0273 401 084); SW Thames Regnl Health Authy, 40 Eastbourne Terrace, London W2 3QR (☎ 071 262 8011, fax 071 258 3908)

CUMING, Hon Mrs (Christine Veronica Helen); *née* Robertson; da of 1 Baron Robertson of Oakridge, GCB, GBE, KCMG, KCVO, DSO, MC, DL; *b* 3 Aug 1927; *m* 13 Aug 1949, Col (Robert) Hugh Cuming, MBE, JP, DL, The Royal Scots Greys, er s of late Hugh Philip Cuming, of Doms, Stansted Mountfitchet, Essex; 2 s, 1 da; *Style—* The Hon Mrs Cuming; Hill Farm, Bragenham, Beds LU7 0EE

CUMING, Frederick George Rees; s of Harold Albert Cuming (d 1976), of Welling, Kent; and Grace Madeleine, *née* Rees; *b* 16 Feb 1930; *Educ* Sidcup Sch of Art, RCA; *m* Oct 1962, Audrey, da of Eric Lee, of Ashton-under-Lyme; 1 s (Daniel Lee b 5 Nov 1964), 1 da (Rachel Joanna b 25 Aug 1971); *Career* Nat Serv Sgt RAEC 1949-51; artist and painter; gp shows incl: Royal Soc of Portrait Painters, John Moores Liverpool, Leicester Gallery, Pictures for Schools, 12 Royal Academicians Chichister, Little Studio NY; one mans shows: New Metropole Arts Centre Folkestone 1972-75, Jonleigh Guildford 1975, Thackeray London 1976, Chichester 1976, Grafton London 1983/85/87/88/90, Drew Canterbury 1983-86, Easton Rooms Rye 1983; works in collections incl: Royal Acad, Miny of Works, Monte Carlo Museum, Brighton and Hove Museum, St Johns and Worcester Colls Oxford, New Metropole Arts Centre, Farringdon Tst; winner grand prix fine art Monaco Ingot Industl Expo; adviser New Metropole Arts Centre Folkestone, tstee Rye Art Gallery and Eastern Rooms Gallery; memb: Nat Tst, New English Arts Club 1960; ARCA 1964, elected Royal Academician 1974; *Recreations* reading, music, travelling, walking; *Clubs* Chelsea Arts, Dover St Arts; *Style—* Frederick Cuming, Esq; The Gables, Wittersham Rd, Iden, Rye, E Sussex TN31 7UY (☎ 07978 322)

CUMING, Col (Robert) Hugh; MBE (1960), JP (1972), DL (Bucks 1976); er s of Hugh Philip Cuming (d 1959), of Doms, Stansted Mountfitchet, Essex and Monica Mary Josephine, *née* MacIntyre (d 1975); *b* 10 Sept 1920; *Educ* The Oratory Sch, Army Staff Coll Camberley; *m* 13 Aug 1949, Hon Christine Veronica Helen, da of Gen Robertson, of Oakridge, GCB, GBE, KCMG, KCVO, DSO, MC, DL; 2 s, 1 da; *Career* cmmnd 1940 Seaforth Highlanders, served N Africa with Phantom, then Sicily and NW Europe, transferred Royal Scots Greys 1949, ret 1962, Col 1976; chm: Quarantine Kennels Assoc 1969-, Bucks Cncl of Voluntary Youth Serv 1975-77, Milton Keynes bench 1980-84, Bucks Co Cts Ctee 1982-84; memb: Exec Cncl ACFA 1976-85, Thames Valley Police Authy 1979-82; *Recreations* shooting, fishing; *Clubs* Cavalry and Guards, Kennel; *Style—* Col Hugh Cuming, MBE, JP, DL; Hill Farm, Bragenham, Leighton Buzzard, Beds (☎ 052 527 257)

CUMINGS, Alison; da of Arthur William Cumings, of Reigate, and Shirley Joan, *née* Williams; *b* 18 Nov 1961; *Educ* Oxted Co (Nat Schs Hockey Champion, jr co hockey player, nationally ranked javelin thrower); *Career* professional squash player; junior introduction 1975, junior Nat squash champion 1978-79, Eng debut 1978 (49 Eng caps), memb GB tour of Aust and NZ 1979, sr Nat squash champion 1982-83; world team champions: Dublin 1985, NZ 1987, Holland 1989; Br doubles champion 1983 1984 1985, Nat Super League Team winner 1990; *Recreations* art, music, design, cars, all sports; *Style—* Ms Alison Cumings; c/o Mrs S Cumings, 74 Raglan Rd, Reigate, Surrey RH2 OET (☎ 0737 243874)

CUMMING; *see*: Gordon-Cumming

CUMMING, (John) Alan; CBE (1983); s of John Cumming; *b* 6 March 1932; *Educ* George Watson's Coll Edinburgh; *m* 1958, Isobel Beaumont, *née* Sked; 3 s; *Career* Woolwich Building Society: chief exec 1969-86, dir 1978-, exec vice chm 1986-; chm: Bldg Soc Assoc 1981-83, Cavendish Wates First Assured plc, Woolwich Homes Ltd; pres Euro Community Mortgage Fedn 1984-87, chm Thamesmead Town, chm Utd Reformed Church Tst, pres Int Union of Housing Fin Institutions 1990-; dir: Value and Income Tst plc; dir: Nat Kidney Res Fndn; *Recreations* bridge, golf; *Clubs* Caledonian; *Style—* Alan Cumming, Esq, CBE; 8 Prince Consort Drive, Chislehurst, Kent (☎ 081 467 8382); Woolwich Building Society, Corporate Headquarters, Watling St, Bexleyheath, Kent DA6 7RR (☎ 081 854 2400)

CUMMING, Prof Gordon; s of Charles Gordon Cumming (d 1982), and Clara, *née* Wright (d 1980); *b* 31 May 1922; *Educ* Worcestershire Co HS, Univ of London (BSc), Univ of Birmingham (BM BS, PhD, DSc), Columbia Univ New York; *m* 19 July 1951, Jean Edith, da of Arthur Dyke Peasnell (d 1983); 4 s ((Alasdair) Duncan Gordon b 4 Aug 1952, Bruce b 14 Jan 1960, Robert (twin), Andrew b 4 Aug 1962), 1 da (Fiona b 17 July 1956); *Career* house physician Med Professorial Unit Queen Elizabeth Hosp Birmingham 1956, house surgn Sorrento Maternity Hosp Birmingham 1957, asst MO Gen Hosp Birmingham 1957, registrar Royal Postgraduate Med Sch 1958, lectr in med Univ of Birmingham 1959, res fell Coll of Physicians and Surgns NY 1960; Univ of Birmingham: lectr in med 1962-65, sr lectr 1965-67, reader in med 1967; conslt physician United Birmingham Hosps 1965, med dir Midhurst Med Res Inst 1973-, faculty prof of clinical sci Univ of Surrey 1977, sr lectr Univ of London Cardiothoracic Inst 1979, treas MRS 1979, prof of thoracic med Univ of London 1984; visiting prof: Univ of Tokyo, Univ of Orange Free State, Univ of Natal; memb: Physiological Soc, MRS, Euro Soc of Clinical Investigation, Assoc of Physicians of GB and NI, Société Francaise de la Tuberculose et des Maladies Respiratoires, Fleischner Soc, Breathing Club, Mass Spectrometer Soc of Japan, American Physiological Soc; treas and memb Cncl Br Lung Fndn, chm Visitors RCP Ctee on Postgraduate Educn; memb Editorial bd: American Jl of Physiology 1968-72, Clinical Sci and Molecular Med 1970-75, Jl of Applied Physiology 1973-76, Lung 1980-88; over 100 articles published in learned jls; FRICS 1966 (ARICS 1944), FRCP 1972 (MRCP 1964); *Books* The Medical Management of Acute Poisoning (1961), Structure and Function in the Human Lung (with L B Hunt 1964), Disorders of the Respiratory System (with S Semple 1970 and 1979), The Scientific Foundations of Respiratory Medicine (with J G Scaddin 1979), The Pulmonary Circulation in Health and Disease (with G Bonsignore 1980), The Lung in its Environment (with G Bonsignore 1982), Cellular Biology of the Lung (with G Bonsignore), Drugs and the Lung (with G Bonsignore 1983), Smoking and the Lung (with G Bonsignore 1984); *Recreations* skiing, making violins, music, business; *Style—* Prof Gordon Cumming; Cedar House, Gorehill, Petworth, W Sussex GU28 0JJ (☎ 0798 43066); Midhurst Medical Research Institute, Research Park, University of Surrey, Guildford (☎ 0482 301092)

CUMMING, John Stuart; s of Stuart F M Cumming, MC, FFA (d 1961); *b* 18 March 1928; *Educ* Marlborough, Corpus Christi Coll Cambridge; *m* 1956, Iseult Margaret, da of late Carl W Mercer; 1 s, 3 da; *Career* Lt RAOC; dir Hambros Bank Ltd 1977-88; dir Br Merchant Banking and Securities Houses Assoc 1989-; vice chm of govrs Rose Hill Sch Tunbridge Wells; MICAS; *Recreations* travel, gardening, opera; *Clubs* Sloane; *Style—* John Cumming Esq; Cheyne House, Langton Green, Tunbridge Wells, Kent TN3 0HP (☎ 0892 862066, office 071 796 3606)

CUMMING, (William James) Kenneth; s of Wallace Cumming, of Manchester, and Kathleen Margurite, *née* Lavery; *b* 29 Aug 1946; *Educ* The Royal Belfast Acad Inst, The Queen's Univ of Belfast (BSc, MB BCh); *m* 13 July 1971, Ruth Christina, da of Duncan Beaumont (d 1971); 2 da (Emma b 27 Dec 1973, Claire b 25 Aug 1975); *Career* registrar and sr registrar Newcastle upon Tyne 1972-79, conslt neurologist Withington Hosp Univ of Manchester 1979-; pres NW Myasthenic Assoc, sec Manchester Med Soc, treas N of E Neurological Soc, chm Manchester Regional Imaging PLC; Hon MD The Queens Univ Belfast 1979, BAO 1971, FRCP, FRCPI; *Recreations* golf, skiing; *Clubs* East India; *Style—* Kenneth Cumming, Esq; 370 Chester Road, Woodford, Cheshire; The Beeches Consulting Centre, Mill Lane, Cheadle, Cheshire SK8 2PY (☎ 061 428 1072)

CUMMING, Ronald Patrick; s of John Alexander Cumming (d 1951), of Golspie, Sutherland, and Annabella, *née* Thomson (d 1972); *b* 15 Aug 1923; *Educ* Golspie Secdy Sch, Univ of Aberdeen (MB ChB); *m* 1 Oct 1947, Norma Gladys, da of Norman Kitson (d 1962), of Aberdeen; 2 s (Peter b 12 Sept 1948, Roy b 1 Sept 1953); *Career* asst in gen practice Huntly Aberdeenshire 1945-47, asst in Dept of Anatomy Univ of Aberdeen 1947-49, asst in gen practice Rhynie Aberdeenshire 1949-50, jr surgical offr Ronkswood Hosp Worcester 1950-51, sr house offr and registrar in surgery Victoria Hosp Burnley 1951-53 registrar and sr registrar in surgery Aberdeen Hosps 1953-57, conslt Shetland Hosp 1957-85; memb Lerwick Town Cncl and Shetland CC 1967-75, hon Sheriff and JP Shetland Is, hon pres Shetland Fiddlers Soc 1975-85; memb: Grampian Ctee for Employment of Disabled People (former chm Shetland Ctee), Aberdeen Medico-Chirurgical Soc; fell BMA 1982, sr fell Assoc of Surgns of GB and Ireland; FRCSEd 1952; *Books* Aspects of Health and Safety in Oil Development (jt ed, 1973), Aberdeen Medico-Chirurgical Society Bicentennial History (contrib, 1989);

Recreations golf, gardening, reading, music; *Style—* Ronald Cumming, Esq; 62 Hammerfield Avenue, Aberdeen AB1 6LJ (☎ 0224 313192); Clach Ruadh, Main St, Golspie, Sutherland KW10 6RA (☎ 04083 3112)

CUMMING-BRUCE, Hon Alexander (Alec) Pascoe Hovell-Thurlow; OBE (1960); yst s of 6 Baron Thurlow (d 1952); *b* 26 Oct 1917; *Educ* Shrewsbury, Trinity Coll Cambridge (BA, MA); *m* 21 Feb 1942, Catherine Agnes, da of Rev Hamilton Blackwood, of Scalby, Yorks; 2 s, 1 da; *Career* Colonial Admin Serv 1941-60, Home Civil Serv 1961-78; *Style—* Hon Alec Cumming-Bruce, OBE; Leazes Cottage, Leazes Place, Durham City

CUMMING-BRUCE, Edward Simon; s of Rt Hon Sir Roualeyn Cumming-Bruce, and Lady Sarah Cumming-Bruce, *née* Savile (d 1991); *b* 7 June 1958; *Educ* Ampleforth, Magdalen Coll Oxford (MA); *m* 1984, Antonia, da of CS Gaisford- St Lawrence, of Howth Castle, Dublin, Eire; 2 s (Michael b 1985, William b 1987), 1 da (Isabelle b 1990); *Career* Laurence Prust & Co (and successor firms); trainee 1980-, dir Laurence Prust Corporate Finance Ltd 1984, ptnr Laurence Prust & Co 1986, dir CCF Laurence Prust Ltd 1989; dir Schroder Securities Ltd 1990-, non-exec dir Interlink Express plc 1990-; memb Int Stock Exchange 1986; *Recreations* fishing, shooting; *Style—* Edward Cumming-Bruce, Esq; Schroder Securities Limited, 120 Cheapside, London EC2 (☎ 071 382 3000, fax 071 382 3057)

CUMMING-BRUCE, Rt Hon Sir (James) Roualeyn Hovell-Thurlow; PC (1977); 3 s (twin) of late 6 Baron Thurlow; *b* 9 March 1912; *Educ* Shrewsbury, Magdalene Coll Cambridge (BA); *m* 4 Aug 1955, Lady (Anne) Sarah Alethea Marjorie Savile (d 1991), yst da of 6 Earl of Mexborough (d 1945); 2 s, 1 da; *Career* called to the Bar Middle Temple 1937, judge of High Court Family Div 1964-77, presiding judge NE Circuit 1971-74, a Lord Justice of Appeal 1977- 85 (ret); kt 1964; *Clubs* Pratt's, United Oxford and Cambridge; *Style—* The Rt Hon Sir Roualeyn Cumming-Bruce; 1 Mulberry Walk, London SW3 (☎ 071 352 5754)

CUMMINGS, Constance; CBE (1974); da of Dallas Vernon Halverstadt (d 1922), of Seattle, USA, and Kate Logan, *née* Cummings (d 1957); *b* 15 May 1910; *Educ* St Nicholas Girls' Sch USA, Univ of London; *m* 3 July 1933, Benn Wolfe Levy, s of Octave George Levy (d 1947), of London; 1 s (Jonathan Cummings b 1949), 1 da (Jemima Madge b 1951); *Career* theatre, film, TV and radio actress; plays incl: Mme Bovary 1938, Goodbye Mr Chips 1939, Romeo and Juliet, St Joan (Old Vic) 1939-40, organised many troop shows during the war years, Peter and the Wolf (Albert Hall) 1951, Lysistrata 1957, Rape of the Belt 1957, Who's Afraid of Virginia Woolf? 1964, Fallen Angels 1967; NT: Long Day's Journey into Night, The Cherry Orchard, Coriolanus; The Circle (Hong Kong Arts Festival), Mrs Warren's Profession (English-Speaking Theatre Vienna); NY: The Chalk Garden, Wings; memb: Lab Pty, Arts Cncl, Cncl Br Actors' Fraternity, Exec Ctee Actors Charitable Tst, RSA; *Recreations* anthropology, music, horticulture; 68 Old Church Street, London SW3 (☎ 071 352 0437)

CUMMINGS, John Scott; MP (Lab) Easington 1987-; s of George Cummings, and Mary *née* Cain; *b* 6 July 1943; *Educ* Murton Cncl Sr Sch; *Career* colliery electrician Murton Colliery 1958-87, sec Murton Colliery Mechanics 1967-87; memb: Easington Rural and District Cncls (leader 1979-87), Northumbrian Water Authy 1977-83, Peterlee and Aycliffe Devpt Corp 1980-87; vice chm Coalfield Community Campaign 1984-87; *Recreations* Jack Russell terriers, walking, travel; *Clubs* Murton Victoria, Murton Demmi, Murton Ex Servicemans, Thornley Catholic, Peterlee Lab; *Style—* John Cummings, Esq, MP; 18 Grasmere Terrace, Murton, Seaham, Co Durham; House of Commons, London SW1A 0AA

CUNARD, Peter John; s of Basil Charles Henry Cunard (d 1962), of London, and Christine May, *née* Tremer; *b* 21 Aug 1945; *Educ* Latymer Fndn; *m* 1970, Susan Margaret Ethel, da of James Coleridge; 2 s (Nicholas Peter b 30 Oct 1971, Sebastian James b 29 Dec 1972), 1 da (Catherine Jane b 27 Nov 1976); *Career* press offr Assoc Television 1964-69, press and PR offr English Stage Co Royal Court Theatre 1969, PR advsr Duke of Bedford 1969-73, head of PR Trust House Forte 1973-76, dir Durden-Smith Communications 1976-80, fndr and md Granard Communications 1980-90, chief exec The Rowland Co (after merger of Granard Communications with Kingsway PR) 1990-, memb Exec Ctee Rowland Worldwide Ltd; tstee Sick Childrens Trust 1984; MIOD 1980, MCIM, vice chm Devpt Ctee Public Relations Consultants Assoc 1985; *Books* Public Relations Case Book (1990); *Recreations* travel, photography, theatre studies, vintage cars, cricket; *Style—* Peter Cunard, Esq; The Rowland Company, 67-69 Whitfield St, London W1P 5RL (☎ 071 436 4060, fax 071 255 2131)

CUNDALL, Geoffrey Percival; s of William Percival Cundall (d 1967), of York, and Dorothy Mary, *née* , Barker (d 1985); *b* 14 Oct 1924; *Educ* Bootham Sch York, Univ of Leeds (BSc); *m* 16 June 1950, Rachel, da of Edward Holmes Horner (d 1960), of Settle, Yorks; 3 da (Ruth Lillian b 1953, Heather Clare b 1956, Joanna Christine b 1959); *Career* former lectr: UMIST, Univ of Sheffield; fndr ptnr Cundall Johnston & Ptnrs; author of numerous papers (particularly on energy); registering offr Newcastle monthly meeting Religious Soc of Friends, chm Newcastle Cncl for Vol Serv 1987-; FIEE, FIMechE, FCIBSE, MConsE; *Recreations* fell walking, skiing, photography, debating; *Style—* Geoffrey Cundall, Esq; 14 Towers Avenue, Jesmond, Newcastle upon Tyne NE2 3QE (☎ 091 281 1407); Cundall, Johnston & Partners, Horsley House, Regent Centre, Gosforth, Newcastle upon Tyne NE3 3LU (☎ 091 213 1515, fax 091 213 1701, telex 23152)

CUNDY, Clifford Benjamin; s of Walter Augustus Cundy (d 1956), of Immingham, Lincs, and Esme Miriam, *née* Spiers (d 1970); *b* 19 Dec 1927; *Educ* Humberstone Fndn Sch Clee, Magdalen Coll Oxford; *m* 23 Dec 1950, Hazel Patricia, da of Benjamin Hazelwood (d 1946), of Rangoon, Burma; *Career* sculptor and painter; since 1973 has regularly exhibited his work at galleries incl: Upper Street Gallery Islington, Wills Lane Gallery St Ives, Alwin Gallery London, Armstrong Davis Gallery Arundel, Arts Centre Hong Kong, Caldwell Gallery Belfast and Dublin, Bath Arts Festival, Chapman Gallery London, Avivson Gallery Milwaukee; memb Nat Soc of Painters; *Clubs* Sketch; *Style—* Clifford Cundy, Esq; 32 Cambrian Rd, Richmond, Surrey TW10 6JQ (☎ 081 940 8494)

CUNEO, Terence Tenison (Terry); OBE (1987); s of Cyrus Cincinnata Cuneo (d 1916) and Nell Marian Tenison (d 1953); *b* 1 Nov 1907; *Educ* Sutton Valence; *m* 1934, Catherine Mayfield (d 1979), yr da of Maj Edwin George Monro, CBE; 2 da (Linda, Carole); *Career* portrait and figure painter, ceremonial, mil and engrg subjects; served WWII RE and as war artist; has painted extensively in N Africa, S Africa, Rhodesia, Canada, USA, Ethiopia, Far East; one-man exhibitions: RWS Galleries London 1954 and 1958, Sladmore Gallery 1971, 1972, 1974; retrospective exhibition Mall Galleries 1988; RGI *Major works incl:* Coronation of HM The Queen Westminster Abbey (Royal Collection 1953), equestrian portrait of HM The Queen as Col-in-Chief Grenadier Gds (cmmnd 1963), Garter Ceremony St George's Chapel Windsor (cmmnd by HM 1964), Sir Winston Churchill's Lying in State (1965), Rt Hon Edward Heath (1971), Field Marshal Viscount Montgomery of Alamein (1972), Duke of Beaufort (commemorating 40 years as Master of the Horse), King Hussein of Jordan (1980), Col H Jones, VC (1984), Fortieth Anniversary of D-Day (1984); *Books* The Mouse and his Master (autobiog 1977), The Railway Painting of Terence Cuneo, Terence Cuneo Railway Painter of the Century (1980); *Recreations* travel, riding, writing; *Style—* Terry Cuneo, Esq, OBE; Fresh Fields, 201 Ember Lane, East Molesey, Surrey (☎ 081 398 1986/ 7981)

CUNINGHAME; *see*: Montgomery Cuninghame

CUNINGHAME; *see*: Fairlie-Cuninghame

CUNINGHAME; *see*: Fergusson-Cuninghame of Caprington

CUNINGHAME, Lady (Marjorie) Joan Mary; *née* Wentworth-Fitzwilliam; 2 da of Lt-Col 7 Earl Fitzwilliam, KCVO, CBE, DSO, JP, DL (d 1943); *b* 19 Oct 1900; *m* 1, 4 Nov 1925 (m dis 1949), Maj Grismond Picton Philipps, CVO (Knt 1953), Grenadier Gds (d 1967); 1 s; 1 da; m 2, 6 Oct 1949, Lt-Col William Wallace Smith Cuninghame, DSO, JP, DL, late Life Gds, 16 Laird of Caprington (d 1959); *Style—* Lady Joan Cuninghame; Homestead, Vallee des Vaux, St Helier, Jersey CI

CUNLIFFE, Prof Barrington Windsor (Barry); s of George Percival Windsor (d 1942), and Beatrice Emma, *née* Mersh; *b* 10 Dec 1939; *Educ* Northern GS Portsmouth, St Johns Coll Cambridge (BA, MA, PhD, LittD); *m* 1, 1962 (m dis 1979), Frances Ann, *née* Dunn; 1 s (Daniel b 1962), 1 da (Charlotte b 1967); m 2, 4 Jan 1979, Margaret, da of late Robert Herdman, of Brockworth, Glos; 1 s (Thomas b 1981), 1 da (Anna b 1984); *Career* asst lectr Univ of Bristol 1963-66, prof of archaeology Univ of Southampton 1966-72, prof of euro archaeology Univ of Oxford 1972-; memb: Roman Soc, Soc Medieval Archaeology, Royal Archaeological Inst; vice pres: Soc of Antiquaries 1982-85, Prehistoric Soc 1983-86; Hon: DLitt Univ of Sussex 1983, DSc Univ of Bath 1984; FSA 1964, FBA 1979, correspondent memb Deutschen Archaologischen Instituts; *Books* The Cradle of England (1972), Rome and the Barbarians (1975), Rome and her Empire (1978), The Celtic World (1979), Roman Bath Discovered (1984), The City of Bath (1986), Greeks, Romans and Barbarians (1988); *Clubs* Athenaeum; *Style—* Prof Barry Cunliffe; Institute of Archaeology, 36 Beaumont St, Oxford (☎ 0865 278240)

CUNLIFFE, Sir David Ellis; 9 Bt (GB 1759), of Liverpool, Lancashire; s of Sir Cyril Henley Cunliffe, 8 Bt (d 1969); *b* 29 Oct 1957; *Educ* St Alban's GS for Boys; *m* 1983, Linda Carol, da of John Sidney Batchelor, of Harpenden; 2 da (Emma Mary b 1986, Katherine Alice b 1990); *Heir* bro, Andrew Cunliffe; *Career* sales representative; *Style—* Sir David Cunliffe, Bt; Sunnyside, Burnthouse Lane, Needham, nr Harleston, Norfolk IP20 9LN (☎ 0379 853 866)

CUNLIFFE, Hon Henry (Harry); s and h of 3 Baron Cunliffe; *b* 9 March 1962; *Educ* Eton; *Style—* The Hon Harry Cunliffe

CUNLIFFE, Lawrence Francis; MP (Lab) Leigh 1979-; *b* 25 March 1929; *Educ* St Edmund's RC Sch Worsley Manchester; *m* 1950, Winifred, da of William Haslem; 3 s, 2 da; *Style—* Lawrence Cunliffe Esq, MP; House of Commons, London SW1

CUNLIFFE, Hon Merlin; yr s of late 2 Baron Cunliffe; *b* 29 April 1935; *Educ* Eton; *m* 1, 23 April 1960 (m dis), Deborah Rutherford, yst da of Harold Thornton Grimwade, MBE, of Urara, Lismore, Victoria, Australia; 1 da (and 1 da decd); m 2, 1978, Mrs Amanda June Foster, da of Samuel Rogers; *Style—* The Hon Merlin Cunliffe; Wills Rd, Dixon's Creek, Vic 3775, Australia

CUNLIFFE, 3 Baron (UK 1914); Roger Cunliffe; s of 2 Baron Cunliffe (d 1963), and his 1 w, Joan Catherine, da of late Cecil Lubbock (n of 1 Baron Avebury); *b* 12 Jan 1932; *Educ* Eton, Trinity Coll Cambridge (BA, MA), Architectural Assoc (AADipl), Open Univ; *m* 27 April 1957, Clemency Ann, da of late Maj Geoffrey Benyon Hoare, of Clover House, Aldeburgh, Suffolk; 2 s, 1 da; *Heir* s, Hon Henry Cunliffe; *Career* consltg architect; dir Exhibition Consultants Ltd; asst Worshipful Co of Goldsmiths; *Books* Office Buildings (with Leonard Manasseh, 1962); *Recreations* making bread, planting trees, cycling; *Style—* The Rt Hon Lord Cunliffe; The Broadhurst, Brandeston, Woodbridge, Suffolk IP13 7AG (☎ 072 882 751)

CUNLIFFE, William James; s of William Cunliffe, and Bertha, *née* Longworth; *b* 28 Dec 1939; *Educ* Univ of Manchester (BSc, MB ChB), Univ of London (MD); *m* 3 June 1963, (Elizabeth) Janet, da of Arthur Wheeler Wood; 2 s (David Neil b 14 May 1964, Timothy Peter b 28 April 1970), 1 da (Susan Deborah b 20 June 1967); *Career* sr registrar dermatology dept Royal Victoria Infirmary Newcastle Upon Tyne 1966-69 (registrar 1964-66), consIt dermatologist Gen Infirmary at Leeds 1969-, chm and dir Leeds Fdn for Dermatological Res 1981-; chm: Br Soc of Investigated Dermatology 1976-79, Yorkshire Dermatologists, Br Assoc of Dermatology and Therapy Sub Gp; sec and pres Euro Soc of Dermatological Res 1985-89; *Recreations* walking, gardening; *Style—* William Cunliffe, Esq; 47 Tredgold Avenue, Bramhope, Leeds LS16 9BS (☎ 0532 672326); Department of Dermatology, The General Infirmary at Leeds, Great George St, Leeds LS1 3EX (☎ 0532 432799)

CUNLIFFE-LISTER, Hon Nicholas John; s of late Maj the Hon John Yarburgh Cunliffe-Lister, eld s of 1 Earl of Swinton, GBE, CH, MC, MP; raised to the rank of an Earl's son 1974; hp of bro, 2 Earl; *b* 4 Sept 1939; *Educ* Winchester, Worcester Coll Oxford; *m* 19 Feb 1966, Hon (Elizabeth) Susan, da of 1 Viscount Whitelaw, CH, MC, PC, *qqv*; 2 s, 1 da; *Career* late 2 Lt WG; slr 1966; *Style—* Hon Nicholas Cunliffe-Lister; Glebe House, Masham, Ripon, Yorks

CUNLIFFE-LISTER, Hon Mrs Nicholas; Hon (Elizabeth) Susan; *née* Whitelaw; eldest da of 1 Viscount Whitelaw, *qv*; *b* 2 Nov 1944; *m* 19 Feb 1966, Hon Nicholas John Cunliffe-Lister, *qv*; 2 s, 1 da; *Style—* The Hon Mrs Nicholas Cunliffe-Lister; Glebe House, Masham, Ripon, Yorkshire

CUNNINGHAM, Andrew Edward Tarrant; s of Will Edward Dennis Cunningham (d 1980), and Muriel Iris, *née* Tarrant (d 1987); *b* 15 March 1945; *Educ* The King's Sch Canterbury; *m* 24 March 1973, Mary Vivien Swainson; 2 s (Anthony Paul b 6 Aug 1974, John Roger b 17 Nov 1976); *Career* ptnr Moore Stephens 1972- (articled clerk 1963, mangr 1971); Liveryman City Livery of Upholders 1977, Freeman Worshipful Co of Goldsmiths 1977; FCA 1974 (ACA 1969); *Recreations* golf, music, collecting wine; *Clubs* Piltdown Golf Sussex; *Style—* Andrew Cunningham, Esq; Moore Stephens, St Paul's House, Warwick Lane, London EC4P 4BN (☎ 071 248 4499, fax 071 248 3408, car 0836 652714)

CUNNINGHAM, Sir Charles Craik; GCB (1974, KCB 1961, CB 1946), KBE (1952), CVO (1941); s of late Richard Yule Cunningham, of Abergeldie, Kirriemuir, Angus, and Isabella, *née* Craik; *b* 7 May 1906; *Educ* Harris Acad Dundee, Univ of St Andrews (MA, BLitt, LLD); *m* 1934, Edith Louisa (d 1990), da of late Frank Coutts Webster, OBE; 2 da (Isobel, Margaret); *Career* joined Scot Office 1929, private sec to Sec of State for Scot 1935-39, Scot Home Dept 1939-57 (sec 1948-57); perm under sec Home Office 1957-66, dep chm UKAEA 1966-71; chm: Radiochemical Centre Ltd 1971-74, Uganda Resettlement Bd 1972-74; dir Securicor 1971-81; *Clubs* Reform, New (Edinburgh); *Style—* Sir Charles Cunningham, GCB, KBE, CVO; Bankside, Peaslake, Surrey GU5 9RL (☎ 0306 730402)

CUNNINGHAM, David; CB (1983); s of Robert Cunningham, of 15 Buchanan Drive, Bearsden, Dunbartonshire (d 1956), and Elizabeth *née* Shields (d 1983); *b* 26 Feb 1924; *Educ* High Sch of Glasgow, Univ of Glasgow (MA, LLB); *m* 26 Aug 1955, Ruth Branwell, da of Rev Thomas James Campbell Crawford (d 1955), of Barony Manse, West Kilbride, Ayrshire; 1 s (Robert Campbell (Keith) b 1956), 2 da (Isabel Sharon b 1958, Aileen Shields Branwell b 1962); *Career* capt Cameronians (seconded Intelligence Corps and Control Commn Germany) 1942-47; deputy slr to Sec of State for Scotland 1978-80, slr to Sec of State for Scotland 1980-84; *Recreations* hill walking, reading, motor cars, theatre; *Style—* David Cunningham Esq, CB; The Green Gates,

Innerleithen, Peeblesshire EH44 6NH (☎ 0896 830436)

CUNNINGHAM, Hon Mrs (Edith Louise); *née* MacDermott; da of Baron MacDermott, MC, PC, (Life Peer) (d 1979); *b* 12 Jan 1930; *Educ* Wycombe Abbey, Queen's Univ Belfast (MB BCh); *m* 30 April 1955, Samuel Barbour Cunningham, er s of Col James Glencairn Cunningham, OBE, DL, of Ballytrim, Co Down; 2 s (James, Samuel), 2 da (Anna, Rachel); *Career* GP ret 1990; MRCGP until 1990; *Recreations* gardening; *Style—* The Hon Mrs Cunningham; Ballytrim House, 10 Ballytrim Road, Killyleagh Downpatrick, Co Down BT30 9TH

CUNNINGHAM, George; s of Harry Cunningham, and Christina, *née* McKay; *b* 10 June 1931; *Educ* Manchester and London Univs (BA, BSc); *m* 6 July 1957, Mavis, *née* Walton; 1 s, 1 da; *Career* 2 Lt RA 1954-56; with CRO 1956-63, 2 sec UK High Cmmn Canada 1958-60; cwlth offr Labour Party 1963-66, with Miny of Overseas Devpt 1966-69; contested Henley 1966; MP SW Islington 1970-74, MP Islington S and Finsbury 1974-83; MEP 1978-79; Lab to Dec 1981, Ind 1981-82, SDP from 1982; oppn front bench spokesman Home Affrs 1979-81; chief exec The Library Assoc 1984-; FBIM 1989; *Books* The Management of Aid Agencies (1974), Careers in Politics (1984); *Clubs* National Liberal; *Style—* George Cunningham, Esq; 28 Manor Gdns, Hampton, Middx TW12 2TU (☎ 081 979 6221); Library Association, 7 Ridgmount St, London WC1E 7AE (☎ 071 636 7543, fax 071 436 7218)

CUNNINGHAM, Lt-Gen Sir Hugh Patrick; KBE (1975, OBE 1966); s of Sir Charles Banks Cunningham, CSI (d 1967), of Campbelltown, Argyll and Grace, *née* Macnish; *b* 4 Nov 1921; *Educ* Charterhouse; *m* 1955, Jill, da of J S Jeffrey (d 1978), of E Knoyle, Wilts; 2 s, 2 da; *Career* 2 Lt RE 1942, GOC SW Dist 1971-74, ACGS (OR) MOD 1974-75, Lt-Gen 1975, Dep Chief of Def Staff (OR) 1976-78, ret; Col Cmdt RE 1976-81, Col Queen's Gurkha Engrs 1976-81, Col Bristol Univ OTC 1977-87; HM Lt Tower of London 1983-86; dir: Fairey Holdings 1978-87, Fairey Engineering 1981-86, MEL 1982-89, Trend Communications Ltd 1983-86; chm: LL Consultans 1983-89, The Trend Group 1986-89; Master Worshipful Co of Glass Sellers 1980-81; pres Old Carthusian Soc 1982-87; *Clubs* Army and Navy, MCC; *Style—* Lt-Gen Sir Hugh Cunningham, KBE; Brickyard Farm, East Knoyle, Salisbury, Wilts SP3 6BP (☎ 074 783 281); 607 Howard House, Dolphin Square, London SW1 (☎ 071 8217960); Trend Group, High Wycombe, Bucks (☎ 06285 24977)

CUNNINGHAM, Lady Jill; da of J S Jeffrey (d 1977), of Little Leigh, E Knoyle, Salisbury; *b* 7 May 1930; *m* 27 July 1955, Lt-Gen Sir Hugh Cunningham, s of Sir Charles Banks Cunningham, CSI (d 1967); 2 s (John Charles b 1958, Richard Hugh b 1960), 2 da (Susan Grace b 1956, Caroline Mary (Mrs Praze) b 1962); *Career* chm: Life Anew Tst, Alcohlism and Drug Dependancy Treatment Centre; tstee Chemical Dependency Centre; *Recreations* gardening, opera; *Style—* Lady Cunningham; Brickyard Farm, East Knoyle, Salisbury, Wiltshire SP3 6BP (☎ 074 783 281)

CUNNINGHAM, Dr John Anderson; MP (Lab) Copeland 1983-; s of Andrew Cunningham; *b* 4 Aug 1939; *Educ* Jarrow GS, Bede Coll Univ of Durham; *m* 1964, Maureen; 1 s, 2 da; *Career* former research chemist Durham (PhD 1966), then schoolmaster and Trades Union official; memb Chester-Le-St Dist Cncl (chm Fin Ctee 1969-74), MP (Lab) Whitehaven, Cumbria 1970-1983, PPS to James Callaghan when PM 1972-76, Parly under sec of state Dept of Energy 1976-79, front bench oppn spokesman: Industry 1979-Nov 1983, Environment and memb Shadow Cabinet Nov 1983-, shadow ldr House of Commons and Lab Nat Campaigns coordinator 1989-; *Recreations* gardening, fell walking, fly fishing, music, books, ornithology; *Style—* Dr John Cunningham, MP; House of Commons, London SW1

CUNNINGHAM, John Roderick; s of John Cunningham (d 1952), of Kent, Millicent, *née* Seal (d 1929); *b* 13 May 1926; *Educ* Beckenham Sch Kent, Queen's Univ Belfast N Ireland (BSc); *m* 1964, Monica Rachel, da of Cedric Robert Seymour George (d 1964), of Horley, Surrey; 1 s (Roderick b 1965), 2 da (Meryl b 1955 (from previous marriage), Clare b 1970); *Career* dir Coutts and Co 1980-87, chm Nikko Bank plc 1987-; memb Bd of Govrs of Cordwainers Coll, chm City Branch Royal Soc of St George; vice chm: City Branch IOD, Tonbridge Cons Assoc; Master Worshipful Co of Loriners 1984; FCIB, FRSA; *Recreations* gardening in Southern Spain, City of London activities; *Clubs* IOD, Overseas Bankers, City Livery; *Style—* John R Cunningham, Esq; Oak Lodge, 126 Pembury Road, Tonbridge, Kent TN9 2JJ; The Nikko Bank (UK) plc, 17 Godliman Street, London EC4V 5BD (☎ 071 528 7070)

CUNNINGHAM, Mark James; s of James Arthur Cunningham, and Carole Kathleen, *née* Wood; *b* 6 June 1956; *Educ* Stonyhurst, Magdalen Coll Oxford (BA), Poly of Central London (Dip Law); *m* 19 July 1980, Jane, da of Prof Victor Lambert (d 1981); 2 s (Charles b 1984, Edward b 1989), 2 da (Clementine b 1981, Susannah b 1985); *Career* called to the Bar Inner Temple 1980; *Recreations* tennis, cricket, hunting, gardening, food; *Style—* Mark Cunningham, Esq; 5 New Square, Lincoln's Inn, London WC2 3RJ (☎ 071 404 0404, fax 071 831 6016)

CUNNINGHAM, Samuel Barbour; DL (Co Down); s of Col James G Cunningham, OBE, of Glencairn Lodge, Tullykinlough RD, Killyleagh, Co Down, and Mollie Barbour, *née* Pears; *b* 7 Dec 1929; *Educ* Stowe; *m* Hon Edith Louise, da of Baron MacDermott (Lord Chief Justice of N Ireland), of Glenburn, Cairnburn Rd, Belfast (d 1979); 2 s (James MacDermott b 16 Oct 1957, Samuel Clarke b 5 May 1962), 2 da (Anna Louise b 16 April 1956, Rachel Edith b 19 March 1964); *Career* gen mangr Dalgety Agriculture Ltd N Ireland; *Recreations* county pursuits; *Clubs* Ulster Reform (Belfast); *Style—* Samuel Cunningham, Esq, DL; 10 Ballytrim Rd, Killlyleagh, Downpatrick, Co Down BT30 9TH (☎ 0396 828 057)

CUNYNGHAME; *see*: Blair-Cunynghame

CUNYNGHAME, Sir Andrew David Francis; 12 Bt (NS 1702) of Milncraig, Ayrshire; s of Sir (Henry) David St Leger Brooke Selwyn Cunynghame, 11 Bt (d 1978) and Hon Lady (Pamela) Cunynghame, da of late 5 Baron Stanley of Alderley; *b* 25 Dec 1942; *Educ* Eton; *m* 1, 1972, Harriet Ann, da of Charles Thomas Dupont, of Montreal, Canada; 2 da (Ann Marie b 1978, Tania b 1983); m 2, 19 Aug 1989, Isabella, da of late Edward Everett Watts, Jr; *Heir* bro, John Cunynghame; *Career* former chm City Vintagers Ltd; senior ptnr Chipchase Cunynghame; FCA; *Clubs* Brooks's; *Style—* Sir Andrew Cunynghame, Bt; 69 Hillgate Place, London W8 7SS; Chipchase Cunynghame, 54-58 Caledonian Road, London N1 9RN (☎ 071 278 7992)

CUNYNGHAME, John Philip Henry Michael Selwyn; s of late Sir (Henry) David St Leger Brooke Selwyn Cunynghame, 11 Bt; hp of bro, Sir Andrew Cunynghame, 12 Bt; *b* 9 Sept 1944; *Educ* Eton; *m* 1981, Marjatta, da of Martti Markus, of Muhos, Finland; 1 s (Alexander b 1985), 1 da (Niina b 1983); *Career* dir Griersons; *Style—* John Cunynghame Esq; Griersons, 430 High Rd, London NW10 2HA (☎ 081 459 8011, telex : 923 540)

CUNYNGHAME, Hon Lady (Pamela Margaret); 2 da of 5 Baron Stanley of Alderley, KCMG (d 1931); *b* 6 Sept 1909; *m* 7 Oct 1941, Sqdn Ldr Sir (Henry) David St Leger Brooke Selwyn Cunynghame, 11 Bt, RAFVR (d 1978); 3 s; *Career* actress; *Style—* The Hon Lady Cunynghame; 83 Clarendon Street, Leamington Spa, Warwickshire

CUPITT, Rev Don; s of Robert Cupitt, of Wendover, Bucks, and Norah Cupitt; *b* 22 May 1934; *Educ* Charterhouse, Trinity Hall Cambridge (BA), Westcott House Cambridge; *m* 28 Dec 1963, Susan Marianne, da of Frank Cooper Day (d 1941); 1 s (John b 1965), 2 da (Caroline b 1966, Sally b 1970); *Career* Nat Serv 2 Lt Royal Signals 1956-57; curate St Phillip's Salford 1959-62, vice princ Westcott House Cambridge 1962-65; Emmanuel Coll Cambridge: dean 1965-, asst lectr 1968-73, lectr 1973-; Hon DLitt Univ of Bristol 1985; *Books* Christ and the Hiddeness of God (1971), Crisis of Moral Authority (1972), The Leap of Reason (1976), Jesus and the Gospel of God (1979), The Debate about Christ (1979), Taking Leave of God (1980), The Sea of Faith (1984, BBC TV series 1984), Only Human (1985), The Long-Legged Fly (1987), The New Christian Ethics (1988), Radicals and the Future of the Church (1989), The Worlds of Science and Religion (1976), Who Was Jesus (with Peter Armstrong, 1977, BBC TV documentary, 1977) The Nature of Men (1979), Explorations in Theology (1979), The World to Come (1982), Life Lines (1986), Creation out of Nothing (1990); *Recreations* hill-walking; *Style—* The Rev Don Cupitt; 62 Humberstone Road, Cambridge CB4 1JF; Emmanuel College, Cambridge CB2 3AP (☎ 0223 334267)

CURIEL, Raul Morris; s of Isaac Curiel Segura, of Montevideo, Uruguay, and Clara, *née* Margounato; *b* 31 March 1946; *Educ* Colegio Nacional Jose P Varela Scdy Sch Montevideo Uruguay, Univ de la Republica Montevideo Uruguay, Iowa State Univ USA (BArch), Univ of Minnesota USA (MArch); *m* 26 May 1976, Linda, da of Ronald Webb; 2 da (Alessandra Stephanie b 5 May 1985, Melanie Jane b 30 May 1989); *Career* formerly architect Sao Paulo Brazil, ptnr The Fitzroy Robinson Partnership UK 1983- (architectural asst 1978-83); major architectural projects incl: The Standard Chartered Bank, Sedgwick House, HQ for the Moscow Narodny Bank, interiors for London HQ of Drexel Burnham Lambert, a mixed conservation/new office building at 75 King William St, numerous business parks; awarded: AIA merit award, selected design Sch of Architecture ISU 1971, selected design UNESCO's Int Design Competition 1972, Mason's award 1990 and Tiler's and Bricklayer's award 1990 for building at 75 King William St; memb: IAB 1977, RIBA 1979; *Recreations* theatre, reading, swimming, viewing buildings, sketching; *Style—* Raul Curiel, Esq; The Fitzroy Robinson, Partnership, 77 Portland Place, London W1N 4EP (☎ 071 636 8033)

CURL, Prof James Stevens; s of George Stevens Curl (d 1974), of Hillhall, Co Down, and Sarah, *née* McKinney; *b* 26 March 1937; *Educ* Campbell Coll, Queen's Univ, Belfast Coll of Art, Oxford Sch of Architecture, UCL; *m* Jan 1960 (m dis 1986), Eileen Elizabeth, da of John Blackstock (d 1984), of Glendale Park, Belfast; 2 da (Astrid b 1962, Ingrid b 1964); *Career* architect, town planner, antiquarian, architectural historian; architectural ed Survey of London 1970-73, conslt architect to Scottish Ctee for European Architectural Heritage 1975, 1973-75; currently dir of hist architecture Res Unit Dept of Architecture Leicester, author of numerous articles and reviews; Liveryman Worshipful Co of Chartered Architects; FSA, memb RIBA, MRTPI, ARIAS, FSAScot; *Books* The Victorian Celebration of Death (1972), Victorian Architecture (1973), The Erosion of Oxford (1977), A Celebration of Death (1980), The Egyptian Revival (1982), The Life and Work of Henry Roberts 1803-76 (1983), English Architecture (1987), The Londonderry Plantation 1609-1914 (1986), Victorian Architecture (1990), The Art and Architecture of Freemasonry (1991); *Recreations* music, opera, travel, literature, food, wine, poetry, painting; *Clubs* Art Workers Guild; *Style—* Prof James Stevens Curl, FSA; 2 The Coach House, Burley-on-the-Hill, Oakham, Rutland LE15 7SJ (☎ 0572 755880); Department of Architecture, PO Box 143, Leicester LE1 9BH (☎ 0533 551551, ext 7432)

CURLE, Sir John Noel Ormiston; KCVO (1975, CVO 1956), CMG 1966; s of Maj William Sidney Noel Curle, MC (d of wounds 1918), of Melrose; *b* 12 Dec 1915; *Educ* Marlborough, New Coll Oxford; *m* 1, 1940 (m dis 1948), Diana, da of Cdr Ralph H Deane, RN; 1 s, 1 da; m 2, 1948, Pauline, da of Hylton Welford, of Hylton, Co Durham, and wid of Capt David Roberts; 1 step-s (decd), 2 step-da; *Career* served WWII Irish Gds Capt 1941; entered Dip Serv 1939; ambass to: Liberia 1967-70, Guinea 1968-70, the Philippines 1970-72; vice marshal of the Diplomatic Corps 1972-75, ret; dir of protocol Hong Kong 1976-85; advsr for Coronation of the King of Swaziland 1986; *Recreations* skiing; *Clubs* Cavalry and Guards, Beefsteak; *Style—* Sir John Curle, KCVO, CMG; Appletree House, nr Aston-le-Walls, Daventry, Northants NN11 6UG (☎ 029 586 211)

CURLING, David Antony Brian; s of Bryan William Richrd Curling, of Fullerton Manor, nr Andover, Hants, and Elizabeth Mary, da of Maj Sir Eric Bonham, 3 Bt, CVO, JP (d 1937), and sis of Sir Antony Bonham, 4 Bt (UK 1852), DL, *qv*; *b* 27 Jan 1943; *Educ* Eton; *m* 19 Oct 1970, Jennifer, da of John Samuel Schlesinger; 2 da (Charlotte Chloe b 18 April 1972, Antonia Jesscia b 20 March 1974); *Career* asst audit mangr Dixon Wilson Tubbs & Gillet (now Dixon Wilson) 1966 (articled clerk 1962-65), audit mangr Peat Marwick Mitchell Johannesburg 1967-68, asst mangr Corp Fin Dept Union Acceptances Pty Ltd Johannesburg 1970 (accountant to Mutual Fund 1969); Williams de Broe plc (formerly Williams de Broe Hill Chaplin & Co): res analyst 1971, institutional salesman 1972-84, appointed dir 1974, head Foreign Institutional Dept 1985-89, head Private Client and Fund Mgmnt Dept 1989-; dir: William de Broe (Holdings) Ltd, Banque Bruxelles Lambert (Jersey) Ltd, Banque Bruxelles Lambert Trust Co (Jersey) Ltd; *Recreations* sailing, skiing, shooting; *Clubs* Royal Yacht Squadron, Bembridge Sailing (cdre 1985-86); *Style—* David Curling, Esq; Williams De Broe, 6 Broadgate, London EC2M 2RP (☎ 071 588 7511, fax 071 588 1702)

CURLING, David Richard Michael; s of Lt-Col Richard Robinson Curling, DSO (d 1953), and Victoria Margaret (d 1965), 2 da of Sir William Michael Curtis, 4 Bt; *b* 9 May 1923; *Educ* Gordonstoun; *m* 1954, Olive Marigold, da of Douglas Cory-Wright, CBE, and gda of Sir Arthur Cory-Wright, 2 Bt; 1 s, 2 da; *Career* Midshipman RNR Atlantic, Indian Ocean; advertiser; dir J Walter Thompson Co Ltd, High Sheriff of Bucks 1980-81; memb Automobile Assoc Ctee; *Recreations* sailing, shooting; *Clubs* Royal Yacht Squadron, Boodle's, Garrick, Royal Ocean Racing; *Style—* David R M Curling, Esq; The Rosary, Coleshill, nr Amersham, Bucks (☎ 0494 726431)

CURLING, Hon Mrs (Melissa); *née* Llewelyn-Davies; da of Baron Llewelyn-Davies (Life Peer); *b* 1 June 1945; *m* 1974, Christopher Desmond Curling, 2 s of Bryan William Richard Curling, VRD, of Conford Park, Liphook, Hants, and Elizabeth Mary, o da of Sir Eric Henry Bonham, 3 Bt; 1 s (Richard b 1983), 1 da (Rosa b 1979); *Style—* The Hon Mrs Curling; 3 Richmond Crescent, London N1

CURNOCK, Dr David Anthony; s of George Henry Reginald Curnock, of Bramcote Hills, Nottingham, and Vera Marjorie, *née* Bucknell; *b* 17 Aug 1946; *Educ* Chigwell Sch Essex, St John's Coll Cambridge (MA, MB BChir), Charing Cross Hosp Med Sch; *m* 13 Nov 1971, Anne Elizabeth, da of John Ruff, of Holmbury-St-Mary, Surrey; 1 s (Michael b 1982), 3 da (Ruth b 1972, Elizabeth b 1974, Esther b 1980); *Career* lectr in child health Univ of Benin Nigeria 1977-79, sr registrar of paediatrics Derbys Children's Hosp and Nottingham City Hosp 1979-82, conslt paediatrician Nottingham City Hosp 1982-; chm Southwell Diocesan Cncl Family Care; FRCP 1989; *Recreations* printing, railway history; *Style—* Dr David Curnock; 39 Sevenoaks Crescent, Bramcote Hills, Nottingham NG9 3FP; Dept of Paediatrics, City Hospital, Nottingham NG5 1PB (☎ 0602 691169)

CURPHEY, Dr (Robert) Norman; s of John Cubbon Curphey (d 1966), of 7 Auckland Terrace, Parliament St, Ramsey, Isle of Man, and Isabel Margaret, *née* Killip; *b* 18 May 1943; *Educ* Ramsey GS, Charing Cross Hosp Med Sch Univ of London (MB BS); *m* 21 Sept 1968, Jennifer, da of Roy Skudder (d 1982), of 31 Old Church Rd, Playing Place, Truro; 2 da (Juliet b 1972, Sarah b 1973); *Career* sr registrar Leeds Gen Infirmary 1973-76, conslt radiologist Royal Cornwall Hosp Teliske 1976-; memb Ctee

Breast Gp RCR, dir Cornwall Breast Screening Serv, SW Reg radiologist quality assurance mangr of breast screening; MRCS 1966, LRCP 1966, FRCR 1975; *Recreations* golf, gardening; *Style—* Dr Norman Curphey; Chy-an-Gwens, Moresk Road, Truro, Cornwall TR1 1BW (☎ 0872 77908); Mammography Unit, Royal Cornwall Hospital (Treliske), Truro, Cornwall TR1 3LJ (☎ 0872 74242)

CURRAN, Kevin Malcolm; s of Kevin Patrick Curran, of Carolina Farm, Rusape, Zimbabwe, and Sylvia, *née* Ziehl; *b* 7 Sept 1959; *Educ* Marandellas HS; *Career* professional cricketer; Rhodesian Schs 1977, Gloucestershire CCC 1985-90 (awarded county cap 1985), Northamptonshire CCC 1991-; Natal cricket XI SA 1988-89, World XI tour W Indies 1985; Zimbabwe: debut 1980, played in ICC Trophy 1982, played in Prudential World Cup 1983 and 1987, also represented nat Rugby team 1979-81; Rhodesian Army 1978-79, tobacco buyer and grower 1979-84; *Recreations* deepsea and freshwater fishing, squash, tennis, golf; *Style—* Kevin Curran, Esq; c/o Northamptonshire County Cricket Club, County Ground, Wantage Road, Northampton NN1 4TJ (☎ 0604 32917, fax 0604 232855)

CURRAN, Paul; s of Stanley Curran, of 34 Richardson Rd, Thornaby, Cleveland, and Hilda Veronica, *née* Collins; *b* 15 Jan 1961; *m* 28 Oct 1989, Jacquie Ann, da of Henry Gilbert Driscoll, of 66 King James Ave, Cuffley, Herts; *Career* professional cyclist; winner Star trophy 1985-88, Cwlth Games 1986: road race champion, team time trial champion; Br amateur road race champion 1987, Br professional circuit race champion 1989; Professional Cycling Assoc; *Recreations* cold water tank fish; *Clubs* Manchester Wheelers, Stockton Wheelers; *Style—* Paul Curran, Esq; 8 Hurn Walk, Stainsby Hill, Thornaby, Cleveland

CURRAN, Sir Samuel Crowe; s of John Hamilton Curran (d 1959); *b* 23 May 1912; *Educ* Univ of Glasgow (MA, BSc, PhD, DSc), Univ of Cambridge (PhD); *m* 1940, Joan Elizabeth, da of Charles Millington Strothers (d 1975); 4 children; *Career* scientist and educationalist; former chief scientific advsr to Sec of State for Scotland, chief scientist UKAEA 1955-59; princ: Royal Coll of Sci and Technol 1959-64, Univ of Strathclyde 1964-80; visiting prof in energy studies Univ of Glasgow 1980-; FRS, FRSE, FEng; Cdr Order of St Olav Norway 1965, Cdr Polonia Restituta Poland 1970, kt 1970; *Recreations* golf, horology; *Clubs* Caledonian; *Style—* Sir Samuel Curran, FRS, FRSE; 93 Kelvin Court, Glasgow G12 0AH (☎ 071 334 8329)

CURRAN, Stephen William; s of Dr Richard Desmond Curran, CBE (d 1985, Capt RNVR), and Marguerite Claire, *née* Gothard; *b* 9 March 1943; *Educ* Marlborough, Wellington, RMA Sandhurst; *m* 21 June 1969, Anne Beatrice, da of Harry Grumbar, of Rats Castle, Roughway, nr Tonbridge, Kent; 1 s (Charles b 1972), 1 da (Louise b 1979); *Career* Lt 1 The Queens Dragoon Gds 1963-66; Permutit Co Ltd 1966-67, Bowater Co Ltd 1967-71, analyst Grumbar and Sec 1971-75, managing conslt Coopers and Lybrand Assocs 1975-79, project fin mangr NCB Pension Funds 1979-81, dep chief exec Candover Investmts plc 1981-; FCCA 1973; *Recreations* skiing, swimming, tennis, running; *Clubs* Cavalry and Guards, Hurlingham; *Style—* Stephen Curran, Esq; Candover Investments plc, 20 Old Bailey, London EC4M 7LN (☎ 071 489 9848)

CURREY, Hon Mrs (Heather Mary); *née* Drummond of Megginch; 2 da of 15 Baron Strange (d 1982), and Margaret Violet Florence (d 1975), da of Sir Robert William Buchanan Jardine, 2 Bt; was co-heiress with her sisters to the Barony of Strange (*see* Baroness Strange); *b* 9 Nov 1931; *Educ* Hatherop Castle; *m* 11 Aug 1954, Lt-Cdr Andrew Christian Currey, RN, o s of Rear Adm Philip Currey, CB, OBE (d 1979), of Pond Cottage, Newton Valence, Hants; 2 s (Robert James Drummond b 1955, John Andrew Fairbridge b 1959), 1 da (Arabella Mary Christian b 1958); *Clubs* Army and Navy; *Style—* The Hon Mrs Currey; The Mill House, Santon, Isle of Man (☎ 0624 824053)

CURRIE, Prof Sir Alastair Robert; s of John Currie (d 1948), of Isle of Islay, and Maggie Mactaggart (d 1972); *b* 8 Oct 1921; *Educ* Glasgow HS, Univ of Glasgow (BSc, MB); *m* 1949, Jeanne Marion, da of Edward Colin Clarke (d 1954), of Bournemouth; 3 s, 2 da; *Career* pathologist; regius prof of pathology Univ of Aberdeen 1962-72, prof of pathology Univ of Edinburgh 1972-86 (emeritus prof 1986-); Hon DSc: Univ of Birmingham 1983, Univ of Aberdeen 1985; Hon LLD Univ of Glasgow 1987; FRCP (London, Edinburgh, Glasgow), FRCSE, FRCPath, FRSE; kt 1979; *Clubs* New (Edinburgh); *Style—* Prof Sir Alastair Currie; 42 Murrayfield Ave, Edinburgh EH12 6AY (☎ 031 337 3100); Grianan, Strathlachlan, Argyll (☎ 036 986 769)

CURRIE, Andrew Buchanan; s of Buchanan Currie, of 8 Bollards Lane, Sutton Bonington, Loughborough, Leics LE12 5PA, and Wilma Drysdale, *née* Livingston; *b* 16 April 1954; *Educ* Loughborough GS, Univ of Birmingham (BA); *Career* employment res exec Inst of Dirs 1983-86, sr account exec Profile Public Relations 1986-88, head of res Shopping Hours Reform Cncl 1988-; ed Making Sense of Shopping 1988-; *Recreations* opera, reading, writing; *Style—* Andrew Currie, Esq; 115 Northside, Clapham Common, London SW4 9SW; The Shopping Hours Reform Council, 36 Broadway, London SW1H 0BH (☎ 071 233 0366, fax 071 222 5258)

CURRIE, Brian Murdoch; s of William Murdoch Currie (d 1984), and Dorothy, *née* Holloway; *b* 20 Dec 1934; *Educ* Blundells, Oriel Coll Oxford (MA); *m* 21 Oct 1961, Patricia Maria, da of Capt Frederick Eaton-Farr (d 1945); 3 s (Murdoch b 1964, Lachlan b 1967, Gregor b 1975), 1 da (Lucinda b 1966); *Career* Subaltern BAOR RTR 1957-59; CA 1962; ptnr Arthur Andersen & Co 1970, fin memb HMSO Bd 1972-74, managing ptnr Arthur Andersen and Co London 1977-82; inspr Dept of Trade 1978-81, memb Restrictive Practices Ct, memb Cncl and chm Parly and Law Ctee Inst of CAs, chm Public Sector Liaison Gp of Accounting Standards Ctee 1984-86; tstee Oriel Coll Devpt Tst 1980, fell Br Prod and Inventory Control Soc (memb Nat Cncl 1970-73); FIMC; *Recreations* natural history; *Clubs* Reform; *Style—* Brian Currie, Esq; Westbrook House, Bampton, Devon EX16 9HU (☎ 0398 331418)

CURRIE, Prof David Anthony; s of Kennedy Moir Currie (d 1972), of London, and Marjorie, *née* Thompson; *b* 9 Dec 1946; *Educ* Battersea GS, Univ of Manchester (BSc), Univ of Birmingham (M Soc Sci), Univ of London (PhD); *m* 9 July 1975 (m dis), Shaziye, da of Hussein Gazioglu, of Nicosia, Cyprus; 2 s (James Mehmet b 9 April 1978, Timothy Timur b 8 may 1982); *Career* Hoare and Govett Co 1971- 72, Econ Models 1972; prof of econs QMC London 1981-88 (lectr 1972-79, reader 1979-81), prof of econs dean of res and dir of Centre for Econs Forecasting London Business Sch 1988-; memb Royal Econ Soc; *Books* Advances in Monetary Economics (ed, 1985), The Operation and Regulation of Financial Markets (ed, 1986), Macroeconomic Interactions between North and South (ed, 1988), Macroeconomic Policies in an Interdependent World (ed, 1989); *Recreations* music, literature, running, swimming; *Clubs* Reform; *Style—* Prof David Currie; London Business School, Sussex Place, Regents Park, London NW1 4SA (☎ 071 262 5050, telex 27461 LONBISKOL G, fax 071 724 6069)

CURRIE, Sir Donald Scott; 7 Bt (UK 1947); s of George Donald Currie (d 1980), and Janet, *née* Scott; suc unc, Sir Alick Bradley Currie, 6 Bt (d 1987); *b* 16 Jan 1930; *m* 1, 1948 (m dis 1951), Charlotte, da of Charles Johnstone, of Mesa, Arizona, USA; 1 s, 2 da (twins); m 2, 30 April 1952, Barbara Lee, da of A P Garnier, of California; 1 s, 2 da; *Heir* s, Donald Mark Currie b 1949; *Career* US Dept of the Interior; US Nat Park Serv; *Style—* Sir Donald Currie, Bt

CURRIE, Edwina; MP (C) S Derbyshire 1983-; *b* 13 Oct 1946; *Educ* Liverpool Inst, St Anne's Coll Oxford (MA), LSE (MSc); *m* 1972, Raymond Frank Currie; 2 da; *Career* teacher and lectr 1972-81, head Dept of Business Studies Bromsgrove Sch 1978-81; city cncllr Birmingham 1975-86; memb: Birmingham AHA 1975-82, Birmingham Community Rels Cncl 1979-83; chm: Birmingham Social Servs Ctee 1979-80, Central Birmingham Health Authy 1981-83, Housing Ctee 1982-83; memb Select Ctee on Social Servs 1983-86, vice pres Fedn Cons Students 1984-85, memb Gen Advsy Cncl BBC 1985-86, Parly private sec to Keith Joseph Sec of State for Educn 1986, Parly under sec DHSS, Min for Womens Health 1986-88; columnist Today Newspaper 1990-; Assoc of Speakers Clubs Speaker of the Year 1990; *Books* Life Lines (1989), What Women Want (1990); numerous articles and short stories; *Recreations* family, writing, domestic arts; *Clubs* Swadlincote Cons (Derbys); *Style—* Mrs Edwina Currie, MP; House of Commons, London SW1A OAA

CURRIE, Ian Hamilton; s of John Currie (d 1984), and Vera Matilda Currie, *née* Lea; *b* 9 March 1948; *Educ* Portsmouth Northern GS; *m* 22 Feb 1972, Catherine Helen, da of Ernest William Fish (d 1983); 2 da (Victoria Catherine b 1979, Jacqueline Neoma b 1983); *Career* fin dir Gieves Gp plc, dir Bookpoint Ltd; chm: Roundabout Garages Ltd, Pullinger Interiors and Furnishings Ltd, Merlin Publishing Ltd; FCA (England and Wales) 1970; *Recreations* cruiser sailing; *Clubs* Portchester Sailing (vice cdre); *Style—* Ian Currie, Esq, FCA; 2 Church Rd, Hayling Island, Hants (☎ 0705 462966, fax 0705 461240, car 0836 270166)

CURRIE, James McGill; s of late David Currie, of Kilmarnock (Scotland), and Mary, *née* Smith; *b* 17 Nov 1941; *Educ* St Joseph's Sch Kilmarnock, Blairs Coll Aberdeen, Royal Scots Coll, Valladolid (Spain), Univ of Glasgow (MA); *m* 27 June 1968, Evelyn Barbara, da of Alexander Malcolm Macintyre, of Glasgow; 1 s (Alister John b 1971), 1 da (Jennifer b 1973); *Career* civil servant; asst princ Scot Home and Health Dept 1968-72, Scot Educn Dept 1972-75; asst sec: Tport Policy 1977-80, Industl Devpt 1981-82; cnsllr for Social Affrs and Tport at UK Perm Representation to EEC in Brussels 1982-86, dir Euro Regnl Devpt Fund in Regnl Policy Directorate of Euro Cmmn (Brussels) 1987-89, chef de cabinet to Sir Leon Brittan 1989-; *Recreations* guitar, tennis, good food; *Style—* James M Currie, Esq; EEC Commission, 200 Rue De La Loi, 1040 Brussels, Belgium (☎ 010 322 236 0125)

CURRIE, Joseph Austin; s of John Currie (d 1979), of Mullaghmarget, Dungannon, Co Tyrone, and Mary Currie, *née* O'Donnell (d 1984); *b* 11 Oct 1939; *Educ* Edendork PES; St Patrick's Acad, Dungannon; Queen's Univ Belfast (BA); *m* 13 Jan 1968, Annita, *née* Lynch; 2 s (Dualta b 1971, Austin b 1974), 3 da (Estelle b 1968, Emer b 1979, Caitriona b 1970); *Career* lectr, conslt, writer, broadcaster; MP N Ireland 1964-72, memb N Ireland Assembly 1973-75, min of Housing Local Govt and Planning 1974; memb: NI Constitutional Convention 1975-76, NI Assembly 1980-84; elected Dail Eireann for Dublin West 1989, appointed to Anglo-Irish Inter Parly Gp 1989, Irish presidential candidate 1990; *Recreations* golf, snooker, Gaelic football; *Style—* J A Currie, Esq; 35 Tullycullion Rd, Tullydraw, Donaghmore, Dungannon, Co Tyrone

CURRIE, Kenneth Alexander (Ken); s of Alexander Currie, of Barrhead, and Georgina, *née* Ruddie; *b* 9 March 1960; *Educ* Barrhead HS, John Nielson Sch Paisley, Paisley Coll of Technol, Glasgow Sch of Art (Elizabeth Greenshields Fnd scholar, Cargill scholar, BA, Dip of Postgrad Studies, Newberry medal); *Career* artist; solo exhibitions: Art and Social Commitment (with Keith Ross, Glasgow Arts Centre) 1982, New Work from Glasgow (Arnolfini, Bristol) 1986, Third Eye Centre Glasgfow 1988, Raals Galerie Berlin 1988, The Story of Glasgow (Kelvingrove Museum, Galsgow) 1990, Raals Gallery London 1991; gp exhibitions incl: New Image Glasgow (Third Eye Centre and tour) 1985-86, New Art New World (Christie's London, for Save the Children Fund) 1986, A Cabinet of Drawing (Gimpels Fils London) 1986, The Vigourous Imagination (Scottish Nat Gallery of Modern Art) 1987, Art History (Hayward Gallery) 1987, Obsessions (Raals Gallery) 1987, The Lion Rampant: New Scottish Paintings & Photography (Artspace, San Francisco) 1988-89, Scottish Art since 1900 (Scottish Nat Gallery of Modern Art and Barbican Art Gallery) 1989-90, Metamorphosis (Raals Gallery London) 1989-90, Glasgow's Great British Art Exhibition (Art Gallery and Museum Kelvingrove) 1990, Mischaire le Carte Immague Speculare (Gian Ferrari Arte Contemporanea) 1990-91; works in public collections of: Contemporary Arts Sco London, Scottish Arts Cncl Edinburgh, Br Cncl London, Aberdeen Art Gallery, Nottingham Castle Museum, City of Manchester Art Gallery, Glasgow Museums and art galleries; *Style—* Ken Currie, Esq; Raab Gallery, 6 Vauxhall Bridge Rd, London (☎ 071 828 2588, fax 071 976 5041)

CURRIE, Raymond Frank (Ray); s of William Murdoch Currie (d 1984), and Dorothy, *née* Holloway, of South Molton, Devon; *b* 11 May 1945; *Educ* Blundell's The Loomis Sch Windsor Connecticut, Corpus Christi Coll Cambridge (exhibitioner, BA); *m* 1 July 1972, Edwina, da of Simon Cohen; 2 da (Deborah Josephine b 30 Oct 1974, Susannah Elizabeth b 19 May 1977); *Career* Arthur Andersen & Co: articled clerk 1967-70, qualified 1970, London 1970-73, fndr Birmingham practice 1973-79, dir of training 1979-; memb Bd of Accreditation of Educn Courses CCAB 1985-; ICAEW: chm Dist Training Bd 1986-90, memb Educ and Training Directorate 1989-, chm Examination Devpt Ctee 1991-; memb Business & Mgmnt Studies Ctee CNAA 1986-; FCA 1974 (ACA 1970), MITD 1983, MIPM 1987; *Recreations* all sports - playing some slowly following all enthusiastically, reading, cinema; *Clubs* Reform, MCC, Swadlincote Conservative; *Style—* Ray Currie, Esq; The Tower House, Findern, Derby DE6 6AJ; Flat 1 EE, 1 Carlisle Place, London SW1P 1NP (☎ 071 828 6057); Arthur Andersen & Co, 1 Surrey St, London WC2R 2PS

CURRIE, Prof Ronald Ian; CBE (1977); s of Ronald Wavell Currie, and Elizabeth, *née* Paterson; *b* 10 Oct 1928; *Educ* Univ of Glasgow (BSc), Univ of Copenhagen; *m* 10 July 1956, Cecilia, da of William A de Garis, of Le Grand Douit, St Saviours, Guernsey; 1 s (Crawford b 1960), 1 da (Susan b 1957); *Career* RN Scientific Serv 1949, William Scoresby Expedition to S Atlantic Ocean 1950, Discovery II Expedition to Antarctic 1951; head of Biology Dept Nat Inst of Oceanography 1961 (worked in N Atlantic 1953-62), chm biological planning Int Indian Ocean Expedition 1960, sec and dir Scottish Marine Biology Assoc 1966-87, professorial fell Univ of Edinburgh 1988-90; hon sec Challenger Soc 1956-88, FRSE 1969, FIBiol 1967; *Books* The Benguela Current (1960), Antarctic Oceanography (1968); *Recreations* gardening, cooking, oil painting; *Clubs* Royal Overseas, Trout; *Style—* Prof Ronald Currie, CBE, FRSE; Kilmore House, Kilmore by Oban, Argyll PA34 4XT (☎ 063 177 248)

CURRIE-CATHEY, (Vernon Howard) Peter; s of Edward Stanley Currie-Cathey, and Eileen Peggy, *née* Fryer; *b* 21 Aug 1941; *Educ* Sloane GS; *m* 2 Feb 1963, Jean Sylvia, *née* Rice; 2 s (James Vernon b 24 April 1967, Stuart Alex b 25 Sept 1969); *Career* ptnr Nigel Rose & Ptnrs (chartered quantity surveyors); Freeman City of London, memb Worshipful Co of Arbitrators; FRICS 1964, FCIArb 1973; *Recreations* badminton; *Style—* Peter Currie-Cathey, Esq; 6 Broad St, Wokingham, Berks RG11 1AB (☎ 0734 774 702, fax 0734 774 829)

CURRIE OF BALILONE, William McMurdo; Feudal Baron of Balilone; s of John Currie of Balilone (d 1943), and Helen Dick, *née* McMurdo (d 1955); *b* 28 Nov 1916; *Educ* Hyndland Sch, Royal Coll of Sci and Technol (BSc); *m* 23 Oct 1954, Irene Frances, da of Robert Hugh Semple Brierton (d 1970); *Career* WWII Br Special Servs 1939-45; conslt Br Cellophane Ltd 1951-53, textile conslt to Br jute trade 1953-68; cultural and diplomatic advsr to US Navy, 14 Submarine Sqdn, Holy Loch, Scotland, ambassador-at-large for free Polish govt in exile; memb Royal Archaeological Inst;

Order of Virtuti Militari (Poland) 1943, Cross of Valour (Poland) 1944, Cdr (with star) Order of Polonia Restituta 1981, Polish Cross of Merit with Crossed Swords 1945, Belgian Médaille d'Honneur (Silver) 1944, Croix Alliés 1946, Companion Mil Order of the Loyal Legion of USA 1977, awarded right to wear Gold Dolphins of US submarine force 1977; GCSMOM 1983, FSAS 1953; *Books* A History of the Curries of Cowal (1973), With Sword and Harp (1977), An Historical Description of Loch Lomond and District (1979); *Recreations* music, reading, fishing, hill-walking; *Clubs* Garrick, Glasgow Highland Officers'; *Style*— The Much Honoured Baron Currie of Balilone; 78 Highburgh Road, Glasgow G12 9EN (☎ 041 339 8901)

CURRY, David Maurice; MP Skipton and Ripon (Con) 1987, MEP (EDG) NE Essex 1979-89; s of Thomas Harold Curry and Florence Joan, *née* Tyerman; *b* 13 June 1944; *Educ* Ripon GS, CCC Oxford, Harvard (Kennedy Sch of Govt on Kennedy Scholarship); *m* 1971, Anne Helene Maud Roullet; 1 s, 2 da; *Career* reporter: Newcastle Journal 1967-70, Financial Times (trade ed, international companies ed, Brussels correspondent, Paris correspondent, European news ed) 1970-79; sec Anglo-American Press Assoc of Paris 1978-79; fndr Paris Cons Assoc 1977; chm Agric Ctee 1982-84 (yst ctee chm in European Parl's history); Conservative spokesman Budget Ctee 1984-; Rapporteur Gen EEC Budget 1987, Parly sec Miny of Agric Fish and Food 1989-; *Books* The Food War: the EEC-US Conflict in Food Trade (1982); *Recreations* digging, wind-surfing; *Style*— David Curry, Esq, MP MEP; Newland End, Arkesden, Essex CB11 4HF (☎ (079 985) 368); Constituency office: 19 Otley St, Skipton, N Yorks BD19 1DY (☎ 0756 792092)

CURRY, Jilly Mary; d of Thomas Peter Ellison Curry, QC, of Hurlands, Dunsfold, Surrey GU8 4NP, and Pamela Joyce, *née* Holmes; *b* 29 Nov 1961; *Educ* Royal Naval Sch Haslemere, Queen Anne's Sch Caversham; *m* 1990, Robin Wallace, skier; *Career* freestyle skier; memb of freestyle ski team 1984, first Br girl to win a world cup skiing event, Gold medal for the combined freestyle event at World Cup La Clusaz France 1990; *Recreations* tennis, squash, water-skiing, trampolining, foreign languages; *Style*— Miss Jilly Curry; Garden Flat, 61 Inverness Terrace, London W2 (☎ 071 243 8222)

CURRY, John Arthur Hugh; s of Col Alfred Curry (d 1975); *b* 7 June 1938; *Educ* KCS Wimbledon, St Edmund Hall Oxford (MA), Harvard Graduate Sch of Business Admin (MBA); *m* 1962, Anne Rosemary, *née* Lewis; 3 s, 1 da; *Career* chm ACAL plc, non-exec dir Unitech plc; FCA; *Recreations* tennis, rugby, travel; *Clubs* All England Lawn Tennis and Croquet (chm), Int Lawn Tennis Club of GB; *Style*— John Curry, Esq; New Place, The Ridges, Finchampstead, Berks

CURRY, QC (1973) (Thomas) Peter Ellison; s of Maj FRP Curry, RA (d 1955), and Sybil, *née* Woods; *b* 22 July 1921; *Educ* Tonbridge, Oriel Coll Oxford (MA); *m* 30 March 1950, Pamela Joyce, da of Gp Capt AJ Holmes, AFC (d 1950); 2 s (Guy b 1952, Iain b 1953), 2 da (Fleur b 1956, Jilly b 1959, *qv*); *Career* WWII, enlisted 1939, offr Cadet 1940, OCTU Bangalore and Deolali India 1941; 1941-44: 1 Indian Field Regt, Indian Artillery (India, North West Frontier, Burma, Assam); air training course Peshawar 1944, Capt Air Force Devpt Centre Amesbury 1944, air directorate War Office GSO 3 1945-46; called to Bar Middle Temple 1953, QC 1966 (resigned 1967), slr Freshfields 1967, returned to Bar 1970, QC 1973, pres Aircraft and Shipbuilding Industries Arbitration Tribunal 1978-80; bencher Middle Temple 1979; running Olympic Games 1948, Br 3000m steeplechase champion 1948, winner Oxford and Cambridge Cross Country 1947 and 1948; squash: represented Army, Oxford Univ, Sussex; asst scoutmaster Stepney Sea Scouts 1946; chm: Walston House Boys and Girls Club 1951, Cobham Cons Assoc 1958; vice chm Barristers Benevolent Assoc 1990- (treas 1964-71 and 1984-90), chm Chancery Bar Assoc 1980-85, trustee Stable Lads Welfare Tst 1986-; *Recreations* lawn tennis, gardening, farming; *Clubs* Army & Navy; *Style*— Peter Curry, Esq, QC; Hurlands, Dunsfold, Surrey (☎ 356 727 5730); 5 Victoria Grove Mews, London W8; 4 Stone Buildings, Lincolns Inn, London WC2 (☎ 071 242 5524, fax 071 831 9152/048 649 356, telex 892 2300)

CURRY, Stephen Robert; s of Stanley Curry (d 1964), of Clitheroe, Lancashire, and Norah, *née* Rowlinson; *b* 17 Oct 1942; *Educ* Clitheroe Royal GS, Manchester Coll of Commerce (journalism course); *m* Angela, *née* Blackshaw; 1 s (Michael b 27 Jan 1970); *Career* journalist; The Blackburn Times 1959-62, Lancashire Evening Post 1963, sports reporter Head Office United Newspapers London 1964-66, chief football writer Daily Express 1980- (football reporter 1966-80); *Style*— Stephen Curry, Esq; Daily Express, Ludgate House, 245 Blackfriars Rd, London SE1 9UX (☎ 071 928 8000/071 922 7141, car 0831 237 057)

CURRY-TOWNELEY-O'HAGAN, Hon Mrs (Helen Frances Alice Towneley); *née* O'Hagan; da of 3 Baron O'Hagan (d 1961); *b* 3 March 1912; *m* 23 May 1940, Capt Ian Desmond Curry, RA, who assumed by deed poll 1942 the surname of Curry-Towneley-O'Hagan (d 3 July 1969), 2 s of Thomas David Curry, of Upminster, Essex; 1 s; *Style*— The Hon Mrs Curry-Towneley-O'Hagan; 24 Burgh St, Islington, N1

CURTEIS, Ian Bayley; s of John Richard Jones, of Lydd, Kent, and late Edith Marion Pomfret Cook, *née* Bayley; *b* 1 May 1935; *Educ* Slough GS, Univ of London; *m* 1, 8 July 1964 (m dis 1985), Mrs Joan MacDonald; 2 s (Tobit b 1966, Mikol b 1968); m 2, 12 April 1985, Joanna (aka the novelist Joanna Trollope), da of AGC Trollope, of Overton, Hants; 2 step da (Louise b 1969, Antonia b 1972); *Career* TV playwright, dir, actor; and BBC TV script reader 1956-63, staff dir drama BBC and ATV; dir plays by: John Betjeman, John Hopkins, William Trevor and others 1963-67; chm Ctee on Censorship Writers Guild of GB 1981-85; tv plays incl: Beethoven, Sir Alexander Fleming (BBC entry at Prague Festival 1973), Mr Rolls and Mr Royce, Long Voyage out of War (trilogy), The Folly, The Haunting, Second Time Round, A Distinct Chill, The Portland Millions, Philby, Burgess and Maclean (Br entry Monte Carlo Festival 1978, BAFTA nomination Best Play of the Year), Hess, The Atom Spies, Churchill and the Generals (Grand Prize for Best Programme of 1981 New York Int Film and TV Festival and BAFTA nomination Best Play of the Year), Suez 1956 (BAFTA Nomination Best Play of the Year), Miss Morison's Ghosts (British entry Monte Carlo Festival), BB and Lord D, The Mitford Girls; screenplays: Andre Malraux's La condition Humaine (1982), Lost Empires (adapted from J B Priestley), Graham Green's The Man Within (TV), The Nightmare Years (TV 1989), The Zimmerman Telegram (1990), Mikhail and Raisa (1990); published plays: A Personal Affair, Long Voyage out of War (1971), Churchill and the Generals (1979), Suez 1956 (1980), The Falklands Pay (1987); FRSA 1984; *Recreations* avoiding television; *Clubs* Garrick, Beefsteak; *Style*— Ian Curteis, Esq; The Mill House, Coln St Aldwyns, Cirencester, Gloucestershire (fax 028 575 551)

CURTIN, William George; s of Charles Martin Curtin (d 1970), and Lily, *née* Feasey; *b* 17 Sept 1921; *Educ* Buckingham Gate Central Sch, Univ of Liverpool (MEng), UMIST (PhD); *m* Ella Alice, da of William Gentis; 1 da (Nicola Jane b 9 Aug 1954); *Career* Cubbitts Contractors: office boy and jr draughtsman 1934-35, draughtsman 1935-36, detailer 1936-38, site engr 1938-44; design engr Sir Frederick Snow & Ptnrs 1944-48, engr London CC 1948-49, lectr Brixton Sch of Building 1949-51, sr lectr Liverpool Polytechnic 1951-60, conslt Curtins Consulting Engineers plc 1981- (sr ptnr 1960-81); Henry Adams Bronze medal 1980 and 1981, Oscar Faber Dip 1980, Civil Engrg Innovation award 1981; FIStructE 1958, memb Assoc of Consulting Engrs 1959, FICE 1978, FEng 1989; *Books* Structual Masonry Designers Manual, Structural Masonry Detailing, Design of Reinforced and Prestressed Masonry; *Recreations* mountaineering (rock climbing, skiing, hill walking), reading, gardening; *Style*— William G Curtin, Esq; Curtins Consulting Engineers plc, 19 Rodney St, Liverpool L1 9EQ (☎ 051 709 9596, fax 051 708 9762)

CURTIS, Prof Adam Sebastian Genevieve; s of Herbert Lewis Curtis, DSM (d 1974) of 24 Lingfield Rd, London SW19, and Nora, *née* Stevens (d 1954); *b* 3 Jan 1934; *Educ* Aldenham, King's Coll Cambridge (BA, MA), Univ of Edinburgh (PhD); *m* 3 May 1958, Ann, da of William Park, of 33 Castle Terr, Berwick upon Tween; 2 da (Penelope Jane b 1961, Susanna Clare b 1984); *Career* lectr in zoology UCL 1962-67 (hon res asst Dept of Anatomy 1957-62), prof of cell biology Univ of Glasgow 1967-; pres Scot Sub-Aqua Club 1972-75, memb RSE 1983-86, vice pres Soc for Experimental Biology 1988-; FIBiol 1968, FRSE 1969; *Books* The Cell Surface (1967), Cell-cell Recognition (ed, 1978); *Recreations* gardening, sports diving, making mosaics; *Style*— Prof Adam Curtis; 2 Kirlee Circus, Glasgow G12 0WT (☎ 041 339 2152); Dept of Cell Biology, University of Glasgow, Glasgow G12 8QQ (☎ 041 330 5147, fax 041 330 4501)

CURTIS, Andrew Grant; s of Brigadier Francis Cockburn Curtis (d 1986), and Dorothy Joan Curtis, *née* Grant (d 1990); *b* 1 Aug 1939; *Educ* Wellington, Trinity Hall Cambridge (MA); *m* 17 Oct 1964, Theresa Loraine, da of Theodore D Shephard; 1 s (Nicholas Simon b 1966), 2 da (Johanna Loraine b 1969, Jessica Martha b 1972); *Career* exec local dir Barclays Bank plc: Bristol 1969, Darlington 1973, Manchester 1978 (retail dir 1989); *Recreations* sailing, squash, tennis; *Clubs* Orford Sailing; *Style*— Andrew G Curtis, Esq; Tanyard Farm, Pickmere, Knutsford, Cheshire WA16 0JP (☎ 0565 893219); Barclays Bank plc, Regional Office, 51 Mosley St, Manchester M60 2AU (☎ 061 228 3322)

CURTIS, Anthony Samuel; s of Emanuel Curtis (d 1979), of London, and Eileen, *née* Freedman; *b* 12 March 1926; *Educ* Midhurst GS, Merton Coll Oxford (BA, MA); *m* 3 Oct 1960, Sarah, da of Dr Carl Myers; 3 s (Job b 1961, Charles b 1963, Quentin b 1965); *Career* served RAF 1945-48; lectr Br Inst of Sorbonne 1950-51, freelance journalist and critic (The Times, New Statesman, BBC) 1952-55, on staff Times Educnl Supplement (asst ed 1955-58), Harkness fell in journalism at Yale and elsewhere USA 1958-59, literary ed Sunday Telegraph 1960; Financial Times: arts and literary ed 1970-72, literary ed 1972-89, literary corr and critic 1989-; numerous broadcasts on Radio 3 and 4, author of features and radio plays, reg appearances on Critics Forum; Br Cncl lectr France & India; memb Soc of Authors (tstee pension fund), treas Royal Lit Fund; FRSA (1990); *Publications include* The Pattern of Maugham (1974), Somerset Maugham (biography, 1977), The Rise and Fall of the Matiné Idol (ed, 1977), The Critical Heritage: Somerset Maugham (ed with John Whitehead, 1987), The Nonesuch Storytellers: Somerset Maughan (ed and intro, 1990); *Recreations* correspondence chess, backgammon, draughts; *Clubs* Garrick, Travellers', Beefsteak; *Style*— Anthony Curtis, Esq; The Financial Times, Number One, Southwark Bridge, London SE1 9HL (☎ 071 873 3000, fax 071 236 9764)

CURTIS, Prof Charles David; s of Flt-Lt Charles Frederick Curtis, and Kate Margaret, *née* Jackson (d 1988); *b* 11 Nov 1939; *Educ* High Storrs GS Sheffield, Imperial Coll London, Univ of Sheffield (BSc, PhD); *m* 24 Nov 1963, Diana Joy, da of Lionel Sidney Saxty (d 1990), of Holmfirth Grove, Sheffield; 2 da (Sarah b 1965, Kate b 1968); *Career* Univ of Sheffield 1965-88 (lectr, reader, prof), visiting prof UCLA 1970-71, industl fell Marathon Oil Co Denver 1973, CSPG visiting prof Univ of Calgary 1981, visiting prof Tongji Univ Shanghai China 1984, res assoc Br Petroleum Res Centre 1987-88, conslt BP Research International 1988-, head of Dept Univ of Manchester 1989 (prof 1988-89); various pubns in jls; memb: Scientific and Educn Ctees Royal Soc, Natural Environment Res Cncl, Cncl for Nat Academic Awards, Geological Socs; FGS 1977; *Recreations* mountaineering, gardening, writing; *Style*— Prof Charles Curtis; Townhead Cottage, Edale Road, Hope S30 2RF; Department of Geology, University of Manchester, Oxford Rd, Manchester M13 9PL (☎ 061 275 3802)

CURTIS, Cllr Christopher Irvin (Chris); s of Harold George Curtis, of Norwich, and Gwendoline Lillian, *née* Ireland; *b* 24 Feb 1948; *Educ* Thorpe GS, Thorpe St Andrews Norwich; *m* 1, 30 April 1968 (m dis 1979), Wendy Diane, *née* Simmonds; 2 s (Simon b 1968, Patrick b 1970); m 2, 18 Aug 1979 (m dis 1991), Janet Elizabeth, *née* Gregory; *Career* order clerk Jarrold & Sons Ltd Norwich 1969-73, estimator and cost exec Creaseys of Hertford 1973-74, political agent to John Pardoe MP 1974, print estimator, Chapel River Press Andover 1975-77, sr prodn controller Macmillan Publishers Basingstoke 1977-83, self-employed print prodn conslt trg as CIC Print Tadley 1984-88, in partnership with Valerie A Shepard Prima Partnership (ed servs and print prodn conslt) 1988-; memb Basingstoke and Deane Borough Cncl 1990-; Hants CC: memb 1981-89, leader Lib/Alliance/Social and Lib Democrat Gp 1983-89; chm Tadley Town Cncl 1984-86 and 1987- (memb 1983); memb: ACC 1985-89, Local Govt Int Bureau Policy Bd 1988-89, Rep Body Cmmn Local Admin England (local Ombudsman); sch govr: Burnham Copse Co Infant and Jr Schs 1981-88, Hurst Community Sch 1985-90, Tadley Co Prim Sch 1988-; Bishopswood Infant Sch 1990-; Tadley and Dist Community Assoc 1982-(chm 1986 and 1987, pres 1988-); Tadley and Dist Citizens Advice Bureau Mgmnt Ctee 1985-; *Recreations* reading, walking; *Style*— Cllr Chris Curtis; 51 Stephens Rd, Tadley, Basingstoke, Hampshire RG26 6RS (☎ 0734 815682, fax 0734 816392)

CURTIS, Deborah; da of Jeremy Curtis, and Dianne Curtis; *b* 24 May 1965; *Educ* King Alfred Sch, Brooklande Coll; *Career* dental technician; Westminster Hosp (under Mrs Karen Horton), travelled and worked in Middle East, various laboratories London, fndr prosthetics dental laboratory Harley St (specialist in balanced articulations for prosthetic work); *Recreations* competitive show jumping on Our Sir Lancelot; *Style*— Miss Deborah Curtis; Dentalform Laboratory, 118 Harley Street, London W1N 1AG (☎ 071 224 1384)

CURTIS, Maj Edward Philip; s of late Maj Gerald Edward Curtis, of Cwmbach Lodge, Glasbury-on-Wye, via Hereford; hp of kinsman, Sir William Curtis, 7 Bt; *b* 25 June 1940; *Educ* Bradfield, RMA Sandhurst; *m* 1978, Catherine Mary, da of Henry Armstrong, of Christchurch, NZ; 2 s (George b 1980, Patrick b 1986), 2 da (Henrietta, Clementine); *Career* Maj 16/5 The Queen's Royal Lancers, served Germany BAOR, Far E, Mid E, UK; Staff Offr 7 Armd Bde 1968-70, Adj 16/5 Lancers 1971, Sqn Ldr 16/5 Lancers 1971-73, Co Cdr RMA Sandhurst 1973-75, Staff Offr HQ 38 Gp RAF 1976-77, ret 1977; stockbroker Harris Allday Lea and Brooks; *Recreations* shooting, fishing, cricket, squash, philately, bridge; *Clubs* MCC, Free Foresters, I Zingari, Salmon and Trout; *Style*— Maj Edward Curtis; Lower Court, Bitterley, Ludlow, Shropshire SY8 3HP (☎ 0584 891052, office: 0584 872391)

CURTIS, Most Rev (Ernest) Edwin; CBE (1976); s of Ernest John Curtis (d 1937), of Stalbridge, Dorset, and Zoe, *née* Tite (d 1927); *b* 24 Dec 1906; *Educ* Foster's Sch Sherborne, Univ of London, Royal Coll of Science (BSc, Dip Ed), Wells Theol Coll; *m* 1, 24 Dec 1937, Dorothy Anne (d 1965), da of John Hill; 1 s (Robert b 17 April 1940), 1 da (Audrey (Mrs Buckingham) b 16 Dec 1938); m 2, 7 Feb 1970, Evelyn Mary, da of Herbert Josling; *Career* sr maths master Lindisfarne Coll Westcliff-on-Sea 1928-31, civil chaplain and princ St Paul's Theol Coll Mauritius 1937-45; vicar: All Saints Portsea 1947-55, St John's Lockheath 1955-66; rural dean Alverstoke Portsmouth 1965-66; bishop: Mauritius and Seychelles 1966-73, Mauritius 1973-76; archbishop of Anglican

Province of Indian Ocean 1973-76; *Style—* The Most Rev Archbishop Edwin Curtis, CBE; 5 Elizabeth Gardens, Havenstreet, Ryde, Isle of Wight PO33 4DU (☎ 0983 883049)

CURTIS, Lady; Joan Margaret; *née* Nicholson; o da of Reginald Nicholson, TD, JP (d 1952), and Lady Laura Margaret (d 1959), yr da of 9 Earl Waldegrave; *b* 19 May 1912; *m* 7 July 1934, Sir Peter Curtis, 6 Bt (d 1976); 1 s, 2 da; *Style—* Lady Curtis; Oak Lodge, Bank St, Bishops Waltham, Hants

CURTIS, John Gilbert; s of late Col A G Curtis; *b* 2 Oct 1932; *Educ* Charterhouse, Worcester Coll Oxford; *m* 1963, Susan Judith, *née* Whitefield; 2 s; *Career* Lt Royal Green Jackets; dir Matheson and Co Ltd 1967-; *Clubs* Gresham, Oriental; *Style—* John Curtis, Esq; Clayhurst, Odiham, Hants; Matheson and Co Ltd, 3 Lombard St, London EC3V 9AQ (☎ 071 528 4000)

CURTIS, Ken E; s of James Curtis (d 1932), and Rosina, *née* Hartley-Beaton (d 1975); *b* 8 May 1919; *Educ* Eldon Sch, Hornsey Sch of Art, Instituto del Arte Florence Italy; *m* 21 June 1947, Anne, da of James Scully (d 1966); 1 s (Glenn b 14 Feb 1953), 1 da (Kim b 6 Oct 1956); *Career* WWII RCSTA Royal Mountain Regt and Med Regts 1939-46 (despatches Ita 1944); advertising agent Dorland Advertising (subsid) 1933-39, gen mangr Scientific Publicity 1946-48, md Skingle of the Strand and We Design It Ltd 1948-68; dir: (jt) SF Partners 1968-80, Leberl Advertising 1987-; account dir Smedley McAlpine 1980-87; memb RA Comrades Assoc; Freeman City of London 1961, Liveryman Worshipful Co of Carmen 1961; MIPA; Polish Order of Merit (War Serv Polish Army in Italy 1944); *Recreations* writing, wildlife; *Clubs* City Livery, World Trade Centre; *Style—* Ken Curtis, Esq; 35 Brabourne Rise, Park Langley, Beckenham BR3 2SQ; Leberl Advertising, 7 Brooks Court, Kirtling St, London SW8 5BX (☎ 071 720 1966)

CURTIS, Lawrence Wesley; DFC (1943 and bar 1944); s of Alfred Curtis (d 1973), and Elizabeth, *née* Powell; *b* 10 May 1921; *m* 11 May 1945, Barbara Mary, da of late Alfred Craven; 3 s (Ian b 1950, Martin b 1953, Simon b 1955); *Career* served Sqdn-Ldr RAF 1939-46, bomber cmd (UK), RAF serv flew with various Bomber Cmd Sqdns, inc 617 Sqdn (The Dam Busters); chm and md Curtis (Wool) Holdings Ltd 1979- (dir 1958-), dir Curtis (Wool) Holdings Ltd (and assoc cos) Gore NZ 1988; winner Queen's Award for Export Achievement; *Recreations* golf; *Clubs* RAF; *Style—* Lawrence Curtis, Esq, DFC; Greaghlone, East Morton, W Yorkshire; Curtis (Wool) Holdings Ltd, Auckland House, Bailey Hills Rd, Bingley, W Yorkshire (☎ 0274 561317)

CURTIS, Dr Leonard Frank; OBE (1989); s of Richard Herbert Curtis (d 1927), and Sarah Ann Maud *née* Miller (d 1969); *b* 2 Sept 1923; *Educ* Crypt Sch Gloucs, Univ of Southampton, Univ of Bristol (BSc, PhD); *m* 29 Dec 1953, Diana Elizabeth Dorothy, da of Charles Thomas Oxenham (d 1968); 2 da (Sarah b 31 Oct 1954, Ruth b 14 Aug 1961); *Career* RAF 1942-46, cmmnd Navigator Flying Branch 1943, 89 Sqdn 1944-46, (sr India, Burma, Malaya); sr sci offr Soil Survey of England and Wales 1951-56, reader in geography and head of Jt Schs Botany and Geography Univ of Bristol 1956-78, chief offr Exmoor Nat Park 1978-88; vice chm European Assoc of Remote Sensing Laboratories 1987- (sec gen 1985-87); memb: Remote Sensing Soc, Br Soil Sci Soc, Sci Faculty Cncl Poly SW; hon sr res fell Univ of Bristol 1979; FRGS; *Books* Introduction to Environmental Remote Sensing (with E C Barrett, second edn, 1982), Soils in the British Isles (1976), Environmental Remote Sensing (1974 and 1977); *Recreations* gardening, walking; *Style—* Dr Leonard Curtis, OBE; Ley Croft, Bossington Lane, Porlock, Somerset TA 24 8HD

CURTIS, Dr Michael; s of Sidney Curtis, of Wallsend, Tyne and Wear, and Cynthia, *née* Daniel; *b* 14 Dec 1954; *Educ* Dame Allan's Sch Newcastle upon Tyne, Univ of Dundee (MB ChB); *Career* lectr in pathology Univ of Newcastle upon Tyne 1979-86, conslt pathologist N Manchester Gen Hosp 1986-88, sr lectr in forensic med Univ of Glasgow 1988-; MRCPath 1985; *Recreations* flying; *Style—* Dr Michael Curtis; Ardfern, 20 Glen Road, Lennoxtown, Glasgow G65 7JX (☎ 0360 310632); Department of Forensic Medicine and Science, University of Glasgow, Glasgow G12 8QQ (☎ 041 330 4574, fax 041 330 4602)

CURTIS, Penelope Jane Hamilton (Mrs Christopher Crouch); da of Thomas Curtis, of Buckland, Surrey, and Nancy Frances Mary, *née* Pearson; *b* 20 Feb 1957; *Educ* St Michael's Sch Oxted Surrey, Univ of Exeter (LLB, Lloyd Parry prize, Maxwell law prize); *m* 22 Aug 1987, Christopher Charles Crouch, s of Francis Harry Anson Crouch; *Career* Freshfields: articled clerk 1979-81, slr 1981-87; N M Rothschild: head Compliance Dept 1987-, dir 1989-; memb City of London Slrs Co, Freeman City of London; memb Law Soc; *Recreations* theatre, opera, walking; *Style—* Ms Penelope Curtis; N M Rothschild & Sons Ltd, New Court, St Swithin's Lane, London EC4P 4DU (☎ 071 280 5000, fax 071 929 1643)

CURTIS, Brig (John Henry) Peter; MC (1943); s of Maj-Gen Henry Osborne Curtis, CB, DSO, MC (d 1964), of Trokes Coppice, Lytchett Minster, Dorset, and Jean Mackenzie, *née* Low (d 1977); *b* 7 Jan 1920; *Educ* Eton, RMC Sandhurst; *m* 1 March 1944, Diana Gabrielle, da of Lt-Col Cecil Campbell (d 1966), of Chicksgrove Manor, Tisbury, Wilts; 3 da (Elizabeth b 1946, Susan b 1948, Lucy b 1951); *Career* 2 Lt 60 Rifles KRRC 1939, Co 2 Green Jackets KRRC 1961-62, CO 8 Infantry Brigade Catterick 1965-67, ret 1967; hon local sec Badenoch and Strathspey BFSS 1970-; dir Spey Fishing Trust Ltd 1978-88; *Recreations* shooting, fishing; *Clubs* Army and Navy; *Style—* Brig Peter Curtis, MC; c/o Lloyds Bank plc, 6 Pall Mall, London SW1Y 5NH

CURTIS, Richard Alexander John; s of Dato Richard John Froude Curtis (d 1987), and Marjorie, *née* Snow; *b* 20 Nov 1951; *Educ* King's Sch Canterbury, Univ of Bristol (LLB), London Business Sch; *Career* slr: Norton Rose Botterell & Roche London 1976-79, Jardine Matheson & Co Hong Kong 1979-83; dir Jardine Offshore Gp Singapore 1983-86, md Vase Ltd; vice chm Jermyn St Assoc; memb Law Soc; *Recreations* squash, tennis, golf, ceramics, water skiing; *Clubs* Oriental, RAC; *Style—* Richard Curtis, Esq; Vase Limited, 10 Clifton Road, London W9 1SS (☎ 071 286 2535, 071 266 2427)

CURTIS, His Hon Judge Richard Herbert; QC (1977); s of Norman James Curtis, JP (d 1983), and Dorothy Mary, *née* Willison; *b* 24 May 1933; *Educ* Shrewsbury, Oxford Univ (MA); *m* 1958, Gillian Morton, da of John Morton Cave (d 1969); 4 s (Rupert, Alexander, Jonathan, Benedict); *Career* called to the Bar Inner Temple 1958, rec Crown Ct 1974-89; hon rec City of Hereford 1981, bencher Inner Temple 1985, a pres Mental Health Review Tbnls 1983, rec City of Birmingham and sr circuit judge Oxford and Midland Circuit 1989; formerly Lt The Sherwood Foresters (ME); *Recreations* viticulture, golf; *Style—* His Hon Judge Curtis, QC; 1 Kings Bench Walk, Temple, London EC4 (☎ 071 353 8436)

CURTIS, Timothy Stephen (Tim); s of Bruce Curtis, of 10 Denison Close, Malvern, Worcs, and Betty Holliday, *née* Roebuck; *b* 15 Jan 1960; *Educ* Royal GS Worcester, Hatfield Coll Durham, Magdalene Coll Cambridge (Cricket blue); *m* 21 Sept 1985, Philippa Neild, da of David Neild Cornock-Taylor; 1 da (Jennifer May b 9 Feb 1991); *Career* professional cricketer; Worcestershire CCC: first class debut 1979, awarded county cap 1984, vice capt 1990-; England NCA under 19 tour Canada 1979; 5 Test match appearances: 2 v W Indies (Headingley, Oval) 1988, 3 v Aust (Edgbaston, Old Trafford, Trent Bridge) 1989; honours: Co Championship 1988 and 1989, Refuge Assurance League 1987 and 1988, runners up Nat West Trophy 1988; schoolmaster Royal GS Worcester during two winter terms, chm Professional Cricketers' Assoc 1989-; *Recreations* all sports, gardening, reading novels, socialising; *Style—* Tim Curtis, Esq; Worcestershire CCC, County Ground, New Road, Worcester(☎ 0905 422694)

CURTIS, Very Rev Wilfred Frank; s of Wilfrid Arnold Curtis, MC (d 1984), and Flora May, *née* Burbidge (d 1980); *b* 24 Feb 1923; *Educ* Bishop Wordsworths Sch Salisbury, Kings Coll London (AKC); *m* 1951, Muriel, da of Henry William Dover (d 1974); 2 s (Ian, Michael), 2 da (Hazel, Christine); *Career* Army 1941-47, Maj RA 1946, India 1943-46; ordained 1952; area sec Church Missionary Soc, advsr in rural work 1955-65, home sec Church Missionary Soc 1965-74, provost of Sheffield 1974-88 (provost emeritus 1988-), rural dean Okehampton 1989-; hon fell Sheffield City Poly 1980, hon canon Butere Cath Kenya 1982-; *Recreations* walking, natural history, photography; *Style—* The Very Rev Frank Curtis; Ashplant's Fingle Cottage, Drewsteignton, Exeter, Devon EX6 6QX (☎ 0647 21253)

CURTIS, Sir William Peter; 7 Bt (UK 1802), of Cullands Grove, Middlesex; s of Sir Peter Curtis, 6 Bt (d 1976); *b* 9 April 1935; *Educ* Winchester, Trinity Coll Oxford, RAC Cirencester; *Heir* kinsman, Maj Edward Curtis; *Career* late 16/5 Lancers; *Style—* Sir William Curtis, Bt; Oak Lodge, Bank St, Bishop's Waltham, Hants

CURTISS, Air Marshal Sir John Bagot; KCB (1980, CB 1979), KBE (1982); s of Maj E F B Curtiss, RFC; *b* 6 Dec 1924; *Educ* Radley, Wanganui Collegiate Sch NZ, Worcester Coll Oxford; *m* 1946, Peggy Drughorn, da of Edward Bowie; 3 s, 1 da; *Career* RAF 1942, flying 1942-74, dir gen RAF 1975-77, Cmdt Staff Coll 1977-80, AOC No 18 Gp 1980-83; dir and chief exec Soc of Aerospace Cos 1984-89; memb: Meml Fund For Disaster Relief 1990-, Exec Ctee Air League 1985-, pres Aircrew Assoc 1986-; FRAeS, FRSA; *Clubs* RAF, MCC, Pilgrims, Royal Lymington Yacht, Air League; *Style—* Air Marshal Sir John Curtiss, KCB, KBE; c/o Coutts and Co, 1 Old Park Lane, London W1Y 4BS

CURTOIS, Brian Richard; s of Leslie Howard Curtois, of Leigh-on-Sea, Essex, and Marjorie Joyce Louise, *née* Fenton (d 1966); *b* 30 Dec 1936; *Educ* Dulwich; *m* 29 Sept 1962, Brenda Rosemary, da of late Donald Osman Copeland; 1 s (Martin Ralph b 25 Nov 1964), 1 da (Jennifer b 18 Feb 1967); *Career* journalist; Hornchurch News 1957, Ilford Recorder 1957-59, Nottingham Evening News 1959-61, Press Association 1961-64; BBC: gen reporter 1964-70, political reporter 1970-74, dep political ed later chief political corr 1974-88, memb BBC Commons TV Project team 1988-89, chief Parly commentator 1988-; *Recreations* cricket, music, theatre, walking; *Clubs* Essex County Cricket; *Style—* Brian Curtois, Esq; BBC Westminster, No 4 Millbank, London SW1 (☎ 071 973 6210)

CURWEN, David Christian; s of John Ernest Curwen (d 1942), of Kent, and Blanche Lydia, *née* Whittaker (d 1972); *b* 30 Nov 1913; *Educ* Kings Sch Canterbury; *m* 1, 29 Jan 1944 (m dis 1949), Margaret Forsyth; 1 s adopted (Christopher b 1941); m 2, 23 Sept 1950, Helen Barbara Anne, da of Kyrle W Willans (d 1973); *Career* engr; Short Bros Rochester 1938-39; fndr: David Curwen Ltd 1946, Curwen and Newbery Ltd 1952; conslt engr 1965-; *Recreations* fly-fishing, building steam engines; *Style—* David C Curwen, Esq; The Cottage, Rectory Lane, All Cannings, nr Devizes, Wilts (☎ 038 086 204)

CURWEN, Michael Jonathan; s of Dr Montague Curwen, and Thelma, *née* Freiberger; *b* 13 Nov 1943; *Educ* Clifton, Queen's Coll Oxford (BA); *m* 28 June 1970, (Helena) Sandra, da of Dr Charles Norman Faith; 1 s (Robert b 1974), 1 da (Nicola b 1971); *Career* called to the Bar Inner Temple 1966, rec SE Circuit 1989; *Recreations* theatre, golf, gardening; *Style—* Michael Curwen, Esq; 10 Raeburn Close, London NW11 6UG; 6 Pump Court, Temple, London EC4Y 7AR (☎ 071 583 6013, fax 071 353 0464)

CURWEN, (David) Niel; s of Brian Murray Curwan (d 1954), and Dorothy, *née* Powell (d 1943); *b* 22 Jan 1930; *Educ* Rugby, Gloucs Coll of Agric; *Career* Nat Serv Rifle Bde 1948-50; farmer; chm NFU Glos 1971, NFU rep Jt Advsy Ctee Cotswold Area of Outstanding Nat Beauty 1972-, chm Area Trg Ctee Gloucs and N Avon 1974-90;memb: Bristol Avon Local Land Drainage Ctee Wessex Water Authy 1974-89, Cncl Gloucs Tst for Nature Conservation 1976-, Bristol Avon Local Flood Def Ctee (NRA Wessex Region), Thames Agric Trg Bd 1990-, Severn Regnl Ctee Nat Tst 1990-; govr Gloucs Coll of Agric 1978-, chm Nat Tst Local Ctee of Mgmnt for Minchinhampton Commons 1980-, pres Gloucs Farming and Wildlife Advsy Gp 1985- (chm 1980-85); dir: Three Avons Region Group Traders' Assoc Ltd 1970-87, Brown's Estate Ltd 1981- (alternate dir 1964-81, chm 1988-), Farming and Wildlife Trust Ltd 1989-; *Recreations* squash; *Style—* Niel Curwen, Esq; Yew Tree Cottage, Boundary Court, Woodchester, Stroud, Glos GL5 5PL (☎ 0453 873580)

CURZON, Hon (Christian) Avril; da of Hon Francis Nathaniel Curzon (3 s of 4 Baron Scarsdale and yr bro of 1 and last Marquess Curzon of Kedleston, who was also cr Viscount Scarsdale) by his w Winifred Phyllis, da of Capt Christian and Lady Jane Combe (da of 3 Marquess Conyngham); yr sis of 3 Viscount Scarsdale; raised to rank title and precedence of Viscount's da 1980; *b* 24 April 1923; *Educ* Downham Hatfield Heath Herts; *Career* Pathology Dept Royal Northern Infirmary Inverness 1942-45; The British Racehorse 1949-57; E D O'Brien Orgn (PR) 1961-77; *Recreations* photography, racing, gardening; *Style—* The Hon Avril Curzon; The House of the Pines, Virginia Ave, Virginia Water, Surrey (☎ 0344 843151)

CURZON, Hon David James Nathaniel; s (by 1 m) of 3 Viscount Scarsdale; *b* 3 Feb 1958; *Educ* Stowe; *m* 1981, Ruth, da of John Ernest Linton (d 1966), of Wavertree, Liverpool; 1 s (Andrew b 1986), 1 da (Emma b 1983); *Career* dir David Curzon Ltd; *Recreations* the arts, golf, tennis; *Clubs* Lansdowne; *Style—* The Hon David Curzon; Chilton House, Lingfield Rd, Wimbledon Village, London SW19 4PZ

CURZON, Jane Victoria (Enid); da of late Malcolm Mackenzie Fergusson, of Toronto, Canada, and Enid Marie, *née* Forsythe (d 1953); *m* 1950 (m dis 1965), as his 2 w, Cdr George William Chambré Penn Curzon, RN (d 1976), s of Hon Frederick Graham Curzon (2 s of 3 Earl Howe); 1 s (7 Earl Howe), 1 da (Emma); *Career* serv WRNS 1943-45; radio actress, businesswoman; *Style—* Mrs Jane Curzon; Windsor Croft, Windsor Lane, Great Missenden, Bucks

CURZON, Prof Martin Edward John; s of Stanly Arthur Curzon, of Selsdon, Surrey, and Antoinette Carmela, *née* Davies; *b* 11 May 1940; *Educ* Univ of London (BDS, PhD), Univ of Rochester (MS); *m* 29 Aug 1964, Jennifer Anne; 3 s (Richard Martin b 1967, Thomas Paul b 1972, Neil Simon b 1974); *Career* external Govt of BC 1965-66, lectr Univ of Bristol 1968-70, sr dental offr Govt of Canada 1970-73, chm Oral Biology Eastman Dental Center 1973-83 (fell 1966-68), prof Univ of Leeds 1983-; pres Br Paedodontic Soc 1987-77; memb: BDA, ORCA, CAPD, AAPD, IADR; *Books* Trace Elements and Dental Disease (1983); *Recreations* fell walking, gardening; *Style—* Prof Martin Curzon; 3 Claremont Court, Headingley, Leeds (☎ 0532 784 864); Dept Child Dental Health, University of Leeds, Clarendon Way, Leeds LS2 9LU (☎ 0532 336138)

CURZON, Hon Peter Ghislain Nathaniel; s (by 1 m) and h of 3 Viscount Scarsdale; *b* 6 March 1949; *Educ* Ampleforth College; *m* 1983, Mrs Karen Lynne Osbourne, *née* Jackson; 1 da (Danielle b 1983); *Career* landowner (50 acres); *Recreations* The Cresta Run, skiing, golf; *Style—* The Hon Peter Curzon; Battle Barn Stud Farm, Sedlescombe, E Sussex

CUSACK, Cyril James; s of James Walter Cusack (d 1953), of Durban, SA, and Alice

Violet, *née* Cole (d 1974); *b* 26 Nov 1910; *Educ* St Thomas Coll Newbridge Co. Kildare, Univ Coll Dublin, Nat Univ of Ireland; *m* 1, 5 April 1945, Maureen (d 1977), da of late James Kiely, of Derry, Ireland; 2 s (Paul, Padraig), 4 da (Sinead, Sarcha, Niamh, Catherine); m 2, 18 Nov 1979, Mary Rose; *Career* Little Willie Caryle in East Lynne at Clanmel 1916; Abbey Theatre Dublin: Malcolm in Macbeth 1934, Marchbanks in Candida 1935, The Fool in Baile's Strand 1938, The Covey in The Plough and the Stars 1938, Christy Mahan in The Playboy of the Western World 1938, Denis in The Whiteheaded Boy 1942, Conn in The Shaughraun 1967, title role in Hadrian VII 1969, title role in the Vicar of Wakefield 1974, Walter in You Never Can Tell 1978; Cusack Prodns Gaiety Theatre Dublin: Romeo in Romeo and Juliet 1944, Dick Dudgemin in The Devil's Disciple 1947, Louis Dubedat in The Doctors's Dilemma 1947, Bluntshli in Arms and The Man 1953, Christy Mahan in The Playboy of The Western World 1953, Codger in The Bishops Bonfire, 1955, title role in Androcles and the Lion 1956, title role in Hamlet 1957, Roger Casement in Casement 1958, title role in The Temptation of Mr O 1961; Int Theatre Festival Paris The Playboy of the Western World; France and Euro cities Arms and the Man and Krapp's Last Tape; Olympia Theatre Dublin and Newhaven Boston USA, Irish President in Goodwill Ambassador; films incl: Knocknagow, My Left Foot, Little Dorrit, Danny Champion of the World, The Fool 1916-89; Hon LLD Nat Univ of Ireland 1977, Hon DLitt Trinity Coll Univ of Dublin 1980, Hon DLitt New Univ of Ulster 1982; hon memb Royal Dublin Soc; *Books* Taries An Aifreann (1942), The Temptation of Mr O (1961), Timepieces (1970), The Humour is On Me (1980), Between The Acts; *Clubs* United Arts Dublin, Arts Belfast (Hon); *Style—* Cyril Cusack, Esq

CUSACK, Mark Paul John; s of Capt Robert Joseph Cusack, of Dublin, and Olive Mary, *née* Byrne; *b* 28 Feb 1958; *Educ* St Paul's Sch Dublin, Trinity Coll Dublin (BBS); *m* July 1990, Susan Jane Williams; *Career* CA; Arthur Andersen & Co 1979-83, dir and head UK res Hoare Govett Securities 1988-90 (conglomerates analyst 1985-88, construction analyst 1983-85), dir Hoare Govett Corporate Finance 1990-; *Recreations* squash, tennis; *Clubs* Queens, Fitzwilliam (Dublin); *Style—* Mark P Cusack, Esq; 1 Tideway Wharf, 153 Mortlake High Street, London SW14 8SW; 4 Broadgate, London EC2M 7LE (☎ 071 601 0101, fax 071 374 1403, telex 297801)

CUSANI, David Anthony; s of Derek Herbert Cusani, of Wigan, and Marie Patricia, *née* Hawkins; *b* 16 July 1959; *Educ* St Johns Rigby Orrell, Padgate Coll Warrington, Liverpool Poly; *m* 4 May 1985, Julie, da of Frederick Bernard; 2 c (Dominic Alessandro Carlo b 5 May 1987, Daniel Gianluca b 4 April 1990); *Career* Rugby Union lock and No 8 Orrell RUFC and England (1 cap); clubs: Wigan RUFC 1978-80, Orrell RUFC 1980-88 and 1989-, Liverpool St Helens FC 1988/89, Barbarians RFC; rep: Lancashire 1980- (Co Champions: 1981, 1988, 1990), North of Eng (Divnl Champions 1987 and 1988), Eng U23 1982, Eng B (debut v Ireland B 1983), Eng XV v Italy 1990; England: tour SA 1984, debut v Ireland 1987; dir Rugbyclass Tours, prodn mangr Sol Sports; *Recreations* eating out, all sports, history; *Style—* David Cusani, Esq; 20 Carr Rd, Clayton-le-Woods, Chorley, Lancs PR6 7QD (☎ 0772 34967, 0625 618700, fax 0625 501148); Orrell RUFC, Edgehall Rd, Orrell, Wigan WN5 8TL

CUSENS, Prof Anthony Ralph; OBE (1989); s of James Henry Cusens (d 1964), and May Edith, *née* Thomas (d 1988); *b* 24 Sept 1927; *Educ* St John's Southsea, UCL (BSc, PhD); *m* 25 July 1953, Pauline Shirin, da of Herbert James German (d 1973); 3 da (Deborah b 1954, Rebecca b 1955, Sarah b 1962); *Career* res engr Br Cast Concrete Fedn 1952-56; sr lectr: Royal Military Coll of Sci Shrivenham 1954-56, Univ of Khartoum 1956-60; prof of structural engrg Asian Inst of Technol Bangkok 1960-65; prof of civil engrg: Univ of Dundee 1965-78, Univ of Leeds 1979-; FICE 1966, FIStructE 1967, FRSE 1974, FEng 1988; *Books* Bridge Deck Analysis (1975); *Recreations* golf; *Clubs* East India, Pannal Golf; *Style—* Prof Anthony Cusens, OBE; Old Hall Cottage, Bramham, Wetherby, W Yorks LS23 6QR (☎ 0937 845527); Department of Civil Engineering, University of Leeds, Leeds LSW 9JT (☎ 0532 332267, fax 0532 332265)

CUSHING, Peter Wilton; OBE (1989); s of George Edward Cushing (d 1956), and Nellie Maria, *née* King (d 1961); *b* 26 May 1913; *Educ* Shoreham GS Sussex, Purley Co Secdy Sch Surrey; *m* 10 May 1943, Violet Helene ((Helen) d 1971), da of Ernest Beck (d 1951); *Career* actor; in repertory 1936, Hollywood 1939-41, toured Forces camps with ENSA 1942-44, Old Vic tour of Australasia with Sir Laurence Olivier 1948 (Richard Skin of Our Teeth, The School for Scandal) and Olivier's Festival Season 1951 (Caesar and Cleopatra, Anthony and Cleopatra); TV incl: Nineteen Eighty Four (1954), Sherlock Holmes series 1969; Films incl: Chumps at Oxford 1939, Hamlet 1948, Star Wars 1977, Top Secret 1982; Hammer Films 1957-73 incl: Curse of Frankenstein 1957, Dracula 1958, Hound of the Baskervilles 1959, Frankenstein Must Be Destroyed 1969, The Satanic Rites of Dracula 1973; *Books* Peter Cushing, An Autobiography (1986), Past Forgetting - Memoirs of the Hammer Yea (1988); *Recreations* painting, reading; *Style—* Peter Cushing, Esq, OBE; c/o John Redway & Assoc, 5 Denmark St, London WC2H 8LP

CUSHING, Robert; JP (W Sussex 1959); s of Arthur Robert Cushing (d 1956), of Silverdale, Rowlands Rd, Worthing, and Ethel Florence, *née* Jarvis (d 1976); *b* 19 July 1918; *Educ* Hardenwick Sch Harpenden Herts, Wykeham House Sch Worthing, Brighton Coll; *Career* admitted slr Supreme Court of Judicature 1946; sr ptnr Dixon Holmes & Cushing Slrs 1959- (articled clerk 1936); Worthing Area Guild for Voluntary Servs (formerly Worthing and Dist Cncl of Social Servs): hon slr 1946-, chm 1964-75, vice pres 1975, elected chm of Bench Worthing Petty Sessional Div 1985-88 (former as and dep chm); govr and tstee Queen Alexandra Hosp Home for Disabled Ex-Servicemen (hon slr to tstees), hon life vice pres Lawn Tennis Assoc 1988, pres Sussex Co Lawn Tennis Assoc; memb: Sussex Law Soc, Worthing Law Soc (pres 1958-59); memb Law Soc; *Recreations* lawn tennis; *Clubs* W Worthing (pres); *Style—* Robert Cushing, Esq, JP; 31 Balcombe Court, W Parade, Worthing, Sussex BN11 3SW (☎ 0903 206557); Dixon Holmes & Cushing, 18 Liverpool Gardens, Worthing, Sussex BN11 1RY (☎ 0903 38273, fax 0903 823014)

CUSINE, Prof Douglas James; s of James Fechney Cusine (d 1987), of Johnstone, Renfrewshire, and Catherine, *née* McLean (d 1975); *b* 2 Sept 1946; *Educ* Hutchesons' Boys' GS Glasgow, Univ of Glasgow (LLB); *m* 21 July 1973, Marilyn Calvert, da of George Ramsay (d 1988), of Johnstone, Renfrewshire; 1 s (Graeme b 2 Jan 1984), 1 da (Jane b 19 Sept 1981); *Career* admitted slr 1971; lectr in private law Univ of Glasgow 1974-76, head Dept of Conveyancing Univ of Aberdeen 1987- (lectr 1976-82, sr lectr in conveyancing 1982-90, prof 1990-); memb and examiner for Law Soc of Scotland 1988-; memb: Lord President's Advsy Cncl for Messengers at Arms and Sheriff Offrs 1989-, Cncl of the Law Soc; chm Bd of Examiners Soc of Messengers at Arms and Sheriff Offrs 1990-; *Books* The Impact of Marine Pollution (jt ed, 1980), Scottish Cases and Materials in Commercial Law (jt ed, 1987), A Scots Conveyancing Miscellany (ed, 1988), New Reproductive Techniques: A Legal Perspective (1988), Law and Practice of Diligence (jtly, 1990); *Recreations* swimming, walking, bird watching; *Style—* Prof Douglas Cusine; Dept of Conveyancing and Professional Practice of Law, University of Aberdeen, Taylor Building, Old Aberdeen AB9 2UB (☎ 0224 272415, fax 0224 272442, telex 73458 UNIABNG)

CUSSINS, Peter Ian; s of Philip Cussins (d 1976), of Newcastle upon Tyne, and Doreen Cussins; *b* 18 March 1949; *Educ* Bootham Sch York, Univ of London (BSc); *m* 18 Sept 1973, Vandra Jean, da of Maynard Stubley, of Alnmouth, Northumberland; 1 s (Jabin b 1980), 3 da (Abigail b 1976, Alexandra b 1978, Lydia b 1983); *Career* chm: Lemmington Estates Ltd 1973-, Cussins Investmt Properties Ltd 1981-, Cussins Commercial Devpts Ltd 1981-, Cussins Property Gp plc 1981, Cussins Green plc 1986; *Recreations* golf, fishing; *Style—* Peter I Cussins, Esq; Morwick Hall, Acklington, Morpeth, Northumberland NE65 9DG; Purley Hall, Pangbourne, Berks RG8 HDJ; Cussins Property Gp plc, 1/2 Rutland Gdns, London SW1 (☎ 071 584 1424)

CUSSONS, Jeremy Alexander; s of Alexander Stockton Cussons (d 1986), and Wendy Grace Cussons; *b* 2 Sept 1950; *Educ* Marlborough; *m* 1, 5 Feb 1970, Renee Elizabeth, da of Arnold Hossman (d 1974); 1 s (Leo b 1971), 1 da (Angela b 1973); m 2, 4 Sept 1982, Rebecca Ann, da of Reginald Mercado, OBE (d 1985); 1 s (Sebastian b 1983); *Career* farmer; estate mangr; *Recreations* reading, tennis, charity fundraising; *Style—* Jeremy Cussons, Esq; Ballacotch Manor, Crosby, IOM (☎ 0624 851712)

CUST, Hon Peregrine Edward Quintin; s and h of 7 Baron Brownlow; *b* 9 July 1974; *Style—* The Hon Peregrine Cust

CUSTIS, Patrick James; CBE (1981); er s of Alfred William Custis (d 1945), of Dublin and Amy Custis; *b* 19 March 1921; *Educ* The High Sch Dublin; *m* 1954, Rita, yr da of Percy William Rayner (d 1968), of Bognor Regis; 1 s; *Career* CA; Josolyne Miles Co CA's 1946-51, RTZ 1951-55, Glynwed International 1956-67, fin dir Worldwide Group Guest Keen and Nettlefolds (GKN) 1974-81 (joined 1967), ret; dir: New Court Property Fund Managers Ltd (Rothchilds Co) 1978-, Lloyds Bank Midlands and N Wales Regnl Bd 1979-, Prisons Bd (Home Office) 1980-85, Associated Heat Services plc 1981-90, Wolseley plc 1982-90, Leigh Interests (dep chm) 1982-, Birmingham Technology Ltd 1983-, MCD plc Group (chm) 1983-86, Wyko Group plc 1985-, Benford Concrete Machinery plc 1985-86; chm Midlands Indust Gp of Fin Dirs 1977-80, co-opted memb Cncl ICAEW 1979-85, memb Monopolies and Mergers Cmmn 1981-82; Liveryman Worshipful Co of Chartered Accountants in England and Wales; FCA, FCMA, FCIS, JDipMA, FRSA; *Recreations* gardening, walking, reading; *Clubs* Royal Overseas League, Lansdowne; *Style—* Patrick Custis, Esq, CBE, FRSA; West Barn, Westmancote, Tewkesbury, Glos GL20 7ES (☎ 0684 72865)

CUSWORTH, Leslie (Les); s of Cecil Cusworth (d 1982), and Jean, of Normanton, West Yorkshire; *b* 31 July 1954; *Educ* Normanton GS; *m* 24 July 1976, Marcia Jean Ann, da of Norman Hobbs; 2 da (Hannah Jean b 14 Dec 1982, Sara b 28 Dec 1987); *Career* Rugby Union fly half Leicester FC and England (12 caps); clubs: Leicester FC 1978- (365 appearances, 946 points scored, record no of drop goals in a season (25) 1975), Barbarians RFC 1978-90; England: debut v NZ 1979, Five Nations debut v France 1982; physical educn teacher 1976-83, dir P & G Bland Insurance Brokers 1983-; *Recreations* golf, snooker, squash; *Style—* Les Cusworth, Esq; 14 Stoughton Drive, Evington, Leicester LE5 6AN (☎ 0533 738030); Leicester Football Club, Aylestone Rd, Leicester (☎ 0533 541607, fax 0533 541607)

CUSWORTH, (George Robert) Neville; s of George Ernest Cusworth (d 1966), of Bad Homburg, Germany, and Violet Helene, *née* Cross (d 1969); *b* 14 Oct 1938; *Educ* St Paul's, Keble Coll Oxford (BA, MA), Courtauld Inst of Art History (Cert in Euro Art), Stanford Univ California USA; *m* 6 Sept 1963, (Vivien) Susan, da of Philip Glynn Grylls, of Worthing, Sussex; 1 s (Nicholas b 20 March 1964), 1 da (Juliet b 30 Jan 1966); *Career* dir: Professional Div Reed International Books Ltd 1990- (chief exec), Reed Publishing Ltd 1989-, chm: Butterworth Group 1990- (chief exec 1987-90), Bowker-Saur Ltd 1989-, Butterworth-Heinemann Ltd 1990-; dir Int Electronic Publishing Res Centre 1985-88, memb Cncl Publishers Assoc 1988-, chm Bd Book House Trg Centre 1989-; tstee Camden Festival Tst 1986-; Freeman City of London 1982, Liveryman Worshipful Co of Stationers and Newspapers 1984; FRSA, FInstD; *Recreations* theatre, heraldry, art history, walking; *Clubs* Garrick; *Style—* Neville Cusworth, Esq; 4 Old Dock Close, Kew Green, Richmond, Surrey TW9 3BL; Oaklands, Herodsfoot, Liskeard, Cornwall PL14 4QX

CUTHBERT, Barry Gordon; *b* 21 Dec 1953; *Career* CA; co sec Grange Motors (Brentwood) Ltd 1980 (dir 1981); AICA, FICA; *Style—* Barry G Cuthbert, Esq; 225 Ingrave Rd, Brentwood, Essex CM13; Grange Motors (Brentwood) Ltd, Brook Street, Brentwood, Essex (☎ 0277 216 161, fax 0277 220 187)

CUTHBERT, Mark William Harcourt; s of Nicholas Harcourt Cuthbert, of Dorking, Surrey, and Pauline Barbara, *née* Pledge (d 1984); *b* 14 Aug 1954; *Educ* City of London Freemen's Sch, Kingston Poly Sch of Architecture (BA, Dip Arch); *m* 10 May 1986, Moya Christine, da of John Patrick Grey Walsh (d 1986); *Career* architect and designer; memb RIBA; *Recreations* musician (classical guitar), painter; *Style—* Mark W H Cuthbert, Esq; 3 Ivy Cottage, Hampstead Lane, Dorking, Surrey (☎ 0306 888467); 80 High St, Ewell, Surrey (☎ 081 393 4644)

CUTHBERT, Michael William; s of Thomas Cuthbert (d 1977), of Coventry, and Thelma Josephine, *née* O'Hehir; *b* 6 July 1956; *Educ* Archbishop Ullathorne RC Comp Sch, UCL (LLB); *m* 29 July 1989, Stephanie Edith, da of David Henry Tate, of Leigh, Surrey; *Career* slr; Slaughter and May: articled clerk 1978-80, asst slr 1980-82; Clifford Turner: asst slr 1982-86, ptnr 1986-87; Clifford Chance: London 1987-89, ptnr New York 1989; memb: Law Soc 1980, City of London Solicitor's Co; Slr of the Supreme Ct of: the Judicature of Eng and Wales 1980, Hong Kong 1986; *Recreations* opera, food and wine, the cinema; *Clubs* Raffles; *Style—* Michael Cuthbert, Esq; 11 Tryon Street, London SW3 3LG; New York, 525 East 72nd St, Apartment 28E, New York, New York 10021, USA (☎ 212 439 9758); Clifford Chance, Manhatten Tower, 101 East 52nd Street, New York, New York 10022, USA (☎ 212 750 1440, fax 212 758 6625, telex 429391); Clifford Chance, Royex House, Aldermanbury Square, London EC2V 7LD (☎ 071 600 0808, fax 071 726 8561, telex 8959991)

CUTHBERT, Stephen Colin; s of Colin Samuel Cuthbert (d 1975), formerly of Sanderstead, Surrey, and Helen Mary Cuthbert, *née* Scott (d 1986); *b* 27 Oct 1942; *Educ* Trinity Sch of John Whitgift, Univ of Bristol (BSc); *m* 1, 22 Feb 1969, Jane Elizabeth (m dis 1986), da of David Bluett (decd), of Sydney Australia; 2 s (Simon b 1974, Ian b 1974), 1 da (Nicola b 1971); m 2, 27 Oct 1987, Susan Melanie, da of Kenneth Gray, of Brighton; stepchildren 1 s (Christopher b 1982), 2 da (Joanna b 1971, Nicola b 1974); *Career* md Brent Chemicals International plc 1980- (dir 1976); vice chm CBI Southern Region 1990; *Recreations* cruising sailing, family interests; *Style—* Stephen Cuthbert, Esq; Ridgeway, Iver, Bucks SL0 9JJ (☎ 0753 651812, fax 0753 652460)

CUTHBERT, Lady Victoria Lucy Diana; *née* Percy; 2 da of 10 Duke of Northumberland, KG, GCVO, TD, PC (d 1988); *b* 19 April 1949; *m* 1975, (John) Aidan Cuthbert; 1 s (David Hugh b 1987), 3 da (Alice Rose b 1978, Lucy Caroline b 1982, Mary Belinda b 1984); *Style—* Lady Victoria Cuthbert; Beaufront Castle, Hexham, Northumberland

CUTHBERTSON, Eric Ian; WS (1963); s of Ranald Ker Cuthbertson (d 1983), of Ravelston Brae, Ravelston Dykes Rd, Edinburgh, and Agnes Thomson, *née* Mitchell (d 1967); *b* 17 Nov 1934; *Educ* Edinburgh Acad, Sedbergh, Univ of Edinburgh; *m* 17 Nov 1962, Shona Campbell Aitken, da of Francis Aitken Wright (d 1959); 1 da (Fiona b 1967); *Career* slr 1963-; dir: Scottish Equitable Life Assurance Society, Scottish Building Society (chm), Inverteviot Properties (Edinburgh) Ltd; *Recreations* shooting, fishing, mountain walking, gardening; *Clubs* Bruntsfield Links Golf; *Style—* Eric I

Cuthbertson, Esq, WS; 102 Ravelston Dykes, Edinburgh (☎ 031 337 7629); 21 Melville Street Lane, Edinburgh EH3 7QB (☎ 031 225 7500, fax 031 220 1231)

CUTHILL, Bruce Douglas; s of Alexander Cuthill, and Irene, *née* Coupar; *b* 29 July 1960; *Educ* Menzieshill HS; *m* 22 Sept 1989, Karen Anne, da of George Gallagher Welsh; *Career* hockey player; capt: Menzieshill Hockey Club (indoor and outdoor teams), Scotland (indoor and outdoor teams, 60 outdoor Caps, 71 indoor); Glenfiddich Int Player of the Tournament 1987-88, Scottish Player of the Year 1988-89, Intercity Tournament-Player of the Tournament 1988-89; *Style*— Bruce Cuthill, Esq; 33 Seymour Street, Dundee, Tayside DD2 1HA (☎ 0382 644273)

CUTLER, (John) Derek; s of (Joseph) Thomas Cutler (d 1962), of Oldbury, Worcs, and Winifred, *née* Skidmore (d 1984); *b* 2 Aug 1932; *Educ* Oldbury GS, Birmingham Sch of Architecture; *m* 5 May 1958, Peggy Maureen, da of Herbert William Merrett (d 1984), of Bordon, Hants; 2 s (Timothy John b 1962, James Ewen b 1967), 1 da (Jacqueline Ann b 1960); *Career* Nat Serv RE 1958-60; architect; sr ptnr Phillips Cutler Troy 1985-87 (ptnr 1962-85), md PCPT Architects Ltd 1987-; memb Birmingham Architectural Assoc, fndr memb Cheviot Housing Assoc, memb Cncl Midlands New Town Soc, memb RIBA 1958, FRSA 1966; *Recreations* jazz, theatre; *Style*— Derek Cutler, Esq; Kontur, Mount Road, Tettenhall Wood, Wolverhampton WV6 8HR; PCPT Architects Ltd, 178 Birmingham Rd, West Bromwich, West Midlands B70 6QG (☎ 021 553 6251, fax 021 553 4232, telex 338024, car 0836 713124)

CUTLER, Sir Horace Walter; OBE (1963), DL (Gtr London 1981); eldest s of Albert Benjamin Cutler, and Mary Ann Cutler; *b* 28 July 1912; *Educ* Harrow GS; *m* 1957, Christiane, da of Dr Klaus Muthesius; 1 s, 3 da (and 1 s from previous m); *Career* former Mayor of Harrow, ldr of oppn GLC 1974-77 (dep ldr 1964-67 and 1973-74), memb Harrow West 1964-; ldr: GLC 1977-81, oppn 1981-82, contested (C) Willesden East 1970; kt 1979; *Books* The Cutler Files (autobiog, 1982); *Style*— Sir Horace Cutler, OBE, DL; Hawkswood, Hawkswood Lane, Gerrards Cross, Bucks (☎ 3182)

CUTLER, The Hon Peregrine Cust Ivor; *m* (m dis); 2 s (Jeremy, Daniel); *Career* RAF (VR) 1942-43, trained as air navigator (grounded for dreaminess); humorist; aged 6 sang My Love is Like a Red Red Rose by Robert Burns and won sch prize, apprentice fitter Rolls Royce 1940, first aid and storeman Winsor Engrg Co 1943-45, teacher 1948-80 (A S Neill's Summerhill 1950-51, ILEA 1952-80), first gig at Blue Angel London 1957 (unmitigated failure), started writing poetry aged 42 (wasn't any good until 48); music: 270 songs, music for Ken Russell's Diary Of A Nobody BBC2; records: Dandruff (with Phyllis King, 1974), Velvet Donkey (with Phyllis King and Fred Frith, 1975), Jammy Smears (with Phyllis King, 1976), Women Of The World (1984), Privilege (with Linda Hirst, David Toop and Steve Beresford, 1984), Gruts (1986), Prince Ivor (1986), Life In A Scotch Sitting Room Volume 2 (Speakout); TV: The Acker Bilk Band Show, Magical Mystery Tour, Offbeat for Tired Music Lovers, Up Sunday, Dave Allen in search of the great British eccentric, Innes Book of Records, Old Grey Whistle Test; radio: Monday Night At Home, John Peel 1970-, Start The Week, Andy Kershaw, Pye Radio Award for Humour 1980-81; BBC Radio 3 plays 1979-85 incl: Silence, Ivor Cutler & The Mermaid, Ivor Cutler & The Mole, Ivor Cutler & The Princess, Ivor Cutler & His Dad, Ivor Cutler & A Barber, A Miner Is Approached by Ivor Cutler, A Sheet Metalworker is Approached by Ivor Cutler; performances incl: The Royal Festival Hall, Coliseum, Rainbow, Theatre Royal Drury Lane, a tour with Van Morrison; cartoons: Observer, Private Eye, Sunday Times, International Times; Poetry: Many Flies Have Feathers (1972), A Flat Man (1977), Private Habits (1981), Large et Puffy (1984), Flesh Carpet (1986), A Nice Wee Present From Scotland (1988); Short Stories (illustrated by Martin Honeysett): Life in a Scotch Sitting Room (Vol 2 1984), Gruts (1986), Fremsley (1987), Glasgow Dreamer (1990); Short Stories (illustrated by author): Gruts (1962), Cockadoodledon't!!! (1966); Children's Stories (illustrated by Helen Oxenbury): Meal One (1971), Balooky Klujypop (1973), The Animal House (1976); Herbert-Five Stories (illustrated by Patrick Benson, 1988), Grape Zoo (illustrated by Jill Barton, 1991); quotes about Ivor Cutler incl: The demeanour and voice of the weariest human ever to be cursed with existence (Music Week), Ivor Cutler spends a lot of time in his bedroom (Observer Magazine); ambition to disappear without any help; memb: PRS, MCPS, PPL, PLR , LPS, NPS; *Style*— Ivor Cutler; BBC, London W1A 1AA

CUTLER, Keith Charles; s of Henry Walter Cutler, of Woburn Sands, Bucks, and Evelyn Constance, *née* Butcher; *b* 14 Aug 1950; *Educ* Rickmansworth GS, Cedars Sch, Univ of Bristol (LLB); *m* 30 Aug 1975, Judith Mary, da of Ronald Philip Haddy (d 1974); 1 s (James b 1982), 1 da (Anna b 1985); *Career* called to the Bar Lincoln's Inn 1972; asst rec 1989; memb Hon Soc Lincoln's Inn; FSJ; *Clubs* RAC; *Style*— Keith Cutler, Esq; 3 Pump Court, Temple, London EC4Y 2AJ (☎ 071 353 0711, fax 071 353 3319)

CUTTING, Dr John Charles; s of Dr Charles Latham Cutting of Bath, and Frances Cutting (d 1946); *b* 31 Oct 1946; *Educ* Hymers Coll Hull, Guy's Hosp (MB BS, MD, MPhil); *m* 1 (m dis 1981), Elizabeth Ann, *née* Murgatroyd; 2 s (Roger Kenneth b 21 July 1975, Graham John b 4 Oct 1977); m 2, 22 Sept 1984, Rosemary Catherine Anne, da of Ralph Ivor Charlish (d 1982); *Career* sr lectr KCH 1979-83, conslt psychiatrist Bethlem Royal and Maudsley Hosps London 1983-; memb Ed Bd Journal of Neurology, Neurosurgery and Pschiatry; FRSM 1973, memb assoc BR neurologists 1982; *Books* The Psychology of Schizophrenia (1985), The Clinical Roots of the Schizophrenia Concept (with M Shepherd, 1987); *Recreations* reading, gardening, tennis, bridge; *Style*— Dr John Cutting; Mill Wood, Wall Hill, Forest Row, E Sussex RH18 5EG (☎ 034 2823335)

CUTTLE, Geoffrey; s of Ralph Cuttle (d 1972), of Essex, and Ethel Maud, *née* Piper (d 1988); *b* 16 Oct 1933; *Educ* Malvern, Downing Coll Cambridge (MA); *m* 30 Sept 1961, Elizabeth Mary, da of Thomas James Copeland, of Essex; 1 s (Edward William John b 1967), 2 da (Mary Linsdell b 1964, Elizabeth Ann b 1966); *Career* held various mgmnt and consultancy positions within STC Gp and ICL 1956-90, computer conslt 1991-; FBCS, FIQA, CEng, MBIM; *Publications include* Exec Programs and Op Systems (1970); *Recreations* croquet, wine, collecting; *Clubs* Royal Inst of GB; *Style*— Geoffrey Cuttle, Esq; Lynwood, 35 Mount Hermon Rd, Woking, Surrey GU22 7UN (☎ 0483 762808)

CUTTS, Katherine; *b* 30 Oct 1942; *m* 23 March 1963, (George) Nigel Cutts; 3 da (Sara Christabel b 14 Feb 1964, Louise Victoria b 8 Jan 1966, Charlotte Emma b 31 Aug 1968); *Career* chm and co sec Clover Properties 1985-; memb: Indust Tbnl Panel 1986, Quorn Hunt Pony Club, Notts Bldg Preservation Tst Ltd, Parish Cncl 1972-79, Rushcliffe BC 1979-89, Notts CC 1989; Cons; *Recreations* hunting, conservation, politics; *Style*— Mrs Katherine Cutts; Normanton House, Old Melton Rd, Normanton-on-the-Wolds, nr Plumtree, Notts NG12 5NN (☎ 0602 2495); Castle House, 74 St James's St, Nottingham NG1 6FJ

CUVELIER, Nicola; *née* Lockey; da of Zoe-Linsley Thomas; *Educ* Christ's Hosp Hertford, Kings Cross Tech Coll, Birkbeck Coll London (BA), London Coll of Printing; *m* Aug 1990, Pierre-Yves Aloys Dorémieux De St Vaast Cuvelier, s of Yves Cuvelier; *Career* communications and marketing consultant; filing clerk Bassett's Sweeet Factory Clapham, stylist to advtg photographers 1975-76, copywriter J Walter Thompson 1976-77, ed Commercials Section Broadcast Magazine 1980-82 (reporter 1977-80), creative and mktg conslt to various advtg agencies New York 1982-84, fndr Foresight Communications Ltd London 1985- (currently chairwoman); memb Think Tank on Communication with Women for the Lab Party 1987, co-author Design Policy Lab Party 1990; UK columnist Millimeter (American film jl), US corr for UK media jnls 1982-84, contrib on communications to various other jnls, co-writer film Say Say Say 1983, author various health educn and mgmnt trg films; MInstD; *Recreations* flying, art, travel, politics, mythology, physics, eastern philosophies; *Style*— Mrs Nicola Cuvelier; Foresight Communications Ltd, 48 Lexington St, London W1R 3LH (☎ 071 734 6691/9, fax 071 734 2359)

CYMERMAN, Anthony; s of Alfred Cymerman, of Highgate, London, and Annette, *née* Loufer; *b* 4 Dec 1944; *Educ* La Sainte Union Convent, Hargrave Park Sch, Dame Allan's Sch, Univ of Leeds (BChD); *m* 28 March 1976, Cherry, da of Maj R Keal, MBE; 1 s (James Alexander b 9 June 1977), 1 da (Kate Elizabeth b 28 Dec 1981); *Career* qualified from Leeds Dental Sch 1970, assoc London 1970-72, started own private practice in Harley St 1971 (second practice in NW London 1974); conslt BUPA and Private Patients Plan 1982; memb: Camden and Islington FPC (now FHSA), Camden and Islington Local Dental Ctee, Camden and Islington Dental Serv Ctee, Dental Advsy Ctee UCH, Fedn London Area LDCS; hon tutor UCH Dental Sch 1986; memb: BDA 1970, RSM 1987; *Recreations* cricket, clay pigeon shooting; *Clubs* MCC; *Style*— Anthony Cymerman, Esq; 25 Dartmouth Park Hill, London NW5 1HP (☎ 071 485 2505); 44 Harley St, London W1 (☎ 071 637 3234, 0860 68 3861)

CYPRUS AND THE GULF, Bishop of 1987-; Rt Rev John Edward Brown; s of Edward Brown and Muriel Brown; *b* 13 July 1930; *Educ* Wintringham GS Grimsby, Kelham Theol Coll (BD); *m* 1956, Rosemary, *née* Wood; 1 s; *Career* ordained: deacon 1955, priest; master St George's Sch Jerusalem, curate St George's Cath Jerusalem, chaplain Amman Jordan 1954-57, curate i/c All Saints Reading 1957-60, missionary and chaplain All Saints Cath Khartoum Sudan 1960-64; vicar: Stewkley Buckingham 1964-69, St Luke's Maidenhead 1969-73, Bracknell Berks 1973-77; rural dean Sonning 1974-77, archdeacon of Berks 1978-86, episcopal canon St George's Cath Jerusalem 1987-; *Recreations* walking, Middle East and African studies; *Style*— The Rt Rev the Bishop of Cyprus and the Gulf; P O Box 2075, Nicosia, Cyprus

CZERNIN, Hon Mrs ((Mary) Hazel Caridwen); *née* Scott-Ellis; eldest da of 9 Baron Howard de Walden and 5 Baron Seaford and Lady Howard de Walden, *née* Countess Irene Harrach (d 1975); *b* 12 Aug 1935; *m* 20 Nov 1957, Joseph Czernin, s of late Count Franz Josef Czernin (of the family granted title of Count (*Reichsgraf*) of the Holy Roman Empire by the Emperor Ferdinand III 1652 with the predicate 'Hoch und Wohlgeboren (High and well-born)'); 1 s, 5 da; *Career* co-heiress to Barony of Howard de Walden; *Style*— The Hon Mrs Czernin; White Oak House, Highclere, Newbury, Berks RG15 9RJ; 47 Queens Gate Gardens, London SW7 5ND

CZERNIN, Maud, Countess; Maud Sarah; da of Ronald Hamilton, OBE (d 1958; s of Rt Hon Lord George Hamilton, GCSI, JP, 3 s of 1 Duke of Abercorn, KG, PC; Lord George Hamilton m Lady Maud Lascelles, CI, da of 3 Earl of Harewood), and Florence Marguerite (the actress 'Sarah Brooke', d 1959), da of Maj John Hannah; *b* 4 April 1917; *m* 4 Nov 1939 (m dis 1947), Count Manfred Maria Edmund Czernin, DSO, MC, DFC (d 1962), yst s of Count Otto Czernin; 1 s, 1 da; *Style*— Maud, Countess Czernin; 50 Hartismere Road, London SW6

CZIRJÁK, Gyula; s of Gyula Czirják (d 1975), and Etelka, *née* Ruber (d 1982); *b* 7 Jan 1929; *Educ* Piarist GS Budapest, Univ of Econs Budapest; *m* 19 March 1955, Marta, da of Ferenc Voros (d 1971); *Career* asst to prof Univ of Econs Budapest 1951-54, various posts Nat Bank of Hungary Budapest 1954- (latterly gen mangr), dep chm Hungarian Int Bank Ltd London 1973-77 and 1983-; memb Foreign Banks Assoc London; *Recreations* photography, gardening, reading; *Clubs* RAC; *Style*— Gyula Czirjak, Esq; 22 Southacre, Hyde Park Crescent, London W2 2QB; Princes House, 95 Gresham St, London EC2V 7LU (☎ 071 606 5371, fax 071 606 8565, telex 887206)

D

D'AETH, Prof Richard; s of Walter D'Aeth, and Marion Edith Turnbull; *b* 3 June 1912; *Educ* Bedford Sch, Emmanuel Coll Cambridge (PhD), Harvard Univ (AM); *m* 1943, Pamela Straker; 2 da; *Career* prof of educn Univ Coll of West Indies 1952-58, Univ of Exeter 1958-77; pres Hughes Hall Cambridge 1978-84; *Style*— Prof Richard D'Aeth; Hughes Hall, Cambridge CB1 2EW (☎ 0223 352866)

D'ALBIAC, James Charles Robert; s of Air Marshal Sir John D'Albiac, KCVO, KBE, CB, DSO (d 1963), and Lady Sibyl Mary, *née* Owen; *b* 14 Oct 1935; *Educ* Winchester, Magdalen Coll Oxford (BA); *m* 2 May 1964, Carole Ann, da of Robert Percy Garner (d 1988); 1 da (Jane Sibyl b 22 Sept 1966); *Career* Nat Serv 2 Lt Lincolnshires serv Malaya 1954-56; stockbroker, ptnr Rowe & Pitman stockbrokers London 1968-86, dir Mercury Asset Mgmnt 1986-; memb Int Stock Exchange, AMSIA; *Recreations* golf, chess; *Clubs* Berkshire Golf, United Oxford & Cambridge Univ; *Style*— James D'Albiac, Esq; 65 Pont Street, London SW1; Mercury Asset Management, 33 King William Street, London EC4 (☎ 071 280 2197, 0844 278 961, fax 0844 279 106, car 0836 242 306)

D'AMBRUMENIL, Christopher Hugh; s of Lewis d'Ambrumenil (d 1968); *b* 17 Jan 1926; *Educ* Wellington; *m* 1962, Cathleen Marion; *Career* WW II Capt Coldstream Gds; memb Hexham RDC 1964-74, chm Gen Purposes Ctee Northumberland CC 1971-81, memb Northern RHA 1979-83, chm Pyman Bell & Co 1980-86, hon alderman Northumberland CC 1981; *Clubs* Cavalry and Guards', Norfolk (Norwich); *Style*— Christopher d'Ambrumenil, Esq; Church Court, Kettlestone, Norfolk NR21 0AU (☎ 032 877 783)

D'ARCY, Robert John Bruce; s of Cecil Vivian Robert D'Arcy, of Hunterswood, Holbrook, Ipswich, Suffolk, and Margery Mary, *née* Bailey (d 1987); *b* 12 Aug 1942; *Educ* Marlborough, Univ of Munich, Coll of Estate Management; *m* 22 Nov 1969, Janet Maxwell, da of Maxwell Heron Matheson (d 1978), of Widelands, Waldringfield, Woodbridge, Suffolk; 2 s (Justin b 6 Sept 1971, Toby b 26 Jan 1977), 2 da (Annabel (twin) b 6 Sept 1971, Charlotte b 12 Jan 1973); *Career* chartered surveyor; Chestertons 1966-68, Donaldsons 1968-69, ptnr James Crichton and Co 1979-, exec dir London Anglia Developments plc 1985; FRICS; *Recreations* sailing, shooting; *Clubs* Royal Thames Yacht; *Style*— Robert D'Arcy, Esq; The Old Rectory, Bredfield, Woodbridge, Suffolk IP13 6AX (☎ 0394 385223); Number 6, 10 Palace Gate, London W8 5NF (☎ 071 589 1131, fax 071 581 9336, car 0836 213066)

D'ASCOLI, Bernard; s of Georges d'Ascoli, of Aubagne, France, and Marcelle, *née* Thermes; *b* 18 Nov 1958; *Educ* Marseille Conservatoire; partner, Eleanor Harris; *Career* pianist; debuts: Queen Elizabeth Hall, Barbican and Royal Festival Hall 1982, Concertgebouw Amsterdam 1984, Houston USA 1985, The Proms Royal Albert Hall 1986, Tokyo 1988, Paris 1989; performed as soloist with: RPO, LPO, Philharmonia, BBC Symphony Orch, CBSO, Chamber Orch of Euro; played under conductors incl: Paavo Berglund, Andrew Davis, Sergiu Comissiona, Kurt Sandeling, Sir Yehudi Menuhin, Andrew Litton, Yevgeny Svetlanov, Michel Plasson, Sir John Pritchard; various int tours; *Recordings* Liszt Sonata, La Legierezza; Franck: Prelude Chorale and Fugue (1982); Schuman: Carnaval, Papillons, Fantasie Stücke op 111 (1989); Chopin: 4 Ballades, Nocturne in C Sharp Minor, Berceuse, Tarantelle, Andante Spianato and Grande Polonaise (1990); *Awards* Best Young Talent in France 1976, First Prize Int Maria Canals Competition Barcelona 1978, Chopin Prize Santander 1980, Third Prize Leeds Int Piano Competition; prize winner: Marguerite Long Competition Paris, Bach Competition Leipzig, Chopin Competition Warsaw; *Recreations* philosophy, psychology, technology and engineering, sport; *Style*— Bernard d'Ascoli, Esq; Van Walsum Management, 26 Wadham Rd, London SW15 2LR (☎ 081 874 6344, fax 081 877 0077)

D'CRUZ, Trevlyn Raphael; s of Samuel Patrick D'Cruz (d 1961), Kathlyn, *née* Bellett (d 1965); *b* 30 Aug 1938; *Educ* Goethals Sch; *m* 4 Jan 1964, Jill Ann, da of John Hudson Rogers; 1 s (Jaimie Simon b 20 Nov 1964), 1 da (Emma Claire b 27 Aug 1966); *Career* articled clerk to N N Pampel 1955-60, chartered accountant Baker Todman & Co 1961-65, Morgan Crucible Co 1966-70; publisher: New English Library 1970-81, Hodder & Stoughton 1981-84; md Accountancy Business Group 1985-; chm Merton Women's Aid (refuge) 1987-; FCA 1966; *Recreations* reading, opera; *Style*— Trevlyn D'Cruz, Esq; 9 Allfarthing Lane, London SW18 2PG (☎ 081 874 1951); Institute of Chartered Accountants in England and Wales (ICAEW), Accountancy Business Group, 40 Bernard St, London WC1N 1LD (☎ 071 833 3291)

D'EYNCOURT; see Tennyson d'Eyncourt

D'JANOEFF, Alexander Constantine Basil; s of Constantine V D'Janoeff (d 1986), of Windsor, and Margarita, *née* Rotinoff; *b* 27 March 1952; *Educ* Eton, Strasbourg Univ France, Oxford Poly; *Career* qualified CA 1977; Cooper & Lybrand Deloitte: joined 1972, Paris 1977-80, London 1980-85, seconded Schroder Ventures (Mgmnt Buy Out Fund) 1985-, Corp Fin Dept 1986-, ptnr 1986-, dir mergers and acquisitions Europe 1989-; FCA, FRSA; *Recreations* mountain walking in Switzerland; *Clubs* Brooks's, Annabel's, Guards Polo; *Style*— Alexander D'Janoeff, Esq; Coopers & Lybrand Deloitte, Plumtree Court, London ECA 4HT (☎ 071 822 8560, fax 071 822 8500)

D'OLIVEIRA, Damian Basil; s of Basil D'Oliveira (the former Test Cricketer), and Naomi, *née* Brache; *b* 19 Oct 1960; *Educ* Blessed Edward Oldcorne Secdy Modern; *m* 26 Sept 1983, Tracey Michele, da of Malcolm John Davies; 2 s (Marcus Damian b 27 April 1986, Dominic James b 29 April 1988); *Career* professional cricketer; Worcestershire CCC 1982-: first class debut v Zimbabwe 1982, awarded county cap 1985, over 150 appearances; English Cos tour to Zimbabwe 1984-85; achievements with Worcs: Britannic Assurance champions 1988 and 1989, Refuge Assurance League winners 1987 and 1988 (runners up 1989), Refuge Assurance Cup Final runnrs up 1988, Nat West Trophy runners up 1988, Benson & Hedges Cup runners up 1990; man of the match awards: Benson & Hedges 1984 and 1986, Nat West 1983 and 1986; *Style*— Damian D'Oliveira, Esq; Worcestershire CCC, New Rd, Worcester WR2 4QQ (☎ 0905 422694)

D'OYLY, Hadley Gregory; s and h of Maj Sir Nigel D'Oyly, 14 Bt; *b* 1956; *Educ* Milton Abbey; *Career* sales and mktg dir and md D'Oyly Coulson Holdings; *Recreations* squash; *Style*— Hadley D'Oyly, Esq; 37B New North Rd, Islington, London N1 6JB (☎ 071 490 0443)

D'OYLY, Sir Nigel Hadley Miller; 14 Bt (E 1663) of Shottisham, Norfolk; s of Sir Hastings D'Oyly, 11 Bt (d 1950), and his 2 w Evelyn; suc half bro Sir John Rochfort D'Oyly, 13 Bt (d 1986); *b* 6 July 1914; *Educ* Radley, Sandhurst; *m* 27 Oct 1939, Dolores (d 1971), da of Robert Gregory, of New Lodge, Crowhurst, Sussex; 1 s (Hadley b 1956), 2 da (Carol b 1942, Sherry b 1946); *Heir* s, Hadley Gregory, *qv*; *Career* served WW II, Maj, The Royal Scots, Hong Kong, France, War Office; civil engr, md OPS (London) & Co; *Recreations* rugby, tennis, swimming, photography; *Clubs* SCGB, Knights'; *Style*— Sir Nigel D'Oyly, Bt; Woodcote, Crowhurst, nr Battle, E Sussex TN33 9AB (☎ 042 483 589)

D'SOUZA, Mavis Mathilda Ursula; da of John Paul Martin D'Souza (d 1982), of London, and Mildred Amelia, *née* Fernandes; *b* 14 March 1947; *Educ* St Joseph's Convent Sch Dar-Es-Salaam Tanzania, Univ of London (LLB); *Career* called to the Bar Middle Temple 1975, ed Lloyd's Law Reports 1976-; memb: Bar Assoc of Commerce, Fin and Indust 1976, Int Bar Assoc 1986, Inst of Chartered Shipbrokers 1987; *Recreations* country walking, reading; *Style*— Miss Mavis D'Souza; Lloyd's of London Press, 1 Singer St, London EC2A 4LQ (☎ 071 250 1500)

DABORN, Alan Francis; OBE (1966), TD (1963), JP (1970), DL (1971); s of Alwyne Victor Daborn (d 1969); *b* 20 Feb 1923; *Educ* KCS Wimbledon; *m* 1949, Thelma Elizabeth, da of Samuel Greenwood (d 1948); 2 s; *Career* serv WWII Para Regt, TA with 4 Bn KSLI and Bde HQ Col; chartered surveyor; ptnr Alwyne Daborn & Son (amalgamated with John German 1970); *Recreations* bookbinding, reading; *Clubs* Naval and Military; *Style*— Alan Daborn, Esq, OBE, TD, JP, DL; 15 Dogpole, Shrewsbury, Shropshire SY1 1EN (☎ 0743 56176)

DACEY, Lionel Ivor Herbert (Lyn); s of John William Archer Dacey (d 1966), and Esther Ann Rees (d 1982); *b* 9 Sept 1932; *Educ* Newport HS; *m* 9 Dec 1959, Patricia Ann, da of Leonard George Kinsey Black (d 1984); 1 s (Paul b 1971); *Career* gp planning exec Dobson Park Industs plc, md Markon Engineering Co Ltd, dir Dobson Park Industs plc 1984-89, chm and chief exec Kango Wolf Power Tools Ltd 1984-89; chm and dir: Kango Wolf Power Tools Ltd UK, Kango Wolf Int Inc Canada, Kango Wolf Power Tools Pty Ltd Australia, Kango Wolf Tools Inc USA, Kango Ltd 1988-89; dir Ralliwolf Ltd India 1985-; *Recreations* golf, shooting; *Clubs* Luffenham Heath Golf; *Style*— Lyn Dacey, Esq; Toll Bar House, Burley, Oakham LE15 7TA (☎ 0572 755606, fax 0572 724 807)

DACIE, Sir John Vivian; s of John Charles Dacie; *b* 20 July 1912; *Educ* King's Coll Sch, King's Coll Hosp (MD); *m* 1938, Margaret Kathleen Victoria, *née* Thynne; 3 s, 2 da; *Career* sr lectr then reader Br Postgrad Medical Sch 1946-57, prof of haematology London Univ 1957-77; author; FRS 1967, Hon FRSM 1984; kt 1976; *Books* Haemolytic Anaemias, Practical Haematology; *Recreations* entomology, music; *Style*— Sir John Dacie, FRS; 10 Alan Rd, Wimbledon, London SW19 (☎ 081 946 6086)

DACRE, Nigel; s of Peter Dacre, and Joan, *née* Hill; *b* 3 Sept 1956; *Educ* Univ Coll Sch Hampstead London, St John's Coll Oxford (MA); *m* Dr Jane Elizabeth Dacre, da of Peter Verrill; 1 s (Robert b 1989), 1 da (Claire b 1986); *Career* graduate trainee BBC 1978,, BBC Bristol 1980, TV journalist News at Ten ITN 1982, assoc ed budget progs ITN 1984-86, prog ed world news ITN 1987, newsroom ed ITN General Election Special 1987, ed Euro Elections Special 1989, exec prodr News At One (ed 1989-90) and News at 5.40 1990-; *Books* ITN Budget Factbook (ed, 1985); *Recreations* jazz piano, walking; *Style*— Nigel Dacre, Esq; 52 Cholmeley Cres, Highgate, London N6 5HA (☎ 071 341 2134); Independent Television News, 48 Wells St, London W1P 4DE (☎ 071 637 2424)

DACRE, Paul Michael; s of Peter Dacre, and Joan, *née* Hill; *b* 14 Nov 1948; *Educ* Univ Coll Sch London, Univ of Leeds (BA); *m* Kathleen, da of Charles James Thomson; 2 s (James Charles b 21 May 1984, Alexander Peter b 6 Aug 1987); *Career* Daily Express: reporter Manchester 1970-71, reporter, feature writer and assoc features ed London 1971-76, NY corr 1976-79; Daily Mail: bureau chief NY 1980, dep news ed London 1981, news ed 1983, asst ed news and foreign 1986, asst ed features 1987, exec ed 1988, assoc ed 1989-; ed Evening Standard 1991-; *Style*— Paul Dacre, Esq; c/o The Evening Standard, Northcliffe House, 2 Derry Street, London W8 5EE (☎ 071 938 6000)

DACRE, Baroness (E 1321); Hon Rachel Leila; *née* Brand; da of 4 Viscount Hampden, who was also 26 Baron Dacre, following whose death (1965) the Viscountcy passed to his bro while the Barony fell into abeyance between the two surviving daughters, till terminated in favour of Rachel, the elder, 1970; *b* 24 Oct 1929; *m* 26 July 1951, Hon William Douglas-Home, *qv*; 1 s, 3 da; *Heir* s, Hon James Thomas Archibald Douglas-Home b 16 May 1952; *Style*— The Rt Hon Lady Dacre; Kilmeston, Alresford, Hants

DACRE LACY, Alastair de Saumarez; s of Edward Dacre Lacy (d 1969); *b* 29 Nov 1928; *Educ* Bradfield Coll; *m* 1960, Avril, da of Edward Frederick Ranger (d 1982); 2 da; *Career* chm and md Technicare International Newbury 1972- (Queens's award for Export 1979, 1983), Thor Engrg Services Ltd Poole; dir: Turriff Corp plc, Value Engrg Australasia Pty Ltd (Perth Australia), Technicare 1983, Sendirian Berhad (Kuala Lumpur), Bellman Computing Ltd, Kuwait British Technical Services Ltd, Technicare Group Ltd, Technicare Avionics Ltd, Chermont Turriff Ltd, Express Insulation Ltd, Technicare Snd Bhd (State of Brunei), Chelgrave Contracting Pty Ltd Aust, Amarit Technicare Ltd Thailand, Waleed Technical Services (LLC) Oman, ARC Insulation Ltd, Technicare Holdings Ltd, Staffwise Employment Agency Ltd, Terotechnology Ltd; chm ME and N Africa Ctee London C of C, memb Exec Ctee ME Assoc; memb Worshipful Co of Gunmakers; *Clubs* Royal Thames Yacht, Oil Industries; *Style*— Alastair Dacre Lacy, Esq; Coombe Lodge, Farnborough, nr Wantage, Oxon OX12 8NP

DACRE OF GLANTON, Baroness; Lady Alexandra Henrietta Louisa; *née* Haig; da of Field Marshal 1 Earl Haig; *m* 1, 10 June 1941 (m dis 1954), Rear Adm Clarence Dinsmore Howard-Johnston, CB, DSO, DSC; 2 s, 1 da; m 2, 4 Oct 1954, Hugh Trevor-Roper, *see* Dacre of Glanton, Baron; *Career* chm: Music Therapy Charity 1969-82, Edinburgh Festival Guild 1960-80, Border Regn; organiser Oxford Subscription Concerts 1962-80; patron Cambridge Univ Opera Society; *Recreations* music, painting, interior decoration, gardening; *Style*— The Rt Hon the Lady Dacre of Glanton; The Old Rectory, Didcot, Oxon

DACRE OF GLANTON, Baron (Life Peer UK 1979), of Glanton, Co Northumberland; Hugh Redwald Trevor-Roper; s of Dr Bertie William Edward Trevor-Roper; *b* 15 Jan 1914; *Educ* Charterhouse, Ch Ch Oxford; *m* 4 Oct 1954, Lady Alexandra Haig, da of Field Marshal 1 Earl Haig, the WWI Gen; *Career* sits as Cons in House of Lords; former tutor Ch Ch Oxford, regius prof modern history Oxford 1957-80, nat dir Times Newspapers 1974, master Peterhouse Cambridge 1980-87; *Clubs* United Oxford & Cambridge Univ, Beefsteak; *Style*— The Rt Hon the Lord Dacre of Glanton; The Old Rectory, Didcot, Oxon OX11 7EB

DADA, Feroze Ahmad; s of Ahmad Valimohamed Dada, of Pakistan, and Halima; *b* 21 April 1952; *Educ* St Patrick's Sch Karachi, Univ of Karachi (BCom); *m* 4 Feb 1984, Farida, da of HLA Maung, of Burma; 1 da (Sumaya b 1986); *Career* ptnr Freeman & Partner chartered accountants 1981-; dir: Reyker Securities Ltd 1984-, FSI Group plc 1986-; FCA 1983, assoc Inst of Taxation 1978; *Books* Interest Relief for Companies (1981); *Recreations* cricket; *Clubs* Brondesbury Cricket; *Style*— F A Dada, Esq; 25 Coppice Walk, Totteridge, London N20 8DA (☎ 081 446 7846); 30 St James's St, London SW1A 1HB (☎ 071 925 0770, fax 071 925 0726)

DAFFERN, Allan Lister; s of Lister Daffern, of Keighley, and Anne Marguerite, *née* Stewart; *b* 8 Aug 1939; *Educ* Bellevue GS Bradford; *m* 14 Sept 1963, Madeleine, da of late Albert Cyril Yeo; 1 s (Richard b 25 Oct 1969), 2 da (Jane b 24 Aug 1964, Sarah 29 April 1967); *Career* Nat Serv RAEC 1960-62; trainee Royal Insurance 1955-60, md: Life & Pensions Co Bartlett Insurance Brokers 1972-85 (joined 1963), life & pensions brokerage Rattray Daffern & Partners Ltd (co sold to Willis Coroon 1987) 1985-87; regnl md Willis Wrightson Financial Planning Ltd 1988-89, chief exec Willis Consulting Ltd (operating dir of Willis Coroon plc) 1989-; dep chm Fin Servs Ctee Br Insurance & Investmt Brokers Assoc 1984-89; FCII 1960, Assoc Pensions Mgmnt Inst 1983; *Recreations* golf, fell walking, travel, Yorkshire cricket; *Clubs* Yorkshire CCC; *Style*— Allan Daffern, Esq; The Carrs, Darley, Harrogate, N Yorkshire HG3 2QQ (☎ 0423 780384); Willis Consulting Ltd, 30 Park Place, Leeds LS1 2SP (☎ 0532 459077, fax 0532 426824)

DAFFERN, Antony Richard; s of late Edward William Daffern; *b* 14 May 1934; *Educ* King Edward VI Sch Nuneaton, Manchester Univ; *m* 1959, Freda, *née* Appleby; 2 da; *Career* co dir; asst md Telefusion plc 1978-83, dep chm 1983-; memb NTRA Cncl 1978-; *Style*— Antony Daffern, Esq; 27 Rowland Lane, Cleveleys, Blackpool FY5 2QX (☎ 0253 854562)

DAFTER, Raymond Maurice (Ray); s of Maurice Henry Dafter, of Swindon, Wilts, and Dorothy Joan, *née* Vincent; *b* 22 April 1944; *Educ* Marlborough GS, The Coll Swindon, Harvard Univ; *m* 25 Sept 1965, Christine, da of William Charles Richard Franklin (d 1976), of Swindon, Wilts; 2 da (Yvonne Louise b 5 May 1968, Claire Rachel b 13 Dec 1970); *Career* journalist: Evening Advertiser Swindon 1961-64, Evening Post Bristol 1964-70, Financial Times London 1970-83; central dir Public and Overseas Relations Electricity Cncl London 1983-88, dep chief exec and head of consultancy Valin Pollen Ltd 1988-90, corp affairs dir Enterprise Oil plc 1990-; memb Cncl Br Inst of Energy Econ; FInstPet 1978, MIPR 1988; *Books* Running Out of Fuel (1978), Scraping the Barrel (1980), Winning More Oil (1982); *Recreations* sailing, music, flying, walking; *Style*— Ray Dafter, Esq; Wolsey Oast, Claygate Rd, Laddingford, Kent (☎ 089 273 376)

DAGGER, John Frederick Hannay; s of Richard Leslie Dagger (d 1973), of Newcastle upon Tyne, and Iris, *née* Hannay (d 1973); *b* 13 July 1927; *Educ* Uppingham; *m* 19 June 1948, Patricia Anne, da of Charles Edward Thompson (d 1979), of Sheffield; 1 s (Richard b 1950), 1 da (Sarah b 1953); *Career* Capt Coldstream Gds 1945-52 (Malaya 1948-50); tea planter S India 1952-56; Hopfactors (UK) Ltd 1957 (dir 1963-86); genealogist; memb AGRA 1984; *Recreations* walking, looking up old relatives; *Style*— John Dagger, Esq; Oak House, Horsmonden, Tonbridge, Kent TN12 8LP (☎ 0892 722272)

DAGLESS, Prof Erik Leslie; s of Alec W Dagless, and Johanne, *née* Petersen (d 1976); *b* 4 Nov 1946; *Educ* Orton Longueville GS, Univ of Surrey (BSc, PhD); *m* 23 Aug 1969, Christine Annette, da of Leslie Lansbury; 2 s (Niels b 1973, Stephen b 1975), 1 da (Helen b 1972); *Career* lectr Univ Coll Swansea 1971-78, sr lectr UMIST 1981 (lectr 1978-81), dean of engrg Univ of Bristol 1988- (prof 1982-, head of dept 1985-88, hon ed Part E IEE Proceedings; memb: Exec Ctee UCNS, Sub Ctee SERC; FIEE; *Books* Introduction to Microprocessors (1979); *Style*— Prof Erik Dagless; Department of Electrical and Electronic Engineering, University Walk, University of Bristol, Avon BS8 1TR (☎ 0272 303030 ext 3260)

DAGWORTHY PREW, Wendy Ann; da of Arthur Sidney Dagworthy (d 1972), of Gravesend, Kent, and Jean Annie, *née* Stubbs; *b* 4 March 1950; *Educ* Northfleet Secdy Sch for Girls, Medway Coll of Design, Hornsey Coll of Art (BA); *m* 4 Aug 1973, Jonathan William Prew, s of Capt William Sidney Augustus Prew (d 1961), of Somerset and Africa; 1 s (Augustus b 1987); *Career* designer/dir Wendy Dagworthy Ltd 1972-; lectr various colls, coll external assessor BA Hons degree fashion and textiles; current assessor: St Martin's Sch of Art, Trent Poly, Leicester Poly, Squire Coll, Hong Kong Poly; course dir Fashion BA Hons Degree Central St Martin's Coll of Art & Design 1989-; dir London Designer Collections 1982, conslt CIYAA Fashion/Textiles Bd 1982-, judge Art and Design Projects various mfrs, memb RSA Bd; participating designer Fashion Aid Albert Hall; exhibitor VRA; seasonal exhibitor: London, Milan, NY, Paris; various TV appearances; Fil D'Or Int Linen Award; memb Br Fashion Cncl; *Recreations* dining out, theatre, horse racing, reading, painting, cooking; *Clubs* Chelsea Arts, Groucho; *Style*— Ms Wendy Dagworthy Prew; 18 Melrose Terrace, London W6 (☎ 071 602 6676); 15 Poland St, London W1 (☎ 071 437 6105)

DAHRENDORF, Sir Ralf; KBE (1982); s of Gustav Dahrendorf (d 1954), and Lina, *née* Witt (d 1980); *b* 1 May 1929; *Educ* Hamburg Univ (DPhil), LSE (PhD); *m* 1980, Ellen Joan; *Career* lectr Saarbrücken 1957; prof sociology: Hamburg 1958-60, Tübingen 1960-64, Konstanz 1966-69 (vice-chm Funding Ctee Konstanz Univ 1964-66); Parly sec of state W German FO 1979-70, memb EEC Cmmn Brussels 1970-74, dir LSE 1974-84, warden St Antony's Coll Oxford 1987-; memb: Hansard Soc Cmmn on Electoral Reform 1975-76, Royal Cmmn on Legal Servs 1976-79; tstee Ford Fndn 1976-88; FBA, FRSA, hon MRIA; Hon fell: Imperial Coll, LSE; Hon DLitt: Reading, Dublin; Hon LLD: Manchester, Wagner Coll NY, York (Ontario), Columbia NY; Hon DHL: Kalamazoo Coll, John Hopkins Univ Baltimore; Hon DSc: Ulster, Bath; Hon DUniv: Open Univ, Maryland, Surrey; Hon Dr: Université Catholique de Louvain; Hon DSSC: Queens Belfast, Univ of Birmingham; Gr Cross de l'Ordre du Mérite (Sénégal) 1971, Gr Bundesverdienstkreuz mit Stern und Schulterband (FDR) 1974, Gr Croix de l'Ordre du Mérite (Luxembourg) 1974, gr goldenes Ehrenzeichen am Bande für Verdienste (Austria) 1975, Gr Croix de l'Ordre de Léopold II (Belgium) 1975; *Clubs* Reform, Garrick; *Style*— Sir Ralf Dahrendorf, KBE; St Antony's College, Oxford OX2 6JF

DAICHES, David; s of Salis Daiches (d 1945), and Flora Levin (d 1983); *b* 2 Sept 1912; *Educ* George Watson Coll Edinburgh, Univ of Edinburgh (MA, Vans Dunlop Scholar, Eliot Prize) Balliol Coll Oxford (DPhil, Elton exhibitioner); *m* 1, 28 July 1937, Billie Isobel Janet (d 1977), da of William Mackay (d 1941), of Scotland; 1 s (Alan Harry b 1939), 2 da (Jennifer Rachel b 1941, Elizabeth (Mrs Mackay) b 1946); m 2, 22 Dec 1978, Hazel Margaret Newman (d 1986); *Career* HM Dip Serv; second Sec Br Embassy Washington DC USA 1943-46; Bradley fell Balliol Coll Oxford 1936-37, prof of English Cornell Univ USA 1946-51, lectr in English and fell Jesus Coll Cambridge 1951-61, prof of English and dean Sch of English and American Studies Univ of Sussex 1961-77, dir Inst for Advanced Studies in the Humanities Univ of Edinburgh 1981-86; former pres: Soc of Authors in Scotland, Assoc for Scottish Literary Studies, Saltire Soc (now hon pres); Hon LittD Brown Univ 1968, Docteur de l'Universite Sorborne 1973; Hon DLitt: Univ of Edinburgh 1976, Univ of Sussex 1978, Univ of Stirling 1980, Univ of Glasgow 1987, Univ of Bologna 1989, Guelph Univ 1990; hon fell Sunderland Poly 1977; FRSE, FRSL; *Books* The Novel and The Modern World (1939), The King James Bible: A Study of its Sources and Development (1941), Robert Burns (1950), A Critical History of English Literature (1960), The Paradox of Scottish Culture (1964), Walter Scott and his World (1971), God and the Poets (1984); *Recreations* music, talking; *Clubs* Scottish Arts, New Club (Edinburgh); *Style*— Prof David Daiches, FRSE; 12 Rothesay Place, Edinburgh EH3 7SQ

DAICHES, Lionel Henry; QC (Scotland 1956); s of Rev Dr Salis Daiches (d 1945), of Edinburgh, and Flora Levin (d 1983); *b* 8 March 1911; *Educ* George Watson's Coll Edinburgh, Univ of Edinburgh (MA, LLB); *m* 1947 (m dis 1973), Dorothy Bernstein; 2 s (Michael, Nicholas); *Career* N Staffs Regt 1940-46, Maj J A G Staff, 1 Army N Africa, Italy (including Anzio Beachhead); admitted to faculty of advocates 1946, standing jr counsel Bd of Control Scotland 1950-56; fell Int Acad of Trial Lawyers 1976; *Books* Russians at Law (1960); *Recreations* talking, globe trotting; *Clubs* New, Scottish Arts, Puffins (Edinburgh); *Style*— Lionel Daiches, Esq, QC; 10 Heriot Row, Edinburgh EH3 6HU (☎ 031 5564144); Parliament Hse, Parliament Sq, Edinburgh EH1 1RF (☎ 031 2262881)

DAIN, David John Michael; s of late John Gordon Dain, and Gladys Ellen, *née* Connop; *b* 30 Oct 1940; *Educ* Merchant Taylors', St John's Coll Oxford (MA); *m* 28 June 1969, Susan Kathleen, da of J Richard F Moss, OBE, of Stapleford, Cambridge; 1 s (Christopher b 1977), 4 da (Sarah b 1974, Penelope b 1979, Tessa b 1981, Sophie (twin) b 1981); *Career* HM Dip Serv 1963-: Sch of Oriental and African Studies (Persian Studies), Br Embassy Tehran 1964, Oriental Sec Kabul 1965-68, Cabinet Office 1969-72, Bonn 1972-75, FCO 1975-78, Head of Chancery Athens 1978-81, dep high cmmr Nicosia 1981-85, Head Western Euro Dept FCO 1985-89, attached to Office of the Min for the Civil Serv 1989-90, high cmmr Cyprus 1990-; fell Inst of Linguists; memb Frant Church Ctee; Royal Order of Merit Norway 1988; *Recreations* tennis, bridge, walking, sailing, natural history, fishing; *Clubs* United Oxford and Cambridge Univ, Oxford Union; *Style*— David Dain, Esq; Foreign and Cwlth Office, Whitehall, London SW1

DAINTITH, Prof Terence Charles; s of Edward Daintith (d 1942), and Irene, *née* Parsons; *b* 8 May 1942; *Educ* Wimbledon Coll, St Edmund Hall Oxford (BA, MA), Univ of Nancy (Leverhulme Euro scholar); *m* Christine Anne, da of Sqdn Ldr Charles Edward Bulport; 1 s (Edward Charles b 1967), 1 da (Alexandra b 1968); *Career* assoc in law Univ of Calif 1963-64, lectr in constitutional law Univ of Edinburgh 1964-72 (dir of studies in law 1970-72), visiting prof Faculty of Law Univ of Aix Marseilles III France 1975, prof of pub law and head Dept of Pub Law Univ of Dundee 1972-83 (fndr and dir Centre for Petroleum and Mineral Law Studies 1977-83), prof of law Euro Univ Inst Florence 1981-87, hon visiting prof Univ of Dundee 1983-, dir Inst of Advanced Legal Studies and prof of law Univ of London 1988-, external prof Euro Univ Inst Florence Italy 1988-, Parsons scholar Univ of Sydney 1988; memb: Editorial Bd Modern Legal Studies 1974-, Academic Advsy Gp Section of Energy and Nat Resources Law Int Bar Assoc 1982-, Conseil d'Administration, Association Internationale de Droit Economique (Louvain) 1985-; ed Jl of Energy and Nat Resources Law (Vol 1, 1983-); tstee: Hamlyn Tst 1988-, Petroleum and Mineral Law Educn Tst 1989-; barr Lincoln's Inn 1966-, memb Academia Europaea 1989-; *Publications* Report on the Economic Law of the United Kingdom (1974), United Kingdom Oil and Gas Law (with G D M Willoughby, 1977, 2 edn 1984), The Legal Character of Petroleum Licences (ed and contrib, 1981), European Energy Strategy: The Legal Framework (with L Mancher, 1986), Contract and Organisation: Social Science Contributions to Legal Analysis (with G Teubner 1986), The Legal Integration of Energy Markets (with S Williams, 1987), Law as an Instrument of Economic Policy: Comparative and Critical Approaches (1988); *Recreations* cycling, curling and carpentry; *Clubs* Athenaeum; *Style*— Prof Terence Daintith; Institute of Advanced Legal Studies, 17 Russell Square, London WC1B 5DR (☎ 071 637 1731, fax 071 436 8824, telex 269400)

DAINTON, Baron (Life Peer UK 1986), of Hallam Moors in South Yorkshire; Sir Frederick Sydney Dainton; s of George Whalley, and Mary Jane Dainton; *b* 11 Nov 1914; *Educ* Central Sch Sheffield, St John's Coll Oxford (MA, BSc), Sidney Sussex Coll Cambridge (PhD, ScD); *m* 1942, Barbara Hazlitt, JP, PhD, o da of late Dr W B Wright, of Manchester; 1 s (Hon John Bourke b 10 Sept 1947), 2 da (Hon Mary Crawford (Hon Mrs Whitehead) b 15 Feb 1950, Hon Rosalind Hazlitt (Hon Mrs Conway) b 11 April 1952); *Career* fell and praelector St Catharine's Coll Cambridge 1945-50, H O Jones lectr in Physical Chemistry Univ of Cambridge 1947-50, vice chllr Univ of Nottingham and hon dir Cookridge High Energy Radiation Res Centre Univ of Leeds 1965-70 (prof of physical chemistry 1950-65), Dr Lee's prof of chemistry Univ of Oxford 1970-73, chllr Univ of Sheffield 1979-; chm: Nat Libraries Ctee 1969-70, Cncl Scientific Policy Advsy Bd for the Res Cncls 1969-73, Univ Grants Ctee 1973-78, Harkness fellowship UK Selection Ctee 1974-81, Nat Radiological Protection Bd 1978-85, Br Library Bd 1978-85, Royal Postgrad Med Sch 1979-89, Edward Boyle Meml Tst 1982-; govr: Henley Admin Staff Coll 1974-89, LSE 1980-; tstee: Br Museum (natural history) 1976-82, Wolfson Fndn 1979-88; cmmr Museums and Galleries 1983-; hon fell: St Catharine's Coll Cambridge, St John's Coll Oxford, RCP, Royal Soc of Chemistry, RCR, Br Inst of Radiology, Library Assoc, LSE, QMC (now Queen Mary and Westfield Coll), Birkbeck Coll, Goldsmith's Coll, RPMS; prime warden Worshipful Co of Goldsmiths 1982-83; FRSC 1938, FRS 1957; kt 1971; *Books* Chain Reactions (1956, 1966, in Polish and Chinese translations), Photochemistry and Reaction Kinetics (jt ed and contrib, 1967), Choosing a British University (1980), Universities and the National Health Service (1983); *Recreations* walking, colour photography; *Clubs* Athenaeum; *Style*— The Rt Hon Lord Dainton, FRS; Fieldside, Water Eaton Lane, Oxford OX5 2PR (☎ 08675 5132)

DAINTY, Hon Mrs (Priscilla); *née* Wolfenden; da of Baron Wolfenden, CBE (d 1985); *b* 1937; *m* 1959, Col F L Dainty; *Style*— The Hon Mrs Dainty; Thump Head Cottage, 22 Boobery, Sampford Peverell, Devon

DAKERS, Dr Lionel Frederick; CBE (1983); s of Lewis Dakers (d 1978), and Eleanor, *née* Hooper (d 1976); *b* 24 Feb 1924; *Educ* Rochester Cathedral Choir Sch, pupil of Sir Edward Bairstow (organist of York Minster), Royal Acad of Music; *m* 21 April 1951, Mary Elisabeth, da of Rev Claude Williams (d 1963); 4 da (Rachel, Mary, Juliet, Felicity); *Career* WWII, served RAEC 1942-47; asst organist St George's Chapel Windsor 1950-54, asst music master Eton 1952-54; organist: Ripon Cathedral 1954-57, Exeter Cathedral 1957-72; dir Royal Sch of Church Music 1972-89; Hon DMus Lambeth 1979; FRCO 1945, FRAM 1962, FRCM 1980; *Books* Church Music at the Crossroads (1970), A Handbook of Parish Music (1979), Making Church Music Work (1978), Music and the Alternative Service Book (ed, 1980), The Chorister's

Companion (ed, 1980), The Psalms - Their Use and Performance Today (1980), The Church Musician as Conductor (1982), Church Music in a Changing World (1984), Choosing - and Using - Hymns (1985); *Recreations* book collecting, gardening, continental food, travel; *Clubs* Athenaeum; *Style*— Dr Lionel Dakers, CBE; 6 Harcourt Terrace, Salisbury, Wiltshire SP2 7SA (☎ 0722 24880)

DAKIN, Christopher John; s of George Frederick Dakin, CBE (d 1969), and Helena May, *née* Samuels (d 1973); *b* 20 Aug 1931; *Educ* Haileybury, Gonville and Caius Coll Cambridge (MA); *m* 1956, Maureen, da of Albert George Seymour (d 1977); 2 s (Gervase, Simon), 1 da (Samantha); *Career* dir: Plessey Research (Caswell) Ltd 1982-85, Stromberg-Carlson Corporation USA 1984-85, Plessey Major Systems Ltd 1985-86; chief exec and dir Plessey Public Networks Ltd 1984-85, BICC Cables Ltd 1987; FIEE; *Recreations* bricklaying; *Style*— C John Dakin, Esq; Stack Polly, Woodbank Lane, Chester CH1 6JD (☎ 0244 880035); BICC Cables Ltd, Heronsway, Chester Business Park, Wrexham Rd, Chester CH4 9PZ (☎ 0244 688400)

DAKIN, Robert Baxter; s of John Dakin (d 1975), and Gladys Ivy, *née* Reakes (d 1972); *b* 6 Oct 1934; *Educ* Monkton Combe Sch; *m* 28 May 1960, Dieuwertje Matthea Johanna, da of Jan Hendrik Berkhout, of Beverwyk, Holland; 2 s (Mark b 1962, John b 1973), 1 da (Joanna b 1961); *Career* Mil Serv 2 Lt Somerset LI and W India Regt in Jamaica 1957-60; CA 1957; Price Waterhouse & Co 1964-67, currently in private practice in Cambridge; played hockey for Jamaica; lay reader C of E 1965-; FCA; *Recreations* golf, hockey, tennis; *Style*— Robert Dakin, Esq; 48 Lantree Crescent, Trumpington, Cambridge (☎ 0223 840040)

DALAL, Maneck Ardeshir Sohrab; s of Khan Bahadur Ardeshir Sohrab Dalal, OBE (d 1958), and Amy Nanavutty (d 1940); *b* 24 Dec 1918; *Educ* Barnes HS Deolali India, Trinity Hall Cambridge; *m* 1947, Kathleen Gertrude, da of Frank Richardson (d 1971); 3 da (Christina, Susan, Caroline); *Career* called to the Bar Middle Temple 1945; pres: Indian Chamber of Commerce in GB 1959-62, Indian Mgmnt Assoc of UK 1960-63; regional dir Air India London 1959-77; chm: Foreign Airlines Assoc of UK 1965-67, Indian YMCA in London 1972-, Bharatiya Vidya London 1975-; min for Tourism of Civil Aviation High Cmmn of India 1973-77, md Tata Ltd London 1978-, gp dir Tata Industries Bombay 1980-; vice pres Friends of Vellore 1979-, vice chm Festival of India GB 1980-81, dep chm Royal Overseas League 1981-, (chm 1985); memb: Inst of Travel of Tourism, Br Cncl of Churches, LCCI London and Regional Affairs Ctee, Int Bd of Utd World Colleges; FCIT, FBIM; *Recreations* tennis, squash rackets (captained Cambridge Univ in both games); *Clubs* Royal Over-Seas League, Hurlingham; *Style*— M A S Dalal, Esq; Tall Trees, Marlborough Rd, Hampton, Middlesex (☎ 081 979 2065); Tata Ltd, 18 Grosvenor Place, London SW1X 7HS (☎ 071 235 8281, telex 21501 or 917422)

DALAL, Dr Shashichandra Dhirajlal (Shashi); s of Dhirajlal Sarupchand Dalal (d 1944), and Motiben, *née* Choksey (d 1934); *b* 16 April 1923; *Educ* Babu Panalal Puranchand Jain HS, Univ of Bombay (MB BS, MD), Univ of Copenhagen (DA); *m* 21 Dec 1951, Vatsala Shashichandra, da of Motilal Sivchand Jhaveri (d 1988); 1 s (Gautam b 1955), 2 da (Shreedevi b 1952, Sandhya b 1956); *Career* various med posts Bombay Hosps 1947-52; Govt of Tanzania: MO 1952-62, Miny of Health 1952-67, specialist anaesthetist 1963-67; conslt anaesthetist: HH Aga Khan Hosp Dar Es Salaam 1967-71, N Middx Hosp London 1974-90, NE Thames Regnl Health Authy 1974-90; FFARCS; *Recreations* reading, walking; *Clubs* Lions (Enfield); *Style*— Dr Shashi Dalal; 38 Partridge Road, St Albans, Hertfordshire AL3 6HH; Dept of Anaesthesia, North Middlesex Hospital, Sterling Way, Edmonton, London N18 1QX (☎ 081 807 3071 ext 2221)

DALE, Antony; OBE (1973); s of Maj Claude Henry Dale, CMG, OBE (d 1946), and Dorothy, *née* Liddell (d 1974); *b* 12 July 1912; *Educ* Brighton Coll, Oriel Coll Oxford (BA, BLitt, MA); *m* 10 May 1941, Yvonne Chevallier, da of Douglas Arthur Macfie; 1 da (Madeline Heather (Mrs Rijndorf)); *Career* admitted slr 1938; chief investigator of historic bldgs DOE 1961-76 (investigator 1946-61); hon sec Regency Soc of Brighton and Hove 1945-, pres Sussex Archaeological Soc 1979-80; Fell Soc of Antiquaries 1953; *Books* Fashionable Brighton (1946), The History and Architecture of Brighton (1948), About Brighton (1951), Brighton Old and New (1953), James Wyatt (1956), Brighton Town and Brighton People (1976), The Theatre Royal Brighton (1980), The Wagners of Brighton (with Sir Anthony Wagner, 1982), Brighton Churches (1989); *Clubs* Athenaeum; *Style*— Antony Dale, Esq, OBE; 38 Prince Regent's Close, Brighton BN2 5JP

DALE, Celia Marjorie (Mrs Guy Ramsey); da of James Dale (d 1985), of London, and Marguerite, *née* Adamson (d 1981), of London; *Educ* privately; *m* 1938, Guy Ramsey (d 1959), s of Cecil Ramsey; 1 s (Simon b 1944); *Career* reviewer, publishers' advsr, author; *books*: The Least of These (1943), To Hold the Mirror (1945), The Dry land (1952), The Wooden O (1953), Trial of Strength (1955), A Spring of Love (1960), Other People (1964), A Helping Hand (1966), Act of Love (1969), A Dark Corner (1971), The Innocent Party (1973), Helping with Inquiries (1979), A Personal Call and Other Stories (1986), Sheeps Clothing (1988); author of numerous short stories, radio, and television recordings; winner Crime Writers Assoc Veuve Cliquot Short Story award; memb Crime Writers Assoc 1979; *Recreations* reading, conversation, travel; *Style*— Ms Celia Dale; Curtis Brown, 162-168 Regent St, London W1R 5TB (☎ 071 872 0331, fax 071 872 0332)

DALE, David Kenneth Hay; CBE (1976); s of Kenneth Hay Dale, and Francesca Susanna Hoffman; b 27 Jan 1927; *Educ* Dorchester GS; *m* 1956, Hanna Szydlowska; 1 s; *Career* dep govr Seychelles 1975, (sec to Cabinet 1976), FCO 1977-80, govr Montserrat 1980-85; *Style*— David Dale, Esq, CBE; Chatley Cottage, Batcombe, Nr Shepton Mallet, Somerset, BA4 6AF

DALE, Iain Leonard; OBE (1989); s of Leonard H Dale, CBE, DL (d 1986), and Doris Anne Smithson (d 1984); fndr of Dale Electric International plc Group 1935; *b* 9 June 1940; *Educ* Scarborough Coll Yorkshire; *m* Maria, da of Josef Lanmuller (d 1973), of Pottendorf-Landegg, Lower Austria, Austria; 3 s (Jonathan Iain b 1963, Paul Josef b 1967, David Leonard b 1969); *Career* creative dir Streets Advertising 1969-71, md Hicks Oubridge Public Affairs 1971-74; dir: Dale Electric International plc 1971 (chief exec 1986-), Dale Electric of GB Ltd, Comptoir Gen Impex (France), Ottomotores Dale Sa De Cv (Mexico), Dale Electric Power Systems Ltd (Thailand), Erskine Systems Ltd (UK), Houchin Ltd (UK), (non-exec) TR Pacific Investment Trust plc 1990-; chm South East Asia Trade Advsy Gp 1988-; assoc Br Generating Set Manufacturers 1984-85 memb: Nat Cncl Confedn Br Industs (CBI) 1984-, NEDO Generating Set Sub Gp 1982-87, Latin American Trade Advsy Gp 1985-; CBIM, FRSA; memb Co Merchant Adventurers of City of York; *Recreations* walking, photography; *Clubs* Royal Over-Seas League; *Style*— Iain L Dale, Esq, OBE; Grove House, Low Marishes, Malton, N Yorks YO17 0RQ (☎ 065 386 223, fax 065 386 544); Dale Electric International plc, Electricity Buildings, Filey, N Yorks YO14 9PS (☎ 0723 514141)

DALE, John Howard; s of Rev David Howard Dale, of St Ives Huntingdonshire, and Betty Margureta (Betty), *née* Rosser; *b* 18 July 1951; *Educ* King Henry VIII GS for Boys, Bretton Hall Coll Univ of Leeds (Cert Ed); *m* 25 Aug 1979, Mary Elizabeth, da of Joseph Frank Waterhouse, of Birmingham; 1 s (Joseph), 1 da (Charlotte); *Career* actor 1971-73: Hull, Sheffield, Brighton; artistic dir Community Arts Centre Brighton 1973-75, asst dir Royal Ct Theatre London 1975-77, writer and dir BBC TV Children's Dept 1977-80, conslt Industl Personnel Depts 1981-82, exec prodr Children's and Young People's Dept TVS 1983-86; devised Saturday ITV formats: Number 73, Motormouth; head of late evening progs TVS, devised POV 1986-87; head Special Projects TVS; prodr and dir: 6 hours network adult drama, 27 hours children's drama incl Knights of God ITV; freelance writer, dir and prodr in TV and theatre; memb Bd: Artswork Ltd, Polka Theatre; dir J & M Prodns; *Recreations* children, pubs, writing; *Style*— John Dale, Esq; J & M Productions, 32 Court Rd, London SE9 5NU

DALE, Peter Grenville Hurst; s of Thomas Calvert Dale (d 1964), of Ambleside, N Brunton, Gosforth, Newcastle upon Tyne, and Phyllis, *née* Addison; *b* 14 Feb 1935; *Educ* Dame Allan's Boys Sch, Rutherford Coll, King's Coll Univ of Durham (Dip Arch); *m* 1 (m dis 1985), Dr Marion Ishbel Dale, *née* Duncan; 3 s (Ruarigh b 1966, Patrick b 1968, Robert b 1971); m 2, 14 Sept 1988, Elizabeth Josephine Mary, da of Lt Cdr Reginald Galer, RN (ret), of 10 Tudor Close, Pembroke, Dyfed; *Career* architect; former posts in: Kingston upon Thames, Surrey Co, Gateshead Borough, Newcastle City; asst dir Lothian Region 1974-77, co architect Humberside 1977-87, assoc lectr Leeds and Huddersfield Sch of Architecture 1987-, self employed architect 1987-; author of RIBA open learning packages in practise mgmnt and tendering procedures; former memb Cncl SCALA and RIAS; RIBA: hon treas, vice pres, former chm Yorks Region, twice former pres Humberside Branch, memb coordinating ctee, memb Professional Conduct Ctee; memb Br Architectural Library Tst, chair Finance and Resources Cmmn; ret JP, former dep chm Lothian Region Children's Panels; memb Worshipful Co of Chartered Architects 1988, Freeman City of London 1990; memb RIBA 1961, FRIAS 1971, ACIArb 1987; *Recreations* painting, golf, fishing, shooting; *Style*— Peter Dale, Esq; 8 West End Rd, Cottingham, N Humberside HU16 5PA (☎ 0482 845693)

DALE, Stephen Hugh; s of Frederick Francis George Dale, of Lewes Sussex, and Margaret, Brenda Nancy, *née* Beales; *b* 12 July 1955; *Educ* Bolton Sch, Univ of Manchester (BA); *m* 7 April 1979, Susan Maria, da of Reginald Pearman, of Newland Park, Hull; *Career* chartered accountant Deloitte Haskins & Sells Manchester 1976-80 (articled clerk 1976-79); Price Waterhouse: joined Tax Dept Manchester 1980, specialised in VAT and transfd to London office 1983, ptnr 1989-; memb: ICAEW 1980- (memb Tax Ctee, chm VAT Ctee), Vat Practitioners Gp 1983- (memb Exec Ctee), jt VAT Consultative Ctee; *Books* Advanced VAT Planning Property and Financial Services (1989); *Recreations* walking, golf; *Style*— Stephen Dale, Esq; Price Waterhouse, 32 London Bridge St, London SE1 9SY (☎ 071 939 8254, fax 071 378 1072)

DALE, Thomas Edward (Tom); s of Leonard George Dale (d 1964), of St Osyth, Essex, and Sybil Eileen Mary, *née* Stevenson (d 1988); *b* 14 March 1931; *Educ* Gosfield Sch Halstead, LSE (BSc), Inst of Educn Univ of London (PGCE); *Career* Nat Serv RA 1950-52; teacher 1952-54, warden Cambridge Int Centre 1960-66; organising sec Liberal International (Br Gp) 1967-, PA to Ldr of Lib Pty 1967-76, int offr Lib Pty 1977-85; dir: TEAM Promotions Ltd 1986-, Mercialodge Ltd 1987-; Parly candidate: (Lib) Harwich 1959 1964 1966 and 1969, (Alliance) Centl Suffolk 1987; pres Harwich Lib Assoc (now SLD), former chm E Regnl Lib Pty, former memb ELDRE Brussels, pres Univ of London Union 1957-58, sec LSE SU 1955-56, govr LSE 1981-87; memb Essex CC (rep Brightlingsea Div) 1965-67 (also 1973-77 and 1981), ldr SLD Gp 1989- (dep ldr 1981-89), spokesman on highways and agric estates 1981-89; chm ACC Consumer Affrs Ctee 1986-87 and 1988-89; overseas fund raising dir Fight for Sight Appeal 1990-; memb: Tendring DC 1979-, St Osyth PC 1979-87, E Anglia Tourist Bd 1986-, Kent and Essex Sea Fisheries Cmmn 1986-; govr: Gosfield Sch (former chm), Colchester Inst; sec: Hampden Educnl Tst, Herbert Samuel Fndn; *Recreations* theatre, films, travel; *Clubs* National Liberal; *Style*— Tom Dale, Esq; Flat 1, 2 Barking Road, London E6 3BP (☎ and fax 081 470 8640, telex 8956 551); Springmead, Ladysmith Ave, Brightlingsea, Colchester, Essex CO7 0JD (☎ 020630 5552)

DALE, Sir William Leonard; KCMG (1965); s of late Rev William Dale; *b* 1906; *Educ* Hymers Coll Hull; *m* 1, 1948 (m dis 1953), Elizabeth Romeyn, da of Prof Adolph Elwyn, of NY; m 2, 1966, Mrs Gloria Finn, *née* Spellman; 1 da; *Career* barr 1931; entered Colonial Office 1935; legal advsr: Govt of Libya 1951-53, Miny of Educn 1954; sec of state for Cwlth Rels 1961-66; int legal conslt; *Books* Law of the Parish Church, Legislative Drafting:A New Approach, The Modern Commonwealth; *Clubs* Travellers'; *Style*— Sir William Dale, KCMG; 20 Old Buildings, Lincoln's Inn, WC2A 3UP (☎ 071 242 9365)

DALE, William Paterson; s of John Robert Dale (d 1969), of Auldhame, N Berwick, E Lothian, and Mary Waugh, *née* Paterson (d 1980); *b* 2 March 1923; *Educ* Sedbergh Sch; *m* 1, 5 March 1947, Kathleen Ann (d 1977), da of William David Simpson of Highfield, N Berwick, E Lothian; 2 s (Robert b 1956, Alec b 1958), 3 da (Anne b 1948, Mary b 1949, Cynthia b 1953); m 2, Rosemary Joy, widow of Arthur Harrison and da of Stewart Paton, of Templeton Burn, Kilmarnock; *Career* Nat Serv WWII served HG and Coast Guard 1939-45; farmer: Lochhouses, Dunbar 1944-84, Myreton Aberlady 1966-79, Setonmains Longniddry 1966-84, The Holmes, St Boswells and Hoebridge, Melrose 1979-; dir: Myreton Motor Museum Aberlady 1966-, Melrose Motor Museum 1983-; er Church of Scotland; *Recreations* vintage car rallies; *Clubs* Bentley Drivers, Bullnose Morris; *Style*— William P Dale, Esq; The Holmes, St Boswells, Melrose, Roxburghshire TD6 OEL (☎ 0835 22356)

DALE-THOMAS, Philippa Mary; da of Peter Alan Dale-Thomas, of Taunton, Somerset, and Riole Wynette Alpha, *née* Tribe; *b* 5 March 1960; *Educ* Cheltenham Ladies' Coll, Cambridge Coll of Arts and Technol (HND); *Career* Bd dir Edelman Public Relations 1989- (joined 1982); IPR awards; pub affairs 1987, commerce and indust 1989 and 1990, internal communications 1989; MIDA 1988, memb IOD 1989; *Recreations* horse riding, playing the piano; *Style*— Miss Philippa Dale-Thomas; Edelman Public Relations Worldwide, Kingsgate House, 536 King's Road, London SW10 0TE (☎ 071 835 1222, fax 071 351 7676)

DALES, Richard Nigel; s of Kenneth Richard Frank Dales, TD (d 1989), of Southwold, Suffolk, and Olwen Mary, *née* Preedy; *b* 26 Aug 1942; *Educ* Chigwell Sch, St Catharine's Coll Cambridge (MA); *m* 10 Sept 1966, Elizabeth Margaret, da of Edward Owen Martin (d 1966), of Loughton, Essex; 1 s (Jeremy b 1973), 1 da (Eleanor b 1976); *Career* entered FO 1964, third sec Yaoundé Cameroon 1965-67, FCO 1968-70, second sec 1969, second (later first) sec Copenhagen 1970-73, asst private sec to Sec of State for Foreign and Cwlth Affrs 1974-77, first sec Head of Chancery and HM Consul Sofia 1977-81, asst S Asian Dept FCO 1981-82, cnsllr Copenhagen 1982-86, dep high cmmr Harare 1986-89, Head of Central and Southern African Dept FCO 1989-; *Recreations* music, walking; *Style*— Richard Dales, Esq; c/o Foreign and Commonwealth Office, King Charles St, London SW1A 2AH

DALEY, Michael John William; s of Desmond William Daley, of Cockfosters, Herts, and Alma Joan, *née* Ellen; *b* 23 Sept 1953; *Educ* Hatfield Sch; *Career* S G Warburg & Co Ltd 1973-77, Credit Suisse First Boston Ltd 1977-86 (asst mangr 1979, mangr 1982), dir Credit Suisse First Boston Asset Management Ltd 1985, vice pres and head Fixed Income Group Morgan Stanley International 1986-, exec dir Morgan Stanley Asset Management Ltd 1988-; FInstD 1984, MBIM 1986; *Recreations* golf, skiing, mountaineering, motoring; *Clubs* RAC; *Style*— Michael Daley, Esq; Morgan Stanley

Int, Kingsley House, Wimpole St, London W1 (☎ 071 709 3513, fax 071 283 4455, telex 917141)

DALGARNO, Frederick George Scott; s of Frederick Dalgarno; *b* 17 June 1943; *Educ* Robert Gordon's Coll Aberdeen Univ of Aberdeen, Univ of Strathclyde; *m* 1969, Moyra, da of William Ellis; 1 s, 2 da; *Career* dir: Murray Johnstone Ltd 1986-, Richards plc 1984-, Lasalle Ltd; *Recreations* golf, soccer, swimming; *Clubs* Royal Northern and Univ (Aberdeen), Royal Aberdeen Golf; *Style*— Fred Dalgarno, Esq; 14 Westfield Terr, Aberdeen (☎ 0224 642470)

DALGETY, Hugh Barkly Gonnerman; Lord of the Manors and patron of the livings of Lockerley and E Tytherley; s of Arthur William Hugh Dalgety (d 1972), of Lockerley Hall, and Wanzie, *née* Rodgers (d 1990); ggs of Frederick G Dalgety the fndr of Dalgety plc; *b* 16 Aug 1943; *Educ* Milton Abbey, RAC Circencester; *m* 1976, Margaret Anne, da of Desmond Charles Nigel Baring, of Ardington, Oxon; 2 s (Richard b 1977, Thomas b 1984), 1 da (Katherine b 1979); *Career* MFH Tedworth 1964-65, Hursley 1975-78, Portman 1978-82, S & W Wilts 1986-88; *Recreations* field sports, travel; *Clubs* White's; *Style*— Hugh Dalgety, Esq; Millards Hill House, Trudoxhill, Frome, Somerset BA11 5DW (☎ 037384 229)

DALGETY, Ramsay Robertson; QC (Scot 1986); s of James Robertson Dalgety, of Dundee, and Georgia Alexandra, *née* Whyte; *b* 2 July 1945; *Educ* Dundee HS, Univ of St Andrews (LLB); *m* 13 Nov 1971, Mary Margaret, da of Rev Neil Cameron Bernard, of Edinburgh; 1 s (Neil b 1975), 1 da (Caroline b 1974); *Career* Advocate at the Scottish Bar 1972-85; dir and chm: Archer Tport Ltd and Archer Tport (London) Ltd 1982-85, Venture Shipping Ltd 1983-88; dir Scot Opera Glasgow 1980-90; memb: Faculty of Advocates 1972, IOD 1982-89; cncllr City of Edinburgh DC 1974-80, dep chm and tstee Opera Singers' Pension Fund London 1983-, dir Scottish Opera Theatre Tst Ltd Glasgow 1987-90, temp sheriff 1987-91, dep traffic cmmr for Scotland 1988-, dep chm Edinburgh Hibernian Shareholders' Assoc 1990-; *Recreations* boating, golf, opera, travel; *Style*— Ramsay R Dalgety, Esq, QC; 196 Craigleith Rd, Edinburgh EH4 2EE (☎ 031 332 1417); Faculty of Advocates, Advocates Library, Parliament Hse, Edinburgh EH1 1RF (☎ 031 226 5071, 226 2881, fax 031 225 3642, telex 727856 FACADV G)

DALHOUSIE, 16 Earl of (S 1633); Simon Ramsay; KT (1971), GCVO (1979), GBE (1957), MC (1944), JP (Angus 1967), DL (1951); also Lord Ramsay of Dalhousie (S precedence of 1618), Lord Ramsay and Keringtoun (S 1633) and Baron Ramsay of Glenmark (UK 1875); s of 14 Earl of Dalhousie (d 1928), and Lady Mary Heathcote-Drummond-Willoughby (d 1960), da of 1 Earl of Ancaster; suc bro, 15 Earl of Dalhousie 1950; *b* 17 Oct 1914; *Educ* Eton, Ch Ch Oxford; *m* 26 June 1940, Margaret Dalhousie, CStJ, da of Brig-Gen Archibald Stirling of Keir, JP, DL, MP (d 1931); 3 s, 2 da; *Heir* s, Lord Ramsay, *qv*; *Career* 4/5 Bn Black Watch, Maj 1942; Lieut Royal Co of Archers (Queen's Body Guard for Scotland) 1956; MP (C) Angus 1945-50, Cons whip 1946-48, Lord-Lt 1967-89; govr gen Fedn of Rhodesia and Nyasaland 1957-63; lord chamberlain to HM Queen Elizabeth The Queen Mother 1965-; chllr Univ of Dundee 1977-; *Recreations* gardening, fishing; *Clubs* White's; *Style*— The Rt Hon the Earl of Dalhousie, KT, GCVO, GBE, MC, JP, DL; 5 Margaretta Terrace, London SW3 (☎ 071 352 6477); Brechin Castle, Brechin, Angus (☎ 035 62 2176)

DALITZ, Prof Richard Henry; s of Frederick William Dalitz (d 1959), of Melbourne, Aust, and Hazel Blanche, *née* Drummond (d 1970); *b* 28 Feb 1925; *Educ* Scotch Coll, Ormond Coll Melbourne (BA,BSc), Trinity Coll Cambridge (PhD); *m* 8 August 1946, Valda, da of William Victor Giffen Suiter (d 1970), of Melbourne, Aust; 1 s (Rodric b 10 Nov 1947), 3 da (Katrine b 4 Aug 1950, Heather b 22 March 1960, Ellyn b 24 March 1964); *Career* res asst in physics Univ of Bristol 1948-49, reader in mathematical physics Univ of Birmingham 1955-56 (lectr 1949-55), prof of physics Enrico Fermi Inst for Nuclear Studies Univ of Chicago 1956-66, Royal Soc res prof Univ of Oxford 1963-; fell: All Souls Coll Oxford 1964-90, American Physical Soc 1959; corr memb Australia Acad Sci 1978, foreign memb Polish Acad Sci 1980; FRS 1960; *Books* K Mesons and Hyperons: Reports on Progress in Physics (1957), Strange Particles and Strong Interactions (1962), Nuclear Interactions of the Hyperons (1965), Quark Models for the Elementary Particle: High Energy Physics (1966), Nuclear Energy Today and Tomorrow (contrib 1971); *Recreations* biographical researches, study of Sorbian (Wendish) language, history and emigration, travelling hopefully; *Style*— Prof Richard Dalitz, FRS; 28 Jack Straws Lane, Oxford, Oxon OX3 ODW (☎ 0865 62531); Dept of Theoretical Physics, 1 Keble Rd, Oxford OX1 3NP (☎ 0865 273966, fax 0865 273418, telex 83295 NUCLOX G)

DALKEITH, Countess of; Lady Elizabeth Marian Frances; *née* Kerr; 4 da of 12 Marquess of Lothian, KCVO, *qv*; *b* 8 June 1954; *Educ* London Sch of Economics (BSc); *m* 31 Oct 1981, Earl of Dalkeith, *qv*; 2 s, 1 da; *Career* radio journalist BBC; chm The Scot Ballet 1990-, memb Dumfries and Galloway Health Bd 1989-90, patron CRUSAID Scotland; *Recreations* music, reading, theatre, television; *Style*— Countess of Dalkeith; Dabton, Thornhill, Dumfriesshire; 24 Lansdowne Road, London W11

DALKEITH, Earl of; Richard Walter John Montagu Douglas Scott; s and h of 9 and 11 Duke of Buccleuch and Queensberry, KT, VRD, JP, *qv*; *b* 14 Feb 1954; *Educ* Eton, Christ Church Oxford; *m* 31 Oct 1981, Lady Elizabeth Marian Frances Kerr, 4 da of 12 Marquess of Lothian; 2 s, (Lord Eskdaill, Hon Charles David Peter b 1987), 1 da (Lady Louisa b 1982); *Heir* s, Walter John Francis Montagu Douglas Scott (Lord Eskdaill) b 2 Aug 1984; *Career* dir Border Television 1989-90; dist cncllr Nithsdale 1984-90, memb Nature Conservancy Cncl 1989-; nat memb for Scot: IBA 1990, Ind TV Cmmn; pres East of Eng Agric Soc 1990-91; *Style*— Earl of Dalkeith; D.L. Dabton, Thornhill, Dumfries (☎ 0848 30467); 24 Lansdowne Rd, London W11 3LL (☎ 071 727 6573)

DALLAS, John Eastwood; s of Sidney John Dallas (d 1979), of Rodhuish, Somerset, and Joan Constance Evelyn, *née* Griffiths; *b* 21 Nov 1942; *Educ* Winchester, New Coll Oxford (MA); *m* 3 April 1985, Vivette, da of Isak Francko (d 1984), of Geneva, Switzerland; *Career* co dir: Security Tag Systems Inc 1983, Fountmill Ltd 1986, G Modiano Ltd 1988; *Recreations* travel, walking, theatre; *Style*— John E Dallas, Esq; Fountmill Ltd, 27 Sloane Ave, London SW3 3JB (☎ 071 589 1582)

DALLING, Robert; s of John Dalling, and Mary Watson, *née* Youngson; *b* 17 Nov 1942; *Educ* Ardrossan Acad, Univ of Glasgow (MB ChB); *m* 27 March 1972, Lorna MacLean, da of John Stoddart; 1 s (Jonathan b 8 May 1979), 2 da (Claire b 2 March 1974, Jane b 22 Dec 1976); *Career* conslt surgn Stobhill Hosp Glasgow 1978-; Burgher of City of Glasgow, memb of Incorporation of Tailors Glasgow; FRCSEd 1972, FRCS Glasgow 1984; *Style*— Robert Dalling, Esq; 287 Southbrae Drive, Glasgow G13 1TR Scotland (☎ 041 959 2338); Department of Surgery, Stobhill Hospital, Glasgow G21 3UW (☎ 041 558 0111)

DALLMEYER, Hon Mrs (Ursula Nina); *née* Balfour; da of 2 Baron Kinross (d 1939), and Caroline Elsie (d 1969), da of Arthur M Johnstone-Douglas, DL; *b* 12 March 1914; *m* 14 Sept 1939, Col Christopher James York Dallmeyer, DSO and bar, WS; 3 s, 1 da; *Style*— The Hon Mrs Dallmeyer; Green Corner, Tyninghame, Dunbar, E Lothian EH42 1XL (☎ 0620 860394)

DALLOW, Peter Raymond; s of Henry Pownall Dallow (d 1969), and Annie Louise, *née* Taylor (d 1928); *Educ* Bishop Vesey's GS Sutton Coldfield; *m* 1945, Margaret Doreen Brandwood; 1 s (John Roderick b 4 Jan 1948), 1 da (Sally Ann (Mrs Kirkman) b 24 Sept 1955); *Career* served WWII Capt RA in UK Egypt and Italy 1940-46, Maj Army Cadet Force 1948-56, paymaster TA, Maj The Queen's Own Warwickshire and Worcestershire Yeomanry 1960-67; qualified chartered accountant H H Sherwood & Co 1948 (ptnr 1951-67), sr ptnr Sherwood Thompson & Co Tamworth Staffs 1967-87; fndr chm Acocks Green Young Cons 1949-52; Solihull Cons Assoc: memb 1955-, hon treas 1971-72, chm 1972-75, vice pres and tstee 1990-; memb: Yardley Cons Assoc 1948-55, Cncl ICAEW 1977-87, Nat Cncl and Fin Ctee The Carr-Gomm Soc Ltd, Fin Ctee The Nat Assoc of Decorative and Fine Arts Soc; pres: The Birmingham and W Midlands Soc of Chartered Accountants 1976-77 (memb Ctee 1966-87), The Birmingham Chartered Accountant Students Soc 1978-79; The Assoc of Accounting Technicians: fndr memb and memb Cncl 1980-88, pres 1983-84; FCA; *Recreations* music, opera; *Clubs* Naval & Military, The Birmingham; *Style*— Peter R Dallow, Esq; The Coppice, Elmdon Park, Solihull, West Midlands B92 9EJ (☎ 021 742 0942)

DALLY, Dr Ann Gwendolen (Mrs Philip Egerton); da of Claud Mullins (d 1968), and Gwendolen Mullins; *b* 29 March 1926; *Educ* Oxford HS, Somerville Coll Oxford (exhibitioner, BA, MA), St Thomas' Hosp London (MB BS), (DObstRCOG); *m* 1, 1950 (m dis 1969), Peter John Dally, s of Capt Arthur John Dally, RN; 6 c (Simon b 1951, d 1989, Mark b 1952, Emma b 1954, Jane b 1956, John b 1959, Adam b 1961); m 2, 1959, Philip Wellsted Egerton, s of Arthur Egerton; *Career* St Thomas' Hosp, St James' Hosp Balham, Wandsworth Hosp Group, private practice 1956-; ed Maternal And Child Care 1965-70, pres Assoc of Ind Doctors in Addiction, res assoc Wellcome Inst for the History of Medicine 1990-; *Awards* Research prize 1956; memb: BMA 1950-, RSM 1958-; *Books* A Child is Born (1966), Intelligent Person's Guide to Modern Medicine (1966), Cicely, the Story of a Doctor (1968), Mothers, their Power and Influence (1976), The Morbid Streak (1977), Why Women Fail (1978), Inventing Motherhood: The Consequences of an Idea (1981), A Doctor's Story (1990), Women Under The Knife (1991); *Recreations* country, family life; *Clubs* RSM, BMA; *Style*— Dr Ann Dally

DALLY, Brian John Michael; RD; s of David Charles Dally (d 1971), and Eileen, *née* Oates (d 1936); *b* 11 Oct 1930; *Educ* UCS Hampstead, Silcoates Sch Wakefield; *m* 21 Sept 1957, Philida Susan, da of Lt Cdr Kenneth McIver Woods, RN (ka 1940); 2 s (David b 1960, Jonathan b 1962); *Career* Lt Cdr RNR 1952-76; slr of Supreme Ct, ptnr Taylor Joynson Garrett, advocate and slr High Cts of Singapore and Malaysia, ptnr Donaldson and Burkinshaw Singapore 1961-66, dir Rutland Tst plc; hereditary Freeman Borough of Pembroke 1963, Freeman City of London; *Recreations* sailing, skiing, squash, opera; *Clubs* Royal Lymington Yacht, Tanglin (Singapore); *Style*— Brian J M Dally, Esq, RD; 20 St Mary's Road, Wimbledon, London SW19 (☎ 081 946 0408); 180 Fleet Street, London EC4 (☎ 071 430 1122)

DALLY, Harold Roy; s of William Dally (d 1941), and Sarah, *née* Carver (d 1966); *b* 1 Nov 1928; *Educ* Midsomer Norton, Kent Hort Inst, Royal Botanic Gdns Kew; *m* 4 Sept 1954, Sybil Efan, da of William John (d 1970); 1 da (Rohan b 1956); *Career* horticulturist; Botany Dept Univ Coll Cardiff 1953-57, Fisons Ltd 1957-63, States of Guernsey 1963-68, currently md Kenilworth Vineries Ltd Guernsey; dir Les Nicolles Vineries Ltd, chm Guernsey Grower Co-operative Ltd; *Recreations* gardening, carving, photography; *Style*— Harold Dally, Esq; Val au Vallee, La Rue de la Falaise, Guernsey (☎ 0481 38139); Kenilworth Vineries Ltd, Route Militaire, Vale, Guernsey (☎ 0481 44774, fax 0481 47698, telex 4191317 KENVIN)

DALMENY, Lord; Harry Ronald Neil Primrose; s and h of 7 Earl of Rosebery; *b* 20 Nov 1967; *Style*— Lord Dalmeny

DALRYMPLE; *see*: Hamilton-Dalrymple

DALRYMPLE, Lady Antonia Marian Amy Isabel; *née* Stewart; only da of Lt-Col 12 Earl of Galloway (d 1978); *b* 3 Dec 1925; *m* 5 April 1946, Sir (Charles) Mark Dalrymple, 3 Bt, who d 1971, when the title became ext; *Style*— The Lady Antonia Dalrymple; Newhailes, Musselburgh, Midlothian

DALRYMPLE, Hon Colin James; JP, DL (Midlothian); 4 and yst s of Lt-Col 12 Earl of Stair, KT, DSO, JP, DL (d 1961); *b* 19 Feb 1920; *Educ* Eton, Trinity Coll Cambridge; *m* 1, 25 Aug 1945 (m dis 1954), Pamela Mary, only da of Maj Lamplugh Wickham, CVO; 1 da; m 2, 12 March 1956, Fiona Jane, only da of late Adm Sir Ralph Alan Bevan Edwards, KCB, CBE; 1 s, 2 da; *Career* served WWII, Italy, Scots Gds, ret Maj; vice pres Scottish Landowners, Fedn, memb Queen's Body Guard for Scotland (Royal Co of Archers); *Recreations* landowning and farming; *Clubs* New (Edinburgh); *Style*— The Hon Colin Dalrymple, JP, DL; Oxenfoord Mains, Dalkeith, Midlothian, Scotland

DALRYMPLE, Hon Hew North; TD, DL (Ayrshire); s of 12 Earl of Stair (d 1961); bro of 13 Earl of Stair, *qv*; *b* 27 April 1910; *Educ* Eton; *m* 1, 20 June 1938, Mildred Helen (d 1980), da of Hon Thomas Henry Frederick Egerton (d 1953), 3 s of 3 Earl of Ellesmere (5 Earl became 6 Duke of Sutherland); 1 s (Robert Hew b 1946); m 2, 20 Jan 1983, Helen M W Phillips; *Career* formerly Capt 2 Bn Black Watch (TA), served N Africa and Burma (twice wounded); memb Queen's Body Guard for Scotland (Royal Co of Archers); *Style*— The Hon Hew Dalrymple, TD, DL; Castlehill, Ballantrae, Ayrshire KA26 0LA

DALRYMPLE, Viscount; John David James Dalrymple; s and h of 13 Earl of Stair, KCVO, MBE; *b* 4 Sept 1961; *Career* short serv commission with Scots Gds 1982-; *Style*— Viscount Dalrymple

DALRYMPLE, Robert Gordon; s of Ian Murray Dalrymple (d 1989), and Joan Margaret, *née* Craig; *b* 1 March 1943; *Educ* Rugby, Trinity Coll Cambridge (MA); *m* 17 Oct 1970, Diana Elizabeth Kennet, da of David Arthur Williams (d 1979); 1 s (Alexis Murray Lucien b 1974), 2 da (Friday Alexandra Sophie Kennet b 1972, Miranda Victoria-Jane b 1975); *Career* journalist: United Newspapers 1969, City and Industrial Publicity Services 1969-72; business and fin affrs mangr BL Motor Corp 1972-75, sec gen Indust Ctee For Packaging And The Environment 1975-76; dir: Universal McCann 1976-81, Grandfield Rork Collins 1981-; writer and journalist as Robert Pilgrim; former chm Ealing Arts Cncl, memb Cncl World Wide Fund For Nature; *Books* Education In England (1970), England Is A Foreign Country (1971), How African Was Egypt ? (ed, 1973), The Political Pound (ed, 1983), Robert Pilgrim's London (1987), Robert Pilgrim's Endangered Species (1988), Resuming The Egg (1989); *Recreations* cricket, broadcasting, writing; *Clubs* Naval and Military; *Style*— Robert Dalrymple, Esq; Grandfield Rork Collins, Prestige Hse, 14-18 Holborn, London EC1N 2LE (☎ 071 242 2002, fax 071 405 2208)

DALRYMPLE-CHAMPNEYS, Lady; Norma Hull; da of late Col Richard Hull Lewis and wid of A S Russell, MC, DSc; *Educ* Univ of Oxford (MA); *m* 1974, as his 2 w, Capt Sir Weldon Dalrymple-Champneys, 2nd Bt, CB, DM, FRCP (d 14 Dec 1980, when title became extinct); *Career* hon res fell (formerly fell and librarian) Somerville Coll Oxford, hon fell Oriel Coll, Oxford; *Books* The Notebook of Thomas Bennet (1956), Bibliography of William Cowper (1963), Poems of William Cowper (1967), The Complete Poetical Works of George Crabbe, 3 vols (1987); *Style*— Lady Dalrymple-Champneys

DALRYMPLE-HAMILTON OF BARGANY, Capt North Edward Frederick; CVO (1961, MVO 1954), MBE (1953), DSC (1943), JP (1980), DL (Ayrshire 1973); s of Adm Sir Frederick Hew George Dalrymple-Hamilton of Bargany, KCB (d 1974, gs of 10 Earl of Stair, KT, JP, DL) by his w Gwendolen, 3 da of Sir Cuthbert Peek, 2 Bt; *b*

17 Feb 1922; *Educ* Eton; *m* 1, 23 July 1949, Hon Mary Helen (d 1981), da of Rt Hon David John Colville, GCIE, TD, PC, 1 Baron Clydesmuir (d 1954); 2 s (North John Frederick b 1950, James Hew Ronald b 1955); m 2, 9 April 1983, Geraldine Inez Antoinette, da of late Maj Frank Harding (who m 1, 1955, Maj Rowland Beech, MC (d 1972); 2 da); *Career* entered RN 1940, served WWII and Korea, Cdr 1954, cmdg HMS Scarborough 1958, exec offr HM Yacht Britannia 1959-60, Capt 1960, Capt (F) 17 Frigate Sqdn 1963, dir Naval Signals MOD 1965, Capt Adm Surface Weapons Estab 1967, ret 1970; ensign Queen's Bodyguard for Scotland (Royal Co of Archers); *Clubs* New (Edinburgh), Pratt's, MCC; *Style—* Capt North Dalrymple-Hamilton of Bargany,CVO,MBE,DSC,JP,DL,RN; Lovestone House, Bargany, Girvan, Ayrshire KA26 9RF (☎ 046 587 227)

DALRYMPLE-HAMILTON, Christian Margaret; MBE (1989), DL (District of Wigtown 1982); er da of Adm Sir Frederick Hew George Dalrymple-Hamilton, of Bargany, KCB (whose f, Col Hon North D-H, MVO, was 2 s of 10 Earl of Stair, KT, JP, DL), by his w Gwendolen, 3 da of Sir Cuthbert Peek, 2 Bt; *b* 20 Sept 1919; *Style—* Miss Christian Dalrymple-Hamilton, MBE, DL; Cladyhouse, Cairnryan, Stranraer, Wigtownshire

DALRYMPLE-HAY, Sir James Brian; 6 Bt (GB 1798) of Park Place, Wigtownshire; s of Lt-Col Brian George Rowland Dalrymple-Hay (d 1943); suc cous, 5 Bt (d 1952); *b* 19 Jan 1928; *Educ* Blundell's; *m* 12 April 1958, Helen Sylvia, da of late Stephen Herbert Card, of Reigate, Surrey; 3 da (Fiona, Charlotte, Lucie); *Heir* bro, John Hugh Dalrymple-Hay; *Career* Lt RM 1948; ptnr in firm of Estate Agents 1968-85; *Style—* Sir James Dalrymple-Hay, Bt; The Red House, Church St, Warnham, nr Horsham, W Sussex

DALRYMPLE-HAY, John Hugh; s of Lt-Col Brian Dalrymple-Hay (d 1943); hp of bro Sir James Dalrymple-Hay, 6 Bt; *b* 16 Dec 1929; *Educ* Blundell's; *m* 6 Oct 1962, Jennifer Phyllis Roberta, da of Brig Robert Johnston, of 44 Exeter House, Putney Heath, London SW15; 1 s (Malcolm John Robert April 1966); *Career* late Capt Royal Scots Fusiliers; *Recreations* golf, skiing, sailing; *Style—* John Dalrymple-Hay, Esq; Little Meadow, Forty Green Rd, Knotty Green, Beaconsfield, Bucks HP9 1XL

DALRYMPLE-WHITE, Sir Henry Arthur Dalrymple; 2 Bt (UK 1926) of High Mark, Co Wigtown; DFC (1941) and bar (1942); s of Lt-Col Sir Godfrey Dalrymple Dalrymple-White, 1 Bt (d 1954, s of Gen Sir Henry Dalrymple White, KCB, who cmd 6 Inniskilling Dragoons throughout Crimean War and was maternal gs of Sir Hew Dalrymple, 1 Bt), by his w Hon Catherine Mary, da of 12 Viscount Falkland; *b* 5 Nov 1917; *Educ* Eton, Magdalene Coll Cambridge, London Univ; *m* 17 Sept 1948 (m dis 1956), Mary, only da of Capt Robert Henry Cuncliffe Thomas, 8th Royal Hus, by his wife Cynthia, 2nd da of Capt Francis Sandford; 1 s; *Heir* s, Jan Hew Dalrymple-White; *Career* Wing-Cdr RAFVR, served WW II; *Style—* Sir Henry Dalrymple-White, Bt, DFC; c/o Aero Club of East Africa, PO Box 40813, Nairobi, Kenya

DALRYMPLE-WHITE, Jan Hew; s and h of Sir Henry Arthur Dalrymple Dalrymple-White, 2 Bt; *b* 26 Nov 1950; *Educ* Stowe, Huddersfield Polytechnic, Univ of Stirling; *Style—* Jan Dalrymple-White, Esq

DALTON, Sir Alan Nugent Goring; CBE (1969), DL (Cornwall 1982); s of Harold Goring Dalton, and Phyllis Marguerite, *née* Ash; *b* 26 Nov 1923; *Educ* King Edward VI Sch Southampton; *Career* md: English Clays, Lovering and Pochin and Co Ltd 1961-84; dep chm Eng China Clays plc 1968-84 (chm 1984-89); dir: Sun Alliance and London Assurance Gp 1976-89, (Western regnl bd) Nat Westminster Bank Ltd 1977-; chm BR (Western) Bd 1978-, dir Westland plc 1980-85, chm Devon & Cornwall Development Co 1988-; CBIM, FRSA; kt 1977; *Recreations* sailing, painting, reading; *Clubs* Royal Yacht Squadron, Royal Western Yacht Eng; *Style—* Sir Alan Dalton, CBE, DL; English China Clays plc, John Keay House, St Austell, Cornwall

DALTON, Andrew Searle; s of Frederick James Searle Dalton (d 1953), of Derby, and Mary, *née* Whittaker (d 1973); *b* 18 May 1949; *Educ* Oundle, Magdalen Coll Oxford; *m* 16 Oct 1982, Jennie Kelsey, da of Edward Webb Keane, of New York; 2 s (Frederick b 1986, Benjamin (twin) b 1986), 1 da (Abigail b 1985); *Career* SG Warburg Gp plc 1972-, chm Warburg Asset Management, dir Mercury Asset Management Group plc 1986-; memb Cncl: Lindley Lodge Educnl Tst, Kingham Hill Tst; Liveryman Worshipful Co of Grocers; *Clubs* Carlton; *Style—* Andrew Dalton, Esq; 9 Lansdowne Crescent, London W11 2NH (☎ 071 221 9335); Warburg Asset Management, 33 King William St, London EC4R 9AS (☎ 071 280 2800, fax 071 280 2820)

DALTON, Vice Adm Sir Geoffrey Thomas James Oliver; KCB (1986); s of Jack Roland Thomas Dalton (d 1981), of Epsom, Surrey, and Margaret Kathleen, *née* Oliver (d 1978); *b* 14 April 1931; *Educ* Reigate GS, RNC Dartmouth; *m* 30 March 1957, Jane Hamilton, da of Colin Hamilton Baynes (d 1976), of Suffolk; 4 s (Alastair b 1964, David b 1966, Richard b 1970, Antony b 1971); *Career* joined RN 1949; cmd: HMS Maryton 1958-60, HMS Relentless 1966-67, Cdr 1966, HMS Nubian 1969-70, Capt 1972, HMS Jupiter and Seventh Frigate Sqdn 1977-79, HMS Dryad (Sch of Maritime Ops) 1979-81; Rear Adm 1981, Asst Chief of Naval Staff (Policy) 1981-84, Vice Adm 1984, Dep Supreme Allied Cdr Atlantic 1984-87; sec gen MENCAP 1987-90; Freeman City of London 1953, Liveryman Worshipful Co of Drapers 1957; FBIM 1987; *Recreations* tennis, gardening, walking; *Clubs* Royal Overseas League; *Style—* Vice Adm Sir Geoffrey Dalton, KCB; Farm Cottage, Catherington, Hants PO8 OTD (☎ 0705 592369)

DALTON, Patrick Michael; s of Jack Rowland Thomas Dalton (d 1984), and Kathleen Margaret, *née* Oliver (d 1978); *b* 4 Oct 1941; *Educ* Whitgift Sch; *m* 7 June 1967, (Elizabeth) Gillian Vera, da of Charles Claude Allan, of Shawburn, by Selkirk, Scotland; 2 s (Barnaby John Allan b 10 April 1971, Nicko Alexander Neale b 17 Nov 1972); *Career* RNC Dartmouth, gen serv HMS Kemerton, HMS Wakeful 1960-65, Fleet Air Arm 1965-73; Mullens & Co 1973-78; ptnr: Capel-Cure Myers 1978-88, ANZ McCaughan 1988-89, Dalton Associates 1989-; memb Small Farms Orgn; Freeman City of London, Liveryman Worshipful Co of Drapers; FCIS; *Recreations* farming, skiing, tennis, sailing; *Clubs* Western (Glasgow); *Style—* Patrick Dalton, Esq; Millwood Farm, Hartfield, East Sussex (☎ 089 277 619); ANZ-McCaughan, 65 Holborn Viaduct, London EC1 (☎ 071 236 5101)

DALTON, Robin Ann; da of Dr Robert Agnew Eakin (d 1965), of Sydney, Aust, and Lyndall Everad, *née* Solomon (d 1950); *b* 22 Dec 1920; *Educ* Frensham NSW Aust, SOAS London Univ; *m* 1, 8 Oct 1940 (m dis 1942), Ian (John) Gordon Spencer, of Queensland, Aust; m 2, 1 May 1953, Emmet Michael Dalton (d 1957), s of Maj-Gen James Emmet Dalton, MC (d 1978), of Dublin; 1 s (Seamus Emmet b 1956), 1 da (Lisa Maria b 1954); *Career* special advsr and press offr Thai govt 1953-58; literary agent Robin Dalton Assocs Ltd 1965-87, dir Int Famous Agency (now ICM) 1972-75; entered film indust 1984, project developer Nineteen Eighty-Four 1984, exec prodr Emma's War 1985, prodr Madame Sousatzka 1988; life memb Anglo-Thai Soc, memb BAFTA; *Books* Aunts up the Cross (as Robin Eakin 1963, reprinted 1980), Australia Fair? (chapter in anthology, 1984), numerous magazine and newspaper articles; *Style—* Mrs Robin Dalton; 127 Hamilton Terrace, London NW1 9QR (☎ 071 328 6169)

DALY, Barbara Susan (Mrs Laurence Tarlo); da of Philip Daly (d 1985), and Eva, *née* Sapherson (d 1971); *b* 24 March 1944; *Educ* Leeds Coll of Art; *m* 16 March 1982, Laurence Joel Frederic Tarlo, s of William Tarlo, of Long Island, NY; *Career* make-up artist: BBC 1964-68, freelance 1968-86; md Colourings Ltd 1986-, films incl A Clockwork Orange, make-up conslt to HRH The Princess of Wales; patron Skin Treatment and Res Tst Westminster Hosp, ctee memb Orgn for Trg, patron Nat Assoc Drama for Visually Handicapped; memb BAFTA 1987; *Books* Daly Beauty, Make-up Made Easy, New Looks From Barbara Daly; *Recreations* eastern philosophy, swimming; *Clubs* RAC; *Style—* Ms Barbara Daly; Colourings Ltd, 4 Albion Place, Galena Rd, London W6 OLT (☎ 081 741 8090, fax 081 741 2951)

DALY, Most Rev Cahal Brendan; *see*: Armagh, Archbishop of

DALY, Lt-Col Denis James; s of Maj Denis Bowes Daly, MC (d 1984), of The Glen House, Ballingarry, Co Limerick, Eire, and Diana, *née* Lascelles (d 1971); *b* 23 May 1930; *Educ* Eton; *m* 20 Feb 1954, Valerie Margaret, yst da of Maj Rae Crawford Stirling-Stuart (d 1977), of Cowbridge Lodge, Malmesbury, Wilts; 2 s (Anthony b 1959 d 1982, Christopher b 1964), 1 da (Phillipa Jane b 1957); *Career* cmmnd RHG 1949, cmd Household Cavalry Regt 1969-72, def advsr Br High Cmmn Malawi 1973-75, cmd Driving and Maintenance Sch RAC Centre 1978-80, ret 1983; COI 1983-85, Capt of Invalids Royal Hosp Chelsea 1986-; *Recreations* field sports; *Clubs* Cavalry and Gds, Royal Cwlth Soc; *Style—* Lt-Col Denis Daly; 41B Warwick Gardens, London W14 8PL; Royal Hosp, Chelsea, London SW3 4SR (☎ 071 730 0161)

DALY, Francis D; s of Edward M Daly, of Montenotte, Cork (d 1983), and Clare, *née* Egan (d 1987); *b* 16 Sept 1943; *Educ* Glenstal Abbey, Univ Coll Cork (BCL); *m* 21 Feb 1970, Patricia Mary, da of the late H P O'Connor, of Cork; 2 s (Teddy b 14 Nov 1970, Ken b 22 April 1972), 2 da (Aiveen b 14 Nov 1973, Alex b 6 Oct 1976); *Career* admitted slr 1966; ptnr Ronan Daly Jermyn 1970-(joined 1966); chm Allied Metropole Hotel plc, memb Cncl Inc Law Soc (chm Fin Ctee); *Recreations* golf, sailing; *Clubs* Cork Golf, Cork & County, Schull Sailing; *Style—* Francis D Daly, Esq; Cleveland, Blackrock Rd, Cork; Corthna, Schull, Co Cork (☎ 021 294 279); 12 South Mall, Cork (☎ 021 272 333, fax 021 273 521, telex 76165)

DALY, Lawrence; s of James Daly (d 1950), of Glencraig, and Janet, *née* Taylor (d 1975); *b* 20 Oct 1924; *Educ* St Columba's RC Sch, Loretto, Cowdenbeath Tech Coll; *m* 26 March 1949, Reñee May, da of George Baxter (d 1970), of Worcester; 4 s (Rannoch b 1949, Kerran b 1953, Shannon b 1961, Cavan b 1963), 1 da (Morven b 1951); *Career* coal miner 1938-64, agent Fife Area NUM 1964-66, sec NUM Scotland 1966-69, sec NUM Britain 1969-75; memb: Gen Cncl TUC, Fife CC, Lochgelly DC, Int War Crimes Tribunal (Bertrand Russel and Vietnam); sec NUM Glencraig Colliery Fife; TVC Gold Badge 1976; *publications* pamphlets: A Young Miner sees Russia (1946), The Miners and The Nation (1968); *Recreations* cycling, music, poetry; *Style—* Lawrence Daly, Esq; Glencraig, 45 Hempstead Lane, Potten End, Berkhamsted, Herts (☎ 0442 864332)

DALY, Margaret Elizabeth; MEP Somerset Dorset West 1984-; da of Robert Bell (d 1978), of Belfast, and Evelyn Elizabeth, *née* McKenna; *b* 26 Jan 1938; *Educ* Methodist Coll Belfast; *m* 1964, Kenneth Anthony Edward Daly, s of Edward Joseph Daly (d 1983), of Ireland; 1 da (Denise b 1971); *Career* Trade Union official ASTMS 1959-70, conslt CCO 1976-79, dir Cons Trade Union Orgn 1979-84; *Style—* Mrs Margaret Daly, MEP; The Old School House, Aisholt, Bridgwater, Somerset; European Parliament Strasbourg (☎ 027 867 688)

DALY, Prof Michael de Burgh; s of Dr Ivan de Burgh Daly, CBE, FRS (d 1974), of Long Crendon, Bucks, and Beatrice Mary, *née* Leetham (d 1976); *b* 7 May 1922; *Educ* Loretto, Gonville and Caius Coll Cambridge (MA, MD, ScD), St Bartholomew's Hosp London; *m* 4 Sept 1948, (Beryl) Esmé, da of Wing Cdr Alfred James Nightingale (d 1948), of London; 2 s (Colin de Burgh b 10 Sept 1950, Nigel de Burgh b 20 March 1954); *Career* house physician St Bartholomew's Hosp London 1947-48, lectr in physiology UCL 1948-54, pt/t extramural contract Miny of Supply (now MOD) Porton Wilts 1949-51, Rockefeller Fndn travelling fell in med Univ of Pennsylvania USA 1952-53, Locke res fell Royal Soc at Dept of Physiology UCL 1955-58, chair of physiology Univ of London at St Bartholomew's Hosp Med Sch London 1958-84, visiting prof physiology Univ of NSW Aust 1966, Ethel Mary Baillieu fell Baker Med Res Inst Melbourne 1976, distinguished visitor in physiology Royal Free Hosp Sch of Med 1984-; many pubns in sci jls, film William Harvey and the Circulation of the Blood (awarded Gold Medal of BMA); treas St Bartholomew's Hosp Med Sch 1983-84 (govr 1970-), ed Journal of Physiology 1956-63 and 1984-89, chm Monographs Bd of Physiological Soc 1981-87 (memb 1979-87); awarded: Schafer Prize in Physiology UCL 1953, Thruston medal Gonville and Caius Coll Cambridge 1958, Sir Lionel Whitby medal Univ of Cambridge 1963; memb Underwater Physiology Sub Ctee of Med Res Cncl RN Personnel Res Ctee 1975-, chm Advsy Panel and Ethical Ctee for Underwater Personnel Res Miny of Def (RN) (memb 1975-) memb: Physiological Soc 1951-86 (hon memb 1986-), Soc of Experimental Biology 1965-, Undersea and Hyperbaric Med Soc 1972-88, Euro Undersea Biomed Soc 1972-, Br Heart Fndn Res Fund Ctee 1982-85; FRCP, FRSM 1958-; *Recreations* model engineering; *Clubs* RSM; *Style—* Prof Michael Daly; 7 Hall Drive, Sydenham, London SE26 6XL (☎ 081 778 8773); Dept of Physiology, Royal Free Hosp Sch of Med, Rowland Hill St, London NW3 2PF (☎ 071 794 0500)

DALY, Michael Francis; CMG; s of late William Thomas Daly, and Hilda Frances Daly; *b* 7 April 1931; *Educ* Downside, Gonville and Caius Coll Cambridge; *m* 1, 1963, Sally Malcolm Angwin (d 1966); 1 da; m 2, 1971, Juliet Mary Siragusa, *née* Arning; 1 step da; *Career* Transreef Indust & Investmt Co SA 1955-66, Gen Electric Co London 1966; HM Dip Serv: first sec FCO 1967, first sec (commercial) Rio de Janeiro 1969, first sec (info) and head of chancery Dublin 1973, asst head Cultural Rels Dept FCO 1976, cnsllr consul gen and head of chancery Brasilia 1977-78, ambass Ivory Coast Upper Volta and Niger 1978-83, head W African Dept FCO and non resident ambass Chad 1983-86, ambass Costa Rica and non resident ambass to Nicaragua 1986-89, ambass Bolivia 1989-91; *Style—* Michael Daly, Esq, CMG; Foreign and Commonwealth Office, King Charles St, London SW1 2AH (☎ 071 233 4576)

DALYELL, Hon Mrs (Kathleen Mary Agnes); *née* Wheatley; da of Baron Wheatley (Life Baron) (d 1988); *b* 17 Nov 1937; *Educ* Convent of Sacred Heart, Queens Cross Aberdeen, Univ of Edinburgh; *m* 26 Dec 1963, Tam Dalyell, MP, *qv*; 1 s, 1 da; *Career* teacher of history; memb Historic Buildings Cncl of Scotland 1975-87, memb Ancient Monuments Bd of Scotland 1989-, chm Bo'ness Heritage Tst, tstee Paxton Tst; *Recreations* reading, travel, hill walking; *Style—* The Hon Mrs Dalyell; The Binns, Linlithgow EH49 7NA

DALYELL, Tam; MP (Lab) Linlithgow 1962-; s of Lt-Col Gordon Dalyell, CIE, and Eleanor Dalyell; *b* 9 Aug 1932; *Educ* Eton, King's Coll Cambridge, Univ of Edinburgh; *m* 26 Dec 1963, Kathleen Mary Agnes, da of Baron Wheatley, QC, *qv*; 1 s (Gordon b 26 Sept 1965), 1 da (Moira b 25 May 1968); *Career* Nat Serv Royal Scots Greys 1950-52; memb: Public Accounts Ctee, Select Ctee on sci and tech 1965-68, Nat Exec Ctee of Lab Pty 1986-87, Educ Inst of Scot; weekly columnist New Scientist 1967-; *Books* Case for Ship Schools (1960), Ship School Dunera (1962), Devolution: the End of Britain ? (1978), One Man's Falklands (1983), A Science Policy for Britain (1983), Misrule How Mrs Thatcher Misled Parliament (1987), Dick Crossman: A Portrait (1989); *Style—* Tam Dalyell, Esq, MP; Binns, Linlithgow, Scotland

DALZEL-JOB, Lt Cdr Patrick; DL (1979); s of Capt Ernest Dalzel Job (ka 1916), and Ethel, *née* Griffiths (d 1970); *b* 1 June 1913; *Educ* Berkhamsted Sch, Switzerland; *m* 26 June 1945, Bjorg (d 1986), da of Erling Bangsund (d 1977), of Tromso, Norway; 1

s (Iain b 1946); *Career* Lt Cdr (removed whole civilian population from Narvik before German bombing, received personal thanks of King of Norway), special ops in enemy-occupied territory, ret 1956; writer; youth organiser Duke of Edinburgh's Award; Knight (1 class) Royal Norwegian Order of St Olav with Swords; Arctic Snow to Dust of Normandy (1991); *Recreations* sailing (to Arctic Russia in 1939), skiing; *Clubs* Special Forces; *Style—* Lt Cdr Patrick Dalzel-Job, DL; Nead-an-Eoin, by Plockton, Ross-shire, Scotland (☎ 059984 244)

DALZELL, Ian Robert; s of Thomas Leon Dalzell (d 1958), and Barbara, *née* Curnock; *b* 22 Nov 1949; *Educ* The Heath Sch, Univ of Lancaster (MA); *m* 13 Dec 1974, Susan Amy, da of Percy Phillips (d 1971); 2 s (Ross Phillip b 1981, James Lean b 1984); *Career* CA 1971; res offr Int Centre for Res in Accounting 1972-76, princ lectr Lancashire Poly 1976-87, ptnr Ross Dalzell Grange-over-Sands 1987-, dir Grange Investment Services 1987-; pres NW Soc of CA 1982-83; *Recreations* swimming, fell-walking, bird watching, antiques; *Style—* Ian Dalzell, Esq; Badgers' Sett, Windermere Rd, Grange-over-Sands, Cumbria LA11 6JT; Ross Dalzell, Main St, Grange-over-Sands, Cumbria LA11 6DP (☎ 05395 34320, fax 05395 35096)

DALZELL, Lady Muriel Marjorie; *née* Dalzell; da of late 13 Earl of Carnwath; *b* 22 Sept 1903; *m* 18 Jan 1927, Lt-Col John Norton Taylor, who assumed, by Royal Licence, surname and arms of Dalzell on marriage; o s of late James Taylor, Lisnamallard, to Tyrone; 1 s; *Style—* The Lady Muriel Dalzell; Sand House, Wedmore, Somerset (☎ 0934 712224)

DALZIEL, Ian Martin; s of John Calvin Dalziel (d 1983), and Elizabeth Roy, *née* Bain; *b* 21 June 1947; *Educ* Daniel Stewart's Coll Edinburgh, St John's Coll Cambridge, Université Libre de Bruxelles, London Business Sch; *m* 1972, Nadia Maria Iacovazzi; 4 s; *Career* Mullens & Co 1970-72, Manufacturers Hanover Ltd (London and NY) 1972-83, co fndr and dep md Adam & Co Gp plc 1983-, chm Continental Assets Trust plc; Lepercq-Amcur Fund NV; memb Richmond upon Thames Cncl 1978-79; MEP (EDG) Lothians 1979-84; *Recreations* golf, shooting; *Clubs* New (Edinburgh), Royal and Ancient Golf (St Andrews); *Style—* Ian Dalziel, Esq; 42 Pall Mall, London SW1Y 5JG (☎ 071 839 4615)

DALZIEL, Malcolm Stuart; CBE (1984); s of Robert Henderson Dalziel (d 1979), and Susan Aileen, *née* Robertson (d 1981); *b* 18 Sept 1936; *Educ* Banbury GS, St Catherine's Coll Oxford (MA); *m* 1961, Elizabeth Anne, da of Major Philip Collins Harvey (d 1977); 1 s (Rory b 1974), 2 da (Caroline, Annabel); *Career* Nat Serv 1955-57, Lt The Northamptonshire Regt; The British Cncl: educn offr Lahore Pakistan 1961-63, regnl dir Penang Malaysia 1963-67, regnl rep Lahore Pakistan 1967-70, rep Sudan 1970-74, dir Mgmnt Serv Dept and dep controller Estabs Div 1974-79, controller Higher Educn Div 1983-87; cncllr cultural affairs The British Embassy Cairo 1979-83, sec Int Univ and Poly Cncl 1983-87; dep chm Cncl for Educn in the Cwlth 1990- (memb Exec Ctee 1983-), affiliate Queen Elizabeth House Int Devpt Centre Oxford Univ; assoc conslt dir CERES (Conslts in Econ Regeneration in Europe Servs) 1988-90 (assoc conslt 1988-); memb Court Univ of Essex 1983-88; *Recreations* theatre, ballet, rugby football, walking; *Clubs* United Oxford and Cambridge, Northampton CCC (vice pres); *Style—* Malcolm Dalziel, Esq, CBE; 368 Woodstock Rd, Oxford OX2 8AE (☎ 0865 58969)

DAMANT, David Cyril; s of William Alexander Arthur Damant (d 1983), and Mary Edith Damant; *b* 15 March 1937; *Educ* Queens' Coll Cambridge; *Career* former ptnr: Investmt Res Cambridge, Quilter Goodison Co 1982-86; md Paribas Assistant Management (UK) Ltd 1987-; pres Euro Fedn of Fin Analysts Socs 1974-76, chm Soc of Investmt Analysts 1980-82 (fell 1986), memb Bd Int Accounting Standards Ctee 1986-, memb UK Accounting Standards Ctee 1987-90, co chm Int Co-ordinating Ctee Fin Analysts Assocs; *Recreations* opera, food & wine; *Clubs* Beefsteak, Garrick, City of London; *Style—* David Damant, Esq; Agar House, 12 Agar St, London WC2 (☎ 071 379 6926); 16 Orchard St, Cambridge (☎ 0223 357768); Paribas Asset Management (UK) Ltd, 68 Lombard St, London EC3V 9LJ (☎ 071 621 1161, fax 621 9108, telex 886055)

DAMANT, Maj John Louis; s of Cdr Eric Louis Baxter Damant (d 1964), and Sybil Alice, *née* Joy (d 1989); *b* 13 April 1930; *Educ* Cheltenham, RMA Sandhurst; *m* 8 Oct 1960 (m dis 1974), Gillian, da of John Harvey; 2 s (Patrick John Charles, Charles Francis), 1 da (Louisa Jane); m 2, 8 Feb 1979, Jane Garrett; *Career* cmmnd 7 (QO) Hussars 1950: Korea 1952 (ADC Gen Mike West), Hong Kong, Malaya 1954-56, UN Cyprus 1964, withdrawal Aden 1967, ret 1968; fndr Food for Thought restaurant Covent Garden London 1977; ret to France in 1983 (leaving restaurant under charge of step da) to continue painting, studied in Paris Atelier Goetz and Cours De Ville Montparnasse 1974; *Recreations* racing, roulette, art exhibitions; *Clubs* Lansdowne, Charlie Chesters; *Style—* Maj John Damant; La Vernelle, Monsaguel, Issigeac 24560, France (☎ 53 58 71 48)

DAMERELL, Lady Mary Barbara; *née* Carnegie; yr da of 13 Earl of Northesk, *qv*; *b* 10 Feb 1953; *Educ* Oak Hall Haslemere, Heathfield Ascot; *m* 1977, William Patrick Sterling Damerell; 3 s (Charles b 1980, Thomas b 1982, Robert b 1985); *Style—* The Lady Mary Damerell; 2 Kempson Road, Fulham, London SW6 4PV

DAMPNEY, Major Theo Douglas; TD (1960), JP (Dorset 1964); s of Douglas Reeks Dampney (d 1974), and Kathleen Mary, *née* Hall (d 1972); *b* 4 March 1922; *Educ* Blundells; *m* 4 Sept 1957, Joan Elizabeth Mary, da of Roy Dry, of Dorset; 3 s (Trelawney b 1958, Tristram b 1960, Piers b 1962), 1 da (Alexandra b 1964); *Career* Royal Wilts Yeo 1939, cmmnd Sandhurst 1942, 3 Hussars ME and Italy 1942-46, Royal Wilts Yeo 1948-60, ret Maj; former memb Cncl RASE 1976 (dep chm and chm Hants Agric Exec Ctee 19 memb Cncl NFU 1961-79 (chm Hants 1957); *Recreations* sailing, shooting; *Clubs* Cavalry and Guards, Farmers'; *Style—* Maj Theo Dampney, TD, JP; Parley Court, Hurn, Christ Church, Dorset BH23 6BB (☎ 0202 573361)

DANCE, Brian David; s of Leonard Harold Dance (d 1964), of E Molesey, and Marjorie Greenfield Swain (d 1978), (formerly Mrs Dance), *née* Shrivelle; *b* 22 Nov 1929; *Educ* Kingston GS, Wadham Coll Oxford (BA, MA), Univ of London; *m* 17 Aug 1955, Chloe Elizabeth, da of John Frederic Allan Baker, CB, (d 1987); 2 s (David b 1956, Richard b 1959), 2 da (Amanda b 1962, Sarah b 1964); *Career* Nat Serv 1948-49, Flt Lt RAFVR (T) 1954-61; asst master Kingston GS 1953-59; sr history master: Faversham GS 1959-62, Westminster City Sch 1962-65; headmaster Cirencester GS 1965-66, princ Luton Sixth Form Coll 1966-73, headmaster St Dunstans Coll Catford 1973-; memb Cambridge Local Examinations Syndicate 1968-73, fndr chm Lewisham Environmental Tst 1987-88, govr Bromley HS 1983-; memb: HMC 1973, SHA 1965- (formally Headmasters Assoc) (cncl memb 1968-76, Nat Exec Ctee 1972-76); author of various articles for Times Educational Supplement and Headmasters' Association Review; *Recreations* theatre, music, watching but no longer playing ball games; *Clubs* East India, Devonshire, Sports and Public Sch; *Style—* Brian Dance, Esq; The Headmaster's House, St Dunstan's College, London SE6 4TY (☎ 081 690 1277); St Dunstan's College, Stanstead Road, Catford, London SE6 4TY (☎ 081 690 1274/7)

DANCE, Charles Walter; s of Walter Dance (d 1950), of Birmingham, and Eleanor, *née* Perks (d 1985); *b* 10 Oct 1946; *Educ* Widey Tech Sch Plymouth, Plymouth Sch of Art, Leicester Coll of Art and Design; *m* 18 July 1970, Joanna Elizabeth Nicola Daryl, da of Francis Harold Haythorn, of Plymstock, Devon; 1 s (Oliver b 1974), 1 da (Rebecca b 1980); *Career* actor 1970-; seasons at repertory theatres: Leeds, Oxford, Windsor, Swindon, Chichester, Greenwich; joined Royal Shakespeare Company 1975; roles incl: Catesby in Richard III, Oliver in As You Like It, Lancaster in Henry IV, title role in Henry V, Aufidius and title role in Coriolanus; television: Seigfried Sasson in The Fatal Spring, Truman in Rainy Day Women, Harry Maxim in The Secret Servant, Guy Perron in The Jewel in the Crown (nomination for Best Actor), Forester in First Born, Gerry in Out On A Limb, The Phantom in Phantom of the Opera; films: Plenty, The Macguffin, The Golden Child, Good Morning Babylon, Hidden City, White Mischief, Pascali's Island, China Moon, Alien III; *Style—* C W Dance, Esq; c/o Caroline Dawson Associates, 47 Courtfield Rd, London SW7 (☎ 071 370 0708)

DANCY, Dr (Christopher) Mark; s of Prof John Christopher Dancy, of Mousehole, Cornwall, and Angela Dawn, *née* Bryant; *b* 16 July 1948; *Educ* Winchester, Trinity Coll Oxford, St Thomas's Hosp London (BA, BM BCh); *m* 30 June 1974, Susanna, da of Lt Cdr Cedric Collingwood Wake-Walker, of Rogate, nr Petersfield, Hants; 1 s (Luke b 1983), 2 da (Arabella b 1977, Martha b 1979); *Career* dir of med Central Middx Hosp 1989 (conslt cardiologist 1987); MRCP 1976; *Recreations* sailing, choral singing; *Style—* Dr Mark Dancy; Central Middx Hosp, Acton Lane, London NW10 7NS (☎ 081 965 5733, fax 081 965 1837)

DANDO, John Penstone; s of Lionel Victor Dando (d 1935), and Winifred Kate, *née* Penstone (d 1970); *b* 17 Feb 1935; *Educ* Wembley County Sch; *m* 18 April 1960, Patricia Anne, da of Henry Gammel Lee (d 1977); 1 s (Gavin b 1967), 2 da (Stella b 1963, Karen b 1964); *Career* dir: F Bolton & Co (Aviation) Ltd 1967-85, F Boulton & Co (Foreign) Ltd 1973-85, Matheson Bolton & Co Ltd 1973-74, F Boulton & Co (Holdings) Ltd 1975-87, Frizzell International Ltd 1990-, Frizzell Insurance Brokers Ltd 1991- ; md: F Bolton International Ltd 1975-80 (chm 1980-89), F Boulton & Co Ltd 1980-84, Frizzell DEP Ltd 1983-; *Recreations* trombone playing, wildlife, reading, walking, boating, wine; *Style—* John P Dando, Esq; College Farm House, Ferry Road, South Stoke, Oxon RG8 0JP; Frizzell D E P Ltd, 14-22 Elder Street, London E1 (☎ 071 247 6595)

DANDONA, Dr Paresh; s of Som Nath Dandona, and Sham, *née* Mehra; *b* 25 May 1943; *Educ* Scindia Sch India, Univ of Allahabad India (BSc), All India Inst of Med Scis (MB BS), Univ of Oxford (Rhodes scholar DPhil); *m* 8 Oct 1970, Nilu, da of Kvldip Kapoor; 2 s (Sonny b 1974, Kabir b 1977); *Career* Wellcome res fell Univ of Oxford 1969-71, house offr Brompton Hosp and Nat Hosp Queens Sq 1972-73; Royal Free Hosp: sr registrar 1973-75, dir metabolic unit and sr lectr 1978-, physician in charge diabetic serv 1985-; FRCP 1988 (MRCP 1974), memb Br and American Diabetic Assocs; *Recreations* music, architecture; *Style—* Dr Paresh Dandona; Lydbrook, 44 Hampstead Lane, London N6 4LL (☎ 081 341 3558); Metabolic Unit, Royal Free Hosp, London NW3 2QG (☎ 071 794 0500/ 3481, fax 071 348 5242)

DANDY, David James; s of James Dandy, of Gt Shelford, Cambs, and Margaret, *née* Coe (d 1984); *b* 30 May 1940; *Educ* Forest Sch, Emmanuel Coll Cambridge, London Hospital Med Coll, (MA, MD, BChir, FRCS); *m* 17 Sept 1966, (Stephanie) Jane, da of Harold Vaughan Essex (d 1985), of Wellington, Somerset; 1 s (James b 1971), 1 da (Emma b 1973); *Career* sr fell Toronto Gen Hosp Canada 1972-73, conslt orthopaedic surgn Addenbrook's Hosp Cambridge and Newmarket Hosp 1975-, assoc lectr Faculty Clinical Med Univ of Cambridge 1975-, civilian advsr in knee surgery RN and RAF 1980-; James Berry prize RCS 1985; memb Int Arthroscopy Assoc 1973 (pres 1989-), fell Br Orthopaedic Assoc 1975; memb: Int Soc of Knee, Euro Soc of Knee and Arthroscopy 1984; Freeman: City of London, Worshipful Soc of Apothecaries 1987; FRCS; *Books* Arthroscopy of the Knee (1973), Arthroscopic Surgery of the Knee (1981), Arthroscopy of the Knee; A Diagnostic Atlas (1984), Essentials of Orthopaedics and Trauma (1989); *Recreations* gardening, writing; *Style—* David Dandy, Esq; Addenbrooke's Hospital, Hills Rd, Cambridge CB2 2QQ (☎ 0223 216231)

DANDY, (Robert) Michael; s of John Dandy, DL, of Bedford, and Mary, *née* Simkins (d 1978); *b* 11 May 1954; *Educ* Wellingborough Sch, Coll of Law Guildford; *m* 12 April 1980, Eithne Bridget, da of Dr J J Holloway, of Northampton (d 1967); 1 s (Peter John b 1982), 1 da (Eleanor Mary b 1984); *Career* slr Messrs C C Bell and Son Bedford 1980-87; co sec Gibbs and Dandy plc 1980-86 (dir 1984, md 1986); dir: Assoc Heating Equipment Distributors Ltd, Gibbs and Dandy Pension Trustees Ltd Luton 1986-; *Recreations* cricket, soccer; *Clubs* MCC; *Style—* Michael Dandy, Esq; Gibbs and Dandy plc, PO Box 17, 226 Dallow Rd, Luton LU1 1JG (☎ 0582 21233)

DANEMAN, Paul Frederick; s of Frederick Daneman (d 1930), and Dorothy, *née* Almenrader; *b* 26 Nov 1925; *Educ* Haberdashers' Aske's, Sir William Borlase's Sch Marlow, Univ of Reading; *m* 1, 1952 (m dis 1965), Susan, *née* Courtnay; m 2, 10 Oct 1965, Meredith Frances, da of late Thomas Kinmont; 2 da (Sophie b 1965, Flora b 1973); *Career* RAF bomber cmd 1943-47; actor; first professional appearance 1947, Bristol Old Vic 1950, Birmingham Rep 1951-52, Old Vic 1953-55 (Toby Belch, Tullus Aufidius in Coriolanus, Justice Shallow in Henry IV, Malcolm in Macbeth), original Vladimir in Waiting for Godot 1955, Old Vic 1957-58 (Henry VI, Fool in King Lear), Cusins in Major Barbara Royal Court 1958, Old Vic 1961-62 (Dr Faustus, Bastard in King John, Richard III, Malvolio in Twelfth Night), Arthur in Camelot (Drury Lane) 1965, Captain Hook in Peter Pan 1967, Rolfe in Hadrian VII (Haymarket) 1969, Don't Start Without Me (Garrick) 1971, Double Edge (Vaudeville) 1975, title role in Macbeth 1976, Shut Your Eyes and Think of England (Apollo) 1979; films incl: Zulu 1966, How I Won the War 1967, Oh What a Lovely War 1966; tv incl: Richard III in An Age of Kings 1960, Not in Front of the Children 1970, Spy Trap 1972-74, Never a Cross Word 1971, Stay with Me till Morning 1980, Two Gentleman of Verona 1983, Antigone 1984-85, Hold the Dream 1987, Roman Holiday 1987, Perfect Spy 1988, Blore MP 1989; *Recreations* painting, reading; *Style—* Paul Daneman, Esq; 81 Deodar Rd, London SW15 2NU; c/o Chatto & Linnit, Prince of Wales Theatre, Coventry St, London W1 (☎ 071 930 6677, fax 071 930 0091, telex 881 1630)

DANESH, Booth J; s of Nasir Danesh (d 1988), and Fakhreya Danesh (d 1988); *b* 15 March 1942; *Educ* Univ of Baghdad (MB ChB), Univ of Dundee (PhD); *m* Feb 1980, Avril, da of Colin Campbell; 1 s (Darius b 19 Dec 1980), 1 da (Aria b 1 Nov 1983); *Career* doctor of medicine, physician and gastroenterologist; currently at Stobhill Gen Hosp Glasgow; author of scientific pubns in med jls incl The Lancet; LAH, FRCP 1989; *Books* Extracorporeal Circulation for the study of the Preterum Factus (with C H M Walker), The Mammalian Factus in Vitro (contrib, 1973); *Recreations* skiing, wind surfing, swimming; *Style—* Booth Danesh, Esq; 3 Ledcameroch Rd, Bearsden, Glasgow G61 4AA (☎ 041 942 7170); Stobhill General Hospital, Glasgow G21 3UW (☎ 041 558 0111)

DANG, Mohinder Singh; s of Mohan Singh, of 56 RB Prakash Chand Rd, Amristar, Punjab, India, and Shakuntal, *née* Kaur; *b* 2 April 1946; *Educ* Med Coll Amristar (MB BS), Punjab Univ (MS Ophth), Univ of Dublin (DO); *m* 5 Dec 1975, Sona Singh, da of Aya Ram (d 1989); 1 s (Rickey b 21 Oct 1979 d 1979), 2 da (Neetika b 24 Jan 1977, Tarana b 11 May 1982); *Career* sr house offr: Charing Cross Hosp London 1973, Canterbury Hosp 1973-74; registrar ophthalmology: Birkenhead Hosp 1974-78, Bournemouth Hosp 1978-80; sr registrar ophthalmology Manchester Royal Eye Hosp 1980-83, conslt ophthalmology Darlington Meml Hosp 1983-; author of numerous articles in jls; chm Med Exec Ctee Memorial Hosp Darlington 1990; memb Exec: Sikh Community Gp Darlington, Overseas Doctors Assoc UK, Indian Doctors of Cleveland; hon res fell Indian Cncl of Medical Res 1970-72; Masters in Surgery (ophth) 1973;

FRCSEd 1979, fell Coll of Ophthalmologists UK 1988; *Recreations* walking, reading, travel, golf; *Style—* Mohinder Singh Dang, Esq; Mussoorie House, Compton Grove, Darlington, Co Durham (☎ 0325 486371); Consultant Ophthalmic Surgeon, Memorial Hospital, Darlington, Co Durham (☎ 0325 380100)

DANGAN, Elizabeth, Viscountess; Elizabeth Anne; da of late Lt-Col Pelham Rawstorn Papillon, DSO (d 1940), of Crowhurst Park, Sussex; *b* 14 May 1920; *m* 1, 16 July 1938, Flt Lt Stephen Alers Hankey, RAF (ka 1943); 2 da (Stephanie (Mrs Roger Parkman Griswold) b 1939, Caroline (Mrs Lawrence Smith Huntington) b (posthumously) 1944); m 2, 17 Nov 1944 (m dis 1950), Denis Arthur, Viscount Dangan (later 5 Earl Cowley, d 1968); 1 s (Richard Francis, 6 Earl Cowley b 1946 d 1975); m 3, 11 Dec 1953, Freeman Winslow Hill, of Bermuda; 1 da; *Style—* Elizabeth, Viscountess Dangan; PO Box 285, Paget, Bermuda

DANGAN, Viscount; Garrett Graham Wellesley; s (by 1 m) and h of 7 Earl Cowley; *b* 30 March 1965; *m* 30 June 1990, Claire L, o da of Peter Brighton, of Stow Bridge, Norfolk; *Career* Traded Options, Hoare Govett Ltd; *Clubs* 151 Club, Brooks's; *Style—* Viscount Dangan

DANIEL, David Albiston; JP (Cheshire 1960); s of Norman Albiston Daniel (d 1965), of Gandria, Congleton, Cheshire, and Evelyn Mary, *née* Congdon (d 1987); *b* 16 Dec 1928; *Educ* Trent Coll; *m* 17 Sept 1955, Joyce, da of George Beach Aylett (d 1964), of Bodelwyddan, Clwyd; 1 s (Julian Albiston b 1963), 1 da (Sara Caroline Bostock b 1957); *Career* slr; dep coroner Cheshire 1960-74, chm SE Cheshire Petty Sessional Div 1967-74; pres N Staffs Law Soc 1987-88; *Style—* David Daniel, Esq, JP; Copperfields, Peel Lane, Astbury, Congleton, Cheshire CW12 4RE (☎ 0260 273180); 8-10 West St, Congleton, Cheshire CW12 1JS (☎ 0260 272777, fax 0260 274243)

DANIEL, Gerald Ernest; s of Alfred Ernest Daniel (d 1932), of Taunton, Somerset, and Beata May, *née* Perrott (d 1967); *b* 7 Dec 1919; *Educ* Huish's GS Taunton; *m* 11 April 1942, Ecila Roslyn, da of Joshua Patmore Dillow, RM (d 1966), of Stoneyhead, Wrantage, Somerset; 1 s (Nigel Adrian b 15 Nov 1954), 1 da (Carole Sandra (Mrs Jackson) b 11 Feb 1943); *Career* Somerset LI (TA) 1939-45; appts in borough treasy depts 1935-68, city treas Nottingham 1968-74, co treas Nottinghamshire 1974-84, dir Horizon Travel plc 1975-85; pub sector advsr Pannell Kerr Forster CAs 1984-; memb IPFA 1949- (pres 1983-84); Freeman of City of London 1984; FCA, IRRV, SAT, FRSA; *Recreations* music (organist), gardening, skiing; *Clubs* Royal Over-Seas League; *Style—* Gerald Daniel, Esq; Brookvale, Star Lane, Blackboys, Uckfield, East Sussex TN22 5LD (☎ 0825 890712)

DANIEL, Sir Goronwy Hopkin; KCVO (1969), CB (1962); s of David Daniel; *b* 21 March 1914; *Educ* Pontardawe Secdy Sch, Amman Valley Co Sch, UCW Aberystwyth, Jesus Coll Oxford; *m* 28 March 1940, Lady Valerie Lloyd George, *qv*; 1 s, 2 da; *Career* lectr Dept of Econs Univ of Bristol 1940-41, clerk House of Commons (attached to Select Ctee Nat Expenditure) 1941-43, Miny of Town & Country Planning 1943-47, chief statistician Miny of Fuel and Power 1947, under sec 1955-64, perm under sec of state Welsh Office 1964-69; princ UCW Aberystwyth 1969-79, vice chllr Univ of Wales 1977-79; dep chm Commercial Bank of Wales 1984-90 (dir 1972-); HM Lt for Dyfed 1979-89; former chm HGTAC; former memb: Gen Advsy Cncl BBC, Welsh Languange Cncl, SSRC; chm Welsh Fourth TV Channel Authy 1981-86; dep chm Prince of Wales Ctee 1980-86; Hon Freeman City of London; hon fell: Jesus Coll Oxford, Univ of Wales; Hon LLD Wales; *Clubs* Travellers'; *Style—* Sir Goronwy Daniel, KCVO, CB; Cae Ffynnon, 67 St Michael's Road, Llandaff, Cardiff (☎ 0222 553150)

DANIEL, His Hon Judge Gruffydd Huw Morgan; s of Prof John Edward Daniel (d 1962), and Catherine Megan Parry-Hughes (d 1972); *b* 16 April 1939; *Educ* Ampleforth, Univ Coll of Wales (LLB), Inns of Court Sch of Law; *m* 10 Aug 1968, Phyllis Margaret Bermingham, da of Walter Ambrose Bermingham, of Clifden, Connemara, Eire (d 1988); 1 da (Antonia Siwan Bermingham); *Career* Nat Serv 1958-60 (volunteered) served 24 Foot, the South Wales Borderers, cmmnd 2 Lt 23 Foot the Royal Welch Fusiliers, Capt 6/7 RWF 1965, served MELF (Cyprus) and UK; called to the Bar Gray's Inn 1967, rec 1980-86, in practice Wales and Chester circuit, circuit jr 1975, asst parly boundary cmmnr for Wales 1981-82 (Gwynedd Enquiry) and in 1985, liaison judge for Gwynedd 1988- (dep liaison judge 1984-88), circuit judge 1986; *Recreations* shooting, sailing, gardening; *Clubs* Reform, Royal Anglesey Yacht; *Style—* His Hon Judge Daniel; Rhiw Gôch, Halfway Bridge, Bangor, Gwynedd; The Castle, Chester

DANIEL, (Reginald) Jack; OBE (1958); s of Reginald Daniel Daniel, and Florence Emily, *née* Woods; *b* 27 Feb 1920; *Educ* Royal Naval Engrg Coll Keyham, RNC Greenwich; *Career* warship and submarine designer; dir Submarine Design and Prodn 1970-74, dir gen Ships and head of RCNC MOD 1974-79, bd memb Br Shipbuilders and dir of technol Warships 1979-84, conslt and Canadian project dir VSEL plc 1984-; FEng, FRINA, FIMarE, RCNC; *Style—* Jack Daniel, Esq, OBE; Meadowland, Cleveland Walk, Bath; VSEL plc, Upper Borough Walls, Bath BA1 1RG (☎ 0225 61 177)

DANIEL, Peter; s of Lt-Col H O Daniel (d 1953), and Margery, *née* Thomas (d 1974); *b* 6 Nov 1924; *Educ* St Paul's Sch London, King Williams Coll IOM, Univ of Liverpool (BArch, MCD); *m* 6 Sept 1951 (m dis 1971), Helen, da of C W Cockrell (d 1977), of Liverpool; 1 s (William b 1954), 2 da (Sarah b 1958, Tacye (adopted) b 1956); *Career* RN 1943-46, Sub Lt RNVR served Russian Convoys and Far East Fleet; former dep chief architect Peterlee Newtown 1960, chief architect and planner Livingston New Town 1962, private practice as conslt landscape architect and planner 1965-; *Recreations* art, music, gardening; *Clubs* Univ of Edinburgh Staff; *Style—* Peter Daniel, Esq; Church House, Foulden, by Berwick-upon-Tweed TD15 1UH (☎ 0289 86307, fax 041 332 7520)

DANIEL, Philip Louis; 2 s of Oscar Louis Wood Moore (d 1931), and Louisa Ann, *née* à Court (d 1919); name changed by Deed Poll from à Court Moore 1945; *b* 23 June 1919; *Educ* Cardinal Vaughan Meml Sch Kensington, LSE (BA); *Career* OTC (RA) Univ of London 1937-39, cmmnd RA 1940, Capt 1942, served Burma and India 1942-45, Maj 1944, SO HQ SEAC 1944-45 (Supreme Allied Cdr's Commendation 1945), Maj RARO 1945-69; asst princ Civil Serv; Miny of Food: joined 1948, served Overseas Food Corp Tanganyika, private sec to Sir Laurence Helsby and others 1950-52; Air Miny 1953, asst sec Dept Econ Affrs 1965, dep chm SE Econ Planning Bd 1968; DOE: head London Geographical Planning Div 1972-78, New Towns Div 1978-79, memb planning inspectorate 1980-89; chm: Int Ctee Newman Assoc GB 1960-84 (pres 1969-71), Issues Ctee Catholic Union GB 1980-, Clifton Episcopal Cmmn of Inquiry 1989; memb Cncl Town and Country Planning Assoc 1982-89; treas Reigate and Banstead Heritage Tst 1980-, memb Cncl Reigate Soc; hon memb Phi Kappa Theta Fraternity Fairfield Conn USA 1971; Freeman City of London 1972 (memb Guild of Freeman 1974), Liveryman Worshipful Co of Scriveners 1978; FBIM 1980; KSG (HH Pope Paul VI) 1975, Knight Order of Holy Sepulchre of Jerusalem 1980 (Cdre 1985); *Books* articles incl: Can World Poverty Be Abolished? (World Justice Vol XI A Nation's Shame, Three Decades of London Housing (1971); reports incl: London Manpower Study (1976), Building Confidence in London's Inner City (1988); *Recreations* motoring, fencing, theatre, historical and economic writing; *Clubs* Army and Navy, Players Theatre; *Style—* Philip Daniel, Esq; Meadhouse, 37 Somerset Rd, Redhill, Surrey RH1 6LT; Rendel Planning, 61 Southwark St, London SE1 1SA (☎ 071 620 1484)

DANIEL, Dr Reginald; s of Reginald Daniel (d 1988), and Alice, *née* Youell; *b* 7 Dec 1939; *Educ* Palmers Sch Grays Essex, Univ of London, Westminster Hosp Med Sch (MB BS, LRCP, FRCS, fell Coll of Ophthalmologists, DO, AKC, ECFMG); *m* Carol; 1 s (Lorne Piers b 23 July 1968), 1 da (Claire Suzanne b 2 Dec 1969); *Career* conslt ophthalmic surgn: Guy's Hosp, St Thomas' Hosp; ophthalmic private practice in Harley Street and lectr Univ of London; Freeman City of London, Liveryman Worshipful Co of Spectacle Makers; memb BMA; author of many ophthalmic papers in professional jls; *Recreations* golf, tennis, skiing; *Style—* Dr Reginald Daniel; 152 Harley St, London W1N 1HH (☎ 071 935 3834, fax 071 224 2574)

DANIEL, Ruth; da of Rev Richard William Bailey Langhorne (d 1944); whose forebears incl Daniel Langhorne the antiquary (d 1681), Richard Langhorne a victim of Titus Oates (executed 1679) and among American cousins Lady (Nancy) Astor, *née* Langhorne; da of Victoria Winifred Helen, *née* Poole (d 1968); *b* 5 July 1915; *Educ* Maynard Sch Exeter, St Anne's Coll Oxford (MA); *m* 12 Sept 1946, Glyn Edmund Daniel (d 1986), s of John Daniel (d 1948), of Glamorgan; *Career* served WWII in photographic intelligence, Flight Offr WRAF 1941-46; prodn ed Antiquity (a review of archaeology) 1956-86; *Recreations* music, watching cricket; *Clubs* United Oxford & Cambridge Univ (Lady Associate Memb); *Style—* Mrs Glyn Daniel; The Flying Stag, 70 Bridge Street, Cambridge CB2 1UR

DANIEL, Lady Valerie Davidia; *née* Lloyd George; da of 2 Earl Lloyd George of Dwyfor; *b* 14 Feb 1918; *m* 28 March 1940, Sir Goronwy Daniel, KCVO, CB, *qv*; 1 s, 2 da; *Style—* The Lady Valerie Daniel; Ridge Farm, Letterston, Dyfed (☎ 0348 840586); 67 St Michael's Rd, Llandaf, Cardiff (☎ 0222 553150)

DANIEL, William Wentworth; s of George Taylor Daniel, and Margaret Elizabeth, *née* Hopper; *b* 19 Nov 1938; *Educ* Univ of Manchester (BA, MSc); *m* 22 Sept 1961 (m dis 1974), Lynda Mary, *née* Garrett; *Career* asst lectr Univ of Manchester 1962-63, directing staff Ashorne Hill Mgmnt Coll Warwickshire 1963-65, res offr Res Servs Ltd London 1965-67, res fell Univ of Bath 1967-68, dir The Policy Studies Inst (formerly Political and Economic Planning London) 1986- (res fell 1968-83, dep dir 1983-86); *Books* incl: Racial Discrimination in England (1968), The Right to Manage? (1972), Sandwich Courses in Higher Education (1975), Where Are They Now?: a follow up survey of the unemployed (1977), Maternity Rights: the experience of women (1980), Workplace Industrial Relations in Britain (1983), Workplace Industrial Relations and Technical Change (1987), The Unemployed Flow (1990); *Recreations* golf, tennis; *Clubs* Reform, Bude & North Cornwall Golf; *Style—* William Daniel, Esq; Chyvarton, Higher Upton, Bude, North Cornwall; Flat 2, 64 Queensway, London W2 3RL; Policy Studies Institute, 100 Park Village East, London NW1 3SR (☎ 071 387 2171, fax 071 388 0914)

DANIELL, Col Antony Piers de Tabley; OBE (1960), MC (1944), TD (1945); s of Henry Thesiger Whiteman Daniell (d 1935), of Pencraig, Llangefni, Anglesey, and Maud Edith Thesiger, *née* Phibbs (d 1953); *b* 19 June 1913; *Educ* Greshams, Trinity Coll Cambridge (MA); *m* 30 Sept 1947, Noreen Mary Alison, da of Col Alexander John Cruickshank, DSO (d 1978), of Innage House, Shifnal, Salop; 1 s (John b 1950 d 1990); *Career* TA RE 1937, enlisted 1939, Capt 1940, Maj 1942; OC 59 Field Co RE in 4 Br Div: N Africa 1 Army 1943, Italy 1944, RE Newark 1944, demobbed 1945; rejoined TAas Lt-Col 1947 (Col 1956); civil engrg contractor; dir Wilson Lovatt & Sons Ltd 1955-71 (joined 1935), chm The Network 1982-89; memb: Ironbridge Gorge Devpt Tst 1971-78, Shropshire Conservation Devpt Tst 1981-; DL: Staffs 1962, Shropshire 1974; FICE 1960 (memb 1939); *Publications* Mediterranean Safari (1943-44); *Recreations* walking, bird watching, gardening; *Clubs* Naval and Military; *Style—* Col Antony Daniell, OBE, MC, TD; Cottage Farm House, Frodesley, Shrewsbury SY5 7HD (☎ 06944 626)

DANIELL, Gillian Mary; da of John Averell Daniell, of The Springs, Stoney Hollow, Lutterworth, Leicestershire and Nancy Helen Law; *b* 23 Feb 1947; *Educ* The Sch of Sts Mary and Anne Bromley, Loughborough Coll of Art, Slade Sch of Fine Art, Goldsmiths Coll of Art (BA), RCA (MA); *m* 1972 (m dis 1987), Vaughan, da of Herman Grylls; 1 da (Sarah Hope b 22 June 1979); *Career* theatre designer and artist; exhibitions incl: Young Contemporaries 1969, mixed show (RCA) 1970 and 1971, mixed show (Trinity Coll Cambridge) 1971, Art Spectrum (Alexandra Palace London) 1971, Past students of the Environmental Media Dept (RCA Gallery) 1972, mixed staff show (Croydon Coll of Art) 1973, Art Into Landscape exhibition (Serpentine Gallery) 1974 (awarded second prize); Scaling Up (Guild Hall Manchester) 1986; co-designer and dir The Zoo Story (Royal Ct Theatre, Theatre Upstairs) 1970; designer: As Cuecas (The Bloomers) (German Inst Lisbon Portugal) 1975 and 1985, The Winter Dances (Royal Ct Theatre, Theatre Upstairs) 1977, Up In Sweden (King's Head Theatre) 1980, Third Flight (CV One Theatre Co Bush Theatre and tour) 1980, Benefit Gala for The American Theatre Co (Theatre Royal Drury Lane) 1981; freelance designer for Durham Theatre Co Darlington: Janet and John and The Boon Dogglers 1982-83, Aladdin 1982-83, Pitmatic Times 1983, Dick Whittington 1983, The Bloomers 1985, The Magic Island 1984, Oh What A Lovely War 1984, The Land of Hope and Glory Boys 1985; designer: Hollywood Or Bust (Thames TV) 1984, Robin Hood (BBC Playschool) 1984, Diary of A Somebody-The Orton Diaries (NT) 1987, Monopoly (The Old Red Lion) 1987, Two Acts Of Love (Prince of Wales Theatre) 1987, The Orton Diaries (The Kings Head Theatre) 1987, Rat In The Skull (The Liverpool Playhouse) 1987, Every Good Boy Deserves Favour (Queen Elizabeth Hall) 1987, This Savage Parade (The Kings Head Theatre) 1987, Second Lady(The Liverpool Playhouse) 1988, Macbeth (The Liverpool Playhouse) 1988, Of Mice And Men (The Liverpool Playhouse and UK tour) 1989, A Slice of Saturday Night (The Kings Head Theatre and The Arts Theatre) 1989, Getting In (The Bridge House Theatre) 1989, The Manchurian Candidate (New Vic Touring Co) 1991; TV documentary prodr, formed own TV prodn co 1982; clients incl: Zandra Rhodes and Gina Fratini 1981-82, Kangol Hats 1982, Midland Bank 1983, Chrysalis Records 1983, PW Forte Fashion 1983, London Borough of Brent 1983, Lewis's Stores 1983-84, Haverstock School-The Movie (dir) 1990; fndr Calliope Theatre Co Williamstown Mass, co-dir and designer Fallen Woman 1985; memb CNAA (examiner for fine art BA Hons) 1984-87; *Awards* nomination for Best Design in Charrington London Fringe award (for Slice of Saturday Night) 1990; memb Soc of Br Theatre Designers 1989-; pt/t lectr variously at: Portsmouth Poly, Croydon Coll of Art, Homerton Coll Cambridge, London Coll of Printing, Kingston Poly, Heatherley Sch of Art, Central St, Martins Coll of Art; *Style—* Ms Gillian Daniell; Felix De Wolfe, 376-378 The Strand, London WC2R OLB (☎ 071 379 5767, fax 071 836 0337)

DANIELL, Hon Mrs (Mary Elizabeth Jill Rodd); da of 2 Baron Rennell (d 1978); *b* 1932; *m* 1, 13 Nov 1954, Michael Langan Dunne; 2 s (John b 1957, Stephen b 1961), 3 da (Mary Jemima (Mrs Lord) b 1955, Teresa b 1962, Miranda b 1966); m 2, 7 March 1985, Christopher Bridges Daniell; *Style—* The Hon Mrs Daniell; 6 Leinster Square, London W6; Ashley Farm, Stansbatch, Pembridge, Herefordshire

DANIELL, Col Patrick John; CBE (1987); s of Brigadier AJ Daniell, CBE, DSO, of Oaklodge, Hillside St, Hythe, Kent, and Phyllis Kathleen Rhona, *née* Grove Annesley; *b* 15 Dec 1939; *Educ* Wellington, RMA Sandhurst; *Career* 7 Parachute Regt RHA 1962-66 and 1975-77, Br Army Trg Team Kenya 1966-69, Staff Coll 1969-72, Cwlth

Liaison Mission UN Cmd Korea 1972, Nat Def Coll 1978, Cdr The Sultan of Oman's Artillery 1979-82, MOD 1982-87; personnel and industl rels dir Macmillan Publishers Ltd 1987-90; the Sultan of Oman's Medal for Distinguished Service (WKIM) 1980; *Recreations* horticulture, fishing; *Style*— Col Patrick Daniell, CBE; Abbey Cottage, Itchen Abbas, Winchester, Hants SO21 1BN; Macmillan Publishers Ltd, Houndmills, Basingstoke, Hampshire RG21 2XS (☎ 0256 29242)

DANIELL, Sir Peter Averell; TD (1950), DL (Surrey 1976); s of late Roger Henry Averell Daniell; *b* 8 Dec 1909; *Educ* Eton, Trinity Coll Oxford (MA); *m* 18 July 1935, Leonie Mayne, da of late Henry Beauchamp Harrison; 2 s (Roger b 1939, James b 1949), 1 da (Celia (Mrs Prideaux) b 1936); *Career* KRRC 1939-45; sr ptnr Mullens and Co, ret 1973; sr govt broker 1963-73; kt 1971; *Clubs* Brooks's, Alpine; *Style*— Sir Peter Daniell, TD, DL; Glebe House, Buckland, Surrey (☎ 073 784 2320)

DANIELLS-SMITH, Roger Charles; s of Charles Frederick Daniells-Smith, of Harlow, Essex, and Marie, *née* Daniells; *b* 26 Aug 1952; *Educ* Newport GS, King's Coll London (LLB); *m* 26 May 1979, Annette Louise, da of Stefan Kazimiercz Wacnik, DSO (d 1986); 2 da (Helena Elizabeth b 1981, Sophie Anne b 1983); *Career* called to Bar Middle Temple 1974; *Recreations* gardening, motoring, watersports, antiques; *Style*— Roger Daniells-Smith, Esq; 92 Devenay Rd, Stratford, London E15 (☎ 081 555 5792); 8 King's Bench Walk, Temple, London EC4 (☎ 071 353 7851)

DANIELS, (David) Donald; s of Leon Daniels (d 1964), of London, and Anna, *née* Kettelapper (d 1964); *b* 27 Jan 1911; *Educ* Holborn GS, London Poly; *m* 1, 1937 (m dis 1947), Elizabeth Phillips; 1 s (Paul b 22 Feb 1943); m 2, 8 Aug 1950, Miriam (Mimi), da of Morris Aarons (d 1965), of London; 1 da (Linda b 6 June 1952); *Career* RAC 1941, Intelligence Corps (counter espionage interrogator in Euro languages) 1944, demobbed 1946; dep chm S Daniels Co Ltd London 1973 (co-fndr 1946), underwriting memb at Lloyds London; hosp visitor Br Heart Fndn; memb Nat Exec Ctee Br Assoc of Food Importers and Distributors; vice pres College of Driver Educn; former: chm Trades Advsy Cncl, vice chm ROSPA Advanced Drivers Assoc, memb Grocers Inst, pres Portsoken Ward Club, memb London C of C; Freeman: City of London 1950, Worshipful Co of Basket Makers; *Recreations* golf, bird breeding, music, travelling; *Clubs* Verulam Golf (St Albans), City Livery (memb Cncl), United Wards London (memb Governing Body); *Style*— Donald Daniels, Esq; South Quay Plaza, 183 Marsh Wall, London E14 (☎ 071 538 0188, fax 071 410 0067, telex 28837 DAN PLC)

DANIELS, George; MBE (1982); s of George Daniels, and Beatrice, *née* Cadou; *b* 19 Aug 1926; *m* 1964, Juliet Anne, *née* Marryat; 1 da; *Career* served 2 Bn E Yorks Regt 1944-47; author, watchmaker, horological consultant; began professional horology 1947-, restoration of historical watches 1956-, hand watch-making to own designs 1969-; master Worshipful Co of Clockmakers 1980; Victor Kullberg Medal Stockholm Watch Guild 1977, Gold Medal Br Horological Inst 1981, Tompion Gold Medal 1981, City & Guilds Insignia Award (Hons) 1986, City & Guilds Gold Medal for Craftmanship 1991; hon fell and Gold Award of American Watchmakers Inst 1987; *Books* English and American Watches (1965), The Art of Breguet (1975, 2nd edition 1978), Watchmaking (1981), Sir David Salomons Collection (1981); *Recreations* vintage cars, fast motorcycles, opera, Scotch whisky; *Style*— George Daniels, Esq, MBE; 34 New Bond St, London W1A 2AA

DANIELS, Karl; s of Harold George Daniels of Ipswich (d 1965); *b* 1 Dec 1935; *Educ* Ipswich Sch; *m* 1960, Janice Margaret, da of Vernon Billing; 2 s; *Career* pension scheme consultant; md Noble Lowndes Pensions Ltd 1979-, dir Lowndes Associated Pensions Ltd, English Pension Tstees Ltd, Lowndes Mgmnt Incentives Ltd, dir Scottish Pension Tstees Ltd 1976-; *Clubs* RAC; *Style*— Karl Daniels, Esq; Church Cottage, Church Rd, Lingfield, Surrey (☎ 0342 832023)

DANIELS, Patrick Deane; s of Gerald Ernest Deane Daniels (d 1942), and Marcelle Barbara Mary Daniels; *b* 20 April 1940; *Educ* St George's Coll Weybridge Surrey, Univ of Durham (LLB), Coll of Law; *m* Heide Marie, da of Friedrich Mumm (d 1944); 1 s (Mark Frederick), 1 da (Nina Marie); *Career* asst slr Bulcraig and Davis 1965-66 (articled clerk 1962-65), attended course in German law and worked in Germany 1966-67, asst slr Freshfields 1968-72, ptnr Simmons and Simmons 1973- (asst slr 1972-73); freeman and liveryman City of London slrs' Co 1990; memb: Law Soc, BR Inst of Int and Comparative Law; Tolley's Company Law (contrib), Management of Interest Rate Risk, Management of Currency Risk (1989); *Recreations* walking, swimming, arts, wine; *Clubs* Carlton; *Style*— Patrick Daniels, Esq; Herons, Herons Lane, Fyfield, Nr Ongar, Essex CM5 0RQ (☎ 0277899205); Simmons and Simmons, 14 Dominion St, London EC2M 2RJ (☎ 071 628 2020, 071 588 4129)

DANIELS, (Newton Edwards) Paul; s of Handel Newton Daniels, and Nancy, *née* Lloyd; *b* 6 April 1938; *Educ* Sir William Turner's GS Coatham Redcar ; *m* 1, 26 March 1960 (m dis 1975); 3 s (Paul Newton b 9 Sept 1960, Marti b 19 Aug 1963, Gary b 15 March 1969); m 2, 2 April 1988, Debbie, *née* McGee; *Career* Nat Serv Green Howards 1957-59, served Hong Kong; magician and entertainer; clerk (later internal auditor) local govt, mobile grocery business (later shop owner), turned professional 1969, TV debut Opportunity Knocks 1970; subsequent TV series incl: The Paul Daniels Magic Show, Odd One Out, Every Second Counts, Wizbit (childrens series); theatre: It's Magic (Prince of Wales) 1980-82, An Evening With Paul Daniels (Prince of Wales) 1983; Christmas season Savoy 1989; summer seasons: Great Yarmouth 1979, Bournemouth 1980, Blackpool 1983; appeared in 5 Royal Variety Shows; winner: Magician of the Year award, Hollywood's Acad of Magical Arts Golden Rose of Montreux trophy 1985 (for Paul Daniels Easter Magic Show BBC); memb Inner Magic Circle; *Books* Paul Daniels Magic Book (1980), More Magic (1981), Paul Daniels Magic Annual (1983), 77 Popular Card Games and Tricks (1985); *Recreations* photography, golf, tennis; *Clubs* The Magic Circle; *Style*— Paul Daniels, Esq; P O Box 250, Uxbridge, Middx UB9 5DX (☎ 0302 321 233, fax 0895 834 891)

DANIELS, Prof Peter George; s of Frederick James Daniels, of Ilford, Essex, and Eileen Bertha, *née* Galley; *b* 30 Sept 1950; *Educ* Ilford Co HS, Univ of Bristol (BSc), UCL (PhD); *m* 12 July 1975, Anne Elizabeth, da of Robert Latham, of Hammersmith, London; 1 s (Geoffrey b 1989), 1 da (Katherine b 1986); *Career* head of Dept of Mathematics City Univ 1987- (lectr 1977, reader 1981, prof of applied mathematics 1985); *Recreations* soccer, gardening; *Style*— Prof Peter Daniels; Department of Mathematics, City University, Northampton Square, London EC1V 0HB (☎ 071 253 4399, fax 071 250 0837)

DANIELS, Raymond Alfred; MC (1946); s of late Alfred Daniels; *b* 15 July 1923; *Educ* Bedford Modern Sch; *m* 1954, Helen, *née* Clark; 3 s; *Career* md William Press & Son 1975-; *Style*— Raymond Daniels Esq, MC; Greystock, 64 Merrybent, Darlington, Co Durham (☎ 0325 74 238)

DANIELS, Robert George Reginald; CBE (1984), JP (Essex and Ongar, 1969), DL (Essex 1980); s of Robert Henry Daniels, and Edith, *née* Brignall; *b* 17 Nov 1916; *Educ* private and state; *m* 26 Oct 1940, Hancock; 1 da (Patricia Ann b 1942); *Career* Mil Service (despatches twice); insur rep Prudential Assurance 1938-76, ret; memb: Theydon Bois Parochial Cncl 1952- (chm 1969-), Epping RDC 1952-55; Epping and Ongar RDC: memb 1955-74, vice chm 1958-59 and 1964-65, chm 1959-60 and 1965-66; memb Epping Forest DC 1974-79; Essex CC: memb 1965-, alderman 1969, vice chm 1977-80, chm 1980-83; Dartford Tunnel Jt Ctee: memb 1968-, vice chm 1970-74, chm 1974-; gen cmmr of Income Tax Epping Div 1970-; pres: Theydon Bois Br Legion 1985- (chm 1973-85), Outward Bound Tst Essex 1985; memb Chelmsford Engrg Soc 1980-; *Recreations* reading; *Clubs* Essex; *Style*— Robert Daniels, Esq, CBE, JP, DL; 42 Dukes Avenue, Theydon Bois, Epping, Essex (☎ 037 881 3123)

DANILOVICH, Hon Mrs (Irene); *née* Forte; 3 da of Baron Forte (Life Peer), *qv*; *b* 15 Dec 1956; *m* 19 March 1977, John Joseph Danilovich, *qv*; 1 s (John Charles Amadeus b 14 Sept 1981), 1 da (Alice Irene Angelica b 4 Jan 1985); *Style*— The Hon Mrs Danilovich; 37 Carlyle Square, London SW3 6HA

DANILOVICH, John Joseph; s of John George Danilovich (d 1988), of California, and Alice Marie, *née* Walsh (d 1984); *b* 25 June 1950; *Educ* The Choate Sch, Stanford Univ (BA), Univ of S California (MA); *m* 19 March 1977, The Hon Irene, da of Lord Forte of Ripley; 1 s (John Charles Amadeus b 14 Sept 1981), 1 da (Alice Irene Angelica b 4 Jan 1985); *Career* dir: IBEX Mutual Insur Co 1972-77, Colocotronis Chartering Ltd 1972-77; ptnr The Eisenhower Gp Washington DC, conslt Atlas/ Interocean Shipping Gp; chm: George Bush for Pres (Europe), Choate Rosemary Hall Alumni (Europe); memb: Republican Nat Fin Ctee, bd of dirs The Panama Canal Cmmn; co chm Republicans Abroad; *Recreations* shooting, skiing, theatre; *Clubs* Buck's, Queen's, Pacific-Union (San Francisco); *Style*— John Danilovich, Esq; 37 Carlyle Square, London SW3 6HA (☎ 071 352 6315); c/o Pegasus House, 37-43 Sackville St, London W1X 2AH (☎ 071 439 9721, fax 071 437 1156)

DANKS, Hon Mrs (Serena Mary); *née* Gifford; da of 4 Baron Gifford (d 1937), and Anne Maud, da of Bt-Col William Aitchison, JP, DL, of Drumore; *b* 30 Sept 1919; *m* 1, 28 Sept 1940 (m dis 1945), Patrick de Gruchy Vignoles Crawshay Warren; 1 s; m 2, 17 Oct 1951, Arthur Reginald Danks, MBE, TD, *qv*; 1 s, 1 da; *Style*— The Hon Mrs Danks; Loscombe, Sydling St Nicholas, Dorchester, Dorset DT2 9PD

DANKWORTH, Jacqueline Caryl; da of Jonathan Dankworth, of The Old Rectory, Wavendon, Milton Keynes, and Clemantina Diana, *née* Campbell; *b* 5 Feb 1963; *Educ* St Paul's Girls London, The Guildhall Sch of Music and Drama London; *Career* actress; roles incl: Liza in My Fair Lady (Cheltenham Everyman), Abigail in The Crucible and Constanza in Amadeus (Belgrade Theatre Coventry), chrous in Creon and Calphurnia in Julius Caeser (Haymarket Theatre Co Br Cncl India Tour), Hero in Much Ado About Nothing and Nerissa in The Merchant of Venice (RSC National Westminster Tour), Sonya in Uncle Vanya (Tour of Britain), Emily in Liaisons Dangereuse (Ambassadors Theatre West End), Cinderella in Into the Woods (Phoenix Theatre West End); film appearances incl: street singer in 1871, Alexander's sister in 1919; TV appearances incl: The Bill, Jackanory Playhouse, South Bank Show, Stephen Sondheim's Masterclass; concert appearances incl: LSO Barbican Centre, BBC Concert Orchestra Croydon; other performances incl: It's Better with a Band Late Night Review (Show People Donmar Warehouse), Lorca's Women RSC Early Stages, Suitcase Fair (The Stables Warendon); *Recreations* walking with my dog, swimming; *Style*— Ms Jacqueline Dankworth; Jean Merylese/Laurne Mansfield, International Artistes Representation, Mezannine Floor, 235 Regent St, London W1R 8AX (☎ 071 439 8401, fax 071 409 2070)

DANKWORTH, John Philip William; CBE (1974); *b* 20 Sept 1927; *Educ* Monoux GS, RAM, Berklee Coll; *m* 18 March 1958, Clementina Dinah (Cleo Laine); 1 s (Alex b 1960), 1 da (Jackie b 1963); *Career* musician, closely involved with post war devpt of Br jazz 1947-60; cmmnd compositions incl: Improvisations (with Matyas Seiber) 1959, Escapade (Northern Sinfonia Orchestra) 1967, Tom Sawyers Saturday (Farnham) 1967, String Quartet 1971, Piano Concerto (Westminster festival) 1972, Grace Abounding 1980, The Diamond and The Goose 1981, Reconciliation (for silver jubilee of Coventry Cathedral) 1987, Lady in Waiting (Houston Ballet), Man of Mode (RSC), Edward II (Nat Theatre); film scores incl: We Are the Lambeth Boys, The Criminal, Saturday Night Sunday Morning 1964, Darling, The Servant 1965, Modesty Blaise, Sands of Kalahari, Morgan, Return From the Ashes (Academy Award nomination) 1966, Accident 1969, Salt and Pepper 1969, Fathom 1969, 10 Rillington Place 1971, The Last Grenade 1971; musical theatre incl: Boots with Strawberry Jam (with Benny Green) 1968, Colette (starring Cleo Laine) 1979; TV theme for the Avengers series; numerous records incl: Echoes of Harlem, Misty, Symphonic Fusions; Variety Club of GB show business personality award (with Cleo Laine); Hon MA Open Univ 1975, Hon DMus Berklee Sch 1982; FRAM 1973; *Recreations* driving, household maintenance; *Style*— John Dankworth, Esq, CBE; c/o International Artistes Ltd, 235 Regent St, London W1A 2JT (☎ 071 439 8401, fax 071 409 2070)

DANN, Clifford Thomas; s of George Dann (d 1971), of Hellingly, Sussex, and Grace Sophia, *née* Hook (d 1970); *b* 17 July 1927; *Educ* Hailsham Co Sch, Univ of London (BSc); *m* 1, 14 Aug 1948 (m dis 1988), Bronwen Annie, da of the late Gordon Gauld, of Coventry; 1 s (Vyvian b 1959), 1 da (Angela b 1951); m 2, 21 Nov 1988, Patricia Anne Purdon, da of The Very Rev Ivan Delacherois Neill, CB, OBE; *Career* chartered surveyor; RICS: chm Jr Orgn 1957-58, Cncl 1958-61 and 1973-87, chm Sussex branch 1973-74, chm Public Affrs Ctee 1975-80, chm Policy Review Ctee 1980-82, pres 1983-84; Int Fedn of Surveyors: UK del 1958-82, memb London Congress Ctee 1967-70, chm Town Planning Cmmn 1974-75; lectr on arbitration practice; fndr and sr ptnr Clifford Dann & Ptnrs 1956; dir: Individual Life Insurance Co 1972-76, Network Date Ltd 1981-83; chm: Lewes Round Table 1958, Sussex Area World of Property Housing Tst 1965-72, League of Friends of Chailey Heritage (physically disabled children) 1978-; vice chm Chailey Heritage Sch Govrs 1985-; memb: The Speaker's Appeal for St Margaret's Westminster Ctee, Friends of Lewes Ctee 1957-63, Lewes Old Peoples' Welfare Ctee 1962-68; govr Lewes Tech Coll 1967-73 (vice chm 1971-73), pres Lewes C of C 1965, memb Surrey and Sussex Rent Assessment Panel 1965-72, govr Brighton Poly 1989-; Freeman City of London 1979, Liveryman Worshipful Co of Chartered Surveyors; memb FIABCI 1960-85, ARICS 1949, FRICS 1957; *Books* author of numerous articles in professional jls incl International Economic Factors in Urban Devpt (1962), Community Land Scheme (1971-75); *Recreations* music, organ, choir training, gardening, DIY, travelling abroad; *Style*— Clifford Dann, Esq; The Old Jewellers, 176 High St, Uckfield, Sussex; Albion House, Lewes, Sussex (☎ 0273 477022)

DANN, Jill; da of Maj Harold Norman Cartwright, MC (d 1955), of Solihull, Warwicks, and Marjorie Alice, *née* Thornton (d 1972); *b* 10 Sept 1929; *Educ* Solihull HS for Girls, Univ of Birmingham (LLB), St Hilda's Coll Oxford (BCL); *m* 12 July 1952, Anthony John Dann (Tony), s of Sydney William Henry Dann (d 1988), of Chippenham, Wilts; 3 s (Christopher b 1954, Michael b and d 1956, Timothy b 1961), 2 da (Jennie b 1957, Rachel b 1961); *Career* barr; broadcaster and dir Wiltshire Radio; vice chm House of Laity Gen Synod, church cmmnr, tstee Church Urban Fund, former Mayoress of Chippenham, pres St Paul and St Mary Colls Cheltenham; *Recreations* family, grandchildren; *Clubs* Royal Cwlth Soc; *Style*— Mrs Jill Dann; The Riverbank, Reybridge, Lacock, Wiltshire SN15 2PF (☎ 0249 73205, fax 0249 443412)

DANSON, Hon Barnett Jerome; PC (Canada); s of Joseph B Danson, and Saidie W Danson (both decd); *b* 8 Feb 1921; *Educ* Toronto Public Sch, Toronto HS; *m* 1943, Isobel, da of J Robert Bull of London; 4 s; *Career* served WWII, Queen's Own Rifles of Canada (wounded Normandy 1944, ret as Lt, appointed Hon Lt-Col 1974); consul gen for Canada in Boston 1944-46; fndr and pres Danson Corporation Ltd (Scarborough) 1953-74; MP (Lib) York N 1968-79, Parly sec to PM Trudeau 1970-72, min of state urban affrs 1974-76, min of nat def 1976-79; chm of bd de Havilland

Aircraft of Canada Ltd 1982-84, dir Ballet Opera House Corp; dir: Algoma Central Railway, Urban Transportation Development Corporation UTDC Int, General Steelwares Ltd, Winchester Group Ltd, chm GSW Thermoplastics Co; chm: Inst for Political Involvement, Arms Control Centre; dir: Canadian Cncl of Christians and Jews, Empire Club of Canada, Ballet Opera House Corp; dir emeritus Canadian Cncl for Native Business; *Recreations* fishing, skiing, music; *Clubs* Donalda (Toronto), Craigleith Ski (Collingwood Ontario); *Style—* The Hon Barnett J Danson; 1106-561 Avenue Rd, Toronto M4V 2J8, Canada (☎ 416 323 3274)

DANTER, Maj John Trevor; s of William Herbert Danter (d 1955), of Gloucester, and Kathrine Louise, *née* Rudge; *b* 30 July 1930; *Educ* The Crypt Sch Gloucester, RMA Sandhurst, RAC Cirencester; *m* 12 April 1955, Heather Maud, da of Richard Judd (d 1984), of Cambridgeshire; 1 s (Alistair b 1957); *Career* cmmnd South Staffs Regt 1951-68; served: N Ireland, Cyprus, Germany, Aden, Kenya, UK; ret Maj; agent to Trinity Coll managing The Trimley Estate Felixstowe Suffolk 1970-87; ptnr Bidwells Chartered Surveyors 1980, md Bidwells and King Perth 1987, dir Perth Enterprise Co 1989; chm Suffolk Coastal Cons Assoc 1985-87; *Recreations* fly-fishing, horse racing, walking, music, reading; *Clubs* Army & Navy; *Style—* Maj John Danter; Annfield, Glenalmond, Perthshire PH1 3SE (☎ 073 888 267); Bidwells, 5 Atholl Place, Perth (☎ 0738 26 178)

DANTZIC, Roy Matthew; s of David A Dantzic, of Whitecraigs, Glasgow, and Renee, *née* Cohen; *b* 4 July 1944; *Educ* Brighton Coll Sussex; *m* 3 June 1969, Diane, da of Abraham Clapham (d 1984), of Whitecraigs, Glasgow; 1 s (Toby Alexander b 15 Feb 1975), 1 da (Emma Lucy b 23 Sept 1973); *Career* Coopers & Lybrand 1962-69, Kleinwort Benson Ltd 1970-72, Drayton Corporation Ltd 1972-73, Samuel Montagu & Co Ltd 1974-80 (dir 1975), fin dir Britoil plc (formerly Br National Oil Corporation) 1980-84; dir: Pallas Group SA 1984-85, Wood Mackenzie & Co 1985-89, Stanhope Properties plc 1989-; non exec chm Premier Portfolio Group plc 1985-, non-exec dir: Br Nuclear Fuels plc 1987-, Moor Park (1958) Ltd 1980-90, Saxon Oil plc 1984-85; govr Brighton Coll 1990-, pt/t memb CEGB 1984-87; FICAS 1969; *Recreations* golf, theatre, sitting in the shade; *Clubs* MCC, Moor Park Golf; *Style—* Roy Dantzic, Esq; Moor Park, Northwood, Middlesex; Lansdowne House, Berkeley Square, London, W1X 6BP

DANVERS, Ivor Colin; s of Charles Danvers (d 1948), of London, and Violet, *née* Broughton (d 1970); *b* 14 July 1932; *Educ* Central Sch of Speech and Drama; *m* 3 Sept 1956, Henrietta, da of John Bruce Holmes (d 1968), of London; 1 s (Thomas Asher b 1 Sept 1965), 1 da (Lindsey b 24 Aug 1958); *Career* Nat Serv RAF 1950; actor; theatre incl: The Mousetrap (Ambassadors) 1960, Robert and Elizabeth (Lyric) 1964, The Waiting Game (Arts) 1965, Give a Dog a Bone (Westminster) 1967, Norman Conquests (Globe and Apollo) 1975, Journey's End (Mermaid and Cambridge) 1972, Touch of Danger (Whitehall) 1989, Me and My Girl (Adelphi) 1990, many regnl prodns; dir Richmond Theatre Surrey 1966-70; tv incl: The Little Door, Minder, Terry and June, Love from Italy, No Place like Home, Angels, Softly Softly, The World Walk, Purple People Eater, Gerald Urquhard in Howards Way 1985-90; active supporter SPARKS and Aid for the Crippled Child, pres Stage Golf Club 1987; *Recreations* chess, bridge, golf; *Clubs* Richmond Golf, Stage Golf; *Style—* Ivor Danvers, Esq; c/o April Young Ltd, The Clockhouse, 6 St Catherines Mews, Milner St, London SW3 2PU (☎ 071 584 1274)

DANVILLE, Comte Norbert Leon; s of Comte André Danville, Croix de Guerre (d 1986), of Paris, and Valentine, *née* de Topolsky (d 1979); *b* 26 Nov 1947; *Educ* Ecole Alsacienne Paris, Law Sch (Paris Panthéon), Sciences PO Paris; *m* 1 (m dis 1988), Annick Jousset; m 2, 24 Oct 1988, Madame Ines Voute, da of Jean Sapinno, of Geneva, Switzerland; 1 step da (Melissende Voute b 1980), 1 da (Anne-Laure b 1989); *Career* 19 Sqdn Cavalry Regt at Les Invalides, Paris 1973-74; with Compagnie Finançière Edmond de Rothschild, Paris 1974-78; Barclays Bank SA France 1978-82; BAII (London) 1982-89, Union Finances Grain 1990-, md Acteon (Paris) 1990-; cncllr Franco-British Chamber of Commerce; memb: Franco-Swiss Chamber, Geneva; The French Benevolent Soc, London; FIOD; *Clubs* Overseas Bankers', RAC; Union Finance Grain, 17 Ave George V F75008 Paris; *Style—* Comte Norbert Danville; BAII, 2 rue Thalberg, 1208 Geneva, Switzerland

DARANYI-FORBES-SEMPILL, Hon Mrs (Kirstine Elizabeth); *née* Forbes-Sempill; changed names by deed poll 1986 to Daryani-Forbes-Sempill; da of 19 Lord Sempill (d 1965) by 2 w, Cecilia, *née* Dunbar-Kilburn; half-sis of Lady Sempill, *qv*; *b* 9 Aug 1944; *m* 1, 1 June 1968 (m dis 1985), John Michael Forbes-Cable (who assumed by deed poll 1968 the additional name of Forbes), second s of late Richard Cable, of Woodhill Compton, Wolverhampton, Staffs; 2 s (William Richard Craigievar b 1970, Malcolm Dunbar Craigievar b 1972); m 2, 1990, Bela Peter de Daranyi, s of late Bela de Daranyi and late Countess Margit de Daranyi Haller de Hallerkeo, of Budapest, Hungary; *Style—* The Hon Mrs Daranyi-Forbes-Sempill; Flat 8, 17-20 Embankment Gardens, London SW3 (☎ 071 351 2125)

DARBOURNE, John William Charles; CBE (1977); s of late William Leslie Darbourne, and Violet Yorke; *b* 11 Jan 1935; *Educ* Battersea GS, UCL (BArch), Harvard (MLA); *m* 1960, Noreen Fifield (d 1988); 1 s, 3 da; *Career* ptnr John Darbourne Partnership (architects, landscape architects and planners); RIBA, assoc Inst of Landscape Architects; *Style—* John Darbourne, Esq, CBE; 6 The Green, Richmond, Surrey (☎ 081 940 7182)

DARBY, Prof Sir (Henry) Clifford; CBE (1978, OBE 1946); s of Evan Darby (d 1955), of Resolven, Wales, and Jennie, *née* Thomas (d 1957); *b* 7 Feb 1909; *Educ* Neath Co Sch, St Catharine's Coll Cambridge (BA, PhD, MA); *m* 26 Dec 1941, Eva Constance, da of William Thomson (d 1935), of Wood Green, London; 2 da (Jennifer Elizabeth b 1944, Sarah Caroline b 1951); *Career* Capt Intelligence Corps 1940-41, Naval Intelligence Div Admty 1941-44; lectr in geography Univ of Cambridge 1931-45; prof of geography: Univ of Liverpool 1945-49, UCL 1949-66, Univ of Cambridge 1966-76 (emeritus 1976-); visiting prof: Chicago Univ 1952, Harvard Univ 1959 and 1964-65, Univ of Washington Seattle 1963; memb: Royal Cmmn on Historical Monuments 1953-77, Nat Parks Cmmn 1958-63, Water Resources Bd 1964-68; author geographical and historical pubns; fell King's Coll Cambridge 1932-45 and 1966-81 (hon fell 1983), hon fell St Catharine's Coll Cambridge 1960; Hon DUniv: Chicago 1967, Liverpool 1968, Durham 1970, Hull 1975, Ulster 1977, Wales 1979, London 1987; FBA 1967; kt 1988; *Books* The Medieval Fenland (1940), The Domesday Geography of England (7 vols, ed and contributor), The Changing Fenland (1983); *Style—* Prof Sir Clifford Darby, CBE; 60 Storey's Way, Cambridge CB3 0DX (☎ 0223 354745)

DARBY, Dr David James William; s of William Darby (d 1971), of Cairo, and Sylvia Aitken (d 1975); *b* 14 June 1935; *Educ* Downside, Royal London Hosp Med Sch Univ of London (MB BS, DO, MRCS, LRCP, memb Univ of London Boxing Team); *m* 1, 1958 (m dis 1966), Fern Linker; 2 s (Mark Benedict b 1958, Hugh David b 1960), 1 da (Fiona Fern Mary b 1962); m 2, 1975, Charlotte Elizabeth, da of Leslie Baines, OBE; *Career* St John's Hosp Jerusalem 1963; opthalmologist: Royal London Hosp 1964-70, Westminster Hosp 1965-84, Moorfield Eye Hosp 1969-; in private practice 1970-; med offr ABA 1975-; memb BMA 1960, FRSM 1970, MCOphth 1989; author of Common Causes of Visual Loss in the Elderly (Br Jl of Geriatric Med, 3 Vols, 1983); *Recreations* shooting, fishing, boating, golf; *Clubs* The Royal Society of Medicine, The Cricketers, The Benedicts, Saints & Sinners, Harlequin RFC, Richmond Golf; *Style—* Dr David Darby

DARBY, (Elizabeth Ann) Foxy; *née* Foxon; da of Lt-Col Arthur Denham Foxon, DSO, TD, of Orford, Suffolk, and Vera Mae, *née* Newsome; *b* 2 Feb 1952; *Educ* Westonbirt Sch, Kingston Coll of Art (DipAD), RCA (MA); *m* 1 Oct 1983, Keith Harry Darby, s of Harry Darby (d 1970), of Hagley, Worcs; 3 s (Harry b 1986, Randel b 1987, Edward b 1990); *Career* personal design asst to John Stefanidis 1977-79, dir: Fanny Foxon Ltd (interior design) 1979-83, Country Fittings Ltd 1983-91; design dir Triumph Holdings Ltd 1986-91; *Recreations* Jack Russell terriers, horse-riding, designing, reading books on architecture, houses and gardens; *Style—* Mrs Keith Darby; Warnell Hall, Sebergham, Cumbria; 8 Gerald Rd, London SW1 (fax 0228 514645)

DARBY, Dr Francis John; TD (1964); s of late Col John Francis Darby, TD, CBE, and Georgina Alice Darby; *b* 24 Feb 1920; *Educ* Nottingham HS, Edinburgh Acad, Univ of Edinburgh (MB ChB); *m* 1969, Pamela Elizabeth, da of Sidney Hill (d 1970); 3 s; *Career* served 1939-46 Capt Royal Signals (despatches); hospital and gen practice 1950-64; DHSS 1964-82: dep chief med advsr Social Security 1978-80, chief med advsr 1980-82; chief med offr and conslt physician Cayman Islands 1983-85; hon physician to HM The Queen 1980-84; memb Worshipful Soc of Apothecaries of London 1978, Freeman City of London 1979; MFOM, MRCGP, DIH, DMJ, FRSM; *Recreations* sailing, swimming; *Clubs* Royal Lymington Yacht, Royal Signals Yacht; *Style—* Dr Francis Darby, TD; Ruardean, Captains Row, Lymington, Hants SO41 9RP (☎ 0590 677119)

DARBY, The Rt Rev Harold Richard; *see*: Sherwood, Bishop of

DARBY, John Oliver Robertson; s of Ralph Darby (d 1968), and Margaret, *née* Robertson (d 1978); *b* 5 Jan 1930; *Educ* Charterhouse; *m* 17 Sept 1955, Valerie, da of Louis Wilfred Leyland Cole (d 1987); 3 s (Simon b 1958, William Nicholas b 1960, James b 1966); *Career* Nat Serv RAF PO 1953-55; Arthur Young (now Ernst & Young) 1955-87: ptnr 1959-74, chm 1974-87; chm: Nat Homes Loans 1985-, Property Lending Tst 1987-, BREL Gp 1989- (dir 1987-89), Ultramar plc 1988- (dir 1988); dir St Edmund's Sch Ltd 1975, tstee Devpt Tst for Young Disabled; Freeman City of London; MICAEW, FCA 1953; *Recreations* horse-racing, golf, theatre; *Clubs* Garrick, Royal Thames Yacht, Royal and Ancient Golf (St Andrews); *Style—* John Darby, Esq; Ultramar plc, 141 Moorgate, London EC2M 6TX (☎ 071 256 6080, fax 071 256 8556, telex 885444)

DARBY, Hon Mrs (Meriel Kathleen); *née* Douglas-Home; da of Baron Home of the Hirsel; *b* 27 Nov 1939; *m* 30 March 1964, Adrian Marten George Darby; 1 s, 1 da; *Career* Acupuncturist; *Style—* The Hon Mrs Darby; Kemerton Court, nr Tewkesbury, Glos

DARBY, Dr Michael Douglas; s of Arthur Douglas Darby, of The Old Rectory, Ilketshall St Margaret, Nr Bungay, Suffolk, and Ilene Doris, *née* Eatwell (d 1986); *b* 2 Sept 1944; *Educ* Rugby, Univ of Reading (PhD); *m* 26 Aug 1977, Elisabeth Susan, da of Lesley Robert Done; *Career* asst to Barbara Jones 1963; V & A: Textiles Dept 1964-72, prints and drawings 1973-76, exhibitions offr 1977-83, dep dir 1984-87; Surveyor gen Carroll Fndn 1990-; memb: Crafts Cncl 1984-87, IOW Advsy Ctee English Heritage 1986-, Cncl The Nat Tst 1989-, Cncl Royal Entomological Soc 1988-90; FRES 1977, FRSA 1979, FRGS 1984, AMA 1990; *Books* Stevengraphs (jtly, 1968), Marble Halls (jtly, 1973), Early Railway Prints Victoria and Albert Museum (1974, 1979), The Islamic Perspective (1983), British Art in the V and A (1983), John Pollard Seddon (1983), and author of numerous articles in popular and learned jls; *Recreations* books, beetles, drawing; *Style—* Dr Michael Darby; Carroll Foundation, Carroll House, 2-6 Catherine Place, London SW1E 6HF

DARBY, Dr Peter George; s of Cecil George Darby (d 1987), and Ethel Mary, *née* Steele (d 1985); *b* 21 June 1934; *Educ* Pinner Co Sch, Univ of London St Georges Hosp Med Sch (MB BS), Univ of Liverpool (DMRD); *m* 31 Oct 1959, Sheila Karen Rosemary, da of Hans Marius Kjeldsen (d 1982), of Wallingford, Berks; 2 s (Simon b 1961, Christopher b 1963), 1 da (Naomi (Mrs Watkins) b 1967); *Career* Nat Serv Capt RAMC 1959-61, Regtl MO LI Somerset and Cornwall; house surgn St Georges Hosp 1958, GP 1961-70, registrar radiology Liverpool Hosps 1970-73, sr registrar Bristol Hosps 1973-76, conslt radiologist Swindon 1976-; memb Ctee: Wessex RHA, Swindon DHA; memb: Parish Church S Cerney, Harnhill Centre Christian Healing Cirencester; MRCR 1973 (memb Ctee) LRCP, MRCS; *Style—* Dr Peter Darby; Meadow View, Cricklade Rd, S Cerney, Cirencester, Glos (☎ 0285 860328); Dept of Diagnostic Radiology, Princess Margaret Hosp, Okus Rd, Swindon, Wilts SN1 4JU (☎ 0793 536231)

DARBY, Sir Peter Howard; CBE (1973), QFSM (1970); s of the late William Cyril Darby, and Beatrice, *née* Colin; *b* 8 July 1924; *Educ* Coll of Advanced Technol Birmingham; *m* 1948, Ellen Josephine, *née* Glynn; 1 s, 1 da; *Career* chief offr London Fire Brigade 1977-80; HM's chief inspr of Fire Servs 1980-87, dir Argus Alarms; chm: Certifire, FS Nat Examinations Bd, govrs of St James Secdy Modern Sch Barnet; Freeman City of London, Liveryman Worshipful Co of Basketmakers; FIFireE 1968, CBIM 1983; CStJ 1982; kt 1985; *Recreations* golf, fishing, sailing; *Clubs* Livery, Candlewick Ward, City of London; *Style—* Sir Peter Darby, CBE, QFSM; 10 Moor Lane, Rickmansworth, Herts WD3 1LG

DARBYSHIRE, (John) Anthony Charles; s of (Leslie) Noel Darbyshire (d 1981), of Carnfield Hall, Normanton, Derbyshire, and Marjorie Darbyshire (d 1947); *b* 7 May 1939; *Educ* Uppingham, Keble Coll Oxford (BA, MA), McGill Univ Montreal; *m* 1, 3 June 1967 (m dis 1982), (Faith) Lorraine, da of Noel William Hempsall, of Furze Court Farm, Walesby, Notts; 1 s (Markham Noel Charles b 10 June 1968); m 2, 28 Aug 1982, Sheena Nanette Mabel, da of Capt Thomas Wilson Taylor, of Barnby Moor House, Barnby Moor, Retford, Notts; 1 s (John) Hamish McGregor b 26 Sept 1984), 1 da (Keturah Mona Ellen b 8 Dec 1986); *Career* prodn mangr John Darbyshire & Co Ltd 1964-66, conslt Urwick Orr & Ptnrs 1966-67, chm AH Turner Gp Ltd 1967-90; memb: Mgmnt Ctee Br Vehicle Rental & Leasing Assoc 1980-90, Cncl CBI 1982-90 (Smaller Firms Cncl 1979-89, E Midlands Regnl Cncl 1980-90); chm Bassetlaw Industry Assoc 1986-89 (memb Mgmnt Ctee 1986-90), memb Nat Exec Bd Young Enterprise 1989-90 (chm Notts area Bd 1986-90), chm N Notts Trg and Enterprise Cncl 1989-90; FID 1976, FRSA 1988, CBIM 1989 (MBIM 1971, FBIM 1983); *Recreations* skiing, golf, gardening and preserving the quality of life; *Style—* Anthony Darbyshire, Esq; Barnby Moor House, Barnby Moor, Retford, Notts DN22 8QX (☎ 0777 700440)

DARBYSHIRE, David Glen; s of Thomas Leslie Darbyshire (d 1979), and Alice, *née* Moss; *b* 20 May 1944; *Educ* Wigan GS, Liverpool Coll of Art, Univ of Newcastle upon Tyne (BA, BArch); *m* 7 July 1973 (sep 1987), Jane Helen; 1 da (Kate); *Career* architect Ryder and Yates Ptnrs 1972-75, princ architect Washington Devpt Corp 1975-79, ptnr Jane and David Darbyshire 1979-87; Civic Tst Award for Dukes Cottages Backworth; Civic Tst Commendation for: Church St Cramlington, St Johns Green Percy Main; winner of: St Oswald's Hospice Special Category Regnl Ltd Competition and Civic Tst Award, RIBA Nat Award Building of the Year 1988, The Times/RIBA Community Enterprise Scheme Commendation, Housing Design Award for Sollingwood Ct Morpeth 1989; princ Darbyshire Architects 1987-; MRIBA;

Recreations music, mechanical engineering, fine art; *Clubs* Bristol Owners; *Style*— David Darbyshire, Esq; 10 Lily Crescent, Jesmond, Newcastle upon Tyne (☎ 091 281 0501); Hawthorn Cottage, Hawthorn Rd, Gosforth, Newcastle upon Tyne NE3 4DE (☎ 091 284 2813)

DARBYSHIRE, David Stewart; s of Wing Cdr Rupert Stanley Darbyshire (ka 1941), and Ann, *née* Todd; *b* 14 Nov 1940; *Educ* Radley, Oriel Coll Oxford (MA); *m* 24 Jan 1970, Elizabeth, da of Eric Watts; 1 s (Rupert b 1975), 2 da (Sophie b 1973, Alice b 1978); *Career* Capt SAS AVR 1964-70; called to the Bar 1965-66; Arthur Andersen & Co: London 1966-72, Paris 1972-79, ptnr 1976, Leeds 1979-85, London 1985-; cncl memb Hakluyt Soc 1989; vice pres Federation des Experts Comptables Européens 1990, memb Ordre des Experts Comptables and Compagnie des Commissaires aux Comptes 1977; FCA 1970, ATII 1971; *Recreations* sailing, hill-walking; *Clubs* Special Forces, Sea View Yacht; *Style*— David Darbyshire, Esq; 11 Warwick Sq, London SW1V 2AA; Hutton Mount, Ripon, N Yorks HG4 5DR; Arthur Andersen & Co, 1 Surrey St, London WC1R 2PS (☎ 071 438 3731, fax 071 831 1133, telex 8812711)

DARBYSHIRE, Jane Helen; *née* Wroe; da of Gordon Desmond Wroe, of Brixham, S Devon, and Patricia, *née* Keough; *b* 5 June 1948; *Educ* Dorking GS, Univ of Newcastle (BA, BArch); *m* 7 July 1987 (m dis), David Glen Darbyshire, s of Thomas Darbyshire (d 1980), of Wigan, Lancs; 1 da (Kate b 1979); *Career* chartered architect; in private practice, sr ptnr Jane and David Darbyshire 1979-87, princ Jane Darbyshire & Associates 1987-; works: exhibitor at RIBA 'Women in Architecture' 1983, winner of St Oswalds Hospice Design Competition 1981, exhibitor DLI Museum Durham 1981; Civic Tst: award for restoration 1982, commendation for Cramlington Housing 1983, commendation flat refurbishment Percy Main 1986, award St Oswalds Hospice Gosforth Newcastle upon Tyne 1987; award for Housing Design, Morpeth 1988, Nat RIBA award 1988, Building of the Year award 1988, Nat Housing Design award 1989; features: Channel 4 Design Matters, BBC Townscape; Civic Tst assessor, RIBA awards assessor 1984-; *Recreations* music, art, history of architecture; *Style*— Ms Jane Darbyshire; 27 Brandling Place South, Jesmond, Newcastle upon Tyne; Jane Darbyshire Assocs, Millmount, Ponteland Rd, Newcastle upon Tyne

DARCY DE KNAYTH, Baroness (18 in line, E 1332); Davina Marcia Ingrams; *née* Herbert; da of 17 Baron Darcy de Knayth (*née* Hon Mervyn Herbert, 2 s of 4 Earl of Powis by his w (Violet) Countess of Powis, in whose favour the abeyance existing in the Barony of Darcy de Knayth was terminated in 1903) and Vida, da of late Capt James Harold Cuthbert, DSO; *b* 10 July 1938; *m* 1 March 1960, Rupert George Ingrams (k in a motor accident 28 Feb 1964), s of Leonard St Clair Ingrams, OBE, and bro of Richard Ingrams, *qv*; 1 s, 2 da; *Heir* s, Hon Caspar Ingrams; *Career* sits as Independent peeress in House of Lords; *Style*— The Rt Hon Lady Darcy de Knayth; Camley Corner, Stubbings, Maidenhead, Berks (☎ 062 882 2935)

DARE, Barry Stanton; s of Clifford Stanton Dare (d 1985), and Doris Muriel, *née* Geeson (d 1988); *b* 29 July 1936; *Educ* St Paul's, UCL (BSc); *m* 16 June 1962, Wendy Angela Vivien, da of Flt Lt Walter Wilkins (d 1986); 2 s (Clifford Stanton b 1967, Jocelyn Stanton b 1970); *Career* sr accountant Tansley Witt 1958-62, co sec predecessor to Thorn Security 1962-65, mgmnt conslt (later ptnr) John Tyzack & Ptnrs 1965-69, gp chief exec Conduit Holdings 1969-71, diversified interests incl mgmnt consultancy and specialised account practice 1971-, dir several cos and md Unwins Seeds Ltd; FCA, FBIM; *Recreations* cricket, fishing, dry stone walling; *Clubs* The Carlton; *Style*— Barry S Dare, Esq; 61 Kingston Lane, Teddington, Middx; Old Mill Dene, Blockley, Moreton in Marsh, Gloucester; 23 Regatta Ct, Oyster Row, Cambridge; Unwins Seeds Ltd, Histon, Cambridge

DARE, John Ashton; *b* 15 Nov 1938; *Educ* Stanford Univ (BA, MBA); *m* Christine Lesley; 1 da (Elizabeth Gordon b 1967); *Career* US Navy 1960-62; First Nat City Bank 1964-70; dir: London Multinational Bank 1970-77, Baring Bros & Co Ltd 1977; *Recreations* sailing; *Clubs* Royal Yacht Sqdn, Royal Ocean Racing (cdre), Hurlingham; *Style*— John Dare, Esq; Baring Brothers & Co Ltd, 8 Bishopsgate, London EC2N 4AE (☎ 071 280 1000)

DARE, Hon Mrs (Phyllida Anne); da of Baron Benson (Life Peer), GBE; *b* 1943; *m* 1967, Simon John Dare; *Style*— The Hon Mrs Dare; 10 Bowerdean St, London SW6

DARE, Wendy Angela Vivien; da of Walter Wilkins (d 1985), of Teddington, Middx, and Majorie Vivien, *née* Williams (d 1974); *b* 10 Feb 1942; *Educ* Twickenham County GS, Kingston Poly (BA); *m* 16 June 1962, Barry Stanton Dare, s of Clifford Stanton Dare (d 1986), of Teddington, Middx; 2 s (Clifford Roderick b 1967, Jocelyn David b 1970); *Career* recruitment specialist, Dare recruitment; raising children; chm Teddington Soc, chm Richmond and Kingston Young Enterprise Bd; *Recreations* gardening, looking at gardens, reading about gardens; *Clubs* Univ Women's, Network, WIM; *Style*— Mrs Wendy Dare; 61 Kingston Lane, Teddington, Middx (☎ 081 977 2502); Old Mill Dene, Blockley, Moreton-in-Marsh, Glos (☎ 0386 700 457)

DARELL, Guy Jeffrey Adair; s and h of Sir Jeffrey Lionel Darell, 8 Bt, MC; *b* 8 June 1961; *Educ* Eton, RMC Sandhurst; *Career* cmmnd Coldstream Guards 1981; insur broker with Minets London Lloyds 1984-; *Style*— Guy Darell Esq; 23 Coleford Rd, London SW18 (☎ 081 874 8432); Denton Lodge, Harleston, Norfolk (☎ 098 686 206)

DARELL, Brig Sir Jeffrey Lionel; 8 Bt (GB 1795), of Richmond Hill, Surrey, MC (1945); s of Col Guy Marsland Darell, MC (d 15 April 1947), 3 s of 5 Bt; suc cous, Sir William Darell, 7 Bt (d 10 Feb 1959); *b* 2 Oct 1919; *Educ* Eton, RMC Sandhurst; *m* 30 June 1953, Bridget Mary, da of Maj-Gen Sir Allan Adair, 6 Bt, GCVO, CB, DSO, MC; 1 s, 2 da; *Heir* s, Guy Jeffrey Adair Darell (*qv*); *Career* Brig (ret) Coldstream Guards, served WWII 1939-45, Lt-Col 1957, cmd 1 Bn Coldstream Guards 1957-59, AAG War Office 1959-61, Cdr RMA Sandhurst 1961-64, regimental Lt-Col cmdg Coldstream Guards 1964, vice pres Regular Commissions Bd 1968, Cmdt Mons Officer Cadet Sch 1970-72; tstee and memb London Law Trust 1981-; High Sheriff of Norfolk 1985-86; *Clubs* Army and Navy; *Style*— Brig Sir Jeffrey Darell, Bt, MC; Denton Lodge, Harleston, Norfolk (☎ 098 686 206)

DARELL-BROWN, Hon Mrs (Christina Louise); *née* Vanneck; da of 6 Baron Huntingfield; *b* 26 Jan 1946; *m* 8 July 1967, Anthony Darell-Brown, son of late Col Mark Darell-Brown, DSO, of 10 Queen's Elm Sq, SW3; 2 s, 1 da; *Style*— The Hon Mrs Darell-Brown; The Old Rectory, Witnesham, Ipswich, Suffolk

DARESBURY, 3 Baron (UK 1927), of Walton, Co Chester; Sir Edward Gilbert Greenall; 4 Bt (UK 1876); o s of 2 Baron Daresbury (d 1990), and his 2 w, Josephine (d 1958), da of Brig-Gen Sir Frederick Laycock, KCMG, DSO, and Katherine, 3 da of Hon Hugh Hare, 4 s of 2 Earl of Listowel, KP; *b* 27 Nov 1928; *Educ* Eton; *m* 1, 7 Feb 1952, Margaret Ada, yst da of Charles John Crawford (d 1940), and Ella, sis of Sir Denis Anson, 4 Bt; 3 s (Hon Peter Gilbert b 1953, Hon Gilbert b 1954, Hon John Edward b 1960), 1 da (Hon Susan Rosemary (Hon Mrs Haden-Taylor) b 1956); m 2, 1986, Mary Patricia, da of Lewis Parkinson (d 1977); *Heir* s, Hon Peter Gilbert Greenall b 1953; *Career* chm: Randall & Vautier Ltd, Grunhalle Lager International; *Recreations* boating; *Style*— The Rt Hon the Lord Daresbury; Crossbow House, Trinity, Jersey, CI (☎ 0534 63316)

DARGAN, Dr Michael Joseph; *b* 14 Sept 1918; *Educ* Patrician Brothers Ballyfin Co Meath, Trinity Coll Dublin; *m* Catherine (Blanche) O'Rourke; 2 s, 3 da; *Career* former chm: Aer Lingus (and chief exec), CRH plc, Bank of Ireland Fin Ltd, Intercontinental Hotels (Ireland) Ltd, Fitzwilton Gp, Pigs & Bacon Cmmn, Posts and Telegraphs Review Gp, Irish Mgmnt Inst; former dir: Bank of Ireland, Burlington Industs Inc (USA); chm: Robert J Goff plc, Int Bloodstock Hldgs, Klopman Int Ltd, Atlantic Mills Ltd; owner Athasi Stud, ptnr Eyrefield House Stud, sr steward Turf Club; life fell Int Acad of Mgmnt; *Clubs* Irish Turf, Links (NY); *Style*— Dr Michael Dargan; Lime Hill, St Doolagh's, Dublin 17 (☎ 0001 477526, fax 0001 472169)

DARKAZALLY, Mamoun; s of Abdul Hadi (d 1986), and Farizeh Arabi; *b* 9 Oct 1942; *Educ* Univ of New York (BS), New York Univ Graduate Sch of Business (MBA); *m* 2 June 1971, Vivian, da of William Ram (d 1968); 1 s (Anwar b 1973); *Career* Chase Manhattan Bank: NY 1973-74, Beirut 1974-75; Commercial Bank of Qatar 1975-79, dep gen regnl mangr Al Saudi Banque London 1981- (Paris 1979-81), dep gen mangr and head Private Banking Banque Française de l'Orient 1990-; memb IOD; dir Arab Bankers Assoc, chm Syrian Arab Assoc UK 1988-; *Style*— Mamoun Darkazally Esq; 7A Inverness Gardens, London W8 (☎ 071 221 1874); 31 Berkeley Square, London W1 (☎ 071 493 8942, fax 071 493 7193, telex 23875)

DARKE, Geoffrey James; s of Harry James Darke (d 1983), and Edith Annie Darke (d 1973); *b* 1 Sept 1929; *Educ* Prince Henry's GS Worcs, Birmingham Sch of Architecture (Dip Arch); *m* 1959, Jean Yvonne, da of Edwin Rose (d 1971); 1 s (Christopher), 2 da (Elizabeth, Sarah); *Career* cmmnd RE 1954-56, Malaya; sr architect Stevenage New Town Devpt Corp 1952-58, private practice 1958-61, ptnr Darbourne & Darke, Architects and Landscape Planners 1961-, work incl several large cmmns, particularly public housing (also commercial and civic bldgs); successes in nat and int competitions incl: Stuttgart 1977, Hanover 1979, Bolzano 1980, Hanover (Misburg) 1982; fndr Geoffrey Darke Assoc 1987; memb Cncl RIBA 1977-83, chm Competitions Working Gp RIBA 1979-84; memb Aldebrugh Festival Snape Maltings Fndn 1979-; ARIBA, FRSA; numerous medals and awards for architectural work; co-recipient (with John Darbourne) Fritz Schumacher Award Hamburg 1978 for servs to architecture and town planning; *Recreations* music; *Clubs* Reform; *Style*— Geoffrey Darke Esq; Geoffrey Darke Assoc, EBC House, Kew Rd, Richmond, Surrey TW9 2NA (☎ 081 332 1551, telex 268821 EBC GD, fax 081 332 2448)

DARKE, Marjorie Sheila; *b* 25 Jan 1929; *Educ* Worcester GS for Girls', Leicester Coll of Art and Technol; *m* 12 July 1952; 2 s (b 1955 and 1957) 1 da (b 1959); *Career* textile designer John Lewis Partnership 1950-54, writer 1962-; *books incl* for young adults: Ride the Iron Horse (1973), The Star Trap (1974), A Question of Courage (1975), The First Midnight (1977), A Long Way to Go (1978), Comeback (1981), Tom Post's Private Eye (1982), Messages and Other Shivery Tales (1984), A Rose From Blighty (1990); for children: Mike's Bike (1974), What Can I Do? (1975), Kipper's Turn (1976), The Big Brass Band (1976), My Uncle Charlie (1977), Carnival Day (1979), Kipper Skips (1979), Imp (1985), The Rainbow Sandwich (1989), Night Windows (1990); memb: Soc of Authors, Int PEN; *Style*— Ms Marjorie Darke; c/o Rogers Coleridge & White Ltd, Literary Agency, 20 Powis Mews, London W11 1JN (☎ 071 221 3717)

DARKE, Simon Geoffrey; s of Dr Geoffrey Darke, of 5 Grenfell Rd, Leicester, and Margaret Winifred, *née* Wadsworth (d 1987); *b* 14 Dec 1941; *Educ* Downside, London Hosp Med Coll (MB BS, MS); *m* 31 Jan 1970, Patricia Elizabeth, da of Philip Wreaks Mason, CBE (d 1975); 2 s (Nicholas Gregory Simon b 18 June 1974, Christopher Michael Mason b 4 June 1977), 1 da (Tiffanie Jane b 18 Aug 1972); *Career* London Hosp: house surgn 1965, rotating surgical resistrar 1969-71, lectr to surgical unit 1971-72, sr registrar 1973-76, lectr professional surgical unit 1976-77; Addenbrooke's Hosp Cambridge: accident offr 1967-68, sr house offr 1968; surgical registrar Bethnal Green Hosp 1968-69; sr registrar: Whipps Cross Hosp 1972-73, London Hosp 1973-75; conslt vascular and gen surgn: E Dorset Health Authy, Royal Victoria Hosp, Boscombe and Poole Gen hosp 1977-; numerous presentations and lectures to learned socs, numerous pubns in med jls; memb and former sec Vascular Sugical Soc GB and Ireland, fndr exec memb and current treas Euro Soc Vascular Surgery; MRCP, LRCS 1965, FRCS 1970, MS 1977; memb: Assoc Surgns, BMA; *Books* contrib book chapters on vascular surgery; *Recreations* tennis, fishing, shooting, skiing; *Style*— Simon Darke, Esq; Oaks, 6 Leicester Rd, Branksome Park, Poole, Dorset BH13 6BZ (☎ 0202 761870; Royal Victoria Hosp, Shelley Rd, Boscombe, Bournemouth, Dorset, (☎ 0202 35201)

DARLEY, Kevin Paul; s of Clifford Darley, of Wolverhampton, West Midlands, and Dorothy Thelma, *née* Newby; *b* 5 Aug 1960; *Educ* Colton Hills Comp Sch; *m* 22 Nov 1982, Debby Ford, da of Donald Ford; 2 da (Lianne Kerry b 1983, Gemma Louise b 1988); *Career* flat race jockey; apprenticed to Reg Hollinshead 1976, rode out claim 1978, Champion apprentice 1978 (70 winners), retained by owner Peter Savill 1989-; first winner Dust Up Haydock 1977, first group winner Borushka Gp 2 Park Hill Stakes; Cock of the North 1990 (83 winners); *Recreations* gardening, listening to music (Phil Collins & Genesis), DIY, shooting, fishing; *Style*— Kevin Darley, Esq; Liagem, Stonefield Avenue, Easingwold, York YO6 3NR (☎ 0347 22588)

DARLING, Alistair Maclean; *b* 28 Nov 1953; *Career* slr 1978-82; advocate 1984-; memb Lothian Regnl Cncl 1982-87; *Style*— Alistair Darling, Esq; 53 GEO VI Bridge, Edinburgh (☎ 031 220 0108, fax 031 220 4231)

DARLING, Hon Sir Clifford; MP (Bahamas); s of Charles and Aremelia Darling; *b* 6 Feb 1922; *Educ* Acklins Public Sch, several public schs in Nassau; *Career* senator 1964-67, dep speaker House of Assembly 1967-69, Min of State 1969, Min of Labour and Welfare 1971, present Min of Labour and National Insur; kt 1977; *Style*— The Hon Sir Clifford Darling, MP; C H Bain Building, POB 1525, Nassau, Bahamas

DARLING, Lt Cdr Gerald Ralph Auchinleck; RD (1968), QC (1967, Hong Kong 1968), DL (Co Tyrone 1990); s of Lt-Col Ralph Reginald Auchinleck Darling (d 1958), of NI, and Moira Freda Bessie, *née* Moriarty (d 1983); *b* 8 Dec 1921; *Educ* Harrow, Hertford Coll Oxford (MA); *m* 1954, Susan Ann, da of Brig Mervyn Hobbs, OBE, MC; 1 s (Patrick), 1 da (Fiona (Mrs Torrens-Spence)); *Career* served RNVR 1940-46, Fleet Fighter Pilot, Med, Test Pilot Eastern Fleet, Chief Test Pilot Br Pacific Fleet, served with RNR to 1968; called to the Bar Middle Temple 1950; bencher 1970; Lloyd's appeal arbitrator 1978-, judge of Admiralty Ct of Cinque Ports 1978-, wreck cmmr, landowner (242 acres); tstee Royal Naval Museum Portsmouth 1985-90; Freeman City of London; *Recreations* fly-fishing, shooting; *Clubs* Naval and Military, Tyrone Co; *Style*— Lt Cdr Gerald Darling, RD, QC, DL; Crevenagh House, Omagh, Co Tyrone, N Ireland BT79 0EH (☎ 0662 242138); Queen Elizabeth Building, Temple, London EC4Y 9BS (☎ 071 353 9153, telex 262762 INREM G)

DARLING, Hon (Robert) Julian Henry; s and h of 2 Baron Darling; *b* 29 April 1944; *Educ* Wellington, RAC Cirencester; *m* 1970, Janet Rachel, da of J Mallinson; 2 s, 1 da; *Career* farmer; FRICS; *Recreations* fishing; *Clubs* Norfolk; *Style*— The Hon Julian Darling; Trematon Castle, Saltash, Cornwall PL12 4QW (☎ 0752 843778)

DARLING, Gen Sir Kenneth Thomas; GBE (1969, CBE 1957), KCB (1963, CB 1957), DSO (1945); eld s of (George) Kenneth Darling, CIE (d 1964), of Dial House, Aldeburgh; *b* 17 Sept 1909; *Educ* Eton, RMC; *m* 1941, Pamela Beatrice Rose (d 1990), eld da of Maj Henry Denison-Pender, DSO, OBE, MC (d 1967), of Hook, Hants; *Career* 2 Lt 7 Royal Fus 1929, served WWII, 6 Airborne Div NW Europe (wounded), cmd 5 Parachute Bde Java 1946, cmd Airborne Forces Depot 1948, cmd 16 Independent Parachute Bde 1950, COS 1 Corps 1955, COS 2 Corps 1956, Dep Dir of Staff Duties WO 1957, Maj-Gen 1958, Dir of Ops Cyprus 1958-60, Dir of Inf WO

1960-62, Lt-Gen 1962, GOC 1 Corps 1962-63, Col Royal Fus 1963-68, GOC-in-C Southern Cmd 1964-66, Gen 1967, Col Cmdt Para Regt 1965-67, C-in-C Allied Forces N Europe 1967-69, Col Royal Regt of Fus 1968-74, ADC (Gen) to HM The Queen 1968-69; *Recreations* riding, hunting; *Clubs* Army & Navy; *Style—* Gen Sir Kenneth Darling, GBE, KCB, DSO; Vicarage Farmhouse, Chesterton, Bicester, Oxon OX6 8UQ (☎ 0869 252092)

DARLING, 2 Baron (UK 1924); Robert Charles Henry Darling; DL (Somerset 1972, Avon 1974); s of Maj Hon John Darling, DSO (s of 1 Baron); suc gf 1936; *b* 15 May 1919; *Educ* Wellington, Sandhurst; *m* 15 Aug 1942, Bridget Rosemary Whishaw, da of Rev Francis Cyprian Dickson; 1 s, 2 da; *Heir* s, Hon Julian Darling, FRICS; *Career* served WWII, Italy, Maj; chief exec Royal Bath and West & South Counties Soc 1961-79; dir Bristol Waterworks 1978-90; regnl dir Lloyds Bank 1979-89; *Recreations* fishing, gardening; *Style—* The Rt Hon Lord Darling, DL; Puckpits, Limpley Stoke, Bath, Avon (☎ 0225 722146)

DARLING, Vera Hannah; OBE (1985); da of Leonard William Henry Darling, of Surrey, and Rosy Louise, *née* Whybrow; *b* 18 July 1929; *Educ* Varndean Sch for Girls Brighton, Brunel Univ; *Career* inspr: Nurse Trg Sch, The Gen Nursing Cncl for Eng and Wales 1968-73 (examinations offr 19 princ offr The Jt Bd of Clinical Nursing Studies 1978-83, prof offr (educn and trg) The Eng Nat Bd for Nursing Midwifery and H Visiting 1984; dir The Lisa Sainsbury Fndn 1985-; RGN, RNT, OND, BTAC; *Books* Research for Practising Nurses (contrib with Jill Rogers, 1986), Ophthalmic Nursing (with Margaret Thorpe, 2 edn 1981); *Style—* Miss Vera H Darling, OBE; The Lisa Sainsbury Foundation, 8-10 Crown Hill, Croydon, Surrey CR0 1RY (☎ 081 686 8808)

DARLINGTON, Instr Rear Adm Sir Charles Roy; KBE (1965); s of Charles Arthur Darlington (d 1962), of Stoke-on-Trent, and Alice, *née* Edwards, of Prestatyn (d 1919); *b* 2 March 1910; *Educ* Orme Sch Newcastle-under-Lyme, Univ of Manchester (BSc); *m* 1935, Nora Dennison, da of James Wright, of Maulds Meaburn, Westmorland; 1 s, 1 da; *Career* joined RN 1941, served WWII, HMS Valiant in Med and E Indies, HMS Excellent, Instr Capt 1956, Instr Rear Adm 1960, dir Naval Educ Serv 1960-65, ret; memb staff of Haileybury 1965-75; *Recreations* maths, cricket, hill walking; *Style—* Rear Adm Sir Charles Darlington, KBE; 11 Freestone Rd, Southsea, Hants (☎ 0705 825974)

DARLINGTON, Gavin Leslie Brook; s of Arthur Brook Darlington, and Pamela Leslie, *née* Roberts; *b* 27 June 1949; *Educ* Rugby, Downing Coll Cambridge (LLB); *m* 11 April 1977, Pavla Ann, da of Karel Kucek; 1 s (Nicholas James b 7 Jan 1986), 1 da (Georgina Ruth b 19 Nov 1989); *Career* ptnr Freshfields 1980- (articled clerk 1972-74, asst slr 1974-80); memb: Law Soc, Int Bar Assoc; *Recreations* gardening, golf, swimming, theatre, cinema; *Style—* Gavin Darlington, Esq; Hollist House, Hollist Lane, Easebourne, Midhurst, West Sussex, GU29 9RS; Whitefriars, 65 Fleet St, London EC4Y 1HT

DARLINGTON, Stephen Mark; s of John Oliver Darlington, MBE, and Bernice Constance Elizabeth, *née* Murphy; *b* 21 Sept 1952; *Educ* King's Sch Worcester, ChCh Oxford (MA); *m* 12 July 1975, Moira Ellen, da of Noel Edward Lionel Hill; 3 da (Rebecca b 1979, Hannah b 1981, Olivia b 1985); *Career* asst organist Canterbury Cathedral 1974-78, master of music St Albans Abbey 1978-85, artistic dir Int Organ Festival 1979-85, organist and student in music ChCh Oxford and lectr Univ of Oxford 1985-; FRCO; *Recreations* travel, wine, canoeing; *Style—* Stephen Darlington, Esq; Christ Church Oxford OX1 1BY (☎ 0865 276195)

DARLOW, Paul Manning; s of Brig Eric William Townsend Darlow, OBE, of New Inn Cottage, East End, Witney, Oxon, and Joan Elsie Darlow, JP, *née* Ring; *b* 7 Feb 1951; *Educ* St Edwards Sch Oxford, Mt Hermon Sch Massachusetts, Kings Coll London (LLB); *Career* called to the Bar Middle Temple 1973; *Style—* Paul Darlow, Esq; St John's Chambers, Small Street, Bristol BS1 1DW (☎ 0272 213456, fax 0272 294821); 1 Temple Gardens, London EC4Y 9BD (☎ 071 353 0407)

DARNLEY, 11 Earl of (I 1725); Adam Ivo Stuart Bligh; sits as Baron Clifton of Leighton (E 1608); also Baron Clifton of Rathmore (I 1721), Viscount Darnley (I 1723); s of 9 Earl of Darnley (d 1955), and his 3 w, Rosemary, da of late Basil Potter; suc half-bro, 10 Earl, 1980; *b* 8 Nov 1941; *Educ* Harrow, Ch Ch Oxford; *m* 14 Oct 1965, Susan Elaine, JP, da of Sir Donald Forsyth Anderson (d 1973), by his w Margaret, sis of Sir Harry Llewellyn, 3 Bt, CBE (*qv*); 1 s, 1 da (Lady Katherine Amanda b 1971); *Heir* s, Lord Clifton of Rathmore; *Style—* The Rt Hon Earl of Darnley; Netherwood Manor, Tenbury Wells, Worcs WR15 8RT(☎ 08854 221)

DARRAGH, Dr Paul Mervyn; TD; *b* 20 Feb 1947; *Educ* Queen's Univ Belfast (MD, PhD), Univ of Edinburgh (MSc, Dip Comm Med); *m* April 1973, Heather Isobel; 1 s (Peter Edward John b 1979), 1 da (Alison Jane b 1977); *Career* princ in gen practice NI 1975, asst chief administrative med offr Eastern and Social Servs Bd NI 19 sr lectr The Queen's Univ Belfast and conslt in pub health med Royal Victoria Belfast 1980-; prison visitor, chm Bd of Govrs Edenbrooke PS; sec Townsend St Presbyterian Church, chm Townsend Outreach Centre, co-dir Townsend Enterprise Park; FRCP (Ireland) 1989, FFPHM (RCP) 1989; *Recreations* sailing; *Style—* Dr Paul Darragh, TD; The Queen's University Belfast, Royal Victoria Belfast, Grosvenor Rd, Belfast (☎ 0232 240503)

DARROCH, Donald Ewen Dugald MacInness; s of Donald Darroch, of Feolin Ferry, Isle of Jura, and Isabella, *née* MacInnes; *b* 10 June 1956; *Educ* Craighouse Secdy Jura; *m* 24 Feb 1984, Dorothy Jill, da of Thomas Rankin Kimble, of Clarkston, Glasgow; 1 s (Ruaridh b 30 April 1989), 1 da (Dawn b 1 June 1987); *Career* mangr and advsr to Sir William Lithgows Estates Jura 1980; proprietor Darroch: Farming 1983-, Property & Shipping 1983-, Cosmetics 1987-, Mktg 1988-; ptnr Darroch Crafts 1988-; *Recreations* fishing, stalking, shooting, skiing, reading; *Clubs* CGA; *Style—* Donald Darroch, Esq; Inver Lodge, Craighouse, Isle of Jura, Argyll, Scotland PA60 7XX (☎ 049682 223); PO Box 1, Craighouse, Isle of Jura, Argyll, Scotland PA60 7XX (☎ 049682 223, fax 049 632 346, telex 934999 T G/MBX 049682223)

DARROCH OF GOUROCK, Captain Duncan; 7 of Gourock, Lord of the Barony of Gourock (Renfrewshire), Chief of the name of Darroch; er s of Lt-Col Duncan Darroch, 6 of Gourock, Lord of the Barony of Gourock (d 1960), and RoseMary Lillian Helena, *née* Henderson (d 1989); descended from Duncan Darroch (d 1823), who purchased the estate and barony of Gourock 1784; each successive head has borne the name of Duncan and, with one exception, served in the army (*see* Burke's Landed Gentry, 18 edn, vol 1, 1965); *b* 12 Oct 1931; *Educ* Harrow, RMA Sandhurst; *m* 24 March 1956, Nicola Jeanne, o da of Robert George Seidl, of Zürich, Switzerland; 7 da (Claire Nicola (Mrs Darroch-Thompson) b 1956, Laura Jenny (Mrs Gilbert) b 1959, Louise Rosemary (Mrs Burk) (twin) b 1959, Melanie Jeanne (Mrs Knight) b 1960, Melissa Carolyn (Baroness Bernard de Haldevang) b 1963, Christine Joanna (Mrs Frazer) b 1965, Alexandra Marguerite b and d 1967); *Career* cmmnd The Argyll and Sutherland Highlanders 1952, ADC 1955-56, Capt 1957, ret 1958; memb Lloyd's; FLIA 1964; *Recreations* swimming, windsurfing; *Clubs* Army and Navy; *Style—* Capt Duncan Darroch of Gourock; The Red House, Branksome Park Road, Camberley, Surrey (☎ 0276 23053)

DARTMOUTH, 9 Earl of (GB 1711); Gerald Humphry Legge; also Baron Dartmouth (E 1682) and Viscount Lewisham (GB 1711); s of 8 Earl, CVO, DSO, RN (d 1962), and Roma, Countess of Dartmouth, *qv*; *b* 26 April 1924; *Educ* Eton; *m* 1, 21 July 1948 (m dis 1976), Raine, da of Alexander George McCorquodale (d 1964), and who m 2, 1976, 8 Earl Spencer, LVO, *qv*; 3 s, 1 da; m 2, 1980, Mrs Gwendoline May Seguin, da of late Charles René Seguin; *Heir* s, Viscount Lewisham; *Career* served WWII, Capt Coldstream Guards (despatches); chm: Ocean Wilsons Holdings plc, Scottish Cities Investment Trust plc, Lancashire & London Investment Trust plc, Anglo-Brazilian Soc, Royal Choral Soc; Hon LLD Dartmouth Coll USA; FCA; *Clubs* Buck's, Naval and Military; *Style—* The Rt Hon Earl of Dartmouth; The Manor House, Chipperfield, King's Langley, Herts (☎ 09277 64498)

DARTMOUTH, Roma, Countess of; Roma Ernestine; da of Sir Ernest Burford Horlick, 2 Bt (d 1934), by his 1 w Jane Shillaber (who m 2, 1931, Sir Francis Oppenheimer, KCMG, who d 1961), da of Col Cunliffe Martin, CB, Bengal Cav; *b* 25 Nov 1903; *m* 10 April 1923, Humphry, 8 Earl of Dartmouth (d 1962); 1 s (9 Earl, Gerald Humphry), 1 da (Lady Heather Mary Margaret, Baroness Herschell, w of 3 Baron); *Style—* The Rt Hon Roma, Countess of Dartmouth; 15b Bedford Towers, Brighton, Sussex

DARVAS, Theodore Frederic (Teddy); s of Simon Darvas (d 1969), and Aurelia, *née* Zahler (d 1970); *b* 1 June 1925; *Educ* Highgate Sch; *m* 21 March 1959, Ramona Beryl, da of Capt Algernon Augustus Henry Stracey (d 1940); 2 da (Jane Caroline b 1 Jan 1963, Anna Judith b 27 Nov 1966); *Career* film ed; credits incl: Heavens Above 1963, Woman Times Seven 1966, Assasination Bureau 1969, The Railway Children 1971 (GBFE award for best editing), Amazing Mr Blunden 1973, Woman of Substance 1984, Letters to an Unknown Lover 1985, Hold the Dream 1986, Judgement in Berlin 1987, Act of Will 1989; has edited films in Paris, India and Berlin; memb: ACCT, BAFTA; *Recreations* music, watching cricket; *Clubs* MCC, Savage, Lord's Taverners; *Style—* Teddy Darvas, Esq

DARWALL-SMITH, Lucy Ellen; da of Herbert Francis Eade, and Anne Barbara, *née* Forbes; *b* 1 June 1955; *Educ* Micklefield Sch for Girls; *m* 5 Aug 1978, (Randle) Philip Ralph Darwall-Smith, s of Randle Frederic Hicks Darwall-Smith; 1 da Daisy (b 26 Nov 1985); *Career* assoc dir Lopex 1979-81, md DSA Ltd 1981-; memb IOD, PRCA; *Recreations* theatre, ballet, food, friends; *Clubs* Commonwealth, Sloane; *Style—* Mrs Lucy Darwall-Smith; Middleham House, Ringmer, nr Lewes, East Sussex BN8 5EY (☎ 0273 813503, fax 0273 814019)

DARWEN, 2 Baron (UK 1946) of Heys-in-Bowland; Cedric Percival Davies; s of 1 Baron Darwen (d 1950); *b* 18 Feb 1915; *Educ* Sidcot Sch, Univ of Manchester (BA); *m* 14 July 1934, Kathleen Dora, da of the late George Sharples Walker, of Pendleton, Manchester; 3 s, 1 da; *Heir* s, Hon Roger Michael Davies; *Career* sat as Lab peer in House of Lords until 1982 when he joined Lib Pty; chm and md Darwen Finlayson Ltd 1954-73, pres Independent Publishers' Guild 1973-87; former schoolmaster; *Style—* The Rt Hon Lord Darwen; White Lodge, Sandelswood End, Beaconsfield, Bucks (☎ 049 46 3355)

DARWENT, Rt Rev Frederick Charles; JP; *see*: Aberdeen and Orkney, Bishop of

DARWIN, George Erasmus; e s of William Robert Darwin (d 1970; gs of Charles Darwin); *b* 11 Feb 1927; *Educ* Winchester, Trinity Coll Cambridge (MA); *m* 5 Oct 1956, Shuna Mary, da of George Ronald Service, of Kinfauns House, by Perth (d 1961); 2 s, 1 da; *Career* Babcock & Wilcox Ltd 1957-78, chief exec Richardsons Westgarth Gp 1978-82, chm Home Grown Produce (Hldgs) 1979-; *Recreations* sailing, bridge; *Clubs* Savile; *Style—* G E Darwin, Esq; 3A Pembroke Gardens, London W8 (☎ 071 602 6474); Home Grown Produce (Hldgs) Ltd, Greenhill House 90/93 Cowcross St, London EC1M 6BH (☎ 071 251 1089, fax 071 251 4758)

DARWIN, Henry Galton; CMG 1977; s of Sir Charles Galton Darwin KBE, FRS, of Newnham Grange, Cambridge, and Katharine, *née* Pember; *b* 6 Nov 1929; *Educ* Marlborough, Trinity Coll Cambridge (MA); *m* 5 July 1958, Jane Sophia, da of John Traill Christie (d 1980), princ of Jesus Coll Oxford; 3 da (Sophia b 1961, Emma b 1964, Carola b 1967); *Career* 2 legal advsr FCO 1984-89, called to the Bar Lincoln's Inn 1953; asst legal advsr and later legal cnsllr and dep legal advsr 1954-60, 1963-67, 1970-73 and 1976-84, legal advsr Br Embassy Bonn and UK Mission to the UN 1960-63 and 1967-70, dir gen Legal Serv Cncl Secretariat EC Brussels 1973-76; contrib to books on peaceful settlement of int disputes and int sett of frontier disputes; *Clubs* Athenaeum; *Style—* Henry G Darwin, Esq, CMG; 30 Hereford Square, London SW7 4NB (☎ 071 373 1140)

DARWIN, Philip Waring; s of William Robert Darwin (d 1971), and Sarah Monica, *née* Slingsby (d 1987); *b* 23 Oct 1929; *Educ* Winchester, Trinity Coll Cambridge (BA); *Career* Nat Serv 2 Lt 3 The Kings Own Hussars 1948-49; CA 1955; Moores Carson & Watson 1952-55, Schweppes Ltd 1955-57, Schweppes (USA) Ltd 1957-60 (vice pres 1958-60); Laurence Prust & Co: ptnr 1962-83, sr ptnr 1974-83, dir 1986-90, chm gp devpt Capital Trust plc; memb Cable Authy; Freeman Worshipful Co of Drapers; *Clubs* Savile; *Style—* P W Darwin, Esq; 4 Gore St, London SW7 5PT (☎ 071 584 8842); Chairman Group Development, Capital Trust plc, 125 High Holborn, London WC1V 6PY (☎ 071 242 1148, fax 071 831 7187)

DARWISH, Dr Darwish Hassan; s of Hassan Darwish, of Khartoum, The Sudan, and Mariam Ali Malass'i; *b* 23 July 1946; *Educ* Secdy Sch Khartoum Sudan, Univ of Alexandria Egypt (MB ChB), Univ of Liverpool (PhD); *m* 1 Jan 1970, Samia Tahia Ali, da of Taha Ali Saafan (d 1952); 1 s (Samy b 24 July 1972), 1 da (Cleopatra b 29 Oct 1977); *Career* MO Khartoum Civil Hosp Sudan 1969-71, sr house offr Liverpool Maternity and Women's Hosps 1971; registrar 1972-75: Liverpool Maternity Hosp, St Catherine's Hosp Wirral, Broadgreen Hosp; lectr in obstetrics and gynaecology Univ of Liverpool 1976- (res fell 1975), conslt obstetrician and gynaecologist Mersey RHA for the Wirral 1980-; memb Br Soc of Med and Dental Hypnosis, Br Soc for Colposcopy and Cervical Pathology, Liverpool Med Inst; pres Wallasy Med Soc; MRCOG 1975; *Books* How to Prevent Pregnancy (1979); *Style—* Dr Darwish Darwish; Hortiack, Kings Dr, Caldy, Wirral, Merseyside L48 2JH (☎ 051 625 2456); BUPA Murrayfield Hospital, Holmwood Drive, Thingwall, Wirral, Merseyside L61 1AU (☎ 051 648 7000); Arrowe Park Hospital, Arrowe Park Rd, Upton, Wirral, Merseyside L49 5LN (☎ 051 678 5111)

DAS, Dr Sankar Kumar; s of D Das (d 1974), of Calcutta, India, and late Nilima, *née* Roy Chondbury; *b* 1 Dec 1933; *Educ* Univ of Calcutta (MB BS); *m* 26 Nov 1977, Enakshi, *née* Roy, da of P K Roy (d 1976); 1 s (Shumit b 1 June 1979), 1 da (Priya b 27 Feb 1984); *Career* med registrar Victoria Hosp Blackpool 1964-66, fell internal and chest med, nuclear med and asst instr med VA Hosp Milwaukee Wisc USA 1966-69, sr med registrar King's Coll Hosp and St Francis Hosp London 1970-74 conslt physician: geriatric med Manor Hosp Derby and Derby City Hosp 1974-77, St Helier Gp Hosp and London Borough of Sutton 1977-; hon sr lectr Univ of London 1977-, recognised teacher St George's Hosp Tooting 1977-; inventor: hind paddle walker Mk I, II, III, exercising machine, DAK mobile Mk I, II walking frames, disc computor for analytical prog on geriatric med and clinical audi urinary incontinence gadgets (male and female); conslt Specialist Assoc; memb: Panel on Residential Accomodation Sutton Borough, Br Geriatric Soc, American Coll of Chest Physicians, scrutiniser for local candidates; memb and fell RSH 1966; memb: Br Geriatric Soc 1966, Royal Inst GB; fell: Int Biographical Assoc 1980, Int Youth in Achievement 1980; *Books* Lecture Notes on Medical Infirmities, Europe (1981), Fits, Faints and Falls (1985), contrib to med jls and author of papers on computers in medicine; *Recreations* flying, polo, horse riding, cricket; *Style*— Dr Das; 62 Rose Hill, Sutton, Surrey SM1 3EX (☎ 081 644 1639); St Helier Hosp, Wrythe Lane, Carshalton, Surrey SM5 1AA (☎ 081 644 4343)

DAS NEVES, Hon Mrs (Amanda Mary Alnwick); *née* Grey; only da of Baron Grey of Naunton, GCMG, GCVO, OBE (Life Peer), *qv*; *b* 23 Jan 1951; *Educ* St Mary's Sch Calne, Bedford Coll, Univ of London; *m* 1975, José das Neves; *Style*— The Hon Mrs das Neves; 18 Wakehurst Rd, London SW11

DASHWOOD, Cyril Francis; s of Cyril Russell Dashwood, CBE (d 1962), of Slough, and Laura Louise, *née* Steward (d 1959); *b* 15 March 1925; *Educ* Cranleigh Sch; *m* 20 Sept 1958, Prudence Elizabeth, da of Arnold George Oliver Williams, of Amersham; 2 s (Richard b 1961, William b 1968), 1 da (Joanna b 1964); *Career* Flt Lt RAF 1943-47; CA; sr ptnr Moores Rowland; vice pres Hockey Assoc 1988- (hon treas 1983-), memb Cncl English Sinfonia Orchestra 1982-, chm Amersham and Chesham Bois Choral Soc, former chm Broad St Ward Club; Freeman: City of London 1985, Worshipful Co of CAs 1986; FCA 1950; *Recreations* music, sport, gardening; *Clubs* Carlton, Wig and Pen, MCC; *Style*— Cyril Dashwood, Esq; Ruthwell, Oakway, Chesham Bois, Bucks HP6 5PQ (☎ 0494 725103); Cliffords Inn, Fetter Lane, London EC4A 1AS (☎ 071 831 2345, fax 071 831 6123, telex 886504 MARCA)

DASHWOOD, Edward John Francis; s (by 1 m) and h of Sir Francis John Vernon Hereward Dashwood, 11 Bt, *qv*, by his 1 w; *b* 25 Sept 1964; *Educ* Eton, Univ of Reading (BSc); *m* 10 April 1989, Lucinda Nell, da of G H F Miesegaes and Mrs D Parker; *Career* land agent, landowner; ARICS; *Recreations* shooting, fishing, tennis; *Style*— E J F Dashwood, Esq; West Wycombe Park, Bucks (☎ 0494 24411)

DASHWOOD, Sir Francis John Vernon Hereward; 11 Bt (Premier Bt of GB, cr 1707), of West Wycombe, Buckinghamshire; s of Sir John Dashwood, 10 Bt, CVO (d 1966); *b* 7 Aug 1925; *Educ* Eton, ChCh Oxford, Harvard Business Sch; *m* 1, 3 May 1957, Victoria Ann Elizabeth Gwynne (d 1976), da of Maj John Frederick Foley, Baron de Rutzen (d 1944) (whose ancestor Augustus, Col in the Army of the Grand Duchy of Lithuania, obtained an acknowledgement of nobility from King Wladislaw IV of Poland *ante* 1677), of Slebech Park, Pembrokeshire, by his w Sheila Victoria Katrin (now Lady Dunsany), da of Sir Henry Philipps, Bt, of Picton Castle; 1 s, 3 da (Emily b 1958, m 1981 Charles Naper, Georgina b 1960, Caroline b 1962); m 2, 1977, Marcella Teresa Guglielmina Maria, formerly w of Giuseppe Sportoletti Baduel, wid of Jack Frye, CBE, and da of Marcellino Scarafia; 1 stepson (Marco Sportoletti Baduel b 1966); *Heir* s, Edward John Francis; *Career* landowner and farmer; Lloyd's underwriting agent and memb; Parly candidate (C) W Bromwich 1955 and Gloucester 1957; High Sheriff Bucks 1976; chm Bucks Branch CLA 1980; *Books* The Dashwoods of West Wycombe; *Recreations* shooting, windsurfing; *Clubs* White's; *Style*— Sir Francis Dashwood, Bt; West Wycombe Park, High Wycombe, Bucks HP14 3AJ (☎ 0494 23720); Knollys House, 47 Mark Lane, London EC3 (☎ 071 929 0811)

DASHWOOD, Sir Richard James; 9 Bt (E 1684), of Kirtlington Park, Oxfordshire, TD (1987); s of Sir Henry George Massy Dashwood, 8 Bt (d 1972), by his w, Susan Mary (d 1985), da of late Maj Victor Robert Montgomerie-Charrington; *b* 14 Feb 1950; *Educ* Eton; *m* 1984, Kathryn Ann, er da of Frank Mahon, of Berkshire; 1 s; *Heir* s, Frederick George Mahon Dashwood b 29 Jan 1988; *Career* Lt 14/20 King's Hussars 1969, TA & VR 1973- (Brevet Major 1987); *Style*— Sir Richard Dashwood, Bt; Ledwell Cottage, Sandford St Martin, Oxon OX5 4AN (☎ 060 883 267)

DAUBENY, (Charles) Niel; s of Richard Louis Daubeny (d 1968), of Miri Sarawak, and Madeleine Florence *née* Marsh; *b* 4 Aug 1937; *Educ* Wellington; *m* 23 Sept 1967, Mary Rose, da of Sir Alan Cumbrae Rose McLeod, KCVO (d 1981), of London; 1 s (Richard b 1977), 2 da (Victoria b 1969, Louise b 1972); *Career* Nat Serv RN 1958-60, TA 22 SAS 1960-63; Price Waterhouse & Co 1960- 66, dep gp chief accountant Mercantile and Gen Reinsur Co 1970-74, gp fin controller Bank of America Int Ltd 1974-78, dir and gp fin dir Scandinavian Bank Gp plc 1978-90, gp fin dir Skandinaviska Enskilda Banken, London 1990-; FCA 1974; *Recreations* squash, gardening; *Clubs* IOD; *Style*— Niel Daubeny, Esq; Halnacker Hill, Bowlhead Green, Godalming, Surrey GU8 6NN (☎ 0428 682170); Scandinaviska Enskilda Banken, 2-6 Cannon St, London EC4 6XX (☎ 071 236 6090)

DAUBNEY, Christopher Paul; s of Kenneth Crocker Daubney, of 40 Rookswood, Alton, Hants, and Evelyn Blanche Daubney (d 1987); *b* 14 Sept 1942; *Educ* Clifton, St Johns Coll Cambridge (MA); *Career* various posts BBC 1964-73; IBA: princ engr quality control 1973-81, head of quality control 1981-83, head Engrg Info Servs 1984-87, head Engrg Secretariat 1987, asst dir engrg (policy and projects) 1987-88; chief engr Channel 4 1988-; CEng, FIEE, MIOA; *Style*— Christopher Daubney, Esq; Channel 4 TV, 60 Charlotte St, London W1P 2AX (☎ 071 631 4444)

DAUKES, Lt-Col John Clendon; s of Lt-Col Sir Clendon Turberville Daukes, CIE (d 1947), of Sevenoaks, and Lady Dorothy Maynard, *née* Lavington Evans (d 1968); *b* 20 Nov 1916; *Educ* Charterhouse, RMA Woolwich; *m* 2 Sept 1944, Elizabeth, da of Capt Cosmo Alec Onslow Douglas, DSO (d 1971), of Berks; 2 s (Clendon Douglas, David Jeremy Gordon), 1 da (Jennifer Ann); *Career* cmmnd 1937, Lt Col RA, Dunkirk evacuation 1940, Normandy landing D-Day, (despatches), Staff Coll Camberley 1942, instr 1944-45, RN Staff Coll Greenwich 1951, Brevet Lt-Col 1955, ret 1958; gen asst Int Pipeline Agency Paris (CEOA) 1958 (exec asst 1962), personnel mangr Dep Dir Admin, Int Staff NATO Paris then Brussels 1967-69, bursar Charterhouse and clerk to the Governing Body 1969, chm Schs Bursars Assoc 1975-78, ret 1981; memb: Ct of Assts of Sons of the Clergy Corp 1975, memb Ctee of the Clergy Orphan Corp 1980-, governing bodies Assoc Exec Ctee 1982-84; tstee Carthusian Tst 1979-; memb governing body: St Margaret's Bushey 1980-89, St Edmund's Canterbury 1980-89, Farlington Horsham 1980-86, Tormead Guildford 1980-86; memb Governing Bodies Assoc Exec Ctee 1982-84; *Recreations* skiing & many games; *Style*— Lt-Col John C Daukes; 4 Burford Lodge, Elstead, Godalming, Surrey GU8 6HU (☎ 0252 703030)

DAULBY, Charles William (Bill); s of Philip Daulby (d 1989), of Foulridge, Lancs, and Mary, *née* Wilkinson; *b* 8 June 1947; *Educ* Colne GS, Univ of Sheffield (BA); *m* 4 Aug 1970, Christine Anne, da of Fred Spencer (d 1987), of Colne, Lancs; 2 da (Emma b 1974, Kate b 1977); *Career* dir: Nissan UK Holdings Ltd 1989-, AFG Holdings Ltd 1989-; md Automotive Leasing Ltd 1990-; *Recreations* golf; *Style*— Bill Daulby, Esq; Nissan UK Holdings Ltd, Nissan House, Columbia Drive, Durrington, Worthing, W Sussex (☎ 0903 68561, fax 0903 66623, car 0860 339969)

DAULTRY, Joseph George; s of Joseph Daultry (d 1954), of St Georges Rd, London SE11, and Gladys Mary, *née* Dudley (d 1968); *b* 24 Aug 1916; *Educ* Archbishop Temples Central Sch, Gibson & Weldon Sch of Law; *m* 24 March 1941, Lily, da of John Benjamin Butterfield (d 1962), of Dewsbury Rd, Leeds; 2 da (Jennifer Linda (Mrs Roberts) b 1948, Susan Josephine (Mrs Simpson) b 1952); *Career* Nat Serv WWII Flt Sgt RAF 1940-46; admitted slr 1949, practised in London (ret 1983); vice pres RAF Assoc, appointed by Lord Chllr as pres Mental Health Review Tbnl (NE Thames Area) 1979-88; Freeman: City of London 1961, Worshipful Co of Butchers 1961; memb Law Soc 1949; *Recreations* bowls; *Clubs* Selborne and Bounds Green, Bush Hill Park Golf; *Style*— Joseph Daultry, Esq; 33 Eversley Crescent, Winchmore Hill, London N21 1EL (☎ 081 360 1730); 109-111 Cecil Rd, Enfield, Middx EN2 6TN (☎ 081 366 6387)

DAUNCEY, Brig Michael Donald Keen; DSO (1945), DL (Gloucester 1983); s of Thomas Gough Dauncey (d 1965), of Crowthorne, Berks, and Alice, *née* Keen (d 1988); the name Dauncey was first recorded in Uley, Glos, c1200s; *b* 11 May 1920; *Educ* King Edward's Sch Birmingham; *m* 1945, Marjorie Kathleen, da of Hubert William Neep (d 1967); 1 s (John), 2 da (Gillian, (Margaret) Joy); *Career* cmmnd 22 Cheshire Regt 1941, seconded to Glider Pilot Regt 1943, Arnhem 1944 (wounded, taken prisoner, later escaped), MA to GOC-in-C Greece 1946-47, seconded to Para Regt 1947-49, Staff Coll 1950, instr RMA Sandhurst 1957-58, CO 1 Bn 22 Cheshire Regt 1963-66 (BAOR and UN Peace-keeping Force Cyprus), DS Plans JSSC 1966-68, Cmdt Jungle Warfare Sch 1968-69, Cmdt Support Weapons Wing Sch of Inf Netheravon 1969-72, Brig 1973, def and mil attaché Br Embassy Madrid 1973-75, ret from Army 1976; Col 22 Cheshire Regt 1978-85, Hon Col 1 Cadet Bn Glos Regt (ACF) 1981-90; *Recreations* rough shooting, travelling, tennis, under-gardener; *Clubs* Army & Navy; *Style*— Brig Michael Dauncey, DSO, DL; Uley Lodge, Uley, nr Dursley, Glos GL11 5SN (☎ 0453 860216)

DAUNT, Patrick Eldon; s of Dr Francis Eldon Daunt (d 1953), of Hastings, and Winifred Doggett, *née* Wells; descendant of Daunt family of Owlpen Manor Gloucs, and Kilkascan Castle, Co Cork; *b* 19 Feb 1925; *Educ* Rugby, Wadham Coll Oxford (BA, MA); *m* 1958, Jean Patricia, da of Lt-Col Percy Wentworth Hargreaves (d 1983), of Herts; 3 s (William, Thomas, Francis), 1 da (Caroline); *Career* housemaster Christ's Hosp 1961, headmaster Thomas Bennett Comp Sch Crawley 1965-73; princ admin Educn Dept Cmmn of Euro Communities 1974-82, head of bureau for action in favour of disabled people Cmmn of Euro Communities 1982-87, visiting fell London Inst of Educn 1988-91, vice-chm Cerebral Palsy Overseas 1989, chm Assoc Spina Bifida 1990; *Books* Comprehensive Values (1974); *Recreations* botanizing, books; *Clubs* United Oxford and Cambridge; *Style*— Patrick Daunt, Esq; 4 Bourn Bridge Rd, Abington, Cambridge (☎ 0223 891485)

DAVE, Dr Narendra Pranlal Girdharlal; s of Pranlal Girdharlal Dave (d 1968), of Nairobi, Kenya, and Yasumati, *née* Vyas; *b* 2 Nov 1951; *Educ* HH The Aga Khan Sch Mombasa Kenya, Middx Hosp Med Sch Univ of London (MB BS, DRCOG); *m* 10 April 1978, Bhavna, da of Jagdish Natwarlal Bhatt (d 1984), of London; 1 da (Punita b 1983); *Career* Capt RAMC (TA) 1981; physician; Cleveland Vocational Trg Scheme for Gen Practice Univ of Newcastle upon Tyne 1979-82; med offr: Govt of Tristan Da Cunha 1982-84, Yorkshire Clinic Bingley 1984-85, Govt of Anguilla W Indies 1985-88, MOD 1989-; fell Soc of Community Med; memb: Biochemical Soc, Royal Soc of Health; FRSM, FRIPH; *Recreations* golf; *Style*— Dr Narendra P G Dave; 27 Stoneway, Hartwell, Northampton, NN7 2JY

DAVENPORT; *see*: Bromley-Davenport

DAVENPORT, Brian John; QC (1980); s of late Robert Cecil Davenport, FRCS, and Helen Elizabeth, *née* Mayfield (d 1990); *b* 17 March 1936; *Educ* Bryanston Sch, Worcester Coll Oxford; *m* 1969, Erica Tickell, yr da of Prof E N Willmer; 2 s, 1 da; *Career* called to the Bar (Grays Inn) 1960; jr counsel to: ECGD 1970-74, Dept of Employment 1972-74, Bd of Inland Revenue 1974-80; law cmmr 1981-88; joined Inner Temple (ad eundem) 1978, bencher of Grays Inn 1984; *Style*— Brian Davenport, Esq, QC; 43 Downshire Hill, London NW3 1NU (☎ 071 435 3332)

DAVENPORT, Maj David John Cecil; CBE (1989), DL (Hereford and Worcester 1974); Lord of the Manors of Mansel Lacy, Wormsley, Yazor and Bishopstone; s of Maj John Lewes Davenport, TD, JP, DL (d 1964), and Louise Aline (d 1987), da of Col Cecil John Herbert Spence-Colby, CMG, DSO, TD, of Donnington Hall, Ledbury; *b* 28 Oct 1934; *Educ* Eton, RMA Sandhurst, RAC Cirencester; *m* 1, 1959 (m dis 1970), Jennifer, *née* Burness; 2 da; m 2, 1971, Lindy, *née* Baker; 1 s; *Career* Grenadier Gds 1954-67, ret Maj; chm Leominster DC 1975-76; memb Forestry Cmmn Nat Advsy Ctee for Eng 1974-87, chm COSIRA 1982-88 (rural devpt cmmr 1982-90); High Sheriff Hereford and Worcester 1989-90; *Clubs* Boodle's, MCC; *Style*— Maj David Davenport, CBE, DL; Mansel House, Mansel Lacy, Hereford HR4 7HQ (☎ 098 122 224)

DAVENPORT, Hugo Benedick; s of Arthur Nigel Davenport, of Belgravia, London, and Helena Margaret, *née* White (d 1979); *b* 6 June 1953; *Educ* Westminster, Univ of Sussex (BA); *m* 10 Aug 1988, Sarah, da of Hugh Mollison; 1 s (Bram b 10 Aug 1986); *Career* syndication asst Visnews Ltd 1976-77, trainee reporter rising to feature writer Liverpool Daily Post and Echo 1977-80, freelance journalist 1980-81 (worked for Guardian, Financial Times, Evening Standard, Catholic Herald), NI corr The Observer 1984-85 (reporter and feature writer 1981-84), feature writer Mail On Sunday 1985-87, film critic Daily Telegraph 1990-91 (news feature writer 1987-90); prize for population and environmental reporting Population Inst Washington 1989; *Recreations* reading, walking, drawing, music; *Style*— Hugo Davenport, Esq; The Daily Telegraph, 181 Marsh Wall, Isle of Dogs, London E14 9SR (☎ 071 538 5000, fax 071 538 3810)

DAVENPORT, James Kinder (Jamie); s of John Grenville Kinder Davenport, of Falkirk, Scotland, and Audrey Willis, *née* Kirby; *b* 18 July 1955; *Educ* George Heriot's Sch Edinburgh, Trinity Coll Cambridge (BA); *m* 7 July 1979, (Deborah) Sian, da of Dr J Quentin Hughes; 2 s (Benjamin Kinder b 31 Oct 1981, John James (decd) b 9 July 1987), 2 da (Gemma Louise b 21 May 1984, Lily Clare b 30 Jan 1989); *Career* advertising exec; account exec Grey Advertising 1977-79; account exec then assoc dir: Geers Gross Ltd 1979-84, Foote Cone & Belding 1984-86; TBWA (TBWA-Holmes Knight Ritchie since 1990): dir 1986-87, client service dir 1987-89, chief exec UK 1989-90, dir TBWA/HKR 1990-; MIPA; *Recreations* family, friends and the dinner table; *Style*— Jamie Davenport, Esq; TBWA-Holmes Knight Ritchie, 8 Crinan St, London N1 9UF (☎ 071 883 5544, fax 071 833 8751, mobile 0836 204003)

DAVENPORT, John Martin; s of Eric Davenport, of Ridge Acre, Hook Heath, Woking (d 1961), and Winifred Mary, *née* Elder; *b* 16 Oct 1931; *Educ* Uppingham, Oriel Coll Oxford (MA); *m* 14 Sept 1957, Wendy Angela, da of Claude Wyatt, of 8 Milner Rd, West Overcliff Drive, Bournemouth; 2 s (Philip b 1961, Peter b 1966); *Career* exec dep chm F & C Pacific Investmt Tst plc 1966-89, exec dir Foreign & Colonial Mgmnt Ltd 1970-89, investmt mangr, dir Community Hosps Gp plc 1981-, exec dir Granville Investmt Mgmnt 1989-; FCA; *Recreations* railways, gardening; *Clubs* Gresham; *Style*— John Davenport, Esq; Mint House, 77 Mansell St, London E1 8AF (☎ 071 488 1212)

DAVENPORT, Montague; CBE (1972, OBE 1959); s of Hayward Montague Davenport (d 1959); *b* 26 May 1916; *Educ* Sherborne, Pharmaceutical Soc Coll (PhC); *m* 1952, Olive Margaret, da of Donald Frank Brabner (d 1948); 2 s; *Career* WWII Lt Cdr RNVR; asst sec FCO 1971-78 (joined 1946), govr dir J T Davenport Ltd 1959-; *Style*— Montague Davenport, Esq, CBE; Chalcots, Orchard Way, Esher, Surrey (☎ 0372 462384)

DAVENPORT, (Arthur) Nigel; s of Maj Arthur Davenport, MC, of Sidney Sussex Coll, Cambridge; *b* 23 May 1928; *Educ* Cheltenham, Trinity Coll Oxford; *m* 1, 1951 (m dis 1962) Helena (d 1978); 1 s (Hugo), 1 da (Laura); m 2, 1972 (m dis 1980; she m 1, 1968, Richard Durden-Smith), Maria Penelope Katharine (b 1945), da of Sir William Aitken, KBE, MP (d 1964, n of 1 Baron Beaverbrook), and sis of Jonathan Aitken, MP; 1 s (Jack); *Career* served RASC and with Br Forces Network in Germany 1946-48; late memb OUDS; actor 1951-; memb original English Stage co Royal Court Theatre (appearing in 14 prodns); tv appearances incl: George III in The Prince Regent, South Riding, Howards Way, Trainer; film appearances incl: A Man for All Seasons, Virgin soldiers, Mary Queen of Scots, Chariots of Fire; co dir; pres Equity 1987- (vice pres 1978-81); *Recreations* gardening, travel; *Clubs* Garrick; *Style*— Nigel

Davenport, Esq; c/o Green & Underwood, 2 Conduit St, London W1

DAVENPORT, Peter; s of Herbert Charles William Davenport, of 12 St Seiriol Grove, Birkenhead, Merseyside, and Kathleen, *née* Murphy; *b* 24 March 1961; *Educ* Corpus Christi HS; *m* 5 Dec 1988, Lesley Jayne, da of Gerald and Phyllis Reid; *Career* professional footballer: Nottingham Forest 1982-1986 (118 appearances, 54 goals), Manchester United 1986-88 (83 appearances, 26 goals), Middlesbrough 1988-90 (60 appearances, 8 goals), Sunderland 1990-; 1 full England cap (v Eire 1985), 1 England B appearance (v NZ 1984); civil servant Land Registry Department 1979-81; *Recreations* golf, cricket, tennis, marine art, antiques, home computer; *Style—* Peter Davenport, Esq; c/o Sunderland A F C, Roker Park, Sunderland (☎ 091 514 0332)

DAVENPORT, Robert Simpson; s of Richard Simpson Davenport, and Dorothy Mary, *née* Evans; *b* 7 Jan 1941; *Educ* Canford; *m* 1970, Patricia, *née* Temple; 2 s; *Career* Singleton Fabian & Co (later merged with Binder Hamlyn) 1958-62, Peat Marwick Mitchell & Co (later KPMG Peat Marwick McLintock) 1963-67, S G Warburg & Co Ltd 1968-88 (exec dir 1975-88), exec dir Hill Samuel Bank 1988-; govr Elliott Sch Putney 1982-88; *Clubs* Hurlingham; *Style—* Robert Davenport, Esq; 1 Genoa Ave, London SW15 6DY; Eaton House, Dolmans Hill, Lytchett Matravers, Nr Poole, Dorset BH16 8HP

DAVENPORT-HANDLEY, Sir David John; OBE (1962), JP (Rutland 1948), DL (Leics 1974); s of John Davenport-Handley (d 1943); *b* 2 Sept 1919; *Educ* RNC Dartmouth; *m* 1943, Leslie Mary, da of Wing Cdr Sydney Mansfield Goldsmith, RAF; 1 s, 1 da; *Career* Lt RN, ret 1947; chm: Clipsham Quarry Co Ltd 1947-, Rutland and Stamford Cons Assoc 1952-65, Rutland Petty Sessional Div 1957-84, E Mids Area Cons Assoc 1971-77 (treas 1965-71), Nat Union of Cons and Unionist Assocs 1979-80 (vice chm 1977-79); Vice-Lt Rutland 1972 (High Sheriff 1954, DL 1962); tstee Oakham Sch 1970-86, memb Parole Bd 1981-84, pres E Mids Area Cons Cncl 1987-, chm Rutland Historic Churches Preservation Tst 1987-, pres Nat Union of Cons and Unionist Assocs 1990-91; kt 1980; *Recreations* gardening, music; *Clubs* English Speaking Union; *Style—* Sir David Davenport-Handley, OBE, JP, DL; Clipsham Hall, Oakham, Rutland, Leics (☎ 0780 410204)

DAVENTRY, 3 Viscount (UK 1943); Francis Humphrey Maurice Fitzroy Newdegate; JP (Warwickshire 1960), DL (1970); father assumed by Royal Licence the additional surname of Newdegate 1936; s of Cdr the Hon John Maurice FitzRoy Newdegate, RN (d 1976), s of 1 Viscountess Daventry (d 1962), and Hon Mrs John FitzRoy Newdegate, *qv*; *b* 17 Dec 1921; *Educ* Eton; *m* 1959, Hon Rosemary, da of Lt-Gen 1 Baron Norrie, GCMG, GCVO, CB, DSO, MC (d 1977); 2 s, 1 da; *Heir* s Hon James Fitzroy Newdegate; *Career* Capt Coldstream Gds 1943, ADC to Viceroy of India 1946-48; High Sheriff Warwicks 1970, Vice Lord-Lt 1974-90, Lord-Lt Warwickshire 1990-; *Clubs* Boodle's; *Style—* The Rt Hon the Viscount Daventry, JP, DL; Temple House, Arbury, Nuneaton, Warwicks CV10 7PT (☎ 0203 383514)

DAVENTRY, Viscountess; Rosemary; *née* Norrie; da of late 1 Baron Norrie, GCMG, GCVO, CB, DSO, MC; *b* 1926; *m* 1959, 3 Viscount Daventry, JP, *qv*; 2 s, 1 da; *Style—* The Rt Hon the Viscountess Daventry; Temple House, Arbury, Nuneaton, Warwicks CV10 7PT (☎ 0203 383514)

DAVEY, Maj Christopher Julian Tudor; s of Maj-Gen Basil Charles Davey, CB, CBE (d 1959), and Enid Sanford, *née* Tudor (d 1989); *b* 9 April 1942; *Educ* Eton, Jesus Coll Cambridge (MA); *m* 6 Jan 1979, Deborah Ann, da of Rev Canon H Rhodes Cooper, of Halifax , Nova Scotia; 1 s (Dominic b 1981), 1 da (Colette b 1983); *Career* cmmnd 2 Royal Tank Regt 1964, ret 1983; private pilots licence balloons 1974, world time record flight Yeovil to Angers 1975, transatlantic flt St Johns to Biscay and received Royal Aero Club gold medal from HRH Prince Charles 1978, first N Sea crossing into Europe Hull to Osann 1980; pres Cambridge Boat Club 1964 (winning Blue 1962 & 1964); *Recreations* rowing, ballooning, viticulture, house building; *Clubs* Leander, British Balloon & Airship, Inst of Advanced Motorists; *Style—* Maj Christopher Davey; The Wine House, Bathsprings Vineyard, Bailbrook Lane, Bath BA1 7AB (☎ 0225 852131)

DAVEY, Hon Mrs (Heather Mary); *née* Grasmere; only da of Baron Morris of Grasmere (Life Peer, d 1990); *b* 17 Aug 1925; *m* 1, 1946 (m dis 1972), Tom Berry Caldwell, son of William Caldwell, of Wigan, Lancs; 1 s, 2 da; m 2, 1972, Alfred G Davey; *Style—* The Hon Mrs Davey; Coach House, Kirk Hammerton, York

DAVEY, Col John Patrick; OBE (1989), TD (1965, and Bar 1971), DL (1983); s of Algernon George Davey (d 1938), of Trimley St Mary nr Ipswich, and Nora, *née* Sneezum (d 1980); *b* 7 Oct 1923; *Educ* Framlingham Coll Suffolk; *m* 29 March 1951, Kathleen, da of Harry Farrow; 2 s (Charles St John b 4 May 1953, James St John b 11 Sept 1957); *Career* WWII volunteered RB 1942-43, RA 1943-44, 5 Regt RHA 1944-45, served France, Germany and Berlin 1944-45, adj Sch of Artillery India 1945-47, demobbed as Capt 1947; articled clerk Bland Fielden & Co Colchester 1941-42; Scrutton Goodchild & Sanderson Ipswich: joined 1947, ptnr 1952-87, sr ptnr 1987-89; dir RC Edmondson Group 1989-, dir Sadler Holdings Group 1989-; Suffolk and Norfolk Yeomanry RA (TA): Lieut 1953-56, Capt 1956-59, Maj 1959-67; Lt-Col cmdg Suffolk and Cambridge Regt 1967-70, TA Col East Anglia 1970-74, ret 1974; sec and chief exec Ipswich and Suffolk C of C Indust and Shipping 1971-1990, dir Ipswich Enterprise Agency 1985-, chm Bd Govrs Suffolk Coll 1986; FCA 1954 (ACA 1949), FInstT 1954 (ATII 1949); *Recreations* rugby, squash, tennis, swimming, gardening; *Style—* Col John Davey, OBE, TD, DL; 1 St Edmunds Road, Ipswich, Suffolk IP1 3QY (☎ 0473 254989); Scrutton Bland, Sanderson House, Museum St, Ipswich, Suffolk IP1 1HE (☎ 0473 259201, fax 0473 231643)

DAVEY, Jon Colin; s of Frederick John Davey, and Dorothy Mary, *née* Key (d 1969); *b* 16 June 1938; *Educ* Raynes Park GS; *m* 1962, Ann Patricia, da of Maj Stanley Arthur Streames (d 1977); 2 s (Simon b 1964, Jonathan b 1967), 1 da (Jennifer b 1972); *Career* asst sec Broadcasting Dept HO 1981-85 (asst sec of Franks Ctee on Official Secrets 1971-72, sec of Williams Ctee on Obscenity and Film Censorship 1977-79, sec of Hunt Inquiry into Cable Expansion and Broadcasting Policy 1982); dir gen Cable Authy 1985-90, dir of Cable Independent Television Commission 1991-; *Recreations* music, lawn-making, English countryside; *Style—* Jon Davey, Esq; 71 Hare Lane, Claygate, Esher, Surrey KT10 0QX (☎ 0372 462078); Independent Television Commission, 70 Brompton Road, London SW3 1EY (☎ 071 584 7011)

DAVEY, Prof Kenneth Jackson; s of Reginald Alfred Davey (d 1962), and Vera Elizabeth, *née* Jackson (d 1973); *b* 7 Dec 1932; *Educ* Silcoates Sch, Merton Coll Oxford (MA), Univ of Birmingham (MSocSc); *m* 18 Aug 1962, Beryl Joyce, da of John Iliff Herbert (d 1975); 2 s (Guy b 1964, Julian b 1966), 1 da (Stephanie b 1971); *Career* RA 1954-56: 2Lt 1955, Lt 1956; HM Overseas Admin Serv in Uganda 1957-69, dir of studies E African Staff Coll 1970-72, Inst of Local Govt Studies Univ of Birmingham 1972- (assoc dir 1974-83, prof of devpt admin 1981-, dir 1983-89); conslt to govts of: Kenya 1975-76, Indonesia 1978-, Pakistan 1981-82, Jordan 1984-85, Bangladesh 1989, Mexico 1989-, Hungary 1990; conslt to World Bank on urban fin 1982-; memb: Solace Overseas Devpt Panel 1980-89, Malvern Coll Cncl 1986-; vice chm: Worcester Diocesan Ctee For Mission 1986-, Powick Parochial Church Cncl 1986-; FRSA 1988; *Books* Taxing a Peasant Society (1974), Financing Regional Government (1983), Strengthening Municipal Government (1989); *Recreations* choral singing, walking; *Style—* Prof Kenneth Davey; Cross House, Powick, nr Worcester WR2 4RP (☎ 0905 830286); Institute of Local Government Studies, University of Birmingham, PO Box 363, Birmingham B15 2TT (☎ 021 414 5011, fax 021 414 4989, telex 3337 UOBHAM)

DAVEY, Hon Mrs (Margaret Wilmett); only da of Baron Helsby (Life Peer, d 1978), by his w Wilmett (*see* Baroness Helsby); *b* 6 Nov 1939; *m* 1, 1960, (John Frederick) Keith St Pier, eldest son of Nurse Frederick St Pier, of Purley, Surrey; m 2, 1976, Brian Davey; *Style—* The Hon Mrs Davey; 7 Holmlea Court, Chatsworth Road, East Croydon CRO 1HA

DAVEY, Nigel Thomas; s of Leslie Douglas, and Elsie Alice, *née* Hummerston; *b* 8 May 1947; *Educ* Ilford Co HS, Trinity Coll Cambridge (MA); *m* 19 Aug 1972, Ruth Mary; 3 s (James b 1975, Andrew b 1977, Richard b 1979); *Career* CA; ptnr: Spicer & Oppenheim 1980, Touche Ross & Co 1990; FCA 1972; *Books* The Business of Partnerships (with PJ Oliver, 1986), Partnership Taxation (with EE Ray, 1987); *Recreations* badminton, tennis, music; *Style—* Nigel Davey, Esq; 31 Middleton Rd, Shenfield, Brentwood, Essex CM15 8DJ (☎ 0277 211954); Touche Ross & Co, Friary Court, 65 Crutched Friars, London EC3N 2NP (☎ 071 480 7766, fax 071 480 695, telex 884257 E)

DAVEY, Norman Thomas; s of Edward Thomas Davey (d 1979), of Torquay, Devon, and Kathleen Taylor, *née* Griffiths; *b* 28 Sept 1925; *Educ* Homelands Central Sch, Torquay, Torquay Sch of Art, S Devon Tech Coll, Oxford Sch of Arch (Dip Arch); *m* 11 Feb 1962, Anne Felicity, da of Rev Arthur Douglas Young (d 1965); 3 s (Geoffrey b 1963, Benedict b 1965, Clement b 1968); *Career* RN 1943-47 (AB, radar, gunnery); architect; private practice (chiefly concerned with church architecture) 1964, memb Guildford Diocesan Advsy Ctee for Care of Churches and Churchya tstee Soc for the Maintenance of the Faith, co-opted memb Governing Cncl of Chichester Theol Coll 1983-89; RIBA 1953; *Recreations* reading, musical appreciation, countryside, villages, pubs, churches, naval history, current naval affairs; *Style—* Norman Davey, Esq; The Cottage, 2 Heatherley Rd, Camberley, Surrey GU15 3LW (☎ 0276 64615)

DAVEY, Peter John; s of John Davey (d 1981), and Mary, *née* Roberts; *b* 28 Feb 1940; *Educ* Oundle, Univ of Edinburgh (BArch); *m* 1968, Carolyn Frances, da of Maj Francis Hervey Pulford (d 1978); 2 s (Pelham Francis John b 1977, Meredith William Thorold b 1979); *Career* architect; ed Architectural Review 1982-, managing ed Architect's Jl 1978-; MRIBA 1970; *Books* Arts and Crafts Architecture (1982); *Clubs* Athenaeum; *Style—* Peter Davey, Esq; 44 Hungerford Rd, London N7 9LP; Architectural Review, 9 Queen Anne's Gate, London SW1 (☎ 071 222 4333, fax 071 222 5196)

DAVEY, Richard H; s of Hubert H Davey, and May, *née* Harding; *b* 22 July 1948; *Educ* Lancing, Lincoln Coll Oxford (BA); *m* (Anna b 17 Jan 1974, Edward b 30 July 1981, Nicholas b 10 Feb 1984, Benedict b 31 Aug 1989); *Career* Slater Walker 1970-76, NM Rothschild & Sons 1976-83, dir Exco International plc 1983-87; md: Merrill Lynch International 1987-89, NM Rothschild & Sons 1989-; *Style—* Richard Davey, Esq; N M Rothschild & Sons Limited, New Court, St Swithins Lane, London EC4 (☎ 071 280 5071)

DAVEY, Dr Ronald William; s of Frederick George Davey, and Cecilia Beatrice, *née* Lawday; *b* 25 Oct 1943; *Educ* Trinity Sch of John Whitgift, Kings Coll London, Kings Coll Hosp Med Sch; *Career* princ in NHS 1970-77, dep md dir Pharmakon Clinics 1977-79, private med practice 1980, clinical asst Royal London Homeopathic Hosp and Tunbridge Wells Homeopathic Hosp 1981-85, hon med dir Blackie Fndn Tst, consltg physician in homeopathy and electro stimulation, physician to HM Queen Elizabeth II 1986-; tstee conslt and vice chm of Res Cncl for Complementary Medicine 1987-89; lectr: Faculty of Homeopathy, Poly of E London, Missionary Sch of Medicine; visiting res fell 1978-79, Marie Curie Meml Fndn, Blackie fell Nat Heart and Lung Inst 1978-90 (currently visiting res fell); memb: Homeopatric Med Res Cncl, Exec Br Homeopathy Res Gp, Academic Advsy Bd Univ of Exeter; memb Soc of Free Radicat Res, FRSM, memb BMA, assoc Br Med Acupuncture Soc; *Books* contrib numerous articles to various med pubns (1979-90); *Recreations* riding, skiing, reading, music, ballet and opera; *Clubs* RSM; *Style—* Dr Ronald Davey; 1 Upper Wimpole St, London W1M 7TD (☎ 071 580 5489, fax 071 224 1094)

DAVEY, (Margaret) Rowena; da of Edward Smith Thomas Davies (d 1938), of Easton, Dunmow, Essex, and Muriel Davies, *née* Gaunt (d 1938); *b* 14 Nov 1917; *Educ* Cheltenham Ladies Coll, Queen's Coll Harley St; *m* 19 Oct 1940, late Norris Gerald Davey, MC, TD, s of Edward Octavius Davey (d 1937), of Tower House, Dunmow; 1 s (John Edward Norris b 1946), 1 da (Mary Rubina b 1943); *Career* memb: Dunmow RDC 1956-74, Essex CC 1961-82 (chm Health and Children's Ctees), Ctee of Inquiry into the Care and Supervision of Maria Colwell 1973, NE Thames Regnl Authy 1974-82; chm: East Anglian Children's Regnl Planning Ctee 1969-79, West Essex Health Authy 1982-86; hon life vice pres Saffron Walden Constituency Cons Assoc; *Recreations* starting things and watching them grow, reading, sewing, being at home; *Style—* Mrs Rowena Davey; Tower House, Dunmow, Essex CM6 3BA (☎ 0371 872162)

DAVEY, Trevor Ian; s of George Edward Gordon Davey, of 17 Dyke Road Avenue, Hove, Sussex, and Patricia, *née* Routledge; *b* 30 June 1956; *Educ* Windlesham Sch, Eastbourne Coll; *m* 21 Oct 1978, Christina Margaret, da of Edward Victor Axford; 1 s (Alan Trevor James b 4 Sept 1981), 2 da (Emma Margaret b 14 Feb 1986, Katy Patricia b 26 July 1990); *Career* dir James Davey Sites Limited 1981-85 (joined 1972); chm: Capital Matters 1980-, Coastway Services 1984-, Regal Display Limited 1986-, Hassocks Amenity Association 1990- (vice chm 1987-90); fireman West Sussex Fire Brigade 1989-, dir Hills 1990-; *Recreations* Jack and Jill Windmill Soc, Amenity Assoc, Fire Brigade and Rescue Serv; *Style—* Trevor Davey, Esq; Regal Display Ltd, Trevina House, 42 Lodge Lane, Keymer, Hassocks, West Sussex BN6 8LX (☎ 07918 3319/ 0273 561350, fax 0273 550868)

DAVID, Brian Rhodri; TD (and three bars); s of Herbert Cyril David (d 1978), and Enid Mary, *née* Rees (d 1968); *b* 20 Sept 1917; *Educ* Mill Hill Sch; *m* 30 Dec 1939, Joan Margaret (Peggy), da of HG Kemp (d 1938); 1 s (Nicholas Brian b 27 March 1942), 1 da (Sally Margaret b 30 Sept 1944); *Career* cmmnd RA TA 1936, Capt 1940, Maj July 1941, 2 i/c HAA Regt, ret 1953; Robinson David & Co Ltd: joined 1936, dir 1941, asst md 1949, resigned 1968; dir Burts & Renton Ltd 1968-74, chm Principality Building Soc 1981- (dir 1958-, dep chm 1976-81); memb Indust Tbnl 1978-87, gen cmmr for Income Tax 1979-; pres: Cardiff C of C 1962, Newport and Gwent C of C 1974; *Recreations* watching rugby football; *Clubs* Cardiff and Co, Glamorgan Wanderers Rugby Football; *Style—* Brian David, Esq, TD; 20 Mill Rd, Llanishen, Cardiff CF4 5XB (☎ 0222 752 514); PO Box 89, Principality Buildings, Queen St, Cardiff CF1 1UA (☎ 0222 344 188, fax 0222 314 567)

DAVID, Elizabeth; CBE (1986, OBE 1976); 2 da of Rupert Sackville Gwynne, MP (d 1924), and Hon Stella Ridley (who m 2, 1933, Capt John Hamilton, Extra ADC to Gov of Jamaica, and d 1973), 2 da of 1 Viscount Ridley (d 1904); *b* 1913; *m* 30 Aug 1944 (m dis 1960), Lt-Col Ivor Anthony David, IA; *Career* author of numerous cookery books; FRSL 1982; Hon DUniv Essex 1980, DLit Univ of Bristol 1990; Chev du Mérite Agricole (Fr) 1977; *Books* A Book of Mediterranean Food (1950), French Country Cooking (1951), Italian Food (1954), Summer Cooking (1955), French Provincial Cooking (1960), English Cooking, Ancient and Modern; vol I, Spices, Salts and

Aromatics in the English Kitchen (1970), English Bread and Yeast Cookery (1977) An Omelette and a Glass of Wine (1984); *Style—* Mrs Elizabeth David, CBE; c/o Penguin Books, Harmondsworth, Middx

DAVID, Hugh Housdon; s of James Frederick David, and Marjorie Grace, *née* Housdon; *b* 22 May 1954; *Educ* GS, Stockwell Coll, Inst of Educn Univ of London (BEd); *Career* English teacher Ramsden Sch Orpington Kent 1976-82, dir Fulcrum Theatre 1982-84; freelance writer 1982-; play: Coping (London 1982, BBC Radio 1985); documentary: The Last Night Forever (BBC Radio 1983); contribs: The Times, The Independent, The Independent on Sunday, Times Educational Supplement, London Evening Standard; memb Awards Panel Royal TV Soc 1986 and 1988; *Books* The Fitzrovians (1988); *Recreations* reading, theatre, wine; *Style—* Hugh David, Esq; Flat D, 37 Albert Square, London SW8 1BY (☎ 071 587 0935, mobile 0860 301501)

DAVID, Joanna; da of Maj John Almond Hacking, and Davida Elizabeth, *née* Nesbitt; *b* 17 Jan 1947; *Educ* Altrincham GS, Elmhurst Ballet Sch, Royal Acad of Dancing, Webber Douglas Acad of Dramatic Art; partner since 1972, Edward Charles Morice Fox, *qv*; 1 s (Frederick Samson Robert Morice b 5 April 1989), 1 da (Emilia Rose Elizabeth b 31 July 1974); *Career* actress; Chichester Festival Theatre 1971, Family Reunion 1973 and Uncle Vanya 1977 Royal Exchange Manchester, Cherry Orchard 1983 and Breaking the Code 1986 Theatre Royal Haymark TV appearances incl: War and Peace, Sense and Sensibility, Last of the Mohicans, Duchess of Duke Street, Rebecca, Carrington and Strachey, Fame is the Spur, First Among Equals, Paying Guests, Unexplained Laughter, Hannay, Children of the North; memb ctee: Ladies Theatrical Guild, Unicorn Theatre for Children; *Style—* Miss Joanna David; c/o Peter Browne Management, Pebro House, 13 St Martins Road, London SW9 (☎ 071 737 3444)

DAVID, Joseph; OBE (1983); s of Morris David (d 1955), of Glamorgan, and Goldie Freedman; *b* 22 March 1928; *Educ* Pontypridd Boys Sch, Manchester Univ (BSc); *m* 1959, Shirley, da of Hyman Selbey, of London; 1 s (Alun b 1964), 2 da (Keren b 1963, Deborah b 1968); *Career* chartered textile technologist; co dir 1968, chm and md Catomance Ltd 1977-; pres: Br Pest Control Assoc 1976-78, Br Wood Preserving Assoc 1986-; FTI; *Recreations* conservation and restoration, theatre, reading; *Style—* Joseph David, Esq, OBE; 1 Coneydale, Welwyn Garden City, Herts AL8 7RX (☎ 0707 326625); Catonance Ltd, 96 Bridge Road, East Welwyn, Garden City, Herts AL7 1JW (☎ 0707 324373, telex 267418, fax 0707 372191)

DAVID, Hon Nicholas Christopher; er s of Richard William David and Baroness David (Life Peer), *qv*; *b* 1937; *m* 1, 1962 (m dis 1975), Hilke Hennig; m 2, 1977 (m dis 1982), Iva Williams; m 3, Judy Sterner; *Style—* The Hon Nicholas David; Dept of Archaeology, Univ of Ibadan, Nigeria

DAVID, Baroness (Life Peer UK 1978), of Romsey, City of Cambridge; Nora Ratcliff David; JP (Cambridge City 1965); da of George Blockley Blakesley, JP (d 1934); *b* 23 Sept 1913; *Educ* Ashby-de-la-Zouch Girls' GS, St Felix Southwold, Newnham Coll Cambridge (MA); *m* 1935, Richard William David, s of late Rev Ferdinand Paul David; 2 s, 2 da; *Career* sits as Lab Peer in House of Lords, dep chief oppn whip 1983-87 and oppn spokesman for environment/local in Lords 1983-86, oppn spokesman for educn 1986- (and 1979-83); former Cambridge city cnllr, Cambs co cnllr 1974-79; memb Bd Peterborough Devpt Corp 1976-78; Baroness-in-Waiting to HM The Queen 1978-79; hon fell: Newnham Coll Cambridge 1986, Anglia Higher Educn Coll 1989; *Recreations* swimming, theatre, reading; *Style—* The Rt Hon Lady David, JP; 50 Highsett, Cambridge CB2 1NZ (☎ 0223 350376); Cove, New Polzeath, nr Wadebridge, Cornwall (☎ 020 886 3310); House of Lords, London SW1 (☎ 071 219 3159)

DAVID, Hon Richard Sebastian David; s of Richard William David, CBE, and Baroness David, *qqv*; *b* 1940; *m* 1963, Eva Ross; *Career* FRCS; surgn, gen practitioner Fort Macleod Alberta 1975-; FRCS; *Style—* The Hon Richard David; Box 820, Fort Macleod, Alberta, Canada

DAVID, Richard William; CBE (1967); s of Rev FP David (d 1955), and Mary W David; *b* 28 Jan 1912; *Educ* Winchester Coll, CCC Cambridge (MA); *m* 1935, Nora (Baroness David, *qv*); 2 s, 2 da; *Career* publisher 1936-74; London mangr CUP 1948-63, sec to the Syndics 1963-70, univ publisher 1970-74; pres Botanical Soc of the Br Isles 1979-81; *Books* The Janus of Poets (1935), Love's Labour Lost (ed Arden Shakespeare edn 1951), Shakespeare in the Theatre (1978), Review of the Cornish Flora (co-author 1981), Sedges of the Br Isles (1982); *Clubs* Garrick; *Style—* Richard David, Esq, CBE; 50 Highsett, Cambridge CB2 1NZ (☎ 0223 350376)

DAVID, Lady; Sheila Jane Yorke; *née* Hardy; da of Maj Arthur Yorke Hardy (d 1951), and Agnes, *née* Green (d 1956); *b* 29 Aug 1914; *Educ* Challoners Sch, Courtauld Inst; *m* 1, 15 Oct 1953, Sir Percival Victor David Ezekiel David, 2 and last Bt (d 1964); m 2, 6 Oct 1968, Dr John Douglas Riddell (d 1976); has reverted to her former style of Lady David; *Career* curator and librarian Sir Percival David Collection of Chinese Art 1932-40, assisted with Int Exhibition of Chinese Art Burlington House 1935-36, involved with aircraft prodn of the De Haviland Mosquito 1940-41 (interned Shanghai 1941, exchanged 1942), curator Sir Percival David Fndn of Chinese Art 1950-59 (fndn estab 1950, opened to pub 1952); FRPSL; memb: RIIA, Oriental Ceramic Soc 1935; *Books* Precisely Dated Chinese Antiquities (1970); *Recreations* ballet, opera, music, international affairs; *Style—* Lady David

DAVID, Tudor; s of Thomas David (d 1941), of Barry, Wales, and Blodwen, *née* Jones (d 1988); *b* 25 April 1921; *Educ* Barry GS, Univ of Manchester (BA), Univ of Oxford; *m* 1, Jan 1943, Nancy (d 1984), da of Robert Ramsay (d 1948), of Crook, Co Durham; 1 s (Martyn b 1946), 1 da (Glenwyn b 1947); m 2, 21 Feb 1987, Margaret, da of Glyndwr Dix (d 1978), of Glynneath, Glamorgan; *Career* cmmnd tech branch RAF 1942, Staff Offr Flying Trg Cmd 1943-45, Sqdn Ldr Air HQ India 1945-46; extra mural lectr Univ of Newcastle 1946-48; local govt offr Lincolnshire 1949-53; asst ed Education 1953-74; ed: The Teacher 1974-79, Education 1979-86, Journal of Oil and Gas Accountancy 1986-; freelance journalist 1986-; memb Cncl Hon Soc of Cymmrodorion, memb Welsh Acad; FCP, FRSA; *Books* Perspectives in Geographical Education (1973), Education: The Wasted Years? (1988); *Recreations* opera, rugby; *Style—* Tudor David, Esq; 21 Pointers Close, Isle of Dogs, London E14 3AP (☎ 071 987 8631)

DAVID, Wayne; MEP (Lab) S Wales 1989-; s of David Haydn David, of Claren House, Cefn Rd, Cefn Cribwr, Bridgend, Mid Glam, and Edna Amelia, *née* Jones; *b* 1 July 1957; *Educ* Cynffig Comp Sch, Univ Coll Cardiff (BA, PGCE, further educn, Charles Morgan prize in welsh history), Univ Coll Swansea; *Career* teacher of history Brynteg Comp Sch 1983-85, tutor organiser Workers' Educn Assoc Mid Glamorgan 1985-89, treas Euro Parly Lab Party (formerly Br Lab Gp) 1989-; vice pres Cardiff Br UN Assoc; memb: Anti-Apartheid Movt, Nicaraguan Solidarity Campaign; *Recreations* music, reading; *Style—* Wayne David, Esq, MEP; Claren House, Cefn Rd, Cefn Cribwr, Bridgend, Mid-Glam CF32 0AE (☎ 0656 741142); South Wales Euro Office, 199 Newport Rd, Cardiff, South Glam (☎ 0222 490215, fax 0222 488758)

DAVID, William Nigel; s of Idris Thomas David, of 31 Somerset Rd, Barry, S Glamorgan, and Joan, *née* Morgan (d 1986); *b* 13 May 1951; *Educ* Kent Coll Canterbury, St Edmund Hall Oxford (MA); *m* 5 April 1975, Karen Susan, da of John Kenneth William Phipps; 1 s (Thomas Morgan b 1 Jan 1984), 1 da (Sarah Louise b 29 Jan 1982); *Career* Simon & Coates 1973-74, Touche Ross & Co 1975-80, Quotations Dept The Stock Exchange 1980-83, dir of corp fin Hoare Govett 1983; FCA 1981; *Recreations* cricket, golf, rugby, gardening, reading; *Clubs* Vincents (Oxford); *Style—* William David, Esq; Hoare Govett Corporate Finance, 4 Broadgate, London EC2M 7LE (☎ 071 374 1856, fax 071 374 1388)

DAVIDGE, Christopher Guy Vere; OBE (1982); s of (Cecil) Vere Davidge (d 1981), of Little Houghton, Northants, and his 1 w, (Ursula) Catherine (d 1948), yr da and co-heir of Christopher Smyth, JP, DL (d 1934); *see* Burke's Landed Gentry, 18 edn, vol II, 1969; *b* 5 Nov 1929; *Educ* Eton, Trinity Coll Oxford (MA); *m* 1 Feb 1963, Winifred Marian, da of John Stanley Crome; *Career* dir Mixconcrete (Holdings) plc 1964-82 (md 1964-69), chm various private cos 1960-; memb Cncl Lloyds 1982-, dir Lloyds of London Press Ltd 1985- (chm 1989-); High Sheriff of Northants 1988-89; rowed for GB 1952-63, steward Henley Royal Regatta 1967-, FISA medal of Honour 1973; chm Leander Club 1968-78, hon treas Cwlth Games Cncl 1969-74 (vice chm 1974-90, vice pres 1990 chef de mission GB team Olympic Games 1976, vice pres Br Olympic 1976- (vice chm 1972-76), pres Amateur Rowing Assoc 1977-85; chm of govrs and tstee: Maidwell Hall Sch Northampton 1979-, Three Shires Hosp Northampton 1981-; govr St Andrew's Hosp Northampton 1969-; memb Cncl FISA (chm Regattas Cmmn 1976-90); Freeman: City of London, Worshipful Co of Waterman; *Recreations* rowing, gardening, restoration of old houses; *Clubs* Leander, Vincents; *Style—* Christopher Davidge, Esq, OBE; Little Houghton House, Northampton (☎ 0604 890234)

DAVIDOVITZ, Robert Hyman Colin; BEM (1954); s of Lambert Samuel Davidson, and Rose-Marie Davidson; *b* 18 Aug 1930; *Educ* Tynecastle Secdy Sch Edinburgh; *m* 20 Sept 1958, Catherine, da of Archibald Callaghan; 2 s (Philip b 1961, Robert b 1964), 2 da (Judith b 1959, Theresa b 1963); *Career* RN: boy telegraphist 1946, telegraphist 1948, leading telegraphist (special) 1951, PO telegraphist (PROV) 1954; Assoc-Rediffusion telerecordist 1955, sr engr Scottish TV 1957; Southern TV: sr engr 1958, prodn mangr 1964, prodn controller 1975; West Midland studio controller ATV/Central 1981, dir ops TV AM 1987-; pres Catenians Southampton 1976; *Recreations* photography, painting, yachting; *Style—* Robert Davidovitz, Esq, BEM; 55 Kingsway, Chandlers Ford, Hants SO5 1FH (☎ 0703 251 342); TV-am Breakfast Television Centre, Hawley Crescent, Camden Town, London (☎ 071 267 4300, car 0836 262010)

DAVIDSON, Alan Ingram; s of late Joseph Davidson, of 642 Holburn St, Aberdeen, and late Jean, *née* Dunbar; *b* 25 March 1935; *Educ* Robert Gordon's Coll Aberdeen, Univ of Aberdeen (MB ChB, ChM); *m* 14 Oct 1967, Margaret Elizabeth, da of McKay Eric Robertson, of Caputh, 5A Darnaway Rd, Inverness, Scotland; 2 s (Ranald b Nov 1968, Lindsay b April 1970); *Career* Nat Serv Capt RAMC 1960-62; conslt surgn and hon sr lectr Aberdeen Royal Infirmary 1974; DObstRCOG 1963, FRCSEd 1968; *Recreations* gardening; *Clubs* University, Royal Northern; *Style—* Alan Davidson, Esq; Green Roofs, 20 Hillview Rd, Cults, Aberdeen, Scotland (☎ 0224 867347) Aberdeen Royal Infirmary, Foresterhill, Aberdeen, Scotland (☎ 0224 681818)

DAVIDSON, Andrew Scott Rutherford; s of Andrew Rutherford Davidson of Edinburgh (d 1967), and Jean, *née* McKenzie (d 1983); *b* 18 Nov 1929; *Educ* Merchiston Castle Sch, Edinburgh; *m* 2 Sept 1960, Dorothy Mowat Proudfoot, da of Dr Charles Crighton Robson, MC (d 1958); 1 s (Charles b 1966), 2 da (Katharine b 1962, Sarah b 1964); *Career* Capt the Royal Scots 1950; joined Bank of Scotland 1951, gen mangr (England) 1977-89; non-exec dir: The Br Linen Bank Ltd 1978-89, Kellock Ltd 1981-, The Canada Life Assurance Co of GB Ltd 1990-, Canada Life Unit Tst Mngrs Ltd 1990-, Bank of Scotland London Bd 1989-; chm Bankers Benevolent Fund 1980-89; memb The Lombard Assoc; Freeman City of London 1978; FIB (Scotland); *Recreations* golf, fishing, rugby, birdwatching; *Clubs* City of London, MCC, Walton Heath Golf; *Style—* Andrew Davidson, Esq; Dawes Mead, Leigh, Reigate, Surrey RH2 8NN (☎ 030678 281)

DAVIDSON, Anthony Beverley; s of Dr Ronald Beverley Davidson (d 1972), and Edna Robina Elizabeth, *née* Cowan; *b* 25 Dec 1947; *Educ* Morgan Acad Dundee, Univ of St Andrews (MA); *m* 21 Dec 1971, Avril Rose, da of John Pearson Duncan, of 10 Barnes Ave, Dundee; 2 s (Ronald John b 1975, Duncan Anthony b 1982), 2 da (Amanda Beverley b 1977, Laura Rose b 1979); *Career* CA 1974; mangr Deloitte Haskins & Sells (Edinburgh) 1970-75, sr mangr Whitelaw Wells & Co 1975-76, chief accountant Highways Dept Lothian Regnl Cncl 1976-77, chief inspr TSB (Tayside and Central Scotland) 1977-79, head Inspection Div TSB Gp 1979-82, gen mangr TSB (Tayside and Central Scotland) 1982-83, sr exec dir TSB Scotland plc 1987-90 (gen mangr 1983-87); dir Provincial Insurance plc 1990-, memb Co of Merchants of City of Edinburgh 1986; FCMA 1975, FIB (Scot) 1984; *Recreations* golf, photography, skiing; *Clubs* Gullane Golf, Wentworth and Windermere golf; *Style—* Anthony Davidson, Esq; The Whim, Victoria Rd, Windermere, Cumbria LA23 2DL (☎ 096 62 6271); Provincial Insurance plc, Stramongate, Kendal LA9 4BE (☎ 0539 740762, fax 0539 740762)

DAVIDSON, Arthur; QC (1978); *b* 7 Nov 1928; *Educ* Liverpool Coll, King George V Sch Southport, Trinity Cambridge; *Career* MP (Lab) Accrington 1966-83; principal oppn front bench spokesman Legal Affrs 1982-83 (dep oppn spokesman Legal Affrs 1981-82); PPS to Slr-Gen 1968-70, fought Blackpool S 1955, Preston N 1959, Parly Sec Law Offrs Dept 1974-79; memb Nat Exec of Fabian Soc; former: chm PLP Home Affrs Gp, memb Consumers' Assoc Cncl; Home Affrs Select Ctee 1980-; *Style—* Arthur Davidson Esq, QC; 11 South Sq, Gray's Inn, London WC1R 5EU

DAVIDSON, Hon Lord; Charles Kemp Davidson; s of Rev Donald Davidson, DD (d 1970), of Edinburgh, and Charlotte Davidson; *b* 13 April 1929; *Educ* Fettes, Univ of Oxford (MA), Univ of Edinburgh (LLB); *m* 1960, Mary, da of Charles Mactaggart, MC (d 1984), of Argyll; 1 s (Donald), 2 da (Caroline, Louise); *Career* Nat Serv 2 Lt Argyll Sutherland Highlanders 1953-55; Faculty of Advocates: admitted 1956, keeper Advocates Library 1972-76, vice dean 1979-83, dean 1977-79; QC (Scot) 1969; procurator to Gen Assembly of the Church of Scot 1972-83, senator of the Coll of Justice 1983-, dep chm Boundary Cmmn for Scot 1985, chm Scot Law Cmmn 1988-; FRSE; *Style—* The Hon Lord Davidson, FRSE; 22 Dublin Street, Edinburgh (☎ 031 556 2168)

DAVIDSON, Christopher William Sherwood (Bill); s of Thomas Leigh Davidson, of Iddesleigh, Queens Road, Ilkley, W Yorks, and Donaldine, *née* Brown (d 1982); *b* 29 July 1940; *Educ* Uppingham, Univ of Nottingham (BA); *Career* articles with R K Denby (later Sir Richard Denby) 1962-65, admitted slr 1966; asst slr: Winkworth & Pemberton Westminster 1966-67, Coward Chance 1968-70; ptnr Ashton Hill & Co Nottingham 1971-75, gp slr and co sec NUS Services Ltd 1975-77; co sec: Endsleigh Insurance Services Ltd 1968- (legal advsr 1966-), NUS Services Ltd 1984-; fndr (later sr ptnr) Christopher Davidson & Co 1977-; memb Law Soc; *Recreations* cooking and crime fiction; *Style—* Bill Davidson, Esq; The Old Rectory, Kemerton, Nr Tewkesbury, Gloucestershire GL20 7HY (☎ 0242 9689 244); 2/3 Oriel Terr, Oriel Rd, Cheltenham, Gloucestershire GL20 7HY (☎ 0242 581481, fax 0242 221 210)

DAVIDSON, Clare Louise; da of Dr Walter Eardley Freeling Davidson, (d 1984) and Viola Joan, *née* Howard of London; *b* 30 May 1943; *Educ* Ashford HS for Girls, LAMDA; *m* 1969 (m dis 1986), Viggo Richard Kihl, 1 s (Thomas Eardley b 1972), 1 da (Emily Broun b 1974); partner, Johann Valentyn Budding; *Career* freelance dir, acting and voice coach: LAMDA, privately, Riverside Studios, Morley Coll, The

Actors Centre; lectr: Guildhall, RADA; voice coach to: Sting, Lulu, Dudley Moore, Bob Hoskins; dialogue coach on numerous films incl: Chitty Chitty Bang Bang, Brimstone and Treacle, The Bride, Accident; fndr own acting studio 1990, currently dir Fndn Course British American Drama Acad (dean 1988-89), theatre dir 1973-; prodns incl: Up in Sweden (King's Head Theatre), The Maids (Dublin Festival and the Lyric Theatre Hammersmith), Happy Days (Belfast Festival and Warehouse Theatre London), Boesman and Lena (Field Day Theatre Co and Hampstead Theatre Club), Miss Julie (The Lyric Hammersmith then Duke of Yorks Theatre), Little Eyolf (The Lyric) 1985, Five Finger Exercise (Cambridge Theatre Company), Hedda Gabler (Rogeland Theatre Stavenger then Bloomsbury Theatre London) 1986, Peer Gynt (Cambridge Theatre Co) 1987, Atonement (Lyric Theatre Hammersmith) 1987, Alpha Beta (Man in the Moon Theatre) 1988, Shona (Pentameters) 1989, A Midsummer Night's Dream 1990, Hay Fever 1990; memb Equity 1963-, Directors Guild 1983- (fndr memb Cncl 1983-85); *Style*— Ms Clare Davidson

DAVIDSON, Duncan Lewis Watt; s of Lewis Davidson, CBE, DD (d 1981), and Jean Davidson; *b* 16 May 1940; *Educ* Knox Coll Jamaica, Univ of Edinburgh (BSc, MB ChB); *m* 22 July 1964, Anne Veronica McDougall, da of Dr Arthur Maiden, OBE, of Little Brooksby, Queens Terrace, St Andrews, Fife KY16 9ER; 4 s (Simon Lewis Tweedie b 9 July 1965, Mark Oliver Tweedie (twin) b 9 July 1965, (Julian) Anthony b 6 Feb 1967, Peter Duncan b 2 June 1970), 1 da (Kathleen Anne b 2 Jan 1978); *Career* various appts in med and neurology in Edinburgh and Montreal Canada 1966-76, conslt neurologist Tayside Health Bd and hon sr lectr in med Univ of Dundee 1976-; hon sec and treas Scottish Assoc for Neurological Sciences; FRCPE 1979; *Books* Neurological Therapeutics (with Jar Lenman, 1981); *Recreations* golf, gardening, photography; *Style*— Duncan Davidson, Esq; Brooksby, Queens Terrace, St Andrews, Fife KY16 9ER (☎ 0334 76108); Department of Neurology, Dundee Royal Infirmary, Dundee DD1 9ND (☎ 0382 23125)

DAVIDSON, Hon Mrs (Elizabeth Maud); *née* Younger; da of 2 Viscount Younger of Leckie (d 1946), and Maud (d 1957), er da of Sir John Gilmour, 1 Bt; *b* 22 May 1913; *m* 31 March 1937, Lt-Col Kenneth Bulstrode Lloyd Davidson, only s of late Col Charles John Lloyd Davidson, DSO, of The Manor House, Eglinton; 4 s, 1 da; *Style*— The Hon Mrs Davidson; The Manor House, Eglinton, Co Londonderry, N Ireland BT47 3AA (☎ 0504 810222)

DAVIDSON, Erick Stanley; s of Stanley Davidson, of East Allenby House, Horncliffe, Northumberland, and Agnes Sanderson Turnbull, *née* Mackay; *b* 10 Feb 1949; *Educ* Berwick-upon-Tweed GS, Hull Sch of Architecture, Newcastle Coll of Art (Business Studies and Design Dip); *m* 1977, Yvonne Jean Grace, da of Archibald Dickson (d 1981); 2 da (Carolyne b 1 May 1978, Linsey b 2 April 1982); *Career* mangr Marks & Spencer 1971-72, asst to md pubns RIBA 1972-74, business mangr The Jenkins Gp 1974-76, mktg dir Ads Graphics 1976-78, fndr chm and jt md The Tayburn Gp Ltd 1978-; memb Merchant Co of Edinburgh; MCSD; *Recreations* golf; *Clubs* Dun Whinny, Gleneagles, Dunbar; *Style*— Erick Davidson, Esq; Beech House, Dalrymple Crescent, Edinburgh EH9 2NX (☎ 031 667 7421); 15 Kittle Yards, Causewayside, Edinburgh EH9 1PJ (☎ 031 622 0662, fax 031 622 0606, car 0836 330614)

DAVIDSON, Judge Ian Thomas Rollo; QC (1977); s of Dr Robert Davidson (d 1970), and Margaret Miller Davidson (d 1980); *b* 3 Aug 1925; *Educ* Fettes, Corpus Christi Coll Oxford (BA); *m* 1, 1954, Gyöngyi (m dis 1982), da of Prof Csaba Anghi; 1 s (Stuart), 1 da (Amanda); m 2, 1984, Barbara Ann, da of Jack Watts; 1 s (Alasdair); *Career* War Serv RAC 1943-47, Lt Derbyshire Yeo; called to the Bar Gray's Inn 1955, asst lectr UCL 1959-60, dep rec Nottingham 1971, rec of the Crown Ct 1974, circuit judge 1984-; *Recreations* music, golf, photography; *Clubs* Forty, Notts Servs, Muswell Hill Golf, Notts Golf; *Style*— His Hon Judge Ian Davidson, QC; 15 Park Valley, The Park, Nottingham NG7 1BS (☎ 0602 470 672)

DAVIDSON, James Patton; CBE (1980); s of Richard Davidson (d 1971), and Elizabeth Ferguson, *née* Carnichan; *b* 23 March 1928; *Educ* Rutherglen Acad, Univ of Glasgow (BL); *m* 1, 1953, Jean Stevenson Ferguson, da of John B Anderson (d 1979); 2 s (Euan b 1958, Hamish b 1963); m 2, 1981, Esmé Evelyn, da of Robert Reuben Ancill, JP (d 1966); *Career* Lt RASC 1948-50; chm: Ardrossan Harbour Co 1976-83, Clydeport Stevedoring Services 1977-83, Rhu Marina 1976-80, Clydeport Authority 1980-83 (md 1966); dir Iron Trades Insurance Group 1981; chm: Nat Assoc of Port Employers 1974-79, Br Ports Assoc 1980-82, Pilotage Cmmn 1983-; FRSA, FCIT, CBIM; *Recreations* sailing, golf, reading, music, bridge; *Clubs* Oriental, Cambuslang Golf; *Style*— James Davidson, Esq, CBE; 44 Guthrie Court, Gleneagles, Perthshire PH3 1SD

DAVIDSON, Jim; *b* 1953; *Educ* St Andrew's Sch Charleton; *Career* popular entertainer, comedian; TV appearances incl: New Faces (debut ITV) 1976, What's On Next, The Jim Davidson Show (five series, TV Times award Funniest Man on TV 1980) 1979-, Up The Elephant And Round The Castle, Home James, Stand Up Jim Davidson, Jim Davidson Special 1984, Jim Davidson's Falkland Specials 1985, Jim Davidson In Germany 1986, Jim Davidson's Comedy Package 1987, Wednesday At Eight 1988, Telethon 1988; stage performances incl: Britannia Pier Great Yarmouth 1986 and 1989, Princess Theatre Torquay 1987, 1988 and 1990 Cardiff 1987, Cinderella (Apollo Oxford, Hippodrome Bristol, Alhambra Theatre Bradford) 1985, 1986 and 1989, Back on The Road Tour 1990; many cabaret and club engagements; videos incl The Un-Editied Jim Davidson Live; LPs incl: The Jim Davidson Album, A Dirty Weekend with Jim Davidson, Another Dirty Weekend; books incl: Too Risky, Too Frisky, Jim Davidson Gets Hooked; *Style*— Jim Davidson, Esq

DAVIDSON, 2 Viscount (UK 1937); John Andrew Davidson; s of 1 Viscount Davidson, GCVO, CH, CB, PC (d 1970), and Hon Dame Frances Davidson, DBE (Baroness Northchurch, d 1985); *b* 22 Dec 1928; *Educ* Westminster, Pembroke Coll Cambridge; *m* 1, 30 June 1956 (m dis 1974), Margaret Birgitta (who m 2, 1974, as his 2 w, 4 Viscount Colville of Culross), da of Maj-Gen Cyril Henry Norton, CB, CBE, DSO; 4 da (incl Hon Mrs Oldfield and Lady Edward Somerset, *qqv*); m 2, 1975, Pamela Joy Dobb, da of John Vergette; *Heir* bro, Hon Malcolm Davidson; *Career* served with Black Watch and 5 Bn KAR 1947-49; dir strutt & Parker (Farms) Ltd 1960-75; lord-in-waiting 1985-86; Capt Queen's Body Guard of the Yeomen of the Guard (dep chief whip in House of Lords) 1986-; memb: Cncl CLA 1965-75, RASE 1973-75; *Style*— The Rt Hon Viscount Davidson; House of Lords, London SW1A 9PW

DAVIDSON, Prof John Frank; s of John Davidson, and Katie Davidson; *b* 7 Feb 1926; *Educ* Heaton GS Newcastle, Trinity Coll Cambridge (BA, PhD, ScD); *m* 1948, Susanne Hedwig Ostberg; 1 s, 1 da; *Career* Mechanical Devpt Dept Rolls Royce Derby 1947-50 (apprentice 1947); Univ of Cambridge: res fell Trinity Coll 1949-53, res in Engrg Laboratory 1950-52, univ demonstrator in chemical engrg 1952-54, univ lectr 1954-75, fell and steward Trinity Coll 1957, prof of chemical engrg and head Dept of Chemical Engrg 1975-78, Shell prof of Chemical Engrg 1978-; visiting prof: Univ of Delaware 1960, Univ of Sydney 1967, MIT 1981, Univ of Delaware 1981 (also Oregon and Houston), Univ of Notre Dame Indiana 1988; visiting lectr Univs of Cape Town and Johannesburg 1964, Wilhelm lectr Princeton 1988; memb: Ct of Enquiry for Flixborough Disaster 1974-75, Advsy Ctee on Safety of Nuclear Instalations HSE 1977-87, Advsy Cncl for Applied Res and Devpt 1980 (memb Jt Working Pty on Biotechnology), Governing Body AFRC Inst of Engrg Res 1982, Advsy Bd AFRC Inst of Food Res 1986; foreign assoc US Nat Acad of Engrg 1976, fell Indian Nat Sci Acad 1990; FIChemE (pres 1970-71), MIMechE, fndr FEng 1976 (memb Acid Emmissions Ctee 1985), FRS 1974 (vice pres 1989); Hon DSc Univ of Aston 1989; Docteur Honoris Causa de l'Institut National Polytechnique de Toulouse 1979, Int Fluidization Award of Achievement (Engrg Fndn Conf Banff) 1989; *Books* Fluidization Particles (with D Harrison, 1963), Fluidization (1971, 2 edn with R Clift and D Harrison, 1985); *Recreations* hill walking, gardening, mending bicycles and other domestic artifacts; *Style*— Prof John Davidson; 5 Luard Close, Cambridge CB2 2PL (☎ 0223 246104); University of Cambridge, Dept of Chemical Engineering, Pembroke St, Cambridge CB2 3RA (☎ 0223 334799)

DAVIDSON, Dr John Knight; OBE (1990); s of John Rose Davidson (d 1973), of Edinburgh, and Edith Jane, *née* Good (d 1965); *b* 17 Aug 1925; *m* 25 June 1955, Edith Elizabeth, da of Archibald McKelvie (d 1963), of Edinburgh; 2 s (Alastair b 1958, Neil b 1959), 1 da (Fiona b 1956); *Career* conslt radiologist in admin charge Western Infirmary and Gartnavel Gen 1967-90, Nat Hyperbaric Centre Aberdeen 1990-; conslt: US Navy 1974-89, French Navy 1978, several diving cos; MRC Decompression Sickness Panel 1965-; cncl memb Med and Dental Def Union of Scotland 1971-; RCR: cncl memb 1971-74 and 1984-87, chm Examining Bd 1976-79, chm Standing Scot Ctee 1985-89, Scot Sub Ctee on Distinction Awards 1982-84; Rohan Williams prof Australasia 1977, Aggarwal Meml Oration India 1988; dep pres and memb BRCS Glasgow 1988-, med advsy gp BBC Scot 1988-; hon fell Royal Aust Coll Radiology 1979, RCR, BMA, BIR, FRCPEd, FRCPS; *Books* Aseptic Necrosis of Bone (1976), numerous radiology pubns; *Recreations* golf, bridge, painting, hill-walking, skiing; *Clubs* R&A, Glasgow Art, Pollok Golf; *Style*— Dr John Davidson, OBE; 31 Newlands Rd, Glasgow G43 2JG (☎ 041 632 3113); Lifewatch, 5/6 Park Terrace, Glasgow G3 6BY (☎ 041 332 8010)

DAVIDSON, Dr (William) Keith Davidson; CBE (1982); s of James Fisher Keith Davidson (d 1978), Bearsden, Glasgow, and Martha Anderson, *née* Milloy (d 1956); *b* 20 Nov 1926; *Educ* Coatbridge Secdy Sch, Univ of Glasgow; *m* 6 Feb 1952, Dr Mary Waddell Aitken, da of Dr George Jamieson (d 1967), Chryston; 1 s (Keith b 1954), 1 da (Mhairi b 1956); *Career* Med Offr 1 Bn RSF 1950, Maj 2 i/c 14 Field Ambulance 1950-51, Med OIC Holland and Belgium 1952; chm: Glasgow Local Med Ctee 1971-75, Scottish Gen Med Servs Ctee 1972-75-, dep chm Gen Med Servs Ctee (UK) 1975-79; memb: Scottish Med Practices Ctee 1968-80, Scottish Health Serv Policy Bd 1985-; chm Scottish Health Serv Planning Cncl 1984-; BMA: memb Cncl 1972-81, fell 1975, chm scottish Cncl 1978-81, vice pres 1983-; hon pres Glasgow Eastern Med Soc 1984-85, pres Scottish Midland and Western Med Soc 1985-86; JP (Glasgow) 1962, SBSTJ 1976; elder Church of Scotland 1956-, session clerk Stepps Parish Church 1983-; memb Bonnet Makers and Dyers Craft 1964; BMA 1949, DPA 1967, FRCGP 1980, RSM 1988; *Recreations* gardening, caravanning; *Clubs* RSAC; *Style*— Dr Keith Davidson, CBE; Dunvegan, Stepps, Glasgow G33 6DE (☎ 041 774 2103); 67 Gilbertfield Street, Ruchazie, Glasgow G33 3TU (☎ 041 774 5987, car 0035 240 221)

DAVIDSON, Malcolm Alexander; s of Robert Stanley Davidson (d 1987), and Hilda, *née* Capewell (d 1975); *b* 30 Nov 1933; *Educ* Prescot GS; *m* 31 July 1958, Patricia Edna, da of Raymond Parker Lenton (d 1982); 1 s (Alasdair Malcolm b 1965), 1 da (Fiona Sarah b 1967); *Career* Nat Serv Queen's Own Cameron Highlanders 1952-54; md Littlewoods Pools 1987-, dir The Littlewoods Orgn 1987-; *Recreations* shooting, golf, tennis, swimming, music; *Style*— Malcolm A Davidson, Esq; Littlewoods Pools, Walton Hall Ave, Liverpool L67 1AA (☎ 051 525 3677, 051 342 3920)

DAVIDSON, Hon Malcolm William Mackenzie; s of 1 Viscount Davidson; *b* 28 Aug 1934; *Educ* Westminster, Pembroke Coll Cambridge; *m* 1970, Mrs Evelyn Ann Carew Perfect, da of William Blackmore Storey; 1 s (Nicholas b 1971), 1 da (Sophie b 1973); *Clubs* White's, Pratt's, Bath & County, Puffins (Edinburgh); *Style*— The Hon Malcolm Davidson; Las Cuadras, Monte de la Torre, Los Barrios 11370, Prov de Cadiz, Spain (☎ and fax 9 56 630 234)

DAVIDSON, Dr Neil McDonald; s of John Mackinnon Davidson (d 1980), and Alice Mary Stewart, *née* McDonald; *b* 15 May 1940; *Educ* Merton Coll Oxford (MA, DM), St Thomas's Hosp London; *m* 31 Dec 1963, Jill Ann, da of Ernest Ripley; 3 s (Angus b 1966, Alastair b 1970, Calum b 1981), 1 da (Fiona b 1967); *Career* lectr then sr lectr in med Ahmadu Bello Univ Zaria Nigeria 1969-74, conslt physician Eastern Gen Hosp Edinburgh 1979-, hon sr lectr Univ of Edinburgh 1979- (lectr then sr lectr in med 1975-79), asst dir of studies in med Edinburgh Postgrad Bd for Med 1985-; author of papers on peri-partum cardiac failure, endocrinology and metabolism, tropical diseases; memb GMC 1989, FRCPE 1982, FRCP 1984; *Recreations* collecting antique maps, munro-bagging; *Style*— Dr Neil Davidson; 43 Blackford Rd, Grange, Edinburgh EH9 2DT (☎ 031 667 3960); Eastern General Hospital, Seafield St, Edinburgh EH6 7LN (☎ 031 554 4444)

DAVIDSON, (Charles) Peter Morton; s of Dr William Philip Morton Davidson (d 1978), of Northumberland, and Muriel Maud, *née* Alderson (d 1987); *b* 29 July 1938; *Educ* Harrow, Trinity Coll Dublin (MA, LLB); *m* 15 Sept 1966, Pamela Louise, da of Harry Campbell-Rose, of Natal; *Career* called to Bar Inner Temple 1963; contested (C) N Battersea Gen Election 1966, chm London Rent Assessment Panel 1973-84, pt/t immigration appeals adjudicator 1976-84; memb London Borough cncl: Wandsworth 1964-68, Merton 1968-71; met stipendiary magistrate 1984-; *Recreations* music, travel; *Style*— Peter Davidson, Esq; Camberwell Green Magistrates Court, 15 D'Eynsford Rd, London SE5 7UP

DAVIDSON, Richard John; s of Arthur Vincent Davidson, of Folkestone, Kent, and Mary Anne Rutter, *née* Douglas; *b* 2 Sept 1946; *Educ* Fettes, Worcester Coll Oxford (BA, MA); *m* 30 April 1977, Alison Elizabeth, *née* Wager; 2 s (Thomas Henry b June 1980, Peter John b Feb 1982); *Career* slr; Baker & McKenzie London: articled clerk 1968-70, slr 1970-72, assoc (Chicago) 1972-74, ptnr 1975-, memb Exec Ctee 1990; memb Law Soc; *Recreations* painting, sculpting; *Clubs* Arts, Dover St; *Style*— Richard Davidson, Esq; Baker & McKenzie, Aldwych House, Aldwych, London WC2B 4JP (☎ 071 242 6531)

DAVIDSON, Prof Robert; s of George Braid Davidson (d 1970), and Gertrude May, *née* Ward (d 1978); *b* 30 March 1927; *Educ* Bell Baxter Sch Cupar Fife, Univ of St Andrews (MA, BD); *m* 22 Aug 1952, Elizabeth May, *née* Robertson; 4 s (Robert Ward b 1953, Donald George b 1955, John Alexander b 1970, Scott b 1973), 3 da (Joyce Elizabeth b 1958, Olive May b 1962, Elizabeth May b 1966); *Career* lectr: biblical studies Univ of Aberdeen 1952-60, Hebrew and Old Testament Univ of St Andrews 1960-66, Old Testament Univ of Edinburgh 1966-72; prof of Old Testament language and literature Univ of Glasgow 1972-; (princ Trinity Coll 1982-, Kerr lectureship 1983); Edward Cadbury lectureship Univ of Birmingham 1988-89; DD Univ of Aberdeen 1985; FRSE 1989, Moderator of Gen Assembly of the Church of Scot 1990-; *Books* The Bible Speaks (1959), Pelican Guide to Modern Theology (vol 3, 1970), The Old Testament (1964), The Bible in Religious Education (1979), The Courage to Doubt (1983), Ecclesiastes and Song of Songs (1986); Commentaries: Genesis (1-11, 1973), Genesis (12-50, 1979), Jeremiah (1, 1983), Jeremiah (2, 1985), Wisdom and Worship (1990); *Recreations* music, gardening; *Style*— Prof Robert Davidson; 30 Dumgoyne Dr, Bearsden, Glasgow G61 (☎ 041 942 1810); Dept of Biblical Studies, Univ of Glasgow, G12 8QQ (☎ 041 339 8855 ext 4607)

DAVIDSON, Roderick Macdonald; JP (1976); s of Dr Stephen Moriarty Davidson, of Bristol, and Kathleen Flora, *née* Macdonald; *b* 2 Jan 1938; *Educ* Clifton, St John's Coll Cambridge; *m* 17 June 1961, Jane Margaret, da of Dr Basil Stanley Kent, of Kingsclere; 1 s (Michael b 1965), 2 da (Emma b 1963, Juliet b 1969); *Career* Nat Serv RM 1956-58, cmmnd 1957; dir Albert E Sharp & Co (stockbroker); Bristol City Cncllr 1969-74; memb Cncl: Clifton Coll, St Peters Hospice Bristol, Clifton Zoo; membership sec Antient of St Stephens Ringers Dolphin Canynges; tax cmmr 1978, High Sheriff of Avon 1981-82; memb: Int Stock Exchange, Worshipful Co of Curriers, The Securities Assoc; *Recreations* golf, fishing, music; *Clubs* MCC, Clifton, Thurlestone Golf; *Style—* Roderick Davidson, Esq, JP; Albert E Sharp & Co, Spectrum, Bond St, Bristol BSI 3DE (☎ 0272 260051)

DAVIDSON, Hon Mrs (Sheila Anne); yr da of 2 Baron Greenhill, MD, DPH (d 1989); *b* 1951; *m* 1979, Robert Davidson, of Edmonton; *Style—* The Hon Mrs Davidson; 10336 Villa Avenue, Edmonton, Alberta, Canada T5N 3T9

DAVIDSON, Air Vice-Marshal Rev Sinclair Melville; CBE (1968); s of James Stewart Davidson (d 1961), and Anne Sinclair, *née* Cowan (d 1938); *b* 1 Nov 1922; *Educ* Bousfield Sch Kensington, RAF Cranwell, RAF Tech Coll, Chichester Theol Coll; *m* 1944, Jean Irene, *née* Flay; 1 s (and 1 s decd); *Career* served WWII, RAF (despatches), psa 1956, air staff Air Miny 1957-60, JSSC 1960, Asst Cmdt RAF Locking 1963-64, chm Jt Signal Bd (Middle East) 1965, idc 1968, dir Signals (Air) MOD 1969-71, Air Offr Wales and Station Cdr RAF St Athan 1972-74, asst chief Def Staff (Signals) 1974-75; sec Inst of Electronic and Radio Engrs 1977-82; ordained 1982, priest i/c Parish of Holy Trinity High Hurstwood 1983-88; *Recreations* parish affairs, maintenance of home and garden; *Clubs* RAF; *Style—* Air Vice-Marshal Rev Sinclair Davidson, CBE; Trinity Cottage, High Hurstwood, Uckfield, East Sussex (☎ 0825 812151)

DAVIDSON DAVIS, Philomena Mary; da of Thomas Oliver Grant Davidson (d 1985), and Mary Bridget Bourke; *b* 24 March 1949; *Educ* Convent of Jesus & Mary Willesden London, Isleworth Poly, Hammersmith Coll of Art and Building (pre Dip in Art), City & Guilds of London Art Sch (Edward Stott travel scholarship, Dip in Sculpture), Royal Acad Schs London (RAS Dip in Sculpture, Gold Medal for Sculpture, Bronze medal for work from the figure); *m* 7 Dec 1974, Michael Frank Davis, s of Samuel Harold Davis; 2 da (Lucy Victoria b 3 June 1977, Ruth Alexandra b 18 Jan 1982); *Career* teacher of English as a foreign language and student of Japanese language arts and architecture Japan 1973-76; maintained small studio in London 1976-80, opened Bronze Foundry Milton Keynes 1980, work on prodns of Aliens and Little Shop of Horrors films at Pinewood Studios 1985-86, opened current studio Hanslope 1987; works incl: Flying Carpet ride, Dream Flight, High Flyer (life-size bronzes Queens Court Shopping Centre Milton Keynes), Mary and Boy Christ in high relief (St Augustine's RC Milton Keynes), Mary and Christ as a Baby (St Augustine's RC Milton Keynes); exhibitions: Royal Acad (Summer Show), Royal West of England Acad (Annual Show), Westminster City Gallery, Bircham Gallery, Moya Bucknall Fine Art Gallery Solihull, Anna Mei Chadwick Gallery London; chm Milton Keynes Craft Guild 1988-90; memb Soc of Women Artists 1987, first woman pres Royal Soc of Br Sculptors 1990 (assoc 1984, fell 1990), FRSA 1990; *Recreations* swimming, reading biographies; *Clubs* Arts; *Style—* Ms Philomena Davidson Davis; The Bronze Foundary, St James St, New Bradwell, Milton Keynes, Bucks (☎ 0908 315841)

DAVIDSON-HOUSTON, Maj Aubrey Claud; s of Lt-Col Wilfred Bennett Davidson-Houston, CMG (d 1960), and Annie Henrietta, *née* Hunt (d 1941); *b* 2 Feb 1906; *Educ* St Edward's Sch Oxford, RMC Sandhurst, Slade Sch of Fine Art; *m* 29 Sept 1938, Georgina (Nina) Louie Ethel (d 1961), da of Capt Harold Dobson (ka 1915); 1 da (Sarah (Madame Jacques Arragon) b 1941); *Career* served WWII Europe and post-war Germany, Maj, ret 1949; portrait painter 1952-; royal portraits include: HM The Queen (for RWF), The Duke of Edinburgh (for 8 King's Royal Irish Hussars, Duke of Edinburgh's RR, House of Lords, Oxford and Cambridge Univ Club), Queen Elizabeth the Queen Mother (for Black Watch of Canada), The Prince of Wales (twice for Royal Regt of Wales), Mary Princess Royal (for WRAC), Henry Duke of Gloucester (for Royal Inniskilling Fusiliers, Scots Gd Trinity House), Duchess of Kent (for Army Catering Corps); other portraits for regiments, city livery cos, Oxford and Cambridge Univs; *Recreations* painting; *Clubs* Buck's, MCC, Naval and Military; *Style—* Maj Aubrey Davidson-Houston; Hillview, 42 West End Lane, Esher, Surrey KT10 8LA (☎ 0372 464769); 4 Chelsea Studios, 412 Fulham Rd, London SW6 1EB (☎ 071 385 2569)

DAVIDSON KELLY, Charles (Norman); s of Frederick Nevil Davidson Kelly (d 1976), of Edinburgh, and Mary Lyon Campbell, *née* MacLeod; *b* 2 June 1945; *Educ* Edinburgh Acad, Univ of Oxford (BA), Univ of Edinburgh (LLB); *m* 2 Sept 1972, Annabella Daphne Pitt, da of Herbert Alasdair Pitt Graham, of the Bahamas; 1 s (John b 1977), 1 da (Suzanna b 1979); *Career* slr with Ivory & Sime Edinburgh, co sec Oil Exploration (Holdings) Ltd 1974-79, corp devpt dir LASMO plc 1986-; *Recreations* sheep breeding; *Clubs* Puffins; *Style—* Norman Davidson Kelly, Esq; Little Boarhunt, Liphook, Hants GU30 7EE; 100 Liverpool Street, London EC2M 2BB (☎ 071 943 4545)

DAVIE; *see*: Ferguson Davie

DAVIE, Alan; CBE (1972); *b* 28 Sept 1920; *Educ* Edinburgh Coll of Art (DA); *m* 1947, Janet Gaul, 1 da; *Career* painter, poet, musician, silversmith and jeweller; many one-man and mixed exhibitions world-wide 1946-, incl: London, Edinburgh, New York, Paris, Florida, Perth, Japan; work included: in Br Painting 1700-1960 Moscow, Br Painting and Sculpture 1960-70 Washington, Br Paintings 1974 Hayward Gallery, and 25 years of Br Art, RA London 1977; many works in public collections world-wide; external assessor Art Degrees 1967-; music concerts and broadcasts with Tony Oxley Sextet 1974-75; Gregory fell Leeds Univ; voted Best Foreign Painter, VII Bienal de Sao Paulo 1963, Saltire Award 1977; FRSA; *Books* Alan Davie (edited by Alan Bowness, Lund Humphries 1967); *Recreations* sailing, underwater swimming, music; *Style—* Alan Davie, Esq, CBE; Gamels Studio, Rush Green, Hertford

DAVIE, Belinda Mary; da of Wing Cdr Minden Vaughan Blake, DSO, DFC (d 1981) of Virginia Water, Surrey, and Mary Jessie Blake; *b* 18 June 1951; *Educ* St Margarets Sch Bushey Herts, Univ of Bristol (BSC), INSEAD Fontainebleu France (MBA); *m* 13 Sept 1986, Jonathan Richard Davie, s of Richard Davie of Wimbledon London; 1 da (Samantha Jane b 4 Jan 1991); *Career* with Hill Samuel Investment Management Ltd 1972-79, INSEAD France 1979-80, dir Mercury Asset Management plc 1988- (joined 1980); *Recreations* golf, tennis, skiing; *Clubs* Berkshire Golf, Royal Wimbledon Golf; *Style—* Mrs Belinda Davie

DAVIE, (Stephen) Rex; s of Sydney Charles Davie (d 1986); *b* 11 June 1933; *Educ* Ilfracombe GS; *m* Sept 1955, Christine; 1 s (Stephen Mark), 1 da (Ruth Nicola); *Career* exec offr Inland Revenue 1951, Office of Minister for Science 1962, NEDO 1967, Civil Serv Dept 1970, asst sec 1979, sr sec Security Cmmn 1979-89, under sec Cabinet Office 1989 (joined 1983); *Recreations* reading, motoring, gardening; *Style—* Rex Davie, Esq; Cabinet Office, Government Offices, Great George St, London SW1P 3AL (☎ 071 270 6030, fax 071 270 6136)

DAVIE, Prof Ronald; s of Thomas Edgar Davie (d 1956), and Gladys May, *née* Powell; *b* 25 Nov 1929; *Educ* King Edward VI GS Aston Birmingham, Univ of Reading (BA), Univ of Manchester (CertEd, Dip in Teaching the Deaf), Univ of Birmingham (Dip in Educnl Psychology), Univ of London (PhD); *m* 3 Aug 1957, Kathleen, da of William Wilkinson (d 1976); 1 s (Neil Adrian John b 1961), 1 da (Alison Catherine (Mrs Gray) b 1960); *Career* county educnl psychologist Isle of Wight 1961-64, co-dir Nat Child Devpt Study 1968-71, dep dir and dir of res Nat Children's Bureau 1972-73 (princ res offr 1965-68), prof of educnl psychology Univ Coll Cardiff 1974-81, dir Nat Children's Bureau 1982-90, consulting psychologist 1990-, visiting prof Oxford Poly 1991-; pres: Child Devpt Soc, Kent Paediatric and Child Health Soc; vice pres: Young Minds, Br Assoc for Early Childhood Educn; chm Nat Curriculum Cncl's Steering Ctee on Severe Learning Difficulties Project; memb: Nat Curriculum Cncl's Whole Curriculum and Curriculum Review Ctees, BBC/IBA Central Appeals Advsy Ctee 1973; FBPsS, hon memb BPA 1985; *Books* 11,000 Seven-Year-olds (1966), Living with Handicap (1970), From Birth To Seven (1972), Children Appearing Before Junvenile Courts (1977), Change in Secondary Schools (1985), Child Sexual Abuse: The Way Forward After Cleveland (1989); photography, antiques; *Style—* Prof Ronald Davie; 3 Grange Grove, Canonbury, London N1 2NP (☎ 071 226 3761)

DAVIE-THORNHILL, Capt Humphrey Bache Christopher; JP (1954), DL (Derbys 1981); Lord of the Manor of Stanton-in-Peak and patron of 2 livings; s of Lt-Col Bertie George Davie (d on active service 1917), by his w Flora Helen Frances, Lady of the Manor of Stanton-in-Peak (d 1958), only da and heiress of Maj Michael M'Creagh (who assumed by Royal Lic 1882, additional surname of and arms of Thornhill on the s of his wife to the Stanton-in-Peak estate); *b* 5 Feb 1905; *Educ* Eton, Trinity Hall Cambridge; *m* 12 Nov 1930, Anna Elizabeth (d 1976), da of Sir John Barlow, 1 Bt, JP (d 1932); 2 s, 1 da; *Career* served WWII 1939-45, RA Armaments Inspection Dept, Capt 1942; High Sheriff Derbys 1955; Freeman of Barnstaple; AIMechE; *Clubs* Naval & Military; *Style—* Capt Humphrey Davie-Thornhill, JP, DL; Stanton Hall, Matlock, Derbys (☎ 0629 636216)

DAVIES, Cdre Alan; s of Maj David Robert Davies, MBE, RA (d 1973), of Northumberland, and Olive, *née* English; *b* 23 Feb 1922; *Educ* Dame Allens Sch Newcastle upon Tyne, Sir John Cass Coll London; *m* 14 Dec 1948, (Mary) Joyce, da of Ernest Bowes (d 1979), of Consett; 2 s ((Alan) Martin b 28 May 1950, Richard Michael b 17 Aug 1953), 1 da (Alison Joyce b 4 Sept 1951); *Career* Br Tanker Co: apprentice 1937, Cdr 1951, Cdre 1973, ret 1978; churchwarden St Barts Whittingham, lay reader, sec Cons Assoc branch; Royal Inst Navigation (life memb); *Recreations* gardening, winemaking; *Style—* Cdre Alan Davies; Lime Trees Cottage, Whittingham, Alnwick, Northumberland NE66 4RA (☎ 066 574 615)

DAVIES, Air Marshal Sir Alan Cyril; KCB (1979, CB 1974), CBE (1967); s of Richard Davies, of Maidstone; *b* 31 March 1924; *m* 1949, Julia Elizabeth Ghislaine, da of James Russell, of Forres; 2 s (and 1 s decd); *Career* joined RAF 1941, cmmnd 1943, cmd Jt Anti-Submarine Sch Flight 1952-54, cmd Air Sea Warfare Devpt Unit 1958-59, Cmd No 201 Sqdn 1959-61, Air Warfare Coll 1962, dep dir Operational Requirements MOD 1964-66, cmd RAF Stradishall Suffolk 1967-68, dir Air Plans MOD 1969-72, asst Chief of Air Staff MOD 1972-74, dep COS HQ Allied Air Forces Central Europe 1974-77, dep C-in-C RAF Strike Command 1977, dir Int Mil Staff NATO Brussels 1978-81, head RAF Support Area Economy Review Team 1981-83; co-ordinator Anglo/American Rels MOD 1984; *Clubs* RAF; *Style—* Air Marshal Sir Alan Davies, KCB, CBE; c/o Lloyds Bank Limited, PO Box 1190, 7 Pall Mall, London SW1Y 5NA

DAVIES, Alun Grier; CBE (1980); s of Thomas Davies (d 1957), of Beth-Horon, Penygroes, Llanelli, and Sarah Ann, *née* Edwards (d 1978); *b* 16 Sept 1914; *Educ* Amman Valley GS, UCW Aberystwyth (BA); *m* 29 June 1940, Claudia Eleanor, da of John Evans (d 1948), of Penygraig, Aberdyfi, Gwynedd; 1 s (Gareth); *Career* called to the Bar Gray's Inn 1945, HM inspr of taxes Inland Revenue 1936-47, taxation controller Consolidated Zinc Corp 1947-65, exec dir RTZ Corp plc 1965-79, int conslt 1979-87; memb Audit Ctee UCW 1990- (memb Ct 1973 and 1980-, hon treas 1980), memb of Central Fin Bd Methodist Church 1960-88; pres: Christian Assoc of Business Execs 1977-82, Int Fiscal Assoc 1979-83; cncl memb: IOD 1966-84, CBI 1970-73; chm of Tax Ctees: IOD 1965-78, CBI 1970-73; Freeman City of London 1975, Liveryman Worshipful Co of Loriners 1975; FInstD, FTII; *Books* Man the World Over (1947), Render unto Caesar (1966); *Recreations* wine tasting, freelance journalism; *Clubs* Caledonian, RAC; *Style—* Alun Davies, Esq, CBE; 7 Craigleith, Grove Rd, Beaconsfield HP8 1PT (☎ 0494 671 601); The Toft, Aberdovey, Gwynedd, Wales

DAVIES, Sir Alun Talfan; QC (1961); s of Rev William Talfan Davies, of Gorseinon, Swansea; *b* 22 July 1913; *Educ* Gowerton GS, University Coll of Wales Aberystwyth (LLB), Gonville and Caius Coll Cambridge (MA, LLB); *m* 1942, Eiluned Christopher, da of Humphrey R Williams, of Stanmore Middx; 1 s, 3 da; *Career* called to the Bar Gray's Inn 1939, bencher 1969; recorder of: Merthyr Tydfl 1963-68, Swansea 1968-69, Cardiff 1969-71; a recorder of the Crown Court 1972-86, hon recorder of Cardiff 1972-86, judge of Court of Appeal Jersey and Guernsey 1969-83; memb Criminal Injuries Compensation Bd 1976-85; pres: Royal Nat Eisteddfod of Wales 1979-82, Ct Welsh Nat Opera 1978-1981, Welsh Centre of Int Affrs 1986-90; chm Bank of Wales 1991- (dep chm 1973-91, dir 1971-73); former vice chm HTV (Gp) Ltd and chm Welsh Bd, chm Tstees Aberfan Fund; hon prof fell UCW Aberystwyth 1971; Hon LLD UCW (Aberystwyth) 1973, pres Welsh Centre of Int Affrs; kt 1976; *Style—* Sir Alun Davies, QC; 10 Park Rd, Penarth, S Glam (☎ 0222 701341)

DAVIES, Prof Alwyn George; s of Rev John Lewis Davies (d 1986), of Hunstanton, Norfolk, and Victoria May, *née* Rowe; *b* 1926; *Educ* Hamonds GS Swaffham Norfolk, (BSc, PhD, DSc); *m* 11 Aug 1956, Margaret, da of Geoffrey Drake (d 1980), of Menai Bridge, Anglesey; 1 s (Stephen b 1960), 1 da (Sarah b 1958); *Career* lectr Battersea Poly 1949, prof chemistry UCL 1969 (lectr 1953, reader 1964); FRSC, FRS 1989; *Books* Organic Peroxides (1961); *Style—* Prof Alwyn Davies, FRS; 26 South Approach, Moor Park, Northwood, Middx HA6 2ET (☎ 09274 23528); Chemistry Dept UCL, 20 Gordon St, London WC1H 0AJ (☎ 071 387 7050, fax 071 380 7463, telex 28722 UCPHYS G)

DAVIES, Rear Adm Anthony; CB (1964), CVO (1972); s of James Arthur Davies (d 1939), and Margaret Davies (d 1971); *b* 13 June 1912; *Educ* RNC Dartmouth, Open Univ (BA); *m* 1940, Lilian Hilda Margaret (d 1980), da of Sir Harold Martin Burrough, GCB, KBE, DSO (d 1977); 2 s, 2 da; *Career* joined RN 1926, dep dir RN Staff Coll 1956-57, Far East Fleet Staff 1957-59, dep dir Naval Intelligence 1959-62, head Br Def Liaison Staff Canberra Australia 1963-65; warden St George's House Windsor Castle 1966-72; *Style—* Rear Adm Anthony Davies, CB, CVO; 11A South St, Aldbourne, Marlborough, Wilts (☎ 0672 40418)

DAVIES, Capt Anthony John (Taff); s of Albert Joseph Davies, of Princes Street, Metherington, Lincolnshire, and Gladys, *née* Blackbourn; *b* 29 Oct 1936; *Educ* The Minster Sch Southwell; RN Colls: Dartmouth, Manadon, Greenwich; *m* 12 Sept 1959, Mary Josephine, da of Leonard John Crook (d 1983), of Paignton, Devon; 2 s (Timothy John Peter b 1964, Roderick James Lindsay b 1967); *Career* RN: joined 1953, Cdr 1972, Capt 1979, fleet weapon engr offr 1981-83, RCDS 1984, dir ship refitting policy MOD(N) 1985-87, Capt HMS Collingwood 1987-88; md Davies Consultancy Ltd 1989-, dir Applied Systems Consultants Ltd 1989-; memb: Royal Utd Servs Inst, US Naval Inst, MENSA; CEng, FIMarE 1977, FIEE 1980, FBIM 1985, EurIng, FEANI 1990;

Recreations climbing, sailing, golf; *Clubs* RN Sailing Assoc, West Wittering Sailing, Batti-Wallah's Soc, RN Royal Marines Mountaineering; *Style—* Capt Taff Davies, RN; North House, Chapel Lane, West Wittering, Chichester, West Sussex PO20 8QG (☎ 0243 513414, fax 0243 511373, car 0831 491166)

DAVIES, Ashwynne; s of David Iwan Davies (d 1951), of Conwil, Dyfed, and Margaretta, *née* Jones (d 1982); *b* 16 June 1931; *Educ* Queen Elizabeth GS Carmarthen, Cardiff Coll Univ of Wales (BSc); *m* 1 Jan 1955, Valmai, da of William Jones (d 1970), of Tan-y-Gored, Cwmgiedd, Ystradgynlais, Brecknochshire; 1 s (Stephen), 1 da (Bethan); *Career* ptnr CDC Braine and Partners 1968-74, fndr ptnr Freeman Fox Braine and Partners 1974-84, chm Freeman Fox Wales Ltd 1985-86 (md 1984-86), dir Freeman Fox Ltd 1984-86, md Acer Freeman Fox Wales Ltd 1986-; memb Bethany Church Rhiwbina Cardiff; CEng, FICE 1974, FIWEM 1987, MConsE 1974; *Style—* Ashwynne Davies, Esq; 77 Heol Briwnant, Rhiwbina, Cardiff CF4 6QH (☎ 0222 620583); Acer Wales, Shand House, 2 Fitzalan Place, Cardiff CF2 1ED (☎ 0222 488887)

DAVIES, Barbara; da of Mr W Jennings, of 35 Hyperion Rd, Stourton, Stourbridge, W Midlands, and Ruby Annie Jennings; *b* 22 June 1947; *Educ* Haden Hill Sch Old Hill, Dudley Girls HS; *m* 2 Aug 1968, John Herbert Simeon, s of Mr A C Davies (d 1967); 2 s (Chris b 1970, Mike b 1973); *Career* dir and co sec: BSC (Contracts) Ltd, Bloomfield Steel Construction Co Ltd; *Recreations* golf, skiing; *Clubs* Enville GC; *Style—* Mrs Barbara Davies; Bloomfield Rd, Tipton, West Midlands DY4 9HB

DAVIES, Dr Bethan; da of Ben Davies (d 1980), of Gravesend, Kent, and Enid, *née* Thickens (d 1974); *b* 15 Sept 1927; *Educ* GS for Girls Gravesend, UCL W London Hosp Med Sch (MRCS, LRCP), Univ of Manchester (MEd); *m* 1, 8 April 1950 (m dis 1965), Ralph Schwiller, s of Isidore Schwiller (d 1956), of London; 1 s (John b 28 Oct 1953); m 2, 6 Sept 1986, Prof (Henry John) Valentine Tyrrell; *Career* CMO and SC MO Southampton 1960-72, conslt in audiological med Charing Cross Hosp 1974-; pres W London branch NDCS, jt pres BACDA; memb: BSA, BAAP; *Recreations* book collecting (antiquarian children's); *Style—* Dr Bethan Davies; Fair Oaks, Coombe Hill Rd, Kingston on Thames, Surrey KT2 7DU (☎ 081 949 6623); Charing Cross Hospital, Fulham Palace Rd, London W6 (☎ 081 846 1020)

DAVIES, Betty Alicia; JP (Nottingham 1971); da of Charles William Pearl (d 1975), of Nottingham, and Alice, *née* Stevenson; *b* 13 April 1934; *Educ* Haywood Sch Nottingham, London Guildhall Sch of Music and Drama; *m* 3 April 1954, Barry Douglass Davies, s of Cecil Vivien Davies (d 1972), of Bidston, Cheshire; *Career* fashion and textile designer; chm and md Campus Clothes Ltd 1966-89, chm and design dir Betty Davies Acad Collection 1987-, princ Betty Davies Fashion International 1990, chm Hebridean Trading Co Ltd 1990; memb Ct Univ of Nottingham, public memb Press Cncl 1983-, memb Bd of Govrs Nottingham Girls HS 1987-, govr Edinburgh Coll of Art 1989-, chm Nottingham Cncl for Voluntary Serv 1981-84; MBIM 1982; *Recreations* musical, theatrical, collects paintings of contemporary woman artists, seal watching; *Style—* Mrs Betty Davies, JP; Baileys's Garden, Nottingham NG3 5BW (☎ 0602 621555/604412); 27 Royal Mile Mansions, Edinburgh EH1 1QN (☎ 031 225 6065, fax 0602 506 023)

DAVIES, Air Vice-Marshal (David) Brian Arthur Llewelyn; Honorary Physician To Her Majesty The Queen; s of Cyril Graham Vincent Davies (d 1978), of Dyfed, and Iris Ann Thomas; *b* 4 Feb 1932; *Educ* UCL, Univ Coll Hosp Med Sch (BSc, MB BS); *m* 24 May 1958, Jean Mary, da of Edwin Rupert Goaté (d 1978), of Beccles, Suffolk; 2 s (Christopher b 1959, Nicholas b 1961); *Career* dep dir med personnel Miny of Def 1980-82, OC RAF(H) Wegberg W Germany 1982-85, cmdt Central Med Estab 1985-87, dep PMO Strike Cmd 1987-89, PMO RAF Support Cmd 1989-; memb: BMA, Faculty of Pub Health Med; MFOM; *Recreations* skiing, gardening, travel; *Clubs* RAF; *Style—* Air Vice-Marshal Brian Davies; Principal Medical Officer, Headquarters, Royal Air Force Support Command, Brampton, Huntingdon, Cambridgeshire

DAVIES, Prof (John) Brian; s of John Kendrick Davies (d 1966), and Agnes Ada Davies (d 1971); *b* 2 May 1932; *Educ* Univ of Cambridge (MA), Univ of London (MSc, PhD, DSc); *m* 11 Aug 1956, Shirley June, da of Frederick Ralph Abrahart; 1 s (Jeremy b 1960), 2 da (Fiona b 1961, Nicola b 1970); *Career* res scientist Mullard Res Laboratories 1955-63; Univ of Sheffield: lectr 1963-67, sr lectr 1967-70, reader 1970-85, prof 1985-; dean of engrg UCL 1989-91; FIEE 1982, FEng 1988; *Books* Electromagnetic Theory (vol 2, 1972); *Recreations* cross country skiing, music, mountaineering; *Style—* Prof Brian Davies; 14 Gaveston Dr, Berkhamsted, Herts HP4 1JE (☎ 0442 864954); Dept of Electrical Engrg, Univ Coll, Torrington Place, London WC1E 7JE (☎ 071 387 7050, fax 071 387 4350, telex 296273)

DAVIES, (James) Brian Meredith; s of late Dr G Meredith Davies, and Caroline Meredith Davies; *b* 27 Jan 1920; *Educ* Bedford Sch, Med Sch St Mary's Hosp Univ of London (MD, DPH); *m* 1944, Charlotte, *née* Pillar; 3 s; *Career* hon lectr in (preventive) paediatrics Univ of Liverpool 1964-84; dir Social Services City of Liverpool 1971-82; FFPHM; *Books* Community Health Preventive Medicine and Social Services (5 ed 1983), Community Health and Social Services (5 ed 1991), The Disabled Child and Adult (1982); *Recreations* skiing, fishing, golf; *Style—* Brian Meredith Davies, Esq; Tree Tops, Church Rd, Thornton Hough, Wirral, Merseyside (☎ 051 336 3435)

DAVIES, Bryan; s of George William Davies (d 1989), and Beryl Davies; *b* 9 Nov 1939; *Educ* Redditch Co HS, UCL (BA), Inst of Educn, LSE (BSc); *m* 1963, Monica Rosemary Mildred, da of Jack Shearing (d 1980); 2 s (Roderick Gareth b 1964, Gordon Huw b 1966), 1 da (Amanda Jane b 1969); *Career* teacher Latymer Sch 1962-65, lectr Middx Poly 1965-74, MP (Lab) Enfield North 1974-79; sec Parly Lab Pty 1970-; PPS: to Dep PM 1975-76, Educn 1976, Treasy 1977; memb: Select Ctee on Overseas Devpt 1975-78, Select Ctee on Pub Expenditure 1975-78, Med Res Cncl 1977-79; govt whip 1979; *Recreations* literature, sport; *Style—* Bryan Davies, Esq; House of Commons, Westminster SW1 (☎ 071 219 4266)

DAVIES, Christopher Henry; s of William Henry Davies (d 1976); *b* 6 Nov 1939; *Educ* Wolverhampton GS, Univ of Durham (BA); *m* 1968, Elisabeth, da of Leo Thalmann (d 1947); 2 children; *Career* md Forbo-Nairn Ltd 1983-87, chief exec Sea Fish Indust Authy 1988-; *Style—* Christopher Davies, Esq; 7 West Carnethy Ave, Colinton, Edinburgh EH13 0ED; Nairn Floors Ltd, PO Box 1, Kirkcaldy KY1 2SB (☎ 0592 261111); Sea Fish Indust Authy, 10 Young St, Edinburgh EH2 4JQ (☎ 031 225 2515)

DAVIES, Cyril James; CBE, DL; s of James Davies (d 1967), of Newcastle-upon-Tyne, and Frances Charlotte, *née* Baker (d 1960); *b* 24 Aug 1923; *Educ* Heaton GS Newcastle-upon-Tyne; *m* Elizabeth Hay Leggett, da of James William Hay (d 1954), of Newcastle; 2 s (Nigel b 1950, Chistopher b 1954), 2 da (Elizabeth b 1952, Julia b 1958); *Career* WWII Lt (A) RNVR Fleet Air RN 1942-46; city treas: Newcastle upon Tyne 1969-74, Tyne and Wear 1974-80; chief exec Newcastle-upon-Tyne 1980-86; memb Newcastle Univ Cncl; dir: N Housing Assoc, Theatre Royal Tst, Tyne Theatre Tst, Northern Art; tstee: William Leech Charity, Rothley Charity, Newcastle Cathedral Tst; *Recreations* gardening, music, theatre, walking; *Clubs* Naval; *Style—* Cyril Davies, Esq, CBE, DL; 36 Lindisfarne Close, Jesmond, Newcastle-upon-Tyne NE2 2HT (☎ 091 281 5402)

DAVIES, David; s of David Sydney Davies, of Crickhowell, Powys, and Annie Elizabeth, *née* Wlliams; *b* 8 March 1936; *Educ* The GS for Boys Brecon, Univ of Wales Coll of Cardiff (BA); *m* 7 Aug 1962, Ann Meylek, da of Alfred maylek Griffiths; 1 s (Justin Alexander b 12 May 1970), 1 da (Juliet Susannah Elizabeth b 22 Aug 1972); *Career* articled clerk Alban & Lamb Chartered Accountant Cardiff 1959-62, audit sr Fryer White Hill London 1962-63, qualified CA 1963, accountant Coopers & Lybrand London and Rotterdam 1963-65, ptnr Alban & Lamb 1966-78 (joined 1965); Spicer & Pegler: assoc responsible for audit devpt 1972-78, memb and audit rep 1978-86, ptnr i/c insolvency practice 1980-90; ptnr Touche Ross 1990- (following merger); memb: Dist Soc ICAEW 1970-72, Fin Ctee Prince of Wales Tst 1980, Cncl All Saints Church Penarth 1984-86; dir: Borough of Taff Ely Enterprise Agency 1988-90, People Versus Severely Handicapped 1987-89; FCA (ACA 1963), Licenced Insolvency Practitioner; *Recreations* now involved in sport as spectator, church work, bridge; *Clubs* Cardiff & County Glamorgan CCC (vice president), Cardiff RFC; *Style—* David Davies, Esq; High Cliff, 157 Plymouth Rd, Penarth, South Glamorgan, Wales CF6 2DG (☎ 0222 711838); Touche Ross, Chartered Accountants, Blenheim House, Newport Rd, Cardiff (☎ 0222 48111)

DAVIES, David Cyril; s of D T Davies, and Mrs G Davies, JP; *b* 7 Oct 1925; *Educ* Lewis Sch Pengam, UCW Aberystwyth (LLB); *m* 1952, Joan Rogers; 2 children; *Career* headmaster: Greenway Sch Bristol 1964-67, Woodberry Down Sch ILEA 1967-71, Crown Woods Sch 1971-84; pres Inverliever Tst 1971-84; *Style—* David Davies, Esq; 9 Plaxtol Close, Bromley, Kent (☎ 081 464 4187)

DAVIES, Hon David Daniel; yr s of Baron Davies of Penrhys (Life Peer), *qv*; *b* 1944; *m* 1969, Cheryl, da of Thomas Herbert, of Tylorstown, Rhondda; 1 s; *Style—* The Hon David Davies

DAVIES, 3 Baron (UK 1932), of Llandinam, Co Montgomery; David Davies; s of 2 Baron Davies (ka 1944), by his w, Ruth Eldrydd (d 1966), da of Maj W M Dugdale, CB, DSO, of Glanyrafon Hall, Llanyblodwell, Shropshire; *b* 2 Oct 1940; *Educ* Eton, King's Coll Cambridge; *m* 1972, Beryl, da of W J Oliver; 2 s (Hon David Daniel, Hon Benjamin Michael Graham b 7 July 1985), 2 da (Hon Eldrydd Jane b 1973, Hon Lucy b 1978); *Heir* s, Hon David Daniel Davies b 23 Oct 1975; *Career* chm Welsh National Opera Co 1975-; CEng, MICE; *Style—* The Rt Hon the Lord Davies; Plas Dinam, Llandinam, Powys

DAVIES, Dr David Denison; s of Samuel Davies (d 1958), and Ethel Mary, *née* Dennison (d 1980); *Educ* Salt GS, Univ of Leeds (MRCS, LRCP), Univ of London (PhD); *m* 26 Feb 1977, Kay; 1 s (Edward b 1978), 1 da (Philippa b 1980); *Career* conslt anaesthetics Central Middx Hosp London 1970-, res fell Anaesthetics Res Dept RCS London (1967-70); FFARCS; memb: Anaesthetic Res Soc, Pain Soc; fell RSM; numerous publications on gas chromatography, pharmacokinetics of anaesthetic agents, morbidity and mortality in anaesthesia and pain therapy; *Books* Gas Chromatography in Anaesthesia: Thesis (1975); *Recreations* history, painting; *Style—* Dr David Denison Davies; 10 Beaufort Place, Bray, Maidenhead, Berks SL6 2BS (☎ 0628 71003); Dept of Anaesthetics, Central Middx Hosp, Acton Lane, London NW10 (☎ 081 965 5733); 144 Harley St, London W1N 1AF (☎ 071 935 0023)

DAVIES, David Evan Naunton; CBE (1986); s of David Evan Davies (d 1935), and Sarah, *née* Samuel (d 1982); *b* 28 Oct 1935; *Educ* West Monmouth Sch, Univ of Birmingham (MSc, PhD, DSc); *m* 21 July 1962, Enid (d 1990), da of James Edwin Patilla; 2 s (Christopher James b 1965, Michael Evan b 1967); *Career* lectr and sr lectr Univ of Birmingham 1961-67, hon sr princ sci offr Royal Radar Estab Malvern 1966-67, asst dir Res Dept BR Derby 1967-71, vice provost UCL 1986-88 (prof of electrical engrg 1971-86), vice-chllr Univ of Loughborough 1988-; Rank Prize for Optoelectronics 1984, Callendar Medal (Inst Measurement and Control) 1984, Centenial Medal (Inst of Electrical and Electronic Engrs USA) 1984, Faraday Medal (IEE) 1987; memb and chm of numerous ctees of: MOD, DES, Cabinet Office; FIEE 1967, FEng, FRS 1984; author of over 150 publications mainly concerned with radar and fibre optics; *Style—* Prof David Davies, CBE; Tall Trees, The Ridgeway, Rothley, Leicestershire LE7 7LE; 5 Prince Regent Mews, Netley St, London NW1; Vice Chancellor, Univ of Loughborough, Loughborough, Leicestershire (☎ 0509 222 000, fax 0509 610 723)

DAVIES, Sir David Henry; s of David Henry Davies; *b* 2 Dec 1909; *Educ* Brierley Hill Sch Ebbw Vale; *m* 1934, Elsie May, da of Joseph Battrick; 1 s, 1 da (and 1 da decd); *Career* gen sec Steel Trades Confedn 1967-75 (asst gen sec 1953-66); hon sec Br Section Int Metalworkers Fedn 1960-, hon treas Br Lab Party 1965-67 (chm 1963), vice chm Nat Dock Labour Bd 1966-68, chm Euro Coal and Steel Community Consultative Ctee 1973; memb: Gen Cncl TUC 1967-75, English Industl Estates Corp 1971-75, Industl Arbitration Bd 1974; first chm Welsh Devpt Agency 1976-79; kt 1973; *Style—* Sir David Davies; 82 New House Park, St Albans, Herts (☎ 0727 56513)

DAVIES, David Levric; CB (1982), OBE (1962); s of Benjamin Davies (d 1955), and Elizabeth, *née* Jones (d 1985); *b* 11 May 1925; *Educ* Llanrwst GS, Univ of Wales Aberystwyth (LLB); *m* 1955, Beryl Justine, da of Charles Clifton Newman, of Dorset; *Career* Sub Lt RNVR served in France, Belgium, Holland, Iceland 1943-46; called to the Bar Middle Temple 1949, colonial legal serv 1950-64: Aden 1950-56 (crown counsel), Tanganyika 1956-64, asst to Law Offrs 1956, Parly draftsman 1958, slr gen 1961; Home Civil Serv 1964-82: sr legal asst Parly Counsel Office 1964-72, seconded Jamaica as sr Parly counsel 1965-69, seconded Seychelles as attorney gen 1970-72; under sec (legal) head of Advsy Div HM Treasy Slrs Office 1977- (asst treasy slr 1973-77); *Style—* David Davies, Esq, CB, OBE; Greystones, Breach Lane, Shaftesbury, Dorset (☎ 0747 51224)

DAVIES, David Michael (Dai); *b* 10 June 1947; *Educ* Monmouth GS London, Bartholomew's Hosp (MB BS, MRCS, LRCP, cert for higher educn surgical trg in plastic surgery); *m* 3 c; *Career* conslt plastic surgn; house physician Bart's London 1971; sr house offr Birmingham Accident Hosp 1972; lectr Dept of Anatomy Bart's Med Sch 1973; sr house offr Bart's 1973-74; registrar gen surgery and orthopaedics St Albans City Hosp 1974-76; plastic surgery Queen Victoria Hosp East Grinstead 1976-78 (Burns res fell hon sr registrar 1976-77); registrar NE Thames Regnl Plastic Surgery Unit St Andrew's Hosp Billericay 1978-79; sr registrar Dept of Plastic Surgery Frenchay Hosp Bristol 1979-81, overseas visiting fell in microsurgery Royal Melbourne Hosp 1979-81; conslt plastic surgn: W Middx Univ Hosp Isleworth 1981-88, Hammersmith Hosp 1981- (also hon sr lectr), St Mary's Hosp 1987-, Charing Cross Hosp Fulham 1988- (also hon sr lectr); teacher Univ of London 1985-; sec: Plastic Surgical Section RSM 1985-86, NW Thames Advsy Ctee on Plastic Surgery 1988-; ed plastic surgery section of Surgery jl 1987-; FRCS 1975, FRS; memb: BMA, Br Assoc of Plastic Surgns, Br Assoc of Aesthetic Plastic Surgns (memb Cncl 1988-90, archivist 1989), Br Microsurgical Soc (sec 1984), Assoc of Head & Neck Oncologists of GB, Joseph Soc (Euro Acad of Facial Surgery); Thackray scholar in microvascular surgery (Br Assoc of Plastic Surgns) 1978; *Books* ABC of Plastic Surgery (1985); author of numerous papers in Br Jl of Surgery, Br Med Jl and Br Jl of Plastic Surgery; *Style—* Dai Davies, Esq; 53 Ormond Ave, Hampton, Middx TW12 2RY (☎ 081 941 5031); 55 Harley St, London W1N 1DD (☎ 071 631 3927)

DAVIES, Rev Prof David Protheroe; s of Rev Canon William John Davies (d 1987), and Mary Annie Maureen, *née* Lewis; *b* 19 July 1939; *Educ* Christ Coll Brecon, Corpus Christi Cambridge (MA), CCC Oxford (MA, BD); *m* 23 July 1963, Brenda

Lloyd, da of late William Huw Owen; 1 da (Siwan Eleri b 1972); *Career* ordained: deacon 1964, priest 1965; asst curate St Mary's Swansea 1964-67; St David's Univ Coll Lampeter: lectr 1967-76, sr lectr 1976-86, dean Faculty of Arts 1977-81, dean Faculty of Theology 1981- (previously 1975-77), prof of theology 1986-, dep princ 1988-; memb Ct and Cncl Univ of Wales; chm and dir Cwmni'r Gannwyll (ind TV Co), memb Central Religious Advsy Ctee (BBC and IBA); *Books* Yr Efengylau A'r Actau (1978), Diwinyddiaeth Ar Waith (1984); *Recreations* sport, acting; *Style—* The Rev Prof David Davies; Nantaeron, Peniel, Carmarthen, Dyfed SA32 7HS (☎ 0267 234552); Dept of Theology and Religious Studies, St David's University College, Lampeter, Dyfed SA48 1ED (☎ 0570 422351, fax 0570 423423, telex 48475)

DAVIES, David Thurston; s of Edward Andrew Davies (d 1959), of London W1, and Mabel Cordelia, *née* Parket (d 1985); *b* 21 May 1926; *Educ* Sherborne, Law Soc's Sch of Law; *m* 1954, Pauline Mary, da of John Henry Allen Wilkins; 2 s (Andrew John b 1955, Simon Henry b 1957), 1 da (Emma Mary Elizabeth (now Mrs Moore) b 1961); *Career* Navy 1944-47 with final rank of Sub Lt RNVR (later Lt Cdr RNR RD); Penningtons: articled 1947, slr 1950, ptnr 1953, sr ptnr 1974-; memb Law Soc 1950, fell Inst of Taxation 1985; *Books* The Will Draftsman's Aid Oyez (1971), Will Precedents and Inheritance Tax (1st edn 1978, 3rd edn 1988), Butterworths' Wills Probate and Administration Service (gen ed, 1990-); *Recreations* reading, travel, playing squash, watching cricket, visiting churches and National Trust properties; *Style—* David T Davies, Esq; The Barn, Shortgrove, Newport, Essex CB11 3TX (☎ 0799 40455); Penningtons Clement House, 99 Aldwych, London WC2B 4LJ (☎ 071 242 4422)

DAVIES, David Yorwerth; s of Hywell Morris Davies (d 1985), and Marjory Winnifred Davies (d 1970); *b* 24 Feb 1939; *Educ* Grove Park GS Wrexham, Univ of Durham (Dip Arch); *m* 31 May 1969, Angela, da of Jack Theed (d 1966); 2 s (Andrew b 1970, Gareth b 1972); *Career* fndr D Y Davies Association of Chartered Architects 1969, exec chm D Y Davies plc 1986-; cmmnd bldgs incl: Heathrow Terminal 3, Blue Circle Industs HQ Aldermaston; dir Docklands Development Corp 1988; Freeman Worshipful Co of Blacksmiths 1975; RIBA (vice pres 1987), hon fell AIA, CIArb; *Recreations* golf, food, wine; *Clubs* RAC, Sunningdale Golf, Royal and Ancient Golf of St Andrews, Merion Golf (Pennsylvania); *Style—* David Davies, Esq; 36 Paradise Road, Richmond, Surrey, TW9 1SE (☎ 081 948 5544)

DAVIES, Rt Hon (David John) Denzil; PC (1978), MP (Lab) Llanelli 1970-; s of G Davies; *b* 9 Oct 1938; *Educ* Queen Elizabeth GS Carmarthen, Pembroke Oxford; *m* 1963, Mary Ann Finlay, of Illinois, USA; 1 s, 1 da; *Career* barrister Gray's Inn 1964; taught Chicago Univ 1963, law lecturer Leeds Univ 1964; memb Public Accounts Ctee 1974-, pps to Sec of State Wales 1974-76, min of state Treasury 1976-79; oppn front bench spokesman: Treasury Matters 1979-81, Defence and Disarmamemt 1981-88, shadow Welsh sec 1983, chief opposition spokesman on defence 1985-; *Style—* The Rt Hon Denzil Davies, MP; House of Commons, London SW1A 0AA (☎ 071 219 5197)

DAVIES, Derek; s of John Davies (d 1965), and Alice, *née* Heap; *b* 27 Oct 1933; *Educ* Bolton Sch, Trinity Hall Cambridge (MA, MB BChir); *m* 2 May 1959, Barbara Jean, da of William Helsby (d 1969); 2 s (Christopher b 1960, Timothy b 1969), 2 da (Alison b 1964, Amanda b 1967 d 1980); *Career* sr med house offr Manchester Royal Infirmary 1960-62 (resident clinical pathologist 1959-60); med registrar: Derbyshire Royal Infirmary 1962-63, UCH 1963-65; lectr and sr lectr clinical endocrinology Victoria Univ of Manchester 1968-88 (hon conslt 1972-88), conslt physician Manchester Royal Infirmary 1988; FRSM, FRCP, fell Manchester Med Soc; *Style—* Derek Davies, Esq; 32 Barrow Bridge Rd, Smithills, Bolton, Lancs BL1 7NJ (☎ 0204 47129); Department of Clinical Endocrinology, Manchester Royal Infirmary, Oxford Rd, Manchester M13 9WL (☎ 061 276 4256)

DAVIES, Derek Lewis; s of Glyndwr Lewis, and Lily May, *née* Jones; *b* 28 Sept 1933; *Educ* Birmingham Central Coll of Tech; *m* 4 Oct 1954, Barbara Joy, da of Charles Barwick; 2 s (Jeremy b 1960, Robert b 1966); *Career* Lt Royal Mil Police 1954-56; GEC: student apprentice Birmingham 1950-54, chief engr Pakistan 1958-62, dir Overseas Servs 1973-81, dir Electrical Projects 1981-86; sales mangr Foster Transformers Ltd 1962-67, sales dir Ottermill Switchgear 1967-73, chm Drake & Scull Holdings plc 1986-89, dir Simon Engineering plc 1987-; memb NEDO Airports Ctee 1985, chm UK Airports Gp 1984-86; Freeman Worshipful Co of Feltmakers; FRSA, ARAeS; *Recreations* rugby, golf; *Clubs* Athenaeum; *Style—* Derek Davies, Esq; Simon House, PO Box 31, Stockport, Cheshire (☎ 061 428 3600, fax 061 428 1634)

DAVIES, Diana Clare; da of William Roy Elliott (d 1990), of Rushden, Northants, and Maureen Winifred, *née* Pridmore; *b* 7 May 1961; *Educ* Chichele Girls Sch Rushden; *m* 25 Aug 1984, Peter David Davies, s of John Davies; 1 da (Lauren Jacqueline b 30 Sept 1990); *Career* athlete; life memb Leicester Corinthian Athletics Club, jr UK int 1978, full UK int 1978-; achievements at high jump: UK champion 1984, 1986, 1987, 1988, WAAA champion 1984, 1985, 1986, 1989, represented GB Olympic Games 1984 and 1988; UK high jump record holder 1982-; office sec 1977-84, audio-typist 1984-85, asst manageress Olympus Sport International Ltd 1988-; *Recreations* netball, swimming; *Clubs* International Athletics; *Style—* Mrs Diana Davies; c/o Olympus Sport International Ltd, Murrayfield Rd, Braunstone, Leicester

DAVIES, Donald; CBE (1978, OBE 1973); s of Wilfred Lawson Davies (d 1972), and Alwyne Davies; *b* 13 Feb 1924; *Educ* Ebbw Vale GS, Univ Coll Cardiff (BSc); *m* 1948, Mabel, da of John Henry Hellyar (d 1960); 2 da; *Career* civil engr; memb National Coal Bd 1973-84 (area dir 1967-73); chm: NCB Opencast Exec 1973-83, NCB Ancillaries 1979-87; conslt mining engineer; FIMinE; *Recreations* golf, fishing; *Clubs* RAC; *Style—* Donald Davies, Esq, CBE; Wendy Cottage, Dukes Wood Ave, Gerrard's Cross, Bucks (☎ 0753 885083; business 071 235 2020)

DAVIES, Douglas Arthur Douglas Arthur Douglas A; s of Joseph Davies (d 1932), and Ellen Dewhurst, *née* Penswick (d 1975); *b* 16 Sept 1927; *Educ* Waterloo GS; *m* 1953, Jean, da of Walter Marsh (d 1978); 2 s (Alan Robert and Duncan James b 1962 (twins)), 1 da (Ruth Louise b 1965); *Career* mgmnt conslt; dir Riverside Court Management (Chester) Ltd; *Recreations* fly fishing, travel, boating, antique glass; *Style—* Douglas A Davies, Esq; The Old House, Checkley, Hereford HR1 4ND

DAVIES, Hon Edward David Grant; 2 s of 1 Baron Davies (but er s by his 2 w); *b* 30 Jan 1925; *Educ* Gordonstoun, King's Cambridge; *m* 1, 1949, Patricia, yr da of Clifford Roberts Musto, of Salisbury, Rhodesia; 1 s, 3 da; m 2, 1975, Shirley, da of Le Grew Harrison and former w of Johnny Gaze; *Career* chm London Tst; dir Globe Investment Tst; *Style—* The Hon Edward Davies; 30 Southacre, Hyde Park Crescent, London W2; Ingestone, Foy, Ross-on-Wye, Herefordshire

DAVIES, Elidir Leslie Wish; s of late Rev Thomas John Landy Davies, and Hetty Boucher, *née* Wish; *b* 3 Jan 1907; *Educ* Colchester Sch, Bartlett Sch of Architecture, London Univ; *m* 1, Vera, *née* Goodwin (d 1974); m 2, 1976, Kathleen, *née* Burke-Collis (d 1989); *Career* chartered architect Elidir L W Davies and Partners; FRIBA, FRSA; *Style—* Elidir Davies Esq; Burrswood, Groombridge, Kent

DAVIES, Emrys Thomas; s of Evan William Davies (d 1954), and Dinah, *née* Jones; *b* 8 Oct 1934; *Educ* Parmiters Fndn Sch London, Sch of Slavonic Studies Cambridge, Sch of Oriental & African Studies London; *m* 1960, Angela Audrey, da of Paul Robert Buchan May (d 1952); 1 s (Robert), 2 da (Victoria, Elizabeth); *Career* RAF 1953-1955, served Peking and Shanghai 1956-59, FO 1959-60, Political Residence Bahrain 1960-62, UN Gen Assembly NY 1962, FO 1962-63, asst political advsr to Hong Kong Govt 1963-68, Br High Cmmn Ottawa 1968-71, FCO 1972-76, commercial cnsllr HM Embassy Peking 1976-78; (charge 1976 and 1978), Univ of Oxford Business Summer Sch 1977; NATO Defense Coll Rome 1979, dep high cmmr Ottawa 1979-82; Diplomatic Serv Overseas inspr 1982-83, dep perm rep to OECD Paris 1984-87, HM ambass Hanoi Vietnam 1987-; *Books* Albigensians and Cathars (transl.); *Recreations* tennis, walking; *Clubs* Royal Cwlth Soc; *Style—* Emrys Davies, Esq; His Excellency, British Embassy, 16 Pho Ly Thuong Kiet, Hanoi, Vietnam

DAVIES, Dr Ernest Arthur; JP (Lancs and Inner London 1962); s of Dan Davies (d 1935), and Ada, *née* Smith (d 1957); *b* 25 Oct 1926; *Educ* Coventry Jr Tech Sch, Westminster Coll London (CertEd), Univ of St Andrews (BSc), St Johns Coll Cambridge (PhD); *m* 1, 28 July 1956 (m dis 1967), Margaret Stephen Tait, da of Henry Gatt, of Oldham; m 2, 20 Oct 1972 (m dis 1980), Patricia, da of Sidney Bates (d 1981); *Career* aircraft apprentice 1 Signals Sch RAF Cranwell 1942-43 (med discharge); sr res scientist GEC 1957-63, physics lectr UMIST 1963-66, MP (Lab) Stretford 1966-70 (PPS to Sec of State for Foreign Affrs 1968-69, UK Parly rep 24 gen assembly UN 1969, Parly sec Miny Technol 1969-70, mgmnt conslt and lectr 1970-87, ret 1987; cncllr: Borough of Stretford 1961-67, London Borough of Southwark 1974-82; resigned Lab pty 1982; memb: Nat Tst, Friends of Royal Acad; MInstP 1959, CPhys; *Recreations* gardening, enjoyment of music and art, travel; *Style—* Dr Ernest Davies, JP; 5 Rye Hill Park, London SE15 3JN (☎ 071 732 3904)

DAVIES, Hon Francis William Harding; s of Rt Hon John Emerson Harding Harding-Davies, who was nominated a Life Peer 16 June 1979, but who d 4 July 1979 before the Peerage was cr; raised to rank of a Baron's s 1980; *b* 22 Nov 1946; *Educ* Windlesham House Sch, The Nautical Coll Pangbourne, Strasbourg Univ; *m* 1972, Lynda Margaret Mae, *née* Squires; 3 c; *Career* asst mangr int EMI Records 1966-68, int export mangr Liberty Records 1968-70; pres: Love Productions Ltd 1970-78, Partisan Music Productions Inc 1978-82, ATV Music Group Canada 1982-85, TMP - The Music Publisher 1986; *Recreations* photography, music; *Style—* The Hon Francis Davies; PO Box 615, Don Mills, Ontario M3C 2T6, Canada

DAVIES, Frank John; s of Lt-Col F H Davies, of Lincoln, and Veronica Josephine Davies (d 1943); *b* 24 Sept 1931; *Educ* Monmouth Sch, UMIST; *m* 1956, Sheila Margaret, da of Geoffrey Bailey (d 1938); 3 s (James, Stephen, Jonathan); *Career* chief exec and md Rockware Gp plc, chm Rockware Glass Ltd, dir Ir Glass plc, pres Glass Mfrs Fedn 1986 and 1987; memb: Oxon Health Authy 1983, cncl CBI 1986-; pres Fedn Européene de Verre D'Emballage 1989, tstee Banbury Orthopaedic Rehabilitation Tst 1988; OstJ 1979; Freeman: City of London, Worshipful Co of Basketmakers, Worshipful Co of Glass Sellers; CBIM, FRSA; *Recreations* gardening, music, theatre; *Clubs* Carlton; *Style—* Frank Davies, Esq; Stonewalls, Castle St, Deddington, Oxon OX5 4TE (☎ 0869 38131); 5 Chandos St, London W1M 9DG (☎ 071 637 0369, fax 071 636 4639)

DAVIES, Gareth; s of Lewis Davies (d 1985), of S Devon, and Margaret Ann, *née* Jones; *b* 13 Feb 1930; *Educ* King Edward's GS Aston Birmingham; *m* 12 Sept 1953, Joan Patricia, da of Edmond Charles Prosser (d 1986), of NZ; 1 s (Mark b 1959); *Career* chm and gp chief exec Glynwed International plc and subsidiary co's 1986- (joined 1969); dir: Raglan Property Trust plc 1985-, The BTS Gp plc 1987-; non-exec dir: Barclays Bank Regnl Bd, Midlands Electricity Board 1989; FCA, CBIM; *Recreations* music, opera; *Style—* Gareth Davies, Esq; 4 Beech Gate, Roman Road, Little Aston, W Midlands; Headland House, 54 New Coventry Road, Sheldon, Birmingham B26 3AZ (☎ 021 742 2366, telex 336608, fax 021 742 0403)

DAVIES, (David) Gareth Griffiths; s of Tudor Griffiths Davies, of Preston, and Dilys Katherine, *née* Davies; *b* 29 Oct 1951; *Educ* Winchester, Downing Coll Cambridge (BA, MA); *m* 30 July 1977, Daphne Sarah, da of Edward Chambre Dickson, TD, DL; 1 s (Nicholas b 1981), 1 da (Philippa b 1984); *Career* called to the Bar Inner Temple 1975, in practice N Circuit 1976-81; admitted slr 1983, ptnr Rawsthorn Edelstons 1985-; memb Law Soc 1983; *Recreations* gardening; *Clubs* MCC, Naval; *Style—* Gareth Davies, Esq; Green House, Balderstone, nr Blackburn, Lancashire BB2 7LL (☎ 0254 812 334); 7 Station Rd, Hesketh Bank, Preston PR4 6SN (☎ 0772 814 921, fax 0772 815 008)

DAVIES, (David) Garfield; s of David John Davies (d 1976), of Bridgend, Glamorgan, and Lizzie Ann, *née* Evans; *b* 24 June 1935; *Educ* Heolgam Secdy Modern Bridgend, Bridgend Tech Coll, Port Talbot Sch of Further Educn; *m* 12 March 1960, Marian, da of Raymond Jones, of Trelewis, nr Trewallis, Glamorgan; 4 da (Helen Claire b 16 Jan 1961, Susan Karen b 22 May 1962, Karen Jayne b 16 June 1965, Rachel Louise b 24 Jan 1969); *Career* Nat Service Sr Aircraftsman RAF 1956-58; jr operative British Steel Corp 1950-51, apprentice electrician 1951-56, electrician 1958-69; area organiser Union of Shop Distributive and Allied Workers (USDAW) 1969-73, dep divnl offr 1973-78, nat offr 1978-86, gen sec 1986-; memb TUC Gen Cncl 1986-; cncllr Penybont RDC 1966-69; JP Ipswich 1972-78; *Style—* Garfield Davies, Esq; 64 Dairyground Road, Bramhall, Stockport, Cheshire SK7 2QW (☎ 061 439 9548); Union of Shop, Distributive & Allied Workers, 188 Wilmslow Road, Fallowfield, Manchester M14 6LJ (☎ 061 224 2804, fax 061 257 2566)

DAVIES, Gavyn; s of W J F Davies, of Southampton, and M G Watkins; *b* 27 Nov 1950; *Educ* Taunton's Sch Southampton, St John's Coll Cambridge (BA), Balliol Coll Oxford; *m* 1989, Susan Jane Nye; 1 da (Rosie b 31 Jan 1990); *Career* econ advsr Policy Unit 10 Downing St 1974-79, UK economist Phillips and Drew 1979-81, chief UK economist: Simon and Coates 1981-86, Goldman Sachs 1986-; visting prof LSE 1988; *Recreations* sport; *Style—* Gavyn Davies, Esq; 5 Old Bailey, London EC3M 7AH (☎ 071 248 6464, fax 071 489 2968)

DAVIES, (Ernest Walter) Geoffrey; s of Rupert Davies (d 1979), and Beryl, *née* Lewis (d 1971); *b* 18 Sept 1930; *Educ* West Monmouth Sch, St Catharine's Coll Cambridge (MA), St Mary's Hosp London (MB BChir, FCOphth, DO); *m* 6 Sept 1958, Joy Avril, da of Charles Brocklehurst Pinnock; 2 s (James b 15 June 1959, Peter b 6 June 1963), 2 da (Adele b 17 Nov 1960, Juliet b 16 Aug 1965); *Career* ophthalmic surgeon; trained at Moorfields Eye Hosp and Guy's specialising in retinal surgery & diabetic conditions of the eye, conslt ophthalmic surgeon Kings Coll Hosp 1969-; FRCS; memb: RSM 1962, BMA 1965, Club Jules Gonin 1972, Coll of Ophthalmologists 1988; *Recreations* rifle shooting, cliff walking; *Style—* Geoffrey Davies, Esq; 127 Harley St, London W1N 1DJ (☎ 071 580 1631)

DAVIES, Captain Geoffrey Franklin; TD (1964); s of Franklyn George Davies (d 1952), of Kidderminster, Worcs, and Doris, *née* Thatcher (d 1987); *b* 13 Jan 1930; *Educ* King Charles I Sch Kidderminster, King Edward VI Sch Stourbridge, Univ of Birmingham (LLB); *m* 1, 19 June 1954 (m dis 1970), Barbara Mary, da of Maj William Horace Cooper (d 1965), of The Old Rectory, Hagley, W Midlands; 1 s (Nigel William b 16 Nov 1956), 1 da (Jayne Elizabeth b 1 Sept 1958); m 2, 31 Oct 1970 (m dis 1972), Barbara Jean, da of James Skillen, of USA; 1 s (James Skillen b 12 Aug 1971); m 3, 30 July 1977, Barbara (Bobby) Joyce, da of Harold Williams (d 1959), of Chaddesley, Corbett, Worcs; *Career* cmmnd 2 Lt RASC 1953, Capt RASC later RCT 1956, serv with 110 Tport Column until 1964; admitted slr 1952; ptnr: Thursfield Adams Westons 1956-, Desmond & Holder Worcester 1987-; former chm WM Cooper & Sons (Builders), sec John Brecknell Charity 1956-, cases sec and/or chm NW and SE

Shropshire Branch NSPCC 1956-, memb Kidderminster Borough Cncl (chm two ctees) 1970-76, chm Kidderminster Cons 200 Club 1970-83, form prov Aide de Campe Knights Templar Worcs, vice pres Stourport Boat Club, former prov sr Grand Warden Worcs; memb Law Soc (1952); *Recreations* rowing, golf; *Clubs* Leander, Worcester Rowing, Kidderminster Golf; *Style*— Capt Geoffrey F Davies; Drayton Lodge, Drayton, Belbroughton, nr Stourbridge, W Midlands (☎ 0562 730 240); 14 Church St, Kidderminster, Worcestershire (☎ 0562 820 575, fax 0562 66 783, telex 337 837 THURSF G)

DAVIES, Geoffrey Walter; s of Sir David Davies, of 82 New House Park, St Albans, Herts, and Lady Alice May, *née* Battrick; *b* 12 Aug 1943; *Educ* St Albans GS for Boys, Poly of N London; *m* 1 (m dis 1985), Delia Faith, *née* Goodchild; 1 s (Haydn Gareth b 5 Aug 1970); m 2, 29 April 1987, Catherine Susan, da of Maurice Hoare; 1 da (Hannah Fern b 28 Sept 1988); *Career* architect; Hubbard Ford Ptnrship, Clifford Culpin & Ptnrs, GMW Int, appointed by Milton Keynes Devpt Corpn with special responsibility for design and devpt of industrial and commercial bldgs 1970, private practice 1974; memb Architects Registration Cncl UK; memb RIBA, fell Faculty of Bldg; *Books* System Building for Industry (1973); *Recreations* rugby football, cricket, shooting; *Clubs* Northants County Cricket, Woburn Syndicate, Leighton Buzzard RFC; *Style*— Geoffrey Davies, Esq; Wells Cottage, Church Lane, Great Brickhill, Milton Keynes MK17 9AE (☎ 052526 685); Brickhill House, 701 South Fifth St, Witan Gate East, Central Milton Keynes MK9 2PR (☎ 0908 664551, fax 0908 678368)

DAVIES, George Raymond (Gerry); OBE (1977); s of George John Davies (d 1935); *b* 3 Oct 1916; *Educ* East Ham GS; *m* 1945, Sylvia, *née* Newling; 1 s, 1 da; *Career* dep city librarian Cambridge 1953-55; The Booksellers Assoc of GB and Ireland: gen sec 1955-64, dir 1964-66 and 1970-81, hon life memb 1981-; md Bowker Publishing Co Ltd 1966-69, dep ed The Bookseller 1969-70, chm BA service House Ltd 1977-82; pres Int Fedn 1978-81 (hon memb 1988); Book Trade Benevolent Soc: dir 1956-86, pres 1986-89, patron 1989-; fell Library Assoc (life memb 1981); *Books* jt ed: Books are Different, A Mortal Craft, Books and Their Prices; *Recreations* words, music, estate management; *Clubs* Savile; *Style*— Gerry Davies Esq, OBE; Crotchets, Mayfield, E Sussex (☎ 0435 872356)

DAVIES, George William; s of George Davies (d 1987), of Southport, Lancs, and Mary, *née* Wright; *b* 29 Oct 1941; *Educ* Bootle GS, Univ of Birmingham; *m* 1, 25 Sept 1965 (m dis 1985), Anne Margaret, da of Maj Donald Dyson Allan, of Hants; 3 da (Melanie b 8 Aug 1966, Emma b 23 Sept 1968, Alexandra b 7 Sept 1973); m 2, 7 Dec 1985, Mrs Elzbieta (Liz) Krystyna Devereux-Batchelor, da of Stanislaw Ryszard Szadbey; 2 da (Lucia b 22 May 1988, Jessica b 2 June 1989); *Career* stock merchandise controller Littlewoods Stores 1967-72, School Care (own business) 1972-75, Party Plan and Pippadee Lingerie 1975-81; joined J Hepworth & Son 1981-: responsible for launch of Next Feb 1982, jt gp md 1984, chief exec 1985, chm and chief exec 1987-88; chm and md The George Davies Partnership plc 1989; memb Ct Univ of Leics 1988-; Hon Liverpool Poly 1989; FRSA 1987, sr fell RCA 1988; *Books* incl: What Next? (1989); *Recreations* golf, tennis, squash; *Clubs* Formby Golf, Rothley Golf (Leicester), Leicester Squash; *Style*— George Davies, Esq; The George Davies Partnership plc, Magna House, Magna Park, Watling Street, Lutterworth, Leicestershire LE17 4JQ

DAVIES, Geraint Talfan; s of Aneirin Talfan Davies OBE (d 1980), of Cardiff and Mary Anne, *née* Evans (d 1971); *b* 30 Dec 1943; *Educ* Cardiff HS For Boys , Jesus Coll Oxford (MA); *m* 9 Sept 1967, Elizabeth Shan, da of Thomas Vaughan Yorath of Cardiff; 3 s (Matthew b 1969, Rhodri b 1971, Edward b 1974); *Career* asst ed Western Mail 1974-78, head of news and current affairs HTV Wales 1978-82, asst controller of programmes HTV Wales 1982-87, dir of programmes Tyne Tees TV 1987-90, controller BBC Wales 1990; chm Newydd Housing Assoc 1975-78; tstee: Tenovus Cancer Appeal 1984-87, Br Bone Marrow Donor Appeal 1987-; memb: Mgmnt Ctee Northern Sinfonia 1989-90, Cncl of Inst of Welsh Affairs 1988-; dir: Northern Stage Co 1989-90, The Newcastle Initiative 1989-; *Style*— Geraint Talfan Davies, Esq; BBC Wales, Broadcasting House, Llandaff, Cardiff CF5 2YQ (☎ 0222 572880, fax 0222 555286, telex 265781)

DAVIES, (Edward) Glyn; s of Thomas Davies (d 1976); *b* 16 Feb 1944; *Educ* Llanfair Caereinion HS; *m* 26 July 1969, Bobbie, da of Austen Roberts, of Welshpool; 3 s (Edward b 1970, Patrick b 1973, Tim b 1980), 1 da (Sally b 1976); *Career* farmer; dist cnclr Montgomeryshire Cncl 1976-88 (chm 1985-88), chm Devpt Bd for Rural Wales 1989-, bd memb Wales Tourist Bd 1989-; *Recreations* squash, running; *Style*— Glyn Davies, Esq; Cil Farm, Berriew, Montgomeryshire, Mid-Wales (☎ 0686 640247); Chairman's Office, Development Board for Rural Wales, Ladywell House, Newton, Montgomeryshire (☎ 0686 626965)

DAVIES, Gp Capt (Hubert) Gordon; CBE (1965), AE (1946); s of Hubert Offen Davies (d 1948); *b* 25 July 1919; *Educ* Purley GS, Regent St Polytechnic; *m* 1941, Alice Rhoda (d 1990), da of late Philip Lawrence; 1 s, 1 da; *Career* CO Univ of Hull Air Sqdn 1950-53, asst Air Force advsr UK, high cmmr Ottawa 1954-56, chief instr No 2 Flying Sch Syerston Notts 1958-60, Gp Capt orgn and plans HQ NEAF Cyprus 1962-65, dir Mgmnt and Staff Training MOD 1965-67, CO RAF Tern Hill Shropshire 1967-70, dep dir War Coll Greenwich 1972-74; sr mgmnt devpt advsr HCITB Wembley 1974-77, regnl mangr S and E HCITB 1977-83, asst head of training HCITB 1983-84; *Recreations* travel; *Clubs* RAF; *Style*— Gp Capt H Gordon Davies, CBE, AE; Pantiles, 18 Garnet Drive, Ratton, Eastbourne, E Sussex BN20 9AE (☎ 0323 507207)

DAVIES, Prof Graeme John; DL (Merseyside); s of Harry John Davies, and Gladys Edna, *née* Pratt; *b* 7 April 1937; *Educ* Sch of Engrg Univ of Auckland NZ, Univ of Cambridge (MA, ScD); *m* Florence Isabelle; 1 s (Michael b 1960), 1 da (Helena b 1961); *Career* lectr Dept of Metallurgy and Materials Sci Univ of Cambridge 1962-77, fell St Catharine's Coll 1967-77, prof Dept of Metallurgy Univ of Sheffield 1978-86, vice-chllr Univ of Liverpool 1986-; memb: Cncl of Ctee of Vice-Chllrs and Principals, Exec Cncl Assoc of Cwlth Univs, Cncl The Industl Soc, The Michaelmas Gp, Steering Ctee Business Opportunities on Merseyside Initiative, Cncl Liverpool Sch of Tropical Med, Merseyside Enterprise Forum; dir: Univs Superannuation Scheme Ltd, BNF Metals Technol Centre Ltd, Univ of Liverpool Energy Co, Univ of Liverpool China Business Consultancy; tstee: Nat Museums and Galleries on Merseyside, Bluecoat Soc of Arts, Liverpool Festival Tst, Mersey Heritage Tst (also chm), Merseyside Bldgs Preservation Tst, Liverpool Community Tst, Univ of Liverpool Pension Fund; pres: Liverpool Econ and Statistical Soc, Liverpool and District Sci Industl and Res Library Advsy Cncl; vice pres Liverpool and Merseyside Branch ESU; author and co-author of more than 120 sci papers on forming processes, welding, solidification and casting, mechanical properties of materials; Rosenbaum Medal Inst of Metals 1982, Freeman City of London 1987, Liveryman Worshipful Co of Ironmongers 1989; CEng, FIM, FIMechE, FRSA, FEng 1988; *Books* Solidification and Casting (1973), Texture and the Properties of Materials (co-ed, 1976), Solidificacao e Fundicao das Metals e Suas Ligas (jtly, 1978), Hot Working and Forming Processes (co-ed, 1980), Superplasticity (jtly, 1981), Essential Metallurgy for Engineers (jtly, 1985); *Recreations* birdwatching; *Clubs* Athenaeum, Athenaeum (Liverpool); *Style*— Prof Graeme Davies, DL; University of Liverpool, Senate House, Abercromby Square, Liverpool L69 3BX (☎ 051 794 2003, telex UNILPLG, fax 051 708 7092)

DAVIES, Graham Penry; s of Alcwyn Penry Davies (d 1958); *b* 16 Sept 1925; *Educ* City of London Sch, Peterhouse, Cambridge; *m* 1953, Rosemary Graham, *née* Down; 1 s, 2 da; *Career* Sub-Lt (A) (AE) RNVR; chm Erith plc 1985; pres Soc of Builders Merchants 1978-80, memb Cncl RNVR Offrs Assoc 1976; MIMC; *Recreations* golf, yacht racing (yacht 'Fleur Vigueur II'); *Clubs* Naval, Parkstone Yacht, Parkstone Golf; *Style*— Graham Davies Esq; 66 Anthonys Ave, Poole, Dorset (☎ 0202 707 298)

DAVIES, Gwilym Prys; s of William and Mary Matilda Davies; *b* 8 Dec 1923; *Educ* Towyn Sch, Univ Coll Wales Aberystwyth; *m* 1951, Llinos Evans; 3 da; *Career* ptnr Morgan Bruce and Nicholas Slrs Cardiff Pontypridd and Porth 1957; *Style*— Gwilym Davies Esq; Lluest, 78 Church Rd, Tonteg, Pontypridd, Mid Glam (☎ 0443 2462)

DAVIES, Handel; CB (1961); s of Henry John Davies (d 1960), of Llwydcoed, Aberdare, Mid Glamorgan, and Elizabeth, *née* Howells (d 1968); *b* 2 June 1912; *Educ* Aberdare GS, Univ Coll Cardiff, Univ of Wales (BSc, MSc); *m* 28 March 1942, Mary Graham, da of Prof R G Harris (d 1964), of Manor Rd, Farnborough; *Career* sr princ sci offr Royal Aircraft Estab Farnborough 1949-52, chief supt Aeroplane and Armament Experimental Estab 1952-55, sci advsr Air Miny 1955-56, dir gen sci res (Air) Miny of Supply 1956-59, dep dir Royal Aircraft Estab 1959-63, dep controller R & D (Air) Miny of Technol 1963-69, gp tech dir BAC 1969-77, chm Standing Conf on Schs of Sci and Tech 1978-81; govr Woking Sixth Form Coll; pres Royal Aeronautical Soc 1976-77; FAIAA 1960, Hon FRAeS 1980, FEng 1981; *Recreations* sailing, skiing; *Clubs* RAF Yacht; *Style*— Handel Davies, Esq, CB; Keel Cottage, Woodham Rd, Horsell, Woking, Surrey GU21 4DL (☎ 0483 714192)

DAVIES, Hereward Scott; s of George Frederick Davies (d 1986), of Aldeburgh, Suffolk, and Florence, *née* Scott (d 1987); *b* 1 Aug 1935; *Educ* Berkhamsted Sch; *m* 7 June 1958 (m dis 1988), Sara Brigid, da of Cdr William John Adlam Willis, CGM, MVO, QPM, RN (d 1984), of Dovercourt; 1 s (Simon b 1959), 1 da (Claire b 1961); *Career* Nat Serv RAF 1958-60; ptnr Hereward Scott Davies CAs 1960-; former chm N London CAs Gp; FCA 1958; *Recreations* Nat Hunt horse racing, good food and wine; *Clubs* Rotary Club (Friern Barnet & Whetstone); *Style*— Hereward Davies, Esq; 89 Monks Avenue, New Barnet, Herts EN5 1DA (☎ 081 441 1227); Prospect House, 2 Athenaeum Rd, London N20 9AE (☎ 081 446 4371, fax 081 446 7606)

DAVIES, Howard John; s of Leslie Powell Davies, of Rochdale, Lancs, and Marjorie, *née* Magowan; *b* 12 Feb 1951; *Educ* Manchester GS, Memorial Univ of Newfoundland, Merton Coll Oxford (MA), Stanford Univ Calif (MS in Mgmnt Sci); *m* 30 June 1984, Prudence Mary, da of Eric Phillipps Keely, CBE (d 1988), of Findon; 2 s (George b 1984, Archibald b 1987); *Career* FO 1973-74, private sec to HM Ambass Paris 1974-76, HM Treasy 1976-82, McKinsey and Co 1982-85, special advsr to Chllr of the Exchequer 1985-86, McKinsey and Co 1986-87, controller of audit The Audit Cmmn 1987-; *Recreations* cricket, writing; *Clubs* Barnes Common Cricket; *Style*— Howard Davies, Esq; 1 Vincent Sq, London SW1 (☎ 071 828 1212, car 0836 282797)

DAVIES, Brig (David) Hugh; MC (1944); s of David John Davies, JP (d 1938), of Carmarthen, Dyfed, Wales, and Catherine Jane, *née* Philipps (d 1963); *b* 17 Aug 1918; *Educ* Cathedral Sch Hereford, RMC Sandhurst; *m* 20 March 1943, Audrey, da of Jesse James Smith (d 1954), of Tenterden, Kent; 1 da (Jane Caroline (Mrs Cookson) b 15 Nov 1945); *Career* cmmnd KORR 1938, active serv Palestine 1938-39 (wounded), WWII serv 107 Regt RAC (Adj, Sqdn Ldr, Actg CO), Holland (wounded 1944), Staff Coll Haifa Palestine 1945, GS02 1 Div and Actg GS01 Palestine 1946-48, transferred 7 QOH, Adj 1948-49 (despatches 1949), DAAG AG 17 WO 1949-51, Sqdn Ldr and 2 i/c 7 Hussars 1951-53, instr Staff Coll Camberley 1956-58, CO 1958-61 asst dir plans Jt Planning Staff MOD 1961-63, Cdr 5 Inf Bde Gp 1963-65, Col QOH 1964-72, Brig RAC HQ Western Cmd 1966-68; chm: Rose Smith & Co (Fuel) Ltd 1978-84 (non-exec dir 1968-75), Kent Royal Br Legion; pres Ashford Valley Foxhounds, Rolvenden and Tenterden Branches Royal Br Legion; treas Rolvenden Cons Assoc; Hon Freeman Carmarthen 1950; *Recreations* hunting, fishing; *Clubs* Cavalry and Guards', Army and Navy; *Style*— Brig Hugh Davies, MC; Barton Wood, Rolveden, Cranbrook, Kent (☎ 0580 241 294)

DAVIES, Hugh Llewelyn; s of Vincent Ellis Davies, OBE, of 12 St Swithuns Close, East Grinstead, Sussex, and Rose Trench, *née* Temple; *b* 8 Nov 1941; *Educ* Rugby, Churchill Coll Univ of Cambridge (BA); *m* 21 Sept 1968, Virginia Ann, da of Hugh Lucius; 1 s (Jonathan b 1973), 1 da (Charlotte b 1970); *Career* Dip Serv FO 1965, Chinese language studies Hong Kong 1966-68, second sec and HM consul Peking 1969-71, China Desk FCO 1971-74, first sec (econ) Br Embassy Bonn 1974-77, head of chancery Br High Cmmm Singapore 1977-79, asst head Far Eastern Dept FCO 1979-82, secondment Barclays Bank Int 1982-83, commercial cnsllr Br Embassy Peking 1984-87, dep perm UK rep OECD Paris 1987-90, head Far East Dept FCO 1990-; *Recreations* sports, art, gardens; *Style*— Hugh Davies, Esq; c/o FCO, King Charles St, London SW1A 2AH

DAVIES, Hugh Seymour; s of Harold Escott Davies, of Wanborough, Wilts, and Joan Mary, *née* Seymour; *b* 23 April 1943; *Educ* Westminster, Univ of Oxford (BA); *m* 5 Sept 1981, Pamela Judith, da of Anthony Michael Bailey (d 1957); 1 da (Rebecca b 1986); *Career* composer, instrument inventor, performer and musicologist; asst to the composer Karlheinz Stockhausen in Cologne (1964-66), conslt researcher Electronic Music Studio Goldsmiths' Coll Univ of London 1986- (dir 1967-86), conslt Music Dept Gemeentemuseum The Hague 1986-; compositions incl: Shozyg I + II 1968, Meldoci Gestures 1978, Strata 1987; major performances incl: Stockhausen's performing gp 1964-66, BBC Promenade Concerts 1969 and 1986, Stockholm Festival for Electroacoustic Music 1989; ctee memb: Macnaghten Concerts 1968-71, Arts Cncl New Activities 1969-70, Electroacoustic Music Assoc 1977-88; memb Bd of Dirs Artist Placement Gp 1975-89; Hon citizenship City of Baltimore USA 1988; *Books* International Electronic Music Catalog (1968); chapters in: Poésie Sonore International (1979), Electronic Music for Schools (1981), Nuova Atlantide (1986), Echo-The Images of Sound (1987), Vitalité et contradictions de l'avant-garde: Italie-France 1909-1924 (1988), Nordic Music Days 100 Years (1988); The New Grove Dictionary of Musical Instruments (300 entries 1984); *Style*— Hugh Davies, Esq; 25 Albert Rd, London N4 3RR (☎ 071 272 5508)

DAVIES, (Edward) Hunter; s of John Davies (d 1958),of Carlisle, and Marion, *née* Brechin (d 1987); *b* 7 Jan 1936; *Educ* Creighton Sch Carlisle, Carlisle GS, Univ of Durham; *m* 1960, Margaret Forster, *qv*; 1 s, 2 da; *Career* author of over 30 books; journalist Sunday Times 1960-84, ed Sunday Times Magazine 1975-77, columnist Punch 1979-89, presenter BBC Radio Four's Bookshelf 1983-86; *Books Incl:* Here We Go Round the Mulberry Bush (1965), The Good Guide to the Lakes (publisher 1984); *Style*— Hunter Davies, Esq; 11 Boscastle Rd, London NW5 (☎ 071 485 3785); Grasmoor House, Loweswater, Cockermouth, Cumbria

DAVIES, Huw Humphreys; s of William Davies (d 1984), of Llangynog, and Harriet Jane, *née* Humphreys; *b* 4 Aug 1940; *Educ* Llandovery Coll, Pembroke Coll Oxford (MA); *m* 1966, Elizabeth Shân, da of William Harries; 2 da (Elin Mari b 24 April 1969, Catrin Humphreys b 23 Sept 1971); *Career* prog dir and prodr TWW 1964-68; HTV Wales: programme dir and prodr 1968-78, asst controller of programmes 1978-79, controller of programmes 1979-81, dir of programmes 1981-89, chief exec 1987-; govr Welsh Coll of Music and Drama, memb Gorsedd of Bards; FRSA 1989; *Recreations* walking, reading, swimming; *Style*— Huw Davies, Esq; HTV, TV Centre, Cardiff CF5

6XJ (☎ 0222 590323)

DAVIES, His Hon Judge Ian Hewitt; TD; s of Rev John Robert Davies (d 1968), and Gwendoline Gertrude, *née* Garling (d 1978); *b* 13 May 1931; *Educ* Kingswood Sch, St John's Coll Cambridge (MA); *m* 31 July 1962, Molly Cecilia, da of Brig Charles Hilary Vaughan Vaughan, DSO (d 1978); *Career* Nat Serv 1950-51, cmmnd KOYLI 3 Bn Parachute Regt, TA 1951-71, Lt-Col; called to the Bar Inner Temple 1958, circuit judge 1986; *Recreations* lawn tennis, sailing; *Clubs* Boodles, MCC, Hurlingham; *Style—* His Hon Judge Davies, TD; c/o Middlesex Crown Court, Parliament Square, London

DAVIES, Ian Leonard; CB (1983); s of Harry Leonard Davies, of Barry, S Glamorgan (d 1966), and Janet Doris, *née* Hellings (d 1986); *b* 2 June 1924; *Educ* Barry County Sch, Univ Coll of S Wales & Monmouth Cardiff, St John's Coll Cambridge (BA, MA); *m* 22 Sept 1951, Hilary, da of Rear Adm Sir Oswald Henry Dawson, KBE (d 1950), of Cheltenham; 2 s (Roger b 1954, James b 1966), 2 da (Siriol Hinchliffe b 1956, Barbara du Preez b 1962); *Career* MOS: TRE 1944-46, BLEU 1946-47; RRE: head of Quantum and Microwave Electronics Div 1960-63, head of Airborne Radar Dept 1963-69; IDC 1970; MOD: asst chief scientific advsr (projects) 1971-72, PE deputy controller Electronics 1973, PE deputy controller Air Systems 1973-75; dir Admiralty Underwater Weapons Estab Portland 1975-84, advsr MMC 1986, memb Cncl IEE 1974-77, chm Electronics Divnl Bd 1975-76; chm: Weymouth Music Club 1986-, Weymouth CAB 1987-90; FIEE 1966 (memb 1952); *Recreations* music, walking, DIY; *Clubs* Athenaeum; *Style—* Ian L Davies, Esq, CB; 37 Bowleaze Coveway, Weymouth, Dorset DT3 6PL

DAVIES, Hon Islwyn Edmund Evan; CBE (1986), JP (Powys), DL (Powys 1983); s of 1 Baron Davies; *b* 10 Dec 1926; *Educ* Gordonstoun; *m* 1959, Camilla Anne, elder da of Col Lawrence William Coulden, of Hadley Wood, Herts; 3 s; *Career* Hon LLD (Wales); FRAgs; *Style—* The Hon Islwyn Davies, CBE, JP, DL; Perthybu, Sarn, Newtown, Powys (☎ 068 688 620)

DAVIES, Dr Ivor John; s of David Howell Davies, of Penarth, S Glam, and Gwenllian, *née* Phillips (d 1990); *b* 9 Nov 1935; *Educ* Penarth Co Sch, Cardiff Coll of Art (NDD), Swansea Coll of Art, Univ of Lausanne, Univ of Edinburgh (PhD); *Career* artist; teacher of art and craft Little Ealing Secdy Modern Boys Sch London 1957-59, asst teacher of Eng Univ of Lausanne and Gymnases 1959-61, pt/t lectr in history of art Extra Mural Dept Cardiff 1961-63, lectr in history of art and head School of Cultural Studies Faculty of Art and Design Gwent Coll of Higher Educn Newport 1978-88; lectr and external examiner for numerous bodies; solo exhibitions 1963- incl: Oriel (Welsh Art Cncl Gallery Cardiff) 1974, City Art Gallery Leeds 1975, Talbot Rice Art Centre Univ of Edinburgh 1972, 1973, 1974 and 1977, Holsworthy Gallery New King's Road London 1980 and 1981, Newport Museum and Art Gallery 1987, Max Rutherson/Roberts Gallery Bond St London 1989; numerous gp exhibitions nationally and internationally 1953-90; pub collections incl: Welsh Arts Cncl, Scottish Arts Cncl, City Art Gallery Leeds, Nat Museum of Wales, Arts Cncl of GB, Newport Museum and Art Gallery; author of various articles and involved in multi-media and experimental theatre; *Clubs* Les Amis du Vin; *Style—* Dr Ivor Davies; 99 Windsor Rd, Penarth, South Glamorgan, Wales CF6 1JF (☎ 0222 703492)

DAVIES, Jack Gale Wilmot; OBE (1946); s of Langford George Davies, and Lily Barnes Davies; *b* 10 Sept 1911; *Educ* Tonbridge, St John's Coll Cambridge; *m* 1949, Georgette O'Dell, *née* Vanson; 1 s; *Career* formerly: exec dir Bank of England, dir Portals Water Treatment Ltd; *Style—* Jack Davies, Esq, OBE; 31 Wingate Way, Cambridge (☎ 0223 841284)

DAVIES, Rev Jacob Arthur Christian; s of Jacob S Davies, and Christiana Davies; *b* 24 May 1925; *Educ* Univ of Reading (BSc), Selwyn Coll Cambridge, Imperial Coll of Tropical Agric; *m* Sylvia Onikeh Cole; 2 s, 2 da; *Career* high cmmr for Sierra Leone in London 1972-74; non-resident ambass to Denmark, Sweden and Norway 1972-74; dir Personnel Div FAO 1976- (formerly dep dir Agric Operations Div); *Style—* The Rev Jacob Davies; Agricultural Operations Division, FAO, Viale Delle Terme di Caracalla, Rome, Italy

DAVIES, Hon Mrs (Joan Mary); *née* Royle; da of Baron Royle (Life Peer, d 1975); *b* 17 Dec 1920; *m* 1, 1942 (m dis 1963), Gordon Dixon; 1 s; m 2, 1975, Albert Roberts (d 1980); m 3, 1987, Rev John Atcherley Davies; *Style—* The Hon Mrs Davies; The Vicarage, Hyde, Fordingbridge, Hants SP6 2QJ (☎ 0452 53216)

DAVIES, John; s of John Charles Davies (d 1987), of Birmingham, and Kathleen Anne, *née* Snipe; *b* 12 July 1946; *Educ* Bournville Boys Tech Sch Birmingham; *m* 6 Nov 1971, Jacqueline, da of William Springall Wheeler; 1 s (Charles William b 26 Nov 1974), 3 da (Alison Jane b 29 April 1976, Nicola Kate b 23 March 1978, Lucy Anne b 25 June 1980); *Career* trainee investment analyst Midland Assurance Ltd Birmingham 1964-67; investment analysis: J M Finn & Co (Stockbrokers) 1968-71, Nat Coal Bd Pension Fund 1971-73; Confederation Life Insurance Co: asst mangr equity investmt 1973-74, mangr pension investmts 1974-76, mangr segregated funds investmts 1976-79, dep investmt mangr 1979-82; investmt mangr 3i Group plc 1982-84, md 3i Portfolio Management Ltd 1984-; govr and trustee St Michael Sch Sunninghill; AMSIA 1970; *Recreations* music, reading, hill walking; *Clubs* Girt Clog Climbing; *Style—* John Davies, Esq; 3i Portfolio Management Ltd, 91 Waterloo Road, London SE1 8XP (☎ 071 928 3131, fax 071 928 0058)

DAVIES, Prof John Christopher Hughes (Christie); s of Christopher George Davies (d 1984), and Marian Eileen, *née* Johns (d 1975); *b* 25 Dec 1941; *Educ* Dynevor Sch, Emmanuel Coll Cambridge (BA, MA); *Career* tutor in economics Univ of Adelaide Aust 1964, radio prodr BBC Radio 3 prog 1967-69, lectr in sociology Univ of Leeds 1969-72, visiting lectr in sociology Indian univs incl Univ of Bombay and Univ of Delhi 1973-74, prof of sociology Univ of Reading 1984- (lectr then sr lectr then reader 1972-84), distinguished scholars interdisciplinary lectr Inst of Humane Studies George Mason Univ Virginia 1986; *Books* Wrongful Imprisonment (with R Brandon, 1973), Permissive Britain (1975), Censorship and Obscenity (with R Dhavan, 1978), Ethnic Humor Around the World (1990); *Recreations* travel, solitude, jokes; *Clubs* Union Soc (Cambridge); *Style—* Prof Christie Davies; Dept of Sociology, University of Reading, Whiteknights, Reading, Berks RG6 2AA (☎ 0734 318518, fax 0734 314404, telex 947813)

DAVIES, (David) John; s of J N J Davies (d 1978), of Epsom, and P Davies, *née* Williams (d 1983); *b* 17 March 1933; *Educ* Christ's Coll Cambridge (MA); *m* 29 Oct 1960, Pauline Margot, s of E R Owen (d 1955), of Ashtead; 2 s (Gordon Howard b 1964, Richard James b 1967, d 1988); *Career* analyst Cazenove and Co 1968-71, managing ptnr and md Quilter Goodison Co 1981-86 (joined 1971, ptnr 1973), dep md Paribas Ltd 1987-; Freeman: City of London, Worshipful Co of Upholders; memb Stock Exchange 1973, MBIM, FRSA, fell IOD; *Recreations* water sports; *Clubs* Carlton; *Style—* John Davies, Esq; Paddock Cottage, Downsway, Tadworth, Surrey KT20 5DH (☎ 073 781 3226); Paribas Ltd, 33 Wigmore St, London W1H OBN (☎ 071 355 2000, fax 081 895 2544)

DAVIES, Dr John Douglas (Jack); s of Maj William Herbert Douglas Davies (d 1987), and Ethel Mary Sheila, *née* Smith (d 1984); *b* 10 Aug 1936; *Educ* St Pauls, Univ of London (MB BS, MD); *m* 1 June 1963, (Patricia) Maureen, da of Thomas Addison (d 1969); 1 s (William Alexander Douglas b 1967), 3 da (Penelope Jane b 1964, Rachel Laura b 1966, Anthonia Ruth b 1969); *Career* sr registrar Bart's 1966-72, conslt sr lectr in pathology Univ of Bristol and Bristol Royal Infirmary 1972-, dir Regional Breast Pathology Unit Southend Hosp, lectr in cellular pathology Bristol Poly 1975-; external examiner: RCS, RCPath, Univs of Manchester and Wales 1982-, Worshipful Society of Apothecaries London 1990-; over 200 medico-scientific papers on breast and elastic pathology; vice pres Academicals CC, memb Editorial Bd W of Eng Med Jl 1989-, chm Information Gp Breast Pathology Advsy Ctee, memb Ctee Pathological Soc GB 1983-87, chm SW regnl Histopathology Gp 1983-88, memb RCPath Acad Activity Ctee, memb cncl and post graduate educn sec Assoc Clinical Pathologists 1984-, pres Wessex ACP 1990-; memb Worshipful Soc of Apothecaries 1990; LRCP 1961, MRCPath 1969, FRCPath 1980, MRCS 1961, FRSM 1969; *Books* Periductal Mastitis (1971), Vascular Disturbances in AG Stansfeld's Lymph Node Biopsy Interpretation (1985), Guidelines for Course Organisers (1990); *Recreations* fly-fishing, dog walking, wood watching; *Style—* Dr Jack Davies; 20 Clifton Park, Clifton, Bristol BS8 3BZ (☎ 0272 734294); 70 The Watton, Brecon, Powys LD3 7EL (☎ 0874 5926); Regional Breast Pathology Unit, Southmead Hospital, Bristol BS10 5NB (☎ 0272 505050 ext 4169, fax 0272 509690)

DAVIES, Prof John Duncan; OBE (1984); s of Ioan Davies, and Gertrude Davies; *b* 19 March 1929; *Educ* Pontardwe Sch, Treforest Sch of Mines, Univ of London (PhD, DSc); *m* 1949, Barbara, *née* Morgan; 3 da; *Career* formerly prof of civil engrg and dean Univ Coll Swansea, princ W Glam Inst of Higher Educn 1976-77, dir Poly of Wales 1978; memb: OU Delegacy 1978-83 (Visiting Ctee 1986-89), MSC Ctee Wales 1979-83, Wales Advsy Body for Higher Educn 1982-88, Cncl for Nat Academic Awards (CNAA) 1985-; *Style—* Prof John Davies, OBE; Polytechnic of Wales, Treforest, Pontypridd, Mid Glam, Wales (☎ 0443 405133)

DAVIES, John Howard; CBE (1984), DL (Clwyd 1986); s of Rev William Hugh Davies (d 1981), of Cardiff, and Mary Eunice, *née* Thomas (d 1971); *b* 6 May 1926; *Educ* Holyhead Co Sch, UCW, Poitiers Univ France (BA, DipEd); *m* 5 Oct 1954, Elizabeth, da of James Jenkins, JP (d 1965), of Carmarthen; 3 s (Jonathan b 1956, Mark b 1958, Timothy b 1960); *Career* Capt Royal Welch Fusiliers 1944-48, cmmnd Indian Mil Acad; served: India, Burma, Malaya, Sumatra; Colonial Educn Serv North Nigeria 1952-56, dist educn offr Notts 1957-58, dep dir of educn Montgomeryshire 1958-66; Flintshire: dep dir of educn 1966-70, dir of educn 1970-74; Clwyd 1974-85; chm: Welsh Fourth Channel Authy (S4C) 1986, Cncl UCW Bangor, Clwyd Appeal Fund for Hosp Scanner Equipment; memb: Cncl and Ct UCW, Cncl UCW (Coll of Med), Cncl and Ct Nat Library of Wales, N Wales Arts Cncl; hon memb Gorsedd of Bards 1985; FRSA 1980; *Recreations* golf, gardening; *Style—* John Howard Davies, Esq, CBE, DL; Staddle Stones, Hendy Rd, Mold, Clwyd (☎ 0352 700110); S4C, Sophia Close, Cardiff (☎ 0222 343421, fax 0222 341643, telex 9401 7032 SIAN G)

DAVIES, John Howard; s of Jack Davies; *b* 9 March 1939; *Educ* Haileybury, Imperial Service Coll, Grenoble Univ; *Career* child film actor 1948: Oliver in Oliver Twist, The Rocking Horse Winner, Tom in Tom Brown's Schooldays; BBC: prodn asst 1967, prodr 1969, head of comedy 1977-82, head of Light Entertainment Gp 1982-85; controller of light entertainment Thames TV 1988- (prodr and dir 1985-); BBC credits incl: The World of a Beachcomber, All Gas and Gaiters, The Goodies, Steptoe and Son, Monty Python's Flying Circus, The Good Life, Fawlty Towers, The Other One; Thames TV credits incl: Executive Stress, We'll Think Of Something, Andy Capp, Mr Bean, No Job For A Lady; winner: two BAFTA awards, Golden Rose of Montreux, The City of Montreux prize, Press prize; *Style—* John Howard Davies, Esq; c/o Michael Whitehall, 125 Gloucester Rd, London SW7 4TE (☎ 071 244 8466, fax 071 244 9060)

DAVIES, Wing Cdr John Irfon; MBE (1963); s of Thomas Mervyn Davies, of Porthcawl, and Mary Margaret, *née* Harris (d 1988); *b* 8 June 1930; *Educ* Stanley Sch, Croydon Poly; *m* 20 Dec 1950, Jean Marion, da of late John Bruce Anderson , of Darlington; 1 da (Jane b 1957); *Career* RAF 1948, cmmnd 1950, Flying Coll 1956, Staff Coll 1963, Coll of Air Warfare 1970, MOD 1970-72 (and 1964-66), Cabinet Office 1972-74; Welsh Office: princ Housing Div 1974-76, private sec to Sec of State for Wales 1976-78, asst sec agric policy 1978-82, asst sec housing policy 1983-84, under sec housing health and social policy 1985-86, under sec and head Agric Dept 1986-90; dir Sallingburybasy (Wales) 1990-; lay memb GMC 1990-, sec Univ of Wales Review Bd 1990-; *Recreations* golf, music, fishing; *Clubs* Farmers, Radyr Golf, RAF; *Style—* Wing Cdr John Davies, MBE; Friston, 15 Windsor Rd, Radyr, Cardiff CF4 8BQ (☎ 0222 84267)

DAVIES, John Kenyon; s of Harold Edward Davies (d 1990), of Cardiff, and Clarice Theresa, *née* Woodburn (d 1989); *b* 19 Sept 1937; *Educ* Manchester GS, Wadham Coll Oxford (BA), Merton Coll Oxford (MA), Balliol Coll Oxford (DPhil); *m* 1, 8 Sept 1962 (m dis 1978), Anna Elbina Laura Margherita, da of A Morpurgo (d 1939), of Rome; m 2, 5 Aug 1978, Nicola Jane, da of Dr R M S Perrin; 1 s (Martin b 1979), 1 da (Penelope b 1981); *Career* Harmsworth scholar Merton Coll Oxford 1960-63, jr fell Centre for Hellenic Studies Washington DC 1961-62, Dyson jr fell Balliol Coll 1963-65, lectr in ancient history Oriel Coll Oxford 1968-77, Rathbone prof of ancient history and classical archaeology Univ of Liverpool 1977-, pro vice chllr Univ of Liverpool 1986-90; ed: Journal of Hellenic Studies 1973-77, Archaeological Reports 1972-74; chm: St Patrick's Isle (IOM) Archaeological Tst 1982-85, NW Archaeological Tst 1982-; FBA 1985, FSA 1986, FRSA 1988; *Books* Athenian Propertied Families 600-300BC (1971), Democracy and Classical Greece (1978), Wealth and the Power of Wealth in Classical Athens (1981), The Trojan War: its historicity and context (jt ed with L Foxhall, 1984); *Recreations* choral singing; *Style—* Prof John R Davies, FSA; 20 North Rd, Grassendale Park, Liverpool L19 0LR (☎ 051 427 2126); School of Archaeology Classics and Oriental Studies, University of Liverpool, Abercromby Square, P O Box 147, Liverpool L69 3BX (☎ 051 794 2400, fax 051 708 6502, telex 027 0 UNILPL G)

DAVIES, John Michael; s of Vincent Ellis Davies, of W Sussex; *b* 2 Aug 1940; *Educ* Kings Sch Canterbury, Peterhouse Cambridge; *m* 1971, Amanda Mary, da of Hedley Wilton Atkinson, of Devon; 2 s (William b 1976, Harry b 1982), 1 da (Anna b 1973); *Career* clerk Parliament Office House of Lords 1964, private sec Leader of House & Chief Whip House of Lords 1971; sec: to Chm of Ctees and Establishment Offr 1974, Statute Law Ctee 1974-83; princ clerk Overseas & European Office 1983, clerk Private Bills and Examiner of Petitions for Private Bills 1985, reading clerk and clerk of Public Bills 1988, clerk asst 1991, sec of Soc of Clerks-at-the-Table in Cwlth Parliaments (joint ed of The Table) 1967-83; *Style—* Michael Davies, Esq; 26 Northchurch Terrace, London N1 4EG; House of Lords, SW1 (☎ 071 219 3000)

DAVIES, Jonathan; s of Leonard Davies (d 1976), of Trimsaran, and Diana, *née* Rees; *b* 24 Oct 1962; *Educ* Gwendraeth GS; *m* 11 Aug 1984, Karen Marie, da of Byron J Hopkins; 1 s (Matthew Scott b 20 July 1988); *Career* Rugby League threequarters Widnes RLFC and Great Britain (6 caps), former Rugby Union outhalf Llanelli RFC and Wales (27 caps); clubs: Trimsaran, Neath RFC, Llanelli RFC, Barbarians RFC, Irish Wolfhounds RFC, Scottish Co-optimists RFC, Welsh Cravshays RFC, Widnes RLFC; Wales: debut v Eng 1985, memb World Cup Squad (6 appearances) 1987, memb Triple Crown Winning team 1988, tour NZ (2 test appearances) 1988; selected for Br Lions 1988 (did not tour), joined Widnes RLFC for World record signing fee 1989, GB tour NZ 1990; *Books* Jonathan (1989); *Recreations* any sport; *Style—* Jonathan Davies, Esq; Widnes Rugby League Football Club,

Naughton Park, Lower House Lane, Widnes, Cheshire (☎ 051 4952250, fax 051 423 2720)

DAVIES, Hon Jonathan Hugh; s of 2 Baron Davies; *b* 25 Jan 1944; *Educ* Eton, Univ Coll Oxford; *m* 15 Oct 1966, (Mary) Veronica, da of Sir (William) Godfrey Agnew, KCVO; 2 s, 4 da; *Career* memb Museums and Galleries Cmmn 1985-; *Style—* The Hon Jonathan Davies; Stonehill House, Abingdon, Berks

DAVIES, Keith Laurence Maitland; s of Wyndham Matabele Davies, QC (d 1972), and Enid Maud Davies (d 1971); *b* 3 Feb 1938; *Educ* Winchester, ChCh Oxford (MA); *m* 20 June 1964, Angela Mary, da of C D Fraser Jenkins; 1 s (Julian b 1973), 2 da (Claire b 1967, Annabel b 1968); *Career* called to the Bar Inner Temple 1962, private practice 1962-84, met stipendiary magistrate 1984-; *Style—* Keith Davies, Esq; c/o 1 Paper Buildings, London EC4

DAVIES, Kenneth Seymour; s of George Seymour Davies, of Eastcote, Middx, and (Isobel) Dorothy, *née* Corfield; *b* 11 Feb 1948; *Educ* St Nicholas GS Northwood; *m* 15 May 1971, Brenda Margaret, da of William George Cannon (d 1987), of Ruislip, Middx; 4 s (Mark b 1972, Peter b 1974, Robert b 1976, Trevor b 1982), 1 da (Kirsty b 1980); *Career* CA 1970; ptnr Pannell Kerr Forster 1974-; hon treas Willing Wheels Club (cancer charity); FCA; *Recreations* gardening, walking; *Style—* Kenneth Davies, Esq; Braunston, 15 Berks Hill, Chorleywood, Herts WD3 5AG (☎ 0923 282156); Pannell Kerr Forster, 78 Hatton Garden, London EC1N 8JA (☎ 071 831 7393, fax 071 405 6737, telex 295928)

DAVIES, Laura Jane; MBE (1988); da of David Thomas Davies, and Rita Ann, *née* Foskett; *b* 5 Oct 1963; *Educ* Fullbrook Co Secdy Sch; *Career* golfer; memb Curtis Cup Team 1984, Br Open Ladies Golf Champion 1986, US Open Champion 1987, 15 Tournament wins in professional career 1985-; memb Golf Fndn; *Recreations* all sport, music; *Style—* Miss Laura Davies, MBE

DAVIES, (Robert) Leighton; s of Robert Brinley Davies (d 1978), of Cwmparc, Rhondda, Mid Glamorgan, and Elizabeth Nesta , *née* Jones; *b* 7 Sept 1949; *Educ* Rhondda County GS Porth, CCC Oxford (BA, BCL); *m* 25 Aug 1979, Linda Davies, da of David Fox, of Park Rd, Cwmparc, Rhondda, Mid Glamorgan; 1 s (Rhoss b 30 May 1980), 1 da (Rhia b 12 Nov 1985); *Career* called to the Bar Gray's Inn 1975; practising barr in Cardiff 1975-, appointed asst rec 1990; memb: Greenpeace, The Criminal Bar Assoc 1988; *Recreations* fly fishing, gardening, watching rugby football; *Style—* Leighton Davies, Esq; Bryn Corun, Glyncoli Road, Treorchy, Rhondda, Mid-Glamorgan (☎ 0443 774559); 34 Park Place, Cardiff CF1 3TN (☎ 0222 382731, fax 0222 222542)

DAVIES, Maldwyn Thomas; s of Mervyn Davies (d 1985), of Merthyrtydfil, Mid Glam, S Wales, and Ceinwe, *née* Williams (d 1983); *b* 24 Oct 1950; *Educ* Welsh Coll of Music and Drama Cardiff (B Mus), Royal Acad of Music (LRAM); *m* 5 August 1978, Christine Margaret, da of Howard Jestyn Powell; 2 da (Bethan Catherine b 18 January 1985, Elin Angharad b 22 March 1987); *Career* singer; appearances at festivals: Edinburgh, Leeds, Bath, Cheltenham, Fishguard, Windsor, Hong Kong, Florence, Bergen, Vienna; concerts: Bach Choir, Huddersfield Choral Soc, BBC Welsh Symphony, LSO Scot Nat Orchestra, BBC Philharmonic, The Philharmonia, Acad of St Martin-in-the Fields; contract player Royal Opera House Covent Garden 1980-82 (small roles in Billy Budd and Alceste); other opera performances incl: Cosi Fan Tutti (Lyric Opera of Old), L'Isola Disabitata (Wexford Festival), Das Rheingold (The Ring Cycle Bayreuth Festival), The Seraglio (Kent Opera), Alceste (Geneva), The Seraglio, The Magic Flute and Cosi Fan Tutti (Scot Opera), debut A Midsummer Marriage (ENO); records exclusively for the BBC; recordings: Boughton's The Immortal Hour, Bridge's The Christmas Rose, The Haydn Nelson Mass, The Messiah, Alcina, Stainer's The Crucifixion, Mozart's Requiem; silver medal Welsh Coll of Music and Drama; ARCM; *Recreations* horse and ponies, fishing, films; *Style—* Maldwyn Davies, Esq; Lies Askonas Ltd, 186 Drury Lane, London WC2B 5RY (☎ 071 405 1808)

DAVIES, Prof Margaret Constance (Mrs E W J Mitchell); da of Capt Harry Brown (d 1925), of Manchester, and Margaret Hilda *née* Croft; *b* 4 May 1923; *Educ* Queen Mary Sch Lytham, Somerville Coll Oxford (MA), Sorbonne Paris (Doctorat de L'Universite de Paris); *m* 1; 1 s (Martin b 1949), 1 da (Philippa b 1953); m 2, 25 Jan 1985, Prof Sir (Edgar) William John Mitchell, CBE, FRS, *qv*, s of Edgar Mitchell (d 1964); *Career* lectr Westfield Coll London 1962-64; Univ of Reading: lectr 1964-70, reader 1970-75, prof 1975-88, emeritus prof 1988-, Univ of Nottingham special prof 1989-; govr Queen Anne Sch Reading; memb: Assoc Internationale des Etudes Françaises, Soc French Studies, Assoc of Univ Profs of French, Academia Europaea; *Publications* Two Gold Rings (1954), Colette (1958), Appolinaire (1962), Une Saison en Enfer de Rimbaud (1975), various articles on modern French poetry; *Recreations* music, opera, reading, good food, cooking, travel; *Style—* Prof Margaret Davies

DAVIES, Mark Edward Trehearne; s of Denis Norman Davies, of Slinfold, Sussex, and Patricia Helen, *née* Trehearne; *b* 20 May 1948; *Educ* Stowe; *m* 1, 8 June 1974 (m dis 1984), Serena Barbara, *née* Palmer; m 2, 20 Nov 1987, Antonia Catherine, da of Jeremy Barrow Chittenden, of Lytes Cary Manor, Somerset; 1 s (Hugo b 5 Oct 1989), 1 da (Sophia b 13 May 1988); *Career* commodity broker Ralli Int 1969, fndr Inter Commodities 1972 (awarded Queens Award for Export Achievement 1981), md GNI Ltd (formerly Inter Commodities Ltd) 1972; dir: GNI Holdings Ltd 1976, Inter Commodities Trading Ltd 1976, Tweseldown Racecourse Ltd 1979; chm GNI Freight Futures Ltd 1981; dir: ICV Information Systems Ltd 1981, Inter Commodities Ltd 1982, Gerrard and Nat Holdings plc 1985, Guy Morrison Ltd 1986, GH Asset Management Ltd 1988; chm GNI Wallace Ltd 1986; memb London Metal Exchange; *Books* Trading in Commodities (co-author, 1974); *Recreations* hunting, racing; *Clubs* Lansdowne; *Style—* Mark Davies, Esq; 25 Mulberry Walk, London SW3; Colechurch House, 1 London Bridge Walk, London SE1 2SX (☎ 071 378 7171, fax 071 407 3848, car 0860 519 400)

DAVIES, Lady (Mary Bailey); *née* Liptrot; da of Henry Liptrot, of Aberstwyth; *m* 1933, Rt Hon Sir (William) Arthian Davies, (d 1979); 1 da; *Style—* Lady Davies; Ballinger Lodge, Great Missenden, Bucks

DAVIES, Mel John; s of William John Davies, of 45 Parkwood Drive, Rhiwderin, Gwent, and Ruby Rosalie Davies; *b* 27 Aug 1948; *Educ* Duffryn Comp Sch, Newport Tech Coll; *m* 6 Sept 1980, Rosalie Rhonda, da of James Iorwerth James; 2 s (Gregory James b 12 Sept 1987, Jonathan William b 24 Jan 1990); *Career* racehorse owner; total 25 race wins, 17 by Barnbrook Again: Queen Mother Champion 2m chase (twice), Arlington Premier Final, Gerry Fielden Hurdle, Ladbroke Hurdle Leopardstown, Comton Brothers Chase, Hurst Park Chase, 5 times winner Newbury, 5 times winner Cheltenham incl South Wales Showers Caradon Mira Silver Trophy; records held by Barnbrook Again: 2m course Newbury, 2 1/2m course Cheltenham; sponsor of 5 races Cheltenham and 3 races Chepstow, presenter Channel 4 racing Newmarket 1990; apprentice plumber then plumber, fndr md South Wales Shower Supplies; raised money towards res into children's cancer illnesses and for Spinal Injuries Assoc; nominated for S Wales Young Businessman award 1988; *Recreations* horse-racing, former Newport County FC devotee, various charities; *Style—* Mel Davies, Esq; 11 Bridewell Gardens, Undy, Magor, Gwent NP6 3JZ; Unit 4, Court Rd, Cwmbran, Gwent NP44 3AS (☎ 0633 872828, fax 0633 872264)

DAVIES, (Albert) Meredith; CBE (1982); s of Rev E A Davies; *b* 30 July 1922; *Educ* Stationers Co's Sch, Keble Coll Oxford, RCM, Accademia di St Cecilia Rome; *m* 1949, Betty Hazel, *née* Bates; 3 s, 1 da; *Career* conductor: Royal Choral Soc 1972-85, Leeds Philharmonic Soc 1975-83; princ Trinity Coll of Music 1979-88; *Style—* Meredith Davies, Esq, CBE; 40 Monmouth St, Bridgwater, Somerset TA6 5EJ

DAVIES, Prof (Cyril Thomas) Mervyn; s of Cyril Thomas Davies, of Bridgnorth, Shropshire, and Florence Davies (d 1985); *b* 2 Dec 1933; *Educ* Univ of London (BSc), Univ of Edinburgh (PhD, DSc); *m* 30 March 1963, Jacqueline Grace, da of Raymond John Morgan, of Lyme Regis; 2 s (Jonathan b 16 March 1965, James Davies b 26 April 1966), 1 da (Susanna Davies b 17 Oct 1970); *Career* lectr Univ of Edinburgh 1962-65, lectr and res scientist MRC 1965-79, visiting prof Univ of Milan 1968-69, conslt WHO 1969, prof of physiology Dar es Salaam Tanzania 1970-72, visiting res prof Stockholm Sweden 1973, visiting prof Copenhagen Denmark 1975, dir Med Res Cncl Unit Queens Med Centre Nottingham 1979-85, fndn prof of sport and exercise scis Univ of Birmingham 1986-; sec Int Paediatric Work Physiology Gp 1976, physiological conslt to Sports Cncl 1977-78, ed Bd of European Jl of Applied Physiology 1977; memb Physiological Soc; *Recreations* gardening, bridge, squash racquets, reading; *Clubs* Edgbaston Priory (Birmingham); *Style—* Prof Mervyn Davies; The Coach House, Pumphouse Lane, Barnt Green, Bromsgrove, Worcs B60 1QW (☎ 021 445 4745); PO Box 363, The University of Birmingham B15 2TT (☎ 021 414 4113)

DAVIES, Hon Justice (David Herbert) Mervyn; MC (1944), TD (1946); s of Herbert Bowen and Esther Davies; *b* 17 Jan 1918; *Educ* Swansea GS; *m* 1951, Zita Yollanne Angelique Blanche Antoinette, da of Rev E A Phillips, of Bale, Norfolk; *Career* served WWII 18 Bn Welch Regt, 2 London Irish Rifles in Africa and Europe; admitted slr 1939, called to the Bar Lincoln's Inn 1947, QC 1967, circuit judge 1978-82, high court judge chancery 1982-; kt 1982; *Style—* The Hon Mr Justice Mervyn Davies, MC, TD; 7 Stone Buildings, Lincoln's Inn, WC2 (☎ 071 242 8061); The White House, Great Snoring, Norfolk (☎ 0328 820 575)

DAVIES, Sir (Alfred William) Michael; s of Alfred Edward Davies (d 1958), of Stourbridge, Worcs; *b* 29 July 1921; *Educ* King Edward's Sch Birmingham, Birmingham Univ; *m* 1947, Margaret, da of Robert Ernest Jackson, of Sheffield; 1 s, 3 da; *Career* barrister Lincoln's Inn 1948, QC 1964, leader Midland Circuit 1968, dep chm Northants Quarter Sessions 1963-71; recorder: Grantham 1963-65, Derby 1965-71, Crown Ct 1972; judge of the High Ct of Justice (Queen's Bench Div) 1973-91; chm Mental Health Review Tribunal for Birmingham Area 1965-71, chllr Diocese of Derby 1971-73, chm Hospital Complaints Procedure Ctee 1971-73; kt 1973; *Style—* Sir Michael Davies; Royal Courts of Justice, London WC2

DAVIES, (Angie) Michael; *b* 23 June 1934; *Educ* Shrewsbury, Queens' Coll Cambridge (MA); *m* 1960, Jane Priscilla; 2 children; *Career* CA; former chm and chief exec Imperial Foods and dir Imperial Gp (to May 1982); chm: Tozer Kemsley and Millburn Hldgs 1985-86 (non-exec dir 1982-86), Worth Investmt Tst 1986 (non-exec dir 1984), Bredero Properties 1986, Perkins Foods 1987, Calor Gp 1988 (non-exec dir 1987), Berk Ltd 1988, Wiltshier plc 1988; dep chm: TI Group 1990 (non-exec dir 1984), Manpower 1989 (non-exec dir 1987); non-exec dir: British Airways 1983, Avdel 1983, Littlewoods Orgn 1982-88, TV-am 1983-89; *Style—* A Michael Davies Esq; Little Woolpit, Ewhurst, Cranleigh, Surrey (☎ 0483 277344); 7 Lowndes Close, London SW1 (☎ 071 235 6134)

DAVIES, (John) Michael; s of Vincent Ellis Davies, OBE, of Bentley Lodge, E Grinstead, Sussex and Rose Trench, *née* Temple; *b* 2 Aug 1940; *Educ* King's Sch Canterbury, Peterhouse Cambridge (BA); *m* 1971, Amanda, da of Hedley Wilton Atkinson, of Shaldon, Devon; 2 s (William b 1976, Harry b 1982), 1 da (Anna b 1973); *Career* private sec to ldr of House of Lords and chief whip 1971-74, princ clerk Overseas and Euro Off 1983-85, clerk of private bills House of Lords 1985; *Recreations* cricket, France; *Style—* Michael Davies Esq; 26 Northchurch Terrace, London N1 4EG; House of Lords, London SW1 (☎ 01 219 3233)

DAVIES, Prof (John) Michael; s of Alfred Ernest Davies (d 1975), of Walsall, and Mavies Muriel, *née* Wildgoose (d 1979); *Educ* Queen Mary's GS Walsall, Univ of Manchester (BSc, PhD, DSc); *m* 24 June 1967, Anthea Dorothy, da of Rex Henry Percy, MBE, DL, of Guildford; 1 s (Peter b 18 Nov 1972), 1 da (Claire b 16 Oct 1974); *Career* lectr Univ of Manchester 1962-65, engr Ove Arup & Partners Edinburgh 1965-70, visiting prof Univ of Karlsruhe 1980-81, chm Civil Engrg Dept Univ of Salford 1988- (reader 1971-80, prof 1981); memb: Br Standards Ctees, Ctee Euro Convention for Constructional Steelwork; ctee coordinator Int Bldg Cncl 1985-89; FIStructE 1976, FICE 1977; *Books* Manual of Stressed Skin Diaphragm Design (with E R Bryan, 1982); *Recreations* tennis, golf, skiing; *Clubs* Ski Club of GB, Didsbury Golf, Hale Lawn Tennis; *Style—* Prof Michael Davies; 83 Park Road, Hale, Altrincham, Cheshire WA15 9LQ (☎ 061 980 2838); Department of Civil Engineering and Construction, University of Salford, Salford M5 4WT (☎ 061 736 5843, fax 061 745 5060)

DAVIES, Norman Thomas; MBE (1970), JP (Hants 1984); s of Edward Ernest Davies (d 1937), and Elsie, *née* Scott; *b* 2 May 1933; *Educ* Holywell, RMA Sandhurst, Open Univ (BA); *m* 1961, Penelope Mary, da of Peter Graeme Agnew, of Cornwall; 1 s (Peter), 1 da (Clare); *Career* cmmnd RA 1954, served Malaya, Germany and UK 1954-64, mil asst to COS Northern Army Gp 1968-69, cmd C Battery RHA, 2 i/c 3 Regt RHA 1970-72, GSO I (DS) Staff Coll Camberley and Canadian Land Forces Cmd and Staff Coll 1972-74, cmd 4 Field Regt RA 1975-77, mil dir of studies RMC of Sci Shrivenham 1977-80 (Col 1977); registrar Gen Dental Cncl 1981; memb EEC Advsy Ctee on the Trg of Dental Practitioners 1983; *Recreations* golf, gardening, wine, household maintenance; *Style—* Norman Davies, Esq, MBE, JP; Lowfields Cottage, London Rd, Hartley Wintney, Hamps (☎ 025 126 3303); General Dental Council, 37 Wimpole St, London W1M 8DQ

DAVIES, Sir Oswald; CBE (1973), DCM (1944), JP (1969); s of George Warham Davies, and Margaret, *née* Hinton; *b* 23 June 1920; *Educ* Central Schs Sale, Manchester Coll of Technol; *m* 1942, Joyce, da of Thomas Henry Eaton; 1 s, 1 da; *Career* dir Fairclough Construction Group (chief exec 1965-78, chm 1965-83), chm Amec plc 1983-85 (dir 1985); CBIM, FIHT, FCIOB, FFB, FRGS, FRSA; kt 1984; *Style—* Sir Oswald Davies, CBE, DCM, JP; c/o Amec plc, Sandiway House, Northwich, Cheshire CW8 2YA (☎ 0606 883885)

DAVIES, Owen Mansel; s of D Mansel Davies, of Penarth, South Glamorgan, and Margaret Phyllis, *née* Hunt; *b* 3 June 1934; *Educ* Swansea GS, Clifton Coll, Peterhouse Cambridge (BA, MA); *m* 1960, Elisabeth Jean Leedham; 1 s (Timothy Mansel b 8 May 1963), 2 da (Catherine Elisabeth b 30 July 1961, Susan Margaret b 12 July 1966); *Career* Nat Serv Lt RA 1953-55; BP International technologist Aden Petroleum Refinery 1960-64, process engr London 1965-68, project engr BP Italia Rome 1969, mangr Catalytic Branch BP Trading Ltd 1970-72, mangr Projects Div Refineries Dept BP Trading Ltd 1972-75, md BP SE Asia Singapore 1975-78, pres Sohio Construction Co San Francisco 1978-80, gen mangr Projects London 1981-88, gen mangr Business Services BP Engineering London 1988-; FInstPet 1978, FIChemE 1985, FEng 1989, CEng, Eur Ing; *Recreations* sailing, gardening, photography; *Style—* Owen Davies, Esq; BP Engineering, Uxbridge One, 1 Harefield Rd, Uxbridge, Middx UB8 1PD (☎ 0895 25501)

DAVIES, Patrick Taylor; CMG (1978), OBE (1967); s of Andrew Taylor Davies (d

1983), and Olive Kathleen Mary, *née* Hobson (d 1972); *b* 10 Aug 1927; *Educ* Shrewsbury, St John's Coll Cambridge (BA), Trinity Coll Oxford; *m* 1959, Marjorie Eileen, da of late Arthur Wilkinson; 2 da (Jennifer, Susan); *Career* entered HM Colonial Admin Serv Nigeria 1952, perm sec Kano State 1970-79, chief inspr Area Cts 1972-79; *Style—* Patrick Davies, Esq, CMG, OBE; Rose Cottage, Childs Ercall, Salop TF9 2DB (☎ 095 278 255)

DAVIES, Prof Paul Charles William; s of Hugh Augustus Robert Davies, of London, and Pearl Vera, *née* Birrell; *b* 22 April 1946; *Educ* Woodhouse GS Finchley, UCL (BSc, PhD); *m* 1, 13 July 1968 (m dis 1972), Janet Elaine, *née* Hammill; m 2, 28 July 1972, Susan Vivien Corti, da of Corti Woodcock (d 1958); 1 s (Charles Hugh Aidan b 1981), 1 da (Annabel Eleanor b 1977); *Career* former prof Dept of Physics Univ of Newcastle upon Tyne, currently prof Dept of Physics and Mathematical Physics Univ of Adelaide S Aust; former govr Dame Allan's Schs Newcastle upon Tyne, vice pres Teilhard de Chardin Centre; FInstP 1984, FAIP 1990; *Books* The Physics of Time Asymmetry (1974 and 1977), Space and Time in the Modern Universe (1977), The Forces of Nature (1979, 2 edn 1986), The Search for Gravity Waves (1980), The Runaway Universe (1978), The Edge of Infinity (1981), The Accidental Universe (1982), Quantum Fields in Curved Space (with N D Birrell, 1982), God and the New Physics (1983), Quantum Mechanics (1984), Superforce (1984), The Ghost in the Atom (with J R Brown, 1986), The Cosmic Blueprint (1987), Superstrings (with J R Brown, 1988), The New Physics (ed, 1989); fiction: Fireball (1987); numerous tech papers incl: Scalar Particle Production in Schwarzschild and Rindler Metrics (1975), The Thermodynamic Theory of Black Holes (1977), Perturbation Technique for Quantum Stress Tensors in a General Robertson-Walker Spacetime (with WG Unruh, 1979), Journey through a Black Hole (with I G Moss, 1989); *Recreations* travel, making radio and television programmes; *Style—* Prof Paul Davies; The University of Adelaide, Dept of Physics & Mathematical Physics, Box 498, GPO Adelaide, South Australia 5001 (☎ 08 228 5685, fax 08 224 0464, telex UNIVAD AA 89141)

DAVIES, Peter Donald; s of Stanley Davies, of Aberystwyth, Dyfed, and Dorothy Margaret, *née* Addicott (d 1987); *b* 14 May 1940; *Educ* Ardwyn Sch Aberystwyth, Guy's Hosp Univ of London (MB BS); *m* 23 May 1965 (m dis 1989), Penelope Anne, da of Wilfred Reginald Dawes; 2 da (Lucy Bronwen b 1969, Emma Sian b 1971); *Career* lectr in experimental opthalmology Inst of Opthalmology London 1967-70, resident Moorfields Eye Hosp 1970-74, sr registrar Middx Hosp and Moorfields Eye Hosp 1974-78, conslt opthalmic surgn Norwich Health Dist 1978-, initiated the devpt of out-patient cataract surgery in the UK 1983-, author of pubns on opthalmology and corneal surgery; FRCS 1973; *Recreations* horse riding, shooting; *Style—* Peter Davies, Esq; Consulting Rooms, Hill House, Old Watton Rd, Colney, Norwich NR4 7SZ (☎ 0603 56181 ext 408)

DAVIES, Peter Douglas Royston; s of Douglas Frederick Davies, of Christchurch, Dorset, and Edna Matilda, *née* Dingle; *b* 29 Nov 1936; *Educ* Brockenhurst Co HS Hants, LSE (BSc); *m* 28 Jan 1967, Elizabeth Mary Lovett, da of Dr Leslie Williams (d 1956); 1 s (Simon Leslie Peter b 1968), 2 da (Eleanor Catherine b 1971, Jane Olivia b 1974); *Career* FCO: FO 1964-66, second sec Nicosia 1966-67, FO 1967-68, first sec Budapest 1968-71, FCO 1971-74, consul Rio de Janiero 1974-78, cnsllr The Hague 1978-82, dep high cmmr Kuala Lumpur 1982-85, RCDS 1986, head Arms Control and Disarmament Dept FCO 1987; *Recreations* reading, walking; *Style—* Peter Davies, Esq; FCO, King Charles St, London SW1A 2AH (☎ 071 270 2242)

DAVIES, (Roger) Peter Havard; OBE (1978); s of Arthur William Davies (d 1926), of Berkswell, and Edith Mary, *née* Mealand (d 1966); *b* 4 Oct 1919; *Educ* Bromsgrove Sch, St Edmund Hall Oxford (MA); *m* 1956, Ferelith Mary Helen, da of Maj John McLaughlin Short (d 1969); 2 s (Mark, Simon), 2 da (Jessica, Lucy); *Career* served WWII, Capt RA (AOP); offr Br Cncl 1949-80: served Hungary, Israel, Sarawak, Finland, Chile and India, dir Drama and Music Dept 1965-69, Info 1974-75; dir: Anti-Slavery Soc 1980-87, Project Mala (India); vice chm: Exec Cncl Int Serv for Human Rights Geneva, Human Rights Sub-Ctee UN Assoc; *Books* Human Rights (1988); *Recreations* music, golf, walking, family life; *Clubs* Royal Cwlth Soc, Union (Oxford), Bengal (Calcutta); *Style—* Peter Davies Esq, OBE; Ley Cottage, Elmore Rd, Chipstead, Surrey CR3 3SG (☎ Downland 253905); United Nations Association, 3 Whitehall Court, London SW1A 2EL

DAVIES, Peter Lewis Morgan; OBE 1978; s of David Morgan Davies (d 1962), and Annie Lee, *née* Jones (d 1983); *b* 15 Feb 1927; *Educ* Fishguard Co Sch; *m* 23 May 1953, Gwenith, da of Thomas Devonald Thomas Cilgerran (d 1969), of Cilgerran; *Career* Lt Welch Regt and Royal Welch Fusiliers 1944-48; Midland Bank plc 1943-51; Barclays Bank Int Ltd: Bahamas 1952-55, Nigeria 1955-67, Libya 1968-70, Zambia 1970-79, mangr Kaunda Square Kitwe (northern area mangr), alternate dir Barclays Zambia Ltd; team ldr World Bank Mission to Indonesia 1979-80, md Pembrokeshire Business Initiative 1983-86, business cncllr Welsh Devpt Agency 1986-89, Br Exec Serv Overseas Fiji 1990 (Turks and Caicos Is 1982-83); memb: TAVRA Wales Regnl Ctee and Assoc, Nat Employers Liaison Ctee Wales; county treas Royal Br Legion Pembrokeshire, hon patron 4 Bn Royal Regt of Wales, memb Bd Fishguard Music Festival; FBIM 1973; *Recreations* photography, philately; *Style—* Peter Davies, Esq, OBE; Court House, Tower Hill, Fishguard, Pembrokeshire SA65 9LA (☎ 0348 873 793)

DAVIES, Prof Peter Owen Alfred Lawe; s of Archdeacon David John Davies (d 1935), of Sydney, NSW, Aust, and Grace Augusta Lawe (d 1984); *b* 24 Oct 1922; *Educ* Canberra GS, Univ of Sydney (BE), Trinity Coll Cambridge (PhD); *m* 1, 15 June 1950, Meg (d 1979), da of Capt Arthur Goodhart Pite, MC (d 1938), of Cheltenham; 1 s (Edward b 1953), 4 da (Marianne b 1951, Helen b 1955, Janet b 1958, Katherine b 1960); m 2, 5 Oct 1982, Shirley Coleman, da of John Green (d 1976); *Career* RAAF 1940-45: cmmnd radar offr 1941, PO, Flying Offr then Flt Lt; RAF Cambridge Univ Sqdn 1948-49: PO, voluntary res serv, flying trainee; RAAF Adelaide Univ Sqdn 1952-56, voluntary res serv as engrg flight cdr; Charles Kolling travelling scholar 1948-50, lectr then sr lectr in fluid mechanics Adelaide Univ 1950-56, reader in sound and vibration Univ of Southampton 1962-72 (sr res fell 1957-62), prof of experimental fluid dynamics Univ of Southampton 1972-88; contrib chapters to many learned texts, papers and scientific jls; memb Southampton Deanery Synod; CEng 1947, FIMechE 1962, MIOA 1975; *Books* Introduction to Dynamic Analysis and Automatic Control (1965); *Recreations* singing, playing music, sailing; *Clubs* Keyhaven Yacht, Hurst Castle Sailing; *Style—* Prof Peter Davies; 80 Highfield Lane, Southampton SO2 1RJ (☎ 0703 555396); Institute of Sound and Vibration Research, University of Southampton SO9 5NH (☎ 0703 592292, fax 0703 553033, telex 47661 SOTON U)

DAVIES, Maj-Gen Peter Ronald; s of Lt-Col Charles Henry Davies, of Crookham Village, Hants, and Joy, *née* Moore; *b* 10 May 1938; *Educ* Llandovery Coll, Welbeck Coll, RMA Sandhurst; *m* 12 Sept 1960, (Rosemary) Julia, da of David Felice (d 1961), of Douglas, IOM; 1 s (Tristan David Henry b 1961), 1 da (Cecily Harriet (Mrs Eaton) b 1963); *Career* cmmnd Royal Signals 1958, served BAOR Berlin, Cyprus, Borneo and UK 1958-68, RMCS 1969, Staff Coll Camberley 1970, OC Artillery Bde Signal Sqdn 1971-72, Bde Maj 20 Armd Bde 1973-74, instr Staff Coll Camberley 1975-76, CO 1 Armd Div Signal Regt 1976-76, Col GS SD HQ UKLF 1979-82, Bde Cdr 12 Armd Bde 1982-84, RCDS 1984, Dep Cmdt Army Staff Coll 1985-86, Col King's Regt (8th, 63rd, 96th) 1986-, chm Regtl Cncl and King's Liverpool and Manchester Regts' Assoc 1986-, Cdr Communications BAOR 1987-90, GOC Wales 1990-, Col Cmdt Royal Signals 1991-; govr Welbeck Coll 1980-81; *Recreations* rugby, music, wine, literature, art medals; *Clubs* Army and Navy, London Rugby, Cardiff and County; *Style—* Maj-Gen Peter Davies; RHQ The King's Regiment, Graeme House, Derby Square, Liverpool L2 7SD

DAVIES, Ven Philip Bertram; s of Rev Bertram Davies (d 1970), and Nancy Jonsson, *née* Nicol (d 1978); *b* 13 July 1933; *Educ* Lancing Coll, Cuddesdon Theol Coll; *m* 29 June 1963, (Elizabeth) Jane, da of The Ven John Farquhar Richardson, *qv*; 2 s (Simon Philip b 1964, Matthew James b 1968), 2 da (Sarah Jane b 1966, d 1973, Eleanor Mary b 1974); *Career* supt Travancore Tea Estates Co S India 1957-58 (asst supt 1954-57), asst sales mangr Lewis's Ltd Manchester 1959-61; asst curate St John the Baptist Atherton Lancs 1963-66, vicar St Mary Magdalen Winton Eccles 1966-71, rector St Philip with St Stephen Salford 1971-76, vicar Christ Church Radlett Herts 1976-87, rural dean Aldenham 1979-87, archdeacon of St Albans 1987; *Recreations* fishing, gardening, bridge; *Style—* The Ven the Archdeacon of St Albans; 6 Sopwell Lane, St Albans, Herts AL1 1RR (☎ 0727 57973)

DAVIES, Maj-Gen Philip Middleton; OBE (1974); s of Hugh Davies (d 1942); *b* 27 Oct 1932; *Educ* Charterhouse; *m* 1956, Mona, da of Richard Wallace (d 1980); 2 c; *Career* CO 1 Bn The Royal Scots 1973-76, Cdr 19 Airportable Bde and 7 Field Force 1977-79, Cdr Land Forces Cyprus 1981-83, Maj-Gen 1983, GOC NW Dist 1983, ret 1986; md Utd Aircraft Industs Ltd 1986-88; *Recreations* flyfishing, tennis, gardening; *Clubs* Army and Navy; *Style—* Maj-Gen Philip Davies, OBE; c/o National Westminster Bank, Warminster, Wilts

DAVIES, Quentin; MP (C) Stamford and Spalding 1987; s of Dr Michael Ivor Davies, and Thelma Davies; *b* 29 May 1944; *Educ* Dragon Sch, Leighton Park, Gonville and Caius Coll Cambridge (BA), Harvard (Frank Knox Fell); *m* 1983, Chantal, da of Lt-Col R L C Tamplin, Military Knight of Windsor; 2 s (Alexander, Nicholas); *Career* HM Dip Serv 1967-74: 3 sec FCO 1967-69, 2 sec Moscow 1969-72, 1 sec FCO 1973-74; Morgan Grenfell & Co Ltd: mangr, subsequently asst dir 1974-78, rep France, dir gen and pres Morgan Grenfell France S A 1978-81 (dir 1981-87); *Recreations* reading, walking, riding, skiing, travel; *Clubs* Beefsteak, Travellers, Constitutional (Spalding), S Lincs Cons (Bourne), Travellers (Paris); *Style—* Quentin Davies, Esq, MP; c/o House of Commons, London SW1

DAVIES, Dr Rachel Bryan; da of John Edwards (d 1960), and Gweno, *née* Davies Bryan (d 1981); *b* 6 Oct 1935; *Educ* Friends' Sch Sibford, Friends' Sch Sidcot, Univ Coll of Wales Aberystyth (LLB), QMC London (LLM), King's Coll London (PhD); *m* 1958, Geraint Tim Davies, s of David Evan Davies; 1 s (Siôn Bryan b 1967), 4 da (Angharad Bryan b 1960, Crisiant Bryan b 1963, Manon Bryan b 1965, Rhianon Bryan b 1968); *Career* called to the Bar Gray's Inn 1965-; res asst Law Faculty Melbourne Univ 1958-62, lectr in law Kingston Polytechnic 1965-67, law reporter The Times 1975-81, commercial law reporter Financial Times 1981-; chm: Rent Tribunals 1981-86, Industl Tribunals 1986-; exec and consultative ed Kluwer Law Publishing 1985-89; De Lancey and De La Hantey prize for medico-legal journalism 1981; FRSA 1990; *Recreations* walking, music, reading; *Style—* Dr Rachel Davies; Gelli Eblyg, Llangynwyd, nr Maesteg, Mid Glamorgan CF34 0DT (☎ 0656 739115); The Financial Times, 1 Southwark Bridge, London SE1 9HL (☎ 071 873 4863, fax 071 407 5700)

DAVIES, Prof (Robert) Rees; s of William Edward Davies (d 1967), of Corwen, Gwynedd, and Sarah Margaret, *née* Williams (d 1986); *b* 6 Aug 1938; *Educ* Ysgol y Berwyn Bala, UCL (BA), Merton Coll Oxford (D Phil); *m* 29 July 1966, Carys, da of Ifor Lloyd Wynne (d 1970), of Wrexham, Clwyd; 1 s (Prys b 11 April 1972), 1 da (Manon b 25 May 1968); *Career* lectr: Univ Coll Swansea 1961-63, UCL 1963-76; prof and head of Dept of History Univ Coll of Wales Aberystwyth 1976- (princ 1988-), asst and review ed History 1963-73, James Ford special lectr Univ of Oxford 1988, Wiles lectr Queen's Univ Belfast 1988; memb: Ancient Monuments Bd for Wales 1978-, Cncl Nat Museum of Wales 1987-, Cncl Historical Assoc 1990-; chm Nat Curriculum History Ctee for Wales 1988-, convenor History at Univs Def Gp 1990-; Winner (Jt) Wolfson Literary award for History 1987; FRHistS 1968 (vice pres 1988-), FBA 1987; *Books* Lordship and Society in the March of Wales (1978), Conquest, Coexistence and Change: Wales 1063-1415 (1987), Domination and Conquest: The experience of Ireland, Scotland and Wales 1100-1300 (1990), Welsh Society and Nationhood (ed, 1985), The British Isles 1100-1500 (ed, 1988); *Recreations* walking, music; *Style—* Prof Rees Davies; Dept of History, Univ College of Wales, Aberystwyth, Dyfed (☎ 0970 622662, fax 0970 611446)

DAVIES, (William) Rhodri; s of His Hon Judge (Lewis) John Davies, QC, and Janet Mary, *née* Morris; *b* 29 Jan 1957; *Educ* Winchester, Downing Coll Cambridge (BA); *m* 28 July 1984, Hon Victoria Catherine (Vicky), da of Stewart Platt, of Writtle nr Chelmsford, Essex; 3 da (Rachael b 1985, Joanna b 1987, Jessica b 1990); *Career* called to the Bar Middle Temple 1979, practising in London 1980-; *Recreations* walking, cross-country running; *Clubs* Thames Hare & Hounds; *Style—* Rhodri Davies, Esq; 1 Essex Ct, Temple, London EC4Y 9AR (☎ 071 583 2000, fax 071 583 0118)

DAVIES, Prof (Eurfil) Rhys; CBE (1990); s of Daniel Haydn Davies (d 1957), and Mary, *née* Jenkins (d 1961); *b* 18 April 1929; *Educ* Rhondda GS, Llandovery Coll, Clare Coll Cambridge (BA, MA, MB BChir), St Mary's Hosp London; *m* 15 Dec 1962, Zoë Doreen, da of Stanley Ivan Victor Chamberlain (d 1984); 3 s (Matthew b 1966, Huw b 1968, Timothy (twin) b 1968); *Career* Nat Serv Capt RAMC 1954-56, regtl MO 24 Regt 1955-56; conslt radiologist Utd Bristol Hosps 1966-81, prof of radiodiagnosis Univ of Bristol 1981-, civilian conslt in radiodiagnosis to the RN 1988-; pres Br Nuclear Med Soc 1972-74; memb: Admin of Radioactive Substances Advsy Ctee, Bristol and Weston 1984-86; Royal Coll of Radiologists: registrar 1976-81, warden 1984-86, pres 1986-89; memb GMC 1989-; memb Ct Univ of Bath; hon fell Faculty of Radiologists RCSI 1976; FRSM, FFR 1964, FRCPE 1972, FRCR 1976, Fell Faculty of Dental Surgns RCS 1989; memb: BMA, Br Inst of Radiology; *Books* Radionuclides in Radiodiagnosis (jtly 1974), Nuclear Medicine: Applications in Surgery (ed with G Thomas, 1988); *Recreations* walking, theatre, wine; *Style—* Prof Rhys Davies, CBE; 19 Hyland Grove, Westbury on Trym, Bristol BS9 3NR (☎ 0272 501532)

DAVIES, Sir Richard Harries; KCVO (1984, CVO 1982), CBE (1962); s of Thomas Henry Davies (d 1964) and Minnie Oakley, *née* Morgan (d 1964); *b* 29 June 1916; *Educ* Porth Co Sch, Cardiff Tech Coll (BSc); *m* 1, 15 April 1944, Hon Annie (Nan) Butcher (d 1976), er da of 1 Baron Macpherson of Drumochter (d 1965); 2 s, 2 da; m 2, 1979, Mrs Patricia P Ogier; *Career* Scientific Civil Serv 1939-46, Br Air Cmmn Washington DC 1941-45; vice pres Ferranti Electric Inc NY 1948-63, dir Ferranti Ltd 1970-76, pres Br American C of C NY 1959-62, vice pres Manchester C of C 1976; HRH Duke of Edinburgh's Household: asst private sec 1977-82, treas 1982-84, Extra Equerry 1984; pres Radio Soc of GB 1988; FIEE; *Recreations* gardening, sailing, amateur radio; *Clubs* Athenaeum, Pratt's; *Style—* Sir Richard Davies, KCVO, CBE; Haven House, Thorpeness, Leiston, Suffolk IP16 4NR

DAVIES, Richard James Guy; s of George Glyn Davies, MBE, of Frinton-On-Sea, Essex, and Cynthia Joan, *née* Franklin; *b* 7 Dec 1953; *Educ* Felsted Sch Essex, St Catharine's Coll Cambridge (MA); *m* 19 July 1980, Michele Clarke, da of Michael C

Lipscomb (d 1981); 2 s (Michael b 1985, Christopher b 1987); *Career* Lazard Bros & Co Ltd 1976-(dir 1986-), seconded to Korea Merchant Banking Corp Seoul Korea 1978-80; *Recreations* sailing, music, literature; *Clubs* Royal Burnham Yacht; *Style—* Richard Davies, Esq; 262 Trinity Rd, London SW18 (☎ 081 874 1442); Lazard Brothers & Co Ltd, 21 Moorfields, London EC2P 2HT (☎ 071 588 2721, fax 071 628 2485, telex 886438)

DAVIES, Prof Robert; s of Thomas Stephen Davies (d 1985), of Abercynon, Glam, and Winifred Gertrude, *née* Taylor (d 1985); *b* 5 Jan 1935; *Educ* Mountain Ash GS, Univ of Birmingham; *m* 30 March 1959, (Sylvia) Meriel, da of Richard Westwood Rhodes (d 1985), of Hagley, W Midlands; 1 da (Sylvia Anne (Mrs Warwick)); *Career* tech offr ICI 1957-60, dep chief engr Bilston Foundaries 1960-61; Univ of Birmingham: lectr 1965-71, sr lectr 1971-78, reader in engrg plasticity 1978-82, prof of mechanical engrg 1982-, dep dean faculty of engrg 1987-90; author of 80 papers on: metal forming, powder metallurgy, adhesive bonding, laser technol; memb Nat Tst; CEng 1965, MIMechE 1965, MIM 1975, memb RSPB; *Books* Developements in High Speed Metal Forming (1970); *Recreations* antiques, ornithology; *Style—* Prof Robert Davies; School of Manufacturing & Mechanical Engineering, The University, PO Box 363, Birmingham B15 2TT (☎ 021 414 4140, fax 021 414 3958, telex 3389 SPAPHY G)

DAVIES, Prof Robert James; s of Canon Dilwyn Morgan Davies, of 6 Manor Barn, Ilmington, Warwickshire, and Kate, *née* Maltby (d 1987); *b* 24 Feb 1943; *Educ* St John's Sch Leatherhead, St Catharine's Coll Cambridge (MA, MB BS,MD); *m* 22 Dec 1969 (m dis 1979), Katharine Lindsay, da of Harold Sydenham, of Dunchurch, Rugby; 2 s (Mark b 10 Oct 1972, James b 26 May 1975); m 2, 6 June 1980, Karen Barbara, da of Denis Henley, of Love Lane, Bexley; *Career* res fell Brompton Hosp 1971-73, lectr in med St Thomas's Hosp 1973-76, med res Univ of Tulane New Orleans USA 1976-77; St Bartholomew's Hosp: conslt physician 1977-, dir asthma and allergy res dept 1981-, reader in respiratory med 1983-, conslt in charge dept of respiratory med 1987-; Pres Br Soc for Allergy and Clinical Immunology; Medal of faculty of med Univ of Montpellier France 1981; FRCP 1982, fell American Acad of Allergy and Immunology 1984; *ed:* Respiratory Medicine (1988-), Allergy The Facts (1989); *Recreations* hill walking, wind surfing, skiing; *Clubs* Athenaeum; *Style—* Prof Robert Davies; 96 Vanbrugh Park, Blackheath, London SE3 7AL; Dept of Respiratory Med, St Bartholomews Hosp, West Smithfield, London EC1A 7BE (☎ 01 601 8436, fax 01 601 8444, car 0836 638874)

DAVIES, Robert John; s of William Edward Davies (d 1956), of Wimbledon, and Esther Emily, *née* Weeks (d 1982); *b* 28 May 1926; *m* 24 Aug 1957, Pamela Margaret, da of Hugh Hume Dixon, CBE, of Majorca; 2 s (Stephen b 1959, Martin b 1960), 1 da (Alison b 1966); *Career* coastal cmd air sea rescue servs RAFVR 1943-47; American Express Bank: vice-pres and gen mangr India and Pakistan 1967-73, vice-pres and gen mangr Greece 1973-76, md Italy (SPA) 1976-80, vice-pres and gen mangr UK (Ltd) 1981-84, vice-pres gen mangr and head of Military Banking Div for UK Iceland (Ltd) 1985-89, ret 1990; MInstD, FCIB 1970, FCIS 1972; Cavaliere Ufficiale of the Order Al Merito Della Repubblica Italiana 1980; *Recreations* golf, cycling, reading; *Clubs* Oriental, Wig and Pen, Badgemore Country; *Style—* Robert Davies, Esq; Lynmas, The Hamlet, Gallowstree Common, South Oxfordshire

DAVIES, Robert John; s of Prof William Davies (d 1988), of Aberystwyth, and Janet, *née* Robinson; *b* 12 Oct 1948; *Educ* King Edward VII Sch Sheffield, HS of Stirling, Univ of Edinburgh (LLB); *m* 28 Aug 1971, Eileen Susan, da of George Littlefield (d 1952); 1 s (Christopher b 1978); *Career* fin dir Ford Motor Company Spain 1983-85 (various positions UK and USA 1970-83), dir and mgmnt conslt Coopers & Lybrand Associates 1985-87, fin dir Wedgwood Limited 1987-88, gp chief fin offr Waterford Wedgwood plc 1989-, currently dir Waterford Wedgwood UK plc; FCMA 1976; *Recreations* golf; *Style—* Robert Davies, Esq; Waterford Wedgwood plc, Barlaston, Stoke-on-Trent ST12 9ES (☎ 0782 204141, fax 0782 204402, telex 36170, car 0860 620393)

DAVIES, Robert Stephen; s of Richard George Davies (d 1968), and Megan, *née* Matthews; *b* 23 Feb 1945; *Educ* Bridgend GS; *m* 25 July 1970, Philippa Mary, da of Herbert Woodley (d 1971); 2 s (Charles b 1972, Nicholas b 1975), 2 da (Lucy b 1982, Katy b 1982); *Career* audit mangr Mann Judd 1969-71 (articled clerk 1965-69), mgmnt conslt 1971-72, supervisor budgets and planning Gulf Oil Int London 1974-76 (sr fin analyst 1972-74), mangr fin and servs Gulf Oil Refining Ltd 1976-78; fin dir: Gulf Oil Switzerland AG 1978-80, Gulf Oil (GB) Ltd 1980-; fndr memb Jaguar Car Club, memb Cncl Cheltenham Ladies Coll; FCA 1969; *Recreations* music, antique collecting, vintage cars, tennis; *Clubs* Bentley Drivers; *Style—* Robert Davies, Esq; The Quadrangle, Imperial Sq, Cheltenham, Glos (☎ 0242 225 302, fax 0242 573 059)

DAVIES, Prof Rodney Deane; s of Holbin James Davies, of Loveday St, Naracoorte, S Aust, and Rena Irene, *née* March (d 1982); *b* 8 Jan 1930; *Educ* Adelaide HS, Univ of Adelaide (BSc, MSc), Univ of Manchester (PhD, DSc); *m* 3 Jan 1953, (Valda) Beth, da of Arthur Roy Treasure (d 1988); 2 s (Warwick b 1953 d 1977, Stewart b 1960), 2 da (Rosalyn b 1955, Claire b 1957); *Career* Univ of Manchester: asst lectr 1953-56, lectr 1956-63, sr lectr 1963-67, reader 1967-76, prof of radio astronomy 1976-, dir Nuffield Radio Astronomy Laboratories 1988-; visiting astronomer Radio Physics Div CSIRO Sydney Australia 1963 (res offr 1951-53); memb various bds and ctees SERC, pres Royal Astronomical Soc 1987-89 (sec 1978-86), memb various ctees Int Astronomical Union; FRAS 1956, FInstP, CPhys 1972; *Books* Radio Studies of the Universe (with H P Palmer, 1959), Radio Astronomy Today (with H P Palmer and M I Large, 1963), The Crab Nebula (co ed with F G Smith, 1971); *Recreations* gardening and fell walking; *Style—* Prof Rodney Davies; Parkgate House, Fulshaw Park, Wilmslow, Cheshire SK9 1QG (☎ 0625 523592); University of Manchester, Nuffield Radio Astronomy Laboratories, Jodrell Bank, Macclesfield, Cheshire SK11 9DL (☎ 0477 71321, fax 0477 71618, telex 36149)

DAVIES, (Anthony) Roger; s of (Richard) George Davies of Bridgend, Glamorgan (d 1968), and Megan, *née* Matthews; *b* 1 Sept 1940; *Educ* King's Coll Univ of London (LLB, AKC); *m* 23 Sept 1967, Clare, da of Cdr William Arthur Walters, RN; 2 s (George b 1974, Hugo (twin) b 1974), 1 da (Antonia b 1972); *Career* called to the Bar Gray's Inn 1965; Lord Justice Holker sr scholar, in practice South Eastern Circuit, met stipendiary magistrate 1985; *Recreations* music, history, reading; *Clubs* Travellers; *Style—* Roger Davies, Esq; c/o Horseferry Rd, Magistrates Court, London SW1

DAVIES, Roger Guy; s of Cyril Graham Davies, OBE (d 1974), and Hettie Susannah, *née* Lewis; *b* 5 Nov 1946; *Educ* Kingswood Sch, Fitzwilliam Coll Cambridge (MA); *m* 30 May 1970, Diana June, da of Harold Charles Perks (d 1967); 3 s (Tom b 23 Sept 1973, William b 8 Nov 1974, Edward b 18 Dec 1977), 1 da (Georgina b 18 Oct 1982); *Career* ptnr Allen & Overy 1976- (articled clerk 1970-72, asst slr 1972-76); Freeman Worshipful Co of Slrs; memb: Law Soc, ctee City of London Law Soc; *Recreations* golf, tennis, shooting, music; *Clubs* Ashridge Golf, Oxford and Cambridge Golfing Soc, Hawks; *Style—* Roger Davies, Esq; Corner Farm, Gaddesden Row, Hemel Hempstead, Herts HP2 6HN (☎ 0442 211055); Allen & Overy, 9 Cheapside, London EC2V 6AD (☎ 071 248 9898, fax 071 236 2192, telex 8812801)

DAVIES, Ronald; MP (Lab) Caerphilly 1983-; s of late Ronald Davies; *b* 6 Aug 1946; *Educ* Bassaleg GS, Portsmouth Polytechnic, Univ Coll of Wales Cardiff; *m* 1981, Christina Elizabeth Rees; *Career* former tutor and organiser WEA, sponsored by NUPE, memb Rhymney Valley District Cncl 1969, Mid-Glamorgan CC educn offr; *Style—* Ronald Davies, Esq, MP; House of Commons, London SW1

DAVIES, Hon (Francis) Ronald; s of 1 Baron Darwen; *b* 29 March 1920; *Educ* Bootham Sch; *m* 1942, Margaret Phyllis, da of John George Cockworth; 2 s, 1 da; *Career* called to the barr Gray's Inn 1948; *Style—* The Hon Ronald Davies; 39 Parkside, Mill Hill, NW7

DAVIES, Rt Rev Roy Thomas; *see*: Llandaff, Bishop of

DAVIES, (Robert) Russell; s of John Gwilym Davies, of Knowle, West Midlands and Gladys, *née* Davies; *b* 5 April 1946; *Educ* Manchester GS, St John's Coll Cambridge (scholar, BA, Tiarks German award); *m* 23 March 1972, Judith Anne, da of Noel Stephen Slater; 1 s (Steffan John b 5 Feb 1979); *Career* freelance journalist and broadcaster; TV actor and presenter (5 Series) 1970-71, cartoonist Liberal News 1971, caricaturist Times Literary Supplement 1972-74; The Observer: football reporter 1973-76, film critic 1973-78, contracted writer 1983-88; sports columnist New Statesman 1978-79 (reporter 1973-), TV critic Sunday Times 1979-83 (columnist 1978-), dep ed Punch 1988 (contributer 1976-), sports columnist and feature writer Sunday Telegraph 1989-; broadcasting credits incl: documentaries on American culture for Radio 3, biographies of jazz figures, plays for radio, Midweek 1979-81, sports documentaries; TV credits incl: What The Papers Say, What The Papers Say Annual Awards 1989-91, presenter Saturday Review, presenter Jazz Week and Jazz On a Summer's Day weekend BBC2, music documentaries BBC2 (Laughing Louie, Duke Ellington And His Famous Orchestra, Le Jazz Hot, The Lowest Of The Low, Buddy Bolden's Children, A Musical Nation?, The Honky Tonk Professor); formerly: Librettist, Love And The Ice Cream Vendor (Roundhouse and South Bank Show LWT), Actor Charles Charming's Challenges (recorded album with Clive James, *qv*, Apollo Theatre), The World of Buddy Bolden (with Humphrey Lyttelton) 1986; memb: NUJ, Br Actors Equity, Punch Table; *Books* Peregrine Prykke's Pilgrimage (illustrator, 1976), Vicky (with Liz Ottaway, 1987), Ronald Searle (1990); *Recreations* jazz and jazz history, trombone, tuba, bass saxophone and piano playing, comic art, cartooning, tidying up; *Style—* Russell Davies, Esq; c/o Peters, Fraser and Dunlop, 5th Floor, The Chambers, Chelsea Harbour, Lots Road, London SW10 0XF

DAVIES, Ryland; s of Gethin Davies, and Joan Davies; *b* 9 Feb 1943; *Educ* Royal Manchester Coll of Music; *m* 1, 1966 (m dis 1981), Anne Elizabeth Howells; m 2, 1983, Deborah Rees; 1 da (Emily); *Career* int opera singer (tenor); performed at Int Opera houses throughout the world including: Convent Garden, Glyndebourne, NY Met, Milan, Paris, Vienna, Bonn; also many recordings and work in radio, TV and film; fell Royal Manchester Coll of Music; *Style—* Ryland Davies Esq; Milestone, Broom Close, Esher, Surrey

DAVIES, Sharron Elizabeth; da of Terry Davies, and Sheila, *née* Conybeare; *b* 1 Nov 1962; *Educ* Kelly Coll Devon; *Career* memb Br Olympic Team 1976 (youngest memb), and 1980 (Silver medallist); Cwlth Record holder and double champion 1978; Sportswoman of the Year 1978 and 1980; Cwlth Silver and Bronze medallist 1990; TV personality; *Style—* Sharron Davies

DAVIES, (John) Simon; s of Arthur Rees Davies (d 1982), of Newcastle-Emlyn, Dyfed, and Catherine Elizabeth, *née* Jones; *b* 12 March 1937; *Educ* Cardigan GS, Coll of Estate Mgmnt (pres SU); *m* 24 Oct 1959 (m dis 1989), Anja Ilse, da of Gerhard Körner (d 1965), of Munich; 1 s (Michael Stephen b 1 April 1960, d 1978), 1 da (Kathleen Anja b 1 June 1964); m 2, March 1990, Sheila Jane, da of Reginald Henderson; *Career* princ and sr ptnr Kemp and Hawley CS; hon memb Gorsedd of Bards; Freeman City of London; FRICS; *Recreations* rugby, opera; *Style—* Simon Davies, Esq; 47 Upper Montagu St, London W1H 1FQ (☎ 071 262 4305); 13 Monmouth St, London WC2H 9DA (☎ 071 405 8161, fax 071 836 2214)

DAVIES, Stan Gebler; s of Max Davies (d 1965), of Toronto, and Olive Margaret, *née* Gebler; *b* 16 July 1943; *Educ* educated in Dublin and Toronto; *m* 1966, Janet, da of Frank Collis; 1 da (Clancy b 24 Oct 1966); *Career* journalist and author; worked on Londoner's Diary Evening Standard 1965-82; contrib to: Evening Standard, Independent, Spectator, Sunday Telegraph, Irish Sunday Independent, and other Br and Irish magazines; contested (unsucessfully) Cork SW as a Conservative and Unionist in 1987 Irish gen election; *Books* James Joyce: A Portrait of the Artist (with Robin Moore, 1974), The Kaufmann Snatch (1976), Our Missile's Missing (1977), The Twilight Reich (1979); *Recreations* music, television, shooting, drinking; *Clubs* Chelsea Arts, Colony Room; *Style—* Stan Davies, Esq

DAVIES, Hon Stephen Humphrey; s of 2 Baron Darwen; *b* 3 Oct 1945; *Educ* Royal GS High Wycombe; *m* 1968, Kathleen Prestwood; 2 s (Timothy b 1970, Peter b 1980), 2 da (Ruth b 1972, Rachel b 1976); *Style—* The Hon Stephen Humphrey Davies; c/o Rt Hon Lord Darwen, White Lodge, Sandelswood End, Baconsfield, Bucks

DAVIES, Dr Stevie; da of Henry James Davies (d 1974), of Swansea, and Mona Joan Davies; *b* 2 Dec 1946; *Educ* Priory Girls' GS Shrewsbury, Univ of Manchester (BA, MA, PhD); *m* 1, 1 s (Robin Harry b 1980), 2 da (Emily Jane b 1977, Grace Hannah (twin) b 1980); m 2, 1990, Frank Regan; *Career* lectr in English lit Univ of Manchester 1971-84; author and pt/t tutor 1984-; *Books* literary criticism: Emily Bronte: The Artist as a Free Woman (1983), Images of Kingship in 'Paradise Lost' (1983), The Idea of Woman in Renaissance Literature (1986), Emily Bronte (1988), Virginia Woolf's 'To the Lighthouse' (1989); novels: Boy Blue (1987, Fawcett Soc Book prize 1989), Primavera (1989); memb Milton Soc of America; memb CND and involved with Green issues, the Peace Movement and Feminism; *Recreations* playing piano, listening to music, reading; *Style—* Dr Stevie Davies

DAVIES, Stewart Lyn; s of Edward Lyn Davies, and Alexandria Scott Milligan; *b* 5 Jan 1969; *Educ* Tomlinscote Secdy Sch, Farnborough Coll of Technol; *Career* Rugby Union hooker Rosslyn Park FC; clubs: Farnborough RFC, Camberley RFC, Rosslyn Park FC 1987- (Div 1 debut v Wasps FC 1989, 52 appearances); rep: Eng U21 debut v Netherlands 1990, reserve Eng B; mechanical engr, recruitment conslt, business communications conslt RPL Telecommunications; *Recreations* deep sea diving, scuba diving; *Style—* Stewart Davies, Esq; 38 Regent Way, Frimley, Camberley, Surrey GU16 5NT (☎ 0276 28017); c/o Rosslyn Park FC, Priory Lane, Roehampton, London SW15

DAVIES, Susan Elizabeth (Sue); OBE; da of Stanworth Wills Adey (d 1980), and Joan Mary Margaret Charlesworth (d 1967); *b* 14 April 1933; *Educ* Nightingale-Bamford NY USA, Eothen Caterham Surrey, Triangle Secretarial Coll; *m* 11 Sept 1954, John Ross Twiston Davies, s of John Harold Twiston Davies (d 1990); 2 da (Joanna Lyn Twiston b 27 Dec 1955, Stephanie Jane Twiston b 27 March 1956, d 1988); *Career* photography; Municipal Jl 1953-54, various voluntary jobs, Artists Placement Gp 1966-67, ICA 1967-70, fndr and dir Photographers' Gallery 1971- (first photography gallery in Europe); Progress medal Royal Photographic Soc 1982, Kulturpreis German Photographic Soc 1990; Hon FRPS 1980; memb: CNAA Photography Ctee 1982-86, CNAA Design Panel 1986-88; *Recreations* jazz, gardens, grandchildren; *Clubs* Chelsea Arts; *Style—* Mrs Sue Davies, OBE; Photographers' Gallery, 5 Great Newport St, London WC2H 7HY (☎ 071 831 1772, fax 071 836 9704)

DAVIES, Hon Mrs (Teresa Katherine); *née* David; er da of Richard William David, CBE, and Baroness David (*qqv*); *b* 1944; *m* 1967, Llewelyn Anthony Davies; *Style—*

The Hon Mrs Davies; 50 Clarence Rd, Birmingham 13

DAVIES, Thomas; s of David Charles Davies (d 1967), and Henrietta Florence, *née* Sutton (d 1984); *b* 25 June 1932; *Educ* Pinner County GS; *m* 1959, Ursula Jane, da of Leonard Theodore Freeman; 3 da (Virginia Jane (Mrs Stevens) b 1962, Gillian Karina b 1964, Kristina Louise b 1968); *Career* Sydenham & Co Chartered Accountants: articled clerk 1952-57, qualified 1958, opened Hereford office 1960, ptnr 1967-; ptnr i/c Hereford office Kidsons Impey (following merger); ACA 1958; *Recreations* game fishing, walking, ornithology, crosswords; *Style—* Thomas Davies, Esq; Hunters Moon, Breinton, Hereford HR4 7PB (☎ 0432 266746); Kidsons Impey, Elgar House, Holmer Rd, Hereford HR4 9SF (☎ 0432 352222, fax 0432 269367)

DAVIES, Hon Thomas Barratt (Barry); 2 s of 1 Baron Darwen (d 1950); *b* 4 June 1916; *Educ* Bootham Sch, Coll of Art Liverpool; *m* 8 March 1941, Doreen, da of Arthur James Allen, of Portsmouth; 1 s (Alan b 1949), 3 da (Barbara b 1944, Hilary b 1947, Judith (twin) b 1949); *Career* lectr in art education Univ of Reading 1948-65; *Style—* The Hon T Barry Davies; 56 Old Street, Upton-upon-Severn, Worcs WR8 0HW (☎ 06846 3088)

DAVIES, Trevor Glyn; s of William Gerald Davies (d 1985), and Freda Grace Davies, *née* Sewell; *b* 9 Dec 1955; *Educ* St Albans Sch, Univ of Nottingham (BA); *m* 25 Sept 1982, Nicole Elizabeth, da of Derek Vernon Coulson, of Malta; 1 s (Timothy b 1986), 1 da (Jessica b 1988); *Career* called to the Bar Gray's Inn 1978; *Recreations* golf, tennis; *Clubs* Northampton Co; *Style—* Trevor Davies, Esq; 2 Dr Johnsons Buildings, Temple, London EC4Y 7AY (☎ 071 353 5371)

DAVIES, Tudor Griffith; s of Griffith Davies, of Barry, Glamorgan, and Rhiannon, *née* Martin; *b* 2 Dec 1951; *Educ* Barry Boys GS, Manchester Univ (BSc); *m* 26 July 1980, Julia Alison, da of John William Harvey, of Trentham, Staffs; 3 s (William, Gwyn, Rhodri), 1 da (Sally); *Career* dir: Thurman Publishing Gp 1978-80, CBS Architectural Ironmogery 1980-84; corporate recovery ptnr Arthur Young CAs 1984-88; ACA; *Recreations* fishing, shooting, rugby football, walking; *Clubs* United Service (Cardiff); *Style—* Tudor Davies, Esq; Netherton Hse, Fintry, Stirlingshire, Scotland G63 0YH (☎ 036086 242); 173 City Rd, Cardiff, S Glam (☎ 0222 497 138, car 0836 702 357)

DAVIES, Lady Venetia Constance Kathleen Luz; *née* Hay; da of 14 Earl of Kinnoull; *b* 1929; *m* 1953, Maj Joseph Trevor Davies; 2 da (Nicola b 1957, Sally b 1960); *Style—* The Lady Venetia Davies; 14 Old School Court, Grimston Gardens, Folkestone, Kent CT20 2UA

DAVIES, (William) Vivian; s of Walter Percival Davies, of 88 Elgin Rd, Pwll, Llanelli, Dyfed, and Gwenllian, *née* Evans; *b* 14 Oct 1947; *Educ* Llanelli GS, Jesus Coll Oxford (BA, MA), Queen's Coll Oxford (Randall-MacIver student in archaeology); *m* 30 Oct 1970, Janet Olwen May, da of Laurie Frederick Foat, of Nant Cottage, 51 Llwynhendy Rd, Llwynhendy, Llanelli, Dyfed; 1 s (Thomas Dafydd Robert b 30 June 1974), 1 da (Elen Mai b 24 May 1971); *Career* egyptologist; dep keeper Dept of Egyptian Antiquities Br Museum 1981-88 (asst keeper 1974-81), visiting prof of Egyptology Univ of Heidelberg 1984-85, keeper of Egyptian Antiquities Br Museum 1988-; *Books* Egyptian Sculpture (with T G H James, 1983), Saqqara Tombs (with A B Lloyd and A J Spencer, 1984), Problems and Priorities in Egyptian Archaeology (ed with J Assmann and G Burkard, 1987), Egyptian Hieroglyphs (1987), Catalogue of Egyptian Antiquities in the British Museum VII Axes (1987), Egypt and Africa Nubia from Prehistory to Islam (ed, 1991); FSA 1980; *Style—* Vivian Davies, Esq, FSA; Department of Egyptian Antiquities, British Museum, London WC1B 3DG (☎ 071 323 8306, fax 071 323 8480)

DAVIES, Prof Wendy Elizabeth; da of Douglas Charles Davies, of Toronto, and Lucy, *née* Evans; *b* 28 Aug 1942; *Educ* Maynard Sch, Univ of London (BA, PhD); *Career* historian; lectr Univ of Birmingham 1970-76; UCL: lectr 1977-81, reader 1981-85, prof 1985-, head of dept 1987-; visiting fell All Souls Coll Oxford 1986; memb Cncl Soc for Medieval Archaeology 1983-86; FRHistS 1979, FSA 1988; *Books* An Early Welsh Microcosm (1978), The Llandaff Charters (1979), Wales in the Early Middle Ages (1982), Small Worlds, The Village Community in Early Medieval Brittany (1988), Patterns of Power (1990); *Recreations* gardening, singing; *Style—* Prof Wendy Davies, FSA; History Department, University College, Gower Street, London WC1E 6BT (☎ 071 387 7050)

DAVIES, Rev Dr William Rhys; s of Rhys Thomas Davies (d 1936), and Alice, *née* Swift; *b* 31 May 1932; *Educ* Blackpool GS, Hartley Victoria Theol Coll Manchester, Univ of Manchester (MA, PhD), BD (London External); *m* 9 Nov 1955, Barbara Constance, da of Allan Topping (d 1978); 1 s (Michael b 27 June 1957), 1 da (Helen b 20 Feb 1964); *Career* methodist minister: Middleton Manchester 1955-60, Fleetwood 1960-65, Stockton on Tees 1965-66, Warrington (serving as sr lectr in religious studies Padgate Coll 1966-79); supt methodist minister Bradford Mission 1979-83, princ Cliff Coll Calver Sheffield 1983-, pres Methodist Conf 1987-88, moderator Free Church Federal Cncl 1991-92; memb Cncl of Mgmnt Evangelical Alliance 1985-91; *Books* Gathered into One (1975), Spirit Baptism and Spiritual Gifts in Early Methodism (1973), What About the Charismatic Movement? (1980), Rocking the Boat (1986); *Recreations* reading, sport; *Style—* The Rev Dr William Davies; Cliff College, Calver, Sheffield S30 1XG (☎ 0246 582321)

DAVIES-COOKE, Capt (Philip) Peter; s of Col Philip Ralph Davies-Cooke, CB (d 1974), of Gwysaney Hall, Mold, Clwyd, and Kathleen Mabel Davies-Cooke, OBE; *b* 4 July 1925; *Educ* Eton; *m* 1, 6 July 1957, Jane (d 1981), da of Edmund George Coryton (d 1981), of Linkincom, Yelverton, Devon; 3 s (Richard b 1 July 1960, Paul b 30 March 1962, Michael b 2 Nov 1965); m 2, 24 Sept 1985, Zinnia Mary Arfwedson, da of late Col RB (Reggie) Hodgkinson, MC; *Career* 1 Royal Dragoons 1945-54; landowner; *Recreations* fishing, shooting; *Clubs* Cavalry and Guards; *Style—* Capt Peter Davies-Cooke; Gwysaney Hall, Mold, Clwyd

DAVIES OF PENRHYS, Baron (Life Peer UK 1974), of Rhondda, Co Mid-Glamorgan; Gwilym Elfed Davies; s of David Davies (d 1942); *b* 9 Oct 1913; *Educ* Tylorstown Boys' Sch; *m* 1940, Gwyneth, da of Daniel Rees, of Trealaw, Rhondda; 2 s Hon Gwynfor b 1942, Hon David Daniel b 1944), 1 da (Hon Beryl (Hon Mrs Powell) b 1947); *Career* memb St John Ambulance Bde 1926-46; memb Glamorgan CC 1954-61, chm Local Govt Ctee 1959-61, MP (L) Rhondda (E) 1959-74; PPS: Min of Labour 1964-68, Min of Power 1968; *Style—* The Rt Hon the Lord Davies of Penrhys; Maes-y-Ffrwd, Ferndale Rd, Tylorstown, Ferndale, Rhondda, Glamorgan (☎ 0443 730 254)

DAVIES-SCOURFIELD, Brig Edward Grismond Beaumont; CBE (1966, MBE 1951), MC (1945), DL (1984); s of Henry Gwyn Davies-Scourfield (d 1934), of Sussex, and Helen Mary, *née* Newton (d 1973); *b* 2 Aug 1918; *Educ* Winchester, RMC Sandhurst; *m* 24 Nov 1945, Diana Lilias, da of Sir Nigel Davidson, CBE (d 1961), of Sussex; 1 s (Gwyn b 1959), 1 da (Susan b 1948); *Career* army offr, ret 1973; cmmnd 2 Lt KRRC 1938, CO 1 Bn Rifle Bde 1960 (Lt-Col), Bde Col Royal Green Jackets 1962, Brig Cdr Br Jt Servs Trg Team Ghana 1964, Dep Cdr Nearelf 1966, cmd Salisbury Plain Area 1970; gen sec Nat Assoc of Boys Clubs (vice pres) 1973-82, memb E Hants Ctee CPRE, chm Hants Army Benevolant Fund, tstee regtl funds 1971-89, church warden 1975-88; *Recreations* racing, shooting, tennis, walking; *Clubs* Army and Navy, Mounted Infantry; *Style—* Brig E G B Davies-Scourfield, CBE, MC, DL; Old Rectory Cottage, Medstead, Alton, Hants GU34 5LX (☎ 0420 62133)

DAVIS; *see*: Lovell-Davis

DAVIS; *see*: Hart-Davis

DAVIS, Albert Edward; s of Albert Ellerd Davis (d 1954), of 27 Church St, Luton, Beds, and Kate Elizabeth, *née* Sell (d 1962); *b* 15 July 1928; *Educ* Luton GS; *m* 1 March 1952, Rhona, da of Walter Maurice Temple-Smith (d 1980), of 21 Park Mount, Harpenden, Herts; 1 s (Andrew Albert b 1956); *Career* sr ptnr Davis & Co (certified accountants) 1964- (joined 1945, jr ptnr 1950-64); memb: City of London Branch Royal Soc of St George, United Wards Club City of London; Freeman City of London 1984, Liveryman Worshipful Co of Arbitrators 1984; FTII 1951, FCCA 1952, FCIArb 1968; *Recreations* music, walking, travel, horticulture; *Clubs* City Livery; *Style—* Albert Davis, Esq; Hamilton House, 1 Temple Ave, Temple, London EC4Y 0HA (☎ 071 353 4212, fax 071 353 3325)

DAVIS, Lady Alison Elizabeth; yst da of 1 Earl Attlee (d 1967); *b* 14 April 1930; *m* 8 March 1952, Richard Lionel Lance Davis, s of late Maj Arthur Owen Lance Davis, of Hinckley, Leics; 3 da (Jennifer (Mrs Lochen) b 1953, Tessa (Dr Dormon) b 1955, Belinda (Mrs Johnston) b 1957); *Style—* The Lady Alison Davis; Westcott, 8 Beacon Rise, Sevenoaks, Kent TN13 2NJ

DAVIS, Sir (William) Allan; GBE (1985); s of Wilfred Egwin Davis (d 1953), and Annie Ellen, *née* Fraser (d 1978); *b* 19 June 1921; *Educ* Cardinal Vaughan Sch Kensington; *m* 1944, Audrey Pamela, da of Lionel Arthur Louch (d 1966); 2 s (Michael, Paul), 1 da (Jane); *Career* served WWII pilot RNVR 1940-44; joined Barclays Bank 1939, apprentice Dunn Wylie & Co 1944 (ptnr 1952, sr ptnr 1972-76), sr ptnr Armitage & Norton London 1979-87 (ptnr 1976); dir: Catholic Herald Ltd, City of London Heliport Ltd, Crowning Tea Co Ltd, Dunkelman & Son Ltd, Fiat Auto UK Ltd, Internatio-Muller UK Ltd and UK subsids, Victory NRG Hldgs Ltd and UK subsids; common councilman Ward of Queenhithe 1971-76, Alderman Ward of Cripplegate 1976, Sheriff City of London 1982-83, Lord Mayor of London 1985-86, HM Lt City of London 1986; chm: Port and City of London health ctee and social servs ctee 1974-77, mgmnt ctee London Homes for the Elderly 1975-88; memb Ct HAC 1976, chm City of London Centre St John's Ambulance Assoc 1987 (hon treas 1979-82 and 1983-84, vice pres 1985); govr: Bridewell Royal Hosp 1976, Cripplegate Fndn 1976 (chm 1981), Cardinal Vaughan Memorial Sch 1968-81 and 1985-88, Lady Eleanor Holles Sch 1979 (chm 1989-91); tstee: Sir John Soane's Museum 1979, Morden Coll 1982; chm: govrs Research into Ageing 1987-89 (vice pres 1989-), tstees Winged Fellowship 1987-89 (vice patron 1989); special tstee Jt Bartholomew's and St Mark's Hosps 1988; dep pres Publicity Club of London; memb Cncl: Young Enterprise, Order of St John for London 1986-89, City Univ London 1986-; Liveryman Worshipful Co of Painter Stainers 1959 (hon treas 1962, memb Ct 1962-); Hon Liveryman: Worshipful Co of CAs, Worshipful Co of Launderers, Worshipful Co of Constructors 1989; KCSG 1979; FCA, FRSA, FTII, memb ICEAW, CBIM; Order of Merit Qatar (Class 1) 1985, Cdr Isabel the Catholic 1986, Cdr Order of Merit FRG 1986; *Clubs* City Livery and Oriental; *Style—* Sir Allan Davis, GBE; 168 Defoe House, Barbican EC2Y 8DN (☎ 071 638 5354)

DAVIS, (Richard) Anthony; s of Joseph David Davis (d 1970), of King's Court, Talley, Dyfed, and Blanche Marie, *née* Stephenson; *b* 20 May 1945; *Educ* Ruthin Sch Clywd; *m* 11 July 1981, Wendy Hilary, da of Eric Curme, of Rodborough, Gloucestershire; *Career* marketing conslt; law articles in private practice Birmingham 1963-66, personnel mgmnt Britannic Assurance Birmingham 1966-70; mktg communications: Rentokil E Grinstead 1970-71, Camping and Caravanning Club London 1971-73; private practice 1973-; ed British Commercial and Industrial Property 1974-76, press offr Silver Jubilee Expo Hyde Park London 1977, jt fndr Davenport Communications 1982-; Parly candidate (Lib) Solihull Gen Election 1970; visiting lectr Coll for Distributive Trades London 1976-83; memb Cncl Inst PR 1988- (memb 1974-); Freeman City of London 1988-; *Recreations* music, classical guitar, watercolours, gardening, food, photography, swimming, walking; *Style—* Anthony Davis, Esq; Davenport Communications, Clerkenwell House, 45-47 Clerkenwell Green, London EC1R 0HT (☎ 071 251 6859, fax 071 608 1350)

DAVIS, Anthony Ronald William James; s of Donald William Davis, of Barnes, and Mary Josephine, *née* Nolan-Byrne; *b* 26 July 1931; *Educ* Ratcliffe, The Oratory, Regent St Poly; *Career* Nat Serv Army 1953-55; architectural asst Housing Dept Middx Co Architect's Dept 1956-58, sub ed The Builder 1959; ed: Official Architecture and Planning 1964-70, Building 1970-74 (dir 1972-77); editorial dir: New World Publishers Ltd 1983-86 (ed in chief 1978-83), Middle East Construction and Saudi Arabian Construction 1983-86; bd memb: Architecture and Planning Publications Ltd 1966, Building (Publishers) Ltd 1972; ed World Property 1986-90, currently independent media conslt; memb Cncl Modular Soc 1970-71; JP Berks 1973-81; *Recreations* collecting porcelain, music and dreaming architecture; *Style—* Anthony Davis, Esq; 8 Blake Close, Dowles Green, Wokingham, Berks RG11 1QH (☎ 0734 785046)

DAVIS, Col Anthony Wilmer; MBE (1972); s of Brig Thomas William Davis, OBE (d 1982), of Sea Point, South Africa, and Margot Caddy, *née* Mackie (d 1983); *b* 11 Aug 1930; *Educ* Bryanston; *m* 28 June 1957, Susan Ward, da of Stephen Edgar Hames (d 1985), of Prestbury, Cheshire; 1 s (Simon b 1959), 1 da (Fiona b 1961); *Career* RMA Sandhurst 1949-51, cmmnd Manchester Regt 1951, Staff Coll Camberley 1961, Armed Forces Staff Coll Norfolk Virginia USA 1968, Bde Maj Berlin Inf Bde 1969-71, CO King's Regt 1972-74, Directing Staff Nat Def Coll Latimer 1975-77, Col GS Staff Coll Camberley 1978-81; Comptroller and Sec Forces Help Soc and Lord Roberts Workshops 1982-; *Recreations* golf, classical music; *Style—* Col A W Davis, MBE; c/o Midland Bank plc, Knightsbridge Branch, London SW1X 9RG

DAVIS, (John) Barry; s of Wilfred John Davis (d 1973), of Birmingham, and Edna Olive, *née* Chester (d 1988); *b* 6 Jan 1936; *Educ* George Dixon GS Birmingham; *m* 10 Sept 1960, Brenda Margaret, da of William Henry Barnes; 1 da (Elizabeth Jayne b 20 Jan 1972); *Career* articled clerk Jacob Cavenagh & Skeet Chartered Accountants Birmingham 1952-57, qualified 1958, ptnr Neville Russell (formerly Dixon Hopkinson Birmingham) 1965- (sr ptnr 1958-64); methodist local preacher; hon consul Finland; FCA (ACA 1958), MIPA, LLCM, ALCM; *Recreations* classical music, opera, ballet, gardening; *Clubs* Birmingham Consular Association, Birmingham Organists Association; *Style—* Barry Davis, Esq; Neville Russell, Britannia House, 50 Great Charles St, Queensway, Birmingham B3 2LY (☎ 021 236 7711, fax 021 236 2778)

DAVIS, Hon Mrs (Beatrice Margaret); da of 1 Viscount Mills (d 1968), and Winifred Mary (d 1974), da of George Conaty, of Birmingham; *b* 21 July 1916; *Educ* Edgbaston C of E Coll for Girls Birmingham; *m* 20 Dec 1941, Walter Goodwin Davis (d 1973), s of Goodwin Julian Davis (d 1940); 2 s (Patrick b 1947, Andrew b 1950), 1 da (Jane b 1957); *Career* antique dealer; *Style—* The Hon Mrs Davis; Chantry House, Sheep Street, Stow-on-the-Wold, Glos G54 1AA (☎ 0451 30450)

DAVIS, Maj-Gen Brian William; CB (1985), CBE (1980, OBE 1974); s of late Edward William Davis, MBE, and Louise Jane, *née* Webber; *b* 28 Aug 1930; *Educ* Weston super Mare GS, Mons Offr Cadet Sch Aldershot; *m* 1954, Margaret Isobel Jenkins; 1 s, 1 da; *Career* cmmnd RA 1949, Lt-Col Staff Coll Camberley 1969-71, CO 32 Light Regt RA serving in BAOR NI and UK 1971-74, Col logistic plans and ops HQ BAOR 1975, Brig 1975, Cdr RA 3 Div 1976-77, RCDS 1978, COS NI 1979-80, C-in-C Mission to Soviet Forces Germany 1981-82, Maj-Gen 1982, COS Logistic Exec

(Army) MOD 1982-83, Vice QMG 1983-85, ret 1985; head of public affairs RO plc 1985-; *Recreations* rugby, cricket, fishing; *Clubs* Army & Navy, Special Forces, HAC, MCC, Somerset CCC, Piscatorial Soc; *Style*— Maj-Gen Brian Davis, CB, CBE; c/o Williams and Glyn's Bank, Laurie House, Victoria Rd, Farnborough, Hants

DAVIS, Calum; s of Roy Albert George Davis, of Pigeon House Corner, Rockford, Ringwood, Hants, and Catherine Jessie Davis; *b* 18 June 1951; *Educ* Taunton Sch, Canterbury Sch of Architecture (Dip Arch); *m* 20 Aug 1977, Joan Anne, da of John Alfred Stevens; 1 s (Jamie b 1981), 1 da (Josie b 1984); *Career* architect; princ and fndr Architon Gp Practice CAS and Planning Consultants; dir: Cabvesquare Ltd 1984, Architon Services Ltd 1986, Mainstreet Designs Ltd 1986, Architects Registration Cncl UK 1979; England trialist U19 Rugby 1969, RIBA; *Recreations* golf, skiing, windsurfing, conservation of historic buildings; *Style*— Calum Davis, Esq; Cotmandene House, Dene St, Dorking, Surrey RH4 2BZ; Architon Gp Practice, 525 London Rd, N Cheam, Surrey SM3 8JR (☎ 081 330 6069, fax 081 330 7374, car 0860 331349)

DAVIS, Carl; *b* 28 Oct 1936; *m* Jean Boht; 2 da (Hannah b 1 Jan 1972, Jessie b 6 May 1974); *Career* composer and conductor; studied with: Paul Nordoff and Hugo Kauder NY, Per Norgaad Copenhagen; asst conductor New York City Opera 1958; *musical theatre* Diversions (Obie Prize Best Review) 1958, Twists (Arts Theatre London) 1962, The Projector and Cranford (Theatre Royal Stanford East), Pilgrim (Edinburgh Festival), The Wind in the Willows (Haymarket) 1985; *incidental music for theatre incl* The Prospect Theatre Co, The National Theatre, The Royal Shakespeare Co, The London Contemporary Dance Co, Saddlers Wells Royal Ballet, Northern Ballet Theatre; *ballet* A Simple Man (Northern Ballet) 1987, Lipizzaner 1989, Madly, Badly Sadly, Gladly (London Contemporary Ballet), David and Goliath, Dances of Love and Death, The Picture of Dorian Gray (Saddlers Wells Royal Ballet) 1987; *music for TV incl* The Snow Goose (BBC TV) 1971, The World at War (Thames TV, Emmy Award) 1972, The Naked Civil Servant (Thames TV) 1975, Our Mutual Friend (BBC TV) 1978, Churchill - The Wilderness Years (Southern TV) 1981, Hollywood (Thames TV) 1980, Silas Marner (BBC TV) 1985, Hotel du Lac (BBC TV) 1986, The Accountant (BAFTA Award) 1990, The Secret Life of Ian Fleming 1989; *operas for TV* The Arrangement, Who Takes You to The Party, Orpheus in the Underground, Peace; *film music* The Bofors Gun 1969, The French Lieutenant's Woman 1981, Champions 1984, The Girl in a Swing 1988, Rainbow 1988, Scandal 1988, Frankenstein Unbound 1990; *concert works* Music for the Royal Wedding, Variations on a Bus Route, Overture on Australian Themes, Clarinet Concerto, Line on London Symphony 1984, Fantasy for Flute and Harpsichord 1985, The Searle Suite for Wind Ensemble, Fanfare for Jerusalem 1987, Norwegian Brass Music 1988, Variations for a Polish Beggar's Theme 1988, Pigeons Progress 1988, Jazz Age Fanfare 1989, Liverpool Oratorio (by Paul McCartney) 1991; *recordings* Christmas with Kiri, Beautiful Dreamer (with Marylin Horne), The Silents, Ben Hur, A Simple Man, The Town Fox and Other Musical Tales (text by Carla Lane); Chevalier des Arts et des Letrres 1988; *Style*— Carl Davis, Esq

DAVIS, Sir Charles Sigmund; CB (1960); s of Maurice Davis (d 1943); *b* 22 Jan 1909; *Educ* Trinity Coll Cambridge; *m* 1940, Pamela Mary, da of Kenneth Dawson, OBE (d 1957); 2 da (Caroline, Elizabeth); *Career* HG 1940-45; called to the Bar Inner Temple 1930, legal advsr to MAFF and The Forestry Cmmn 1957-74, counsel to the Speaker House of Commons 1974-83; chm of cncl Nat Soc for Cancer Relief 1983-85 (tstee 1983-89), vice pres Cancer Relief Macmillan Fund 1989-; LRAM, ARCM; kt 1965; *Recreations* music; *Style*— Sir Charles Davis, CB; The Little House, 43 Wolsey Rd, E Molesey, Surrey KT8 9EW (☎ 081 979 6617)

DAVIS, Chloë Marion; *née* Pound; OBE (1975); da of Richard Henry Pound; *b* 15 Feb 1909; *m* 1928, Edward Thomas Davis; 1 s; *Career* memb: Consumer Consultative Ctee EEC 1973-76, Cncl on Tribunals 1970-79, Consumer Standards Advsy Ctee of Br Standards Instn 1965-78 (chm 1970-73); chm Consumer Affrs Gp of Nat Organisations 1973-; *Style*— Mrs Edward Davis, OBE; Auberville Cottage, 246 Dover Rd, Walmer, Kent

DAVIS, Clive Timothy; s of Sherman Alexander Davis, of Bath, and Betty Mavis, *née* Savery; *b* 8 Oct 1959; *Educ* Culverhay Comp Sch, St Catherine's Coll Oxford (BA, Bullock prize); *m* 2 May 1986, Mohini, da of Mohanbhai Patel; 1 s (Shivan Clive b 7 Sept 1990); *Career* journalist; books ed West Indian World newspaper 1981-85 (gen reporter and arts ed 1981-82), BBC News trainee 1982-84, sub ed BBC Radio News 1984-86, book reviewer New Statesman 1984-, freelance arts writer and gen reporter The Guardian 1985-86, arts feature writer London Daily News 1986-87, book reviewer New Society 1987-89, arts writer and music critic The Times 1987-, fiction and non-fiction reader Chatto & Windus 1988-89, contrib Sunday Telegraph 7 Days Magazine 1989-90, writer and presenter Richard Wright - A Native Son (Radio 4 documentary); *Recreations* walking, piano, cricket; *Style*— Clive Davis, Esq; The Times, 1 Pennington St, London E1 9XN

DAVIS, Sir Colin Rex; CBE (1965); s of Reginald George Davis (d 1944), of Weybridge, Surrey, by his w Lillian; *b* 25 Sept 1927; *Educ* Christ's Hosp, Royal Coll of Music; *m* 1, 1948 (m dis 1964), April Cantelo; 1 s, 1 da; m 2, 1964, Ashraf Naini, da of Abeolvahab Naini Assar (d 1978); 3 s, 2 da; *Career* formerly conductor: BBC Scottish Orchestra, Sadler's Wells (musical dir 1961-65); chief conductor BBC Symphony Orchestra 1967-71, conducted Bayreuth 1977, musical dir Royal Opera House Covent Garden 1971-86; princ guest conductor: Boston Symphony Orchestra 1972-84, LSO 1974-; music dir Bayerischer Rundfunk Orchestra Munich 1983-; hon conductor Dresden Stattskapelle 1990, Commendatore of Republic of Italy 1976, Chev de la Legion d'Honneur 1982, Cdr's Cross of the Order of Merit of Fed Republic of Germany 1987, Cdr L'Ordre des Lettres (France) 1990; kt 1980; *Recreations* reading, gardening; *Clubs* Athenaeum; *Style*— Sir Colin Davis, CBE; c/o 7A Fitzroy Park, London N6 6HS; c/o Columbia Artists Mgmnt Inc, 165 W 57th St, New York, NY 10019, USA

DAVIS, David; *b* 14 June 1935; *Educ* William Ellis Sch Highgate, Univ of London (BSc); *m* 2 July 1958; *Career* ptnr Cohen Arnold & Co (chartered accountants) 1961-70, fin advsr and lectr 1970-; non-exec dir 1970-: Daejan Holdings plc, City & Country Properties plc, Metropolitan Properties Ltd; headmaster Pardes House GS E Finchley 1979-85, memb House Ctee Bearsted Meml Hosp; FCA, ATTI; *Recreations* walking, kiting, gardening, computer studies; *Style*— David Davis, Esq; 158-162 Shaftesbury Ave, London WC2 (☎ 071 836 1555)

DAVIS, David Henry; s of Harry Joseph Davis (d 1986), of London, and Madge May, *née* Rosen; *b* 25 July 1936; *Educ* Streatham GS, Brighton Coll, Pitmans Coll; *m* 21 June 1959, Beryl Maureen, da of Harry Lancer; 1 s (Jonathan Anthony Bruce b 19 March 1963); *Career* trainee South London Advertiser 1952-53; reporter: Croydon Times 1953-56, Kentish Express 1956-57; sub ed Press Assoc/Reuters 1957-62, chief sub ed Universal News Services 1962-64, business reporter The Times 1964-68; Daniel J Edelman Ltd (PR): dir 1968, dep md 1969-76, md 1976-80, chm 1980-85; chm Daniel J Edelman Europe Ltd 1985-; MIPR 1982, vice chm PR Conslt Assoc 1985; *Recreations* watching sport, my family; *Clubs* The Carlton, Press (Paris); *Style*— David Davis, Esq; 67 Albion Gate, Albion St, Hyde Park, London W2 (☎ 071 402 1913); Daniel J Edelman Europe Ltd, Kingsgate House, 536 King's Rd, London SW10 OTE (☎ 071 835 1222, fax 071 351 7449)

DAVIS, David Michael; MP (C) Boothferry 1987-; s of Ronald Alexander Davis, and Elizabeth *née* Brown; *b* 23 Dec 1948; *Educ* Bec GS, Univ of Warwick (BSc), London Business Sch (MSc), Harvard Univ (AMP); *m* 28 July 1973, Doreen, da of Alfred John Cook; 1 s (Alexander b 1987), 2 da (Rebecca b 1974, Sarah b 1977); *Career* dir: Tate & Lyle plc 1987 (non exec dir 1987-90), Globe Investment Trust plc 1989-90; *Recreations* flying, mountaineering, writing; *Clubs* Reform; *Style*— D M Davis, Esq, MP; House of Commons, Westminster, London SW1

DAVIS, David William; s of George Henry Davis, of Beaconsfield, and Lucy Ada, *née* Tylee (d 1959); *b* 29 Oct 1942; *Educ* Emanuel Sch; *m* 25 Nov 1967, Jennifer, da of Wilfred Snell; 1 s (Kenneth b 28 May 1971), 1 da (Jacqueline b 25 Feb 1970); *Career* CA 1966; ptnr: Fryer Sutton Morris & Co 1967-, Fryer Whitehill & Co 1971-, Clark Whitehill 1982-; FCA 1975, MBIM 1975; *Recreations* badminton, bridge; *Style*— David Davis, Esq; Elm End House, Henton, Oxon OX9 4AH (☎ 0844 521 64); Clark Whitehill, 25 New Street Sq, London EC4A 3LN (☎ 071 353 1577, fax 071 583 1720, telex 887 422, car 0860 632 382)

DAVIS, Derek Richard; s of Stanley Lewis Davis, OBE, of Malta, and Rita Beatrice Rachel, *née* Rosenheim; *b* 3 May 1945; *Educ* Clifton, Balliol Coll Oxford (BA); *m* 25 Jan 1987, Diana, da of Ellis Levinson, of Chelsea; 1 s (Joshua b 1990), 1 da (Rebecca b 1988); *Career* asst princ Bd of Trade 1967, princ DTI 1972, head Oil and Gas Div Dept Energy 1987- (asst sec 1977, under sec and head Gas Div 1985); *Style*— Derek Davis, Esq; Department of Energy, 1 Palace St, London SW1 5HE (☎ 071 238 3099)

DAVIS, Donald Conway; s of George Davis (d 1981), of Liverpool, and Edna Ruth, *née* Conway; *b* 19 March 1932; *Educ* Quarry Bank HS; *m* 1965, Edwina Margaret Lawson, da of Edwin Lawson Spence (d 1955), of Lancs; 1 s (Simon b 1971), 3 da (Alexandra b 1966, Lucinda b 1968, Emily b 1986); *Career* 2 Lt Army 1955-57; CA; gp dir: Liverpool Daily Post & Echo Ltd (publishing and printing) 1962-69, Harrison & Son Ltd (printing) 1969-73; gp md Pitman plc (publishing and printing) 1973-82, exec chm Security Holdings Ltd (printing) 1983-86, md Hunter Print Group plc (printing) 1986-89; chm: Balding & Mansell plc, Contemporary Printers Ltd, TH Brickell & Son Ltd (The Blackmore Press); dir: Bath Press Gp Ltd, Thamesmouth Printing Gp plc; Liveryman Worshipful Co of Stationers and Newspaper Makers; FCA; *Recreations* sailing, golf, shooting, cricket and rugby, photography; *Clubs* Hon Artillery Co, Royal Thames Yacht, Marylebone Cricket, Beaconsfield Golf, Royal Southampton Yacht, Wasps Rugby Football, Lancs Co Cricket, RSA; *Style*— Donald Davis, Esq; Austenwood, Austenwood Common, Gerrards Cross, Buckinghamshire SL9 8NL

DAVIS, Prof Donald Henry; s of Henry William Davis (d 1978), and Georgina Rose, *née* Marshall (d 1984); *b* 28 Nov 1934; *Educ* Sir George Monoux GS, UCL (BSc, PhD); *m* 2 Sept 1961, Anne Elizabeth, da of Harold Thomas Grinstead (d 1988); 1 s (Timothy John), 1 da (Claire Elizabeth); *Career* res assoc Univ of Chicago 1961-62; UCL: res asst Physics Dept 1959-61 and 1962-63, lectr 1963-72, reader Physics and Astronomy Dept 1972-86, prof 1986-; memb: RSPB, WWF; CPhys, FInstP 1971; *Recreations* bridge, photography, gardening; *Style*— Prof Donald Davis; Department of Physics and Astronomy, University College London, Gower Street, London WC1E 6BT (☎ 071 380 7151, fax 071 380 7145, telex 28722 U G)

DAVIS, Prof Edward Arthur; s of Edward Davis (d 1988), and Elizabeth, *née* Smith; *b* 26 Nov 1936; *Educ* Univ of Birmingham (BSc), Univ of Reading (PhD), Univ of Cambridge (MA); *m* 30 Oct 1960, Christine Elizabeth, da of Philip Edwyn Riley (d 1987); 2 s (Philip b 1962, Andrew b 1964); *Career* res asst prof Physics Dept Univ of Illinois USA 1963-64, scientist Xerox Corp Rochester NY USA 1964-67, lectr Physics Dept Univ of Cambridge 1973-80 (Royal Soc Mr and Mrs John Jaffé Donation res fell Cavendish Laboratory 1968-73), dean Faculty of Sci Univ of Leicester 1987- (prof of experimental physics 1980-); chm Tilton Parish Cncl; CPhys, FInstP, fell American Physical Soc; *Books* Electronic Properties of Non-Crystalline Materials (with N F Mott, 1971, 2 edn 1979); *Recreations* flying light aircraft, fell walking, rock climbing, golf; *Style*— Prof Edward Davis; The Mill House, Tilton-on-the-Hill, Leics LE7 9LG (☎ 053754 242); Physics Dept, University of Leicester, University Rd, Leicester LE1 7RH (☎ 0533 523571/0, fax 0533 550182, telex 341664 LUXRAY G)

DAVIS, Frank; JP; s of Julius Davis (d 1970), of Hampstead Garden Suburb, and Dinah, *née* Benjamin; *b* 8 June 1920; *Educ* London Poly, Inns of Ct Sch of Law; *m* 4 Jan 1945, Irene, da of Isaac Lipman (d 1964); 2 s (Malcolm, Richard); *Career* Special Servs; memb Lloyds of London 1979, md various companies; cnclr Finchley Borough Cncl 1956-65, ldr Finchley Cncl, cnclr London Borough of Barnet 1964-71 and 1990; Parly candidate Finchley 1966, Acton 1968; changed name temporarily to Frank Liberal Davis, forcing amendment to Representation of the People Act 1949, which prohibited appearance of party affiliations on ballot papers; resigned from Lib Party 1970, joined Conservative Party 1987; chm Wingate Charity Tst, fndr Wingate FC, govr Tel Aviv Univ, vice pres Maccabi Assoc, memb Trades Advsy Cncl 1951-87; magistrate for Inner London 1963- (dep chm), memb Appeals Tbnls Dept of Social Servs & Dept of Employment, lay judge of Crown Ct (appeals), Mayor of Finchley 1963-64; memb: Arsenal FC, The Hon Soc of Grays Inn 1953; Order of Independence Uganda 1964; *Recreations* travel, horticulture; *Clubs* Rotary Int; *Style*— Frank Davis, Esq, JP; 20 Connaught Drive, Finchley, London NW11 6BJ

DAVIS, Grahame Watson; s of William Henry, of Chatham, Kent (d 1944), and Georgina, *née* Watson (d 1985); *b* 9 Sept 1934; *Educ* King's Sch Rochester; *m* 29 Aug 1963, Wendy Lovelace Davis, JP, da of Antony Lovelace Wagon, of Rochester (d 1978); 1 s (Piers b 1971), 1 da (Helena b 1966); *Career* slr; sr ptnr Hextall Erskine; Co of London dir: Complete Security Serv Ltd, Elmswood Commercial Conslts Ltd, Ashley Communications UK Ltd, Cheapside Conslts Ltd, Retail Discount Vouchers Ltd; memb The Law Soc; *Recreations* golf, cricket; *Clubs* Wig and Pen, Castle; *Style*— Grahame W Davis, Esq; 79 Eccleston Square, London SW1V 1PW (☎ 071 828 7011); 52-54 Leadenhall St, London EC3A 2AP (☎ 071 488 1424, fax 071 828 8341, car 0860 351311)

DAVIS, Herbert Edmund (Bert); s of Edmund Christopher Davis (d 1936), of Woodford Green, Essex, and Emily Maud, *née* Curran (d 1949); *Educ* Business Coll; *m* 5 June 1937, (Lydia) Mary Elizabeth, da of Frank Henry Sturges (d 1942), of Surbiton, Surrey; 2 s (John Anthony b 30 Sept 1947, Charles Edmund b 29 Dec 1949), 1 da (Jane Ellen b 20 Aug 1938); *Career* served HG until 1941; RAOC: Lt 1941, Capt 1943, served 51 Div 1943-46, Maj 1945, demobbed 1946; chm Esher Laundry Ltd 1988-(md 1942-88); vice pres Inst Br Launderers 1961-62; fndr memb Worshipful Co Launderers 1960, Freeman City of London 1978 ; Knight of the Order Orange Nassau with Swords Holland 1946; *Recreations* golf; *Clubs* Coombe Wood Golf (former Capt 1973); *Style*— Bert Davis, Esq; 14 Berystede, Kingston upon Thames, Surrey KT2 7PQ (☎ 081 549 8631); Esher Laundry Ltd, Kingston upon Thames, Surrey KT1 3DT (☎ 081 546 6266)

DAVIS, Sir (Ernest) Howard; CMG (1969), OBE (1960); s of Edwin Howard Davis; *b* 22 April 1918; *Educ* Christian Bros Sch Gibraltar, Coll of St Joseph Blackpool, Univ of London; *m* 1948, Marie, da of Gustave Bellotti; 2 s; *Career* dep govr Gibraltar 1971-78; kt 1978; *Style*— Sir Howard Davis, CMG, OBE; Flat 6, Mount Pleasant, South Barrack Rd, Gibraltar (☎ A 70358)

DAVIS, Dr Ian Robert; s of David Davis (d 1988), of Paignton, S Devon, and Theodora, *née* Rawson; *b* 2 March 1937; *Educ* Northern Poly (DipArch), Georgia Inst of Technol, Univ Coll Univ of London (PhD); *m* 8 July 1961, Judith Margaret, da of Roy Cardwell (d 1975), of Bognor, Sussex; 1 s (Simon b 1969), 2 da (Amanda b 1962, Caroline b 1964); *Career* architect in practice 1961-70, princ lectr Sch of Architecture Oxford Poly 1970-89; advsr UN Post-Disaster Shelter Provision 1975-91, memb Nat Acad of Sci Int Ctee on the Implications of Disaster Assistance Washington DC 1976-79, ldr Housing and Hazards Section Int Karakovam Expedition, chm Int Panel on Disaster Risk Reduction 1981-86, dir Disaster Mgmnt Centre 1982-89; memb Nat Ctee on the Int Decade for Nat Disaster Reduction 1990-; RIBA, FRGS; *Books* Shelter and Disaster (1978), Disasters and Small Dwelling (ed, 1982), Dunroamin - The Suburban Semi and It's Enemies (with P Oliver and I Bentley, 1982); *Recreations* photography, painting, travel; *Style—* Dr Ian Davis; 97 Kingston Rd, Oxford OX2 6RL (☎ 0865 56473); Disaster Management Centre, Oxford Polytechnic, Headington, Oxford OX3 0BP (☎ 0865 819210, fax 0865 819073, telex G 83147 VIA)

DAVIS, Ivor John Guest; CB (1983); s of Thomas Henry Davis (d 1963); *b* 11 Dec 1925; *Educ* Devonport HS, Univ of London (external BSc); *m* 1954, Mary Eleanor, da of Robert Porter Thompson (d 1974); 2 c; *Career* comptroller-gen patents, trade marks and designs Patent Office 1978-85, pres Admin Cncl Euro Patent Office 1981-84, dir Common Law Inst of Intellectual Property 1986; *Recreations* music, gardening; *Style—* Ivor Davis, Esq, CB; 5 Birch Close, Eynsford, Dartford, Kent (☎ 0322 862725)

DAVIS, James Gresham; CBE (1988); s of Col Robert Davis, OBE, JP (d 1963), and Josephine *née* Edwards; *b* 20 July 1928; *Educ* Bradfield, Clare Coll Cambridge (MA); *m* 24 Nov 1973, Adriana Johanna (Hanny), da of Evert Verhoef (d 1977), of Rhoon, Holland; 3 da (Mariske b 1974, Katrina b 1978, Charlotte b 1980); *Career* RN 1946-49; P & OSN Co 1952-72: Calcutta 1953-54, Kobe (Japan) 1954-56, Hong Kong 1956-57; dir: P & O Lines 1967-72, Kleinwort Benson Ltd 1973-88, DFDS Ltd 1975-, Pearl Cruises of Scandinavia Inc 1982-86, Rodskog Shipbrokers (Hong Kong) Ltd 1983-88; memb advsy bd: J Lauritzen A/S Copenhagen 1981-85, DFDS A/S Copenhagen 1981-85; advsr Tjaeborg (UK) Ltd 1985-87; chm Friends of the World Maritime University 1985-, pt/t memb Br Transport Docks Bd 1981-83, memb Cncl Missions to Seamen 1981-; memb Cncl Bureau Veritas 1989-; pres: CIT 1981-82, World Ship Soc 1969 (1971, 1984, 1985, 1986), Inst of Freight Forwarders Ltd 1984-86, Inst of Chartered Shipbrokers 1990-; vice pres: Br Maritime League 1984-89, Inst of Chartered Shipbrokers 1988-90; memb: Baltic Exchange 1973, Greenwich Forum 1982; govr Queenswood Sch; Freeman City of London 1986, Liveryman and Asst to the Court Worshipful Co of Shipwrights, Younger Brother Trinity House; FCIT 1969, Hon FNI 1985, Hon FInstFF 1986, FRSA 1986; *Recreations* golf, family, ships; *Clubs* Brooks's, Hurlingham, Golfers, Harwich and Dovercourt Golf, Royal Calcutta Golf, Fanlingerers, Holland Park Lawn Tennis; *Style—* James Davis, Esq, CBE; 115 Woodsford Sq, London W14 8DT (☎ 071 602 0675); Summer Lawn, Dovercourt, Essex CO12 4EF (☎ 0255 502981)

DAVIS, James Patrick Lambert; s of Walter Patrick Carless Davis, and Jane, *née* Lamert (d 1988); *b* 23 Sept 1946; *Educ* Charterhouse, Balliol Coll Oxford; *m* 18 May 1974, Sally Anne, da of Noel Kemball; 1 s (Andrew b 23 March 1978), 3 da (Nicola b 23 March 1980, Sarah b 9 June 1982, Clare b 30 June 1986); *Career* Freshfields: articled clerk 1969, ptnr 1976-, ptnr i/c Singapore Office 1980-84; *Recreations* fishing, golf; *Clubs* MCC, Singapore Cricket, Berkshire Golf; *Style—* James Davis, Esq; Freshfields, Whitefriars, 65 Fleet St, London EC4Y 1HS (☎ 071 936 4000, fax 071 832 7001)

DAVIS, John; s of Alfred Davis (d 1972), and Amelia Redman (d 1951); *b* 27 Aug 1934; *m* 20 March 1954, Jean Doris, da of Horace George Newson (d 1964); *Career* served WWII Fleet Air Arm 1942-46; film prodr and dir; entered films 1950, formed View Finder Films Ltd 1960, writer and dir of documentaries and TV commercials, prodn assoc Go To Blazes, assoc prodr The Quare Fellow; prodr: Girl in the Headlines, Daylight Robbery; dir Cry Wolf, prodn coordinator Murphy's War, prodr and dir Danger Point; co-writer: Obsession, The Linsky Witness; prodn mangr: The Beast Must Die, Sherlock Holmes, Murder By Degree, Can I Help You?, Silver Dream Racer, Rememberance; writer: Grand Babylon Hotel, The End of Love; prodn supervisor: Gilbert and Sullivan Operas, Indiana Jones and The Temple of Doom, Lace II, The Two Mrs Grenvilles; prodn mangr: Never Say Never Again, King David; assoc prodr: Nineteen Eighty Four, Half Moon Street, Taffin; line prodr Spooks, prodr Indiscreet; assoc prodr: Inspector Morse, Moi General de Gaulle; prodn supervisor About Face, rep Completion Bd Fifty Fifty; dir: Bryanston Films Ltd, Bryanston Seven Arts Ltd; *Clubs* Saville; *Style—* John Davis, Esq; 20 Brockley Ave, Stanmore, Middlesex HA7 4LX (☎ 081 958 6115); Higher Hayne, Roadwater, West Somerset (☎ 0984 40555); Goldcrest Elstree Film Studios, Shenley Rd, Borehamwood, Elstree, Herts WD6 1JG (☎ 081 953 1600 ext 208, fax 071 953 6740)

DAVIS, John; s of William Davis (d 1954), and Elsie Elizabeth Davis (d 1959); *b* 29 Aug 1943; *Educ* Cardiff HS, Univ of S Wales and Monmouthshire Cardiff (BSc Econ), Univ of Lausanne; *m* 3 June 1967, Gillian Mary; 3 s (Barnaby Simon b 22 March 1972, Dominic James b 16 Aug 1974, Matthew Jonathan b 21 Feb 1978), 1 da (Sophie Angharad Louise b 23 Sept 1981); *Career* admitted slr 1970; asst slr: Slaughter and May 1970-76, Osborne Clarke 1976-77; ptnr and dep managing ptnr Osborne Clarke 1977-, Notary Public 1984-; vice chm Bd of Govrs and fndn govr Stoke Bishop C of E VC Primary Sch, managing tstee Stoke Bishop Educnl Charity, hon pres Target MS, memb Bristol Clifton and West of England Zoological Soc, hon legal advsr Somerset and Avon Vergers Guild; memb: Bd of Dirs Bristol Initiative, Devpt and Fin Ctee Bristol and Avon Groundwork Tst; memb: Law Soc, Bristol Medico Legal Soc, Ecclesiastical Law Soc, The Notaries Soc; *Recreations* golf, skiing, theatre, music, conservation; *Clubs* The Clifton, Bristol & Clifton Golf; *Style—* John Davis, Esq; St Davids, 6 Ivywell Rd, Sneyd Park, Bristol BS9 1NX (☎ 0272 686425); 30 Queen Charlotte St, Bristol BS99 7QQ (☎ 0272 230220, fax 0272 279209, telex 44734)

DAVIS, Prof John Allen; s of Maj H R Davis, MC, RA, and Mary, *née* Allen; *b* 6 Aug 1923; *Educ* Blundell's, St Mary's Hosp London Univ (MB BS), Harvard Univ, Nuffield Inst Oxford, MD, FRCP; *m* 1957, Madeleine Elizabeth Vinnicombe, da of Wing Cdr Charles Harry Norman Ashlin, RAF; 3 s (Henry b 1958, Arthur b 1959, William b 1963), 2 da (Mary b 1961, Elizabeth b 1967); *Career* 1948-50, serv BAOR; house physician St Mary's Hosp London 1946-47, house physician Hosp for Sick Children Great Ormond St London 1949-50, course Int Children's Centre, registrar Paediatric Dept St Mary's Hosp 1951-52, exchange sr asst Children's Hosp Med Centre Boston and teaching fell 1953, sr registrar Paediatric Unit St Mary's Hosp 1957-59 (unit home care scheme 1954-57), res fell Nuffield Oxford 1959-60, sr lectr Postgrad Med Sch Hammersmith, reader in paediatrics Inst of Child Health Univ of London, childrens physician Hammersmith Hosp 1967, prof of paediatrics Univ of Manchester 1967-79, prof of paediatrics Univ of Cambridge 1979-88; external examiner Univs: Sheffield, Oxford, Newcastle, London, Leicester, Hong Kong, Singapore; memb Bd Royal Coll of Midwives 1975-; patron Soc for Reproductive and Infant Psychology, former vice pres RCP; *Recreations* collecting and painting watercolours, gardening, reading, music; *Style—* Prof John Davis; Fourmile House, 1 & 3 Cambridge Road, Gt Shelford, Cambridge CB2 5JE

DAVIS, John Burton; s of Percy Oliver Davis (d 1980); *b* 20 Oct 1922; *Educ* Trinity Sch of John Whitgift, Croydon; Queen Mary Coll London Univ (BSc); *m* 1944, Irene Margaret, da of late William Victor Reid; 1 s, 1 da; *Career* Lt REME; sr exec Lead Industries Gp Ltd; dir: Assoc Lead Mfrs Ltd, Assoc Lead Mfrs (Pty) Ltd SA, Frys Metals (Pty) Ltd SA, Waldies Ltd Calcutta India, Tewin Wood Roads Ltd; *Style—* John Davis, Esq; 5 Bishops Rd, Tewin Wood, Welwyn, Herts (☎ 043 879 597)

DAVIS, John David Tremaine; s of Sqdn Ldr Clarence Tremaine Davis RFC, RAF (d 1966) and Doris Mary, *née* Songhurst; *b* 23 Jan 1927; *Educ* King Edward VI Sch Stafford; *Career* chartered architect, chartered surveyor; Co Borough of Eastbourne 1958-64, E Sussex CC 1964-69, Civil Serv 1969-87; design mangr Multi Professional Gp, planning offr Naval Base Chatham, establishment mangr (Navy) Portsmouth, chm Regnl Design Feedback Ctee, mangr Regnl Conslts Coordinating Gp; completed projects: Central Library and Municipal Offices Eastbourne Co Hall ESCC Lewes, Paymaster Generals Office Crawley, Portsmouth Crown Ct, Maidstone Crown Ct; ARICS 1949, RIBA 1958; *Recreations* sailing; *Style—* John Davis, Esq; Hurstbourne, West Down Rd, Bexhill-on-Sea, East Sussex TN39 4DY (☎ 0424 211566)

DAVIS, Sir John Gilbert; 3 Bt (UK 1946); s of Sir Gilbert Davis, 2 Bt (d 1973); *b* 17 Aug 1936; *Educ* Oundle, RNC Dartmouth; *m* 16 Jan 1960, Elizabeth Margaret, da of Robert Smith Turnbull, of Falkirk; 1 s (Richard b 1970), 2 da (Wendy, Linda); *Career* exec vice pres Abitibi Price Inc Toronto until 1990, former chm Abitibi Price Sales Corporation NY; currently developing support businesses to the pulp and paper indust in Canada; *Recreations* squash, golf, reading, piano; *Clubs* Toronto, Rosedale Golf, Donalda; *Style—* Sir John Davis, Bt; 5 York Ridge Road, Willowdale, Ontario M2P 1R8, Canada

DAVIS, Sir John Henry Harris; CVO (1985); s of Sydney Myering Davis, of London, and Emily, *née* Harris; *b* 10 Nov 1906; *Educ* City of London Sch; *m* 1, 1926, Joan Buckingham; 1 s; m 2, 1947, Marion Gavid; 2 da; m 3, 1954 (m dis 1965), Dinah Sheridan; m 4, 1976, Mrs Felicity Rutland; *Career* Br Thomson Houston Gp 1931-38; joined Odeon Theatres Ltd (later The Rank Org) 1938, pres The Rank Org 1977-83 (chief exec 1962-74, chm 1962-77); dir Eagle Star Insur Co Ltd 1948-82, chm Southern TV Ltd 1968-76, jt pres Rank Xerox 1972-83, chm Nat Centre of Films for Children 1951-80; dir The Rank Fndn 1953, chm and tstee The Rank Prize Funds 1972; Hon DTech Univ of Loughborough 1975; Commandeur de l'Ordre de la Couronne (Belgium), KStJ; kt 1971; *Recreations* gardening, reading, travel, music; *Clubs* RAC; *Style—* Sir John Davis, CVO; 4 Selwood Terrace, London SW7 3QN

DAVIS, John Patrick; s of Ralph Patrick Davis, of The Beacon, Pilgrims Way, Chaldon, Surrey, and Vivian Hilda, *née* Braund; *b* 12 June 1944; *Educ* Tonbridge, Univ of Nottingham (BSc); *m* 5 Aug 1972, Fenella Irene, da of Guy Charles Madoc, CBE, KPM, of Close Foillan, Ramsey, Isle of Man; 1 s (Michael b 23 June 1975), 1 da (Rosemary b 11 June 1976); *Career* gen mangr mech engrg Redpath Dorman Long Ltd 1979-83; chm Aerospace Engrg plc 1990- (chief exec and gp md 1985-90); churchwarden; memb: CEng 1971, FIEE 1986, MIWeldE 1983; *Recreations* mountain walking, bee keeping; *Style—* John Davis, Esq; The Old Vicarage, Bourton, Swindon, Wiltshire SN6 8HZ; Aerospace Engineering plc, PO Box 25, South Marston Industrial Estate, Swindon, Wiltshire SN3 4TR (☎ 0793 827000, fax 0793 827578)

DAVIS, Jonathan Lewis; s of Cyril Harris Davis, BEM, of London N10, and Caroline, *née* Rubens; *b* 11 Nov 1948; *Educ* Clifton City Univ (BSc), Cranfield Sch of Mgmnt (MBA); *m* 23 July 1972, Elizabeth, da of late Louis Natali; 2 s (Neil Louis b 1976, Andrew Henry b 1978), 1 da (Emma Rachel b 1983); *Career* prodn engr Reliance Cords and Cables 1972-74 (prodn mangr 1974-77, dir 1978-81); ind conslt 1981-82; The Guidehouse Group plc 1982- (dir 1984-), md Guidehouse Ltd 1985-; Freeman City of London, Liveryman Worshipful Co of Musicians; MIProdE, MBIM; *Recreations* walking, scuba diving, reading, music, sailing; *Clubs* RAC; *Style—* Jonathan Davis, Esq; The Guidehouse Group Plc, Durrant House, 8-13 Chiswell St, London EC1Y 4UP (☎ 071 628 5858, fax 071 628 4473)

DAVIS, Dr Julian Richard Edgley; s of Robert Gordon Davis, and Patricia Davis; *b* 10 July 1954; *Educ* George Heriot's Sch, Univ of Edinburgh (BSc, MB ChB) Univ of Birming (PhD); *m* 10 July 1984, Ann, da of Denis Taylor; 3 s (William Michael b 8 Dec 1982, Jonathan Morgan b 31 Oct 1990, Nicholas Julian (twin) b 31 Oct 1990), 1 da (Sally Nicola b 8 July 1988); *Career* lectr med Dept Med Univ of Birmingham 1986-88 (Med Res Cncl training fell 1983-86), sr lectr med Dept Med Univ of Manchester 1988-, hon conslt physician Manchester Royal Infirmary; memb Clinical Endocrinology Ed Bd RCP UK 1981; licentiate RAM 1985; *Recreations* music (piano and chamber music esp 20th century), mountain walking; *Style—* Dr Julian Davis; Manchester Royal Infirmary, Dept of Med, Oxford Rd, Manchester M13 9WL (☎ 061 276 4256, fax 061 275 5584)

DAVIS, Kenneth John; s of Kenneth John Davis, of Marine Drive, Saltdean, Sussex, and Ethel Viola, *née* Miller; *b* 10 March 1943; *Educ* Addey and Stanhope GS; *m* 18 Feb 1967, Janette Doreen, da of John Henry Lighton; 1 s (Anthony Lee b 1971), 1 da (Elizabeth Ann b 1974); *Career* Alexander Stenhouse Ltd: regnl dir 1982-85, mktg dir 1985-86, chief operating offr (all UK and Eire branches) 1986-87, chief exec offr 1988-; dir Cawick Hall Insur Servs 1983-; Freeman City of London, memb Worshipful Co of Insurers; FCII; *Books* Marketing Insurance a Practical Guide (jtly, 1986); *Recreations* sailing; *Clubs* Little Ship; *Style—* Kenneth Davis, Esq; Alexander Stenhouse Ltd, 10 Devonshire Sq, London EC2M 4LE (☎ 071 621 9990, fax 071 621 9950, telex 920368 ASLDN G)

DAVIS, Lucinda Jane; s of Dennis Michael Davis, of W Sussex, and Wendy Francis, *née* Odgear; *b* 22 March 1958; *Educ* Haywards Heath GS, Kings Coll London Univ (LLB); *Career* called to the Bar Grays Inn 1981, SE Circuit; memb Hon Soc Grays Inn 1980; *Style—* Ms Lucinda Davis; Chichester Chambers 3 East Pallant Chichester W Sussex PO19 1TR (☎ 0243 784 538)

DAVIS, Margaret Ann McLeod Leo (Meg); da of John Alexander Bede McLeod Davis (d 1976), of Montréal, Quebec, and Barbara Ann Davis; *b* 26 Sept 1957; *Educ* École Classique Sécondaire Villa Maria, McGill Univ (BA); *Career* Pheonix Theatre Montréal 1978-80, dir MBA Literary Agents 1988- (joined 1984); co fndr Paradox Theatre Montréal; trombonist: York Symphony Orch, Tudor Orch London; *Recreations* trombone, cigars, late night philosophy; *Style—* Ms Meg Davis; MBA Literary Agents Ltd, 45 Fitzroy St, London W1P 4HR (☎ 071 387 2076, fax 071 387 2042)

DAVIS, Prof Mark Herbert Ainsworth; s of Christopher Ainsworth Davis (d 1951), and Frances Emily, *née* Marsden, JP, of Loughborough, Leics; *b* 1 May 1945; *Educ* Oundle, Clare Coll Cambridge (BA, MA, ScD), Univ of Calif Berkeley (MS, PhD); *m* 15 Oct 1988, Jessica Isabella Caroline, da of Robert Sinclair Smith, of Broadstairs, Kent; *Career* res asst Electronics Res Laboratory Univ of California Berkeley 1969-71; Imperial Coll London: lectr 1971-79, reader 1979-84, prof of system theory 1984-; visiting prof: Harvard Univ, MIT, Univ of Oslo; FSS 1985; *Books* Linear Estimation and Stochastic Control (1977), Stochastic Modelling and Control (1985); *Recreations* classical music (violin and viola); *Style—* Prof Mark Davis; 11 Chartfield Ave, London SW15 6DT (☎ 081 789 7677); Dept of Electrical Engrg, Imperial Coll, London SW7 2BT (☎ 071 589 5111 ext 5200)

DAVIS, Martin Mitchell; s of Kenneth Bertram Davis (d 1983), of Alcester, Warwickshire, and Emily Mary Tillett, MBE, *née* Gateley; *b* 30 May 1943; *Educ* Ampleforth, Univ Coll Oxford (MA); *m* 21 June 1975, Caroline Ann, da of John James

Yorke Scarlett (d 1984), of Kingsbridge, S Devon; 3 s (Edmund b 1976, Leo b 1977, Thomas b 1979), 1 da (Agnes b 1982); *Career* slr; ptnr Wiggin & Co Cheltenham 1974-77, fndr Davis & Co; chm Cheltenham Cncl of Churches 1977-78, pres Cheltenham Legal Assoc 1987-88, ctee memb Glos and Wilts Law Soc; *Recreations* gardening, walking, photography, listening to music, cycling, recycling; *Clubs* Pax Christi, Newman Assoc; *Style—* Martin Davis, Esq; Syreford, nr Andoversford, Cheltenham, Glos (☎ 0242 820474); 25 Rodney Rd, Cheltenham (☎ 0242 235202, fax 0242 224716, telex 437244 CMINTL G)

DAVIS, Sir Maurice Herbert; OBE (1953), QC (1965); *b* 30 April 1912, St Kitts; *m* Kathleen; 1 s, 5 da; *Career* memb Exec Cncl St Kitts, dep pres Gen Legve Cncl and memb Fed Exec Cncl, chief justice W Indies Assoc States Supreme Ct and Supreme Ct of Grenada 1975-80; kt 1975; *Style—* Hon Sir Maurice Davis, OBE, QC; PO Box 31, Basseterre, St Kitts, W Indies

DAVIS, Dr Michael; Geof Harry Tyrrell Davis, of London, and Joan, *née* Latcham; *b* 8 July 1943; *Educ* Charterhouse, St Thomas's Hosp Med Sch Univ of London (MB BS, MD, MRCP); *m* 5 Dec 1970, Elizabeth Maureen, da of Hedley Victor Billing (d 1984); 2 s (Justin b 10 May 1974, Julian b 29 Jan 1978), 1 da (Joelle b 18 May 1972); *Career* jr hosp posts 1967-74, sr lectr and conslt physician Liver Unit Kings Coll Hosp 1974-82; conslt physician: Dudley Rd Hosp Birmingham 1982-86, Royal United Hosp Bath 1986-; author scientific papers and chapters med textbooks relating to gastroenterology; memb Br Soc Gastroenterology 1972, FRCP 1984; *Books* Drug Reactions and the Liver (1981), Therapy of Liver Disease (1989); *Recreations* music, walking, stained glass; *Style—* Dr Michael Davis; Royal United Hospital, Combe Park, Bath BA1 3NG

DAVIS, Michael (Mike); s of S H S Davis (d 1989), of Watlington, Oxon, and B H Davis, *née* Back; *b* 6 Jan 1948; *Educ* Winchester, Sorbonne; *m* 1975 (m dis 1985), Angela, *née* Fortune; 2 da (Kate b 1978, Sophie b 1981); *Career* advtg exec; Foote Long & Belding London 1967-70; Young & Rubicam: Milan Italy 1970, London 1971-76, Tokyo Japan 1976-78, dir London 1978-81; dir Holdings Bd Wight Collins Rutherford & Scott plc 1981-84, dir of client servs TBWA London 1984-87, founding ptnr and md Leagas Shafron Davis Chick 1987-, work consists of managing nat and int advtg campaigns incl UK govt's AIDS campaign; MIPA, memb Mktg Soc; *Recreations* fly fishing, tennis, music; *Style—* Michael Davis, Esq; Leagas Shafron Davis Chick, 1 Star St, London W2 1QD (☎ 071 262 0874, fax 071 706 1549, car 0860 608004)

DAVIS, Michael Edward; s of Capt Raymond Norris Davis, of Sevenoaks, Kent, and Margaret, *née* Pierce; *b* 14 Aug 1951; *Educ* Sevenoaks Sch, Univ of London (BA); *m* 17 Aug 1974, Helen Frances, da of William Podmore; OBE JP, of Consall Hall, Wetley Rocks, Stoke on Trent, Staffs; 1 s (Paul Michael William b 4 July 1983), 1 da (Laura Helen Margaret b 6 Feb 1986); *Career* admitted slr 1977, ptnr Herbert Smith 1986- (joined 1975); Freeman Worshipful Co of Slrs; memb: Law Soc, Int Bar Assoc, Acad of Experts, Soc of Construction Law; *Recreations* horse riding, water skiing, travel, landscaping, rugby football; *Style—* Michael Davis, Esq; Herbert Smith, Exchange House, Primrose St, London EC2A 2HS (☎ 071 374 8000)

DAVIS, Norman Harold; s of Tobias Davis (1990), of Edgware, Middx, and Sybil, *née* Bernstein (d 1984); *b* 16 July 1931; *Educ* Strodes Fndn Egham Surrey; *m* 10 June 1956, Evelyn, da of Harry Lester (d 1954), of Finchley, London; 1 s (Robin b 1961); *Career* CA, sr ptnr Lane Heywood Davis CAs 1955-, fin dir Yale & Valor plc 1969-87, chm Dixor Strand plc 1978-1986, dir Apollo Watch Products plc 1989-; former chm: Lighting and Leisure Industries plc, George H Hurst plc; former dir: Henara plc, Phoenix Mining and Finance plc; vice chm Jewish Blind Soc; *Clubs* Oriental; *Style—* Norman H Davis, Esq; 30 Church Mount, Hampstead Garden Suburb, London N2 0RP (☎ 081 455 8977); Lane Heywood Davis, Anchor Brewhouse, 50 Shad Thames, Tower Bridge City, Tower Bridge, London SE1 2YB (☎ 071 403 4403, fax 071 357 6357, telex 892596, car 0836 596 614)

DAVIS, Penelope Jane; da of Anthony John Davis, of Cambridge, and Jean Margaret, *née* Stone; *b* 25 July 1960; *Educ* Cambridgeshire HS For Girls, Cambridge Coll Arts and Tech, Univ of Lancaster (BA), Central London Poly; *m* 1990, Geoffrey Robert Isitt; *Career* mangr Siggi Hats 1984, weekly columnist Fashion Weekly 1988-, md Davis & Hesbacher Ltd 1988-; *Recreations* riding, cooking, reading, cinema; *Style—* Miss Penelope Davis; 7 Racton Rd, Fulham, London SW6 1LW (☎ 071 381 9462)

DAVIS, Peter John; s of John Stephen Davis, and Adriantie, *née* de Baat; *b* 23 Dec 1941; *Educ* Shrewsbury; *Career* mgmnt trainee and salesman Ditchburn Orgn 1959-65, mktg and sales Gen Foods Ltd 1965-72, Fitch Lovell Ltd 1973-76, mktg dir Key Markets 1973-76, dir and asst md J Sainsbury plc 1976-86, chief exec Reed Int plc 1986-, dir Granada Gp 1987-; dep chm fin Devpt Bd NSPCC, govr Duncombe Sch Hertford; *Recreations* sailing, swimming, opera, ballet, wine; *Clubs* Trearddur Bay Sailing (Cdre 1982-84); *Style—* Peter Davis, Esq; Reed House, 6 Chesterfield Gardens, London W1A 1EJ (☎ 071 491 8279)

DAVIS, Peter Kerrich Byng; s of Frank C Davis, MC (d 1979), and Barbara, *née* Hartshorne; *b* 4 May 1933; *Educ* Felsted, Univ of London, St Thomas' Hosp Med Sch (MB BS); *m* 24 April 1965, Jennifer Anne, da of Brig-Gen (Creemer) Paul Clarke (d 1971); 1 s (Paul b 14 Aug 1966), 1 da (Emma b 9 Aug 1968); *Career* sr registrar in plastic surgery Churchill Hosp Oxford 1968-71; conslt plastic surgn 1971-: St Thomas' Hosp London, Queen Marys' Hosp Roehampton, Kingston Hosp, St Stephen's Hosp London; Br Assoc of Aesthetic Plastic Surgns: memb 1977-, vice pres 1981, pres 1982-84, hon sec 1988-; memb: BMA 1959, BAPS 1971, RSM 1971, ICPRS 1971, ISAPS 1979; *Books* Operative Surgery (contrib, 1982), Maxillo - Facial Injuries (contrib, 1985); *Recreations* fishing; *Style—* Peter Davis, Esq; 97 Harley St, London W1 (☎ 071 486 4976, car 0860 333 472)

DAVIS, Philip; s of David Davis (d 1949), of Forest Gate, and Amelia, *née* Rees (d 1949); *b* 14 Dec 1919; *Educ* Clarkes Coll; *m* 19 Aug 1968, Barbara Edith, da of Alfred Millward, of Kidderminster; *Career* RSC TA 1938, mobilised BEF 1939, evacuated from Dunkirk 1940, Home Serv WO Signals 1941, demobbed 1946; md own company controlling chain of retail fish and poultry shops; chm London Fish and Poultry Retailers Assoc 1968, pres Nat Fedn of Fishmongers 1973, buyer and mangr Fish Dept Barkers of Kensington 1977, fish conslt J Sainsbury 1982-89; town cncllr Staines 1956-57, chm numerous ctees, memb Staines CC; Freeman City of London 1956, Liveryman Worshipful Co of Fishmongers 1959; *Recreations* chess; *Style—* Philip Davis, Esq; Flat 5, Sunset Lodge, 30 The Avenue, Branksome Park, Poole, Dorset BH13 6HG (☎ 0202 766096)

DAVIS, Reginald; *m* 20 June 1948, Audrey Fields; 1 da; *Career* served RN and Fleet Air Arm WWII as photographer, active serv Far East; photographer specialising in Royalty and celebrities; has accompanied the Br Royal Family on more than fifty state visits and has photographed membs of eighteen Royal familes, has an int colour library comprising 37,000 photographs; first and second Encylopaedic Britannica awards for colour photography 1962, first prize Rothmans award for colour photography 1971, Order of Taj (Iran) 1978; memb: FRPS (1971), fell Br Inst (1975), FBIPP, fell Master Photographers Assoc (1980); *Books* Royalty of the World (1969), Princess Anne A Girl of Our Time (1973), Elizabeth Our Queen (1977), Royal Families of the World (1978), The Prince of Wales (1978), Monarchy in Power (1978), The Persian Prince (1979), The Royal Family of Thailand (1981), The Royal Family of Luxembourg (1989); *Recreations* gardening, rotary; *Clubs* Hendon Rotary (pres 1989-90); *Style—* Reginald Davis, Esq; 64 Totteridge Village, London N20 8PS (☎ 081 445 3131, fax 081 446 8886)

DAVIS, Hon Mr Justice; Sir (Dermot) Renn; OBE (1971); s of Capt Eric Renn Davis, OBE (d 1945), of Highlands Hotel, Molo, Kenya, and Norah Alexandrina, *née* Bingham (d 1967); *b* 20 Nov 1928; *Educ* Prince of Wales Sch Nairobi, Univ of Oxford (BA); *m* 1984, Mary Helen Farquharson, da of Brig Thomas Farquharson Ker Howard, DSO (d 1963), of Goldenhayes, Woodlands, Hants, and wid of William James Pearce; *Career* barr; crown counsel Kenya 1956-62, attorney gen Solomon Is and legal advsr Western Pacific High Cmmn 1962-73, Br Judge Anglo-French Condominium of the New Hebrides 1973-76; chief justice: Solomon Is and Tuvalu 1976-80, Gilbraltar 1980-86, Falkland Is 1987; justice of appeal Ct of Appeal for Gibraltar 1989-; judge Br Atlantic Territory 1988-; kt 1981; *Clubs* United Oxford and Cambridge, Univ Muthaiga Country (Nairobi); *Style—* Sir Renn Davis, OBE; Ivy House, Shalbourne, nr Marlborough, Wilts SN8 3QH

DAVIS, Richard Henry; s of Ralph Davis, of Cornwall, and Joyce Amelia, *née* Danziger, of London; *Educ* Univ Coll Sch, Ealing Coll of Higher Educ; *m* 11 Sept 1974, Suzanne Jane, da of Cyril Roy Biggs; 1 s (Mark Walton b 26 Dec 1976), 1 da (Charlotte Anne Mary b 6 Dec 1983); *Career* Connaught Hotel 1966-67, accounts clerk Grand Metropolitan 1968-69; Rank Hotels: Royal Lancaster 1969-74 (trainee, purchasing mangr, sr asst mangr); EMI Leisure Ltd 1975-79 (banqueting mangr and food & beverage mangr Selfridge Hotel, gen mangr Royal Westminster Hotel, mgmt conslt IHLC 1980-82, md Dukes Hotel 1982-89, mgmnt conslt RH Davies 1990-; UK team Culinary Olympics Budapest 1968; Master Innholder 1987, Freeman City of London 1987; FHCIMA; *Recreations* sailing, swimming, riding, reading, music; *Clubs* RAC; *Style—* Richard Davis, Esq; 22 Belsize Rd, London NW6 4RD (☎ 071 722 9691)

DAVIS, Robert Aston; s of Percy Robert Davis (d 1970), of Kingston upon Thames, Surrey, and Florence Blanche, *née* Aston; *b* 11 June 1937; *Educ* Kingston GS; *m* 5 Sept 1959 (m dis 1976), Madge, da of George Albert Free, of Coltishall, Norwich, Norfolk; 2 da (Alison Julia b 1965, Heather Anneliese (Mrs Hill) b 1968); *Career* 2 Lt RA Colchester 1956, Lt Hong Kong 1958; sales mangr Plastics Div Imperial Chemical Industries PLC 1972-81, ptnr Alexander-Davis Assocs Advertising Agency 1982-; hockey: played for Hertfordshire 1962-76 (winners 1974), rep E of England 1975 and 1976; vice pres: Eastern Counties Hockey Assoc, Hertfordshire Co Hockey Assoc, Broxbourne Hockey Club; *Recreations* hockey, travel; *Clubs* Broxbourne Sports; *Style—* Robert Davis, Esq; 6 The Spinney, Beechwood Close, Hertford, Herts SG13 7JR (☎ 0992 581331); Alexander-Davis Associates, 41 Chambers St, Hertford, Herts SG14 1PL (☎ 0992 552300, fax 0992 552452, telex 818288 ADWARE G)

DAVIS, Air Vice-Marshal Robert Leslie; CB (1984); s of Sidney Davis; *b* 22 March 1930; *Educ* Woolsingham GS, Bede Sch Collegiate Sunderland Co Durham; *m* 1956, Diana, *née* Bryant; 1 s, 1 da; *Career* Cdr RAF Staff and air attaché, Br Defence Staff Washington DC 1977-80, administrator of the Sovereign Base Areas and Cmdr Br Forces and AOC Cyprus 1980-83, ret 1983; *Clubs* RAF; *Style—* Air Vice-Marshal Robert Davis, CB; High Garth Farm, Witton-le-Wear, Co Durham

DAVIS, Robert Michael Pennick; *b* 26 July 1942; *Educ* Brighton Coll; *m* 11 March 1973, Suzanne Margaret; 2 s (Steven David Pennick b 2 Aug 1974, Mark Richard b 5 Aug 1976); *Career* dir Smith New Court plc (formerly Smith Bros) 1973- (joined 1960); membership sec Totteridge Manor Assoc; memb Stock Exchange 1965; *Recreations* golf, cricket; *Clubs* MCC, Gresham; *Style—* Robert Davis, Esq; Smith New Court House, 20 Farringdon Rd, London (car 0836 234 658)

DAVIS, Rodney Colin; s of (Arthur) Cyril Gordon Davis, of 13 Glenleigh Park, Warblington, Havant, Hants, and Phyllis Eleanor Margaret Griffiths, *née* Roberts (d 1977); *b* 9 July 1940; *Educ* Churcher's Coll Petersfield, King's Coll London (LLB), Tulane Univ New Orleans USA (LLM); *m* 4 Sept 1965, Elizabeth Jeanne, da of Arthur William Richards of Englefield, Sturminster Newton, Dorset; 1 s (Ian b 1968), 1 da (Sarah b 1970); *Career* asst slr Durham CC 1965-70, asst clerk Berks CC 1970-74; ptnr: Coward Chance 1979-87 (asst slr 1974-79), Clifford Chance 1987-; memb City of London Slrs Co; *Recreations* gardening; *Style—* Rodney Davis, Esq; Bridge House, Thames Road, Goring, Reading RG8 9AH (☎ 0491 872207); Blackfriars House, 19 New Bridge St, London EC4 (☎ 071 353 0211, fax 071 489 0046)

DAVIS, Roger O'Byrne; s of Paul Patterson Davis (d 1984), of Burnham Market, Norfolk, and Mabel Beryl Davis; *b* 1 Aug 1943; *Educ* Wrekin Coll Wellington Shropshire; *Career* articled clerk Chantrey Button & Co 1960-66; Cooper Brothers & Co (now Coopers & Lybrand Deloitte): joined 1966, ptnr 1975, seconded to HM Treasy 1975-77, currently head of accounting practice; FCA; *Books* Adding Value To The External Audit (1990); *Recreations* walking, sailing, music; *Style—* Roger Davis, Esq; 15 Blackheath Park, London SE3 9RW (☎ 081 852 7339); Crafers Barn, Morston Rd, Langham, Holt, Norfolk NR25 7DG (☎ 0328 830677); Coopers & Lybrand Deloitte, Plumtree Court, London EC4A 4HT (☎ 071 822 4531)

DAVIS, (Richard) Simon; s of Peter Richard Davis, DSC, of Busby Lodge, Chartridge Lane, Chesham, Bucks, and Evelyn Janet Hill, *née* Richmond; *b* 29 July 1956; *Educ* Wellington Sch Somerset, Leicester Univ (LLB); *m* 26 July 1980, Caroline Jane, da of Hugh Robert Neal, of Bucks; 2 s (Toby b 1987, Guy b 1989), 1 da (Imogen b 1990); *Career* called to the Bar 1978; *Recreations* rugby, squash, swimming, tennis; *Style—* Simon Davis, Esq; 36 Essex St, Temple, London (☎ 071 413 0353, fax 071 413 0374)

DAVIS, Prof Stanley Stewart; s of William Stanley Davis, of Warwick, and Joan, *née* Lawson; *b* 17 Dec 1942; *Educ* Warwick Sch, Univ of London (BPharm, PhD, DSc); *m* 24 Nov 1984, Lisbeth, da of Erik Illum (d 1986), of Denmark; 3 s (Benjamin b 1970, Nathaniel b 1974, Daniel b 1984); *Career* lectr Univ of London 1967-70, sr lectr Univ of Aston 1970-75, Lord Trent prof of pharmacy Univ of Nottingham 1975-; FRSC, fell Royal Pharmaceutical Soc; *Books* Imaging in Drug Research (1982), Microspheres in Drug Therapy (1984), Site Specific Drug Delivery (1986), Delivery Systems for Peptides (1987), Polymers for Controlled Drug Delivery (1987); *Recreations* skiing, tennis, painting; *Style—* Prof Stanley Davis; 19 Cavendish Crescent North, The Park, Nottingham NG7 1BA; Department of Pharmaceutical Sciences, Univ of Nottingham, University Park, Nottingham (☎ 0602 484848 ext 3217)

DAVIS, Steven Ilsley; s of Lt-Col George Ilsley Davis, of Tinmouth, Vermouth, USA, and Marion Brown Davis; *b* 6 Nov 1934; *Educ* Phillips Acad Mass USA, Amherst Coll Mass USA (BA), Harvard Business Sch (MBA); *m* 27 Feb 1960, Joyce Ann, da of Theodore S Hirtz (d 1962), of NY; 2 s (Andrew Tinmouth b 1962, Christopher Stamer b 1963), 1 da (Stephanie b 1975); *Career* private US Army Reserve 1958; asst vice pres JP Morgan & Co 1959-66, US Agency for Int Devpt 1966-68, first vice pres Bankers Trust Co 1968-72; md: First International Bankshares Ltd 1972-79, Davis Int Banking Conslts 1979-; asst dir US Govt Agency for Int Devpt 1966-68; Hon Phi Beta Kappa Amherst Coll; *Books* The Eurobank (1975), The Management of International Banks (1979), Excellence in Banking (1985), Managing Change in the Excellent Banks (1989); *Recreations* skiing, tennis, hiking; *Clubs* Roehampton; *Style—* Steven Davis, Esq; 66 South Edwardes Sq, London W8 (☎ 071 602 6348); 15 King St, London SW1 (☎ 071 839 9255, fax 071 839 9250)

DAVIS, Mrs André; Sue; *see*: Thomson, Sue

DAVIS, Terence Anthony Gordon (Terry); MP (Lab) Birmingham, Hodge Hill 1983-; s of Gordon Davis; *b* 5 Jan 1938; *Educ* King Edward VI GS Stourbridge, UCL, Univ of Michigan; *m* 1963, Anne, *née* Cooper; 1 s, 1 da; *Career* Parly candidate (Lab): Stechford March 1977 (by-election), Bromsgrove 1970, 1971, 1974 (twice); MP (Lab): Bromsgrove 1971-74, Stechford 1979-83; oppn front bench spokesman: Health Serv 1981-83, Treasy and Econ Affrs 1983-86, Indust 1986-87; memb Public Accounts Ctee 1987-; memb MSF, former memb Yeovil RDC, business exec (MBA) and motor indust mangr; *Style*— Terry Davis, Esq, MP; c/o House of Commons, London SW1

DAVIS, Sir Thomas Robert Alexander Harries; KBE (1980); s of Sidney Thomas Davis; *b* 11 June 1917; *Educ* King's Coll Auckland, Otago Univ Med Sch (MB ChB), Sch of Tropical Medicine Sydney Univ; Harvard Sch of Public Health (Master of Public Health); *m* 1, 1940, Myra Lydia Henderson; 3 s; m 2, 1979, Pa Tepaera Arika; *Career* MO and surgical specialist Cook Islands Med Serv 1945-52 (chief MO 1948); Dept Nutrition Harvard Sch 1952-55, chief Dept Environmental Med Fairbanks 1955-56; dir: Environmental Med Fort Knox 1956-61, Natick 1961-63; res exec Arthur D Little Inc 1963-71; formed Democratic Party of Cook Islands 1981; patron: Cook Islands Sports Assoc (Men's Olympic Ctee), Boxing Assoc; visiting dir Bishop Museum Husii; Pa Tu Te Rangi Ariki 1979; premier Cook Islands 1978; FRSTM and H , FRSH; memb Royal Soc Med (1960); Silver Jubilee Medal; Order of Merit Fed Repub of Germany 1978; *Books* Doctor to the Islands (1954), Makutu (1956), author of numerous scientific pubns; *Clubs* Avatiu Sports (patron), Lions (pres), Harvard (Boston USA), Rarotonga Yacht (patron), Avastim Cricket (patron), Wellington (NZ); *Style*— Sir Thomas Robert Davis, KBE; Aremango, Rarotonga, Cook Islands

DAVIS, William; *b* 6 March 1933; *Educ* City of London Coll; *m* 1967, Sylvette Jouclas; *Career* former financial ed: Evening Standard, Sunday Express, The Guardian; presenter BBC TV's Money Programme 1967-69, ed Punch 1969-79, dir Fleet Hldgs and Morgan Grampian 1979-81, ed-in-chief Financial Weekly 1980-81, ed High Life (Br Airways in-flight magazine) 1973, chm Br Tourist Authy and the Eng Tourist Bd 1990, dir Thomas Cook; broadcaster, columnist, author; *Books* Three Years Hard Labour, Merger Mania, Money Talks, Have Expenses Will Travel, It's No Sin to be Rich, The Best of Everything (ed), Money in the 1980's: How to make it, how to keep it, The Rich, Fantasy, The Corporate Infighters Handbook, The Supersalesman's Handbook, The Innovators, Children of the Rich; *Style*— William Davis, Esq

DAVIS, Hon William Grenville; QC (Canada); s of Albert Grenville; *b* 30 July 1929; *Educ* Brampton HS, Univ Coll, Univ of Toronto, Osgoode Hall Law Sch; *m* 1, 1953, Helen, *née* Macphee (d 1962); m 2, 1963, Kathleen Louise, *née* Mackay; 2 s, 3 da; *Career* called to Bar of Ontario 1955; memb (C) Provincial Parliament; min of education 1962-71, min of univ affairs 1964-71; premier of Ontario and pres of the Council Ontario 1971; leader Progressive (C) Party of Ontario; *Style*— The Hon William Davis, QC; Office of the Premier of Ontario, Parliament Buildings, Toronto, Ontario, Canada; 61 Main St South, Brampton, Ontario, Canada

DAVIS-GOFF, Sir Robert William; 4 Bt (UK 1905); s of Sir Ernest Davis-Goff, 3 Bt (d 1980); *b* 12 Sept 1955; *Educ* Cheltenham; *m* 1978, Nathalie Sheelagh, da of Terence Chadwick, of Lissen Hall, Swords, Co Dublin; 3 s (William b 1980, Henry b 1986, James b 1989), 1 da (Sarah b 1982); *Career* picture dealer, property mgmnt; *Recreations* shooting; *Clubs* Kildare Street & University (Dublin); *Style*— Sir Robert Davis-Goff, Bt; office: 17 Duke Street, Dublin 2, Repub of Ireland

DAVISON; *see*: Biggs-Davison

DAVISON, Prof Alan Nelson; s of Alfred Nelson Davison (d 1950), of Leigh On Sea, Essex, and Ada Elizabeth, *née* Dahl (d 1985); *b* 6 June 1925; *Educ* Westcliff HS, Univ Coll Nottingham (B Pharm), Birkbeck Coll London (BSc); *m* 3 July 1948, Patricia Joyce, da of Ernest Frederick Pickering (d 1932); 1 s (Andrew Nelson b 1957), 2 da (Heather Jane (Mrs Gilbert) b 1952, Ann Catherine (Mrs Jenkins) b 1954); *Career* MRC Toxicology Unit 1950-54, MRC exchange fell Sorbonne Paris 1954- 55, Roche Prods Welwyn Gdn City 1955-57, res fell Dept of Pathology Guy's Hospital Med Sch 1957-60, prof of biochemistry Charing Cross Hosp Med Sch 1965-71, prof of neurochemistry and chemical pathology Inst of Neurology 1971-90; former sec Biochemical Soc, chief ed Jl of Neurochemistry, memb editorial bd of several learned jls; Churchwarden; Freeman: City of London 1988, Worshipful Co of Pewterers 1988; FRCPath; memb: Biochemical Soc, Euro and Int Neurochemical Soc; *Books* Biochemistry of Neurological Diseases (1976), Myelination (1970), Biochemical Correlates of Brain Structure and Function (1977), Applied Neurochemistry (1968); *Recreations* choral singing, painting; *Style*— Prof Alan Davison; Senior Research Fellow, Dept of Pathology, Hunterian Institute, London WC2A 3PN (☎ 071 405 3474, fax 071 831 9438)

DAVISON, Dr Alexander Meikle (Sandy); RD (1985); s of John Christal Davison, of Riding Mill, Northumberland, and Alison Meikle, *née* Goodfellow; *b* 31 Jan 1940; *Educ* Daniel Stewarts Coll Edinburgh (BSc, MB ChB, MD); *m* 10 June 1960, Marion Elizabeth Stewart, da of James George Somerville; 2 s (Andrew b 1960, Iain b 1967), 1 da (Pamela b 1965); *Career* Surgn Lt Cdr RNR princ med offr HMS Ceres 1987; conslt renal physician St James' Univ Hosp 1974-, sr clinical lectr Univ of Leeds 1984-; ed-in-chief Nephrology Dialysys Transplatation monthly jl, contrib to Davidsons Textbook of Med; memb: Cncl of Euro Dialysis and Transplantation Assoc, Exec Ctee on Int Soc for Artificial Organs, Medical Appeal Tbnl; FRCPEd, FRCP; *Books* Dialysis Review (ed, 1978), Synopsis of Renal Diseases (1981), Mainstream Medicine, Nephrology (1988); *Recreations* shooting; *Style*— Dr Sandy Davison, RD; 9 Lidgett Park Road, Leeds LS8 1EE (☎ 0532 661042); Dept of Renal Medicine, St James's University Hospital, Leeds LS9 7TF (☎ 0532 433144, fax 0532 428870)

DAVISON, Arthur Clifford Percival; CBE (1974); s of Arthur MacKay Davison (d 1970), of Montreal, Canada, and Hazel Edith, *née* Smith (d 1978); *b* 25 Sept 1918; *Educ* McGill Music Conservatory Montreal, Conservataire de Musique Montreal, RAM; *m* 1, 1950 (m dis 1977), Barbara June, *née* Hildred; 1 s (Darrell Richard), 2 da (Beverley Ann Hildred, Lynne Barbara); m 2, 2 March 1978, Elizabeth, da of Richard Blanche; *Career* a dir and dep leader London Philharmonic Orch 1957-65, asst conductor Bournemouth Symphony Orch 1965-66; musical dir and conductor: Royal Orchestral Soc 1956-, Little Symphony of London 1964-, Virtuosi of England 1970-; guest conductor of orchs 1964-: London Philharmonic, London Symphony, Philharmonia, Royal Philharmonic, BBC Orchs, Birmingham Symphony, Bournemouth Symphony and Sinfonietta, Ulster, Royal Liverpool Philharmanic, New York City Ballet, CBC Radio and Television Orchs, Royal Danish Ballet; dir and conductor Nat Youth Orch of Wales 1966-90, fndr Arthur Davison Family Concerts 1966, conductor and lectr Goldsmith's Coll London 1971-85, conductor Welsh Coll of Music and Drama Symphony Orch 1973-84 (govr to 1989), orchestral dir Birmingham Conservatoire of Music (formerly Birmingham School of Music) 1981-83; EMI/CFP award for sale of half a million classical records 1973, Guild for Promotion of Welsh Music Award for long and distinguished service 1976, Gold Disc for sale of one million classical records 1977, European tour recorded for BBC TV; articles in various musical jls; M Mus Wales Univ 1974; FRAM 1966, FRSA 1977; *Style*— Arthur Davison, Esq, CBE; Glencairn, Shepherd's Hill, Merstham, Surrey RH1 3AD (☎ 0737 642206 and 4434)

DAVISON, Barry George; s of William Davison; *b* 12 Dec 1935; *m* 1960, Jean Doreen; 3 da (Tracy b 1962, Katharine b 1964, Joanne b 1970); *Career* 2 Lt RA; chm and md Foster Bros Clothing plc 1978-85; chm Non Foods Policy Ctee Retail Consortium 1981-85; dir chm Crossland Lighting plc 1987-89, chm John Partridge Sales Ltd 1986; dir: Neville Industrial Securities Ltd 1986, M V Imports & Exports Ltd 1987, Midlands Residential Corporation plc 1988, Action Apparal Ltd 1989; memb Midlands Industl Cncl 1983; FCA; *Recreations* golf; *Clubs* Blackwell Golf, Thurlestone Golf; *Style*— Barry Davison, Esq; The Firs, Lovelace Ave, Solihull, West Midlands (☎ 021 705 2850); 7 Links Court, Thurlestone, Devon (☎ 054 857 770)

DAVISON, Belinda Jane; da of William Patrick John Davison, of Lichfield, Staffordshire, and Judith Ann Davison; *b* 25 Oct 1964; *Educ* Adcote Sch Shropshire, St Mary and St Annes, Sutton Coldfield Tech Coll, LAMDA; *Career* actress; theatre: Nana (Alemeida 1987, Mermaid 1988), Taming of the Shrew (Mercury Theatre Colchester) 1988, The Circle (Mercury Theatre Colchester) 1988, Morte D'Arthur (Lyric Theatre) 1990; tv: Casualty 1989; *Style*— Miss Belinda Davison; Talent Artists Ltd, 1 Charlotte St, London W1P 1DH (☎ 081 340 7090)

DAVISON, Clive Phillip; s of Maj Laurence Napier Davison (d 1966), and Rosa Rachel Louisa, *née* Parker; *b* 14 March 1944; *Educ* Grange Sch Christchurch Dorset, Poly of the South Bank, Thames Poly; *m* 30 March 1968 (m dis 1982), Sandra, da of Thomas Keith Lord of Billericay Essex; ptnr, Jane Elise, da of Roger Howorth, of West Moors, Dorset; 1 s (Alexander Napier), 1 da (Hannah Louise b 26 Jan 1990); *Career* chartered architect, assoc Trehearne & Norman Preston & Partners 1974-77, ptnr Trehearnes 1977-79, co sec and dir I M Coleridge Ltd 1987, design and site supervisor of Min of P T T Riyadh 1977-83, princ Davison Assoc; RIBA; *Recreations* squash, guitar, reading, skiing; *Clubs* CGA, Christchurch and Kingston Rowing, Sandown Park; *Style*— Clive Davison, Esq; 3 Croft Rd, Christchurch, Dorset BH23 3QQ (☎ 0202 479341); Priory Chambers, 6 Church St, Christchurch, Dorset (☎ 0202 470176)

DAVISON, Derek Harold; CBE (1985); s of John George Davison (d 1959), and Lillian, *née* Riley (d 1966); *b* 26 July 1923; *Educ* Queen Elizabeth GS, Univ of Southampton; *m* 1, 1946, Germaine, da of Emile Riffard (d 1970), of Egypt; 2 s (John b 1947, Guy b 1949); m 2, 1979, Lavinia, da of Roland Wellicome (d 1960), of Bournemouth; *Career* RAF 1941-46; pilot bomber cmd and pathfinder sqdn M East, communication sqdn Heliopolis Egypt Italy; Br S American Airways Corpn-BOAC 1947-53, Pakistan Int Airlines 1953-57, El Al 1957-62; Britannia Airways: chief pilot 1962, ops dir and chief pilot 1965, asst md and chief pilot 1973, md 1976, chm and chief exec 1982, ret 1988; non exec dir Thomson Travel Ltd 1988; Britannia & Euro Ind Airlines formed Assoc des Compagnies Aériennes de la Communauté Européenne (ACE), pres ACE 1980, 1981 and 1990-, nat dir ACE UK 1982-88; chm emeritus and memb Airworthiness Requirements Bd 1985, pres Int Air Carrier Assoc (IACA), chm Br Air Tport Assoc 1988-90; Queen's Commendation for Valuable Servs in the Air 1977; *Recreations* private flying, sailing, skiing, swimming; *Clubs* RAF, Southampton Yacht; *Style*— Derek Davison, CBE; ACE Abelag, PO Box 36, Brussels Airport, Zaventeng, Belgium (☎ 010 02 720 5880, fax 010 02 721 2288)

DAVISON, Hon Mrs (Elizabeth Slater); da of Baron Slater, BEM (Life Peer d 1977); *b* 1934; *m* 1955, Frank Davison; *Style*— The Hon Mrs Davison; 1 Seymour Grove, Eaglescliffe, Cleveland

DAVISON, (George) Gordon; s of George Robert Davison (d 1984), and Winifred Margaret, *née* Collie (d 1982); *b* 30 Nov 1934; *Educ* Kings Sch Tynemouth, Kings Coll Univ of Durham (BSc); *m* 1, 30 Dec 1961, Anne; 1 da (Susan b 1970), 1 s (Peter b 1974); m 2, 4 July 1969, Judith Agnes; *Career* chm Berghaus Ltd 1966-; *Recreations* climbing, skiing, windsurfing, diving, squash; *Style*— Gordon Davison, Esq; 1 Dene Grange, 23 Lindisfarne Rd, Jesmond, Newcastle upon Tyne NE2 2HE (☎ 091 281 4151); 34 Dean St, Newcastle upon Tyne NE1 1PG (☎ 091 232 3561, fax 091 216 0922, telex 537728 BGHAUS G)

DAVISON, Ian Frederic Hay; *b* 30 June 1931; *Educ* London Sch of Economics & Political Sci (BSc), Univ of Michigan; *Career* managing ptnr Arthur Andersen & Co 1966-82, dep chm and chief exec Lloyds of London 1983-86; chm: Hong Kong Securities Review Ctee 1987-88, Credit Lyonnais Capital Markets 1988-, Laing & Cruickshank, Storehouse plc; non-exec dir: Cadbury Schweppes plc, The Independent, Chloride Group plc; tstee V&A Museum; FCA, memb Cncl ICAEW; *Books* A View of the Room, Lloyd's, Change and Disclosure (1987); *Recreations* music, opera, gardening; *Clubs* Arts, Athenaeum; *Style*— Ian Hay Davison, Esq; Credit Lyonnais Capital Markets, Broadwalk House, 5 Appold St, London EC2A 2DA (☎ 071 588 4000, fax 071 588 0301)

DAVISON, Hon (William) Kensington; DSO, DFC; yr s of 1 Baron Broughshane, KBE (d 1953); *b* 1914; *Educ* Shrewsbury, Magdalen Coll Oxford; *Career* WWII Wing Cdr RAFVR; barr Inner Temple; *Clubs* Garrick; *Style*— The Hon Kensington Davison DSO, DFC; 3 Godfrey St, London SW3 3TA (☎ 071 352 7826)

DAVISON, Dr William; TD (1966, Clasps 1978-84); s of Thomas Kirkup Davison (d 1953), of Sunderland, and Mary, *née* Atkinson (d 1939); *b* 12 Sept 1925; *Educ* Bede GS, Univ of Edinburgh (MB ChB); *m* 15 Feb 1954, Lilas, da of William Grief (d 1973), of Sunderland; 1 s (Ian b 1962), 2 da (Valerie b 1960, Helen b 1964); *Career* Nat Serv MO RAMC 1949-51; RAMC (TA) 1952-85 (QHP (TA) 1983 and 1984), Col Cmdg 308 (County of London) Gen Hosp 1981-85; conslt geriatric med Addenbrooke's Hosp 1960-; fndr chm Br Assoc for Serv to Elderly, pres Age Concern Cambridgeshire, tstee Cambridge Talking News; FRCPE 1969; *Books* Ageing the Facts (with N Coni and S Webster, 1984), The Geriatric Prescriber (with N Coni and B Reiss, 1987), Lecture Notes on Geriatrics (with N Coni and S Webster, 1988); *Recreations* eating, drinking and talking; *Style*— Dr William Davison, TD; Melbourne House, 53 Gilbert Road, Cambridge CB4 3NX (☎ 0223 354300); Department of Geriatric Medicine, Addenbrooke's Hospital, Cambridge CB2 2QQ (☎ 0223 217543)

DAVOUD, Raymond Israel; s of Benjamin Davoud (d 1982), and Lilly, *née* Ely; *b* 27 Dec 1931; *Educ* St Pauls, Trinity Coll Cambridge (MA), McGill Univ Montreal (MCOMM); *m* 31 March 1960, Nicole Matilde, MBE, da of Isaac Samuel Gellert, of 247 Avenue Winston Churchill, 1180 Brussels; 1 s (Alexander Joseph); *Career* Ind Mktg Conslt 1964-; registered conslt Chartered Inst of Mktg DTI Initiative; memb Mktg Soc, MRS; *Recreations* bridge, gardening, classic cars; *Clubs* Marketing; *Style*— Raymond Davoud, Esq; Raymond Davoud & Associates, 22 Kingsgate Ave, London N3 3BH (☎ 081 346 4879/2179, car 0860 464323)

DAVSON; *see*: Glyn, Bt, Sir Anthony

DAVSON, Christopher Michael Edward; s of Sir Edward Davson, 1 Bt, KCMG (d 1937); hp to bro Sir Anthony Glyn, 2 Bt, *qv*; *b* 26 May 1927; *Educ* Eton; *m* 1, 2 June 1962 (m dis 1972), Evelyn, *née* Wardrop; 1 s (George Trenchard Simon b 1964); m 2, 1975, Kate, da of Ludo Foster, of Greatham Manor, Pulborough, Sussex; *Career* Capt, formerly Welsh Guards; formerly fin dir of cos in the Booker McConnell Gp; dir Kate Foster Ltd; Liveryman Worshipful Co of Musicians; FCA; *Recreations* archaeology; *Style*— Christopher Davson, Esq; 5 Market Rd, Rye, Sussex

DAVY; *see*: Arthington-Davy

DAVY, Horace George; MBE (1970); s of Charles Horace (d 1972), and Florence Maude, *née* Weedon (d 1960); *b* 25 Feb 1927; *Educ* Sir John Cass Fndn Sch, Alleyn's Coll, City of London Coll; *m* 2 July 1955, Gabrielle Mary, da of Thomas Joseph Reginald Scotman (d 1971); 1 s (Christopher b 1957), 1 da (Kim b 1959); *Career*

RAFVR 1944-45, RNVR 1945, RASC 1946-48, Warrant Offr ME, City of London Yeo (Rough Riders) TA 1950-53; UK Chamber of Shipping: joined 1941, asst sec 1960, sec 1963, asst gen mangr 1966, gen mangr 1969; Gen Cncl Br Shipping:dep DG 1975, dir 1980, dep DG and sec 1987-89; gen mangr Br Motor Ship Owners Assoc 1981-86, dir BOSVA 1985; author of articles on merchant shipping and def incl Brassey's Guide; organiser 1 Tanker Safety Conf 1967, sec Br Ship Fedn 1987, hon fell Inst of Chartered Shipbrokers 1989; *Recreations* Abbotsbury Shetland Pony Stud; *Clubs* Baltic Exchange, The Anchorites; *Style—* Horace Davy, Esq, MBE; Highcroft Paddocks, Hempstead Rd, Bovingdon, Herts HP3 0HE (☎ 0442 832653); British Offshore Support Vessels Assoc, 30-32 St Mary Axe, London EC3A 8ET (☎ 071 283 2922)

DAWBARN, Sir Simon Yelverton; KCVO (1980), CMG (1976); s of Frederic Dawbarn, and Maud Louise, *née* Mansell; *b* 16 Sept 1923; *Educ* Oundle, CCC Cambridge; *m* 1948, Shelby Montgomery, *née* Parker; 1 s, 2 da; *Career* WWII Reconnaissance Corps; FCO 1949-53 and 1961-71; served: Brussels, Prague, Tehran, Algiers, Athens; FCO 1971-75, head of W African Dept and non-resident ambass to Chad 1973-75, consul-gen Montreal 1975-78, ambass to Morocco 1978-82; *Style—* Sir Simon Dawbarn, KCVO, CMG

DAWBER, George Arthur; s of Arthur Dawber (d 1986), of Calgary Canada, and Gladys, *née* Garrett (1989); *b* 15 Sept 1939; *Educ* Alma Park, UMIST; *m* 19 March 1966, Glenys, da of Eric Ernest Whalley; 1 s (Howard Jason b 20 May 1972), 2 da (Zoë Cordelia b 29 July 1970, Aimie Camilla b 9 March 1980); *Career* professional photographer: nat serv station photographer RAF, trained in photographic transmissions 1956-59, professional cricketer Lancashire CCC 1959-60, industl photographer 1960-70, general photographer 1970-75, freelance with own studio 1975- (specialising in wedding, portrait and PR photography), princ lectr Fuji Professional Sch of Photography UK (has lectured widely UK and Overseas); memb Admissions and Qualifications Bd BIPP (nat pres BIPP 1983-84); *Awards* winner Kodak Bride of the Year Competition, awarded Craftsmen Degree of Professional Photographers of America and Presidential award for services to his profession 1984; FBIPP, FMPA, FRSA, ARPS; *Style—* George Dawber, Esq; The Cottage, 159 Dialstone Lane, Offerton, Stockport, Cheshire SK2 6AU (☎ 061 483 3114); G A & G Dawber Ltd, The Garden Studio, 159 Dialstone Lane, Offerton, Stockport, Cheshire SK2 6AU (☎ 061 483 3114, fax 061 483 6063)

DAWE, Roger James; CB (1988), OBE (1970); s of Harry James, and Edith Mary, *née* Heard; *b* 26 Feb 1941; *Educ* Hardye's Sch Dorchester, Fitzwilliam House Cambridge; *m* 1965, Ruth Day, da of Frederic Jolliffe; 1 s (Mark b 1968), 1 da (Caroline b 1971); *Career* joined Miny of Lab 1962; private sec to: PM 1966-70, Sec of State for Employment 1972-74; under sec MSC 1981-84, dep sec Dept of Employment 1985-88, dir gen Trg Agency 1988-; *Recreations* tennis, soccer, theatre, music; *Style—* Roger Dawe, Esq, CB, OBE; Training Enterprise and Education Directorate, Rm 766, Caxton House, Tothill St, London SW1H 9NF (☎ 071 837 2795)

DAWES, Prof Edwin Alfred; s of Harold Dawes (d 1939), of Goole, Yorks, and Maude, *née* Barker (d 1967); *b* 6 July 1925; *Educ* Goole GS, Univ of Leeds (BSc, PhD, DSc); *m* 19 Dec 1950, Amy, da of Robert Dunn Rogerson (d 1980), of Gateshead; 2 s (Michael b 1955, Adrian b 1963); *Career* lectr in biochemistry Univ of Leeds 1950 (asst lectr 1947-50), sr lectr in biochemistry Univ of Glasgow 1961-63 (lectr 1951-61); Univ of Hull: Reckitt prof of biochemistry 1963-, dean of sci 1968-70, pro vice chllr 1977-80, dir Biomedical Res Unit 1981-; ed Biochemical Journal 1958-65, ed in chief Journal Gen Microbiology 1976-81, pubns mangr Fedn of Euro Microbiological Socs 1982-90 (ed in chief F Microbiology Letters), chm Sci Advsy Ctee Yorks Cancer Res Campaign 1978- (campaign dep chm 1987-); visiting lectr Biochemical Soc Aust and NZ 1975, American Med Alumni lectr Univ of St Andrews 1980-81; hon vice pres The Magic Circle London (memb 1959-, historian 1987-), hon life pres Scot Conjurers Assoc 1973-, pres Br Ring Int Brotherhood of Magicians 1972-73, pres Hull Lit and Philosophical Soc 1976-77 (cncl memb 1973-); FRSC 1956, FIBiol 1964; *Books* The Great Illusionists (1979), Isaac Fawkes: Fame and Fable (1979), Quantitative Problems in Biochemistry (6 edn, 1980), Biochemistry of Bacterial Growth (jtly, 3 edn 1982), The Biochemist in a Microbial Wonderland (1982), Vonetta (1982), The Barrister in The Circle (1983), The Book of Magic (1986), Microbial Energetics (1986), The Wizard Exposed (1987), Philip Larkin: the Man and His Work (contrib, 1989), Henri Robin: Expositor of Science and Magic (1990), Novel Biodegradable Microbial Polymers (ed, 1990); *Recreations* conjuring, book-collecting; *Clubs* Savage; *Style—* Prof Edwin Dawes; Dane Hill, 393 Beverley Road, Anlaby, N Humberside HU10 7BQ (☎ 0482 657998); Department of Applied Biology, University of Hull, Hull, N Humberside HU6 7RX (☎ 0482 465316, fax 0482 466443, telex 5925 KHMAIL G, f a o HULIB 375)

DAWES, Ewan David; JP (1975 Northumberland); s of Joseph Dawes (d 1965), of Ashington, Northumberland, and Florence, *née* Woodgate (d 1982); *b* 6 Nov 1937; *Educ* King Edward VI GS Morpeth, Univ of Manchester (Dip Arch); *m* 8 Aug 1963, Joan Elizabeth, da of James Bland Tomlin (d 1978), of Ashington Northumberland; 2 da (Jan b 1966, Lyn b 1967); *Career* ptnr in sundry private practices 1960; memb Jt Technical Ctee Working Gp on Design and Build Tendering Procedures 1981-82; ARIBA 1963; memb: UMIST 1960, Architects in Industry and Commerce 1972; FRSA 1983, FBIM 1983; *Recreations* golf; *Style—* Ewan D Dawes, Esq, JP; Millard Design Partnership, Ilex House, 7 Holly Avenue West, Newcastle upon Tyne NE2 2AR (☎ 091 281 5297, fax 091 281 4286)

DAWES, Prof Geoffrey Sharman; CBE (1980); s of Rev W Dawes; *b* 21 Jan 1918; *Educ* Repton, New Coll Oxford (BA, BSc, BM BCh, DM); *m* 1941, Margaret Monk; 2 s, 2 da; *Career* Rockerfeller travelling fell 1946, dir Nuffield Inst for Medical Res Oxford 1948-85; author of numerous scientific pubns; chm: Physiological Systems and Disorders Bd MRC 1978-80, Lister Inst of Preventive Med 1988; vice pres Royal Soc 1977 and 1979, memb MRC 1978-82, chm Bd of Govrs Repton 1971-84 (govr 1959-87); Max Weinstein Award 1963, Gairdner Found Award 1966, Maternité Award of European Assoc Perinatal Medicine 1976, Virginia Apgar Award, American Acad of Pediatrics 1980; FRCOG, FRCP, Hon FACOG; *Books* Foetal and Neonatal Physiology (1968); *Style—* Prof Geoffrey Dawes, CBE; 8 Belbroughton Rd, Oxford (☎ 0865 58131)

DAWES, Howard Anthony Leigh; s of George Roland Dawes (d 1965), of Weatheroak Hall, nr Alvechurch, Worcs, and (Phyllis) Kathleen, *née* Reeves; *b* 4 Aug 1936; *Educ* Uppingham; *m* 13 July 1962 (sep 1983), (Yvonne) Anne, da of Baron Rex Joseph (d 1987); 1 s (Christopher b 1965), 3 da (Catherine b 1967, Domini b 1970, Imogen b 1972); *Career* chm and chief exec: Dawes Trust Ltd 1965-, Neville Industrial Securities 1965-88; dir Velcourt Gp plc 1968-; chm: Epag International Ltd 1976-, WB Technology Ltd 1990-, Nuffield Hosp 1984-89; past chm Ctee of Friends of Birmingham Museums and Galleries, hon treas Birmingham Cons Assoc 1968-76, memb Midland Industl Cncl 1977-, hon sec Scientific Instrument Soc 1984-; Freeman City of London, Liveryman Worshipful Co of Glaziers; FCA, FRAS 1960, FRSA 1975; *Recreations* history of sci; *Clubs* Kildare Street (Dublin); *Style—* Howard Dawes, Esq; Craycombe House, nr Fladbury, Worcestershire WR10 2QS (☎ 0386 860 692); P O Box 15, Pershore, Worcestershire WR10 2RD (☎ 0386 861 075, fax 0386 861 074)

DAWES, John Garlfield; s of John Desmond Dawes, of Northwich, Cheshire, Lancashire, and Lena Dawes (d 1979); *b* 13 Feb 1942; *Educ* Cadishead Secdy Modern Sch, Manchester Coll of Technol (City and Guilds in photography); *m* 1962, Marion, da of Clifford Hewson; 1 s (John Desmond b 16 March 1970), 2 da (Brendan Jay b 17 Oct 1966, Amanda Jane b 1 May 1972); *Career* sports photographer; signed to Wolverhampton FC aged 15, Chester FC 1957-58, joined John Mountfield Photo Agency Warrington, Liverpool Weekly News, Mercury Press Agency, Daily Express Manchester, chief sports photographer Daily Star; winner various awards incl: Sports Photographer of the Year, Northern Sports Photographer of the Year, News Photographer of the Year, News Sequence of the Year; memb NUJ, AIPS; *Recreations* golf; *Style—* John Dawes, Esq; Daily Star, Ludgate House, 245 Blackfriars Rd, London SE1 9UX (☎ 071 928 8000)

DAWICK, Viscount; Alexander Douglas Derrick Haig; s and h of 2 Earl Haig, OBE; *b* 30 June 1961; *Educ* Stowe, Cirencester; *Style—* Viscount Dawick; The Third, Melrose, Roxburghshire TD6 9DR (☎ 057 36287)

DAWID, Prof (Alexander) Philip; s of Israel Dawid, and Rita, *née* Abel; *b* 1 Feb 1946; *Educ* City of London Sch, Trinity Hall and Darwin Coll Cambridge (BA, MA, Dip Maths and Statistics); *m* 18 March 1974, (Fatemeh) Elahe, da of Mohamed Ali Madjd; 1 s (Jonathan b 10 May 1975), 1 da (Julie b 29 July 1979); *Career* prof of statistics The City Univ 1978-81, prof UCL 1982- (lectr 1969-78, readr 1981-82); medicines cmmr 1988-; memb Int Statistical Inst 1978, Fell Inst of Mathematical Statistics 1979; *Recreations* music; *Style—* Prof Philip Dawid; Department of Statistical Science, University College London, Gower St, London WC1E 6BT (☎ 071 380 7190)

DAWKINS, Dr Ceridwen Elizabeth; da of Dr Herbert Charles Cole, of Abingdon, Oxon, and Elsie May, *née* Williams; *b* 22 June 1952; *Educ* St Helen & St Katharine Sch Abingdon, Univ of Bristol (BSc, MB ChB); *m* 16 July 1977 (m dis 1989), Dr Richard William Spence, s of Dr William Ormerod Spence (d 1977), of Bristol; 3 da (Dawn b 1980, Michaela (twin) b 1980, Eleanor b 1983); m 2, 29 Sept 1990, Martin Scott Dawkins, s of Thomas George Desmond Dawkins, of Somerset; *Career* conslt chem pathologist Dept of Chem Pathology Frenchay Hosp Bristol 1986-; ACB 1979, MRCPath 1984, ACP 1986; *Recreations* skiing, fell walking, gardening; *Style—* Dr Ceridwen Dawkins; Dept of Chemical Pathology, Frenchay Hospital, Bristol BS16 1LE (☎ 0272 701212 ext 2781)

DAWKINS, Simon John Robert; s of Col William John Dawkins, and Mary, *née* King; *b* 9 July 1945; *Educ* Solihull Sch, Univ of Nottingham (BA), Queens' Coll Cambridge (PGCE), Birkbeck Coll London (MA); *m* 25 July 1968, Janet Mary, da of Gordon Harold Stevens; 1 s (Thomas Peter James b 16 Nov 1974), 1 da (Sarah Mary Louise b 2 Oct 1972); *Career* head of econs and housemaster Dulwich Coll, headmaster Merchant Taylors' Sch Crosby Liverpool; *Recreations* sport, gardening; *Clubs* E India; *Style—* Simon Dawkins, Esq; Brackenwood, St George's Rd, Hightown, Liverpool (☎ 051 929 3546); Merchant Taylors' School, Crosby, Liverpool L23 (☎ 051 928 3508)

DAWNAY, Lady Angela Christine Rose; *née* Montagu Douglas Scott; 5 da of 7 Duke of Buccleuch and Queensberry, KT, GCVO (d 1935), and sis of HRH Princess Alice, Duchess of Gloucester; *b* 26 Dec 1906; *m* 28 April 1936, Vice Adm Sir Peter Dawnay, KCVO, CB, DSC, *qv*; 1 s, 1 da; *Style—* The Lady Angela Dawnay; The Old Post Cottage, Wield, Alresford, Hants (☎ 0420 63041)

DAWNAY, Caroline Margaret; da of Capt Oliver Payan Dawnay, CVO (d 1988), of Longparish and Wexcombe, and Lady Margaret Boyle, da of 8 Earl of Glasgow; *b* 22 Jan 1950; *m*; 1 s (Hugo Ronald Alexander MacPherson b 28 Jan 1980); *Career* dir A D Peters & Co Ltd Writers' Agents 1981- (joined 1977, merger to form Peters Fraser & Dunlop 1988); *Clubs* 2 Brydges Place; *Style—* Miss Caroline Dawnay; 14 Sterndale Rd, London W14 0HS; Peters Fraser & Dunlop, Fifth Floor, The Chambers, Chelsea Harbour, Lots Rd, London SW10 0XF (☎ 071 376 7676)

DAWNAY, Hon Mrs (Iris Irene Adele); *née* Peake; LVO (1959); da of 1 Viscount Ingleby (d 1966), and Lady Joan, *née* Capell, Vicountess Ingleby (d 1979); *b* 23 July 1923; *m* 25 March 1963, as his 2 w, Oliver Payan Dawnay, CVO (d 1988), s of Maj-Gen Guy Dawnay, CB, CMG, DSO, MVO (d 1952), of Longparish House, Hants, *see* Viscount Downe; 1 da (Emma b 1964); *Career* lady-in-waiting to HRH The Princess Margaret 1952-62; *Style—* The Hon Mrs Dawnay, LVO; Wexcombe House, Marlborough, Wilts (☎ 026 489 229); Flat 5, 32 Onslow Sq, London SW7 (☎ 071 584 3963)

DAWNAY, (Charles) James Payan; s of Capt Oliver Payan Dawnay, CVO (d 1988), and Lady Margaret Stirling Aird, *née* Boyle; *b* 7 Nov 1946; *Educ* Eton, Trinity Hall Cambridge (MA); *m* 10 June 1978, Sarah, da of Edgar David Stogdon, MBE, of Little Mead, Witchampton, Wimborne, Dorset; 1 s (David b 1985), 3 da (Alice b 1979, Olivia b 1981, Fenella b 1988); *Career* dir Mercury Asset Mgmnt Gp plc 1987-, chm Mercury Fund Managers Ltd 1987-; *Recreations* fishing, collecting; *Clubs* Brooks, Pratts; *Style—* C J P Dawnay, Esq; 85 Elgin Crescent, London W11 (☎ 071 229 5940); 33 King William St, London EC4 (☎ 071 280 2800)

DAWNAY, Hon James Richard; s of 10 Viscount Downe; *b* 8 Sept 1937; *m* 1976, Gillian, yst da of Major James Dance, MP (d 1971), of Moreton Morrell, Warwicks, and formerly w of Capt Simon George Melville Portal, *see* Baronetage, Portal; 1 s (Thomas b 1978); *Style—* The Hon James Dawnay; 31 Eaton Mansions, London SW1 (☎ 071 730 2471)

DAWNAY, Lady Katharine Nora de la Poer; *née* Beresford; 2 da of 6 Marquess of Waterford; *b* 23 Dec 1899; *m* 14 Oct 1926, Maj-Gen Sir David Dawnay, KCVO, CB, DSO (d 1971), *see* Peerage, Viscount Downe; 2 s (Hugh b 1932, Peter (twin) b 1932), 2 da (Blanche b 1928 d in a motor accident in Copenhagen 1953, Rachel b 1929 d 1983); *Style—* The Lady Katharine Dawnay; Whitfield Court, Waterford, Eire

DAWOOD, Nessim Joseph; s of late Yousef Dawood and Muzli, *née* Toweg; *b* 27 Aug 1927; *Educ* Univ of Exeter, Univ of London; *m* 1949, Juliet, *née* Abraham; 3 s; *Career* Arabist; md The Arabic Advertising and Publishing Co Ltd London 1958; dir: Contemporary Translations Ltd (London) 1962, Bradbury Willienson (graphics) 1975-76, ME conslt; fell Inst of Linguists; *Books* The Thousand and One Nights (ed, 1954), The Koran (trans 1956, 35 edn 1990), Aladdin and Other Tales (trans 1957), The Muqaddimah of Ibn Khaldun (trans 1967), Tales from the Thousand and One Nights (trans 1973, 16 edn 1990), Arabian Nights (illustrated children's edn 1978), Sinbad the Sailor, Aladdin and Other Tales (1989), The Koran (trans with Arabic parallel text, 1990); *Book Translations* The Muqaddimah of Ibn Khaldun (1967), The Thousand and One Nights (1954), The Koran (1956, 33 edn 1988), Aladdin and Other Tales (1957), Tales from the Thousand and One Nights (1973, 15 edn 1988), Arabian Nights (illustrated children's edn 1978); *Recreations* theatre; *Clubs* Hurlingham; *Style—* Nessim J Dawood, Esq; Berkeley Square House, Berkeley Square, London W1X 5LE (☎ 071 409 0953)

DAWS, Andrew Michael Bennett; s of Victor Sidney Daws (d 1978), and Doris Jane Daws; *b* 11 March 1943; *Educ* King's Sch Grantham, Univ of Exeter (LLB), Coll of Law; *m* 1, 1969 (m dis 1979), Edit, *née* Puskas; m 2, 27 Aug 1981, Phoebe, da of Clifford Hughes (d 1955); 2 s (Harry Arthur Victor Bennett b 1986, Guy Cromwell George Bennett b 1990), 1 da (Constance Clemency Jane Bennett b 1984); *Career* slr 1967, ptnr Denton Hall Burgin and Warrens 1975-; *Recreations* golf, squash; *Clubs* Royal Mid-Surrey GC, Roehampton; *Style—* Andrew M B Daws, Esq; 5 Chancery Lane, London, WC1A 1LF (☎ 071 242 1212, fax 071 404 0087, telex 263567

BURGIN G)

DAWSON, Anthony Michael; s of Leslie Joseph Dawson, and Mable Annie, *née* Jayes; bro of J L Dawson, *qv*; *m* 1956, Barbara Anne Baron, da of late Thomas Forsyth, MD; 2 da; *Career* physician: St Bartholomew's Hosp, King Edward VII Hosp for Officers, physician to HM The Queen 1982- (formerly to the Royal Household); vice chm Mgmnt Ctee King's Fund for London 1979, treas RCP 1985-, head of Med Household 1988-; FRCP; *Style—* Anthony Dawson, Esq; 35 Meadowbank, Primrose Hill Rd, London NW3 3AY

DAWSON, Bruce Amager; *b* 17 Dec 1928; *Educ* Univ of Edinburgh (MA); *Career* advsr Kuwait Investmt Office London 1990- (fndr memb 1963-), chm London Sinfonietta, vice chm Torras Hostench SA; dir: Ercros SA, Granfel PLC, Matrix Investments, Prima Immobiliaria SA, Hays Group; *Recreations* arts, sport; *Clubs* Hon Co of Edinburgh, Sunningdale, Valderrama (Spain); *Style—* Bruce Dawson, Esq; c/o St Vedast House, 150 Cheapside, London EC2V 6ET

DAWSON, Lady; Caroline Jane; only child of William Antony Acton, of La Foscarina, Komeno, Gouvia, Corfu; *b* 12 May 1933; *m* 7 July 1955, Sir (Hugh Halliday) Trevor Dawson, 3 Bt (d 14 Feb 1983); 2 s (*see* Dawson, Sir Hugh M T, Bt); *Style—* Lady Dawson

DAWSON, Lt-Col Herbrand Vavasour; DL (N Yorks 1988); s of Maj John Vavasour Dawson (d 1935), and Charlotte Gerda, *née* Romilly (d 1980); *b* 13 June 1918; *Educ* Winchester, RMA Sandhurst; *m* 19 Dec 1942, Grizelda Louise, da of Maj George Mitchell Richmond (d 1957), of Kincairney, Murthly, Perthshire; 1 s (Christopher b 1943), 1 da (Catherine b 1944); *Career* cmmnd Queens Own Cameron Highlanders 1938; served: France 1939-40, Sicily 1943, Holland & Germany 1944-45, GSO III HQ BAOR 1946-48; student Staff Coll 1950, Bde-Maj 155 Inf Bde 1951-53, DAAG HQ Scottish Cmd 1957-60, cmd 4/5 Bn Queens Own Cameron Highlanders 1960-62, AAG HQ Northern Cmd, ret Lt-Col 1968; N Yorks CC: chm 1989-, vice chm 1985, elected 1973; chm Public Protection Ctee 1981; *Recreations* skiing; *Style—* Lt-Col Herbrand Dawson, DL; Weston Hall, Otley, Yorks (☎ 0943 462430)

DAWSON, Sir Hugh Michael Trevor; 4 Bt (UK 1920), of Edgwarebury, Co Middlesex; s of Sir (Hugh Halliday) Trevor Dawson, 3 Bt (d 1983), and Lady Dawson, *qv*; *b* 28 March 1956; *Educ* at home; *Heir* bro, Nicholas Dawson, *qv*; *Style—* Sir Hugh Dawson, Bt; 11 Burton Court, Franklin's Row, London SW3

DAWSON, John Leonard; s of late Leslie Joseph Dawson, and Mabel Annie Jayes; *b* 30 Sept 1932; *Educ* King's Coll Hosp London (MB MS); *m* 1958, Rosemary Brundle; 2s, 1 da; *Career* surgn: Bromley Hosp, King Edward VII Hosp for Offrs, King's Coll Hosp, to HM's Royal Household 1975-83, to HM The Queen 1983-90 (sergeant surgn 1990-); dean Faculty of Clinical Med Kings Coll Sch of Med and Dentistry; FRCS; *Style—* John Dawson, Esq; 107 Burbage Rd, Dulwich, London SE21 7AF

DAWSON, (Archibald) Keith; s of Wilfred Joseph Dawson, MBE, of Scarborough, and Alice Marjorie Dawson (d 1985); *b* 12 Jan 1937; *Educ* Scarborough HS for Boys, Nunthorpe GS, Queen's Coll Oxford (BA, DipEd); *m* 16 Dec 1961, Marjorie, da of Arthur George Blakeson (d 1977), of Wetherby; 2 da (Eleanor Margaret b 1965, Katharine Elizabeth b 1967); *Career* Nat Serv RAF 1955-57; teacher Ilford Co HS For Boys 1961-63; headmaster: The John Mason Sch Abingdon 1971-79, Haberdashers' Aske's Sch 1987- (teacher 1963-65, head of history 1965-71); princ: Scarborough Sixth Form Coll 1979-84, King James's Coll of Henley 1984-87; memb Headmaster's Conf; FBIM 1987; *Books* Society and Industry in the Nineteenth Century - A Documentary Approach (with Peter Wall, 1968), The Industrial Revolution (1971); *Recreations* walking, swimming, cricket, theatre, music; *Clubs* East India, Public Schools; *Style—* Keith Dawson, Esq; (☎ business 081 207 4323, fax 081 207 4439)

DAWSON, Leslie (Les); s of Leslie Dawson, of Unsworth, Bury (d 1973), and Julia Helen (d 1956); *b* 2 Feb 1934; *m* 1, Margaret Rose (decd); 1 s Stuart Jason b 3 March 1969), 2 da (Julie Helen b 9 May 1965, Pamela Jayne b 20 July 1971); m 2, 1989, Tracy; *Career* comedian, entertainer, actor; entered show business as musician in clubs, theatre and cabaret venues; worked in radio as entertainer and writer; tc incl: Sez Les (Yorkshire TV) 1968-79, Les & Lulu (BBC) 1980, The Dason Watch (BBC) 1980-82, host of Blankety Blank 1985-90; appearances on Parkinson, Wogan and The Generation Game; straight acting role in La Mona (BBC2) 1990; Club Mirror award for Best Entertainer, Variet Club award for Radio Personality of the Year, five Royal Variety performances; actively involved with: Variety Club of GB, Grand Order of Water Rats (Past King Rat); *Books* Hitler Was My Mother-in-Law, Card For The Club (1971), Dawson's Lancashire (1974), A Clown Too Many (1986), A Time Before Genesis (1987), Come Back With The Wind (1990); *Recreations* golf, writing articles, music (piano); *Clubs* St Annes District (pres), Lancashire Automobile (hon pres); *Style—* Les Dawson, Esq

DAWSON, Mark Patrick; s of Douglas George Damer Dawson; *b* 19 Oct 1941; *Educ* Wellington; *m* 1, 1970 (m dis 1983), Carol Anne, da of John Dudley Groves; 2 s; m 2, 1987 (Constance) Clare Power, *née* Mumford; *Career* Lt Essex Yeo; former chm and md Pickford Dawson & Holland Ltd; md: Jardine Matheson Insur Brokers UK Ltd 1978-79, Jardine Matheson Underwriting Agencies Ltd 1979, Jardine Glanvill Underwriting Agencies Ltd (re-named Jardine Ltd, Lloyd's Underwriting Agents); *Clubs* Boodle's, City of London; *Style—* Mark Dawson, Esq; Cooks Green, Lamarsh, Bures, Suffolk C08 5DY

DAWSON, Michael John; OBE (1986); *b* 20 Jan 1943; *Educ* King James' GS Knaresborough; *m* ; 2 da; *Career* trainee and cost and accounting asst Cawood Wharton Limited 1960-64, asst mgmnt accountant Yorkshire Dyeware Limited 1964; mgmnt accountant: Belzona Molecular Metal Limited 1964-67, Denys Fisher Toys Limited 1967-70; chm Tunstall Group plc 1970-, currently non-exec dir Yorkshire Fund Management Limited; chm The Prince's Youth Business Tst N Yorks, dir N Yorks Trg Enterprise Cncl, memb Bd and past chm Assoc of High Technol and Related Growth Industs of N Yorks (YORTEK); FCCA 1970; *Recreations* game fishing, shooting, gardening, cookery; *Clubs* Reform, IOD, Merchant Adventurers (York), Merchant Taylors' (York), Yorkshire (York); *Style—* Michael Dawson, Esq, OBE; The Doctor's House, Askham Bryan, York YO2 3QS (☎ 0904 706373)

DAWSON, Nicholas Antony Trevor; s of Sir (Hugh Halliday) Trevor Dawson, 3 Bt (d 1983); hp of bro, Sir Hugh Dawson, *qv*; *b* 17 Aug 1957; *Style—* Nicholas Dawson Esq

DAWSON, Dr Peter; s of Frederick Dawson, of Sheffield, and May, *née* Pierrepoint; *b* 17 May 1945; *Educ* Firth Park Sch Sheffield, King's Coll London (BSc, PhD), Westminster Med Sch (MB BS); *m* 20 July 1968, Hilary Avril, da of Kenneth Reginald Sturley, of Amersham, Bucks; 1 s (James b 1978), 1 da (Kate b 1976); *Career* sr house offr in: gen and renal med Hammersmith Hosp 1979-80, medical oncology Royal Marsden Hosp 1980; registrar in radiology Guy's Hosp 1980-82, sr registrar radiology Middx Hosp 1982-85, reader and hon conslt Royal Postgrad Med Sch and Hammersmith Hosp 1985-; author of various scientific med res papers; MInstP 1966, MRCP 1980, FRCR 1984; *Recreations* grand opera, wine, snooker; *Style—* Dr Peter Dawson; Beeches, Green Lane, Chesham Bais, Amersham, Bucks HP6 5LQ (☎ 0494 728222); Hammersmith Hosp, Dept of Radiology, Du Cane Rd, London W12 0HS (☎ 081 740 3123, fax 081 743 5409)

DAWSON, Rev Peter; OBE (1986); s of Richard Dawson (d 1963), of London, and Henrietta Kate, *née* Trueman (d 1984); *b* 19 May 1933; *Educ* Beckenham Tech Sch, Beckenham GS, LSE (BSc), Westminster Coll (PGCE); *m* 20 July 1957, Shirley Margaret Pentland, da of William James Johnson (d 1983); 2 da (Miriam b 6 June 1959, Paula b 24 May 1961); *Career* RAF Nat Serv 1951-53, Mauripur Pakistan; sch master London and Liverpool 1957-70; sch master fell commoner: Keble Coll Oxford 1969, CCC Cambridge 1979; headmaster Eltham Green Sch London 1970-80; ordained Methodist Minister 1985; gen sec Prof Assoc of Teachers 1980-; *Books* Making a Comprehensive Work (1981), Teachers and Teaching (1984); *Recreations* reading, golf, family activities; *Clubs* Carlton; *Style—* The Rev Peter Dawson, OBE; 72 The Ridings, Ockbrook, Derby DE7 3SF (☎ 0332 672669); Prof Assoc of Teachers, St James's Ct, 77 Friar Gate, Derby DE1 1EZ (☎ 0332 372 337, fax 0332 290 310/292 7431)

DAWSON, Ven Peter; s of late Leonard Smith Dawson, and Cicely Alice Dawson; *b* 31 March 1929; *Educ* Manchester GS, Keble Oxford, Ridley Hall Cambridge; *m* 1955, Kathleen Mary Sansome; 1 s, 3 da; *Career* rector of Morden (dio of Southwark) 1968-77, rural dean of Merton 1975-77, archdeacon of Norfolk 1977; *Style—* The Ven the Archdeacon of Norfolk; Intwood Rectory, Norwich, Norfolk (☎ 0603 51946)

DAWSON, (Joseph) Peter; s of Joseph Glyn Dawson (d 1980), and Winifred Olwen, *née* Martin (d 1957); *b* 18 March 1940; *Educ* Bishop Gore GS Swansea, UC Swansea (BSc); *m* 1964, Yvonne Anne Charlton, da of Charlton Smith (d 1974), of London; 1 s (Alex b 1972), 1 da (Jo-Anne b 1969); *Career* Trade Union official; negotiating sec: Assoc of Teachers in Tech Insts 1974-75, Nat Assoc of Teachers in Further and Higher Educn 1976-79 (gen sec 1979-89, asst sec (membership) 1989-; memb: Euro Ctee World Confedn of Organisation of Teaching Profession 1983-, Exec Bd of Euro Trade Union Ctee for Educn 1984-90; hon fell Coll of Preceptors 1984; *Recreations* theatre, cricket, assoc football; *Clubs* Surrey CCC; *Style—* Peter Dawson, Esq; 27, Britannia Street, London WC1X 9JP (☎ 071 837 3636)

DAWSON, Robin Peter; s of Harry (Henry) Leonard Dawson, of 14 Woodhurst South, Maidenhead, Berks, and Marian, *née* Crosland; *b* 11 March 1947; *Educ* Slough GS, Univ of Bradford (BTech), S Bank Poly (BSc); *m* 15 Aug 1969, Gillian Mary, da of John Rhodes Aspden (d 1975); 2 s (Paul Derek b 1972, Martin Stuart b 1975); *Career* engrg trg with Rolls Royce Ltd, UKAEA and C&CA; ptnr H L Dawson and Ptnrs 1970-; consultancy retains cmmns for engrg design of royal and other palaces, castles, museums, art galleries and gen industl projects; Freeman City of London, Liveryman Worshipful Co of Engrs; Eur Ing, CEng, MIM, MIES (NA), MConsE, FIMechE, FIEE, FCIBSE, FIHospE, FRSA; *Recreations* aeronautical history, industl and other archaeology; *Clubs* City Livery, Royal Over-Seas League; *Style—* Robin Dawson, Esq; Waylands, Kings Oak Close, Monks Risborough, Aylesbury, Bucks HP17 9LB (☎ 08444 6534); H L Dawson and Partners, 5 Queen Victoria Rd, High Wycombe, Bucks HP11 1BA (☎ 0494 34646, fax 0494 465032)

DAWSON, Prof Sandra June Noble; *née* Denyer; da of Wilfred Denyer, of Corton Denham, Sherborne, Dorset, and Joy Victoria Jeanne, *née* Noble; *b* 4 June 1946; *Educ* Dr Challoners Sch Amersham Bucks, Univ of Keele (BA); *m* 23 Aug 1969, Henry Richards Currey Dawson, s of Horace Dawson (d 1952), of Sotik, Kenya; 1 s (Tom Stephen John b 1983), 2 da (Hannah Louise Joy b 1976, Rebecca Annie Brenda b 1978); *Career* Imperial Coll London: res offr 1969-70, lectr and sr lectr 1971-80, prof of organisational behaviour 1990-, dep dir Mgmnt Sch; memb Issues Gp Diocesan Bd of Social Responsibility, Policy Devpt Ctee Inst of Occupational Health, Br Sociological Assoc 1970-; *Books* Analysing Organisations (1986), MacMillan Safety at Work: The Limits of Self Regulation (1988); *Recreations* music, walking; *Style—* Prof Sandra Dawson; The Management School, Imperial College, 53 Princes Gate, Exhibition Rd, London SW7 2PG (☎ 071 589 5111, ext 7015)

DAWSON, Air Chief Marshal Sir Walter Lloyd; KCB (1954, CB 1945), CBE (1943), DSO (1948); s of Walter James Dawson, of Sunderland; *b* 6 May 1902; *Educ* privately, RAF Cranwell; *m* 1927, Elizabeth Leslie (d 1975), da of late D V McIntyre, of Cotherstone; 1 s, 1 da; *Career* enlisted in RAF as boy mechanic 1919, cmmnd from Cranwell 1922, Wing Cdr 1939, served WWII Coastal Cmd and Air Miny as dir Anti-U-Boat Ops and dir Plans, Gp Capt 1944, Air Cdre 1946, AOC Levant 1946-48, Air Vice-Marshal 1948, Cmdt Sch of Land-Air Warfare 1948-50, dir IDC 1950-52, dep COS SHAPE 1953-56, Air Marshal 1953, Inspr Gen RAF 1956, Air Chief Marshal 1956, air memb Supply and Orgn Air Miny 1958-60, ret 1960; chm Handley Page Ltd 1966-69, dir Southern Electricity Bd 1961-72; *Clubs* RAF; *Style—* Air Chief Marshal Sir Walter Dawson, KCB, CBE, DSO; Woodlands, Heathfield Ave, Sunninghill, Berks

DAWSON, William Strachan; s of John Oliver Hanbury Dawson, of South Cadbury, Somerset, and Elizabeth Sutherland, *née* Strachan; *b* 10 Sept 1955; *Educ* Winchester, Selwyn Coll Cambridge (MA); *m* 8 Sept 1984, Alison Jill, da of John Eric Aldridge, of Bentley Wood, Halland, nr Lewes, E Sussex; 1 s (Henry b 1988), 1 da (Lucinda b 1986); *Career* admitted slr 1980, ptnr Simmons & Simmons 1986-; chm Conduit Mead Co Ltd 1989-; *Books* contrib Tolley's Practical Guide to Company Acquisitions (1989); *Recreations* golf, skiing, food, classical music; *Style—* William Dawson, Esq; 84 Church Road, Richmond, Surrey TW10 6LW (☎ 081 940 9790); Simmons & Simmons, 14 Dominion St, London EC2M 2RJ (☎ 071 628 2020, fax 071 588 4129, telex 888562 SIMMON G)

DAWSON-DAMER, Hon Lionel John Charles Seymour; yr s of George Lionel Seymour, Viscount Carlow (ka 1944, s and h of 6 Earl of Portarlington), and Peggy, *née* Cambie (d 1963); *b* 12 Oct 1940; *Educ* Eton; *m* 10 Dec 1965 (m dis 1975), Rosemary Ashley Morrett (who m 1977 (m dis 1983), as his 3 w, 7 Marquess of Northampton), da of P G M Hancock; m 2, 1982, Ashley Judith, da of Gp Capt W Mann, of Perth, W Australia; *Style—* The Hon John Dawson-Damer; Oran Park, Narellan, NSW 2567, Australia

DAWSON-GOWAR, Hon Mrs; Hon Judith Margaret; *née* Gordon Walker; er da of Baron Gordon-Walker, CH, PC (Life Peer, d 1980); *b* 1936; *Educ* N London Collegiate Sch, Lady Margaret Hall Oxford (MA), Univ Coll London (BA, PhD); *m* 1, 1957 (m dis 1975), Graham Carleton Greene, *qv*, s of Sir Hugh Carleton Greene, KCMG, OBE; m 2, 1981, Prof Norman William Dawson-Gowar, s of Harold James Dawson-Gowar; 1 step s, 1 step d; *Career* lectr in psychology Birkbeck Coll London Univ 1966-76, prof of psychology Open Univ 1976; *Publications* (under name Judith Greene) Psycholinguistics: Chomsky and Psychology (1972), Thinking and Language (1975), Learning to use Statistical Tests in Psychology (with M d'Oliveira 1982), Basic Cognitive Processes (with Carolyn Hicks, 1984), Language Understanding (1986); *Style—* Prof the Hon Judith Dawson-Gowar; The Homestead, Cuddington, Bucks

DAWSON PAUL, Anthony; s of Joseph Dawson Paul (d 1976), and Eugenie Flavie, *née* Ozanne (d 1968); *b* 17 June 1935; *Educ* Charterhouse; *m* 22 Nov 1969, Merrill Anne, da of Brig Herbert Anthony Brakes, MBE (d 1987); 2 s (Andrew b 2 July 1972, Nicholas b 9 Aug 1974); *Career* sr ptnr Dennis Murphy Campbell Stockbrokers 1984 (joined 1955, ptnr 1961), dir The Average Tst plc; memb Ctee London Regnl Assoc of the Int Stock Exchange; chm and vice pres of the Putney Soc, memb City of London Livery Ctee 1987-89; memb Ct The Worshipful Co of Salters 1984; FCIS; *Clubs* City of London; *Style—* Anthony Dawson Paul, Esq; 14 Dover Park Drive, Roehampton, London SW15 5BG (☎ 081 789 0011); Dennis Murphy Campbell, 6 Broad Street Place, London EC2M 7DA (☎ 071 638 0033, fax 071 638 1318)

DAWTRY, Sir Alan; CBE (1968, Mil MBE 1945), TD (1948); s of Melancthon

Dawtry, of Sheffield; *b* 8 April 1915; *Educ* King Edward VII Sch Sheffield, Univ of Sheffield; *Career* served WWII, France, N Africa and Italy (despatches twice), Lt-Col; admitted slr 1938, asst slr Sheffield 1938-48; dep town clerk: Bolton 1948-52, Leicester 1952-54; town clerk: Wolverhampton 1954-56, Westminster 1956-77; memb Metrication Bd 1969-74, Clean Air Cncl 1960-75; chm Sperry RAND Ltd 1977-86, Sperry RAND (Ireland) Ltd 1977-86, pres London Rent Assessment Panel 1979-86; FBIM, FRSA; awarded numerous foreign decorations; kt 1974; *Style—* Sir Alan Dawtry, CBE, TD; 901 Grenville House, Dolphin Square, London SW1 (☎ 071 798 8100)

DAY, Bernard Maurice; CB (1987); s of Maurice James Day (d 1959), of Chingford, Essex, and May Helen, *née* Spicer (d 1972); *b* 7 May 1928; *Educ* Bancroft's Woodford Green Essex, LSE (BSc); *m* 11 Feb 1956, (Ruth Elizabeth) Betty, da of Richard Stansfield (d 1957), of Walton-on-Thames; 2 s (Keith b 1961, Geoffrey b 1965), 1 da (Christine b 1959); *Career* Intelligence Corps and RA 1946-48, cmmnd RA 1948; cabinet sec Cabinet Office 1959-61, sec Meteorological Office 1965-70, estab offr Cabinet Office 1970-72; MOD: head air staff sec 1972-74, under sec appts central staffs and air force 1974-84, under sec fleet support 1985-88, ret 1988; panel chm Civil Serv Selection Bd 1988-(res chm 1984-85), parish church cncllr St Mary Oatlands, memb Mental Health Assoc; *Recreations* swimming, change ringing; *Clubs* Cwlth Tst; *Style—* Bernard Day, Esq, CB; 2 Farmleigh Grove, Walton-on-Thames, Surrey KT12 5BU (☎ 0932 227416)

DAY, Dr Christopher Duncan; s of Roger William Elmsall Day (d 1984), and Kathleen Margaret, *née* Bell; *b* 19 July 1941; *Educ* Hymers Coll Hull, Kings Coll Univ of Durham (MB BS); *m* 1, 5 Nov 1966, Pamela (d 1979), da of William Corbet Barnsley (d 1981), of Newcastle upon Tyne; 1 s (William b 1977), 1 da (Elizabeth b 1972); m 2, 21 Aug 1982, Rosemary Ann, da of Charles Darby, of Datchet, Berks; *Career* house offr in surgery and med Newcastle upon Tyne Gen Hosp 1964-65, sr house offr in anaesthetics Dudley Rd Hosp Birmingham 1965-66, registrar and sr registrar in anaesthetics Sheffield Hosps 1966-70, conslt in anaesthetics N Derbs Health Authy 1970-; memb: CSA, AAGBI; *Style—* Dr Christopher Day; Alghero, 44 Matlock Rd, Walton, Chesterfield, Derbs S42 7LE (☎ 0246 270942); Chesterfield and N Derbyshire Royal Hospital, Chesterfield Rd, Calow, Chesterfield, Derbs S44 5BL (☎ 0246 277271)

DAY, Sir Derek Malcolm; KCMG (1984, CMG 1973); s of Alan W Day (d 1968), and Gladys, *née* Portlock (d 1974); *b* 29 Nov 1927; *Educ* Hurstpierpoint Coll, St Catharine's Coll Cambridge (MA); *m* 1955, Sheila, da of George Nott (d 1955), of Newnhan Bridge, Worcs; 3 s (William, Richard, Nicholas), 1 da (Katharine); *Career* HM Foreign Serv 1951: 3 sec Br Embasssy Tel Aviv 1953-56, private sec to Ambass Rome 1956-59, 2 then 1 sec FO 1959-62, 1 sec HM Embassy Washington 1962-66, 1 sec FO 1966-67, asst private sec to Sec of State for Foreign Affrs 1967-68, head of Personnel Ops Dept FCO 1969-72, cnsllr Br High Cmmn Nicosia 1972-75, HM ambass to Ethiopia 1975-78, asst under sec FCO 1979, dep under sec of state FCO 1980, chief clerk 1982-84, Br high cmmr Ottawa 1984; dir Monenco Ltd Canada; cncl memb Canada-UK C of C, cmmr Cwlth War Graves Cmmn, vice chm BRCS, chm and govr Hurstpierpoint Coll, govr Bethany Sch; *Clubs* Hawks (Cambridge), United Oxford & Cambridge; *Style—* Sir Derek Day, KCMG; Etchinghill, Goudhurst, Kent

DAY, John Eddy; s of Charles William Day (d 1965), of Exeter, and Elizabeth Jane, *née* Williams (d 1956); *b* 1 March 1922; *Educ* Exeter Sch; *m* 30 Aug 1946, Pamela Winifred, da of Douglas Hamilton Beckett (d 1956), of Dolgelley; *Career* RM 1940-51: cmmnd Probationary 2 Lt 1940, 1 Bn 1941-42, HMS Howe 1942-43 served Arctic and Med, 45 RM Commando 1944-45 served France Holland Germany (wounded twice, despatches 1945), Br Mil Mission France 1946-47, instr French Commando Sch Algeria, HQ Plymouth Gp 1947-48, Instr Offrs Sch 1948-51; Malayan Civil Serv 1951-58: cadet Telok Anson Perak 1951, sec to Br advsr Perak 1951-52, asst dist offr Kroh Perak 1952-53, asst sec Def Dept Kuala Lumpur 1953-54, dist offr Pekan Pahang 1955-58; UK Security Serv 1958-82; French Croix de Guerre 1944; *Books* The Story of 45 RM Commando (1948); *Recreations* reading, walking my dogs; *Clubs* Naval & Military; *Style—* J E Day, Esq

DAY, Dr Kenneth Arthur; s of Arthur Day (d 1989), and Irene Laura, *née* Pope; *b* 18 July 1935; *Educ* Greenford Co GS, Bristol Univ Med Sch (MB ChB, DPM); *m* 27 June 1959, Sheila Mary, da of Albert Torrance (d 1971); 2 s (Paul Vincent b 1961, Matthew Charles b 1964), 1 da (Caroline b 1960); *Career* registrar Barrow Hosp Bristol 1962-66, registrar and sr registrar Dept of Psychiatry Univ of Newcastle 1966-69, conslt psychiatrist Northern RHA and Newcastle Health Authy 1969-, sr lectr Dept of Psychiatry Univ of Newcastle 1986-, Mental Health Act cmmr 1988-; sec Int Assoc Sci Study of Mental Deficiency 1985-, vice chm Mental Retardation Section World Psychiatric Assoc 1989- (sec 1983-89); DHSS: memb Hosp Advsy Serv 1972, sci advsr 1981-87, memb Standing Med Advsy Ctee 1984-88, memb Nat Devpt Team 1977-86, med memb Mental Health Review Tbnl 1988-; RCPsych: memb cncl and numerous ctees, chm Section for Psychiatry of Mental Handicap 1983-87; Winston Churchill Meml Fellowship 1972, Burden Gold medal and Res prize 1985-86, Blake Marsh lectr RCPsych 1989, WHO Fellowship 1990; writer and presenter The Special Child YTV 1977 and The Special Child Teenage Years YTV 1979; conslt and writer BBC TV series incl: Homes from Home 1976, Accident of Birth 1978, Aspects of Mental Handicap 1979, The Handicapped Family 1979, Lets Go 1979, 1980 and 1982; winner Animal Portraits category Wildlife Photographer of the Year 1989, pres Northern Region Mencap 1978-; Freeman City of London 1989, Yeoman Worshipful Soc of Apothecaries 1988; FRCPsych 1978 (fndn memb 1972), FRSM 1983; *Publications* The Special Child (1977), The Special Child - The Teenage Years (1979), Behaviour Problems in Mental Handicapped: An Annotated Bibliography (1988), author of numerous scientific papers and chapters on mental handicap; *Recreations* squash, badminton, tennis and other sports, natural history, painting, carving, photography; *Style—* Dr Kenneth Day; 28 Percy Gardens, Tynemouth, Tyne & Wear; Northgate Hospital, Morpeth, Northumberland NE61 3BP (☎ 0670 512281)

DAY, Lance Reginald; s of Reginald Day (d 1974), of Welwyn Garden City, Herts, and Eileen, *née* McKeone; *b* 2 Nov 1927; *Educ* Sherrardswood Sch Welwyn Garden City, Alleyne's GS Stevenage, Northern Poly, UCL (BSc, MSc); *m* 3 Jan 1959, Mary Ann, da of late John Sheahan, of Dublin; 1 s (Nicholas b 1960), 2 da (Anneliese b 1959, Caroline b 1972); *Career* Sci Museum: res asst 1951-62, sr res asst 1962-64, asst keeper 1964-69, asst keeper Dept of Chemistry 1970-74, keeper Dept of Electrical Engrg and Communications 1974-76, library keeper 1976-87; sec Nat Railway Museum Ctee 1973-75, memb Cncl: Newcomen Soc for the Study of the History of Engrg and Technol 1989- (hon sec 1973-82), Library Ctee New Forest Museum 1989-, hon organiser RNIB Welwyn Garden City 1968-86; *Books* Broad Gauge (1985), An Encyclopaedia of the History of Technology (contrib to chapters on printing and chemical industry, 1990); *Style—* Lance Day, Esq; 12 Rhinefield Close, Brockenhurst, Hants SO42 7SU (☎ 0590 22079)

DAY, Lucienne; da of Felix Conradi (d 1957), of Croydon, Surrey, and Dulcie Lilian, *née* Duncan-Smith; *Educ* Convent Notre Dame De Sion Worthing Sussex, Croydon Sch of Art, RCA; *m* 5 Sept 1942, Robin Day, OBE, *qv*, s of Arthur Day (d 1956), of High Wycombe, Bucks; 1 da (Paula b 1954); *Career* teacher Beckenham Sch of Art 1942-47, freelance designer 1948- (dress fabrics, furnishing fabrics, carpets, wallpapers, table-linen); cmmnd by: Heal's Fabrics, Edinburgh Weavers, Cavendish Textiles, Tomkinsons, Wilton Royal, Thos somerset, firms in USA Scandinavia and Germany; designed china decoration for Rosenthal china Bavaria 1956-68, currently designing silk mosaic tapestries; conslt (with Robin Day) John Lewis Partnership 1962-87; work in permanent collections incl: V & A, Trondheim Museum Norway, Cranbrook Museum Michigan, Röhsska Museum Gothenburg Sweden, Musée des Arts Decoratifs Montreal, Art Inst of Chicago; awards incl: Design Cncl 1957, 1960 and 1968, American Inst of Dirs first award 1950; Triennale Di Milano: Gold medal 1951, Gran Premio 1954; memb: Rosenthal Studio-Line Jury 1960-68, ctee Duke of Edinburgh Prize for elegant Design 1960-63, Cncl RCA 1962-67, design bursary juries RSA; RDI 1962 (Master 1987-89), ARCA 1940, FSIAD 1955; *Recreations* plant collecting in Mediterranean regions, gardening; *Style—* Mrs Lucienne Day; 49 Cheyne Walk, Chelsea, London SW3 5LP (☎ 071 352 1455)

DAY, Margaret Lucy; da of Robert Manley Day (d 1968), of The Grange, Great Brington, Northampton, and Mary Elizabeth, *née* Evans (d 1986); *b* 12 Dec 1941; *Educ* E Haddon Hall and Mon Fertile Switzerland; *Career* farmer; *Recreations* hunting, racing, country pursuits; *Style—* Miss Margaret Day; Mill House, East Haddon, Northampton NN5 8DV (☎ 0604 770243)

DAY, Martin James; s of Flt Lt Clifford Day, RAFVR (d 1961), and Molly, *née* Dale; *b* 12 April 1944; *Educ* City of London Sch, Univ of Durham (BA), Christ's Coll Cambridge (LLM); *m* 1, 1970 (m dis 1976), Elizabeth Mary, da of Sqdn Ldr Thomas H Sykes, RAFVR; m 2, Loraine Frances, da of Frank Leslie Hodkinson (d 1984), of Langton Green, Tunbridge Wells, Kent; 1 s (James b 1978), 1 da (Philippa b 1983); *Career* admitted slr 1969, articled clerk Austin Wright & Co 1966-68, ptnr Linklaters & Paines 1976- (asst slr 1969-76); chm: Tstees of the Hampton Arts Tst 1969-72, Thameside Arts Tst 1973, Westminster Children's Charitable Fndn 1976-90, Kibogora Hosp Tst 1989-; memb: Ct of Common Cncl (Ward of Aldersgate) 1977-79 and 1986-87, Governing Body SOAS Univ of London 1978-79; Liveryman City of London Slrs Co 1976; dir Slrs Benevolent Assoc 1988-; memb: Law Soc, American Bar Assoc, Canadian Bar Assoc, Int Bar Assoc, Union Internationale des Arocats; FRGS (1965); *Books* Unit Trusts: The Law and Practice (with P I Harris, 1974); *Recreations* collecting contemporary art and furniture; *Clubs* Carlton; *Style—* Martin J Day, Esq; Barrington House, 59-67 Gresham St, London, EC2V 7JA (☎ 071 606 7080, fax 071 606 5113, telex 884349 and 888167)

DAY, Mervyn Richard; s of Albert Richard Day (d 1973), of Chelmsford, Essex, and Peggy Jean, *née* Mann; *b* 26 June 1955; *Educ* King Edward VI GS; *m* 27 Oct 1975, Moira Ann, da of Robert Richardson; 2 s (Richard Mervyn b 25 Jan 1979, James Edward b 15 April 1985), 1 da (Rebecca Louise b 23 Sept 1976); *Career* professional footballer; West Ham Utd 1971-79: apprentice 1971-73, professional 1973-, league debut v Ipswich 1973, 232 appearances; 188 appearances Orient 1979-83, 33 appearances Aston Villa 1983-85, 265 appearances Leeds Utd 1985-; 5 England under 23 caps 1974-76; honours: FA Cup West Ham Utd 1975, Euro Cup-Winners Cup runners-up West Ham United 1976, Div 2 Championship Leeds United 1990; Young Player of the Year Professional Footballers' Assoc 1975; full coaching licence FA 1986, asst FA programme for excellence, currently asst FA Nat Sch Lilleshall; *Recreations* golf, cricket, reading; *Style—* Mervyn Day, Esq; Leeds United FC, Elland Rd, Leeds, West Yorkshire LS11 OES (☎ 0532 716037)

DAY, Prof Michael Herbert; s of Herbert Arthur Day (d 1962), and Amy Julienne, *née* Bradwin (d 1970); *b* 8 March 1927; *Educ* Sevenoaks Sch, Royal Free Hosp Sch of Med Univ of London (MB BS, PhD, DSC)); *m* 12 April 1952, José Ashton, da of Joseph Hankins (d 1985); 1 s (Jeremy Paul); *Career* RAF 1945-48, served England and ME; prof of anatomy and dir dept St Thomas's Hosp Med Sch 1972-89; invited lectures incl: Harvard Univ Cambridge Mass, Yale Univ New Haven Conn, The Leakey Fndn for Anthropological Res, Univ of Surrey, LSE, The Royal Free Hosp Sch of Med; named lectures; The Bennett lecture of Leicester Literary and Philosophical Soc 1977, The Osman Hill Meml lecture 1978, The Louis Leakey Meml lecture 1984; Chartered Soc of Physiotherapy: Fellowships Advsy Bd 1977-88, memb Cncl 1977-, memb Working Pty on Rules of Professional Conduct and Ethics 1983-86; memb and nat del Exec Ctee of Perm Cncl Int Union of Anthropological and Ethnological Sciences 1983-, pres World Archaelogical Congress 1986-, numerous undergrad and postgrad examinerships at home and abroad; chm: The Bill Bishop Meml Tst, The Leakey Tst, Govrs Int Students House 1990- (govr 1984-90); FRSM (pres Section of Med Educn 1978-79); fell: Royal Anthropological Inst (pres 1979-83), The Linnean Soc; memb: Anatomical Soc of GB and I (vice pres 1980), Soc for the Study of Human Biology, BMA, Primate Soc of GB (pres 1976-79), Int Primatological Union, American Assoc of Physical Anthropology; MRCS 1954, LRCP 1954; *Books* Guide to Fossil Man (4 edn 1986); *Recreations* real tennis, fly fishing, sub-aqua diving; *Clubs* Athenaeum, MCC; *Style—* Prof Michael Day; 26 Thurlow Road, Hampstead, London NW3 5PP (☎ 071 435 0899); The Machan, Carradale, Argyll, Scotland; The Manyatta, Emerald Ridge, St Peter, Barbados, W Indies; Dept of Palaeontology, Natural History Museum, Cromwell Rd, London SW7 5BD (☎ 071 938 9314, telex 94015932=MDAY G)

DAY, Michael John; *b* 6 Feb 1944; *Educ* Univ of Liverpool (BA); *m* 26 Feb 1966, Susan, *née* McCallum; 1 s (Philip John b 21 Sept 1970), 1 da (Tanya Jane b 22 April 1969); *Career* actuary; ptnr Duncan C Fraser & Co 1972-86, chm Heywood & Ptnrs Ltd 1983-, dir William M Mercer Fraser Ltd 1986-; FIA 1970; *Style—* Michael Day, Esq; William M Mercer Fraser Ltd, 30 Exchange Street East, Liverpool L2 3QB (☎ 051 236 9771, fax 051 236 1831, telex FRASER 627110 CHACOM G, car 0836 266131)

DAY, Michael John; OBE (1980); s of Albert Day, of London, and Ellen Florence, *née* Itter (d 1973); *b* 4 Sept 1933; *Educ* Univ Coll Sch, Selwyn Coll Cambridge, LSE; *m* 30 July 1960, June Marjorie, da of Dr John William Mackay (d 1958), of Whitehaven, Cumberland; 1 s (Christopher b 1965), 1 da (Lisa (Mrs Gordon Clark) b 1963); *Career* Nat Serv RA; probation offr: Surrey 1960-64, sr probation offr W Surrey 1964-67; asst princ probation offr Surrey 1967-68; chief probation offr: Surrey 1968-76, W Midland 1976-88; chm: Chief Probation Offr Conference 1974-77, Assoc of Chief Offr of Probation 1983-88, Cmmn for Racial Equality 1988-; *Recreations* countryside, gardening, music, books; *Style—* Michael Day, Esq, OBE; Thornhill, Oldbury, Bridgnorth, Shropshire (☎ 071 828 7022, fax 071 630 7605)

DAY, Prof Nicholas Edward; s of John King Day, of 1 Pearson Rd, Holt, Norfolk, and Mary Elizabeth, *née* Stinton; *b* 24 Sept 1939; *Educ* Greshams Sch, Univ of Oxford (BA, Jr Univ prize), Univ of Aberdeen (PhD); *m* 19 Sept 1961, Jocelyn Deanne, da of Henry George Broughton (d 1988); 1 s (Owen John b 5 May 1965), 1 da (Sheenagh Louise b 4 April 1963); *Career* res fell Univ of Aberdeen 1962-66, fell Australian Nat Univ 1966-69, statistician then head Unit of Biostatistics and Field Studies Int Agency for Res on Cancer Lyon 1969-86, cancer expert Nat Cancer Inst USA 1978-79, dir MRC Biostatistics Unit Cambridge 1986-89 (hon dir 1989-), prof of public health Univ of Cambridge 1989-; chm MRC Ctee on the Epidemiology and Surveilance of Aids; fell Royal Statistical Soc; *Books* Statistical Methods in Cancer Research Vol 1 (1980) and Vol 2 (1988), Screening For Cancer of the Uterine Cervix (1986), Screening For Breast Cancer (1988); *Recreations* sea fishing, tree growing; *Style—* Prof Nicholas

Day; Porch House, Haddenham, Ely, Cambs CB6 3TJ (☎ 0353 740472); Department of Community Medicine, University of Cambridge, Hills Rd, Cambridge (☎ 0223 336818, fax 0223 62553)

DAY, Robin; OBE; s of Arthur Day (d 1956), of High Wycombe, Buckinghamshire, and Mary, *née* Shersby (d 1956); *b* 25 May 1915; *Educ* High Wycombe Sch of Art, RCA; *m* 5 Sept 1942, Lucienne, da of Felix Conradi (d 1957), of Croydon, Surrey; 1 da (Paula b 1954); *Career* princ of own design practise 1940-; seating design: Royal Festival Hall 1951, Shakespeare Meml Theatre, Barbican Arts Centre and other major bldgs; interior design Super VC10 aircraft; Gold medal for Design Triennale Exhibition 1951, SIAD Design medal 1957, Design Centre award 1957, 1961, 1965 and 1966, Royal Designer Indust 1959; served on juries of nat and int design competitions; design colls lectr and assessor of diploma work; ARCA; *Recreations* walking, mountaineering, ski touring; *Clubs* Alpine, Climbers, Eagle Ski; *Style—* Robin Day, Esq, OBE; 49 Cheyne Walk, London SW3 5LP (☎ 071 352 1455)

DAY, Sir Robin; s of late William Day; *b* 24 Oct 1923; *Educ* Bembridge Sch, St Edmund Hall Oxford (pres Oxford Union 1950); *m* 1965 (m dis 1986), Katherine Mary, *née* Ainslie, of Perth, W Australia; 2 s; *Career* called to the Bar 1952, TV broadcaster and journalist; presenter: Panorama BBC 1967-72, World at One 1978-87, BBC Radio 1978-87, Question Time BBC TV 1979-89; chm Hansard Soc for Parly Govt 1981-83; hon bencher Middle Temple, hon fell St Edmund Hall; kt 1981; *Clubs* Garrick, Athenaeum; *Style—* Sir Robin Day; c/o BBC TV Studios, Lime Grove, London W12

DAY, Roger Cooper; OBE (1989); s of Frank Edward Cooper Day (d 1941), of Chalfont-St-Giles, Bucks, and Mary, *née* Stretch (d 1986); *b* 4 June 1933; *Educ* Geelong CEGS Victoria Aust; *m* 14 Sept 1964, Rita Anna, da of Alfredo Giollo-Sartori, of Bellinzona, Switzerland; 3 da (Monique b 16 April 1966, Daniela b 29 Feb 1968, Alexandra b 8 Jan 1971); *Career* 2 Lt Royal Signals 1955, Lt TARO 1958; apprentice EMI Ltd 1952-55, sales engr Redifon Ltd 1957-60, mangr Africa Westrex Corp (USA) 1960-62, PDG Litton France 1963, controller Serv Spares Mfrg Decca Radar 1965-74, gp md SE Labs 1978 (md 1974-78), md Cambridge Instruments 1979, chm Monotype Corp plc 1984 (md 1980); chm: ATD Fourth World 1980 (tstee 1975), EG Housing Assoc 1980 (sec and treas 1967), Queen Alexandra's House 1987 (memb Cncl 1980); memb Cncl and hon treas PIRA 1987; AMIEEE 1964; *Recreations* music (organ), walking, gardening, machinery; *Clubs* Commonwealth; *Style—* Roger Day, Esq, OBE; 33 Emperor's Gate, London SW7 4JA (☎ 071 373 0570); The Corner House, High St, Melbourn, Royston, Herts SG8 6ER (☎ 0763 260 469); The Monotype Corporation plc, Salfords, Redhill, Surrey RH1 5JP (☎ 0737 765959, fax 0737 769243, telex 917125)

DAY, Rosemary; da of Albert Rich (d 1985), and Alice, *née* Wren; *b* 20 Sept 1942; *Educ* Christ's Hosp, Bedford Coll Univ of London (BA); *m* (m dis); *Career* asst dir gen GLC 1979-82 (joined 1964), dir Admin London Tport 1983-87, chief exec Data Networks plc 1986-88; non-exec dir: Nationwide Anglia Building Society 1983-88, London Buses Ltd 1988-, Manpower (Watford) Ltd 1989-, RCGP enterprizes 1990-; exec dir Allied Dunbar Assurance plc 1988-; memb London Trg and Enterprise Gp 1990-; chm Joyful Co of Singers 1987 (Sainsbury's Choir of the Year 1990); ATII 1980, FRSA 1983, CBIM 1988; *Recreations* singing, conversation, the arts, gardening, woking; *Style—* Mrs Rosemary Day; Allied Dunbar Assurance plc, Allied Dunbar Centre, Swindon SN1 1EL (☎ 0793 514514, fax 0793 610359)

DAY, Stephen Peter; CMG (1989); s of Frank William Day (d 1956), and Mary Elizabeth Day (d 1968); *b* 19 Jan 1938; *Educ* Bancroft's Sch Essex, CCC Cambridge (MA); *m* 24 Feb 1965, Angela Doreen, da of William Attwood Waudby, of Kenya; 1 s (Richard b 1972), 2 da (Belinda b 1966, Philippa b 1968); *Career* HMOCS; political advsr South Arabian Fedn 1961-67, first sec Political Adviser's Office Singapore 1970, first sec (press) UK mission to UN New York 1972-75, cnsllr Beirut 1977-78, consul-gen Canadian Prairie Provinces 1979-81, ambass Doha 1981-84, head of ME Dept FCO 1984-86, attached to household of HRH The Prince of Wales 1986; ambass Tunis 1987-; *Recreations* walking, reading; *Clubs* Athenaeum; *Style—* Stephen Day, Esq, CMG; British Embassy, Tunis, Tunisia (☎ 010 216 1 245100, fax 010 216 1 354877, telex 14007)

DAY, Stephen Richard; MP (C) Cheadle 1987; s of late Francis Day, and Annie, *née* Webb; *b* 30 Oct 1948; *Educ* Otley Secdy Mod Sch, Park Lane Coll of Further Educ, Leeds Poly; *m* 2, 25 Nov 1982, Frances, da of late James Raywood Booth, of 7 Upper Green Lane, Hove Edge, Nr Brighouse, W Yorks; 1 s by previous m (Alexander b 1973); *Career* sales clerk William Sinclair & Sons 1965-70 (asst sales mangr 1970-77); sales rep: Larkfield Printing Co 1977-80, A H Leach & Co 1980-84; sales exec: PPl Chromacopy 1984-86, Chromagene Ltd 1986-87; conslt Chromagene Photo Labs 1987; former memb: Otley Town Cncl, Leeds City Cncl; Parly candidate (Cons) Bradford gen election 1983; successfully sponsored Motor Vehicles - Wearing of Seat Belts by Children Act 1988; graduate memb Inst of Export 1972-, conslt NALGO 1990-; *Recreations* music, films, Roman history; *Clubs* Royal Wharfedale, Cheadle and Gatley Cons, Cheadle Hulme Cons; *Style—* Stephen Day, Esq, MP; House of Commons, Westminster SW1A OHA (☎ 071 428 6349, 071 219 6200)

DAY, Timon Richard; s of Peter Leonard Day, and Lois Elizabeth, *née* Stockley; *b* 16 March 1951; *Educ* St Paul's, Univ of Exeter (BA); *m* 31 March 1979, Zuzannah; 1 s (Matthew Peter b 15 Aug 1988); *Career* mkt res trainee RSGB Ltd until 1974, mkt res Mass Observation 1974-76, teacher at French Lycée Paris 1976-78, fin journalist Investors Review 1978-80, freelance journalist 1980-81; fin journalist: Financial Info Co 1981-83, Scotsman Newspapers 1983-87, Mail on Sunday 1987-89 (business ed 1989-); winner NFSE Small Business Journalist of the Year award 1990; *Recreations* tennis, walking, cycling, cinema; *Clubs* Campden Hill Lawn Tennis; *Style—* Timon Day, Esq; Mail on Sunday, City Office, Temple House, Temple Ave, London EC4

DAY-LEWIS, Sean Francis; s of Cecil Day-Lewis, Poet Laureate 1967-72 (d 1972), of London, and Constance Mary, *née* King (d 1975); *b* 3 Aug 1931; *Educ* Allhallows Sch Devon; *m* 1960, Gloria Ann (Anna), da of James Henry Mott (d 1980); 1 s (Finian b 1966), 1 da (Keelin b 1963); *Career* Nat Serv RAF 1949-51; ed: Bridport News 1952-53, Southern Times Weymouth 1953-54, Herts Advertiser St Albans 1954-56, Express and Star Wolves 1956-60; arts ed Socialist Commentary 1966-71, TV and radio ed Daily Telegraph 1970-86 (ed 1960), TV ed London Daily News 1986-87; freelance writer and commentator on broadcasting matters 1987-; *Books* Bulleid, Last Giant of Steam (1964), An English Literary Life (1980), One Day In The Life of Television (ed, 1989); *Recreations* music, ball games, country life; *Style—* Sean Day-Lewis, Esq; 52 Masbro Rd, London W14 0LT (☎ 071 602 3221); Restorick Row, Rosemary Lane, Colyton, Devon (☎ 0297 53039)

DAYKIN, Dr Andrew Philip; s of Philip William Daykin, of 11 Cunningham Ave, St Albans, Herts, and Eileen Elizabeth, *née* Sales (d 1985); *b* 27 Dec 1950; *Educ* St Albans Sch, Univ of Oxford (MA), St Mary's Hosp Med Sch (MB BS); *m* 10 Sept 1977, Chrystal Margaret, da of Anthony George Mitsides, of 70 Cissbury Ring S, London; 2 da (Eleni b 1981, Ariana b 1983); *Career* sr house offr Whittington Hosp London 1977, sr house offr and registrar in anaesthetics St Mary's Hosp London 1978-81, sr registrar Winchester and Southampton Hosps 1981-86, clinical fell in anaesthesia Ottawa Childrens Hosp Canada 1984, conslt in anaesthesia and intensive care Taunton and Somerset Hosp 1986; MRCP 1978, FFARCS 1980; *Recreations* canoeing, sailing; *Style—* Dr Andrew Daykin; Priors Lodge, Blagdon Hill, Taunton, Somerset TA3 7SH (☎ 0823 42588); Musgrove Park Hospital, Taunton, Somerset TA1 5DA (☎ 0823 333444)

DAYKIN, Christopher David; s of John Francis (d 1983), and Mona, *née* Carey; *b* 18 July 1948; *Educ* Merchant Taylors', Pembroke Coll Cambridge (BA, MA); *m* 1977, Kathryn Ruth, da of Harold William Tingey; 2 s (Jonathan b 1982, Jeremy b 1984), 1 da (Rachel b 1981); *Career* Govt Actuary's Dept: 1970, 1972-78 and 1980, princ actuary 1982-84, directing actuary 1985-89, actuary 1989-; princ (Health and Social Servs) HM Treasy 1978-80; FIA 1973; VSO Brunei 1971; *Recreations* travel, photography, language; *Style—* Christopher Daykin, Esq; Government Actuary's Dept, 22 Kingsway, London WC2B 6LE (☎ 071 242 6828)

DAYMOND, Dr Terence John; s of Deric Alfred Daymond, of Verwood, Dorset, and Ethel Anne, *née* Bird; *b* 24 Feb 1942; *Educ* Rutlish Sch, Univ of Edinburgh (MB ChB, MRCP), (RCOG Dip Obst), (Dip Phys Med); *m* 18 Jan 1969, Jacqueling Mary, da of Bernard Joffre Martin, of Wisbech, Cambridgeshire; 1 s (Benjamin b 1983), 3 da (Carolyn b 1969, Joanna b 1971, Charlotte b 1986); *Career* acting CMO Dhariwal nr Amritsar Punjab India 1969-70, med registrar Kings Lynn Norfolk 1971-73, rheumatology registrar Aylsham Norfolk 1973-76, sr registrar rheumatology Royal Victoria Infirmary Newcastle upon Tyne 1976-79, conslt rheumatology and rehabilitation Dist Gen Hosp Sunderland 1979, lectr in med Univ of Newcastle upon Tyne, hon lectr Dept of Pharmacy Sunderland Poly, hon physician Sunderland Spastic Soc; pres: Sunderland Branch Nat Back Pain Soc, Washington Branch Arthritis Care; FRCP 1987; memb BMA, BSR; *Books* Treatment in Clinical Medicine Rheumatic Disease (with Hilary H Capell, T J Daymond, W Carson, 1983); *Recreations* swimming; *Style—* Dr Terence Daymond; Ivy Lodge, 25 Front St, Whitburn, Sunderland SR4 7JB (☎ 091 529 3912); Department of Rheumatology, District General Hospital, Kayll Rd, Sunderland SR2 7TP (☎ 091 565 6256)

DAZELEY, Peter William; s of William Henry George Dazeley, of W London, and Freda Kathleen, *née* Ward; *b* 29 June 1948; *Educ* Holland Park Comp; *m* (m dis); *Career* left sch aged 15, worked in advtg photography, set up own studio 1976, moved to personally designed studio Fulham 1984, now specialising in prodn of creative images for leading advtg and design cos; memb NUJ, life memb Assoc of Photographers (formerly AFAEP); *Recreations* golf, squash; *Clubs* Queens, Coombe Hill Golf, Coombe Wood Golf; *Style—* Peter Dazeley, Esq; Peter Dazeley, The Studios, 5 Heathmans Rd, Parsons Green, Fulham, London SW6 4TJ (☎ 071 736 3171, fax 071 736 3356)

DE BENE, Dr John William; s of Reginald Burton De Bene (d 1988), of Cranbrook, Kent, and Anthea Mary, *née* Halliday; *b* 5 April 1945; *Educ* Univ Coll of Rhodesia, Univ of Birmingham (MB ChB, distinction and Wolfson medal for social med), Univ of Glasgow (Nuffield travelling scholar); *m* 1, 1969 (m dis 1988), Monae Mary McCall-Smith; 2 da (Jessica b 27 April 1977, Harriet b 27 June 1978); m 2, Sept 1989, Jill Elizabeth, da of Brian Fairhead; *Career* Capt TA Med Corps Rhodesia 1971; Univ Coll of Rhodesia 1969-71 (jr and sr house offr posts in med, surgery, obstetrics, gynaecology, cardiothoracic surgy), princ in gen practice Maidstone 1973-90; pt/t unit gen mangr Maidstone: Maternal and Child Health Serv 1985-, Acute and Community Servs 1990-; full time unit gen mangr Maidstone Acute and Community Unit 1990-; *Style—* Dr John de Bene; 8 Wytherling Close, Bearsted Park, Maidstone, Kent ME14 4QB (☎ 0622 35186); Maidstone District General Hospital, Maidstone Health Post Graduate Centre, Hermitage Lane, Maidstone, Kent ME16 9QQ (☎ 0622 729000 ext 4752, fax 0622 720807)

DE BONO, Edward Francis Charles Publius; s of late Prof Joseph Edward de Bono, CBE, of St Julian's Bay, Malta, and Josephine, *née* Burns; *b* 19 May 1933; *Educ* St Edward's Coll Malta, Royal Univ of Malta (BSc, MD), Ch Ch Oxford (Rhodes Scholar) (D Phil Oxon, PhD); *m* 1971, Josephine Hall-White; 2 s; *Career* asst dir of res Dept of Investigative Med Univ of Cambridge 1963-76, lectr in med 1976-83; dir Cognitive Res Tst Cambridge 1971-83; *Books* The Use of Lateral Thinking (1967), Lateral Thinking; a text book of creativity (1970), Wordpower (1977), de Bono's Thinking Course (1982); *Style—* Dr Edward de Bono; Cranmer Hall, Fakenham, Norfolk

DE BOTTON, Gilbert; *b* 16 Feb 1935; *Educ* Victoria Coll Alexandria Egypt, Columbia Univ USA (MA); *m* 1, 6 July 1962 (m dis 1988) Jacqueline, *née* Burgauer; 1 da (Miel de Botton b 27 Feb 1968), 1 s (Alain de Botton b 20 Dec 1969); m 2, 17 Dec 1990, Hon Mrs Janet Green, da of Lord Wolfson of Marylebone, formerly wife of Michael Green; *Career* UFITEC SA Union Financiére (Zurich) 1960-68, md Rothschild Bank AG (Zurich) 1968-82, chm Global Asset Management London 1983-; tstee Tate Gallery 1985-, chm Int Cncl Tate Fndn; *Recreations* art, literature; *Clubs* Carlton; *Style—* Mr Gilbert de Botton; 1 Eaton Close, London SW1W 8JX; Suot Mulin, St Moritz, Switzerland; Global Asset Management Ltd, GAM House, 12 St James's Place, London SW1A 1NX (☎ 071 493 9990, fax 071 493 0715, telex 296099 GAMUK G, car 0860 31 6111)

DE BUNSEN, Hon Mrs (Alexandra); *née* Carrington; da of 6 Baron Carrington; *b* 11 April 1943; *m* 8 Sept 1965, Maj Peter Noel de Bunsen, Coldstream Guards (ret), eldest s of late Charles de Bunsen, of Fincastle, Pitlochry, Perth (gs Sir (Thomas) Fowell Buxton 3rd Bt, GCMG) 2 s (Charles b 1970, James b 1973), 1 da (Victoria b 1968); *Style—* The Hon Mrs de Bunsen; The Old Rectory, Kirby Bedon, Norwich, Norfolk

DE BUNSEN, Ronald Lothar; s of Lothar Henry George de Bunsen (d 1950), and Victoria Alexandrina (d 1953), da of Sir (Thomas) Fowell Buxton, 3 Bt, GCMG; *b* 19 Feb 1910; *Educ* Westminster, Trinity Coll Cambridge (BA, MA); *m* 29 Nov 1941, Margaret Forester (d 1989), da of Cdr Morris Edward Cochrane, DSO, RN; 3 da (Margaret b 1943, Emma b 1944, Helen b 1949); *Career* Nat Serv WWII Flying Offr RAFVR; bank offr Barclays Bank Ltd; *Clubs* Travellers'; *Style—* Ronald L De Bunsen, Esq; Burgess Farm, Upshire, Waltham Abbey, Essex EN9 3TG

DE BURGH, Chris John (*né* Davison); s of Charles John Davison, of Wexford, Ireland, and Maeve Emily, *née* de Burgh; *b* 15 Oct 1948; *Educ* Marlborough, Trinity Coll Dublin (MA); *m* Diane Patricia, da of Arthur Morley; 2 s (Hubie Christopher b 29 March 1988, Michael Charles Arthur b 30 Oct 1990), 1 da (Rosanna Diane b 17 April 1984); *Career* singer and songwriter; has released 13 albums to date from debut album Far Beyond These Castle Walls (released 1975) to High on Emotion-Live from Dublin (released 1990); The Lady in Red (single, released 1986) attained number 1 status in UK, USA and elsewhere as did the album it was taken from Into the Light and its follow-up album Flying Colours; has achieved int status and toured the world extensively covering Europe, Aust, Japan, UK and Ireland with sales of singles and albums reaching into millions worldwide; winner of over 80 Gold, Silver and Platinum awards since 1976 from USA, Canada, England, Ireland, W Germany, Belgium, Holland, Switzerland, Austria, Norway, Sweden, Spain, S Africa, Aust, Hong Kong, Brazil, Denmark, France and Israel; other awards incl: Beroliner award (W Germany), Bambi award (W Germany), Midem Int Trophy (France), ASCAP award (UK and America, 1987 and 1988), IRMA awards (Ireland 1985-1990); *Recreations* swimming, scuba diving, golf, fine wine collecting, antiques, persian rugs; *Style—* Chris De Burgh, Esq; Mismanagement, 754 Fulham Rd, London SW6 5SH (☎ 071 731 7074, fax 071

736 8605)

DE BURGH, Lydia Anne; da of Capt Charles De Burgh, DSO, RN (d 1973), of Seaforde, and Isabel Caroline Berkeley, *née* Campbell (d 1969); *b* 3 July 1923; *Educ* privately, Byam Shaw Sch of Art; *Career* WRNS 1942 (ULTRA), Br Red Cross 1943-45; professional portrait wildlife and landscape painter; exhibitions at: Royal Soc Portrait Painters, Royal Soc Br Artists, Royal Birmingham Soc, Royal Ulster Acad, Glasgow Inst of Fine Arts, Soc Wildlife Artists London, Soc Equestrian Artists, Ulster Water Colour Soc; cmmns incl: Princess Alice HRH The Duchess of Gloucester 1954, HM The Queen 1955 (1956 and 1959), The Late Marquess and Marchioness of Headfort, African wildlife in Kenya for Rowland Ward Ltd, Crossroads of Sport - Sportsmans Gallery NY 1960-70, Maze Prison 1972; one person shows incl: NI Office, Vose Gallery Boston Mass 1957, HQ NI 1975 and 1978, Gordon Gallery London, Wildlife Gallery Eastbourne; lectr worldwide, numerous interviews on BBC; assoc: RUA 1956-85, HRUA 1985-, Ulster Water Colour Soc, Chelsea Art Soc 1956-72; *Recreations* travelling, reading, gardening, fine arts, fashion; *Style—* Ms Lydia De Burgh, HRUA; Coolattin Lodge, Seaforde, Downpatrick, Co Down, BT30 8PD

DE CABARRUS, Lady Caroline Mary; *née* Percy; eldest da of 10 Duke of Northumberland, KG, GCVO, TD, PC, JP (d 1988); *b* 3 May 1947; *m* Jan 1974, Count Pierre de Cabarrus; 2 da (Chiara b 1974, Diana b 1977); *Style—* The Lady Caroline de Cabarrus; Syon House, Brentford, Middlesex TW8 8JF

DE CHAIR, Lady (Anne) Juliet Dorothea Maud; *née* Wentworth-Fitzwilliam; o child of 8 Earl Fitzwilliam (k in a flying accident in France 1948); *b* 24 Jan 1935; *Educ* St Hilda's Coll Oxford; *m* 1, 23 April 1960 (m dis 1972), as his 2 w, 6 Marquess of Bristol (d 1985); 1 s (Lord Nicholas Hervey b 1961); m 2, 1974, as his 4 w, Capt Somerset Struben de Chair, s of Adm Sir Dudley de Chair KCB, KCMG, MVO; 1 da (Helena b 1977); *Style—* The Lady Juliet de Chair; St Osyth's Priory, St Osyth, nr Clacton-on-Sea, Essex CO16 8MZ; Bourne Park, Bishopsbourne, nr Canterbury, Kent CT4 5BJ

DE CLIFFORD, 27 Baron (E 1299); John Edward Southwell Russell; er s of 26 Baron de Clifford, OBE, TD (d 1982), by his 1 w, Dorothy Evelyn, da of Ferdinand Meyrick, MD, of Kensington Court, London, and Kate Meyrick the nightclub owner; *b* 8 June 1928; *Educ* Eton, RAC Cirencester; *m* 27 June 1959, Bridget Jennifer, yst da of Duncan Robertson, of Llantysilio Hall, Llangollen, by his w Joyce (sis of Sir Watkin Williams-Wynn, 10th Bt, CBE, *qv*); *Heir* bro, Hon William Russell; *Career* farmer; *Clubs* Naval & Military; *Style—* The Rt Hon Lord de Clifford; Cliff House, Sheepy, Atherstone, Warwicks CV9 3RQ (☎ 0827 880280)

DE COURCY, Anne Grey; da of Maj John Lionel Mackenzie Barrett (d 1940), of Tendring, Essex, and Evelyn Kathleen Frances, *née* Porter; *Educ* Wroxall Abbey, Leamington Spa, Warwick; *m* 1, Michael de Courcy (decd); m 2, 24 Jan 1959, Robert Armitage, s of Gen Sir Clement Armitage, KCB, CMG, DSO, DL, of Downington House, Lechlade, Glos; 1 s (John b Dec 1959), 2 da (Sophy b June 1961, Rose b March 1964); *Career* Evening News: writer, columnist, woman's ed 1972-80; Evening Standard: writer, columnist, section ed 1982-; *Books* Kitchens (1973), Starting From Scratch (1975), Making Room at the Top (1976), A Guide to Modern Manners (1985), The English in Love (1986), 1939 The Last Season (1989); *Recreations* reading, writing, swimming; *Style—* Ms Anne de Courcy; Evening Standard, North Cliffe House, 2 Derry St, London W8 (☎ 071 938 7584, fax 9372648)

DE COURCY, Nevinson Russell; s of Nevinson William de Courcy (d 1919), and Grace, *née* Russell (d 1967); ggs of Adm Hon Michael de Courcy, 3 s of 25(20) Baron Kingsale; hp to kinsman, 30 Baron, Premier Baron of Ireland; *b* 21 July 1920, (posthumously); *m* 23 July 1954, Nora Lydia, da of James Plint, of Great Crosby, Lancs; 1 s (Nevinson Mark, b 11 May 1958), 1 da (Katherine Grace, b 26 April 1955); *Career* MA, MICE, MNZIE; *Style—* Nevinson de Courcy Esq; 15 Market Rd, Remuera, Auckland 5, NZ

DE COURCY HUGHES, Rosemary Margaret; da of Col Edward Guy Lethbridge Thurlow (d 1966), and Margaret Merry, *née* Vaughan (d 1952); *b* 19 June 1919; *Educ* Royal Sch Bath; *m* 1, 14 Feb 1947, Maj Jasper John Ogilvie; 2 s (Philip b 1948, David b 1952); m 2, Lt Cdr James Henry de Courcy Hughes; *Career* offr ATS 1943-47; Territorial Efficiency Medal; *Recreations* gardening, travelling; *Clubs* Army & Navy; *Style—* Mrs Rosemary de Courcy Hughes; The Old Rectory, Hinton St George, Somerset (☎ 0460 73031)

DE COURCY LING, John; CBE (1990); s of late Arthur Norman Ling (d 1973), and Veronica, *née* de Courcy (d 1987); *b* 14 Oct 1933; *Educ* King Edward's Sch Edgbaston, Clare Coll Cambridge (MA); *m* 4 July 1959, Jennifer Rosemary, da of Stanley Haynes (d 1957); 1 s (Adam b 12 Aug 1960), 3 da (Julia b 31 Oct 1961, Patricia b 15 Jan 1963, Catherine b 16 Jan 1965); *Career* served HM Dip Serv 1959-78, cnsllr HM Embassy Paris 1974-77; MEP (EDG) Midlands Central 1979-89, chm Euro Parly Delgn to Israeli Knesset 1979-81, Cons chief whip until 1983; farmer and landowner 1978-; vice chm Devpt Aid Ctee 1984; memb Cncl: Lloyds 1986-88, RIIA 1990-; *Recreations* yacht racing, skiing, opera; *Clubs* Beefsteak, Travellers'; *Style—* John de Courcy Ling, Esq, CBE; 31 Chapel St, London SW1 (☎ 071 235 5655); Lamb House, Bladon, Oxon OX7 1RS (☎ 0993 811654)

DE DARANYI, Hon Mrs (Kirstie Elisabeth); *née* Forbes-Sempill; da of 19 Lord Sempill, AFC (d 1965), and his 2 w, Cecilia Alice, *née* Dunbar-Kilburn (d 1984); *b* 9 Aug 1944; *m* 1, 1968 (m dis 1989), John Michael Forbes-Cable (who assumed the additional surname of Forbes by Deed Poll 1968); 2 s (William Richard Craigievar b 1970, Malcolm Dunbar Craigievar b 1972); m 2, 17 Feb 1990, Bela P de Dranyi, 2 s of late Bela de Daranyi and late Countess Margit Daranyi-Haller de Hallerkeo, of Budapest, Hungary; *Style—* The Hon Mrs de Daranyi; Wingham Barton Manor, Westmarsh, nr Canterbury, Kent CT3 2LW

DE FALBE, Christian Vigant William; s of Brig-Gen Vigant William de Falbe, CMG, DSO, DL, JP (d 1940), of Whittington House, nr Lichfield, and Amy Rhona, *née* Hanbury (d 1947); *see* Burke's Landed Gentry, 18 edn, vol III, 1972; *b* 1 Jan 1923; *Educ* Eton; *m* 12 June 1954, Jane, da of Maj Rowland Arthur Marriott, OBE, of Cotesbach Hall, Lutterworth, Leics; 3 s ((Charles) Christian b 1957, John Vigant Tuxen b 1963, (William) Frederick b 1966), 3 da ((Emma) Sophia (Mrs Thomas Newton) b 1959, Clarissa (Mrs Julian Coles) b 1961); *Career* served KRRC 1941-46, wounded N Africa 1942, Major; dir H Clarkson and Co (Insur) Ltd 1953-73; underwriting memb Lloyds 1953-88; *Clubs* Cavalry and Guards'; *Style—* Christian V W de Falbe, Esq; Saffins, Bicknoller, nr Taunton, Somerset

DE FONBLANQUE, Brig Hugh Barrington; s of Maj-Gen E B de Fonblanque, CB, CBE, DSO (d 1981), and Elizabeth Flora Lutley *née* Sclater; *b* 22 Oct 1937; *Educ* Ampleforth, RMA Sandhurst; *m* 3 Nov 1984, Fiona Elizabeth, da of Brigadier T P Keene (d 1980); 1 da (Philippa Alice b 1985), 1 step s (Timothy Patrick Frederick Myatt b 1971), 2 step da (Emma Louise Myatt b 1969, Antonia Sarah Myatt b 1973); *Career* co the Kings Troop RHA 1973-76, co 19 Field Regiment RA 1977-79, cdr Sultan of Oman's Artillery 1984-87, Regtl Brig RA 1988-90; *Recreations* mountaineering, sailing and equestrian sports; *Clubs* Army and Navy; *Style—* Brigadier Hugh De Fonblanque; The Old Rectory, Bathealton, Taunton, Somerset TA4 2AN (☎ 0984 23320)

DE FONBLANQUE, John Robert; s of Maj-Gen Edward Barrington de Fonblanque, (d 1982), of The Cottage, Bank, Lyndhurst, Hants, and Elizabeth Flora Lutley, *née* Sclater; *b* 20 Dec 1943; *Educ* Ampleforth, King's Coll Univ of Cambridge (MA), LSE (MSc); *m* 24 March 1984, Margaret, da of Harry Prest, of 158 Cannock Rd, Stafford; 1 s (Thomas b 1985); *Career* HM Dip Serv since 1968: second sec Jakarta 1969-71, first sec UK rep to EC 1971-77, princ HM Treasy 1977-79, FCO 1979-83, asst sec Cabinet Office 1983-85, cnsllr Delhi 1986-87, UK rep to Euro Community 1988-; *Recreations* mountain walking; *Style—* John R de Fonblanque, Esq; UK Permanent Representation to the EC, Brussels

DE FRANCIA, Prof Peter Laurent; s of Laurent Fernand de Francia (d 1937) of Paris, and Alice, *née* Groom; *b* 25 Jan 1921; *Educ* Univ of London (BA), Slade Sch; *m* 1980 (m dis 1988), Jenny Franklin; *Career* Army Service 1940-45; Canadian Govt Exhibition Commision Ottowa 1948-50, prodr BBC TV London 1952-54, Dept of Art History St Martin's Sch London 1954-61, Dept of Art History RCA 1961-69, princ Dept of Fine Art Goldsmiths Coll 1970-72, prof of painting RCA 1972-86; exhibitions 1958-80 incl: Milan, London, Amsterdam, Prague, New York, Edinburgh, London; recent exhibitions: Forum Gallery NY 1983, Camden Arts Centre London 1987, Pomeroy Purdy Gallery London 1989, London Frith St Gallery 1989; contrib to Art History Exhibition Hayward Gallery London 1987-88; works in pub collections: V & A, Br Museum, Tate Gallery London, Museum of Modern Art New York, Graves Art Gallery Sheffield, City Gallery Birmingham, Museum of Modern Art Prague; FRCA; *Books* Léger, the Great Parade (1969), The Life and Work of Ferdinand Léger (1983), Untitled (1989); *Style—* Prof Peter de Francia; 44 Surrey Square, London SE17 2JX (☎ 071 703 8361); Lacoste, Vaucluse, France (☎ 010 33 90 75 91 12)

DE FREITAS, Lady; Helen Graham; da of Laird Bell, Hon KBE, Hon LLD Harvard, of Chicago; *m* 1938, Rt Hon Sir Geoffrey de Freitas, KCMG (d 1982, MP Central Nottingham, Lincoln and Kettering, Parly under-sec Air and Home Office, high cmmr Ghana 1961-63, Kenya 1964; 3 s, 1 da; *Style—* Lady de Freitas; 34 Tufton Court, Tufton St, London SW1 (☎ 071 799 3770)

DE FREYNE, 7 Baron (UK 1851); KM Francis Arthur John French; s of 6 Baron, JP, DL (d 1935), by Victoria, da of Sir John Arnott, 2 Bt; *b* 3 Sept 1927; *m* 1, 30 Jan 1954 (m dis 1978), Shirley Ann, da of late Douglas Rudolph Pobjoy; 2 s (Hon Fulke b 1957, Hon Patrick b 1969), 1 da (Hon Vanessa b 1958); m 2, 1978, Sheelin Deirdre, da of Col Henry O'Kelly, DSO, of Co Wicklow, and wid of William Walker Stevenson; *Heir* s, Hon Fulke Charles Arthur John French, *qv*; *Style—* The Rt Hon Lord De Freyne; The Fendal Baron of Coolavin, Boyle, High Lake, Costello, Roscommon, Lemy, Carberry and Kilcoleman; c/o The House of Lords, Westminster, London SW1

DE GELSEY, Alexander Henry Marie; CBE (1989); s of Baron Henry de Gelsey (d 1963), and Marguerite, *née* Lieser (d 1965); *b* 24 June 1924; *Educ* RC Univ Sch Budapest, Trinity Coll Cambridge; *m* 5 Feb 1969, Romy, da of Frederick Edgar Cairns (d 1972), of Oxford; 1 da (Annabel b 1975); *Career* chm Sericol Int Ltd 1955-, memb SE Thames RHA 1984-88, chm E Kent Enterprise Agency 1985-; memb: Kent Economic Devpt Bd 1986-, Kent Investments Ltd 1986-, Southern Bd BR 1988-, Special Health Authy 1989-, Governing Cncl Univ of Kent 1989-; govr: Cobham Hall Sch, W Heath Sch; hon consul of the Republic of Hungary 1990-; *Recreations* shooting, boating, travelling, walking; *Style—* Alexander de Gelsey, Esq, CBE; 22 South Terrace, London SW7 2TD (☎ 071 581 2541, fax 071 584 4156); Boughton Church House, Faversham, Kent ME13 9NB (☎ 0227 751202, fax 0227 750962)

DE GELSEY, William Henry Marie; s of Baron Henry de Gelsey (d 1963), formerly of Hungary, and Marguerite, *née* Lieser (d 1965); *b* 17 Dec 1921; *Educ* Roman Catholic Univ Public Sch Budapest, Trinity Coll Cambridge (MA); *Career* investment banker; exec dir Hill Samuel and Co Ltd 1959-71, md Orion Bank Ltd 1971-80, dep chm Orion Royal Bank Ltd 1980-; *Recreations* travelling; *Clubs* Annabel's, Mark's, Harry's Bar; *Style—* William de Gelsey, Esq; Orion Royal Bank Ltd, Hibiya Kokusai Building, 2-3 Uchisaiwaicho 2-Chome, Tokyo 100, Japan (☎ 010 813 501 6431, fax 010 813 501 7833)

DE GERLACHE DE GOMERY, Baron (Belgium 1924, by King Albert I); Philippe; LVO (1963); s of Baron de Gerlache de Gomery (cr Baron 1924, Polar explorer, the first to winter in the Antarctic, d 1934), gn of Baron (Etienne Constantin) de Gerlache (cr 1844), who was Pres of the Belgian Congress and led the Delegation that offered the Belgian crown to Prince Leopold of Saxe-Saalfeld-Coburg; a second Barony (cr 1885, the first having become extinct 1883) is held by a senior branch of the family; a common ancestor of both lines was Jean Louis de Gerlache, Seigneur de Gomery, who received a confirmation of nobility from the Empress Maria Theresa 1751; *b* 12 Nov 1906; *Educ* Bedales Sch, Decroly (Brussels), Univ of Antwerp; *m* 1937, Yvonne, da of Maurice Verhoustraeten; 1 s; *Heir* s, Baron Jean de Gerlache de Gomery b 20 Dec 1952; *Career* Capt Cdr Belgian Artillery 1940; head Belgian Econ Mission London 1946-47, special cnsllr Belgian Embassy London 1948-73, sec Anglo-Belgian Club 1974 (exec chm 1982); *Recreations* painting, walking, reading; *Clubs* Anglo-Belgian; *Style—* Baron de Gerlache de Gomery, LVO; 3 Upper Cheyne Row, SW3 5JW (☎ 071 352 3343)

DE GREY, Hon Mrs (Amanda Lucy); *née* Annan; elder da of Baron Annan, OBE (Life Peer), *qv*; *b* 13 June 1952; *m* 1977, Spencer Thomas de Grey, s of Roger de Grey, PRA; 1 da (Georgia Catherine b 1988); *Style—* The Hon Mrs de Grey; 56 Clapham Manor St, London SW4

DE GREY, Dr Roger; s of Nigel de Grey, CMG, OBE (d 1951), and Florence Emily Frances, *née* Gore; nephew of the artist Spencer Gore; *b* 18 April 1918; *Educ* Eton, Chelsea Sch of Art; *m* 1942, Flavia Hatt, *née* Irwin; 2 s, 1 da; *Career* WWII, Royal West Kent Yeo and RAC; artist; teacher and master of painting King's Coll Univ of Newcastle 1947-53, reader in painting (former first sr tutor) RCA 1953, princ City and Guilds of London Art Sch Kennington 1973; one man shows incl: New Art Centre, The Leicester Galleries, Agnews and Gallery 10; private and public collections Br and abroad incl: HM The Queen, The Tate Gallery, The Arts Cncl, Govt Art Collections Fund, The Queensland Gallery (Brisbane), Birmingham and Carlisle galleries; awarded prize for most distinguished exhibit (Marennes) at Summer Exhibition 1979; tstee: Nat Portrait Gallery, Royal Acad Tst, American Assocs of Royal Acad Tst, Open Coll of Arts; pres: Artists' Gen Benevolent Tst, Kent Fedn of Amenity Assocs; former memb: SE Regnl Ctee Nat Tst, Cathedrals' Advsy Ctee, Stamps' Advsy Cncl; Hon Fell RCA 1985, pres Royal Acad of Arts 1985 (assoc 1972, academician 1969, treas 1976), Hon Dr of Civil Law Univ of Kent 1989; *Books* Reynolds Lecture (1986); *Style—* Dr Roger de Grey, PRA; Royal Academy of Arts, Piccadilly, London W1V 0DS (☎ 071 439 7438, fax 071 434 0837)

DE GUINGAND, Anthony Paul; s of Paul Emile De Guingand (d 1976), and Olwyn Doreen, *née* Witts; *b* 7 Aug 1947; *Educ* Ampleforth; *m* 24 Nov 1973, Diana Mary, da of John Harrington Parr; 2 s (Marcus b 1977, Peter b 1982), 1 da (Emily b 1979); *Career* exec dir International Commodities Clearing House Ltd 1973-86; md: London Traded Options Mkt, Int Stock Exchange 1986-; memb Ctee London Soc of CAs (chm City Gp); FCA; *Recreations* rugby, golf; *Style—* Anthony de Guingand; The International Stock Exchange, London EC2N 1HP (☎ 071 588 2355, fax 071 374 0451)

DE HAAS, Margaret Ruth; da of Joseph de Haas, of 33 Chessington Court, Charter

Way, London, and Lisalotte Herte, *née* Meyer; *b* 21 May 1954; *Educ* Townsend Girls Sch Bulawayo Zimbabwe, Univ of Bristol (LLB); *m* 18 May 1980, Iain Saville Goldrein, s of Neville Clive Golrein, of Torreno, 18 St Andrews' Rd, Blundellsands, Crosby, Liverpool; 1 s (Alastair Philip b 1 Oct 1982), 1 da (Alexandra Ann b 22 Feb 1985); *Career* called to the Bar Middle Temple 1977, practising N Circuit; memb Family Law Bar Assoc; *Books* Property Distribution on Divorce (second edn with Iain S Goldrein, 1985), Personal Injury Litigation (with I Goldrein, 1985), Domestic Injunctions (1987), Butterworths Personal Injury Litigation Service (second edn with I Goldrein, 1988); *Recreations* family, swimming, law, theatre; *Style—* Miss Margaret de Haas; 4 Linden Ave, Blundellsands, Crosby, Liverpool L23 8UL (☎ 051 924 2610); 5th Floor, Coin Exchange, Fenwick St, Liverpool L2 7LQ (☎ 051 227 5009, fax 051 227 5488, car 0836 583 257)

DE HALPERT, Cdr Simon David; s of Lt Cdr Michael Francis de Halpert, DSC, RN, of Petersfield, Hants, and (Eleanor) Anne Love, *née* White; *b* 27 Dec 1945; *Educ* Cranford, BRNC Dartmouth; *m* 19 Dec 1970, Katherine Marie Lafferty, da of James Daly, of Havant, Hants; 2 s (Michael b 1974, Christopher b 1975), 1 da (Natasha b 1972); *Career* Midshipman HMS Highburton 1965, Midshipman and Sub Lt HMS Tiger 1966, Sub Lt HMS Llandaff 1966-67, Sub Lt and Lt HMS Mohawk 1968-70, Lt HMS Upton 1970-71, HMS Brighton 1972-73, Warfare Course HMS Dryad 1973-74, HMS Charybdis 1974-75, Advanced ASW Course HMS Vernon 1976, seconded US Navy 1976-78 (Lt and Lt Cdr), Lt Cdr HMS Lowestoft 1979-80, HMS Diomede 1980, HMS Dryad 1981-82, HMS Cleopatra 1983-84, Cdr and OC HMS Argonaut 1985-86, Cdr HMS Dryad 1987-89; *Recreations* squash, real tennis, cricket, gardening, music; *Style—* Cdr Simon de Halpert

DE HOGHTON, Sir (Richard) Bernard Cuthbert; 14 Bt (E 1611), DL (Lancs); s of Sir Cuthbert de Hoghton, 12 Bt (d 1958), and half-brother of Sir (Henry Philip) Anthony Mary de Hoghton, 13 Bt (d 1978); *b* 26 Jan 1945; *Educ* Ampleforth, McGill Univ Montreal (BA), Birmingham Univ (MA); *m* 1974, Rosanna Stella Virginia, da of Terzo Buratti, of Florence; 1 s, 1 da; *Heir* s, Thomas de Hoghton b 1980; *Career* landowner; investment banker with Brown Shipley & Co 1990-, Turner and Newall & Co Ltd 1967-71, sr exec: Vickers da Costa & Co 1971-77, de Zoete & Bevan & Co 1977-89 (ptnr 1984-86); dir BZW Secs Ltd 1986-89; Kt SMO Malta, Kt Constantinian Order of St George; Assoc European Soc of Investment Analysts; *Recreations* shooting, tennis; *Clubs* Royal Overseas League; *Style—* Sir Bernard de Hoghton, Bt, DL; Hoghton Tower, Hoghton, Preston, Lancs (☎ 025 485 2986)

DE JONGH, Nicholas; s of Cyril Windsor de Jongh (d 1981), of Esher, Surrey, and Margaret, *née* Whitelaw (d 1990); *b* 13 Jan 1938; *Educ* St Edward's Sch Oxford; *m* 7 June 1975, Elizabeth Jane, da of Dr Richard Norman (d 1961), of Fakenham, Norfolk; 1 s (Alexander b 1977), 1 da (Miranda b 1982); *Career* Nat Serv Army 1956-58; dir Engrg Employers Fedn 1979- (joined 1975); memb various orgns involved in promotion of careers in engrg; FRSA 1986; *Recreations* writing, gardening, pictures; *Clubs* Carlton; *Style—* Nicholas de Jongh, Esq; 22 Campion Rd, London SW15 6NW (☎ 081 785 6928); Netherfield, The Street, Sharrington, Norfolk NR24 2AB; The Engineering Employers' Federation, Broadway House, Tothill St, London SW1H 9NQ (☎ 071 222 7777, fax 071 222 2782)

DE JONQUIERES, Guy; s of Maurice de Fauque de Jonquières, of London, and late Pauline de Jonquières; *b* 14 May 1945; *Educ* Lancing, Exeter Coll Oxford; *m* 1977, Diana Elizabeth, da of T V N Fortescue; 2 s (Alexander b 1981, Julian b 1983); *Career* graduate trainee Reuters 1966-68; Financial Times: staff corr 1968-80 (Paris, Washington, Saigon, NY, Brussels), electronics indust corr 1980-86, int business ed 1986-; *Recreations* reading, travel; *Style—* Guy De Jonquières Esq; 2 Rochester Terrace, London NW1 9JN (☎ 071 485 5870); The Financial Times, 1 Southwark Bridge, London SE1 9HL (☎ 071 873 3651, fax 071 405 5700)

DE KLEE, Col Murray Peter; OBE (1974); s of Lt-Col Frederick Bertram de Klee (d 1963), and Violet Virginia, *née* Guthrie (d 1988); *b* 3 Jan 1928; *Educ* Wellington; *m* 6 July 1955, Angela Moira Jean, da of Patrick Stormonth-Darling (d 1960); 3 s (Rupert b 1956, Hugo b 1957, Richard b 1960), 1 da (Nichola b 1959); *Career* Scots Gds 1945-83, regtl duty incl tours with the Parachute Regt and SAS Regt interspersed with staff appointments, active serv Malaya 1948 (despatches 1950 and 1956), Near East 1956, Cyprus 1956, Borneo 1965, S Arabia 1968, Malay Peninsula 1969, NI 1970, Lt Col Cmdg Scots Gds 1975; Croix de Guerre 1956; *Recreations* stalking, skiing; *Style—* Col Murray de Klee; Auchnacraig, Isle of Mull, Argyll

DE L'ISLE, Lord William Philip Sidney; 9 Bt (UK 1806 & 1818), of Castle Goring, Sussex, and 7 Bt of Penshurst Place, Kent, respectively, VC (1944), KG (1968), GCMG (1961), GCVO (1963), PC (1951); 1 Viscount (UK 1956), also Baron De L'Isle and Dudley (UK 1835); s of 5 Baron De L'Isle and Dudley, JP (d 1945), and Winifred (d 1959), da of Roland Yorke Bevan and Hon Agneta, da of 10 Lord Kinnaird; *b* 23 May 1909; *Educ* Eton, Magdalene Coll Cambridge; *m* 1, 8 June 1940, Hon Jacqueline Corinne Yvonne Vereker (d 1962), o da of Field Marshal 6 Viscount Gort (I) and 1 Viscount Gort of Hamsterley (UK 1946), VC, GCB, CBE, DSO, MVO, MC (d 1946); 1 s, 4 da (Hon Elizabeth (Hon Mrs Abel Smith) b 1941, Hon Catherine (Hon Mrs Villiers) b 1942, Hon Anne (Hon Mrs Harries) b 1947, Hon Lucy (Hon Mrs Willoughby) b 1953); m 2, 24 March 1966, Margaret, da of Maj-Gen Thomas Shoubridge, CB, CMG, DSO, and wid of 3 Baron Glanusk, DSO; *Heir* s, Maj the Hon Philip John Algernon Sidney, MBE, b 21 April 1945; *Career* served Grenadier Gds Reserve 1929 and WWII; Barclays Bank 1936-39; sits as Cons peer in House of Lords; MP (C) Chelsea 1944-45, Parly sec Miny of Pensions 1945, sec of state for Air 1951-55, govr gen Aust 1961- 65; former dir various public cos incl: Lloyds Bank plc, British Match Co plc, Schweppes plc, Phoenix Assurance plc (chm 1966-79), Manufacturers Hanover Trust plc, Continental Insurance Co of New York plc; chm No 1 Poultry Ltd, Palmerston Property Developments Plc; pres: Freedom Assoc 1984- (chm 1975-84), SE England Tourist Bd; chm Winston Churchill Memorial Tst, dep pres Victoria Cross and George Cross Assoc; former tstee: British Museum, Nat Portrait Gallery, RAF Museum, Royal Armouries Museum; hon bencher Gray's Inn 1982; hon memb Grocers' Co 1987; Hon LLD: Sydney Univ, Hampden Sydney Coll Virginia; hon fell: Magdalene Coll Cambridge, Australian Inst of Architecture; hon FRIBA; FCA 1934; KStJ; *Recreations* painting, gardening, shooting; *Clubs* White's; *Style—* The Rt Hon Viscount De L'Isle, VC, KG, GCMG, GCVO, PC; Penshurst Place, Tonbridge, Kent (☎ 0892 870223); Glanusk Park, Crickhowell, Brecon

DE L'ISLE BUSH, Lt Cdr (Christopher) Godfrey; s of Lt Hugh Godfrey de L'Isle Bush, MC, Glous Regt (d 1918); *b* 10 Dec 1916; *Educ* Abberley Hall, RNC Dartmouth; *m* 1950, Christine, da of Clifford Exell, of Little Court, Hardenhuish, Chippenham, Wilts; 4 children; 9 gchildren; *Career* Lt Cdr RN, cmd HM Destroyers Leamington, Newmarket, Farndale and Hambledon WW II; chm Reytex Oil and Gas Inc; *Recreations* salmon fishing, picture restoration; *Style—* Lt Cdr Godfrey de L'Isle Bush; Frampton Lodge, Frampton-on-Severn, Gloucester GL2 7EX (☎ 0452 740246)

DE LA BEDOYERE, Comtesse Michael; Charlotte; *née* Halbik; *b* 24 Nov 1931; *Educ* The Old Palace Mayfield Sussex; *m* 1961, as his 2 w, Comte Michael de la Bédoyère, sometime ed Catholic Herald and gs through his f of Alexis Huchet, Marquis de la Bédoyère (who m 1869 Hon Mildred Greville-Nugent, da of 1 Baron Greville); Charles Huchet de la Bédoyère was cr Comte 1710 and was Procureur-Général of the Bretagne Parlement, while another Huchet was cr Comte 1815 by Napoleon; Bertrand Huchet, Seigneur de la Huchetais and Sec of State to Jean V, Duke of Brittany, m c 1420 Jeanne de la Bédoyère, Dame de la Bédoyère; Comte Michael was gs through his mother of Dr A Thorold, sometime Bishop of Winchester; 2 c; *Career* md Search Press Ltd, Burns & Oates Ltd (publishers to the Holy See 1842-); *Recreations* gardening, swimming, photography; *Clubs* Hurlingham; *Style—* Comtesse Michael de la Bédoyère; Spey House, Mayfield, E Sussex; Wellwood, North Farm Rd, Tunbridge Wells, Kent TN2 3DR (☎ 0892 510850)

DE LA BEDOYERE, Count Quentin Michael Algar; s of Count Michael de la Bedoyere (d 1973), and Catherine, *née* Thorold (d 1959); *b* 23 Nov 1934; *Educ* Beaumont Coll Old Windsor Berks, LAMDA; *m* 28 July 1956, Irene Therese Philippa, da of late Martyn Gough; 2 s (Guy Martyn Thorold b 28 Nov 1957, Raoul Maurice Greville b 20 Aug 1959), 3 da (Catherine Christina Mansel b 20 April 1961, Camilla Louise Nugent b 27 Sept 1963, Christina Sibyl Montagu b 15 April 1966); *Career* Nat Serv 2 Lt RASC 1953-55; Jacqmar Ltd 1956-57; Sun Life of Canada: sales rep 1957, field mgmnt 1960, London Head Office 1972, field trg offr 1972-76, mktg offr 1976-79, dir mktg devpt and PR 1980, vice pres individual product mktg 1984, vice pres planning and devpt 1987-90, vice pres product mgmnt 1990-, dir Sun Life of Canada Unit Managers Limited 1990-; *Books* The Doctrinal Teaching of the Church (1963), The Family (1975), Barriers and Communication (1976), The Remaking of Marriages (1978), Managing People and Problems (1988), How to Get Your Own Way in Business (1990); *Recreations* freelance writing, public speaking, motorcycling, grandchildren; *Style—* Count de la Bedoyere; Sun Life of Canada, Basing View, Basingstoke, Hampshire RG21 2DZ (☎ 0256 841414, fax 0256 811129)

DE LA BERE, Adrian; s of Sir Rupert De la Bère, 1 Bt (d 1978); hp of bro, Sir Cameron De la Bère, 2 Bt, *qv*; *b* 17 Sept 1939; *Style—* Adrian De la Bère Esq

DE LA BERE, Sir Cameron; 2 Bt (UK 1953); s of Sir Rupert De la Bère, 1 Bt, KCVO (d 1978), Lord Mayor of London 1952-53, and Marguerite (d 1969), eldest da of Lt-Col Sir John Humphery; *b* 12 Feb 1933; *Educ* Tonbridge and abroad; *m* 20 June 1964, Clairemonde, only da of Casimir Kaufmann, of Geneva; 1 da (Rejane b 1965); *Heir* bro, Adrian De la Bère; *Career* jeweller; Liveryman Worshipful Co of Skinners; *Clubs* Société Litéraire (Geneva), Hurlingham; *Style—* Sir Cameron De la Bère Bt; 1 Avenue Theodore Flournoy, 1207 Geneva, Switzerland (☎ 010 41 22 786 00 15)

DE LA MARE, Prof Albinia Catherine; da of Richard Herbert Ingpen de la Mare (d 1986), and Amy Catherine, *née* Donaldson (d 1968); *b* 2 June 1932; *Educ* Queens Coll Harley St London, Lady Margaret Hall Oxford (BA, MA), Warburg Inst Univ of London (PhD); *Career* asst librarian Bodleian Library Oxford 1964-88 (temp cataloguer 1962-64), prof of palaeography King's Coll London 1989-, Civil Def Corps 1965-68, memb Nat Voluntary Civil Aid Oxford 1968; memb Comité International de Paléographie Latine 1986, FRHistS, FBA 1987, FSA 1990; *Books* Catalogue of the Italian Manuscripts of Major J R Abbey (with J Alexander, 1969), Catalogue of the Lyell Manuscripts of Bodleian Library of Oxford (1971), Handwriting of Italian Humanists I (1973), Miniatura Fiorentina del Rinascimento (contrib, 1985); *Recreations* gardening, listening to music, travel; *Style—* Professor Albinia de la Mare, FSA; Department of Palaeography, King's Coll, Strand, London WC2R 2LS

DE LA MARE, Sir Arthur James; KCMG (1968, CMG 1957), KCVO (1972); s of Walter de la Mare, of Jersey; *b* 15 Feb 1914; *Educ* Victoria Coll Jersey, Pembroke Coll Cambridge; *m* 1940, Katherine Sherwood; 3 da; *Career* FO 1936; served: Tokyo, San Francisco, Seoul; head Security Dept FO 1953-56, cnsllr Washington 1956-60, head Far Eastern Dept FO 1960-63; ambass: Afghanistan 1963-65, Thailand 1970-73; asst under sec FO 1965-67, high cmmr Singapore 1968-70; chm: Anglo-Thai Soc 1976-82, Royal Soc Asian Affrs 1978-84, Jersey Soc in London 1980-85; *Style—* Sir Arthur de la Mare, KCMG, KCVO; Havre de Grace, Rue des Fontaines, Trinity, Jersey JE3 5AQ CI

DE LA MARE, (Walter) Giles Ingpen; s of Richard Herbert Ingpen de la Mare (d 1986), of Much Hadham, Herts, and Amy Catherine, *née* Donaldson (d 1968); *b* 21 Oct 1934; *Educ* Eton, Trinity Coll Oxford (MA); *m* 10 Aug 1968, Ursula Alice, da of Nigel Oliver Willoughby Steward, OBE, of Cullompton, Devon; 1 s (Joshua b 1969), 1 da (Catherine b 1971); *Career* Nat Serv RN 1953-55, Midshipman RNVR 1954 (Sub Lt 1955); dir: Faber and Faber Ltd 1969-, Faber Music Ltd 1977-87, Geoffrey Faber Holdings Ltd 1990-; Publishers' Assoc: chm Univ Coll and Professional Publishers Cncl 19 memb PA Cncl 1982-85, chm PA Copyright Ctee 1988; memb Stefan Zweig Ctee Br Library 1986-, literary tstee Walter de la Mare 1982-; *Books* The Complete Poems of Walter de la Mare (ed, 1969); *Recreations* music (performance and listening), art and architecture, photography, exploring remote places; *Clubs* Garrick; *Style—* Giles de la Mare, Esq; Faber and Faber Ltd, 3 Queen Sq, London WC1N 3AU (☎ 071 465 0045)

DE LA RUE, Sir Andrew George Ilay; 4 Bt (UK 1898), of Cadogan Square, Chelsea, Co London; s of Sir Eric Vincent de la Rue, 3 Bt (d 1989), and his 1 w, Cecilia (d 1963), da of Maj Walter Waring, DL, MP (d 1930); *b* 3 Feb 1946; *m* 1984, Tessa, er da of David Dobson, of Stragglethorpe Grange, Lincoln; 2 s (b 1986, b 1989); *Heir* s, b 25 Nov 1986; *Style—* Sir Andrew de la Rue, Bt; Caldra, Duns, Berwickshire (☎ 0361 3294)

DE LA TOUR, Frances; da of Charles De La Tour (d 1983), and Moyra Silberman, *née* Fessas; family of the painter Georges De La Tour (d 1652); *b* 30 July 1945; *Educ* Lycee Francais De Londres, Drama Centre London; *m* 1 s (Josh Kempinski b 7 Feb 1977), 1 da (Tamasin Kempinski b 12 Nov 1973); *Career* actress: Standard award Best Actress 1980 for Duet for One, Critics award Best Actress 1980, SWET award Best Actress in a new Play 1980 for Duet for One; SWET award Best Actress in a Revival 1983 for Moon for the Misbegotten; nominated for BAFTA award Best Actress 1985 for Duet for One; *Style—* Ms Frances De La Tour

DE LA WARR, Anne, Countess; Anne Rachel; *née* Devas; o da of late Capt Geoffrey Charles Devas, MC, of Cawdor, and Joan, *née* Campbell-Bannerman; *m* 18 May 1946, 10 Earl De La Warr, DL (d 1988); 2 s (11 Earl, Hon Thomas Sackville, MP), 1 da (Lady Arabella)

DE LA WARR, Sylvia, Countess; Sylvia Margaret; DBE (1957); da of William Reginald Harrison, of Liverpool, and sister of Rex Harrison, actor; *m* 1, 15 April 1925, first and last Earl of Kilmuir, PC, GCVO (d 1967); 2 da (Lady Pamela Blackmore, Lady Miranda Cormack and Lalage b 1926 d 1944); m 2, 1 March 1968 as his 2 w, 9 Earl De La Warr, PC, GBE (d 1976); *Style—* The Rt Hon Sylvia, Countess De La Warr, DBE; Ludshott Manor, Bramshott, Hants GU30 7RD (☎ 0428 724668)

DE LA WARR, 11 Earl (GB 1761); William Herbrand Sackville; also Baron De La Warr (E 1299 and 1570), Viscount Cantelupe (GB 1761), and Baron Buckhurst (UK 1864); er s of 10 Earl De La Warr, DL (d 1988); *b* 10 April 1948; *Educ* Eton; *m* 1978, Anne, *née* Leveson, former w of Earl of Hopetoun (s of 3 Marq of Linlithgow); 2 s (Lord Buckhurst, Hon Edward b 1980); *Heir* s, William Herbrand Thomas, Lord Buckhurst b 13 June 1979; *Career* farmer and stockbroker; Mullens & Co 1976-81, Laing & Crookshank 1981-; *Style—* The Rt Hon the Earl De La Warr; Buckhurst Park, Withyam, E Sussex (☎ 0892 770790)

DE LASZLO, Damon Patrick; only s of Patrick David de Laszlo (d 1980), and Deborah, *née* Greenwood, da 1 Viscount Greenwood PC, KC, and gs of Philip de

Laszlo (d 1937), the portrait painter; *b* 8 Oct 1942; *Educ* Gordonstoun; *m* 1972, Hon Sandra Daphne, da of 2 Baron Hacking (d 1971); 2 s (Robert b 1977, William b 1979), 1 da (Lucy b 1975); *Career* memb Lloyds; co dir; chm Economic Res Cncl 1980-; *Recreations* shooting, scuba diving, economics; *Clubs* Boodle's, Carlton, City of London; *Style*— Damon de Laszlo, Esq; A2 Albany, Piccadilly, London W1V 9RD (☎ 071 437 1982); Pelham Place, Newton Valance, Alton, Hampshire GU34 3NQ (☎ 0420 58212)

DE LÈZARDIÈRE, Alec; *b* 16 Dec 1948; *Educ* Ecole Polytechnique Paris, Univ of Stanford (MBA); *m* Isabelle; 2 s (Charles b 13 June 1980, Joachim b 16 May 1984), 2 da (Angelique b 17 Jan 1983, Ludivine b 16 Jan 1989); *Career* md Paribas Ltd 1989- (joined 1974); *Recreations* opera, golf, shooting, skiing; *Clubs* Jockey (Paris), Automobile (Paris), Wentworth; *Style*— Comte Alec de Lèzardiére, Esq; Chief Executive, Paribas Capital Markets Group, 33 Wigmore St, London W1H 0BN (☎ 071 895 2606, fax 071 895 2447)

DE LISLE, Everard John Robert March Phillipps; DL (Leics 1980); s of Maj John Adrian Frederick March Phillipps de Lisle, DL (d 1961), of Stockerston Hall, Leics, and Elizabeth Muriel Smythe, *née* Guinness (d 1974); *b* 8 June 1930; *Educ* Eton, RMA Sandhurst; *m* 2 April 1959, Hon Mary Rose, da of Osbert Peake, 1 Viscount Ingleby, PC (d 1966), of Snilesworth, Northallerton, Yorks; 2 s (Charles b 1960, Timothy b 1962), 1 da (Rosanna b 1968); *Career* cmmd RHG (The Blues) 1950, Capt 1954, Maj 1960, demob 1962; Stock Exchange 1963- (memb 1965); High Sheriff Leics 1974, vice Lord Lt Leics 1990; *Recreations* shooting, tennis, swimming; *Clubs* MCC, Leicestershire; *Style*— Everard de Lisle, Esq, DL; Stockerston Hall, Oakham, Leics LE15 9JD (☎ 0572 822404); 4 Hereford Mansions, Hereford Rd, London W2 5BA (☎ 071 229 4120)

DE LISLE, Hon Mrs (Mary Rose); *née* Peake; da of 1 Viscount Ingleby (d 1966), and Lady Joan Rachel de Vere, *née* Capell (d 1979), da of 7 Earl of Essex; *b* 23 April 1940; *Educ* Queens Coll London; *m* 2 April 1959, Everard John Robert March Phillipps de Lisle, DL (Leics 1980), RHG (ret), *qv*, eld s of Major John de Lisle, DL (d 1961), of Stockerston Hall, Uppingham, Leics; 2 s (Charles b 1960, Timothy b 1962), 1 da (Mary Rosanna b 1968); *Career* lay canon Leicester Cathedral 1989; *Recreations* tennis, writing, family history; *Style*— The Hon Mrs de Lisle; Stockerston Hall, Oakham, Leics (☎ 0572 822404); 4 Hereford Mansions, Hereford Rd, London W2 5BA (☎ 071 229 4120)

DE LONGUEMAR, Vicomte Pierre; s of Col Vicomte de Longuemar and Odette, *née* Cesbron Lavau; *b* 9 May 1929; *Educ* Ecole des Hautes Etudes Commerciales Paris; *m* 7 Feb 1955, Armelle, da of Comte Michel de Beaumont; 2 s (Thierry b 1955, Geoffroy b 1957), 1 da (Diane-Marie b 1961); *Career* Int Dept Banque Paribas Paris 1954-66, International Finance Corporation Washington 1966-69, sous-directeur Banque Paribas Paris 1969 (directeur adjoint 1977, directeur 1984), md Banque Paribas London 1987-90; non-exec dir: Paribas Ltd 1987, Banque Franco-Yougoslave; *Clubs* Overseas Bankers', Jockey (Paris); *Style*— Vicomte Pierre de Longuemar; Banque Paribas, 3 Rue D'Antin, 75002 Paris, France (☎ 42 98 12 34)

DE LONGUEUIL, 11 Baron (sole title in Peerage of Canada, cr 1700); Raymond David Grant; s of 10 Baron (d 1959, whose half unc, 7 Baron, received recognition of cr of Louis XIV by Queen Victoria in 1880 under terms of Treaty of Quebec which ceded sovereignty of Canada from Fr to GB), and Ernestine (d 1981), da of Hon Ernest Bowes-Lyon, 3 s of 13 Earl of Strathmore, formerly wife of Francis Winstone Scott; *b* 3 Sept 1921; *m* 1946, Anne, da of late Patrick Brough Maltby; 1 s; *Heir* s, Michael Charles b 1947; *Style*— Baron de Longueuil; 64190 Navarrenx, France

DE LOS ANGELES, Victoria; *b* 1 Nov 1923; *Educ* Escoles Milá i Fontanals de la Generlitat de Catalumya Barcelona, Conservatorio de Liceo Barcelona (hons grad completed the 6 year course in 3 years); *m* 1948, Enrique Magriná (dec'd); 2 s; *Career* lyric soprano, opera 2 concert arisite; concert debut de la Musica Catalana Barcelona 1944, opera debut Gran Teztro del Liceo Barcelona 1945, concert and opera tours of Europe, N Central and S America, SA, ME, Far East, Aust, NZ, Thailand, Korea, Philippines, Singapore, Hong Kong and most E Euro countries 1945-; repertoire of German lieder, French art songs and Spanish songs exceeding 1000; operatic repertoire incl: Marriage of Figaro, Lohengrin, Tannhouser, Meistersinger, Trautatz, Cavelleriz Rusticana, I Pagliacci, La Boheme, Madame Butterfly, Manon; 1 prize concord Int Geneva 1947, Gold medal Barcelona 1958, medal Premio Roma 1969, numerous French, Italian and Dutch awards; Gold disc for 5 million records sold FB; Hon Doctorate Univ of Barcelona; Cross of Lazo de Dama Spain, Condecoracion Bancla de la Order Civil de Alfubiox Spain; *Style*— Miss V De Los Angeles; Avenide de Pedralbos 57, 08034 Barcelona, Spain; Basil Douglas Artists Management, 8 St George's Terrace, London NW1 8XJ (☎ 071 722 7142, fax 071 722 1841)

DE LOTBINIERE *see also*: Joly de Lotbinieṙe

DE MARÉ, Eric Samuel; s of Bror August Erik de Maré (d 1948), timber broker of London, and Ingrid Inga-Brita, *née* Tellander (d 1964); genealogy traced to first Crusade from France; Jean de Maré, Huguenot, assassinated the Duc de Guise; Jacques Le Bel de Maré, refugee, taught the King of Sweden how to wield the epée; gf, govr of Dalarna Province, Sweden; cous, Rolf de Maré, founder of Swedish Ballet Company and Museum of Dance, Stockholm; bro Dr Patrick de Maré, pioneer of Group Psychotherapy; *b* 10 Sept 1910; *Educ* St Paul's, Architectural Assoc Sch of Architecture London; *m* 1, 1936, Vanessa Burrage (d 1972); m 2, 1974, Enid Verity, artist and colour conslt, da of Edward Hill (d 1970), of London; *Career* freelance architectural writer and photographer; ed Architects' Journal 1943-46, hon treas Social Credit Pty 1938-46; *Books* incl: Canals of England, Bridges of Britain, Time on the Thames, Penguin Photography, Scandinavia, London's Riverside, London 1851, Wren's London, Architecture and Photography, Victorian Woodblock Illustrators (Yorks Post award 1980), Swedish Crosscut: The Story of the Göta Canal, A Matter of Life or Debt (The Douglas Social Credit Creed in the Light of the Micro-Chip Revolution), Eric de Maré, Builder with Light (Architectural Assoc Monograph, 1990); *Recreations* philosophising with friends, bashing the Money Mafia; *Style*— Eric de Maré Esq; The Old Chapel, Tunley, nr Sapperton, Cirencester, Glos GL7 6LW (☎ 028 576 382)

DE MARFFY VON VERSEGH, Hon Mrs (Pelline Margot); *née* Lyon-Dalberg-Acton; da of 3 Baron Acton; *b* 24 Dec 1932; *m* 30 June 1953, Lazlo de Marffy von Versegh; 6 s (Denis b 1954, Miklos b 1956, Joseph b 1957, Paul b 1958, Robert b 1962, Stephen b 1965), and 1 s decd, 1 da (Gabriella b 1960); *Style*— Hon Mrs de Marffy von Versegh; Ealing Farm, PO Box 29, Umvukwes, Zimbabwe

DE MAULEY, 6 Baron (UK 1838); Gerald John Ponsonby; s of 5 Baron de Mauley (d 1962); *b* 19 Dec 1921; *Educ* Eton, Ch Ch Oxford (BA, MA); *m* 1954, Helen, widow of Lt-Col Brian Abdy Collins, OBE, MC, and da of Hon Charles Sholto Douglas (d 1960, 2 s of 19 Earl of Morton); *Heir* bro, Hon Thomas Maurice Ponsonby, *qv*; *Career* Lt Leics Yeo, Capt RA, served 1939-45 (France); called to the Bar Middle Temple; *Style*— The Rt Hon Lord de Mauley; Langford House, Little Faringdon, Lechlade, Glos

DE MEYER, Lady Susan Ankaret; *née* Howard; da of 11 Earl of Carlisle (d 1963), of Naworth Castle, Carlisle and his 2 w Esmé Mary Shrubb, Countess of Carlisle, *née* Iredell; *b* 13 Nov 1948; *Educ* Benenden; *m* 1, 9 Sept 1967 (m dis 1978), Charles James Buchanan-Jardine, s of Capt Sir John William Buchanan-Jardine, 3 Bt (d 1969); 1 da (Flora b 1971); m 2, 1978, Count Hubert Charles Guillaume de Meyer, s of Count Hervé Marie de Meyer, of Fribroug, Switzerland; 1 s (Alexander b 1978); *Style*— The Lady Susan de Meyer; 37 Lennox Gardens, London SW3 (☎ 071 584 9474); Little Fosse Farm, Nettleton, nr Chippenham, Wilts, Castlecombe (☎ 0249 782315) Oxford OX5 3PG (☎ 0869 40239)

DE MONTALT, John Derek; s of James Leonard Moult, BEM, and Mary Jane, *née* Payne (d 1985); assumed the surname of de Montalt as a direct descendant of Eustace de Montalt, Chief Baron of Chester and Hereditary Steward to the Earls of Chester 1071; *b* 18 Nov 1932; *Educ* Yorks Army Sch, Private Army Higher Educn Schs, Wolsey Hall Coll Oxford; *m* 23 March 1957, Joy Mary, da of William Edward Humphrey; 2 da (Sharon May b 4 Feb 1958, Deborah Joy b 31 March 1961); *Career* podiatrist and chiropodist; sr Eastbourne Health Dist 1964-; memb: Nat Health Advsy Ctee for Eastbourne dist 1974, Co Gentleman's Assoc, Derbyshire Record Soc; knighthood of St Colombus 1988; LCh, SRCh, memb: Harl Soc, Inst of Chiropodists 1964 (sec Hosp and Pub Appts Ctee 1964-69), MRSH 1964-69; *Recreations* genealogical research, photography, gardening, walking; *Style*— John de Montalt, Esq; St Anthony's Grange, 33 St Anthony's Ave, Eastbourne, East Sussex BN23 6LN (☎ 0323 34268); Winnifred Lee Health Centre, Wartling Rd, Eastbourne (☎ 0323 20555 ext 140)

DE MONTMORENCY, Sir Arnold Geoffroy; 19 Bt (I 1631), of Knockagh, Co Tipperary; s of James Edward Geoffrey de Montmorency (d 1934); suc cous, Sir Reginald d'Alton Lodge de Montmorency, 18 Bt, 1979; *b* 27 July 1908; *Educ* Westminster, Peterhouse Cambridge (MA, LLM); *m* 20 April 1949 (m annulled 1953), and remarried, 1972, Nettie Hay, da of William Anderson of Morayshire; *Career* War Serv RASC 1939-45 (Maj 1944-45); called to the Bar Middle Temple 1932, chm (pt/t) Industl Tbnls 1975-81, chm Contemporary Review Cmmn 1962; Parly candidate (Lib): Cambridge 1959, Cirencester and Tewkesbury 1964; fndr and pres Friends of Peterhouse; *Books* Integration of Industrial Legislation (1984); *Clubs* Nat Liberal; *Style*— Sir Arnold de Montmorency, Bt; 2 Garden Ct, Temple, London EC4Y 9BL

DE NORMANN, John Anthony; OBE (1989); s of Sir Eric de Normann, KBE, CB (d 1982), of Surrey, and Winifred Scott, *née* Leigh (d 1968); *b* 25 Jan 1923; *Educ* Westminster, ChCh Oxford (MA); *m* 1959, Diana, da of Charles Phipps (d 1960), of Wilts; 2 s (Roderick b 1959, Anthony b 1961); *Career* Capt RA Far East 1942-45; ICI 1947-80, chm Farrow Gp 1970-80; cncllr: Economic and Social Consultative Assembly, European Community Brussels 1982-90; dir: BSI, Nat Cncl of Building Material Prodrs; *Recreations* book collecting, gardening, travel, motoring; *Clubs* White's; *Style*— John A de Normann, Esq, OBE; Lower Leaze, Box, nr Corsham, Wilts (☎ 0225 742 786)

DE PELLEGRINO FARRUGIA, Dr Joseph Francis; s of Don Romeo Farrugia (d 1951), and Donna Angela dei Nobili Pellegrino (d 1975); *b* 21 March 1924; *Educ* Lyceum, Univ of St Andrews (MB ChB); *m* 2 June 1966, Margaret Constance, da of Johan Arvid North (formerly von Johannson), of Hull and Turku; 2 s (Adrian b 1967, Guy b 1969), 1 da (Giuliana-Augusta b 1974); *Career* cmmnd 1941: Weapon Trg Offr 1942, Maj 1943-48, dir PW Intelligence Bureau E A Cmd; RAMC 1956; specialist in Psychiatry RARO 1966, rotating internships W Cornwall Hosps 1956-58, MO Menston Psychiatric Hosp 1968-63, princ in family med 1963-86, dir surgery and sr examiner St John's Ambulance Bde 1965-80, MO Nat Blood Transfusion Serv 1987; *Recreations* architecture, books, wine, opera; *Clubs* The Challoner (fndr memb), Landsdowne; *Style*— Dr Joseph De Pellegrino Farrugia; Top Lodge, Broughton, Skipton, N Yorks BD23 3AE (☎ 0756 799585); Coutts & Co, Hanover St Branch; Lindley Hse Nursing Home, Otley Rd, Shipley, W Yorks (☎ 0274 580502)

DE PEYER, Gervase; *b* 11 April 1926; *Educ* King Alfred's London, Bedales, Royal Coll of Music; *m* 1, 1950 (m dis 1971), Sylvia Southcombe; 1 s, 2 da; m 2, 1971 (m dis 1979), Susan Rosalind Daniel; m 3, 1980, Katia Perret Aubry; *Career* dir London Symphony Wind Ensemble, fndr and conductor Melos Sinfonia, fndr memb Melos Ensemble of London, solo clarinettist Chamber Music Soc of Lincoln Center NY 1969; Gold medal Worshipful Co of Musicians 1948; ARCM, Hon ARAM; *Style*— Gervase de Peyer, Esq; Porto-Vecchio 1250, SO Washington St, Alexandria, Virginia 22314 USA

DE PIRO, His Hon Judge; Baron Alan Caesar Haselden; QC (1965); s of Joseph William de Piro (killed 1942), of Singapore; *b* 31 Aug 1919; *Educ* Repton, Trinity Hall Cambridge (MA); *m* 1, 1947, Mary Elliot (decd); 2 s; m 2, 1964, Mona Addington; 1 step s, 1 step da; *Career* Capt, served W Africa; barr 1947, dep chm Warwicks QS and Bedford QS 1967-72, master of the Bench Middle Temple 1971-, rec 1972-82, circuit judge (Midland and Oxford Circuit) 1983-91; vice pres Union Internationale des Avocats 1969-71, memb Cncl Int Bar Assoc 1967-86; *Recreations* canals, gardening, conversation; *Clubs* Hawks (Cambridge); *Style*— His Hon Judge de Piro, QC; Toll House, Bascote Locks, Leamington Spa, Warwicks

DE RAMSEY, 3 Baron (UK 1887); Ailwyn Edward Fellowes; KBE (1974), TD, DL (Huntingdon and Peterborough 1973, Cambs 1974); s of Capt Hon Coulson Churchill Fellowes (d 1915), s of 2 Baron and Lady Rosamond, *née* Spencer-Churchill, sis of 8 Duke of Marlborough; suc gf, 2 Baron, 1925; *b* 16 March 1910; *Educ* Oundle; *m* 27 July 1937, Lilah Helen Suzanne (d 1987), da of late Francis Anthony Labouchere, of 15 Draycott Ave, London SW3, by his w Evelyn Mary, da of Sir Walter Stirling, 3 Bt (ret 1934); 2 s, 2 da; *Heir* s, Hon John Ailwyn Fellowes; *Career* Capt (135 Field Regt) Herts Yeo RA (TA) 1939; patron of four livings; Ld-Lt: of Huntingdonshire 1947-65, of Huntingdon and Peterborough 1965-68; pres Country Landowners' Assoc 1963-65; *Style*— Rt Hon Lord De Ramsey, KBE, TD, DL; Abbots Ripton Hall, Huntingdon (☎ 048 73 234)

DE RENUSSON D'HAUTEVILLE, Comtesse Gérard; Hon Joanna Phoebe; *née* Rodd; er da of 2 Baron Rennell, KBE, CB (d 1978); *b* 4 July 1929; *Educ* Westonbirt Sch for Girls, Friend's Acad Long Island USA; *m* 2 July 1966, Comte Gérard de Renusson d'Hauteville, Offr de la Légion d'Honneur, Croix de Guerre, s of Marquis de Renusson d'Hauteville (d 1949), of Croissy-sur-Seine, France; *Career* bookseller; *Recreations* reading, writing, pedigree dogs; *Clubs* Ebury Court; *Style*— Comtesse Gérard d'Hauteville; The Allianes Francaise Paris; 10 rue François Mouthon, 75015 Paris; 9 rue Puget, 06100 Nice, Alpes Maritimes, France; The British Institute of Florence, Florence, Italy

DE ROS, 28 Baron (E 1264); Peter Trevor Maxwell; Premier Baron of England; s of 27 Baroness de Ros (d 1983) and Cdr David Maxwell, RN, *qv*; gs of Hon Mrs (Angela) Horn (*qv*); *b* 23 Dec 1958; *Educ* Headfort Sch Kells, Stowe, Down HS Downpatrick; *m* 5 Sept 1987, Angela Siân, da of late Peter Campbell Ross; 1 s (Finbar James b 14 Nov 1988), 1 da (Katharine Georgiana Maxwell b 26 oct 1990); *Heir* s, Hon Finbar James Maxwell b 14 Nov 1988; *Style*— The Rt Hon the Lord de Ros

DE ROSNAY, Baroness Joël; Hon Stella Candida; *née* Jebb; yr da of 1 Baron Gladwyn, GCMG, GCVO, CB; *b* 7 Dec 1933; *m* 12 Dec 1959, Baron Joël de Rosnay; 1 s (Alexis b 1967), 2 da (Tatiana b 1961, Cecilia b 1963); *Style*— Baroness Joël de Rosnay; 146 rue de l'Universite, Paris VII, France

DE ROTHSCHILD; *see*: Rothschild

DE ROTHSCHILD, Edmund Leopold; TD (and 2 Bars); s of Maj Lionel Nathan de Rothschild, OBE, JP (d 1942), of Exbury House, Exbury, nr Southampton, and Marie-Louise, *née* Beer; *b* 2 Jan 1916; *Educ* Harrow, Trinity Coll Cambridge (MA); *m*

1, 22 June 1948, Elisabeth (d 1980), da of Marcel Lentner, of Vienna; 2 s (Nicholas David b 10 Oct 1951, David Lionel (twin) b 28 Nov 1955), 2 da (Katherine Juliette b 11 July 1949, Charlotte Henrietta b 28 Nov 1955); m 2, 26 April 1982, Anne Evelyn, JP, widow of J Malcolm Harrison, OBE; *Career* Maj RA (TA), served WWII, BEF, BNAF, CMF, France, N Africa, Italy (wounded); merchant banker; non-exec dir N M Rothschild & Sons 1975- (ptnr 1946-, sr ptnr 1960-70, chm 1970-75); chm AUR Hydropower Ltd; dep chm British Newfoundland Corp Canada 1963-69 (dir 1953-63); dep chm Churchill Falls (Labrador) Corpn (Canada); pres: Assoc of Jewish Ex-Service Men and Women, Res into Ageing, Care Britain; tstee: Freedom from Hunger Campaign 1965, Queens Nursing Inst; memb: Asia Ctee BNEC 1970-71 (chm 1971), Cncl Royal Nat Pension Fund for Nurses; Freeman City of London, Liveryman Worshipful Co of Fishmongers 1949; Hon LLD Memorial Univ of Newfoundland 1961, Hon DSc Salford 1983; Order of the Sacred Treasure (1 class) Japan 1973; *Books* Window on the World (1949); *Recreations* fishing, gardening, golf; *Clubs* White's, Portland; *Style*— Edmund de Rothschild, Esq, TD; New Court, St Swithin's Lane, London EC4P 4DU (☎ 071 280 5000, fax 071 929 1643, telex 888031) Exbury House, Exbury, nr Southampton, Hants SO4 1AF (☎ 0703 893145)

DE ROTHSCHILD, Baron Eric Alain Robert David; s of Baron (James Gustave Jules) Alain de Rothschild (d 1982), and Mary Germaine, *née* Chauvin du Treuil; *b* 3 Oct 1940; *Educ* Lycée Janson de Sailly Paris France, Polytechnicum of Zürich; *m* 21 Dec 1983, (Donna) Maria Beatrice, da of Don Alfonso Cracciolo di Forino (d 1990); 1 s (James Alain Robert Alexandro b 7 Dec 1985), 1 da (Anna Saskia Esther b 29 April 1987); *Career* managing ptnr Chateau Lafite Rothschild 1974-; chm: Paris Orleans SA 1975-, Rothschild Continuation Ltd London 1977-; dir: N W Rothschild & Sons Ltd London 1978, M M Warburg-Brickmann Wirtz & Co Hamburg 1978-, Cinzano Group Geneva 1989-, N M Rothschild Asset Management Ltd London 1989-, Chalone Inc San Francisco 1989-; admin La Fundiaria Assicurazione Florence 1989; *Style*— Baron Eric de Rothschild; Rothschild & Co Banque, 17 Avenue Matignon, 75008 Paris, France (☎ 1 40 74 40 74, fax 1 45 63 78 86)

DE ROTHSCHILD, Sir Evelyn Robert Adrian; s of Anthony de Rothschild, DL (d 1961, 3 s of Leopold de Rothschild, CVO, JP, 1 cousin Edmund de Rothschild, *qv*), and Yvonne, da of late Robert Cahen d'Anvers, of Paris; *b* 29 Aug 1931; *Educ* Harrow, Trinity Coll Cambridge; *m* 1, 1966 (m dis 1971), Jeanette (d 1981), da of Ernest Bishop; m 2, 1973, Victoria, da of Lewis Schott; 2 s (Anthony b 1977, David b 1978), 1 da (Jessica b 1974); *Career* chm: N M Rothschild & Sons, Economist Newspaper 1972-89 (currently dir), United Racecourses Ltd 1977-; kt 1989; *Style*— Sir Evelyn de Rothschild; Ascott, Wing, Leighton Buzzard, Beds; N M Rothschild & Sons, New Court St, St Swithin's Lane, London EC4P 4DU (☎ 071 280 5000)

DE SALABERRY, Count Pascal; s of Comte de Salaberry, of Le Bailly, Nemours, France, and Gilberte, *née* Burrus; *b* 15 Nov 1941; *Educ* Univ of Paris, Univ of Geneva; *Career* Banque Transatlantique Paris 1969-77, Ivory & Sime plc Edinburgh 1978-; chm: Sumitrust Ivory & Sime Ltd 1989 (md 1987), Instate plc 1989; non-exec dir: Personal Assets Trust plc 1983, Continental Assets Trust plc 1990; *Recreations* sports, bridge, backgammon, antiques; *Clubs* Dean Tennis (Edinburgh); *Style*— Count Pascal de Salaberry; 8 Great Stuart St, Edinburgh EH3 7TN (☎ 031 225 5060); One Charlotte Square, Edinburgh EH2 4DZ (☎ 031 225 1357, fax 031 225 2375, telex 72724

DE SALIS, 9 Count (Holy Roman Empire 1748, cr by Francis I); John Bernard Philip Humbert de Salis; TD; also Hereditary Knight of the Golden Spur (1571); s of 8 Count de Salis (Lt-Col Irish Gds), of Lough Gur, Co Limerick (d 1949, descended from Peter 1 Count de Salis-Soglio, Envoy of the Grisons Republic to Queen Anne at the time of the Treaty of Utrecht; Jerome, 2 Count de Salis, was naturalised Br by Act of Parliament 1731 following his marriage to Mary, da and co-heiress of the last Viscount Fane); an earlier member of the family, Feldzeugmeister Rudolph von Salis, was cr a Baron of the HRE by the Emperor Rudolf II in 1582 for gallantry against the Turks; through Sophia, da of Adm Francis William Drake, w of Jerome, 4 Count de Salis, the family is heir-gen of the great Sir Francis; the 8 Count's mother was Princess Hélène de Riquet, da of Prince Eugène de Caraman-Chimay (Prince of Chimay 1527 HRE by Maximilian I, Belgium 1889 by Leopold II), a descendant of Jean de Croy killed at Agincourt 1415, and gs of Thérèse de Cabarrus (Madame Tallien); *b* 16 Nov 1947; *Educ* Downside, CCC Cambridge (LLM); *m* 1, 1973 (m dis and annulled); m 2, Marie-Claude, 3 da of Col René-Henri Wüst, Swiss Army, of Zürich and Geneva; 1 s (Count John-Maximilian Henry b 3 Nov 1986); *Heir* s, Count John-Maximilian Henry de Salis b 3 Nov 1986; *Career* late Brevet Maj 9/12 Royal Lancers (Prince of Wales's), Panzergrenadier Swiss Army; called to the Bar Gray's Inn; delegate Int Ctee Red Cross Missions in Middle East, Africa, and head of delgn Iraq, Thailand, special envoy in Lebanon 1982; ptnr Gautier, Salis et Cie Geneva; ambass of Order of Malta to Thailand; Kt of Honour and Devotion Sov Mil Order Malta 1974, Kt of Justice Constantinian Order of St George; *Recreations* melancholia; *Clubs* Cavalry and Guards', Travellers', Beefsteak, Royal Bangkok Sports; *Style*— The Count de Salis, TD; Maison du Bailli, CH-1422 Grandson, Switzerland (☎ 024 241466); office: Gautier, Salis & Cie, 14 rue Etienne Dumont, CH-1204 Geneva, Switzerland (☎ 022 213030)

DE SALIS, Timothy Stephen Fane; s of Rev Andrew Augustine Fane De Salis (d 1962), of Honiton, Devon, and Violet Eileen Charlotte, *née* Higgens; *b* 2 Sept 1936; *Educ* Allhallows Sch Devon; *m* 11 June 1966, Penelope Elisabeth, da of the Very Rev Michael John Nott, of Southsea, Hants; 2 s (Mark b 1967, Jonathan b 1971), 1 da (Nicola b 1969); *Career* dir: CGA Insur Brokers Ltd 1978 (md 1986), County Gentlemen's Assoc plc 1986, CGA Financial Servs Ltd 1987; *Recreations* reading, walking; *Style*— Timothy S De Salis, Esq; 21 Broadwater Avenue, Letchworth, Herts SG6 3HF (☎ 0462 684182); Country Gentlemens Assoc plc, Icknield Way West, Letchworth, Herts SG6 4AP (☎ 0462 480011, fax 0462 481407)

DE SAUMAREZ, 7 Baron (UK 1831); Eric Douglas Saumarez; er twin s of 6 Baron de Saumarez (d 1991), and Joan (Julia) Beryl, *née* Charlton; *b* 13 Aug 1956; *Educ* Milton Abbey, Nottingham Univ, RAC Cirencester; *m* 14 July 1982, Christine Elizabeth, yr da of Bernard Neil Halliday, OBE, of Woodford Green, Essex; 2 da (Claire b 1984, Emily b 1985); *Heir* bro, Hon Victor Saumarez b 13 Aug 1956; *Career* farmer; *Recreations* shooting, fishing, flying, driving, sailing; *Style*— The Rt Hon the Lord de Saumarez; Vicarage Farm, Coddenham, Suffolk (☎ 044 979 573)

DE SAUMAREZ, Hon Louisa; *née* Saumarez; only da of 6 Baron de Saumarez (d 1991); *b* 7 March 1955; *m* 4 Sept 1982 (m dis), Duncan W MacGregor, o s of Alasdair MacGregor, of Tregaer Mill, Monmouth; *Style*— The Hon Louisa de Saumarez; c/o Shrubland Vista, Coddenham, Ipswich, Suffolk

DE SAVARY, Peter John; *Educ* Charterhouse; *m* 1 (m dis), Marcia; 2 da; m 2, 1985 (m dis 1986), Alice, *née* Simms; m 3 1986, Lucille Lana, *née* Paton; 2 da; *Career* America's Cup Challenger 1983; dir of various int cos; *Style*— Peter de Savary Esq; Littlecote House, Hungerford, Berks

DE SILVA, (George) Desmond Lorenz; QC (1984); s of Edmund Frederick Lorenz de Silva, MBE, of Kandy, Sri Lanka, and Esme Norah Gregg, *née* Nathanielsz (d 1982); *b* 13 Dec 1939; *Educ* Dulwich, Trinity Coll Kandy Sri Lanka; *m* 5 Dec 1987, HRH Princess Katarina of Yugoslavia, o da of HRH Prince Tomislav of Yugoslavia, ggggda of Queen Victoria; *qv*; *Career* called to the Bar Middle Temple 1964, Sierra Leone 1968, Gambia 1981; memb Home Affrs Standing Ctee Bow Gp 1982, Editorial Advsy Bd Crossbow; vice pres St John Ambulance London (Prince of Wales Dist) 1984, Cnclman City of London (ward of Farringdon Without); landowner (Taprobane Island in the Indian Ocean); Freeman City of London, memb Worshipful Co of Fletchers; CStJ 1985 (OStJ 1980); *Recreations* politics, shooting, travel; *Clubs* Carlton, City Livery, Orient (Colombo); *Style*— Desmond de Silva Esq, QC; 28 Sydney Street, London SW3; Villa Taprobane, Taprobane Island, off Sri Lanka; 2 Paper Buildings, Temple, London EC4Y 7ET (☎ 071 353 9119)

DE SILVA, Harendra Aneurin Domingo; s of Annesley De Silva (d 1978), of Colombo, Sri Lanka, and Mahar De Silva (d 1989); *b* 29 Sept 1945; *Educ* Millfield, Queen's Coll Cambridge (MA, LLM); *m* 10 June 1972, Indira; 1 s (Nihal Ceri b 17 Jan 1979), 1 da (Ayesha Annette b 30 July 1975); *Career* called to the Bar Middle Temple, asst rec; *Recreations* golf, bridge, tennis; *Clubs* Roehampton; *Style*— Harendra De Silva, Esq; 2 Paper Buildings, Temple, London EC4Y 7ET (☎ 071 936 2611)

De SILVA, Dr Stephane Gwendoline; da of Muthumadinage Piyasena, of Sri Lanka, and Esther, *née* Dabare (d 1989); *b* 11 Dec 1938; *Educ* Methodist Coll Colombo Sri Lanka, Med Sch Univ of Colombo Sri Lanka; *m* 19 Oct 1967, Ariyapala De Silva, s of K A De Silva (d 1971), of Sri Lanka; 1 da (Tania Gitanjali b Aug 1968); *Career* conslt psychiatrist Leavesden Hosp 1981- (sr registrar 1978-80), clinical tutor and regnl tutor for NW Thames RHA 1985; chairperson Med Exec Ctee Leavesden Hosp 1988; memb BMA, MRCPsych; *Style*— Dr Stephanie De Silva; 12 Grove Road, Northwood, Middlesex (☎ 09274 21356); Leavesden Hospital, College Rd, Abbots Langley, Herts (☎ 0923 674090 ext 21)

DE SPON, Baron (Holy Roman Empire and Bavaria, cr by Charles VII, with appellation *Wohlgeboren*, 1742); John Seymour; also Noble of the HRE (Matthias, 1612), Baron of France (Louis XV 1743); s of John, Baron de Spon (d 1966, ggs of François Nicolas, Baron de Spon, premier président du Conseil Souverain d'Alsace 1776-90, who emigrated to England 1792, in his turn s of Jean François, Baron de Spon, Comte zu Forbach, Imperial and Bavarian ambass to Frederick the Great 1743-47); *b* 28 Dec 1913; *Educ* Lower Sch of John Lyon Harrow, King's Coll London; *m* 1 May 1948 (m dis 1953), Florence, *née* Shaw; *Career* ret journalist; formerly with: Western Morning News, Rand Daily Mail, Daily Mirror, News of the World, Sunday Times, Daily Telegraph, Sunday Telegraph; ed Burke's Peerage and Burke's Landed Gentry 1941-46; Parly candidate (Lib) N Kensington 1935, LCC candidate W Islington 1937; patron L'Orchestre du Monde 1988; Freeman City of London 1963, Liveryman Worshipful Co of Stationers 1985 (Freeman 1982); FRGS 1963; kt of Sacred Military Order of Constantine of St George (conferred by HRH Prince Ferdinand de Bourbon de Deux-Siciles 1981); *Recreations* shooting, book collecting; *Clubs* Travellers'; *Style*— Baron de Spon; 17 Goodwood Court, Devonshire St, London W1 (☎ 071 636 2649)

DE STACPOOLE, 6 Duke (Papal title, conferred 1831 by Gregory XVI); George Geoffrey Robert Edward de Stacpoole; also Count Stacpoole (French cr of Louis XVIII 1818) and Marquis de Stacpoole (Papal title conferred by Leo XII 1826); s of 5 Duke, JP (d 1965); The Stacpooles have resided in Ireland from the twelfth century, the family name is taken from a feudal lordship in Pembrokeshire; *b* 21 June 1917; *Educ* Downside; *m* 15 July 1947, Dorothy Anne, o da of late Richard Edmund Dease, RAFVR, of Rath House, Co Leix; 2 s (George Richard b 1948, David Henry Oliver b 1951), 1 da (Valerie Brigid Dorothy (Mrs Jeremy Richardson) b 1950); *Career* Maj late Royal Ulster Rifles, served WWII; *Style*— Major the Duke de Stacpoole; Hempsted Corner Cottage, Benenden, Cranbrook, Kent TN17 4ET (☎ 0580 240634)

DE STEMPEL, Sophie Christina; da of Baron Michael De Stempel, of Crosfield Road, Hampstead, and Cristina MacDonald; *b* 31 Dec 1960; *Educ* Lady Eden's Sch London, Convent of the Sacred Heart Woldingham, City and Guilds Sch of Art Kennington; *Career* artist; exhibitions incl: Gallery 24 Powis Terrace 1985, Conway Hall 1986, Albermarle Gallery 1987, The Mall Galleries 1988, and many mixed shows; most important works: The Unmade Bed 1986 (Saatchi collection), Profile of Gillian Melling 1988 (Catherine Parma collection), interior 1989 (Berry collection), Interior Bathroom 1989 (Saatchi collection), India Jane Birley 1990 (Pigoztsi collection), India Jane in an Interior 1990-91 (Saatchi collection); *Style*— Sophie De Stempel; Pippi Houldsworth (Houldsworth Fine Art), 46 Bassett Rd, London W10 (☎ 081 969 8197)

DE SWIET, Dr Michael; s of John de Swiet, of Trewen Pentrych, Cardiff, and Mary Marguerite, *née* Smith; *b* 15 Aug 1941; *Educ* Cheltenham, Univ of Cambridge (MD); *m* 12 Sept 1964, Eleanor Jane, da of Richard Miles Hawkins, of Weston Hill House, Broadwas on Teme, Worcs; 2 s (Thomas Michael b 12 May 1970, Charles Richard John b 12 Dec 1972), 1 da (Harriet Kate b Aug 1968); *Career* sr house offr Nat Hosp for Nervous Diseases 1968; UCH: house physician 1966-67, sr house offr 1967-68, res fell 1968-70; res fell Univ of California San Francisco 1970-71, registrar Radcliffe Infirmary Oxford 1971-73; consIt physician 1973-: Queen Charlotte's Hosp, Brompton Hosp, UCH; academic sub dean Royal Postgrad Med Sch Inst of Obstetrics and Gynaecology; MRCP 1968, FRCP 1981; *Books* Medical Disorders in Obstetric Practice (2 edn, 1989), Basic Science in Obstetrics 7 Gynaecology (co-ed, 1986); *Recreations* the arts, gardening, woodwork, walking; *Style*— Dr Michael de Swiet; 60 Hornsey Lane, London N6 5LU (☎ 071 272 3195); High Blean Cottage, Raydaleside, Leyburn, N Yorks DL8 3DJ (☎ 0969 50362); Queen Charlotte's Hospital, Goldhawk Rd, London W6 0XG (☎ 081 740 3905, fax 081 740 3922, car 042 691 441

DE TRAFFORD, Sir Dermot Humphrey; 6 Bt (UK 1841), of Trafford Park, Lancs; VRD; s of Sir Rudolph de Trafford, 5 Bt, OBE (d 1983), by his 1 w, June Isabel, MBE (d 1977), only da of Lt-Col Reginald Chaplin; *b* 19 Jan 1925; *Educ* Harrow, ChCh Oxford (MA); *m* 1, 26 June 1948 (m dis 1973), Patricia Mary, da of late Francis Mycroft Beeley, of Long Crumples, nr Alton, Hants; 3 s, 6 da; m 2, 1974, Xandra Carandini, da of Lt-Col Geoffrey Trollope Lee, and former w of Roderick Walter; *Heir* s, John Humphrey de Trafford ;*Career* md GHP Gp Ltd 1961 (chm 1966-77), dep chm Imperial Continental Gas Assoc 1972-87 (dir 1963-87), chm Low & Bonar plc 1982-90 (dep chm 1980); memb IOD, CBIM, FRSA; *Recreations* gardening, golf; *Clubs* White's, Royal Ocean Racing; *Style*— Sir Dermot de Trafford, Bt, VRD; The Old Vicarage, Appleshaw, nr Andover, Hants (☎ 0264 772357)

DE TRAFFORD, John Humphrey; er s and h of Sir Dermot de Trafford, 6 Bt, VRD, *qv*, and his 1 w, Patricia; *b* 12 Sept 1950; *Educ* Ampleforth, Univ of Bristol (BSc); *m* 1975, Anne, da of Jacques Faure de Pebeyre; 1 s (Alexander Humphrey b 1978), 1 da (Isabel b 1980); *Career* vice pres American Express Europe Ltd 1987-; *Clubs* Royal Ocean Racing; *Style*— John de Trafford, Esq; 30 Norland Square, London W11 4PU

DE TRAFFORD, Katherine, Lady; Katherine; eldest da of William Walter Balke, of Cincinnati, USA; *m* 1, Sebastiano Lo Savio; m 2, 2 Feb 1939, as his 2nd w, Sir Rudolph Edgar Francis de Trafford, 5 Bt, OBE (d 1983); *Style*— Katherine, Lady de Trafford; 70 Eaton Sq, London SW1

DE VALOIS, Dame Ninette (Edris); CH (1980), DBE (1951, CBE 1947); 2 da of Lt-Col Thomas Robert Alexander Stannus, DSO, JP (d of wounds 1917) (Anglo-Irish Protestant family settled in Ireland ca 1618), and Elizabeth Graydon, *née* Smith (d 1961); *b* 6 June 1898; *m* 5 July 1935, Dr Arthur Blackall Connell; *Career* fndr: dir Royal Ballet 1931-63 (previously Sadler's Wells Ballet), Royal Ballet Sch; former ballerina; prima ballerina Covent Garden Royal Opera Season 1919 and 1928, with Diaghilev's Ballet Russes 1923-26; choreographer: Rake's Progress, Checkmate, Don Quixote; pres London Ballet Circle until 1981; Chev of the Legion of Honour (France) 1950; Royal Albert medal 1963, Erasmus prize Fndn Award 1974; *Books* Invitation to the Ballet (1937), Come Dance With Me (1957), Step By Step (1977); *Style*— Dame Ninette de Valois, CH, DBE; c/o Royal Ballet School, 153 Talgarth Rd, London W14 (☎ 081 748 6335/3123)

DE VASCONCELLOS, Josephina; MBE (1985); da of late H H de Vasconcellos, and Freda, *née* Coleman; *Educ* Royal Acad Schs; *m* 1930, Delmar Banner (d 1983); *Career* sculptor; works incl: High Altar and Statue (Varengeville Normandy) for Bristol Cathedral) 1948, Nat War Meml (St Bee's Sch) 1955, life size Mary and Child and design gp of 11 sculptures by 11 sculptors (St Paul's Cathedral) 1955, Flight into Egypt (for St Martin in the Fields, now in Cartmel Priory) 1958, Winged Victory Crucifix (Clewer Church and Canongate Kirk Edinburgh) 1964, life size Virgin and Child (Blackburn Cathedral) 1974, Reredos (Wordsworth Chapel) 1988, Lord Denning (portrait in bronze) 1969; fndr memb Soc of Portrait Sculptors, fndr Out Post Emmaus; projects: Adventure Base for Deprived Youngsters, The Harriet Tst; Hon DLitt Univ of Bradford 1977; FRBS, memb IPI; *Recreations* dance, musical composition; *Clubs* Reynolds; *Style*— Ms Josephina de Vasconcellos, MBE; The Old Wash House Studio, Peggy Hill, Ambleside, Cumbria LA22 9EG (☎ 05394 33794)

DE VERE, Anthony Charles Mayle; CMG (1986); *b* 23 Jan 1930; *Educ* St John's Coll Cambridge; *m* 1, 1959, Geraldine Gertrude Bolton (d 1980); m 2, 1986, Rosemary Edith Austin; *Career* Army Infantry Officer Malaya 1950-52; Colonial Serv (later HMOCS): joined provincial admin Tanganyika 1953, Kibondo 1953-56, i/c Kondoa-Irangi Devpt Scheme 1957-59, resident magistrate Singida 1959, dist cmmr Tunduru 1960-61 and Kigoma 1961-62, head of Local Govt Western Region 1962-63; HM Dip Serv: joined FO (later FCO) 1963, first sec Lusaka 1967-70, first sec NY 1972-74, cncllr Washington 1982-86, FCO 1986; *Recreations* riding, most things rural, sculpture, music, books; *Clubs* Athenaeum; *Style*— Anthony de Vere, Esq, CMG; Haddiscoe Hall, Norfolk NR14 6PE; 40 Ashburn Place, SW7 4JR

DE VESCI, 7 Viscount (I 1776); Thomas Eustace Vesey; 9 Bt (I 1698); also Baron Knapton (I 1750); s of 6 Viscount de Vesci (d 1983), by his w Susan Ann (d 1986), da of late Ronald Owen Lloyd Armstrong-Jones, MBE (and sis of Earl of Snowdon, *qv*); *b* 8 Oct 1955; *Educ* Eton, Univ of Oxford; *m* 5 Sept 1987, Sita-Maria Arabella, o da of Brian de Breffny (d 1989), of Castletown Cox, Co Kilkenny, and Maharaj Kumari Jyotsna Devi Dutt, da of late Maharajadhiraj Bahadur Uday Chand Mahtab, KCIE, of Burdwan; 1 s (Damian Brian John b 1985), 1 da (Cosima Frances b 1988); *Heir* s, Hon Damian Brian John Vesey b 1985; *Career* bloodstock agent, stud farmer; *Clubs* White's; *Style*— The Rt Hon the Viscount de Vesci; Abbey Leix, Co Leix, Ireland (☎ 0502 31101/31162)

DE VIBRAYE, Comtesse Honor Cecilia; *née* Paget; da of Adm Sir Alfred Paget, KCB, KCMG, DSO (2 s of Gen Lord Alfred Paget, CB, MP, 5 s of 1 Marquess of Anglesey), and Viti, da of Rt Hon Sir William Macgregor, GCMG, CB, PC; *b* 18 June 1907; *m* 1, 25 April 1928 (m dis 1930), Lt-Cdr Vivian Russell Salvia Bowlby, RN (ret), s of Col Robert Bowlby; m 2, 15 April 1936 (m dis 1946), Ralph Gledhill, of Portland, Oregon; m 3, 11 Nov 1952 (m dis 1957), Comte François Hurault de Vibraye (presumably a collateral of the Huraults, anciently (c 1479) Seigneurs of, among other fiefs, Cheverny (Loir-et-Cher), la Grange, and Vibraye, and descended from a Seigneur of St Denis-sur-Loire c 1340, a member of this family being cr Marquis by Louis XIII 1625, while the 6 Marquis had conferred on him again the title of Marquis (having already been cr a *Pair de France* (Peer) 1815) by Louis XVIII 1817); *Style*— Comtesse Honor de Vibraye

DE VIGIER, William Alphonse; Hon CBE (1978); s of Dr Wilhelm de Vigier (decd); *b* 22 Jan 1912; *Educ* La Chataigneraie Coppet Switzerland; *m* 1939, Betty Kendall; 2 da; *Career* former chm and fndr Acrow plc; memb: Bd Vigier Cement, BA 1973-78; chm: Acrow Corp of America, Acrow Canada, Acrow Zimbabwe, Acrow Botswana, Acrow SA, Vigierhof AG Switzerland Aust; kt Star of the North (Sweden), GC Order of Star of Africa; *Clubs* East India, Devonshire, The Metropolitan (NY); *Style*— William A de Vigier, Esq; Suite 33, St James's Square, London SW1Y 4JH; Sommerhaus, Solothurn, Switzerland

DE VILLIERS, Hon Alexander Charles; s and h of 3 Baron de Villiers; *b* 29 Dec 1940; *m* 1966; *Style*— The Hon Alexander de Villiers

DE VILLIERS, 3 Baron (UK 1910); Arthur Percy de Villiers; s of 2 Baron de Villiers (d 1934); *b* 17 Dec 1911; *Educ* Diocesan Coll SA, Magdalen Coll Oxford; *m* 9 Nov 1939 (m dis 1958), Edna Alexis Lovett, da of Dr A D MacKinnon, of Wilham Lake, BC, Canada; 1 s, 2 da; *Heir* s, Hon Alexander Charles de Villiers; *Career* called to the Bar Inner Temple 1938; Auckland Supreme Ct 1949; farmer, ret; *Style*— The Rt Hon the Lord de Villiers; PO Box 66, Kumeu, Auckland, New Zealand (☎ 010 64 9 411 8173)

DE VINK, Peter Henry John; s of Dr Ludovicus Petrus Hendricus Josephus De Vink (d 1987), and Catharina Louisa Maria, *née* Van Iersel; *b* 9 Oct 1940; *Educ* Univ of Edinburgh (BCom); *m* 27 May 1967, Jenipher Jean, da of Ranald Malcolm Murray-Lyon, MD (d 1969); 1 s (Patrick b 1971), 1 da (Natalie b 1970); *Career* Nat Serv 1961-63, cmmnd Dutch Army; dir Ivory & Sime 1975 (joined 1966, ptnr 1969), fndr Edinburgh Fin & Gen Holdings Ltd 1978; dir: Viking Resources Oil & Gas Ltd 1972-88, Viking Resources Tst plc 1972-88, Wereldhave NY 1973-90, Benline Offshore Contractors Ltd 1974, Edinburgh Fin & Gen Holdings Ltd 1978, Albany Oil & Gas Ltd 1987, Capital Copiers (Edinburgh) Ltd 1989-90; memb: Exec Scot Cncl (Devpt and Ind), Inst of Offshore Engrg at Heriot Watt Univ; *Recreations* shooting, golf, fishing; *Clubs* New (Edinburgh); *Style*— Peter H J De Vink, Esq; Cotswold, 46 Barnton Ave, Edinburgh EH4 6JL (☎ 031 336 2004); Edinburgh Financial & General Holdings Ltd, 7 Howe St, Edinburgh EH3 6TE (☎ 031 225 6661, fax 031 556 6651, car 083 956, portable 0836 702 335)

DE VOIL, Paul Walter; s of late Pfarrer Paul Vogel, and late Maria Christine, *née* Hurfeld; adopted s of late Very Rev Walter Harry de Voil, of Carnoustie; *b* 29 Sept 1929; *Educ* Fettes, Hertford Coll Oxford; *m* 26 July 1952, Sheila, da of late William George Danks, of Elsecar; 1 s (Nicholas b 1962), 1 da (Sally b 1960); *Career* Flying Offr RAF 1950-53; taxation conslt and lectr: Inland Revenue 1953-60, Ford Motor Co 1960-63, Herbert Smith & Co 1964-69, Baker Sutton & Co 1969-78, Lonrho plc 1978-87, Arthur Young (now Ernst & Young) 1987-89, Paul de Voil & Co 1990-; churchwarden and reader; Freeman: City of London 1969, Worshipful Co of Slrs 1969; memb: FTII 1964, Law Soc 1967; *Books* de Voil on Tax Appeals (1969), de Voil on Value Added Tax (1972); *Recreations* wine, music, statues, bright-eyed love; *Clubs* RAF; *Style*— Paul de Voil, Esq; Water Lane Barn, Denston, Newmarket, Suffolk (☎ 0440 820 181)

DE VRIES, Edo Barend Philip; s of Philip De Vries (d 1954), of Hilversum, Netherlands, and Ella, *née* Troetel (d 1980); *b* 13 Nov 1925; *Educ* Gymnasium Haganum, Prinses Beatrix Lyceum Glion Switzerland, Univ of Utrecht (LLM); *m* 1, 2 Dec 1949 (m dis 1961), Anne Eliza, da of Hary Hyman Tels (d 1940), of Rotterdam; 2 da (Harriet (Mrs Hermans) b 1950, Elizabeth (Baroness Van Utenhove) b 1954); m 2, Mary McHugh (d 1968); 1 s (Philip b 1966); m 3, 1969 (m dis 1988), Sonya Beasley; 1 da (Clare b 1969); *Career* voluntary WWII serv 1944-45; barr; mangr Int Legal Dept Royal Dutch-Shell Group Venezuela (various positions 1949-68); practicing memb Tax Bar; *Books* Taxation of Trades in the United Kingdom (1975); *Recreations* sailing, piano playing, DIY, music; *Clubs* RAF Yacht; *Style*— Edo de Vries, Esq; 1 Appleton Road, Catisfield, Fareham, Hampshire PO15 5QH (☎ 0329 47711, fax 0329 47706)

DE WAAL, Sir Henry (Constant Hendrik); KCB (1989, CB 1977), QC (1988); 3 s of late Hendrik de Waal; *b* 1 May 1931; *Educ* Tonbridge, Pembroke Coll Cambridge; *m* 1964, Julia Jessel; 2 s; *Career* called to the Bar Lincoln's Inn 1953, bencher 1989, Law Cmmn 1969-71, Parly Counsel 1971-81, second Parly counsel 1981-86, first Parly Counsel 1987; *Style*— Sir Henry Waal, KCB, QC; 62 Sussex St, London SW1

DE WAAL, The Rev Canon Hugo Ferdinand; s of Bernard Hendrik de Waal, of 4 Sherford Court, Taunton, and Albertine Felice, *née* Castens; *b* 16 March 1935; *Educ* Tonbridge, Pembroke Coll Cambridge (MA), Munster Univ Germany, Ridley Hall Cambridge; *m* 4 April 1961, Brigit Elizabeth Townsend, da of Rev John Massingberd-Mundy, of 79 Wolverton Rd, Newport Pagnell; 1 s (Bernard b 1967), 3 da (Katharine b 1962, Joanna b 1964, Penelope b 1966); *Career* curate St Martin's-in-the-Bull-Ring Birmingham 1960, chaplain Pembroke Coll Cambridge 1964, priest i/c Dry Drayton Diocese of Ely (rector 1967), anglican minister Ecumenical Church Bar Hill Cambs, vicar Blackpool Parish Church 1974, princ Ridley Hall 1978-; hon canon Ely Cathedral 1985; *Recreations* music, squash, fly fishing, walking; *Style*— The Rev Canon Hugo de Waal; The Principal's Lodge, Ridley Hall, Cambridge (☎ 0223 353 040)

DE WEND FENTON, (Michael Richard) West; o s of Maj William Ross de Wend Fenton, TD (d 1951), of Underbank Hall and Ebberston Hall, Yorkshire, and Margaret Constance Millicent, *née* Dunn (d 1965); descended from William Fenton (d 1743), who acquired Underbank by his marriage to Frances, o da and heiress of Capt Richard West, whose ancestors had held it since early 16 century, and whose descendant another William Fenton was murdered by robbers in Spain 1855, leaving the life interest of his estate to his four sisters, of whom the third, Jessey, m Maj James Douglas de Wend and conveyed the estate to her descendants (*see* Burke's Landed Gentry, 18 edn, vol III, 1972); *b* 2 Feb 1927; *Educ* Eton, RAC Cirencester; *m* 23 April 1955, Margaret Annora Mary, eldest da of Reginald Arthur Lygon (d 1976), of 3 Embankment Gardens, London SW3; 2 s (Jonathan Lygon West b 28 July 1958, Ross Matthew Mark b 9 July 1960), 2 da (Rosalie Marye Margaret b 21 June 1957, Clarissa Emily b 4 Sept 1962); *Career* served Scots Guards, KSLI and French Foreign Legion; farmer; pioneered minibus tours of Russia and Eastern Europe; memb Ebberston Church and Parish Cncls; *Recreations* shooting, travelling, teasing; *Style*— West de Wend Fenton, Esq; Ebberston Hall, Scarborough, N Yorkshire (☎ 0723 85516)

DE WICHFELD, Lady (Angela Alice) Maryel; *née* Drummond; da of 16 Earl of Perth (d 1951); *b* 5 March 1912; *m* 1, 14 June 1937 (m dis 1959), Count Alessandro Augusto Giovanni Giacinto Barnaba Manassei di Collestatte (d 1962); 2 s (John b 1937, Michael b 1947), 1 da (Francesco Montesi Righetti); m 2, 26 Sept 1960, Viggo Dmitri de Wichfeld; *Style*— The Lady Maryel de Wolfe de Wichfeld; 41 Lennox Gdns, London SW1

DE WOLFE, Earl Felix; s of Meyer De Wolfe (d 1976), and Regina, *née* Van Leer (d 1979); *b* 18 July 1914; *Educ* UCS; *m* 23 June 1967, Brenda, da of Bernard Duggleby (d 1980), of Hull; 2 da (Victoria b 1965, Caroline b 1968); *Career* WWII Flt-Lt RAF 1941-45; theatrical and literary agent 1938; chm Personal Mangrs Assoc 1970-77; *Style*— Earl De Wolfe, Esq; Flat C, 10 Hyde Park Mansions, London NW1 5BG (☎ 071 723 3508); Mansfield House, 376-9 Strand, London WC2R 0LN (☎ 071 379 5767, fax 836 0337)

DE ZULUETA, Hon Lady (Marie-Louise); *née* Hennessy; eldest da of 2 Baron Windlesham (d 1962); *b* 9 March 1930; *m* 14 Sept 1955, Sir Philip Francis de Zulueta (d 1989); 1 s (Francis b 1959), 1 da (Louise b 1956); *Style*— The Hon Lady de Zulueta; 3 Westminster Gdns, Marsham St, London SW1P 4JA

DE ZULUETA, Capt Paul Gerald; *see*: Torre Diaz, Count of

DEACON, Hon Mrs (Elizabeth Anne); *née* Vane; 2 da of 11 Baron Barnard, TD, JP, by his w, Lady Davina, *née* Cecil, da of 6 Marquess of Exeter; *b* 17 May 1956; *m* 1982, Glyn Deacon, eldest s of late A Deacon; 2 da (Jessica Anne b 1982, Laura Sophie b 1984); *Style*— The Hon Mrs Deacon; 91 The Green, Headlam, Gainford, Darlington, Durham DL2 3HA

DEAKIN, Maj-Gen Cecil Martin Fothergill; CB (1961), CBE (1956); s of William R Deakin; *b* 20 Dec 1910; *Educ* Winchester; *m* 1934, Evelyn Mary Frances (d 1984), da of Sir Arthur Grant, 10 Bt of Monymusk, CBE, DSO (d 1931); 1 s, 1 da; *Career* cmmnd Grenadier Gds 1931, served WWII; Cdr: 2 Bn Grenadier Gds 1945-46, 1 Bn 1947-50, 32 Gds Bde 1953-55, 29 Inf Bde 1955-57, Suez; BGS 1957-59, dir of Mil Trg 1959, GOC 56 London Div (TA) 1960, dir TA 1960-62, Cmdt Jt Servs Staff Coll 1962-65, ret 1965; dir Mental Health Fndn 1966-90, pres Grenadier Gds' Assoc 1966-82; *Clubs* Royal Yacht Sqdn; *Style*— Maj-Gen Cecil Deakin, CB, CBE; Lettre Cottage, Killearn, Stirlingshire G63 9LE

DEAKIN, John; s of Keith John Deakin, of Bedford, and Kathleen Irene, *née* Stenning; *b* 4 March 1965; *Educ* Sharnbrook Sch Beds, Bedford Coll of Higher Educn, South Notts Coll West Bridgford; *Career* rowing cox; began coxing Star Club Bedford 1978-79, coxed fastest club eight from the provinces 1982-84, joined Notts Co Rowing Assoc 1986-, rep GB in lightweight eights and placed fifth at World Championships Copenhagen 1987, won lightweight competitions 1987 (Mannheim, Amsterdam, Nottingham and Bronze at Lucerne), won lightweights 1989 (Nottingham), Ladies Plate Henley in re-row against Harvard in record time, competitions won 1990 (Thames Cup Henley Royal Regatta, Silver medal Lucerne, Bronze medal World Championships Lake Barrington Tas); course record 6mins 11secs Ladies Plate Henley 1989, lightweight eight record 5mins 40secs Lucerne Int Regatta, Br lightweight eight record 5mins 37secs World Championships 1990; asst contracts engr 1984-86, rowing coach and casual work 1986-88, sales rep A R Wilson Nottingham 1989- (delivery driver 1988-89); ARA Instructors award for coaching 1988; *Recreations* theatre, cinema, arts and crafts, collecting books; *Style*— John Deakin, Esq; 39 Exchange Rd, West Bridgford, Nottingham; Nottinghamshire County Rowing Association, National Watersports Centre, Holme Pierrepont, Nottingham (☎ 0602 821212)

DEAKIN, Michael; s of Sir William Deakin, and Margaret Beatson Bell; *b* 21 Feb 1939; *Educ* Bryanston Universite d'Aix Marseilles, Emmanuel Coll Cambridge (MA); *Career* writer, documentary and film maker; fndr ptnr Editions Alecto (fine art publishers) 1960-64, prodr BBC Radio Current Affairs Dept 1964-68, prodr then editor Documentory Unit Yorkshire TV 1968-81; prodns incl: Out of Shadow into the Sun - The Giger, Struggle for China, Whicker's World - Way Out West, Johnny Go Home (Br Acad award, 1976), David Frost's Global Village, The Frost Interview - The Shah, Act of Betrayal 1987, Not a Penny More, Not a Penny Less 1989, Secret Weapon 1990; fndr memb TV-am Breakfast Time Consortium 1980; TV-am: dir of progs 1982-84, memb Bd 1984-85, conslt 1984-87; dir Griffin Productions Ltd 1985-, sr vice pres Paramount/Revcom 1987; *Books* Restif de la Bretonne - Les Nuits de Paris (translated with Nicholas Deakin, 1968), Gaetano Donizetti (1968), Tom Grattan's War (1970), The Children on the Hill (1972, 9 edn 1982), Johnny Go Home (with John Willis, 1976), The Arab Experience (with Antony Thomas, 1975, 2 edn 1976), Flame in the Desert (1976), I Could Have Kicked Myself (with David Frost, 1982), Who Wants to be Millionaire (with David Frost, 1983), If You'll Believe That You'll Believe

Anything... (1986); *Recreations* motorcyling, eating, music, dalmations; *Clubs* BAFTA; *Style—* Micheal Deakin, Esq; Paramount/Revlom, Balfour House, 54 Gt Tichfield St, London W1 2LP (☎ 071 636 5066, fax 0714 436 3232)

DEAKIN, Hon Mrs (Rose Albinia); *née* Donaldson; er da of Baron Donaldson of Kingsbridge, OBE (Life Peer); *b* 4 Nov 1937; *m* 16 Dec 1961, Nicholas Deakin, s of Sir William Deakin, DSO, *qv*; 1 s, 2 da; *Style—* The Hon Mrs Deakin; 126 Leighton Rd, London NW5

DEAKIN, Sir (Frederick) William Dampier; DSO (1943); s of Albert Witney Deakin, of Aldbury, Tring, Herts; *b* 3 July 1913; *Educ* Westminster Sch, Ch Ch Oxford; *m* 1, 1935 (m dis 1940), Margaret Ogilvy, da of Sir Nicholas Beatson Bell, KCSI, KCIE (d 1936); 2 s; m 2, 1943, Livia Stela, da of Liviu Nasta, of Bucharest; *Career* fell and tutor Wadham Coll Oxford 1936-49, first sec HM Embassy Belgrade 1945-46, res fell Wadham Coll 1949, warden St Antony's Coll Oxford 1950-68, ret; hon fell: Wadham Coll 1961, St Antony's Coll 1969; hon student Ch Ch Oxford 1979; Grosse Verdienstkreuz 1958, Chev de la Légion d'Honneur 1953; Hon FBA 1981; kt 1975; *Clubs* Beefsteak, White's, Brooks's; *Style—* Sir William Deakin, DSO; 83330 Le Beausset, Le Castellet, Var, France

DEAKINS, Eric Petro; s of Edward Deakins (d 1970), of 19 Strode Rd, London, and Gladys Frances, *née* Townsend (d 1964); *b* 7 Oct 1932; *Educ* Tottenham GS, LSE (BA); *Career* Nat Serv 2 Lt RASC 1953-55; memb Tottenham Borough Cncl 1958-61 and 1962-63; MP (Lab): West Walthamstow 1970-74, Walthamstow 1974-87; Parly under sec: Trade 1974-76, Health & Social Security 1976-79; divnl gen mangr FMC Ltd 1969-70 (exec 1959-69), political and trade conslt 1987-, dir Consumer Watch 1988-; memb Cncl: World Devpt Movement 1980-, Population Concern 1983-; *Books* A Faith to Fight For (1964), You and Your MP (1987), What Future for Labour? (1988); *Recreations* writing, cinema, squash, football; *Style—* Eric Deakins, Esq; 36 Murray Mews, London NW1 9RJ (☎ 071 267 6196)

DEAKINS, Peter John; s of William Amos Deakins (d 1955), and Ethel Sarah, *née* Pigeon (d 1975); *b* 15 March 1934; *Educ* Torquay GS; *m* 3 June 1966, Wendy Patricia, da of Henry Martin Finn (d 1946); 3 s (Sasha b 1967 d 1969, St John b 1968, Guy b 1970); *Career* memb Conservation and Preservation Gp for: Albert Bridge 1968, Addington Sq 1968, Battersea Sq 1970, Clapham Junction 1971; fndr memb Intentionally Moderate Size Housing Assoc 1968, memb Bd S London Family Housing Assoc 1978-; ARIBA; *Books* South London Parks, Gardens and Open Spaces; *Recreations* sailing, walking, travel; *Style—* Peter J Deakins, Esq; 34 Albany Mansions, Albert Brige Rd, London SW11 4PG (☎ 071 223 5999); Studio 57, 140 Battersea Park Rd, London SW11 (☎ 071 223 5999)

DEALTRY, Prof (Thomas) Richard; s of George Raymond Dealtry (d 1966), of York, and Edith, *née* Gardener (d 1990); *b* 24 Nov 1936; *Educ* Cranfield Inst of Advanced Technol (MBA); *m* 17 Sept 1963 (m dis 1982), Pauline Sedgwick; 1 s (Roger Paul b 7 June 1968), 1 da (Claire Elizabeth b 1 Nov 1972); *Career* Nat Serv 1959-61, Capt RAEC 1960; under sec Scottish Office and Industl Advsr for Scotland 1977-78, regnl dir and conslt industl advsr Gulf Orgn for Industl Consulting Arabian Gulf Territories Orgn 1978-82, business and mgmnt devpt conslt 1982-, company broker and prof in strategic mgmnt at Int Mgmnt Centre Buckingham 1982-; CEng, MIMIE, FIMC, MCIM; *Recreations* golf, rugby union; *Style—* Prof Richard Dealtry; 43 Huntstanton Ave, Harbourne, Birmingham B17 8SX (☎ 021 429 8995, fax 021 420 3498)

DEAN, Beryl (Mrs Phillips); MBE (1975); da of Herbert Charles Dean (d 1950), of Bromley, Kent, and Marion, *née* Petter (d 1946); *b* 2 Aug 1911; *Educ* Bromley HS, Royal Sch of Needlework, Bromley Sch of Art, RCA; *m* 22 June 1974, Wilfrid Maurice Phillips, s of Capt William George Phillips (d 1968), of Northampton; *Career* actg head Eastbourne Sch of Art 1939-45, designer and maker of ballet costumes 1939-46, tutor Hammersmith Coll of Art 1947-66, freelance ecclesiastical designer and embroiderer 1956-89; designs: Chelmsford Cathedral 1954-86 (red frontal, vestments, goldbanner, large hanging), Emmanuel Coll Cambridge 1961 (altar frontal), Guildford Cathedral 1965 (cope, mitre), Canterbury Cathedral 1966- (cope, mitre, copes for Dean and Chapter), St George's Chapel Windsor Castle 1970-75 (five large panels), Resurrection cope and mitre 1980, large panel Twelfth Night 1987; lectr Stanhope Inst of Adult Educn 1964-78; examples of work exhibited in GB and USA, Royal exhibitioner RCA, organiser Exhibition Br Ecclesiastical Embroidery St Paul's Cathedral Crypt 1990; FSDC, ARCA; *Books* Ecclesiastical Embroidery (1958), Church Needlework (1961), Ideas for Church Embroidery (1968), Creative Appliqué (1970), Embroidery in Religion and Ceremonial (1981), Church Embroidery (1982), Church Needlework (new edn, 1990); *Recreations* gardening; *Style—* Beryl Dean, MBE; 59 Thornhill Square, London N1 1BE (☎ 071 607 2572)

DEAN, Brenda; da of Hugh Dean, of 35 Consett Ave, Thornton, Cleveleys, Lancs; *b* 29 April 1945; *Educ* St Andrews Eccles, Stretford GS; *Career* admin sec Manchester Branch SOGAT 1959-71 (asst branch sec 1971, sec 1976), pres SOGAT 1983 (gen sec 1985); memb: Women's Nat Cmmn (co chm 1975-78), Nat Econ Devpt Cncl 1985-, BBC Gen Advsy Cncl 1985-, TUC Gen Cncl 1985-, TUC Econ Ctee 1987-; Hon MA Univ of Salford 1986; *Recreations* reading, cooking, sailing; *Style—* Ms Brenda Dean; SOGAT House, 274-288 London Road, Hadleigh, Benfleet, Essex SS7 2DE (☎ 0702 554111)

DEAN, Brian; s of Thomas Brown Dean (d 1959), of Jarrow, and Florence, *née* Shaw; *b* 10 July 1937; *Educ* Dame Allan's Boys Sch Newcastle, Univ of Edinburgh (MB ChB), Univ of Liverpool (MCh); *m* 24 March 1962, (Catherine) Margaret, da of Thomas Day McNeill Scrimgeour, MBE (d 1969), of Burntisland Fife; 3 da (Rosalyn Gresham b 1962, Alison b 1966, Joanna b 1970); *Career* conslt surgn Fife Orthopaedic Serv 1970-; memb Aberdeen Angling Club (pres 1980-81), memb Rotary Club (pres of Dunfermline 1980-81), pres Fife Branch BMA 1982-83; memb: RCSEd, BMA, FRCS, fell BOA; *Recreations* game fishing, yachting, modelling; *Style—* Brian Dean, Esq; Dunfermline and West Fife Hospital, Reid Street, Dunfermline, Fife (☎ 0383 737777)

DEAN, Ian Hall; s of George William Dean (d 1972) and Irene Violet Alice, *née* Hall (d 1990); *b* 19 Sept 1944; *Educ* Kilburn GS, Eastbourne GS; *m* 1, 3 Sept 1966, Jacqueline Mary, da of Alan Maurice Rayne, of 3 Spencer Rd, Eastbourne, E Sussex; 2 da (Carole b 1969, Catherine b 1971); m 2, 2 Sept 1976, Diane, da of Leslie Ambrose Nicol, of 192 Seven Sisters Road, Eastbourne, E Sussex; 1 s (Richard b 1978); *Career* deputy underwriter S C Lloyd Haine & Co 1974 (joined 1963, claims settler 1970), dep chm and dir of reinsurance Excess Insurance Group 1980-81 (dir of underwriting 1979, dep 1977, mangr 1974, underwriter 1974), chm Sphere Drake Insurance Group plc 1982-; directorships incl: Arpel Trimark Agencies Ltd, Dai Tokyo Insur (UK) Ltd, Sphere Drake Insurance plc and subsidiaries; *Recreations* walking, tennis, reading; *Style—* Ian H Dean, Esq; Winster House, Forest Rd, Forest Row, East Sussex RH18 5NA (☎ 0342 822472); Sphere Drake Insurance Group plc, 52-54 Leadenhall St, London EC3A 2BJ (☎ 071 480 7340, fax 071 481 3828, telex 935015, 0860 712530)

DEAN, James Patrick; s of Sir Patrick Henry Dean, GCMG, of London, and Patricia Wallace, *née* Jackson; *b* 30 Jan 1949; *Educ* Rugby; *m* 31 July 1982, Jill Suzanne; *Career* cmmnd Royal Green Jackets 1968; called to the Bar Lincoln's Inn 1977; *Recreations* walking, swimming; *Clubs* Brooks's; *Style—* James Dean, Esq; Flat 2, 1 Montagu Place, London W1H 1RG (☎ 071 935 6707); 1 Verulam Buildings, Gray's Inn, London WC1R 5LQ (☎ 071 242 7646)

DEAN, Hon Mrs (Jenefer); *née* Mills; da of 5 Baron Hillingdon (by 1 m); *b* 6 April 1935; *m* 7 April 1962, His Honour Judge Joseph Jolyon Dean, *qv*, s of Basil Dean, CBE (d 1978); 1 s (Ptolemy Hugo b 1967), 2 da (Antigone Lucy b 1963, Tacita Charlotte b 1965); *Career* mangr Ashford Citizens Advice Bureau; *Style—* The Hon Mrs Joseph Dean; The Hall, West Brabourne, Ashford, Kent

DEAN, John Ronald; s of Canon Desmond Keable Dean, and Constance Bertha, *née* Penfold; *b* 27 May 1935; *Educ* William Hulme's GS Manchester, Battersea GS; *m* 18 July 1959, Yvonne Mavis Gale, da of Arthur Frederick Homer; 1 s (Jonathan Stephen Homer b 21 March 1963), 1 da (Nicola Yvette Clare (Mrs Jeynes) b 16 Feb 1966); *Career* accountant Hovis McDougall 1953-57, ptnr KPMG Peat Marwick McLintock 1979- (articled clerk 1957-62); ACIS 1960, FCA 1974 (ACA 1963); *Recreations* choral singing, theatre, mountain walking; *Style—* John Dean, Esq; KPMG Peat Marwick McLintock, 1 Puddle Dock, Blackfriars, London EC4V 3PD (☎ 071 236 8000 ext 6365, fax 071 583 1938)

DEAN, His Hon Joseph Jolyon; s of Basil Dean, CBE (d 1978), and Esther Bagger, *née* Van Gruisen, formerly Dean (d 1983); *b* 26 April 1921; *Educ* Harrow, Univ of Oxford (MA); *m* 7 April 1962, Hon Jenefer, *née* Mills, *qv*, da of 5 Baron Hillingdon, MC (d 1982), of the Tod House, Seal, Kent; 1 s, 2 da; *Career* Mil Serv RA 1941-46, Capt 51 Highland Div, Western Desert, Sicily, Normandy, Holland, Germany; barr 1947, bencher Middle Temple 1972, circuit judge 1976 (ret 1987); chm E Ashford Rural Tst 1988; *Books* Hatred Ridicule or Contempt, A Book of Libel Cases (1953); *Clubs* Army and Navy; *Style—* His Hon Joseph Dean; The Hall, West Brabourne, Ashford, Kent

DEAN, (Wilfred) Martin Vernon; s of Basil Dean, CBE (d 1978), of London, and Esther Bagger, *née* Van Gruisen (d 1983); *b* 18 March 1920; *Educ* Harrow, Brasenose Coll Oxford (MA); *m* 20 April 1949, Nancy Clare, da of Joseph Victor Lynch, OBE (d 1962); 3 s (Anthony b and d 1955, Christopher b and d 1957, John b 1963), 4 da (Patricia b 1950, Rosemary b 1952, d 1956, Theresa b 1954, Mia b 1958); *Career* RE 1940-45, cmmnd 1941, attached KGVO Bengal Sappers & Miners 1942-45, Capt 1944; admitted slr 1948, conslt Blount Petre & Co (slrs) 1988- (ptnr 1951-87); memb Law Soc 1948; *Recreations* gardening, photography, bridge; *Clubs* Garrick; *Style—* Martin Dean, Esq; 23 St Petersburgh Place, London W2 4LA (☎ 071 229 5505)

DEAN, Sir Patrick Henry; GCMG (1963, KCMG 1957, CMG 1947); s of Prof Henry Roy Dean (d 1961); *b* 16 March 1909; *Educ* Rugby, Gonville and Caius Coll Cambridge; *m* 1947, Patricia Wallace, da of T Frame Jackson; 2 s; *Career* barr 1934, asst legal advsr FO 1939-45, head German Political Dept FO 1946-50, min Rome 1950-51, sr civilian instr IDC 1952-53, asst under sec FO 1953-56, dep under sec 1956-60, perm UK rep to UN 1960-64, ambass advsr Washington 1965-69, memb Dept Ctee to examine operation Section 2 Official Secrets Act 1971; chm Cambridge Petroleum Royalties 1975-82; dir: Ingersoll-Rand Holdings 1971-81, Amex Bank 1976-81 (int advsr American Express 1969-); conslt Taylor Woodrow 1986- (dir 1969-84); chm Governing Body Rugby Sch 1972-84, vice pres English-Speaking Union 1983-(chm 1973-83) tstee Economist 1973-90; hon fell: Gonville and Caius Cambridge, Clare Coll Cambridge (fell 1932-35); hon bencher Lincoln's Inn 1965; Hon LLD: Univ of Columbia, William and Mary Coll and additional US Univs; KStJ; *Recreations* walking; *Clubs* Brooks's; *Style—* Sir Patrick Dean, GCMG; 5 Bentinck Mansions, Bentinck St, London W1 (☎ 071 935 0881)

DEAN, Dr Paul; CB (1981); s of Sydney Dean (d 1969), and Rachel, *née* Kurshirsky; *b* 23 Jan 1933; *Educ* Hackney Downs GS, QMC London (BSc, PhD); *m* 10 Oct 1961, Sheila Valerie, da of Reuben Gamse (d 1973); 1 s (Grahame Clive b 29 Aug 1965), 1 da (Andrea Rachel b 14 Sept 1962); *Career* Nat Physics Laboratory: theoretical physicist 1955-66, head Central Computer Unit 1967, supt Div Quantum Metrology 1969-74, dep dir 1984-76, dir 1977-90; under sec Dept of Indust 1976-77 (pt/t head Div 1979-81); writer and advsr; memb Int Ctee Weights and Measures 1985-90; chm: Conslt Ctee on Ionizing Radiation 1987-90; pres Br Measurement and Testing Assoc 1990; chm EUROMET 1988-90, fell QMC 1984 (then QM and Westfield Coll); FInstP 1970, FIMA 1969; *Recreations* chess, music, computing, bridge, mathematics, astronomy; *Style—* Dr Paul Dean, CB; Bushy House, Teddington, Middlesex TW11 0EB

DEAN, Sir (Arthur) Paul; MP (C) Woodspring 1983-; s of Arthur Dean; *b* 14 Sept 1924; *Educ* Ellesmere Coll, Exeter Coll Oxford (MA, BLitt); *m* 1, 1957, Doris (d 1979), da of Frank Webb, of Sussex; m 2, 1980, Peggy, *née* Parker; *Career* WWII Capt Welsh Gds, ADC to Cdr 1 Corps BAOR; former farmer; CRD 1957, resident tutor Swinton Cons Coll 1958-62, asst dir CRD 1962-64, Parly candidate (C) Pontefract 1962, MP (C) N Somerset 1964-83, front bench oppn spokesman Health and Social Security 1969-70, Parly under-sec DHSS 1970-74, chm Cons Health and Social Security Ctee 1979-82; memb: Commons Servs Select Ctee 1979-82, Exec Ctee Cwlth Parly Assoc UK Branch 1975-, Commons Chm's Panel 1979-82; second dep chm House of Commons and dep chm Ways and Means 1982-87, first dep chm Ways and Means and dep speaker 1987-; formerly: memb Church in Wales Governing Body, govr BUPA, chm Cons Watch-Dog Gp for Self-Employed; dir: Charterhouse Pensions, Watney Mann and Truman Hldgs; govr Cwlth Inst 1981-89, pres Oxford Univ Cons Assoc; kt 1985; *Clubs* Oxford Carlton (pres); *Style—* Sir Paul Dean, MP; House of Commons, London SW1A 0AA

DEAN, Peter Henry; s of Alan Walduck Dean, and Gertrude, *née* Bürger; *b* 24 July 1939; *Educ* Rugby, Univ of London (LLB); *m* 31 July 1965, Linda Louise, da of The Rev William Edward Keating; 1 da (Amanda b 1967); *Career* admitted slr 1962; RTZ Corp plc: joined 1966, sec 1972-74, dir 1974-85; freelance business conslt 1985-; non-exec dir: Assoc Br Ports Holdings plc 1980-, Liberty Life Assurance Co Ltd 1986-; dep chm Monopolies and Mergers Cmmn 1990- (memb 1982-), chm Cncl of Mgmnt Highgate Counselling Centre 1991- (memb 1985-); chm English Baroque Choir 1985-89; memb Law Soc; *Recreations* music (especially choral singing), skiing; *Clubs* Ski Club of GB, Kandahar; *Style—* Peter Dean, Esq; 52 Lanchester Road, Highgate, London N6 4TA (☎ 081 883 5417)

DEAN, Raymond Frank (Ray); s of Mario Frank Dean (d 1957), and Leah Marsh Shannon; *b* 29 July 1936; *Educ* Britannia HS Vancouver, Guildford Coll of Art Surrey; *m* 26 Oct 1971, Anne Elisabeth, da of Capt Stanley Young, RN (d 1989); *Career* engine room aprentice RCN 1953-56; draughtsman Alcan Canada 1956-59 (chief shop steward Utd Steelworkers of America); photographer 1961-; assignments incl: still photography for Oscar winning documentary Dylan Thomas by Jack Howells, first exhibition Wig & Pen Club, work published by Br Jl of Photography and Photography Magazine; theatre and ballet photography incl: The Royal Opera House, Nureyev, Fonteyn, Marcel Marceau, Le Coq Mime, Comedie Francaise; design work for Derek Jarman incl: The Devils, Jazz Calendar; jt fndr Job Magazine 1973-84; Int industl photographer; clients incl: Shell International, Elf Oil, Buitoni, Honeywell, Design Magazine, British Steel, Coutts Bank, Hill Samuel, Lloyd's, Alcan, Michelin, ICI; *Recreations* France and Scotland, eating, drinking, taking pictures; *Style—* Ray Dean, Esq; 27 Fishers Lane, Chiswick, London W4 1RX; Barmollach House, Grogport, nr Carradale, Mull of Kintyre; Ray Dean Photography, 27 Fishers Lane, Chiswick,

London W4 1RX (☎ 081 994 0779)

DEAN, (Cecil) Roy; s of Arthur Dean (d 1989), of Herts, and Flora Clare Dean (d 1980); *b* 18 Feb 1927; *Educ* Watford GS, London Coll of Printing and Graphic Arts (dip), Coll for the Distributive Trades (MIPR); *m* 1954, Heather, da of Sydney Sturtridge (d 1981); 3 s (Jonathan, Nicholas, Charles); *Career* RAF India and Pakistan 1945-48, COI 1948-58; HM Dip Serv: Colombo 1958-62, Vancouver 1962-64, Lagos 1964-68, FCO 1968-71 and 1973-76, Houston 1971-73, dir Arms Control and Disarmament Res Unit 1976-83, dep Br high cmmnr Accra Ghana 1983-86, ret; memb UN Sec-Gen's Expert Gp on Disarmament Insts 1980-81; tstee Urbanaid 1986; writer and broadcaster, author of numerous pamphlets and articles on int affrs, BBC radio series The Poetry of Popular Song; *Recreations* crosswords (Times Nat Champion 1970 and 1979), light verse, songwriting; *Style—* Roy Dean, Esq; 14 Blyth Rd, Bromley, Kent BR1 3RX (☎ 081 460 8159)

DEAN, Hon Mrs (Thalia Mary); *née* Shaw; da of late 2 Baron Craigmyle; *b* 7 Aug 1918; *m* 4 Sept 1939, Winton Basil Dean, s of Basil Dean, CBE (d 1978); 1 s, 2 da (both decd), 1 adopted da; *Style—* The Hon Mrs Dean; Hambledon Hurst, Godalming, Surrey

DEAN, Winton Basil; s of Basil Herbert Dean, CBE (d 1978), of London, formerly of Little Easton Manor, Dunmow, Essex, and Esther, *née* Van Gruisen (d 1983); *b* 18 March 1916; *Educ* Harrow, King's Coll Cambridge (MA); *m* 4 Sept 1939, Hon Thalia Mary Shaw, da of 2 Baron Craigmyle (d 1944); 1 s (Stephen b 1946), 2 da (Brigid b 1943, d 1945, Diana b and d 1948), 1 adopted da (Diana b 1955); *Career* Admlty (Naval Intelligence) 1944-45; memb: Music Panel Arts Cncl 1957-60, Ctee Handel Opera Soc 1955-60, Cncl Royal Musical Assoc 1965- (vice pres 1970-); Ernest Bloch prof of music 1965-66, Regent's lecturer Univ of California Berkeley 1977, Matthew Matthew Vassar lecturer Vassar Coll Poughkeepsie NY 1979; memb Mgmnt Ctee Halle Handel Soc 1979-; kuratorium Göttingen Handel Festival 1981-; translated libretto of Weber's opera Abu Hassan (performed Cambridge Theatre 1938), ed (with Sarah Fuller) Handel's opera Julius Caesar (performed Birmi 1977); Hon RAM 1971; FBA 1975; corresponding memb American Musicological Soc 1989; *Books* The Frogs of Aristophanes (translation of songs and choruses to music by Walter Leigh, 1937), Bizet (1948, 3 revised edn 1975), Shakespeare and Opera (in Shakespeare and Music, 1964), Handel and The Opera Seria (1969), Beethoven and Opera (in The Beethoven Companion, 1971), Handel, Three Ornamented Arias (ed, 1976), The Rise of Romantic Opera (jt ed with E J Dent, 1976), The New Grove Handel (1982), Handel's Operas 1704-1726 (with J M Knapp, 1987), Essays on Opera (1990), French Opera, Italian Opera and German Opera in the Age of Beethoven 1790-1830 (in New Oxford History of Music vol VIII, 1982); *Recreations* shooting, naval history; *Clubs* English Speaking Union; *Style—* Winton Dean, Esq; Hambledon Hurst, Godalming, Surrey GU8 4HF (☎ 0428 682644)

DEAN OF BESWICK, Baron (Life Peer UK 1983), of West Leeds in the Co of West Yorks; Joseph Jabez Dean; s of John and Annie Dean, of Manchester; *b* 3 June 1922; *m* 1945, Helen, da of Charles Hill; issue; *Career* MP (Lab) Leeds W 1974-83; *Style—* The Rt Hon Lord Dean of Beswick; House of Lords, London SW1

DEANE, John Woodforde; s of Lt-Col Michael Wallace Blencowe Deane (d 1973), and Eileen Haslewood, *née* McNish Porter (d 1968); *b* 2 Aug 1929; *Educ* Winchester; *m* 8 Jan 1966, Gillian Merriman, da of Humphrey Morgan Hughes (d 1965); 2 s (Nicholas b 1967, Michael b 1972), 2 da (Lucy b 1968, Rebecca b 1969); *Career* RMC Sandhurst 1947-48, Lancs Fusiliers and Royal Regt Fusiliers 1949-71; sr princ DOE 1981-85 (princ 1971-81), Property Servs Agency 1985-89, Bursar Micklefield Sch Seaford; memb: New Sussex Opera, E Sussex Chorale; chm Ripe and Chalvington Flower Show Ctee; *Recreations* golf, gardening, chess, cycling, bell ringing, choral singing; *Clubs* Army and Navy; *Style—* John Deane, Esq; Lovers' Farmhouse, Chalvington, nr Hailsham, E Sussex (☎ 032 811 207); Micklefield School, Sutton Avenue, Seaford, E Sussex (☎ 0323 892457)

DEANE, Hon Robert Fitzmaurice; s and h of 8 Baron Muskerry; *b* 26 March 1948; *Educ* Sandford Park Sch Dublin, Trinity Coll Dublin; *Style—* The Hon Robert Deane; 15 Glenroy Rd, Manor Gardens, 4001 Durban, S Africa

DEANS, Rodger William; CB (1977); s of Andrew Deans, and Elizabeth Deans; *b* 21 Dec 1917; *Educ* Perth Acad, Univ of Edinburgh; *m* 1943, Joan Radley; 1 s, 1 da; *Career* WWII Maj RA and REME, mil prosecutor Palestine 1945-46; Sec of State for Scotland and HM Treasy Scotland: legal asst 1947-50 sr legal asst SO 1951-62, asst slr 1962-71, slr 1971-80; conslt ed Green & Son Edinburgh 1981-82, sr chm Supplementary Benefit Appeal Tbnls 1982-84, regnl chm (Scotland) Social Security Appeal Tbnls and Med Appeal Tbn (1984-90; *Recreations* hill walking, gardening; *Clubs* Scottish Arts (Edinburgh), Univ of Edinburgh Staff; *Style—* Rodger Deans, Esq, CB; 25 Grange Rd, Edinburgh 9 (☎ 031 667 1893)

DEAR, Geoffrey James; QPM (1982), DL (1985); s of Cecil William Dear, and Violet Mildred, *née* Mackney; *b* 20 Sept 1937; *Educ* Fletton GS, UCL (LLB); *m* 1958, Judith Ann, da of J W Stocker (d 1972), of Peterborough; 1 s (Simon b 1963), 2 da (Catherine b 1961, Fiona b 1966); *Career* joined Peterborough Combined Police after cadet serv 1956, inspr to Supt Mid Anglia Constabulary 1965-72, asst chief constable Nottinghamshire Constabulary 1972, dep asst cmmnr Met Police 1980-81, asst cmmr Met Police 1981-85, chief constable West Midlands Police 1985-90, HM inspr of constabulary 1990-; fell UCL 1990; FRSA 1989; *Recreations* field sports, rugby football, fell walking, music, reading; *Clubs* Naval and Military; *Style—* Geoffrey Dear, Esq, QPM, DL; Government Buildings, Whittington Rd, Worcester WR5 2PA (☎ 0905 359 564)

DEAR, Nick; s of Peter Dear, of Portsmouth, and Joan, *née* Loud; *b* 11 June 1955; *Educ* Taunton's Coll Southampton, Univ of Essex (BA); *partner*, Penny, da of Fred Downie, of Townsville, Aust; 1 s (Finnegan Downie Dear b 1 April 1990); *Career* playwright in residence Royal Exchange Theatre Manchester 1987-88; plays: Temptation (1984), The Art of Success (1986, John Whiting award 1987), Pure Science (1986), A Family Affair (1988), In the Ruins (1989), The Last Days of Don Juan (1990); Pye Radio award (for Matter Permitted) 1981; memb Writers' Guild of GB; *Recreations* music; Rosica Colin Ltd, 1 Clareville Grove Mews, London, SW7 5AH (☎ 071 370 1080, fax 071 244 6441)

DEAR, Simon James Kirksey; s of Geoffrey James Dear, and Judith Ann Dear; *b* 30 Jan 1963; *Educ* Southwell Minster GS Southwell Notts; *m* 26 Sept 1987, Helen Margaret Frances, da of Bernard Ensor Jay; 1 s (Thomas James Kirksey b 16 Nov 1990); *Career* Rugby Union player Rosslyn Park FC; clubs: Chingford RFC 1981-82, Richmond FC 1982-84, Metropolitan Police RFC 1984-88, Rosslyn Park FC 1988-; rep: Middx, London Division, Br Police, Br Police and Combined Servs, Penguins, Public Sch Wanderers, Eng B (debut v Namibia 1990); toured: USA, Canada, Aust, NZ, Spain, Portugal, France, Germany, Holland, Belgium, Italy; *Recreations* windsurfing, away trips; *Style—* Simon Dear, Esq; Rosslyn Park FC, Upper Richmond Road, Roehampton, London SW15 (☎ 081 876 1879)

DEARDEN, James; s of Basil Dearden; *b* 1949; *Educ* New Coll Oxford (BA); *Career* started as prodn asst in film indust 1967, cutting room trainee rising to film editor in commercials and documentaries 1971-76; writer prodr and dir: The Contraption 1978 (first short film), Diversion (Gold plaque Chicago Film Festival 1980); writer and dir: The Cold Room 1983 (Special Jury prize Oxford Film Festival 1984), Pascali's Island 1987 (selected as an offical Br entry 1988 Cannes Film Festival), A Kiss Before Dying 1991; writer of several screenplays incl Fatal Attraction (Academy Award nomination); *Style—* James Dearden, Esq; c/o Duncan Heath/ICM, 162 Wardour St, London W1

DEARDEN, Dr (Norman) Mark; s of Norman Gerald Dearden, of Droitwich, and Mary Isobel Emily, *née* Mosby; *b* 30 June 1953; *Educ* Lord William's GS, Univ of Leeds (BSc, MB ChB); *m* 6 Sept 1986, Margaret Ruth, da of Eric Burkinshaw; 2 s (Paul b 1988, Richard b 1989); *Career* jr doctor Leeds 1977-81, lectr in anaesthetics Univ of Leeds 1981-84, conslt neuro anaesthetist and pt/t sr lectr in anaesthetics Edinburgh 1985-; contrib: Lancet, Br Jl of Anaesthesia, Br Jl of Hospital Medicine, Jl of Neurosurgery; Brit rep of the Intensive Care Gp of The World Fedn of Neurology; memb: Yorks Soc of Anaesthetists 1980, Intensive Care Soc 1983, Scottish Soc of Anaesthetists 1985, E of Scotland Soc of Anaesthetists 1985, World Fedn of Neurologists 1988, Euro Intensive Care Soc 1989; *Books* Brain Protection (1983), The Clinical Use of Hypnotic Drugs in Head Injury (contrib); *Recreations* horticulture, DIY; *Style—* Dr Mark Dearden; 11 East Camus Place, Fairmilehead, Edinburgh EH10 6QZ (☎ 031 445 1271); Dept of Clinical Neurosciences, Western General Hosp, Crewe Rd, Edinburgh EH4 2XU (☎ 031 332 2525)

DEARDEN, Neville; s of Maj Issac Samuel Dearden (d 1979), and Lilian Anne, *née* Claxton (d 1983); *b* 1 March 1940; *Educ* Rowlinson Tech Sch Sheffield, King Alfred Coll Winchester, Univ of Southampton; *m* 1, 4 April 1963, Jean Rosemary, da of Walter Francis Garratt, of Sheffield; 2 s (Adrian b 1968, David b 1970), 1 da (Karen b 1966); m 2, 3 May 1980, Eileen Bernadette, da of Dr William John Sheehan; 4 s (Michael b 1981, Patrick b 1984, Ciaran b 1987, Liam b 1990); *Career* head of Science Dept Lafford Sch Lincolnshire 1961-67; md: W Garratt & Son Ltd 1972-78, M & H Fabrications Ltd 1972-77; chief exec S W Fabrications Ltd 1980-84, md Sheffield Brick Group plc 1982-87, chief exec Pan Computer Systems Ltd 1982-85; chm: Parker Winder and Achurch Ltd 1983-85, C H Wood Security Ltd 1983-, Smith Widdowson Eadem Ltd 1983- (md 1986-); md F G Machin Ltd 1983-; chief exec: JCL Engineering Services Ltd, Crompton Engineering (Lancs) Ltd 1989, gp manufacturing dir Comyn Ching Ltd 1990-; FBIM, FIIM, FICE; *Recreations* game and sea fishing, boating, practical craft work; *Clubs* Birmingham Press, De La Salle Assoc, Sheffield RUFC, Royal Yachting Assoc; *Style—* Neville Dearden, Esq; Comyn Ching Ltd, 110 Golden Lane, London EC1 (HO); 296 Penistone Rd, Sheffield S6 2FT (☎ 0742 852201, fax 0742 852531, telex 547545)

DEARING, (Ian) Barry; s of Ernest Dearing, of Read, and Winifred Mary, *née* Roberts; Lord of the Manor of Balderstone; *b* 24 July 1947; *Educ* Burnley GS (Edward Livesey Scholar), Leeds Univ (LLB); *m* 11 Sept 1974, Jennifer, da of John Harrison Woodward, MBE, of Glengarry, Lytham; 3 s (Richard b 1978, Peter b 1981, Edward b 1984); *Career* slr 1971; notary public 1987; *Recreations* fishing, books; *Clubs* Law Soc; *Style—* Barry Dearing, Esq; Brookside, Read, Lancs (☎ 025482 2295); Stanley House, Clitheroe, Lancs (☎ 0200 26811, telex 635170, fax 0200 28223)

DEARING, Sir Ronald Ernest (Ron); CB (1979); s of Ernest Henry Ashford Dearing (d 1941), and M T Dearing; *b* 27 July 1930; *Educ* Doncaster GS, Univ of Hull (BSc), London Business Sch; *m* 1954, Margaret Patricia, *née* Riley; 2 da; *Career* regnl dir N Region DTI 1972-74, under sec DTI and Dept of Industry 1972-76, dep sec Dept of Industry 1976-80, chm PO 1981-87 (dep chm 1980); gp chm Nationalized Industs Chairmen's Gp 1983-84; non-exec dir: Prudential Corp 1987-, Whitbread Co plc 1988-, Ericsson Ltd 1988-, Br Coal Corp 1988-, IMI plc 1988-; chm Review Ctee on Accounting Standards and chm designate Fin Reporting Cncl; chm: Co Durham Devpt Co 1987-, CNAA 1987-88, Polys and Colls Funding Cncl 1988-, Northern Devpt Co 1990-, Fin Reporting Cncl 1990-; kt 1984; *Recreations* music and gardening; *Clubs* City Livery; *Style—* Sir Ron Dearing, CB; 28 Westhawe, Bretton, Peterborough PE3 8BA

DEARNLEY, Dr Christopher Hugh; LVO; s of Rev Charles Dearnley; *b* 11 Feb 1930; *Educ* Cranleigh, Worcester Coll Oxford (MA, DMus); *m* 1957, Bridget, *née* Wateridge; 3 s, 1 da; *Career* organist and master of the Choristers Salisbury Cathedral 1957-68, organist and dir of music St Paul's Cathedral 1968-90, pres Inc Assoc of Organists 1968-70; chm: Friends of Cathedral Music 1971-90 (vice pres 1990-), Percy Whitlock Tst 1982-89 (pres 1989-); memb Cncl RCO 1980-89; dir: Eng Hymnal Co 1970-, Harwich Festival 1981-89 (pres 1989-); acting dir of music Christ Church St Lawrence Sydney 1990-91; patron Nat Accordian Orgn 1989-, hon govr Corp of the Sons of the Clergy 1989-; Dr of Fine Arts Westminster Coll Fulton USA 1989; FRCO; *Books* The Treasury of English Church Music Vol III (1965), English Church Music 1650-1750 (1970); *Style—* Dr Christopher Dearnley, LVO; Challacombe, Lower Marine Parade, Dovercourt, Essex CO12 3SR; c/o Cattai PO, NSW 2756, Australia (☎ 01061 045 750453)

DEAS, Roger Stewart; s of George Stewart (d 1983), of Motherwell, and Winifred Mary, *née* Ogden; *b* 1 Aug 1943; *Educ* The HS of Glasgow, Univ of Glasgow (BSc); *m* 27 June 1970, Carole, da of Percy Woodward, of Nottingham; 2 da (Angela Elizabeth b 1972, Wendy Jane b 1974); *Career* fin dir: Brown Bros Ltd 1974-81, Currys Gp plc 1981-85, Heron Corporation plc 1985-86; nat fin ptnr Coopers & Lybrand Deloitte 1986-; ACMA 1974, FCMA 1986; *Recreations* sailing; *Clubs* Royal Motor Yacht, N Haven Yacht; *Style—* Roger Deas, Esq; Fairways, Park Rd, Farnham Royal, Bucks SL2 3BQ (☎ 02814 2377); Coopers & Lybrand Deloitte, St Andrews House, 20 St Andrew St, London EC4A 3AD (☎ 071 583 5000)

DEATH, Basil; s of Charles Death (d 1943), of Herts, and Carrie Helena, *née* Piper (d 1961); *b* 18 Jan 1916; *Educ* Downside, Pembroke Coll Cambridge; *Career* Irish Gds 1939-45, served NW Europe, ret 1945 with rank of Maj; dir R K Harrison & Co Ltd 1947-57; memb Lloyd's; pres Int Gundog League (Retriever Soc), chm The Labrador Club; *Recreations* stalking, shooting, fishing, gardening; *Clubs* Brooks's, Kennel; *Style—* Basil Death, Esq; Dunellan House, Strathtay, Perthshire PH9 0PJ (☎ 08874 221)

DEAVE, John James; s of Charles John Deave (d 1970), of London, and Gertrude Debrit, *née* Hunt (d 1972); *b* 1 April 1928; *Educ* Charterhouse, Pembroke Coll Oxford (MA); *m* 16 Aug 1958, Gillian Mary, now Rev G M Deave (Deacon 1987), da of Adm Sir Manley Power, KCB, CBE, DSO (d 1981), of Norton Cottage, Yarmouth, IOW; 1 s (Jonathan b 1959), 1 da (Victoria b 1961); *Career* called to the Bar Gray's Inn 1952, rec, chm Med Appeal Tbnl; *Recreations* gardening, history; *Clubs* Notts United Services; *Style—* John Deave, Esq; Greensmith Cottage, Stathern, Melton Mowbray, Leics (☎ 0949 603 40); 1 High Pavement Chambers, Nottingham (☎ 0602 418218)

DEAVILLE, Timothy John Norfolk; s of Rev Robert Deaville (d 1972), and Phyllis Eleanor, *née* Laycock; *b* 3 Aug 1933; *Educ* Marlborough, Christ's Coll Cambridge (MA); *m* 26 Aug 1961, Jette, da of Dr Odont Frode Hilming, of Copenhagen, Denmark; 2 da (Caroline b 1965, Georgina b 1971); *Career* Nat Serv 2 Lt REME 1955-57, TA Lt Staffs Yeomanry 1957-63; devpt engr Rolls Royce Ltd 1957-59, project engr Ind Coope Ltd 1959-62, mgmnt conslt P-E Consulting Gp Ltd 1962-64, md Troman Bros Ltd and two other subsidiaries of Cope Allman Int Ltd 1964-66, divnl gen mangr Mobbs Miller Ltd 1969-71, owner and ptnr Hatchers Poultry 1971-1989; *Recreations* sailing, opera; *Clubs* Royal Southern Yacht, Royal Yachting Assoc; *Style—* Timothy Deaville, Esq; Hatchers Farm, Farley, Salisbury, Wilts SP5 1AQ (☎ 072 272 356, fax 072 272 356); Casa Coniglio, Sao Clemente, Vale Formoso, Almansil, 8100

Loulé, Portugal (☎ 089 95098)

DEBARGE, Hon Mrs (Robina Jane); *née* Cayzer; da of 2 Baron Rotherwick; *b* 24 Jan 1953; *Educ* St George's Switzerland; *m* 4 July 1981, Olivier Debarge, s of Albert Emile Joseph Debarge (d 1972), of Paris; 2 da; *Career* chm Robina Cayzer Ltd; *Recreations* skiing; *Style—* The Hon Mrs Debarge; 3 Redesdale St, London SW3 4BL (☎ 071 352 6955)

DEBENHAM, Hon Mrs (Daphne Joan); *née* Godber; da of 1 and last Baron Godber (d 1976); *b* 17 Aug 1923; *m* 20 June 1942, Archibald Ian Scott Debenham, DFC, AE; 2 s, 2 da; *Style—* The Hon Mrs Debenham; Bowerland Farm, Bowerland Lane, Lingfield, Surrey RH7 6DF (☎ 0342 832878)

DEBENHAM, Sir Gilbert Ridley; 3 Bt (UK 1931) of Bladen, Co Dorset; s of Sir Ernest Ridley Debenham, 1 Bt, JP (d 1952); suc bro, Sir Piers Kenrick Debenham, 2 Bt, 1964; *b* 28 June 1906; *Educ* Eton, Trinity Coll Cambridge; *m* 1 April 1935, Violet Mary, da of His Honour Judge (George Herbert) Higgins (d 1937); 3 s (George Andrew b 1938, d 1991, William Michael b 1940, Paul Edward b 1942), 1 da (Virginia Mary (Mrs Purchon) b 1936); *Heir* gs, Thomas Adam Debenham b 1971; *Career* consultant psychiatrist NHS 1949-; farmer; ret; *Style—* Sir Gilbert Debenham, Bt; Tonerspuddle Farm, Dorchester, Dorset (☎ Bere Regis 471 245)

DEBENHAM, Michael George Scott; s of Archibald Ian Scott Debenham, DFC, of Bowerland Farm, Bowerland Lane, Lingfield, Surrey, and Daphne Joann, *née* Godber; *b* 12 Oct 1943; *Educ* Haileybury, ISC, Univ of St Andrews (BSc); *m* July 1966 (m dis 1980), Janine Elizabeth, da of Anthony Davies, of Crockham Hill, Edenbridge, Kent; 3 da (Sarah b 14 April 1968, Anna b 27 March 1970, Tessa b 11 April 1974); m 2, 6 March 1981, Roberta, da of Luigi Courir, of Genova, Italy; *Career* Br Inspecting Engrs Ltd: dir Material Control Ltd 1971, dir International Ltd 1976, dir Pipelines Ltd 1982, md 1987, dir Holdings UK Ltd 1987; memb Tandridge PCC 1976-77; Liveryman Worshipful Co of Merchant Taylors; MIHT 1968, MICE 1971, CEng 1971, AWeldI 1985, FIQA 1986; *Recreations* tennis, squash, gardening; *Style—* Michael Debenham, Esq; British Inspecting Engineers Ltd, Bank of America House, Elmfield Rd, Bromley, Kent (☎ 081 464 3434, fax 081 290 0701, telex 919 572)

DEBENHAM, (Alfred) Thomas Keeys (Tom); MBE; s of Alfred Edward Debenham (d 1944), of 20 Harns Court, London SW1, and May, *née* Penson (d 1940); *b* 6 March 1910; *Educ* Marlborough; *m* 30 Aug 1935, Mary Elizabeth, da of Arthur Raymond Land (d 1947), of Croydon; 1 s (John Keeys b 1944), 1 da (Mary Anne b 1955); *Career* pre-war RA, TA; WWII ME 1941, Egypt, Cyprus, Palestine, Staff Offr SORA 1943, Staff Offr Eastern Cmd RA; Maj TA 1948; former oil co exec; rifle shooting: England int, shot for GB against Australia, NZ and Canada; pre-war racing driver at Brooklands; memb Royal Br Legion; *Recreations* field sports, ocean racing; *Clubs* Royal Ocean Racing; *Style—* Tom Debenham, Esq, MBE

DEBENHAM TAYLOR, John; CMG (1967), OBE (1959), TD (1967); s of John Francis Taylor (d 1941), and Harriett Beatrice, *née* Williams (d 1973); *b* 25 April 1920; *Educ* Whitgift, Aldenham; *m* 1966, Gillian May, da of Cyril Bernard James (d 1981), of Sussex; 1 da (Catherine Jessica b 1972); *Career* Maj RA (TA) Finland, Middle East and SE Asia 1939-45; HM Dip Serv: FO 1946, control cmmn Germany 1947-49, second sec Bangkok 1950, acting consul Songhkla 1951-52, vice consul Hanoi 1952-53, FO 1953-54, first sec Bangkok 1954-56, FO 1956-58, Singapore 1958-59, FO 1960-64, cnsllr Kuala Lumpur 1964-66, FO 1966-69, cnsllr Washington 1969-72 and Paris 1972-73, FCO 1973-77, ret 1977; industl conslt 1978-87; *Recreations* walking, reading, history; *Clubs* Naval and Military; *Style—* John Debenham Taylor, Esq, CMG, OBE, TD; c/o Lloyds Bank, 1 Butler Place, London SW1H 0PR

DEBERE, (Greville) David; s of David Debere (d 1937), of London, and Patricia, *née* Crone; *b* 22 Aug 1935; *Educ* Lancing; *m* 4 Nov 1967, Margaret Anne Silvester, da of Sir Cyril Haines, KBE (d 1988); 1 s (Nicholas b 1972), 1 da (Stephanie b 1970); *Career* admitted slr 1959, asst slr Coward Chance 1960-67, ptnr Brecher & Co 1969-82, currently asst dir Slrs Complaints Bureau of Law Soc (joined 1983-); memb Assoc Cricket Umpires; memb Law Soc 1960; *Recreations* sport, cricket umpiring, bridge; *Clubs* MCC, Middx CC; *Style—* David Debere, Esq; Solicitors Complaints Bureau, Portland House, Stag Place, London SW1E 5BL (☎ 071 834 2288, fax 071 828 3099)

DEBY, John Bedford; QC (1980); s of late Reginald Bedford Deby, and late Irene, *née* Slater; *b* 19 Dec 1931; *Educ* Winchester, Trinity Coll Cambridge (MA); *Career* called to the Bar Inner Temple 1954; rec of the Crown Ct 1977-, bencher Inner Temple 1986; *Style—* John Deby, Esq, QC; 11 Britannia Rd, London SW6 2HJ (☎ 071 736 4976)

DECIES, 6 Baron (I 1812); Arthur George Marcus Douglas de la Poer Beresford; only s of 5 Baron Decies, DSO, PC (d 1944; ggs of 1 Baron Decies who was bro of 1 Marquess of Waterford), by his 1 w, Vivien (d 1931), da of George Jay Gould, of New York, USA; *b* 24 April 1915; *Educ* Bryanston, Bonn Univ; *m* 1, 21 Oct 1937, Ann (d 28 March 1945), da of late Sidney Walter Trevor, of Camperdown, Victoria, Australia; m 2, 12 Sept 1945, Diana, widow of Maj D W A Galsworthy, Royal Fus, and da of Wing-Cdr G Turner-Cain; 1 s, 2 da; *Heir* s, Hon Marcus Hugh Tristam de la Poer Beresford; *Career* served 1939-45 as Flying Offr RAFVR; DFC (USA); *Style—* The Rt Hon The Lord Decies; Ballydavid House, Woodstown, Co Waterford, Ireland

DEE, Michael James Damian; s of Kenneth William Dee (d 1977), of Bath, and Dorothy Josephine, *née* Whittern-Carter; *b* 12 June 1946; *Educ* Dovai Coll, Univ of Edinburgh (BSc); *m* 28 April 1973, Pamela Sarah, da of Cecil George Moore, of Jersey; 4 da (Samantha b 1974, Joanna b 1976, Nicola b 1977, Belinda b 1980); *Career* dir Damian Investment Tst 1972-73, md Europlan Financial Servs 1976-, chm Europlan Holdings Ltd 1984-; tstee Nat Childrens Orch; FInstD; *Recreations* sailing, golf; *Clubs* Royal Channel Islands Yacht, La Moye Golf; *Style—* Michael Dee, Esq; Sous Le Moulin, Rozel St Martin, Jersey, Channel Islands; Lister House, The Parade, St Helier, Jersey, Channel Isands (☎ 0534 38500, telex 4192334 wyvern G, fax 0534 38690)

DEEDES, Maj-Gen Charles Julius (John); CB (1968), OBE (1953), MC (1944); s of Gen Sir Charles Deedes, KCB, CMG, DSO (d 1968), of Budleigh Salterton, Devon, and Eve Mary, *née* Dean-Pitt; *b* 18 Oct 1913; *Educ* Oratory Sch, RMC Sandhurst; *m* 4 Sept 1939, Beatrice Elaine (Betty), da of H M Murgatroyd (d 1961), of Brockfield Hall, York; 3 s (Charles (Michael) Julius b 1941, Christopher b 1944, Jeremy b 1955); *Career* cmmnd KOYLI 1933, regtl appts 1939-44, serv NW Europe, Caribbean, Italy (wounded), asst mil sec GHQ ME 1946-48, CO Glider Pilot Regt 1949-50, GSO 1 WO 1951-54, CO 1 Bn KOYLI 1954-56, serv Kenya, Aden, Cyprus, Col Gen Staff WO 1957-59, Bde Cdr 150 Inf Bdes TA 1959-62, dep dir staffs duties MOD 1963-65, chief of staff HQ Eastern Cmd 1965-68, Col KOYLI 1966-70, COS HQ Southern Cmd 1968, Dep Col (Yorks) LI 1970-72; treas: Thirsk and Malton Cons Assoc, Ryedale Cons Assoc; FBIM 1968; Norwegian Military Cross 1940; *Recreations* foxhunting, horticulture, tennis; *Style—* Maj-Gen John Deedes, CB, OBE, MC; Lea Close, Brandsby, York YO6 4RW (☎ 034 75 239)

DEEDES, Jeremy Wyndham; s of The Rt Hon Lord Deedes, MC, DL, PC, *qv*, and Evelyn Hilary, *née* Branfoot; *b* 24 Nov 1943; *Educ* Eton; *m* 1973, Anna Rosemary, da of late Maj Elwyn Gray; 2 s (George William b 28 Feb 1976, Henry Julius b 8 June 1978); *Career* reporter Daily Sketch 1966-69 (Kent & Sussex Courier 1963-66), dep ed Daily Express 1976-79, managing ed Evening Standard 1979-85 (ed Londoner's Diary 1970-76), managing ed Today 1985-86, exec ed Daily and Sunday Telegraph 1986-; *Recreations* cricket, racing, cabinet making; *Clubs* Boodles; *Style—* The Hon Jeremy Deedes; Hamilton House, Compton, Newbury, Berkshire RG16 0RJ (☎ 0635 578 695); The Daily Telegraph, 181 Marsh Wall, London E14 (☎ 071 538 5000)

DEEDES, Baron (Life Peer UK 1986), of Aldington, Co Kent; William Francis; MC (1944), PC (1962), DL (Kent 1962); s of Herbert William Deedes, JP, of Saltwood Castle (which was sold 1925) and Sandling Park (which was sold 1897), and Melesina Gladys, JP, 2 da of Philip Chenevix Trench, gs of Richard Chenevix Trench, yr bro of 1 Baron Ashtown; *b* 1 June 1913; *Educ* Harrow; *m* 1942, Evelyn Hilary, da of Clive Branfoot, of Stonegrave, Yorks; 1 s (Hon Jeremy Wyndham b 1943) and 1 s decd (Julius Brook b 1947 d 1970), 3 da (Hon Juliet Evelyn Mary b 1948, Hon Victoria Frances Jill (Hon Mrs Southey) b 1950, Hon Lucy Rose (Hon Mrs Crispin Money-Coutts) b 1955); *Career* served WWII Maj KRRC (TA); ed The Daily Telegraph 1974-85; memb Historic Bldgs Cncl England 1958-62, MP (C) Ashford 1950-74, min without portfolio 1962-64, Parly under sec Home Office 1955-57, Parly sec Miny Housing and Local Govt 1954-55; *Clubs* Carlton, Beefsteak, Royal and Ancient; *Style—* The Rt Hon Lord Deedes, MC, DL, PC; New Hayters, Aldington, Kent (☎ 023 372 269)

DEEHAN, James Patrick (Jim); s of James Deehan, and Bridget, *née* Murrin; *b* 1945; *Educ* St Ignatius Coll London, Univ of Durham (BA); *m* Christine; 1 s (James); *Career* articled clerk Vinney Merretts; Price Waterhouse: joined 1970, ptnr (Zambia) 1985-88, ptnr (UK) 1980-; chm W of England CAs Trg Bd, memb Ct Univ of Bath; FCA; *Recreations* squash, Spurs; *Style—* Jim Deehan, Esq; Price Waterhouse, Clifton Heights, Triangle West, Clifton, Bristol BS8 1EB (☎ 0272 293701)

DEELEY, Michael; s of John Hamilton-Deeley (d 1979), and Josephine Frances Anne, *née* Deacon; *b* 6 Aug 1932; *Educ* Stowe; *m* 1, 1955 (m dis 1967), Teresa Harrison, 1 s (Manuel b 4 Jan 1964), 2 da ((Catherine) Anne b 26 Aug 1956, Isobel b 16 July 1957); m 2, 16 Jan 1970, Ruth Vivienne Emilie, da of Vivian George Stone-Spencer of Brighton, Sussex; *Career* Nat Serv 1950-52, 2 Lt IRWK serv Malaya 1951-52; film prodr; md: Br Lion Films 1972-76, EMI Films Ltd 1976-79; pres EMI Films Inc (USA) 1977-79, chm and chief exec offr Consolidated Entertainment Inc 1984-; prodr more than thirty motion pics incl: The Deer Hunter (Best Film Oscar 1978), The Italian Job, Convoy, Murphy's War, The Man Who Fell to Earth, Blade Runner, Robbery; NAACP Image Award for 'A Gathering of Old Men'; dep chm Br Screen Advsy Cncl, fndr memb: PM's Working Party on the Film Indust (1974), Interim Action Ctee on the Film Indust; memb Motion Picture Acad Arts & Sciences (US), ACTT; *Recreations* sailing; *Clubs* Garrick, Wianno YC; *Style—* Michael Deeley, Esq; Little Island, Osterville, Mass 02655, USA; 9000 Sunset Boulevard, 415, Los Angeles, CA 90069, USA (☎ 213 275 5719, fax 213 275 5786)

DEELEY, Peter Anthony William; s of George William Deeley (d 1985), of Warwicks, and Bridie Deeley, of Balsall Common, nr Coventry; *b* 30 Aug 1942; *Educ* Ratcliffe Coll Leics, Coventry Poly; *m* 9 July 1966, Patricia Ann, da of Walter Edgar Jones (d 1983), of Coventry; 3 da (Eleanor Elizabeth Jude b 28 Sept 1976, Anna Shahida Jude b 10 Aug 1982, Rosemary Lucy Jude b 27 Nov 1984); *Career* dep md GW Deeley Ltd 1968 (joined 1958); chm: Deeley Group Ltd 1985, Coventry and Warwicks Jt Trg Ctee for Construction Indust 1980-; pres Builder Employers Confedn (Coventry) 1970-; vice chm: Coventry Hosps Tst, Coventry Tech Coll 1990-; memb Cncl Coventry C of C and Trade; Freeman City of Coventry 1963; memb Inst of Bldg; *Recreations* golf, walking; *Clubs* N Warwicks Golf; *Style—* Peter Deeley, Esq; Icarus, Vicarage Rd, Stoneleigh, nr Coventry CV8 3DH (☎ 0203 414436); Deeley Group Ltd, William Hse, Torrington Ave, Coventry (☎ 0203 462521, fax 0203 469533, telex 311765)

DEERE, Col Edward George; GSM (NI, 1974); s of Sydney Charles Deere, of Newton Aycliffe, Co Durham, and Rose Mary, *née* Bennett (d 1981); *b* 4 Sept 1942; *Educ* Duke of York's Royal Mil Sch Dover, Guy's Hosp London (BDS); *m* 27 Feb 1965, Angela Mary, da of John Holmes (d 1989), of Shoreham-by-sea, Sussex; 1 s (Robert Edward John b 1966), 1 da (Harriet Mary Rose b 1970); *Career* cmmnd 2 Lt RADC 1961, Capt 1964, Maj 1969, Lt-Col 1977, Col 1987; sr specialist dental offr BMH Iserlohn W Germany 1975, sr registrar in oral surgery Charing Cross Hosp 1978; conslt dental offr: BMH Munster W Germany 1979, BMH Iserlohn W Germany 1980, Queen Elisabeth Mil Hosp Woolwich 1982, BMH Munster W Germany 1985, 22 Field Hosp RAMC 1988; specialist orthodontic private practice Horsham 1989-; FDSRCS 1973, FDSRCSEd 1973, D'ORTH RCS 1975; *Recreations* photography, golf, computing, gardening; *Clubs* RSM; *Style—* Col Edward Deere; 9 Bonar Place, Chislehurst, Kent BR7 5RJ (☎ 081 4671377)

DEERHURST, Viscount; Edward George William Omar Coventry; s (by 1 m) and h of 11 Earl of Coventry; *b* 24 Sept 1957; *Style—* Viscount Deerhurst; 18 Tanjenong Place, Burleigh Heads, Qld 4220, Australia

DEERING, Peter Henry; s of William John Deering (d 1962), and Margaret Florence Deering; *b* 25 Feb 1931; *Educ* N London Poly Sch of Architecture; *m* 9 Aug 1952, Fay Constance, da of Walter Frederick Sermons (d 1984); *Career* Nat Serv 1955-56; assoc Martin Hutchinson (architect) 1949-67, ptnr David Hogg and Ptnrs (architects) 1973-; magistrate (chm Haringey div); fndr chm Forty Hill (Enfield) Conservation Area Study Gp; memb: Enfield Preservation Soc, Middx Justices Advsy Ctee, 1990-; chm Bd of Visitors Pentonville Prison; *Recreations* cricket, bowls; *Clubs* MCC, Cricketers Club of London, Myddelton House CC Enfield (pres); *Style—* Peter Deering, Esq; 11 Lambourne Gardens, Enfield, Middx EN1 3AD (☎ 081 363 4093); David Hogg and Ptnrs, 20 Crawford Place, London W1H 1JE (☎ 071 724 5720)

DEERY, Dr Alastair Robin Stewart; s of Sgt-Major Michael John Stewart Deery, MM, and Isabella Stout, *née* Murray; *b* 5 Oct 1953; *Educ* Alleynes Sch, Univ of London (BSc, MB BS); *m* 24 Dec 1981, Dr Clare Constantine Davey, da of Dr Charles James Constantine Davey; *Career* house offr UCH London 1979, sr house offr Manchester 1980, registrar in histopathology Western Infirmary Glasgow 1981-83, sr registrar in histopathology and cytopathology Charing Cross Hosp London 1984-86, conslt, hon sr lectr histopathology and cytopathology and dir cytopathology unit Royal Free Hosp London 1986-; memb: Br Soc of Clinical Cytology, Pathological Soc of UK; memb: BMA, Royal Coll of Pathologists 1987; *Recreations* collecting writing instruments, skiing; *Style—* Dr Alastair Deery; 70 Princes Square, London W2 4NY; Cytopathology Unit, Academic Dept of Histopathology, Royal Free Hosp Sch of Medicine, Pond St, Hampstead, London NW3 2QG (☎ 01 435 1008)

DEGNI, Raffaele Giuseppe; s of Antonio Degni, and Francesca, *née* Caressa; *b* 18 Aug 1954; *Educ* St John Adamson HS, Univ of Witwatersrand S Africa (BAcc); *Career* articled clerk Karlin Isaacs & Co (S Africa) 1972-77, audit mangr Deloitte Haskins & Sells (S Africa) 1977-78; Grey Advertising (S Africa): accountant 1978, gp systems analyst 1980-82, gp fin controller 1983-86, gp fin dir 1986-89; gp fin dir Acsis Group plc (London) 1989-; memb: S Africa Inst of CAs 1978, Pub Accountants and Auditors Bd 1978, IOD (S Africa) 1984, Inst of Mktg Mgmnt 1989, IOD (London) 1990; *Recreations* theatre, cinema, reading; *Clubs* Wanderers (Johannesburg); *Style—* Raffaele Degni, Esq; Acsis Group plc, 6 Derby St, London W1Y 7HD (☎ 071 499 8433, fax 071 629 3017, car 0836 356 936, mobile 0860 760817)

DEHN, Conrad Francis; QC (1968); s of Curt Gustav Dehn (d 1948), of London, and Cynthia Doris, *née* Fuller (d 1987); *b* 24 Nov 1926; *Educ* Charterhouse, Ch Ch Oxford (BA, MA); *m* 1, 1954, Sheila, da of William Kilmurray Magan (d 1967), of London; 2 s (Hugh b 1956, Guy b 1957), 1 da (Katharine b 1959); m 2, 1978, Marilyn, da of Peter Collyer (d 1979), of Oxon; *Career* RA 1945-48, best cadet Mons OCTU 1946, 2 Lt 1947; called to the Bar Gray's Inn 1952, rec 1974, bencher 1977; dir Bar Mutual Insur Fund 1988; *Recreations* theatre, travel, walking; *Clubs* Reform; *Style—* Conrad Dehn, Esq, QC; Fountain Court, Temple, London EC4Y 9DH (☎ 071 583 3335, telex 8813408 FONLEG G, fax 071 353 0329)

DEHN, Thomas Clark Bruce; s of Harold Bruce Dehn, and Jean Margaret Henderson, *née* Ewing; *b* 6 March 1949; *Educ* Harrow, St Bartholomew's Hosp Med Coll London (MB BS, MS, FRCS, LRCP); *m* 4 Sept 1984, (Dorothea) Lorraine, da of Gilbert Maurice Baird, of Dunbartonshire; 2 da (Henrietta b 1986, Emily b 1988); *Career* gen surgn; conslt gen surgn Royal Berkshire Hosp Reading, clinical lectr in surgery Nuffield Dept of Surgery John Radcliffe Hosp Oxford 1984-88, lectr in surgery St Bartholomew's Hosp Med Coll 1980-84; conslt surgn Royal Berks Hosp Reading 1990-; memb Hosp Jr Staff Ctee 1987-88; Freeman City of London, Liveryman Worshipful Co of Distillers; *Recreations* flying; *Style—* Thomas Dehn, Esq; Dept of Surgery, Royal Berkshire Hospital, Reading, Berkshire RG1 5AN

DEIGHTON, Robert John Greenway; s of Col John Harold Greenway Deighton, OBE, MC, of Ennis, Co Clare, and Maureen Hunt, of Co Limerick; *b* 5 Sept 1948; *Educ* Wellington, Univ of Durham (BA); *m* 1 May 1971, Olivia Jane Nikola, da of Lt-Col Leslie Garrick Young (d 1984); 2 s (Jamie b 1976, Harry b 1980), 1 da (Clare b 1974); *Career* dir Doyle Dane Bernbach 1976-80, dep md Foote Cone Belding 1980-83, chm and chief exec Kirkwoods 1983-86, chm Deighton & Mullen 1987-; *Recreations* cricket, squash, shooting; *Clubs* MCC, Naval and Military; *Style—* Robert J G Deighton, Esq; Deighton & Mullen, 41 Gt Pulteney St, London W1R 3DE (☎ 071 434 0040, fax 071 439 1590, telex 8955246)

DEITH, Geoffrey Wilson; s of Leslie Herbert Deith (d 1973), and Mary Elizabeth May, *née* Holt; *b* 15 Jan 1935; *Educ* Stand GS Whitefield Lancs, Royal Tech Coll Salford (HNC); *m* 15 Aug 1959 (m dis), Mavis Ann, da of James Payne, of Mudeford, Bournemouth; 2 s (Christopher b 1960, Ivan b 1965), 1 da (Gillian b 1962); *Career* Nat Serv Army 1951-53; process and devpt engr Unilever, Birds Eye Foods 1959-63; md: RE Ingham & Co 1963-80, Rank Organisation Int Indust Div, Toshiba Corpn, Rank Toshiba TV Manufacture 1980-84; dir: Waterford Glass Gp plc, Waterford Crystal Inc; chm: Waterford-Aynsley (UK) Ltd 1984-87, Aynsley Group plc, Concepts Devpt Ltd; dir COAB Ltd; *Recreations* skiing, horse riding; *Style—* Geoffrey Deith, Esq; Coachman's Cottage, Coach House Mews, Blithfield, Rugeley, Staffs WS15 3NL (☎ 0889 500500); Aynsley Group plc, Portland Works, Longton, Stoke-on-Trent, Staffs ST3 1HS (☎ 0782 599499, fax 0782 599498, telex 36423)

DEL MAR, Michael Bernard; s of Richard Oscar Del Mar, of Milford-on-Sea, Hants, and Millicent, *née* Shewell; *b* 6 June 1946; *Educ* Marlborough Coll, Univ of Birmingham (BSc); *m* 9 Jan 1971, Anthea Noël, da of Paul Ian Van Der Gucht, of Herriard, Hants; 3 s (Dominic b 7 Dec 1972, Sam b 11 April 1974, Oliver b 1 Oct 1976); *Career* ptnr L Messel 1978-86, exec dir Shearson Lehman Hutton Securities 1988-90, dir SG Warburg Securities; *Recreations* fishing, gardening; *Style—* Michael Del Mar, Esq; Avenue Farm, Herriard, Hampshire

DEL MAR, Norman René; CBE (1975); s of M Del Mar, of 12 Kidderpore Gdns, NW3; *b* 31 July 1919; *Educ* Marlborough, RCM; *m* 1947, Pauline Joy, da of G C Mann, of Chigwell; 2 s (Jonathan, Robin); *Career* conductor; asst to Sir Thomas Beecham 1947, princ conductor Eng Opera Gp 1949-55, prof of conducting GSM 1953-60; conductor: Yorks Symphony Orch 1955-56, BBC Scottish Orch 1960-65; princ guest conductor Gothenburg Symphony Orch 1969-73, conductor RAM 1973-77, princ conductor Acad of the BBC Bristol 1974-77, conductor and prof of conducting RCM 1972-, artistic dir Norfolk and Norwich Triennial Festival 1979-82, princ guest conductor Bournemouth Sinfonietta 1982-85, artistic dir and princ conductor Aarhus Symphony Orch 1985-88, currently conductor of Honour in Aarhus, freelance conductor in UK and abroad; FRCM, FGSM; *Books* Richard Strauss: 3 vols (1962-72), Mahler's Sixth Symphony A Study (1980), Orchestral Variations (1981), Anatomy of the Orchestra (1981), Companion to the Orchestra (1987); *Style—* Norman Del Mar, Esq, CBE; Witchings, Hadley Common, Barnet, Herts

DELACOMBE, Maj-Gen Sir Rohan; KCMG (1964), KCVO (1970), KBE (1961, CBE 1951, MBE 1939), CB (1957), DSO (1944); s of Lt-Col Addis Delacombe, DSO (d 1941), of Shrewton Manor, nr Salisbury, Wilts; *b* 25 Oct 1906; *Educ* Harrow, RMC and Staff Coll Camberley; *m* 15 Feb 1941, Eleanor Joyce, da of Robert Lionel Foster, JP (d 1952), of Egton Manor, York; 1 s, 1 da; *Career* 2 Lt Royal Scots 1926; served: Egypt, N China, India; WWII served: France, Norway, Normandy, Italy; active serv 1937-39 (Palestine, despatches), Lt-Col cmdg 2 and 8 Bns Royal Scots 1943-45, GSO (1) 2 Inf Div S E Asia 1945-47, Col (GS) HQ BAOR 1949-50, cmd 5 Inf Bde 1950-53, dep mil sec War Office 1953-55, GOC 52 (Lowland) Div and Lowland Dist 1955-58, Maj-Gen 1956, GOC Berlin (Br Sector) 1959-62, Col Royal Scots 1956-64, Hon Col 1 Armoured Regt to 1974, Hon Air Cdre RAAF; govr of Victoria, Aust 1963-74; Hon Freeman City of Melbourne, Hon LLD Melbourne and Monash, admin of the Cwlth of Aust on four occasions 1971-72 and 1973; memb Royal Co of Archers (Queen's Bodyguard for Scot), pres Royal Br Legion (Wilts); FRAIA, KStJ; *Style—* Maj-Gen Sir Rohan Delacombe, KCMG, KCVO, KBE, CB, DSO; Shrewton Manor, nr Salisbury, Wilts SP3 4DB (☎ 0980 620253)

DELACOTE, Jacques; *Educ* Paris Conservatory, Musikakademie Vienna (under Aof Swarowsky); *Career* conductor; debut Bruckner Symphony No 9 with NY Philharmonic 1972; has conducted maj int orchestras incl: Vienna Philharmonic, Israel Philharmonic, Orchestre de Paris, Orchestre National de France, San Francisco Symphony, Montreal Symphony, London Symphony, Cleveland Orchestra, Scot Nat and Chamber Orchestra; opera debut at Vienna State Opera; has worked with: Deutsche Oper am Rhein (Un Ballo in Maschera, La Trainata, Carmen), Zurich Opera (Der Freischutz), Royal Danish Opera (Falstaff), Royal Opera House Covent Garden (Faust, La Traviata, Tales of Hoffman, Werther, Carmen, Turandot), Chatelet Theatre Paris (Ernani, Cendrillon), Paris Opera (Dialogues of the Carmelites), Hamburg State Opera (Le Cid, Guillaume Tell, Aida, Carmen, Tales of Hoffman, La Boheme), Munich State Opera (Aida), Scottish Opera (La Boheme, Die Fledermaus), WNO (Eugene Oriegin), Teatro Liceo Barcelona (Romeo et Juliet, Herodiade), Denver Opera (Tales of Hoffmann); recent operatic appearances incl: Turandot and Samson et Dalila (on tour in Japan and Korea with Royal Opera House Covent Garden), Faust, Cavalleria Rusticana and Pagliacci (with ENO), Werther (in Buenos Aires), Turandot (in Pittsburgh), Don Giovanni and Massenet's Don Quichotte (in Bordeaux), Faust (in Montreal), Carmen (Earls Ct London, Japan), Samson et Delila (in Barcelona with Baltsa and Domingo); debut Henry Wood Promenade Concerts 1986; has made recordings of operatic arias with Samuel Ramey and Jose Carreras for EMI; *Style—* Jacques Delacote, Esq; Lies Askonas Ltd, 186 Drury Lane, London WC2B 5RY (☎ 071 405 1808, fax 071 242 1831, telex 265914 ASKONA G)

DELACOURT-SMITH OF ALTERYN, Baroness (Life Peeress UK 1974); Margaret Rosalind; da of F J Hando; *b* 5 April 1916; *Educ* Newport High Sch, St Anne's Coll Oxford; *m* 1939, Lord Delacourt-Smith, PC (Life Peer, d 1972); 1 s, 2 da; m 2, 1978, Prof Charles Blackton; *Career* cncllr of Royal Borough of New Windsor 1962-65, JP 1962-67; *Style—* The Rt Hon The Lady Delacourt-Smith of Alteryn; 56 Aberdare Gardens, London NW6 (☎ 071 624 1728)

DELAFIELD, Air Cdre John; s of Geoffrey E Delafield (former Cdr RNVR, d 1985), and Joan, *née* Hamblin; *b* 31 Jan 1938; *Educ* Monkton Combe Sch, RAF Coll Cranwell; *m* 12 Oct 1963, (Patricia) Jane, da of Maj G M Blake, RM; 1 s (Richard John b 17 Jane 1968), 1 da (Margaret b 4 Sept 1965); *Career* RAF Offr; formerly Pilot and flying instr, station cdr RAF Newton 1980-82, staff MOD 1982-; gliding: 7 times nat champion, 3 times Br Gliding Team; MRAeS; *Books* Gliding Competitively (1982); *Recreations* gliding; *Clubs* RAF Gliding and Soaring Assoc; *Style—* Air Cdre John Delafield; Ministry of Defence, Lacon House, Theobalds Rd, London WC1 (☎ 071 430 6445)

DELAHUNT, Anthony Henry; s of Henry John Delahunt (d 1962), of London, and Mary Lanegan; *b* 2 Sept 1940; *Educ* St Ignatius Coll; *m* 1967, Veronica, da of Brian Farrell, of Ireland; 3 s (Ian b 1968, Graham b 1970, Stephen b 1972); *Career* fin dir Noble Lowndes & Ptnrs Ltd 1985; FCA; *Recreations* cricket, reading, theatre; *Clubs* Royal Automobile, Catenian Assoc; *Style—* Anthony Delahunt, Esq; Wembury, 4A Green Lane, Purley, Surrey CR2 3PG (☎ 01 660 2190); Noble Lowndes & Ptnrs Ltd, PO Box 144, Norfolk House, Wellesley Road, Croydon CR9 3EB (☎ 081 686 2466, fax 081 680 7998)

DELAMAIN, Capt Nicholas Sinclair; o s of Lt-Col Walter Thomas Delamain (d 1976), of Trevellyan Cottage, Barrington, nr Ilminster, Somerset, and Philippa Anne, *née* Clifford (d 1966); *b* 24 Nov 1931; *Educ* Rugby, RMA Sandhurst; *m* 1, 30 May 1959 (m dis 1965), Juliet, da of Capt Charles Kendall, of Kent; 2 s (Rupert b 1959, Charles b 1960); m 2, 16 Dec 1968 (m dis 1975), Alix, da of Col Harold Brigham, of Cork; 1 s (Julian b 1972), 1 da (Georgina b 1969); m 3, 31 Aug 1985, Juliet Flora, da of Capt Alan J M Richardson, of Southrop Manor, Southrop, Lechlade, Glos (d 1965); *Career* cmmnd 10 Royal Hussars (PWO) 1952-60; served: Germany, Jordan, Australia (ADC to Govr of W Australia), Royal Wilts Yeo 1960-64; jt md: Hill & Delamain Ltd 1966-84, H & D Walford Ltd 1984-86; md: Sinclair Marine Ltd, Pelican Airways Ltd 1980-84; *Recreations* racing, hunting; *Clubs* Turf, Cavalry and Guards, MCC; *Style—* Capt Nicholas Delamain; Grove Farm House, Cold Aston, nr Cheltenham, Glos GL54 3BN (☎ 0451 20651, work ☎ 0451 21967, telex 427214)

DELAMERE, 5 Baron (UK 1821); Hugh George Cholmondeley; s of 4 Baron Delamere (d 1978, whose gf 2 Baron was fifth cous of 1 Marquess of Cholmondeley) and his 1 w, Phyllis, da of Lord George Montagu Douglas Scott (3 s of 6 Duke of Buccleuch); *b* 18 Jan 1934; *Educ* Eton, Magdalene Coll Cambridge (MA Agric); *m* 1964, Ann Willoughby, da of Sir Patrick Renison, GCMG, and formerly w of Michael Tinné; 1 s; *Heir* s, Hon Thomas Patrick Gilbert Cholmondeley b 19 June 1968; *Career* farmer; sr settlement officer Kinangop 1962-63; landowner (57,000 acres); *Recreations* racing, shooting, flying; *Clubs* Pitt, Muthaiga Country, Jockey (Kenya); *Style—* The Rt Hon the Lord Delamere; Soysambu, Elmenteita, Kenya; Delamere Estates Ltd, Private Bag, Nakuru, Kenya (☎ Elmenteita 28)

DELAMORE, Irvine William; s of William Delamore (d 1968), and May, *née* Wright; *b* 16 July 1930; *Educ* Spalding GS, Univ of Edinburgh (MB ChB, PhD); *m* 8 Dec 1955, (Hilda) Rosemary, Edgar Frank Thomas (d 1984); 2 da (Catherine b 1957, Wendy b 1958); *Career* surgn Lt RNVR 1955-57; Damon Runyon res fell Yale Univ Med Sch 1960-61, Baroda Med Sch India 1963-64; conslt physician: Blackburn Royal Infirmary 1966-69, Manchester Royal Infirmary; memb: Br Soc for Haematology, Royal Soc of Apothecaries; FRCPE 1968, FRCPath 1974, FRCP 1981; *Books* Haematological Aspects of Systemic Disease (1990), Myeloma and other Paraprotein Disorders (1986), Leukaemia (1986); *Recreations* golf, gardening, photography, reading; *Style—* Dr Irvine Delamore; Fisher House, Rivington, Bolton BL6 7SL (☎ 0204 969437); Bupa Hospital, Russell Rd, Whalley Range, Manchester M16 8AJ (☎ 061 226 0112)

DELANEY, Francis James Joseph (Frank); 5 s of Edward Joseph Delaney (d 1968), of Tipperary, Ireland, and Elizabeth Josephine, *née* O'Sullivan; *b* 24 Oct 1942; *Educ* Abbey Schs Tipperary, Rosse Coll Dublin; *m* 1, 1966 (m dis 1980), Eilish, *née* Kelliher; 3 s (Edward b 1968, Bryan b 1971, Owen b 1976); m 2, 1988, Susan, *née* Collier; *Career* writer, broadcaster, TV, Radio, Journalism; chm Nat Book League and Book Tst 1984-86; *Books* James Joyce's Odyssey (1981), Betjeman Country (1983), The Celts (1986), A Walk in the Dark Ages (1988), My Dark Rosaleen (novella 1989), Legends of the Celts (1989); *Clubs* Athenaeum; *Style—* Frank Delaney, Esq; 43 Old Town, London SW4

DELANEY, Gerald Palmer; JP (Northumberland 1981); s of Francis Harold Delaney (d 1961), of Moncton, Canada, and Ruth Amanda McKenzie (d 1980); *b* 2 July 1925; *Educ* Moncton HS; *m* 26 March 1947, Cecily Patricia, da of Albert Edward Murrell, MBE, RN; 2 s (Patrick b and d 1951, Stephen b 1953), 2 da (Geraldine b 1950, Marion b 1957); *Career* Canadian Army 1941-45; Corpl: France, Belgium, Holland, Germany; Health Serv admin, gp sec St George's Hosp Morpeth 1968-73, area admin N Tyneside Health Authy 1973-80; AHSM; *Style—* Gerald Delaney, Esq, JP; Hillside, Burnhouse Rd, Wooler, Northumberland (☎ 0668 81237)

DELANEY, Dr John Christopher; s of John Lawrence Delaney (d 1985), and Isabel, *née* Garroch; *b* 16 Feb 1941; *Educ* St Anselms Coll Birkenhead, Univ of Liverpool (MB Chb); *m* 24 July 1965, Julia Margaret, da of Ernest Emmett Cotter, of Liége House, Upton, Wirral; 2 s (Andrew John b 1968, Simon Gerard James b 1971), 1 da (Susan Mary b 1966); *Career* appointed conslt physician 1976-, dist tutor RCP 1986, pubns on asthma and aspirin sensitivity; chm: Wirral Dist Conslts Ctee, med bd Wirral Hosps; memb: Br Thoracic Soc: BMA; FRCP 1984 (MRCP 1971); *Recreations* golf, gardening, reading; *Style—* Dr John Delaney; Chelline, 12 West Close, Noctorum, Birkenhead, Merseyside (☎ 051 677 2500); Arrowe Park Hospital, Upton, Wirral (☎ 051 678 5111, car 0860 596747)

DELAP, Hon Mrs (Anastasia Diana); *née* Noble; 3 da of Baron Glenkinglas (Life Peer, d 1984), and Baroness Glenkinglas, *qv*; *b* 17 Jan 1948; *m* 7 Oct 1967, Jonathan Sinclair Delap, s of William Frederick Delap, of Kalou, Kenya; 2 s; *Style—* The Hon Mrs Delap; Little Armsworth, Alresford, Hants

DELBRIDGE, Richard; s of Tom Delbridge, and Vera, *née* Lancashire; *b* 21 May 1942; *Educ* LSE (BSc), Univ of California Berkeley (MBA); *m* 19 Mar 1966, Diana Genevra Rose, da of H W Bowers-Broadbent; 1 s (Mark b 1973), 2 da (Roseanna b 1970, Cressida b 1982); *Career* CA 1966; Arthur Andersen and Co: articled clerk 1963-66, mgmnt conslt 1968-, ptnr 1974-76; sr vice pres and gen mangr London office Morgan Guaranty Tst Co of New York 1987- (int op 1976-79, comptroller 1979-85, asst gen mangr 1985-87), gp fin dir Midland Bank plc 1989-; bd memb The Securities Assoc 1988-89; FCA 1972; *Recreations* walking, reading; *Style—* Richard Delbridge, Esq; 48 Downshire Hill, London NW3 1NX; Midland Bank plc, Poultry, London EC2

DELDERFIELD, Antony D; s of Stanley William Delderfield, of Bromley; *b* 10 May 1925; *Educ* Quernmoore Coll; *m* 1948, Hella Marie Anna; 3 children; *Career* Lloyd's broker, Lloyd's Underwriting memb; chm Wigham Poland Marine Far East Ltd 1981-; dir Wigham Poland Holdings Ltd 1981-; *Recreations* sailing, music; *Clubs* Lloyds Yacht; *Style—* A D Delderfield Esq; 10 Burnsall St, Chelsea, London SW3 (☎ 01 481 0505); Wigham Poland Holdings, 24 Minories, London EC3 (☎ 01 481 0505)

DELEVINGNE, Hon Mrs (Angela Margo Hamar); *née* Greenwood; da of 1 Viscount Greenwood, KC, PC, and Margery, DBE (d 1968), da of Rev Walter Spencer (d 1948); *b* 8 July 1912; *m* 1937, (Edward) Dudley Delevingne (d 1974), s of late Edward Charles Delevingne; 2 s (Edward Hamar, Charles Hamar), 2 da (Venetia (d 1988),Caroline); *Style—* The Hon Mrs Delevingne; 22 Ovington St, London SW3

DELEVINGNE, Charles Hamar; s of (Edward) Dudley Delevingne (d 1974), and Hon Angela Margo Hamar, *née* Greenwood, *qv*; *b* 25 June 1949; *Educ* Embley Park; *m* 18 June 1983, Pandora Anne, da of Jocelyn Greville Stevens, *qv* of Testbourne, Hampshire; 2 da (Chloe b 1984, Poppy b 1986); *Career* chm of Property Investmt Co; *Recreations* shooting, fishing; *Clubs* Buck's; *Style—* Charles Delevingne, Esq; 95 Albert Bridge Road, London SW11 (☎ 01 585 0301); Testbourne Lodge, Hampshire (☎ 026 472 569); Kimbolton Lodge, Fulham Road, SW3 (☎ 01 589 1126)

DELFONT, Baron (Life Peer UK 1976), of Stepney in Greater London; Bernard Delfont; s of Isaac Winogradsky (d 1936), of Odessa, Russia, and Olga Winogradsky (d 1981); *b* 5 Sept 1909,Tokmak, Russia; *Educ* Rochelle St Sch London; *m* 1946, Helen Violet Carolyn (formerly an actress under the name Carole Lynne), da of Victor Cecil Haymen, and formerly w of late Derek Farr; 1 s (Hon David, *qv*), 2 da (Hon Mrs Meddings, Hon Mrs Morse, *qqv*); *Career* chm and chief exec: EMI Film and Theatre Corp 1969-80 (later chief exec EMI), Trusthouse Forte Leisure 1981-82, First Leisure Corp 1983-; dir of various cos; life pres Entertainment Artists Benevolent Fund, pres Entertainment Charities Fund, former pres Printers' Charitable Corp, former chief Barker Variety Club of Gt Britain; Companion Rat Grand Order of Water Rats; kt 1974; *Style—* The Rt Hon Lord Delfont; House of Lords, London SW1

DELFONT, Hon David Stephen; only s of Baron Delfont (Life Peer), *qv*; *b* 1953; *Educ* Millfield; *m* 1982, Sarah Louise, da of Peter Edgington; 2 s (Joseph b 1983, Alexander b 1985); *Style—* The Hon David Delfont

DELFOSSE, Jean-Marie Michel Joseph; LVO (1986), MVO (1966); s of Antoine Delfosse (d 1980), and Odette, *née* Eustace (d 1977); *b* 21 Oct 1920; *Educ* Univ of Liege (D Law); *m* 15 April 1947, Huguette, da of Georges Van Roye; 3 s (Philippe b 2 April 1948, Bernard b 31 Aug 1950, Vincent b 14 Oct 1952), 1 da (Jamin Claire b 10 Sept 1951); *Career* Nat Serv Cmdt 1942-42; barrister Court of Appeal Liege; Belgian: Officier de l'Ordre de Leopold, Croix de Guerre avec Palmes, Croix des Evadés, 1940 war medal; *Style—* Jean-Marie Delfosse, Esq, LVO, MVO; British Consulate, HM Honorary Consul, 45 Rue Beeckman, 400 Liege, Belgium (☎ 01 041 23 58 32, fax 01 041 23 77 11)

DELL, David Michael; CB (1986); s of Montague Roger Dell (d 1980), and Aimée Gabrielle, *née* Gould (d 1964); *b* 30 April 1931; *Educ* Rugby, Balliol Coll Oxford (MA); *Career* 2 Lt Royal Signals, serv Egypt and Cyprus 1954-55; Admty 1955-60, MOD 1960-65, Miny of Technol 1965-70; DTI 1970-; dir: Industl Devpt Unit 1984-87, Euro Investmt Bank 1984-87; chief exec Br Overseas Trade Bd 1987; *Clubs* St Stephen's Constitutional, Leeds (Leeds); *Style—* David M Dell, Esq, CB; 1 Victoria St, London SW1

DELL, Rt Hon Edmund Emanuel; PC (1970); s of Reuben and Frances Dell; *b* 15 Aug 1921; *Educ* Owen's Sch London, Queen's Coll Oxford (MA); *m* 1963, Susanne Gottschalk; *Career* Lt RA serv Euro 1944-45; memb Manchester City Cncl 1953-60, pres Manchester and Salford Trades Cncl 1958-61, MP (Lab) Birkenhead 1964-79, Parly sec Miny of Technol 1966-67, Parly under sec of state Dept of Econ Affrs 1967-68; min of state: BOT 1968-69, Dept of Employment and Productivity 1968-70; chm Commons Public Accounts Ctee 1973-74 (acting chm 1972-73), paymaster-gen 1974-76, sec of state trade and pres BOT 1976-78, memb Ctee Three Wise Men appointed by Euro Cncl to review procedures 1978-79; chm: Hansard Soc Cmmn on Paying for Politics 1979-80, Ctee on Int Business Taxation 1982, Working Pty on Co Political Donations 1985 (Hansard Soc and Const Reform Centre); chm and chief exec Guinness Peat Group 1979-82, chm C4 TV Co Ltd 1980-87, dir Shell Transport and Trading Co plc; chm: Pub Fin Fndn 1984, Prison Reform Tst 1988, London C of C and Indust, Commercial Educn Tst 1989, LCCI 1990-; dep chm Govrs Imperial Coll 1988; hon fell Fitzwilliam Coll Cambridge 1986 F; *Publications* The Good Old Cause (ed with JEC Hill, 1949), Brazil: The Dilemma of Reform (Fabian pamphlet, 1964), Political Responsibility and Industry (1973), Report on European Institutions (with B Biesheuvel and R Marjolin, 1979) The Politics of Economic Independence (1987), The Making of Economic Policy, 1974-76; articles in learned journals; *Recreations* listening to music; *Style—* The Rt Hon Edmund Dell, PC; 4 Reynolds Close, NW11 7EA (☎ 081 455 7197)

DELL, Dame Miriam Patricia; DBE (1980, CBE 1975), JP (1975); da of Gerald Wilfred Matthews (d 1940, family arrived NZ 1824) and Ruby Miriam, *née* Crawford (d 1948); *b* 14 June 1924; *Educ* Epsom Girls' GS, Auckland Univ (BA), Auckland Teachers' Training Coll (Teaching Cert); *m* 1946, Dr Richard Kenneth Dell, QSO; 4 da; *Career* teacher 1945-47, 1957-58 and 1961-71; nat chm Young Wives 1956-58; memb: Exec Cncl for Equal Pay and Opportunity 1966-76, various sub ctees Standards Assoc 1967-70, Joint Ctee on Womens Employment Nat Devpt Cncl 1969-74; convener and tutor Hutt Valley Marriage Guidance Cncl 1971 (tutor 1964-70); memb: Exec Environment and Conservation Organisation 1971-78 (chm 1988-), Ctee of Inquiry into Equal Pay 1971-72, Nat Exec Nat Marriage Guidance Cncl 1972-76; fndr memb Hutt Valley Branch Fedn Univ Women, chairwoman Ctee on Women 1974-81; memb: Nat Cmmn for UNESCO 1974-85, Nat Cncl Urban Devpt Assoc 1975-78, Steering Ctee and consIt Nat Cmmn for IYC 1977-79, Social Security Appeal Authority 1974-; pres Inter-Church Cncl of Public Affairs 1982- (vice-pres 1979-82); Nat Cncl of Women of NZ: rep for Mothers' Union Wellington Branch 1957, fndr memb Hutt Valley Branch 1958, pres 1966-68, vice pres Bd of Offrs 1967-70, nat pres 1970-74, convener Physical Environment Standing Ctee 1974-78, convener Status of Women Standing Ctee 1978-79; co-opted memb Parly Watch Ctee 1974-, vice convener Standing Ctee on Physical Environment Int Cncl of Women 1973-76 (pres 1979-86, vice pres 1976-79); has organised numerous workshops, leadership training courses and seminars and has represented NZ at many overseas conferences; Adele Ristori prize 1976, Queen's Silver Jubilee medal 1977, New Zealand Commemorative medal 1990; *Recreations* gardening, handcraft; *Style—* Dame Miriam Dell, DBE, JP; 98 Waerenga Rd, Otaki, NZ (☎ 47 267), 24 Townsend Rd, Wellington, NZ (☎ 888 726)

DELL, Ven Robert Sydney; s of Sydney Edward Dell (d 1957); *b* 20 May 1922; *Educ* Harrow Co Sch, Emmanuel Coll Cambridge, Ridley Hall; *m* 1953, Doreen Molly, da of William Layton (d 1957); 1 s, 1 da; *Career* ordained 1948, vice-princ Ridley Hall Cambridge 1957-65, vicar of Chesterton Cambridge 1966-73, archdeacon of Derby 1973-, hon canon of Derby Cathedral and examining chaplain to Bishop of Derby 1973, canon residentiary of Derby Cathedral 1981-; memb of the Gen Synod of the Church of Eng 1978-85; *Style—* The Ven the Archdeacon of Derby; 72 Pastures Hill, Littleover, Derby, DE3 7BB (☎ 0332 512700); Derby Church Hse, Full St, Derby DE1 3DR (☎ 0332 382233)

DELLA GRAZIA, Duchessa; Lady Hermione Gwladys; *née* Herbert; only da of 4 Earl of Powis (d 1974), and Hon Violet Ida Eveline (Baroness Darcy de Knayth in her own right); *b* 17 Sept 1900; *m* 6 Nov 1924, Conte Roberto Lucchesi Palli, 11 Duca della Grazia, and 13 Principe di Campofranco (recognised by King Umberto I 1891), who d 1979; 1 da; *Style—* Duchessa della Grazia; Hotel Beaurivage, 1006 Lausanne, Switzerland

DELLBORG, Rolf Gudmund; s of J George DellBorg (d 1961), and D Harriett, *née* Kjeallman (d 1948); *b* 20 Aug 1929; *Educ* Univ of Upsala (LLB); *m* 20 Oct 1949, Elison Mary Christine; 1 s (Richard b 1954); *Career* 2 Lt Swedish Army; banker, advocate and fin consIt; md Hambros Bank 1966-79 (ret); dir: Nat Bank of Sharjah Sharjah UAE, BT Rolatruc Sweden; chief Exec Wesley Investments Ltd, chm Scarab Investment Management Co Ltd; *Recreations* fishing, golf, shooting; *Clubs* Royal Batchelors Gothenburg, Addington Golf (Surrey), Wisley Golf; *Style—* Rolf G DellBorg, Esq; Flat 15, 22 St James's Square, London SW1Y 4JH

DELLIÈRE, John Peter; s of Robert Fernand George Dellière, of Haslemere, Surrey, and Elaine Gorton, *née* Hobbs; *b* 6 Aug 1944; *Educ* Whitgift Sch; *m* 28 June 1969, Elizabeth Joan, da of Gordon Keith Harman, of Lower Kingswood, Surrey; 3 s (Christian John b 10 Jan 1972, James Peter b 26 Aug 1976, Michael Robert Gordon b 2 Oct 1979); *Career* Mellors Basden & Co (City Accountants) 1963-68, Arthur Anderson & Co 1968-70, dir The White House (Linen Specialists) Ltd 1970, jt md The White House Ltd and subsidiary cos 1982 (dir 1980, md 1985); memb Cncl Bond St Assoc 1977 (Chm 1981-83); ACA 1967, FCA 1979, ATII 1967; *Recreations* golf, tennis; *Clubs* RAC, St James's; *Style—* John Dellière, Esq; Stable Cottage, Mill Lane, Ripley, Surrey GU23 6QT (☎ 0483 224975); The White House Ltd, 51 New Bond St, London W1Y 0BY (☎ 071 629 3521, fax 071 629 8269, mobile tel 083 362, telex 299 815 WYTOWZ G)

DELLIPIANI, Dr Alexander William; s of William Alexander Dellipiani (d 1965), of Gibraltar, and Lourdes, *née* Pallas (d 1982); *b* 25 Oct 1934; *Educ* Gibraltar GS, Univ of Edinburgh (MB ChB, MD); *m* 29 Sept 1962, Dorothy Sheila Lenore, da of Allan Inglis, CMG (d 1984), of Edinburgh; 1 s (John b 13 Jan 1973), 3 da (Elizabeth b 7 May 1964, Jane b 27 April 1968, Louise b 7 Dec 1970); *Career* house offr The Royal Infirmary Edinburgh 1959-60, sr lectr The Med Sch Baroda India 1965-66, lectr Dept of Therapeutics Univ of Edinburgh 1964-68 (res fell 1960-64), consIt physician N Tees Gen Hosp 1968-; univ postgrad med tutor N Tees Dist 1973-76, regnl advsr RCP(Ed) 1976 (examiner MRCP II 1970-), consIt physician Cleveland Constabulary 1986; memb Vocational Trg Sub-Ctee Med Newcastle; chm: N Tees Dist Med Exec Ctee 1976-78, Gen Hosp Staff Ctee 1980-84; memb: N Regnl Res Ctee 19820, Northern RHA 1982-90, N Regnl Med Ctee 1982-90; fell RMS Edinburgh 1959, MBSG 1964, memb British Soc of Digestive Endoscopy 1972-; FRCP, FRCPE; *Books* contrib: Disease of the Gut and Pancreas (1987), Coronary Care in The Community (1977), Intestinal Stomas (1978); *Style—* Dr Alexander W Dellipiani; Lynton, 17 Maltby Rd, Thornton, Middlesborough, Cleveland TS8 9BU (☎ 0642 590470); North Tees General Hospital, Hardwick, Stockton on Tees, Cleveland TS19 8PE (☎ 0642 672122)

DELLOW, Jeffrey; s of Earnest Dellow (d 1963), of Heworth, County Durham, and Edith, *née* Greenwal; *b* 19 Jan 1949; *Educ* Bill Quay Sch, St Martins Sch of Art, Maidstone Coll of Art, Slade Sch of Fine Art (Cheltenham Fellowship); *m* June 1976, Paula Jean Alison, da of Lt Col Roy Cleasby, MBE; 1 da (Bryony Grace b 27 Jan 1987); *Career* artist; exhibitions incl: John Moores 10 (Liverpool) 1976, Drawing in Action (Arts Cncl Touring Show) 1978-79, Open Attitudes (MOMA Oxford) 1979, Small Works by Younger Br Artists 1980, Small Works (Roehampton Inst) 1980, Sculpture and Painting from the Greenwich Studios (Woodlands Gallery Blackheath) 1981, Opening Show (Hull Artists Assoc) 1982, Small Works (Newcastle upon Tyne Poly Gallery) 1982, Whitechapel Open 1983-90, Marseille Art Present (Artis Gallery Marseille, Maison du Peuple Gardance France) 1983, 100 Artists (The Showroom Gallery London) 1984, Drawings and Watercolours (Hull Coll of Art) 1984, Greenwich Festival Studio Open 1985-90, Summer in the City (Ikon Gallery Birmingham) 1985, Three Painters (Arteast Gallery collective) 1986, solo show New Paintings (Castlefield Gallery) 1987, Three Abstract Painters (Todd Gallery) 1987, Art for Sale (Minories Gallery) 1988 Idylls (Todd Gallery Summer Show) 1989, Bath Art Fair 1989, John Moores 16 (Liverpool) 1989, Art 90 (Islington Art Fair) 1990, Todd Soho Gallery 1990, Olympia Art Fair 1990, Creative Assets (Harris Museum Preston) 1990, Works on Paper (Todd Gallery) 1990, Pachipamwe III (Nat Gallery of Zimbabwe Harare) 1990, Broadgate Art Week 1990; work in collections: Art Cncl of GB, Unilever, James Capel, Cooper & Lybrand, Arthur Anderson & Co, BASF UK; *Awards* Boise travelling scholarship, Arts Cncl of GB minor bursary, prizewinner Athena Art award (Barbican, 1988); lectr: Hull Coll of Art 1977-86, Roehampton Inst London 1978-80, N E London Poly 1978-86, Slade Sch of Fine Art (postgrad painters) 1980-82, Winchester Sch of Art 1982-86, Central Sch of Art 1982-84; head of painting and print lectr: Hull of Coll of Art 1986-88, Kingston Poly 1988-; visiting artist: RAF Bruggen W Germany 1974-75, Hull Coll of Art 1977, NE London Poly 1978, Roehampton Inst London 1978, Maidstone Coll of Art 1979, Slade Sch of Fine Art 1979, Manchester Poly Fine Art 1980, Norwich Sch of Art 1981, Winchester Sch of Art 1981; *Style—* Jeffrey Dellow, Esq; Todd Gallery, 326 Portobello Rd, London W10 5OU (☎ 071 960 6209)

DELMAR-MORGAN, Michael Walter; s of Curtis Delmar Morgan (d 1987), and Susan Henrietta, *née* Hargreaves Brown; *b* 1 March 1936; *Educ* Eton; *m* 17 Feb 1962, Marjorie, da of John Kennedy Logan (d 1984); 1 s (Benjamin b 1966), 2 da (Katharine b 1968, Alexandra b 1971); *Career* banker; dir Brown Shipley & Co Ltd 1966-88; *Recreations* sailing; *Clubs* Royal Yacht Sqdn; *Style—* Michael W Delmar-Morgan, Esq; Swaynes, Rudgwick, nr Horsham, Sussex RH12 3JD

DELTEIL, Christian Claude; s of Roger Delteil, and Catherine, *née* Fluxa; *b* 13 May 1954; *m* 9 Jan 1978, Geneviève Petit-Roche; 1 s (Sébastien b 31 Dec 1985), 1 da (Lauriane b 19 May 1979); *Career* Military Serv as chef of Admiral Brest; apprentice in Caborg France, commis then chef de partie Le Gauroche London 1975-76, chef de partie The Connaught 1976-77, sous chef then head chef Chewton Glen Hotel New Milton Hants 1978-82, chef and proprieter L'Arlequin 1982-; awards: one Michelin Star 1983, two stars Egon Ronay 1983, Restaurant of the Year Egon Ronay 1989; memb Academic Culinaire; *Recreations* karate, deep sea diving; *Style—* Christian Delteil, Esq; L'Arlequin Restaurant, 123 Queenstown Rd, London SW8 (☎ 071 622 0555, fax 071 498 7015)

DELVE, Sir Frederick William; CBE (1942); s of Frederick John Delve, of Brighton, and Eleanor Maria, *née* Brown; *b* 28 Oct 1902; *Educ* Brighton; *m* 9 Feb 1924, Ethel Lillian Morden (d 1980); *Career* RN 1918-23; joined Fire Serv 1923, chief offr Croydon Fire Bde 1934-41, dep inspr-in-chief NFS 1941-43, chief regnl fire offr London Regn NFS 1943-48, chief offr London Fire Bde 1948-62; hon pres Securicor Ltd; KPFSM 1940; kt 1962; *Style—* Sir Frederick Delve, CBE; 53 Ashley Court, Grand Ave, Hove, E Sussex (☎ 0273 774605)

DELVIN, Dr David George; s of William Delvin, of Ayrshire, and Elizabeth, *née* Falvey; *b* 28 Jan 1939; *Educ* St Dunstan's Coll, King's Coll Hosp Univ of London; *m* 1 (m dis), Kathleen, *née* Sears; m 2, Christine Campbell Webber; *Career* TV doctor and writer; memb GMC, med consIt to FPA, consIt ed of Gen Practitioner, vice chm Med Journalist Assoc, winner Best Book award of American Med Writers' Assoc, Consumer Columnist of the Year; LRCP, MRCS, DRCOG, MRCGP; Médaille de la Ville de Paris; *Recreations* scuba, running, opera; *Clubs* Royal Soc of Medicine; *Style—* Dr David Delvin; c/o Coutts & Co, 2 Harley St, London W1

DELVIN, Lord; Sean Charles Weston Nugent; does not at present use courtesy title; s and h of 13 Earl of Westmeath; *b* 16 Feb 1965; *Educ* Ampleforth; *Career*

computer programmer; *Style*— Sean Nugent, Esq

DEMARCO, Richard; OBE (1984); s of Carmine Demarco (d 1975), of Edinburgh, and Elizabeth Valentine Fusco (d 1982); *b* 9 July 1930; *Educ* Holy Cross Acad Edinburgh Coll of Art, Moray House Teachers Coll; *m* 1956, Anne Carol, da of Robert Muckle; *Career* artist, arts organiser, bdcaster, lectr; art master Duns Scotus Acad Edinburgh 1956-67; illustrator of BBC pubns 1958-61, fndr memb and vice chm Traverse Theatre Club 1963-67, dir Traverse Art Gallery 1963-67, artistic dir Richard Demarco Gallery 1966-; introduced avant-garde visual art to Edinburgh Festival Prog 1967 and presented avant-garde art from abroad 1968-84; responsible for promotion of nat and int art and theatre; visiting lectr at over 150 schs of art and univs; artist represented in over 1600 collections; reg broadcaster TV and Radio in Britain, N America and Poland; progs incl: One Man's Week (1971), The Demarco Dimension-Art In A Cold Climate (1988), The Green Man (1990), Images (5 progs, 1974); pubns incl: The Artist as Explorer (1978), The Road to Meikle Seggie (1978), The Celtic Consciousness; weekly columnist Edinburgh and Lothian Post 1987-89, Sunday Times (Scotland) 1988; dir Sean Connery's Scot Int Educn Tst 1972, memb Bd of Govrs Carlisle Sch of Art 1973-77, contrib ed Studio International 1982-84; external examiner: Stourbridge Sch of Art 1987-89, Wolverhampton Sch of Art 1990; Scot Arts Cncl award for services to the Arts in Scotland 1975; The Gold Order of Merit of the Polish Peoples Republic 1976, The Order of Cavaliere della Republica D' Italia 1988; hon fell RIAS 1991; *Recreations* exploring The Road to Meikle Seggie towards the Hebrides, in the footsteps of the Roman Legions, St Servanus and the Celtic Saints, and the medieval scholars, onwards into the Mediterranean and Eastern Europe; *Clubs* Scottish Arts (Edinburgh), Polish; *Style*— Cav Richard Demarco, OBE; 23A Lennox St, Edinburgh EH4 1PY (☎ 031 343 2124); The Richard Demarco Gallery Ltd, 17-21 Blackfriars St, Edinburgh EH1 1NB (☎ 031 557 0707 and 031 557 5707, fax 031 552 5972)

DEMELLO DIAS, Angela Joy; da of Malcolm Squire Cox (d 1968), and Joyce, *née* Oatley; *b* 12 Aug 1959; *Educ* Royal Ballet Sch (White Lodge and Upper); *m* 3 March 1984, Mario Antonio Demello Dias, s of Tancredo Dias (d 1982); *Career* entered Royal Ballet 1977, many roles in the repertoire of the Royal Ballet Covent Garden, joined Eng Nat Ballet 1991; *Style*— Mrs Angela Demello; Markova House, Jay Mews, London; c/o English National Ballet

DEMERY, Edward Peter; s of Peter Demery, and Cecilia Gwyneth Nepean, *née* Clifford-Smith; *b* 12 Dec 1946; *Educ* Bradfield; *m* 16 Jan 1971, Alexandra, da of Harold Paillet Rodier of Overdale, St Nicholas Hill, Leatherhead, Surrey; 1 s (Rupert b 1972), 1 da (Miranda b 1973); *Career* dir Clifford-Smith (underwriting agencies) Ltd 1976-85, joined Justerini & Brooks Ltd wine merchants 1967 (dir 1977, sales dir 1986-); memb Worshipful Co of Vintners; *Recreations* golf, cricket, tennis; *Clubs* Izingari, Band of Brothers, R & A, Royal St George's Golf; *Style*— Edward Demery, Esq; 72 Vineyard Hill Rd, Wimbledon, London SW19 7JJ (☎ 081 946 7056); 61 St James's St, London SW1A 1LZ (☎ 071 493 8721, telex 264 470 WINEJB G)

DEMPSEY, (James) Andrew Craig; s of James Dempsey (d 1982), and Gladys, *née* Cook; *b* 17 Nov 1942; *Educ* Ampleforth, Univ of Glasgow; *m* 4 April 1966, Grace, da of Dr Ian MacPhail; 1 s (Colin b 1971), 1 da (Catherine b 1976); *Career* exhibition organiser Arts Cncl of GB 1966-71, keeper Dept of PR Victoria & Albert Museum 1971-75, asst dir Hayward Gallery 1975-; *Recreations* reading, walking; *Style*— Andrew Dempsey, Esq; Hayward Gallery, South Bank Centre, London SE1 (☎ 071 921 0876, fax 071 928 0063)

DEMPSEY, Dr Brenda Mary; da of George Kenneth Price (d 1972), of 24 Curzon Rd, Prenton, Birkenhead, Cheshire, and Doris Hamill, *née* Crawford (d 1977); *b* 22 July 1927; *Educ* Birkenhead HS, GPDST, Univ of Liverpool Med Sch (MB ChB); *m* 1, 26 Jan 1952, John Anthony Dempsey (d 1982), s of George Barlow Dempsey, MC (d 1959), of Hanslope, Street Hey Lane, Willaston, Wirral, Cheshire; 2 s (David C b Aug 1956, Christopher John b Aug 1964), 2 da (Alison M b April 1958, Carolyn M b Oct 1961); m 2, June 1985, Barry Walker Kay; *Career* Royal Free Hosp: resident anaesthetist 1952, registrar anaesthetist 1954-57, sr registrar 1957; resident anaesthetist Queen Charlotte's Maternity Hosp and Chelsea Hosp for Women 1952-53, anaesthetist The Nethersole Hosp Hong Kong 1958-60; conslt anaesthetist: Elizabeth Garret Anderson Hosp 1961-72, Prince of Wales Hosp Tottenham 1961-72, Ashford Dist Gen Hosp Ashford Middx 1972; memb Rotary Inner Wheel Staines; FFARCS 1955; *Recreations* managing a livery stables and riding school, swimming; *Style*— Dr Brenda Dempsey; Lyfords Meadow, 127 Lock's Ride, Ascot, Berks SL5 8RX (☎ 0344 882129); Ashford District General Hospital, Ashford, Middlesex (☎ 0784 251188)

DEMPSTER, Lady Camilla Dorothy Godolphin; *née* Osborne; da of 11 Duke of Leeds (d 1963); *b* 14 Aug 1950; *m* 1, 1971 (m dis 1976), Robert Julian Brownlow Harris; 1 da; m 2, 1977, as his 2nd w, Nigel Richard Patton Dempster, the columnist; 1 da; *Style*— The Lady Camilla Dempster; 11 Neville Terrace, London SW7

DEMPSTER, Ian Tom; s of Tom Roberts Dempster (d 1972), of Broxbourne, Herts, and Mary, *née* Parry (d 1984); *b* 2 April 1934; *Educ* Charterhouse; *m* 1, Judith Clare (d 1971), da of Kenneth Bernard Pearce, of Hertford; 2 da (Ellen b 1967, Victoria b 1969); m 2, 2 Jan 1978, Elizabeth Mary, da of Robert Muir Meek (d 1960), of Girvan, Ayrshire; 1 da (Clare b 1979); *Career* Pilot Offr RAF (pilot GD Branch) 1957-58; CA Chalmers Impey and Co 1952-63, chm Sign and Metal Industries plc (now Acme Signs plc) 1964-, vice chm Cheshunt Building Society 1989- (dir 1979-); fin offr London N Euro Constituency Cons Cncl, chm Enfield Dist Mfrs Assoc 1973 (dir 1988-), pres Electric Sign Mfrs Assoc 1975; dir Cncl Br Sign Assoc Ltd 1988-; FCA; *Recreations* golf, gardening; *Clubs* October; *Style*— Ian Dempster, Esq; The White House, Greyhound Lane, South Mimms, Potters Bar, Herts EN6 3NX (☎ 0707 43 183); Acme Signs plc, Sewardstone Rd, Waltham Abbey, Essex (☎ 0992 719 662, fax 0992 710 101, telex 267444)

DEMPSTER, John William Scott; s of Dr David Dempster (d 1981), of Plymouth, and Mary Constance, *née* Simpson (d 1985); *b* 10 May 1938; *Educ* Plymouth Coll, Oriel Coll Oxford; *Career* civil servant; dep sec Dept of Tport, princ private sec to the Sec of State for the Environment 1976-77, finance offr Dept of Tport 1977-81, princ establishment and finance offr Lord Chancellor's Dept 1981-84, head of marine directorate Dept of Tport 1984-89, princ establishment and fin offr Dept of Tport 1989-; *Recreations* mountaineering, sailing (part owner of yacht Carolina); *Clubs* Royal Southampton Yacht, Swiss Alpine; *Style*— John Dempster, Esq; Dept of Transport, 2 Marsham Street, London SW1P 3EB (☎ 071 276 5219)

DEN BRINKER, Carl Siegmund; s of Hermanus Maria den Brinker (d 1975); *b* 29 March 1930; *Educ* St Franciscus Coll Rotterdam, Univ of Bath (MSc); *m* 1965, Margaret, da of Frank Todd (d 1990); 1 s, 3 da; *Career* physicist Texas Instruments Ltd 1961-75, dir Mackintosh Conslts 1976-78, tech dir Redifon Ltd 1978-90, Scientific conslt 1990-; memb Cncl Nat Academic Awards 1978-84, vice-pres IERE 1984-87, Def Scientific Advsy Cncl (Comm Tech Ctee) 1984-90, dir Rediffusion Electronics 1985-89; Freeman City of London, Master Elect Worshipful Co of Scientific Instrument Makers; CPhys, CEng, FInstP, FIEE, FInstD; *publications* author of several scientific papers and patents; *Recreations* music, theatre, saxon church architecture; *Clubs* IOD; *Style*— Carl den Brinker Esq; 55 Underhill Rd, London SE22 0QR (☎ 081 693 5970)

DENBIGH AND DESMOND, Betty, Countess of; Verena Barbara; da of William Edward Price (d 1966), of Hallgates, Cropston, nr Leicester; *b* 1 March 1904; *m* 1, 1923, Lt-Col Thomas Paget Fielding Johnson (decd); 1 da; m 2, 17 May 1940, 10 Earl of Denbigh and Desmond (d 1966); 1 s (11 Earl), 1 da (Lady Clare Simonian); *Style*— The Rt Hon Betty, Countess of Denbigh and Desmond; Newnham Paddox, nr Rugby, Warwicks (☎ 0788 832173)

DENBIGH AND DESMOND, 11 and 10 Earl of (E 1622 and I 1622); William Rudolph Michael Feilding; also Baron Feilding, Viscount Feilding (both E 1620), Baron Feilding, Viscount Callan (both I 1622), and Baron St Liz (E 1663); s of 10 and 9 Earl of Denbigh and Desmond (d 1966); 2 cousin seven times removed of Henry Feilding the novelist and magistrate); *b* 2 Aug 1943; *Educ* Eton; *m* 2 Sept 1965, Caroline Judith Vivienne, da of Lt-Col Geoffrey Cooke; 1 s, 2 da (Lady Samantha b 1966, Lady Louisa b 1969); *Heir* s, Viscount Feilding, *qv*; *Career* sits as Liberal peer in House of Lords; *Style*— The Rt Hon Earl of Denbigh and Desmond; 21 Moore Park Rd, SW6 (☎ 01 736 0460); Pailton House, Newnham Paddox, Rugby, Warwicks (☎ 832176)

DENCER, Geoffrey Hargreaves; s of late Charles Dencer; *b* 20 Sept 1928; *Educ* Stockport GS, Manchester Univ (BSc); *m* 1981, Patricia, *née* Crocome; children by previous m; *Career* chartered civil engineer, construction dir IDC Construction Ltd Stratford 1970- (formerly with Charles Tennet & Son Stockton on Tees); *Style*— Geoffrey Dencer, Esq; 138 Bridgetown Rd, Stratford-upon-Avon, Warwickshire CU37 7JH

DENCH, Dame Judith Olivia (Dame Judi Williams); DBE (1988, OBE 1970); da of Reginald Arthur Dench and Eleanora Olave Dench; *b* 9 Dec 1934; *Educ* The Mount Sch York, Central Sch of Speech and Drama; *m* 1971, Michael Williams, actor; 1 da (Tara b 1972); *Career* actress; assoc memb RSC 1969-; numerous performances for: RSC, The Old Vic Co, NT, and in West End; films and television; pres Festival of Br Theatre 1983-; SWET Best Actress of the Year Award 1977, 1980 and 1984, Variety Club Actress of the Year Award 1982, Bdcasting Press Guild TV and Radio Award for Best Actress, The *Standard* Best Actress Award 1983, Plays and Players Best Actress Award 1984, Olivier Award 1987, Evening Standard Best Actress Award 1987, BAFTA Best Supporting Actress Award 1987 and 1989; Hon DLitt: Univ of York 1978, Univ of Warwick 1980, Univ of Birmingham 1989; *Style*— Dame Judi Dench, DBE

DENHAM, 2 Baron (UK 1937); Sir Bertram Stanley Mitford Bowyer; 10 Bt (E 1660), of Denham, and 2 Bt (UK 1933), of Weston Underwood; PC (1981), KBE (1991); s of 1 Baron Denham (d 1948), and Hon Daphne Freeman-Mitford, da of 1 Baron Redesdale; suc to Btcy of Denham on death of kinsman 1950; *b* 3 Oct 1927; *Educ* Eton, King's Coll Cambridge; *m* 14 Feb 1956, Jean, da of Kenneth McCorquodale, MC, TD; 3 s, 1 da; *Heir* s, Hon Richard Grenville George Bowyer; *Career* late Lt Oxford and Bucks LI; a lord in waiting to HM The Queen 1961-64 and 1970-71, Capt of Yeomen of the Gd (dep chief whip in House of Lords) 1971-74, Capt Hon Corps Gentlemen-at-Arms 1979- (govt chief whip House of Lords), oppn dep chief whip 1974-78, oppn chief whip 1978-79; *Books* The Man Who Lost His Shadow (1979), Two Thyrdes (1983), Foxhunt (1988); *Clubs* White's, Pratt's, Buck's, Carlton; *Style*— The Rt Hon the Lord Denham, PC, KBE; The Laundry Cottage, Weston Underwood, Olney, Bucks (☎ 0234 711535)

DENHAM, Dowager Baroness; Hon Daphne; *née* Freeman-Mitford; da of late 1 Baron Redesdale, GCVO, KCB; *b* 3 Sept 1895; *m* 27 Feb 1919, 1 Baron Denham, MC (d 1948); 2s (1 ka), 1 da; *Style*— The Rt Hon the Dowager Lady Denham; Dunsland, Shrublands Rd, Berkhamsted, Herts HP4

DENHAM, Dr Michael John; s of Ernest William Denham (d 1989), and Lila Beatrice, *née* Sword (d 1974); *b* 17 March 1935; *Educ* King Edward VI Sch Norwich, City of Norwich Sch, Downing Coll Cambridge, Westminster Med Sch (MA, MD, FRCP); *m* 31 Oct 1965, Sheila Ann, da of David Rodger (d 1976); 1 s (Nicholas b 1973), 2 da (Tessa b 1970, Susan b 1976); *Career* conslt physician in geriatric med Northwick Park Hosp and Clinical Res Centre 1973-; RCP examiner: for membership 1985-, for Dip of Geriatric Med 1989-; lectr and examiner: for health visitors Stevenage Coll 1979-88, for health visitors and dist nurses Hatfield Poly 1989-; ed jl Cave of the Elderly 1989-, author numerous articles on care of the elderly; sec Br Geriatrics Soc 1979-81, annual secondments to NHS Advsy Serv 1981-, med advsr to Research into Ageing 1983-90; *Books* Treatment of Medical Problems in the Elderly (ed 1980), Blood Disorders in the Elderly (jt ed 1985), Infections in the Elderly (ed 1986), Drugs in Old Age (jt ed 1990); *Recreations* swimming, reading, DIY, air shows, gardening; *Style*— Dr Michael Denham; Northwick Park Hospital, Watford Rd, Harrow, Middx HA1 3UJ (☎ 01 864 3232)

DENHOLM, (James) Allan; s of James Denholm (d 1959), and Florence Lily Keith, *née* Kennedy (d 1972); *b* 27 Sept 1936; *Educ* Hutchesons' Boys GS Glasgow; *m* 10 Sept 1964, Elizabeth Avril, da of John Stewart McLachlan, of Duni, South Broomage Ave, Larbert, Stirlingshire FK5 3ED; 1 s (Keith b 7 Sept 1966), 1 da (Alison b 24 May 1969); *Career* dir: William Grant and Sons Ltd 1975-, Scottish Mutual Assur Soc 1987-; dir Scottish Cremation and Burial Reform Soc 1980-; chm: E Kilbride Devpt Corpn 1983- (memb 1979-), Glasgow Jr C of C 1972-73; pres 49 Wine and Spirit Club of Scotland 1983-84, tstee Scottish Cot Death Tst 1985-, vice pres ICAS 1989-; visitor Incorp of Maltmen in Glasgow 1980-81, dir of Weavers' Soc of Anderson 1987; CA 1960, FSA Scotland 1987; *Recreations* shooting, golf; *Clubs* Royal Scottish Automobile; *Style*— J Allan Denholm, Esq; Greencroft, 19 Colquhoun Drive, Bearsden, Glasgow G61 4NQ (☎ 041 942 1773); William Grant & Sons Ltd, 208 West George St, Glasgow G2 2PE (☎ 041 248 3101, fax 041 248 2795, telex 778314)

DENINGTON, Baroness (Life Peer UK 1978), of Stevenage, Herts; Dame Evelyn Joyce Denington; DBE (1974, CBE 1966); da of Philip Charles Bursill, of Woolwich; *b* 9 Aug 1907; *Educ* Blackheath HS, Bedford Coll London; *m* 1935, Cecil Dallas Denington, s of Richard Denington, of Wanstead; *Career* journalist 1927-31, teacher 1933-50; gen sec Nat Assoc Lab Teachers 1937-47; memb: St Pancras Borough Cncl 1945-59 (chm Staff Ctee, Planning Ctee Purposes Ctee), LCC 1946-65 (vice-chm Housing Ctee 1949-60, chm Dvpt & Mgmnt Sub-Cte 1949-60, chm New & Expanding Towns Ctee 1960-65), GLC 1964-77 (chm Cncl 1975-76, dep ldr opposition 1967-73, chm Ho Ctee 1964-67, chm Tport Ctee 1973-75), Stevenage Devpt Corpn 1950-80 (chm 1966-80), Central Housing Advsy Ctee 1955-73 (memb sub-ctee producing Park Morris report and chm sub-ctee producing Our Older Homes Report), SE Econ Planning Ctee 1966-79; memb and chm of various bds of mgmt and govr of schs in St Pancras and Islington 1945-73, chm London Coll for the Garment Trades (Coll of Fashion), memb and chm of govrs Ardale Sr Boys' Approved Sch, chm Hornchurch Childrens' Home; memb: Sutton Dwellings Housing Tst 1976-82, Shackleton Housing Assoc 1976-82, N Br Housing Assoc 1976-88, St Pancras Assoc 1977-78, Gtr London Secdy Housing Assoc 1978-83, Sutton (Hastoe) Housing Assoc 1981-88, St Edward's Housing Assoc 1983-87; memb and a vice-chm Town & Co Planning Assoc; Freeman City of London; Hon FRIBA, Hon MRTPI; *Style*— The Rt Hon Baroness Denington, DBE; Flat 3, 29 Brunswick Square, Hove, E Sussex

DENISON, (Alan) David; s of Wing Cdr Amos Allen Denison MBE, MC (d 1976), and Mary Myfanwy Blakeman, *née* Roberts; *b* 7 May 1945; *Educ* William Ellis Sch Highgate, RAF Cranwell; *m* 9 Sept 1972, Virginia Jane, da of Reinhold Anton Wassman (d 1971) of Br Columbia, Canada; 3 s (Nicolas, Mungo, Barnaby); *Career* PO RAF 1964-67; CA; Coopers & Lybrand 1967-72, Baring Bros & Co Ltd 1972-82, md BASE Int Hldgs plc 1984-; *Recreations* flying, collecting first editions; *Clubs* RAF; *Style*— David Denison, Esq; Midsummer House, Midsummer Boulevard, Central Milton Keynes, MK9 3BN (☎ 0908 664 315, fax 0908 665 312)

DENISON, Edward Allan Kitson; OBE (1986), TD (and clasp); s of Wing Cdr Amos Allan Denison MBE, MC (d 1976), of Devon, and Margery, *née* Morton (d 1975); *b* 13 Sept 1928; *Educ* St Peter's York, Brasenose Coll Oxford (MA, BCL); *m* 18 May 1957, Mary Hey, da of William Peacock, of Eshersykes, Malton, N Yorks; 1 s (Mark b 1960) 1 da (Clare b 1962); *Career* cmmnd W Yorks Regt 1947, served occupation of Austria TA 1948-67, Lt-Col 3 Prince of Wales Own, Yorks and Humberside TA and AVR Assoc; slr and sr ptnr in private practice; formerly head of Legal Dept to Shepherd Building Group and first chm legal group to Bldg Employers Confedn; former chm and pres Thirsk and Malton and Ryedale Cons Assoc, chm London York Fund Mangrs Ltd; non-exec dir: Ben Johnson & Co Ltd 1978-85, Equity & General plc 1984-86, Univ of Leeds Fndn and many private cos; public appts: N Riding CC 1970-74, N Yorks CC 1973-81 (ldr 1977-81); memb: ACC Fin Ctee 1977-81, Yorks & Humberside Econ Planning Cncl, Yorks Humberside & E Midlands Industl Devpt Bd; pres York Euro Cons Assoc; vice chm Bd of Govrs St Peters Sch; boxed for Oxford Univ 1950-51, memb Headingley RUFC 1950-56; *Recreations* shooting, skiing, tennis, travel; *Clubs* Army and Navy, Yorkshire, Vincents; *Style*— Edward A K Denison, Esq, OBE, TD; The Old Vicarage, Bossall, York; Chancery Hse, 141-143 Holgate Rd, York (☎ 0904 610820, fax 0904 656972)

DENISON, John Law; CBE (1960, MBE Mil 1945); s of Rev Herbert Bouchier Wiggins Denison (d 1968), of Bexhill, Sussex; *b* 21 Jan 1911; *Educ* Brighton Coll, Royal Coll of Music, St George's Sch Windsor Castle; *m* 1, 1936 (m dis 1946), Anne Claudia Russell, da of Col Claude Russell Brown, CB, DSO (d 1939); m 2, 1947, Evelyn Donald (d 1958), da of John Moir; 1 da; m 3, 1960 Audrey Grace Burnaby (d 1970), da of Brig-Gen Frederick Gilbert Bowles, RE (d 1947); m 4, 1972, Françoise Henriette Mitchell (d 1985), da of Maître Garrigues; *Career* served WWII 1939-45 (despatches); music dir Arts Cncl of GB 1948-65, dir South Bank Concert Halls 1965-76; chm: Cultural Programme, London Celebrations, Queen's Silver Jubilee 1977; hon treas Royal Philharmonic Soc 1976-89; chm: Royal Concert (in aid of musical charities) 1976-87, Arts Educn Schs; memb Cncl Royal Coll of Music; FRCM, Hon RAM, Hon GSM; Cdr Order of Lion (Finland), Chev dans l'Ordre des Arts et des Lettres (France); *Clubs* Garrick; *Style*— John Denison, Esq, CBE; 22 Empire House, Thurloe Place, London SW7 2RU

DENISON, (John) Michael Terence Wellesley; CBE (1983); s of Gilbert Dixon Denison (d 1959), and Marie Louise, *née* Bain (d 1915); maternal gf A W Bain on Kimberley diamond rush 1871, founded A W Bain & Sons Insurance Brokers Leeds 1874 (now Bain-Clarkson), Lord Mayor of Leeds 1913; *b* 1 Nov 1915; *Educ* Wellesley House Broadstairs, Harrow (entrance exhibitioner), Magdalen Coll Oxford (BA); *m* 29 April 1939, Dulcie Winifred Catherine (the actress Dulcie Gray, *qv*), da of Arnold Savage Bailey, CBE (d 1935); *Career* Army 1940-46; Capt Intelligence Corps: NI, ME, Greece, UK; actor; cncllr Equity 1949-77 (vice pres 1952, 1961-63, 1974); dir: Allied Theatre Prodns 1966-75, Play Co of London 1970-74, New Shakespeare Co 1971-; 112 theatrical prodns of which 50 in London, 15 films, innumerable radio and TV plays (including 80 as Boyd QC); Queen's Jubilee Medal 1977; FRSA; *Books* The Actor and His World (1964), Overture and Beginners (1973), Double Act (1985); articles for the Dictionary of National Biography on Sir Noel Coward, Sir Peter Daubeny and Peter Bridge (1985-86); *Recreations* golf, painting, watching cricket, gardening, motoring; *Clubs* MCC, Richmond Golf; *Style*— Michael Denison, Esq, CBE; Shardeloes, Amersham, Buckinghamshire HP7 0RL

DENISON-PENDER, Hon Robin Charles; yr s of 2 Baron Pender, CBE (d 1965) and bro of 3 Baron; *b* 7 Sept 1935; *Educ* Eton; *m* 7 May 1966, Clare Nell, only da of Lt-Col James Currie Thomson, MBE, TD, JP, DL, of Stable Court, Walkern, Herts; 2 s, 1 da; *Career* late 2 Lt 11 Hussars 1954-56; memb of London Stock Exchange; vice pres Royal Albert Hall 1970-83, chm The Knole Club 1985-; *Recreations* golf, gardening, tennis; *Clubs* White's; *Style*— The Hon Robin Denison-Pender; Jessups, Mark Beech, Edenbridge, Kent TN8 5NR (☎ 0342 850684)

DENMAN, 5 Baron (UK 1834); Sir Charles Spencer Denman; 2 Bt (UK 1945), of Staffield, Co Cumberland; CBE (1976), MC (1942), TD; s of Hon Sir Richard Denman, 1 Bt (d 1957); suc cous, 4 Baron, 1971; *b* 7 July 1916; *Educ* Shrewsbury; *m* 11 Sept 1943, Sheila Anne (d 1987), da of Lt-Col Algernon Bingham Anstruther Stewart, DSO; 3 s, 1 da; *Heir* s, Hon Richard Thomas Stewart Denman; *Career* served WW II Duke of Cornwall's LI (TA), Maj 1943, served India, M East, Mediterranean; contested Leeds Central (C) 1945; dir (formerly chm) Marine & General Mutual Life Assurance Soc; formerly dir Consolidated Gold Fields and other cos; vice-pres Middle East Assoc; memb: Ctee of Middle East Trade, Ctee on Invisible Exports; tstee: Kitchener Memorial Fund, Arab Br Charitable Fndn; formerly govr Windlesham House School; now chm: Arundell House plc, Cox & Bell Ltd; dir: Close Bros Gp, British Water, Wastewater Ltd; chm Saudi British Soc; pres Royal Soc for Asia Affairs; cncl memb Inst for Study of Conflict; *Clubs* Brooks's; *Style*— The Rt Hon Lord Denman, CBE, MC, TD

DENMAN, Prof Donald Robert; s of Robert Martyn Denman (d 1915), of Belfast, and Letitia Kate, *née* Barnes (d 1968); *b* 7 April 1911; *Educ* Christ's Coll Finchley, Univ of London (BSc, MSc, PhD), Univ of Cambridge (MA); *m* 12 April 1941, (Jessie) Hope, da of Richard Henry Prior (d 1919); 2 s (Jonathan b 1949, Richard b 1951); *Career* WWII serv Air Miny RAF (Civil) 1939-41, dep exec Cumberland War Agric Ctee 1941-46; chartered surveyor in private practice 1937-39; Univ of Cambridge: land agent 1946-48, lectr 1948-68, head Dept of Land Econ 1962-78, prof land econ 1968-78, fell Pembroke Coll 1962-78, emeritus prof and fell 1978-; established land econ tripos and dept at Univ of Cambridge, undertook similar pioneering work in other univs UK and overseas; patron Small Farmers' Assoc; memb: Land Decade Educnl Cncl, ctees RICS, ctees Cwlth Assoc of Surveying and Land Econ; chm Cwlth Human Ecology Cncl, memb advsy panel Aims of Indust, fndr Human Ecology Fndn, advsr Govt of Iran 1968-74; memb: Agric Improvement Cncl, Cncl Nat Academic Awards, Nat Cmmn UNESCO, Ecology Cmmn, Int Union for Conservation of Nature; memb Ely Church Assembly; Hon DSc Univ of Kumasi 1979, Hon fell Royal Swedish Acad of Forestry and Agric 1971, Hon fell Ghana Inst of Surveyors 1970; FRICS (gold medallist); Distinguished Order of Hamayoun, Imperial Ct of Persia 1974; *Books* over 40 publications incl: Origins of Ownership (1958), Land use and the Constitution of Property (1969), Land Use: an Introduction to Proprietary Land Use Analysis (1976), The Place of Property (1978), Land in a Free Society (1980), Markets Under the Sea (1983), After Government Failure (1987); *Recreations* travel; *Clubs* Carlton, Farmers; *Style*— Prof Donald Denman; 12 Chaucer Road, Cambridge CB2 2EB (☎ 0223 357 725)

DENMAN, Lady Frances Esmé; *née* Curzon; 2 da of 5 Earl Howe (d 1964), by his 2 w, Joyce Mary McLean, da of Charles McLean Jack, of Johannesburg, S Africa; *b* 1939; *m* 1, 1962, Derek Alan Whiting, yr s of William Thomas Whiting, of Beckenham, Kent; 2 s; m 2, 1976, Harold Denman, yr bro of 5 Baron Denman; 1 s; *Style*— The Lady Frances Denman; Wybarnes, Ticehurst, E Sussex

DENMAN, Harold; s of Hon Sir Richard Denman, 1 Bt (d 1957); *b* 26 Jan 1922; *Educ* Repton, Balliol Oxford; *m* 1976, Lady Frances Esmé Curzon, da of 5 Earl Howe; 1 s (Roland Sebastian Richard b 1 June 1977); *Career* Capt RA 1939-45; dir Tennant Budd Ltd 1959; *Style*— Harold Denman, Esq; Wybarnes, Ticehurst, E Sussex TN5 7DL (☎ 200332)

DENMAN, Hon James Stewart (Jamie); s of 5 Baron Denman, MC; *b* 7 Aug 1954; *Educ* Summerfields, Stowe, The Mill Climping, Warsash; *m* 6 July 1989, Philippa Jane Emma, da of Lewis Ronald Frederick Trowbridge (d 1990), of Winchester; *Style*— The Hon James Denman; c/o Macmillans, 351 Fulham Road, London SW6 (☎ 071 351 2939)

DENMAN, Hon (Christopher) John; s of 5 Baron Denman, MC; *b* 5 Sept 1955; *Educ* Millfield, The Mill Littlehampton; *m* 1984, Jenny B, only da of Rupert Allen, of Willaston in Wirral, Cheshire; 1 s (Alexander b and d 1987); *Style*— The Hon John Denman

DENMAN, Hon Richard Thomas Stewart; s and h of 5 Baron Denman, MC; *b* 4 Oct 1946; *Educ* Milton Abbey; *m* 18 April 1984, (Lesley) Jane, da of John Stevens, of 2 Shakespear Drive, Hinckley, Leics; 2 da (Natasha Anne b 1986); *Career* chartered accountant; articled to Deloitte 1966; ACA; *Clubs* Brooks's; *Style*— The Hon Richard Denman

DENMAN, Sir (George) Roy; KCB (1977, CB 1972), CMG (1968); s of Albert Denman, of 20 River Park, Marlborough, Wilts; *b* 12 June 1924; *Educ* Harrow, St John's Coll Cambridge; *m* 1966, Moya, da of John M Lade; 1 s, 1 da; *Career* served WW II as Maj Royal Signals, BOT 1948, served in HM Embassies Bonn and UK delgn to Geneva 1957-61 and 1965-67, under-sec BOT 1967-70; memb: negotiating delgn EEC 1970-72, BOTB 1972-75; dep sec: DTI 1970-74, Dept of Trade 1974-75; second perm sec Cabinet Off 1975-77, dir-gen External Affairs EEC 1977-82, head of delegation cmmn of EC to US 1982-; *Style*— Sir Roy Denman, KCB, CMG; 2100 M Street, NW (Suite 707), Washington DC, 20037 USA (☎ 010 1 202 862 9500)

DENMAN, Sylvia Elaine; da of Alexander Yard, of Barbados, and Eileen, *née* Alleyne (d 1966); *Educ* Queens Coll of Barbados; *m* 20 Dec 1962 (m dis 1975), Hugh Denman; 1 da (Sophia b 24 Aug 1971); *Career* called to the Bar Lincoln's Inn, lectr and sr lectr Oxford Poly 1966-76, sr lectr and tutor Univ of the W Indies 1977-82, Fullbright fell NY Univ 1982-83, princ equal opportunities ILEA 1983-86, pro asst dir Poly of the S Bank 1986-89, dep dir of educn ILEA 1989-90; former memb: Race Relations Bd, Equal Opportunities Cmmn, Lord Chllr's Advsy Ctee on Legal Aid; currently: Leverhulme fell, tstee Runnymede and John Hunt and Erro/Barrow Award Tsts, govr Haverstock Sch, lawyer and chm London Rent Assessment Panel; FRSA; *Recreations* music, walking, theatre; *Style*— Mrs Sylvia Denman; 32 Belsize Park Gardens, London NW3 4LH (☎ 071 586 1734)

DENNEHY, Constance Mauguerita; da of Dennis Franklyn Dennehy (d 1944), of Christchurch, NZ, and Constance, *née* Dennehy; *b* 29 Dec 1931; *Educ* Villa Maria Convent, Canterbury Univ Coll NZ, Univ of Otago NZ (MB ChB); *Career* conslt child psychiatrist Hosps for Sick Children 1971-, hon lectr St Bartholomews Hosp 1972-; FRCPE, MRCPsych, DPM, FRSM, FRGS; *Style*— Miss Constance Dennehy; 18 Montpelier Grove, London NW5 2XD (☎ 071 485 4210); Queen Elizabeth's Hospital for Children, Hackney Rd, London E2 8PS; 14 Devonshire Place, London W1

DENNES, John Mathieson; s of Norman Dennes, BSc (d 1964), formerly of Middle Green, Poulshot, Devizes, Wilts, and Muriel Evelyn Thomas (d 1985); *b* 19 May 1926; *Educ* Rugby, Christ's Coll Cambridge (MA); *m* 5 April 1961, Verity Ann Mary, da of Lt-Col Leslie Rushworth Ward, MC, RA (d 1977), of Caltofts, Harleston, Norfolk; 4 s (Jonathan b 1962, Thomas b 1963, Adam b 1964, William b 1966); *Career* Mil Serv 1944-47, Intelligence Corps (Far East); slr; sr ptnr Waltons & Morse (ret); non exec dir 1989: Holman Franklin Ltd, Holman MacLeod Ltd, Holman Managers Ltd, Newgreen (Underwriting Agencies) Ltd; non exec dir 1990: David Evers Ltd, Eversure Underwriting Agency Ltd; elected Annual Subscriber to Lloyd's 1989; *Recreations* choral music, industrial archaeology, driving, good food and wine; *Style*— John M Dennes, Esq; Church House, Wellow, Bath, Avon BA2 8QS

DENNETT, Angelina Brunhilde; da of Leonard Arthur Dennett (d 1978), and Antonia Augustine Elizabeth Dennett; *b* 11 June 1956; *Educ* Ridgeway Secdy Sch, West Kent Coll, City of London Poly (BA), Univ of London (LLM); *m* 15 Aug 1989, David Thomas Fish; *Career* called to the Bar Middle Temple 1980; awards incl: Middle Temple Blackstone Pupillage award 1981, Malcolm Wright Pupillage award 1981; memb Family Law Bar Assoc; *Style*— Ms Angelina Dennett; Manchester House Chambers, 18-22 Bridge St, Manchester M3 3B7 (☎ 061 834 7007, fax 061 834 3462, DX 1853 Manchester 3)

DENNING, Baron (Life Peer UK 1957), of Whitchurch, Co Southampton; Alfred Thompson Denning; PC (1948), DL (Hants 1978); s of Charles Denning (d 1941), of Whitchurch, Hants, and Clara, *née* Thompson; *b* 23 Jan 1899; *Educ* Andover GS, Magdalen Coll Oxford; *m* 1, 28 Dec 1932, Hilda Mary Josephine (d 22 Nov 1941), da of late Rev Frank Northam Harvey; 1 s; m 2, 27 Dec 1945, Joan Daria, da of John Vinings Elliott-Taylor, and wid of John Matthew Blackwood Stuart, CIE; *Career* barr Lincoln's Inn 1923, KC 1938, bencher 1944; chllr: Dio of Southwark 1937-44, London 1942-44; rec of Plymouth 1944, judge of the High Ct of Justice 1944-48, Lord Justice of Appeal 1948-57, Lord of Appeal in Ordinary 1957-62, Master of the Rolls 1962-82, ret; hon master of the bench: Middle Temple 1972, Gray's Inn 1979, Inner Temple 1982; chm Royal Cmmn on Historical Manuscripts to 1982, pres Nat Marriage Guidance Cncl to 1983; conducted Profumo Inquiry 1963; treas Lincoln's Inn 1964; hon fell: Magdalen Coll Oxford, Univ Coll London; author, broadcaster; kt 1944; *Publications* Smith's Leading Cases (joint ed, 1929), Bullen and Leake's Precedents (1935), Freedom under the Law (Hamlyn Lectures, 1949), The Changing Law (1953), The Road to Justice (1955), The Discipline of Law (1979), The Due Process of Law (1980), The Family Story (1981), What Next in the Law (1982), The Closing Chapter (1983), Landmarks in the Law (1984), Leaves From My Library (1986); *Clubs* Athenaeum; *Style*— The Rt Hon Lord Denning, PC, DL; The Lawn, Whitchurch, Hants (☎ 025 682 2144)

DENNING, (Charles Henry) David; s of late Lt-Gen Sir Reginald Denning, KCVO, KBE, CB, of Delmonden Grange, Hawkhurst, Kent, and Lady Eileen Violet Denning, OBE, *née* Currie; *b* 1 May 1933; *Educ* Winchester; *m* 21 June 1958, Patricia Margaret, da of Cdr Nigel Loftus Henry Fane (d 1974); 2 s (James Henry b 1959, Guy William b 1962), 2 da (Sophia Jane b 1964, Venetia Mary b 1966); *Career* cmmnd 11 Hussars 1952, demob 1954, Territorial Offr City of London Yeo 1954-57; underwriting memb Lloyds 1960-; dir: B W Noble Ltd Insurance Brokers 1968-74, C T Bowring Insurance Ltd 1973-74; md The Copenhagen Reinsurance Co UK Ltd 1974-, dep chm Reinsurance Offices Assoc 1987- (memb Exec Ctee); *Recreations* shooting, farming; *Clubs* The Gresham; *Style*— David Denning, Esq; Bewl Bridge Farm, Lamberhurst, Kent TN3 8JJ (☎ 0892 890876)

DENNING, (Michael) John; s of Frederick Edward Denning (d 1985), of Bath, and Linda Agnes Albertine, *née* Young (d 1953); *b* 29 Nov 1934; *Educ* Benedicts; *m* 12 March 1966, Elizabeth Anne, da of Ralph William Beresford, of High Clere, Ben Rhydding, Ilkley, Yorks; 1 s (Simon b 1969), 2 da (Jacqueline b 1968, Nicola b 1972);

Career owner of historic 13 century Burghope Manor; fndr The Heritage Circle of Historic Country Houses, lectr and after-dinner speaker on the stately homes of GB, organiser of tours for overseas gps to visit and stay in stately homes; *Recreations* shooting, travel; *Style—* Michael Denning, Esq; Burghope Manor, Winsley, Bradford-on-Avon, Wiltshire BA15 2LA (☎ 0225 723557/722695)

DENNING, Dr the Hon Robert Gordon; only child of Baron Denning, PC; *b* 3 Aug 1938; *Educ* Winchester, Magdalen Coll Oxford (MA, PhD); *m* 30 Dec 1967, Elizabeth Carlyle Margaret, da of E R Chilton, of Oxford; 2 children; *Career* 2 Lt KRRC 1957-58; fell and tutor in Inorganic Chemistry, Magdalen Coll Oxford 1968-; *Style—* Dr the Hon Robert Denning; Magdalen College, Oxford OX1 4AU

DENNINGTON, Dudley; s of John Dennington (d 1962), and Beryl, *née* Hagon (d 1944); *b* 21 April 1927; *Educ* Clifton, Imperial Coll London (BSc); *m* 1951, Margaret Patricia, da of Andrew Mackenzie Stewart (d 1976); 2 da; *Career* 2 Lt RE; mangr George Wimpey 1959-65, traffic cmmr and dir of devpt GLC 1970-72 (chief engr 1965-70), sr ptnr Bullen & Partners 1988- (ptnr 1972-88); visiting prof King's Coll London 1978-80; vice pres ICE 1990-92; FCGI, FEng, FICE, FIStructE, FHKIE; *Recreations* painting; *Clubs* Reform; *Style—* Dudley Dennington, Esq; 25 Corkran Rd, Surbiton, Surrey (☎ 081 399 2977); Bullen and Partners, 188 London Rd, Croydon (☎ 081 686 2622, telex 8811965)

DENNIS, Maj-Gen Alastair Wesley; CB (1985), OBE (1973); s of Ralph Dennis, and Helen, *née* Henderson; *b* 30 Aug 1931; *Educ* Malvern, RMA Sandhurst; *m* 1957, Susan Lindy Elgar; 1 s, 2 da; *Career* Col GS Cabinet Off 1974-75, Cdr 20 Armd Bde 1976-77, Dep Cmdt Staff Coll 1978-80, dir Def Policy (B) MOD 1980-82; dir Mil Assistance Overseas MOD 1982-85; sec Imperial Cancer Res Fund 1985-, chm Assoc Med Res Charities 1987-, govr Malvern Coll 1987-; *Recreations* golf, gardening, bees; *Style—* Maj-Gen Alastair Dennis, CB, OBE; c/o Barclays Bank, 2 Market Place, Wallingford, Oxon OX10 0EJ

DENNIS, Lt-Col Delwyn Distin; OBE (1943); s of Claude Distin Dennis (d 1968), of Weston-super-Mare, and Annie Gertrude Dennis; *b* 11 Jan 1914; *Educ* Bristol GS; *m* 26 Feb 1938, Madge Josephine, da of John Nelson Phillips (d 1930), of Weston-super-Mare; 1 s (Barrie Distin George b 1945 (decd)); *Career* Mil Serv: France 1939-40, N Africa 1942-44, Lt-Col Normandy-Germany (despatches) 1944-45; sr vice pres and gen mangr (UK and Ireland) Canada Life Assurance Co (hon vice pres and non exec dir 1979-); dir: Canada Life Assurance Co of GB Ltd, Canada Life Unit Trust Managers Ltd, Trinity Estates plc (chm); Freeman : Worshipful Co of Blacksmiths, Worshipful Co of Marketers; *Recreations* golf, skiing; *Clubs* RAC, Burhill Golf, City Livery; *Style—* Lt-Col Delwyn Dennis, OBE; Shelmerdene, 27 Ashley Drive, Walton-on-Thames, Surrey KT12 1JT (☎ 0932 227 590); 97-101 Cannon St, London BC4N 5AD (☎ 071 283 9871)

DENNIS, Prof Ian Howard; s of Flt Lt Bernard Cecil Dennis (d 1982), of Altrincham, Cheshire, and Jean Harrison, *née* Dennis; *b* 17 Sept 1948; *Educ* Manchester GS, Queens' Coll Cambridge (MA); *m* 17 July 1982, Dr Susan Mary Bower, da of Ivan William Bower (d 1989), of Southsea, Hants; 1 s (Robert William b 1984), 1 da (Katherine Mary b 1986); *Career* called to the Bar Gray's Inn 1971; lectr in law Cncl of Legal Educn 1971-73; UCL: lectr 1974-82, reader 1982-87, prof 1987-; special conslt Law Cmmn 1986-87 (memb criminal codification team 1981-89), memb Cncl Soc of Pub Teachers of Law; *Books* Odgers Principles of Pleading and Practice (with D B Casson, 1975), Codification of the Criminal Law, a Report to the Law Commission (with J C Smith and E J Griew, 1985); *Recreations* chess, swimming, wine, mountain walking; *Style—* Prof Ian Dennis; Faculty of Laws, University College London, Bentham House, Endsleigh Gardens, London WC1H 0EG (☎ 071 387 7050)

DENNIS, Rt Rev John; *see*: St Edmundsbury and Ipswich, Bishop of

DENNIS, John Francis; s of Peter Kirton Dennis, and Anne Seward Francis, *née* Burrowes; *b* 23 Nov 1948; *Educ* Harrow; *m* 16 Aug 1976, Katina June, da of Maj (Stephen) Charles Selwyn, MBE, ERD, DL, of Bembridge, IOW; 1 s (William b 1987), 4 da (Anna b 1977, Mollie b 1979, Francesca b 1982, Kitty b and d 1984); *Career* fndr The Crowood Press 1982, currently chm and publisher The Crowood Press Ltd; *Recreations* travel, country sports, chess, golf, farming; *Clubs* Naval and Military; *Style—* John Dennis, Esq; Crowood House, Ramsbury, Marlborough, Wiltshire SN8 2HE (☎ 0672 20242); 9 Cheyne Row, London SW3 5HR (☎ 071 351 4283); The Crowood Press Ltd, Gipsy Lane, Swindon, Wiltshire SN2 6DQ (☎ 0793 496493)

DENNIS, Peter; *b* 2 Sept 1934; *Educ* Toxteth Sch Liverpool; *Career* Nat Serv RA 1952-54; taxation offr Inland Revenue Liverpool 1954-57; Martins Bank/Barclays Bank: various appts rising to section leader Martins Bank Taxation Office Liverpool 1957-64, controller Taxation Section Brimingham Trust Co Office 1964-68, asst mangr Liverpool Taxation Office 1968-71, mangr Cambridge Taxation Office 1971-73, mangr Personal Fin Planning Service Dept 1973-78, sr mktg mangr Barclays Unicorn Group 1978-83, market services dir Barclays Investment Management Ltd 1983-84, sales and mktg dir Barclays Unicorn Group 1984-86, dir Barclays Financial Services Ltd 1986-89, md Barclays Unicorn 1989-, dir Barclays Financial Services 1989-, chm various assoc offshore cos 1989-; ACIB; *Recreations* golf, swimming, soccer, ornithology; *Style—* Peter Dennis, Esq

DENNIS, Raymond Andrew; s of Sir Raymond Dennis, KBE (d 1939), of Grafham Grange, Bramley, Surrey, and Sybil Margaret, eldest da of Sir Leonard Wilkinson Llewelyn, KBE, JP (d 1924), controller Munitions Supply WWI; *b* 30 Nov 1936; *Educ* Down House; *m* 1968, Penelope Anne, da of Col John Lugard (d 1969), and cous of Baron Lugard, GCMG, CB, DSO, PC (extinct 1945), of Priory Court, Duns Tew, Oxon; 1 s, 1 da; *Career* underwriting agent and farmer; memb Lloyd's 1961-, dir R L Glover & Co Underwriting Agents Ltd 1970-; Freeman City of London; *Recreations* fishing, painting; *Clubs* City of London (life memb Guild of Freemen of City of London); *Style—* Raymond Dennis, Esq; 8 Canning Place, London W8 (☎ 071 584 8636, office 071 623 9104); Berry House, Shillingford, Tiverton, Devon (☎ 039 86 275)

DENNIS, Dr Richard Benson; s of Alfred Benson Dennis, of Weymouth, Dorset, and Valentine Betty, *née* Smith; *b* 15 July 1945; *Educ* Weymouth GS, Univ of Reading (BSc, PhD); *m* 17 Dec 1971, Beate, da of Wilhelm Stamm (d 1974), of W Germany; 2 da (Andrea b 1974, Angela b 1976); *Career* Alexander von Humboldt fell Munich Univ W Germany 1976-78, sr lectr Heriot-Watt Univ 1978- (lectr 1971), fndr Miltek GmbH W Germany 1980, md Edinburgh Instruments Ltd 1983-, dir Edinburgh Sensors Ltd 1987-; memb: Cncl of Mgmnt UK Trade Assoc for Lasers and Electro-optics, chm Sch Bd Balerno HS; *Recreations* bridge, golf; *Clubs* Carlton Bridge, Dalmahoy Country; *Style—* Dr Richard Dennis; Moorside, 8 Ravelrig Hill, Balerno, Edinburgh EH14 7DJ (☎ 031 449 5392); Edinburgh Instruments Ltd, Riccarton, Currie, Edinburgh EH14 4AS (☎ 031 449 5844, fax 031 449 5848, telex 7255 EDINST)

DENNISON, Dr Brian; s of John Dennison, of Whitburn, Tyne & Wear, and Ethel, *née* Heppell (d 1957); *b* 27 Jan 1938; *Educ* Robert Richardson GS Ryhope, Univ of St Andrews (MB ChB); *m* 1, 5 April 1966 (m dis 1978), Taniya Louise Norah, da of Sqdn Ldr Phillip Lindley Hanson-Lester (d 1984), of Malaga, Spain; 1 da (Taniya Elizabeth Sarah b 30 July 1969); m 2, 1 Sept 1978, Sara Geraldine, da of Kenneth Bertram Hutchings, of Newport, Gwent; *Career* maj, served 23 Parachute Field Ambulance, RMU 3Bn Parachute RAMC 1964-69, Surgn Lt Cdr RNR 1984-; med dir Dubai Petroleum Co 1969-76, specialist anaesthetist Lismore Base Hosp NSW Aust 1977-81, conslt anaesthetist S Tees Health Authy 1981- (chm Div of Anaesthesia 1986-89); memb: BMA, Assoc of Anaesthetists, Obstetric Anaesthetists Assoc, Euro Soc of Regnl Anaesthesia, Euro Undersea Biomedical Soc, Airbourne Med Soc; MRCGP 1974, FFARCS 1980; *Recreations* scuba diving, walking, flying; *Style—* Dr Brian Dennison; Rosehill, Newton Rd, Great Ayton, N Yorks (☎ 0642 723897); Sehit Ahmet Kemal Cad, Lapta, Mersin 10, Turkey; South Cleveland Hospital, Marton Rd, Middlesbrough, Cleveland (☎ 0642 850850)

DENNISTON, Rev Robin Alastair; s of late Alexander Guthrie Denniston, CMG, CBE; *b* 25 Dec 1926; *Educ* Westminster, ChCh Oxford (BA); *m* 1, 1950, Anne Alice Kyffin (d 1985), da of Dr A Geoffrey Evans (d 1951); 1 s, 2 da; m 2, 1987, Rosa Susan Penelope Beddington; *Career* 2 Lt 66 Airborne Light Regt RA, serv UK; md Hodder & Stoughton Ltd 1968-72 (previously promotion mangr, editorial dir), dep chm George Weidenfeld & Nicolson 1973; non-exec chm A R Mowbray & Co 1974-; chm: Sphere Books 1975-76, Thomas Nelson & Sons 1975-78, Michael Joseph 1975-78, George Rainbird Ltd 1975-78; dir Thomson Pubns Ltd and Hamish Hamilton Ltd 1975-78, acad publisher 1978; Oxford Univ Press, Oxford publisher 1983-88; ordained: deacon 1978, priest 1979; priest i/c Gt and Little Tew 1987-; *Books* Partly Living (1967); *Recreations* farming, music; *Clubs* Oxford and Cambridge; *Style—* The Rev Robin Denniston; 16A Inverleith Row, Edinburgh E3 5LS (☎ 031 556 8949)

DENNY, Sir Alistair Maurice Archibald; 3 Bt (UK 1913), of Dumbarton, Co Dunbarton; s of Sir Maurice Edward Denny, 2 Bt, KBE (d 1955); *b* 11 Sept 1922; *Educ* Marlborough; *m* 18 April 1949, Elizabeth, da of Maj Sir (Ernest) Guy Richard Lloyd, 1 Bt, DSO (d 1987); 2 s (and 1 s decd); *Heir* s, Charles Alistair Maurice Denny; *Career* served with Fleet Air Arm 1944-46; *Recreations* golf, music, photography, gardening; *Clubs* Royal and Ancient Golf; *Style—* Sir Alistair Denny, Bt; Crombie Cottage, Abercrombie, Anstruther, Fife KY10 2DE (☎ 033 37 631)

DENNY, Sir Anthony Coningham de Waltham; 8 Bt (I 1782), of Castle Moyle, Kerry; s of Rev Sir Henry Lyttelton Lyster Denny, 7 Bt (d 1953); *b* 22 April 1925; *Educ* Clayesmore, Anglo-French Art Centre, Regent St Polytech Sch of Architecture; *m* 1 Sept 1949, Anne Catherine, er da of late Samuel Beverley; 2 s, 1 adopted da; *Heir* s, Piers Anthony de Waltham Denny b 14 March 1954; *Career* serv RAF (air crew) 1943-47; designer; ptnr in Verity and Beverley, Architects and Designers, WIM Offr in London, Tetbury, Gloucestershire and Lisbon, Portugal; hereditary Freeman of Cork; MCSD, FRSA; *Style—* Sir Anthony Denny, Bt; Daneway House, Sapperton, nr Cirencester, Glos (☎ 028 576 232)

DENNY, Charles Alistair Maurice; s and h of Sir Alistair Denny, 3 Bt; *b* 7 Oct 1950; *Educ* Wellington, Univ of Edinburgh; *m* 1981, Belinda (Linda), yr da of J P McDonald, of Dublin; 1 s (Patrick Charles Alistair b 1985), 1 da (Georgina Mary b 1989); *Recreations* golf, gardening; *Clubs* Royal and Ancient Golf St Andrews; *Style—* Charles Denny, Esq

DENNY, Edward Joseph; s of John Denny, of Sydney, NSW Australia, and Anne, *née* Conlon; *b* 20 Nov 1962; *Educ* Macleod Tech Coll Melbourne, Newry Catering Coll (City & Guilds Certs), Leeds Poly (DipHH); *m* 21 Oct, Alison Sheila Macintyre, da Alexander Macintyre; *Career* commis de cuisine Royal Hotel Kilkeel Co Down NI 1980-82, Chef de partie then sous chef Restaurant L'Auberge Edinburgh 1982-84; Box-Tree Restaurant: chef de partie 1984, head chef 1986, co-dir 1986-; top listings in all maj food guides incl: 1 Rosette (AA Guide), 4/5 for cooking (Good Food Guide), Rosette (Michelin Guide); *Recreations* spending time with my wife, dining out, cinema; *Style—* Edward Denny, Esq; The Box-Tree Restaurant Ltd, Church St, Ilkley, W Yorksihre LS29 9DR (☎ 0943 608484)

DENNY, James Frederick Lowndes; yr s of late John Anthony Denny (d 1943), and Eileen Alice Maud, da of Col Meyrick Edward Selby-Lowndes, of Mursley Grange, Bucks; *b* 1925; *Educ* Hawtreys, Eton; *m* 1 April 1950, Mary Clare, only da of late Col Francis William Wilson-FitzGerald, DSO, MC, of Purton House, Wilts; 1 s (John William b 27 Oct 1958), 2 da (Sarah Elizabeth b 10 Feb 1953, Lucinda Clare b 4 April 1954); *Career* chm: E M Denny (Holdings) Ltd, Denny Meat Trading Ltd and E M Denny & Co Ltd; dir Coey Ltd and the Ulster Farmers' Ltd, ret; conslt UK Provision Trade Fedn; *Recreations* painting; *Clubs* Boodle's; *Style—* James Denny, Esq; The Old Farm House, Goring-on-Thames, Reading, Berks RG8 9HD (☎ 0491 872323)

DENNY, John Ingram; s of Thomas Ingram Denny, of Macclesfield, Cheshire, and Claire Dorothy, *née* Lewis; *b* 28 May 1941; *Educ* Normain Coll Chester, Poly of N London (DipArch), Univ of Reading (MSc); *m* 2 June 1967, Carol Ann Frances, da of Walter James Hughes, of St Leonards, Bournemouth, Hants; 1 s (Paul b 7 Oct 1969), 2 da (Louise b 23 July 1971, Sarah b 31 Jan 1974); *Career* currently princ ptnr Cecil Denny Highton chartered architects (joined 1970, elected ptnr 1971); responsible for following cmmns: the refurbishment remodelling and restoration of the FO Whitehall and the Old WO, the interior design for the Home Sec's Office Queen Anne's Gate, over 20 projects for V & A and Natural History and Sci Museums, Customer Accounting Centre for Thames Water Authy, Swindon; memb Assoc of Conslt Architects, ARIBA, ACIArb; *Recreations* golf, photography; *Style—* John Denny, Esq; Minstrels, 1 Broadway, Gustard Wood, Wheathampstead, Hertfordshire AL4 8LW (☎ 0438 832397); Cecil Denny Highton, Axtell House, 23/24 Warwick St, London W1R 5RB (☎ 071 734 6831, fax 071 734 0508, car 0860 303265)

DENNY, Jonathan Molesworth; s of Maj Noel Nigel Molesworth Denny, MC, of 82 Barkham Rd, Wokingham, Berks, and Margaret Louise Denny; *b* 28 Aug 1953; *Educ* Charterhouse, Univ of Southampton (LLB); *m* 20 May 1978, Annette Clare, da of Peter Raymond Underwood Easteal (d 1986); 2 s (Timothy Peter Noel b 1985, James Rupert Simon b 1990), 1 da (Charlotte Lois Clare b 1983); *Career* admitted slr 1977; managing ptnr Cripps Harries Hall 1990- (joined 1980, ptnr 1982); memb Law Soc; *Recreations* cricket, tennis, skiing, viticulture; *Style—* Jonathan Denny, Esq; Cripps Harries Hall, 84 Calverley Rd, Tunbridge Wells, Kent TN1 2UP (☎ 0892 515121, fax 0892 515444)

DENNY, Linda May; *née* Magnun; da of Maximilian Magnun, of Calcutta, India, and Suzi Kathleen, *née* Allen; *b* 22 Feb 1950; *Educ* Bath Acad of Art; *m* 1, 19 Aug 1968, William Jones; 1 s (Stephen William Magnun b 1967); m 2, 24 Aug 1984, Richard William Geoffrey Denny, *qv*, s of Rev Sir Henry Littleton Lyster Denny, 7 Bt (d 1952), of Tralee Castle, Co Kerry; *Career* dir: Management Publishing Ltd, Management Ltd, Results Training Ltd; horse breeder, commenced breeding and showing Irish Draught (endangered breed) 1987, and British Sport Horse; *Recreations* skiing, painting, farm interest, conservation, hunting with Royal Artillery and Heythrop; *Clubs* Sloane; *Style—* Mrs Richard Denny; Coldicote Farm, Moreton-in-Marsh, Glos (☎ 0680 50515); Management House, 20 Northgate St, Devizes, Wilts SN10 1JT (☎ 0380 77555)

DENNY, Piers Anthony de Waltham; er s and h of Sir Anthony Denny, 8 Bt; *b* 14 March 1954; *Educ* King Alfred Sch, Westfield Coll London; *m* 1978, Ella Jane, o da of Peter P Huhne, of Earls Court; 2 da (Matilda Ann b 1988, Isabel Margaret b 1990); *Style—* Piers Denny, Esq

DENNY, Richard William Geoffrey; s of Rev Sir Henry Lyttleton Lyster Denny, 7 Bt (d 1952), of Co Kerry, and Joan Dorothy Lucy, *née* Denny (d 1976); bro Sir Anthony Denny, 8 Bt, *qv*, architect to Royal Household, and Robyn Denny, distinguished modern painter; *b* 4 Feb 1940; *Educ* Royal Masonic Sch Bushey Herts, Plumpton Coll of Agric Sussex; *m* 1, 24 Feb 1961 (m dis 1978), Andrée Suzanne Louise, eldest da of Marcel Louis Parrot; 4 s (Lyster b 1961, Walter b 1963, Giles b 1964, Julius b 1966); m 2, 24 Aug 1984, Linda May, *qv*, da of Maximilian Magnun, of Calcutta, India; *Career* int conference speaker on motivation; md Denny Farms Ltd 1967-, co-fndr and dir Leadership Devpt Ltd 1974, lectured round the world on selling, motivation and people mgmnt 1974-79; fndr, md and chm Results Training Ltd, Man Management Publishing Ltd, Man Management Ltd 1979-; writer and presenter world's first video sales course on professiona selling 1983, toured Aust and NZ 1985, recorded Dare to be Great 1986, writer and presenter The Professional Manager world's largest video course; author of Selling to Win (1988); *Recreations* sheep breeding, farming, sailing, squash, hunting, photography, skiing; *Clubs* Sloane; *Style—* Richard Denny, Esq; Coldicote Farm, Moreton-in-Marsh, Gloucestershire; Man Management Ltd, Management House, 20 Northgate St, Devises, Wilts (☎ 0380 77555)

DENNY, Ronald Mackinnon; s of Frank Herbert Denny (d 1947), of Enfield, Middx, and Gladys Amy, *née* Mackinnon (d 1976); *b* 23 Dec 1920; *Educ* Edmonton GS, RAF Coll, Univ of London (Dip TS), Univ of Kent (MA), Univ of Birmingham; *m* 14 Feb 1945, Gwenllian Audrey Caroline, da of Brinley Richard Cound (d 1948), of Burryport, S Wales; 2 da (Diane Meryl b 1948, Sally Shan b 1953); *Career* RAFVR 1939, cmmnd Pilot Offr Tech Radar Branch 1943, Offr i/c Flt Lt Airborne Radar Honiley 1944-46, demob 1946 Flt Lt; asst airport mangr Heathrow Airport 1953-56; seconded to: NATO Paris 1958-60, Chateauroux France 1960-64; controller Eastern Rd Construction Unit 1968-73, asst sec Dept of Tport 1974-80, dep dir-gen Br Property Fedn 1981-87, mgmnt conslt 1988-, chm Bain Clarkson Property Insurance Ltd 1989-; AAA Champion 120 yards high hurdles Middx and Southern Counties 1939, chm Farningham Parish Cncl 1989-, govr Anthony Roper Primary Sch 1989-; FBIM 1971, FIHT 1980, MCIT 1981, Hon Fell Architectural Assoc 1981; *Recreations* travel, gardening; *Clubs* RAF; *Style—* Ronald Denny, Esq; Maplescombe Oasts, Farningham, Kent DA4 0JY (☎ 0322 864 363); 35 Catherine Place, London SW1E 6DY (☎ 071 828 0111, fax 071 834 3442)

DENNY, Ronald Maurice; s of Maurice Ellis Louis Denny (d 1981), and Ada Beatrice, *née* Bradley; *b* 11 Jan 1927; *Educ* Gosport County Sch; *m* 7 Nov 1952, Dorothy, da of William Hamilton (d 1933); 1 s (Andrew b 1964), 2 da (Jane b 1957, Elizabeth b 1958); *Career* chartered engineer; chief exec Rediffusion plc 1979-89 (chm 1985, ret 1989); dir: Bet plc 1982-89 (ret), Thames Television 1980-89, Electrocomponents plc 1984; memb Philharmonia Orchestra Tst 1984; FIEE 1975, FRSA 1985, Hon RCM 1984; *Recreations* music, reading; *Clubs* Athenaeum, Arts; *Style—* Ronald Denny, Esq; 19 Nichols Green, London W5 2QU (☎ 081 998 3765); Electrocomponents plc, 21 Knightsbridge, London SW1X 7LY (☎ 071 245 1927, fax 071 235 4458, telex 9419777)

DENNYS, Hon Mrs (Lavinia Mary Yolande); *née* Lyttelton; yst da of 9 Viscount Cobham (d 1949); *b* 21 Aug 1921; *m* 1, 15 Feb 1945, Capt Cecil Francis Burney Rolt, 23 Hussars (ka 6 April 1945); m 2, 12 Dec 1949, Maj John Edward Dennys MC (d 1973); 1 s; *Career* Subaltern ATS 1941-45; *Style—* The Hon Mrs Dennys; Cannon Cottage, Fore St, Budleigh Salterton, Devon (☎ 039 54 3100)

DENNYS, Nicholas Charles Jonathan; s of John Edward Dennys, MC (d 1973), and Hon Lavinia Yolande Lyttelton; *b* 14 July 1951; *Educ* Eton, BNC Oxford (BA); *m* 19 Feb 1977, Frances Winifred, da of Rev Canon Gervase William Markham, of Morland Penrith Cumbria; 4 da (Harriet b 5 Feb 1979, Sophie b 2 Feb 1981, Romilly b 31 March 1984, Katharine b 14 July 1986); *Career* called to the Bar Middle Temple 1975; *Recreations* golf, windsurfing, reading; *Style—* Nicholas Dennys, Esq; 1 Atkin Bldgs, Gray's Inn, London WC2 (☎ 071 404 0102)

DENNYS, Rodney Onslow; CVO (1981, MVO 1969), OBE (Mil 1943); Arundel Herald of Arms Extraordinary; s of Frederic Onslow Brooke Dennys, and Florence Claire, da of Rudolph Hermann Wolfgang Leopold de Paula; *b* 16 July 1911; *Educ* Canford, LSE; *m* 12 Jan 1944, Elisabeth Katharine, da of Charles Henry Greene and sister of Graham Greene, the novelist, *qv*; 1 s, 2 da; *Career* serv WWII Intelligence Corps (Lt-Col 1944) and RARO 1946; serv FO 1937-41 and 1947-57 (The Hague, Egypt, Turkey, Paris); asst to Garter King of Arms 1958-61, Rouge Croix Pursuivant 1961-67, Somerset Herald of Arms 1967-82 (serv on Earl Marshal's Staff for State Funeral of Sir Winston Churchill 1965, and Investiture of HRH Prince of Wales 1969), Arundel Herald of Arms Extraordinary 1982-; High Sheriff of E Sussex 1983/4; dir: Heralds' Museum 1983- (dep dir 1978-83), Arundel Castle Tstee Ltd 1977-87; memb CPRE 1972-: memb Nat Exec 1973-78, chm Sussex Branch 1972-77 (vice pres 1977); chm Cncl Harleian Soc 1977-83; Freeman City of London, Liveryman and Freeman Worshipful Co of Scriveners; FSA, FRSA, FSG; *Books* The Heraldic Imagination (1975), Heraldry and the Heralds (1982); *Recreations* ornithology, heraldry; *Clubs* Garrick, Sussex, City Livery; *Style—* Rodney Dennys, Esq, CVO, OBE, Arundel Herald of Arms; Heaslands, Steep, nr Crowborough, Sussex; College of Arms, Queen Victoria Street, London EC4 (☎ 071 248 1912)

DENOON DUNCAN, Russell Euan; s of Douglas Denoon Duncan (d 1955), of Johannesburg, and Ray, *née* Reynolds (d 1981); *b* 11 March 1926; *Educ* Michaelhouse Natal S Africa; *m* 28 Jan 1956, Caroline Jane Lloyd, da of Noel Wynne Spencer Lewin (d 1980), of London; 2 s (James b 1957, Angus b 1960); *Career* SA Artillery 1943-45; serv: Egypt, Italy; admitted slr 1961; ptnr Webber Wentzel Johannesburg 1952-61; Cameron Markby Hewitt (formerly Markbys): ptnr 1963-90, sr ptnr 1987-90, conslt 1990-; chm National Australia Group Limited 1987-; chm Br Polish Legal Assoc 1991- (vice chm 1989-91); Freeman Worshipful Co of Slrs 1987; *Recreations* mountain walking, tennis, painting; *Clubs* City of London, City Law, Royal Tennis Ct, Rand; *Style—* Russell Denoon Duncan, Esq; Rose Cottage, Watts Rd, Thames Ditton, Surrey KT7 OBX (☎ 081 398 5193, fax 081 398 9282); Cameron Markby Hewitt, Sceptre Court, 40 Tower Hill, London EC3N 4BB (☎ 071 702 2345, fax 071 702 2303, telex 925779 CAMLAW G)

DENSON, John Boyd; CMG (1972), OBE (1965); s of George Denson (d 1965), of Cambridge, and Alice, *née* Boyd; *b* 13 Aug 1926; *Educ* Perse Sch Cambridge, St John's Coll Cambridge (BA, MA); *m* 1957, Joyce Myra, da of Charles Henry Symondson (d 1973), of Bucks; *Career* Capt Intelligence Corps RA Malaya 1944-47; Dip Serv 1951-83: chargé d'affaires Peking 1969-71, RCDS 1972, cncllr Athens 1973-77, ambass Kathmandu 1977-83, ret; memb Univs China Ctee 1987-; Gorkha Dakshina Bahu First Class (Nepal) 1980; *Recreations* wine, theatre, pictures; *Clubs* Royal Overseas League, Achilles; *Style—* John Denson, Esq, CMG, OBE; Little Hermitage, Pensile Rd, Nailsworth, Stroud, Glos GL6 0AL (☎ 045 383 3829)

DENT, Hon Mrs (Ann Camilla); *née* Denison-Pender; da of 2 Baron Pender, CBE (d 1965); *b* 18 June 1931; *m* 2 Oct 1952, Robin John Dent, *qv*; 2 da (Annabel Jane b 1954, m 1981 James John Meade, Jennifer Ann b 1957, m 1982 Andrew Everard Martin Smith); *Style—* The Hon Mrs Dent; 44 Smith St, London SW3 (☎ 071 352 1234)

DENT, Hon Mrs (Anne Elizabeth); *née* Taylor; da of Baron Ingrow, OBE, TD (Life Baron 1982); *b* 1951; *m* 1975, Charles Jonathan Dent, elder s of John Harker Dent; 1 s (James Geoffrey b 1980), 1 da (Sarah Louise b 1984); *Style—* The Hon Mrs Dent; Ribston Hall, Wetherby, Yorks

DENT, Hon Mrs (Diana Mary); *née* Taylor; da of Baron Ingrow, OBE, TD (Life Baron 1982); *b* 1953; *Educ* Benenden Sch; *m* 1979, John Patrick Dent, yr s of John Harker Dent; 1 s (b 1984), 1 da (b 1986); *Style—* The Hon Mrs Dent; Clock Farm, Hunsingore, Wetherby, Yorks

DENT, Evelyn Robert Wilkinson; s of Sir Robert Annesley Wilkinson Dent, CB (d 1983), of Maulds Meaburn, Penrith, Cumbria (High Sheriff of Westmorland 1959), and Elspeth Muriel, *née* Tritton (d 1988); *b* 16 May 1934; *Educ* Eton, Trinity Coll Camb (MA); *m* 15 June 1963, (Celia) Margaret, da of Douglas Hazard Harris, of Steep, Petersfield, Hants; 2 s (Julian b 1964, Nicholas b 1970), 1 da (Caroline b 1966); *Career* admitted slr 1960; pres W Surrey Law Soc 1973-74; ret from practice 1984; chm Rent Assessment Ctee (SE area) 1984-; Freeman of the City of London 1955, Liveryman of the Grocers' Co 1964; *Style—* Evelyn Dent, Esq; Meaburn Edge, Petworth Road, Haslemere, Surrey

DENT, Jeremy Francis; s of Cdr Adrian James Dent, of Sway, Hants, and Diane Elizabeth, *née* Buxton; *b* 24 Jan 1952; *Educ* Bradfield Coll, Univ of Southampton (BSc); *Career* trainee accountant Peat Marwick McLintock 1974-77; lectr in accounting: Univ of Southampton 1977-82, London Business Sch 1982-88 (prof 1988-90); reader in accounting LSE 1991-; FCA 1977; *Style—* Jeremy Dent, Esq; 2 Keble House, Manor Fields, London SW15 3LS (☎ 081 785 2828); London School of Economics & Political Science, Houghton St, London WC2A 2AE (☎ 071 405 7686, fax 071 242 0392, telex 24655)

DENT, Sir John; CBE (1976, OBE 1968); s of Harry F Dent; *b* 5 Oct 1923; *Educ* King's Coll Univ of London (BSc); *m* 1954, Pamela Ann, da of Frederick G Bailey; 1 s; *Career* chm CAA 1982-6; dir: Engineering Group Dunlop Ltd Coventry 1968-76, Dunlop Holdings Ltd 1970-82, Industrie Pirelli Spa 1978-81, Dunlop AG 1979-82, Pirelli Gen 1980, Pirelli Ltd 1985; md Dunlop 1978-82; pres: Inst of Travel Mgmnt 1986-, Int Fedn of Airworthiness 1987-89; FEng, CEng; kt 1986; *Style—* Sir John Dent, CBE; Hellidon Grange, Hellidon, Daventry, Northants (☎ 0327 60589)

DENT, Robin John; s of Rear Adm John Dent, CB, OBE (d 1973); *b* 25 June 1929; *Educ* Marlborough; *m* 2 Oct 1952, Hon Ann Camilla Denison-Pender, da of 2 Baron Pender, CBE (d 1965); 2 da (Annabel Jane (Mrs Meade) b 15 Oct 1954, Jennifer Ann (Mrs Martin Smith) b 27 May 1957); *Career* Bank of England 1949-51, M Samuel & Co 1951-65, dir Hill Samuel & Co Ltd 1965-67, md Baring Bros & Co Ltd 1967-86; dir: TR City of London Tst plc 1977-, Barings plc 1985-89; chm Mase Westpac Ltd 1989-, memb Bd Cancer Res Campaign 1967-, treas King Edward's Hosp Fund for London 1974-; memb: Advsy Ctee Hon Kong & Shanghai Banking Corp 1974-81, Deposit Protection Bd 1982-85; dep chm Export Guaranty Advsy Cncl 1983-85; chm: Exec Ctee Br Bankers Assoc 1984-85, chm Public Works Loan Bd 1990-, special tstee St Thomas's Hosp 1988-; *Clubs* White's; *Style—* Robin Dent, Esq; 44 Smith St, London SW3 4EP (☎ 071 352 1234); Mase Westpac Ltd, Westpac House, 75 King William St, London EC4N 7HA (☎ 071 621 7800, fax 071 283 4254, telex 884491)

DENT, Hon Rosamond Mary (Sister Ancilla, OSB); da of William Herbert Shelley Dent, MC, and 19 Baroness Furnivall (d 1969, when the Barony became abeyant between Sister Ancilla and Hon Mrs Bence, *qv*); co-heiress to Barony, renounced right in favour of sister; *b* 3 June 1933; *Educ* Holy Child Convent Mayfield; *Style—* Sister Ancilla, OSB; Minster Abbey, Minster, nr Ramsgate, Kent

DENT, Lady Rosanagh Elizabeth Angela Mary; *née* Taylour; er da of 6 Marquess of Headfort, by his 1 w (*see* Hon Mrs Knight); *b* 20 Jan 1961; *Educ* St Mary's Convent Ascot, Oxford Poly (BA); *m* 30 July 1983, Andrew Congreve Dent, eldest s of Robin Dent, of Olivers, Painswick, Glos; 1 s (Michael b 1989); *Career* dir DMD Ltd 1987-; *Recreations* polo; *Style—* The Lady Rosanagh Dent; Shipton Glebe, Woodstock, Oxon

DENT, Hon Mrs (Sarah); *née* Douglas-Home; eldest da of Baroness Dacre and Hon William Douglas-Home; *b* 4 July 1954; *m* Dec 1978, Nicholas Charles Dent, yst s of Maj T C Dent, of 51 Addison Rd, London W14; 1 s, 2 da; *Style—* The Hon Mrs Dent; Derry House, Kilmeston, Alresford, Hants

DENT, Hon Mrs (Tatiana Ines Alexandra); *née* Wilson; 2 da of 4 Baron Nunburnholme; *b* 17 Sept 1960; *m* 5 March 1988, Nigel L Dent, s of Robin Dent, of Painswick, Glos; 2 s (Freddie b 10 March 1989, Harry Barnaby Nigel b 3 Jan 1991); *Style—* The Hon Mrs Dent; 15 Ewald Road, London SW6

DENT, William Alan; s of Fred Dent, MBE (d 1977), of Hill House, Locharbriggs, Dumfriesshire, and Freda Mary, *née* Taylor (d 1972); *b* 3 Dec 1926; *Educ* Carlisle GS, Univ of Leeds (Dip Arch); *m* 31 July 1950, Mary, da of Norris Walker (d 1970), of Cliffe Ash, Golcar, West Riding, Yorkshire; 3 s (James b 1951, Andrew b 1955, Peter b 1962); *Career* RN 1944-47; local authys' educnl and recreational bldgs 1951-71, princ private practice 1972-86, diocesan architect Church of I Diocese of Clogher; conslt Scotch-Irish Tst; hon architect Access for the Disabled Omagh; ARIBA 1951; *Recreations* gardening, antiquarian research, woodwork; *Clubs* Tyrone County; *Style—* William Dent, Esq; 71 Millcroft, Whiteclosegate, Carlisle, Cumbria

DENT-YOUNG, David Michael; CBE (1977); s of Lt Col John Dent-Young, TD (d 1955), of Nutley, North Rd, Bath, and Olivette, *née* De Bruyn (d 1939); *b* 25 March 1927; *Educ* St Aibans Coll Grahamstown SA, Camborne Sch of Mines Cornwall (ACSM); *m* 12 July 1951, Patricia, da of James Edward McKeon, of 9 Lansdown Rd, Bath; 3 da (Jane b 1952, Sarah b 1954, Nicola b 1964); *Career* mining engr Nigerian Alluvials Ltd 1951-53; AO Nigeria Ltd: mining engr 1953-57, area engr 1957-65, dist supt 1964-67, sr supt 1967-71; chm and md Amalgamated Tin Mines of Nigeria Ltd 1973-80 (md 1980-83), dir Bisichi Mining plc 1983-; govr Jos Sch of Mines; memb: Nigerian Chamber of Mines, Nigerian Employers Consultative Assoc, Nigerian Mining Employers Assoc, Consultative Ctee Restoration & Reclamation, Bd of Mgmnt Kaduna Poly Nigeria; pres Plateau Horticultural Soc (Nigeria); CEng, FIMM; Nigerian medal of Independance 1961; *Recreations* gardening, photography, swimming; *Clubs* Royal Cwlth Soc, Cdr Rayfield Sailing (Nigeria), vice pres Plateau Turf (Nigeria); *Style—* David Dent-Young, Esq, CBE; The Cloisters Cottage, Perrymead, Bath BA2 5AY (☎ 0225 837677); Bisichi Mining plc, 30-34 New Bridge St, London EC4V 6LT (☎ 071 236 3539, fax 071 248 2850)

DENTON, Charles Henry; s of Alan Denton; *b* 20 Dec 1937; *Educ* Reading Sch, Bristol Univ (BA); *m* 1961, Eleanor Mary, *née* Player; 1 s, 2 da; *Career* dir of progs: ATV, Central Indep TV; md Black Lion Films, chief exec Zenith; chm The Producers Assoc; *Style—* Charles Denton, Esq; Gordon House, West Tytherley, nr Salisbury, Wilts

DENTON, Prof Sir Eric James; CBE (1974); s of George Denton; *b* 30 Sept 1923; *Educ* Doncaster GS, St John's Coll Cambridge (ScD), UCL; *m* 1946, Nancy Emily, da of Charles Wright; 2 s, 1 da; *Career* lectr physiology Univ of Aberdeen 1948-56, physiologist Marine Biological Assoc Laboratory Plymouth 1956-74 (dir 1974-87), res prof Royal Soc Univ of Bristol 1964-74; FRS; kt 1987; *Style—* Prof Sir Eric Denton, CBE, FRS; Fairfield House, St Germans, Saltash, Cornwall PL12 5LS (☎ 0503 30204); The Laboratory, Citadel Hill, Plymouth, Devon PL1 2PB (☎ 0752 222772)

DENTON, Jean; CBE; da of Charles Moss, and Kathleen, *née* Tuke; *Educ* Rothwell GS, LSE (BSc); *Career* info exec BBC News Div (Home and Overseas) 1958, communications exec Proctor & Gamble 1959-61, mktg conslt and asst ed Retail Business Economist Intelligence Unit 1961-64, market investigations Women's

Magazines Div IPC 1964-66, res Hotel and Catering Dept Univ of Surrey 1966-68, professional racing/rally driver 1968-71 (competed in Europe & Middle East, successfully completed London-Sydney Marathon and World Cup Rally to Mexico, twice British Women Racing Driver's Champion); mktg dir: Huxford Gp 1971-78, Heron Motor Gp 1978-80; md Herondrive 1980-85, dir external affairs Austin Rover Gp 1985-86, dir Burson-Marsteller 1986-, dep chm Black Country Development Corporation 1987-; memb Bd: British Nuclear Fuels plc, Triplex Lloyd plc, London & Edinburgh Insurance Gp, Think Green; memb: Interim Advsy Ctee on Teachers Pay and Conditions, The Engrg Cncl (chm Fin Ctee), The RSA Cncl; chm: FORUM UK, Women on the Move Against Cancer; former chm Mktg Gp of GB; former memb Hansard Soc's Cmmn on Women at the Top; memb Worshipful Co of Markestors, Freeman City of London 1982; FCInstM 1972, FIMI 1974, FRSA 1987, CBIM 1988; *Clubs* Reform, British Women Racing Drivers (vice pres); *Style—* Mrs Jean Denton, CBE

DENTON, Kenneth Raymond; s of Stanley Charles Denton (d 1957), of Rochester, and Lottie Bertha Rhoda, *née* Dorrington (d 1972); *b* 20 Aug 1932; *Educ* Rochester Tech and Sch of Art, Medway Coll of Art and Design; *m* 5 Oct 1957, Margaret, da of Thomas Nesbitt (d 1969), of Crossnenagh, Keady, Co Armagh, NI; 3 s (Colin b 1959, Martin b 1960, Nigel b 1961); *Career* Nat Serv RASC, transferred to REME 1952-54; freelance designer and decorative artist 1954-63; designs incl: domestic interiors and furniture, interiors and inn-signs for major brewing cos, Bd Room for Grants of St James; lectr 1963-67: Royal Sch Mil Engrg, Maidstone Coll of Art, Medway Coll of Design, Erith Coll of Art; landscape and marine artist 1967-; exhibitions in UK, Europe, Canada, USA; 30 one man shows; two man exhibitions with: Patrick Hall, Leslie Moore, Enzo Plazzotta; work in many private and public collections, numerous TV and radio appearances; FBID 1963, RSMA 1976, FCSD 1987, FRSA 1989; *Recreations* classical music, piano playing; *Clubs* Rotary; *Style—* Kenneth Denton, Esq; Priory Farm Lodge, Sporle, Kings Lynn, Norfolk PE32 2DS (☎ 0760 22084)

DENTON-CLARK, Jeremy; s of Bryan Sandford Clark, of Geneva, Switzerland, and Jenifer Lambie, *née* Neil (d 1971); *b* 7 Sept 1944; *Educ* Cheltenham; *m* 30 Oct 1971, Catherine Enrica, da of Timothy James O'Leary; 2 s (James Anthony b 2 Nov 1974, Nicholas Edward b 28 June 1977); *Career* dir SDS Bank Ltd 1984-86, md City Merchants Bank Ltd 1986-; *Recreations* family; *Style—* Jeremy Denton-Clark, Esq; City Merchants Bank Ltd, 13 Austin Friar, London EC2N 2AJ (☎ 071 638 3511, fax 071 638 2187, telex 886532)

DENYER, Prof Peter Brian; s of Robert Ralph Denyer, of Littlehampton, Sussex, and Evelyn May, *née* Swinbank; *b* 27 April 1953; *Educ* Worthing Tech HS, Loughborough Univ of Technol (BSc), Univ of Edinburgh (PhD); *m* 20 July 1977, Fiona Margaret Lindsay, da of Ernest William Reoch, of Edinburgh; 2 da (Kate b 1982, Kirsty b 1984); *Career* design engr Wolfson Microelectronics Inst Edinburgh 1976-80; Univ of Edinburgh: lectr 1981-86, reader 1986, prof advent chair of integrated electronics 1986-; chm DTI SERC Sub Ctee for Microelectronic Design; *Books* Introduction to MOSLSI Design (1983), VLSI Signal processing-A Bit Serial Approach (1985), Bit-Serial VLSI Computation (1988); *Recreations* hill walking, young family, plumbing; *Style—* Prof Peter Denyer; 91 Colinton Rd, Edinburgh EH10 5DF (☎ 031 337 3432); The University of Edinburgh, Dept of Electrical Engineering, Mayfield Rd, Edinburgh EH9 3JL (☎ 031 650 5594, fax 031 662 4358)

DENYER, Roderick Lawrence; QC (1990); s of Oliver James Denyer (d 1982), and Olive Mabel, *née* Jones; *b* 1 March 1948; *Educ* Grove Park GS for Boys Wrexham, LSE (LLM); *m* 21 April 1973, Pauline; 2 da (Hannah b 4 March 1978, Alexandra b 10 Feb 1981); *Career* barr; lectr in law Univ of Bristol 1971-73, called to the Bar 1973; various pubns in legal jls; *Recreations* cricket, 1960's pop music; *Style—* Roderick Denyer, Esq, QC; St John's Chambers, Small Street, Bristol BS1 1DW (☎ 0272 213456, fax 0272 294821)

DENYER, Stephen Robert Noble; s of Wilfred Denyer, of Sherborne, Dorset, and Joy Victoria Jeanne, *née* Noble; *b* 27 Dec 1955; *Educ* Fosters GS Sherborne, Univ of Durham (BA); *m* 3 Sept 1988, Monika Maria, da of Heinrich Christoph Wolf, of Lübeck, W Germany; *Career* slr; ptnr Allen & Overy (specialising in corp fin work) 1986-; Freeman Worshipful Co of Slrs 1986; memb Law Soc 1980; *Recreations* walking, travel, gardening; *Style—* Stephen Denyer, Esq; Allen & Overy, 9 Cheapside, London EC2V 6AD (☎ 071 248 9898, fax 071 236 2192, telex 8812801

DENZA, Eileen; CMG (1984); da of Alexander Young, of Aberdeen, and Ellen Duffy (d 1981); *b* 23 July 1937; *Educ* Univ of Aberdeen (MA), Univ of Oxford (MA), Harvard Univ (LLM); *m* 1966, John Denza, s of Luigi Carlo Denza; 2 s (Mark b 1969, Paul b 1971), 1 da (Antonia b 1967); *Career* asst lectr in law Univ of Bristol 1961-63, called to the Bar Lincoln's Inn 1963, asst legal advsr FCO 1963-74, legal cnsllr FCO 1974-86, legal advsr to UK Representation to Euro Community 1980-83, pupillage and practice at Bar 1986-87, second counsel to the Chm of Ctees, counsel to Euro Communities Ctee House of Lords 1987-; *Books* Diplomatic Law (1976); contributor to: Satow, Diplomatic Practice, Essays in Air Law; *Recreations* music; *Style—* Mrs Eileen Denza, CMG

DERAMORE, 6 Baron (UK 1885); Sir Richard Arthur de Yarburgh-Bateson; 7 Bt (UK 1818); yr s of 4 Baron Deramore (d 1943), and bro of 5 Baron (d 1964); *b* 9 April 1911; *Educ* Harrow, St John's Coll Cambridge (MA), Architectural Assoc Sch; *m* 28 Aug 1948, Janet Mary, da of John Ware, MD; 1 da; *Heir* none; *Career* serv 1940-45, Fl Lt, RAFVR; chartered architect; ptnr Arthur William Kenyon 1938-39, memb Cncl Architectural Assoc 1951-54, ptnr Cherry and Deramore 1965-70, practised as Arthur Deramore in Bucks, then Yorks 1970-82; FRIBA (ARIBA 1937); *Recreations* water colour painting, cycling, golf, motoring, writing; *Clubs* RAF, RAC; *Style—* Rt Hon Lord Deramore; Heslington House, Aislaby, Pickering, N Yorks (☎ 0751 73195)

DERBY, 18 Earl of (E 1485); Edward John Stanley; 12 Bt (E 1627), MC (1944), DL (Lancs 1946); also Baron Stanley of Bickerstaffe (UK 1832) and Baron Stanley of Preston (UK 1886); s of Capt Rt Hon Lord Stanley (as he was styled), PC, MC (d 1938, s of 17 Earl, KG, PC, GCB, GCVO (d 1948), himself gs of 14 Earl, Conservative PM), and Sibyl Louise Beatrix (d 1969), da of Henry Arthur Cadogan, Viscount Chelsea; *b* 21 April 1918; *Educ* Eton, Magdalen Coll Oxford; *m* 22 July 1948, Lady Isobel, JP (d 1990), da of Hon Henry Augustus Milles-Lade, JP (d 1937), and sis of 4 Earl Sondes; *Heir* nephew, Edward Richard William Stanley, *qv*; *Career* chm Aintree Tst 1982-; pres Caravan Club; CO 5 Bn King's Regiment TA 1947-51; chm NW Area TA Assoc 1979-83; pres: Rugby Football League 1948-, Professional Golfers' Assoc 1964-; PGA European Tour 1976-; late Maj Grenadier Gds (Res); Hon Col Liverpool Scottish 1964-67, Hon Col 5/8 Bn, King's Regt 1975-88, (Cmdg) 5 Bn 1947-51 (Hon Col 1951-67), Hon Col 4(V)Bn The Queen's Lancashire Regt 1975-87, TA&VR Hon Col 1 and 2 Bns Lancastrian Vols 1967-75, Hon Capt Mersey Div RNR 1952-89; Hon LLD Liverpool and Lancaster, pres of Merseyside Chamber of Commerce 1972-; Ld-Lt of Co Lancaster 1951-68; pro chllr of Univ of Lancaster 1964-71; constable of Lancaster Castle 1972-; *Clubs* White's, Jockey; *Style—* The Rt Hon the Earl of Derby, MC, DL; Knowsley, Prescot, Merseyside L34 4AF (☎ 051 489 6147); Stanley House, Newmarket, Suffolk CB8 7DF (☎ 0638 663011)

DERBY, Peter Jared; s of Samuel Jonathan James Derby, of 22 Harberton Drive, Belfast (d 1974), and Frances Emma, *née* Leckie; *b* 21 Feb 1940; *Educ* Inchmarlo Sch, Royal Belfast Academical Inst, Queens Univ Belfast (BSc); *m* 3 Aug 1968, Rosemary Jane, da of Charles Euan Chalmers Guthrie (d 1985), of Swanston Cottage, 36 Gamekeepers Road, Edinburgh; 1 s (Andrew b 1971), 2 da (Lucy b 1969, Polly b 1973); *Career* jt asst actuary Scot Widows Fund 1965-67 (joined 1961), ptnr Wood Mackenzie and Co 1970-86 (joined 1967); dir: Hill Samuel and Co Ltd 1986-88, Ashton Tod McLaren 1988-89, Quilter Goodison Co Ltd; sidesman Christ Church Shamley Green; memb Guildry of Brechin Angus 1973; Freeman: City of London, Worshipful Co of Actuaries 1979-; FFA (1965), AIA (1968), memb Stock Exchange (1970); *Recreations* golf, tennis, squash, skiing, music; *Clubs* Travellers', New (Edinburgh), Woking Golf; *Style—* Peter J Derby, Esq; Haldish Farm, Shamley Green, Guildford GU5 0RD (☎ 0483 898 461); Quilter Goodison Co Ltd, St Helen's, 1 Undershaft, London EC3A 8BB (☎ 071 600 4177, fax 071 726 8826, telex 883719)

DERBY, Bishop of 1988-; Rt Rev Peter Spencer Dawes; s of late Jason Spencer Dawes, and late Janet, *née* Blane; *b* 5 Feb 1928; *Educ* Aldenham, Hatfield Coll Univ of Durham (BA); *m* 4 Dec 1954, Ethel; 2 s (Michael b 1959, Daniel b 1964), 2 da (Janet b 1956, Mary b 1968); *Career* ordained: deacon 1954, priest 1955; curate: St Andrew Islington, St Ebbes Oxford 1954-60; tutor Clifton Theological Coll 1960-65, vicar Good Shepherd Romford 1965-80, examining chaplain to Bishop of Chelmsford 1970, archdeacon West Ham 1980-88; memb: Gen Synod 1970, Standing Ctee 1975; *Style—* The Rt Rev the Bishop of Derby; 6 King Street, Duffield, Derby DE6 4EU

DERBY, Richard Outram Walker; s of Maj John Derby, TD (d 1964), and Marie Enid Derby (d 1982); *b* 27 April 1940; *Educ* Harrow; *m* 1, 1963, Sarah Mary, only da of late Lt-Col P J Luard, DSO, OBE; 1 s (Edward), 2 da (Amanda, Henrietta); m 2, 1979, Anthea Mary Boyd, da of Lt-Col J R Roberts, RA, of Wincanton, Somerset; *Career* sr ptnr Godfray, Derby & Co (stockbrokers), dir Capel-Cure Myers Ltd; ptnr and memb Cncl of the Int Stock Exchange; *Recreations* fox hunting; *Style—* Richard Derby, Esq; College Green Manor, East Pennard, Somerset (☎ 0458 50240); Capel-Cure Myers, 1 Northumberland Buildings, Queen Square, Bath

DERBYSHIRE, Sir Andrew George; s of late Samuel Reginald Derbyshire; *b* 7 Oct 1923; *Educ* Chesterfield GS, Queen's Coll Cambridge (MA), Architectural Assoc (AADip); *m* Lily Rhodes, *née* Binns, widow of Norman Rhodes; 3 s, 1 da; *Career* physicist and architect; pres RMJM Ltd; Hon DUniv York; FRIBA, FRSA; kt 1986; *Style—* Sir Andrew Derbyshire; 83 Paul St, London EC2A 4NQ (☎ 071 251 5588); 4 Sunnyfield, Hatfield, Herts AK9 5DX (☎ 265903)

DERBYSHIRE, Prof Edward; s of Edward Derbyshire, of 2103 Pine Valley Drive, Timonium, Maryland, USA, and Kathleen, *née* Wall; *b* 18 Aug 1932; *Educ* Alleyne's GS Stone Staffs, Univ of Keele (BA, Dip Ed), McGill Univ (MSc), Monash Univ (PhD); *m* 2 June 1956, Maryon Joyce, da of Arthur John Lloyd, of 34 The Village, Keele, Staffs; 3 s (Edmund Lloyd b 20 Jan 1959, Edward Arthur b 13 April 1965, Dominic Giles b 17 Nov 1968); *Career* RAEC 1954-56; lectr in geography Univ of New South Wales Aust 1960-62, sr lectr in geography Monash Univ Aust 1965-66 (lectr 1963-65), prof of geomorphology Univ of Keele 1984 (lectr in physical geog 1967-70, sr lectr 1970-74, reader 1974-84); Univ of Leicester: prof of physical geography 1985-90, res prof 1990-; chm Br Geomorphological Res Gp 1982-83 (hon sec 1971-75), pres section E Br Assoc for the Advancement of Science 1989-90; FGS (1974), FRGS (1980); Antarctic Serv Medal USA 1974; *Books* The Topographical Map (1966), Climatic Geomorphology (ed, 1973), Geomorphology and Climate (ed, 1976), Geomorphological Processes (with JR Hails and KJ Gregory, 1980); *Recreations* photography, music, poetry, painting; *Style—* Prof Edward Derbyshire; 24 Norfolk Road, Brighton, E Sussex BN1 3AA; Centre for Loess Research, University of Leicester, Leicester LE1 7RH (☎ 0533 523821, telex LEICUN G, fax 0533 522200)

DERING, Lady (Betty Bridgett); *née* Powys Druce; only da of late Lt-Col Vere Powys Druce, of Charminster, Dorset; *b* 15 May 1916; *Educ* Beaufront, Camberley, Surrey; *m* 17 April 1940, Lt-Col Sir Rupert Anthony Yea Dering, 12 Bt (d 1975, when the title became extinct); 1 da; *Recreations* croquet, horse racing, travel; *Style—* Lady Dering; Bellings, Midhurst, Sussex

DERMOTT, William; CB (1984); s of William and Mary Dermott; *b* 27 March 1924; *Educ* Univ of Durham (MSc); *m* 1946, Winifred Joan Tinney; 1 s, 1 da; *Career* agric scientist Univ of Durham and Wye Coll Univ of London 1943-46, MAFF 1976- (sr SG specialist and dep chief sci specialist 1971-76), head of Agric Sci Serv 1976-84, pres Br Soc of Soil Sci 1981-82, actg dir gen ADAS 1983-84; *Style—* William Dermott, Esq, CB; 22 Chequers Park, Wye, Ashford, Kent TN25 5BB (☎ 0233 812694)

DERRICK, John; s of John Raymond Derrick, of Aberdare, and Megan Irene Derrick; *b* 15 Jan 1963; *Educ* Blaengdanr Comp Sch Aberdare; *m* 20 April 1985, Anne Irene, *née* Jenkins; 1 s (Liam Kyle b 3 April 1987), 1 da (Joanna Louise b 30 Jan 1990); *Career* professional cricketer; Glamorgan CCC: joined 1982, first class debut 1983, awarded county cap 1988; spent winters in Aust and NZ 1984-; represented Welsh Schools at under 11 under 15 and under 19 levels, Lords groundstaff 3 years; *Recreations* watching all sports, cooking and washing up; *Style—* John Derrick, Esq; 27 Broniestyn Terrace, Trecynon, Aberdare, Mid Glamorgan (☎ 0685 883283); Glamorgan CCC, Sophia Gardens, Cardiff (☎ 0222 343478)

DERRINGTON, John Anthony; CBE; s of late John Derrington; *b* 24 Dec 1921; *Educ* Battersea Poly (BSc), Imperial Coll London (DIC); *m* 1971, Beryl June, *née* Kimber; 1 s, 3 da; *Career* chartered civil engineer conslt; formerly dir Sir Robert McAlpine & Sons; *Recreations* gardening, travel, reading; *Style—* John Derrington, Esq, CBE; 3 Gorham Ave, Rottingdean, Sussex

DERRY, Anthony Edward (Tony); s of Wilfred Francis Derry (d 1976); *b* 18 April 1933; *Educ* Hereford GS; *m* 1951, Marie Elaine, da of Reginald Edwards (d 1981); 3 children; *Career* chm and md Long John Scotch Whisky 1982- (previously sales dir Arthur Bell & Sons, int sales dir Whyte & Mackay); md James Burrough Distillers plc (following merger of Long John Int Ltd and James Burrough plc) 1987; chm 1989: James Burrough Distillers plc, Whitbread N America; *Recreations* private flying, rugby; *Style—* Tony Derry, Esq; c/o Long John International plc, 20 Queen Anne's Gate, London SW1 (☎ 071 222 7060); 3 Laleham Abbey, Laleham Park, nr Staines, Middx (☎ 0784 63244); James Burrough Distillers plc, 60 Montford Place, Kennington Lane, London SE11 5DF (☎ 071 735 8131)

DERVAIRD, Hon Lord; John Murray; QC (Scotland 1974); s of John Hyslop Murray (d 1984), of Beoch, Stranraer, and Mary, *née* Scott; *b* 8 July 1935; *Educ* Cairnryan Sch, Edinburgh Acad, CCC Oxford (MA), Univ of Edinburgh (LLB); *m* 30 July 1960, Bridget Jane, 2 da of Sir William Maurice Godfrey, 7 Bt (d 1974); 3 s (Alexander Godfrey b 12 Feb 1964, William John b 21 Oct 1965, David Gordon b 4 June 1968); *Career* Lt Royal Signals 1954-56; advocate 1962, memb Scottish Law Cmmn 1979-88; chm: Agric Law Assoc 1981-85 (vice pres 1985-), Scottish Cncl of Law Reporting 1978-88, Scottish Lawyers Euro Gp 1975-78, Med Appeal Tribunals 1978-79 and 1985-88, Scottish Ctee on Arbitration 1986-, Scot Cncl for Arbitration 1989-; Lord of Session (Senator of the Coll of Justice) 1988-89, Dickson Minto prof of co and commercial law; hon pres Advocates Business Law Gp 1988-; chm Scottish Ensemble (formerly Scottish Baroque Ensemble), vice pres Comité Européen de Droit Rural 1989-; *Books* Stair Encyclopedia of Scots Law - Title 'Agriculture' (1987); *Recreations* music, farming, gardening, birdwatching; *Clubs* New (Edinburgh), Puffins (Edinburgh); *Style—* The Hon Lord Dervaird, QC; 4 Moray Place, Edinburgh EH3 6DS (☎ 031 225

1881); Fell Cottage, Craigcaffie, Stranraer DG9 8QS (☎ 0776 3356); Wood of Dervaird Farm, Glenluce, Wigtownshire (☎ 05813 222)

DERVISH, Djemal; s of Dervish Djemal (d 1979), of Harrow, Middx, and Nazire, *née* Abdullah; *b* 21 Oct 1944; *Educ* Lymington Sch Hampstead, Univ of London (BSc); *m* 16 Sept 1972, Meral, da of Mehmet Selcuk, of Cyprus; 2 s (Serkan b 1974, Tarhan d 1985); *Career* sci res asst 1969-70; admitted slr 1974, sr ptnr Fletcher Dervish & Co 1979; memb: Slrs Complaints Negligence Panel 1986, Slrs Complaints Intervention Panel 1989-; chm Trainee Slrs Monitoring Panel 1987, pres N Middx Law Soc 1988; hon legal advsr CAB: Tottenham, Wood Green, Edmonton, Hornsey; hon legal advsr Religious Charity; memb: Law Soc 1972, N Middx Law Soc 1977; *Recreations* gardening, reading, walking; *Clubs* The Portman, The Belfry; *Style—* Djemal Dervish, Esq; 389 Cockfosters Rd, Hadley Wood, Herts (☎ 081 449 7573); Principal Office, 582/4 Green Lanes, Harringey, London N8 ORP (☎ 081 800 4615, fax 081 802 2273 or 081 808 1504, car 0836 776 201)

DERWENT, 5 Baron UK (1881); Sir Robin Evelyn Leo Vanden-Bempde-Johnstone; 7 Bt (GB 1796), LVO (1957); s of 4 Baron Derwent, CBE (d 1986), and Marie Louise, *née* Picard (d 1985); *b* 30 Oct 1930; *Educ* Winchester, Clare Coll Cambridge (MA); *m* 12 Jan 1957, Sybille Marie Louise Marcelle, da of Vicomte de Simard de Pitray (d 1979); 1 s (Hon Francis Patrick Harcourt b 1965), 3 da (Hon Emmeline Veronica Louise (Hon Mrs Winterbotham) b 1958, Hon Joanna Louise Claudia b 1962, Hon Isabelle Catherine Sophie b 1968); *Heir* s, Hon Francis Patrick Harcourt b 1965; m 1990, Cressida Bourke; *Career* 2 Lt Kings Royal Rifle Corps 1949-50, Lt Queen Victoria's Rifles (TA Res) 1950-53; second sec FO 1954-55 (and 1958-61 private, sec to Br Ambass Paris 1955-58; second sec Mexico City 1961-65; first sec: Washington 1965-68; FO 1968-69; N M Rothschild & Sons Ltd 1969-85, md Hutchison Whampoa (Europe) Ltd 1985-; dir: F and C (Pacific) Investment Trust, Cluff Resources plc, Genfin Ltd, Tanks Consolidated Investments plc; chm London & Provincial Antique Dealers' Assoc (LAPADA); Chev Legion of Hon 1957, Officier de l'Ordre Nationale du Mérite (France) 1978; *Recreations* shooting, fishing; *Clubs* Boodle's, Beefsteak; *Style—* The Rt Hon the Lord Derwent, LVO; Hackness Hall, Scarborough, N Yorks; 30 Kelso Place, London W8 5QG

DESAI, Prof Meghnad Jagdishchandra; s of Jagdishchandra Chandulal Desai (d 1984), of Baroda, India, and Mandakini, *née* Majmundar (d 1989); *b* 10 July 1940; *Educ* Univ of Bombay (BA, MA), Univ of Pennsylvania (PhD); *m* 27 June 1970, Gail Graham, da of George Ambler Wilson, CBE (d 1978), of London; 1 s (Sven b 18 Sept 1975), 2 da (Tanvi b 12 April 1972, Nuala b 2 jan 1974); *Career* assoc specialist Dept of Agric Econ Univ of California 1963-65; LSE: lectr 1965-77, sr lectr 1977-80, reader 1980-83, prof 1983-, head of devpt studies 1990-; memb Cncl Royal Econ Soc, chm Exec Ctee Fabian Soc; Islington South and Finsbury Constituency Lab Pty 1986-, pres Assoc of Univ Teachers in Econ 1987-89; *Books* Marxian Economic Theory (1974), Applied Econometrics (1976), Marxian Economics (1979), Testing Monetarism (1981), Cambridge Economic History of India vol 2 (co-ed, 1983), Agrarian Power & Agricultural Productivity in South Asia (co-ed, 1984), Lectrs on Advanced Econometric Theory (ed, 1988), Lenin's Economic Writings (ed, 1989); *Recreations* reading, politics; *Style—* Prof Meghnad Desai; 51 Ellington Street, London N7 8PN (☎ 071 607 5391); 5 Rue de La Pie, Montaigu de Quercy, 82150 France; London School of Economics, Houghton St, London WC2A 2AE (☎ 071 405 7686, telex 24655 BLPESG)

DESAI, Dr Shrivatsa Pandurangrao; s of Dr Pandurangrao Bhimarao Desai (d 1974), of Shriniketana, Saptapur, Dharwad, India, and Satyabhama, *née* Subhadra Sali; *b* 3 Jan 1946; *Educ* Karnatak Coll, Karnatak Med Coll Hubli (MB BS), Univ of Bombay (MS); *m* 28 Jan 1974, Vani Shrivatsa, da of Kanakapura Subbarao Rangarao, of Davangere, India; 1 s (Chetan b 1975), 1 da (Deepti b 1980); *Career* conslt opthalmologist 1982-; fell Coll of Opthalmologists, FRCSEd; *Recreations* photography, gardening; *Clubs* Kannada Balaga (UK); *Style—* Dr Shrivatsa Desai; Consultant Ophthalmologist, Doncaster Royal Infirmary, Armthorpe Rd, Doncaster DN2 5LT (☎ 0302 366666)

DESCH, Stephen Conway; QC (1980); s of Dr Harold Ernest Desch, (d 1978); *b* 17 Nov 1939; *Educ* Dauntsey's Sch, Magdalen Coll Oxford (MA, BCL), Northwestern Univ Chicago; *m* 1973, Julia Beatrice, da of John Geoffrey Little, OBE, RN, ret (d 1975); 2 da; *Career* called to the Bar Gray's Inn 1962, lectr in law Magdalen Coll Oxford 1963-65, joined Midland Circuit 1964, rec of the Crown Ct 1979-; *Style—* Stephen Desch, Esq, QC; 2 Crown Office Row, Temple, London EC4Y 7HJ (☎ 071 353 9337)

DESMOND, Denis Fitzgerald; CBE (1989); s of Maj James Fitzgerald Desmond, JP, DL, of Ballyarton House, Killaloo, Londonderry, and Harriet Ivy, *née* Evans (d 1972); *b* 11 May 1943; *Educ* Castle Park Dublin, Trinity Coll Glenalmond Perthshire; *m* 25 July 1965, Annick Marie Marguerite Francoise, da of M Jean Faussemagne, of Nancy, France; 1 da (Stephanie b 1970); *Career* 2 Lt and Lt RCT (TA) 1964-69; chm and md Desmond & Sons Ltd Londonderry 1970- (dir 1966-70), chm Adria Ltd Strabane 1976-81, dir Ulster Development Capital Ltd Belfast 1985-90, regnl dir Nationwide Anglia Building Society 1986-90, Ulster Bank Ltd 1990-; High Sheriff Co Londonderry 1974, ADC to Govr NI 1967-69; Hon DSc Queen's Univ Belfast 1987; *Recreations* fishing, tennis; *Style—* Denis Desmond, Esq, CBE; Desmond & Sons Ltd, Drumahoe, Londonderry BT47 3SD (☎ 0504 44901, fax 0504 48447/47331, car 0860 747839, telex 74402)

DESMOND, Denis John; s of Patrick Desmond, of Worcester, and Doreen Desmond (d 1985); *b* 30 Oct 1949; *Educ* Ratcliffe Coll Leicester, Univ of Liverpool (BA); *m* 30 March 1973, Elizabeth Mary, da of Gerard Corcoran, of Altrincham, 1 s ((Christopher) Liam), 1 da (Laura Jane); *Career* called to the Bar Middle Temple 1974; *Style—* Denis Desmond, Esq; 6 Fountain Court, Steelhouse Lane, Birmingham (☎ 021 2333282, fax 021 2363600, car 0860 631111)

DESSELBERGER, Ulrich; s of Dr Hermann Desselberger (d 1985), and Henriette Albers; *b* 22 July 1937; *Educ* Ludwig Georgs Gymnasium Darmstadt Germany, Free Univ Berlin (MD); *m* 15 April 1965, Elisabeth Martha Maria, da of Bernhard Wieczorek (d 1976); 2 s (Malthias b 1967, Jona b 1969), 2 da (Susanne b 1966, Mirjam Ruth b 1971); *Career* res asst Dept of Pathology Virchow Hosp and Klinikum Westend W Berlin 1967-69, res asst and consIt dept of virology Hanover med sch 1970-76, Fulbright res fell and visiting res asst prof Dept of Microbiology Mount Sinai Med Center NY 1977-79, sr lectr Dept of Virology Univ of Glasgow, hon consIt Greater Glasgow Health Bd UK 1979-88, consIt virologist and dir regional virus laboratory E Birmingham Hosp 1988-; memb: NY Acad of Sciences, American Soc for Microbiology, American Soc for Virology, Soc for Microbiology UK, Deutsche Gesellschaft für Hygiene und Mikrobiologie of Germany; MRCPath, FRCPS; *Style—* Ulrich Desselberger, Esq; Regional Virus Laboratory, East Birmingham Hospital, Birmingham B9 5ST (☎ 021 771 0396, fax 021 766 8602)

DETHRIDGE, David John; s of Thomas Henry John Dethridge, and Eileen Elizabeth, *née* Pain; *b* 25 June 1952; *Educ* Kingston GS, King Edward's Sch Bath, Queen's Coll Oxford (MA); *m* 13 Aug 1988, Alexandra, da of Peter Neville Metcalfe; 1 s (Christopher b 27 Jan 1990); *Career* called to the Bar Lincoln's Inn 1975; head of Chambers 12 Old Square Lincoln's Inn 1986-91 (memb 1977), barr Gray's Inn; memb Cncl Latimer House Oxford Church Soc, former memb Nat Ctee Lawyers Christian Fellowship; *Style—* David Dethridge, Esq; 1 Verulan Buildings, Gray's Inn, London WC1R 5LQ (☎ 071 242 7646)

DETSINY, (Anthony) Michael; s of Rudolph Detsiny, JP (d 1987), and Edith, *née* Scheff; *b* 25 July 1941; *Educ* Highgate; *m* 2 Dec 1967, Angela Hazel, da of Francis Charles Cornell (d 1977); 2 s (Warren Rodney b 1969, Stephen Charles b 1978), 1 da (Hazel Karen b 1972); *Career* dir: Cadbury Ltd 1977-83, Allied Breweries 1983-86, Creative Business Communications plc 1986-; md The Creative Business Ltd; *Recreations* gardening, reading; *Clubs* RAC; *Style—* Michael Detsiny, Esq; The Willows, Moor End Common, Frieth, nr Henley-on-Thames, Oxon (☎ 0494 881176); The Creative Business Ltd, 37 Dean Street, London W1V 5AP (☎ 071 434 2631, telex 8952165, fax 071 437 0194)

DEUTSCH, Antonia Sara; da of Ronald Leopold Deutsch, of Ilmington, Warwickshire, and Jill Patricia, *née* Davis; *b* 24 June 1957; *Educ* The Abbey Sch Worcestershire, The Sorbonne; *m* 31 May 1980, Colin David Guy, s of Guy Martyn Robinson; 1 s (Oscar Charles Thomas Robinson b 4 Nov 1989); *Career* photographic asst 1981-84, freelance photographer specialising in people landscapes and black and white images 1984-; awards incl: AFAEP Silver award 1989, Ilford Print of the Year award 1989, two AFAEP Award nominations 1991; memb AFAEP 1988; *Recreations* photography, independent rough travel, family; *Style—* Ms Antonia Deutsch; 14A Hesper Mews, London SW5 OHH (☎ 071 244 8772, mobile 0836 344 972)

DEUTSCH, David Leonard; s of Oscar Deutsch (d 1941), of Birmingham, and Lily, *née* Tanchan (d 1983); *b* 10 Jan 1926; *Educ* Stanley House Sch Edgbaston Birmingham, Lawrences Coll Birmingham, Queen Mary Coll Univ of London; *m* 7 April 1960, Clare, da of Andrew Daniel Cory James (d 1979), of Wimbledon, London SW19; 1 s (Alexander b 31 Jan 1964); *Career* Sgt Intelligence Corps 1946-48; assoc prodr J Arthur Rank Film Prodns 1956 films incl: High Tide at Noon, The One That Got Away, The Floods of Fear; dir Sydney Box Assocs Ltd, prodr Blind Date, exec i/c of prodn Anglo-Amalgamated Film Distributors Ltd 1960-69; prodns incl: Nothing But the Best 1964, Catch Us If You Can 1965, Interlude 1967, Lock Up Your Daughters 1968, A Day in the Death of Joe Egg 1970; co prodr The Day of the Jackel; TV prodns incl: Shakespear Lives! 1983, Reflections 1984, The Chain 1985, Mr Knowall, The Verger, The Colonel's Lady; screenplays incl: The Blue Train, The Jacaranda Tree, Berlin Berlin, memb BAFTA; *Recreations* photography; *Style—* David Deutsch, Esq; 26b Thorney Crescent, Morgan's Walk, London SW11 3TR (☎ 071 585 1592)

DEUTSCH, Renee; da of Maurice Deutsch, and Matilda Deutsch; *b* 2 Aug 1944; *Educ* Hendon Co GS, Northern Poly Sch of Architecture; *m* (m dis); *Career* architecture and design for 10 years, mgmnt consultancy for 6 years; appeals coordinator (3 years): Almeida Theatre, Half Moon Theatre, London Contemporary Dance; head of consumer PR Dennis Davidson Assocs, vice pres and md Consumer Products Division The Walt Disney Co Ltd; md consumer prods UK Walt Disney Co Ltd; *Recreations* performing arts, visual, arts, reading, watching tennis; *Clubs* Groucho; *Style—* Ms Renee Deutsch; The Walt Disney Co (UK), 31-32 Soho Square, London W1V 6AP (☎ 071 734 8111, 071 586 3504, fax 071 439 8741, 21532)

DEVAS, Michael Campbell; MC (1945); only s of Geoffrey Charles Devas, MC (d 1971; whose mother was Edith, da of Lt-Col Hon Walter Campbell, 3 s of 1 Earl Cawdor), by his w Joan (d 1975), great niece of Rt Hon Sir Henry Campbell-Bannerman, the Liberal PM (1906-08); *b* 6 June 1924; *Educ* Eton; *m* 1, 28 June 1952 (m dis 1966), Patience Merryday, da of late Sir Albert Gerald Stern, KBE, CMG (d 1966); 1 s, 1 da; m 2, 12 Oct 1967, Gillian Barbara, da of late Col H M P Hewett, of The Court House, Chipping Warden, nr Banbury, and formerly w of Charles Arthur Smith-Bingham; 1 s; *Career* served Welsh Gds NW Europe 1942-47; banker; chm Colonial Mutual Life Assurance (London Bd) 1982-, joined M Samuel & Co Ltd 1947, dir 1960; dir Kleinwort Benson Ltd 1965-86 (ret), chm Kleinwort Charter Investment Trust plc, dir Dover Corporation (USA); *Recreations* sailing, skiing; *Clubs* White's, Royal Yacht Sqdn; *Style—* Michael Devas, Esq, MC; Hunton Court, Maidstone, Kent (☎ 06272 307); work: 24 Lugdate Hill, London EC4P 4BD

DEVENPORT, Martyn Herbert; s of Horace Devenport (d 1944), and Marjorie Violet, *née* Fergusson (d 1973); *b* 11 Jan 1931; *Educ* Maidstone GS, Gonville and Caius Coll Cambridge (MA); *m* 1957, Mary Margaret, da of Percy Vincent Lord (d 1984); 3 s (Andrew, William, Edward), 1 da (Kate); *Career* asst master Eton Coll 1957-67, headmaster Victoria Coll 1967-; memb Headmasters' Conf 1967-; pres: Jersey Festival Choir 1983-, Jersey Assoc of Headteachers 1988-89; *Recreations* sailing (yacht 'Con Brio'), photography; *Clubs* Public Schs; *Style—* Martyn Herbert Devenport, Esq; Sans Souci, Faldouet, Gorey, Jersey, CI (☎ 0534 52795); Victoria Coll, Jersey, CI (☎ 0534 37591)

DEVERALL, Philip Brook; s of William James Deverall, of 7 Blue Waters Drive, Lyme Regis, Dorset, and Marion, *née* Brook (d 1983); *b* 30 April 1937; *Educ* Lymm GS Cheshire, UCL (MB BS); *m* 10 June 1961, Ann Beaumont, da of Frank Henry Drury (d 1961); 2 s (Stephen Charles b 16 July 1962, James Joseph b 6 March 1976), 1 da (Helen Catherine b 10 Feb 1965); *Career* house physician and surgn UCH London 1960-61, sr house surgn Barnet Hosp 1961-63, cardio vascular fell Univ of Alabama USA 1968-70, conslt heart surgn Leeds Hosp 1970-77 (registrar in surgery 1963-65, registrar 1965-68, chm and dir Cardiac Dept), conslt heart surgn Guy's Hosp 1977; author of numerous scientific articles and chapters in books; memb: Br Cardiac Soc, American Heart Assoc, Soc of Thoracic Surgns, Soc of Thoracic Surgns USA; hon memb Soc of Cardiovascular Surgns of Asia 1987; *Recreations* travel, theatre, music; *Style—* Philip Deverall, Esq; 3 Northfield Close, Bromley, Kent BR1 2WZ (☎ 081 467 5418); Flat 11, 22 Park Crescent, London W1N 3PD (☎ 071 636 0641); 21 Upper Wimpole St, London W1M 7TA (☎ 071 935 2847, telex 266549 PBDEV G)

DEVERELL, Sir Colville Montgomery; GBE (1963, OBE 1946), KCMG (1957, CMG 1955), CVO (1953); s of George Robert Deverell, of Kilencoole, Castle Bellingham, Co Louth, and Maud, *née* Cooke; *b* 21 Feb 1907; *Educ* Portora Sch Enniskillen Ulster, Trinity Coll Dublin (LLB), Trinity Coll Cambridge; *m* 5 Oct 1935, Helen Margaret, da of Dallas A Wynne Willson, of St Mary's Lodge, Kidlington, Oxford; 3 s; *Career* entered Colonial Admin Serv 1931; asst dir Civil Affrs Branch E Africa Cmd HQ 1941-46, memb Earl de la Warr's delegation to Ethiopia 1944, sec Devpt and Reconstruction Authy Kenya 1946-49, admin sec Kenya 1949-52, colonial sec Jamaica 1952-55, govr the Windward Islands 1955-59, govr and C-in-C of Mauritius 1959-62, sec gen Int Planned Parenthood Fedn 1964-69; KStJ; *Style—* Sir Colville Deverell, GBE, KCMG, CVO; 123 Greys Road, Henley-on-Thames, Oxon RG9 1TE

DEVERELL, Brig (John Freegard) Jack; OBE (1987, MBE 1979); s of Harold James Frank Deverell (d 1986), of Bath, and Joan Beatrice, *née* Carter; *b* 27 April 1945; *Educ* King Edwards Sch Bath, RMA Sandhurst, RNC Greenwich; *m* 15 Dec 1973, Jane Ellen, da of Gerald Tankerville Norris Solomon, of Hindon, Wilts; 1 s (Simon b 21 Oct 1978), 1 da (Emma b 23 Nov 1976); *Career* RMA Sandhurst 1964-65, cmmnd Somerset and Cornwall Light Infantry 1965, cmd 3 Bn Light Infantry 1984-86, dir Staff Royal Mil Coll of Sci 1986-88, Cdr UK Mobile Force 1988-90; *Recreations* cricket, rugby, golf, rackets, riding; *Clubs* 1 Zingari, Free Foresters, Mounted Infantry; *Style—* Brig Jack Deverell, OBE

DEVEREUX, Alan Robert; CBE (1980), DL; s of Donald Charles Devereux, and

Doris Louie Devereux; *b* 18 April 1933; *Educ* Colchester Sch, Clacton Co HS, Mid-Essex Tech Coll; *m* 1, 1959, Gloria Alma, *née* Hair (d 1985); 1 s (Iain b 1964); m 2, 1987, Elizabeth; *Career* dir: Scottish Mutual Assurance Society 1972-, Walter Alexander plc 1980-90, Solsgirth Investment Trust Ltd 1981-90, Hambros Scotland Ltd 1984-90; int dir Gleneagles Group PLC 1990-; chm: CBI (Scotland) 1977-79, Hambro Legal Protection (Scotland) Ltd 1985-90, Scottish Tourist Bd 1980-90, Quality Scotland Fndn 1991- ; memb Br Tourist Authy 1980-90; CBIM; *Recreations* reading, work, running for aeroplanes; *Clubs* E India, Devonshire, Sports and Public Schools; *Style—* Alan Devereux, Esq, CBE, DL; Viewfield, 293 Fenwick Rd, Glasgow G46 6UH (☎ 041 638 2586, fax 041 638 7656)

DEVEREUX, Richard; s of Austin Augustus Devereux (d 1970), of Lincoln, and Vera Evelyn, *née* Whylde; *b* 3 April 1956; *Educ* Bishop King Sch Lincoln, Portsmouth Coll of Art (scholar, DipAD); *m* 20 Aug 1977, Christine Anne, da of Stanley Holmes; 1 da (Hannah Galadriel b 22 March 1988); *Career* sculptor; solo exhibitions: Recent Works (Axis Gallery Brighton) 1979, Recent Works (Hiscock Gallery Portsmouth) 1980, Circles (Usher Art Gallery Lincoln) 1984, Assembled Rites (Artsite Bath) 1987, On Sacred Ground (Cairn Gallery Glos) 1988, Beyond the Hall of Dreams (New Art Centre London) 1989; gp exhibitions incl: Rufford Arts Centre Notts 1982, Ogle Gallery Cheltenham 1984, Sculpture to Touch (Usher Gallery Lincoln, Ferens Gallery Hull, Normanby Hall Scunthorpe) 1986, 20th Century Br Sculpture (Roche Court Wilts) 1988-90, New Art Centre London 1989-90, Southampton City Art Gallery 1990; collections incl: Tate Gallery, Bodleian Library Oxford, Nat Library of Scotland, Trinity Coll Dublin, various private collections UK and abroad; published limited edn books: Quiet Flame (1986), Assembled Rites (1987), The Bowl of Grain (1989-90); *Style—* Richard Devereux, Esq; 21 North Parade, Lincoln, Lincolnshire LNI 1LB (☎ 0522 542776)

DEVEREUX, Robert Charles Debohun; s of Herbert Morris Devereux (d 1949), and Fanny Rosemary Devereux (d 1980); *b* 15 Dec 1928; *Educ* Repton, Univ of Cambridge (MA); *m* 23 Oct 1954, Anna-Mary, da of Henry Edmund Theoderic Vale (d 1969); 1 s (Charles b 3 June 1956), 2 da (Christina b 13 April 1958, Jane b 12 June 1961); *Career* Nat Serv RE 1947-49 Egypt; Wellcome plc: joined 1953, chief engr 1958, gen prodn mangr 1964-69, ops dir 1972-; memb Chem Industs Assoc Trade Affrs Bd 1959-69, pres NW Kent Post Grad Med Centre 1972-77; CEng, MIMechE, FBIM; *Recreations* reading, gardening; *Clubs* RAC; *Style—* Robert Devereux, Esq; Wellcome plc, Temple Hill, Dartford, Kent DA1 5AH (☎ 0322 223488, fax 0322 228564)

DEVEREUX, Vanessa Gay; da of Edward James Branson, of Cakeham Manor, West Wittering, West Sussex, and Eve Huntley, *née* Flindt; *b* 3 June 1959; *Educ* Box Hill Sch, New Acad of Art Studies; *m* 1983, Robert Devereux, s of Humphrey Devereux; 1 s (Noah Edward b 1987), 1 da (Florence b 1989); *Career* with: Posterbrokers 1981-83, Picturebrokers 1983-86; proprieter Vanessa Devereux Gallery 1986-; fndr Portobello Contemporary Art Festival; *Recreations* theatre, cinema, sport, food; *Style—* Mrs Vanessa Devereux; 98 Oxford Gardens, London W10 (☎ 081 968 5612); 11 Blenheim Crescent, London W11 2EE (☎ 071 221 6836, fax 071 221 6481)

DEVEY, John Michael; s of William James Devey (d 1966), of Wolverhampton, and Ada Florence, *née* Lawson; *b* 19 Feb 1938; *Educ* St Peter's Collegiate Sch Wolverhampton; *m* 25 Oct 1962, Brenda, da of John Arthur Whitehead (d 1977), of Wolverhampton; 1 s (Paul), 1 da (Jacqueline); *Career* CA; ptnr Campbell & Co Wolverhampton; non-exec dir Wolverhampton Health Authy; pres Wolverhampton Lawn Tennis and Squash Club; FCA 1961; *Recreations* golf, squash, tennis; *Clubs* South Staffs Golf; *Style—* John Devey, Esq; Deepdale Cottage, Stratford Brook, Hilton, Bridgnorth, Shrops (☎ 07464 588); Campbell & Co, 87 Tettenhall Rd, Wolverhampton (☎ 0902 21441)

DeVILLE, Sir (Harold Godfrey) Oscar ; CBE (1979); s of Harold DeVille (d 1980); *b* 11 April 1925; *Educ* Burton-on-Trent GS, Trinity Coll Cambridge (MA); *m* 1947, Pamela Fay, da of late Capt Rowland Ellis; 1 s; *Career* Lt RNVR 1943-46; personnel mangr Ford Motor Co 1949-65; BICC Ltd: gen mangr central personnel rels 1965-70, dir 1971, exec vice chm 1978-80, exec dep chm 1980-84; chm Meyer Int plc 1987- (dir 1984); memb: Cmmn on Industl Rels 1971-74, Central Arbitration Ctee 1976-77, Cncl ACAS 1976-, Cncl CBI 1977-85; memb Cncl and fell: Inst Manpower Studies 1971-, Indust Soc 1977-84; chm: Iron and Steel Econ Devpt Ctee 1984-86, Govt Review of Vocational Qualifications 1985-86, memb Bd BR 1985-91; memb Cncl Univ of Reading 1985-, chm Nat Cncl for Vocational Qualifications 1986-90; CBIM, FIPM; kt 1990; *Recreations* genealogy, fell-walking; *Style—* Sir Oscar DeVille, CBE; Meyer International PLC, Villiers House, 41-47 Strand, London WC2N 5JG

DEVINE, (John) Hunter; s of John Hunter Devine (d 1982), of Lenzie, Scot, and Joan Margaret, *née* Hislop; *b* 1 Dec 1935; *Educ* Lenzie Acad; *m* 25 Jan 1964 (m dis 1989), Gillian, da of Edwin John Locke (d 1982), of Chester; 2 s (Oliver John Hunter b 1968, Gavin Richard b 1970); *Career* footballer: int Scottish amateur 1956-60, GB Olympic Team Rome 1960; London sec Scottish Amicable Life Assurance Soc 1964-70 (actuarial trainee 1953-64), pension sales mangr Scottish Amicable 1971-75, dir Leslie & Godwin (Life and Pensions) Ltd 1975-78, Godwins Ltd 1978-86; md: Godwins Central Servs Ltd 1978-81, Godwins Central Ltd 1982-86, Godwins Ltd 1987-; memb Worshipful Co of Actuaries 1982, Freeman City of London 1983; FFA 1964, FPMI 1977, ASA 1980, FIOD 1988; *Recreations* football, golf, theatre, travel; *Clubs* Queens Park Football, Hindhead Golf; *Style—* Hunter Devine, Esq; Godwins Ltd, Briarcliff House, Kingsmead, Farnborough, Hants GU14 7TE (☎ 0252 544 484, fax 0252 522 206, car 0836 211 735, telex 858241)

DEVITT, James Hugh Thomas; s and h of Sir Thomas Gordon Devitt, 2 Bt, of 49 Lexden Rd, Colchester, Essex, and his 3 w, Janet Lilian, da of late Col Hugh Sidney Ellis, CBE, MC; *b* 18 Sept 1956; *Educ* Sherborne, Corpus Christi Coll Cambridge (MA); *m* 20 April 1985, Susan Carol, da of Dr (Adrian) Michael (Campbell) Duffus, of Woodhouse Farm, Thelbridge, Crediton, Devon; 2 s (Jack Thomas Michael b 1988, William James Alexander b 1990), 1 da (Gemma Florence b 1987); *Career* chartered surveyor; Savills PLC; ARICS; *Clubs* Ipswich Town Football; *Style—* James Devitt, Esq; Black Ditches, Little Hormead, Buntingford, Herts

DEVITT, Wing Cdr Peter Kenneth; AE (1950); s of Howson Foulger Devitt (d 1949); *b* 4 June 1911; *Educ* Sherborne; *m* 1, 12 Sept 1935 (m dis 1950), Eunice Stephanie, yst da of Sir Charles Sheriton Swan (d 1944); 1 s, 3 da; m 2, 20 Jan 1950 (m dis 1953), Joan Elizabeth, da of late T Forbes Robertson, of Santa Barbara, California; m 3, 1953 (m dis 1965), Eunice Stephanie, his former w; *Career* served 1939-45 War with RAuxAF (Battle of Britain, despatches Burma), Actg Gp Capt, Wing Cdr 1944; Lloyd's broker and underwriting memb; govr Royal Merchant Navy Sch 1946 (chm 1956-62, vice pres 1967-80, vice patron 1980); former co dir; former vice chm Surrey Territorial and Air Force Assoc; master Worshipful Co of Skinners 1962-63; former DL Surrey; *Recreations* golf, croquet, shooting, painting; *Clubs* RAF; *Style—* Wing Cdr Peter Devitt, AE; Upper Sherbrook, Sherbrook Hill, Budleigh Salterton, E Devon

DEVITT, Lt-Col Sir Thomas Gordon; 2 Bt (UK 1916), of Chelsea, Co London; s of Arthur Devitt (d 1921), s of 1 Bt; suc gf, Sir Thomas Lane Devitt, 1 Bt, 1923; *b* 27 Dec 1902; *Educ* Sherborne, Corpus Christi Coll Cambridge; *m* 1, 21 June 1930 (m dis 1936), Joan Mary, 2 da of late Charles Reginald Freemantle; m 2, 25 Jan 1937 (m dis 1953), Lydia Mary, da of late Edward Milligen Beloe; 2 da; m 3, 12 Dec 1953, Janet Lilian, da of late Col Hugh Sidney Ellis, CBE, MC; 1 s, 1 da; *Heir* s, James Hugh Thomas Devitt; *Career* reg Army 1926-30; ptnr Devitt and Moore; former chm: Sharmans Garages Ltd, Macers Ltd, govrs Nautical Coll Pangbourne; govr Sherborne Sch, chm Nat Serv for Seafarers; *Clubs* MCC; *Style—* Lt-Col Sir Thomas Devitt, Bt; 5 Rembrandt Close, Holbein Place, London SW1W 8HS; 49 Lexden Rd, Colchester, Essex CO3 3PY (☎ 0206 577958)

DEVLIN, (Hugh) Brendan; s of Maj John Joseph Devlin, OBE, and Kathleen Claire, *née* Maxey (d 1966); *b* 17 Dec 1932; *Educ* Trinity College Dublin (BA, MB BCh, BAO, MA, MD, MCh), St Thomas' Hosp London; *m* 13 Sept 1958, Ann Elizabeth, da of Maj Robert Arthur Heatley (d 1947); 5 s (Timothy Robert MP, qv, John Paul (d 1972), James Brendan, Peter Leonard, Brendan Michael William); *Career* demonstrator in anatomy Trinity Coll Dublin 1958, surgical registrar Sir Patrick Dun's Hosp Dublin 1959, sr surgical registrar St Thomas' Hosp London 1963, conslt surgn N Tees Gen Hosp 1970, lectr in clinical surgery Univ of Newcastle upon Tyne 1970, Arris and Gale lectr RCS 1970, Colles lectr RCSI 1985; vice chm Br Jl of Surgery, memb Cncl RCS, memb Ct of Examiners RCSI, sec Nat Confidential Enquiry into Perioperative Deaths, memb Mgmnt Ctee King Edwards Hosp Fund for London, memb Jt Conslts Ctee Dept of Health; Hon Fell Assoc of Surgns of Poland (Rydygier medal 1989), Hon Fell Assoc of Surgns of India (Chatterjee lectr 1984); FRCSI 1960, FRCS 1961, FACS 1985, FRCSEd 1988; *Books* Stoma Care Today, Medicine (1985), Management of Abdominal Hernias (1988), The Report of a Confidential Enquiry into Perioperative Deaths (1988; *Recreations* gardening, walking, music; *Clubs* RSM; *Style—* Brendan Devlin, Esq; Fir Tree House, Hilton, Yarm, Cleveland TS15 9JY (☎ 0642 590246); North Tees General Hospital, Hardwick, Stockton-on-Tees, Cleveland TS19 8PE (☎ 0642 603571, fax 0642 602995)

DEVLIN, Lt-Col Brian; OBE (1963, MBE 1959); s of Dr Francis Joseph Devlin (d 1965), of Liverpool, and Selina Mary, *née* Allan (d 1973); *b* 30 June 1919; *Educ* St Francis Xavier's Coll Liverpool, Stonyhurst Coll, Univ of Liverpool (MB ChB, DPH); *m* 1 Jan 1948, Dr Esther Margaret, da of Michael Joseph Carr (d 1948), of Dundalk, Co Louth; 3 s (Hugh b 1951, Mark b 1955, Patrick b 1965), 1 da (Fiona b 1949); *Career* RAMC: Lt 1942, Capt 1943, Maj 1946, Lt-Col 1959; 1 Airborne Div (served N Africa, Italy, Holland, Norway) 1943-45, SMO Br Mil Mission to Saudi Arabia 1946-49, DADAH Singapore 1952-55, WO 1955-58, PMO MOD Malaya 1958-62, RAMC (TA) 1966-72, MO MPNI, MSS, DHSS 1963-71; adjudicating med practitioner DHSS 1984-89 (SMO 1971-84); memb Somerset CC 1985-89; *Recreations* golf, bridge, fishing; *Clubs* RAMC HQ Officers Mess; *Style—* Lt-Col Brian Devlin, OBE; Rectory Stables, Mells, Frome, Somerset BA11 3PT (☎ 0373 812 951)

DEVLIN, Hon Dominick; 2 s of Baron Devlin, PC (Life Peer); *b* 2 Dec 1942; *Educ* Winchester, UCL (LLB); *m* 27 May 1967, Carla, da of Lamberto Fulloni, of Rome; 2 s (Daniel b 1968, Christopher b 1972), 1 da (Maddalena b 1969); *Style—* The Hon Dominick Devlin; Bâtiment A, Verger de la Tour, 01210 Ornex, Ferney Voltaire, France

DEVLIN, Hon Gilpatrick; eldest s of Baron Devlin, PC (Life Peer); *b* 26 Dec 1938; *Educ* Winchester; *m* 25 Feb 1967, Glenna, da of John Parry-Evans, MRCS, of Colwyn Bay, Denbighshire; 1 s (Benedick b 1967); *Style—* The Hon Gilpatrick Devlin; 6 Millfield Lane, London N6 6JD

DEVLIN, James Alexander; s of James Alexander Devlin (d 1971), of Prince Albert Drive, Glasgow, and Eleanor, *née* Porter (d 1988); *b* 1 May 1934; *Educ* Possil Sch; *m* 2 May 1964, Caroline Ann Whitaker, da of Bernard John Austin; 1 s (David James b 1966, Ann Fiona b 1968); *Career* directorships 1984-87 (ret): Shell Overseas Services Ltd, Shell Co of Turkey Ltd, Shell Co of Qatar Ltd, Shell Mkts (ME) Ltd, Shell Trading (ME) Ltd, Shell Oman Trading Co Ltd, Saudi Arabian Markets and Shell Lubricants Co Ltd, NV Turkse Shell, AL Jomaih and Shell Lubricating Oil Co, Shell Exploration (Libya) Ltd, Sirtica Shell Ltd, Shell Co of Burma, Shell Co of India, Shell Co of Pakistan, Shell Co of Sri Lanka, Abu Dhabi Petroleum Co Ltd, Iranian Oil Participants Ltd, Iranian Oil Services (Hldgs) Ltd, Iraq Petroleum Co Ltd, Petroleum Servs ME Ltd, Qatar Shell Service Co Ltd, Iraq Petroleum Pensions Ltd, Petromin Shell Refinery Co, The Shell Co of Kuwait Ltd; hon sec and treas Wigtownshire Branch SSAFA; FCIS; *Recreations* golf, travel; *Style—* James A Devlin, Esq; Chapel Rossan, Ardwell, Stranraer, Galloway DG9 9NA (☎ 0776 86208)

DEVLIN, His Hon Judge Keith Michael; s of Francis Michael Devlin, of Goring, Sussex, and Norah Devlin; *b* 21 Oct 1933; *Educ* Price's Sch, Univ of London (LLB, MPhil, PhD); *m* 12 July 1958, Pamela Gwendoline, da of Francis James Phillips (d 1984), of Inverkeithing, Fife, Scotland; 2 s (Stephen b 1964, Philip b 1966), 1 da (Susan b 1968); *Career* cmmnd Nat Serv 1953-55; called to the Bar Gray's Inn 1964; dep chief clerk Met Magistrates Cts Serv 1964-66, various appts as a dep met stipendiary magistrate 1975-79; asst rec 1980-83, rec 1983-84, circuit judge 1984, liaison judge Beds 1990-; Brunel Univ: lectr in law Brunel Univ 1966-71, reader in law 1971-84, assoc prof of law 1984-, memb of Univ Ct 1984-88; fell Netherlands Inst for Advanced Study in the Humanities and Social Sciences Wassenaar 1975-76, memb Consumer Protection Advsy Ctee 1976-81; Magistrates' Assoc (memb of Legal Ctee 1974-88, vice chm 1984-88, co-opted memb of Cncl 1980-88); JP Inner London (Juvenile Ct Panel) 1968-84, (chm 1973-84); jt fndr and ed Anglo-American Law Review 1972-84; Liveryman Worshipful Co of Feltmakers; Memb Royal Inst (memb Fin Ctee 1987-); FRSA; *Publications* Sentencing Offenders in Magistrates' Courts (1970), Sentencing (Criminal Law Library No5, with Eric Stockdale, 1987), articles in legal journals; *Recreations* Roman Britain, watching cricket, fly-fishing; *Clubs* Athenaeum, MCC, Hampshire Cricket; *Style—* His Hon Judge Keith Devlin; Crown Court, St Albans, Hertfordshire AL1 3XE (☎ 0727 834481)

DEVLIN, Hon Matthew; 4 and yst s of Baron Devlin, PC (Life Peer); *b* 8 June 1946; *Educ* Winchester, New Coll Oxford; *m* 25 July 1969, Rosemary Joan Boutcher, 3 da of Lt-Col E C Van der Kiste, of The Old Rectory, Durrington, Wilts; 2 s (William b 17 March 1972, Edward b 21 April 1975), 2 da (Beatrice b 16 May 1970, Mary b 10 Jan 1977); *Career* banker Citibank NA; *Style—* The Hon Matthew Devlin; Ruffway, Platt Common, St Mary's Platt, Sevenoaks, Kent (☎ 0732 885380)

DEVLIN, Baron (Life Peer UK 1961); Patrick Arthur Devlin; PC (1960); s of William J Devlin; *b* 25 Nov 1905; *Educ* Stonyhurst, Christ's Coll Cambridge; *m* 12 Feb 1932, Madeleine, da of Sir Bernard Oppenheimer, 1 Bt; 4 s, 2 da; *Career* called to the Bar Gray's Inn 1929, bencher 1947, treas 1963; KC 1945; justice of the High Ct (Queen's Bench Div) 1948-60, lord justice of Appeal 1960-61, lord of Appeal in Ordinary 1961-64; chm: Bedford Coll for Women 1953-59, Ctee of Inquiry into Dock Labour Scheme 1955-56, Nyasaland Cmmn of Inquiry 1959, Press Cncl 1964-69; high steward Univ of Cambridge 1966-91, kt 1948; *Style—* Rt Hon Lord Devlin, PC; West Wick House, Pewsey, Wilts

DEVLIN, Roger William; s of William Devlin, of Lancs, and Edna, *née* Cross; *b* 22 Aug 1957; *Educ* Manchester GS, Wadham Coll Oxford (MA); *m* 1983, Louise Alice Temlett, da of John Frost Tucker, of Somerset; 1 da (Sophie Victoria Temlett b 29 Nov 1989); *Career* merchant banking; dir Hill Samuel & Co Ltd 1986-; *Recreations* golf, horse racing; *Clubs* Worplesdon, Royal St George's Golf; *Style—* Roger Devlin,

Esq; 87 Portland Road, Holland Park, London W11 4LN (☎ 071 243 1916); Hill Samuel & Co Ltd, 100 Wood Street, London EC2P (☎ 071 628 8011)

DEVLIN, Stuart Leslie; AO (1988), CMG (1980); *b* 9 Oct 1931; *Educ* Gordon Inst of Technol Geelong, Royal Melbourne Inst of Technol, RCA; *m* 1986, Carole; *Career* goldsmith, silversmith and designer; Royal Warrant as Goldsmith Jeweller to HM The Queen 1982; Freeman City of London 1966, memb Ct of Assts Worshipful Co of Goldsmiths 1986, DesRCA (Silversmith), DesRCA (Industl Design-Engrg); *Style—* Stuart Devlin, Esq, AO, CMG; Southbourne Court, Copsale, Southwater, West Sussex (☎ 0403 733000)

DEVLIN, Hon Timothy; 3 s of Baron Devlin, PC (Life Peer), *qv*; *b* 28 July 1944; *Educ* Winchester, Univ Coll Oxford; *m* 31 Jan 1967, Angela, er da of A J G Laramy; 2 s (Sebastian b 1973, Fabian b 1975), 2 da (Miranda b 1969, Esmeralda b 1971); *Career* journalist; former news ed TES, reporter The Times 1971-73 (educn corr 1973-77), nat dir ISIS 1977-84, PR dir IOD 1984-86, assoc dir Charles Barker Traverse-Healy 1986-89, fndr Tim Devlin Enterprises (PR consultancy); *Style—* The Hon Timothy Devlin; Ramsons, Maidstone Rd, Staplehurst, Kent TN12 0RD (☎ 0580 893176)

DEVLIN, Timothy Robert (Tim); MP (C) Stockton South 1987-; s of H Brendan Devlin, and Ann Elizabeth, *née* Heatley; gf Dr J J Devlin, OBE; *b* 13 June 1959; *m* 1987 (m dis 1989), Jacqueline, da of George Bonner; *Career* memb of the Cons Res Dept 1981; accountant 1981-84; called to the Bar Lincoln's Inn 1985; former chm LSE Cons, chm Islington N Cons Assoc 1986 (sec 1985); memb: Stockton-on-Tees Cons Assoc, Soc of Cons Lawyers; Bow Gp; chm Northern Gp Cons MPs, sec Cons Backbench Small Business Ctee, Parly sec on Charity Law, campaigner for Family Cts; memb: Franco-Br Parly Gp, All Pty Disablement Gp, IPU, Br-American Parly Gp, All Pty Arts and Heritage Gp, All Pty Clubs Gp; dep chm for Affrs Forum; memb R11A; patron: Opera Nova, Stockton Vocal Union, Stockton Music Festival; govr Yarm Sch; *Style—* Tim Devlin, Esq, MP; 2 Russell St, Stockton-on-Tees, Cleveland TS18 1NS (☎ 0642 603035)

DEVNEY, (Constance) Marie; CBE (1978, OBE 1973); da of Dr Richard Swanton Abraham; *b* 1 April 1934; *Educ* Pendleton HS, Bedford Coll London; *m* 1, 1960 (m dis 1976), Thomas Michael Valentine Patterson; m 2, 1984, Barrie Spencer Devney; *Career* TGWU: nat woman officer 1963-76, nat officer 1976-84; chm Gen Cncl of TUC 1974-75 and 1977 (memb 1963-84); memb: Hotel and Catering Training Bd 1966-86, Central Arbitration Ctee 1975-, Equal Opportunities Cmmn (pt/t) 1976-84, Legal Aid Advsy Ctee 1986-90; dir Remploy 1968-; *Style—* Mrs Marie Devney, CBE; 34 York House, Upper Montagu St, London W1

DEVON, 17 Earl of (E 1553); Sir Charles Christopher Courtenay; 13 Bt (I 1644), JP (Devon 1950); patron of four livings; s of Rev the 16 Earl of Devon, MA (d 1935); *b* 13 July 1916; *Educ* Winchester, RMC; *m* 29 July 1939, Sybil Venetia, da of Capt John Vickris Taylor, JP (d 1956), and formerly wife of 6 Earl of Cottenham; 1 s, 1 da; *Heir* s, Lord Courtenay, *qv*; *Career* Capt Coldstream Gds (RARO), WWII 1939-43 (wounded, despatches), Actg Maj 1942; *Style—* The Rt Hon the Earl of Devon, JP; Stables House, Powderham Castle, Exeter EX6 8JQ (☎ 0626 890253)

DEVONALD, Hon Mrs (Charlotte Elizabeth Ann); da of 2 Baron Croft, *qv*; *b* 1952; *Educ* Benenden; *m* 4 June 1975, Emrys Thomas Devonald; 1 s (James b 1979), 1 da (Jennifer b 1977); *Style—* The Hon Mrs Devonald; Enderley, Stony Lane, Little Kingshill, Great Missenden, Bucks

DEVONPORT, Viscountess; Sheila Isabel; da of Col Charles Hope-Murray (d 1938), of Morishill, Beith, Ayrshire; *Educ* St Leonards, Sch, Univ of St Andrews; *m* 12 March 1938, 2 Viscount Devonport (d 1973); 1 s (3 Viscount), 1 da; *Style—* The Rt Hon the Viscountess Devonport; The Old Vicarage, Peasmarsh Place, nr Rye, E Sussex TN31 6XB

DEVONPORT, 3 Viscount (UK 1917); Sir Terence Kearley; 3 Bt (UK 1908); also Baron Devonport (UK 1910); s of 2 Viscount Devonport (d 1973); *b* 29 Aug 1944; *Educ* Aiglon Coll Switzerland, Selwyn Coll Cambridge (BA, DipArch, MA), Univ of Newcastle (BPhil); *m* 7 Dec 1968 (m dis 1979), Elizabeth Rosemary, 2 da of late John G Hopton, of Chute Manor, Andover; 2 da (Hon Velvet b 1975, Hon Idonia b 1977); *Heir* kinsman, Chester Dagley Hugh Kearley; *Career* architect: David Brody NY USA 1967-68, London Borough of Lambeth 1971-72, Barnett Winskill Newcastle upon Tyne 1972-75; landscape architect Ralph Erskine Newcastle 1977-78, in private practice 1979-84; forestry mangr 1973-, farmer 1978-; md Tweedswood Enterprises 1979; dir various other cos 1984-; chm Millhouse Developments Ltd 1898-; memb: Lloyd's 1976-, Int Dendrology Soc 1978-, TGEW Northern Advsry Ctee 1978-, TGUK Nat Land Use and Environment Ctee 1984-87, CLA Northern Advsry Ctee 1980-85; vice pres: Arboricultural Assoc 1987-, Forestry Cmmn ref panel 1987-; ARIBA, ALI; Order of Mark Twain (USA) 1977; *Recreations* nature, travel, the arts, good food, trees, music, country sports; *Clubs* Beefsteak, Farmers', RAC, MCC, Northern Counties (Newcastle); *Style—* The Rt Hon the Viscount Devonport; Ray Demesne, Kirkwhelpington, Newcastle upon Tyne, Northumberland NE19 2RG

DEVONSHIRE, 11 Duke of (E 1694); Andrew Robert Buxton Cavendish; MC (1944), PC (1964); also Baron Cavendish of Hardwicke (E 1605), Earl of Devonshire (E 1618), Marquess of Hartington (E 1694), Earl of Burlington and Baron Cavendish of Keighley (both UK 1831); s of 10 Duke of Devonshire, KG, MBE, TD (d 1950), and Lady Mary Gascoyne-Cecil, GCVO, CBE (d 1988), da of 4 Marquess of Salisbury, KG, PC; *b* 2 Jan 1920; *Educ* Eton, Trinity Coll Cambridge; *m* 19 April 1941, Hon Deborah Mitford (*see* Devonshire, Duchess of); 1 s, 2 da (Lady Emma Tennant, Lady Sophia Morrison, *qqv*); *Heir* s, Marquess of Hartington; *Career* served WWII as Capt Coldstream Gds; contested Chesterfield (C) 1945 and 1950 (pres Chesterfield Cons Assoc 1982); Parly under sec of state for Cwlth Rels 1960-62, min of state Cwlth Rels Office 1962-1964, min of state Colonial Affrs 1963-64; former exec steward Jockey Club, memb Horserace Totalisator Bd 1977-86; vice lord-lt Derbys 1957-87, chllr Univ of Manchester 1965-86; chm Grand Cncl Br Empire Cancer Campaign 1956-81; pres: Royal Hosp and Home Putney, National Assoc for Deaf Children; former pres Lawn Tennis Assoc, former nat pres Cons Friends of Israel; KStJ; *Books* Park Top: A Romance of the Turf (1976); *Clubs* Brooks's, White's, Pratt's; *Style—* His Grace the Duke of Devonshire, MC, PC; Chatsworth, Bakewell, Derbyshire (☎ 024 658 2204); 4 Chesterfield St, London W1X 7HG (☎ 071 499 5803)

DEVONSHIRE, Duchess of; Hon Deborah Vivien; *née* Mitford; 6 da of 2 Baron Redesdale (d 1958), and sis of Nancy, Pamela, Unity and Jessica Mitford (*see* Treuhaft, Hon Mrs), also of Hon Lady Mosley, *qv*; *b* 1920; *Educ* private; *m* 1941, 11 Duke of Devonshire, *qv*; 1 s, 2 da; *Career* dir: Chatsworth House Tst, Cavendish Hotel Baslow, Devonshire Arms Hotel Bolton Abbey; non-exec dir: Tarmac plc, W & FC Bonhams Ltd; chm Chatsworth Food Ltd, ptnr Chatsworth Carpenters; pres many local charitable orgns; *Books* The House: A Portrait of Chatsworth (1982), The Estate: A View From Chatsworth (1990); *Style—* Her Grace the Duchess of Devonshire; Chatsworth, Bakewell, Derbyshire DE4 1PP

DEVONSHIRE, John Warrick; VRD (1956); s of Ernest Warrick Devonshire (d 1954), and Mabel Cecily Woods (d 1982); gggs of Adm Sir John Ferris Devonshire, KCH (d 1839) one of Lord Nelson's Captains; *b* 21 Dec 1912; *Educ* Sutton Valence; *m* 28 July 1949, Elizabeth, da of Col Frederick George Glanville Weare (d 1975); 2 da (Sally b 1953, Penelope b 1955); *Career* WWII Cdr RNVR served Atlantic convoys, Narvik, Mediterranean, Indian Ocean (last convoy to Singapore), staff of Adm Sir Philip Vian, mentioned in despatches 1944 and 1946; banker, regnl dir Lloyds Bank 1975-81 (regnl gen mangr 1970-74, joined 1931); *Recreations* cricket, golf, gardening, tracing ancestry; *Clubs* MCC, The Naval, The County Guildford; *Style—* John W Devonshire, Esq, VRD; Langhurst Place, Chiddingfold, Surrey GU8 4XP (☎ 042868 4572)

DEVONSHIRE, Michael Norman; TD (1969); s of Maj Norman George Devonshire (d 1983), of Tunbridge Wells, and Edith, *née* Skinner (d 1965); *b* 23 May 1930; *Educ* The Kings Sch Canterbury; *m* 31 March 1962, Jessie Margaret, da of Meirion Roberts (d 1974), of Tywyn Merioneth; *Career* 2 Lt RA 1953-55; TA 1956-69: Queen's Own Royal West Kent Regt, Queen's Regt; admitted slr 1953, Master of Supreme Ct (Taxing Office) 1979, rec of Crown Ct 1987; pres London Slrs Litigation Assoc 1974-76, cdre Boughbeach Sailing Club 1976-79, memb Rotary Club of the Pantiles Tunbridge Wells, treas SE Regnl Assoc RYA, memb Cncl RYA 1978-, vice chm Int Regulations Ctee Int Yacht Racing Union; *Books* Taxation of Contentious Costs (1979), Greenslade on Costs (conslt ed); *Recreations* sailing; *Style—* Michael Devonshire, Esq, TD; 17 Chestnut Avenue, Southborough, Tunbridge Wells, Kent TN4 OBS (☎ 0892 28672); Royal Courts of Justice, Strand, London WC2 (☎ 071 936 6526)

DEWAR; *see*: Beauclerk-Dewar

DEWAR, Dr Albert Duncan (Bill); s of Alexander Dewar (d 1947), of Smeaton, Midlothian and Dover, Kent, and Bertha Jane, *née* Mortby (d 1962); *b* 30 March 1915; *Educ* Dover GS, Univ of London (BSc, PhD); *m* 16 July 1955, Ann Vallack, da of Dr Clive Vallack Single, DSO (d 1931), of Sydney, Australia; *Career* WWII Civil Def London 1939-45; Physiology Dept Br Drug Hosp London 1937-45, demonstrator physiology Univ of Liverpool 1945-48, sr lectr in physiology Univ of Edinburgh 1945-82 (hon fell 1982-85), res pubn on physiology of reproduction, developer The Edinburgh Masker Anti-Stammering Device; restorer: Old Kirk of Weem Perthshire (Heritage Year award 1975), Castle Menzies Weem; ed Clan Menzies Magazine; memb: Physiological Soc, Soc for Endocrinology; *Recreations* scottish architectural history and restoration work; *Style—* Dr Bill Dewar; 1 Belford Pl, Edinburgh EH4 3DH (☎ 031 332 3607); Smithy Cottage, Camserney, By Aberfeldy, Perthshire

DEWAR, Donald Campbell; MP (Lab) Glasgow Garscadden 1978-; s of Dr Alasdair Dewar, of Glasgow; *b* 21 Aug 1937; *Educ* Glasgow Acad, Glasgow Univ; *m* 1964 (m dis 1973), Alison Mary, da of Dr James S McNair, of Glasgow; 1 s, 1 da; *Career* MP (Lab) Aberdeen South 1966-70, PPS to Pres BOT 1967, front bench oppn spokesman Scottish Affrs 1981- (chm Commons Select Ctee Scottish Affrs 1979-81), re-elected to Shadow Cabinet Nov 1983; *Style—* Donald Dewar Esq, MP; 23 Cleveden Rd, Glasgow G12 0PQ (☎ 041 334 2374)

DEWAR, Lady Elisabeth Jeronima; *née* Waldegrave; 3 da of 12 Earl Waldegrave; *b* 4 April 1936; *m* 17 Oct 1963, Hon John Dewar, s of 3 Baron Forteviot; 1 s, 3 da; *Style—* The Lady Elisabeth Dewar; Aberdalgie House, Perth

DEWAR, Hamish Richard John; s of Richard John Gresley Dewar, of Hay Hedge, Bisley, Nr Stroud, Glos, and Andrena Victoria Dewar; *b* 15 Jan 1956; *Educ* Sherborne, Downing Coll Cambridge (MA); *m* 21 May 1983, Anna Maria, da of Patrick Cloonan of Sawbridgeworth, Herts; 1 s (Lachlan b 18 July 1987), 1 da (India b 3 Jan 1989); *Career* specialist in conservation and restoration of paintings; studied under Richard Maelzer at Edward Speelman Ltd 1977-81, own practice 1982-; main restoration works incl: David with Head of Goliath by Guido Ren, Seed of David (alter piece from Llandaff Cathedral) by Rossetti, Hope by G F Watts, Bubbles by Sir John Everett Millais; *Recreations* golf, racing; *Clubs* Sunningdale Golf; *Style—* Hamish Dewar, Esq; 23 Clapham Manor St, London SW4 6DN (☎ 071 622 0309); 9 Old Bond St, London W1X 3TA (☎ 071 629 0317, car 0860 622 537)

DEWAR, Ian Peter Furze; s of late John Thompson Dewar, and Joan Eileen, *née* Knott; *b* 2 March 1947; *Educ* Eltham GS, Coll for Distributive Trades (Dip Mktg); *m* 1 Feb 1975, Wendy Jane, da of Brian Palmer; 2 s (Oliver John b 1985, Francis James b 1987); *Career* Brunnings Yorks 1979-82, dir THB & W 1982-84, dir O & M Direct 1984-85, Grey Direct 1989-; fndr Dewar Coyle Maclean 1985-89; MInstM 1970, MIPA 1989; *Recreations* food and drink; *Clubs* Pinball Owners Assoc; *Style—* Ian Dewar, Esq; 48 Palace Rd, East Molsey, Hampton Ct, Surrey KT8 9DW ; Westminster House, Kew Rd, Richmond, Surrey TW9 2ND (☎ 081 948 4131, fax 081 940 7788)

DEWAR, Ian Stewart; JP (Glamorgan 1985); s of William Stewart Dewar, of Penarth (d 1955); *b* 29 Jan 1929; *Educ* Penarth County Sch, Univ Coll Cardiff, Jesus Coll Oxford (MA); *m* 1968, Nora Stephanie, da of Stephen House (d 1970), of Kettering; 1 s, 1 da; *Career* civil servant 1953-83: private sec to Min of Labour 1956-58, asst civil service cmmr 1961-62, dir Manpower Res Unit 1965-66, under sec Welsh Office 1973-83, planning inspr 1983-85; cncllr Glamorgan 1985- (vice chm 1990-91); memb Governing Bodies: Univ of Wales, Nat Museum of Wales; *Recreations* hill walking, historical research, book collecting; *Clubs* Civil Service, United Services Mess (Cardiff); *Style—* Ian Dewar, Esq, JP; 59 Stanwell Rd, Penarth, South Glamorgan CF6 2LR (☎ 0222 703255)

DEWAR, Hon John James Evelyn; s and h of 3 Baron Forteviot, MBE; *b* 5 April 1938; *Educ* Eton; *m* 17 Oct 1963, Lady Elisabeth Jeronima, 3 da of 12 Earl Waldegrave, KG; 1 s, 3 da; *Style—* The Hon John Dewar; Aberdalgie House, Perth

DEWAR, Robert James; CMG (1969), CBE (1964); s of Dr Robert Scott Dewar (d 1939); *b* 1923; *Educ* Glasgow HS, Univ of Edinburgh, Wadham Coll Oxford; *m* 1947, Christina Marianne, da of late Olaf August Ljungberger of Stockholm; 2 s, 1 da; *Career* chief conservator of forests 1960-64, perm sec Natural Resources Malawi 1964-69, memb staff World Bank 1969-84, chief of Agric Div Regnl Mission for E Africa 1974-84, conslt to the World Bank 1984-86; *Recreations* golf, angling, gardening; *Clubs* Royal Cwlth Soc; *Style—* Robert Dewar Esq, CMG, CBE; Hawkshaw, Comrie Rd, Crieff, Perthshire PH7 4BJ (☎ 0764 4830)

DEWAR, Hon Simon Thomas; s of 3 Baron Forteviot, MBE and Cynthia Monica Starkie; *b* 11 Feb 1941; *Educ* Bradfield; *m* 1970 (m dis 1973), Helen Bassett; m 2, 1979, Jennifer Alexandra, da of John Edward St John Hedge, Avoca, NSW (d 1982), 3 da (Fiona b 1980, Alexandra b 1982, Mary b 1984); *Career* landowner (16,000 acres); *Recreations* game fishing, 'Samantha D'; *Clubs* Union, Imperial Services (Sydney); *Style—* The Hon Simon Dewar; Terling Pk, Moree, NSW 2400, Australia, (☎ 067 548 620)

DEWAR DURIE, Christian Frances; da of Lt-Col Raymond Varley Dewar Durie of Durie, of Pewsey, Wilts, *qv*, and Frances, *née* St John Maule; *b* 6 Aug 1945; *Educ* Downe House Newbury, Belfast Coll of Art, St Martin's Sch of Art (DipAD); *Career* asst designer H & M Rayne 1966-70, gp designer Euromanik Ltd 1970-73, fashion co-ordinator AndréPeters-Louis Ferraud 1974-75, fashion dir Nigel French Enterprises Ltd 1975-78, managing ed Prism Fashion Publications 1978-81, owner and dir Parasol Assocs 1981-; Winston Churchill Memorial Tst Travel Fellowship 1969; FRSA 1967; *Recreations* skiing, travel, theatre, literature, art; *Style—* Miss Christian Dewar Durie; Parasol Associates, 3 King's House, 400 King's Road, London SW10 0LL (☎ 071 351 3236)

DEWAR-DURIE, Andrew Maule; s of Lt-Col Raymond Varley Durie, of Durie, of Court House, Pewsey, Wiltshire, and Wendy, *née* Frances St John Maule; *b* 13 Nov 1939; *Educ* Cheam Sch Berks, Wellington Coll Berks; *m* 25 Aug 1972, Marguerite

Jamila, da of Graf Kunata Kottulinsky, of Vienna, Austria; 2 s (James Alexander b 26 April 1978, Philip Antony b 29 Aug 1986), 1 da (Nicola Louise b 19 Sept 1974); *Career* cmmnd Argyll & Sutherland Highlanders 1958-68, served: UK, BAOR, SE Asia, Aden; ret Capt 1968; White Horse Distillers 1968-83: dir 1973-82, sr export dir 1982-83; int sales dir Long John International (Whitbread & Co plc) 1983-88; James Burrough Distillers: Euro sales dir 1988, dep md 1988-89, md 1989-90, chief exec offr 1990-; Liveryman Worshipful Co of Distillers 1986; *Recreations* sailing, tennis, rough shooting, skiing; *Clubs* Army & Navy, The Cresta, Woodroffes; *Style—* Andrew Dewar-Durie, Esq; Woolfield Farm, Froxfield, nr Petersfield, Hants GU32 1DF (☎ 0730 88 201); James Burrough Ltd, 60 Montford Place, Kennington Lane, London SE11 5DF (☎ 071 735 8131, fax 071 793 0228, telex 262 647

DEWAR OF THAT ILK AND VOGRIE (THE DEWAR), Lt-Col (Kenneth) Malcolm Joseph; OBE; Chief of the Name and Arms of Dewar; o s of Vice Adm Kenneth Gilbert Balmain Dewar, CBE (d 1964), sometime ADC to HM King George V, and Gertrude Mary (d 1969), da of Frederick Annesley Stapleton-Bretherton and Hon Isabella Mary, da of 12 Baron Petre; recognised 1989 by the Lord Lyon King of Arms as Dewar of that Ilk and Vogrie, Chief of the Name and Arms of Dewar, as Representer of the Dewars of that Ilk (a style last used in 1618 and dating back to 1296) and of the Baronial House of Dewar of Vogrie, Midlothian; *b* 13 Aug 1915; *Educ* Beaumont; *m* 19 Oct 1940, Alice Maureen, da of Rev John James O'Malley, of Camberley, Surrey; 1 s (Michael Kenneth O'Malley Dewar of that Ilk and Vogrie, Younger b 1941, *qv*), 1 da (Melanie b 1948); *Career* cmmnd 2 Lt The Suffolk Regt 1936, Lt-Col 1958, ret 1966; *Style—* Lt-Col Malcolm Dewar of that Ilk and Vogrie, OBE; The Dower House, Grayshott, Hindhead, Surrey (☎ 042 873 5592)

DEWAR OF THAT ILK AND VOGRIE, YOUNGER, Col Michael Kenneth O'Malley; o s and h of Lt-Col (Kenneth) Malcolm Joseph Dewar of that Ilk and Vogrie, OBE, Chief of the Name and Arms of Dewar, *qv*, and Alice Maureen, *née* O'Malley; *b* 15 Nov 1941; *Educ* Downside, Pembroke Coll Oxford (BA, MA), RMA Sandhurst; *m* 6 July 1968, Lavinia Mary, o da of late Dr Jack Souttar Minett, of Stony Stratford, Bucks; 3 s (Alexander Malcolm Bretherton b 1970, James Michael Bretherton b 1973, Edward Jack Bretherton b 1978), 1 da (Katharine Victoria Lavinia b 1981); *Career* cmmnd 2 Lt The Royal Green Jackets 1962, psc, Lt-Col 1982, CO Light Division Depot 1985-87, Col 1987, Col Defence Studies Staff Coll Camberley 1987-90 (ret); dep dir Int Inst for Strategic Studies 1990-; Kt of Honour and Devotion SMO Malta 1988; *Books* Internal Security Weapons and Equipment of the World (1978), Brush Fire Wars, Campaigns of the British Army since 1945 (1984, revised 1987), The British Army in Northern Ireland (1985), Weapons and Equipment of Counter-Terrorism (1987), The Art of Deception in Warfare (1989), The Defence of the Nation (1989), An Anthology of Military Quotations (1990), Ragged War (1990), Northern Ireland Scrapbook (jtly, 1986), Campaign Medals (jtly, 1987); *Clubs* Naval and Military; *Style—* Col Michael Dewar of that Ilk and Vogrie, Younger; c/o Barclays Bank plc, 50 Jewry St, Winchester, Hants SO23 8RG

DEWDNEY, Prof John Christopher; s of William Alfred Ernest George Dewdney (d 1980), of Bloxham, Banbury, Oxfordshire, and Irene Matilda, *née* Hitchman (d 1976); *b* 8 June 1928; *Educ* Baines GS Poulton le Fylde Lancs, Univ of Edinburgh (MA); *m* 21 April 1956, Euphemia Jean Duffie, da of John Sinclair (d 1975), of Kirkcaldy, Fife; 3 s (Peter John b 8 Aug 1958, Nicholas b 20 Jan 1964, Alexander b 7 April 1970); *Career* RAF 1946-48; prof of geography Univ of Sierra Leone 1965-67, prof of geography Univ of Durham 1986- (lectr 1952-68, sr lectr 1968 reader 1971-86); FRSGS; *Books* A Geography of Turkey (1971), USSR in Maps (1982), A Geography of the Soviet Union (3 edn, 1979); *Recreations* fell-walking, philately; *Style—* Prof John Dewdney; 48 South St, Durham DH1 4QP (☎ 091 386 4885); Dept of Geography, Science Laboratories, South Rd, Durham DH1 3LE (☎ 091 374 2458, fax 091 374 3740, telex 537351)

DEWE, Roderick Gorrie; s of Douglas Percy Dewe (d 1978), and Rosanna Clements Gorrie (d 1971); *b* 17 Oct 1935; *Educ* abroad, Univ Coll Oxford (BA); *m* 1964, Carol Anne, da of Michael Beach Thomas (d 1941), of Herts; 1 s (Jonathan 1967), 1 da (Sarah b 1965); *Career* chm Dewe Rogerson Group Ltd; *Recreations* golf, travel; *Clubs* City of London; *Style—* Roderick Dewe, Esq; 55 Duncan Terrace, London N1 8AG (☎ 071 359 7318); Booking Hall, Southill Station, nr Biggleswade, Beds (☎ 0462 811 274); 3 1/2 London Wall Buildings, London Wall, EC2M 5SY (☎ 071 638 9571, fax 071 628 3444, telex 883610)

DEWE MATHEWS, Bernard Piers; TD (1965); s of Denys Cosmo Dewe Mathews (d 1985), of 1 Park Village West Regents Park London, and Elizabeth Jane, *née* Davies (d 1937); *b* 28 March 1937; *Educ* Ampleforth, Harvard Business Sch; *m* 10 Feb 1977, Catherine Ellen, da of Senator John Ignatius Armstrong (d 1977) of NSW Aust; 1 s (Charles-Frederick (Freddie) b 1985), 3 da (Jacqueline b 1978, Laura b 1979, Chloe b 1982); *Career* Nat Serv 2 Lt serv Malaya 1956-57, TA Maj 21 SAS Regt 1957-67; Edward Moore & Sons CAs 1957-62, BP Co Ltd 1962-65, Coopers & Lybrand & Assocs 1965-69; dir: Head of Project Fin J Henry Schroder Wagg & Co Ltd 1978- (joined 1969-), Thames Power Ltd 1988-; govr St Paul's Girls' Prep Sch, cncl memb London C of C 1986-87; memb: SEATAG 1985-89, OPB 1989-; FCA 1972 (ACA 1962); *Recreations* music, opera, skiing, landscape gardening; *Clubs* Roehampton; *Style—* Bernard Dewe Mathews, Esq, TD; 112 Castelnau, Barnes, London SW13 9EU (☎ 081 741 2592); J Henry Schroder Wagg & Co Ltd, 120 Cheapside, London EC2V 6DS (☎ 071 382 6682, fax 071 382 3950, telex 885029)

DEWEY, Sir Anthony Hugh; 3 Bt (UK 1917), JP (1961); s of Maj Hugh Grahame Dewey, MC (d 1936), and gs of 2 Bt (d 1948); *b* 31 July 1921; *Educ* Wellington, RAC Cirencester; *m* 22 April 1949, Sylvia, da of late Dr Ross MacMahon; 2 s, 3 da; *Heir* s, Rupert Grahame Dewey; *Career* Capt RA NW Europe 1940-46; farmer Somerset; *Clubs* Army and Navy; *Style—* Sir Anthony Dewey, Bt, JP; The Rag, Galhampton, Yeovil, Somerset (☎ 0963 40213)

DEWEY, Prof John Frederick; s of John Edward Dewey (d 1982), of London, and Florence Nellie Mary, *née* Davies; *b* 22 May 1937; *Educ* Bancrofts Sch, Univ of London (BSc, DIC, PhD), Univ of Cambridge (MA, ScD), Univ of Oxford (MA, DSc); *m* 4 July 1961, Frances Mary, da of William Blackhurst (d 1971), of Wistow, Cambs; 1 s (Jonathan Peter 1965), 1 da (Ann Penelope b 1963); *Career* lectr: Univ of Manchester 1960-64, Univ of Cambridge 1964-70; prof: Albany Univ New York 1970-82, Univ of Durham 1982-86, Univ of Oxford 1986-; FGS 1960, FRAS 1983, FRS 1985; *Recreations* water colour painting, model railways, tennis, skiing, cricket; *Clubs* Athenaeum; *Style—* Prof John Dewey, FRS; Sherwood Lodge, 93 Bagley Wood Rd, Kennington, Oxford OX1 5NA (☎ 0865 735525); Dept Earth Sciences, Parks Rd, Oxford OX1 3PR (☎ 0865 272021)

DEWEY, Rupert Grahame; s and h of Sir Anthony Dewey, 3 Bt; *b* 29 March 1953; *m* 23 Oct 1978, Suzanne Rosemary, da of late Andrew Lusk, of Fordie Comrie, Perthshire; 2 s (Thomas Andrew b 1982, Oliver Nicholas b 1984), 1 da (Laura Kate b 1988); *Career* slr Wood & Awdry Bath; *Style—* Rupert Dewey, Esq; Church Farm House, Wellow, Bath BA2 8QS

DEWHIRST, Alistair Jowitt; CBE (1987); s of Capt Stanley Dewhirst (d 1955); *b* 23 Nov 1921; *Educ* Worksop Coll; *m* 1948, Hazel Eleanor, da of Ernest Reed (d 1979); 3 children; *Career* Maj 14 Army Burma (despatches 1945); chm I J Dewhirst Hldgs plc (clothing manufacturers); *Recreations* sailing, golf; *Clubs* Army and Navy, Royal Ocean Racing, Royal Yorks Yacht, Royal London Yacht, Ganton Golf, The Leeds; *Style—* Alistair Dewhirst Esq, CBE; Nafferton Grange, Driffield, E Yorks; c/o I J Dewhirst Holdings plc, Duwear House, Westgate, Driffield, N Humberside (☎ 0377 42561)

DEWHIRST, Timothy Charles; DL (N Humberside); s of Alistair Jowitt Dewhirst, CBE, of Driffield, N Humberside, and Hazel Eleanor, *née* Reed; *b* 19 Aug 1953; *Educ* Worksop Coll; *m* 15 July 1978, Prudence Rosalind, da of Frank Geoffrey Horsell, of Knaresborough, N Yorks; 1 s (Charles Alistair Geoffrey b 4 June 1980), 1 da (Samantha Prudence b 26 June 1983); *Career* chief exec Dewhirst Group plc (clothing and toiletry mfrs) 1986-, vice chm BCIA 1990-; *Recreations* hockey, shooting; *Style—* Timothy C Dewhirst, Esq, DL; Nafferton Heights, Nafferton, nr Driffield, N Humberside YO25 0LD (☎ 0377 44400); Dewhirst Group plc, Dewhirst House, Westgate, Driffield, N Humberside YO25 7TH (☎ 0377 42561, telex 527530, fax 0377 43814, car ☎ 0836 620832)

DEWHURST, Prof Sir (Christopher) John; s of late John Dewhurst; *b* 2 July 1920; *Educ* St Joseph's Coll Dumfries, Victoria Univ Manchester; *m* 1952, Hazel Mary Atkin; 2 s, 1 da; *Career* formerly prof of obstetrics and gynaecology Univ of London at Queen Charlotte's Hospital for Women, dean Inst of Obstetrics and Gynaecology 1979-85; Hon DSc Sheffield, Hon MD Uruguay; Hon FACOG, Hon FRCSI, Hon FCOG (SA), Hon FRACOG, FRCOG, FRCSE; kt 1977; *Style—* Prof Sir John Dewhurst; 21 Jack's Lane, Harefield, Middx UB9 6HE (☎ 089 582 5403)

DEWHURST, William; s of William Dewhurst (d 1967); *b* 12 Jan 1921; *Educ* Bolton Poly; *m* 1940, Emily, da of Thomas Edward Horridge; 2 s; *Career* chartered engr; joined Br Reinforced Concrete Engrg Co Ltd Stafford 1949, works dir 1969, dir subsid Spencer Mesh Ltd (Wakefield) 1972-; MIMechE; *Recreations* golf; *Clubs* Wolstanton (Newcastle-under-Lyme), Brocton Hall Golf (Stafford); *Style—* William Dewhurst, Esq; Evesham, Old Coach Lane, Brocton, Stafford

DEWS, Peter; s of John Dews (d 1961), and Edna, *née* Bloomfield (d 1976); *b* 26 Sept 1929; *Educ* Queen Elizabeth GS Wakefield, Univ Coll Oxford (BA, MA); *m* 1960, Ann, da of Arthur Stanley Rhodes (d 1982); *Career* schoolmaster 1952-54; dir sound and TV BBC 1954-64; dir: Ravinia Festival Chicago 1964 and 1971, Birmingham Repertory Theatre 1966-72, Hadrian VII Birmingham 1967, London 1968, NY 1969, Chichester Festival Theatre 1978-80, Stratford Ontario 1984 (1973, 1981); awarded: Antoinette Perry (Tony) award Broadway 1969, Guild of TV Drama Prodrs and Dirs award for best drama prodn (An Age of Kings 1960); Hon DLitt Univ of Bradford; *Style—* Peter Dews, Esq; 8 Capstan Row, Deal, Kent CT14 6NE (☎ 0304 368937)

DEXTER, Bunny Katharine Weston; da of M W Dexter, and H L Taylor Dexter; *Educ* Walnut Hill, Bryn Mawr Coll (BA), NYU Film Sch; *Career* journalist (sci, political, travel), writer of numerous film scripts incl Flora (best short subject film Chicago Film Festival); dir Euro Games Agency 1988, invented board games: SHRINK 1988, The Worm Turned 1990; produced short film in France (Death); mangr political campaign NY State senator election; memb Ctee SOS for the Homeless; memb BAFTA; *Clubs* Chelsea Arts Academy; *Style—* Ms Bunny Dexter; 37 Lennox Gardens, London SW1X 0DF

DEXTER, Colin; *b* 29 Sept 1930; *Educ* Stamford Sch, Christ's Coll Cambridge (MA); *m* 30 March 1956, Dorothy; 1 s (Jeremy b 1962), 1 da (Sally b 1960); *Career* Nat Serv; author; sr asst sec Univ of Oxford Delegacy of Local Examinations 1966-87; five times crossword champion of Ximenes and Azed Competitions; hon MA by incorporation Univ of Oxford 1966; memb: Crime Writers Assoc, Detection Club; *Books* Inspector Morse Crime Novels: Last Bus to Woodstock (1975), Last Seen Wearing (1976), The Silent World of Nicholas Quinn (1977), Service of All The Dead (Silver Dagger award CWA, 1979), The Dead of Jericho (Silver Dagger award CWA, 1981), The Riddle of the Third Mile (1983), The Secret of Annexe 3 (1986), The Wench is Dead (Gold Dagger award CWA, 1989); *Recreations* crosswords, reading; *Style—* Colin Dexter, Esq; 456 Banbury Rd, Oxford OX2 7RG (☎ 0865 54385)

DEXTER, Edward Ralph; s of Ralph Marshall Dexter (d 1974), and Elise Genevieve, *née* Dartnall (d 1974); *b* 15 May 1935; *Educ* Radley, Jesus Coll Cambridge; *m* 1963, Susan Georgina, da of Thomas Cuthbert Longfield; 1 s (Thomas), 1 da (Genevieve); *Career* Nat Serv 2 Lt 11 Hussars Malaya; dir Edward & Susan Dexter Ltd (PR); cricket capt Cambridge, Sussex and England 1960-65, chm England Ctee TCCB; Parly candidate (C) Cardiff 1965; Malaya Campaign Medal; *Recreations* golf; *Clubs* Sunningdale Golf, Royal & Ancient Golf; *Style—* Ted Dexter, Esq; 20a Woodville Gardens, Ealing, London W5 2LQ (☎ 081 998 6863)

DEXTER, Prof (Thomas) Michael; s of Thomas Richard Dexter (d 1976), and (Gertrude) Agnes, *née* Depledge; *b* 15 May 1945; *Educ* Manchester Central GS, Univ of Salford (BSc, DSc), Univ of Manchester (PhD); *m* 10 Aug 1966 (m dis 1978), (Frances) Ann, da of John Sutton, of Lawer Swanscoe Farm, Hurdsfield, nr Macclesfield; 2 s (Alexander Michael b 1972, Thomas b 1987), 2 da (Katrina Ann (twin) b 1972, Rachel b 1985); *Career* visiting fell Sloan Kettering Inst NY USA 1976-77, sr scientist Paterson Laboratories Manchester 1977-87 (scientist 1973), life fell Cancer Res Campaign 1978-, head of Dept of Experimental Haemotology Paterson Inst for Cancer Res Manchester 1982-, prof of haemotology (personal chair) Univ of Manchester 1985-, pres Int Soc for Experimental Haematology 1988-89, author 222 papers in jls; memb: Scientific Ctee Leukaemia Res Fund 1985-88, Grants Ctee Cancer Res Campaign 1986-, Ctee on Effects of Ionising Radiation 1988-; MRCPath 1987; *Recreations* folk-singing, poetry & gardening; *Style—* Prof Michael Dexter; Bridge End, Pedley Hill, Adlington, Cheshire SK10 4LB; Paterson Institute for Cancer Research, Christie Hospital & Holt Radium Institute, Withington, Manchester M20 9BX (☎ 061 446 2596, telex 9349999 TXLINK G - quote MBX 614458123 as first line of text, fax 061 4347728)

DEXTER, Sally Julia; da of Edward Dexter, of Sonning Common, Reading, and Retha Joan, *née* Roginson; *b* 15 April 1960; *Educ* Chiltern Edge Sch Sonning Common, King James Coll Henley on Thames, Nat Youth Theatre, LAMDA; partner, Mark Lockyer; *Career* actess; *roles incl* Bunny in Babes in Arms (LAMDA) 1984, Princess Winnifred in Once Upon A Mattress (Watermill Theatre, Newbury) 1985; Royal Nat Theatre 1985-88: Hermione in The Winter's Tale, Octavia in Antony and Cleopatra, Sarah Eldridge in Entertaining Strangers, Fanny Margolies in The American Clock, Mizi in Dalliance, Polly Peachum in The Threepenny Opera, Miss Prue in Love for Love; Open Air Theatre Regent's Park 1989: Acerbita in The Swaggerer, Olivia in Twelfth Night, Titania in A Midsummer Night's Dream; Lady Betty in Lady Betty (Cheek by Jowl) 1989; Royal Shakespeare Co 1990-91: Catalena in The Last days of Don Juan, Regan in King Lear, Helen in Troilus and Cressida; winner Lawrence Olivier award for the Most Promising Newcomer in Theatre 1986; *Recreations* walking, talking, eating, hot baths, horse riding; *Style—* Ms Sally Dexter; c/o Duncan Heath Associates Ltd, Paramount House, 162-170 Wardour Street, London W1V 3AT (☎ 071 439 1471 and 071 439 2111, fax 071 439 7274)

DHANDSA, Narinder S; s of Shiv Dhandsa (d 1971), and Samitar Dhandsa; *b* 29 Feb 1956; *Educ* Gillingham GS Kent, St Thomas' Hosp Med Sch (MB, BS); *Career* jr hosp doctor NHS 1979-82, chm and chief exec Associated Nursing Services plc 1984-; currently dir: Rickshaw Restaurants Ltd, Vigour Ltd; *Recreations* skiing, golf, art; *Style—* Dr Narinder Dhandsa; Associated Nursing Services plc, Meadbank, 12 Parkgate Rd, London SW11 4NN (☎ 071 924 3026, car 0836 724592)

DHASMANA, Janardan Prasad; s of Govind Ram Dhasmana, of Dehradun, India, and Savitri Dhasmana; *b* 15 Jan 1942; *Educ* Lucknow Univ India (BSc, MB BS, MS); *m* 2 Dec 1965, Lakshmi, da of Ram Prasad Joshi (d 1986); 1 s (Devesh b 6 Oct 1973), 1 da (Divya b 27 July 1970); *Career* surgical registrar The Wellingdon Hosp New Delhi 1968-71; Bristol Royal Infirmary: registrar in cardiothoracic surgery 1975-78, sr registrar 1978-85, conslt 1986-; clinical res fell Univ of Alabama 1980-81, sr registrar in cardiac surgery Royal Hosp for Sick Children Gt Ormond St London 1982-83; memb Soc of Thoracic and Cardiovascular Surgeons of GB and Ireland, Br Cardiac Soc, BMA; FRCS 1975, FRCSEd 1975; *Recreations* photography, sports watching, music; *Style—* Janardan P Dhasmana, Esq; Consultant Cardiothoracic Surgeon, Bristol Royal Infirmary, Bristol BS2 8HW (☎ 0272 230000 ext 3182)

DHESI, Paul Gurkirpal; s of J S Dhesi, and J K Dhesi; *b* 9 Dec 1951; *Educ* Univ of Bradford (BTech); *m* 17 Sept 1976, Valerie; 2 da (Yasmin b 25 Feb 1979, Lisa b 6 Feb 1981); *Career* component quality engr Thorn Consumer Electronics Bradford 1976-78, field sales engr Texas Instruments Ltd Bedford 1978-81; Microvitee plc: sales and mktg dir 1981-84, md 1984-87, chief exec 1987-; govr Rhodesway Upper Sch Bradford, dir Steering Ctee Trg and Enterprise Cncl Bradford 1989; MInstD; *Clubs* IOD; *Style—* Paul Dhesi, Esq; Microvitee plc, Futures Way, Bolling Rd, Bradford, W Yorks BD4 7TU (☎ 0274 390011, fax 0274 841423, telex 517717)

DHILLON, Amar Paul; s of Dharm Singh Dhillon, and Amar Kaur, *née* Johl; *b* 7 Nov 1951; *Educ* Gateway Boys' GS Leicester, St Johns Coll Cambridge (MD), Middx Hosp Med Sch (BA, MA, MB BChir); *m* 21 Dec 1974, Gouri, da of Nirmal Singh Hoon, of 127 Church Rd, Hanwell, London; 3 s (Arjun b 1980, Ashok b 1983, Achal b 1984); *Career* lectr Bland-Sutton Inst of Pathology Middx Hosp Med Sch 1978-85, sr lectr and hon conslt Royal Free Hosp Sch of Med 1985-; res in diseases of gut, endocrine system and related tumours; MRCP 1979, MRCPath 1983; *Books* The Digestive System (1989); *Recreations* squash, tennis; *Style—* Amar Dhillon, Esq; 121 Church Rd, Hanwell, London W7 3BJ (☎ 081 567 3260); Department of Histopathology, Royal Free Hospital School of Medicine, University of London, Rowland Hill St, London NW3 2PF (☎ 071 794 0500 ext 3279)

DHILLON, Tarlochan Singh; s of Darshan Singh Dhillon, of W Midlands, and Parkash Kaur Dhillon, *née* Uppal; *b* 27 Nov 1949; *Educ* King Edward VI GS Birmingham; *m* 17 July 1971, Ravinderjit Kaur, da of Bakshish Singh Randhawa, of India; 1 s (Bal Navjot Singh b 1983), 4 da (Tribhavanjit b 1973, Inderpreet b 1977, Gurmeet b 1980, Harjeet b 1981); *Career* CA; Russell Durie Kerr Watson & Co (later Spicer & Pegler), audit supervisor Price Waterhouse & Co 1974-78, divnl mgmnt accountant Truflo Ltd 1978-79, mgmnt accountant Durapipe Ltd 1980-84; in private practice as Dhillon & Co, dir Birmingham Credit Union Development Agency Ltd; memb of social, cultural and charitable societies: Sandwell Community Relations Cncl 1982-84, treas Sandwell Cncl for Voluntary Serv; chm Supervisory Ctee W Midlands Punjabee Savings Credit Union Ltd; FCA, MBIM; *Recreations* reading, chess; *Style—* Tarlochan S Dhillon, Esq; 15 Arden Grove, Langley, Oldbury, Warley, W Midlands B69 4SU (☎ 021 544 6426); 33 Broad St, Wolverhampton, W Midlands WV1 1HZ

DHRANGADHARA, Maharaja Sriraj of Makharan-; His Highness Mahamandlesvar Maharana Sriraj Meghrajji III Jhaladhipati; 45th Regnant and Head of the Jhalla-Makhavan Clan and of the Shaktimant Order, &c; s of HH M Sriraj Ghanashyamsinhji, GCIE, KCSI, and suc 4 February and enthroned 15 February 1942; *b* 3 March 1923; *Educ* Local Rajput Hostel, Dhrangadhara Rajdham Shala (Palace School) which was moved to UK and became Millfield Somerset, Heath Mount and Haileybury, St Joseph's Acad, Dehra Dun, Sivaji Mil School Poona, Christ Church, Ruskin School of Drawing, and Institute of Social Anthropology Oxford (Dip with distinction and BLitt); *m* 1943, Princess Brijrajkunvarba, da of HH the Maharaja of Marwar-Jodhpur; 3 s; *Heir* s, Yuvaraj of Dhrangadhara, Jhalavrit Maharajkumar Shri Sodhsalji; *Career* governed 1942-48; agrarian, social and constitutional reformer; acceded to India 9 August 1947; ceded powers to Saurashtra 1948; Upa-Rajpramukh and Acting Rajpramukh of Saurashtra 1948-52; Oxford 1952-58: elected to Gujarat Legve Assembly and from Jhalavad (Gujarat) to Parliament (Lok Sabha) 1967; promoter and intendant gen Consultation of Rulers of Indian States in Concord for India 1967; KCSI, FRAS, FRAI, ARHistS, BLitt (Oxon); *Recreations* Research in sociology, social history, ethnography; *Style—* His Highness The Maharaja Sriraj of Dhrangadhara; 108 Malcha Marg, New Delhi-110021

DI PALMA, Vera June; da of William di Palma (d 1949), and Violet May, *née* Pryke; *b* 14 July 1931; *Educ* Haverstock Central Sch, Burghley Girls Sch; *m* 4 July 1973, Ernest Brynmor Jones; *Career* accountant in public practice 1947-64, tax accountant Dunlop plc 1964-67, sr lectr City of London Poly 1967-71, tax conslt 1971-80, chm Mobile Training Ltd 1978-; dep chm Air Travel Tst Ctee, public works loan cmmr, memb VAT Tbnl; FCCA 1956 (pres 1980-81), FTII 1960; *Books* Capital Gains Tax (1972), Your Fringe Benefits (1978); *Recreations* tennis, dog walking, gardening; *Style—* Ms Vera di Palma, OBE; Temple Close, Sibford Gower, Banbury, Oxon OX15 5RX (☎ 0295 78 222); Mobile Training Ltd, Africa House, 64/78 Kingsway, London WC2B 6AH (☎ 071 242 3067, fax 071 831 6234, car 0860 374343)

DIAMAND, Peter; Hon CBE (1972); *b* 1913; *Educ* Schiller-Realgymnasium Berlin, Univ of Berlin; *m* 1, 1948 (m dis 1971), Maria Curcio; m 2 (m dis 1979), Sylvia Rosenberg; 1 s; *Career* dir: Holland Festival 1948-65, Edinburgh Int Festival 1965-78; conslt: Orchestre de Paris 1976-, Teatro alla Scala (Milan) 1977-78; dir and gen mangr RPO 1978-81, dir Mozart Festival Paris 1981-87; Hon LLD Univ of Edinburgh; Offr des Arts et des Lettres France 1985; *Style—* Peter Diamand, Esq, CBE; 28 Eton Court, Eton Ave, London NW3 3HJ (☎ 071 586 1203)

DIAMOND, His Hon Judge Anthony Edward John; ,QC; s of Arthur Sigismund Diamond (d 1978), and Gladys Elkah Diamond (d 1945); *b* 4 Sept 1929; *Educ* Rugby Corpus Christi Coll Cambridge (MA); *m* 21 Dec 1965, Joan Margaret, da of Thomas Gee; 2 da (Emma b 1966, Lucy b 1971); *Career* 2 Lt RA 1948-49; called to the Bar Gray's Inn 1953; practised as barr at commercial bar 1958-90, dep high ct judge 1982-90, head of chambers 4 Essex Court 1984-90, rec Crown Ct 1985-90, bencher Gray's Inn 1985, Circuit judge 1990; memb: Independent Review Body under colliery review procedure 1983-90, chm of Appeal Tbnl under Banking Act 1985-90, circuit judge 1990; *Recreations* the visual arts; *Style—* His Hon Judge Anthony Diamond, QC; 1 Cannon Place, London NW3 1EH (☎ 071 435 6154)

DIAMOND, Prof Aubrey Lionel; s of Alfred Diamond (d 1951), of London, and Millie, *née* Solomons (d 1963); *b* 28 Dec 1923; *Educ* Central Fndn Sch London, LSE (LLM); *m* 26 Nov 1955, Eva Marianne, da of Dr Adolf Bobasch (d 1976), of London; 1 s (Paul b 1960), 1 da (Nicola b 1958); *Career* RAF 1943-47; Law Dept LSE 1957-66, ptnr Lawford & Co 1959-71 (conslt 1986-), law prof QMC London 1966-71, law cmmr 1971-76, dir Inst Advanced Legal Studies 1976-86, hon fell LSE 1984, fell QMC 1984, law prof Notre Dame Univ (USA) 1987-, co dir London Law Centre 1987-; visiting prof: Stanford Univ, Univ of Virginia, Tulane Univ, Melbourne Univ, Univ of East Africa; memb Latey Ctee on Age of Majority 1965-67, vice pres Inst Trading Standards Admin 1975-, chm Hamyln Tst 1977-88, advsr on security interests DTI 1986-88; cncl memb Law Soc 1976-; Hon MRCP 1990; *Books* The Consumer, Society and the Law (with Sir Gordon Borrie, 1963), Introduction to Hire-Purchase Law (1967), Commercial and Consumer Credit (1982), A Review of Security Interests in Property (1989); *Style—* Prof Aubrey Diamond; University of Notre Dame, London Law Centre, 7 Albemarle St, London W1X 3HF (☎ 071 493 9002, fax 071 408 4465)

DIAMOND, Derek Robin; s of Lord John Diamond, of Little Chalfont, Bucks, and Sadie, *née* Lyttleton; *b* 18 May 1933; *Educ* Harrow County GS, Univ of Oxford (MA), Northwestern Univ of Illinois (MSc); *m* 12 Jan 1957, Esme Grace, da of Richard Bryant Passmore (d 1982); 1 s (Andrew Richard b 1961), 1 da (Stella Ruth b 1963); *Career* lectr in geography Univ of Glasgow 1957-68, prof of geography (specialising in urban and regnl planning) LSE 1982- (reader in regnl planning 1968-82), hon prof of human geography Inst of Geography Beijing (PRC) 1990; vice pres Town and Country Planning Assoc, hon pres Regional Studies Assoc, hon memb RTPI 1989, MIBG, FRGS; *Books* Regional Policy Evaluation (1983), Infrastructure & Industrial Costs in British Industry (1989); *Recreations* philately; *Clubs* Geographical; *Style—* Prof Derek Diamond; 9 Ashley Drive, Walton-on-Thames, Surrey KT12 1JL (☎ 0932 223280); London School of Economics and Political Sciences (☎ 071 955 7586, fax 071 955 7412)

DIAMOND, Col (Clifford) Hugh; s of George Clifford Diamond, OBE (d 1985), of The Cathedral Green, Llandaff, Cardiff, and Beryl, *née* Jones (d 1984); *b* 1 Jan 1934; *Educ* Cardiff HS, RMA Sandhurst, Nat Def Coll; *m* Feb 1960, Susan Jane Mayo, da of Gerald Mayo Meates (d 1944); 1 s (Jonathan b 1963); *Career* Army; cmmnd The Welch Regt 1954 (amalgamated into Royal Regt of Wales 1969), seconded to 2 KEO Gurkha Rifles 1962-65; serv: BAOR, Middle East, Far East, Aust, Turkey, Africa, UK; def and mil attaché Khartoum and Mogadishu; OStJ 1973; *Recreations* shooting, social tennis, gardening, reading, music; *Clubs* Army and Navy, MCC; *Style—* Col Hugh Diamond; Moor Farm Cottage, Bodenham Moor, Herefordshire (☎ 056 884 398)

DIAMOND, Baron (Life Peer UK 1970); John Diamond; PC (1965); s of late Rev Solomon Diamond, of Leeds, and Henrietta Diamond; *b* 30 April 1907; *Educ* Leeds GS; *m* 1, 1932 (m dis 1947); 2 s, 1 da; m 2, 1948, Julie; 1 da; *Career* former dir: Sadlers Wells Trust Ltd, London Opera Centre; MP (Lab) Manchester 1945-51, Gloucester 1957-70; chief sec to the Treasury 1964-70 (memb of Cabinet 1968-70); dep Chm of Ctees House of Lords 1974; chm: Royal Cmmn on the Distribution of Income and Wealth 1974-79, Indust and Parliament Tst 1976-; tstee Cncl for Social Democracy 1981-; hon treas Fabian Soc; elected SDP Leader in House of Lords 1982; *Style—* Rt Hon Lord Diamond, PC; Aynhoe, Doggetts Wood Lane, Chalfont St Giles, Bucks

DIAMOND, Peter Michael; s of William Howard Diamond (d 1979), and Dorothy Gladys Diamond, *née* Powell (d 1961); *b* 5 Aug 1942; *Educ* Bristol GS, Queens' Coll Cambridge (MA); *m* 1968, Anne Marie; 1 s (Benjamin b 1969), 1 da (Candida b 1972); *Career* chief arts & museums offr Bradford 1976-80, chm Yorkshire Sculpture Park 1978-81, memb of Craft Cncl 1981-84, dir Birmingham Museums & Art Gallery 1980-, memb of Cncl Aston Univ 1983-; *Style—* Michael Diamond, Esq; 40 Jordan Rd, Four Oaks, Sutton Coldfield, W Midlands B75 5AB (☎ 021 308 3287); City Museum & Art Gallery, Chamberlain Square, Birmingham B3 3DH (☎ 021 235 2833)

DIBB-FULLER, Edwin; *b* 1946; *Educ* Brixton Sch of Building London; *Career* sr engr Alan Marshall and Partners Consulting Engineers (responsible for design of numerous public sector commercial and hosp) 1970-77, project leader and sr structural engr BBC (responsible for design of regnl television studios in Manchester, Bristol, Glasgow and Belfast) 1977-85, responsible for the design of several commercial projects incl London HQ Morgan Guarantee Company of NY; Building Design Partnership 1985- (ptnr, profession chm for Southern Region); CEng, FIStructE; *Style—* Edwin Dibb-Fuller, Esq; Building Design Partnership, PO Box 4WD, 16 Gresse Street, London W1A 4WD

DIBBEN, Kenneth Francis; s of Stanley Cyril Dibben (d 1978), and Edna Florence, *née* Hobbs (d 1977); *b* 13 Feb 1929; *Educ* King Edward VI Sch Southampton, Worcester Royal GS, Univ of Southampton (BCom); *m* 1962, Dora Mary Bower, *née* Tunbridge; 1 s (Gye b 1975); *Career* former dir Hambros Bank Ltd, chm Kalamazoo PLC; former Cons Party candidate; dir: Chilworth Centre, Univs Superannuation Scheme; memb Univs Authorities Panel, treas Univ of Southampton; hon treas: Wider Shareownership Cncl, Fountain Soc, Furniture History Soc; Freeman City of London, Liveryman Worshipful Co of Chartered Accountants; FCA, CBIM, FCT; *Clubs* Carlton, Hong Kong (HK); *Style—* Kenneth Dibben, Esq; 3 Marsham Court, Marsham Street, London SW1P 4JY (☎ 071 821 9153, fax 071 630 8273); Naish Priory, East Coker, Somerset BA22 9HQ (☎ 093 586 2201)

DIBBLE, Robert Kenneth; s of Herbert William Dibble (d 1973), and Irene Caroline Dibble; *b* 28 Dec 1938; *Educ* Westcliff HS for Boys; *m* 26 Aug 1972, Teresa Frances, da of James Vincent MacDonnell; 4 s (William b 5 July 1973, Thomas b 12 April 1975, Edward b 7 Feb 1979, Matthew b 31 Dec 1980); *Career* RNC Dartmouth 1955-58, HMS Belton 1958-59, Lt HM Yacht Britannia 1959-60, HMS Caesar 1961-62, Russian interpreter's course 1962-64, mixed manned ship USS Claude V Ricketts 1964-65, long communications course 1965-66, Sqdn Communications Offr HMS Ajax 1966-67, Lt Cdr HMS Hampshire 1967-68, head of electronic warfare HMS Mercury 1968-70, def fell Kings Coll London 1970-71, Staff Ops Offr to Sr Naval Offr W Indies 1971-72, Cdr naval staff MOD 1972-75, i/c HMS Eskimo 1975-76, DS Maritime Tactical Sch 1976-77; admitted slr 1980; slr Linklaters and Paines 1980-81 (articled clerk 1978-80), ptnr Wilde Sapte 1982; Freeman: City of London, City of London Solicitor Co, Worshipful Co of Shipwrights; *Recreations* family, tennis, music, reading, languages; *Style—* Robert Dibble, Esq; Wilde Sapte, Queensbridge House, 60 Upper Thames St, London EC4V 3BD (☎ 071 236 3050, fax 071 236 9624, telex 887793

DIBELA, Sir Kingsford; GCMG (1983, CMG 1978); s of Norman Dibela and Edna Dalauna; *b* 16 March 1932; *m* 1952, Winifred Tomolaria; 2 s, 4 da; *Career* teacher primary sch 1956-63; pres: Weraura Local Govt Cncl Milne Bay 1963-77, Milne Bay Area Authy 1073-77; memb Nat Parl 1975-82 (speaker 1977-80), govr-gen Papua New Guinea 1983-89, chm MBB Finance (PNG) Ltd 1989-; *Style—* Sir Kingsford Dibela, GCMG; PO Box 113, Port Moresby, Papua New Guinea

DICE, Brian Charles; s of Frederic Dice, MC, of Minehead, Somerset (d 1979); *b* 2 Sept 1936; *Educ* Clare Coll Cambridge (MA); *m* 22 May 1965, Wendy, da of De Warrenne Harrison (d 1983); 2 da (Nicola b 1968, Melissa b 1971); *Career* Cadbury Schweppes plc 1960-86 (dir 1979-86), chief exec Br Waterways Bd 1986-; *Style—* Brian Dice, Esq; Stratton Wood, Beaconsfield, Bucks HP91HS

DICK, (John) Antony; s of Cdre John Mathew Dick, CB, CBE (d 1981), and Anne Moir, *née* Stewart; *b* 23 March 1934; *Educ* Trinity Coll Glenalmond, Worcester Coll Oxford (BA); *m* 15 May 1967, Marigold Sylvia, da of Rev Cecil B Verity; 1 s (Crispin b 1971), 2 da (Amy-Clare b 1972, Jasmine b 1974); *Career* RN 1952-54; qualified CA 1956; investmt mangr: Iraq Petroleum Co Ltd 1961-67, J Henry Schroder Wagg and Co Ltd 1967-68; md Kingsdrive Investment Management Ltd 1969-70; dir GT Management plc 1970-; non-exec dir: USDC Investment Trust 1987, Nordic Investment Trust 1985, GT Investment Fund SA 1980, Thornton Pan European Investment Trust 1987, F & C Eurotrust 1989; memb: Advsy Ctee to Local Authy Mutual Investmt Tst; *Recreations* sailing, psychological astrology; *Style—* Antony Dick, Esq; 26 Chalcot Square, London NW1 8YA (☎ 071 722 5126); GT Management plc, 8 Devonshire Square, London EC2M 4YJ (☎ 071 283 2575, fax 071 626 6176, telex

886100)

DICK, Brian Booth; s of James Dick, and Doris Ethel, *née* Booth; *b* 20 Dec 1943; *Educ* Kilmarnock Acad; *m* 19 Oct 1966, Caryl Anne, da of James McClure; 1 s (Alistair b 25 Oct 1972), 2 da (Laura b 26 Oct 1967, Susanna b 19 May 1969); *Career* sec: Crown Continental Merchant Bank Jamaica 1971-74, Caribbean Bank 1974-76; fin dir and sec: Lyle Shipping plc 1980-83, Noble Grossart Ltd 1983-; involved with: Morningside Baptist Church, Holy Corner Church Centre; MICAS; *Recreations* hockey, golf, curling, refereeing hockey; *Style—* Brian Dick, Esq; 2 Ravelston House Rd, Edinburgh EH4 3LW (☎ 031 332 1120); Noble Grossart Ltd, 48 Queen St, Edinburgh EH2 3NR (☎ 031 226 7011, fax 031 226 6032)

DICK, Brig (Raphael) Christopher Joseph; CBE; s of Capt Henry Pfeil Dick (d 1951), and Marie Louise Armandine Cornslie, *née* Van Cutsem; *b* 3 July 1935; *Educ* Downside; *Career* cmmnd RTR 1954, IRTR 1954-60, Staff Coll 1965-67 (staff 1972-76), Sqdn ldr 13/18 Hussars 1968-70, CO 3 RTR 1976-78, Col 1981-83, Brig 1984-88; dir Linguaphone Inst 1988-; memb RUSI; *Recreations* skiing, swimming, walking, sailing; *Clubs* Naval and Military; *Style—* Brig Christopher Dick, CBE; 14 Rivermill, 15 Grosvenor Road, London SW1V 3JN; Linguaphone Institute Ltd, St Giles House, 50 Poland St, London W1 (☎ 071 439 4222, fax 071 734 0469, telex 261352)

DICK, Prof David Andrew Thomas; s of David McCulloch Dick (d 1963), and Elizabeth Alexander, *née* Forrest (d 1941); *b* 11 June 1927; *Educ* Hillhead HS Glasgow, Univ of Glasgow (MB ChB), Balliol, Merton and St Cross Colls Oxford (MA, DPhil, DSc); *m* 15 Aug 1958, Dr Elizabeth Graham, da of Maj Bryson Kynoch Reid; 3 s (James Graham b 1960, Andrew Bryson b 1961, Peter Reid b 1963); *Career* Capt RAMC, RMO 2 RTR 1950-52; demonstrator anatomy: Univ of Glasgow 1953-55, Univ of Oxford 1955-58; res fell Copenhagen 1958-59, lectr in anatomy Univ of Oxford 1959-67, visiting prof of physiology and US Public Health Serv res fell Duke 1966-67, pt/t prof of anatomy Univ of Dundee 1988- (Cox prof of anatomy 1968-88); memb: Anatomical Soc (vice pres 1987), Physiological Soc; *Books* Cell Water (1966); *Recreations* hill walking, poetry (reading and writing); *Style—* Prof David Dick; Department of Anatomy and Physiology, University of Dundee, Dundee DD1 4HN (☎ 0382 23181)

DICK, Frank William; OBE (1989); s of Frank Dick, of 33 Pearce Ave, Corstorphine, Edinburgh, and Diana May, *née* Sinclair; *b* 1 May 1941; *Educ* Royal HS Edinburgh, Loughborough Coll (DLC), Univ of Oregon (BSc); *m* 1, 1970 (m dis 1977), Margaret Fish; 1 s (Frank Sinclair Shacklock b 3 Oct 1972); m 2, 18 Feb 1980, Linda Elizabeth, da of Frank Brady; 2 da (Erin Emma Louise b 18 July 1981, Cara Charlotte Elizabeth b 18 may 1985); *Career* dep dir of physical educn Worksop Coll 1965-69, nat athletics coach Scotland 1970-79, dir of coaching Br Amateur Athletics Bd 1979-; athletics coach: Euro Cup 1979-89, Olympic Games 1980-88, Euro Championships 1982-90, World Championships 1983-87; coach to: Daley Thompson (athletics) 1983-, Boris Becker (conditioning tennis) 1986-89, Jeff Thompson (conditioning karate) 1986-; chm Br Assoc of Nat Coaches 1985-86, pres Euro Athletics Coaches Assoc 1985-; FBISC 1989; *Books* Training Principles (1980 and 1989); *Recreations* music, public speaking, jogging; *Style—* Frank Dick, Esq, OBE; 3 The Windings, Sanderstead, Surrey CR2 0HW (☎ 081 651 4858); 3 Duchess Place, Hagley Rd, Edgbaston, Birmingham (☎ 021 454 3912, telex 334253 BAABG, fax Business: 021 456 4061, Home: 081 657 3247, car 0860 751705)

DICK, Gavin Colquhoun; s of John Dick (d 1949), of Motherwell, Lanarkshire, and Catherina MacAuslan, *née* Henderson (d 1983); *b* 6 Sept 1928; *Educ* Hamilton Acad, Univ of Glasgow (MA), Balliol Coll Oxford (MA), SOAS, Univ of London (cert in Turkish); *m* 20 Dec 1952, (Elizabeth) Frances, da of Jonathan Hutchinson (d 1972), of Haslemere, Surrey; 2 da (Helen b 1953, Catherine b 1956); *Career* Lt 3 RTR 1952-54; Civil Serv DTI (formerly Bd of Trade): asst princ 1954-58, princ 1958-67, UK trade cmmr Wellington NZ 1961-64, asst sec 1967-75, jt sec Review Ctee on Overseas Representation 1968-69, under sec 1975-84, govr Coll of Air Trg Hamble 1975-80; memb Bd English Estates 1982-84, conslt Office of Telecoms 1984-87, conslt Radio Communications Div 1987-89; vice chm Mobile Radio Trg Tst 1990-; *Recreations* linguistics; *Clubs* United Oxford and Cambridge University; *Style—* Gavin Dick, Esq; Fell Cottage, Bayley's Hill, Sevenoaks, Kent TN14 6HS (☎ 0732 453704)

DICK, Prof George Williamson Auchinvole; s of Rev David A Dick (d 1965), of Ramsay Gardens, Edinburgh, and Blanche, *née* Spence (d 1945); *b* 14 Aug 1914; *Educ* Royal HS Edinburgh, Univ of Edinburgh (MD, DSc), John Hopkins Univ Baltimore USA; *m* 6 June 1941, Brenda Marian, da of Samuel Cook; 2 s (Bruce b 3 Feb 1948, John-Mark b 24 Aug 1953), 2 da (Alison b 18 June 1950, Caroline b 14 April 1952); *Career* WWII Lt RAMC 1940, Capt RAMC graded specialist 1941, E Africa Cmd 1942-46 (Maj, specialist pathology, OC Mobile Lab Br and Italian Somaliland and reserved areas, mobile res unit), Lt-Col OC Med Div No IEA Gen Hosp; pathologist Colonial Med Res Serv 1946-51; fell 1947-48: Rockefeller Fndn, John Hopkins Univ (res fell 1948-49); scientific staff MRC 1951-54, prof of microbiology Queen's Univ Belfast 1955-65, dir Bland-Sutton Inst 1966-73, Bland-Sutton prof of pathology Middlesex Hosp Med Sch Univ of London 1966-73; 1973-81: asst dir Br Postgrad Med Fedn 1973-81, postgrad dean SW Thames RHA 1973-81, prof of pathology Univ of London 1973-81, hon lectr and hon conslt Inst Child Health 1973-81, chm MARC ltd; pres Inst Med Laboratory Technol 1966-76, treas RCPath 1973-78, pres Rowhook Med Soc 1975-; memb: Mid Downs Health Authy W Sussex 1981-84, Jt Bd Clinical Nursing Studies 1982-85; chm DHSS/Regnl Librarians Ctee 1982-, examiner Med Schs (UK, Dublin, Nairobi, Kampala, Riyadh, Jeddah), assessor HNS and CMS S London Coll; Liveryman Worshipful Co Apothecaries; memb RSM, BMA, Int Epidemiol Soc, Pathology Soc GB (and Ireland) FRCPE, FRCP, FRCPath, MPH, FLA; *Books* Immunisation (1978, (re-issued as Practical Immunisation, 1986), Immunology of Infectious Diseases (ed, 1979), Health on Holiday and other Travels (1982); author of over 200 scientific papers on yellowfever, arbor viruses, polio, hepatitis, multiple sclerosis and others; *Recreations* epidemiology of infectious diseases and prevention, travel, gardening, natural history; *Style—* Prof George Dick

DICK, John Alexander; MC (1944), QC (Scotland) 1963; yr s of Rev David Auchinvole Dick, and Blanche Hay Spence; *b* 1 Jan 1920; *Educ* Waid Acad Anstruther, Univ of Edinburgh; *m* 1951, Rosemary Benzie, *née* Sutherland; *Career* cmmnd Royal Scots 1942, served Italy 1944, Palestine 1945-46; called to the Bar (Scots) 1949, lectr in public law Univ of Edinburgh 1953-60, jr counsel in Scotland to HM Cmmrs of Customs and Excise 1956-63, cmmr under Terrorism (NI) Order 1972-73; Sheriff the Lothians and Borders at Edinburgh 1968-78, Sheriff princ N Strathclyde 1978-82, Sheriff princ Glasgow and Strathkelvin 1980-86; Hon LLD Univ of Glasgow 1987; *Recreations* hillwalking; *Clubs* Royal Scots (Edinburgh); *Style—* Sir John Dick, MC, QC; 3 St Margaret's Court, North Berwick, East Lothian EH39 4QH (☎ 0620 5249)

DICK, (John) Kenneth; CBE; s of late John Dick, and Beatrice May, *née* Chitty; *b* 5 April 1913; *Educ* Sedbergh; *m* 1942, Pamela Madge, *née* Salmon; 3 s (1 decd); *Career* CA; ptnr Mann Judd & Co 1947 (joined 1936); Mitchell Cotts Gp Ltd: jt md 1957, md 1959, dep chm 1964, chm 1966-78; chm: Hume Hldgs Ltd 1975-80, NM Rothschild (Leasing) Ltd 1978-; dir: NM Rothschild and Sons Ltd 1978-, Esperanza Ltd 1978-80, Sinclair Res Ltd 1983-; memb: Cwlth Devpt Corpn 1967-80, Br Nat Export Ctee 1968-71, Covent Garden Market Authy 1976-82; chm Ctee for ME trade 1968-71, pres ME Assoc 1971-81 (vice pres 1970); FCA, FRSA; *Recreations* golf; *Style—* Kenneth Dick, Esq, CBE; Overbye, 18 Church St, Cobham, Surrey, (☎ 071 280 5000)

DICK, Stewart John Cunningham; s of John David Cunningham Dick, of Edinburgh (d 1990), and Jessie Anderson Calder (d 1985); *b* 14 Jan 1946; *Educ* George Watson's Coll Edinburgh, Univ of Edinburgh; *m* 12 April 1974, Alison Aileen Mackintosh, *née* Dickson; *Career* Wallace and Sommerville (became Whinney Murray) 1968-72; Brown, Shipley and Co Ltd: joined 1972, dir Corporate Banking 1980-, head Credit Ctee 1986-; MICAS 1972; *Recreations* gardening, golf; *Clubs* Caledonian, RAC; *Style—* Stewart Dick, Esq; Ardmore, Woodlands Road, West Byfleet, Surrey KT14 6JW (☎ 0932 342755); Brown, Shipley & Co Ltd, Founders Court, Lothbury, London EC2R 7HE (☎ 071 606 9833)

DICK-LAUDER, Lady; Hester Marguerite; da of Lt-Col George Cecil Minett Sorell-Cameron, CBE (d 1947), by his w Marguerite Emily (d 1968), elder da of Hon Hamilton James Tollemache; *b* 1920; *m* 13 Nov 1945, Maj Sir George Andrew Dick-Lauder, 12 Bt (d 1981); 2 s, 2 da; *Style—* Lady Dick-Lauder; Firth Mill House, by Auchendinny, Roslin, Midlothian

DICK-LAUDER, Mark Andrew; s of Sir George Dick-Lauder, 12 Bt (d 1981); bro and hp of Sir Piers Dick-Lauder, 13 Bt; *b* 3 May 1951; *m* 1970 (m dis 1982), Jeanne, *née* Mullineaux, of Bolton; 1 s (Martin b 1976); *Style—* Mark Dick-Lauder, Esq

DICKENS, Barnaby John; s of Archie Bernard Dickens, and June Mary McNeile; *b* 9 June 1954; *Educ* Dulwich, Trinity Coll Cambridge (scholar, MA); *m* 13 Oct 1983, Lucy Anne, da of Sir Oliver Nicholas Millar, GCVO; 2 s (Roland Oliver Porter b 9 April 1979, Max John Porter b 27 Aug 1981), 1 da (Marnie Dickens b 13 Nov 1985); *Career* account exec: The Creative Business 1977-78, WS Crawford 1978-79; Public Advertising Cncl LA 1980, account dir Marsteller 1984 (account mangr 1981), Bd account dir GGK London 1986-; *Recreations* badminton, my family; *Style—* Barnaby Dickens, Esq; GGK London Ltd, 76 Dean St, London W1V 5HA (☎ 071 734 0511)

DICKENS, Dr Diana Margaret; da of Frederick George Young, OBE (d 1981), of Bath, Somerset, and Nora Evelyn, *née* Evans; *b* 7 April 1938; *Educ* Sheffield HS, Univ of Bristol (MB ChB); *m* 6 June 1964, Anthony John Gilmore Dickens, s of George Edward Dickens, of Bristol, Avon; 1 s (Stephen James Gilmore b 4 June 1970), 1 da (Sandi b 23 Aug 1967); *Career* conslt psychiatrist Leavesden Hosp Watford 1974-85, gen mangr Rampton Hosp Retford Notts 1989- (med dir 1985-89); vice pres RCPsych, memb Standing Med Advsy Ctee; FRSM, FRCPsych; *Recreations* golf, music, literature, art and design; *Style—* Dr Diana Dickens; Rampton Hospital, Retford, Notts DN22 0PD (☎ 077 784 321)

DICKENS, Prof (Arthur) Geoffrey; CMG (1974); s of Arthur James Dickens (d 1957), of Hull, and Gertrude Helen, *née* Grasby (d 1979); *b* 6 July 1910; *Educ* Hymers Coll Hull, Magdalen Coll Oxford (BA, MA), Univ of London (DLit); *m* 1 Aug 1936, Molly (d 1978), da of Capt Walter Bygott, RE (d 1959); 2 s (Peter Geoffrey b 1940, Paul Jonathan b 1945); *Career* served RA 1940-45, 2 Lt 1941, Lt 1942, Capt 1943; fell of Keble Coll Oxford 1933-49; prof of history: Univ of Hull 1949-62 (pro vice chllr 1959-62), King's Coll London 1962-67 (FKC 1967), Univ of London 1967-77; dir Inst of Hist Res 1967-77, foreign sec Br Acad 1968-78; pres: Central London Branch Hist Assoc 1980-, Hornsey Hist Soc 1982-, German History Soc 1980-89; hon vice pres Royal Hist Soc 1977-, The Hist Assoc 1978-; author 17 books and numerous articles on the Renaissance and Reformation period and local history, mainly Yorkshire; Hon D Litt: Kent, Sheffield, Leicester, Liverpool, Hull (all 1977); FBA 1966, FSA 1963, FRHistS 1947; Order of Merit (Cdr's Class) of Federal Republic of Germany 1980; *Books* 17 books and numerous articles on the Renaissance and Reformation period and local history, mainly Yorkshire; *Recreations* studying modern British painting (ca 1900-50); *Clubs* Athenaeum; *Style—* Prof A G Dickens, CMG; Institute of Historical Research, Senate House, London WC1E 7HU (☎ 071 636 0272)

DICKENS, Geoffrey Kenneth; JP (St Albans, Barnsley then Oldham 1968), MP (C) Littleborough and Saddleworth 1983-; s of John Wilfred Dickens (d 1979); *b* 26 Aug 1931; *Educ* E Lane Sch Wembley, Harrow Tech Coll, Acton Tech Coll; *m* 1956, Norma Evelyn, *née* Boothby; 2 s; *Career* Nat Serv RAF; co dir; MP (C) Huddersfield West 1979-83 (contested Teeside Middlesbrough Feb 1974 and Ealing North Oct 1974); hon alderman City and Dist of St Albans 1976; chm: Sandridge Parish Cncl 1968-69 (memb 1960-73), St Albans Rural Dist Cncl 1970-71 (memb 1967-74); memb: Herts CC 1970-75, Royal Humane Soc Testimonial on Vellum for Bravery Saving Lives, Parly Select Ctee on Energy; tstee Childwatch (child protection); treas Assoc of Cons Clubs, vice pres Lancs Fedn of Cons Clubs; *Clubs* Conservative; *Style—* Geoffrey Dickens Esq, JP, MP; House of Commons, Westminster, London SW1A 0AA (☎ 071 219 6224)

DICKENS, Air Cdre Sir Louis Walter; DFC (1940), AFC (1938), DL (Berks 1966); s of C H Dickens; *b* 28 Sept 1903; *Educ* Clongowes Wood Sch, Cranwell Cadet Coll; *m* 1939, Ena Alice (d 1971), da of F J Bastable; 1 s, 1 da; *Career* RAF: Bomber Cmd 1940 and 1943-44, Flying Instr Canada 1941-42, SHAEF France 1944-45, ret 1947; chm Berks CC 1965-68 (memb 1952-74, alderman 1959-73); kt 1968; *Style—* Air Cdre Sir Louis Dickens, DFC, AFC, DL; Wayford, Bolney Ave, Shiplake, Henley, Oxon

DICKENS, Monica Enid (Mrs R O Stratton); MBE (1981); da of late Henry Charles Dickens; *b* 10 May 1915; *Educ* St Paul's Girls' Sch Hammersmith; *m* 1951, Cdr Roy Olin Stratton, USN; 2 da; *Career* writer; fndr of US Samaritans; *Books* One Pair of Hands, Mariana, One Pair of Feet, The Fancy, Thursday Afternoon, The Happy Prisoner, Joy and Josephine, Flowers on the Grass, My Turn to Make the Tea, No More Meadows, The Winds of Heaven, The Angel in the Corner, Man Overboard, The Heart of London, Cobbler's Dream, Kate and Emma, The Room Upstairs, The Landlord's Daughter, The Listeners, The House at World's End, Summer at World's End, Follyfoot, World's End in Winter, Dora at Follyfoot, Spring Comes to World's End, Talking of Horses, Last Year When I was Young, The Horse at Follyfoot, Stranger at Follyfoot, The Messenger, Ballad of Favour, The Haunting of Bellamy 4, Cry of a Seagull, Miracles of Courage, Dear Doctor Lily (1988), Enchantment (1989), Closed at Dusk (1990), The Scar (1991), An Open Book (autobiog); *Style—* Miss Monica Dickens, MBE (Mrs R O Stratton); Lavender Cottage, Brightwalton, Berks RG16 0BY (☎ 048 82 302)

DICKENSON, Sheena Margaret; *née* Ross; da of Duncan Cameron Ross, and Elsie, *née* McKenzie; *b* 29 July 1948; *Educ* Dingwall Acad, Univ of Edinburgh (BSc, MB ChB); *m* 12 July 1986, Robert Graham Dickenson, s of John Edward Dickenson (d 1985); 1 da (Eleanor Anne b 16 July 1988); *Career* conslt anaesthetist Huntingdon Health Authy 1983-, dir J E Dickenson (Wellingborough) Ltd 1987-; memb: Assoc of Anaesthetists, Br Med Acupuncture Soc; fell Faculty of Anaesthetists RCS; *Recreations* gardening, cookery, skiing, walking; *Style—* Dr Ross (Mrs Dickenson); Ayrfield, 131 Huntingdon Rd, Thrapston, Northants NN14 4NG (☎ 08012 3066); Hinchingbrooke Hosp, Hinchingbrooke Park, Huntingdon, Cambs (☎ 0480 456131)

DICKER, Col Geoffrey Seymour Hamilton; CBE (1965), TD (1953), DL (1963), DCL (1985); s of Capt Arthur Seymour Hamilton Dicker, MBE (d 1974), of Oakley House, Acle, Norfolk, and Margaret Kathleen, *née* Walley (d 1971); *b* 20 July 1920; *Educ* Haileybury, King's Coll Cambridge; *m* 1942, Josephine Helen, da of F G Penman (d 1963), of Inwood, Bushey, Herts; 1 s, 2 da (1 decd); *Career* joined Royal Signals

1940, Adj 6 Armoured Divnl Signals 1943-45, GSO (2) AFHQ Caserta 1945-46 (MBE, despatches), cmmnd TA 1948, Hon Col 54 (E Anglian) Signal Regt (TA) 1960-67, Hon Col 36 (E) Signal Regt (V) 1979-85, ADC (TA) to HM The Queen 1965-70, vice chm Cncl of TA and VR Assocs 1975-80, Hon Col Cmdt RCS 1970-80, chm Reserve Forces Assoc 1976-83, vice pres (UK) Inter-Allied Confed of Reserve Offrs 1976-83; CA 1950; treas Univ of East Anglia 1973-85, pro chllr and chm of Council 1985-90, chm Eastern Region Bd Eagle Star Insur Co 1969-86, pres Great Yarmouth Cons Assoc 1969-86, ptnr Lovewell Blake and Co, Gt Yarmouth, Lowestoft, Norwich and Thetford (ret 1983); treas Scientific Exploration Soc 1987-90; FRSA 1985; *Recreations* sailing (yachts 'Skal III', 'Camberwell Beauty', motor cruiser 'Leomina'; *Clubs* Norfolk, Army and Navy, Royal Norfolk and Suffolk Yacht (Cdre 1978-80), Norfolk Broads Yacht (Cdre 1959-62); *Style—* Col Geoffrey Dicker, CBE, TD, DL; The Hollies, Strumpshaw, Norwich NR13 4NS (☎ 0603 712357)

DICKIE, Brian James; s of Robert Kelso Dickie and Harriet Elizabeth, *née* Riddell (d 1969); *b* 23 July 1941; *Educ* Haileybury, Trinity Coll Dublin; *m* 1968, Victoria Teresa Sheldon, da of Edward Christopher Sheldon Price, of Glos; 2 s (Patrick b 1969, Edward b 1974), 1 da (Eliza b 1970); *Career* artistic dir Wexford Festival 1967-73, administrator Glyndebourne Touring Opera 1967-81, gen administrator Glyndebourne 1981-; *Clubs* Garrick; *Style—* Brian Dickie, Esq; c/o The Canadian Opera Co, 227 Front St East, Toronto, Ontario M5A 1E8, Canada

DICKIE, Col Charles George; TD (1975), DL (Merseyside 1983-88); s of Rev Robert Pittendreigh Dickie (d 1934), of The Manse, Longriggend, Lanarks, and Margaret, *née* Brock (d 1964); *b* 21 Jan 1932; *Educ* Uddington GS; *m* 5 Oct 1956, Jane Mitchell, da of William Marshall (d 1971); 1 s (Stuart b 28 Feb 1963), 2 da (Dianne b 8 May 1961, Susan b 6 Feb 1965); *Career* Nat Serv, RA 1950-52; TA 1952-56 and 1963-82, RARO 1983-; RASC to 1965, then RCT, then staff appts SOI Liaison, US Logistics Tport Branch NW Dist Col (TA) Non-infantry HQ NW Dist; ADC (TA) to HM The Queen 1980-83; co sec Liverpool Building Society (Birmingham Midshires Building Society 1982-) 1972-; treas Mersey Synod Utd Reform Church 1980-84, pres CBSI 1989-91 (dep pres 1988-89, cncl memb 1980-), civil rep W Midlands Reg Forces Employment Assoc, vice chm TA & VRA NW Eng; FCBSI, FIBScot; *Clubs* Army & Navy, Inst of the RCT; *Style—* Col C G Dickie, TD; The Malthouse, Folley Rd, Ackleton, Shropshire, WV6 7JL (☎ 07465 420); Birmingham Midshires Bldg Soc, PO Box 81, 35/49 Lichfield St, Wolverhampton WV1 IEL (☎ 0902 710710, fax 0902 28849, car 08 732663)

DICKIE, Rev Prof Edgar Primrose; MC; s of William Dickie; *b* 12 Aug 1897; *Educ* Dumfries Acad, Edinburgh Univ, Ch Ch Oxford, New Coll Edinburgh, Marburg Tubingen; *m* 1927, Ishbel Graham Holmes; *Career* emeritus professor of divinity St Mary's Coll, St Andrews Univ 1967- (prof 1935-67); extra chaplain to the Queen in Scotland 1967- (chaplain 1956-67); *Style—* The Rev Prof Edgar Dickie, MC; Craigmont Nursing Home, St Andrews, Fife (☎ 0334 73608)

DICKIE, Dr Nigel Hugh; s of John Dickie, of Oxshott, Surrey, and Inez Campbell, *née* White; *b* 4 Oct 1956; *Educ* King's Coll Sch Wimbledon, Queen Elizabeth Coll Univ of London (BSc, The Copping prize in Nutrition, PhD); *m* 24 Aug 1986, Alison Susan May, da of John Michael Duffin: 2 s (Andrew James John b 27 Feb 1988, Alexander Stuart b 8 Oct 1990); *Career* nutritionist Van den Berghs and Jurgens Ltd 1982-83, conslt nutritionist Slimming Magazine, Slimming Magazine Clubs and various leading Food Companies 1983-85, dir Counsel Ltd (PR co) 1985-; Freeman City of London 1989; memb: Nutrition Soc 1978, Br Dietetic Assoc 1985, soc of Chem Indust 1985, Royal Soc of Health 1986; fell Inst Food Science & Technol 1991; *Recreations* good food and wine, family and home; *Style—* Dr Nigel Dickie; Counsel Ltd, 15-17 Huntsworth Mews, London NW1 6DD (☎ 071 402 2272)

DICKIN, Malcolm Donald; s of Donald Arthur Swingler Dickin (d 1981), and Ethel Ada, *née* Bennett (d 1965); *b* 5 May 1939; *Educ* William Hulme's GS Manchester; *m* 1 s (Andrew Malcolm b 1969), 1 da (Sally Nicola b 1972); *Career* solicitor; *Style—* Malcolm D Dickin, Esq; 18 Coppice Close, Woodley, Stockport SK6 1JH (☎ 061 494 9812); 1 Market St, Denton, Manchester M34 3BX (☎ 061 336 5031)

DICKINS, Julian Grahame; s of Grahame John Dickins, of 48 Wendan Rd, Newbury, Berks, and Claire Daisy, *née* Myers; *b* 31 Dec 1957; *Educ* St Bartholomew's Sch Newbury, Univ of Southampton (LLB), Coll of Law Guildford; *Career* admitted slr 1983; ptnr Pennington Ward Bowie 1986- (slr 1983-86); memb Law Soc 1983-; *Recreations* amateur dramatics, church organ, piano; *Style—* Julian Dickins, Esq; Southfork, 66 Lipscombe Close, Newbury, Berkshire RG14 5JW (☎ 0635 36305); Penningtons, 9-19 London Rd, Newbury, Berkshire RG13 1JL (☎ 0635 523344, fax 0635 523444)

DICKINSON, (Vivienne) Anne (Mrs David Phillips); da of Oswald Edward (d 1956), of Mapperley Park, Nottingham, and Ida Ismay Harris (d 1984); *b* 27 Sept 1931; *Educ* Nottingham Girls HS; *m* 1, 15 March 1951 (m dis 1961), John Kerr Large, s of Maj Thomas Large (d 1959), of Cotgrave, Notts; m 2, 22 June 1979, David Hermas Phillips (d 1989); *Career* exec Crawford 1960-64; promotions ed: Good Housekeeping 1964-65, Harpers Bazaar 1965-67; dir: National Magazine Co 1967-68, Benson PR Ltd 1968-70 (md 1970-71); bought Kingsway PR Ltd (formerly Benson PR) 1971 (sold to Saatchi & Saatchi 1985), exec chm Rowland Co 1990 (ret); chm Woman of the Year Lunch 1983-85 (vice chm 1987-90), vice chm PRCA 1978-82 and 1990, PR Professional of the Year 1988, chm Family Welfare Assoc 1990; Freeman: City of London 1990, Worshipful Co of Marketors 1990; FIPR 1986, CBIM 1986, FIOD 1987, MInstM 1979; *Recreations* riding; *Clubs* Civil Service Riding; *Style—* Miss Anne Dickinson; 26 Bedford Gardens, Kensington, London W8; St Mary's Cottage, Church Sqaure, Rye, Sussex

DICKINSON, Antony Havergal; s of Adolphus Havergal Dickinson (d 1946), of Gosforth, Newcastle upon Tyne, and Sophia Hamilton, *née* Woods (d 1947); *b* 27 Nov 1901; *Educ* Loretto Sch Musselburgh Scotland, Pembroke Coll Cambridge (MA); *m* 16 Sept 1930, Eunice Louisa, da of Thomas George Mylchreest, of Eltofts Thorner, nr Leeds, Yorks; 1 da (Catherine Elisabeth (Mrs Pestell) b 1934); *Career* CD Controller Tyne & Wear Sub-Regn Area West; slr and NP: admitted slr 1927, former sr ptnr Ingledew Mather and Dickinson (formerly Mather and Dickinson) slrs and notaries Newcastle, conslt Ingledew Bolterell (memb Eversheds); vice pres Nat Hist Soc of Northumbria, vice pres Ponteland CC Northumberland; memb: Law Soc, Soc of NP's, Newcastle upon Tyne Law Soc, Slrs Benevolent Soc; *Recreations* fishing and squash racquets; *Clubs* Northern Counties, hon memb Northumberland Golf; *Style—* Antony Dickinson, Esq; Riftswood, Woolsington Bridge, Newcastle upon Tyne NE13 8BL (☎ 091 2869186); Ingledew Botterell, Milburn House, Dean St, Newcastle upon Tyne NE1 1NP (☎ 091 2611661, telex 53598 INGLAW)

DICKINSON, Brian Henry Baron; s of Alan E F Dickinson (d 1978), and Ethel M Dickinson (d 1980); *b* 2 May 1940; *Educ* Leighton Park Sch Reading, Balliol Coll Oxford (BA); *m* 26 May 1971, Sheila Minto; *Career* asst sec Dept of Prices and Consumer Protection 1975; MAFF: asst princ 1964, princ 1968, asst sec 1978, grade 3 1984; *Style—* Brian Dickinson, Esq; Ministry of Agriculrure, Fisheries and Food, Ergon House, 17 Smith Square, London SW1P 3HX (☎ 071 238 6429)

DICKINSON, Bruce Bradbury; s of Harold Raymond Dickinson, of Australia, of Isobel Flora Dickinson, *née* Bremner; *b* 2 July 1934; *Educ* Manly Boys High, Queensland Univ; *m* 1961, Dorothy Yvonne, da of Gerald George Carpenter, of Swansea; 1 s (Mark b 1969), 2 da (Fiona b 1963, Claire b 1965); *Career* banker; sr gen mangr Australia & New Zealand Banking Gp, md Grindlays Bank plc; *Recreations* golf; *Clubs* Union, Royal Sydney Yacht Sqdn, Metropolitan golf, Royal Blackheath Golf; *Style—* Bruce Dickinson, Esq; 4 Woodhall Avenue, Dulwich, London SE21 7HL (☎ 081 693 6636); PO Box 7, Montague Close, London SE1

DICKINSON, Clive Havelock Maplesden; s of Richard Havelock Dickinson, of Oxfordshire, and Betty Evelyn, *née* Maplesden; *b* 1 Oct 1953; *Educ* Lord Williams GS Thame, Wadham Coll Oxford (MA); *m* 30 Aug 1980, Claire Marguerite Amey, da of Edward Algernon Richardson (d 1970); 1 s (Ralph b 1986), 1 da (Jennifer b 1989); *Career* writer; in best sellers listing (under various names) 1980, 1986, 1987; co-fndr Travellers Press 1988; FRGS; *Recreations* architectural restoration, skiing; *Clubs* Vincent's (Oxford); *Style—* Clive H M Dickinson, Esq; Wootton Farm, Checkley, Herefordshire HR1 4NA (☎ 0432 890422)

DICKINSON, Hon David Christopher; 4 s of Hon Richard Sebastian Willoughby Dickinson, DSO (d 1935, only s of 1 Baron Dickinson), of Washwell House, Painswick, Glos; granted 1944 title, rank and precedence of the son of a baron, which would have been his had his father survived to succeed to the title; *b* 29 Jan 1935; *Educ* Eton, Trinity Coll Oxford; *m* 1970, Caroline Mary, da of late Arthur Denton Toosey, and formerly w of late Peter Yeoward; *Style—* The Hon David Dickinson; Nanneys Bridge, Church Minshull, Nantwich, Cheshire

DICKINSON, Prof Harry Thomas; s of Joseph Dickinson (d 1979), and Elizabeth Stearman, *née* Warriner (d 1979); *b* 9 March 1939; *Educ* Gateshead GS, Univ of Durham (BA, DipEd, MA), Univ of Newcastle (PhD), Univ of Edinburgh (DLitt); *m* 26 Aug 1961, Jennifer Elizabeth, da of Albert Galtry, of Kilham, E Yorks; 1 s (Mark James b 1967), 1 da (Anna Elizabeth b 1972); *Career* Earl Grey fell Univ of Newcastle 1964-66; Univ of Edinburgh: asst lectr 1966-68, lectr 1968-73, reader 1973-80, prof of Br history 1980-; concurrent prof of history Nanjing Univ China 1987-; author of many historical essays and articles; FRHistS; *Books* The Correspondence of Sir James Clavering (1967), Bolingbroke (1970), Walpole and the Whig Supremacy (1973), Politics and Literature in the Eighteenth Century (1974), Liberty and Property (1977), Political Works of Thomas Spence (1982), British Radicalism and the French Revolution (1985), Caricatures and the Constitution (1986), Britain and the French Revolution (1989); *Style—* Prof Harry Dickinson; 44 Viewforth Terr, Edinburgh EH10 4LJ (☎ 031 229 1379); History Department, Univ of Edinburgh, Edinburgh EH8 9JY (☎ 031 650 3785)

DICKINSON, Very Rev the Hon Hugh Geoffrey; s of Hon Richard Sebastian Willoughby Dickinson, DSO (d 1935), of Washwell House, Painswick, Glos; raised to the rank of a baron's son, which would have been his had his father survived to succeed to the title, 1944; *b* 17 Nov 1929; *Educ* Westminster, Trinity Coll Oxford, Cuddesdon Theol Coll; *m* 29 June 1963, Jean Marjorie, da of Arthur Storey, of Leeds; 1 s, 1 da; *Career* ordained 1956; chaplain: Trinity Coll Cambridge 1958-63, Winchester Coll 1963-69; bishop's advsr for adult education Coventry Diocese 1969-77, vicar of St Michael's St Albans 1977-86, dean of Salisbury 1986-; *Style—* The Very Rev the Hon Hugh Dickinson; The Deanery, 7 The Close, Salisbury, Wilts SP1 2EF (☎ 0722 322457)

DICKINSON, Hon Mrs (Jessica Rosetta); *née* Mancroft; da of 2 Baron Mancroft, KBE, TD (d 1987); *b* 10 May 1954; *m* 15 Oct 1983, Simon C Dickinson, eld s of Peter Dickinson, of Newbrough, Northumberland; 1 s (Milo Clervaux Mancroft b 1989), 2 da (Phoebe Victoria b 1984, Octavia Jessica b 1986); *Style—* The Hon Mrs Dickinson; Wortley House, Wotton-under-Edge, Glos (☎ 0453 843174)

DICKINSON, Prof (Christopher) John; s of Reginald Ernest Dickinson (d 1978), of London, and Margaret, *née* Petty (d 1983); *b* 1 Feb 1927; *Educ* Berkhamsted Sch, Univ of Oxford (BSc, MA, DM), UCH Med Sch; *m* 26 June 1953, Elizabeth Patricia, da of William Patrick Farrell (d 1985), of London; 2 s (Mark John b 1956, Paul Tabois b 1965), 2 da (Emma Elizabeth b 1955, Caroline Margaret b 1958); *Career* Capt RAMC (jr med specialist) 1955-56; house appts UCH 1953-54; Middx Hosp: med registrar 1957-58, res fell 1959-60; Rockefeller fell Cleveland Clinic USA 1960-61; UCH 1961-75: lectr, sr lectr, conslt; prof of med St Bartholemew's Hosp Med Coll 1975-; memb: Med Res Cncl 1986-90, Assoc of Physicians; former chm: Med Res Soc, Assoc Clinical Profs of Med; former vice pres RCP; former sec: Harveian Soc, Euro Soc Clinical Investigation; MRCP 1956, FRCP 1968, ARCO 1987; *Books* Electrophysiological Technique (1950), Clinical Pathology Data (1951 & 1957), Clinical Physiology (1959, 5 edn, 1985), Neurogenic Hypertension (1965), Computer Model of Human Respiration (1977), Software for Educational Computing (1980), Neurogenic Hypertension II (1990); *Recreations* theatre, opera, playing the organ; *Clubs* Garrick; *Style—* Prof John Dickinson; Griffin Cottage, 57 Belsize Lane, London NW3 5AU (☎ 071 431 1845); Medical College of St Bartholomew's Hospital, W Smithfield, London EC1A 7BE (☎ 071 601 7531, fax 071 601 7024)

DICKINSON, Prof John Philip; s of George Snowden Dickinson (d 1974), of Morecambe, and Evelyn, *née* Stobbart; *b* 29 April 1945; *Educ* Univ of Cambridge (BA, MA), Univ of Leeds (MSc, PhD); *m* 17 Feb 1968, Christine, da of Maurice Houghton (d 1980), of Morecambe; 1 s (Anthony), 2 da (Rachel, Vanessa); *Career* lectr: Univ of Leeds 1968-71, Univ of Lancaster 1971-75; sr lectr: Univ of Western Aust 1975-80, Univ of Dundee 1980-81; prof of accounting Univ of Stirling 1981-85; Univ of Glasgow: prof of accounting and fin 1985-, head Dept of Accounting and Fin 1987, dir Glasgow Business Sch 1987-89, dean of Law and Fin Studies 1989-; dist organiser Christian Aid; CPA, FASA 1976, FBIM 1980, FRSA 1980, ACIS 1976; *Books* Statistics for Business Finance and Accounting (1976), Portfolio Theory (1974), Risk and Uncertainty in Accounting and Finance (1974), Portfolio Analysis and Capital Markets (1976), Management Accounting: An Introduction (1988), Statistical Analysis in Accounting and Finance (1990); *Recreations* photography, travel, languages, poetry; *Style—* Prof John Dickinson; 7 Rowan Gdns, Dumbreck, Glasgow G41 5BT (☎ 041 427 0414); Univ of Glasgow, Dept of Accounting and Finance, 65 Southpark Ave, Glasgow G12 4LE (☎ 041 330 5428, fax 041 330 4442, telex 777070 UNIGLA)

DICKINSON, Lorna; da of Michael Eugene Dickinson, of the Sussex Guest House, Sidmouth, Devon, and Barbara, *née* Benfield; *b* 20 Dec 1958; *Educ* Homelands Sch Derby, Univ of Warwick (BA); *m* 4 June 1983, Michael Ingham; *Career* prodr: BBC Radio Derby 1980-81, BBC Radio Nottingham 1981-82; res LWT 1982-83: Sunday Sunday, The Late Clive James, An Audience with Mel Brooks; assoc prodr LWT 1984-87: An Audience with Billy Connolly, The World According to Smith and Jones, Clive James meets Katharine Hepburn, The Dame Edna Experience; prodr LWT 1988-: Aspel and Company, The Trouble with Michael Caine (Gold Award New York Int Film & TV Festival), The Trouble with Joan Collins, The Trouble with Agatha Christie; *Style—* Ms Lorna Dickinson; London Weekend Television, South Bank Television Centre, London SE1; (☎ 071 261 3719, fax 071 261 3527)

DICKINSON, Hon Martin Hyett; er s and h of 2 Baron Dickinson; *b* 30 Jan 1961; *Style—* The Hon Martin Dickinson

DICKINSON, Hon Mrs Richard; May Southey; *née* Lovemore; *m* 15 May 1924, Hon Richard Sebastian Willoughby Dickinson, DSO (d 1935), only s of 1 Baron Dickinson; 4 s (2 Baron Dickinson, *qv*, Hon Peter b 1927, Very Rev Hon Hugh b

1929, Hon David b 1935); *Career* JP; sculptor and painter; *Style—* The Hon Mrs Richard Dickinson; The Poultry Court, Painswick, Stroud, Glos GL6 6QT (☎ 0452 812273)

DICKINSON, Patric Laurence; s of John Laurence Dickinson, and April Katherine, *née* Forgan, of Stroud, Glos; *b* 24 Nov 1950; *Educ* Marling Sch, Exeter Coll Oxford (MA); *Career* res asst Coll of Arms 1968-78, Rouge Dragon Pursuivant of Arms 1978-89, Richmond Herald 1989-; called to the Bar Middle Temple 1979; hon treas: English Genealogical Congress 1975-, Bar Theatrical Soc 1978-; hon sec and registrar Br Record Soc 1979-, vice pres Assoc of Genealogists and Record Agents (AGRA) 1988-; *Recreations* music, cycling, swimming, walking, talking, attending memorial services; *Style—* P L Dickinson, Esq; College of Arms, Queen Victoria St, London EC4V 4BT (☎ 071 236 9612)

DICKINSON, Prof Peter; s of Frank Dickinson (d 1978), and Muriel, *née* Porter; *b* 15 Nov 1934; *Educ* The Leys Sch, Queens' Coll Cambridge (MA), Juilliard Sch of Music NY; *m* 29 July 1964, Bridget Jane, da of Lt Cdr Edward Philip Tomkinson, DSO (ka 1942); 2 s (Jasper b 1968, Francis b 1971); *Career* composer; recorded works incl: piano concerto and organ concerto, Outcry, Mass of the Apocalypse, The Unicorns, Rags, Blues and Parodies, Soncycles; pianist; recorded works largely with sister Meriel Dickinson (mezzo); academic posts incl prof Univ of Keele 1974-84 (now emeritus); numerous contribs to books periodicals and BBC radio; bd memb Trinity Coll of Music 1984; memb: Assoc of Professional Composers, Sonneck Soc USA, RSM; LRAM, ARCM, FRCO, FRSA; *Books* Twenty British Composers (ed, 1975), The Music of Lennox Berkeley (1989); *Recreations* rare books; *Style—* Prof Peter Dickinson; c/o Novello & Co, 8 Lower James St, London W1R 4DN

DICKINSON, Hon Peter Malcolm de Brissac; s of Hon Richard Sebastian Willoughby Dickinson, DSO (s of 1 Baron Dickinson); raised to the rank of a Baron's s 1944; *b* 16 Dec 1927; *Educ* Eton, King's Coll Cambridge; *m* 25 April 1953, Mary Rose, elder da of Vice Adm Sir Geoffrey Barnard, KCB, CBE, DSO (d 1988), of Bramdean, Alresford, Hants; 2 da (Philippa Lucy Ann b 1955, Polly b 1956), 2 s (John Geoffrey Hyett b 1962, James Christopher Meade b 1963); *Career* author; asst editor Punch 1952-69; chm Mgmnt Ctee Soc of Authors 1978-80; has published numerous children's books and detective novels; *Style—* The Hon Peter Dickinson; 61a Ormiston Grove, London W12

DICKINSON, 2 Baron (UK 1930); Richard Clavering Hyett Dickinson; s of Hon Richard Sebastian Willoughby Dickinson, DSO (d 1935) and gs of 1 Baron (d 1943); *b* 2 March 1926; *Educ* Eton, Trinity Coll Oxford; *m* 1, 1957 (m dis), (Margaret) Ann, da of late Brig Gilbert R McMeekan, CB, DSO, OBE, JP; 2 s; m 2, 1980, Rita Doreen Moir; *Heir* s, Hon Martin Hyett Dickinson; *Style—* Rt Hon Lord Dickinson; Painswick House, Painswick, Stroud, Glos (☎ 0452 813204)

DICKINSON, Stephen; s of Rev Arthur Edward Dickinson (d 1989), and Ada Violet, *née* Hickey (d 1972); *b* 12 Oct 1934; *Educ* Aysgaith, St Edward's Sch Oxford, Kings Coll Newcastle, Univ of Durham (BA); *m* 23 March 1968, Mary Elisabeth, da of Maj Richard Quintin Gurney (d 1980), of Bawdeswell Hall, East Dereham, Norfolk; 2 s (Michael Edward b July 1969, James Stephen b May 1971); *Career* Nat Serv Flying Offr RAF 1957-59; chartered accountant; CA Br Virgin Islands 1963-74, md Grainger Trust plc Newcastle upon Tyne; ACA 1962; *Recreations* field sports, farming; *Clubs* Whites, Northern Counties, RAF; *Style—* Stephen Dickinson, Esq; Crow Hall, Bardon Mill, Hexham, Northumberland (☎ 0434 344495); Grainger Trust plc, Chaucer Buildings, 57 Grainger St, Newcastle upon Tyne (☎ 091 261 1819, fax 091 232 7874)

DICKINSON, Capt Trevor Gledhill; s of Percy Parkin Dickinson (d 1972), and Winifred Jane Dickinson, *née* Gledhill (d 1985); *b* 29 Aug 1924; *Educ* Bradford GS, Kings Coll Cambridge; *m* 18 Dec 1954, Pauline, da of Archie Seymore Pearce; 2 da (Penelope b 1956, Zöe-Jane b 1962); *Career* served WWII UK and E Africa, Capt RA and RE 1943-47; slr; sr ptnr Geoffrey Parker & Bourne Leamington Spa, dep dist judge Co and High Ct Midland and Oxford Circuit 1984-; past pres Warwick Avon Rotary Club, Dist 106 alumni offr Rotary Int (past Dist 106 Fndn chm); *Recreations* music, Rotary Int; *Clubs* Army and Navy; *Style—* Captain Trevor G Dickinson; 5 Elliotts Orchard, Barford, Warwick CV35 8ED (☎ 0926 624565); Geoffrey Parker & Bourne, 124 The Parade, Leamington Spa CV32 4BU (☎ 0926 427211, fax 0926 450287)

DICKS, Terence Patrick; MP (C) Hayes and Harlington 1983-; s of Frank and Winifred Dicks; *b* 17 March 1937; *Educ* LSE, Oxford Univ; Min of Labour 1959-66; *m* (m dis); 1 s, 2 da; *Style—* Terence Dicks, Esq, MP; House of Commons, London SW1

DICKSON, Alec (Alexander) Graeme; CBE (1967, MBE 1945); s of late Norman Bonnington Dickson, OBE, of Struan, Wimbledon Park, SW19, and late Anne, *née* Higgins; *b* 23 May 1914; *Educ* Rugby, New Coll Oxford; *m* 1951, Mora Agnes, da of Laurence Hope Robertson; *Career* fndr and first dir VSO 1958-62, fndr Community Serv Vols 1962, conslt to Cwlth Secretariat 1974-77; hon conslt Int Baccalaureat 1984-, hon chm Nat Youth Leadership Cncl 1984-; *Style—* Alec Dickson Esq, CBE; 19 Blenheim Rd, London W4 1UB (☎ 081 994 7437)

DICKSON, Dr Donald Harold Wauchope; s of William Hamilton Dickson (d 1966), of Belfast, and Marie, *née* Hayes (d 1963); *b* 16 Oct 1924; *Educ* Belfast Royal Acad, Queen's Univ Belfast (PhD); *m* 15 Sept 1951, (Verena) Audrey, da of Leonard Edwin Arthur Naylor (d 1972), of Iver, Bucks; 1 s (Andrew Charles Patrick b 11 July 1956); *Career* res chemist Glaxo Laboratories Ltd London 1950-54, mgmnt liaison exec and prodn controller Parke Davis & Co London 1954-60, head Dept of Chemistry Malvern Coll 1960-64, princ N Antrim Further Educn Area 1964-85; CP Snow fell Univ of Texas at Austin USA 1987- (Humanities Res Cente Award 1991); Abbeyfield Soc: area chm N Antrim and N Derry 1968-85, memb Nat Cncl UK 1975-86, memb Fin and Gen Purposes Ctee UK 1981-86; Assoc of Principals of Colls: memb Salaries Superannuation and Servs UK 1974-85, chm NI 1979-80, memb UK Nat Cncl 1983-85 (1977-80), hon memb UK 1986; govr Belfast Royal Acad 1977-79, memb Bd of Educn Centre New Univ of Ulster 1977-84; FRSC 1964; *Books* Principles of Chemistry (1969); *Recreations* writing, veteran athletics (active), rugby football; *Clubs* Savage, MCC, XL, Leprechauns, Royal Portrush Golf, Crustaceans (Edinburgh); *Style—* Dr Donald Dickson; 3 Meldreth, Coley Ave, Woking, Surrey GU22 7BS (☎ 0483 761106)

DICKSON, Prof Gordon Ross; s of Thomas Winston Dickson (d 1962), and Florence, *née* Carruthers (d 1978); *b* 12 Feb 1932; *Educ* Tynemouth HS, King's Coll Durham (BSc, DPhil); *m* Dorothy Olive (d 1989), da of (John) Wilfred Stobbs (d 1958); 2 s (Stephen Ross b 1957, John Raymond b 1962), 1 da (Kay b 1964); *Career* tutorial res student Univ Sch Agric King's Coll Newcastle upon Tyne 1953-56, asst farm dir Cncl King's Coll Nafferton Stocksfield-on-Tyne 1956-58, farms mangr Fitzalan-Howard Estates Arundel W Sussex 1958-71, princ Royal Agric Coll Cirencester 1971-73, prof of agric Univ of Newcastle upon Tyne 1973-; chm: North of England Advsy Ctee of Forestry Cmmn 1987-, Agric Wager Bd England & Wales 1981-84; dep chm Home-Grown Cereals 1983-; memb: Agric & Vet Sci Sub Ctee UGC 1974-86, Min of Agric Advsy Cncl 1976-79, Centre for Mgmnt in Agric; memb and dep chm Central Cncl Agric & Hort Co-op 1972-82; fell RAS; *Recreations* sport, art; *Clubs* Farmers' (London); *Style—* Prof Gordon Dickson; The West Wing, Bolam Hall, Northumberland NE61 3ST (☎ 0661 881 696); Dept of Agriculture, The University, Newcastle upon Tyne, NE1 7RU (☎ 091 222 6869, fax 091 222 6720)

DICKSON, Dr James Holmes; s of Peter Dickson (d 1973), and Jean, *née* Holms (d 1951); *b* 29 April 1937; *Educ* Bellahouton Acad Glasgow, Univ of Glasgow (BSc), Univ of Cambridge (MA, PhD); *m* 6 June 1964, Camilla Ada, da of George Bruce Lambert (d 1970); 1 s (Peter b 1965), 1 da (Kate b 1968); *Career* fell (former res fell) Clare Coll Cambridge 1963-70, sr res asst Univ of Cambridge 1961-70, sr lectr (former lectr) in botany Univ of Glasgow 1970-; botanist Royal Soc expedition to Tristan da Cunha 1961, ldr Trades House of Glasgow expedition to Papua New Guinea 1987; pres: Nat History Soc Glasgow, Botanical Soc Edinburgh, conslt to Britoil Exhibition Glasgow Garden Festival 1988; FLS 1964; *Books* Bryophytes of the Pleistoscene (1973); *Recreations* gardening; *Style—* Dr James Dickson; 113 Clober Rd, Milngavie, Glasgow, Scotland (☎ 041 956 4103); Botany Department, University of Glasgow (☎ 041 339 8855 ext 4363)

DICKSON, Jeremy David Fane; s of Lt Col J D L Dickson, MC (d 1959), and Elizabeth Daphne, *née* Fane; *b* 23 June 1941; *Educ* Marlborough, Emmanuel Coll Camb (MA); *m* 9 Oct 1965, Patricia, da of Laurence Cleveland Martin (d 1980); 1 s (James David Laurence b 30 Jan 1970), 1 da (Lucy Camilla b 25 June 1971); *Career* ptnr Cooper's & Lybrand Deloitte 1977, chm Insur Gp, chm Insur Ctee Fedn des Experts Comptables Euro; FCA; *Recreations* golf, cricket, shooting, philately; *Clubs* MCC, Royal Wimbledon Golf; *Style—* Jeremy Dickson, Esq; 8 Alan Rd, Wimbledon, London SW19 7PT (☎ 081 946 5854); PO Box 207, 128 Queen Victoria St, London EC4P 4JX (☎ 071 456 5854, fax 071 248 0413)

DICKSON, John Abernethy; CB (1970); s of John Dickson (d 1918); *b* 19 Sept 1915; *Educ* Robert Gordons Coll Aberdeen, Aberdeen Univ; *m* 1942, Helen Drummond, da of Peter Drummond Jardine (d 1974); 2 da; *Career* Forestry Cmmn: joined 1938, head of harvesting and mktg 1965-68, dir gen and dep chm 1968-76; chm: Cwlth Forestry Assoc 1972-75 Forest Thinnings Ltd 1981-86 (dir 1978-86); *Style—* John Dickson Esq, CB; 56 Oxgangs Rd, Edinburgh (☎ 031 445 1067)

DICKSON, Hon Mrs (Lynda Mary Kathleen); *née* Aitken; da (by 2 w) of Sir Max Aitken, Bt (d 1985; 2 Baron Beaverbrook, who disclaimed his peerage 1964); *b* 1948; *m* 1, 1969 (m dis 1974), Nicolas Saxton, s of Robert Saxton, of La Jolla, Calif; m 2, 1977, Jonathan James Dickson; 2 s (Joshua James b 1977, Leo Casper b 1981); *Style—* The Hon Mrs Dickson; 45 Broomwood Road, London SW11

DICKSON, Murray Graeme; CMG (1961); s of late Norman Bonnington Dickson, OBE, and late Anne Dickson, *née* Higgins; bro of Alec Dickson (*qv*); *b* 19 July 1911; *Educ* Rugby, New Coll Oxford (MA), Univ of London (DipEd); *Career* ordinary seaman MN 1934-35, War Serv with Force 136 SE Asia, Maj; Prison Serv (Borstals) 1935-40, joined Educn Dept Govt of Sarawak 1947, dir of educn Sarawak 1955-66, UNESCO advsr on educn to Govt of Lesotho 1967-68; *Books* A Sarawak Anthology-Understanding Kant's Critique of Pure Reason (19 Tales from Herodotus (1989); *Clubs* Royal Cwlth Soc; *Style—* Murray Dickson, Esq, CMG; 1 Hauteville Court Gardens, Stamford Brook Ave, London W6 0YF

DICKSON, Hon Mrs (Paula Mary); *née* Tordoff; da of Baron Tordoff (Life Peer); *b* 1960; *m* 1987, Brian Dickson, of Wanaka, New Zealand; *Style—* The Hon Mrs Dickson

DICKSON, Ruth Marjorie; MBE, JP; da of Col Randolf Nelson Greenwood, MC, JP (d 1977), and Beatrice Marion, *née* Montfort-Bebb (d 1949); *b* 9 Feb 1923; *Educ* St Margarets Welwyn Herts, Eastbourne Coll (Dip Domestic Econ); *m* 12 May 1944, Col David D Livingstone Dickson, TD, DL (d 1984), s of Frederick Livingstone Dickson (d 1960); 2 s (Duncan Charles Livingstone b 1945, Malcolm James Livingstone b 1949); *Career* ATS 1940, cmmnd 1941, discharged 1943; fndr Ruth Dickson Tst for Disabled 1974-; pres: Stone Handicapped Club, Stafford Multiple Sclerosis Club; former memb and chm Stone RDC (joined 1958), memb Stafford Bor Cncl 1974-, Mayor 1974-75; *Recreations* gardening, gundogs; *Style—* Mrs Ruth Dickson, MBE, JP; Hill Cottage, Barlaston, Stoke on Trent (☎ 078 139 2434)

DIDSBURY, (Michael) Peter Townley; s of William Didsbury (d 1975), and Edith Pomfrett, *née* Brown; *b* 10 April 1946; *Educ* Hymers Coll Hull, Balliol Coll Oxford (Elton exhibition), Univ of Durham (MPhil); *m* Patricia Ann, da of Leonard Cooley; 1 da (Sarah Louise b 10 June 1983); *Career* schoolmaster Humberside Educn Authy 1974-80, archaeologist Humberside CC Archaeology Unit 1987-; *books* The Butchers of Hull (1982), The Classical Farm (1987); *awards* Poetry Book Soc Recommendation for The Classical Farm 1987, The Cholmondely award for Poetry 1989; *Style—* Peter Didsbury, Esq; c/o Bloodaxe Books, PO Box 1SN, Newcastle upon Tyne NE99 1SN

DIEHL, His Hon Judge John Bertram Stuart; QC (1987); s of Ernest Henry Stuart Diehl, of Swansea and Caroline Pentreath *née* Lumsdaine; *b* 18 April 1944; *Educ* Bishop Gore Sch Swansea, UCL Aberystwyth (LLB); *m* 29 July 1967, Patricia; 2 s (Robert b 1973, Stephen b 1975); *Career* asst lectr and lectr Univ of Sheffield 1965-69, called to the Bar Lincoln's Inn 1968, rec 1984, circuit judge 1990-; *Recreations* squash, sailing; *Clubs* Bristol Channel Yacht; *Style—* His Hon Judge J B S Diehl, QC; Underhill House, Newton Rd, Mumbles, Swansea SA3 4SW

DIEHL, Hon Mrs (Sybil Diana); 3 da (only child by 2 m) of 3 Baron Tollemache (d 1955); *b* 1 May 1930; *m* 24 Nov 1966, Harold Diehl; *Style—* The Hon Mrs Diehl

DIEPPE, Prof Paul; *b* 20 May 1946; *Educ* Caterham Sch, St Bartholomews Hosp London; *m* 14 Aug 1971, Elizabeth Anne; 2 da (Clare Rachel b 29 April 1974, Victoria Louise b 30 April 1977); *Career* registrar Guys Hosp 1973-74, sr registrar Barts 1976-78 (res fell 1974-76), ARC prof of rheumatology Univ of Bristol 1987- (sr lectr in med 1978-86); chm Heberden Ctee Br Soc for Rheumatology, chm Res Ctee Arthritis and Rheumatism Cncl; FRCP 1983; *Books* Crystals and Joint Disease (1983), Rheumatological Medicine (1985), Slide Atlas of Rheumatology (1985), Arthritis (1988); *Recreations* sailing; *Style—* Prof Paul Dieppe; Rheumatology Unit, Bristol Royal Infirmary, Bristol BS2 8HW (☎ 0272 230701, fax 0272 253665)

DIERDEN, Kenneth Norman (Ken); s of Norman William Dierden (d 1984), of Havant, and Marjorie Harvey, *née* Nicholas; *b* 26 Feb 1952; *Educ* Bancrofts Sch Woodford Green, Univ of Southampton (BA); *m* 28 Aug 1976, Margaret Ann, da of Walter Roland Charles Hayward, of Stoke-on-Trent; 1 da (Isabella b 1988); *Career* Freshfields Slrs 1980- (ptnr 1987-); memb Worshipful Co of Slrs; memb Law Soc, ATII; *Books* Tolley's Company Law (contrib, 1988); *Recreations* hockey, squash; *Style—* Ken Dierden, Esq; Freshfields, Whitefriars, 65 Fleet St, London EC4Y 1HT (☎ 071 936 4000, fax 071 248 3487/8/9, telex 889292)

DIGBY, Baroness; Dione Marian; *née* Sherbrooke; DL (Dorset 1983); da of Rear Adm Robert St Vincent Sherbrooke, VC, CB, DSO (d 1972), of Oxton Lodge, Notts, and Rosemary Neville, *née* Buckley; *b* 23 Feb 1934; *Educ* Southover Manor Sch; *m* 18 Dec 1952, 12 Baron Digby, *qv*; 2 s, 1 da; *Career* chm: Dorset Assoc of Youth Clubs 1966-75, Dorset Community Cncl 1977-79, Standing Conference of Rural Community Cncls and Cncls of Voluntary Service 1977-79, Dorset Small Industries Ctee of COSIRA 1982-85; govr Dorset Coll of Agric 1977-83; W Dorset Dist cnsllr representing Cerne Valley 1976-86; memb: Wessex Water Authority 1983-89 (chm Avon and Dorset Customer Consultative Ctee), BBC/IBA Central Appeals Advsry Ctee 1975-80, SW Arts Management Ctee 1980-86, Bath Festival Cncl of Management 1971- (chm 1976-81), Arts Cncl of GB 1982-86 (chm Trg Ctee, vice chm Dance Panel, memb Music Panel), South Bank Bd 1985-88 (govr 1988-90); non-exec dir National Westminster Bank Western Advsry Bd 1986-; memb: Bd Nat Rivers Authority 1989- (chm Wessex Regnl Advsry Bd), Univ of Exeter Cncl 1981-; tstee Royal Acad of

Music Fndn 1985-; chm South and West Concerts Bd 1989-; memb Western Orchestral Soc Bd of Management 1989-; govr Sherborne Sch 1987-; fndr, chm and hon sec Summer Music Soc of Dorset 1963-; pres: Dorset Opera, Dorset Craft Guild; *Recreations* skiing, sailing, tennis; *Style—* The Rt Hon the Lady Digby, DL; Minterne, Dorchester, Dorset DT2 7AU (☎ 0300 341370)

DIGBY, 12 Baron (I 1620 and GB 1765); Edward Henry Kenelm Digby; JP (1959); s of 11 Baron, KG, DSO, MC (d 1964), and Hon Pamela, *née* Bruce (d 1978), da of 2 Baron Aberdare; bro-in-law of late Averell Harriman; *b* 24 July 1924; *Educ* Eton, Trinity Coll Oxford, RMC; *m* 18 Dec 1952, Dione Marian, DL (Dorset 1983), yr da of Rear Adm Robert St Vincent Sherbrooke, VC, CB, DSO; 2 s, 1 da; *Heir* s, Hon Henry Noel Kenelm Digby, *qv*; *Career* Capt Coldstream Gds 1947, ADC to C-in-C Far E Land Forces 1950-51; memb Dorchester RDC 1962; memb Dorset CC 1966-81 (vice chm 1974-81); Lord-Lt for Dorset 1984- (DL 1957), vice Lord-Lt 1965-84; dep chm SW Econ Planning Cncl, pres Cncl of St John for Dorset 1984, pres Royal Bath and W Soc 1976, chm RAS of the Cwlth 1967-79, dir C H Beazer (Hldgs) plc, pres Wessex Branch Inst of Dirs; dir: Gifford-Hill Inc, (Dallas) Kier Int Ltd; churchwarden St Andrew's Minterne Magna; KStJ 1984; *Recreations* skiing, tennis; *Clubs* Pratt's; *Style—* The Rt Hon the Lord Digby, JP; Minterne, Dorchester, Dorset DT2 7AU (☎ 030 03 370)

DIGBY, Hon Henry Noel Kenelm; s and h of 12 Baron Digby; *b* 6 Jan 1954; *Educ* Eton; *m* 12 July 1980, Susan E, er da of Peter Watts, of 6 Albert Terrace Mews, SW1; 1 s (Edward St Vincent Kenelm b 5 Sept 1985), 1 da (Alexandra Jane Kira b 13 March 1987); *Career* gp fin controller Jardine Davies (Manila) 1980-81, asst treas Jardine Matheson & Co Ltd 1981-84, investmt mangr Jardine Fleming & Co Ltd Hong Kong 1984-, dir Jardine Fleming Investmt Mgmnt Ltd 1989; ACA; *Recreations* skiing, tennis; *Style—* The Hon Henry Digby; Minterne, Dorchester, Dorset; office: Jardine Fleming Hldgs Ltd, 47th Floor, Connaught Centre, Hong Kong

DIGBY, Hon Rupert Simon; yr s of 12 Baron Digby; *b* 21 Aug 1956; *Educ* Eton, Southampton Univ (BSc); *m* 2 Aug 1986, Charlotte Fleury, yr da of late Robert Hirst, of Hamstead Mill, Marsh Benham, Berks; 1 da (Arabella b 26 Sept 1989); *Career* electronic design engineer; *Style—* The Hon Rupert Digby; Rookwood Farm House, Stockcross, Newbury, Berks

DIGBY, Hon Zara Jane; only da of 12 Baron Digby; *b* 27 May 1958; *Educ* Cobham Hall, Le Vieux Chalet Chateau d'Oex Switzerland; *Career* dress designer; *Recreations* skiing, tennis, cooking, sailing, the arts; *Style—* The Hon Zara Digby; 82 Horder Rd, London SW6 5EE (☎ 071 736 2872)

DIGBY-BELL, Christopher Harvey; s of Lt-Col Horatio Arthur Digby-Bell, of Chichester, Sussex, and Elizabeth Margaret Ann, *née* Cochrane; *b* 21 June 1948; *Educ* Marlborough; *m* 7 Sept 1974, Claire, da of Stephen Sutherland Pilch, of Finchampstead, Berkshire; 2 s (Timothy b 1981, William b 1984), 1 da (Melissa b 1980); *Career* admitted slr 1972; Taylor & Humbert 1966-82, managing ptnr Taylor Garrett 1987-89 (joined 1982), Frere Cholmeley 1989-; legal advsr Down's Syndrome Assoc 1990; memb Law Soc 1972; *Recreations* cricket, golf, swimming, collecting cricket prints, photography, cinema, pop music, playing the drums, watching American football; *Clubs* MCC, Leander, Stewards (Henley), Berkshire Golf; *Style—* Christopher Digby-Bell, Esq; 28 Lincoln's Inn Fields, London WC2A 3HH (☎ 071 405 7878, fax 071 405 9056, telex 27623 G)

DIGGLE, Dr James; s of James Diggle, and Elizabeth Alice, *née* Buckley; *b* 29 March 1944; *Educ* Rochdale GS, St John's Coll Cambridge (Henry Arthur Thomas scholar, Pitt scholar, Browne scholar; winner: Hallam prize, Members' Latin Essay prize, Montagu Butler prize, Browne medals for Greek elegy and Latin epigram, Porson prize, Chllrs Classical medal; Craven student, Allen scholar, BA, MA, PhD, LittD); *m* 8 June 1974, Sedwell Mary, da of Preb Frederick Alexander Routley Chapman (d 1989); 3 s (Charles James b 1975, Julian Alexander b 1977, Nicholas Marcel b 1978); *Career* Univ of Cambridge: fell Queens' Coll 1966-, librarian Queens' Coll 1969-77, asst lectr in classics 1970-75, praelector Queens' Coll 1971-73 and 1978-, lectr in classics 1975-89, univ orator 1982-, reader in Greek and Latin 1989-; librarian Faculty of Classics 1975-81, hon sec Cambridge Philological Soc 1970-74 (jt ed Proceedings 1970-82), hon treas Classical Jls Bd 1979-, jt ed Cambridge Classical Texts and Commentaries 1977-, chm Faculty of Classics 1989-90; FBA 1985; *Books* The Phaethon of Euripides (1970), Flavii Cresconii Corippi Iohannidos... Libri VIII (jt ed, 1970), The Classical Papers of A E Housman (jt ed, 1972), Studies on the text of Euripides (1981), Euripidis Fabulae (vol 2 1981, vol 1 1984), The Textual Tradition of Euripides' Oresteia (1991); *Recreations* family life, reading Balzac; *Style—* Dr James Diggle; Queens' College, Cambridge CB3 9ET (☎ 0223 335527)

DIGGLE, Maj James; TD; s of James Stanley Diggle (d 1973), Dorothy Mary Mellalieu (d 1961); *b* 20 Aug 1915; *Educ* Canford Sch, St John's Coll Cambridge (MA); *m* 1 Oct 1938, Margaret, da of Henry Hood (d 1941); 3 s (Richard James b 1947, Peter Hood b 1950), 2 da (Julia b 1940, Lorna b 1944); *Career* WWII served 42 Dir RASC as Maj; memb Manchester Stock Exchange 1937, sr ptnr Charlton Seal Dimmock 1981, now conslt Charlton Seal Ltd; *Recreations* golf, fishing, gardening, masonry; *Clubs* Prestbury Golf; *Style—* Maj James Diggle, TD; White Cottage, 33 Castle Hill, Prestbury, Cheshire SK10 4AS (☎ 0625 829328)

DIGGLE, Maj Peter John; s of Lt-Col Wadham Heathcote Diggle, DSO, OBE, MC (d 1958), of Eden House, Malton, Yorks, and Nancy, *née* Conran (d 1958); *b* 17 July 1921; *Educ* Stowe, Trinity Coll Cambridge; *m* 17 Sept 1959, Anna Sylvia, da of Freiherr von der Lancken-Wakenitz (d 1956), of Seidlitzhof, Krefeld; 2 s (Richard b 1961, William b 1962); *Career* Maj Gren Gds 1940-52, serv NW Europe and Malaya; dir: J M Potter Ltd 1953-62, R C Carr Ltd, J Senior Ltd and J Haig Ltd 1962-66, City Jewellers Ltd 1965-66; fndr Diamond Investment Concept 1968, dir Inter Diamond Brokers SA 1972-76, chm Amalgamated Diamond Brokers 1976-86, dir Pub Servants Housing Fin Assoc Homeownership Club 1984-, dir Minibars (UK) Ltd 1989-; patron Harrogate Abbeyfield Soc, pres Household Div Assoc Yorks Branch, chm Sydney Smith Appeal; *Recreations* tennis, shooting, equitation; *Clubs* Army and Navy, Shikar; *Style—* Maj Peter Diggle; The Old Brewery, Thornton le Clay, York YO6 7TE (☎ 065381 334); 100 Park Lane, London W1Y 4AR (☎ 071 408 0534, fax 071 491 2483)

DIGNAN, Maj-Gen Albert Patrick; CB (1978), MBE (1952); s of Joseph William Dignan (d 1964), and Rosetta Weir (d 1978); *b* 25 July 1920; *Educ* Christian Brothers Sch Dublin, Trinity Coll Dublin (MA, MD); *m* 1952, Eileen, da of James John White (d 1956); 2 s, 1 da; *Career* Brig and Consulting Surgeon FARELF 1969-71, sr consultant surgeon and asst prof of Military Surgery Queen Alexandra Military Hosp Millbank 1972-73, dir Army Surgery and consulting surgeon to the Army 1973-78, QHS 1974-78, hon consultant surgeon Royal Hosp Chelsea, hon consultant Oncology and Radiotherapy Westminster Hosp 1975-78, consultant in Accident and Emergency Medicine Ealing Hosp 1978-79; fell Assoc of Surgns of GB and Ireland, FRCS, FRCSI, FRSM; *Recreations* gardening, golf; *Style—* Maj-Gen Albert Dignan, CB, MBE; 37 Queens Rd, Beckenham, Kent (☎ 081 658 7690)

DILHORNE, 2 Viscount (UK 1964); Sir John Mervyn Manningham-Buller; 5 Bt (UK 1866); also Baron Dilhorne (UK 1962); s of 1 Viscount Dilhorne, sometime Lord High Chllr and Lord of Appeal in Ordinary (d 1980, ggs of Sir Edward M-B, 1 Bt, who was bro of 1 Baron Churston) by his w Lady Mary Lindsay (4 da of 27 Earl of Crawford and Balcarres); *b* 28 Feb 1932; *Educ* Eton, RMA Sandhurst; *m* 1, 8 Oct 1955 (m dis 1973), Gillian Evelyn, er da of Col George Cochrane Stockwell, JP; 2 s, 1 da (Hon Mary b 1970); m 2, 17 Dec 1981, Susannah Jane (*see* Eykyn, Dr Susannah Jane), da of late Cdr W C Eykyn, RN, and former w of Colin Gilchrist; *Heir* s, Capt Hon James Edward Manningham-Buller; *Career* Lt Coldstream Gds 1952-57, served Egypt, Germany, Canal Zone; CCllr Wilts 1964-66; barrister 1979; md Stewart Smith (LP&M) Ltd 1970-74; memb Jt Parly Ctee on Statutory Tribunals 1981-; fellow Inst of Taxation (memb Cncl 1969-82); *Recreations* skiing, opera singer (bass), shooting; *Clubs* Buck's, Pratt's, Royal St George's, Swinley Forest Golf; *Style—* The Rt Hon Viscount Dilhorne; 164 Ebury St, London SW1W 8UP

DILHORNE, Dowager Viscountess; Lady Mary Lilian; *née* Lindsay; 4 da of 27 Earl of Crawford and Balcarres (d 1940); *b* 27 Sept 1910; *m* 18 Dec 1930, 1 Viscount Dilhorne (d 1980); 1 s (present peer); 3 da; *Style—* The Rt Hon the Dowager Viscountess Dilhorne

DILKE, Sir John Fisher Wentworth; 5 Bt (UK 1862) of Sloane Street, Chelsea; s of Sir Fisher Wentworth Dilke, 4 Bt, Major (TA), Lloyd's underwriter (d 1944), of Lepe Point, Exbury, Hants, and Ethel Lucy (d 1959), e da of W K Clifford, FRS; *b* 8 May 1906; *Educ* Winchester, New Coll Oxford; *m* 1, 15 Sept 1934 (m dis 1949), Sheila, o da of Sir William Seeds, KCMG (d 1973), sometime ambass to Brazil and Russia; 2 s; m 2, 28 Dec 1951, Iris Evelyn, only child of late Ernest Clark, of 99 Torrington Park, N12; *Heir* s, Rev Charles John Wentworth Dilke; *Career* HM Foreign Service 1929-32, sub-editor and foreign correspondent for The Times 1936-39, rejoined Foreign Service 1939, head Br Official Wireless News 1942, political correspondent COI 1945, BBC External Dept 1950; Lloyd's underwriter 1944-; *Clubs* Royal Thames Yacht; *Style—* Sir John Dilke, Bt; Ludpits, Etchingham, E Sussex (058 081 383)

DILKES, Frank Pool; OBE (1989); s of Frank Pool Dilkes (d 1926), and Bridget, *née* Ryan (d 1966); *b* 30 April 1918; *Educ* High Pavement Secdy Sch Nottingham, Univ of London (LLB); *m* 13 Aug 1955, Audrey Helen, da of Donald Leslie Tyler (d 1957); 3 s (Paul b 1957, David b 1961, Simon b 1963), 1 da (Teresa b 1959); *Career* RAOC, REME India and Burma, 1 year attached to IA (despatches); asst sec Dewsbury and West Riding Building Society 1957; West Bromwich Building Society: asst mangr 1958, gen mangr 1961, md 1965-83, chm 1983-90; Midland Assoc of Building Socs (now Midlands and West Assoc of Building Socs): treas 1961-69, chm 1970-71, vice pres 1984-90, pres 1990-; nat pres Chartered Building Socs Inst 1972-73; pres Sandwell Assoc of Indust and Commerce 1979-80; FCIS 1949, FCBSI 1949, FRSA 1980, CBIM 1970, FID 1970; *Recreations* reading, music, walking; *Style—* Frank P Dilkes, OBE; 282 Broadway North, Walsall, W Midlands WS1 2PT (☎ 0922 23924)

DILKS, Prof David Neville; s of Neville Ernest Dilks, and Phyllis, *née* Follows; *b* 17 March 1938; *Educ* Worcester Royal GS, Hertford Coll Oxford (BA), St Antony's Coll Oxford; *m* 15 Aug 1963, Jill, da of John Henry Medlicott (d 1971), of Shrewsbury; 1 s (Richard b 1979); *Career* res asst: Sir Anthony Eden (later Earl of Avon) 1960-62, Marshal of the RAF Lord Tedder 1963-65, Rt Hon Harold Macmillan (later Earl of Stockton) 1964-67; asst lectr then lectr LSE 1962-70; Univ of Leeds: prof of int history 1970-, chm Sch of History 1974-79, dean of the Faculty of Arts 1975-77, dir Inst for Int Studies 1989, memb Univs Funding Cncl 1989-; tstee: Imperial War Museum 1983-90, Edward Boyle Meml Tst 1981-, Heskel and Mary Nathaniel Tst 1985-89, Lennox-Boyd Meml Tst 1984-; Freeman City of London 1979, Liveryman Worshipful Co of Goldsmiths 1983; FRHistS, FRSL; *Books* Curzon in India (vol 1 1969, vol 2 1970), The Diaries of Sir Alexander Cadogan (ed 1971), The Conservatives (contrib, 1977), Neville Chamberlain (vol 1, 1984); *Clubs* Brooks's, Royal Cwlth Soc; *Style—* Prof David Dilks; Wits End, Long Causeway, Leeds LS16 8EX (☎ 0532 673466); School of History, The University, Leeds LS2 9JT (☎ 0532 333584/5/6)

DILL, Sir (Nicholas) Bayard; CBE (1951), JP; s of late Col Thomas Melville Dill, of Devonshire, Bermuda, and Ruth Rapalje Neilson Dill; *b* 28 Dec 1905; *Educ* Saltus GS Bermuda, Trinity Hall Cambridge; *m* 1930, Lucy Clare, da of Sir Henry William Watlington, OBE, of Bermuda (d 1942); 2 s; *Career* memb Colonial Parl Bermuda (Devonshire Parish) 1938-68, memb HM Exec Cncl 1944-54; former chm (Bermuda): Bd of Trade, Bd of Educn, Bd of Works, Bd of Civil Aviation, Bermuda Trade Devpt Bd; memb Legislative Cncl Bermuda 1968-73; sr ptnr Conyers Dill & Pearman (Barristers-at-Law) 1928-; chllr Anglican Church 1951-84; kt 1955; *Clubs* Royal Bermuda Yacht, Royal Thames Yacht, Royal Amateur Dinghy, Canadian and Met (NY); *Style—* Sir Bayard Dill, CBE, JP; Newbold Place, Devonshire, Bermuda (010 1 809 2 292 4463); office (☎ 010 1 809 2 295 1422, telex 3213)

DILLON, Rt Hon Lord Justice; Sir (George) Brian Hugh Dillon; PC (1982); s of Capt George Crozier Dillon, RN (d 1946); *b* 2 Oct 1925; *Educ* Winchester, New Coll Oxford; *m* 1954, Alisoun Janetta Drummond, da of Hubert Samuel Lane, MC (d 1962); 2 s, 2 da; *Career* called to the Bar Lincoln's Inn 1948, QC 1965, bencher Lincoln's Inn 1973, high court judge (Chancery) 1979-82, Lord Justice of Appeal 1982-, memb Supreme Ct Rule Ctee 1986-; *Style—* Rt Hon Lord Justice Dillon; Bridge Farm House, Grundisburgh, Woodbridge; Royal Courts of Justice, WC2

DILLON, Brian Patrick; s of John Desmond Dillon, MBE (d 1956), of Blackheath, London SE3, and Mary Josephine, *née* Ryan (d 1970); *b* 21 April 1930; *Educ* Beaumont Coll Old Windsor Berks, St Mary's Hosp Med Sch Univ of London (MB BS); *m* 1 (m dis), Jane Lesley, da of John Macleod; m 2, Linda Whitaker Larby, da of Ian Macaulay; *Career* Nat Serv Coldstream Gds 1948-50, served Malayan Emergency; sr house offr St Mary's Hosp 1957-59, Gp Singapore 1959-61, registrar in obstetrics and gynaecology St Mary's 1961-63, visiting registrar Salisbury Univ of Rhodesia 1964, registrar in obstetrics and gynaecology St Mary Abbot's Hosp 1965-66, Med offr PDO (Shell) Oman 1967-68, visiting sr registrar Lusaka Univ of Zambia 1969-70, sr registrar in obstetrics and gynaecology St George's Hosp London 1971-74; conslt in obstetrics and gynaecology 1975-: Barnet Gen Hosp, Edgware Gen Hosp Middx, Finchley Meml Hosp London, Victoria Maternity Hosp Barnet, PPP Med Centre New Cavendish St London; memb: Med Soc, Hunterian Soc, BMA; MRCOG 1966, FRCS 1971, FRCOG 1982; *Recreations* cricket, sailing, shooting; *Clubs* Guards, MCC, Lords Taverners; *Style—* Brian Dillon, Esq; Highfield, Totteridge Green, London N20 8PE (☎ 081 445 6348); Pen-y-Frith, Hafod Elwy, Mynydd Hiraethog, Clwyd, N Wales; 40 Harley St, London W1N 1AB (☎ 071 636 7922)

DILLON, Hon Mrs (Erica Helen Susan); *née* Rollo; only da of 13 Baron Rollo; *b* 12 Dec 1939; *m* 1970, Valentine Edward Dillon; *Style—* The Hon Mrs Dillon; 45 Sandford Rd, Dublin

DILLON, 22 Viscount (I 1622); Henry Benedict Charles Dillon; also Count Dillon (Fr cr of Louis XIV 1711 for Hon Arthur Dillon, 3 s of 7 Viscount and father of 10 and 11 Viscounts, who was Col proprietor of the Dillon Regt, promoted to Lt-Gen in the Fr service, govr of Toulon, and cr titular Earl Dillon 1721/22 by the Chevalier de St Georges, otherwise known as the Old Pretender or, to his supporters, James III); s of 21 Viscount Dillon (d 1982); *b* 6 Jan 1973; *Heir* unc, Hon Richard Dillon, *qv*; *Style—* Rt Hon the Viscount Dillon; 83 Talfourd Rd, London SE15 (☎ 071 701 5931)

DILLON, Irène, Viscountess; Irène Marie France; *née* Merandon du Plessis; da of René Merandon du Plessis, of Whitehall, Mauritius and Jeanne Cecile, *née* de Bricqueville; *Educ* Queen's Coll; *m* 4 Dec 1939, 20 Viscount Dillon (d 1979); 4 s (21

Viscount (d 1982), Richard, Patrick, Michael), 4 da (Hon Isabelle (Hon Mrs Cobbe) b 1942, Hon Ines b 1952, Hon Rosaleen b 1953 d 1960, Hon Magdalen b 1957); *Career* painter; *Style—* Rt Hon Irène, Viscountess Dillon; 14 St Mary's Cottages, Drogheda, Co Louth, Ireland

DILLON, Viscountess; (Mary) Jane; da of late John Young, of Castle Hill House, Birtle, Lancs; *m* 1972, 21 Viscount Dillon (d 1982); 1 s (Henry, 22 Viscount Dillon, *qv*), 1 da (Beatrice Ines Renee b 28 Dec 1978); *Career* designer; *Style—* Rt Hon Viscountess Dillon; 28 Canning Cross, London, SE5 8BH

DILLON, Martin; s of Gerard Dillon, and Maureen, *née* Clarke; *b* 2 July 1949; *Educ* St Finians Belfast, Montfort Coll Hants, St Malachy's Coll Belfast; *m* 1, Aug 1973 (m dis 1984), Mildred Matilda, da of Albert Smyth; m 2, 1986, Katherine, da of Patrick Bannon; 1 da (Nadia b Feb 1987), 1 step s (Crawford Anderson); *Career* journalist Belfast Telegraph 1972-73, arts prodr BBC 1975-78 (news reporter 1974-75); ed topical features: Radio 1986-88 (ed gen progs 1979-86), TV 1988-; plays written TV and Radio incl: The Squad, The Waiting Room, The Dog; *Books* Political Murder in NI (1973), Rogue Warrior of the SAS: A Biography of Lt-Col Paddy 'Blair' Mayne (1987), The Shankill Butchers: A Case Study of Mass Murder (1989); The Dirty War (1990); *Recreations* flyfishing; *Style—* Martin Dillon, Esq; Ardara House, Bally Gowan Rd, Comber, Co Down; BBC Broadcasting House, Ormeau Ave, Belfast, N I (☎ 0232 244400)

DILLON, Hon Michael Edmund; 4 s (twin) of 20 Viscount Dillon; *b* 29 Oct 1957; *Educ* Glenstal Abbey Sch Co Limerick, Hampshire Coll of Agric Sparsholt; *m* 1 Oct 1983, Henrietta Catherine, yr da of Charles Elwell, of Bottrells Close, Chalfont St Giles; 1 s (Charles b 1985), 2 da; *Style—* The Hon Michael Dillon

DILLON, Hon Mrs (Priscilla Frances); yr da of 2 Baron Hazlerigg; *b* 30 July 1952; *m* 1975, Hon Richard Dillon, *qv*, 2 s of 20 Viscount Dillon; 1 s, 1 da; *Style—* The Hon Mrs Dillon; 5 Edith Grove, London SW10

DILLON, Hon Richard Arthur Louis; 2 s of 20 Viscount Dillon; hp to n, 22 Viscount Dillon; *b* 23 Oct 1948; *Educ* Downside, RAC Cirencester; *m* 1975, Hon Priscilla (Scilla) Frances, da of 2 Baron Hazlerigg; 1 s (Thomas Arthur Lee b 1 Oct 1983), 1 da (Charlotte Frances b 1978); *Career* served RHG 1966-69; FSVA; *Style—* The Hon Richard Dillon

DILLON, Lady; (Elia) Synolda Augusta; *née* Cholmondeley Clarke; o da of Cecil Butler Cholmondeley Clarke (d 1924), of The Hermitage, Holycross, Co Tipperary, and Fanny Ethel (d 1971), er da of Maj Edward Augustus Carter, of Theakston Hall, Yorks; *b* 19 March 1916; *Educ* Alexandra Coll Dublin; *m* 11 Feb 1947, Sir Robert William Charlier Dillon, 8 Bt (d 1982, when the title became extinct, also Baron Holy Roman Empire cr 1782) s of Robert Arthur Dillon, of Folkstone; *Style—* Lady Dillon; Lismullen, 174 Glebemount, Wicklow, Co Wicklow, Ireland

DILLON, Terence John; *b* 16 July 1939; *Educ* St Joseph's Coll Upper Norwood; *m* 10 Aug 1968, Claire; 2 da (Jennifer Joan b 1973, Susan Jane b 1975); *Career* fin and planning BP 1963- (Investmt Dept 1973-); FCA 1961; *Recreations* tennis, chess, lepidoptera, antiquarian books; *Style—* Terence Dillon, Esq; British Petroleum Pension Trust, Britannic House, Moor Lane, London EC2Y 9BU (☎ 071 920 4279)

DILLOWAY, Clifford Charles (Cliff); *b* 22 April 1926; *Educ* Wanstead Co HS; *m* Ada Lilian; 1 s (Graham b 1953), 1 da (Hilary b 1957); *Career* Sgt Air Gunner RAF; arbitrator and expert witness in computer disputes, ed of Computer Books Review; dir: Dilloway and Son Ltd, Endispute Ltd; dir and gen mangr Package Programs Ltd, mangr Computer Centre Ford Motor Co Ltd; memb Intellectual Property Ctee, Br Computer Soc; FCMA, FBCS, JDipMA, FCIArb, MIDPM; *Recreations* assisting in his wife's bed and breakfast business; *Style—* Cliff Dilloway, Esq; Highcroft, Gunhouse Lane, Stroud, Glos GL5 2DB (☎ 0453 763387, fax 0453 751528)

DILLWYN-VENABLES-LLEWELYN *see also*: Venables-Llewelyn

DILLWYN-VENABLES-LLEWELYN, Lady Delia Mary; da of Capt Michael Hugh Hicks-Beach, MP (Viscount Quenington, s of 1 Earl St Aldwyn, and who was ka 1916, vp); raised to the rank of an Earl's da 1920; *b* 2 Aug 1910; *m* 3 Dec 1934, Brig Sir (Charles) Michael Dillwyn-Venables-Llewelyn, 3 Bt, MVO, (d 1976); 1 s, 1 da; *Style—* The Lady Delia Dillwyn-Venables-Llewelyn; Llysdinam, Hall, Llandrindod Wells, Powys (☎ 059 789 200)

DILS, Prof Raymond Ronald; s of Francoise Gommaire Dils, of Birmingham (d 1968), and Minnie Dils (d 1968); *b* 16 March 1932; *Educ* Univ of Birmingham (BSc, PhD, DSc); *m* 29 Oct 1966, Joan Agnes, da of George Crompton (d 1945), of Stoke-on-Trent; 2 da (Ruth, Rachael); *Career* lectr Dept of Biochemistry Univ of Birmingham 1962-69, sr lectr then reader Dept of Biochemistry Univ of Nottingham Med Sch 1969-76, prof Dept of Biochemistry and Physiology Univ of Reading 1976-; author of numerous papers in jls; vice pres: Univ of Reading Branch AUT, Thames Valley Branch WEA; memb: Cncl AUT, Nutrition Soc, Biochemical Soc, Soc for Endocrinology; FRIC, FIBiol, CChem, CBiol; *Recreations* theatre, reading, travel; *Style—* Prof Raymond Dils; Department of Biochemistry and Physiology, School of Animal and Microbial Sciences, University of Reading, Whiteknights, PO Box 228, Reading RG6 2AJ (☎ 0734 318015, fax 0734 310180)

DILWORTH, Prof Jonathan Robin; s of Robert Arnold Dilworth, OBE, and Jean Marion Dilworth; *b* 20 Aug 1944; *Educ* Trinity Sch Croydon, Jesus Coll Oxford (MA), Univ of Sussex (DPhil, DSc); *m* 7 Aug 1971, Nicola Jane, da of Leonard Still (d 1980); 2 da (Jane b 1974, Emma b 1978); *Career* PSO unit of Nitrogen Fixation Univ of Sussex 1967-84 (ASO 1967), Dept of Chemistry and Biological Chemistry Univ of Essex 1985-; FRCS 1985; *Recreations* golf, tennis, badminton, squash; *Style—* Prof Jonathan Dilworth; 8 Baronia Croft, Highwoods, Colchester CO4 4EE (☎ 0206 841432); Department of Chemistry and Biological Chemistry, University of Essex, Colchester CO4 3SQ (☎ 0206 872119)

DILWORTH, Stephen Patrick Dominic; s of Patrick Dilworth, of London, and Ida Dilworth; *b* 20 Oct 1951; *Educ* St Josephs Acad Blackheath, Open Univ (BA); *m* 12 April 1975, Susan Carolyn, da of Patrick Joseph Stopps, of Herts; 1 s (Nicholas b 1981), 1 da (Laura b 1982); *Career* regnl mangr Leeds Permanent Building Soc: Thames Valley 1982-86, London 1986-88; asst gen mangr of mktg Town and Country Building Soc 1988-; dir: Soho Ltd, Link Interchange Network Ltd; memb Ctee Soho Housing Assoc, assoc memb Borehamwood Operatic Soc; FCBSI 1977; *Books* More Than A Building Society (1987); *Recreations* squash, golf, films, football, history, economics; *Clubs* RAC; *Style—* Stephen Dilworth, Esq; 215 The Strand, London WC2 (☎ 071 353 1399, fax 071 353 1398)

DIMBLEBY, David; s of Richard Dimbleby, CBE (d 1965), and Dilys, da of late A A Thomas; *b* 28 Oct 1938; *Educ* Charterhouse, ChCh Oxford, Paris Univ, Perugia Univ; *m* 1967, Josceline Rose, da of Thomas Gaskell; 1 s, 2 da; *Career* freelance broadcaster, newspaper proprietor; news reporter BBC Bristol 1960-61, presenter and interviewer on network programmes incl: religion (Quest), science for children (What's New?), politics (In My Opinion), Top of the Form 1961-63; reporter BBC2 (Enquiry) and dir of films incl: Ku-Klux-Klan, The Forgotten Million, Cyprus: The Thin Blue Line 1964-65; special corr CBS News New York, documentary film (Texas-England) and film reports for '60 minutes' 1966-, commentator Current Events 1969, presenter BBC1 24 Hours 1969-72, chm The Dimbleby Talk-In 1971-74, films for Reporter at Large 1973, Election Campaign Report 1974, BBC Election and Results programmes 1979, film series The White Tribe of Africa 1979 (Royal TV Soc Supreme Documentary award); md Wandsworth Borough News Ltd 1979-86 (chm 1986); presenter: Panorama BBC1 1974-77, 1980-82 (reporter 1967-69), People and Power 1983, General Election Results programmes 1983-87, This Week Next Week 1984-86; chm family firm Dimbleby and Sons Ltd 1986- (md 1966-86); presenter An Ocean Apart 1988; *Books* An Ocean Apart 1988; *Style—* David Dimbleby, Esq; 14 King St, Richmond, Surrey TW9 1NF

DIMBLEBY, Jonathan; s of Richard Dimbleby, CBE (d 1966), and Dilys, *née* Thomas; *b* 31 July 1944; *Educ* UCL (BA); *m* 1968, Bel Mooney; 1 s, 1 da; *Career* freelance journalist, broadcaster and author; TV and radio reporter BBC Bristol 1969-70, BBC Radio World at One 1970-71; for Thames TV: This Week 1972-78 and 1986-88, prodr and presenter Jonathan Dimbleby in South America 1979, Jonathan Dimbleby in Evidence: The Police 1980, The Bomb 1980, The Eagle and the Bear 1981, The Cold War Game 1982, The American Dream 1984, Fours Years On - The Bomb 1984; assoc ed and presenter First Tuesday series 1982-85, ed documentary series Witness 1986-88; presenter and ed Jonathan Dimbleby on Sunday TV-am 1985-86; for BBC TV: presenter On the Record 1988-; writer and presenter: Review of the Year 1989 and 1990, Russia at the Rubicon 1990; interview with President Gorbachev 1990; for BBC Radio: chm Any Questions? 1987-, presenter Any Answers? 1988-; awards incl Soc of Film and TV Arts Richard Dimbleby Award (for most outstanding contrib to factual TV) 1974; memb: bd Int Broadcasting Tst, Nat AIDS Tst, VSO, Richard Dimbleby Cancer Fund; *Books* Richard Dimbleby (1975), The Palestinians (1979); *Recreations* music, sailing, tennis; *Style—* Jonathan Dimbleby, Esq; c/o David Higham Associates Ltd, 5-8 Lower John St, London W1R 4HA

DIMES, Francis Gordon; s of John Francis Arthur Dimes, OBE (d 1966), of New Malden, Surrey, and Elizabeth, *née* Larkey; *b* 17 June 1920; *Educ* Tiffin Sch, Chelsea Coll Univ of London (BSc), Kingston Poly (NCAA, MSc); *m* 8 Sept 1945, Ellen Margaret, *née* Archibald; 3 da (Susan b 1946, Gina b 1948, Jane b 1949); *Career* WWII, conscripted 1942, Bombadier signal Trg RA 1943; 2 Oban (air landing) Anti-Tank Regt RA: 1 Airborne Div 1945, Army Educn Corps 1946, WO 1946, discharged 1947; before war serv was with Dept of Palaeontology Geological Survey and Museum; curator of bldg and deco stones Collections 1960-81; vice pres Palaeontographical Soc (former sec), chm Friends of the Orton Tst, memb Palaeontological Assoc; Freeman City of London, Liveryman Worshipful Co of Masons; FGS; *Books* Stone in Building (with John Ashurst, 1977), Fossil Collecting (with Richard V Melville, 1979), Conservation of Building and Decorative Stone (with John Ashurst and Honeyborne, 1989); *Clubs* City Livery, Tetrapods; *Style—* Francis G Dimes, Esq; 31 Bowness Crescent, Kingston Vale, London SW15 3QN (☎ 081 546 2079)

DIMMICK, (Alexander) Mark; s of Roland George Alexander Dimmick (d 1980), late of Bilton Rugby, and late Margaret Jayne, *née* Lodge; *b* 17 Oct 1939; *Educ* Rugby Sch, St John's Coll Cambridge (MA); *m* 15 Oct 1962, Josephine Mary, da of Neville Holmes, of Spa Ct, Ripon, N Yorks; 1 s (Alexander b 1970); *Career* chemical engr (chartered); sr ptnr Amplan Mgmnt Systems-Information Tech in Agric, dir Eric Garner & Partners Ltd; Trade Assoc AEA; ICI Wilton 1968-81, Kimberly Clark Ltd Maidstone 1962-68, Nat Sci Pt I, chem engr Pt II 1962, Comp Sci 1982; *Recreations* antique collecting, music; *Clubs* Inst of Chem Engrs, Br Computer Soc, Nat Art Collections Fund, Old Rugbean Soc, CGA; *Style—* Mark Dimmick, Esq; Beck House, Thirlby, Thirsk, Yorks YO7 2DJ (☎ 0845 597330)

DIMMOCK, Prof Nigel John; s of Herbert Douglas Dimmock (d 1987), of Brookwood Surrey, and Doreen Agnes, *née* Robinson (d 1984); *b* 14 April 1940; *Educ* Woking GS, Univ of Liverpool (BSc), Univ of London (PhD); *m* 1, 27 April 1963 (m dis), Jennifer Ann, da of John Glazier of Bulawayo, Zimbabwe; 2 s (Nicholas b 1 Feb 1964, Simon b 26 Dec 1965), 1 da (Samantha b 1 Nov 1967); m 2, 30 Oct 1987, Jane Elizabeth Mary, da of Dr Samuel Ballantine, of Leicester (d 1985); *Career* virologist and teacher; MRC Salisbury 1961-66, Aust Nat Univ Canberra 1966-71; Univ of Warwick: lectr 1971, sr lectr 1975, reader 1982, prof 1986; visiting res fell: Melbourne 1977, Munich 1979, Vancouver 1981, Perth Aust 1987; memb: Med Advsy Ctee Multiple Sclerosis, Soc for Gen Microbiology; ed Jl of Gen Virology 1980-88; *Books* Introduction of Modern Virology 1987 (with S B Primrose 1987); *Recreations* theatre, books, working with wood, road running; *Style—* Prof Nigel Dimmock; Dept of Biological Sciences, University of Warwick, Coventry CV4 7AL (☎ 0203 523593, fax 0203 523701)

DIMMOCK, Rear Adm Roger Charles; CB (1988); s of Frank Charles Dimmock, and Ivy Annie May, *née* Archer (d 1989); *b* 27 May 1935; *Educ* Price's Sch; *m* 1958, Lesley Patricia Reid; 3 da (Sandra b 1959, Jacqueline b 1960 d 1987, Nicola b 1963); *Career* entered RN 1953; pilot's wings FAA 1954, USN 1955, qualified flying instr 1959; Master Mariner Foreign Going Cert of Serv 1979; served RN Air Sqdns and HM Ships Bulwark, Albion, Ark Royal, Eagle, Hermes, Anzio, Messina, Murray, Berwick (i/c), Naiad (i/c); CSO to FO Carriers and Amphibious Ships 1978-80; cmd RNAS: Culdrose 1980-82, HMS Hermes 1982-83; dir Naval Air Warfare MOD 1983-84, Naval Sec 1985-87, Flag Offr Naval Air Cmd 1987; chm tstees Fleet Air Arm Museum 1987-88; dir Archer Mullins Ltd 1990-; chm United Servs Hockey Club Portsmouth 1983-87; pres: RN Hockey Assoc 1985-90, Combined Services Hockey Assoc 1987-, Denmead-Hambledon Branch RNLI 1981-; memb Ctee of Mgmnt RNLI 1987-; *Recreations* hockey umpire, cricket, squash, golf, family and friends; *Clubs* Royal Cwlth, RN; *Style—* Rear Adm Roger Dimmock, CB; Beverley House, 19 Beverley Grove, Farlington, Portsmouth, Hants PO6 1BP

DIMOND, Bronwyn Vivienne Sylvia; TD (1990); *Educ* Rugby HS for Girls, Univ of London (Dip Nursing); *m* m, 1 da; *Career* trained Hosp of St Cross Rugby 1061-64 (SRN winner of Gold medal for academic achievement), theatre staff nurse Sheffield Royal Infirmary 1964; theatre sister: Utd Sheffield Hosps 1964-68 (staff nurse 1964), Childrens Hospital (sister i/c of cardiac-thoracic theatres) 1964-68, theatre superintendent Duchess of Kent Children's Orthopaedic Hosp Sandy Bay Hong Kong 1968-71, head Dept of Biology Greengates Int Sch Mexico City 1971-74, theatre sister Royal Surrey County Hosp Guildford 1974-75, nursing offr St Luke's Hops Guildford 1975-76, sr nursing offr (1 Res) West Surrey & NE Hampshire Dist 1976-77, area nurse serv planning offr Surrey Area Health Authy 1977-80, acting dist nursing offr (on secondment) N Surrey Health Dist 1979-80, regnl nurse, serv planning and res Oxford Regnl Health Authy 1980-81, chief nursing offr Portsmouth and SE Hampshire Health Authy 1981-83, nurse advsr regnl liaison DHSS Regnl Liaison Serv Planning Nursing Div 1983-86; unit gen mangr servs Dartford and Gravesham Health Authy: priority case servs 1987-90, acute servs 1990-; memb: Royal Coll of Nursing, Inst of Health Serv Mgmnt, TA (Maj); *Recreations* horses (cross country and hunting), opera, ballet, cooking, entertaining; *Style—* Mrs Bronwyn Dimond, TD; Meadowbank, 5 Hasteds, Hollingbourne, Kent ME17 1VQ (☎ 0622 880 510, office 0322 27211 ext 357)

DIMSON, Prof Elroy; s of David Dimson, of London, and Phyllis, *née* Heilpern; *b* 17 Jan 1947; *Educ* Univ of Newcastle upon Tyne (BA), Univ of Birmingham (MCom), Univ of London (PhD); *m* 1 July 1969, Dr Helen Patricia, da of Max Sonn, of Whitley Bay; 3 s (Jonathan Ashley b 1971, Benjamin Simon b 1979, Daniel Marc b 1986), 1 da (Susanna Rachel b 1973); *Career* Tube Investmts 1969-70, Unilever Ltd 1970-72, London Business Sch 1972- (dean MBA Progs 1986-90); dir: The German Investment

Trust plc, superannuation arrangements Univ of London; bd memb: Journal of Banking and Finance, Investing, MBA Review; visiting prof: Chicago Univ, California Univ (Berkeley), Hawaii Univ, Euro Inst Brussels, Bank of England; advsr: SIB, Int Stock Exchange; *Books* Risk Measurement Service (with Paul Marsh, 1979-) Cases in Corporate Finance (with Paul Marsh, 1988), Stock Market Anomalies (1988), author of numerous published papers; *Style*— Prof Elroy Dimson; London Business School, Sussex Place, Regents Park, London NW1 4SA (☎ 071 262 5050, fax 071 724 7875, telex 27461)

DIMSON, Gladys Felicia; CBE (1976); da of late I Sieve; *Educ* Laurel Bank Sch Glasgow, Univ of Glasgow, LSE; *m* Dr S B Dimson; 1 da; *Career* memb: GLC for Battersea North 1970-85 (former chm GLC Housing Ctee), ILEA 1970-85, Bd Shelter, Cncl of Toynbee Hall 1983-; chm: Toynbee Housing Assoc 1976-88, E London Housing Assoc 1979-; tstee: Sutton Housing Tst 1982-90, Shelter Housing Aid Centre; *Style*— Mrs Gladys Dimson, CBE

DIN, Russhied Ali; s of Matab Ali Din, of Rawalpindi, Pakistan, and Hilda Rose, *née* Dring (d 1985); *b* 8 April 1956; *Educ* Ordsall Secdy Modern, Salford Coll of Technol, Birmingham Poly (BA); *Career* designer: City Industrial Shopfitters 1978, Fitch & Co 1979, Italy Studies Giardi Rome 1980, Thomas Saunders Architects 1981, Peter Glynn Smith Assoc 1982-84 (BAA Gatwick refurbishment 1983), Allied Int Designers 1984-86; formed Din Assocs 1986 (became Ltd Co 1988), design conslt to Next Retail plc 1987, top office exhibition 1988, Dept X concept completed Oxford St 1988, designed theatre set and costumes for Leicester Haymarket Theatre 19 Young Business Person of the Year (Observer and Harvey Nichols) 1990 MCSD; *Recreations* equestrian pursuits, tennis; *Style*— Russhied Din, Esq; Bushell Rd, Balham, London (☎ 071 673 0276); 6 South Lambeth Place, Vauxhall, London SW8 (☎ 071 582 0777, Fax 071 582 3080)

DINAN, Lady Charlotte Elizabeth Anne; *née* Curzon; da of 6 Earl Howe, CBE; *b* 5 July 1948; *m* March 1988, Barry Dinan; 1 s (Richard); *Style*— Lady Charlotte Dinan; Chalkpit House, Knotty Green, Beaconsfield, Bucks

DINARDO, Carlo; s of Nicandro Dinardo, and Rosaria, *née* Iannacone; *b* 5 July 1939; *Educ* St Patrick's High Coatbridge Scotland, Paddington Tech Coll, Tech Coll Coatbridge Scotland, Univ of Strathclyde; *m* 30 Aug 1962, Irene Rutherford, da of William James Niven (d 1977), of Helensburgh; 1 s (Mark b 27 April 1967), 2 da (Karen b 24 Oct 1965, Lorraine b 7 Aug 1973); *Career* fndr ptnr Roxburgh Dinardo & Ptnrs consulting engrs 1969, princ Dinardo & Ptnrs 1978-; dir: Scottish Conslts Int 1987-, Dinardo Properties Ltd 1988-; paper published for Inst of Petroleum 1977; Inst of Structural Engrs: paper published on educn 1987, and on structural repairs at Uniroyal 1988, ctee memb of Educn Eask Gp Inst Struet E 1987-; ctee memb of Industl Trg Advsy Bd at Paisley Coll of Technol; memb Bd of Govrs of Westbourne Sch for girls Glasgow 1984-; C Eng 1965, MIStructE 1965, MICE 1967, FIStrucE 1976, FICE 1976, MIHT 1979, FInstPet 1979, ACIArb 1980, FGS 1982, FIHT 1982, MConsE 1984, FEANI; *Recreations* golf, skiing, fishing, rugby, curling, historical travels; *Clubs* Royal Northern & Univ (Aberdeen), Buchanan Castle Golf (Drymen), Glasgow Golf, Royal Aberdeen Golf; *Style*— Carlo Dinardo, Esq; Tighness, Main St, Killearn G63 9NB (☎ 0360 50298); Dinardo and Partners, Mirren Court, 119 Renfrew Rd, Paisley, Renfrewshire PA3 4EA (☎ 041 889 1212, fax 041 889 5446, car 0860 836 757, telex 265871 84 DAPOO1)

DINEEN, Michael Laurence; s of John Leonard Dineen, of Kendal, and Nancy Margaret, *née* Carter; *b* 17 July 1949; *Educ* Brockenhurst GS, Keble Coll Oxford (BA), Magdalene Coll Cambridge (LLB); *Career* lectr Dorset Inst of Higher Educn 1974-78, called to the Bar Inner Temple 1977 (practising barr 1978-); wine treas Western Circuit 1990-; *Recreations* wine and food, talking, walking, skiing, amateur dramatics; *Clubs* Reform, Hampshire (Winchester); *Style*— Michael Dineen, Esq; 17 Carlton Crescent, Southampton, Hampshire S09 5AL (☎ 0703 639001, fax 0703 339625)

DINELEY, Prof David Lawrence; s of Leonard Wilfrid Dineley, Croix De Guerre (d 1960), of Birmingham, and Hilda Nellie, *née* Lawrence (d 1976); *b* 24 Aug 1927; *Educ* Yardley GS, Univ of Birmingham (BSc, PhD); *m* 23 July 1953, Nancy Margaret, da of Ivon Stanley Moore (d 1981); 2 da (Frances Gillian (Mrs Dickins) b 1955, Rachel Margaret b 1957); *Career* lectr: Univ Coll Exeter 1950-59, Univ of Bristol 1959-60; prof Univ of Ottawa Canada 1960-68, Chaning Wills prof of geology Univ of Bristol 1968-90; govr Bristol Old Vic, tstee The Exploratory Bristol; FGS 1950, memb Inst Geology 1972; *Books* Earth's Voyage Through Time (1973), Fossils (1979), Rocks (1977), Aspects of a stratigraphic system - the Devonian (1984); *Recreations* listening to music, theatre, DIY; *Style*— Prof David Dineley; Treetops, 12 Hyland Grove, Westbury on Trym, Bristol BS9 3NR (☎ 0272 500951); Dept of Geology, Univ of Bristol, Wills Memorial Bldg, Bristol BS9 3NR (☎ 0272 303030, fax 0272 253385)

DINGEMANS, Rear Adm Peter George Valentin; CB (1990), DSO; s of Dr George Albert Dingemans, of Grenofen, Steyning, Sussex, and Marjorie Irene, *née* Spong; *b* 31 July 1935; *Educ* Brighton Coll; *m* 25 March 1961, Faith Vivien, da of Percy Michael Bristow (d 1986); 3 s (Timothy George b 1962, James Michael b 1964, Piers Anthony b 1966); *Career* entered RN 1953; jr offr 1953-58: Vanguard, Superb, Ark Royal ; 1 Lt Woolaston 1958-60, torpedo anti-sub offr HMS Yarmouth 1963, OIC Leading Rating's Leadership Course 1964, CO HMS Maxton 1965-67, RAF staff course Bracknell 1968, 1 Lt HMS Torquay 1969-70, staff of Flag Offr 2 i/c Far East Fleet, MOD Directorate of Naval Plans 1971-73, CO HMS Berwick and HMS Lowestoft 1973-74, MOD staff asst COS (policy) 1974-76; Capt: Fishery Protection, Mine Counter Measure 1976-78; RCDS 1979, CO HMS Intrepid Falkland Islands Conflict 1980-82, Cdre Amphibious Warfare, Rear Adm 1985, Flag Offr Gibraltar 1985-87, COS to C in C Fleet 1987-90; dir Argosy Asset Management Plc 1990-; Freeman City of London, Liveryman Worshipful Co of Coachmakers and Coach Harnessmakers; *Recreations* family and friends, tennis, shooting; *Clubs* Naval and Military, City Livery; *Style*— Rear Adm Peter Dingemans, CB, DSO; c/o Lloyds Bank Ltd, Steyning, Sussex

DINGLE, Dr John Thomas; s of T H Dingle (d 1990), and Violet, *née* Tolman; *b* 27 Oct 1927; *Educ* King Edward Sch Bath, Univ of London (BSc, DSc), Univ of Cambridge (PhD); *m* 11 July 1953, Dorothy Vernon; 2 s (Jonathan b 1957, Timothy b 1959); *Career* Mil Serv RN 1946-49; res asst Royal Nat Hosp for Rheumatic Diseases Bath 1951-59; Strangeways Research Laboratory: sr res asst 1959, head Physiology Dept 1969, dep dir (MRC external staff) 1971-79, chm Pathophysiology Laboratory 1976-, dir 1979-; Corpus Christi Coll Cambridge: fell 1968-, warden of Leckhampton 1981-86, steward of Estates 1987-; chm Editorial Bd The Biochemical Jl 1976-82, pres Br Connective Tissue Soc 1980-86, treas Cambridge Univ Rugby Union Football Club 1983-90 (pres 1990-; *Awards* Heberden medal 1978, Steindler award 1980; author of numerous papers in scientific learned jls; *Recreations* rugby, sailing; *Clubs* Hawks, Farmers; *Style*— Dr John Dingle; Walnut Tree Cottage, 38 Church St, Gt Shelford, Cambridge; Strangeways Research Laboratory, Worts Causeway, Cambridge CB1 4RN (☎ 0223 243231, fax 0223 411609)

DINGLEY, Gerald Albert; s of Albert Dingley, and Cecélia, *née* Frost; *Educ* Henry Compton Sch for Boys, LSE; *m* 1957, Christine, da of Alexander Wait; 1 s (Mark), 1 da (Tina); *Career* RAF; md Pentax UK Ltd 1979-, pres dir gen Pentax France SA 1982-, chm Euro Mgmnt Ctee Pentax 1990-; *Style*— Gerald Dingley, Esq; c/o Pentax UK Ltd, Pentax House, South Hill Ave, South Harrow, Middx (☎ 081 864 4422)

DINGWALL, Lady; *see*: Lucas of Crudwell, Baroness

DINGWALL-FORDYCE, Andrew; s of James Alexander Dingwall-Fordyce, TD (d 1988), and Edith May, *née* Leather; *b* 22 Feb 1957; *Educ* Rugby, Scotland Coll of Agric (OND), Webber Douglas Acad of Dramatic Art; *m* 28 June 1986, Lucinda Mary-Jane, da of Col Francis John Kevin Williams, CBE, TD, DL, of Brimstage, Merseyside; 1 da (Charlotte Mar b 11 June 1990); *Career* actor 1976-78; farmer and landowner; sporting agent; vice chm East Aberdeenshire Conservatives, regnl sec Game Conservancy 1983-, chm NE Region Scottish Landowners Fedn 1989-, memb Club of Deir Aberdeenshire; pres: New Deer Agric Assoc Aberdeenshire, Highland Gundog Club; *Recreations* shooting, golf, skiing, theatre, bridge, drink, squash; *Clubs* Royal Northern and Univ (Aberdeen); *Style*— Andrew Dingwall-Fordyce of Brucklay; Brucklay House, Maud, Peterhead, Aberdeenshire (☎ 077 14 253); Brucklay Estate Office, Sheuado, Maud, Peterhead, Aberdeenshire

DINGWALL-SMITH, Ronald Alfred; CB (1977); *b* 24 Feb 1917; *Educ* Alleyn's Sch, LSE; *m* 1 June 1946, (Margaret) Eileen; 1 s (Richard b 1951), 1 da (Gillian (Mrs Waters) b 1947); *Career* WWII serv Maj gen list 1939-47; clerical offr MOT 1934-35, auditor Exchequer and Audit Dept 1936-47; Scottish Educn Dept: asst princ 1947-49, admin princ 1949-56, asst sec 1956-65; under sec Scottish Devpt Dept 1965-70, princ fin offr Scottish Office 1970-78; sr res fell Univ of Glasgow 1979-81; memb Bd: St Vincent Drilling 1979-80; chm Hanover (Scotland) Housing Assoc Ltd 1988- (memb 1979-); memb: Hanover (Scotland Housing Assoc Charitable Tst 1982, Heritage Housing Ltd 1982-, Hanover (Caol) Housing Assoc Ltd 1985-; memb Cmmn Local Authy Accounts in Scotland 1980-85, govr Moray House Co of Educn Edinburgh 1980-87; memb Royal Cwlth Soc; *Recreations* golf, bowls, gardening; *Clubs* Braid Bowling (Edinburgh); *Style*— Ronald Dingwall-Smith, CB; 3 Frogston Terrace, Edinburgh EH10 7AD (☎ 031 445 2727); Hanover Housing Group, 36 Albany St, Edinburth EH1 3QH (☎ 031 557 0598, fax 031 557 1280)

DINKEL, Emmy Gerarda Mary; da of John Jacob Keet (d 1937), of Orsett, Grays, Essex, and Mary, *née* Hartoch (d 1951); *b* 5 Sept 1908; *Educ* Palmer's Coll Grays Essex, Southend-on-Sea Coll of Art, RCA; *m* 25 Oct 1941, Prof Ernest Michael Dinkel (d 1983), s of Charles Dinkel (d 1944), of Huddersfield, Yorks; 2 s (John Michael Antony b 9 Oct 1942, Philip Charles Christian b 3 Oct 1946); *Career* teacher of embroidery and design to Evening Insts London 1932-34, arts and crafts teacher Sherborne Sch for Girls 1934-37, freelance illustrator and designer 1937-39, sr instr Coll of Art Gt Malvern 1939-41, supply teacher Edinburgh 1957-61; princ works incl: Dream Children, Funeral of Mozart, Babe Eternal, Jane Eyre, Hungarian Peasant Women, Precious Bane, Flight to Freedom and Peace, The Dream Cloud, Aconites in Duntisbourne; exhibitions incl: RA, RSA, RWA and other galleries; memb Cirencester Civic Soc; RWA 1987, ARCA 1933; *Style*— Mrs E G M Dinkel; 1 The Mead, Cirencester, Glos GL7 2BB (☎ 0285 653682)

DINKEL, Philip Charles Christian; s of late Ernest Michael Dinkel, and Emmy Dinkel; *b* 3 Oct 1946; *Educ* Ampleforth; *m* 3 Oct 1981, Lucia, *née* Stevens; 2 s (Henry b 1988, Theodore b 1990), 1 da; *Career* architect; Sir Hugh Casson project architect for Hobhouse Ct Trafalgar Square 1973-77 (Civic Trust award 1981), in private practice specialising in conservation work, commercial and residential 1977-; AA Year prize 1970; memb RIBA; *Recreations* the arts, cello, conservation matters; *Clubs* Roehampton, RAC; *Style*— Philip Dinkel, Esq; 4 Ravenna Rd, London SW15 6AW (☎ 071 789 6669, fax 071 789 6476)

DINKIN, Anthony David; s of Hyman Dinkin, of London, and Mary, *née* Hine; *b* 2 Aug 1944; *Educ* Henry Thornton GS Clapham, Coll of Estate Mgmnt Univ of London (BSc); *m* 20 Oct 1968, Derina Tanya, da of Benjamin Green; *Career* called to the Bar Lincolns Inn 1968, examiner in law Univ of Reading 1985, rec Crown Court 1989; memb Anglo-American Real Property Inst; *Recreations* gardening, theatre, music, travel; *Clubs* Players; *Style*— Anthony Dinkin, Esq; 8 New Sq, Lincolns Inn, London WC2 (☎ 071 242 4986, fax 071 405 1166)

DINSDALE, Reece; s of Alan Dinsdale, and Sally, *née* Walker; *b* 6 Aug 1959; *Educ* Normanton GS; *Career* actor; theatre appearances: Beethoven's Tenth (W End) 1983, Red Saturday (Royal Ct) 1984, Observe the Sons of Ulster (Hampstead) 1986, Woundings (Royal Exchange Manchester) 1986, Don Carlos (Royal Exchange Manchester) 1987, Old Years Eve (Royal Shakespeare Co) 1987-88, Boys Mean Business (Bush) 1989, Wild Oats (West Yorkshire Playhouse) 1990, Playboy of the Western World (West Yorkshire Playhouse) 1991; TV appearances: Threads (BBC) 1984, Home To Roost (YTV), Coppers (BBC) 1987, Storyteller 1987, Take Me Home 1988, Haggard (YTV), Young Catherine 1990; film appearances: Winter Flight 1984, A Private Function 1984; *Style*— Reece Dinsdale, Esq; Louis Hammond Management Ltd, Golden House, 29 Great Pulteney St, London W1R 3DD (☎ 071 734 1931)

DINWIDDIE, Ian Maitland; s of Lauderdale Maitland Dinwiddie (d 1978), and Frances Lilian Pedrick; *b* 8 Feb 1952; *Educ* Sherborne Sch Dorset, Exeter Univ (BA); *m* 1978, Sally Jane, da of Leslie Ronald Croydon; 1 s (Andrew b 1984), 1 da (Laura b 1981); *Career* audit mangr Arthur Young & Co 1972-82; fin controller Arbuthnot Savory Milln Hldgs Ltd 1982-86; gen mangr Savory Milln Ltd 1986; finance dir Arbuthnot Latham Bank Ltd 1987; *Recreations* sailing; *Style*— Ian Dinwiddie, Esq; Arbuthnot Latham Bank Ltd, 131 Finsbury Pavement, Moorgate, London EC2A 1AY (☎ 071 628 9876, fax 071 638 1545, telex 885970)

DINWIDDIE, Dr Robert; s of Noel Alexander Williamson Dinwiddie, of Dumfries, Scotland, and May Stirling, *née* Kennedy; *b* 23 Feb 1945; *Educ* Dumfries Acad, Univ of Aberdeen (MB ChB); *m* 23 Oct 1971, Mary McCalley, da of James Saunderson (d 1984), of Dumfries, Scotland; 1 s (Robert b 1973), 1 da (Jane b 1974); *Career* conslt paediatrician: Queen Charlotte's Maternity Hosp London 1977-86, the Hosp for Sick Children Gt Ormond St London 1977-; hon sr lectr Inst of Obstetrics and Gynaecology and Child Health Univ of London 1977-; scientific pubns on paediatric and neonatal problems esp cystic fibrosis and the chest, contrib Parents magazine; memb Cncl RSM, parent govr Rutlish Sch for Boys Merton Park London, hon med advsr Central London Branch Cystic Fibrosis Res Tst; pres: Section of Paediatrics RSM; memb: Br Paediatric Assoc, Neonatal Soc, DCH; FRCP; *Books* The Diagnosis and Management of Paediatric Respiratory Disease (1990); *Recreations* gardening, walking, running; *Clubs* RSM; *Style*— Dr Robert Dinwiddie; 1 Circle Gardens, Merton Park, London SW19 3JX; The Hospital For Sick Children, Great Ormond St, London WC1N 3JH (☎ 071 405 9200, fax 071 289 8643)

DIRKSE-VAN-SCHALKWYK, Hon Mrs ((Lilian) Anne Grenville); da of Rev Hon Louis Chandos Francis Temple Morgan-Grenville, Master of Kinloss (d 1944) and yr sis of Lady Kinloss, *qv* (raised to the rank of a Baron's da 1947); *b* 8 June 1924; *m* 1, 25 Jan 1951, Ernest Frederick Harris, CBE (d 1965); m 2, 10 June 1965, Maurice Emile Deen (d 1971); m 3, 1973, Willem Dirkse-van-Schalkwyk (retired S African ambass to Canada, France and Italy); *Style*— The Hon Mrs Dirkse-van-Schalkwyk; 26 Boulevard des Moulins, Monte Carlo, MC 98000, Monaco

DISCHE, Dr Frederick Ephraim; s of Harry Dische (d 1972), of Ilford, Essex, and Lilian, *née* Fogel; *b* 8 March 1924; *Educ* Ilford Co HS Essex, Middx Hosp Med Sch (MB BS, MD); *m* 6 Sept 1953, Sylvia, da of Louis Goldberg (d 1932), of SA; 1 s (Geoffrey b 1954), 1 da (Rosalind b 1957); *Career* Nat Serv MO, Flt Lt RAF 1948-50;

conslt histopathology Dulwich and King's Coll Hosps London 1958-89, hon sr lectr in pathology King's Coll Sch of Med and Dentistry and Inst of Urology Univ of London; recognised teacher Univ of London, examiner in pathology RCS and RCP; FRCPath 1970, FRCP 1977; *Books* Concise Renal pathology (1987); *Recreations* fellwalking, skiing, mountain biking, photography; *Style—* Dr Frederick Dische; c/o Midland Bank plc, 66 Lordship Lane, East Dulwich, London SE22 8HL

DISLEY, John Ivor; CBE (1979); s of Harold Disley, and Marie Hughes; *b* 20 Nov 1928; *Educ* Oswestry HS, Loughborough Coll; *m* 1958, Sylvia Cheeseman; 2 da; *Career* former Br steeplechase record holder and former Welsh mile record holder; Bronze Medal winner Helsinki Olympics 1952, Sportsman of the Year 1955; vice chm Sports Cncl 1974-82; dir: London Marathon Ltd, Reebok UK Ltd, Silva UK Ltd; memb Royal Cmmn on Gambling; *Books* Tackle Climbing, Orienteering, Expedition Guide, Your way with Map & Compass; *Recreations* mountaineering, running; *Clubs* Climbers, Ranelagh Harriers; *Style—* John Disley, Esq, CBE; Hampton House, Upper Sunbury Rd, Hampton, Middlesex (☎ 081 979 1707)

DISPENZA, Adriano; s of Mario Dispenza, of St Laurent du Var, France, and Lina, *née* Inzirillo; *b* 24 Sept 1948; *Educ* Queen Mary Coll (BSc), Paris (Dip Faculte de Droit et Sciences Economiques); *m* 12 March 1979, Rallia Jean, da of John Adam Hadjipateras, of Greece; 1 da (Carolina b 5 March 1981); *Career* Morgan Grenfell & Co Ltd 1973-77, Amex Bank Ltd 1977-79, md First Chicago Ltd 1979-88, exec dir Merrill Lynch Int Ltd; *Recreations* reading, travel, crosswords; *Clubs* RAC; *Style—* Adriano Dispenza, Esq; Merrill Lynch Int Ltd, Ropemaker Place, 25 Ropemaker St, London EC2Y 9LY (☎ 071 867 4882, fax 071 867 4455); Via Manzoni 31, 10121 Milano, Italy (☎ 02 2900 1178, fax 02 2900 2899)

DISS, Eileen (Mrs Raymond Everett); da of Thomas Alexander Diss, and Winifred, *née* Irvine; *b* 13 May 1931; *Educ* Ilford Co HS, Central Sch of Art and Design; *m* 18 Sept 1953, Raymond Terence Everett, s of Elmo Terence Everett; 2 s (Timothy Patrick b 1959, Matthew Simon Thomas b 1964), 1 da (Danielle Claire b 1956); *Career* BBC TV designer 1952-59, freelance designer 1959-; TV designs for BBC incl: Maigret, Cider with Rosie; TV designs for ITV incl: The Prime of Miss Jean Brodie, Porterhouse Blue, Jeeves and Wooster; theatre designs for Nat Theatre and W End Theatres; feature films: A Doll's House, Betrayal, 84 Charing Cross Road, A Handful of Dust; BAFTA awards 1961, 1965, 1974; RDI, FRSA; *Style—* Miss Eileen Diss; 4 Gloucester Walk, London W8 4HZ (☎ 071 937 8794)

DITTMERS, Manuel Ludwig; s of Helmuth Dittmers (film dir), and Karin, *née* Volquartz (former actress); descends from one of the five oldest German families, Margrave of Dithmarschen (Theutmarsi) since 4 Sep 929; *b* 15 April 1961; *Educ* LSH-Holzminden, Studio Sch Cambridge, Davies's Tutorial Coll London, Mander Portmann Woodward London, Eurocentre Paris, Univ of Nice, Univ of Lille, Univ of Buckingham, US Int Univ (BA, MEd), LSE (MSc); *Career* Dimen Corp: conslt 1985-86, mgmnt conslt 1986-87, sr mgmnt conslt 1987-89, sr strategic mgmnt conslt 1990, head of corp strategy 1991-; fndr of World Wide Peace 1984 (registered in 92 countries) responsible for Middle East Peace Plan 1986, Amazonas & Sahara World Park Project 1987, World Citizen Passport 1989, fndr of WWP Animal Rights 1987; memb: PEN 1987, Convocation Univ of London 1990-; helmsman in 122 races (9 Nat, 2 Euro, 4 World Championships) winning 38; FRSA 1990, MBIM 1990, PHI DELTA KAPPAN San Diego Chapter 1989; *Books* Charter of World-Wide-Peace (1984), The Green Party in West Germany (1986), World and Environment (1989), Impressions of Fuerteventura (1990), European Poems (1990), Crisis Management (1991), Sieseby und Schwansen (1991); *Recreations* sailing, golf, motor racing, photography, painting; *Clubs* Royal Ocean Racing, Silverstone Racing, LSH-Bund, Norddeutscher Regatta Verein, Alster Piraten; *Style—* Manuel Dittmers, Esq; 4 Remus House, Castle St, Buckingham MK18 1BS (☎ 0280 815859, fax 0280 824080)

DIVER, Hon Sir Leslie Charles; s of J W Diver; *b* 4 Nov 1899; *m* 1, 1922, Emma, *née* Blakiston; 1 s, 2 da; *m* 2, 1971, Mrs Thelma Evans; *Career* farmer and grazier; memb Legislative Cncl WA (Co Pty) for Central Province 1952-74, pres Legislative Cncl WA 1960-74; kt 1975; *Recreations* bowls; *Clubs* Manning Memorial Bowling; *Style—* The Hon Sir Leslie Diver; 48 Sulman Ave, Salter Point, Como, WA 6152, Australia

DIX, Alan Michael; OBE (1985); s of late Cdr Charles Cabry Dix, CMG, DSO, RN, and Ebba Sievers; *b* 29 June 1922; *Educ* Stenhus Kostskole Denmark; *m* 1955, Helen Catherine McLaren; 1 s, 1 da; *Career* escaped from Nazi occupied Denmark to Scotland 1943; cmmnd RAF 1944; pres Capitol Car Distribs Inc USA 1958-67, gp vice pres Volkswagen of America 1967-68, md Volkswagen (GB) Ltd 1968-72, pres Mid-Atlan Toyota Inc USA 1972-73, dir of mktg BL Int 1973-74, proprietor Alan M Dix Assocs 1974-76, chm Motor Agents Pensions Admins Ltd 1976-85, dir HP Info Ltd 1977-85, dir-gen The Motor Agents Assoc Ltd London 1976-85; contrib to auto trade jnls; King Christian X War Medal 1947; Freeman and Liveryman Worshipful Co of Coachmakers and Coach Harness-Makers 1980; FMI, FInstM, FIMH, FBIM; *Recreations* yachting, photography, study of professional mgmnt (int speaker on mgmnt and orgn); *Clubs* Danish, RAF, Burkes, RAF Yacht (Hamble); *Style—* Alan Dix, Esq, OBE; Tigh Na Failte, 1 Firhills, Letham Grange, nr Arbroath, Angus DD11 YRL Scotland (☎ 0241 89421)

DIX, Anthony Arthur William; JP (Wimbledon 1981); s of Lt-Col Harold A G Dix (d 1961), of Charlwood, and Olga A J, *née* Appleby (d 1989); *b* 5 Nov 1930; *Educ* Tonbridge, Univ of London (BSc Econ), Brünel Univ (MA); *m* 18 July 1959, Ellen; 3 da (Angela b 1960, Bettina b 1961, Catherine b 1964); *Career* Nat Serv 2 Lt KAR 1950; called to the Bar Lincoln's Inn 1956; memb Stock Exchange 1962; Parly candidate: (Lib) S Kensington 1964, (Lab) Bridlington 1974; princ S Chelsea Coll 1985-89; Bd of Visitors Wandsworth Prison, Howard League; treas New Bridge; *Recreations* sailing; *Style—* Anthony Dix, Esq, JP; 9 Margin Drive, Wimbledon, London SW19 (☎ 081 946 1479); Keith Bayley Rogers & Co, 93-95 Borough High St, London SE1 1NL (☎ 071 378 0657)

DIX, Prof Gerald Bennett; s of Cyril Dix (d 1984), and Mabel Winifred, *née* Bennett (d 1970); *b* 12 Jan 1926; *Educ* Altrincham GS, Univ of Manchester (BA, Dip TP), Harvard (Master Landscape Arch); *m* 1, 1956 (m dis 1963); 2 s (Stephen b 1957, Graham b 1959); m 2, 1963, Lois, da of John Noel Nichols (d 1966); 1 da (Kate b 1964); *Career* RAF 1944-47; asst lectr Univ of Manchester 1951-53 (studio asst in arch 1950-51), chief asst to Sir Patrick Abercrombie and city planning offr Addis A 1954-56, sr planning offr Singapore 1957-59, acting planning advsr Singapore 1959, sr res fell Ghana 1959-63, sr planner BRS/ODA UK Govt 1963-65, prof of planning Univ of Nottingham 1970-75 (lectr then sr lectr 196 Univ of Liverpool: Lever prof 1978-88, pro vice chllr 1984-87, hon sr fell 1988-; memb: E Midlands Econ Planning Cncl 1973-75, Historic Areas Advsy Ctee English Heritage 1986-88; pres World Soc for Ekistics 1987-91; ARIBA 1950-87, FRTPI; *Books* Ecology and Ekistics (ed, 1977), Third World Planning Review (fndr ed, 1978-90); *Recreations* travel, photography; *Clubs* Athenaeum; *Style—* Prof Gerald Dix; 13 Friars Quay, Norwich NR3 1ES (☎ 0603 632 433); Dept of Civic Design, Univ of Liverpool, P O Box 147, Liverpool L69 3BX (☎ 051 794 3121, fax 051 708 6502, telex 62709 UNILPL G)

DIX, Wing Cdr Kenneth John Weeks; OBE (1975), AFC (1958), QC (1967); s of Eric John Dix (d 1982), of Dorset, and Kate, *née* Weeks; *b* 12 Sept 1930; *Educ* HMC Canford Dorset, RAF Colls Cranwell, Bracknell, Manby (PSC, AWC); *m* 1, 1963 (m dis); m 2, 19 July 1969, Susan Mary, da of Lt Cdr C Sharp (d 1954); 1 s (Michael b 1956), 1 da (Linda b 1954); *Career* RAF 1948-83 (Europe, ME, Far E, USA), ret with rank of Wing Cdr; business devpt mangr of electronic def systems and mil advsr Marconi Def Systems Ltd, specialist in aviation, navigation, weapons and reconnaissance systems, dir Electronic Def Assoc; represented RAF and Combined Servs at rugby and athletics; Queens Commendation 1967; MRAes, MBIM, MIEE, memb BHS; *Recreations* fly fishing, horse riding, shooting, study antiques; *Clubs* RAF; *Style—* Wing Cdr Kenneth J W Dix, OBE, AFC, QC, RAF (ret); 41 Lincoln Park, Amersham, Bucks (☎ 0494 72 5562); Marconi Def Systems, The Grove, Warren Lane, Stanmore, Middx (☎ 081 954 2311)

DIXIE, Lady (Dorothy Penelope); da of E King-Kirkman; *m* 7 Dec 1950, as his 2 wife, Sir (Alexander Archibald Douglas) Wolstan Dixie, 13 Bt (d 1975, when title became dormant or extinct); 2 da (Eleanor b 1952, Caroline b 1960); *Style—* Lady Dixie; Bosworth Park, Leics

DIXON, Prof Anthony Frederick George (Tony); s of George Edward Dixon (d 1988), and Rose Emma, *née* Middlemiss (d 1986); *b* 4 May 1932; *Educ* E Ham GS, UCL (BSc), Jesus Coll Oxford (DPhil); *m* 20 Aug 1957, (Theodora) June, da of Michael Phil Theodore White, of E Harling, Norfolk; 1 s (Keith b 1965), 1 da (Fiona b 1963); *Career* sr lectr Univ of Glasgow 1969-74 (asst lectr 1957-59, lectr 1959-69, prof of biology Univ of East Anglia 1974-; MBES 1952, FIBiol 1975, FRES 1979; *Books* Biology of Aphids (1973), Simulation of Lime Aphid Population Dynamics (with ND Barlow, 1980), Cereal Aphid Populations: Biology Simulation and Prediction (with N Carter and R Rabbinge, 1982), Aphid Ecology (1985); *Recreations* reading; *Style—* Prof Tony Dixon; 20 Newfound Drive, Cringleford, Norwich, Norfolk NR4 7RY; School of Biological Sciences, University of East Anglia, Norwich NR4 7TJ (☎ 0603 592260, telex 975334)

DIXON, Dr Bernard; s of Ronald Dixon (d 1962), and Grace Peirson; *b* 17 July 1938; *Educ* Queen Elizabeth GS Darlington, King's Coll Univ of Durham (BSc), Univ of Newcastle upon Tyne (PhD); *m* 1963 (m dis 1987), Margaret Helena Charlton; 2 s, 1 da; *Career* formerly res fell Univ of Newcastle, dep ed World Medicine 1966-68; ed New Scientist 1969-79 (dep ed 68-69); European ed: The Sciences 1980-85, Science 1980-86, The Scientist 1986-89; Biotechnology 1989-, ed Med Sci Res 1989-; columnist Br Med Jl, Biotec (Italy); conslt ed Scientific Research in Europe project; memb Bd Speculations in Sci and Technol, Mircen Jl; vice pres Gen Section Br Assoc for Advancement of Sci, vice chm Cncl for Sci and Soc; memb Cncl: Panos Inst London, European Environmental Res Organisation; memb Bd Edinburgh Int Festival; CSS (1982); FIBiol (1982) CBiol (1984); *Books* What is Science For (1973), Beyond the Magic Bullet (1978), Invisible Allies (1976), Health and the Human Body (1986), Ideas of Science (1984), How Science Works (1989), Science and Society (1989), From Creation to Chaos (1989); *Style—* Dr Bernard Dixon; 139 Cornwall Rd, Ruislip Manor, Middx HA4 6AW (☎ 0895 632 390)

DIXON, Bernard Tunbridge; s of Archibald Tunbridge Dixon; *b* 1928; *Educ* Owen's Sch, UCL (LLB); *m* 1962, Jessie Netta Watson, *née* Hastie; 1 s, 3 da; *Career* admitted slr 1952; former ptnr Dixon & Co, sr legal asst with Charity Cmmrs 1970-74, dep charity cmmr 1975-81, charity cmmr 1981-84; *Style—* Bernard Dixon, Esq; T J Smith & Son, 14 Castle St, Liverpool L2 0SG

DIXON, Brian Ringrose; s of Reginald Ernest Dixon (d 1978), of Market Weighton, and Marianne, *née* Ringrose; *b* 4 Jan 1938; *Educ* Pocklington Sch; *m* 8 Oct 1966, Mary Annette, da of Sidney Robertson (d 1982), of Hawick; 2 s (James b 1971, John b 1973); *Career* Barclays Bank plc: asst mangr Scarborough 1971-73, asst mangr Grimsby 1973-76, asst dist mangr York dist 1976-79, mangr Berwick upon Tweed 1979-83, regnl dir Scot 1983-; bd dir Strathclyde Innovation; cncl memb Scot Enterprise Fndn; memb: Governing Cncl Scot Business in the Community, Royal Highland and Agric Soc of Scot; ACIB; *Recreations* rugby, cricket; *Style—* Brian R Dixon, Esq; 90 St Vincent St, Glasgow G2 5UB (☎ 041 221 9585, fax 041 221 1714, telex 777286)

DIXON, Christopher John Arnold; TD; s of Hubert John Dixon, MC (d 1972), of Wimbledon, and Mary Frances (d 1958); *b* 17 Aug 1928; *Educ* Rugby; *m* 8 Oct 1955, Ethelwyn Ada, da of Lt-Col J H Mousley, DSO, TD (d 1959), of Middleton Tyas, Yorks; 3 s (Anthony b 1958, Timothy b 1962, Michael b 1963), 1 da (Phyllida b 1960); *Career* Nat Serv and Short Serv Cmmn 2 Lt RA 1947-50, Maj TA 1951-60; Norton Rose 1951-88: ptnr 1960-81, dep sr ptnr 1981-; memb Law Soc 1955; *Recreations* sailing; *Clubs* City Univ, RA Yacht; *Style—* Christopher Dixon, Esq, TD; Norton Rose, Kempson House, Camomile St, London EC3A 7AN (☎ 071 283 2434, fax 071 588 1181, telex 883652)

DIXON, Colin Steele; s of Oliver Colin Dixon, MBE, TD, of The Four Winds, Thorsway, Caldy, Wirral, and Kathleen Mary, da of Peter Gray; ggf founded paper firm of L S Dixon & Co Ltd 1876; *b* 3 May 1952; *Educ* Ampleforth; *m* 16 Aug 1975, Penelope Jane, da of Wing-Cdr James Eric Storrar, DFC, AFC, AE, of The Tower House, Chester; 1 s (Charles Lanty b 1985), 2 da (Rozanne, Laura b (twins) 1980); *Career* md L S Dixon Gp Ltd 1987, chm Walter Scott Motors; dir: Slater Harrison Co Ltd, Dean Valley Ltd; *Recreations* racing, shooting, tennis; *Clubs* Turf; *Style—* Colin Dixon, Esq; The Old Post House, Woodmancott, nr Winchester, Hants SO21 3BL (☎ 025 675 541)

DIXON, David Michael; CVO (1991); s of Rev James Eric Dixon, MC (d 1955), of Surrey, and Florence, *née* Pye (d 1980); *b* 1 May 1926; *Educ* Whitgift Sch, Univ of Oxford (MA), Harvard Law Sch; *m* 1953, Alison Mary, da of Sir Leonard Sinclair (d 1984), of Surrey; 2 s, 1 da; *Career* RAFVR 1944-47; slr, conslt Withers 1991- (ptnr 1957-90, sr ptnr 1982-86), hon legal advsr Br Olympic Assoc 1977-; hon sec Cwlth Games Fedn 1982-; chm ELF UK plc; *Recreations* sport, travel; *Clubs* Brooks's, Hurlingham, Achilles, Vincent's; *Style—* David Dixon, Esq, CVO; 10 Peek Crescent, London SW19 5ER (☎ 081 946 4125); Mains of Panholes, Blackford, Perthshire (☎ 076 482 351); 197 Knightsbridge, London SW7 1RZ (☎ 071 225 5555, telex 919156, fax 071 225 5197)

DIXON, Donald; MP (Lab) Jarrow 1979-; s of late Christopher Albert Dixon, and Jane Dixon; *b* 6 March 1929; *Educ* Ellison Street Elementary Sch Jarrow; *m* Doreen Morad; 1 s, 1 da; *Career* shipyard worker 1947-74, branch sec GMWU 1974-79, cllr S Tyneside MDC 1963-; *Style—* Donald Dixon, Esq, MP; 1 Hillcrest, Jarrow, Tyne and Wear NE32 4DP (☎ 0632 897635)

DIXON, Hugh Hume; CBE; s of Clement Dixon, of NZ, and Mary Emmeline, *née* Hume; *b* 9 Oct 1902; *Educ* Milton Sch Bulawayo Rhodesia, Rhodes Univ Coll Grahamstown SA, Rugby Tech Coll Night Sch, Oriel Coll Oxford (MA); *Career* apprentice British Thomson-Houston Co Rugby 1920-22, Rhodes scholar 1922-25, pupil of Henry Howard Humphreys 1925-27, asst engr and res engr 1927-30, dep res engr 1930-36 (N Wales viaduct and tunnels) , res engr Haifa Palestine Water Supply Investigation 1936-37, sr engr and res engr 1936-39, engrg inspr Dept of Health Scotland 1939-45, ptnr Howard Humphreys & Sons (ptnr responsible for various nat and int projects 1945-68, sr ptnr on ret 1968, conslt 1968-73, chief res engr for construction of Lefkara Dam and Kirokiti Water Treatment Works Cyprus 1971-74, helped Cyprus Nat Ctee on Large Dams to organise an ICOLD study tour 1974; main fields of interest: siting of and design of large dams and the associated hydrology and soil mechanics, roads, bridges, tunnels; numerous tech papers in professional jls and at confs; memb Panel Inst of Engrs qualified under Reservoirs (Safety Provisions) 1930, chm BNCOLD 1968-71, rep Br Ctee on Large Dams Cncl of Br Nat Ctee of Irrigation and Drainage, memb cncl ACE, island chm UK Citizens Assoc Cyprus 1974-75, vice pres for Eur ICOLD 1971-74; fell: American Soc of Civil Engrs, Rhodesian Inst of Engrs, Inst of Pub Health Engrs; memb: Br Geotech Soc, Jamaican Inst of Engrs, E African Inst of Engrs, ACE; FICE (George Stephenson Gold Medal), FIWES, FInstHE, CEng, FRSA; *Recreations* rugby, cricket, rowing, tennis; *Style*— Hugh Dixon, Esq, CBE; Woodbury House, Jouldings Lane, Farley Hill, Reading, Berks RG7 1UR

DIXON, Ian Leonard; CBE (1991); s of late Leonard Frank Dixon; *b* 3 Nov 1938; *Educ* S W Essex Co Tech Sch, Harvard Business Sch; *m* 1961, Valerie Diana, da of late Alexander Barclay; 2 s, 1 da; *Career* chartered builder; jt chm and chief exec Willmott Dixon Ltd 1971-, cncllr Beds 1977-85, tstee The Bedford Charity 1977-86; chm: N Herts Health Authy 1984-87, CBI Eastern Region 1988-90, Riverside Health Authy 1990-; pres Chartered Inst of Bldg 1989-90, Beds Trg and Enterprise Cncl 1990-; FCIOB, CBIM, FRSA; *Recreations* shooting, philately; *Clubs* The Carlton; *Style*— Ian Dixon, Esq, CBE; Penthouse, No1 Bickenhall Mansions, Bickenhall Street, London W1H 3LB

DIXON, James Wolryche; s of late Michael Wolryche Dixon, of Withy Fold, Cook's Corner, Crowborough, Sussex, and Barbara Mary, *née* Eccles; *b* 20 Feb 1948; *Educ* Lancing, CCC Oxford (MA); *Career* RAFVR actg PO Univ of Oxford Air Sqdn 1966-69; articled with Barton Mayhew & Co 1969, ptnr Ernst & Young 1984-; FCA 1972, FRSA 1988; *Books* Vat Guide and Casebook (conslt ed, 1 edn), Tax Case Analysis (contrib), Vat Planning (contrib); *Recreations* cycling, photography, bridge, cooking; *Clubs* United Oxford and Cambridge Univ; *Style*— James Dixon, Esq; 48 Lytton Grove, Putney, London SW15 2HE (☎ 081 788 6717); Ernst & Young, Becket House, 1 Lambeth Palace Rd, London SE1 7EU (☎ 071 928 2000, fax 071 928 1345)

DIXON, John Graham; s of Francis Brian Dixon (d 1985), of Bramhall, Cheshire, and Doris Brenda, *née* Leigh; *b* 2 July 1946; *Educ* The King's Sch Macclesfield; *Career* CA; Thornton Baker (now Grant Thornton) Manchester 1964-70; Peat Marwick Mitchell (now KPMG Peat Marwick McLintock): London 1971-74, Manchester 1974-, ptnr 1976; pres Lancashire and Cheshire Fauna Soc; FCA; *Recreations* ornithology, golf; *Clubs* St James's (Manchester), Manchester Literary and Philosphical Soc; *Style*— John Dixon, Esq; KPMG Peat Marwick McLintock, 7 Tib Lane, Manchester M2 6DS (☎ 061 832 4221, fax 061 832 7265)

DIXON, John Watts; s of John David Dixon, of Liverton, Devon, and Carol Emmie Lucinda Dixon, JP, *née* Watts; *b* 27 Sept 1951; *Educ* Harrow, The Queen's Coll Oxford (MA); *m* 11 Oct 1980, Catherine Barbara, da of Guy Neville Borton, of Penshurst, Kent; 3 da (Annabel b 1982, Elizabeth b 1985, Sarah b 1988); *Career* called to the Bar 1975, memb Hon Soc of the Middle Temple; Freeman City of London 1977; *Recreations* gardening; *Style*— John W Dixon, Esq; 2 Harcourt Buildings, Temple, London EC4Y 9DB (☎ 071 353 6961, fax 071 353 6968)

DIXON, Sir Jonathan Mark; 4 Bt (UK 1919), of Astle, Chelford, Co Palatine of Chester; s of Capt Nigel Dixon, OBE, RN (d 1978), and Margaret Josephine, da of late Maurice John Collett; suc unc, Sir John George Dixon, 3 Bt (d 1990); *b* 1 Sept 1949; *Educ* Winchester, Oxford Univ (MA); *m* 1978, Patricia Margaret, da of James Baird Smith; 2 s (Mark Edward b 1982, Timothy Nigel b 1987), 1 da (Katherine Anne b 1980); *Heir* s, Mark Edward Dixon b 29 June 1982; *Recreations* fishing; *Style*— Sir Jonathan Dixon, Bt; 19 Clyde Road, Bristol BS6 6RJ

DIXON, Kenneth Herbert Morley; s of Arnold Morley Dixon (d 1975); *b* 19 Aug 1929; *Educ* Cranbrook Sch Sydney Aust, Univ of Manchester (BA), Harvard Business Sch (AMP); *m* 1955, Patricia Oldbury, *née* Whalley; 2 s (Michael, Giles b 1969); *Career* Lt Royal Signals BAOR Cyprus 1947-49; Calico Printers Association Ltd 1952-56; Rowntree & Co: joined 1956, mktg UK Confectionery Div 1966, dir Rowntree Mackintosh Ltd and dep chm UK Confectionery Div 1970, chm UK Confectionery Div 1973, dep chm Rowntree Mackintosh Ltd 1978, chm Rowntree Mackintosh plc (Rowntree plc from 1987) 1981-89; vice chm Legal and General Group plc 1986- (dir 1984-), dir Yorkshire Television Holdings plc 1989-, dep chm Bass PLC 1990- (dir 1988-); memb: Cncl for Indust and Higher Educn 1986-, Cncl Nat Forum for Mgmnt Educn and Devpt 1987-; pt/t memb British Railways Bd 1990-; Univ of York: memb Hon Degrees Cteee 1983-, memb Fin Ctee 1986, chm Jt Ctee on Jarratt Report 1986, memb Policy and Resources Ctee 1987-, memb Ctee on Appts to Court and Cncl 1988-, pro chllr 1987-, chm Cncl 1990 (memb Cncl 1983); chm Open Univ Visiting Ctee 1990; FRSA, CBIM; *Recreations* reading, music, fell walking; *Style*— Kenneth Dixon, Esq; c/o PO Box 206, York YO1 1XY (☎ 0904 612261)

DIXON, (James) Maurice Dixon; s of William Dixon (d 1988), and Mary, *née* Sunter; *b* 29 Sept 1936; *Educ* Queen Elizabeth GS, Kirkby Lonsdale, Coll of Electronics Malvern, Univ of Southampton; *m* Janet Kathleen, da of Frederick Elcox (d 1958); 1 s (Andrew John), 2 da (Lynne Julia, Helen Sara (Mrs Shambrook); *Career* design engr Kelvin Hughes 1959-61, sr design engr (chief inspector, prodn controller, engrg mangr), Kollsman Instrument Ltd 1961-71 (responsible for design of aircraft instruments incl Concorde), exec director Penny and Giles Int plc 1971-; md Penny & Giles Transducers Ltd; chm: Penny & Giles Avionic Systems Ltd, Penny & Giles Sensors & Systems Ltd, Graham N Russell Precision Ltd; govr Grange Comp Sch Christchurch, memb Ctee Highcliffe jr choir; MIEE 1962, MI Mech E 1969, FBIM 1985, CEng; *Recreations* walking, gardening, old cars, photography; *Style*— Maurice Dixon, Esq; Heathside, Manchester Road, Sway, Lymington, Hants SO41 6AS; 4 Airfield Way, Christchurch, Dorset BH23 3TH (☎ 0202 476621, telex 41566, fax 0202 470070)

DIXON, Hon Peter Herbert; s of 2 Baron Glentoran; *b* 15 May 1948; *Educ* Eton, Grenoble Univ; *m* 1975, Jane Blanch, da of Eric Cutler; 2 da (Louise Vyvyan Mary b 1977, Rose Clare b 1980); *Career* chartered accountant; *Recreations* tennis, shooting; *Clubs* Boodle's; *Style*— The Hon Peter Dixon; The Old Rectory, Yattendon, Newbury, Berks

DIXON, Peter John; s of George Edward Dixon, and Violet Jose, *née* Bell; *b* 4 Feb 1949; *Educ* King Edward VI GS, Wellingborough GS, LSE (BSc), London Inst of Educn (postgrad CertEd), Brunel Univ (MEd); *m* 28 July 1973, (Elizabeth) Susan, da of Joseph Arthur Butterworth; 2 s (Simon Peter b 29 Sept 1979, Nicholas Jonathan b 8 Nov 1981); *Career* head of history and integrated studies Hayes Co GS 1972-80, chef and proprietor White Moss House Cumbria 1980-; winner of food and wine awards in all leading guide books; Master Chef of GB; *Recreations* walking, squash, wine tasting, bridge, chess; *Style*— Peter Dixon, Esq; White Moss House, Rydal Water, Grasmere, Cumbria LA22 9SE (☎ 09665 295)

DIXON, Peter Richard Hamilton; ERD (1963); s of Arthur Frederick William Dixon, CSI, CIE (d 1947), of Church Crookham, Hants, and Gwendolen Mary, *née* Hamilton (d 1952); *b* 3 Oct 1931; *Educ* Shrewsbury, Christs Coll Cambridge (MA, LLB); *m* 17 Dec 1966, Christine Mary, da of Alderman Edward Francis Gethin (d 1959), of Shrewsbury; 1 s (John Peter Christian b 25 Jan 1970); *Career* Nat Serv RCS 1950-52, army emergency res RCS 1952-70, 81 Signal Sqdn OC (V) 1967-70 (Hon Col (V) 1981-87); slr 1959; sr ptnr Radcliffes & Co 1982-90 (ptnr 1961-90); Liveryman Worshipful Co of Makers of Playing Cards, memb Soc of Knights of the Round Table; memb Law Soc 1959; *Recreations* rowing, travel; *Clubs* East India, Leander; *Style*— Peter Dixon, Esq, ERD; 25 Victoria Grove, London W8 5RW (☎ 071 584 7954); Flat C2, The Court, St Mary's Place, Shrewsbury; 15 Great College St, Westminster, London SW1P 3SJ (☎ 071 222 7040)

DIXON, Peter Vibart; s of Meredith Vibart Dixon (d 1967), of Surrey, and Phyllis Joan, *née* Hemingway (d 1982); *b* 16 July 1932; *Educ* Radley, King's Coll Cambridge (MA); *m* 1955, Elizabeth Anne Howie, da of Dr Max Davison (d 1970), of Surrey; 3 s (Patrick, Henry, Nigel); *Career* Nat Serv RA 1950-51; various posts in: HM Treasy, Office of the Lord Privy Seal, Colonial Office, Civil Serv Cmmn; econ cncllr Br Embassy Washington 1972-75, press sec and head of Info Div HM Treasy 1975-78, under sec (industl policy) HM Treasy 1978-82, sec to NEDC 1982-87; dir of planning and admin Turner Kenneth Brown (slrs) 1987-; FRSA, FBIM; memb Royal Inst of Public Admin; *Clubs* Utd Oxford & Cambridge Univ; *Style*— Peter Dixon, Esq; 17 Lauriston Rd, Wimbledon, London SW19 4TJ (☎ 081 946 8931); 100 Fetter Lane, London EC4A 1DD (☎ 071 242 6006)

DIXON, Piers; s of Sir Pierson Dixon (d 1965), by his w (Alexandra) Ismène (d 1987); *b* 20 Dec 1928; *Educ* Eton, Magdalene Coll Cambridge (MA), Harvard Business Sch; *m* 1, 1960 (m dis 1973), Edwina, da of Lord Duncan-Sandys; 2 s (Mark, Hugo); m 2, 1976 (m dis 1981), Janet, wid of 5th Earl Cowley and da of Ramiah Doraswamy Aiya, of Wales; m 3, 1984, Anne, da of John Cronin; 1 s (Piers b 1981); *Career* 2 Lt Grenadier Gds 1948-49; merchant banking London and NY 1954-64, ptnr Sheppards and Chase (stockbrokers) 1964-81, MP (C) Truro 1970-74, sec Cons Backbenchers' Finance Ctee 1970-71 (vice chm 1972-74); sponsor Rehabilitation of Offenders Act 1974; *Books* Double Diploma (1968), Cornish Names (1973); *Recreations* tennis, modern history; *Clubs* Beefsteak, Brooks's, Pratt's; *Style*— Piers Dixon, Esq; 22 Ponsonby Terrace, London SW1 (☎ 071 821 6166, telex 895 1859 BASIL G)

DIXON, Prof Richard Newland; s of Robert Thomas Dixon (d 1985), of Borough Green, Kent, and Lilian, *née* Newland (d 1973); *b* 25 Dec 1930; *Educ* Judd Sch Kent, Kings Coll London (BSc), St Catharines Coll Cambridge (PhD, ScD); *m* 18 Sept 1954, Alison Mary, da of Gilbert Arnold Birks (d 1966), of Horsforth, Leeds; 1 s (Paul b 1959), 2 da (Joan b 1961, Sheila b 1962); *Career* post doctoral fell Nat Res Cncl of Canada 1957-59, ICI fell lectr in chem Univ of Sheffield 1959-69, Sorby res fell Univ of Sheffield 1964-69, pro-vice chllr Univ of Bristol 1989- (prof of chem 1969-, dean of sci 1979-82), visiting scholar Stanford Univ USA 1982-83; memb: Faraday Cncl of Royal Soc of Chem (vice pres 1989-), SERC Ctees; CChem 1976, FRSC 1976, FRS 1986; *Books* Spectroscopy and Structure (1965), Theoretical Chemistry (Vol 1 1971, Vol 2 1973, Vol 3 1975); *Recreations* mountain walking, travel, theatre, concerts, photography; *Style*— Prof Richard Dixon, FRS; 22 Westbury Lane, Bristol BS9 2PE (☎ 0272 681691); School of Chemistry, University of Bristol, Cantock's Close, Bristol BS8 1TS (☎ 0272 303030 ex 4270)

DIXON, Hon (Thomas) Robin Valerian; MBE (1969), DL (1979); er s of 2 Baron Glentoran, KBE, PC, *qv*, and Lady Diana Wellesley, da of 3 Earl Cowley; *b* 21 April 1935; *Educ* Eton; *m* 1, 12 Jan 1959 (m dis 1975), Rona, da of Capt George C Colville, of Bishop's Waltham; 3 s; m 2, 1979 (m dis 1988), Alwyn Gillian, da of Hubert A Mason, of Donaghadee Co Down; m 3, 1990, Margaret Anne Murphy; *Career* 2 Lt Grenadier Gds 1954, Capt 1958, Maj 1966; md Redland of N Ireland 1972-; *Recreations* sailing (yacht 'Lazy Life'), squash, skiing; *Clubs* Kildare St Univ (Dublin); *Style*— The Hon Robin Dixon, MBE, DL; Drumadarragh House, Ballyclare, Co Antrim, N Ireland; c/o Redland of N Ireland Ltd, 61 Largy Rd, Crumlin, Co Antrim, N Ireland BT29 4RR (☎ 084 94 22791)

DIXON, Roger Harry Vernon; s of Thomas Frank Dixon (d 1943), of Letchworth, Hertfordshire, and Marjorie, *née* Vernon (d 1985); *b* 19 June 1929; *Educ* Christ's Hosp Sch, St Catharine's Coll (open exhibition, BA, MA); *m* 18 June 1955, Mary Kathleen, da of Roderick James Barr; 1 s (David Anthony James b 30 April 1956), 2 da (Jill Elizabeth (Mrs Shepherd) b 9 Dec 1958, Ann Katherine b 9 Oct 1961); *Career* Travers Smith Braithwaite (solicitors): articled clerk 1953-57, asst slr 1957-61, ptnr 1962-; Freeman of City of London; City of London Solicitors Co: Liveryman, memb Ct, sr warden; memb: Law Soc, Int Bar Assoc; *Recreations* travel, music, theatre; *Clubs* City of London, MCC; *Style*— Roger Dixon, Esq; Travers Smith Braithwaite, 10 Snow Hill, London EC1A 2AL (☎ 071 248 9133, fax 071 236 3728)

DIXON, Roy; s of Tom Dixon (d 1972), and Gladys, *née* Walsh (d 1988); *b* 9 Feb 1938; *Educ* King William's Coll IOM; *m* 25 March 1961, Shirley; 1 s (Andrew b 1964), 1 da (Amanda b 1962); *Career* slr; md Poco Properties Ltd 1972-86, dir McArd Holdings Ltd 1986-; *Recreations* motor sports, skiing; *Style*— Roy Dixon, Esq; Newhaven Shore Rd, Port St Mary, IOM (☎ 0624 832233); Church Rd, Port Erin, IOM (fax 0624 833011, car phone 0860 640 014)

DIXON, Dr Stanley; s of Sidney Dixon (d 1962), of Walsall, Staffs, and Rose, *née* Forrester (d 1975); *b* 19 May 1927; *Educ* Queen Marys GS Walsall, Univ of Birmingham (BSc, PhD); *m* 12 July 1951, Diana Joyce, da of Alfred Kendrick; 2 da (Wendy b 1955, Valerie b 1959); *Career* res scientist and supervisor Ei Du Pont Inc 1951-61; sales mangr 1968-71, Du Pont UK Ltd (lab dir 1963-68); div dir Geneva Du Pont Int 1971-83, md Benzole Producers Ltd 1983-; memb SIGMA X1; *Recreations* golf; *Clubs* Sandy Lodge, Oriental; *Style*— Dr Stanley Dixon; Nantucket, Violet Way, Loudwater, Rickmansworth, Herts WD3 4JP (☎ 0923 776139); 44 Lowndes St, London SW1X 9BB (☎ 071 235 6895, fax 071 245 6796, telex 21574 B)

DIXON, Victoria Jane; da of John Thompson Dixon, of 9 Black Moss Lane, Ormskirk, Lancs, and Elizabeth Jean, *née* Capstick; *b* 5 Aug 1959; *Educ* Ormskirk GS, Univ of Cambridge (MA); *Career* int hockey player; memb GB team: World Cup 1983 and 1990, European Cup 1984 and 1987, Olympic Games 1988; selected for world XI by int press after Seoul Olympics, voted player of the year 1988-89 by GB hockey press; *Recreations* tennis, reading, theatre; *Style*— Miss Victoria Dixon; 99 Stonefield, Bar Hill, Cambridge CB3 8TE (☎ 0954 780331); Netherhall Sch, Gunhild Way, Cambridge (☎ 0223 242931)

DIXON-GREEN, Anthony Joseph; s of Joseph Dixon Green, MBE (d 1963), and Lilian May Dixon (d 1972); *b* 12 Sept 1926; *Educ* Stowe; *m* 1, 6 Oct 1955, Angela Dawn Holley, da of Major Kenneth Herbert Holley, of Herts; 1 s (Simon Anthony), 1 da (Melanie Clare); m 2, 11 July 1981, Susan Faulkner; *Career* Capt Royal Hampshire Regt (Palestine 1946-47); chm L S Dixon Group Ltd 1987; dir: Walter Scott Motors Ltd 1977, Dean Valley Ltd 1952, Hurcott Paper Mills Ltd 1952, Walter Scott Motors (London) Ltd 1978; *Recreations* sailing, hunting, skiing; *Clubs* Royal Yacht Sqdn, Royal Ocean Racing; *Style*— Anthony Dixon-Green, Esq; Sunbeam Cottage, Church Oakley, Basingstoke, Hants RG23 7LJ; L S Dixon Gp Ltd, Octagon House, Rectory Road, Oakley, Hants RG23 7LJ (☎ 0256 782106)

DIXON SMITH, Robert William (Bill); DL (1986); s of Mr Dixon Smith, of Lascelles, Thistley Green Rd, Bocking, Braintree, Essex, and Alice Winifred, *née* Smith (d 1976); *b* 30 Sept 1934; *Educ* Oundle, Writtle Agric Coll; *m* 13 Feb 1960, Georgina Janet, da of George Cook, of Firview, Tidings Hill, Halstead, Essex; 1 s (Adam William George b 11 Jan 1962), 1 da (Sarah Jane b 16 Dec 1960); *Career* Nat Serv 2 Lt King's Dragoon Gds 1955-57; farmer; chm Essex CC 1986-89 (memb 1965-

), vice chm Assoc of CCs 1989-; Freeman Worshipful Co of Farmers 1988; *Style*— Bill Dixon Smith, Esq, DL; Houchins, Coggeshall, Essex CO6 1RT (☎ 0376 561448); c/o County Hall, Chelmsford, Essex

DOBASH, Dr Rebecca Emerson; da of I M Emerson, and Helen, *née* Cooper; *b* 3 Feb 1943; *Educ* Arizona State Univ (BA, MA), Washington State Univ (PhD); *m* 5 June 1965, Russell P Dobash, s of Paul Dobash; *Career* lectr and reader Univ of Stirling 1972-, co fndr and co dir Inst for the Study of Violence; memb: Int Sociological Assoc, Br Sociological Assoc, American Sociological Assoc, Soc for the Study of Social Problems; award for outstanding research and pubns Int Soc of Victimology; *Books* Violence Against Wives (1979), The Imprisonment of Women (1986), Women, Violence and Social Change (1990); *Recreations* travel; *Style*— Dr Rebecca Dobash; Glenesk, Perth Rd, Dunblane, Scotland FK15 0HA; Institute for the Study of Violence, Department of Sociology and Social Policy, University of Stirling, Stirling FK9 4LA (☎ 0786 73171, fax 0786 63000, telex 777557 STUNIV G)

DOBB, Erlam Stanley; CB (1963), TD; s of Arthur Erlam Dobb (d 1957); *b* 16 Aug 1910; *Educ* Ruthin Sch, Univ Coll of N Wales; *m* 1937, Margaret, da of Percy Williams (d 1955), of Colwyn Bay; *Career* Royal Welch Fus Maj TA; asst and land cmmr Miny of Agric Fisheries and Foods 1935-47, Agric Land Serv 1947-71 (dir 1959-70), dir-gen ADAS 1973-75; govr Royal Agric Coll 1960-75, chm Thomas Phillips Price Tstees 1971-83 (tstee and memb 1984), memb Agric Res Cncl 1973-75; *Clubs* Farmer's; *Style*— Erlam Dobb, Esq, CB, TD; Churchgate, Westerham, Kent (☎ 0959 62294)

DOBBS, Sir Richard Arthur Frederick; KCVO (1991), JP (Co Antrim 1956); o s of Maj Arthur Frederick Dobbs, JP, DL (d 1955), of Castle Dobbs, memb Senate of N Ireland 1923-33 and 1937-55, and Hylda Louisa, *née* Higginson (d 1957); descended from Robert Dobbs, of Batley, Yorkshire, whose gs John Dobbs went to Ireland in 1596 (*see* Burke's Irish Family Records); *b* 2 April 1919; *Educ* Eton, Magdalene Coll Cambridge (BA, MA); *m* 28 Aug 1953, Carola Day, da of Gp Capt Christopher Clarkson, of Old Lyme, Connecticut, USA; 4 s ((Richard Francis) Andrew b 28 May 1955, Nigel Christopher b 19 March 1957, Matthew Frederick b 5 July 1959, Nicholas Arthur Montagu b 12 Feb 1973), 1 da (Sophia Carola b 27 Aug 1965); *Career* T/Capt Irish Gds (Supplementary Reserve), served WWII; called to the Bar Lincoln's Inn 1947, memb Midland circuit 1951-55; HM Lord Lt Co Antrim 1975- (DL 1957-59, Lt 1959-75); *Clubs* Cavalry and Guards'; *Style*— Sir Richard Dobbs, KCVO, JP; Castle Dobbs, Carrickfergus, Co Antrim, Northern Ireland (☎ 0960 372238)

DOBBS, Prof (Edwin) Roland; s of Albert Edwin Dobbs (d 1961), and Harriet, *née* Wright; *b* 2 Dec 1924; *Educ* Ilford County HS, Queen Elizabeth's GS Barnet, UCL (BSc, PhD, DSc); *m* 7 April 1947, Dorothy Helena, da of late Alderman A F T Jeeves, of Stamford, Lincs; 2 s (Richard Alexander Edwin b 1952, Jeremy Francis Roland b 1964), 1 da (Helena Jane b 1949); *Career* radar res offr Admty 1943-46; lectr in Physics Queen Mary Coll Univ of London 1949-58, assoc prof of physics Brown Univ USA 1959-60 (res assoc in applied maths 1958-59), AEI fell Cavendish Laboratory Univ of Cambridge 1960-64, prof of physics and head of Dept of Physics Univ of Lancaster 1964-73; Univ of London: Hildred Carlisle prof of physics Bedford Coll 1973-85, prof and head Dept of Physics Royal Holloway and Bedford New Coll 1985-90, vice dean Faculty of Sci 1986-90, dean Faculty of Sci 1988-90, emeritus prof of physics 1990; visiting prof: Brown Univ 1966, Wayne State Univ 1969, Univ of Tokyo 1977, Univ of Delhi 1983, Cornell Univ USA 1984, Univ of Florida 1989, Univ of Sussex 1989-; memb: Physics Ctee SRC 1970-73, Nuclear Physics Bd SRC 1974-77; chm Solid State Physics Sub Ctee Sci and Engrg Res Cncl 1983-86; FInstP 1964 (hon sec 1976-84), FIOA 1977 (pres 1976-78); *Books* Electricity and Magnetism (1984), Electromagnetic Waves (1985); *Recreations* travel, gardening, music; *Clubs* Athenaeum; *Style*— Prof Roland Dobbs; School of Mathematical and Physical Sciences, University of Sussex, Falmer, Brighton BN1 9QH (☎ 0273 606755, fax 0273 678097)

DOBBY, David Lloyd; s of William Lloyd Dobby, of Walmer, Deal, Kent, and Susan Kathleen, *née* Jobson (d 1986); *b* 6 April 1936; *Educ* St Dunstan's Coll Catford, Regent St Poly (Dip Arch); *m* 17 March 1967, Lesley Madeline, da of Frederick William Herron, of Walmer, Deal, Kent; 2 da (Anna b 19 March 1969, Liz b 27 July 1971); *Career* architect 1965; CWS 1957-59, Ronald Ward & Partners 1959-61, Raymond Spratley & Partners 1961-63, Douglas Marriott & Partners 1963-65, James Munce Partnership 1965-68, Rush & Tompkins Group 1968-73; ptnr private practice 1973-86: John Floydd Partnership, Dobby Foard & Ptnrs, DY Davies Dobby Foard; dir practice DY Davies plc 1986-88, md Sargent & Potiriadis 1988-89, mgmnt conslt Practice and Quality Assurance 1990-; exec assoc Watkins Gray International 1990-; House of the Year Design award 1970 and 1972; designs incl: First Bush Bank W Africa, theme park Florida, new railway village Ashford Kent, Rush & Tompkins HQ offices Sidcup, Chatham House Duke of York St St James's; parish cncllr 1978-86; treas local ballet sch 1980-85, memb Dover Girls GS PTA 1980-86, Freeman City of London 1981, Liveryman Worshipful Co of Joiners and Ceilers 1981-; RIBA 1965, LicIQA 1990; *Recreations* golf, reading; *Clubs* Royal Cinque Ports, East India, Folio Soc; *Style*— David Dobby, Esq; 10 Jarvist Place, Kingsdown, nr Deal, Kent CT14 8AL (☎ 0304 373331)

DOBELL, Anthony Russell; s of Thomas Russell Dobell, MBE, TD, of Cheshire, and Fiona Helen, *née* Barrett (d 1974); *b* 15 Sept 1948; *Educ* Rugby; *m* 15 April 1983, Hilary, da of Ronald Shaw, of Cheshire; 2 s (Richard b 1985, Myles b 1987); *Career* CA 1971; ptnr: Robson Rhodes Manchester 1978-88, A R Dobell & Co 1988-; hon sec Manchester Soc of CA's 1986-90; memb Over Peover Parish Cncl 1985-, hon sec Friends of Manchester Northern Hosp 1975-; FCA; *Recreations* family, gardening, walking, most sports; *Clubs* St James's Manchester, Knutsford Golf, Alderley Edge Tennis and Squash; *Style*— Anthony R Dobell, Esq; Pear Tree Farm, Peover Heath, Cheshire (☎ 0625 861454); 13 Hyde Rd, Denton (☎ 061 320 4111)

DOBELL, Hon (Sarah) Camilla; da of 6 Baron Heytesbury; *b* 20 May 1965; *m* 19 July 1989, James T C Dobell, twin of Mrs Jenny Dobell, of London; *Style*— The Hon Mrs Dobell

DOBIE, Alan Russell; s of Robert George Dobie (d 1985), and Sarah, *née* Charlesworth (d 1965); *b* 2 June 1932; *Educ* Wath GS, Barnsley Art Sch, London Old Vic Theatre Sch; *m* 1, 1955 (m dis 1961), Rachel Roberts; m 2, 1963 (m dis 1985) Maureen Stobie; 3 da (Casey b 1964, Emelia b 1966, Natasha b 1968); *Career* actor; 41 prodns with Old Vic Assoc London and Bristol 1952-56; to date 108 stage prodns incl: Jimmy Porter in Look Back in Anger (Royal Court and tour) 1957, Bill Walker in Major Barbara (Royal Court) 1958, Col in Live Like Pigs (Royal Court) 1958, Bernard Ross in No Concern of Mine (Westminster) 1958, Private Hurst in Sergeant Musgraves Dance (Royal Court) 1959, Ulrich Brendal in Rosmersholme (Comedy Theatre) 1960, Louis Flax in Tiger and the Horse (Queens) 1960, Macbeth in Macbeth (Ludlow Castle) 1961, Donald Howard in The Affair (Strand) 1961, Thomas Becket in Curtmantle (RSC Aldwych) 1962, Corporal Hill in Chips with Everything (Royal Court and Broadway) 1963, Bill Maitland in Inadmissible Evidence (Wyndham) 1965, Benito Cereno in Benito Cereno (Mermaid) 1967, Thomas More in Man For All Seasons (Manitoba) 1968, Hamlet in Hamlet (Manitoba) 1973, Prospero in The Tempest (Edinburgh Festival) 1978, Bottom in Midsummer Nights Dream (Edinburgh Festival) 1978, Stephan Von Sala in The Lonely Rd (London Old Vic) 1984, Atticus Finch in To Kill A Mockingbird (Mermaid) 1989, Haakon Werle in The Wild Duck (Phoenix) 1990, Nat in I'm Not Rappaport (tour) 1991; numerous tv roles incl: Face in The Alchemist (BBC) 1961, Faustus in Dr Faustus (BBC) 1961, David Corbet in The Planemakers (ATU) 1964, Kurt in Dance of Death (ATU) 1965, The Brothers in The Corsican Brothers (ATV) 1965, William The Conqueror in Conquest (BBC) 1966, Neckludou in Ressurection (BBC) 1968, Robespierre in Danton (BBC) 1970, Andrei Bolkonski in War & Peace (BBC) 1971, Synavski in Trial of Synavski & Daniel (CBC) 1974, Martin Ellis in Double Dare (BBC) 1976, Stephen Blackpool in Hard Times (Granada) 1976, Cribb in Waxwork (Granada) 1978, Judge Brack in Hedda Gabler (YTV) 1980, Charles Clement in Gericault (BBC) 1982, Rabbi Moses in The Disputation (Channel 4) 1984; contrib to 56 radio progs and 160 documentary commentaries; has appeared in 7 films incl: Charge of the Light Brigade (as Mog) 1967, A Long Days Dying (as Helmut) 1967; *Recreations* art work, skiing, DIY; *Style*— Alan Dobie, Esq; Vernon Conway Ltd, 5 Spring St, London W2 3RA (☎ 071 262 5506/7)

DOBIE, Brig Joseph Leo; CBE (1969); s of David Walter Dobie (d 1943); *b* 26 Sept 1914; *Educ* Tynemouth HS, Univ of Durham (BSc), Mil Coll of Sci; *m* 1940, Joan Clare, da of Frank Watson (d 1982); 1 s, 3 da; *Career* 2 Lt RE (TA) 1937, Tyne Electrical Engrs RE (TA), Lt RAOC 1938, REME 1942, served WWII; Cmdt Army Apprentices' Sch Aborfield 1962-65 (Col), DDEME 1 Br Corps Germany 1965-66 (Brig), inspr of REME MOD 1966-69 (Brig); exec external rels and mktg ERA 1970-74; dir: external activities and exec special projects IEE London 1974-82, Michael Shortland Assocs (conslts in computer aided engrg) 1982-87; CEng, FIEE; *Recreations* golf, gardening; *Clubs* Liphook Golf; *Style*— Brig Joseph Dobie, CBE; Findings, Tower Rd, Hindhead, Surrey GU26 6ST (☎ 042 873 5469)

DOBIE, Margaret Graham Campbell; OBE (1989); da of Robert Latta, JP (d 1936), of Kirkudbrightshire, and Janet Annie, *née* Campbell (d 1964); *b* 2 Dec 1928; *Educ* Dumfries Acad, Univ of Edinburgh (MA); *m* 27 June 1953, James Tait Johnstone Dobie, DSC, s of William Gardiner Murchie Dobie, MBE; 3 s (Robert b 23 July 1955, Alan b 24 Feb 1958, James b 14 Aug 1964); *Career* chair Children's Panel Advsy Gp 1985-88, memb Broadcasting Cncl for Scotland 1987-, vice chair Scottish Assoc for the Study of Delinquency 1989-, memb Br Fedn of Univ Women; *Recreations* tennis, skiing, travel; *Clubs* Crosby hall, Chelsea; *Style*— Mrs Margaret Dobie, OBE; Mansepark, Kirkgunzeon, Dumfries, Scotland DG2 8LA (☎ 038 776 661)

DOBKIN, Ronald; s of Morris Dobkin (d 1940), of Bethnal Green, London, and Anne, *née* Goodman; *b* 15 Feb 1909; *Educ* Davenant Fndn GS Whitechapel E London; *m* 1, 2 Nov 1958 (m dis 1983), Marian, *née* Green; 1 s (Jonathan Michael b 3 March 1964), 1 da (Elaine b 25 Nov 1965); m 2, 13 Dec 1986, Marion Joan (Lee), da of Arthur Roland Shutler, of Hythe, Southampton; *Career* CA; trainee Viney Price & Goodyear 1956-62, gen mangr Craven House Securities 1963-67, chief accountant Macmillans 1967-72, princ Ronald Dobkin & Co 1973-76; ptnr: Dobkin Smallman & Co 1976-80, Dobkin Northover 1980-; treas: Winchester RFC 1969-80, The Bollinger Boys Luncheon Club 1984-; chm The Lords Taverners Hampshire and Surrey Region 1986-89 (memb Hants Region 1986-); FCA 1962; *Recreations* bridge, chess, rugby football; *Style*— Ronald Dobkin, Esq; 36-40 St George's St, Winchester SO23 8BE (☎ 0962 841616, fax 0962 841611)

DOBLE, Denis Henry; s of Percy Claud Doble, of Canterbury, and Dorothy Grace, *née* Petley; *b* 2 Oct 1936; *Educ* Dover GS, New Coll Oxford (MA); *m* 18 July 1975, Patricia Ann, da of Peter Robinson (d 1985), 1 s (Robin b 1981), 1 da (Katie b 1979); *Career* Colonial Office 1960-65; HM Dip Serv 1965-: second sec Br Embassy Brussels 1966-68, first sec (devpt) Br High Cmmn Lagos 1968-72, S Asian Dept FCO 1972-75, first sec (econ) Br Embassy Islamabad 1975-78, first sec Br Embassy Lima 1978-82, E African Dept FCO 1982-84, actg dep high cmmr Bombay 1985, dep high cmmr Calcutta 1985-87, dep high cmmr Kingston 1987-, SBStJ 1972; *Recreations* tennis, cricket; *Clubs* MCC; *Style*— Denis Doble, Esq; Foreign and Commonwealth Office, King Charles St, London SW1A 2AH

DOBLE, John Frederick; OBE (1981); s of Cdr Douglas Doble, RN (d 1972), of Ashbrittle, Somerset, and Marcella, *née* Cowan; *b* 30 June 1941; *Educ* Sunningdale Sch, Eton, RMA Sandhurst, Hertford Coll Oxford (BA); *m* 1 Dec 1975, Isabella Margaret Ruth, da of Col W H Whitbread, TD, of Haslemere, Surrey; 1 da (Iona) Louisa b 20 July 1977); *Career* Capt 17/21st Lancers 1959-69, (on exchange with Lord Strathcona's House, Royal Canadians 1967-69); HM Dip Serv: FCO Arabian Dept 1969-72, Beirut 1972-73, UK delgn NATO Brussels 1973-77, FCO Cwlth Coordination Dept 1977-78, Maputo 1978-81, FCO Info Dept 1981-83; Barclays Bank International 1983-85; consul gen: Edmonton 1985-89, Johannesburg 1990-; Liveryman of the Worshipful Co of Merchant Taylors 1971; *Recreations* horse and water sports, history, manual labour; *Clubs* Royal Cwlth, Poplar Blackwell and Dist Rowing; *Style*— John Doble, Esq, OBE; British Consulate General, PO Box 10101, Johannesburg 2000, South Africa (☎ 010 27 11 337 7270)

DOBREE, John Hatherley; er s of Hatherley Moor Dobrée, OBE (d 1956), and Muriel, *née* Hope, (d 1960), of Stanford-le-Hope, Essex; *b* 25 April 1914; *Educ* St Bart's Hosp Univ of London (MS); *m* 16 Sept 1941, Evelyn Maud, da of Thomas Francis Smyth (d 1950), of Dublin; 2 s (Charles b 1947, Robert b 1950); *Career* Capt RAMC, MEF 1942-46; ophthalmic surgn; conslt: St Bart's Hosp London, N Middx Hosp London; vice pres Ophthalmic Soc UK, dep master Oxford Ophthalmic Congress, hon sec Sect of Ophthalmology RSM; FRCS; *Books* The Retina (with Sir Stewart Duke Elder), Blindness (with Eric Boulter); *Style*— John Dobree, Esq

DOBREE BELL, Hon Mrs (Astrid Signe); *née* Williamson; da of 3 Baron Forres (d 1978), and Gillian Ann Maclean (now Mrs Miles H de Zoete), da of late Maj John M Grant, RA; *b* 20 Dec 1951; *m* 1976, Peter Karl Dobree Bell, 1 s (Hugh John b 1982), 1 da (Lucy Claire b 1984); *Style*— The Hon Mrs Dobree Bell; 15 Third Street Abbotsford, 2192, SA

DOBSON; *see*: Howard-Dobson

DOBSON, Hon Mrs (Anne Mary); *née* Hope; only da of 3 Baron Rankeillour (d 1967); *b* 20 Dec 1936; *m* 5 July 1958, John Stephen Dobson, JP (*qv*); 1 s, 2 da; *Style*— The Hon Mrs Dobson; Papplewick Lodge, Notts

DOBSON, Prof (Richard) Barrie; s of Richard Henry Dobson (d 1967), and Mary Victoria Dobson; *b* 3 Nov 1931; *Educ* Barnard Castle Sch, Wadham Coll Oxford (BA, DPhil); *m* 19 June 1959, Narda, da of Maurice Leon (d 1981); 1 s (Richard Mark b 1 Dec 1961), 1 da (Michelle Jane b 19 Feb 1963); *Career* lectr in medieval history Univ of St Andrews 1958-64; Univ of York: lectr, sr lectr, reader 1964-76; prof: of history Univ of York 1978-88, of medieval history Univ of Cambridge 1988-; pres: Jewish Historical Soc of England 1990-91, Surtees Soc 1987-, Ecclesiastical History Soc 1991-92; memb Merchant Taylor's Co City of York 1979; FRHistS 1974, FSA 1979, FBA 1988; *Books* The Peasants Revolt of 1381 (1971), Durham Priory 1400-1450 (1973), The Jews of York and the Massacre of 1190 (1974), York City Chamberlains Accounts 1396-1500 (1980); *Recreations* hill walking, swimming; *Style*— Prof Barrie Dobson, FSA; Christ's College, Cambridge CB2 3BU (☎ 0223 334900)

DOBSON, Vice Adm David Stuart; s of Eric Walter Dobson, and Ethel, *née* Pethurst; *b* 4 Dec 1938; *Educ* RNC Dartmouth; *m* 22 Dec 1962, Joanna Mary, da of late A T Counter; 2 s (Ben b 1964 Shaun b 1966), 1 da (Rebecca b 1970); *Career* RN: CO HMS Amazon 1975-76; Cdr Fleet Air Arm Appointer 1976-78; Capt Naval and Air Attache Athens 1979-82; SNO Falkland Islands 1982-83; CO HMS Southampton and

Capt 5th destroyer sqdn 1983-85; Capt of the Fleet 1985-88; Rear Adm 1988-90; Vice Admin 1991; memb MIPM; *Recreations* hill walking, choral singing; *Clubs* Army and Navy; *Style—* Vice Admiral David Dobson; c/o Lloyds Bank, The Square, Petersfield

DOBSON, Sir Denis William; KCB (1969, CB 1959), OBE (1945), QC (1971); s of William Gordon Dobson, of Newcastle upon Tyne; *b* 17 Oct 1908; *Educ* Charterhouse, Trinity Coll Cambridge; *m* 1, 1934 (m dis 1947), Thelma, da of Charles Swinburne, of Newcastle upon Tyne; 1 s, 1 da; m 2, 1948, Mary Elizabeth, da of Capt J A Allen, of Haywards Heath; 2 s, 1 da; *Career* served WWII with RAF (UK, W Desert, Italy), Wing Cdr 1944; admitted slr 1933, called to the Bar Middle Temple 1951, bencher 1968, dep clerk of the Crown in Chancery Lord Chllr's Office 1954-68, clerk of the Crown in Chancery and perm sec to Lord Chllr 1968-77; *Clubs* Athenaeum; *Style—* Sir Denis Dobson, KCB, OBE, QC; 50 Egerton Crescent, London SW3 2ED (☎ 071 589 7990)

DOBSON, Frank Gordon; MP (Lab) Holborn and St Pancras 1983-; s of James William Dobson, and Irene Shortland, *née* Laley; *b* 15 March 1940; *Educ* Archbishop Holgate's GS York, LSE; *m* 1967, Janet Mary, da of Henry Alker; 3 children; *Career* former administrator CEGB and Electricity Cncl; asst sec Cmmn for Local Admin 1975-79; memb exec Chile Solidarity Campaign 1979-, NUR sponsored MP (Lab) Holborn and St Pancras South 1979-1983, oppn front bench spokesman: Educn 1981-83, shadow health mini 1983-87, shadow leader of the house and campaign co-ordinator 1987-; *Style—* Frank Dobson, Esq, MP; 22 Great Russell Mansions, Great Russell Street, London WC1B 3BE

DOBSON, Geoffrey John; s of Gilbert Petch Dobson, of Farnham, Surrey, and Eva, *née* Wrigglesworth; *b* 31 Dec 1945; *Educ* Ashville Coll Yorks; *m* 28 April 1973, Ann Kathleen, da of Edward Meredith Smith; 2 s (Christopher b 1976, Philip b 1978); *Career* accountant; co sec LJ Hydleman & Co Ltd 1971-74 (joined 1970), Euro fin dir Engelhard Ltd 1983- (joined 1974); FCA 1970; *Recreations* sailing, skiing, squash, swimming; *Clubs* RAC; *Style—* Geoffrey Dobson, Esq; Engelhard Ltd, Chancery House, St Nicholas Way, Sutton, Surrey SM1 1SB (☎ 081 643 8080)

DOBSON, John Chaytor; s of William Ernest Dobson (d 1952), and Lilian, *née* Stephen (d 1974); *b* 28 Oct 1928; *Educ* RNC Dartmouth; *Career* steel indust 1950-56, Baltic Exchange 1956-58, oil exec int oil co 1958-90; elected memb GLC 1970-86 (vice chm 1979-80); Freeman City of London, Liveryman Worshipful Co of Fletchers; *Recreations* formerly played Surrey county cricket club 2 X1; *Clubs* Carlton, Hurlingham, City Livery, United and Cecil, MCC; *Style—* John Dobson, Esq; 55 Richmond Court, 200 Sloane St, London SW1X 9QU (☎ 071 235 2603)

DOBSON, John Stephen; JP (1962); elder s of John Dobson (d 1960), of The Old Vicarage, Farnsfield, Notts; *b* 19 July 1932; *Educ* Ampleforth; *m* 5 July 1958, Hon Anne Mary, *née* Hope, da of 3 Baron Rankeillour (d 1967); 1 s, 2 da; *Career* textile mfrg chm 1964-; dist cnllr 1974-; High Sheriff Notts 1975-76; pres: Ashfield Cons Assoc, Dist Scouts; *Recreations* hunting, sailing, skiing, tennis; *Clubs* Army & Navy, Aldeburgh Yacht, Royal Thames Yacht; *Style—* J Stephen Dobson, Esq, JP; Papplewick Lodge, Notts (☎ 0602 632975); 14 Fawcett Rd, Aldeburgh, Suffolk (☎ 072 845 3485); 209 Lillie Rd, London SW6 7LW (☎ 071 385 4872)

DOBSON, Michael William Romsey; s of Sir Denis Dobson, KCB, OBE, QC, of 50 Egerton Crescent, London SW3, *qv*, and Lady Mary Elizabeth, *née* Allen; *b* 13 May 1952; *Educ* Eton, Trinity Coll Cambridge (MA); *Career* Morgan Grenfell 1973-: NY 1978-80, dir Investmt Servs London 1980-84, md NY 1984-88, head of Int Investmt London 1985-86, md Asset Mgmnt 1987-, chm Asset Mgmnt 1988-; gp chief exec Morgan Grenfell Group; dir: Anglo and Overseas Trust plc 1987-, The Overseas Investmt Trust plc 1987-; *Recreations* tennis, golf; *Clubs* Brooks, Turf, Queens, Hurlingham, New York Racquet & Tennis; *Style—* Michael Dobson, Esq; 61 Onslow Sq, London SW3 (☎ 071 584 1956); 23 Great Winchester St, London EC2 (☎ 071 588 4545, fax 071 588 5598, telex 8953511)

DOBSON, Nigel Hewitt; s of George Hewitt Dobson (d 1984), of Beckenham, Kent, and Ethel Grace, *née* Boxshall; *b* 13 Aug 1949; *Educ* St Dunstan's Coll; *Career* Whinney Murray & Co (now Ernst & Young) 1968-: Ernst & Ernst St Louis Missouri 1974-75, Corporate Advsy Servs Div Whinney Murray 1976-, seconded Corporate Fin Dept Midland Bank 1978-80, ptnr corporate reconstruction 1981-; FCA (ACA 1972); *Recreations* sailing, gardening, reading; *Style—* Nigel Dobson, Esq; 5 Samuel Court, 44 Kelsey Park Ave, Beckenham, Kent BR3 2UN (☎ 081 658 3115); Minnis Bay, Birchington, Kent; Ernst & Young, Becket House, 1 Lambeth Palace Rd, London SE1 7EU (☎ 071 928 2000)

DOBSON, Peter Holliday; DL (W Yorks); s of Alfred Dobson (d 1963), of Tynwald Thorner nr Leeds, and Edith Maud, *née* Holliday (d 1960); *b* 7 April 1917; *Educ* Bradfield; *m* 20 Aug 1940, Joan, da of Ernest Thomas Seymour; 2 da (Katharine Elizabeth (Mrs Whitaker) b 17 Feb 1945, Judith Caroline (Mrs James) b 10 Jan 1947); *Career* articled clerk Beevers & Adgie Leeds 1935-39, ptnr: Alfred Dobson & Co 1947-60, Whinney Smith & Whinney 1960- (following merger), Whinney Murray & Co (following Merger), Ernst & Whinney (following merger), ret 1980; memb: Cncl ICAEW 1960-80, Appeal Ctee ICAEW; JP Leeds 1955-87; Freeman City of London, past master Worshipful Co of Chartered Accountants in England & Wales; FCA (ACA 1947); *Recreations* golf, gardening, reading; *Style—* Peter Dobson, Esq; Robin Hill, Sicklinghall Rd, Wetherby, W Yorks LS22 4AA (☎ 0937 581850)

DOBSON, Sir Richard (Portway); s of Prof John Frederic Dobson (d 1948); *b* 11 Feb 1914; *Educ* Clifton Coll, King's Coll Cambridge; *m* 1946, Mrs Emily Margaret Carver, da of J R Herridge; 1 step da; *Career* served in China 1936-40, Flt-Lt RAF 1941-45 (pilot); with Br-American Tobacco Co Ltd in China, Rhodesia and London 1946 (dir 1955, chm 1970-76, pres 1976-79); dir: Exxon Corp, Davy Int 1975-84, Lloyds Bank Int 1976-84; non-exec chm BL 1976-77; kt 1976; *Clubs* United Oxford and Cambridge Univ; *Style—* Sir Richard Dobson; 16 Marchmont Rd, Richmond upon Thames, Surrey (☎ 081 940 1504)

DOBSON, Susan Angela (Sue); da of Arthur George Henshaw, and Nellie, *née* Flower (d 1978); *b* 31 Jan 1946; *Educ* Holy Family Convent, Assumption Convent Ramsgate, Ursuline Convent Westgate on Sea, NE London Poly (BA, Dip HE); *m* 1966 (m dis 1974), Michael Dobson; *Career* fashion, cookery and beauty ed Femina 1965-69, contributing ed Fair Lady 1969-71; ed: SA Inst of Race Rels 1972, Wedding Day and First Home 1978-81, Successful Slimming 1981, Woman & Home 1982-; *Books* The Wedding Day Book (1981, 1989); *Recreations* travel, books, photography, theatre, music, exploring countryside around home in Kent; *Style—* Ms Sue Dobson; IPC Magazines, Kings Reach Tower, Stamford St, London SE1 9LS (☎ 071 261 5423)

DOCHERTY, Peter Thomas Christopher; s of Dr Joseph Francis Docherty (d 1975), and Sylvia, *née* Kinnamont; *b* 1 Sept 1939; *m* 6 Aug 1966, Eleanor, da of Brian Bolgar, of Ireland; 4 s (Ian b 1967, Bruce b 1972, Duncan b 1971, Brian b 1977); *Career* conslt Ophthalmic Surgeon Derbyshire Royal Infirmary; designer of a cannula used worldwide for cataract surgery; author of many articles in medical journals; FRCS, FRCSI, LRCPI & LM, DO, DOMS RCPST; *Recreations* golf, scuba diving; *Clubs* Irish Graduates Soc, Mickleover Golf; *Style—* Peter Docherty, Esq; Shamrock Lodge, 9 Farley Road, Derby DE3 6BY; Derbyshire Royal Infirmary, London Road, Derby DE1 2QY (☎ 0332 47141, ext 328)

DOCKER, Rt Rev Ivor Colin; *see*: Horsham, Bishop of

DOCKERTY, John Samuel; s of Edgar Samuel Dockerty (d 1973), of Berkswell, nr Coventry, and Olive Irene, *née* Manger (d 1982); *b* 2 Nov 1929; *Educ* King Henry VIII Coventry; *m* 17 March 1956, Jean Ann, da of William Arthur James Brick (d 1975), of Stamford, Lincs; 2 s (Christopher b 1960, Andrew b 1967), 2 da (Deborah b 1957, Nicola b 1963); *Career* co dir of timber importer J O Walker & Co plc 1960 (dep chm 1973); chm E Anglian Timber Trade Assoc 1986-88; *Recreations* cricket, gardening, travelling abroad; *Style—* John Dockerty, Esq; Broadlawns, Barton Rd, Wisbech, Cambs (☎ 0945 583614); J O Walker & Co plc, Nene Quay, Wisbech (☎ 0945 582215)

DOCKRAY, Brian; s of George Arthur Dockray, of Kendal, Cumbria, and Dorothy Mary, *née* Mason (d 1985); *b* 18 Oct 1930; *Educ* Leeds Sch of Architecture; *m* 21 July 1956, Edith Emilie, da of Olaf Friestad (d 1987), of Kristiansand, Norway; 1 s (David Olaf b 1964); *Career* cmmnd RE Chatham 1954, Capt RE TA; sr ptnr Gill Dockray and Ptnrs Chartered Architects Kendal Kirkby Lonsdale and Ambleside 1961-; winner of over 30 Civic Tst Awards and 4 Euro Heritage Awards; rep in cross country and atheletics events for: Br Army 1954-56, Yorkshire 1955-57; FRIBA; *Recreations* golf, walking lakeland hills, water colours; *Clubs* Ulverston Golf, Kendal Golf; *Style—* Brian Dockray, Esq; Skewbarrow Top, High Tenterfell, Kendal, Cumbria LA9 4PQ (☎ 0539 721684); 45 Highgate, Kendal, Cumbria LA9 4EE (☎ 0539 722656)

DODD, David Kilburn; s of Thomas K Dodd (d 1988), and Florence, *née* Marks (d 1980); *b* 31 Oct 1932; *Educ* Kingswood Sch, Yale Univ (BA), Harvard Univ (MBA); *Career* US Navy 1954-56, Lt USS Ticonderoga Atlantic Sixth Fleet; Merrill Lynch 1958-79: corp fin New York 1958-73, UK regnl dir 1973-76, chief fin offr 1973-79; int mktg dir Cedel 1979-81, dep dir County Bank 1981-84, dep md Mitsui Finance 1985-90, sr conslt D C Gardner 1990-; various pubns in jls; memb: Bond Club of New York, Investmt Assoc of NY, NY Soc of Security Analysts; *Recreations* tennis, beginners golf, skiing, travel (historic sights); *Clubs* Yale, Harvard, Hurlingham, Mark's; *Style—* David K Dodd, Esq; Two Lexham House, 9c Thistle Grove, Chelsea, London SW10 9RR (☎ 071 373 5451)

DODD, Air Vice-Marshal Frank Leslie; CBE (1968), DSO (1944), DFC (1944), AFC (1943, and bars 1955 and 1959), AE (1945); s of Frank Herbert Dodd (d 1944), of Dunston, Staffs; *b* 5 March 1919; *Educ* King Edward VI Sch Stafford, Univ of Reading; *m* 1942, Joyce Lilian, da of George Claxton Banyard (d 1957), of Thetford, Norfolk; 1 s, 3 da; *Career* joined RAFVR 1938, photo-recce Mosquitos 1944-45, Station Cdr RAF Coningsby 1961-63, Cmdt Central Flying Sch 1965-68, Air Cdre 1966, dir RAF Estabs 1968-70, DG Special Air Def Project 1970-74, Air Vice-Marshal 1970, ret 1974; admin MacRobert Tst 1974-85; LRPS (1987); *Recreations* golf, photography; *Clubs* RAF; *Style—* Air Vice-Marshal Frank Dodd, CBE, DSO, DFC, AFC, AE; c/o Barclays Bank plc, Market Square, Stafford ST16 2BE

DODD, Ian Wilfred; s of William Ogilvy Dodd, of 9 Whitethorn Drive, Brighton, and Margery Lillian, *née* Harper (d 1942); *b* 14 July 1942; *Educ* Brighton Coll, RNC Dartmouth; *m* 1, 25 Sept 1965 (m dis 1979), Marilyn Grace, da of Jack Smith, of Brighton; 3 s (Andrew Ogilvy b 1967, Alexander Mark b 1969, Alistair Ian Paul b 1974); m 2, 20 Dec 1986, Patricia Marian, *née* Keeling; *Career* slr Eastbourne Borough Cncl 1966-67, ptnr then sr ptnr Griffith Smith Slrs (formerly Griffith Smith Dodd 1967-; scout cmmr Brighton (ret), hon slr Brighton Hove and Dist Samaritans, vice pres Mencap (Brighton Hove and Dist), fndr pres Rotary Club of Brighton and Hove Soiree, Int chm Rotary Dist 125, hon sec and tstee Muttinat Ctee of Polioplus; govr: Brighton Coll, Queens Park Co Primary Sch; memb Law Soc; *Recreations* reading, music, gardening, walking, sailing and skiing, dining well; *Style—* Ian Dodd, Esq; 47 Old Steyne, Brighton BN1 1NW (☎ 0273 24041, fax 0273 203796, telex 878112)

DODD, John; s of Albert Victor Jack Dodd (d 1971), and Marjorie Violet, *née* Lowenhoff; *b* 3 June 1934; *Educ* Lawrenceville Sch New Jersey USA, Chiswick Poly, Coll Of Law Univ of London (LLB); *m* 1, 24 June 1961 (m dis 1985), Wendy Patricia, da of Patrick George Channell (d 1987); 4 s (Paul b 3 May 1963, Benjamin b 19 Dec 1969, James b 7 April 1972, Timothy b 2 July 1975), 1 da (Samantha b 21 Feb 1965); m 2, 30 Nov 1985, Yvonne Myvanwy, da of Albert John Thomas Purdue; 2 step s (Graeme b 21 March 1987, Neil b 2 March 1980), 1 step da (Caroline b 3 Oct 1973); *Career* Nat Serv RA: England, Korea, Hong Kong; admitted slr 1961; ptnr: Hair & Co 1963-77, Young Jones Hair & Co 1977-79, Devonshires 1980-; memb: Adoption Panel LDS Soc Servs Adoption Agency 1984-88, Advsy Bd LDS Soc Servs; area cncl Church of Jesus Christ of Latter-Day Saints 1987- (regnl ldr 1965-); memb Law Soc Admission Panel; Freeman City of London, Liveryman City of London Slrs Co; *Recreations* skiing, swimming, water sports; *Style—* John Dodd, Esq; Devonshires; Salisbury House, London Wall, London EC2M 5QY (☎ 071 628 7576, fax 071 256 7318)

DODD, Ken - Kenneth Arthur; OBE (1982); s of Arthur Dodd, by his w Sarah; *b* 1931; *Educ* Holt HS Liverpool; *Career* singer, comedian, actor, entertainer; *Style—* Kenneth Dodd Esq, OBE; 76 Thomas Lane, Knotty Ash, Liverpool

DODD, Martin William Lindsay; TD (1976); s of Sir John Samuel Dodd Kt, TD (d 1973), of Les Fraises, Rozel, Jersey, CI, and Margaret MacDougal, *née* Hamilton; *b* 22 Oct 1939; *Educ* Eton, L'Ecole Superieure De Commerce Au Rouen; *Career* inf HAC 1959-73, Maj RHA HAC 1973-76; dir: Lyon Estates Br Heating Engrs 1961-73, Alkmay Builders 1967-71; fin dir: Southern Extrusions Crittal McKinney 1972-74, Crittali Components Crittal Galvanising Southern Extrusion 1974-76, CEGO Engrg 1976-78; md Security Computing Servs 1978-82; fin dir: Hygena 1982, AG Tiles 1982-87; parish cnllr 1972-82, church warden 1975-82, treas Saffron Waldron Lib Constituency Assoc 1978-82; Liveryman: Worshipful Co of Vintners 1966, Worshipful Co of Painter Stainers 1976; FCA 1964; *Recreations* Br Show Jumping Assoc judge, national carriage driving official, art, music, horseriding; *Clubs* HAC; *Style—* Martin Dodd, Esq, TD; Woodcote, Hall Orchard, Bramshall, Nr Uttoxeter, Staffs ST14 5DF (☎ 08895 66436); Haileybury and Imperial Service College, Hertford SG13 7NU (☎ 0992 462 507, fax 0992 463 603)

DODD, Col Norman Lavington; s of Ralph Harry Dodd (d 1962), of Moorcroft, Beaconsfield Rd, Four Oaks, Sutton Coldfield, and Marion Edith Dodd (d 1959); *b* 23 June 1917; *Educ* St Peter's Sch York, RMA Woolwich; *m* 18 Sept 1942, Eileen Charlotte, da of Maj George Gibbs (d 1940), of Wellington, NZ; 1 da (Maureen (Mrs Judge) b 16 Oct 1946); *Career* cmmnd RA 1937, 1 Field Regt RA India 1937-39, 4 RHA Egypt 1940, Capt Surrey Yeo 1940, SO RA Nigeria 1940, Maj OC 3 Light Batt W African Artillery Nigeria and Burma 1941-45, 2 i/c 101 Lt Regt Artillry 1945, MID 1945, 2 i/c and A/Lt-Col Dorset Yeo 1945, Staff Coll 1945, DAAG 4 Armd Bde 1946, BM 69 AA Bde 1947-49, Batt cmd and staff Nigeria 1949-52, Batt cmd locating batt 1953-56, NATO HQ Fontainbleau 1956-58, Lt-Col CO 280 (City of Glasgow) Field Regt RA TA 1958-60, local Col SBLO USA REUR Heidelberg 1960-62, staff AFNORTH Oslo 1962-64, Col Head Br Def Intelligence Liaison Staff Washington USA 1964-67, Chief of PR AFCENT Holland 1967-70, ret 1970; def corr in numerous int def jls 1970-89; pres Sidmouth Branch Royal Br Legion 1980-(Cullompton branch 1971-80 memb Burma Star Assoc 1970-79, co sec ACC (Int) Devon Scouts, contrib to Scouting Magazine; memb: Inst of Journalists 1969-88, RUSI until 1989; *Recreations* shooting, travel, riding, painting, skiing; *Style—* Col Norman Dodd; Byways, 23 Cotlands, Cotmaton Rd, Sidmouth, Devon EX10 8SP (☎ 0395 514 693)

DODD, William Atherton; CMG (1983); s of Frederick Dodd (d 1979) of Mayfield, Newton Lane, Chester, and Sarah, *née* Atherton (d 1976); *b* 5 Feb 1923; *Educ* City GS Chester, Christs Coll Cambridge (MA, Cert Ed); *m* 10 Aug 1949, Marjorie, da of Maj Reginald Charles Penfold, MC (d 1970), of Reckerby, Queens Park, Chester; 2 da (Patricia b 1954, Janet b 1957); *Career* WW11 Capt 8 Gurkha Rifles 1942-45; sr history master Ipswich Sch 1947-52, educn offr Miny of Educn Tanganyika/Tanzania 1952-65, under sec ODM 1980-83 (advsr 1970-77, educn advsr 1978-83), conslt Univ of London Inst of Educn 1983- (lectr 1965-70), chm Sir Christopher Cox Meml Fund, UK rep UNESCO Exec Bd 1983-85; *Books* Primary School Inspection in New Countries (1968), Society Schools and Progress in Tanzania (with J Cameron, 1970), Teacher at Work (1970); *Recreations* walking, music, watching cricket; *Clubs* MCC, Kent CR, Sevenoaks Vine; *Style—* William Dodd, Esq, CMG; 20 Bayham Rd, Sevenoaks, Kent TN13 3XD (☎ 0732 454238); Inst of Education, Univ of London, 20 Bedford Way, London WC1H 0AL (☎ 071 636 1500 ext 734)

DODDS, Denis George; CBE (1977); s of Herbert Yeaman Dodds (d 1941), of Newcastle upon Tyne, and Violet Katherine Dodds (d 1928); *b* 25 May 1913; *Educ* Rutherford Coll Newcastle upon Tyne, Armstrong Coll Univ of Durham, Univ of London (LLB); *m* 27 Feb 1937, Muriel Reynolds (Pearly), da of Edward Smith (d 1950), of Durham; 2 s (Michael Edward b 9 Sept 1937, Gareth Yeaman b 26 June 1943), 3 da (Philippa Helen b 30 Aug 1944, Jaqueline Eira b 4 March 1947, Stephanie Eileen b 20 Feb 1951); *Career* Lt RNVR 1940-46, served: destroyers, light coastal forces, naval trg; admitted slr 1936; dep town clerk Cardiff 1946-48, sec and slr S Wales Electricity Bd 1948-57, industl relations advsr Electricity Cncl 1957-60, chm Merseyside and N Wales Electricity Bd 1962-77 (dep chm 1960-62); memb Electricity Cncl 1962-77: chm Nat Jt Ctee for managerial pay and conditions, vice chm Nat Jt Industl Cncl for pay and conditions of manual employees; chm: Port of Preston Advsy Bd 1977-79, Br Approval Serv for Electric Cables Ltd 1981-, Merseyside C of C and Indust 1976-78; memb: CBI Cncl Wales 1962-78, NW Econ Planning Cncl 1971-79, Nat Advsy Cncl for Employment of Disabled People 1981-; cmmr for Boy Scouts Penarth S Wales 1950-57, gen sec Bristol Free Churches Housing Assoc 1983-, memb Westbury-on-Trym PCC 1984-87; CIEE 1960-, FBIM 1960-77; *Recreations* music, gardening; *Clubs* Cwlth Soc; *Style—* Denis Dodds, Esq, CBE; Corners, 28 Grange Park, Westbury-on-Trym, Bristol BS9 4BP (☎ 0272 621440)

DODDS, Jacqueline Ann; da of Ronald Woolley (d 1982), of Hoddesdon, Herts, and Gladys, *née* Wilderspin; *b* 8 Feb 1947; *Educ* Netteswell GS, Turnford Coll of Further Ed; *m* 2, 1986, Joseph Peter Dodds, s of Robert Horne Dodds; 1 s (Robert Lloyd b 26 June 1984); *Career* civil servant Export Credits Guarantee Dept 1965-67, audit/accounts clerk Trevor Jones & Co (chartered accountants) Waltham Cross 1967-69; Everett Pinto & Co (now merged with Finnies): trainee accountant 1967-69, ptnr 1978, i/c Branch Office Buntingford 1980-83; founded own sole practice J A Kennion & Co 1983-; pres Beds Bucks and Herts Dist Soc of Chartered Accountants 1990-91 (memb 1981-); FCA 1981 (ACA 1976); *Style—* Mrs Jacqueline Dodds; J A Kennion & Co, Hillside Farm, Newmarket Road, Royston, Hertfordshire SG8 7LZ (☎ 0763 245663, fax 0763 245194)

DODDS, Nigel Alexander; s of Joseph Alexander Dodds, of Enniskillen, Co Fermanagh, and Doreen Elizabeth, *née* McMahon; *b* 20 Aug 1958; *Educ* Portora Royal Sch, St John's Coll Cambridge (univ scholarship and McMahen studentship, BA, Winfield prize for law), Inst of Professional Legal Studies Belfast; *m* 17 Aug 1985, Diana Jean, da of James Harris, of Loughbrickland, Banbridge, Co Down; 2 s ((Nigel Andrew) Mark b 5 Aug 1986, Andrew James Joseph b 5 Jan 1990); *Career* called to the Bar NI 1981; memb Secretariat of Euro Parl 1983-; elected memb Belfast City Cncl 1985-, Lord Mayor of Belfast 1988-89; vice pres Assoc of Local Authorities of NI 1988-89; memb senate Queens Univ Belfast 1988-; spokesman UDUP; patron Kegworth Air Disaster Appeal Fund; *Style—* Nigel Dodds, Esq; City Hall, Belfast (☎ 0232 320202)

DODDS, Sir Ralph Jordan; 2 Bt (UK 1964), of W Chiltington, Co Sussex; s of Sir (Edward) Charles Dodds, 1 Bt, MVO, (d 1973); *b* 25 March 1928; *Educ* Winchester, RMA Sandhurst; *m* 9 Oct 1954, Marion, da of Sir Daniel Thomas Davies, KCVO (d 1966), of 36 Wimpole St, London; 2 da; *Career* Capt 13/18 Royal Hussars; underwriting memb of Lloyd's 1964; insur broker: Bray Gibb & Co (later Stewart Wrightson (UK) Ltd 1958-83), Willis Faber & Dumas 1983-90; *Clubs* Cavalry & Guards, Hurlingham; *Style—* Sir Ralph Dodds, Bt; 49 Sussex Square, London W2

DODDS, Richard David Allan; OBE (1990); s of Allan Edward Russell Dodds, of Winchester, and Mary Pattinson, *née* Johnson; *b* 23 Feb 1959; *Educ* Kingston GS, St Catharine's Coll Cambridge (Hockey blue), St Thomas's Hosp Med Sch London; *m* 28 Sept 1985, Doon Laura, da of Patrick Lovett; 1 da (Hannah Frances Emma b 22 Aug 1989); *Career* hockey player; Cambridge Univ 1978-81 (capt 1980-81), Southgate Hockey Club 1981-89; England caps: 6 under 18 and under 19 1976, 26 under 21 1977-80 (capt 1980), 79 full; 65 GB caps; honours: Bronze medal Olympic Games LA 1984, Silver medal World Cup London 1986, Silver medal Euro Cup Moscow 1987, Gold medal Olympic Games Seoul 1988; qualified doctor 1984, currently registrar in orthopaedic surgery Nuffield Orthopaedic Centre Oxford; FRCS 1989; *Recreations* cricket, golf, squash; *Style—* Richard Dodds, Esq, OBE; c/o The hockey Association, 16 Northdown St, London N1 9BG

DODDS-PARKER, Sir (Arthur) Douglas; only s of Arthur Percy Dodds-Parker (d 1940); sr rep of jr line of Parker of Little Norton, Co Derby (the Parkers became ironmasters and made much of the cannon used against the Americans and Napoleon, William Parker being master cutler 1761); assumed additional surname and arms of Dodds by Royal Licence 1908; the name Dodds comes from Sir Douglas' father's godfather, Ralph Dodds, sometime Lord Mayor of Newcastle; has inherited through maternal gf (Wise) the feudal right to collect dung from the streets of Dundee; by his w Mary (d 1934), da of Joseph Alexis Patrick Wise, JP, of Belleville Park, Cappoquin, Co Waterford; *b* 5 July 1909; *Educ* Winchester, Magdalen Coll Oxford (MA); *m* 6 April 1946, Aileen Beckett, only da of Norman Beckett Coster (d 1929), of Paris, and wid of Capt Ellison Murray Wood, IG; 1 s; *Career* served WWII Grenadier Gds (despatches), specifically employed in Special Operations 1940-45, special ops 1940-45, with Sudan Political Serv 1930-1939; co dir 1946-; MP (C) Oxfordshire (Banbury Div) 1945-59, MP (C) Cheltenham 1964-74; under sec of state for Foreign and Cwlth Affrs 1953-57, chm Cons Parly Foreign and Cwlth Ctee 1970-73, UK memb of Euro Parl Strasbourg 1973-74; Légion d'Honneur (Fr), Croix de Guerre avec Palme (Fr); kt 1973; *Recreations* fishing, walking; *Clubs* Carlton, Leander, Vincent, Special Forces (chm and pres 1975-81); *Style—* Sir Douglas Dodds-Parker; 9 North Court, Great Peter St, London SW1; The Lighthouse, Westport, New York, NY 12993, USA

DODGE, Paul William; s of Ralph William Dodge, of 5 Squires Ride, Leics, and Greta, *née* Rogerson; *b* 26 Feb 1958; *Educ* Roundhill HS Thurmaston, Wreake Valley Coll Syston; *m* 12 April 1981, Julia, da of Herbert Alan Bown; 2 s (Alexander William b 17 Nov 1984, Oliver Paul b 27 Aug 1987); *Career* Rugby Union centre three quarter Leicester FC and England (32 caps); Leicester FC 1975- (420 appearances); England: debut v Wales 1978, won Grand Slam 1980, toured Argentina 1981 (2 test appearances), toured Fiji Tonga Japan, toured SA 1984, toured NZ 1985 (2 test appearances), most capped centre (32 caps 1978-85); Br Lions: toured SA 1980 (2 test appearances); runs family restoration and bookbinding business; *Recreations* tennis, golf, swimming, reading, gardening; *Style—* Paul Dodge, Esq; Leicester Football Club, Welford Road, Leicester

DODGEON, David Charles; s of Walter Dodgeon (d 1968), of Singapore, and Anne Elizabeth, *née* Mills; *b* 21 Nov 1952; *Educ* King's Sch Bruton, Chelmer Inst of Higher Educn (HND); *m* 28 Feb 1976, Yvonne Christine, da of Anthony Vernon Hollington, of Clacton-on-Sea; *Career* accountant P&O steam Navigation Co Ltd 1976-78, co sec Hedger Mitchell Stark 1978-81, gp fin controller Grandfield Rork Collins Ltd 1981-86, fin dir Rowland Ltd 1986-88; dir The Rhino Communications Gp; ICSA 1976, MBIM 1978; *Recreations* sport incl golf, squash, photography; *Clubs* RAC, Pall Mall; *Style—* David Dodgeon, Esq; Great Braxted Hall Barn, Great Braxted, Essex CM8 3EN (☎ 0621 892999), 14 Blacklands Terrace, London SW3 2SP (☎ 071 584 7666, fax 071 225 3409)

DODGSON, Paul; s of Flt Lt Reginald Dodgson, RAF, and Kathleen Slyvia, *née* Jay; *b* 14 Aug 1951; *Educ* Tiffin Sch Kingston, Univ of Birmingham; *m* 20 Feb 1982, Jan, da of Geoffrey Hemingway (d 1966); 2 da (Eleanor b 17 Sept 1984, Laura b 22 July 1986); *Career* called to the Bar Inner Temple 1975; in practice criminal law; *Recreations* sailing; *Clubs* Hardway Sailing, Bar Yacht, Surrey Cricket; *Style—* Paul Dodgson, Esq; 2 Garden Court, Temple, London EC4 (☎ 071 583 0434, fax 071 353 3987)

DODMAN, Alan Victor; s of C V Dodman (d 1949), of Byfleet, Surrey, and A M Dodman, *née* Matcham (d 1985); *b* 12 July 1924; *Educ* Woking GS for Boys Surrey; *m* 17 Sept 1949, Hazel, da of Alfred Reeves (d 1937); 3 s (Eric Alan b 13 Jan 1952, John Richard b 17 Nov 1961, Philip Andrew b 18 Sept 1964); *Career* Nat Serv WWII RAF Warrant Offr and Pilot; sales dir TF Firth and Sons Ltd 1963-77, md Firth Carpets Ltd 1977-83, exec dep chm Readicut International plc 1988- (md 1983-88), dir and chm of various Readicut subsidiary cos 1983-; *Recreations* cricket and interest in most other sports; *Clubs* Yorks Co Cricket; *Style—* Alan Dodman, Esq; Peper Harow, 113 Pannal Ash Rd, Harrogate, N Yorks HG2 9JL (☎ 0423 504 298); Readicut International plc, Clifton Mills, Brighouse, Yorks HD6 4ET (☎ 0484 721 223, fax 0484 716 135, telex 517457)

DODSON, Hon Christopher Mark; s and h of 3 Baron Monk Bretton, *qv*; *b* 2 Aug 1958; *Educ* Eton, Univ of S Calif (MBA); *m* 1988, Karen, o da of B J McKelvain, of Fairfield, Conn, USA; 1 s (Benjamin b 1989), 1 da (Emma b 1990); *Career* pres and fndr Applied Digital Technology Beverly Hills California USA; *Style—* The Hon Christopher Dodson

DODSON, Sir Derek Sherborne Lindsell; KCMG (1975, CMG 1963), MC (1945), DL (Lincoln 1987); s of Charles Sherborne Dodson, MD (d 1956), of Leadenham, Lincoln, and Irene Frances, *née* Lindsell (d 1977); *b* 20 Jan 1920; *Educ* Stowe, RMC Sandhurst; *m* 29 Nov 1953, Julie Maynard, o child of Hon Maynard Bertram Barnes (d 1970), of Washington DC, USA; 1 s (Gerald b 1957), 1 da (Caroline b 1955); *Career* served 1939-48 in RSF, mil asst to Br Cmmr Allied Control Cmmn for Bulgaria 1945-46; private sec to Min of State FO 1955-58, consul Elisabethville 1962-63, cnsllr and consul-gen Athens 1966-69; ambass: Hungary 1970-73, Brazil 1973-77, Turkey 1977-80; special rep to Sec of State for Foreign and Cwlth Affairs 1980-; chm Anglo Turkish Soc 1982-, Beaver Guarantee Ltd 1984-86, dir Benguela Railaway Co 1984-; Grand Cross of Cruzeiro do Sul (Brazil) 1976; *Recreations* walking, reading, history; *Clubs* Boodle's, Travellers'; *Style—* Sir Derek Dodson, KCMG, MC, DL; 47 Ovington St, London SW3 (☎ 071 589 5055); Gable House, Leadenham, Lincoln (☎ 0400 72212)

DODSON, Hon Henry George Murray; s of 3 Baron Monk Bretton; *b* 11 Feb 1960; *Educ* Eton, CNAA (BSc); *Career* assoc dir John D Wood Commercial Ltd 1988-; ARICS 1986; *Style—* The Hon Henry Dodson

DODSON, Jane Leila; da of Maj Michael Bedell Dodson, of Northington Down, nr Alresford, Hants, and Leila Mary, *née* Downer; *b* 20 Feb 1950; *Educ* Sorbonne, Birkbeck Coll London (BA); *m* 4 Oct 1986, Mervyn Peter Michael Walker, s of Dr Richard Hillier Walker, of The Old Parsonage, Galmpton, nr Kingsbridge, S Devon; 1 s (Alexander Michael Luke Wolfe b 24 Feb 1988); *Career* dir and shareholder Benjamin Benjamin Assocs 1976-82, dir and owner The Kinnerton Street Design Co Ltd 1980 (Interior designers and decorators); memb Save the Rhino Appeal; *Recreations* theatre, music, reading, art, languages, antiques, sculpture, skiing, tennis, swimming, sailing, cooking, entertaining, gardening; *Style—* Miss Jane Dodson; 45 Wilton Crescent, London SW1 (☎ 071 235 7031); The Kinnerton St Design Co Ltd, 36 Kinnerton St, Knightsbridge, London SW1X 8ES (☎ 071 235 9315, fax 071 823 1595, car phone 0831 458791)

DODSON, Richard Charles; s of John Summerville Dodson, of 17 Saville Court, Woodford Green, Essex, and Muriel Edith, *née* Bunce; *b* 2 Jan 1951; *Educ* Buckhurst Hill County HS, UCL (BSc); *m* 14 April 1979, Barbara, da of Allan Carrington, of 21 Clarkes Ave, Kenilworth, Warwickshire; 1 s (Lee b 1968); *Career* media res dir Foote Cone and Belding ltd 1984-87 (media res mangr 1972), md Telmar Communications Ltd 1988-, pres Telmar Gp Inc NY 1989-; treas Woodford Green CC; FIPA 1987; *Recreations* racing horses, cricket, bridge; *Style—* Richard Dodson, Esq; 15 Fairlight Ave, Woodford Green, Essex IG8 9JP (☎ 081 504 6193); Curlew Cottage, Talland St, Polperro, Cornwall; Telmar Communications Ltd, Southbank Technopark, 90 London Rd, London SE1 6LN (☎ 071 922 8816, fax 071 261 9724, car 0860 463232)

DODSWORTH; *see*: Smith-Dodsworth

DODSWORTH, Geoffrey Hugh; JP (York 1961, later Herts); s of late Walter J J Dodsworth, and Doris, *née* Baxter; *b* 7 June 1928; *Educ* St Peter's Sch York; *m* 1, 1949, late Isabel Neale; 1 da (Helen b 1958); m 2, 1971, Elizabeth Ann, da of Dr Alan W Beeston, of Cumbria; 1 s (Simon b 1972), 1 da (Mary b 1974); *Career* dir Grindlays Bank Ltd 1976-80, chief exec Grindlay Brandts Ltd 1977-80, chm Oceanic Fin Servs Ltd 1985-86 (pres and chief exec 1982-85), dep chm Oceanic Fin Corp Ltd 1985-86 (pres and chief exec 1982-85), pres Jorvik Fin Corp Ltd 1986-, dir Co Properties Gp plc 1987-88, currently chm Dodsworth & Co Ltd (formed 1988), dir of other cos; memb York City Cncl 1959-65, MP (Cons) Herts SW 1974-79; FCA; *Recreations* riding; *Clubs* Carlton; *Style—* Geoffrey Dodsworth Esq, JP; Well Hall, Well, Bedale, N Yorks DL8 2PX (☎ 0677 70223); 78, Cliffords Inn, Fetter Lane, London EC4A 1BX (☎ 071 831 8926)

DODSWORTH, Prof (James) Martin; s of Walter Edward Dodsworth, and Kathleen Ida, *née* MacNamara; *b* 10 Nov 1935; *Educ* St George's Coll Weybridge, Univ of Fribourg, Wadham Coll Oxford (BA, MA); *m* 14 April 1968, Joanna, da of Wiktor Slawosz Rybicki; 1 s (Samuel James b 1968); *Career* lectr in Eng Birkbeck Coll Univ of London 1961-67, lectr then sr lectr then prof of Eng Royal Holloway Coll Univ of London (now Royal Holloway and Bedford Coll) 1967-, poetry reviewer The Guardian 1969-88, ed English 1976-87; chm: The English Assoc 1987-, Cncl for Univ Eng (co fndr with Dr Gordon Campbell); *Books* The Survival of Poetry (ed, 1970), Hamlet Closely Observed (1985), English Economise'd (1989); *Style—* Prof Martin Dodsworth; 59 Temple Street, Brill, Buckinghamshire HP18 9SU (☎ 0844 237106); Royal Holloway & Bedford New College, Egham Hill, Egham, Surrey TW20 0EX

DODSWORTH, Robert Leslie; DL; s of Harold Dodsworth; *b* 7 Sept 1936; *Educ*

Barnard Castle Sch, Univ of Durham; *m* 1964, Hazel Joan, *née* Moyse; 2 s; *Career* CA; gp chief exec Ransomes plc engrs Ipswich 1977-; *Recreations* golf, squash; *Clubs* Ipswich & Suffolk, Woodbridge Golf, Ipswich Golf; *Style—* Robert Dodsworth, Esq, DL; 223 Rushmere Rd, Ipswich, Suffolk (☎ 0473 724974); Ransomes plc, Ipswich (☎ 0473 270000)

DODWELL, Christina; da of Christopher Bradford Dodwell, of Sussex, and Evelyn, *née* Beddow; *b* 1 Feb 1951; *Educ* Southover Manor Lewes, Beechlawn Coll Oxford; *Career* explorer and author; 3 year journey through Africa by horse 1975-78; 2 year journey through Papua New Guinea by horse and canoe 1980-81, presenter BBC film River Journey-Waghi 1984 (winner BAFTA award); memb Madagascar Consulate; Freedom Sepik River region of Papua New Guinea 1984; FRGS 1982, FRSA 1985; *Books* Travels with Fortune 1979, In Papua New Guinea 1982, An Explorers Handbook 1984, A Traveller in China 1986, A Traveller on Horseback 1987, Travels with Pegasus 1989; *Recreations* fossil hunting, walking; *Style—* Ms Christina Dodwell; 16 Lanark Mansions, Pennard Road, London W12 8DT; Hodder & Stoughton, 47 Bedford Sq, London WC1B 3DP (☎ 071 636 9851, fax 071 746 0134, telex 885887)

DODWELL, Prof (Charles) Reginald; s of William Henry Walter (d 1969), of Cheltenham, and Blanche, *née* Mudway (d 1965); *b* 3 Feb 1922; *Educ* Pates Sch Cheltenham, Gonville and Caius Coll Cambridge (MA, PhD, LittD); *m* 5 Dec 1942, Sheila Juliet, da of James Henry Fletcher (d 1981), of Cheshire; 1 s (David b 8 July 1955), 1 da (Jane b 5 Dec 1951); *Career* Lt RNVR 1941-45; fell Gonville and Caius Coll Cambridge 1950-53, sr fell Warburg Inst 1950-53, librarian Lambeth Palace 1953-58; fell, lectr and librarian Trinity Coll Cambridge 1958-66; Pilkington prof history of art Univ of Manchester 1966-89, dir Whitworth Art Gallery 1966-89; FBA 1960; *Books* Canterbury School of Illumination (1954), Theophilus De Diversis Artibus (1961), Reichenau Reconsidered (1965), Painting in Europe 800-1200 (1971), Anglo-Saxon Art (1982), The Pictorial Arts of the West 800-1200 (1991); *Recreations* opera, Shakespeare, badminton; *Style—* Prof Reginald Dodwell; The Old House, 12 Park Rd, Cheadle Hulme, Cheshire SK8 7DA (☎ 061 485 3923); Univ of Manchester, Oxford Rd, Manchester M13 9PL (☎ 061 275 3311)

DOE, Canon Francis Harold; s of Spencer F Doe (d 1922), and Ellen Mary, *née* Yerrill (d 1968); *b* 2 June 1922; *Educ* Secdy & Southwark Ordination Course; *m* 3 Sept 1955, (Elinor) Jill, da of Capt David Houseman (d 1956), of Middlesex; 1 s (Michael b 3 March 1959), 1 da (Amanda 24 Oct 1960); *Career* curate: Sompting 1971-74, Stopham and Hardham 1974-78, priest i/c Sutton Bignor and Barlavington 1978-81, vicar Warnham 1981-87, rector Stopham and Fittleworth 1987-, rural dean Petworth 1988-, canon and prebendary Chichester Cathedral 1989-; govr Chichester Prebendal Sch, vice chm Fittleworth Sch; *Recreations* watching cricket, sailing; *Clubs* Forty, Sea View Yacht; *Style—* The Rev Canon Francis Doe; Fittleworth Rectory, Pulborough, W Sussex RH20 1JG (☎ 079882 455)

DOEGAR, Rakesh Chandar; s of Hans Raj Doegar, of New Delhi, India, and Kamla Sood (d 1946); *b* 10 Jan 1945; *Educ* Dehra Sch, Queens Coll, Punja State Univ, (BA Econ); *m* 31 July 1971, Anne Marilyn, da of James William Herbert, of Moonrakers, Elveley Drive, W Ella, Hull, E Yorks; 1 s (Chand-Edward b 1982), 2 da (Hemione b 1973, Evemala b 1978); *Career* CA; sr ptnr R C Doegar & Co 1985, sr ptnr Jackson Taylor 1986, chm: M E I Engrg plc 1985, Sheppee Engrg Ltd 1986, Wiltex Ltd 1987; FICA; *Recreations* swimming, moor and fell walking, landscape gardening; *Clubs* Groucho; *Style—* Rakesh Doegar, Esq; Walton House, Walton on the Hill, Tadworth, Surrey KT20 7UJ; 159 Putney High St, London SW15 1RT

DOGGART, Anthony Hamilton (Tony); s of James Hamilton Doggart (d 1989), of Albury, Surrey, and his 2 w Leonora Margaret, *née* Sharpley; *b* 4 May 1940; *Educ* Eton, King's Coll Cambridge (MA); *m* 1 May 1964, Caroline Elizabeth, da of Nicholas Gerard Voute, of Flat 2, Huize Boschzicht, Neuhuyskade 2, 2596 XL The Hague; 1 s (Sebastian Hamilton b 6 April 1970), 1 da (Nike Henrietta b 16 March 1972); *Career* head of Special Business Dept Save & Prosper Gp 1970-74, pres First Investment Annuity Co of America 1974-78, int exec vice pres Insur Co of N America 1978-80, fin dir Save & Prosper Gp 1986- (sales dir 1980-86); called to the Bar Middle Temple 1962(memb Lincoln's Inn); chm Tax Ctee Unit Trust Assoc, memb The Crafts Cncl, memb Ctee Iris Fund for the Prevention of Blindness, involved with Waterboatmen Ltd; *Books* Tax Havens and Offshore Funds (Economist Intelligence Report, 1972); *Recreations* skiing, water skiing, wild mushrooms, oak furniture; *Clubs* Garrick, Brooks's, City of London, Hurlingham; *Style—* Tony Doggart, Esq; 23 Ovington Gardens, London SW3 1LE (☎ 071 584 7620); Save & Prosper Gp Ltd, 1 Finsbury Ave, London EC2M 2QY (☎ 071 588 1717, fax 071 247 5006/071 377 5213, 883838)

DOGGART, John Victor; s of John Doggart, of Macclesfield, and Sara Doggart; *b* 9 May 1941; *Educ* Uppingham, Clare Coll Cambridge (MA), UCL (MA); ptnr Zoë, da of Air Cdre James Coward, of Canberra Australia; 1 da (Tamzin b 1973); *Career* architect: Robert Matthew Johnson Marshall 1962, Urban Resources Administration (NY) 1966, Richard and Su Rogers (now Richard Rogers Assocs) 1967-69; energy conslt Milton Keynes Development Corp 1970-80, ptnr ECD Partnership (architects and energy conslts) 1980-; former memb Dept of Energy Solar Heating Ctee, memb Nat Energy Rating Ctee; CEng, MInstE; *Recreations* canoeing, sailing, skiing, jigsaws, reading; *Style—* John Doggart, Esq; The ECD Partnership, 11-15 Emerald St, London WC1N 3QL (☎ 071 405 3121, fax 071 405 1670)

DOHERTY, Dr Ciaran Conor; s of John Doherty, and Kathleen, *née* Hunter; *b* 29 March 1948; *Educ* St Marys CBS GS Belfast, Queens Univ of Belfast (MB, MD); *m* Kathleen Mary Collins, da of John Michael Collins, of 12 Denewood Park, Belfast; 1 s (Conor b 1981), 2 da (Karen b 1978, Catherine b 1981); *Career* NI kidney res fell 1976-78, clinical fell in nephrology med centre Univ of S California 1979-81, conslt renal physician Belfast City Hosp and Royal Victoria Hosp 1981-, special lectr dept of med Queens Univ of Belfast 1983-, (jr tutor 1973-75, clinical teacher in nephrology 1981-), post grad clinical tutor Belfast Post Grad Med Centre 1985; author of 30 papers on kidney disease transplantation and diuretics; pres I Nephrology Soc 1986-88, NI rep and cncl memb Nat Assoc of Clinical Tutors 1986; MRCP 1975, memb Assoc of Physicians of GB and NI 1988, fell Royal Acad of Med in Ireland 1990; *Books* Peptic Ulcer and Chronic Renal Failure (1978); *Clubs* Corrigan; *Style—* Dr Ciaran Doherty; 17 Deramore Park South, Belfast, Northern Ireland BT9 5JY; Regional Nephrology Unit, Belfast City Hospital Tower, Lisburn Rd, Belfast BT9 5JY (☎ 0232 329241)

DOHERTY, Dr Michael; s of Donald Doherty, of Upton, Devon, and Eileen Mary, *née* Fairchild (d 1980); *b* 7 March 1951; *Educ* City of London Freemens Sch, St John's Coll Cambridge (BA, MA, MB BChir, MD, MRCP); *m* 27 Sept 1980, Sally Anne; 2 da (Emma b 1982, Jill b 1983); *Career* conslt sr lectr rheumatology Univ of Nottingham 1985-; chm Arthritis and Rheumatism Educn Sub-Ctee, assoc ed Annals of Rheumatic Diseases, ed-in-chief International Monitor-Rheumatology; Freeman City of London 1984; *Books* Rheumatological Medicine (1985), Pyrophosphate Arthropathy - A Clinical Study (1988); *Recreations* cinema, opera, osteology, art; *Style—* Dr Michael Doherty; Rheumatology Unit, City Hospital, Nottingham NG5 1PB (☎ 0602 691412)

DOHERTY, Michele; da of Michael John Doherty, of 31 Manor Crescent, Standlake, Witney, Oxon, and Kitty Doreen, *née* Watters; *b* 28 May 1964; *Educ* Henry Box Sch Witney Oxon; *Career* memb Br Barefoot Water Ski Team 1977-79 and 1984- (Capt 1989), Euro Gp II ladies champion 1977, 1979 and 1986-89, Nat ladies champion 1978 and 1984-89, Euro ladies Challenge 1985-89, World ladies jump champion 1986; currently: Nat and Euro ladies trick record holder, Nat and Euro ladies slalom record holder, Nat ladies forwards and backwards speed record holder; Southern Region barefoot water ski coach; memb BWSF; *Recreations* whippet racing, golf; *Clubs* 3 T's Water Sports (Standlake); *Style—* Miss Michele Doherty; 31 Manor Crescent, Standlake, Witney, Oxon OX8 7RX (☎ 0865 300852); Barclays Bank plc, 30 Market Sq, Witney, Oxon OX8 7BJ (☎ 0993 776611, fax 0993 773610)

DOHERTY, Prof Peter Charles; s of Eric C Doherty, and Linda M Doherty; *b* 15 Oct 1940; *Educ* Univ of Queensland (BVSc, MVSc), Univ of Edinburgh (PhD); *m* 1965, Penelope Stephens; 2 s; *Career* veterinary surgeon; veterinary offr Animal Res Inst Brisbane 1963-67, scientific offr then sr scientific offr Dept of Experimental Pathology Moredun Res Inst Edinburgh 1967-71, postdoctoral fell then res fell Dept of Microbiology John Curtin Sch of Med Res ANU Canberra (1972-75, (prof and head Dept of Experimental Pathology 1982-88), assoc prof then prof Wistar Inst Philadelphia 1975-82, chm Dept of Immunology (Michael F Tamer chair of Biomedical Res) St Jude Children's Res Hosp Memphis 1988-; licentiate RCVS; memb: American Assoc of Immunologists, American Assoc of Pathologists, Neuroimmunology Soc; FAA 1983, FRS 1987; Paul Ehrlich Prize (West Germany) 1983, Gairdner Int Award for Med Sci (Canada) 1986; memb various editorial boards; *Publications* author of numerous articles in learned journals, book chapters and reviews; *Recreations* walking, skiing, reading; *Style—* Prof Peter Doherty, FRS; 1389 Vinton Avenue, Memphis, Tennessee 38104, USA FOREIGN (☎ 901 725 9522); Department of Immunology, St Jude Children's Research Hospital, 332 North Lauderdale, Memphis, Tennesse 38101-0318 (☎ 901 522 0470, fax 901 527 6616)

DOIG, Caroline May; da of Lt George William Lowson Doig (d 1942); *b* 30 April 1938; *Career* house offr and registrar Dundee, gen surgery trg Darlington and Durham, sr house offr in paediatric surgery Glasgow, further paediatric surgery trg Hosp for Sick Children Gt Ormond St London and Hosp for Sick Children Edinburgh; currently sr lectr in paediatric surgery Univ of Manchester, conslt Booth Hall Children's Hosp and St Mary's Hosp Manchester; memb: Admissions Ctee Univ of Manchester, paediatric speciality trg gp NHS 1976-78, Surgical Div Manchester DHA, paediatric surgery rep Central Manchester Dist Surgical Ctee, N Manchester AHA 1990, Cncl of Manchester Med Soc 1980, 1983, 1990- (memb Cncl of Surgical Section 1982), Cncl of Paediatric Section RSM 1984-87, Cncl RCSEd 1984- (examiner primary 1980-, examiner part II 1982-, memb Sci and Educn Sub Ctee 1985-89 and 1990-, examiner in Singapore 1987, Kuwait 1989, Kuala Lumpur 1990, Hong Kong 1990), Med Advsy Bd Br Cncl 1990; nat pres Med Women's Fedn 1985-86 (memb 1962-, memb Cncl 1980-, memb Exec 1981-, memb Sub Ctee on Postgrad Trg, memb Med Educn and Ethical Ctee, Manchester Liason offr); memb: Br Assoc of Paediatric Surgns, Assoc of Surgns of GB and I, Br Soc of Gastroenterology, Br Paediatric Soc of Gastroenterology, Scot Paediatric Surgical Soc, Manchester Med Soc, Manchester Paediatric Club; FRSA; *Recreations* golf, swimming, theatre, ballet and cooking; *Style—* Miss Caroline Doig; 11 Kersal Crag, Singleton Road, Salford M7 0WL; Booth Hall Children's Hospital, Charlestown Rd, Blackley, Manchester M9 2AA (☎ 061 741 5198)

DOIG, Robertson Lindsay; s of Isaac Doig (d 1977), of Dundee, and Jean Ann Durno, *née* Robertson (d 1986); *b* 30 Aug 1938; *Educ* Univ of St Andrews (MB ChB), Univ of Dundee (ChM); *m* 24 Sept 1966, Roslyn, da of James Mayo Buchanan (d 1989), of Toorak, Melbourne; 3 s (Geoffrey b 1971, Roger b 1974, Colin b 1978); *Career* lectr in surgery and sr surgical registrar St Thomas' Hosp 1968-76, surgn to the Gen Infirmary Leeds and hon sr lectr in surgery Univ of Leeds 1976-; former tutor RCS; fell: Assoc of Surgns, Vascular Surgical Soc, RSM; memb: Br Assoc of Endocrine Surgns, Leeds Medico-legal Soc (vice pres and memb Ctee), Leeds Medico-Chirurgical Soc; Freeman City of London 1978, Liveryman Worshipful Soc of Apothecaries; FRCS Ed 1967, FRCS 1969; *Recreations* shooting, history, fine arts, music; *Clubs* Cheselden; *Style—* R Lindsay Doig, Esq; Strathleven, 439 Harrogate Road, Leeds, W Yorkshire LS17 7AB (☎ 0532 680053); General Infirmary at Leeds LS1 3EX (☎ 0532 432799); Mid-Yorkshire Nuffield Hospital, Leeds LS18 4HP (☎ 0532 588756); BUPA Hospital Leeds LS8 1NT (☎ 0532 693939)

DOIMI de LUPIS, Countess (Thyra) Ingrid Hildegard; da of Nils Andreas Detter (d 1961), and Thyra Carin, *née* Hellberg; *b* 24 Nov 1939; *Educ* Lyceum Stockholm, Mon Fertile Lausanne, Univ of Oxford (DPhil), Univ of Stockholm (Jur Kand, Jur Lic, Jur Dr), Univ of Paris (lic en droit), Univ of Turin (CHEE, Dip Euro Law); *m* 2 April 1968, Count Louis Doimi de Lupis, s of Count Peter Doimi (d 1964); 3 s (Count Peter b 1971, Count Nicholas b 1975, Count Lawrence b 1977), 2 da (Paola b 1969, Christina b 1973); *Career* asst judge Stockholm Central and Civil and Criminal Court 1962-63, barr Middle Temple and Lincoln's Inn 1977-; Univ of Oxford: fell St Antony's Coll 1963-64, tutor Merton Coll 1963-64, fell Lady Margaret Hall 1964-68, lectr 1964; res prof of law of Euro communities Swedish State Cncl 1968-72, prof of int law Univ of Uppsala 1974-76, visiting prof LSE 1980- (lectr 1972-74), Lindhagen Prof of int law Univ of Stockholm 1988-, DG Inst for Studies in Environmental Law 1989-; memb: Br Inst of Int Comparative Law 1965-, Royal Inst Int Affrs 1976-; memb: Nat Exec Stockholm Int Law Asoc 1976- (memb Exec Bd London 197 chm Ctee Maritime Neutrality 1989-, Int Inst for Strategic Studies 1985-, Union Int des Avocats 1986-, Energy Ctee Int Bar Assoc 1987-, Int Inst for Space Law Paris 1989-, Euro Space Agency Law Centre Paris 1989- (fndr); fell Int Acad of Astronautics 1990-; *Books* incl: Law Making by International Organisations (1965), The East African Community and the Common Market (1971), International Law and the Independent State (1973, 2 edn, 1987), The Law of Economic Integration (1976), The Law of War (1987), International Law (1989); *Recreations* music, skiing; *Clubs* Hurlingham; *Style—* Countess Doimi de Lupis; 10 Wellington Court, 116 Knightsbridge, London SW1X 7PL (☎ 071 589 0413); 1 Hare Court, Temple, London EC4 (☎ 071 351 3171, fax 071 166 477)

DOLBY, Dr Richard Edwin; s of James Edwin Dolby, of 3 Neal Close, Northampton, and Kathleen Florence, *née* Clarke (d 1978); *b* 7 July 1938; *Educ* Northampton GS, Selwyn Coll Cambridge (BA, MA, PhD); *m* ; 2 da (Catherine Julia b 30 Aug 1965, Elizabeth Jane b 1 July 1968); *Career* Nat Serv REME 1956-58, graduate trainee Alcan Industries 1962-63, GEC Hurst Research Laboratories 1963-65, The Welding Institute: joined as res metallurgist 1965, head of Materials Dept 1978-80, res mangr 1980-86, dir Research & Technol 1986-; Pfeil prize Inst of Metals 1972, Sir William Larke Medal The Welding Inst 1982, Brooket Medal The Welding Inst 1990; chm Materials Engrg Div and vice pres Inst of Metals 1988-; chm: Res Strategy Study Gp Int Inst of Welding 1989-, Ctee on the Structural Integrity of Fast Breeder Ractors UKAEA 1989-; FIM 1977, fell The Welding Inst 1977, FEng 1987; *Recreations* golf, philately, gardening; *Style—* Dr Richard Dolby; 25 High St, Burwell, Cambridgeshire CB5 OHD (☎ 0635 741305); The Welding Institute, Abington Hall, Abington, Cambridge CB1 6AL (☎ 0223 891162)

DOLE, John Anthony; s of Thomas Stephen Dole (d 1974), of Faversham, Kent, and Winifred Muriel, *née* Henderson; *b* 14 Oct 1929; *Educ* Berkhamsted Sch; *m* 1952, Patricia Ivy, da of Victor Clements, of Kent; 2 s (Nicholas, Marcus); *Career* admin The Sports Cncl 1972-75, dir Sr Staff Mgmnt DOE and Tport 1978-82, controller of the Crown Suppliers 1982-86, controller and chief exec HM Stationery Office 1987-89, ret; *Recreations* writing, philately; *Style*— John Dole, Esq

DOLL, Prof Sir (William) Richard Shaboe; OBE (1956); s of Henry William Doll, and Amy Kathleen, *née* Shaboe; *b* 28 Oct 1912; *Educ* Westminster, St Thomas's Hosp (DM, MD, DSc); *m* 1949, Joan Mary Faulkner, da of Charles William Duncan Blatchford; 1 s, 1 da; *Career* served WWII RAMC; dir Statistical Res Unit MRC 1961-69, Regius prof of med Oxford 1969-79, first warden Green Coll Oxford 1979-83; chm: Adverse Reaction Sub Ctee Ctee for the Safety of Medicines 1970 UK Coordinating Ctee Cancer Research 1972-77; vice pres Royal Soc 1970-71; memb: MRC 1970-74, Royal Cmmn on Environmental Pollution 1973-79, Standing Cmmn Energy and Environment 1978-82; RCP lectr: Milroy 1953, Marc Daniels 1969; orator Harveian 1982; hon fell 1982-: LSHTM, RSM; Hon DSc: Reading, Newcastle, Newfoundland, Belfast, Stoney Brook, Harvard, London, Oxford; Hon DM Tasmania; Royal Soc's Buchanan medal, Royal Soc's Royal medal 1986, RIPH&H Gold medal, BMA Gold medal 1983; FRCP, FRCGP; kt 1971; *Style*— Prof Sir Richard Doll, OBE; 12 Rawlinson Rd, Oxford OX2 6UE (☎ 0865 58887)

DOLLEY, Christopher; s of late Dr Leslie George Francis Dolley; *b* 11 Oct 1931; *Educ* Bancrofts Sch, CCC Cambridge; *m* 1966, Christine Elizabeth Cooper, 3 s; *Career* chm Penguin Books 1971-73 (former export mangr, dir, md); dir book devpt IPC 1973-77; chm Damis Group Ltd 1971-; *Style*— Christopher Dolley Es; Elm Place, 54 St Leonards Rd, Windsor, Berks (☎ 66961)

DOLLING, Frank - Francis Robert (Frank); s of Frederick Dolling; *b* 21 Jan 1923; *Educ* Tottenham County Sch; *m* 1949, Maisie Noquet; 2 da; *Career* served WWII RAF; joined Barclays Bank Int 1947; chm: Barclays Merchant Bank 1980-, Barclays Bank Int 1983-; dep chm Barclays Bank 1983-; *Style*— Frank Dolling Esq; Rowan Cottage, The Ridgway, Pyrford, Surrey (☎ 093 23 43362); Barclays Bank International Ltd, 54 Lombard St, London EC3P 3AH (☎ 071 283 8989)

DOLLOND, Steven; s of Charles Dollond; *b* 28 Nov 1943; *Educ* Quintin Sch, Lincoln Coll Oxford (MA), Harvard Business Sch (MBA); *Career* barr Middle Temple; private office of Ldr of the Opposition 1968-70, contested (C) Eton and Slough Feb and Oct 1974; mgmnt conslt Arthur D Little 1972-77, mktg dir Br Technol Gp 1977-86, md Strategy International 1988-; *Recreations* exotic travel; *Clubs* Carlton; *Style*— Steven Dollond, Esq; 804 Grenville House, Dolphin Square, London SW1V 3LR (☎ 071 798 8089)

DOLMAN, James William; s of Victor William Dolman (d 1989), of Ilminster, Somerset, and Dorothy Edith, *née* Angell (d 1973), of Calne Wiltshire; *b* 26 April 1934; *Educ* Ilminster GS, St John's Coll Cambridge (MA, LLM); *m* 28 Dec 1957, Jean, da of Harry Angles (d 1966), of Ipswich; 1 s (Edward James b 1960), 3 da (Elizabeth (Mrs Page) b 1961, Katherine b 1963, Emily b 1966); *Career* Nat Serv cmmnd RAF 1952; admitted slr; sr ptnr Bircham & Co, hon slr King Edward VII's Hosp for Offrs; hon fell Purcell Sch of music, chm Samuel Gardner Meml Tst; memb: Law Soc 1960, City of Westminster Law Soc; *Recreations* arts, cycling, rough sports; *Style*— James Dolman, Esq; 15 Spencer Walk, Putney, London SW15; 1 Dean Farrar St, Westminster, London SW1 (☎ 071 222 8044)

DOLMAN, Julian Henry; s of Arthur Frederick Dolman (d 1976), of Newport, Monmouthshire, and Margaret Mary, *née* McKinnon; *b* 16 Sept 1939; *Educ* Sherborne, St Catherine's Coll Cambridge (MA); *m* 1, 29 Nov 1962 (m dis 1974), Juliet, da of James White, of Charmouth; 2 da (Catherine b 1964, Sarah b 1966); m 2, 21 Sept 1974, Susan Jennifer, da of Roy Frederick Palmer, of Little Aston, Sutton Coldfield; 2 s (Charles b 1975, Edward b 1976); *Career* admitted slr 1966, ptnr Wall James and Davies; author of numerous articles on town planning law; Freeman City of London 1979; memb Law Soc 1966; *Recreations* Africana 1840-52, history, gardening; *Style*— Julian Dolman, Esq; Forge Mill Farm, Shelsley Beauchamp, Worcs WR6 6RR; Wall James and Davies, 19 Hagley Road, Stourbridge, W Mids DY8 1QW (☎ 0384 371 622, fax 0384 374 057)

DOLMETSCH, Carl Frederick; CBE (1953); s of Dr (Eugène) Arnold Dolmetsch, Chev de la Légion d'Honneur (d 1940), and Mabel, *née* Johnston (d 1963); *b* 23 Aug 1911; *Educ* privately, studied violin under Carol Flesch and Antonio Brosa; *m* 24 Feb 1937 (m dis 1961), Mary Douglas, da of James Alexander Ferguson, of Over Courance, by Lockerbie, Dumfriesshire; 2 s (François b 1940, Richard b 1945 d 1966), 2 da (Jeanne b 1942, Marguerite b (twin) 1942); *Career* musician; first public concert at 7 and first tour at 8; tours incl: Alaska, Australia, Austria, Belgium, Canada, Colombia, Denmark, France, Germany, Italy, Japan, Netherlands, NZ, Sweden, Switzerland, USA; dir: Soc of Recorder Players 1937-, Haslemere Festival of Early Music and Instruments 1940-, Dolmetsch Int Summer Sch 1971-; md Arnold Dolmetsch Ltd 1940-76 (chm 1963-78), chm Dolmetsch Musical Instruments 1982-; memb Art Workers Guild 1953- (Master 1988); hon fell Trinity Coll of Music 1950; Hon DLitt Univ of Exeter 1960; hon fell London Coll of Music 1963; ISM; *Books* author of many edns of Music, books on recorder playing (1957, 1962, 1970, 1977); *Recreations* ornithology, natural history; *Style*— Carl Dolmetsch, Esq, CBE; Jesses, Grayswood Rd, Haslemere, Surrey GU27 2BS (☎ 0428 643818); Dolmetsch Musical Instruments, 107 BRI, Haste Hill, Haslemere, Surrey GU27 3AY (☎ 0428 3235, fax 0428 56808, telex 858485 DEVCOM G)

DOLMETSCH, Mary Douglas; *née* Ferguson; da of James Alexander Ferguson (d 1963), of Dumfriesshire, and Janet Weir (d 1964); *b* 16 Feb 1916; *Educ* Dumfries Acad, Abbots Hill Hemel Hempstead, Glasgow Coll of Domestic Sci; *m* 24 Feb 1937, Carl Frederick, s of Eugene Arnold Dolmetsch (d 1940), of Haslemere, Surrey; 2 s (François b 1940, Richard b 1945 decd), 2 da (Jeanne b 1942, Marguerite (twin) b 1942); *Career* dir Arnold Dolmetsch Ltd Early Musical Instruments 1938-81; life memb Dolmetsch Fndn, (hon organising sec 1947-61); Br Red Cross Peeblesshire 1966-73; Nat Dip Housewifery, ret; *Recreations* gardening, reading, travel, music, theatre; *Clubs* The Caledonian, (Edinburgh); *Style*— Mrs Mary D Dolmetsch; Easter Greybield, Peebles, Scotland EH45 9JB

DOLTON, David John William; s of Walter William Dolton (d 1969), and Marie Frances Duval, *née* Rice; *b* 15 Sept 1928; *Educ* St Lawrence Coll Kent; *m* 1, 1959, Patricia Helen, da of late Maj Ernest G Crowe; 1 s (Kevin b 1964), 1 da (Catherine b 1961); m 2, 1986, Rosalind Jennifer, da of Harold Victor Chivers, of Bath, Avon; *Career* Delta Metal Gp 1950-76: commercial dir Extrusion Div, dir admin and personnel Rod Div 1967-76, also various non-exec directorships; chief exec Equal Opportunities Cmmn 1976-78, asst gen mangr UK National Employers Mutual General Insurance Ltd 19 dir and asst gen mangr NEM Business Services Ltd 1980-89; mgmnt conslt 1989-; reader Diocese of Gloucester; Liveryman Worshipful Co of Gold and Silver Wyre Drawers; FCIS, FBIM, FIPM; *Recreations* music, reading, hill walking, swimming, travel, photography; *Style*— David Dolton, Esq; 85 Corinium Gate, Cirencester, Glos GL7 2PX (☎ 0285 657739)

DOLTON, Nigel Timothy; s of Robert Hugh Dolton, of Walton-on-Thames, Surrey, and Vera Florence, *née* Hemming; *b* 21 Feb 1944; *Educ* Bradfield Coll; *m* 17 May 1969, Jutta, da of Herr Roderich Hans Emil Dittmar; 1 s (Timothy b 1974), 1 da (Sally b 1976); *Career* advertising exec; dir Smedley McAlpine Saward Ltd 1980-; *Recreations* golf, theatre; *Clubs* Burhill Golf; *Style*— Nigel T Dolton, Esq; Balaton, Oatlands Close, Weybridge, Surrey; 140 Camden Street, London NW1 9DB (☎ 071 267 7070, fax 071 267 2707)

DOMINGO, Rashid; MBE (1987); s of late Achmat Domingo, of Cape Town, SA, and Rukea Domingo; *b* 24 June 1937; *Educ* Trafalgar HS Cape Town, Univ of Cape Town (BSc); *m* 1962, Moreeda, *née* Maureen Virginia Sheffers; 1 s, 1 da; *Career* prodn mangr: Seravac Laboratories 1961-67, Miles Seravac Laboratories 1967-71; md Biozyme Laboratories Ltd 1971-; MIBiol, CChem, CGIA, FRCS, FBS, FInstD, FInstM; *Style*— Rashid Domingo, Esq, MBE; The Beeches, Pen-y-Pound, Abergavenny, Gwent (☎ 0873 79460, work tel 0495 790678)

DOMINIAN, Dr (Jacob) Jack; s of Charles Joseph Dominian, and Mary, *née* Scarlatou; *b* 25 Aug 1929; *Educ* Lycee Leonin Athens, St Mary's HS Bombay, Stamford GS, Fitzwilliam House Cambridge (MA, MB BChir), Exeter Coll Oxford (MA); *m* 23 June 1955, Edith Mary, da of John Smith (d 1961), of 5 Brighton Grove, N Shields; 4 da (Suzanne Mary b 1957, Louise Regina b 1958, Elise Aline (Mrs Milne) b 1961, Catherine Rene b 1964); *Career* Nat Serv RAOC 1948-49; conslt physician then sr house offr Radcliffe Infirmary 1957-58, sr registrar Maudsley Hosp 1958-64, conslt physician Central Middlesex Hosp 1965-88; dir One Plus One Marriage & Partnership Research 1971-; memb: Catholic Marriage Advsy Cncl, Church of England's Cmmn on Marriage; Hon DSc Univ of Lancaster 1976; memb: BMA, RSM; FRCPEd, FRC Psych; *Books* Christian Marriage (1967), Marital Breakdown (1968), The Church and the Sexual Revolution (1971), Cycles of Affirmation (1975), Authority (1975), Proposals for a New Sexual Ethic (1977), Marriage Faith Love (1981), The Capacity to Love (1985), Sexual Integrity (1987), God, Sex and Love (with Hugh Montefiore, 1989); *Recreations* writing, music, theatre; *Style*— Dr Jack Dominian; Pefka, The Green, Croxley Green, Rickmansworth, Herts (☎ 0923 720 972); 2 Devonshire Place, London W1

DOMINICZAK, Dr Marek Henryk; s of Dr Tadeusz Dominiczak, of Gdansk, Poland, and Dr Aleksandra Dominiczak; *b* 12 March 1951; *Educ* Copernicus HS Gdansk, Med Acad of Gdansk Poland (MB, PhD); *m* 26 Dec 1976, Dr Anna Felicja Dominiczak, da of Prof Jakub Penson (d 1971); 1 s (Peter b 1985); *Career* conslt pathologist St Luke's Hosp Malta 1979-82, registrar and sr registrar Glasgow Royal Infirmary 1982-85, conslt biochemist Western Infirmary Glasgow 1985-, hon lectr Univ of Glasgow 1986-; special professional at: Univ of Oslo 1974, Rockerfeller Univ NY 1989; memb: Br Diabetic Assoc, Assoc Clinical Biochemists, Br Hyperlipidlaemia Assoc, American Assoc for Clinical Chem; MRCPath; *Recreations* tennis, photography; *Clubs* Bearsden Tennis; *Style*— Dr Marek Dominiczak; 27 Dunkeld Drive, Bearsden, Glasgow G61 2AR (☎ 041 942 3742); Dept of Biochemistry, Western Infirmary, Glasgow G11 6NT (☎ 041 339 8822 ext 4788, fax 041 339 2628)

DON, Andrew George; s of Air Vice-Marshal Francis Percival Don, OBE (d 1964), of Elmham House, E Dereham, Norfolk, and Angela Jane, *née* Birkbeck; *b* 23 Aug 1934; *Educ* Eton, Trinity Coll Cambridge (MA); *m* 30 May 1974, Diana Susan, da of John Edward Dykes, of 48 Chesil Court, London SW3 and Haverthwaite, Cumbria; *Career* called to the Bar Inner Temple 1960; local chm Social Security Appeal Tbnls 1984, dep chm Agric Land Tbnl 1986, chm Med Appeal Tbnls (N London Region); memb Norfolk CC 1969-77; steward Gt Yarmouth and Fakenham Racecourses, churchwarden Little Dunham; *Recreations* fishing, shooting, racing, travel; *Clubs* Cavalry and Guards, Norfolk (Norwich); *Style*— Andrew Don, Esq; The Old Rectory, Little Dunham, Kings Lynn, Norfolk PE32 2DG (☎ 0760 22584); 48 Chesil Court, London SW3; Octagon House, 19 Colegate, Norwich (☎ 0603 623186)

DON, Robert Seymour; s of Air Vice-Marshal Francis Percival Don, OBE, DL (d 1964), of Elmham House, North Elmham, Norfolk and Angela Jane, *née* Birkbeck; *b* 5 April 1932; *Educ* Eton, Trinity Coll Cambridge (MA); *m* 2 July 1955, Judith Henrietta, da of Geoffrey Nicholas Holmes, of the Old Rectory, Shotesham All Saints, Norfolk; 4 da (Charlotte b 1956, Joanna b 1958, Fiona b 1962, Henrietta b 1965); *Career* Nat Serv 1 The Royal Dragoons 1950-52, TA Fife and Forfar Yeomanry 1953-54; John Harvey & Sons Ltd 1957-65, RS Don Ltd and Hicks & Don Ltd Wine Merchants (chm 1966), owner Elmham Park Vineyard & Winery 1970-; vice chm English Vineyards Assoc, former chm Norfolk Fruit Growers Assoc; Master of Wine; *Books* Teach Yourself Wine (1968), Off the Shelf (1967); *Recreations* shooting, fishing, deer stalking, skiing, photography; *Clubs* The Cavalry & Guards; *Style*— Robert Don, Esq; Elmham House, North Elmham, Dereham, Norfolk NR20 5JY (☎ 036 281 363)

DON, Robin Cameron; s of John Buttercase Don (d 1970), of Newport-on-Tay, Fife, Scotland, and Elizabeth Seath, *née* Fairbairn (d 1986); *b* 9 June 1941; *Educ* Bell Baxter HS Cupar Fife; *Career* theatre designer; trained to be a blacksmith and engr; apprentice to theatre designer Ralph Koltai 1967-71; *Designer* Open Space Theatre 1971-77: Four Little Girls, Othello, Tooth of Crime, How Beautiful with Badges, The Taming of the Shrew, And They Put Handcuffs on the Flowers, Sherlock's Last Case, Measure for Measure, Hamlet, The Merchant of Venice; Mary Queen of Scots (Scot Opera) 1977, Bartholomew Fair (Round House) 1978, Les Mamelles de Tiresias (RAM/Opera North) 1978, Les Mamelles de Tiresias (ENO) 1979, Eugene Onegin (Aldeburgh) 1979, The Marriage of Figaro (Opera North) 1979, A Midsummer Night's Dream (Aldeburgh) 1980, The Flying Dutchman (Opera North) 1980, The Ticket of Leave Man (NT) 1981, Shakespeare's Rome (Mermaid) 1981, Hotel Paradiso (NT of Iceland) 1981, The Trumpet Major (RNCM and WNO) 1981, The Last Elephant (Bush) 1981, Cosi Fan Tutti(NIOT Belfast) 1981, The Birthday Party (Pitlochry) 1981-82, Song and Dance (Palace London) 1982, Madame Butterfly (Opera North) 1982, L'Elisir d' Amore (NIOT Belfast) 1982, The Midsummer Marriage (San Francisco Opera) 1983, Peter Grimes (WNO) 1983, Eugene Onegin (Ottawa) 1982, Twelfth Night (RSC Stratford) 1983 and (RSC Barbican) 1984, The Boy Friend (Old Vic) 1984, Tamerlano (Opera de Lyon) 1984, When I Was a Girl I Used to Scream and Shout (Bush) 1984, Giasone (Buxton Festival) 1984, Kiss of the Spiderwoman (Bush) 1985, When I Was A Girl...(Edinburgh Festival) 1985, On The Edge (Hampstead) 1985, Chicago (NT of Iceland) 1985, Man of Two Worlds (Westminster) 1985, Peter Grimes (Aust Opera Sydney) 1986, A Midsummer Night's Dream (ROH Covent Garden) 1986, Don Quixote (NY City Opera) 1986, Eugene Onegin (San Francisco Opera) 1986, When I Was A Girl...(Sydney and Whitehall) 1986, More Light (Bush) 1987, Norma (ROH) 1987, Carmen (Sydney) 1987, La Forza del Destino (Toronto) 1987, Fat Pig (Haymarket Leicester) 1987, Spookhouse (Hampstead) 1987, The Brave (Bush) 1988, Ziegfeld (London Palladium) 1988, A Walk in the Woods, (Comedy) 1988, Cavalleria Rusticana (Sydney) 1989, Hidden Laughter (Vaudeville) 1990, The Rocky Horror Show (Piccadilly) 1990, Macbeth (Sanitago Ballet) 1991; *Awards* winner Golden Troika (for Eugene Onegin) at Prague Quadriennale 1979; dir Int Scenography Course Central St Martin's London 1990-; memb: Exec Ctee Soc of Br Theatre Designers 1975-, British Theatre Design 1979-1983, British Theatre Design 1983-1987; *Recreations* exploration of natural phenomena; *Style*— Robin Don, Esq

DON, Stuart Warren; s of Stuart M Don (d 1931); *b* 14 Sept 1914; *Educ* Hotchkiss Sch, Princeton Univ USA (BA); *m* 1, 1938, Elsie Burke (d 1983), da of Herbert H Foster (d 1962); 3 da; m 2, 1984, Ann Margaret Frances, o da of late Lt-Col Robert George Barlow, widow of Roger Thornycroft, DSC, and previously of Capt John Rupert Dupree, and formerly w of Hon William Gladstone Bethell; *Career* Lt-Col US Army; exec recruitment John Courtis and Ptnrs 1976-, vice pres Chemical Bank 1959-69, Chase Manhattan Bank 1954-59, dir American Chamber of Commerce (UK) 1958- (pres 1967-69), US/UK Educnl Cmmn 1968-, tstee American Sch in London 1969-, exec cmmr Br-American Associates 1970-; Bronze star 1945, Croix de Guerre 1945; *Recreations* foxhunting; *Clubs* Boodle's, City of London, Buck's, American, Monday Luncheon (co-chm 1972-), Ends of the Earth (exec commissioner 1976-); *Style—* Stuart Don, Esq; The Green, Kingham, Oxon; 15 Portman Square, London W1H 9HD (☎ 071 935 6704)

DON-WAUCHOPE, Sir Roger Hamilton; 11 Bt (NS 1667), of Newton; elder s of Sir Patrick George Don-Wauchope, 10 Bt (d 1989), and Ismay Lilian Ursula, *née* Hodges; *b* 16 Oct 1938; *Educ* Hilton Coll Natal, Durban Univ; *m* 14 Dec 1963, Sallee, yr da of Lt-Col Harold Mill-Colman, OBE, ED, of Durban, S Africa; 2 s, 1 da; *Heir* s, Andrew Craig Don-Wauchope b 18 May 1966; *Career* CA; Deloitte Haskins & Sells 1959- (ptnr 1972-); *Style—* Sir Roger Don-Wauchope, Bt; Newton, 53 Montrose Drive, Pietermaritzburg 3201, Natal, S Africa (☎ 010 27 0331 471107)

DONAGHY, Michael John; s of Patrick Joseph Donaghy (d 1985), of New York City, and Eveline Christine, *née* Sheehy (d 1972); *b* 24 May 1954; *Educ* St Raymond's HS New York, Fordham Univ New York (Regent's scholarship, BA), Univ of Chicago (MA); *Career* ed Chicago Review 1978-85, freelance writer of poetry and reviews 1985-; *publications:* Slivers 1985, Shibboteth 1988; *Awards:* Nat Poetry Competition 1988, Whitbread Prize for Poetry 1989, Geoffrey Faber Meml Award 1990; *Style—* Michael Donaghy, Esq; 51 Burgoyne Rd, London N4 (☎ 081 341 1469)

DONAGHY, Roger; s of George Gerald Donaghy (d 1989), and Florence, *née* Thompson; *b* 10 Feb 1940; *Educ* Portadown Tech Coll, Univ of Adelaide; *m* 17 Nov 1962, Rachael, da of Joseph Watson, of Portadown, Co Armagh, NI; 1 da (Nina Dianne b 1968); *Career* reporter and feature writer Portadown Times 1955-61, feature writer Advocate Newspapers Tasmania 1961-63, TV reporter and industl corr Aust Broadcasting Corp Adelaide 1961-65; BBC World Serv News 1966-; journalist, duty ed, newsroom ed; FDR memb Rotary Club of Danson; *Recreations* golf, travel, reading, photography; *Style—* Roger Donaghy, Esq; 41 Bean Rd, Bexleyheath, Kent (☎ 081 303 5109); BBC, Bush House, Strand, London WC2 (☎ 081 240 3456)

DONALD, Dr Alastair Geoffrey; OBE (1982); s of Dr Pollok Donald (d 1955), of Whitehouse Rd, Edinburgh, and Henrietta Mary, *née* Laidlaw (d 1975); *b* 24 Nov 1926; *Educ* Edinburgh Acad, CCC Cambridge (MA), Univ of Edinburgh (MB ChB); *m* 3 April 1952, (Edna) Patricia, da of Richard Morrison, WS, of Ireland (d 1944), of 12 Mortonhall Rd, Edinburgh; 2 s (Ian Pollok b 1955, William b 1960), 1 da (Patricia Mary b 1953); *Career* Sqdn-Ldr med branch RAF 1952-54; GP Edinburgh 1954-, lectr Dept Gen Practice Univ of Edinburgh 1960-70; RCGP: vice chm Cncl 1976-77, chm Bd of Censors 1979-80, chm Cncl 1979-82, chm Int Ctee 1987-; past chm and provost SE Scotland Faculty, radio doctor BBC Scotland 1976-78; chm: UK Conf of Postgrad Advrs in Gen Practice 1978-80, Court of Dirs The Edinburgh Acad 1978-85 (dir 1957-85), Jt Ctee on Postgrad Trg for Gen Practice 1982-85, Armed Servs Gen Practice Approval Bd 1986-, Scottish Ctee Action on Smoking and Health 1986-, Med Advsy Gp BBC Scotland 1988-; specialist advsr to House of Commons Social Servs Ctee 1986-87; James MacKenzie medal RCP Edinburgh 1983, James MacKenzie lectr RCGP 1985, Bruce Meml lectr 1987; pres: Rotary Club Leith 1957-58, Edinburgh Academical Club 1978-81; FRCGP 1971, FRCPE 1981; *Recreations* golf; *Clubs* Hawks (Cambridge), Univ of Edinburgh Staff; *Style—* Dr Alastair Donald, OBE; 30 Cramond Rd North, Edinburgh EH4 6JE (☎ 031 336 3824); Leith Mount, 46 Ferry Rd, Edinburgh EH6 4AE (☎ 031 554 0558)

DONALD, Hon Mrs (Angela Caroline); da of Baron McFadzean, kt (Life Peer); *b* 5 Dec 1942; *Educ* Benenden; *m* 21 Sept 1963, Robin Vyvyan Carter Donald, s of Norman Donald, of Newbury, Berks; 3 children; *Recreations* reading, tennis; *Style—* The Hon Mrs Donald; Osborne House, Bathampton, Bath, Avon BA2 6SW (☎ 0225 464212)

DONALD, Craig Reid Cantlie; CMG (1963), OBE (1959); s of Rev Francis Cantlie Donald (d 1974), of Lumphanan, Aberdeenshire, and Mary, *née* Reid (d 1945); *b* 8 Sept 1914; *Educ* Fettes, Emmanuel Coll Cambridge (BA, MA); *m* 2 June 1945, Mary Isabel (d 1989), da of John Speid (d 1912), of Sidpore Tea Estate, India; 1 da (Rosemary Ann (Mrs John) b 1946); *Career* WWII Lt-Col MEF and CMF 1940-46; admin offr Cyprus 1937; cmmr Famagusta 1948, registrar Co-op Socs 1951, dep fin sec Uganda 1951, sec to the Treasy 1956-63 (memb Legislative Cncl 1954-62), Bursar Malvern Coll 1964-79; govr Ellerslie and Downs Colwall Schs; *Recreations* gardening; *Clubs* Travellers'; *Style—* C R C Donald, Esq, CMG, OBE; 55 Geraldine Rd, Malvern, Worcs WR14 3NU (☎ 0684 561446)

DONALD, David Mitchell Cooke; WS; *b* 29 Sept 1914; *Educ* Aberdeen GS, Aberdeen Univ (LLB); *m* 1941, Mary Catherine; *Career* served 21 Army Gp, Maj, DAAG; merchant banker 1960; chm: Fleming Claverhouse Investmt Tst plc, Fleming Fledgeling Investmt Tst plc, Fleming Universal Investmt Tst plc, Mercantile and General Reinsurance Co plc; non-exec dir: Robert Fleming Hldgs Ltd, Prudential Corp plc; *Recreations* gardening; *Clubs* Carlton; *Style—* David Donald Esq, WS; Downs House, Plumpton, Sussex BN7 3DH (☎ 0273 890465); Robert Fleming Holdings Ltd, 8 Crosby Sq, London EC3A 6AN (☎ 01 638 5858)

DONALD, Ian Francis; s of Harold Gordon Donald (d 1975), of Capetown, SA, and Jean Dorian, *née* Graham (d 1947); *b* 20 Aug 1928; *Educ* St Peter's Coll Adelaide S Aust; *m* 20 Nov 1958, Sonia Evelyn, da of James Bruce Leask, CBE (d 1980), of Pangbourne, Berks; 1 s (Adrian Francis b 1963), 1 da (Caroline Bruce b 1968); *Career* jt md Firth Cleveland Ltd 1960-72, dep chm Guest Keen & Nettlefolds plc (now GKN plc) 1972-88; chm: Allen West Ltd Ayr 1985-89, United Engineering Steels Ltd 1986-; dir Hall Engineering (Holdings) plc 1987-; chm Hayward Fndn, chm Charles Hayward Tst; FIOD; *Recreations* shooting, fishing, sailing; *Clubs* Royal Thames Yacht, RAC; *Style—* Ian Donald, Esq; Rockfield Farm, Monmouth NP5 4NH, (☎ 0600 3217, fax 0600 4715)

DONALD, John Alistair; *b* 6 Dec 1928; *Educ* Farnham GS, Farnham Sch of Art, RCA (travel scholarship); *m* (m dis); 4 s, 1 da; *Career* Nat Serv 1947-49; self-employed designer goldsmith and silversmith; design conslt: Hadley Co 1956-75, Antler Luggage 1958-68, Halex hairbrushes 1960-65; exhibitor with Goldsmiths Co NY 1960, fndr own workshop Bayswater 1960; proprietor: retail shop and workshop Cheapside 1968-, retail shop (with Tecla Pearls) Bond St London 1969-72, additional workshop Sussex 1970; external assessor to various maj arts and crafts schs, chief assessor Chamber of Mines jewellery competition SA 1972 and 1973; work incl: civic and presidential regalia, silver for Birmingham Cathedral, Oxford & Cambridge Colls and City Livery Cos; work in the private collections of: HRH The Queen Mother, HRH Princess Margaret, HRH Prince Charles, Duchess of Gloucester, Queen Margarethe of Denmark, Rt Hon Mrs Thatcher; former offices incl: Sheriff of Nottingham, Mayor of Lincoln, Sheriff City of London; Warden Worshipful Co of Goldsmiths (Freeman 1959, Liveryman 1972); *Recreations* golf; *Style—* John Donald, Esq; 120 Cheapside, London EC2 (☎ 071 606 2675)

DONALD, Dr John Robin; TD (1968); s of Robert Rintoul Donald (d 1979), of Philadelphia, USA, and Jean Bonnar, *née* Philp (d 1984); *b* 2 April 1929; *Educ* Hillhead HS Glasgow, Univ of Glasgow (MB ChB); *m* 19 Oct 1957 (m dis 1975), Sarah (Sally), *née* Johnstone; 2 s (Iain, Ross); *Career* MO: 1 Bn Kings Own 1953-55, 1 Bn Glasgow Highlanders 1955-67, 1 Bn Lowland Vols 1972-84; conslt in neuroanaesthesia 1969-, author of various papers on blood loss during surgery; chm property mgmnt ctee of 34 Cranworth St, sec Crangeorge Residents' Assoc, memb Scottish Nat Blood Transfusion Ctee; Fell Coll of Anaesthetists 1963; *Recreations* TA, hill walking, history; *Style—* Dr John Donald, TD; 34 Cranworth St, Glasgow G12 8AG (☎ 041 334 2218); Dept of Neuroanaesthesia, Institute of Neurological Sciences, Southern General Hospital, Glasgow G51 4TF (☎ 041 445 2466)

DONALD, William Sainsbury; *b* 30 May 1933; *Educ* Aberdeen GS, Aberdeen Coll of Agric; *m* 1956, Bertha Mary; 2 children; *Career* md Donald-Russell Ltd; former pres Scottish Assoc of Wholesale Meat Salesmen; *Recreations* shooting, fishing, squash; *Clubs* Farmers', Directors'; *Style—* William Donald, Esq; Binghill House, Milltimber, Aberdeen (☎ 0224 732554); Donald & Russell, Inverurie, Aberdeenshire (☎ 0467 22601)

DONALDSON, Antony Christopher; s of Sqdn Ldr John William Donaldson (ka 1940), and Sheila Richardson, *née* Atchley; *b* 2 Sept 1939; *Educ* Charterhouse, Regent Street Poly, Slade Sch UCL, UCL, Harkness Fellowship USA; *m* 1960, Patricia Anne, da of Charles William Marks; 2 s (Matthew John b 1961, Lee b 1963); *Career* artist; teacher Chelsea Sch of Art 1962-66; recents cmmns incl: bronze and iron screen Yohji Yamamoto London 1987, fountain Horselydown Square Michael Baumgarten for Berkley House 1988-91 and torso Anchor Ct Horselydown Square 1989-91, aquarium wall and doors Arnold Chan Isometrics London 1990, wall piece Emmanuelle Khanh Paris 1990; solo exhibitions incl: Rowan Gallery London 1963, 1965, 1966, 1968, 1970, 1979 and 1981, Nicholas Wilder Gallery Los Angeles 1968, Galleria Milano Milan 1971, Galerie du Luxembourg Paris 1973, 1976 and 1977, Bonython Gallery Adelaide Australia 1983, Juda Rowan Gallery London 1984, Daniel Gervis Paris 1985, Corcoran Gallery Los Angeles 1985, Mayor Rowan Gallery London 1989; gp exhibitions incl: Young Contemporaries (London) 1958, 1959, 1960 and 1961, John Moores Open (Walker Art Gallery Liverpool) 1963, The New Generation (Whitechapel Art Gallery) 1964, 4ieme Biennale des Jeunes Artistes Musee d'Art Moderne Paris 1965, Recent British Painting (Peter Stuyvesant Fndn Collection) 1967, Art for Industry (RCA) 1969, Pittsburgh Int 1967, Contemporary Prints (Ulster Museum Belfast) 1972, Graphics by Gallery Artists (Mayor Rowan Gallery London), 1978, British Pop Art (Birch and Conran Fine Art London) 1987, Gallery Artists (Rowan Gallery London) 1991; pub collections incl: Arts Cncl of GB, Bradford City Art Gallery, Contemporary Art Soc London, Govt Art Collection, Olinda Museum Brazil, Tate Gallery, Ulster Museum Belfast, Walker Art Gallery Liverpool; films: Soft Orange 1969, Pix 1972; *Style—* Antony Donaldson, Esq; c/o A Gregory-Hood, Mayor Rowan Gallery, 31A Bruton Place, London W1 (☎ 071 499 3011, fax 071 355 3486)

DONALDSON, (William) Blair MacGregor; s of Dr William Donaldson, of 11 Crawfurd Rd, Edinburgh, and Janet Thompson, *née* Orr (d 1970); *b* 24 Dec 1940; *Educ* The Edinburgh Acad, Univ of Edinburgh (MB ChB); *m* 27 July 1966, Marjorie Stuart, da of Hugh Gordon Mackay (d 1958); 1 da (Lesley Elizabeth b 1972); *Career* jr hosp appts in Tasmania and Scotland 1966-79, conslt ophthalmic surgn, sr univ lectr 1979- (special interest in microsurgical instrument design and devpt); memb: BMA, SOC, MECA; FRCSE, FCOphth; *Recreations* skiing, tennis, golf, shooting, oil painting, silversmithing; *Style—* Blair Donaldson, Esq; Kindrochit Lodge, Braemar, Deeside, Aberdeenshire; 45 Carlton Place, Aberdeen (☎ 0224 641166)

DONALDSON, Dr David Abercrombie; s of Robert Danaldson, of Coatdyke, Coatbridge, and Margaret, *née* Cranston (d 1982); *b* 29 June 1916; *Educ* Coatbridge Sr Secdy Sch, Glasgow Sch of Art; *m* 1, 1942 (m dis 1947), Kathleen Boyd, da of Jo Maxwell (d 1983); 1 s (David Lennox b 15 July 1944); m 2, 8 Sept 1948, Maria (Marysia) Krystyna, da of Maj Leon Witold Mora-Szorc (d 1984), of Carcavelos, Portugal; 2 da (Sally Mora b 23 Nov 1950, Caroline Mary b 14 Sept 1956); *Career* painter; head drawing and painting Glasgow Sch of Art 1967-81; sitters incl: Dame Jean Roberts, Lord Binning, Rev Lord McLeod, Mrs Winifred Ewing, MEP, Earl of Haddo, Cameron of Lochiel, Sir Samuel Curran, Sir Norman MacFarlane, Rt Hon Margaret Thatcher, Rt Hon David Steel, Sir Alwyn Williams, HM The Queen for the Palace of Holyroodhouse; painter of landscapes still life and composition; maj exhibitions incl: Retrospective (Glasgow, Edinburgh, Dundee, London) 1983, Donaldson At 70 (fine Arts Soc Glasgow and Edinburgh); works in collections worldwide; appointed by Royal warrant painter and limner to HM The Queen in Scotland 1977-; memb Ctees Scot Arts Cncl; Hon LLD Univ of Strathclyde 1971, Hon DLitt Univ of Glasgow 1988; ARSA 1951, memb RSA 1962, RP 1964, RGI 1977; *Recreations* music, cooking; *Clubs* Glasgow Art; *Style—* Dr David Donaldson; 5 Cleveden Drive, Glasgow G12 0SB (☎ 041 334 1029); 7 Chelsea Manor Studios, Flood St, London SW3 (☎ 071 352 1932); St Roman de Malegarde, Vaucluse, Provence 84290, France (☎ 010 33 90289265)

DONALDSON, David Torrance; QC (1984); s of Alexander Walls Donaldson, of Glasgow, and Margaret Merry, *née* Bryce; *b* 30 Sept 1943; *Educ* Glasgow Acad, Gonville and Caius Coll Cambridge (MA), Univ of Freiburg (DrJur); *m* 31 Dec 1985, Therese Marie Madeleine, da of Pierre Arminjon; *Career* fell Gonville and Caius Coll Cambridge 1965-1969, called to Bar Gray's Inn 1968; *Style—* David Donaldson, Esq, QC; 2 Hare Court, Temple, London EC4Y 7BH (☎ 071 583 1770, fax 071 583 9269, telex 27139)

DONALDSON, Frances; da of Frederick Lonsdale (d 1954), and Leslie Brook Hoggan; *b* 13 Jan 1907; *m* 20 Feb 1935, John George Stuart, Baron Donaldson, s of Stuart Donaldson; 1 s (Thomas b 1 June 1935), 2 da (Rose b 4 Nov 1937, Catherine b 18 Nov 1945); *Career* author; *Books*: Approach to Farming (1942), Four Years Harvest (1945), Milk Without Tears (1955), Freddy Lonsdale (1957), Child of the Twenties 1959, The Marconi Scandal (1962), Evelyn Waugh: Portrait of a Country Gentleman (1967), Edward VIII (1974, Wolfson history award 1975), P G Wodehouse (authorised biography, 1982), The British Council: the first fifty years (1984), The Royal Opera House in The Twentieth Century (1988); FRSL 1975; *Style—* Frances Donaldson; 17 Edna St, London SW11 3DP (☎ 071 223 0259)

DONALDSON, Hamish; s of James Donaldson (d 1983), of Ferring, Sussex, and Marie Christine Cormack, *née* Smith; *b* 13 June 1936; *Educ* Oundle, Christ's Coll Cambridge (MA); *m* 18 Dec 1965, Linda, da of Dr Leslie Challis Bousfield (d 1980), of Billingshurst, Sussex; 3 da (Fiona b 1968, Sally b 1969, Catherine b 1973); *Career* dir Hill Samuel & Co Ltd 1978-85, md Hill Samuel Merchant Bank (SA) 1985-86, chief exec Hill Samuel Bank Ltd 1987-, dir TSB Group plc 1990; Freeman: Worshipful Co of Info Technologists 1988, City of London 1988; *Books* A Guide to the Successful Management of Computer Projects (1978), Designing a Distributed Processing System (1979); *Recreations* amateur operatics, golf; *Style—* Hamish Donaldson, Esq; Edgecombe, Hill Road, Haslemere, Surrey GU27 2JN (☎ 0428 4473)

DONALDSON, Hugh Montgomery; s of Dr Ian Montgomery Kerr Donaldson (d 1968), of Glasgow, and Annie Meek May, *née* Ferrier; *b* 21 Dec 1941; *Educ* Kelvinside Acad Glasgow, Univ of Glasgow (BSc), Univ of Strathclyde (MSc); *m* 8 Oct 1965, (Shirley) Rosemary, da of Shirley Edwin McEwan (Sem) Wright; 2 s (Richard Ian Montgomery b 14 Oct 1966, Nicholas Phillip Kerr b 19 Sept 1968), 1 da (Susannah Jane b 29 Nov 1971); *Career* sandwich apprentice Fairfield Shipbuilding and Engineering Co Ltd 1959-63; ICI: various maintenance research jobs Nobel Div until 1971 (joined as engr 1964), Organics Div 1971-73, area engr Huddersfield works 1973-76, project gp mangr Engrg Dept 1976-78, works engr Huddersfield Works

1978-81, chief engr ICI plc Engrg Dept NW and Fine Chemicals 1981-85, ops dir ICI Organics Div and Fine Chemicals Manufacturing Organisation 1985-90, gen mangr (personnel) ICI plc 1991-; dir Atic Industries Bombay 1988-; memb Inst Chem Engrs 1985, FEng 1989, FIMechE 1989; *Recreations* sailing, golf, jogging, gardening; *Style—* Hugh Donaldson, Esq; ICI plc, 9 Millbank, London SW1P 3JF (☎ 071 834 4444, fax 071 834 2042, car 0860 558550)

DONALDSON, Prof John Dallas; s of John Donaldson (d 1988), of Elgin, and Alexandrina Murray Ross, *née* Dallas (d 1985); *b* 11 Nov 1935; *Educ* Elgin Acad, Univ of Aberdeen (BSc, PhD), Univ of London (DSc); *m* 22 March 1961, Elisabeth Ann, da of George Edmond Forrest, of Eastbourne; 1 s (Richard b 1969), 2 da (Claire b 1962, Sarah b 1965); *Career* asst lectr Univ of Aberdeen 1958-61, chemistry lectr Chelsea Coll London 1961-72, reader in inorganic chemistry Univ of London 1972-80; The City Univ: prof of industl chemistry 1980-90, dir Industl & Biological Chemistry Res Centre 1988-; prof of chemistry Brunel Univ 1990-; chm: J D Donaldson Res Ltd 1984-, Hopeman Associates (Scientific & Environment Consultants) Ltd 1991-; memb Nat Ctee for Chemistry 1985-; tstee Zimbabwe Tech Mgmnt Trg Tst 1983-, memb Chemistry Ctee Int Tin Res Inst; Freeman City of London 1982, Liveryman Worshipful Co of Pewterers 1983 (Freeman 1981); FRSC 1959, CChem, FRSA 1986, fell Soc of Industl Chemistry; *Books* Symmetry & Sterochemistry (with S D Ross, 1972), Cobalt in Chemicals (with S J Clarke and S M Grimes, 1986), Cobalt in Medicine Agriculture and the Enviroment (with S J Clarke and S M Grimes, 1986), Cobalt in Electronic Technology (with S J Clarke and S M Grimes, 1988); *Style—* Prof John Donaldson; 21 Orchard Rise, Richmond, Surrey TW10 5BX (☎ 081 876 6534); Dept of Chemistry, The City, Univ Northampton Sq, London EC1V 0HB (☎ 071 253 4399, fax 071 250 0837)

DONALDSON, Dame (Dorothy) Mary; GBE (1983), JP (Inner London 1960); da of Reginald George Gale Warwick (d 1956), and Dorothy Alice Warwick (d 1979); *b* 29 Aug 1921; *Educ* Portsmouth HS for Girls (GPDST), Wingfield Morris Orthopaedic Hosp, Middx Hosp (SRN); *m* 1945, Rt Hon Lord Donaldson, of Lymington, *qv*; 1 s, 2 da; *Career* chm Women's Nat Cancer Control Campaign 1967-69; memb: Inner London Juvenile Ct Panel 1960-65, Ct of Common Cncl 1966-75, ILEA 1968-71, City Parochial Fndn 1969-75, NE Met Regnl Hosp Bd 1970-74, Cities of London and Westminster Disablement Advsy Ctee 1974-, NE Thames RHA 1976-81, Governing Body Charterhouse Sch 1980-84, Automobile Assoc Ctee 1985-89; vice pres Br Cancer Cncl 1970, Counsel and Care for the Elderly 1980-; govr: London Hosp 1971-74, City of London Sch for Girls 1971-, Berkhampstead Schs 1976-80, Gt Ormond Street Hosp for Sick Children 1978-80; chm: Cncl Banking Ombudsman 1985, Interim Licensing Authy In Vitro Fertilisation and Human Embryology 1985; Sheriff City of London 1981-82, Lord Mayor of London 1983-84; hon fell Girton Coll Cambridge 1983; memb Guild of Freemen City of London, alderman City of London (Coleman St Ward) 1975-, Freeman City of Winnipeg, Liveryman Worshipful Co of Gardeners', Hon Freeman Worshipful Co of Shipwrights 1985, Hon Liveryman Worshipful Co of Fruiterers 1985; Hon DSc City Univ; hon memb CIArb; Order of Oman 1981, IPR President's medal 1984, Grand Officier de L'Ordre National du Mérite 1984, DStJ 1983; *Recreations* sailing, skiing, gardening; *Clubs* Royal Cruising, Royal Lymington Yacht, Bar Yacht; *Style—* Dame Mary Donaldson, GBE, JP; c/o The Guildhall, P O Box 270, London EC2P 2EJ (☎ 071 588 6610)

DONALDSON, Hon Michael John Francis; o s of Baron Donaldson of Lymington, PC (Life Peer), *qv*; *b* 16 Nov 1950; *Educ* Stanbridge Earls; *m* 11 Nov 1972, Judith Margaret, da of Edgar William Somerville, *qv*, of Stone House, Garsington, Oxford; 2 s (William Michael Somerville b 29 Aug 1977, James John Francis (twin) b 29 Aug 1977); *Career* negotiator with Knight Frank & Rutley London 1969-71; dir: Edwood Property Co Ltd 1972-75, Nab Properties Ltd 1972-80; md and chm Marquis & Co, commercial property surveyors and valuers 1975-; chm SW London branch Incorporated Soc of Valuers and Auctioneers 1982-85; memb Nat Cncl of Incorporated Soc of Valuers and Auctioneers 1985-; memb Prof Practice Ctee 1985-; Freeman City of London, Liveryman Worshipful Co of Cutlers; ASVA, ARVA, ACIArb 1973, FSVA, IRRV 1981; *Recreations* sailing, skiing, walking; *Clubs* Royal Southampton Yacht, Guildford Coastal Cruising; *Style—* The Hon Michael Donaldson; The Old Coach House, Westwood Rd, Windlesham, Surrey GU20 6LT (☎ 0344 26909); 61 Richmond Rd, Twickenham, Middx TW1 3AW (☎ 081 891 0222, fax 081 891 1767)

DONALDSON, Dr (James) Roy; s of James Donaldson (d 1979), and Ellen Hill, *née* Burnside; *b* 24 Dec 1927; *Educ* Bearsden Acad Dunbartonshire, West of Scotland Agric Coll (Nat and Coll Dip in Dairying), Glasgow Univ (BChir), Royal Coll of Pathologists (Dip), London Univ Sch of Tropical Med and Hygiene (Dip in Bacteriology); *m* 25 July 1956, Flora, da of John MacDonald (d 1968); 1 s ((James) Graham), 1 da (Lynne Marie); *Career* Maj RAMC 1965, 2 i/c 24 Field Ambulance Aden 1965-67; pathologist David Bruce Laboratories Wilts 1967-68, Br Mil Hosp Minister BAOR 1968-70, Herbert Hosp Woolwich 1970-71; clinical pathologist: US Army Med Res Unit, Inst of Med Res Kuala Lumpur 1971-74; Lt-Col 1972, pathologist Cambridge Mil Hosp Aldershot 1974-76, conslt pathologist and co offr David Bruce Laboratories Wilts 1976-81, awarded The Herbert Parkes & Tulloch Medals for First in Order of Merit, Army Health & Pathology 1965, Tri-Serv Alexander Gold Medal for Res 1974, Gen Serv Medal South Arabia 1967, Silver Jubilee Medal Queen Elizabeth II 1977; dairy bacteriologist 1948-50, surgical med and obstetric house offr 1957-59; princ gen med practice: Birmingham (partnership) 1959-61, Scotland 1961-65; conslt microbiologist: Greater Glasgow Bd, The Bacteriology & Serology of Gen Practice, Obstetric & Neonatal Paediatric Patients, The Bacteriology of Public Health and the Environment; memb: Scottish Food Coordination Ctee, Greater Glasgow Environmental Health Sub-Ctee; hon clinical lectr Glasgow Univ; memb Royal Coll of Pathologists 1975 (fell 1987), Hosp Infection Soc, Br Soc for Study of Infection; *Recreations* trout fishing, occasional golf, gardening, the philosophy of man's inhumanity; *Style—* Dr Roy Donaldson; Bacteriology Laboratory, Wolfson Centre (Level 5), Taylor St, Glasgow G4 0NA (☎ 041 552 1991)

DONALDSON, Hon Thomas Hay; o s of Baron Donaldson of Kingsbridge, OBE (Life Peer), and Lady Donaldson of Kingsbridge, *qqv*; *b* 1 June 1936; *Educ* Eton, Cincinnati Univ USA, Trinity Coll Cambridge (BA); *m* 1962, Natalie, da of late Basil Wadkovsky, of Miami Beach; 2 s, 4 da; *Career* with Empire Trust Co NY 1958-62, W E Hutton and Co NY 1962-63, Morgan Guaranty Trust Co of NY London Office 1963- (vice pres 1972-90, Euro credit offr 1982-91, md 1990-, chm Euro credit political communication 1991-); FCIB; *Books* Lending in International Commercial Banking, The Medium Term Loan Market (with J A Donaldson), Understanding Corporate Credit, How to Handle Problem Loans, Thinking About Credit, Credit Risk and Exposure in Securitisation and Transactions; *Recreations* bridge, reading, writing; *Clubs* Brooks's; *Style—* The Hon Thomas Donaldson; The Old Lodge, Mayertorne, Wendover Dean, Wendover, nr Aylesbury, Bucks HP22 6QA (☎ 0296 696486)

DONALDSON, (Charles) William; s of Charles Glen Donaldson (d 1957), of Sunningdale, Berks, and Elizabeth Jane Stockley (d 1955); *b* 4 Jan 1935; *Educ* Winchester, Magdalene Coll Cambridge (BA); *m* 1, 1958, Sonia Iris, da of Edward Avory; 1 s (Charles b 1960); m 2, 1967 (m dis 1975), Claire Evelyn Gordon; m 3, 1986, Cherry Jane Hatrick; *Career* author: Nat Serv RN 1953-55, cmmnd as Sub Lt, served in 5 Submarine Sqdn; theatrical producer 1958-70; shows incl: The Ginger Man, Beyond the Fringe, The Bedsitting Room; books incl: The Henry Root Letters, The English Way of Doing Things, Is This Allowed?; *Recreations* watching television, reading Martin Amis; *Style—* William Donaldson, Esq; 139 Elm Park Mansions, Park Walk, London SW10 (☎ 071 352 9689)

DONALDSON OF KINGSBRIDGE, Baroness; Frances Annesley; da of Frederick Lonsdale (d 1954), the playwright, and Leslie Brooke, *née* Hoggan; *b* 13 Jan 1907; *m* 20 Feb 1935, Baron Donaldson of Kingsbridge, *qv*; 1 s, 2 da; *Career* author; *Books* Approach to Farming (1941), Four Years Harvest (1945), Milk Without Tears (1955), Freddy Lonsdale (1957), Child of the Twenties (1959), The Marconi Scandal (1962), Evelyn Waugh: Portrait of a Country Neighbour (1967), Actor Managers (1970), Edward VIII (1974, Wolfson History Award 1975), King George VI and Queen Elizabeth (1977), Edward VIII: the Road to Abdication (1978), P G Wodehouse: a Biography (1982), The British Council: the first fifty years (1984), The Royal Opera House In The Twentieth Century (1988), Yours Plum, The Letters of PG Wodehouse (ed, 1990); *Style—* The Rt Hon the Lady Donaldson of Kingsbridge; 17 Edna Street, Battersea, London SW11 3DP (☎ 071 223 0259)

DONALDSON OF KINGSBRIDGE, Baron (Life Peer UK 1967); John George Stuart Donaldson; OBE (1944); s of Rev Stuart Alexander Donaldson (d 1915), master of Magdalene Coll Cambridge, by his wife Lady Albinia Frederica Hobart-Hampden (d 1932), sis of 7th Earl of Buckinghamshire; *b* 9 Oct 1907; *Educ* Eton, Trinity Coll Cambridge; *m* 20 Feb 1935, Frances Annesley Lonsdale, *qv*; 1 s, 2 da; *Career* sits as Lib Democrat in House of Lords; Parly under-sec of state (Lab) N Ireland 1974-76, min for the arts Dept of Educn and Science 1976-79; dir: Royal Opera House Covent Garden 1958-74, Sadler's Wells Opera 1962-74; chm: Nat Cncl for the Care and Resettlement of Offenders 1965-74, Fedn of Zoos 1971-74; chm: Hotels Catering NEDO 1972-74, Confedn of Art & Design Instns 1982-84; *Clubs* Brooks's; *Style—* The Rt Hon the Lord Donaldson of Kingsbridge, OBE; 17 Edna St, Battersea, London SW11 3DP (☎ 071 223 0259)

DONALDSON OF LYMINGTON, Baron (Life Peer UK 1988), of Lymington in the County of Hampshire; John Francis Donaldson; PC (1979), QC (1961); s of Malcolm Donaldson (d 1973), by his 1 w, Evelyn Helen Marguerite, eld da of late Maj Alistair Gilroy, 11 Hussars; *b* 6 Oct 1920; *Educ* Charterhouse, Trinity Coll Cambridge (MA); *m* 1945, (Dorothy) Mary (*see* Donaldson, Dame Mary); 1 s (Michael b 1950), 2 da (Margaret-Ann b 1946, Jennifer b 1948); *Career* .erved WW II Royal Signals and Gds Armd Div Signals, Control Cmmn for Germany (legal Div); called to the Bar Middle Temple 1946, High Court judge (Queen's Bench) 1966-79, lord justice of appeal 1979-82, master of the rolls and chm Lord Chllr's advsy cncl on Public Record 1982-, pres Br Maritime Law Assoc 1979-; govr Sutton's Hosp in Charterhouse 1981-85; visitor: Nuffield Coll Oxford and UCL 1982-, London Business Sch 1987-; former memb Gen Cncl Bar, dep chm Hants QS, memb Cncl on Tbnls, pres Nat Industl Rels Court; FCIArb, pres Chartered Inst of Arbitrators 1980-83; Hon DUniv Essex 1983; Hon LLD Sheffield 1984, hon fell Trinity Coll Cambridge; kt 1966; *Style—* The Rt Hon the Lord Donaldson of Lymington, PC; Royal Courts of Justice, Strand, London WC2 (☎ 071 936 6002, home 071 588 6610)

DONCASTER, Archdeacon of; *see*: **Carnelley, The Ven Desmond**

DONCASTER, Bishop of, 1982-; Rt Rev William Michael Dermot Persson; s of Leslie Charles Grenville Alan Persson (d 1948), and Elizabeth Mercer, *née* Chambers; *b* 27 Sept 1927; *Educ* Monkton Combe Sch, Oriel Coll Oxford (MA); *m* 27 April 1957, Ann, da of Reginald Charles Ward Davey (d 1983), of Heronsgate; 2 s (Matthew b 1960, Adam b 1966), 1 da (Rachel b 1958, m Lt Cdr Charles Anthony Johnstone-Burt, RN); *Career* Royal Signals 1944-48, served in Germany, cmmnd 2 Lt; deacon 1953, priest 1954, vicar Christ Church Barnet 1958-67, rector of Bebington 1967-79, vicar of Knutsford 1979-82, bishop of Doncaster 1982-; proctor in convocation 1975-82, examining chaplain to Bishop of London 1981-82, del to WCC Vancouver Assembly 1983; memb: BCC Assembly 1977-80 and 1984-90, chm C of E Cncl for Christian Unity 1991; *Clubs* National Liberal; *Style—* Rt Rev the Bishop of Doncaster; Bishop's Lodge, Hooton Roberts, Rotherham, S Yorkshire S65 4PF (☎ 0709 853370)

DONEGALL, 7 Marquess of (I 1791); Dermot Richard Claud Chichester; LVO; sits as Baron Fisherwick (GB 1790); also Viscount Chichester of Carrickfergus and Baron Chichester of Belfast (I 1625), Earl of Donegall (I 1647), Earl of Belfast (I 1791), Baron Templemore (UK 1831); Hereditary Lord High Admiral of Lough Neagh and Govr of Carrickfergus Castle; s of 4 Baron Templemore, KCVO, DSO, OBE, PC, JP, DL (d 1953), and Hon Clare Meriel Wingfield (d 1969), da of 7 Viscount Powerscourt; suc kinsman, 6 Marquess of Donegall 1975, having suc as 5 Baron Templemore 1953; *b* 18 April 1916; *Educ* Harrow, RMC; *m* 16 Sept 1946, Lady Josceline Gabrielle Legge, *qv*, da of 7 Earl of Dartmouth, GCVO, TD (d 1958); 1 s, 2 da; *Heir* s, Earl of Belfast; *Career* 2 Lt 7 Hussars 1936, (POW 1941-44), Maj 1944, served in Egypt, Libya, Italy; one of HM Bodyguard, Hon Corps of Gentlemen at Arms 1966; grand master Masonic Order Ireland, sr grand warden England, grand warden United Grand Lodge (Masonic) 1982-, Standard Bearer HM Body Guard of Hon Corps of Gentleman at Arms 1984-86; *Recreations* shooting, fishing; *Clubs* Cavalry & Guards', Kildare St (Dublin); *Style—* Most Hon Marquess of Donegall LVO; Dunbrody Park, Arthurstown, Co Wexford, Eire (☎ 010 353 51 89104)

DONEGALL, Marchioness of; Lady Josceline Gabrielle; *née* Legge; 5 and yst da of 7 Earl of Dartmouth, GCVO, TD (d 1958), and Lady Ruperta Wynn-Carrington (d 1963) (da of 1 and last Marquess of Lincolnshire), whereby Lady Donegall is 1 cous once removed to Lord Carrington; *b* 22 May 1918; *m* 16 Sept 1946, 7 Marquess of Donegall; 1 s, 2 da; *Career* first aid Nurse Yeo; *Style—* The Most Hon the Marchioness of Donegall; Dunbrody Park, Arthurstown, Co Wexford, Eire

DONEGALL, Maureen, Marchioness of; Maureen; da of Maj Geoffrey C Scholfield, MC, of Birkdale, Lancs; *m* 1, Douglas McKenzie; m 2, 17 Aug 1968, as his 2 w, 6 Marquess of Donegall (d 1975); *Career* served in WRNS, SEAC; *Style—* The Most Hon Maureen, Marchioness of Donegall; 5 Lake View Court, Wimbledon Park Road, London SW19

DONERAILE, Melva, Viscountess; Melva Jean; *née* Clifton; da of George W Clifton, of St Louis, MO, USA; *m* 1945, 9 Viscount Doneraile (d 1983); 3 s, 2 da; *Style—* Rt Hon Melva, Viscountess Doneraile; 405 Eve Circle, Placentia, California 92670, USA

DONERAILE, 10 Viscount (I 1785); Richard Allen St Leger; also Baron Doneraile (in the process of establishing right to the Peerages at time of going to press); s of 9 Viscount Doneraile (d 1983), and Melva, Viscountess Doneraile, *qv*; *b* 17 Aug 1946; *Educ* Orange Coast Coll California; *m* 1969, Kathleen Mary, da of Nathaniel Simcox; 1 s, 1 da (Hon Maeve b 1974); *Heir* s, Hon Nathaniel St Leger b 13 Sept 1971; *Career* air traffic control specialist Missippi Univ; *Style—* Rt Hon Viscount Doneraile; 405 Eve Circle, Placentia, California 92670, USA

DONGER, Alan David; TD; s of William James Donger (d 1957), of Courtenay Rd, Winchester, and Hilda Marion, *née* Markham (d 1954); *b* 21 Oct 1919; *Educ* Charterhouse; *m* 9 Sept 1949, Annette Strathern, da of Air Chief Marshal Sir Douglas C S Evill, GBE, KCB, DSC, AFC (d 1971); 1 s (William Alan b 1953), 1 da (Alison Sophie b 1951); *Career* joined TA Hamps Carabiniers Yeo 1938, mobilised Munich

Crisis 1938, WWII served N Africa, Italy (despatches) 1945, mil govt Austria 1945-46, Lt Col, cdr Hamps Carabiniers Yeo 1952-55, 295 HAA Regt RATA; chartered surveyor 1948, sr ptnr Pink & Arnold (later Pink Donger & Lowry) 1977-84, conslt Dreweatt Neate 1984-; JP (Winchester) 1951-89; memb Lord Chllrs Panel of Agric Arbitrators 1967-86, mangr Home Office Approved Sch 1952-72, memb Advsy Ctee Local Authy Community Home 1972-79, conslt valuer to Dean and Chapter of Winchester 1975-84, receiver to Hosp of St Cross and Almhouse of Noble Poverty 1975-84; ARICS 1948, FRICS 1954; *Recreations* gardening; *Style—* Alan Donger, Esq, TD

DONKIN, Dr Robert Arthur; s of Arthur Donkin (d 1967), of Loansdean, Morpeth, Northumberland, and Elisabeth Jane, *née* Kirkup (d 1969); *b* 28 Oct 1928; *Educ* Univ of Durham (BA, PhD), Univ of Cambridge (MA); *m* 13 Sept 1970, Jennifer, da of Joseph Edward Kennedy (d 1968), of Michael's Fold, Grasmere, Westmorland; 1 da (Lucy b 1977); *Career* Nat Serv Lt RA 1953-55; King George VI Meml fell Univ of Calif Berkeley 1955-56, asst lectr Dept of Geography Univ of Edinburgh 1956-58, lectr Dept of Geography Univ of Birmingham 1958-70, Leverhulme res fell 1966, visiting prof of geography Univ of Toronto 1969; Univ of Cambridge: fell Jesus Coll 1972-, tutor Jesus Coll 1975-85, lectr in geography and Latin America 1971-90, reader in historical geography 1990-; memb Hakluyt Soc 1967; FRAI 1969, FRGS 1975, FBA 1985; *Books* The Cistercian Order in Europe: a bibliography of printed sources (1969), Spanish Red: an ethnogeographical study of cochineal and the opuntia cactus (1977), The Cistercians: studies in the geography of medieval England and Wales (1978), Agricultural Terracing in the Aboriginal New World (1979), Manna: an historical geography (1980), The Peccary: with observations on the introduction of pigs to the New World (1985), The Muscovy Duck, Cairina Moschata Domestica (1989), Meleagrides: an historical and ethnogeographical study of the Guinea fowl (1991); *Style—* Dr Robert Donkin; 13 Roman Hill, Barton, Cambridge (☎ 0223 262 572); Jesus College, Cambridge

DONLEAVY, (James Patrick) Michael; s of (John) Patrick Donleavy (d 1957), of NY, and Margaret Mary, *née* Walsh (d 1987); *b* 23 April 1926; *Educ* Fordham Prep Sch NYC, Roosevelt HS Yonkers, Manhattan Prep Sch NYC, Trinity Coll Dublin; *m* 1, 1949 (m dis 1969), Valerie, da of John McMichael Heron (d 1950), of Ilkley, Yorks and Port-e-Villen, IOM; 1 s (Philip b 22 Oct 1951), 1 da (Karen b 31 March 1955); m 2, 1969 (m dis 1988), Mary Wilson Price; 1 s (Rory b 27 July 1980), 1 da (Rebecca b 28 Dec 1979); *Career* WWII US Navy 1944-46; author and playwright; novels: The Ginger Man 1955, Fairy Tales of New York 1961, A Singular Man 1963, The Saddest Summer of Samuel S 1966, The Beastly Beatitudes of Balthazar B 1968, The Onion Eaters 1971, The Destinies of Darcy Dancer Gentleman 1977, Schultz 1980, Leila 1983, JP Donleavy's Ireland In All Her Sins and Some of Her Graces 1986, A Singular County 1987, Are You Listening Rabbi Löw 1987, That Darcy Dancer Gentleman 1990; plays: What They Did in Dublin with The Ginger Man (with introduction) 1961, Fairy Tales of New York 1960, A Singular Man 1964, The Saddest Summer of Samuel S 1967, The Beastly Beatitudes of Balthazar B 1981; short stories: Meet My Maker The Mad Molecule 1964; manuals: The Unexpurgated Code: A complete manual of survival and manners, De Alfonce Tennis: The Superlative Game of Eccentric Champions, Its History, Accountrements, Rules, Conduct and Regimen 1984; painting exhibitions Anna-Mel Chadwick Gallery 1989; *Recreations* farming; *Clubs* Kildare St and Univ (Dublin), NY Athletic; *Style—* Michael Donleavy, Esq; Levington Park, Mullingar, Co Westmeath, Ireland (☎ 044 48903, fax 044 48351)

DONNACHIE, Prof Alexander; s of Cdr John Donnachie, RNVR (d 1979), of Kilmarnock, Scotland, and Mary Ramsey, *née* Adams; *b* 25 May 1936; *Educ* Kilmarnock Acad, Univ of Glasgow (BSc, PhD); *m* 9 April 1960, Dorothy, da of Thomas Paterson (d 1979), of Kilmarnock, Scotland; 2 da (Susan b 1963, Lynn b 1965); *Career* lectr UCL 1963-65 (DSIR res fell 1961-63), res assoc CERN Geneva 1965-67, sr lectr Univ of Glasgow 1967-69; Univ of Manchester: prof of physics 1969-, head of theoretical physics 1975-85, dean Faculty of Sci 1985-87; dir Physical Laboratories 1989-; CERN: chm SPS Ctee 1988-, memb Res Bd, memb Scientific Policy Ctee, memb Cncl; sec C11 Cmmn IUPAP 1987-90, chm Nuclear Physics Bd SERC 1989- (memb Cncl 1989-); FInstP; *Books* Electromagnetic Interactions of Hadrons Vols 1 and 2 (1978); *Recreations* sailing, walking; *Style—* Prof Alexander Donnachie; Physics Department, University of Manchester, Manchester M13 9PL (☎ 061 275 4200, fax 061 273 5867, telex JODREL G36149)

DONNACHIE, Ian Louis; *b* 4 June 1947; *Educ* DBA, MMS, MHSM, DipHSM, Graduate Program Hosp Mgmnt Chicago; *m* (m dis); 2 da (Samantha, Elspeth); *Career* chief exec St James's Univ Hosp NHS Tst Leeds, memb Nat Cncl Inst of Health Servs Mgmnt 1983-, tstee and memb Bd NHS Mgmnt Advsy Serv, editioral advsr Journal of Health Care Management, memb HRH Duke of Edinburgh's Sixth Cwlth Study Conf Australia, dir and memb Bd Martin House Childrens Hospice; *Recreations* sculpture, theatre, opera, reading; *Style—* Ian Donnachie, Esq; 30 Victoria St, Leeds LS7 4PB (☎ 0532 698 354); St James's University Hospital, Beckett St, Leeds LS7 9TF (☎ 0532 433144 ext 5835, fax 0532 426496)

DONNE, David Lucas; s of late Dr Cecil Lucas Donne, of Wellington, NZ, by his w Marjorie Nicholls Donne; *b* 17 Aug 1925; *Educ* Stowe, Ch Ch Oxford, Syracuse Univ; *m* 1, 1957, Jennifer Margaret Duncan (d 1975); 2 s, 1 da; m 2, 1978, Clare, da of Maj F J Yates; *Career* called to the Bar Middle Temple 1949; chm: Dalgety 1977-86 (dep chm 1975-77), Crest Nicholson 1973-, Steetley 1983- (dep chm 1979-83), Argos plc 1990; dir Royal Trust Bank; *Style—* David Donne Esq; PO Box 53, Brownsover Rd, Rugby CV21 2UT

DONNE, Sir Gaven (John); KBE (1979); s of Jack Alfred Donne, and Mary Elizabeth Donne; *b* 8 May 1914; *Educ* Palmerston North Boys' HS, Hastings HS, Victoria Univ Wellington NZ, Auckland Univ NZ; *m* 1946, Isabel Fenwick, da of John Edwin Hall; 2 s, 2 da; *Career* barr and slr 1938; stipendiary magistrate 1958-75, Puisne judge Supreme Court of Western Samoa 1970-71, chief justice Western Samoa 1972-75; chief justice: Niue 1974-82, the Cook Islands 1975-82; memb Court of Appeal Western Samoa 1975-82, rep of HM The Queen in the Cook Islands 1975-84; chief justice: Nauru 1985-, Tuvalu 1985-; memb Court of Appeal of Kiribati 1986-; *Style—* Sir Gaven Donne, KBE; Supreme Court Nauru; Otaramarre, RD4, Rotorua, NZ

DONNE, Sir John Christopher; s of Leslie Victor Donne (d 1960), of Hove, and Mabel Laetitia Richards, *née* Pike; *b* 19 Aug 1921; *Educ* Charterhouse; *m* 1945, Mary Stuart, da of George Stuart Seaton (d 1938); 3 da; *Career* admitted slr 1949, Notary Public; conslt Donne Mileham & Haddock 1985-91; pres Sussex Law Soc 1969-70; chm: SE Regnl Hosp Bd 1971-74, SE Thames RHA 1973-83, NHS Trg Authy (for England and Wales) 1983-86; govr: Guy's Hosp 1971-74, Guy's Hosp Med Sch 1974-83; governing tstee Nuffield Provincial Hosp Tst 1975-; memb: Ct Univ of Sussex 1979-87, Mgmnt Ctee King Edward Hosp Fund for London 1982-84; memb Ct of Assts Worshipful Co of Broderers (Master 1983-84); FRSA, FRSM; kt 1976; *Recreations* music, photography, gardening; *Clubs* Pilgrims, MCC, Army and Navy, Butterflies; *Style—* Sir John Donne; The Old School House, Acton Burnell, Shrewsbury, Shropshire SY5 7PG (☎ 06944 647)

DONNELLAN, Declan Michael Dominic Martin; s of Thomas Patrick John Donnellan, of Ballinlough, Co Roscommon, Eire, and Margaret Josephine, *née* Donnellan; *b* 4 Aug 1953; *Educ* St Benedict's Ealing, Queens' Coll Cambridge (MA); *Career* called to the Bar Middle Temple 1977; artistic dir Cheek By Jowl Theatre Co 1981-, assoc dir of Royal Nat Theatre 1989; prodns: Macbeth and Philoctetes for Finnish Nat Theatre, Fuente Ovejuna and Peer Gynt for Royal Nat Theatre; dir of the year Drama and Olivier Awards 1988, Olivier Award for Outstanding Achievement 1990; *Style—* Declan Donnellan, Esq; Cheek By Jowl, Alford House, Aveline St, London SE11 5DQ (☎ 071 793 0153/4, fax 071 735 1031)

DONNELLY, Alan John; MEP (Lab) Tyne & Wear 1989; s of John Donnelly, of Jarrow, and Josephine, *née* Anderson; *b* 16 July 1957; *Educ* Springfield Comprehensive Sch, Sunderland Polytechnic; *m* 1979 (m dis 1982), Hazel Cameron; 1 s (Jonathan Alan b 21 July 1980); *Career* nat fin dir GMB 1987-89 (regnl offr 1978-87), dir Unity Trust Bank 1987-89; memb: Lab Party 1974, South Tyneside Met Borough Cncl 1980-84, Fabian Soc; *Recreations* tennis, swimming, music; *Style—* Alan Donnelly, Esq, MEP; 1 South View, Jarrow, Tyne & Wear (☎ 091 4897643); European Parliament, Rue Belliard, Brussels (☎ 010 322 284 5404)

DONNELLY, (Joseph) Brian; s of Joseph Donnelly (d 1986), and Ada Agnes, *née* Bowness (d 1971); *b* 24 April 1945; *Educ* Workington GS, Queen's College Oxford (BA, MA), Univ of Wisconsin (MA); *m* 20 Aug 1966 (m dis 1987), Susanne; 1 da (Kathryn Charlotte b 27 Oct 1970); *Career* 2 sec Republic of Ireland Dept FCO 1973, 1 sec UK mission to UN NY 1975, head of chancery Br High Cmmn Singapore 1979, asst head Personnel Policy Dept FCO 1982, deputy to chief scientific advsr Cabinet Office 1985, cnsllr and consul gen Br Embassy Athens 1988, Royal Coll of Defence Studies 1990-; *Recreations* travel, reading, watching any sports, cinema; *Clubs* MG Owners, Hash House Harriers; *Style—* Brian Donnelly, Esq; c/o Foreign Commonwealth Office, King Charles St, London SW1A 2AH (☎ 071 235 1091, fax 071 235 0876)

DONNELLY, James Thomas; s of Thomas Donnelly, and Margaret, *née* Nugent; *b* 21 Aug 1931; *Educ* Kilashee, Castleknock Coll, Trinity Coll Dublin (MA); *m* 31 April 1966, Lelia Ann, da of James Ivan McGuire, QC; 3 s (Christopher b 3 Aug 1970, Nicholas b 1 June 1972, James b 13 May 1976), 1 da (Lelia 15 May 1979); *Career* md: J & J Hunter Belfast 1956, Bryanstown Holdings 1962, Whitecliff Holdings 1963; chm Downtown Radio 1979, dir Radio 2000 Dublin 1989; underwriting memb Lloyds 1979; Cncl memb Belfast C of C; *Recreations* sailing, golf; *Clubs* Royal Irish Yacht, Royal Belfast Golf, Royal Alfred Yacht; *Style—* James Donnelly, Esq; Crawfordsburn, Co Down, Northern Ireland (☎ 0247 853255); J & J Hunter Ltd, Balmoral Rd, Belfast, Northern Ireland BT12 6PX (☎ 0232 618535)

DONNELLY, John; s of Thomas Donnelly, of Elgin St, Bolton, and Mary Elizabeth, *née* Prescott; *b* 20 Dec 1934; *Educ* Thornleigh Salesian Coll Bolton; *m* 22 May 1961, Jean, da of James Mullineux; 3 s (Robert b 17 Feb 1962, Julian b 30 Oct 1963, Andrew b 16 Feb 1970), 1 da (Kathryn b 18 May 1966), 1 adopted s ((Robert) Paul b 2 Feb 1987); *Career* Nat Serv RAF 1958-60; articled clerk Cooper and Cooper CAs, office mangr Greenhalgh Son and Dutton CAs 1960-62, co sec WHS Taylor & Co Ltd 1962-74, fndr and now sr ptnr J F Donnelly CAs 1974-; dir: Hartnell and Rose Ltd, Melrose Projects Ltd, Heath Moss Ltd; govr: Broadfield Special Sch Lancs, St John's Primary Sch Bolton; interview chm NW Eng Project Tst, chm Mgmnt Ctee Barl Youth Club Lancs CC; FCA; *Recreations* cycling, walking, swimming, interest in all sports; *Style—* John Donnelly, Esq; 9 Greenacres, Turton, Bolton BL7 0QG (☎ 0204 852127); J & F Donnelly, Peel House, 2 Chorley Old Road, Bolton BL1 3AA (☎ 0204 381712)

DONNELLY, Maurice John; s of James Heenan Donnelly (d 1965), and Mary Agnes Donnelly (d 1985); *b* 31 May 1933; *Educ* Stonyhurst Coll, Univ of Durham (BSc); *m* 1980, June, da of F W Donohue (d 1967; sr res engr and memb of Res Team on The Davis Escape; decorated by HM King George VI for work on poisonous gases), of Morecambe; 3 da (Nicola, Caroline, Linsey), 1 step s (Michael J Steward), 1 step da (Mrs Gail Prill); *Career* Nat Serv RM 1955; chief exec Lunesdale Farmers Ltd 1966-74; joined Tube Investmts 1975 (sales dir 1980, business devpt dir 1983); dir Br Red Cross Cumbria branch 1987; *Recreations* golf, squash; *Clubs* Morecambe Golf, Vale of Lune Rugby; *Style—* Maurice Donnelly Esq; Eden Vale, 338 Marine Rd, Morecambe, Lancs LA4 5AB (☎ 0524 415544)

DONNELLY, Peter Lane; Baron of Duleek (Feudal Barony), Co Meath, Ireland; Lord of the Manor of Rushmere, Suffolk; s of Paul J Donnelly Jr, of Laurel Cove Road, Oyster Bay, Long Island, New York, USA, and Marian, *née* Kinsly; *b* 18 March 1947; *Educ* Georgetown Univ Washington DC (BSFS), Fordham Univ NY (Juris Doctor); *m* 1 (m dis 1982), Joyce Arbon; m 2, 23 May 1983, Georgina Mary, da of late Dennis Dallamore, of Johannesburg, SA; 2 s (Sebastian Peter Sumner b 1986, Octavian Xavier b 1989); *Career* vice pres The European-American Bank & Tst Co NY 1969, ptnr Kuhn Loeb Lehman Brothers Int NY 1977, md Int The First Boston Corp NY 1982, md (Europe) Prudential-Bache Capital Funding London 1986; memb NY Bar Assoc; Baron of Duleek Co Meath Eire, Lord of the Manor of Rushmere Suffolk; *Recreations* tennis, painting; *Clubs* Piping Rock (NY), Union (NY), Annabel's, Inanda (Johannesburg), Doubles (NY); *Style—* Peter Donnelly; 8 Cresswell Gardens, London SW5; 118 East 93rd Street, New York, NY, USA; Hyla Brook Farm, Reading, Vermont, USA; Prudential Bache Securities UK (Inc), 9 Devonshire Square, London EC2M 4HP (☎ 071 548 4076, fax 071 548 4641)

DONNER, Clive; s of Alex Donner (d 1981), of London, and Deborah, *née* Taffel (d 1976); *b* 21 Jan 1926; *m* 1971, Jocelyn Rickards, da of Bertie Rickards; *Career* film and theatre dir; asst film ed 1941, freelance film dir 1956-; films incl: Scrooge 1951, The Card, Meet Me Tonight, Genevieve 1952, The Million Pound Note 1953, The Purple Plain, I Am A Camera 1955, Some People 1962, The Caretaker (Silver Bear Berlin Film Festival) 1963, Nothing But The Best 1963, What's New Pussycat? (Jean Georges Auriol/Paul Gilson award) 1965, Luv 1967, Here We Go Round the Mulberry Bush 1967, Alfred the Great 1969, Oliver Twist 1981, The Scarlet Pimpernel 1982, Arthur the King 1983, A Christmas Carol 1984, Dead Man's Folly 1986, Babes in Toyland 1986, Best Kept Secret (Motor Neurone Assoc) Silver award Br Med Cncl; Stealing Heaven 1988, Not A Penny More Not A Penny Less 1989, Coup de Foudre (Love at First Sight) 1990, Arividerci Roma 1990, First Love Second Chance 1990, Gumshoe Waltz 1990; theatre incl: The Formation Dancers (Arts & Globe Theatre) 1964, Notts Playhouse Shakespeare and Pinter 1970-71, The Front Room Boys (Royal Court Theatre) 1971, Kennedy's Children (Kings Head Arts Theatre, The Golden Theatre NY) 1975, The Picture of Dorian Gray (adapted by John Osborne, Greenwich Theatre) 1975; *Recreations* classical music (particularly opera) popular music, reading, walking anywhere from the streets of London to the Australian sea shore; *Style—* Clive Donner, Esq

DONNER, John Melville; s of Gerald Melville Donner (d 1964), and Pearl, only da of Sir Frank Bernard Sanderson, 1 Bt (d 1965); *b* 18 July 1930; *Educ* Stowe, RMA Sandhurst; *m* 1952, Patricia Mary, da of Barnet Thomas Jenkins (d 1941); 1 s (Rupert b 1955), 1 da (Annabel b 1958); *Career* Coldstream Gds 1948-53 and 1956 (Suez), T/Capt; entered Lloyd's 1955 (Arbon Langrish), elected memb 1964; dir Fenchurch Insurance Holding 1969 (md 1969-74); chm: Donner Underwriting Agencies Ltd 1976-90 (pres 1990) (Queen's Award for Export 1983 and 1988), JD Underwriting Agencies Ltd 1979-90, RD Underwriting Agencies 1980, CD Underwriting Agencies Ltd 1983; Stirling Underwriting Agencies 1988; dir: Alexander Syndicate Mgmnt Ltd

1982-, West Somerset Railway PLC 1991; chm Western Bloodstock Ltd; chm bd of govrs St Michael's Sch Tawstock; Freeman City of London 1977, Liveryman Worshipful Co of Plaisterers; *Recreations* old vehicles, gardening, travel, food and wine; *Clubs* Carlton, Bentley Drivers, Rolls Royce Enthusiasts; *Style—* John Donner, Esq; 39 Bramerton St, London SW3 (☎ 071 352 9964); Quarkhill, Crowcombe, Taunton, Somerset TA4 4BJ (☎ 098 48 651)

DONNET, Hon Gavin Alexander; s of Baron Donnet of Balgay (Life Peer; d 1985); *b* 2 Oct 1950; *Educ* Hyndland Secdy Sch Glasgow; *m* 1976, Margaret Louise, *née* Scott; 2 c; *Style—* The Hon Gavin Donnet; 9 Scotscraig Place, Broughty Ferry, Dundee DD5 3JU

DONNET, Hon Stephen Christopher; s of Baron Donnet of Balgay, CBE, JP (Life Peer, d 1985), and Mary, *née* Black; *b* 31 Dec 1960; *Educ* Jordanhill Coll Sch, Univ of Strathclyde (BA); *m* 1 April 1989, Deborah Rae, da of Edward James Campbell; *Career* CA 1989; asst investmt mangr Scottish Amicable Life Assurance Soc 1989-; accounting mangr Scottish Amicable Investment Managers Ltd 1990-; *Style—* The Hon Stephen Donnet; Flat E, 259 Kelvindale Road, Glasgow G12 0QU (☎ 041 337 2481)

DONNET OF BALGAY, Baroness; Mary; da of Gavin Mitchell Black; *m* 1945, Baron Donnet of Balgay (Life Peer; sometime pres Scottish TUC; d 1985); 2 s, 1 da; *Style—* Rt Hon Lady Donnet of Balgay; 8 Jordanhill Drive, Glasgow G13 (☎ 041 954 8188)

DONOHOE, Peter Howard; s of Harold Steven Donohoe (d 1974), and Marjorie, *née* Travis; *b* 18 June 1953; *Educ* Chetham's Sch, Univ of Leeds (BA), Royal Northern Coll of Music (B Mus), Paris Conservatoire of Music, Tchaikowsky Conservatory of Music Moscow; *m* 23 Oct 1980, Elaine, da of William Geoffrey Burns; 1 da (Jessica b 21 April 1986); *Career* int concert pianist; London debut 1979, US debut 1983, recording debut 1982; appearances in major festivals and with major orchs incl annual visits to Henry Wood Promenade Concerts London 1979-; winner seventh int Tschaikovsky Competition Moscow 1982; exclusive recording artist with EMI/Angel label, recordings incl Tschaikovsky Piano Concerto Number 2 (winner Concerto Record of the Year Award 1988); hon fell Royal Northern Coll Music 1983; *Style—* Peter Donohoe, Esq; Saint Just, 82 Hampton Lane, Solihull, West Midlands B91 2RS (☎ 94082242 MSTRO G); c/o Harold Holt Ltd, 31 Sinclair Rd, London W14 0NS (☎ 071 603 4600/5148, fax 071 603 0019, telex 22 339 Hunter)

DONOUGHMORE, Jean, Countess of; (Dorothy) Jean; MBE (1947); eldest da of John Beaumont Hotham (d 1924), clerk of the Senate and asst clerk of the Parliament of N Ireland; *b* 12 Aug 1906; *m* 27 July 1925, 7 Earl of Donoughmore (d 1981); 2 s (8 Earl, Hon Mark Hely-Hutchinson), 1 da (Lady Sara Collins); *Career* SSStJ; *Style—* The Rt Hon Jean, Countess of Donoughmore; High Coodham, Symington, Ayrshire, Scotland KA1 5SJ (☎ 0563 830253 1301)

DONOUGHMORE, 8 Earl of (I 1800); Richard Michael John Hely-Hutchinson; sits as Viscount Hutchinson of Knocklofty (UK 1821); also Baron Donoughmore of Knocklofty (I 1783) and Viscount Donoughmore of Knocklofty (I 1797); s of Col 7 Earl of Donoughmore (d 1981), and Jean, Countess of Donoughmore, MBE, *qv*; *b* 8 Aug 1927; *Educ* Winchester, New Coll Oxford (BM BCh); *m* 1 Nov 1951, Sheila, da of late Frank Frederick Parsons and Mrs Roy Smith-Woodward; 4 s; *Heir* s, Viscount Suirdale; *Career* Capt RAMC; fin conslt, co dir; chm: Headline Book Publishing plc, St Luke's Oxford (charity); *Recreations* fishing, shooting, racing; *Clubs* Hurlingham, Jockey (Paris); *Style—* The Rt Hon the Earl of Donoughmore; The Manor House, Bampton, Oxon OX8 2LQ

DONOUGHUE, Baron (Life Peer UK 1985), of Ashton, Co Northants; Bernard Donoughue; s of Thomas Joseph Donoughue and Maud Violet, *née* Andrews; *b* 8 Sept 1934; *Educ* Northampton GS, Lincoln Coll Oxford (BA), Nuffield Coll Oxford (MA, DPhil); *m* 1959 (m dis 1990), Carol Ruth, da of late Abraham Goodman; 2 s (Hon Paul Michael David b 1969, Hon Stephen Joel b 1969), 2 da (Hon Rachel Anne b 1965, Hon Kate Miriam b 1967); *Career* lectr, sr lectr, reader LSE 1963-74, sr policy advsr to PM 1974-79, devpt dir Econ Intell Unit 1979-81, asst ed The Times 1981-82, head of res and investmt policy Grieveson Grant & Co 1984-86 (ptnr 1983), dir Kleinwort Benson Securities 1986-88, exec vice-chm London and Bishopsgate Int Investmt Hldgs 1988-; memb: advsy bd Wissenschaftzentrum Berlin 1978, cncl LSE; assoc memb Nuffield Coll Oxford; hon fell: Lincoln Coll Oxford, LSE; chm Exec LSO; *Books* Trade Unions in a Changing Society (1963), British Politics and the American Revolution, The People into Parliament (with W T Rogers, 1964), Herbert Morrison: portrait of a politician (with G W Jones, 1973), Prime Minister (1987); *Style—* The Rt Hon the Lord Donoughue; 11 Bloomfield Terrace, London SW1

DONOVAN, Hon Hugh Desmond; s of Baron Donovan, PC (Life Peer, d 1971); *b* 23 Feb 1934; *Educ* Harrow, New Coll Oxford; *m* 26 July 1968, Margaret, da of Hugh Forbes Arbuthnott (ggs of 8 Viscount of Arbuthnott); 1 s (Charles Edward b. 1974); *Career* served RN as Midshipman; barr; *Recreations* golf, photography; *Clubs* Royal Wimbledon Golf; *Style—* The Hon Hugh Donovan; 40 Felden St, SW6 (☎ 071 731 4001)

DONOVAN, Ian Alexander; s of Ivar Kirkwood Donovan (d 1983), and Marion Sutherland, *née* Esslemont; *b* 19 Dec 1945; *Educ* Malvern, Univ of Birmingham (MB ChB, MD); *m* 3 May 1975, Rosamund Mary, da of Reginald Vickors, of the Crescent, Hagley, Worcs; 1 s (Robert b 1985), 2 da (Amy b 1980, Lorna b 1982); *Career* sr lectr in surgery Univ of Birmingham 1979-87, conslt surgn W Midlands RHA 1987-; memb: Cncl Assoc of Surgns GB and Ireland, Advsy Ctee Admin of Radioactive Substances DHSS; hon sec W Midland Surgns Soc; memb: Surgical Res Soc, Br Soc of Gastroenterology; FRCS; *Recreations* golf, photography, family; *Clubs* Edgbaston Golf; *Style—* Ian Donovan, Esq; Edgbaston Nuffield Hosp, Edgbaston, Birmingham (☎ 021 456 2000)

DONOVAN, Ian Edward; s of John Walter Donovan (d 1986), and Ethel Molyneux Studdy Hooper (d 1990); *b* 2 March 1940; *Educ* Leighton Park Sch Reading; *m* 26 July 1969, Susan Betty da of William Harris, of Abbotsbury, Dorset; 2 s (Christopher George b 1971, James William b 1974); *Career* fin dir: Lucas Girling Koblenz 1978-81, Lucas Electrical 1982-84; gp dir fin and central servs CAA 1985-88, memb for fin CAA 1986-88, dir and gp controller Smiths Industs Aerospace & Def Systems Ltd 1988-; *Recreations* sailing, music; *Style—* Ian E Donovan, Esq; Lawn Farm, Church Lane, Tibberton, Droitwich, Worcs WR9 7NW; 11 Sussex House, 220 Kew Rd, Kew, Richmond, Surrey

DONOVAN, Jason Sean; s of Terence Patrick Donovan, of Melbourne, Australia, and Susan Margaret, *née* Menlove (now Mrs McIntosh); *b* 1 June 1968; *Career* actor and singer; tv work: first appearance Skyways (Network 7 Aust) 1979, I Can Jump Puddles (Aust Broadcasting Corp) 1979, Neighbours 1985-89, Heroes 1988, Shadows of the Heart 1990; hit singles: Nothing Can Divide Us 1988, Especially For You (duet with Kylie Minogue) 1988, Too Many Broken Hearts 1989, Sealed With A Kiss 1989, Everyday 1989, Hang On To Your Love 1990, Another Night 1990, Rythym of the Rain 1990, Doing Fine 1990; albums: Ten Good Reasons (platinum disc) 1989, Between the Lines 1990; concert tours: Aust, Far East, Europe; Logies awards (Aust): Best New Talent 1987, Most Popular Actor 1988, Most Popular Actor in a Mini Series 1990; Smash Hits awards: Most Fanciable Male 1989, Best Album 1989, Best Male Singer 1989, Best Male Artist of the Year 1990; sold more singles in the UK than any other act 1989, singer on Band aid single Do They Know It's Christmas 1989; *Recreations* surfing, reading biographies; *Style—* Jason Donovan, Esq; Richard East Productions Pty Ltd, 38 Arthur St, South Yarra, Victoria 3141, Australia (☎ 0101 61 3 827 6377, fax 01061 3 827 5165)

DONOVAN, John Edward; s of late Leslie Donovan, Maj RE; *b* 24 Sept 1930; *Educ* Wimbledon Coll; *m* 1957, Margaret Bridget, *née* O'Brien; 1 s (twin), 2 da; *Career* Flying Offr RAF Nat Serv; CA; in private practice; fin dir Lovelace Investment Ltd; hon treas: Handicapped Children's Pilgrimage Tst, To Romania with Love, Hosanna House Tst; FCA, ATII; *Recreations* music, reading; *Style—* John Donovan, Esq; St Josephs, 56 Molesey Park Rd, East Molesey, Surrey KT8 0JZ

DONOVAN, Judith; da of Ernest Nicholson, of Bradford, and Joyce, *née* Finding; *b* 5 July 1951; *Educ* St Josephs Coll Bradford, Woking Girls GS, Univ of Hull (BA); *m* 12 Nov 1977, John Patrick Donovan, s of William Donovan, of Darlington; *Career* mktg trainee Ford Motor Co 1973-75, account mangr J Walter Thomson 1976, advertising mangr Grattan 1977-82, md Judith Donovan Assocs 1982; chm Bradford TEC, dep chm Bradford Breakthrough, cncl memb Bradford C of C, CBI rep on Ct of Univ of Bradford, past pres Bradford Jr C of C (cncl memb), govr Friends of Bradford Art Galleries & Museums, past chm Bradford Business Club, fndr patron Women Mean Business, patron Small Business Bureau, memb Westminster Dining Club; MInstM 1977, MBIM 1978, MCAM 1979; memb: IOD 1983, Mktg Soc 1987; *Recreations* reading, the Western Front, pets; *Style—* Mrs Judith Donovan; 42 Heaton Grove, Bradford, W Yorks BD9 4EB (☎ 0274 543 966); Judith Donovan Assocs, Phoenix House, Rushton Avenue, Bradford, W Yorkshire BD3 7BH (☎ 0274 656222, fax 0274 656167, car 0836 610683)

DONOVAN, Prof Robert John; s of Francis Alexander Donovan, of Sandbach, Cheshire, and Ida, *née* Brooks; *b* 13 July 1941; *Educ* Sandbach Sch, UCW (BSc), Univ of Cambridge (PhD); *m* 20 June 1964, Marion, da of William Colclough (d 1952); 1 da (Jane Frances); *Career* res fell Gonville and Caius Coll 1966-70; Univ of Edinburgh: lectr in physical chemistry 1970, reader 1974, appointed to personal chair of physical chemistry 1979, head Dept of Chemistry 1984-87, appointed to chair of chemistry 1986); visiting scientist Max-Planck Inst für Strömungsforshung Göttingen 1975, JSPS sr visiting fell Inst of Molecular Sci Okazaki Japan 1982 (visiting fell 1983 and 1989); author numerous pubns; chm Laser Facility Ctee SERC 1988-; FRSE 1976, FRSC 1980; *Recreations* riding, skiing and hill walking; *Style—* Prof Robert Donovan, FRSE; Dept of Chemistry, University of Edinburgh, West Mains Rd, Edinburgh EH9 3JJ (☎ 031 650 4722, fax 031 662 4054)

DOOLEY, Wade Anthony; s of Geoffrey Dooley, of Warrington, Cheshire, and Ethel Beatrice, *née* Wright; *b* 2 Oct 1957; *Educ* Bolton Boys Sch, Beamont Boys' Sch Warrington, Lancashire Police Cadet Coll Preston; *m* 25 Oct 1980, Sharon Diane, da of late Sydney Corrie; 1 da (Sophie Helen b 14 Nov 1989); *Career* Rugby Union lock forward Preston Grasshoppers RUFC and England (38 caps); clubs: Preston Grasshoppers RUFC 1975-, Fylde RUFC, Barbarians RFC; rep: British Police, Lancashire B, Lancashire North; England: debut v Romania 1985, Five Nations debut v France 1985, memb World Cup squad 1987, toured Argentina 1990, most capped England lock forward; memb Br Lions tour Aust 1989 (2 test appearances); police offr Blackpool 1975-; *Recreations* music (everything except jazz and country & western), eating out, fell walking, passion for gardening and relaxing with wife and baby and pet airedale Janna; *Style—* Wade Dooley, Esq; c/o Preston Grasshoppers RUFC, Lightfoot Lane, Fulwood, Preston, Lancashire (☎ 0772 863027)

DOOTSON, Thomas; s of Samuel Dootson (d 1970), of Fulham, London, and Ethel, *née* Boardman (d 1946); *b* 16 July 1941; *Educ* Blackburn Tech HS, Sir Christopher Wren Sch of Bldg & Art London; *m* 7 Dec 1963, Margaret Katherine May, da of William Windsor Connell (d 1964), of Thornton Heath; 1 s (Alistair William Samuel b 8 Nov 1971), 2 da (Sarah Louise b 13 April 1970, Charlotte Elizabeth b 14 March 1973); *Career* dir: Abbeygate Securities Ltd 1979-86, Connell-Menzies Partnerships 1979-86, Peel Holdings plc 1983-86, TAM Holdings IOM Ltd 1987, Peregrine International Ltd 1987, Cresta Holdings Ltd 1988 (listed London Stock Exchange), Abbeygate Securities IOM Ltd; chm Cresta Properties 1988-91; *Recreations* sailing, diving, golf; *Style—* Thomas Dootson, Esq; Winterbourne, Hillberry Green, Douglas, Isle of Man; PO Box 145, Douglas, Isle of Man (☎ 0624 663797 fax 0624 67732, car 0860 640020)

DORAN, Dr Barry Reginald Harewood; s of Walter Reginald Doran (d 1987), of Worcester Park, Surrey, and Dorothy Maud, *née* Harewood (d 1986); *b* 11 Feb 1940; *Educ* Raynes Park Co GS, St Bartholomew's Hosp Univ of London (MB BS); *m* 25 March 1966, Sheila, da of George Batterby, of Brundall, Norwich; 3 s (Andrew b 1966, Timothy b 1970, Michael b 1971); *Career* res asst RCS 1971-72, hon lectr in anaesthetics Victoria Univ of Manchester 1972-, dir Intensive Therapy Unit Manchester Royal Infirmary 1977- (conslt anaesthetist 1972-); inaugural chm Northern Critical Care Soc; memb: Anaesthetic Res Soc, Intensive Care Soc, Manchester Med Soc; FFARCS 1969; *Books* contrib: Surgery of the Mouth and Jaws, Cash's Textbook of Physiotherapy, Practical Anaesthesia for Surgical Emergencies; *Recreations* shooting; *Clubs* Ollerton; *Style—* Dr Barry Doran; Intensive Therapy Unit, Manchester Royal Infirmary, Oxford Rd, Manchester M13 9WL (☎ 061 276 4715)

DORAN, Frank; MP (Lab) Aberdeen S 1987-; s of Francis Doran, and Betty, *née* Hedges; *b* 13 April 1949; *Educ* Leith Acad, Univ of Dundee (LLB); *m* 1967, Patricia Ann Doran (Pat), *née* Govan; 2 s (Frank, Adrian); *Career* admitted slr 1977; shadow spokesman on oil and gas 1988-; fndr memb Scottish Legal Action Gp, fndr memb and former chm Dundee Assoc for Mental Health; *Recreations* cinema, football, art, sport; *Clubs* Aberdeen Trades Council; *Style—* Frank Doran, Esq, MP; 12 Laurelbank, Dundee (☎ 0382 27086); House of Commons, London SW1A 0AA (☎ 01 219 3588); Constituency: 44 King Street, Aberdeen AB2 3AX (☎ 0224 640531, fax 0224 643613)

DORE, Brian James; s of Albert Dore (d 1979), of Oxford, and Cissie, *née* Barratt; *b* 16 March 1935; *Educ* City of Oxford HS for Boys; *m* 14 June 1958, Mary Roberta, da of Henry Hansford (d 1977), of Oxford; 2 s (Andrew Michael b 1961, Trevor John b 1965); *Career* accountant; sr ptnr Weller Messenger & Kirkman Oxford (ret) memb Chartered Assoc of Certified Accountants and Taxation, ICAEW; *Recreations* ornithology, travel; *Clubs* Clarendon; *Style—* Brian J Dore, Esq; c/o National Westminster Bank, Comlomberle, Jersey; Weller Messenger & Kirkman, 8 King Edward St, Oxford OX1 4HL (☎ 0865 723131)

DORÉ, Katharine Emma; da of Robert Edward Frederick Dorè, of West Somerset, and Estelle Margaret, *née* Smith; *b* 13 Feb 1960; *Educ* St Brandon's Sch for Girls, Central Sch of Speech & Drama; *Career* freelance stage mangr and admin; cos worked for 1981-88 incl: Leicester Haymarket, Whirligig Children's Theatre, Scottish Ballet, English Touring Opera (now City of Birmingham Opera), Watermans Arts Centre; co dir (with Matthew Bourne) Adventures in Motion Pictures (modern dance co) 1988-; winner Barclays New Stages award for Adventures in Motion Pictures 1990; *Recreations* contemporary arts; *Style—* Ms Katharine Doré; AMP, Sadlers Wells, Rosebery Ave, London EC1R 4TN (☎ 071 278 6563, fax 071 837 0965)

DOREY, Prof Anthony Peter (Tony); s of HW Dorey, of Wishford, Wilts, and N E Dorey, *née* Fancy; *b* 16 July 1938; *Educ* Brockenhurst GS, Univ of Cambridge; *m* 24 Sept 1960, Valerie; 1 s (Mark b 1963), 1 da (Juliet (Mrs Burd) b 1965); *Career* res physicist Philips 1960-65, lectr in physics Univ of Loughborough 1965-67, lectr and sr lectr electronics Univ of Southampton 1967-83; memb Inst of Physics, FIEE, MIEEE

(USA); *Books* contrib to: Moderne Methoden Und Hilfsmittel Der Ingenieur Ausbidlung (ed G Buzdugan, 1978), VLSI 89 (ed G Musgrave, 1989), Design and Test for VLSI and WSI Circuits (ed R Massara, 1989), Developments in Integrated Circuit Testing (ed D Miller, 1987); *Recreations* fell walking, singing; *Style—* Prof Tony Dorey; Honeytrek, Post Horse Lane, Hornby, Lancs LA2 8RH; Engineering Dept, Univ of Lancaster, Bailrigg, Lancaster LA1 4YR (☎ 0524 65201, fax 0524 381707, telex 65111 LANCUL G)

DOREY, Geoffrey Richard; s of Conseiller John Dorey (d 1984), and Blanche Flere, *née* Bichard; *b* 28 Aug 1944; *Educ* Elizabeth Coll Guernsey, City of London Coll Moorgate; *m* 1969 (m dis 1990), Evelyne Genevieve, da of Col Renaud Sabattier, of France; 2 s (Olivier b 1972, Pascal b 1976), 1 da (Sophie b 1974); *Career* md Fruit Export Group 1978-83 (dir 1972); dir: BD Holdings Ltd 1983-, Island Insurance Co Ltd 1978-, Group Channel TV 1985-; Douzainier de la Paroisse du Castel 1987, Sénéchal Fief Le Comte 1987; *Recreations* period cars, wine, vernacular architecture, badminton; *Clubs* United, Guernsey; *Style—* Geoffrey Dorey, Esq; Les Queux, Castel, Guernsey; BD Holdings Ltd, PO Box 350 , St Peter Port, Guernsey (☎ 0481 723881, fax 714204)

DOREY, Graham Martyn; s of late Martyn Dorey, and late Muriel, *née* Pickard; *b* 15 Dec 1932; *Educ* Kingswood Sch Bath, Ecole des Roches Verneuil, Univ of Bristol (BA), Univ of Caen (Cert d'Ètudes Juridiques); *m* 5 Sept 1962, Penelope Cecile, da of late Maj E A Wheadon, ED; 2 s (Robert b 1970, Martyn b 1972), 2 da (Suzanne b 1963, Jane b 1964); *Career* advocate of the Royal Court 1960, slr-gen Guernsey 1973, attorny-gen Guernsey 1977, dep bailiff Guernsey 1982-; people's dep States of Guernsey 1970-73; *Recreations* sailing; *Style—* Graham Dorey, Esq; Royal Court, Guernsey (☎ 0481 26161)

DORIGO, Anthony Robert (Tony); s of Roberto Dorigo, and Rosemary Anne, *née* Stankovic; *b* 31 Dec 1965; *Educ* Thornton Park HS Adelaide Aust, Seacombe HS Adelaide Aust; *m* 14 Feb 1988, Heather, da of Nicol Rystant Morris; 2 s (Luke b 28 July 1988, Todd Robert b 3 Jan 1991); *Career* professional footballer; 111 league appearances Aston Villa 1984-87 (signed as apprentice July 1982), transfered to Chelsea for a fee of £475,000 1987-, over 170 appearances; England caps: 11 under 21, 4 B, 5 full incl third/fourth place play-off v Italy World Cup 1990; player of the year: Aston Villa 1986-87, Chelsea 1987-88; *Recreations* golf; *Style—* Tony Dorigo, Esq; Chelsea FC, Stamford Bridge, Fulham Road, London SW6 1HS (☎ 071 385 5545)

DORIN, Geoffrey Stephen Neilson; s of Stephen Dorin (d 1972), and Lily, *née* Miller (d 1988); *b* 21 Dec 1925; *Educ* Whitley Bay HS, King's Coll Durham, Open Univ (BA); *m* 2 April 1955, Patricia Margaret, da of James Norman Adamson (d 1966); 1 s (Andrew James Neilson b 1961), 1 da (Julia Ruth b 1963); *Career* Nat Serv 1946 RAPC (Capt); former md: Smith & Barnes Ltd, John W & S Dorin Ltd; admin dir St Oswald's Hospice Newcastle upon Tyne 1982-; *Recreations* country pursuits, travel, gardening; *Style—* Geoffrey S N Dorin, Esq; Oak Tree Cottage, West Rainton, Houghton-le-Spring, Wearside (☎ 091 584 9070); Silverdale Cottage, Snitter, Rothbury (☎ 0669 21084); St Oswald's Hospice, Regent Avenue, Newcastle upon Tyne NE3 1EE (☎ 091 285 0063)

DORJI, Hon Mrs (Manjula); *née* Sinha; er da of 3 Baron Sinha, *qv*; *b* 1947; *m* (m dis), Tobgye Dorji, s of late Jigme Dorji, prime min of Bhutan; 1 s (Jigme); *Style—* Hon Mrs Dorji; 7 Lord Sinha Rd, Calcutta

DORKING, Bishop of 1986-; Rt Rev David Peter Wilcox; s of John Wilcox (d 1961), and Stella May, *née* Bower (d 1977); *b* 29 June 1930; *Educ* Northampton GS, St John's Coll Oxford (MA), Lincoln Theological Coll; *m* 11 Aug 1956, Pamela Ann, da of Herbert Leslie Hedges; 2 s (Peter b 1961, Christopher b 1968), 2 da (Sara b 1957, Frances b 1959); *Career* asst curate St Helier Morden Southwark 1954-56, staff sec Student Christian Movement and asst curate Univ Church Oxford 1956-59; Theological Coll posts: Lincoln 1959-64, Bangalore S India 1964-70; vicar Gt Gransden and rector Lt Gransden Ely 1970-72, canon Derby Cathedral and warden E Midlands Jt Ordination Scheme 1972-77, princ Ripon Coll Cuddesdon and vicar Cuddesdon Oxford 1977-86; *Recreations* walking, music, art, theatre; *Style—* The Rt Rev the Bishop of Dorking; Dayspring, 13 Pilgrims Way, Guildford, Surrey GU4 8AD (☎ 0483 570829)

DORMAN, Lt-Col Sir Charles Geoffrey; 3 Bt (UK 1923), of Nunthorpe, York, MC (1942); o s of Sir Bedford Lockwood Dorman, 2 Bt, CBE (d 1956); *b* 18 Sept 1920; *Educ* Rugby, BNC Oxford; *m* 22 Dec 1954 (m dis 1972), Elizabeth Ann, CStJ, o da of late George Gilmour Gilmour-White, OBE, JP; 1 da; *Heir* kinsman, Philip Dorman; *Career* served 3 The Kings Own Hussars 1941-47, Capt 1942, 13/18 Royal Hussars 1947-70, Maj 1954, Lt-Col 1961, GSO (1) (ADSR) AORE 1961-64, GSOI (W), IFVME 1964, ret 1970; *Recreations* gliding; *Style—* Lt-Col Sir Charles Dorman, Bt, MC; Hutton Grange Cottage, Gt Rollright, Chipping Norton, Oxon (☎ 0608 737535)

DORMAN, John Douglas; s of Sir Maurice Dorman, GCMG, GCVO, of The Old Manor, W Overton, nr Marlborough, Wilts, and Florence Monica, *née* Churchward Montagu-Smith; *b* 30 Sept 1939; *Educ* Sedbergh, Magdalene Coll Cambridge (BA); *m* 20 July 1974, Pauline Anne; 1 s (Rory b 1976), 2 da (Arabella b 1975, Shara b 1979); *Career* trainee mangr Bunge and Co Ltd 1962-64, trainee offr then vice pres The Chase Manhattan Bank NA 1964-73, gen mangr and dir First Int Bancshares Ltd 1973-79, conslt Orion Bank Ltd 1980-81, gen mangr London branch Bank of New England NA 1981-; *Recreations* skiing, sailing, tennis, bicycling, travel; *Clubs* Hurlingham, Anabel's, Hayling Island Sailing; *Style—* John Dorman, Esq; 21 Narborough St, London SW6 (☎ 071 731 1717); Dexter House, 2 Royal Mint Ct, London EC3N 4QN (☎ 071 481 8181, fax 071 481 4111)

DORMAN, Sir Maurice Henry; GCMG (1961, KCMG 1957, CMG 1955), GCVO (1961), DL (Wilts 1978); s of John Ehrenfried Dorman (d 1957), of 77 Eastgate, Stafford, and Madeleine Louise, *née* Bostock (d 1978); *b* 7 Aug 1912; *Educ* Sedbergh, Magdalene Coll Cambridge (MA); *m* 4 Dec 1937, (Florence) Monica Churchward, DStJ, da of Montague George Smith (d 1947), of Torquay, Devon; 1 s (John b 1939), 3 da (Joanna (Mrs Oswin) b 1941, Elisabeth (Mrs Latham) b 1943, Sibella (Mrs Laing) b 1949); *Career* admin offr Tanganyika Territory 1935, clerk cncls Tanganyika 1940-45, asst to Lt Govr Malta 1945, princ asst sec Palestine 1947, seconded to Colonial Office 1948, dir Social Welfare and Community Devpt Gold Coast 1950, colonial sec Trinidad and Tobago 1952-56 (acting govr Trinidad 1954-55); govr gen: Sierra Leone 1961-62 (govr, C-in-C and Vice Adm 1956-61 independence), Malta 1964-71 (govr and C-in-C 1962-64 independence); ret; dep chm Pearce Cmmn on Rhodesian Opinion 1971-72, chm Br Observer Gp at Zimbabwe Independence Elections 1980; chm: Swindon Hosp Mgmnt Ctee 1972-74, Swindon Health Authy 1981-88, West of England (previously Ramsbury) Building Soc 1983-87 (dir 1972-83); tstee Imperial War Museum 1972-85, vice pres Badminton Sch Bristol, life govr Monkton Combe Sch Bath; lord prior Ven Order St John 1980-85 (chief cdr St John Ambulance 1975-80, almoner Order St John 1972-75), GCStJ 1978 (KStJ 1957); Hon DCL (Durham) 1962, Hon LLD (Malta) 1964; *Recreations* golf, gardening, grandchildren; *Clubs* Athenaeum, Casino Maltese (Valletta); *Style—* Sir Maurice Dorman, GCMG, GCVO, DL; The Old Manor, Overton, nr Marlborough, Wilts SN8 4ER (☎ 067 286 600)

DORMAN, Philip Henry Keppel; s of Richard Dorman (d 1976), gs of 1 Bt; hp of kinsman, Sir Charles Dorman, 3 Bt, MC; *b* 19 May 1954; *Educ* Marlborough, Univ of St Andrews; *m* 12 April 1982, Myriam Jeanne Georgette, da of late René Bay of Royan, France; 1 da (Megan Bay Keppel b 1984); *Career* tax conslt; *Recreations* golf; *Clubs* MCC, Waterhall Golf (Brighton); *Style—* Philip Dorman Esq

DORMAN, Richard Bostock; CBE (1984); s of John Ehrenfried Dorman (d 1957), of Stafford, and Madeleine Louise Bostock (d 1975); *b* 8 Aug 1925; *Educ* Sedbergh, St John's Coll Cambridge (BA); *m* 1950, Anna, da of Maj Frank Illingworth (d 1977), of Surrey; 1 s (Paul b 1963), 2 da (Julia b 1953, Deborah b 1959); *Career* HM Dip Serv: first sec Nicosia 1960-64, dep high cmmr Freetown 1964-66, NATO Def Coll Rome 1968-69, cnsllr Addis Ababa 1969-73, commercial cnsllr Bucharest 1974-77, cnsllr South Africa 1977-82, high cmmr Port Vila 1982-85; ret; *Recreations* chm British Friends of Vanuatu; *Clubs* Royal Cwlth Soc; *Style—* Richard Dorman, Esq, CBE; 67 Beresford Rd, Cheam, Surrey SM2 6ER (☎ 081 642 9625)

DORMAND OF EASINGTON, Baron (Life Peer UK 1987), of Easington, Co Durham; John Donkin Dormand; s of Bernard and Mary Dormand, of Haswell, Co Durham; *b* 27 Aug 1919; *Educ* Bede Coll Durham, Loughborough Coll, St Peter's Coll Oxford, Harvard Univ; *m* 1963, Doris, da of Thomas Robinson, of Houghton-le-Spring, Co Durham; 1 step s, 1 step da; *Career* chm PLP 1981-87; former teacher, educn advsr & dist educn offr; asst govt whip 1974, ld cmmr of Treasury 1974-79; memb: Peterlee Lab Club, Easington Workingmen's Club; MP (Lab) Easington 1970-87; *Style—* The Rt Hon the Lord Dormand of Easington; House of Lords, London SW1A OPW

DORMANDY, John Adam; s of Paul Szeben, and Klara, *née* Engel; *b* 5 May 1937; *Educ* St Paul's, Univ of London (MB BS); *m* 29 Jan 1983, Klara Dormandy, da of Prof I Zarday; 1 s (Alexis b 1969), 1 da (Xenia b 1972); *Career* conslt surgn; awarded: Fahreus Medal, Hamilton Bailey Prize, Hunterian Professorship of RCS; chm: section on clinical measurement RSM, Venous Forum RSM; conslt vascular surgn St George's Hosp, hon sr lectr surgery Univ of London, ed jls on various aspects of circulatory disease; chm Euro Consensus on Critical Limb Ischaemia; DSc 1990; FRCSE 1974, FRCS 1975; *Books* Clinical Haemorheology (1987), Critical Limb Ischaemia (1990); *Recreations* skiing, squash; *Style—* John Dormandy, Esq; Department of Vascular Surgery, St James' Wing, St George's Hospital, Blackshaw Rd, London SW17 (☎ 081 672 1255, fax 081 767 8346)

DORMER, 16 Baron (E 1615); Sir Joseph Spencer Philip Dormer; 16 Bt (E 1615); s of Capt 14 Baron Dormer, CBE, JP, DL, RN (d 1922); suc bro, 15 Baron Dormer, 1975; *b* 4 Sept 1914; *Educ* Ampleforth, Ch Ch Oxford; *Heir* cous, Lt Cdr Geoffrey Henry Dormer, RN; *Career* served WW II, Capt Scots Gds, NW Europe; sits as Cons peer in the House of Lords; pres Warwick and Leamington Cons Assoc 1983; hon vice pres Worcestershire Branch Grenadier Guards Assoc; landowner and farmer; Kt of Honour and Devotion of the SMO of Malta; *Recreations* shooting, fishing, gardening; *Clubs* Cavalry & Guards; *Style—* Rt Hon Lord Dormer; Grove Park, Warwick CV35 8RF (☎ (0926) 498838)

DORMER, Michael Henry Stanhope; o child of Robert Stanhope Dormer (d 1960), and Ebba (d 1961), widow of Sir Everard Hambro, KCVO, and da of Charles Cecil Beresford Whyte, JP, DL, of Hatley Manor, co Leitrim; he is descended through the Counts Buttlar from the 'Blood-Countess' Elisabeth Báthory (walled-up alive and d 1614); *b* 8 Dec 1930; *m* 21 Jan 1959, Daphne Margaret, elder da and co-heiress of Capt Oswald James Battine (d 1938), and his w Gwendoline who was eldest da and co-heiress of Col Sir Colin MacRae of Feoirlinn (d 1952), by his w Lady Margaret (d 1954), da of 3 Marquess of Bute; 1 s, 2 da; *Career* Kt of Honour and Devotion SMO Malta, Kt of Justice of the Constantinian Order of St George; *Recreations* gardening, genealogy, painting; *Clubs* Turf, Beefsteak; *Style—* Michael Dormer Esq; Bowdown House, Greenham, Newbury, Berks (☎ 0635 43311)

DORMER, Robin James; s of Dudley James Dormer (d 1983), and Jean Mary, *née* Brimacombe; *b* 30 May 1951; *Educ* Int Sch of Geneva Switzerland, Univ Coll of Wales Aberystwyth (LLB); *Career* Coward Chance 1976-80; admitted slr 1980, memb legal staff Law Cmmn 1980-87, asst Parly Counsel Office 1987-90, memb Solicitor's Office Dept of Health 1990-; *Style—* Robin Dormer, Esq; Office of the Solicitor, Department of Health, New Court, 48 Carey St, London WC2A 2LS (☎ 071 972 1300, fax 071 972 1554)

DORMER, Hon Rosamund Jane; JP (Warwicks 1948); yst da of 14 Baron Dormer, CBE (d 1922); *b* 15 April 1911; *Career* Jr Cdr ATS 1942; *Style—* The Hon Rosamund Dormer, JP; School House, Spetchley, Worcs

DORREEN, Dr James M; s of late Ernest James Dorreen, civil engr, and late Margaret Dorothy Dorreen; *b* 11 Jan 1916; *Educ* Univ of New Zealand (MSc), Imperial Coll London (PhD); *m* Ruth Sinclair; 3 s (Peter James, Mark Sinclair, Adrian Luke); *Career* Capt NZ Engrs 2 NZEF 1939-45; int oil conslt; formerly with Exxon in Australasia, S America, Far East, Europe and N Africa; ret as pres and md Esso Morocco, Exploration & Production Inc; dir: Texas Pacific Oil, Premier Consolidated Oilfields, Falcon Resources; *Books* papers in scientific journals; *Recreations* geology; *Clubs* American (London), Royal Over-seas League; *Style—* Dr James Dorreen; The Woodlands, Cavendish Road, St George's Hill, Weybridge, Surrey KT13 0JY

DORRELL, Stephen James; MP (Cons) Loughborough 1979-; s of Philip Dorrell; *b* 25 March 1952; *Educ* Uppingham, BNC Oxford; *m* 1980, Penelope Anne Wears, da of James Taylor, of Windsor; *Career* PA to Rt Hon Peter Walker MP 1974; export dir family clothing firm; Parly candidate (C) Kingston-upon-Hull E Oct 1974; PPS to Rt Hon Peter Walker MP Sec of State Energy 1983-, asst govt whip 1987, Parly under sec of state for health 1990-; *Recreations* walking; *Style—* S J Dorrell, Esq, MP; House of Commons, London SW1

DORRIEN-SMITH, Lady Emma; *née* Windsor-Clive; da of 3 Earl of Plymouth; *b* 13 Feb 1954; *m* 1975, Robert Arthur (Smith-Dorrien-Smith, eldest s of late Lt Cdr Thomas Mervyn Smith-Dorrien-Smith, RN, of Tresco, Isles of Scilly, and Tamara, Lady O'Hagan; 2 s (Adam b 1978, Michael b 1987), 1 da (Frances b 1980); *Style—* Lady Emma Dorrien-Smith; Tresco Abbey, Isles of Scilly

DORSET, Archdeacon of; *see*: Walton, Ven Geoffrey Elmer

DORWARD, David Campbell; s of David Gardyne Dorward (d 1971), of Craigton House, Monkie, and Margaret Edward, *née* Boyle; *b* 7 Aug 1933; *Educ* Morgan Acad, Univ of St Andrews (MA), RAM (GRSM); *m* 11 June 1968, Janet, da of Donald Offord; 1 s (Alan Michael b 15 Aug 1978), 2 da (Helen Marianne b 19 Nov 1972, Frances Imogen b 15 July 1974); *Career* Royal Philharmonic Soc prizewinner 1958, music prodr BBC Edinburgh 1962-; composed: concerto for wind and percussion 1960, symphony number 1 1961, four string quartets 1963-72, violin concerto 1965, cello concerto 1966, piano concerto 1976, viola concerto 1981; arts advsr Lamp of Lothian 1967-, memb Scottish Arts Cncl 1972-78, conslt dir Performing Rights Soc 1985-; ISM; memb: Composers' Guild Soc of Professional Composers, Scottish Soc of Composers; *Recreations* drawing and painting, photography, trying to program home computers, being alone, reading, walking; *Style—* David Dorward, Esq; 10 Dean Park Crescent, Edinburgh EH4 1PH (☎ 031 332 3002); BBC, 5 Queen St, Edinburgh EH2 1DY (☎ 031 225 3131)

DOSSETOR, Dr Jonathan Francis Bryan; s of Rev Roberts Francis Dossetor, of Salisbury, Wilts, and Joan Alicia, *née* Knott; *b* 6 Jan 1944; *Educ* St John's Sch Leatherhead, St Catharine's Coll Cambridge, UCH; *m* 29 July 1967, Susan P, da of L

A Willmott (d 1967); 1 s (Nicholas b 15 Dec 1975), 2 da (Alice b 10 May 1970, Joanna b 1 March 1972); *Career* sr registrar paediatrics Ahmadu Bello Univ Hosp Zaira Nigeria 1973-7 lectr paediatrics The Royal Hosp for Sick Children Yorkhill Glasgow 1977-81, conslt paediatrician The Queen Elizabeth Hosp Kings Lynn 1981-; FRCP 1987; *Recreations* birdwatching, fishing, beekeeping; *Style—* Dr Jonathan Dossetor; 57 Castle Rising Road, South Wootton, Kings Lynne, Norfolk POE30 3JA (☎ 0553 671576); The Queen Elizabeth Hosp, Gayton Rd, King's Lynn, Norfolk PE30 4ET (☎ 0553 766266)

DOSSETUR, Dr Jonathan Francis Bryan; s of Rev Roberts Francis Dossetor, of Salisbury, Wilts, and Joan Alicia, *née* Knott; *b* 6 Jan 1944; *Educ* St John's Sch, Leatherhead, St Catherine's Coll Cambridge, UCH; *m* 29 July, da of L A Willmott (d 1967); 1 s (Nicholas b 15 Dec 1975), 2 da (Alice b 10 May 1970, Joanna b 1 March 1972); *Career* sr registrar paediatrics Ahmadu Bello Univ Hosp Zaire Nigeria 1973-76, lectr paediatrics The Royal Hosp for Sick Children Yorkhill Glasgow 1977-81, conslt paediatrcian The Queen Elizsabeth Hosp Kings Lynn 1981-; FRCP 1987; *Recreations* birdwatching, fishing, beekeeping; *Style—* Dr Jonathan Dossetor; 57 Castle Rising Rd, South Wootton, King's Lynn, Norfolk PE30 3JA (☎ 0553 671576); The Queen Elizabeth Hosp, Gayton Rd, King's Lynn, Norfolk PE30 4ET (☎ 0553 766266)

DOTRICE, Roy; s of Louis Dotrice and Neva, *née* Wilton; *b* 26 May 1925; *Educ* Dayton Acad, Intermediate Sch Guernsey; Elizabeth Coll; *m* 1946, Kay Newman; 3 da (Michéle (m 1987 Edward Woodward, the actor) Karen (m 1986 Alex Hyde White, actor s of Wilfrid Hyde White), Yvette (m 1985, John E R Lumley)); *Career* actor; 9 years with Royal Shakespeare Co; over 30 West End performances; 6 Broadway appearances including 2 one-man shows *viz* Abraham Lincoln and Brief Lives, Emmy Award the latter in Guinness Book of World Records as longest running solo performance (1,700); best actor award TV England 1969 (Brief Lives), America 1966 (The Caretaker); Tony nomination as best Broadway actor 1981; latest films Amadeus, Corsican Brothers, The Eliminators; latest American TV: A Team, The Wizard, Magnum PI, Beauty and the Beast; *Recreations* fishing, riding, golf; *Clubs* Garrick, Players; *Style—* Roy Dotrice Esq; c/o Bernard Hunter, Leading Players, 31, Kings Road, London SW3

DOUBLE, Michael Stockwell; s of Cyril William Stockwell Double (d 1942), and Alice Elizabeth Ellen, *née* Smith (d 1987); *b* 3 March 1935; *Educ* Christ's Hosp, Pembroke Coll Cambridge (MA); *m* 26 Feb 1966, Julia, da of Harold Ashwell Westrope (d 1961); 2 da (Lucy b 1967, Clare b 1970); *Career* Nat Serv Royal Corps of Signals; CA; dir: The Tussaud's Group Ltd 1981-, Warwick Castle Ltd 1987-, Chessington World of Adventures Ltd 1987-; FCA; *Recreations* sailing, theatre, walking; *Clubs* Island Cruising; *Style—* Michael Double, Esq; The Tussaud's Group Ltd, Marylebone Rd, London NW1 5LR (☎ 071 935 6861, fax 071 465 0864)

DOUBLEDAY, Lt-Col Garth Leslie; TD (1950), JP (Kent 1956), DL (1965); s of Sir Leslie Doubleday (d 1975), by his w Nora, da of William Foster, of Tunbridge Wells; *b* 13 July 1913; *Educ* Charterhouse, Clare Coll Cambridge; *m* 1946, May Alison, da of Frank Hann; 3 s, 3 da; *Career* served 1939-45 RA, Middle East, cdr 516 LAA regt (TA) 1949-52; gen cmmr of Income Tax 1970; High Sheriff 1976-77; master Worshipful Co of Fruiterers 1968; *Clubs* Farmers', MCC; *Style—* Lt-Col Garth Doubleday, TD, JP, DL; Rodmersham House, Rodmersham, Sittingbourne, Kent (☎ 0795 423545)

DOUBLEDAY, John Vincent; s of Gordon Vincent Doubleday, of Essex, and Margaret Elsa Verder, *née* Harris; *b* 9 Oct 1947; *Educ* Stowe, Goldsmith's Coll Sch of Art; *m* 1969, Isobel Jean Campbell, da of Maj Frederick Robert Edwin Durie, of Argyll; 3 s (Robert b 1974, Edwin b 1977, James b 1979); *Career* artist; exhibitions incl: Waterhouse Gallery 1968-69 and 1970-71, Richard Demarco Gallery Edinburgh 1973, Laing Art Gallery Newcastle, Bowes Barnard Castle 1974, Pandion Gallery NY, Aldeborough Festival 1983; portraits incl: Baron Ramsey of Canterbury 1974, King Olav of Norway 1975, Prince Philip Duke of Edinburgh, Earl Mountbatten, Golda Meir 1976, Ratu Sukuna 1977, Regeneration 1978, Maurice Bowra 1979, Charlie Chaplin (Leicester Square), Lord Olivier, Mary and Child Christ (Rochester Cathedral), Caduceus (Harvard Mass), Isambard Kingdom Brunel (two works in Paddington and Bristol), Charlie Chaplin (Vevey 1982, and London), Beatles (Liverpool), Dylan Thomas (Swansea 1984 and Phoenix 1985), Commando Memorial 1986, Sherlock Holmes (Town Square Meiringen) 1988, Arthur Mourant (St Helier Museum Jersey) 1990; works in public collections: Ashmolean, Br Museum, Herbert F Johnson NY, Tate Gallery, V & A, Nat Museum of Wales; *Recreations* cross-country skiing; *Style—* John Doubleday, Esq; Lodge Cottage, Goat Lodge Rd, Gt Totham, Maldon, Essex (☎ 0621 892085); Torrdarroch, Ardrishaig, Argyll, Scotland

DOUBLEDAY, (Richard) Noel; s of John Frederick Doubleday, and Ivy Muriel Mitchell (d 1957); gs of pioneer of Public Library System; *b* 27 May 1930; *Educ* Rossall Sch, King Edward's Edgbaston, Downing Coll Cambridge (MA); *m* 13 April 1982, Catherine Mary, da of The Ven Philip L C Price (d 1983); *Career* former dir of devpt Keston Coll 1983-86; dir: Open Doors (UK) 1968-75, Living Bibles Int (UK) 1986-; freelance prodr and contributor to BBC; *Recreations* swimming, walking, dining out, classical music; *Clubs* Athenaeum; *Style—* Noel Doubleday, Esq; 22 Forest Rd, Bordon, Hampshire GU35 0BH (☎ 0420 477668)

DOUEK, Ellis Elliot; s of Cesar Douek, of London, and Nelly, *née* Sassoon; *b* 25 April 1934; *Educ* English Sch Cairo Egypt, Westminster Med Sch (MRCS, LRCP); *m* 22 March 1964, Nicole Iris, da of Robert Galante (d 1984); 2 s (Daniel b 1965, Joel b 1967); *Career* Capt RAMC 1960-62; registrar ENT Royal Free Hosp 1965, sr registrar Kings Coll Hosp 1968, conslt otologist Guys Hosp 1970; FRCS 1967, RSM, BAO; *Books* Sense of Smell and It's Abnormalities (1974), contrib chapters in: Textbook of Otology and Laryngology 1988, Robbs Surgery 1976; *Recreations* painting; *Clubs* Athenaeum; *Style—* Ellis Douek, Esq; 1-24 Reynolds Close, London NW11 (☎ 081 455 6047); 2 Silerchie, Camaiore, Italy; 97 Harley St, London W1 (☎ 071 935 7828, 071 487 4695)

DOUGAL, Malcolm Gordon; s of Eric Gordon Dougal (d 1970), and Marie, *née* Wildermuth; *b* 20 Jan 1938; *Educ* Ampleforth, Queen's Coll Oxford (MA); *m* 14 Sept 1964, Elke, da of Hans Urban, of Essen, W Germany; 1 s (Gordon b 17 June 1982); *Career* 2 Lt Royal Sussex Regt served Korea and Gibraltar 1956-58; De Havilland Aircraft 1961-64, Ticket Equipment Ltd (Plessey) 1964-66, Harris Lebus 1967-69, FCO London 1969-72; first sec: Br Embassy Paris 1972-76, Br Embassy Cairo 1976-79; FCO London 1979-81, HM Consul Gen Lille France 1981-85, Dep High Comm Br High Cmmn Canberra Aust 1986-89, Royal Coll of Def Studies London 1990-; memb: RSPB, Nat Tst; *Recreations* natural history, books, wine, history; *Style—* Malcolm Dougal, Esq; Foreign & Commomnwealth Office, Whitehall, London SW1A 2AH

DOUGHTY, Dr Andrew Gerard; s of Samuel Henry Doughty (d 1963), and Ella Cadman, *née* Scott (d 1970); *b* 2 Sept 1916; *Educ* Beaumont Coll Berks, St Thomas's Hosp Med Sch Univ of London (MB BS); *m* 8 Oct 1949, Peggy, da of Frank Harvey Giles (d 1979); 1 s (Gerard Francis Peter b 1955), 1 da (Catherine Mary b 1952); *Career* Lt RAMC 1942, transferred IMS 1942, serv India, Burma, Borneo, demobbed Maj specialist in anaesthetics 1946; conslt anaesthetist: Kingston Hosp Surrey 1950-80, St Teresa's Maternity Hosp Wimbledon 1951-82; estab course of practical instruction in epidural analgesia in childbirth Kingston Hosp; FRSM (pres anaesthetic section 1977), FFARCS, pres Obstetric Anaesthetists Assoc 1979-81, FRCOG (ad eundem); *Books* Symposium on Epidural Analgesia in Obstetrics (ed, 1972), Epidural Analgesia in Obstetrics a second symposium (ed, 1980); *Recreations* music, ensemble and solo singing; *Clubs* RSM, London Sketch; *Style—* Dr Andrew Doughty; 10 River Avenue, Thames Ditton, Surrey KT7 ORS (☎ 081 398 3408)

DOUGLAS, Alasdair Ferguson; s of George Douglas, of Perth, Scotland, and Christina, *née* Ferguson; *b* 16 March 1953; *Educ* Perth Accd, Univ of Edinburgh (LLB) QMC London (LLM); *m* Kathryn Veronica Cecile, da of Cecil Kennard, OBE (d 1971); 1 s (Robert Ferguson), 1 da (Alice Jane); *Career* admitted slr 1981; ptnr Travers Smith Braithwaite 1985-; memb Worshipful Co of Slrs; memb: Law Soc, Law Soc of Scotland; *Books* contrib: Tolley's Tax Planning, Tolley's Company Law; *Recreations* reading, cooking; *Style—* Alasdair Douglas, Esq; 10 Snow Hill, London EC1A 2AL (☎ 071 248 9133, fax 071 236 3728, telex 887117)

DOUGLAS, Prof Alexander Shafto (Sandy); CBE (1985); s of Maj Quentin Douglas, RE (d 1974), of Kensington, London, and Edith Dorothy, *née* Ingram (d 1965); *b* 21 May 1921; *Educ* Marlborough, Coll of Estate Mgmnt (BSc), Trinity Coll Cambridge (BA, MA, PhD); *m* 16 Dec 1945, Audrey Mary Brasnett, da of Reginald George Parker (d 1983), of Mildenhall, Suffolk; 1 s (Malcolm b 1956), 1 da (Shirley (Mrs Mauger) b 1953); *Career* WWII Royal Signals: Signalman 1941, offr cadet 1942, 2 Lt India 1943, Lt 1943 (served 2 Div Kohima), released 1946; visiting prof Univ of Illinois USA 1953-57, fell and jr bursar Trinity Coll Cambridge 1954-55, dir Univ of Leeds Computing Laboratory 1957-60, tech dir CEIR UK Ltd (now SD - SCICON) 1960-68, chm Leasco Systems and Res Ltd 1968-69, prof LSE 1969-84 (emeritus prof 1984-), chm Buxton Douglas & Ptnrs Ltd (consulting and litigation support) 1971, non-exec dir The Monotype Corp 1973-78, pt/t visiting prof Middx Business Sch Middx Poly 1987-; govr Int Cncl for Computers and Communications 1981-, dir UK Cncl for Computers for Devpt 1987-90, advsr Sci and Technol Parly Ctees 1970-76; memb Def Sci Advsy Cncl 1971-88, sci Advsy Ctee Br Cncl 1978-88; Freeman City of London 1965, Liveryman Worshipful Co of Wheelwrights 1965, memb Worshipful Co of Info Technologists 1986; FBCS (fndr memb 1956, pres 1972), FIMA 1964, ACIArb 1986, MBAE 1988, CEng 1990; *Books* Second Report of the Secretary General on the Application of Compute to Development (jtly 1973); *Recreations* tennis, bridge, philately; *Clubs* City Livery (memb cncl 1989-); *Style—* Prof Alexander Douglas, CBE; 9 Woodside Ave, Walton-on-Thames, Surrey KT12 5LQ (☎ 0932 224 923); The Buxton Douglas Partnership, 116 Temple Chambers, Temple Ave, London EC4Y 0DT (☎ 071 583 1379)

DOUGLAS, Anthony Jude (Tony); s of Arthur Sydney Douglas (d 1976), and Margaret Mary, *née* Farey; *b* 14 Dec 1944; *Educ* Cardinal Vaughan GS, Univ of Southampton (BA); *m* 24 Aug 1968, Jacqueline, *née* English; 2 da (Amy Jane b 2 Oct 1978, Laura Claire b 28 May 1984); *Career* Lintas Advertising: graduate trainee 1967, various account mgmnt posts, client serv dir 1980; D'Arcy McManus & Masius (D'Arcy Masius Benton & Bowles since merger 1985): gp account dir 1982, jt md 1985, jt chm and chief exec 1987-; FIPA, memb Mktg Soc; *Recreations* jogging, walking, reading, travel; *Clubs* RAC, St James's; *Style—* Tony Douglas, Esq; D'Arcy Masius Benton and Bowles, 2 St James's Square, London SW1 (☎ 071 839 3422)

DOUGLAS, (William) Barry; s of Barry Douglas (d 1988), and Sarah Jane, *née* Henry; *b* 23 April 1960; *Educ* RCM (with John Barstow, further study with Maria Curcio); *Career* concert pianist; debut London 1981, Gold medal Tchaikovsky Int Piano Competition 1986; worldwide concert career; tours: USA, Japan, Far East, USSR, Europe; subject of TV documentary After The Gold, exclusive recording contract RCA BMG; Hon DMus Queens Univ Belfast; FRCM; *Recreations* driving, reading, food and wine; *Style—* Barry Douglas, Esq; Terry Harrison Artists Management, 9A Penzance Place, London W11 4PE (☎ 071 221 7741, fax 071 221 2610, telex 25872)

DOUGLAS, Hon Charles James Sholto; yr s of 21 Earl of Morton; *b* 14 Oct 1954; *m* 1981, Anne, da of late William Gordon Morgan, of Waikato, New Zealand; 1 s (James William Sholto b 1984), 2 da (Rebecca Katherine b 1982, Jilian Rosomond Florence b 1986); *Career* ptnr Dalmahoy Farms; *Style—* Hon Charles Douglas; Dalmahoy, Kirknewton, Midlothian

DOUGLAS, Desmond Hugh; MBE (1987); s of Vincent Wesley Douglas (d 1980), and Irene, *née* McCleish; *b* 20 July 1955; *Educ* Gower St Boys Secondary Modern Sch, Lozells Birmingham; *Career* table tennis player; 11 times English closed champion, Welsh Open champion, twice English Open champion, Euro top twelve champion 1987, Hungarian Open team champions 1989, Cwlth singles winner, Cwlth team winner 1989; *Style—* Desmond Douglas, Esq, MBE; 92 Norman Road, Walsall, West Midlands WS5 3QN

DOUGLAS, Donald Macleod; s of Alexander Douglas (d 1973), of Falkirk, Scotland, and Florence, *née* Breakspear (d 1974); *b* 7 March 1933; *Educ* Falkirk HS, Edinburgh Coll of Art (travelling scholarship), RADA (scholarship); *m* 1968, Angela, *née* Galbraith; 3 da (Amy b 1971, Eliza b 1973, Joanna b 1975); *Career* actor; stage debut RSC 1960; repertory cos incl: Glasgow Citizens, Bristol Old Vic, Birmingham, Manchester, Leatherhead, Newcastle; West End Plays: Poor Bitos (Duke of York's), Boys in the Band (Wyndham's) Savages (Comedy), Gotcha (Shaw); RSC 1978-79: Merchant of Venice, Wild Oats, The Churchill Play; Mr Cinders (Fortune) 1983, The Three Estates (Edinburgh Festival 1986, Warsaw), tv incl: Rob Roy, Red Gauntlet, Middlemarch, Sense and Sensibiltity, War and Peace, Poldark; films incl: A Bridge Too Far, Give My Regards to Broad Street, She's Been Away; recent appearances incl: Stephen Joseph Co (The Revengers Comedies, June Moon) 1989, Absurd Person Singular (Whitehall) 1990-91; has appeared as orator with various orchs notably at the Albert Hall Promenade concert for Sir Arthur Bliss's Requiem (with the composer conducting); *Recreations* gardening, riding, painting; *Style—* Donald Douglas, Esq; Joan Brown, Brunskill Management, 3 Earl Rd, London SW14 7JH (☎ 081 876 9448)

DOUGLAS, Sir Donald MacLeod; MBE (1943); s of William Douglas; *b* 28 June 1911; *Educ* Madras Coll, Univ of St Andrews (ChM), Minnesota Univ (MS Minn); *m* 1945, Margaret Diana Whitley; 2 s, 2 da; *Career* asst surgn Edinburgh Municipal Hosps 1945, reader in experimental surgery Univ of Edinburgh 1945-51; surgn Ninewells Hosp Dundee 1951-76, prof of surgery Univ of Dundee (formerly Queen's Coll) 1951-76, emeritus 1977, dean of Faculty of Medicine Univ of Dundee 1969-70; pres: RCSE 1970-73, Assoc of Surgns of GB and Ireland 1964; surgn to HM The Queen in Scotland 1965-76, extra surgn to HM The Queen in Scotland 1977-; FRCSE, FRCS, FRSE, Hon FACS, Hon FRCS (SA), Hon FRCSI, Hon DSc St Andrews; kt 1972; *Style—* Sir Donald Douglas, MBE, FRSE; The Whitehouse of Nevay, Newtyle, Angus (☎ 022 85 315)

DOUGLAS, Gavin Stuart; RD (1970), QC (Scot 1971); s of late Gilbert Georgeson Douglas and Rosena Campbell Douglas; *b* 12 June 1932; *Educ* South Morningside Sch, George Heriot's Sch, Univ of Edinburgh (MA, LLB); *Career* Nat Serv RNVR; admitted slr 1955; admitted Faculty of Advocates 1958, pt/t sub-ed The Scotsman 1957-61, memb Lord Advocate's Dept London (Parly draftsman) 1961-64, resumed practice at Scottish Bar 1964, jr counsel to BOT 1965, counsel to Scottish Law Cmmn 1965-, chm Industl Tbnls 1966-78, counsel to Sec of State for Scotland under Private Legislation Proce (Scotland) Act (1936) 1969-75 (sr counsel under that Act 1975-), ed Session Cases (7 volumes) 1976-82; Hon Sheriff in various Sheriffdoms 1965-71, Temp

Sheriff 1990-; *Recreations* skiing, golf; *Clubs* Univ Staff (Edinburgh), Army and Navy; *Style*— Gavin Douglas, Esq, RD, QC; Parliament House, Parliament Sq, Edinburgh 1 (☎ 031 226 5071)

DOUGLAS, Lord Gawain Archibald Francis; s of 11 Marquess of Queensberry (d 1954), by his 3 w (*qv* Mimi, Marchioness of Queensberry); *b* 23 May 1948; *Educ* Downside, Royal Acad of Music (LRAM); *m* 1971, Nicolette, da of Col Frank Eustace (d 1976), of Hong Kong; 1 s (Jamie b 1975), 5 da (Dalziel b 1971, Elizabeth b 1974, Natasha b 1976, Margarita b 1978, Mary-Anne b 1981); *Career* former prof of pianoforte Blackheath Conservatoire of Music, music prof Kent Rural Music Sch Canterbury, concert recitalist, accompanist and duettist in company with wife; *Recreations* tennis, swimming, writing short stories and poems, books; *Clubs* Polish Hearth; *Style*— The Lord Gawain Douglas; 2 Archery Square, Walmer, Deal, Kent (☎ 0304 375813)

DOUGLAS, (John) Graham; s of Dr Keith Douglas, of Menston, nr Ilkley, and Mavis Douglas; *b* 20 Oct 1949; *Educ* Bradford GS, Univ of Edinburgh (BSc, MB ChB), MRCP 1977, FRCP 1988, FSAS; *m* 1 Oct 1977, Alison, da of John Menzies, of Dalkeith, Edinburgh; 1 s (Jamie b 5 Oct 1980), 1 da (Catriona Douglas b 7 June 1983); *Career* jr med and surgical house offr Edinburgh Royal Infirmary 1974-75, SHO and registrar in gen medicine, gastroenterology and renal medicine Eastern Gen Hosp and Edinburgh Royal Infirmary 1975-81, sr registrar in chest med and infection Edinburgh Royal Infimary and Northern Gen Hosp 1981-86, conslt physician with an interest in thoracic med and infection Aberdeen 1986-; author of 60 publications on subjects incl gen and thoracic med and infection; *Recreations* cycling, skiing, vegetable gardening, DIY, golf, history; *Style*— Dr Graham Douglas; Rhicuillin, 9 Golfview Road, Bieldside, Aberdeen AB9 1AA (☎ 0224 861435); Thoracic Medicine Unit, City Hospital, Urquhart Rd, Aberdeen (☎ 0224 681818 ext 58305)

DOUGLAS, Henry Russell; s of Russell Douglas (d 1975), and Jeannie, *née* Drysdale (d 1977); *b* 11 Feb 1925; *Educ* Lincoln Coll Oxford (MA); *m* 1951, Elizabeth Mary, da of Ralph MacHattie Nowell, CB (d 1973), of Wimbledon; 2 s (James, Alexander), 3 da (Jane, Catherine, Dominica); *Career* Lt RNVR (submarines) 1943-46; journalist; features ed, ldr writer and dep ed Liverpool Daily Post 1950-69, ldr writer The Sun 1969-76, legal mangr News Gp 1976-89; chm Newspaper Pres Fund 1990-91; fell Inst of Journalists (pres 1972); *Recreations* chess, motoring; *Clubs* Utd Oxford and Cambridge Univ; *Style*— Henry Douglas, Esq; Austen Croft, Austen Rd, Guildford, Surrey GU1 3NP (☎ 0483 576960)

DOUGLAS, Prof Ian; s of Prof Ronald Walter Douglas, of West Hill, Ottery St Mary, Devon and Edna Maud, *née* Cadle; *b* 2 Dec 1936; *Educ* Merchant Taylors', Balliol Coll Oxford (BLitt, MA), Aust Nat Univ (PhD); *m* 16 Nov 1963, Maureen Ann, da of Frank Bowler (d 1988); 2 s (David b 1965, d 1981, Aidan b 1967), 1 da (Fiona b 1972); *Career* Nat Serv Bombardier RA 1956-58; lectr Univ of Hull 1966-71, prof of geography Univ of New England Armidale NSW Aust 1971-78, prof of physical geography Univ of Manchester 1979-; pres Inst of Aust Geographers 1978, chm Br Geomorphological Res Grp 1980-81, organiser first Int Conf On Geomorphology Manchester 1985; MIWEM 1975; *Books* Humid Landforms (1977), The Urban Environment (1983), Environmental Change and Tropical Geomorphology (co-ed, 1985); *Recreations* walking in rainforests, swimming, gardening; *Style*— Prof Ian Douglas; 21 Taunton Road, Sale, Cheshire M33 5DD (☎ 061 973 1708); School of Geography, University of Manchester M13 9PL (☎ 061 275 3642)

DOUGLAS, James; s of James Douglas (d 1936), of Edinburgh, and Margaret Helen Douglas (d 1933); *b* 4 July 1932; *Educ* Heriot Watt Coll, Paris Conservatoire, Mozarteum Salzburg, Hochschule Munich; *m* 1, 12 July 1959, Mary Henderson Irving (d 1967); 2 s (Stephen James b 1961, Gavin John b 1962); m 2, 16 April 1968, Helen Torrance, da of S W Fairweather of 20 Murrayfield Drive, Edinburgh EA12; 1 da (Katharine Helen b 1971); *Career* composer, accompanist, organist; dir Eschenbach Editions and Caritas Records; compositions incl: 9 symphonies, 9 string quartets, 17 orchestral works, chamber music, piano music, organ music, over 200 songs; dir of music Christ Church Edinburgh; memb: ISM 1964; RCO 1986; *Books* The Music of Hermann Reutter (1966); *Recreations* reading, cloud watching; *Clubs* RCO; *Style*— James Douglas, Esq; 28 Dalrymple Crescent, Edinburgh EH9 2NX (☎ 031 667 3633)

DOUGLAS, Dr James Frederick; s of Capt Rev James Douglas CF (ka 1944), and Annie Hildegarde, *née* Harte; *b* 22 Sept 1938; *Educ* Portora Royal Sch Enniskillen, Wadham Coll Oxford (MA, BMBCh, BCL), Queens Univ of Belfast (MB BCh); *m* 27 Apr 1973, Giselle Sook An Lim; 4 s (Jeremy b 1975, Timothy b 1978, Andrew b 1981, Stephen b 1983, d 1984); *Career* lectr Coll of Law 1963-64, called to the Bar Middle Temple 1964, houseman Royal Victoria Hosp Belfast 1969-70, nephrologist 1972, conslt Belfast City and Royal Victoria Hosps 1975, sr nephrologist Belfast City Hosp 1988-, author of various pubns on: renal transplantation, renal failure, renal toxicology, the law and renal failure; memb Renal Assoc, FRCP 1987 (MRCP 1973); *Recreations* astronomy, equestrianism; *Style*— Dr James Douglas; Department of Nephrology, Belfast City Hospital, Lisburn Rd, Belfast (☎ 0232 329241 ext 2218/3010)

DOUGLAS, James Murray; CBE (1985); da of Herbert Douglas (d 1968), and Amy Crawford Murray (d 1976); *b* 26 Sept 1925; *Educ* Morrisons Acad Crieff, Univ of Aberdeen (MA), Balliol Coll Oxford (BA); *m* 1950, Julie, da of Hermann Kemmner (d 1969); 1 s (Michael b 1952), 1 da (Kathleen b 1954); *Career* RAF Fl Lt 1944-47; entered Civil Serv 1950, Treasy 1960-63, asst sec Miny Housing and Local Govt 1964, sec Royal Cmmn on Local Govt 1966-69, dir CLA 1970-90; vice pres Confedn of Euro Agric 1971-88, chm Enviroment Ctee 1988-90; wrote various articles on local govt and landowning; sec Euro Landowning Orgns Gp 1972-87; memb: Econ Devpt Ctee for Agric 1972-90, Cncl CBI 1986-89, NW Kent Branch Oxford Univ Soc, N Kent Decorative and Fine Arts Soc; *Publications* various articles on local govt and landowning; *Recreations* golf, music, reading, films, theatre; *Clubs* Utd Oxford & Cambridge Univ, Chislehurst Golf; *Style*— James Douglas, Esq, CBE; 1 Oldfield Close, Bickley, Kent BR1 2LL (☎ 081 467 3213)

DOUGLAS, John Robert Tomkys; s of Sir Robert McCallum Douglas, OBE, and Millicent Irene Tomkys, *née* Morgan (d 1980); *b* 24 July 1930; *Educ* Oundle, Univ of Birmingham (BSc 1951); *m* 12 Oct 1957, Sheila Margaret, da of Miles Varey (d 1963), of Liverpool); 2 s (Philip b 1960, Jonathan b 1962), 1 da (Alison b 1958); *Career* Nat Serv RE 1953-55, 2 Lt 1954; civil engr; dir various cos in Douglas Group 1953-, md Robert M Douglas Holdings plc 1976-87 (chm 1978-); dir: Birmingham Heartlands Ltd 1987-, Heartlands Development Services Ltd 1989-, Construction Indust Trg Bd 1990-; ldr Sutton Coldfield Crusaders 1956-81, gen cmmr for Income Tax 1968-, memb Ct of Govrs Univ of Birmingham 1972-, vice pres Birmingham Chamber of Indust and Commerce 1990- (memb Cncl 1981), tstee TSB Foundation for England and Wales 1986-, pres Fedn of Civil Engrg Contractors 1987-90 (chm 1974-75); Freeman Worshipful Co of Paviors; FIHT (MIHT 1967), FCIOB 1973, FRSA 1982, CBIM 1983; *Recreations* music, theatre, sailing; *Clubs* Caledonian, Royal Engineer Yacht; *Style*— John Douglas, Esq, OBE; Robert M Douglas Holdings plc, 395 George Rd, Erdington, Birmingham, West Midlands B23 7RZ (☎ 021 344 4888, fax 021 344 4801, telex 3 RMDBHM G, car 0831 205203)

DOUGLAS, Keith Humphrey; s of Arthur Ernest Douglas (d 1977), and Gladys Kittie, *née* Dyson (d 1926); *b* 11 May 1923; *Educ* Claremont Sch, Leamington Tech Coll; *m* 1944, Joan Lilian, da of Henry Sheasby (d 1976), of Leamington Spa; 2 s (Russell b 1948, Alistair b 1957); *Career* chm and md Keith Douglas (Motor Sport) 1964-, dir GKN Gp 1966-85, princ Keith Douglas & Associates 1985-, conslt Auto Sports Int Conference, sr assoc de Montfort Mgmnt, assoc PE Int; commentator: Silverstone 1962-, ITV 1964-66; advsr to the Bd Guthrie Douglas Ltd, pres Nottingham Sports Car Club 1966-71, dir RAC Motor Sports Assoc 1975-, vice chm RAC Br Motorsports Cncl 1975-, vice pres Br Motor Racing Marshals Club 1975-, chm RAC MSC Race Ctee 1980-, tstee RAC ACU Motor Sports Trg Tst; *Recreations* motor sport commentating, game fishing, music, charity work for motor industry fund (BEN), (Life Govr 1989); *Clubs* RAC, BRDC, JDC, JCC, Guild of Motoring Writers, Thursday (organiser); *Style*— Keith Douglas, Esq; 281 Four Ashes Rd, Dorridge, Solihull, W Midlands (☎ 0564 773202)

DOUGLAS, Kenneth; s of John Carr Douglas (d 1948), and Margaret Victoria, *née* Allen (d 1980); *b* 28 Oct 1920; *Educ* Sunderland Tech Coll, (Dip Naval Arch); *m* 1942, Doris, da of Thomas Henry Southern Lewer (d 1958); 1 s (Colin), 2 da (Gloria, Sally); *Career* tech asst Ship Div NPL 1945-46, mangr Vickers Armstrong Naval Yard 1946-53, dir and gen mangr William Gray & Co 1953-58; md: Austin & Pickersgill 1958-69 and 1979-83, Upper Clyde Shipbuilders 1969-73; chm: Simons Lobnitz, UCS Training Co, Douglas (Kilbride) Ltd 1972-77; dep chm Govan Shipbuilders 1971-73, chm and md Steel Structures Ltd 1974-76, ship repair mktg dir Br Shipbuilders 1978-79, chm Kenton Shipping Services Darlington 1968-77; chm of govrs Sunderland Poly 1982-; memb: Tyne and Wear Residuary Bd 1985-88, Bd Polys and Colls Employees Forum 1987-90; fell Sunderland Poly 1980-; FRSA 1987; *Clubs* Sunderland, Ashbrooke; *Style*— Kenneth Douglas, Esq; 7 Birchfield Rd, Sunderland, Tyne and Wear SR2 7QQ; Monks Cottage, Romaldkirk, Barnard Castle, Co Durham

DOUGLAS, Margaret Elizabeth; *b* 22 Aug 1934; *Career* BBC: joined as sec 1951, later worked in Current Affairs Dept, chief asst to Dir Gen 1983-87, chief political advsr 1987-; *Style*— Miss Margaret Douglas; BBC, Broadcasting House, London W1A 1AA (☎ 071 927 4563)

DOUGLAS, Richard Giles; MP (Lab) Dunfermline West 1983-; *b* 4 Jan 1932; *Educ* Govan HS, Cooperative Coll Stanford Hall Loughborough, Univ of Strathclyde, LSE; *m* 1954, Jean Gray, da of Andrew Arnott; 2 da; *Career* Co-op Pty sponsored, AEU, econ conslt; Parly candidate (Lab): S Angus 1964, Edinburgh W 1966, Glasgow Pollok (by-election) 1967; MP (Lab): Stirlingshire E and Clackmannan 1970-Feb 1974 (contested same in Oct 1974), Dunfermline 1979-1983; resigned from Lab Pty March 1990, joined SNP Oct 1990; memb: Def Select Ctee 1983-87; *Style*— Richard Douglas Esq, MP; Braehead House, High Street, Auchtermuchty, Fife

DOUGLAS, Rodney Hugh Rovery; s of Hugh Rovery Douglas, of Egham, Surrey, and Florence Alice, *née* Haggerty; *b* 18 Nov 1933; *Educ* Willesden Co GS, UCL (BSc); *m* 4 June 1960, Elise Margaret, da of Capt Bertram Vautier (d 1970), of Egham; 2 s (Graham b 1962, Adrian b 1964), 1 da (Heather b 1970); *Career* cmmn RAF 1956-59, Flt-Lt (airfield construction); serv 5001 sqdn: Malta, Libya, Cyprus, Aden; cmmnd Maj RE (TA, Engr and Tport Staff Corps) 1985, Lt-Col 1989; Mersey River Bd 1954-56, dir responsible for airport highway and public health projects Sir Frederick Snow & Ptnrs Ltd (conslt engrs) 1959-; former pres Woking and Dist Scot Soc; CEng (civil), FICE, FInstHT, MConsE; *Recreations* yacht cruising, Scottish dancing; *Clubs* RAF, Cruising Assoc; *Style*— Rodney Douglas, Esq; Saltwood, Onslow Crescent, Woking, Surrey GU22 7AU (☎ 0483 772637); Sir Frederick Snow and Partners Ltd, Ross House, 144 Southwark St, London SE1 OSZ (☎ 071 928 5688, fax 071 928 1774, telex 917478 Snowmen London)

DOUGLAS, Dr (William) Stewart; s of William Douglas (d 1988), of Beith, Ayrshire, and Jane Goldie, *née* Guy; *b* 21 Feb 1945; *Educ* Spier's Sch, Univ of Glasgow (MB ChB); *m* 10 Jan 1986, Margaret Ross, da of James Russell Scott (d 1986), of Giffnock, Glasgow; *Career* conslt dermatologist; house offr: in med Ballochmyle Hosp 1968-69, in surgery Royal Infirmary Dumfries 1969; Ure scholar Univ of Glasgow Dept of Med 1969-70; Glasgow Royal Infirmary: sr house offr in med 1970-72, registrar in dermatology 1972-73 and 1974-75; lectr Univ of Nairobi Kenya 1973-74, sr registrar Aberdeen Royal Infirmary 1975-77, lectr Univ of Aberdeen 1975-77, conslt dermatologist to Lanarkshire Health Bd 1977-; hon sec Scottish Dermatological Soc 1981-83; MRCP 1972, FRCPG 1982; *Recreations* sailing, skiing, cycling; *Style*— Dr Stewart Douglas; 102 Brownside Road, Cambuslang, Glasgow G72 8AF; Dept of Dermatology, Monklands District General Hospital, Airdrie MI 60JS Lanarkshire (☎ 0236 69344)

DOUGLAS, Rt Hon Sir William Randolph; KCMG (1983), PC (1977); s of William P Douglas; *b* 24 Sept 1921; *Educ* Bannatyne Sch, Verdun HS Quebec, McGill Univ (BA), LSE (LLB); *m* 1951, Thelma Ruth, da of Ernest Gershon Gilkes; 1 s, 1 da; *Career* called to the Bar Middle Temple 1947, slr-gen Jamaica 1962 (formerly asst attorney-gen), Puisne Judge (Jamaica) 1962, chief justice (Barbados) 1965-; kt 1969; *Style*— The Rt Hon Sir William Douglas, KCMG; Leland, Pine Gdns, St Michael, Barbados (☎ 010 1809 2030); Chief Justice's Chambers, Supreme Court, Coleridge St, Bridgetown, Barbados (☎ 010 1809 3461)

DOUGLAS AND CLYDESDALE, Marquess of; Alexander Douglas Douglas-Hamilton; s and h of 15 Duke of Hamilton and (12 of) Brandon; *b* 31 March 1978; *Style*— Marquess of Douglas and Clydesdale

DOUGLAS-HAMILTON, Lord David Stephen; 5 and yst s of 14 Duke of Hamilton and (11 of) Brandon, KT, GCVO, AFC, PC (d 1973); *b* 26 Dec 1952; *Educ* Eton; *Style*— Lord David Douglas-Hamilton

DOUGLAS-HAMILTON, Lord Hugh Malcolm; 3 s of 14 Duke of Hamilton and (11 of) Brandon, KT, GCVO, AFC, PC (d 1973); *b* 22 Aug 1946; *Educ* Eton; *m* 1971, June Mary Curtis; 1 s, 1 da; *Clubs* Scottish Arts; *Style*— The Lord Hugh Douglas-Hamilton; Begbie Farmhouse, Haddington, E Lothian (☎ 062 082 3141)

DOUGLAS-HAMILTON, Lord James Alexander; MP (C) Edinburgh W, Oct 1974-; 2 s of 14 Duke of Hamilton and Brandon, KT, GCVO, AFC, PC (d 1973); *b* 31 July 1942; *Educ* Eton, Balliol Coll Oxford (MA), Univ of Edinburgh (LLB); *m* 1974, Hon (Priscilla) Susan (Susie), *née* Buchan, *qv*, da of 2 Baron Tweedsmuir; 4 s (John Andrew b 1978, Charles Douglas b 1979, James Robert b 1981, Harry Alexander (twin) b 1981); *Career* offr TA 6/7 Bn Cameronians Scottish Rifles 1961-66, TAVR 1971-73, Capt 2 Bn Lowland Volunteers; Parly under sec of state for Home Affrs, Local Govt and Environment for Scottish Office 1987-90, advocate Parly under sec of state for home affrs and environment with responsibility for the Arts 1990-; advocate (Scots) 1968-74; Parly candidate (C) Hamilton Feb 1974; Scottish Cons whip 1977, Scots govt whip and lord cmmr Treasy 1979-81, memb Scottish Select Ctee Scottish Affrs 1981-83; hon sec: Cons Parly Constitutional Ctee, Cons Parly Aviation Ctee 1983-; chm Scottish Parly All-Pty Penal Affrs Ctee 1983, PPS to Malcolm Rifkind MP, min FO 1983-86, Sec of State for Scotland 1986-87; hon pres Scottish Amateur Boxing Assoc 1975-; Oxford Boxing blue 1961, pres Oxford Union Soc 1964; pres Royal Cwlth Soc (Scotland) 1979-87, Scottish Nat Cncl UN Assoc 1981-87; life memb Nat Tst for Scotland (memb Cncl 1977-82); *Books* Motive for a Mission: The Story Behind Hess's Flight to Britain (1971), The Air Battle for Malta: the Diaries of a Fighter Pilot (1981), Roof of the World: Man's First Flight over Everest (1983); *Recreations* golf, forestry, debating, history, boxing; *Style*— The Lord James Douglas-Hamilton, MP; House of

Commons, London SW1A 0AA (☎ 071 219 4399, fax 071 219 4206)

DOUGLAS-HAMILTON, Lady Malcolm; Natalie Wales; CBE; da of Maj Nathaniel Brackett Wales, of New York and Boston, and late Mrs Charles E Greenough, of New York City; *b* 8 Aug 1909; *Educ* private NY; *m* 1, late Kenelm Winslow; 2 da (Natalie Wales Winslow Burnett (decd), Mrs Mary-Chilton Winslow Mead); m 2, late Edward Latham; m 3, late Edward Bragg Paine; m 4, as his 2 w Lord Malcolm Douglas-Hamilton, OBE, DFC, MP Inverness (k in air crash 1964; he was 3 s of 13 Duke of Hamilton); *Career* fndr and pres: Bundles for Br Inc, The Ctee to Unite America Inc, The American-Scottish Fndn Inc; *Style—* Lady Malcolm Douglas-Hamilton, CBE; Apartment 10E, 174 E 74th St, New York, NY 10021, USA; The American-Scottish Fndn Inc, PO Box 537, Lenox Hill Station, NY City, NY 10021, USA (☎ 212 249 5556)

DOUGLAS-HAMILTON, Lord Patrick George; 4 s of 14 Duke of Hamilton and (11 of) Brandon, KT, GCVO, AFC, PC (d 1973); *b* 2 Aug 1950; *Educ* Eton; *Style—* Lord Patrick Douglas-Hamilton; Flat 3, 136 Ebury St, SW1 (☎ 071 730 3760); Lennoxlove, Haddington, E Lothian (☎ 062 082 2156)

DOUGLAS-HAMILTON, Lady James; Hon (Priscilla) Susan; *née* Buchan; o child of 2 Baron Tweedsmuir, CBE, CD, and Baroness Tweedsmuir of Belhelvie (cr Life Peeress 1970, d 1978); *b* 22 Aug 1949; *Educ* St Margaret's Sch Aberdeen, Hatherop Castle Glos; *m* 1974, Lord James Alexander Douglas-Hamilton, MP, *qv*; 4 s (incl twins); *Style—* Lady James Douglas-Hamilton

DOUGLAS-HOME, Hon (Lavinia) Caroline; DL (Berwicks 1983); eldest da of Baron Home of the Hirsel, KT, PC; *b* 11 Oct 1937; *Career* woman of the bedchamber (temp) to HM Queen Elizabeth The Queen Mother 1963-65, lady-in-waiting (temp) to HRH The Duchess of Kent 1966-67; tstee Nat Museum of Antiquities of Scotland 1982-85; FSAS; *Recreations* antiquities, fishing; *Style—* The Hon Caroline Douglas-Home, DL; Dove Cottage, The Hirsel, Coldstream, Berwickshire TD12 4LP (☎ 0890 2834)

DOUGLAS-HOME, Hon David Alexander Cospatrick; CBE (1991); only s of Baron Home of the Hirsel and h to Earldom of Home (disclaimed by his father 1963, from 1951 to which date Hon David D-H was known as Lord Dunglass); *b* 20 Nov 1943; *Educ* Eton, Christ Church Coll Oxford; *m* 1972, Jane Margaret, yr da of Col John Williams-Wynne, *qv*; 1 s (Michael David Alexander b 1987), 2 da (Iona Katherine b 1980, Mary Elizabeth b 1982); *Career* dir: Morgan Grenfell & Co Ltd 1974-, Morgan Grenfell (Scotland) 1978-, Morgan Grenfell (Hong Kong) Ltd and Morgan Grenfell Asia Holdings Pt 1989-, Morgan Grenfell Thai Company Ltd 1990-, Economic Forestry Group 1981-, Agricultural Mortgage Corporation 1979-; chm: Morgan Grenfell Int Ltd 1987, Morgan Grenfell (Scotland) Ltd 1986 and Ctee for M E Trade 1986; The Ditchley Fndn: govr and memb Cncl of Mgmnt 1976-; ECGD: memb Export Guarantee Advsy Cncl, memb Country and Fin Ctee 1988-; memb Projects Ctee 1989; govr Cwlth Inst 1988-; memb Offshore Industry Export Advsy Gp 1989-; Cncl RASE; *Recreations* outdoor sports; *Clubs* Turf; *Style—* The Hon David Douglas-Home, CBE; 99 Dovehouse St, London SW3

DOUGLAS-HOME, Hon Edward Charles; s of 14 Earl of Home, KT, TD (d 1951); *b* 1 March 1920; *Educ* Eton; *m* 24 July 1946, Nancy Rose, da of Sir Thomas Dalrymple Straker-Smith (d 1970), of Carham Hall, Cornhill-on-Tweed, Northumberland; 3 s; *Career* 2 Lt 155 Field Regt RA; *Style—* The Hon Edward Douglas-Home; Westnewton, Kirknewton, Wooler, Northumberland

DOUGLAS-HOME, Hon Mrs Henry; Felicity Betty; da of late Maj Aubrey Thomas Jonsson, RIR, of Cranford, Winterskloof, Natal, S Africa; *m* 1, 28 July 1948 (m dis 1962), the Hon (Victor) Patrick Hamilton Wills; 2 s, 1 da; m 2, 16 Feb 1966, as his 3 w, Maj the Hon Henry Montagu Douglas-Home, MBE (d 1980), 2 s of 13 Earl of Home, KT, TD; 1 s; *Style—* Hon Mrs Henry Douglas-Home; Old Greenlaw, Berwickshire, Scotland

DOUGLAS-HOME, Hon James Thomas Archibald; only s of Hon William Douglas-Home and Baroness Dacre; h to the Barony of Dacre; *b* 16 May 1952; *m* 1979, Christine, da of William Stephenson, of The Ridings, Royston, Herts; 1 da (Emily b 1983); *Style—* The Hon James Douglas-Home; c/o Rt Hon Baroness Dacre, Derry House, Kilmeston, nr Alresford, Hants

DOUGLAS-HOME, Lady (Alexandra) Margaret Elizabeth; da of 6 Earl Spencer (d 1922); *b* 4 July 1906; *m* 7 July 1931 (m dis 1947), Maj Hon Henry Montagu Douglas-Home (d 1980); 2 s (both decd), 1 da; *Style—* Lady Margaret Douglas-Home; Trimmers, Burnham Market, King's Lynn, Norfolk (☎ 0553 243)

DOUGLAS-HOME, Hon William; 3 s of 13 Earl of Home, KT, TD (d 1951); *b* 3 June 1912; *Educ* Eton, New Coll Oxford; *m* 26 July 1951, Baroness Dacre, *qv*; 1 s, 3 da; *Career* 2 Lt The Buffs 1941, Capt 1943; author and playwright; *Style—* The Hon William Douglas-Home; Derry House, Kilmeston, nr Alresford, Hants

DOUGLAS-MANN, Bruce Leslie Home; s of late Leslie Douglas-Mann, MC, of Torquay, and Alice Home Douglas-Mann; *b* 23 June 1927; *Educ* Upper Canada Coll Toronto, Jesus Coll Oxford; *m* 1955, Helen, da of Edwin Tucker, of Dulwich; 1 s, 1 da; *Career* admitted slr 1954; sr ptnr Douglas-Mann & Co 1964-; MP (Lab): Kensington N 1970-74, Merton Mitcham and Morden 1974-82 (resigned from Lab Pty 1981), joined SDP, sat as Ind Social Democrat, res seat 1982; refought on SDP/Lib Alliance ticket: 1982, 1983, 1987; chm SHELTER 1990- (chm Exec Ctee 1987-, Memb Bd 1974-), vice pres Bldg Socs Assoc 1973-, pres or vice pres Social Environmemt and Resources Assoc 1973-80; chm: PLP Housing and Construction Gp 1974-79, PLP Environment Gp 1979-81 (vice chm 1972-79), Parly Select Ctee on Environment 1979-82, chm Soc of Lab Lawyers 1974-80; former memb Kensington & Chelsea Cncl; chm Arts Cncl Tst for Special Funds; *Style—* Bruce Douglas-Mann, Esq; 33 Furnival St, London EC4A 1JQ (☎ 071 405 7216)

DOUGLAS MILLER, Robert Alexander Gavin; s of Maj Francis Gavin Douglas Miller (d 1950), and Mary Morison, *née* Kennedy; *b* 11 Feb 1937; *Educ* Harrow, Oxford Univ (MA); *m* 9 March 1963, Judith Madeleine Smith, da of Richard Michael Desmond Dunstan, OBE, of Pear Tree Cottage, Firbeck, nr Worksop, Notts; 3 s (Andrew Gavin b 30 Sept 1963, Robert Peter b 15 Jan 1965, Edward James b 20 May 1966), 1 da (Emma Lucy Jane b 8 Jan 1969); *Career* served in 9 Lancers 1955-57; joined Jenners Edinburgh 1962: md 1972, chm and md 1982-; chm and md Kennington Leasing; dir: First Scottish American Investmt Tst, Northern American Tst, Bain Clarkson Ltd, Edinburgh C of C; chm: Game Conservancy (Scotland), Outreach Tst; memb Cncl: Atlantic Salmon Tst, Kyle of Sutherland Fishery Bd; treas Royal Co of Archers (Queen's Body Guard for Scotland); landowner (5850 acres); *Recreations* fishing, shooting, gardening; *Clubs* New (Edinburgh); *Style—* Robert Douglas Miller, Esq; Bavelaw Castle, Balerno, Midlothian (☎ 031 449 3972); Jenners, 48 Princes St, Edinburgh EH2 2YJ (☎ 031 225 4791)

DOUGLAS OF KIRTLESIDE, Baroness; Hazel; 2 da of late George Eric Maas Walker, of Mill Hill, London, and widow of Capt W E R Walker; *m* 2, 28 Feb 1955, as his 3 wife, 1 Baron Douglas of Kirtleside (d 1969, when title became extinct); 1 da (Hon Katharine Douglas); *Style—* Rt Hon Lady Douglas of Kirtleside; Misbourne Cottage, Denham Village, Bucks

DOUGLAS PENNANT, Lady Janet Marcia Rose; *née* Pelham; only da of 6 Earl of Yarborough (d 1966), and Hon Pamela Douglas Pennant (d 1968), 2 da of 3 Baron Penrhyn; *b* 17 Oct 1923; *m* 20 March 1948, John Charles Harper (s of Sir Charles Henry Harper, KBE, CMG), who assumed by Royal Licence the surname Douglas Pennant in lieu of his patronymic 1950; 2 s (Richard b 1955, Edmond b 1960); *Style—* The Lady Janet Douglas Pennant; Penrhyn, Bangor, Gwynedd (☎ 0248 370 286)

DOUGLAS-PENNANT, Hon Nigel; yr s of 5 Baron Penrhyn (d 1967), by his 2 w, and hp of bro, 6 Baron Penrhyn, DSO, MBE; *b* 22 Dec 1909; *Educ* Eton, Clare Coll Cambridge; *m* 1, 6 Sept 1935, Margaret Dorothy (d 1938), da of Thomas George Kirkham; 1 s; m 2, 20 July 1940, Eleanor Stewart (d 1987), eldest da of late Very Rev Herbert Newcome Craig, Dean of Kildare; 1 s, 1 da; *Career* formerly Maj RM; *Style—* The Hon Nigel Douglas-Pennant; Brook House, Glemsford, Sudbury, Suffolk

DOUGLAS-PENNANT, Hon Susan Victoria; 3 and yst da of 5 Baron Penrhyn (only da by 2 w); *b* 24 May 1918; *Educ* Owlstone Croft Cambridge, St Bartholomew's Hosp London; *Career* SRN, SCM; *Style—* The Hon Susan Douglas-Pennant; Adam's Cottage, Horningsham, Warminster, Wilts

DOUGLAS-SCOTT-MONTAGU, Hon Mary Rachel; da of 3 Baron Montagu of Beaulieu by 1 wife; *b* 16 Nov 1964; *Educ* Central Sch of Art and Design (BA); *Career* designer; *Style—* The Hon Mary Douglas-Scott-Montagu

DOUGLAS-SCOTT-MONTAGU, Hon Ralph; s (by 1 m) and h of 3 Baron Montagu of Beaulieu by 1 wife; *b* 13 March 1961; *Educ* Millfield, Brockenhurst Sixth Form Coll, Central Sch of Art and Design; *Career* graphic designer; *Books* The Producers' Guide to Graphics (book and video) (1986), The Graphics Guide (1988); *Clubs* BBC; *Style—* The Hon Ralph Douglas-Scott-Montagu; Palace House, Beaulieu, Brockenhurst, Hants SO42 7ZN

DOUGLASS OF CLEVELAND, Baroness; Edith; da of Charles Amer; *m* 1926, Baron Douglass of Cleveland (Life Peer, d 1978); 1 da (Hon Mrs Long); *Style—* Rt Hon Lady Douglass of Cleveland; 5 The Chase, Stanmore, Middx HA7 3RX (☎ 081 954 2101)

DOULTON, Alfred John Farre; CBE (1973, OBE (Mil) 1946), TD (1954); s of Hubert Victor Doulton (d 1942), of Dulwich, and Constance Jessie Farre (d 1965); *b* 9 July 1911; *Educ* Dulwich, Brasenose Coll Oxford (MA); *m* 14 June 1940, Vera Daphne, da of Ronald Angus Wheatley (d 1973), of Esher; 4 s (John b 1942, Angus b 1944, Peter (twin) b 1944, Roger b 1949), 1 da (Valerie b 1949); *Career* serv WWII 1940-46, active serv: Burma, Malaya, Java (despatches twice), AAQMG (Lt-Col) 23 Indian Div; schoolmaster, house master Uppingham Sch 1946-54 (asst master 1934-40), headmaster Highgate Sch 1955-74, statistician Ind Schools Info Serv 1974-80; alderman and vice chm Educn Ctee Haringey Cncl 1968-71; *Recreations* music, cricket, reading, dinghy sailing, ornithology, gardening; *Clubs* Athenaeum, MCC; *Style—* Alfred J F Doulton, Esq, CBE, TD; Field Cottage, Beadon Lane, Salcombe, Devon TQ8 8JS (☎ 054 884 2316)

DOULTON, John Herbert Farre; s of Alfred John Farre Doulton, CBE, TD, of Field Cottage, Beadon Lane, Salcombe, Devon, and Vera Daphne, *née* Wheatley; *b* 2 Jan 1942; *Educ* Rugby, Keble Coll Oxford (BA); *m* 26 April 1986, Margaret Anne, da of Rev Cecil Ball (d 1959); *Career* asst master and housemaster Radley Coll 1966-88, princ Elizabeth Coll Guernsey 1988-; memb: Guernsey Deanery Synod, Admiralty Interview Bd; *Recreations* walking, travel, architecture, photography, boats, gardening, DIY; *Style—* John Doulton, Esq; Brantwood, Forest Rd, St Martin's, Guernsey, Channel Islands (☎ 0481 38995); Elizabeth College, Guernsey, CI (☎ 0481 726544, fax 0481 714839)

DOULTON, Roger Stewart; s of Lt Col Alfred John Farre Doulton, CBE, TD, of Salcombe, Devon, and Daphne Vera, *née* Wheatley; *b* 28 March 1949; *Educ* Rugby, Univ of Oxford (MA); *m* June 1978 (m dis 1988), Shonni Doulton; 2 s (Ben b 30 Dec 1979, Jem b 25 April 1983); *Career* asst slr: Herbert Smith & Co 1976-81, Davies Arnold & Cooper 1981-84; ptnr Winward Fearon & Co 1986-; ctee memb and legal corr Br Insur Law Assoc; memb Br Acad of Experts; *Recreations* french horn playing, the arts generally, politics, sport; *Clubs* Wig and Pen, City Forum, Salcombe Yacht; *Style—* Roger Doulton, Esq; Winward Fearon, 35 Bow Street, London WC2E 7AU (☎ 071 836 9081)

DOUNE, Lord; John Douglas Stuart; s and h of 20 Earl of Moray; *b* 29 Aug 1966; *Style—* Lord Doune

DOURO, Marquess of; Arthur Charles Valerian Wellesley; s and h of 8 Duke of Wellington, KG, LVO, OBE, MC; *b* 19 Aug 1945; *Educ* Eton, Ch Ch Oxford; *m* 3 Feb 1977, Antonia (chm Guinness Trust, tstee Getty Nat Gallery Endowment Fund), da of HRH Prince Frederick von Preussen (d 1966, s of HIH Crown Prince Wilhelm, s and h of Kaiser Wilhelm II), and Lady Brigid Ness, *qv*; 1 s, 3 da (Lady Honor b 25 Oct 1979, Lady Mary b 16 Dec 1986, Lady Charlotte b 8 Oct 1990); *Heir* s, Earl of Mornington b 31 Jan 1978; *Career* dep chm Guinness Mahon Holdings plc, dir Transatlantic Holdings plc, Sun Life Corporation plc, GAM Worldwide Inc, Eucalyptus Pulp Mills 1979-88, Rothmans International plc; chm: Deltec Securities (UK) Ltd 1985-89; dep chm: Deltec Panamerica SA 1985-89, Thames Valley Broadcasting 1975-84, Dunhill Holdings plc; MEP (C) for Surrey West 1979-89, Parly candidate Islington N (C) 1974; *Style—* Marquess of Douro; The Old Rectory, Stratfield Saye, Reading RG7 2DA; Apsley House, Piccadilly, London W1V 9FA

DOUSE, Anthony Clifford; s of Clifford Redvers Douse (d 1968, of Nottingham, and Lilian Beatrice, *née* Wells (d 1952); *b* 18 Aug 1939; *Educ* Mundella GS Nottingham, RADA; *m* 6 July 1968, Diana Margaret, da of Walter Stanley Thompson; 1 da (Diana Helen b 1 Dec 1984); *Career* actor; NT: State of Revolution, Strife, Macbeth, Richard III, The Fruits of Enlightenment, Danton's Death, Lorenzaccio, Major Barbara, The Fawn, Antigone, Wild Honey, Neaptide, Man Beast and Virtue, Once in a While the Odd Thing Happens; Royal Court: A Collier's Friday Night, The Duchess of Malfi, King Lear; other theatre incl: RSC (1991), Major Barbara (Chichester Festival), Timon of Athens (Leicester), various work in repertory; TV incl: Lovejoy (1990), Van der Valk; films incl Prick Up Your Ears; memb editorial staff Howard Baker Amalgamated Press (early 1960's); *Recreations* reading; *Style—* Anthony Douse, Esq; Carol Martin Personal Management, 19 Highgate West Hill, London N6 6NP (☎ 081 348 0847)

DOUSE, Raymond Andrew; s of Reginald Conrad Raymond Douse, of Eastbourne, and Patricia *née* Heatherley; *b* 10 May 1947; *Educ* Downside, New Coll Oxford (BA); *m* 2 Nov 1974, Christine Lesley, da of Maurice Hayes, of Melbourne, Aust; 2 s (Nicholas b 1977, Christopher b 1986), 1 da (Olivia b 1980); *Career* investment banker; dir Hill Samuel & Co Ltd 1980-85; md: MMG Patricof & Co Ltd 1985-89, Daiwa Europe Strategic Advisors (Corp servs) Ltd; *Recreations* music, horse racing; *Style—* Raymond A Douse, Esq; 94 Arthur Rd, Wimbledon, SW19; 5 King William St, London EC4N 7AX (☎ 071 548 8251)

DOUTHWAITE, Charles Philip; s of Alfred George Douthwaite, of Saffron Walden, Essex, and Margaret, *née* Rose; *b* 23 March 1949; *Educ* Kingswood Sch, Jesus Coll Cambridge (MA); *m* 14 Feb 1976, Margaret Ann, da of Derek Linford, MBE (d 1975), of Stanford-Le-Hope, Essex; 1 s (Henry b 1980), 1 da (Harriet b 1982); *Career* called to Bar Grays Inn 1977; *Style—* Charles Douthwaite, Esq; Field Cottages, Chrishall Grange, Heydon, Royston, Herts SG8 7NT (☎ 0763 838 061); 2 Crown Office Row, Temple, London EC4Y 7HJ (☎ 071 583 8755, fax 071 583 1205)

DOVE, Anthony Charles; s of Ian Mayor Dove (d 1972), of Blackpool, and Joan Beatrice, *née* Hadley; *b* 22 July 1945; *Educ* Rugby, St John's Coll Cambridge (MA, McMahon studentship); *m* 1 June 1974, Susan Elizabeth, da of Joseph Cant; 3 da

(Caroline Jane b 4 Aug 1977, Charlotte Elizabeth b 25 Oct 1982, Rebecca Joan b 8 March 1984); *Career* Simmons & Simmons: articled clerk 1967-69, asst slr 1969-73, ptnr 1973-; memb Law Soc; *Recreations* music, the creation of value; *Clubs* Barbican Health & Fitness; *Style*— Anthony Dove, Esq; Simmons & Simmons, 14 Dominion St, London EC2M 2RJ (☎ 071 628 2020, fax 071 588 4129, car 0831 582498)

DOVE, Hon Mrs (Elizabeth); *née* Carington; only da of 5 Baron Carrington (d 1938); *b* 4 June 1917; *m* 13 Nov 1943, Capt William Lionel Dove, RAMC, s of late Edward William Dove; 2 s; *Style*— The Hon Mrs Dove; 6 Woolton Hill Road, Liverpool L25 6HX

DOVE, Jack Richard; s of William Jack Dove (d 1978), and Hannah Elizabeth Dove (d 1973); *b* 16 June 1934; *Educ* Berkhamsted Sch; *m* 18 Dec 1958, Janet Yvonne, da of Melville Clarke (d 1985), of Kingsthorpe, Northampton; 1 s (Ian William b 31 Dec 1963); *Career* Nat Serv RAF 1956-58; CA; fndr Dove Naish & Ptnrs; chm Northants Business Ctee of Rural Devpt Cmmn; tstee: Lamport Hall Preservation Tst, Northampton FC (The Saints); chm Friends of Northampton Gen Hosp; FCA 1956, ATII 1957; *Recreations* music, gardening, rugby football, country pursuits; *Clubs* Cheyne Walk Northampton, Northampton Cons; *Style*— Jack R Dove, Esq; 29 Abington Park Cres, Northampton NN3 3AD (☎ 0604 36918); Eagle Hse, 28 Billing Rd, Northampton NN1 5AJ

DOVE, John; s of Leonard Ernest Dove, 23 Stambourne Way, West Wickham, Kent, and Florence May, *née* Shipley; *b* 13 Sept 1942; *Educ* Beckenham GS, St Thomas's Med Sch (MB BS); *m* 17 Sept 1966, Philippa Jill, da of John Stephen Brown (d 1967); 4 s (Stephen b 1972, Michael b 1976, Jane b 1977, Benjamin b 1980), 1 da (Rebecca b 1970); *Career* Sqdn Ldr RAF med offr 1966-76; conslt orthopaedic surgn; dir Stoke-on-Trent serv 1980-, sec and treas Br Scoliosis Soc; Freeman City of Liverpool; LRCP, FRCS; *Books* Spinal Deformity by Stagnara (translated from French); *Recreations* wine, reading, music, mountaineering; *Style*— John Dove, Esq; 31 Quarry Ave, Hartshil, Stoke-on-Trent ST4 7EW

DOVE, John; s of Anthony Dove, and Betty Margaret, *née* Curran; *b* 24 July 1944; *Educ* Ampleforth, Univ of Durham (BA), Univ of Manchester (Dip in Drama); *Career* theatre dir; Arts Cncl trainee dir under Philip Hedley Birmingham 1971-72, assoc dir to Jane Howell Northcott 1973-74 (co dir Bingo), freelance dir 1974-84 (worked with Richard Eyre at Nottingham, Richard Cotterell at Bristol Old Vic, Tony Robertson at Old Vic), assoc dir Hampstead Theatre 1984- (prodns incl: A Little Like Drowning (Plays and Players award), Ask for the Moon, The Daughter in Law, The Awakening, Hedda Gabler); other recent prodns incl: Rafts and Dreams (Royal Court), Goodnight Siobhan (Royal Court), A Muse of Fire (Edinburgh Festival), adaptation of Angelic Avengers for The Danish Co; *Recreations* painting, music, athletics, writing; *Style*— John Dove, Esq; Hampstead Theatre, Swiss Cottage Centre, London NW3 (☎ 081 722 9224)

DOVE, John Edward; JP (Cheshire 1975, currently Hampshire); s of Rev Frederick John Dove (d 1976), and Lesley, *née* Robson (d 1981); *b* 1 March 1922; *Educ* Owen's Sch London, Northern Poly London; *m* 28 June 1952, Ann Nomori, da of John Ireson (d 1968); 2 s (Robert b 1953, Martin b 1959), 1 da (Sally (Mrs Grunwell) b 1956); *Career* teacher of music and maths Akeley Wood Sch Buckingham 1940-45, surveyor (later dir) Dove Bros Ltd (builders) 1948-62, regnl mangr H Fairweather & Co Ltd 1963-67, mktg mangr Taylor Woodrow Construction Midlands Ltd 1967-70, dir John Finlan Ltd (property developers) 1970-73; md: Jartay Developments Ltd 1973-80, Ward Dove Ltd 1981-; Royal Cwlth Soc: joined 1940, memb Cncl 1954-, vice pres 1986; chm Emsworth Resident' Assoc, memb Langstone Cons Club; Freeman City of London 1949; Liveryman: Worshipful Co of Tylers and Bricklayers 1949 (Master 1977 Worshipful Co of Leathersellers 1951; FCIOB; *Recreations* music, lawn tennis, public speaking; *Clubs* City Livery, Emsworth Sailing; *Style*— John Dove, Esq, JP; Tadworth Lodge, 25 Park Cres, Emsworth, Hants PO10 7NT (☎ 0243 373520)

DOVE, Leonard Ernest; CBE (1969); s of Alfred Dove (d 1955); *b* 10 Feb 1913; *Educ* Wilson's GS Camberwell; *m* 1938, Florence May, da of William Humphrey Shipley (d 1942); 1 s (and 1 s decd), 2 da; *Career* accountant and comptroller Gen Bd of Customs and Excise 1963-73; hon treas Methodist Church (overseas div) 1972-84, memb Kent Ecumenkal Cncl 1983-; *Style*— Leonard Dove, Esq, CBE; 23 Stambourne Way, West Wickham, Kent BR4 9NE (☎ 081 777 5213)

DOVE, Martin David John; s of John Edward Dove, and Ann Nomori, *née* Ireson; *b* 29 April 1959; *Educ* Helsby GS, Adams GS, Kings Coll Univ of London (BA, AKC); *m* 11 April 1987, Sharon Rose Elizabeth, da of Roy William Rogers Edmonds; 1 da (Rachael Alice Rose b 1 Sept 1989); *Career* Coopers and Lybrand London 1980-86, Cwlth Devpt Corpn London 1986-89 Industl Venture Co Ltd Thailand 1989-; memb Woodmansterne Baptist Church; Freeman City of London, Liveryman Worshipful Co of Leathersellers; ICAEW 1983; *Recreations* squash, hockey; *Style*— Martin Dove, Esq; Industrial Venture Co Ltd, 67/11 Saisuan Plu, South Sathorn Rd, Bangkok 10120 Thailand (☎ 010 662 213 1254/5, fax 010 662 213 1163, telex 20606 TH)

DOVER, Den; MP (C) Chorley 1979-; s of Albert Dover (d 1971), and Emmie, *née* Kirk (d 1971); *b* 4 April 1938; *Educ* Manchester GS, Univ of Manchester (BSc); *m* 1959, Anne Marina, da of Jeffrey Wright (d 1952); 1 s, 1 da; *Career* civil engr; chief exec Nat Building Agency 1971-72, projects dir Capital and Counties Property plc 1972-75, contracts mangr Wimpey Laing Iran 1975-77, dir of Housing Construction GLC 1977-79; *Recreations* cricket, hockey, golf; *Style*— Den Dover, Esq, MP; 30 Countess Way, Euxton, Chorley, Lancs; 166 Furzehill Rd, Boreham Wood, Herts

DOVER, Sir Kenneth James; s of Percy Henry James Dover (d 1978) and Dorothy Valerie Anne Healey (d 1973); *b* 11 March 1920; *Educ* St Paul's, Balliol Coll Oxford (MA, DLitt), Merton Coll Oxford; *m* 1947, Audrey Ruth, da of Walter Latimer (d 1931); 1 s, 1 da; *Career* served WWII RA; Univ of St Andrews: prof of Greek 1955-76, dean Faculty of Arts 1960-63 and 1973-75, chllr 1981; Sather visiting prof Univ of California 1967, prof-at-large Cornell 1983-89, prof of classics Stanford Univ California (Winter Quarter) 1987-; hon fell Balliol Coll Oxford 1977 (fell 1948-55), hon fell Merton Coll Oxford 1980; hon foreign memb American Acad of Arts and Sciences 1979-, foreign memb Royal Netherlands Acad of Arts and Sciences 1979-; pres: Soc for Promotion of Hellenic Studies 1971-74, Classical Assoc 1975, Corpus Christi Coll Oxford 1976-86 (hon fell 1986), Br Acad 1978-81, FRSE, FBA; Hon LLD: Birmingham 1979, St Andrews 1981; Hon DLitt: Bristol, London 1980, St Andrews 1981, Liverpool 1983, Durham 1984; Hon DHL Oglethorpe 1984; kt 1977; *Books* Greek Word Order (1960), Greek Popular Morality in the time of Plato & Aristotle (1974), Commentaries on various classical Greek Literature, Greek Homosexuality (1978); papers in learned journals; *Recreations* historical linguistics; *Clubs* Athenaeum; *Style*— Sir Kenneth Dover; 49 Hepburn Gdns, St Andrews, Fife KY16 9LS (☎ 0334 73589)

DOVER, Michael Grehan; s of Maj E J Dover (d 1983), of Ireland, and Ida, *née* Grehan; *b* 22 Oct 1948; *Educ* King's Sch Canterbury, Trinity Coll Dublin (BA); *m* 1972, Ruth, da of Capt T A Pearson (d 1972), of Ireland; 2 s (Alexander b 1975, Linden b 1983), 1 da (Katherine b 1979); *Career* publisher Weidenfeld Publishers Ltd 1987 (ed dir 1982); *Clubs* Chelsea Arts; *Style*— Michael Dover, Esq; 27 Fulham Park Gdns, London SW6 4JX (☎ 071 731 0818); Weidenfeld and Nicolson, 91 Clapham High St, London SW4 7TA (☎ 071 622 9933)

DOVER, Bishop of, 1980-; Rt Rev Richard Henry McPhail Third; s of Henry McPhail Third (d 1952), and Marjorie Caroline Third (d 1982); *b* 29 Sept 1927; *Educ* Alleyn's Sch, Reigate GS, Emmanuel Coll Cambridge (MA); *m* 4 June 1966, (Constance) Helen, da of William George Illingworth, of Lyminge; 2 da (Christine b 1967, Hilary b 1969); *Career* ordained: deacon 1952, priest 1953; curate: St Andrew Mottingham 1952-55, Sanderstead i/c of St Edmund Ruddlesdown 1955-59; vicar: Sheerness 1959-67, Orpington 1967-76; hon canon Rochester Cathedral 1974-76, bishop of Maidstone 1976-80; Hon DCL Univ of Kent 1990; *Recreations* music, walking; *Style*— The Rt Rev the Bishop of Dover; Upway, St Martin's Hill, Canterbury CT1 1PR (☎ 0227 464537); Diocesan House, Lady Wootton's Green, Canterbury CT1 1NQ (☎ 0227 459382, fax 0227 450 964)

DOVER, Prof William Duncan; s of Joseph Dover (d 1938), and Sarah Jane Graham, *née* Wilson (d 1989); *Educ* Bishopshalt Sch, Univ of Surrey (Dip Tech), UCL (PhD); *m* 27 July 1968, Dilys, da of John Richard Edwards (d 1989); 1 s (James William b 1973), 1 da (Elizabeth Mary b 1976); *Career* asst Faculté Polytechinque De Mons Belgium 1966-67, lectr City Univ London 1967-69, Shell prof of mechanical engrg UCL 1987- (lectr 1969-78, reader 1978-83, prof of mechanical engrg 1983-87); dir: Dover & Partners Ltd 1979-, UCL Underwater NDE Centre 1985, TSC Ltd 1985; visiting prof City Univ 1985; MIMechE, CEng, FINDT; *Books* Fatigue of Offshore Structures (ed, 1989), Fatigue of Large Scale Threaded Connections (ed, 1989); 180 tech and sci papers; *Recreations* tennis, jogging, skiing; *Style*— Prof William Dover; Coniston House, Orchehill Avenue, Gerrards Cross, Buckinghamshire SL9 8QH (☎ 0753 886097), NDE Centre, Dept of Mechanical Engineering, University College London, Torrington Place, London WC1E 7JE (☎ 071 380 7184, fax 071 383 0831, telex 296273)

DOW, (John) Christopher Roderick; s of Warrender Begernie Dow (d 1950), of Shoreham-by-Sea; *b* 25 Feb 1916; *Educ* Bootham Sch York, Brighton, Hove, Sussex GS, UCL; *m* 1960, Clare Mary Keegan; 1 s, 3 da; *Career* economist; dep dir Nat Inst of Econ and Social Res 1954-62, sr econ advsr HM Treasy 1962-63 (econ advsr 1945-54), asst sec-gen Orgn for Econ Co-operation and Devpt 1963-73, dir Bank of England 1973-81, advsr to Govr of Bank of England 1981-84; visiting fell Nat Inst of Econ and Social Res 1984-; *Clubs* Reform; *Style*— Christopher Dow, Esq; c/o Reform Club, 104 Pall Mall, London SW1

DOW, Hon Mrs (Jessica Catherine); 3 and yst da of 2 Baron Stamp (d 1941, as result of enemy action during European War); *b* 21 Sept 1936; *Educ* Univ of London (BA); *m* 9 Sept 1961, John Edward Chalmers Dow; 2 da (Charlotte b 1963, Juliette b 1966); *Style*— The Hon Mrs Dow; 30 Norfolk Farm Rd, Pyrford, Woking, Surrey GU22 8LH (☎ 0483 722710)

DOWD, George Simon Edmund; s of George Francis Edmund Dowd, of 67 Rothbury St, Scarborough, Yorks, and Lily, *née* Clay; *b* 9 Nov 1946; *Educ* Scarborough HS for Boys, Univ of Liverpool Med Sch (MB ChB, FRCS, MCh (Orth), MD); *m* Angela Christine, da of John Anthony Sedman; 3 da (Olivia Jayne b 13 Oct 1975, Caroline Suzanne b 19 Oct 1977, Charlotte Louise b 12 Nov 1980); *Career* house surgn and physician David Lewis Northern Hosp Liverpool 1971-72, lectr in orthopaedics Univ of Liverpool 1978-81; sr lectr and conslt orthopaedic surgn: Royal Liverpool Hosp and Royal Liverpool Children's Hosp 1981-82, Univ of London and Royal Nat Orthopaedic Hosp 1982-87, conslt orthopaedic surgn St Bartholomew's Hosp and Homerton Hosp London 1987-; Huntarian prof RCS 1985; ABC travelling fell, Heritage visiting prof Calgary Canada 1986; Norman Roberts medal 1978, President's medal BR Orthopaedic Res Soc 1986; memb BMA, Br Orthopaedic Assoc, Br Orthopaedic Res Soc; *Publications* author of Multiple Choice Questions In Orthopaedics and Trauma (1987), papers on trauma, arthritis and knee disorders in leading med jls; *Recreations* sailing, tennis and travel; *Style*— George Dowd, Esq; St Bartholomews Hospital, West Smithfield, London EC1A 7BE (☎ 071 601 8888); 134 Harley St, London W1N 1AH (☎ 071 486 7912)

DOWDEN, Richard George; s of Peter John Dowden, of Fairford, Gloucs, and Eleanor Isabella, *née* Hepple; *b* 20 March 1949; *Educ* St Georges Coll, Bedford Coll London (BA); *m* 3 July 1976, (Mary Catherine) Penny, da of Stanley William Mansfield (d 1977); 2 da (Isabella Catherine b 1981, Sophie Elizabeth b 1983); *Career* sec Cmmn for Int Justice and Peace RC Bishops Conf 1972-75, ed Catholic Herald 1976-79, journalist The Times 1980-86, Africa ed The Independent 1986-; *Style*— Richard Dowden, Esq; 7 Highbury Grange, London N5; 40 City Rd, London EC1Y 2DB (☎ 071 253 1222)

DOWDESWELL, Lt-Col (John) Windsor; MC (1943), TD (1947), DL (1976); s of Maj Thomas Reginald Dowdeswell (d 1967), and Nancy Olivia, *née* Pitt (d 1966); *b* 11 June 1920; *Educ* Malvern; *m* 1948, Phyllis Audrey, da of Donald Gomersal Horsfield (d 1972); 1 s (Patrick), 1 da (Bridget); *Career* WWII, RA, 50 Div, France and Belgium 1940, ME 1941-43, Sicily 1943, NW Europe 1944-46; Lt Col cmdg 272 (N) Fd Regt RA(TA) 1963-66, Hon Col 101 (N) Field Regt RA (V) 1981-86; md Engineering Co 1960-63; magistrate Gateshead 1955-90, chm Gateshead Health Authy 1984-; Vice Lord-Lt Tyne and Wear 1987-; *Clubs* Northern Counties, Newcastle; *Style*— Lt-Col Windsor Dowdeswell, MC, TD, DL; 40 Oakfield Rd, Gosforth, Newcastle NE3 4HS (☎ 091 2852196)

DOWDING, 2 Baron (UK 1943); Wing Cdr Derek Hugh Tremenheere Dowding; only s of Air Chief Marshal of the RAF 1 Baron Dowding, GCB, GCVO, CMG (d 1970); *b* 9 Jan 1919; *Educ* Winchester, Cranwell; *m* 1, 17 Feb 1940 (m dis 1946), Joan Myrle, da of Donald James Stuart, of Nairn; m 2, 7 May 1947 (m dis 1960), Alison Margaret, da of James Bannerman, of Norwich, and widow of Maj R W H Peebles, BCS; 2 s; m 3, 17 Dec 1961, Mrs Odette L M S Hughes, da of Louis Joseph Houles; *Heir* s, Hon Piers Dowding; *Career* Pilot Offr 1939 74 (F) Sqdn, UK Mid East WW II, Co No 49 (B) Sqdn 1950, Wing Cdr 1951; *Style*— Rt Hon The Lord Dowding; 501 Gilbert House, Barbican, EC2 (☎ 071 628 8547)

DOWDING, Fergus James Edward; s of Cecil John Dowding (d 1988), and Ruth Mary, *née* Arnold; *b* 10 Oct 1960; *Educ* Sherborne, Seale-Hayne Agric Coll; *Career* farmer 1982-85; dir: Shepton Farms Ltd 1978-89, Montague Organic Gardens 1989-; antique furniture dealer Pelham Galleries Chelsea London 1985-; *Recreations* calligraphy, genealogy, palaeology, architecture, snorkeling; *Style*— Fergus Dowding, Esq; 17 Glenfield Rd, London SW12 (☎ 081 673 7180); Orchard House, Shepton Montague, Wincanton, Somerset (☎ 0749 813319)

DOWDING, Muriel, Baroness; Muriel; da of late John Albino; *Educ* Walthamstow Hall Sevenoaks, Convent of the Holy Child Sussex; *m* 1, 1935, June Maxwell Whiting, RAF (ka 1944); 1 s; m 2, 25 Sept 1951, as his 2 w, Air Chief Marshal 1 Baron Dowding, GCB, GCVO, CMG (d 1970); *Career* vice pres RSPCA to 1981-83; pres Nat Anti-Vivisection Soc, trustee of Ferne Animal Sanctuary, pres Nat Animal Rescue Kennels, hon tres Int Assoc Against Painful Experiments on Animals, founder and chm Beauty Without Cruelty 1959, resigned 1981; *Books* Beauty not the Beast (1980); *Recreations* theosophy, spiritualism, astrology, all occult subjects; *Style*— The Rt Hon Muriel, Lady Dowding; Ashurst Lodge, Speldhust Rd, Langton Green, Tunbridge Wells, Kent TH3 0JF

DOWDING, Hon Piers Hugh Tremenheere; s and h of 2 Baron Dowding by 2 wife; *b* 18 Feb 1948; *Educ* Fettes; *Style*— The Hon Piers Dowding

DOWELL, Anthony James; CBE (1973); s of Arthur Henry Dowell (d 1976), and

Catherine Ethel, *née* Raynes (d 1974); *b* 16 Feb 1943; *Educ* Hants Sch, Royal Ballet Sch; *Career* princ dancer Royal Ballet, assoc dir Royal Ballet, dir Royal Ballet 1986-; *Clubs* Marks; *Style—* Anthony Dowell, Esq, CBE; The Royal Opera House, Covent Garden, London, WC2E 7QA (☎ 071 240 1200)

DOWELL, Prof John Derek; s of William Ernest Dowell, of Ellistown, Leicester, and Elsie Dorothy, *née* Jarvis; *b* 6 Jan 1935; *Educ* Coalville GS Leicestershire, Univ of Birmingham (BSc, PhD); *m* 19 Aug 1959, Patricia, da of Lesley Clarkson, of Maltby, Yorkshire; 1 s (Simon Jeremy b 1964), 1 da (Laura b 1962); *Career* res fell Univ of Birmingham 1958-60, res assoc CERN Geneva 1960-62, lectr in physics Univ of Birmingham 1962-68, visiting scientist Argonne National Laboratory USA 1968-69, sr lectr Univ of Birmingham 1970-73 (lectr 1969-70) scientific assoc CERN Geneva 1973-74, prof of elementary particle physics Univ of Birmingham 1980- (sr lectr 1974-75, reader 1975-80), scientific assoc CERN Geneva 1985-87; chm SERC Particle physics ctee 1981-85 (memb Nuclear Physics Bd 1974-77 and 1981-85), memb CERN Scientific Policy Ctee 1982-90, UK memb Euro Ctee for Future Accelerators 1989-; memb American Physical Soc, FRS 1986, FInstP 1987 (Rutherford medal and prize 1988), CPhys 1987; *Books* Over 100 papers in scientific jls; *Recreations* piano, amateur theatre, squash, skiing; *Style—* Prof John Dowell, FRS; 57 Oxford Road, Moseley, Birmingham B13 9ES (☎ 021 449 3332); School of Physics and Space Research, The Universtiy of Birmingham, Birmingham B15 2TT (☎ 021 414 4658, fax 021 414 6709, 33 89 38)

DOWELL, Richard Gough; s of Richard Stanley Dowell (d 1943), and Dorothy Gough (d 1919); *b* 5 Jan 1915; *Educ* Rugby, Magdalene Coll Cambridge (MA) 1948; *m* 9 May 1942, Diana Vera, da of John Percy Tilley (d 1951), of Ranworth Oxshott, Surrey; 4 da (Susan b 1943, Carolyn b 1945, Wendy b 1947, Jane b 1950); *Career* wartime RAF VR Pilot, Flight Lt in UK and Europe; co dir of 8 private cos 1945 down to 3 in 1987; JP for Surrey 1964-81; GCIT for Surrey 1968-81; FZS 1945; *Recreations* real tennis, other sports; *Clubs* Royal Tennis Court Hampton Court Palace, RAF, Piccadilly, MCC; *Style—* Richard Dowell, Esq; The Gables, South Walk, Middleton-on-Sea, Sussex (☎ 0243 584107)

DOWER, Robert Charles Philips (Robin); s of John Gordon Dower (d 1947), and Pauline, *née* Trevelyan, CBE, JP; *b* 27 Oct 1938; *Educ* The Leys Sch Cambridge, St John's Coll Cambridge (MA), Univ of Edinburgh (BArch), Univ of Newcastle (DipLD); *m* 4 Nov 1967, Frances Helen, da of Henry Edmeades Baker, of Owletts, Cobham, Kent; 1 s (Thomas b 1971), 2 da (Beatrice b 1974, Caroline b 1976); *Career* architect, landscape designer; Yorke Rosenberg Mardall London 1964-71, in private practice as princ Spence & Dower (chartered architects) Newcastle-upon-Tyne 1974-; memb: Cncl for Protection of Rural England, Northumberland and Newcastle Soc 1971-, Northern Cncl for Sport and Recreation 1976-86, Countryside Cmmn for England and Wales 1982-; minister's nominee to Northumberland Nat Park 1978-81; ARIBA 1965; *Recreations* wood engraving, lettering inscriptions, walking, gardening; *Style—* Robin Dower, Esq; Cambo House, Cambo, Morpeth, Northumberland NE61 4AY (☎ 067 074 297); c/o Spence & Dower, 1 Osborne Road, Newcastle-upon-Tyne NE2 2AA (☎ 091 281 5318)

DOWIE, Iain; s of Robert Dowie, of Hatfield, Hertfordshire, and Ann, *née* Taylor; *b* 9 Jan 1965; *Educ* Onslow Sch Hatfield, Hatfield Poly (MMechE); partner, Deborah Ann Scattergood; *Career* professional footballer; schoolboy player Southampton, over 50 appearances Luton Town 1989-; 5 caps Northern Ireland; environmental engr Air Weapons Div British Aerospace 1983-88; *Recreations* poetry, golf, travel, music, movies; *Style—* Iain Dowie, Esq; Luton Town FC, Kenilworth Stadium, 1 Maple Road, Luton, Bedfordshire LU4 8AW (☎ 0582 411622)

DOWLEY, (Laurence) Justin; s of Laurence Edward Dowley, of Leicestershire, and Virginia, *née* Jorgensen; *b* 9 June 1955; *Educ* Ampleforth, Balliol Coll Oxford (MA); *m* 10 Oct 1986, Emma Louise, da of Martin Lampard, of Theberton, Suffolk; 1 s (Myles b 1989), 1 d (Laura b 1987); *Career* CA; Price Waterhouse 1977-80, Morgan Grenfell 1981- (currently dir), non-exec dir Filmtrax 1989-90; govr St Francis of Assisi Sch Notting Hill; ACA 1980; *Recreations* fishing, tennis, shooting; *Clubs* Royal West Norfolk Golf, MCC, Boodles; *Style—* Justin Dowley, Esq; Morgan Grenfell & Co Ltd, 23 Great Winchester St, London EC2P 2AX (☎ 071 5884545, fax 071 8266180)

DOWLING, Kenneth; CB (1985); s of Alfred Morris Dowling (d 1963), and Maria Theresa Dowling, *née* Berry (d 1952); *b* 30 Dec 1933; *Educ* King George V GS Lancs; *m* 1957, Margaret Frances, da of Alfred Cyril Bingham (d 1974); 2 da (Angela, Catherine); *Career* called to the Bar Grays Inn 1960; asst dir Public Prosecutions 1972, 1978 and 1982-85; *Recreations* golf, reading; *Clubs* Wyke Green Golf (Middlesex); *Style—* Kenneth Dowling Esq, CB; 4-12 Queen Anne's Gate, London SW1H 9AZ (☎ 071 213 6026)

DOWLING, Prof Patrick Joseph; s of John Dowling (d 1951), of Dublin, and Margaret, *née* McKittrick; *b* 23 March 1939; *Educ* Christian Brothers Sch Dublin, Univ Coll Dublin (BE), Imperial Coll London (DIC, PhD); *m* 14 May 1966, Dr Grace Carmine Victoria Dowling, da of Palladius Mariano Agapitus Lobo, of Zanzibar; 1 s (Tiernan b 7 Feb 1968), 1 da (Rachel b 8 March 1967); *Career* bridge engr Br Constructional Steelwork Assoc; Imperial Coll London: res fell 1966-74, reader 1974-79, BSC prof 1979-; fndr ptnr Chapman & Dowling 1981, head Civil Engrg Dept Imperial Coll 1985-, memb Exec Ctee and Cncl Steel Construction Inst 1985-, conslt KML Conslt Engrs 1988-, memb Cncl Royal Holloway and Bedford New Coll 1989-; Gustave Trasenster Medal, Assoc des Ingénieurs Sortis de L'Université de Liege; FIStructE 1978, FICE 1979, FEng 1981, FRINA 1985, FGGI 1989; *Publications include* ed: Journal of Constructional Steel Research, Steel Plated Structures (1977), Buckling of Shells in Offshore Stuctures (1982), Design of Steel Structures (1988); *Recreations* reading, travelling, sailing; *Clubs* Athenaeum, Chelsea Arts; *Style—* Prof Patrick Dowling; Imperial Coll, Civil Engineering Dept, London SW7 2BU (☎ 071 589 5111, ext 4709, fax 071 581 1263, telex 918351)

DOWN, Sir Alastair (Frederick); OBE (1944, MBE 1942), MC (1940), TD (1951); s of Capt Frederick Edward Down (d 1959); *b* 23 July 1914; *Educ* Marlborough; *m* 1947, Maysie Hilda (Bunny), da of Capt Vernon Mellon; 2 s, 2 da; *Career* WW11 despatches twice, with 8 Army and 1 Canadian Army as Lt-Col and Col; CA 1938; dep chm and md BP Co Ltd 1962-75, pres BP Group in Canada 1957-62, chm and chief exec Burmah Oil Co Ltd 1975-83; kt 1978; *Recreations* shooting, golf, fishing; *Style—* Sir Alastair Down, OBE, MC, TD; Brieryhill, Hawick, Roxburghshire TD9 7LL Scotland

DOWN, Ashley Gordon; s of John Ernest Frank Down (d 1959), of Sydney, Aust, and Lois Marie, *née* Whitelaw; *b* 17 Nov 1938; *Educ* Brisbane Boys Coll, Univ of Queensland (BEcon), Harvard Business Sch; *m* 1, 21 April 1970 (m dis 1983) Ferelith Alison, da of Maj Mark Palmer, of Surrey; 1 s (John Mark Palmer b 1979), 1 da (Selina Eleanor b 1975); m 2, 8 Oct 1984, Christine Stanton *née* McRoberts; *Career* sec Brisbane Stock Exchange 1959-67 (asst sec 1957-59), White Weld & Co (NY) 1967-69, ptnr i/c corp fin James Capel & Co (London) 1969-83, chm Prudential Bache Capital Funding (London) 1983-89, dir M&G Group plc 1979-; treas Esmee Fairbairn Charitable Tst, memb Cncl Wildfowl and Wetland Tst; *Recreations* country sports; *Clubs* Brooks's, City of London, MCC, Australian; *Style—* Ashley Down, Esq; Dor Knap House, Middle Hill nr Broadway, Worcs WR12 7LA (☎ 0386858797); 43 Bedford Gardens, London W8; 79 The Esplanade, Balmoral, Sydney NSW, Australia; 9 Devonshire Square, London EC2 M4HP (☎ 071 548 4044, fax 071 548 4642)

DOWN, Lesley-Anne; da of P J Down, of London, and Isabella, *née* Gordon-Young; *b* 17 March 1955; *Educ* Professional Childrens Sch; *m* 1, 1982 (m dis 1985), William Friedkin; 1 s (Jack b 1982); m 2, 1986, Don Fauntleroy, s of Don Fauntleroy; *Career* actress 1967-; theatre work incl: The Marquise, Hamlet, Great Expectations; tv work incl: The Snow Queen, Upstairs Downstairs, The One and Only Phyliss Dixie, Heartbreak House, Unity Mitford, The Hunchback of Notre Dame, The Last Days of Pompeii, Arch of Triumph, North And South Book 1, North And South Book 2, Indiscreet, Ladykillers, Shivers, Nightwalk, Frog Girl; film work incl: The Smashing Bird I Used to Know, All the Right Noises, Countess Dracula, Assault, Salawag, Tales from Beyond The Grave, Brannigan, The Pink Panther Strikes Again, The Betsy, Hanover Street, The Great Train Robbery, Rough Cut, Sphinx, Scenes from A Goldmine, Nomads; nomiee Golden Globe Best Actress for North And South; winner: Evening Standard award Best New Actress for The Pink Panther Strikes Again, Bravo German award Best Actress for North And South; *Style—* Ms Lesley-Anne Down; c/o Pam Prince, CAA, 9830 Wilshire Boulevard, Beverly Hills 90210, USA (☎ 0101 213 288 4545)

DOWN, Michael Kennedy; s of John Down (d 1952), and Irene Beryl, *née* Kennedy (d 1982); *b* 4 Feb 1930; *Educ* Sevenoaks Sch; *m* Barbara Joan, *née* West; 1 s (Ian b 1962), 2 da (Clare b 1958, Laura b 1960); *Career* Nat Serv RAF 1948-50; CA 1955; Edward Moore & Sons: articled clerk 1950-55, ptnr 1960, jt managing ptnr 1974-80, dir (formerly non-exec) 1980- (now Moores Rowland International); tstee Across Tst; Freeman City of London, Liveryman Worshipful Co of Glovers; FCA, FInsTD, FBIM; *Recreations* travel, country life, local politics; *Style—* Michael Down, Esq; Moores Rowland, Cliffords Inn, Fetter Lane, London EC4A 1AS (☎ 071 831 2345)

DOWN, Peter Ashford; s of late Ernest Augustus Down, of 47 Boscombe Overcliff Drive, Bournemouth, and (Dorothy Irene) Audrey, *née* Sparkes; *b* 12 Sept 1928; *Educ* Clayesmore Sch Blandford Dorset, Queens' Coll Cambridge (MA); *m* 24 June 1954, Ann, da of late John Cater Crawshaw; 1 s (Andrew John b 1963), 2 da (Sally Ann b 1957, Frances Elizabeth b 1960); *Career* works servs RE 1947-49; architect; ptnr E A Down & Son 1957-60, Jackson Greenen Down & Partners 1960-87, dir Jackson Greenen Down Ltd 1987-89 (div of of D Y Davies plc); former chm: Hants and Isle of Wight Architectural Assoc, local RIBA branch; former pres Bournemouth 41 Club, memb Bournemouth Rotary; FRIBA 1957; *Books* Environment and the Industrial Society (jtly, 1976); *Recreations* travel, painting, photography; *Style—* Peter Down, Esq; 1 Kinross Rd, Bournemouth BH3 7DE (☎ 0202 553163)

DOWN, Rt Rev William John Denbigh; s of Willliam Leonard Frederick Down (Flying Offr, RAFVR), of 10 Haldon Ave, Teignmouth, Devon, and Beryl Mary, *née* Collett; *b* 15 July 1934; *Educ* Farnham GS, St John's Coll Cambridge (BA, MA), Ridley Hall Theol Coll Cambridge; *m* 29 July 1960, Sylvia Mary, da of Martin John Aves (d 1985); 2 s (Andrew b 1962, Timothy b 1975), 2 da (Helen (Mrs Burn) b 1964, Julia b 1968); *Career* chaplain: RANR 1972-74, HMAS Leeuwin Fremantle W Aust 1972-74; ordained: deacon 1959, priest 1960; asst curate St Paul's Church Fisherton Anger Salisbury, asst chaplain The Missions to Seamen S Shields 1963-64 (sr chaplain 1964-65), port chaplain The Missions to Seamen Hull 1965-71, sr chaplain The Missions to Seamen Fremantle W Aust 1971-74, dep gen sec The Missions to Seamen London 1975 (gen sec 1976-90), chaplain St Michael, paternoster Royal City of London 1976-90; Hon Canon: Holy Trinity Cath Gibraltar 1985, St Michael's Cath Kobe Japan 1987; bishop of Bermuda 1990-; Freeman City of London 1981; Hon Chaplain: Worshipful Co of Carmen 1978 (Hon Liveryman 1981), Worshipful Co of Farriers 1983 (Hon Liveryman 1986), Worshipful Co of Innholders 1983-90, Hon Memb Hon Co of Master Mariners 1989; *Books* On Course Together (1989); *Recreations* golf, watching cricket, ships and seafaring, walking; *Clubs* Royal Bermuda Yacht, Royal Hamilton Dinghy, Royal Cwlth Soc; *Style—* The Rt Rev the Bishop of Bermuda; Bishop's Lodge, PO Box HM 769, Hamilton HMCX, Bermuda (☎ 010 809 292 2967 fax 010 809 292 5421)

DOWN AND DROMORE, 96 Bishop of 1986-; Rt Rev Gordon McMullan; s of Samuel McMullan (d 1952, professional footballer); *b* 31 Jan 1934; *Educ* Queen's Univ Belfast (BSc, PhD), Ridley Hall Cambridge (Dip Relig Studies), Trinity Coll Dublin (MPhil), Geneva Theol Coll (THD); *m* 1957, Kathleen, da of Edward Davidson (d 1965); 2 s; *Career* ordained 1962, archdeacon of Down 1979-80, bishop of Clogher 1980-86; chm BBC Religious Advsy Ctee (N Ireland), memb Central Religious Advsy Cncl for Bdcasting (BBC/IBA); *Books* A Cross and Beyond (1976), We Are Called... (1977), Everyday Discipleship (1979), Reflections on St Mark's Gospel (1984), Growing Together in Prayer (1990); *Recreations* association football, rugby football, cricket; *Style—* The Rt Rev the Bishop of Down and Dromore; The See House, 32 Knockdene Park South, Belfast BT5 7AB, N Ireland (☎ 0232 471973)

DOWNE, 11 Viscount (I 1681); John Christian George Dawnay; sits as Baron Dawnay of Danby (UK 1897); er s of 10 Viscount Downe, OBE, JP, DL (d 1965); *b* 18 Jan 1935; *Educ* Eton, Christ Church Coll Oxford; *m* 16 Sept 1965, Alison Diana, da of Ian Francis Henry Sconce, OBE, TD, of Brasted Chart, Kent; 1 s, 1 da (Hon Sarah Frances b 2 April 1970); *Heir* s, Hon Richard Henry Dawnay b 9 April 1967; *Career* serv as Lt Grenedier Gds 1954; vice Lord Lt N Yorks 1982-, industl mangr electronics indust, tstee The Science Museum 1985-; Hon Col 150 Northumbrian Regt RCT (V) 1984-; *Recreations* analogue circuit design and railways (selectively); *Clubs* Pratt's; *Style—* The Rt Hon the Viscount Downe; Wykeham Abbey, Scarborough, N Yorks (☎ 0723 862404); 5 Douro Place, W8 (☎ 071 937 9449)

DOWNER, Prof Martin Craig; s of Dr Reginald Lionel Ernest Downer (d 1937), of Shrewsbury, and Eileen Maud Downer, *née* Craig (d 1962); *b* 9 March 1931; *Educ* Shrewsbury, Univ of Liverpool (LDS, RCS), Univ of London (DDPH, RCS), Univ of Manchester (PhD, DDS); *m* 1961, Anne Catherine, da of R W Evans, of Cheshire; 4 da (Stephanie b 1962, Caroline b 1965, Diana b 1968, Gabrielle b 1972); *Career* area dental offr Salford 1974-79; chief dental offr: Scottish Home and Health Dept 1979-83, DHSS 1983-90; prof of dental health policy Eastman Inst of Dental Surgery 1990-; hon sr lectr Univs of Edinburgh and Dundee 1979-83; memb: WHO, Expert Panel on Oral Health; *Books* contributor: Cariology Today (1984), Strategy for Dental Caries Prevention in European Countries (1987), Evolution in Dental Care (1990); *Style—* Prof Martin Downer; Department of Policies, London Institute of Dental Surgery, 256 Gray's Inn Rd, London WC1X 8LD (☎ 071 837 3646)

DOWNER, Sorrel Louise; da of Robert Downer (d 1988), of Hastings, and Cecile Jessie, *née* Groves; *b* 31 Oct 1961; *Educ* Namhuga Sch Uganda, Bruton Sch for Girls Somerset, Univ of Newcastle upon Tyne (BA); *Career* journalist; freelance work 1985-88, feature writer 1988-89 (Smash Hits, Just 17, Melody Maker, Blitz); freelance on shifts: Daily Star, The Sun, Daily Mirror, Evening Standard; ed style and music page Metropolis Evening Standard 1989-; *Recreations* riding, travelling, water skiing, writing; *Style—* Ms Sorrel Downer; Metropolis, Evening Standard, Northcliffe House, 2 Derry St, London W8 5EE (☎ 071 938 7698, fax 071 937 2648)

DOWNES, George Robert; CB (1967); s of Philip George Downes (d 1919), of Burnham on Crouch, and Isabella, *née* Webster (d 1967); *b* 25 May 1911; *Educ* King Edward's GS Birmingham, Grocers' London; *m* 24 May 1947, Edna Katherine, da of William Longair Millar (d 1969), of Ringwood; 2 da (Alison b 1948, Marianne b 1951); *Career* RNVR in destroyers 1942-45 (Lt 1943); GPO: asst surveyor 1937, asst princ

1939, princ 1946; princ private sec Lord Pres of Cncl 1948-50, Lord Privy Seal 1951, asst sec 1951, Imperial Defence Coll 1952; GPO: dep regnl dir London 1955, dir London postal regn 1960, dir postal servs 1965, dir ops and overseas 1967-71; dir of studies Royal Inst of Public Admin 1973-, vice pres Abbeyfield N London Ex Care Soc 1990- (chm 1977-90); *Recreations* music, gardening; *Style—* George Downes, Esq, CB; Orchard Cottage, Frithsden, Berkhamstead, Herts HP4 1NW (☎ 0442 866620)

DOWNES, Justin Alasdair; s of Patrick Downes (d 1978), and Eileen Marie, *née* Mackie; *b* 25 Sept 1950; *Educ* The Oratory; *Career* dir: Fin Strategy 1980-85, Street Fin Strategy 1985-86; md Fin Dynamics Ltd 1986-; memb Somerset CC 1976-; memb Cncl Family Holidays Assoc 1990; *Style—* Justin Downes, Esq; 30 Furnival Street, London EC4A 1JE

DOWNES, Prof (John) Kerry; s of Ralph William Downes, and Agnes Mary, *née* Rix (d 1980); *b* 8 Dec 1930; *Educ* St Benedict's Ealing, Courtauld Inst of Art (BA, PhD); *m* 1962, Margaret, da of John William Walton (d 1963); *Career* librarian: Barber Inst of Fine Arts, Univ of Birmingham 1958-66; prof of history of art Univ of Reading 1978- (lectr 1966, reader 1971); memb Royal Cmmn on Historical Monuments of Eng 1981-; FSA 1962; *Books* Hawksmoor (1959 and 1969), Vanbrugh (1977 and 1987), Wren (1971, 1982 and 1988), Rubens (1980), English Baroque Architecture (1966); *Recreations* music, drawing, microchips, contemplation; *Style—* Prof Kerry Downes, FSA; Dept of History of Art, Univ of Reading, Reading, RG1 5AQ, (☎ 0734 318891)

DOWNEY, Sir Gordon Stanley; KCB (1984, CB 1980); s of Capt Stanley William Downey (d 1940), of London, and Winifred, *née* Dick (d 1970); *b* 26 April 1928; *Educ* Tiffin's Sch, LSE (BSc); *m* 7 Aug 1952, Jacqueline Norma, da of Samuel Goldsmith (d 1972), of London; 2 da (Alison b 1960, Erica b 1963); *Career* 2 Lt RA 1946-48; Miny of Works 1951-52, on loan to Miny of Health 1961-62, Treasy 1952-78, dep head of Central Policy Review Staff 1978-81, comptroller and auditor gen 1981-87; special advsr to Ernst & Young (formerly Ernst & Whinney) 1988-90; complaints cmmr Securities Assoc 1989-90; chm delegacy King's Coll Med and Dental Sch 1989-, chm FIMBRA 1990-; memb bd of Business Performance Gp LSE 1989-, readers' rep Independent 1990-; memb Cncl CIPFA 1982-87; *Recreations* visual arts, tennis; *Clubs* Army and Navy; *Style—* Sir Gordon Downey, KCB; Chinley Cottage, 1 Eaton Park Road, Cobham, Surrey KT11 2JG (☎ 0932 67878)

DOWNEY, Maurice Edmund; s of late Edmund Downey, author (as F M Allen) (d 1937); *b* 2 April 1930; *Educ* Waterpark Coll; *m* 1956, Marie, da of late Timothy Flynn; 5 c; *Career* CA; ptnr Reynolds Cooper McCarron 1973-87, conslt Ernst & Young 1987-, dir Irish Lee Assurance Co 1978-87, chm Waterford Harbour Cmmrs 1976-88, Mayor of Waterford 1970-71, former cncl memb Inst of Chartered Accountants in Ireland; *Recreations* rugby, walking, travel; *Style—* Maurice Edmund Esq; Milltown Grove, Milltown, Dublin (☎ 0001 697236); Fairview, Newtown, Waterford, Eire (☎ 051 74191)

DOWNHILL, Ronald Edward; s of John Edward Downhill (d 1986), of Burghfield Common, Berkshire and Lily, *née* Darraugh; *b* 11 Aug 1943; *Educ* Hyde Co GS Cheshire; *m* 1969, Olwen Elizabeth, da of Ronald Siddle; 3 da (Helen Louise b 1972, Rebecca Clare Elizabeth b 1975, Victoria Ruth b 1984); *Career* called to the Bar 1968; admitted slr 1974; Inland Revenue: Chief Inspector's Branch 1960-64, Estate Duty Office 1964-69, Slr's Office 1969-74; self employed tax conslt in ptnrship 1977-82, head of Tax and Tst Dept Berwin Leighton (joined 1974, ptnr 1976-77 and 1982-); conslt ed Tax Cases Analysis; memb Revenue Law Ctee of Law Soc 1989; memb Law Sol 1974, ATII 1978; *Recreations* watching soccer, model railways, reading; *Style—* Ronald Downhill, Esq; Berwin Leighton Solicitors, Adelaide House, London Bridge, London EC4R 9HA (☎ 071 623 3144, fax 071 623 4416)

DOWNIE, Prof Robert Silcock; s of Capt Robert Mackie Downie (d 1980), of Glasgow, and Margaret Barlas, *née* Brown (d 1974); *b* 19 April 1933; *Educ* HS of Glasgow, Univ of Glasgow (MA), Queen's Coll Oxford (BPhil); *m* 15 Sept 1958, Eileen Dorothea, da of Capt Wilson Ashley Flynn (d 1942), of Glasgow; 3 da (Alison, Catherine, Barbara); *Career* Russian linguist Intelligence Corps 1955-57, lectr in philosophy Univ of Glasgow 1959-69, visiting prof of philosophy Syracuse NY USA 1963-64, prof of moral philosophy Univ of Glasgow 1969-, Stevenson lectr in medical ethics 1986-88; FRSE; *Books* Government Action and Morality (1964), Respect for Persons (1969), Roles and Values (1971), Education and Personal Relationships (1974), Caring and Curing (1980), Healthy Respect (1987), Health Promotion (1990); *Recreations* music; *Style—* Prof Robert Downie; 17 Hamilton Drive, Glasgow G12 8DN; Kilnaish, By Tarbert, Argyll (☎ 041 339 1345); Dept of Philosophy, Glasgow Univ, Glasgow G12 8QQ (☎ 041 339 8855 ext 4273)

DOWNING, Dr Anthony Leighton; s of Sydney Arthur Downing, and Frances Dorothy Downing; *b* 27 March 1926; *Educ* Arnold Sch Blackpool, Univ of Cambridge, Univ of London; *m* 1952, Kathleen Margaret Frost; 1 da; *Career* dir Water Pollution Res Laboratory 1966-73, ptnr Binnie & Partners Consulting Eng 1974-86, self-employed consultant 1986-; FIChemE, FIBiol, Hon FIWEM, MIE (Malaysia), FRSA; *Recreations* golf; *Clubs* Knebworth Golf, United Oxford and Cambridge Univ; *Style—* Dr Anthony Downing; 2 Tewin Close, Tewin Wood, Welwyn, Herts (☎ 043 879 474)

DOWNING, Dr David Francis; s of Alfred William Downing (d 1963), and Violet Winifred, *née* Wakeford (d 1989); *b* 4 Aug 1926; *Educ* Bristol GS, Univ of Bristol (BSc, PhD), Univ of California Los Angeles; *m* 1948, Margaret, da of Raymond Llewellyn (d 1958); 1 s (Jonathan b 1962), 1 da (Anna b 1961); *Career* Army Lt Royal Welsh Fusiliers 1944-48; fell Univ of California Los Angeles 1955-57, lectr Dept of Agric and Horticulture Univ of Bristol 1957-58, Chem Def Establ MOD 1958-63 and 1966-68, scientific liason offr Br Embassy Washington DC USA 1963-66, cnsllr (scientific) Br High Cmmn Ottawa Canada 1968-73, asst dir Royal Armaments R & D Estab MOD 1973-78; cnsllr (scientific) Br Embassy Moscow USSR 1978-81, asst dir resources and programmes MOD 1981-83, attaché (Def R & D) Br Embassy Washington DC USA 1983-87, pt/t chm Civil Serv Cmmn Recruitment Bd, lay chm Cncl Salisbury Cathedral, chm of Govrs Salisbury and Wells Theol Coll; FRSA; *Recreations* cross country skiing, arctic art, bird watching; *Clubs* Army & Navy; *Style—* Dr David Downing; 13 The Close, Salisbury, Wilts SP1 2EB

DOWNING, John Cottrill Ralph; DL (1981); s of Dr Charles Cottrill Ralph Downing (d 1962), of Cardiff, and Ruby, *née* Elliot (d 1980); *b* 22 May 1931; *Educ* Felsted, Pembroke Coll Cambridge (MA); *m* 1959, Muriel Maureen, da of Leslie Webb (d 1983), of Cardiff; 2 da (Caroline b 1961, Nicola b 1963); *Career* ar dir Lyddon Stockbrokers; dir: National Investment Group plc, Capel-Cure Myers Capital Management Ltd; memb Int Stock Exchange; *Recreations* golf, collecting watercolours, stage musicals; *Clubs* Brooks's, Constitutional, Windsor, Cardiff and County, Royal Porthcawl; *Style—* John Downing, Esq, DL; North Lodge, Court Colman, Pen-y-fai, nr Bridgend, Mid Glamorgan CF31 4NG (☎ 0656 721208); National Westminster Bank Building, 113 Bute St, Cardiff CF1 1QS (☎ 0222 473111)

DOWNING, Paul Nicholas; s of Sydney Edward Downing (d 1982), of Berkhamsted, and Glady *née* Miles; *b* 9 March 1947; *Educ* Berkhamsted Sch, Univ of Essex; *m* 19 June 1971, Suzanne Mary (d 1989), da of Dr Howel Norman Rees (d 1983), of Port Talbot, S Wales; 1 da (Charlotte); *Career* slr; ptnr Clifford Chance 1980-90, managing ptnr Pinsent and Co London 1991-; memb: Law Soc, Int Bar Assoc; *Recreations* riding, scuba diving, skiing; *Clubs* Ski of GB, Br Sub-Acqua; *Style—* Paul Downing, Esq; 22 Parkside Gardens, Wimbledon, London SW19 5EU (☎ 081 946 7331); Blackfriars House, 19 New Bridge Street, London EC4V 6BY (☎ 071 353 0211, fax 071 489 0046, telex 887847 LEGIS G)

DOWNING, Richard; s of John Clifford Downing, of 40 Clifton St, Stourbridge, and Greta Irene, *née* Kelley; *b* 8 Feb 1951; *Educ* King Edward VI Sch Stourbridge, Univ of Birmingham (BSc, MB ChB, MD); *m* 24 July 1976, Stella Elizabeth, da of Steve Kolada, of Woodrow, Chaddesley Corbett, Worcs; 2 s (Benjamin b 1978, Thomas b 1982), 1 da (Alice Elizabeth Gwendoline b 1984); *Career* res assoc Washington Univ St Louis USA 1977-78; surgical registrar: Birmingham AHA 1979-80, Worcester Royal Infirmary 1980-83; sr lectr and hon conslt surgery Univ of Birmingham 1986-90 (lectr 1983-86), conslt vascular surgn Worcester Royal Infirmary 1990-; author of pubns on vascular surgery and pancreatic islet transplantation; examiner Faculty Dental Surgery RCS, advsr in surgery Int Hosps Gp 1987-90; memb: BMA, Br Diabetic Assoc, Br Transplantation Soc, Euro Soc Vascular Surgery, Pancreatic Soc GB and Ireland, Surgical Vascular Soc GB and Ireland; FRCS 1980; *Recreations* second-hand book collecting, rambling; *Style—* Richard Downing, Esq; Deptartment of Surgery, Worcester Royal Infirmary, Rankswood, Worcester WR5 1HW (☎ 0905 763333 ext 34341)

DOWNS, Barry; s of Samuel Downs (d 1964), of Stockport, and Hilda, *née* Barlow (d 1947); *b* 6 Sept 1931; *Educ* Dial Stone Sch, Heaton Moor Coll; *m* 20 July 1957, Kay, da of Frank Etchells, of Bramway High Lane, Stockport; 1 s (Simon Paul b 1960), 1 da (Philippa Anne b 1963); *Career* CA 1957, in practice B Downs & Co 1969; sec S Casket plc 1960-64, lectr Textile Cncl Productivity Centre 1964-69; dir: Jones Travel (Urmston) Ltd 1969, Sun Island Holidays Ltd 1975, Happiday Travel Ltd 1984, Royal Exchange Theatre Catering Ltd 1981; chm govrs Offerton HS; *Recreations* cricket, golf, politics, theatre; *Clubs* Grange, Bramhall Golf; *Style—* Barry Downs, Esq; The Old Vicarage, 5 Egerton Rd, Davenport, Stockport (☎ 061 483 4617); B Downs & Co, 67 Wellington Rd, S Stockport (☎ 061 480 0845)

DOWNS, Sir Diarmuid; CBE (1979); s of John Downs, and Ellen *née* McMahon; *b* 23 April 1922; *Educ* Gunnersbury Catholic GS, City Univ London; *m* 1951, Mary Carmel, *née* Chillman; 1 s, 3 da; *Career* chm and md Ricardo Consulting Engineers plc 1976-87, dir Gabriel Communications Ltd (formerly Universe Publications Ltd); pres IMechE 1978-79, memb Bd of Br Cncl 1987-; kt 1985-; *Recreations* theatre, literature, music; *Clubs* St Stephen's, Hove (Hove); *Style—* Sir Diarmuid Downs, CBE; The Downs, 143 New Church Rd, Hove, E Sussex BN3 4DB (☎ 0273 419 357)

DOWNS, Donald Alexander Primrose; s of David Alexander Downs (d 1969), of Westerham, Kent, and Harriet Helsdon, *née* Plumbly (d 1935); *b* 22 May 1924; *Educ* Sevenoaks Sch, The Polytechnic (Dip Arch), NAC (Cert); *Career* Lt 3 Carabiniers (Prince of Wales's Dragoon Gds) 1944-47, served Burma; architect 1955-84: Pite Son & Fairweather, Raglan Squire & Partners, PSA DOE; ed Journal of the Flyfishers Club 1975-80; contrib to: Flyfishers Journal, Salmon and Trout Association Magazine, Trout and Salmon Magazine, Journal of the Flydressers Guild; pres The Fly Dressers Guild, sec Assoc of Professional Game Angling Instrs, examiner Nat Anglers Cncl; Friend of Save The Children 1988; ARIBA 1955, APGAI 1974; *Books* with John Veniard: Fly-tying Problems and their Answers (1970), Fly-tying Development Progress (1972), Modern Fly-tying Techniques (1973); *Recreations* angling, beagling, writing verse, cartooning; *Clubs* The Flyfishers; *Style—* Donald Downs, Esq; The Mead, Hosey, Westerham, Kent TN16 1TA

DOWNS, Richard Hudson; s of Arthur Stanley Downs (d 1931); *b* 19 July 1920; *Educ* West Leeds HS, London Poly, Bradford Tech; *m* 1942, Mary; 1 s; *Career* Flt Lt UK and India; chm: Cindex Ltd 1976-82, Cindico plc 1982-84, Medop Ltd 1982-88; *Recreations* aviation; *Style—* Richard Downs Esq; Point Neptune, Fort George, Guernsey, CI (☎ 0481 726525, fax 0481 726528)

DOWNSHIRE, 8 Marquess of (I 1789); (Arthur) Robin Ian Hill; also Earl of Hillsborough (I 1751 and GB 1772, which sits as), Viscount Hillsborough (I 1717), Viscount Fairford (GB 1772), Viscount Kilwarlin (I 1771), Baron Harwich (GB 1756), and Baron Hill (I 1717); Hereditary Constable of Hillsborough Fort; s of Capt Lord (Arthur) Francis Henry Hill, The Greys Reserve (d 1953, s of 6 Marquess of Downshire), and Sheila (d 1961), yst da of Lt-Col Stewart MacDougall of Lunga; suc uncle, 7 Marquess, 1989; *b* 10 May 1929; *Educ* Eton; *m* 1, 5 Oct 1957, Hon Juliet Mary Weld-Forester (d 1986), da of 7 Baron Forester; 2 s (Earl of Hillsborough b 1959, Lord Anthony Ian b 1961), 1 da (Lady Georgina Mary b 1964); m 2, 18 Sept 1989, Mrs Diana Marion Hibbert, 2 da of Rt Hon Sir Ronald Hibbert Cross, 1 and last Bt, PC, KCMG, KCVO (d 1968), and former w of James Richard Emery Taylor; *Heir* s, Earl of Hillsborough, *qv*; *Career* 2 Lt Royal Scots Greys; CA; *Recreations* tennis, golf, shooting; *Clubs* White's; *Style—* The Most Hon the Marquess of Downshire; Clifton Castle, Ripon, N Yorks (☎ 0765 89326); 27 Cranmer Court, Whiteheads Grove, London SW3 (☎ 071 589 4085)

DOWNTON, Dr Christine Veronica; da of Henry Devereux Downton (d 1962), and Christina Vera, *né e* Threadgold; *b* 21 Oct 1941; *Educ* Caerphilly GS, LSE (BSc, Phd); *m* 1981, Joseph Chubb, s of Percy Chubb II (d 1983), of New Jersey; *Career* investmt banker; chief exec offr: Archimedes Assocs, Co Nat-West Investmt Mgmnt; sr conslt to the pres Fed Res Bank of NY, asst dir N M Rothschild, asst advsr Bank of England; *Recreations* reading, walking; *Style—* Dr Christine V Downton; 21 Belgrave Mews South, London SW1; 110 Riverside Drive, NY, USA; Fenchurch Exchange, London EC3

DOWNTON, Paul Rupert; s of George Charles Downton, of Sevenoaks, Kent, and Jill Elizabeth, *née* Goodban; *b* 4 April 1957; *Educ* Sevenoaks Sch, Univ of Exeter (LLB); *m* 19 Oct 1985, Alison Christine, da of Walter Dennis Naylor (d 1987); 1 s (Jonathan George Denis b 20 Sept 1989), 1 da (Phoebe Alice b 16 Dec 1987); *Career* professional cricketer; capt cricket and rugby teams Sevenoaks Sch 1975 (most capped rugby player in sch history); Kent CCC 1976-79, awarded county cap 1979; Middlesex CCC 1980-: debut 1980, awarded county cap 1981, benefit 1990; England: vice capt young cricketers' tour W Indies 1976, 30 Test matches 1980-88, 28 one-day Ints; England tours: NZ and Pakistan 1977-78, W Indies 1980 and 1986, India and Aust 1984-85, World Cup India and Pakistan 1987; County Championship winners Kent 1977 and 1978; honours with Middlesex CCC: County Championship 1980, 1982, 1985, 1990, Benson & Hedges Cup 1978, 1983, 1986, Gillette Cup 1980, Natwest Trophy 1984 and 1988; stockbroker James Capel & Co off-seasons 1986-; *Recreations* most sports particularly golf, reading when time; *Style—* Paul Downton, Esq; Middlesex CCC, Lords Cricket Ground, London NW8 8QN (☎ 071 289 1300)

DOWNWARD, Maj-Gen Peter Aldcroft; CB (1979), DSO (1967), DFC (1952); s of Aldcroft Leonard Downward (d 1969), and Mary Rigby, *née* Halton (d 1978); *b* 10 April 1924; *Educ* King William's Coll IOM; *m* 1, 1953, Hilda Hinckley Wood (d 1976); 2 s (Jeremy, Julian); m 2, 1980, Mary Boykett Procter, *née* Allwork; *Career* enlisted The Rifle Bde 1942, cmmnd S Lancs Regt (PWV) 1943, seconded Parachute Regt, NW Europe 1944-45, India and SE Asia 1945-46, Palestine 1946, Berlin Airlift 1948-49, Army pilot Korea 1951-53, as Cdr 1 Bn The Lancs Regt (PWV) South Arabia 1966-67, Cdr Berlin Inf Bde 1971-74, Cdr Sch of Infantry 1974-76, GOC W Midland Dist 1976-78; Col The Queen's Lancashire Regt 1978-83, Col Cmdt The King's Div 1979-83; Hon Col Liverpool Univ OTC 1979-89; Lt-Govr Royal Hosp Chelsea 1979-84;

dir Oxley Devpts Co 1984-89; chm Museum of Army Flying 1984-88; pres Br Korean Veteran's Assoc 1987; pres Assoc of Service Newspapers 1987-; govr Military Knights of Windsor 1989-; *Recreations* sailing, shooting, skiing; *Clubs* Army & Navy; *Style*— Maj-Gen Peter Downward, CB, DSO, DFC; The Mary Tudor Tower, Windsor Castle, Berks SL4 1NJ (☎ 0753 868286)

DOWNWARD, Sir William Atkinson; JP (1973), DL (Lancs 1971); s of George Thomas Downward (d 1915); *b* 5 Dec 1912; *Educ* Manchester HS, Manchester Coll of Technol; *m* 1946, Enid, da of late Alderman Charles Wood; *Career* memb Manchester City Cncl 1946, Lord Mayor of Manchester 1970-71, alderman Manchester 1971-74, Lord Lt Greater Manchester 1974-77; memb Ct of Govrs Univ of Manchester 1969, chm Manchester Overseas Students Welfare Conference 1972-87, dir Manchester Royal Exchange Theatre Co 1976-89; pres Greater Manchester Fedn of Boys Clubs 1978-; Hon LLD Manchester 1977; kt (1977); *Style*— Sir William Downward, JP, DL; 23 Kenmore Rd, Northenden, Manchester M22 4AE (☎ 061 998 4742)

DOWSE-BRENAN, Lt Col Anthony Edward Francis; JP (1972); s of Maj Frederick Esmonde Dowse-Brenan, OBE (d 1955), of Longdown Lodge, Sandhurst, Berks, and Frances Sarah, *née* Crecy (d 1965); *b* 24 April 1923; *Educ* Peter Symonds Sch, Winchester, King's Coll Durham; *m* 13 April 1952, Elizabeth, da of George Chartis Wood Homer (d 1953), of Bardolf Manor, Dorchester, Dorset; 2 da (Frances Elizabeth Christine b 5 Nov 1955, Annette Caroline (Mrs Davies) b 21 April 1959); *Career* cmmnd RA 1942, HQ 6 Armd Div N Africa 1943-44, 152 Field Regt (Ayreshire Yeo) Italy and Austria 1944-45,Capt 1 RHA ACD to Gen Sir Charles Loewen Italy and Palestine, instr RAC Bovington 1949-51, Adj 81 HAA Regt 1952-53, instr RMA Sandhurst 1953, student Staff Coll Camberley 1954, WO 1955-56, Maj 18 Medium Regt 1957-58, Bde Maj RA 43 Div 1959-60, battery cdr 3 RHA 1961-, 255 Medium Regt, Lt-Col Somerset Yeo and LI 1967-68; headmaster St Martins Sch Crewkerne 1966-84; memb RIIA 1955-82, dep ldr and chm educn Somerset CC 1977-81; chm: Cncl Colleges of Further and Higher Educn 1983-84, Crewkerne Town Cncl 1984-87, Cncl Educnl Fndn For Visual Aids 1986-87; vice chm Cncl Appaloosa Horse Soc 1988-89; pres Crewkerne Ctees: Civic, Twinning, Conservative; govr and vice chm Yeovil Coll; *Recreations* athletics, breeding appaloosa horses; *Clubs* Farmers; *Style*— Lt-Col Anthony Dowse-Brenan; Moorlands House, Merriott, Somerset; Old Manor Farm (Alder Stud) Buckland St Mary, Somerset, (☎ 0460 72442); Toraine Services, Oxen Rd, Crewkerne, Somerset, (☎ 0460 74111, fax 0460 77101)

DOWSETT, Prof Charles James Frank; s of Charles Aspinall Dowsett (d 1957), and Louise, *née* Stokes (d 1983); *b* 2 Jan 1924; *Educ* Owen's Sch Islington, St Catherine's Soc Oxford, Peterhouse Cambridge (MA, PhD), École Nationale des Langues Orientales Vivantes Paris, Institut Catholique Paris; *m* 23 Sept 1949, Friedel (d 1984), da of Friedrich Lapuner (d 1958), of Kalweitschen, East Prussia; *Career* reader in Armenian SOAS London 1965 (lectr 1954-65), Calouste Gulbenkian prof of Armenian studies Univ of Oxford and fell Pembroke Coll 1965-; visiting prof Univ of Chicago 1976; cncl memb: Royal Asiatic Soc 1972-76, Philological Soc 1973-77; bd memb Marjory Wardrop Fund for Georgian Studies; contrib of various articles to specialist and learned pubns; FBA 1978; *Books* The History of the Caucasian Albanians by Movses Daskhurantzi (1962), The Penitential of David of Gandjak (1962), Kütahya tiles and pottery from the Armenian Cathedral of St James Jerusalem Vol 1 (with John Carswell, 1972); *Style*— Prof Charles Dowsett; 21 Hurst Rise Rd, Cumnor Hill, Oxford OX2 9HE

DOWSON, Antony Peter; s of John Robert Dowson, and Sheila Margret, *née* Horstead; *b* 27 Jan 1958; *Educ* Royal Ballet School, White Lodge Richmond Park; *m* 17 March 1990, Fiona Jane, *née* Chadwick; *Career* princ dancer Royal Ballet Co; leading roles since 1985 incl: Romeo and Juliet, Manon, Sleeping Beauty, La Fille Mal Gardee, Prince of the Pagodas; *Recreations* watching football, Chelsea FC, listening to music, cooking; *Style*— Antony Dowson, Esq; c/o Royal Ballet Company, Royal Opera House, Covent Garden, London WC2 (☎ 071 240 1200)

DOWSON, Prof Duncan; CBE (1989); s of Wilfrid Dowson (d 1970), of Kirkymoorside, Yorks, and Hannah, *née* Crosier (d 1987); *b* 31 Aug 1928; *Educ* Lady Lumley's GS Pickering Yorks, Univ of Leeds (BSc, PhD, DSc); *m* 15 Dec 1951, Mabel, da of Herbert Strickland (d 1961), of Kirkbymoorside, Yorks; 2 s (David Guy b 1953, Stephen Paul b 1956, d 1968); *Career* Sir W G Armstrong Whitworth Aircraft Co 1952-54; Dept Mechanical Engrg Univ of Leeds 1954-: lectr 1954-63, sr lectr 1963-65, reader 1965-66, prof of fluid mechanics and tribology 1966-, dir Inst of Tribology 1967-86, head of dept 1967-, pro vice chllr 1983-85, dean for int relations 1988-; visiting prof Univ of NSW Sydney 1975; memb: Educn and Sci Working Pty on Lubrication Educn and Res 1972-76, Orthopaedic Implant Ctee DHSS 1974-77, Regnl Sci Ctee YRHA 1977-80, Res Ctee Arthritis and Rheumatism Cncl 1977-85, SERC ctees 1987-; memb Cncl IMechE 1988- (vice pres 1988-); Hon DTech Chalmers Univ of Technol Göteborg Sweden 1979; FIMechE 1973, FEng 1982, FRS 1987, FRSA; Fell: ASME, ASLE; memb Royal Swedish Acad of Engrg Sci 1986; *Books* Elastohydrodynamic Lubrication (second edn, 1977), History of Tribology (1979), Biomechanics of Joints and Joint Replacements (1981), Ball Bearing Lubrication (1981); *Recreations* walking; *Style*— Prof Duncan Dowson, CBE, FRS; Ryedale, 23 Church Lane, Adel, Leeds LS16 8DQ (☎ 0532 678933); Dept of Mechanical Engineering, The University of Leeds, Leeds LS2 9JT (☎ 0532 332153, fax 0532 424611, telex 556473 UNILDS G)

DOWSON, Graham Randall; s of late Cyril James Dowson, by his w late Dorothy Celia, *née* Foster; *b* 13 Jan 1923; *Educ* Alleyn Court Sch, City of London Sch, Ecole Alpina Switzerland; *m* 1, 1954 (m dis 1974), Fay Weston; 2 da; m 2, 1975, Denise, da of Sydney Shurman; *Career* serv WWII Sqdn Ldr pilot Coastal Cmd; dir: A C Neilsen Co Oxford 1953-58, Southern Television 1958-75; chief exec Rank Organisation Ltd 1972-74 (dep 1960-72), chm Erskine House Investments 1975-83; dir: Carron Co (Holdings) Ltd 1976-82, Carron Investments Ltd 1976-82, Cambridge Communications Ltd 1978-79, R C O Holdings Ltd 1979-; dep chm: Nimslo International Ltd, Nimslo Ltd, Nimslo European Holdings and Nimslo Corporation 1978-84; chm: Pincus Vidler Arthur Fitzgerald (advertising agency) 1979-84, Marinex Petroleum Ltd, Marinex Petroleum USA Inc and Marinex Petroleum Holdings 1980-84; dir Filmbond 1985-87, dep chm Paravision (UK) 1988- (dir 1987-); pres Euro League for Econ Co-operation (Br Section) 1983- (chm 1972-83); dep chm and vice pres Nat Playing Fields Assoc; chm: Graham Dowson Assoc 1975-, Teltech plc 1984-85, Migraine Tst 1986-88, Dowson-Salisbury Assoc 1987-, Premier Speakers 1988-; *Recreations* sailing; *Clubs* Royal London Yacht (Cdre 1978-80), Royal Southern Yacht, RAF, Distillers Livery, Carlton; *Style*— Graham Dowson Esq; 193 Cromwell Tower, Barbican, London EC2Y 8DD

DOWSON, Dr Jonathan Hudson; *b* 19 March 1942; *Educ* The Leys Sch Cambridge, Queens' Coll Cambridge (MA, MB, BChir, MD), St Thomas' Hosp, Univ of Edinburgh (DPM, PhD); *m* 29 Dec 1965, Lynn Susan, *née* Dothie; 2 s (James b 1968, Jonathan b 1972), 1 da (Emma b 1967); *Career* lectr in psychiatry Univ of Edinburgh 1973-75 (lectr in anatomy 1969-72), conslt psychiatrist Addenbrookes Hosp Cambridge 1977-, lectr in psychiatry Univ of Cambridge 1977-, visiting prof Univ of Florida 1983; examiner: Univ of Cambridge 1988-, RCPsych 1981- (regnl advsr 1990-); papers on ageing, brain lipopigment, personality disorders and drugs in psychiatry; fell commoner Queens' Coll Cambridge 1985; *Books* Treatment and Management In Adult Psychiatry (co-ed and contrib, 1983); *Recreations* squash, theatre; *Clubs* United Oxford and Cambridge Univ; *Style*— Dr Jonathan Dowson; Old Vicarage, Church Lane, Sawston, Cambridge; Department of Psychiatry, Level 4 Addenbrooke's Hospital, Hills Rd, Cambridge CB2 2QQ (☎ 0223 336965)

DOWSON, Sir Philip Manning; CBE (1969); s of Robert Manning Dowson, of Geldeston, Norfolk; *b* 16 Aug 1924; *Educ* Gresham's Sch Holt, Univ Coll Oxford, Clare Coll Cambridge (MA); *m* 1950, Sarah Albinia, da of Brig Wilson Theodore Oliver Crewdson, CBE (d 1961), by his w Albinia Joane, 2 da of Sir Nicholas Henry Bacon, 12 Bt, of London; 1 s, 2 da; *Career* Sub-Lt RNVR; architect; Ove Arup and Partners 1953, fndr ptnr Arup Associates Architects and Engrs 1963; memb Royal Fine Art Cmmn 1970-, tstee The Thomas Cubitt Tst 1978-, memb Bd of Tstees Royal Botanic Gardens Kew 1983-, tstee The Armouries 1984-89; Royal Gold medal for Architecture 1981, AA Opl; hon fell: American Inst of Architects, RCA; Royal Acad of Arts 1979; ARIBA, FSIAD; kt 1980; *Style*— Sir Philip Dowson, CBE, RA; 2 Dean Street, London W1V 6QB (☎ 071 734 8494); 1 Pembroke Studios, Pembroke Gdns, London W8

DOXAT, Charles; s of John Nicholas Doxat, of Camberley, Surrey, and Margaret Jane, *née* Weston; *b* 12 March 1942; *Educ* Westminster; *m* 16 March 1963, Susan, da of John Eric Moore; 1 s (Jake b 23 June 1965), 1 da (Colette b 18 Aug 1963); *Career* trainee rising to account rep J Walter Thompson London 1960-67, mktg mangr Food Brokers Ltd 1967-68, md Sunquick Soft Drinks Ltd 1968-70, account dir J Walter Thompson London 1970-73, dir client servs and planning Dorland Advertising Ltd 1973-84; md: Foote Cone & Belding Ltd 1984-86, Doxat Chapman & Partners Ltd 1986-88; dep chm Burton Wiggard Doxat Ltd 1988-; holder several British titles and records swimming incl Masters Swimming Champion; *Recreations* triathlon, golf; *Clubs* Otter Swimming, Wig & Pen, Lansdowne, Royal Wimbledon Golf; *Style*— Charles Doxat, Esq; 6 Molyneux St, London W1H 5HU; Burton Wisgard Doxat Ltd, 16 Rupert St, London W1V 7FN (☎ 071 439 0146, fax 071 434 2591)

DOYE, Paul Frederick; s of Herbert Walter Charles Doye (d 1946), and Hilda Katie Louise, *née* Edwards; *b* 6 July 1940; *Educ* Hassenbrook Sch Essex; *m* 15 Sept 1962, Brenda Marion Kelway, da of Henry Tongeman (d 1975), of Stanford-le-Hope, Essex; 3 s (Stephen b 1964, Philip b 1967, Jonathan b 1971), 1 da (Ruth b 1966); *Career* dir: Keyser Ullmann Ltd 1969-81, Petrocon Gp plc 1972-88, Lonrho plc 1979-83, Charterhouse Bank Ltd 1980-; *Recreations* family, Christian activities; *Style*— Paul F Doye, Esq; 22 Monkhams Drive, Woodford Green, Essex (☎ 081 505 1418); Charterhouse Bank Ltd, 1 Paternoster Row, London EC4 (☎ 071 248 4000)

DOYLE, Anthony Paul; MBE (1988); s of Bernard James Doyle, of 33, Dane Rd, Ashford, Middx, and Agnes, *née* Laker; *b* 19 May 1958; *Educ* Salesian Coll Chertsey Surrey; *m* 9 Feb 1980, Anne Margaret, da of O P D'Rozairo; *Career* professional cyclist; world professional pursuit champion 1980 and 1986; European Madison champion: 1984, 1985, 1987, 1988, 1989 and 1990; Omnium champion 1988 and 1989; 12 UK nat titles, 4 Silver and 3 Bronze medals World Championships, 2 Bronze medals Cwlth Games 1978, respresented UK Olympic Games Moscow 1980; chm Clarence Wheelers Cycling Club; *Style*— Anthony Doyle, Esq, MBE

DOYLE, (Frederick) Bernard; s of James Hopkinson Doyle, and Hilda Mary, *née* Spotsworth; *b* 17 July 1940; *Educ* Univ of Manchester, Harvard Business Sch (MBA); *m* Ann, *née* Weston; 2 s (Stephen Francis, Andrew John), 1 da (Elizabeth Ann); *Career* chartered engr; mgmnt conslt 1967-72: London, Brussels, USA; Booker McConnell 1973-81 (dir 1979, chm Engrg Div to 1981); chief exec: SDP 1981-83, Welsh Water Authy 1983-87; dir public sector ops MSL Int (UK) Ltd 1988-90; dir mgmnt servs Bristol & West Building Soc 1990-; CBIM, FICE, FIWES, FRSA; *Recreations* reading, theatre, bird watching, walking, sailing; *Style*— Bernard Doyle, Esq; 15 Oldfield Place, Hotwells, Bristol B58 4QJ

DOYLE, David; RD (1973, and bar 1983); s of Edward Doyle, of 19 Mountcastle Loan, Edinburgh, and Mary Stephenson, *née* Shand; *b* 28 Sept 1937; *Educ* George Heriot's Sch Edinburgh, Univ of Edinburgh (MD); *m* 24 Oct 1964, Janet Caryl (d 1984), da of late Stanley Maurice Gresham Potter, of Nottingham; 5 s (Michael b 1966, Stanley b 1968, Edward b 1970, Arthur b 1972, Quintin b 1977); *Career* RAF VR 1958-61, Univ of Edinburgh Air Sqdn, R (Aux) AF 1962-67, RNR 1967-; house offr in med and surgery Edinburgh Royal Infirmary 1961-62, anatomy demonstrator Univ of Edinburgh 1962-63, sr house offr in surgical neurology Edinburgh 1963, appts in academic pathology and neuropathology 1963-71: Edinburgh, King's Coll Hosp London; conslt neuropathologist Glasgow 1971-; FRCPathl; *Recreations* Highland bagpiping, sailing, flying; *Clubs* RN, RSM, Royal Scottish Piping Assoc; *Style*— Dr David Doyle, RD; Institute of Neurological Sciences, Glasgow G51 4TF (☎ 445 2466 ext 3771)

DOYLE, Ian Thomas; s of James Doyle, of Glasgow, and Catherine Forgie Workman (d 1989); *b* 13 March 1940; *Educ* Whitehill Sr Secondary Sch Glasgow; *m* 2 Sept 1961 (m dis 1980), Maureen Marshall, da of Samuel Sunderland; 1 s (Lee Grant Marshall b 30 March 1968), 1 da (Gillian Stuart b 10 April 1967); m 2, 15 Oct 1982, Irene Dick Scott, da of Peter Dick; *Career* fndr and dir Doyle Cruden Group 1967-, fndr and chm Cuemasters Ltd 1988-; mangr Stephen Hendry since 1985; stable incl Mike Hallett and Joe Johnson; *Recreations* motor racing, golf and sport generally; *Style*— Ian Doyle, Esq; Cuemasters Ltd, Kerse Rd, Stirling FK7 7SG (☎ 0786 62634, fax 0786 50068)

DOYLE, Hon Mrs (Katharine Alexandra); *née* McClintock-Bunbury; eldest da of 4 Baron Rathdonnell (d 1959), and Pamela, *née* Drew; *b* 19 Feb 1940; *m* 1960, James Joseph Doyle, s of Timothy Doyle, of Tobinstown, Co Carlow; *Style*— The Hon Mrs Doyle; Coole Stables, Rathvilly, Co Carlow

DOYLE, Prof Peter; s of Archibald Edward Doyle (d 1979), of Widnes, and Mary, *née* Hemlet; *b* 23 June 1943; *Educ* West Park GS, Univ of Manchester (MA), Carnegie-Mellow Univ USA (MSc, PhD); *m* 8 Sept 1973, Sylvia Mary, da of Jeremiah Augustus Kenny, of Canley; 2 s (Benjamin Hollis b 6 Nov 1978, Hugo William b 8 June 1985); *Career* lectr London Business Sch 1971-73, prof of mktg Univ of Bradford 1973-84, prof INSEAD 1978-79, prof of mktg and strategic mgmnt Univ of Warwick 1984-; author of over 100 articles and books on mktg and business strategy; FInstM, fell Cam Fndn; *Books* Inflation (with R J Ball, 1969), Case Studies in International Marketing (1982), Marketing Management (1974); *Recreations* tennis, running; *Clubs* Lansdowne; *Style*— Prof Peter Doyle; Hurst House, Stratford Road, Henley-in-Arden, Warwickshire B95 6AB (☎ 05642 2960); 41 Gloucester Walk, London; Warwick Business School, University of Warwick, Coventry CU4 7AL (☎ 0203 523911, fax 0203 523719, car 0836 76743

DOYLE, Sir Reginald Derek Henry; CBE (1980); s of John Henry Doyle (d 1966), and Elsie, *née* Palmer; *b* 13 June 1929; *Educ* Aston Commercial Coll; *m* 12 Dec 1953, June Magretta, da of Bertram Stringer (d 1940); 2 da (Amanda Jayne b 3 May 1959, Wendy Louise b 13 March 1963); *Career* RN 1947-54; Fire Serv 1954-84: chief fire offr Worcestershire, Hereford and Worcester 1974 and Kent 1977, Fire Serv Inspectorate 1984-, currently HM Chief Inspr of Fire Services; memb Rotary Club Kent; memb Guild of Fire Fighters; CBIM 1989, FIFireE 1973; *Recreations* badminton, shooting, swimming; *Style*— Sir Reginald Doyle, CBE; Home Office, Queen Annes St, London SW1H 9AT (☎ 071 273 3561)

DOYLE, Prof William; s of Stanley Joseph Doyle (d 1973), of Scarborough, Yorks, and Mary Alice, *née* Bielby; *b* 4 March 1942; *Educ* Bridlington Sch, Oriel Coll Oxford

(BA, MA, DPhil); *m* 2 Aug 1968, Christine, da of William Joseph Thomas (d 1969), of Aberdare, Glam; *Career* sr lectr in history Univ of York 1978-81, (asst lectr 1967-69, lectr 1969-78), prof modern history Univ of Nottingham 1981-85, prof of history Univ of Bristol 1986-; visiting prof: Columbia S Carolina 1969-70, Bordeaux 1976, Paris 1988; Hon DUniv Universife de Bordeaux III France; FRHistS; *Books* The Parlement of Bordeaux and the End of the Old Regime 1771-90 (1974), The Old European Order 1660-1800 (1978), Origins of the French Revolution (1980), The Ancien Regime (1986), The Oxford History of the French Revolution (1989); *Recreations* books, decorating, travelling about; *Clubs* Athenaeum, United Oxford and Cambridge Univ; *Style—* Prof W Doyle; 2 Beaufort East, Bath, Avon BA1 6QD (☎ 0225 314341); Department of History, University of Bristol, 13 Woodland Rd, Bristol BS8 1TB (☎ 0272 303429)

DOYNE, Capt Patrick Robert; s of Col Robert Harry Doyne (d 1965), of Somerset, and Verena Mary, *née* Seymour (d 1979); *b* 9 Oct 1936; *Educ* Eton; *m* 7 Dec 1963, Sarah Caroline, da of Brig James Erskine Stirling, DSO, DL (d 1968), of Inverness-shire; 1 s (Timothy b 1966), 1 da (Lucinda b 1964); *Career* Capt Royal Green Jackets 1955-69, serv in Kenya, Malaya, Germany, Cyprus, USA; broker Lloyds 1969-74, Lloyds underwriter 1968-, food indust 1974-83, investment advsr Hill Samuel 1988; dir Stacks Relocation 1988; sec SCGB 1983-86; High Sheriff Warwickshire 1987; *Recreations* country sports, cricket; *Clubs* Boodle's, Pratt's, MCC; *Style—* Capt P R Doyne; Woodlands, Idlicote, Shipston-on-Stour, Warwickshire CV36 5DT (☎ 0608 61594)

DRABBLE, Margaret; da of His Honour John Frederick Drabble, QC (d 1982), by his w Kathleen, *née* Bloor; *b* 5 June 1939; *Educ* The Mount Sch York, Newnham Coll Cambridge; *m* 1, 1960 (m dis 1975), Clive Walter Swift; 2 s, 1 da; m 2, 1982, Michael Holroyd, CBE (*qv*); *Career* author of many books; Hon DLitt Univ of Sheffield; *Style—* Ms Margaret Drabble; c/o Peters Fraser & Dunlop, 5th Floor, The Chambers, Chelsea Harbour, London SW10 0XF

DRABBLE, Phil Percey Cooper; s of Dr Edward Percy Drabble, and Madeline Ursula, *née* Steele; *b* 14 May 1914; *Educ* Bromsgrove, Univ of London; *m* 6 Sept 1939, Jessie Constance, da of George Thomas; *Career* engrg indust 1938-61, dir George Salter & Co Ltd; author and broadcaster 1961-; best known for One Man and His Dog 1975-; contrib to jls: Country Times, Country, Derbyshire Life, Trust, Burton Daily Mail; lectr Foyles Lecture Agency 1964-, professional naturalist managing a wildlife reserve of 90 acres (specialising in badgers and herons); author of over 20 books on rural and naturalist topics; *Recreations* natural history; *Style—* Phil Drabble, Esq; Goat Lodge, Abbots Bromley, Rugeley Staffs WS15 3EP (☎ 0283 840 345)

DRABBLE, Richard John Bloor; s of His Hon Frederick John Drabble, QC (d 1982), and Kathleen Marie, *née* Bloor (d 1984); *b* 23 May 1950; *Educ* Leighton Park Sch Reading, Downing Coll Cambridge (BA); *m* 31 May 1980, Sarah Madeleine Hope, da of Lt Cdr John David Walter Thomas Lewis (d 1966); 3 s (William b and d 1981, Frederick b 1982, Samuel b 1985); *Career* called to the Bar Inner Temple 1975; *publications* Halsburys Laws Social Security (contrib), numerous articles; *Recreations* reading, walking; *Style—* Richard Drabble, Esq; 2 Paper Buildings, Temple, London EC4Y 7ET (☎ 071 353 5835, fax 071 583 1390, telex 885358

DRABU, Yasmin Jeelani; *née* NAQUSHBANDI

DRACUP, Michael Henry Empsall; s of George Robinson Dracup, of Ilkley; *b* 9 Oct 1930; *Educ* Denston Coll; *m* 1957, Jean Shirley, da of Albert Knight (d 1974); 3 c; *Career* dir: Robinson & Peel Ltd 1957-77, Colonial Combing Co (Lana) Ltd 1961-77, Sir James Hill & Son Ltd 1967-77 (md 1968-77), Woolcombers Mutual (vice chm 1972-77), Hallcroft Estate Co 1971-; dir and chief exec Lister & Co plc 1977-; chm: Woolcombers Employers' Fedn 1969-71, Br Wool Confedn 1973-75; *Recreations* golf; *Clubs* Bradford Golf, Otley RUFC; *Style—* Michael Dracup, Esq; Beech House, 78 Cleasby Rd, Menston, nr Ilkley (☎ 0943 72552); Lister & Co plc, Manningham Mills, Bradford, Yorks

DRAGUN, Richard Eugejusz; s of Jan Dragun, of Anlaby, nr Hull, and Genowefa, *née* Hulnicka (d 1990); *b* 13 May 1951; *Educ* Marist Coll Hull, London Coll of Printing (DipAD); *Career* designer Nat Car Park Ltd 1973-74, dir Design Research Unit Ltd 1980-89 (designer 1974-80, assoc 1980-89); seconded pt/t: conslt and designer British Mass Transit Consultants 1986-87, sr designer Baghdad Metro project 1981-84; ptnr BDP Design 1989-; exhibition and museum design incl: Nat Sound Archive London (permanent exhibition), Spaceworks (Nat Maritime Museum London), History and Culture of Oman (Smithsonian Inst Washington DC), Gulf Cooperation Cncl (Summer Conf Exhibition Oman), Nat History Museum and Travelling Exhibitions for Miny of Heritage and Culture (Sultanate of Oman, TV Gp Pavillion Dar Es Salaam), Int Trade Fair 1990 (1 prize for best overall pavillion design, 3 prize for Motor Trade Presentation); work selected for pubn and exhibition in CIK Graphic Design 1984-85, Modern Publicity, Graphics Packaging, Graphics Diagrams (Switzerland), Design (Republic of China), World Graphic Design (Japan); author of various articles; memb Governing Body of Southwark Coll, chm Art and Design Consultative Ctee, MCSD 1978; *Recreations* swimming, squash, flying, modern prints, books; *Style—* Richard Dragun, Esq; Building Design Partnership, PO Box 4WD, 16 Gresse St, London W1A 4WD (☎ 071 631 4733, fax 071 631 0393)

DRAIN, Geoffrey Ayrton; CBE (1981), JP (1966); s of Charles Henry Herbert Drain, MBE, of Lee-on-Solent, Hants; *b* 26 Nov 1918; *Educ* Skipton GS, Queen Mary Coll London (BA, LLB); *m* 1950 (m dis 1959), Dredagh Joan Rafferty; 1 s; *Career* served as Staff Capt Paiforce and India; gen sec NALGO 1973-83 (dep gen sec 1958-73); dir: The Bank of England 1978-86, Collins-Wilde plc 1985-89; chm Home Bridging plc 1986-89, visiting prof Imp Coll Univ of London 1983-88, dep chm Euro Movement 1982-89; memb: Employment Appeal Tbnl 1982-89, Engrg Cncl 1982-84; treas Vol Centre 1983-; tstee Community Projects Fndn 1974-; fell and govr Queen Mary Coll Univ of London 1980-, chm Norman Hart Meml Fund 1989-; *Recreations* cricket, football, walking, birdwatching, bridge; *Clubs* Reform, MCC; *Style—* Geoffrey Drain Esq, CBE, JP; Flat 3, Centre Heights, Swiss Cottage, London NW3 6JG (☎ 071 722 2081)

DRAKAKIS-SMITH, David William; s of William Smith (d 1966), of Liverpool, and Jessica, *née* Hughes; *b* 18 Nov 1942; *Educ* Univ of Wales (BA, MA), Univ of Hong Kong (PhD); *m* 29 Dec 1967, Angela, da of Emmanuel Jean Drakakis, of Cardiff; 1 s (Emmanuel David b 1976), 1 da (Chloe b 1974); *Career* univ lectr: Glasgow 1967-88, Hong Kong 1968-73, Durham 1973-75; res fell Aust Nat Univ 1975-80, prof Univ of Keele 1980-; chm Inst Br Geographers, Developing Areas Res Gp; FRSA; *Books* Urbanisation Housing and the Development Process (1981), Urbanisation in the Developing World (ed and contrib, 1986), Multinationals and the Third World (co-ed, 1986), The Third World City (1987), Cities and Economic Development in the Periphery and Semi-Periphery (ed, 1989); *Recreations* golf, walking, football, art; *Style—* Prof David Drakakis-Smith; Dept of Geography, University of Keele, Staffordshire ST5 5BG (☎ 0782 621111, telex 36113 UNKLIGB, fax 0782 613847)

DRAKE; *see*: Rivett-Drake

DRAKE, Dr Brian John; s of Frederick William Drake (d 1953), of Cambridge, and Grace Emily, *née* Ayers (d 1971); *b* 13 July 1926; *Educ* Perse Sch, St John's Coll Cambridge (MA), Balliol Coll Oxford (MA, BM BCh); *m* 30 May 1960 (m dis 1977), Vibeke Engelbrekt-Pedersen, da of Willi Engelbrekt (d 1982), of Denmark; 2 s (Laurence Karsten b 1963, Marcus John b 1966); *Career* GP in Histon 1957-89 and conslt genit-urinary med Bedford Gen Hosp 1966-; pres Cambridge Med Soc 1985-86; MSSVD; *Recreations* music, playing organ and piano; *Clubs* MSSVD; *Style—* Dr Brian Drake; Lavernock, 45 Station Rd, Histon, Cambridge CB4 4LQ

DRAKE, Prof Charles Dominic; s of William Drake (d 1952), of Co Durham, and Eleanor, *née* Molloy (d 1976); *b* 1 Jan 1924; *Educ* St Cuthbert's GS Newcastle Upon Tyne, Univ of Cambridge (MA, LLM); *m* 20 July 1957, Mary, da of James Whelan (d 1967), of Sunderland; 1 s (Christopher William b 1959), 1 da (Marion Elizabeth b 1962); *Career* WWII serv Northumberland Fus 1942-46; barr 1950-54, sr lectr Univ of Durham, prof Univ of Leeds (dean 1977-80, head of dept 1980-83); visiting prof: Univ of S Carolina 1978-79, Vanderbilt Univ 1985-86; memb Soc Public Teachers of Law, head Law Sch Ctee 1980-83, arbitrator and chm Bds of Arbitration for ACAS, memb Legal Studies Bd CNAA; *Books* incl: Law Partnership (1982), Labour Law (1981), Employment Protection (with D B Bercusson 1983), Health and Safety (with F Wright, 1982); *Recreations* piano, jogging, walking; *Style—* Prof Charles Drake; 4 North Lane, Roundhay, Leeds LS8 2QJ (☎ 0532 659835), Faculty of Law, University of Leeds, Leeds LS2 9JT (☎ 0532 335010)

DRAKE, Sir (Arthur) Eric Courtney; CBE (1952), DL (Hants 1983); s of Dr (Arthur William) Courtney Drake (d 1964); *b* 29 Nov 1910; *Educ* Shrewsbury, Pembroke Coll Cambridge (hon fell); *m* 1, 1935 (m dis) , Rosemary, da of late P L Moore, of Swansea; 2 da; m 2, 1950, Margaret Elizabeth, da of late Ralph Goodbarne Wilson, of Walford Court, Ross-on-Wye, Herefordshire; 2 s; *Career* md Br Petroleum Co Ltd 1958 (chm 1969-75), dep chm P & O 1976-81, pres Cncl Chamber of Shipping in UK 1964; life memb of Court City Univ 1969, hon petroleum advsr Br Army 1971-, elder brother Trinity House 1975-, chm Mary Rose Trust 1979-83; one of HM Lts for City of London; Hon DSc Univ of Cranfield 1971; kt 1970; *Recreations* sailing (owns ketch 'Shimran'), shooting; *Clubs* Royal Yacht Sqdn, Leander; *Style—* Sir Eric Drake, CBE, DL; The Old Rectory, Cheriton, nr Alresford, Hants (☎ 0962 771334)

DRAKE, (John) Gair; s of John Nutter Drake (d 1980), and Anne, *née* Waddington (d 1988); *b* 11 July 1930; *Educ* Univ Coll Sch, The Queen's Coll Oxford (MA); *m* 1957, Jean Pamela, da of William George Bishop (d 1990), of Sussex; 1 s (Paul), 1 da (Susan); *Career* chief registrar and chief accountant Bank of England 1983-90, govr South Bank Poly 1987; *Recreations* sport, family; *Clubs* Chaldon Cricket, Limpsfield Chart Golf; *Style—* Gair Drake, Esq; 114 Stanstead Road, Caterham, Surrey CR3 6AE (☎ 0883 346130)

DRAKE, Hon Mr Justice; Hon Sir (Frederick) Maurice Drake; DFC (1944); s of Walter Charles Drake (d 1980), of Harpenden; *b* 15 Feb 1923; *Educ* St George's Sch Harpenden, Exeter Coll Oxford; *m* 1954, Alison May, da of William Duncan Waterfall, CB (d 1970), of Harpenden; 2 s, 3 da; *Career* served WWII, Flt Lt RAF; called to the Bar Lincoln's Inn 1950, bencher 1976, QC 1968, dep chm Beds QS 1966-71, rec of the Crown Court 1972-78, standing sr counsel to Royal Coll of Physicians 1972-78, judge of the High Court (Queen's Bench Div) 1978-, presiding judge Midland and Oxford Circuit 1979-83; memb of Parole Bd 1984-86, (vice chm 1985-86); hon alderman St Albans DC; kt 1978; *Recreations* music, opera, gardening; *Style—* The Hon Mr Justice Drake, DFC; Royal Courts of Justice, Strand, London WC2 2LL (☎ 071 936 6259)

DRAKE, Robert Geoffrey (Geoff); s of Robert Ronald Drake, and Alice, *née* Simcox (d 1973); *b* 6 April 1937; *Educ* Tonypandy GS, UCW Swansea (BA, DipEd); *m* 15 Aug 1959, Marion Elaine; da of William John Jones (d 1944); 1 s (Jonathan b 5 Sept 1968), 2 da (Heather b 22 Aug 1963, Alison b 22 Jan 1964); *Career* fndr Drake Group of Companies 1971 (currently chm and md); memb: SDP Nat Ctee, CBI and CBI Smaller Firms Cncl; chm SDP Cncl for Wales, parly candidate SDP Alliance Cardiff West 1987, former exec memb Br Educnl Equipment Assoc; *Recreations* tennis; *Clubs* Cwlth Tst; *Style—* Geoff Drake, Esq; 4 Llwyn Drysgol, Radyr, Cardiff CF4 8DN (☎ 0222 842064), 89 St Fagans Rd, Fairwater, Cardiff CF5 3AE (☎ 0222 5060333, fax 0222 554909)

DRAKE, Hon Mrs (Rosemary Etheldreda); *née* Adderley; eldest da of 6 Baron Norton (d 1961 as a result of a fall from his horse), and Elizabeth, *née* Birkbeck (d 1952); *b* 17 Oct 1913; *m* 29 Sept 1949, Rev John Paul Drake, s of Canon Frederick William Drake (d 1930), of Eastchurch Rectory, Isle of Sheppey; 1 s (Simon b 1956), 1 da (Catherine b 1950); *Career* memb Chartered Soc of Physiotherapy; in charge of Dept of Physiotherapy Westminster Hosp 1947-50; *Style—* The Hon Mrs Drake; 3 The Cloisters, Welwyn Garden City, Herts AL8 6DU (☎ 0707 325379)

DRAKE-BROCKMAN, Hon Sir Thomas Charles; DFC (1944); s of Robert J Drake-Brockman; *b* 15 May 1919; *Educ* Guildford GS; *m* 1, May 1942 (m dis), Edith Sykes; 1 s, 4 da; m 2, 1972, Mary McGinnity; *Career* 10 Light Horse Regt (CMF) 1938-40, RAAF 1941-45, serv Aust, Euro, Middle East, Malta; farmer 1938-40 and 1946-59; exec memb Farmers Union of W Aust 1952-58 (Wool Section pres 1955-58), vice pres Aust Wool and Meat Prodrs Fedn 1957-58; former Aust min for Air, min for Admin Servs and min for Aboriginal Affrs, former dep pres of Senate, senator (Country Pty) for W Aust 1958-78, ldr Nat Country Pty in Senate 1969-75, actg ldr of govt in Senate on several occasions, gen pres Nat Country Pty (WA) Inc 1978-81, fed pres Nat Country Pty of Aust 1978-81; state pres Aust-Br Soc 1982-90; kt 1979; *Style—* The Hon Sir Thomas Drake-Brockman, DFC; 80 Basildon Rd, Lesmurdie, WA 6076, Aust

DRAKES, David Hedley Foster; s of Donald Frank Drakes (d 1986), and Kathleen, *née* Caldecott; *b* 20 Sept 1943; *Educ* Wyggeston GS for Boys Leicester, St Catharine's Coll Cambridge (exhibitioner, MA); *m* Patricia Margaret Mary, da of Edward Henshall; *Career* advtg account mangr: Doyle Dane Bernbach London 1966-70, Aalders Marchant Weinreich London 1970-72; fndr and dir Intellect Games 1973-76, md Marketing Solutions Limited 1977-82, fndr manging ptnr and majority Shareholder The Marketing Partnership Limited 1983-; past chm: Inst Sales Promotion, The Sales Promotion Conslts Assoc; memb: Mktg Soc 1978, MRS 1989; *Recreations* opera, ballet, theatre, playing squash; *Clubs* RAC; *Style—* David Drakes, Esq; The Marketing Partnership Ltd, 69 Hatton Garden, London EC1N 8JT (☎ 071 831 9190, fax 071 831 1852)

DRAKES, Paul William Foster; s of Donald Frank Drakes (d 1986), and Kathleen, *née* Caldicott; *b* 6 Nov 1950; *Educ* Wyggeston GS; *m* 1, 1973 (m dis 1980), Janet Bell; 2 s (Oliver b 30 Dec 1975, William b 3 Jan 1979); m 2, 1981, Stephanie Anne, da of Melvyn Moffatt; 2 s (Jonathan b 18 Dec 1986, Harry b 4 July 1989); *Career* trainee Sun Life Co Leicester 1967, mgmnt trainee Dunlop Leicester 1967, trainee media planner and buyer Gee Advertising Leicester 1968, media planner and buyer C R Cassons London 1969, Media Gp Allardyce Hampshire 1970, media gp head The Media Department Ltd 1973-; Primary Contact Ltd: media mangr 1973, media dir and Bd dir 1976, account gp head 1986, dir of client servs 1988-; MIPA; *Recreations* with 4 sons and 2 at boarding school (Radley) little time for hobbies, watching sons is main occupation; *Style—* Paul Drakes, Esq; 109 Panewell Park, East Sheen, London SW14 8JT (☎ 081 878 0899); Primary Contact Ltd, Porters Place, 33 St John St, London EC1M 4AA (☎ 071 253 2800, fax 071 490 3101, car 0831 123753)

DRAPER, Alan Gregory; s of William Gregory Draper (d 1973), of Leeds, W Yorks, and Ada Gertrude, *née* Davies (d 1982); *b* 11 June 1926; *Educ* Leeds GS, Queen's Coll Oxford (MA); *m* 1, 1953 (m dis), Muriel, da of Arthur Tremlett Cuss (d 1974); 3 s (Nicholas b 1955, Timothy b 1957, Jeremy b 1961); m 2, 1977, Jacqueline, da of Leandre Gubel (d 1990); 1 da (Pascale b 1966); *Career* Sub-Lt RNVR 1945-47, def civil servant 1950-85; UK Delgn to NATO: first sec 1964-66, asst sec 1966-84 (counsellor 1974-77); chm NATO Budget Ctees 1977-81; Royal Ordnance 1982-: dir gen personnel 1982-84, dir trg 1985; sr lectr 1986, RMCS Shrivenham, dir Defence Procurement Management Group Royal Military Coll of Sci 1988-; *Recreations* reading, music, amateur dramatics, travel, golf; *Style—* Alan Draper, Esq; c/o RMCS Shrivenham (☎ 0973 782551, ext 2492 or 2555)

DRAPER, Gerald Carter; OBE (1974); s of Alfred Henderson Draper (d 1962), and Mona Violanta, *née* Johnson (d 1982); *b* 24 Nov 1926; *Educ* Avoca Sch, Trinity Coll Dublin (MA); *m* 1951, Winifred Lilian, *née* Howe; 1 s (Alan), 3 da (Valerie, Hilary, Shirley); *Career* dir commercial ops BA 1978-82, md BA Intercontinental Servs Div May-Aug 1982; dir: BA Associated Cos 1972-82, Br Intercontinental Hotels Ltd 1976-82; chm Br Airtours Ltd 1978-82, ret from BA Bd 1982, chm Silver Wing Surface Arrangements Ltd 1971-82; dep chm: Tst Houses Forte Travel Ltd 1974-82, ALTA Ltd 1977-82; chm: Govt Advsy Ctee on Advertising 1978-83, Draper Assocs Ltd 1983-87; govr Coll of Air Training 1983-84; memb: Bd Communications Strategy Ltd 1983-86, Marketors Livery Co, Bd AGB (TRI) Ltd 1983-85, Hoverspeed UK Ltd 1984-86; Centre for Airline and Travel Marketing Ltd; chm: Outdoor Advertising Assoc of Gt Britain 1985-, Br Travel and Educnl Tst Ltd, BR (southern) Bd 1990-; Master Worshipful Co of Marketers; FCIM, FRSA; *Recreations* shooting, golf, sailing; *Clubs* Burhill Golf, City Livery; *Style—* Gerald Draper, Esq, OBE; Old Chestnut, Onslow Rd, Burwood Park, Walton-on-Thames, Surrey (☎ 0932 228612; office: 071 935 4426); 13B La Frenaie, Cogolin, Var, France

DRAPER, Dr Ivan Thomas; s of Thos George Draper (d 1966), and Ethel Alice, *née* Pearson (d 1962); *b* 11 Sept 1932; *Educ* Bemrose Sch, Univ of Aberdeen (MB ChB); *m* 4 July 1956, Muriel May, da of John Monro (d 1955); *Career* res fell Dept of Med John Hopkins Hosp Baltimore USA 1962-63, sr conslt neurologist Inst Neurological Scis Glasgow (conslt neurologist 1965-); hon asst curate St Bride's Episcopal Church Glasgow, former pres Scottish Ornithologists Club, memb Cncl Scottish Cncl for Spastics, FRCPE 1966, FRCPG 1976; *Books* Lecture Notes on Neurology (6 edn, 1986); *Recreations* fishing, books, ornithology; *Style—* Dr Ivan Draper; Dept of Neurology, Institute of Neurological Sciences, Southern General Hospital Glasgow (☎ 041 4452466)

DRAPER, Richard Donald; s of Richard Jack, of Trefeinon Farm, Talgarth, Brecon, Powys, and Margaret Alice, *née* Snook (d 1990); *b* 14 Sept 1934; *Educ* Sherborne; *m* 23 April 1959, Nicole, da of Prof Lucien Lefort (d 1979), of Cours Vitton, Lyons, France; 1 s (Nicolas b 1960), 1 da (Frances b 1962); *Career* chm and md R J Draper and Co Ltd Glastonbury Somerset; former pres Mid Somerset Agric Soc; pres: Wells RFC, Horrington CC; *Recreations* golf, cricket, rugby, football; *Style—* Richard Draper, Esq; The Manor House, E Horrington, Wells, Somerset BA5 3EA (☎ 0749 72512); R J Draper & Co Ltd, PO Box 3, Chilkwell St, Glastonbury, Somerset BA6 8YA (☎ 0458 31420, telex 449427, fax 0458 35355)

DRAPER, Prof Ronald Philip; s of Albert William Draper, and Elsie, *née* Carlton; *b* 3 Oct 1928; *Educ* Nottingham Boys HS, Univ of Nottingham (BA, PhD); *m* 19 June 1950, Irene Margaret; 3 da (Anne Elizabeth b 1957, Isobel Frances b 1959, Sophia Mildred b 1964); *Career* PO-Flying Offr RAF 1953-55; lectr in Eng Univ of Adelaide 1955-56; Univ of Leicester: asst lectr 1957-58, lectr 1958-68, sr lectr 1968-73; Univ of Aberdeen: Regius Chalmers prof of Eng 1987-, head of dept 1984-, prof of Eng 1973-; *Books* DH Lawrence (1964), DH Lawrence The Critical Heritage (ed, 1970), Hardy the Tragic Novels (ed, 1975) George Eliot 'The Mill on the Floss' and 'Silas Marner' (ed, 1978), Tragedy Developments in Criticism (ed, 1980), Lyric Tragedy (1985), Shakespeare: 'The Winter's Tale' Text and Performance (1985), DH Lawrence 'Sons and Lovers' (1986), Thomas Hardy Three Pastoral Novels (ed, 1987), Shakespeare's Twelfth Night (1988), The Literature of Region and Nation (ed, 1989), An Annotated Critical Bibliography of Thomas Hardy (with Martin Ray, 1989), The Epic Developments in Criticisms (ed, 1990); *Dramatic scripts*: The Canker and the Rose (with PAW Collins, Mermaid Theatre 1964), DHL A Portrait of DH Lawrence (with Richard Hoggart, Nottingham Playhouse 1967, New End Theatre, Hampstead 1978, BBC TV 1980); *Recreations* reading, walking, listening to music; *Style—* Prof Ronald Draper; 50 Queen's Rd, Aberdeen AB1 6YE (☎ 0224 318 735); University of Aberdeen, Taylor Buildings, King's College, Old Aberdeen AB9 2UB (☎ 0224 272 623)

DRAYCOTT, Douglas Patrick; QC (1965); s of George Draycott, and Mary Ann, *née* Burke; *b* 28 Aug 1918; *Educ* Wolstanton GS, Oriel Coll Oxford (MA); *m* 1 (m dis 1974), Elizabeth Victoria, da of F H Hall; 2 s (Philip b 1947, Simon b 1950), 3 da (Julia b 1954, Charlotte b 1957, Emma b 1961); m 2, 2 March 1979, Margaret Jean Brunton, da of Andrew Watson Speed; *Career* RTR Europe 1939-46, liaison offr to War Cabinet (Historical Section); called to the Bar Middle Temple 1950, master of the Bench 1972, leader Midland and Oxford circuit 1979-83; *Recreations* inland waterways; *Style—* Douglas Draycott, Esq, QC; 11 Sir Harry's Rd, Edgbaston, Birmingham B15 2UY (☎ 021 440 1050); 4 Kings Bench Walk, London EC4Y 7DL (☎ 071 353 3581); 5 Fountain Court, Birmingham B4 6DR (☎ 021 236 5771)

DRAYCOTT, Gerald Arthur; s of late Arthur Henry Seely Draycott, and late Maud Mary Draycott; *b* 25 Oct 1911; *Educ* King Edwards Sch Stratford-on-Avon; *m* 1, Phyllis Moyra, da of late Ralph Evans, of Norfolk; 2 s (Richard, Hugh), 1 da (Lucy); *Career* Sqdn Ldr RAF 1939-46 (despatches); barr Middle Temple, practiced SE Circuit, dep recorder of Bury St Edmunds 1966, recorder Crown Ct 1972-86; chm: Local Appeal Tbnl, Med Appeal Tbnl, Vaccine Damage Tbnl, Rent Assessment & Nat Insur Ctees; *Recreations* gardening; *Clubs* Norfolk County; *Style—* Gerald A Draycott; Nethergate House, Saxlingham Nethergate, Norwich NR15 1PB (☎ 0603 623186); Octagon House, Colegate, Norwich

DRAYSON, Robert Quested; DSC (1943); s of Frederick Louis Drayson (d 1963), of Kent, and Elsie Mabel, *née* West (d 1971); *b* 5 June 1919; *Educ* St Lawrence Coll Ramsgate, Downing Coll Cambridge (BA, MA); *m* 1943, Rachel, da of Stephen Spencer Jenkyns (d 1956); 1 s (Nicholas), 2 da (Gillian, Elizabeth); *Career* RNVR 1939-46, Lt in cmd HM Motor Torpedo Boats; asst master and housemaster St Lawrence Coll 1947-50, asst master Felsted 1950-55; headmaster: Reed's Sch Cobham 1955-63, Stowe 1964-79; appointed lay reader 1979, res lay chaplain to Bishop of Norwich 1979-84; govr: Parkside 1958-63, Beachborough 1965-79, Bilton Grange 1966-79, Beechwood Park 1967-79, Monkton Combe Sch 1976-85, St Lawrence Coll 1976-, Felixtowe Coll 1981-84; chm of Govrs Riddlesworth Hall Sch 1980-84; memb: HMC Ctee 1973-75 (chm Midland Div 1975), Gen Cncl S American Missionary Soc (chm Selection Ctee 1980-), Allied Schs Cncl 1980-, Cncl McAlpine Educn Endowments Ltd 1982-, Ctee Ind Schs' Travel Assoc 1982-, Cncl Martyr's Meml & C of E Tst 1983-; elected to Band of Brothers 1987; FRSA; *Recreations* hockey (Cambridge Blue 1946-47), Kent XI (capt 1947-56, Final Eng trial 1950), watching cricket, golf, walking; *Clubs* Hawks (Cambridge); *Style—* Robert Drayson, Esq, DSC; Three Gables, Linkhill, Sandhurst, Cranbrook, Kent TN18 5PQ (☎ 0580 850447)

DRAYSON, Hon Mrs (Shirley Joan Bailey); granted title, rank and precedence of a Baron's da; 2 da of Hon Herbert Crawshay Bailey, JP (d 1936); sis of 4 Baron Glanusk; *b* 28 April 1912; *m* 31 Jan 1946, George Dupin Drayson (d 1969); 1 s (Charles Dupin b 1947); *Style—* The Hon Mrs Drayson; Rectory Cottage, Rectory Lane, Ashington, W Sussex

DRESCHER, Derek Peter; s of Clifford Drescher (d 1966), and Joan Ringrose, *née* Jackson; *b* 13 March 1940; *Educ* Pocklington Sch, Univ of Birmingham; *m* 11 April 1966, Gillian Mary, da of Ronald Harry Eden, of Oxford; 2 da (Lucy, Alison); *Career* lighting designer Lincoln and Oldham Repertory Theatre Cos 1961-63, music prodr BBC Radio 1971- (studio mangr 1963-71); documentaries incl: Constant Lambert, Jelly Roll Morton, Charlie Parker, Little Titch, Max Roach, Miles Davis (The Phoenix); series incl: Man-Woman of Action, Desert Island Discs (1976-86), Jazz Today, Concerto, Highway to Heaven, Before the Blues (won Sony award for best specialist music prog 1988), This Week's Composer, Duke Ellington, Third Ear; *Books* Desert Islands Lists (with Roy Plomley, 1984); *Recreations* theatre, music, travel, books, photography; *Style—* Derek Drescher, Esq; 10 Fortismere Ave, Muswell Hill, London N10 3BL (☎ 081 883 8081); BBC, Broadcasting House, Portland Place, London W1A 1AA (☎ 071 927 4327)

DRESSER, Hilary Sarah; da of Clive Dresser, and Wihelmina, *née* Stratton; *b* 12 April 1968; *Educ* Millfield, Kingston Poly; *Career* sprint canoeist; former nat champion and holder of Br course record for 500 m, world championships Bulgaria 1989, Silver medal Nottingham Int Regatta 1989, Bronze medal Mechelen Int Regatta Belgium 1989, memb Br Olympic trg squad; *Recreations* Mensa tests, clarinet and piano; *Clubs* The Royal Canoe; *Style—* Miss Hilary Dresser

DREVERMAN, Hon Mrs (Sarah Jane Moira); *née* Nivison; yr da of 3 Baron Glendyne; *b* 1 May 1957; *m* 21 April 1979, Ian Dreverman, eldest s of A H Dreverman, of Gordon, NSW, Australia; *Style—* The Hon Mrs Dreverman; Hurdcott, Barford St Martin, Salisbury, Wilts

DREW, Sir Arthur Charles Walter; KCB (1964, CB 1958); er s of Arthur Drew (d 1920), of Mexico City, and Louisa *née* Schulte Uemmingen (d 1974); *b* 2 Sept 1912; *Educ* Christ's Hosp, King's Coll Cambridge (MA); *m* 9 Jan 1943, Rachel Anna, er da of Guy William Lambert, CB; 1 s (Walter Guy Arthur b 23 March 1949), 3 da (Harriet (Mrs Bretherton) b 16 Feb 1944, Philippa b 1 May 1946, Marian (Mrs Mollett) b 30 Nov 1953); *Career* asst principal War Off 1936, permanent sec 1963-64, permanent sec MOD (War Dept) 1964-68; JP (Richmond 1963 and 1973-82); memb: Admty, Army & Air Force Bds 1968-72, Cncl Nat Tst 1974-84, Historic Bldgs Cncl 1982-84; tstee: Natural History Museum 1972-82, Br Museum 1973-85, Imperial War Museum 1973-84, RAF Museum 1976-, Nat Army Museum 1981-; chm: Standing Cmmn Museums and Galleries 1978-85 (memb 1973-85), Ancient Monuments Bd England 1978-86, Cncl of Voluntary Welfare Work 1979-89, QMC London 1982-89; pres Museums Assoc 1984, re-elected 1985; Worshipful Co of Master Drapers 1977-78; hon FMA 1986; *Clubs* Reform; *Style—* Sir Arthur Drew, KCB; 2 Branstone Rd, Kew, Surrey TW9 3LB (☎ 081 940 1210); Authers Cottage, Cotleigh, Honiton, Devon

DREW, Christopher Thomas; s of (John) Sydney Wallace Drew, of Whitstable, Kent, and (Edith) Rosemary, *née* Hamilton; *b* 13 Feb 1947; *Educ* Trinity Sch of John Whitgift Croydon, LSE (LLB); *m* 18 Dec 1971, Cheryl, da of Simon Welcoop (d 1989), of Knightsbridge; *Career* called to the Bar Gray's Inn 1969; standing counsel to DTI SE circuit 1989-; Freeman City of London 1977; *Recreations* opera, book collecting; *Clubs* Royal Automobile, Pall Mall; *Style—* Christopher Drew, Esq; 11 Chapel Street, Belgrave Square, London SW1X 7BY

DREW, Dan Hamilton; s of Daniel Edward Drew (d 1974), of Petworth, Sussex, and Rena Frayer, *née* Hamilton (d 1990); *b* 31 Jan 1938; *Educ* Stubbington House and Tonbridge; *m* 1, 1963 (m dis), Carol Ann, da of Dr Robert Gibson Miller, of Helston, Cornwall; 1 s (Angus b 1967), 1 da (Xanthe b 1966); m 2, 1976, Beverley, da of Alan Lestocq Roberts (d 1981), of Graffham, Sussex; 1 da (Frances b 1979); *Career* CA; gp fin dir Interlink Express plc 1982-; *Recreations* shooting, fishing; *Style—* Dan Drew, Esq; Lower Poswick, Whitbourne, Worcester WR6 5SS (☎ 0886 21275); Unit 21, Hartlebury Trading Estate, Kidderminster DY10 4JB (☎ 0299 250697, fax 0299 251174, car 411530)

DREW, Dorothy Joan; da of Francis Marshall Gant (d 1956), of Reading, Berkshire, and Wilhelmina Frederica, *née* Dunster (d 1982); *b* 31 March 1938; *Educ* The Sch of St Helen and St Katharine, Univ of London (LLB); *m* 12 Dec 1959, Patrick Keith Drew, s of Alec Charles Drew (d 1967), of Reading, Berks; 2 s (Dean Patrick b 1961, Jon Philip Francis b 1967), 1 da (Jane Caroline b 1964); *Career* called to the Bar Grays Inn 1981, pt/t chm Social Security Appeal Tbnls sitting at Central London 1986-; magistrate Reading Bench 1975, memb Kensington Social Security Appeal Tbnl 1984-86, pt/t Adjudicator Immigration Appeals Tbnl sitting at Central London 1989; *Recreations* music, theatre, gardening, tennis; *Style—* Mrs Dorothy Drew; Handpost, Swallowfield, Berks RG7 1PY; 13 Draycott Ave, London SW3

DREW, Jane Beverly; *b* 24 March 1911; *Educ* Croydon; *m* 1 (m dis); 2 da; m 2, 1942, Edwin Maxwell Fry; *Career* architect; ptnr Fry Drew & Ptnrs 1946-; author; FRIBA; *Style—* Ms Jane Drew; West Lodge, Cotherstone, Barnard Castle, Co Durham DH12 9PF (☎ 0833 50217)

DREW, Joanna Marie; CBE (1985); *b* 28 Sept 1929; *Career* Arts Council of GB 1952-88: asst dir Exhibitions 1970, dir of Exhibitions 1975, dir of Art 1978-86; dir Hayward and regnl exhibitions South Bank Centre 1987-; memb Cncl RCA 1979-82; Officier L'Ordre des Arts et Lettres 1988 (Chevalier 1979); *Style—* Miss Joanna Drew, CBE; South Bank Centre, Royal Festival Hall, London SE1 8XX (☎ 071 921 0600, telex 626 226 SBBG)

DREW, John Sydney Neville; s of John William Henry Drew (d 1989), and Kathleen Marjorie, *née* Wright; *b* 7 Oct 1936; *Educ* King Edward's Sch Birmingham, St John's Coll Oxford (MA), Fletcher Sch of Law and Diplomacy, Tufts Univ (AM); *m* 22 Dec 1962, Rebecca Margaret Amanda, *née* Usher; 2 s (Jason b 1965, David b 1972), 1 da (Emma b 1967); *Career* Lt Somerset LI 1955-57; HM Dip Serv 1960-73, dir of mktg and exec programmes London Business Sch 1973-79, dir of corp affairs Rank Xerox 1979-84, dir of euro affrs Touche Ross Int 1984-86, visiting prof of Euro mgmnt Imperial Coll of Sci and Technol 1987-90, head of UK Offices of the Euro Cmmn 1987-; assoc fell Templeton Coll Oxford 1982-87; *Books* Doing Business in the European Community (1979), Europe 1992-Developing an Active Company Approach to the European Market (1988); *Recreations* travel, reading, golf, family life; *Style—* John Drew, Esq; 49 The Ridgeway, London NW11 8PQ (☎ 081 455 5054); Commission of the European Communities, Jean Monnet House, 8 Storey's Gate, London SW1P 3AT (☎ 071 222 8122, fax 071 222 0900/8120, telex 23208 EURUK G)

DREWITT, Brian; s of Albert Edward Drewitt, and Dorothy Aida Tyler, *née* Cullum; *b* 9 Dec 1940; *Educ* St Olaves GS London, Gonville and Caius Coll Cambridge (MA); *m* 8 Feb 1964 (m dis 1984); 2 da (Alison Sarah b 1965, Emma Louise b 1967); *Career* ammnd RAF 1962-81, diverse appts incl operational helicopter pilot Malaya 1965-68; engrg mgmnt project offr (avionics) for Tornado aircraft in MOD (procurement exec) 1972-76, NATO MRCA mgmnt agency Munich 1976-80; ret Sqdn Ldr 1981; Messerschmitt-Bölkow-Blohm (MBB) Munich; currently sales mangr helicopter div; MRAeS, CEng; *Recreations* squash, skiing, music; *Clubs* RAF; *Style—* Brian Drewitt,

Esq; MBB Helicopter Gp, PO Box 801140, D-8000 Munich, West Germany (fax 010 4989 6000 8720)

DREWITT, Timothy Paul Geoffrey; s of Lt-Col Geoffrey Bernard Drewitt, TD, DL (d 1987), and Elma Alberta Joan, *née* Thomas; *b* 16 May 1943; *Educ* Blundell's, The Architectural Assoc Sch of Architecture (AA Dip); *m* 19 Dec 1970, Marie Josée, da of Dr Campbell Davoine (d 1964), of Mauritius; 1 s (Campbell b 21 May 1973), 1 da (Zoe b 27 April 1972); *Career* architect: principal in own practice with wife 1967-; past projects include: Burne House Telephone Exchange Marylebone 1970, The Round House Chalk Farm 1985-87; present projects: new archive and reading room GT Smith St Library Westminster 1987-, restoration of Prideaux Place (the house dates from Elizabeth I) Padstow Cornwall 1987-; *Recreations* shooting, sailing, music; *Clubs* Royal Ocean Racing, St James's Place; *Style*— Timothy Drewitt, Esq; 28 Upper Park Rd, London NW3 (☎ 071 586 0671)

DREWRY, Dr David John; s of Norman Tidman Drewry (d 1984), of Grimsby, Lincs, and Mary Edwina, *née* Wray; *b* 22 Sept 1947; *Educ* Havelock Sch Grimsby, Queen Mary Coll London (BSc), Emmanuel Coll Cambridge (PhD); *m* 10 July 1972, Gillian Elizabeth, da of Clifford Francis Holbrook (d 1978); *Career* Cambridge Univ: Sir Henry Strakosh fell 1972, sr asst in res 1978-83, asst dir of res 1983; dir Scott Polar Res Inst, dir Br Antartic Survey 1987-; Polar medal 1986; memb Int Glaciological Soc 1969 (vice pres 1990), chm Cncl of Mangrs of Nat Antarctic Programmes 1989-; vice pres: Comité Arctique Int 1989-, Royal Geographical Soc 1990-; FRGS 1972; US Antartic Serv medal 1979; *Books* Antarctica: Glaciological and Geophysical Folio (1983), Glacial Geologic Processes; *Recreations* music, walking, gastronomy; *Style*— Dr David Drewry; British Antarctic Survey, High Cross, Madingley Rd, Cambridge CB3 0ET (☎ 0223 61188, fax 0223 62616)

DREXEL, Hon Mrs ((Mildred Sophia) Noreen Stonor); yr da of 5 Baron Camoys (d 1968), by his w Mildred (d 1961), da of late William Watts Sherman, of New York and Rhode Is; *b* 1922; *m* 3 Feb 1941, John R Drexel III, only s of late John R Drexel, of New York and Philadelphia; 1 s, 2 da; *Style*— The Hon Mrs Drexel; Stonor Lodge, Bellevue Ave, Newport, Rhode Island, USA

DREYER, Adm Sir Desmond Parry; GCB (1967, KCB 1963, CB 1960), CBE (1957), DSC (1940), JP (Hants 1968), DL (Hants 1985); s of Adm Sir Frederic Charles Dreyer, GBE, KCB (d 1956), of Winchester, by his w Una Maria, da of Rev J T Hallett; *b* 6 April 1910; *Educ* RNC Dartmouth; *m* 1, 1934, Elisabeth (d 1958), da of Sir Henry Getty Chilton, GCMG (d 1954); 1 s, 1 da (and 1 s decd); m 2, 12 Dec 1959, Marjorie Gordon (widow of Hon Ronald George Whiteley, OBE, yr s of 1 Baron Marchamley), da of Ernest Jukes, of Rickmansworth; *Career* RN 1924, served HMSS Ajax, Coventry, Cairo and Duke of York and at Admlty WWII, Capt 1948, COS to C-in-C Med 1955-57, Rear-Adm 1958, ACNS 1958-59, Flag Offr (Flotillas) Med 1960-61, Vice-Adm 1961 Flag Offr Air (Home) 1961-62, Cdr Far E Fleet 1962-65, Adm 1965, Second Sea Lord and chief Naval Personnel 1965-67, chief advsr (personnel and logistics) to Sec of State for Def 1967, ret 1968; first and princ Naval ADC to HM The Queen 1965-68; memb: Nat Bd for Prices and Incomes 1968-71, Armed Forces Pay Review Bdy 1971-79; pres RN Benevolent Tst 1970-78; memb: Not Forgotten Assoc 1973-, Regular Forces Employment Assoc 1978-82, Offrs' Pension Soc 1978-84; Gentlemen Usher to the Sword of State 1973-80; High Sheriff Hants 1977; *Recreations* dry fly fishing, golf; *Clubs* Army & Navy; *Style*— Adm Sir Desmond Dreyer, GCB, CBE, DSC, JP, DL; Brook Cottage, Cheriton, Nr Alresford, Hants (☎ 096 279 215)

DREYER, Capt Jeremy Chilton; RN; s of Adm Sir Desmond Dreyer, GCB, CBE, DSC, DL, of Brook Cottage, Cheriton, Alresford, Hants, and Elisabeth, *née* Chilton (d 1958); *b* 24 May 1935; *Educ* Winchester; *m* 6 Aug 1960, Antoinette Marion (Toni), da of William Cornwall Stevens (d 1983), of Trevessa, Princes Risborough, Bucks; 2 s (Michael b 20 March 1963, Benjamin b 13 July 1967), 2 da (Katherine b 9 Nov 1961, d 1980, Sophie b 3 May 1970); *Career* RN 1953, qualified Signal Communications 1963; cmd: HMS Falmouth 1970-72, HMS Exeter 1980-82; capt 5 Destroyer Sqdn, Cdre Dep Chief Allied Staff to C-in-C Eastern Atlantic 1982-85, ret 1985; asst clerk of course Ascot Racecourse 1985-; *Recreations* shooting, fishing, golf, tennis, skiing; *Style*— Capt Jeremy Dreyer, RN; Old Mill Cottage, Droxford, Hants SO3 1QS (☎ 0489 877208); Ascot Racecourse, Ascot, Berks SL5 7JN (☎ 0990 22211)

DRIFE, Prof James Owen; s of Thomas John Drife, of Bourach, The Knowe, Ancrum, Jedburgh, and Rachel Coldwell, *née* Jones (d 1986); *b* 8 Sept 1947; *Educ* Muirkirk JS Sch, Cumnock Acad, Univ of Edinburgh (BSc, MB ChB, MD); *m* 16 June 1973, Diana Elizabeth, da of Prof Ronald Haxton Girdwood, of 2 Hermitage Drive, Edinburgh; 1 s (Thomas b 20 Dec 1975), 1 da (Jennifer b 23 Nov 1977); *Career* house offr Edinburgh Royal Infirmary 1971-72, MRC res fell Edinburgh 1974-76, registrar Eastern Gen Hosp Edinburgh 1976-79, lectr Univ of Bristol 1979-82, sr lectr Univ of Leicester 1982-90, prof of obstetrics and gynaecology Univ of Leeds 1990-, hon conslt obstetrician and gynaecologist Leeds Gen Infirmary 1990-; UK ed European Journal of Obstetrics and Gynaecology, co-ed Contemporary Reviews in Obstetrics and Gynaecology; hon sec Blair-Bell Res Soc, convenor of study gps RCOG, memb Cases Ctee Med Protection Soc; MRCOG 1978, FRCSEd 1981, FRCOG 1990; *Books* Dysfunctional Uterine Bleeding and Menorrhagia (ed, 1989), Micturition (co-ed, 1990), HRT and Osteoporosis (co-ed,1990); *Recreations* songwriting; *Clubs* RSM, National Liberal; *Style*— Prof James Drife; Department of Obstetrics and Gynaecology, D Floor, Clarendon Wing, Belmont Grove, Leeds LS2 9NS (☎ 0532 432799)

DRING, Lt-Col Sir (Arthur) John; KBE (1952), CIE (1943), JP (Hants 1954), DL (1972); s of Sir William Arthur Dring, KCIE, VD (d 1912), by his w Jane Reid Greenshields, widow of W L Alston; *b* 4 Nov 1902; *Educ* Winchester, RMC Sandhurst; *m* 1, 13 Oct 1934, Marjorie Wadham (d 1943), da of late J C Wadham, of Green Orchard, Lindfield, Sussex; 2 da; m 2, 20 March 1946, Alice Deborah, wid of Maj-Gen John Stuart Marshall, CB, DSO, OBE, and only da of Maj-Gen Gerald Cree, CB, CMG (d 1932); *Career* joined Guides Cavalry IA 1923, Maj 1939, transferred Political Serv 1927, dep sec Viceroy's Exec Cncl 1936, sec to govr NWFP 1937-40, political agent S Waziristan 1940 (despatches), dir of Civil Supplies NWFP 1943-47, chief sec 1947; prime minister to Nawab of Bahawalpur 1948-52, advsr on plebiscites to Govrs and Govrs-Gen of Gold Coast 1955-56, Nigeria 1959; *Recreations* gardening, riding; *Style*— Lt-Col Sir John Dring, KBE, CIE, JP, DL; Ava Cottage, Purbrook, Porsmouth, Hants PO7 5RX (☎ 070 14 263000)

DRINKWATER, Sir John Muir; QC (1972); s of John Drinkwater, OBE, Cdr RN (d 1971), and Edith Constance St Clair, *née* Muir (d 1978); *b* 7 March 1991; *Educ* RN Coll Dartmouth; *m* 10 Oct 1952, Jennifer Marion, da of Edward Fitzwalter Wright (d 1956), of Morley Manor, Derby; 1 s (Jonathan Dominick St Clair b 1956); 4 da (Jane Fairrie b 1954, Joanna Elizabeth b 1958, Juliet Caroline Leslie b 1961, Jessanda Katharine Jemima b 1964); *Career* HM Submarines 1943-47, Flag Lt to C-in-C Portsmorth and first Sea Lord 1947-50, Lt Cdr 1952, invalided 1953; called to the Bar Inner Temple 1957, rec Crown Ct 1972, memb Parly Boundary Cmmn for England 1975-79, Income Tax cmmr, bencher Inner Temple; dir BAA plc; kt 1988; *Clubs* Garrick, Pratt's; *Style*— Sir John Drinkwater, QC; Meysey Hampton Manor, Cirencester, Gloucestershire; 27 Kilmaine Rd, London SW6; Le Moulin De Lohitzun, 64120 St Palais, France; 2 Harcourt Bldgs, Temple, London EC4 (☎ 071 353 8415)

DRINKWATER, (Collingwood) Peter; s of Roddam Collingwood Drinkwater (d 1965), of Kirby, Isle of Man, and Dorothy Mary Adeney; *b* 2 Sept 1931; *Educ* Eton, Sandhurst; *m* 22 June 1956, Belinda Rennie, da of Albert Cyril Sharwood (d 1976), of Ballater, Aberdeenshire; 2 s (James b 1963, Richard b 1965), 2 da (Carolyn b 1958, Nicola b 1960); *Career* served Coldstream Gds 1949-58, Capt; chm E Austin plc and Gp Cos 1959-86; *Recreations* shooting; *Style*— Peter Drinkwater, Esq; Kirby, Isle of Man (☎ 0624 75411, work: 0624 20333)

DRISCOLL, Fiona Elizabeth Lawrence; da of James P Driscoll, and Jeanne L Williams; *b* 27 April 1958; *Educ* Sorbonne (Diploma), Somerville Coll Oxford (MA); *Career* mktg advsr Republican Campaign NY 1976, fin servs broker FPC 1976-79, mgmnt conslt Deloitte Haskins and Sells 1980-85, account dir Collett Dickenson Pearce 1985-87, sr conslt Lowe Bell Communications 1987-; memb Nat Youth Cncl 1975, librarian (vice pres) Oxford Union 1979; *Style*— Ms Fiona Driscoll; Lowe Bell Communications, 7 Hertford St, Mayfair, London W1Y 7DY (☎ 071 495 4044, fax 071 629 1279)

DRISCOLL, James Patrick; s of Henry James Driscoll (d 1965), of Cardiff, and Honorah, *née* Flynn (d 1962); *b* 24 April 1925; *Educ* Coleg Sant Illtyd Cardiff, Univ Coll Cardiff (BA); *m* 16 April 1955, Jeanne Lawrence, da of James Idris Williams; 1 s (Jonathan James b 20 Sept 1961), 1 da (Fiona Elizabeth b 27 April 1958); *Career* asst lectr and fell Univ Coll Cardiff 1951-53, res fell Cncl of Europe 1953, Br Iron & Steel Fedn 1953-67 (latterly econ dir), md corp strategy Br Steel Corp 1967-80, dir Nationalised Industs' Chairmen's Gp 1975-90, chm and md Woodcote Consits Ltd 1980-, sr ptnr Woodcote Consultancy Services 1990-; chm Lifecare NHS Tst 1990-; policy advsr Nationalised Industries Chairmen's Gp 1990-; Parly candidate (Cons) Rhondda West 1950; nat dep chm Young Cons 1950, dep chm Univ Cons Fedn 1949-50, dep chm Nat Union of Students 1951-53; memb: Ct of Govrs Univ Coll Cardiff (now Univ of Wales Coll of Cardiff) 1970-, CBI Cncl 1970-; observer NEDC 1975-, chm Econ Ctee Int Iron & Steel Inst 1972-74; FREconS, FRSA; *Recreations* travel, reading; *Style*— James Driscoll, Esq; Foxley Hatch, Birch Lane, Purley, Surrey CR8 3LH (☎ 081 668 4081); The Lifecare NHS Trust, St Lawrence's Hospital, Coulsdon Road, Caterham-on-the-Hill, Surrey CR3 5YA (☎ 0883 346411, fax 0883 347822)

DRISCOLL, Mark Robert; s of Leo Driscoll, and Katherine Driscoll; *b* 5 Oct 1949; *Educ* Colston's Sch Bristol, King's Coll London (BA); *m* 9 Oct 1981, Elspeth Margaret, da of David Cayley, of Cirencester, Gloucester; 1 s (William), 1 da (Anna); *Career* BBC: studio mangr 1971, exec prodr World Service 1986, ed for assignments Newsnight 1990; *Recreations* athletics, mountaineering, fishing; *Style*— Mark Driscoll, Esq; BBC Television, London W12

DRISCOLL, Peter John; s of Cornelius Driscoll (d 1978), of St Michael's on Sea, Natal, SA, and Helen, *née* Ball; *b* 4 Feb 1942; *Educ* St David's Marist Coll Johannesburg, Univ of the Witwatersrand Johannesburg (BA); *m* 14 Jan 1967, Angela Mary, da of Lester Harry Hennessy; 2 da (Justine Helen b 13 July 1971, Miranda Deborah b 4 Aug 1975); *Career* reporter Rand Daily Mail Johannesburg 1959-67, news ed Post Newspapers Johannesburg 1967-68, script writer and sub ed ITN 1969-73, freelance author journalist and bdcaster Dublin 1974-89, chief sub ed RTE News 1990-; novels: The White Lie Assignment (1971), The Wilby Conspiracy (1973), In Connection with Kilshaw (1974), The Barboza Credentials (1976), Pangolin (1979), Heritage (1982), Spearhead (1988), Secrets of State (1991); The Babysitters (TV play, RTEH, 1980); numerous TV documentary scripts, radio broadcasts, book reviews, feature articles; *Recreations* swimming, fishing, walking; *Style*— Peter Driscoll, Esq; c/o David Higham Associates Ltd, 5-8 Lower John St, Golden Square, London W1R 4HA (☎ 071 437 7888, fax 071 437 1072)

DRIVER, Sir Antony Victor; s of Arthur William Driver (d 1966), and Violet Clementina, *née* Brown (d 1986); *b* 20 July 1920; *Educ* King's Coll London (BSc); *m* 16 Oct 1948, Patricia, da of Alfred Tinkler (d 1950); 3 s (Andrew Charles b 1952, James Antony b 1954, Robert Patrick b 1957); *Career* WWII Lt Ra 1 Airlanding Light Regt 1 Airborne Div 1941-45; dir BP Oil Ltd 1978-80, chm Hoogovens (UK) Ltd 1986-88 (dir 1980-88); memb Ctee of Mgmnt Inst of Cancer Res, chm SW Thames RHA 1982-88; Liveryman Worshipful Co of Tallow Chandlers 1972-, Freeman City of London; CEng, FIMechE, FInstPet, FBIM; *Recreations* travel, wine, gardening, pyrotechnics; *Style*— Sir Antony Driver

DRIVER, Charles Jonathan (Jonty); s of Rev Kingsley Ernest Driver (d 1964), and Mrs Phyllis Edith Mary Baines, *née* Gould; *b* 19 Aug 1939; *Educ* St Andrews Grahamstown, Univ of Cape Town (BA, BEd), Trinity Coll Oxford (MPhil); *m* 1967, Ann Elizabeth, da of Dr Bernard Albert Hoogewerf, of Chislehurst (d 1958); 2 s (Dominic b 1968, Thackwray b 1969), 1 da (Tamlyn b 1972); *Career* pres Nat Union of S African Students 1963-64; house master Int Sixth Form Centre Sevenoaks Sch 1968-73, dir of Sixth Form Studies Matthew Humberstone Sch 1973-78, princ Island Sch Hong Kong 1978-83, headmaster Berkhamsted Sch 1983-89, master Wellington Coll Berks 1989; FRSA; *Books* Elegy for a Revolutionary (1968), Send War in Our Time, O Lord (1969), Death of Fathers (1971), A Messiah of the Last Days (1973); poetry: I Live Here Now (1973), Occasional Light (with Jack Cope, 1980), Hong Kong Portraits (1986); biography: Patrick Duncan, S African and Pan-African (1980); *Recreations* long-distance running, rugby, reading; *Style*— C J Driver, Esq; The Master, Wellington College, Crowthorne, Berks RG11 7PU (☎ 0344 772261)

DRIVER, Christopher Prout; s of late Dr Arthur Driver; *b* 1 Dec 1932; *Educ* Rugby, ChCh Oxford; *m* 1958, Margaret Elizabeth, *née* Perfect; 3 da; *Career* writer and ed; Guardian staff 1960-68, ed The Good Food Guide 1969-82, food and drink ed The Guardian 1984-88 (co-ed personal page 1988-); *Books* A Future for the Free Churches? (1962), The Disarmers (1964), The Exploding University (1971), The British at Table 1940-80 (1983), Pepys at Table (1984), Twelve Poems (1985); *Style*— Christopher Driver, Esq; 6 Church Rd, Highgate, London N6 4QT (☎ 081 340 5445); The Book In Hand, Bell St, Shaftesbury, Dorset

DRIVER, David John; s of Denis Alan Driver (d 1968), of Cambridge, and Mona Eileen, *née* Scott; *b* 4 Aug 1942; *Educ* Perse Sch Cambridge, Cambridge Sch of Art; *m* 27 Nov 1976, Sara Penelope, da of Ashley Rock; 1 s (Paul Robert Thomas b 28 Dec 1979, Helen Rachel b 5 April 1984); *Career* freelance illustrator and designer for various publications 1963 incl: Town, Queen, Vogue, Penguin Books, Observer Magazine, Sunday Times, Harpers Bazaar (re-design 1969), The Listener (re-design 1980); art ed Farm and Country (Thomson Organisation) 1963-67, asst art ed Womans Mirror (IPC) 1967-68, art dir Cornmarket Press 1968-69, art ed and dep ed Radio Times 1969-81, freelance art dir Francis Kyle Gallery 1979-, head of design and asst ed The Times (News International)1981-; winner various awards incl: Gold & Silver awards for Radio Times D&AD 1976, Editorial Award of Excellence Soc of Newspaper Design Awards (USA) 1987 and 1989, Features Design award Br Press Awards 1989; *Books* The Art of Radio Times (ed, compiler and designer, 1981); designer: Garham Greene Country (by Paul Hogarth and Graham Greene), The Windsor Style (by Suzy Menkes), The Mediterranean Shore (by Paul Hogarth and Laurence Durrell); *Recreations* cricket; *Style*— David Driver, Esq; The Times, Times Newspapers Ltd, 1 Pennington St, London E1 9XN (☎ 071 782 5000)

DRIVER, (James) Donald; s of John Driver (d 1970), of Lancs, and Dorothea (Leslie) Driver (d 1987); *b* 20 Dec 1924; *Educ* Clitheroe Royal GS, Univ of Manchester; *m* 1948, Delia Jean, da of James Wilkinson, of Clitheroe; 1 s (John b 1952), 2 da (Susan b

1950, Joanna b 1957); *Career* Lt HM RM 1942-46; admitted slr 1948, private practice until 1970; gp legal advsr Investors in Industry plc (3i) 1973-83; dir: Meggitt plc (chm 1985-), Data Guild Ltd (chm 1984-), Travellers Fare Ltd (chm 1989-), Dollar Air Services Ltd; *Recreations* sailing, cycling; *Style*— Donald Driver, Esq; Littlefield, Dedswell Drive, West Clandon, Guildford, Surrey GU4 7TQ (☎ 0483 222 518, fax 0483 225 313)

DRIVER, Sir Eric William; s of William Weale Driver and Sarah Ann Driver; *b* 19 Jan 1911; *Educ* Strand Sch London, King's Coll London; *m* 1, 1938 (m dis), Winifred Bane; 2 da; m 2, 1972, Sheila Mary Johnson; *Career* civil engr; ICI Ltd 1938-, chief civil engr Mond Div to 1973; chm Mersey Regional Health Authy 1973-82; kt 1979; *Style*— Sir Eric Driver; Chapel House, Crowley, Northwich, Cheshire (☎ 056 585 361)

DRIVER, Mrs John Michael; Olga Lindholm; *see*: Aikin, Olga Lindholm

DROGHEDA, 12 Earl of (I 1661); Henry Dermot Ponsonby Moore; also Baron Moore (I 1616 and UK 1954, by which latter title he sits in House of Lords) and Viscount Moore (I 1621); s of 11 Earl of Drogheda, KG, KBE (d 1989), and Joan Eleanor, *née* Carr (d 1989); *b* 14 Jan 1937; *Educ* Eton, Trinity Coll Cambridge (BA); *m* 1, 15 May 1968 (m dis 1972), Eliza, da of Stacy Barcroft Lloyd, Jr, of Philadelphia; m 2, 1978, Alexandra, da of Sir Nicholas Henderson, GCMG; 2 s (Benjamin Garrett Henderson, Viscount Moore b 1983, Hon Garrett Alexander b 1986), 1 da (Lady Marina Alice b 1988); *Heir* s, Viscount Moore b 21 March 1983; *Career* Lt Life Gds 1957; photographer (professional name Derry Moore); *Books* The Dream Come True, Great Houses of Los Angeles (with Brendan Gill, 1980), Royal Gardens (with George Plumptre, 1982), Stately Homes of Britain (with Sybilla Jane Flower, 1982), Washington, Houses of the Capital (with Henry Mitchell, 1982), The English Room (with Michael Pick, 1984), The Englishwoman's House (with Alvilde Lees-Milne, 1984), The Englishman's Room (with Alvilde Lees-Milne, 1986); *Clubs* Garrick, Brooks's; *Style*— The Rt Hon the Earl of Drogheda; 40 Ledbury Rd, London W11 2AB

DROMGOOLE, Jolyon; s of Nicholas Arthur Dromgoole, of 68 Meopham Rd, Mitcham, Surrey, and Violet Alice Georgina Brookes (d 1959); *b* 27 March 1926; *Educ* Christ Hosp, Dulwich, Univ Coll Oxford (MA); *m* 10 March 1956, Anthea, da of Sir Antony Bowlby, 2 Bt, of The Old Rectory, Ozleworth, nr Wootton-under-Edge, Glos; 5 da (Emma b 1957, Julia b 1961, Rose, Susanna, Belinda (identical triplets) b 1964); *Career* dir Cncl Secrétariat ICE 1985, deputy under-sec of state (Army) 1984 MOD, entered HM Forces 1944, cmmnd 14/20 King's Hussars 1946; Univ Coll 1948-50; entered administrative Civil Service; assigned to WO 1950, private sec to Permanent Under-Sec 1953, princ 1955, priv sec to Sec of State 1964-65, asst sec 1965, cmmnd sec HQ FARELF Singapore 1968-71, RCDS 1972, under-sec Broadcasting Dept Home Office 1973-76, asst under-sec of state Gen Staff 1976-79, personnel and logistics 1979-84 MOD, dep under-sec of state (Army) 1984 MOD, dir Cncl Secretariat ICE; *Recreations* polo, literature; *Clubs* Athenaeum, Royal Commonwealth, Tidworth Polo; *Style*— Jolyon Dromgoole, Esq; 13 Gladstone St, London SE1 6EY (☎ 071 928 2162); Montreal House, Barnsley, Glos (☎ 028 574 331); Institution of Civil Engineers, Great George St, London SW1P 3AA (☎ 071 222 7722, fax 222 7500)

DROMGOOLE, Nicholas; s of Nicholas Arthur Dromgoole, and Violet Alice Georgina, *née* Brookes; *b* 3 Dec 1935; *Educ* Dulwich, St Edmund Hall Oxford (MA), Sorbonne (Dip); *m* (m dis 1988), Lesley Collier; *Career* headmaster: Belmont Coll N Devon (formerly asst mangr), Grenville Coll N Devon, Pierrepont Sch Surrey; head of dept (formerly dean of Arts Faculty twice) City of London Polytechnic 1961-; dance critic Sunday Telegraph 1965-; contrib of features to: Daily Telegraph, Country Life, Dancing Times, Dance and Dancers; chm Inst of Choreology 1969-87, Dance Section Critics Circle 1980-86; memb: Drama Advsy Ctee British Council, Dance and Performing Arts Ctees, Council for National Academic Awards; hon fell Inst of Choreology; *Books* Sibley and Dowell (1976); *Clubs* Garrick; *Style*— Nicholas Dromgoole, Esq; Sunday Telegraph, Peterborough Court at South Quay, 181 Marsh Wall, London E14 9SR (☎ 071 538 5000)

DROMGOOLE, Patrick Shirley Brookes Fleming; s of Nicholas Arthur Humphrey Dromgoole, and Violet Dromgoole; *b* 30 Aug 1930; *Educ* Dulwich, Univ Coll Oxford (MA); *m* 1960, Jennifer Veronica Jill, da of S O Davis of Weymouth; 2 s (Sean, Dominic), 1 da (Jessica); *Career* actor and variously employed London and Paris 1947-51; BBC drama producer/dir 1954-63; freelance theatre, film and TV dir 1963-69; programme controller HTV Ltd 1969, asst md 1981, md 1987, ch exec HTV Gp plc 1988; dir: Bristol Hippodrome Tst, English Shakespeare Co; FRTS; *Recreations* travel, breeding Dexter cattle, swimming; *Clubs* Savile, Clifton (Bristol), Lotos (New York), Castel's (Paris); *Style*— Patrick Dromgoole, Esq; 38 Petersham Place, London SW7 51U (☎ 071 584 2237); 99 Baker Street, London W1M 2AJ (☎ 071 486 4311 ext 275, fax 071 935 6724; car ☎ 0836 217044, telex , 264357)

DRON, Melville James; s of James Tod Dron (d 1950), and Jean Paterson, *née* McIntyre; *b* 1 Dec 1934; *Educ* Hutchesons' Boys' GS Glasgow; *m* 5 April 1963, Hazel Mary, da of Thomas Evelyn Caldecott, of Malpas, Ches; 3 s (James Melville Thomas, Andrew Donald McIntyre, Angus Richard Tod); *Career* Nat Serv Coldstream Gds 1953-55; ptnr Peat Marwick McLintock 1969-; FCA, FCCA, ACMA; *Recreations* golf, gardening, piping; *Clubs* Caledonian; *Style*— Melville Dron, Esq; Backfield House, Wotton Rd, Iron Acton, Bristol BS17 1XD (☎ 045422 509); 40 Andrewes House, Barbican, London EC2Y 8AX (☎ 071 638 3144); Peat Marwick McLintock, 1 Puddle Dock, Blackfriars, London EC4V 3PD (☎ 071 236 8000, fax 071 248 6552, telex 8811541 PMMLO4 G)

DRONKE, Prof (Ernst) Peter Michael; s of AHR Dronke, and MM Dronke, *née* Kronfeld; *b* 30 May 1934; *Educ* Victoria Univ NZ (MA), Magdalen Coll Oxford (MA), Univ of Cambridge (MA); *m* 1960, Ursula Miriam, *née* Brown; 1 da; *Career* res fell Merton Coll Oxford 1958-61; Univ of Cambridge: lectr in medieval Latin 1961-79, fell Clare Hall 1964-, reader 1979-89, prof of medieval Latin lit 1989-; guest lectr Univ of Munich 1960, guest prof Centre d'Etudes Médiévales Poitiers 1969, Leverhulme fell 1973, WP Ker lectr Univ of Glasgow 1976, guest prof Univ Autónoma Barcelona 1977, visiting fell Humanities Res Centre Canberra 1978, visiting prof of medieval studies Westfield Coll 1981-86, Matthews lectr Birkbeck Coll 1983; co ed: Mittellateinisches Jahrbuch 1977-, Premio Internazionale Ascoli Piceno 1988; author of essays in learned jls and symposia; hon pres Int Courtly Literature Soc 1974, corresponding fell Real Academia de Buenas Letras 1976; FBA (1984); *Books* Medieval Latin and the Rise of the European Love-Lyric (2 volumes, 1965-66), The Medieval Lyric (1968), Poetic Individuality in the Middle Ages (1970), Fabula (1974), Abelard and Heloise in Medieval Testimonies (1976), Barbara et Antiquissima Carmina (with Ursula Dronke, 1977), Bernardus Silvestris Cosmographia (ed, 1978), Introduction to Francesco Colonna Hypnerotomachia (1981), Women Writers of the Middle Ages (1984), The Medieval Poet and his World (1984), Dante and Medieval Latin Traditions (1986), Introduction to Rosvita, Dialoghi Drammatici (1986), A History of Twelfth Century Western Philosophy (1988), Hermes and the Sibyls (1990); *Recreations* music, film, Brittany; *Style*— Prof Peter Dronke; 6 Parker Street, Cambridge (☎ 0223 359942)

DRUCKER, Dr Henry Matthew; s of Arthur Drucker (d 1980), and Frances, *née* Katz; *b* 29 April 1942; *Educ* Rutherford HS New Jersey USA, Allegheny Coll USA (BA), LSE (PhD); *m* 29 March 1975, Nancy Livia, da of Edwin Harold Newman, of NY; *Career* sr lectr in politics Univ of Edinburgh 1979-86 (lectr 1967-78); dir: Development Office Univ of Oxford 1987-, Campaign for Oxford 1988-; memb: Political Studies Assoc, Hansard Soc, Inst of Charity Fund-Raising Mangrs; *Style*— Dr Henry Drucker; University Offices, Wellington Square, Oxford OX1 (☎ 0865 270222, fax 0865 270225)

DRUMALBYN, Baroness; Rita Macpherson; *m* 1, Harry Edmiston (decd); m 2, 1985, as his 2 w, 1 and last Baron Drumalbyn, KBE, PC (d 1987); 2 step da (Hon Lady Weatherall, Hon Mrs Wilson, *qqv*); *Style*— The Rt Hon Lady Drumalbyn; 108 Montagu Mansions, London W1H 1LE

DRUMLANRIG, Viscount; Sholto Francis Guy Douglas; s and h of 12 Marquess of Queensberry; *b* 1 June 1967; *Style*— Viscount Drumlanrig

DRUMM, David Andrew Francis; s of Owen Eugene Drumm, and Kathleen Mary Drumm (d 1986); *b* 18 Feb 1949; *Educ* Univ of Sussex (BA); *m* 6 Sept 1975, Veronica Kaye, da of Arthur Aubrey; 1 s (Simon b 1980), 1 da (Jacqueline Jane b 1983); *Career* Lazard Brothers & Co Ltd 1971-78, Gulf International Bank Bahrain 1979-86, branch mangr Gulf International Bank London 1987-; *Recreations* tennis, photography; *Style*— David Drumm, Esq; Rays Court Hall, Friary Rd, South Ascot, Berks SL5 9HD (☎ 0344 26028); Gulf Int Bank, 2/6 Cannon St, London EC4M 6XP (☎ 071 248 6411, fax 071 248 6411 ext 281, telex 8812889)

DRUMM, Liam Joseph; s of Christopher Austin Drumm, of Belfast, N Ireland, and Josephine, *née* Ormsby; *b* 23 Aug 1951; *Educ* St Mary's GS Belfast N Ireland; *m* 29 Aug 1974, Kathleen, da of Thomas Rooney (d 1979), of Belfast; 1 s (Cathal Liam Austin), 1 da (Ciara Theresa Josephine); *Career* accountant, fin controller Elders Grain Europe; dir: Elders Grain Europe Ltd, Elders Malt Ltd; *Recreations* theatre, music, parachute jumping, mountaineering, golf; *Clubs* City and Counties, Peterborough, Rumpole's; *Style*— Liam Drumm, Esq; 6 Curlew Walk, Deeping St James, Peterborough (☎ 0778 346683); Peterscourt, City Road, Peterborough (☎ 0733 310880)

DRUMM, Rt Rev Walter Gregory; s of Owen Drumm, and Kathleen, *née* Garrett (d 1986); *b* 2 March 1940; *Educ* St Aloysius' Coll Highgate, Balliol Coll Oxford (MA), Beda Coll Rome; *Career* tutor 1962-66, ordained 1970, asst priest St Paul's Wood Green 1970-73, chaplain Univ of Oxford 1973-83, parish priest Our Lady of Victories' Church Kensington 1983-87, rector Beda Coll Rome 1987-, prelate of honour to HH The Pope; *Clubs* Oxford and Cambridge; *Style*— The Rt Rev Mgr Walter Drumm; Pontifical Beda College, Viale de San Paolo 18, 00146 Roma, Italy (☎ 396 556 1700)

DRUMMOND, David James; s of James Drummond, of Edinburgh, and Audrey Joan, *née* Morrison; *b* 4 Aug 1956; *Educ* George Watsons Coll Edinburgh, Edinburgh Univ (BMus), RNCM Manchester; *m* 25 June 1983 (m dis 1988), Jane Caroline, da of Derek Tregilges, of Perranporth, Cornwall; *Career* staff conductor and chorus master Stora Teatern Gothenburgh Sweden 1982-84 (conducted Katerina Ismailova, Turn of the Screw, Don Giovanni, Spöket Paå Canterville, Lo Sposo Senza Moglie), asst chorus master Eng Nat Opera 1984-88 (conducted: Die Fledermaus, Mikado, Magic Flute), chorus master Scottish Opera 1988- (conducted Street Scene); *Recreations* squash, golf, hill-walking, football, languages, travel; *Style*— David Drummond, Esq; 1 Archer Road, South Norwood, London SE25 4JN (☎ 081 656 8796), Scottish Opera, 39 Elmbank Crescent, Glasgow G2 4PT (☎ 041 3346722, 041 2484567)

DRUMMOND, Lady Elizabeth Helen; *née* Kennedy; only da of 7 Marquess of Ailsa, OBE, *qv*; *b* 23 Feb 1955; *m* 1976, Rev Norman Walker Drummond, MA, BD; 2 s (Andrew b 1977, Christian b 1986), 2 da (Margaret b 1980, Marie Clare b 1981); *Style*— Lady Elizabeth Drummond; Headmaster's House, Loretto, Musselburgh, Midlothian EH21 7RA

DRUMMOND, Hon James David; s and h of Viscount Strathallan; *b* 24 Oct 1965; *Style*— The Hon James Drummond

DRUMMOND, Hon James Reginald; yr s of 17 Earl of Perth, PC; *b* 28 July 1938; *Educ* Downside, Trinity Coll Cambridge; *m* 1, 24 July 1961 (m dis 1985), Marybelle, da of late Capt Charles Gordon, of Park Hill, Aberdeen; m 2, 25 May 1988, Ferelith Alison, da of Mark Palmer, of Stanners Hill House, Chobham, Surrey; *Style*— The Hon James Drummond; 76 Holland Park, London W11 3SL; Churchill House, Dinder, Wells, Somerset BA5 3RW

DRUMMOND, Hon John Humphrey Hugo; 3 and yst s of Capt Humphrey Drummond of Megginch, MC, and Lady Strange, *qqv*; *b* 26 June 1966; *Educ* Eton, St John's Coll Cambridge; *Style*— The Hon John Drummond; Megginch Castle, Errol, Perth PH2 7SW (☎ 08212 222); 160 Kennington Rd, London SE11 6QR (☎ 071 735 3681)

DRUMMOND, John Richard Gray; CBE (1990); s of late Capt A R G Drummond, by his w Esther (*née* Pickering), of Perth, W Australia; *b* 25 Nov 1934; *Educ* Canford, Trinity Coll Cambridge; *Career* joined BBC 1958; former asst head Music and Arts; dir Edinburgh Int Festival 1978-83; vice chm Br Arts Festival Assoc 1981; FRSA; *Style*— John Drummond, Esq, CBE; 61c Campden Hill Court, London W8 7HL (☎ 071 937 2257)

DRUMMOND, Maldwin Andrew Cyril; OBE (1990), JP (1963), DL (Hampshire 1976); s of Maj Cyril Augustus Drummond, JP, DL (d 1945), of Cadland House, and Mildred Joan, *née* Humphreys (d 1976); *b* 30 April 1932; *Educ* Eton, RAC Cirencester, Univ of Southampton; *m* 1, 1955 (m dis 1977), Susan, da of Sir Kenelm Cayley; 2 da (Frederica (Mrs Templer) b 1957, Annabella (Mrs Robinson) b 1959); m 2, 1 Jan 1978, Gillian Vera (Gilly), da of Gavin Clark, of Menton, S France; 1 s (Aldred b 1978); *Career* Nat Serv The Rifle Bde 1950-52, Capt Queen Victoria's Rifles TA 1952-65; farmer and owner Manor of Cadland; dir: Rothsay Seafoods 1968-, Ocean Sound Ltd 1985-, Southampton Harbour Bd and Br Tports Docks Bd 1965-75, Southern Water Authy 1983-86; chm: Bldg Ctee STS Sir Winston Churchill 1964-66, Sail Trg Assoc 1967-72, Warrior (formerly Ships) Reservation Tst 1979-, Maritime Tst 1980-89, Boat Ctee RNLI 1984-, New Forest 9th Centenary Tst 1987-, New Forest Ctee 1990-, Heritage Coast Forum 1988-; pres: Hampshire Field Club and Archaeological Soc, Shellfish Assoc of GB and NI 1987-; tstee: Mary Rose Tst 1976-, Royal Naval Museum 1986-; memb Ctee of Mgmnt RNLI 1971-; memb: New Forest DC 1957-65, Hampshire CC 1965-75; verderer of the New Forest 1961-90, countryside cmmr 1980-86, High Sheriff of Hampshire 1980-81; Freeman City of London 1986, memb Ct Worshipful Co of Fishmongers 1986; FRGS, FRSA; *Books* Conflicts in an Estuary (1973), Secrets of George Smith Fisherman (ed and illustrator, 1973), Tall Ships (1976), Salt-Water Palaces (1979), The Yachtsman's Naturalist (with Paul Rodhouse, 1980), The New Forest (with Philip Allison, 1980), The Riddle (1985); *Recreations* sailing; *Clubs* Royal Yacht Squadron, Royal Cruising, Whites, Pratts, Leander Rowing; *Style*— Maldwin Drummond, Esq, OBE, JP, DL; Cadland Hse, Fawley, Southampton (☎ 0703 891 543); Manor of Cadland, Cadland Hse, Fawley, Southampton SO4 1AA (☎ 0703 892 039); Wester Kames Castle, Isle of Bute (☎ 0700 3983)

DRUMMOND, Prof Michael Frank; s of Kenneth John Drummond (d 1973), and Ethel Irene, *née* Spencer; *b* 30 April 1948; *Educ* Atherstone GS, Univ of Birmingham (BSc), Univ of Birmingham (MCom), Univ of York (DPhil); *m* 8 June 1973, Margaret, da of James Brennan, of Tamworth, Staffs, 1 s (Thomas b 1980), 1 da (Kate b 1987); *Career* Univ of Birmingham: lectr 1978-84, sr lectr 1984-86, prof of health services management 1986-90; memb: North Warwickshire Health Authy 1982-90, Med Comm 1988-; *Books* Principles of Economic Appraisal in Health Care (1980), prof of economics Univ of York 1990; Studies in Economic Appraisal in Health Care (1981), Economic Appraisal of Health Technology in the European Community (1987), Methods for the Economic Evaluation of Health Care Programmes (1987); *Recreations* running, travel; *Style*— Prof Michael Drummond; Centre for Health Economics, University of York, Heslington, York YO1 5DD (☎ 0904 433709, fax 0904 433644)

DRUMMOND, Rev Norman Walker; s of Edwin Payne Drummond, of Renfrewshire (d 1971), and Jean Drummond, *née* Walker; *b* 1 April 1952; *Educ* Crawfordton House Dumfriesshire, Merchiston Castle Edinburgh, Fitzwilliam Coll Cambridge (MA), New Coll Edinburgh (BD); *m* 1976, Lady Elizabeth Helen Kennedy, da of 7 Marquess of Ailsa; 2 s (Andrew b 1977, Christian b 1986), 2 da (Margaret b 1980, Marie Clare b 1981); *Career* ordained as minister of the Church of Scot, cmmnd to serv as Chaplain to HM Servs Army 1976; chaplain: Depot Parachute Regt and Airborne Forces 1977-78, 1 Bn The Black Watch (Royal Highland Regt) 1978-82, Fettes Coll 1982-84, to Moderator of Gen Assembly of Church of Scot 1980; headmaster Loretto Sch 1984-; memb: Queens Body Guard for Scotland Royal Co of Archers, memb Ct Heriot Watt Univ; chm: Musselburgh and DC of Social Serv, Ronald Selby Wright Christian Leadership Tst; memb Scot Cncl Duke of Edinburgh award Scheme; *Books* The First 25 Years - the Official History of the Kirk Session of The Black Watch (Royal Highland Regiment); *Recreations* rugby football, cricket, golf, curling, traditional jazz, Isle of Skye; *Clubs* MCC, Free Foresters, New (Edinburgh), Hawks (Cambridge); *Style*— The Rev Norman Drummond; Headmaster's House, Loretto Sch, Musselburgh, East Lothian, Scotland

DRUMMOND, Rhona Jean; da of David John Drummond, of Crieff, Scotland, and Mary Lorna, *née* Miller; *b* 25 Sept 1953; *Educ* Regis Sch Staffordshire, Univ of Edinburgh (MA), Int House (TEFL, DipCam); *Career* child therapy offr Newcastle upon Tyne 1976-77; teacher: St Mary's Coll St Lucia West Indies 1977-79, EFL London 1979; classified field sales Express Newspapers London 1979-82; The Observer: display sales exec 1982-84, int sales exec 1984-85, newspaper advertisement mangr 1985-88, publisher Observer Communications 1988-; memb Int Press Inst 1988-; *Books* Alternative Scotland (asst ed, 1976); *Recreations* sailing, horse riding, skiing, tennis, painting; *Clubs* Antigua Yacht; *Style*— Ms Rhona Drummond; 231 Ladbroke Grove, London W10 6HG; The Observer Newspaper, Chelsea Bridge House, Queenstown Rd, London SW8 4NN (☎ 071 350 3232, fax 071 627 5570)

DRUMMOND, Robert Malcolm; s of Guy Malcolm Dixon Drummond, OBE, of Cheshire, and Daphne, *née* Flawn; *b* 3 June 1945; *Educ* Rugby, Univ of St Andrews (LLB), Manchester Business Sch (MBA); *m* 1970 (m dis), Brenda; 1 da (Alison b 1975); m 2, 1981, Lorraine, da of Thomas Kitchiner Aymes; *Career* regnl dir and asst gen mangr ICFC (later Investors In Indust 3i's) Leeds and London 1972-84, ptnr of Venture Capital Partnership Alta Berkeley Assocs 1984-85, md County Nat West Ventures Ltd (Ventures and Devpt Capital) 1985-89; vice chm Electra Kingsway Ltd 1989-90 (investmt mgmnt Venture Capital), non-exec dir Southnews plc (newspaper publisher) 1986, md Grosvenor Venture Managers Ltd 1990, dir Grosvenor Development Capital plc; FCA; *Recreations* golf, skiing; *Style*— Robert Drummond, Esq; 14 Connaught Square, London W2 2HG (☎ 071 724 2702); Grosvenor Venture Managment, 2-6 Bath Rd, Slough SL1 3RZ (☎ 0753 811812, fax 0753 811813)

DRUMMOND, Capt Spencer Heneage; DSC (1943); s of Algernon Cecil Heneage Drummond (d 1975), and Janetta, *née* Vandfleur (d 1958); *b* 2 June 1922; *Educ* RN Coll Dartmouth, Univ of Southampton (MPhil); *m* 17 Dec 1949, Patricia Keane, da of Col Michael Keane, OBE, of Ireland; 2 s (Crispin b 1955, Hereward b 1959), 3 da (Deirdre b 1953, Ianthe b 1960, Helena b 1963); *Career* WWII served RN Med; ret as Dep Chief of Allied Staff to NATO C in C with rank of Cdre; memb: RORC, Sail BSC Round World; *Recreations* yacht racing; *Clubs* Royal Ocean Racing; *Style*— Capt Spencer Drummond, DSC; Keepers Cottage, Petersfield, Hampshire

DRUMMOND-HAY, Lady Bettina Mary; *née* Lindsay; elder da of 29 Earl of Crawford and (12 of) Balcarres; *b* 26 June 1950; *Educ* Camden Sch for Girls, Goldsmith's Coll; *m* 1975, Peter Charles Drummond-Hay, s of John Hay-Drummond-Hay, gs of Sir Robert Drummond-Hay, CMG, who added the first 'Hay' to his name; 1 s (Thomas Auriol b 20 Nov 1989), 3 da; *Career* school teacher; *Style*— The Lady Bettina Drummond-Hay; Balcarres, Colinsburgh, Leven, Fife

DRUMMOND-HAY, Lady Margaret; *née* Douglas-Hamilton; 2 da of 13 Duke of Hamilton and (10 of) Brandon (1940); *b* 13 Oct 1907; *m* 1 Feb 1930, Maj James Drummond-Hay (d 1981); 2 s, 4 da; *Style*— The Lady Margaret Drummond-Hay; c/o Mrs R T Whiteley, Hall Farm, Evenley, Brackley, Northants NN13 5SH

DRUMMOND-MORAY OF ABERCAIRNY, William George Stirling Home; Laird of Abercairny from time immemorial, since the lands came to the Morays as dowry with a daughter of the Earls of Strathearn 'by the Indulgence of God' (who, alone among the Counts in Christendom, nominated their own bishops), successors to the ancient Kings of Strathearn; 2 (but eldest surviving) s of Maj James Drummond-Moray, twenty-first of Abercairny, and of Ardoch, Perthshire, JP, DL, by his w Jeanetta (twin da of Lt-Col Lord George Scott, OBE, JP, DL, 3 s of 6 Duke of Buccleuch & (8 of) Queensberry); *b* 22 Aug 1940; *Educ* Eton, RAC Cirencester; *m* 7 Jan 1969, (Angela) Jane, da of Lt-Cdr Michael Baring, RN (d 1954); 3 da (Anne b 1971, Frances b 1974, Georgia b 1979); *Career* estate mangr; *Recreations* shooting, polo; *Style*— William Drummond-Moray of Abercairny; Abercairny, Crieff, Perthshire (☎ Crieff 0764 3114)

DRUMMOND-MURRAY OF MASTRICK, Hon Mrs (Barbara Mary Hope); 4 and yst da of 2 Baron Rankeillour, GCIE, MC (d 1958); *b* 21 Feb 1930; *Educ* private; *m* 12 June 1954, (William Edward) Peter Louis Drummond-Murray of Mastrick, *qv*; 4 s, 1 da; *Style*— The Hon Mrs Drummond-Murray of Mastrick; 67 Dublin Street, Edinburgh, EH3 6NS (☎ 031 556 2913)

DRUMMOND-MURRAY OF MASTRICK, William Edward Peter Louis; s of Edward John Drummond-Murray of Mastrick (d 1976), and Eulalia Ildefonsa Wilhelmina Heaven (d 1988); *b* 24 Nov 1929; *Educ* Beaumont Coll; *m* 1954, Hon Barbara Mary, *qv*; 4 s, 1 da; *Career* dir Utd and Gen Tst and other cos; chief exec Hosp of St John and St Elizabeth London 1978-82, Slains Pursuivant of Arms to the Lord High Constable of Scotland the Earl of Erroll 1981-; Kt of Hon and Devotion SMOM 1971, Grand Cross of Obedience 1984, Chllr Br Assoc SMOM 1977-89, Delegate of Scotland 1989-; CStJ 1977, KStJ 1988; *Recreations* archaeology, genealogy, heraldry, baking, brewing, bookbinding; *Clubs* Beefsteak, Whites, New (Edinburgh), Puffin's (Edinburgh); *Style*— Peter Drummond-Murray of Mastrick; 67 Dublin St, Edinburgh, EH3 6NS (☎ 031 556 2913)

DRUMMOND OF MEGGINCH, Hon Catherine Star Violetta; da of Capt Humphrey Drummond of Megginch, MC, and Baroness Strange, *qqv*; *b* 15 Dec 1967; *Educ* Heathfield, Dundee Coll of Commerce; *Recreations* travel, photography, gardening; *Style*— The Hon Catherine Drummond of Megginch; Megginch Castle, Errol, Perthshire (☎ 082 12 222)

DRUMMOND OF MEGGINCH, Hon Charlotte Cherry; da of Capt Humphrey Drummond of Megginch, MC, and The Lady Strange; *b* 14 May 1955; *Educ* Heathfield; *Style*— The Hon Charlotte Drummond of Megginch; Tresco, 160 Kennington Rd, London SE11 (☎ 071 735 3681); 2500 'Q' St NW, Washington DC 20007, USA (☎ 202 342 5318)

DRUMMOND OF MEGGINCH, Capt Humphrey; MC (1945); formerly Humphrey ap Evans, changed name by decree of Court of Lord Lyon 1966; s of Maj James John Pugh Evans, MBE, MC (d 1974), of Lovesgrove, Aberystwyth; *b* 18 Sept 1922; *Educ* Eton, Trinity Coll Cambridge; *m* 2 June 1952, Cherry Drummond, Lady Strange (16th holder of the peerage); 3 s, 3 da; *Career* serv 1940-45 with 1 Mountain Regt; Indian Political Serv 1947; gen sec Cncl for Preservation of Rural Wales 1947-51, Welsh rep of Nat Tst 1949-54; Gold Staff Offr coronation of HM Queen Elizabeth II; author and magazine contributor; chm Soc of Authors (Scot) 1975-81; proprietor: The Historical Press, Scottish Salmon Fisheries; *Books* Our Man in Scotland, The Queen's Man, The King's Enemy, Falconry, Falconry For You, Falconry in the East; *Clubs* Garrick; *Style*— Capt Humphrey Drummond of Megginch, MC; Tresco, 160 Kennington Rd, London SE11 (☎ 071 735 3681); Megginch Castle, Errol, Perths PH2 7SE (☎ 08212 222)

DRUMMOND YOUNG, James Edward; QC (1988); s of Duncan Drummond Young, MBE, DL, of Edinburgh and Annette, *née* Mackay; *b* 17 Feb 1950; *Educ* John Watson's Sch Edinburgh, Sidney Sussex Coll Cambridge (BA), Harvard Law Sch (Joseph Hodges Choate Meml fell, LLM), Univ of Edinburgh (LLB); *Career* admitted to Faculty of Advocates 1976, standing jr counsel Bd of Inland Revenue 1986-88; *Books* The Law of Corporate Insolvency in Scotland (with JB St Clair, 1988), Stair Memorial Encyclopaedia of the Laws of Scotland (contrib, 1989); *Recreations* music, travel; *Clubs* New (Edinburgh); *Style*— James Drummond Young, Esq, QC; 14 Ainslie Place, Edinburgh EH3 6AS (☎ 031 225 7031); Advocates' Library, Parliament House, Edinburgh EH1 1RF (☎ 031 226 5071, fax 031 225 3642, telex 727856 FACADV 6)

DRURY, Rev John Henry; s of Henry Drury, and Barbara Drury; *b* 23 May 1936; *Educ* Bradfield, Trinity Hall Cambridge (MA), Westcott House Cambridge; *m* 1972, (Frances) Clare, da of Rev Prof Dennis Eric Nineham, of Bristol; 2 da; *Career* curate St John's Wood London 1963; chaplain: Downing Coll Cambridge 1966, and fell Exeter Coll Oxford 1969; resident canon Norwich Cathedral and examining chaplain to Bishop of Norwich 1973, vice dean Norwich 1978, lectr in religious studies Univ of Sussex 1979-82, dean of chapel King's Coll Cambridge 1983-; *Books* Tradition and Design in Luke's Gospel (1976), The Parables in the Gospels (1985), Critics of the Bible (1989), The Burning Bush (1990); *Recreations* music, drawing; *Style*— The Rev John Drury; King's Coll, Cambridge (☎ 0223 350411)

DRURY, John Kenneth; s of John Kenneth Drury, of Paisley and Elizabeth Laird McNeil, *née* Pattison; *b* 23 Jan 1947; *Educ* Paisley GS, Univ of Glasgow (MB ChB, PhD); *m* 16 July 1974, Gillian Ruth Alexandra, da of Dr Thomas Gilmore, of Paisley; 1 s (Colin b 1981), 1 da (Sarah b 1978); *Career* res fell Inst of Physiology Univ of Glasgow, conslt gen surgn with interest in peripheral vascular surgery Victor Infirmary Glasgow 1987-, hon clinical lectr Univ of Glasgow 1987-, examiner in fellowship RCS Glasgow, author of papers on gen and vascular surgery; memb: Ctee Paisley RNLI, Cncl Southern Med Soc; FRCS 1978; memb: Vascular Soc GB 1987, European Soc, Vascular Surgery; *Recreations* yachting, squash, golf, skiing; *Style*— John Drury, Esq; 17 Lanfine Rd, Paisley, Renfrewshire PA1 3NJ (☎ 041 8894512); Dept of Surgery, Victoria Infirmary, Langside, Glasgow G42 9TY (☎ 041 6494545)

DRURY, Martin Dru; s of Walter Neville Dru Drury, TD, of Little Brookstreet, Edenbridge, Kent, and Rae, *née* Sandiland; *b* 22 April 1938; *Educ* Rugby; *m* 5 Jan 1971, Elizabeth Caroline, da of The Hon Sir Maurice Bridgeman, KBE (d 1980), of The Glebe House, Selham, Sussex; 2 s (Matthew b 8 Aug 1972, Joseph b 18 June 1977), 1 da (Daisy b 6 Sept 1974); *Career* 2 Lt 3 The King's Own Hussars 1957, Lt The Queen's Own Hussars 1958, Capt Army Emergency Reserve 1966; broker at Lloyds 1959-65, assoc dir Mallett & Son (Antiques) Ltd 1965-73; The Nat Tst: historic bldgs rep and advsr on furniture 1973-81, historic bldgs sec 1981-; vice chm Attingham Summer Sch, memb Exec Ctee The Georgian Gp; dir: Landmark Trust, Arundel Castle Tst Ltd; Liveryman Worshipful Co of Goldsmiths; *Recreations* walking, travel, gardening; *Clubs* Brooks's, Pratt's; *Style*— Martin Drury, Esq; 3 Victoria Rise, London SW4 0PB (☎ 071 622 1411); 18 The Street, Stedham, Sussex; The National Trust, 36 Queen Anne's Gate, London SW1 (☎ 071 222 9251, telex 8950997 NTRUST G)

DRURY, Prof Sir (Victor William) Michael; OBE (1978); s of George Leslie Drury (d 1936), of Bromsgrove, and Trixie, *née* Maddox; *b* 5 Aug 1926; *Educ* Bromsgrove Sch, Univ of Birmingham (MB ChB, MRCS, LRCP); *m* 7 Oct 1950, Joan, da of Joseph Williamson, of Winsford, Cheshire; 3 s (Mark b 9 May 1952, Simon b 17 March 1958, James b 27 July 1960), 1 da (Linda b 19 July 1954); *Career* Capt (surgical specialist) RAMC 1951-53, civilian consIt to Army 1985-; travelling fell Nuffield 1965, GP Bromsgrove 1953-, sr clinical tutor Dept of Med Univ of Birmingham 1973-80 (prof gen practice 1980), visiting prof Canterbury NZ 1984, Jeffcote professorship Westminster and Charing Cross 1989-; memb: GMC 1984-, SCOPME 1989-; pres RCGP, hon memb Br Paediatric Assoc 1989; FRCGP 1970, FRCP 1988, FRACGP 1988; kt 1989; *Books* Medical Secretary's Handbook (5 edn, 1986), Introduction to General Practice (1979), Treatment A Handbook of Drug Therapy (43 instalments 1978-91), The Receptionist (1987), Treatment & Prognosis (1989), The New Practice Manager (1990); *Recreations* gardening, bridge, talking; *Style*— Prof Sir Michael Drury, OBE; Rossall Cottage, Church Hill, Belbroughton, nr Stourbridge, W Mids DY9 ODT (☎ 0562 730229); The Medical Sch, University of Birmingham, Birmingham (☎ 021 414 3758)

DRURY, Dr Paul Leslie; s of Maj Frederick Leslie Drury, of Danbury, Essex, and Joan Susan; *b* 11 June 1947; *Educ* St Albans Sch, Queens' College Cambridge (MA, MB BChir); *m* 1980, Dr Susan Ruth Rudge; *Career* lectr Bart's 1978-86, conslt physician 1986-; pubns in endocrinology and diabetes; sec Med and Scientific Section Br Diabetic Assoc; MRCP 1975; *Books* Diabetes and Its Management (with Watkins and Taylor, 4 edn 1990); *Recreations* gardening, running; *Style*— Dr Paul Drury; King's College Hospital, London, SE5 9RS (☎ 071 326 3241); Greenwich District Hospital, London SE10 9HE (☎ 081 858 8141, fax 081 293 4030)

DRURY, Ruth Elizabeth; da of Lt-Col George Richard Johnston, RA (d 1974), of Wood Corner, Lank Hills Rd, Winchester, Hants, and Unity Ussher, *née* Quicke (d 1980); *b* 19 June 1927; *Educ* privately; *m* 11 Dec 1948, Denis Gordon de Courcy Drury, s of Gordon de Courcy Drury, MC (d 1947), of Kenya and London; 2 s (Robert b 20 Feb 1950, Gordon b 13 Nov 1951), 2 da (Caroline b 12 March 1954, Rosemary b 7 March 1957); *Career* fashion photography; memb: Central London Branch Parkinson's Disease Soc, Cncl White Lion Soc Royal Coll of Arms, Exec Ctee Soc for Individual Freedom, Ctee Poppy Ball in Aid of Royal Br Legion, Guild of Freemen City of London, Royal Society of St George City of London Branch, United Wards Club City of London, City of London Cripplegate Ward Club, Royal Henley Regatta, Lady Taveners; Freeman City of London; *Recreations* Genealogy; *Clubs* City Livery, St Stephens Constitutional; *Style*— Mrs Denis Drury; 8 Evelyn Mansions, Carlisle Place, Westminster, London SW1P 1NH (☎ 071 828 0665)

DRURY, Stephen Patrick; s of Patrick Keith Drury, of The Spinney, Leigh Place, Cobham, Surrey, and Anne Rosemary, *née* Major-Lucas; *b* 20 May 1954; *Educ* Charterhouse, Oriel Coll Oxford (MA); *m* 25 June 1983, Deborah Ann, da of late

Wilfred McBrien Swain, OBE; 1 s (Patrick b 1984), 1 da (Frances b 1987); *Career* called to the Bar 1977, admitted slr 1980, admitted slr Hong Kong 1984, ptnr Holman Fenwick & Willan 1985- (joined 1978); memb Cncl: Amateur Rowing Assoc 1980-84, Hong Kong Amateur Rowing Assoc 1984-87; Freeman City of London, Liveryman Worshipful Co of Merchant Taylors 1988; *Books* Arrest of Ships (vol 6, 1987); *Recreations* rowing, golf; *Clubs* Kingston Rowing, Royal Hong Kong Yacht, Effingham Golf, Lansdowne; *Style—* Stephen Drury, Esq; Holman Fenwick & Willan, Marlow Hse, Lloyds Ave, London EC3N 3AL (☎ 071 488 2300, fax 071 481 0584, telex 8812247)

DRURY-LOWE, Capt Patrick John Boteler; s of Lt-Col John Drury Boteler Packe-Drury-Lowe (d 1960), of Prestwold Hall, Loughborough, Leicestershire, and Rosemary Marguerite, *née* Hope-Vere (d 1990); *b* 9 Aug 1931; *Educ* Eton; *m* 1, 12 Oct 1959 (m dis 1968), Belinda Mary, da of Sir Hardman A Mort Earle Bt (d 1979), of Kensington Sq, London; 2 da (Lucy b 1961, Candida b 1963); m 2, 2 Nov 1968 (m dis 1972), Mrs Pamela Estelle Cayzer; *Career* serv Scots Guard 1949-58, ADC to Govr S Australia 1955-58; cmmr St John Ambulance Bde Derbyshire 1962-71, cdr and cmmr St John Ambulance Bde Derbyshire 1971-72, vice pres and vice chm St John Cncl of Derbyshire; county cncllr Derbyshire 1961-64; jt master Meynell and S Staffs Hunt 1970-75; KStJ; *Recreations* shooting; *Clubs* White's, Pratt's; *Style—* Capt Patrick Drury-Lowe; Locko Park, Derby, DE2 7BW (☎ 0322 673 517); Estate Office, Locko Park, Derby, DE2 7BW (☎ 0332 662 785)

DRYBURGH, Dr Frances Joan; da of Thomas Stewart Neilson (d 1980), of Largs, Scot, and Alice Smith, *née* Nicol; *b* 16 Nov 1938; *Educ* Stirling HS, Univ of Glasgow (BSc, MB ChB); *m* 2 July 1965, Eric Campbell Dryburgh, s of James Dryburgh (d 1987); 2 s (Keith b 1967 d 1983, Gordon b 1969); *Career* conslt clinical biochemist Glasgow Royal Infirmary 1981- (sr registr 1973-80); former pres Scot Western Assoc Med Womens Fedn, memb Soroptimist Int GB and Ireland, memb Nat Assoc of Clinical Biochemists; FRCP (Glasgow) 1990; *Style—* Dr Frances Dryburgh; 19 Quadrant Rd, Newlands, Glasgow G43 2QP (☎ 041 637 3509); Department of Pathological Biochemistry, Royal Infirmary, Castle St, Glasgow (☎ 041 552 3535, fax 041 553 1703, telex 779234 HLAGLA)

DRYDEN, Sir John Stephen Gyles; 11 Bt (GB 1733) of Ambrosden, Oxfordshire and 8 Bt (GB 1795) of Canons-Ashby, Northamptonshire; s of Sir Noel Percy Hugh Dryden, 10 Bt (d 1970; 6 in descent from Sir Erasmus Dryden, 6 Bt, bro of the poet John Dryden); *b* 26 Sept 1943; *Educ* Oratory Sch; *m* 1970, Diana Constance, da of Cyril Tomlinson, of New Zealand; 1 s, 1 da; *Heir* s, John Frederick Simon Dryden b 26 May 1976; *Style—* Sir John Dryden, Bt; Spinners, Fairwarp, Uckfield, Sussex

DRYDEN, Rosamund, Lady; Rosamund Mary; *née* Scrope; eldest da of Stephen Francis Eustace Scrope (d 1936), and Ethelburga Mary Magdalen Pega, yst da of Edmund Waterton, JP, DL, of Deeping Waterton, Lincs, Privy Chamberlain to HH Pope Pius IX; *b* 13 July 1915; *m* 22 Aug 1941, Sir Noel Percy Hugh Dryden, 10 Bt (d 1970); 1 s (Sir John Dryden, 11 and present Bt); *Style—* Rosamund, Lady Dryden; Spinners Cottage, Fairward, Uckfield, E Sussex

DRYHURST, Michael John; s of Edward Dryhurst, 0-9, Northwood Lane, Highgate, London, and Lilian Mae, *née* Roberts (d 1956); *b* 22 March 1938; *Educ* Brighton Coll; *m* 2 Nov 1975, Anna, da of Thomas Manscier (d 1940); 3 da (Lorraine Horder, Deborah Cottrell, Samantha Lester); *Career* camera asst Pinewood Studios 1955-60; asst dir: Aspect Prodns Ltd (tv commercials) 1960-64, Shepperton Studios (over 40 films) 1964-73; moved to Hollywood 1973, prodn assoc The Stone Killer for Dino de Laurentiis, assoc (line) prodr The Terminal Man for Warner Bros; recent films incl: Excalibur, Amityrille II, Superman III, Never say Never Again, The Emerald Forest, Harem (mini-series), Hope and Glory (5 Oscar Nominations 1988); completed screenplay Redmayne West 1988; memb: BFI, ACTT; *Books* London Bus and Tram Album (1963, 67, 79), The London Trolleybus (1987); *Recreations* reading, cinema, photography, music, driving old double decker buses; *Clubs* Groucho; *Style—* Michael Dryhurst, Esq; Orchard Bay House, St Lawrence, Isle of Wight PO38 1NU (☎ 0983 852 038); 502 San Vincente Boulevard £202, Santa Monica, CA 90402, USA (☎ 010 1 213 395 0462); Michael Dryhurst Productions Ltd, 9056 Santa Monica Boulevard, Suite 307, Los Angeles, California 90069, USA

DRYLAND, Michael Hubert; s of Maj Hubert Dryland, MBE, and Eva May, *née* Farrant, JP; *b* 24 Jan 1927; *Educ* Worksop Coll Notts, Exeter Coll Oxford (MA); *m* 17 April 1954, Wendy, da of Neville Gilbert Sparkes (d 1988); 2 s (Timothy Michael b 31 Aug 1956, Jonathan Charles b 28 Sept 1959); *Career* RN 1945-48; admitted slr, conslt Ware & Peters of York, chm Yorkshire Rent Assessment Panels and Rent Tbnls; former Master Worshipful Co of Merchant Taylors (York); memb Law Soc 1952; *Recreations* music, tennis, walking; *Style—* Michael Dryland, Esq; Linden Cottage, Huntington, York

DRYSDALE, Andrew Watt; s of Sir Matthew Drysdale (d 1963), of 46 Onslow Square, London SW3, and Nesta, *née* Lewis (d 1964); *b* 15 Feb 1932; *Educ* Eton, Magdalene Coll Cambridge (LLB); *m* 3 Jan 1956, Merida, da of Maj-Gen Sir Julian Gascoigne, KCMG, KCVO, CB, DSO; 3 da (Laura b 28 April 1958, Helena b 6 May 1960, Alexandra b 26 Sept 1962); *Career* Nat Serv 2 Lt 60 Rifles 1950-52, TA Queens Westminster Rifles, Capt Queens Royal Rifles, ret 1962; called to the Bar Lincolns Inn, underwriter Lloyds 1956-; jt master Surrey Union Hunt; memb Worshipful Co of Merchant Taylors; *Recreations* hunting, fishing, sailing; *Clubs* Boodles, City of London; *Style—* Andrew Drysdale, Esq; Ferriers Grange, Hookwood, Horley, Surrey (☎ 0293 783 218); Andrew Drysdale Underwriting Ltd, Jamacia Bldgs, St Michaels Alley, London EC3 (☎ 071 626 2324)

DRYSDALE, Neil; s of Stuart Drysdale, of Crieff, and Sigrid Drysdale, *née* Waldmann; *b* 4 Sept 1955; *Educ* Morrison's Acad Crieff, Aberdeen Univ (LLB); *m* 28 Feb 1980, Miriam Clare, da of Rev James Ekron Little, of Perthshire; 2 s (Anthony Lewis b 1980, Mark b 1983); *Career* ptnr Drysdale Mickel & Anderson W S 1979-; dir: Grampian Light Industries Ltd 1980, Crieff Visitors Centre Ltd 1985, Perthshire Paperweights Ltd 1986, A W Buchan & Co Ltd 1988; *Recreations* tennis, golf, gardening; *Style—* Neil Drysdale, Esq; Newmilne, Fowlis Wester, by Crieff, Perthshire (☎ 0764 83 362, fax 0764 2903, car 0860 410 830)

DRYSDALE WILSON, John Veitch; s of Alexander Drysdale Wilson (d 1949), and Winifred Rose, *née* Frazier (d 1972); *b* 8 April 1929; *Educ* Solihull Sch, Guildford Tech Coll; *m* 27 March 1954, Joan Lily, da of John and Lily Cooke, of Selsey, Sussex; 1 s (Alexander b 30 June 1958), 1 da (Jane b 7 July 1962); *Career* Nat Serv Capt on staff of CREME 6 Armd Div; Dennis Bros Ltd Guildford: apprentice engr 1946-50, MIRA res trainee 1949-50, jr designer 1950-51; mgmnt trainee BET Fedn Ltd 1953-55; Esso Petroleum Co Ltd: tech sales engr 1955-59, head of Mechanical Laboratories 1959-66; Edwin Cooper Ltd (prev Burmah Oil Trading Ltd, formerly Castrol Ltd) chief engr R & D 1966-77; Inst Mechanical Engrs: projects and res offr 1977-79, dep sec 1979-90; dir Mechanical Engrg Pubns Ltd 1979-90, dir Professional Engrs Insur Bureau Ltd 1989-90; author of numerous papers on engine lubrication; Freeman City of London; Liveryman: Worshipful Co of Engrs, Worshipful Co of Arbitrators; CEng, FIMechE, FCIArb; *Recreations* travel; *Clubs* East India, Caravan; *Style—* John Drysdale Wilson, Esq

DU BREUIL, Lady Joanna Edwina Doreen; *née* Knatchbull; elder da of 7 Baron Brabourne and Countess Mountbatten of Burma, *qqv*; *b* 5 March 1955; *Educ* Atlantic Coll, Univ of Kent, and Columbia Univ USA; *m* 3 Nov 1984, Baron Hubert Henry François du Breuil, yr s of Baron and Baronne du Breuil of Paris; 1 da (Eleuthera b 1986); *Style—* Lady Joanna du Breuil; 16 Bishop's Rd, London SW6 (☎ 071 385 3684)

DU CANE, John Peter; OBE (1964); 4 s of Charles Henry Copley Du Cane (d 1938), late of Braxted Park, Essex, and his 2 wife Mathilde (d 1961), da of Henri Allain, of Dinard, France; *b* 16 April 1921; *Educ* Canford; *m* 12 Nov 1945, Patricia Wallace, da of James Desmond, of Townsville, Qld, Aust; 2 s; *Career* served WW II, RN Air Arm; chm: Selection Tst Ltd 1978-81 (dir 1966-81, md 1975-81), Seltrust Hldgs (Aust) 1978-81, Selco Mining Corp (Canada) 1978-81, Consolidated African Selection Tst 1978-81; dir: Amax Inc 1966-, BP Int 1980-81 (chief exec BP Minerals Int 1980-81), Aust Consolidated Minerals 1981-85 (dep chm 1983-85), Ultramar plc 1983-87; FRSA; *Recreations* sailing, fishing, photography; *Clubs* Royal Naval Sailing Assoc, The Mining Club (New York); *Style—* John Du Cane Esq, OBE; Castel Du Prieure, 8 Avenue De Bizeux, 35801 Dinard, France

DU CANN, Charlotte Jane Lott; da of Richard Dillon Lott Du Cann, QC, and Charlotte Mary *née* Sawtell; *b* 20 June 1956; *Educ* Felixstowe Coll, Birmingham Univ (BA); *Career* shopping ed Vogue 1979-81; freelance writer 1981-: The Observer, Sunday Express mag, Time Out, Harpers & Queen; features writer The World of Interiors 1984, style ed The Magazine 1984-85, shopping and beauty ed Tatler 1986-87, contributing ed Elle 1987-88, fashion ed Independent 1988-90; currently writing for: Elle, Sunday Times, The Guardian, New Statesman, Society; *Books* Offal and The New Brutalism (1984), Vogue Modern Style (1988); *Recreations* poetry and cooking; *Style—* Ms Charlotte Du Cann; 223 Westbourne Park Rd, London W11 (☎ 071 243 0121)

DU CANN, Rt Hon Sir Edward Dillon Lott; KBE (1985), PC (1964); er s of Charles Garfield Lott du Cann (d 1983); er bro of Richard du Cann, QC, *qv*; *b* 28 May 1924; *Educ* Colet Court, Woodbridge Sch, St John's Coll Oxford; *m* 1962 (m dis 1990), Sally Innes, da of James Henry Murchie (d 1967), of Ainways, Caldie, Cheshire; 1 s, 2 da; *Career* Parly candidate (C): W Walthamstow 1951, Barrow in Furness 1955; MP (C) Taunton Div of Somerset Feb 1956-87, econ sec Treasy 1962-63, min of state BOT 1963-64; dir Bow Group Publications 1979-84; memb Select Ctee: House of Lords Reform 1962, Privilege 1972-87; chm Select Ctee: Pub Expenditure 1971-73, Pub Accounts 1974-79, Treasy and Civil Serv Affrs 1979-83; chm: 1922 Ctee 1972-84, Liaison Ctee Select Ctee 1974-83; vice chm Br American Parly Gp 1978-81, chm all pty Maritime Affrs Gp 1984-87, fndr chm Pub Accounts Cmmn 1984-87, pres Cons Parly EC Reform Gp 1985-87; former chm: Cons Pty Orgn, Burke Club; former memb Lord Chllr's Advsy Ctee Pub Records; former jt sec: UN Parly Gp, Cons Parly Fin Gp; fndr Unicorn Group Unit Trusts 1957; chm: Unicorn Gp 1957-62 and Unicorn 1957-, Assoc Unit Tst Mangrs 1961, Keyser Ullman 1972-75, Cannon Assurance 1972-80, Lonrho plc 1984- (dir 1972-); dep chm Family Planning Int Ctee, vice chm Wider Share Ownership Ctee 1970-; pres: Anglo-Polish Cons Soc 1972-74, Nat Union Cons Unionist Assocs 1981-82; vice pres Br Insur Brokers 1978-, govr Hatfield Coll Univ of Durham 1988; visiting fell Univ of Lancaster Business Sch 1970-82; Hon Col 155 Wessex Regt RCT (Vols) 1972-82, retains hon rank of Col, hon life memb Inst of RCT 1983; Freeman Taunton Deane Borough 1977; *Clubs* Carlton, Pratt's, Royal Thames Yacht, House of Commons Yacht (Cdre 1962, Adm 1974), Royal Western Yacht Club of England, Somerset Co; *Style—* Rt Hon Sir Edward du Cann, KBE; 9 Tufton Court, Tufton St, London SW1 (☎ 071 222 1922); Lonrho plc, Cheapside House, London EC2V 6BL (☎ 071 606 9898)

DU CANN, Lady; Jenifer Patricia Evelyn; da of Evelyn King, Embley Manor, Romsey, Hants, and Hermoine, *née* Crutchley; *b* 5 May 1945; *Educ* Fritham House, Queens Sec Coll; *m* 30 July 1966, Sir Robert Cooke (d 1987), s of Robert Victor Cooke (d 1979), of Bristol; 1 s (Patrick b 1967), 1 da (Louise b 1970); m 2, 25 May 1990, Sir Edward Du Cann; *Career* interior decorator 1981-87, owner of Athelhampton historic house and gdns (open to public); chm Historic Houses Assoc Wessex, memb Dorset and Somerset Theatre Co; *Books* Athelhampton Guide Book (1989); *Recreations* reading, walking, music; *Style—* Lady Du Cann; Athelhampton, Dorchester, Dorset DT2 7LG (☎ 0305 848 363)

DU CANN, Richard Dillon Lott; QC (1975); yr s of Charles du Cann (d 1983), and bro of Edward du Cann, *qv*; *b* 27 Jan 1929; *Educ* Steyning GS, Clare Coll Cambridge; *m* 1955, Charlotte Mary Sawtell; 2 s, 2 da; *Career* barrister Gray's Inn 1953 (bencher 1980), treasury counsel Inner London QS 1966-70, treasury counsel Centl Criminal Court 1970-75, chm Criminal Bar Assoc 1977-80, chm Bar of England and Wales 1980/81, recorder S E Circuit 1982-; *Style—* Richard du Cann Esq, QC; 29 Newton Rd, London W2 (☎ 071 229 3859)

DU CROS, Sir Claude Philip Arthur Mallet; 3 Bt (UK 1916) of Canons, Middx; s of Sir Philip Harvey du Cros, 2nd Bt (d 1975); *b* 22 Dec 1922; *m* 1, 1953 (m dis 1974), Mrs Christine Nancy Tordoff (d 1988), da of F E Bennett; 1 s; m 2, 1974, Margaret Roy, da of late Roland James Frater; *Heir* s, Julian Claude Arthur Mallet du Cros; *Career* farmer; *Style—* Sir Claude du Cros, Bt; Longmeadow, Ballaugh, Glen, Ramsey, Isle of Man

DU CROS, Julian Claude Arthur Mallet; s and h of Sir Claude Mallet, 3 Bt; *b* 23 April 1955; *Educ* Eton; *m* 1984, Patricia M, o da of Gerald A Wyatt, of Littlefield School, Liphook, Hants; 1 s (Alexander Julian Mallet b 25 Aug 1990), 1 da (Henrietta Mary b 1988); *Style—* Julian du Cros Esq

DU CROS, Rosemary, Lady; Rosemary Theresa; MBE (1945); only da of Sir John David Rees, 1 Bt, KCIE, CVO, MP (d 1922); *b* 23 Sept 1901; *m* 3 Nov 1950, as his 2 w, Capt Sir Philip Harvey du Cros, 2 Bt (d 1975); *Career* Capt ATA; dame pres Cons Assoc (Torrington Parly constituent), patron Cons Assoc (Torridge and W Devon Parly constituent); *Books* ATA Girl, Memoirs of a Wartime Ferry Pilot, contributions to The Aeroplane and Flight; *Clubs* Naval & Military; *Style—* Rosemary, Lady du Cros, MBE; Bocombe, Parkham, Bideford, N Devon

DU-FEU, Vivian John; s of Colin William Percy Du-Feu, of 57 Pullman Drive, Bargate Wood, Godalming, Surrey, and Jean Betty, *née* Borne; *b* 17 March 1954; *Educ* Priory Secdy Boys Sch Newport IOW, Guildford Co Tech Coll (OND), Univ Coll of Cardiff (LLB); *m* 1 Oct 1977, Lynda Barbara, da of Eric William Wren, of 1 Hayley Close, Hythe, Southampton SO4 6RT; *Career* admitted slr 1979; ptnr John Loosemoore & Co 1981, pt/t lectr in labour law Univ Coll Cardiff 1983-86, ptnr Phillips & Buck 1984- (asst slr 1983-84); mmeb Law Soc, MIPM 1988; *Books* Conduct of Proceedings Before Industrial Tribunals (1988); *Recreations* music, squash; *Style—* Vivian Du-Feu, Esq; Philips & Buck Solicitors, Fitzalan House, Fitzalan Rd, Cardiff CF2 1XZ (☎ 0222 471147, fax 0222 464347, telex 497625, car 0860 540004)

DU PARCQ, Hon John Renouf; s of Baron du Parcq (Life Peer, d 1949); *b* 9 June 1917; *Educ* Rugby, Exeter Coll Oxford (MA); *m* 16 Nov 1940, Elizabeth, da of Evan Skull Poole; 1 s (Richard b 1943), 1 da (Elizabeth b 1947); *Career* chartered electrical engr, ret 1972; MIEE; *Recreations* joinery; *Style—* The Hon John du Parcq; 10 Anchor Quay, Norwich NR3 3PR (☎ 0603 667782)

DU PRÉ, Ian Alastair; s of Gareth Kirkham du Pré, of Jersey, CI, and Elisabeth Sheila Mary, *née* Dodd; *b* 30 Oct 1945; *Educ* Sherborne; *m* 5 Dec 1981, Sabine, da of Guy de Brabandère; 1 da (Pascale b 5 March 1983); *Career* articled clerk Ernst &

Young 1964-69, accountant Lippincott & Margulies 1969-70, dir Douglas Llambias Associates 1970-77, ptnr Coopers & Lybrand Deloitte 1977-; FCA (ACA 1969); *Recreations* sport; *Clubs* MCC; *Style*— Ian du Pré, Esq; Coopers & Lybrand Deloitte, Plumtree Court, London EC4A 4HT (☎ 071 583 5000, fax 071 822 4652)

DU PREEZ, Hon Mrs (Carina Gillian); *née* Hacking; da of 2 Baron Hacking (d 1971); *b* 28 May 1956; *Educ* Benenden Sch; *m* 1981, Jac Jacobus du Preez; *Recreations* swimming, tennis, walking; *Style*— The Hon Mrs du Preez; 8 Winters Wynd, Newlands 7700, Cape Province, S Africa (☎ 010 27 21 619324)

DU SAUTOY, Peter Francis; CBE (1971, OBE 1964); s of Col E F du Sautoy, OBE, TD, DL (d 1964), and Mabel, *née* Howse (d 1973), descended from Pierre François du Sautoy, a French officer (a supporter of the Young Pretender) who while a POW on parole in England married Mary Abbot in 1758 and founded the English branch of the family; *b* 19 Feb 1912; *Educ* Uppingham, Wadham Coll Oxford (MA); *m* 1937, Phyllis Mary (Mollie), da of Sir Francis Floud, KCB, KCSI, KCMG (d 1965); 2 s (Bernard, Stephen); *Career* asst educn offr City of Oxford 1937-40, served with RAF 1940-45 (Sqdn Ldr, Air Miny); chm: Faber and Faber Ltd 1971-77 (dir 1946-77), Faber Music Ltd 1971-77 (dir 1965-77); memb Cncl Aldeburgh Festival Fndn 1976-87 (dep chm 1982-87); pres Publishers Assoc 1967-69; *Clubs* Garrick; *Style*— Peter du Sautoy Esq, CBE; 31 Lee Rd, Aldeburgh, Suffolk IP15 5EY (☎ 0728 452838)

DU VIVIER, Richard Adolphe Charles; CBE (1973, MBE 1945); s of James du Vivier, of Belgium; *b* 27 Dec 1911; *Educ* Malvern, King's Coll Cambridge; *m* 1936, Margaret, da of Sir Robert Aske, 1 Bt; 2 s, 2 da; *Career* Maj WW II (served N Africa, Italy, NW Europe); ret schoolmaster, Br Cncl Rep Uruguay & Mexico 1951-55 & 1970-73; *Recreations* tennis, golf; *Clubs* Hurlingham, Sudbury Golf; *Style*— Richard du Vivier Esq, CBE; 45 Chatsworth Rd, London W5

DUBOWITZ, Prof Victor; s of Charley Dubowitz, and Olga, *née* Schattel; *b* 6 Aug 1931; *Educ* Beaufort W Central HS S Africa, Univ of Cape Town (BSc, MB ChB, MD), Univ of Sheffield (PhD); *m* 10 July 1960, Lilly Magdalena Suzanne, *née* Sebok; 4 s (David b 1963, Michael b 1964, Gerald b 1965, Daniel b 1969); *Career* res assoc histochemistry Royal Postgrad Med Sch 1958-60, clinical asst Queen Mary's Hosp for Children Carshalton 1958-60, lectr clinical pathology Nat Hosp for Nervous Diseases 1960-61, lectr child health Univ of Sheffield 1961-65 (sr lectr 1965-67), reader child health and developmental neurology Univ of Sheffield 1967-72, prof of paediatrics Univ of London 1972-, hon consIt paediatrician Hammersmith Hosp 1972-, dir Jerry Lewis Muscle Res Centre 1972-; FRCP 1972; Cdr Order Constantine the Great 1980, Arvo Ylppo Gold Medal Finland 1982; *Books* Developing and Diseased Muscle A Histochemical Study (1968), The Floppy Infant (2nd edn, 1980), Muscle Biopsy: A Modern Approach (2nd edn, 1985), Gestational Age of the Newborn: A Clinical Manual (1977), Muscle Disorders in Childhood (1978), Neurological Assessment of the Preterm and Full-term Infant (1981), A Colour Atlas and Muscle Disorders in Childhood (1989); *Recreations* sculpting, hiking; *Style*— Prof Victor Dubowitz; Dept of Paediatrics, Royal Postgrad Med Sch, Ducane Rd, London W12 (☎ 081 740 3295)

DUBRAS, Bernard Louis; s of Leon Dubras, and Binda Blampied; *b* 10 Jan 1926; *Educ* De La Salle Coll Jersey; *m* 19 Sept 1957, Molly, da of Samuel James Baughen; 2 da (Louise Adele b 8 Dec 1960, Charlotte Mary b 29 Feb 1964); *Career* Lloyds Bank plc 1940-47, CH Dubras Ltd 1947-52, chm Dubras Holdings Ltd, md Chandis Ltd; non-exec dir: Jersey Electricity Co Ltd, S G Warburg (Jersey) Ltd; dir CH Dubras Ltd, md St John's Pharmacy Ltd; former chm Jersey Cheshire Home Fndn, Procureur du Bien Public (tstee) Municipality of St Helier, chm Care Ctee Parish of St Helier, memb and former pres Jersey Circle Catenian Assoc; former pres: Rotary Club of Jersey, Jersey C of C and Indust; former chm: Jersey Cncl for Safety and Health at Work, Advsy Cncl BBC local radio; former memb Cncl Jersey Milk Mktg Bd; FIOD; *Recreations* boating, gardening; *Style*— Bernard Dubras, Esq; Clos Des Chênes, Route De La Vallee, St Peter, Jersey (☎ 0534 81 871); 5 Great Union Rd, St Helier, Jersey (☎ 0534 36 401, fax 0534 68 442)

DUCAT-AMOS, Air Cmdt Barbara Mary; CB (1974), RRC (1971); da of Capt George William Ducat-Amos (d 1942), master mariner, and Mary, *née* Cuthbert (d 1974); *b* 9 Feb 1921; *Educ* The Abbey Sch Reading, Nightingale Training Sch, St Thomas's; *Career* trained SRN and CMB (pt 1) St Thomas's Hosp, dep matron RAF Hosp Nocton Hall 1967-68, sr matron RAF Hosp Changi Singapore 1968-70, princ matron MOD (RAF) 1970-72 (Queens Hon Nursing Sister 1972-78), matron-in-chief Princess Mary's RAF Nursing Serv and dir RAF Nursing Servs 1972-78; nursing offr (sister) Cable and Wireless plc 1978-85; nat chm Girls Venture Corps 1982-; CStJ 1975; *Recreations* music, theatre, travel; *Clubs* RAF; *Style*— Air Cmdt Barbara Ducat-Amos, CB, RRC; c/o Barclays Bank, Wimbledon Common, Wimbledon High St, London SW19

DUCE, Edward Harold; s of Nathan Duce (d 1960), and Ellen, *née* Picton; *b* 14 April 1911; *Educ* Reading Sch; *m* 25 Aug 1973, Sheila Grace Ellen, da of Arthur Edward Paine (d 1986); *Career* RNVR 1943-46, Lt (S) 1944; admitted slr 1936; ptnr: Ratcliffe & Duce Reading 1940-57, Ratcliffe Duce & Gammer 1957-76; pres: Berks Bucks & Oxon Incorp Law Soc 1960-61 (sec 1949-75), Mental Health Review Tbnls 1960-73; first chm Legal Aid Area Ctee (S Area) 1950-53; sec: Southern Area Assoc of Law Socs 1950-75, Jt Ctee with the Bar 1970-75; chm Assoc Prov Law Socs; memb Reading C of C; treas: Maidenhead Civic Soc, Thames Reach Residents Assoc; memb: Berks Playing Fields Assoc, Law Soc 1936-; Freeman: City of London 1966, Worshipful Co of Upholders 1966; *Books* History of Berks Bucks & Oxon Law Society (1989); *Recreations* music, model railway; *Style*— Harold Duce, Esq; The Lodge, 2(B) College Avenue, Maidenhead, Berks SL6 6AJ; Eastgate House, 1 & 2 High St, Wallingford, Oxon OX10 OBJ (☎ 0491 34400, fax 0491 33740)

DUCHESNE, Brig (Peter) Robin; OBE (1978); s of Herbert Walter Duchesne (d 1978), of Dyffryn, Conway Rd, Mochdre, Clwyd, and Irene, *née* Cox (d 1979); *b* 25 Sept 1936; *Educ* Colwyn Bay GS, RMA Sandhurst, RMC of Sci, Royal Navy Staff Coll; *m* 30 March 1968, Jennifer MacLean, da of Brian Elphinstone Gouldsbury, of 1 Whites Close, Piddlehinton, Dorset; 1 s (Charles b 7 April 1974), 1 da (Emma b 1 Oct 1977); *Career* cmmnd RA 1956, 101 Airborne Div USA 1963-64, Capt instr RMA Sandhurst 1965-67, CO 49 Field Regt RA 1975-77, Dir Staff Army Staff Coll Camberley 1977-79, Cdr Mil Advsy Team Ghana 1979-81, Cdr Arty 1 Armd Div Brig 1981-83, D/Cdr and COS UN Force Cyprus 1984-86; memb UN Assoc, vice chm Sailing Ctee Sail Trg Assoc Cncl, sec gen RYA 1986-, skipper jt serv entry Whitbread Round the World Race 1978; FBIM 1987; *Recreations* sailing, walking, most sports; *Clubs* RORC; *Style*— Brig Robin Duchesne, OBE; Lake Lodge, Farnham, Surrey GU10 2QB (☎ 025 125 3901); Royal Yachting Association, Romsey Rd, Eastleigh, Hants (☎ 0703 629 962, fax 0703 629 924, telex 47393 BOATIN G)

DUCIE, 6 Earl of (UK 1837); Basil Howard Moreton; also Baron Ducie (GB 1763) and Baron Moreton (UK 1837); s of Hon Algernon Howard Moreton (d 1951), 2 s of 4 Earl of Ducie; suc unc 1952; *b* 15 Nov 1917; *Educ* C of E GS Brisbane Queensland; *m* 15 April 1950, Alison May, da of Leslie Atkins Bates, of Brisbane, Queensland; 3 s, 1 da; *Heir* s, Lord Moreton; *Career* patron of 2 livings; served 1941-45 with 62 A I Bn and 2/3 A I Bn New Guinea and Islands; *Style*— Rt Hon Earl of Ducie; Tortworth House, Tortworth, Wotton-under-Edge, Glos

DUCKER, Bernard John; s of Arthur John Ducker (d 1972), of Blackheath, and Ella Maud, *née* Jermy (d 1953); *b* 26 July 1922; *Educ* Roan Sch; *m* 7 May 1949, Dr Daphne Mary, da of Edward Harry Norris Dowlen (d 1977); 3 s (Adrian John b 11 June 1951, Gerard Bernard b 28 Feb 1954, Roderick Edward John b 2 Aug 1956); *Career* WWII Flt Lt RAF 1942-46; qualified CA 1949; ptnr: E C Brown & Batts 1949-81, Callingham Crane 1981-87; dir: Nicholas Reinsurances Ltd, Pillinger Air Ltd; memb Worshipful Co of Scriveners; *Recreations* sailing, vintage and veteran cars; *Clubs* RAF; *Style*— Bernard Ducker, Esq; Merrileas, Leatherhead Rd, Oxshott, Surrey KT22 0EZ; 526 Purley Way, Croydon, Surrey (☎ 081 680 770, fax 081 680 2345, telex 291312 PILAIR)

DUCKWORTH, Anthony John Stanhope; 3 and yst s of Sir George Herbert Duckworth, CB (d 1934), of Dalingridge Pl, Sharpthorne, Sussex, half-bro of Virginia Woolf; *b* 2 Oct 1913; *Educ* Eton, Trinity Cambridge; *m* 23 April 1941, Audrey Diana, da of Johannes Nicolaas Tollenaar, of 74 Chester Sq, SW1; 2 s, 1 da; *Career* sr ptnr Fielding Newson-Smith Stockbrokers 1970-77, dir Eagle Star Trust Co Ltd (former chm), Moet & Chandon (London) Ltd, Parfums Christian Dior (UK) Ltd; *Recreations* shooting, golf; *Clubs* Bucks; *Style*— Anthony Duckworth Esq; 2 Eaton Place, SW1 (☎ 071 235 4776); Southacre House, Southacre, nr Kings Lynn, Norfolk (☎ 076 05 272)

DUCKWORTH, His Hon Judge; Brian Roy; s of Eric Roy Duckworth (d 1972); *b* 26 July 1934; *Educ* Sedbergh, Univ of Oxford (MA); *m* 1964, Nancy Carolyn, da of Christopher Holden (d 1972); 3 s, 1 da; *Career* barr 1958, rec Crown Court 1972-83, Circuit Judge (Northern Circuit) 1983-; hon pres S Cumbria Magistracy 1987-; *Recreations* golf, sailing, gardening; *Clubs* Pleasington Golf; *Style*— His Hon Judge Duckworth; c/o The Crown Court, Lancaster Road, Preston, Lancs

DUCKWORTH, Edward Richard Dyce; s and h of Sir Richard Duckworth, 3 Bt; *b* 13 July 1943; *Educ* Marlborough, Cranfield; *m* 1976, Patricia, only da of Thomas Cahill, of Eton, Berks; 1 s, 1 da; *Career* engineer and management conslt; *Recreations* tennis, fishing; *Style*— Edward Duckworth Esq

DUCKWORTH, Dr (Walter) Eric; OBE (1991); s of Albert Duckworth (d 1947), and Rosamund, *née* Biddle (d 1978); *b* 2 Aug 1925; *Educ* Waterloo GS, Queens' Coll Cambridge (MA, PhD); *m* 16 April 1949, Emma, da of Thomas Cowan (d 1980); 1 s (Stephen b 1951); *Career* asst dir BISRA 1960-69, md Fulmer Ltd (formerly Fulmer Res Inst) 1969-90; dir: Ricardo Consulting Engineers plc 1978-87, Fleming International High Income Investment Trust 1984-90; memb Standing Ctee on Industry Engrg Cncl, tstee Comino Fndn; memb: Worshipful Co of Scientific Instrument Makers 1984, Worshipful Co of Engrs 1984; Hon DTech Brunel Univ 1976, Hon DUniv Univ of Surrey 1980; FIM 1963, FEng 1980; *Books* A Guide to Operational Research (1962, 3 edn 1977), Statistical Techniques in Technological Research (1968), Electroslag Refining (1969), Manganese in Ferrous Metallurgy (1976); *Recreations* gardening, photography; *Clubs* Stoke Poges Golf; *Style*— Dr Eric Duckworth, OBE; Orinda, Church Lane, Stoke Poges, Slough SL2 4PB

DUCKWORTH, Geoffrey Keith; s of Gordon Trevor Duckworth, of 46 Shearwater Rd, Offerton, and Mary, *née* Hoskin (d 1976); *b* 14 Feb 1941; *Educ* Kings Sch Macclesfield; *m* 27 Jan 1967, Christine Mary, da of Frank Parker Wilson; 2 s (Martin Keith b 18 Oct 1968, Peter Robert b 23 Oct 1970), 1 da (Alison Jane b 6 Feb 1974); *Career* ptnr Booth Ainsworth 1970- (articled clerk 1968); ACA 1968; *Recreations* keen sportsman; *Clubs* Mellor Lacrosse, Mellor Cricket; *Style*— Geoffrey Duckworth, Esq; Booth Ainsworth, 19 Hollins Lane, Marple, Stockport SK6 6AW (☎ 061 427 6265, fax 061 426 0293)

DUCKWORTH, Brig Geoffrey Loraine Dyce; CBE (1978); s of Capt Arthur Dyce Duckworth, RN (d 1973), of Aldershaw House, Southborough, Kent, and Grace Ella Mary, *née* Pontifex; *b* 24 May 1930; *Educ* Stowe; *m* 16 Dec 1961, Philippa Ann, da of Sir Percy Rugg, JP, DL (d 1986); 1 s (Jeremy b 1963), 1 da (Juliet b 1964); *Career* cmmnd RTR 1950, Staff Coll Camberley 1961, Lt-Col 1968, GSO1 directing staff Aust Staff Coll 1968-70, CO 2 RTR 1970-72, COS 2 Armd Div 1973-75, Cdr Br Army Trg Unit Suffield Canada 1975-77, Regtl Col RTR 1978-80, Brig 1980, Dep Fortress Cdr Gibraltar 1980-83, vice pres Regular Cmmns Bd 1983-85; ADC to HM The Queen 1982-85; admin mangr Quilter Goodison Stockbrokers London 1986, head of admin The Game Conservancy Fordingbridge 1987; memb: local PCC, Salisbury Music Soc; pres Army Cadet League Battersea; Freeman City of London 1957, Ct Asst Worshipful Co of Armourers and Brasiers 1988; Kt of the Hon Soc of Knights of The Round Table 1988; *Recreations* fly fishing, gardening, making music; *Style*— Brig Geoffrey Duckworth, CBE; Weir Cottage, Bickton, Fordingbridge, Hants SP6 2HA (☎ 0425 655813); The Game Conservancy, Fordingbridge, Hants SP6 1EF (☎ 0425 652381)

DUCKWORTH, John Clifford; s of late Harold Duckworth, and A H Duckworth, *née* Woods; *b* 27 Dec 1916; *Educ* KCS Wimbledon, Univ of Oxford; *m* 1942, Dorothy Nancy, *née* Wills; 3 s; *Career* md National Research Development Corporation 1959-1970; chm Lintott Contral Equipment Ltd; tstee Sci Museum; *Style*— John Duckworth, Esq; Suite 33, 140 Park Lane, London W1 (☎ 071 499 0355, telex 27314)

DUCKWORTH, Hon Mrs ((Mary) Katharine Medina); *née* Chatfield; OBE (1946); da of Adm of the Fleet 1 Baron Chatfield, GCB, OM, KCMG, CVO, PC (d 1967), and Lilian Emma Chatfield, CStJ, *née* Matthews (d 1977); *b* 1911; *m* 22 Sept 1947, Henry George Austen de L'Etang Herbert Duckworth, RA, s of late Sir George and Lady Margaret Duckworth; 2 da; *Career* WVS 1939-46; *Style*— The Hon Mrs Duckworth, OBE; Dalingridge Place, Sharpthorne, Sussex (☎ 0342 810411)

DUCKWORTH, Maj Peter Alexander; s of Evelyn Poole Duckworth (d 1930), of Darjeeling, India, and Muriel Bowen, *née* Dobbie (d 1979); *b* 16 July 1923; *Educ* Royal Masonic Sch; *m* 30 Sept 1950, Ann, da of Lt Cdr George Cuthbert Irwin Ferguson (d 1941), of Copythorne, nr Southampton; 3 s (Luke b 1954, Rollo b 1957, Rufus b 1961), 1 da (Georgia b 1966); *Career* served 5 Royal Inniskilling Dragoon Gds: France, Germany BLA 1944-45, Korea 1951, Egypt 1953; Br Modern Pentathlon Champion 1949 and 1951, army epee champion 1951, Br Olympic Modern Pentathlon team mangr 1960; chm Hart Dist Cncl 1983-85, rep of Hants Dist Cncls on Serplan, chm Hants Branch Assoc of Dist Cncls; head gardener Bramshot House Fleet; *Recreations* swimming, croquet, gardening, hide and seek; *Clubs* Epee, Milocarian; *Style*— Maj Peter Duckworth; Bramshot House, Fleet, Hants (☎ 0252 617304)

DUCKWORTH, Sir Richard Dyce; 3 Bt (UK 1909), of Grosvenor Place, City of Westminster; s of Sir Edward Dyce Duckworth, 2 Bt (d 1945); *b* 30 Sept 1918; *Educ* Marlborough; *m* 5 Sept 1942, Violet Alison, da of Lt-Col George Boothby Wauchope, DSO (d 1952), of Highclere, Newbury, by his wife Violet Adelaide, widow of Capt Merveyn Crawshay (ka 1914), da of Capt Edward von Mumm; 2 s; *Heir* s, Edward Duckworth; *Career* Retired East India merchant; *Style*— Sir Richard Duckworth, Bt; Dunwood Cottage, Shootash, Romsey, Hants

DUCKWORTH, Roger Peter Terence; s of Ronald Duckworth (d 1966), of Blackburn, Lancs, and Bessie, *née* Smith (d 1980); *b* 16 Jan 1943; *Educ* Accrington GS; *m* 12 June 1965, Marion, da of William Henry Holden (d 1981), of Blackburn, Lancs; 1 s (Myles b 1972), 1 da (Laurel b 1970); *Career* chm and chief exec offr Netlon Ltd and the Netlon Group of Cos; ACMA; *Recreations* music, fell walking, theatre; *Clubs* Farmers; *Style*— Roger Duckworth, Esq; Netlon Ltd, Blackburn, Lancs (☎ 0254 62431, telex 63313, fax 0254 680008)

DUCKWORTH, Stephen Roger; s of Edwin Bateman Duckworth, of 24 Kigsway,

Ansdell, Lytham St Annes, Lancs, and Brenda Doreen, *née* Stoate (d 1980); *b* 19 June 1939; *Educ* Bootham Sch York, King's Coll Cambridge (MA); *m* 29 July 1967, Elisabeth Moira, da of Edward Thomas Harvey (d 1964), of Exeter, Devon; 2 da (Anita b 1968, Beverley b 1970); *Career* princ fin offr Nat Ports Cncl 1966-73, fin dir Paddington Churches Housing Assoc 1973-82, head of housing fin Nat Fedn of Housing Assoc 1982-; former chm: mangrs Barlby Primary Sch N Kensington, Fin and Staff Ctee N Kensington Amenity Tst, Kensington Amnesty Gp; former treas Notting Hill Social Cncl; memb Mgmnt Ctee: Circle 33 Housing Tst, Shepherds Bush Housing Assoc; circuit treas Notting Hill Methodist Church; FCA 1964; *Books* Understanding Accounts (1987), Private Finance Manual (ed, 1988); *Recreations* travel, fell walking, swimming, photography; *Style—* Stephen Duckworth, Esq; National Federation of Housing Association, 175 Grays Inn Rd, London WC1X 8UP (☎ 071 2786571)

DUCKWORTH-CHAD, Anthony Nicholas George; s of A J S Duckworth of Southacre House, King's Lynn, Norfolk; *b* 20 Nov 1942; *Educ* Eton, RAC Cirencester; *m* 6 May 1970, Elizabeth Sarah, da of Capt C B H Wake-Walker of East Bergholt Lodge, Suffolk; 2 s (James b 1972, William b 1975), 1 da (Davina b 1978); *Career* farmer and landowner; memb: Walsingham RDC 1963-74, North Norfolk DC 1974- (chm 1987-89); chm Norfolk branch Country Landowners Assoc 1977-78, govr Greshams Sch 1974-; Liveryman Worshipful Co of Fishmongers Co; *Recreations* country sports; *Clubs* Whites, Pratts; *Style—* Anthony Duckworth-Chad, Esq; 5 Cumberland St, London SW1V 4LS; Pynkney Hall, East Rudham, King's Lynn, Norfolk

DUDBRIDGE, Bryan James; CMG (1961); s of Walter Dudbridge, OBE, and Anne Jane, *née* Baker; *b* 2 April 1912; *Educ* King's Coll Sch Wimbledon, Selwyn Coll Cambridge; *m* 29 Oct 1943, (Audrey) Mary, da of W B Heywood; 2 s (John b 1945, Simon b 1953), 1 da (Josephine b 1949); *Career* Colonial Admin Serv: cadet Tanganyika Territory 1935 (sundry sub dists and dist 1939-52), sec Land Utilization Ctee Southern Highland Province 1952; actg prov cmmr: i/c Southern Province 1953 (sr dist offr 1953), local govt in secretariat 1955; prov cmmr i/c Western Province 1957, min for prov affrs 1959-60, ret 1961; Christian Aid (overseas charity arm of Br Cncl of Churches): assoc dir 1963, later dep dir, actg dir 1970, ret 1972; parish cncllr High Halden; memb: CAB Ashford, Wye Coll Beagles, Stoke Hill Beagles; *Clubs* Royal Cwlth Soc; *Style—* Bryan Dudbridge, Esq, CMG; Red Rock Bungalow, Elm Grove Rd, Topsham, Exeter EX3 0EJ (☎ 0392 874468)

DUDBRIDGE, Glen; s of George Victor Dudbridge, and Edna Kathleen, *née* Cockle; *b* 2 July 1938; *Educ* Bristol GS, Magdalene Coll Cambridge (BA, MA, PhD), New Asia Inst of Advanced Chinese Studies Hong Kong; *m* 16 Sept 1965, Sylvia Lo Fung-Young, da of Lo Tak-Tsuen (d 1981); 1 s (Frank b 1967), 1 da (Laura b 1968); *Career* Nat Serv RAF 1957-59; jr res fell Magdalene Coll Cambridge 1965, fell Wolfson Coll Oxford 1966-85 (emeritus fell 1985); visiting assoc prof: Yale Univ 1972-73, Univ of California at Berkeley 1980; prof Chinese Univ of Cambridge 1985-89, fell Magdalene Coll Cambridge 1985-89, prof of Chinese Univ of Oxford 1989- (lectr modern Chinese 1965-85), fell Univ Coll Oxford 1989-; FBA 1984; *Books* The Hsi-yu chi: a study of antecedents to the 16th century Chinese novel (1970), The legend of Miao-shan (1978, Chinese edn 1990), The Tale of Li Wa: study and critical edn of a Chinese story from the 9th century (1983); *Style—* Prof Glen Dudbridge; Oriental Inst, Pusey Lane, Oxford, OX1 2LE (☎ 0865 278200, fax , 0865 278190)

DUDDERIDGE, John Webster; OBE (1962); s of William George Dudderidge (d 1945), of Cheddon Fitzpaine, Somerset, and Mary Ethel, *née* Webster (d 1962); *b* 24 Aug 1906; *Educ* Magnus GS Newark-on-Trent, University Coll Nottingham (BSc); *m* 25 July 1936, (Gertrude Louisa) Evelyn, da of Rev Frederick S Hughes (d 1920) of N China Mission, Peking, China; 2 s (John b 1937, Philip b 1949), 2 da (Ruth b 1938, Hilary b 1944); *Career* asst master Manor House Sch London 1929-31, asst master and house master Haberdashers' Aske's Sch 1931-69; memb: Cambridge Wildlife Tst, Cncl for the Protection of Rural Eng, Nat Tst; BOA: cncl member 1949-69, exec ctee memb 1969-73, dep chm 1973-77, vice pres 1977-; Br Canoe Union: fndr memb 1936, sec for racing 1936-49, gen sec 1939-59, pres 1959-77, hon life pres 1977-, Award of Honour 1961; Int Canoe Fedn: memb Bd 1938-80, vice pres 1946-48, hon memb 1980-; Award of Honour 1962, Gold medal 1980; sec/treas Cwlth Canoeing Fedn 1968-84; memb Cncl for Eng Cwlth Games Fedn 1976-83; memb Ctee of Advsrs Sports Aid Fndn 1976-80; memb Br Olympic Canoe Team 1936, mangr Br Canoe Racing Team 1938-58, int official 1948-81; author of numerous articles on canoes and canoeing for magazines, jls, almanacks and encyclopaedias; *Recreations* canoeing, walking, gardening, reading; *Clubs* Royal Canoe, Canoe Camping; *Style—* John Dudderidge, Esq, OBE; Tyros, 15 Lacks Close, Cottenham, Cambridge, CB4 4TZ (☎ 0954 51752)

DUDDERIDGE, Philip Stephen; s of John Webster Dudderidge, OBE, of North Leigh, Oxon, and Gertrude Louisa Evelyn, *née* Hughes; *b* 6 Feb 1949; *Educ* Haberdashers' Aske's Sch; *m* 1973, Jennifer Anne, da of Terence W Hayes; 5 s, 1 da; *Career* sound engr and artistes' mangr; fndr, chm and md Soundcraft Electronics Ltd 1973-89 (Queen's Award for Export 1979 and 1985); chm and md Focusrite Audio Engineering Ltd 1989-; dir Assoc of Professional Recording Servs; *Recreations* flying; *Style—* Philip Dudderidge, Esq; Chilterns, Grimms Hill, Great Missenden, Bucks; Focusrite Audio Engineering Ltd, 2 Bourne End Business Centre, Coves End Rd, Bourne End, Bucks SL8 5AJ (☎ 0628 819456)

DUDGEON, Gus; s of Patrick Boyd Dudgeon, and Elizabeth Louise, *née* Crighton; *b* 30 Sept 1942; *Educ* Haileybury and Imperial Service, Summerhill; *m* 3 April 1965, Sheila, da of George Arthur Bailey; *Career* record prodr (formerly sound engr); founded own prodn co 1968; hits incl: Space Oddity (David Bowie), Je T'Aime (Sounds Nice), co-produced with Paul McCartney The Urban Spaceman (Bonzo Dog Doo Dah Band); prodr of all Elton John records 1969-76 and 1986-; singles incl: Your Song, Rocket Man, Crocodile Rock, Daniel, Saturday Night's Alright for Fighting, Yellow Brick Road, Don't Go Breaking My Heart, Nikita; has produced for other artists incl: Joan Armatrading, Chris Rea, Elkie Brooks, Jennifer Rush, Kiki Dee; Silver discs: Run for Home 1978, Back and Fourth 1978, Magic in the Air 1978; Gold disc Whatever Happened to Benny Santini 1978; Platinum disc (Germany) for Heart over Mind 1987 and all Elton John Records; NME Best British Produced Record 1973, Top Albums Producer 1974 and 1975, NOI Pop Producer Billboard magazine 1975; *Recreations* theatre, gardening, collecting rhinos, water-skiing, excellent food, Mercedes, Aston-Martins, and of course music; *Style—* Gus Dudgeon, Esq; c/o Chris Gilbert, Rockmasters Ltd, 110 Westbourne Grove, London W2 52U (☎ 071 727 8636, fax 071 229 4061)

DUDLEY, Anne Jennifer; da of William James Beckingham, of Brighton, and Dorothy Thelma Beckingham; *b* 7 May 1956; *Educ* Eltham Hill GS, RCM (performer's Dip, BMus), King's Coll London (MMus); *m* 1978, Roger Dudley, s of Leonard William Dudley; *Career* musician, composer, arranger, prodr; keyboard player and arranger with: ABC (Lexicon of Love album), Wham! (Young Guns, Bad Boys and Everything She Wants), Malcolm McLaren (co-wrote Buffalo Gals and other tracks on Duck Rock), Frankie Goes to Hollywood (Two Tribes and The Power of Love); fndr memb Art of Noise (performed, wrote and co-produced all five albums); freelance arranger and musician with: Phil Collins, Paul McCartney, Wet Wet Wet, Dusty Springfield, Wham, Lisa Minelli, Lloyd Cole, Jaz Coleman of Killing Joke (songs From the Victorious City 1990); composer of soundtracks for cinematic feature films incl: Hiding Out, Buster, Wilt, Silence Like Glass, Say Anything, Mighty Quinn, Dragnet, Disorderlies, The Miracle; composer of soundtrack music for tv: BSB Channel Identification Themes (1990), Jeeves and Wooster (1990), Krypton Factor, Max Headroom, Rory Bremner; composer of music for tv and cinema commercials incl: Britvic (Citrus Spring), Bols, Revlon, Brylcream, World Wildlife Fund, Mars (Galaxy); *Style—* Mrs Anne Dudley; Mark Anders, Polar Union, 119-121 Freston Rd, London W11 (☎ 071 243 0011, fax 071 221 2722)

DUDLEY, Bishop of 1977-; Rt Rev Anthony Charles (Tony); s of Lt Charles Frederick Dumper, MC (d 1965), and Edith Mary, *née* Ribbins (d 1966); *b* 4 Oct 1923; *Educ* Surbiton GS, Christ's Coll Cambridge (BA, MA), Westcott House Cambridge; *m* 5 June 1948, Sibylle Anna Emilie, da of Paul Hellwig (d 1945), of Germany; 2 s (Peter Nicholas b 1951, Michael Richard Thomas b 1956), 1 da (Hildegard Sarah Sibylle b 1954); *Career* ordained 1947, archdeacon N Malaya 1955-64, dean Singapore 1964-70, rural dean Stockton on Tees 1970-77; memb: CND, Dudley Borough Educn Ctee; *Books* Vortex of the East (1962); *Recreations* walking, gardening, reading; *Style—* The Rt Rev the Bishop of Dudley; 366 Halesowen Rd, Cradley Heath, W Midlands (☎ 021 550 3407)

DUDLEY, Baroness (14 in line, E 1439); Barbara Amy Felicity Wallace; *née* Lea-Smith; da of 12 Baron Dudley (d 1936); suc bro, 13 Baron, 1972; *b* 23 April 1907; *m* 1929, Guy Raymond Hill Wallace (d 1967); 3 s, 1 da; *Heir* s, Hon Jim Wallace; *Style—* The Rt Hon the Lady Dudley; Hill House, Napleton Lane, Kempsey, Worcs (☎ (0905) 820253)

DUDLEY, Hon Mrs (Betty); *née* Montague; da of 1 Baron Amwell (d 1966); *b* 15 Oct 1920; *m* 1941, John Forbes Dudley; 1 da; *Style—* The Hon Mrs Dudley; 76 Eastcourt Rd, Burbage, Wilts

DUDLEY, Charles Edward Steele; s of Col Stewart Dudley, MC (d 1977), of Tiverton, Devon, and Gertrude Alexandra, da of Maj-Gen Sir SB Steele, KCMG, CB, MVO; *b* 4 Sept 1935; *Educ* St Andrews Coll Grahamstown, RMA Sandhurst; *m* 29 March 1965, Marianne, da of Douglas Sandford Kemp, of Belize and Brazil; 2 da (Charlotte Elaine b 1969, Lucie Elizabeth b 1973); *Career* cmmnd KSLI 1956; Sultans Armed Forces Oman 1965; farming and business 1971; chm The Free Angola Campaign (a UK Gp supporting the Nat Union for the Total Independence of Angola) 1987- (fndr memb), admin sec Cons Friends of Angola 1990-; dir Research and Analysis International Ltd; resided and travelled extensively throughout Africa and M E; *Recreations* long distance riding, Elizabethan history, freelance writing, port wines; *Style—* Charles Dudley, Esq; The Free Angola Campaign, PO Box 380, Reading, Berkshire RG3 6GR (☎ 0734 410998, fax 07354 4339)

DUDLEY, Grace, Countess of; Grace Maria Kolin; *m* 1, Prince Stanislas Radziwill; m 2, 1961, as his 3 w, 3 Earl of Dudley (d 1969); *Style—* The Rt Hon Grace, Countess of Dudley; Greycliff, Nassau, Bahamas

DUDLEY, Prof Hugh Arnold Freeman; CBE (1988); s of Walter Lionel Dudley (d 1944), and Ethel Marion, *née* Smith (d 1938); *b* 1 July 1925; *Educ* Heath GS Halifax , Univ of Edinburgh (MB ChB, ChM); *m* 17 July 1947, Jean Bruce Lindsay, da of James Johnston (d 1966), of Keltneyburn, Aberfeldy, Perthshire; 2 s (Raymond James Desomeri b 1948, Nigel Hugh Desomeri b 1951), 1 da (Iona Mary Bruce Lindsay); *Career* Lt and Capt RAMC 1948-50, Maj (Actg Lt Col) RAAMC 1968-72; lectr Univ of Edinburgh 1954-58, sr lectr Univ of Aberdeen 1958-62, Fndn prof Monash Univ 1962-72, prof St Mary's Hosp London 1972-88; pres: Surgical Res Soc of Australia, Surgical Res Soc of GB and Ireland, Biological Engrg Soc of GB; chm Br Journal of Surgery Soc; hon fell: SA Coll of Surgns, American Surgical Assoc; Medal of Merit S Vietnam 1971; FRCSE 1951, FRACS 1964, FRCS 1974; *Recreations* shooting; *Style—* Prof Hugh Dudley, CBE; Broombrae, Glenbuchat, Strathdon, Aberdeenshire AB36 8UA (☎ 097 5641341)

DUDLEY, Maurice; s of Samuel Geoffrey Dudley (d 1933), and Evelyn Horton (d 1986); *b* 19 Jan 1925; *Educ* secondary sch, night sch, correspondence coll; *m* 17 Dec 1949, Rose Eileen Esther, da of James Sidney Massey (d 1978); 2 s (Paul Maurice b 1955, Mark Ian b 1958); *Career* WWII RAF aircrew with 2 Tactical Airforce; CA; md Dismantling & Engineering Gp Ltd; dir: Dismantling & Engineering Ltd, Kidderminster Steel Ltd, Deks Clear Ltd; former pres: Nat Fedn of Demolition Contractors, Euro Demolition Assoc; former chm Demolition Indust Register, memb Drafting Ctee for Code of Practice for Demolition & Dismantling Standards Inst; *Recreations* golf, swimming; *Clubs* Sutton Coldfield Golf (past capt); *Style—* Maurice Dudley, Esq; Grey Gables, 16A Le More, Four Oaks, Sutton Coldfield, West Midlands (☎ 021 308 4351); Lion House, Mucklow Hill, Halesowen, West Midlands (☎ 021 550 9041, fax 021 501 3023, telex 338063, car 0836 590330)

DUDLEY, 4 Earl of (UK 1860); William Humble David Ward; also Baron Ward of Birmingham (E 1664) and Viscount Ednam (UK 1860); s of 3 Earl of Dudley, MC (d 1969), by his 1 w, Lady Rosemary, *née* Sutherland-Leveson-Gower, RRC (d 1930), da of 4 Duke of Sutherland; *b* 5 Jan 1920; *Educ* Eton, Christ Church Oxford; *m* 1, 1946 (m dis 1961), Stella, da of Miguel Carcano, KCMG, KBE, sometime Argentinian Ambass to UK; 1 s, 2 da (twins); m 2, 1961, Maureen Swanson; 1 s, 5 da; *Heir* s, Viscount Ednam; *Career* sits as Cons in House of Lords; 2 Lt 10 Hussars 1941, Capt 1945; A D C To The Viceroy of India 1942-43; dir: Baggeridge Brick Co Ltd, Tribune Investment Trust Ltd; *Clubs* White's, Pratt's, Royal Yacht Sqdn; *Style—* The Rt Hon The Earl of Dudley; Vention House, Putsborough, Georgeham, N Devon (☎ 0271 890631/890632); 6 Cottesmore Gdns, London W8 (☎ 071 937 5671)

DUDLEY, William Stuart; s of William Stuart Dudley, and Dorothy Irene, *née* Stacey; *b* 4 March 1947; *Educ* Highbury GS, St Martins Sch Art (BA), Slade Sch of Art UCL (Post Grad Dip Fine Art); *Career* res stage designer Nat Theatre 1970-; prodns incl: The Mysteries, Lark Rise, Undiscovered Country, The Critic, Cat on a Hot Tin Roof, The Shaughraun, The Changeling; stage designs RSC incl: Richard III, A Midsummer Night's Dream; stage designs Royal Opera House incl: Don Giovanni, Tales of Hoffman, Der Rosen Kavalier; designer of The Ring at Bayreuth 1983; fndr memb folk band Morris Minor and the Austin Seven 1980, hon pres Tower Theatre 1988, hon dir Irish Theatre Co London; memb Soc Br Theatre Designers; *Recreations* playing the concertina and the cajun accordian; *Style—* William Dudley, Esq; 30 Crooms Hill, Greenwich, London SE10 (☎ 081 858 8711)

DUDLEY EDWARDS, Ruth; da of Robert Walter Dudley Edwards (d 1988), and Sheila, *née* O'Sullivan (d 1985); *b* 24 May 1944; *Educ* Sacred Heart Convent Dublin, Sandymount HS Dublin, Univ Coll Dublin (BA, MA, DLitt), Girton and Univ Colls (now Wolfson Coll) Cambridge, City of London Poly (dip Business Studies); *m* 1, 31 July 1965 (m dis 1975), Patrick John Cosgrave, s of Patrick Joseph Cosgrave (d 1952); m 2, Jan 1976, John Robert Mattock, s of John Leonard Mattock (d 1986); *Career* principal DOI 1975-79, freelance writer 1979-, company historian The Economist 1982-; memb Exec Ctee Br Irish Assoc 1981-, chm Br Assoc for Irish Studies 1986-; *Books* An Atlas of Irish History (1973), Patrick Pearse: the triumph of failure (1977), James Connolly (1981), Corridors of Death (1981), Harold MacMillan: a life in pictures (1983), The Saint Valentine's Day Murders (1984), Victor Gollancz: a biography (1987), The School of English Murder (1990); *Recreations* friends; *Clubs* Academy,

Reform; *Style*— Miss Ruth Dudley Edwards; 40 Pope's Lane, Ealing, London W5 4NU (☎ 081 579 1041)

DUDLEY-SMITH, Rt Rev Timothy; *see*: Thetford, Bishop of

DUDLEY-WILLIAMS, Sir Alastair Edgcumbe James; 2 Bt (UK 1964), of City and Co of the City of Exeter; s of Sir Rolf Dudley Dudley-Williams, 1 Bt (d 1987); *b* 26 Nov 1943; *Educ* Pangbourne Nautical Coll; *m* 1972, Diana Elizabeth Jane, twin da of Robert Henry Clare Duncan, of Haslemere, Surrey; 3 da (Marina Elizabeth Catherine b 1974, Lorna Caroline Rachel b 1977, Eleanor Patricia Rosemary b 1979); *Heir* bro, Malcolm Philip Edgcumbe Dudley-Williams, *qv*; *Career* field salesman Hughes Tool Co Texas 1962-64, oil well driller Bay Drilling Corp (Louisiana) 1964-65; driller: Bristol Siddeley Whittle Tools Ltd 1965-67, Santa Fe Drilling Co (N Sea and Libya) 1967-72, Inchcape plc 1972-86, Wildcat Conslts 1986-; *Recreations* gardening, fishing, shooting; *Clubs* Royal Cornwall Yacht; *Style*— Sir Alastair Dudley-Williams, Bt; The Corner Cottage, Brook, Godalming, Surrey

DUDLEY-WILLIAMS, Helen, Lady; (Margaret) Helen; *née* Robinson; er da of late Frederick Eaton Robinson, OBE, of Enfield, Middx; *m* 25 May 1940, Sir Rolf Dudley Dudley-Williams, 1 Bt (d 1987); 2 s; *Style*— Helen, Lady Dudley-Williams; The Old Manse, South Petherton, Somerset TA13 5DB

DUDLEY-WILLIAMS, Malcolm Philip Edgcumbe; yr s of Sir Rolf Dudley Dudley-Williams, 1 Bt (d 1987); bro and hp of Sir Alastair Edgcumbe James Dudley-Williams, 2 Bt, *qv*; *b* 10 Aug 1947; *Educ* Pangbourne Nautical Coll; *m* 1973, Caroline Anne Colina, twin da of Robert Henry Clare Duncan, of The Wall House, High Street, Haslemere, Surrey; 2 s (Nicholas Mark Edgcumbe b 1975, Patrick Guy Edgcumbe b 1978), 1 da (Clare Helen Colina b 1982); *Style*— Malcolm Dudley-Williams, Esq

DUERDEN, Prof Brian Ion; s of late Cyril Duerden, of Seedhill, 13 Westbury Close, Burnley, Lancs, and Mildred, *née* Ion; *b* 21 June 1948; *Educ* Nelson GS, Univ of Edinburgh (BSc, MB ChB, MD); *m* 5 Aug 1972, Marjorie, da of Thomas Blakey Hudson, of 5 Birtwhistle Close, Brierfield, Burnley, Lancs; *Career* house offr thoracic surgery and infectious diseases City Hosp Edinburgh 1972-73, lectr and hon registrar in bacteriology Univ of Edinburgh Med Sch 1973-76; Univ of Sheffield Med Sch: lectr and hon sr registrar in med microbiology 1976-79, sr lectr and hon conslt in med microbiology 1979-83; prof and hon conslt microbiologist and infection control doctor Children's Hosp Sheffield 1983-90; Univ of Wales Coll of Med: prof of med microbiology 1991-, dir Public Health Laboratory 1991-, dir med microbiology S Glamorgan 1991-; chm Ed Bd Jl of Med Microbiology 1987- (ed in chief 1982-), memb Ed Ctee Reviews Med Microbiology; hon sec Assoc Profs of Med Microbiology 1989-; memb: Pathological Soc GB and Ireland (memb Ctee 1981-), Nat Quality Assur Advsy Panel 1986-, Microbiology Advsy Ctee 1988-, Jt Dental Ctee MRC 1989-, Assoc Med Microbiologists 1983- (hon sec 1984-87); MRCPath 1978 (memb Cncl 1986-89 and 1990-, examiner 1981-, memb Exec Ctee 1990-), FRCPath 1990, corr fell Infectious Diseases Soc of America, chm Soc of Anaerobic Microbiology 1989- (memb 1976-); *Books* Short Textbook of Medical Microbiology (fifth edn, 1983), A New Short Textbook of Microbial and Parasitic Infection (1987), Topley and Wilson's Principles of Bacteriology, Virology and Immunity (contrib 7 edn, 1983-84, ed and contrib 8 edn 1990); *Recreations* cricket, photography, travel, music; *Style*— Prof Brian Duerden; Pendle, Crossway Green, Chepstow, Gwent NP6 5LU; Department of Medical Microbiology, University of Wales College of Medicine, Heath Park, Cardiff CF4 4XN (☎ 0222 742168)

DUFF, Alistair David Buchanan; s of Maj David Kerr Duff (d 1963), of Tighnabruaich House, Argyll and Muriel Kerr, *née* Cavaghan (d 1988); *b* 19 July 1928; *Educ* George Watson's Sch Edinburgh, Univ of Edinburgh; *m* 1 Feb 1958, Cynthia Mary, da of Maurice Stork Hardy (d 1974), of Cleughhead, Annan, Dumfriesshire; 1 s (Roderick b Oct 1963), 1 da (Carolyn b Aug 1962); *Career* Nat Serv RA Malaya 1947-49; vice chm Cavaghan & Gray Ltd Carlisle 1977-88 (dir 1957-63, and md 1963-77); chm: Br Bacon Curers Fedn 1975-76, TSB Lancs and Cumbria 1976-83 (memb Central Bd 1976-86, tstee Eng and Wales 1983, dep chm NW Regnl Bd 1984-89); dir Carlisle Race Course Co 1978-; *Recreations* shooting, horse racing, sailing; *Clubs* Farmers, Border and County; *Style*— Alistair Duff, Esq; Monkcastle, Southwaite, Carlisle, Cumbria CA4 OPZ (☎ 069 74 73 273)

DUFF, Rt Hon Sir (Arthur) Antony; GCMG (1980, KCMG 1973, CMG 1964), CVO (1972), DSO (1944), DSC (1943), PC (1980); yr s of Adm Sir Arthur Allan Morison Duff, KCB, JP, DL (d 1952, ggs of Robert William Duff, whose mother was Lady Helen Duff, da of 1 Earl of Fife, ancestor of Dukes of Fife. Robert's f was Vice Adm Robert Duff of Logie and Fetteresso, one of 23 children of Patrick Duff of Craigston by his 2nd wife (he had 36 altogether)); *b* 25 Feb 1920; *Educ* RNC Dartmouth; *m* 1944, Pauline Marion, da of Capt R H Bevan, RN, and widow of Flt-Lt J A Sword; 1 s, 1 step s, 2 da; *Career* served RN 1937-46; entered Foreign Service 1946; first sec: FO 1952, Paris 1954; counsellor Bonn 1962-64, ambass to Nepal 1964-65, Cwlth Office 1965-68, dep high cmmr Kuala Lumpur 1969-72, high cmmr Kenya 1972-75, dep under sec of State FCO 1975-80, dep to Perm Under Sec of State 1977-80; dep govr Southern Rhodesia 1979-80, dep sec Cabinet Office 1980-87 (ret); *Clubs* Army and Navy; *Style*— The Rt Hon Sir Antony Duff, GCMG, CVO, DSO, DSC; c/o National Westminster Bank, 17 The Hard, Portsea, Hants

DUFF, Gordon Ray; s of Maj David Kerr Duff (d 1963), of Tighnabruaich House, Argyll, and Muriel, *née* Cavaghan (d 1988); *b* 17 March 1930; *Educ* George Watson's Coll Edinburgh, Open Univ (BA); *m* 23 May 1959, Willa Mary, da of James Glover (d 1967), of Arinagour, Isle of Coll, Argyll; 4 s (David, Ian, Ranald, Alistair); *Career* enlisted RE 1949, cmmnd 1950, Capt 1953, 4 Bn Border Regt (TA) on transfer to RARO 1961; regnl dir Scottish subsids of Cavaghan of Gray Group 1959-69, mgmnt conslt 1969-88 (Cumbria & Inverness-Shire), currently conslt Crown Estates Cmmrs Scot; memb: Lochaber Presbytery, Bd of Stewardship and Fin Church of Scot, Cncl BIM (Chm Scot Ctee); FBIM 1980, MMS 1986, FIMC 1986; *Recreations* shooting, fishing; *Clubs* Highland; *Style*— Gordon Duff, Esq; Highbridge, Spean Bridge, Inverness-shire PH34 4EX (☎ 0397 81 391); 101 High Street, Fort William, Inverness-shire PH33 6DG (☎ 0397 5924, fax 0397 5030)

DUFF, Prof Michael John Benjamin; s of George Benjamin Duff (d 1976), and Joan Emily, *née* Reynolds; *b* 17 Jan 1933; *Educ* Emanuel Sch Wandsworth, UCL (BSc, PhD); *m* 20 April 1963, Susan Mary, da of Alfred Jones (d 1986); 1 s (Robert Michael b 1967), 1 da (Charlotte Fiona b 1964); *Career* devpt engr EMI Electronics Ltd 1956-58, prof of applied physics Dept of Physics and Astronomy UCL 1985- (res asst 1958-62, lectr 1962-77, reader 1977-84); hon sec Br Pattern Recognition Soc 1976-84, chm BPRA 1984-86, pres Int Assoc for Pattern Recognition 1990- (sec 1984-90); CEng 1966, FIEE 1981, FRSA 1986; *Books* numerous pubns incl: Conference on Recent Developments in Cloud Chamber and Associated Techniques (ed with N Morris, 1956), Computing Structures for Image Processing (ed, 1983), Modern Cellular Automata (with K Preston, 1984), Intermediate-Level Image Processing (ed, 1986); *Recreations* travelling, music, gardening, photography; *Style*— Prof Michael Duff; Bramham Cottage, 66 Westow Park, Thames Ditton, Surrey KT7 0HL

DUFF, Samuel; s of Rev Samuel Noel Duff, and Emily McKinney, *née* Douther; *b* 20 Feb 1946; *Educ* Rainey Endowed Sch Edinburgh, Univ of Edinburgh; *m* 8 Nov 1969, Patricia Katherine Fleming, da of Donald Morris Miller (d 1961), of Dale, Halkirk, Caithness; 2 s (Innes Noel b 1975 (decd), Andrew Samuel b 1977), 2 da (Louise Emma Jane b 1971, Iona Katherine b 1971); *Career* vet; asst: RS Cowie Ptnrs Keith 1970-77, AE Orr 1977-78; ptnr Orr Duff and Howat 1978-; pres Scottish Metropolitan Div BVA 1990-91; memb BVA; *Style*— Samuel Duff, Esq; Redriggs, Ceres, Fife (☎ 033482 345)

DUFF, Timothy Cameron; s of Timothy Duff (d 1974) of Tynemouth, and Marjory Magdalene, *née* Cameron; *b* 2 Feb 1940; *Educ* Royal GS Newcastle upon Tyne, Gonville and Caius Coll Cambridge (MA, LLM); *m* 23 June 1966, Patricia, da of Capt John Munby Walker DLI (d 1955), of N Shields; 2 s (John b 1968, James b 1970), 1 da (Emma b 1973); *Career* admitted slr 1965; sr ptnr Hadaway and Hadaway (N Shields and Whitley Bay) 1988-; sec and clerk to tstees Tyne Mariners Benevolent Inst 1984, dir Tynemouth Bldg Soc 1985; memb Ecclesiastical Law Soc (1988); *Recreations* sailing, reading, outdoor pursuits; *Clubs* Green Wyvern Yacht; *Style*— Timothy Duff, Esq; 58 Howard St, North Shields, Tyne & Wear, NE30 1AL (☎ 091 257 0382, fax 091 296 1904)

DUFF GORDON, Sir Andrew Cosmo Lewis; 8 Bt (UK 1813), of Halkin, Ayrshire; s of Sir Douglas Frederick Duff Gordon, 7 Bt (d 1964, whose ggf, Sir William Duff Gordon, 2 Bt, was paternal gs of 2 Earl of Aberdeen); *b* 17 Oct 1933; *m* 1, 1967 (m dis 1975), Grania Mary, da of Fitzgerald Villiers-Stuart, of Dromana, Villerstown, Co Waterford; 1 s; m 2, 1975, Eveline (Evie) Virginia, da of Samuel Soames, of Boxford House, Newbury; 3 s; *Heir* s, Cosmo Henry Villiers Duff Gordon b 18 June 1968; *Career* dir Nelson Hurst-Marsh Agencies Ltd; *Clubs* City Univ, Sunningdale Golf, Kington Golf; *Style*— Sir Andrew Duff Gordon, Bt; 27 Cathcart Rd, London SW10; Downton House, Walton, Presteigne, Powys (☎ 054 421 223)

DUFF-ASSHETON-SMITH, Hon Lady (Millicent) Joan Marjoribanks; da of 3 Baron Tweedmouth (decd); *b* 1906; *m* 1935 (m dis 1937), Sir Charles Michael Robert Vivian Duff-Assheton-Smith, Bt (d 1980); *Style*— The Hon Lady Duff-Assheton-Smith; 45 Westminster Gdns, London, SW1

DUFFELL, Michael Royson; s of Roy John Duffell (d 1979), of Lenham, Kent, and Ruth Doris, *née* Gustaffson; *b* 19 June 1939; *Educ* Dulwich; *m* 1963, Gisela, *née* Rothkehl; 1 s (Christian Royson b 2 Feb 1964), 1 da (Julie Royson b 20 Oct 1969); *Career* reception mangr Hyde Park Hotel 1966-69, gen mangr Grosvenor Hotel Chester 1969-76, controller of the Household to HM King Hussein of Jordan 1976-80, dir and gen mangr The Ritz 1980-84; md: Cunard Hotels and The Ritz 1984-88, Hotel Atop the Bellevue Philadelphia USA 1988-90; pres Service Concepts Marketing Inc Palm Beach Florida 1990; *Recreations* tennis, skiing; *Style*— Michael Duffell, Esq; 26 Brechin Place, London SW7 4QA; 19 Via Del Corso, Palm Beach Gardens, Florida 33418 (☎ 407 624 3624)

DUFFELL, Brig Peter Royson; CBE (1988, OBE 1981), MC (1966); s of Roy John Duffell (d 1979), of Lenham, Kent, and Ruth Doris, *née* Gustaffson; *b* 19 June 1939; *Educ* Dulwich Coll; *m* 9 Oct 1982, Ann Murray, da of Col Basil Bethune Neville Woodd (d 1975), of Rolvenden, Kent; 1 s (Charles Basil Royson b 20 Oct 1986), 1 da (Rachel Leonie Sylvia b 9 April 1985); *Career* cmmnd 2 KEO Gurkha Rifles 1960, attended Staff Coll Camberley 1971, Brigade Maj 5 Brigade 1972-74, MA to C in C UKLF 1976-78, Cmdt 1 Bn 2 KEO Gurkha Rifles 1978-81, Col GS MOD 1981-83, Cdr Gurkha Field Force 1984-5; CoS 1 (BR) Corps 1986-87, RCDS 1988, Cdr Br Forces Hong Kong 1989-; FRGS 1975; *Recreations* golf, reading, writing, travel; *Clubs* Travellers', Hong Kong; *Style*— Brig Peter Duffell, CBE, MC; HQ British Forces Hong Kong, BFPO 1 (☎ office: 010 852 58633300, home: 010 852 58496371)

DUFFERIN AND AVA, Marchioness of; Lindy - Serena Belinda Rosemary; *née* Guinness; da of Gp Capt Loel Guinness, OBE (d 1988), and his 2 w, Lady Isabel Manners, yr da of 9 Duke of Rutland; *b* 25 March 1941; *m* 21 Oct 1964, 5 and last Marquess of Dufferin and Ava (d 1988); *Career* writer and artist; *Recreations* gardening, nature conservation; *Style*— The Most Hon the Marchioness of Dufferin and Ava; Clandeboye, Bangor, Co Down, N Ireland; 4 Holland Villas Rd, London W14

DUFFERIN AND CLANDEBOYE, 10 Baron (I 1800); Sir Francis George Blackwood; also 11 Bt (I 1763) of Ballyleidy, and 7 Bt (UK 1814); s of late Capt Maurice Baldwin Raymond Blackwood, DSO, RN (d on active serv 1941) and Dorothea (d 1967), da of late Hon G Bertrand Edwards, of Huon Park, Sydney, NSW; suc to cousin's baronetcy 1979; s to barony of Dufferin and Clandeboye and baronetcy of Ballyleidy 1988 on death of 5 and last Marquess of Dufferin and Ava; *b* 20 May 1916; *Educ* Knox GS Wahroonga, Sydney Tech Coll; *m* 1941, Margaret, da of Hector Kirkpatrick, of Lindfield, NSW, Aust; 2 s, 1 da; *Heir* s, Hon John Francis Blackwood, *qv*; *Career* former chemical engr, now consulting engr in private practice; FIEAust, ARACI; *Style*— The Rt Hon Lord Dufferin and Clandeboye; Uambi, 408 Bobbin Head Rd, N Turramurra, NSW 2074 Australia

DUFFETT, Christopher Charles Biddulph; s of Capt Charles Henry Duffett, CBE, DSO (d 1981), and Leonora Biddulph; *b* 23 Aug 1943; *Educ* Bryanston, Peterhouse Cambridge (MA), Wharton Sch Univ of Pennsylvania (MBA); *m* 1973, Jennifer Edwards; 2 s (Samuel Owen Salisbury b 1975, Daniel Charles William Biddulph b 1977); *Career* asst economist Nat Devpt Office 1965-67, Exec Banking Dept S G Warburg and Co Ltd 1969-71, area fin mangr Inco Ltd NY 1971-74, treas Inco Europe Ltd 1974-77, gp treas Rank Organization Ltd 1977-79, gp fin dir The Economist Newspaper Ltd 1979-88, md The Law Debenture Corp plc 1988-; FCT; *Recreations* gardening, sailing, walking; *Clubs* Royal Ocean Racing; *Style*— Christopher Duffett, Esq; Princess House, 95 Gresham St, London EC2V 7LY (☎ 071 606 5451)

DUFFETT, Michael Terence; s of Francis Duffett, of Beckenham Kent, and Marjorie, *née* McCarthy (d 1988); *b* 1 Aug 1939; *Educ* Hill Scholl Stillness, Central Poly, London Coll of Printing and Graphic Art; *m* Janet, da of Stanley Spencer; 4 da (Rachel b 1 Dec 1966, Emma b 24 Feb 1968, Rebecca b 9 May 1969, Sarah b 19 April 1970); *Career* photographer (photography of Fine Art, Museum and Gallery Photographic Mgmnt); med photographer Royal Nat Orthopaedic Hosp 1959, photographer for Tate Gallery 1962, freelance commercial photographer and design conslt 1967-70, conslt to Slater Walker 1970; advsr on creation of new Photographic Dept Tate Gallery 1974, princ photographer Photographic Dept Tate Gallery 1977-, began collection of photographic equipment (1860-1960) 1977, lectr 1979-; chief Govt photographer 1985-, organiser and mangr photographic recording prog of 30,000 Turner watercolours and drawings for the Clore Gallery 1985-, undertook complete photographic survey of entire collection Dulwich Picture Gallery 1988; conslt Bournemouth and Poole Coll of Art and Design 1990; judge: Kodak Ltd Exposure Project 1989, Kodak Ltd Exposure Project Number Two 1990, BIPP Nat Print Competition 1990, Inst of Med and Biological Illustrators 1990; chm and fndr Assoc of Hist and Fine Art Photographers 1986 (host and princ speaker Autumn Seminar); exhibitions incl: Guildhall 1961, Gallery Las 1963, Kings Gallery 1964, Kings Road Gallery 1972; ARPS 1965, FRSA 1987, FBIPP 1988; *Style*— Michael Duffett, Esq; 1 Queens Rd, Beckenham, Kent BR3 4JN (☎ 081 650 2944); Tate Gallery, MillBank, London SW1P 4RG (☎ 071 821 1313, fax 071 931 7512)

DUFFIELD, George Peter; s of Charles Duffield, of Wakefield and Elsie, *née* Berry; *b* 30 Nov 1946; *Educ* Stanley Secdy Sch Wakefield Yorks; *m* Nov 1971, Gillan Marjorie, da of late George Hughes; 1 s (Nick George b 18 Jan 1973), 1 da (Nathalie Jane b 28 July 1975); *Career* flat race jockey; apprenticed to A J Waugh 1962, started race riding

1967, runner up Apprentice Championships 1968 and 1969, turned professional 1970 (after riding 75 winners); represented GB at Sandown Int Races and in Barbados, rider of over 2000 winners worldwide; winner: Sussex Stakes (Gp 1), Solario Stakes (Gp 3), Jersey Stakes, Seaton Delavil, Child Stakes, two gp winners France, gp 3 Germany, Great Metropolitan, Royal Hunt Cup, Ascot Stakes, Manchester November Handicap (twice), Zetland Gold Cup (twice), Newmarket Challenge Stakes, Van Geest, Newbury Autumn Cup, Bovis Handicap Ascot (twice), Lockinge Stakes The Oakes Calcutta India, The Army Cup Calcutta, top 2 year olds race Calcutta; rider of over 100 winners in Jamaica, 13 victories on Spindrifter in a season, rode Noalcholic when champion miler of Europe, 5 times Jockey of Mouth, Scottish & Yorkshire racing clubs Jockey of Year, guest of honour Racing Press Dinner Scotland; *Recreations* hunting, shooting, fishing; *Style*— George Duffield, Esq; Cedar Cottage, Burrough Green, Newmarket, Suffolk CB8 9NE (☎ 0638 507544); D Ellis, 6 Cardigan St, Newmarket, Suffolk (☎ 0638 668484)

DUFFUS, Sir Herbert George Holwell; s of William Alexander Duffus, JP (d 1963), and Emily Henrietta Mary, *née* Holwell (d 1961), a direct descendant of John Zephaniah Holwell, HEICS, one of the 23 survivors of the Black Hole of Calcutta; *b* 30 Aug 1908; *Educ* Cornwall Coll Jamaica; *m* 1939, Elsie Mary, da of Richard Leslie Hollinsed, JP (d 1950), of Barbados; *Career* Capt Jamaica Local Forces 1940-46; slr Supreme Ct: of Jamaica 1930-55, of England 1948-55; barr Lincoln's Inn 1956, Puisne judge Jamaica 1958-62, judge of appeal Jamaica 1962-64, pres Ct of Appeal Jamaica 1964-68, chief justice of Jamaica 1968-73, actg govr-gen Jamaica 1973, chllr of the Church (Anglican) in Jamaica 1973-76; chm cmmn: Enquiry into Prisons in Jamaica 1954, Operations of Private Land Developers in Jamaica 1975-76, Police Brutality and The Admin of Justice in Grenada 1973-74, Barbados Govt's Private Enterprises 1977-78, Local Govt Elections in Jamaica 1986; kt 1966; *Recreations* chm of several charitable instns and fndns; *Style*— Sir Herbert Duffus; 6 Braywick Rd, PO Box 243, Kingston 6, Jamaica (☎ 809 92 70171); 119 Main St, Witchford, nr Ely, Cambs (☎ 0353 3281)

DUFFUS OF DALCLAVERHOUSE, James Coutts; s of James Montague Coutts Duffus of Dalclaverhouse and of the Mansion of Claverhouse, by Dundee, Angus (d 1947); *b* 3 June 1919; *Educ* Arnhall Coll Sch Dundee; *Career* Corps of RE (TA) (despatches) WW II; holder in life-rent of the superiority of the lands, estate and feudal fief of Dalclaverhouse, Co Angus; recognised in present name and style by Lord Lyon King of Arms 1955; archivist; FRSA, FSA Scot; *Style*— James Duffus of Dalclaverhouse Esq; 68 New Cavendish St, London W1 (☎ 071 580 5152)

DUFFY, Bryan Scott Alan; s of Francis Duffy (d 1966); *b* 21 March 1943; *Educ* Hull Univ (BSc Econ); *m* 1968, Krystyna Elizabeth Maria, da of Bohden Bitner, of Cracow, Poland; 2 children; *Career* chm Brown & Jackson plc 1977-; tstee The Marriage & Family Trust; chm of appeals Nat Marriage Guidance Cncl; FCA; *Recreations* tennis, golf, opera; *Clubs* Vanderbilt; *Style*— Bryan Duffy Esq; Dane End House, Dane End, Herts SG12 0LR; Brown & Jackson plc, Battle Bridge House, 300 Gray's Inn Rd, London WC1 (☎ 071 278 9635)

DUFFY, Carol Ann; da of Francis Duffy, and Mary, *née* Black; *b* 23 Dec 1955; *Educ* St Joseph's Convent Stafford, Stafford Girls' HS, Univ of Liverpool (BA); *Career* freelance writer; *Books* Standing Female Nude (1985), Selling Manhattan (1987), The Other Country (1990); awards: Eric Gregory award 1984, C Day Lewis fellowship 1982-84, Somerset Maugham award 1988, Dylan Thomas award 1990, Scottish Arts Cncl Book award of merit 1985 and 1990; *Style*— Ms Carol Ann Duffy

DUFFY, Dr Francis Cuthbert; s of John Austin Duffy (d 1944), and Annie Margaret, *née* Reed; *b* 3 Sept 1940; *Educ* St Cuthberts GS Newcastle upon Tyne, Architectural Assoc Sch London (AADip, Hons), Univ of California (MArch), Princeton (MA, PhD); *m* 4 Sept 1965, Jessica Mary, da of Phillip Bear, of Chiddingstone, Kent; 3 da (Sibylla b 1966, Eleanor b 1969, Katya b 1970); *Career* asst architect Nat Bldg Agency 1964-67, Harkness fell of the Cwlth Fund 1967-70 (in USA), estab and head London Office of JFN Assoc 1971-74, fndr and chm Bldg Use Studies 1980-88, fndr and chief ed Facilities (newsletter) 1984-90; Duffy Eley Giffone Worthington (DEGW) architects: estab 1974-, fndr ptnr, chm; conslt on the working environment to many cos and insts, vice pres RIBA; ARIBA; *Books* Planning Office Space (jtly, 1976), The Orbit Study (princ author, 1984), Orbit 2 (jtly, 1985), The Changing City (jtly, 1989), The Changing Workplace (1997); *Clubs* Princeton, New York, Architectural Assoc London; *Style*— Dr Francis Duffy; 195 Liverpool Rd, London N1 0RF (☎ 071 837 3064); 3 The Terrace, Walberswick, Suffolk (☎ 0502 723814)

DUFFY, Hazel Marion; *b* 9 April 1941; *Educ* Univ of London (BSc Econ); *m* (sep); 1 s (Jonathan b 2 Aug 1969), 1 da (Siobhan b 7 Oct 1966); *Career* Review of Indust the Times 1964-66; industl corr The Guardian 1973-78 (Investors 1972-73), industl corr and regnl affairs corr Financial Times 1978-90; *Recreations* gardening in County Cork; *Style*— Ms Hazel Duffy; 4a Victoria Works, Graham Street, Birmingham, West Midlands B1 3PE (☎ 021 236 1670)

DUFFY, John Rutherford; s of Thomas Leo Duffy (d 1972), of Rugby, and Mary Agnes, *née* Collins; *b* 16 Aug 1932; *Educ* Lawrence Sheriff Sch Rugby, Rugby; *m* 23 June 1959, Muriel Hamilton, da of John Birkett (d 1966), of Rugby; *Career* slr, sr ptnr Bretherton Turpin & Pell Rugby; chm Social Security Appeal Tbnl Coventry 1985-88; govr Lawrence Sheriff Sch Rugby 1970- (chm 1985-); capt Northamptonshire Co Golf Club 1982; chm: Rugby Round Table 1967-68, Area 45 Round Table 1969-70; *Recreations* golf, fishing; *Clubs* Northamptonshire County Golf; *Style*— John R Duffy, Esq; 19 Hillmorton Road, Rugby (☎ 0788 565260); 16 Church Street, Rugby (☎ 0788 73431)

DUFFY, Mark Peter; s of Arthur Peter Duffy, and Mary Louise Duffy; *b* 8 Nov 1956; *Educ* Liverpool Inst, Peterhouse Cambridge (MA); *Career* investmt analyst W Greenwell and Co 1980-85, dir S G Warburg Securities 1985-; *Publications* Rothmans International (1984), Bat and Financial Services (1985), RJR Nabisco - Profile of a New Group (1986), Tobacco Stocks and Diversification (1988), Bat the Dollar and Farmers Group (1988), Unilever and Personal Products (1989); *Style*— Mark Duffy, Esq; S G Warburg Securities, 1 Finsbury Ave, London EC2M 2PA (☎ 382 4383, fax 382 4292)

DUFFY, Maureen Patricia; da of Grace Wright; *b* 1933; *Educ* Trowbridge HS, Sarah Bonnell HS for Girls, King's Coll London (BA); *Career* author, playwright and poet; co fndr Writers' Action Gp; chm: Authors Licensing and Collecting Soc 1980-, Br Copyright Cncl 1989-; pres Writers Guild of GB 1986-89 (jt chm 1977-88), vice pres Beauty Without Cruelty; FRSL; *Style*— Ms Maureen Duffy; 18 Fabian Rd, London SW6 7TZ

DUFFY, (Albert Edward) Patrick; MP (Lab) Sheffield Attercliffe 1970-; s of James Duffy (d 1973); *b* 17 June 1920; *Educ* LSE (BSc, PhD), Columbia Univ NY (PhD); *Career* Lt Fleet Air Arm RN 1940-46; economist; lectr Univ of Leeds; MP (Lab) Colne Valley Yorks 1963-66, parly under-sec of state for Def (Navy) 1976-79, former chm Lab Parly Econ Affairs Fin Gp; oppn spokesman: Def 1979-80 and 1983-, Disarmament 1983-; pres: Lab Def Gp, North Atlantic Assembly 1988- (memb 1979-, vice-pres 1987); *Clubs* Trades & Labour (Doncaster), Naval; *Style*— Patrick Duffy, Esq, MP; 153 Bennetthorpe, Doncaster; House of Commons, London SW1A 0AA

DUFFY, Patrick G; s of Dr J B Duffy, and Mrs E C Duffy; *b* 8 Jan 1949; *Educ* (BCh, BOA); *m* 13 July 1987, Dr Zara Anne, *née* McClenahan; 1 s (Frederick b 16 July 1989); *Career* conslt paediatric urologist The Hosps for Sick Children Gt Ormond St London, sr lectr paediatric urology Inst of Urology London; memeb: BMA, RSM, FRCSI; *Recreations* sailing, squash, music; *Style*— Patrick Duffy, Esq; 8 Legard Rd, London N5 1EE (☎ 071 359 1068), Private Consulting Rooms, 29 Orde Hall St, London WC1N 3JL (☎ 071 405 9791)

DUFFY, Terence John; s of John Edward Duffy (d 1989), of Birkenhead, Cheshire, and Theresa, *née* Williamson (d 1963); *b* 24 Aug 1947; *Educ* St Anselm's Coll Cheshire, Jesus Coll Cambridge (BA, MA), New Coll Oxford (BM BCh); *m* 6 Aug 1971, Rowena Siriol, da of Henry Vaughan-Roberts, BM, of Conwy, N Wales; 1 s (Elliot Edward Vaughan b 1977), 1 da (Alexandra Margaret Theresa (Sasha) b 1983); *Career* house appts Bedford and Oxford 1972-73, demonstrator in anatomy Univ of Cambridge 1973-74 (supervisor Jesus Coll 1973-74), sr house offr and registrar Bedford and Cambridge Hosp 1974-78, registrar Swansea 1978-79, Wellcome res fell Cambridge 1979-80, lectr in surgery Univ of Cambridge 1980-84 (fell Jesus Coll 1980-84), conslt in gen and transplant surgery N Staffs Hosp 1984-, sr lectr in surgery Univ of Keele 1984-89; numerous pubns on gen and transplant surgery 1978-; memb: Br Transplant Soc, W Midlands Surgical Soc, BMA 1969, BTS 1980; FRCS 1977, FRSM 1989; *Recreations* music, sport; *Style*— Terence Duffy, Esq; North Staffordshire Hosp Centre, City General Hosp, Newcastle Rd, Stoke-on-Trent, Staffs (☎ 0782 621133)

DUFTY, (Arthur) Richard; CBE (1971); s of Thomas Ernest Dufty (d 1915); *b* 23 June 1911; *Educ* Rugby, Liverpool Sch of Architecture; *m* 1937, Kate Brazley (d 1991), da of Charles Ainsworth (d 1928); 1 s, 2 da; *Career* served WWII, Lt RNVR, North Sea; sec and gen ed to Royal Cmmn on Historical Monuments (E) 1962-72 (memb 1975-85); Master of the Royal Armouries in HM Tower of London 1963-76; pres Soc of Antiquaries 1978-81; chm London Diocesan Advsy Ctee 1973-84; memb: Standing Ctee on Conservation of West Front of Ely Cathedral 1974-85, Farnham (Bldgs Preservation) Tst 1968- (received Times Conservation award 1986), Br Ctee of Corpus Vitrearum Medii Alvi 1970-84, vice chm Cathedrals Advsy Cmmn 1981-88; tstee: Coll of Arms Tst, Marc Fitch Fund; memb: Ancient Monuments Bd for Eng 1962-73 and 1977-80, Cncl for Places of Worship 1976-81, Cncl Nat Army Museum 1963-83, London Conservation award 1984; DLitt Lambeth 1988; Hon Liveryman Worshipful Co of Glaziers and Worshipful Co of Armourers and Brasiers; hon memb Art Workers' Guild; *Books* W Morris's Cupid and Psyche Armamenta Armamentaria (with FH Cripp-Day), Morris Embroideries; *Recreations* appreciation of architecture, William Morris and the arts and crafts movement, gardens, music; *Clubs* Athenaeum, Arts, Naval; *Style*— Richard Dufty, Esq, CBE; 46 Trafalgar Court, Farnham, Surrey; Church Cottage, Kelmscott, Oxfordshire

DUGDALE, Hon David John; s of 1 Baron Crathorne, PC, TD (d 1977); *b* 4 May 1942; *Educ* Eton, Trinity Coll Cambridge; *m* 1972, Susan Louise, da of Maj L A Powell (d 1972); 1 s, 1 da; *Career* farmer and engr; *Recreations* building, photography, shooting; *Style*— The Hon David Dugdale; Park House, Crathorne, Yarm, Cleveland (☎ 0642 700225, work: 700295)

DUGDALE, Rev Canon Dennis (Tim); OBE (1978); s of Brian Dugdale (d 1955), of Wetherby, Yorks, and Beatrice Mary, *née* Mountain (d 1922); *b* 22 March 1919; *Educ* King James' GS Knaresborough Yorks, Worcester Ordination Coll; *m* 15 Sept 1945, Angel Honor, 3 offr WRNS, da of Capt James Alexander Pollard Blackburn, DSC (d 1979), of Eastbourne; 1 da (Juliet b 1946); *Career* Midshipman RNR 1938, Sub Lt 1940, Lt 1942, Lt Cdr 1950, survivor of HMS Rawalpindi 1939, POW in Germany 1939-45, resigned cmmn 1955; cadet Clan Line Steamer's Ltd 1935-39, second offr Trg Ship Arethusa 1946-48, marketing exec Massey-Harris-Ferguson Ltd 1949-64; Ordination Coll 1965-68, ordained Guildford Cathedral (deacon 1968, priest 1969); curate St Mary the Virgin Shalford Surrey 1968-71, rector Sandon Wallington and Rushden Herts 1971-74, anglican chaplain Ghent and Ypres Belgium 1974-84, canon Pro-Cathedral Brussels 1982; *Recreations* walking and countryside pursuits; *Style*— The Rev Canon Tim Dugdale, OBE; 12 High Trees, Carew Road, Eastbourne BN21 2JB (☎ 0323 26661)

DUGDALE, John Robert Stratford; s of Sir William Francis Stratford Dugdale, 1 Bt (d 1965), bro of Sir William Dugdale, 2 Bt, *qv*; *b* 10 May 1923; *Educ* Eton, Ch Ch Oxford; *m* 1956, Kathryn Edith Helen, DCVO, JP, *qv*; 2 s, 2 da; *Career* CC Salop 1969-81, Lord-Lt 1975-; chm Telford Development Corporation 1971-75; KStJ; *Clubs* Brooks's, White's; *Style*— John Dugdale, Esq; Tickwood Hall, Much Wenlock, Salop TF13 6NZ (☎ 0952 882644)

DUGDALE, Dame Kathryn Edith Helen; DCVO (1984, CVO 1973), JP (Salop 1964); da of Col Rt Hon Oliver Frederick George Stanley, MC, PC, MP (d 1950), and Lady Maureen Vane Tempest Stewart (see Londonderry); gda of 17 Earl of Derby; and Lady Alice Montagu, da of Duke of Manchester; *b* 4 Nov 1923; *m* 1956, John Robert Stratford Dugdale, *qv*; 2 s, 2 da; *Career* woman of the bedchamber to HM The Queen 1955- (temporary extra 1961-71); *Style*— Dame Kathryn Dugdale, DCVO, JP; Tickwood Hall, Much Wenlock, Salop TF13 6NZ (☎ 0952 882644)

DUGDALE, Keith Stuart; JP (1967); s of George Dugdale (d 1954), of Norwich, and Dorothy Elizabeth, *née* Parherson (d 1970); *b* 27 Sept 1930; *Educ* Gresham's Sch Holt, Magdalen Coll Oxford (MA); *m* 1957, Angela Marion, *née* Willey; 2 s (Christopher John b 1966, Jeremy Keith b 1969), 1 da (Hilary Ruth b 1964); *Career* CA; Martin & Acock: articled clerk 1951, ptnr 1956; FCA 1955; *Recreations* book collecting, music, gardening; *Clubs* Norfolk; *Style*— Keith Dugdale, Esq, JP; Beck House, Kelling, Holt, Norfolk NR25 7EL (☎ 026 370 389); Martin and Acock, 2 The Close, Norwich NR1 4DJ (☎ 0603 612311, fax 0603 613210)

DUGDALE, (William) Matthew Stratford; s and h of Sir William Stratford Dugdale, 2 Bt; *b* 22 Feb 1959; *Style*— Matthew Dugdale, Esq

DUGDALE, Peter Robin; CBE (1987); s of Dr James Norman Dugdale, and Lilian, *née* Dolman; *b* 12 Feb 1928; *Educ* Canford, Magdalen Coll Oxford (MA); *m* 1957, (Esme) Cyraine, da of L Norwood Brown; 3 s (Mark b 1958, Luke b 1961, Paul b 1967); *Career* joined Union Insurance Soc of Canton Ltd Hong Kong 1949 (merged with Guardian Assurance Co Ltd 1960); marine and aviation mangr and chief underwriter Guardian Assurance Co Ltd/Guardian Royal Exchange Assurance Ltd 1965-73; pres Guardian Insurance Co of Canada 1973-76; gen mangr Guardian Royal Exchange Insurance Ltd 1976-78; md Guardian Royal Exchange Assurance Ltd/plc 1978-; dep chm British Assurance Assoc 1979; chm: Trade Indemnity plc 1980-, British Insurance Assoc 1981-82, Aviation and Gen Insurance 1982-84, Assoc of British Insurers 1987-89; govr of Canford Sch; Master Worshipful Co of Insurers 1989-; CBIM 1984; *Recreations* flat coated retrievers; *Clubs* Oriental; *Style*— Peter Dugdale, Esq, CBE; 68 King William St, London EC4N 7BU (☎ 071 283 7101, fax 071 623 0217, telex 883232)

DUGDALE, Sir William Stratford; 2 Bt (UK 1936) of Merevale and Blyth, Co Warwick; CBE (1982), MC (1943), JP (Warwicks 1951), DL (1955); s of Sir William Francis Stratford Dugdale, 1 Bt (d 1965), and bro of John R S Dugdale, *qv*; *b* 29 March 1922; *Educ* Eton, Balliol Coll Oxford; *m* 1, 13 Dec 1952, Lady Belinda Pleydell-Bouverie (d 1961), da of 7 Earl of Radnor, KG, KCVO; 1 s, 3 da; m 2, 17 Oct 1967, Cecilia Mary, da of Lt-Col Sir William Mount, 2 Bt, ED, DL; 1 s, 1 da; *Heir* s William Matthew Stratford Dugdale; *Career* Capt Grenadier Gds 1944, served in Africa and Italy (despatches); slr 1949; chm: Trent River Authy 1965-73, Severn Trent Water Authy 1974-84, Nat Water Cncl 1982-84; dir Phoenix Assur 1985 (and other cos);

High Sheriff Warwicks 1971-72; High Steward of Stratford-upon-Avon 1976-; *Clubs* Brooks's, White's, MCC, Jockey; *Style*— Sir William Dugdale, Bt, CBE, MC, JP, DL; Blyth Hall, Coleshill, Birmingham B46 2AD (☎ 0675 462203); Merevale Hall, Atherstone, Warwicks (☎ 082 771 3143); 24 Bryanston Mews West, London W1 (☎ 071 262 2510)

DUGDALE SYKES, Hon Mrs (Betty Charlotte); *née* Deane; o da of 8 Baron Muskerry, *qv*; *b* 3 July 1951; *Educ* Alexandra Coll Dublin, Trinity Coll Dublin (BA); *m* 1974, Jonathan Martin Dugdale Sykes, s of Martin Colin Dugdale Sykes, of 1 Churchill Close, W Coker, Yeovil, Somerset; 1 s (Daniel b 1980), 1 da (Karen b 1985); *Career* business woman; *Recreations* tennis, gardening; *Style*— The Hon Mrs Dugdale Sykes; The Kennels, Springfield, Dromcollogher, Co Limerick, Eire

DUGGAN, Prof Arthur William; s of Bernard Morgan Duggan, of Sydney, Australia, and Margaret, *née* Bell; *b* 14 June 1936; *Educ* Univ of Queensland (BSc, MB BS, MD), Aust Nat Univ (PhD); *m* 4 July 1961, (Gwyndolyn) Helen, da of William Nathan Randall (d 1980); 2 s (Peter b 1962, Richard b 1964), 1 da (Anne b 1969); *Career* med practice Queensland Aust 1961-67 (med res 1968-70), CJ Martin fell Nat Health Med Res Cncl of Aust 1971-73, sr fell in pharmacology Inst of Advanced Studies Aust Nat Univ 1974-87, prof of vet pharmacology Univ of Edinburgh 1987-, RSM Fndn visiting prof 1989-; pres Aust Pain Soc; *Recreations* golf; *Style*— Prof Arthur Duggan; 5C Strathalmond Rd, Edinburgh EH4 8AB; Dept of Preclinical Vet Sciences, University of Edinburgh, Summerhall, Edinburgh EH9 1QH (☎ 031 667 1011)

DUGGAN, Shaun Walker; s of Francis Rupert Duggan, MD (d 1959), and Mary Elinor, *née* Walker (d 1981); *b* 30 March 1940; *Educ* Christ's Hosp; *m* 19 June 1965, Lavinia Debonnaire Hope, da of Maj Ian McIntyre Stevens (d 1964); 1 s (Charles b 1966), 2 da (Emma b 1968, Victoria b 1972); *Career* CA 1964; stockbroker: Laing & Cruickshank 1967-84 (ptnr 1972), Capel-Cure Myers 1987-88, ANZ McCaughan 1988-89, ind investmt advsr 1990-; memb Stock Exchange 1971; *Recreations* skiing, the Times crossword; *Clubs* Buck's, City of London; *Style*— Shaun W Duggan, Esq; The Grove, Turners Hill, West Sussex RH10 4SF (☎ 0342 716146)

DUGUID, Ian McIver; s of John Duguid (d 1980), and Georgina, *née* McIver (d 1983); *b* 16 April 1926; *Educ* Aberdeen GS, Univ of Aberdeen (MB ChB, MD), Univ of London (DO, PhD); *m* 16 Dec 1961, Yvonne Jean, da of William Michie (d 1959), of Aberdeen; 2 s (Graham b 1963, Stewart b 1967); *Career* sr ophthalmic surgn: Moorfields Eye Hosp London, Charing Cross and Westminster Hosps London; FRCS 1961, FCOpth 1988; Offr de L'Ordre National Du Merite (1986); *Recreations* rugby, cars; *Style*— Ian Duguid, Esq; 30 Chester Close North, London NW1 4JE; 73 Harley St, London W1N 1DE (☎ 071 935 5874)

DUGUID, Keith Paris; s of John Paris Duguid (d 1971), of Walsall, Staffs, and Gladys May, *née* Cooksey (d 1985); *b* 19 Jan 1942; *Educ* Chuckery Secdy Sch Walsall, Wednesbury Tech Coll Staffs, Manchester Coll of Sci & Technol; *m* 11 Sept 1965, Ann Moll, da of Charles Davis; 1 s (Angus John Paris b 3 June 1975), 2 da (Sally Ann b 22 Jan 1969, Rebecca b 15 June 1971); *Career* trainee then medical photographer Dept of Medical Illustration Manchester Royal Infirmary 1958-63; Dept of Medical Illustration and AV Services Westminster Hosp Medical Sch 1966-85 (med photographer, sr med photographer, dep to dir, head of Dept), dir Dept of Medical Illustration Univ of Aberdeen 1985-; lectr in UK USA and ME, examiner in med photography and AV to RPS, BIPP and Inst of Med Illustrators, ed Journal of Audiovisual Media in Medicine, memb Editorial Bd Journal of Educational Technology Abstracts, author of over 40 papers; awards: Presidential award for 1990 BIPP, Norman K Harrison award Inst of Med Illustrators, Harold E Louis Research Film award BMA; FRPS, FBIPP, Assoc Inst of Med Illustrators; *Books* Essential Clinical Signs (jtly, 1990); *Recreations* gardening, painting; *Style*— Keith Duguid, Esq; University of Aberdeen, Dept of Medical Illustration, Polwarth Building, Forester Hill, Aberdeen AB9 2ZD (☎ 0224 681818 ext 52805)

DUGUID, Hon Mrs ((Sandra) Lillias); *née* Donnet; da of Baron Donnet of Balgay (Life Peer d 1985); *b* 1947; *m* 1971, Dr Nigel Duguid; 2 s (Douglas, David), 1 da (Andrea); *Style*— The Hon Mrs Duguid; 8 Sackville Street, St John's, Newfoundland A1A 4R3, Canada

DUHIG, (Robert) Ian; s of Robert Augustine Duhig (d 1983), and Margaret Mary, *née* Torpey (d 1985); *b* 9 Feb 1954; *Educ* Cardinal Vaughan GS, Univ of Leeds (BA, PGCE); *m* 12 June 1981, Jane, da of Derek Alfred Tony Vincent (d 1980); 1 s (Owen b 1986); *Career* Rehabilitation of Metropolitan Addicts (ROMA) 1977-79, Extern Belfast 1979-80, Short-Stay Young Homeless Project 1980-81, Leeds Young Person's Housing Tst 1982-85, Leeds Housing Concern 1985-88, York City Cncl Housing Dept 1988-; poetry published in various national and local pubns incl TLS and Ir Review, winner 1987 Nat Poetry Competition; *Style*— Ian Duhig, Esq; 16 Pasture Terrace, Leeds LS7 4QR (☎ 0532 696255); 1 Museum St, York (☎ 0904 613161)

DUKE, Prof Chris; s of Frederick Alexander Duke, of Manchester, and Edith *née* Page; *b* 4 Oct 1938; *Educ* Eltham Coll, Jesus Coll Cambridge (BA, Cert Ed, MA), King's Coll London (PhD); *m* 1, (m dis 1981), Audrey Ann, *née* Solomon; 3 s (Stephen b 1968, Alex b 1978, Paul b 1981), 2 da (Annie b 1970, Cathy b 1972); m 2, Jan 1982, Elizabeth Ann, da of E Lloyd Sommerlad, of Sydney, Aust; *Career* lectr: Woolwich Poly 1961-66, Univ of Leeds 1966-69; fndr dir of continuing educn Australian National Univ 1969-85, fndn prof and chm of continuing educn and dir of open studies Univ of Warwick 1985-, ed Int Jl of Univ Adult Educn 1971-, author of various books; hon sec Univs Cncl for Adult and Continuing Educn and other int and local continuing educn positions; Hon DLitt Keimyung Univ Korea; FACE, FRSA; *Recreations* gardening, bird-watching, living; *Style*— Prof Chris Duke; 91 Upper Holly Walk, Leamington Spa, Warwickshire CV32 4JS; Dept of Continuing Education, University of Warwick, Coventry CV4 7AL (☎ 0203 523835)

DUKE, Maj-Gen Sir Gerald William; KBE (1966, CBE 1945), CB (1962), DSO (1945), DL (Kent 1970); s of late Lt-Col Arthur A G Duke, IA; *b* 12 Nov 1910; *Educ* Dover Coll, RMA Woolwich, Jesus Coll Cambridge; *m* 1946, Mary Elizabeth, *née* Burn (d 1979); 1 s, 1 da; *Career* 2 Lt RE 1931, served with MEF 1936-44, Lt-Col 1942, Brig 1944, NW Europe 1944-45, SEAC 1945-46 (despatches), Maj-Gen 1959; attaché Cairo 1952-54, engr-in-chief WO 1963, Army dept MOD 1964-65, ret; Col Cmdt Military Provost Staff Corps 1961-67, Col Cmdt RE 1966-75; govr Dover Coll 1961-, vice pres Hockey Assoc 1965-, chm SS & AFA Kent 1973-85, pres Scout Assoc Kent 1974-85; *Clubs* Royal Ocean Racing, Rye Golf; *Style*— Maj-Gen Sir Gerald Duke, KBE, CB, DSO, DL; Little Barnfield, Hawkhurst, Kent (☎ 0580 753214)

DUKE, Lawrence Kenneth; s of Dr Marvin L Duke, of Tokyo, and Judith Anne, *née* Jackoway; *b* 7 March 1956; *Educ* Monterey HS, Mass Inst of Technol (BS), Univ of NY State (BS), Harvard Business Sch (MBA); *Career* US Navy Offr Nuclear Power Program and Civil Engrg Corps 1978-82 (Navy Achievement medal 1981); portfolio mangr Citibank NA, Treasy Dubai UAE 1984-86, chief dealer Futures and Options Gp Treasy Midland Bank London 1986, dep gen mangr Treasy Nomura Bank International London 1986-90, vice pres and global head of new prod devpt State Street Bank and Trust Company London 1990-; tutor in fin Evening MBA Prog City Univ Business Sch 1989-; memb Int Forex Assoc 1984; *Recreations* jogging, basketball; *Style*— Lawrence Duke, Esq; 30 Prospect Place, Wapping Wall, London E1 9SP (☎ 071 480 6786)

DUKE, Neville Frederick; DSO (1943), OBE (1953), DFC (1942 and two bars 1943, 1944), AFC (1948); s of Frederick Herbert Duke; *b* 11 Jan 1922; *Educ* Convent of St Mary, Judd Sch Tonbridge; *m* 1947, Gwendoline Dorothy, da of Sydney Fellows; *Career* RAF fighter pilot and test pilot 1940-48; served WWII: UK, W Desert, N Africa; CO 145 Sqdn Italy 1944, Sqdn Ldr, ret RAF 1948; CO 615 Sqdn RAuxAF 1950-51; chief test pilot Hawker Aircraft Ltd 1948-56, md Duke Aviation, mangr Aircraft Operating Unit Dowty Group, tech advsr conslt and chief test pilot Miles Aviation Ltd; test pilot: Brooklands Aerospace Group, Lovaux Ltd, Croplease Ltd, Aeronautic Ltd; MC (Czech) 1946; Queen's Commendation 1955; *Recreations* flying, fishing, sailing; *Clubs* RAF, Royal Cruising, Royal Naval Sailing Assoc, Royal Lymington Yacht; *Style*— Neville Duke, Esq, DSO, OBE, DFC, AFC; 14 Kensington Park, Milford-On-Sea, Lymington, Hants

DUKE-WOOLLEY, Hon Mrs (Elizabeth Alice Cecilia); *née* Jolliffe; da of 3 Baron Hylton (d 1945); *b* 1906; *m* 1, 1928 (m dis 1937), Lt-Col Edmond Joly de Lotbinière (kt 1964); 2 s; m 2, 1938 (m dis 1946), Hilary Beecham Duke-Woolley, DFC, RAF; *Style*— The Hon Mrs Duke-Woolley; Cedar Cottage, Alfriston, Polegate, E Sussex BN26 5XH

DULAKE, Thomas Anthony; s of Thomas Sowerby Dulake (d 1961), and Hilda Mary Anderson, *née* Crass (d 1984); *b* 9 July 1945; *Educ* Kings Sch Bruton; *m* 7 Oct 1978, (Linda) Robin, da of John Derek Willcox (d 1980); 4 s (Thomas b 1979, George b 1980, Edward b 1982, Bartholomew b 1985); *Career* md HMS Warrior, chm Royal Stafford China Co Ltd; building advsr Landmark Tst, dep chm Warship Tst, dir Portmouth Naval Heritage Tst; *Clubs* Reform; *Style*— Thomas Dulake, Esq; 7 Gayfere St, Westminster, London SW1

DULSON, Robert P (Bob); s of Henry Dulson (d 1985), of Newcastle-Under-Lyme, and Irene May, *née* Walley, MBE; *b* 31 July 1946; *Educ* Newcastle HS Staffordshire; *m* 2 Feb 1974, Angela, da of Albert Askey, of Leek, Staffordshire; *Career* journalist Northcliffe Newspapers 1970-78; BBC: publicist 1978, sr publicity offr 1985-88, chief press offr 1988-89, head of press and info 1989; *Recreations* music, theatre, gardening, DIY; *Style*— Bob Dulson, Esq; Room 2006, BBC Television Centre, Wood Lane, London W12 7RJ (☎ 071 576 1865, fax 071 7497554, telex 265781 BBCHQ G)

DULVERTON, 2 Baron (UK 1929); Sir Frederick Anthony Hamilton Wills; 3 Bt (UK 1897), CBE (1974), TD, DL (Glos 1979); s of 1 Baron Dulverton, OBE (d 1956), and Victoria Wills, OBE, da of Rear Adm Sir Edward Chichester, 9 Bt, CB, CMG; *b* 19 Dec 1915; *Educ* Eton, Magdalen Coll Oxford (MA); *m* 1, 1939 (m dis 1960), Judith Betty (d 1983), da of Lt-Col Hon Ian Leslie-Melville, TD, s of 11 Earl of Leven and (10 of) Melville; 2 s, 2 da; m 2, 1962, Ruth Violet Mary, da of Sir Walter Randolph Fitzroy Farquhar, 5 Bt, and formerly w of Maj R G Fanshawe; *Heir* s, Hon (Gilbert) Michael Hamilton Wills; *Career* sits as Cons in House of Lords; jt master: N Cotswold 1950-56, Heythrop 1967-70; 2 Lt Lovat Scouts 1936 (Maj 1944); pres: Timber Growers' Orgn Ltd 1976-78, Bath and West and Southern Counties Agric Soc 1973, Three Counties Agric Soc 1975, Br Deer Soc (ret), Gloucestershire Tst for Nature Conservation; hon pres Timber Growers of UK ; former memb: Home Grown Timber Advsy Ctee, Scottish Advsy Ctee to Nature Conservancy Cncl; memb Red Deer Cmmn (ret); chm Dulverton Tst, former tstee World Wildlife Fund; hon life fell The Wildfowl Trust, Waynflete fell Magdalen Coll Oxford; film-maker on wildlife subjects; Gold medal of Royal Forestry Soc of England, Wales and NI 1982; Cdr of the Order of the Golden Ark (Netherlands); *Style*— The Rt Hon the Lord Dulverton, CBE, TD, DL; Batsford Park, Moreton-in-Marsh, Glos (☎ 0608 50303); Fassfern, Kinlocheil, Fort William, Inverness-shire (☎ 039 783 232)

DUMA, Alexander Agim; s of Dervish Duma, of West Horsley, Surrey, and Naftali, *née* Andoni (d 1966); *b* 30 March 1946; *Educ* UCL (LLB); *m* 1980 (m dis 1983), Mary Gertrude, da of Surgn-Col E W Hayward, of Oxon; *Career* called to the Bar Gray's Inn 1969; Parly candidate (C) 1979, GLC candidate Bermondsey (C) 1977; dir: Blackfriars Settlement 1977-84 and 1986-89, Barclays Merchant Bank Ltd 1983-87, Chase Investment Bank Ltd 1987-89, Smith New Court Corporate Finance Ltd 1989-, Oldavon Ltd 1988- (chm), Equity & Gen plc 1987-90, Torday & Carlisle plc 1988-; memb Cncl Newcomen Collett Fndn 1977-, pres Bermondsey Cons Assoc 1979-83; *Clubs* Carlton, Gresham; *Style*— Alexander Duma, Esq; 13 Coulson St, London SW3 (☎ 071 823 7422); Smith New Court Corporate Finance Ltd, Chetwynd House, St Swithins Lane, London EC4 (☎ 071 528 8367)

DUMAS, Henry Raymond; s of Henry Dumas, CBE, MC, of The Old Rectory, Orcheston St Mary, Wilts, and Hester, *née* Lenton; *b* 18 Sept 1952; *Educ* Radley Coll, Bristol Univ (BSc); *m* 21 Sept 1979, Marina Helene, da of Allan Hayman QC, of Sidbourne Estate, Orford, Suffolk; 1 s (Henry Frederick b 1986), 2 da (Caroline Sophie b 1981, Lucy Emily b 1983); *Career* insurance broker Willis Faber & Dumas 1976-81, dir and active underwriter Wellington Underwriting Agencies 1986- (with co 1981-); *Recreations* golf, tennis, opera; *Clubs* MCC, Harequins RF; *Style*— Raymond Dumas, Esq; Coldharbour Farm, Wick, Avon BS15 5RJ

DUMAS, Col (John) Jeremy; s of Lt-Col John Roger Dumas, Mount Cottage, Wherwell, Andover, Hants, and Hermione Elizabeth, *née* Parry; *b* 6 June 1942; *Educ* Radley; *m* 26 Feb 1966, Elizabeth Jane, da of Maj-Gen W Odling, CB, OBE, MC, DL, of Fingringhoe, Colchester, Essex; 1 s (Richard John b 19 Dec 1967), 2 da (Alethea (Leafy) b 7 Jan 1970, Emily b 13 Jan 1972); *Career* Mons OCS 1962, cmmnd RA 1962, 2 Lt (later Lt) 1962-67, Lt Junior Leaders Regt RA 1967-68, Capt 1969, 1 RHA 1969-71, 307 Batty 1972-73, instr RMAS 1973-74, Army Staff Coll 1975, Maj 1976, GSO2 MOD 1976-77, OC 4 (Sphinx) Field Batty RA 1978-80, GSO2 HQ NI 1980, SO2 G3 OS HQ 38 Gp RAF 1981-82, Lt-Col 1983, SO1 Nigerian Cmd and Staff Coll 1983-85, SO1 MOD 1985-88, DA Beirut 1989-90, Col 1991, DA Damascus 1991; *Recreations* offshore sailing, skiing; *Style*— Col Jeremy Dumas; c/o Ministry of Defence, Whitehall, London

DUMAS, Markham Cresswell (Mark); s of Lt-Col P A E Dumas, (d 1990), of Matfield, Kent, and Betty, *née* Hine; *b* 27 March 1951; *Educ* Pangbourne Coll; *m* 16 June 1973, Nicola, da of Herbert Bradley (d 1981), of Dublin; 3 s (Christopher b 1975, Charles b 1977, Patrick b 1980); *Career* commodity broker; md ED&F Man (Coffee) Ltd 1982- (joined 1968); govr Amesbury Sch Hindhead Surrey; *Recreations* golf, tennis, opera; *Clubs* MCC, Harlequins RF; *Style*— Mark Dumas, Esq; ED&F Man (Coffee) Ltd, Sugar Quay, Lower Thames St, London EC3R 6DU (☎ 071 626 8788, 885431)

DUMFRIES, Earl of; John Colum Crichton-Stuart; s and h of 6 Marquess of Bute, *qv*; *b* 26 April 1958; *Educ* Ampleforth; *m* 1984, Carolyn, da of Bryson Waddell (d 1975); 1 s (John, Viscount Mount-Stuart b 21 Dec 1989), 2 da (Lady Caroline b 1984, Lady Cathleen b 1986); *Career* motor racing driver as Johnny Dumfries 1980-; Br Formula Three Champion, runner-up in FIA European Formula Three Championship 1984; contracted to Ferrari grand prix team as test driver 1985; number two driver for John Player Special Team Lotus 1986; 1st place Le Mans 1988; *Style*— Earl of Dumfries

DUMMETT, Prof Michael Anthony Eardley; s of George Herbert Dummett (d 1970), and Mabel Iris, *née* Eardley-Wilmot (d 1980); *b* 27 June 1925; *Educ* Sandroyd Sch, Winchester, ChCh Oxford; *m* 1951, Ann Chesney; 3 s, 2 da (1 s and 1 da decd); *Career* Univ of Oxford: fell All Souls Coll 1950-79 (sr res fell 1974-79), reader philosophy of mathematics 1962-74, Wykeham prof of logic 1979-, fell New Coll Oxford

1979-; author of books on philosophy and tarot; FBA 1968-81; *Books Incl:* : Truth and Other Enigmas (1978), The Game of Tarot (1980); *Recreations* playing exotic card games; *Style—* Prof Michael Dummett; 54 Park Town, Oxford (☎ 0865 58698); New College, Oxford (☎ 0865 271972)

DUMPER, Anthony Charles; *see:* Dudley, Bishop of

DUNALLEY, 6 Baron (I 1800); Henry Desmond Graham Prittie; s of 5 Baron Dunalley, DSO (d 1948); *b* 14 Oct 1912; *Educ* Stowe, RMC; *m* 23 April 1947, (Mary) Philippa, o da of Maj Hon Philip Plantagenet Cary (d 1968), s of 12 Viscount Falkland, JP, DL; 2 s, 1 da; *Heir* s, Hon Henry Francis Cornelius Prittie b 30 May 1948; *Career* 2 Lt Rifle Bde 1933, served E Africa, ME, Italy and SEAC 1939-46, attached 4 KAR 1937-41, instr Staff Coll 1943, 2 KRRC 1951-52, Lt-Col, ret 1953; *Recreations* fishing; *Clubs* Kildare Street and University, Greenjackets, Christchurch (NZ, hon memb); *Style—* The Rt Hon the Lord Dunalley; Church End House, Swerford, Oxford OX7 4AX (☎ 0608 730005)

DUNANT, Sarah; da of David Dunant, and Estelle, *née* Joseph; *Educ* Godophin and Latymer Girls Sch, Newnham Coll Cambridge (BA); *m* ; 2 da (Za b 12 March 1987, Georgia b 30 Dec 1990); *Career* prodr BBC Radio Three and Four 1974-76; freelance journalist writer and broadcaster 1976-: BBC Radio Four, World Serv, Radio London, Capital Radio, The Listener; lectr Goldsmith's Coll 1985-86, presenter The Late Show BBC Two TV, co-writer Thin Air BBC One TV; *Books* Exterminating Angels (jtly, 1983), Intensive Care (jtly, 1986), Snow Storms In A Hot Climate (1988), Birth Marks (1991); *Recreations* travel; *Style—* Ms Sarah Dunant

DUNBAR; *see:* Hope-Dunbar

DUNBAR, Sir Archibald Ranulph; 11 Bt (NS 1700), of Northfield, Moray; s of Maj Sir (Archibald) Edward Dunbar, 10 Bt, MC (d 1969); *b* 8 Aug 1927; *Educ* Wellington, Pembroke Coll Cambridge, Imperial Coll of Tropical Agric Trinidad; *m* 1974, Amelia Millar Sommerville, da of H C Davidson, of Currie, Midlothian; 1 s, 2 da; *Heir* s, Edward Horace Dunbar b 18 March 1977; *Career* entered Colonial Serv 1953, agric offr Uganda, ret 1970; Hon Sheriff Sheriff's Ct Dist of Moray; Kt of Honour and Devotion SMOM 1989; *Books* A History of Bunyoro-Kitara (1965), Omukama Chwa II Kabarega (1965), The Annual Crops of Uganda (1969); *Recreations* cross-country running, model railway; *Clubs* New (Edinburgh); *Style—* Sir Archibald Dunbar, Bt; The Old Manse, Duffus, Elgin, Scotland IV30 2QD (☎ 0343 830270)

DUNBAR, Sir Drummond Cospatrick Ninian; 9 Bt (NS 1698) of Durn, Banffshire; MC (1943); s of Sir George Alexander Drummond, 8 Bt (d 1949); *b* 9 May 1917; *Educ* Radley, Worcester Coll Oxford; *m* 1957, Sheila Barbara Mary, da of John B de Fonblanque; 1 s; *Heir* s, Robert Drummond Cospatrick Dunbar; *Career* served WWII Maj Black Watch; served: Middle E 1942-43, N Africa 1943, Sicily 1943, Normandy 1944 (twice wounded); Maj Black Watch, ret 1958; *Clubs* Naval and Military; *Style—* Sir Drummond Dunbar, Bt, MC

DUNBAR, Sir Jean Ivor; 13 Bt (NS 1694), of Mochrum, Wigtownshire; s of Sir Adrian Ivor Dunbar, 12 Bt (d 1977); *b* 4 April 1918; *m* 1944, Rose Jeanne Hertsch; 2 s, 1 da; *Heir* s, Capt James Michael Dunbar, USAF b 17 Jan 1950; *Career* late Sgt Mountain Engineers, USA Army; *Style—* Sir Jean Dunbar, Bt; Mochrum Park, Kirkcowan, Wigtownshire

DUNBAR, John Greenwell; s of John Dunbar; *b* 1 March 1930; *Educ* UCS London, Balliol Oxford (MA); *m* 1974, Elizabeth Mill Blyth; *Career* sec Royal Cmmn on the Ancient and Historical Monuments of Scotland 1978-90; memb Ancient Monuments Bd for Scotland 1978-90; FSA, FSA Scot, hon FRIAS; *Books* The Architecture of Scotland (revised edn 1978), Accounts of the Masters of Works 1616-1649 (vol 2, jt ed 1982); *Clubs* New (Edinburgh); *Style—* John Dunbar, Esq, FSA; Patie's Mill, Carlops, by Penicuik, Midlothian (☎ 0968 60250)

DUNBAR, Robert Drummond Cospatrick; s and h of Sir Drummond Dunbar, 9 Bt; *b* 17 June 1958; *Educ* Harrow, Ch Ch Oxford; *Career* investment mangr; *Style—* Robert Dunbar, Esq

DUNBAR, William John; OBE (1986); s of Capt William George Dunbar (d 1980), and Margaret May, *née* Probin (d 1939); *b* 19 May 1931; *Educ* Prior Park Bath; *m* 8 Feb 1958, Maureen Ann, da of Col C Harris, OBE, MC (d 1966); 2 s (Simon b 1959, Richard b 1960), 2 da (Catherine b 1961 d 1983, Anna b 1964); *Career* Nat Serv 2 Lt Trieste Italy 1953-55, chief fin offr Olayan Saudi Hldgs 1978-80, chief exec BSC Ind Ltd 1980-85, gp md BETEC plc 1985, dir Clayhithe plc 1986-; FCMA, FBCS, FBIM; *Recreations* tennis, squash, skiing; *Clubs* IOD; *Style—* W J Dunbar, Esq, OBE; BETC plc, Mandeville Rd, Aylesbury, Bucks HP21 8AB (☎ 0296 395911, telex 83210, fax 0296 82424)

DUNBAR OF HEMPRIGGS, Dame Maureen Daisy Helen; Btss (NS 1706), of Hempriggs, Caithness-shire; da of Courtenay Edward Moore (decd), s of late Jessie Mona Duff (decd), (who m Rev Canon Courtenay Moore), da of de jure 5 Bt; suc kinsman, Sir George Cospatrick Duff-Sutherland-Dunbar, 7 Bt, 1963; assumed name of Dunbar 1963, and recognised in the name of Dunbar of Hempriggs by Lyon Court 1965; *b* 19 Aug 1906; *Educ* Headington Sch Oxford, RCM (LRAM); *m* 1940, Leonard James Blake (d 1989), former dir of music Malvern Coll; 1 s, 1 da; *Heir* s, Richard Francis Dunbar of Hempriggs, yr; *Career* music teacher; *Style—* Lady Dunbar of Hempriggs, Btss; 51 Gloucester St, Winchcombe, Cheltenham, Glos (☎ 0242 602122)

DUNBOYNE, 28 Baron (18 by Patent) (I 1324 and 1541) Patrick Theobald Tower Butler; VRD; s of 27 Baron (d 1945), and Dora Isolde Butler (d 1977), da of Cdr F F Tower, OBE, RNVR; *b* 27 Jan 1917; *Educ* Winchester, Trinity Coll Cambridge (MA); *m* 29 July 1950, Anne Marie, o da of late Sir Victor Alexander Louis Mallet, GCMG, CVO; 1 s, 3 da; *Heir* s, Hon John Fitzwalter Butler; *Career* 2 Lt (Supp Res) Irish Gds 1939, Lt 1940-44 (POW 1940-43, King's Badge), Refugee Dept Foreign Office 1945-46; called to the Bar: Middle Temple 1949, Inner Temple 1962, King's Inns Dublin 1966; practised from London 1949-71, rec Hastings 1961-71; dep chm: Kent QS 1963-71, Middx QS 1962-65, Inner London QS 1971; circuit judge 1972-86, Archbishop of Canterbury's commissary gen for Canterbury Diocese 1959-71; pres and fell Irish Genealogical Res Soc; *Books* The Trial of J G Haigh (Notable British Trials Series, 1953), Recollections of the Cambridge Union 1815-39 (jtly, 1953), Butler Family History (1966, 7 edn 1990), Happy Families (1983); *Recreations* lawn tennis, Butler genealogies; *Clubs* Irish, All England Lawn Tennis of GB, Int Lawn Tennis (pres 1973-83), 45 (pres 1974-), Union (Cambridge, pres 1939), Pitt (Cambridge); *Style—* His Hon The Rt Hon Lord Dunboyne, VRD; 36 Ormonde Gate, London SW3 4HA (☎ 071 352 1837)

DUNCAN, Alexander John (Alex); s of Alexander Gideon Duncan (d 1963), and Ada Emmie Jervis, of Newcastle, Staffs; *b* 5 Feb 1925; *Educ* Newcastle-under-Lyme HS Staffs, Univ of Birmingham (BComm); *m* 29 Oct 1962, Elsie Jeannette, da of George William Pember (d 1969); *Career* treas Birmingham Univ Guild of Undergraduates 1950-51; pres North Staffordshire Soc of CAs 1980-81; memb: Newcastle-under-Lyme Conservative Club; Stoke-on-Trent Repetory Players, ACA 1957, ACCA; *Recreations* listening to jazz and other music, theatre; *Style—* Alex Duncan, Esq; Wychways, 28 Parkway, Trentham, Stoke-on-Trent (☎ 0782 657951), Alex G Duncan & Co, 31 Hartshill Rd, Stoke-on-Trent (☎ 0782 44808)

DUNCAN, Andrew Raymond; s of Arthur Raymond Duncan, and Olwyn, *née* Williams; *b* 19 Nov 1947; *Educ* Hutchesons Boys' GS Glasgow; *m* 18 June 1971, Carol Ann, da of Maj Edwin Ralph Duggan (d 1987); 1 s (Charles b 6 April 1976), 1 da (Jane b 15 Nov 1972); *Career* CA; ptnr Frame Kennedy and Forrest 1972-89, started own practice 1989; Highland Area Inst of CA's: sec 1977-87, memb Cncl 1987-89, memb Finance and Gen Purpose Ctee 1987-89; memb joint working party Scottish and English Inst CA; sec Highland Craft Point to Promote Scottish Crafts and Craftsmen 1980-; MICAS; *Recreations* fishing, walking, reading, music; *Style—* Andrew Duncan, Esq; Enrick House, Balnain, Glenurquhart, Invernes-shire IV3 6TJ (☎ 04564 352); Andrew Duncan & Co, Chartered Accountants, 2 Culduthel Rd, Inverness IV2 4AB (☎ 0463 711178, fax 0463 238076)

DUNCAN, Prof Archibald Alexander McBeth; s of Charles George Duncan (d 1978), of Edinburgh, and Christina Helen, *née* McBeth (d 1973); *b* 17 Oct 1926; *Educ* George Heriot's Sch Edinburgh, Univ of Edinburgh, Balliol Coll Oxford; *m* 21 Aug 1954, Ann Hayes, da of William Ewart Hayes Sawyer (d 1969); 2 s (Alastair David b 1958, Ewen James b 1960), 1 da (Beatrice Jane b 1956); *Career* lectr Balliol Coll Oxford 1950-51; lectr in history: Queen's Univ Belfast 1951-53, Univ of Edinburgh 1953-62; Leverhulme res fell 1961-62, prof of Scottish history and literature Univ of Glasgow 1962-; clerk of Senate Univ of Glasgow 1978-83; memb Royal Cmmn on the Ancient and Historical Mounuments of Scotland 1969-; FRHistS 1960, FRSE 1982, FBA 1987; *Books* Scotland, The Making of the Kingdom (1975), Scotland from Earliest Times to 1603 (by W C Dickinson, revised by A A M Duncan 3 edn 1977), Regesta Regum Scotorim V, The Acts of Robert I 1306-29 (1988); *Style—* Prof Archibald Duncan, FRSE; 17 Campbell Drive, Bearsden, Glasgow G61 4NF (☎ 041 942 5023); Department of Scottish History, 9 University Gardens, Glasgow G12 8QH (☎ 041 339 8855 5349, fax 041 330 4808)

DUNCAN, Prof Archibald Sutherland; DSC (1943); s of Rev Henry Cecil Duncan, KIH (d 1963), of Darjeeling, India, and (Rose) Elsie, *née* Edwards (d 1958); *b* 17 July 1914; *Educ* Merchiston Castle Sch, Univ of Edinburgh (MB ChB); *m* 12 April 1939, Barbara, da of John Gibson Holliday, JP (d 1955), of Penrith, Cumbria; *Career* WWII Surgn Lt Cdr RNVR Med and UK; jr hosp appts in Royal Infirmary Edinburgh and Gt Ormond St London 1936-41, temp obstetrician and gynaecologist Inverness 1945-46, lectr and pt/t conslt obstetrician and gynaecologist Univ of Aberdeen 1946-50, sr lectr Univ of Edinburgh and conslt Western Gen Hosp Edinburgh 1950-53, prof of obstetrics and gynaecology Univ of Wales 1953-66, conslt Utd Cardiff Hosps 1953-66, exec dean Faculty of Med and prof of med educn Univ of Edinburgh 1966-76; chm Scot Cncl on Disability 1977-80, vice pres Inst of Med Ethics 1985-, Gen Cncl Assessor Ct Univ of Edinburgh 1979-83; hon pres: Br Med Students Assoc 1965-66, Univ of Edinburgh Graduates' Assoc; memb: Lothian Health Bd 1977-83 (vice chm 1981-83), James IV Assoc of Surgns, Gen Med Cncl 1974-78; hon memb Alpha Omega Alpha Hon Med Soc (USA); Hon MD Univ of Edinburgh 1984; memb: BMA, Assoc for Study of Med Educn; FRCS (Edinburgh) 1939, FRCOG 1955, FRCP (Edinburgh) 1969; *Books* Dictionary of Medical Ethics (ed jtly, second edn 1981); *Recreations* photography, mountains; *Clubs* New (Edinburgh); *Style—* Prof Archibald Duncan, DSC; 1 Walker St, Edinburgh EH3 7JY (☎ 031 225 7657)

DUNCAN, Lady; Beatrice Mary Moore; da of Thomas O'Carroll and widow of Maj Philip Blair-Oliphant; *m* 1960, as his 2 w, Sir James Alexander Lawson Duncan, 1 Bt (d 1974); *Style—* Lady Duncan; Jordanston, by Alyth, Perthshire

DUNCAN, Prof Christopher John; s of Jack William Duncan (d 1982), Selsdon, and Muriel Agnes, *née* Kirlew (d 1966); *b* 23 Feb 1932; *Educ* Trinity Sch of John Whitgift Croydon, Queen Mary Coll London (BSc, PhD); *m* 6 Sept 1958, Jennifer Jane, da of Ernest John Powell (d 1964), of Bickley, Kent; 3 s (Stephen b 1959, James b 1962, Alastair b 1962); *Career* reader in animal physiology Univ of Durham 1964-70, prof of zoology Univ of Liverpool 1970- (lectr in zoology 1958-64); memb Cncl symposium convener and pubn offr Soc for Experimental Biology, govr Liverpool Poly 1985-89, memb Cncl and chm NW Gp Inst of Biol; FIBiol 1980, scientific fell Zoological Soc of London 1980, FRSA 1989; *Books* Molecular Properties and Evolution of Excitable Cells (1967), Calcium in Biological Systems (ed, 1976), Secretory Mechanisms (ed, 1979); *Recreations* sailing, gardening, reading; *Clubs* Dee Sailing; *Style—* Prof Christopher Duncan; 3 Eddisbury Road, West Kirby, Wirral, Merseyside L48 5DR (☎ 051 632 1261), Dept of Environmental Biology, School of Life Sciences, University of Liverpool, PO Box 147, Liverpool L69 3BX (☎ 051 7944987, fax 051 7086502, telex 627095 UNILPL G)

DUNCAN, Rev Dr Denis MacDonald; s of Reginald Duncan (d 1951), of Edinburgh, and Clarice Ethel, *née* Hodgkinson (d 1967); *b* 10 Jan 1920; *Educ* George Watson's Coll Edinburgh, Univ of Edinburgh (MA, BD), Univ of Somerset (PhD); *m* 21 March 1942, Henrietta Watson Mackenzie, da of Capt John Barclay Houston, RN (d 1940), of Edinburgh; 1 s (Raymond Denis b 1942), 1 da (Carol Louise Watson (Mrs Pyle) b 1945); *Career* minister: St Margaret's Juniper Green Edinburgh 1944-50, Trinity Duke St Glasgow 1950-57; ed British Weekly 1958-70 (managing ed 1962-70); assoc dir and trg supervisor Westminster Pastoral Fndn 1972-79, dir The Churches' Cncl for Health and Healing 1983-88; md Arthur James Ltd (Publishers) 1983-; chm World Assoc for Pastoral Care and Counselling 1977-79; writer and interviewer Scott TV 1974-79; chm: Highgate Counselling Centre London 1970-, St Barnabas Ecumenical Centre for Christian Counselling and Healing Norwich; pres Green Pastures Home of Healing; memb Inst of Journalists; fell: Int Inst of Community Serv, Int Biographical Assoc; *Books* Creative Silence, A Day at a Time, Love, The Word that Heals, The Way of Love, Victorious Living, Here is my Hand! Health and Healing: A Ministry to Wholeness; ed: Through the Year with William Barclay, Through the Year with JB Phillips, Everyday with William Barclay, Marching Orders, Marching On; *Clubs* Arts; *Style—* The Rev Dr Denis Duncan; 1 Cranbourne Rd, London N10 2BT (☎ 081 883 1831, fax 081 883 8307); 4 Broadway Rd, Evesham, Worcs WR11 (☎ 0386 446566, fax 0386 446566)

DUNCAN, Derek Cecil; s of Joseph Hugh Duncan (d 1960), of Farnham, Surrey, and Hilda Madeleine, *née* Pickford (d 1989); *b* 10 June 1932; *Educ* Rugby, Univ of Cambridge (MA); *m* 17 Feb 1973, Yvonne Louise, da of Ernest Stanley Crisp (d 1981), of Rustington, Sussex; *Career* Lt 33 Parachute FD Regt RA 1953; admitted slr 1960, asst sec Stock Exchange 1964, sr asst sec Law Soc 1976, area dir Southern Legal Aid 1980, ret 1989; memb: Law Soc 1960, Oxford and Cambridge Golf Soc 1963; Liveryman Worshipful Co of Grocers 1968; *Books* In Alpine Pastures (1963); *Recreations* golf, photography, sitting in the sun; *Style—* Derek Duncan, Esq; Heather Way, Lower Bourne, Farnham, Surrey (☎ 025 125 4291)

DUNCAN, Lady Eileen Elizabeth; *née* Hope Johnstone; da of Maj Percy Wentworth Hope Johnstone, RA (TA), *de jure* 10 Earl of Annandale and Hartfell (d 1983), by his 2 w, Margaret (*see* Dowager Countess of Annandale and Hartfell); *b* 3 Oct 1948; *m* 1969, Andrew Walter Bryce Duncan, son of Sir Arthur Bryce Duncan (d 1984); 3 s; *Style—* The Lady Eileen Duncan; Newlands, Kirkmahoe, Dumfries and Galloway

DUNCAN, Lady; Etelka de Vangel; *m* 1958, Sir (Charles Edgar) Oliver Duncan, 3 and last Bt (d 1964); *Style—* Lady Duncan; Horsforth Hall, Guiseley, W Yorks

DUNCAN, George; s of William Duncan (d 1966), and Catherine Gray, *née* Murray; *b* 9 Nov 1933; *Educ* Holloway Co GS, LSE (BSc), Wharton Sch of Fin, Pennsylvania Univ (MBA); *m* 1965, Frauke Ulricke; 1 da (Fiona b 1969); *Career* chief exec: Truman Habury Buxton Ltd 1967-71, Watney Mann Ltd 1971-72, Yule Catto & Co Ltd 1973-

75; vice chm International Distillers & Vintners Ltd 1972; chm: Lloyds Bowmaker Ltd 1976-86 (dir 1973), ASW Holdings plc 1986-, HMC Group plc 1986-, Whessoe plc 1987- (dir 1986), Humberside Financial Group Ltd 1987; dir: BET plc 1981-, Lloyds Bank 1982-87, Haden plc 1974-85 (dep chm 1984-85), TR City of London Trust plc 1977-, Associated British Ports Holdings plc 1986-, Newspaper Publishing plc 1986-, Dewe Rogerson Group Ltd 1987, Calor Group plc 1990-; chm CBI Cos Ctee 1980-83, memb President's Ctee CBI 1980-83; Freeman City of London 1971; FCA, CBIM; *Recreations* tennis, skiing, opera; *Style—* George Duncan, Esq; c/o Granville House, 132 Sloane St, London SW1X 9AX (☎ 071 730 0491)

DUNCAN, Ian Alexander; s of late Kenneth George Duncan, and Peggy Pauline, *née* Stuchbury; *b* 21 April 1946; *Educ* Central GS Birmingham, Coll of Commerce Birmingham; *m* Carol Hammond, da of William Wilford Smith, of Bucks; 2 s (Adam Harvey b 1966, Alexander James b 1975), 1 da (Tavira Caroline b 1975); *Career* certified accountant, founding fell Assoc of Corp Treasurers, formerly fin dir Pentos plc (resigned Pentos and all subsids 1984); fin dir Tomkins (and subsids and assocs) 1984-; *Recreations* travel, flying helicopters, DIY, gardening, music, reading; *Style—* Ian A Duncan, Esq; The Tudor House, Devonshire Avenue, Amersham-on-the-Hill, Bucks HP6 5JF; East Putney House, 84 Upper Richmond Rd, London SW15 2ST (☎ 081 871 4544, fax 081 874 3882)

DUNCAN, Ian McIntosh; *b* 25 Nov 1931; *Educ* Royal HS Edinburgh; *m* 14 June 1958, Marjorie Anne, da of Robert Brown (d 1968); 3 s (Callum b 1960, Neil b 1962, Andrew b 1964); *Career* Imperial Chemical Industries 1957-72 (various appts from works accountant to head Profits and Forecasting Group), Cavenham Ltd 1972-82 (various appts from gp controller to dir), GO Holdings Management Inc 1983-88 (chm, pres and chief exec), md fin and admin Guiness plc 1990-, non-exec dir Era Group plc 1990-; *Recreations* tennis, golf, badminton; *Style—* Ian Duncan, Esq; Guiness plc, 39 Portman Square, London W1H 9HB (☎ 071 486 0288, fax 071 486 4968, telex 23368)

DUNCAN, Sir James Blair; s of John Duncan, and Emily MacFarlane Duncan; *b* 24 Aug 1927; *Educ* Whitehall Sch Glasgow; *m* 1974, Betty Psaltis; *Career* chm Transport Development Group Ltd 1975-; memb LTE (pt/t) 1979-82, vice pres Scottish Cncl 1983- (memb 1976-); chm: London Exec Ctee 1983-, London C of C 1986-88; pres Inst of Rd Tport Engrs 1984-88, Chartered Inst of Tport 1980-1981; CA (Scotland), FCIT, CBIM, FRSA (1977); kt 1981; *Books* Papers on Transport matters; *Recreations* travel, reading, walking, swimming, theatre; *Clubs* Caledonian; *Style—* Sir James Duncan; 17 Kingston House South, Ennismore Gdns, London, SW7

DUNCAN, Kathleen Nora; da of George James Denis Dale (d 1983), and Nellie Logan, *née* Jamieson; *b* 26 Sept 1946; *Educ* Christs Hosp, St Aidans Coll Durham (BA), Poly of Central London (Dip Arts Admin); *m* 11 Jan 1975 (m dis 1983), Neil Stuart Duncan; *Career* head of arts servs London Borough of Havering 1971-73, dep dir SE Arts 1974-76, chief exec Composers and Authors Soc of Hong Kong 1977-79, gen mangr Archer Travel Hong Kong 1979-82, int mktg dir Boosey & Hawkes Music Publishers Ltd 1983-86, mktg dir Order of St John 1986-89, mktg conslt The Performing Right Soc Ltd 1989-90, DG TSB Foundation for England and Wales; almoner and govr Christs Hosp; MinstD; *Recreations* music, travel, walking; *Style—* Mrs Kathleen Duncan; 148 Cranmer Ct, London SW3 3HF (☎ 071 589 6777); TSB Foundation for England and Wales, 25 Milk St, London EC2V 8LU (☎ 071 606 7070, fax 071 606 0510)

DUNCAN, Dr Kenneth Playfair; CB (1985); s of Rev John Henry Duncan (d 1951), and Sophia, *née* Ritchie (d 1985); *b* 27 Sept 1924; *Educ* HS of Dundee, Univ of St Andrews (BSc, MB ChB); *m* 1950, Gillian, da of Dr Douglas Arthur Crow (d 1944); 4 da (Janet, Sally, Mary, Lucy); *Career* chief MO UKAEA 1958-69, head of health and safety Br Steel 1969-75, visiting prof London Sch of Hygiene 1976-80, dep dir gen HSE 1982-85 (dir med servs 1975-81), asst dir biological med NRPB 1985-89; FRCPE, FRCP; *Recreations* gardening, walking; *Style—* Dr Kenneth Duncan, CB; Westfield, Steeple Aston, Oxon (☎ 0869 40277)

DUNCAN, Kenneth Sandilands (Sandy); OBE; s of Dr William Arthur Duncan (d 1946), of 3 Wilmington Terrace, Eastbourne, Sussex, and Ethel Mary, *née* Edwards (d 1969); *b* 26 April 1912; *Educ* St Andrew's Eastbourne, Malvern, New Coll Oxford (BA); *m* 1, 4 June 1941, Katharine Beatrice, *née* Darwall (d 1955); 1 s (Andrew Duncan b 1943); m 2, June 1957 (m dis 1966), Dorothy, *née* Wentworth; *Career* WWII 2 Lt 176 Field Battery RA 1940, lectr OCTU Ilkley Yorks 1942-44, Asst Staff Capt, RA 3 Br Inf Div 1944-45, lectr WO Sch of Mil Admin No 1 Trg Wing, Maj (non substantive) reverting to Capt; master Bradfield 1935-38, gen sec Univs Athletics Union 1949-51, hon sec Achilles Club (Oxford and Cambridge blues and half blues) 1948-87, gen sec Cwlth Games Cncl for Eng 1948-72, hon sec Cwlth Games Fedn 1948-82, gen sec Br Olympic Assoc 1948-75 (conslt/librarian); Double Blue (Oxon) Athletics 1931, Soccer 1935, competed GB Int Athletics 1932-37; winner: Silver medal 4 x 110 yds relay Cwlth Games 1938, Gold medal 4 x 110 yds World Univ Games (Paris) 1937; Chef de Mission of 12 GB Olympic Teams (summer and winter) 1952-72; Olympic Order 1984, The White Rose and Lion of Finland 1952; *Books* The Oxford Book of Athletic Training (1957), Athletics - Do it This Way (1952); *Clubs* East India, Over-Seas League; *Style—* Sandy Duncan, Esq, OBE; Flat 1, 57 Gloucester Rd, South Kensington, London SW7 4QN (☎ 071 584 4012); The British Olympic Association, 1 Wandsworth Plain, London SW18 1EN (☎ 081 871 2677, fax 081 871 9104, telex 932312

DUNCAN, Michael Greig; s of Alec Greig Duncan (d 1979), and Betty, *née* Shaw; *b* 9 Sept 1957; *Educ* King Williams Coll IOM, Downing Coll Cambridge (BA); *m* 2 July 1983, Fiona Helen, da of Michael John Carlisle Glaze, CMG; 2 s (Rory b 8 March 1985, Adam b 12 June 1989), 1 da (Chloe b 14 Oct 1986); *Career* admitted slr 1981, ptnr Allen & Overy 1987- (asst slr 1981-86); memb City of London Law Soc; *Style—* Michael Duncan, Esq; 9 Cheapside, London EC2V 6AD (☎ 071 248 9898, fax 071 236 2192, telex 881 2801)

DUNCAN, Dr Nicholas Hugh; s of Maj Dr Peter Duncan (d 1979), of Wyle Cop, Hyde Rd, Gorton, Manchester, and Pauline May, *née* Hughes; *b* 9 Sept 1954; *Educ* William Hulme's GS, Royal Victoria Med Sch Manchester (MB ChB); *m* 25 June 1984, Claire, da of Dennis Cooper (d 1980), of Hillview, Hollowood Rd, Malpas, Cheshire; 1 s (Ashley James b 1986); *Career* sr registrar in anaesthesia Ahmadu Bello Univ Kaduna Nigeria 1982-83, sr registrar in anaesthesia Univ of Cambridge 1983-85, conslt in anaesthesia and intensive care Queen Elizabeth Hosp Kings Lynn Norfolk 1986-; FFARCS 1982; *Recreations* shooting, skiing, windsurfing; *Style—* Dr Nicholas Duncan; Dept of Anaesthesia, Queen Elizabeth Hospital, Gayton Rd, King's Lynn, Norfolk PE30 4ET (☎ 0553 766266)

DUNCAN, Dr Peter Watson; s of Arthur Alexander Watson Duncan, of Edinburgh, and Catherine Bowes, *née* Williamson; *b* 14 April 1954; *Educ* George Heriots Sch, Univ of Edinburgh (MB ChB); *m* 16 April 1983, Fiona Margaret, da of Arthur Murray Grierson, of Tetbury, Glos; 1 s (Ian b 27 Feb 1987), 2 da (Meg b 3 April 1985, Jane b 18 Aug 1989); *Career* registrar in anaesthetics Royal Infirmary of Edinburgh 1979-82; sr registrar in anaesthetics: Newcastle upon Tyne 1982-85, Univ of Natal Durban 1983-84; conslt in anaesthetics and intensive care Royal Preston Hosp 1985-; memb Intensive Care Soc; FFARCS 1981; *Recreations* photography, music; *Style—* Dr Peter Duncan; Royal Preston Hospital, Sharoe Green Lane, Preston, Lancs (☎ 0772 710555)

DUNCAN, Roderick Kenneth; s of Kenneth George Duncan, DCM (d 1979), and Peggy Pauline, *née* Stutchbury; *b* 9 Feb 1949; *Educ* Central GS for Boys Birmingham, Birmingham Coll of Commerce; *m* 23 Sept 1972, Susan Deborah, da of Lionel William Lane, of Solihull; 2 s (Matthew James b 9 May 1978, Alistair Scott b 19 Nov 1980); *Career* sales dir Company Unit Trusts Ltd 1985-87, investmt sales dir Aetna International (UK) Ltd 1987-, dir Aetna Unit Trusts Ltd 1987-, dep md Schroder Unit Trusts Ltd 1989; ACIS 1972; *Recreations* golf, militaria, golf memorabelia; *Style—* Roderick Duncan, Esq; Amberley, Orchard Rd, Shalford, Surrey GU4 8ER; Shroder Unit Trusts Ltd, Gutter Lane, London EC2

DUNCAN, (Harry) Roy; s of Harry William Duncan, and Olive, *née* Jackson (d 1969); *b* 29 June 1948; *Educ* Truro Sch Cornwall; *m* 27 Oct 1973, Barbara Alison, da of Peter Vincent James, of 10 Grassholm Close, Milford Haven, Dyfed; 2 da (Armorel b 1977, Bryony b 1978); *Career* Army Intelligence Corps 1965; former Church of Eng reader, former lifeboatman, magistrate, pres local branch Br Heart Fndn, chm Cncl of the Isles of Scilly 1985- (memb 1969-); *Recreations* ornithology, drumming, golf; *Style—* Roy Duncan, Esq; The Biggal, St Mary's, Isles of Scilly, Cornwall TR21 OPT (☎ 0720 22648)

DUNCAN, His Excellency Stanley Frederick St Clare; CMG (1983); s of Stanley Gilbert Scott Duncan; *b* 13 Nov 1927; *Educ* Latymer Upper; *m* 1967, Jennifer Bennett; 2 da; *Career* India Office 1946; CRO 1947-67; Diplomatic Service 1967-, head Consular Dept FCO 1977-80, Canadian Nat Def Coll Kingston Ontario 1980-81, Br ambass Bolivia 1981-85; Br high cmmr Malta 1985-; *Style—* His Excellency Mr Stanley Duncan, CMG; 7 St Anne Street, Floriana, Valletta, Malta; c/o Foreign and Commonwealth Office, King Charles St, London SW1A 2AH

DUNCAN, Hon Mrs (Doreen) Synolda Tower Butler); da of 27 Baron Dunboyne (decd); *b* 17 Feb 1918; *m* 1945, Maj Atholl Duncan, MC, RA (d 1983); 2 s, 2 da; *Style—* The Hon Mrs Duncan; 9 Marland House, 28 Sloane St, London SW1X 9NE

DUNCAN MILLAR, Ian Alastair; CBE (1978), MC (1945), JP (1952), DL (1960); s of late Sir James Duncan Millar; *b* 22 Nov 1914; *Educ* Gresham's, Univ of Cambridge (MA); *m* 1945, Louise Reid, da of W McCosh (d 1937); 2 s, 2 da; *Career* served Corps of Royal Engrs 1940-45, Maj; contested (Lab) Parly elections Banff 1945, Kinross and W Perthshire 1949 and 1963; Perthshire and Kinross: cncllr 1946-79, convenor 1975-78; regnl cncllr and convenor Tayside 1974-78; dir Macdonald Fraser and Co 1961-86, Tay Dist Salmon Fisheries Bd 1962-80 and 1986-; chm: United Auctions (Scot) Ltd 1967-74, conslt ctee on Freshwater and Salmon Fisheries Act 1981-; vice pres Scot Landowners Fedn 1985-90; memb Royal Co of Archers (Queen's Bodyguard for Scotland) 1956-; MICE 1939, CEng, FIFM 1988; *Books* A Countryman's Cog (1990); *Recreations* learning about and catching salmon, meeting people; *Clubs* Royal Perth Golfing Soc; *Style—* I A Duncan Millar Esq, CBE, MC, JP, DL; Reynock, Remony, Aberfeldy, Perthshire PH15 2HR (☎ 088 73 400)

DUNCAN-SANDYS *see also*: Sandys

DUNCAN-SANDYS, Hon Laura Jane; 3 and yst da of Baron Duncan-Sandys, CH, PC (Life Peer; d 1987), and only da by his 2 w Marie-Claire, *née* Schmitt; *b* 1964; *Educ* Queen's Coll Harley St; *Career* dir Newton Sandys Ltd (mktg consultancy), conslt to traders in Eastern Block; sr parly offr Consumers Assoc 1989-90, fndr Laura Sandys Assoc 1990-; *Style—* The Hon Laura Duncan-Sandys; 30 Hesper Mews, London SW5 (☎ 071 373 7421)

DUNCOMBE; *see*: Pauncefort-Duncombe

DUNCOMBE, (Nicholas) Guy; s of Roy Duncombe, and Joan Thornley, *née* Pickering; *b* 1 Sept 1952; *Educ* Abbotsholme Sch Derbyshire; *m* 14 Jan 1973; 2 da (Kirsty Nicola b 1974, Zoe Louise b 1975); *Career* CA; dir: Finance & Equity Ltd, Heritage Leisure Gp Ltd; *Recreations* sailing, flying, shooting, skiing; *Clubs* Naval and Military; *Style—* Guy Duncombe; Bramble Cottage, Osbaston, Nuneaton, Warks (☎ 0455 291007); Quorn House, 21 Station Rd, Hinckley, Leics (☎ 0455 611044)

DUNCOMBE, Roy; VRD (1957); *b* 7 June 1925; *Educ* Hinckley GS; *m* 6 May 1946, Joan Thornley; 1 s, 2 da; *Career* Pilot Fleet Air Arm, Lt Cdr (A) RNR; chm Nationwide Anglia Bldg Soc (former dep chm), fin dir Ferry Pickering Gp plc 1943-87; *Recreations* walking, swimming, boating, ornithology; *Clubs* Naval and Military; *Style—* Roy Duncombe, Esq, VRD; Westways, Barton Rd, Market Bosworth, Nr Nuneaton, Warwickshire CV13 0LQ (☎ 0455 291728, work 071 242 8822, car 0836 621167)

DUNCUMB, Dr Peter; s of late William Duncumb , and Hilda Grace, *née* Coleman; *b* 26 Jan 1931; *Educ* Oundle, Clare Coll Cambridge; *m* 1955, Anne Leslie, *née* Taylor; 2 s, 1 da; *Career* dir and gen mangr TI Group Res Laboratories 1979-87, dir Res Centre in Superconductivity Univ of Cambridge 1988-89; hon prof Univ of Warwick 1990-; FRS; *Style—* Dr Peter Duncumb, FRS; 5 Woollards Lane, Great Shelford, Cambridge (☎ 0223 843064)

DUNDAS, (Robert) Alexander; sixteenth representative of the Robertsons of Auchleeks dating from 1530; s of Ralph Dundas (d 1982), of Airds, Appin, Argyll, and Margaret Beryl, *née* Maclean of Ardgour, *qv*; ggs of Ralph Dundas and Emily Bridget (d 1934), da of Robert Robertson, 10 of Auchleeks (d 1872); twelfth in male line descent from Sir William Dundas, 15 of Dundas (ka 1513 at Flodden Field); *b* 12 June 1947; *Educ* Harrow, Ch Ch Oxford; *m* 9 July 1977, Sarah Rosalind, da of (William) Simon Wilson, of Ballochmorrie, Barrhill, Girvan, Ayrshire, and Ann, da of Sir James Lithgow, 1 Bt; 1 s (Ralph b 1988), 1 da (Catriona b 1985); *Career* Grieveson, Grant & Co stockbrokers 1970-79 (portfolio mangr Far East 1974-79), dir and investmt mangr Japan G T Management Asia Ltd 1980-, dir GT Management plc 1984- (chm Investmt Ctee 1988-90); *Recreations* Scottish history, art objects, gastronomy, shooting, armchair cricket; *Clubs* Boodle's, Pratt's, Puffin's (Edinburgh), Royal Hong Kong Jockey; *Style—* Alexander Dundas, Esq; 6 Eldon Rd, London W8 5PU; G T Mgmnt plc, Eighth Floor, 8 Devonshire Square, London EC2M 4YJ (☎ 071 283 2575, fax 071 626 6176, telex 886100 GT)

DUNDAS, Lord (Richard) Bruce; yst s of 3 Marquess of Zetland, DL (d 1989); *b* 6 Jan 1951; *Educ* Harrow; *m* 1, 1974 (m dis 1981), Jane Melanie, yst da of Ernest Frederick Wright, of 47 Montrose Place, London; 1 s (Max b 1978), 1 da (Emily Louisa b 1980); m 2, 1983, Sophie Caroline, o da of Henry Giles Francis Lascelles, and Caroline, *née* Baring; 2 da (Flora b 1986, Tallulah b 1988); *Style—* The Lord Bruce Dundas; 49 Stephendale Road, London SW6

DUNDAS, Lord David Paul Nicholas; 2 s of 3 Marquess of Zetland, DL (d 1989); *b* 2 June 1945; *Educ* Harrow, Central Sch of Speech and Drama; *m* 1971, Corinna, da of Denys Scott, of 11 Glebe Place, Chelsea, London SW3; 1 s (Harry Thomas Jango b 1981), 1 da (Daisy Star b 1975); *Career* song writer; *Style—* The Lord David Dundas; 17 Mandeville Courtyard, 142 Battersea Park Rd, London SW11 4NB

DUNDAS, Hugh McKenzie; s of Hon Richard Serle Dundas (d 1968, 3 s of 6 Viscount Melville), and his 1 w, Lydia Catherine, *née* McKenzie (d 1922); hp to Viscountcy of Melville; *b* 3 June 1910; *Educ* Saskatchewan Univ; *m* 29 Sept 1939, Catherine Sanderson, da of late John Wallace, of Edinburgh; 1 s ((Hugh) Robert Sanderson b 1943), 1 da (Catherine b 1948); *Clubs* Toronto Royal Canadian Military Inst, Pembroke Curling; *Style—* Hugh Dundas, Esq; 298 Alfred St, Pembroke, Ontario K8A 3A6, Canada (☎ 613 732 3116, work 613 732 8581)

DUNDAS, Gp Capt Sir Hugh Spencer Lisle; CBE (1977), DSO (1944, and Bar

1945), DFC (1941), DL (Surrey 1969); 2 s of Frederick Dundas (himself s of Hon John Dundas, sometime MP for Richmond, Yorks, and yr bro of 3 Earl and 1 Marquess of Zetland) Sylvia, da of Hugh March Phillipps; *b* 22 July 1920; *Educ* Stowe; *m* 1950, Hon (Enid) Rosamond, *qv*; 1 s, 2 da; *Career* served RAF WWII UK fighter cmd and Med, ret 1947; chm: BET plc 1982-87 (md 1973-82, dep chm 1981-82), Thames TV 1981-87, Rediffusion 1978-85, Rediffusion TV 1978-85, BET Omnibus Servs 1978-85, BET Investments 1978-85; formerly with Beaverbrook Newspapers Ltd; chm: Cancer Relief Macmillan Fund 1987-, The Prince's Youth Business Tst 1987-90; kt 1987; *Clubs* White's, RAF; *Style—* Gp Capt Sir Hugh Dundas, CBE, DSO, DFC, DL; The Schoolroom, Dockenfield, Farnham, Surrey (☎ 025 125 2331); 55 Iverna Court, London W8 (☎ 071 937 0773)

DUNDAS, Lady; Isabel; da of Charles Goring, of Wiston Park, Steyning, Sussex; *m* 1933, Maj Sir Thomas Calderwood Dundas, 7 and last Bt, MBE (d 1970); 2 da (Alice Kirsty (Lady Pilkington) b 1937, Davina Margaret (Mrs Martin Charles Findlay) b 1939); *Style—* Lady Dundas; 6 The Green, Slaugham, Handcross, Sussex

DUNDAS, James Frederick Trevor; s of Sir Hugh Dundas, CBE, DSO, DFC, *qv*, and Hon Lady Dundas; *b* 4 Nov 1950; *Educ* Eton, New Coll Oxford, Inns of Court Sch of Law; *m* 27 June 1979, Jennifer Ann, da of John Daukes; 1 s, 2 da; *Career* called to the Bar Inner Temple 1972, dir Morgan Grenfell & Co Ltd 1981; *Style—* James Dundas, Esq; 23 Great Winchester St, London EC2P 2AX (☎ 071 588 4545)

DUNDAS, Margaret Beryl; *née* Maclean of Ardgour; da of Lt-Col Alexander John Hew Maclean of Ardgour, JP, DL (d 1930), of Ardgour, Argyllshire, and Hon Muriel Annette Burns, OBE, JP (d 1969), yr da of 3 Baron Iverclyde; *b* 20 July 1923; *Educ* Oxenfoord Castle; *m* 16 July 1946, Ralph Dundas (d 1982), s of Robert William Dundas, MC (d 1928); 2 s ((Robert) Alexander, *qv*, b 1947, Hew Ralph b 1953); *Career* WWII ATS 1942-45; Argyll Girl Guides: memb 1960-82, pres 1982-90; *Style—* Mrs Ralph Dundas; Ambleside, St Catherine's Place, Elgin, Moray (☎ 0343 54 1256)

DUNDAS, Hon Lady ((Enid) Rosamond); da of 3 Baron Trevethin and 1 Baron Oaksey (d 1971); sis of 2 Baron Oaksey, *qv*; *b* 1924; *m* 1950, Gp Capt Sir Hugh (Spencer Lisle) Dundas, *qv*; 1 s (James b 1950), 2 da (Sarah b 1953, Amanda b 1956); *Style—* The Hon Lady Dundas; The Schoolroom, Dockenfield, Farnham, Surrey; 55 Iverna Court, London W8 (☎ 071 937 0773)

DUNDEE, 12 Earl of (S 1660); Alexander Henry Scrymgeour of Dundee; also Viscount Dudhope (S 1641), Lord Scrymgeour (S 1641), Lord Inverkeithing (S 1660), Baron Glassary (UK 1954); Baron of Barony of Wedderburn; Hereditary Royal Standard Bearer for Scotland; s of 11 Earl of Dundee (d 1983), and Patricia, Countess of Dundee, *qv*; *b* 5 June 1949; *Educ* Eton, St Andrews Univ; *m* 1979, Siobhan Mary, da of David Llewellyn, of Sayers, Gt Somerford, Wilts; 1 s, 3 da (Lady Marina Patricia Siobhan b 21 Aug 1980, Lady Flora Hermione Vera b 30 Sept 1985, Lady Lavinia Rebecca Elizabeth b 5 Nov 1986); *Heir* s, Lord Scrymgeour, *qv*; *Career* contested (C) Hamilton by-election 1978; *Style—* The Rt Hon the Earl of Dundee; Farm Office, Birkhill, Cupar, Fife

DUNDEE, Patricia, Countess of; Patricia Katharine; da of Lt-Col Lord Herbert Andrew Montagu Douglas Scott, CMG, DSO (decd), (5 s of 6 Duke of Buccleuch and Queensberry); *m* 1, 1931, Lt-Col Walter Douglas Faulkner, MC, Irish Gds (ka 1940); 1 s, 1 da (*see* Lady Moncreiffe of that Ilk); m 2, 1940, Lt-Col Hon David Scrymgeour Wedderburn, DSO, Scots Gds (d 1944 of wounds received in action); 2 da; m 3, 1946, 11 Earl of Dundee (d 1983); 1 s (12 Earl of Dundee, *qv*); *Recreations* painting; *Clubs* Caledonian; *Style—* The Rt Hon Patricia, Countess of Dundee; Coultra Farm House, Newport-on-Tay, Fife

DUNDERDALE, Sue; da of John Mason Dunderdale (d 1988), of Lytham St Anne's, and Dorothy, *née* Alderson; *b* 6 Sept 1947; *Educ* Morecombe GS, Univ of Manchester; *Career* fndr and first artistic dir Pentbus Theatre Co 1973-78; freelance theatre dir 1978-84; artistic dir: Solo Poly Theatre 1984-88, Greenwich Theatre 1988-89, BBC drama dir's course 1989; dir: Nativity Blues BBC 2 1988, Killing The Cat (by David Spencer) Royal Court Upstairs 1990; co-chm Dirs Guild of GB 1986-87; *Style—* Ms Sue Dunderdale; c/o Pauline Asper, Noel Gay Organisation, 24 Denmark St, London WC2H 8NJ (☎ 071 836 3941)

DUNDONALD, Dowager Countess of; Ann Margaret; *née* Harkness; da of Sir Joseph Welsh Park Harkness, CMG, OBE (d 1962), and Florence Margaret, *née* Furniss; *b* 3 Aug 1924; *m* 1 (m dis), C F Edward Staib; 1 s (John, *see* STAIB, Hon Mrs), 2 da; m 2, 1978, 14 Earl of Dundonald (d 1986); *Career* served WVS 1942-43, WRNS 1943-46; *Recreations* travel, painting; *Clubs* Caledonian, Sloane; *Style—* The Rt Hon the Dowager Countess of Dundonald; Beau Coin, La Haule, Jersey, Channel Islands

DUNDONALD, 15 Earl of (S 1669); Iain Alexander Douglas Blair; also Lord Cochrane of Dundonald (S 1669), Lord Cochrane of Dundonald, Paisley and Ochiltree (S 1669), and Marquis of Maranhão (Empire of Brazil 1823 by Dom Pedro I for 10 Earl); s (by 1 m) of 14 Earl of Dundonald (d 1986); *b* 17 Feb 1961; *Educ* Wellington, Royal Agric Coll (Dip Ag); *m* 4 July 1987, (M) Beatrice (L), da of Adolphus Russo, of Gibraltar; *Heir* Kinsman Lord Cochrane of Cults; *Career* dir: Arthurstone Developments plc, Duneth Securities Ltd, New Capital and Scottish Properties Ltd; *Recreations* skiing, sailing, shooting, fishing; *Style—* The Rt Hon the Earl of Dundonald; Lochnell Castle, Ledaig, Argyll

DUNFORD, Campbell Edward; *b* 24 Dec 1944; *Educ* St Edmund Hall Oxford (MA); *m* 18 Nov 1974, Karen Christian, da of Isaac Henry Thompson (d 1983), of Market Overton, Rutland, Leics; *Career* dir and gen mangr Guthrie Trading (UK) Ltd 1979-81, trade fin dir Midland Bank 1981-1988, gen mangr Moscow Narodny Bank Ltd 1988-89, int fin conslt 1989-, chm Trade-Aide Financial Services Ltd; chm Br Exporters Assoc, chm Export Fin Ctee London C of C, memb Cncl LCCI, chm Aid Funded Advsy Serv; *Recreations* squash, classical music, gardening; *Style—* Campbell Dunford, Esq; Great Down Farm, Marnhull, Dorset DT10 1JY

DUNFORD, David John; s of Alfred George Dunford (d 1962), and Kate, *née* Spearman; *b* 30 Jan 1948; *Educ* Univ of Essex (BA); *m* 7 Sept 1978, Anne Wilson, da of James Fleming (d 1981); *Career* asst ed then dep chief sub ed Essed Co Newspapers 1973-78; BBC 1978-; sub ed, chief sub ed and duty ed BBC Radio News, fin journalist for radio TV and World Service, currently ed Gen News Serv providing comprehensive news and current coverage to local and regnl stations and the Br Forces Broadcasting; *Recreations* golf, trivial pursuit; *Clubs* Warren Golf, Maldon Essex; *Style—* David Dunford, Esq; 3 Avenue Road, Great Baddow, Chelmsford, Essex (☎ 0245 356484), Room 3051, BBC Broadcasting House, London W1A 1AA (☎ 071 9274010, fax 071 5807725)

DUNFORD, Neil Roy; s of Charles Roy Dunford, and Joyce Ellen Dunford; *b* 16 Jan 1947; *Educ* Edinburgh Acad, Sedbergh, Univ of St Andrews (MA); *m* 24 April 1976, Gillian; *Career* Deloitte & Co 1968-72, J Henry Schroder Wagg 1972-81, Scottish Widows Fund 1981-85, Morgan Grenfell Asset Mgmnt 1985-; *Style—* Neil Dunford, Esq; 21 Ashley Drive, Walton-on-Thames, Surrey KT12 1JL (☎ 0932 246 496); Morgan Grenfell Asset Mgmnt, 20 Finsbury Circus, London EC2M 1NB (☎ 071 256 7500, fax 071 826 0331, telex 920286 NGAM G)

DUNGEY, Roger Harvey (aka Roger Harvey); s of William Arthur Dungey (d 1978), and Norah Isabella, *née* Harvey; *b* 27 Sept 1939; *Educ* Lingfield Co Secdy Sch Surrey, Writtle Agric Coll Essex; *m* 30 Jan 1965, Kathleen Anne Bootherstone; 2 s (Graham b 1968, Stephen b 1971), 1 da (Suzanne Louise b 1973); *Career* horticulturist; dir: Rochford House Plants 1965-76, Roger Harvey Ltd 1976; memb Inst of Horticulture; *Recreations* walking, gardening, travelling; *Style—* Roger Dungey, Esq; The Farm House, Bragbury Lane, Stevenage, Herts SG2 8TJ (☎ 0438 814979); Roger Harvey Garden World, Bragbury Lane, Stevenage, Herts SG2 8TJ (☎ 0438 811777); Mazoe, Main St, Walberswick, Suffolk (☎ 0502 722432)

DUNGLASS, Lord; *see*: Home of the Hirsel, Baron

DUNHAM, John Wilfred; s of William Henry Dunham (d 1953), of London, and Emma Eleanor, *née* Mack (d 1981); *b* 22 April 1923; *Educ* St Georges Coll, Hornsey Coll of Art; *m* 28 March 1945, Rosa Margaret, da of Gaetano d'Angelo (d 1966); 1 s (Geoffrey Michael b 1963, d 1972); *Career* insur broker Lloyds of London 1939-; Freeman City of London, Liveryman The Worshipful Co of Fruiterers 1979; *Clubs* Oriental, MCC, Wig & Pen; *Style—* John Dunham, Esq; Dunham Financial Servs Ltd, 54 London Fruit Exchange, Brushfield St, London E1 6EU (☎ 071 247 6751, 037 27 27959)

DUNHAM, Sir Kingsley Charles; s of Ernest Pedder Dunham, of Brancepeth, Co Durham (d 1974), and Edith Agnes, *née* Humphreys (d 1939); *b* 2 Jan 1910; *Educ* Durham Johnston Sch, Univ of Durham (DSc, PhD), Univ of Harvard (MS, SD); *m* 1936, Margaret, da of William Young, of Choppington, Northumberland; *Career* New Mexico Bureau of Mines 1935, geologist with HM Geological Survey of GB 1935-50, prof of geology Univ of Durham 1950-66, dir Inst of Geological Sciences 1967-75, consulting geologist 1976-, dir Weardale Minerals Ltd 1982-86; foreign sec Royal Soc 1971-76; hon doctorates from 11 UK and US univs; FRS, FRSE, FEng; kt 1972; *Recreations* music, gardening; *Clubs* Geological Soc, Probus (Durham); *Style—* Sir Kingsley Dunham, FRS, FRSE; Charleycroft, Quarryheads Lane, Durham DH1 3DY (☎ 091 384 8977)

DUNHAM, Simon Peter; s of Maj Peter Browning Dunham, of Coltishall, Norfolk, and Constance Amy Margerita, *née* Young; *b* 10 Oct 1939; *Educ* Bedales, Architectural Assoc Sch (DipArch); *m* 18 March 1967, Dorothy Patricia, da of George Robert Broomhead (d 1985); 1 s (Martyn Fitzroy b 23 Jan 1969); *Career* qualified architect 1964; ptnr Charter Bldg Design Gp 1966-82, dir Charter Ptnrship 1982 (chm 1982-); conslt architect Royal Architectural Soc 1980-, vice chm Architect in Agric 1980-87; memb Round Table 1962-79; ARIBA; *Recreations* sailing, skiing; *Style—* Simon Dunham, Esq; The Charter Partnership Ltd, St Mary's House, 15 Cardington Rd, Bedford MK42 0BP (☎ 0234 42551, fax 0234 60055, car 0860 258245)

DUNHILL, Richard; s of Vernon Dunhill (d 1938), and Helen, *née* Field Moser (d 1984); Co Alfred Dunhill formed by gf 1907; *b* 27 Oct 1926; *Educ* Beaumont Coll; *m* 5 April 1952, Patricia Susannah, da of Henry B Rump (d 1965); 3 s (Christopher John b 1954, (Alfred) Mark b 1961, Jonathan Henry b 1962), 1 da (Susan Mary b 1953); *Career* army conscript 1944-48; joined Alfred Dunhill Ltd 1948: dir 1961, dep chm 1967, chm 1977; chm Dunhill Holdings plc 1981 (pres 1989); Barker Variety Club of GB; Master Worshipful Co of Pipemakers and Tobacco Blenders 1987-88; *Recreations* gardening, backgammon; *Clubs* RAC; *Style—* Richard Dunhill, Esq; 30 Duke Street, St James's, London SW1Y 6DL (☎ 071 499 9566, fax 071 499 6471)

DUNKEL, Arthur; *b* 28 Aug 1932; *Educ* Univ of Lausanne (BSc Econ); *m*; 2 children; *Career* Federal Office for Foreign and Econ Affrs: Dept of Public Economy Bern 1956-60, head of section for OECD Affrs 1960-64, head of Section for Cooperation with Developing Countries 1964-71, head of section for World Trade Policy Min Plenipotentiary (appointed 1973) and permanent rep to GATT 1971-76; del and ambass Plenipotentiary for Trade Agreements of the Swiss Govt 1976-80; in charge of: world trade policy matters, multilateral econ and trade rels with developing countries industrialisation, trade in agriculture and primary products, bilateral trade rels with various trading ptnrs of Switzerland; head of the delegation of Switzerland 1976-80 to: GATT Multilateral Trade Negotiations (Tokyo Round), UNCTAD IV, UNIDO, commodity confs; DG GATT 1980-; sr lectr Univs of Geneva and Fribourg; various studies, articles and reports published in econ reviews, winner Max Schmidheiny Fndn Freedom prize St Gallen Switzerland 1989 and Consumers for World Trade award (USA); vice chm and rapporteur UNCTAD Intergovernmental Gp on Supplementary Financing 1968, rapporteur UNCTAD Bd 1969, chm GATT Ctee of Balance of Payments Restrictions 1972-75, chm UN Conf of a New Wheat Agreement 1978; Hon Dr Univ of Fribourg 1980; *Style—* Arthur Dunkel, Esq; GATT Centre William Rappard, 154 rue de Lausanne, Geneva 21, Switzerland (☎ 010 41 22 7395111)

DUNKELD, Bishop of, 1981-; Rt Rev Vincent Paul Logan; s of Joseph Logan (d 1975), and Elizabeth, *née* Flannigan; *b* 30 June 1941; *Educ* Blairs Coll Aberdeen, St Andrew's Coll Drygrange Melrose, CCC London (DipRE); *Career* ordained priest Edinburgh 1964; asst priest: St Margaret's Davidsons Mains Edinburgh 1964-66, CCC London 1966-67; chaplain St Joseph's Hosp Rosewell Midlothian 1967-77, advsr in religious educn Archdiocese of St Andrews and Edinburgh 1967-77, parish priest St Mary's Ratho Midlothian 1977-81, episcopal vicar for educn Archdiocese of St Andrews and Edinburgh 1978-81; *Style—* The Rt Rev the Bishop of Dukeld; Bishop's House, 29 Roseangle, Dundee DD1 4LS (☎ 0382 24327)

DUNKLEY, Christopher; s of Robert Dunkley, and Joyce Mary, *née* Turner; *b* 22 Jan 1944; *Educ* Haberdashers' Aske's; *m* 1967, Carolyn Elizabeth, s of Lt-Col Arthur Philip Casey Lyons (d 1976), of Hampstead; 1 s (Damian b 1969), 1 da (Holly b 1971); *Career* journalist and broadcaster; feature writer and news ed UK Press Gazette 1965-68, reporter then specialist correspondent and critic The Times 1968-73, TV critic Financial Times 1973-, presenter of Feedback BBC Radio 4 1986-; winner: Br Press Awards Critic of the Year 1976 and 1986, TV-am Broadcast Journalist of the Year 1989; *Books* Television Today and Tomorrow: Wall to Wall Dallas?; *Recreations* motorcycling, collecting, books, eating Italian food; *Style—* Christopher Dunkley, Esq; 38 Leverton St, London NW5 2PG (☎ 071 485 7101)

DUNLEATH, 4 Baron (UK 1892); Charles Edward Henry John Mulholland; TD; s of 3 Baron Dunleath, CBE, DSO (d 1956), and Henrietta, da of Most Rev C F D'Arcy, Archbishop of Armagh; *b* 23 June 1933; *Educ* Eton, Univ of Cambridge; *m* 1959, Dorinda Margery, da of late Lt-Gen Arthur Percival, CB, DSO, OBE, MC; *Heir* cous, Maj Sir Michael Mulholland, 2 Bt; *Career* 11 Hussars, cmd North Irish Horse, actg Lt-Col 1967-69, Capt Ulster Def Regt 1971-73; Hon Col North Irish Horse 1981-86; nat govr (NI) BBC 1967-73; memb: and asst speaker NI Legislative Assembly 1973-75 and 1982-86, NI Constitutional Convention 1975-76, Ards Borough Cncl 1977-81, NI Parly Assembly 1982-86 (formerly asst speaker); assoc memb Anglo Irish Inter-Parly Body 1989-; chm: Carreras Rothmans (N Ireland) Ltd 1974-84, N Ireland Independent TV Ltd, Dunleath Estates Ltd, Ulster & General Holdings Ltd; dir Northern Bank Ltd; currently Vice Lt Co Down (DL 1964); CBIM; *Style—* The Rt Hon The Lord Dunleath, TD; Ballywalter Park, Newtownards, Co Down, N Ireland (☎ 024775 8203)

DUNLOP, Andrew James; s of Robert Jack Donlop, of Port Appin, and Dorothy Shirley, *née* Dixon; *b* 21 June 1959; *Educ* Trinity Coll Glenalmond, Glasgow Acad, Univ of Edinburgh (MA); *Career* Midland Bank Int 1981-82, Cons Res Dept 1982-86, special advsr to Sec of State for Def George Younger 1986-88, PMs Policy Unit 1988-; memb Glasgow Incorporate of Bankers, Glasgow Incorporation of Hammermen, Inst of

Bankers; *Recreations* music, skiing, sailing, walking, tennis; *Clubs* St Stephen's Constitutional, Royal Thames Yacht; *Style—* Andrew Dunlop, Esq; 10 Downing St, London SW1 (☎ 071 930 4433)

DUNLOP, Rear Adm Colin Charles Harrison; CB (1972), CBE (1963), DL (Kent 1976); s of Rear Adm Samuel Harrison Dunlop, CB (d 1950), of Surrey, and Hilda Dunlop (d 1965); *b* 4 March 1918; *Educ* Marlborough; *m* 1941, Moyra Patricia O'Brien, da of John Albert Gorges (d 1968); 3 s (Angus, Robin (d 1946), Graham); *Career* RN 1935-74, served WWII HM Ships Kent, Valiant, Diadem, Orion, in Far East, Med and Atlantic; cmd HMS Pembroke 1964-66, dir Def Policy 1968-69, Rear Adm 1969, cmd Br Naval Staff Washington 1969-71, Flag Offr Medway 1971-74 (ret 1974); dir gen Cable TV Assoc and Nat TV Rental Assoc 1974-83; *Recreations* cricket, country pursuits; *Clubs* Army and Navy, MCC, I Zingari, Free Foresters, Band of Bros; *Style—* Rear Adm CCH Dunlop, CB, CBE, DL; Chanceford Farm, Frittenden, nr Cranbrook, Kent (☎ 058 080 242)

DUNLOP, Frank; CBE (1977); s of Charles Norman Dunlop, and Mary, *née* Aarons; *b* 15 Feb 1927; *Educ* Kibworth Beauchamp GS, Univ Coll London (BA); *Career* theatre dir: Old Vic, NT (former asst dir and admin dir), RSC, Royal Ct; Young Vic: fndr 1969, dir 1969-83, conslt 1978-80; dir Edinburgh Int Festival 1984-1991; Hon Fell UCL 1979, Hon Doctorate Philadelphia Coll of Performing Arts 1978; Hon DUniv: Heriot Watt 1989, Edinburgh 1990; Chev Order of Arts and Letters (France) 1987; *Style—* Frank Dunlop, Esq, CBE; Edinburgh International Festival, 21 Market Street, Edinburgh EH1 1BW (☎ 031 226 4001, telex 728115 EDFEST)

DUNLOP, (Norman) Gordon Edward; CBE; s of Ross Munn Dunlop (d 1947); *b* 16 April 1928; *Educ* Trinity Coll Glenalmond; *m* 1952, Jean, da of George Fyfe Taylor (d 1975); 1 s, 1 da; *Career* CA; former chief exec Commercial Union Assurance Co Ltd 1972-77, Inchcape Berhad Singapore 1979-83, chief fin offr Br Airways 1982-89, memb bd Br Airways 1983-89, chm Ferrum Holdings plc 1989-; memb Cncl of Lloyds 1990-; *Recreations* skiing, fishing, gardening; *Clubs* Caledonian, Buck's; *Style—* Gordon Dunlop, Esq, CBE; 28 Brunswick Gardens, London W8 4AL (☎ 071 221 5059)

DUNLOP, Rev Ian Geoffrey David; s of Walter Nigel Usher Dunlop (d 1988), and Marguerite Irene, *née* Shakerley (d 1965); *b* 19 Aug 1925; *Educ* Winchester, New Coll Oxford (MA), Univ of Strasbourg; *m* 2 Nov 1957, Deirdre Marcia, da of Archibald Marcus De La Maziere Jamieson (d 1981); 1 s (Robin Alastair *b* 6 July 1966), 1 da (Harriet Elizabeth *b* 28 Nov 1967); *Career* Lt Irish Gds 1944; vicar Bures Suffolk 1962-71, chllr Salisbury Cathedral 1971-; memb: Gen Synod 1975-85, Cathedral's Advsy Cmmn 1980-85; tstee Historic Churches Preservation Tst 1969; contrib to: The Connoisseur, Country Life, The Field, The Church Times; FSA 1965; *Books* Versailles (1956, 2 edn 1970), Palaces and Progresses of Elizabeth I (1962), Châteaux of the Loire (1969), Companion Guide to the Ile De France (1979), The Cathedrals Crusade (1982), Royal Palaces of France (1985), Thinking It Out (1986), Burgundy (1990); *Recreations* birdwatching; *Clubs* Army and Navy; *Style—* The Rev Canon Ian Dunlop, FSA; 24 The Close, Salisbury, Wilts SP1 2EH (☎ 0722 336 809)

DUNLOP, Dr James Montgomery; s of Gabriel Dunlop (d 1944), of Ormiston, Newburgh, Fife, and Margaret Louise, *née* Leiper; *b* 25 Aug 1930; *Educ* Bell-Baxter Sch Cupar, Trinity Coll Dublin (MA, BCh, BAO), Univ of Glasgow (DPH, DPA); *m* 15 Sept 1960, Dr Joyce Lilian Dunlop, *qv*, da of William Strangman Hill (d 1968), of Ounavarra, Lucan, Co Dublin; 2 s (Jonathan *b* 1961, Douglas *b* 1966), 1 da (Joanne *b* 1964); *Career* RAF 1948-49; chief asst co MO N Riding of Yorks 1966-70, dep MOH Hull 1970-74, port MO Hull and Goole Port Health Authy 1970-, med referee Hull Crematorium 1970-, currently dir of pub health Hull Health Authy (dist community physician 1974-82, dist MO 1982-89); numerous leading and other articles in professional jls; book reviews for: Medical Officer, Public Health, British Medical Journal; chm: Charitable Tsts BMA (fell 1978, memb 1959), Conjoint Ctee Epsom Coll; memb Cncl Soc of Public Health; FFCM (now Faculty of Public Health Med) 1978 (member 1972, treas 1990-), FRMS 1953 (member 1949); *Recreations* stamp collecting, writing, sailing, farming; *Clubs* Rugby, Royal Philatelic Soc; *Style—* Dr James Dunlop; Sungates, 136 Westella Rd, Kirkella, North Humberside HU10 7RR (☎ 0482 655680), Victoria House, Park St, Hull HU2 8TD (☎ 0482 223191, fax 229668)

DUNLOP, John Leeper; s of Dr John Leeper Dunlop (d 1959), and Margaret Frances Mary, *née* Fiffett (d 1972); *b* 10 July 1939; *Educ* Marlborough; *m* 22 June 1965, Susan Jennifer, da of Gerard Thorpe Page (d 1985), of The Old Rectory, Harpole, Northants; 3 s (Timothy *b* 1966 d 1987, Edward *b* 1968, Harry *b* 1976); *Career* Nat Serv 2 Lt Royal Ulster Rifles 1959-61; racehorse trainer 1964-, trained Derby winner and 1600 other winners; memb Ctee: Nat Trainers Fedn, Stable Lads Welfare Tst, Br Racing Sch; *Recreations* coursing, breeding racehorses, owning show horses; *Clubs* Turf; *Style—* John Dunlop, Esq; House on the Hill, Arundel, Sussex (☎ 0903 882106); Castle Stables, Arundel, Sussex (☎ 0903 882194, fax 0903 884173, car tel 0860 339805, telex 87475 RACDEL)

DUNLOP, Dr Joyce Lilian; da of William Strangman Hill (d 1968), of Ounavarra, Lucan, Co Dublin, Ireland, and Doris Irene, *née* Odlum (d 1972); *b* 14 April 1933; *Educ* Glengara Park Sch Kingston Co Dublin Ireland, Trinity Coll Dublin (MA, MB BCh, BAO); *m* 15 Sept 1960, Dr James Montgomery Dunlop, *qv*, s of Gabriel Dunlop, of Ormiston, Newburgh, Fife, Scotland; 2 s (Jonathan *b* 1961, Douglas *b* 1966), 1 da (Joanne *b* 1964); *Career* sr house offr in anaesthetics Dumfries and Galloway Royal Infirmary 1959-61, sr registrar in psychiatry Kingston Gen Hosp Hull 1976-77, conslt psychiatrist De La Pole Hosp Hull 1978-; conslt advsr to Relate and Cruse Hull; memb BMA 1958, MRCPsych 1976, DObstRCOG; *Books* contribs incl: Practitioner (1978), British Journal of Psychiatry (1979), British Medical Journal (1984), When Doctors Get Sick (1988), British Journal of Sexual Medicine (1989); *Recreations* gardening, stamp collecting, tennis; *Style—* Dr Joyce Dunlop; Sungates, 136 Westella Rd, Kirkella, North Humberside HU10 7RR (☎ 0482 655680), De La Pole Hospital, Willerby, Hull HU10 6ED (☎ 0482 875875)

DUNLOP, Robert Fergus; AE (1956); s of Maj A Fergus Dunlop, OBE, TD (d 1980), and Gwendolen Elizabeth, *née* Coit; *b* 22 June 1929; *Educ* Marlborough, St John's Cambridge, MIT; *m* 1966, Jane Clare, da of Lt-Col George Hervey McManus (d 1959), of Canada; 1 s, 2 da; *Career* cmmnd 2 Lt RA, later Flt Lt 501 (Co of Glos) Fighter Sqdn RAuxAF; Sloan fell 1960; Bristol Aeroplane Co Ltd and subsids Br Aircraft Corp 1952-66, Westland Aircraft Ltd 1966-70, dir Lonrho plc 1972- (joined 1970); CEng, MRAeS; *Recreations* windsurfing, gardening; *Style—* Robert Dunlop, Esq, AE; 42 Woodsford Square, London W14 8DP (☎ 071 602 2579)

DUNLOP, Thomas; s and h of Sir Thomas Dunlop, 3 Bt; *b* 22 April 1951; *Educ* Rugby, Univ of Aberdeen (BSc); *m* 1984, Eileen, da of Alexander Henry Stevenson (d 1990); 1 da; *Style—* Thomas Dunlop, Esq; Bredon Croft, Bredon's Norton, nr Tewkesbury, Glos GL20 7HB

DUNLOP, Sir Thomas; 3 Bt (UK 1916) of Woodbourne, Co Renfrew; s of Sir Thomas Dunlop, 2 Bt (d 1963); *b* 11 April 1912; *Educ* Shrewsbury, St John's Coll Cambridge; *m* 1947, Adda Mary Alison, da of Thomas Arthur Smith (d 1952); 1 s, 1 da (and 1 da decd); *Heir* s, Thomas Dunlop; *Career* ptnr Thomas Dunlop and Sons, former chm of Savings Bank of Glasgow, govr Hutchesons Sch 1957-80; CA; OStJ 1965; *Recreations* fishing, shooting and golf; *Clubs* Western Glasgow; *Style—* Sir Thomas Dunlop, Bt; The Corrie, Kilmacolm, Renfrewshire (☎ 0505 87 3239)

DUNLOP, Prof William; s of Alexander Morton Dunlop, and Annie Denham Rennie, *née* Ingram; *b* 18 Aug 1944; *Educ* Kilmarnock Acad, Univ of Glasgow (MB ChB), Univ of Newcastle upon Tyne (PhD); *m* 25 March 1968, Sylvia Louise, da of Dr Irwin Krauthamer; 1 s (Keith *b* 1972), 1 da (Emma *b* 1973); *Career* various jr posts in Obstetrics and Gynaecology Dept, Regius prof Univ of Glasgow 1969-74, seconded as lectr Univ of Nairobi 1972-73, MRC scientific staff Newcastle 1974-75, visiting assoc prof Med Univ of S Carolina 1980, prof and head of Dept Obstetrics and Gynaecology Univ of Newcastle upon Tyne 1982- (sr lectr 1975-82); chm Blair-Bell Res Soc, ed in chief Foetal Med Review; FRCSEd 1971, FRCOG 1984 (MRCOG 1971); *Recreations* music, drama, literature; *Style—* Prof William Dunlop; Department of Obstetrics and Gynaecology, University of Newcastle upon Tyne, Princess Mary Maternity Hospital, Newcastle upon Tyne NE2 3BD (☎ 091 281 6177)

DUNLUCE, Viscount; *see*: Earl of Antrim

DUNMORE, Anne, Countess of; Anne Augusta Murray; da of Thomas Clouston Wallace, of Holodyke, Dounby, Orkney; *b* 18 June 1943; *Educ* Downe House Newbury; *m* 1967, 9 Earl of Dunmore (d 1980); 2 da (Lady Kate *b* 1969, Lady Rebecca *b* 1970); *Career* dir Edinburgh Tapestry Company Ltd, conslt Harris Tweed Assoc; *Style—* The Rt Hon Anne, Countess of Dunmore; 14 Regent Terrace, Edinburgh EH7 5BN

DUNMORE, Helen; da of Maurice Ronald Dunmore, and Betty, *née* Smith; *b* 12 Dec 1952; *Educ* Nottingham HS for Girls, Univ of York (BA); *m* 24 Oct 1980, Francis Benedict Charnley; 1 s (Patrick Maurice *b* 28 July 1981), 1 step s (Oliver Benjamin *b* 13 Feb 1977); *Career* poet; writer-in-residence: Poly of Wales 1990-91, Brighton Festival 1991; tutor various residential poetry courses Arvon Fndn; works incl: The Apple Fall (1983), The Sea Skater (1986, winner Poetry Soc's Alice Hunt Bartlett award 1987), The Raw Garden (1988, Poetry Book Soc Choice winter 1988-89), Short Days, Long Nights, New and Selected Poems (1991); various short stories, poetry for children, and songs in magazines, anthologies and broadcasts on Radio 3 and 4 (work also featured on BBC TV's Artswest); winner Cardiff Int Poetry Competition 1990; *Recreations* family life and friendships, freshwater swimming; *Style—* Ms Helen Dunmore; c/o Lisa Eveleigh, A P Watt Ltd, 20 John St, London WC1N 2DR (☎ 071 405 6774, fax 071 831 2154)

DUNMORE, 11 Earl of (S 1686); Kenneth Randolph Murray; JP (Beaconsfield Municipality Tasmania 1962); also Viscount Fincastle, Lord Murray of Blair, Moulin and Tillimet (Tullimet; both S 1686); 2 s of Arthur Charles Murray (d 1964); suc er bro 1981; the Earls of Dunmore descend from the 2 s of 1 Marquess of Athole; *b* 6 June 1913; *m* 1938, Margaret Joy, da of late P D Cousins, of Burnie, Tasmania; 2 s; *Heir* s, Viscount Fincastle; *Career* late Sgt 12/50 Bn Australian Inf; former Master Tamar Valley Masonic Lodge 42 Tasmanian Constitution 1957-58; patron: Exeter RSL Bowls Club, Combined Scottish Soc of NSW Australia; *Style—* The Rt Hon the Earl of Dunmore, JP; Gravelly Beach, 7276 W Tamar, Tasmania, Australia

DUNN, Angus Henry; s of Col Henry George Mountfort Dunn (d 1969), and Catherine Mary (d 1986); *b* 30 Dec 1944; *Educ* Marlborough, King's Coll Cambridge (MA), Pennsylvania Univ; *m* 1973, Carolyn Jane, da of Alan Bartlett, of The Oast, High Tilt, Cranbook, Kent; 2 s (Thomas *b* 1974, James *b* 1977), 1 da (Eliza *b* 1983); *Career* HM Diplomatic Service 1968-73 (FCO, Kuala Lumpur, Bonn); joined Morgan Grenfell & Co Ltd 1972- (dir 1978-88), exec deputy chm Morgan Grenfell (Asia) Ltd Singapore 1983-85; dir: Julianas Hldgs plc 1983-85, Manufacturers Hanover Ltd 1988-; *Books* Export Finance (co-author, 1983), Personal Accountant (software pubn, 1990); *Recreations* riding, sailing; *Clubs* Royal Thames Yacht; *Style—* Angus Dunn, Esq; Dower House, Oxon Hoath, Tonbridge, Kent

DUNN, Douglas Eaglesham; s of William Douglas Dunn (d 1980), and Margaret, *née* McGowan; *b* 23 Oct 1942; *Educ* Renfrew HS, Camphill Sch Paisley, Scottish Sch of Librarianship, Univ of Hull (BA); *m* 1, Lesley Balfour, *née* Wallace (d 1981); *m* 2, 10 Aug 1985, Lesley Jane, da of Robert Bathgate (d 1979); 1 s (William Robert Bathgate *b* 5 Jan 1987), 1 da (Lillias Ella Bathgate *b* 18 June 1990); *Career* writer; fell in creative writing Univ of St Andrews 1989-; books of poetry incl: Terry Street (1969), The Happier Life (1972), Love or Nothing (1974), Barbarians (1979), St Kilda's Parliament (1982), Elegies (1985), Selected Poems (1986), Northlight (1988); Secret Villages (short stories, 1985), Andromache (translation, 1990), Poll Tax: The Fiscal Fake (1990), The Essential Browning (ed, 1990); Somerset Maugham Award 1972, Geoffrey Faber Meml prize 1975, Hawthornden prize 1982, Whitbread Book of the Year award for 1985 (1986), Cholmondeley award 1989; Hon LLD Dundee 1987, hon prof Univ of Dundee 1987, hon fell Humberside Coll; FRSL 1981; *Recreations* music, gardening; *Style—* Douglas Dunn, Esq; c/o Faber & Faber Ltd, 3 Queen Square, London, WC1N 3AU

DUNN, Geoffrey Herbert; MBE (1959); s of Philip Ryland Dunn (d 1980), and Barbara Julia, *née* Burrow; *b* 24 Jan 1938; *Educ* Liverpool Coll, St John's Coll Cambridge (MA); *m* 31 Aug 1963, Cathleen (Kay) Jennifer Reay, da of Clifford William Merrick (d 1985); 2 s (Simon *b* 1964, Matthew *b* 1973), 1 da (Alison *b* 1966); *Career* 1 Bn 22 (Cheshire) Regt 1956-58 (2 Lt 1957); Telephone Cables Div BICC 1963-67; dir and gen mangr: Malayan Cables Berhad 1970-76 (works mangr 1967-70), BICC Connollys Ltd 1976-81, Home Sales Div BICC 1982-86; dir: quality and customer serv BICC Cables Ltd 1986-, British Approvals Serv for Electric Cables (BASEC); FBIM 1979, CEng 1981, FIEE 1981; *Recreations* golf; *Clubs* The Royal Birkdale Golf; *Style—* Geoffrey Dunn, Esq, MBE; 40 Merrilocks Rd, Blundellsands, Liverpool L23 6UN (☎ 051 924 2366); BICC Cables Ltd, Heronsway, Chester Business Park, Chester CH4 9PZ (☎ 0244 688400, fax 0244 688401)

DUNN, Geoffrey Richard; s of Kenneth Grayson Dunn, of 7 Woodlands, Pound Hill, Crawley, Sussex, and Nila Jane, *née* Griffiths; *b* 10 July 1949; *Educ* Ifield GS, Univ of Manchester (BSc, MSc), Manchester Business Sch (Dip); *m* 26 July 1973, Patricia Ann, da of John Thompson, of 8 Craiglands, Lightcliffe, nr Halifax , W Yorks; *Career* investmt controller ICFC Ltd 1975-78, corp fin exec SG Warburg & Co Ltd 1978-80, asst gp treas GKN plc 1980-83, head of fin and planning Midland Bank plc 1984-87, gp fin dir Exco Int plc 1987-; memb MCT 1982; *Recreations* mountaineering, skiing, opera and music; *Clubs* Alpine, London Mountaineering; *Style—* Geoffrey Dunn, Esq; 5 Church Walk, Highgate, London N6 6QY (☎ 081 348 4893); EXCO Int plc, 80 Cannon St, London EC4N 6LJ (☎ 071 623 4040, fax 071 283 8450, telex 887198)

DUNN, (William) Hubert; QC (1982); s of William Patrick Millar Dunn (d 1964), of Tudor Hall, Holywood, Co Down, and Isobel, *née* Thompson (d 1954); *b* 8 July 1933; *Educ* Winchester, New Coll Oxford (BA); *m* 23 Sept 1971, Maria Henriquetta Theresa D'Arouje Perestrella, da of George Hoffacker de Moser, 3 s of Count de Moser in the nobility of Portugal; 1 s (Sebastian *b* 29 Aug 1973), 1 da (Eugenia *b* 27 May 1972); *Career* 2 Lt The Life Gds 1956-57, Household Cavalry Res of Offrs 1957-64; called to the Bar Lincoln's Inn 1958; local govt cmmr 1963; rec of the Crown Court 1980; chm City of London and Westminster S Lib Pty 1976-79; *Recreations* travel, literature; *Clubs* Boodle's; *Style—* Hubert Dunn, Esq, QC; 19 Clarendon St, London SW1; Tudor Hall, Hollywood, Co Down

DUNN, John Churchill; s of John Barrett Jackson Dunn (d 1984), and Dorothy Dunn, *née* Hiscox; *b* 4 March 1934; *Educ* Christ Church Cathedral Choir Sch, Oxford; The King's Sch, Canterbury; *m* 19 April 1958, Margaret, da of Stanley Farrand Jennison (d

1982); 2 da (Joanna b 1960, Emma b 1963); *Career* broadcaster BBC staff 1956-76; freelance radio 2, programmes incl: Breakfast Special, Late Night Extra and numerous others; currently hosts own show 1976-; *Recreations* working, skiing, sailing, wine; *Style*— John C Dunn, Esq

DUNN, Prof John Montfort; s of Col Henry George Montfort Dunn (d 1970), and Catherine Mary, *née* Kinloch (d 1986); *b* 9 Sept 1940; *Educ* Winchester, Millfield, King's Coll Cambridge (BA); *m* 1, 1965 (m dis 1971), Susan Deborah, *née* Fyvel; m 2, 1973 (m dis 1987), Judith Frances Bernal; *Career* Univ of Cambridge: fell Jesus Coll 1965-66, fell King's Coll 1966-, lectr in political science 1972-77, reader in politics 1977-87, prof of political theory 1987-; visiting prof: Univ of Ghana, Univ of Br Columbia, Univ of Bombay, Tokyo Met Univ, Tulane Univ; FBA 1989; *Books* The Political Thought of John Locke (1969), Modern Revolutions (1972), Dependence and Opportunity (with A F Robertson, 1973); Western Political Theory in the Face of the Future (1979), Political Obligation in its Historical Context (1980), The Politics of Socialism (1984), Rethinking Modern Political Theory (1985), Interpreting Political Responsibility (1990); *Style*— Prof John Dunn; The Merchant's House, 31 Station Rd, Swavesey, Cambridge CB4 5QJ (☎ 0954 31451); King's College, Cambridge CB2 1ST (☎ 0223 350411)

DUNN, Baroness (Life Peer UK 1990), of Hong Kong Island in Hong Kong and of Knightsbridge in the Royal Borough of Kensington and Chelsea; Lydia Selina Dunn; DBE (1989, CBE 1983, OBE 1978), JP (1976); da of Yenchuen Yeh Dunn (d 1965); *b* 29 Feb 1940; *Educ* St Paul's Convent Sch, Univ of California at Berkeley (BS); *Career* chm: Swire & Maclaine Ltd 1982- (exec trainee 1963, dir 1973, md 1976), Swire Loxley Ltd 1982-, Camberley Enterprises Ltd, Swire Marketing Ltd, The Eagle's Eye International Ltd 1988-, Swire Source America Inc 1988-, Asian American Mangers Inc 1988-, Christie's Swire (Hong Kong) Ltd 1989-, Swires Rsources Ltd 1989-; dir: Swire Trading (Taiwan) Ltd 1969-88, John Swire & Sons (HK) Ltd 1978-, Hongkong and Shanghai Banking Corp 1981-, Cathay Pacific Airways Ltd 1985-, Christie's Swire (Holdings) Ltd 1989-, Hong Kong Seibu Enterprise Co Ltd 1989-; exec dir Swire Pacific Ltd 1982-; pres Carroll Reed International Ltd 1990-; chm: Hong Kong Trade Devpt Cncl 1983-; dep chm: Exec Ctee Cwlth Parly Assoc (Hong Kong Branch) 1985-88; sr memb Exec Cncl Hong Kong 1988- (memb 1982-88), memb Legislative Cncl Hong Kong 1976-85 (sr memb 1985-88, memb Fin Ctee 1976-), memb Int Cncl of the Asia Soc and Hong Kong Assoc; memb Cncl: Chinese Univ 1978-90, Trade Policy Res Centre London 1980-89; memb Cncl Volvo Int Advsy Bd 1984; Hon LLD 1984; *Recreations* collecting antiques; *Clubs* Hong Kong, Hong Kong Country, World Trade Centre, The Royal Hong Kong Jockey; *Style*— The Rt Hon The Baroness Dunn, DBE, JP; John Swire & Sons (HK) Ltd, 5th Floor, Swire Hse, 9 Connaught Rd, Central Hong Kong (☎ 8408888); John Swire & Sons Ltd, Swire Hse, 59 Buckingham Gate, London SW1E 6AJ (☎ 071 834 7717)

DUNN, Lady Mary Helen Alma Graham; da of 6 Duke of Montrose; *b* 11 April 1909; *m* 1, 21 April 1931, Maj John Percival Townshend Boscawen, MBE, Gren Gds (d 1972), s of Townshend Evelyn Boscawen; 2 s; m 2, 1975, as his 2 w, Brig Leslie C Dunn, TD, DL (d 1990), s of William Lawrie Dunn, of Kilmacolm, Renfrewshire; *Style*— The Lady Mary Dunn

DUNN, Lady Mary Sybil; *née* St Clair-Erskine; da of 5 Earl of Rosslyn; *b* 9 May 1912; *m* 1, 1933 (m dis 1944), Philip Gordon Dunn (afterwards 2 Bt); 2 da (*see* Dunn, Nell); m 2, 5 Oct 1945 (m dis 1959), as his 2 w, Robin Francis Campbell, CBE, DSO (d 1985); m 3, 5 Oct 1962 (m dis 1969), Charles Raymond McCabe; re-m 4, 1969, Sir Philip Gordon Dunn, 2 and last Bt (d 1976); *Style*— Lady Mary Dunn; Draycot Fitzpayne Manor, Marlborough, Wilts

DUNN, Neil; s of Robert Dunn (d 1980), and Jean Hendrie Dunn, *née* Ramage (d 1987); *b* 15 Dec 1949; *Educ* Leith Acad Sch, Heriot Watt Univ (BA); *m* 1970, Dianne Isabella Mary, da of Robert Gilchrist Burgess (d 1965); 2 da (Elissa Lucienne b 1974, Chrisanna Amy b 1976); *Career* dir until 1989: Ivory & Sime plc (and various sudsids), Nippon Assets Investments SA; dir: Trenwick Inc, Clydesdale Group plc 1989-, Castle Cairn Investment Trust 1990-; ptnr N Dunn & Co 1989-; *Recreations* reading, fishing, walking; *Style*— Neil Dunn, Esq; St Johns, Temple, Midlothian; 14 Learmonth Place, Edinburgh EH3 1PG (☎ 031 337 8592, fax 031 313 2200)

DUNN, Nell Mary; yr da of Sir Philip Dunn, 2 Bt (d 1976), and Lady Mary Dunn, *qv*; *b* 9 June 1936; *m* 1957 (m dis 1979), Jeremy Christopher (writer), s of Christopher Sandford, of Eye Manor, Leominster; 3 s (Roc b 1957, Reuben b 1964, Jem b 1967); *Career* author; *Works include* Poor Cow, Up the Junction, Steaming (play); *Style*— Miss Nell Dunn

DUNN, Air Marshal Sir Patrick Hunter; KBE (1965, CBE 1950), CB (1956), DFC (1941); s of late William Alexander Dunn, of Ardentinny, Argyllshire; *b* 31 Dec 1912; *Educ* Glasgow Acad, Loretto, Univ of Glasgow; *m* 1939, Diana Ledward Smith; 2 da (*see* Sir Nigel Marsden, Bt); *Career* cmmnd RAF 1933; served WWII Egypt, Libya, Sudan, Air Miny and Fighter Cmd; ADC to HM The Queen 1953-58, Cmdt RAF Flying Coll Manby 1956-58, Air Vice Marshal 1959, AOC No 1 Gp Bomber Cmd 1961-64, AOC-in-C Flying Training Cmd 1964-66, Air Marshal 1965, ret 1967; dir Mgmnt Servs British Steel Corp 1967-68, dep chm British Eagle International Airlines 1968, vice pres UK NATO Def Coll Assoc 1969, chm Eagle Aircraft Services Ltd 1969, dir Gloucester Cricklewood Kingston and Coventry Trading Estates Ltd 1969-81; tstee and govr Loretto Sch 1959-81; pres: Fettesian Lorettonian Club 1972-75, Lorettonian Society 1980-81; memb: Ctee Assoc of Governing Bodies of Public Schools 1976-79, Br Atlantic Ctee 1976-; FRAeS; *Style*— Air Marshal Sir Patrick Dunn, KBE, CB, DFC; Little Hillbark, Cookham Dean, Berks SL6 9UF (☎ 062 84 5625)

DUNN, Paula; da of Paul Kenneth Dunn, and Louise, *née* Brissett; *b* 3 Dec 1964; *Career* athlete (sprinter); UK champion 100m and 200m: 1986, 1987 and 1988; WAAA champion 100m and 200m: 1987, 1988 and 1989; Cwlth Games 1986: Silver medallist 100m, Gold medallist 4 x 100m relay; Olympic Games 1988: quarter-finalist 100m, semi-finalist 200m, semi-finalist 4 x 100m relay; Silver medallist Europa Cup 100m and 200m 1989 ; Silver medallist Cwlth Games 1990, Bronze medallist European Championship 1990; athletic devpt offr and med clerical offr, also involved with local schs and sports clubs; *Recreations* athletics, reading; *Clubs* Stretford AC; *Style*— Miss Paula Dunn; 4 Salisbury Road, Chorlton-cum-Hardy, Manchester M21 1SL (☎ 061 881 6068); Belle Vue Athletic Centre, Recreational Services, Pink Bank Lane, Longsight, Manchester, M12 5GL

DUNN, Richard Johann; s of Maj Edward Cadwalader Dunn, MBE, TD (d 1985), of Burgh, Suffolk, and Gudlaug, *née* Johannesdóttir; *b* 5 Sept 1943; *Educ* Forest Sch, St John's Coll Cambridge (MA); *m* 20 June 1972, Virginia Gregory, da of Norman Joseph Gaynor (d 1967), of Canton, Ohio; 2 s (Andrew Glover Gaynor b 1980, William Edward Gaynor b 1986), 1 da (Elizabeth Page Gaynor b 1987); *Career* media - visual; writer and prodr Assoc British Pathe 1967-72; dir: Swindon Viewpoint Ltd 1972-76, EMI Films 1976-77, Thames TV 1978 (md 1985), ITN Ltd 1985- (dep chm 1990), Starstream Ltd 1986-, Ind Broadcasting Telethon Tst 1986-, Thames Help Tst 1986-, SES (Astra) 1987-, Channel Four TV Co Ltd 1989-; chm: Thames TV Int 1985-, ITV Assoc 1988-, Euston Films Ltd, Cosgrove Hall Prodns; govr: Nat Film and TV Sch, Forest Sch; pres Battersea Arts Centre; vice pres Royal TV Soc; *Clubs* Hawks (Cambridge), RAC; *Style*— Richard Dunn, Esq; 14 Bolingbroke Grove, London SW11 6EP; Thames TV plc, 306 Euston Rd, London NW3 (☎ 071 387 9494)

DUNN, Robert John; MP (C) Dartford 1979-; s of Robert Dunn (d 1986); *b* 14 July 1946; *Educ* State Schs; *m* 1976, Janet Elizabeth, da of Denis Wall (d 1983); 2 s; *Career* former sr buyer with Sainsbury's; Parly candidate (C) Eccles 1974 (vice pres Eccles Cons Assoc 1974-), jt sec Cons Backbench Educn Ctee 1980-82, advsr to Prof Assoc of Teachers 1982-83; PPS: DES until 1982, Cecil Parkinson (as Chm Cons Pty) 1982-83; under sec of State DES 1983-88, chm Cons Back Bench Social Security Ctee 1988-89, memb 1922 Ctee 1988-; pres Young Conservatives: Dartford 1976-, SE Area 1989; chm Cons Backbench Tport Ctee 1990; *Clubs* Carlton; *Style*— Robert Dunn, Esq, MP; House of Commons, London SW1 (☎ 071 219 5209)

DUNN, Rt Hon Sir Robin Horace Walford; MC (1944), PC (1980); s of Brig Keith Frederick William Dunn, CBE, DL (d 1985), and his 1 w, Ava, *née* Kays; *b* 16 Jan 1918; *Educ* Wellington, RMA Woolwich; *m* 1941, Judith Allan, da of Sir Gonne St Clair Pilcher, MC (d 1966); 1 s, 1 da (and 1 da decd); *Career* cmmnd RA 1938, RHA 1941; served WWII France, Belgium, Libya, Normandy, NW Europe (despatches twice), Staff Coll 1946, ret Hon Maj 1948; Hon Col Cmdt RA 1981-1984, Hon Col 1984; called to the Bar Inner Temple 1948, jr counsel Registrar of Restrictive Trading Agreements 1959-62, memb Gen Cncl of the Bar 1959-63 (treas 1967-69), QC 1962, bencher Inner Temple 1969, judge High Ct of Justice Family Div 1969-80, presiding judge Western Circuit 1974-78, Lord Justice of Appeal 1980-84, ret; kt 1969; *Clubs* Cavalry and Guards'; *Style*— Rt Hon Sir Robin Dunn, MC; Lynch Mead, Allerford, Somerset TA24 8HJ (☎ 0643 862509)

DUNN, (George) Roger; s of George Dunn, and Marjorie Rose, *née* Brown; *b* 10 Jan 1936; *Educ* Tettenhall Coll, Univ of Bristol (BSc); *m* 22 Aug 1970, (Patricia) Jane, da of Frank J R Law (d 1972), of Churchill, Worcs; 3 da (Sarah b 1972, Claudia b 1975, Juliet b 1977); *Career* Tube Investmts 1958-67, AIC Ltd 1967-75, chm and md Arcontrol Ltd 1975-; memb: SE Regnl Cncl of CBI, Engrg Cncl Regnl Orgn, Ct Bristol Univ; chm GAMBICA Ctee (for mfrg electrical switchgear and centl gear assemblies); FIEE, MIMechE, FInstD; *Recreations* swimming, playing the flute, private flying; *Style*— Roger Dunn, Esq; Ancontrol Ltd, Borough Green, Kent TN15 8RD (☎ 0732 883151, fax 0732 885982, telex 95580)

DUNN, Stephen; s of William Thomas Corbett Dunn, of 36 Sherfield Drive, Cochrane Park Estate, Newcastle upon Tyne, and Margaret, *née* Brennan; *b* 22 June 1960; *Educ* Heaton Comp Sch, Newcastle upon Tyne Coll of Art (HND DipAD); *Career* advertising art dir; Boase Massimi Pollit 1979; Leagas Delaney: joined 1982, head art dir 1985, memb Bd 1988; awards: 3 Design and Art Direction Silver awards, 3 Gold and 15 Silver Campaign Press awards, 4 Silver Campaign Poster awards, 4 Gold and 1 Silver One Show awards (US), 8 Gold and 6 Silver Creative Circle awards; memb Design and Art Directors Assoc; *Style*— Stephen Dunn, Esq; Leagas Delaney, 233 Shaftsbury Ave, London WC2 (☎ 071 836 4455)

DUNN, Lt-Col Sir (Francis) Vivian; KCVO (1969), OBE (1960), RM; s of Capt W J Dunn, MVO, MC, RHG; *b* 24 Dec 1908; *Educ* Peter Symonds Sch Winchester, Konservatorium der Musik Cologne, RAM; *m* 1938, Margery Kathleen Halliday; 1 s, 2 da; *Career* int conductor and composer; principal dir of Music RM, ret 1968; Liveryman and Master Worshipful Co of Musicans 1989-; ARAM, FRAM, FRSA; *Style*— Lt-Col Sir Vivian Dunn, KCVO, OBE, RM; 16 W Common, Haywards Heath, Sussex (☎ 0444 412987)

DUNN-MEYNELL, Hugo Arthur; s of Arthur James Dunn (d 1959), of London, and Mary Louise Maude, *née* Meynell (d 1945); *b* 4 April 1926; *Educ* John Fisher Sch Purley; *m* 1, 1952 (m dis 1980), Nadine Madeleine, da of late Percy Denson; 3 s, 1 da; m 2, 1980, Alice Wooledge, da of Dr Pierre Joseph Salmon, of Hillsborough, California; *Career* wine and food writer and conslt; pres Lonsdale Advertising International 1978-89, chm International Wine and Food Soc 1978-80 (exec dir 1983-); Liveryman Worshipful Co of Innholders; Grand-Officier Les Chevaliers du Tastevin; FRGS, FIPA; *Recreations* wine and travel; *Clubs* Athenaeum; *Style*— Hugo Dunn-Meynell, Esq; 125 Mount St, London W1Y 5HA (☎ 071 629 2647); International Wine and Food Society, 108 Old Brompton Rd, London SW7 3RA (☎ 071 370 0909, fax 071 373 5377)

DUNNE, Lady Miranda; *see*: Lowther

DUNNE, Thomas Raymond; JP (Hereford and Worcester 1977); s of Philip Dunne, MC (d 1965), of The Old Parsonage, East Clandon, Surrey, and Margaret Ann Dunne, CBE, *née* Walker; *b* 24 Oct 1933; *Educ* Eton; *m* 17 July 1957, Henrietta Rose, da of Cosmo Stafford Crawley (d 1989); 2 s (Philip b 1958, Nicholas b 1970), 2 da (Camilla (Hon Mrs Rupert Soames) b 1960, Letitia b 1965); *Career* RMA Sandhurst 1951-53, cmmnd RHG 1953-59, Hon Col 4 (volunteer) Bn The Worcestershire and Sherwood Foresters Regt 1987- (formerly 2 Bn Mercian Volunteers); memb Hereford CC 1962-68; High Sheriff Herefordshire 1970, DL Hereford and Worcester 1974 (Herefordshire 1973), HM Lord Lieutenant Hereford and Worcester 1977-, Custos Rotularum 1977-; pres Three Counties Agric Soc 1977, nat vice pres Royal Br Legion 1982, dir W Midland Regnl Bd Central TV, chm Tstees Dyson Perrins Museum 1985; KStJ 1977; *Recreations* travelling; *Style*— Thomas Dunne, Esq, JP; County Hall, Spetchley Road, Worcester

DUNNE, W Peter; s of William Joseph Dunne (d 1985), and Mary Anne, *née* Hynes (d 1958); *b* 6 Nov 1936; *Educ* Dublin; *m* 29 Nov 1969, Fionuala Anne, da of James Joseph Fox (d 1989), of Dublin; *Career* chief exec offr (confs and travel): Cwlth Econ Ctee 1961-66, Cwlth Secretariat 1966-; *Recreations* antiquarian books, music, cricket; *Clubs* MCC, Nat Lib, Royal Over-Seas League, RDS (Dublin); *Style*— W Peter Dunne, Esq; The Nuik, 55 Bodley Rd, New Malden, Surrey KT3 5QD, (☎ 081 942 1434); 11 Martello Mews, Dublin 4; Cwlth Secretariat, Marlborough Hse, Pall Mall, London SWIY 5HX (☎ 071 839 3411, fax 071 930 0827, telex 27678)

DUNNET, Prof George Mackenzie; OBE (1986); s of John George Dunnet (d 1983), of Aberdeen, and Christina Isabella, *née* Mackenzie (1978); *b* 19 April 1928; *Educ* Peterhead Acad, Univ of Aberdeen (BSc, PhD, DSc); *m* 5 Jan 1953, Margaret Henderson, da of James Thomson (d 1957), of Longside, Aberdeen; 1 s (Ian Thomson b 1956), 1 da (Karen Elizabeth b 1960), 1 da decd (Judith Ann b 1954, d 1980); *Career* res offr Wildlife Section CSIRO Aust 1953-58, lectr/sr in zoology and dir Culterty Field Station Univ of Aberdeen 1958-71, sr res fell Animal Ecology Div DSIR NZ 1968-69; Univ of Aberdeen: prof of zoology 1971, regius prof of natural history 1974-, dean Faculty of Science 1984-87; former memb: Scot Ctee The Nature Conservancy, The Natural Environment Res Cncl, The Br Tst for Ornithology, The Br Cncl; chm: Shetland Oil Terminal Environmental Advsy Gp 1977-, Salmon Advsy Ctee 1986-91, The Nature Conservancy Cncl for Scot 1991-92, Fish Farming Advsy Ctee; memb The Nature Conservancy Cncl 1990-; former chm: Review Gp on Badgers and Bovine Tuberculosis, advsy ctees for Protection of Birds; FRSE 1970, FIBiol 1974, FRSA (1981); Monograph of the Fleas of Australia (1974); *Recreations* croquet; *Clubs* Royal Cwlth; *Style*— Prof George Dunnet, OBE, FRSE; Whinhill, Inverebrie, Ellon, Aberdeen AB4 9PT (☎ 03587 215); Zoology Department, University of Aberdeen, Aberdeen AB9 2TN (☎ 0224 272876, fax 0224 272396, telex 73458 UNIABN-G)

DUNNETT, Lady; Clarisse; *b* 7 May 1924; *Educ* Budapest Hungary, Bristol; *m* 1, Grantley Loxton-Peacock (decd); 1 s, 1 da (*see* Osborne, Sir Peter, Bt); m 2, 1979, as his 2 w, Sir Anthony Grover, sometime chm Lloyds and Lloyds Register of Shipping (d

1981); m 3, 1983, Sir James Dunnett, GCB, CMG, *qv*; *Career* painter (known as Clarisse Loxton Peacock); fifteen one-man exhibitions, London, New York and Dusseldorf; *Recreations* gardening; *Style—* Lady Dunnett; 85 Bedford Gdns, London W8 (☎ 071 727 5286)

DUNNETT, Denzil Inglis; OBE (1962), CMG (1966); s of Sir James Dunnett, KCIE (d 1957), of Edinburgh, and Annie Sangster (d 1955); *b* 21 Oct 1917; *Educ* Edinburgh Acad, Oxford (MA); *m* 1946, Ruth (d 1973), da of Laurence Rawcliffe (d 1948), of Lancs; 2 s (Roderick b 1946, James b 1948), 1 da (Ursula b 1950); *Career* RA 1939-46 (Maj India, Germany); HM Dip Serv 1947-77; ambass 1972-75 to: Senegal, Mali, Mauretania, Guinea, Guinea-Bssau; London rep of the Scottish Devpt Agency 1978-82; dir The Sea Vegetable Co 1985-; *Publications include* Bird Poems (1989); *Recreations* fountains, golf; *Clubs* Caledonian; *Style—* Denzil Dunnett, Esq, OBE, CMG; 11 Victoria Grove, London W8 5RW (☎ 071 584 7523)

DUNNETT, (William Herbert) Derek; s of William Herbert Dunnett (d 1978), of Surrey, and Lilian Agnes, *née* Waugh (d 1968); *b* 9 Feb 1921; *Educ* The Manor House Horsham, Rugby; *m* 14 Dec 1950, Peggy Cummins; 1 s (William b 1954), 1 da (Margaret b 1962); *Career* dir Carters Tested Seeds Ltd 1946-62 (md 1962-67); md Raynes Park Securities Ltd 1969-; memb of Lloyds (external) 1978-; rackets champion: public schools (doubles 1939, singles 1938), services singles 1955, Open Invitation doubles 1951; FID; *Recreations* sport, racing, arts; *Clubs* Queens, MCC; *Style—* Derek Dunnett, Esq; 105 Comeragh Rd, West Kensington, London W14 9HS

DUNNETT, Dorothy; da of late Alexander Halliday, and late Dorothy, *née* Millard; *b* 25 Aug 1923; *Educ* James Gillespie's HS for Girls Edinburgh; *m* 1946, Alastair Mactavish Dunnett; 2 s (Ninian, Mungo); *Career* civil servant 1940-55; portrait painter 1950-, novelist 1961-; dir Scot TV plc 1979-; tstee: Scot Nat War Meml 1962-, Nat Library of Scot 1986-; dir Edinburgh Book Festival 1990-; *Books* Game of Kings (1961), Queens' Play (1964), The Disorderly Knights (1966), Dolly and the Singing Bird (1968), Pawn in Frankincense (1969), Dolly and the Cookie Bird (1970), The Ringed Castle (1971), Dolly and the Doctor Bird (1971), Dolly and the Starry Bird (1973), Checkmate (1975, Scottish Arts Cncl Award 1976), Dolly and the Nanny Bird (1976), King Hereafter (1982), Dolly and the Bird of Paradise (1983), Niccolò Rising (1986), The Spring of the Ram (1987), The Highlands of Scotland (with A M Dunnett, 1988), Race of Scorpions (1989), Moroccan Traffic (1991); *Recreations* travel, sailing, music, ballet, mediaeval history; *Clubs* New (Edinburgh), Caledonian; *Style—* Mrs Alastair Dunnett; 87 Colinton Rd, Edinburgh EH10 5DF (☎ 031 337 2107, fax 031 346 4140)

DUNNETT, Jack; *b* 24 June 1922; *Educ* Whitgift Middle Sch Croydon, Downing Coll Cambridge; *m* 1951, Pamela Lucille; 2 s, 3 da; *Career* served WWII, Royal Fusiliers and Cheshire Regt (Capt); slr 1949; memb GLC 1964-67; MP (Lab): Nottingham Central 1964-74, Nottingham East 1974-83; PPS to: Sec of State Defence and Min of Defence (Army) 1964-66, Min of Aviation 1966-67, Min of Transport 1969-70; vice pres Football Assoc 1981-89, pres Football League 1981-89; *Style—* Jack Dunnett, Esq; Whitehall Court, London SW1

DUNNETT, Sir (Ludovic) James; GCB (1969, KCB 1960, CB 1957), CMG (1948); s of Sir James Dunnett, KCIE (d 1953), bro of Sir George Sangster Dunnett; *b* 12 Feb 1914; *Educ* Edinburgh Acad, Univ Coll Oxford; *m* 1, 1944, Olga Adair (d 1980), m 2, 1983, Clarisse, Lady Grover; *Career* joined Air Miny 1936, transferred to Miny of Civil Aviation 1945 (asst sec 1945, under-sec 1948-51), under-sec (Air) Miny of Supply 1951-53 (dep sec 1953-58), dep sec Miny of Transport 1958 (permanent sec 1959-62), permanent sec Miny of Labour 1962-66, permanent under-sec of state MOD 1966-74; chm Int Maritime Industs Forum 1974-79; pres Institute of Manpower Studies 1977-80, memb SSRC 1977-83; visiting fell Nuffield Coll Oxford 1960-68; *Clubs* Reform; *Style—* Sir James Dunnett, GCB, CMG; 85 Bedford Gardens, London W8

DUNNETT, Pamela Dawn Hamilton; da of Claude Hamilton Johnson (d 1967), and Elsie Muriel, *née* Street (d 1972); *b* 4 Nov 1925; *Educ* St Dominics Priory, Port Elizabeth SA; *m* 26 Oct 1946, Hanbury William Dunnett, s of Hanbury Dunnett (d 1961); 1 s (Geoffrey b 21 April 1950), 1 da (Gillian b 10 Nov 1947); *Career* WWII SAAF 1943-45; dir Dunnetts (Birmingham) Ltd 1971-; memb Cons Assoc, former ctee memb Sunshine Homes for Blind Children, former govr Knowle Hill Approved Sch Kenilworth; *Recreations* golf, bridge, painting; *Clubs* Coventry Golf, Warwick Boat; *Style—* Mrs Pamela Dunnett; Barons Lodge, Hareway Lane, Barford, Warwick (☎ 0926 624 034); Dunnetts (Birmingham) Ltd, Vanguard Works, Kings Rd, Tyseley, Birmingham (☎ 021 706 0271, fax 021 706 6169)

DUNNILL, Michael Simpson; s of Arthur Hoyle Dunnill (d 1958), of Bristol, and Florence Simpson, *née* Rollinson (d 1984); *b* 26 March 1928; *Educ* Bristol GS, Univ of Bristol (MB ChB, MD), Univ of Oxford (MA); *m* 30 Oct 1952, Hilda, da of H Eastman (d 1939), of Bristol; 2 s (Phillip Arthur Simpson b 1956, Michael Giles Simpson b 1964); *Career* Nat Serv MO RAMC Highland Light Infantry 1952-54; jr clinical pathologist Bristol Royal Infirmary 1954-55 (house physician and surgn 1951-52), demonstrator Univ of Bristol 1955-56; Univ of Oxford: joined 1956, lectr in pathology 1961, dir of clinical studies 1966-72, fell Merton Coll 1967-; res assoc Dept of Med Univ of Columbia 1961-62, conslt pathologist Oxford 1961-, examiner RCP 1972-80, memb Cncl RCPath 1977-80 (examiner 1977); FRCP 1971 (memb 1956), FRCPath 1972; *Books* Pathological Basis of Renal Disease (1976), Pulmonary Pathology (1982), Morphometry (jtly, 1982); *Recreations* walking, fly fishing; *Clubs* Athenaeum, MCC; *Style—* Michael Dunnill, Esq; Histopathology Department, John Radcliffe Hospital, Headington, Oxford OX3 9DU (☎ 0865 817252)

DUNNILL, Prof Peter; s of Eric Dunnill (d 1980), of Rustington, Sussex, and Majorie (d 1985); *b* 20 May 1938; *Educ* Willesden Tech Sch, UCL (BSc), Royal Inst (PhD); *m* 11 Aug 1962, Patricia Mary, da of Sidney Lievesley, of Winchmore Hill, London; 1 s (Paul b 2 April 1971); *Career* staff MRC Royal Inst 1963-64, prof of biochemical engrg 1984- (lectr 1964-79, reader 1976-84); memb: Biotechnology Advsy Gp to the Heads of Res Councils 1987-90, Biotechnology Joint Advsy Bd 1989-; FRSC 1979, FIChemE 1981, FEng 1985; *Books* Fermentation and Enzyme Technology (1979), Enzymic and Non-enzymic Catalysis (1980); *Recreations* music; *Style—* Prof Peter Dunnill; SERC Centre for Biochemical Engineering, Dept of Chemical & Biochemical Engineering, UCL, Torrington Place, London WC1E 7JE (☎ 071 380 7368, fax 071 388 0808, telex 29627 ENGG)

DUNNING, Prof Eric Geoffrey; s of Sydney Ernest Dunning (d 1981), and Florence Daisy, *née* Morton (d 1987); *b* 27 Dec 1936; *Educ* Acton Co GS for Boys, Univ of Leicester (BSc, MA); *m* 1, 12 July 1962 (m dis 1965), Ellen Adrienne, da of Col Nathaniel Sweets (d 1988), of St Louis, Missouri; m 2, 17 July 1969 (m dis 1986), (Ursula) Judith Clare Hibbert; 1 s (Michael James b 1976), 1 da (Rachel Clare b 1978); *Career* prof of sociology Univ of Leicester 1988- (asst lectr 1962, lectr 1963, sr lectr 1972); dir Sir Norman Chester Centre for Football Res 1987-; visiting lectureships: Univ of Warwick 1966-69, Univ of Nottingham 1974; visiting professorships: Brooklyn Coll NY 1964, Univ of Minnesota 1968, State Univ of NY 1970; memb Br Sociological Assoc; *Books* The Sociology of Sport (1971), Barbarians Gentlemen and Players (1979), Hooligans Abroad (1984), Quest For Excitement (1986), The Roots of Football Hooliganism (1988), Football on Trial (1990), Sport and Leisure in the Civilizing Process (1991); *Recreations* music, theatre; *Style—* Prof Eric Dunning; Sir Norman Chester Centre for Football Research, Dept of Sociology, University of Leicester, Leicester LE1 7R4 (☎ 0533 522736)

DUNNING, Graham; s of Maj James Edwin Dunning, of Romsey Hants, and Jane Priscilla, *née* Hunt; *b* 13 March 1958; *Educ* King Edward VI Sch Southampton, Emmanuel Coll Cambridge (MA), Harvard Law Sch (LLM); *m* 26 July 1986, Claire Abigael, da of Dr W S C Williams, of Oxford; *Career* short serv cmmn 3 RTR 1977; called to the Bar Lincoln's Inn 1982; *Recreations* swimming, squash, golf, film, theatre and wine; *Style—* Graham Dunning, Esq; 50 Gibson Square, Islington, London N1 (☎ 071 359 0777), 4 Essex Ct, Temple, London (☎ 071 5839191, fax 071 353 3421, telex 888465 COMCAS)

DUNNING, Prof John Harry; s of John Murray Dunning (d 1966), and Anne Florence, *née* Baker (d 1965); *b* 26 June 1927; *Educ* Lower Sch of John Lyons Harrow, City of Coll, UCL (BSc), Univ of Southampton (PhD); *m* 1, (m dis 1975); 1 s (Philip John b 1957); m 2, 4 Aug 1975, Christine Mary, da of Ernest Stewart Brown; *Career* Sub Lt RNVR 1945-48; lectr and sr lectr in econs Univ of Southampton 1952-64; Univ of Reading: fndn prof of econs 1964-75, Esmee Fairbairn prof of int investmt and business studies 1975-88; ICI res prof in int business 1988-; prof of int business Rutgers Univ 1989-; chm Econs Advsy Gp Ltd; conslt to UK Govt depts, OECD, UN Centre on Transnational Corps; memb: Royal Econ Soc, Acad of Int Business, pres AIB 1987-88; Dr hc Universidad Autonome Madrid 1990, Hon PhD Uppsala Univ Sweden 1975; *Books* incl: American Investment in British Manufacturing Industry (1958), British Industry: Change and Development in the Twentieth Century (w Thomas, 2 edn 1963), The Economics of Advertising (with D Lees and others, 1967), An Economic Study of the City of London (with E V Morgan, 1971), Readings in International Investment (1972), Economic Analysis and the Multinational Enterprise (1974), The World's Largest Industrial Enterprises 1962-77 (1981), International Capital Movements (with John Black, 1982), Multinational Enterprises, Economic Structure and International Competitiveness (1985), Japanese Participation in British Industry (1986), Explaining International Production (1988), Multinationals, Technology and Competitiveness (1988), Structural Change in the World Economy (with Allan Webster, 1990); *Recreations* gardening, walking; *Clubs* Athenaeum; *Style—* Prof John H Dunning; Dept of Econs, Univ of Reading, Whiteknights, Reading, Berks RG6 2AA (☎ 0734 318159, fax 0734 750236)

DUNNING, Kathleen, Lady; Kathleen Lawrie Cuthbert; da of J Patrick Cuthbert, MC; *m* 1936, Sir William Leonard Dunning, 2 Bt (d 1961); *Style—* Kathleen, Lady Dunning; Barclayhills, Guildtown, Perth

DUNNING, Norman Moore; s of Lt Frank Dunning, of 30 Hawthorne Drive, Sandbach, Cheshire, and Jean, *née* Anderson; *b* 15 April 1950; *Educ* Sandbach Sch, Jesus Coll Oxford (BA), Univ of Manchester (Adv Dip Social Admin and Social Work); *m* 8 April 1972, Diana Mary, da of Capt Eustace Russell Tansley, of Rectory House, Astbury, Cheshire; 2 s (Matthew James b 27 Oct 1976, Michael Richard b 27 June 1978); *Career* probation offr Manchester and Salford 1973-75, social worker NSPCC 1975-77, div mangr RSSPCC 1987- (ldr Overnewton Centre 1978-87); former chm Br Assoc for the Study and Prevention of Child Abuse and Neglect 1986-89, vice chm Scottish Child Law Centre; memb: Cncl and professional Advsy Gp Childline; *Recreations* running, cycling, swimming; *Style—* Norman Dunning, Esq; 7 The Ness, Dollar, Clackmannanshire FK14 7EB (☎ 0259 43354); 36 Park Terrace, Stirling FK2 6JR (☎ 0786 51248, car 0836 700790)

DUNNING, Sir Simon William Patrick; 3 Bt (UK 1930) of Beedinglee, Lower Beeding, Sussex; s of Sir William Leonard Dunning, 2 Bt (d 1961); *b* 14 Dec 1939; *Educ* Eton; *m* 1975, Frances Deirdre Morton, da of Maj Patrick William Morton Lancaster; 1 da; *Heir* none; *Career* insurance broker and underwriting memb of Lloyd's; *Clubs* Turf, Western (Glasgow); *Style—* Sir Simon Dunning, Bt; Low Auchengillan, Blanefield, by Glasgow, G63 9AU (☎ 0360 70323)

DUNNINGTON, Philip Graham; s of John Dunnington, of Bath, and Barbara Helen, *née* Clague; *b* 10 March 1947; *Educ* Windsor GS, Univ of Bristol (BA); *m* 4 Dec 1976, Jane Anne, da of John Cater (d 1987); 1 s (Nicholas b 1982), 3 da (Hannah b 1983, Fiona b 1985, Philippa b 1988); *Career* assoc dir of mktg ITEL Air 1977-79, sales and mktg mangr Aircraft Short Bros Ltd 1979-83, md Saab-Fairchild International 1983-85, dir of sales and mktg Cameron Balloons Ltd 1985-, examiner commercial balloon licences CAA 1989; *Recreations* hot air balloon and airship expeditions; *Clubs* British Balloon & Airship; *Style—* Philip Dunnington, Esq; Mulberry House, Front Street, Churchill, Bristol BS19 5NB (☎ 0934 852359); Cameron Balloons Ltd, St John's St, Bedminster, Bristol BS3 4HN (☎ 0272 637216, fax 0272 661168, telex 44825 GASBAG)

DUNNINGTON-JEFFERSON, Isobel, Lady; (Frances) Isobel; da of Col Herbert Anderson Cape, DSO, of Thorganby, York; *m* 1938, Lt-Col Sir John Alexander Dunnington-Jefferson, DSO, 1 Bt (d 1979); 1 s, 1 da; *Style—* Isobel, Lady Dunnington-Jefferson; Rectory Cottage, Escrick, York YO4 6LE (☎ 0904 87 686)

DUNNINGTON-JEFFERSON, Sir Mervyn Stewart; 2 Bt (UK 1958); s of Lt-Col Sir John Alexander Dunnington-Jefferson, 1 Bt, DSO (d 1979); *b* 5 Aug 1943; *Educ* Eton; *m* 1971, Caroline Anna, da of John Bayley, of Hillam Hall, Monk Fryston, Yorks; 1 s, 2 da; *Heir* s, John Alexander Dunnington-Jefferson b 23 March 1980; *Career* ptnr Marldon Construction; *Recreations* sport; *Clubs* MCC, Queen's; *Style—* Sir Mervyn Dunnington-Jefferson, Bt; 7 Bolingbroke Grove, London SW11 (☎ 081 675 3395)

DUNPARK, Hon Lord Alastair McPherson Johnston; TD (1948), QC (1958); s of Rev Alexander McPherson Johnston (d 1957), of Stirling, and Eleanora Guthrie, *née* Wyllie (d 1966); *b* 15 Dec 1915; *Educ* Merchiston Castle Sch, Univ of Cambridge (BA), Univ of Edinburgh (LLB); *m* 1, 16 Dec 1939, Katharine Margaret, *née* Mitchell (d 1983); 3 s (Alan Charles Macpherson b 13 Jan 1942, (Alastair) Bryan Mitchell b 9 March 1948, Colin Lindsay Wyllie b 23 Oct 1952); m 2, 29 Sept 1984, Kathleen Elizabeth Sarah Macfie, *née* Welsh; *Career* advocate 1946, jr counsel Miny of Food and Miny of Tport, sheriff princ Dumfries and Galloway 1966-68, Scottish Law Cmmn 1968-71, senator Coll of Justice and Lord of Session Scotland 1971-90; pres: Lothian Marriage Counselling Serv 1974-87, Scottish Univ's Law Inst 1977-91; chm: Edinburgh Legal Dispensary 1961-, RA Assoc Scotland 1962-76, Cockburn Assoc (The Edinburgh Civic Tst) 1969-74, St George's Sch for Girls Edinburgh 1973-89; *Publications* Walton on Husband and Wife (jt ed 3 edn), Gloag & Henderson's Introduction to the Law of Scotland (jt ed 7 edn); *Recreations* reading; *Clubs* New (Edinburgh), Honourable Company of Edinburgh Golfers; *Style—* The Hon Lord Dunpark, TD; 17 Heriot Row, Edinburgh EH3 6HP (☎ 031 556 1896); Parliament House, Edinburgh

DUNPHIE, Maj-Gen Sir Charles Anderson Lane; CB (1948), CBE (1942), DSO (1943); s of Sir Alfred Dunphie, KCVO; *b* 20 April 1902; *Educ* RNCs Osborne and Dartmouth, RMA Woolwich; *m* 1, 1931, Eileen (d 1978), da of Lt-Gen Sir Walter Campbell, KCB, KCMG, DSO; 1 s, 1 da; m 2, 1981, Susan, widow of Col P L M Wright, of Roundhill, Wincanton; *Career* cmmnd RH and RFA 1921, served WWII (despatches) Brig RAC 1941, Cdr 26 Armoured Bde 1942-43, dep dir RAC WO 1943-45, dir gen Armoured Fighting Vehicles 1945-48, ret 1948; chm Vickers Ltd 1962-67; memb HM's Hon Corps Gentlemen-at-Arms 1952-62; Cdr Legion of Merit USA, Silver Star USA; kt 1959; *Clubs* Army and Navy; *Style—* Maj-Gen Sir Charles Dunphie, CB, CBE, DSO; Roundhill, Wincanton, Somerset BA9 8HH (☎ 0963 33278)

DUNPHIE, Brig Christopher Campbell; MC (1972); s of Maj-Gen Sir Charles Dunphie, CB, CBE, DSO, *qv*, of Roundhill, Wincanton, Somerset, and Eileen, *née* Campbell (d 1978); *b* 29 March 1935; *Educ* Eton, RMA Sandhurst; *m* 28 Sept 1963, Sonia Diana, da of Brig R C H Kirwan, DSO, OBE (d 1989); 1 s (Charles b 1970); *Career* cmmnd Rifle Bde 1955 (later Royal Green Jackets), Regtl Serv in Kenya, Malaya, BAOR and Cyprus 1955-67, Staff Coll 1968, MA to CGS 1969-71, Co Cmd 3 RGJ served UN Force Cyprus and NI 1971-73, instr Staff Coll 1973-76 (Lt-Col), CO 3 RGJ Berlin, UK and NI 1976-78, asst dir of def policy MOD 1979-82, COS to LANDEP C-in-C Fleet Falklands Op 1982, Cmdt Tactics Wing Sch of Inf 1983-85, Div Brig Light Div 1985-87, ret 1988; memb: Queens Body Guard for Scotland (The Royal Co of Archers); *Books* Brightly Shone the Dawn (with Garry Johnson, 1980); *Recreations* cricket, skiing, field sports, music; *Clubs* I Zingari, Free Foresters, Perth; *Style—* Brig Christopher Dunphie, MC; Wester Cloquhat, Bridge of Cally, Blairgowrie, Perthshire PH10 7JP (☎ 025 086 320)

DUNRAVEN AND MOUNT-EARL, Nancy, Countess of; Nancy; da of Thomas Burks Yuille, of Halifax Co, Virginia, USA; *m* 1934, as his 2 w, 6 Earl of Dunraven and Mount-Earl, CB, CBE, MC (d 1965); 1 s (7 Earl), 2 da (Lady Melissa Brooke, w of Maj Sir George B, 3 Bt, MBE; Marchioness of Waterford, w of 8 Marquess); *Style—* The Rt Hon Nancy, Countess of Dunraven and Mount-Earl; Kilgobbin, Adare, Co Limerick

DUNRAVEN AND MOUNT-EARL, 7 Earl of (I 1822); Sir Thady Windham Thomas Wyndham-Quin; 7 Bt (GB 1781); also Baron Adare (I 1800), Viscount Mount-Earl (I 1816), Viscount Adare (I 1822); s of 6 Earl of Dunraven and Mount-Earl, CB, CBE, MC (d 1965; one of the small number of families of Celtic antecedents in the Irish peerage. Lord Dunraven and Mount-Earl's ancestors were chiefs of a clan situated long before even the Norman invasions of Ireland in Co Clare and the O'Quins are the origin of the name of the Barony of Inchiquin); *b* 27 Oct 1939; *Educ* Ludgrove, Le Rosey Switzerland; *m* 1969, Geraldine, da of Air Cdre Gerard W McAleer, CBE; 1 da (Lady Ana b 1972); *Heir* none; *Career* farming and property Devpt; *Clubs* Kildare Street (Dublin); *Style—* The Rt Hon The Earl of Dunraven and Mount-Earl; Kilcurley House, Adare, Co Limerick, Ireland (☎ 061 86201)

DUNROSSIL, 2 Viscount (UK 1959); John William Morrison; CMG (1981); s of 1 Viscount, GCMG, MC, PC, QC (d 1961); *b* 22 May 1926; *Educ* Fettes, Oriel Coll Oxford; *m* 1, 1951 (m dis 1969), Mavis, da of A Llewellyn Spencer-Payne; 3 s, 1 da; m 2, 1969, Diana Mary Cunliffe, da of C M Vise; 2 da (Hon Joanna Catherine b 25 April 1971, Hon Mary Alison b 12 Dec 1972); *Heir* s, Hon Andrew William Reginald Morrison; *Career* served RAF 1945-48; CRO 1951, private sec to Sec of State 1952-54, second sec Canberra Australia 1954-56, first sec and dep actg high cmmr E Pakistan 1958-60, first sec Pretoria Capetown 1961-64 (seconded to Foreign Service 1961), Diplomatic Service Admin Office 1965, on loan to Intergovernmental Maritime Consultative Orgn (IMCO) 1968-70, cnsllr and head of Chancery Ottawa 1970-75, cnsllr Brussels 1975-78, high cmmr Fiji, Republic of Nauru, and Tuvalu 1978-82, high cmmr Barbados and (concurrently but non-resident) Antigua & Barbuda, St Vincent & The Grenadines, St Lucia, Cwlth of Dominica, Grenada and also Br Govt rep WI Assoc State of St Kitts-Nevis 1982-83, govr and C-in-C of Bermuda 1983-; KStJ 1983; *Style—* The Rt Hon the Viscount Dunrossil, CMG; c/o Foreign and Commonwealth Office, Downing Street, London SW1; Government House, Hamilton, Bermuda

DUNSANY, 19 Baron (I 1439); Lt-Col Randal Arthur Henry Plunkett; s of 18 Baron Dunsany, the author (d 1957), and Lady Beatrice (d 1970), *née* Child-Villiers, da of 7 Earl of Jersey; hp to Barony of Killeen (*see* 12 Earl of Fingall); *b* 25 Aug 1906; *Educ* Eton; *m* 1, 1938 (m dis 1947), da of Senhor G De Sà Sottomaior, of São Paulo, Brazil; 1 s; m 2, 1947, Sheila Victoria Katrin, da of Sir Henry Philipps, 2 Bt, and widow of Maj John Frederick Foley, Baron de Rutzen, Welsh Gds; 1 da; *Heir* s, Hon Edward Plunkett; *Career* joined 16/5 Lancers (SR) 1926, transfd IA 1928, Guides Cavalry Indian Armoured Corps, ret 1947; *Style—* Lt-Col The Rt Hon The Lord Dunsany; Dunsany Castle, Co Meath, Ireland (☎ 046 25198)

DUNSDON, Graham Eric; s of Walter Eric Dunsdon (d 1985), of Horsham, W Sussex, and Dorothy Edith, *née* Hawkins (d 1975); *b* 13 Sept 1944; *Educ* Collyer's GS Horsham; *m* 18 Sept 1965, Mary, da of Joseph Nathaniel Bradley (d 1984); 1 s (Simon b 1967), 2 da (Helen b 1969, Lucy b 1973); *Career* insurance and banking, ACII; asst gen mangr TSB Trust Co Ltd 1975-82; dir: TSB Insurance Services Ltd 1981-82, Household International (UK) Ltd 1984-, HFC Bank plc 1989-; md: FIMS Ltd 1982-83, Hamilton Insurance Co Ltd 1983-90 (dir 1983-), Hamilton Life Assurance Co Ltd 1983-90 (dir 1983-); chm Hamilton Financial Planning Services Ltd 1986-90; *Recreations* church activities, family; *Style—* Graham Dunsdon, Esq; c/o HFC Bank plc, North Street, Winkfield, Windsor, Berkshire SL4 4TD (☎ 0344 892203)

DUNSEATH, Robert William (Robin); s of William Hamilton Dunseath (d 1946), of Bangor, NI, and Barbara, *née* Brown; *b* 14 June 1907; *Educ* Campbell Coll Belfast, Concord HS Massachussets USA, Queen's Univ Belfast, Manchester Univ (BSc, Dip Tech Sci); *m* 19 May 1962, Hazel Mary, da of Peter Copsey, Peterborough; 1 s (Ashley b 1964), 1 da (Elizabeth b 1971); *Career* dir Royal Lyceum Theatre Edinburgh 1984-, world pres The World Haggis Hurling Soc 1978; FInstD; *Recreations* restoring old cottages, cars; *Style—* Robin Dunseath, Esq; 16 Maybury Road, Edinburgh; The Coach House, Dundonnachie, Dunkelp, Scotland; 5 Castle Terrace, Edinburgh, Scotland (☎ 031 228 6992, fax 031 228 6889, car ☎ 0860 326552)

DUNSIRE, Thomas; WS (1950); s of Thomas Dunsire (d 1976), of 30 Fairford Rd, Highbridge, Somerset, and Joan, *née* Duncan (d 1985); *b* 16 Nov 1926; *Educ* George Watson's Coll Edinburgh, Morrison's Acad Crieff, Univ of Edinburgh (MA, LLB); *m* 17 Dec 1966, Jean Mary, da of John Bellwood Wright (d 1961), of Studley Rd, Middlesborough; *Career* War Serv 1944-47, Ordinary Seaman RN; admitted slr 1950; conslt J & J Milligan WS (now Morton Fraser Milligan WS) 1988-90 (ptnr 1951, sr ptnr 1983-88); chm Morrisons Acad 1984 (govr 1972); *Style—* Thomas Dunsire, Esq, WS; 40 Liberton Brae, Edinburgh

DUNSTAN, Hon Maj Harry Bernard (Hal); TD 1964; s of Bernard Mainwaring Dunstan (d 1946), of Warrington, Lancs, and Nellie Dunstan, *née* Sneyd (d 1956); *b* 21 July 1918; *Educ* Bolton Sch; *m* 10 April 1948, Dorothy Mary Johnston, da of John Gordon (d 1952), of Scotland; 2 s (Michael John b 1953, Peter Gordon b 1954), 1 da (Christine Mary b 1950); *Career* Duke of Lancasters Own Yeo TA 1939-40 and 1948-67, cmmnd 40 Bn RTR 1941, HQ 8 Armd Div 1941-42, 3 Kings Own Hussars 1942-46; served: N Africa, Italy, Palestine, res cmmn TARD 1967 and granted hon rank of Maj; worked in Coal Indust 1934-82 (ret as mktg mangr NCB 1982); *Recreations* travel, gardening; *Clubs* Army & Navy; *Style—* Hon Maj Hal Dunstan, TD; Denstone Hse, Lincoln Rd, Tuxford, Notts NG22 0HP (☎ 0777 870380)

DUNSTER, Francis Henry; s of Henry Frank Dunster (d 1960), and Elsie, *née* Whitehorn; *b* 24 Aug 1935; *Educ* Leighton Park Sch, Coll of Estate Mgmnt; *m* 19 Oct 1963, Maria Patricia, da of George Walsh (d 1983); 2 s (James b 1967, Charles b 1970), 1 da (Sarah b 1964); *Career* Healey & Baker: assoc ptnr 1965, equity ptnr 1969-, ptnr i/c Glasgow Office 1982-88; FRICS, ACIarb; *Recreations* tennis, golf, rugby; *Clubs* MCC, Royal Scottish Automobile, Reading Rugby, Maidenhead Golf; *Style—* Francis Dunster, Esq; 29 St George St, Hanover Sq, London W1A 3BG (☎ 071 629 9292)

DUNSTER, (Herbert) John; CB (1978); s of Herbert Dunster (d 1980); *b* 27 July 1922; *Educ* UCS, Imperial Coll of Science and Technol; *m* 1945, Rosemary Elizabeth, *née* Gallagher; 1 s, 3 da; *Career* scientist (radiology); Royal Naval Scientific Serv 1942, scientist UK Atomic Energy Authority 1946-71, asst dir Nat Radiological Protection Bd 1971-76, dep dir gen Health and Safety Exec 1976-; ARCS; *Recreations* music, photography, work; *Style—* John Dunster Esq, CB; Hill Cottage, 65 Castlebar Rd, W5 (☎ 081 997 0439)

DUNTHORNE, John William Bayne; s of Philip Bayne Dunthorne, of Alton, Hants, and Ruth Mabelle, *née* Sturch; *b* 26 Aug 1946; *Educ* Abingdon Sch, Oxford Sch of Architecture (Dip Arch); *m* 16 Aug 1974, Maggie Alice, da of John Edgar Taylor (d 1988), of Blofield, Norfolk; 1 s (Oliver b 1983), 1 da (Joanna b 1981); *Career* assoc ptnr Chapman Lisle Assocs 1972-74, jt sr ptnr Dunthorne Parker Architects & Designers 1978-88, dir DPSL 1985-88; RIBA, MCSD; *Books* An Airport Interface (with M P Parker, 1971); *Recreations* cricket, golf, snow skiing; *Clubs* MCC, Forty, Lord Gnome's CC; *Style—* J W B Dunthorne, Esq; 5 Aspley Rd, London SW18 2DB (☎ 081 874 4904); Dunthorne Parker, Architects & Designers, 8 Seymour Place, London W1H 5WF (☎ 071 258 0411)

DUNTZE, Dowager Lady Nesta; da of late T R P Herbert; *m* 1, Godfrey Ariel Evill; m 2, 1966, as his 2 w, Sir George Edwin Douglas Duntze, 6 Bt, CMG (d 1985); *Style—* The Dowager Lady Duntze; 25 Ennismore Gardens, London SW7

DUNWICH, Bishop of 1980-; Rt Rev Eric Nash Devenport; s of Joseph Samuel Devenport (d 1964), and Emma Devenport (d 1947); *b* 3 May 1926; *Educ* St Chad's Sch, Open Univ, Kelham Theol Coll; *m* 19 April 1954, Jean Margaret, da of Cliff Richardson (d 1985); 2 da (Rachel Mary b 1956, Clare Helen b 1962); *Career* curate: St Mark Leicester 1951-54, St Matthew Barrow-in-Furness 1954-56; succentor Leicester Cathedral 1956-59; vicar: Shepshed 1959-64, Oadby 1964-73; leader of mission Leicester 1973-80, hon canon Leicester 1973-80, area chaplain Actors' Church Union 1980- (chaplain 1973-); chm Hospital Chaplaincies Cncl, diocesan communications offr; Liveryman Worshipful Co of Framework Knitters 1980-; *Recreations* theatre, painting; *Clubs* Royal Commonwealth Soc; *Style—* The Rt Rev the Bishop of Dunwich; The Old Vicarage, Stowupland, Stowmarket, Suffolk IP14 4BQ

DUNWICH, Viscount; Robert Keith Rous; s (by 1 m) and h of 6 Earl of Stradbroke, *qv*; *b* 17 Nov 1961; *Style—* Viscount Dunwich

DUNWOODY, Hon Mrs (Gwyneth Patricia); MP (Lab) Crewe and Nantwich 1983-; o da of Baroness Phillips (Life Peer) and Morgan Phillips (d 1963), sometime Gen Sec Labour Pty; *b* 12 Dec 1930; *Educ* Fulham County Secdy Sch, Convent of Notre Dame; *m* 1954 (m dis 1975), Dr John Elliot Orr Dunwoody; 2 s, 1 da; *Career* former journalist for Fulham local newspaper and writer for radio, also former memb Totnes Cncl; MP (Lab): Exeter 1966-70, Crewe 1974-1983; Parly sec Bd of Trade 1967-70, UK memb of Euro Parl 1975-79, memb Lab NEC 1981-, chm NEC Local Govt Sub-Committee Nov 1981-, oppn front bench spokesman Health Service 1981-, memb Lab Home Policy Ctee 1982-89; dir Film Prodn Assoc of Gt Britain 1970-74; responsibility for co-ordinating Lab Party campaigns 1983-89, memb Select Ctee Tport, chm Lab Friends of Israel; *Style—* The Hon Mrs Dunwoody, MP; House of Commons, London SW1

DUPLESSIS, Hugo Jules; s of Capt Gerald Duplessis (d 1949), of Newtown Park, Lymington, and Kathleen, *née* McCalmont 1971, gd of Baron of Kingsale); *b* 30 June 1923; *Educ* Beaumont Coll, Southampton Univ; *m* Oct 1952, Joyce (m dis 1979), da of Capt C Percy Keevil (d 1969), of Cockfosters, Herts; 1 s (Christopher b 1963), 1 da (Primrose b 1962); *Career* WWII Fleet Air Arm RN 1942-46; Admty Scientific Serv 1950-52, project ldr Decca Radar 1952-54; md: Newtown Industs 1954-, Fibreclad Ltd and Ropewalk Boatyard 1958-61; dir Koloplas Ltd 1962-71, Irish Atlantic Charters 1977-; conslt on fibreglass boats, yacht surveyor and designer 1954- (semi-ret 1985); Irish del to EEC Ctee on Fibreglass Boats 1982; memb: New Forest RDC 1963-71, Boldre Parish Cncl 1956-71, New Forest Assoc of Parish Cncls 1958-71 (chm 1964-67), Hants Assoc of Parish Cncls 1962-67; memb: RINA, Plastics and Rubber Inst, Irish Fedn of Marine Industs, Inst of Oceanography, Soc of Plastics Engrs, Irish Boat Rentals Assoc; author of numerous tech papers and articles on nautical matters including fibreglass boats; *Recreations* cruising, country pursuits, saving the world from extermination; *Clubs* Royal Cruising, Irish Cruising, Ocean Cruising, Bantry Bay SC (Cdre 1975-78, Vice Cdre 1984-88); *Style—* Hugo Duplessis, Esq; Ballylickey, Bantry, Co Cork, Ireland; Irish Atlantic Charters, Bantry, Co Cork, Ireland

DUPPLIN, Viscount; Charles William Harley Hay; s and h of 15 Earl of Kinnoull, Arthur William George Patrick Hay, and Countess of Kinnoull, Gay Ann Hay, *née* Lowson; *b* 20 Dec 1962; *Educ* Eton, Ch Ch Oxford (MA), City Univ, Inns of Court Sch of Law; *Career* called to the Bar Middle Temple 1990; investmt banker with Credit Suisse First Boston Ltd 1985-88; fine art underwriter with Roberts & Hiscox Ltd at Lloyd's 1990; *Recreations* skiing, squash, philately, motor cars, racing; *Clubs* Turf, MCC, Lansdowne, Oxford and Cambridge; *Style—* Viscount Dupplin; 59 Scarsdale Villas, London W8 (☎ 071 938 4265)

DUPRÉ, Sophie (Mrs Clive Farahar); *née* Dupré; da of Desmond John Dupré, lutenist (d 1974), and Catherine Lane, novelist, of Oxford; *b* 6 Jan 1955; *Educ* Convent of the Sacred Heart Tunbridge Wells; *m* 12 April 1980, Clive Robert Farahar, antiquarian bookseller; 2 s (Henry Robert b 1981, Austin James b 1988) and 2 s decd (Frederick James b 1984 d 1985, Theodore Austin b and d 1987), 1 da (Emily Alexandra b 1979); *Career* specialist in autographed letters and manuscripts, runs int business supplying private collectors and Insts; *Recreations* travel; *Style—* Miss Sophie Dupré; XIV The Green, Calne, Wilts SN11 8DQ

DUPREE, Gordon John Felix; OBE (1978); s of Gordon Dupree (d 1950), and Rose Winifred Kate Dupree (d 1977); *b* 14 Oct 1929; *Educ* Lime Grove Sch of Building, Arts & Crafts; *m* 20 Oct 1951, Jeanette Gladys, da of Stanley Woodcock; 3 s (Kevin, Martin, Neil), 1 da (Susan Diane); *Career* chm and chief exec LA Rumbold Ltd; *Recreations* bowls, football, racing; *Clubs* Sutton Bowling and Bracknell; *Style—* Gordon Dupree Esq, OBE; Stonesteep, 210 Upper Chobham Road, Camberley, Surrey (☎ 0276 28471); L A Rumbold Ltd, Doman Road, Camberley Surrey (☎ 0276 66456)

DUPREE, Harry William; s of Harry Dupree (d 1932), of Tunbridge Wells, and Kate Evelyn, *née* Gilliam (d 1967); *b* 20 Jan 1913; *Educ* Tonbridge Sch; *m* 30 Oct 1939, Joanne Gwendoline, da of Hugh Philip Bishop (d 1986); 1 s (Michael b 1943), 2 da (Philippa b 1948, Lucy b 1954); *Career* WWII Sqdn Ldr RAF (Airfield Construction Branch) 1944-47; sr engr Kuwait Oil Co 1947-49, chief engr Basildon Development Corporation 1949-61; Sir Owen Williams and Ptnrs: ptnr 1961-77, conslt 1977-87; CEng, FICE, FIHT, MConsE; *Books* Urban Transportation: The New Town Solution (1987); *Clubs* RAF; *Style—* Harry Dupree, Esq; Broadway House, The Broadway, Amersham, Buckinghamshire (☎ 0494 726 464)

DUPREE, Sir Peter; 5 Bt (UK 1921); s of Sir Victor Dupree, 4 Bt (d 1976); *b* 20 Feb 1924; *m* 1947, Joan, da of late Capt James Desborough Hunt; *Heir* kinsman, Thomas William James David Dupree b 5 Feb 1930; *Style—* Sir Peter Dupree, Bt; 15 Hayes Close, Chelmsford, Essex CM2 0RN

DURACK, Dame Mary; DBE (1978, OBE 1966), AC (1989); da of Michael Patrick Durack, and Bessie Ida Muriel, *née* Johnstone (d 1980); *b* 20 Feb 1913; *Educ* Loreto

Convent Perth; *m* 1938, Horace Clive (d 1980), s of John Pettigrew Miller; 2 s, 2 da (and 2 da decd); *Career* author, playwright and historian; former memb of staff W Aust Newspapers Ltd; dir Aust Stockman's Hall of Fame and Outback Heritage Centre (patron Branch); hon life memb: fellowship of Aust Writers (pres Waust Branch 1958-63 Int PEN Sydney (memb Waust branch); memb: Aust Soc of Authors, Nat Tst, Royal Waust Historical Soc, Aust Soc of Women Writers (presented with the Alice award 1982); patron Friends of the Battye Library Waust, former exec memb Aboriginal Cultural Fndn; Cwlth Literary Grants 1973 and 1977, Aust Res Grant 1980 and 1984-85, emeritus fellowship Lit Bd of the Aust Cncl 1987- (1983-86), fndn fell Curtis Univ of Technol 1987; author of numerous scripts for ABC Drama Dept; Hon DLitt Univ of Waust 1978; *Books* Keep Him My Country (1955), Kings in Grass Castles (1959), To Ride a Fine House (1963), Kookanoo & Kangaroo (1963), The Australian Settler (1963), The Courteous Savage (1964), The Rock and the Sand (1969), To Be Heirs Forever (1976), Sons in the Saddle (1983); *Plays inc* The Ship of Dreams (1968), Swan River Saga (1972); *Style—* Dame Mary Durack, DBE; 12 Bellevue Ave, Nedlands, W Australia 6009 (☎ 010 61 386 1117)

DURAND, Rev Sir (Henry Mortimer) Dickon Marion St George; 4 Bt (UK 1892); s of Lt-Cdr Mortimer Henry Marion Durand, RN (d 1969), 4 s of 1 Bt; suc unc, Brig Sir Alan Algernon Marion Durand, 3 Bt, MC, 1971 descends from Ducal House of Northumberland; gggs of Bishop Heber famous hymn writer; The Durand line (border of India (now Pakistan), Afghanistan & Russia) was created by grandfather and great uncle, Sir Henry & Sir Mortimer Durand; Archbishop E W Benson (d 1896), originated Service of Nine Lessons with Carols, c 1880 one of the best loved Anglican services; *b* 19 June 1934; *Educ* Wellington Coll, Sydney Univ (Aus), Salisbury Theological Coll; *m* 1971, Stella Evelyn, da of Capt Christopher L'Estrange, of Lisnalurg, Sligo (d 1984); 2 s (Edward b 1974, David b 1978), 2 da (Rachel b 1972, Madeleine b 1980); *Heir* s, Edward Alan Christopher Percy Durand b 21 Feb 1974; *Career* clergyman (Anglican) Church of Ireland; ordained 1969, priest-in-charge St Benedict's Ashford Common (dio London) 1975-79, Bp's curate in charge Kilbixy Union of Parishes (dio Meath) 1979-82, rector Youghal Union of Parishes (dio Cork Cloyne & Ross); *Recreations* history, railways, heraldry, philately, militaria; *Style—* Rev Sir Dickon Durand, Bt; The Rectory, Youghal, Co Cork, Republic of Ireland

DURANT, Sir (Robert) Anthony Bevis; MP (C) Reading West 1983-; s of Capt Robert Michael Durant (d 1962), of Woking, and Violet Dorothy, *née* Bevis; *b* 9 Jan 1928; *Educ* Bryanston; *m* 1958, Audrey Stoddart; 2 s, 1 da; *Career* agent Clapham Cons Office 1958-62, nat organiser Young Cons Movement, CCO 1962-67, dir Br Indust and Scientific Film Assoc 1967-70, dir AVCAS 1970-72, gen mangr and co sec Talking Pictures Ltd 1972-84, memb Woking Urban Cncl 1968-74 (chm Educn Ctee 1969-74), (C) Rother Valley 1970, MP (C) Reading North Feb 1974-1983, memb Select Ctee Parly Cmmn for Admin 1974-83, former vice chm Parly Gp for World Govt; former chm All-Pty Ctees: Inland Waterways, Widows and Single-Parent Families; former conslt: Delta Electrical Ltd, Br Film Prod Assoc - GB; asst govt whip 1984-86, Lord Cmmr of the Treasy and govt whip 1986-90, Crown Estates Paving cmmr 1987-90, chm Cwlth Parly Assoc (UK Branch) 1987-90; vice chamberlain HM Household 1988-90; kt 1991; *Recreations* boating, golf; *Clubs* Golfers; *Style—* Sir Anthony Durant, MP; Hill House, Surley Row, Caversham, Reading, Berkshire

DURANTE, Viviana; da of Giulio Durante, and Anna Maria Durante; *b* 8 May 1967; *Educ* White Lodge, Royal Ballet School; *Career* ballet dancer; princ dancer with Royal Ballet Company; performances incl: Swan Lake, Sleeping Beauty, Romeo and Juliet, Cinderella, The Nutcracker, Violin Concerto, Bayadere, Manow Requiem, Rhapsody, Ondine; awarded The Evening Standard award, The Time Out award; *Recreations* reading, swimming, tennis, relaxing; *Style—* Miss Viviana Durante; Royal Opera House, Covent Garden, London WC2E 9DD (☎ 071 240 1200)

DURBAN, Donald Desmond; CBE (1986); s of Douglas Ernest Durban (d 1937); *b* 25 July 1924; *Educ* Roan GS; *m* 1948, Daphne Olliver, da of Eric May (d 1973), of Australia; 1 s (David), 1 da (Susan); *Career* Served WWII Lt RN (Air Arm), pilot in FAA; dep chief exec and gp co sec Trusthouse Forte (50 years with the co from RN serv), ret from exec duties 1986; chm Nat Cncl of British Hotel Restaurants & Catering Assoc; 1988-89; memb: Hotel and Catering NEDO 1972-79 (chm Ctee on Hotel Prospects), Cncl STA; Freeman City of London, Master Worshipful Company of Chartered Secretaries and Administrator; *Recreations* golf, family; *Clubs* MCC, Royal Blackheath Golf (former capt), Caterpillar, Spitfire Soc (fndr memb), Naval; *Style—* Donald Durban, Esq, CBE; 54 Foxes Dale, Blackheath, London SE3 (☎ 081 852 1907); Chalkstones, Park Lane Cherhill, Wilts (☎ 0249 813 091)

DURBIN, Prof James; s of George William Durbin (d 1970), and Lucy Winifride, *née* Coffey (d 1948); *b* 3 June 1923; *Educ* Wade Deacon GS Widnes, St Johns Coll Cambridge (BA, MA); *m* 22 March 1958, Anne Dearnley, da of Philip Outhwaite (d 1984), of Spofforth; 2 s (Richard b 1960, Andrew b 1962), 1 da (Joanna b 1964); *Career* Army Operational Res Gp 1943-45; Boot and Shoe Trade Res Assoc 1945-47, Dept of Applied Econ Cambridge 1948-49; LSE: asst lectr then lectr 1950-53, reader in statistics 1953-61; prof of statistics 1961-88; visiting prof: Univ of N Carolina 1959-60, Stanford Univ 1960, Univ of Calif Berkeley 1970, Univ of Capetown 1978, UCLA 1984, UC Santa Barbara 1989, Nat Univ of Singapore 1990; pres: ISI 1983-85, RSS 1986-87; *Books* Distribution Theory for Tests Based on the Sample Distribution Function; *Recreations* skiing, mountain walking, travel, opera, theatre; *Style—* Prof James Durbin; 31 Southway, London NW11 6RX (☎ 081 458 3037)

DURBIN, Leslie Gordon James; CBE (1976), MVO (4 class, 1943); s of Harry Durbin (d 1918); *b* 21 Feb 1913; *Educ* Central Sch of Arts and Crafts; *m* 1940, Phyllis Ethel, da of Arthur James Ginger; 1 s, 1 da; *Career* served RAF 1940-45 (Allied Central Interpration Unit making topographical target models), indefinite leave to make Stalingrad Sword (given by King George VI to Stalingrad) 1943; silversmith; apprenticed to Omar Ramsden 1929-38, travelling scholarship and full time scholarship awarded by Worshipful Co of Goldsmiths 1938-40, tutor Central Sch 1945-50, Royal Coll of Art 1945-60; own workshop in partnership with Leonard Moss 1945-76, designed Silver Jubilee hallmark; 50 Years Silversmith Retrospective Exhibition at Goldsmiths' Co 1982, Royal Mint accepted designs of four regions for new one pound coin 1983; Liveryman Worshipful Co of Goldsmiths; Hon LLD Univ of Cambridge; *Style—* Leslie Durbin, Esq, CBE, MVO; 298 Kew Rd, Richmond, Surrey TW9 3DU

DURBIN, Col Peter Charles; OBE (1987), TD (1976); s of Frederick Charles Durbin, and Susan Grace, *née* Norton; *b* 29 April 1941; *Educ* Marlborough; *m* 22 Jan 1972, Linda Susan; 1 s (Andrew Charles b 22 Aug 1977), 1 da (Elizabeth b 11 Feb 1980); *Career* TA: enlisted 10 Bn Parachute Regt 1964, cmmnd 1967, transfd RCT 1968, Capt 1971, Maj 1976, Lt-Col 1983, Col 1990; admitted slr 1964; asst solicitor Farrer and Co 1964-68; ptnr: Shelly and Johns 1969-80 (asst solicitor 1968-69), Foot and Bowden 1981-; advocacy in Magistrates' and Co Cts; memb W Wessex Territorial Aux and Vol Res Assoc; Freeman City of London 1984, memb Worshipful Co of Carmen 1984; memb Law Soc 1965, MBIM; *Recreations* territorial army, shooting, sailing, walking; *Clubs* Royal Western Yacht (Plymouth), Rotary (Saltash); *Style—* Col Peter Durbin, OBE, TD; Warraton Lodge, 72 Oaklands Drive, Saltash, Cornwall PL12 4LU (☎ 0752 844369); 70-76 North Hill, Plymouth PL4 8HH (☎ 0752 663416, fax 0752 671802, telex 0752 45223)

DURCAN, Paul; s of John James Durcan (d 1988), and Shelia MacBride of Dublin; *b* 16 Oct 1944; *Educ* Gonzaga Coll Dublin, Univ Coll Cork (BA); *m* 1 Aug 1967 (sep), Nessa, *née* O'Neill; 2 da (Sarah O'Neill b 22 June 1969, Siabhra O,Neill b 20 July 1970); *Career* poet; O West Port In The Light of Asia Minor (1975), Teresa's Bar (1976), Sam's Cross (1978), Selected Poems (1982), The Berlin Wall Cafe (Poetry Society Choice, 1985), Going Home To Russia (1987), Jesus and Angela (1988), Daddy, Daddy (Whitbred Poetry award, 1990); Patrick Kavanagh award 1974, Irish American Cultural Institute Poetry award 1989; memb Aosdàa 1981; *Recreations* walking; *Style—* Paul Durcan, Esq; 14 Cambridge Ave, Dublin 4

DURDEN-SMITH, Neil; s of Anthony James Durden-Smith (d 1963), of Middx, and Grace Elizabeth, *née* Neill (d 1938); *b* 18 Aug 1933; *Educ* Aldenham, RNC; *m* 1964, Judith Rosemary Locke, da of David Norman Chalmers (d 1952), of Cheshire; 1 s (Mark b 1968), 1 da (Emma b 1967); *Career* RN 1952-63; prodr BBC Outside Bdcasts Dept (special responsibility 1966 World Cup) 1963-66; radio and TV bdcasting incl: Test Match and Co Cricket, Olympic Games 1968 and 1972, Trooping the Colour, Royal Tournament, Money Matters, Sports Special; dir Ruben Sedgwick 1987-; chm and md Durden-Smith Communications 1974-81; chm: The Lord's Taverners 1980-82, Sport Sponsorship Int 1982-87, The Altro Gp 1982-, Expedier 1990-; dir The Anglo-American Sporting Clubs 1969-74; vice pres: Eng Schools Cricket Assoc, Eng Indoor Hockey Assoc; Freeman City of London; memb Lloyd's 1983; *Books* Forward for England (1967), World Cup '66 (1967); *Recreations* theatre, current affrs, cricket, golf, tennis, reading the newspapers; *Clubs* MCC, Lord's Taverners, I Zingari, Wig & Pen, Free Foresters, Lords and Commons CC, County Cricketers GS; *Style—* Neil Durden-Smith, Esq; 28 Hillway, Highgate, London N6 6HH (☎ 081 348 2340)

DURHAM, Earldom of (UK 1833); *see*: Lambton, Lord (Anthony Claud Frederick)

DURHAM, Archdeacon of; *see*: Perry, The Ven Michael Charles

DURHAM, The Rt Rev; 92 Bishop (cr 635) 1984-, David Edward Jenkins; patron of 101 livings, the Archdeaconries of Durham and Auckland, and all the Canonries in his Cathedral (the see was first established at Holy Island 635, but on the invasion of the Danes removed to Chester-le-Street and finally to Durham); er s of Lionel Charles Jenkins, and Dora Katherine, *née* Page; *b* 26 Jan 1925; *Educ* St Dunstan's Coll Catford London, Queen's Coll Oxford (MA); *m* 1949, Stella Mary, da of Henry Leonard Peet (d 1976); 2 s (Christopher, Timothy), 2 da (Deborah, Rebecca); *Career* temp cmmn RA 1943-47, Capt; priest 1954, succentor Birmingham Cathedral 1953-54, fell chaplain and praelector in theology The Queen's Coll Oxford 195 dir humanum studies World Cncl of Churches Geneva 1969-73, dir William Temple Fndn Manchester 1979-, prof of theology Univ of Leeds 1979-84, chm SCM Press 1989; tstee Trinity Press Int (Philadelphia) 1989; Hon DD: Univ of Durham 1987, Trinity Coll Toronto 1989, Aberdeen 1990; *Books* Guide to the Debate about God (1966), The Glory of Man (1967, republished 1984), Living with Questions (1969), Man Fallen and Free (contrib, 1969), What is Man? (1970), The Contradiction of Christianity (1976, republished 1985), God, Miracles and the Church of England (1987), God, Politics and the Future (1988), God, Jesus and Life in the Spirit (1988), Still Living With Questions (1990, revised version of Living With Questions), Free to Believe (with Rebecca Jenkins, 1991); *Recreations* music (opera), walking, travel books; *Style—* The Right Rev the Bishop of Durham; Auckland Castle, Bishop Auckland, Co Durham DL14 7NR (☎ 0388 602576)

DURHAM, Baron; Edward Richard Lambton; s and h of Lord Lambton, *qv*; *b* 19 Oct 1961; *m* 1983, Christabel Mary, yst da of Rory McEwen (decd), of Bardrochat; 1 s (b 23 Feb 1985); *Style—* (known as) Lord Durham

DURHAM, Sir Kenneth; s of late George Durham, and Bertha, *née* Aspin; *b* 28 July 1924; *Educ* Queen Elizabeth GS Blackburn, Univ of Manchester (BSc); *m* 1946, Irene Markham; 1 s, 1 da; *Career* served WWII RAF; chm: BOCM Silcock 1971, Unilever 1982- (joined 1950, vice chm Unilever Ltd 1978-82, dir Unilever NV and Unilever 1974-86), Woolworth Hldgs plc 1986-; dir: Br Aerospace 1980- (dep chm 1986), Delta Gp plc 1984, Morgan Grenfell Gp plc 1986; tstee Leverhulme Tst; kt 1985; *Style—* Sir Kenneth Durham; Woolworth Holdings plc, North West House, 119 Marylebone Rd, London NW1 5PX (☎ 071 724 7749, telex 267007)

DURHAM, Michael Victor Hugh; s of George Ernest Durham, of Great Crosby, Liverpool, and Violet, *née* Tongue (d 1953); *b* 30 Nov 1941; *Educ* Merchant Taylors Boys Sch Crosby, Univ of Bristol (BSc); *m* 20 April 1968, Barbara Jessica, da of Robert Nimmo, of Formby, Lancs; 2 s (Fraser James b 21 April 1973, Mark Sinclair b 4 Oct 1974), 1 da (Suzanna Louise b 3 July 1978); *Career* Lt Royal Engrs TA 1963-65; construction dept GEC Turbine Generators Ltd 1964-79, res engr Yosu Power Station S Korea 1975-77; Ewbank Preece Ltd 1979-: dir Tenaga Ewbank Preece Malaysia 1983-85, dir 1985-, ptnr Co Union Tst 1989-; memb Inst of Directors; C Eng, MI Mech E, MIE Malaysia; *Recreations* bridge, crosswords, golf, tennis; *Clubs* Inst of Directors, West Worthing Tennis; *Style—* Michael Durham, Esq; Little Foxes, Mill Lane, High Salvington, Worthing, W Sussex BN13 3DJ (☎ 0903 692505); Ewbank Preece Ltd, Prudential House, North St, Brighton E Sussex BN1 1RW (☎ 0273 724533, telex 878102, fax 0273 200483, car 0860 644048)

DURIE, Sir Alexander Charles; CBE (1973); s of Charles Durie (d 1948); *b* 15 July 1915; *Educ* Queen's Coll Taunton; *m* 1941, Joyce May, da of late Lionel Richard Hargreaves; 1 s (Alistair b 1944), 1 da (Juliet (Hon Mrs John Greville Napier) b 1942); *Career* serv WWII, Lt-Col; dir: Shell Co (Aust) Ltd 1954-56, Shell-Mex and BP Ltd 1962-64 (joined 1933, md 1963-64), Mercantile Credit 1973-80, Thomas Cook Group 1974-79, Private Patients Plan Ltd 1977-87, H Clarkson Holdings 1978-85, Chelsea Building Soc 1979-87; vice pres: Br Assoc Industl Eds 1959-71, Alliance Int de Tourisme 1965-71 (pres 1971-77), Ind Schs Careers Orgn 1973 (chm 1969-73), AA 1977- (DG 1964-77), Br Road Fedn 1978 (memb 1962-), Ashridge Coll 1978- (govr 1963-78), Surrey CC 1980- (memb Ctee 1970-80, pres 1984-85); memb Govt Inquires into: Civilianisation of Armed Forces 1964, Cars for Cities 1964, Rd Haulage Operators' Licensing 1978; memb: Cncl Motor and Cycle Trades Benevolent Fund 1959-73, Nat Rd Safety Advsy Cncl 1965-68, Advsy Cncl on Road Res 1965-68, Mktg Ctee BTA 1970-77, Advsy Cncl Traffic and Safety Tport and Road Res Lab 1973-77, Int Road Fedn (London); gen cmmr Income Tax 1960-85; FCIT, Hon FInstHE, FBIM (memb Cncl 1962-73, vice chm 1962-67, chm Exec Ctee 1962-65, ch Fells 1970-73); Freeman City of London; memb Cncl Imperial Soc of Knights Batchelor 1978- (chm 1988); kt 1977; *Style—* Sir Alexander Durie, CBE; The Garden House, Windlesham, Surrey (☎ 0276 72035)

DURIE, David Robert Campbell; s of Frederick Robert Edwin Durie, of Ardrishaig, Argyll, and Joan Elizabeth Campbell, *née* Learoyd; *b* 21 Aug 1944; *Educ* Fettes, Christ Church Oxford (BA, MA); *m* 27 July 1966, Susan Frances, da of Arthur Leighton Hume Weller (d 1953); 3 da (Rosamund Clare b 1969, Madeleine Rachqel b 1971, Eleanor Louise b 1975); *Career* asst princ Miny of Technol 1966, princ DTI 1971 (asst princ 1970), first sec UK Delgn to OECD Paris 1974; asst sec: DPCP 1978 (princ 1977), Dept of Trade 1980, Cabinet Office 1982, DTI 1984; under sec (GD3) DTI 1985-, head of Investigations Div DTI 1989-; *Recreations* moderately strenuous outdoor exercise, theatre, family, music; *Style—* David Durie, Esq; Department of Trade and Industry, 123 Victoria St, London SW1 (☎ 071 215 6426, fax 071 215 6894)

DURIE, Joanna Mary (Jo); da of John Durie (d 1984), of Bristol, and Diana Nell *née* Ford; *b* 27 July 1960; *Educ* Clifton HS; *Career* tennis player: winner under 12 and under 14 Nat Championships, won all three Nat Championships at age of 16, ranked 5 in the World 1984, ranked GB no 1 1983, 1984, 1985, 1987; semi-finalist US Open and French Championships 1983, winner of the Wimbledom mixed doubles title (with Jeremy Bates) 1987; winner numerous tournaments worldwide; represented GB in Wightman Cup 1980 and Federation Cup 1981-; *Recreations* golf (handicap 20), skiing; *Style—* Miss Jo Durie; Winchmore Hill, London

DURIE OF DURIE, Lt-Col Raymond Varley Dewar; MID (1943); s of Robert Nugent Dewar Durie, OBE, MC (d 1959), and Ida Pollexfen Varley (d 1972); illustrious forebear George Durie, last Abbot of Dunfermline 1480-1573, 2 cousin of W B Yeats; *b* 10 Aug 1905; *Educ* Blundell's, Sandhurst; *m* 1, 1932, Joan (d 1934), da of R Dolbey (d 1933); m 2, 1938, Frances, da of Col H N st J Maule, CMG, of Bath; 1 s (Andrew b 1939), 2 da (Diana b 1934, Christian b 1945); *Career* Regular Army Offr Argyll and Sutherland Highlanders, Lt-Col China; *Recreations* cricket, hockey, tennis, shooting, polo; *Style—* Lt-Col Raymond Durie of Durie, MID; Court House, Pewsey, Wiltshire SN9 5DL (☎ 0672 63452)

DURKIN, Dr Christopher John; s of Air Marshal Sir Herbert Durkin, KBE, CB, of Willowbank, Drakes Drive, Northwood, Lady Dorothy Hope Durkin, *née* Johnson; *b* 21 March 1952; *Educ* St Edmunds Coll Ware, Watford, GS, Emmanuel Coll Cambridge, (MA), KCH Med Sch (MB BChir); *m* 29 July 1978, Clare Margaret, da of Denis Bernard Jarvis, of 43 Ferndale Rd, Lichfield, Staffs; 3 da (Helen b 1982, Charlote b 1985, Olivia b 1987); *Career* sr house offr Nottingham 1977-78, registrar Sutton Coldfield 1978-80, sr registrar geriatric and gen med Oxford Teaching GP and Amersham 1980-83; conslt physician geriatric and gen med: Aylesbury Vale Health Authy, Stoke Mandeville Hosp; dist clinical tutor Univ of Oxford Aylesbury Vale Healthy Authy; memb Aylesbury Vale Health Authy, chm Oxford region Br Geriatrics Soc; chm Thame and Dist Round Table; MRCP 1978; *Recreations* Round Table, golf, skiing; *Style—* Dr Christopher Durkin; 52 Elm Trees, Long Crendon, Aylesbury, Bucks HP18 9DF (☎ 0296 84111 ext 3406)

DURKIN, Air Marshal Sir Herbert; KBE (1976), CB (1973); s of Herbert Durkin (d 1968); *b* 31 March 1922; *Educ* Burnley GS, Emmanuel Coll Cambridge; *m* 1951, Dorothy Hope, da of Walter Taylor Johnson; 1 s, 2 da; *Career* joined RAF 1941, served WWII in Europe and India, Gp-Capt 1962, Air Cdre 1967, dir of Eng Policy (RAF) MOD 1967, Air Vice Marshal 1971, Air Marshal 1976, ret 1978; pres Inst of Electrical Engrs 1980-81, pres Assoc of Lancastrians in London 1988-89; *Recreations* golf; *Clubs* RAF; *Style—* Air Marshal Sir Herbert Durkin, KBE, CB; Willowbank, Drakes Drive, Northwood, Middx (☎ 092 74 23167)

DURKIN, Dr Michael Anthony Patrick; s of John Durkin (d 1986), of Cheltenham, Glos and Wimbledon, Surrey, and Philomena, *née* O'Shea; *b* 26 July 1950; *Educ* Whitefriars Sch Cheltenham Glos, Univ of London Middx Hosp Med Sch (MB BS); *m* 19 July 1978, Susan Claire, da of Lawrence Paul Cotterell, of Cheltenham, Glos; 3 s (Luke b 1979, Jack b 1981, James b 1983); *Career* registrar in anaesthesia St Thomas' Hosp London 1976-79, res registrar Middx Hosp London 1980-81, sr registrar S Western RHA 1981-85, conslt in annaesthesia and intensive care Gloucestershire Royal Hosp 1985-, visiting assoc faculty Yale Univ Sch of Med 1989 (asst prof 1982-84), articles in jls on anaesthesia, intensive care and monitoring; ctee memb: Soc of Anaesthetists of S Western Regn, Gloucester Dis Med Advsy Ctee, Regnl Ctee for Higher Specialist Trg (anaesthesia); tstee Intensive Care Charity; memb; Euro Intensive Care Soc, Int Anaesthesia Res Soc, Intensive Care Soc, Assoc of Anaesthetists GB; FFARCS 1981, fell Coll Anaesthetists, memb BMA; *Books* Post Anaesthetic Recovery (2 edn 1989); *Recreations* skiing, tennis and now as rugby spectator; *Clubs* Lilleybrook; *Style—* Dr Michael Durkin; Little Ashley, Ashley Road, Battledown, Cheltenham GL52 6QE (☎ 0242 516249), Glouchestershire Royal Hospital, Gloucester GL1 3NN (☎ 0452 28555)

DURLACHER, Nicholas John; s of John Sydney Durlacher MC; *b* 20 March 1946; *Educ* Stowe, Magdalene Coll Cambridge; *m* 1971, Mary Caroline, da of Maj G L I McLaren (d 1978); 1 s; *Career* memb London Stock Exchange, ptnr Wedd Durlacher Mordaunt & Co 1971-86, dir Barclays de Zoete Wedd Futures Ltd 1986-; *Recreations* skiing, tennis, golf, shooting; *Clubs* City of London; *Style—* Nicholas Durlacher, Esq; Archendines Fordham, nr Colchester, Essex (☎ 0206 240 627)

DURLACHER, Peter Laurence; s of Adm Sir Laurence Durlacher, KCB, OBE, DSC (d 1986), of Mas Tournamy, Mougins, France 06, and Rimma Durlacher, *née* Sass-Tissovsky, MBE; *b* 27 April 1935; *Educ* Winchester, Inst of Political Sci Paris, Magdalene Coll Cambridge; *m* 1, 14 March 1959 (m dis 1976), Jennifer Ann, da of Hugh Blauvelt (d 1967), of Drumnadrochit, Inverness; 2 s (Christopher b 1963, Julian b 1966), 2 da (Fenella b 1961, Sophie b 1968); m 2, Mary Cresswell-Turner, da of Richard Girouard (d 1989), of Colville Rd, London W11; *Career* md Henry Ansbacher 1970-72 (merchant banker 1957-66, dir 1966-), i/c Overseas Dept Wedd Durlacher Mordaunt 1972-76; conslt 1976-80: Stock Exchange, IMF; ptnr Laurie Milbank Stockbroker 1981-86; tstee Schoolmistresses and Governesses Benevolent Inst 1968-, hon treas Nat Youth Bureau 1977-89; Liveryman Worshipful Co of Cutlers; *Recreations* gardening, fox hunting; *Clubs* City of London; *Style—* Peter Durlacher, Esq; The Pump House, Wymondham, Melton Mowbray, Leics (☎ 057 284 508); 5 Rayners Rd, London SW15 (☎ 081 785 9894); Durlacher West Ltd, 3 Cleary Court, 21/23 St Swithins Lane, London EC4 (☎ 071 623 2001)

DURMAN, David John; s of John Bloyd Durman, and Joan Winifred Durman; *b* 10 July 1948; *Educ* Sutton High Sch Plymouth, Univ of Leeds (BA); *m* 6 Jan 1973, Hilary Pamela Durman; *Career* ed Woman Magazine 1988-; *Style—* David Durman, Esq; Woman, King's Reach Tower, Stamford St, London SE1 9LS (☎ 071 261 6452)

DURRANCE, Philip Walter; s of Arthur Durrance (d 1960), of Ilkley, Yorkshire, and Marguerite Grace, *née* Rotheray (d 1966); *b* 30 June 1941; *Educ* Harrow, Oriel Coll Oxford (MA); *m* 16 Sept 1966 (m dis), Francoise Genevieve Jeanne, da of Marcel Tiller; 1 s (Christopher b 29 July 1967), 1 da (Genevieve b 8 Sept 1968); *Career* admitted slr June 1965, ptnr Withers 1968-; dir: F Bender, Henkel Chemicals, Leo Laboratories; FInstD, memb Law Soc; *Recreations* theatre, cinema, art, tennis, squash, cricket; *Style—* Philip Durrance, Esq; 5/14 Fairhazel Gdns, London NW6 (☎ 081 328 6590); 20 Essex St, London WC2 (☎ 071 836 8400, fax 071 240 2278, telex 24213)

DURRANI, Prof Tariq Salim; s of Mohammed Salim Khan Durrani (d 1980), of London, and Bilquis Jamal; *b* 27 Oct 1943; *Educ* EPUET Dacca Bangladesh (BEng), Univ of Southampton (MSc, PhD); *m* 6 Aug 1972, Clare Elizabeth, da of late Howard Kellas; 1 s (Jamiel Tariq b 1986), 2 da (Monise Nadia b 1977, Sophia Jasmine b 1981); *Career* res fell Univ of Southampton; Univ of Strathclyde: lectr, sr lectr, prof signal processing, chm Dept Electronic and Electrical Engrg, dep princ (info technol); chm Professional Gp on Signal Processing (chm: Scottish Transputer Centre SERC/DTI, Scottish Electronics Technol Gp, Parallel Signal Processing Centre DTI; FIEE 1983, FIEEE 1989; *Books* Laser Systems in Flow Measurements (with C Greated, 1977), Geophysical Signal Processing (with E A Robinson, 1986), Signal processing (co-ed J L Lacoume and R Stora, 1987), Mathematics and Signal Processing (ed, 1987); *Recreations* swimming; *Clubs* Ross Priory; *Style—* Prof Tariq Durrani; 14 Duchess Park, Helensburgh, Dunbartonshire G84 9PY (☎ 0436 76590); University of Strathclyde, Department of Electronic and Electrical Engineering, 204 George St, Glasgow G1 1XW (☎ 041 552 4400, ext 2540, fax 041 552 2487, tele 77472 UNISLIB G)

DURRANT, Anthony Harrisson; s of Frank Baston Durrant (d 1952), of London, and Irene Maude, *née* Drury (d 1985); *b* 3 Jan 1931; *Educ* Sir Joseph Williamson's Mathematical Sch Rochester Kent; *m* 30 June 1956, Jacqueline, da of John Ostroumoff (d 1945); 1 s (Max), 2 da (Caroline, Julia); *Career* admitted slr 1956; sr ptnr Horwood & James 1975, pres Bucks Berks and Oxon Incorporated Law Soc 1977-78, rec 1987; dep chm S Western area Agric Land Tbnl 1987, hon slr: Br Paraplegic Sports Stadium Stoke Mandeville (memb exec ctee), Stoke Mandeville Hosp Post Grad Soc and memb exec cncl; memb: Law Soc, Agric Law Assoc; *Recreations* reading, boating; *Clubs* Phyllis Court, Henley-on-Thames, Law Soc; *Style—* Anthony Durrant, Esq; Little Kimble House, Little Kimble, Bucks HP17 0UF (☎ 0296 613712); 7 Temple Square, Aylesbury, Bucks HP20 2QB (☎ 0296 87361)

DURRANT, Roy Turner; s of Francis Henry Durrant (d 1957), and Edna May, *née* Turner; *Educ* Lavenham Sch Suffolk, Camberwell Art Sch (NDD); *m* 7 March 1959, Jean , da of Harold Malcolm Lyell (d 1982); 4 s (Francis b 11 Jan 1960, Timothy b 30 May 1962 (d 1964), John b 31 July 1964, Edward b 17 Feb 1966); *Career* Suffolk Regt 1944-47; exhibitions incl: Beaux Arts Gallery London 1950, Roland Browse and 1959, Artists Int Assoc Gallery 1969 (1953, 1957), Loggia Gallery London 1984 (1973, 1975, 1981), Gallerie of Br Art Lausanne Switzerland 1988; works in public collection incl: The Tate, dept of biochemistry Univ of Cambridge, Usher Gallery Lincoln, Imperial War Museum, Bury St Edmunds Town Cncl, City of Bradford Art Gallery, Carlisle Art Gallery, Bertrand Russell Fndn Nottingham, Castle Museum Norwich, Univ of Adelaide Aust, WA Art Gallery Perth, Univ of Massachuetts Amherst USA, Worthing Art Gallery, RAF Museum Hendon, Hove Museum and Art Gallery; admin post Vickers Ltd 1956-63, dir Heffer Gallery Cambridge 1963-76; FRSA, FFPS, memb NEAC; *Books* A Rag Book of Love (1960); *Recreations* reading, radio; *Style—* Roy Turner Durrant, Esq; 38 Hurst Park Avenue, Cambridge CB4 2AE (☎ 0223 61730)

DURRANT, William Alexander Estridge; JP; s and h of Sir William Durrant, 7 Bt; *b* 26 Nov 1929; *m* 1953, Dorothy Croker, BA; 1 s, 1 da; *Career* farmer and grazier; Capt 12/16 Hunter River Lancers; *Style—* William Durrant, Esq, JP; Spring Pk, Gaspard, via Quirindi, NSW 2343, Australia

DURRANT, Sir William Henry Estridge; 7 Bt (GB 1784), JP (NSW 1940); s of Sir William Henry Estridge Durrant, 6 Bt (d 1953); *b* 1 April 1901; *m* 1927, Georgina Beryl Gwendoline (d 1968), da of Alexander Purse; 1 s, 1 da; *Heir* s, William Alexander Estridge; *Career* serv WWII; CA; assoc with the formation of the film indust in NSW 1930's and construction of film studios; former pres and life patron NSW Justices Assoc, memb: UN Orgn Aust, cncl Royal Cwlth Soc NSW; *Style—* Sir William Durrant, Bt, JP; 1634 Pacific Highway, Wahroonga, NSW, Australia

DURRELL, Gerald Malcolm; OBE (1982); s of Lawrence Durrell, and Louisa Florence, *née* Dixie; *b* 7 Jan 1925; *Educ* privately in Greece; *m* 1, 1951 (m dis 1979), Jacqueline Sonia; m 2, 1979, Lee Wilson; *Career* student keeper Zoological Soc of Whipsnade Park London 1945, organiser and leader of numerous zoological expeditions worldwide 1946-, fndr zoological park Jersey Channel Islands 1959, fndr and hon dir Jersey Wildlife Preservation Tst 1963-; fndr Wildlife Preservation Tst: Int USA 1973, Canada 1985; books incl: The Overloaded Ark (1953), My Family And Other Animals (1956), A Zoo In My Luggage (1960), The Whispering Land (1962), The Donkey Rustlers (1968), Birds, Beasts and Relatives (1969), Beasts In My Belfry (1973), The Stationary Ark (1976), The Mockery Bird (1981), The Fantastic Flying Journey (1987), The Ark's Anniversary (1990); films produced for BBC TV include: Two In The Bush (1962), A Bull Called Marius (1966), The Stationary Ark (1974), Ark On The Move (1981), Durrell in Russia (1986), Ourselves and Other Animals (1987); Dr of Humane Letters Yale 1977, Univ of Durham DSc 1988, Univ of Kent DSc 1989; *Style—* Gerald Durrell, Esq, OBE; Les Augres Manor, Trinity, Jersey, Channel Islands (☎ 64666)

DURRELL, Prof Martin; s of Leslie Hay Durrell (d 1972), of Coltishall, Norfolk, and Audrey Lillian, *née* Easton; *b* 6 Nov 1943; *Educ* Manchester GS, Jesus Coll Cambridge (BA, MA), Univ of Manchester (DipLing), Univ of Marburg (DPhil); *m* 30 Aug 1969, Ruth, da of Geoffrey Loy Barlow (d 1977), of Bury, Lancs; 1 s (John b 1975), 1 da (Ann b 1979); *Career* sr lectr (former lectr) Univ of Manchester 1970-86, guest prof Univ of Alberta 1983-84; prof of German Univ of London 1986-90, Univ of Manchester 1990-; corresponding memb Academic Cncl Institut für Deutsche Sprache 1984-, memb Cncl Philogical Soc 1989-; *Recreations* music, theatre, ornithology; *Style—* Prof Martin Durrell; Manchester Univ, Manchester (☎ 061 275 3182)

DURRINGTON, Dr Paul Nelson; s of Alec Edward Durrington, of Hurst Green, E Sussex, and May Ena, *née* Nelson; *b* 24 July 1947; *Educ* Chislehurst and Sidcup GS, Univ of Bristol (BSc, MB, ChB, MD); *m* 13 Dec 1969, Patricia Joyce, da of Capt Alfred Newton Gibbs, MC, of Aldwick, W Sussex; 1 s (Mark Christopher Newton b 1977), 2 da (Hannah Jane b 1975, Charlotte Lucy b 1987); *Career* house offr and sr house offr appts 1972-76; Bristol Royal Infirmary, Bristol Royal Hosp for Sick Children, Frenchay Hosp Bristol; travelling fell: Br Heart Fndn, American Heart Assoc Univ of California San Diego 1979-80; sr lectr in med Univ of Manchester 1982- (lectr 1976-82), hon conslt physician Manchester Royal Infirmary and Univ of South Manchester 1982-; memb Stockport Health Authy, memb Ctee Br Hyperlipidaemia Assoc, med advsr to Family Heart Assoc; FRCP 1987; *Books* Hyperlipidaemia Diagnosis and Management (1989); *Recreations* angling; *Clubs* Errwood Fly Fishing; *Style—* Dr Paul Durrington; University of Manchester, Dept of Medicine, Manchester Royal Infirmary, Oxford Rd, Manchester M13 9WL (☎ 061 2764226)

DURWARD, Alan (Scott); s of Archibald Durward (d 1964), and Dorothy, *née* Westlake (d 1978); *b* 30 Aug 1935; *Educ* St John's Coll Cambridge (MA); *m* 1962, Helen, da of Joseph Gourlay; 2 s (Giles b 1964, Hugo b 1966); *Career* ops gp chief exec Alliance & Leicester Building Society 1989- (chief gen mangr 1986-); formerly with Imperial Tobacco and Rowntree; *Style—* Scott Durward, Esq; Alliance & Leicester Building Society, 49 Park Lane, London W1Y 4EQ (☎ 071 629 6661)

DUSSEK, Julian Eric; s of Lt-Cdr Eric Albert Dussek, of Plaxtol, Kent, and Ivy Marion, *née* Wynne; *b* 12 April 1944; *Educ* St Lawrence Coll Ramsgate, Univ of London (MB BS); *m* 6 Sept 1969, (Margot) Vanessa Tryce, da of Lt-Cdr Edward Guy Tryce Morgan (d 1964); 1 s (John b 1976), 1 da (Nicola b 1973); *Career* conslt thoracic surgn: The Brook Regnl Cardiothoracic Unit 1981-89, Guys Hosp 1981-, Brighton Health Authy 1981-, St Thomas Hosp 1989-; author of contribs to books on cardiothoracic and oesophageal surger memb Plaxtol Parish Cncl, sec Soc of Cardiothoracic Surgns of GB; FRCS 1974; *Recreations* cooking and the history of eating; *Style—* Julian Dussek, Esq; Tebolds, The Street, Plaxtol, Sevenoaks, Kent TN15 0QJ (☎ 0732 810489); The Cardiothoracic Unit, Guys Hospital, London SE1 9RT (☎ 071 955 4322)

DUTFIELD, William Henry (Harry); s of John Hubert Dutfield, and Janie Scott, *née* Blair; *b* 12 Dec 1908; *Educ* King Charles I GS Kidderminster, Worcs; *m* 2 June 1938, Daisy Iris (Bobby), *née* Huxter; 1 s (Simon John b 1946), 1 da (Susan Jane (Mrs Standerwick) b 1944); *Career* carpet mfr in attic at home 1925-27, moved to new premises and formed Dutfield & Quayle 1928-37, started Axminster Carpets Ltd 1937-

(ceased carpet mfr and produced aircraft parts for Rolls Royce etc 1940-45); acquired woollen mill now Buckfast Spinning Co Ltd 1950, fndr Marlin Carpets Ltd Christchurch NZ 1960, pres and fndr Game Fishing Co of Fiji 1965, dir Fiji Resorts Ltd; first importer from NZ of Drysdale sheep (world's finest carpet wool; *Books* Harry Dutfield, Carpet Manufacturer & Fisherman (1974); *Recreations* big game fishing, golf, salmon fishing; *Style—* Harry Dutfield, Esq; Little Cloakham, Axminster, Devon (☎ 0297 32158); Porthsawl, Portscatho, nr Truro, Cornwall; Axminster Carpets Ltd, Axminster, Devon (☎ 0297 32244, fax 0297 35241, telex 42923)

DUTHIE, Prof Robert Buchan; CBE (1984); s of James Andrew Duthie (d 1964), and Elizabeth Jean, *née* Hunter (d 1967); *b* 4 May 1925; *Educ* Aberdeen GS, King Edward VI GS Chelmsford, Heriot-Watt Coll Edinburgh, Univ of Edinburgh Med Sch (MB ChB, ChM); *m* June 1956, Alison Ann Macpherson, da of Harold James Kittermaster; 2 s (Alasdair b 1960, Malcolm b 1966), 2 da (Catriona b 1959, Gillian b 1962); *Career* served Malaya RAMC 1948-49; house Physician Western Gen Hosp Edinburgh 1949, registrar Royal Infirmary Edinburgh 1951-53 (house surgn 1948-49); res fell: Scottish Hosps Endowment Res Tst Edinburgh 1953-56, Nat Cancer trst Bethseda USA 1956-57; external memb MRC and sr registrar Inst Orthopaedics London 1957-58, prof Orthopaedic Surgery Univ Sch Med and Dentistry 1958-66, surgn-in-chief Univ of Rochester Med Centre USA 1958-66, Nuffield prof orthopaedic surgery Oxford 1966-, surgn Nuffield Orthopaedic Centre Oxford 1966-, hon civil conslt in orthopaedic surgery to RN 1974-; govr Oxford Sch for Boys; Hon Dsc Rochester NY 1982; FRCSE, FRCS, FACS (hon) 1987; Royal Sovreigns Order Malta; *Books* Textbook of Orthopaedic Surgery (jtly, 1982), Management of Haemophilia (1984); *Recreations* family, tennis; *Clubs* Oxford and Cambridge; *Style—* Prof Robert Duthie, CBE; Barna Brow, Harberton Mead, Headington, Oxford (☎ 0865 62745); Nuffield Orthopaedic Centre, Windmill Rd, Headington, Oxford OC3 7LD (☎ 0865 227377, fax 0865 742348)

DUTHIE, Sir Robin Grieve; CBE (1978); s of George Duthie, and Mary, *née* Lyle; *b* 2 Oct 1928; *Educ* Greenock Acad; *m* 5 April 1955, (Violetta) Noel, da of Harry Maclean; 2 s (David b 1956, Peter b 1959), 1 da (Susan b 1962); *Career* Nat Serv 1946-49; apprentice CA Thomson Jackson Gourlay & Taylor 1946-51, qualified CA 1952; chm: Black & Edgington plc 1972-83 (md 1962-80), Bruntons (Musselburgh) plc 1984-86, Britoil plc 1988-90, Capital House plc 1988-, Tay Residential Investments plc 1989-; dir: British Asset Trust plc 1977-, Royal Bank of Scotland plc 1978-, Insight Group plc 1983-90 (formerly Black and Edgington), Investors Capital Trust plc 1985-, Carclo Engineering Gp plc 1986-, Royal Bank of Scotland Group plc 1986-, Sea Catch plc 1987-, Tay Residential Investments plc 1989-, British Polythene Industries plc 1988-; treas Nelson St EU Congregational Church Greenock 1970-, cmmr Scottish Congregational Ministers Pension Fund; memb: Scottish Econ Cncl 1980-, Governing Cncl Scottish Business in the Community 1987-, Ct Univ of Strathclyde 1988-; Hon LLD Univ of Strathclyde 1984, Hon DTech Napier 1989; CBIM 1975, FRSA 1983, FScotVEC 1988, FRIAS 1989; kt 1987; *Recreations* curling, golf; *Clubs* Greenock Imperial; *Style—* Sir Robin Duthie, CBE; Fairhaven, 181 Finnart St, Greenock, (☎ 0475 22642); BP Scotland, 301 St Vincent St, Glasgow G2 5DD, (☎ 041 225 5143, fax 041 225 2263, telex 777633)

DUTT, Trevor Peter; s of Dr Bishnu Pada Dutt (d 1970), of Mitcham, Surrey, and Phyllis Ida, *née* Roche; *b* 14 Sept 1943; *Educ* Dulwich, St Barts Hosp Med Coll (MB BS, LRCP); *m* 27 May 1986, Pauline Deirdre, da of Walter Edward Chapman, of Chigwell, Essex; 1 step s (Damien Nicholas Edward Caracatsanis b 2 May 1974); *Career* Surgn Cdr RNR (London Div), SMO Royal Marines Res City of London 1988-90; jr med staff posts 1965-80: St Barts, Whipps Cross, Royal Northern, City of London Maternity and Charing Cross Hosps; conslt obstetrics and gynaecology Royal Northern and Whittington Hos 1980; Freeman City of London 1967, Liveryman Worshipful Soc of Apothecaries 1967; MRCS, FRCOG 1988 (memb 1975); *Recreations* sailing, sub-aqua diving, horse riding; *Clubs* Athenaeum, Savage; *Style—* Trevor Dutt, Esq; 129 Mount View Rd, London N4 4JH (☎ 081 348 7054); 28 Weymouth St, London WIN 3FA (☎ 071 580 1723, car 0860 625 431 and 0860 7 868)

DUTTINE, John; s of Josef Duttine (d 1956), of Barnsley, Yorkshire, and Caroline Edith, *née* Hampton (d 1983), of Bradford, Yorkshire; *b* 15 March 1949; *Educ* Buttershaw Comprehensive Sch Bradford, Drama Centre London; ptnr, common law wife, Carolyn Margaret, da of Donald Hutchinson; 1 s (Oscar James b 15 Sept 1980); *Career* actor; entered profession Glasgow Citizens Theatre 1970; tv credits incl: A Pin to see the Peepshow (1973), Spend Spend Spend (1976), Saturday, Sunday, Monday (1977), People Like Us (1977), The Devils Crown (1978), The Mallens (1979), Wuthering Heights (1979), To Serve them all My Days (1980), Day of the Triffids (1981), The Outsider (1982), Woman of Substance (1983); films incl: Zeffirelli's Jesus of Nazareth (1976), Who Dares Wins (1982); theatre incl: Hamlet (1984), Richard II (1987), The Browning Version (1988), The Woman in Black (1989); winner of TV Times best actor award 1980; *Style—* John Duttine, Esq; c/o Derek Webster, AIM, 5 Denmark St, London W1 (☎ 071 836 2001)

DUTTON, Brig Bryan Hawkins; CBE (1990, OBE 1984, MBE 1978); s of George Ralph Neale Dutton (d 1983), and Honor, *née* Morris; *b* 1 March 1943; *Educ* Lord Weymouth Sch, RMA Sandhurst, Royal Military College of Science, Staff College Camberley; *m* 15 July 1972, Angela Margaret, da of Harold Keith Wilson (d 1970); 1 s (Charles b 1974), 1 da (Sophie b 1977); *Career* commissioned into Devonshire and Dorset Regt 1963; regtl serv 1963-73, NI, Germany, Libya, Nr Guiana, UK, Belize; C-in-C's Mission to Soviet forces in E Germany 1976-78, regtl duty NI and BAOR 1978-79, staff security coordinator NI 1979-81, instructor Staff Coll Camberley 1981-82, mil asst to Adj-Gen 1982-84, CO 1 Bn Devonshire and Dorset Regt NI and Berlin 1984-87, UKLF overseas ops 1987, cmd 39 Infantry Brigade Ulster 1987-89 dir Public Relations (army) 1990; *Recreations* offshore sailing, country pursuits, wildlife, music, history; *Style—* Brig Bryan Dutton, CBE; Ministry of Defence, Main Building, Whitehall, London SW1 1AA

DUTTON, Hon Mrs George; Pauline Stewart; da of Maj Stewart Robinson; *m* 1959, as her 2 husband, Hon George Dutton (d 1981), yr s of 6 Baron Sherborne; *Style—* The Hon Mrs George Dutton; Westerley, Kingsthorne, Herefordshire (☎ 0981 540 309)

DUTTON, Richard Odard Astley (Dickie); s of William Astley Dutton (d 1959), of 73 Iverna Ct, London, and Alice Margaret, *née* Halls; *b* 9 Sept 1935; *Educ* Lancing, RMA Sandhurst; *m* 2 Dec 1961, Susan Kathleen, da of Maj JR O'B Warde, TD, JP, DL (d 1976), of Squerryes Ct, Westerham, Kent; 1 s (Rodney Henry Odard Ralph b 1967), 2 da (Sarah b 1965, Harriet b 1972); *Career* cmmnd KOYLI 1956: Capt and Adj 1 Bn 1962-63, Mons Offr Cadet Sch 1963-65; sales mangr Ross Foods 1965-66, classified ad mangr The Times 1967-70, vice chm Marlar International 1972-79, dir The Butterfield Ptnrship 1989-90, Dutton Exec Search 1990-; *Recreations* long distance cycling, singing; *Clubs* Arts, Canada; *Style—* Dickie Dutton, Esq; 61 Ellerby St, London SW6 6EU (☎ 071 736 2899); Dutton Executive Search, Hamilton House, Victoria Embankment, 1 Temple Avenue, London EC4Y 0HA (☎ 071 353 4212)

DUTTON, Robert William; s of Wilfred Harry (d 1982) and Florence Amy, *née* Monk; *b* 17 Feb 1949; *Educ* Manchester Business Sch (MBA); *Career* CA; merchant banker: Hill Samuel & Co Ltd 1973-84; corp fin dir Co Nat West Ltd 1985-88 (previously Co Bank); fin dir Co Nat West Securities Ltd (incorporating Wood MacKenzie & Co Ltd 1988-); FCA; *Recreations* music, theatre, skiing, mountain walking, travel; *Style—* Robert Dutton, Esq; Drapers Gdns, 12 Throgmorton Ave, London EC2P 2ES (☎ 071 382 1000, telex : 916 041, fax : 071 638 2152)

DUTTON, Timothy James; s of James Derek Dutton, JP, of Richmond, N Yorks, and Joan Rosemary, *née* Parsons; *b* 25 Feb 1957; *Educ* Repton, Keble Coll Oxford (BA); *m* 1 April 1987, Saffia, da of B Rasheed, of Washington USA; 1 da (Leila b 4 June 1988); *Career* called to the Bar Middle Temple 1978; jr SE circuit 1982, faculty memb Nat Inst of Trial Attorneys USA 1987; *Clubs* Oxford and Cambridge; *Style—* Timothy Dutton, Esq; 33 Culmstock Road, London SW11 (☎ 071 233 0350), East Lodge, Poltalloch, Kilmartin, Argyll, (☎ 054 65292), Farrars Building, Temple, London EC5Y 7BD (☎ 071 583 9241, fax 071 583 0090)

DUVAL, Derrick Brian; s of Harold Smith (d 1985), and Florence Gertrude Smith, *née* Osborne (d 1960); *b* 1 Jan 1935; *Educ* Wednesbury Tech Coll, Birmingham and Portsmouth Schs of Architecture (Dipl Arch); *m* 20 Aug 1960, Pauline, da of Horace Cockley; 1 s (Spencer Gavin b 1970); *Career* Nat Serv with RA (air reconnaissance intelligence); architect, princ Duval Brownhill Ptnrship, architects to the Close in Lichfield and cnslts to English Heritage and num heritage orgns; dir property co; *Recreations* political work, elected cncllr; *Clubs* Rotary; *Style—* Derrick Duval; 23 Dam St, Lichfield, Staffs WS13 6AE (☎ 0543 264303); Georgian House, 24 Bird St, Lichfield, Staffs WS13 6PT (☎ 0543 254257)

DUVAL, Robin Arthur Philip; s of Arthur Edward Bickersteth Duval (d 1976), of Exeter, Devon, and Jane Elizabeth, *née* Evans; *b* 28 April 1941; *Educ* King Edward's Sch Birmingham, UCL (BA), Univ of Michigan; *m* 20 Dec 1968, Lorna Eileen, da of Robert Watson, of Cardiff; 1 s (Sam b 1976, d 1978), 4 da (Polly b 1969, Sophie b 1971, Daisy b 1982, Martha b 1983); *Career* radio studio mangr BBC 1964-65, TV prodr J Walter Thompson 1965-68, princ Home Office 1981-83, head of UK prodn COI 1983-85 (TV prodr 1968-81), chief asst TV IBA 1985-90, dep dir of progs Independent Television Cmmn 1991-; memb RTS 1986; *Recreations* music, Aston Villa, theatre, church architecture, food; *Style—* Robin Duval, Esq; Independent Television Commission, 70 Brompton Rd, London SW3 1EY (☎ 071 584 7011, telex 24345)

DUVOLLET, Hon Mrs (Sheila Helen); *née* Parnell; 3 da of 6 Baron Congleton (d 1932), and Hon Edith Mary Palmer Howard (d 1979), da of Baroness Strathcona and Mount Royal; *b* 1923; *m* 1959 (m dis 1976), Roger Henry Duvollet; 1 da (Annette Frances b 1961 d 1982); *Style—* The Hon Mrs Duvollet; Burton Lodge, Burton Bradstock, Bridport, Dorset

DWEK, Joseph Claude (Joe); s of Victor Joseph Dwek; *b* 1 May 1940; *Educ* Carmel Coll, Univ of Manchester (BSc, BA); married with 2 children; *Career* chm and md Bodycote Int plc and subsids; chm: KM Kledingbedrijven Ehco NV, Vetements Professionels France, Panelflex Hldgs plc; memb: Ct of Univ of Manchester, Ct UMIST, Public Purchasing Ctee CBI, Consultative Taxation Ctee CBI, Dept of Indust NW Advsy Bd, NW Regnl Cncl CBI; dir Dunham Forest Golf and Country Club Ltd; FTI, AMCT; *Recreations* golf; *Style—* Joe Dwek, Esq; The Coppins, Hill Top, Hale; Bodycote Int plc, 140 Kingsway, Manchester M19 1BA (☎ 061 257 2345, telex 667072, fax 061 257 2353)

DWEK, Prof Raymond Allen; s of Victor Joseph Dwek (d 1988), of Manchester, and Alice, *née* Liniado; *b* 10 Nov 1941; *Educ* Carmel Coll, Univ of Manchester (BSc, MSc), Lincoln Coll Oxford (DPhil), Exeter Coll Oxford (DSc); *m* 21 June 1964, Sandra, da of Dr David I Livingstone, of Manchester; 2 s (Robert b 14 July 1967, Joshua b 23 March 1978), 2 da (Juliet b 19 Dec 1965, Deborah b 3 Oct 1974); *Career* lectr in biochemistry Trinity Coll Oxford 1976-84 (res lectr in physical chemistry ChCh 1966-68, lectr in organic chemistry ChCh 1968-75, departmental demonstrator for Dept of Biochemistry Oxford 1969-74, res lectr in biochemistry ChCh 1975-76; visiting Royal Soc Res fell at Weizmann Inst Rehovot Israel 1969, Royal Soc Locke Res fell 1974-76; visiting professorships: Duke Univ N Carolina 1968 (seconded to Inst of Exploratory Res fort Monmouth NJ), Univ of Trieste Italy 1974, Univ of Lund Sweden 1977, Inst of Enzymology Budapest Hungary 1980; author various articles in books and jls on physical chemistry, biochemistry and med; memb of various scientific ctees incl: Oxford Enzyme Gp 1971-88, Oxford Oligosaccharide Gp 1983, MRC AIDS Antiviral Steering Ctee 1987, dir and founding memb scientist Oxford Glycosystems Ltd 1988-; *Books* Nuclear Magnetic Resonance in Biochemistry (1973), Physical Chemistry Principles and Problems for Biochemists (jtly, 1975), Nuclear Magnetic Resonance (jtly 1977), Biological Spectroscopy (with Benjamin Cummings, 1984); *Style—* Prof Raymond Dwek; Ambleside, Vernon Ave, N Hinksey, Oxford OX2 9AU (☎ 0865 242065); Glycobiology Univ, Dept of Biochemistry, University of Oxford, South Parks Rd, Oxford OX1 3QU (☎ 0865 275343, fax 0865 275259)

DWORKIN, Paul David; *b* 7 April 1937; *Educ* Hackney Downs GS London, LSE (BSc Econ); *m* 1959, Carole Barbara Burke; 2 s; *Career* E Africa High Cmmn Dar es Salaam Tanganyika 1959, E African Common Servs Orgn Nairobi Kenya 1961, asst statistician BOT 1962 (statistician 1965); chief statistician: DTI 1972, Dept of Employment 1977; under-sec: DTI 1977-81, Central Statistical Office 1982-83; dir of statistics Dept of Employment 1983-89, asst dir Central Statistical Office 1989-; FSS; *Recreations* golf, skiing, theatre; *Clubs* Civil Service, Ski Club of GB, Stanmore Golf; *Style—* Paul Dworkin, Esq

DWORKIN, Prof Ronald Myles; s of David Dworkin; *b* 11 Dec 1931; *Educ* Harvard Coll, Oxford Univ, Harvard Law Sch; *m* 1958, Betsy Celia Ross; 1 s, 1 da; *Career* professor of jurisprudence Oxford Univ 1969, fell Univ Coll 1969-; FBA; *Style—* Prof Ronald Dworkin; University Coll, Oxford

DWYER, Mark Peter; s of James Dwyer, and Philomena, *née* King; *b* 9 Aug 1963; *Educ* Christian Brothers; *Career* Nat Hunt jockey; *Recreations* golf, tennis; *Style—* Mark Dwyer, Esq

DYAS, Anthony Rodney Joseph; s of Charles Joseph Henry Dyas, of Northolt, Middlesex, and Dorothy Ada, *née* Hutchinson; *b* 14 Aug 1940; *Educ* Greenford County GS; *m* 16 March 1963, Vivien Ann, da of William Alec George Herbert (d 1982); 3 da (Jennifer (Jenny) b 1966, Kristina (Tina) b 1968, Suzanne (Suzi) b 1970); *Career* certified accountant: Pearl Assurance Co Ltd 1957-59, Ass Br Foods Ltd 1959-69, Singer and Friedlander Ltd 1969- (dir 1974); FCCA 1964; *Recreations* running, motor cars; *Clubs* Ruislip 41; *Style—* Anthony Dyas, Esq; 18 the Avenue, Ickenham, Uxbridge UB10 8NP (☎ 0895 632343); 21 New St, Bishopsgate, London EC2M 4HR (☎ 071 623 3000, fax 071 623 2122, telex 886977)

DYBLE, John Maxwell; s of Bertram Dyble (d 1979), of Liverpool, and Mabel, *née* Owen (d 1969); *b* 28 April 1929; *Educ* Quary Bank Liverpool; *m* 1948, Eileen, da of Wing Cdr Harry Proudlove; 1 s (John Christopher b 27 April 1950), 1 da (Penelope Jane b 23 Feb 1956); *Career* apprenticeship in photography Liverpool 1945, mangr Stewart Bale London 1949-68, in own practice London 1968-, sr ptnr Doran Dyble Photography Hemel Hempstead 1981-; FBIPP 1970 (MBIPP 1948), FRPS 1971 (MRPS 1968); *Recreations* research, photographic history and equipment; *Style—* John Dyble, Esq; 13 Highclere Drive, Longdean Park, Hemel Hampstead, Hertfordshire HP3 8BT (☎ 0442 65360); Doran Dyble Photographŷ, 31 High St, Hemel Hempstead, Herts HP1 3AA (☎ 0442 54467, fax 0442 212236)

DYER, Chief Constable Alan; QPM; s of William Arthur Butt (d 1949), of Doncaster, and Dorothy Ann, *née* Hunter; *b* 4 Jan 1934; *Educ* Henry Melish GS Nottingham, Univ of Nottingham; *m* 31 Dec 1955, Penelope Jane, da of Capt Oswald Henry Peel Cox (d 1961), of Nottingham; 1 s (Jonathon Mark b 1959), 1 da (Sally Anne b 1957); *Career* able seaman RN 1952-54; Notts Constabulary 1954-80, Durham Constabulary 1980-82, Bedfordshire Police 1982-; memb: Bedfordshire St John Cncl, Rotary Club of Kempston Bedford, Assoc of Police Offrs 1980-; OStJ; *Style—* Chief Constable Alan Dyer; Police Headquarters, Woburn Road, Kempston, Bedford MK43 9AX (☎ 0234 841212)

DYER, Lt Cdr Anthony Gascoyne (Tony); MBE (1983); s of Joseph Bernard Dyer (d 1983), of Tewkesbury, Glos, and Lymington, Hants, and Rosetta Elizabeth, *née* Brading (d 1966); *b* 19 March 1933; *Educ* Tewkesbury GS, Britannia RN Coll Dartmouth; *m* 19 March 1966, Sally Joan, da of William Metcalfe (d 1986), of Taunton, Somerset; 1 s (Richard b 24 Feb 1971), 1 da (Caroline b 29 Jan 1974); *Career* RN 1951-83, Hydrographic Dept 1983-84, harbour master Cattewater Harbour Plymouth 1984-; sec Port of Plymouth Marine Liaison Ctee 1977-83; memb Ctee: Royal Western YC of England, Trans-Altantic Race Ctee, Round Britain Race Ctee; fell Royal Inst of Navigation 1978 (memb Cncl 1975-78 and 1982-83), fell Nautical Inst 1981 (memb Cncl 1981-83), memb Soc for Nautical Res 1973; *Recreations* yacht racing and cruising, moor walking, gardening; *Clubs* Naval Royal Western YC of England; *Style—* Lt Cdr Tony Dyer, MBE, RN; White Cottage, 119 Priory Rd, Lower Compton, Plymouth, Devon PL3 5EX; 2 The Barbican, Plymouth, Devon PL1 2LR (☎ 0752 669534, fax 0752 669691)

DYER, Charles; s of James Dyer (d 1980), and Florence, *née* Stretton (d 1975); *b* 7 July 1928; *Educ* Highlands Cncl Sch Ilford, Queen Elizabeth's GS Barnet; *m* 1960, Fiona, da of Elizabeth Thomson; 3 s (John, Peter, Timothy); *Career* Flying Offr RAFVR, navigator 512 Sqdn Europe and 243 Sqdn Pacific, demobbed 1948; playwright, author, actor, director; has acted in 250 plays and films, has appeared at 120 theatres; made West End debut as Duke in Delderfield's Worm's Eye View (Whiteh Theatre 1948); has written plays for Royal Shakespeare Co; his works, mostly duologues, are in constant prodn; latest prodns incl: L'Escalier (Theatre de L'Oeuvre Paris 1985-86), Sottoscala (Satiri Theatre Rome 1987-88), Mother Adam (Rome Festival 1988), Lovers Dancing (Albery Theatre London 1983-84); his Loneliness Trilogy (Rattle of a Simple Man, Staircase, Mother Ad been translated into most languages; *Style—* Charles Dyer Esq; Old Wob, Gerrards Cross, Bucks SL9 8SF

DYER, Geoffrey John; s of Arthur John Dyer, and Philys Mary, *née* Tudor; *b* 5 June 1958; *Educ* Cheltenham GS, Corpus Christi Coll Oxford (BA); *Career* author; *Books* Ways of Telling: The Work of John Berger (1986), The Colour of Memory (1989), But Beautiful: A Book about Jazz (1991); *Style—* Geoffrey Dyer, Esq

DYER, Lois Edith; OBE (1984); da of Richard Morgan Dyer (d 1961), and Emmeline Agnes Dyer, *née* Wells (d 1976); *b* 18 March 1925; *Educ* Richmond Co Sch, Middlesex Hosp Sch of Physiotherapy; *Career* physiotherapist Middlesex Hosp London 1945-47, sr physiotherapist Coronation Non-Euro Hosp Johannesburg SA 1948-51; supt physiotherapist: Johannesburg Gp of Hosps 1951-56, Westminster Hosp London 1958-61, Roy Nat Orthopaedic Hosp Stanmore Middlesex 1963-72; physiotherapy offr DHSS London 1976-85; freelance conslt physiotherapist; MCSP 1945, FCSP 1986; Physiotherapy Practice (co-ed, 1985-89); *Books* numerous publications in jls and books; *Recreations* country pursuits, music, bridge, animal welfare, conservation; *Style—* Miss Lois Dyer, OBE, FCSP; Garden Flat, 6 Belsize Grove, London NW3 4UN (☎ 071 722 1794)

DYER, Prof Sir (Henry) Peter Francis Swinnerton-; 16 Bt (E 1678), of Tottenham, Middx; KBE; s of Sir Leonard Schroeder Swinnerton Dyer, 15 Bt (d 1975), and Barbara, *née Brackenbury*; *b* 2 Aug 1927; *Educ* Eton, Trinity Coll Cambridge; *m* 25 May 1983, Dr Harriet Crawford, er da of Rt Hon Sir Patrick Browne, OBE, TD, *qv*; *Heir* kinsman, Richard Dyer-Bennet, *qv*; *Career* Cwlth Fund fell Univ of Chicago 1954-55, res fell Trinity Coll Cambridge 1950-54 (fell 1955-73, dean 1963-73); master St Catharine's Coll Cambridge 1973-83; prof of mathematics Cambridge Univ 1971-88 (lectr 1960-71, univ lectr Cambridge Maths Lab 1960-67); vice chllr Cambridge Univ 1979-81; visiting prof Harvard 1971; chm: Ctee on Academic Orgn (London Univ) 1980-82, Steering Gp responsible for planning inst to replace New Univ of Ulster and Ulster Poly 1982-84; fellow Eton 1981-, dir Prutec 1981-86, chm Univ Grants Ctee 1983-89, chief exec Univs Funding Cncl 1989-91, chm CODEST 1987-91 (memb 1984-91); Hon DSc Bath 1981; hon fell: Worcester Coll Oxford, Trinity Coll Cambridge, St Catharine's Coll Cambridge; FRS; *Recreations* destructive gardening; *Style—* Prof Sir Peter Dyer, Bt, KBE, FRS; The Dower Hse, Thriplow, Cambs (☎ 076 382 220); University Funding Council, 14 Park Crescent, London W1 (☎ 071 636 7799)

DYER, Simon; s of Maj-Gen G M Dyer, CBE, DSO (d 1979), of Richmond, and Evelyn Mary, *née* List; *b* 19 Oct 1939; *Educ* Ampleforth, Univ of Paris, Univ of Oxford (BA, MA); *m* 21 Jan 1967, (Louise) Gay, da of Anthony Lister Walsh, (d 1968), of Headley; 2 da (Jemima b 1970, Louise b 1973); *Career* AA: chief accountant 1967-72, dir 1972-, md 1982-87, dir-gen 1987-; Freeman City of London, Liveryman Coachmakers and Coachharnessmakers (1984); FCA 1978; *Recreations* gardening, tennis, skiing; *Clubs* Cavalry and Guards, Hurlingham; *Style—* Simon Dyer, Esq; The Automobile Association, Fanum House, Basingstoke, Hants (☎ 0256 20123)

DYER-BENNET, Richard; s (by 1 w) of Maj Richard Stewart Dyer-Bennet (d 1983, gggs of Sir Thomas Swinnerton Dyer, 9 Bt); hp of kinsman, Sir (Henry) Peter Francis Swinnerton-Dyer, 16 Bt, *qv*; *b* 1913; *m* 1, 1936 (m dis 1941), Elizabeth Hoar Pepper; 2 da; m 2, 1942, Melvene Ipcar; 2 da; *Career* musician; *Style—* Richard Dyer-Bennet Esq; Star Route 62, Box 29, Great Barrington, Mass 01230, USA

DYKE; *see*: Hart Dyke

DYKE-COOMES, Martin; s of Ernest Thomas Dyke-Coomes, and Gladys Dorothy, *née* Bignell; *b* 14 Aug 1948; *Educ* Sarah Robinson Secdy Modern, Ifield GS, Architectural Assoc; *m* 24 June 1978, Margaret, *qv*, da of George Herbert Pinhorn; 1 s (Ned Alexander b 1981), 1 da (Amy Elizabeth b 1983); 2 adopted s (Anthony b 1967, Claude b 1973); *Career* architect ARCUK 1973; set up CGHP Architects in 1979; worked from 1976-79 in Covent Garden for the Community Assoc opposin changing the GLC plans for the area; fndr Dyke Coomes Assocs 1989; principle works: Hoxton St London N1 Regeneration (Times/RIBA award Jubilee Hall Redevelopment 1984-87 (Times/RIBA award 1988), Holland and Thurstan Dwellings 1982-86; participant in 1986 RIBA 40 under 40's exhibition; *Recreations* sleeping, dreaming, drinking, scheming, fishing; *Clubs* Manchester United, 7 Dials Social Centre; *Style—* Martin Dyke-Coomes, Esq; Dyke Coomes Associates Architects, 89-93 Shepperton Rd, London N1 3DF (☎ 071 359 8230)

DYKES, Andrew Christopher; s of John Christopher Dykes (d 1981), of London, and Mollie Theresa, *née* Cheesman; *b* 7 June 1954; *Educ* Westminster, Trinity Coll Cambridge (MA); *m* 24 April 1982, Christina Anne, da of Lt-Col James Malcolm Harrison, OBE, TD (d 1979), of Bickerton, Cheshire; 2 s (Barnaby b 1987, Thomas (twin) b 1987); *Career* called to the Bar Inner Temple 1977, Thomas R Miller & Son 1977-87; dir: Thomas Miller P & I 1985-87, Int Tankers Owners Pollution Federation Ltd 1986-87; md: Victor O Schinnerer and Company Ltd 1990-, Encon Underwriting Ltd 1990-; Sloan fell London Business Sch 1988; Freeman City of London 1977, Liveryman Worshipful Co of Coopers 1977; *Recreations* fishing, sailing; *Clubs* Travellers'; *Style—* Andrew Dykes, Esq; The Forge, Exbury, nr Southampton SO4 1AH (☎ 0703 894717)

DYKES, David Wilmer; s of Capt David Dykes, OBE (d 1978), and Jenny, *née* Thomas (d 1971); *b* 18 Dec 1933; *Educ* Swansea GS, Corpus Christi Coll Oxford (MA), Univ of Wales (PhD); *m* 22 Sept 1967, Margaret Anne, da of Harvey Clifford George (d 1969); 2 da (Elizabeth Anne b 28 July 1972, Rosemary Louise b 29 July 1978); *Career* cmmnd RN 1955-58; civil servant Bd of Inland Revenue 1958-59, admin appts Univ of Bristol and Univ Coll of Swansea 1959-63, dep registrar Univ Coll of Swansea 1963-69, registrar Univ of Warwick 1969-72; Nat Musuem of Wales: sec 1972-86, actg dir 1985-86, dir 1986-89; memb Cncl Royal Inst of South Wales 1962-69 and 1985-, hon lectr in history Univ Coll Cardiff (later Univ of Wales Coll of Cardiff) 1975-, chllr Order of St John Priory for Wales 1991-; awarded Parkes - Weber prize and medal 1954; Freeman City of London 1985, Liveryman Worshipful Co of Tin Plate Workers 1985; FRNS 1958, FRHistS 1965, FSA 1973, FRSA 1990; *Books* Anglo-Saxon Coins in the National Museum of Wales (1977), Alan Sorrell: Early Wales Recreated (1980), Wales in Vanity Fair (1989); author of articles and reviews in numismatic, historical and other jls; *Recreations* numismatics, writing, gardening; *Clubs* Athenaeum, United Oxford & Cambridge Univ, Cardiff & County, Bristol Channel Yacht Swansea; *Style—* Dr David Dykes, FSA; Cherry Grove, Welsh St Donats, nr Cowbridge, South Glamorgan CF7 7SS

DYKES, Hugh John; MP (C) Harrow East 1970-; s of Richard Dykes of Weston-super-Mare, Somerset; *b* 17 May 1939; *Educ* Weston-super-Mare GS, Pembroke Coll Cambridge; *m* 1965, Susan Margaret, da of Elwand Smith of Wakefield, Yorks; 3 s; *Career* investment analyst and stockbroker: ptnr Simon & Coates 1968-78, assoc memb Quilter Goodison & Co (formerly Quilter, Hilton, Goodison) 1978; contested (C) Tottenham 1966, research sec Bow Gp 1965-66, PPS to: parly under secs Defence 1970-, parly under sec Civil Service Dept, UK memb European Parl 1974-, chm Cons Parly European Ctee 1979-80 (former sec, v-chm), vice pres Cons Gp for Europe 1982 (chm 1979-1980), dir Dixons plc Far Eastern Div; *Clubs* Beefsteak, Garrick, Carlton; *Style—* Hugh Dykes Esq, MP; House of Commons, London SW1

DYKSTRA, Ronald Gerrit Malcolm (Ronnie); s of Cdr Gerrit Abe Dykstra (d 1978), of Wilmslow, and Margaret Kirk (d 1970); *b* 4 March 1934; *Educ* Edinburgh Acad; *m* 1, 28 April 1960 (m dis), Jennifer Mary, da of James Cramer (d 1964), of Manchester; 3 s (Peter b 1961, Richard b 1963, Paul b 1966); m2, 6 Sept 1986, Sonia, da of Arthur Hughes, of Hereford; *Career* admitted slr 1957, sr ptnr Addleshaw Sons & Latham Manchester 1987- (asst slr 1957-61, ptnr 1961-87); hon slr Wilmslow Green Room Soc, pres Soc of Construction Arbitrators; memb Law Soc (1961); FCIArb; *Recreations* swimming, walking, amateur drama; *Style—* Ronnie Dykstra, Esq; 7 Racecourse Rd, Wilmslow, Cheshire SK9 5LF (☎ 0625 525 856); Dennis House, Marsden St, Manchester M2 1JD (☎ 061 832 5994)

DYMOKE, Lt-Col John Lindley Marmion; MBE (1960), DL (Lincs 1976); thirty-fourth Queen's Champion (in full: The Honourable the Queen's Champion and Standard Bearer of England); s of Lionel Marmion Dymoke (d 1963), and Rachel Isabel (d 1989), da of Hon Lennox Lindley (3 s of 1 Baron Lindley); *b* 1 Sept 1926; *Educ* Christ's Hosp; *m* 1953, Susan Cicely, eldest da of Lt Francis Fane, RN (himself ggggs of 8 Earl of Westmorland), of The Manor, Fulbeck, Lincs; 3 s (Francis, m 1982, Rosalie, da of Maj Anthony Goldingham; Philip, m 1982, Arabella, da of Sir Ralph Dodds, 2 Bt; Charles, m 1990, Kathry da of Rex Topham); *Career* Lt-Col Royal Anglian Regt, served Royal Lincolnshire Regt, instr RMA Sandhurst 1962, cmmnd 3 Bn Royal Anglian Regt 1966-69, ret 1972; landowner (3000 acres) and farmer; High Sheriff of Lincs 1979; chm Lincs Branch CLA 1982-85; Master Worshipful Co of Grocers 1977; *Clubs* Army and Navy; *Style—* Lt-Col John Dymoke, MBE, DL; The Estate Office, Scrivelsby Court, Horncastle, Lincs (☎ 0507 523325)

DYMOND, Dr Duncan Simon; s of Dr Sydney Cyril Dymond (d 1978), and Adele, *née* Spector (d 1977); *b* 25 Feb 1950; *Educ* St Paul's, Bart's Med Sch Univ of London (MB BS, MD); *m* 26 March 1977, Roberta Laura, da of Fiorenzo Bazzi, of Milan, Italy; 1 s (Daniel b 1982), 1 da (Francesa b 1979); *Career* asst prof med and cardiology Mount Sinai Med Sch Univ of Wisconsin 1980-81, sr registrar in cardiology 1981-86, conslt cardiologist Bart's 1987-; fndr Br Nuclear Cardiology Gp, memb Cncl Br Cardiovascular Intervention Soc Scientificc Ctee, hon asst sec Br Cardiac Soc 1990-; memb: Br Nuclear Med Soc 1979, Br Cardiology Soc 1980, MRS 1981, fell American Coll of Cardiology 1983, fndr fell Euro Soc of Cardiology 1989; *Recreations* cricket, tennis, skiing, pianoforte, Italian opera, watercolours; *Clubs* MCC; *Style—* Dr Duncan Dymond; Cardiac Dept, St Bartholomew's Hosp, London EC1A 7BE (☎ 071 726 6233), 114 Harley St, London W1N 1AG (☎ 071 935 6789, car 0836 297007)

DYNES, John Brian; s of John Dynes; *b* 17 Oct 1933; *Educ* Portadown Tech Coll, Queen's Univ Belfast; *m* 1961, Alice Mary, *née* Graham; 1 s, 1 da; *Career* md Henry Denny & Sons (Ulster) Ltd 1977-87, dir Henry Denny & Sons Ltd 1978-87, ACMA; *Recreations* golf, bridge, amateur radio; *Clubs* Farmers'; *Style—* John Dynes, Esq; 30 Breagh Rd, Portadown, Co Armagh, N Ireland (☎ 0762 338360); H Denny & Sons (NI) Ltd, Obins Street, Portadown, Co Armagh (☎ 0762 334914)

DYNEVOR, 9 Baron (GB 1780); Richard Charles Uryan Rhys; s of 8 Baron Dynevor, CBE, MC (d 1962, fifth in descent from Baroness Dynevor, herself da of 1 and last Earl Talbot, of the same family as the Earls of Shrewsbury); *b* 19 June 1935; *Educ* Eton, Magdalene Coll Cambridge; *m* 1959 (m dis 1978), Lucy Catherine King, da of Sir John Rothenstein, CBE; 1 s, 3 da; *Heir* s, Hon Hugo Griffith Uryan Rhys b 19 Nov 1966; *Style—* The Rt Hon the Lord Dynevor; The Walk, Carmarthen Rd, Llandeilo, Dyfed SA19 6RS

DYOTT, Richard Burnaby Kennedy; s of Maj William Boyd Kennedy Shaw (d 1979), and Eleanor, *née* Dyott (d 1982); *b* 6 Feb 1945; *Educ* Radley, RAC Cirencester (MRAC); *m* 1981, Sara Jane Modwena, da of Robert Westby Perceval, of Staffordshire; 1 s (William b 1987), 1 da (Caroline b 1985); *Career* chartered surveyor; High Sheriff of Staffordshire 1983; FRICS; *Recreations* forestry, shooting; *Clubs* Boodle's; *Style—* Richard Dyott, Esq; Freeford Manor, Lichfield, Staffs (☎ 0543 262300); Godfrey-Payton, Old Bablake, Hill St, Coventry (☎ 0203 226684)

DYSART, Countess of (eleventh holder of title, S 1643); Rosamund Agnes; also Lady Huntingtower (S 1643); da of Maj Owain Edward Whitehead Greaves, JP, DL (d 1941), and Countess of Dysart (tenth holder, d 1975); *b* 15 Feb 1914; *Heir* sister, Lady Katherine Grant, *qv*; *Style—* The Rt Hon the Countess of Dysart; Bryn Garth, Grosmont, Abergavenny, Gwent

DYSON, John Michael; s of Eric Dyson; *b* 9 Feb 1929; *Educ* Bradfield, CCC Oxford; *Career* admitted slr 1956; ptnr Field Roscoe & Co (subsequently Field Fisher & Co, then Field F Martineau) 1957-73; master of the Supreme Ct of Judicature (Chancery Div) 1973-, asst rec of the Crown Court; *Style—* J M Dyson Esq; 20 Keats Grove, London NW3 2RS (☎ 071 794 3389)

DYSON, Prof Robert Graham; s of Jack Dyson (d 1970), of Saddleworth, Oldham, and Sylvia, *née* Schofield; *b* 6 Sept 1942; *Educ* Hulme GS Oldham, Univ of Liverpool (BSc), Univ of Lancaster (PhD); *m* 31 July 1965, Dorothy, da of Daniel Prestwich (d 1987), of Oldham; 1 s (Michael), 1 da (Joanne); *Career* sr systems technologist Pilkington Bros plc 1968-70 (res mathematician 1964-68); Univ of Warwick: lectr

1970-77, sr lectr 1977-84, prof operational res and systems 1984-, pro-vice chllr 1989-; chm Warwick Business Sch 1978-81; memb: OR Panel SERC 1985-89, Operational Res Soc (former cncl memb Educn Res Ctee and chm awards: President's Medal (Operational Res Soc), Pergamon Prize (for articles in jl of Operational Res Soc); *Books* Strategic Planning: Models and Analytical Techniques (1989); *Recreations* cricket (played for Uppermill, Southport & Birkdale and Leamington CC's), theatre, rugby union (passive); *Style—* Prof Robert Dyson; Warwick Business School, University of Warwick, Coventry CV4 7AL (☎ 0203 523775)

DYSON, Prof Roger Franklin; s of John Franklin Dyson (d 1969), of Oldham, Lancs, and Edith Mary, *née* Jobson (d 1981); *b* 30 Jan 1940; *Educ* Counthill GS Oldham, Univ of Keele (BA), Univ of Leeds (PhD); *m* 8 Aug 1964, Anne Elizabeth, da of Travis Edward Greaves (d 1985), of Oldham; 1 s (Mark Franklin b 1965), 1 da (Miranda Jane b 1967); *Career* lectr econ and industl rels Univ of Leeds 1966-74 (asst lectr 1963-66), Univ of Keele: sr lectr industl rels and dep dir adult educn 1974-76 prof and dir adult educn 1976-89, dir Clinical Mgmnt Unit Centre for Health Planning and Mgmnt 1989-; dir Mercia Pubns Ltd 1984-, ed Health Servs Manpower Review 1975-86; conslt advsr to sec of state at DHSS 1979-81, chm North Staffs Health Authy 1982-86; RSM 1982; *Recreations* gardening, gastronomy; *Clubs* Carlton, Royal Soc of Med; *Style—* Prof Roger Dyson; Elendil, Newcastle Rd, Ashley Heath, Market Drayton, Shropshire TF9 4PH (☎ 063 087 2906); Centre for Health Planning and Management, The Science Park, University of Keele, Staffs ST5 5BG (☎ 0782 621111, fax 0782 613847, telex 36113 UNKL

DYSON, Timothy John Bruce; s of Michael Bruce Dyson (d 1966), and Joyce Mary, *née* Simpson; *b* 3 Dec 1960; *Educ* Mirfield HS, Greenhead Coll, Univ of Loughborough (BSc); *Career* Text 100: joined as graduate trainee 1984, account mangr 1986-87, assoc dir 1987-89, co dir 1989-90, dir Text 100 International 1990-; MIPR, MInstD; *Recreations* skiing, windsurfing, sailing; *Style—* Timothy Dyson, Esq; Text 100, Network House, Wood Lane, London W12 7SL (☎ 081 740 4455, fax 081 749 4456, car 0836 564 038)

DZIKUNU, George Kwame; s of Robert Dzikunu-Toh (d 1976), of Ghana, and Jessie, *née* Jacobson (d 1974); *b* 2 July 1946; *Educ* Ebenezer Secdy Sch, Inst of African Studies Ghana; *m* 17 Oct 1980, Nancy, da of James Nii Okai; 1 s (James Kwashi b 7 Oct 1979), 2 da (Jessie Ami b 3 Dec 1977, Joyce Esi b 25 Oct 1988); *Career* lead dancer and instr Ghana Nat Dance Ensemble 1970-73, leader and tutor Sakofa Dance Troupe Ghana 1974, dance instr Steel & Skin Arts London 1978-79, master drummer and dance tutor Ekome Arts Bristol 1980-82, freelance drumming and dancing tutor 1983, sr supervisor community project Manpower Service Cmmn 1984, fndr and exec artistic dir Adzido Pan African Dance Ensemble 1984-; winner: Choreographic Innovation award Black Dance Devpt Tst 1988, Outstanding Creative Achievement award Dance Umbrella and Time Out 1988; *Recreations* music, videoing, cooking; *Style—* George Dzikunu, Esq; 25 Ryecroft Rd, Lewisham, London SE13 6EZ

E

EABORN, Prof Colin; s of Tom Stanley Eaborn (d 1964), of Wrexham, Clwyd, and Caroline, *née* Cooper (d 1974); *b* 15 March 1923; *Educ* Ruabon GS, Univ Coll of N Wales Bangor (BSc, PhD, DSc); *m* 30 Aug 1949, Joyce, da of David Thomas, of Newcastle Emlyn, Dyfed; *Career* reader in chemistry Univ of Leicester 1954 (asst lectr 1947, lectr 1950), ed Jl of Organometallic Chemistry 1964-, pro-vice chllr sci Univ of Sussex 1968-72 (prof of chemistry 1962), contrib Jl of the Chemical Soc and Jl of Organometallic Chemistry (ed 1964-), Robert Welch visiting scholar Rice Univ Texas 1961-62, Erskine fell Univ of Canterbury NZ 1965, distinguished prof New Mexico State Univ 1973, Canadian Cwlth fell and visiting prof Univ of Victoria BC 1976, Gilman lectr State Univ 1978; FS Kipping Award of American Chem Soc 1964; Royal Soc Chemistry: Organometallic award 1975, Ingold medal 1976, Main Gp Element Award 1989; hon sec Chem Soc 1964-71, chm Br Cmmn on Chem Educn 1967-69, vice pres Dalton Div Royal Soc of Chemistry 1971-75; memb: Italy UK Mixed Cultural Ctee 1972-80, Cncl Royal Soc 1978-80 and 1988-89; Hon DSc Sussex 1990; FRSC, FRS 1970; *Books* Organosilicon Compounds (1960); *Style—* Prof Colin Eaborn, FRS; School of Chemistry and Molecular Sciences, University of Sussex, Brighton BN1 9QJ (☎ 0273 606755)

EADE, Robert Francis; s of Stanley Robert Eade, of Hulverstone, Isle of Wight; *Educ* Bromsgrove, London External (BSc); *m* 1965, Mary Lindsay, da of Sidney John Coulson, of Stratton-on-the-Fosse, Somerset; 3 children; *Career* dir: Commercial Technology 1983-85, md Internat THORN EMI plc 1985-, Metal Industries Ltd, James G. Biddle Co, Thorn Mod. Barbados Ltd, Evershed & Vignoles France, SA, INMOS Int plc, THORN EMI (USA) Inc, THORN EMI South Africa (Pty) Ltd, THORN EMI New Zealand Ltd, THORN EMI (Australia) Ltd, THORN EMI Licht Organschaft, THORN EMI AB; memb cncl British Electrical and Allied Mfrs' Assoc (BEAMA); pres Scientific Instrument Manufacturers' Assoc (SIMA, fed memb of BEAMA) 1981-82; pres GAMBICA (assoc for the instrumentation, control and automation industry) 1982-84; CEng, FIEE, FRS; *Style—* Robert Eade, Esq, FRS; Furnace Lodge, Furnace Farm Road, Felbridge, East Grinstead, W Sussex RH19 2PU; Thorn EMI House, Upper St Martin's Lane, London WC2H 9ED (☎ 071 836 2444)

EADES, Capt Geoffrey Alan; CBE (1989); s of Harry William Eades (d 1969), and Violet Eades (d 1985); *b* 14 Dec 1938; *Educ* Portsmouth GS, Britannia RNC; *m* 13 Aug 1966, Julia Marion, da of Richard Bastow (d 1978); 1 s (James b 1971), 1 da (Joanna b 1969); *Career* RN 1957-89: Cdr 1974, Capt 1979, Cdre RN Staff Coll 1984-86, SNO ME 1988; cmd of HM Ships: Greatford 1965, Russell 1972-74, Avenger 1977-79, Battleaxe 1983-84, Beaver and First Frigate Sqdn 1987-88; ADC to HM Queen 1987-89; nautical assessor to House of Lords 1991; MNI 1977; FBIM 1988; *Recreations* sailing, genealogy, maritime history; *Clubs* Emsworth Sailing; *Style—* Capt Geoffrey Eades, CBE, RN; Ferranti International, Western Rd, Bracknell, Berks RG 12 1RA (☎ 0344 483232)

EADES, Dr Sheila Mary; da of Lt-Col John Henry Eades (d 1971), of Burrington, Bristol, and Evelyne Guli, *née* Goodbody (d 1955); *b* 19 Feb 1930; *Educ* Stanstead Coll Quebec Canada, Kambala Sch Sydney Aust, Redland HS Bristol, Royal Free Med Sch London (MB BS); *Career* paediatric registrar: Plymouth Hosp 1959, Bristol Children's Hosp 1960, Queen Elizabeth Hosp 1962; sr paediatric registrar Royal Free Hosp London 1965 (house offr 1956); conslt paediatrician: N Devon 1968, Cornwall and Is of Scilly 1972; memb Nat Assoc Welfare of Children in Hosp; FRCPEd; *Recreations* gardening, travelling; *Style—* Dr Sheila Eades; Royal Cornwall Hospital (Treliske), Truro, Cornwall (☎ 0872 74242)

EADIE, Alastair Gordon; s of Col James Alister Eadie, DSO, TD, DL (d 1961), of Vernons Oak, Sudbury, Derbyshire; *b* 25 June 1940; *Educ* Eton; *m* 14 April 1966, Hon Jaqueline, *qv*; 3 s (James b 1967, Christopher b 1969, Edward b 1972); *Career* dir: International Distillers & Vintners UK Limited, Gilbeys Wines and Spirits Ltd, Morgan Furze of Brick Street Ltd, Strategic Sporting (Berwickshire) Ltd, Saccone & Speed Ltd, Juterini & Brooks UK Ltd; memb: Wine & Spirit Assoc of GB and NI, Wine Promotion Bd; *Recreations* shooting and stalking; *Clubs* Cavalry & Guards; *Style—* Alastair Eadie, Esq; Bourne Orchard, Brickendon, Hertford, SG13 8NU

EADIE, Alex(ander); BEM (1960), JP (Fife 1951), MP (Lab) Midlothian 1966-; s of Robert Eadie; *b* 23 June 1920; *Educ* Buckhaven Sr Secdy Sch; *m* 1941, Jemima, da of T Ritchie, of Wemyss; 1 s; *Career* former coal miner, chm Fife Housing Ctee; memb: Educn Ctee, Scot Cncl Lab Pty Exec Ctee, Scot NUM; fought Ayr 1959 and 1964, former PPS to Min for Social Security (Miss M Herbison), Parly under sec Energy 1974-79, oppn front bench spokesman Energy 1973-74, 1979-85 and 1986-87; chm: PLP Power and Steel Gp, Miners' Parly Gp; vice chm Parly Trade Union Gp, sec Miners' Parly Gp 1983-85 and 1986-87; *Style—* Alex Eadie, Esq, BEM, JP, MP; Balkerack, The Haugh, East Wemyss, Fife (☎ 0592 71 3636)

EADIE, Craig Farquhar; s of Donald Eadie, of Hazeldene, Seaford, E Sussex, and Maureen, *née* Irwing; *b* 22 April 1955; *Educ* Canford, Worcester Coll Oxford (BA), Aix-Marseilles Univ France (DES); *m* 3 Oct 1987, Deborah Ann, da of Leslie Burnett, of W Wycombe, Bucks; *Career* admitted slr 1980; ptnr Frere Cholmeley 1986-; dir: Inst of Contemporary British History, Watside Charities; legal advsr Kentish Town CAB; *Style—* Craig Eadie, Esq; 10 Denmark Rd, Wimbledon, London SW19 4PG; Frere Cholmeley Slrs, 28 Lincoln's Inn Fields, London WC2A 3HH (☎ 071 405 7878, fax 071 405 9056, telex 27623)

EADIE, Douglas George Arnott; s of Herbert Arnott Eadie (d 1932), of Leeds, and Hannah Sophia, *née* Wingate (d 1974); *b* 16 June 1931; *Educ* Epsom Coll, The London Hosp Med Coll (MB BS, MS); *m* 7 May 1957, Gilliam Carlyon, da of Maj Sydney Baron Coates, MC (d 1953); 2 s (Simon George Arnott b 1959, James Raymond b 1952), 2 da (Victoria Hannah Arnott b 1958, Lucy Jane Arnott b 1966); *Career* Capt Short Serv Cmmn RAMC 1957-60, served Far East Land Forces; Hugh Robertson exchange fell presbyterian St Lukes Hosp Chicago USA 1963-64, conslt surgn King Edward VII Hosp of Offrs 1978-, examiner in surgery Univ of London 1973-88; The London Hosp: surgical registrar 1963-67, sr lectr surgery 1968-69, conslt surgn 1969-88, hon consltg surgn 1988; memb: Bd of Govrs Epsom Coll 1973-77, Cncl GMC 1983-88; treas Med Protection Soc 1986-90 (chm cncl 1976-83), chm Med Advsy Bd The Cromwell Hosp; Master Worshipful Soc of Apothecaries 1989; memb Vascular Soc of GB & I (past hon sec); FRCS; *Recreations* golf, country pursuits; *Clubs* The Athenaeum, MCC; *Style—* Douglas Eadie, Esq; 7 Hillsleigh Rd, London W8 6PU (☎ 071 229 5242); 18 Upper Wimpole St, London W1M 7TB (☎ 071 487 3285)

EADIE, Hon Mrs (Jacqueline Noel); yr da of 5 Baron Ashtown, OBE (d 1979), by his wife Ellen Nancy, *née* Garton (d 1949); *b* 22 Dec 1940; *m* 14 April 1966, Alastair Gordon Eadie, *qv*; 3 s (James b 1967, Christopher b 1969, Edward b 1972); *Style—* The Hon Mrs Eadie; Bourne Orchard, Brickendon, Hertford SG13 8NU

EADIE, John Harold Ward; s of Harold George Eadie, CBE, and Marjorie Sanborn, *née* Ward; *b* 29 May 1909; *Educ* Cheltenham Coll; *m* 1946, Ellice Aylmer, CBE, *qv*; *Career* Maj RASC and Combined Operations, chm Gilbertson & Page Ltd and Gilbertson & Page (Can) Inc; *Recreations* cricket, golf; *Clubs* Royal and Ancient, MCC; *Style—* John Eadie, Esq; 74 Roebuck House, Palace St, SW1 (☎ 01 828 6158)

EADIE, Paul James McGregor; s of Hugh Russell McGregor Eadie (d 1960), and Helen, *née* Kondorgeorgeakis; *b* 18 Feb 1943; *Educ* Oundle, Geneva, Munich, Grenoble, Madrid, Perugia; *m* 1965, Victoria Cynthia, da of Frederick Gutwein (d 1969), of USA; 2 s (Russell Paul b 1967, James Cameron b 1969), 2 da (Holly Katherine b 1971, Charlotte Léonie b 1977); *Career* Macclesfield UDC 1976-82, cncllr, chm and chief exec Eadie Bros & Co Ltd 1982-, chief exec Eadie Hldgs Ltd 1982-85, dep chm Eadie Hldgs plc 1985-87, dir BRT Ltd India 1979-; dir Manchester C of C; dep chm: Br Textile Machinery Assoc, Latin American Trade Advsy Gp; town cncllr Wilmslow Dean Row and Lacey Green; AIL; *Recreations* theatre, cinema, reading; *Style—* Paul Eadie, Esq; The Pole Mews, Pole Lane, Antrobus, Cheshire CW9 6NN (☎ 0606 891522); Victoria Works, PO Box 22, Paisley PA1 1PD (☎ 041 889 4126); Hillside, Brook St, Knutsford, Cheshire WA16 8EB (☎ 0565 54871)

EADIE, Sam; s of late George Eadie; *b* 12 March 1935; *Educ* Trinity Coll Glenalmond, Exeter Coll Oxford; *m* 1958, Fiona Stewart, *née* Gillies; 1 s, 2 da; *Career* RNVR 1953-57; Royal Dutch Shell 1957-77, res conslt 1978-, dir Energy Advice Ltd 1987-; *Recreations* squash, skiing, music, travel, languages; *Style—* Sam Eadie, Esq; 4 Wotton Way, Cheam, Surrey (☎ 081 393 4230)

EADY, Anthony James; s of John James Eady, and Doris Amy, *née* Langley (d 1988); *b* 9 July 1939; *Educ* Harrow, Univ of Oxford (MA); *m* 23 June 1973, Carole June, da of Cyril Albert James Langley (d 1957); 2 s (Jeremy b 1974 d 1975, Nigel b 1976), 1 da (Joanna b 1978); *Career* Theodore Goddard and Co 1962-66, admitted slr 1966, J Henry Schroder Wagg and Co Ltd 1966-79, sec Lazard Bros and Co Ltd 1979-; Liveryman Worshipful Co of Slrs 1979; *Recreations* Hertford Soc, road running; *Clubs* Thames Hare and Hounds, United Oxford and Cambridge University; *Style—* Anthony Eady, Esq; Lazard Bros and Co Ltd, 21 Moorfields, London EC2P 2HT (☎ 071 588 2721, fax 071 628 2485)

EADY, David; QC (1983); s of Thomas William Eady (d 1978), and Kate, *née* Day; *b* 24 March 1943; *Educ* Brentwood Sch, Trinity Coll Cambridge (MA, LLB); *m* 1974, Catherine Hermione, yr da of Joseph Thomas Wiltshire, of Little Clarendon, North Rd, Bathwick, Bath; 1 s (James b 1977), 1 da (Caroline b 1975); *Career* called to the Bar Middle Temple 1966; rec 1986, memb Ctee on Privacy and Related Matters (The Calcutt Ctee) 1989-90; *Books* The Law of Contempt (jtly, with A J Arlidge, QC); *Recreations* music, watching cricket; *Style—* David Eady, Esq, QC; Goodshill Ho, Tenterden, Kent TN30 6UN (☎ 058 06 3644); 1 Brick Ct, Temple, London EC4Y 9BY (☎ 071 353 8845)

EADY, David Max; s of Sir Wilfrid Eady, GCMG, KCB, KBE (d 1962), of Rodmell, Sussex, and Margaret Elisabeth, *née* Laistner (d 1969); *Educ* Westminster, Trinity Coll Cambridge (BA); *m* 28 Aug 1954, Giséle Jeanne, da of Col Alfred Vacher (d 1966), of Gemozac, France; *Career* Capt Intelligence Corps 1943-45; writer and dir of: feature films, TV drama, commercials, documentaries; twice winner childrens jury award Los Angeles Childrens Film Festival; BISFA awards: gold, silver, bronze; winner Bronze Bear Berlin Film Festival, Acad Award nomination USA; memb: BAFTA 1955, Guild of Film Prodn Execs 1978; *Recreations* music, theatre, swimming; *Clubs* BAFTA; *Style—* David Eady, Esq; 59a Albert Drive, London SW19 6LB (☎ 081 785 2355); 14 Rue de Liberation, Gemozac, France 17 260 (☎ 010 334 694 55060)

EAGLE, Ronald Arthur; s of Charles Henry Eagle (d 1986), and Marjorie Isobel Eagle; *b* 8 Feb 1950; *Educ* Gravesend Technical High Sch; *m* 1, 12 April 1971, Pauline, da of Frederick Benton of Gravesend Kent; m 2, 7 Sept 1978, Sandra, da of Kenneth Minchin of Peregrin Road Sunbury on Thames Middlesex; 1 s (Jonathan Charles b 1980), 1 da (Alexandra Katherine b 1982), 1 step (Nicholas Reddick b 1974); *Career* statistics clerk Daily Mail 1966, media buyer Hobson Bates & Partners 1966-68, media planner Ogilvy & Mather 1968-71, sales gp head Border TV Ltd 1971-76, sales controller HTV Ltd 1976-84; sales dir Tyne Tees TV 1984-; dir: Tyne Tees Holdings plc, Tyne Tees TV Ltd, Nucleus Healthcare Productions Ltd, Tube Productions Ltd; chief exec Vision Marketing Ltd; *Recreations* reading, swimming, caravanning, travel; *Style—* Ron Eagle, Esq

EAGLES, Brian; s of David Eagles (d 1982), of London, and Anne, *née* Estrin; *b* 4 Feb 1937; *Educ* Kilburn GS, Univ of London (LLB); *m* 30 May 1961, Marjorie, da of Leopold Weiss (d 1983), of London; 2 s (Simon b 1965, Paul b 1967), 1 da (Karen b 1963); *Career* slr; ptnr: J Sanson & Co 1960-67, Herbert Oppenheimer Nathan & Vandyk 1967-88, S J Berwin & Co 1988-; arbitrator American Film Mkt Assoc 1986; memb N Middx Mgmnt Ctee Nat Marriage Guidance Cncl 1972-75, hon slr Celebrities Guild of GB 1983-; memb Law Soc 1960; regular contributor of articles to legal and entertainment industry publications; *Recreations* music, film, theatre, bridge (master), skiing, tennis, walking; *Style—* Brian Eagles, Esq; Montague House, 107 Frognal, Hampstead, London NW3 6XR; Les Anemones, Villars-Sur-Ollon, Switzerland; Les Hermes, Tournamy Les Mougins, France; S J Berwin & Co, 236 Grays Inn Rd, London WC1X 8HB (☎ 071 278 0444, fax 071 833 2860, telex 8814928 WINLAW)

EAGLES, Lt-Col (Charles Edward) James; LVO (1988); s of Maj Charles Edward Campbell Eagles, DSO, RMLI (ka 1918), and Esmé Beatrice, *née* Field (d 1965); *b* 14 May 1918; *Educ* Marlborough; *m* 1941, Priscilla May Nicolette, da of Brig Arthur Cottrell, DSO, OBE (d 1962), of Boughton Aluph Cottage, Ashford, Kent; 1 s (Anthony), 3 da (Susan, Jane, Mary); *Career* RM 1936-65; Civil Serv, MOD 1965-83; HM Body Gd of Hon Corps of Gentlemen-at-Arms: memb 1967-88, Harbinger 1981-86, Standard Bearer 1986-88; *Recreations* shooting; *Clubs* Army and Navy; *Style—* Lt-Col James Eagles, LVO; Fallowfield, Westwell, Ashford, Kent (☎ 0233 712552)

EAMES, (Cecil) Blair William; s of Cecil Harold Percival Eames (d 1929), and Catherine Maria, *née* Sewell (d 1969); *b* 9 June 1923; *Educ* St Albans Sch, Univ of London; *m* 1 June 1946, Sheila Nancy, da of Eric Waldemar Ling (d 1954); 1 s (Mark b 16 May 1956); *Career* cmmnd RAF Branch Pilot 1942-48, retired Sqdn Ldr; dir and gen mangr Sells PR Ltd 1954-64, sec gen World Packaging Orgn 1964-72; dir: Godbolds Advertising Ltd 1973-82, Harpenden Building Soc 1980-; md Social Serv Advertising Ltd 1983-; memb: Round Table Movement 1950-60, St Albans Arts Cncl 1960-70; Liveryman Worshipful Co of Distillers 1959-; MCIM, MIPA, MICFM; *Recreations* food, wine, gardening, music; *Clubs* RAF, MCC; *Style*— Blair Eames, Esq; Parkside Coach House, 60 Mill Lane, Welwyn, Herts AL6 9ES; Social Service Advertising Ltd, Farringdon House, The Parade, St Albans Road East, Hatfield, Herts AL10 0ET (☎ 0707 275533, fax 0707 268357)

EARDLEY-WILMOT *see also*: Wilmot

EARDLEY-WILMOT, Sir John Assheton; 5 Bt (UK 1821) of Berkswell Hall, Warwickshire; LVO (1956), DSC (1943); s of Cdr Frederick Neville Eardley-Wilmot (d 1956), and n of Maj Sir John Eardley-Wilmot, 4 Bt (d 1970); *b* 2 Jan 1917; *Educ* Stubbington, RNC Dartmouth; *m* 23 June 1939, Diana Elizabeth, yr da of late Cdr Aubrey Moore, RN; 1 s, 1 da; *Heir* s, Michael John Assheton Eardley-Wilmot; *Career* Cdr (RN) ret 1967; on staff Monopolies Cmmn 1967-82; Liveryman Paviors' Co; FRSA (1970); *Recreations* fishing; *Clubs* Wig and Pen; *Style*— Sir John Eardley-Wilmot, Bt, LVO, DSC; 41 Margravine Gdns, London W6 8RN (☎ 01 748 3723)

EARL, Donald George Monk; s of Lt-Col Stanley Albert Earl (d 1955), and Elsie, *née* Pitt (d 1979); *b* 10 Aug 1921; *Educ* Wolverhampton Sch, Wrexham GS, Norwich GS; *m* 10 July 1945, Patricia, da of Harold Williamson (d 1956); 1 s (Michael John b 1951); *Career* banker; pres Banking Insur Finance Union 1970-72 (vice pres 1968-70); memb: Industl Tbnls 1975-89, Business and Technicians Trg Cncl (GB & NI) 1979-82 and 1985-88; FCIB (memb Cncl 1971-82); *Recreations* golf, gardening; *Style*— D G M Earl, Esq; 6 Arden Road, Dorridge, Solihull, W Midlands B93 8LG (☎ 0564 774229)

EARL, Hon Mrs (Edith Honor Betty); *née* Maugham; 2 da of 1 Viscount Maugham (d 1958) (former Lord Chancellor), and 2 Viscountess Maugham, *née* Helen Mary Romer (d 1950); *b* 24 March 1901; *m* 25 April 1925, Sebastian Earl (d 1983), s of Alfred Earl, of Chepstow Villas, W4; 2 s (Julian, Stephen); *Career* portrait painter; *Style*— The Hon Mrs Earl; Flat 6, 6 Onslow Square, London SW7 3NP (☎ 071 589 4758); The Flat, Chilland Ford, Martyr Worthy, nr Winchester, Hants (☎ 0962 78329)

EARL, Kimble David; s of Leonard Arthur Earl, of Surrey, and Margaret Lucy, *née* Pulker; *b* 29 Nov 1951; *Educ* Caterham Sch Surrey; *Career* dep chief exec Argus Press Gp, chief exec Newspaper Div and Consumer Publishing Div Argus Press Ltd; chm: Reading Newspaper Co Ltd, Windsor Newspaper Co Ltd, London and North Surrey Newspapers Ltd, Surrey and South London Newspapers Ltd, South London Press Ltd, Argus Specialist Pubns, Trident Press, Reading Newspaper Printing Co Ltd, Thames Valley Publishing, Argus Consumer Magazines Ltd, Argus Books, Argus Specialist Exhibitions; dir: SM Distribution Ltd, Argus Press Hldgs Inc, Team Argus Inc, Argus Business Pubns Ltd, Argus Retail Services Ltd, Great Western Newspapers Ltd; *Recreations* walking, motor coach driving, travel; *Style*— Kimble Earl, Esq; Argus Press Gp, PO Box 700, Yateley, Camberley, Surrey GU17 7UA (☎ 0252 875075)

EARL, Peter Richard Stephen; s of Peter Richard Walter Earl, and Patricia *née* Lee; *b* 20 Jan 1955; *Educ* City of London Sch, Worcester Coll Oxford (open exhibitioner, MA, Rowing blue), Harvard Univ (Kennedy scholar, memb Rowing team); *m* Emma Elizabeth, *née* Saunders; 1 s (Peter Richard William John b 10 March 1987), 1 da (Amelia Rose Elizabeth b 8 July 1985); *Career* conslt Boston Consulting Group 1978-79, assoc Blyth Eastman Dillon Inc 1979-80, mangr Orion Bank 1980-82, dir ABC International Ltd 1982-85, vice-pres Arab Banking Corporation 1982-85, chm Tranwood Earl Co Ltd (formerly Ifincorp Earl & Co Ltd) 1985-, chief exec Tranwood plc 1988-; fndr: Demerger Corporation plc 1985, Analysis Corporation plc 1986; hon treas The Journal of Roman Studies; International Mergers & Acquisitions (1986); *Recreations* marathons, skiing, geriatric rowing, corporate rescues, book reviews; *Clubs* Vincent's, Brooks's; *Style*— Peter Earl, Esq; Tranwood Plc, 123 Sloane St, London SW1X 9BW (☎ 071 730 3412)

EARL, Roger Lawrence; s of Lawrence William Earl, of 44 Ventnor Villas, Hove, Sussex, and Doris Florence, *née* Copelin; *b* 4 Oct 1940; *Educ* St Christophers Sch Kingswood Surrey, Hollingbury Ct Brighton Sussex, St Pauls; *m* 22 July 1968, Lynda Marion, da of Harold Frederick Waldock, of 16 Tynemouth Drive, Enfield; 2 da (Meredith Louise b 12 June 1970, Alexandra Kirsten b 20 July 1972); *Career* jr broker Arbon Langrish & Co (Lloyds brokers) 1957-65; Bland Welch & Co/Bland Payne & Co (Lloyds brokers): asst dir 1966-70, exec dir 1970-73, bd dir and md North American div 1973-79; md and chief exec Fenchurch Group (Lloyds brokers) 1979-, dir GPG plc 1987-89; memb: Kew Soc, Lloyds 1970; *Recreations* motor sport, swimming, scuba diving, tennis; *Clubs* IOD, Hurlingham, Riverside, Ferrari Owners, Annabels; *Style*— Roger Earl, Esq; 4 Cumberland Road, Kew, Surrey TW9 3HQ (☎ 081 948 1714); 9E Barkston Gardens, London, SW5 (☎ 071 370 0387); Flouquet, Lacour de Visa, Tarn et Garonne, France; La Carabela, 46 Via Del Bosque, Canyamel, Mallorca, Spain; Fenchurch Insurance Group Ltd, 136 Minories, London EC3N 1QN (☎ 071 488 2388/ 01 481 3863, fax 071 481 9467, c 0836 232758, telex 8870047 LOQOTE G/884442 LOQOTE LONDON)

EARLAM, Richard John; s of Francis Earlam, MD (d 1959), of Mossley Hill, Liverpool, and Elspeth, *née* Skippers; *b* 26 March 1934; *Educ* Liverpool Coll, Uppingham, Trinity Hall Cambridge (MA, MChir), Univ of Liverpool; *m* 6 Sept 1969, Roswitha, da of Alfons Teuber, of Munich (d 1971), playwright; 2 da (Melissa b 1976, Caroline b 1979); *Career* Capt RAMC 1960-62, surgical specialist Br Mil Hosp Hong Kong, TA MO 359 Field Regt RA; conslt gen surgn The London Hosp 1972, Fulbright scholar 1966, Alexander Von Humboldt fellowship W Germany 1968; chm: NE Thames Regnl Advsy Ctee in Gen Surgery, MRC Sub Ctee on Oesophageal Cancer; memb MRC: Cancer Therapy Ctee, Manpower Ctee; examiner RCS 1982-86, res asst Mayo Clinic USA 1966-67, clinical asst to Prof Zenker Munich 1968; memb RSM, FRCS; *Books* Clinical Tests of Oesophageal Function (1976); author of chapters and papers on abdominal surgery, oesophagus, stomach and gallbladder disease, epidemiology, surgical audit and coding; *Recreations* tennis, mountains summer and winter, beekeeping; *Clubs* Association of Surgeons; Collegium Internationale Chirurgiae Digestivae, Furniture History Soc; *Style*— Richard John Earlam, Esq; 4 Pembroke Gardens, London W8 6HS (☎ 071 602 5255); 55 Harley St, London W1 (☎ 071 637 4288)

EARLE, Col David Eric Martin; OBE (1969); 2 s of Brig Eric Greville Earle, DSO (d 1965), of Bucks, and Noel, *née* Downes-Martin (d 1975; family originated from Stockton, Cheshire 15 century; gggf created a Bt 1869 (*see* Sir Hardman Earle, 6 Bt); *b* 14 Aug 1921; *Educ* Stowe, ChCh Oxford; *m* 8 April 1947, Betty Isabel, yst da of Lawford Shield (d 1964), of Glos; 2 s (Charles b 1951, George b 1953), 2 da (Victoria b 1952, Charlotte b 1959); *Career* RA 1944; WWII 1940-45 in UK, India, Ceylon and Malaya; instr in gunnery, airborne artillery, DS Staff Coll Camberley, CO 32 Heavy Regt RA and Station Cmd Hildesheim; sec for studies, NATO Def Coll; Col GS MOD Offr Trg; ret 1974; entered Civil Serv by way of Principals Competition; DOE, served in several HQ directorates and as regnl admin offr PSA Bristol 1979-82; chm: Bath Centre for Voluntary Serv 1986-87, Relate N and W Wilts Marraige Guidance, N Wilts and Thamesdown Gp Cncl for Protection of Rural Eng; memb Community Cncl for Wiltshire 1990; FBIM 1973; *Recreations* photography, archaeology; *Style*— Col David E M Earle, OBE; Sheepways, Church Lane, Kington Langley, Chippenham, Wilts SN15 5NR (☎ 024975 274)

EARLE, Sir (Hardman) George (Algernon); 6 Bt (UK 1869), of Allerton Tower, Woolton, Lancs; s of Sir Hardman Alexander Mort Earle, 5 Bt (d 1979), and Maie, Lady Earle, (d 1986); *b* 4 Feb 1932; *Educ* Eton; *m* 24 Jan 1967, Diana Gillian Bligh, da of Col Frederick Ferris Bligh St George, CVO (d 1970), ggs of Sir Richard Bligh St George, 2 Bt; 1 s, 1 da; *Heir* s, Robert George Bligh Earle, b 24 Jan 1970; *Career* Nat Serv Ensign in Grenadier Gds; memb of London Metal Exchange 1962-73; *Recreations* fox hunting, sailing; *Clubs* Royal Yacht Sqdn; *Style*— Sir George Earle, Bt; Abington, Murroe, Co Limerick, Eire (☎ 061 386 108)

EARLE, Dr James Henry Oliver; s of John James Earle (d 1942), of Worcester Park, Surrey, and Constance Mary, *née* Gardner; *b* 5 June 1920; *Educ* Tiffin GS Kingston-upon-Thames, Kings Coll London, Westminster Med Sch (MD, BS); *m* 1, 26 Dec 1942 (m dis 1976), Jean Bessell, da of Edmund Bessell Whalley (d 1968), of Rogate, Sussex; 1 s (Nigel James b 1948), 1 da ((Mary) Jane b 1944); m 2, 7 Sept 1976, Lady Helen Norah, wid of Rt Hon Lord Runcorn, TD (d 1968), da of Sir Crosland Graham (d 1946), of Clwyd Hall, Ruthin, N Wales; *Career* lectr and sr lectr clinical pathology Westminster Med Sch 1949-53, asst conslt pathologist Royal Marsden Hosp 1953-56, conslt pathologist and dir laboratories Royal Masonic Hosp 1956-63, conslt pathologist Teaching Gp Westminster Hosp 1963-85; memb: Cncl and Exec Ctee Marie Curie Fndn (Cancer Care) 1953-, Academic Bd Westminster Med Sch (subsequently Charing Cross Med Sch) 1970-85, Bd Govrs Westminster Hosp 1972-74; rep Univ of London Kingston and Richmond Health Authy 1974-82 (vice chm 1978-82), chm DMT and Area Scientific Ctee Roehampton Health Dist 1974-82; Silver Jubilee medal 1977; Freeman City of London 1978, Liveryman Worshipful Co Apothecaries 1977; FRSM, FRCPath, MRCS, LRCP; *Recreations* fishing, gardening, opera, photography; *Style*— Dr James Earle; 18 Hillside, Wimbledon SW19 4NL (☎ 081 946 3507)

EARLE, Joel Vincent (Joe); s of James Basil Foster Earle, of Kyle of Lochalsh, Ross-shire, and Mary Isabel Jessie, *née* Weeks; *b* 1 Sept 1952; *Educ* Westminster, New Coll Oxford (BA); *m* 10 May 1980, Sophia Charlotte, da of Oliver Arbuthnot Knox, of London; 2 s (Leo b 1981, Martin b 1984); *Career* V & A Museum: keeper Far Eastern Dept 1983-87 (res asst 1974-77, asst keeper 1977-83), head of public servs 1987; maj exhibitions: Japan Style 1980, Gt Japan Exhibition 1981, Toshiba Gallery of Japanese Art 1986; tstee: Chiddingstone Castle Kent, The Design Museum, The Oriental Museum Durham; memb Ctee Japan Festival 1991; *Books* An Introduction to Netsuke (1980), An Introduction to Japanese Prints (1980), The Great Japan Exhibition (contrib, 1981), The Japanese Sword (translater, 1983), Japanese Art and Design (ed, 1987); *Style*— Joe Earle, Esq; 123 Middleton Rd, London E8 4LL; c/o Harrison Parrott Ltd, 12 Penzance Place, London W11 4PA (☎ 071 229 9166, fax 071 221 5042)

EARLE, Michael George; s of Henry George Earle (d 1984), of Hambleden, nr Henley-on-Thames, Oxon, and Elizabeth Mary, *née* Wheeler (d 1953); *b* 30 July 1944; *Educ* Sir William Borlase's Sch; *Career* dir: Keene Game Products (UK) Ltd 1978-, Keene Game Products (Overseas) Ltd 1978-; md & dir British & General Tube Co Ltd 1977-84; dir Globelion Ltd 1984-, md Barnham Press Ltd 1985-, dir Barfields Ltd 1990-; *Recreations* shooting; *Style*— Michael Earle, Esq; 227 Marlow Bottom, Marlow, Bucks (☎ 0628 471618), Barnham Press Ltd, Marlborough Trading Estate, High Wycombe, Bucks HP11 2LB (☎ 0494 450631)

EARLE, Col Peter Beaumont; MC (1945), DL (1967); s of Loftus Earle (d 1949); *b* 9 April 1917; *Educ* Eton, RMA Sandhurst; *m* 1, 1940, Ursula, da of late Maj F W Warre, OBE, MC; 1 s, 1 da; m 2, 1971, Judith, da of late Dr G T MacKinnell Childs; *Career* KRRC 1937-58, mil asst to CIGS War Office 1943-45, Col 1958; FO (PID) 1945-46, MOD (JIB) 1947-48, memb Def Res Bd Canada 1948-49, dir Henry Kendall and Sons Ltd 1959-; warden St George's Hanover Sq London 1962-; Croix de Guerre (France) 1945; FRSA 1947; Cdr Order of Merit (Peru) 1964; *Clubs* Brooks's; *Style*— Col Peter Earle, MC, DL; Stairs Hill House, Empshott, Selborne, Hants GU33 6HY (☎ 042 07 284)

EARLE, Peter Desmond Noel; s of late Brigadier E G Earle, DSO, of Walton Hall, Bletchley, Bucks, and late Noel Fielding-Johnson *née* Downs-Martin; *b* 20 Nov 1923; *Educ* Wellington, Ch Ch Oxford; *m* 6 Sept 1953, Hope, da of Wallace Sinclair Macgregor, of Vancouver, BC; 1 s (Robert b 1959), 2 da (Heather b 1960, Melanie b 1964); *Career* served RN 1942-47 home waters, South Atlantic, Indian Ocean and Pacific (Far East) LT RNVR exec officer, navigator; company dir; pres The Country Gentlemen's Associations plc (chief exec 1972-86, chm 1983-86); editor CGA magazine and guide to country living (Hutchinson & David Charles); *Recreations* gardening, writing, swimming, tennis, skiing, yachting; *Clubs* Naval, Dwits; *Style*— Peter Earle, Esq; Stow Bedon House, Attleborough, Norfolk (☎ 095 383 284)

EARLE, Richard Greville; DL (1984); s of John Greville Earle, JP (d 1933), and Jacobina Reid, *née* Clark (d 1970); *b* 12 Nov 1925; *Educ* Winchester, Trinity Coll Cambridge (MA); *m* 19 Jan 1956, Joanna Mary, JP, da of Cdr Henry Kelsall Beckford Mitchell, RN, CBE, JP, DL, of Sherborne, Dorset; 2 da (Elizabeth b 1957, Susan b 1959); *Career* RNVR 1943-47, Sub Lt (A); farmer and landowner; dir: Wessex Grain Ltd, Henstridge Grain Services Ltd 1985-; chm: Dorset NFU 1964, Dorset Small Industs Ctee (COSIRA) 1972-81, Standing Conf on Oil and Gas Exploration English Channel 1980-84, Leonard Cheshire Fndn Appeal in W Dorset 1985-88, W Dorset Family Support Serv 1987-, Community Cncl of Dorset 1987-90, Dorset CLA 1988-90; memb: Dorset CC 1967-85, Cncl of Country Landowners Assoc 1985-; govr Dorset Coll of Agric and Horticulture 1990-; High Sheriff 1983; *Recreations* countryside; *Clubs* Farmers; *Style*— Richard Earle, Esq, DL; Frankham Farm, Ryme Intrinseca, Sherborne DT9 6JT (☎ 0935 872304)

EARLES, Prof Stanley William Edward; s of William Edward Earles (d 1984), of Birmingham, and Winnifred Anne, *née* Cook (d 1959); *b* 18 Jan 1929; *Educ* King's Coll London (BSc, PhD, AKC), Univ of London (DSc); *m* 23 July 1955, Margaret Isabella, da of John Brown (d 1988), of Wormley, Hertfordshire; 2 da (Melanie Jane b 1962, Lucy Margaret b 1964); *Career* scientific offr Admiralty Engrg Laboratory 1953-55; Dept of Mechanical Engrg QMC: lectr 1955-69, reader 1969-75, prof 1975-76; King's Coll London: prof of mechanical engrg 1976-, head of Mechanical Engrg Dept 1976-90, head of Sch of Physical Scis and Engrg 1990-; dean of engrg Univ of London 1986-90; govr: Goff's Sch Hertfordshire 1964-88, Turnford Sch Hertfordshire 1970-87, Hatfield Poly Hertfordshire 1989-; FIMechE 1976; *Recreations* real tennis, gardening; *Style*— Prof Stanley Earles; Woodbury, Church Lane, Wormley, Broxbourne, Herts EN10 7QF (☎ 0992 464 616); Division of Engineering, Mechanical Engineering, King's Coll, Strand, London WC2R 2LS (☎ 071 836 5454, fax 071 836 1799)

EARNSHAW, (Thomas) Roy; CBE (1977, OBE 1971); s of Godfrey Earnshaw (d 1962), and Edith Annie, *née* Perry (d 1962); *b* 27 Feb 1917; *Educ* Marlborough Coll Liverpool; *m* 2 Sept 1953, Edith, da of Willie Rushworth (d 1976), of Rochdale; 2 da (Rachel Catherine (Mrs Tsirigotakis) b 17 Nov 1957, Hilary Jane (Mrs Jacobs) b 3 May

1960); *Career* WWII Inf 1940-46, Lance Corpl rising to Maj and second i/c 1 Bn Lancs Fusiliers; shipping and shipbroking Liverpool 1933-39, various appts subsid cos of Turner & Newhall Ltd, export appts (latterly export sales mangr) Turner Brothers Asbestos 1939-40 and 1946-53, dir AM & FM Ltd Bombay 1954-59, export dir Ferodo Ltd 1959-66, dir and divnl gen mangr TBA Industl Products Ltd 1966-76, memb advsy cncl BOTB 1975-82 (Export Year and Export Utd advsr 1976- dir: Actair Int Ltd 1979-83, Act Hldgs Ltd 1979-83, Unico Fin Ltd 1979-81; London econ advsr to Merseyside CC 1980-82, visiting fell Henley Mgmnt Coll 1981-90, conslt and lectr in int mgmnt 1982-; former pres Rochdale C of C, chm NW Region C of C, UK and del Euro C of C, memb Bd of Mangrs Henley YMCA; MICS 1937, MIEx 1948, FRSA 1980; *Recreations* painting, sketching, music, walking; *Clubs* Leander; *Style*— Roy Earnshaw, Esq, CBE

EARP, Denis Nigel Warriner; s of Fred Stanley Earp, of 14-16 Belle Vue Road, Clevedon, Avon, and Ethel Marjorie, *née* Warriner (d 1974); *b* 11 Oct 1929; *Educ* Bootham Sch York, King's Coll Cambridge (Exhibitioner, State Scholar, MA); *m* 1, 18 Sept 1954, Audrey Patricia, da of Arthur Percival Winsor; 2 s (Roger David b 20 Jan 1959, Michael John b 10 July 1960); m 2, 19 Dec 1975, Jean Mary Robbins, da of Gilbert George Francis Malpass; *Career* asst engr Binnie & Partners Consulting Engineers 1952-62, sr engr South Staffordshire Waterworks Co 1962-70, dep chief engr Colne Valley Water Co 1970-74, tech dir Welsh Water Authority 1984-86 (div mangr 1974-84), divnl dir Binnie & Partners Chester 1986-; panel AR engr DOE 1978-; memb Ctee: Inst of Civil Engrs, Int Congress on Large Dams, Br Dam Soc, BSI, Nat Water Cncl, Water Authys Assoc, Inst of Water Engrs and Scientists, BIM; elder United Reformed Church, hon treas Cmmn of Covenanted Churches in Wales; FIWEM 1970, FICE 1971 (MICE 1956), FEng 1988; *Recreations* travel, theatre, music, reading, voluntary work; *Style*— Denis Earp, Esq; 16 Percy Road, Handbridge, Chester CH4 7EZ (☎ 0244 678086); 3 The Dell, Gower Rd, Killay, Swansea SA2 7DX (☎ 0792 204902); Binnie & Partners, 25 Newgate St, Chester CH1 1DE (☎ 0244 317044, fax 0244 347256, car 0860 710364)

EASON, Dr John; s of Reginald Eason, of Bristol, and Helena, *née* Morgans; *b* 3 April 1951; *Educ* St Brendan's Coll Bristol, St Catharines Coll Cambridge (MB BChir, MA); *m* 3 Jan 1987, Janene Alice, da of Ian Jeffrey Ridley, of Melbourne, Australia; *Career* gen med Whipps Cross Hosp 1982-83; anaesthetics: London Hosp 1978-82, Kings Coll Hosp 1983-; FFARCS 1981, MRCP 1983; *Books* Contrib Anaesthesia Review Number Seven (1989); *Recreations* geology, carpentry; *Style*— Dr John Eason; Dept Anaesthesia and Intensive Care, King's Coll Hosp, Denmark Hill, London SE5 9RS (☎ 01 274 6222)

EASSON, Prof Angus; s of William Coleridge Easson (d 1987), and Olive Mary, *née* Hornfeck (d 1962); *b* 18 July 1940; *Educ* William Ellis GS, Univ of Nottingham (BA), Univ of Oxford (DPhil); *Career* lectr English: Univ of Newcastle upon Tyne 1965-71, Royal Holloway Coll Univ of London 1971-77; chm Modern Languages Dept Univ of Salford 1989- (prof of English 1977-, dean Soc Sci's and Arts 1986-89); *Books* Elizabeth Gaskell (1979); *Recreations* opera; *Style*— Prof Angus Easson; University of Salford, Modern Languages Department, Salford M5 4WT (☎ 061 745 5029)

EASSON, Malcolm Cameron Greig; s of Prof Eric Craig Easson (d 1983), of Cheshire, and Moira McKechnie, *née* Greig; *b* 7 April 1949; *Educ* Marple Hall GS, Univ of Manchester; *m* 6 July 1972, Gillian, da of Stanley Oakley, of Cheshire; 1 s (James b 1979), 1 da (Helen b 1982); *Career* princ of firm of CAs specialising in taxation and finance for doctors of med, regular contrib of fin articles to medical jls; FICA; *Recreations* golf, gardening, reading, music; *Style*— Malcolm C G Easson, Esq; Frith Knoll, Eccles Road, Chapel-el-le-Frith, Derbyshire SK12 6RR; Rex Buildings, Wilmslow, Cheshire SK9 1HZ (☎ 0625 527351)

EAST, David Edward; s of Edward William East, of London, and Joan Lillian East; *b* 27 July 1959; *Educ* Hackney Downs Sch, Univ of East Anglia (BSc); *m* 1984, Jeanette Anne, da of Leonard Frank Smith (d 1985), of Loughton, Essex; 1 s (Matthew David b 1986); *Career* professional cricketer Essex CCC 1981-; *Style*— David East, Esq; c/o Essex CCC, New Writtle St, Chelmsford, Essex CM1 0PG (☎ 0245 25242)

EAST, Gerald Reginald Ricketts; s of Reginald Butterfill East (d 1960), of Littleton, Winchester, and Dora Harriet Kate, *née* Ricketts; *b* 17 Feb 1917; *Educ* Peter Symonds Sch, St Edmund Hall Oxford (MA); *m* 7 June 1944, Anna Elder, da of Robert Smyth (d 1969), of Cullybackey, Co Antrim; 1 s (Gerald Robert), 2 da (Jane Elisabeth, Anne Maureen); *Career* enlisted RA 1939, cmmnd 1940, Maj 1944; served: UK, France and Germany; asst princ WO 1947, private sec Sec of State 1954-55, inspr of estabs 1958, princ estab offr 1970, Civil Serv cmmr 1974, ret 1977; chm Incorporated Froebel Educnl Inst and pres Froebel Assoc 1978-89; *Recreations* travel; *Style*— Gerald East, Esq; Appleden, 4 Dibdale Road, Neasham, Co Durham DL2 1PF (☎ 0325 720577)

EAST, Grahame Richard; CMG (1961); 2 s of William Robert East (d 1938), and Eleanor Maude Beatrice East (d 1971); *b* 10 Feb 1908; *Educ* Bristol GS, Corpus Christi Coll Oxford (MA); *m* 1937, Cynthia Mildred, da of Adam Louis Beck, OBE (d 1964); 2 s (Richard, John), 2 da (Rosalind, Celia); *Career* asst master Royal Belfast Academical Instn 1929; civil serv 1930-, asst sec Bd of Inland Revenue 1941-, special cmmnr of Income Tax 1962-, ret 1973; *Style*— Grahame East, Esq, CMG; 44 Devonshire Rd, Sutton, Surrey SM2 5HH

EAST, John Hilary Mortlock; s of Grahame Richard East, CMG, and Cynthia Mildred, *née* Beck; *b* 6 March 1947; *Educ* St Paul's, BNC Oxford; *m* 22 Aug 1970, (Dorothy) Diane, da of Roy Cuthbert Tregidgo; 2 s (Richard b 1976, Jonathan b 1985), 2 da (Tamsyn b 1974, Emily b 1978); *Career* admitted slr 1972; ptnr Clifford Chance 1976-; govr Seaton House Sch Ltd Sutton Surrey; Freeman Worshipful Co of Slrs; memb Law Soc; *Recreations* rugby fives, squash, cricket, cinema, reading, theatre; *Clubs* Singapore Cricket, Jesters; *Style*— John East, Esq; Clifford Chance, Royex House, Aldermanbury Sq, London EC2V 7LD (☎ 071 600 0808, fax 071 726 8561)

EAST, John Richard Alan; s of Bertram David (Barry) East, of Eaton Square, London, and Gladys, *née* Stone (d 1957); *b* 14 May 1949; *Educ* Westminster; *m* 1, 14 May 1971 (m dis 1986), Judith Adrienne, da of Clive Hill, of Horshall, Surrey; 2 s (Robin b 1974, Christopher b 1978); m 2, 12 July 1986, Charlotte Sylvia, da of Lt Cdr Peter Gordon Merriman, DSC, RN (d 1965); *Career* Speechly Bircham (Slrs) 1967-70, Mitton Butler Priest & Co Ltd 1971-73, Panmure Gordon & Co 1973-77; Margetts & Addenbrooke (formerly Margetts & Addenbrooke East Newton, Kent East Newton & Co) 1977-86: sr ptnr 1977-80, managing ptnr 1980-86, sr ptnr 1983-86; dir: National Investment Group plc 1986-87, Guidehouse Group plc and subsids 1987-; md Guidehouse Securities Ltd 1987-, chief exec Guidehouse Group plc 1990-; memb Stock Exchange 1974; tstee and memb Ctee The Square Mile Charitable Tst; *Recreations* music, the playing and recording of electronic musical instruments, travel; *Clubs* Carlton; *Style*— John East, Esq; Hermiston, 110 Victoria Drive, Wimbledon, London SW19 6PS (☎ 081 789 4918); Durrant House, 8-13 Chiswell St, London EC1Y 4UP (☎ 071 628 5858, fax 071 628 4473)

EAST, Prof Robin Alexander; s of Percy Alexander East (d 1981), of Romsey, Hants, and Winifred May, *née* Southwell; *b* 11 Dec 1935; *Educ* Barton Peveril GS, Univ of Southampton (BSc, PhD); *m* 6 Oct 1962, June, da of George Henry Slingsby (d 1977), of Sheffield; 1 da (Jennifer Lynn b 1963); *Career* apprentice Vickers Supermarine 1953-57, visiting res fell Aust Nat Univ at Canberra 1973; Univ of Southampton: Sir Alan Cobham res fell 1960-63, lectr, sr lectr and reader in aeronautics 1963-85, prof and head of Aeronautics Dept 1985-90; memb various ctees and former chm Southampton Branch RAeS; memb Space Engrg Panel SERC; MAIAA 1969, CEng 1983, FRAeS 1985; *Books* around 70 pubns on hypersonic aerodynamics and experimental facilities in int jls and conf proceedings; *Recreations* gardening, photography, ornithology, walking; *Style*— Prof Robin East; East Croft, North Common, Sherfield English, Romsey, Hants SO51 6JT (☎ 0794 40444); Dept of Aeronautics & Astronautics, Univ of Southampton, Southampton, Hants SO9 5NH (☎ 0703 592324, telex 47661)

EAST, Stephen John; s of Charles William East, of Croydon, Surrey, and Olive Lillian, *née* East; *b* 3 March 1958; *Educ* Selhurst GS Croydon, Loughborough Univ of Technol (BSc); *Career* Binder Hamlyn Chartered Accountants 1979-83; Redland plc: asst treas 1983-84, dep treas 1984-87, gp treas 1987-; vice chm Programme Ctee Assoc Corporate Treas, memb Croydon South Cons Assoc; ACA 1982, MCT 1986; *Style*— Stephen East, Esq; 34 Lower Barn Rd, Sanderstead, Surrey CR8 1HQ (☎ 081 660 1602); Redland House, Reigate, Surrey RH2 0SJ (☎ 0737 233 307, fax 0737 223 797, telex 28626, car 0836 290 180)

EAST ANGLIA, Bishop of 1976-; Rt Rev Alan Charles Anthony Clark; s of William Thomas Durham Clark (d 1977), and Ellen Mary Clark, *née* Compton (d 1950); *b* 9 Aug 1919; *Educ* Westminster Choir Sch, Junior Seminary for Southwark Diocese at Mark Cross, English Coll Rome (scholar), Gregorran Univ Rome (STD); *Career* ordained Parish of St Joseph's Bromley 1945, vice rector Ven English Coll Rome 1954-64, consecrated titular bishop of Elmham and auxiliary of Northampton 1969, transferred to See of East Anglia 1976-; peritus (expert advsr) Second Vatican Cncl 1960-65, co-chm Anglican and Roman Catholic Int Cmmn 1969; chm Dept of Mission and Unity Roman Catholic Episcopal Conf of England and Wales 1984 (pres Nat Cmmn for Ecurmenism 1970), co-chm Jt Working Gp of World Cncl of Churches and the Holy See (Vatican) 1985; Freeman City of London 1968; Knight Cdr Equestrial Order of Holy Sepulchre; *Publications* Dialogue in Faith (Publication of address to Gen Synod of (of E, 1974); *Recreations* music, literature; *Style*— The Rt Rev the Bishop of East Anglia; The White House, 21 Upgate, Poringland, Norwich NR14 7SH (☎ 05086 2202, car 05086 5358)

EASTAWAY, Nigel Antony; s of Kenneth George Eastaway, and Muriel Angus; *b* 17 Nov 1943; *Educ* Chigwell Sch; *m* 17 Aug 1968, Ann, da of Cecil Douglas Geddes; 1 s (James Nigel Andrew b 18 May 1983), 1 da (Suzanne Emma Louise b 4 July 1980); *Career* CA; conslt Moores Rowland 1990- (tax ptnr until 1989); non-exec dir: International Fiscal Services Ltd, Nevern Daries Ltd; author of books on taxation: Moores Rowland's Yellow Tax Guide 1990/91, Moores Rowland's Orange Tax Guide 1990/91, Handbook on the Capital Gains Tax 1979, Tax and Financial Planning for Medical Practitioners, Practical Share Valuation, Share Valuation Cases, Utilising Personal Tax Losses and Reliefs, Tax Aspects of Company Reorganisations, Intellectual Property Law and Taxation, Allied Dunbar Expatnate Tax and Investment Guide, Taxation of Lloyds Underwriters, Principles of Capital Transfer Tax; memb: Taxation Ctee London C of C and Indust, Tech Ctee and Admin Ctee Inst of Taxation, Cncl Inst of Taxation; FCA, FCCA, FCIS, FTII, fell Hong Kong Soc of Accountants, hon fell Hong Kong Inst of Taxation, fell Offshore Inst, memb Int Tax Planning Assoc; *Books* Soviet Aircraft Since 1918 (ed), Aircraft of the Soviet Union (contrib), Mikoyan MiG-21 (contrib), The Soviet Air Force (contrib), Janes All the World's Aircraft (contrib); *Recreations* russian aircraft, playing with old cars, Bentleys, Jaguars and Morgans; *Style*— Nigel Eastaway, Esq; Moores Rowland, Cliffords Inn, Fetter Lane, London EC4A 1AS (☎ 071 831 2345, fax 071 831 3004, mobile 0860 328500)

EASTERLING, Prof Patricia Elizabeth; da of Edward Wilson Fairfax (d 1978), and Annie, *née* Smith (d 1989); *b* 11 March 1934; *Educ* Blackburn HS for Girls, Newnham Coll Cambridge (BA, MA); *m* 22 Dec 1956, (Henry) John Easterling, s of Rev Claude Easterling (d 1962); 1 s (Henry Thomas Fairfax b 1963); *Career* asst lectr Univ of Manchester 1957-58; Newnham Coll Cambridge: asst lectr 1958-60, fell and lectr 1960-87, vice princ 1981-86, hon fell 1987-; univ lectr Univ of Cambridge 1969-87, prof of Greek and head of dept UCL 1987-; pres Classical Assoc 1988-89; chm: Ctees of Jt Assoc of Classical Teachers, Cncl of Univ Classical Depts 1991-; *Books* Ovidiana Graeca (with E J Kenney, 1965), Sophocles Trachiniae (ed, 1982), Cambridge History of Classical Literature I (jt ed B M W Knox, 1985), Greek Religion and Society (jt ed J V Muir, 1985); *Recreations* walking; *Style*— Prof P E Easterling; Department of Greek and Latin, University College London, Gower St, London WC1E 6BT (☎ 071 380 7493, fax 071 387 8057)

EASTERMAN, Nicholas Barrie; s of Cyril Saul Herman Easterman, of Lausanne, Switzerland, and Sheila, *née* Cope (d 1983); *b* 11 April 1950; *Educ* Millfield, UCL (LLB); *Career* called to the Bar Lincoln's Inn 1975; memb: Lincoln's Inn 1969, Cncl of Legal Educn; *Recreations* photography, driving, good wine and cognac; *Clubs* RAC; *Style*— Nicholas Easterman, Esq; 4 Brick Court, Temple EC4 7AD (☎ 071 353 1492)

EASTHAM, Kenneth; MP (Lab) Manchester Blackley 1979-; s of late James Eastham; *b* 11 Aug 1927; *Educ* Openshaw Tech Coll; *m* 1951, Doris, da of Albert Howarth; *Career* former planning engr GEC Trafford Park, memb: NW Econ Planning Cncl 1975-79, Manchester City Cncl 1962-80 (sometime dep ldr, chm Educ Ctee), AUEW sponsored, memb Employment Select Ctee; *Style*— Kenneth Eastham, Esq, MP; House of Commons, London SW1

EASTHAM, Hon Mr Justice; Hon Sir (Thomas) Michael; yst s of His Hon Sir Tom Eastham, QC, JP, DL (d 1967), and Margaret Ernestine, *née* Smith; *b* 26 June 1920; *Educ* Harrow, Trinity Hall Cambridge; *m* 1942, Mary Pamela, o da of late Dr H C Billings, of Shere, Surrey; 2 da (and 1 da decd); *Career* WWII Capt Queen's Royal Regt 1940-46; called to the Bar Lincoln's Inn 1947; QC 1964; rec of: Deal 1968-71, Cambridge 1971; hon rec Cambridge 1972, bencher Lincoln's Inn 1972, rec Crown Ct 1972-78, judge of the High Ct of Justice Family Div 1978-; kt 1978; *Style*— The Hon Mr Justice Eastham; 7a Porchester Terrace, London W2 (☎ 071 723 0770)

EASTICK, Barrington Richard; s of Douglas Martineau Eastick (d 1957), of Berkshire, and Sylvia, *née* Weddle (d 1934); *b* 17 July 1934; *Educ* St Andrew's Sch Eastbourne, Uppingham; *m* 15 Jan 1966, Madeleine Anne, da of John Nathaniel Preston (d 1982), of Co Meath; 2 s (James b 1966, Benjamin b 1971), 1 da (Tara b and d 1969); *Career* RAF FO ME 1952-55; md Ragus Sugars and assoc cos 1957-87 (conslt and dir 1988-); motor driver 1952-77, sec and reformer ERA Club 1958 (team mangr 1958-60); memb ctee Bentley Drivers Club 1965-79 (memb Competitions Ctee, WO B Meml Fund co-ordinator); *Recreations* vintage and classic cars, military history, Switzerland; *Clubs* Leander, Henley Rowing, Bentley Drivers', ERA, Vintage Sports Car; *Style*— Barrington R Eastick, Esq; Fawley Lodge, Fawley, Henley-on-Thames, Oxfordshire RG9 3AJ (☎ 0491 571763); Ragus Sugars, Sugar Manufacturers, 193 Bedford Ave, Trading Estate, Slough, Berkshire SL1 4RT (☎ 0753 75353, fax 0753 691514)

EASTMAN, Brian Ralph; s of Leonard Eastman (d 1969), of Ashtead, Surrey, and Edith, *née* Beakhurst; *b* 31 May 1940; *Educ* Glyn Sch Epsom, Kingston Coll of Art (DArch); *m* 16 May 1964, (Dorothy) Mary, da of Arthur Randall (d 1973), of Ashtead, Surrey; 2 s (Andrew b 5 May 1965, Mark b 18 June 1966), 1 da (Ruth b 10 Aug

1972); *Career* consIt architect Wandsworth Borough Cncl 1963-, princ Philip Goodhew Ptnrship (chartered architects) 1979- (assoc 1960-74, ptnr 1974-79), consIt architect City of Westminster 1987-; chm Crawley Planning Gp 1975-78, churchwarden Ifield Team 1984-89, ldr Scout Assoc; MRIBA 1965; *Clubs* Sloane; *Style—* Brian Eastman, Esq; 182 Buckswood Drive, Crawley RH11 8PS (☎ 0293 529414); Philip Goodhew Ptnrship, Chartered Architects, 54 Warwick Square, Westminster SW1V 2AJ (☎ 071 828 1042, fax 071 630 0270)

EASTMAN, Lady Mary Agatha; *née* Campbell; yr da of 4 Earl Cawdor (d 1914); *b* 6 Jan 1905; *m* 5 Feb 1931, Brig Henry Claude Warrington Eastman, DSO, MVO, late RA (d 1975), s of Thomas Eastman, MA, of Northwood Park, Winchester; 1 s, 1 da; *Style—* The Lady Mary Eastman; Pandy Newydd, Halfway Bridge, Bangor, Gwynedd

EASTMENT, Peter John; s of Alexander John Eastment, of Setters Glade, Holcombe, Bath, and Kathleen Mary, *née* Blackmore; *b* 26 April 1947; *Educ* Wells Cathedral Sch; *m* 6 Sept 1975, Linda Loraine, da of Patrick Gould (d 1987); 1 s (Mark b 1978), 1 da (Rebecca b 1980); *Career* graduate Nat Inst of Hardware 1968; Casswells Ltd: dir 1973, sec 1980, md 1986; former: vice chm Young Cons, govr Wrighlington Sch Avon; *Recreations* travel, golf; *Clubs* Fosseway-Country; *Style—* Peter Eastment, Esq; Casswells Ltd, 6-9 High St, Midsomer Norton, Bath, Avon (☎ 0761 413 331)

EASTMOND, Dr Clifford John; s of Charles John Henry Eastmond (d 1980), and Hilda, *née* Horrocks; *b* 19 Jan 1945; *Educ* Audenshaw GS, Univ of Edinburgh Med Sch (BSc, MB ChB, MD); *m* 25 March 1967, Margaret, da of Stanley Wadsworth (d 1976); 2 s (Nigel b 1970, Timothy b 1972), 1 da (Heather b 1975); *Career* house physician Northern Gen Hosp Edinburgh 1969, house surgn Royal Infirmary Edinburgh 1970, sr house offr Sefton Gen Hosp Liverpool 1970, registrar Liverpool Hosps 1971-74, res fell Univ of Liverpool Med Sch 1974-76, sr registrar Rheumatism Res Unit Leeds Univ and Gen Infirmary 1976-79, consIt rheumatologist Grampian Health Bd 1979-, clinical sr lectr Univ of Aberdeen 1979-; elder Skene Parish Church, pres Westhill and Dist Rotary Club 1989-90, memb Cairngorm Mountaineering Club; FRCPE 1984, FRCP 1990; memb Br Soc Rheumatology (cncl memb 1987-90); *Recreations* scottish mountaineering, skiing, music; *Style—* Dr Clifford Eastmond; Whinmoor, 34 Leslie Cres, Westhill, Skene, Aberdeen AB32 6UZ (☎ 0224 741009); City Hosp, Dept of Rheumatology, Urquhart Rd, Aberdeen (☎ 0224 681818, fax 0224 685307)

EASTOE, Prof John Eric; s of Eric Wilfred Eastoe (d 1979), of Rudgwick, Sussex, and Winifred Mabel, *née* Trundel; *b* 3 Nov 1926; *Educ* Minchenden Sch Southgate, Imperial Coll London (BSc, ARCS, PhD, DIC), RCSE (DSc); *m* 14 April 1951, Beryl, da of Stanley Walter Musson (d 1987), of Corby Glen, Lincs; 1 s (Richard b 1954), 1 da (Sally b 1952); *Career* chemist and dental res offr, pioneered analysis of collagen and human growth hormone 1951, discovered amelogenins 1960; res offr Br Gelatine and Glue Res Assoc 1950-57, Leverhulme and Freemasons' fell RCS 1957-80, prof of oral biology Univ of Newcastle upon Tyne 1980-90; pres Br Soc Dental Res 1988-90; memb: Biochemical Soc 1953, Soc Applied Bacteriology 1956; IADR 1958, ORCA 1965, FDSRCS 1986; *Books* Practical Analytical Methods for Connective Tissue Proteins (1963), Practical Chromatographic Techniques (1964), Biochemistry and Oral Biology (1977 and 1988); *Recreations* walking, travel, photography, music, art history; *Clubs* Artefact; *Style—* Prof John Eastoe; 15 Campus Martius, Heddon on the Wall, Newcastle upon Tyne NE15 0BP (☎ 0661 852767)

EASTON, Hon Mrs (Caroline Ina Maud); *née* Hawke; eldest da of 9 Baron Hawke (d 1985); *b* 13 Feb 1937; *Educ* Hatherop Castle Glos; *m* 6 Aug 1960, John Francis Easton, o s of late Rev Cecil Gordon Easton, Vicar of Littlewick Green, Berks; 1 s, 1 da; *Career* called to the Bar Middle Temple 1959 (not practising now); *Recreations* music, sport; *Style—* The Hon Mrs Easton; The Old Hall, Barley, nr Royston, Herts (☎ 076 384 368)

EASTON, David John; s of Air Cdre Sir James Alfred Easton, KCMG, CB, CBE (d 1990), and Anna Mary, *née* McKenna (d 1977); *b* 27 March 1941; *Educ* Stowe, Balliol Coll Oxford (MA); *m* 16 May 1964, (Alexandra) Julie, da of Kenneth Woodburn Clark, of London; 2 s (James b 1969, Edward b 1974), 2 da (Sophie b 1965, Charlotte b 1972); *Career* TA 1959, 2 Lt OUOTC 1962, Lt Inns of Ct & City Yeo 1964; FO: entered 1963, third sec Nairobi 1965-66, second sec UK Mission Geneva 1967-70, MECAS Lebanon 1970-72, first sec FCO 1972, first sec Br Embassy Tripoli 1973-77, first sec FCO (Def Dept) 1977-80, first sec later cnsllr Br Embassy Amman 1980-83, cnsllr FCO 1986-89; political cnsllr New Delhi; *Recreations* swimming, tennis, travel, antiquities and antiques; *Style—* David Easton, Esq; Foreign & Commonwealth Office, Downing Street, London SW1 (☎ 071 210 6877)

EASTON, Dendy Bryan; s of Leslie Herbert Easton (d 1962), of Tadworth, Surrey, and Dora, *née* Napper (d 1969); *b* 13 March 1916; *Educ* Cranleigh Sch, Univ of Reading (Dip Hort); *m* 28 June 1941, Iris Joan, da of Albert Edward Keyser (d 1979), of Hove, Sussex; 2 s (Timothy b 1943, Dendy b 1950), 2 da (Ann b 1942, Jane b 1947); *Career* cmmnd 1939, BEF France 1939-40, UK and PAIFORCE 1944-45 RARO 1946, Capt and Adj 6 CRASC; nurseryman; chm and md Meare Close Nurseries Ltd (family business 1938-); MI Hort; *Recreations* gardening, fly fishing, motoring, preservation of common land; *Clubs* Vintage Sports Car, Aston Martin Owners; *Style—* Dendy Easton, Esq; Hunters Hall, Tadworth, Surrey KT20 5SB; Meare Close Nurseries Ltd, Tadworth Street, Tadworth, Surrey KT20 5RQ (☎ 0737 812449)

EASTON, James; OBE (1986); s of John Easton, and Helen, *née* Whitney; *b* 1 Sept 1931; *Educ* Saints' John and Cantius Sch Broxburn; *m* 1960, Rosemary Hobbin; 1 s, 2 da; *Career* served HM Forces 3 Hussars 1952-55; served Admiralty 1957-60; Dip Serv: FO 1960, Br Embassy Prague 1960-62, Br Embassy Paris 1963-65, FO 1965-68, vice consul Br Embassy Belgrade 1968-71, vice consul Br Embassy La Paz 1971-74, second sec Br Consulate NY 1974-78, first sec FCO 1978-83, first sec Br Embassy Rome 1983-87, HM Consul Gen Brussels 1987-89, ret 1989; *Style—* James Easton, Esq, OBE; 6 Cedar Gardens, Sutton, Surrey SM2 5DD

EASTON, Dr John Archibald; s of Robert William Easton (d 1965), and Jessie Hardie, *née* Leitch (d 1977); *b* 16 Aug 1930; *Educ* St Pauls, St Thomas Hosp Med Sch (MB BS); *m* 31 Aug 1957, Susan, da of Lt-Col Paul Hodder-Williams, OBE, TD, of Court House, Exford, Somerset; 3 s (Anthony b 1959, David b 1962, Graham b 1966); *Career* Nat Serv RAMC 1949-51; lectr in clinical pathology St Thomas Hosp Med Sch 1963-66, consIt clinical pathologist Windsor Gp Hosp Mgmnt Ctee 1966-74; East Berks Health Authy: consIt haematologist 1974-90, dir pathology 1986-90; chm Hosp Med Advsy Ctee East Berks Hosps 1983-85; FRCPath 1976; memb: Assoc Clinical Pathologists 1962, Br Soc Haematology 1963; *Recreations* walking, ornithology, music; *Clubs* Royal Cwlth Soc; *Style—* Dr John Easton; Frenham, Beaconsfield Rd, Farnham Common, Bucks SL2 3LZ (☎ 0753 643979)

EASTON, John Francis; s of Rev Cecil Gordon Easton (d 1959), of The Vicarage, Littlewick Green, Maidenhead, Berks, and Nora Gladys, *née* Hall; *b* 20 Aug 1928; *Educ* City of London Sch, Keble Coll Oxford (MA); *m* 6 Aug 1960, Hon Caroline Ina Maude, da of 9 Baron Hawke (d 1985), of Faygate Place, Faygate, Horsham, Sussex; 1 s (Nicholas John b 1961), 1 da (Ina Frances b 1964); *Career* Nat Serv RASC 1951-53; called to Bar Middle Temple 1951; slr Inland Revenue Office 1955-88, pt/t chm VAT Tbnls 1988; reader Dioc St Albans; *Recreations* languages, swimming; *Style—* John Easton, Esq; The Old Hall, Barley, Royston, Herts SG8 8JA (☎ 076 384 8368)

EASTON, Dr (Alfred) Leonard Tytherleigh; s of Leonard Tytherleigh (d 1945), and Maria Adelaida Bertran de Lis (d 1973); *b* 11 July 1921; *Educ* Harrow, Pembroke Coll Cambridge (MD); *m* 29 July 1945, Mary Josephine Latham, da of John Latham (d 1962); 1 s (Edward b 1949 d 1966), 1 da (Claire b 1947); *Career* Sqdn Ldr (Med) RAF ME 1947-49; surgn, obstetrician and gynaecologist; consIt London Hosp 1958-82, King George Hosp Ilford 1958-73, ret 1986; hon consIt surgn London Hosp; FRCS, FRCOG; *Recreations* arts, theatre, opera, cricket; *Clubs* Garrick, MCC; *Style—* Dr Leonard Easton; 612 Gilbert House, Barbican, London EC2Y 8BD (☎ 071 638 0781)

EASTON, Sir Robert William Simpson; CBE; *Career* chm and md Yarrow Shipbuilders; kt 1990; *Style—* Sir Robert Easton, CBE

EASTON, Timothy Nigel Dendy; s of Dendy Bryan Easton, of Tadworth, Surrey, and Iris Joan Easton; *b* 26 Aug 1943; *Educ* Mowden Sch, Christ Coll Brecon, Kingston Coll of Art, Scholarship Heatherley Sch of Art London; *m* 5 April 1967, Christine Margaret, da of Flt Lt James William Darling (d 1984); 2 da (Lucy Kathryn Rebecca b 1969, Isabella b 1971); *Career* artist/sculptor; works incl: mural Church of the Good Shepherd Tadworth 1969-71, mural Theological Coll Salisbury 1967-73, (drawings for Salisbury mural exhibited Chicago and Kansas USA 1968); first London exhibition Young Artists Upper Grosvenor Gallery 1970, began exhibiting sculptures in bronze 1971; various exhibitions of paintings and sculptures since 1970 in: England Germany, Luxembourg, America; Chris Beetles Gallery London 1990; portraits incl: Dr Glyn Simon as Archbishop of Wales, Gen Sir Geoffrey Musson; cmmn for Surgeons of Queen Victoria Hosp E Grinstead 1989; Elizabeth Greensfields Meml Fndn Award Montreal Canada 1973; sec Debenham Local Hist Gp, lectr Cambridge Extra Mural Bd; *Books* An Historical Atlas of Suffolk (contributor, 1988); *Recreations* vernacular architecture in Suffolk; *Style—* Timothy Easton, Esq; Bedfield Hall, Bedfield, Woodbridge, Suffolk IP13 7JJ (☎ 0728 76 380)

EASTWOOD, (Noel) Anthony Michael; s of Edward Norman Eastwood (d 1984), of Headingley, Yorks, and Irene, *née* Dawson (d 1979); *b* 7 Dec 1932; *Educ* The Leys Sch Cambridge, Christ's Coll Cambridge (MA); *m* 1965, Elizabeth Tania Gresham, da of Cdr Thomas Wilson Boyd, CBE, DSO, DL (d 1987); 3 s (Rupert b 1967, James b 1969, Alexander b 1972); *Career* Lt RA 1951-54, Pilot Offr RAFVR 1954-56; De Havilland Aircraft Co 1956-60, RTZ Group 1960-61, AEI Group 1961-64; dir: Charterhouse Japhet Ltd 1964-79, Daniel Doncaster & Sons Ltd 1971-81, The Barden Corporation 1971-81, SWB Fishing Ltd (Falklands) 1980-, Falcon Publishing (Bahrain) 1981-84, Caribbean Publishing Co 1981-84, Hawk Publishing Co (UAE) 1981-86, IDP Interdata (Aust) 1984-, Ergo Communication Services Ltd 1987-, Spearhead Communications Ltd 1988-, European Public Policy Advisers Group SA 1989, Witte-Boyd Holdings Ltd 1990- Community Trade Advsrs (SA) 1989; chm Interdata Group 1981-, pres Charterhouse Japhet Texas Inc 1974-77; memb London Ctee Yorkshire and Humberside Devpt Assoc 1975-, sec Royal Aeronautical Soc 1982-83; *Recreations* skiing, sailing (Daydream), travel, family; *Clubs* Royal Thames Yacht; *Style—* Anthony Eastwood, Esq; Palace House, Much Hadham, Herts SG10 6HW (☎ 0279 842409)

EASTWOOD, (John) Hugo; s of John Francis Eastwood, OBE, KC (d 1952), of 5 Sloane Ct East, London SW3, and Dorothea Constance Cecil, *née* Butler (d 1961); *b* 10 Dec 1935; *Educ* Eton; *m* 1, 15 Dec 1956 (m dis 1965), Susan Elizabeth, da of Cdr Peter Harry Cator (d 1979), of St Mary's Happisburgh, Norwich; 2 s (John Fabian b 20 Jan 1958, (Thomas) Edmund b 4 Dec 1960); m 2, 8 Feb 1966, Davina Naldera, da of Maj Edward Dudley Metcalfe, MVO, MC (d 1957), of London; 1 s (Philip Hugo b 17 Sept 1966), 1 da (Emma Alexandra b 12 Feb 1969); *Career* memb London Stock Exchange 1963-69, farmer 1970-; dir: Anglers Co-op Assoc Tstee Co, John Eastwood Water Protection Tst; memb cncl Anglers Co-op Assoc; *Recreations* fishing, shooting, growing rhododendrons; *Clubs* Brooks's, Fly Fishers; *Style—* Hugo Eastwood, Esq; The Pheasantry, Bramshill Park, Bramshill, Hants RG27 0JN (☎ 025 126 2343); 4 Lydon Rd, Clapham Old Town, London SW4

EASTWOOD, (William) James Michael; s of William Walter Rashleigh Eastwood (d 1941), and Mabel Caroline, *née* Ellershaw (d 1959); *b* 13 June 1917; *Educ* Wellington; *m* 8 May 1954, (Katherine) Gillian, da of C Maurice Champness (d 1960), of Orchardleigh, Purley; 3 da (Diana (Mrs Kenchington), Miranda (Mrs Hilton), Annie (Mrs Dixon)); *Career* KRRC 1940-46; serv: India, Burma, China; with Dunlop Rubber Co 1935-39 and 1946, Beecham Group 1953-58, C Shippam Ltd 1959-80; dir James Eastwood & Assocs 1980- (consIts in food indust Europe to Australasia), Veeraswamy's Food Products 1988-; chm: Chichester Branch Euro Movement 1983-88, Food Mfrs Export Ctee 1969-73, Aust and NZ Trade Advsy Ctee 1969-89; Liveryman Worshipful Co of Merchant Taylors 1946; *Recreations* cricket, gardening, travel; *Clubs* MCC, RAC, Aust; *Style—* James Eastwood, Esq, MBE; office: Little Mandage, Funtington, Chichester, West Sussex (☎ 0234 575 409, fax 0234 786 930, telex 86402 FOR J)

EASTWOOD, Sir John Bealby; DL (Notts 1981); s of William Eastwood and Elizabeth Townroe, *née* Bealby; *b* 9 Jan 1909; *Educ* Queen Elizabeth's GS Mansfield; *m* 1, 1929, Constance Mary Tilley (d 1981); 2 da; m 2, 1983, Mrs Joan Mary McGowan, *née* Hayward (d 1986); *Career* chm Adam Eastwood & Sons (builders) 1946-; OStJ; kt 1985; *Style—* Sir John Eastwood, DL; Adam Eastwood & Sons, Burns Lane, Warsop, Mansfield, Notts

EASTWOOD, (Anne) Mairi; *née* Waddington; da of John Waddington (d 1979), and Helen Cowan, *née* MacPherson; *b* 11 July 1951; *Educ* St Leonards Sch, Imperial Coll Univ of London (BSc); *m* 10 Aug 1974 (m dis 1987), James William Eastwood, s of late Donald Smith Eastwood; 1 s (Donald James b 1983), 1 da (Joanna b 1980); *Career* Arthur Young: chartered accountant 1976, ptnr in charge computer servs consultancy 1985-87, recruitment ptnr 1985-87, nat staff ptnr 1988-89; chief exec Eastwood Consulting Ltd 1989-; memb Alumni Bd Imperial College; FCA 1981; *Clubs* Reform, IOD, Lansdowne; *Style—* Mrs Mairi Eastwood; Appledore Cottage, 4 Brewers Court, Winsmore Lane, Abingdon, Oxon OX14 5BG; Eastwood Consulting Ltd, 22-25 Sackville St, London W1X 1DE (☎ 071 287 3670)

EASTWOOD, (John) Stephen; s of Rev John Edgar Eastwood (d 1972), of Over Wallop, Hants, and Elfreda, *née* Behrendt (d 1962); *b* 27 April 1925; *Educ* Denstone Coll Staffs, Open Univ (BA); *m* 11 June 1949, Nancy, da of Samuel Charles Gretton (d 1988), of Felpham, Sussex; 1 s (David b 1955), 2 da (Elizabeth (Mrs Chamberlain) b 1954, Gillian (Mrs Wright) b 1957); *Career* WWII coder RN 1943-46; admitted slr 1949, asst slr Salop CC 1950-53 (Leics CC 1949-50), sr asst slr Northants CC 1953-58, ptnr Wilson and Wilson Kettering 1958-76; chm Industl Tbnls 1976-82, regnl chm Industl Tbnls Nottingham 1982-; asst rec 1981-87, rec 1987-; pres: Northants Law Soc 1986-87, Kettering Rotary Club 1973-74 (memb 1963-77), Kettering Huxloe Rotary Club 1983-84 (memb 1983-); chm: Kettering Round Table 1963-64 (memb 1961-66), Abbeyfield (Kettering) Soc 1974-; memb Law Soc; *Recreations* painting, reading, music, walking, gardening; *Style—* Stephen Eastwood, Esq; 20 Gipsy Lane, Kettering, Northants NN16 8TY (☎ 0536 85612); Regional Office of the Industrial Tribunals, Birkbeck House, Trinity Sq, Nottingham (☎ 0602 475701)

EASTWOOD, Dr Wilfred; s of Wilfred Andrew Eastwood (d 1977), and Annice Gertrude, *née* Hartley (d 1985); *b* 15 Aug 1923; *Educ* Hemsworth GS, Sheffield Univ (BEng), Aberdeen Univ (PhD); *m* 1947, Dorothy Jean, da of Charles St George Gover, of 40 Grange Court, Totley, Sheffield; 1 s (Richard), 1 da (Janet); *Career* conslt engr; sr ptnr Eastwood and Ptnrs 1972-; prof of civil engrg Univ of Sheffield 1964-70, pres IStructE 1976-77; chm: Cncl of Engrg Insts 1983-84, Cwlth Engrg Cncl 1983-85; Hon DEng (Sheffield) 1984; FEng; *Recreations* watching cricket from third man and gardening; *Clubs* Yorks CC; *Style*— Dr Wilfred Eastwood; 45 Whirlow Park Rd, Sheffield S11 9NN (☎ 0742 364645); office: St Andrew's House, 23 Kingfield Rd, Sheffield S11 9AS (☎ 0742 554554, fax 554330)

EASTWOOD, William Harry; s of Harry Eastwood (d 1950), and Hilda Eastwood (d 1987); *b* 15 March 1946; *Educ* Worksop Coll, St Catherine's Coll Oxford (MA), Technische Hochschule Aachen, INSEAD Fontainebleau (MBA); *m* 28 Aug 1970, Angela, *née* Nieme; 1 s (Thomas Harry b 5 June 1975), 1 da Natasha Hildegarde b 1 Aug 1978); *Career* md: JB Eastwood Ltd 1970-79, Eastwood Heating Developments Ltd 1979-82, Eastwood Anglo-European Investment plc 1983-; chm: Continuous Stationary plc 1986-, Tyzack plc 1987-89, Eurovein Ltd 1989-; *Recreations* hunting (hon sec Grove & Rufford), skiing; *Clubs* Farmers'; *Style*— William Eastwood, Esq; The Old Kennels, Rufford, Newark, Notts NG22 9DF (☎ 0623 822826); Green Lane Works, Green Lane, Sheffield S3 8ST (☎ 0742 720030, fax 0742 726368)

EASTY, Prof David; s of Arthur Victor Easty, and Florence Margaret Easty; *b* 6 Aug 1933; *Educ* King's Sch Canterbury, Univ of Manchester (MD); *m* 14 Jan 1963, Božana, da of Milan Martinović (d 1968); 3 da (Valerie, Marina, Julia); *Career* Capt RAMC 1959-62; Moorfields Eye Hosp City Rd London 1966-72; memb: BMA, Int Soc for Eye Res; FRSM, FRCS, FCOpth; *Books* Virus Diseases of The Eye (1984), External Eye Disease (ed, 1985), Immediate Eye Care (1990), Current Opthalmic Surgery (1990); *Recreations* squash, jogging, fishing; *Clubs* Army & Navy; *Style*— Prof David Easty; 42 Clifton Park Rd, Clifton, Bristol BS8 3HN; Department of Ophthalmology, Bristol University, Bristol Eye Hospital, Lower Maudlin St, Bristol BS1 2LX (☎ 0272 230060, fax 0272 251141)

EATOCK TAYLOR, Prof (William) Rodney; s of William Taylor, of Hadley Wood, Herts, and Norah O'Brien, *née* Ridgeway; *b* 10 Jan 1944; *Educ* Rugby, King's Coll Cambridge (BA, MA), Stanford Univ California (MS, PhD); *m* 16 Jan 1971, Jacqueline Lorraine Cannon, da of Desmond Cannon Brookes (d 1981); 2 s (Thomas b 1973, Henry b 1976); *Career* engr; Ove Arup and Partners 1968-70; UCL 1970-89: assoc res asst 1970-72, lectr 1972-80, reader 1980-84, prof of ocean engrg 1984-89, dean of engrg 1988-89; prof of mechanical engrg Univ of Oxford 1989-; author of numerous articles in jls; fell St Hugh's Coll Oxford 1989-; FRINA 1986 (MRINA 1979), FIMechE 1989, FEng 1990; *Recreations* music; *Clubs* Athenaeum; *Style*— Prof Rodney Eatock Taylor; University of Oxford, Department of Engineering Science, Parks Rd, Oxford OX1 3PJ (☎ 0865 273144, fax 0865 273010, telex 83295 NUCLO

EATON, Arthur Raymond; s of Arthur Albert Eaton (d 1954), of Teddington, Middlesex, and Enid Bell (d 1973); *b* 13 March 1930; *Educ* Maiden Earleigh Berkshire, Ardingly Coll Haywards Heath Sussex; *m* 2, 2 Nov 1973, Pamela Winifred, da of Richard Weston (d 1982), of The Bear, Stock, Essex; 2 s (Nicholas b 1958, Andrew b 1964), 2 da (Caron b 1956, Jacqueline b 1957), 1 step da (Tracy b 1964); *Career* Nat Serv RHG, Festival of Br Staff Admin 1950-51; Ardath Tobacco Co 1951-68, licensee 1968; *Recreations* rowing, horse riding, music, theatre; *Style*— Arthur Eaton, Esq; 19 Swann Grove, Holt, Norfolk NR25 6DP

EATON, Charles Le Gai; s of Charles Eaton (d 1921), and Ruth Frances Eaton, *née* Muddock (d 1973); *b* 1 Jan 1921; *Educ* Charterhouse, King's Coll Cambridge (MA); *m* 1, 1944, Katharine Mary, *née* Clayton; 1 s (Leo Francis b 1945); m 2, 1956, Corah Keturah, *née* Hamilton; 1 s (Maurice Le Gai b 1959), 2 da (Judith Layla Ruth b 1957, Corah Ann b 1961); *Career* journalist and lectr in West Indies and Egypt 1945-54; COI 1955-59; dir UK Info Servs: Jamaica 1959-64, Madras 1964-66; grade 6 offr FCO 1967-69, first sec (Info) Br High Cmmn Trinidad 1969-73, Cwlth Coordination Dept 1973-76, ret 1977; conslt Islamic Cultural Centre London 1978-; author, broadcaster and lectr; *Books* The Richest Vein: Eastern Religions and Modern Thought (1950), King of the Castle: Choice and Responsibility in the Modern World (1977, reprinted 1990), Islam and the Destiny of Man (1985, German and French translations); *Recreations* photography, gardening; *Clubs* The Travellers; *Style*— Gai Eaton, Esq; 35 Riddlesdown Rd, Purley, Surrey CR8 1DJ (☎ 081 660 1252); Islamic Cultural Centre, Park Road NW8 7RG (☎ 071 724 3363)

EATON, Donald Stuart; s of Arthur Edward Eaton (d 1930), of Heaton Chapel, Cheshire, and Lillie, *née* Lord (d 1974); *b* 30 March 1923; *Educ* King Edward VII Sch Lytham Lancs; *m* 23 April 1949, Margaret Hibbert, da of Harold Slater (d 1937), of Lytham St Annes, Lancs; 1 s (David b 1959), 2 da (Hazel b 1953, Rachel b 1956); *Career* Civil Def 1940-42; dep accountant Rank Orgn 1945-47, asst gen mangr Metro Goldwyn Mayer 1947-51; gp fin dir: Caxton Publishing Group plc 1951-61, Pratt Standard Range plc 1961-66; fndr and sr ptnr Eaton & Partners CAs 1945-81, ret; memb: Ctee Assoc of Lancastrians in London 1961-81 (chm 1976), Freedom Assoc (chm Middx 1971-81); parental govr Richmond upon Thames Coll 1978-79; Freeman: City of London 1971, Worshipful Co of Plumbers 1971, Worshipful Co of Chartered Acountants 1978; FCA 1945 (prizewinner), FTII 1945, MBIM 1967, FFB 1975; *Recreations* cricket, filming and video, photography, sailing; *Clubs* City Livery, United Wards; *Style*— Donald S Eaton, Esq

EATON, Guy Ashley; s of Paul Eaton, of Maidenhead, Berks, and Elizabeth Ann Eaton (d 1971); *b* 27 April 1951; *Educ* Oundle Sch, Univ of Bristol; *m* 21 Sept 1983, Ulker, da of Tarik Sagban, of Bursa, Turkey; 1 da (Natalia b 1987); *Career* CA; banker; FICA; *Recreations* music, photography; *Clubs* RAC; *Style*— Guy A Eaton, Esq; 30 Bracewell Rd, London W10; Richard House, 30/32 Mortimer St, London W1

EATON, Peter; *b* 24 Jan 1914; *Educ* Manchester; *m* 1, Ann Wilkinson; m 2, Valerie Carruthers; 2 s (Russell, Rupert); m 3, 1952, Margaret, da of Henry Gordon Taylor (d 1980); 2 da (Ruth, Diana); *Career* antiquarian bookseller, fndr and dir Peter Eaton (Booksellers) Ltd; artist; publisher and author of: A History of Lilies, Marie Stopes, A Preliminary Checklist of her Writings; Peter Eaton Library on Robert Owen & Co-op Movement, named after him now in Japanese Univ; pres Private Library Assoc; *Recreations* collecting works of pre-raphaelites, reading, music; *Clubs* Reform; *Style*— Peter Eaton, Esq; Lilies, Weedon, Aylesbury, Bucks HP22 4NS (☎ 0296 641393)

EATON, Philip Bromley; s of Percy Eaton, of N Wales, and Ethel Mary, *née* Swindell; *b* 3 June 1925; *Educ* Sir John Talbot's Sch, Univ of Liverpool Sch of Architecture (BArch); *m* 3 April 1953, Joan, da of William Frederick Welch, MBE; 1 s (Mark b 1956); *Career* Capt KSLI served: Egypt, Palestine, Cyprus; fndr Eaton Manning Wilson architectural practice 1961; chm Shrops Soc of Architects 1986-88, hon pres Ludlow Constituency Liberal Democrats 1982; ARIBA; *Recreations* travelling, gardening, music and the arts; *Style*— Philip B Eaton, Esq; Scotsmansfield, Burway, Church Stretton, Shrops; 6 High St, Shrewsbury (☎ 0743 67744)

EATON, Stuart John; JP (West Bromwich 1972); s of Leslie Yates Eaton (d 1970), and Beatrice Nancy, *née* Jevon (d 1983); *b* 26 Nov 1927; *Educ* Dudley GS, Dudley Tech Coll; *m* 29 May 1950, Doreen May, da of Horace Enoch Dickens (d 1969); 2 s (Robert, Christopher); *Career* writer RN 1945-47 served: Aust, Colombo, Hong Kong; Tipton & Coseley Building Society: clerk and cashier 1941, chief clerk and cashier 1950, chief exec 1958-87, dir 1981-87, non-exec dir 1987-; pres: Tipton Harriers, Tipton Scout Cncl; treas and tstee Tipton Med Tst; memb: Ctee Tipton Cons and Unionist Club, Tipton Rotary Club (former pres), Fellowship Ltd Dudley Castle Mess (past chm); MBIM 1971, FBIM 1980; *Recreations* walking, jogging, choral singing; *Clubs* Tipton Cons; *Style*— Stuart Eaton, Esq, JP; 215 Northway, Sedgley, Dudley DY3 3RG (☎ 09073 3046)

EATON, Capt Thomas Christopher; OBE (1962), TD (1946), DL (1971); s of Frederic Ray Eaton (d 1962), of Norwich; *b* 13 Oct 1918; *Educ* Stowe; *m* 1958, Robin Elizabeth, da of Alexander Berry Austin (Ka 1943); 1 s, 2 da; *Career* Nat Serv 4 Bn Royal Norfolk Regt (TA) 1936-50, served WWII (wounded, despatches, POW Singapore 1942-45); admitted slr and NP 1947; memb Norwich City Cncl 1949-74 (ldr 1969-70), Lord Mayor of Norwich 1957-58, Parly candidate (Cons) Norwich N 1951 and 1955; tstee E Anglian Tstee Savings Bank 1957-80; govr Theatre Royal (Norwich) Tst Ltd 1972-85, chm Meml Tst 2 Air Div USAAF 1975-; *Recreations* theatre and travel; *Clubs* Norfolk; *Style*— Capt Thomas Eaton, OBE, TD, DL; 3 Albemarle Rd, Norwich, Norfolk NR2 2DF (☎ 0603 53962)

EATON, (Robert) William; s of Robert James Eaton of Algarve, Portugal, and Anne Margaret, *née* Poole; *b* 6 Nov 1953; *Educ* Tettenhall Coll Wolverhampton, Wolverhampton Poly (LLB); *m* 21 June 1978, Elaine Dianne, da of Lawrence Raymond Oliver (d 1979); 1 da (Caroline b 1988); *Career* dir Robert Eaton Ltd Hotel and Garage Pty 1971-75, law student and articled clerk 1975-81; asst then ptnr: Manby & Stewart Wolverhampton 1981-87, asst then ptnr Bond Pearce Plymouth 1988-89; memb: Port of Plymouth Jr C of C, Law Soc; *Recreations* football, cycling, sailing, building model railways; *Clubs* Plymouth Royal Corinthian Yacht; *Style*— William Eaton, Esq; 17 Thornhill Rd, Mannamead, Plymouth, Devon PL3 5NF (☎ 0752 674227); Bond Pearce Solicitors, 1 The Crescent, Plymouth PL1 3AE (☎ 0752 266633, fax 0752 225350, telex 45404)

EATS, Richard John Drake; s of Thomas John Drake Eats (d 1978), of Effingham, Surrey, and Alma, *née* Holdham; *b* 11 Sept 1945; *Educ* Dulwich, Emmanuel Coll Cambridge (MA), Cranfield Sch of Mgmnt (MBA); *m* 1980, Hilary Martelli, da of Eric Vernon Dawson; 2 s (Thomas Martin Drake b 1981, Matthew James Drake b 1986); *Career* inspr of taxes Inland Revenue 1968-69, Save & Prosper Ltd 1969-71, Britannia Group 1971-74, mktg dir Chieftain Trust Managers 1976-84, md GT Unit Managers 1989- (mktg dir 1984-89); memb Exec Ctee Unit Tst Assoc 1990; *Recreations* golf, child rearing; *Clubs* Roehampton; *Style*— Richard Eats, Esq; 2 Muncaster Rd, London SW11 6NT (☎ 071 228 9009); Gt Unit Managers Ltd, 8 Devonshire Square, London EC2M 4YJ (☎ 071 283 2575, fax 071 626 6176)

EATWELL, Dr John Leonard; s of Harold Jack Eatwell, of Swindon, Wilts, and Mary, *née* Tucker (d 1987); *b* 2 Feb 1945; *Educ* Headlands GS Swindon, Queens' Coll Cambridge (BA, MA), Harvard Univ (AM, PhD); *m* 24 April 1970, Hélène, da of Georges Seppain, of Marly-le-Roi, France; 2 s (Nikolai b 1971, Vladimir b 1973), 1 da (Tatyana b 1978); *Career* teaching fell Harvard Univ 1968-69; Univ of Cambridge: res fell Queens' Coll 1969-70, fell and dir of studies in econs Trinity Coll 1970-, univ lectr in econs 1977- (asst lectr 1975-77); visiting prof of econs New School for Social Research NY 1980-; econ advsr to Rt Hon Neil Kinnock MP 1985-; memb: Cambridge Constituency Lab Pty, Royal Econ Soc, American Econ Asoc; *Books* An Introduction to Modern Economics (with Joan Robinson, 1973), Keynes's Economics and the Theory of Value and Distribution (with Murray Milgate, 1983), Whatever Happened to Britain? (1982), The New Palgrave Dictionary of Economics (with Murray Milgate and Peter Newman, 1987); *Recreations* watching ballet, modern dance and rugby football; *Style*— Dr John Eatwell; Trinity College, Cambridge CB2 1TQ (☎ 0223 338406)

EBAN, Hon Mrs (Rosemary); *née* Inman; da of 1 and last Baron Inman, PC (d 1979); *b* 26 Feb 1933; *m* 1, 19 Feb 1955 (m dis), Nicholas Milton Kollitsis, MD, FRCS, s of Miltiades Kollitsis, of Kythrea, Cyprus; 1 s, 2 da; m 2, 1982, Dr Raphael Eban, FRCP, FRCR; *Style*— Hon Mrs Eban; Parsonage House, Goosey, Oxon SN7 8PA

EBBISHAM, 2 Baron (UK 1928); Sir Rowland Roberts Blades; 2 Bt (UK 1922), TD; s of 1 Baron Ebbisham, GBE (d 1953, sometime MP (C) Epsom, treasurer Conservative Party and Lord Mayor of London), and Margaret, MBE, OStJ, Officier de la Légion d'Honneur(d 1965), da of Arthur Reiner, of Sutton, Surrey; *b* 3 Sept 1912; *Educ* Winchester, Ch Ch Oxford; *m* 26 Oct 1949, Flavia Mary, yst da of Charles Francis Meade, JP (d 1975) (gs of 3 Earl of Clanwilliam), and Lady Aileen (d 1970), *née* Brodrick, da of 1 Earl of Midleton; 3 da; *Career* served WWII, Lt 98 Surrey & Sussex Yeo Field Regt RA, POW; common councilman City of London Candlewick Ward 1948-83, pres London C of C 1958-61, pres Assoc of Br Chambers of Commerce 1968-70, Master Mercers' Co 1963-64, one of HM Lieuts for City of London, chm City Lands Ctee and chief commoner Corpn of London 1967-68; pres Br Importers' Confedn 1978-80, chm Anglo-Dal plc, dir Williams Lea plc, vice pres London Record Soc, memb Euro Trade Ctee BOTB 1973-82; hon treas Br Printing Industs Fedn 1971-81; former Capt Surrey Second Eleven (cricket); Hon DSc The City Univ 1984; Order of Yugoslav Flag with Gold Wreath, Cdr Order of Orange Nassau; *Style*— The Rt Hon Lord Ebbisham, TD; St Ann's, Church Street, Mere, Wilts BA12 6DS (☎ 0747 860376)

EBBRELL, John; s of Keith Ebbrell, of 7 Gorsefield Avenue, and Rosalind, *née* Cain; *b* 1 Oct 1969; *Educ* Wirral GS; *Career* professional footballer; selected for FA Nat Sch of Excellence Lilleshall; Everton 1986-: apprentice then professional, debut 1988, over 50 appearances; England caps: under 15, under 16, under 18, under 19, under 21; *Style*— John Ebbrell, Esq; Everton FC, Goodison Park, Liverpool L4 4EL (☎ 051 521 2020)

EBDON, Howard Tom; s of Tom Ebdon (d 1931), and Ellen Ebdon (d 1961); *b* 1 June 1919; *m* 22 Oct 1961, Grace, da of William Thomas Bond (d 1951), of Monmouthshire; *Career* with Miny of Agric, surveyor, lectr in valuations and law of dilapidations; memb Nat Art Collection Fund; assoc of Croquet Assoc of London, sidesman St Woolos Cathedral Newport Gwent, friend of RA; *Recreations* arts; *Clubs* Royal Overseas, St James London; *Style*— Howard T Ebdon, Esq; Harlyn, 56 Bryngwyn Rd, Newport, Gwent NP9 4JT

EBDON, Thomas John; s of Thomas Dudley Ebdon, and Hilda Minnie, *née* Hayward, both of Rustington, W Sussex; *b* 3 April 1940; *Educ* Wallington GS, Brixton Sch of Bldg (HND); *m* 27 March 1965, Janet Wendy, da of Herbert Noel Cobley (d 1982); 1 s (Robert John b 1965), 1 da (Elizabeth Wendy b 1967); *Career* dep md James Longley and Co Ltd 1987- (joined 1963, dir 1972), dir James Longley Holdings Ltd 1989-, dir Heating & Ventilation Southern Ltd 1974, chm Pennthorpe Sch Tst Ltd 1979-89, fndr memb St Catherine's Hospice Crawley 1979 (chm 1989-), churchwarden Horsham (Diocese of Chichester) 1974-79; Freeman: City of London 1980, Worshipful Co of Paviors 1982; *Recreations* cricket, photography, philately, walking; *Clubs* MCC; *Style*— John Ebdon, Esq; James Longley & Co Ltd, East Park, Crawley, West Sussex RH10 6AP (☎ 0293 561212, fax 0293 564564)

EBERLE, Adm Sir James Henry Fuller; GCB (1981, KCB 1979); s of Victor Fuller Eberle (d 1974), of Bristol, and Joyce Mary Eberle; *b* 31 May 1927; *Educ* Clifton, RNC Dartmouth; *m* 1950, Ann Patricia (d 1988), da of E Thompson, of Hong Kong; 1 s, 2 da; *Career* RN 1941-83; served WWII, Capt 1965, Rear-Adm 1971, asst chief Fleet Support 1972-74; flag offr: Sea Training 1974-75, Aircraft Carriers and Amphibious Ships 1975-77; chief of Fleet Support 1977-79, C-in-C Fleet and Allied C-in-C Channel and E Atlantic 1979-81, C-in-C Naval Home Cmd 1981-82, Flag ADC to HM The Queen 1981-82; dir Royal Inst of Int Affrs 1983-90; Hon LLD Univ of Bristol

1989; *Clubs* Farmers'; *Style*— Adm Sir James Eberle, GCB

EBERLIN, Richard Harold; JP (1970); s of Capt Albert Edgar Eberlin, MC (d 1977), and Edith Annie Eberlin (d 1965); *b* 15 Aug 1926; *Educ* Sedbergh, Univ of Nottingham (Dip Arch); *m* 10 May 1952, Christine Russell, da of Dr Edward Russell Trotman (d 1984), of Nottingham; 4 s (David Richard, Jonathan Russell, (decd) Michael Anthony, Andrew William); *Career* RAF WWII; princ ptnr Eberlin and Ptnrs; flag offr Trent Valley Sailing Club 1963-65, memb Nottingham Derby and Lincoln Soc of Architects (pres 1967), fndr Royal Yachting Assoc E Mids regn (chm 1968); memb: Water Recreation Ctee of the E Midlands Sports Cncl (vice chm 1969), Royal Yachting Assoc Cncl 1971-78 Nottingham Derby and Lincoln Jt Consultative Bd Craftsmanship Award Panel 1972-, Magistrates Cts Ctee 1979, Police Ctee 1983; chm: Nat Facilities Ctee Royal Yachting Assoc for England and Wales, Bramcote Conservation Soc; pres Nottingham City Business Club 1972; Freeman City of London; ARIBA 1956, FRIBA 1964; *Recreations* sailing, bowls; *Clubs* Naval and Military, Nottingham and Notts United Servs, Trent Valley Sailing, ICC Salcombe Yacht, Queen Anne's Bowling; *Style*— Richard Eberlin, Esq, JP; The Orchard, Moss Drive, Bramcote, Notts NG9 3HH (☎ 0602 258325)

EBERSTEIN, (Robert) David; s of Douglas Eberstein, of Drill Hall Cottage, Southwold; *b* 12 Feb 1941; *Educ* Wellington; *m* 1968, Rosemary Margaret, da of Charles Capper Hemming, of Great Chesterford; 1 s, 2 da; *Career* fin dir Smith Kline & French Laboratories Ltd 1973-, vice pres Smith Kline & French Int Co 1980- (regnl dir 1979); FCA; *Style*— David Eberstein Esq; Smith Kline & French International Co, Mundells, Welwyn Garden City, Herts (☎ 0707 325111); Hyde House, Firs Drive, Gustardwood, Herts (☎ 0438 832909)

EBERT, Peter; s of Prof Carl Ebert, CBE (d 1980), of Calif, USA, and Lucie Oppenheim; *b* 6 April 1918; *Educ* Salem Sch Germany, Gordonstoun; *m* 1, 1944, Kathleen Havinden; 2 da; m 2, 1951, Silvia Ashmole; 5 s, 3 da; *Career* theatre dir; dir of productions Scottish Opera 1964-76, Opera Sch Toronto Univ 1967-68; intendant: theatres in Augsburg 1968-73, Bielefeld 1973-75, Wiesbaden 1975-77; gen admin Scottish Opera 1977-80; Hon Doctor of Music St Andrew's Univ 1979; *Style*— Peter Ebert, Esq; Col di Mura, Lippiano, 06010 (PG), Italy

EBERTS, John David (Jake); s of Edmond Howard Eberts (d 1977), and Elizabeth Evelyn, *née* MacDougall; *b* 10 July 1941; *Educ* Bishops Coll Sch Quebec, McGill Univ (BChemE), Harvard Business Sch; *m* 1968, Fiona Louise, da of John Baillie Hamilton Leckie (d 1978); 2 s (Alexander b 1973, David b 1975), 1 da (Lindsay b 1979); *Career* investmt banker and md Oppenheimer & Co Ltd 1972-76, fndr Goldcrest Films Ltd 1976-83, Embassy Communications Ltd 1984-85, Goldcrest Films and TV Ltd 1985-87, Allied Filmmakers 1985-; *Recreations* tennis, ski-ing, photography; *Clubs* Queens; *Style*— Jake Eberts, Esq; Katevale Productions Ltd, 3A Walmer Courtyard, 225/227 Walmer Road, London W11 4EY (☎ 071 229 9173, fax 071 229 9798)

EBRAHIM, Sir (Mahomed) Currimbhoy; 4 Bt (UK 1910), of Bombay; s of Sir (Huseinali) Currimbhoy Ebrahim, 3 Bt (d 1952); *b* 24 June 1935; *m* 15 Nov 1958, Dur-e-Mariam, da of Minuchehir Ahmud Nurudin Ahmed Ghulam Ally Nana, of Karachi; 3 s, 1 da; *Heir* s, Zulfiqar Ali Currimbhoy Ebrahim; *Career* memb Standing Council of Baronetage; *Style*— Sir Currimbhoy Ebrahim, Bt; Baitullah 33, Bait-ul-Amen Mirza Kalig Beg Rd, Jamshed Quarters, Karachi

EBRAHIM, Zulfiqar Ali Currimbhoy; eldest s and h of Sir Currimbhoy Ebrahim, 4 Bt; *b* 5 Aug 1960; *Educ* Habib Public Sch, DJ Science Coll; *m* 1984, Adila, da of Akhtar Halipota; 1 s (Mustafa b 22 Sept 1985); *Career* aeronautical engr 1982-; *Recreations* swimming, athletics; *Style*— Zulfiqar Ali Currimbhoy Ebrahim, Esq; Baitullah 33, Bait-ul-Amen Mirza Kalig Beg Rd, Jamshed Quarters, Karachi

EBRINGTON, Viscount; Charles Hugh Richard Fortescue; s (by 1 m) and h of 7 Earl Fortescue; *b* 10 May 1951; *Educ* Eton; *m* 1974, Julia, er da of Air Cdre J A Sowrey; 3 da (Hon Alice Penelope b 8 June 1978, Hon Kate Eleanor b 25 Oct 1979, Hon Lucy Beatrice b 29 April 1983); *Style*— Viscount Ebrington; Ebrington Manor, Chipping Campden, Glos

EBSWORTH, Her Hon Judge; Ann Marian; da of Arthur Ebsworth, OBE, BEM, RM (ret), and late Hilda Mary Ebsworth; *b* 1937; *Educ* London Univ; *Career* called to the Bar Gray's Inn 1962, recorder Crown Court 1978-83, circuit judge (Northern Circuit) 1983-; *Style*— Her Hon Judge Ebsworth; 33 Warren Drive, Wallasey, Cheshire

EBSWORTH, Prof Evelyn Algernon Valentine; s of Brig Wilfred Algernon Ebsworth, CB, CBE, (d 1978) of Cambridge, and Cynthia, *née* Blech (d 1975); *b* 14 Feb 1933; *Educ* Marlborough, Univ of Cambridge (BA, MA, PhD, ScD); *m* 20 Aug 1955, Mary (d 1987), da of Frank Reyner Salter, OBE, (d (Jonathan b 1962), 3 da (Nicolette b 1958, Rachel b 1960, Lucy b 1964 d 1987); m 2 1990, Rose, *née* Stinson, wid of Prof J J Zuckerman; *Career* Univ of Cambridge: fell Kings Coll 1957-59, fell Christs Coll 1959-67, demonstrator 1959-64, lectr 1964-67, tutor Christs Coll 1964-67; Crum Brown prof of chem Univ of Edinburgh 1967-90, vice chllr and Warden Univ of Durham 1990-; author of numerous papers published in learned jls; former memb Scot Examinations Bd, corresponding memb Acad of Sciences Göttingen; FRSC, FRSE; *Books* Volatile Silicon Compounds (1963), Structural Methods in Inorganic Chemistry (jtly, 1988); *Recreations* opera, gardening; *Style*— Prof Evelyn Ebsworth, FRSE; Univ of Durham, Old Shire Hall, Durham DH1 3HP (☎ 091 374 2000)

EBURNE, Sir Sidney Alfred William; MC (1944); s of Alfred Edmund Eburne, and Ellen Francis Eburne; *b* 26 Nov 1918; *Educ* Downhills Sch; *m* 1942, Phoebe Freda, *née* Beeton Dilley; 1 s, 1 da; *Career* served WWII Capt RA; dir: Morgan Grenfell 1968-75 (joined 1946), Morgan Grenfell Holdings 1971-75, Abbey Capital Holdings Ltd; md Crown Agents 1976 (dir of finance 1975), sr crown agent and chm Crown Agents for Overseas Govts and Admins 1978-83; dir Peachey Property Corporation plc 1983-88; govr Peabody Tst 1983; kt 1982; *Clubs* Carlton; *Style*— Sir Sidney Eburne, MC; Motts Farm, Eridge, E Sussex TN3 9LJ

EBURY, Denise, Baroness; Hon Denise Margaret; *née* Yarde-Buller; 2 da of late 3 Baron Churston, MVO, OBE (d 1930); *b* 24 Oct 1916; *m* 21 Nov 1941 (m dis 1954), as his 2 w, 5 Baron Ebury (d 1957); 2 s (Hon William Grosvenor, Hon Richard Grosvenor), 2 da (Hon Mrs Cross, Hon Ms Vane Percy); *Style*— Denise, Lady Ebury; 10 Froxfield, Woburn Park, Eversholt, Milton Keynes MK17 9DP

EBURY, 6 Baron (UK 1857); Francis Egerton Grosvenor; s of 5 Baron Ebury, DSO (d 1957, whose ggf, 1 Baron, was yr bro of 2 Marquess of Westminster and 2 Earl of Wilton; thus Lord Ebury is hp to 7 Earl of Wilton and ultimately, since Lord Wilton is himself hp to all the 6 Duke of Westminster's titles except the Dukedom, might inherit those honours too), by his 1 w, Anne, da of Herbert Acland-Troyte, MC (gn of Sir Thomas Acland, 10 Bt); *b* 8 Feb 1934; *Educ* Eton; *m* 1, 10 Dec 1957 (m dis 1962), Gillian Elfrida Astley, o da of Martin Soames, and Myra Drummond, niece of 16 Earl of Perth; 1 s; m 2, 8 March 1963 (m dis 1973), Kyra, o da of L L Aslin; m 3, 1974, Suzanne, da of Graham Suckling, of NZ; 1 da (Hon Georgina Lucy b 1973); *Heir* s, Hon Julian Grosvenor; *Recreations* ornithology, horology, photography; *Clubs* Hong Kong, Melbourne, Melbourne Savage; *Style*— The Rt Hon Lord Ebury; 8B Branksome Tower, 3 Tregunter Path, Hong Kong

EBURY, Dowager Baroness; Sheila Winifred; *née* Dashfield; da of Arthur Edward Dashfield, of Oxford; *b* 28 April 1925; *m* 1, - Anker; m 2, 12 Oct 1954, as his 3 w, 5 Baron Ebury (d 1957); *Style*— The Rt Hon the Dowager Lady Ebury; 37 Linkside Ave, Oxford OX2 8JE

ECCLES, 1 Viscount (UK 1964); David McAdam Eccles; CH (1984), KCVO (1953), PC (1951); also 1 Baron Eccles (UK 1962); s of William McAdam Eccles, FRCS (d 1946), and Anna Coralie, *née* Anstie (d 1930); *b* 18 Sept 1904; *Educ* Winchester, New Coll Oxford; *m* 1, 10 Oct 1928, Hon Sybil Frances Dawson (d 1977), eldest da of 1 & last Viscount Dawson of Penn, GCVO, KCB, KCMG, PC (d 1945); 2 s, 1 da; m 2, 26 Sept 1984, Mary, widow of Donald Hyde, of Four Oaks Farm, Somerville, NJ, USA; *Heir* s, Hon John Dawson Eccles CBE; *Career* sits as Conservative in House of Lords; MP (C) Chippenham Wilts 1943-62, min of Works 1951-54, min of Education 1954-57, pres Bd of Trade 1957-59, min of Educn 1956-62, chm of Tstees Br Museum 1966-70; Paymaster Gen 1970-73, chm Br Library Bd 1973-78, pres World Crafts Cncl 1974-78; *Style*— The Rt Hon Viscount Eccles, CH, KCVO, PC; Dean Farm, Chute, nr Andover, Hants (☎ 026 470 210); 6 Barton Street, London SW1 (☎ 071 222 1387)

ECCLES, Jack Fleming; CBE (1980); s of Thomas Eccles (d 1962), of Manchester; *b* 9 Feb 1922; *Educ* Chorlton HS Manchester, Univ of Manchester (BA); *m* 24 May 1952, Hon Milba Hartley, *qv*; 1 s, 1 da; *Career* served Burma in ranks 1944-45; trade union official GMBATU 1948-86, chm and pres TUC 1984-85; dir Remploy Ltd 1976-90; memb Eng Industl Estates Corp 1976-, chm Plastics Processing Indust Trg Bd 1982-88, non-exec dir British Steel plc; *Recreations* cine-photography; *Style*— Jack Eccles, Esq, CBE; Terange, 11 Sutton Rd, Alderley Edge, Cheshire SK9 7RB

ECCLES, Prof Sir John Carew; s of William James Eccles, of Melbourne, and Mary Eccles; *b* 27 Jan 1903; *Educ* Melbourne Univ, Magdalen Coll Oxford; *m* 1, 1928 (m dis 1968), Irene Frances, da of Herbert Miller, of Motueka, NZ; 4 s, 5 da; m 2, 1968, Helena Táboříková; *Career* air Kanematsu Inst Sydney Hosp 1937-43, prof of physiology Otago Univ NZ 1944-51, prof of physiology ANU Canberra 1951-66, Chicago Res Inst 1966-68, prof of neurobiology State Univ Buffalo New York 1968-75, emeritus 1975-; Baly Medal RCP 1961, Royal Medal Royal Society 1962, Cothenius Medal Deutsche Akademie der Naturforscher Leopoldina 1963, Nobel Prize for Medicine (jtly) 1963, Order of Rising Sun with Gold and Silver Stars, AC 1990; FRS, FAA, FRACP; kt 1958; *Books* incl: Physiology of Nerve Cells (1957), Physiology of Synapses (1964), The Inhibitory Pathways of the Central Nervous System (1969), Facing Reality (1970), The Understanding of the Brain (1973), The Self and its Brain (jtly, 1977), The Human Mystery (1979), The Human Psyche (1980), The Wonder of Being Human (jtly, 1984), Evolution of the Brain: Creation of the Self (1989); *Style*— Prof Sir John Eccles, FRS; Ca' a la Gra', CH 6646 Contra (Locarno), Ticino, Switzerland (☎ 093 67 2931)

ECCLES, Hon John Dawson; CBE (1985); s and h of 1 Viscount Eccles, CH, KCVO, PC, and his 1 w Hon Sybil Frances Dawson (d 1977), da of 1 Viscount Dawson of Penn; *b* 20 April 1931; *Educ* Winchester, Magdalen Coll Oxford (BA); *m* 29 Jan 1955, Diana Catherine (Baroness Eccles of Moulton, *qv*), 2 da of Raymond Wilson Sturge, of Ashmore, nr Salisbury; 1 s, 3 da; *Career* Capt TA; Head Wrightson & Co Ltd 1955-77; dir: Glynwed Int plc 1972-, Investors in Industry plc 1974-88, Davy Int plc 1977-81; chm Chamberlin & Hill plc 1982-; memb Monopolies & Mergers Cmmn 1976-85 (dep chm 1981-85); memb Cwlth Devpt Corp 1982-85, (gen mangr 1985-;) chm: Bd of Tstees Royal Botanic Gdns Kew 1983-, The Georgian Theatre Royal Richmond Yorks; Hon DSc Silsoe Coll Cranfield Inst of Technology 1989; *Recreations* gardening, theatre; *Clubs* Brooks's; *Style*— The Hon John Eccles, CBE; Moulton Hall, Richmond, Yorks (☎ 0325 77 227); 6 Barton Street, London SW1P 3NG (☎ 071 222 7559)

ECCLES, Hon Mrs (Milba Hartley); da of Baron Williamson (Life Peer, d 1983), and Hilda, *née* Hartley (d 1988); *b* 19 June 1926; *m* 24 May 1952, Jack Fleming Eccles, CBE, *qv*; 1 s, 1 da; *Style*— The Hon Mrs Eccles; Terange, 11 Sutton Rd, Alderley Edge, Cheshire SK9 7RB

ECCLES, (Hugh William) Patrick; QC (1990); s of Gp Capt Hugh Haslett Eccles, of 16 York Mansions, Prince of Wales Drive, London, and Mary, *née* Cunnane; *b* 25 April 1946; *Educ* Stonyhurst, Exeter Coll Oxford (scholar, MA), Middle Temple London (Winston Churchill Pupillage prize); *m* 15 April 1972, (Rhoda) Ann, da of Patrick Brendon Moroney; 3 da (Katherine Ann b 15 July 1974, Clare b 18 Oct 1976, Fiona b 18 Oct 1980); *Career* called to the Bar Middle Temple 1968, head of Chambers 1985, rec of Crown Ct 1987; memb County Ct Rule Ctee 1987; memb Hon Soc of the Middle Temple 1964; *Recreations* tennis, wine & P G Wodehouse; *Style*— Patrick Eccles, Esq, QC; Grapevine Cottage, High Street, Long Wittenham, Nr Abingdon, Oxon OX14 4QQ (☎ 086730 7436); 2 Harcourt Buildings, Temple, London EC4Y 9DB (☎ 071 353 6961); Harcourt Chambers, Churchill House, St Aldates Courtyard, 38 St Aldates, Oxford OX1 1BN (☎ 0865 791559)

ECCLES, Brig Ronald; DSO (1972); s of Rowland Eccles (d 1976), and Penelope May Kerr Sinnatt, *née* Thom (d 1975); *b* 23 Aug 1928; *Educ* Barnard Castle Sch, RMA Sandhurst; *m* 25 July 1953, Glenys Mary Walker, da of Gareth Walton Budden (d 1959); 2 da (Sarah b 1955, Karen b 1957); *Career* York and Lancaster Regt 1948, seconded Parachute Regt 1952-54, cmd 1 Green Howards 1969-72, def advsr New Delhi 1980-82, Col York and Lancaster Regt 1979-87; Clerk to Worshipful Co of Fruiterers 1986-88; *Style*— Brig Ronald Eccles, DSO

ECCLES, Hon Simon Dawson; yr s of 1 Viscount Eccles; *b* 11 Sept 1934; *Educ* Repton; *m* 17 Oct 1961 (m dis 1986), Sheelin Lorraine; 1 s, 1 da; *Career* Capt Royal Fusiliers; *Recreations* tobogganing, music; *Style*— Hon Simon Eccles; 27 Chestnut Street, Boston, Massachusetts 02108, USA

ECCLES, Hon William David; o s of Hon John Dawson Eccles, CBE, and Baroness Eccles of Moulton (Life Peer), *qqv*; *b* 9 June 1960; *m* 1984, Claire Margaret Alison, da of Brian Seddon, of 77 Lawn Road, Hampstead, London NW3; 2 s (Peter David b 1987, Tom b 1988); *Style*— The Hon William Eccles

ECCLES OF MOULTON, Baroness (Life Peer UK 1990), of Moulton in the Co of N Yorks; Diana Catherine Eccles; 2 da of late Raymond Wilson Sturge, of Lords Mead, Ashmore, Salisbury, Wilts; *m* 29 Jan 1955, Hon John Dawson Eccles, CBE, er s and h of 1 Viscount Eccles, CH, KCVO, PC; 1 s (Hon William David b 1960), 3 da (Hon Alice Belinda (Hon Mrs Ward) b 1958, Hon Catherine Sara (Hon Mrs Gannon) b 1963, Emily Frances b 1970); *Career* chm Ealing Dist Health Authy; *Style*— The Rt Hon Lady Eccles of Moulton; Moulton Hall, Moulton, Richmond, N Yorks DL10 6QH; 6 Barton St, London SW1P 3NG

ECCLES-WILLIAMS, Hilary a'Beckett; CBE (1970); s of The Rev Cyril Archibald Eccles-Williams (d 1952), of Summer Fields, nr Oxford, and Hermione a'Beckett, *née* Terrell (d 1984); *b* 5 Oct 1917; *Educ* Eton, BNC Oxford (MA); *m* 21 Sept 1943, Jeanne Marjorie, da of W J Goodwin, of 36 St Bernard's Rd, Solihull, W Mids; 2 s (Simon b 1955, Mark b 1959), 4 da (Virginia b 1946, Tamare b 1947, Sherry b 1949, Sophie b 1963); *Career* Nat Serv WWII Maj RA 1939-45, served Dunkirk and Normandy; consul: Cuba 1953-61, Nicaragua 1951-59, Bolivia 1965-82, Costa Rica 1964-; chm and dir various cos; ldr govt trade missions Czechoslovakia and Canada 1965; chm: Br Export Houses Assoc 1958-60, Br Heart Fndn Midland Ctee 1973-76, Asian Christian Colls Assoc 1966-70, Guardians Birmingham Assay Office 1979-88, Birmingham Cons Assoc 1976-79 (pres 1979-84), W Midlands Met Ctee of Cons Party 1980-86, Latin American Forum Cons Foreign and Overseas Cncl 1985-88, Golden Jubilee Appeal Ctee Queen Elizabeth Hosp Birmingham 1987-89; pres: Birmingham C of C 1965-66, Assoc of Br Cs of C 1970-72, Birmingham Consular Assoc 1973-74, Birmingham E Euro Constituency 1984-, Sparkbrook Constituency Cons Assoc 1988-; vice pres W Mids Cons Cncl 1985-, memb Nat Union Exec Ctee Cons Pty 1975-85, gen cmmr Income Tax 1966-70, govr Univ of Birmingham 1967-, pres Cons Pty One Nation Forum W Mids Area 1990-; Hon Capt Bolivian Navy 1964-; Freeman City of London; *Recreations* golf, walking; *Clubs* N Warwickshire Golf; *Style—* Hilary Eccles-Williams, Esq, CBE; 36 St Bernard's Road, Solihull, W Midlands B92 7BB

ECCLESHARE, (Christopher) William; s of Colin Forster (d 1989), and Elizabeth, *née* Bennett; *b* 26 Oct 1955; *Educ* William Ellis Sch Highgate, Trinity Coll Cambridge (BA); *m* 1980, Carol Ann, da of Arnold W Seigel; 2 s (Thomas Christopher b 1984, Charles David b 1986), 1 da (Rose Judith b 1989); *Career* J Walter Thompson Company Limited: joined as graduate trainee 1978, assoc dir 1983, sr assoc dir 1985, main bd dir 1986, head of account mgmnt 1988, dep md 1991-; accounts handled incl: Rowntree Mackintosh, Elida Gibbs, Golden Wonder, Kellogg, Brooke Bond Foods, ITV Association, Harveys of Bristol, Nuclear Electric plc; MIPA; *Recreations* politics, music, theatre; *Style—* William Eccleshare, Esq; 5 Northolme Rd, London N5 2UZ (☎ 071 359 4241); J Walter Thompson Company Limited, 40 Berkeley Square, London W1X 6AD (☎ 071 499 4040, fax 071 493 8432, car 0836 315085)

ECCLESTON, Harry Norman; OBE (1979); s of Harry Norman Eccleston (d 1971), of Coseley, Staffs, and Kate, *née* Pritchard (d 1978); *b* 21 Jan 1923; *Educ* Bilston Sch of Art, Birmingham Coll of Art (Dip Painting, Art Teachers Dip), RCA Engraving Sch; *m* 5 Aug 1948, Betty Doreen, da of Wilfrid Gripton (d 1954), of Bilston, Staffs; 2 da (Judith Elizabeth (Mrs Park) b 1950, Jennifer Margaret (Mrs Stanbridge) b 1954); *Career* RN 1942-46, temp cmmn RNVR 1943; artist, lectr in illustration and printmaking SE Essex Tech Coll 1951-58, artist designer Bank of England Printing Works 1958-83 (designer of series of banknotes with historical portraits £1 Newton, £5 Wellington £10 Nightingale, £20 Shakespeare, £50 Wren), conslt Bank of England Printing Works 1983-86; exhibited prints and watercolours home and abroad 1948-; ARE 1948, RE 1961 (pres 1975-89), RWS 1975, memb Art Workers Guild 1984, FRSA 1972, hon memb Royal Birmingham Soc of Artists 1989; *Clubs* Arts; *Style—* Harry Eccleston, Esq, OBE; 110 Priory Rd, Harold Hill, Romford, Essex RM3 9AU (☎ 04023 40275)

ECCLESTON, Simon Antony Sudell; JP (1977); s of James Thomas Eccleston, of Shropshire, and Kathleen Mary, *née* Cryer (d 1964); *b* 4 April 1944; *Educ* Denstone Coll Staffs; *m* 4 Oct 1967, Angela Penelope Gail, da of Noel Harrison (d 1988), of Wolverhampton; 2 s (Piers Edward Dominic b 1971, Crispin Benedict Chad b 1982), 2 da (Cressida Sophie Heloise b 1974, Candida Annalee Gabriel b 1981); *Career* md Conveyor Systems Ltd; memb: Wolverhampton Health Authy 1987-89, Cncl (regnl and small firms) CBI, Staffs Shrops Euro Cons Exec, S Staffs Cons Assoc Exec 1972-, PCC, Black Country Steering Gp CBI; bd memb: Industl Devpt Bd DTI 1988-, Walsall Trg and Enterprise Cncl 1989-, Exec Staffs and Shrops Magistrates Assoc, Ctee W Midlands Branch IOD 1988-; chm Cons Assoc branch 1971-79 and 1980, pres Walsall C of C and Indust 1986-87; Freeman City of London 1989; *Recreations* trout fishing, shooting, riding, ocean sailing, landscape gardening; *Clubs* City Livery; *Style—* Simon Eccleston, Esq, JP; Chatwell Court, Great Chatwell, Shrops; Conveyor Systems Ltd, Kings Hill, Wednesbury, W Midlands (☎ 021 526 4971)

ECCLESTON, Prof William; s of Henry Eccleston, of Preston, Lancs, and Bertha, *née* Wilson; *b* 3 March 1941; *Educ* Harris Coll Preston, Chelsea Coll (MSc, PhD); *m* 12 April 1966, Catherine Yvonne, da of Joseph Daley, of Preston (d 1989); 2 s (John b 25 Jan 1967, Daniel b 13 July 1969); *Career* sr princ sci Plessey Res Laboratories 1966-71; Univ of Liverpool: lectr 1971-81, sr lectr 1981-85, prof of electronics 1985-86, Robert Rankin professor of electronic engrg 1986-, head Dept of Engrg Electronics 1986-; numerous pubns in learned jls, memb SERC/DTI Silicon Technology Sub-Ctee 1989-91; Freeman Borough of Preston (Hereditary); FIEE 1985, CEng 1985; *Recreations* music, football, walking, cricket; *Clubs* Lancashire Cricket, Lab Pty; *Style—* Prof William Eccleston; Thornhill, 8 College Ave, Formby, Liverpool L37 3JL (☎ 07048 71009); Dept of Electrical Engineering & Electronics, University of Liverpool, Liverpool L69 3BX (☎ 051 794 4502)

ECHENIQUE, Dr Marcial Hernan; s of Marcial Echenique, of Santiago, Chile, and Rosa, *née* Talavera; *b* 23 Feb 1943; *Educ* Catholic Univ Santiago Chile, Barcelona Univ Spain (Dip Arch, D Arch), Cambridge Univ (MA); *m* 23 Nov 1963, Maria Louisa, da of Ernesto Holzmann (d 1978), of Santiago, Chile; 2 s (Marcial Antonio b 16 July 1964, Martin Jose b 25 Nov 1965), 1 da (Alejandra b 1 Aug 1969); *Career* asst lectr in urbanism Univ of Barcelona Spain 1963-65, reader in architecture and urban studies Cambridge Univ 1980- (lectr in architecture 1970-80), chm Marcial Echenique & Ptnr Ltd (architectural and planning conslts) 1990-, memb bd Banco de Bilbao y Vizcaya Spain 1988; memb: Civic Soc Huntingdon & Godmanchester 1979, RSA 1986; ARCUK 1988; *Books* Urban Development Models (jtly, 1975), Modelos de la Estructura Espacial Urbana (1975), La Estructura Del Espacio Urbano (jtly, 1975); *Recreations* music; *Style—* Dr Marcial Echenique; Farm Hall, Godmanchester, Cambs; 49-51 High St, Trumpington, Cambridge (☎ 0223 840 704, fax 0223 840 84, telex 817 977 MEPOLA G)

ECHLIN, Sir Norman David Fenton; 10 Bt (I 1721); s of Sir John Frederick, 9 Bt (d 1932); *b* 1 Dec 1925; *Educ* Masonic Boys' Sch Clonskeagh Co Dublin; *m* 8 Dec 1953, Mary Christine, o da of John Arthur, of Oswestry, Salop; *Style—* Sir Norman Echlin, Bt; Nartopa, Marina Av, Appley, Ryde, Isle of Wight

ECKERSLEY, Thomas (Tom); OBE (1948); s of John Eckersley, and Eunice, *née* Hilton; *b* 30 Sept 1914; *Educ* Salford Coll of Art; *Career* in partnership with Eric Lombers 1934-39, graphic work for: London Transport, Shell Mex, General Post Office, BBC, Austin Reed; visiting lectr in graphic design Westminster Sch of Art 1937-39, RAF cartographer and designer of posters for General Post Office, Royal Soc for Prevention of Accidents and RAF 1940-45, head of Graphic Design Dept London Coll of Printing 1958-76; exhibitions: Shell Posters (Shell Mex House London) 1938, International Posters (Univ of Washington DC) 1940, Eight British Designers (National Museum Stockholm) 1952, Graphic Art from Britain (Amercian Inst of Graphic Arts New York) 1956, European Design (Univ of California) 1962, Documenta III (Kassel) 1964, Polish Poster Biennale (Warsaw) 1972-74, Homage to Tom (London Coll of Printing and Paperpoint Gallery) 1975, Brno Bienalle (Czechoslovakia) 1978, Thirties - British Art and Design Before the War (Hayward Gallery London) 1979, British Arts Centre Yale (USA) 1980, London Transport Museum 1985; regualar exhibitions with Alliance Graphique Internationale; work in public collections: Museum of Modern Art (NY), Imperial War Museum, V & A Museum, London Transport Museum, Nat Gallery of Australia, Library of Congress (USA); awards: Royal Designer for Industry (RSA) 1963, Chartered Soc of Designers Medal for outstanding work over 60 years 1990; memb Alliance Graphique Internationale 1950; fell: Soc of Artists and Designers 1961, Soc of Typographic Designers 1961; hon fell Manchester Coll of Art and Design 1961; *Books* Poster Design (1954); *Style—* Tom Eckersley, Esq, OBE; 53 Belsize Park Gardens, London NW3 (☎ 071 586 3586)

ECKERSLEY, Tobias William Hammersley (Toby); MBE (1989); s of Timothy Huxley Eckersley (d 1980), and Penelope Anne, *née* Hammersley; *b* 22 July 1941; *Educ* Charterhouse, St John's Coll Oxford (MA), LSE (MSc); *Career* HM Foreign Serv 1964-67, IMF 1967-71, Williams & Glyn's Bank 1971-75, ICI 1976-; Parly candidate (C) Peckham 1983, chm Dulwich Cons Assoc 1988-90, memb Cons Pty Policy Gp for London 1983-86; London Borough of Southwark: ldr of oppn 1979-85, ldr Cons Gp 1990-, cncllr 1977-86 and 1990-, memb Ministerial Advsy Panel on Abolition of GLC and Met Counties 1984-86, fndr and sec London Assoc for Saving Homes 1974-77; *Recreations* tree cultivation; *Style—* Tobias Eckersley, Esq, MBE; Imperial Chemical Indust plc, Millbank, London SW1 (☎ 071 798 5118)

ECKERSLEY-MASLIN, Rear Adm David Michael; CB (1984); eldest s of Cdr C E Eckersley-Maslin, OBE, RN, of Tasmania, and Mrs L M Lightfoot, of Bedford; *b* 27 Sept 1929, Karachi; *Educ* RNC Dartmouth; *m* 1955, Shirley Ann, da of late Capt H A Martin, DSC, RN; 1 s, 1 da; *Career* Capt: HMS Eastbourne 1966-68, HMS Euryalus 1971-72, HMS Fife 1975, HMS Blake 1976, RCDS 1977; DOR RN 1978-80, flag offr Sea Trg 1980-82, ACNS (Falklands) 1982, Def Staff (Signals) 1982, Def Staff (CIS) 1983-84; asst dir: Cmd Control and Communications Systems, Int Mil Staff NATO HQ Brussels 1984-86, DG NATO Communications and Informations Systems Agency Brussels 1986-; int vice pres AFCEA; *Recreations* cricket, tennis, squash, golf; *Clubs* MCC, Royal Cwlth Soc, RN Cricket; *Style—* Rear Adm David Eckersley-Maslin, CB; Dunningwell Hall Court, Shedfield, Southampton, Hants (☎ Wickham 0329 832350, office Brussels 246 8267)

ECROYD, (Edward) Peter; s of William Edward Bedingfeld Ecroyd (d 1951), of Armathwaite, Cumberland, and Iris Bloxsome, *née* Day; *b* 24 Nov 1932; *Educ* Harrow, Royal Agric Coll; *m* 25 April 1957, Felicity Anne Graham, er da of Frederick Graham Roberts, OBE (d 1981); 1 s (Edward Charles b 1959), 2 da (Emma Lucinda (Mrs Paul Dorahy) b 1961, Susanna Victoria (Mrs Jeremy Ball) b 1963); *Career* landowner; High Sheriff of Cumbria 1984-85; memb; Regnl Fisheries Ctee N W Water Authy 1974-89, Fisheries Ctee N W area Nat Rivers Authy 1989-; chm: Eden & District Fisheries Ctee 1974-80, N Area Fisheries Ctee 1980-83, Eden and District Fisheries Assoc 1970-83 (pres 1984); vice chm Salmon and Trout Assoc 1988-91 (memb Cncl 1970-), memb Salmon Advsy Ctee 1987-90, fndr and chm Eden Owners Assoc 1986-, chm Cumberland Branch Country Landowners Assoc 1988-90 (pres 1990-); *Recreations* fishing, shooting; *Style—* Peter Ecroyd, Esq; Low House, Armathwaite, Carlisle, Cumbria CA4 9ST (☎ 06992 242)

EDBROOKE, Dr David Louis; s of Edward John Edbrooke, of Skelton, York, and Doris Edbrooke (d 1984); *b* 29 Nov 1946; *Educ* St Peter's Sch York, Guy's Hosp Med Sch; *m* 22 March 1975, Judith Anne, da of Douglas Rex Whittaker (d 1956); 1 s (Nicholas Robert), 1 da (Claire Diane); *Career* conslt anaesthetist Rotherham Dist Gen Hosp 1979-82, dir Intensive Care Unit Royal Hallamshire Hosp 1982-, clinical advsr Inst of Biomedical Equipment Evaluation and Servs; numerous articles in learned jls; nat examiner in Extended Ambulance Aid for NHS Trg Authy, memb Steering Ctee for Extended Trg for Ambulance Aid for S Yorks Met Ambulance Serv, chm Southern Sector Div of Anaesthesia; memb Intensive Care Soc 1982, memb Casualty Surgns Assoc 1984; memb BMA 1971, fell Royal Coll of Anaesthetists 1976, FFARCS, LRCP, MRCS; *Books* Basic Concepts for Operating Room and Critical Care Personnel (with S J Mather and D L Edbrooke, 1982), Multiple Choice Questions for Operating Room and Critical Care Personnel (with S J Mather and D L Edbrooke, 1983), Prehospital Emergency Care (with S J Mather and D L Edbrooke, 1986); *Recreations* golf; *Clubs* Lindrick Golf Notts; *Style—* Dr David Edbrooke; High Noon, Hollinberry Lane, Howbrook, High Green, Sheffield S30 7EL (☎ 0742 848305); Intensive Care Unit, Royal Hallamshire Hospital, Glossop Road, Sheffield S10 2JF (☎ 0742 766222)

EDDERY, Paul Anthony; s of James Eddery (d 1989), and Josephine (Jude) Eddery of Newmarket; *b* 14 July 1963; *Educ* Burford GS Oxfordshire; *m* 14 Nov 1987, Sally, da of Charles Guest; *Career* jockey; apprentice jockey (with Reg Hollinshead) 1979-84, first ride in public 1979, first win in public on Tufu at Wolverhampton 1979; best horses ridden: Oh So Sharp, Most Welcome, Cadeaux Genereux Inchmurrin; finished second on: Untold in 1986 Oaks on first classic ride, Most Welcome in 1987 Derby on first Derby ride; big races won incl: July Cup (1989) Gp 1, Lockinge Stakes Gp 2, Cork & Orrey Stakes Gp 3, Ebor Handicap, Northumberland Plate; *Recreations* golf, waterskiing and tennis; *Style—* Paul Eddery, Esq; Jane McKeown, Saint Marina, Snailwell Rd, Newmarket, Suffolk (☎ 0638 661589, fax 0638 510746)

EDDISON, Roger Tatham; s of Edwin Eddison (d 1917), of Leeds, and Hilda Muriel, *née* Leadam (d 1963); *b* 16 Sept 1916; *Educ* Charterhouse, Univ of Cambridge (MA); *m* 10 May 1941, Rosemary Christine, da of Cdr Charles B Land, RN (d 1947); 2 s (Charles b 1942, Hugh b 1949), 1 da (Sally b 1944); *Career* Maj RA 1939-46; head of Operational Res, BISRA 1948-55, NAAFI 1955-61; pres (fndr memb and Silver medallist) Operational Res Soc 1966-67; dir Science in Gen Mgmnt Ltd, memb Cncl Metra Int Paris 1961-70, Novy Eddison & Ptnrs 1970-; M Harland & Son Ltd 1968-86; visiting prof Univ of Sussex 1968-74; *Clubs* Athenaeum; *Style—* Roger T Eddison, Esq; Horstedpond Farm, Uckfield TN22 5TR (☎ 0825 762636); Novy Eddison & Ptnrs, 1 Frayslea, Uxbridge UB8 2AT (☎ 0895 57791)

EDDLESTON, Prof Adrian Leonard William Francis; s of Rev William Eddleston, of 25 Springfields, Colyford, Colyton, Devon, and Kathleen Brenda, *née* Jarman; *b* 2 Feb 1940; *Educ* Queen Elizabeth's GS Blackburn, St Peter's Coll Oxford (MA, BM BCh, DM), Guy's Hosp; *m* 10 Sept 1966, Hilary Kay, da of Kenneth Radford (ka 1942); 3 s (Stephen b 1969, Andrew b 1972, Paul b 1974), 1 da (Carolyn b 1968); *Career* conslt physician King's Coll Hosp 1976-, vice dean King's Coll Sch of Med and Dentistry 1987- (prof liver immunology 1982-, sub dean curriculum 1984-89); memb Camberwell Health Authy 1986-; sec Euro Assoc Study of Liver 1982-84, euro rep Cncl Int Assoc for Study of Liver 1984-88; FRCP 1974, memb Assoc Physicians GB and Ireland 1974; *Books* Immunology of Liver Disease (1979); *Recreations* electronics, computing, model aircraft, music; *Style—* Prof Adrian Eddleston; Liver Unit, King's College School of Medicine and Dentistry, Denmark Hill, London SE5 9RS (☎ 071 326 3066, fax 071 274 7246)

EDE, Maurice Gordon; s of William Gordon Ede, of 17 Beverley Gardens, Ashburton, Devon, and Phyllis Maud; *b* 12 Dec 1946; *Educ* Weymouth GS; *m* 1969, Margaret Anne, da of Robert Lockhart; 1 s (Simon Maurice b 1973), 1 da (Catherine Jane b 1976); *Career* articled clerk Butterworth Jones & Co Weymouth Dorset, CA Coopers & Lybrand, ptnr Finn-Kelcey and Chapman 1976 (joined 1975); memb: Ctee S Eastern Soc of CAs 1980- (pres 1987-88), Cncl Inst of CAs 1988; FICE 1969; *Recreations* amateur dramatics, dancing; *Style—* Maurice Ede, Esq; Finn-Kelcey and Chapman, Ashford House, The Tufton Centre, Ashford, Kent TN23 1YB (☎ 0233 629255, fax 0233 643901)

EDELL, Stephen Bristow; s of Ivan James Edell (d 1958), and Hilda Pamela Edell (d 1976); *b* 1 Dec 1932; *Educ* Uppingham, Univ of London (LLB); *m* 20 Sept 1958, Shirley, da of Leslie Ross Collins (d 1984); 2 s (Philip b 1969, Nicholas b 1973), 1 da (Theresa b 1964); *Career* Nat Serv RA 2 Lt 1951-53; admitted slr 1958; ptnr: Knapp-Fishers 1959-75, Crossman Block & Keith 1984-87; law cmmr 1975-83, Bldg Soc Ombudsman 1987-; *Books* Inside Information on The Family and The Law (1969), The Family's Guide To The Law (1974); *Recreations* family life, music, opera, theatre, golf, tennis; *Clubs* City Livery; *Style—* Stephen B Edell, Esq; Office of the Building Societies Ombudsman, Grosvenor Gardens House, 35-37 Grosvenor Gardens, London SW1X 7AW (☎ 071 931 0044)

EDELMAN, Colin Neil; s of Gerald Bertram Edelman (d 1955), and Lynn Queenie, *née* Tropp; *b* 2 March 1954; *Educ* Haberdashers' Aske's, Clare Coll Cambridge (MA); *m* 26 Oct 1978, Jacqueline Claire, da of Hardy Wolfgang Seidel, of London; 1 s (James Simon b 14 Jan 1984), 1 da (Rachel Laura b 17 Sept 1982); *Career* called to the Bar Middle Temple 1977, Midlands and Oxford Circuit; *Recreations* badminton, skiing; *Style—* Colin Edelman, Esq; Devereux Chambers, Devereux Ct, London WC2R 3JJ (☎ 071 353 7534, fax 071 353 1724)

EDELMAN, David Laurence; s of Gerald Edelman (d 1955), and Lynn, *née* Tropp, JP; *b* 7 April 1948; *Educ* Haberdashers' Aske's, Univ of Leeds (B Com); *m* 4 July 1971, Sandra Marice, da of Ephraim Freeman; 1 s (Jonathan b 1984), 2 da (Emma b 1976, d 1979, Tanya b 1981); *Career* tax ptnr Edelman & Co (CAs) 1976-81, dir City Trust Ltd (bankers) 1981-86, jt md Moorfield Estates plc 1983-; chm London Borough of Hillingdon Wishing Well Appeal for Great Ormond St Hosp 1987-89; FCA 1972; *Recreations* skiing, art, music; *Style—* David Edelman, Esq; 34 Links Way, Northwood, Middx HA6 2XB; Moorfield Estates plc, Shern House, 16 Melbourne Road, Bushey, Herts WD2 3LN (☎ 081 950 9556, fax 081 950 8886, car phone 0836 274964)

EDELMAN, Dr Jack; CBE (1987); s of Samuel Edelman (d 1971), and Netta, *née* Smith (d 1989); *b* 8 May 1927; *Educ* Sir George Monoux GS, Imperial Coll London (BSc), Univ of Sheffield (PhD), Univ of London (DSc); *m* 15 Aug 1958, Joyce Dorothy; 2 s (Alex b 1959, Daniel b 1961), 1 step s (Simon b 1954), 1 step da (Jane b 1950); *Career* reader in enzymology Imperial Coll London 1956-64, prof of botany Univ of London 1964-73, visiting prof Univs of Nottingham and London 1975-83; dir Ranks Hovis McDougall plc 1982-88, chm Marlow Foods 1987-90; chm Br Industl Biological Res Assoc 1978-83, chm The Latymer Fndn 1990- (govr 1983-), vice pres Inst of Biology 1984-86, chm Nutrition Ctee and tstee Rank Prize Funds 1984-, vice pres Br Nutrition Fndn 1989-; Queen Elizabeth Coll London 1979-85, Industl Consultative Ctee on Biotechnology DTI 1983-, Univ of Kent at Canterbury 1983-, King's Coll London 1985-; memb of many industl and govt ctees, chm MAFF/DTI Link programme 1988-; author of various text books and children's science books; *Clubs* Athenaeum; *Style—* Dr Jack Edelman, CBE; 55 Black Lion Lane, London W6 9BG (☎ 081 748 8299, fax 081 563 0459)

EDELMAN, Keith Graeme; *b* 10 June 1950; *Educ* Haberdashers' Aske's, UMIST (BSc); *m* 29 June 1974, Susan Margaret; 2 s (Daniel b 3 April 1978, Nicholas b 1 July 1980); *Career* dir Ladbroke Group plc 1986, chm Texas Homecare; *Recreations* skiing, tennis, collecting antiques, cooking; *Style—* Keith Edelman, Esq; 4 Heathside Close, Moor Park, Northwood, Middlesex HA6 2EQ; Ladbroke Group plc, 10 Cavendish Place, London W1M 9DL (☎ 071 323 5000, fax 071 436 1310, telex 291268)

EDELSHAIN, Martin Bernard; s of Norman Israel Edelshain, of Israel, and Monna Annette Carlish; *b* 18 Dec 1948; *Educ* Clifton, Jesus Coll Cambridge (BA); *m* 1984, Yasuko, da of Yukitane Okada, of Japan; 1 s (Benjamin b 1986), 1 da (Deborah b 1987); *Career* dir: S G Warburg & Co Ltd 1983-86, S G Warburg, Akroyd, Rowe & Pitman, Mullens Securities Ltd 1986-88, S G Warburg & Co Ltd 1988-; *Recreations* cricket, skiing; *Clubs* MCC; *Style—* Martin B Edelshain, Esq; 8 Wellington Place, London NW8 9JA (☎ 071 289 8733); S G Warburg & Co (Japan) Ltd, Tokyo Branch, New Edobashi Building, 172 Nihombashi-Honcho, Chuo-ku, Tokyo 103 (☎ 010 81 03 3246 4151); 1 Finsbury Avenue, London EC2M 2PA (☎ 071 860 1090)

EDEN, John Forbes; s of late Thomas Eden, of 57 Hillpark Ave, Edinburgh, and Eleanor Dundas, *née* Harford; *b* 9 March 1929; *Educ* St Peter's Coll Adelaide Aust, St John's Coll Cambridge (MA); *m* 9 May 1959, Mary Caroline, da of Denis Piercy Prowse, of Portishead, Avon (d 1977); 1 s (Charles b 1963), 3 da (Caroline (Mrs Green) b 1960, Alison (Mrs Stacey) b 1962, Suzanne b 1965); *Career* 2Lt RA 1951-52, TA 1952-61, Maj OC Gloucester Vol Artillery 1959-60; admitted slr 1956, conslt Bevan Ashford Exeter, Bristol, Swindon, Taunton, Tiverton; pres: Assoc SW LAw Socs 1968-69, Devon and Exeter Inc Law Soc 1988-89; inspr DTI 1987-89; clerk Dean and Chapter Exeter 1966-89, memb of Ct Univ of Exeter 1968-, registrar Archdeaconry Exeter 1968-87, dep registrar High Ct and Co Ct 1977-, memb Lord Chllrs Judicial Review Ctee Devon 1989-, tstee Exeter Cathedral Preservation Tst 1988-; memb Law Soc 1956; *Recreations* music, badminton; *Style—* John Eden, Esq; 25 West Ave, Exeter, Devon EX4 4SD (☎ 0392 559 55); Curzon House, Southernhay West, Exeter, Devon EX4 3LY (☎ 0392 411 111)

EDEN, Prof Richard John; OBE (1978); s of James Arthur Eden, and Dora M Eden; *b* 2 July 1922; *Educ* Hertford GS, Peterhouse Cambridge; *m* 1949, Mrs Elsie Jane Greaves, da of late Herbert Edwards; 1 s, 1 da, and 1 step da; *Career* Nat Serv WWII, Capt REME Airborne Forces Europe and India; reader in theoretical physics 1964-83, head Energy Res Gp Cavendish Laboratory Univ of Cambridge; visiting prof and scientist at various univs in USA and Europe 1954; Univ of Cambridge: prof of energy 1983-89, emeritus prof 1989-, fell Clare Hall (emeritus fell 1989-); chm Caminus Energy Ltd, memb Eastern Electricity Bd 1985-; *Recreations* reading, painting; *Clubs* Army and Navy; *Style—* Prof Richard Eden, OBE; 6 Wootton Way, Cambridge, CB3 9LX

EDEN, Hon Robert Frederick Calvert; s (by 1 m) and h to baronetcies of Baron Eden of Winton, 9 and 7 Bt, PC; *b* 30 April 1964; *Style—* The Hon Robert Eden

EDEN, Hon Robert Ian Burnard; s and h of 9 Baron Auckland; *b* 25 July 1962; *Educ* Blundell's Sch Tiverton; *m* May 1986, Geraldine; *Style—* The Hon Robert Eden; c/o Tudor Rose House, 30 Links Rd, Ashtead, Surrey KT21 2HF

EDEN, Hon Roger Quentin; yr s of 6 Baron Henley (d 1962), and Lady Dorothy Georgiana Howard (d 1968), da of 9 Earl of Carlisle; *b* 18 June 1922; *Educ* Rugby; *m* 26 June 1946, Carys Wynne (d 1990), da of Ifi Hywi Dyfed Davies (d 1973), of Camwy, Penrhyndeudraeth, Gwynedd; 2 s (Morton, Elvyn), 2 da (Carol, Jane); *Career* Flying Offr RAF 1944; Shell Int Petroleum 1950-81 (head of automotive fuels devpt 1975-80); CEng, MRAeS; *Style—* The Hon Roger Eden; 29A Hamilton Terrace, St John's Wood, London NW8 9RE; Askerton Castle, Brampton, Cumbria

EDEN, Hon Ronald John; yr s of 8 Baron Auckland, MC (d 1957); *b* 5 March 1931; *Educ* Glenalmond, ChCh Oxford; *m* June 1957, Rosemary Dorothy Marion, yr da of Sir John Frederick Ellenborough Crowder (d 1961), of 116 Ashley Gardens SW1; 2 s; *Career* former stockbroker; *Books* Going to The Moors; *Recreations* reading, writing; *Style—* The Hon Ronald Eden; Cromlix, Dunblane, Perthshire (☎ 0786 822125)

EDEN OF WINTON, Baron (Life Peer UK 1983), of Rushyford, Co Durham; Rt Hon Sir John Benedict Eden; 9 Bt (E 1672), of West Auckland, Durham, and 7 Bt (GB 1776), of Maryland, America, PC (1972); s of Sir Timothy Calvert Eden, 8 and 6 Bt (d 1963), and Patricia Eden, *née* Prendergast (d 1990); *b* 15 Sept 1925; *Educ* Eton, St Paul's Sch USA; *m* 1, 28 Jan 1958 (m dis 1974), Belinda Jane, da of late Sir (Frederick) John Pascoe; 2 s, 2 da; m 2, 1977, Margaret Ann, da of late Robin Gordon, former w of Viscount Strathallan, *qv*; *Heir* (to baronetcies only) s, Hon Robert Frederick Calvert Eden; *Career* served WWII, Lt RB, 2 Gurkha Rifles 1943-47, Adj The Gilgit Scouts; MP (C) Bournemouth West Feb 1954-83; oppn front bench spokesman for Power 1968-70, min of state Miny of Technol June-Oct 1970, min for indust 1970-72, min of post and telecommunications 1972-74; memb Trade and Indust Sub Ctee of Commons Expenditure Ctee 1974-76; chm: Select Ctee European Legislation 1976-79, Select Ctee Home Affrs 1979-83; pres: Ind Schs Assoc 1969-71, Wessex Area of Nat Union of Cons and Unionist Assocs 1974-77; chm: Lady Eden's Schools Ltd, Wonder World plc 1982-, Gamlestaden plc 1987-, The Bricorn Group Ltd 1990-; chm: Bd of Tstees Royal Armouries 1986-, The British Lebanese Association Ltd 1989-; *Recreations* gardening; *Clubs* Boodle's, Pratt's; *Style—* The Rt Hon Lord Eden of Winton, PC; 41 Victoria Rd, London W8 5RH; Knoyle Place, East Knoyle, Salisbury, Wilts SP3 6AF

EDENS, Joanne Marie (Jo); da of Bryan Ivor Whitworth, of King's Lynn, Norfolk, and Shirley Frances, *née* Slater; *b* 1 Oct 1967; *Educ* Lynn Grove HS, East Norfolk Sixth Form Coll, Univ of Warwick (BSc); *m* 5 Aug 1989, Stuart David Edens, s of Alan David Edens, of Thatcham, Berks; *Career* 5 place in jr Euro and Med Archery Championships 1983, 7 place in archery event Seoul Olympics 1988, 11 place in Archery World Championships 1989, world record holder 30m distance with score of 357 Euro Championships 1990 (5 place overall); Br Ladies Target Archery Champion 1987, 1988 and 1989; Br Ladies Field Archery Champion 1988 and 1989; memb Christians in Sport; *Clubs* Leamington Spa Archery; *Style—* Mrs Stuart Edens; c/o Grand National Archery Society, 7th Street, National Agricultural Centre, Stoneleigh, Kenilworth, Warwickshire CV8 2LG

EDES, Brian; s of Eric Donald Edes, of 6 Walmer Close, Southwater, Horsham, W Sussex, and Pamela Jean, *née* Darvill; *b* 12 July 1957; *m* 5 April 1980, Jacqueline Anne, da of Donald Arthur Swift; 1 s (Mathew b 24 July 1988), 1 da (Lauren b 16 Feb 1985); *Career* asst architect Barton Myers Assocs Toronto Ontario Canada 1981-84, architect Foster Associates (for Stansted Airport) London 1984-87, private practice 1987-; ARCUK 1984, memb RIBA 1988; *Recreations* skiing, swimming; *Style—* Brian Edes, Esq; 11A Finsbury Park Rd, London N4 2LA (☎ 071 359 8866)

EDES, (John) Michael; CMG (1981); s of late Lt-Col N H Edes, and Louise Edes; *b* 19 April 1930; *Educ* Blundell's, Clare Coll Cambridge (BA), Yale Univ (MA); *m* 1978, Angela Mermagen; 2 s; *Career* Diplomatic Serv, ret; ambass to Libya 1980-83; head UK Delegation to Conference on Security and Disarmament in Europe Stockholm 1983-86; visiting fell Int Inst for Strategic Studies 1987; head UK Delegation (with personal rank of ambass) to negotiations on Conventional Armed Forces in Europe and on Confidence and Security Building Measures Vienna 1989-90; *Recreations* gardening, listening to music; *Clubs* Athenaeum, Hawk's, Cambridge; *Style—* Michael Edes, Esq, CMG; Foreign and Commonwealth Office, King Charles St, London SW1

EDEY, Harold Cecil; s of Cecil Edey (d 1971), and Elsie Norah, *née* Walmsley (d 1965); *b* 23 Feb 1913; *Educ* HS for Boys Croydon, LSE (pt/t, BCom); *m* 1944, Dilys Mary Pakeman, da of Richard Idris Jones: 1 s (David Peter b 1949), 1 da (Nerys Elizabeth b 1946); *Career* cmmnd RNVR 1940-46; articled clerk John Baker Sons and Bell 1930-35; staff memb: Deloitte Plender Griffiths and Co 1935-36, S Pearson and Son Group 1936-40 and 1946-49; LSE: lectr in accounting and fin 1949-55, reader in accounting 1955-62, prof of accounting 1962-80, pro-dir 1967-70, emeritus prof 1980-, hon fell 1986; fndr govr of London Business Sch 1965-71; memb: Cncl of CNAA 1965-73, Senate Univ of London 1975-80; hon prof UCW 1980-; laureate Chartered Accountants Founding Socs Centenary award 1987, Silver Jubilee medal 1977; Freeman City of London 1986, Hon Liveryman Worshipful Co of Chartered Accountants in England and Wales 1986; Hon LLD CNAA 1972; ACA 1935 (memb Cncl 1969-80); *Books* National Income and Social Accounting (with A J Peacock, 1954), Business Budgets and Accounts (1959), Introduction to Accounting (1963), The Companies Act 1981 (with L H Leigh, 1981), Accounting Queries (1982); *Recreations* walking; *Style—* Harold Edey, Esq

EDEY, Russell Philip; s of Lt-Col Anthony Russell Edey, of S Africa, and Barbara Stephanie Ann, *née* Rees-Jones; *b* 2 Aug 1942; *Educ* St Andrew's Coll Grahamstown S Africa; *m* 8 June 1968, Celia Ann Malcolm, da of James Bisdee Malcolm Green, of Colchester, Essex; 2 s (Philip b 1971, Anthony b 1975), 1 da (Kate b 1973); *Career* CA; md N M Rothschild & Sons Ltd 1990 (dir 1981-), Northern Foods plc 1988; dir The New Shakespeare Company Ltd 1990-, memb Cncl of Mgmnt The Br Lung Fndn 1990-; *Recreations* tennis, theatre, current affairs, wine; *Clubs* Australian, Melbourne; *Style—* Russell Edey, Esq; Starling Leeze, Coggeshall, Essex, CO6 1SL; N M Rothschild & Sons Ltd, New Court, St Swithins Lane, London EC4P 4DU

EDGAR, Anthony Samuel; s of Robert Rex Samuel Edgar (d 1979), and Esme Sophie, *née* Levy (d 1988); *b* 7 Sept 1937; *Educ* Harrow; *m* 1 (m dis), Roberta Hilary Ann Holbrook; 1 s (Maximilian Halbrook Samuel); m 2, 29 July 1983, Sarah; 1 step s (Christopher Samuel Konig); *Career* chm H Samuel Ltd; master: Exmoor Foxhounds, Hargate Hunt, W Dulvert Foxhounds; Freeman: City of London, Worshipful Co of Clockmakers, Worshipful Co of Goldsmiths; *Recreations* hunting, shooting, fishing, skiing, sailing; *Clubs* Carlton, East India, Oriental; *Style—* Anthony Edgar, Esq; Lower Green Farm, Hawkley, Liss, Hants (☎ 0730 84411); 36 Montpelier Walk, London SW7; Higher Blackland, Withypool, Minehead, Somerset; Garynahine, Isle of Lewis

EDGAR, Prof (William) Michael; s of Benjamin Frederic Edgar (d 1987), of Elvaston Rd, Hexham, Northumberland, and Marion, *née* Golightly (d 1979); *b* 10 June 1940; *Educ* Newcastle Royal GS, Univ of Newcastle (BDS, BSc, PhD, DDSc); *m* 4 Aug 1965, Christine Lesley, da of Alfred Leslie Tinwell (d 1983), of 26 Dene Rd, Tynemouth, Northumberland; 2 s (Thomas b 1970, James b 1974), 1 da (Abigail b 1967); *Career* sr lectr oral physiology Univ of Newcastle 1977-81 (lectr 1968-77); visiting scientist: Eastman Dental Centre Rochester NY 1972, Nat Inst Dental Res NIH Bethesda MD 1979; prof dental sci Univ of Liverpool 1982-; *Recreations* music, walking; *Style—* Prof Michael Edgar; Dept of Clinical Dental Sciences, University of Liverpool, PO Box 147, Liverpool L69 3BX (☎ 051 706 5261/2); 14 Hougoumont Ave, Waterloo, Liverpool L22 0LL

EDGCUMBE, Piers Valletort; 2 surviving s of George Edgcumbe (d 1977), but er by his 2 w, Una Pamela, da of Edward Lewis George, of Perth, W Australia; hp to half-bro, 8 Earl of Mount Edgcumbe; *b* 23 Oct 1946; married and divorced; *Style—* Piers Edgcumbe Esq

EDGE, Dr David Owen; s of Stephen Rathbone Holden Edge (d 1955), and Kathleen Edith, *née* Haines; *b* 4 Sept 1932; *Educ* The Leys Sch Cambridge, Gonville and Caius Coll Cambridge (BA, MA, PhD); *m* 21 Feb 1959, Barbara, *née* Corsie; 2 s (Alastair Clouston b 23 Nov 1963, Gordon b 2 Oct 1966), 1 da (Aran Kathleen (Mrs Woodfin) b 23 June 1960); *Career* Nat Serv Corpl wireless instr RAF 1950-52; physics master Perse Sch Cambridge 1959, prodr Sci Talks BBC London 1959-66, dir Sci Studies Unit Univ of Edinburgh 1966-89 (reader 1979-), ed Social Studies of Sci 1970-, pres Soc for Social Studies of Sci 1985-87; advsr HQ Scout Assoc Scot 1967-85, memb various Ctees and Panels CNAA 1972-89, pres Scout and Guide Graduate Assoc (former chm), chm Bd Science Policy Support Gp 1989-; FRAS 1960, FRSA 1972, FAAAS 1989; *Books* Meaning and Control (ed with JN Wolfe, 1973), Astronomy Transformed: The Emergence of Radio Astronomy in Britain (with M Mulkay, 1976), Scientific Images and Their Social Uses (with I Cameron, 1979), Science in Context: Readings in the Sociology of Science (ed with B Barnes, 1982); *Recreations* hill walking, travel, enjoying music and sport; *Clubs* Baden-Powell House; *Style—* Dr David Edge; 25 Gilmour Rd, Edinburgh EH16 5NS (☎ 031 667 3497, fax 031 668 4008); Science Studies Unit, Edinburgh University, 34 Buccleuch Place, Edinburgh EH8 9JT (☎ 031 650 4261/4256, telex 727442 UNNED G, fax 031 667 9801)

EDGE, Geoffrey; s of John Edge (d 1977), of Tividale, Warley, W Midlands, and Alice

Edith, *née* Rimell (d 1986); *b* 26 May 1943; *Educ* Rowley Regis GS, LSE, Univ of Birmingham (BA); *Career* asst lectr geography Univ of Leicester 1967-70, lectr geography Open Univ 1970-74, res fell Birmingham Poly 1979-80, sr res fell Preston and Northeast London Polys 1980-84; New Initiatives coordinator Copec Housing Tst 1984-87, sr assoc PE International 1987-; chm Planning Ctee Bletchley UDC 1972-74, vice chm Planning Ctee Milton Keynes Borough Cncl 1973-76, MP (Lab) Aldridge Brownhills 1974-79 (Parly private sec, Dept Educn Science and Privy Cncl Office), chm Econ Devpt Ctee W Midlands CC 1981-86, chm W Midlands Enterprise Bd 1982-, leader Walsall Met Borough Cncl 1988- (chm Policy and Resources Ctee) 1988-90; memb: Town and Country Planning Assoc, Regnl Studies Assoc, Geographical Assoc, Assoc of Univ Teachers; MIGB; *Books* Regional Analysis & Development (jt ed, 1973); *Recreations* gardening, walking, travel, reading, listening to classical music; *Style—* Geoffrey Edge, Esq; 31 Dudley Rd West, Tividale, Warley, W Midlands; 18 Harringworth Court, Lichfield Rd, Shelfield, Walsall, W Midlands (☎ 021 557 3858); West Midlands Enterprise Board, Wellington House, 31/34 Waterloo St, Birmingham B2 5JT (☎ 021 236 8855, fax 021 233 3942 telex 021 23

EDGE, Prof Gordon Malcolm; *Educ* Brunel Univ (DTech); *m* Nikki; 2 s (Tom, Matthew), 1 da (Lucy); *Career* md Cambridge Consultants Ltd 1961-69; PA Technoloy: fndr and chief exec 1970-86, memb Int Bd 1974-86, memb Bd Stockholm 1977-86; fndr Generics Holding Corporation 1986-; currently non-exec dir: Peek plc, Wharfdale plc; speaker at seminars and conferences, contrib to books and jls; res visitor Dept of Zoology Univ of Cambridge 1982-85, visiting memb King's Coll, visiting prof Brunel Univ 1985-; memb: Ericsson Sci Cncl Stockholm 1983-, ACARD 1984-86, Cncl BTG 1985-, Bd ADAS 1985-, Ctee on Emerging Technols ACOST 1986-89 (chm Sub Gp on Advanced Mfrg 1988-); advsr on R&D mgmnt to Volvo AB 1985-; fell Royal Swedish Acad of Engrg Scis 1989; CEng, MIEE; *Books* Technology Management (ed Wild, 1990); *Clubs* Athenaeum; *Style—* Prof Gordon Edge; Peek plc, 207 Radley Rd, Abingdon, Oxon OX14 3XA (☎ 0235 528271, fax 0235 532836)

EDGE, Capt (Philip) Malcolm; s of Stanley Weston Edge (d 1977), and Edith Harriet, *née* Liddell; *b* 15 July 1931; *Educ* Rock Ferry HS, HMS Conway, Liverpool Nautical Coll; *m* 18 Feb 1967, Kathleen Anne, da of Richard Nelson Alfred Greenwood (d 1986); 1 s (David b 1977), 1 da (Caroline b 1974); *Career* i/c Shipping subsidiary BP 1969 (apprentice 1949, jr offr 1951); Corp of Trinity House: elder bro and memb Bd 1978-, dep master and chm Bd 1988-; memb Port of London Authy 1980-, dir Standard Protection & Indemnity Assoc Ltd 1988-; Freeman City of London 1980; Liveryman: Hon Co of Master Mariners 1980 (Hon Freeman 1988-), Worshipful Co of Shipwrights 1990; Freeman and memb of Court Watermans Co of River Thames 1983; FNI 1979; *Recreations* sailing, DIY; *Clubs* Royal Thames Yacht; *Style—* Capt Malcolm Edge; Hillside, Layters Way, Gerrards Cross, Bucks SL9 7QZ (☎ 0753 887937); Trinity House, Tower Hill, London (☎ 071 480 6601, fax 071 480 7662, telex 987526 NAVAID G)

EDGE, Stephen Martin; s of Harry Hurst Edge, of Bolton, Lancs, and Mary, *née* Rigg; *b* 29 Nov 1950; *Educ* Canon Slade GS Bolton, Univ of Exeter (LLB); *m* 6 Sept 1975, Melanie, da of Eric Stanley Lawler, of Hassocks, Sussex; 2 da (Charlotte Louise b 1982, Katharine Sarah b 1987); *Career* admitted slr 1975; ptnr (specialising in corporate tax) Slaughter and May 1973-; various contribs to pubns and articles on tax; *Clubs* MCC; *Style—* Stephen Edge, Esq; 35 Basinghall St, London EC2V 5DB (☎ 071 600 1200, 071 726 0038)

EDGE (THE), (David Evans); s of Garvin Evans, of Dublin, and Gwenda; *b* 8 Aug 1961; *Educ* Mount Temple Sch; *Career* guitarist and fndr memb U2 1978-; U2 formed in Dublin with Bono, *qv* (vocals, guitar), Larry Mullen, *qv* (drums) and Adam Clayton, *qv* (bass); U2 played first London dates and released U23 (EP 1979, CBS Ireland) 1979, band signed to Island Records and released Boy (LP 1980) and three singles 1980, toured UK, US, Belguim and Holland 1980, released October (LP 1981, Silver disc) which entered UK charts at No 11 and three singles Fire, Gloria and A Celebration giving the band their first UK charts entries 1981-82, band toured extensively in UK, US, Ireland and Europe 1981-83, New Year's Day (single 1983) gave band their first UK Top Ten hit, War (LP 1983, US Gold disc) entered UK charts at No 1 and US Top Ten, band toured US and UK 1983, Under A Blood Red Sky (live album 1983, UK Platinum disc) entered UK charts at No 2, voted Band of the Year Rolling Stone Writers Poll 1984, Pride (In the Name of Love) single produced by Brian Eno and Daniel Lanois reached No 3 in UK charts gaining Silver disc 1984, band toured Aust, NZ and Europe, The Unforgettable Fire (LP 1984) entered UK charts at No 1, Unforgettable Fire (single 1985) entered UK charts at No 8; played: Madison Square Garden NY, Longest Day Festival Milton Keynes Bowl, Croke Park Dublin, Live Aid Wembley (Best Live Aid Performance Rolling Stone Readers Poll 1986) 1985; voted Best Band Rolling Stone Readers Poll 1986 (joint No 1 Critics Poll); played: Self Aid Dublin, A Conspiracy of Hope (Amnesty Int Tour) 1986; The Joshua Tree (LP 1987, Grammy award Album of the Year, 12 million worldwide sales) entered UK charts at No 1 as fastest selling album in Br music history and reached No 1 in US charts; With Or Without You (single 1987), I Still Haven't Found What I'm Looking For (single 1987), Where The Streets Have No Name (single 1987) released and entered UK charts; first three singles from The Joshua Tree reached No 1 in US charts; world tour (opened Arizona) 1987; 100 shows in US and Europe incl: Wembley Stadium, Madison Square Gardens NY, Sun Devil Stadium Arizona and Croke Park Dublin (winners Grammy award Best Rock Performance 1987-88); Desire (single 1988) gives U2 their first No 1 single, Rattle & Hum (LP 1988) entered UK charts at No 1, U2 played Smile Jamaica (Dominion Theatre) in aid of hurricane disaster relief 1988, world premiere U2 Rattle & Hum (film 1988) Dublin, Angel of Harlem (single 1988) entered UK charts at No 10; Grammy awards: Best Rock Performance (Desire) 1989, Best Video (Where The Streets Have No Name) 1989; When Love Comes to Town (single 1989), All I Want Is You (single 1989) released, band toured Aust 1989, New Year's Eve 1989 concert at Point Depot Dublin (broadcast live to Europe and USSR, 500 million estimated audience), recorded Night & Day for Aids benefit LP (Red, Hot & Blue) 1990; *Style—* The Edge; c/o Principle Management, 30-32 Sir John Rogersons Quay, Dublin 2, Ireland (☎ 0001 777 330, fax 0001 777 276)

EDGE-PARTINGTON, (James) Patrick Seymour; s of Rev Canon Ellis Foster Edge-Partington, MC, Queen's Chaplain (d 1957), and Esther Muriel, *née* Seymour (d 1948); *b* 16 March 1926; *Educ* Marlborough; *m* 1951, Monica Madge, da of Howard Philip Smith (d 1964); 2 s (Julian, Simon), 1 da (Jane); *Career* Coldstream Gds 1944-47, T/Capt Palestine; CA 1951; chm Crown House plc 1963-, Tilbury Gp plc 1975-; FCA, CBIM; *Clubs* RAC; *Style—* Patrick Edge-Partington, Esq; c/o Crown House plc, 2 Lygon Place, SW1 (☎ 071 730 9287, telex 918602)

EDGERTON, William (Bill) Pieter; s of Capt Eric William Edgerton (d 1981), of 43 Darling St, Balmain, Sydney, NSW, Aust, and Hetty, *née* Wessels; *b* 13 Oct 1951; *Educ* Scots Coll Sydney, Univ of NSW Sydney; *m* 19 Nov 1982, Sarah Alysha Grey, da of David William Stansfeld (d 1987); 2 s (Rory Pieter Wyon b 3 March 1983, Sean David William b 20 Sept 1984); *Career* full time int competitive sailor 1973-87; two ton world champion 1981, crew mangr of Yacht of the Year 1983, navigator winning team Southern Cross Cup 1985, S Aust challenge for def of Americas Cup 1985-87; coach: Br Nat Keelboat 1987-, Br Adm's Cup Team first place 1989 (second 1987), Br Team Southern Cross Cup 1989; memb Tech Ctee Royal Ocean Racing Club and Royal Lymington Yacht; *Recreations* skiing, gardening; *Clubs* ROR, RLY, BRS; *Style—* William Edgerton, Esq; Royal Yachting Association, RYA House, Romsey Road, Eastleigh, Hants SO5 4YA (☎ 0703 629962, fax 0703 629924)

EDGLEY, Colin Ronald; s of Andrew Charles Edgley, and Doreen, *née* Major; *b* 13 Dec 1945; *Educ* Haberdashers' Aske's; *m* 9 Aug 1969, Carole, da of Alexander Cornish (d 1981), of Wallington; 1 s (Simon Alexander Charles b 1972), 1 da (Alison Charlotte b 1975); *Career* various directorships Spillers Foods Ltd 1981-88 incl: Gland Supplies Ltd, Manor Produce Ltd, Suir Endocrine Ltd; chm: Spillers Foods Ltd 1982-84 and 1986-88, Castlefield Foods Ltd 1986-88; chief exec Homepride Foods Ltd 1988-; FCCA 1976; *Recreations* rugby, golf; *Style—* Colin Edgley, Esq; Thurlow House, Long Thurlow, Suffolk IP31 3JA (☎ 0359 259539); Compass House, 80 Newmarket Rd, Cambs (☎ 0223 461600, car 0860 725742, telex 818878)

EDGSON WRIGHT, Paul; s of Hugh Edgson Wright, MM (d 1979), of Folkestone, Kent, and Diana Christine, *née* Smith; *b* 3 March 1935; *Educ* Marlborough; *m* 11 June 1960, Gillian Elspeth, da of Sidney Leonard Shaw, of Santiago, Chile; 2 s (Mark b 1963, (Andrew) Peter b 1967), 1 da (Kathryn b 1961); *Career* articled Barton Mayhew & Co CAs 1953-59, Riddell Stead Graham & Hutchinson CAs Montreal PQ Canada 1959-61, Stanhay (Ashford) Ltd Gp 1961-72 (taken over by Hestair plc 1971) (appointed fin dir and co sec 1970), chm Stanhay (Autos) Ltd 1972-76, gp chief accountant MacBlast gp of cos 1976-77, Rothman Pantall & Co CAs 1978-84, formed Shaws CAs (reg insolvency practitioner) specialising in insolvency and investigations 1985; FCA; *Recreations* shooting, fishing, sailing, ornithology; *Style—* Paul Edgson Wright, Esq; Clareville House, 26/27 Oxendon St, London SW1Y 4EP (☎ 071 930 2217, telex 893715 ROTHCO G, fax 071 930-9849)

EDINBURGH, Bishop of 1986-; Rt Rev Richard Frederick Holloway; s of Arthur Holloway (d 1987), and Mary, *née* Luke (d 1976); *b* 26 Nov 1933; *Educ* Kelham Theological Coll, Edinburgh Theological Coll, Union Theological Seminary New York; *m* 20 April 1963, Jean Elizabeth, da of the Rev Edwin Oliver Kennedy, of Hackett St Own, New Jersey; 1 s (Mark Ramsay b 16 May 1969), 2 da (Ann b 1964, Sara b 1966); *Career* Nat Serv RA 1952-54; priest i/c St Margaret and St Mungo's Glasgow 1963-68; rector: Old St Paul's Edinburgh 1968-80, The Church of the Advent Boston Mass 1980-84; vicar St Mary Magdalen Oxford 1984-86; *Books* Let God Arise (1972), A New Vision of Glory (1974), A New Heaven (1979), Beyond Belief (1981), Signs of Glory (1982), The Killing (1984), The Anglican Tradition (ed, 1984), Paradoxes of Christian Faith and Life (1984), The Sidelong Glance (1985), The Way of the Cross (1986), Seven to Flee, Seven to Follow (1986), Crossfire: Faith and Doubt in an Age of Certainty (1988), When I Get to Heaven (1988), Another Country, Another Kind (1991); *Recreations* walking, reading, films, music; *Clubs* New (Edinburgh); *Style—* The Rt Rev the Bishop of Edinburgh; 3 Eglinton Crescent, Edinburgh EH12 5DH (☎ 031 226 5099); Diocesan Centre, Walpole Hall, Chester St, Edinburgh EH3 7EN

EDINGTON, Paul Tellet; s of Dr Francis Cameron Edington, of Penrith, and Anella Jean, *née* Munro; *b* 24 April 1943; *Educ* Sedbergh, Selwyn Coll Cambridge (MA, MB BCh), St Mary's Hosp Med Sch London; *m* 3 March 1973, Jane Margaret, da of Dr Geoffrey Howard Bulow, of Wellington Heath; 2 s (James b 1976, David b 1978), 1 da (Katherine b 1982); *Career* registrar St Mary's Hosp London 1973-76, exchange registrar Univ of Cape Town 1975-76; sr registrar rotation Newcastle upon Tyne: Newcastle Gen Hosp, Royal Victoria Hosp, Princess Mary Maternity Hosp, Queen Elizabeth Hosp Gateshead; conslt obstetrician and gynaecologist Univ Hosp Nottingham 1981-; LRCP, MRCS, FRCOG 1990 (MRCOG 1974); *Recreations* golf, cricket, squash, gardening, skiing, music; *Style—* Paul Edington, Esq; 1 Baildon Close, Wollaton Park, Nottingham NG8 1BS (☎ 0602 786187); University Hospital, Queen's Medical Centre, Nottingham NG7 2UH (☎ 0602 421421 ext 44596)

EDIS, Richard John Smale; s of Denis Charles Edis, of Willand, Devon, and Sylvia Mary, *née* Smale; *b* 1 Sept 1943; *Educ* King Edward's Sch Birmingham, St Catherine's Coll Cambridge (MA); *m* 3 April 1971, Geneviéve Nanette Suzanne, da of René Marcel Cérisoles, of Palm Beach and Nice; 3 s (Rupert b 1971, Oliver b 1972, Jamyn b 1975); *Career* HM Dip Serv 1966-; served: Nairobi, Lisbon, NY, Geneva; presently HM Cmmr Br Indian Ocean Territory and head E African Dept FCO; kt Mil Order of Christ Portugal 1973; *Recreations* reading, sport; *Clubs* Traveller's; *Style—* Richard Edis, Esq; c/o FCO, London SW1A 2AH

EDLMANN, Stephen Raphael Reynolds; s of Capt Raphael Francis Reynolds (d 1975), and Waltraud Helga Mathilde, *née* Seveeke (d 1984); *b* 13 March 1954; *Educ* Tonbridge, Trinity Hall Cambridge (MA); *m* 14 July 1979, Deborah Catherine, da of Roger John Nimmo Booth, of Co Durham; 4 s (Richard b 1980, Oliver b 1981, Nicholas b and d 1981, Lawrence b 1983); *Career* ptnr Linklaters & Paines slrs 1985- (joined 1977); memb Worshipful Co of Slrs 1985; memb: Law Soc 1979, Int Bar Assoc 1986; *Recreations* entertaining, racing, shooting, golf; *Clubs* Hawks, MCC, Roehampton, Harlequins; *Style—* Stephen Edlmann, Esq; Linklaters & Paines, Barrington House, 59-67 Gresham St, London EC2V 7JA (☎ 071 606 7080, fax 071 606 5113, telex 884349/

EDMENSON, Sir Walter Alexander; CBE (1944); s of late Robert Robson Edmenson, of Monkseaton, Northumberland; *b* 2 Dec 1892; *m* 1918, Doris (d 1975), da of John Davidson; 1 s (ka 1940), 1 da (d 1975); *Career* served WWI with N Irish Horse and RFA (despatches), served WWII NI rep Miny of War Tport 1939-46; N Continental Shipping Co 1948-70, Ulster Tport Authy 1948-61, shipowner, Belfast Harbour Cmmr 1940-61, Clyde Shipping Co 1946-64; pres: The Ulster Steamship Co, G Heyn & Sons; dir various other shipping cos; dir: BEA 1946-63, Gallaher Ltd 1946-66, The Belfast Banking Co 1946-70, Belfast Bank Executor & Trust Co 1946-70, Commercial Insur Co of Ireland 1964-72; chm N Ireland Civil Aviation Advsy Cncl 1946-61; memb Lloyd's Register of Shipping 1949-74; Cncl of Chamber of Shipping 1943-73; cmmr Irish Lights 1950-85; DL Belfast 1951-87; American Medal of Freedom with Palms 1945; kt 1958; *Style—* Sir Walter Edmenson, CBE; 101 Bryansford Rd, Newcastle, Co Down, N Ireland (☎ 02967 22769)

EDMISTON, Robert Norman; s of Vivian Randolph Edmiston and Norma Margaret Edmiston; *b* 6 Oct 1946; *Educ* Abbs Cross Tech, Barking Regnl Coll of Technol; *m* 1967, Patricia Ann, da of Alfred Edward Talbot (d 1962); 1 s (Andrew b 1969), 2 da (Deborah b 1971, Angela b 1975); *Career* fin analyst Ford Motor Co, capital planning mangr Chrysler (mangr fin analysis), fin dir Jensen Motor Co, chm and md IM Group Ltd; *Recreations* church activities, swimming, windsurfing, flying, shooting; *Style—* Robert Edmiston, Esq; IM Group, Ryder Street, West Bromich, West Midlands (☎ 021 557 6200, telex 337554)

EDMONDS, Dr Charles John; s of Charles John Edmonds, of Enfield, Middx, and Lilian, *née* Robertson; *b* 17 April 1929; *Educ* Latymer Sch Edmonton, Univ of London (MD, DSc); *m* 13 March 1965, Gillian Mary, da of Augustus Riggott (d 1988); 3 s (Nicholas, Christopher, Jonathan); *Career* Nat Serv, Flt-Lt RAF Inst of Aviation Med Farnborough Hants 1955-56; clinical scientist MRC 1967-, conslt endocrinologist: UCH London 1967-, Northwick Park Hosp Harrow Middx 1972-; author many scientific pubns; FRCP, memb RSM; *Books* The Large Intestine (1981), Journal of Endocrinology (scientific ed); *Recreations* walking, cycling, gardening, reading; *Style—* Dr Charles Edmonds; Northwick Park Hospital, Watford Rd, Harrow, Middx HA1 3UJ

EDMONDS, David Albert; s of Albert Edmonds, of Kingsley, Cheshire, and Gladys Edmonds; *b* 6 March 1944; *Educ* Helsby GS Cheshire, Univ of Keele (BA); *m* 1966, Ruth, da of Eric Beech, of Christleton, Chester; 2 s (Jonathan, Benedict), 2 da (Jane, Elizabeth); *Career* asst princ Miny of Housing and Local Govt 1966-69 (private sec/ Parly sec 1969-71), princ DOE 1971-73, observer Civil Serv Selection Bd 1973-74, visiting fell Johns Hopkins Univ Baltimore USA 1974-75; DOE: private sec/permanent sec 1975-77, asst sec 1977-79, private sec to Sec of State 1979-83, under sec Inner Cities Directorate 1983-84; chief exec The Housing Corp 1984-, dep chm New Statesman and Society 1988-90; pres Int New Towns Assoc 1988-, dir The Housing Fin Corp 1988-; *Recreations* opera, golf, walking, films; *Clubs* Wimbledon Park Golf, Wimbledon Wanderers CC; *Style*— David Edmonds, Esq; 61 Cottenham Park Rd, Wimbledon, London SW20 0DR (☎ 081 946 3729); The Housing Corp, 149 Tottenham Court Rd, W1P 0BN (☎ 071 357 9466)

EDMONDS, Cdr John Christopher; CMG (1978), CVO (1971); s of Capt Archibald Charles Mackay Edmonds, OBE, RN (d 1961), of Bognor Regis, Sussex; *b* 23 June 1921; *Educ* Kelly Coll; *m* 1, 1948 (m dis 1965), Elena, da of Serge Tornow; 2 s; m 2, 1966, Armine, da of Clement Hilton Williams, MBE (d 1963), of Sonning, Berks; *Career* RN 1939-59, Cdr 1957; staff of: NATO Defence Coll 1953-55, C-in-C Home Fleet 1955-57, CDS 1958-59; Dip Serv 1959-81, cnsllr Br Embassy Ankara 1968-71, Paris 1972-74, head Arms Control and Disarmament Dept FCO 1974-77; leader UK delgn to comprehensive test ban treaty negotiations Geneva (with personal rank of ambassador), 1978-81; visiting fell in int relations Reading Univ 1981-; *Recreations* golf, gardening, travel; *Clubs* Army and Navy; *Style*— Cdr John Edmonds, CMG, CVO, RN; North Lodge, Sonning, Berkshire RG4 0ST

EDMONDS, John Walter; s of Walter Edgar Edmonds (d 1986), and Maude Rose, *née* Edwards; *b* 28 Jan 1944; *Educ* Christ's Hosp, Oriel Coll Oxford (MA); *m* 30 Sept 1967, (Janet) Linden, da of Franklin Arthur Callaby (d 1978); 2 da (Lucinda Jane b 1969, Nanette Sally b 1972); *Career* GMB (formerly GMWU): res asst 1965-67, dep res offr 1967-68, regnl organiser 1968-72, nat offr 1972-85, gen sec 1986-; dir National Building Agency; govr LSE; memb Royal Cmmn on Environmental Pollution; visiting fell Nuffield Coll Oxford; dir Unity Bank; tstee Inst of Public Policy Res; memb Gen Cncl TUC; FRSA 1989; *Recreations* cricket, carpentry; *Clubs* Wibbandune CC; *Style*— John W Edmonds, Esq; 50 Graham Rd, Mitcham, Surrey CR4 2HA; GMB, 22-24 Worple Road, London SW19 4DD (☎ 081 947 3131, fax 081 944 6552)

EDMONDS, (Douglas) Keith; s of (Maxwell) John Edmonds, of Duffield, Derbyshire, and Margaret Agnes, *née* Morrison (d 1977); *b* 23 July 1949; *Educ* Ecclesbourne Sch Derbyshire, Univ of Sheffield Med Sch (MB ChB, capt Rugby Club); *m* 13 Oct 1990, Gillian Linda, da of Cyril Rose; *Career* house physician Rotherham Hosp 1973-74, sr house offr Accident and Emergency Sheffield Hosp 1974-75 (house surgn 1974), lectr Dept of Anatomy Univ of Sheffield 1975, sr house offr Obstetrics and Gynaecology Jessop Hosp for Women Sheffield 1975-77, registrar in obstetrics and gynaecology Southampton Hosp 1977-78; sr registrar in obstetrics and gynaecology: Queen Elizabeth Hosp Aust 1979-80, Southampton and Winchester Hosps 1980-82; conslt obstetrician and gynaecologist to Queen Charlotte and Chelsea Hosp and Hosp for Sick Children 1982-; author of many scientific pubns; memb: Blair-Bell Res Soc, Ovarian Club, Br Fertility Soc (and American), World Cncl of Paediatric and Adolescent Gynaecology; FRSM, FRACOG 1982 (MRACOG 1979), FRCOG 1990 (MRCOG 1979); *Books* Practical Paediatric and Adolescent Gynaecology (1989); *Recreations* tennis, golf; *Clubs* Gynaecological Club of GB, Roehampton; *Style*— Keith Edmonds, Esq; 78 Harley St, London W1N 1AE (☎ 071 636 4797)

EDMONDS, Knowler Gilliam; s of Herbert Southgate Edmonds (d 1950), of Chatham, Kent, and Dorothy Kate, *née* Dunkin (d 1973); *b* 27 July 1922; *Educ* Rochester Tech Coll, Medway Coll of Art and Crafts (Dip); *m* 6 Oct 1945, Gretta Marjorie (d 1988), da of Herbert Lovelady, DFC (d 1976); 1 s (Richard b 1950 d 1967), 1 da (Christine b 1948); *Career* WWII Sgt RAF (radar service) 1942-46; printing estimator C Tinling Co Ltd 1948-50, printing prodn offr Automatic Telephone & Electric Co Ltd 1950-56, printing mangr Hazel Grove Printing & Boxmaking Co Ltd 1956-60, printing conslt and prodr Cross Courtenay Ltd 1960-67, gp publicity mangr A Monk & Co Ltd 1967-83; numerous awards in art, printing and typography; newspaper contrib under pseudonym Edmond Gill; former memb: Printing Hist Soc, Br Assoc Indust Eds; *Recreations* books, photography, sketching, golf; *Style*— Knowler Edmonds, Esq; Kensington, London Road North, Poynton, Cheshire SK12 1BX (☎ 0625 873603)

EDMONDS, Richard Edward Howard; JP; s of late Eric Edmonds; *b* 7 July 1925; *Educ* Wellington, Oriel Coll Oxford; *m* 1958, Sarah Anne, da of Hugh Merriman, DSO, MC, TD, DL; 1 s, 2 da; *Career* Lt Oxfordshire and Bucks LI, served Palestine 1945-47; chm: Clements (Watford) Ltd, Coln Gravel Ltd; High Sherriff Hertfordshire 1991; co dir and farmer; *Recreations* shooting, fishing; *Style*— Richard Edmonds Esq, JP; Micklefield Hall, Rickmansworth, Herts WD3 6AQ (☎ 0923 774747, office 244222)

EDMONDS, Robert Humphrey Gordon (Robin); CMG (1969), MBE (1944); s of Air Vice-Marshal Charles Humphrey Kingsman Edmonds, CBE, DSO (d 1954), and Lorna Karim Chadwick, *née* Osborn (d 1974); *b* 5 Oct 1920; *Educ* Ampleforth, Brasenose Coll Oxford (MA); *m* 1, 1951 (m dis 1975), Georgina, da of late Cdr Anthony Boyce Combe; 4 s (Charles, Dominic, Robert, James); m 2, 1976, Enid Flora, widow of Dr Michael Balint; *Career* Army 1940-46, Maj (despatches); HM Foreign (later Diplomatic) Serv 1946-78; conslt Kleinwort Benson Ltd 1984-86 (advsr 1978-83), ret; memb Cncl Royal Inst of Int Affairs 1986-; *Books* Soviet Foreign Policy - The Brezhnev Years (1983), Setting The Mould - The United States and Britain 1945-50 (1986), The Big Three: Churchill, Roosevelt and Stalin in peace and war (1991); *Clubs* Turf; *Style*— Robin Edmonds, Esq, CMG, MBE; Raven House, Ramsbury, Wiltshire SN8 2PA

EDMONDSON, Hon Anthony James Kinghorn; yr s of 1 Baron Sandford (d 1959), and Edith Elizabeth, *née* Freeman (d 1946); *b* 20 July 1924; *Educ* Eton, Harvard Univ; *m* 1, 26 April 1947 (m dis 1969), Olivia Charlotte, yst da of late Rev Oswald Andrew Hunt; 3 s, 1 da; m 2, 21 Aug 1969, Hilary Pauline, o child of Col E S Trusler, OBE; 1 s (d 1979); *Career* Capt Grenadier Gds (ret); *Style*— The Hon Anthony Edmondson; Upton Manor, East Knoyle, Salisbury, Wilts SP3 6BW (☎ 0747 83 270)

EDMONDSON, Prof Hugh Dunstan Christopher; s of Dr Dunstan Hugh Edmondson (d 1990), and Audrey Mary, *née* Burdon (d 1989); *b* 13 April 1936; *Educ* Stonyhurst, Univ of Birmingham (DDS, BDS, DA, MB ChB); *m* 13 May 1961, Eileen Margaret, da of William Burley; 1 s (Christopher Hugh b 1964), 2 da (Rowena Mary b 1962, Caroline Audrey b 1963); *Career* prof of oral surgery and oral med Univ of Birmingham 1983- (lectr 1971-75 sr lectr 1975-83); chm Dental Formulary Sub Ctee BDA; memb: Advsy Ctee on NHS Drugs, Ctee on Dental and Surgical Materials BDA; fell BAOMS, MRCS, LRCP, LDS RCS, FDS RCS; *Books* A Radiological Atlas of Diseases of the Teeth and Jaws (with R M Bro and P G J Rout, 1983); *Recreations* shooting, fishing; *Style*— Prof Hugh Edmondson; Huddington Court, Huddington, Droitwich, Midlands WR9 7LJ (☎ 090 569 247); Dental Sch, St Chads, Queensway, Birmingham B4 6NN (☎ 021 236 8611)

EDMONDSON, Dr Philip Charles; s of Dr Reginald Edmondson (d 1964), of Dunchurch, Rugby, and Phyllis, *née* Elam; *b* 30 April 1938; *Educ* Uppingham, Christ's Coll Cambridge (MA, MD, MB BChir, MRCP), St Bart's Hosp London; *m* 7 Sept 1968, Margaret Lysbeth, da of Stanley Bayston, of Saxton, Tadcaster, Yorks; 3 da (Camilla b 25 April 1970, Claire b 12 May 1972, Cordelia b 5 Jan 1980); *Career* physician to Westminster Abbey 1979, conslt physician to many major industl cos; Freeman City of London, Liveryman Worshipful Soc of Apothecaries; FRSM, fell Med Soc of London; *Recreations* fishing, country pursuits; *Clubs* Boodles; *Style*— Dr Philip Edmondson; 18 Lennox Gardens, London SW1X 0DG (☎ 071 584 5194); Hornton Lodge, Vicarage Lane, Dunchurch, Rugby (☎ 0788 810 500); 99 Harley St, London W1N 1DF (☎ 071 935 7501)

EDMONDSON, Dr Robert Somerville; s of William Edmondson (d 1974), and Eileen Edmondson (d 1971); *b* 11 Aug 1937; *Educ* Bradford GS, St Bartholomew's Hosp Univ of London (MB BS); *m* 20 July 1962, Brenda Sigrid, da of John Woodhead (d 1964); 2 s (Christopher Somerville b 1965, William Somerville b 1969), 2 da (Sarah Jane b 1964, Ann-Marie b 1967); *Career* conslt anaesthetist Leeds Gen Infirmary 1969- (chairman of faculty 1986-88), hon lectr Univ of Leeds 1969-; sec and treas Yorkshire Soc Anaesthetists 1975-85; FFARCS; *Books* Intensive Care (contrib, 1983), Contemporary Neurology (1984); *Recreations* rowing, sailing, squash, photography, travel; *Style*— Dr Robert Edmondson; Chalforde House, 34 Hall Drive, Bramhope, Leeds LS16 9JE (☎ 0532 842478); Department of Anaesthesia, Leeds Central Infirmary, Leeds (☎ 0532 437172)

EDMONDSON, Simon Andrew; s of The Hon Anthony James Kinghorn Edmondson, of Upton Manor, East Knoyle, Salisbury, Wiltshire, and Olivia Charlotte, *née* Hunt; *b* 29 Aug 1955; *Educ* Shrewsbury, City and Guilds Sch of Art, Kingston Poly (BA), Chelsea Sch of Art (MA), Syracuse Univ NY (MFA); *Career* artist; solo exhibitions: Intrude (Fairbanks Gallery Syracuse NY) 1979, Portraits (Royal Star and Garter Richmond Surrey) 1981, Nicola Jacobs Gallery 1982, 1984, 1986, 1987, 1990, Michael Haas Gallery Berlin 1986, Turske and Turske Gallery Zurich 1986, Long and O'Hara Gallery NY 1986, David Beitzel Gallery NY 1989-91; gp exhibitions incl: Stowells Trophy (Royal Acad London) 1976, Northern Young Contemporaries (Walker Art Gallery Liverpool) 1977, Ogle Gallery Eastbourne 1978, two man exhibition (Fairbanks Gallery Syracuse NY) 1979, MFA '80 (Lowe Art Gallery NY) 1980, Abstract Lyricism (Cheltenham Music Festival) 1981, The Figuratine Exhibition (Nicola Jacob's Gallery) 1981 and 1983, Summer Exhibition (Nicola Jacobs Gallery London) 1982, Painter's Choice (Little Missenden Festival) 1983, The Image as Catalyst (Ashmolean Museum Oxford) 1984, Artists for the 1990's (Paton Gallery London), Reed Stremmel Gallery San Antonio Texas 1986, Long and O'Hara Gallery NY 1986, Kohji Ogura Gallery Nagoya Japan 1986, (The Self-Portrait - A Modern view (Artsite Bath) 1987, British Figurative Painting (Univ Art Gallery Calif State) 1987-88, Mother and Child (Lefevre Gallery London) 1988, British Art-The Literate Link (Asher Faure Gallery L A) 1988, Whitechapel Open (Whitechapel Art Gallery London) 1988, New British Painting (towing USA) 1988-90, Winter '89 and Ten Years at Nicola Jacobs Gallery (Nicola Jacobs Gallery London) 1989, Portfolio Two-Painters in Print (Curwen Gallery London) 1989; work in five public collections; *Awards* Ford Fndn award 1978, 1979, graduate fellowship Syracuse Univ 1979-80, Gtr London Arts Assoc award 1984; *Recreations* travelling, literature, poetry; *Style*— Simon Edmondson, Esq; 105 Carpenter's Rd, London E15 2DU (☎ 081 555 1671); Nicola Jacobs Gallery, 9 Cork St, London (☎ 071 437 3868); David Beitzel Gallery, 102 Prince St NY, NY10012 (☎ 212 219 2863)

EDMONDSON, Stephen John; s of George Edmondson, of Scunthorpe, and Jean Mary, *née* Stanton; *b* 21 Aug 1950; *Educ* Scunthorpe GS, Middx Hosp Med Sch, Univ of London (BSc, MB BS); *m* 17 July 1976, Barbara Bridget Alison, da of Dr Malcolm Nugent Samuel Duncan, TD; 1 s (Adam George b 1984); *Career* conslt cardiothoracic surgn Bart's 1984-; memb: Soc of Thoracic and Cardiovascular Surgns of GB and 1982, Br Cardiac Soc 1984, NE Thames Thoracic Soc; FRCS 1979, MRCP 1980; *Recreations* tennis, golf, squash, football; *Clubs* Vanderbilt Racquet, Ealing Golf, Ulysses FC; *Style*— Stephen Edmondson, Esq; 69 Harley St, London W1N 1DE (☎ 071 935 6375, fax 071 224 3823)

EDMONSTONE, Hon Mrs (Alicia Evelyn); *née* Browne; o da of 5 Baron Kilmaine (d 1946), and Lady Aline Kennedy (d 1957), da of 3 Marquess of Ailsa; *b* 4 Feb 1909; *m* 30 Nov 1936, Cdr Edward St John Edmonstone, RN (d 1983), yr s of Sir Archibald Edmonstone, 5 Bt, CVO (d 1954); 1 s (William), 1 da (Helen); *Style*— Hon Mrs Edmonstone; Barcombe Old Rectory, nr Lewes, Sussex BN8 5TN

EDMONSTONE, Sir Archibald Bruce Charles; 7 Bt (GB 1774), of Duntreath Castle, Stirlingshire; s of Sir Archibald Charles Edmonstone, 6 Bt (d 1954), and Gwendolyn Mary, *née* Field (d 1989); *b* 3 Aug 1934; *Educ* Stowe; *m* 1, 17 Jan 1957 (m dis 1967), Jane, er da of Maj-Gen Edward Charles Colville, CB, DSO (s of Adm Hon Sir Stanley Colville, GCB, GCMG, GCVO); 2 s (Archibald Edward Charles b 4 Feb 1961, Nicholas William Mark b 16 April 1963), 1 da (Philippa Carolyn b 12 June 1959); m 2, 12 June 1969, Juliet Elizabeth, o da of Maj-Gen Cecil Martin Fothergill Deakin, CB, CBE; 1 s (Dru Benjamin Marshall b 26 Oct 1971), 1 da (Elyssa Juliet b 11 Sept 1973); *Heir* s, Archibald Edward Charles Edmonstone (*qv*); *Career* 2 Lt Royal Scots Greys 1954-56; *Recreations* shooting, fishing; *Clubs* White's; *Style*— Sir Archibald Edmonstone, Bt; Duntreath Castle, Blanefield, by Glasgow (☎ 0360 70215)

EDMONSTONE, Archibald Edward Charles; s (by 1 m) and h of Sir Archibald Edmonstone, 7 Bt; *b* 4 Feb 1961; *Educ* Stowe, RMA Sandhurst; *Career* commissioned as 2 Lt Scots Gds 1982; *Style*— Archibald Edmonstone, Esq

EDMONTON, Bishop of (1984-); Rt Rev Brian John Masters; s of Stanley William Masters (d 1965), and Grace Hannah, *née* Stevens; *b* 17 Oct 1932; *Educ* Collyers Sch Horsham, Queens' Coll Cambridge (MA); *Career* insur broker Lloyds 1955-62; asst curate St Dunstan and All Saints Stepney 1964-69, vicar Holy Trinity Hoxton 1969-82, bishop Fulham 1982-84; *Recreations* theatre, squash; *Clubs* United Oxford and Cambridge Univ; *Style*— The Rt Rev the Bishop of Edmonton; 1 Regents Park Terrace, London NW1 7EE (☎ 071 267 4455, fax 071 267 4404)

EDMUND, John Humphrey; s of Charles Henry Humphrey Edmund, of Swansea, and Vera May, *née* Warmington; *b* 6 March 1935; *Educ* Swansea GS, Jesus Coll Oxford (MA); *m* 4 Sept 1965, (Elizabeth Ann) Myfanwy, da of William Lewis Williams, of Newport, Dyfed (d 1975); *Career* Nat Serv RN 1953-55; admitted slr 1961; ptnr Beor, Wilson & Lloyd Swansea; under sheriff W Glam 1983-, Clerk to Gen Cmmrs of Taxes (Swansea Div) 1986-; Law Soc 1962; *Clubs* Vincents (Oxford), Bristol Channel Yacht; *Style*— John Edmund, Esq; 84 Pennard Rd, Pennard, Swansea, West Glamorgan SA3 2AA (☎ 044128 2526); Calvert House, Calvert Terrace, Swansea SA1 6AP (☎ 0792 655 178, fax 0792 467 002)

EDMUND-DAVIES, Baron (Life Peer UK 1974), of Aberpennar, Co Mid-Glamorgan; (Herbert) Edmund Edmund-Davies; PC (1966); assumed additional name of Edmund to patronymic 1974; 3 s of Morgan John Davies, of Mountain Ash, Glam, and Elizabeth Maud Edmunds; *b* 15 July 1906; *Educ* Mountain Ash, King's Coll London, Exeter Coll Oxford; *m* 1935, Sarah Eurwen, da of late John Williams, JP, of Barry; 3 da (Hon Ann (Hon Mrs Worlock) b 1936, Hon Elisabeth (Hon Mrs Large) b 1939, Hon Shân (Hon Mrs Schüffel) b 1940); *Career* called to the Bar Gray's Inn 1929, bencher 1948, treas 1965 and 1966, former rec of Merthyr Tydfil, Swansea, Cardiff, High Court judge (Queen's Bench) 1958-66, Lord Justice of Appeal 1966-74, Lord of Appeal in Ordinary 1974-82; life govr and fellow King's Coll London, pro chllr Univ of

Wales 1974-85; chm Aberfan Inquiry Tribunal 1966; Hon LLD Univ of Buckingham 1989; founded Edmund-Davies Chair in Criminal Law Kings Coll London 1989; kt 1958; *Style—* The Rt Hon Lord Edmund-Davies, PC; 5 Gray's Inn Sq, London WC1

EDMUNDS, Michael John; s of John Harold Edmunds (d 1985), of Cradley, Hereford and Worcester, and Jessica Agnes, *née* Muir (d 1961); *b* 6 Aug 1933; *Educ* Buckingham Coll Harrow, Univ of London (BSc), UCL (Planning Dip); *m* 4 April 1959, Mollie Evelyn, da of John Leslie Butlin (d 1988), of Bexhill, Sussex; 1 s (Andrew b 1973), 2 da (Alison b 1965, Katie b 1966); *Career* RAF Gen Duties Branch 1952-54; surveyor in nat ind and pension funds City Centre Properties Ltd and Settled Estate 1957-68, dir Debenham Tewson and Chinnocks 1987-90 (joined 1968, ptnr 1973); memb Bd Coll of Estate Mgmnt 1983- (hon treas 1983-86), ARICS 1958, FRICS 1978; *Recreations* family, work, profession, enjoying the sun; *Clubs* RAF, Royal Automobile; *Style—* Michael Edmunds, Esq; Dell Cottage, Chartridge, nr Chesham, Buckinghamshire HP5 2TS (☎ 024 020 441)

EDNAM, Viscount; William Humble David Jeremy Ward; s and h of 4 Earl of Dudley; *b* 27 March 1947; *Educ* Eton, ChCh Oxford; *m* 1, 1972 (m dis 1976), Sarah, da of Sir Alastair Coats, 4 Bt; m 2, 1976 (m dis 1980), Debra Louise, da of George Robert Pinney; 1 da; *Style—* Viscount Ednam; Villa Montanet, Les Garrigues, 84220 Goult-Gordes, France

EDNEY, Dr Andrew Thomas Bailey; s of Sydney George Edney (d 1986), and Dorothy Mary, *née* Smith; *b* 1 July 1932; *Educ* Borden Sch, Univ of London, RCVS (BVMS), Open Univ (BA); *Career* Nat Serv 201 Sqdn RAF 950-52; gen practice Odiham Hants 1958-65, MAFF 1966-67, vet advsr in industry Waltham Centre Leics 1968-85, vet ed Pergamon Press plc 1985-, vet conslt author and ed 1985; chm Round Table; BSAVA: sec 1976-77, nat pres 1979-80; WSAVA: sec 1982-86, vice pres 1986-90, pres 1990-; MRCVS 1958, FRSM 1970; *Books* Dog and Cat Nutrition (1982, 1988), Pet Care (1984), Dog and Puppy Care (1985); *Recreations* fine art related to animals, vintage aircraft, gardening; *Clubs* RSM, Kennel; *Style—* Dr Andrew Edney; 22 Crocket Lane, Empingham, Rutland, Leics LE15 8PW

EDRIC, Robert; s of E H Armitage, of Sheffield; *b* 14 April 1956; *Educ* Firth Park GS Sheffield, Univ of Hull (BA, PhD); *m* Helen Sara, *née* Jones; 1 s (Bruce Copley Jones); *Career* novelist; Winter Garden (1985), A New Ice Age (1986), A Lunar Eclipse (1989), In The Days of The American Museum (1990); James Tait Black Fiction prize 1985, runner up Guardian Fiction prize 1986; *Style—* Robert Edric, Esq; c/o Antony Harwood, Curtis Brown Ltd, 162-8 Regent St, London (☎ 071 872 0331, fax 071 872 0332)

EDRIDGE, Olga; da of Col Bernard Alfred Edridge, OBE, of Athens, Greece, and Erica, *née* Mavrommati; *b* 22 March 1951; *Educ* Makris HS for Girls Athens Greece, London Film Sch (Dip in Film Making), Univ of Reading (BA); *Career* BBC: asst film ed and acting ed 1975-79, trainee asst prodr 1979-81, asst prodr and dir 1981-83, prodr of religious progs 1983-86, series prodr of Heart of the Matter 1986-, winner of one Sandford St Martin Tst award 1985 and One world Bdcast Tst award 1987; *Recreations* windsurfing, swimming, theatre, eating with friends; *Style—* Ms Olga Edridge; BBC TV, Room E1019, Television Centre, London W12 7RJ (☎ 081 576 1487)

EDUR, Thomas; s of Enn Edur, of Estoria, and Linda, *née* Mishustina, of Estonia; *b* 20 Jan 1969; *Educ* Tallinn Ballet Sch; *m* 1990, Agnes, da of Juhan Oaks; *Career* ballet dancer; Estonia Ballet Theatre: Coppelia 1987, Giselle 1988, Paquita 1988, Sleeping Beauty 1989, Nostalgia 1989, Romeo and Juliet 1990, Swan Lake 1990, Estonian Ballads; English National Ballet: Coppelia 1990, Nutcraker 1990, Les Sylphide 1990, 3 Preludes 1990, Our Waltzes 1990, Sanguine Fan 1990; Bronze medal and Best Couple prize with his ptnr Agnes Oaks at 1990 Competition in Jackson Mississippi; *Recreations* nature lover; *Style—* Thomas Edur, Esq; English National Ballet, Markova House, 39 Jay Mews, London SW7 2ES (☎ 071 581 1245)

EDWARD, Judge David Alexander Ogilvy; CMG (1981), QC (Scot 1974); s of John Ogilvy Christie Edward (d 1960), of Perth, and Margaret Isabel, *née* MacArthur (d 1989); *b* 14 Nov 1934; *Educ* Sedbergh, Univ Coll Oxford (MA), Univ of Edinburgh (LLB); *m* 22 Dec 1962, Elizabeth Young, da of Terence McSherry, of Edinburgh; 2 s (Giles b 1965, John b 1968), 2 da (Anne b 1964, Katherine b 1971); *Career* Nat Serv Sub Lt RNVR 1955-57; advocate 1962, clerk and treas Faculty of Advocates 1967-77, pres Consultative Ctee of the Bars and Law Socs of the Euro Community 1978-80; tstee Nat Library of Scotland 1966-; memb: Law Advsy Ctee British Cncl 1976-88, Panel of Arbitrators Int Centre for Settlement of Investmt Disputes 1979-89; chm Continental Assets Trust plc 1985-89, dir: Adam & Co Group plc 1983-89, The Harris Tweed Assoc Ltd 1984-89; pres Scottish Cncl for Arbitration, chm Hopetown House Preservation Tst: Salvesen prof of European Inst Univ of Edinburgh 1985-89; Judge of the Court of First Instance of the EC 1989; *Clubs* Athenaeum, New (Edinburgh); *Style—* Judge David Edward, CMG, QC; 32 Heriot Row, Edinburgh EH3 6ES European Court of First Instance, L-2925 Luxembourg (☎ 352 4303 3494)

EDWARD, Hon Mrs (Gillian Margaret); *née* Hunter; da of Baron Hunter of Newington, MBE (Life Peer); *b* 25 May 1948; *Educ* Dundee HS, St Leonards Sch; *m* 1973, Malcolm Greig Edward, s of Oswald Andrew Edward (d 1976); 1 s (Mark b 1979), 1 da (Marisa b 1974); *Career* RGN, SCM; no longer practising; *Style—* The Hon Mrs Edward; 82 Lordswood Rd, Harborne, Birmingham B17 9BY (☎ 021 427 2069)

EDWARDES, Hon Mrs David; Elizabeth; yst da of late Robert Alexander Longman Broadley, of Priest Hill, Limpsfield, Surrey; *m* 22 July 1939, Cdr Hon David Edwardes, DSC (d 1983), 3 s of late 6 Baron Kensington, CMG, DSO, TD, JP, DL; 3 da; *Style—* The Hon Mrs David Edwardes; Carpenter's Yard, Compton Pauncefoot, Yeovil, Somerset

EDWARDES, Leonard Edward (Len); s of Charles James Henry Edwardes (d 1973), of 4 Grove Cottages, High St, Horsell, Woking, Surrey, and Emily, *née* Brown (d 1965); *b* 9 Oct 1931; *Educ* Goldsworth Co Secdy Sch Surrey; *m* 7 June 1954, Sheena, da of Robert George Gray (d 1968); 2 s (Simon b 7 April 1963, Richard b 15 May 1965); *Career* Nat Serv RAF 1950-52; chief engr Debenhams Ltd 1967-75, ptnr Cranage & Perkins (consulting engrs) 1975-80; sr ptnr: Edwardes Friedlander 1980-82, Edwardes Whittle Partnership 1982-; chm and md Nationwide Maintenance Ltd; dir: Falcon Mechanical servs Ltd, E & C Engrg Servs Ltd, Docklands Maintenance Ltd, Falcon Bldg Maintenance Ltd; Freeman: City of London 1981, Worshipful Co of Fanmakers; FBIM 1986; *Recreations* horse racing, golf; *Clubs* Ascot and Fernfell Golf; *Style—* Len Edwardes, Esq; Nationwide Maintenance Ltd, Falcon House, Catteshall Lane, Godalming, Surrey GU7 1JP, (☎ 04868 28674/20556, fax 0483 426987)

EDWARDES, Sir Michael Owen; s of Denys Owen Edwardes, and Audrey Noel, *née* Copeland; *b* 11 Oct 1930; *Educ* St Andrew's Coll Grahamstown S Africa, Rhodes Univ (BA); *m* 1958, Mary Margaret, *née* Finlay; 3 da; *Career* chm and chief exec BL Ltd 1977-82; non-exec chm Chloride Gp plc 1982- (joined 1951, dir 1969-77, chief exec 1972-74, chm and chief exec 1974-77, non-exec dep chm 1977); non-exec chm Hill Samuel South Africa 1982- (non-exec dir Hill Samuel Gp 1980-; memb Judging Panel for Hill Samuel Business Awards 1982); first chm Mercury Communications 1982-1983; exec chm ICL plc 1984-; memb: CBI Cncl 1974-81, CBI President's Ctee 1981-, NEB 1975-77; CBIM (vice chm 1977-80); non-exec dir Int Mgmnt Devpt Inst 1978-; dir A J Gooding Gp 1983-, exec chm Dunlop Hldgs 1984-; Hon FIMechE, Hon LLD Rhodes Univ; kt 1979; *Books* Back From The Brink (1983); *Style—* Sir Michael Edwardes; ICL, Bridge House, Fulham, London SW6 (☎ 071 788 7272)

EDWARDES, Hon (William) Owen Alexander; s and h of 8 Baron Kensington; *b* 21 July 1964; *Style—* The Hon Owen Edwardes; Friar Tuck, Mt West, PO Box 549, Mooi River 3300, Natal, S Africa

EDWARDES, Hon Mrs Michael; Sylvia Inez Pakenham; *née* Johnstone; da of Col Hope Johnstone, CBE (d 1939), and Lilian Ada, *née* Stocker; *m* 1, 21 March 1926 (m dis 1946), Lt-Col Alfred Joseph Thorburn McGaw; 1 da; m 2, 22 Aug 1946, Lt-Col Hon Michael George Edwardes, MBE (d 1985), yst s of 6 Baron Kensington; *Style—* Hon Mrs Michael Edwardes; Ilsom House, Tetbury, Gloucestershire GL8 8RY

EDWARDS, Alan Kenneth Warneford; s of late Trevor James Edwards; *b* 6 June 1927; *Educ* Birkenhead Sch; *m* 1952, Valerie Frances, *née* Burbridge; 3 s, 1 da; *Career* CA; in practice 1954-1961; fin dir Lonsdale Universal Ltd 1962-69, md and dep chm 1969-83, chm Turner Langdale Ltd 1983-; FCA; *Recreations* cricket, motor racing, rugby; *Clubs* MCC; *Style—* Alan Edwards, Esq; Hill Close, Sandy Lane, Cobham, Surrey (☎ 0932 862068)

EDWARDS, Andrew John Cumming; s of John Edwards (d 1977), and Norah Hope, *née* Bevan; *b* 3 Nov 1940; *Educ* Fettes, St John's Coll Oxford (MA), Harvard Univ (AM, MPA); *m* 11 Oct 1969 (m dis 1987), Charlotte Anne, da of Arthur L Chilcot, MBE (d 1981); 1 s (Angus b 1974), 2 da (Hermia b 1972, Madeleine b 1978); *Career* asst master Malvern Coll 1962-63, asst princ HM Treasy 1963-67, private sec to Sir William Armstrong 1966-67, princ HM Treasy 1967-75 (asst sec 1975-84), RCDS 1979, asst sec DES 1984-85, under sec HM Treasy 1985-89 (dep sec (public servs) 1990-); Harkness fell Cambridge Mass 1971-73; conductor: Treasy Singers 1968-84, Acad of St Mary's Wimbledon 1980-; govr Br Inst of Recorded Sound 1975-79, sec Bd of Royal Opera House 1988-; *Books* Nuclear Weapons, the balance of terror, the quest for peace (1986); *Recreations* music, writing, reading, walking; *Style—* Andrew Edwards, Esq; Treasury Chambers, Parliament St, London SW1P 3AG (☎ 071 270 4390)

EDWARDS, Hon Mrs (Ann Cecily Mary); *née* Talbot; da of 8 Baron Talbot de Malahide, MC (d 1975); *b* 22 Dec 1931; *m* 1 Oct 1955, Col Edward Reginald Edwards, s of Edward John Edwards, of Pontypridd, Glamorgan; 3 s; *Style—* Hon Mrs Edwards; Malahide, Whiteway, Litton Cheney, Dorchester, Dorset DT2 9AG

EDWARDS, Hon Mrs (Anna Elizabeth); *née* Turner; da of 2 Baron Netherthorpe; *b* 17 Dec 1961; *Educ* Abbot's Hill Sch; *m* 20 Dec 1986, Simon M Edwards, er s of late Roland Edwards; 1 s (Samuel Alexander b 19 March 1990); *Career* housewife, formerly artist; *Style—* The Hon Mrs Edwards; 31 Sutherland Square, London SE17 3EQ

EDWARDS, Prof Anthony Davies; Gwilym Morgan Edwards (d 1956), of Swansea, and Beryl Eileen, *née* Davies (d 1982); *b* 4 June 1936; *Educ* Bishop Gore GS Swansea, Corpus Christi Coll Cambridge (MA), Univ of London (MPhil), Univ of Exeter (PhD); *m* 16 April 1960, Ann Hopkins, da of William Henry Griffiths, of Penclawdd, Gower; 1 s (Ceri David b 1965), 2 da (Kathryn Jane b 1964, Megan Ruth b 1967); *Career* history teacher: Crown Woods Sch 1957-58, East Ham GS 1959-63, Latymer Upper Sch 1963-66; lectr in educn Univ of Exeter 1966-71, sr lectr Univ of Manchester 1976-79 (lectr in educn 1971-76), currently dean of educn Univ of Newcastle upon Tyne (prof of educn 1979-); memb City of Newcastle Educn Ctee, vice chm Univs Cncl for Educn and Trg of Teachers, educn advsr Univs Funding Cncl; memb: Nat Curriculum Cncl, Curriculum Review Ctee, Br Educnl Res Assoc; *Books* The Changing Sixth Form (1970), Language in Culture and Class (1976), The Language of Teaching (with VJ Furlong, 1978), Investigating Classroom Talk (with D Westgate, 1987), The State and Private Education: an Investigation of the Assisted Place Scheme (with J Fitz and G Whitty, 1989); *Recreations* hill walking, travel, photography, cinema, music; *Style—* Prof Anthony Edwards; 2 Hollin Mill Terrace, Riding Mill, Northumberland NE44 6HR (☎ 0434 682 268); University School of Education, St Thomas' St, Newcastle upon Tyne NE1 7RU (☎ 091 222 6000, fax 091 222 8170)

EDWARDS, Brian; CBE (1988); s of John Albert Edwards (d 1979), of Bebington, and (Ethel) Pat, *née* Davis (d 1980); *b* 19 Feb 1942; *Educ* Wirral GS; *m* 7 Nov 1964, Jean, da of William Cannon, of Neston; 2 s (Christopher b 28 April 1973, Jonathan (twin) b 28 April 1973), 2 da (Penny Adrienne b 27 May 1967, Paula Michelle b 14 Nov 1968); *Career* various hosp posts 1958-69, lectr in health serv studies Univ of Leeds 1969-71, dep gp sec Hull Hosp Mgmnt Ctee 1971-73, dist admin Leeds Dist Health Authy 1973-76, area admin Cheshire AHA 1976-81, regnl gen mangr Trent RHA 1984- (regnl admin 1981-83), visiting prof Univ of Keele 1989; pres Inst of Health Servs Mgmnt 1983; chm: Manpower Advsy Gp NHS 1983-85, Regnl Gen Mangrs Gp England 1986; memb Standing Advsy Ctee on Audit RCP; conslt WHO in: India, Russia, Guyana, Czechoslovakia; ed Health Servs Manpower Review; FHSM 1964, CBIM 1988; *Books* Si Vis Pacem (1973), Planning the Child Health Services (1975), Manager and Industrial Relations (1979), Merit Awards for Doctors (1987); *Recreations* golf; *Clubs* Bakewell Golf (capt 1991); *Style—* Brian Edwards, Esq, CBE; 3 Royal Croft Drive, Baslow, Derbyshire DE4 1SN (☎ 024 658 3459, fax : 024 658 2583); Trent Regional Health Authority, Fulwood, Sheffield, S Yorks (☎ 0742 630 300)

EDWARDS, Hon Mrs (Catherine Gerran); *née* Lloyd; yr da of Baron Lloyd of Kilgerran, CBE, QC (Life Peer, d 1991), and Phyllis Mary, *née* Shepherd; *b* 1 March 1947; *Educ* Roedean; *m* 1972, Philip Gwynfryn Edwards; 1 s, 3 da; *Recreations* tennis; *Clubs* Royal Commonwealth Trust; *Style—* The Hon Mrs Edwards; 2 Woodhill House, Kentish Lane, Essendon, Hertfordshire AL9 6JY

EDWARDS, (David) Cenwyn; s of Alwyn John Edwards (d 1986), of 15 Glasfryn, Pontarddulais, and Edwina Jane, *née* Thomas; *b* 27 Oct 1945; *Educ* Llanelli Boys GS, Univ of N Wales Bangor (BA); *m* 17 April 1971 (m dis 1990), Margaret Eluned, da of Thomas Owen Davies (d 1977); 1 s (Gruffudd b 1979), 1 da (Lowri b 1977); *Career* joined HTV 1969; asst head of news and current affrs 1978-82, head of current affrs 1982-85, asst prog controller and N Wales exec 1985-89, controller of factual and general progs 1989-; memb: Diplomatic and Cwlth Writers Assoc of Br, Nat Eisteddfodd Court; *Recreations* drama, rugby, cricket; *Clubs* Llanelli RFC; *Style—* Cenwyn Edwards, Esq; 28 Denton Rd, Canton, Cardiff; HTV House, Culverhouse Cross, Cardiff (☎ 0222 590157, fax 0222 597183)

EDWARDS, Sir Christopher John Churchill; 5 Bt (1866) of Pye Nest, Yorkshire; s of Sir (Henry) Charles (Serrell Priestly) Edwards, 4 Bt (d 1963), and Daphne, *née* Birt; *b* 16 Aug 1941; *Educ* Frensham Heights Sch, Loughborough Coll; *m* 1972, Gladys Irene Vogelgesang; 2 s (David Charles Priestley b 22 Feb 1974, Ryan Matthew Churchill b 16 April 1979); *Heir* s, David Charles Priestley Edwards; *Career* gen mangr Kelsar Inc (American Home Products, San Diego, Calif) 1979-84, vice pres Valleylab Inc (Pfizer Inc, Boulder Colorado) 1984-89, dir Ohmeda (BOC Group, Louisville, Colorado) 1989-; *Clubs* Ranch Country (Westminster, Colorado); *Style—* Sir Christopher Edwards, Bt; 11637 Country Club Drive, Westminster, Colorado 80234, USA (☎ 0101 30346 93156)

EDWARDS, Prof Christopher Richard Watkin; s of Wing Cdr Thomas Archibald

Watkin Edwards (d 1986), and Beatrice Elizabeth Ruby, *née* Telfer; *b* 12 Feb 1942; *Educ* Marlborough, Univ of Cambridge (MB BChir, MD); *m* 6 April 1968, Sally Amanda Le Blount, da of Sqdn Ldr Gerald Le Bount Kidd, OBE, of Westerham, Kent; 2 s (Adam b 1969, Crispin b 1974), 1 da (Kate b 1971); *Career* sr lectr in med and hon conslt physician St Bartholomew's Hosp London 1975, prof of clinical med Univ of Edinburgh and hon conslt physician to the Lothian Health Bd 1980, chm Dept of Med Western Gen Hosp Edinburgh; memb: Systems Bd and chm Grants Ctee MRC, Physiology and Pharmacology Ctee Wellcome Tst; memb Cncl Soc for Endocrinology; FRCP 1979, FRCPE 1981, FRSE 1990; *Books* Essential Hypertension as an Endocrine Disease (co ed, 1985), Davidson's Principles and Practice of Medicine (co ed, 1987), Recent Advances in Endocrinology and Metabolism (co ed, 1989); *Recreations* golf, painting; *Clubs* Athenaeum; *Style—* Prof Christopher Edwards, FRSE; 2 Ellersly Rd, Edinburgh EH12 6HZ (☎ 031 337 1681); Department of Medicine, Western General Hospital, Edinburgh EH4 2XU (☎ 031 332 2525)

EDWARDS, Sir (John) Clive Leighton; 2 Bt (UK 1921), of Treforis, Co Glamorgan; s of Sir John Bryn Edwards, 1 Bt (d 1922), and Kathleen Ermyntrude, *née* Corfield (d 1975); *b* 11 Oct 1916; *Educ* Winchester; *Career* European War 1940-45 with RASC and as Capt Royal Pioneer Corps; memb: Brooklands Soc, Brooklands Museum; *Recreations* motoring, gardening; *Clubs* Bugatti Owners, Midland Automobile (hon life memb); *Style—* Sir Clive Edwards, Bt; Milntown, Lezayre, nr Ramsey, IOM

EDWARDS, (John) Colin; s of John Henry Edwards (d 1985), of Penzance, and Gwendoline Doris, *née* Sara; *b* 27 Aug 1936; *Educ* Clifton Coll, Lincoln Coll Oxford (MA); *m* 24 Aug 1967, (Daphne) Paulette, da of (Herbert) Peter Bayley, of New Jersey, USA; 1 s (Gavin Perran b 30 March 1973), 1 da (Rebecca b 20 April 1971); *Career* slr 1960; attorney at law Jamaica 1971, dep coroner Truro Dist 1975-, chm Social Security Appeal Tbnl 1980-, dep registrar High and Co Court Western Circuit 1985-; chm Jamaica Rugby Football Union 1972-74 (rep 28 times 1962-72), dep chm Truro Squash Club 1983-87 (Jamaican Champion 1962-72); memb: Law Soc 1960, Jamaica Law Reform Ctee; *Recreations* golf, jogging, squash, reading, gardening; *Clubs* Truro Golf, Truro Squash; *Style—* Colin Edwards, Esq; 15 Nansavallon Road, Truro, Cornwall (☎ 0872 77138); Carlyon & Son, 78 Lemon Street, Truro, Cornwall (☎ 0872 78641, fax 0872 72072)

EDWARDS, David Manning; s of Maj Eric Arthur James Edwards, MC, OBE (d 1983), of Godalming, Surrey, and Sybil Manning, *née* Fenton; *b* 28 April 1947; *Educ* Guilford Sch of Art (BA); *m* 4 May 1974, Linda Jane, da of Norman Arthur Robert Winton, of Clockhouse Mews, Huxley Close, Charterhouse, Godalming, Surrey; 2 s (Adam Harry b 30 Nov 1979, Guy b 30 July 1982); *Career* cartoon film dir and designer; BAFTA Best Animated Cartoon Film 1986 (for Superted); *Recreations* motor racing; *Style—* David Edwards, Esq; Berrymeadow Moorlands, Cowbridge, South Glamorgan CF7 7RQ (☎ 044 634622)

EDWARDS, David Michael; s of Denis Arthur Edwards, of London, and Maude, *née* Cruse; *b* 4 Dec 1947; *Educ* Tulse Hill, London Coll of Printing; *m* 1968, and Christine Nancy, da of John Carzana, of Kent; 2 s (Justin b 1979, Julian b 1981); *Career* publishing Print Buying; chm Paperback Production Gp 1981-82; chm Book Production Gp 1986-87, dir Macdonald & Co Ltd 1981-82; dir (fndr) Century Publishing Co Ltd 1982-85; dir Century Hutchinson Publishing Gp Ltd 1985-88; chm Tashanda Properties Ltd Gibraltar; played football Corinthian Casuals AFC (1st team) 1966-68; *Recreations* golf, tennis, photography; *Style—* David Edwards; 50 Barnfield Wood Rd, Beckenham, Kent BR3 2SU; 12 Marbella Country Club, Nueva Auducia, Marbella, Spain (☎ 9 52 817 150)

EDWARDS, David Michael; CMG (1990); s of Ernest William Edwards, and Thelma Irene, *née* Foxley; *b* 28 Feb 1940; *Educ* King's Sch Canterbury, Univ of Bristol (LLB); *m* 29 Jan 1966, Veronica Margaret, da of Robert Postgate, of Cannes, France; 1 s (Adrian David b 1969), 1 da (Vanessa Louise b 1967); *Career* admitted slr 1964, slr Supreme Court 1964-67, asst legal advsr FO 1967; legal advsr: Br Mil Govt Berlin 1972, Br Embassy Bonn 1974; legal cnsllr 1977, dir legal div IAEA Vienna (on secondment) 1977-79, legal cnsllr FCO 1979, agent of the UK Govt in cases before Euro Cmmn and Court of Human Rights 1979-82, cnsllr and legal advsr UK Mission to UN NY and HM Embassy Washington 1985-88, dep legal advsr FCO 1989-90, sr counsel Bechtel Ltd 1990-, law offr (int law) Hong Kong Govt 1990-; *Recreations* reading, travel, antique clocks, gardening; *Clubs* Royal Over-Seas League, Hong Kong Cricket; *Style—* David Edwards, Esq, CMG; 3 Helene Court, 14 Shouson Hill Rd, Hong Kong

EDWARDS, David St John; s of Capt Herbert Edwards (ka 1917); *b* 16 April 1917; *Educ* Wellington, St John's Coll Cambridge; *m* 1947, Kathleen Mary, da of Surgn Rear Adm Gilbert Syms; 1 s, 2 da; *Career* freight forwarder, dir LEP Transport & Associated Cos 1960-, chm Express Container Transport 1972-; *Recreations* sailing, bridge; *Style—* David Edwards, Esq; Shenley, The Drive, Woking, Surrey (☎ 61535)

EDWARDS, Derek; *b* 28 March 1931; *Educ* Univ of Wales (BSc); *m* Julia Maureen; 1 s (Christopher James), 2 da (Karen Jane, Susan Carolyn); *Career* Nat Serv, flying offr RAF 1952-54; Alcan: UK, W Africa; Pillar Hldgs, dir RTZ Corp, non exec dir TI Gp, non exec dir Bridon Gp: FIM, FEng; *Clubs* East India, MCC; *Style—* Derek Edwards, Esq; RTZ Corp, 6 St James's Sq, London SW1

EDWARDS, (Ronald) Derek Keep; JP (Hants 1978); s of Ronald Allan George Edwards (d 1981), of Hants, and Edith Vere, *née* Keep (d 1974); *b* 22 Nov 1934; *Educ* Winchester; *m* 1, 6 June 1958 (m dis 1984), Sally Anne, da of Patrick Boyle Lake Coghlan, of Fernhurst, West Sussex; 4 s (David b 1959, Simon b 1960, James b 1962, Charles b 1969); m 2, 3 March 1988, Julia Ann; *Career* Kings Dragoon Gds 1953-55, Inns of Ct Regt (TA) 1955-61; memb Stock Exchange 1959; ptnr: R Edwards Chandler & Co 1965-69, Brewin Dolphin & Co 1969-80, AH Cobbold & Co 1980-85; dir Cobbold Roach Ltd 1985; govr Amesbury Sch 1971-86, churchwarden St Mary Aldermary City 1958-80; memb Ctee: Hants Hunt Club, Bassishaw Ward Club (chm 1971); memb Ct of Common Cncl 1978-, Sheriff of London 1989-90; Freeman: City of London 1971, Worshipful Co of Loriners; FBIM, OStJ; *Recreations* field sports, riding, skiing; *Clubs* Cavalry & Guards, City Livery; *Style—* Derek Edwards, Esq, JP; Coneycroft House, Selborne, Hampshire; 2 New Town, Chichester, West Sussex (☎ 071 626 1601/0243 775373)

EDWARDS, Diane Dolores; *b* 17 June 1966; *Career* athlete; memb Sale Harriers Athletics Club, jr UK int 1984, full UK int 1985-; achievements at 800m: English Schs champion 1984, WAAA champion 1986 and 1987, UK Champion 1987, Silver medal Cwlth Games 1986; finallist Olympics Seoul 1988, finallist Euro Championships Split Yugoslavia 1990, Gold medal Cwlth Games Auckland NZ 1990; record holder: Br 600m 1988 (1 minute 26.1 seconds), English 800m 1990 (1 minute 58.6 seconds); ranked No 1 800m UK 1987-; sec Ron Hill Sports; *Style—* Miss Diane Edwards; Amateur Athletic Association, Edgbaston House, 3 Duchess Place, off Hagley Road, Edgbaston, Birmingham B16 8NM (☎ 021 456 4050)

EDWARDS, Duncan John; s of John H C Edwards (d 1973), of Birmingham, and Joan Florence, *née* Battin; *b* 31 Dec 1943; *Educ* Bournville Sch, Birmingham Coll of Commerce; *m* 10 May 1969, Hilary Mary, da of A D Peel (d 1988); 2 s (Robert John b 14 March 1972, Paul Michael b 16 May 1976), 1 da (Joanne Elizabeth b 9 March 1970); *Career* sr admin asst CEGB 1967 (admin trainee 1962-67), admin Worcs CC 1967-71, sr admin United Birmingham Hosp 1971-74, acting asst admin Queen Elizabeth Hosp Birmingham 1974-75, hosp admin Birmingham Children's Hosp 1975-78, hosp sec Royal Hosp Wolverhampton 1978-80, hosp admin Selly Oak Hosp Birmingham 1980-86, unit gen mangr acute servs South Birmingham Health Authy 1986-; gp chm Boy Scout Movement; ACIS, AHSM; *Recreations* gardening, rugby, swimming; *Style—* Duncan Edwards, Esq; Unit General Managers Office, Woodlands Nurses Home, Selly Oak Hospital, Raddlebarn Rd, Birmingham B29 6JD (☎ 021 472 5313)

EDWARDS, Dr (Iorwerth) Eiddon Stephen; CMG (1973), CBE (1968); s of Edward Edwards (d 1944), and Ellen Jane, *née* Higgs (d 1942); *b* 21 July 1909; *Educ* Merchant Taylors', Gonville and Caius Coll Cambridge (MA, LittD); *m* 1938, Annie Elizabeth, yst da of Charles Edwards Lisle (d 1945); 1 s (Philip d 1968), 1 da (Lucy); *Career* keeper of Egyptian antiquities Br Museum 1955-74, jt ed Cambridge Ancient History (3 edn) Vols I-III; author of numerous pubns on Egyptian archaeology and language; FBA; foreign corresponding memb of the Inst de France, Académie des I et Belles-Lettres Paris, ordinary memb of the German Archaeological Inst, corresponding memb of the Fondation Égyptologique Reine Élis Brussels; *Recreations* gardening; *Clubs* Athenaeum; *Style—* Dr Eiddon Edwards, CMG, CBE; Dragon House, Deddington, Oxford OX5 4TT (☎ 0869 38481)

EDWARDS, His Hon Judge (David) Elgan Hugh; s of Howell Dan Edwards, JP (d 1986), of Rhyl, Clywyd, and Dilys, *née* Williams; *b* 6 Dec 1943; *Educ* Rhyl GS, UCW Aberystwyth (LLB); *m* 1, 29 July 1967 (m dis 1981), Jane Elizabeth Hayward; 1 s (Daniel Richard Huw b 1974), 1 da (Kathryn Sian Elizabeth b 1971); m 2, 31 July 1982, Carol Anne, da of Arthur Smalls, of Saughall, Chester; 1 s (Thomas Huw b 1984); *Career* called to the Bar Gray's Inn 1967, rec Wales and Chester Circuit 1982-, attached to Wales and Chester Circuit 1990-; memb Chester City Cncl 1974-84, Sheriff City of Chester 1977-78; *Recreations* swimming; *Clubs* Chester City; *Style—* His Hon Judge Elgan Edwards; c/o Chester Crown Court, The Castle, Chester (☎ 0244 317606)

EDWARDS, Elton Percy (Bill); *b* 25 March 1929; *Educ* Hereford HS for Boys; *m* 3 Sept 1956, Monica Jill; 1 s (Mark William b 3 Aug 1961), 1 da (Elizabeth Jane b 10 June 1958); *Career* CA 1951-; Thompson and Wood Hereford 1951 (articled 1945-50), co sec and accountant Russell Baldwin and Bright 1954-64, ptnr Little Co 1964-86, sr ptnr Edwards Little Co 1986-, established insolvency practice 1967; sec OFFA Group 1988; former chm Hereford Round Table, pres City of Hereford Rotary Club; *Recreations* golf, fishing, swimming, travel; *Clubs* Rotary (Hereford); *Style—* Bill Edwards, Esq; Casita, 7 Yew Tree Gardens, Kings Acre, Hereford (☎ 0432 263040)

EDWARDS, Very Rev (Thomas) Erwyd Pryse; s of Richard Humphreys Edwards (d 1957), and Gwladys, *née* Morgan (d 1973); *b* 26 Jan 1933; *Educ* Machynlleth GS, St David's Univ Coll Lampeter (BD 1956), St Michael's Coll Llandaff; *m* 16 Sept 1961, Mair, da of William Thomas Roberts (d 1988); 2 s (Sion Erwyd b 6 Oct 1965, Huw Thomas b 25 Feb 1969); *Career* ordained deacon 1958, priest 1959, curate Caernarfon 1958-63, asst chaplain St George's Hosp London 1963-66, senior chaplain King's Coll Hospital London 1966-72; vicar: Penmon (Anglesey) 1972-75, Menai Bridge 1975-81, St David's Bangor 1981-86, St James 1986-88; canon Bangor 1988, dean Bangor 1988; chaplain St Davids Hospital Bangor 1981-83, memb of Chaplaincy team Ysbyty Gwynedd 1983-86, area chaplain (Wales) Butlins Holidays Ltd 1982-86; *Recreations* music, DIY, reading; *Style—* The Very Rev the Dean of Bangor; The Deanery, Cathedral Close, Bangor, Gwynedd LL57 1LH (☎ 0248 370693); Cathedral Office, Diocesan Centre, Cathedral Close, Bangor, Gwynedd LL57 1DS (☎ 0248 353983, fax 0248 353882)

EDWARDS, Frank Wallis; CBE (1984); s of Arthur Edwards (d 1962), of Ipswich, and Mabel Lily, *née* Hammond (d 1956); *b* 23 Dec 1922; *Educ* Royal Liberty Sch Essex, Univ of Bradford; *m* 1959, Valerie Ann, da of late Reginald Claude Hitch, of Balcombe; 2 da (Elena, Melinda); *Career* Capt REME 1944-47; Dorr-Oliver Co 1953-70: project and sales engr 1953-59, dir 1959-70, md Euro ops 1966-69, divnl vice pres Int Div 1969-70; H & G Engrg Ltd (formerly Humphreys & Glasgow Ltd) UK 1970-: dir 1971, md 1974, dep chm 1978-; dir: Humphreys & Glasgow Int Ltd 1973-, Process & Energy Conslts Ltd 1974- (chm), MHG Int Ltd 1975-83, Hydreq Ltd 1976-83 (chm 1982-83), Humphreys & Glasgow (Atlantic) Ltd 1976-, Energy Industs Cncl 1976-88, Canatom Heavy Water Ltd 1978-, Humphreys & Glasgow Inc 1981-, Goldmace Ltd 1981-83, Project Evaluation & Implementation Ltd 1982-, INITEC 1982-86, Humphreys & Glasgow (Overseas) Ltd 1982-, Humphreys & Glasgow Pacific Pty Ltd 1984-, Ebasco Humphreys & Glasgow 1984-86; memb Cncl: Br Chemical Engrg Contractors Assoc 1974-83 (chm 1982-83) process plant NEDO 1977-83, Latin America Trade Advsy Gp (BOTB) 1978-84 (chm 1982-84), Sino-Br Trade Cncl (BOTB) 1977- (vice pres 1983-); CEng, FIChemE, MIMechE, FInstD, FRSA (1983); Ordre Du Mono Republic of Togo 1978; *Recreations* gardening, walking, theatre, woodland conservation; *Clubs* Army & Navy, Reform; *Style—* Frank Edwards, Esq, CBE; Spinney Corner, Church Rd, Woldingham, Surrey CR3 7JH (☎ 0883 653360); H&G Engrg Ltd, Enserch House, 8 St James's Square, London SW1Y 4JU (☎ 071 930 7586, telecopy 071 930 8651)

EDWARDS, Gareth Owen; QC (1985); s of Arthur Wyn Edwards (d 1974), and Mair Eluned Jones; *b* 26 Feb 1940; *Educ* Herbert Stratt GS Derbyshire, Univ of Oxford (BA, BCL); *m* 1967, Katharine Pek Har, da of Goh Keng Swee, of Kuala Lumpur, Malaysia; 2 s (David b 1970, John b 1974), 1 da (Kim b 1968); *Career* barr Inner Temple 1963; Capt Army Legal Serv 1963-65, Germany; asst legal advsr Cwlth Office 1965-67, practised Wales and Chester Circuit 1967-; rec Crown Ct 1978; asst cmmr Boundaries Cmmn 1975-80; *Recreations* chess, cricket, tennis, hill walking; *Clubs* Army & Navy; *Style—* Gareth Edwards, Esq, QC; 58 Cache Lane, Chester (☎ 0244 677795); Goldsmith Building, Temple (071 353 7881)

EDWARDS, Sir George Robert; OM (1971), CBE (1952, MBE 1945), DL (Surrey 1981); s of late Edwin George Edwards, of Highams Park, Essex; *b* 9 July 1908; *Educ* SW Essex Tech, Univ of London (BSc); *m* 1935, Marjorie Annie, da of John Lawrence Thurgood; 1 da; *Career* aeronautical engr; Vickers Aviation Ltd: joined design staff 1935, experimental mangr 1940, chief designer Weybridge Works 1945, dir Vickers Ltd 1955-67; chm BAC 1963-75; emeritus pro chllr Univ of Surrey 1979 (pro chllr 1964-79); memb Royal Inst 1971-, FRS; kt 1957; *Style—* Sir George Edwards, OM, CBE, DL, FRS; Albury Heights, White Lane, Guildford, Surrey (☎ 0483 504488)

EDWARDS, Guy Richard Goronwy; QGM (1977), Austrian AC Gold Medal 1977; s of Sqdn Ldr Goronwy Edwards, DFC, RAF, of Liverpool, and Mary Christine Edwards; *b* 30 Dec 1942; *Educ* Liverpool Coll, Univ of Durham (BSc); *m* 26 April 1986, Daphne Caroline, da of William George McKinley, of Co Meath, Ireland; 1 s (Sean) 2 da (Natasha, Jade); *Career* professional racing driver 1965-85, winner 40 int races, drove as team mate to Graham Hill; Grand Prix Formula One: Lola 1974, Lord Hesketh 1976, BRM 1977; drove Le Mans Twenty Four Hour 9 times for Porsche, BMW, Lola (fourth 1985); awarded QGM for helping rescue Niki Lauda from burning Ferrari at German Grand Prix 1976; chm Guy Edwards Racing Ltd (organising sponsorship for motor racing) 1985-, responsible for Jaguar Car Co's commercial sponsorship prog (resulted in them winning 2 world championships 1987 and 1988 and Le Mans 1988 and 1990); Freeman: City of London, Worshipful Co of Coachmakers and Coach Harness Makers; *Recreations* country pursuits, reading, water sports; *Clubs* British Racing Drivers, Club International des Anciens Pilotes de Grand Prix F1 BARC; *Style*— Guy Edwards, Esq, QGM; 38 Tite St, Chelsea, London SW3 4JA (☎ 071 351 6925, 071 351 0303, fax 071 351 3583, telex 941 3119 GERACE)

EDWARDS, Prof Gwynne; s of William Edwards (d 1964), of Clydach Vale, Mid Glamorgan, S Wales, and Rachel Mary Lamb (d 1986); *b* 14 April 1937; *Educ* Porth Co GS, Univ Coll Cardiff, King's Coll London (BA, PhD); *m* 1 Aug 1964, Gillian Marilyn Davies; 1 s (Gareth b 1971), 1 da (Eleri b 1968); *Career* lectr in Spanish Univ of Liverpool 1962-67, head Dept of Romance Languages UCW Aberystwyth 1984-87 (lectr 1967-73, sr lectr 1973-80, reader 1980-83, prof 1983-); professional theatre prodns: Lorca's Blood Wedding 1987, Lorca's Women 1987-88, Mario Vargas Llosa's La Chunga 1988, Lorca's Doña Rosita 1989, Lorca's When Five Years Pass 1989 (winner of Scotsman Fringe First); memb Assoc of Hispanists of England and Wales; *Books* The Prison and the Labyrinth: Studies in Calderonian Tragedy (1978), Lorca: The Theatre Beneath the Sand (1980), The Discreet Art of Luis Bunuel (1982), Dramatists in Perspective: Spanish Theatre in the Twentieth Century (1985), Lorca: Three Plays (1987), Lorca: Plays Two (1990); *Recreations* theatre, music, sport, cinema, travel; *Style*— Prof Gwynne Edwards; 66 Maeshendre, Waun Fawr, Aberystwyth, Dyfed, Wales; Dept of European Languages, University College of Wales, Aberystwyth, Dyfed, Wales (☎ 0970 62 2558)

EDWARDS, Hilary Anne; *née* Skinner; da of Charles Stapleton Skinner (d 1974), and Dorothy Stapleton, *née* Morton (d 1978); *b* 20 Feb 1923; *Educ* Sydenham HS, Bromley HS; *m* 24 May 1947, John May Edwards, s of William May Edwards (d 1961), of Hove, Sussex; 1 s (Simon b 1954), 1 da (Amanda b 1951); *Career* UN Assoc: regnl offr 1968-88, memb Exec Ctee, vice pres Western Region; memb Exec Ctee Soc for Int Devpt 1974-, convener SID UK Chapter Women in Devpt Gp 1981-, vice chm Women's Advsy Cncl of UN 1986-89 (and 1978-84); Gilbert Murray Sr award for work in int affairs; *Recreations* gardening, philosophy, visual arts, writing poetry, travelling; *Clubs* Penn; *Style*— Mrs Hilary Edwards; Assaye, 29 Wellington Road, Parkstone, Poole, Dorset BH14 9LF (☎ 0202 743968)

EDWARDS, Dr Huw; s of Evan Dewi Edwards, of Carmarthen, and Doris Maud, *née* Evans; *b* 22 Dec 1938; *Educ* Queen Elizabeth GS Carmarthen, St Bart's Hosp Med Coll (MB BS, MRCS, LRCP, DPM); *m* 22 June 1963, Brenda Annie, da of Jack Burgess, of Carmarthen; 3 s (Siwan b 1965, Sioned b 1967, Manon b 1972); *Career* sr registrar dept psychological med Welsh Nat Sch of Med 1966-69; conslt psychiatrist 1969-: St David's Hosp, W Wales Gen Hosp, Bronglais Hosp; chm Y Gymdeithas Feddygol (Welsh Med Soc) 1988-; memb: Plaid Cymru, Carmarthen Mind Assoc; FRCPsych 1984; *Books* Wynebu Bywyd (1979), Y Pryfyn Yn Yr Afal (1981); *Recreations* collecting old books, writing, fishing, gardening, botany and archaeology; *Style*— Dr Huw Edwards; Garth Martin, Ffordd Llysonnen, Caerfyrddin, Dyfed, Wales SA33 5EG (☎ 026 782 318); St David's Hosp, Carmarthen, Dyfed SA31 3HB (☎ 0267 237481)

EDWARDS, Jack Trevor; CBE (1985); s of Col Cyril Ernest Edwards, DSO, MC, JP, DL (d 1953), of Bullwood Hse, Hockley, Essex, and Jessie Boyd; *b* 23 June 1920; *Educ* Felsted, Imperial Coll London (BSc); *m* 3 Jan 1959, Josephine (Sally), da of late S W Williams; 1 da (Susan Nicola b 1960); *Career* RAF: Armament Branch 1941-45, Airfield Construction Branch 1945-46, Sqdn Ldr 1946; consulting engr James Williamson & Ptnrs 1946-50; Freeman Fox & Ptnrs: engr 1951-64, ptnr 1965-79, sr ptnr 1980-86; chm Halcrow Fox Assocs 1985-, pres Herongate and Ingrave Preservation Soc, hon sec Brentwood and Dist Branch RNLI, chm Br Conslts Bureau 1983; Liveryman Worshipful Co of Painter-Stainers; memb ACE, FCGI 1982, FICE 1963, FCIT 1976; *Recreations* sailing; *Clubs* St Stephen's Constitutional, Royal Cruising, Royal Burnham Yacht; *Style*— Jack Edwards, Esq, CBE

EDWARDS, Jeffery; Walter Frederick (d 1983), and Hilda, *née* Fenemore; *b* 31 Aug 1945; *Educ* Orange Hill GS, Bushey GS, Leeds Coll of Art and Design (DipAD), RCA (MA, Printmaking prize); *m* 1969, Theresa, da of Cliff Tyrell; 1 s (Roland b 1970), 1 da (Chloë b 1972); *Career* artist 1970; printmaker and painter 1970- (incl murals and advertisments); one person exhibitions: Serpentine Gallery London 1972, New Lane Gallery Bradford 1972, ICA London 1973, Jordan Gallery 1975, Asard and Asard Gallery Stockholm, Thumb Gallery London 1977 and 1980; gp exhibitions incl: Young Contemporaries 1970, Royal Acad 1970, Bradford Print Biennale 1972, 1976, 1979, 1982, International Trieniale of Graphics (Crencher Switzerland) 1973, Camden Arts Centre 1973, Objects (V & A) 1978, Art for Now (Lloyds Bank London) 1981, and Printmaking (Waterloo Gallery) 1982, Artists Choice (RCA) 1984, Angela Flowers Gallery London 1990, Fouts and Fowler Gallery London 1990; pub collections incl: V & A, Tate Gallery, Br Cncl, Brooklyn Museum NY, Bradford City Art Gallery, Whitworth Art Gallery Manchester, Arts Cncl of Great Britain; lectr and internal assessor: Ravensbourne Coll of Art 1971-77, Maidstone Coll of Art 1970-83, Portsmouth Poly 1979-83; sr lectr and internal assessor Printmaking Dept Chelsea Sch of Art 1982-; visiting lectr: RCA, The Slade Sch of Fine Art; *Recreations* rhythm and blues, vintage and thoroughbred cars; *Clubs* Chelsea Arts, Jensen Owners; *Style*— Jeffery Edwards, Esq; Chelsea School of Art, Manresa Rd, London SW3 6LS (☎ 071 351 3844, 071 352 8721)

EDWARDS, Jeremy John Cary; s of William Philip Neville Edwards, CBE, and The Hon Mrs Sheila Edwards, *née* Cary (d 1976); *b* 2 Jan 1937; *Educ* Ridley Coll Ontario Canada, Vinehall Sch Sussex, Haileybury & Imperial Serv Coll Herts; *m* 1, 18 April 1963 (m dis), Jenifer (decd), da of late Capt Langton Mould; 1 s (Julian Peter Cary b 21 Jan 1967), 1 da (Venetia Hester b 16 Aug 1964); m 2, 1974, April Philippa Learmond, da of late Reginald Ernest Harding; 1 s (Benjamin Charles Cary b 17 Dec 1980); *Career* Unilever Ltd 1955-57, Hobson Bates & Co Ltd 1957-59, Overseas Marketing & Advertising Ltd 1959-61, Courtaulds Ltd 1961-63, Vine Products Ltd 1963-66, Loewe SA 1966-68, Jessel Securities Ltd 1968-70, md Vavasseur Unit Tst Management 1970-74, gp md Henderson Administration Group 1974-; hon treas World Wide Fund for Nature UK, memb Cncl C of E Children's Soc (chm Appeals Ctee); *Clubs* Boodle's, City of London; *Style*— Jeremy Edwards, Esq; 37 Oakley Gardens, London SW3 5QQ (☎ 071 351 1953); Henderson Administration Group plc, 3 Finsbury Avenue, London EC2M 2PA (☎ 071 638 5757, fax 071 377 5757, telex 884616 A/B GFRIAR G)

EDWARDS, John; s of late Arthur Leonard Edwards; *b* 2 Jan 1932; *Educ* Wolverhampton Municipal GS; *m* 1, 1954, Nancy Woodcock (d 1978); 1 s, 1 da; m 2, 1979, Brenda Rankin; 1 da; *Career* journalist; editor Yorkshire Post 1969- (joined paper 1961); *Style*— John Edwards Esq; 1 Edgerton Rd, West Park, Leeds LS16 5JD

EDWARDS, John; s of Joseph Edwards, CBE, and Lily, *née* Nager; *b* 6 Nov 1941; *Educ* Kantonsschule Zurich Switzerland, Trinity Coll Cambridge (BA, MA); 5 June 1980, Annemarie Alice Jessica, da of Claude Arpels, Légion D'Honneur, of Rye, NY; 1 s (Luke b 21 Nov 1980), 1 da (Kate b 5 Feb 1984); *Career* admitted slr 1969; ptnr Linklaters and Paines; sr visiting fell Queen Mary Coll Univ of London; memb: Law Soc, Int Bar Assoc; *Recreations* swimming, skiing, music, literature, pictures; *Clubs* Annabel's, Mark's, RAC; *Style*— John Edwards, Esq; 46 Chelsea Pk Gdns, London SW3 (☎ 071 352 5749); Barrington House, 59-67 Gresham St, London EC2V 7JA (☎ 071 606 7080)

EDWARDS, John Andrew Child; s of Arnold Child Edwards (d 1989), and Cathleen Lilian, *née* Cooper; *b* 13 April 1946; *m* May 1967, Virginia Seabourne May; 2 c (Sophie Patricia b 20 Dec 1971, Timothy William Child b 14 Feb 1978); *Career* Nat Hunt trainer; trainer's licence 1967; wins at Nat Hunt Festival Cheltenham incl: Queen Mother Champion Chase (twice), Kim Muir Chase (twice), Grand Annual Chase, Ritz Club Chase, Coral Hurdle; other wins incl: Whitbread Trophy Liverpool, Scottish Grand National Ayr, Martel Cup Liverpool, Charterhouse Chase Ascot, Mackeson Gold Cup Cheltenham; *Recreations* hunting, shooting, fishing; *Style*— John Edwards, Esq; Dason Court, Hentland, Ross-on-Wye, Herefordshire (☎ 098 987 639); Caradoc Court, Sellack, Ross-on-Wye, Herefordshire (☎ 098987 259/315, fax 098987 329)

EDWARDS, John Coates; CMG; s of Herbert John Edwards, and Doris May Edwards; *b* 25 Nov 1934; *Educ* Skinners' Sch Tunbridge Wells, BNC Oxford; *m* 1959, Mary, *née* Harris; 1 s, 1 da; *Career* HM Dip Serv; head: British Devpt Div in the Caribbean 1978-81, West Indian and Atlantic Dept FCO 1981-84; dep high cmmr Br High Cmmn Nairobi Kenya 1984-88, Br high cmmr Maserv Lesotho 1988-; *Clubs* Royal Cwlth Soc, Muthaiga Country (Nairobi); *Style*— John Edwards, Esq, CMG; Fairways, Ightham, Sevenoaks, Kent (☎ 0732 883556); Foreign and Commonwealth Office, King Charles St, London SW1

EDWARDS, John Daniel; s of David Daniel Edwards (d 1954), of Dyfed, and Margaret, *née* Jenkins (d 1964); *b* 23 June 1922; *Educ* Central Sch London, St Martin's Sch of Art, Architectural Assoc; *m* 31 May 1969, Patricia Margaret, da of Randolph Gibson (d 1973), of Bradford; *Career* RAFVR 1941-46; asst publicity mangr Crittall MFG Co Ltd 1947-61, mktg servs mangr Ingersoll-Rand Co Ltd 1962-72, psychologist private practice 1973-; memb Exec Ctee London Welsh Assoc; Freeman City of London 1976, Liveryman Worshipful Co of Marketors 1977; FInstM 1972, FCIM 1989, FNCP 1983; *Recreations* travel, photography, motoring, flying, swimming, walking; *Style*— John Edwards, Esq; Ridgedale, Allison Gardens, Purley on Thames, Reading, Berks RG8 8DF (☎ 0734 422955)

EDWARDS, John David; s of Rev T H D Edwards, of Baymont, Clee Hill Rd, Tenbury Wells, Worcs, and Ann Gollan, *née* Adam; *b* 21 March 1959; *Educ* Haileybury, ISC, Leeds Poly (BA); *m* 25 March 1989, Louise Elisabeth, da of Raymond William Cooper, of Kidderminster, Worcs; *Career* called to the Bar Inner Temple, memb Gen Cncl Bar 1991; memb Gen Exec Ctee Birmingham Fedn Boys Club; *Recreations* tennis, squash, theatre; *Style*— John Edwards, Esq; 8 Fountain Court, Steelhouse Lane, Birmingham B4 6DR (☎ 021 236 5514, fax 021 236 8225)

EDWARDS, Col John David Eric; s of Eric Percy Bowley Edwards, of Melton Mowbray, Leics, and Irene, *née* Green; *b* 16 Oct 1940; *Educ* St Albans Sch, Queen Elizabeth GS Wakefield, Univ of London (BDS); *m* 1, 14 Oct 1967 (m dis 1971), Denise Mary Howard; m 2, 11 Sept 1971, Susan Jane, da of Lt Col Dennis Albert Pearce, of St Leonards, Ringwood, Hants; 3 s (David b 1972, Daniel b 1973, Jonathon b 1976); *Career* 2 Lt RADC 1962, Capt 1965, Maj 1970, Lt Col 1978, Col 1986, served Aden, Hong Kong, Persian Gulf, N Ireland, GB, BAOR, UN Forces Cyprus; principal appts: Dept Cmdt HQ and Trg Centre RADC 1984-86, CO 2 Dental GP NI 1986-87, 2 Dental GP BAOR 1987-89; capt Army Lawn Tennis Team 1984-85; memb Nat Tst; MGDS RCS; *Style*— Col John Edwards; 3/24 Sussex Square, Brighton BN2 5AB; First Avenue House, High Holborn, London WC1V 6HE (☎ 071 430 5688, fax 071 430 5332)

EDWARDS, Prof John Hilton; s of Harold Clifford Edwards, CBE, of Cambridge (d 1989), and Ida Margaret, *née* Phillips (d 1981); *b* 26 March 1928; *Educ* Uppingham, Univ of Cambridge (MA, MB BChir); *m* 18 July 1953, Felicity Clare Edwards, OBE, da of Dr Charles Hugh Christie Toussaint (d 1985), of E Harling, Norfolk; 2 s (Conrad b 1959, Matthew b 1965), 2 da (Vanessa b 1956, Penelope b 1962); *Career* geneticist: unit of population genetics MRC Oxford 1958-59, Children's Hosp Philadelphia 1960; Dept Human Genetics Univ of Birmingham 1961-79 (lectr, sr lectr, reader, prof), conslt WHO 1972-, med genetics NHS Oxford RHA 1979-, prof of genetics Univ of Oxford 1979-; memb Nat Radiological Protection Bd 1987-; associated with Oxford local gp Muscular Dystrophy Gp of GB; FRCP 1972, FRS 1979; *Books* An Outline of Human Genetics (1978); *Recreations* gliding, skiing; *Clubs* Athenaeum; *Style*— Prof J H Edwards, FRS; 78 Old Rd, Headington, Oxford OX3 7LP (☎ 0865 60430); Genetics Laboratory, Dept of Biochemistry, Univ of Oxford, South Parks Rd, Oxford OX1 3QU (☎ 0865 275 317, fax 0865 275 318, telex 83681)

EDWARDS, John Neill Thesen; s of Maj John Herbert Edwards (d 1984), of Pretoria, SA, and Aorea Georgina, *née* Thesen; *b* 2 May 1946; *Educ* St Andrew's Coll Grahamstown SA, Univ of Pretoria (MB ChB); *m* 1 May 1976, Katherine Martine, da of Stanley Douglas Abercrombie, of Poole, Dorset; 4 s (John Patrick Abercrombie b 1978, Charles Thomas Thesen b 1979, Andrew Neill Douglas b 1983, Harison Martin Ashdown b 1988); *Career* registrar in obstetrics and gynaecology John Radcliffe Hosp Oxford, sr registrar in obstetrics and gynaecology, UCH, conslt in obstetrics and gynaecology Poole Gen Hosp 1986; MRCOG 1981, FRCSed 1986; *Recreations* sailing, fishing, shooting; *Clubs* Royal Motor Yacht (Poole), Bournemouth Constitutional; *Style*— John Edwards, Esq; Sarum House, 29 Forest Road, Branksome Park, Poole Dorset BH13 6DQ (☎ 0202 765287)

EDWARDS, John Revill; s of Revill Edwards; *b* 18 July 1947; *Educ* Oundle, Aston Univ, Wharton Graduate Sch of Finance Pennsylvania Univ; *m* 1970, Vienneta Diane, *née* Oxford; 3 s; *Career* marketing dir Edgar Vaughn & Co Ltd; md Evco Chemicals Ltd; dir Houghton Danmark (Denmark); *Style*— John Edwards Esq; Old Birchwood Farm, Hoar Cross, Burton-on-Trent, Staffs (☎ 028 375 381)

EDWARDS, John Robert; s of John Ellis Edwards (d 1981), of 19 Malvern Rd, London, and Lillian Hannah Hall (d 1983); *b* 3 March 1938; *Educ* Willesden Tech Coll, Hornsey Sch of Art, Leeds Inst of Educn, L'Ecole Nationale Superieure d'Architecture et d'Art Visuel Bruxelles (Br Cncl scholar); *m* 1960 (m dis 1973), Jeanette Christine Brown; 3 da (Chloe b 1966, Aphra b 1968, Cassandra b 1971); *Career* artist; sr lectr St Martin's Sch of Art London 1973; visiting artist: Syracuse Univ NY 1976, Sch of Visual Arts New York City 1980; head Dept of Painting and Sculpture St Martin's Sch of Art London 1986-88 (head of painting 1980-86); works in the collections of: Arts Cncl of GB, Br Cncl, Contemporary Art Soc London, Cncl for Nat Academic Awards, Govt Art Collection, Gulbenkian Fndn, Miny of Works Brussels, ICA, Solomon R Guggenheim Museum NY, Towner Art Gallery, Newcastle upon Tyne Poly; commissions: Northwick Park Hosp London 1984, John Hansard Gallery Univ of Southampton 1989; Winston Churchill Travel fell Netherlands and Germany 1989; memb London Group 1987; *Recreations* swimming; *Style*— John Edwards, Esq; 52 Isledon Rd, London N7 7LD (☎ 071 609 7249)

EDWARDS, Joseph Robert; CBE (1963), JP (Oxford 1964); yst s of Walter Smith Edwards; *b* 5 July 1908; *Educ* High Sch Gt Yarmouth; *m* 1, 1936, Frances Mabel Haddon Bourne (d 1975); 3 s, 1 da; m 2, 1976, Joan Constance Mary Tattersall; *Career* joined Austin Motor Co 1928, md British Motor Corp 1966-68; dep chm: Associated Engineering 1969-78, Martin Electrical Equipment (Theale) Ltd 1979-89, Theale Estates Ltd 1989-; chm: Harland & Wolff Ltd 1970, Penta Motors Ltd Reading 1978-87, Canewdon Consultants plc 1985-, Creative Industries Gp Inc (USA) 1985-; dir: Br Printing Corp 1973-81, CSE Aviation 1973-87; *Style*— Joseph Edwards, Esq, CBE, JP; Flat 16, Shoreacres, Banks Rd, Sandbanks, nr Bournemouth, Dorset (☎

0202 709315)

EDWARDS, Keith Harrap; s of Sir Martin Llewllyn Edwards (d 1987), and Lady Dorothy Ward, *née* Harrap (d 1989); *b* 17 Oct 1940; *Educ* Uppingham; *m* 23 May 1964, Susan Eleanore, da of John Walker Clevedon; 3 da (Juliet b 1967, Elizabeth b 1968, Caroline b 1971); *Career* admitted slr 1966; ptnr C and M Edwards Shepherd and Co 1968-78, admin ptnr Edwards Geldard and Shepherd 1979-84, sr ptnr Edwards Geldard 1985- (managing ptnr 1985-90) (Edwards Geldard Solicitors with offices in Cardiff, London, Derby and Monmouth); *Clubs* Cardiff and County, Cardiff Athletic; *Style*— Keith Edwards, Esq; Ivydene, Aberthin, Cowbridge, S Glamorgan (☎ 04463 2788); 16 St Andrews Crescent, Cardiff CF1 3RD (☎ 0222 238239, fax 0222 237268, telex 497913)

EDWARDS, (Alfred) Kenneth; CBE (1989, MBE 1963); s of Ernest Edwards (d 1959), of Carteret House, Westway, London, and Florence May Branch (d 1983); *b* 24 March 1926; *Educ* Latymer Upper Sch, Magdalene Coll Cambridge, Univ Coll London (BSc); *m* 17 Sept 1949, Jeannette Lilian, da of David Louis Speeks, MBE; 1 s (Vaughan b 1951), 2 da (Vivien b 1954, Deryn b 1960); *Career* Flying Offr RAF 1944-47 (RAF Coll Cranwell 1945); HM Overseas Civil Serv Nigeria 1952-63; gp mktg mangr Thorn Electrical Industries Ltd 1964, int dir Brookhirst Igranic Ltd (Thorn Gp) 1967, gp mktg dir Cutler Hammer Europa 1972, chief exec Br Electrical and Allied Manufacturers Associates Ltd (BEAMA) 1976-82; chm: FPM plc 1989-, Business Services Europe 1989-; memb Bd Polar Electronics Ltd 1989-; dep dir gen CBI (memb Cncl 1974 and 1976-82), memb Fin and Gen Purposes Ctee 1977-82, vice chm Eastern Regnl Cncl 1974, dep dir gen Pres's Ctee 1982- (memb 1979-82); memb: Exec Ctee Organisme de Liaison des Industries Metalliques Européennes (ORGALIME) 1976-82, Bd Br Standards Inst (BSI) 1978-82 and 1984-; chm: Br Electrotechnical Ctee and Electrotechnical Divnl Cncl 1981-82, BSI Quality Policy Ctee 1988-; memb Br Overseas Trade Bd (BOTB) 1982-88, memb Salvation Army London Advsy Bd 1982-, dir Business and Technician Educ Cncl (B/TEC) 1983-88, memb BBC Consultative Gp on Industrial and Business Affrs 1983-; pres: European Ctee for Electrotechnical Standardisation (CENELEC) 1977-79 (memb Exec Ctee 1982-, chm Fin Ctee 1983-86), Union des Industries de la Communaute Europeenne (UNICE); memb Ct Cranfield Inst of Technol 1970-75; memb Bd and Exec Ctee Business in the Community 1987-; FRSA 1985; *Recreations* music, books; *Clubs* Athenaeum, RAC, RAF; *Style*— Kenneth Edwards, Esq, CBE; Centre Point, 103 New Oxford St, London WC1A 1DU (☎ 071 379 7400 ext 2153, fax 071 240 1578)

EDWARDS, Malcolm John; CBE (1985); s of John James Edwards (d 1967), of London, and Edith Hannah, *née* Riley (d 1966); *b* 25 May 1934; *Educ* Alleyn's Sch Dulwich, Jesus Coll Cambridge (MA); *m* 2 Dec 1967, Yvonne Sylvia, da of J A W Daniels, of Port Lincoln, Australia; 2 s (Jonathan John b 1970, Mark b 1972); *Career* memb Bd Br Coal 1986 (dir of mktg 1973, commercial dir 1985), memb Fin and Gen Purpose Ctee Southwark Diocesan Bd of Educ; Freeman City of London; CBIM 1988; *Recreations* music, gardening, design 1860-1914; *Style*— Malcolm Edwards, Esq, CBE; Lodge Farm, Moot Lane, Downton, Salisbury, Wilts SP5 3LN (☎ 0725 21538); British Coal, Hobart House, Grosvenor Place, London SW1 (☎ 071 235 2020)

EDWARDS, His Hon Judge; (Charles) Marcus; s of (John) Basil Edwards, CBE, *qv*, and Molly Patricia, *née* Philips (d 1979); *b* 10 Aug 1937; *Educ* Dragon Sch, Rugby, BNC Oxford (BA); *m* 1, 1963, Anne Louise (d 1970), da of Sir Edmund Stockdale, of Hoddington House, nr Basingstoke; m 2, Sandra Edwards (formerly Mrs Wates), da of James Mouroutsos, of Mass, USA; 1 da (Alexandra b 1983); *Career* 2 Lt Intelligence Corps 1955-56; HM Dip Serv 1960-65; third sec: Spain, S Africa, Laos, Whitehall; called to the Bar 1962, practising 1965-86, circuit judge 1986-; chm Pavilion Opera 1986-; *Recreations* gardening, walking, travel; *Clubs* Beefsteak; *Style*— His Hon Judge Edwards; Melbourne House, S Parade, London W4 1JU (☎ 071 995 9146)

EDWARDS, Mark Antony; s of Orville Rudolph Edwards, of NY, USA, and Joan Isabella Carter; *b* 15 Sept 1963; *Educ* Riverside Comp Sch, Lewisham Coll; *m* 16 April, Lucinda Anne, da of Hugh Knock; 1 da (Reanna Isabele b 9 Nov 1990); *Career* amateur boxer; debut 1982, 11 bouts Woolwich St Mary's Club 1982-83, 32 bouts Fitzroy Lodge Club 1983-86, 41 bouts Royal Navy Boxing Assoc 1986-; Amateur Boxing Assoc champion 1988, NATO Cup 1989, Bronze medal Cwlth Games 1990; Royal Marine sportsman of the year 1988; currently serv RN; *Style*— Mark Edwards, Esq; 27 Finch Road, Southsea, Portsmouth, Hants P04 9LT (☎ 0705 851 787); c/o Lt G Palmer, HMS Temeraire, Flathouse Rd, Portsmouth, Hants P01 2HB

EDWARDS, Prof Michael; s of Frank Ernest Walter Edwards, and Irene Louise Dalliston (d 1985); *b* 29 April 1938; *Educ* Kingston GS, Christ's Coll Cambridge (BA, MA, PhD); *m* 7 July 1964, Danielle, da of Jacques Bourdin, of Lamotte-Beuvron, France; 1 s (Paul), 1 da (Catherine); *Career* lectr in French Univ of Warwick 1965-73, sr lectr then reader in lit Univ of Essex 1973-87, prof of English Univ of Warwick 1987-, visiting prof Univ of Paris 1989-90; Medal Collège de France; *Books* La Tragédie Racinienne (1972), To Kindle The Starling (poems, 1972), Eliot/Language (1975), Where (poems, 1975), The Ballad of Mobb Conroy (poems, 1977), Towards a Christian Poetics (1984), The Magic, Unquiet Body (poems, 1985), Poetry and Possibility (1988), Of Making Many Books (1990); *Recreations* walking; *Clubs* Cambridge Union; *Style*— Prof Michael Edwards; 4 Northumberland Rd, Leamington Spa, Warwickshire CV32 6HA (☎ 0926 312205); Department of English and Comparative Literary Studies, University of Warwick, Coventry, Warwickshire CV4 7AL (☎ 0203 523523)

EDWARDS, (John) Michael; CBE (1986), QC (1981); er s of Dr James Thomas Edwards (d 1952), and Constance Amy (d 1985), yr da of Sir John McFadyean; bro of Prof James Griffith Edwards, *qv*; *b* 16 Oct 1925; *Educ* Andover GS, Univ Coll Oxford (BA, BCL, MA); *m* 1, 1951 (m dis 1963), Morna Joyce, *née* Piper; 1 s (James b 1957), 1 da (Caroline (Mrs Martin Pearce) b 1955); m 2, 3 March 1964, Rosemary Ann, da of Douglas Kinley Moore (d 1982); 2 s (Tom b 1967, Owen b 1969); *Career* called to the Bar Middle Temple 1949, practised 1950-55; asst Parly counsel to the Treasy 1955-60; dep legal advsr and dir of certain subsid cos (exporting turn-key plants to E Europe) Courtaulds Ltd 1960-67; BSC: joined 1967, dir of legal servs 1967-69, md (Int) 1968-81, chm and md (Overseas Serv) 1975-81; memb: E Euro Trade Cncl 1973-81, Overseas Project Bd 1973-81, Academic Cncl Inst of Int Business Law and Practice of ICC (Paris) 1982-88, Disciplinary Appeal Ctee Chartered Assoc of Certified Accountants 1983- (chm 1987-90, dep chm 1990-); provost City of London Poly 1981-88; dir: Regnl Opera Tst (Kent Opera) 1981-88 (chm 1983-86), Bell Group International Ltd (formerly Associated Communications Corp) 1982-90 (md 1988-89), Product Innovation Ltd 1983-, Bell Resources Ltd (Aust) 1984-88; chief exec Bond Corp (UK) Ltd 1989-90; memb: Bar Cncl 1971-79 and 1980-83, Senate of Inns of Ct and the Bar 1974-79 and 1980-83 (memb Fin and Exec Ctees), Ctee Bar Assoc for Commerce Fin and Indust 1965- (chm 1972-78, vice pres 1980-82), Educnl Assets Bd 1989-; chm: Eastman Dental Hosp 1983-, Inst of Dental Surgery 1983-; dep chm Ind Appeals Authy for Sch Examinations 1990-; govr Br Post-grad Med Fedn 1987-; Freeman City of London, Memb of Ct Worshipful Co of Ironmongers; CBIM, FCIA 1984; *Recreations* family and friends, driving old cars, making things work; *Clubs* Garrick; *Style*— Michael Edwards, Esq, CBE, QC

EDWARDS, Norman John; s of Ernest Edwards, MBE, and Maude Mary Edwards; *b* 18 Oct 1920; *Educ* Eltham Coll; *m* 14 June 1952, (Isabelle) Margaret Duff, da of Edmond Compton; 1 s (Andrew b 1956), 2 da (Rosalyn b 1954, Gay b 1956); *Career* RE 1940-46, Indian Army 1942-46; ptnr Bernerd Thorpe & Ptnrs 1958-85; govr Eltham Coll (chm Walthamstow Hall 1975-85); memb Worshipful Co of Paviors; memb RICS 1948; *Recreations* gardening, sailing; *Clubs* Oriental, City Livery; *Style*— Norman Edwards, Esq; Westfield, Holbrook Lane, Chislenvest, Kent (☎ 081 467 3458)

EDWARDS, Prof Paul Geoffrey; s of Albert Henry Edwards (d 1964), of Birmingham, and Frances, *née* Dewerson; *b* 31 July 1926; *Educ* St Philip's GS Birmingham, Hatfield Coll Durham (BA), Emmanuel Coll Cambridge (MA); *m* 31 July 1954 (Maj) Ingbritt, da of Nils Nilsson (d 1959), of Lilla Beddinge, Sweden; 2 da (Kristina Alexandra (Mrs Galloway) b 2 Jan 1955, (Anna) Birgitta (Mrs MacDonald) b 26 March 1957); *Career* AC2/GD RAF 1944-48; English teacher St Augustine's Coll Cape Coast Ghana 1954-57, lectr in English Univ of Sierra Leone Freetown 1957-63, prof of English and African lit (personal chair), Univ of Edinburgh 1989 (lectr in English lit 1963, sr lectr 1968, reader 1972); *Books* West African Narrative (1963), Equianos Travels (ed, 1967), The Letter of the late Ignatius Sancho (ed, 1968), Legendary Fiction in Medieval Iceland (with Herman Pálsson, 1972), Egil's Saga (with Herman Pálsson, 1976), Orkneyinga Saga (with Herman Pálsson, 1978), Black Personalities in the Era of the Slave Trade (with James Walvin, 1983), Seven Viking Romances (1985), The Life of Olaudah Equiano (ed, 1988), Eyrbyggia Saga (1989), Vikings in Russia (1989), Magnus Saga (1984); *Recreations* teaching, translating Icelandic literature, chatting; *Clubs* Edinburgh Univ Staff; *Style*— Prof Paul Edwards; 82 Kirk Brae, Edinburgh, Lothian EH16 6JA (☎ 031 664 2574); Department of English Literature, Edinburgh University (☎ 031 667 1011 ext 6226)

EDWARDS, Paul Spencer; s of Alfred Henry Edwards, of 43 Southview Rd, Hornsey, London, and Margery Caroline Edwards (d 1979); *b* 11 Nov 1942; *Educ* Stationer's Company GS; *m* 7 Sept 1963, Maureen Patricia, da of George Gregory, of 45 Augustus Road, Wimbledon SW19; 2 da (Michelle Caroline b 1966, Colette Mary b 1969); *Career* co dir (fin); dir: Albacore Leasing Ltd Bermuda 1986, Commercial Container Transport Ltd 1986, Dolton Shipping Ltd 1983, Furness Travel Ltd 1984, Golden Cross Line Ltd 1984, Johnston Warren Lines Ltd 1985, W Kemp & Co Ltd 1983, Manchester Adamson Ltd 1984, Manchester Liners Ltd 1982, Pacific Steam Navigation Co 1986, Royal Mail Lines Ltd 1986, Shaw Savill & Albion Co Ltd 1982, Stevinson Hardy (Tankers) Ltd 1986; *Recreations* reading, military modelling and DIY; *Style*— Paul Edwards, Esq; 4, Eversley Mount, Winchmore Hill, London N21 1JP; 53 Leadenhall Street, London EC3A 2BR (☎ 071 481 2020)

EDWARDS, Peter Guy; JP (Durham 1960); s of Brig Claud Taylor Edwards, CBE (d 1978), and Maud Harriet (d 1977), da of Charles Hornung, of Oaklands, Horley, Surrey; *b* 9 Feb 1924; *Educ* Clifton, Pembroke Coll Cambridge, Univ of Durham (BSc); *m* 1959, Jill Mary, da of William Devas Everington, of Blakeney, Norfolk; 1 s (Giles b 1961), 2 da (Camilla b 1963, Nicola b 1969); *Career* RE served Europe 1942-45, SEAC 1945-47, resigned Hon Capt 1948; dir Smiths Dock Co 1957-66, chm Tees Div 1965-66, chm Tees side Ctee N Regnl Bd for Indust 1965 (memb 1959-66) dir Dun Elliott 1967-77, chm Brown Bayley Steels Ltd and Dunford Hadfields 1970-77, dir Hunting Petroleum Servs 1978-90, chm Lake & Elliot Ltd 1979-84 (dir 1978-84), north regnl dir Granville & Co 1981-; memb Cncl Univ of Newcastle upon Tyne 1963-67, High Sheriff Co Durham 1968-69; CEng, CBIM; *Recreations* shooting, fishing; *Clubs* Northern Counties; *Style*— Peter Edwards, Esq, JP; Low Walworth Hall, Darlington, Co Durham (☎ 0325 468004)

EDWARDS, Peter John; s of Alfred Edwards (d 1965), of Southend-on-Sea, Essex, and Hilda, *née* Lamb (d 1964); *b* 29 July 1936; *Educ* Thorpe Hall Sch; *m* 29 Aug 1964, Susan, *née* Scott; 1 s (Stuart b 1968), 1 da (Jacqueline b 1971); *Career* sports administrator; sec and gen mangr Essex CCC 1979- (memb 1948-79); table tennis: chm Southend League 1964-72, chm Daventry League 1973-78, chm Northants County Assoc 1976-78 (also county umpire), represented Daventry and Southend Leagues as player; chartered sec: Drayton Group City of London 1953-67, Lifeguard Assurance 1967-76, John Laing 1976-79; ACIS 1957; *Recreations* golf, foreign travel, music, theatre; *Clubs* MCC, Lord's Taverners, Thorpe Hall Golf; *Style*— Peter Edwards, Esq; Essex County Cricket Club, County Ground, New Writtle Street, Chelmsford, Essex CM2 0PG (☎ 0245 252420)

EDWARDS, Peter Robert; s of Robert Edwards, of Worthing, West Sussex, and Doris Edith, *née* Cooper; *b* 30 Oct 1937; *Educ* Christ's Hosp; *m* 1967, Elizabeth Janet, da of Maitland Barrett; 1 s (Simon b 1970), 1 da (Sarah b 1971); *Career* Arthur Young 1955-90 (managing ptnr 1986-90), md Secretan plc 1990-; ind memb Cncl FIMBRA; Freeman City of London 1956, memb Worshipful Co of Merchant Taylors; ICAS 1960; *Recreations* ornithology; *Clubs* Caledonian; *Style*— Peter Edwards, Esq; Glebe Cottage, Church Lane, Bury, Pulborough, West Sussex RH20 1PB (☎ 0798831 774); Secretan Plc, Suite 776, Lloyd's, Lime Street, London EC3M 7DQ (☎ 071 623 8084, fax 071 626 8066)

EDWARDS, Prof Philip Walter; s of Robert Henry Edwards, MC (d 1950), and Bessie, *née* Pritchard (d 1972); *b* 7 Feb 1923; *Educ* King Edward's HS Birmingham, Univ of Birmingham (MA, PhD); *m* 1, 8 July 1947, Hazel Margaret (d 1950), da of late Prof C W Valentine, of Birmingham; m 2, 8 May 1952, Sheila Margaret, da of Reginald Samuel Wilkes (d 1989), of Bloxwich, Staffs; 3 s (Matthew b 1953, Charles b 1956, Richard b 1958), 1 da (Catherine b 1967); *Career* sub Lt RNVR 1942-45; lectr in Eng Univ of Birmingham 1946-60, prof of Eng lit Trinity Coll Dublin 1960-66, prof of lit Univ of Essex 1966-74; Univ of Liverpool: King Alfred prof of Eng lit 1974-90, pro vice chllr 1980-83, emeritus prof of Eng lit 1990-; author of numerous articles; visiting prof: Univ of Michigan 1964-65, Williams Coll Mass 1969, Otago Univ NZ 1980, ICU Tokyo 1989; visiting fell: All Souls Coll Oxford 1970-71, Huntington Library California 1977 and 1983; FBA 1986; *Books* Sir Walter Raleigh (1953), Kyd's The Spanish Tragedy (ed, 1959), Shakespeare and the Confines of Art (1968), Shakespeare's Pericles (ed, 1976), Massinger Plays and Poems (co-ed C Gibson, 1976), Threshold of a Nation (1979), Shakespeare's Hamlet (ed, 1985), Shakespeare: A Writer's Progress (1986), Last Voyages (1988); *Recreations* walking, gardening; *Style*— Prof Philip Edwards; High Gillinggrove, Gillinggate, Kendal, Cumbria LA9 4JB (☎ 0539 721298)

EDWARDS, Rear Adm (John) Phillip; CB (1984), LVO (1971); s of Robert Edwards (d 1981), of Llanbedr, Ruthin, Clwyd, and Dilys Myfanwy, *née* Phillips (d 1947); *b* 13 Feb 1927; *Educ* Brynhyfryd Sch Ruthin, HMS Conway, RN Engrg Coll; *m* 1951, Gwen, da of John Lloyd Bonner (d 1982), of Llandyrnog, Denbigh, Clwyd; 3 da (Susan, Lynn, Siân); *Career* RN 1944-83; Rear Adm serving as DG Fleet Support Policy and Servs 1980-83; currently fell and bursar Wadham Coll Oxford, memb Welsh Health Policy Bd, pres Midland Naval Offrs Assoc, vice pres Oxfordshire SSAFA, pres Oxford Branch RNA; CEng, FIMechE, FBIM; *Recreations* golf; *Clubs* Frilford Heath Golf; *Style*— Rear Adm Phillip Edwards, CB, LVO; Wadham Coll, Oxford OX1 3PN (☎ 0865 277963)

EDWARDS, His Hon Judge Quentin Tytler; QC (1975); s of Herbert Jackson Edwards (d 1950), of Alexandria, Egypt and Burgess Hill, Sussex, and Juliet Hester, *née* Campbell (d 1940); *b* 16 Jan 1925; *Educ* Bradfield; *m* 18 Nov 1948, Barbara Marian, da of Lt-Col Alec Guthrie (d 1952), of Hampstead; 2 s (Adam b 1951, Simon b

1954), 1 da (Charlotte b 1949); *Career* WWII RN 1943-46; called to the Bar Middle Temple 1948, bencher 1972, circuit judge 1982; chllr: diocese of Blackburn 1977-90, diocese of Chichester 1978; fndr memb Highgate Soc 1965-, chm Ecclesiastical Law Soc 1989-(vice chm 1987-89), pres Highgate Literary and Scientific Inst 1988; memb: Bar Cncl 1958-60 and 1977-81, licensed as a reader in the diocese of London 1967-; memb: Legal Advsy Cmmn of Gen Synod C of E 1971-, Diocese Cmmn Gen Synod 1978-; columnist Guardian Gazette 1975-82; Hon MA awarded by Archbishop of Canterbury 1961; *Books* Ecclesiastical Law, (Third Edn), Halsbury's Law of England (with K Macmorran et al 1952); *Recreations* the open air, architecture; *Clubs* Athenaeum; *Style—* His Hon Judge Quentin Edwards, QC; Bloomsbury County Ct, 7 Marylebone Rd, London NW1 5HY (☎ 071 637 8703)

EDWARDS, Prof Richard Humphrey Tudor; s of Hywel Islwyn Edwards, of Llwyn Aeron, Llangollen, and Menna Tudor Edwards (d 1987); *b* 28 Jan 1939; *Educ* Llangollen GS, Middlesex Hosp Med Sch (BSc, MB BS); *m* 23 May 1964, Eleri Wyn, da of J Ernest Roberts; 1 s (Tomos Tudor, d 1982), 1 da (Rhiannon); *Career* resident appts at Middlesex Hosp London 1964, asst RMO Nat Heart Hosp 1965, house physician Hammersmith Hosp 1966, res fell Royal Postgrad Med Sch Hammersmith Hosp London 1966-69 (PhD 1969), Wellcome Swedish res fell Karolinska Inst Stockholm Sweden 1970-71, Wellcome sr res fell in clinical sci Royal Postgrad Med Sch 1971-76, hon conslt Hammersmith Hosp 1972-76, prof of human metabolism Univ Coll Hosp Med Sch 1976-84, head Dept of Med UCL 1982-84; Univ of Liverpool: prof of med, head of Dept of Med 1984-, dir Magnetic Resonance Res Centre 1987-, dir Muscle Res Centre 1988-; pres Euro Soc for Clinical Sci 1982-83, memb RCP Ctee on Ethics of Res in Patients, examiner for membership of RCP London; author of articles on muscle physiology in health and disease in scientific literature; FRCP 1976; *Award* Robert Bing prize of Swiss Acad of Med Sci 1977; *Books* Clinical Exercise Testing (1975); *Recreations* planting trees, mountain walking, gardening in Wales; *Style—* Prof Richard Edwards; Department of Medicine, University of Liverpool, PO Box 147, Liverpool L69 3BX (☎ 051 706 4072, fax 051 706 5802)

EDWARDS, (John) Richard Martin; s of Arthur Crai Edwards, (d 1989) of Stow on the Wold, and Barbara Leslee Mary, *née* Hart; *b* 2 Sept 1941; *Educ* Dulwich; *m* Rowena Gail; da of Cdr George McCracken Rutherford, MBE, DSC, VRD, RNR (ret); 1 s (James Lindsay b 3 Oct 1964), 1 da (Melanie Jane b 13 July 1963); *Career* mgmnt trainee Hyde Park Hotel London 1959-61, trainee Golf Hotel Montreux Switzerland June-Nov 1960, asst banqueting mangr Quaglinos St James 1961-62; Hyde Park Ho☎ reception and accounts April-Nov 1962, asst banqueting mangr 1962-66, banqueting mangr 1966-69; mangr: Continental Hotel (Trust House) Plymouth 1969-70, County Hotel (Trust House Ltd) Taunton 1970-72; Trust House Forte: gen mangr Skyway Southampton June-Nov 1972, gen mangr Post House Southampton 1972-73, dist mangr 20 hotels 1973-74, asst area dir 25 hotels 1974-76; md Chester Grosvenor Hotel (Prestige) 1982-86 (gen mangr 1976-82); dir Exclusive Div Trust House Forte 1986-87, md Forte Classic Hotels 1987-90, quality serv dir Trust House Forte UK Feb - Sept 1990, md Management Services International 1990-; chm: Prestige Hotels 1981 and 1982, Master Innholders 1990-91, Thames & Chilterns Div BHRCA 1989-90, first Hotelier of the Year 1983, Master Innholder 1986; Freeman City of London 1986; Chevalier du Tastevin 1981, FHCIMA 1985, Conseiller Culinaive de Grande Bretagne, Confrerie de la Chaine des Rotisseurs 1989; *Recreations* tennis, gardening, the South of France; *Clubs* Phyllis Court (Henley); *Style—* Richard Edwards, Esq; Management Services International Ltd, PO Box 57, Twyford, Berks RG10 8EJ (☎ 0734 403288, fax 0836 402938, car 0836 628076)

EDWARDS, Robert Charlton (Rob); s of Lawrence Edwin Edwards (d 1977), and Muriel Eugénie, *née* Peel (d 1989); *b* 24 May 1949; *Educ* Worcester Royal GS, Pembroke Coll Oxford, Bristol Old Vic Theatre Sch; *Career* actor; RSC Stratford and the Aldwych 1980-81: Amintor in The Maid's Tragedy, Young Gobbo in The Merchant of Venice, Khomich in Lovegirl and the Innocent by Solzhenitsin, Charles Lamb in The Fool by Edward Bond; Young Vic 1986, 1989 and 1990: Lucio and The Duke in Measure for Measure, Mercutio in Romeo and Juliet; RSC Stratford and Barbican 1990-91: Pericles in Pericles (Barbican only), Pritikin in Barbarians by Maxim Gorky (Barbican only), First Citizen in Coriolanus; Apoo in Topakano's Martyrs' Day (Bush), Hamlet in Hamlet with the London Shakespeare Group (Far Eastern Tours for Br Cncl) 1985 and 1986, Max and Singer in Definitely the Bahamas by Martin Crimp and Angus in No More a-Roving by John Whiting (Orange Tree) 1987; TV: Stephen Lovell in The Fourth Arm (BBC) 1981-82, John Fletcher in By the Sword Divided (BBC) 1983-84 Dr Chris Clarke in The Practice (Granada) 1985, Gilbert Whippet in Campion (BBC) 1988, Prince John in Henry IV Parts I and II and Henry V (BBC); *Recreations* scrambling, mountain walking; *Style—* Rob Edwards, Esq; Marina Martin Management, 6A Danbury St, Islington, London N1 8JU (☎ 071 359 3646)

EDWARDS, Robert John; CBE (1986); s of William Gordon Edwards (d 1938); *b* 26 Oct 1925; *Educ* Ranelagh Sch Bracknell; *m* 1, 1952 (m dis 1972), Laura Ellwood; 2 s, 2 da; m 2, 1977, Brigid O'Neil Forsyth, *née* Segrave; *Career* ed: Tribune 1951-54, Sunday Express 1957-59 (dep), Daily Express 1961 (managing ed 1959-61), Evening Citizen Glasgow 1962-63, Daily Express 1963-65, Sunday People 1966-72, Sunday Mirror 1972-85; dep chm Mirror Gp Newspapers 1985-86; Ombudsman Today 1990-; *Books* Goodbye Fleet Street (1988); *Recreations* reading, sailing; *Clubs* Groucho's, Kennel, Reform; *Style—* Robert Edwards, Esq, CBE; 74 Duns Tew, Oxford OX5 4JL

EDWARDS, Robert Philip (Rob); s of Robert Aelwyn Edwards, of Abbots Langley, Herts, and Kathleen Isobel, *née* Brockbank; *b* 13 Oct 1953; *Educ* Watford Boys GS, Jesus Coll Cambridge (MA); *m* 8 June 1977, Dr Fiona Grant Riddoch, da of Thomas Grant Riddoch; 1 da (Robyn Edwards Riddoch b 20 Feb 1990); *Career* organiser: with the Scot Campaign to Resist the Atomic Menace 1977-78, campaigns with Shelter (Scot) 1978-80; work as freelance researcher, journalist and writer incl: Scot corr Social Work Today 1981-83, res asst to Robin Cook 1980-83, co-ordinator of CND's case at Sizewell Inquiry; Scot corr: New Statesman 1983-89, The Guardian 1989-91, columnist Edinburgh Evening News 1989-91, environment corr Scotland on Sunday 1989-91 (winner of Media Natura Regnl Regional Journalist of the Year in The British Environment and Media Awards 1989); memb NUJ; *Books* Fuelling the Nuclear Arms Race: the Links Between Nuclear Power and Nuclear Weapons (with Sheila Durie, 1982), Britain's Nuclear Nightmare (with James Cutler, 1988); *Recreations* walking, opera, theatre, films and rock music; *Style—* Rob Edwards, Esq; 17 Arden St, Edinburgh EH9 1BR (☎ 031 447 2796, fax 031 447 0647)

EDWARDS, Robert Wynne (Bob); MBE (1986); s of late Edward Thomas Edwards, of Sycharth, Llangedwyn, nr Oswestry, and late Angelena Louise, *née* Morris; *b* 12 Sept 1917; *Educ* Oswestry Boys HS, Shrewsbury Tech Coll; *m* 4 Dec 1948, Joan, *née* Knowles; 1 s (Kenneth b 1951), 3 da (Mary b 1949, Janet b 1953, Jean b 1955); *Career* WWII serv 6 years: Vickers machine gunner trg CI, coastal def Kent and Sussex, Normandy landing; bank clerk 1936-47, currently farms 450 acres at Llangedwyn; Agric Trg Bd: chm Clwyd Trg Ctee 1978, former memb Welsh Conslt Ctee, pres Dyffryn Tanat Trg Gp 1987- (chm 1975-87); NFU: pres Oswestry branch 1982-84 (chm 1968-70), former chm Educn and Trg Panel, former chm Land Use panel; memb Welsh Jt Educn Ctee; chm: Clwyd Rural Enterprise Unit, Bd Govrs Llysfasi Coll, Jt Ctee Welsh Agric Coll; former chm Bd Govrs: Llfyllin HS, Dinas Bran Sch; memb: Regnl Land Drainage Ctee 1985-, Clwyd and Powys Area Manpower BD 1983-88; fndr memb and vice chm: Clwyd Rural Devpt Panel (later Clwydfro), Antur Tanat Cain; dist cncllr Ceiriog 1968-74; cncllr: Denbighshire 1971-74, Clwyd (ind memb) 1974-89; chm: Clwyd CC 1988 (vice chm 1987), Clwyd SW Cons Assoc 1985-88; chm: CLA, NFU; *Style—* Bob Edwards, Esq; Gartheyr, Llangedwyn, Nr Oswestry SY10 9LQ (☎ 069 189 336)

EDWARDS, Hon Robin Ernest; o s of Baron Chelmer, MC, TD (Life Peer), *qv*; *b* 23 Sept 1940; *Educ* privately; *m* 1967, Carol Mayes; 1 da (Charlotte b 1969); *Style—* The Hon Robin Edwards; 14 Augustin Way, Bicknacre, Danbury Way, Essex (☎ 024 541 4321)

EDWARDS, Roger John; s of Flt Lt John Alfred Edwards, of Ewhurst, Surrey, and Melva Joyce, *née* Burrell; *b* 30 Nov 1941; *Educ* Isleworth GS, Univ of Hull; *m* 4 July 1964, Janet Amelia, da of Stanley Victor Holmes (d 1971); 2 s (Nicholas St John b 29 July 1966, Barnaby James (Barney) b 20 Aug 1969); *Career* account mangr McCann Erickson 1964-67, mktg mangr Chesebrough Ponds 1967-70, dir and head of new business Davidson Pearce Ltd 1970-77, chief exec offr Leo Burnett 1979-81 (md 1978-79), chm and chief offr Grey Communications Gp 1985- (md 1982-85), exec dir Grey Euro 1988-; memb: cncl Inst of Practitioners In Advertising, IOD 1984; FIPA 1983; *Recreations* theatre, travel, walking, books, golf; *Clubs* Wisley Golf; *Style—* Roger Edwards, Esq; Grey Communications Group Ltd, 215-227 Great Portland St, London W1 (☎ 01 636 3399, car 0836 523 402)

EDWARDS, Prof Ron Walter; s of Walter Henry Edwards (d 1975), of Birmingham, and Violet Ellen, *née* Groom; *b* 7 June 1930; *Educ* Solihull Sch, Univ of Birmingham (BSc, DSc); *Career* 2 Lt RAOC 1948-50; res scientist: Freshwater Biological Soc 1953-58, Water Pollution Res Laboratory 1958-68; prof and head dept Univ of Wales Inst Sci and Technol 1968-; memb NERC 1970-73 and 1981-84, memb and dep chm Welsh Water Authy 1974-89; Nat Rivers Authy: memb Advsy Ctee 1988-, memb 1989-, chm Wales; memb: Nat Ctee Euro Year of Environment 1987-88 (chm Wales), Prince of Wales Ctee, Cncl RSPB 1988- (chm Wales); chm Nat Parks Review Panel 1989-; FIBiol, FIWEM, FIFM; *Books* Ecology of the River Wye, Conservation and Productivity of Natural Waters, Pollution, Acid Waters; *Recreations* collecting 19 century staffordshire pottery; *Style—* Prof Ron Edwards; Talybont-on-Usk, Brecon, Powys

EDWARDS, Hon Rupert Timothy Guy; o s of Baron Crickhowell, PC (Life Peer); *b* 1954; *Educ* Radley, Trinity Coll Cambridge; *m* 12 May 1990, Olivia Grizel Kirkwood, yr da of Capt (David) Colin Kirkwood Brown, late Gordon Highlanders, and Lady Margaret Nicola Glasse (*qv*), *née* Sinclair, da of 19 Earl of Caithness, CVO, CBE, DSO

EDWARDS, Prof Sir Samuel Frederick (Sam); s of Richard Edwards, of Swansea, and Mary Jane Edwards; *b* 1 Feb 1928; *Educ* Swansea GS, Gonville and Caius Coll Cambridge (MA, PhD), Harvard Univ; *m* 1953, Merriell E M Bland; 1 s, 3 da; *Career* prof of theoretical physics Univ of Manchester 1963-72; Cambridge Univ: fell Gonville and Caius Coll 1972, John Humphrey Plummer prof of physics 1972-84, Cavendish prof of physics 1984-; chm SRC 1973-77, UK del to Sci Ctee NATO 1974-79, memb Cncl Euro Res & Devpt (EEC) 1976-80; Inst of Mathematics and its Applications: memb Cncl 1976-, vice pres 1979, pres 1980-81; chm Def Scientific Advsy Cncl 1977-80 (memb 1973); non exec dir: Lucas Industry 1981-, Steetley plc 1985-; chm and chief scientific advsr Dept of Energy 1983-88 (memb Advsy Cncl on R&D 1974-77), pres BAAS 1988-89 (chm Cncl 1977-82); Hon DSc (Bath, Birmingham, Edinburgh, Salford, Strasbourg, Wales, Sheffield, Dublin), Hon DTech (Loughborough); foreign memb Academie des Sciences, Sheffield, Dublin; FRS, FInstP, FRSC, FIMA; kt 1975; *Books* Technological Risk (1980), Theory of Polymer Dynamics (1986); *Clubs* Athenaeum; *Style—* Prof Sir Sam Edwards, FRS; 7 Penarth Place, Cambridge CB3 9LU (☎ 0223 66610); Cavendish Laboratory, Cambridge (☎ 0223 337259)

EDWARDS, Sandra Mouroutsos; da of James Mouroutsos, of USA, and Joanna, *née* Felopulos; *b* 14 July 1941; *Educ* Bennington HS, Mount Holyoke Coll (BA); *m* 1, 10 Jan 1965 (m dis 1975), Christopher Stephen Wates; 3 da (Melina b 1966, Georgina b 1967, Joanna b 1970); m 2, 21 Nov 1975, His Hon Judge (Charles) Marcus Edwards, *qv*; 1 da (Alexandra b 1983); *Career* ptnr Conspectus Project Management Consultants 1988-89 (conslt 1986-88), dir The Fitzrovia Trust 1989-; nat chm: Fair Play for Children 1972-77, Pre Sch Playgroups Assoc 1974-77; memb: Westminster City Cncl 1974-78, Ealing Borough Cncl 1978-82; chm: Paddington Churches Housing Assoc 1977-, Sutherland Housing Assoc 1977-; Parly candidate Swansea East 1979; chm Knowles Tst 1980-, memb NW Thames RHA 1980-84, dep chm Hammersmith and Queen Charlotte's Special Health Authy 1986- 1984-), dep chm Nat Fedn Housing Assocs Cncl 1989- (memb 1978-81 and 1987-); *Recreations* indoor gardening; *Style—* Mrs Marcus Edwards; Melbourne House, South Parade, London W4 1JU (☎ 081 995 9146)

EDWARDS, Shaun; s of Jack Edwards, of 64 Delph St, Wigan, Lancs, and Phyllis, *née* Johnson; *b* 17 Oct 1966; *Educ* St John Fisher RC Secdy Sch Wigan; *Career* rugby league player; capt all levels under 11 to under 16 Wigan and Lancs, professional Wigan 1983-; England: capt schoolboys (rugby league and rugby union), full debut 1983, 17 appearances; winner 15 major trophies incl playing in 5 Cup Finals; youngest player to appear in a Wembley Cup Final aged 17, youngest player at time to appear in a Test aged 18; Int of the Year award 1989, Man of Steel award for player of year 1990; memb Br Lions Orgn 1988-; *Recreations* golf, athletics (training), music; *Style—* Shaun Edwards, Esq; 64 Delph St, Wigan, Lancashire (☎ 0942 491244); Wigan RLFC, Central Park, Wigan, Lancs

EDWARDS, Sydney Clive; s of late Edward George Edwards; *b* 29 Oct 1935; *Educ* Newton-Le-Willows GS; *m* 1960, Marjorie Eleanor, da of Richard Bryce Fowler; 1 s, 1 da; *Career* CA with Price-Waterhouse (Holland) 1960-65; accountant and dir Alliance Wholesale Grocers and Food Securities 1965-75; fin dir: Mojo Carryway Ltd 1975-77, Lo-Cost Stores Ltd 1977-; FCA; *Recreations* local and family history, music, Welsh; *Style—* S Clive Edwards, Esq; 22 Woodlands Rd, Parkgate, South Wirral, Cheshire (☎ 051 336 1190)

EDWARDS, (Cecil Ralph) Timothy; s of (Herbert Cecil) Ralph Edwards, CBE (d 1978) and Grace Marjorie, *née* Brooke (d 1983); *b* 25 July 1928; *Educ* Westminster, Trinity Coll Cambridge (MA); *m* 1957, Brenda Mary, da of Joseph Henry Vaughan Gibbs; 3 s (Mark b 1957, Simon b 1959, Stephen b 1967), 2 da (Jane b 1961, Katharine (Lady Newman) b 1963); *Career* served Welsh Guards 1947-48, 2 Lt; ptnr Grieveson Grant & Co (stockbrokers); memb Stock Exchange 1961 (Cncl 1980-88), dir The Securities Assoc 1987-89, chm Kleinwort Benson Unit Tst Ltd; dir: Kleinwort Smaller Co's Investmt Tst plc, Ralston Investmt Tst plc; N American Gas Investmt Tst plc, vice pres Nat Museum of Wales 1987-; *Clubs* Brooks's, Leander; *Style—* Timothy Edwards, Esq; Grendon Court, Upton Bishop, Ross-on-Wye HR9 7QP

EDWARDS, Tracy Karen; MBE (1990); da of Antony Herbert Edwards (d 1973), of Purley-on-Thames, Berks, and Patricia Edwards; *b* 5 Sept 1962; *Educ* Highlands Tilehurst, Arts Educn Tring, Gowerton Comp Sch; *Career* yachtswoman; Whitbread Round the World Race: crew memb Atlantic Privateer 1985-86, skipper, navigator and project leader Maiden Royal Jordanian (first all female challenge, first Br win in twelve years) 1989-90, voted Yachtsman of the Year Yachting Journalists Assoc of GB (first woman winner in the award's 35 year history), Daily Express Sportswoman of 1990; i/

c Tracy Edwards Associates Motorsport (Team); Hon Doctorate of Business Admin CNAA; *Books* Maiden (1990); *Recreations* horse riding, helicopter flying; *Clubs* Royal Ocean Racing, Royal Southampton Yacht, RYA; *Style—* Ms Tracy Edwards, MBE; Tracy Edwards Associates Ltd, Port Hamble, Satchell Lane, Hamble, Hampshire (☎ 0703 456079, fax 0703 456254)

EDWARDS, Wilfred Thomas; s of Thomas Edwards (d 1965), of Caverswall, and Bessie Edith, *née* Rooke (d 1981); *b* 6 Jan 1926; *Educ* Newcastle HS, Univ of London (LLB, Dip HA); *Career* Nat Serv 1944-47; inspr of taxes HM Inland Revenue 1948-86 (univ recruitment liason regnl offr Dist and Head Office), tax conslt 1986-; chm Art Club 1974-; memb Bd Dirs English Speaking Union Club 1979- (govr 1972-78), former chm Cncl Staffordshire Soc, voluntary asst Westminster Abbey; Freeman City of London 1971, Liveryman Worshipful Co Loriners 1981; FGS, FRSA; *Recreations* painting, landscape and portrait; *Clubs* Athenaeum, Hurlingham; *Style—* Wilfred Edwards, Esq; Corner Cottage, Brancaster, Norfolk; Friarswood, The Park, Cheltenham, Glos; 18 North Lodge Close, London SW15 6QZ (☎ 01 789 3935)

EDWARDS, William Philip Neville (Bill); CBE (1949); s of Neville Perrin Edwards (d 1956), of Orford, Littlehampton, Sussex, and Margaret Alexandrina Eliza, *née* Connal (d 1960); *b* 4 Aug 1904; *Educ* Rugby, CCC Cambridge (MA), Princeton Univ USA; *m* 1, 8 April 1931, Hon Sheila Cary (d 1976), da of 13 Viscount Falkland, OBE (d 1961); 2 s (Timothy b 1933, d 1987, Jeremy b 1937); m 2, 1976, Joan Ursula, wid of Norman Mullins, da of Capt Reginald Graham Barker; *Career* London Tport Bd (formerly Underground Electric gp of cos) 1927-41, sec to Lord Ashfield, asst outdoor supt of railways 1938, PR offr 1939; asst to Chm of Supply Cncl Miny of Supply 1941-42, head of Industl Info Div Miny of Prodn and dir of info Br Supply Cnc America 1943-45, dir Overseas Info Div Bd of Trade 1945-46, head of Br Info Servs in USA (FO) 1946-49, dir CBI and md Br Overseas Fairs Ltd 1949-66, chm Br Overseas Fairs Ltd 1966-68, UK assoc dir Business Int SA 1968-75, chm PR Indust Ltd 1970-75; Chevalier first class of the Order of Dannebrog Denmark 1955, Cdr of the Order of Vasa Sweden 1962; *Recreations* golf, gardening; *Clubs* Carlton, Walton Heath Golf, West Sussex Golf; *Style—* Bill Edwards, Esq, CBE; Four Winds, Kithurst Lane, Storrington, Sussex RH20 4LP (☎ 0903 744507)

EDWARDS-JONES, Diana Elizabeth; OBE; da of Dr John Cyril Edwards-Jones (d 1964), of Glyncollen House, Morriston, Swansea, and Nancy Gwenllian, *née* Davies (d 1937); *b* 13 Dec 1932; *Educ* Battle Abbey Sch Battle Sussex, Nat Coll of Music and Drama Cardiff, Bristol Old Vic Theatre Sch; *Career* stage mangr Swansea Repertory Co Grand Theatre; ITN 1955-89: prog dir American Election Results 1968-84 and General Election Results 1974-87, dir main news for ITV, helped create News at Ten, coverage of space exploration incl Apollos 14, 15, 16 and 17, prog dir numerous royal occasions, head of prog dirs 1980-89; Royal TV Soc award for General Election Results 1974; chm London Welsh Publicity Soc; memb BAFTA; *Recreations* swimming, music, theatre, travel, reading, skiing, horse racing; *Style—* Miss Diana Edwards-Jones, OBE; 2 Park View, 87 Park Rd, Chiswick, London W4 3ER (☎ 071 994 0904)

EDWARDS-JONES, Ian; QC (1967); s of Col Henry Vaughan Edwards Jones, MC, DL (d 1959), of Swansea, and Mary Catherine, *née* Bloomer (d 1976); *b* 17 April 1923; *Educ* Rugby, Trinity Coll Cambridge (BA); *m* 3 June 1950, Susan Vera Catharine, da of Col Edward Stanley McClintock (d 1975), of Loughlanbridge, Co Carlow; 3 s (Simon b 1952, Mark b 1955, Michael b 1957); *Career* war serv Field Artillery 1942-47 (N Africa, Italy, ME), barr Middle Temple and Lincoln's Inn 1948, practised at Chancery Bar 1949-79, bencher Lincoln's Inn 1975; social security cmmr 1979-85, The Banking Ombudsman 1985-88; fisheries memb: Regnl Fisheries Advsy Ctee and other ctees of Welsh Water Authy 1982-88, Welsh Region Nat Rivers Authy; chm Wye Salmon Fishery Owners' Assoc; *Recreations* fishing, shooting, photography, wine growing; *Clubs* United Oxford and Cambridge Univ; *Style—* Ian Edwards-Jones, Esq, QC; c/o Ground Floor, 7 Stone Buildings, Lincoln's Inn, London WC2 (☎ 071 405 3886)

EDYNBRY, Lance David; s of Ryes Edynbry (d 1960), of Sussex, and Kathleen Janet Whittle, *née* Kidman (d 1990); *b* 21 April 1947; *Educ* Worthing Boys GS, Rose Bruford Coll of Speech and Drama (Dip), Univ of Newcastle (MEd); *m* 3 Sept 1977, Geneviève Marie-Louise Andrée, da of Jean-Joseph Cros, of France; 1 da (Anne-Claire b 1980); *Career* professional repertory actor 1969-70, i/c drama in Lower Sch Thomas Bennett 1970-71, head of drama and sixth form tutor Hayfield CS 1971-76, sr lectr in drama Charlotte Mason Coll of Educn 1976-85; export dir Vignobles Jean Cros France 1985; FRSA; *Recreations* riding, gardening; *Clubs* Farmers; *Style—* Lance Edynbry, Esq; La Janade, Senouillac, 81160 Gaillac, France (☎ 63 41 51 16); Le Mas des Vignes, 81140 Cahuzac/Vere (☎ 63 33 92 62, fax 63 33 92 49, telex 532 691 F)

EDZARD, Christine; da of Dietz Edzard (d 1961), of Paris, and Suzanne, *née* Eisendieck; *b* 15 Feb 1945; *Educ* Cours D'Hulst Paris, Institut D'Etudes Politiques Paris; *m* 23 Dec 1968, Richard Berry Goodwin, s of G Goodwin; 1 da (Sabine Eleanor b 23 Oct 1971); *Career* former asst theatre designer to Lila de Nobili and Rotislav Doboujinsky; designed prodns for: Hamburg Opera, WNO, Camden Town Festival; designer and scripwriter (with Richard Goodwin) Tales of Beatrix Potter; writer and dir: Stories From a Flying Trunk (1979), The Nightingale (Channel 4, 1980), Biddy (1982); film adaptation Little Dorrit (directed with Olivier Stockman) 1987; BAFTA nomination for best screenplay Little Dorrit 1987, Oscar nomination for best screenplay based on material from another source Little Dorrit 1988; memb: ACTT, Directors Guild; *Style—* Ms Christine Edzard; c/o Sands Films, Grices Wharf, 119 Rotherhithe St, London SE16 4NF (☎ 071 231 2209 and 071 231 3645, fax 071 231 2119)

EELEY, Nicholas John; s of Sqdn Ldr (Thomas) Ian Samuel Eeley (d 1979), of Lindfield, Sussex, and Muriel Evelyn, *née* Hockley; *b* 16 April 1936; *Educ* Charterhouse; *m* 28 Sept 1963, Gillian Mary Francis, da of Cyril Joseph Cooke, of Upminster, Essex; 1 da (Harriet Amelia Catherine b 6 Feb 1967); *Career* Nat Serv pilot RAF 1953-55; NM Rothschild & Sons Ltd 1956-83; dir: NM Rothschild Asset Management Ltd 1973-83, Global Asset Management (UK) Ltd 1984-; Freeman City of Oxford 1960; *Recreations* farming, antique furniture; *Style—* Nicholas Eeley, Esq; 33 Chalcot Crescent, London NW1 8YG (☎ 071 586 0366); Gam House, 12 St James's Place, London SW1A 1NX (☎ 071 493 9990, fax 071 493 0715, telex 296099)

EELLS, Hon Mrs (Harriet Elizabeth); *née* Bridges; o da of 2 Baron Bridges, GCMG, *qv*; *b* 28 Nov 1958; *m* 4 July 1981 (m dis), John Charles Eells, s of Prof James Eells, of Wellesbourne, Warwick; *Style—* The Hon Mrs Eells

EELLS, Prof James; s of James Eells (d 1980), of USA, and Mary, *née* Wood (d 1982); *b* 25 Oct 1926; *Educ* Harvard Univ (MA, PhD); *m* 16 June 1950, Anna, *née* Munsell; 1 s (John Charles b 1958), 3 da (Mary Helen b 1951, Elizabeth Munsell b 1953, Emily b 1955); *Career* prof of mathematics Univ of Warwick 1969-; dir mathematics ICTP Trieste 1986-; *Style—* Prof James Eells; Buckle House, Church Walk, Wellesbourne, Warks (☎ 0789 841 417); Maths Institute, University of Warwick, Coventry CV4 7AL (☎ 0203 523523, fax 0203 461 606)

EFFINGHAM, 6 Earl of (UK 1837); Mowbray Henry Gordon Howard; also 16 Baron Howard of Effingham (E 1554); s of 5 Earl of Effingham (d 1946); *b* 29 Nov 1905; *Educ* Lancing; *m* 1, 28 Oct 1938 (m dis 1946), Maria Malvin Gertler; m 2, 12 Aug 1952 (m dis 1971), Gladys Irene Kerry; m 3, May 1972, (Mabel) Suzanne Mingay, da of late Maurice Jules-Marie Le Pen, of Paris, and widow of Wing Cdr Francis Talbot Cragg; *Heir* n, Cdr David Peter Mowbray Algernon Howard, RN; *Career* RA and 3 Maritime Regts WWII; *Recreations* shooting, fishing, philately; *Style—* The Rt Hon Earl of Effingham; House of Lords, London SW1 9DR

EFSTATHIOU, Prof George Petros; s of Petros Efstathiou, of London, and Christina, *née* Parperis; *b* 2 Sept 1955; *Educ* The Somerset Sch London, Keble Coll Oxford (BA), Univ of Durham (PhD); *m* 27 July 1976, Helena Jane (Janet), da of James Lewis Smart, of Poyntzpass, Newry, NI; 1 s (Peter b 1988), 1 da (Zoe b 1986); *Career* res asst Univ of California Berkley 1979-80, sr res fell King's Coll Cambridge 1984-88 (jr res fell 1980-84), asst dir of res Inst of Astronomy Cambridge 1984-88 (SERC res fell 1980-84), Savilian prof of astronomy and head of astrophysics Univ of Oxford 1988-; memb: various ctees SERC, IAU 1980; fell New Coll Oxford 1988-; Maxwell medal and prize Inst of Physics 1990; FRAS 1977; *Recreations* running, playing with my children; *Style—* Prof George Efstathiou; Dept of Physics, Nuclear and Astrophysics Laboratory, Keble Rd, Oxford OX1 3RH (☎ 0865 273300, fax 0865 273418, telex 83295 NUCLO

EGAN, Sir John Leopold; DL (Warwickshire 1989); s of James Edward Egan (d 1982); *b* 7 Nov 1939; *Educ* Imperial Coll London (BSc), London Business Sch (MSc); *m* 1963, Julia Emily, da of George Treble, of Leamington Spa; 2 da; *Career* parts and service dir Leyland Cars 1971-76, corporate parts dir Massey Ferguson 1976-80, chm and chief exec Jaguar Cars Ltd 1980-90, chief exec BAA plc 1990-; non exec dir: Legal & General Gp plc, Foreign and Colonial Investment Trust Ltd; hon fell: Chartered Inst Mktg 1989, Wolverhampton Poly 1989; Int Distinguished Entrepeneur award Univ of Manitoba; kt 1986; *Recreations* skiing, squash, walking, music; *Clubs* Warwick Boat; *Style—* Sir John Egan, DL; BAA plc, 130 Wilton Road, London SW1V 1LQ (☎ 071 932 6707)

EGAN, Lt-Col Leonard John; DL (Clwyd 1982); s of Leonard John Egan (d 1964), and Mary Elizabeth, *née* Donavon (d 1970); *b* 12 March 1924; *Educ* Downside; *m* 1 June 1948, Mina Patience Mary, da of Harry Hickley, of Rowford House, Cheddon Fitzpaine, Taunton Somerset; 1 s (Tom b 1949), 4 da (Harriet b 1950, Joanna b 1954, Mary-Anne b 1956, Naomi b 1962); *Career* cmmnd Royal Welch Fusiliers 1943; served 1943-71: India, Burma, Japan, Malaya, Germany, WI, Malaya, Cyprus, Singapore, Germany, UNF Cyprus, Gulf States; cmd 1 RWF 1966-69 (Lt-Col 1966), ret 1975; dep sec TAVR Assoc Wales 1975-89; memb St John Cncl for Clwyd 1975 (chm 1985); OStJ 1981, CStJ 1987; *Recreations* gardening; *Clubs* St John House; *Style—* Lt-Col Leonard Egan, DL; c/o Lloyds Bank, 2 Silver St, Ilminster, Somerset TA19 0DL

EGAN, Patrick Valentine Martin; s of Eric Egan; *b* 17 July 1930; *Educ* Downside; *m* 1953, Mary Theresa, da of Frederick Hinds Coleman (d 1960); 3 da; *Career* signals instr RA Far E 1949-50; exec dir Unilever plc and Unilever NV 1978-; nominated memb Cncl Lloyd's of London, non-exec dir Fisons plc; *Recreations* riding, hunting, gardening; *Style—* Patrick Egan Esq; Whiteways, Sissinghurst, Cranbrook, Kent (☎ 0580 713201)

EGDELL, Dr (John) Duncan; s of John William Egdell, of Bristol (d 1990), and Nellie Egdell; *b* 5 March 1938; *Educ* Clifton Coll, Univ of Bristol (MB ChB), Univ of Edinburgh (Dip Soc Med); *m* 9 Aug 1963, Dr Linda Mary Egdell, da of Edmund Harold Flint (d 1974), of Barnehurst, Kent; 2 s (Brian, Robin), 1 da (Ann); *Career* house physician and surgn Utd Bristol Hosps 1961-62, in gen practice 1962-65, asst sr med offr Newcastle Regnl Hosp Bd 1968-69 (admin med offr 1966-67), regnl specialist in community med SW RHA 1974-76 (asst sr med offr 1969-72, princ asst sr med offr 1972-74), regnl med offr Mersey RHA 1977-86, community physician and consIt in pub health med Clwyd Health Authy 1986-; FFPHM (1990, FFCM 1979); *Recreations* nature conservation, delving into the past; *Style—* Dr Duncan Egdell; Gelli Gynan Lodge, Llanarmon-yn-Ial, nr Mold, Clwyd CH7 4QX (☎ 08243 345); Clwyd Health Authority, Preswylfa, Hendy Rd, Mold, Clwyd CH7 1PZ (☎ 0352 700227)

EGEE, Dale Richardson; da of Wallace Caldwell Richardson (d 1979), of Vermont, USA, and Corinne Mitchell Richardson (d 1987); *b* 7 Feb 1934; *Educ* Sacred Heart Sch Greenwich Conn USA, Rosemont Coll Pennsylvania USA, Instituto D'Arte Florence Italy; *m* 1, Peter H Lewis (d 1966); 2 s (Anthony b 1960, Adam b 1963), 1 da (Corinna b 1958); m 2, 4 Sept 1966, David Wayne Egee, s of Dr J Benton Egee, of Connecticut, USA; 1 da (Eliza b 1968); *Career* tapestry designer Beirut Lebanon 1968-85; works purchased or commnd by: Lebanese Govt 1972, BCCI Bank 1973 and 1977, Hyatt Hotels 1977, Govt of Qatar 1979, US Govt 1985, 1986 and 1988; art conslt and gallery owner 1979-90 specialising in Middle Eastern African art, co organiser first Contemporary Arab Graphics exhibitions London 1981-83; recent gallery shows incl: Contemporary Islamic Calligraphy, The New Orientalists 1990; conslt to US State Dept for Art Collections for New Embassies 1985-89: Saudi Arabia, Bangladesh, N Yemen, Egypt, Jordan; assisted Br Museum and Jordan Nat Museum in acquisitions of contemporary arab artists; articles in: Arts and the Islamic World 1988, Eastern Art Report 1989; memb: Br Lebanese Assoc, Saudi Br Soc; FRGS 1987; *Recreations* reading, cookery, skiing; *Clubs* Chelsea Arts; *Style—* Ms Dale Egee; 72 Courtfield Gardens, London SW5 (☎ 071 370 3789); 9 Chelsea Manor Studios, Flood St, London SW3 4SR (☎ 071 351 6818, fax 071 376 3510)

EGELAND, Dr Leif; s of Jacob Jacobsen Egeland (d 1946), of Durban, and Ragnhild, *née* Konsmo (d 1965); *b* 19 Jan 1903; *Educ* Durban HS, Natal Univ Coll (BA, MA), Univ of Oxford (BA, BCL, MA); *m* 11 May 1942, (Marguerite) Doreen (d 1984), da of Willem De Zwaan (d 1948), of Pretoria; 1 da (Marguerite Christine (Mrs Suzman) b 9 Aug 1945); *Career* Nat Serv AJAG S African Def Force 1940-43, active serv 6 Armoured Div Middle East 1943; diplomat; S African delegate: San Francisco Conference 1945, final Gen Assembly League of Nations Geneva 1946, Paris Peace Conference 1946, first Gen Assembly UN 1946 (third 1948); S African min to Netherlands and Belgium 1946-47 (Sweden 1944-46), S African high cmmr London 1948-50; politician; MP for Zululand S African House of Assembly 1940-43 (Durban 1933-38); businessman; dir: Johannesburg Consolidated Investment Co 1950-73, S African Breweries 1950-73, Standard Bank of SA 1956-73, Rhodesian Breweries 1956-73, Goodyear Tyre & Rubber Co of SA 1957-76, Standard Gen Insurance Co 1966-83; called to the Bar Middle Temple 1930 (hon bencher hon soc 1948-), advocate Supreme Court of SA 1931-; official fell in law and classics Brasenose Coll Oxford 1927-30 (hon fell 1954-); vice pres Royal Cwlth 1948-, nat pres S African Inst of Int Affrs 1956-78 (hon pres 1978-), pres S African Guide Dogs Assoc for the Blind, chm Smuts Memorial Tst; Hon DCL Univ of Cambridge 1948, Hon LLD Univ of Natal 1990; Knight Cdr of St Olav (with Star) Norway 1943, Knight Grand Cross Order of N Star Sweden 1946, Order of Meritorious Serv (first class Gold) SA 1987; *Books* Bridges of Understanding (1977); *Style—* Dr Leif Egeland; 213 Rivonid Rd, Morningside, Transvaal, S Africa; 41 The Guild, PO Box 651624, Benmore 2010, S Africa (☎ 01027 11 584 5644)

EGERTON, Brian Balguy Le Belward; bro and hp of Sir Philip Grey Egerton, 15 Bt, *qv*; *b* 5 Feb 1925; *Educ* Repton; *Style—* Brian Egerton Esq; Tara, West St, South Petherton, Somerset TA13 5DJ

EGERTON, Cyril Reginald; s of late Hon Francis William George Egerton (2 s of 3 Earl of Ellesmere); hp of 1 cous, 6 Duke of Sutherland; *b* 7 Sept 1905; *Educ* Lancing, Trinity Coll Cambridge; *m* 1, 8 Dec 1934, Mary (d 1949), da of Rt Hon Sir Ronald

Hugh Campbell, GCMG; 1 s (Francis), 3 da (Mrs Michael (Lucy) Pelham, Mrs Frank (Katharine) Watts, Mrs Thomas (Alice) Fremantle); m 2, 29 Jan 1954, Mary Truda (d 1982), o da of late Sir (Thomas) Sydney Lea, 2 Bt; *Career* WWII Capt Hampshire Regt, seconded to RIASC; memb London Stock Exchange 1931-83; Prime Warden Worshipful Co of Dyers 1953-54; *Style—* Cyril Egerton, Esq; Hall Farm, Newmarket, Suffolk (☎ 0638 662557)

EGERTON, Francis Louis; MC; s of Louis Edwin Egerton (2 s of Sir Alfred Egerton, KCVO, CB, by his w Hon Mary Ormsby-Gore, er da of 2 Baron Harlech) and bro of Sir Alfred Egerton, who adopted Francis after his f's death in action 1917; Louis's w was Jane, da of Rev Lord Victor Seymour, 4 s of 5 Marquess of Hertford; *b* 14 Feb 1918; *Educ* Eton, ChCh Oxford; *Career* Capt Welsh Guards; private sec to Sir Alexander Cadogan at Security Cncl New York 1946-47; pres Mallett & Son 1950-; *Recreations* travelling, gardening; *Clubs* White's; *Style—* Francis Egerton, Esq, MC; The Hermitage, Crichel, Wimborne, Dorset (☎ 0258 840 223)

EGERTON, Sir Seymour John Louis; GCVO (1977, KCVO 1970); s of Capt Louis Edwin Egerton (2 s of Sir Alfred Egerton, KCVO, CB, who was sixth in descent from Hon Thomas Egerton, 3 s of 2 Earl of Bridgwater, of an illegitimate line from the ancestors of the Grey-Egerton Bts), and Jane, da of Rev Lord Victor Seymour, 4 s of 5 Marquess of Hertford; *b* 24 Sept 1915; *Educ* Eton; *Career* served WWII Capt Grenadier Gds; banker; chm Coutts & Co 1951-76; Sheriff Gtr London 1968; *Clubs* Boodle's, Beefsteak, Pratt's; *Style—* Sir Seymour Egerton, GCVO; Flat A, 51 Eaton Sq, London SW1W 9BE (☎ 071 235 2164)

EGERTON, Sir Stephen Loftus; KCMG (1988, CMG 1978); s of William le Belward Egerton, ICS (ggs of William Egerton, yr bro of Sir John and Rev Sir Philip Grey-Egerton, 8 and 9 Bts respectively) and Angela Doreen Loftus, *née* Bland; *b* 21 July 1932; *Educ* Eton, Trinity Coll Cambridge (MA); *m* 1958, Caroline, da of Maj Eustace Thomas Cary-Elwes, TD, of Laurel House, Bergh Apton, Norfolk; 1 s, 1 da; *Career* 2 Lt KRRC 1951-53; Dip Serv 1956-: consul gen Rio de Janeiro 1977-80, ambass Iraq 1980-82, asst under sec of state FCO 1982-85; ambass: Saudi Arabia 1986-89, Italy 1989-; Order of King Faisal Bin Abdul Aziz Class 1 1987, Grand Cross Italian Order of Merit 1990; *Clubs* Brooks's, Greenjackets, Eton Ramblers; *Style—* Sir Stephen Egerton, KCMG; c/o FCO (Rome), London SW1

EGERTON-WARBURTON, Hon Mrs (Marya Anne); *née* Noble; da of Baron Glenkinglas (Life Peer, d 1984), and Baroness Glenkinglas, *qv*; *b* 10 Dec 1944; *m* 6 June 1969, as his 3 wife, Peter Egerton-Warburton, *qv*; 1 s, 1 da (twin); *Style—* Hon Mrs Egerton-Warburton; Mulberry House, Bentworth, Alton, Hants GU34 5RB (☎ 0420 62360); 54 Prince's Gate Mews, London SW7 2RB

EGERTON-WARBURTON, Peter; Lord of the Manor of Grafton, patron of the livings of Plemstall and Guilden Sutton; o s of Col Geoffrey Egerton-Warburton, DSO, TD, JP, DL (d 1961; ggs of Rowland Egerton, bro of Sir John Grey-Egerton, 8 Bt, and Rev Sir Philip Grey-Egerton, 9 Bt), and Hon Georgiana Mary Dormer, MBE (d 1955), eldest da of 14 Baron Dormer, CBE, DL; *b* 17 Jan 1933; *Educ* Eton, RMA Sandhurst; *m* 1, 29 Jan 1955 (m dis 1958), Belinda Vera, da of late James R A Young, of Cowdrays, East Hendred, Berks; m 2, 10 Nov 1960 (m dis 1967), Sarah Jessica, er da of Maj Willoughby Rollo Norman (2 s of Rt Hon Sir Henry Norman, 1 Bt); 2 s; m 3, 6 June 1969, Hon Marya Anne, *qv*, 2 da of Baron Glenkinglas, PC; 1 s, 1 da (twin); *Career* cmmnd Coldstream Gds 1953, ret 1962 with rank of Capt; Maj Cheshire Yeo 1963; ptnr John D Wood Estate Agents 1966-86, fndr and chm Egerton Ltd Estate Agents 1986-; landowner; *Clubs* White's, Pratt's, Beefsteak; *Style—* Peter Egerton-Warburton, Esq; 54 Prince's Gate Mews, London SW7 2PR (☎ 071 589 9254); Mulberry House, Bentworth, Alton, Hants GU34 5RB (☎ 0420 62360)

EGGAR, Hon Mrs (Angela Lilian); *née* Mackenzie; only da of 1 Baron Amulree, GBE, PC, KC (d 1942); *b* 16 Jan 1905; *m* 28 Nov 1931, Patrick James Eggar, eldest s of Robert Henry Eggar, of Bentley, Hants; *Style—* The Hon Mrs Eggar; The Barton, Ditcheat, Somerset

EGGAR, Timothy John Crommelin (Tim); MP (C) Enfield North 1979-; s of John Drennan Eggar (d 1983), and Pamela Rosemary Eggar; *b* 19 Dec 1951; *Educ* Winchester, Magdalene Coll Cambridge, London Coll of Law; *m* 1977, Charmian Diana, da of Peter William Vincent Minoprio, late Capt Welsh Guards; 1 s, 1 da; *Career* barr, banker; pa to Rt Hon William Whitelaw 1974, PPS to Min Overseas Devpt 1982-85, dir Charterhouse Petroleum 1983-85, Parly under-sec of state FCO 1985-89; min of State: Dept of Employment 1989-90, Dept of Educn and Science 1990-; *Style—* Tim Eggar, Esq, MP; House of Commons, London SW1 (☎ 071 735 0157)

EGGINGTON, Dr (William Robert) Owen; s of Alfred Thomas Eggington, MC (d 1980), and Phyllis, *née* Wynne (d 1980); *b* 24 Feb 1932; *Educ* Kingswood Sch Bath, Guy's Hosp Med Sch (MB BS, DTM&H, DPH, DIH); *m* 20 Jan 1962, Patricia Mary Elizabeth, da of Maj Henry David Grant, MBE, MC (d 1980), of Cameronians & Palestine Police; 1 s (Patrick Thomas b Oct 1962), 1 da (Claire Mary Ruth b Jan 1964); *Career* RAMC, RMO 2 RHA 1957-60, sr specialist Army Health 1962-73, ret Lt-Col 1973; DHSS Norcross Blackpool: med offr 1973, sr med offr 1979, princ med offr 1984, chief med advsr Social Security; MFCM 1970; *Recreations* Goss heraldic china, mil history, assoc football; *Style—* Dr Owen Eggington; Friars House, 157-168 Blackfriars Rd, London SE1 8EU (☎ 071 972 3286)

EGGINTON, Anthony Joseph; CBE (1991); s of Arthur Reginald Egginton (d 1952), and Margaret Anne, *née* Emslie (d 1951); *b* 18 July 1930; *Educ* Selhurst GS, UCL (BSc); *m* 30 Nov 1957, Janet Leta, da of Albert Herring (d 1966); 2 da (Katharine b 1960, Sarah b 1962); *Career* res assoc: UCL 1951-56, Gen Physics Div AERE Harwell 1956-61; head: Beams Physics Gp, NIRNS Rutherford High Energy Laboratory 1961-65; SRC Daresbury Nuclear Physics Laboratory 1965-88: Machine Gp 1965-72 (Engrg Div SRC Central Office 1972-74), dir engrg and nuclear physics 1974-78, dir sci and engrg 1978-83, dir engrg 1983-88; dir progs and dep chm Sci and Engrg Res Cncl 1988-; *Books* author of various papers and articles in jls and conf proceedings on particle accelerators; *Recreations* sport, cinema, music; *Clubs* Lansdowne; *Style—* Anthony Egginton, Esq, CBE; Witney House, West End, Witney OX8 6NQ (☎ 0993 703502); Science and Engineering Research Council, Polaris House, North Star Avenue, Swindon SN2 1ET (☎ 0793 411139)

EGGINTON, Prof Donald Albert (Don); s of Albert Edward Egginton (d 1943), and Ellen Egginton; *b* 14 March 1934; *Educ* Hamond's GS Swaffham Norfolk, LSE (BSc); *m* 5 Aug 1959, Angela Marion, da of Roy John Shirras; 1 s (David Christopher b 5 Sept 1964), 2 da (Jane Rebecca b 26 Dec 1966, Elizabeth Sarah b 29 May 1970); *Career* Nat Serv RAF 1952-54; Barclays Bank Norfolk 1950-57, Ross Group Westwick Norfolk 1957, articled clerk with Baker Sutton (chartered accountants) London (now merged with Ernst & Young) 1960-63; Univ of Bristol: lectr in accounting 1963-74, sr lectr 1975-80, reader 1980-86, personal professorship 1986, head Dept of Economics 1990-; visiting lectr Univ of Minnesota Minneapolis 1970-71; visiting prof: Univ of Newcastle, Univ of NSW, Aust Nat Univ 1989; Walter Taplin prize for Accounting and Business Res: for paper on Distributable Profit and the Pursuit of Prudence 1982 (with J Forker and M Tippett), for paper on Share Option Rewards and Management Performance 1990; ACIB 1956, FCA 1973 (ACA 1963), memb American Accounting Assoc 1964; *Books* Management Accounting: A Conceptual Approach (with L R Amey, 1973), Accounting for the Banker (1977, 2 edn 1982); *Recreations* painting, swimming; *Style—* Prof Don Egginton; University of Bristol, Department of Economics, 40 Berkeley Square, Bristol, Avon BS8 1HY (☎ 0272 303030, fax 0272 251696)

EGGLESTON, Prof (Samuel) John; s of Edmund Eggleston (d 1959), and Josephine Eggleston (d 1985); *b* 11 Nov 1926; *Educ* Chippenham GS, Univ of London (MA, BSc, DLitt); *m* 1957, Greta Margaret, da of James Patrick (d 1967), of Hereford; 2 s, 2 da; *Career* prof of educn Univ of Keele 1967-84, prof and chm of educn Univ of Warwick 1985-, dir of Res Multi Cultural Educn 1978-; memb Consultative Ctee Assessment of Performance Unit DES 1980-89, memb Trg Ctee Arts Cncl 1983-87, chm Educn Ctee Centl TV 1987-, chm of judges Young Electronics Designer Competition 1986-, govr Design Dimension Tst 1989-, academic advsr Routledge 1977-, dir Trentham Books 1983-; ed: Sociological Review, Design and Technology Teaching; chm Editorial Bd: European Journal of Education, Multicultural Teaching; lectr and examiner many home and overseas univs; FCP 1983; *Books Incl:* The Ecology of the School (1977), Work Experience in Schools (1982), Education for Some (1986); *Recreations* work in design and craft, skiing, riding, travel, gardening; *Style—* Prof John Eggleston; Whitmore Heath, Newcastle-under-Lyme, Staffordshire (☎ 0782 680483); University of Warwick, Warwickshire (☎ 0203 5253848)

EGGLESTON, Hon Sir Richard Moulton; s of John Bakewell Eggleston (d 1932), and Elizabeth Bothwell, *née* McCutcheon (d 1912); *b* 8 Aug 1909; *Educ* Wesley Coll Melbourne, Queen's Coll Melbourne Univ (LLB); *m* 1934, Isabel Marjorie, da of Francis Edward Thom (d 1948); 1 s, 3 da (1 decd); *Career* judge Cwlth Industrial Ct and Supreme Ct ACT 1960-74, judge Supreme Ct Norfolk Island 1960-69, dir Barclays Australia 1974-80; Hon LLD: Melbourne 1973, Monash 1983; kt 1971; *see Debrett's Handbook of Australia and New Zealand for further details*; *Recreations* painting, golf, billiards; *Style—* Hon Sir Richard Eggleston; Willow St, Malvern, Vic 3144, Australia (☎ 822 5215)

EGLESTON, Lady Clarissa; *née* Windsor-Clive; da of 2 Earl of Plymouth (d 1943); *b* 15 Jan 1931; *m* 24 April 1953, Maj Keith Maclean Forbes Egleston, late Rifle Bde, yr s of late Maj Thomas Buchanan Maclean Egleston, MC, of White Hart Lodge, Limpsfield, Surrey; 1 s, 2 da; *Style—* The Lady Clarissa Egleston; 7 Ernest Gdns, London W4 3QU

EGLETON, Lt-Col Clive Frederick William; s of Frederick Egleton (d 1964), of Ruislip, and Rose, *née* Wildman (d 1987); *b* 25 Nov 1927; *Educ* Haberdashers' Aske's; *m* 9 April 1949, Joan Evelyn, da of Thomas Lane (d 1971), of Sandown, IOW; 2 s (Charles Barclay b 13 Aug 1953, Richard Wildman b 7 Jan 1958); *Career* Army serv cmmnd Staffordshire Regt 1945, ret with rank Lt-Col 1975; author; novels: A Piece of Resistance (1970), Last Post For a Partisan (1971), The Judas Mandate (1972), Seven Days To A Killing (1973), The October Plot (1974), Skirmish (1975), State Visit (1976), The Mills Bomb (1978), Backfire (1979), The Winter Touch (1981), A Falcon For The Hawks (1982), The Russian Enigma (1982), A Conflict of Interests (1983), Troika (1984), A Different Drummer (1987), Picture of the Year (1988), Death of a Sahib (1989), In the Red (1990), Last Act (1991); (under pseudonym John Tarrant): The Rommel Plot (1977), The Clauberg Trigger (1979), China Gold (1982); (under pesudonym Patrick Blake): Escape to Athena (1979), Double Griffin (1981); non fiction: The Stealing of Muriel McKay (1978), The Baldau Touch (1982); memb Crime Writers Assoc; *Recreations* gardening, travel; *Clubs* Army and Navy; *Style—* Lt-Col Clive Egleton; c/o Anthony Goff, David Higham Associates Ltd, 5-8 Lower John St, Golden Square, London W1R 5HA

EGLINGTON, Charles Richard John; s of Richard Eglington, and Treena Margaret Joyce Eglington; *b* 12 Aug 1938; *Educ* Sherborne; *Career* dir Akroyd & Smithers plc; Stock Exchange: chm Ctee on Quotations 1978-81, jt dep chm Cncl 1981-84, chm Property and Fin Ctee 1983-86; vice chm: S G Warburg Akroyd Rowe and Pitman, Mullens Securities Ltd; govr: Sherborne Sch, Twyford Sch; *Recreations* cricket, golf; *Clubs* MCC, Walton Heath, Rye, Royal & Ancient; *Style—* Charles Eglington, Esq; S G Warburg Securities, 1 Finsbury Avenue, London EC2M 2PA

EGLINTON, Prof Geoffrey; s of Alfred Edward Eglinton, and Lilian Blackham; *b* 1 Nov 1927; *Educ* Sale GS, Univ of Manchester (BSc, PhD, DSc); *m* April 1955, Pamela Joan Coupland; 2 s (David Geoffrey, Timothy Ian), 1 da decd (Fiona Jayne); *Career* US Public Health fell Ohio State Univ 1951-52, ICI fell Univ of Liverpool 1952-54, reader in organic chemistry Univ of Glasgow 1964-67 (lectr 1954-64); Organic Geochemistry Unit Univ of Bristol: head 1967-, sr lectr 1967-68, reader 1968-73, prof 1973-; adjunct scientist Woods Hole Oceanographic Inst Mass USA 1990-, head Jt Honours Sch of Chemistry and Geology Univ of Bristol 1969-78; visiting prof in Dept of Botany Univ of Texas Austin 1968; conslt: Masspec Analytical Speciality Services Ltd 1975-78 (dir 1978-79); Hazelton Laboratories Europe Ltd 1979-84, Exploration Div BP plc 1981-; managing ed Chemical Geology 1984-89, assoc ed abroad Geochemical Jl Japan 1980-82, res assoc Univ of Calif Space Sciences Laboratory 1970-; memb: Cmmn of Organic Geochemistry of the Int Assoc of Geochemistry and Cosmochemistry 1971-, Interdisciplinary Sci Reviews 1975-, Editorial Bd Origins of Life (D Reidel) 1983-; fndr memb Editorial Bd ADSTRA Jl of Res 1983-, chm Euro Assoc of Organic Geochemists; memb: Sub-Ctee for Space Biology Royal Soc 1970-74, Gen Advsy Cncl of the BBC 1971-77, Planetology Ctee French Govt 1975-77, Sabrina Project Steering Gp Univ of Bristol 1969-80, Cncl Marine Biological Assoc of the UK 1981-84, Nat Ctee on Oceanic Res Royal Soc 1981-87, Cncl NERC 1984-90, Steering Ctee Scientific Info Serv of CIBA Fndn 1984-, Int Exchanges Ctee Royal Soc 1988-91, Marine Sci Ctee WERC 1984-90 (also Earth Sci Ctee); dean graduate studies Univ of Bristol 1985-89; chm: Biomolecular Palaeontology Spacial Topic Steering Gp NERC 1989-, ICPMS Ctee NERC 1990-; memb: American Assoc for Advancement of Sci, Chemical Soc, Geochemical Soc, Geological Soc, Int Soc for Study of the Origins of Life, Academia Europaea, Euro Environmental Res Orgn; FRIC, FRS 1976; NASA Gold medal for Exceptional Scientific Achievement 1973, Alfred E Treibs Medal award (Organic Geochemistry Div Geochemical Soc) 1981, Major Edward D'Ewes Fitzgerald Coke medal (Geological Soc) 1986; *Books* Applications of Spectroscopy to Organic Chemistry (1965), Organic Chemistry: methods and results (1969), Chemsyn (1972, 2 edn 1975); contrib to numerous learned jls; *Recreations* gardeining, walking, sailing; *Clubs* Science (Bristol), Manchester Univ Mountaineering, Rucksack (Manchester); *Style—* Prof Geoffrey Eglinton, FRS; Oldwell, 7 Redhouse Lane, Bristol BS9 3RY (☎ 0272 683833); School of Chemistry, Organic Geochemistry Unit, Cantock's Close, Bristol BS8 1TS (☎ 0272 303671, fax 0272 251295)

EGLINTON AND WINTON, 18 Earl of (S 1507 and UK 1859); Archibald George Montgomerie; Lord Montgomerie (S 1449), Baron Seton and Tranent (UK 1859), Baron Ardrossan (UK 1806); Hereditary Sheriff of Renfrewshire; s of 17 Earl of Eglinton and Winton (d 1966), and Ursula (d 1987), da of Hon Ronald Bannatyne Watson, s of Baron Watson (Life Peer, d 1899); *b* 27 Aug 1939; *Educ* Eton; *m* 7 Feb 1964, Marion Carolina, da of John Henry Dunn-Yarker, of Le Château, La Tour de Peilz, Vaud, Switzerland; 4 s (Lord Montgomerie b 1966, Hon William b 1968, Hon James b 1972, Hon Robert b 1975); *Heir* s, Lord Montgomerie; *Career* dep chm Gerrard & National Holdings plc; *Style—* The Rt Hon the Earl of Eglinton and Winton; The Dutch House, West Green, Hartley Wintney, Hants (☎ 3160); Gerrard and National Holdings plc, 33 Lombard St, London EC3V 9BQ (☎ 071 623 9981, telex

883589)

EGMONT, 11 Earl of (I 1733); Sir Frederick George Moore Perceval; 15 Bt (I 1661); also Baron Perceval (I 1715), Viscount Perceval (I 1722), Baron Lovell and Holland (GB 1762), Baron Arden (I 1770), Baron Arden (UK 1802); s of 10 Earl (d 1932 before establishing claim to Earldom), and Cecilia (d 1916), da of James Burns Moore; *b* 14 April 1914; *m* 31 Aug 1932, Ann Geraldine, da of Douglas Gerald Moodie, of Calgary, Alberta; 1 s (and 2 decd), 1 da; *Heir* s, Viscount Perceval; *Style*— The Rt Hon the Earl of Egmont; Two-dot Ranch, Nanton, Alberta, Canada

EGREMONT, 2 Baron (UK 1963) and 7 Baron Leconfield (UK 1859); (John) Max Henry Scawen Wyndham; s of 6 Baron Leconfield and 1 Baron Egremont, MBE (d 1972; as John Wyndham was private sec to Rt Hon Harold Macmillan, when PM); *b* 21 April 1948; *Educ* Eton, Christ Church Coll Oxford; *m* 15 April 1978, Caroline, da of Alexander Ronan Nelson and Hon Audrey Paget (da of 1 and last Baron Queenborough, s of Lord Alfred Paget, 5 s of 1 Marquess of Anglesey); 1 s (Hon George Ronan Valentine b 31 July 1983), 3 da (Hon Jessica Mary b 27 April 1979, Hon Constance Rose b 20 Dec 1980, Hon Mary Christian b 4 Oct 1985); *Heir* s, Hon George Wyndham; *Career* farmer and writer; memb Royal Cmmn on Historical MSS 1989, chm The Friends of the Nat Libraries 1985-; tstee: The Wallace Collection, The Br Museum 1990-; *Books* The Cousins (1977), Balfour (1980), The Ladies Man (1983), Dear Shadows (1986), Painted Lives (1989); *Style*— The Rt Hon Lord Egremont; Petworth House, Petworth, W Sussex GU28 0AE (☎ 0798 42447)

EGREMONT, (and Leconfield), Dowager Baroness; Pamela; da of Capt Hon Valentine Wyndham Quin (d 1983, 2 s of 5 Earl of Dunraven and Mount-Earl); sis of Lady Roderic Pratt and Marchioness of Salisbury; *b* 29 April 1925; *m* 24 July 1947, 1 Baron Egremont (and 6 Baron Leconfield), MBE (d 1972); 2 s (2 (& 7) Baron Egremont (and Leconfield), Hon Harry Wyndham), 1 da (Hon Mrs Chisholm); *Style*— The Rt Hon the Dowager Lady Egremont; Cockermouth Castle, Cockermouth, Cumbria; 40 Sussex St, London SW1V 4RH (☎ 071 931 9055)

EHRHARDT, Marianne Luise (Mrs Nicholas Stacey); da of Wilhelm Alois Ehrhardt, of Friedrichshafen, West Germany, and Viktoria, *née* Hollenzer; *b* 2 May 1950; *Educ* Graf Zeppelin Gymnasium Friedrichshafen, Staatliche Hochschule fur Musik Freiburg; *m* 10 March 1987, Nicholas Anthony Howard Stacey, *qv*; *Career* flute teacher: Oxford High Sch for Girls 1975-76, ILEA 1976-; fndr and musical dir Ondine Ensemble (classical chamber music ensemble) 1979-, fndr Platform (charitable tst promoting young composers' unpublished works internationally) 1990-; cmmnd and premiered numerous major compositions; major live broadcasts incl: Sudwestfunk Germany 1982, BBC 1983, WGMS Washington DC 1988; foreign tours incl: Germany 1981 and 1982, USA 1984 and 1988; *Recreations* history, skiing; *Style*— Miss Marianne Ehrhardt; 35 Lennox Gardens, London SW1X 0DE

EHRMAN, John Patrick William; s of Albert Ehrman (d 1969), and Rina, *née* Bendit; *b* 17 March 1920; *Educ* Charterhouse, Trinity Coll Cambridge (MA); *m* 1 July 1948, Elizabeth Susan Anne, da of Vice Adm Sir Geoffrey Blake, KCB, DSO (d 1968); 4 s (William b 1950, Hugh b 1952, Richard b 1956, Thomas b 1959); *Career* fell Trinity Coll Cambridge 1947-52, historian Cabinet Office 1948-56, Lees Knowles lectr Cambridge Univ 1957-58, James Ford special lectr Oxford Univ 1976-77; hon treas Friends Nat Libraries 1960-77, vice pres Navy Records Soc 1968-70 and 1974-76, memb Reviewing Ctee on Export of Works of Art 1970-76, tstee Nat Portrait Gallery 1971-85, memb Royal Cmmn Historical Manuscripts 1973-; chm: (advsy) Br Library Reference Div 1975-84, Nat Manuscripts Conservation Fund 1989-; FBA, FSA, FRHistS; *Books* The Navy in the War of William III (1953), Grand Strategy 1943-45 (1956), The British Government and Commercial Negotiations with Europe (1962), The Younger Pitt (vol 1 1969, vol 2 1983), Cabinet Government and War 1890-1940 (1988); *Clubs* Army & Navy, Beefsteak, Garrick; *Style*— John Ehrman, Esq, FSA; The Mead Barns, Taynton, Burford, Oxfordshire

EICHELBERGER, Alyce Faye; da of Albert Clinton McBride (d 1973), and Frances Fay, *née* Mitchell (d 1962); *b* 28 Oct 1944; *Educ* Oklahoma State Univ USA (BSc), Baylor Univ (MA, MSc), Univ of London Inst of Educn (DPMC); *m* 22 Jan 1966, Martin Davis Eichelberger Jr, s of Martin Davis Eichelberger; 2 s (Martin Davis III b 28 Sept 1969, Clinton Charles b 14 March 1973); *Career* teacher secdy sch 1962-69, teaching asst to Dean of Special Educn Baylor Univ 1974-75, educnl psychologist Waco Ind Sch Dist Texas 1975-78, child psychotherapist Notre Dame Clinic 1981-87; teacher: of children with med and emotional problems ILEA 1983-84, in secdy sch for emotionally disturbed children 1980-83; child psychotherapist: Tavistock Clinic, Chalcot Sch; educnl psychologist Educn Records Bureau NY; psychotherapist and psychologist: American Sch of London, American Embassy, Tasis Sch Thorpe Park Surrey; in private practise Harley St; memb: Republicans Abroad, Int Jr League Assoc of Child Psychotherapy 1986; ABPS 1980, fell American Psychological Assoc 1980, fell American Med Psychotherapist Assoc 1987, memb RSM 1988, assoc fell Br Psychological Soc 1988; *Books* Comparative Education of Gifted Children in France (1979), Corporate Education of Gifted Children in the USSR (1979), A Case Study of Maladjusted Children in a London Day School (1983), Another Revolutionary - A Case Study of Psychotherapy With a Five Year Old Rastafarian Boy; *Recreations* jogging, mountain climbing; *Style*— Mrs Alyce Faye Eichelberger

EILLEDGE, Elwyn Owen Morris; s of Owen Eilledge, of Oswestry, Shropshire, and Mary Elizabeth Eilledge (d 1973); *b* 20 July 1935; *Educ* Oswestry Boys HS, Merton Coll Oxford (BA, MA); *m* 30 March 1962; 1 s (Julian Alexander Stephen b 15 June 1970), 1 da (Amanda Gail Caroline b 20 Nov 1968); *Career* qualified CA 1963, sr ptnr Ernst and Young (formerly Ernst and Whinney) 1986- (joined 1965, ptnr 1972-83, managing ptnr 1983-86), chm Ernst and Young Int (formerly Ernst and Whinney Int) 1988-; secondments: Govt of Liberia 1966-68, Hamburg 1968-71; memb Worshipful Co of CA's; FCA; *Recreations* gardening, snooker; *Clubs* Brooks's; *Style*— Elwyn Eilledge, Esq; Whitethorn House, Long Grove, Seer Green, Beaconsfield, Bucks (☎ 0494 676 600); Ernst & Whinney, Becket House, 1 Lambeth Palace Rd, London SE1 7EU (☎ 071 928 2000, fax 071 928 1345, telex 885234)

EILOART, Mildred Joy; da of George Maxwell Eiloart, DFC, RFC (despatches twice; his log book mentions flying gold out to Lawrence of Arabia), of Lyndhurst Gdns Hampstead (d 1964), and Mildred Octavia, *née* Coles (d 1982); niece of Cyril Eiloart, Lt Irish Gds (ka 1918, France), Oswald Eiloart, Actg Capt 1 Bn London Regt (ka 1917, France), and Actg Maj Horace Eiloart, DSO, MC (d 1920 from wounds rec'd in France); gda of F E Eiloart (sr ptnr Watney Eiloart, Inman and Nunn, City Estate Agents and Surveyors); *Career* sec/PA to: Dep Overseas Dir FBI 1958-63, Capt Jaspar Teale, RN, Chief of the Navy Section Ops Div SHAPE Paris; sec/asst librarian to Chief Economist at Rio-Tinto Zinc Corp 1965-81; since when freelance; *Recreations* theatre, ballet, art exhibitions, music, horse racing, reading, walking in the country, European travel; *Clubs* Theatregoers', Euro Assoc of Professional Secs, Nat Tst, Racegoers'; *Style*— Miss Mildred Eiloart; Flat 38, 7 Elm Park Gardens, London SW10 9QG (☎ 071 352 4222)

EILON, Prof Samuel; s of Abraham Joel (d 1974), and Rachel, *née* Deinard (d 1982); *b* 13 Oct 1923; *Educ* Reali Sch Haifa, Technion Haifa (BSc, DipIng), Imperial Coll London (PhD, DSc); *m* 8 Aug 1946, Hannah Ruth, da of Max Samuel; 2 s (Amir, Daniel), 2 da (Romit, Carmel); *Career* Maj Israel Defence Forces 1948-52; engr in indust 1945-48; Imperial Coll London: res asst/lectr 1952-57, reader 1959-63, prof of mgmnt sci 1963-89 (head of Section/Dept 1955-87), sr res fell 1989-; assoc prof Technion Haifa 1957-59, conslt to indust 1957-; Silver Medal The Operational Res Soc 1982; Hon FCGI 1978; FIMechE, FIProdE, CBIM, FEng; *Books* author of 12 books and over 250 papers on management; *Recreations* tennis, walking; *Clubs* Athenaeum; *Style*— Prof Samuel Eilon; Imperial Coll, Exhibition Rd, London SW7 2BX (☎ 071 589 5111 ext 6127)

EINSIEDEL, Andreas J P, Graf von; s of Wittigo Graf von Einsiedel (d 1980), of Frankfurt am Main, Germany, and Walburga, *née* Graefin von Oberndorff; *b* 28 Jan 1953; *Educ* Landschulheim Marquartstein Bavaria, PCL (BA); *m* 2 June 1979, Harriet, da of Henry de L'Etang Duckworth; 3 s (Orlando b 19 Aug 1980, Evelyn b 26 Aug 1982, Robin b 12 April 1988) 1 da (Gwendolen b 24 Jan 1985); *Career* photographer; asst to Dir Interteam (film co) Frankfurt 1977-78, asst to Photographer Jacques Schuhmacher Hamburg 1978-79; farming in Scotland 1979-80; asst to Photographer Norman Gold 1980-81, freelance 1981-, began specialising in photography of interiors and interior design 1983-; regular work for pubns incl: House & Garden, Homes & Gardens, World of Interiors, Madame (Germany), Ambiente (Germany), Madame Figaro (France), Zeit Magazin (Germany), Art Magazin (Germany); photographer for book Classic English Interiors (1990); memb AFAEP 1982-; *Recreations* tennis; *Style*— Andreas Graf von Einsiedel; 72-80 Leather Lane, London EC1N 7TR (☎ 071 242 7674, fax 071 831 3712)

EISLER, Hon Mrs (Jean Mary); 2 da of 1 Baron Layton, CH, CBE (d 1966), and Eleanor Dorothea, *née* Osmaston (d 1959); *b* 14 April 1916; *Educ* St Paul's Girls' Sch London, RCM (ARCM); *m* 12 June 1944, Paul Eisler (d 15 Aug 1966), yr s of Ernst Eisler (d 1951), of Prague; 2 s (John b 1946, Ivan b 1948); *Career* professional musician and music therapist; concert performer and teacher 1941-46; lived in Prague 1948-72; translator of Czech children's books, novels, belles lettres, modern vocal music incl 2 Janáček operas (Osud, Počátek románu); sr music therapist: Goldie Leigh 1976-90, Queen Mary's Hosp for Children Carshalton 1984-, Nordoff/Robbins Music Therapy Centre London 1984-; fndr memb Mgmnt Ctee Nordoff/Robbins Music Therapy Centre; Tagore Gold medal, Nordoff/Robbins Music Therapy Dip 1974; *Style*— Hon Mrs Eisler; Syskon Cottage, 2 Millfield Lane, London N6

EISNER, Hans Gunter; s of Ludwig Eisner (d 1972), of 321 Wilbraham Road, Chorlton-cum-Hardy, Manchester, and Hertha, *née* Buckwitz (d 1976); *b* 4 July 1929; *Educ* Manchester Central High GS, Univ of Manchester Sch of Architecture (BArch); *m* 13 June 1953, (Doreen) Annette Elizabeth, da of Reginald Barker-Lambert, of Tree Tops, Marley Rd, Exmouth, Devon; 2 s (Christopher Paul David b 20 Nov 1954, Andrew James Stephen b 27 May 1961); *Career* architect; Assoc Architects Fairhursts Manchester 1952-53, architect and gp leader Middlesbrough Educn Architects Dept 1954-56, architect i/c Drawing Office Borough of Watford 1956-57, sr assoc architect New School Section Derbyshire Co Architects Dept 1957-62, sr architect i/c R & D Gp Manchester City Housing Dept 1962-63, princ assoc architect SW Regnl Health Authy 1963-75, architect and area building offr Devon Area Health Authy 1975-83, in private practice 1983-; princ projects incl: Ladgate Primary Sch Middlesbrough, Devpt Project for Infant Educn Sawley Infants Sch Long Eaton Derbys, Royal United Hosp Bath Phase I; memb: ARUCK 1953, RIBA 1953, Cncl Assoc of Official Architects 1959-85 (chm 1972-82), RIBA Public Relations TV and Bdcast Ctee 1965-69, RIBA SW Regnl Cncl 1975-78, RIBA Cncl 1975-78, Assoc of Conslt Architects, RIBA Devon and Exeter Branch Exec 1984-89, Rotary Club Exeter (vice pres); *Recreations* walking, music, sketching, travel, gardening; *Clubs* Rotary; *Style*— Hans G Eisner, Esq; Bickleigh House, Edginswell Lane, Kingskerswell, Devon TQ12 5LU (☎ 0803 873597)

EKINS, Eric Walker; s of Thomas Edward Ekins (d 1982), of Barrow-in-Furness, Cumbria, and Janet Walker, *née* Armstrong; *b* 16 June 1938; *Educ* Preston Catholic Coll Lancs; *m* 22 Sept 1962, Patricia Mary, da of Timothy Brendan Laffan, of Eastbourne, E Sussex; 1 da (Clare b 1975); *Career* sr ptnr Ekins and Co CAs; FCA; *Recreations* walking, ornithology, music; *Clubs* North Wilts Rotary; *Style*— Eric Ekins, Esq; 3 Manor Close, Blunsdon, Swindon SN2 4BD (☎ 0793 721 292); Ekins & Co, 31 Victoria Rd, Swindon SN1 3AQ (☎ 0793 642 577)

EL-FALAHI, Sami Dawood; s of Dawood Salman El-Falahi (d 1954), of Baghdad, Iraq, and Munira Abdul, *née* Razzaq (d 1985); *b* 13 Dec 1934; *Educ* Lincoln Coll Oxford (MA), Univ of Loughborough (MSc); *m* 1 (m dis); 2 s (Mohamed Dawood b 30 Dec 1966, Hani b 7 July 1978), 1 da (Daád b 13 Dec 1964); m 2, Emile Murakami; *Career* legal exec various int petroleum cos 1961-72; called to the Bar Inner Temple 1972; currently in practice specialising: settlement of disputes, arbitrations, drafting of commercial agreements and int contracts; FInstPet 1969, FCInstArb 1974; *Books* Arab World Business Law Review (ed), Comparative Guide to Tax Havens of the World; *Recreations* travel, reading, walking, tennis and gardening; *Clubs* Oxford and Cambridge; *Style*— Sami D El-Falahi, Esq; International Law Chambers, ILC House, 77 Chepstow Rd, Bayswater, London W2 5QR (☎ 071 221 5684/4840, fax 071 221 5685, telex 9419395 SDFG)

EL NAHAS, Dr (Abdel) Meguid; s of Hassan Khalil El Nahas (d 1978), of Cairo, Egypt, and Fatma Galal Selim, *née* El Hegazy; *b* 1 Dec 1949; *Educ* Jesuits' Coll Cairo Egypt, Univ of Geneva Med Sch Switzerland, Univ of London (PhD); *m* 30 April 1983, Penelope Anne, da of Henry Denys Hanan, DSC, of Shrewsbury; 2 da (Gemma b 1983, Holly b 1985); *Career* res Mass Gen Hosp Boston USA 1977-78; res fell in nephrology: Paris 1978-79, Royal Postgrad Med Sch London 1979-82; renal registrar Royal Free Hospital London 1982-84, lectr in nephrology Univ of Wales Coll of Med Cardiff 1984-86, conslt renal physician Northern Gen Hosp Sheffield 1986-, dir of res Sheffield Kidney Inst 1986-; FRCP; *Recreations* sports, history, reading, travelling; *Style*— Dr Meguid El Nahas; Sheffield Kidney Inst, Northern General Hospital, Herries Rd, Sheffield S5 7AU (☎ 0742 434343, fax 0742 560472)

ELAM, (John) Nicholas; s of John Frederick Elam, OBE, and Joan Barrington, *née* Lloyd; *b* 2 July 1939; *Educ* Colchester Royal GS, New Coll Oxford, Harvard Univ; *m* 14 Oct 1967, (Florence) Helen, da of Pieter Lentz; 2 s (Peter, Michael), 1 da (Alexandra); *Career* entered HM Dip Serv 1962, FO 1962-64, served Pretoria and Capetown 1964-68, Treasy Centre Admin Studies 1968-69, FCO 1969-71, first sec Bahrain 1971, commercial sec Brussels 1972-76, FCO 1976-79 (dep head News Dept 1978-79), cnsllr and Br Govt rep Salisbury 1979, dep high cmmr Salisbury (later Harare) 1980-83, consul gen Montreal 1984-87, head Cultural Relations Dept FCO 1987-; *Recreations* travel, the arts; *Style*— Nicholas Elam, Esq; Foreign and Commonwealth Office, King Charles St, London SW1A 2AH

ELBORNE, Robert Edward Monckton; s of Sidney Lipscomb Elborne, MBE (d 1986), of Water Newton, nr Peterborough, and Cavil Grace Mary, *née* Monckton (d 1984); *b* 10 Nov 1926; *Educ* Eton, Trinity Coll Cambridge (MA); *m* 25 July 1953, (Leslie) Vivienne, da of Lt Gen Sir Ernest Wood, KCB, CIE, CB, MC (d 1972), of Foxton House, nr Cambridge; 2 s (Mark Edward Monckton b 1958, William Henry Alexander b 1966), 1 da (Charlotte Julia Mary Beare); *Career* Lt Life Gds 1945-47, Lt The Inns of Ct Regt TA 1950-56; called to the Bar Inner Temple Midland Circuit 1950-57, ptnr Waltons & Co 1958-67, sr ptnr Elborne Mitchell & Co 1968-82 (conslt 1982-87); non exec dir: Leicester Building Society 1982-86, Alliance and Leicester

Building Society 1986-, Chancellor Insurance Co Ltd 1988-; external memb Cncl of Lloyd's 1983-87; Freeman City of London, Liveryman Worshipful Soc of Waterman and Lightermen; *Clubs* Boodle's, Beefsteak, City of London; *Style*— Robert Elborne, Esq; Seaton Old Rectory, Oakham, Leicestershire LE15 9HU (☎ 057 287 276); 17 Bettridge Rd, London SW6 3QH (☎ 071 736 9468)

ELCOAT, Rev Canon (George) Alastair; s of George Thomas Elcoat (d 1955), of 137 High View, Wallsend-on-Tyne, and Hilda Gertrude, *née* Bee (d 1962); *b* 4 June 1922; *Educ* Tynemouth Sch, The Queen's Coll Birmingham; *Career* RAF 1941-46; ordained: deacon Newcastle 1951, priest 1952; asst curate Corbridge 1951-55; vicar: Spittal 1955-62, Chatton W Chillingham 1962-70, Sugley 1970-81, Tweedmouth 1981; rural dean: Newcastle West 1977-81, Norham 1982; chaplain to HM The Queen 1982; *Recreations* fell walking, music, photography; *Style*— Rev Canon Alastair Elcoat; The Vicarage, 124 Main St, Tweedmouth, Berwick-on-Tweed TD15 2AW

ELDEN, Jeremy Mark; s of Reginald Elden, and Sheilagh, *née* Carter; *b* 21 June 1958; *Educ* Northgate GS Ipswich, Hertford Coll (BA), Univ of Strathclyde (MSc); *m* 19 Sept 1987, Victoria Mary, *née* Bone; *Career* field engr Schlumberger Overseas SA 1980-82, reservoir engr Britoil 1982-83, oil analyst UBS Phillips & Drew 1984-90, dir oil res BZW 1990-; *Style*— Jeremy Elden, Esq; 74 Andrews House, Barbican, London EC2Y 8AY (☎ 071 588 2995); BZW, 2 Swan Lane, London EC4R 3TS (☎ 071 956 3402, fax 071 956 4615)

ELDER, Prof James Brown; s of David Elder (d 1988), of Linwood, Renfrewshire, Scotland, and Margaret Helen, *née* Cowan (d 1982); *b* 20 May 1938; *Educ* Shawlands Acad Glasgow, Univ of Glasgow (MB ChB, MD); *m* 12 Dec 1964, Sheena Jean Reid Fyfe, da of Colin McLay, of Paisley, Scotland; 3 da (Jacqueline b 1966, Karen b 1967, Alison b 1969); *Career* sr registar in gen surgery Glasgow Western Infirmary 1968-71 (registrar 1965-68), reader in surgery Univ of Manchester Manchester Royal Infirmary 1976-83 (sr lectr and conslt surgn 1971-76), prof of surgery Univ of Keele Sch of Postgraduate Med 1983-, conslt surgn to N Staffs Hosp Centre 1983-; examiner in surgery Univs of: Manchester 1976-83, Glasgow 1981-83, Sheffield 1986-89, Nottingham 1985-89; memb Cncl Br Soc of Gastroenterology, memb Nat Confidential Enquiry into Perioperative Death, memb Senate Univ of Keele, examiner RCPS Glasgow; FRCSEd 1966, FRCS 1966, FRCS Glasgow 1981; *Recreations* hill walking, classical music, reading, photography; *Clubs* British Pottery Manufacturer's Federation (Stoke-on-Trent); *Style*— Prof James Elder; Tara, 182 Seabridge Lane, Westlands, Newcastle-under-Lyme, Staffs ST5 3LS; Department of Surgery, University of Keele, School of Postgraduate Medicine and Biological Sciences, Thornburrow Drive, Hartshill, Stoke-on-Trent (☎ 0782 49144)

ELDER, Mark Philip; CBE (1989); *b* 2 June 1947; *Educ* Bryanston, CCC Cambridge (music scholar, choral scholar, BA, MA); *m* 30 May 1980, Amanda Jane, *née* Stein; 1 da (Katherine Olivia b 13 April 1986); *Career* music dir: English National Opera 1979-, Rochester Philharmonic Orchestra NY 1989-; *Style*— Mark Elder, Esq, CBE; c/o Ingpen and Williams Ltd, 14 Kensington Court, London W8 5DN (☎ 071 937 5158, fax 071 937 4175)

ELDER, Prof Murdoch George; s of Archibald James Elder, of Biggar, Scot, and Lotta Annie Catherine, *née* Craig; *b* 4 Jan 1938; *Educ* Univ of Edinburgh Acad, Edinburgh (MB ChB, MD); *m* 3 Oct 1964, Margaret Adelaide, da of Dr James McVicker (d 1985), of Portrush, Co Antrim, Ireland; 2 s (James b 1968, Andrew b 1970); *Career* Nat Serv Captain RAMC (TA and VR) 1964; lectr Univ of Malta 1969-71, sr lectr and reader Univ of London (Charing Cross Hosp Med Sch) 1971-75, res fell WHO 1976, travelling fell RCOG 1977, prof and head Dept of Obstetrics and Gynaecology Royal Postgraduate Med Sch Univ of London 1978-; dir: Obstetrics and Gynaecology Service Hammersmith, Queen Charlotte's Special Health Authy, WHO Clinical Res Centre 1980-; visiting prof Univs of: California (LA), Singapore, London; examiner Univs of: London, Oxford, Edinburgh, Glasgow, Leeds, Liverpool, Birmingham, Bristol, Malta, Malaysia, Capetown, Singapore; memb Hammersmith and Queen Charlotte's Special Health Authy 1982-90, chm Hosp Med Ctee 1980-85 sec Assoc of Profs (O and G) 1984-86, memb WHO Steering Ctee on Contraception 1980-86; Silver medal Hellenic Obstetrical Soc 1983; FRCS (1968), FRCOG (1978); 200 scientific pubns; *Books* Current Fertility Control (1978), Pre Term Labour (1982), Reproduction, Obstetrics and Gynaecology (1988); *Recreations* golf, travel; *Clubs* Roehampton, 1942; *Style*— Prof Murdoch Elder; 4 Stonehill Rd, London SW14 8RW (☎ 081 876 4332); Hammersmith Hospital, Du Cane Rd, London W12 0HS (☎ 081 743 7171)

ELDER, Walter Brisbane; s of William Johnstone Elder, of Eildon, Strathaven, Lanarkshire, and Jane, *née* Young; *b* 18 Nov 1904; *Educ* Strathaven Acad, Hindenburg Sch; *m* 28 March 1963, Christine Margaret Brisbane, da of William Stewart (d 1972), of Rio de Janeiro, Brazil; *Career* ARP 1939-43, served in France and Germany, RASC 1944-46; dir and chm Hamilton ACasFC 1956-70, chm Elder & Watson 1946-80; pres: Strathaven MIA 1946-56, Glasgow C of C 1946-80; *Recreations* gardening, conservation; *Clubs* Constitutional; *Style*— Walter Elder, Esq; The Spittal House & Lodge, Stonehouse, Lanarkshire (☎ 792224)

ELDERFIELD, Maurice; s of Henry Elderfield (d 1977), and Kathleen Maud, *née* James; *b* 10 April 1926; *Educ* Southgate Co GS; *m* 22 Aug 1953, Audrey June, da of Sydney James Knight (d 1981); 1 s (Christopher b 10 March 1956), 3 da (Sallie b 15 May 1958, Carol (twin) b 15 May 1958, Jacqueline b 11 Oct 1961); *Career* WWII Fleet Air Adm RNVR 1944-47; memb Bd and fin dir Segas 1960-73, fin dir SWA 1973-75, memb Bd of Fin PO 1975-76, fin dir Ferranti Ltd 1977, memb Bd of Fin Br Shipbuilders 1977-80; chm: Throgmorton Trust 1972-84, Sheldon and Partners Ltd, Sheldon Aviation Ltd 1978-90 and 1980-90, Berfield Associates Ltd; tstee East Grinstead Lawn Tennis and Squash Club; FCA 1949; *Recreations* golf, tennis; *Clubs* Gravetye Manor; *Style*— Maurice Elderfield, Esq; Hadleigh, Cansiron Lane, Ashurst Wood, Sussex RH19 3SD (☎ 0342 822638); Sheldon and Ptnrs Ltd, St George's Court, 131 Putney Bridge Rd, London SW15 2PA (☎ 081 874 9953, fax 081 874 9244)

ELDERTON, Prof Richard John; s of Edward Fothergill Elderton (d 1986), and Hilda Mary Irene, *née* Thomas (d 1971); *b* 10 April 1942; *Educ* Lancing Coll Sussex, Univ of London (BDS, PhD); *m* 10 Sept 1966, Pamela Mary, da of Enslie Roy Bater Bolt (d 1987); 2 s (Charles b 1969, Edward b 1971), 1 da (Sophie b 1977); *Career* warrant offr in CCF; in gen dental practice 1965-66, res dental house surgn London Hosp 1966, clinical instr in operative dentistry State Univ of NY Buffalo USA 1966-68, sr lectr in conservative dentistry London Hosp Med Coll 1976-78 (lectr 1968-71, res fell experimental dental care project 1971-76), dir Dental Health Servs Res Unit Univ of Dundee 1979-85, prof of preventive and restorative dentistry and head Dept of Conservative Dentistry Univ of Bristol 1985-; hon scientific advsr to the British Dental Journal 1984-; memb: Expert Advsy Panel on Oral World Health Orgn 1987-, JT Dental Ctee for MRC Health Depts and Serc 1987-; LDS RCS 1965; memb: BDA, IADR, BSDR, BSRD, BASCD; *Books* Positive Dental Prevention (1987), Evolution in Dental Care (1990), the Dentition and Dental Care (1990); *Recreations* running, sailing, wood and metal work, painting, philosophy; *Style*— Prof Richard Elderton; Dept of Conservative Dentistry, Dental School, Lower Maudlin St, Bristol, BS1 2LY (☎ 0272 291900, fax 0272 253724)

ELDON, 5 Earl of (UK 1821); John Joseph Nicholas Scott; Baron Eldon (GB 1799), Viscount Encombe (UK 1821); s of 4 Earl of Eldon, GCVO (d 1976, fifth in descent from the 1 Earl), and Hon Margaret Fraser, OBE (d 1969), da of 16 Lord Lovat; *b* 24 April 1937; *Educ* Ampleforth, Trinity Coll Oxford; *m* 1 July 1961, Countess Claudine, da of Count Franz von Montjoye-Vaufrey and de la Roche (originally a cr of Louis XV of France 1736, confirmed 1743 (also by Louis) and later by Emperor Franz Josef of Austria-Hungary 1888), of Vienna; 1 s, 2 da (Lady Tatiana b 1967, Lady Victoria b 1968); *Heir* s, John Francis Thomas Marie Joseph Columba Fidelis, Viscount Encombe b 9 July 1962; *Career* 2 Lt Scots Gds, Lt Army Emergency Reserve; *Style*— The Rt Hon The Earl of Eldon; c/o House of Lords, London SW1

ELDRED, Dr Vernon Walter; MBE (1970); s of Vernon Frank Eldred (d 1929), of Sutton Coldfield, and Dorothy, *née* Lyon (d 1968); *b* 14 March 1925; *Educ* Bishop Vesey's GS Sutton Coldfield, St Catharine's Coll Cambridge (MA, PhD); *m* 4 Aug 1951, Pamela Mary, da of Arthur Wood (d 1943), of Sutton Coldfield; 2 s (Andrew b 1952, John b 1958), 1 da (Sally b 1956); *Career* Dept Scientific and Industl Res Fuel Res Station Greenwich 1945-47, Atomic Energy Res Establishment Harwell 1947-48, Dept Metallurgy Univ of Cambridge 1948-53, Nelson Res Labs English Electrical Co Stafford 1953-55; Windscale laboratory UAEA: princ scientific offr 1955-59, res mangr metallurgy 1959-76, head of Fuel Examination Div 1976-84, head of Fuel Performance Div and dep head labour 1984-87, head of labour 1987-90; Royal Soc Esso award for Conservation of Energy 1979; memb Cncl Inst Metallurgists 1966-69, chm Ctee Nat Certificates and Dips in Metallurgy 1967-73, memb Bd Br Nuclear Energy Soc 1974-77; fndr memb and first chm West Cumbria Metallurgic Soc; hon fell Inst Nuclear Engrs 1988, pres Gosforth Dist Agric Soc Cumbria 1990; FIM 1968, FEng 1984; *Recreations* beekeeping, fell walking, genealogy, gardening, computers; *Clubs* United Oxford and Cambridge Univ; *Style*— Dr Vernon Walter Eldred, MBE; Fell Gate, Santon Bridge, Holmrook, Cumbria CA19 1UY (☎ 09467 26275)

ELDRIDGE, David John; s of Lt-Col Frederick George Eldridge (ret), of Little Court, Pathfields Close, Haslemere, Surrey, and Irene Mary, *née* Buston; *b* 12 Jan 1935; *Educ* King's Coll Sch Wimbledon; *m* 1, 14 May 1960, Diana Mary (d 1981), da of Eric Copp, of 19 Oval Grange, Hartlepool, Cleveland; 1 s (Charles b 1961), 2 da (Catherine b 1964, Victoria b 1966); m 2, 15 Dec 1984, Anna Maria, da of Jerzy Kowalski, of Warsaw, Poland; *Career* admitted slr 1956; ptnr: Stanley Attenborough & Co 1958-74, Martin & Nicholson 1975-77, Amhurst Brown Colombotti 1977-, Amhurst Brown Warsaw Poland; tstee (since inception 1974) Musuem of Islamic Art Jerusalem; donation govr Christ's Hosp Horsham; Freeman City of London, Liveryman & memb Ct Worshipful Co of Fletchers (Master 1984-86), memb Ct of Assts Guild of Freemen (Master 1983-84); memb Law Soc 1957; *Recreations* fine arts, sport; *Clubs* Royal Automobile, City Livery; *Style*— David Eldridge, Esq; The Coach house, 2c Woodborough Rd, Putney, London SW15 (☎ 081 785 4348); Warsaw, Poland; Amhurst Brown Colombotti, 2 Duke St, St James's, London SW1 (☎ 071 930 2366, fax 071 930 2250, telex 261857 Ambro

ELDRIDGE, Eric William; CB (1965), OBE (1948); o s of William Eldridge (d 1954), of London; *b* 15 April 1906; *Educ* Millfields Central Sch, City of London Coll; *m* 1936, Doris Margaret, da of Peter Kerr (d 1964); 1 s, 1 da; *Career* admitted slr 1934; conslt with Lee and Pembertons Slrs 1971-88, chief admin offr Public Tstee Office 1955-60 (asst public tstee 1960-63, public tstee 1963-71); *Recreations* foreign travel, gardening; *Style*— Eric Eldridge, Esq, CB, OBE; Old Stocks, Gorelands Lane, Chalfont St Giles, Bucks HP8 4HQ (☎ 024 07 2159); Gull Cottage, 249 High St, Aldeburgh, Suffolk

ELDRIDGE, Mark; s of Bernard Derrick Eldridge, of Toronto, Canada (foster f George Hoare, of Liphook, Hants), and Anne May, *née* Murphy (foster mother Eileen Violet, *née* Luff); *b* 9 Aug 1954; *Educ* Churcher's Coll Petersfield Hants, Univ of Lancaster (BA), City Univ (Dip in Law), Inns of Court Sch of Law; *m* 3 July 1982, Alexandra Catherine, da of John Watling Illingworth, of Wellingborough, Northants; 1 s (Joseph b 10 July 1987), 3 da (Charlotte b 27 March 1983, Elizabeth b 27 Sept 1984, Catherine b 31 Jan 1986); *Career* called to the Bar Gray's Inn 1982, memb Inner Temple 1985, elected memb Gen Cncl of the Bar 1985-91, chm Young Bar of England and Wales 1989; govr Thornhill Primary Sch 1986-88, chm Islington South and Finsbury Cons Assoc 1989- (vice chm 1986-89); *Recreations* swimming, golf, tennis; *Clubs* Carlton; *Style*— Mark Eldridge, Esq; 114 Liverpool Rd, Islington, London N1 0RE (☎ 071 226 9863); 10 King's Bench Walk, Temple, London EC4Y 7EB (☎ 071 353 7742, fax 071 583 0579)

ELEGANT, Robert Sampson; s of Louis Elegant (d 1965), and Lillie Rebecca, *née* Sampson (d 1984); *b* 7 March 1928; *Educ* Univ of Pennsylvania (BA), Yale, Columbia Univ (MA, MS); *m* 16 April 1956, Moira Clarissa Brady; 1 s (Simon David Brady b 1960), 1 da (Victoria Ann b 1958); *Career* Far East corr Overseas News Agency 1951-52, war corr Korea 1952-53; corr in Singapore and SE Asia for: Columbia Broadcasting Serv, McGraw-Hill News Serv and North American Newspaper Alliance 1954-55; S Asian corr & chief New Delhi Bureau Newsweek 1956-57, SE Asian corr & chief Hong Kong Bureau Newsweek 1958-61, chief Central Euro Bureau (Bonn-Berlin) Newsweek 1962-64, pub lectr 1964-, chief Hong Kong Bureau Los Angeles Times 1965-69, foreign affrs columnist Los Angeles Times/Washington Post News Serv Munich 1970-72, Hong Kong 1973-76; visiting prof of journalism and int affrs Univ of South Carolina 1976, independent author and journalist 1977-; Pulitzer Travelling fell 1951-52, fell Ford Fndn 1954-55, fell American Enterprise Inst 1976-78, Edgar Allen Poe award Mystery Writers of America 1967, four Overseas Press club awards; *Books non-fiction:* China's Red Leaders (1951), The Dragon's Seed (1959), The Centre of the World (1964), Mao's Great Revolution (1971), Mao vs Chiang: The Battle for China (1972), Pacific Destiny: Inside Asia Today (1990); *novels:* A Kind of Treason (1966), The Seeking (1969), Dynasty (1977), Manchu (1980), Mandarin (1983), White Sun, Red Star (1986); *Recreations* sailing, raising Shih Tzu dogs; *Clubs* Hong Kong Foreign Correspondents, Royal Hong Kong Yacht, Lansdowne; *Style*— Robert Elegant, Esq; The Manor House, Middle Green, Langley, Bucks SL3 6BS (☎ (0753) 20654)

ELEY, Dr Barry Michael; s of Horace Henry Eley (d 1971), and Ena Maud, *née* Cast (d 1975); *b* 6 March 1940; *Educ* St Olave's & St Saviour's GS, The London Hosp Dental Sch (BDS, LDS, RCS); *m* 1 June 1963, Julie Christina, da of Arthur William Rumbold; 1 s (Peter John b 10 Dec 1965), 1 da (Esther Jane b 12 March 1968); *Career* house surgn London Hosp Med Sch 1963; King's Coll Hosp Dental Sch: asst lectr and registrar 1963-65, lectr in conservation dentistry 1965-74, sr lectr in periodontology 1974-80; King's Coll Sch of Med and Dentistry: sr lectr and conslt 1980-89, head of Periodontal Dept 1980-, dir Sch of Dental Hygiene 1980-, reader and conslt in periodontology; author of over 60 scientific papers; FDS RCS 1972; memb: BDA, BSP, BSDR, RMS; *Books* Amalgam Tattoos (1982), Outline of Periodontics (with J D Mason, 2 edn 1989); *Recreations* badminton, golf, listening to music, walking, astronomy; *Style*— Dr Barry Eley; 10 Grosvenor Road, Petts Wood, Orpington, Kent BR5 1QU

ELEY, Piers David Christopher; s of Sir Geoffrey Cecil Ryves Eley, CBE (d 1990); *b* 20 May 1941; *Educ* Sandroyds Sch, Eton, Trinity Coll Cambridge (MA), London Grad Sch of Business Studies (MSc); *m* 1 April 1967, Sarah Cloudesley, da of Lt-Col David E Long-Price, OBE, of Fryerning, Ingatestone, Essex; 1 s (Damian Edward

Piers b 24 Jan 1970), 1 da (Thalia Catherine b 9 Sept 1971); *Career* Norton Rose Botterell & Roche 1964, Hambros Bank Ltd 1964-73; dir: Nordic Bank plc 1973-84, Coopers & Lybrand 1984-89; ptnr Coopers & Lybrand Deloitte Associates 1990-; memb: Inner Temple 1961, London Business Sch Assoc 1969, Business Graduates Assoc 1969; Guildsman of St Brides Fleet St 1984, chm Friends of St Matthias Richmond 1986-; FRSA 1989; *Recreations* painting, gardening, fishing, sailing, shooting, photography, music; *Clubs* Brooks's, Fox, Omar Khayyam, St Mawes Sailing; *Style—* Piers D C Eley, Esq; 35 Montague Rd, Richmond, Surrey TW10 6QJ (☎ 081 940 0788); Coopers & Lybrand Deloitte, Plumtree Court, Farringdon St, London EC4A 4HT (☎ 071 583 5000, fax 071 822 8500, telex 887470)

ELFICK, Richard Stanley; s of Stanley Irving Elfick (d 1971), and Doris May, *née* Whittaker (d 1990); *b* 4 Oct 1934; *Educ* Hounslow Coll; *m* 1968, Hilary Margaret; 1 s (Brian Richard b 1976), 2 da (Sarah Benodet b 1970, Robin Clare b 1972); *Career* Nat Serv 1957-59; trg with Allen Attfield 1951-57; Arthur Andersen: joined 1959, ptnr Arthur Andersen Consulting 1970, Practice Mgmnt 1979-; ACA 1957; *Recreations* sailing, walking; *Clubs* RAC, Royal Ocean Racing, Royal Southern Yacht; *Style—* Richard Elfick, Esq; Wybarton, Moles Hill, Oxshott, Surrey KT22 0DB (☎ 0372 842257); Arthur Andersen, 1 Surrey St, London WC2R 2PS (☎ 071 438 3306)

ELFORD, Colin David; s of Charles John Elford (d 1962), of Tavistock, Devon, and Enid Audrey, *née* Jope; *b* 3 Aug 1936; *Educ* Tavistock Sch; *m* 14 Oct 1966 (m dis 1974), Caroline Margaret, da of Julian Vann (d 1940); 2 s (Julian Charles Colin b 1966, Stuart Michael Paul b 1967); *Career* TA cmmnd 1954-60; ptnr: Mann & Co 1966-69, Hampton & Sons 1969-71; dir Shanning Homes Ltd 1971-77, self-employed 1977-80, dir Mortgage Systems Ltd 1981-86, md City & Provincial Home Loans Ltd 1986-89, self employed 1989-; former cncllr Fleet Urban DC, chm and pres Fleet CC 1968-80, life vice-pres and fndr Fleet Hockey Club, chm Guildford & Godalming Athletic Club 1985-86; AVI 1962, FSVA 1977, FPCS 1981; *Recreations* shooting, angling, squash, cricket; *Clubs* Fleet CC, Fleet Hockey Club, Guildford & Godalming AC; *Style—* Colin Elford, Esq; Brecon House, Ganghill, Guildford, Surrey (☎ 0483 504521)

ELFORD, Hon Mrs (Rowena Frances); eldest da of 2 Viscount St Davids; *b* 7 Aug 1940; *m* 31 Oct 1959 (m dis 1977), David Elford, s of late Richard Elford, of Melbourne, Australia; 1 s, 3 da; *Style—* The Hon Mrs Elford; 4 Holland Court, Oakleigh, 3166 Victoria, Australia

ELGIN AND KINCARDINE, 11 and 15 Earl of (S 1633 and 1647); Andrew Douglas Alexander Thomas Bruce; KT (1981), CD (1985) JP (Fife 1951); also Lord Bruce of Kinloss (S 1604), Lord Bruce of Torry (S 1647), Baron Elgin (UK 1849); 37 Chief of the Name of Bruce; s of 10 Earl of Elgin, KT, CMG, TD (ggs of the 7 Earl who removed to safety the statuary known as The Elgin Marbles from the Parthenon in Athens), and Hon Dame Katherine Elizabeth Cochrane, DBE, da of 1 Baron Cochrane of Cults; *b* 17 Feb 1924; *Educ* Eton, Balliol Coll Oxford (MA); *m* 27 April 1959, Victoria Mary, o da of Dudley George Usher, MBE, TD, of Gallowridge House, Dunfermline; 3 s (Lord Bruce, Hon Adam Robert, Hon Alexander Victor b 1971), 2 da; *Heir* s, Lord Bruce; *Career* served WWII (wounded); chm Nat Savings Ctee Scotland 1972-78; dir: Scottish Amicable Life Assurance Soc (and pres), Royal Highland and Agric Soc 1973-76; pres: Roy Caledonian Curling Club 1968-69, Royal Scottish Automobile Club; Lord High Cmmr to Gen Assembly of Church of Scotland 1980-81; Grand Master Mason of Scotland 1961-65, Ensign Royal Co of Archers (Queen's Body Guard for Scotland); DL Fife 1955; Lord Lt Fife Region 1988-; Hon Col Elgin Regt of Canada (1969); Hon LLD: Dundee 1977, Glasgow 1983; Hon DLitt St Mary's NS 1976; *Style—* The Rt Hon the Earl of Elgin and Kincardine, KT, CD, JP; Broomhall, Dunfermline KY11 3DU (☎ (0383) 872222)

ELIA, Dr Mumtaz Hamid; s of Hamid Elia (d 1959), of Baghdad, Iraq, and Najiba, *née* Yosef (d 1982); *b* 29 Dec 1945; *Educ* Univ of Baghdad Med Sch (MB ChB, DMRT); *m* 30 July 1977, Caroline, da of William Lusk, of Glasgow; *Career* conslt in radiotherapy and oncology Raigmore Hosp Inverness 1983-, dir N Scotland Cancer Registry 1983-, hon sr lectr in radiotherapy and oncology Univ of Aberdeen 1989-; memb: Scotland and Newcastle Lymphoma Gp, Scot Cancer Trials Orgn, Inverness Cancer Self Help Gp; FRCR; *Books* contrib: Atlas of Cancer in Scotland (1985), Cancer Incidence in 5 Continents (1987); *Recreations* swimming, snooker, music; *Clubs* Caledonian; *Style—* Dr Mumtaz Elia; Waterside, Allanfearn, by Inverness IV1 2HY (☎ 0463 713639); 36 Moray Park Ave, Culloden, Inverness IV1 2LS (☎ 0463 792916); Department of Radiotherapy and Oncology, Raigmore Hospital, Inverness (☎ 0463 234151)

ELIAN, Dr Marta; da of Laszlo Steiner (d 1955), of Tel Aviv, Israel, and Magda, *née* Laszlo (d 1985); *b* 14 March 1929; *Educ* Hebrew Univ Hadassa Med Sch Jerusalem; *m* 23 Aug 1949, Dr Ezra Elian (d 1982), s of Dr Henry Eilender (d 1981), of Frankfurt; 2 s (Amnon b 5 Feb 1955, Yoram (twin) b 5 Feb 1955); *Career* sr lectr in neurology Tel Aviv Med Sch 1969, conslt clinical neurophysiologist Old Church Hosp Romford 1981-; author of several papers on epilesy and multiple sclerosis; ABN, ASMT, ABCN; *Style—* Dr Marta Elian; 15 Chalcot Crescent, London NW1 8YE (☎ 071 722 5508); Old Church Hospital, Romford, Essex (☎ 746090 ext 3106); Charing Cross Hospital, Fulham Palace Rd, London (☎ 071 846 1657)

ELIAS, Brian David; s of Albert Murad Elias, and Julie Sophie, *née* Ephriam; *b* 30 Aug 1948; *Educ* St Christopher Sch, RCM, and with Elisabeth Lutyens; *Career* composer: La Chevelure 1969, Peroration 1973, Somina 1979, L'Eylah (cmmnd for BBC Promenade Concerts) 1984, Geranos (cmmnd by Fires of London) 1985, Variations (for solo piano) 1987, Five Songs to Poems by Irina Ratushinskaya (cmmnd by the BBC) 1989; memb Assoc of Professional Composers, New Macnaghten Concerts; *Recreations* reading, gardening, theatre, art; *Style—* Brian Elias, Esq; Chester Music, 8/9 Frith St, London W1V 5TZ (071 434 0066, fax 071 439 2848, telex 21892 MSLDNG)

ELIAS, Dr Elwyn; s of Illtyd Elias (d 1965), and Rachel, *née* Jones; *b* 11 Jan 1943; *Educ* Ardwyn GS, Aberystwyth, Guy's Hosp Med Sch (BSc, MB BS); *m* 3 April 1982, Irene Margaret, da of Rev Reginald Raymond Taylor (d 1977), of Nottingham; 2 s (Gareth b 15 Nov 1983, Joshua b 14 March 1986); *Career* registrar Hammersmith Hosp 1970-72, lectr and hon sr registrar Royal Free Hosp 1973-77, res fell Liver Study Unit, of Chicago Hosp 1977-78, res assoc Univ of Yale Hosp 1978-79, conslt physician Queen Elizabeth Hosp Birmingham 1979-; *Books* Lecture Notes in Gastroenterology (1985); *Style—* Dr Elwyn Elias; Queen Elizabeth Hospital, Edgbaston, Birmingham (☎ 021 472 1311)

ELIAS, Peter Raoul; s of Paul Elias, and Margarethe Rozenzweig; *b* 5 Feb 1933; *Educ* Kilburn GS; *m* 18 July 1953, Betty Ethel Kathleen, da of Joseph Kennedy; 1 s (Roger David b 1957), 1 da (Vivienne Zöe b 1955); *Career* RAF air wireless operator and mechanic; sale dir Training Systems International 1967-69 (export sales mangr 1960-67), princ P R Elias and Assocs 1969-; section offr Thames Valley Special Constabulary 1975-87, Special Constable Dyfed Powys Police 1987-; Police Long Serv medal; *Recreations* golf, motorcycling, linguist, music lover, collecting and riding Harley-Davidsons, writing; *Clubs* Camarthen Golf, Vintage Motorcycle; *Style—* Peter R Elias, Esq; Bryn Cowin, Talog, Carmarthen, Dyfed (☎ 09948 214, fax 09948 573, car 0836 664369)

ELIAS-JONES, Peter John; s of William Peter Jones (d 1973), of Llangefni, Anglesey, and Margaret, *née* Elias; *b* 29 May 1943; *Educ* Llangefni Ysgol Gyfun, Univ of Leeds (BA), Univ of Manchester (Dip); *m* 10 April 1971, Elinor Mair, da of Cyril Owens (d 1988), of Ammanford, Dyfed; 2 da (Elen b 1973, Mari Wyn b 1976); *Career* teacher of music and drama Wallasey GS Cheshire 1966, studio mangr TWW Ltd Cardiff 1967; HTV Ltd Cardiff: dir news 1968, prodr and dir children's progs 1971, head of children's progs 1974, asst prog controller 1981, prog controller entertainment 1988; author of four books for young people and numerous articles; *Style—* Peter Elias-Jones, Esq; HTV, TV Centre, Culverhouse Cross, Cardiff, S Glam CF5 6XJ (☎ 0222 590 590, fax 0222 597183, telex 497703)

ELIBANK, 14 Lord (S 1643); Sir Alan D'Ardis Erskine-Murray; 14 Bt (NS 1628); s of Maj Robert Alan Erskine-Murray, OBE (d 1939), unc of 13 Lord; suc cous 1973; *b* 31 Dec 1923, Wynberg, SA; *Educ* Bedford, Peterhouse Coll Cambridge; *m* 1962, Valerie Sylvia, o da of late Herbert William Dennis, of St Margaret's, Twickenham; 2 s; *Heir* s, Master of Elibank; *Career* barr 1949-59, gen mangr and rep Shell Int Petroleum Co in Qatar 1977-80 (personnel 1955-77), personnel mangr Deminex Oil and Gas Ltd 1981-86; *Style—* The Rt Hon the Lord Elibank; The Coach House, Charters Rd, Sunningdale, Ascot, Berks

ELIBANK, Master of; Hon Robert Francis Alan Erskine-Murray; s and h of 14 Lord Elibank, *qv*; *b* 10 Oct 1964; *Educ* Harrow, Reading Univ (BA); *Career* key account mangr Courage Ltd; *Recreations* soccer, tennis; *Style—* The Master of Elibank; c/o Courage Ltd, Ashby House, 1 Bridge Street, Staines, Middx TW18 4TP (☎ 0784 466199, fax 0784 468131)

ELIOT, Lady Alethea Constance Dorothy Sydney; da of 1 and last Earl Buxton, GCMG, PC (d 1934, sometime Govr-Gen and C-in-C South Africa and gs of Sir Thomas Fowell Buxton, 1 Bt), by his 2 w, Dame Mildred Smith, GBE, JP, sister of 1 Baron Bicester; *b* 2 Aug 1910; *m* 12 July 1934, Canon Peter Charles Eliot, MBE, TD, *qv*; *Style—* The Lady Alethea Eliot; The Old House, Kingsland, Leominster, Herefordshire MR6 9QS (☎ 056 881 285)

ELIOT, Lord; Jago Nicholas Aldo Eliot; s and h of 10 Earl of St Germans; *b* 24 March 1966; *Educ* Millfield; *Style—* Lord Eliot; Port Eliot, St Germans, Cornwall

ELIOT, Ven Canon Peter Charles; MBE (1945), TD (1945); s of Hon Edward Granville Eliot (yst bro of 7 and 8 Earls of St Germans) by his w Clare (herself da of William Phelips, JP, DL, by his 2 w Constance, da of Hon Sir Spencer Ponsonby-Fane, GCB, PC, 6 s of 4 Earl of Bessborough); *b* 30 Oct 1910; *Educ* Wellington, Magdalene Coll Cambridge; *m* 12 July 1934, Lady Alethea, *qv*; *Career* Lt-Col cmdg Kent Yeo RA (TA), served WWII BEF, M East and Italy; admitted slr 1934, practiced until 1953; ordained 1954, rural dean 1960-61, archdeacon of Worcester 1961-75, residentiary canon of Worcester 1965-75; *Recreations* sightseeing, sketching, gardening, amateur theatricals; *Clubs* Travellers'; *Style—* Ven Canon Peter Eliot, MBE, TD; The Old House, Kingsland, Leominster, Herefordshire (☎ 056 881 285)

ELIOT, Hon (Montagu) Robert Vere; s of 8 Earl of St Germans, KCVO, OBE (d 1960); *b* 28 Oct 1923; *Educ* Eton, Ch Ch Oxford; *m* 1983, Marie Frances Richmond Lusk, widow of A R Lusk, of Fordie, Comrie, Perthshire, and da of Geoffrey Mervyn Cooper (d 1984), of Preston Candover, Hants; *Career* a train bearer at Coronation of King George VI, a page of honour to HM 1937-40; served Grenadier Gds 1943-52, Capt (ret), in NW Europe (wounded) 1944, Palestine (medal) 1945-48; ret co dir; memb: Westminster City Cncl 1952-61, Cornwall CC 1977-; Parly Candidate (Cons) Mansfield Notts 1959; provincial grand master for Cornwall, United Grand Lodge of England 1978-; pres Royal Instn of Cornwall 1983-84 (Henwood medal 1990); chm Cornwall Heritage Tst 1984-89, pres Cornwall Family History Soc 1988-; Coronation medal 1937; *Recreations* bridge, reading; *Clubs* Carlton; *Style—* Hon Robert Eliot; Lux Cross House, Pengover Rd, Liskeard, Cornwall PL14 3EL (☎ 0579 42755)

ELIOTT OF STOBS, Sir Charles Joseph Alexander; 12 Bt (NS 1666), of Stobs, Roxburghshire; Chief of the Clan Eliott or Elliot; s of late Charles Rawdon Heathfield Eliott (himself s of half-bro of Sir Arthur Eliott of Stobs, 9 Bt); suc half second cousin, Sir Arthur Eliott of Stobs, 11 Bt (d 1989); *b* 9 Jan 1937; *Educ* St Joseph's Christian Bros Rockhampton nr Brisbane; *m* 1, 1959, Wendy Judith, da of Henry John Bailey, of Toowoomba, Queensland; 1 s (Rodney Gilbert Charles b 1966); m 2, 8 Oct 1988, Andrea Therese Saunders; 1 s (Stephen Charles b 2 Aug 1990) and 1 s decd, 1 da (Cassandra Jane b 1989), 4 da (Elizabeth (Mrs Armanasco) b 1960, Jenny (Mrs Land) b 1961, Josephine (Mrs Grofski) b 1963, Clare Melinda b 1973); *Heir* s, Rodney Gilbert Charles Eliott; *Career* builder (C J & W J Eliott); *Style—* Sir Charles Eliott of Stobs, Bt; 27 Cohoe St, Toowoomba, Qld 4350, Australia (☎ 32 7390)

ELKAN, Walter; s of Hans Septimus Elkan (d 1933), of Hamburg, and Maud Emily, *née* Barden (d 1957); *b* 1 March 1923; *Educ* Frensham Heights, LSE (BSc, PhD); *m* 28 Dec 1946 (m dis 1981), Susan Dorothea, da of Emanuel Jacobs (d 1965); 1 s (David b 1952), 2 da (Ruth b 1954, Jenny b 1955); *Career* served Pioneer Corps and RA 1942-47; sr res fell Makerere Inst Social Res Uganda 1953-60, lectr Univ of Durham 1960 (prof of econs 1965-79), visiting res prof Univ of Nairobi 1972-73, prof of econs Brunel Univ 1979- (emeritus prof 1988); formerly: pres African Studies Assoc, memb Northern Econ Planning Cncl, memb Bd School of Hygiene and Tropical Med; memb: Cncl Royal Econ Soc, Cncl Overseas Devpt Inst, Econ and Soc Ctee for Overseas Res; *Books* An African Labour Force (1959), Economic Development of Uganda (1961), Migrants and Proletarians (1961), Introduction to Development Economics (1973); *Recreations* music, art; *Style—* Prof Walter Elkan; 98 Boundary Rd, London NW8 0RH (☎ 071 624 5102); Brunel University, Dept of Economics, Uxbridge, Middx (☎ 0895 56461 telex 261173)

ELKIN, Alexander; CMG (1976); o s of Boris Elkin (d 1972), and Anna Elkin (d 1973); *b* 2 Aug 1909,St Petersburg; *Educ* Grunewald Gymnasium and Russian Academic Sch Berlin, Univs of Berlin, Kiel and London (DR JUR, LLM); *m* 1937, Muriel, da of Edwin M Solomons (d 1964), of Dublin; *Career* war time Govt Serv 1942-45 (BBC Monitoring Serv 1939-42); called to the Bar Middle Temple 1937, assoc chief Legal Serv UN Interim Secretariat 1945-46, asst dir UN Euro Office Geneva 1946-48, legal advsr to UNSCOB Salonica 1948, dep legal advsr and later legal advsr OEEC (OECD 1960-) 1949-61, UNECA legal conslt formation of African Devpt Bank 1962-64, acting gen counsel of ADB 1964-65, special advsr on Euro Communities Law FCO 1970-79; legal consultancies for: WHO 1948, IBRD 1966, UNDP 1967-68, W African Rgnl Gp 1968, OECD 1975; lectured on Euro Payments System and OECD: Univ of the Saar 1957-60, Univ Inst of Euro Studies Turin 1957-65; lectr on drafting of treaties UNITAR Seminars The Hague, Geneva and NY for legal advsrs and diplomats 1967-84; lectr in language and law: Univ of Bradford 1979-83, Univ of Bath 1979-; hon visiting prof Univ of Bradford 1982-84; memb RIIA; Ford Fndn Leadership Grant 1960; Hon Doctorate in Law Univ of Bath 1990; *Books* contrib: European Yearbook, Journal du Droit Int, Revue Générale du Droit International Public, Survey of Int Affairs 1939-46, Travaux pratiques de L'Institut de Droit Comparé de la Faculté de Droit de Paris; *Recreations* reading, visiting art collections, travel; *Clubs* Travellers'; *Style—* Alexander Elkin, Esq, CMG; 70 Apsley House, Finchley Road, St John's Wood, London NW8 0NZ (☎ 071 483 2475)

ELKIN, Sonia Irene Linda; OBE (1981, MBE 1966); da of Godfrey Albert Elkin (d 1947), and Irene Jessamine Archibald (d 1968); *b* 15 May 1932; *Educ* Beresford House Sch Eastbourne; *Career* overseas sec Assoc of Br C of C 1956, Overseas Dept

Lloyd's Bank 1966; CBI: head W Euro Dept 1967, head Regnl and Small Firms Dept 1972 (dep dir 1973), dir for Smaller Firms 1979-83, dir Regnl Orgn 1983, dir Regions & Smaller Firms 1985-; cmmr Manpower Servs Cmmn 1981-85; *Books* What About Europe? (1967, updated with the co-operation of Mr Angus Hislop and republished in 1971 under the title What About Europe Now?); *Recreations* music; *Clubs* United Oxford & Cambridge Univ (lady associate); *Style*— Miss Sonia Elkin, OBE; CBI, Centre Point, 103 New Oxford St, WC1A 1DU (☎ 071 379 7400, fax 071 497 2597)

ELKINGTON, Robert John; s of late John David Rew Elkington, OBE; *b* 7 Oct 1949; *Educ* Eton, Univ of Exeter (BA); *m* 1, 1974 (m dis 1983), Penelope Josephine, da of late Lt-Col Richard Ian Griffith Taylor, DSO; 1 s; m 2, 1984, Mary Patricia, da of late Maj Hon Antony John Ashley Cooper; 2 da; *Career* banker; md Gerrard and National Holdings plc; *Recreations* tennis, shooting, golf; *Clubs* Boodle's, Pratt's; *Style*— Robert Elkington, Esq; Cranbourne Grange, Sutton Scotney, Winchester, Hants SO21 3NA (☎ 0962 760 494, office 071 623 9981)

ELLAND, William Michael Rodney; s of Percy Elland (d 1960), of London, and Winifred Margaret, *née* Baines; *b* 20 Oct 1947; *Educ* Wimbledon Coll, Balliol Coll Oxford (MA); *Career* called to the Bar Inner Temple 1970, vice chm Bar Euro Gp; memb Worshipful Co of Bakers 1986; *Recreations* bridge, boating; *Clubs* Arts, City Livery; *Style*— William Elland, Esq; 211b Kensington High Street, London W8; Fountain Court, Temple, London EC4Y 9DH (☎ 071 583 3335, fax 071 353 0329/ 1794, telex 88

ELLARD, John Francis; s of (John) Edward Ellard, of Sidbury, Devon, and Marie, *née* Topping; *b* 5 April 1953; *Educ* John Fisher Sch Purley Surrey, King's Sch Chester, Trinity Hall Cambridge (MA); *m* 4 April 1987, Nicola Marigo, da of John David Pugh (d 1973); 2 s ((John) David b 12 Sept 1988, Robert Edward b 8 May 1990); *Career* admitted slr 1977; Linklaters & Paines: articled clerk 1975-77, asst slr 1977-83, ptnr 1983-, resident ptnr NY office 1986-89; memb Law Soc; *Recreations* music, reading, mountain walking, photography; *Clubs* Oxford & Cambridge; *Style*— John Ellard, Esq; 38 Shawfield St, London SW3 4BD; Linklaters & Paines, Barrington House, 59/68 Gresham St, London EC2V 7JA (☎ 071 606 7080, fax 071 606 5113, telex 884349/ 888167)

ELLEN, Eric Frank; QPM (1980); s of Robert Frank Ellen (d 1969), and Jane Lydia Ellen (d 1982); *b* 30 Aug 1930; *Educ* Univ of London (LLB); *m* 1949, Gwendoline Dorothy, da of John Thomas Perkins (d 1937); 1 s (Stephen), 1 da (Susan); *Career* Nat Serv; joined Port of London Police 1950, chief constable 1975, ret 1980; first dir ICC: Int Maritime Bureau 1981, Counterfeiting Intelligence Bureau 1985; Corporate Security Services 1988, chief exec ICC Business Security Services (incorporating IMB, CIB CSS) 1990-; conslt Commmercial Crime Unit, special advsr Int Assoc of Ports and Harbours on port security matters and maritime crime, pres Int Assoc of Airport and Seaport Police 1977-79, chm Euro Assoc of Airport and Seaport Police 1975-78 (now life memb, exec sec 1980-88); chm: Electronic Intelligence Ltd 1985-86, PEBs 1985; memb: Hon Soc of the Middle Temple, Br Acad of Forensic Sciences, Ctee of Cons Lawyers examining Maritime Fraud, Inst of Shipbrokers Ctee on Maritime Fraud; presented or chaired seminars on int commercial fraud and product counterfeiting in over 50 countries, advised Barbados Govt on formation of a new police force for the Barbados Port Authy 1983, reviewed security at ports of Jeddah and Dammam in Saudi Arabia, chm Cambridge Symposia on Commercial Crime 1985-; frequent TV and radio appearances on the subject of marine fraud, terrorism, piracy and product counterfeiting; CBIM; Freeman City of London; Police Long Serv and Good Conduct medal 1 class 1973, Repub of China Police medal 1 class 1979, Queen's Police medal for Distinguished Police Serv 1980; *Books* International Maritime Fraud (co-author), Air and Seaport Security International Reference Book (conslt ed, 1987-89) Violence at Sea (ed, 1987), Piracy at Sea (ed, 1989), Ports at Risk (ed, 1990), published many articles on varied subjects including specialist policemen, marine sabotage, piracy and terrorism, product counterfeiting and fraud; *Recreations* golf; *Clubs* Wig and Pen; *Style*— Eric Ellen, Esq, QPM; International Maritime Bureau, Maritime Ho, 1 Linton Rd, Barking, Essex

ELLENBOROUGH, Dorothy, Baroness; (Helen) Dorothy; da of Harry William Lovatt, late of Co Down; *b* 1901; *m* 31 Jan 1923, 7 Baron Ellenborough MC, JP, DL (d 1945); 2 s (8 Baron, Hon Cecil Law); *Career* DGStJ; *Style*— The Rt Hon Dorothy, Lady Ellenborough, DGStJ; Little Park House, Brimpton, nr Reading, Berks

ELLENBOROUGH, 8 Baron (UK 1802); Richard Edward Cecil Law; s of 7 Baron (d 1945); *b* 14 Jan 1926; *Educ* Eton, Magdalene Coll Cambridge; *m* 9 Oct 1953, Rachel Mary (d 1986), da of late Maj Ivor Mathews Hedley, 17 Lancers; 3 s; *Heir* s, Hon Rupert Law; *Career* sits as Conservative Peer in House of Lords; stockbroker; dir Towry Law & Co; *Style*— The Rt Hon Lord Ellenborough; Withypool House, Observatory Close, Church Rd, Crowborough, East Sussex TN6 1BN (☎ 08926 63139)

ELLERAY, Anthony John; s of Alexander John Elleray, of Waddington, Clitheroe, Lancs, and Sheila Mary, *née* Perkins; *b* 19 Aug 1954; *Educ* Bishop's Stortford Coll, Trinity Coll Cambridge (MA); *m* 17 July 1982, Alison Elizabeth, da of William Goring Potter, DFC, of Twyford, Berks; 1 s (Adam b 22 Sept 1989), 1 da (Harriet b 29 Aug 1985); *Career* called to the Bar Inner Temple 1977, barr Chancery Northern Circuit; memb: Chancery Bar Assoc, Northern Chancery Bar Assoc; *Recreations* bridge, theatre, pictures, wine; *Clubs* Manchester Tennis and Racquets; *Style*— Anthony Elleray, Esq; 4 Amherst Rd, Fallowfield, Manchester M14 6UQ (☎ 061 225 5317); St James' Chambers, 68 Quay St, Manchester M3 3EL (☎ 061 834 7000, fax 061 834 2341)

ELLERTON, Geoffrey James; CMG (1963), MBE (1956); er s of Sir (Frederick) Cecil Ellerton (d 1962), and Dorothy Catherine, *née* Green; *b* 25 April 1920; *Educ* Highgate Sch, Hertford Coll Oxford; *m* 1946, Peggy Eleanor, da of Frederick George Watson (d 1954); 3 s; *Career* Colonial Admin Serv Kenya 1945-63, sec to Cmmns on Mgmnt and Staffing in Local Govt 1964, chm Elder Dempster Lines 1972-74, exec dir Ocean Transport and Trading Ltd 1972-80, chm Electra Group Services 1980-83, dir Globe Investment Trust 1982-86, chm Local Govt Boundary Cmmn for England 1983-; hon treas Hakluyt Soc 1986-; *Recreations* books and music; *Clubs* MCC, Brooks's, Beefsteak; *Style*— Geoffrey Ellerton, Esq, CMG, MBE; Briar Hill House, Broad Campden, Chipping Campden, Glos GL55 6XB (☎ 0386 841003)

ELLERY, Nina; *née* Petrova; da of Alexander Petrov (d 1968), of London, and Lubov Georgivna, *née* Nicholaeva (d 1978); *b* 9 June 1913; *Educ* St Dunstan's Abbey Rd Sch, Plymouth Sch, Carlyle Sch; *m* 31 July 1937, Maj (John) Edgar (Eggi) Ellery, s of James Ellery, OBE (d 1953); *Career* author (writes under name of Nina Petrova); broadcaster for BBC Overseas Serv; sec BRCS, memb Ctee Russian Refugee Relief Assoc (helped after war), sec local Leasehold Assoc 1970-71; memb Soc of Authors; *Books* Russian Cookery (1968), Best of Russian Cookery (1978), wrote for Taste Magazine; *Recreations* reading, making clothes, garden; *Clubs* GB USSR Assoc; *Style*— Mrs Edgar Ellery; 106 Edith Rd, London W14 9AP (☎ 071 603 5106)

ELLES, Baroness (Life Peeress UK 1972), of the City of Westminster; Diana Louie Elles; da of Col Stewart Francis Newcombe, DSO (d 1956), and Elizabeth Chaki; *b* 19 July 1921; *Educ* London Univ (BA); *m* 1945, Neil Patrick Moncrieff Elles, s of Edmund Hardie Elles, OBE; 1 s (Hon James Edmund Moncrieff b 1949), 1 da (Hon (Elizabeth) Rosamund (Hon Mrs Lockhart-Mummery) b 1947); *Career* Flight Offr WAAF 1942-45; called to the Bar 1956; memb Care Ctee Kennington 1956-72; UK delegate UN 1972, MEP 1973-75, memb UN Sub-Cmmn on Discrimination and Minorities 1974-75, oppn front bench spokesman on foreign and euro affrs 1975-79, chm Cons Party Int Office 1973-78, MEP (EDG) Thames Valley 1979-89, vice pres European Parl 1982-87 (chm Legal Affairs Ctee 1987-89); *Style*— The Rt Hon Baroness Elles; 75 Ashley Gdns, London SW1 (☎ 071 828 0175)

ELLES, Hon James Edmund Moncrieff; s of Neil Elles, of 75 Ashley Gardens, London SW1, and Baroness Elles (Life Peeress); *b* 3 Sept 1949; *Educ* Eton, Univ of Edinburgh; *m* 1977, Françoise, da of François Le Bail; 1 s (Nicholas b 22 Aug 1982), 1 da (Victoria b 27 July 1980); *Career* admin external rels EEC 1977-80, asst to Dep DG of Agric EEC 1980-84; MEP for Oxford and Bucks 1984-, memb Budget and External Rels Ctees; *Recreations* skiing, golf, tennis; *Clubs* Royal and Ancient Golf (St Andrews), Carlton; *Style*— James Elles, Esq; c/o Conservative Centre, Church St, Amersham, Bucks HP7 0BD (☎ 02403 21577); 97-113 Rue Belliard, 1040 Bruxelles (☎ 234 2442)

ELLETSON, Lady Alexandra Susan; *née* Marquis; da of 2 Earl of Woolton (d 1969), and his 2 w (Cecily) Josephine (da of Sir Alexander Gordon-Cumming, MC, 5 Bt), now Countess Lloyd-George of Dwyfor; *b* 12 Jan 1961; *m* 27 April 1984, Philip Roger Chandos Elletson, s of Roger Chandos Elletson, *qv*; 1 s (Edward Roger Chandos b 1990), 2 da (Laura b 1985, Sophia b 1986); *Style*— The Lady Alexandra Elletson; The Old Rectory, Huish, Marlborough, Wilts

ELLETSON, Roger Chandos; yr s of Harry Chandos Elletson (d 1928), of Parrox Hall, Preesall, Lancs, and Katherine Helen (d 1970), da of Rev Edward Philips, Rector of Hollington, Staffs; family owned large estates dating back to a gift of 'four oxgangs of land' by King John, ancestors incl a Govr of Jamaica and Dr Ffyfe physician to King Charles II; *b* 4 June 1911; *Educ* Harrow; *m* 1, 18 Nov 1938 (m dis 1949), Simone, da of Joseph Boudard, of Morbihan, France; 1 s (Philip Roger b 23 Dec 1947, *see* Lady Alexandra Elletson), 1 da (Lorraine Joan b 11 March 1946); m 2, 20 Oct 1958, Pamela Mary, da of Leslie Brown, of The Cottage, Little Brington; 1 s (Hope b 13 Feb 1963), 1 da (Anne b 31 July 1960), 1 adopted step s (Anthony Leslie b 26 Feb 1953); *Career* served Army ME, taken prisoner Battle of Crete; md Smith & Philips Witney 1937-39, fndr R C Elletson & Co Ltd 1947, former chm Textile Cos and former dir Humphrey Lloyd & Sons Ltd, Lloyd's underwriter 1961-; pt/t journalist; *Recreations* bridge, golf, skiing; *Clubs* Brooks's, Royal Lytham Golf; *Style*— Roger Elletson, Esq; Grey House, Forton, Preston, Lancs PR3 0AN (☎ 0524 791225)

ELLICOTT, (Mary) Elizabeth; da of John M Robbins (d 1977), and Elizabeth, *née* Rooney; *b* 15 March 1947; *Educ* Pembroke Sch Dublin, London Sch of Journalism; *m* 31 Dec 1976, (William) Drew Ellicott, s of Lt Col C W Ellicott; *Career* asst ed journalist Creation Publications Dublin 1968-69 (trainee journalist 1964), co dir Robbins Assoc (prodn conslts and actors agency) 1969-74, freelance prodr 1974-81, co dir DEE & Co Ltd (TV prog distributors) 1981-; *Recreations* t'ai chi chuan; *Clubs* London Sch of Wu Style T'ai Chi; *Style*— Mrs William Ellicott; 46 Potters Lane, Barnet, Herts EN5 5BE (☎ 081 441 6535); Suite 204, Canalot, 222 Kensal Rd, London W10 5BN (☎ 081 960 2712, fax 081 960 2728, telex 940 128 26 DECO G)

ELLINGTON, Marc Floyd; DL (1984 Aberdeenshire); Baron of Towie Barclay (Feudal Barony), Laird of Gardenstown and Crovie; s of Homer Frank Ellington (d 1984), of Memsie, Aberdeenshire, and Vancouver BC, and Harriette Hannah Kellas; *b* 16 Dec 1945; *m* 21 Dec 1967, Karen Leigh, da of Capt Warren Sydney Streater; 2 da (Iona Angeline Barclay of Gardenstown b 1979, Kirstie Naomi Barclay b 1983); *Career* memb: Nat Ctee Architectural Heritage Soc of Scotland, Historic House Assoc; vice pres Buchan Heritage Soc, tstee Scottish Historic Building Tst, chm Heritage Press (Scot); dir: Aberdeen Univ Research Ltd, Gardenstown Estates Ltd, Soundcraft Audio; ptnr Heritage Sound Recordings; Saltire award 1973, Civic Tst award 1975, Euro Architectural Heritage award 1975; contrib various architectural and historical jls and periodicals, composer and recording artiste, communications conslt, prodr of documentary films and TV progs; memb: Br Heritage Ctee, Performing Rights Soc, Historic Building Cncl for Scotland 1980-, Convention of Baronage of Scotland; serving brother Order of St John; FSA; *Recreations* sailing, historic architecture, art collecting, music; *Style*— Marc Ellington of Towie Barclay, DL; Towie Barclay Castle, Auchterless, Turriff Aberdeenshire AB3 8EP (☎ 08884 347)

ELLINGTON, Paul Robert; *b* 2 Aug 1937; *Educ* Dauntsey's Sch, Univ of Bristol; *m* 30 March 1960, Mireille; 2 s (James, Francis), 1 da (Nicole); *Career* slr; articled clerk: T Weldon Thomson & Co 1958-61, Marcan & Dean 1961-63; Clifford Turner 1963-65, Allen & Overy 1965-68, ptnr McKenna & Co 1970- (slr 1968-70); memb: CBI Co Law Working Gp, CBI Cos Bill Working Gp, Law Soc Insolvency Panel; Freeman Worshipful Co of Slrs; *Recreations* reading, singing, theatre, concerts, walking; *Style*— Paul Ellington, Esq; McKenna & Co, 71 Queen Victoria St, London EC4V 4EB (☎ 071 236 4340, telex 264824, fax 071 236 4485)

ELLINGWORTH, Lady Amanda Patricia Victoria; *née* Knatchbull; da of 7 Baron Brabourne, and Countess Mountbatten of Burma, *qqv*; *b* 26 June 1957; *Educ* Gordonstoun, Univ of Kent, Univ of Peking, Goldsmith Coll London; *m* 31 Oct 1987, Charles V Ellingworth, er s of William Ellingworth, of Laughton, Leics; 1 s (Luke b 27 Jan 1991); *Career* social worker, tstee The Guinness Tst, memb Cncl Caldecott Community; *Style*— The Lady Amanda Ellingworth; Newhouse, Mersham, Ashford, Kent TN25 6NQ

ELLIOT, Alan Christopher; s of Ian Frederick Lettsom Elliot (d 1981), of 142 Pavilion Rd, London SW1, and Madeline Adelaide Mary, *née* Maclachlan (d 1977); *b* 9 March 1937; *Educ* Rugby, Ch Ch Oxford (MA); *m* 20 Jan 1967, Tara Louise Winifred, da of Sir Thomas Brian Weldon, 8 Bt (d 1979), of The Fighting Cocks, West Amesbury, Wilts; 1 s (Dominic b 1975), 3 da (Sacha b 1968, Larissa b 1970, Natalya b 1978); *Career* Nat Serv 1958-60: 2 Lt Welsh Guards cmmnd 1959, sr under offr Mons Offr Cadet Sch; pa to MD Metropole Industries 1960, md Dufay Ltd 1963 (dir 1962), chm Blick Time Recorders 1971- (organised mgmnt buyout from Dufay Ltd 966), chm Blick plc 1986-; *Recreations* shooting, fishing, bridge, skiing; *Clubs* White's, Portland; *Style*— Alan Elliot, Esq; The Old Rectory, Chilton Foliat, Hungerford, Berks RG17 OTF (☎ 0488 682423); 142 Pavilion Road, London SW1 (☎ 071 235 3382); Blick plc, Bramble Rd, Swindon, Wilts (☎ 0793 692 401, fax 0793 618147, car 0831 171387, telex 44332)

ELLIOT, Lady Ann; *née* Child-Villiers; yr da of 8 Earl of Jersey (d 1923); *b* 23 May 1916; *m* 8 June 1937, Maj Alexander Henry Elliot, RA (d 1986), s of Gilbert Compton Elliot (d 1931, gs of Hon Sir George Elliot, KCB, MP, 2 s of 1 Earl of Minto); 1 s, 2 da; *Style*— The Lady Ann Elliot; Broadford, Chobham, Surrey GU24 8EF (☎ 0276 857222)

ELLIOT, David; s of John Elliot, of 78 Farne Drive, Simshill, Glasgow, and Sarah Carroll, *née* Jordan; *b* 13 Nov 1969; *Educ* Holyrood Secdy RC Sch, Open Univ; partner, Audrey, da of Alan McLean; *Career* professional footballer; Garngad Utd Boys' Club, Celtic Boys' Club; Celtic 1987-90: debut v Hamilton Academical 1989, 10 appearances; Partick Thistle 1990-: debut v Falkirk Aug 1990, over 20 appearances, 5 goals; Scotland schoolboy caps: under 15, under 16, under 18; Scottish Football Assoc youth caps: under 16, under 17, under 18 (total 20 caps); Gold medal 100m Scot schs athletics; *Recreations* watching football, supporting Celtic FC, spending time with girlfriend; *Style*— David Elliot, Esq; 78 Farne Drive, Simshill, Glasgow, Scotland G44 5DJ (☎ 041 637 8609); Partick Thistle FC, Firhill Park, Glasgow (☎ 041 946 2673)

ELLIOT, Hon (George Esmond) Dominic; yr s of 5 Earl of Minto (d 1975); *b* 13 Jan 1931; *Educ* Eton, Madrid Univ; *m* 1, 4 May 1962 (m dis 1970), Countess Marie-Anna (Marianne) Berta Felicie Johanna Ghislaine Theodora Huberta Georgina Helene Genoveva, da of Count (Maria) Thomas Paul Esterhazy; 1 s (Esmond b 1965), 1 s decd (Alexander b 1963 d 1985); m 2, 25 June 1983, Jane Caroline, da of Lawrence Reeve, of Sandridge Lodge, Bromham, Wilts; 1 s (George William Hugh b 18 May 1990), 1 da (Violet Elizabeth Marion b 23 Aug 1988); *Career* formerly Lt Scots Gds, served Malaya and London; company director; *Clubs* White's, New (Edinburgh); *Style*— The Hon Dominic Elliot; 88 St James's St, London SW1A 1PW (☎ 071 839 5746); Minto, Hawick, Scotland

ELLIOT, Fiona Jane; da of William James Elliot, and Ruth, *née* Fisher; *b* 10 Dec 1965; *Educ* Colton Hills Sch Wolverhampton; *Career* professional table tennis player 1984-: Cwlth team gold 1985, nat singles and mixed doubles champion 1987, Cwlth team and mixed doubles silver and women's doubles bronze 1989, represented England in two World and two Euro Championships; memb of Women in Table Tennis; *Style*— Miss Fiona Elliot

ELLIOT, Sir Gerald Henry; s of Surgn Capt John Stephen Elliot, RN (d 1972), and Magda Virginia, *née* Salvesen (d 1985); *b* 24 Dec 1923; *Educ* Marlborough, New Coll Oxford (MA); *m* 1950, Margaret Ruth, da of Rev John Stephen Whale; 2 s, 1 da; *Career* served Indian Army 1942-46, Capt; consul for Finland in Edinburgh and Leith 1957-89, sec and chm Scottish Branch Royal Inst of Int Affrs 1963-77; chm: Forth Ports Authy 1973-79, Scottish Arts Cncl 1980-86, Christian Salvesen plc 1981-88 (dep chm and md 1973-81), Scottish Provident Instn 1983-89, Scottish Unit Managers Ltd 1984-88, Biotal 1987-90; memb Ct Univ of Edinburgh 1984; chm: Tstees David Hume Inst 1985-, Princes Scottish Youth Business Tst-, Scottish Opera 1987-, Martin Currie Unit Trusts 1988-90, IOD (Scottish Div) 1989-, Tstees Univ of Edinburgh Devpt Tst 1990-; vice chm Scottish Business in the Community 1987-, tstee Nat Museums of Scotland 1987-, vice pres RSE 1988-; honoris causa Univ of Edinburgh 1989; FRSE 1977; Order of the White Rose of Finland, Kt of First Class 1975; kt 1986; *Style*— Sir Gerald Elliot, FRSE; 8 Howe St, Edinburgh EH3 6TD

ELLIOT, Graeme Arthur; s of Ian Frederick Lettsom Elliot (d 1981), and Madeline Adelaide Mary, *née* Maclachlan (d 1977); *b* 28 Aug 1942; *Educ* Rugby, Magdalene Coll Cambridge (MA); *m* 1, 1966, Hermione, da of Lt-Col John Delano-Osborne, of Hants; 2 da (Alexandra b 1968, Victoria b 1971); m 2, 1983, Nicola Nella Simpson, da of Keith Alexander Taylor, of Queensland; *Career* CA; exec vice chm Slough Estates plc 1986; dir: Bredero plc 1987, Candover Investments plc 1988; FCA; *Recreations* bridge, golf, tennis, skiing; *Clubs* White's, Queen's, Portland, Berks Golf, Royal Melbourne Golf, Sotogrande Golf; *Style*— Graeme Elliot, Esq; Slough Estates plc, 234 Bath Road, Slough, Berks SL1 4EE (☎ 0753 37171)

ELLIOT, Prof Harry; CBE (1975); s of Thomas Elliot (d 1961), of Weary Hall Style, Mealsgate, Cumbria, and Hannah Elizabeth, *née* Littleton (d 1928); *b* 28 June 1920; *Educ* Allhallows Sch, Nelson Sch, Univ of Manchester (BSc, MSc, PhD); *m* 27 May 1943, Betty, da of Henry Leyman (d 1974), of Doddiscombsleigh, Devon; 1 s (Brian b 1944), 1 da (Jean b 1948); *Career* WWII 1941-46; PO Tech (SIGS) RAFVR, served Coastal Cmd incl liaison duties with USAAF and USN, demob Flt Lt 1946; lectr in physics Univ of Manchester 1948-53; Imperial Coll: sr lectr 1953-60, prof 1960-80, sr res fell 1981-90, emeritus prof; Holweck prize and medal Inst of Physics and French Physical Soc; author of numerous papers and articles in learned jls; memb SRC; ARCS Imperial Coll 1961; chm: Astronomy Space and Radio Bd 1971-77, Cncl Royal Soc 1978, Euro Space Agency; FRS 1973, FWAAS 1983, FRAS 1984; *Recreations* painting, gardening, military history; *Style*— Prof Harry Elliot, CBE, FRS; Broadwater Down, Tunbridge Wells TN2 5PE

ELLIOT OF HARWOOD, Baroness (Life Peer UK 1958), of Rulewater, Co Roxburgh; Katharine Elliot; DBE (1958, CBE 1946), JP (Roxburghshire 1967); da of Sir Charles Tennant, 1 Bt (d 1906), and Marguerite, *née* Miles (d 1942); *b* 15 Jan 1903; *Educ* Abbot's Hill Sch Hemel Hempstead; *m* 4 April 1934, as his 2 wife, Rt Hon Walter Elliot, CH, MC, MP, FRS (d 1958), s of William Elliot (d 1928), of Muirglen, Lanark; *Career* sits as Conservative Peer in House of Lords; farmer; memb King George V Jubilee Tst 1936-68, cnllr Roxburghshire 1945-75, contested (C) Kelvingrove Glasgow 1958; chm: Nat Union of Cons and Unionist Assocs 1957-58, Carnegie UK Tst 1965-86 (tstee 1940-86), Consumer Cncl 1963-68; UK delegate to UN Gen Assembly New York 1954-56 and 1957; Hon LLD Univ of Glasgow 1959; Grand Silver Cross Austrian Order of Merit 1961; FRSA; *Recreations* golf, fox hunting; *Style*— The Rt Hon Lady Elliot of Harwood; 17 Lord North St, London SW1 (☎ 071 222 3230); Harwood, Bonchester Bridge, Hawick, Roxburghshire TD9 9TL (☎ 045 086 235)

ELLIOTT, Ann; da of James Albert Hinchliffe, of Highstead, Beck Lane, Bingley, W Yorks, and Josephine, *née* Forster; *b* 12 Sept 1956; *Educ* Bingley GS, Univ of Liverpool (BA); *m* Howard Charles Elliott, s of Donald Elliott; *Career* mktg asst Procter & Gamble 1978-79, account supervisor International Marketing and Promotions 1979-81, brand mangr Buxted Poultry Ltd 1981-83, brand mangr/mktg mangr Whitbread plc 1983-88, mktg dir Pizza Hut (UK) 1988-; *Books* In My Liverpool Home (1988); *Recreations* reading, theatre, interior decoration; *Style*— Mrs Ann Elliott; Pizza Hunt (UK) Ltd, Venture House, Hartley Ave, Mill Hill, London NW7 2HX (☎ 081 959 3677, car 0831 438685)

ELLIOTT, Ann Margaret; da of John Frederick Hildred (d 1976), and Evelyn Rose Collier; *b* 23 Feb 1945; *Educ* Shurnhold Sch Melksham (now George Ward Sch), Chippenham GS, Bath Acad of Art (Dip in Art and Design Graphics), Dept of Educn Univ of Bath (DipEd); *m* 1972, Robert Anthony Elliott; 2 s (b 1978 and 1983), 1 da (b 1980); *Career* art asst Cammell Hudson & Brownjohn Ltd (Films) 1967-68, curatorial asst Sheffield City Art Galleries 1969-72, gallery organiser Gardner Centre Gallery Univ of Sussex 1972-73, exhibition offr Fine Arts Dept Br Cncl 1973-77 and 1985- (temp offr 1972), pt/t res asst Aust Crafts Cncl 1977-78; maj projects incl: J M W Turner Exhibition (Moscow and Leningrad) 1975, Henry Moore Exhibitions (Hong Kong and Japan 1986, India 1988, Moscow and Leningrad 1991), Ben Nicholson Exhibitions (Madrid and Lisbon) 1987, Tony Cragg Venice Biennale 1988; *Recreations* art, running, dogs; *Style*— Mrs Anne Elliott; Vine Cottage, Wisborough Green, nr Billingshurst, West Sussex RH14 OBJ (☎ 0403 700383); The British Council, Visual Arts Dept, 11 Portland Place, London W1N 4EJ (☎ 071 389 3030, fax 071 389 3199)

ELLIOTT, Anthony Charles Raynor; s of Charles Edward Murray Elliott (d 1987), of London, and Lucy Eleanor, *née* Arthur (d 1982); *b* 28 Jan 1937; *Educ* Radley, Trinity Coll Cambridge (MA); *m* 1960, Christina, da of Capt William Theobald Hindson, of Surrey; 2 s (Nicholas Charles Raynor b 1964, Paul William Anthony b 1967); *Career* 2 Lt E Surrey Regt 1955-57; admitted slr 1963; Linklaters & Paines 1963-66; exec dir: RTZ Pillar Ltd (previously Pillar Hldgs Ltd) 1966-76, S G Warburg & Co Ltd 1976-86; non exec dir: Bridon plc, Norcros plc, S G Warburg & Co Ltd; chm St Mary's Hall Brighton 1989 (govr 1967-); *Recreations* classical music, arts, walking, wine; *Style*— Anthony Elliott, Esq

ELLIOTT, Anthony M M (Tony); s of Alan and Katherine Elliott; *b* 7 Jan 1947; *Educ* Stowe, Univ of Keele; *m* 1, Nov 1976 (m dis 1978), Janet, *née* Street-Porter; m 2, June 1989, Jane Laetitia, *née* Cohe; 3 s (Rufus George b 19 April 1988, Bruce Roland b 17 Oct 1990, Lawrence John (twin) b 17 Oct 1990); *Career* fndr and chm Time Out Group 1968-; *Recreations* travel, watching TV, cinema going, eating out with friends, newspapers and magazines, being with family in time left from working; *Style*— Tony Elliott, Esq; Time Out Group, Tower House, Southampton Street, London WC2E 7HD (☎ 071 836 4411, fax 071 836 7118)

ELLIOTT, Anthony Michael; s of late Ernest Elliott, and Sonia Blanche, *née* Organ; *b* 21 April 1944; *Educ* The Forest Sch Horsham Sussex; *m* 1, 1969 (m dis), N Melanie Synge; 1 s (Rupert Francis William b 1 Aug 1970), 1 da (Francesca Elizabeth b 7 Sept 1972); m 2, 1978 (m dis), Maryan Jean MacIntyre: m 3, 21 Dec 1987, Aileen Jennifer Synder, da of David Allan; *Career* trainee Hotel Richmond Geneva Switzerland 1965-66, receptionist Savoy Hotel London 1966-67 (mgmnt trainee 1961-65), asst banqueting mangr Claridges London 1967-70, asst gen mangr Grosvenor Hotel Chester 1970-73, dep gen mangr Royal Garden Hotel London Jan-Aug 1973, gen mangr New Stanley Hotel Nairobi Kenya 1973-75, exec dir Block Hotels Management Nairobi Kenya 1975-78, ptnr Anthony Elliott & Associates London 1978-79, proprietor The Greenway Hotel Cheltenham 1979-, md Granfel Hotels 1985-87; winner Catey award 1988; fndr memb Savoy Gastronomes 1970 (pres 1981), fndr memb and dir Pride of Britain 1982 (chm 1988), Master Innholder 1987 (dep chm 1990); Freeman City of London, memb Worshipful Co of Fanmakers 1979; MHCIMA 1986; *Recreations* cooking, skiing, golf, riding, shooting, swimming; *Clubs* St James's; *Style*— Anthony Elliott, Esq; The Greenway, Shurdington, Cheltenham, Gloucestershire GL51 5UG (☎ 0242 862352); The Greenway Hotel Ltd, Shurdington, Cheltenham, Gloucestershire GL51 5UG (☎ 0242 862352, fax 0242 862780, car 0836 659007/0836 773508)

ELLIOTT, Dr Arnold; OBE (1977); *b* 27 Jan 1921; *Educ* Royal Belfast Academical Inst, Queens Univ Belfast (MB BCh); *m* 8 June 1948, Lee; 2 s (Paul b 1955, Simon b 1957), 1 da (Louise b 1951); *Career* WWI Capt (later actg Maj) RAMC 1944-47; GP; MBMA 1948: memb Gen Med Servs Ctee 1952-, chm Practise Orgn Sub Ctee 1960-86, memb Cncl 1982-, chm Doctors and Social Work Ctee, memb Mental Health Ctee; Gen Med Cncl 1979-89: memb Exec, memb Educn Ctee, memb Health Ctee; pres Soc of Family Practitioner Ctees of England & Wales 1980; memb: Panel of Assessors Dist Nurse Trg 1972-82, Central Cncl for Educn and Trg in Social Work 1974-84; memb: NHS Essex Exec Cncl until 1965, NHS Exec Cncl NE London 1965-74 (chm 1972-74), Redbridge and Waltham Forest Family Practitioner Ctee 1974- (chm 1974-77); sec Redbridge and Waltham Forest Local Med Ctee 1984-, fndr and organiser Ilford and Dist Vocational Trg Scheme for Gen Practice 1977-87, provost NE London Faculty RCGP 1979-82; Freeman City of London 1971, Liveryman Worshipful Soc of Apothecaries 1968-; FRCGP 1976, FRSM; *Recreations* theatre, art, music; *Clubs* RSM; *Style*— Dr Arnold Elliott, OBE; Newbury Park Health Centre, Perrymans Farm Rd, Barkingside, Ilford, Essex IG2 7LE (☎ 081 554 9551)

ELLIOTT, Rev Prof Charles Middleton; s of Joseph William Elliott (d 1982), and Mary Evelyn, *née* Jones (d 1958); *b* 9 Jan 1939; *Educ* Repton, Univ of Oxford (MA, DPhil); *m* 1962, Hilary Margaret, da of Harold Hambling, of Cockfosters, Barnet, Herts; 3 s (Jonathan, Francis, Giles); *Career* asst lectr (later lectr) in pure econs Univ of Nottingham 1963-65, sr res fell UN Res Inst of Social Devpt Geneva 1964-65, reader in econ and head of Dept Univ of Zambia 1965-69, asst sec to res dir Sodepax Geneva 1969-72, sr res assoc Overseas Devpt Gp Univ of E Anglia 1972-75, sr lectr in econ Sch of Devpt Studies Univ of E Anglia 1975-77, dir ODG and md ODG Co Ltd 1976-77, special advsr Parly Select Ctee on Overseas Aid and Devpt 1976-80, prof of Devpt Policy and Planning Univ of Wales 1979-82, dir Centre for Devpt Studies UC Swansea 1979-82, dir Christian Aid 1982-84, GEM Scott fell Univ of Melbourne Australia 1984-85, Benjamin Meaker prof Univ of Bristol 1985-86, prebendary of Lichfield Cathedral 1987-, visiting prof King's Coll London 1987-88, dean Trinity Hall Cambridge 1990-; *Books* Praying the Kingdom (Collins Religious Book Prize, 1985), Comfortable Compassion (1987), Praying Through Paradox (1987), Sword and Spirit: Christianity in a Divided World (1989); *Recreations* fly-fishing, hill walking, sailing; *Style*— The Rev Prof Charles Elliott; Trinity Hall, Cambridge

ELLIOTT, Sir Clive Christopher Hugh; 4 Bt (UK 1917), of Limpsfield, Surrey; s of Sir Hugh Francis Ivo Elliott, 3 Bt, OBE (d 1989); *b* 12 Aug 1945; *Educ* Bryanston, Univ Coll Oxford; *m* 1975, Marie Thérèse, da of Johann Rüttimann, of Hohenrain, Switzerland; 2 s (Ivo Antony Moritz b 1978, Nicolas Johann Clive b 1980); *Heir* s, Ivo Antony Moritz Elliott; *Career* ornithologist; research offr Cape Town Univ (PhD 1973) 1968-75; FAO/UN Regnl Quelea Project Tchad/Tanzania 1975-81, FAO project mangr Arusha, Tanzania 1982-86, Nairobi Kenya 1986-89, country projects offr AGO FAO HQ Rome 1989-; *Recreations* tennis; *Style*— Sir Clive Elliott, Bt; AGOE, FAO, Via delle terre di Caracalla 00100 Rome, Italy

ELLIOTT, David Stuart; s of Arthur Elliott (d 1979), of East Leake, and May, *née* Wright (d 1989); *b* 29 April 1949; *Educ* Loughborough GS, Univ of Durham (BA), Courtauld Inst Univ of London (MA); *m* 23 Feb 1974, Julia Alison, da of Lt Col John Debenham, MC, of Shrivenham, Wilts; 2 da (Joanna b 10 July 1977, Kate b 3 May 1979); *Career* regnl art offr Arts Cncl 1973-76, dir Museum of Modern Art Oxford 1976-; museum winner Sotheby's prize for excellence in the visual arts, Museum of the Year award 1983, winner Nat Art Collections Fund Collect award 1988; advsr VAAC Br Cncl, exec USSR Soc GB, memb London Advsy Bd Central Sch of Speech and Drama, advsr Centre for Int Contemporary Arts NY, exec CIMAM (ICOM); *Books* Alexander Rodchenko (ed 1979), José Clemente Orozco (1981), Tradition and Renewal: Art in the GDR (1984), New Worlds: Art and Society in Russia (1986), Eisenstein at Ninety (ed 1988), 100 Years of Russian Art (1989); *Recreations* collecting art books and art, running; *Style*— David Elliott, Esq; 8 Fairacres Rd, Oxford OX4 1TE; Museum of Modern Art, 30 Pembroke St, Oxford OX1 1BP (☎ 0865 722733, fax 0865 722573, telex MODART 83147 Via GORG)

ELLIOTT, Denholm Mitchell; CBE (1988); s of Myles Layman Farr Elliott, MBE (d 1933), and Nina, *née* Mitchell (d 1967); *b* 31 May 1922; *Educ* Malvern, RADA; *m* 1, 1954 (m dis 1957), Virginia McKenna (actress); m 2, 15 June 1962, Susan Darby, da of Ted Robinson, Jr, of New York, USA; 1 s (Mark b 26 Jan 1967), 1 da (Jennifer b 8 June 1964); *Career* served WWII with RAF Bomber Cmd 1940-45 (prisoner in Germany 1942-45); actor stage and films; plays incl: Ring Round the Moon (New York 1950, Stratford on Avon Season) 1960, The Seagull, The Crucible, Ring Round the Moon (Nat Repertory Co NY) 1963-64; has appeared in 85 films incl: King Rat 1964, Alfie 1966, Here We Go Round the Mulberry Bush 1967, The Seagull 1968, Bad Timing 1980; Brimstone and Treacle, Trading Places 1982, The Missionary 1983, A Private Function 1984; awards incl: BAFTA Best TV Actor, New Standard Best Film Actor 1981, BAFTA Best Supporting Film Actor 1984; *Recreations* gardening; *Clubs* Garrick; *Style*— Denholm Elliott, Esq, CBE; c/o London Management, 235 Regent Street, London W1A 2JT (☎ 071 493 1610)

ELLIOTT, Hon Mrs (Elinor); *née* Spring Rice; eldest (twin) da of 6 Baron Monteagle of Brandon, *qv*; *b* 23 April 1950; *m* 1974, Myles Clare Elliott; 1 s (Thomas b 1977), 2 da (Nina b 1980, Emma b 1983); *Recreations* golf, tennis; *Clubs* Roehampton; *Style*— The Hon Mrs Elliott; 41 Ravenscourt Rd, London W6 0UJ

ELLIOTT, Elizabeth, Lady; Elizabeth Margaret; *née* Phillipson; da of Adolphus George Phillipson (d 1948), of North Finchley; *m* 12 Dec 1939, Sir Hugh Francis Ivo Elliott, 3 Bt, OBE (d 1989); 1 s, 2 da; *Style—* Elizabeth, Lady Elliott; 173 Woodstock Rd, Oxford OX2 7NB

ELLIOTT, Geoffrey Charles; s of Alfred Stanley Elliott (d 1985), of Coventry, and Elsie, *née* Wilday; *b* 10 May 1945; *Educ* Bablake Sch Coventry; *m* 5 April 1969, Lynda Barbara, da of John Arthur Williams (d 1980), of Shipston-on-Stour, Warwicks; 1 s (Nicholas John b 1974), 1 da (Joanne Marie b 1971); *Career* Coventry Evening Telegraph: reporter, feature writer, chief feature writer 1962-72, dep ed 1973-79, ed 1981-90; ed Kent Messenger 1979-80, ed and dir The News Portsmouth 1990-; Guild Br Newspaper Eds: chm Parly and Legal Ctee 1983-86, chm West Midlands 1987-88; memb Press Cncl 1987-90, exec chm Common Purpose Coventry 1989-90; memb Round Table: Rugby Webb Ellis (chm 1977-78), Bearsted Kent, Coventry Mercia; *Recreations* sport, gardening, music; *Style—* Geoffrey Elliott, Esq; Flint Barn, Pook Lane, East Lavant, Chichester, Sussex (☎ 0243 532458); Portsmouth Publishing and Printing Ltd, Hilsea, Portsmouth, PO2 9SX (☎ 0705 664488, fax 0705 673363)

ELLIOTT, Grahame Nicholas; CBE (1991); s of Charles Morris William Elliott (d 1966); *b* 23 Dec 1938; *Educ* Mill Hill Sch; *m* 1968, Zita Catherine, *née* Jones; 2 s, 1 da; *Career* CA, sr ptnr Stoy Hayward (formerly Elliott Templeton Sankey) Manchester; *Clubs* Turf, St James's (Manchester), Racquets (Manchester); *Style—* Grahame Elliott, Esq, CBE; Highbury, Harrop Rd, Hale, Ches (☎ 061 980 4857)

ELLIOTT, Janice; da of Douglas John Elliott, of Fowey, Cornwall, and Dorothy Wilson (d 1968); *b* 14 Oct 1931; *Educ* Nottingham HS for Girls, St Anne's Coll Oxford (BA); *m* 11 April 1959, Robert Eley Cooper, s of James Percy Carfe Cooper; 1 s (Alexander b 3 Feb 1964); *Career* journalist; on editorial staff 1954-62: House & Garden, House Beautiful, Harper's Bazaar (beauty ed), Sunday Times Woman's Page, Sunday Times Colour Magazine; reviewer: Sunday Times, Times, New Statesman, Sunday Telegraph; reg columnist Twentieth Century; writer adult fiction: Cave with Echoes (1962), The Somnambulists (1964), The Godmother (1966), The Buttercup Chain (1967, filmed 1970), The Singing Head (1968), Angels Falling (1969), The Kindling (1970), A State of Peace (1971), Private Life (1972), Heaven on Earth (1975, New Fiction Soc choice), A Loving Eye 1977, The Honey Tree (1978, New Fiction Soc choice), Summer People 1980, Secret Places (1981, Southern Arts award 1981, filmed 1984), The Country of Her Dreams (1982, filmed 1984), Magic (1983), The Italian Lesson (1985), Dr Gruber's Daughter (1986), The Sadness of Witches (1987), Life on the Nile (1989), Necessary Rites (1990); children's fiction: The Birthday Unicorn (1970), Alexander in the Land Mog (1973), The Incompetent Dragon (1982), The King Awakes (1987), The Empty Throne (1988); *Style—* Ms Janice Elliott; Vivien Green, Richard Scott Simon, 43 Doughty St, London WC1N 2LF (☎ 071 405 9351, fax 071 831 2127)

ELLIOTT, Prof John; s of Alfred George Lewis Elliott (d 1989), and Mary Dorothy, *née* Greason; *b* 20 June 1938; *Educ* Ashford GS, Univ of London (MPhil, Dipl in Phil of Educn); *m* 28 July 1967, Jean Marion; 3 da (Dominique, Katherine, Jessica); *Career* sch teacher 1962-67, res offr Schs Cncl Humanities Project 1967-72, tutor Cambridge Inst of Educn 1976-84, prof of educn UEA 1987- (lectr 1972-76, reader in educn 1984-86), memb Univ Cncl for the Educn of Teachers 1987-; tstee Keswick Hall Tst 1987-, pres Cncl of Br Educnl Res Assoc 1989-90 (memb 1987-, vice pres 1988-89); memb Philosophy Educn Soc of GB; FRSA; *Books* Issues in Teaching for Understanding (ed with D Ebbutt, 1985), Case Studies in Teaching for Understanding (ed with D Ebbutt, 1986), Rethinking Assessment and Appraisal (ed with H Simons, 1989), La Investigacion-Accion en Educacion (1989), Action-Research for Educational Change(1991); *Recreations* walking, riding, golf, reading, travel; *Style—* Prof John Elliott; Centre for Applied Research in Education, School of Education, University of East Anglia, Norwich (☎ 0603 56161)

ELLIOTT, John Charles Kennedy; s of Charles Morris William Elliott (d 1967), of Altrincham, Cheshire, and Lesley Margaret, *née* Bush; *b* 13 March 1937; *Educ* Merton House Sch Penmaenmawr, Mill Hill Sch London, Univ of Manchester; *m* 28 July 1962, Angela Mary, da of Col Geoffrey William Noakes OBE, JP, DL; 3 s (Charles Geoffrey b 3 Nov 1963, William James b 10 April 1965, Thomas Richard b 11 May 1969), 1 da (Vanessa Jane b 9 Feb 1967); *Career* admitted slr 1961; articled clerk John Gorna & Co 1956-61, James Chapman & Co 1961-62, Fentons Stansfield & Elliott 1962-68, fndr and sr ptnr Elliott & Co 1968-; dir: Northern Rock Building Society (Northern Bd) 1988-, Hogg Insurance Brokers Ltd (Northern Bd); chm Young Slr's Gp of Law Soc 1973-74, pres Manchester Law Soc 1980; NSPCC: chm Manchester and Salford Branch, chm Gtr Manchester Area Ctee, memb Central Exec Ctee 1980-87; memb Law Soc; *Clubs* The St James's (Manchester), Manchester Tennis and Racquets; *Style—* John C K Elliott, Esq; Bradwall House, Bradwall, Cheshire CW11 9RB (☎ 0270 765 369); Centurion House, Deansgate, Manchester M3 3WT (☎ 061 834 9933, fax 061 832 3693, car 0860 619346)

ELLIOTT, (John) Malcolm; s of Jack Elliot, of 1 Prescott Rd, Wadsley, Sheffield, and Florence Patricia, *née* Hudson; *b* 1 July 1961; *Educ* Myers Grove Sch Sheffield; *Career* cyclist; champion: Nat Schoolboy 1977, RTTC Hillclimb 1980, Cwlth Team Time Trial and Individual Road Race 1982, Br professional Criterium 1984, Br Pursuit 1985, Kelloggs City Centre 1986, Milk Race 1987, Kelloggs Tour of Britain 1988, Tour of Spain 1989 (points); fifth place Moscow Olympics Team Pursuit 1980; *Recreations* travel, motoring; *Style—* Malcolm Elliot, Esq; c/o Mr G Shaw, 5 Birley Rise Crescent, Sheffield 6 (☎ 0742 312223)

ELLIOTT, Mark; CMG (1988); s of William Rowcliffe Elliott, CB, of Farthinghoe, Northants, and Karin Tess, *née* Classen; *b* 16 May 1939; *Educ* Eton, New Coll Oxford (open scholar, BA); *m* 12 Sept 1964, (Hilary) Julian, da of Rev Matthew Richardson (d 1956); 2 s (Justin Mark b 1966, Giles Andrew b 1968); *Career* HM Dip Serv: joined FO 1963, third then second sec Tokyo 1965-69, first sec FCO 1969-73, private sec to Perm Under Sec FCO 1973-75, first sec Nicosia 1975-77, cnsllr Tokyo 1977-81, head Far Eastern Dept FCO 1981-85, under sec NI Office 1985-88, HM ambass Tel Aviv 1988-; *Style—* His Excellency Mark Elliott, CMG; Foreign & Commonwealth Office, King Charles St, London SW1A 2AH

ELLIOTT, Martin John; s of John Elliott, MBE, of Sheffield, and Muriel, *née* Dyson; *b* 8 March 1951; *Educ* King Edward VII GS, Univ of Newcastle upon Tyne (MB BS, MD); *m* 15 Jan 1977, Lesley Rickard, da of Alan Rickard (d 1989), of Puddletown, Dorset; 2 s (Becan b 3 June 1981, Toby b 12 May 1983); *Career* sr registrar and first asst cardiothoracic surgery Freeman Hosp Newcastle on Tyne 1978-83, conslt and sr lectr cardiothoracic surgery Gt Ormond St 1985- (sr registrar 1984-85), sr lectr cardiac surgery RPMS Hammersmith 1988-, visiting paediatric cardial surgn Malta 1989-; exec memb Soc Cardiothoracic Surgns GB and Ireland; FRCS(Eng) 1978; *Style—* Martin Elliott; The Cardiac Wing, The Hosp For Sick Children, Gt Ormond St, London WC1N 3JH (☎ 071 405 9200)

ELLIOTT, Martin John Henry; s of Patrick James Lawrence Elliott, of Blakesley Ave, Ealing, and Beryl Olivia Catherine, *née* Carroll; *b* 26 Aug 1955; *Educ* St Benedicts Sch Ealing, ChCh Oxford (BA); *m* 4 Aug 1984, Rosanna Lina, da of Capt William James Gorard, of Woodville Gardens, Ealing; 2 s (Benedict Edward Henry b 29 Nov 1988, Oliver James Ambrose b 16 Jan 1990); *Career* articled clerk Linklaters & Paines 1977-79; admitted slr 1979; ptnr Linklater & Paines 1985- (slr 1975-85); memb Law Soc; *Recreations* rugby, cricket, tennis, squash, golf, cycling, gardening; *Clubs* MCC; *Style—* Martin Elliott, Esq; Linklaters & Paines, Barrington House, 57-67 Gresham St, London EC2V 7JA (☎ 071 606 7080, fax 071 606 5113, telex 884349/ 888167)

ELLIOTT, Michael Alwyn; s of William Alwyn Edwards and Mrs Jill Elliott, *née* Thornton; assumed stepfather's name; *b* 15 July 1936; *Educ* Raynes Park GS, Insead; *m* 1962, Caroline Margaret, da of John Edward McCarthy; 2 s (Gregory, Dominic), 1 da (Sophie); *Career* dir Kimberly-Clark Ltd 1977-79, gen admin Nat Theatre 1979-85, dir admin Denton Hall Burgin & Warrens (slrs) 1985-88, business conslt 1988-; *Recreations* theatre, golf; *Style—* Michael Elliott, Esq; 149 Forest Rd, Tunbridge Wells, Kent TN2 5EX

ELLIOTT, Sir Norman Randall; CBE (1957, OBE 1946); s of William Randall Elliott, of London, and Catherine Dunsmore; *b* 19 July 1903; *Educ* privately and St Catharine's Coll Cambridge; *m* 1963, late Mrs Phyllis Clarke, da of Mark Markham, of London; *Career* served 21 Army Gp, Col, dep dir of Works; barr 1932; subsequently with: London Passenger Tport Bd, London & Home Counties Jt Electricity Authy (as gen mangr and chief engr), Yorks Electric Power and (as dir) Isle of Thanet Electric Supply Co; chm Howden Gp 1973- (engrg and air-handling, specialising in energy conservation), Electricity Cncl 1968-72; dir: Newarthill & McAlpine Gp 1972-, Schlumberger Ltd 1977-, James Howden & Co; kt 1967; *Style—* Sir Norman Elliott, CBE

ELLIOTT, Patrick James; s of Ernest George Elliott (d 1954), of Brighton, Sussex, and Mary, *née* Keywood (d 1967); *b* 19 Dec 1927; *Educ* Xaverian Coll Brighton; *m* 17 March 1953, Beryl Olivia Catherine (Kate), da of Major Henry Carroll (d 1983), of Brighton; 2 s (Christopher James b 1954, Martin John b 1955), 1 da (Jane Catharine b 1970); *Career* Royal Navy PO 1944-47; property controller Unilever Ltd 1970-72, ptnr Cluttons 1972-78, chief estates offr and md London Tport Exec 1978-83; dir: Priest Marians Holdings plc 1985-1988, City Merchant Developers Ltd 1986, Imry Property Holdings plc 1988-90; memb Mgmnt Ctee: Pan European Property Unit Tst 1979-87, North American Property Unit Tst 1981-; memb Mgmnt Bd Griffin Housing Assoc 1979-; memb Gen Practice Divnl Cncl and other Ctees RICS 1960-; ARICS 1952, FRICS 1963, KSG 1982, FRSA 1989; *Recreations* hill walking, cricket, music; *Clubs* Carlton, MCC; *Style—* Patrick Elliott, Esq; 2 Blakesley Ave, London W5 2DW (☎ 081 998 2266)

ELLIOTT, Peter; MBE; *b* 9 Oct 1962; *Career* athlete; memb Rotherham Athletics Club, England Schs int 1979 (jr 1977), jr UK int 1980-81, full UK int 1983-; winner AAA 800m 1982 and 1987 (1500m 1984); Silver medal Olympic Games Seoul (1500m) 1988; achievements at 800m: UK champion 1983, 1984, 1986, Bronze medal Euro Cup 1983, Silver medal Euro Indoor Championship 1983, Bronze medal Cwlth Games 1986, Silver medal World Championships 1987, fourth Olympic Games Seoul 1988; achievements at 1500m: Cwlth Champion 1990, UK all comers record holder; memb world record 4 x 800m team 1982, UK indoor records at 1500m and 1 mile; joiner 1979-90; *Recreations* golf, fishing, dog walking, movies, football, rugby league; *Clubs* Rotherham Harriers, Roundwood Golf; *Style—* Peter Elliott, Esq, MBE; Amateur Athletic Association, Edgbaston House, 3 Duchess Place, off Hagley Road, Edgbaston, Birmingham B16 8NM (☎ 021 456 4050)

ELLIOTT, Philip Nigel Westbrooke; s of John Stuart Westbrooke Elliott, of Huntmill Farm, Wootton Bassett, and Katherine Briar, *née* Smith; *b* 4 Aug 1958; *Educ* Wootton Bassett Sch; *m* 6 April 1984, Silvia Regina Cavalini, da of Pedro Palmieri, of Colina, S-P, Brazil; 1 da (Stephanie); *Career* polo player: Young Player of the Year 1980, England II 1982 and 1983, challenge Cup (twice), Warwickshire Cup, Br Open Championship, Queen's Cup (twice); rated: 5 handicap England, 6 Handicap Brazil; *Recreations* music, reading; *Clubs* Royal County of Berks Polo, Helvetia Polo & Country (Brazil); *Style—* Philip Elliott, Esq; Haras Taboro, Couna, Brazil, CEP 14770; Garswood, Bracknell, Berks, England

ELLIOTT, Prof Sir Roger James; s of James Elliott (d 1932), and Gladys, *née* Hill; *b* 8 Dec 1928; *Educ* Swanwick Hall Sch Derbys, New Coll Oxford (MA, DPhil); *m* 1952, Olga Lucy, da of Roy Atkinson (d 1940); 1 s (Martin James b 1962), 2 da (Jane Susan b 1955, Rosalind Kira b 1957); *Career* fell St John's Coll Oxford 1957-74, Wykeham prof of Physics Univ of Oxford 1974-88 (sr proctor 1969-70), fell New Coll Oxford 1974-, sec to delegates and chief exec OUP 1988- (delegate 1971-88); chm Computer Bd for Univs and Res Cncls 1983-87, physical sec and vice pres Royal Soc 1984-88, pt/t memb Bd UKAEA 1988-; hon fell St John's Coll Oxford 1988; Hon DSc Paris 1983; FRS 1976; kt 1987; *Clubs* Athenaeum; *Style—* Prof Sir Roger Elliott, FRS; 11 Crick Rd, Oxford OX2 6QL; Oxford University Press, Walton St, Oxford OX2 6DP (☎ 0865 56767)

ELLIOTT, Hon Mrs (Rosemary Aletta); *née* de Villiers; yr da of 3 Baron de Villiers; *b* 20 March 1946; *Educ* Rhodes Univ; *m* 1967, Robin Anderson Elliott, TD; 3 s; *Style—* The Hon Mrs Elliott; 52 St John Rd, Houghton, Johannesburg, S Africa; Sangar Hill Farm, Magaliesburg, Transvaal

ELLIOTT, Hon Mrs (Sophia Anne); *née* Sackville-West; 3 da (by 1 m) of 6 Baron Sackville; *b* 19 July 1957; *m* 17 Dec 1988, Guy R Elliott, o s of Robert Elliott, of Little Ashley Farm, Bradford-on-Avon, Wilts; *Style—* The Hon Mrs Elliott; 11 Sinclair Gardens, London W14

ELLIOTT, Dr (Charles) Thomas; s of Charles Thomas Elliott (d 1970), and Mary Jane, *née* Higgins; *b* 16 Jan 1939; *Educ* Washington Alderman Smith GS, Univ of Manchester (BSc, PhD); *m* Brenda; 1 s (David b 1962), 2 da (Catherine Ann b 1963, Elizabeth Mary b 1966); *Career* asst lectr and lectr Electrical Engrg Dept Univ of Manchester 1963-67, visiting scientist MIT Lincoln Laboratory USA 1970-71; RSRE: sr scientific offr 1967-73, princ scientific offr 1973-79, sr princ scientific offr (individual merit) 1979-86, dep chief scientific offr (individual merit) 1986-, Rank prize for Optoelectronics 1982, The Churchill medal for Engrg, awarded by the Soc of Engrs 1986; FRS 1988, FInstP 1990; *Recreations* reading, golf; *Style—* Dr Charles Elliott, FRS; Royal Signals and Radar Establishment, St Andrews Rd, Malvern, Worcs WR14 3PS (☎ 0684 894820, fax 0684 894540, telex 3397478)

ELLIOTT, Vernon Pelling; s of Harry Vernon Elliott, of Croydon (d 1944), and Florence Edith, *née* Pelling (d 1983); *b* 27 July 1912; *Educ* Selhurst GS, RCM; *m* 25 Sept 1937, Nora Jane, da of Stanley Herbert Mukle (d 1970), of Harrow; 2 da (Naomi b 1938, Bridget b 1939); *Career* Band of the Irish Gds 1940-47; orchestral and solo bassoonist; princ bassoonist: Bournemouth Orch 1936-38, Sadlers Wells Opera & Ballet 1938-39, Philharmonia Orch 1945-75, Royal Opera Covent Garden 1949-53, English Opera Gp and Aldeburgh Festival 1954-60; other orch performances incl: London Philharmonic, London Symphony, Royal Philharmonic; conductor: Royal Philharmonic, Pro Arte Orch, Capriol Orch, Cambridge Symphony Orch, Trinity Coll of Music Orch and Opera, Essex Univ Orch; princ woodwind coach to Kent Youth Orch; prof: RCM 1941-45, Trinity Coll of Music 1945-86, London Coll of Music 1970-72; composed music for BBC TV incl: Ivor the Engine, The Mermaid's Pearls, Noggin the Nog, The Clangers, Pogle's Wood; recordings incl Britten's Turn of the Screw; hon fell Trinity Coll of Music London; memb: Performing Rights Soc, Musicians Union, Mechanical Copyright Soc; Hon TCM; *Recreations* beekeeping, wine making, skiing, sailing; *Clubs* Woodbridge Cruising and Deben Yacht; *Style—* Vernon Elliott, Esq

ELLIOTT, Hon Lord; Walter Archibald; MC (1943), QC (1960); s of Prof Thomas Renton Elliott, CBE, DSO, FRS (d 1961), of Broughton Place, Broughton, Peebleshire, and Martha, *née* M'Cosh; *b* 6 Sept 1922; *Educ* Eton, Univ of Edinburgh; *m* 1954, Susan Isobel, da of late Phillip Mackenzie Ross; 2 s; *Career* Capt Scots Gds Italy, NW Europe WW II; barr and advocate 1950, pres Lands Trbnl for Scotland 1971-, chm of Scottish Land Court with title Lord Elliott 1978-; Brig Queen's Body Guard for Scotland (Royal Co of Archers); *Books* Us and Them, A Study of Group Consciousness (1986); *Recreations* gardening, travel; *Clubs* New (Edinburgh), Scottish Arts (Edinburgh); *Style—* The Hon Lord Elliott, MC; Morton House, Fairmilehead, Edinburgh 10 (☎ 031 445 2548); office: 1 Grosvenor Crescent, Edinburgh (☎ 031 225 7595)

ELLIOTT OF MORPETH, Baron (Life Peer UK 1985), of Morpeth in the Co of Northumberland and of the City of Newcastle-upon-Tyne (Robert) William Elliott; DL (Northumbreland 1983); s of Richard Elliott (d 1957), of Low Heighley, Morpeth, Northumberland, and Mary Elizabeth, da of William Fulthorpe, of Morpeth; *b* 11 Dec 1920; *Educ* King Edward GS Morpeth; *m* 1956, (Catherine) Jane, da of Robert John Burton Morpeth, of Newcastle-upon-Tyne; 1 s (Hon Richard John b 1959), 4 da (Hon Alison Mary (Hon Mrs Campbell Adamson) b 1957, Hon Catherine Victoria (Hon Mrs Taylor) b 1962, Hon Sarah Ann (Hon Mrs Atkinson- Clark) b (twin) 1962, Hon Louise Jane b 1967); *Career* farmer 1939-; chm, vice-pres and pres Northern Area Young Conservatives 1948-55; contested (C) Morpeth 1954 and 1955; MP (C) Newcastle-upon-Tyne N 1957-83; PPS to: Jt Parly Secs Miny of Transport and Civil Aviation 1958-59, Parly Under Sec of State Home Office 1959-60, Min of State Home Office 1960-61, Min for Technical Co-operation 1961-63; asst govt whip 1963-64, opposition whip 1966-70; comptroller of HM Household June-Oct 1970; vice chm Conservative Party Organisation 1970-74; chm Select Ctee on Agriculture, Fisheries and Food 1980-83; kt 1974; *Clubs* Northern Counties; *Style—* The Rt Hon Lord Elliott of Morpeth, DL; Lipwood Hall, Haydon Bridge, Northumberland (☎ 043 484 777); 19 Laxford House, Cundy Street, London SW1 (☎ 071 730 7619)

ELLIOTT-MURRAY-KYNYNMOUND, Hon G E D; *see*: Elliot

ELLIS, Alice Thomas; da of John Lindholm, and Alexandra Lindholm; *b* 9 Sept 1932; *Educ* Bangor County GS for Girls, Liverpool Sch of Art; *m* 1956, Colin Haycraft; 4 s, 1 da (and 1 s, 1 da decd); *Career* writer; *books* (as Anna Haycraft): Natural Baby Food (1977), Darling You Shouldn't Have Gone To So Much Trouble (with Caroline Blackwood, 1980); (as Alice Thomas Ellis): The Sin Eater (1977), The Birds of the Air (1980), The Twenty-Seventh Kingdom (1982), The Other Side of the Fire (1983), Unexplained Laughter (1985), Secrets of Strangers (with Tom Pitt-Aikens, 1986), Home Life (1986), More Home Life (1987), The Clothes in the Wardrobe (1987), The Skeleton in the Cupboard (1988), Home Life Three (1988), Home Life Four (1989), The Loss of the Good Authority (with Tom Pitt-Aikens, 1989), The Fly in the Ointment (1989), The Inn at the Edge of the World (1990), A Welsh Childhood (1990); *Style—* Miss Alice Thomas Ellis; 22 Gloucestor Crescent, London NW1 (☎ 071 485 7408)

ELLIS, Andrew Steven; OBE (1984); s of Peter Vernon Ellis, and Kathleen, *née* Dawe; *b* 19 May 1952; *Educ* St Dunstan's Coll Catford, Trinity Coll Cambridge (BA), Univ of Newcastle (MSc), Newcastle Poly (BA); *m* 13 July 1975 (m dis 1987), Patricia Ann Stevens, da of William Skinner; m 2, 7 July 1990, Helen Prudence Drummond; *Career* proprietor Andrew Ellis (printing and duplicating services) 1973-81, election organiser 1981-85, sec gen Lib Pty 1985-86, chief exec SLD 1988-89; conslt in pub affrs governmental rels and political orgn 1989-, dir Central and Eastern Europe GJW Government Relations Ltd 1990-; vice chm Lib Pty 1980-86; Parly candidate (Lib): Newcastle upon Tyne Central (1974, 1976 by-election, 1979), Boothferry (1983); ldr Lib Gp Tyne and Wear CC 1977-81; *Books* Algebraic Structure (with Terence Treeby, 1971), Let Every Englishman's Home be his Castle (1978); *Clubs* Nat Liberal; *Style—* Andrew Ellis, Esq, OBE; 19 Hayle Road, Maidstone, Kent ME15 6PD (☎ 0622 678 443)

ELLIS, Lady Angela Mary; *née* Shirley; eldest da of 13 Earl Ferrers; *b* 16 June 1954; *m* 1975, Jonathan Ellis, FCA; 1 s (Charles b 1979), 2 da (Louise b 1977, Georgina b 1981); *Style—* The Lady Angela Ellis; The Old Rectory, Thurning, nr Dereham, Norfolk NR20 5QX (☎ 026 387 861)

ELLIS, Anthony John; s of Jack Ellis, of Scunthorpe, S Humberside, and Nancy Doreen, *née* Reed; *b* 15 June 1945; *Educ* Univ of London (BD, MA); *m* 1, 1966 (m dis), Maureen Jane Anne Twomey; 2 da (Kate b 14 Feb 1973, Seònaid b 19 May 1975); m 2, 4 Sept 1980, Alice Anne, da of James Stanley Stewart Findlay, of Helmsdale, Sutherland; 1 da (Bridget b 7 May 1985); *Career* sr lectr Dept of Moral Philosophy Univ of St Andrews 1987- (lectr 1971-1990, chm 1985-89), visiting prof of philosophy Virginia Cwlth Univ Richmond VA 1987-88 (prof 1990-), univ fell of Wollongong 1989; ed and author of various pubns and books; *Recreations* music, hill walking; *Style—* Anthony Ellis, Esq; Dept of Philosphy, Virginia Commonwealth University, 915 W Franklin St, Richmond, Virginia 23284 (☎ 804 367 1224)

ELLIS, Anthony Leonard; s of Leonard William Ellis (d 1975), and Anne Margaret, *née* Todman; *b* 30 March 1943; *Educ* Marlborough Coll Liverpool; *m* 11 March 1978, Joan Isabel, da of Edward Alfred Butler; 1 s (Edward Anthony b 21 March 1987), 1 da (Natalie Joan b 3 Jan 1985); *Career* John Mills (photography) Ltd 1960-; FBIPP 1976 (assoc BIPP 1969); *Recreations* mineral collecting; *Style—* Anthony Ellis, Esq; 37 Holmefield Rd, Liverpool L19 3PE (☎ 051 427 2668); John Mills (photography) Ltd, 11 Hope St, Liverpool L1 9BJ (☎ 051 709 9822, fax 051 709 6585)

ELLIS, Brian William; s of Frank Albert Ernest Ellis (d 1988), and Beryl Christine, *née* Holdsworth (d 1955); *b* 28 Nov 1947; *Educ* Harrow, St Mary's Hosp Med Sch Univ of London (MB BS); *m* 10 July 1976, Loveday Ann, da of David Ernest Pusey (d 1952), of Coleshill, Amersham, Bucks; 1 s (David b 1981), 1 da (Rebecca b 1978); *Career* conslt surgn Ashford Hosp Middlx 1983, hon sr clinical res fell Academic Surgical Unit St Marys Hosp Med Sc of London 1985, clinical advsr to Medical Systems Ltd, dir Medical Software Ltd, chm Hounslow & Spelthorn Health Authy (memb Dist Audit Advsy Ctee), author of various papers on clinical audit and computing; referee for submissions to British Journal of Surgery and British Medical Journal; FRCS 1977; *Books* Hamilton Bailey's Emergency Surgery (jt ed, 12 edn); *Recreations* wine, music, roses; *Style—* Brian Ellis, Esq; Graylands, 124 Brox Road, Ottershaw, Surrey KT16 0LG (☎ 0932 873254); Ashford Hospital, London Rd, Ashford, Middx TW15 3AA (☎ 0784 251188 ext 4429)

ELLIS, Bryan James; s of Frank Elias Ellis, (d 1980) of Harrow, and Catherine Louise (Renée), *née* Samuel (d 1974); *b* 11 June 1934; *Educ* Merchant Taylors, St John's Coll Oxford (Sir Thomas White scholar, BA, MA); *m* 8 Sept 1960, Barbara Muriel, da of Selwyn Leslie Whiteley (d 1960), of Halifax ; 1 s (Mark Richard b 1964), 1 da ((Susan) Rosalind b 1962); *Career* dept of Social Security (formerly DHSS): asst princ 1958-63, princ 1963-71, asst sec 1971-77, undersec 1977-86 and 1990-; chm Civil Serv Selection Bd 1986-87, dep dir Office of Population Censuses and Surveys 1987-90; tstee Leopardstown Park Hosp Tst (chm tstees 1979-84), vice chm of govrs Cleves County Middle Sch Weybridge 1990- (govr 1988-); *Books* Pensions in Britain 1955-75 (1989); *Recreations* theatre, cinema, bridge, walking; *Clubs* MCC; *Style—* Bryan Ellis, Esq; The Adelphi, John Adam St, London WC2N 6HT (☎ 071 962 8073)

ELLIS, Carol Jacqueline (Mrs Ralph Gilmore, JP); QC (1980), JP (West Central Div Inner London 1972); da of Ellis Wallace Ellis (d 1974), of London, and Flora, *née* Bernstein; *b* 6 May 1929; *Educ* Abbey Sch Reading, Univ of Lausanne, UCL (LLB); *m* 6 Jan 1957, (Cyril) Ralph Gilmore; 2 s (Jeremy Charles b 1960, David Emanuel b 1962); *Career* called to the Bar Gray's Inn 1951; law reporter for The Times and legal jls 1952-69; Law Reports and Weekly Law Reports: law reporter 1954-69, asst ed 1969, managing ed 1970, ed 1976; memb Inner London Probation Ctee 1989; *Recreations* travel, music, theatre; *Style—* Miss Carol Ellis, QC, JP; 11 Old Sq, Lincoln's Inn, London WC2A 3TS (☎ 071 430 0341)

ELLIS, Carolyn Noeleen; da of Harold Ellis, of 51 The Boulevard St Annes, Lytham St Annes, Lancs, and Noeleen, *née* Balshaw; *b* 11 March 1960; *Educ* Witton Park HS Blackburn Arts Educnl Sch London; *Career* actress; roles: Aladdin (Southport 1977, Watford 1978), Cinderella (Newcastle) 1979, Cabaret! (England and abroad) 1980-81, Annie (national tour) 1981-84, Consuela in Westside Story (Her Majesty's) 1984-86, Liane in Gigi (Lyric) 1986, Pickwick (Exeter) 1986-87, Miss Silkworm in James and the Giant Peach (Queens Hornchurch and nat tour) 1987, Ruth in Cheeky Chappie (Queen's Hornchurch) 1987, Gloria/Witch in Wizard of Oz (Exeter) 1987, Kings Rhapsody (Churchill Bromley) 1988, Jane Asthon in Brigadoon (Victoria Palace) 1988-89, White Witch in Wizard of Oz (Chichester Festival) 1989-90, Lady Jaqueline in Me and My Girl (Adelphi) 1990-91; concert of Aspects of Love (Sydmonton Festival 1988; *Recreations* walking, swimming, visiting historical places and homes, knitting, teaching dancing and choreography; *Style—* Ms Carolyn Ellis

ELLIS, David; *b* 13 Feb 1934; *Career* Nat Serv Army Special Investigations Branch 1952-55; Crusader Insurance Plc: mgmnt 1956-60, regnl mangr Nigeria 1960-63, city branch mangr 1963-66, PA to Investment and Admin Mangr 1966-69, secondment to US parent gp 1969-70, mangr admin 1971-76, dir and gen mangr 1976-85 (mktg and sales 1976-83, parent group 1983-84, life ops 1984-85); sr vice pres Cigna International Life Group and md Crusader 1986-89, chief exec Lane Clark & Peacock 1989-; memb Worshipful Co of Insurers 1987, Freeman City of London 1987; FICS 1968 (two prizes), FCII 1972, FID 1986; *Recreations* golf, writing, reading, music; *Clubs* ESU; *Style—* David Ellis, Esq; The Old Playhouse, Cuckfield Lane, Warninglid, West Sussex RH17 5SP (☎ 0444 85529); Lane Clark & Peacock, 30 Old Burlington St, London W1X 1LB (☎ 071 439 2266, fax 071 439 0183)

ELLIS, David Raymond; s of Raymond Ellis (d 1986), of Charney Bassett, Nr Wantage, Oxon, and Ethel, *née* Gordon; *b* 4 Sept 1946; *Educ* St Edward's Sch Oxford, ChCh Oxford (MA); *m* 18 December 1974, Cathleen Margaret, da of late Dr Albert Joseph Hawe, CBE, of Accra, Ghana; 1 s (Thomas b 1978), 1 da (Caroline b 1979); *Career* called to the Bar Inner Temple 1970, asst rec 1986; *Clubs* Leander; *Style—* David Ellis, Esq; Lamb Building, Temple, London EC4Y 7AS (☎ 071 353 6701)

ELLIS, Diana Margaret (Di); da of Robert Hall (d 1981), of Twickenham, and Mabel Helen, *née* Steadman (d 1990); *b* 11 April 1938; *Educ* Perivale Girls Sch, Guildford Coll of Technol; *m* 3 Sept 1966, John David Ellis, s of Frederick Henry Ellis; 1 da (Claire Suzanne b 24 Aug 1969); *Career* dist mangr Surrey Co Cncl; competitive career: Middlesex 1954-57, joined St Georges Ladies Rowing Club 1960, coxed winning team Women's Eights Head of River Race 1969, 1971, 1972, 1973 (stroked 1966-68), stroked GB eight Euro Championships 1966, coxed England 1972, Gold medal Nat Championships 1972 (Silver 1973); memb: Women's Rowing Ctee 1977-, Nat Championship Ctee 1977 (chm 1987-89), World Championship Sub Ctee 1986, Ctee Women's Eights Head of River Race 1980, Ctee Gen Training Weekend 1980; dep chm Ctee Women's Henley Regatta 1990, sec Nat Championships of GB 1981-87; chm: Women's Rowing Cmmn 1984-87, rowing events Serpentine Regatta 1987-89, Exec Ctee Amateur Rowing Assoc 1989-; GB team mangr 1988, del FISA Congress 1986-89 and 1990; qualified umpire 1980; *Recreations* guider (brownies, sea rangers), VAD Br Red Cross Soc; *Style—* Mrs Di Ellis; Amateur Rowing Association, 6 Lower Mall, Hammersmith, London W6 9DJ (☎ 081 748 3632, fax 081 741 4658)

ELLIS, (Herbert) Douglas; s of Herbert Ellis; *b* 3 Jan 1924; *Educ* Chester Secdy Sch; *m* 1963, Heidi Marie, da of Rudolph Kroeger; 3 s; *Career* RN 1942-46; chm: Ellis Gp of Cos (Ellmanton Construction Co Ltd, Ellmanton Estates Ltd, Medical Investments Ltd, Ellkar Stud Ltd, Ellmanton Investments Ltd), chm: Aston Villa FC 1968-79 and 1982, Aston Manor Brewery Co Ltd 1985-; memb Lloyd's; *Recreations* football, salmon fishing, foreign travel; *Style—* Douglas Ellis, Esq; 2 Ladywood Rd, Four Oaks, Sutton Coldfield B74 2SN (☎ 021 308 1218)

ELLIS, Geoffrey Albert; s of Albert Edward Ellis (d 1989), of Eaglescliffe, Cleveland, and Alice Isabel, *née* Bell; *b* 20 Sept 1937; *Educ* City of Leicester Boys' Sch, Manchester Univ (Dip Arch); *m* 8 March 1969, Annette Ray Ellis; 2 da (Vanessa Claire b 1975, Verity Fiona b 1981); *Career* architect; asst then sr architect W S Hattrell & Ptnrs Manchester 1961-66, sr architect R Seifert & Ptnrs Manchester 1966-68; ptnr: Gelling Ellis Lomas & Ptnrs Douglas IOM 1968-78, Ellis Brown Ptnrship Douglas IOM 1978-; life memb Douglas Rugby Club, memb IOM Soc of Architects and Surveyors; RIBA 1966, FFAS 1984, FFB 1971; *Recreations* swimming, touring, camping; *Style—* Geoffrey Ellis, Esq; Longlast, Selborne Drive, Douglas, IOM; Ellis Brown, The Rechabite Hall, Allan St, Douglas, IOM (☎ 0624 621375/0624 622692, fax 0624 628465)

ELLIS, Geoffrey Gordon; s of Frederick Ellis (d 1966), of London, and Vera, *née* Clark; *b* 25 July 1940; *Educ* Gravesend GS, Isleworth GS; *m* 16 Sept 1961, Jean Heather, da of Ronald Coles (d 1978), of Bath; 1 da (Kate b 1971); *Career* journalist; Bath Evening Chronicle 1957-68, Thomson Regional 1968-71, The Guardian 1971-79, Now! Magazine 1979-81, The Times 1981-85; dir PR Broad Street Association 1985-89, md Geoffrey Ellis Associates PR Ltd 1989-; *Recreations* wine appreciation, aviation, jazz, books, cooking, France; *Style—* Geoffrey Ellis, Esq; 3-5 Spafield St, Rosebery Avenue, London EC1R 4QB (☎ 071 278 1700, fax 071 837 1311)

ELLIS, Prof Hadyn Douglas; s of Alfred Douglas Ellis, and Myrtle Lillian Ellis; *b* 25 Oct 1945; *Educ* Univ of Reading (BA, PhD), Univ of Aberdeen (DSc); *m* 17 Sept 1966, Diane Margaret, da of Denis Newton, of St Briavels, Glos; 3 s (Stephen David b 1967, Robert Huw b 1980, Jack Richard b 1983); *Career* Univ of Aberdeen: lectr 1970-79, sr lectr 1979-86; prof of applied psychology UWIST 1986-88, prof of psychology UWCC 1988-, head Sch of Psychology 1989-; FBPsS 1986; *Style—* Prof Hadyn Ellis; The Homestead, Castleton, Cardiff CF3 8UN; School of Psychology, UWCC, Cardiff CF1 3YG (☎ 0222 874 867)

ELLIS, Prof Harold; CBE; s of Samuel and Ada Ellis; *b* 13 Jan 1926; *Educ* Univ of Oxford (BM BCh, MCh, DM); *m* 20 April 1958, Wendy, da of Henry Levine; 1 s (Jonathan b 1959), 1 da (Suzanne b 1962); *Career* Capt RAMC 1950-51; res surgical appts 1948-60, sr lectr Univ of London 1960-62, prof of surgery Univ of London at Westminster Hosp 1962-88, univ clinical anatomist Univ of Cambridge 1989-; former vice pres: RCS, RSM; pres Br Assoc of Surgical Oncology; FRCS, FRCOG; *Recreations* medical history; *Style—* Prof Harold Ellis, CBE; 16 Bancroft Ave, London, N2 0AS (☎ 081 348 2720); Dept of Anatomy, University of Cambridge, Tennis Court Rd, Cambridge

ELLIS, Dr (William) Herbert Baxter; AFC (1954); er s of William Baxter Ellis, and Georgina Isabella, *née* Waller; *b* 2 July 1921; *Educ* Oundle, Univ of Durham (BM, BS,

MD); *m* 1, 1948 (m dis), Margaret Mary, da of Frank Limb, OBE (d 1987), of Yorks; 1 s (Christopher b 1954), 1 da (Penny (Mrs Deakin) b 1952); *Career* Surgn Cdr RN 1945-59; qualified Naval Pilot appts incl: RN Hosp Malta 1945-47, RAF Inst of Aviation Med Farnborough 1950-56, US Navy Acceleration Laboratory Johnsville USA 1956-58, RN Air Med Sch Gosport 1958-59; mktg dir Appleyard Gp 1959-64, vice pres Schweppes (USA) 1964-65, dir Bewac 1965-71, dir gen Dr Barnardos 1971-73, med conslt DHSS 1973-, Employment Med Advsy Serv 1973-81, med conslt Plesseys; St John Ambulance: Glos co surgn 1979-87, Glos co cdr 1987-89, chief cdr 1989-; OStJ 1979, CStJ 1987, KStJ 1989; Gilbert Blane Medal 1954; *Books* Hippocrates RN: Memoirs of a Naval Flying Doctor (1988); *Recreations* walking, mending fences; *Clubs* Army and Navy, Naval and Military, St John; *Style—* Dr Herbert Ellis, AFC; 7 Honeywood Hse, Alington Rd, Canford Cliffs, Poole BH14 8LZ

ELLIS, Dr Ian Ogilvie; s of Philip Senior Ellis, of Cranford, 25 Athol Rd, Bramhall, Gtr Manchester, and Anna *née* Ure; *b* 24 Aug 1955; *Educ* Stockport GS, Univ of Nottingham Med Sch (BMed Sci, BM BS); *m* 20 Oct 1979, Jane Elisabeth, da of Dudley John Stevens, of Westbere House, Westbere, Kent; 1 s (James Ogilvie b 1987), 1 da (Sophie Hannah b 1989); *Career* lectr pathology Univ of Nottingham 1980-87, conslt histopathologist specialising in breast disease City Hosp Nottingham 1987-; author of numerous pubns on breast cancer pathology and prognostic factors; memb Working Gp Breast Cancer Screening RCPath, lectr UK Breast Screening Prog Nottingham Trg Centre; MRCPath 1985; *Recreations* game fishing, wine tasting; *Style—* Dr Ian Ellis; Yew Tree House, 2 Kenilworth Rd, The Park, Nottingham (☎ 0602 472186); Dept of Histopathology, City Hospital, Hucknall Rd, Nottingham N55 1PB (☎ 0602 691169, ext 46875)

ELLIS, John; s of Ronald Ernest Ellis, of Hessle N Humberside, and Margaret Sutherland, *née* Insch; *b* 2 Dec 1952; *Educ* Aberdeen GS, Univ of Aberdeen (open bursary, BSc); *m* ; 1 s (Christopher John b 15 March 1983), 1 da (Katherine Elspeth b 20 Feb 1981); *Career* Standard Life Assurance Co 1974-85, Hill Samuel Investment Management 1985-87 (head Client and Investmt Servs, dir Hill Samuel Pensions Investment Management), Wardley Investment Services International Ltd 1987 (dir admin, dir Wardley Unit Trust Managers); Crown Unit Trust Services Ltd: exec mangr 1988, gen mangr 1989, md 1989-; *Recreations* classical music, former memb Edinburgh Festival Chorus, theatre going, armchair sportsman; *Style—* John Ellis, Esq; Crown Unit Trust Services Ltd, Crown House, Crown Square, Woking, Surrey GU21 1XW (☎ 0483 715033, fax 0483 747564)

ELLIS, (Arthur) John; CBE (1986); s of Arthur Ellis, and Freda Jane Ellis; *b* 22 Aug 1932; *Educ* City of London Coll, SW Essex Tech Coll; *m* 1956, Rita Patricia; 2 s, 1 da; *Career* Fyffes Group Ltd: accountant 1954-64, mgmnt accountant 1964-65, chief fin offr 1965-67, fin dir 1967-69, chief exec 1969, chm 1984-; chm: National Seed Development Organisation Ltd 1982-87, Intervention Board for Agricultural Produce 1986-; memb Worshipful Co of Fruiterers; FCCA, MBCS, FCIMA, FICSA; *Recreations* golf, fishing, walking, reading; *Clubs* Reform, Farmers; *Style—* John Ellis, Esq, CBE; Fyffes Group Ltd, 12 York Gate, Regent's Park, London NW1 4QJ (☎ 071 487 4472, fax 071 487 3644, telex 25392)

ELLIS, John Norman; s of Albert Edward Ellis (d 1990), and Margaret, *née* Thomson (d 1986); *b* 22 Feb 1939; *Educ* Osmondthorpe Secdy Mordern Leeds, Leeds Coll of Commerce; *m* 1 (m dis); m 2, 5 Oct 1985, Diane; 1 s (Martin John), 1 da (Karen Elizabeth (Mrs Landricumb)), 2 step s (Graham Anderson, Robert James Anderson); *Career* trade union official; messenger Post Office 1954-57 (postman 1957-58), exec offr MPBW 1967-68 (clerical offr Miny of Works 1958-67); Civil and Public Servs Assoc: full time offr 1968-82, dep gen sec 1982-86, gen sec 1986-; memb Cncl of Civil Servants Nat Whitley Cncl, chm Major Policy Ctee Cncl of Civil Service Unions, memb TUC Gen Cncl (memb various ctees: Econ, Social Insur and Industl Welfare, Educn and Training, Equal Rights, Public Services); *Recreations* DIY, motoring, dog walking, badminton, gardening; *Style—* John Ellis, Esq; 26 Hareston Valley Rd, Caterham, Surrey CR3 6HD (☎ 0883 340449); Civil and Public Services Association, 160 Falcon Rd, London SW11 2LN (☎ 071 924 1840)

ELLIS, Sir John Rogers; MBE (1943); 3 s of late Frederick William Ellis, MD; *b* 15 June 1916; *Educ* Oundle, Trinity Hall Cambridge, London Hosp (MA, MD); *m* 1942, Joan, da of late C J C Davenport; 2 s, 2 da; *Career* dean London Hosp Med Coll 1968-81 (formerly sub dean then vice dean), physician to London Hosp 1951-81; pres Med Protection Soc 1986-89, chm Cncl of Govrs Inst of Educn Univ of London, vice pres Assoc for the study of Med Educn; FRCP; kt 1980; *Recreations* painting, gardening; *Style—* Sir John Ellis, MBE; Little Monkhams, Monkhams Lane, Woodford Green, Essex (☎ 081 504 2292)

ELLIS, Dr Jonathan Richard (John); s of Richard Ellis, of 28 Heath Drive, Potters Bar, Herts, and Beryl Lilian, *née* Ranger (d 1985); *b* 1 July 1946; *Educ* Lochinver House Sch, Highgate Sch, King's Coll Cambridge (BA, PhD); *m* 11 July 1985, Maria Mercedes, da of Alfonso Martinez (d 1982), of Miami Beach, Florida, USA; 1 s (Sebastian b 19 July 1990), 1 da (Jennifer b 17 Jan 1988); *Career* res assoc Stanford Linear Accelerator Centre 1971-72, Richard Chase Tolman fell Calif Inst of Tech 1972-73, ldr Theoretical Studies Div Euro Orgn for Nuclear Res (CERN) Geneva 1988-(staff memb since 1973), Miller prof Univ of California Berkeley 1988; FRS 1984; *Recreations* reading, listening to music, hiking in mountains; *Style—* Dr John Ellis, FRS; 5 Chemin Du Ruisseau, Tannay, 1295 Mies, Switzerland (☎ 010 41 22 776 48 58); Theoretical Studies Division, Cern, 1211-Geneva 23, Switzerland (☎ 010 41 22 767 4142, fax 010 41 22 782 3914)

ELLIS, Dr Julia Peregrine; da of Cecil Montague Jacomb Ellis (d 1942), of London, and Pamela Sage, *née* Unwin; *b* 25 March 1936; *Educ* North Foreland Lodge Sch, Middx Hosp Univ of London (MB BS, DCH); *Career* St George's Hosp London 1966-69, sr registrar dermatology Oxford 1969-74, res dermatology Dept of Dermatology Univ of Miami Med Sch 1974, conslt dermatologist Princess Margaret Hosp Swindon and Wessex Health Authy 1975-; FRCP; former pres St John's Hosp Dermatological Soc London, treas and former pres Dowling Club; *Recreations* fishing; *Style—* Dr Julia Ellis; Princess Margaret Hosp, Okus Rd, Swindon, Wilts SN1 4JU (☎ 0793 536231)

ELLIS, (Dorothy) June; da of Robert Edwin Ellis (d 1963), and Dora, *née* Eden (d 1952); *b* 30 May 1926; *Educ* La Sagesse HS Newcastle upon Tyne, Univ of Durham (BSc), Univ of Newcastle (DipEd, Tennis colours); *Career* sci teacher Darlington and Newcastle 1947-53; St Monica's Sch Essex: head Biology Dept 1953-63, house mistress 1956-63, sr mistress 1959-63; dep head Sibford Sch Oxfordshire 1964-7, headmistress Mount Sch York 1977-86; clerk: Quaker Soc Responsibility and Educn 1986-89 (memb 1978-89), Swerford Parish Cncl 1986-90; govr: Ellerslie Sch Malvern 1987-, Friends Sch Saffron Walden 1990-; memb Cncl and Ctee Woodbrooke Coll 1988-; memb GSA 1977-; *Recreations* the countryside, theatre, reading, cooking, friendships; *Style—* Miss D. June Ellis; Willowside, Swerford, Oxford OX7 4BQ (☎ 0608 737334)

ELLIS, Laurence Edward; s of Dr Edward Alfred Ellis (d 1952), of Great Yarmouth, and the late Ida Ethel, *née* Dawson; *b* 21 April 1932; *Educ* Winchester, Trinity Coll Cambridge (BA, MA); *m* 5 April 1961, Elizabeth, da of Norman James Ogilvie, of Castle Cary; 2 s (Jonathan b 8 May 1962, Simon b 29 Sept 1971), 1 da (Mary b 23 May 1964); *Career* Rifle Bde 1950-52 (S/Lt KRRC 1951-52); housemaster Marlborough Coll 1968-77 (asst master 1955-68), rector (headmaster) Edinburgh Acad 1977-; memb various ctees incl: Business Educn Review Gp 1986-87, MEG (GCSE) Cncl 1986-; AFIMA, FRSA; *Books* SMP Mathematics Course (jtly, 1964-76); *Recreations* lay reader, music, crosswords, woodwork; *Style—* Laurence Ellis, Esq; 50 Inverleith Place, Edinburgh EH3 5QB; The Edinburgh Academy, Henderson Row, Edinburgh EH3 5BL (☎ 031 556 4603)

ELLIS, Mark; s of David Meurig Ellis (d 1960); *b* 27 Sept 1953; *Educ* Llandovery Coll Dyfed, St John's Coll Cambridge (MA, LLB); *Career* barr 1977; mangr of corp fin Arbuthnot Latham Bank 1978-83, dir Polly Peck International plc 1983-, pres PPI (US) Enterprises Inc 1988-; *Recreations* tennis, reading, travel, theatre, cinema; *Style—* Mark Ellis, Esq; PPI Enterprises (US) Inc, 9 W 57 St, Suite 3750, New York NY 10019

ELLIS, Nigel George; s of George Ellis, of Selsey, Sussex, and Ivy, *née* Howell; *b* 19 April 1939; *Educ* Farnborough GS; *m* 31 July 1965, Yvonne Meline Elizabeth, da of Norman Tracy (d 1976), of Crowborough, Sussex; 1 s (Timothy b 1971), 1 da (Victoria b 1968); *Career* co sec City of London Real Property Co 1967-74; dir: Holland America UK Ltd 1974-79, Hammerson Property Devpt and Investmt Corpn 1979-88, BAA plc 1988-; Freeman Worshipful Co of Fanmakers 1984; FCA 1963, FCCA 1985; *Recreations* philately, chess; *Style—* Nigel Ellis, Esq; Woodland Chase, Tennyson's Lane, Haslemere, Surrey (☎ 0428 2428); Fougeryat, Saussignac, 24240 Sigoules, France; BAA plc, 130 Wilton Rd, London SW1 (☎ 071 932 6657, fax 071 932 6734, car 0836 630 753, telex 919268 BAA PLC)

ELLIS, Dr Norman David; s of George Edward Ellis (d 1968), of London, and Annie Leslie, *née* Scarfe (d 1978); *b* 23 Nov 1943; *Educ* Minchenden Sch, Leeds Univ (BA), MA (Oxon), PhD; *m* 1966, Valerie Ann, da of Haddon Fenn, of East Sussex; 1 s (Mark b 1975); *Career* res fell Nuffield Coll Oxford 1971-74; gen sec Assoc First Div Civil Servants 1974-78; under sec British Medical Assoc 1978-; *Recreations* reading, railways, local community affairs; *Style—* Dr Norman Ellis; British Medical Association, BMA House, Tavistock Square, London WC1

ELLIS, Osian Gwynn; CBE (1971); s of Rev Thomas Griffith Ellis (d 1985), of Prestatyn, and Jennie, *née* Lewis (d 1976); *b* 8 Feb 1928; *Educ* Denbigh GS, RAM (Hovey scholar, Dr Joseph Parry prize, Vivian Dunn prize, Harriet Cohen award); *m* 5 Jan 1951, Irene Ellis, da of Richard Hugh Jones (d 1987), of Pwllheli; 2 s (Richard Llywarch b 1956, Tomos Llywelyn b 1959); *Career* concert harpist; played and recorded with: Melos Ensemble London 1954-, Lincoln Center Chamber Music Soc NY 1974-; prof of harp Royal Acad of Music 1959-89, princ harpist LSO 1960-, giver of concerts of poetry and music with Dame Peggy Ashcroft, Paul Robeson, Richard Burton, Lord David Cecil, Dorothy Tutin, Princess Grace and others; worked with Benjamin Britten and Sir Peter Pears 1960-, numerous recital tours with Pears Europe and USA 1974-; works written for him (by Britten): Harp Suite in C Maj 1969, Canticle V (for performance with Pears) 1974, Birthday Hansel 1975; harp concertos written for him by: Alun Hoddinott, William Mathias, Jorgen Jersild, Robin Holloway; solos and chamber music by: Malcolm Arnold, Elizabeth Maconchy, Colin Matthews, Menotti and William Schuman; awards: Grand Prix du Disque, French Radio Critics award; Hon DMus Univ of Wales 1970; FRAM 1960; *Style—* Osian Ellis, Esq, CBE; 90 Chandos Avenue, London N20 9DZ; Arfryn, Yr Ala, Pwllheli, Gwynedd LL53 5BN

ELLIS, Peter Johnson; s of Albert Goodall Ellis (d 1985), and Evelyn, *née* Johnson; *b* 24 Nov 1937; *Educ* Queen Elizabeth GS Wakefield, Trinity Coll Cambridge (MA); *m* 14 July 1960, Janet Margaret, da of Thomas Palmer, of Cambridge; 3 da (Jacqueline b 11 Oct 1961, Christine b 3 July 1964, Rosalind b 4 Jan 1967); *Career* Nat Serv RAF 1955-57; systems analyst IBM (UK) Ltd 1960-64, data processing mangr J & A Scrimgeour 1964-70, jt dep chief exec Grieveson Grant & Co 1982-86 (ptnr 1976-86), dep chm Kleinwort Benson Investment Management 1988- (jt chief exec 1986-88); memb: Soc of Investmt Analysts 1970- (memb Cncl 1976-84), Stock Exchange 1973-; *Recreations* theatre, reading, bridge; *Style—* Peter Ellis, Esq; La Barranca, Tyrrell's Wood, Leatherhead, Surrey (☎ 0372 372343); Kleinwort Benson Investment Management, 10 Fenchurch St, London EC3M 3LB (☎ 071 623 8000, 071 956 7260)

ELLIS, Peter Rowland; s of Capt Frederick Rowland Ellis, MBE (d 1942), and Madge, *née* Wass (d 1988); *b* 4 April 1927; *Educ* Burton-upon-Trent GS, Sidney Sussex Coll Cambridge (MA); *Career* Flying Offr RAF 1948-50; dir Yardley of London Ltd 1975-78; md: Yardley Contracts Ltd 1978-82, Peter Black Toiletries Ltd 1983-87; non-exec dir Peter Black Holdings plc 1987-; *Style—* Peter Ellis, Esq; Rosevine, 391C Ham Green, Holt, Trowbridge, Wilts BA14 6PZ (☎ 0225 782462)

ELLIS, Dr (Francis) Richard; s of (Henry) Francis Ellis, of Halebarns, Cheshire, and Elsie May, *née* Pearson; *b* 3 March 1936; *Educ* Altrincham Co GS, Univ of Manchester (MB ChB), Univ of Leeds (PhD); *m* 9 June 1960, Maureen, da of (Francis) Syndey Statham (d 1983); 1 s ((Angus) Christian b 1963), 1 da (Charlotte (Rebecca) b 1965); *Career* res fell MRC 1966-68, reader in anaesthesia Univ of Leeds 1976- (lectr 1968-71, sr lectr 1971-76); memb: Cncl Coll of Anaesthetists, Bd British Journal of Anesthesia; memb: BMA, RSM, Assoc of Anaesthetists; fell Coll of Anaesthetists, DA, DObstRCOG; *Books* Inherited Disease and Anaesthesia, and Essential Anaesthesia; *Recreations* smallholding, photography, music, engineering; *Style—* Dr Richard Ellis; Dept of Anaesthesia, Clinical Sciences Building, St James's University Hospital, Leeds LS9 7TF (☎ 0532 433144, fax 0532 426496)

ELLIS, Dr Richard MacKay; s of Valentine Herbert Ellis (d 1953), of London, and Angela Peart, *née* Robinson; *b* 9 July 1941; *Educ* Wellington Univ of Cambridge, St Thomas's Hosp; *m* 14 Aug 1976, Gillian Ann, da of Samuel Cole (d 1975), of Reading; 1 s (William b 1978), 1 da (Melissa b 1977); *Career* assoc prof of orthopaedics Univ of Rochester NY USA 1975-80, sr lectr in rehabilitation Univ of Southampton 1980, conslt in rheumatology and rehabilitation Salisbury Hosps 1980; ed jnl of Orthopaedic Med, past pres Inst of Orthopaedic Med; FRCS 1971, FRCP 1989; *Style—* Dr Richard Ellis; 161 Bouverie Avenue South, Salisbury, Wilts SP2 8EB; Wessex Regional Rehabilitation Unit, Odstock Hosp, Salisbury, Wilts SP5 8BJ (☎ 0722 336212)

ELLIS, Prof Richard Salisbury; s of Capt Arthur Ellis, MBE, of Colwyn Bay, Wales, and Marian, *née* Davies; *b* 25 May 1950; *Educ* Ysgol Emrys ap Iwan, UCL (BSc), Wolfson Coll Oxford (DPhil); *m* 28 July 1972, Barbara; 1 s (Thomas Marc b 1978), 1 da (Hilary Rhona b 1976); *Career* princ res fell Royal Greenwich Observatory 1983-, prof of astronomy Univ of Durham 1985- (lectr 1981-), sr res fell SERC 1989- (chm Large Telescope Panel); memb: American Astronomical Soc, Astronomical Soc of Pacific; FRAS; *Books* The Epoch of Galaxy Formation (with C S Frenk, 1988); *Recreations* travel; *Style—* Prof Richard Ellis; Physics Dept, Durham Univ, South Rd, Durham DH1 3LE (☎ 091 374 2163, fax 091 374 3749, telex 537351)

ELLIS, Richard Tunstall; OBE (1970), DL (1967); s of Herbert Tunstall Ellis (d 1925), of Liverpool, and Mary Elizabeth Muriel, *née* Sellers (d 1929); *b* 6 Sept 1918; *Educ* Merchant Taylors' Crosby, Silcoates Sch Wakefield Yorkshire, Univ of Aberdeen (MA, LLB); *m* 2 Jan 1946, Jean Bruce Maitland, da of Maj Richard Reginald Maitland Porter, MC (d 1979), of Aberdeen; 2 s (Keith b 1949, Andrew b 1960), 2 da (Janet (Mrs Baldwin) b 1947, Katharine (Mrs Parker) b 1956); *Career* Royal Signals 51 Div 2 Lt 1939 (POW Germany 1940-45), Lt 1942, Capt 1945; sr ptnr Paull & Williamsons Advocates Aberdeen 1970-83 (ptnr 1949-70); chm: Trustee Savings Bank Scot 1983-86, TSB Scot plc 1986-89; dir TSB Gp plc 1986-89; memb: Scot Bd Norwich Union

Insur Socs 1973-80, Aberdeen Bd Bank of Scot 1972-82, Ct Univ of Aberdeen 1984, Cncl Nat Tst for Scot; chm Scot Div IOD 1988-89; memb: Law Soc of Scot, Law Soc London; *Recreations* golf, hill walking, skiing; *Clubs* Royal Northern (Aberdeen), New (Edinburgh), Army & Navy; *Style—* Richard Ellis, Esq, OBE, DL; 18 Rubislaw Den North, Aberdeen AB2 4AN (☎ 0224 316680)

ELLIS, Ven Robin Gareth; s of Rev Joseph Walter Ellis, and Morva Phyllis, *née* Morgan-Jones; *b* 8 Dec 1935; *Educ* Oldham Hulme GS, Worksop Coll, Pembroke Coll Oxford (BCL, MA); *m* 1964, Anne, da of James Sydney Landers (d 1970); 3 s (Timothy b 1966, Simon b 1968, Dominic b 1971); *Career* asst curate St Peter's Swinton Manchester 1960-63, asst chaplain Worksop Coll 1963-66; vicar: Swaffham Prior with Reach Cambs 1966-74, St Augustine's Wisbech 1974-82, Yelverton 1982-86; archdeacon of Plymouth 1982-; *Recreations* cricket, theatre, prison reform; *Style—* The Ven the Archdeacon of Plymouth; 33 Leat Walk, Roborough, Plymouth (☎ 0752 793 397)

ELLIS, Roger Henry; e s of Francis Henry Ellis (d 1953), of Debdale Hall, Mansfield; *b* 9 June 1910; *Educ* Sedbergh, King's Coll Cambridge (MA); *m* 1939 (Audrey) Honor, o da of late Arthur Baker, JP, DL; 2 da; *Career* WWII Private 1939, Maj 5 Fusiliers 1944, serv Italy and Germany, MFAA offr Italy and Germany 1944-45; Public Record Office: asst keeper 1934, princ asst keeper 1954, conslt ed Catalogue of Seals 1972-86; sec Royal Cmmn on Historical MSS 1957-72, lectr in archive studies UCL 1947-57; Br Records Assoc: ed of Archives 1947-57, chm Cncl 1967-73, vice pres 1971-; pres Soc of Archivists 1964-73 (vice pres Business Archives Cncl 1958-); chm Br Standards Ctee for Drafting BS 5454 1967-72, memb and sec Jt Records Ctee Royal Soc and Royal Cmmn on Historical MSS 1968-75; jt ed Rivista for Br Italian Soc 1946-49; author of articles in Br and foreign jls and collections on care and use of archives and MSS; memb: London Cncl Br Inst in Florence 1947-55, ICA Ctee on Sigillography 1962-77, Advsy Ctee on Export of Works of Art 1964-72, Exec Ctee Friends of the Nat Libraries 1965-88 (hon treas 1977-79); vice pres Royal Inst 1975-76 (mangr 1973-76); corr memb Indian Historical Records Cmmn, FSA, FRHistS; *Publications* Ode on St Crispin's Day (1979), Catalogue of Seals in the Public Record Office, Personal Seals I and II (1979-81) Monastic Seals I (1986), Walking Backwards (1986); *Clubs* Athenaeum; *Style—* Roger H Ellis, Esq; Cloth Hill, 6 The Mount, Hampstead, London NW3

ELLIS, Roger Wykeham; CBE (1983); s of Cecil M J Ellis (d 1942), and Pamela Unwin; *b* 3 Oct 1929; *Educ* Winchester, Trinity Coll Oxford (MA); *m* 25 July 1964, Margaret Jean, da of William H Stevenson (d 1972); 1 s (Alexander b 1967), 2 da (Katherine b 1965, Harriet (twin) b 1967); *Career* Nat Serv 1947-49; Harrow Sch: asst master 1952-61, housemaster 1961-67; headmaster Rossall Sch 1967-72, master Marlborough Coll 1972-86, mangr Graduate Recruitment Barclays Bank 1986-; memb: Harrow Borough Educn Ctee 1956-60, Wiltshire Co Educn Ctee 1975-85; chm Headmasters Conference 1983; *Recreations* golf, fishing; *Clubs* The East India; *Style—* Roger Ellis, Esq, CBE; Barclays Bank plc, 25 Farringdon St, London EC4A 4LP (☎ 071 489 1995)

ELLIS, Sir Ronald; s of William Ellis, and Besse Brownbill; *b* 12 Aug 1925; *Educ* Preston GS, Univ of Manchester (BScTech); *m* 1, 1956, Cherry Hazel, *née* Brown (d 1978); 1 s, 1 da; m 2, 1979 Myra Ann, *née* Lowdon; *Career* dir BL Motor Corpn 1970-76, chm Business Manufacturers Holding Co 1972-76; head of def sales MOD 1976-81; dir: Wilkinson Sword Group 1981-86, Bull Thompson & Associates Ltd; non-exec dir Yarrow 1981-86, non-exec dir Redman Heenan Int 1981-86, pres and md Allegheny International (Industl Div) 1982-85, chm EIDC Ltd; govr and memb Cncl UMIST 1970- (vice pres 1983-); chm EIDC Ltd; FEng, FIMechE, FCIT, CBIM, FRSA; kt 1978; *Recreations* fishing, sailing, reading; *Clubs* Turf, Royal Thames Yacht; *Style—* Sir Ronald Ellis; West Fleet House, Abbotsbury, Dorset DT3 4JF; Flat F, 20 Cornwall Gdns, London SW7

ELLIS, Susan Jacqueline; da of Michael John Irving Ellis, of Bridgwater, Somerset, and Juliette Wendy Scott, *née* Smith; *b* 30 April 1963; *Educ* Leamington Coll for Girls, City Univ Business Sch (BSc); *Career* mgmnt trainee and vacation work Midland Bank International 1981-85 (whilst at univ), graduate trainee National Opinion Polls 1985-86, PR mangr Broad Street Associates 1987-88 (conslt 1986-87); dir Square Mile Communications 1989- (jt fndr and assoc dir 1988-89); *Recreations* sport, cinema, theatre, literature; *Style—* Ms Susan Ellis; Square Mile Communications Limited, Glade House, 52/54 Carter Lane, London EC4V 5EA (☎ 071 329 4496, fax 071 329 0310/11, car 0860 353807)

ELLIS, Maj Thomas Frederick; OBE (1974, MBE 1970); s of Frederick William Ellis (d 1937), and Constance Maude Frances, *née* Sanders; *b* 30 March 1913; *Educ* Oundle, Seale-Hayne Agric Coll, RMC Sandhurst, Mil Staff Coll Quetta (psc); *m* 16 March 1946, Rosanne Mary Laura Curzon, da of Col Alexander Woods, MBE, TD, DL (d 1975); 1 s (Francis William b 1 Feb 1953), 1 da (Philippa Margaret Curzon b 15 Aug 1950); *Career* cmmnd TA Devonshire Regt 1934, cmmnd 2 Punjab Regt Indian Army 1937, served NWFP 1938-41, Staff Capt 44th II Bde 1941-42, Singapore 1942, POW Burma Siam Rly 1942-45, OC 2 Punjab Regt Training Bn Meerut 1946 (despatches 1946), Staff Coll Quetta 1947-48, left India and Pakistan after Independence 1948; Commercial Horticulture Cornwall 1949-54, Colonial Agric Serv 1955-73, dist agric offr Uganda 1960-62, regnl coffee offr Uganda 1962-73, agric conslt ICL with System for Computer Aided Agric Planning and Action 1977-82; pres 2nd Punjab Offrs Assoc; memb of IAA Assoc, pres Hayle Town Tst; memb: CPRE, Royal Inst of Cornwall, Cornwall Heritage Tst, Nat Tst, Cornwall Garden Soc; Bard Gorsedd of Cornwall 1985; *Books* The Functions of Extension Staff (1977); *Recreations* gardening; *Clubs* Royal Overseas League, Corona; *Style—* Maj Thomas Ellis, OBE; Penpol House, Hayle, Cornwall TR27 4NQ

ELLIS, Vivian; CBE (1984); s of Harry Ellis and Maud Isaacson; *Educ* Cheltenham; *Career* Nat Serv RNVR 1939-46 (ret Lt Cdr); composer and author; pres Performing Right Soc 1983-; composer of scores for numerous musicals incl: Mister Cinders (1929, revived 1983), Bless The Bride (1947, revived 1987); songs incl: Spread A Little Happiness, Ma Belle Marguerite, This Is My Lovely Day, I'm On A See-Saw, Other People's Babies; Ivor Novello award 1973 and 1983; Novels: Faint Harmony, Day Out, Chicanery, Goodbye Dollie, I'm on a Seesaw (autobiography); Humorous works: How to Make Your Fortune on The Stock Exchange, How to Enjoy Your Operation, How to Bury Yourself in the Country, How to be a Man About Town; Hon GSM; *Recreations* gardening, painting; *Clubs* Garrick; *Style—* Vivian Ellis, Esq, CBE; c/o Performing Right Society, 29 Berners St, London W1

ELLISON, Adrian Charles; s of Kenneth Charles Ellison, of Knowle, West Midlands, and Joyce, *née* Smith; *b* 11 Sept 1958; *Educ* Solihull Sch, Univ of Reading; *m* 14 May 1988, Clare Louise, da of Carlos Lucien Joseph Heyden; *Career* ox; debut Univ of Reading 1977, int debut 1981; memb: Univ of London Club, Tideway Scullers' Sch Club; major championships: Bronze medallist Men's Pairs (Munich World Championships) 1981, 5 place Men's IVs (Lucerne World Championships) 1982, 11 place Men's VIIIs (Duisberg World Championships) 1983, Gold medallist Mens IVs (Los Angeles Olympics) 1984, 7 place Men's VIIIs (Hazewinkle World Championships) 1985, Gold medallist Men's IVs (Edinburgh Cwlth Games) 1986, 9 place Men's VIIIs (Copenhagen World Championships) 1987, 8 place Men's Lightweight VIIIs (Milan World Championships) 1988, Bronze medallist Men's VIIIs (Bled World Championships) 1989, 4 place Men's VIIIs (Tasmania World Championships) 1990; winner Prince Phillip Challenge Cup for Men's IVs (Henley Royal Regatta) 1982, 1984, 1985 and 1989; World Record holder Men's Pairs (Lucerne Regatta) 1986; currently sole British cox holding World Championship and Olympic medals in Pairs, IVs and VIIIs; diagnostic radiographer 1983-87, fin conslt 1987-; *Style—* Adrian Ellison, Esq

ELLISON, Prof Arthur James; s of Lawrence Joseph Ellison, of Birmingham (d 1978), and Elsie Beatrice Ellison; *b* 15 Jan 1920; *Educ* Solihull Sch, Univ of London (BSc, DSc); *m* 1, 1952, Marjorie (d 1955), da of Walter Cresswell, of Sheffield; m 2, 1963, Marian Elizabeth, da of John Gordon Gumbrell, of London (d 1976); 1 s, 1 da; *Career* design engr: Higgs Motors Ltd 1938-43, Br Thomson-Houston Co Ltd 1947-58 (graduate apprentice 1946); tech asst Royal Aircraft Estab 1943-46, lectr and sr lectr Queen Mary Coll Univ of London 1958-72, hon prof Nat Univ of Engrg Lima Peru 1968, prof of electrical and electronic engrg and Head of Dept City Univ London 1972-85 (prof emeritus 1985-), author of numerous papers and volumes on engrg and psychical res; fndr and chm Int Conf on Electrical Machines 1974-85 (pres of honour pres Soc for Psychical Res 1976-79 and 1981-84); *Books* The Reality of the Paranormal (1988); *Recreations* reading, meditation, parapsychology and travel; *Clubs* Athenaeum; *Style—* Prof Arthur Ellison; 10 Foxgrove Ave, Beckenham, Kent BR3 2BA (☎ 081 650 3801); The City University, Northampton Sq, London EC1V 0HB (☎ 071 253 4399)

ELLISON, Donald Roy; s of Herbert James Ellison (d 1970), of New Milton, Hants, and Marguerite Evelyn, *née* Swapp (d 1976); *b* 20 Jan 1913; *Educ* Solihull Sch, Balliol Coll Oxford (MA); *m* 24 Aug 1954 (m dis 1976), Joan Audrey, da of Joseph Benn Anderson (d 1967), of Cumbria; 1 s (Anthony b 1959), 1 da (Lucy b 1956); *Career* called to the Bar Middle Temple 1940; dep circuit judge and asst rec 1976-83; *Books* Clinical Papers and Essays on Psycho-Analysis by Karl Abraham (jt ed, 1955), Rayden on Divorce (jt ed, 1960); *Recreations* listening to music, theatre going, walking, foreign travel, pursuing useless but interesting knowledge; *Style—* Donald R Ellison, Esq; 27 Wheatsheaf Lane, Fulham, London SW6 6LS (☎ 071 381 5817)

ELLISON, Rt Rev and Rt Hon Gerald Alexander; KCVO (1981), PC (1973); s of late Rev Prebendary John Henry Joshua Ellison, CVO (d 1944), Chaplain in Ordinary to HM Queen Victoria, and Sara Dorothy Graham, *née* Crum; *b* 10 Aug 1910; *Educ* Westminster, New Coll Oxford; *m* 1947, Jane Elizabeth, da of Brig John Houghton Gibbon, DSO (d 1960); 1 s, 2 da; *Career* served chaplain RNVR 1939-43 (despatches); ordained 1935; curate Sherborne Abbey 1935-37, chaplain to Bishop of Winchester 1937-39; chaplain to Archbishop of York 1943-46, vicar St Marks, Portsea 1946-50, canon of Portsmouth 1950, bishop suffragan of Willesden (Dio of London) 1950-55, bishop of Chester 1955-73, bishop of London 1973-81; dean of the Chapels Royal 1973-81, vicar-gen Dio of Bermuda 1983-84; prelate: Order of the Br Empire 1973-81, Imperial Soc of Knights Bachelor 1973-; chaplain and sub-prelate Order of St John 1973-; episcopal canon of Jerusalem 1973-81; pres Actors' Church Union 1973-81; hon bencher Middle Temple 1976; pres Nat Fedn Housing Assocs 1981-; *Books* The Churchman's Duty (1957), The Anglican Communion (1960); *Clubs* Leander, Army and Navy; *Style—* The Rt Rev and the Rt Hon Gerald Ellison, KCVO; Billeys House, 16 Long St, Cerne Abbas, Dorset (☎ 0300 341247)

ELLISON, Prof (Ernest) Graham; s of Ernest Arthur Ellison (d 1987), of Evesham, and Phyllis May Ellison (d 1987); *b* 19 Feb 1932; *Educ* Prince Henry's GS Evesham, UCL (BSc, PhD); *m* 1, Aug 1955 (m dis), Jean, da of E J Williams (d 1988), of Kidwelly; 1 s (Huw Graham b 13 March 1959), 1 da (Karen Jane b 13 Aug 1961); m 2, April 1984, Barbara Janet, da of F Tremlin (d 1980), of Bristol; *Career* Gloster A/C Co 1955-57, Canadair Ltd Montreal Canada 1957-60, lectr QMC London 1960-62, sr res assoc Pratt & Whitney A/C Conn USA 1962-66; Univ of Bristol: lectr, reader, then prof Dept of Mechanical Engrg; author of numerous pubns on res; chm Engrg Profs Cncl; CEng, FIMechE; *Recreations* cricket, golf, enjoying sunshine, food, wine; *Clubs* XL, Optimists Cricket (chm); *Style—* Prof Graham Ellison; 3 Uncombe Close, Backwell, Bristol BS19 3PU; Dept of Mechanical Engineering, University of Bristol, Queens Building, University Walk, Bristol BS8 1TR (☎ 0272 303243)

ELLISON, Ian Keith Casey; CBE (1985); s of Alan Olaf Ellison, of Rugeley, and Joan, *née* Heasman (d 1965); *b* 12 May 1942; *Educ* Hurstpierpoint Coll, Univ of Keele (BA), Reed Coll Portland Oregon USA; *m* 21 March 1970, Mary Joy, da of John East (d 1964); *Career* HM Dip Serv 1965-73 (asst to Dep Govr Gibraltar 1969-71), DTI 1973-75, OFT 1975-78, DOI 1978-79, Cabinet Office 1979, princ private sec to successive Secs of State (Sir K Joseph and Mr P Jenkin) 1979-82, asst sec Telecommunications Div 1982-85; dir Robert Fleming & Co 1986-90, Cable London plc 1987-; md Sectorlink Limited; *Recreations* gardening, music, horses; *Style—* Ian Ellison, Esq, CBE; Beedon Hill House, Beedon, Newbury

ELLISON, Chllr His Hon Judge John Harold; VRD (and clasp); s of Harold Thomas Ellison (d 1940), of Woodspeen Grange, nr Newbury, and Frances Amy, *née* Read (who m again and changed name to Swithinbank 1947 and d 1972), da of Robert John Read, of Norwich; *b* 20 March 1916; *Educ* Uppingham, King's Coll Cambridge (MA); *m* 1952, Margaret Dorothy Maud, da of Maynard Deedes McFarlane, of Sun City, Arizona, USA (d 1984); 3 s (John, Crispin, Francis), 1 da (Jane); *Career* Lt RE (49 W Riding Div TA) 1938-39; RNVR: Offr RNVR 1939-51, HMS Lorna and HMS St Day 1940, Gunnery Specialist HMS Excellent 1940, HMS Despatch 1940-42, Sqdn Gunnery Offr 8 Cruiser Sqdn 1942-44, Trade Div Naval Staff, Staff Offr, Ops to Flag Offr Western Med 1944-45; called to the Bar Lincoln's Inn 1947, practised common law and criminal work Oxford Circuit 1947-71, circuit judge 1972-87; chllr Dioceses of Salisbury and Norwich 1955-, pres SW London Branch of Magistrates Assoc 1974-87, govr Forres Sch Tst Swanage 1974-88; FRAS; *Books* Halsbury's Law of England (3 edn on Courts, 3 and 4 edns on Allotmen and Small Holdings); *Recreations* organs and music, sailing, shooting, skiing, astronomy; *Clubs* Bar Yacht, Ski of GB, Kandahar Ski; *Style—* Chllr His Hon Judge Ellison, VRD; Goose Green House, Egham, Surrey TW20 8PE

ELLISON, Mark Christopher; s of Anthony Ellison (d 1959), and Arlette Maguire, *née* Blundell; *b* 8 Oct 1957; *Educ* Pocklington Sch, Skinners Sch, Univ of Wales (LLB), Inns of Ct Sch of Law; *m* 21 Nov 1981, Kate Augusta, da of Michael Humphrey Middleton, CBE; 1 s, 2 da; *Career* called to the Bar Grays Inn 1979, SE Circuit, specialising in criminal law; *Style—* Mark Ellison, Esq; Queen Elizabeth Building, Temple, London EC4Y 9BS (☎ 071 583 5766)

ELLISON, Richard Mark; s of Peter Richard Maxwell Ellison (d 1968), and Bridget Mary, *née* Horton; *b* 21 Sept 1959; *Educ* Tonbridge, Univ of Exeter (BEd); *m* 1985, Fiona, *née* Dinner; *Career* cricketer; Kent CCC: debut second XI 1971, debut first XI 1981, 140 first class games; Tasmania 1986-87 (7 appearances); England: 11 tests, 14 one day ints, took 10 wickets v Aust Edgbaston 1985; Public School Cricketer of the Year 1978, Wisden Cricketer of the Year 1985, Radio Kent Sport Pesonality of the Year 1985; *Recreations* golf, hockey; *Style—* Richard Ellison, Esq; Kent CCC, St Lawrence Ground, Old Dover Rd, Canterbury, Kent (☎ 0227 456 886)

ELLISON, William Eric; s of Albert Eric Ellison (d 1965), and Alice May, *née* Ineson; *b* 12 Oct 1929; *Educ* Ackworth and Leighton Park Sch, Univ of Leeds (BCom); *m* 1, 29 Aug 1953, Belinda, da of Robert William Theakston (d 1968); 1 s

(David b 1956), 1 da (Polly b 1958); m 2, 5 March 1982, Winifred Mary, da of John William Heaps (d 1965); *Career* sec Leeds Bradford and Dist Soc of CA 1961-65, vice chm Yorks Assoc for Disabled 1982-(treas 1968-82); ptnr Ernst and Whinney (ret 1987); govr Harrogate Int Festival 1975- (treas 1975-80); fin dir Northern Horticultural Soc 1988-; FCA; *Recreations* art, music, travel, computers, golf; *Clubs* The Leeds; *Style—* William E Ellison, Esq; Westfield, Pye Lane, Burnt Yates, Harrogate HG3 3EH (☎ 0423 770 029)

ELLMANN, Lucy Elizabeth; da of Richard David Ellmann (d 1987), and Mary Joan, *née* Donahue (d 1989); *b* 18 Oct 1956; *Educ* Oxford HS for Girls, Falmouth Sch of Art, Canterbury Art Sch, Univ of Essex (BA), Courtauld Inst (MA); *m* 31 Dec 1982 (m dis 1988), Simon Gasquoine; 1 da (Emily Firefly b 1983); *Career* author; winner Guardian Fiction Prize 1987; *Books* Sweet Deserts (1987); *Recreations* cello; *Style—* Ms Lucy Ellmann

ELLS, Eric John; s of Eric Edwin Ells (d 1975); *b* 6 April 1929; *Educ* Blackfen Central; *m* 1952, Amelia Florence, *née* Baulch; 1 s (David), 2 da (Marilyn, Annette); *Career* dir: Rowe Evans Investments plc, Sungkai Holdings Ltd, WJ & H Thompson (Rubber) Ltd; alternate: Bertam Holdings plc, Lendu Holdings plc; *Recreations* travel; *Style—* Eric Ells, Esq; 10 Hurstwood Drive, Bickley, Bromley, Kent BR1 2JF (☎ 081 4676456)

ELLSWORTH, Robert Fred; s of Willoughby Fred Ellsworth (d 1964), and Lucile Rarig (d 1978); Moses Ellsworth (d 1802) was a major supplier to American Army during the American War of Independence; *b* 11 June 1926; *Educ* Univ of Kansas (BSME), Univ of Michigan (JD); *m* 1956, Vivian Esther, da of William A Sies (d 1985); 1 s (Robert), 1 da (Ann); *Career* WWII US Navy 1944-46 served Pacific, Lt Cdr US Navy 1950-53 served Atlantic and Med; investor and co dir; memb of Congress 1961-67, asst to Pres of US 1969, US ambass to NATO 1969-71, asst sec US Dept of Def 1974-75 (dep sec 1975-77), chm Howmet Corp 1983-; pres Robert Ellsworth and Co Inc 1977; dir: Andal Corp 1978-, Price Communications Corp 1982-, Corp of Property Investors 1985-, Fairchild Space and Defence Corp 1989, DBA Systems Inc 1989-; adjunct prof Univ of Maryland Graduate Sch of Public Policy 1990; chm Cncl Int Inst for Strategic Studies London, dir Atlantic Cncl of the US Washington DC, vice chm American Cncl on Germany NYC; landowner; Dept of Defense Medal for Distinguished Public Serv 1975, Presidential Nat Security Medal 1977; *Recreations* hiking, reading, writing, music; *Clubs* Brook (NYC), Army and Navy (Washington DC); *Style—* Mr Robert F Ellsworth; 2001 L Street, NW, Washington DC 20006 (☎ 202 628 1144, fax 202 331 8735, telex 710 0020 RECO)

ELLWOOD, Air Marshal Sir Aubrey Beauclerk; KCB (1949, CB 1944), DSC (1918), DL (Somerset 1960); s of Rev Charles Edward Ellwood, of Cottesmore, Rutland; *b* 3 July 1897; *Educ* Cheam Sch, Marlborough; *m* 1920, Lesley Mary Joan (d 1982), da of late William Peter Matthews, of Walmer, Kent; 1 s, 1 da (and 1 s decd); *Career* with RN Air Service 1916, cmmnd RAF 1919, served India 1919-23 and 1931-36, with RAF Staff Coll, Air Miny and Army Co-operation Cmd during WWII, AOC 18 Gp RAF 1943-44, SASO HQ Coastal Cmd RAF 1944-45, DG Personnel Air Miny 1945-47, Bomber Cmd 1947-50, Air Marshal 1949, AOC-in-C Tport Cmd 1950-52; *Style—* Air Marshal Sir Aubrey Ellwood, KCB, DSC, DL; The Old House, North Perrott, Crewkerne, Somerset

ELLWOOD, Hugh Barton; s of Daniel Ellwood (d 1973), of Clayton-Le-Moors, Accrington, and Josephine, *née* Sharples; *b* 7 March 1938; *Educ* St Bede's Coll Manchester, Gregorian Univ Rome (PhL), Univ of Manchester (BArch); *m* 10 Aug 1966, Marie, da of Frederick Lawson; 2 s (Paul Andrew b 24 Sept 1969, Mark John b 4 Nov 1974), 2 da (Margaret Clare b 21 July 1967, Catherine Ann b 18 March 1980); *Career* architect; Building Design Partnership: architect Preston office 1966-70 (involved in public housing, student accomodation for Univ of Manchester, housing centre in Chorley), assoc Rome Office 1970-72 (involved in private housing in Rome, Lugano, Brussels, planning reports for areas of Calabria), assoc Preston Office 1972-76 (responsible for design and prodn info stages New Gen Infirmary Leeds, devpt plan for Provincial Maternity Hosp Milan), ptnr Preston Office (responsible for New Gen Infirmary at Leeds, Queen's Med Centre Nottingham, hosps in Southport Blackburn and Maghull), chm Preston office 1988-; memb ARCUK 1967, MRIBA 1968; *Style—* Hugh Ellwood, Esq; 16A St Annes Rd East, Lytham St Annes, Lancashire FY8 3HW (☎ 0253 729877); Building Design Partnership, Vernon St, Moor Lane, Preston, Lancashire PR1 3PQ (☎ 0772 59383, fax 0772 201378)

ELLWOOD, Peter Brian; s of Isaac Ellwood (d 1986), of Bristol, and Edith Trotter (d 1981); *b* 15 May 1943; *Educ* King's Sch Macclesfield; *m* 14 Sept 1968, Judy Ann, da of Leonard George Windsor, of Bristol; 1 s (Richard b 23 Sept 1975), 2 da (Elizabeth b 21 April 1970, Rachel b 11 Jan 1973); *Career* Barclays Bristol 1961-89: corp banker and gen mangr's asst to Sr Gen Mangr Head Office London, controller Barclaycards ops 1983-85, chief exec Barclaycard 1985-89; chief exec retail banking TSB 1989-; dir: TSB Bank plc 1989, TSB Gp plc 1990; former chm VDT Ltd; former dir: Visa International, Barclays Bank UK Ltd; tstee Royal Theatre Northampton, memb Coll Ct Nene Coll Northampton; FCIB; *Recreations* theatre, music; *Style—* Peter Ellwood, Esq; Sunderland House, Great Brington, Northants; TSB, 60 Lombard St, London EC3

ELLY, (Richard) Charles; s of Harold Elly, of Sherborne, Dorset, and Dora Ellen, *née* Luing (d 1988); *b* 20 March 1942; *Educ* Sir William Borlase's Sch Marlow, Hertford Coll Oxford (MA); *m* 7 Oct 1967, Marion Rose, da of Bernard Walter Blackwell (d 1987); 1 s (Mark b 1972), 1 da (Frances b 1975); *Career* admitted slr 1966, ptnr Reynolds Parry-Jones & Crawford 1968, sec Southern Area Assoc of Law Socs 1975-82, pres Berks Bucks & Oxon Law Soc 1988-89 (sec 1975-82); Law Soc: memb 1966-, memb Cncl 1981-, chm Legal Aid Ctee 1984-87, chm Standards and Guidance Ctee 1987-90; chm Maidenhead Deanery Synod 1972-79, pres Cookham Soc 1987-, memb Berks CC 1980-82; *Recreations* ornithology, theatre, walking, gardening; *Clubs* Oxford and Cambridge, Sloane; *Style—* Charles Elly, Esq; Court Cottage, Dean Lane, Cookham Dean, Maidenhead, Berks SL6 9AF (☎ 062848 2637); 10 Easton St, High Wycombe, Bucks HP11 1NP (☎ 0494 25941, fax 0494 30701)

ELMES, Paul Nigel; s of Sydney George Elmes (d 1986), and Murzer Doreen, *née* Smith; *b* 12 Dec 1952; *Educ* Westbourne Secdy Modern Ipswich, Ipswich Civic Coll, Royal Dental Hosp London (BDS, LDS, RCS, Med and Surgy prize, Essay Research prize, Dental Material prize); *m* 13 Aug 1977, Amanda Jane, da of Brian Moorhouse; 2 s (Richard Paul b 24 Jan 1979, Christopher Peter b 1 Sept 1980); *Career* residential surgical house surgeon St Georges Hosp London 1977, assoc to Jon Pritchard (Dental Surgeon) Cheltenham 1977-81, princ Dental Clinic West Mersea Colchester 1981-, princ of dental surgy Harley St London 1983; chm NE Essex BDA 1991-92; memb BDA 1977-; *Style—* Paul Elmes, Esq; Deoban, 171 Lexden Rd, Colchester, Essex CO3 3TE (☎ 0206 43516); 102 Harley St, London W1N 1AF (☎ 071 935 2785)

ELMES, Dr Peter Cardwell; s of Capt Florence Romaine Elmes (d 1965), of Culmdavy House, Hemyock, nr Cullompton, Devon, and Lilian Bryham Cardwell (d 1950); *b* 12 Oct 1921; *Educ* Rugby, Ch Ch Oxford (MA, BSc, BM BCh), Western Reserve Univ Cleveland USA (MD); *m* 19 Jan 1957, Margaret Elizabeth Cardwell, da of Henry Sambell Staley (d 1960), of Jabalpur, India; 2 s (John Peter Henry b 1960, David Antony b 1964), 1 da (Ann Elizabeth b 1957); *Career* Capt RAMC 1946-49; registrar, sr registrar and tutor in med Hammersmith Hosp 1950-57; lectr, sr lectr, reader, prof Dept of Therapeutics Queen's Univ Belfast 1958-76; dir MRC Pneumoconiosis Unit 1976-82, conslt in occupational pulmonary disease 1982-; memb Poisons Bd NI, former chm Citizens Advice Bureaux NI, former memb Medicines Cmmn; chm Dinas Powys Civic Tst and Mabon Club; FRCP 1967, FFOM 1982; *Recreations* DIY, gardening; *Style—* Dr Peter Elmes; Dawros House, St Andrews Rd, Dinas Powys, S Glamorgan CF6 4HB (☎ 0222 512 102, fax 0222 515 975)

ELMHIRST, Lady; Marian Louisa; er da of Lt-Col Lord Herbert Andrew Montagu Douglas Scott, CMG, DSO, DL (d 1947; 5 s of 6 Duke of Buccleuch and (8 of) Queensberry), and Marie Josephine Agnes (d 1965), yr da of James Andrew Edwards; *b* 16 June 1908; *m* 1, 1 Nov 1927, Col Andrew Henry Ferguson, The Life Guards (d 4 Aug 1966; his mother was Hon Margaret Brand, eldest da of 2 Viscount Hampden and 24 Baron Dacre), of Polebrook Hall, Oundle; 2 s (John b 1929, d 1939; Ronald b 1931, father of HRH the Duchess of York, *see* Royal Family); m 2, 30 Oct 1968, Air Marshal Sir Thomas Walter Elmhirst, KBE, CB, AFC, DL (d 6 Nov 1982), 4 s of Rev William Elmhirst; *Style—* Lady Elmhirst; No 2 Bungalow, Dummer Down Farm, Dummer, Basingstoke, Hants (☎ 0256 397 267)

ELMHIRST, Roger Thomas; s of Air Marshal Sir Thomas Walter Elmhirst, KBE, CB, AFC (d 1982), and his 1 wife, Katharine Gordon, *née* Black (d 1965); *b* 3 Sept 1935; *Educ* Eton, Trinity Hall Cambridge (MA); *m* 1966, Celia Rozanne, da of Dr H M Jaques (d 1963); 4 children; *Career* Lt Nat Service; pres DG: Charterhouse SA (France) 1978-84, Ermeto SA (France) 1986-; chm: Coloroll Ltd 1982-84, Bradley & Lomas (Electrical) Ltd 1987-; dep md Charterhouse Corporate Investments 1982-84; exec dir Paragon Group Ltd 1984; *Clubs* Cavalry and Guards', Eton Ramblers, Fife Hunt, New Zealand GC; *Style—* Roger Elmhirst, Esq; c/o Paragon Group Ltd, 25 Gilbert Street, London W1Y 2EJ (☎ 071 493 6661,) 15 Ladbroke Grove, London W11 3BD (☎ 071 727 0336); Knowle Cottage, Beaminster, Dorset DT8 3BD (☎ 0308 863038)

ELMSLIE, Kenward Gordon; s of Gordon Forbes Elmslie (d 1955), and Doris Julia, *née* Woollatt (d 1983); *b* 8 April 1927; *Educ* Cheltenham, Jesus Coll Cambridge (MA, LLM); *m* 6 Sept 1958, Jean Elsa, da of Arthur Pearson (d 1959); 2 s (Andrew Gordon b 15 Feb 1960, Ian Forbes b 15 July 1962); *Career* Lt RM 1945-48; barr Inner Temple 1951-55; Colonial Serv Nigeria 1953-55; admitted slr 1956; sr ptnr Richards Butler 1985-88 (ptnr 1960-); memb Cncl Cheltenham Coll 1983-85 and 1987-; *Recreations* opera, swimming; *Clubs* Royal Over-Seas League, Baltic Exchange; *Style—* Kenward Elmslie, Esq; Cedar Lodge, Lilley Drive, Kingswood, Surrey KT20 6JA (☎ 0737 832847); Beaufort House, 15 St Botolph St, London EC3A 7EE (☎ 071 247 6555, fax 071 247 5091, telex 949494 RBLAW G)

ELPHICK, Michael John; s of Herbert Frederick Elphick (d 1970), of Chichester, Sussex, and Joan, *née* Haddow; *b* 19 Sept 1946; *Educ* Lancastrian Sch Chichester, Central Sch of Speech and Drama (scholar); partner, Julia Mary Alexander; 1 da Kate Alexander Elphick; *Career* actor; TV work incl: Holding On (LWT), Private Schultz (BBC), Blue Remebered Hills (BBC), This Year Next Year (Granada), Three Up Two Down (BBC), The Knowledge (Thames), Boon (Central), Crown Court (Granada); theatre work incl: Hamlet (Royal Court, Round House, Broadway NY), Ticket of Leave Man (Nat Theatre), Macbeth (Worcester, Tokyo, Manilla Hong Kong, Chichester Festival Theatre); film work incl: Fraulin Docktor, Buttercup Chain, Cry of the Banshee, Hamlet, Quadrophenia, Elephant Man, Trail of the Pink Panther, Memed my Hawk, The Krays, Privates on Parade, The First Great Train Robbery, Where's Jack, Withnail and I, Buddy's Song, I Bought a Vampire a Motorbike, The Antagonists, Let Them Have It; winner Best Actor Reddifusion TV award 1966; *Recreations* boats; *Clubs* Groucho, Gerry's, Colony; *Style—* Michael Elphick, Esq; Dennis Selinger, ICM 388 Oxford St, London W1

ELPHINSTON, Alexander; s and h of Sir John Elphinston of Glack, 11 Bt; *b* 6 June 1955; *Educ* Repton, St John's Coll Durham; *m* 1986, Ruth Mary Dunnett; 1 s (Daniel John b 24 Sept 1989); *Career* slr; *Recreations* youth work, theatre, jigsaws, cricket; *Style—* Alexander Elphinston, Esq; Maybelle Cottage, Sandford, Crediton, Devon

ELPHINSTON OF GLACK, Sir John; 11 Bt (NS 1701), of Logie, Co Aberdeen; s of Thomas George Elphinston (d 1967; s of de jure 9 Bt), and Gladys Mary, *née* Congdon (d 1973); suc unc, Sir Alexander Logie Elphinstone of Glack, 10 Bt (d 1970); *b* 12 Aug 1924; *Educ* Repton, Emmanuel Coll Cambridge (BA); *m* 29 May 1953, Margaret Doreen, da of Edric Tasker (d 1968), of Cheltenham; 4 s (Alexander b 1955, Charles b 1958, Andrew James b 1961, William Robert b 1963); *Heir* s, Alexander Elphinston, *qv*; *Career* Lt RM 1942-47; chm Lancs, Cheshire and IOM Branches of RICS (Agric Div) 1975; pres Cheshire Agric Valuers' Assoc 1967, memb Lancs River Authy 1969-74, sch govr; estates mangr Mond Div ICI; conslt land agent with Gandy & Son Northwich Cheshire 1983-88; FRICS, FAAV; *Recreations* church, shooting, ornithology, cricket; *Style—* Sir John Elphinston of Glack, Bt; Pilgrims, Churchfields, Sandiway, Northwich, Cheshire CW8 2JS (☎ 0606 883327)

ELPHINSTONE, Sir (Maurice) Douglas Warburton; 5 Bt (UK 1816) of Sowerby, Cumberland, TD; s of Rev Canon Maurice Curteis Elphinstone (d 1969), 4 s of 3 Bt; suc cous, Sir Howard Graham Elphinstone, 4 Bt, 1975; *b* 13 April 1909; *Educ* Loretto, Jesus Coll Cambridge (BA, MA); *m* 30 June 1943, Helen Barbara, da of late George Ramsay Main, of Houghton, Kilmacolm; 1 s, 1 da; *Heir* s, John Howard Main Elphinstone; *Career* served WWII 1939-45 as Maj London Scottish and Sierra Leone Regt RWAFF; life assurance cos and Stock Exchange; FFA, FRSE; *Style—* Sir Douglas Elphinstone, Bt, TD, FRSE; 11 Scotby Green Steading, Scotby, Carlisle, Cumbria CA4 8EH (☎ 0228 513141)

ELPHINSTONE, 18 Lord (S 1509); James Alexander Elphinstone; also Baron Elphinstone (UK 1885); s of Rev Hon Andrew Charles Victor Elphinstone (d 1975; 2 s of 16 Lord and Lady Mary Bowes-Lyon, da of 14 Earl of Strathmore and sis of HM Queen Elizabeth The Queen Mother), and Jean Frances, CVO (who m 3, 1980, Lt-Col John Wilson Richard Woodroffe), da of late Capt Angus Valdimar Hambro, MP, and widow of Capt Hon Vicary Paul Gibbs, Gren Gds; *b* 22 April 1953; *Educ* Eton, RAC Cirencester; *m* 1978, Willa Mary Gabriel, yr da of Maj (George) David Chetwode, MBE, Coldstream Gds; 3 s (Master of Elphinstone, Hon Angus John b 1982, Hon Fergus David b 1985), 1 da (Hon Clementina Rose b 1989); *Heir* s, Hon Alexander Mountstuart, Master of Elphinstone; *Career* ARICS; *Clubs* Turf; *Style—* The Rt Hon Lord Elphinstone; Drumkilbo, Meigle, Blairgowrie, Perths (☎ 082 84 216)

ELPHINSTONE, John Howard Main; s and h of Sir Douglas Elphinstone, 5 Bt, TD, and (Helen) Barbara, *née* Main; *b* 25 Feb 1949; *Educ* Loretto; *m* 20 Oct 1990, Diane Barbara Quilliam, da of Dr Brian Quilliam Callow (d 1973), of Johannesburg, S Africa; *Career* quality assurance management in food processing cos; Express Dairies Maidstone 1980-84, Healds Juices Maidstone 1984-86, Calypsa Coffee Co Ltd Dartford 1986-87, Forrester Foods Bedford 1987-88; ptnr in pest control and timber treatment business Enviroguard (UK) Ltd 1988-; memb: Soc of Chemical Industry 1988, Soc of Food Hygiene Technology 1986; Dip Quality Assurance 1984; *Recreations* DIY, cooking; *Style—* John Elphinstone, Esq; Garden Cottage, 6 Amherst Road, Sevenoaks, Kent TN13 3LS (☎ 0732 459077); Enviroguard (UK) Ltd, Unit 2, Penshurst Enterprise Centre, Penshurst, nr Tonbridge, Kent TN11 8BG (☎ 0892 870164)

ELRICK, Lady Patricia Ruth; *née* Fiennes-Clinton; o da of 18 Earl of Lincoln, *qv*; *b* 1

Feb 1941; *m* 27 Jan 1959 (m dis 1970), Alexander George Stuart Elrick, s of Francis Elrick; 3 s (Nicholas James b 24 Aug 1959, David Wayne b 29 June 1961, Warren Stuart b 4 Dec 1962); *Style*— The Lady Patricia Elrick; 73 Picton Road, Bunbury, W Australia 6230

ELRINGTON, Christopher Robin; s of Brig Maxwell Elrington, DSO, OBE (ka 1945), and Beryl Joan, *née* Ommanney; *b* 20 Jan 1930; *Educ* Wellington, Univ Coll Oxford (MA), Bedford Coll London (MA); *m* 1951, Jean Margaret, da of Col Robert Vernon Maynard Buchanan (d 1969), of Ferndown; 1 s (Giles), 1 da (Judy); *Career* ed Victoria History of the Counties of England 1977-; FSA, FRHistS; *Style*— Christopher Elrington, Esq, FSA; 34 Lloyd Baker St, London, WC1X 9AB (☎ 071 837 4971); Inst of Historical Res, Univ of London WC1E 7HU (☎ 071 636 0272)

ELSON, Edward Elliott; s of Harry Elson (d 1979), and Esther, *née* Cohn; *b* 8 March 1934; *Educ* Phillips Acad Andover Massachusetts, Univ of Virginia (BA), Emory Univ Lamar School of Law (JD); *m* 24 Aug 1957, Suzanne, da of Charles Francis Goodman, of Memphis, Tennessee, USA; 3 s (Charles b 1959, Louis b 1962, Harry b 1965); *Career* chm: Atlanta News Agency Inc 1959-85, Elson's 1973-88, Bank of Gordon Co 1979-83, WH Smith & Sons Holdings (USA) 1985, Majestic Wine Corporation 1988; dir: Citizens & Southern Georgia Corporation 1976-, WH SMith Group plc 1985-, Atlantic American Corporation 1985-, Citizens & Southern Trust Co Inc 1986-, Genesco Inc 1987-, Specialty Coffee Holdings Inc 1990-; tstee (non profit orgns): Talledaga Coll 1973-, Univ of Mid-America 1979-81, Univ of Virginia 1984- (rector 1990-), Brenau Coll 1985- (sec 1990-), Hampton Inst 1985-, Univ of Virginia Med Soc 1986-, Brown Univ 1988-, Emory Univ Bd of Visitors 1986-; American Jewish Ctee (non-profit orgn): memb Bd Govrs 1966-, treas and vice pres 1984-85, chm Bd Tstees 1986- 89; Jewish Historical Soc (non-profit orgn): tstee 1979-, memb Exec Ctee 1979-, vice pres 1980-84; memb Pres Cncl Brandeis Univ 1967-, memb Alumni Cncl Phillips Acad 1975-, co-chm Parents Cncl Brown Univ 1986-88, memb Bd Mangrs Alumni Assoc Univ of Virginia 1982-, pres Jewish Pubn Soc 1987-90 (chm 1990-), memb Exec Ctee Univ of Virgina Med Soc 1987-, vice pres Muscular Dystrophy Assoc America; pres Lyndon B Johnson's Cmmn Obscenity and Pornography 1967-71, vice chm Atlanta-Fulton Co Recreation Authy 1972-80, 1 chm Nat Pub Radio 1976-79, chm Georgia Advsy Ctee to US Civil Rights Cmmn 1976-84; chm Advsy Bd Southeastern Centre Contemporary Art Winston-Salem N Carolina 1976-; chm Bd Visitors Emory Museum Art and Archeology Atlanta Georgia 1985-, memb Bd Bayley Museum Charlottesville Virgina 1986-; tstee American Fedn Arts 1985-, memb Pres Cncl Nat Gallery Washington DC 1986- (tstee Cncl 1990-); Robert B Downs Award Univ of Illinois Graduate Sch Library Sci 1971, American Jewish Ctee's Distinguished Serv award 1975, Nat Radio's Distinguished Serv award 1979, Inst Human Rels award 1982; *Clubs* University (NY), Farmington Country (Virginia), Buckhead (Georgia); *Style*— Edward Elson, Esq; 65 Valley Road, NW, Atlanta, Georgia 30305 (☎ 404 261 4492); 475 Park Ave, New York NY 10022 (☎ 212 593 3963); 69 Eaton Place, London SW1X 8DF (☎ 071 235 8270)

ELSTEIN, David Keith; s of Albert Elstein (d 1983), and Millie Cohen (d 1985); *b* 14 Nov 1944; *Educ* Haberdashers' Aske's, Gonville and Caius Coll Cambridge (BA, MA); *m* 16 July 1978, Jenny, da of Alfred Conway; 1 s (Daniel b 1981); *Career* BBC: The Money Programme, Panorama, Cause for Concern, People in Conflict 1964-68; Thames TV: This Week, The Day Before Yesterday, The World at War 1968-72; Weekend World (LWT) 1972-73; ed This Week, exec prodr documentaries Thames TV 1973-82; md and exec prodr: Brook Productions 1982-86 (Almonds and Raisins, Low), Primetime TV 1983-86 (Seal Morning, Return to Treasure Island, Deliberate Death of a Polish Priest, Double Image); exec prodr Goldcrest TV 1982-83 (Concealed Enemies), dir of progs Thames TV 1986-; *Recreations* cinema, theatre, bridge, reading; *Style*— D K Elstein, Esq; Thames Television, 306 Euston Rd, London NW1 3AZ (☎ 071 387 9494)

ELSTOB, Eric Carl; s of Capt Eric Bramley Elstob, OBE, RN, (d 1949), and Signe Mathilda, *née* Ohlsson (d 1968); *b* 5 April 1943; *Educ* Marlborough, Queen's Coll Oxford (MA); *Career* dir Foreign and Colonial Management Ltd 1969, dep chm F and C Eurotrust plc 1972, GT Japan Investment Trust plc 1972; dir: TR Trustees Corporation plc 1973, The Foreign and Colonial Investment Trust plc (joint mangr 1973-); chm: The Portfolios Fund SIC AV, Foreign and Colonial Reserve Fund; dir Thornton Pan-European Investment Trust plc 1980, dep chm F and C Pacific Investment Trust plc 1984, Bangkok Fund 1986; treas Friends of Christ Church Spitalfields; *Books* Sweden, A Traveller's History (1978); *Recreations* fell walking, canoeing, architecture, history; *Clubs* Cercle Interalliée (Paris); *Style*— Eric Elstob, Esq; 14 Fournier St, Spitalfields, London EC16QE (☎ 071 247 5942); Foreign and Colonial Management, Exchange House, Primrose St, London EC2A 4NY (☎ 071 628 8000, fax 071 828 8188)

ELSTOB, Peter Frederick Egerton; s of Frederick Charles Elstob (d 1974), and Lillian, *née* Page; *b* 22 Dec 1915; *Educ* Michigan Univ; *m* 1, 1937 (m dis 1953), Medora, da of Lionel Leigh-Smith (d 1942); 3 s (Blair b 1940, Michael b 1942, Harry b 1950), 2 da (Ann b 1937, Penelope b 1938 d 1982); m 2, 1953, Barbara, da of Chester Zacheisz (d 1936); 1 s (Mayo b 1951), 1 da (Sukey b 1957); *Career* served WWII RTR Troop Sgt 1940-46 (despatches); author, novelist, mil historian; sec gen Int PEN 1974-82 (vice pres 1982-); md cos incl cosmetic mfrg business and Archive Press Ltd; Bulgarian Commemorative Medal 1982; *Books* Spanish Prisoner (1938, based on his experiences when imprisoned as a suspected spy by the Communists, having volunteered to fly for Spanish Govt during Civil War), military histories and novels; *Recreations* travel, playing the stock exchange; *Clubs* Garrick, Savage; *Style*— Peter Elstob, Esq; Burley Lawn House, Burley Lawn, Hants BH24 4AR (☎ 04253 3406)

ELSTON, Christopher David; s of Herbert Cecil Elston (d 1962), and Ada Louisa Elston, *née* Paige (d 1978); *b* 1 Aug 1938; *Educ* Univ Coll Sch Hampstead, King's Coll Cambridge (BA), Yale Univ USA (MA); *m* 17 Oct 1964, Jennifer Isabel, da of Dr A E Rampling (d 1983); 1 s (Peter b 1966), 2 da (Lucinda b 1968, Elizabeth b 1975); *Career* with Bank of England 1960-, seconded to Bank for Int Settlements Basle Switzerland 1969-71, private sec to govr Bank of England 1976-77, asst to chief cashier 1977-79, seconded HM Diplomatic Service as fin attaché Br Embassy, Tokyo 1979-83, sr advsr (Asia and Australasia) Bank of England 1983-; *Recreations* music, photography, gardening, walking; *Style*— Christopher D Elston, Esq; Bank of England, International Divisions, Threadneedle Street, London EC2R 8AH (☎ 071 601 4265)

ELSTON, John David; s of Lt-Col John William Elston (d 1984), and Alwyn, *née* Fawbert; *b* 2 Aug 1946; *Educ* Norwich Sch, Richmond Sch Yorks, Univ of Newcastle upon Tyne (BA); *m* 27 Sept 1980, Victoria Ann Harding (Vicky), da of Victor William Brown, of 41 Cherry Post Crescent, Etobicoke, Toronto, Canada; 2 s (James b 1982, Henry b 1988), 1 da (Georgina b 1986); *Career* sr exec James Capel & Co 1985- (joined 1973); FCA 1979; *Recreations* squash, tennis, bridge; *Style*— John Elston, Esq; The Dene, 9 Kippington Rd, Sevenoaks, Kent TN13 2LH (☎ 0732 457087); James Capel & Co, James Capel House, PO Box 551, 6 Bevis Marks, London EC3A 7TQ (☎ 071 621 0011, fax 071 621 0496, telex 888866 JC LDN G)

ELSTON, John Scorgie; s of Charles Henry Elston, of 25 Hilbre Court, Westkirby, Merseyside, and Hilda Constance Mary Elston (d 1986); *b* 22 March 1949; *Educ* St Bees Sch Cumberland 1963-67, St Thomas Hosp Med Sch 1967-74 (BSc, MB BS, MD); *Partner* Frederika Estelle Smith; 1 da (Charlotte Rose Scorgie b 10 June 1990); *Career* med practitioner; house jobs in gen med and surgery before specialising in ophthalmology; trg in ophthalmology: St Thomas' Hosp 1975-78, Moorfield's Eye Hosp 1979-87, Hosp for Sick Children 1983-87; conslt ophthalmologist: Nat Hosp for Neurology and Neurosurgery 1987-91, St Marys Hosp London 1987-91, Western Ophthalmic Hosp London 1987-91, Radcliffe Infirmary Oxford 1991-; FRCS 1982, FRSM 1988, FCOphth 1989; *Books* Dystonia II (jtly, 1987), Pediatric Ophthalmology (jtly, 1990), Scientific Basis of Neurosurgery (jtly, 1991), Community Paediatrics (jtly, 1991); *Recreations* golf, tennis, walking, Eng lit; *Clubs* RSM; *Style*— John Elston, Esq; 113 Cumnor Hill, Oxford OX2 9JA (☎ 0865 311522); 8 Upper Wimpole St, London W1M 7TD (☎ 071 486 2257)

ELSWORTH, David Raymond Cecil; s of Violet Kathleen Elsworth; *b* 12 Dec 1939; *m* 20 Dec 1969, Jennifer jane Kimber, da of J K R MacGregor; 2 s (Simon David b 30 May 1972), Ian Robert David b 6 June 1975), 1 da (Jessica b 9 June 1984); *Career* Nat Hunt jockey 1957-72, racehorse trainer 1978-; Nat Hunt winners: Rhyme 'N' Reason (Grand National) 1988, Heighlin (Triumph Hurdle), Barnbrook Again (Queen Mother Champion Chase, twice), Desert Orchid (King George VI Rank Chase 1986 and 1988-90, Whitbread Gold Cup 1988, Cheltenham Gold Cup 1989, Jameson Irish Grand National 1990); trained on the flat: Mighty Flutter (third place, Derby) 1984, In the Groove (winner Goffs Irish One Thousand Guineas, first Classic) 1990; champion Nat Hunt trainer 1987-88; *Recreations* shooting; *Style*— David Elsworth, Esq; Whitsbury Manor Stables, Whitsbury, Fordingbridge, Hampshire (☎ 072 53 589)

ELTIS, Dr Walter Alfred; s of Rev Dr Martin Eltis (d 1968), and Mary, *née* Schnitzer (d 1977); *b* 23 May 1933; *Educ* Wycliffe Coll, Emmanuel Coll Cambridge (BA), Nuffield Coll Oxford (MA); *m* 5 Sept 1959, Shelagh Mary, da of Prebendary Douglas Aubrey Owen (d 1964); 1 s (David b 1963), 2 da (Sarah b 1966, Clare b 1968); *Career* PO navigator RAF 1951-53; Exeter Coll Oxford fell and tutor in econs 1963-88, emeritus fell 1988; DLitt 1990; visiting reader in econs Univ of W Aust 1970-71; visiting prof: Univ of Toronto 1976-77, Euro Univ Florence 1979; gen ed Oxford Econ Papers 1975-81, dir gen Nat Econ Devpt Office 1988 (econ dir 1986-88); memb: Cncl of Govrs Wycliffe Coll 1974-78, CNAA 1987- (chm Social Sci Ctee 1987-88); *Books* Economic Growth: Analysis and Policy (1965), Growth and Distribution (1973), Britain's Economic Problem: Too Few Producers (with Robert Bacon, 19 The Classical Theory of Economic Growth (1984); *Recreations* chess, music; *Clubs* Reform, RAC; *Style*— Dr Walter Eltis; Danesway, Jarn Way, Boars Hill, Oxford OX1 5JF (☎ 0865 735 440); National Economic Development Office, Millbank Tower, London SW1P 4QX (☎ 071 217 4049)

ELTON, Anne, Lady; Anne Frances; eldest da of late Brig Robert Adolphus George Tilney, DSO, TD, DL, and Frances Moore, *née* Barclay; *b* 18 Oct 1933; *m* 18 Sept 1958 (m dis 1979), as his 1 wife, 2 Baron Elton; 1 s, 3 da; *Style*— Anne, Lady Elton; The Hall, Sutton Bonington, Loughborough, Leics (☎ 050 967 2355); 70B Pavilion Rd, London SW1 (☎ 071 581 5967)

ELTON, Antony; s of Jack Elton Williams (d 1971), and Ena Frances, *née* Keeble (d 1967); *b* 3 July 1935; *Educ* Magdalen Coll Oxford, RAM London (LRAM), Univ of Durham (BMus), Univ of Surrey (MMus); *m* 1 (m dis), Barbara Peni; 2 s (Conrad b 1966, Pearce b 1971), 1 da (Serena b 1963); m 2 (m dis), Jean Montanus; 1 da (Joy b 1977); *Career* composer, pianist, lectr, critic, organiser, traveller, anti-cruelty activist; *orginal works incl* pre 1980: Come Away Death, The Exile, Anne, Trombone Quartets, Suite from Nigeria, Prelude to Midsummer, Scottish Sketchbook; post 1980: songs of Women, Polish Symphony, Hungarian Quartet, Balkan Journeys, Sonata for Lefthand, Gifts from Slovakia, Russian Impressions, Fate (dance drama), Heart of Albania, Bulgarian Excursion, Autumn, Decay Doom Delight, Summer Sky Sea, Memories of Portugal, Finnish Suite; NZBC NZ Ballet and NZ Child Welfare 1957-62, ABC, Australian Ballet and Victoria Educn Dept 1962-66; dir of music Durham Tech Coll 1968-77, sr lectr Univ of Nigeria Nsukka 1973-76 (chm Music Dept 1973-75), md Durham Theatre Co, critic Dunham Advertiser; tutor: The Open Univ, Beamish Hall, Billingham coll; concert tours and events for: Amnesty Int, Red Cross, Cancer Research, NSPCC, RSPCA; dir Durham Music Gp, fndr and hon sec The Cox Tst for Young Singers; memb: Performing Rights Soc, Composers Guild, RSP, Labour Party, Charter 88; *Books* Music and Life (1985), Memoirs (1987); *Recreations* swimming, philosophy, history, cricket, dogs, drama; *Style*— Antony Elton, Esq; Mole Cottage, 17 Prospect Terrace, New Brancepeth, Co Durham DH7 7EJ (☎ 091 3732893)

ELTON, Sir Arnold; CBE (1982); s of Max Elton (d 1953), and Ada, *née* Levy (d 1990); *b* 14 Feb 1920; *Educ* UCL (MS); *m* 9 Nov 1952, Billie Pamela, da of John Nathan Briggs; 1 s (Michael Jonathan b 1953); *Career* jr and sr Gold medal in surgery UCH, Gosse res scholarship Charing Cross Hosp 1951; formerly sr surgical registrar Charing Cross Hosp, house surgn, house physician and casualty offr UCH; conslt surgn: Mt Vernon Hosp 1960-70, Harrow Hosp 1951-70, Northwick Pk Hosp 1970-85; memb: Ct of Patrons RCS, Cons Cncl and Nat Exec Ctee, Br Assoc of Surgical Oncology (fndr memb), Govt Ctee on Screening for Breast Cancer, Hunterian Soc Assoc of Surgns; assoc fell Br Assoc of Urological Surgns, memb and chm Court of Examiners to RCS, previously examiner to Gen Nursing Cncl, surgical tutor RCS 1970-82, chm Cons Med Soc 1975-; hon conslt surgeon Northwick Park Hosp 1985-, conslt emeritus surgn Clementine Churchill Hosp; Liveryman: Worshipful Soc of Apothecaries, Worshipful Co of Carmen; Jubilee medal for Community Servs 1977; FRCS; kt 1987; *Recreations* tennis; *Clubs* Carlton, RAC, MCC; *Style*— Sir Arnold Elton, CBE; Carlton Club, 69 St James's Street, London W1; The Consulting Rooms, Wellington Hospital, Wellington Place, London NW8

ELTON, Sir Charles Abraham Grierson; 11 Bt (GB 1717), of Bristol; s of Sir Arthur Hallam Rice Elton, 10 Bt (d 1973); *b* 23 May 1953; *Educ* Eton, Reading Univ; *m* 2 March 1990, Lucy, da of late Lukas Heller and Mrs Caroline Garnham; *Heir* kinsman, Charles Tierney Hallam Elton; *Career* with BBC Publications; *Style*— Sir Charles Elton, Bt; Clevedon Court, Clevedon, Somerset; 34 Pembridge Villas, London NW11

ELTON, Charles Tierney Hallam; s of late Charles Henry Elton (gs of 6 Bt), by 1 w, Edith, da of J F Ward; hp of kinsman, Sir Charles Elton, 11 Bt; *b* 1898; *m* 1924, Helen (d 1963), da of late Capt Frederick Waud; 1 da; *Style*— Charles Elton, Esq

ELTON, David Oatley; s of Jospeh Elton (d 1975), of London, and Ethel Louise Oatley (d 1990); *b* 20 Nov 1943; *Educ* Highgate Sch, Trinity Coll Oxford (MA), London Business Sch (MSc); *m* 17 Feb 1984, Jane Elizabeth, da of Maj Cormack Merrill Jenkins (d 1970), of Surrey; 1 s (Charles b 13 Dec 1984), 1 da (Victoria b 9 Aug 1989); *Career* management conslt Limebeers 1969-70, md Ultramar Golden Eagle 1970-74, pres Ultramar Ontario 1974-76, vice pres Marketing American Ultramar 1978-79, gp mktg coordinator Ultramar plc 1977-87 (dir 1981-); *Recreations* bridge, tennis, opera; *Clubs* Carlton MCC; *Style*— David Elton, Esq; Ultramar plc, 141 Moorgate, London EC2M 6TX (☎ 071 256 6080, fax 071 256 8556, telex 885444)

ELTON, Prof Sir Geoffrey Rudolph; er s of late Prof Victor Leopold Ehrenberg, and Eva Dorothea, *née* Sommer; changed name 1944; *b* 1921; *Educ* Prague, Rydal Schs London (external BA), UCL; *m* 1952, Sheila, *née* Lambert; *Career* formerly history lectr Univ of Glasgow; Univ of Cambridge: history lectr, fell Clare Coll 1954-, prof of constitutional history 1967-83, regius prof of modern history 1983-88; author of books on Tudor England, the Reformation and the Renaissance; FBA; kt 1986; *Style*— Prof Sir Geoffrey Elton; Clare College, Cambridge (☎ 0223 333200); 30 Millington Rd, Cambridge (☎ 0223 352109)

ELTON, Prof George Alfred Hugh; CB (1983); s of Horace William Elton (d 1980), and Violet Elton; *b* 27 Feb 1925; *Educ* Sutton County Sch, Univ of London; *m* 1951, Theodora Rose Edith, da of George Henry Theodore Kingham (d 1965); 2 da; *Career* under sec (food) Miny of Agric Fisheries and Food 1974 (chief scientific advsr 1971-85, dep chief scientist 1972), chm Nat Food Survey 1978-85; memb: Advsy Bd for Res Cncls 1981-85, Agric and Food Res Cncl 1981-85, Natural Environment Res Cncl 1981-85; vice chm EEC Scientific Ctee for Food 1985-, dir Int Life Sciences Inst (Europe) Brussels 1987-; Europa Meda (EC) 1985; Hon DSc Univ of Reading 1984; *Recreations* golf; *Clubs* Savage, MCC; *Style*— Prof George Elton, CB; Green Nook, Bridle Lane, Loudwater, Rickmansworth, Herts WD3 4JH

ELTON, Hon Lucy; yr da of 2 Baron Elton; *b* 19 Dec 1963; *Educ* Central Sch of Art & Design (BA); *Career* sculptress; *Style*— The Hon Lucy Elton

ELTON, Michael Anthony; s of Francis Herbert Norris Elton (d 1976), and Margaret Helen, *née* Gray; *b* 20 May 1932; *Educ* Peter Symonds Sch, Brasenose Coll Oxford (BA, BCL, MA); *m* 16 July 1955, Isabel Clare, da of Thomas Gurney Ryott (d 1965); 2 s (Tim b 1965, Mark b 1970), 2 da (Caroline b 1960, Louise b 1969); *Career* articled 1954-57, admitted slr 1957; asst slr: Cumberland CC 1958-61, Surrey CC 1961-65; asst clerk Bucks CC 1965-70, dep clerk of the Peace for Bucks 1967-70, chief exec ABTA 1970-86, dir gen Nat Assoc of Pension Funds 1987-, dir gen Euro Fedn for Retirement Provision 1987-; former Hants Co Squash player; *Books* Future Perfect (with Gyles Brandreth, 1988), Travelling To Retirement (1989); *Recreations* music, tennis, bridge, gardening; *Clubs* Utd Oxford and Cambridge, Winchester Music, Winchester Lawn Tennis; *Style*— Michael Elton, Esq; 12-18 Grosvenor Gardens, London SW1W 0DH (☎ 071 730 0585, fax 071 730 2595)

ELTON, Michael John; s of John Thomas Humphrey Elton, and Kathleen Margaret, *née* Bird; *b* 20 Dec 1933; *Educ* SW Essex Tech Coll, Royal Naval Electrical Sch; *m* 26 March 1965, Carole Elizabeth, da of William Saunby, of Kettering, Northants; 2 s (James Robert b 1967, Charles Lindsey b 1969); *Career* Nat Serv Sub Lt RNVR 1955-57; serv: 108 Minesweeping Sqdn Malta, base electrical offr Cyprus; Lt RNR 1958-; engrg and sales positions STC London 1957-63, staff of mktg dir ITT Europe Paris 1963-64, mktg mangr STC Data Systems London 1964-69; Control Data 1969-81: mangr int data servs Minneapolis 1969-70 and B 1970-71, md Stockholm 1971-74, chm and md Helsinki 1973-74, gen mangr Brussels 1974-79, gen mangr London 1979-81; vice pres and gen mangr Technitron International Inc 1981-86, md and chief exec Technitron plc 1986-; CEng, FIEE, FBCS, FBIM; *Recreations* swimming; *Clubs* Naval; *Style*— Michael Elton, Esq; Technitron plc, Silwood Park Ascot, Berks SL5 7TQ (☎ 0990 872 821, fax 0990 872 275, telex 848076)

ELTON, Miles Caversham; s of Leo Elton (d 1947), of London, and Minnie, *née* Fleischman (d 1974); *b* 22 Dec 1918; *Educ* St Paul's, Pembroke Coll Oxford (BA, MA), Poly of Central London (DipLaw), Central Cncl for Legal Educn; *m* 8 May 1947, (Evelyn) Marcia, da of Louis Curwen (d 1952), of Liverpool; 1 s (Lionel b 1949), 2 da (Elizabeth (Mrs Roche) b 1954, Caroline (Mrs Franklin) b 1957); *Career* cmmnd RA 1940, served Indian Artillery 1940-45, on secretariat of War Cabinet sub ctee 1945-46, released from Military Serv 1946; chm and md Lead and Alloys Ltd 1955-74 (taken over by Chloride Gp plc 1974), chm Chloride Metals Ltd 1974-75; studied Law 1980-82, called to the Bar Gray's Inn 1982; memb Farriers' Co; *Style*— Miles Elton, Esq; 54 Eyre Court, Finchley Rd, London NW8 (☎ 071 586 1877); Rectory Cottage, Noke, Oxfordshire

ELTON, 2 Baron (UK 1934); Rodney Elton; TD (1970); s of 1 Baron Elton (d 1973), and Dedi (d 1977), da of Gustav Hartmann, of Oslo, Norway; *b* 2 March 1930; *Educ* Eton, New Coll Oxford; *m* 1, 18 Sept 1958 (m dis 1979), Anne Frances, da of late Brig Robert Adolphus George Tilney, DSO, TD, DL; 1 s, 3 da; m 2, 24 Aug 1979, (Susan) Richenda, yst da of late Sir Hugh Gurney, KCMG, MVO; *Heir* s, Hon Edward Paget Elton b 28 May 1966; *Career* formerly: farmer, teacher and lectr; contested (C) Loughborough Leics 1966 and 1970; oppn spokesman Educn and Welsh Affrs 1974-79, dep sec Int Affrs Ctee of Gen Synod of C of E 1976-78, dep chm Andry Montgomery Ltd 1977-79 and 1987-, memb Boyd Cmmn (South Rhodesia elections 1979); Parly under sec of state: NI Office 1979-81, DHSS 1981-82, Home Office 1982-84; min of state Home Office 1984-85, DOE 1985-86; chm: FIMBRA 1987-90, Intermediate Treatment Fund 1990-; pres Bldg Conservation Tst 1990-, tstee City Parochial Fndn & Tst for London; memb: Panel on Takeovers and Mergers 1987-90, Cncl of City & Guilds of London Inst; chm Enquiry into Discipline in Schs 1988, dep chm Assoc of Conservative Peers 1988-, hon vice pres Inst of Trading Standards Administration; *Clubs* Cavalry and Gds, Beefsteak, Pratts; *Style*— The Rt Hon Lord Elton, TD; House of Lords, London SW1

ELVEDEN, Viscount; Arthur Edward Rory Guinness; s and h of 3 Earl of Iveagh; *b* 10 Aug 1969; *Style*— Viscount Elveden

ELVIDGE, John Allan; s of Allan Elvidge (d 1970), and Edith *née* Dallman; *b* 19 March 1946; *Educ* Kingston GS, Downing Coll Cambridge (MA, LLB); *Career* barr 1969-; ldr London Borough of Merton 1988-90, ldr opposition 1990-; fell Dowing Coll Cambridge 1969-75; *Recreations* golf, tennis; *Style*— John Elvidge, Esq; 1 Mitre Court Buildings, Temple, London EC4 (☎ 071 353 0434)

ELWES, Edward Hervey; s of Maj John Elwes, MC (ka 1943), of Farnborough, Hants, and Isabel Pamela Ivy Talbot, *née* Beckwith; *b* 21 March 1941; *Educ* Beaudesert Park, Eton; *m* 18 June 1977, Margaret Frances, da of Dr Robert Joseph House, of Tewkesbury; 2 s (Nicholas b 1979, Toby b 1982); *Career* engr; cncllr Tewkesbury Borough Cncl 1975-81, chm Bushley Parish Cncl 1983-89 (cncllr 1981-); md: Lawrence Elwes Ltd 1974-, Austmark Ltd 1989-; page to late Duke of Northumberland at coronation of Queen Elizabeth II; AMBIM, MIAgE, IEng; *Recreations* shooting, gardening, motor racing; *Clubs* Naval, Sloane; *Style*— Edward H Elwes, Esq; Yew Tree Cottage, Bushley Green, Tewkesbury, Glos GL20 6JB (☎ 0684 294316); Eurocap, High Street, Winchcombe, Cheltenham, Glos GL54 5LJ (☎ 0242 603344, telex 43670, fax 0242 603723)

ELWES, Henry William George; DL (Glos 1982); s of Maj John Hargreaves Elwes, MC, Scots Gds (ka N Africa 1943), and Isabel Pamela Ivy, *née* Beckwith, gda of 7 Duke of Richmond and Gordon; a distant cous of Capt Jeremy Elwes, *qv*; *b* 24 Oct 1935; *Educ* Eton, RAC Cirencester; *m* 8 Sept 1962, Carolyn Dawn, da of Joseph William Wykeham Cripps (d 1958), of Ampney Crucis, Cirencester (3 cous of the post war chllr Sir Stafford Cripps); 3 s (John b 1964, Frederick b 1966, George b 1971); *Career* late Lt Scots Gds; farmer and forester; chm Western Woodland Owners Ltd 1971-85 (pres 1981-), regnl dir Lloyds Bank plc 1985-, dir Colebourne Estate Co; chm: Glos Heritage Tst; tstee dir: Cirencester Benefit Soc, Crickley Hill Tst; tstee: Glos Arthiritis Tst, Barnwood House Tst, Central Telethon Tst; memb: Princes Trust (Glos), Princes Youth Business Trust (Glos), Cirencester Rural Dist Cncl 1959-74, Glos CC 1971- (vice chm 1976-83, chm 1983-85); High Sheriff Glos 1979-80; *Clubs* Confrerie des Chevaliers du Tastevin; *Style*— H W G Elwes, Esq, DL; Colesbourne Park, Cheltenham, Glos GL53 9NP (☎ 024287 262)

ELWES, Hugh Damian; s of Sir Richard Elwes (d 1967), and Freya, eld da of Sir Mark Sykes, Bt, of Sledmere; *b* 27 Sept 1943; *Educ* Ampleforth; *m* 18 April 1973, Susan, da of W J Buchanan (d 1971), of Sydney, Australia; 3 da (Chloe b 1978, Flora b 1981, Sophie b 1984); *Career* publisher; chm Roxby & Lindsey Holdings Ltd and its subsidiary co's; *Style*— Hugh Elwes, Esq; Elm Grove, Henstridge, Somerset BA8 0TQ; 82 Wakehurst Rd, London SW4; Roxby Press Ltd, 126 Victoria Rise, London SW4 0NW (☎ 071 720 8872, fax 071 622 9528)

ELWES, Lady Jean Evelyn; *née* Hope Johnstone; da of Evelyn Wentworth Hope Johnstone (*de jure* 9 Earl of Annandale and Hartfell; d 1964), and Marie (May) Eleanor (d 1969), da of Compton Charles Domvile; *b* 9 July 1917; *m* 4 April 1950, as his 2 wife, Maj Robert Philip Henry Elwes, MBE, MC (d 1976), eldest s of late Robert Hammond Arthur Elwes, JP, of Congham House, Norfolk; 1 da (Mrs Arthur Galbraith b 1951); *Style*— Lady Jean Elwes; Flat 4, 24 Collingham Gardens, London SW5 0HL

ELWES, Capt Jeremy Gervase Geoffrey Philip; DL (Lincs 1969); s of Lt-Col Rudolph Philip Elwes, OBE, MC (d 1962; whose mother was Lady Winefride Feilding, da of 8 Earl of Denbigh, while his f, Gervase Elwes, was Privy Chamberlain to the Pope, and a celebrated tenor), and Helen Hermione, *née* Wright (d 1956); *b* 1 Sept 1921; *Educ* Ampleforth, Sandhurst; *m* 9 July 1955, Clare Mary, er da of Maj-Gen Arthur Joseph Beveridge, CB, OBE, MC; 4 s; *Career* served WWII Capt M East (despatches); farms 1,600 acres in partnership in Lincs from 1949; pres Cncl Preservation Rural England (Lincs) 1979-89 (chm 1962-78); High Sheriff Lincs 1969; fndr Lincs and Humberside Arts Assoc; fndr/chm: Shrievalty Assoc of GB 1971, Elwes Enterprises, Elsham Hall Country Park; vice Lord-Lt for Humberside 1983- (DL 1974), vice chm Environmental Medicine Fndn 1987, co-fndr Scarbank Tst for holidays for handicapped children; *Recreations* natural history, the Arts, handicapped people; *Clubs* Green Jackets, Royal Over-Seas League; *Style*— Capt Jeremy Elwes; Elsham Hall, near Brigg, S Humberside DN20 0QZ (☎ 0652 688738)

ELWES, Jeremy Vernon; CBE (1984); s of Eric Vincent Elwes (d 1985), of Sevenoaks, Kent, and Dorothea, *née* Bilton; *b* 29 May 1937; *Educ* Wirral GS, Bromley GS, City of London Coll (ACIS); *m* 1963, Phyllis Marion, da of George Herbert Harding Relf, of Halstead, Sevenoaks, Kent; 1 s (Jonathan b 1969); *Career* chartered sec; dir Sevenoaks Constitutional Club Co Ltd 1977-; chm Cons Political Centre Nat Advsy Ctee 1981-84, personnel dir Reed Business Publishing Ltd 1982-; chm: Sutton Enterprise Agency Ltd and SE Area Provincial Cncl 1986-, memb Cons Pty Nat Union Exec Ctee 1974-, memb Judge Int Wine and Spirits Competition Ltd 1983-, chm designate St Helier NHS Tst, chm Walthamstow Hall 1984- (govr 1977-), govr Eltham Coll 1977, memb Gp Ctee Gen Cncl Cons Gp for Europe 1990 (1985-89, memb 1977-); Chevalier Ordre des Chevaliers Bretvins (Baillage de GB, Maitre des Ceremonies 1984-88, Chancelier 1986-); *Recreations* wine, food, reading, golf; *Clubs* Carlton, St Stephen's Constitutional, Edenbridge Golf and Country; *Style*— Jeremy Elwes, Esq, CBE; Crispian Cottage, Weald Rd, Sevenoaks, Kent TN13 1QQ (☎ 0732 454208); Reed Business Publishing Group, Quadrant House, The Quadrant, Sutton, Surrey SM2 5AS (☎ 081 661 3019, telex 892084 REEDBP G, fax 081 6 8948)

ELWES, Nigel Robert; s of late Maj Robert Philip Henry Elwes, MBE, MC, of Athry House, Ballinafad, Co Galway, Ireland, and his 1 wife, Vivien Elizabeth Fripp, *née* Martin-Smith; *b* 8 Aug 1941; *Educ* Eton; *m* 22 June 1965, Carolyn Peta, da of Sir Robin McAlpine, CBE, of Aylesfield, Alton, Hampshire; 1 s (Andrew b 1969), 2 da (Serena b 1967, Melisa b 1973); *Career* CA, stockbroker, ptnr Rowe & Pitman 1970-86; Int Stock Exchange: joined 1970, memb Cncl 1983-86 and 1988-, chm Domestic Equity Market Ctee 1988-; fin dir S G Warburg Securities 1986-; FCA; *Recreations* hunting, racing; *Clubs* White's; *Style*— Nigel Elwes, Esq; Aylesfield Farmhouse, Alton, Hants GU34 4BY (☎ 0420 80825); S G Warburg Securities, 1 Finsbury Ave, London EC2M 2PA (☎ 071 606 1066, telex 8952485)

ELWES, Peter John Gervase; s of Lt-Col Simon Edmund Vincent Paul Elwes, RA (d 1975), of Amberley, Sussex, and Hon Gloria Elinor, *née* Rodd (d 1975); *b* 17 Oct 1929; *Educ* Eton, Miles Aircraft Tech Coll, Kingston and Gateshead Colls of Advanced Technol; *m* 7 May 1960, Hon Rosalie Ann, da of Brig James Brian George Hennessy, 2 Baron Windlesham (d 1962), of Askefield, Bray, Ireland; 3 s (Luke b 26 July 1961, Benedict b 4 May 1963, Marcus b 27 Nov 1964), 1 da (Harriet b 3 Dec 1968); *Career* 2 Lt Royal Scots Greys BAOR Germany 1950-52, Lt Northumberland Hussars 1953-56; Vickers Armstrong Ltd Weybridge and Newcastle 1948-53, Ransomes & Rapier Ltd Ipswich 1953-56, Rio Tinto-Zinc Corporation Ltd 1956-73, md Hamilton Bros Oil and Gas Ltd 1973-77, dir Kleinwort Benson Ltd 1977-89, chief exec Enterprise Oil plc 1983-84, md Renown Energy Ltd 1988-89, dep chm and chief exec Hardy Oil & Gas plc 1989; FInstPet; *Recreations* painting, gardening, music; *Clubs* Cavalry and Guards', Hurlingham; *Style*— Peter Elwes, Esq; 75 Murray Rd, Wimbledon, London SW19 4PF; Hardy Oil & Gas plc, 7th Floor, 2 Chalkhill Rd, London W6 8DW (☎ 081 741 7373, fax 081 741 7172, telex 892684)

ELWORTHY, Hon Anthony Arthur; 2 s of Baron Elworthy, KG, GCB, CBE, DSO, LVO, DFC, AFC (Life Peer); *b* 10 March 1940; *m* 1967, Penelope Joy (d 1988), da of E J W Hendry, MBE; 1 s (Alexander Julius b 1973), 1 da (Tracy Lara b 1971); *Style*— The Hon Anthony Elworthy; Box 782404, Sandton 2146, South Africa

ELWORTHY, Hon Christopher Ashton; 3 and yst s of Baron Elworthy, KG, GCB, CBE, DSO, LVO, DFC, AFC (Life Peer), *qv*; *b* 1946; *m* 1968, Ann, da of late Harry Bell Lewis Johnstone; 2 da (Caroline Helen b 1968, Amanda Victoria b 1970); *Style*— The Hon Christopher Elworthy; Gordon's Valley Station, RD2, Timaru, New Zealand

ELWORTHY, John Henry; MBE (1987); s of Henry Elworthy (d 1982), and Hilda Jane, *née* Davey (d 1981); *b* 28 Oct 1923; *Educ* Watford Tech Coll; *m* 5 Jan 1946, Joan Donella Victoria, da of late George Pierce; 2 s (Graham b 1949, Trevor b 1953), 1 da (Penelope b 1960); *Career* WWII Naval Air Arm (Petty Offr); served: E Africa, India, SEAC 1942-46; chm and md Protocol Ltd 1953-, Protocol Engineering plc 1972-, Protocol Corp (USA) 1984-, Protocol Scientific 1985-; pres IPEX 1984, memb Printing Machinery NEDO Sector working party; FIOP; *Recreations* golf, clay pigeon shooting; *Style*— John Elworthy, Esq, MBE; Old Thatch, The Green, Edlesborough, nr Dunstable, Beds; Whaddon Hall, Whaddon, Bucks; Protocol Group of Companies, Northbridge Road, Berkhamsted, Herts (☎ 0442 871122, fax 0442 872251, telex : 826205)

ELWORTHY, Marshal of the RAF Baron (Life Peer UK 1972), of Timaru in New Zealand, and of Elworthy, Co Somerset; Sir Samuel Charles Elworthy; KG (1977), GCB (1962), CBE (1946), DSO (1941), LVO (1953), DFC, AFC; s of late Capt Percy Ashton Elworthy, late 1 Life Gds, and Bertha Victoria, *née* Julius, of Gordons Valley, Timaru, New Zealand; *b* 23 March 1911; *Educ* Marlborough, Trinity Coll Cambridge (MA); *m* 1936, Audrey (d 1986), da of late Arthur Joseph Hutchinson, OBE, of Auckland, New Zealand; 3 s (Hon Timothy b 1938, Hon Anthony b 1940, Hon Christopher b 1946), 1 da (Hon Clare (Hon Mrs Cary) b 1950); *Career* RAF 1935, barr 1935, Chief of Air Staff 1963-67, Chief of Defence Staff 1967-71, Marshal of RAF 1967, constable and govr of Windsor Castle 1971-78, Lord-Lt Gtr London 1973-78; KStJ; *Recreations* fishing; *Clubs* RAF, Leander, Christchurch (NZ), South Canterbury (NZ); *Style*— Marshal of the RAF the Rt Hon Lord Elworthy, KG, GCB, CBE, DSO, LVO, DFC, AFC; Gordon's Valley, RD2, Timaru, New Zealand (☎ 03 684702)

ELWORTHY, Air Cdre the Hon Timothy Charles; CBE (1986); eldest s of Baron Elworthy, KG, GCB, CBE, DSO, LVO, DFC, AFC (Life Peer), *qv*; *b* 27 Jan 1938;

Educ Radley, RAF Coll Cranwell; *m* 1, 1961 (m dis 1969), Victoria Ann, eldest da of Lt-Col H C W Bowring; 2 da (Katharine Emma Victoria b 1963, Lucinda Rose b 1965); m 2, 1971, Anabel, da of late Reginald Ernest Harding, OBE; 1 s (Edward Charles b 1974); *Career* RAF, Air Cdre DOR (Air) 2 MOD; Capt of The Queen's Flight 1989; *Clubs* RAF, Boodle's; *Style—* Air Cdre the Hon Timothy Elworthy, CBE; c/o The Queen's Flight, RAF Benson, Oxon OX9 6AA

ELWYN-JONES, Hon Daniel; o s of Baron Elwyn-Jones, PC, CH (Life Peer, d 1989), and Pearl, *née* Binder (d 1990); *m* Denise ---; *Career* social worker; *Style—* The Hon Daniel Elwyn-Jones; 196 Cable Street, London E1

ELY, 8 Marquess of (I 1801); Sir Charles John Tottenham; 9 Bt (I 1780); sits as Baron Loftus (UK 1801); also Baron Loftus (I 1785), Viscount Loftus (I 1789); s of George Leonard Tottenham (d 1928), and gggs of Rt Rev Lord Robert Ponsonby Tottenham, Bp of Clogher, 2 s of 1 Marquess; suc kinsman 1969; *b* 30 May 1913; *Educ* Queen's Univ Kingston Ontario; *m* 1, 23 June 1938, Katherine Elizabeth (d 1975), da of Lt-Col W H Craig, of Kingston, Ontario; 3 s, 1 da; m 2, 1978, Elspeth Ann, da of late P T Hay, of Highgate; *Heir* s, Viscount Loftus; *Career* headmaster Boulden House, Trinity Coll Sch, Port Hope, Ontario; *Style—* The Most Hon the Marquess of Ely; 20 Arundel Court, Jubilee Place, London SW3 (☎ 071 352 9172); Trinity Coll School, Port Hope, Ontario, Canada

ELY, Michael; s of Harold Ely, of Frinton, Essex and Violet Emily, *née* Bruce; *b* 23 April 1943; *Educ* Suttons Hornchurch Essex; *m* 1, 30 Aug 1965, Christine Mary; 1 s (Jonathan b 1975), 1 da (Jane b 1970); m 2, 25 July 1986, Marion Patricia; *Career* Lloyd's Insur broker; dir: Tennant Budd Ltd 1978-83, Tennant Insur Servs Ltd 1973-83, Cayzer Steel Bowater Int Ltd 1983-88, B&C Insur Brokers Ltd 1988-89, Heath Fielding Insur Broking Ltd 1989-; *Recreations* golf, rotarian, sailing; *Style—* Michael Ely, Esq; Heath Fielding Insurance Broking Ltd, 150 Minories, London EC3

ELY, The Ven Archdeacon of; *see*: Walser, Ven David

ELY, Thea, Marchioness of; Thea Margaret Gordon; da of Lars G Gronvöld (d 1954); *b* 2 May 1911; *m* 5 Sept 1928, 7 Marquess of Ely (d 31 May 1969); 1 da (Anne b and d 1933); *Style—* The Most Hon Thea, Marchioness of Ely; 19 North Pallant, Chichester, W Sussex

ELY, Vernon Newbury; CBE (1972); s of Bernard Ely (d 1947), of Wimbledon, and Anne Maud, *née* Buck (d 1968); *b* 14 Jan 1907; *Educ* King's Coll Sch Wimbledon, Berkhamsted Sch; *m* 1944, Florence Maud (decd), da of Walter Armstrong Higgins (d 1917); 1 s (James); *Career* WWII Wing Cdr RAF 1941-45; Drapers Inst and Cottage Homes: memb Bd of Mgmnt 1938-, chm 1948-50 and 1959-67, treas 1952-59, tstee 1976-, chm tstees 1980-; chm: S London Amateur Athletic Assoc 1935-47 (pres 1947-55), Elys of Wimbledon 1955-90; govr King's Coll Sch 1949-55, ldr Retail Productivity Team to USA 1952, chm Exec Cncl Drapers Chamber of Trade 1955-56 (pres 1975-83), pres Surbiton Lawn Tennis and Squash Club 1968-88, memb employers side Retail Drapery and Outfitting Wages Negotiating Ctee 1960-69 (chm 1970-75), memb Lord Halsbury Ctee of Inquiry on Decimal Currency 1962-63 (favoured ten shilling unit), chm Retails Decimal Ctee 1963-67; memb: Retail Consortium (chm Retail Alliance) 1968-73, Home Office Ctee on Crime Prevention 1971-72, pres Assoc of Retail Distributors 1978-80; FRSA; *Books* Fifty Years Hard (autobiography, 1976); *Recreations* real tennis; *Clubs* Surrey Co Cricket, MCC, Royal Tennis Ct; *Style—* Vernon Ely, Esq, CBE; Elys, Wimbledon, London SW19 (☎ 081 946 9191); 42 West Farm Ave, Ashtead, Surrey

ELYAN, David Asher Gremson; s of Max Elyan, of Castletown, IOM, and Freda, *née* Gremson; *b* 4 Oct 1940; *Educ* Cork GS, Trinity Coll Dublin (BA, BCom, MA); *Career* co sec Gordon & Gotch Holdings plc 1970-74, assoc dir AGB Research plc 1980-87 (co sec 1974-87); dir: Attwood Research of Ireland Ltd 1981-90, Irish TAM Ltd 1981-90, Corporate Lease Management Ltd 1984-, Communication Investments Ltd 1987-, Langton Videotex Ltd 1987-, Elyan Estates Ltd 1987-; hon treas: Trinity Coll Dublin Dining Club 1968-, Friends of Royal Watercolour Soc 1990-; memb: Senate Univ of Dublin 1966-, Corp of Lloyds 1983, Cncl for Br Trinity 400 1987; Freeman City of London, Liveryman Worshipful Co of Chartered Secs 1978; ACCS 1967, ACIS 1969, FCIS 1976, FRSA 1972; *Recreations* bridge, collecting first editions, tennis, squash, art, music; *Clubs* MCC, Kildare St (Dublin), E Gloucestershire (Cheltenham), Union (Malta); *Style—* David Elyan, Esq; 49 Chester Ct, Regent's Pk, London NW1 4BU; 3 Coates Mill, Winchcombe, Glos GL54 5NH; 8th Floor, Queen's House, Holly Rd, Twickenham, Middx TW1 4EG

ELYAN, Prof Sir (Isadore) Victor; s of Jacob Elyan, PC, JP, and Olga Elyan; *b* 5 Sept 1909; *Educ* St Stephen's Green, Trinity Coll Dublin; *m* 1, 1939, Ivy Ethel Mabel Stuart-Weir (d 1965); m 2, 1966, Rosaleen Jeanette, da of William Andrew O'Shea; *Career* served WWII, GSO (2) Mil Sec's Branch (DAMS), Maj IA; called to the Bar: King's Inn 1949, Middle Temple 1952; judge of appeal Ct of Appeal for Basutoland, Bechuanaland Protectorate and Swaziland 1955-66, chief justice Swaziland 1965-70; prof of law and dean Faculty of Law Durban-Westville Univ 1973-77; kt 1970; *Style—* Prof Sir Victor Elyan; PO Box 3052, Durban, Natal, South Africa

ELYSTAN-MORGAN, Baron (Life Peer UK 1981), of Aberteifi, Co Dyfed; (Dafydd) Elystan; s of Dewi Morgan (d 1971), of Llandre, Aberystwyth, Cardiganshire, and Olwen Morgan; *b* 7 Dec 1932; *Educ* Ardwyn GS Aberystwyth, Univ Coll of Wales Aberystwyth; *m* 1959, Alwen, da of William E Roberts, of Carrog, Merioneth; 1 s (Hon Owain b 1962), 1 da (Hon Eleri b 1960); *Career* sat as Lab Peer in House of Lords 1981-87, MP (Lab) Cardiganshire 1966-74, Parly under sec of state Home Office 1968-70, pres Welsh Local Authorities Assoc 1967-73, chm Welsh Parly party 1967-68; called to Bar Gray's Inn 1971 (formerly a slr); rec Wales and Chester Circuit 1983-87, circuit judge 1987-; *Style—* His Hon Judge Lord Elystan-Morgan; Carreg-Afon, Dolau, Bow Street, Dyfed (☎ 097 0828 408)

EMANUEL, Elizabeth Florence; da of Samuel Charles Weiner, of (Croix de Guerre) Honeywood Farm, Warfield, nr Bracknell, Berks, and Brahna Betty, *née* Charkham; *b* 5 July 1953; *Educ* City of London Sch for Girls, Harrow Coll of Art, Royal College of Art (MA); *m* 12 July 1975 (sep 1990), David Leslie Emanuel; 1 s (Oliver b 21 March 1978), 1 da (Eloise b 25 Dec 1979); *Career* fashion designer; opened London Salon 1978, designed wedding gown for HRH Princess of Wales 1981; theatre designs incl: costumes for Andrew Lloyd Webber's Song and Dance 1982, sets and costumes for ballets Frankenstein and The Modern Prometheus (Royal Opera House Covent Garden, La Scala Milan) 1985, costumes for Stoll Moss prodn of Cinderella 1985; costumes for film Diam and Skulls 1990, uniforms for Virgin Atlantic Airlines 1990, appointed design conslt Wensum 1990, launched int fashion label under own name 1991; active involvement with charities: Zoocheck, WWF, Br Divers Marine Life Rescue, Rumanian Angel Appeal, Birthright; FCSD; *Books* Style for All Seasons (with David Emanuel, 1982); *Recreations* music, ballet, cinema; *Style—* Mrs Elizabeth Emanuel; Emanuel, 26a Brook Street, Mayfair, London W1Y 1AE (☎ 071 629 5560/9, fax 071 493 5642)

EMANUEL, Dr Richard Wolff; s of Prof Joseph George Emanuel (d 1958), of 10 Harborne Rd, Edgbaston, Birmingham, and Ethel Miriam Cecelia, *née* Wolff; *b* 13 Jan 1923; *Educ* Bradfield Coll, Oriel Coll Oxford (BA, MA), Middx Hosp Med Sch (BM BCh, DM); *m* 2 Nov 1950, Lavinia, da of George Albert Hoffmann, of Fairhaven, Old Bosham, W Sussex; 3 s (Richard b 8 Nov 1951, Tom b 21 March 1956, Mark b 18 Oct 1961); *Career* Capt RAMC 1948-50; res fell in med Vanderbilt Univ 1956-57, physician National Heart Hosp 1963-90 (asst dir Inst of Cardiology and hon physician 1961-63), physician Middx Hosp 1963-87, advsr in Cardiovascular Disease to Govt of Sudan; chm Med Ctee Nat Heart Hosp 1972-75, memb Academic Bd Middx Hosp Med Sch 1975-77, memb Cncl Middx Hosp Med Sch 1976-77, chm Dist Hosp Med Ctee Middx Hosp 1976-77, sec Working Pty of the RCP to examine the problem of Cardiovasular Fitness of Airline Pilots 1977, sec Working Pty of the RCP and RCS to revise the 1967 Report on A Combined Medical and Surgical Unit for Cardiac Surgery 1977; memb Cncl: Chest Heart and Stroke Assoc 1977-, Br Heart Foundaton 1979-; chm Cardiology Ctee RCP 1979-85 (sec 1973-79); memb: Jt Liaison Ctee DHSS 1980-90, Chairs and Res Gps Ctee Br Heart Fndn, Res Funds Ctee, Br Heart Fndn 1982-85; chm: Physicians Ctee Nat Heart Hosp 1985-90, Cardiac Care Ctee Br Heart Fndn 1987-; tstee Gordon Memorial Tst Fund 1987-; civilian conslt in Cardiology to the RAF 1979-89, advsr in Cardiology to the CAA 1981-; contrib to over 90 publications on cardiovasular disease; memb: Br Acad of Forensic Sci 1960, Assoc of Physicians of GB and I; sec Br Cardiac Soc 1968-70 (memb 1961, asst sec 1966-68, memb Cncl 1981-85); hon memb: Assoc of Physicians of Sudan, Heart Assoc of Thailand; hon fell Phillippine Coll of Cardiology; Grand Commander of the Most Distinguished Order of The Crown of Pahang 1990; *Recreations* fishing, 18 Century glass and ceramics; *Clubs* Oriental; *Style—* Dr Richard Emanuel; 6 Upper Wimpole St, London W1M 7TD (☎ 071 935 3243)

EMBER, Michael George; s of Dr George Leslie Ember (d 1972), and Margaret Ilona, *née* Ungar; *b* 13 May 1935; *Educ* The Gymnasium of Budapest Univ, Hungarian Acad of Drama, Univ of London (BA); *m* 1 April 1967, Elizabeth Ann, da of Sir Charles Sigmund Davis; 3 s (Nicholas Charles b 1969, Thomas Michael b 1972, Philip George b 1973); *Career* chief prodr BBC Radio and originator of: Start the Week, Mid-Week, Stop the Week, In the Psychiatrist's Chair, All in the Mind; *Recreations* tennis, travel; *Style—* Michael Ember, Esq; BBC Broadcasting House, London W1A 1AA (☎ 071 927 4236)

EMBERY, Prof Graham; s of Joseph Henry Embery (d 1987), and Elizabeth Jane; *b* 20 Aug 1939; *Educ* King Edward VI GS, Stourbridge Worchestershire; *m* 14 Jan 1967, Vivienne Lacey, da of William Horace Powell (d 1973); 2 s (Russell Geraint b 25 Nov 1971, James Toby William b 30 Dec 1973), 1 da (Philippa Jane b 24 June 1970); *Career* lectr Queen's Univ Belfast 1968-70, lectr Royal Dental Hosp 1970-73, reader Univ of Liverpool 1984-87 (lectr 1973-77, sr lectr 1977-84), prof of basic sci Univ of Wales Coll of Med Cardiff 1987-; ed Soc for Dental Res, chm Cncl of Euro Study Gp for Res on surface and colloidal phenomena in the oral cavity; memb: Advsy Cncl of Int Soc for Fluoride Res, Int Soc for Dental Res, Br Connective Tissue Soc, Biochemical Soc, Jt Dental Ctee MRC 1991-, Sci and Engrg Res Cncl and Health Authys 1991-; *Recreations* golf, oil painting, classic cars; *Style—* Prof Graham Embery; 16 Townfield Rd, West Kirby, Wirral, Merseyside L48 7EZ (☎ 051 625 5954); Dept of Basic Dental Science, Dental School, University of Wales College of Medicine, Heath Park, Cardiff, South Wales CF4 4XY (☎ 0222 755944 ext 2544, telex 498699 UniHos G, fax 0222 762208)

EMBIRICOS, Epaminondas George; s of George Epaminondas Embiricos (d 1980), of Athens, Greece, and Sophie, *née* Douma; *b* 15 July 1943; *Educ* Philips Exeter Acad New Hamps USA, MIT (BSc, MSc); *m* 19 March 1977, Angela, da of Nicholas Pittas, of London; 2 s (George Epaminondas b 8 May 1978, Nicholas Epaminondas b 8 June 1980); *Career* chm Embiricos Shipping Agency Ltd 1969-; dir: Liberian Shipowners Cncl 1979-84, UK Freight Demurrage and Def Assoc 1984-, Baltic Exchange Ltd 1985-90, Chartering Brokers Mutual Insur Assoc 1986-; vice chm: Greek Shipping Co-op Ctee 1986-, Greek Ctee Det Norske Veritas 1986-; Freeman City of London 1984, Worshipful Co of Shipwrights 1985; *Recreations* sailing, reading; *Clubs* Royal Thames Yacht, Royal Yacht Club of Greece, Royal London Yacht, Island Sailing; *Style—* Epaminondas Embiricos, Esq; Commonwealth House, 1-19 New Oxford St, London WC1A 1NU (☎ 071 831 4388, fax 071 872 9385, telex 920688

EMBLETON, Michael John; s of John James Andrew Embleton, and Georgina Emily Adie, *née* Evans (d 1973); *b* 20 June 1941; *Educ* Kingswood Sch; *m* 30 April 1966, (Leslie) Carol Alfreda, da of Thomas Charles Alan Scribbans (d 1953); 1 s (Philip (Raz)), 1 da (Georgina); *Career* slr; ptnr Pinsent & Co Birmingham and London; memb: The Law Soc, The Birmingham Law Soc; *Recreations* shooting, skiing, sailing; *Style—* Michael Embleton, Esq; Abnalls Cottage, Lichfield WS13 8BN; Pinsent & Co, Post and Mail House, Colmore Circus, Birmingham B4 6BH (☎ 021 200 1050, fax 021 200 1040, telex 33510 PINCOS)

EMBREY, Derek Morris; OBE (1986); s of Frederick Embrey (d 1972), and Ethel May, *née* Morris; *b* 11 March 1928; *Educ* Wolverhampton Poly; *m* 1951, Frances Margaret, da of Arthur Ewart Stephens (d 1971); 1 s (Stephen Adrian), 1 da (Fiona Jacquiline); *Career* Flight Lt RAFVR; group tech dir: AB Electronics Group plc 1973-, AB Systems Ltd, AB Components Ltd, Voice Micro Systems Ltd; chm WAB 1987-90; visiting prof Loughborough Univ of Technol 1977-86; memb: Welsh Industries Bd 1982-85, Engrg Cncl 1982-86, Cncl UWIST 1983-89, NEC 1983-, USITT Bd Univ of Southampton 1988-; vice chm M&D Bd IEE 1990-; CEng, FIEE, FIMechE, MIGasE, FRSA; *Recreations* music, archaeology, piloting and navigating aircraft; *Clubs* RAF London, Birmingham Electric; *Style—* Derek Embrey, Esq, OBE; 21 Rockfield Glade, Parc Seymour, Penhow, nr Newport, Gwent NP6 3JF (☎ 0663 400995); AB Electronic Products Group Ltd, Ynysboeth, Abercynon, Mountain Ash, Mid-Glamorgan (☎ 0443 740331)

EMBUREY, John Ernest; s of John Alfred Emburey (d 1984), and Rose Alice, *née* Roff; *b* 20 Aug 1952; *Educ* Peckham Manor Secondary Sch; *m* 1, 22 Sept 1974 (m dis 1980), Sandra Ann, *née* Ball; m 2, 20 Sept 1980, Susan Elizabeth Anne, da of John Michael Booth, of Melbourne, Aust; 2 da (Clare Elizabeth b 1 March 1983, Chloe Louise b 31 Oct 1985); *Career* cricketer, represented England in 60 test matches and 57 one day internationals: 7 overseas tours, Capt to Sharjah 1987, capt in 2 tests v W Indies 1988, vice capt 1986-89; Middlesex vice capt 1983-: 5 county championships (1976, 1977, 1980, 1982 and 1985), county testimonial 1986, memb unofficial touring team SA 1990; *Books* Emburey - A Biography (1987), Spinning in a Fast World (1989); *Recreations* golf, fishing; *Clubs* MCC; *Style—* John Emburey, Esq; Middlesex County Cricket Club, Lords Cricket Ground, London NW8 8QN (☎ 071 289 1300)

EMERSON, Michael Ronald; s of James Emerson, of Wilmslow, Cheshire, and Priscilla Emerson; *b* 12 May 1940; *Educ* Hurstpierpoint Coll and Balliol Coll Oxford; *m* 1966, Barbara Christine, da of late Harold Brierley; 1 s, 3 da; *Career* dir Macroeconomic Analyses and Policy, directorate-gen for Economic and Financial Affairs EEC Cmmn Brussels 1980- (former economic advsr to president Roy Jenkins); *Style—* Michael Emerson, Esq; 50 Rue Clement Delpierre, 1310 La Hulpe, Belgium (☎ 02 354 3730)

EMERSON, Dr Peter Albert; s of Albert Richard Emerson (d 1979), of Epsom, Surrey, and Gwendoline Doris, *née* Davy (d 1968); *b* 7 Feb 1923; *Educ* Leys Sch, Clare Coll Cambridge (MA, MD), St George's Hosp Med Sch (MB BChir); *m* 22 Nov 1947, Ceris Hood, da of John Frederick Price (d 1943), of Stone, Staffs; 1 s (James Peter b 1949), 1 da (Sally (Mrs Stothard) b 1951); *Career* Sqdn Ldr med branch 1947-51; jr med posts 1947-48, registrar posts 1952-57, asst prof of med State Univ NY

1957-58, conslt physician Westminster Hosp 1958-88, hon conslt physician King Edward VII Hosp Midhurst 1969-88, dean Westminster Med Sch 1981-84; currently: dir of clinical information system Westminster Hosp, hon conslt physician Westminster Hosp, hon conslt physician diseases of the chest to RN; memb BMA, vice pres and sr censor RCP 1985-86; hon fell American Coll of Physicians; FRCP; *Books* Thoracic Medicine (1981); *Recreations* tennis, restoring old buildings; *Clubs* RAF; *Style—* Dr Peter Emerson; Kidlington Mill, Mill End, Kidlington, Oxon OX5 2EG (☎ 08675 2212); 3 Halkin St, Belgrave Sq, London SW1X 7DJ (☎ 071 235 8529)

EMERSON, Ronald Victor; s of Albert Victor Emerson, and Doris, *née* Hird; *b* 22 Feb 1947; *Educ* W Hartlepool GS, Univ of Manchester (BSc), Univ of Durham (MSc); *m* 21 June 1969, Joan Margaret (d 1988), da of James Hubery Willis; 2 s (Christopher Mark b 28 May 1971, Simon Nicholas b 5 March 1975); *Career* De La Rue Group 1970-75, commercial devpt controller Formica International; Bank of America 1975-: head London corp office and UK country mangr 1985-89, head of payment servs and fin insts Europe Middle East and Africa; gen mangr Nomura Bank International 1989-; FRSA; *Recreations* flying, sport, reading; *Style—* Ronald Emerson, Esq; 11 Luckley Wood, Wokingham, Berkshire; Nomura Bank International plc, Nomura House, 1 St Martin's-le-Grand, London EC1A 4NP (☎ 071 929 2366)

EMERSON, Timothy John Peter; s of Col Thomas John Emerson, OBE, TD, DL, of Yelverton, and Rosemary Steeds, *née* White; *b* 14 Feb 1942; *Educ* Kelly Coll Tavistock; *m* 9 June 1984, Susanna Jane, da of Sir Harry Evelyn Battie Rashleigh (d 1984), of Stowford; 1 s (Tom b 2 Sept 1987), 1 da (Charlotte b 9 June 1985); *Career* admitted slr 1965; Stafford clark London 1965-67, Heppenstalls Lyndhurst 1967-73, ptnr Foot & Bowden Plymouth 1973-; clerk to govrs Kelly Coll and St Michael's Sch Tavistock, memb Yelverton Parochial Church Cncl churchwarden 1989, govr Dame Hannah Rogers Sch Ivybridge, tstee Lady Modiford Tst; memb Law Soc 1965; *Recreations* sailing, shooting, skiing, tennis; *Clubs* Royal Western Yacht; *Style—* Timothy Emerson, Esq; Coleraine, Yelverton, Devon PL20 6BN (☎ 0822 852070); Foot & Bowden, 70-76 North Hill, Plymouth PL4 8HH (☎ 0752 663416 fax 0752 671802 telex 45223)

EMERTON, Dame Audrey Caroline; DBE (1989); da of George William Emerton (d 1971), of Tunbridge Wells, and Lily Harriet, *née* Squirrell; *b* 10 Sept 1935; *Educ* Tunbridge Wells GS, Battersea Coll of Technol; *Career* SRN; sr tutor St George's Hosp London 1968, princ nursing offr teaching Bromley HMC 1968-70, chief nursing offr Tunbridge Wells and Leybourne HMC 1970-73, regnl nursing offr SE Thames RHA 1973-; chief nursing offr St John Ambulance Bde 1988- (co nursing offr 1970-84, co cmmr 1984-88); chm: Eng Nat Bd for Nurses Midwives and Health Visitors 1983-85, UK Central Cncl Nursing Midwives and Health Visitors 1985-; Hon DCL Univ of Kent 1989; memb: Royal Coll Nursing, RSM; FRSA; *Style—* Dame Audrey Emerton, DBE; The Corner House, 2 Carlton Rd, Tunbridge Wells, Kent TN1 2JS (☎ 0892 27923); South East Thames RHA, Thrift House, Collington Ave, Bexhill, E Sussex TN39 3NQ (☎ 0424 730073)

EMERTON, Rev Prof John Adney; s of Adney Spencer Emerton (d 1969), of Southgate, and Helena Mary, *née* Quin (d 1964); *b* 5 June 1928; *Educ* Minchenden GS Southgate, Corpus Christi Coll Oxford, Wycliffe Hall Oxford (BA, MA), Univ of Cambridge (MA, BD, DD); *m* 14 Aug 1954, Norma Elizabeth, da of Norman Bennington (d 1986); 1 s (Mark Simon b 1961), 2 da (Caroline Mary b 1958, Lucy Anne b 1966); *Career* ordained: deacon 1952, priest 1953; curate Birmingham Cathedral 1952-53, asst lectr in theology Univ of Birmingham 1952-53, lectr in Hebrew and Aramaic Univ of Durham 1953-55, lectr in divinity Univ of Cambridge 1955-62, visiting prof of Old Testament and Near Eastern studies Trinity Coll Toronto 1960, reader in semitic philology Univ of Oxford 1962-68, fell St Peter's Coll Oxford 1962-68, Regius prof of Hebrew Univ of Cambridge 1968-, fell St John's Coll Cambridge 1970-, visiting fell Inst for Advanced Studies Hebrew Univ of Jerusalem 1983, visiting prof of Old Testament United Theol Coll Bangalore 1986, corresponding memb Göttingen Akademie der Wisseuschaften 1990; ed Vetus Testamentum 1976-; sec Int Orgn for the Study of the Old Testament 1971-89; hon canon St George's Cathedral Jerusalem 1984-; Hon DDUniv of Edinburgh 1977; FBA 1979; *Books* The Peshitta of the Wisdom of Solomon (1959), The Old Testament in Syriac - the Song of Songs (1966); *Style—* The Rev Prof John Emerton; 34 Gough Way, Cambridge CB3 9LN; St John's College, Cambridge CB2 1TP

EMERTON, Philip John; s of Edward Alec Emerton (d 1987), of Springhill House, Goring-on-Thames, and Dorothy Evelyn, *née* East (d 1972); *b* 10 Feb 1935; *Educ* Abingdon Sch; *m* 25 July 1959, Mary Patricia, da of Harold Harvey Creedon (d 1970), of Petersfield; 2 s (Richard b 1960, Mark b 1963); *Career* served RA 1958-60, 2 Lt; ptnr Haines Watts Group 1963- (sr ptnr 1973-); British Legion; FCA 1958, FACCA; *Recreations* fishing, skiing, wine buying; *Style—* Philip Emerton, Esq; Herons Creek, Wargrave, Berks (☎ Wargrave 2642); Leysin, Switzerland; Cagnes-Sur-Mer, France; 27 Couching St, Watlington, Oxon (☎ 049161 3611, fax 049161 3730)

EMERY, Prof Alan Eglin Heathcote; s of Harold Heathcote-Emery (d 1977), and Alice, *née* Eglin (d 1972); *b* 21 Aug 1928; *Educ* Manchester GS, Chester Coll, Univ of Manchester (BSc, MSc, MB ChB, MD, DSc), Johns Hopkins Univ USA (PhD); *m* 13 Oct 1988, Marcia Lynn, da of John Miller (d 1986), of Cleveland, USA; *Career* Nat Serv 14/20 Kings Hussars 1945-47; conslt physician 1966-; emeritus prof Univ of Edinburgh 1983- (prof of human genetics 1968-83), visiting fell Green Coll Oxford 1986-, hon res fell Royal Hosp for Sick Children Edinburgh 1988-, res dir Euro Neuromuscular Centre 1990-; memb: ASH, Res Ctee RCP (London), Scientific Advsy Ctee Brittle Bone Soc, Nat Assoc of Pagets Disease Huntington's Soc, Scientific Ctee Faculty of Community Med; FRCP (Ed) 1970, FRS (Ed) 1972, FLS (1985); *Books* Modern Trends in Human Genetics (vol 1 1970, vol 2 1975), Antenatal Diagnosis of Genetic Disease (1973), Genetic Registers (1976), Psychological Aspects of Genetic Counselling (1984), Introduction to Recombinant DNA (1984), Methodology in Medical Genetics (2 edn, 1986), Duchenne Muscular Dystrophy (1987), Elements of Medical Genetics (7 edn, 1988), Principles & Practise of Medical Genetics (2 edn, 1990); *Recreations* writing poetry, oil painting, marine biology; *Clubs* Scot Arts (Edinburgh); *Style—* Prof Alan Emery, FRS; 1 Eton Terrace, Edinburgh EH4 1QE (☎ 031 343 2262); Medical School, Edinburgh EH8 (☎ 031 667 1011 ext 2505)

EMERY, Anthony Hayward; s of Thomas Frederick Emery (d 1983), *b* 10 July 1930; *Educ* Bablake Sch Coventry, Univ of Bristol (BA), UCL; *Career* formerly chm: Reed Info Servs Ltd, dir Reed Business Publishing Gp; cmmr Historic Bldgs and Monuments for England; *Recreations* architectural historian (author of *Dartington Hall* and papers on late medieval buildings), independent travel, fine arts, Nineteenth Century piano music; *Style—* Anthony Emery, Esq; Willow House, Biddestone, Wilts; Hightrees House, Nightingale Lane, London SW12

EMERY, Brian David; TD (1968, with 3 Bars); s of Alan Joseph Emery (d 1972), of Watford, Herts, and Winifred Houghton, *née* Wells (d 1982); *b* 9 April 1932; *Educ* Watford GS, Queens' Coll Cambridge (BA, MA); *m* 9 Sept 1961, (Margaret) Clare, da of Eric Hurndall (d 1970), of Bushey, Herts; 2 s (Patrick b 1962, Matthew b 1974), 1 da (Vivienne b 1964); *Career* Nat Serv RE 1951-53 (2 Lt 1952), Territorial Serv 1953-86, 122 Field Engr Regt (TA): Lt and Capt 249 FD Sqdn RE (TA) Luton 1953-60, Capt 2 i/c 248 FD Sqdn RE (TA) Bedford 1960-66 (Maj OC 1966-67); transferred Royal Corps of Tport under CVHQ RCT Bedford: Capt 2 i/c 270 Port Sqdn RCT (V) 1967-70, Maj OC 271 Port Sqdn RCT (V) 1970-74, DAQMG 2 TPT Gp RCT 1974-77; CVHQ RCT moved to Grantham becoming HQ RCT TA; Lt-Col CO 161 Ambulance Regt RCT (V) 1977-81, SO1 495 Movement Control Liaison Unit 1981-83, Col Cmd BRSC Liaison & Movements Staff (TA) 1983-86, ret 1986; Equity & Law Life Assur Soc plc 1956-: various appts London and High Wycombe 1956-78; chief accountant 1978-85, pensions mangr 1985-86, dir Equity & Law (Managed Funds) Ltd and Equity & Law (Tstees) Ltd 1985-, asst gen mangr 1986-; half blues Water Polo 1955 and 1956, capt Old Fullerians RFC 1957-60; memb examiners Ctee CII 1983-; FCII 1969, FCIS 1981; *Recreations* walking, swimming, reading; *Style—* Brian Emery, Esq, TD; 8 Stoneleigh Rd, Gibbet Hill, Coventry CV4 7AD (☎ 0203 417 663); Equity & Law Life Assur Soc plc, Equity & Law Ho, Corporation St, Coventry CV1 1GD (☎ 0203 555 424, fax 0203 227 734, telex 311439)

EMERY, David John; s of John Emery, of Tolworth, Surrey, and Joan, *née* Bellenie; *b* 13 Oct 1946; *Educ* Tiffin Sch Kingston; *m* 13 April 1974, Irene Thelma, da of George Board, of Ealing W13; 2 s (Matthew David b 1979, Samuel Jack b 1984), 2 da (Alexandra Lillian b 1976, Georgia Lauren b 1987); *Career* journalist: Surrey Comet 1964-69, Luton Evening News 1969-70, Daily Mail 1970-72, Daily Express 1972-78, Daily Star 1978-82, Daily Express 1982-; sports ed Daily Express 1987 (chief sports writer 1983-87); highly commended in Sports Cncl Awards for Journalism 1987; chm Sports Writers Assoc of GB 1986-89, pres 26.2 Road Runners Club 1984; *Books* Lillian (1971), Waterskiing (with Paul Seaton, 1976), Who's Who of the 1984 Olympics, World Sporting Records (1986); *Recreations* squash, marathon running, cricket, golf; *Clubs* Mid Surrey Squash, 26.2 Road Runners, Claygate Cricket, Surbiton Golf; *Style—* David Emery, Esq; Westwood, 39 Greenways, Hinchley Wood, Surrey KT10 0QH (☎ 081 398 1901); Daily Express, 245 Blackfriars Rd, London SE1 9UX (☎ 071 928 8000, fax 071 922 7974, telex 21841/21

EMERY, Fred; s of Frederick G L Emery (d 1942), and Alice May, *née* Wright (d 1978); *b* 19 Oct 1933; *Educ* Bancroft's Sch, St John's Coll Cambridge (MA, Footlights); *m* 23 Aug 1958, Marianne, da of Nils Nyberg (d 1966); 2 s (Martin b 1960, Alex b 1963); *Career* BBC TV presenter; Nat Serv Fighter Pilot 266 and 234 Sqdns RAF 1951-53 (cmmnd 1952); sch broadcasting Radio Bremen 1955-56; The Times: foreign corr (Paris and Algeria 1961-64, Tokyo SE Asia and Vietnam 1964-67, SE Asia 1967-70), chief Washington corr 1970-77, political ed 1977-81, home ed 1981-82, exec ed 1982; presenter BBC TV: Panorama 1978-80, Platform 1, BBC specials 1980-82, Panorama 1982-; broadcaster BBC World Service (in French) CBC and French TV; *Recreations* tennis, skiing, hill walking; *Clubs* Garrick, OBFC; *Style—* Fred Emery, Esq; 5 Woodsyre, London SE26 6SS; BBC TV, Wood Lane, London W12 7RJ (☎ 081 576 1953)

EMERY, George Edward; CB (1980); s of Frederick Arthur Emery (d 1930), and Florence Emery; *b* 2 March 1920; *Educ* Bemrose Sch Derby; *m* 1946, Margaret, *née* Rice; 2 da; *Career* under sec MOD 1973; dir-gen Defence Accounts (MOD) 1973-80; ret; *Recreations* gardening, amateur dramatics; *Style—* George Emery, Esq, CB; 3 The Orchard, Freshford, Bath (☎ 0225 723561)

EMERY, Gordon Haig; CBE; s of Frank Milwain Emery (d 1947), of Stockport, Cheshire, and Alice, *née* Harrison (d 1919); *b* 11 Nov 1918; *Educ* Manchester Coll of Tech; *m* 1, 1947 (m dis); 2 da (Michelle b 1966, Louise b 1975), 1 adopted da (Joanne(Ms Aylmer) b 1965); m 2, 29 Aug 1980, Josephine Angela, da of John Arthur Thomas (d 1974), of Prestbury, Cheshire; *Career* TA 1939, BEF France 1939-40 and Dunkirk 1940, 8 Army 42 Div 1942-47 in N Africa, Alamein, Tobruk and Tripoli; chm Gordon Emery Gp (bldg contractors, devpt and resource mgmnt): Gordon Emery Ltd, Emery (estate agents) Ltd, Emery Farm Estates Ltd, D & G Emery Ltd, GHE Ltd, Fog Lane Properties Ltd, Hampson and Kemp Ltd, Gordon Emery Inc (USA), Kingfisher Oil Co Ltd, Gold Investmts (Yukon) Ltd; involved with: Stockport Lad's Club 1957 (vice chm 1980), Pendlebury Charitable Tst 1958, Centurion Lacrosse Club 1968, Outward Bound Assoc 1973, Churchill Club 1976, NW Industl Cncl 1979, Manchester Literary and Philosophical Soc 1979, Halle Soc (patron) 1984, NW Regnl Health Authy 1985, Fedn of Boys Clubs 1985, Manchester Young Con's (pres) 1985-87; Stockport Con Assoc: joined 1954, chm 1960-62, pres 1978-81, vice chm 1985-; cncllr Stockport Borough Cncl 1957-63, govr Stockport Sch 1978-88; memb Manchester C of C 1975-, Aims of Indust 1976; FInstD 1979; *Recreations* tennis, swimming, golf; *Clubs* Carlton, St James's (Manchester); *Style—* Gordon Emery, Esq, CBE; 184 Heaton Moor Road, Heaton Moor, Stockport, Cheshire SK4 4DU (☎ 061 432 3460/1713, fax 061 431 0786, car 0860 815 790, telex 666514)

EMERY, John; s of John Emery (d 1981), of Carshalton, Surrey, and Florence Margaret, *née* Hankins; *b* 2 Aug 1938; *Educ* Heath Clark GS, Regent St Poly, City & Guilds (final exam), Inst of Mgmnt Studies (cert in supervisory mgmnt studies); *m* Oct 14 1961, Heather, da of James Lamont; 1 s (Andrew John b 18 July 1977), 1 da (Lisa Jane b 6 July 1971); *Career* Nat Serv litho-camera operator 89 Field Survey Sqdn RE later i/c Photographic Unit operating from The Survey of Kenya Govt offices; professional photographer; served apprenticeship with Fox Photos London, photographic printer Carlton Artists 1959-61, printer/photographer Streets Advertising 1961, chief photographer and mangr Streets Photographic Unit; currently photo-servs mangr Associated Newspapers Ltd (joined 1969 as dep darkroom mangr); FBIPP 1974; *Recreations* shooting, golf, swimming, archery; *Style—* John Emery, Esq; 12 Rutherwyke Close, Stoneleigh, Epsom, Surrey KT17 2NB (☎ 081 393 5451); Associated Newspapers Ltd, Northcliffe House, 2 Derry St, Kensington W8 5TT (☎ 071 938 6391, fax 071 937 3073)

EMERY, Dr (Frank) Michael; s of Rev Frank Emery, of Holyhead, Gwynedd, and Catherine, *née* Smith; *b* 25 April 1937; *Educ* Ellesmere Coll, St Marys Hosp Univ of London (MB BS, DA); *m* 5 Oct 1968, Margaret Anne (Poppy), da of Brig John Ridgeway Reynolds CIE, OBE; 2 da (Kathryn b 1974, Helen b 1977); *Career* sr registrar in anaesthesia Royal Free Hosp 1970-72, unit gen mangr Leighton Hosp Crewe 1985-88 (conslt anaesthetist 1972-, dir pain relief serv 1974-); memb Crewe Dis Health Authy, former Parish Cncllr Acton Nantwich; memb: BMA 1970, Intensive Care Soc 1971, IPS of GB and I 1978, IASP 1988; MRCS, LRCP, FFARCS; *Recreations* tennis, badminton, hockey, sheep breeding; *Style—* Dr Michael Emery; Whitehaven, Whitehaven Lane, Burland, Nantwich, Cheshire CW5 8NH (☎ 0270 74229); Casa Gaynor, Mojacar, Spain; Leighton Hospital, Leighton, Crewe CW1 4QP (☎ 0272 255141, car 0860 527642)

EMERY, Dr Paul; s of Lt Cdr Dr Leonard Lesley Emery RNVR, of Cardiff, and Beryl Olive, *née* Davis; *b* 30 Nov 1952; *Educ* Cardiff HS, Churchill Coll Cambridge (MB BChir, MA, MD), Guys Hosp; *m* 19 July 1980, Shirley Macdonald, da of Sub Lt David Morton Bayne RNVR; 2 da (Lorna Megan b 25 Oct 1987, Joanna Louise b 17 March 1989); *Career* SHO Guys Brompton, med registrar Guys Lewisham 1980, sr registrar Guys 1983, head of rheumatology Walter Eliza Hall and asst physician Royal Melbourne Hosp 1985, conslt and sr lectr Dept of Rheumatology Univ of Birmingham 1988; memb: Br Soc of Rheumatology, Br Soc Immunology, BMA; MRCP 1979; *Books* contrib: The Role of Cytokines in Rheumatological Inflammation Autoimmunregation and Autoimmune Disease (1987), Autoimmune Reactions to D-penicillamine Autoimmun Toxicol (1989), Rheumatoid Arthritis Oxford Textbook of

Renal Medicine (1990); *Recreations* golf, squash; *Clubs* Edgbaston Priory, Edgbaston Golf; *Style*— Dr Paul Emery; 40 St Peters Road, Harborne, Birmingham (☎ 021 427 3793); Dept of Rheumatology, University of Birmingham, Edgbaston, Birmingham B15 2TT (☎ 021 414 6778)

EMERY, Sir Peter Frank Hannibal; MP (C) Honiton 1967-; s of Frank George Emery (d 1960), of Highgate; *b* 27 Feb 1926; *Educ* Scotch Plains N J USA, Oriel Coll Oxford; *m* 1, 1954 (m dis), Elizabeth, da of Philip Nicholson, of Dunsa House, Endsor, Derbys; 1 s, 1 da; m 2, 1972, Elizabeth, yst da of G J R Monnington, of Upper Stonham, Lewes, Sussex; 1 s, 1 da; *Career* MP (C) Reading 1959-66; PPS to successive Mins of State for Foreign Affrs incl: Rt Hon David Ormsby-Gore (later 5 Lord Harlech) 1960-61, Rt Hon Joseph Godber (later Lord Godber of Willington) 1961-63; oppn front bench spokesman Treasy Economics and Trade 1964-66, Parly under sec DTI 1972-74, Energy 1974; jt fndr and first sec Bow Gp, chm Select Ctee Procedure, memb Select Ctee Industry and Trade; chm: Shenley Trust Services Ltd, Wing law Group; delegate to Cncl of Europe & WEU 1964-66 and 1970-72, memb North Atlantic Assembly 1983-, chm Science & Technical Ctee NAA 1986-; capt House of Commons Bridge Team; FInstPS; kt 1981; *Recreations* skiing, tennis, theatre, bridge, travel; *Clubs* Leander, Carlton, Turf, Portland; *Style*— Sir Peter Emery, MP; 8 Ponsonby Terrace, London SW1 (☎ 071 222 6666); Tytherleigh Manor, nr Axminster, Devon EX13 7BD (☎ 0460 20309); office: 40 Park St, London W1Y 3PF (☎ 071 437 6666, fax 493-5096)

EMERY-WALLIS, Frederick Alfred John; DL; s of Frederick Henry Wallis (d 1949), and Lillian Grace Emery *née* Coles (d 1963); *b* 11 May 1927; *Educ* Blake's Acad Portsmouth; *m* 22 Aug 1960, Solange, da of William Victor Randall (d 1957), of Mitcham, Surrey; 2 da (Selina b 4 April 1963, Jennette b 5 March 1971); *Career* SCU4 RCS Middle East Radio Security 1945-48; Portsmouth CC: cncllr 1961-74, Lord Mayor 1968-69, Alderman 1969-74; Hampshire CC: cncllr 1973-, vice chm 1975-76, ldr 1976-; chm Southern Tourist Bd 1976-88 (vice pres 1988-); Assoc of CCs: memb Exec Ctee and Policy Ctee, chm ACC Recreation Ctee 1982-85; memb Community Services Ctee 1990-; govr Portsmouth Poly; chm: Hampshire Archives Tst, New Theatre Royal Tst Portsmouth, govrs Portsmouth HS for Girls; tstee: Learning through Landscapes Tst 1990-, Mary Rose Tst 1980-90; RN Museum Portsmouth; dir: Warrior Preservation Tst, Bd of Welsh Nat Opear 1990-; chm Hampshire Sculpture Tst, memb Cncl of the Br Records Assoc 1979-, vice chm Hampshire Gdns Tst 1984-, memb Hampshire Buildings Preservation Tst 1976-, pres of the Friends of Portsmouth City Records Office 1988-; FSA, Hon FRIBA; *Recreations* music, book collecting; *Style*— Frederick Emery-Wallis, Esq, DL, FSA; Froddington, Craneswater Park, Portsmouth, Hampshire PO4 0NR (☎ 0705 731409); Hampshire County Council, The Castle, Winchester, Hampshire SO23 8UJ (☎ 0962 847943, fax 0962 67273, telex 477729)

EMLEY, Miles Lovelace Brereton; s of Col Derek Brereton Emley, OBE, of Tenny's Court, Marnhull, Sturminster Newton, Dorset, and Mary Georgina, *née* Lovelace; *b* 23 July 1949; *Educ* St Edward's Sch Oxford, Balliol Coll Oxford (MA); *m* 26 June 1976, Tessa Marcia Radclyffe, da of Radclyffe Edward Crichton Powell, MBE (d 1985); 2 s (Oliver b 1978, Alexander b 1982), 1 da (Katherine b 1980); *Career* dir: N M Rothschild & Sons Ltd 1982-89 (joined 1972), Virago Press Ltd 1988-90; md UBS Phillips & Drew Securities Ltd 1989-; Liveryman Worshipful Co of Leathersellers 1979; *Style*— Miles Emley, Esq; Whitehall House, Ashford Hill, Newbury, Berks (☎ 0635 268306); UBS Phillips & Drew, 100 Liverpool Street, London EC2 (☎ 071 901 3333)

EMLY, John Richard Keith; s of Charles Richard Lewis Emly (d 1975), of London, and Lillian Villette, *née* Jenner (d 1971); *b* 15 Sept 1941; *Educ* St Dunstan's Coll Catford; *m* 26 July 1969, Maria Joan, da of Frederic Jozef Jan Gumosz (d 1964), of Catford; 2 s (Timothy b 1978, Benjamin b 1980), 2 da (Gillian b 1972, Sarah b 1974); *Career* jt investmt mangr The Law Debenture Corpn Ltd 1971-1975 (joined 1960), dir Robert Fleming Investmt Mgmnt Ltd 1978-88, main bd dir Robert Fleming Hldgs Ltd 1985- (joined 1975), dir Robert Fleming Asset Mgmnt Ltd 1988-, dir Fleming Investmt Mgmnt Ltd 1988-; memb FRICS 1972, AMSIA; *Recreations* family life; *Style*— John Emly, Esq; Robert Fleming Holdings Ltd, 25 Copthall Avenue, London EC2R 7DR (☎ 071 638 5858, fax 071 588 7219, telex 297451)

EMLYN, Viscount; Colin Robert Vaughan Campbell; s (by 1 m) and h of 6 Earl Cawdor; *b* 30 June 1962; *Educ* Eton, St Peter's Coll Oxford; *Style*— Viscount Emlyn; Cawdor Castle, Nairn, Scotland

EMMERSON, Ian Robert; s of late Robert Leslie Emmerson of Lincoln, and Ida Kathleen, *née* Marshall; *b* 18 Feb 1944; *Educ* City GS Lincoln; *m* 23 Nov 1968, Sheila Margaret, da of Ernest Raymond (Dick) Barber (d 1968); 2 s (Nathan Robert b 1972, Richard Ian b 1974); *Career* GPO 1960-83 (asst exec engr BT), currently dir Impsport (Lincoln) Ltd; pres Br Cycling Fedn, chm Velo Club Lincoln; memb: GB Nat Olympic Ctee, Cwlth Games Cncl for Eng, Exec Ctee Federation Internationale Amateur Cyclisme; sheriff of Lincoln 1990-91; *Recreations* cycling, photography, travel; *Style*— Ian Emmerson, Esq; 5 Larkin Avenue, Cherry Willingham, Lincoln LN3 4AZ (☎ 0522 750000); Impsport (Lincoln) Ltd, Whisby Way, Lincoln LN6 3LQ (☎ 0522 500505, fax 0522 500455)

EMMERSON, John Corti; s of Sir Harold Corti Emmerson, GCB, KCVO (d 1984), and Lucy Kathleen, *née* Humphreys (d 1989); *b* 10 Sept 1937; *Educ* Merchant Taylors', Magdalen Coll Oxford; *m* 30 Oct 1970, Pamela Anne, da of Lt-Col James Shaw, TD (d 1970); 1 s (Dominic b 1973), 1 da (Kate b 1975); *Career* Nat Serv, 2 Lt 4 Royal Tank Regt 1956-58, asst princ Air Ministry 1961-63; admitted slr 1967, ptnr McKenna & Co; dir Woodard Schs (Southern Div) Ltd; govr Ardingley Coll; *Recreations* fly-fishing; *Clubs* Brooks's; *Style*— John C Emmerson, Esq; Court Farm House, Wylye, Wilts; McKenna & Co, Mitre House, 160 Aldersgate St, London EC1 (☎ 071 606 9000)

EMMERSON, Prof (Alfred) Michael; s of William Emmerson, and Elsie, *née* Barratt; *b* 17 Oct 1937; *Educ* UCH Med Sch (MB BS); *m* 30 April 1966, Elizabeth Barbara Mary, da of Dr John Lawn (decd), of Binbrook, Lincolnshire; 1 s (Mark b 29 Sept 1972), 1 da (Catherine b 8 Jan 1971); *Career* Nat Serv class 1 mechanical engr and decoder RN 1957-59; trainee microbiologist UCH London 1966-73 (house offr 1965-66), conslt microbiologist Whittington Hosp London 1973-84, prof of clinical microbiology Royal Victoria Hosp Queen's Univ Belfast 1984-89, prof and head of dept Univ of Leicester 1989; chm Microbiology Advsy Ctee DHSS London, chm Br Standards Inst HCC/67 and CEN/TC 204, memb Assoc of Professors in Med Microbiology; Liveryman Worshipful Co of Apothecaries 1975; MRCS, LRCP, FRCPG, FRCPath, FFPath, fell Hunterian Soc 1975, scientific fell Zoological Soc 1975; *Books* The Microbiology and Treatment of Life Threatening Infections (1982); *Recreations* rugby, athletics, London and Belfast marathons; *Clubs* Leicester Football; *Style*— Prof Michael Emmerson; The Old Cottage, 30 Markfield Rd, Groby, Leicester LE6 0FL (☎ 0533 312111); 11 Southwood Mansions, Southwood Lane, Highgate, London N6 5SZ; Microbiology Department, Leicester University, PO Box 138, Medical Sciences Building, University Rd, Leicester LE1 9HN (☎ 0533 522951, fax 0533 523013)

EMMET, Hon Christopher Antony Robert; JP (W Sussex); eldest s of Baroness Emmet of Amberley (Life Peeress, d 1980), and Thomas Addis Emmet (d 1934); *b* 21 Nov 1925; *Educ* Ampleforth, Balliol Coll Oxford; *m* 22 July 1947, Lady Miranda Fitzalan Howard, *qv*; 1 s, 3 da; *Career* W Sussex cncllr (Pulborough) 1952-62; Cdre Arun Yacht Club Littlehampton 1972-73, pres Houghton Bridge and Dist Angling Soc 1960; *Recreations* sailing; *Style*— The Hon Christopher Emmet, JP; Seabeach House, Selhurst Park, Halnaker, Chichester, Sussex (☎ 0243 773156)

EMMET, Hon David Alastair Rennell; 2 s of Baroness Emmet of Amberley (Life Peeress, d 1980), and Thomas Addis Emmet (d 1934); *b* 31 Jan 1928; *Educ* Ampleforth, Worcester Coll Oxford; *m* 22 July 1967, Sylvia Delia, o da of late Willis Knowles, of Buenos Aires; 1 s, 1 da; *Career* memb Br Community Cncl Argentina 1964-68; FRGS; *Style*— The Hon David Emmet; El Aljibe, Garzon, Maldonado, Uruguay

EMMET, (Arthur) Maitland; MBE (1947), TD (1948); s of Rev C W Emmet (d 1923), of Univ Coll Oxford, and Gertrude Julia, *née* Weir (d 1972); *b* 15 July 1908; *Educ* Sherborne, Univ Coll Oxford (MA); *m* 26 April 1972, Emilie Catherine (Katie), da of Alfred Gough (d 1917), of Saffron Walden; *Career* cmmnd TA 1933, Capt 1938, Co Cdr 6 Bn Oxfordshire & Buckinghamshire Light Inf 1940-42, Sr Liaison Offr (Maj) 25 Indian Div 1942-45, Co Lt-Col St Edward's Sch CCF 1947-56; housemaster St Edward's Sch 1949-56 (asst master 1931-56), pt/t headmaster RAF Selection Bd 1957-79, examiner English language London Univ Examinations Bd 1957-79; hon treas 25 Indian Div Offrs Dining Club 1984- (hon sec 1947-84); Stamford Raffles award (Zoological Soc of London) 1981; rowing Univ of Oxford Trial Eights 1929 and 1930; Royal Entomological Soc: memb 1969-, vice pres 1980-81, hon fell 1984; memb: Linnean Soc, Br Entomological and Nat History Soc (pres 1971), Amateur Entomologists Soc (pres 1975); *Books* The Arakan Campaign of the 25th Indian Div (1947), The Smaller Moths of Essex (1981), The Larger Moths and Butterflies of Essex (with G A Pyman, 1985), The Moths and Butterflies of Great Britain and Ireland (ed and contrib 1976-); *Recreations* entomology; *Clubs* Leander; *Style*— Maitland Emmet, Esq, MBE, TD; Labrey Cottage, Victoria Gardens, Saffron Walden, Essex CB11 3AF (☎ 0799 23042)

EMMET, Lady Miranda Mary; *née* Fitzalan Howard; da of 3 Baron Howard of Glossop and sis of 17 Duke of Norfolk (raised to the rank of a Duke's da, 1975); *m* 22 July 1947, Hon Christopher Anthony Robert Emmet, *qv*; 1 s, 3 da; *Career* international judge of Arabian horses, past pres Arabian Horse Society; *Recreations* riding, long distance walking in the fells; *Style*— The Lady Miranda Emmet; Seabeach House, Selhurst Park, Halnaker, nr Chichester, W Sussex PO18 0LX (☎ 0243 773156)

EMMETT, Bryan David; s of Lilian, *née* Emmott (d 1957); *b* 15 Feb 1941; *Educ* Northern GS Portsmouth, Chislehurst & Sidcup and Tadcaster GS; *m* 25 Nov 1960, Moira, da of John Miller (d 1984), of Edinburgh; 1 s (Mark David b 1961); *Career* Miny of Labour and Nat Serv 1958-59, exec offr War Dept 1959-64, asst princ MOP 1965-69 (asst private sec 1968-69), princ Electricity Div DTI 1969-74; Dept of Energy: princ and private sec to Min of State 1974-75, asst sec and princ private sec to Sec of State 1975-76; asst sec Petroleum Engrg Div 1977-80, under sec and princ estab offr 1980-81, princ estab and finance offr 1981-82, chief exec Employment Div of MSC 1982-85, head of Energy Policy Div 1985- 86, head of Oil Div 1986-87; dir-gen Energy Efficiency Office 1987-88, chief exec Educn Assets Bd 1988-90, Dept of Energy 1990-91 (compulsory early retirement); *Recreations* national hunt racing, hacking, snooker; *Style*— Bryan Emmett, Esq; Hayside Farm, Low St, Sancton, E Yorkshire (☎ 0430 827552)

EMMS, David Acfield; s of Archibald George Emms (d 1975), of Lowestoft, Suffolk, and Winifred Gladys, *née* Richards (d 1979); *b* 16 Feb 1925; *Educ* Tonbridge, BNC Oxford (MA); *m* 8 Sept 1950, Pamela Baker, da of Edwin Leslie Speed (d 1970), of Jesmond, Newcastle upon Tyne; 3 s (John b 1952, Richard b 1959, Christopher b 1969), 1 da (Victoria b 1954); *Career* Capt Royal Indian Airborne Artillery 1943, Hon Col 39 (City of London) Signal Regt 1988-; asst master Uppingham Sch 1951-60; headmaster: Cranleigh Sch 1960-70, Sherborne Sch 1970-74; master Dulwich Coll 1975-86; chm: Headmasters' Conf 1984, Jt Educnl Tst 1987-; dir London House for Overseas Graduates 1987-, vice pres Ind Sch Careers Orgn 1973-; dep chm ESU 1983-89; govr: Bickley Park Sch 1978-81, St Felix Sch Southwold 1983-88, Feltonfleet Sch Cobham 1968-87, Tonbridge Sch (exec chm) 1988-, Brambletye Sch East Grinstead 1982-88, Portsmouth GS 1987-; dep pro chllr City Univ 1989-; Freeman City of London 1950, Master Worshipful Co of Skinners' 1987-88; FRSA 1988; *Publications* HMC Schools and British Industry (1981); *Recreations* radical gardening; *Clubs* Vincent's (Oxford), East India, Itchenor Sailing; *Style*— David Emms, Esq; The Director's Flat, London House for Overseas Graduates, Mecklenburgh Square, London WC1N 2AB (☎ 071 837 8888); Seaforth, Spinney Lane, Itchenor, nr Chichester, West Sussex PO20 7DJ

EMMS, Peter Anthony; s of Anthony Hubert Hamilton Emms, and Daphne, *née* Cooper-Lake; *b* 29 June 1949; *Educ* Stoneham GS Reading, City of London Poly (BA); *m* 6 Nov 1981, Susan Gwendolen, da of Harold Kemp; 1 s (Ben b 1975), 1 da (Joanna b 1977); *Career* exec dir mktg Allied Dunbar Assurance plc 1985-; FCII 1975; *Recreations* gardening, reading; *Style*— Peter Emms, Esq; Hatchgate End, Cockpole Green, Wargrave, Berks RG10 8NT; Allied Dunbar Assurance plc, Allied Dunbar Centre, Swindon, Wilts SN1 1EL (☎ 0793 514514)

EMPSON, Adm Sir (Leslie) Derek; GBE (1975), KCB (1973, CB 1969); s of Frank Harold Empson (d 1960), of Four Oaks, Warwickshire, and Madeleine Norah, *née* Burge; *b* 29 Oct 1918; *Educ* Eastbourne Coll, Clare Coll Cambridge; *m* 1958, Diana Elizabeth, da of P J Kelly, of London; 1 s, 1 da; *Career* joined RNVR 1940, served WWII pilot Fleet Air Arm, Cdr 1952, Capt 1957, naval asst to First Sea Lord 1957-59, Rear Adm 1967, flag offr Aircraft Carriers 1967-68, asst Chief of Naval Staff (Ops and Air) 1968-69, cdr Far East Fleet 1969-70, Vice Adm 1969, Second Sea Lord and Chief of Naval Personnel 1971-64, Adm 1972, C-in-C Naval Home Cmd and flag offr Portsmouth Area 1974-75, Flag ADC to HM The Queen 1974-75, ret 1976; Rear Adm of UK 1985-87, Vice Adm of UK 1987-89; conslt Thorn EMI Ltd 1976-86, chm Roymark Ltd 1983-, conslt Astra Holdings plc 1987-90; chm of govrs Eastbourne Coll 1972-89, chm Fedn Against Copyright Theft 1983-88; *Style*— Adm Sir Derek Empson, GBE, KCB; Deepdale, Hambledon, Hants; c/o Roymark Limited, Unit 224, Canalot Production Studios, 222 Kensal Road, London W10 5BN (☎ 081 968 6063)

EMSALL, Keith Fletcher; s of Harold (d 1946), of Manchester, and Lily Fletcher (d 1956); *b* 23 Feb 1937; *Educ* Stand GS Manchester; *m* 5 Oct 1963, Carol Ann Emsall, JP, da of Albert Lee, of Derbyshire; 2 da (Nicola b 1964, Claire b 1967); *Career* RAF 1955-57; retail mktg Mobil Oil Co 1958-90; memb: N Hertfordshire Dist Cncl 1978-86 and 1987- (chm 1984-85), Mgmnt Bd Motor and Cycle Trades Benevolent Fund 1983-89, Bd of Letchworth Garden City Corp 1989-; chm Ben Housing Assoc Ltd 1983-87, tstee Knebworth Tst 1984-85; *Recreations* golf, reading; *Style*— Keith F Emsall, Esq; 8 Field Lane, Letchworth, Herts SG6 3LE (☎ 674543)

EMSDEN, Kenneth Edward Clare; s of Lt-Col Leslie George Emsden OBE, JP (d 1974), of Verandah House, Clare, Suffolk, and Emma Nora, *née* Metcalfe (d 1967); *b* 15 July 1929; *Educ* Wellington Coll, Trinity Hall Cambridge; *m* 25 Aug 1956, Diana Mabel, da of Maj Colin Edward Arthur Grayling; 1 s (Peter Clare b 1961), 2 da (Jennifer Mary b 1959, Gillian Sarah b 1965); *Career* mangr Plastics Div Shell Chemical (UK) Ltd, dir Vencel Resil; Liveryman Worshipful Co of Horners; *Recreations* walking, sailing, gardening; *Style*— Kenneth Emsden, Esq; Gleanings, Spinney Lane, Rabley Heath, Welwyn, Herts AL6 9TF (☎ 0438 813391)

EMSLEY, Kenneth; s of Clifford Briggs Emsley, and Lily, *née* Goldsborough; *b* 7 Dec 1921; *Educ* Bingley GS, Loughborough Coll, St John's Coll Cambridge (MA), Univ of Newcastle upon Tyne (LLM); *m* 14 May 1959, Nancy Audrey, da of Alfred Ernest Slee; *Career* served WWII; chm Smith & Hardcastle Ltd 1955-65; painter of watercolour drawings and miniature paintings, author of books and articles, lectr in law, ret 1980; pres: The Br Watercolour Soc, The Soc of Miniaturists, The Bradford Arts Club until 1985 (former chm); memb: Cncl Yorks Archeaological Soc Leeds, Brontë Soc, Soc Authors; hon sec Wakefield Manorial Ct Rolls Series; FRSA 1945, FCCS 1957, ACIS 1970, MSEng 1948, PBWS 1985, PSM 1985, FRHistS 1989, FRGS 1989; *Books* Tyneside (with CM Fraser, 1973), Northumbria (with CM Fraser, 1979, rewritten 1989), The Courts of the County Palatine of Durham (1984), Wakefield Manorial Court Rolls (with CM Fraser, vol 1 1979 and vol 5 1987); *Recreations* formerly cricket, rugby, tennis; now bowls, art and music; *Clubs* The Bradford, Cambridge Union, Cambridge Univ Cricket; *Style*— Kenneth Emsley, Esq; 34 Nabwood Drive, Shipley, West Yorkshire BD18 4EL; The Yorkshire Archaeological Society, Claremont, Clarendon Rd, Leeds LS2 9NZ

EMSLIE, Hon Derek Robert Alexander; 2 s of Baron Emslie, MBE, PC, QC (Life Peer), *qv*; *b* 21 June 1949; *Educ* Edinburgh Acad, Trinity Coll Glenalmond, Gonville and Caius Coll Cambridge (BA), Edinburgh Univ (LLB); *m* 1974, Elizabeth Jane Cameron, da of Andrew Maclaren Carstairs; 2 children; *Career* advocate; standing jr counsel DHSS 1979-; *Clubs* Hawks; *Style*— The Hon Derek Emslie; 35 Ann St, Edinburgh EH4 1PL (☎ 031 332 6648)

EMSLIE, Baron (Life Peer UK 1979), of Potterton, in the District of Gordon; George Carlyle Emslie; MBE (1946), PC (1972); s of Alexander Emslie, and Jessie Blair Emslie; *b* 6 Dec 1919; *Educ* The HS of Glasgow, Univ of Glasgow (MA, LLB); *m* 1942, Lilias Ann Mailer, da of Robert Hannington, of Glasgow; 3 s (Hon Nigel, Hon Derek, Hon Richard); *Career* advocate Scot 1948, QC Scot 1957, sheriff of Perth and Angus 1963-66, dean of Faculty of Advocates 1965-70, senator of the Coll of Justice, a lord of session with title Lord Emslie 1970, lord justice gen of Scotland and lord pres of the Ct of Session 1972 Hon LLD Univ of Glasgow 1988; FRSE; *Recreations* golf; *Clubs* New (Edinburgh); *Style*— The Rt Hon Lord Emslie, MBE, PC, FRSE; 47 Heriot Row, Edinburgh (☎ 031 225 3657)

EMSLIE, Hon (George) Nigel Hannington; eldest s of Baron Emslie, MBE, PC (Life Peer), *qv*; *b* 1947; *Educ* Edinburgh Acad, Trinity Coll Glenalmond, Gonville and Caius Coll Cambridge (BA), Edinburgh Univ (LLB); *m* 1973, Heather Ann, da of Arthur Frank Davis, of Bristol; issue; *Career* QC; *Style*— Nigel Emslie; 20 Inverleith Place, Edinburgh EH3 5QB

EMSLIE, Hon Richard Hannington; 3 and yst s of Baron Emslie, MBE, PC (Life Peer), *qv*; *b* 28 July 1957; *Educ* Edinburgh Acad, Trinity Coll Glenalmond, Gonville and Caius Coll Cambridge (BA); *Career* wildlife biologist, res into applied grazing ecology of Umfulozi Game Reserve Zululand for PhD Univ of Witwatersrand Johannesberg SA; *Recreations* football, hockey, golf, skiing, squash, tennis, hypnosis, photography, bird-watching; *Clubs* Edinburgh Ski, Umfolozi Country; *Style*— The Hon Richard Emslie; c/o Resource Ecology Group, Botany Department, Witwatersrand University, 1 Jan Smuts Ave, Jo'burg 2001, S Africa; 47 Heriot Row, Edinburgh EH3 6EX (☎ 031 225 3657)

EMSLIE-SMITH, Dr Donald; s of Lt Col Harry Emslie-Smith (d 1946), of Dunfermline, and Maribel, *née* Milne (d 1952); *b* 12 April 1922; *Educ* Trinity Coll, Glenalmond, Univ of Aberdeen (MD ChB); *m* 19 Sept 1959, Ann Elizabeth, da of Col Thomas Milne, CB, DSO, of Milford-on-Sea, Hants; 1 s (Alistair b 1960), 1 da (Sophie b 1963); *Career* Flt Lt (med) RAFVR UK, Egypt and Sudan 1946-48; registrar in cardiology Dundee Teaching Hosps 1953-54, E Wilson Meml res fell Baker Inst Melbourne 1955-56, tutor and sr registrar Royal Postgrad Med Sch and Hammersmith Hosp 1958-61; sr lectr in med: Univ of St Andrews 1961-67, Univ of Dundee 1967-71 (reader 1971-87, hon fell 1989); hon conslt cardiologist Tayside Health Bd 1961-87; sr memb Assoc of Physicians of GB and Ireland (memb Exec Ctee 1977-80); memb professional socs incl: Br Cardiac Soc (chm 1987), Scottish Soc of Physicians, Harveian Soc of Edinburgh (pres 1986-87 and Harveian Orator); SBStJ; FRCP, FRCPE, FSA (Scot); *Books* Text book of Physiology (8-11 edns, jt ed), Accidental Hypothermia (1977), chapters in med text books and papers in med jls mainly on cardiac electrophysiology and hypothermia; *Recreations* music, fishing, sailing; *Clubs* Flyfishers, Royal Lymington Yacht; *Style*— Dr Donald Emslie-Smith; 48 Seafield Road, Broughty Ferry, Angus DD5 3AN; c/o Dept of Medicine, The University, Dundee DD1 4HN

EMSON, Colin Jack; s of Alfred Jack Emson, of Ashford, Kent, and Rose Florence Jobson (d 1987); *b* 25 July 1941; *Educ* Maidstone GS; *m* 14 Sept 1974, Jennifer Claire, da of Lt-Col James Lynch, of Vancouver, Canada; 2 s (Alexander Chase b 1976, Henry James b 1980), 2 da (Annabel Christina b 1975, Camilla Rose b 1985); *Career* fndr ptnr Emson & Dudley 1966-79; md Robert Fraser & Partners Ltd (merchant bankers) 1979-; *Recreations* polo, skiing, tennis; *Clubs* Turf, Naval and Military, Cowdray Park Polo, St Moritz Tobogganing; *Style*— Colin J Emson, Esq; Robert Fraser & Partners Ltd, 29 Albemarle St, London W1 (☎ 071 493 3211)

EMSON, Brig James Bryce; CBE (1986); s of Capt Frederick James Emson, MC (d 1944), of Home Farm, Babraham, nr Cambridge; *b* 14 July 1938; *Educ* Felsted Sch, Nat Def Coll; *m* 24 Jan 1969, Suzanne Pauline, da of Frederick Anthony Evans, CVO, of Bamber Cottage, Lower Froyle, Alton, Hants; 2 s (Benjamin b 1972, Rupert b 1974); *Career* cmmnd: Parachute Regt 1958, The Life Guards 1981-83, Batus 1983-84, Household Cavalry 1986-87; dir Doctrine (Army) 1987-89, asst cmdt RMA Sandhurst 1990-; govr Welbeck Coll 1987-89; *Books* Dinosaurs To Defence (1986); *Recreations* gardening, skiing, shooting, DIY poetry; *Clubs* Cavalry and Guards; *Style*— Brig James Emson, CBE; RMA Sandhurst, Camberley, Surrey, GU15 4PQ; The Old Rectory, Holwell, nr Sherbourne, Dorset DT9 5LB (☎ 0963 23 312); 30 Beaufoy House, Regents Bridge Gdns, Vauxhall, London; c/o Regimental Headquarters, Household Cavalry, Horse Guards, Whitehall, London (☎ 071 930 4466 ext 2391)

EMSON, Air Marshal Sir Reginald Herbert Embleton; KBE (1966, CBE 1946), CB (1959), AFC (1941); s of Francis Reginald Emson, of Hitcham, Bucks; *b* 11 Jan 1912; *Educ* Christ's Hosp, RAF Coll Cranwell; *m* 1934, Doreen Marjory, da of Hugh Duke, of Holyport, Maidenhead, Berks 2 s, 2 da; *Career* joined RAF 1931, served WWII in Aeroplane Armament Experimental Establishment Gunnery Research Unit Exeter, Fighter Cmmd HQ, Centl Fighter Estab; Gp Capt 1943, dir Armament Research and Devpt (Air) Miny of Supply 1956-59; Air Cdre 1958, Cmdr RAF and Air Attaché Br Defence Staffs Washington 1961-63, Air Vice-Marshal 1962, Asst Chief of Air Staff (Operational Requirements) Air Miny 1963, MOD (RAF) 1964-66, Dep Chief of Air Staff 1966-67, Air Marshal 1966, Inspector-Gen RAF 1967-69, ret; *Clubs* RAF; *Style*— Air Marshal Sir Reginald Emson, KBE, CB, AFC; Vor Cottage, Holyport, Maidenhead, Berks (☎ 0628 21992)

ENDACOTT, Charles George; s of John Kinsman Endacott, of London, and Rita, *née* Ellul; *b* 24 Sept 1950; *Educ* St John's Coll Southsea; *m* 1973 (m dis 1983), Hazel, *née* Dawnshort; 1 da (Natalie b 1 Aug 1979); partner, Barbara Joan Jacobs; *Career* messenger E Allan Cooper Advertising 1967-68, studio jr J L Lakings Studio 1968-69, jr designer SF & Partner Advertising 1969-70, freelance designer and visualiser 1970-71, sole proprietor RJB Associates (design and promotions conslts) 1976-83 (fndr ptnr 1971-76), chm RJB Manpower Ltd 1979-83, md Endacott RJB Ltd 1983-89; chm RJB Group Ltd (chm/md various subsids) 1989-; memb: Inst Sales Promotion, Sales Promotion Conslts Assoc; *Recreations* tennis, classic cars, angling; *Clubs* David Lloyd Slazenger, Feltham Piscatorial Soc; *Style*— Charles Endacott, Esq; RJB Group Ltd, 17-18 Great Poulteney St, London W1R 3DG (☎ 071 439 8591, fax 071 437 2447, car 0860 301012)

ENDACOTT, Patricia Ann (Pat); da of William Frederick Williams (d 1985), and Bertha Emma, *née* Sanderson; *b* 5 March 1946; *Educ* Newmarket GS, Univ of Sussex (BSc); *m* 17 June 1972 (m dis 1980), Michael John Endacott, s of Alfred John Endacott; *Career* programmer Pye of Cambridge Ltd 1968-71, programmer Standard Telephones and Cables Ltd 1971-72; Texas Instruments Ltd; customer serv (Croydon) 1972-76, mangr communications (ISD) 1976-80, mangr field serv (DSD) 1980-82; Prime Computer: dir customer serv (UK Ltd) 1982-85, mktg mangr products and systems (EMEA) 1985-86, dir UK software devpt (UK R & D Ltd) 1986-; MInstD 1988; *Recreations* running, reading, music; *Style*— Ms Pat Endacott; Prime Computer (R & D) Ltd, Willen Lake, Milton Keynes MK15 ODB (☎ 0908 666622, fax 0908 674406, car 0836 310626, telex 826157 PRMSMD G)

ENDERBY, (George Edward) Hale; s of George Alfred Enderby (d 1945) of Boston, Lincolnshire, and Gertrude, *née* Hale (d 1930); *b* 9 June 1915; *Educ* Kingswood Sch Bath, St John's Coll Cambridge (MA), Guy's Hosp London (MB BChir Cambridge); *m* 22 June 1940, Dorothy Frances, da of Arthur Watson Grocock (d 1957), of Boston, Lincolnshire; 1 s (David Hale b 1942), 2 da (Diana Frances b 1944, Angela Jane b 1946); *Career* conslt anaesthetist: Maxillo-Facial & Jaw Unit Rooksdown House Basingstoke 1944-50, Met ENT Hosp 1948-68, Royal Nat Orthopaedic Hosp 1948-54, Queen Victoria Hosp E Grinstead 1950-80; dir Collsurg Services Ltd 1979-; FFARCS 1973-83 (memb Bd, examiner for fellowships 1975-82, Faculty medal 1986), pres anaesthetics section RSM 1981-82; *Recreations* golf; *Clubs* Oxford and Cambridge, Royal Ashdown Forest Golf; *Style*— Hale Enderby, Esq; Furzefield Dormans Park, East Grinstead RH19 3NU (☎ 0342 87255); 149 Harley Street, London W1N 2DE (☎ 071 935 4444)

ENDFIELD, Cyril (Cy); s of Benjamin Endfield (d 1954), of Scranton, PA, USA, and Lena, *née* Raker (d 1986); *b* 10 Nov 1914; *Educ* Yale Univ USA; *m* 1956, Maureen Burgoyne, da of Charles Frederick Burgoyne Forshar; 2 da (Suzanne b 1 Oct 1957, Eden b 21 Oct 1960); *Career* War Serv US Army 1943-45; film dir MGM Studios Hollywood 1942; dir and writer: Argyll Secrets, radio scripts for Orson Welles, Edmund O'Brien and Robert Taylor 1946, wrote Underworld Story and Sound of Fury 1950-51, began writing, directing and producing in Eng 1952-; films incl: Hell Drivers (1956), Zulu (1964), Sands of Kalahari (1965); dir stage run Come Blow Your Horn 1963-56, granted patent for original chess-set design as official commemorative set for Spassky-Fisher World Championship 1972, invented small word processor The Microwriter 1978 (further developed as portable pocket data device call Agenda); *awards* BAFTA shortlist nomination (for Sound of Fury) 1952, finalist Prince of Wales award for Industl Innovation (Tomorrow's World, for microwriter invention) 1981, Br Design Cncl award for Product Design (for Agenda) 1990; memb Screen Directors Guild of America 1949-, PRS; *Books* CY Endfield's Entertaining Card Magic (vols 1-3, 1954, 1955 and 1956), Zulu Dawn (1979); *Recreations* magic, squash; *Clubs* Yale (NY City), Hurlingham; *Style*— Cy Endfield, Esq; c/o Microwriter Systems Plc, 2 Wandle Way, Willow Lane, Mitcham, Surrey CR4 4NA

ENERGLYN, Baroness; Jeanie Thompson; da of John Miller, of Cardiff; *m* 15 March 1941, Baron Energlyn, DL (d 1985; Life Peer UK 1968); *Style*— The Rt Hon Lady Energlyn; 7 The Dentons, Denton Rd, Eastbourne, East Sussex BN20 7SW

ENFIELD, Viscount; William Robert Byng; s and h of 8 Earl of Strafford by his 1 wife, Jennifer Mary Denise, *née* May; *b* 10 May 1964; *Educ* Winchester, Durham Univ; *Style*— Viscount Enfield

ENGEL, David Jonathan; s of Felix Benjamin Engel, of Moniaive, Thornhill, Dumfries-shire, and Elizabeth Ann Helen, *née* Gaskell; *b* 13 Dec 1957; *Educ* Eton, Trinity Coll Oxford (BA); *m* 2 June 1990, Fiona Jane, da of Roger Cooper, of Oxshott, Surrey; *Career* copywriter Zetland Advertising 1981-84, sr copywriter Yellowhammer plc 1984-89, gp creative dir Young & Rubicam UK Ltd 1989-; *Recreations* skiing, squash, windsurfing; *Clubs* Lansdowne, Groucho; *Style*— David Engel, Esq; 79 Horder Road, London SW6

ENGEL, Matthew Lewis; s of Max David Engel, of Northampton, and Betty Ruth, *née* Lesser; *b* 11 June 1951; *Educ* Carmel Coll, Univ of Manchester (BA Econ); *m* 27 Oct 1990, Hilary, da of late Laurence Davies; *Career* reporter; Northampton Chronicle and Echo 1972-75, Reuters 1977-79; The Guardian: joined 1979, cricket corr 1982-87, feature writer, sports columnist and occasional foreign corr 1987-; winner Granada Sportswriter of the Year 1985, commended at Br Sports Journalism awards 1987; *Books* Ashes (1985), The Guardian Book of Cricket (ed, 1986), Sportswriter's Eye (1989), The Sportspages Almanac (ed, 1989, 1990); *Recreations* not writing, not watching sport, gardening theoretically, playing pinball; *Clubs* Northamptonshire County Cricket (vice pres); *Style*— Matthew Engel, Esq; The Guardian, 119 Farringdon Rd, London EC1R 3ER (☎ 071 278 2332)

ENGELMAN, Philip; s of Hyman Engelman, of London, and Freda Rita, *née* Jackson; *b* 25 Jan 1955; *Educ* Hasmonean GS London, UCL (LLB); *m* Diane Mary, da of James Craig Rocks, of Essex; 1 da (Rachael Abigail b 4 April 1984); *Career* called to the Bar Grays Inn 1979; memb: Bar Eng and Wales, Ctee Admin Law Bar Assoc 1989-, Eng Speaking Union debating tour USA 1977, pres UCL Union 1976-77; *Recreations* theatre, food & wine, fell walking, socialising; *Clubs* English Speaking Union; *Style*— Philip Engelman, Esq; Cloisters, Temple, London EC4 (☎ 071 583 0303, fax 071 583 2254)

ENGESET, Jetmund; s of Arne Kaare Engeset (d 1973), and Marta, *née* Birkeland; *b* 22 July 1938; *Educ* Slemdal and Ris Skoler Oslo Norway, Univ of Aberdeen (MB ChB, ChM); *m* 3 June 1966, Anne Graeme, da of Allan Graeme Robertson (d 1946); 2 da (Anne-Marie, Nina Katrine); *Career* sr lectr Univ of Aberdeen 1974-87, surgn to HM The Queen in Scot 1985-, conslt surgn Grampian Health Bd 1987- (hon conslt surgn 1974-87); FRCSEd 1970, FRCS (Glas) 1982; *Recreations* skiing, squash, angling, gardening; *Style*— Jetmund Engeset, Esq; Pine Lodge, 315 North Deeside Rd, Milltimber, Aberdeen (☎ 0224 733753); Aberdeen Royal Infirmary, Foresterhill, Aberdeen (☎ 0224 681818)

ENGLAND, Glyn; JP; *b* 19 April 1921; *Educ* Penarth Co Sch, QMC, LSE; *m* 1942, Tania, *née* Reichenbach; 2 da; *Career* served WW II 1942-47; chief operations engr CEBG 1966-71, dir-gen SW Region 1971-73, chm SW Electricity Bd 1973-77, chm Centl Electricity Generating Bd 1977-82 (p/t memb 1975-77); non-exec dir F H Lloyd Hldgs 1982-87; non-exec dir Triplex Lloyd plc 1987-90; conslt to World Bank, chm Cncl for Environmental Conservation 1983-88, dir UK Centre for Econ and Enviromental Devpt 1984-, chm: Dartington Inst 1985-, chm Woodlands Initiatives Ltd 1989-; Freeman City of London; Hon DSc Univ of Bath; CBIM, FEng, FIEE,

FIMechE; *Recreations* actively enjoying the countryside; *Style—* Glyn England, Esq, JP; Woodbridge Farm, Ubley, Bristol (☎ 0761 62479)

ENGLE, Sir George Lawrence Jose; KCB (1983, CB 1976), QC (1983); *b* 13 Sept 1926; *Educ* Charterhouse, Ch Ch Oxford; *m* 1956, Irene, da of Heinz Lachmann (d 1971); 3 da; *Career* called to the Bar Lincoln's Inn 1953, in practice 1953-57 (bencher 1 entered Parly Counsel Office 1957, seconded as first Parly counsel to Fed Govt of Nigeria 1965-67, Parly counsel 1970-80, with Law Cmmn 1971-73, second Parly counsel 1980-81, first Parly counsel 1981-86; pres Cwlth Assoc of Legve Cncl 1983-86; *Publications* Law for Landladies (1955), Ideas (contrib, 1954), O Rare Hoffnung (contrib, 1960), Oxford Companion to English Literature (contrib, 1985), Cross on Statutory Interpretation (co-ed 2nd edn, 1987); *Style—* Sir George Engle, KCB, QC; 32 Wood Lane, Highgate, London N6 5UB (☎ 081 340 9750)

ENGLEDON, Geoffrey; MBE (1982); s of William Engledon, of Birmingham, and Barbara, *née* Wild; *b* 20 May 1936; *Educ* King Edwards Sch Birmingham, Aston Univ (BSc); *m* 12 Aug 1961, Anne Lettice Flora Louise, da of Harry Higton BEM, of Erdington, Birminghan; 1 s (Alex Harry); *Career* former tech dir: Thermalite Hldgs, currently tech dir Bromley Park Ltd; *Recreations* fly-fishing, model making, reading, gardening; *Clubs* Sloane, Royal Over-Seas; *Style—* Geoffrey Engledon, Esq; 31 New Road, Water Orton, Birmingham B46 1QP; Bromley Park Ltd, Water Court, 10A St Pauls Square, Briminghan B3 1QU (☎ 021 233 0058, fax : 021 233 0134)

ENGLEHART, Robert Michael; QC (1986); s of G A F Englehart (d 1969), of London, and of K P Englehart, *née* Harvey (d 1973); *b* 1 Oct 1943; *Educ* St Edward's Sch Oxford, Trinity Coll Oxford (MA), Harvard Law Sch (LLM), Bologna Centre; *m* 2 Jan 1971, Rosalina Mary, da of L A Foster, of Greatham Manor, Sussex; 1 s (Oliver b 1982), 2 da (Alice b 1976, Lucinda b 1978); *Career* assistente Univ of Florence 1967-68, called to the Bar Middle Temple 1969-, rec of the Crown Ct 1987-; chm London Common Law and Commercial Bar Assoc 1989; *Books* Il Controllo Giudiziario: a Comparative Study in Civil Procedure (contrib 1968); *Recreations* shooting, cricket, windsurfing; *Clubs* MCC; *Style—* Robert Englehart, Esq, QC; 2 Hare Court, Temple, London EC4Y 7BH (☎ 071 583 1770, fax 071 583 9269)

ENGLEHEART, Henry Francis Arnold; DL (Suffolk, 1988); s of Francis Henry Arnold Engleheart (d 1963), of The Priory, Stoke by Nayland, Suffolk, and Filumena Mary, *née* Mayne (d 1983); *b* 18 March 1930; *Educ* Ampleforth, Downing Coll Cambridge (MA); *m* 9 June 1979, Victoria, da of Maj Ian Maitland Pelham Burn (d 1985), of Elenge Plat, Colgate, Horsham, Sussex; 1 s (John b 22 Oct 1981), 2 da (Lucy b 8 May 1980, Mary b 28 April 1985); *Career* land agent and chartered surveyor 1955-62, farmer 1957-; chm Suffolk Preservation Soc 1969-72; memb: Melford RDC 1964-74, Babergh DC 1973- (chm 1979-82), High Sheriff of Suffolk 1986; RICS 1956; *Style—* Henry Engleheart, Esq, DL; The Priory, Stoke by Nayland, Suffolk CO6 4RL (☎ 0206 262 216)

ENGLISH, Anthony Charles; s of Wing Cdr R G English, DFC, of St Marys, Sheringham, Norfolk, and Elizabeth, *née* Gilfillan; *b* 28 Nov 1946; *Educ* Brighton Coll, Angers Univ; *m* 1, Feb 1974 (m dis 1980), Jane; 2 s (Toby John Richard b 2 Aug 1977, Berry Charles b 10 June 1979); m 2, 4 May 1988, Sarah-Jane, da of Maj Bruce Urquhart; *Career* currently chm Eng White Shipping Ltd; currently dir: Eng White Hldgs Ltd, TSR Leasing Ltd; AICS 1969; *Recreations* golf, shooting, skiing, tennis; *Clubs* Royal Wimbledon Golf; *Style—* Anthony English, Esq; Worlds End Cottage, Cobham, Surrey KT11 1AG (☎ 0932 63463); 3 St Marks Place, London SW19 (☎ 081 879 7966, telex 8811781, fax 081 947 3555)

ENGLISH, Arthur Leslie Norman; s of Walter Frederich English (d 1978), of Aldershot, and Ethel Parsons (d 1975); *b* 9 May 1919; *Educ* State Sch Aldershot, West End Boys; *m* 1, 1 Feb 1974, Ivy (d 1975), da of late John Martin; 1 s (Anthony b 16 Nov 1942), 1 da (Ann faith b 13 Nov 1941); m 2, 27 July 1977 (m dis 1984), Teresa Avis, da of Alan Mann; *Career* served WWII 1939-46, Royal Hampshire Regt 9 Hamshires 15 RAC, 143 RAG gunnery instructor (tanks) Lulworth, 2 Army Reconaissance Unit Europe, 4/7 Dragoon 79 Reconaissance; actor Windwmill Theatre 1949-51, Royal Variety performances 1952-82; TV: St Pancras Town Hall, Variety, Looks Familiar, Not In Front of the Children, Beauty Box, Are You Being Served, Ghost of Motley, In Sickness and In Health; Freeman: City of London 1986, Borough of Rushmoor 1990; memb Grand Order of Water Rats 1970; pres Aldershot FC; *Books* Through The Mill and Beyond (1984); *Clubs* Royal Aldershot Officers, Rotary, Conservative; *Style—* Arthur English, Esq; 139 Vale Rd, Ash Vale, nr Aldershot, Hants GU12 5HX (☎ 0252 21989)

ENGLISH, Cyril; s of Joseph English, and Mary Hannah English; *b* 18 Feb 1923; *Educ* Ashton-under-Lyne GS; *m* 1945, Mary Brockbank; 2 da; *Career* Nationwide Anglia Building Soc: asst sec 1961, asst gen mangr 1967, gen mangr 1971, dep chief gen mangr 1974, dir 1978-90, chief gen mangr 1981-85, dep chm 1989-90; chm Nationwide Housing Trust Ltd 1987-; memb Building Socs Investor Protection Bd 1987-; CBIM; *Recreations* golf, music; *Clubs* Calcot Park Golf, Reading; *Style—* Cyril English, Esq; Ashton Grange, Cedar Drive, Flowers Hill, Pangbourne, Berks RG8 7BH (☎ 0734 843841); Nationwide Anglia Building Society, Chesterfield House, Bloomsbury Way, London WC1V 6PW (☎ 071 242 8822)

ENGLISH, Sir Cyril Rupert; s of William James English; *b* 19 April 1913; *Educ* Northgate Sch Ipswich; *m* 1936, Eva Violet, da of George Alfred Moore; 2 s; *Career* served RN 1939-46; tech teacher 1935-39; HM inspr of schools: inspr 1946-55, staff inspr 1955-58, chief inspr 1948-65, sr chief inspr 1965-68; dir gen City and Guilds of London Inst 1968-76; kt 1972; *Style—* Sir Cyril English; 12 Pineheath Rd, High Kelling, Holt, Norfolk

ENGLISH, Sir David; *b* 26 May 1931; *Educ* Bournemouth Sch; *m* 1954, Irene Mainwood; 1 s, 2 da; *Career* took over editorial responsibility for Mail on Sunday July-Nov 1982, ed Daily Mail 1971-, Daily Sketch 1969-71 (feature ed 1956-59), assoc ed Daily Express 1967-69 (foreign ed 1965-67, chief US corr 1963-65, Washington corr 1961-63, joined 1960), foreign corr Sunday Dispatch 1959-60, with Daily Mirror 1951-53; kt 1982; *Style—* Sir David English; c/o Daily Mail, Fleet St, London EC4Y 0JA (☎ 071 353 6000)

ENGLISH, Rev Dr Donald; s of Robert Forster English, and Edna Forster English; *b* 20 July 1930; *Educ* Univ of Leicester, Univ of London (BA, DipEd), Univ of Cambridge (MA); *m* 1962, Bertha; 2 s (Richard, Paul); *Career* educn offr, promoted to flying offr RAF 1953-55; pres Methodist Conf 1978-79 and 1990-91, travelling sec Inter Varsity fellowship 1955-58, asst tutor Wesley Coll Headingley 1960-62, ordained into methodist Miny 1962, tutor in New Testament Theology Trinity Coll Cambridge Eastern Nigeria 1962-66, circuit min Cullercoats Northumberland 1966-72, tutor in historical theology Hartley Victoria Coll Manchester (Lord Rank Chair) 1973-82, gen sec Methodist Church Div of Home Mission 1982-, moderator Free Church Fedn Cncl 1986-87; memb: World Methodist Exec 1976-86, Central Religious Advsy Ctee 1987-, hon fell Roehampton Inst of Higher Educn (former chm and govr Southlands Coll), vice chm World Methodist Cncl Exec 1986, pres World Methodism 1981-86, moderator of Standing Ctee on Unions of Univs in N and Midlands; Hon DD Asbury Theological Seminary Kentucky USA; *Books* Evangelism and Worship (1971), God in the Gallery (1975), Christian Discipleship (1977), Windows on Passion (1978), Why Believe in Jesus? Evangelistic Reflections for Lent (1986), Everything in Christ (1988); *Recreations* reading, gardening, spectator sports; *Style—* Rev Dr Donald English

ENGLISH, Sir Terence Alexander Hawthorne; KBE (1991); s of Arthur Alexander English (d 1934), and Mavis Eleanor, *née* Lund (d 1959); *b* 3 Oct 1932; *Educ* Hilton Coll SA, Witwatersrand Univ SA (BSc), Guy's Hosp Med Sch (MB BS), Univ of Cambridge (MA); *m* 23 Nov 1963, Ann Margaret, da of Mordaunt Dicey (d 1964); 2 s (Arthur Alexander b 1968, William Andrew b 1971), 2 da (Katharine Ann b 1967, Mary Eleanor b 1970); *Career* sr surgical registrar Brompton and Nat Heart Hosps 1968-72, conslt cardiothoracic surgn Papworth and Addenbrookes Hosps 1973-, dir Heart Transplant Res Unit Br Heart Fndn 1980-88, conslt cardiac advsr Wellington Hosp London 1982-88; pres Int Soc for Heart Transplantation 1984 and 1985; memb Cncl: RCS 1981, GMC 1983-89, FRCS 1967 (pres 1989-), FACC 1986, MRCP 1987, Hon FRCPS (London) 1990, FRCP 1990; *Recreations* tennis, walking, reading; *Style—* Sir Terence English, KBE; 19 Adams Rd, Cambridge CB3 9AD (☎ 0223 68744); Papworth Hospital, Cambs CB3 8RE; Royal College of Surgeons, 35-43 Lincoln's Inn Fields, London WC2A 3PN

ENGLISH, Terence Michael; s of John Robert English, of Edmonton, London N18, and Elsie Letitia *née* Edwards; *b* 3 Feb 1944; *Educ* St Ignatius Coll Stamford Hill London, Univ of London (LLB external); *m* 23 July 1966, Ivy Joan, da of Charles William Weatherley (d 1959), of Wood Green, London; 1 s (Andrew b 1972), 1 da (Melanie b 1967); *Career* admitted slr Supreme Ct 1970; clerk to justices: Newbury Hungerford & Lambourn (now W Berks) 1977-, Slough and Windsor 1985-86; met stipendiary magistrate 1986-; chm Panel Inner London Juvenile Ct 1989-; *Recreations* philately, golf, watching sport; *Style—* Terence M English, Esq; Tower Bridge Magistrates Court, 211 Tooley St, London SE1 2JY (☎ 071 407 4232)

ENNALS, Baron (Life Peer UK 1983), of Norwich, Co Norfolk; David Hedley Ennals; PC (1970); s of Capt Arthur Ford Ennals, MC (d 1977), and Jessie Edith, *née* Taylor; bro of John Arthur Ford Ennals, former dir UK Immigrants Advsy Service, and Martin Ennals, *qv*; *b* 19 Aug 1922; *Educ* Queen Mary's GS Walsall, Loomis Inst Windsor Connecticut USA; *m* 1, 1950 (m dis 1977), Eleanor Maud, da of Reginald Victor Caddick, of Bath; 3 s, 1 da; m 2, 1977, Mrs Katherine Tranoy; *Career* served WWII Capt RAC; sec Cncl for Educn in World Citizenship 1947-57 and of UNA 1952-55, overseas sec Labour Party 1958-64, parly under sec Labour Party 1958-64; MP (Lab) Dover 1964-70, Norwich North Feb 1974-83; parly under sec of state MOD 1966-67, parly sec Home Office 1967-68; min of state: DHSS 1968-70, FCO 1974-76; sec of state for Social Services 1976-79; chm of the tstees of the Children's Med Charity; pres: Coll of Occupational Therapists 1985-, MIND (Nat Assoc of Mental Health) 1990-, All Party Parly Group on Tibet, Tibet Soc, All Party Group on Alternative and Complementary Med, Parly Food and Health Forum; vice pres UNA 1987-; *Style—* The Rt Hon Lord Ennals, PC; House of Lords, London SW1A 0AA

ENNALS, Kenneth Frederick John; CB (1983); s of Ernest Ennals and Elsie Dorothy Ennals; *b* 10 Jan 1932; *Educ* Alleyn's Sch Dulwich, LSE; *m* 1958, Mavis Euphemia; 1 s, 2 da; *Career* dep sec DOE 1980-87 (asst sec 1970, under-sec 1976-80); memb Local Govt Boundary Cmmn; *Clubs* Royal Cwlth Soc; *Style—* Kenneth Ennals, Esq, CB; Skitreadons, Petworth Road, Haslemere, Surrey (☎ Haslemere 2733)

ENNALS, Martin; s of Capt Arthur Ford Ennals, MC (d 1977), and Jessie Edith, *née* Taylor; bro of Baron Ennals, PC, *qv*; *b* 27 July 1927; *Educ* Queen Mary's Sch Walsall, LSE (BSc); *m* 1951, Jacqueline B Morris; 1 s, 1 da; *Career* int human rights campaigner and conslt UNESCO 1951-59; sec gen : Nat Cncl for Civil Liberties 1959-66, Nat Ctee for Cwlth Immigrants 1966-68; sec gen Amnesty Int 1968-80; conslt to: UNICEF, UNESCO, Cncl of Europe, UN, Greater London Cncl 1980-84; estab "Article 19" (Freedom of Info) 1985 and 1986, sec gen of Int Alert concerned with internal conflict human rights and devpt 1986-91; first chm: Euro Rights Fndn, the Int Human Rights Info and Documentation Systems (HURIDOCS); chm UK Human Rights Network 1974-88; Ariel Sallows prof of human rights Saskatchewan Univ Canada 1991-; *Style—* Martin Ennals, Esq; 157 Southwood Lane, London N6 5TA (☎ 081 341 2566)

ENNISKILLEN, 7 Earl of (I 1789); Andrew John Galbraith Cole; also Baron Mountflorence (I 1760), Viscount Enniskillen (I 1776) and Baron Grinstead (UK 1815); s of 6 Earl of Enniskillen, MBE, JP (d 1989), and his 1 w, Sonia Mary, *née* Syers (d 1982); *b* 28 April 1942; *Educ* Eton; *m* 3 Oct 1964, Sarah Frances Caroline, o da of late Maj-Gen John Keith- Edwards, CBE, DSO, MC, of Nairobi; 3 da (Lady Amanda Mary b 4 May 1966, Lady Emma Frances b 14 Feb 1969, Lady Lucy Caroline b 8 Dec 1970); *Heir* uncle, Arthur Gerald Cole b 1920; *Career* late Capt Irish Guards; co dir; pilot; *Style—* The Rt Hon the Earl of Enniskillen; c/o Royal Bank of Scotland, 9 Pall Mall, London SW1

ENNISKILLEN, Dowager Countess of; Nancy Henderson; *née* MacLennan; da of late Dr John Alexander MacLennan, of 105 Brooklawn Place, Bridgeport, Conn, USA; *m* 7 May 1955, as his 2 w, 6 Earl of Enniskillen, MBE, JP (d 1989); *Career* former Washington and UN corr The New York Times; former asst attaché and vice consul US Foreign Serv; *Books* Florence Court My Irish Home (1972), Amulsee and Its Church (1990); *Style—* The Rt Hon the Dowager Countess of Enniskillen; Kinloch House, Amulree, Dunkeld, Perthshire PH8 OEB

ENNISMORE, Viscount; Francis Michael Hare; s (by 3 m) and h of 5 Earl of Listowel, GCMG, PC; *b* 28 June 1964; *Style—* Viscount Ennismore

ENNOR, George Patrick Francis; s of Patrick George Albert Ennor, of Byfleet, Surrey, and Phyllis Mary Ennor, *née* Veitch; *b* 17 Dec 1940; *Educ* Malvern Coll; *m* 30 April 1966 (m dis), Martha Bridget Liddell, da of Lewis Civval (d 1973), of Ockley, Surrey; 2 s (Julian b 1970, Daniel b 1973), 1 da (Charlotte b 1968); *Career* racing journalist; The Sporting Life 1960-85 (sr corr 1984-85), chief reporter The Racing Post 1985-; pres Horserace Writers and Reporters Assoc 1974-; *Recreations* history, crime, politics, Portsmouth Football; *Style—* George P F Ennor, Esq; 59 Blenheim Rd, Horsham, Sussex (☎ 0403 60 831); The Racing Post, 120 Coombe Lane, London SW20 (☎ 081 879 3377)

ENRIGHT, Dennis Joseph; s of George Roderick Enright (d 1934), of Leamington Spa, and Grace, *née* Cleaver (d 1986); *b* 11 March 1920; *Educ* Univ of Cambridge (BA, MA), Univ of Alexandria Egypt (DLitt); *m* 3 Nov 1949, Madeleine; 1 da (Dominique b 1950); *Career* lectr Univ of Alexandria 1947-50, extra-mural tutor Univ of Birmingham 1950-53, visiting prof Kōnan Univ Japan 1950-53, Br Cncl prof Chulalongkorn Univ Bangkok 1957-59, prof of Eng Univ of Singapore 1960-70, co ed Encounter magazine 1970-72, dir Chatto & Windus (publishers) 1974-82; Hon DLitt Univ of Warwick 1982, Hon DUniv Univ of Surrey 1985; Queen's Gold Medal for Poetry 1981; FRSL 1961; *Books* Academic Year (1955), Memoirs of a Mendicant Professor (1969), The Oxford Book of Death (ed, 1983), The Alluring Problem: An Essay on Irony (1986), Collected Poems 1987 (1987), Fields of Vision (1988), The Faber Book of Fevers and Frets (ed, 1989), The Oxford Book of Friendship (co-ed, 1991), Under the Circumstances: Poems and Proses (1991); *Recreations* work; *Style—* D J Enright, Esq

ENRIGHT, Derek Anthony; s of Lawrence Enright (d 1962), and Helen Smith, *née* Burns; *b* 2 Aug 1935; *Educ* St Michael's Coll Leeds, Wadham Coll Oxford (BA, DipEd); *m* 1963, Jane Maureen, da of late Geoffrey Simmons; 2 s (Duncan b 1964,

Simon b 1969), 2 da (Amanda b 1965, Jacqueline b 1967); *Career* dep headmaster St Wilfrid's HS Featherstone 1970-79; MEP Leeds 1979-84, del of EEC to Guinea Bissau 1985-87, conslt EEC 1988-; Distinção de Merito da Republica da Guinea Bissau; *Style*— Derek Enright, Esq; The Hollies, 112 Carleton Rd, Pontefract, W Yorks

ENSOM, Donald; s of Charles R A W Ensom (d 1953), and Edith, *née* Young (d 1942); *b* 8 April 1926; *Educ* Norbury Manor Sch Surrey; *m* 11 Sept 1951, Sonia Florence, da of John Brockington Sherrard, of Westcott, Surrey; 1 s (Paul Charles b 1952), 1 da (Jacqueline Elizabeth b 1955); *Career* Sgt RA Survey 1943-47, WWII Surrey Yeo 1949-53; conslt Debenham Tewson & Chinnocks (formerly Nightingale Page & Benn) 1986- (ptnr 1958-86); RICS: pres Building Surveyor's Div 1975-76, chm Professional Practice Ctee 1978-83, chm RICS Insurance Services Ltd 1981-83, hon sec 1983-90, vice pres 1988-90; chm Building Conservation Tst 1980-83; pres Univ of Cambridge Land Economy Soc 1990-91; Freeman City of London, Liveryman Worshipful Co of Chartered Surveyors; ARICS 1951, FRICS 1958, FCIArb 1970; *Recreations* opera, music, social and transport history, caravanning, canals; *Clubs* East India; *Style*— Donald Ensom, Esq; Saxons, Grange Rd, Cambridge, CB3 9AA (☎ 0223 329706)

ENSOR, (George) Anthony; s of George Ensor, of Maesgwyn, Ala Road, Pwllheli, Gwynedd, and Phyllis, *née* Harrison; *b* 4 Nov 1936; *Educ* Malvern, Univ of Liverpool (LLB); *m* 14 Sept 1968, Jennifer Margaret (MB ChB), da of Dr Ronald Caile (d 1978), of 7 Waterloo Road, Birkdale, Southport, Lancs; 2 da (Elizabeth b 1972, Jane b 1978); *Career* admitted slr 1961, ptnr Rutherfords 1963- (now Weightman Rutherfords); dep coroner (city of Liverpool) 1966-; dep judge Crown Ct 1979-83, Rec Crown Ct 1983-; pt/t chm Indust Tbnls 1975-; dir Liverpool FC 1985-, tstee Empire Theatre Liverpool 1986-; memb Judicial Studies Bd 1986-89; pres: Artists Club Liverpool 1976, Liverpool Law Soc 1982; *Recreations* golf, theatre; *Clubs* Artists (Liverpool), Formby Golf, Waterloo RUFC; *Style*— Anthony Ensor, Esq; Weightman Rutherfords, Richmond House, 1 Rumford Place, Liverpool L3 9QW (☎ 051 227 2601, fax 051 227 3223, telex 627538)

ENSOR, David; OBE; s of Rev William Walters Ensor (d 1967), and Constance Eva Ensor (d 1987); *b* 2 April 1924; *Educ* Kingswood Sch Bath; *m* 1947, Gertrude Kathleen, da of Herbert Brown (d 1947); 2 s; *Career* WWII Royal Signals, ADC to GOC Bengal Dist SEAC; md: Knapp Drewett & Sons Ltd 1969-79, Croydon Advertiser Ltd 1979-85; vice-pres Methodist Conf 1981; vice chm Press Cncl 1987- (memb 1982-); *Style*— David Ensor, Esq, OBE; Milborne Lodge, Dinton Rd, Fovant, Salisbury, Wilts SP3 5JW (☎ 072 270 521)

ENSOR WALTERS, Peter Hugh Bennetts; OBE (1957); s of Rev Charles Ensor Walters (d 1938), of London, and Muriel Havergal, *née* Bennetts (d 1966); *b* 18 July 1912; *Educ* Manor House Sch, St Peter's Coll Oxford; *m* 19 March 1936, (Ella) Marcia, da of Percival Burdle Hayter; *Career* vol enlistment Army 1940, cmmnd RAPC 1942, invalided out 1943; staff of late Rt Hon David Lloyd George 1935-39, Nat Govt nat agent Wales and W England 1939-40, gen sec Nat Lib Orgn 1951-58 (nat organiser GB 1944-51), PR conslt 1959-89, pres Central Worthing Cons Assoc 1983-89; former MIPR, FInstD; *Recreations* travel; *Clubs* Union Soc Oxford; *Style*— Peter Ensor Walters, Esq, OBE; 2 Hopedene Ct, Wordsworth Rd, Worthing, W Sussex BN11 1TB (☎ 0903 205678)

ENTICKNAP, Dr John Brandon; s of Walter John Enticknap (d 1971), and Dorothy Constance, *née* Silk (d 1972); *b* 28 Feb 1922; *Educ* King Edward VI Royal GS Guildford, Kings Coll London, Charing Cross and Guy's Hosp Med Sch (MD, MB BS, DCP); *m* 1, 27 May 1944, Winifred Morag Graham, da of Andrew Graham Grieve (d 1968); 3 s (Nicholas John b 1947, Jonathan Graham b 1948, Alasdair Franklin b 1950); m 2, 15 Dec 1972, Pauline Mavis, da of Samuel Tickle Meadow (d 1973); *Career* Capt RAMC served W Africa 1947-49; conslt chem pathologist NW Thames RHB 1954-82; coroners pathologist Eastern Dist Gtr London 1954-89; FRCPath 1966, AKC 1990; *Recreations* local history research, handicrafts; *Clubs* Athenaeum; *Style*— Dr John Enticknap; Tinkers, Wesley End, Stambourne, Halstead, Essex CO9 4PG (☎ 044 085 316); 15 Guilford St, London WC1N 1DX (☎ 071 405 0839)

ENTICOTT, Ronald David (Ron); s of Frederick Walter Enticott (d 1972), of Harrow, and Margaret Irene, *née* Boxall (d 1951); *b* 13 Oct 1942; *Educ* Harrow Weald GS; *m* 1, 26 June 1965 (m dis 1990), (Betty) Elizabeth Anne, da of Charles Golding (d 1982), of Harrow, 2 da (Susan Margaret (Mrs Wilkins) b 1966, Jane b 1967); m 2, Gillian Mavis Merrell; *Career* CA; ptnrs asst Pike Russell CA 1968-77 (articled clerk 1962), dir Wickens Building Group Ltd 198-90 (gp sec 1977); chm Productivity South East, pres Chertsey C of C, vice chm Chertsey Agric Assoc, business studies advsr Brookland Tech Coll, govr Abbeylands Sch; FCA 1978 (ACA 1968); *Recreations* swimming; *Style*— Ron Enticott, Esq; 19 Abbey Road, Chertsey, Surrey KT16 8AL (☎ 0932 563028)

ENTWISTLE, John; DL (Lancs 1983); s of Herbert Entwistle (d 1980), and Clara Entwistle (d 1981); *b* 16 July 1932; *Educ* St Mary's RC Central Sch Burnley Lancs; *m* 1962, Kathleen, da of Patrick Mooney (d 1963); 3 s, 1 da; *Career* Br Telecom engr; co cncllr Lancashire; chm Co Cncl 1989-90; active trade unionist, branch sec National Communications Union; *Recreations* cycling (England team 1958), golf; *Style*— John Entwistle, Esq, DL; 47 Pritchard St, Burnley, Lancs BB11 4JT (☎ (0282) 53480); c/o LN13 TEC, Centenery Way, Burnley, Lancs (☎ (0282) 34876)

ENTWISTLE, Prof Kenneth Mercer; s of William Charles Entwistle, and Maude Elizabeth, *née* Hipkiss; *b* 3 Jan 1925; *Educ* Urmston GS; Univ of Manchester (BSc, MSc, PhD); *m* 9 July 1949, (Alice) Patricia Mary, da of Eric Maurice Johnson; 2 s (Martin Patrick b 1954, Peter Maurice b 1958), 2 da (Hilary Jane b 1953, Bridget Mary b 1965); *Career* Univ of Manchester: lectr 1948, sr lectr 1954, reader 1960, prof of metallurgy (UMIST) 1962-90, prof emeritus 1990-, vice princ (UMIST) 1972-74, dean Faculty of Technol 1976-77, pro-vice chllr 1982-85; hon fell Sheffield Poly; chm Materials Ctee CNAA 1972-74, memb Educn Ctee Inst of Metallurgists 1977-79, memb Metallics Sub Ctee SRC 1979-81, chm Technol Sub Ctee UGC 1985-89, memb UGC 1985-89, advsr on engrg Univs Funding Cncl 1989-; CEng, FIM; *Recreations* scottish dancing, choral singing; *Clubs* Athenaeum; *Style*— Prof Kenneth Entwistle; Greenacre, Bridge End Lane, Prestbury, Macclesfield SK10 4DJ (☎ 0625 829269); Manchester Materials Science Centre, UMIST, Grosvenor St, Manchester M1 7HS (☎ 061 200 3554, fax 061 228 7040, telex 666 094)

ENTWISTLE, Sir (John Nuttall) Maxwell; s of Isaac Entwistle (d 1954), of Formby, Liverpool, and Hannah Entwistle; *b* 8 Jan 1910; *Educ* Merchant Taylors' Sch Great Crosby; *m* 1940, Jean Cunliffe McAlpine, da of John Penman, MD ChB (d 1952); 2 s; *Career* served RN 1944-46; admitted slr 1931, Notary Public 1955; City of Liverpool: cncllr 1938-60, alderman 1960-64, ldr CC 1961-63 (when he initiated plans for redevpt of City Centre); chm: Merseyside Devpt Ctee, Mersey Tunnel Ctee; cncllr Cumbria 1979-82; underwriting memb of Lloyd's 1964-; pres: Edge Hill Cons Assoc 1965-70, Old Boys' Assoc 1969-70; govr Boys' and Girls' Schs 1970-75; chm Liverpool Abbeyfield Soc 1970-75, memb Ct and Cncl Univ of Liverpool; kt 1963; *Recreations* gardening; *Style*— Sir Maxwell Entwistle; Stone Hall, Sedbergh, Cumbria (☎ 0587 20700)

ENTWISTLE, Peter John; s of Herbert Entwistle (d 1988), of Bolton, Lancs, and Winifred Alice Lilian, *née* Fullex (d 1963); *b* 3 June 1933; *Educ* St John's Coll Johannesburg SA, Rhodes Univ Grahamstown SA (BSc), Lincoln Coll Oxford (BA); *m* 4 Jan 1958, Pamela, *née* Ashby; 1 s (Timothy b 1961), 1 da (Sarah-Jane b 1959); *Career* Barclays Bank DCO 1960-63, IBM (UK) Ltd 1963-71, Lloyds Bank 1972 (asst gen mangr 1984), dir BACS 1985-89, dir Swift (UK) 1989-; memb Diabetes and Related Diseases Res Assoc; ACIB 1962; *Recreations* gardening, furniture restoration; *Style*— Peter Entwistle, Esq; 1 De Crespigny Park, London SE5; Parc De La Croisette, Bvd Alexandre III, Cannes, France; Lloyds Bank plc, 71 Lombard St, London EC3

ENTWISTLE, Phillida Gail Sinclair; JP (Liverpool 1980); da of Geoffrey Burgess, CMG, CIE, OBE (d 1972), and Jillian Margaret Eskens, *née* Hope; *b* 7 Jan 1944; *Educ* Cheltenham Ladies' Coll, Univ of London (BSc), Univ of Liverpool (PhD); *m* 6 Sept 1968, John Nicholas McAlpine Entwistle, s of Sir (John Nuttall) Maxwell Entwistle, of Stone Hall, Sedbergh, Cumbria; 1 s (Nicholas b 1970), 1 da (Louise b 1971); *Career* dir J Davey & Sons Liverpool Ltd 1983-88, gen cmmr of Inland Revenue 1985-, memb: Mersey RHA 1987-90, Mental Health Act Cmmn 1989-, Liverpool FHSA 1990-; govr Liverpool Poly 1988; FRSA; *Style*— Mrs Phillida Entwistle, JP; Low Crag, Crook, Cumbria LA8 8LE (☎ 04488 268)

EPPEL, Leonard Cedric; s of Dr David Eppel (d 1963), of Bickenhall Mansions, Baker St, London W1, and Vera, *née* Diamond (d 1973); *b* 24 June 1928; *Educ* Highgate Sch; *m* 15 July 1954, Barbara Priscilla, da of Robert Silk, of Dorset House, Gloucester Place, London W1; 1 s (Stuart Neil b 26 March 1959), 1 da (Rochelle Eleanor b 7 Oct 1956); *Career* md Silks Estates Investments Ltd 1968 (dir 1954); chm: Arrowcroft Gp plc 1969, Albert Dock Co Ltd 1983; vice pres British Red Cross Soc (Merseyside), dir Merseyside Tourist Bd Ltd 1986; dir Millwall FC 1971 (chm 1979-83); Freeman City of London, Liveryman Worshipful Co of Fletchers 1984; FVI 1962, FSVA 1968, Fell IOD 1987; *Recreations* jogging, golf; *Clubs* Carlton; *Style*— Leonard Eppel, Esq; 24 Hanover Square, London W1R 9DD (☎ 071 499 5432, fax 071 493 0323, car 0860 623 351)

EPPS, Hon Mrs (Pamela Anne); *née* Moncreiff; yr da of 4 Baron Moncreiff (d 1942); *b* 17 July 1927; *Educ* Dollar Acad, Edinburgh Univ (MB ChB); *m* 1, 24 Sept 1951 (m dis 1973), Edward James White, s of Henry Thomas White, of Edinburgh; 2 s, 2 da; m 2, 1979, Ernest Frederic Epps (d 1987), s of Reginald George Epps (d 1937); *Career* gen med practitioner under name of Dr White, ret 1989; *Style*— The Hon Mrs Epps; 13 Barntongate Ave, Edinburgh EH4 8BQ (☎ 031 667 1577); Ardchoille, Eredine, by Dalmally, Argyll

EPSOM, Dr Joseph Edward; s of Joseph Edward Epsom, of Loughton, Essex (d 1952), and Mary, *née* Woods (d 1971); *b* 8 Aug 1919; *Educ* St Ignatius Coll, QMC London, London Hosp Med Coll, LRCP, DPH, DIH and MFCP Royal Colls of Surgns and Physicians; *m* 2 July 1945, Barbara, da of Henry Swarbrick, of Bradford, Yorks (d 1966); 7 s (Michael b 18 June 1947, Richard b 5 March 1950, Joseph b 8 March 1951, Henry b 16 Nov 1955, Paul b 15 Oct 1956, John b 27 March 1958, Philip b 15 July 1962), 3 da (Susan b 9 April 1946, Ruth b 17 Jan 1949, Barbara b 11 Jan 1953); *Career* Capt RAMC/RASC 1940-46, OC 47 Port and Beach Detachment 21 Army Gp in Normandy France Belgium Holland Germany; house physician and emergency offr London Hosp 1950, asst princ gen practice 1950-53, registrar Radcliffe Infirmary United Oxford Hosps 1953-54, asst MOH Met Borough of Stepney 1954-56, dep MOH Tottenham Borough Cncl 1956-60; MOH: Met Borough of Bermondsey 1960-65, London Borough of Southwark 1965-74; hon conslt community physician Guy's Hosp, princ sch MO Southwark; chm London Food Ctee 1970-74, fndr City of London Med Res Fund, memb of the Court Leet Kings Manor Southwark, hon fell Assoc Port Health Authys; Liveryman Worshipful Co of Loriners 1973; memb of Faculty of Community Med, fell Soc of Community Med; MRCS, FRSH; *Books* Community Screening London Borough Southwark (1970), Modern Trends in Oncology (contrib 1974); *Recreations* sailing; *Clubs* City Livery, Livery Yacht, Cruising Assoc, Royal Cinque Ports Yacht Dover; *Style*— Dr Joseph Epsom

EPSTEIN, David Leslie; s of Samuel Epstein (d 1969), of London, and Bessie, *née* Silver; *b* 31 Aug 1938; *Educ* Tottenham GS; *m* 13 Dec 1964, Adèle, da of Barnet Kosky (d 1985), of Leicester; 1 da (Amanda b 1966); *Career* Nat Serv SAC RAF; jt md Kuoni Travel Ltd 1969-81, dir gen Assoc of Br Travel Agents (ABTA) 1987-; memb of Travel and Tourism 1987; FICA 1966; *Recreations* amateur stage performing (drama and musical); *Style*— David L Epstein, Esq; Dalebrook, 5 Crooked Usage, Finchley, London N3 3HD (☎ 081 346 3244); 55-57 Newman Street, London W1P 4AH (071 637 2444)

EPSTEIN, Hon Mrs (Edwina Maureen); *née* Stanley; da of 6 Baron Stanley of Alderley; *b* 19 Jan 1933; *m* 1, 5 Jan 1953 (m dis 1966), John Dawnay Innes (d 17 July 1966), 2 s of Lt-Col James Archibald Innes, DSO, of Horringer Manor, Bury St Edmunds, Suffolk; 2 s, 1 da; m 2, 25 Oct 1968, Joshua Philip Epstein, s of Dr Samuel Hyman Epstein, of Boston, Mass, USA; *Career* called to the Bar Inner Temple 1974; *Style*— The Hon Mrs Epstein; 146 Benhill Road, London SE5 7LZ

EPSTEIN, Jon; s of David and Sirena Epstein; *Educ* UCS, UMIST (BSc, organiser Bogle Stroll); *m* Ruth; 2 s (Adam, Jeremy); *Career* mgmnt trainee then area sales mangr Desion-Comino International 1975-76, American Express 1976-79 (mgmnt trainee EMEA, asst mktg mangr France, mktg exec UK), sr conslt Marketing Improvements UK and Europe 1979-82, mktg dir Euro Citicorp (Citicorp Servs Div) 1982-85, American Express 1985-90 (mktg dir travel mgmnt servs, database mktg and market res dir), commercial planning dir Coca-Cola & Schweppes 1990-; Inst of Sales Promotion (UK) Golden Jubilee award (fin servs), American Express Int award (for database marketing innovation); memb: Bd BDMA, CIM, MRS, IOD; *Recreations* skiing, music, photography; *Clubs* Down Hill Only; *Style*— Jon Epstein, Esq; Coca-Cola & Schweppes Beverages Ltd, Charter Place, Uxbridge, Middlesex UB8 1EZ (☎ 0895 31313)

EPSTEIN, Owen; s of Dr Morris Epstein, and Nancy, *née* Frysh; *b* 12 May 1950; *Educ* Univ of Witwatersrand Joahannesburg SA (MB BCh); *m* 10 Dec 1972, June, da of D David Armist; 2 s (Daniel b 4 Aug 1976, Marc b 14 June 1979); *Career* med registrar 1977-79, clinical res fell 1979-82, lectr in medicine 1982-85, conslt and clinical postgrad tutor Royal Free Hosp London 1985-; author of several scientific publications; chm gastroenterology Royal Free Hosp, sec London Jewish Med Soc; MRCP 1976, FRCP 1989; *Style*— Owen Epstein, Esq; 1 Cyprus Gardens, Finchley, London N3 1SP; Dept of Medicine, Royal Free Hospital, Pond St, Hampstead, London NW3 (071 794 0500)

ERAUT, Prof Michael Ruarc; s of Lt-Col Ruarc Bertram Sorel Eraut (d 1987), and Frances Hurst (d 1972); *b* 15 Nov 1940; *Educ* Winchester, Trinity Hall Cambridge (BA, PhD); *m* 7 Aug 1964, (Mary) Cynthia, da of Michael William Wynne, of Tunbridge Wells; 2 s (Patrick b 10 May 1968, Christopher b 27 Aug 1971); *Career* Univ of Sussex Centre for Educnl Technol: fell 1967, sr fell 1971, dir 1973-76, reader in educn 1976-86, prof of educn 1986-, dir Inst of Continuing and Professional Educn 1986-; visiting prof of evaluation Univ of Illinois 1980-81 (in educnl tech 1965-67); *Books* incl: Teaching and Learning: New Methods and Resources in Higher Education (1970), Analysis of Curriculum Materials (1975), Curriculum Development in Further Education (1985), Improving the Quality of YTS (1986), International Encyclopedia of Educational Technology (1989), Education and the Information Society-A Challenge for European Policies (1990); *Style*— Prof Michael Eraut; 49 St Annes Crescent, Lewes,

E Sussex BN7 1SD (☎ 0273 475955); Education Development Building, University of Sussex, Falmer, Brighton (☎ 0273 606755)

ERCOLANI, Lucian Brett; DSO, DFC; s of Lucian Randolph Ercolani, OBE (d 1976), and Eva May, *née* Brett; *b* 9 Aug 1917; *Educ* Oundle; *m* 16 June 1941, Cynthia Violet, da of Major James Douglas, MC (d 1938); 1 da (Jane (Mrs Reynolds) b 10 Aug 1950); *Career* WWII RAF 1940-46, PO Flt Lt 214 Sqdn 1941, Sqdn Ldr 99 Sqdn 1942, Sqdn Ldr 355 Sqdn 1943, Wing Cdr OC 99 Sqdn 1944, Wing Cdr OC 159 Sqdn 1944-45; Ercol Furniture Ltd: joined 1934, jt md 1946, chm 1976-; govr Bucks Coll of Higher Educn; Freeman: City of London 1953, Worshipful Co of Furniture Makers 1953 (Master 1980-81), Worshipful Co of Turners 1959; *Recreations* sailing; *Clubs* RAF, Royal Southern Yacht, Royal Cruising; *Style—* Lucian B Ercolani, Esq, DSO, DFC; Neighbours, Radnage, Nr High Wycombe, Bucks HP14 4BY (☎ 024 026 2133); Ercol Furniture Ltd, London Rd, High Wycombe, Bucks HP13 7AE (☎ 0494 21261, fax 0494 462467, telex 83616)

ERDMAN, Edward Louis; s of Henry David Erdman (d 1945), and Pauline, *née* Jarvis (d 1950); *b* 4 July 1906; *Educ* Grocers' Co Sch; *m* 22 Dec 1949, Pamela, da of late John Howard Mason; 1 s (Timothy James b 1953); *Career* 1937 TA KRRC, Capt N Africa and Italy 1939-45; apprenticeship surveyors office 1923, fndr of Edward Erdman surveyors 1934, conslt Warnford Investments plc 1974- (dir 1962), chm Chesterfield Properties 1979 (dir 1960); World of Property Housing Tst (now Sanctuary Spiral Housing Gp) Assoc: memb Central Cncl 1974, chm 1978, pres 1987; memb Property Advsy Panel to Treasy 1975-77; FSVA, FRSA; *Books* People and Property (1982); *Recreations* football, farming, cycling, athletics; *Clubs* IOD, Annabels, Naval and Military; *Style—* Edward Erdman, Esq; 6 Grosvenor St, London W1X 0AD (☎ 071 629 8191, fax 071 409 2757)

EREAUT, Sir (Herbert) Frank Cobbold; s of Herbert Parker Ereaut and May Julia, *née* Cobbold; *b* 6 May 1919; *Educ* Tormore Sch Upper Deal Kent, Cranleigh Sch, Exeter Coll Oxford; *m* 1942, Kathleen FitzGibbon; 1 da; *Career* served WWII RASC, N Africa, Italy, NW Europe; called to the Bar Inner Temple 1947; Jersey: slr gen 1958-62, attorney gen 1962-69, dep bailiff 1969-74, bailiff 1975-85; judge of the Ct of Appeal in Guernsey 1976-89, dir Standard Chartered Bank (CI) Ltd; KStJ 1983 (CStJ 1978); kt 1976; *Recreations* music, gardening, travel; *Style—* Sir Frank Ereaut; Les Cypres, St John, Jersey, CI (☎ 0534 22317)

EREMIN, Prof Oleg; s of Theodore Eremin, of Melbourne, Aust, and Maria, *née* Avramenko (d 1978); *b* 12 Nov 1938; *Educ* Christian Brothers Coll Melbourne Aust, Univ of Melbourne (MB, BS, MD); *m* 17 Feb 1963, Jennifer Mary, da of Ellis Charles Ching (d 1972), of Melbourne, Aust; 2 s (Andrew b 1972, Nicholas b 1973), 1 da (Katherine b 1968); *Career* asst surgn Royal Melbourne Hosp Aust 1971-72 (1965-71: house offr, sr house offr, registrar), sr registrar Combined Norwich Hosps 1972-74, sr res assoc in immunology Dept of Pathology Univ of Cambridge 1977-80 (res asst 1974-77), sr lectr and conslt surgn Edinburgh Royal Infirmary 1981-85, prof of surgery and conslt surgn Aberdeen Royal Infirmary; memb: Assoc of Surgns of GB and I, Surgical Res Soc, James IV Assoc of Surgns; FRACS, FRCSE; *Recreations* classical music, literature, sport; *Clubs* Royal Northern and Univ; *Style—* Prof Oleg Eremin; 3 The Chanonry, Aberdeen AB2 1RP (☎ 0224 484065); Dept of Surgery, Univ Med Bldgs, Foresterhill, Aberdeen AB9 2ZD (☎ 0224 681818, ext 53004)

ERIAN, John; s of Dr Habib Erian (d 1976), of Cairo, and Aida, *née* Mitry; *b* 12 Aug 1948; *Educ* St Georges Coll, Ain-Shams Med Univ Cairo (MB BCh); *m* 7 July 1973, Jennifer, da of Norman Frank Felton, of 2 Oakes Ave, Hanworth, Middx TW13 5JD; 1 s (Michael b 1974), 2 da (Gehanne b 1976, Simonne b 1977); *Career* conslt obstetrician and gynaecologist; W Cumberland Hosp 1975-79, St George's Hosp 1979-82, Queen Charlotte's Hosp and Chelsea Hosp for Women 1982-83, St Thomas Hosp 1983, Guy's Hosp 1983-85, Farnborough Hosp Kent 1985-; fndr of Bromley Dist Colposcopy Serv and Endocrine Unit and Gift Treatment Orpington Lions Club, pioneered yag laser surgery in UK as an alternative to hysterectomy; author of various papers on laser therapy in gynaecology; memb Int Menopause Soc, MRCOG 1981; *Recreations* tennis, table tennis, swimming, theatre, music, skiing, food and wine; *Style—* John Erian, Esq; 17 Oaklands Close, Petts Wood, Kent BR2 1QQ (☎ 0689 890458); Farnborough Hospital, Farnborough Common, Locksbottom, Orpington, Kent (☎ 0689 853333)

ERICKSON, Prof Charlotte Joanne; da of Knut Eric Erickson (d 1965), of Rock Island, Illinois, and Lae Alberta Regina, *née* Johnson (d 1983); *b* 22 Oct 1923; *Educ* Augustana Coll Rock Island Illinois (BA), Cornell Univ NY (MA, PhD); *m* 19 July 1952, (Glen) Louis Watt, s of Thomas Watt (d 1941), of Dover; 2 s (Thomas b 1956, David b 1958); *Career* instr Vassar Coll Poughkeepsie NY 1950-52, res fell NIESR London 1952-55; LSE 1955-83: asst lectr, lectr, sr lectr, reader, prof; Paul Mellon prof of American hist Univ of Cambridge 1983-90; MacArthur prize fell 1990-; FRHS 1970; *Books* American Industry and the European Immigrant (1957), British Industrialists, Steel and Hosiery (1959) Invisible Immigrants (1974), Emigration from Europe, 1815-1914 (1976); *Recreations* music, gardening; *Clubs* CCC Cambridge; *Style—* Prof Charlotte Erickson; 8 High St, Chesterton, Cambridge CB4 1NG (☎ 0223 323 184); History Faculty, West Road, Cambridge CB3 9EF (☎ 0223 335 317)

ERICKSON, Raymond John; s of Lawrence Erickson (d 1968), of Penarth, and Olive Annie (d 1983); *b* 2 Aug 1926; *Educ* Penarth Co Sch; *m* 7 March 1964, Mary Frances, da of Thomas Brian (d 1981), of Barry; 1 da (Lisa b 1964); *Career* Nat Serv 1944-48, India, Burma, Malasia, Singapore, Japan; mgmnt accountant, chm John Curran Ltd, (dir 1976-); *Style—* Raymond J Erickson, Esq; 5 Minehead Ave, Sully, Penarth CF6 2TH; John Curran Ltd, PO Box 72, Curran Road, Cardiff CF1 1TE

ERIKSEN, Gunn; *b* 28 Dec 1956; *Educ* Norway; *m* 9 Aug 1984, Fred Brown; *Career* worked as ceramicist and weaver in Norway and Scot until 1980; self taught chef and part owner Altnaharrie Inn 1980-; awards for cuisine incl: 5 out of 5 Good Food Guide, 2 stars Egon Ronay, 1 star Michelin, one of top estabs in UK Ackerman Guide; *Recreations* reading, sailing, skiing, architectural drawing, music, creating things!; *Style—* Ms Gunn Eriksen; Altnaharrie Inn, Ullapool, Ross-Shire, Scotland IV26 2SS (☎ 085 483 230)

ERITH, Robert Felix; TD (1977); eld s of Felix Henry Erith, FSA, of Vinces Farm, Ardleigh, Colchester, Essex, and Barbara Penelope, *née* Hawken; *b* 8 Aug 1938; *Educ* Ipswich Sch, Writtle Agric Coll; *m* 7 May 1966, Sara Kingsford Joan, da of Dr Christopher Frederick James Muller, of Lion House, Lavenham, Suffolk; 3 s (Charles b 1967, James b 1970, Edward b (twin) 1970); *Career* 10 Hussars: 2 Lt Serv in Aqaba Jordan and Tidworth Hants 1957-58, AVR serv in Aden, Oman, Cyprus, Hong Kong, W Germany, Berlin, UK, 1962-79, Maj 1973; builders merchant salesman and mgmnt trainee 1960-64: GEO Wallis (London), Broad & Co (London), Hechinger Co (Washington DC), Simon Hardware Co (Oakland California), Bunnings Timber (Perth W Aust); bldg specialist Milln & Robinson 1966- (EB Savory Milln & Co 1967-), ptnr then sr ptnr EB Savory Milln & co 1983-; chm: SBCI Savory Milln Ltd 1985-, Swiss Bank Corporation Equities Group 1989-; memb Stock Exchange 1969-; non-exec dir: Erith plc (dep chm), Royal London Mutual Insurance Society Ltd, Secure Trust Group plc, Aspinwall & Co Ltd; church warden Holy Innocents Church Lamarsh; memb: Dedham Vale Soc, Colne Stour Countryside Assoc; Parly candidate (C) Ipswich 1976-79; memb: NEDO Housing Ctee, Centre for Policy Studies; Liveryman Worshipful Co of Builders' Merchants 1987, Freeman City of London 1987; AMSIA 1971, FID 1986; *Books* Britain into Europe (jtly, 1962), The Role of the Monarchy (jtly, 1965), Savory Milln's Building Book (annual edns 1968-83); *Recreations* farming, environmental pursuits, village cricket, tennis, skiing, stamp collecting; *Clubs* Cavalry and Guards', City of London, MCC; *Style—* Robert Erith, Esq, TD; Shrubs Farm, Lamarsh, Bures, Suffolk C08 5EA (☎ 0787 227520, fax 0787 227197); Swiss Bank Corporation Equities Group, Swiss Bank House, 1 High Timber St, London EC4V 3SB (☎ 071 329 0329, fax 071 975 1354, telex 887434, car 0836 245536)

ERNE, 6 Earl of (I 1798); Henry George Victor John Crichton; JP; sits as Baron Fermanagh (UK 1876); also Baron Erne (I 1768) and Viscount Erne (I 1781); s of 5 Earl (ka 1940), and Lady Davidema, da of 2 Earl of Lytton, KG, GCSI, GCIE, PC; *b* 9 July 1937; *Educ* Eton; *m* 1, 5 Nov 1958 (m dis 1980), Camilla Marguerite, da of late Wing Cdr Owen George Endicott Roberts; 1 s, 4 da; m 2, 1980, Mrs Anna Carin Hitchcock (*née* Bjorck); *Heir* s, Viscount Crichton; *Career* page of honour to HM King George VI 1952 and to HM The Queen 1952-54; Lt N Irish Horse 1960-68; Lord Lt Co Fermanagh; *Clubs* White's, Lough Erne Yacht; *Style—* The Rt Hon the Earl of Erne, JP; Crom Castle, Newtown Butler, Co Fermanagh (☎ 036 573 208)

ERRINGTON, Viscount; Evelyn Rowland Esmond Baring; s and h of 3 Earl of Cromer, KG, GCMG, MBE, PC; *b* 3 June 1946; *Educ* Eton; *m* 1971, Plern, da of Dr Charanpat Isarangkul na Ayudhya (d 1978), of Thailand; *Career* md: Inchcape (China) Limited 1977-, Inchcape Vietnam Limited; dep chm: Land-Ocean Inchcape Container Transport Ltd (Shanghai), Motor Transport Company of Guangdong & Hong Kong Ltd (China); *Recreations* diving, climbing; *Clubs* Oriental, Hong Kong, Royal Hong Kong Yacht; *Style—* Viscount Errington; GPO Box 36, Hong Kong (☎ 852 730 7454, 730 0407); office 852 842 4600)

ERRINGTON, Col Sir Geoffrey Frederick; 2 Bt (UK 1963) of Ness, in Co Palatine of Chester; s of Sir Eric Errington, 1 Bt (d 1973), and Marjorie, *née* Grant-Bennett (d 1973); *b* 15 Feb 1926; *Educ* Rugby, New Coll Oxford; *m* 24 Sept 1955, Diana Kathleen Forbes, da of late Edward Barry Davenport, of Edgbaston; 3 s; *Heir* s, Robin Davenport Errington, *qv*; *Career* GSO 3 (Int) HQ 11 Armd Div 1950-52, GSO 3 MI 3 (b) WO 1955-57, Bde Maj 146 Inf Bde 1959-61, Co Cdr RMA Sandhurst 1963-65, mil asst to Adj-Gen 1965-67, CO 1 Bn King's Regt 1967-69, GSO 1 HQ 1 BR Corps 1969-71, Col GS HQ NW District 1971, AAG M1 (Army) MOD 1974-75, ret 1975; Col King's Regt 1975-86; dir personnel servs Br Shipbuilders 1977-78, employer bd memb Shipbuilding ITB 1977-78; chm CPM Search (UK) Ltd 1990-; Freeman City of London 1980, Liveryman Worshipful Co of Coachmakers and Coach Harness Makers; *Recreations* travelling and gardening; *Clubs* Boodle's, United Oxford and Cambridge, Woodroffes's (chm 1987-); *Style—* Col Sir Geoffrey Errington, Bt; 203a Gloucester Place, London NW1; Stone Hill Farm, Sellindge, Ashford, Kent; office: 38 Saville Row, London W1H 1AG (☎ 071 287 9565)

ERRINGTON, Sir Lancelot; KCB (1976, CB 1962); er s of Maj Lancelot Errington (d 1965), of Beeslack, Milton Bridge, Midlothian; *b* 14 Jan 1917; *Educ* Wellington, Trinity Coll Cambridge; *m* 1939, Katharine Reine, o da of T C Macaulay, MC, of Painswick, Glos; 2 s, 2 da; *Career* served WWII RNVR; entered HO 1939, Miny of Nat Insur 1945, asst sec 1953, under sec Miny of Pensions and Nat Insur 1957-65; seconded: Cabinet Office 1965, DHSS 1968; dep under sec of state 1971-73, 2 perm sec DHSS 1973-76; *Style—* Sir Lancelot Errington, KCB; St Mary's, Fasnacloich, Appin, Argyll (☎ 063 173 331)

ERRINGTON, Robin Davenport; s and h of Col Sir Geoffrey Errington, 2 Bt; *b* 1 July 1957; *Educ* Eton; *Recreations* tennis, skiing, music; *Clubs* Boodle's; *Style—* Robin Errington, Esq; Stone Hill Farm, Sellindge, nr Ashford, Kent

ERRINGTON, Roger; s of Roger Errington, CBE, MC, TD, MD (d 1960) of Gosforth, Newcastle upon Tyne, and Margaret Lilian, *née* Appleby (d 1964); *b* 7 April 1927; *Educ* Fettes, King's Coll Newcastle upon Tyne; *m* 4 Feb 1956, (Susan) Margaret, da of George Robert Hodnett, CBE, TD, MA (d 1979); 2 s (Richard b 1957, Charles b 1959), 1 da (Claire b 1961); *Career* farmer 1951-; dir: T Crossling & Co Ltd 1960- (chm 1974-), J T Parrish plc 1978- (chm 1980-86); Castle Morpeth: rural dist cncllr 1954-74, dist cncllr 1974-, dep mayor 1988, mayor 1989-90; *Recreations* sailing, shooting, flying; *Clubs* Northern Counties; *Style—* Roger Errington, Esq; Abbey House, Newminster, Morpeth, Northumberland NE61 2YJ (☎ 0670 514678); T Crossling & Co Ltd, P O Box 5, Coast Rd, Newcastle upon Tyne NE6 5TP (☎ 091 2654166, fax 091 2764839, telex 537559)

ERRINGTON, Stuart Grant; JP (1970); s of Sir Eric Errington, Bt (d 1973), and Marjorie, *née* Grant Bennett (d 1973); *b* 23 June 1929; *Educ* Rugby, Trinity Coll Oxford (MA); *m* 19 June 1954, Anne, da of Eric Baedeker; 2 s (David, Charles), 1 da (Elizabeth (Mrs Corke); *Career* Nat Serv, 2 Lt RA; mangr Ellerman Lines 1952-59, md Astley Industl Tst 1959-70 (former mangr), chm Mercantile Credit 1977-89 (former exec dir 1970-77, chief exec), dir Barclays UK Ltd, Barclays Merchant Bank 1979-80, chair Nat Assoc CAB 1989; chm: Equipment Leasing Assoc 1976-78, Euro Leasing Assoc 1978-80, Fin Houses Assoc 1982-84; Liveryman: Worshipful Co of Broderers, Worshipful Co of Coachmakers and Coach Harness Makers; CBIM; *Recreations* fishing, golf; *Clubs* Boodle's; *Style—* Stuart Errington, Esq, JP; Earleywood Lodge, Ascot, Berks SL5 9JP; Myddleton House, 115-123 Pentonville Rd, London N1 9LZ (☎ 071 833 2181, fax 071 833 4371, car 0836 510663)

ERROLL, 24 Earl of (S 1452); Merlin Sereld Victor Gilbert Hay; 12 Bt (NS 1685), of Moncreiffe, Perthshire; also 28 Hereditary Lord High Constable of Scotland (conferred as Great Constable of Scotland *ante* 1309 and made hereditary by charter of Robert I 1314), Lord Hay (S 1429) and Lord Slains (S 1452); Chief of the Hays; as Lord High Constable, has precedence in Scotland before all other hereditary honours after the Blood Royal; also maintains private officer-at-arms (Slains Pursuivant); s of Countess of Erroll (d 1978) by her 1 husb, Sir Iain Moncreiffe of that Ilk, 11 Bt (d 1985); his gggggf (the 18 Earl)'s w, Elizabeth FitzClarence, natural da of King William IV, whose arms he quarters debruised by a baton sinister; *b* 20 April 1948; *Educ* Eton, Trinty Coll Cambridge; *m* 8 May 1982, Isabelle, o da of Thomas Sidney Astell Hohler (d 1989), of Wolverton Park, Basingstoke; 2 s (Lord Hay, Hon Richard b 14 Dec 1990), 2 da (Lady Amelia b 23 Nov 1986, Lady Laline b 21 Dec 1987); *Heir* s, Harry Thomas William (Lord Hay) b 8 Aug 1984; *Career* computer conslt; memb Queen's Body Guard for Scotland (Royal Co of Archers); Lt Atholl Highlanders; OStJ; *Recreations* skiing, climbing, parachuting, territorials; *Clubs* Turf, White's, Pratt's, Puffin's; *Style—* The Rt Hon the Earl of Erroll; Wolverton Farm, Basingstoke, Hants RG26 5SX (☎ 0635 298267); Old Slains, Collieston, Aberdeenshire

ERROLL OF HALE, 1 Baron (UK 1964), of Kilmun, Co Argyll; Frederick James Erroll; PC (1960), TD; s of George Murison Erroll (d 1926; s of Bergmans Theodor John, of Rotterdam, by his w Margaret Murison (d 1924); he assumed the surname Erroll by deed poll 1914), and Kathleen Donovan Edington (d 1952); *b* 27 May 1914; *Educ* Oundle, Trinity Coll Cambridge; *m* 19 Dec 1950, Elizabeth, da of Richard Sowton Barrow, of Foxholes, Exmouth, Devon; *Career* MP (C) Altrincham and Sale 1945-64; Parly sec Miny of Supply 1955-56, Bd of Trade 1956-58; economic sec to Treasury 1958-59, min of state Bd of Trade 1959-61 (pres 1961-63), min of Power 1963-64, memb NEDC 1962-63; chm: Bowater Corpn 1973-84, Consolidated Gold Fields 1976-83 (pres 1983-), Whessoe plc (engrg gp based in Darlington); chm Automobile Assoc 1973-86 (vice pres 1986-); *Style—* The Rt Hon Lord Erroll of Hale,

PC, TD; House of Lords, London SW1A 0PW

ERSKINE, (Thomas) Adrian; s of Daniel Erskine, and Molly, *née* Balmer (d 1979); *b* 7 Aug 1934; *Educ* St Malachys Coll Belfast, Queen's Univ Belfast (BSc), Imperial Coll London (DIC); *Career* civil engr Dept of Highways Ontario Canada 1957-59, structural engr Ove Arup and Partners London 1960-62, head Ulster branch BRC Engineering Co Ltd 1964-69, assoc i/c civil and structural work Belfast office Building Design Partnership 1969-78, ptnr McGladdery & Partners (consltg, civil and structural engrs) Belfast 1978-; CEng, MICE 1962; *Recreations* squash, golf, cricket; *Clubs* Belfast Boat, Belvoir Golf, Woodvale Cricket; *Style—* Adrian Erskine, Esq; 24 Sandhurst Drive, Belfast BT9 5AY (☎ 0232 668706); McGladdery and Partners, 64 Malone Ave, Belfast BT9 6ER (☎ 0232 660682)

ERSKINE, Barbara; da of Stuart Nigel Rose, of Hay-on-Wye, and Pamela Yvonne, *née* Anding (d 1988); *b* 10 Aug 1944; *Educ* St George's Harpenden, Univ of Edinburgh (MA); *m* 2 s (Adrian James Earl, Jonathan Erskine Alexander); *Career* freelance editor and journalist, short story writer, novelist; pubns: Lady of Hay 1986, Kingdom of Shadows 1988, Encounters 1990; memb Soc of Authors; *Recreations* reading, riding, growing and using herbs, exploring the past; *Style—* Mrs Barbara Erskine; Blake Friedmann Literary Agents, 37-41 Gower St, London WC1E 6HH (☎ 071 631 4331)

ERSKINE, Hon Mrs David; Caroline Mary; yr da of Rt Hon Sir Alan Frederick Lascelles, GCVO, KCB, CMG, MC, (d 1981); *b* 15 Feb 1928; *m* 1, 20 May 1949, 2 Viscount Chandos (d 1980); 2 s, 2 da; m 2, 3 May 1985, Hon David Hervey Erskine, *qv*; *Style—* The Hon Mrs David Erskine; Felsham House, Felsham, Bury St Edmunds, Suffolk IP30 0QG (☎ 0449 736326); 17 Clareville Court, Clarevile Grove, London SW7 5AT (☎ 071 373 4734)

ERSKINE, Hon David Hervey; DL (Suffolk 1983); 3 s of John Francis Ashley, Lord Erskine, GCSI, GCIE (d 1953, himself s of 12 Earl of Mar and (14 Earl of) Kellie), and Lady Marjorie Hervey (d 1967), er da of 4 Marquess of Bristol; *b* 5 Nov 1924; *Educ* Eton, Trinity Coll Cambridge; *m* 1, 5 Dec 1953, Jean Violet (d 1983), da of Lt-Col Archibald Vivian Campbell Douglas of Mains; 3 da; m 2, 3 May 1985, Caroline Mary, widow of 2 Viscount Chandos (d 1980), and da of Rt Hon Sir Alan Lascelles, GCVO, KCB, CMG, MC (d 1981); *Career* War Serv Italy and Palestine 1944-47; called to Bar Inner Temple 1950, JP Suffolk 1971-86, late Capt Scots Gds; cncllr W Suffolk 1969-74 and Suffolk 1974-85; *Recreations* historical study, sightseeing; *Clubs* Brook's; *Style—* The Hon David Erskine, DL; Felsham House, Felsham, Bury St Edmunds IP30 0QG (☎ 0449 736326); 17 Clareville Court, Clareville Grove, London SW7 5AT (☎ 071 373 4734)

ERSKINE, Sir (Thomas) David; 5 Bt (UK 1821), of Cambo, Fife; JP (Fife 1951), DL (1955); s of Lt-Col Sir Thomas Wilfred Hargreaves John Erskine, 4 Bt, DSO, DL (d 1944, third in descent from Sir David Erskine, 1 Bt, natural gs of 9 Earl of Kellie) of Cambo, Kingsbarns, Fife, and Magdalen Janet, da of Sir Ralph Anstruther, 6 Bt of Balcaskie; *b* 31 July 1912; *Educ* Eton, Magdalene Coll Cambridge (BA); *m* 4 Oct 1947, Ann, da of Col Neil Fraser-Tytler, DSO, MC, TD, DL (d 1937), of Aldourie Castle, Inverness, and Mrs (C H) Fraser-Tytler, CBE *qv*; 2 s (Peter, William), 1 da (Caroline d 1976); *Heir* s, Thomas Peter Neil Erskine; *Career* served WWII, M East, India, Malaya as Maj Indian Corps Engrs; with Butterfield & Swire Hongkong & China 1935-41; landed proprietor (approx 1600 acres) & farmer 1946-; Fife cnllr 1953-74, chm Fife CC 1970-73 (vice-chm 1967-70), Fife regnl cncllr 1974-82; vice Lt Fife 1982-87; *Recreations* gardening, shooting, travel; *Clubs* New (Edinburgh); *Style—* Sir David Erskine, Bt, JP; Westnewhall, Kingsbarns, St Andrews, Fife (☎ 0333 50228)

ERSKINE, Donald Seymour; DL (Perth and Kinross 1969); s of Col Sir Arthur Edward Erskine, GCVO, DSO (d 1963), and Rosemary, *née* Baird; *b* 28 May 1925; *Educ* Wellington; *m* 1963, Catharine Annandale, da of late Kenneth T McLelland; 1 s, 4 da; *Career* serv 1943-47 as Capt RA with Airborne Forces (Europe and Palestine); chartered surveyor; factor for CGA 1950-55, ALPF Wallace of Candacraig 1955-61; factor and dep dir Nat Tst for Scotland 1961-89, gen tstee Church of Scot 1989-; memb Queen's Body Guard for Scot (Royal Co of Archers) 1958; *Recreations* shooting, singing; *Clubs* New (Edinburgh); *Style—* Donald Erskine, Esq, DL; Cleish House, Cleish, Kinross (☎ 057 75 232)

ERSKINE, Lord; James Thorne Erskine; s and h of Maj the 13 Earl of Mar (and 15 of) Kellie, JP, *qv*; *b* 10 March 1949; *Educ* Eton, Moray House Coll of Educn Edinburgh (Dip Social Work, Dip Youth & Co Work), Inverness College (Certificate in Bldg); *m* 1974, Mary Irene, da of Dougal McDougal Kirk, of 137 Easter Rd, Edinburgh, and former w of Roderick Mooney; 5 step children; *Heir* bro, Hon Alexander David Erskine; *Career* Flying Offr RAuxAF 1982-86 (2622 Highland Sqdn), memb RN Aux Serv 1985-89; page of honour to HM 1962-63; community serv volunteer York 1967-68, youth and community worker Craig Millar 1971-73; social worker: Sheffield 1973-76, Elgin 1976-77, Forres 1977-78, Aviemore 1979, HM Prison Inverness 1979-81, Inverness West 1981, Merkinch 1982; supervisor Community Serv by Offenders Inverness 1983-87; assoc Abbey Life Assur Co Ltd 1983; bldg technician 1989-; *Recreations* cycling, gardening, elder of Church of Scotland, railways; *Clubs* New; *Style—* Lord Erskine; Erskine House, Kirk Wynd, Clackmannan, FK10 4JF (☎ 0259 212 438)

ERSKINE, Rev the Hon Michael John; s of 13 Earl of Mar and 15 of Kellie; *b* 5 April 1956; *Educ* Eton, Edinburgh Univ; *m* 5 Sept 1987, Jill, er da of late Campbell S Westwood, of 11 Leighton Gdns, Ellon; *Recreations* hillwalking, travel, outdoor sports; *Clubs* New (Edinburgh); *Style—* The Rev the Hon Michael Erskine; c/o Claremont House, Alloa, Clackmannanshire FK10 2JF (☎ 0259 212020)

ERSKINE, (Thomas) Peter Neil; s and h of Sir David Erskine, 5 Bt, JP, DL; *b* 28 March 1950; *Educ* Eton, Univ of Birmingham, Univ of Edinburgh (post grad); *m* 1972, Catherine, da of Col G H K Hewlett; 2 s (Thomas Struan b 1977, James Dunbar b 1979), 2 da (Gillian Christian b 1983, Mary Caroline b 1986); *Career* worked hotel indust Brazil, returned home to estate; opened visitor centre on one of the farms 1982; currently converting the estate to organic farming; chm Scottish Organic Producer Assoc; professional photographer; *Style—* Peter Erskine, Esq

ERSKINE, Hon Robert William Hervey; yst s of late John Francis Ashley, Lord Erskine, GCSI, GCIE (d 1953); *b* 13 Oct 1930; *Educ* Eton, King's Coll Cambridge; *m* 1, 21 May 1955 (m dis 1964), Jennifer Shirley, yr da of L J Cardew Wood, of Farnham Royal, Bucks; m 2, Oct 1969 (m dis 1975), Annemarie Alvarez de Toledo, da of Jean Lattes, of Paris; 1 s (Alistair Robert) ; m 3, 1977, Belinda, da of Raymond Blackburn, of London; 2 s (Thomas Gerald, Felix Benjamin, late Lt Scots Gds); *Career* author, broadcaster; FSA 1990; *Style—* The Hon Robert Erskine, FSA; 100 Elgin Cres, London, W11 2JL (☎ 071 221 6229)

ERSKINE-HILL, Christine, Lady; Christine Alison; o da of late Capt Henry James Johnstone, RN, of Alva; *b* 13 Jan 1924; *m* 7 Aug 1942, Sir Robert Erskine-Hill, 2 Bt (d 1989); 2 s (Sir Alexander Roger, 3 Bt, *qv*, Henry James b 1953), 2 da (Carola Marion b 1943 (*see* Stormonth-Darling, R A), Alison b 1945); *Style—* Christine, Lady Erskine-Hill; Harelea House, Libberton, Carnwath, Lanarkshire ML11 8LX

ERSKINE-HILL, Dr Howard Henry; s of Capt Henry Erskine-Hill, of Malahide, Co Dublin, Eire, and Hannah Lilian, *née* Poppleton; *b* 19 June 1936; *Educ* Ashville Coll, Univ of Nottingham (BA, PhD); *Career* Univ Coll Swansea Univ of Wales 1960-69 (tutor, asst lectr, lectr in Eng); Cambridge Univ: lectr in Eng 1969-83, reader in literary history 1984-, fell Jesus Coll 1969-80, fell Pembroke Coll 1980-; Olin Fell Nat Humanities Center NC USA 1988-89; Hon LittD Cantab 1988; FBA 1985; *Books* Pope: Horatian Satires and Epistles (ed, 1964), Pope: The Dunciad (1972), The Social Milieu of Alexander Pope (1975), The Augustan Idea (1983); *Recreations* walking; *Clubs* Utd Oxford and Cambridge Univ; *Style—* Dr Howard Erskine-Hill; 194 Chesterton Road, Cambridge CB4 1NE; Pembroke College, Cambridge CB2 1RF (☎ 0223 338138)

ERSKINE-HILL, Sir (Alexander) Roger; 3 Bt (UK 1945), of Quothquhan, Co Lanark; er s of Sir Robert Erskine-Hill, 2 Bt (d 1989), and Christine Alison, *née* Johnstone; *b* 15 Aug 1949; *Educ* Eton, Univ of Aberdeen (LLB); *m* 6 Oct 1984, Sarah Anne Sydenham, da of Dr Richard John Sydenham Clarke (d 1970); 1 s (Robert Benjamin b 1986), 1 da (Kirsty Rose b 1985); *Heir* s, Robert Benjamin Erskine-Hill b 6 Aug 1986; *Career* dir: Salestrac Ltd, The Offer Shop Ltd, Map Mktg Ltd; *Style—* Sir Roger Erskine-Hill, Bt; Great Coleford, Stoodleigh, Tiverton, Devon EX16 9QG; Salestrac Ltd, Cowley Bridge Rd, Exeter EX4 5HQ (☎ 0392 210631)

ERSKINE-MURRAY, (Arthur) Sydney Elibank; o s of Lt-Col Arthur Erskine-Murray, CBE, DSO (d 1948), and Ena Nelson, *née* Trestrail (d 1942); *b* 29 March 1909; *Educ* Bedford Sch, Univ of Birmingham (BSc); *m* 29 June 1940, Florence Duncan, da of William Duncan Robertson; 2 da (Ann, Susan); *Career* mgmnt conslt then vice chm Inbucon Ltd 1944-69; dir: Thomas Poole & Gladstone 1973-78, Grindley of Stoke Ltd 1974-78, Bentley Pianos Ltd 1974-78, S Newman Ltd 1973-78; chm Churchill Guns Ltd 1974-76; MICE, MBIM; *Style—* Sydney Erskine-Murray Esq; Myrtle Bank, Great Amwell, Ware, Herts SG13 9SN (☎ 0920 870146)

ERSKINE-MURRAY, Hon Timothy Alexander Elibank; yr s of 14 Lord Elibank; *b* 6 May 1967; *Educ* Eton, Exeter Univ; *Recreations* rugby, golf, tennis, squash, sailing, fives; *Style—* Hon Timothy Erskine-Murray; The Coach House, Charters Rd, Sunningdale, Ascot, Berks SL5 9QB (☎ 0990 22099)

ERSKINE OF RERRICK, Henrietta, Baroness; Henrietta; da of late William Dunnett, of East Canisbay Caithness; *m* 15 Sept 1922, 1 Baron Erskine of Rerrick, GBE (d 1980); 1 s (2 Baron), 1 da (Hon Mrs Butler); *Career* CStJ; *Style—* The Rt Hon Henrietta, Lady Erskine of Rerrick; 8B Churchfields Avenue, Weybridge, Surrey

ERSKINE OF RERRICK, 2 Baron (UK 1964); Maj Sir Iain Maxwell Erskine; 2 Bt (UK 1961); s of 1 Baron (d 1980); *b* 22 Jan 1926; *Educ* Harrow, Ashridge Management Course; *m* 1, 20 July 1955 (m dis 1964), Marie Elisabeth Burton (now Elisabeth, Countess of Caledon), da of late Maj Richard Burton Allen, 3 Dragoon Gds; m 2, 1974 (m dis), Marie Josephine, da of Dr Josef Klupt; 3 da (Hon Henrietta b 1975, Hon Griselda b 1979, Hon Cora b 1981); *Heir* None; *Career* War Serv Air Crew Training RAFVR 1943, 2 Lt Grenadier Gds 1945, ADC to Cmdt RMA Sandhurst 1951-52, comptroller to Govr-Gen of NZ 1960-62, ret as Maj 1963 (Temp Lt-Col 1961); PR offr to Brigade of Guards 1963-65; higher exec offr Civil Serv MOD 1964-66, dir of PR Saward Baker Ltd 1966-72, md Lonrho Ltd Iran 1972-73, dir Wansdyke Security Ltd 1974-85, London mangr Marples Ridgway Construction Ltd 1974-85; chm Strabo Limited and Erskine Associates 1976; currently dir: Tozer Marples (China Ltd), WSTV Productions Limited 1988-, ISICAD Computers 1989-, Kilpatrick Estates Limited Scotland, CDA International Limited (and chm); chm: Caledonian Commodities Limited Edinburgh 1979-82, D K Financial Services 1988-89; professional photographer; life memb: Nat Tst of Scotland, Royal Photographic Soc (and memb Ctee); memb Ctee and dir De Havilland Aircraft Museum (British Aerospace) 1967-88; qualified pilot 1948 (chm Guards Flying Club 1959-65, Col Confederate Air Force 1983); tstee: RAF Museum Hendon (Bomber Command), Stoke Mandeville Hosp (David Tolkien Tst), Transport Tst; patron: Physically Handicapped and Able Bodied, Orchestra of the World; OStJ; Chevalier Legion of Honor (France); MIPR, MCIM, FInstD; *Recreations* fly fishing, aviation, photography, good food; *Clubs* White's, Special Forces; *Style—* Maj The Rt Hon Lord Erskine of Rerrick; c/o House of Lords, London SW1A 0PW

ERVIN, Wilson; CBE (1986); s of Robert John Ervin (d 1966), of 32 Lucerne Parade, Belfast, and Jane, *née* McVeigh (d 1983); *b* 13 Dec 1923; *Educ* Royal Belfast Academical Inst; *m* Joan Catherine, da of John Mercer, of 7 Broughton Park, Belfast; *Career* served in Fleet Air Arm RN (non cmmnd) in Home Waters, Far East, India, Burma and Australia; banker: dir (formerly chief exec) Northern Bank Ltd (ret from active banking 1985, curretnly non-exec dir); chm: TBF Thompson (Garvagh) Ltd, Jas Anderson Ltd; former pres Inst of Bankers in Ireland; FIB; *Clubs* Ulster Reform, Belvoir Park Golf; *Style—* Wilson Ervin, CBE; 29 Broomhill Park, Belfast BT9 5JB

ERVINE-ANDREWS, Lt-Col Harold Marcus; VC (1940); s of Cyril Clark Ervine-Andrews (d 1948), of New Ross Co Wexford Eire, and Margaret Agnes, *née* O'Halloran (d 1948); *b* 29 July 1911; *Educ* Stonyhurst, RMC Sandhurst; *m* 1, 26 Oct 1939 (m dis), (Emily Annabel Grace) Betty (d 1976), da of Robert Ireland Torrie (d 1970), of Chatsford, Waterford Eire; 1 s (Robert Marcus b 28 Oct 1943), 1 da (Felicity Mary b 2 Oct 1941); m 2, Margaret Cecelia Gregory; *Career* E Lancs Regt, (despatches) 1939, GSO 1 Air HQ SW Pacific Area 1942-43, SALO to cmdg Adm 21 Air Craft Carrier Sqdn E Indies 1945, ADPR Rhine Army 1951; *Recreations* fishing; *Style—* Lt-Col Harold Ervine-Andrews, VC; Treveor Cottage, Gorran, St Austell, Cornwall PL26 6LW (☎ 0726 842 140)

ESAM, David Richard; s of Richard Terrell Esam, of Bath, Avon, and Hilda Margaret, *née* Caswell; *b* 29 Jan 1952; *Educ* Highgate, Univ of Warwick (BA); *m* 21 June 1975, Drusilla Mary, da of James Beesley, of Burnham on Sea, Somerset; 1 s (Andrew David b 1987); *Career* slr; ptnr Crawford Owen Bristol; *Recreations* birdwatching; *Style—* David R Esam, Esq; 3 Hughenden Rd, Clifton, Bristol BS8 2TT; Crawford Owen, 43 Queen Square, Bristol BS1 4QR (☎ 0272 251385, fax 0272 251296)

ESDAILE, (James) Edmund Kennedy; er s of Arundell James Kennedy Esdaile, CBE, sec British Museum and pres Lib Assoc (d 1956), and Katherine Ada, *née* McDowall, art historian (d 1950); gs of J K Esdaile, JP, DL, High Sheriff of Sussex, and Florence, *née* Crawshay, and of Andrew McDowall, sec GPDST, and Ada, *née* Benson, sister of the Archbishop; *b* 21 Sept 1910; *Educ* Lancing, Pembroke Coll Oxford (MA, BLitt); *m* 1939, Ellen Jane Sausmarez Carey (d 1984), da of Rev Christopher Sausmarez Carey and gt niece of George Ward Hunt, Chancellor of the Exchequer and First Lord of the Admiralty under Disraeli; 2 da (Julia Susan Ianthe b 1941, Sarah Jane Philomena b 1946); *Career* announcer BBC 1935-1938; schoolmaster and lectr; insurance Legal & General, ret; asst to mother for her publications: English Monumental Sculpture since the Renaissance (1927), The Stantons of Holborn (1929), Temple Church Monuments (1933); contrib: Thieme Becker's Allgemeines Künstler Lexicon (*ca* 1929-1935), Country Life; reviewer TLS; co fndr Men of the Stones 1947; author, poet; *Publications* Monuments in Ely Cathedral (1973); author of many articles on the history of cricket, edited and illustrated in pen and ink A Silver Shape by his ggf George Crawshay (1980); *Recreations* cricket (when young), shooting (unambitiously), watching cricket and rackets; *Clubs* Arundel Park CC; *Style—* Edmund Esdaile, Esq; 61 North Road, Hertford SG14 1NF

ESDALE, Gerald Paton Rivett; s of Charles James August Esdale (d 1949), of Sutton, Surrey, and Avice Mary, *née* Rivett (d 1963); *b* 21 Oct 1929; *Educ* Malvern, Cambridge (MA); *m* 6 May 1957, Patricia Joyce, da of Elliot David Lindop (d 1974); 1 s (Mark b 1958), 1 da (Patricia b 1963); *Career* Nat Serv 2 Lt WG 1948-50; Thames

Liquid Fuels Ltd (dir 1962), Thames Rico, Thames Petroleum Scotland; CEng, MIMechE, FInstPet; *Clubs* MCC; *Style—* Gerald Esdale, Esq; 58 Wildwood Rd, Hampstead, London NW11 6UP (☎ 081 455 5860); 11 Elvaston Place, London SW7 (☎ 071 581 1729)

ESHER, 4 Viscount (UK 1897); Maj Lionel Gordon Baliol Brett; CBE (1970); also Baron Esher (UK 1885); s of 3 Viscount, GBE (d 1963); *b* 18 July 1913; *Educ* Eton, New Coll Oxford; *m* 22 Oct 1935, (Helena) Christian Olive, da of Ebenezer John Lecky Pike, CBE, MC, DL, of Ditcham Park, Petersfield, Hants; 5 s, 1 da; *Heir* s, Hon Christopher Brett; *Career* served WWII RA (despatches); architect and planner Hatfield New Town 1949-59; memb Royal Fine Art Cmmn 1951-69, pres RIBA 1965-67, memb Advsy Bd Victoria & Albert Museum 1967-72, govr London Museum 1970-77, rector and vice-provost Royal Coll of Art 1971-78; chm: Art Panel Arts Cncl of GB 1972-77, Advsy Bd for Redundant Churches to 1983; tstee Soane Museum 1976-; chm Northern Home Counties Nat Tst 1979-85; Hon DLitt Strathclyde 1967, Hon D Univ York 1970, Hon DSc Edinburgh 1981; *Books* (writes as Lionel Brett) Houses (1947), The World of Architecture (1963), Landscape in Distress (1965), York: a Study in Conservation (1969), Parameters and Images (1970), A Broken Wave: the Rebuilding of England 1940-80 (1981), The Continuing Heritage (1982) Our Selves Unknown (1984); *Clubs* Arts; *Style—* Maj The Rt Hon Viscount Esher, CBE; Christmas Common Tower, Watlington, Oxford

ESMONDE, Eithne, Lady; Eithne Moira Grattan; da of late Sir Thomas Henry Grattan Esmonde, 11 Bt; *b* 1902; *m* 9 June 1927, Sir Anthony Charles Esmonde, 15 Bt (d 1981); 3 s, 3 da; *Style—* Eithne, Lady Esmonde; Ballynastragh, Gorey, Co Wexford

ESMONDE, Sir Thomas Francis Grattan; 17 Bt (I 1692); s of His Hon Judge Sir John Esmonde, 16 Bt (d 1987); *b* 14 Oct 1960; *Educ* Sandford Park Sch, Univ of Dublin (MB BCh, BAO, MRCPI, MRCP); *m* 26 April 1986, Pauline Loretto, da of James Vincent Kearns; *Heir* s, Sean Vincent Grattan Esmonde b 8 Jan 1989; *Style—* Sir Thomas Esmonde, Bt; 6 Nutley Avenue, Donnybrook, Dublin 4, Ireland

ESPENHAHN, Peter Ian; s of Edward William Espenhahn, of E Molesey, and Barbara Mary, *née* Winmill; *b* 14 March 1944; *Educ* Westminster, Sidney Sussex Coll Cambridge (MA); *m* 10 Feb 1968, Fiona Elizabeth, *née* Young, Air Vice Marshall Brian Pashley Young, of Diamarton, Glos; 2 d (Sarah b 1971, Caroline b 1975); *Career* Deloitte Haskins & Sells London 1965-72, dir corp fin dept Morgan Grenfell & Co Ltd 1983- (joined 1973); FCA; *Recreations* sailing, rugby, opera; *Style—* Peter Espenhahn, Esq; 79 Mount Ararat Rd, Richmond, Surrey TW10 6PL; Morgan Grenfell & Co Ltd, 23 Great Winchester St, London EC2P 2AX (☎ 071 826 6255, fax 071 826 6180)

ESPLEN, (Sir) John Graham; 3 Bt (UK 1921), of Hardres Court, Canterbury (but does not use title); o s of Sir (William) Graham Esplen, 2 Bt (d 1989), and Aline Octavia, *née* Hedley; *b* 4 Aug 1932; *Educ* Harrow, St Catharine's Coll Camb (BA); *m* 6 Oct 1956, Valerie Joan, yr da of Maj-Gen Albert Percy Lambooy, CB, OBE; 1 s, 3 da (Wendy Anne b 1959, Fiona Mary b 1960, Mary Caroline b 1962); *Heir* s, William John Harry Esplen b 24 Feb 1967; *Style—* John Esplen, Esq; The Mill House, Moorlands Road, Merriott, Somerset TA16 5NF

ESSENHIGH, Bryan Geoffrey; s of Cdr Thomas Roland Essenhigh (d 1975), of Sevenoaks, Kent, and Winifred, *née* Fox (d 1957); *b* 22 March 1927; *Educ* Tonbridge, Univ of Glasgow; *m* 15 Nov 1952, Barbara Mary, da of Charles Stanley Murgatroyd (d 1962), of Otford, Kent; 1 s (Simon b 1955), 2 da (Susan b 1953, d 1954, Mary b 1958); *Career* Naval Airman 1945-47; estate mangr (fin) 1948-; dir: Brydon Fin Ltd 1970-90, Oastbarn Ltd 1981-; Liveryman Worshipful Co of Patternmakers 1981-; *Recreations* philately, usual country pursuits; *Style—* Bryan G Essenhigh, Esq; Knap Farm, Ridge, Chilmark, Salisbury, Wilts SP3 5BS (☎ 0747 870267); Morrison Estate Office, Fonthill Bishop, Salisbury

ESSER, Robin Charles; s of Charles Esser (d 1982), and Winifred Eileen Esser (d 1972); *b* 6 May 1935; *Educ* Wheelwright GS Dewsbury, Wadham Coll Oxford (BA, MA); *m* 1, 5 Jan 1959, Irene Shirley, *née* Clough (d 1973); 2 s (Daniel b 1962, Toby b 1963), 2 da (Sarah Jane b 1961, Rebecca b 1965); m 2, 30 May 1981, Tui, *née* France; 2 s (Jacob b 1986, Samuel b 1990); *Career* cmmnd 2 Lt KOYLI 1955, transferred General Corps 1956, Capt acting ADPR BAOR 1957; freelance reporter 1956; Daily Express: staff reporter 1957-60, ed William Hickley Column 1962, features ed 1963, NY Bureau 1965, northern ed 1969, exec ed 1970; conslt ed Evening News 1977, exec ed Daily Express 1984-86, ed Sunday Express 1986-89, ed conslt 1989-; *Books* The Hot Potato (1969), The Paper Chase (1971); *Recreations* lunching, sailing, talking, reading; *Style—* Robin Esser, Esq; 35 Elthiron Road, London SW6 4BW

ESSEX, Christine, Countess of; Christine Mary; da of late George Frederick Davis, of Handsworth Wood, Warwicks; *m* 1957, as his 4 w, 8 Earl of Essex (d 8 Dec 1966); *Style—* The Rt Hon Christine, Countess of Essex; 16 Ocean Dve, Merimbula, NSW 2548, Australia

ESSEX, David Albert; s of Albert Cook, of Romford, Essex, and Doris, *née* Kemp; *b* 23 July 1947; *Educ* Shipman Secdy Sch E London; *m* 12 March 1971, Maureen Annette, *née* Neal; 1 s (Daniel Lee), 1 da (Verity Leigh); *Career* actor, singer, composer, prodr; theatre performances incl: Jesus in Godspell (Wyndhams Theatre London) 1972-73 (winner Variety Club Award), Che Guevara in Evita (Prince Edward Theatre London) 1978 (winner Variety Club Award), Lord Byron in Childe Byron (Young Vic Theatre) 1981, Fletcher Christian in own musical (with Richard Crane) Mutiny (Piccadilly Theatre London) and recorded concept album with RPO 1985-86; films incl: That'll Be The Day 1973, Stardust 1974, Silver Dream Racer (composed score) 1979-80; given worldwide concerts for 17 years, winner many gold and silver discs; innumerable TV and radio appearances in: UK, Europe, USA, Australia; involved with numerous charities incl Save the Children Fund, ambassador VSO 1990; memb: Br Actors Equity Assoc, Musicians Union, American Fedn of TV and Radio Artists; *Recreations* cricket, flying helicopters (captain), squash; *Clubs* St James, Lord's Taverners; *Style—* David Essex, Esq; (☎ 071 402 5169, fax 071 723 2768)

ESSEX, David Anthony Dampier; *b* 10 May 1946; *Educ* Lancing, City Univ Business Sch (MSc); *m* 29 April 1972, Virginia; 3 da (Harriet b 1974, Polly b 1976, Tiffany b 1979); *Career* CA; fin controller British Aerospace 1982-85 (chief internal auditor 197 ptnr (i/c servs to mfrs) Ernst & Young 1987- (ptnr 1985-); FCA 1969; *Recreations* family, walking, gardening, France; *Style—* David Essex, Esq; 1 Lambeth Palace Rd, London SE1 7EU (☎ 071 928 2000)

ESSEX, Francis; s of Harold Essex-Lopresti (d 1967), (5 in descent from Count Lopresti, of Sicily), and Beatrice Essex-Lopresti (d 1971); *b* 24 March 1929; *Educ* Cotton Coll, N Staffs; *m* 13 Aug 1956, Jeanne, da of John Shires (d 1982); 2 s (Martin, Stephen); *Career* author, composer, prodr, prodr BBC TV (Light entertainment) 1954-60; sr prodr ATV 1960-65; prog controller Scottish TV 1965-69; prodn controller ATV 1969-76 (dir 1974-81, dir of prodns 1976-81); wrote and presented The Bells of St Martins 1953, directed Six of One (Adelphi theatre) 1964; film scripts: Shillingbury Tales, The Silent Scream, The Night Wind, Cuffy (series), Gabrielle and the Doodleman; music scores: Luke's Kingdom, The Seas must Live, The Lightning Tree, Maddie with Love, The Cedar Tree; writer of plays and songs; chm Conservatives Abroad Javea 1990-; FRTS; Br Acad Light Entertainment Award 1964, Leonard Brett Award 1964; *Books* Shillingbury Tales (1983), Skerrymor Bay (1984); *Recreations* blue water sailing, gardening, tennis; *Style—* Francis Essex, Esq; Punta Vista, Aldea de las Cuevas, Benidoleig, Alicante, Spain

ESSEX, Nona, Countess of; Nona Isobel; da of David Wilson Miller, of Christchurch, NZ; *m* 1, Francis Sydney Smythe, of Sussex (decd); m 2, 6 Nov 1957, as his 2 w, 9 Earl of Essex, TD (d 1981); *Style—* The Rt Hon Nona, Countess of Essex; Capell, 3 Leyburne Close, Ledburn, nr Leighton Buzzard, Beds

ESSEX, 10 Earl of (E 1661); Robert Edward de Vere Capell; also Baron Capell of Hadham (E 1641), and Viscount Malden (E 1661); s of Arthur Algernon de Vere Capell (d 1924; gs of Capt Hon Algernon Capell, RN, bro of 6 Earl of Essex), and Alice Mabel, *née* Currie (d 1951); suc kinsman, 9 Earl, 1981, took seat in House of Lords 7 June 1989; *b* 13 Jan 1920; *m* 3 Jan 1942, Doris Margaret, da of George Tomlinson; 1 s; *Heir* s, Viscount Malden; *Career* served WWII, Flt Sgt RAF; *Style—* The Rt Hon the Earl of Essex; 2 Novak Place, Torrisholme, Morecambe, Lancs

ESSEX, William Alexander Wells; s of Norman Arthur Essex, and Jane Rosemary Wells, *née* Tickler; *b* 13 Aug 1958; *Educ* Marlborough, UEA; *m* 24 Sept 1988, Penelope Anne, da of Lt Cdr David McKerrow Baird; 1 da (Clementine b 24 Oct 1990); *Career* joined Financial Times Group 1982, ed Resident Abroad Magazine 1985-; *Style—* William Essex, Esq; Potash Cottage, Strethall, Essex (☎ 0799 23507); 108 Clerkenwell Rd, EC1M 5SA (☎ 071 251 9321, fax 071 251 4686)

ESSINGTON-BOULTON, Hon Mrs (Crystal); *née* Russell; da of 2 Baron Russell of Liverpool, CBE, MC, by his 2 w; *b* 4 Jan 1936; *m* 23 June 1955 (m dis 1969), John Mark Essington-Boulton, s of Maj Clive Essington-Boulton, of Turvey, Beds; 1 s, 1 da; *Career* restaurateur; ptnr in Edward's Poissonnerie Wine Bar and Restaurant Bath Avon; *Recreations* clay-pigeon shooting, skiing, charity fund raising; *Style—* The Hon Mrs Essington-Boulton; Ann Boleyn's Cottage, Grandmother's Rock Lane, Beach, Bitton, nr Bristol, Avon

ESSON-SCOTT, Hon Mrs (Rosemary Sylvia); da of 13 Viscount Falkland, OBE, and aunt of 15 Viscount; *b* 22 Feb 1910; *m* 1, 17 July 1928 (m dis 1936), John de Perigault Gurney Mayhew, er s of late Lt-Col Sir John Dixon Mayhew, TD, JP, DL; 1 s; m 2, 6 Jan 1937, Aubrey Esson-Scott, s of David Esson-Scott, of Ashley Croft, Walton-on-Thames; *Style—* Hon Mrs Esson-Scott; R2 Marine Gate, Brighton, Sussex

ESSWOOD, Paul Lawrence Vincent; s of Alfred Walter Esswood, and Freda, *née* Garratt; *b* 6 June 1942; *Educ* West Bridgford GS Nottingham, Royal Coll of Music (Henry Blower singing prize); *m* 1, (m dis 1990); 2 s (Gabriel Peter b 1968, Michael William b 1971); m 2, 4 Aug 1990, Aimée Desirée; *Career* opera, concert and recital singer (counter-tenor) specializing in Baroque period; operatic debut Berkeley Univ of California 1966; major performances: Zürich (Monteverdi Operas) Köln (A Midsummer Night's Dream by Britten) Stuttgart, Chicago, La Scala (Paradise Lost by Penderecki), Stuttgart (Akhnaten by Glass); solo recitals: Hyperion (Music for a While by Purcell), Hungaroton (Dichterliebe, Liederkreis Op39 by Schumann), Quint/Harmonia Mundi (English lute songs from Orpheus With his Lute); major recordings incl: all Bachs' Cantatas, Matthew Passion, Christmas Oratorio, Dido & Aeneas by Purcell, Brockes Passion by Telemann; recordings of Handel's work: Jeptha, Saul, Belshazzar, Rinaldo, Xerxes, Messiah, Il Pastor Fido; prof: of Singing RCM 1977-80, in Baroque vocal interpretation RAM 1985-; lay-vicar Westminster Abbey 1964-71; ARCM 1964, Hon RAM 1990; *Recreations* gardening (organic); *Style—* Paul Esswood, Esq; Jasmine Cottage, 42 Ferring Lane, Ferring, West Sussex BN12 6QT (☎ & fax 0903 504480)

ESTALL, Prof Robert Charles; s of Estall John Thomas (d 1967), of London, and Hilda Lilian, *née* West (d 1976); *b* 28 Sept 1924; *Educ* St Mary's Coll Twickenham (Teachers Certificate), LSE (BSc, PhD); *m* 2 April 1956, Mary, da of Frederick Willmott (d 1988), of Exeter; 3 s (Simon James b 1959, Martin Robert b 1961, Richard John b 1968), 1 da (Joanna Mary b 1957); *Career* Petty Offr RN 1942-46; visiting prof Clark Univ Mass USA 1958, res fell The American Cncl of Learned Socs 1962-63, visiting prof Univ of Pittsburg PA USA 1967, prof of geography LSE 1988- (lectr in geography 1955-65, reader in econ geography of N America 1965-88); *Books* New England: A Study in Industrial Adjustment (1966), A Modern Geography of the United States (1976), Industrial Activity and Economic Geography (1980); *Recreations* gardening, reading, walking, golf; *Style—* Prof Robert Estall; 48 The Ridings, Berrylands, Surbiton, Surrey KT5 8HQ (☎ 081 399 0430); London School of Economics, Houghton St, London WC2A 2AE (☎ 071 405 7686)

ESTEVE-COLL, Elizabeth Anne Loosemore; da of PW Kingdon and Nora Kingdon; *b* 14 Oct 1938; *Educ* Darlington Girls HS, Birkbeck Coll London (BA); *m* 1960, Jose Alexander Timothy Esteve-Coll; *Career* head learning resources Kingston Poly 1977, univ librarian Univ of Surrey 1982, keeper Nat Art Library and V & A Museum 1985, dir V & A Museum 1988-; *Recreations* reading, music, foreign travel; *Style—* Mrs Elizabeth Esteve-Coll; c/o Victoria & Albert Museum, South Kensington, London SW7 2RL (☎ 071 938 8501)

ETCHELLS, (Dorothea) Ruth; da of Rev Walter Etchells (d 1961), of Lancs, and Ada, *née* Hawksworth (d 1981); *b* 17 April 1931; *Educ* Merchant Taylors Sch for Girls Crosby Liverpool, Univ of Liverpool (BA, DipEd, MA), Univ of London (BD); *Career* head English Dept Aigburth Vale HS 1959, sr lectr and res tutor Chester Coll Educn 1965, sr lectr Univ of Durham 1973 (vice-princ Trevelyan Coll 1972), princ St John's Coll with Cranmer Hall Univ of Durham 1979- (elected fell St John's Coll 1990), ret 1988; first woman princ of C of E Theological Coll; memb: Governing Body Monkton Combe Sch 1979-90, Cncl Univ of Durham 1985-88, Gen Synod 1985-90 (memb Doctrine Cmmn 1985-91), Crown Appts Cmmn 1986-, Cncl Ridley Hall Cambridge 1989-; conslt Lambeth Conf 1988, chm House of Laity Durham Diocese 1988 (memb Bishops Cncl and Standing Ctee 1977-), memb Durham Family Practitioner Ctee (now Family Health Services Authy) 1988- (vice-chm 1990-); *Books* Unafraid To Be (1969), The Man with the Trumpet (1970), A Model of Making (1983); Poets and Prophets: Robert Browning, John Milton, George Herbert, Early English Poets (ed, 1988), Praying with the English Poets (ed, 1990); *Recreations* friends, pets, country walking; *Clubs* Royal Cwlth; *Style—* Miss Ruth Etchells; 12 Dunelm Ct, South St, Durham DH1 4QX (☎ 091 3841497)

ETKIN, Dr Herbert; s of Jack Etkin, of South Africa, and Helen, *née* Steinbuch; *b* 23 March 1935; *Educ* Athlone HS, Witwatersrand SA (MB BCh, DPM); *m* 5 Jan 1965 (m dis 1981), Janet Rosemary; 3 da (Kerrith Anne b 1966, Laura Jane b 1969, Beverly Nan b 1970); *Career* conslt psychiatrist SE Thames and SW Thames RHAs 1974-; Freeman City of London 1987, memb Soc of Apothecaries; FRCPsych 1987; *Recreations* golf, squash, music; *Clubs* Lewes Golf, Southdown (Lewes); *Style—* Dr Herbert Etkin; 2 De Warrenne Rd, Lewes, E Sussex BN7 1BP (☎ 0273 471118); 77 Grand Parade, Brighton, E Sussex BN7 1JA (☎ 0273 606328)

EUGSTER, Christopher Anthony Alwyn Patrick; s of Gen Sir Basil Eugster, KCB, KCVO, CBE, DSO, MC and Bar, DL (d 1984), and Marcia Elaine Smyth-Osbourne (d 1983); *b* 17 March 1941; *Educ* Downside; *m* 12 Nov 1965, Carole Jane, da of Sqdn Ldr John Bouwens, (ka 1941); 2 s (John b 1967, Rupert b 1969); *Career* dir Kleinwort Benson Ltd 1976-; *Recreations* shooting, fishing; *Clubs* White's, Pratt's; *Style—* Christopher Eugster, Esq

EURICH, Richard Ernst; OBE (1980); s of late Frederick William Eurich; *b* 14 March 1903; *Educ* Bradford GS, Bradford Sch of Arts and Crafts, Slade Sch of Art London; *m* 1934, Mavis Llewellyn, *née* Pope; 2 da (1 s decd); *Career* artist; exhibitions incl:

One Man Show of drawings Goupil Gallery 1929, 16 exhibitions of paintings Redfern Gallery, Royal Acad, New English Art Club, London Group, Tooth's Gallery, Fine Art Society Ltd; Retrospective Exhibitions: Bradford 1951, Bradford, Glasgow, London (Fine Art Soc) and Southampton 1980-81; works purchased by Contemporary Art Soc and Chantery Bequest, painting Dunkirk Beach 1940 purchased for Canadian govt, official war artist 1941-45, rep works in various public galleries incl: Tate Gallery, War Museum; Hon DLitt Bradford 1984; ARA 1942, RA 1953; *Recreations* music, gardening; *Style*— Richard Eurich, Esq, OBE; Appletreewick, 4 West Rd, Dibden Purlieu, Southampton, Hampshire (☎ 0703 842291)

EUSTACE, Hon Mrs (Dorothy Anne); yr da of 1 and last Baron Percy of Newcastle (d 1958), and Stella Katherine, *née* Drummond; *b* 21 Sept 1926; *Educ* Univ of Durham (MB BS); *m* 23 March 1957, Maj Thomas Robert Hales Eustace, o s of late Louis Charles Moss Eustace, of The Cliff, Mousehole, Penzance, Cornwall; 1 s (James b 1960), 2 da (Alicia b 1958, Katherine b 1965); *Style*— The Hon Mrs Eustace; Glebe House, Boughton Aluph, Ashford, Kent

EUSTACE, Dudley Graham; s of Albert Eustace, MBE, of Bristol, and Mary, *née* Manning; *b* 3 July 1936; *Educ* The Cathedral Sch Bristol, Univ of Bristol (BA); *m* 30 May 1964, Diane, da of Karl Zakrajsek (d 1974), of Nova Racek, Yugoslavia; 2 da (Gabriella b 1965, Chantal b 1967); *Career* actg PO RAFVR 1955-58; CA 1962; appts Alcan Aluminium Ltd of Canada in: Canada, Argentina, Brazil, Spain, UK (treas Canada, dir of fin UK); dir of fin Br Aerospace plc; memb: Beaconsfield Cons Assoc, Advsy Cncl ECGD, 100 Gp; FCA; *Recreations* philately, gardening, reading; *Clubs* Univ Club of Montreal Canada; *Style*— Dudley G Eustace, Esq; St Anthony's Cottage, Tylers Green, Penn, Bucks, HP10 8EQ (☎ 049 481 2627); 3540 Ave Du Musée, Montreal, Quebec, Canada; 11 Strand, London, WC2N 5JT (☎ 071 389 3933, fax 3986, car 0860 303 272, telex 919 221)

EUSTACE, Gillian Rosemary; da of John William Seeds, of Cheshire, and Ethel Seeds; *b* 3 Feb 1946; *Educ* Loretto Sch Cheshire; *m* 28 Feb 1970, John Malcolm Eustace, s of Malcolm Edmund Fawcett Eustace (d 1982); 2 da (Emma b 1970, Zoe b 1972); *Career* dir Storeforce Ltd 1979-, co fndr and dir Crombre Eustace Ltd 1980-; FInstD 1987, MBA 1989; *Recreations* theatre, tapestry, Georgian restoration, logic puzzles; *Clubs* Network, IOD, Women of the Year Assoc; *Style*— Mrs Gillian R Eustace; 63 St John St, Oxford OX1 2LG (☎ 0865 56528); Wallingford House, Wallingford on Thames, Oxon (☎ 0491 33333)

EUSTON, Earl of; James Oliver Charles FitzRoy; s and h of 11 Duke of Grafton, KG; *b* 13 Dec 1947; *Educ* Eton, Magdalene Coll Cambridge (MA); *m* 1972, Lady Clare Amabel Margaret Kerr (appeal pres Elizabeth FitzRoy Homes), da of 12 Marquess of Lothian; 1 s (Henry Oliver Charles, Viscount Ipswich, b 1978), 4 da (Lady Louise Helen Mary b 1973, Lady Emily Clare b 1974, Lady Charlotte Rose b 1983, Lady Isobel Anne b 1985); *Heir* s, Viscount Ipswich; *Career* page of honour to HM The Queen 1962-63; asst dir J Henry Schroder Wagg & Co 1973-82; exec dir Enskilda Securities 1982-87; dir: Jamestown Investments Ltd 1987-, Central Capital Holdings 1988-, Capel-Cure Myers Capital Management 1988-; FCA; *Style*— Earl of Euston; 6 Vicarage Gdns, London W8 4AH

EVANS *see also*: Gwynne-Evans, Havard-Evans, Tudor Evans

EVANS, (Laurence) Adrian Waring; s of Laurence Ansdell Evans, of Chesworth House, Horsham, Sussex, and Barbara Alice Waring Blount, *née* Gibb; *b* 29 June 1941; *Educ* Stowe, Trinity Coll Cambridge (BA); *m* 1, 18 Aug 1962 (m dis 1981), Caroline Velleman, da of Antony Ireland Baron von Simunich; 1 s (Dominic b 11 Sept 1968, d 1989), 2 da (Kate b 26 Oct 1965, Laura b 23 July 1971); m 2, 25 Nov 1983, Ingela Brita Byng, da of Axel Berglund, of Stockholm; *Career* vice pres Citibank NA NY 1963-71, dir First Nat Finance Corp Ltd 1971-76, md Grindlays Bank plc 1976-85, gp md Benchmark Gp plc 1986-, dir TSB Commercial plc 1986-; chm Cncl of Mgmnt GAP Activity Projects, govr Stowe Sch; *Clubs* Brooks's; *Style*— Adrian Evans, Esq; 17 Elm Park Rd, London SW3 6BP (☎ 071 351 9342); Benchmark House, 86 Newman St, London W1 (☎ 071 631 3313)

EVANS, Alan Baxter; s of Arthur Llewellyn Evans (d 1947), and Ivy Geraldine, *née* Baxter (d 1954); *b* 18 May 1927; *Educ* Queen Elizabeth GS Wimborne, Exeter Coll Oxford (MA); *m* 1, 26 Nov 1949 (m dis 1964), Anne Elizabeth Gorlin; m 2, 14 Aug 1970, Janet Winifred Anne, da of Arthur Chalmers, of Woonona, NSW, Aust; 1 s (Jonathon Mark Arthur b 1973), 1 da (Harriet Francesca b 1971); *Career* Intelligence Corps 1946-48, served Italy and Austria; dir Spearing & Waldron Ltd 1955-59, mangr Du Pont UK Ltd 1959-61; dir: Tyrolia Sporting Goods Ltd, Evans & Co (London) Ltd 1961-70; jt md Hall & Watts Ltd 1971-; FCA; *Recreations* reading, playing tennis, travelling; *Clubs* United Oxford & Cambridge Univ; *Style*— Alan Evans, Esq; Westwinds, Chapman Lane, Bourne End, Bucks SL8 5PA (☎ 06285 29071); Hall & Watts Ltd, 266 Hatfield Rd, St Albans, Herts (☎ 0727 59288, fax 0727 35683, telex 267001 WATTS G)

EVANS, Alan William; s of Harold Evans (d 1980), of London, and Dorothy, *née* Surry; *b* 21 Feb 1938; *Educ* Charterhouse, UCL (BA, PhD), Univ of Michigan; *m* 10 Aug 1964, Jill Alexandra, da of George Otto Brightwell (d 1961), of Vienna; 2 s (Christopher b 1969, Stephen b 1971); *Career* lectr Univ of Glasgow 1967-71, res offr Centre for Environmental Studies 1971-76, lectr LSE 1976-77; Univ of Reading: reader 1977-81, prof 1981-, pro vice chllr 1990-; FCA 1961; *Books* The Economics of Residential Location (1973), Urban Economics (1985), No Room! No Room! (1988); *Recreations* theatre, cinema, reading, travel; *Style*— Alan Evans, Esq; Lianda, Hill Close, Harrow on the Hill, Middlesex HA1 3PQ (☎ 081 423 0767); Department of Economics, Faculty of Urban and Regional Studies, University of Reading, Whiteknights, Reading, Berks RG6 2BU (☎ 0734 318208, fax 0734 313856, telex 847 813)

EVANS, Amanda Louise Elliot (Mrs Andrew Duncan); da of Brian Royston Elliot Evans, of Sevenoaks, Kent, and June Anabella, *née* Gilderdale; *b* 19 May 1958; *Educ* Tunbridge Girls GS Kent; *m* 2 Sept 1989, Andrew Sinclair Duncan, s of Francis Duncan, of London W11; 1 da (Isobel Florence b 20 Oct 1990); *Career* features ed and writer The World of Interiors Magazine 1981-83, dep ed and conslt Mitchell Beazley Publishers 1983-84, ed Homes and Gardens Magazine 1986- (dep ed 1985-86); *Recreations* mountain climbing, eating, vineyards, skiing; *Style*— Ms Amanda Evans; IPC Magazine, King's Reach Tower, Stamford St, London SE1 9LS (☎ 071 261 5678, fax 071 261 6023)

EVANS, Dr Ann Christine; da of Dr Benjamin Penry Evans, and Jane, *née* Maddock (d 1979); *b* 21 May 1945; *Educ* Neath Girls GS, Univ of Manchester (BSc, MB, ChB, DPM); *m* 16 March 1974, Guy Roderick Cocker, s of Geoffrey Cocker (d 1985); 4 s (Daniel b 1977, Benjamin b 1979, Samuel b 1980, Jacob b 1981); *Career* conslt psychiatrist Calderdale Health Authy 1987-; MRC Psych 1973; *Style*— Dr Ann Evans; 2 Heath Villas, Halifax , West Yorkshire HX3 0BB (☎ 0422 367219); Halifax General Hospital, Salterhebble Hill, Halifax , W Yorks (☎ 0422 357171)

EVANS, Anne Elizabeth Jane; da of David Evans (d 1965), of London and Eleanor (d 1988); *b* 20 Aug 1941; *Educ* RCM, Conservatoire de Genève (Boise Fndn Award and Thomas Beecham Operatic scholarship); *m* 1, 1962 (m dis 1981), John Heulyn Jones; m 2, 1981, John Philip Lucas; *Career* opera singer, Geneva debut as Annina in La Traviata 1967, UK debut as Mimi in La Bohème 1968; Sadler's Wells Opera and ENO 1968-90, roles incl: Elsa in Lohengrin, Marschallin in Rosenkavalier, Sieglinde in Die Walküre, Mlada in Dalibor, Countess in Figaro, Fiordiligi in Così, Pamina in Magic Flute, Violetta in Traviata, Kundry in Parsifal, Ariadne in Ariadne auf Naxos; Welsh National Opera 1974-89, roles incl: Senta in Der Fliegender Holländer, Chrysthomis in Elektra, Empress and Dyer's Wife in Die Frau ohne Schatten, Leonore in Fidelio, Brünnhilde in The Ring, Donna Anna in Don Giovanni, Cassandra in The Trojans; foreign debuts: Elsa in Lohengrin (San Francisco) 1978, Chrysthomis in Elektra Rome 1980, Brünnhilde in Der Ring (Paris 1988, Berlin 1989, Washington 1989, Bayreuth 1989); recording of Wagner's Immolation Scene 1987; *Recreations* cooking, antiques; *Style*— Miss Anne Evans; c/o Ingpen and Williams, 14 Kensington Court, London W8 5DN

EVANS, Sir Anthony Adney; 2 Bt (UK 1920); s of Sir Walter Harry Evans, 1 Bt (d 1922), and Margaret Mary, *née* Dickens (d 1969); *b* 5 Aug 1922; *Educ* Shrewsbury, Merton Coll Oxford; *m* 1, 1 May 1948 (m dis 1957), Rita Beatrice, da of late Alfred David Kettle, of Souldern, Oxon, and formerly w of Larry Rupert Kirsch; 2 s, 1 da; m 2, 1958, Sylvia Jean; *Style*— Sir Anthony Evans, Bt; Almer Manor, Blandford, Dorset

EVANS, Anthony David; s of Capt William Price Evans, RE, of Swansea, and Joan Furze, *née* Pitchford; *b* 14 Dec 1946; *Educ* Grove Park Sch Wrexham, Univ Coll Wales Aberystwyth (LLB); *m* 10 Jan 1987, Diane Janet, da of Bernard Pauls, of Leamington, Ontario, Canada; *Career* admitted slr 1971, ptnr MacFarlanes Slrs 1982-; dep chm Swansea W Cons Assoc 1970; chm Lion Boys' Club Hoxton London 1985-; Liveryman Worshipful Co of Coopers 1975, Freeman Worshipful Co of Slrs 1978; memb Law Soc 1971; *Recreations* sailing, climbing; *Style*— Anthony Evans, Esq; 1 Grove Park, London SE5 8LT; Macfarlanes, 10 Norwich St, London EC4A 1BD (☎ 071 831 9222, fax 071 831 9607, telex 296381 MACFAR G)

EVANS, Prof Anthony John; s of William John Evans (d 1965), and Marion Audrey, *née* Young (d 1988); *b* 1 April 1930; *Educ* Queen Elizabeth's Hosp Bristol, Sch of Pharmacy Univ of London (BPharm, PhD), UCL (PG Dip in Librarianship); *m* 21 Aug 1954, Anne, da of John Horwell (d 1960), of Grimsby; 2 da (Jane b 1957, Susan b 1960); *Career* lectr in pharmaceutical engrg sci Sch of Pharmacy Univ of London 1954-57; librarian: Sch of Pharmacy Univ of London 1958-63, Loughborough Univ 1964-; dean School of Educnl Studies Loughborough Univ 1973-76; memb Exec Bd Int Fedn Library Assocs and Insts (IFLA) 1983-89 (treas 1985-89), hon life memb Int Assoc of Technol Univ Libraries (treas 1968-70, pres 1970-75), vice pres Assoc for Info Mgmnt (ASLIB) 1985-87; conslt: Br Cncl, ODA, UNESCO, UNIDO, World Bank in some 17 countries particularly Mexico, Kenya and China; FLA 1969 (Hon FLA 1990); IFLA medal 1989; *Recreations* travel, sport, model railways and 4 grandchildren; *Clubs* Royal Cwlth Soc; *Style*— Professor Anthony Evans; 78 Valley Rd, Loughborough, Leicestershire LE11 3QA (☎ 0509 215670); Pilkington Library, University of Technology, Loughborough, Leicestershire LE11 3TU (☎ 0509 222340, fax 0509 234806, telex 34319 UNITEC G)

EVANS, Sir Athol Donald; KBE (1963, CBE 1954, MBE 1939); s of Henry Alfred Evans, of Indive, S Africa, and Rhoda May, *née* Greenlees; *b* 16 Dec 1904; *Educ* Graeme Coll, Rhodes Univ S Africa (BA, LLB); *m* 12 Sept 1931, Catherine Millar, da of William M Greig, of East London, Cape Province, S Africa; 1 s, 2 da; *Career* joined S Rhodesia Public Service 1928; law offr, legal advsr, memb Public Service Bd, sec for Int Affairs, sec for Home Affrs (Fedn of Rhodesia and Nyasaland); chm: Bd of Tstees Rhodes Nat Gallery, Zimbabwe Nat Tst, Nat Cncl for Care of the Aged; Gold Cross of St Mark (Greece) 1962; *Style*— Sir Athol Evans, KBE; 8 Harvey Brown Ave, Harare, Zimbabwe (☎ 25164)

EVANS, Hon Mrs (Audrey Mary); o da of 1 Viscount Leathers, CH, PC (d 1965); *b* 21 Dec 1915; *Educ* Benenden Sch, Univ of St Andrews; *m* 7 July 1938, Edward Noel Evans (d 1964), s of Edward William Evans; 2 s, 1 da; *Career* publisher; *Recreations* travel; *Style*— The Hon Mrs Evans; Flat 5, 28 Hyde Park Gdns, London W2 2NB (☎ 071 723 2909)

EVANS, Ven (John) Barrie; s of John Brynley Evans (d 1975), of Chepstow, and Maude, *née* Holland (d 1970); *b* 14 July 1923; *Educ* Newport HS, St David's Coll Lampeter (BA), St Edmund Hall Oxford (MA), St Michael's Coll Llandaff; *m* 30 Dec 1951, Joan (d 1987), da of Sydney Morton (d 1973), of Ashtead, Surrey; 2 s (Christopher b 1955, Martin b 1957); *Career* asst curate Trevethin 1951-57; vicar: of Caerwent 1957-64, of Chepstow 1964-79; archdeacon of Monmouth 1977, rector of Llanmartin 1979-86, archdeacon of Newport 1986-; *Recreations* gardening, travel; *Clubs* St Pierre; *Style*— The Ven The Archdeacon of Newport; Draycot, 16 Stow Park Crescent, Newport, Gwent NP9 4HD (☎ 0633 264919)

EVANS, Prof Barry George; s of William Arthur Evans (d 1984), of Dartford, Kent, and Jean Ida, *née* Lipscombe; *b* 15 Oct 1944; *Educ* Univ of Leeds (BSc, PhD); *m* 1 (m dis 1983), Carol Ann, *née* Gillis; 1 s (Robert Iain Lawrie b 1971), 1 da (Lisa Jane b 1969); m 2, 10 March 1984, Rhian Elizabeth Marilyn, da of Russell Lewis Jones (d 1974), of Camarthen; 1 s (Rhys David Russell b 1984), 1 da (Cerian Elizabeth Lucy b 1985); *Career* lectr sr lectr and reader in telecommunications Univ of Essex 1968-83, Satellite Systems Conslts C&W Ltd 1976-80, Alec Harley Reeves prof of info systems engrg Univ of Surrey 1983-, dir: Satconsult, Speka Ltd; ed International Jl of Satellite Communications; author of over 150 papers on telecommunications and satellite systems published; memb: SERC Ctee of Communications, Dist Computing and Info Technol Training, UK CCIR Ctees 5 and 8, UK URSI del Comms, DTI and SERC Link Mgmnt Ctee; CEng, FIEE; *Books* Telecommunications Systems Design (1974), Satellite Systems Design (1988); *Recreations* travel, wine, sport; *Style*— Prof Barry Evans; Department of Electronic & Electrical Engineering, University of Surrey, Guildford GU2 5XH (☎ 0483 509131, fax 0483 34139, telex 859331)

EVANS, Barry John; s of Arthur Evans, of Hinckley, Leics, and Hilary *née* Dixon; *b* 10 Oct 1962; *Educ* John Cleveland Coll Hinckley, Mount Grace HS; *m* 1 July 1990, Sarah, da of William Butterworth; *Career* Rugby Union wing threequarter Leicester and England (2 caps); Leicester FC: debut 1981, 270 appearances, 165 tries scored (club record), finalist Pilkington Cup 1989; rep: Midlands Division, Eng Students, Eng B; England; tour Aust and Fiji 1988, debut v Aust 1988; sales exec Midlands Div Rank Xerox 1983-85, sales mangr Siemens Communications 1985-90, account mangr Compaq Computer Ltd; *Recreations* all sports; *Style*— Barry Evans, Esq

EVANS, Hon Benedict Blackstone; o s of Thomas Charles Evans (d 1985), and Baroness Blackstone, *qv*; *b* 6 Sept 1963; *Educ* William Ellis Sch for Boys, Manchester Poly (BA); *m* Suzanne, *née* Godson; *Career* writer, lectr and researcher; *Recreations* skiing, architecture and design; *Clubs* Chelsea Arts; *Style*— The Hon Benedict Evans; 17 Fournier St, Spitalfields, London E1 (☎ 071 247 1196)

EVANS, Charles Byron; s of Rees Byron Evans, and Pamela, *née* Steinbach (d 1973); *b* 17 Nov 1944; *Educ* Sherborne, Jesus Coll Oxford (MA); *m* 20 Oct 1979, Elizabeth Jane, da of Clement Yorke Morgan, of Radley Coll, Berks; 3 s (Clement b 4 July 1981, Samuel b 5 Oct 1983, Joseph b 19 March 1986); *Career* admitted slr 1971; asst slr Macfarlanes 1971-74, ptnr Osborne Clarke Bristol 1975- (asst slr 1974-75); sec Bristol central branch RNLI; memb Law Soc 1971; *Recreations* music, rugby football, cricket, wine; *Clubs* Clifton (Bristol); *Style*— Charles Evans, Esq; Osborne Clarke, 30 Queen Charlotte St, Bristol BS99 7QQ (☎ 0272 230220, fax 0272 279209); 6-8 Middle St, London EC1A 7JA (☎ 071 600 0155, fax 071 726 2772)

EVANS, Sir (Robert) Charles; o s of late Robert Charles Evans, of Wrexham; *b* 19 Oct 1918; *Educ* Shrewsbury Sch, Univ Coll Oxford (BM BCh, MA); *m* 1957, Denise Nea, da of Jean-Antoine Morin, of Paris; 3 s; *Career* Nat Serv WWII RAMC SE Asia (despatches); surgical registrar United Liverpool Hosps and Liverpool Regnl Hosps 1947-57, Hunterian prof RCS Eng 1953, princ Univ Coll of N Wales Bangor 1958-84, vice chllr Univ of Wales 1965-67 and 1971-73; dep ldr Everest Expedition 1953, ldr Kangchenjunga Expedition 1955; FRCS; kt 1969; *Books* Eye on Everest (1955), On Climbing (1956), Kangchenjunga - The Untrodden Peak (1956); *Clubs* Alpine (pres 1967-70); *Style*— Sir Charles Evans; Ardincaple, Capel Curig, N Wales

EVANS, Charles Wackett; s of David Richard Evans (d 1970), of Essex, and Emily Alice, *née* Wackett (d 1974); *b* 14 May 1914; *Educ* Burlington Coll; *m* 28 Dec 1951, Hazel, da of George Baldam (d 1985), of Dorset; 1 s (Christoper Charles b 13 Aug 1954), 1 da (Hilary Jane b 20 Dec 1952); *Career* Air Miny Aeronautical Inspection Directorate 1940-42, special duties TaTa Aircraft Ltd Bombay 1942-46; tech mangr Air Tport Charter Ltd Jersey 1947-52, chm and fndr Aviation Jersey Ltd 1953-; FRGS 1953; *Recreations* gardening, travel; *Clubs* Special Forces; *Style*— Charles W Evans, Esq; 21 Merton, Avalon Park, St Clement, Jersey, Channel Islands; Aviation Jersey Ltd, Rue Des Pres, St Saviour, Jersey (☎ 0534 25 301, fax 0534 59 449, telex 419 2161 AVIOJY G)

EVANS, Dr Christopher Charles; s of Robert Percy (d 1974), and Nora Carson, *née* Crowther; *b* 2 Oct 1941; *Educ* Wade Deacon GS Widnes Cheshire, Univ of Liverpool (MB ChB, MD); *m* 5 Feb 1966, Dr Susan Evans, da of Dr Heinz Fuld, of Llanarmon Yn Ial, Mold, Clwyd; 1 s (Matthew b 1973), 2 da (Joanne b 1971, Sophie b 1975); *Career* sr lectr in med and hon conslt physician Univ of Liverpool 1974-78, consult physician in gen and thoracic med Liverpool Health Authy 1978, clinical sub-dean Royal Liverpool Hosp 1978-88, consult MO Royal Life plc 1978; vice pres Med Def Union, pres Liverpool Med Inst; memb Cncl Br Thoracic Soc; MRCP 1968, FRCP 1979; *Books* Chamberlain's Symptoms and Signs in Clinical Medicine (with C M Ogilvie, 1987); *Recreations* skiing, tennis, fell walking, watching Liverpool FC; *Style*— Dr Christopher Evans; Lagom, Glendyke Rd, Liverpool L18 6JR (☎ 051 724 5386); Royal Liverpool Hosp, Prescot St, Liverpool L7 8XP (☎ 051 709 0141); Cardio Thoracic Centre, Broadgreen Hosp, Liverpool L14 3LB (☎ 051 228 4878)

EVANS, Hon Mrs (Cicili Carol); *née* Paget; yst da of 1 and last Baron Queenborough, GBE (d 1949) (by 2 w), gs of 1 Marquess of Anglesey; *b* 18 April 1928; *m* 10 Dec 1949, Capt Robert Victor John Evans, Welsh Guards, s of late Brig John Meredith Jones Evans, CBE, MC, of Wishanger, Churt, Farnham, Surrey; 2 s, 1 da; *Style*— The Hon Mrs Evans; Gainsford House, Cowden, Kent TN8 7JD

EVANS, Clifford John; s of Wallace Evans (d 1971), and Elsie Evans (d 1975); *b* 9 Oct 1928; *Educ* Cardiff HS, Gonville and Caius Coll Cambridge; *m* 4 April 1953, Sheila Margaret (Molly), da of James Walker, of Abergavenny, South Wales; 2 s (Christopher b 23 May 1957, Robert b 16 Sept 1959); *Career* chief engr Caribbean Construction Co Ltd Jamaica 1954-61, ptnr Wallace Evans and Ptnrs (consltg engrs) and ptnr of assoc partnerships in Hong Kong and the Caribbean 1962-90 (sr ptnr 1971-90), chm and md Wallace Evans Ltd 1990-; memb: Penarth Rotary Club 1966-, Penarth RNLI Ctee 1986-; attache Welsh team Cwlth Games Jamaica 1966; pres IStructE 1982-83; memb: Cncl CIArb, Panel of Arbitrators of ICE, CIArb and FIDIC, Standing Ctee for Structural Safety 1983-89, Cncl ICE 1984-87 and 1989-, Cncl ACE 1980-83, Ct of Univ of Wales, Coll of Cardiff; convenor President's Ctee for Urban Environment 1987-; Freeman City of London; Liveryman: Worshipful Co of Engineers, Worshipful Co of Arbitrators, Worshipful Co of Constructors; FEng, FICE, FIStructE, FCIArb, FIHT, FIWEM, FHKIE, FASCE, MConsE; *Recreations* sailing, offshore yacht racing, skiing, swimming; *Clubs* Royal Thames Yacht, Royal Ocean Racing, Royal Corinthian Yacht, Royal Jamaica Yacht, Hawks, Cardiff and County, Livery; *Style*— Clifford Evans, Esq; Mariner's Way, Marine Parade, Penarth, South Glamorgan CF6 2BE; Wallace Evans and Partners, Plymouth House, Penarth, South Glamorgan CF6 2YF (☎ 0222 705577, fax 0222 709793)

EVANS, Air Vice-Marshal Clive Ernest; CBE (1982); s of Leslie Roberts Evans (d 1987), and Mary Kathleen, *née* Butcher (d 1978); *b* 21 April 1937; *Educ* St Dunstans Coll Catford; *m* 15 June 1963, Therese, da of Gp Capt Douglas Cecil Goodrich, CBE; 1 s (Guy b 1966), 1 da (Madeleine b 1970); *Career* RAF trg 1955-56, Pilot; flying instr 1960, served on: Vampires, Hunters, Jet Provosts, Canberras, Lightnings, FIII; RAF Staff Coll 1972, PSO to Controller Aircraft 1973, OC 24 Sqdn (Hercules) 1974-76, NDC 1976-77, DS RAF Staff Coll 1977-79, head RAF Presentation Team 1979-81, OC RAF Lyneham 1981-83, RCDS 1984, COS and Dep Cdr Br Forces Falkland Is 1985, DAC; memb PCC St Mary's Sanderstead; *Recreations* reading, cricket, golf, sailing, gardening; *Clubs* RAF; *Style*— Air Vice-Marshal Clive Evans, CBE; 43 Purley Bury Close, Purley, Surrey CR8 1HW; Royal College of Defence Studies, Seaford House, 37 Belgrave Sq, London SW1X 8NS (☎ 071 235 1091)

EVANS, David; *see*: Edge (The)

EVANS, Prof David Alan Price; s of Owen Evans (d 1978), of 28 Montclair Dr, Liverpool, and Ellen, *née* Jones (d 1975); *b* 6 March 1927; *Educ* Univ of Liverpool (BSc, MB ChB, MD, MRCP, PhD, DSc, J Hill Abram prize for Med, Sir Robert Kelly Meml medal for Surgery, Henry Briggs Meml medal for Obstetrics and Gynaecology, Owen T Williams prize); *Career* Nat Serv Capt RAMC 1953-55 (active serv Japan, Singapore, Korea, Malaya); house physician and house surgn Liverpool Royal Infirmary 1951-52, sr house offr Broadgreen Hosp Liverpool 1955-56; med registrar: Stanley Hosp Liverpool 1956-58, Northern Hosp Liverpool 1959-60; res fell John Hopkins Univ Baltimore 1958-59, consult physician Royal Hosp Liverpool (formerly Royal Infirmary) and Broadgreen Hosp Liverpool 1965-85, prof Dept of Med Univ of Liverpool 1968-72 (lectr 1960-62, sr lectr 1962-68), chm and prof Dept of Med and dir Nuffield Unit of Med Genetics Univ of Liverpool 1972-83, dir of med Riyadh Al Kharj Hosp Programme Riyadh Saudi Arabia 1983-, hon prof of med King Saud Univ Riyadh Saudi Arabia 1988-; visiting prof: Karolinska Univ Stockholm, Helsinki Univ, Berne Univ, Ann Arbor Univ Baltimore USA; sci ed Saudi Med Jl 1983-; author numerous articles and chapters in books on pharmacogenetics; memb Assoc Physicians GB and Ireland 1964, life memb John Hopkins Soc of Scholars 1972; FRCP 1968; *Recreations* country pursuits; *Style*— Prof David Price Evans; 28 Montclair Drive, Liverpool L18 0HA (☎ 051 722 3112, fax 051 478 8033); C123 Riyadh Armed Forces Hospital, PO Box 7897, Riyadh 11159, Kingdom of Saudi Arabia (☎ 010986 4777714)

EVANS, Prof David Emrys; s of Evan Emrys Evans (d 1985), of Cross Hands, Dyfed, and Gwynneth Mair Eurfron, *née* Owen (d 1969); *b* 14 Oct 1950; *Educ* Ysgol Ramadeg Dyffrun Gwendraeth, Univ of Oxford (BA, MSc, DPhil); *m* 20 Oct 1984, Pornsawan; *Career* Dublin Inst for Advanced Studies 1975-76, Univ of Oslo 1976-77, Royal Soc exchange fell Copenhagen Univ 1978, SERC res fell Univ of Newcastle upon Tyne 1979, reader Univ of Warwick 1986-87 (lectr 1979-86), prof Univ Coll of Swansea 1987; Jr Whitehead Prize London Mathematical Soc 1989; memb: London Mathematical Soc, American Mathematical Soc; *Books* Dilatious of Irreversible Evolutions in Algebraic Quantum Theory (with J T Lewis, 1977); *Style*— Prof David Evans; Department of Mathematics and Computer Science, University College of Swansea, Singleton Park, Swansea SA2 8PP (☎ 0792 295460, fax 0792 295618)

EVANS, Prof (John) David Gemmill; s of John Desmond Evans (d 1977), and Babette Evans (d 1985); *b* 27 Aug 1942; *Educ* St Edward's Sch Oxford, Queen's Coll Cambridge (BA, MA, PHD); *m* 14 Sept 1974, Rosemary, da of Gweirydd Ellis, of Chifferham; *Career* fell Sidney Sussex Coll Cambridge 1964-78, dean of Faculty of Arts Queen's Univ Belfast 1986-89 (prof of logic and metaphysics 1978-); memb: NI Schools Examination Cncl, Exec Ctee Int Fedn of Philosophical Socs; MRIA 1983; *Books* Aristotle's Concept of Dialectic (1977), Truth and Proof (1979), Aristotle (1987), Moral Philosophy and Contemporary Problems (1987); *Recreations* mountaineering, astronomy, poker; *Style*— Prof David Evans; Spinney View, Carryduff, Co Down, Northern Ireland BT8 8JD; Philosophy Dept, Queen's University, Belfast BT7 INNa (☎ 0232 245133, telex 74487)

EVANS, David John; MP (Cons) Welwyn Hatfield 1987-; *b* 23 April 1935; *m* Janice Hazel *née* Masters; 2 s, 1 da; *Style*— David Evans, Esq, MP; House of Commons, London SW1A 0AA

EVANS, Prof David John; s of Stanley Evans (d 1969), of Llanelli, Wales, and Margaret Ann, *née* King (d 1984); *b* 30 Sept 1928; *Educ* Llanelli GS, Univ Coll Wales Aberystwyth (BSc), Univ of Southampton (MSc), Univ of Manchester (PhD), Univ of Wales (DSc); *m* 6 Aug 1955, Naldera (Derry), da of Michael Owen (d 1983), of Bedford; 1 s (Neil Wyn b 1961), 2 da (Tracy Susanne b 1962 d 1990, Clare Joanne b 1963); *Career* Nat Serv RAF 1950-52; sr mathematician Rolls Royce Ltd Derby 1955-58, res fell Univ of Manchester 1958-64, dir Computing Laboratory Univ of Sheffield 1964-71, prof of computing Loughborough Univ of Technology 1971- (dir Parallel Algorithms Res Centre 1988-); FBCS, FIMA; *Books* Preconditioning Methods Theory and Applications (1983), Parallel Processing Systems (1983), Sparsity and its Applications (1985); *Recreations* music; *Style*— Prof David Evans; Parallel Algorithms Research Centre, Loughborough University of Technology, Loughborough, Leics LE11 3TU (☎ 0509 222670)

EVANS, David Lawrence; s of Arthur Henry Evans, OBE, FRCS (d 1950), of London, and Dorothy, *née* Briant (d 1983); *b* 21 Sept 1919; *Educ* Rugby, Gonville and Caius Coll Cambridge, Westminster Hosp Med Sch; *m* 14 Jan 1950, Betty Joan, da of Dr Hugh Moreland McCrea, OBE (d 1942), of London; 1 s (Timothy b 1955), 3 da (Joanna b 1950, Philippa b 1952, Gillian b 1957); *Career* Surgn Lt RNVR 1943-47; consult orthopaedic surgn: Southend Gen Hosp 1957-59, Westminster Hosp 1959-85, St Stephen's Hosp Chelsea 1960-72, Queen Mary's Hosp Roehampton 1961-85; memb Sch Cncl Westminster Hosp Med Sch 1972-76 (chm Med Ctee 1972-75, memb Bd of Govrs 1972-74); chm Br Ed Bd and Cncl of Mgmnt Journal of Bone and Joint surgery 1975- (memb 1969- and contrib); pres Br Orthopaedic Assoc 1980 (travelling fell USA and Canada 1956, memb Exec Ctee 1964-69, hon sec 1966-67), hon fell Section of Orthopaedics RSM London 1987 (pres 1979); FRCS (memb Cncl 1973, vice pres 1989-91); *Recreations* golf, fishing, bridge; *Clubs* Royal Wimbledon Golf (Captain 1981); *Style*— David Evans, Esq; Lane End, 12 The Drive, Wimbledon, London SW20 8TG (☎ 081 946 4016)

EVANS, His Hon Judge David Marshall; QC (1981); s of Robert Trevor Evans, and Bessie Estelle, *née* Thompson; *b* 21 July 1937; *Educ* Liverpool Coll, Trinity Hall Cambridge (MA, LLM), Univ of Chicago (JD); *m* 1961, (Alice) Joyce, da of Ernest Rogers (d 1961); 2 s (Richard b 1967, James b 1969); *Career* teaching fell Stanford Univ Palo Alto California 1961-62, asst prof Univ of Chicago Illinois 1962-63, lectr UC of Wales Aberystwyth 1963-65; called to the Bar Gray's Inn 1964, in practice Northern circuit, recorder of Crown Ct 1984, circuit judge 1987-; *Recreations* walking, photography, visual arts, motorsport; *Clubs* Athenaeum (Liverpool); *Style*— His Hon Judge D Marshall Evans, Esq, QC; Queen Elizabeth II Law Courts, Derby Square, Liverpool L2 1XA (☎ 051 236 4555)

EVANS, David Mervyn; s of (Edward) Mervyn Evans, of Swansea, and Muriel Hawley, *née* Amison; *b* 18 Sept 1942; *Educ* Clifton, Middx Hosp Med Sch (MB BS); *m* 19 June 1971, Dr Elizabeth Cecily Evans, da of Frederick Hornung (d 1973); 1 s (Daniel b 1975), 1 da (Kate b 1976); *Career* consult plastic surgn Wexham Park Hosp Slough and Guy's Hosp London; hon sec Br Soc for Surgery of the Hand 1986-88, memb Cncl Br Assoc of Plastic Surgns, chm Med Commission on Accident Prevention, asst ed Jl of Hand Surgery (Br vol); FRCS 1969; *Recreations* music, windsurfing, skiing; *Style*— David Evans, Esq; The Hand Clinic, Oakley Green, Windsor SL4 4LH (☎ 0753 831333)

EVANS, Rt Rev David Richard John; s of Maj William Henry Reginald Evans, of Carnbrae, 2 Hindover Road, Seaford, Sussex, and Beatrix Catherine, *née* Mottram; *b* 5 June 1938; *Educ* Christ's Hospital, Gonville and Caius Coll Cambridge (MA); *m* 25 July 1964, Dorothy Evelyn, da of Rev Martin Parsons, of 61 Elmtree Rd, Locking, Weston-Super-Mare, Avon; 1 s (Peter b 16 Sept 1971), 2 da (Hilary b 4 Jan 1966, Caroline b 1 Oct 1967); *Career* 2 Lt Middx Regt 1957-59; ordained St Paul's Cathedral 1965, curate Christ Church Cockfosters 1965-68, asst priest Holy Trinity Lomas De Zamora Buenos Aires 1969-77, gen sec Asociacion Biblica Universitaria Argentina 1971-76, chaplain Good Shepherd Lima Peru 1977-83; bishop of: Peru 1978-88, Bolivia 1982-88; asst bishop of Bradford 1988-; memb Nat Cncl of Church Ministry to Jews, int coordinator of the Evangelical Fellowship of the Anglican Communion; *Books* Encuentro Con Dios (1976); *Recreations* squash, golf; *Style*— The Rt Rev David Evans; 30 Grosvenor Rd, Shipley, W Yorks BD18 4RN (☎ 0274 582033, fax 0274 531689)

EVANS, Hon David Robert Cynlais; s of Baron Evans of Claughton (Life Peer); *b* 1964; *Educ* Birkenhead Sch, UCL (LLB); *Recreations* hockey, rugby, golf, squash, cars, literature; *Style*— Hon David Evans

EVANS, David Robert Howard; s of The Rev Denys Roberts Evans (d 1988), of Oxford, and Beryl Mary, *née* Toye; *b* 27 Feb 1950; *Educ* Magdalen Coll Sch Oxford, Univ of Exeter (LLB), King's Coll and LSE Univ of London (LLM), Brasenose Coll Oxford (DipLaw); *m* 1, 6 Jan 1979 (m dis 1988), Gillian Mary; 1 s (Matthew Charles b 1985); m 2, 7 May 1989, Janet Lea, formerly w of Amos Kollek, of New York, da of Nat T Kanarek; *Career* admitted slr 1976; slr: Freshfields 1975-77, British Railways Bd 1977-79, Linklaters & Paines 1980-82; ptnr: Berwin Leighton 1984-87 (slr 1982-83), D J Freeman & Co 1987-; Freeman City of London 1981, Liveryman Worshipful Co of Slrs 1988; memb Law Soc 1976; *Recreations* playing clarinet, tennis, skiing, horse riding; *Clubs* The Reform, Music Makers Group; *Style*— David Evans, Esq; 51 Drayton Gardens, London SW10 (☎ 071 835 2143); D J Freeman & Co, 1 Fetter Lane, London EC4 (☎ 071 583 5555, fax 071 583 3232, telex 913434)

EVANS, David Stanley; s of (Evan) Stanley Evans, CBE (d 1982), and Muriel Gordon, *née* Henderson (d 1983); *b* 12 May 1935; *Educ* Charterhouse, St Thomas' Hosp Univ of London (MB BS, MS); *m* 18 May 1968, Mary Agnes Christina, da of Dr John Tierney (d 1984); 1 s (James b 1973), 3 da (Katherine b 1972, Charlotte b 1980, Sarah b 1983); *Career* house surgn: St Thomas' Hosp 1960, Royal Post Grad Hosp Hammersmith 1962; sr house offr Hosp for Sick Children Great Ormond St 1963, sr surgical registrar St Thomas' Hosp 1970-74 (surgical registrar 1966-69), consult surgn Royal Shrewsbury Hosp 1974-; Hunterian prof RCS 1971; author various papers on diagnosis of venous thrombosis; memb Shropshire div BMA; memb: RSM, BMA, Assoc of Surgns of GB and Ireland, Vascular Surgical Soc GB and Ireland; *Recreations* golf, shooting; *Style*— David Evans, Esq; Royal Shrewsbury Hospital, Mytton Oak Rd, Shrewsbury (☎ 0743 231122)

EVANS, David Vernon; s of Walter Evans (d 1976), of Osmotherley, N Yorks, and Florence Ethel, *née* Vernon; *b* 8 March 1935; *Educ* Durham Sch, St Catharine's Coll Univ of Cambridge (MA, LLM); *m* 5 May 1962, Sonia Robinson Evans, JP; 1 s (Andrew b 1963), 2 da (Rachel b 1966, Judith b 1967); *Career* slr Crombie Wilkinson & Robinson York 1959-61, managing ptnr Simpson Curtis Leeds 1982- (joined 1961, ptnr 1963); govr Leeds GS, church warden Parish of Leeds City (tstee Leeds Parish Church appeal fund), memb Ctee St Catharine's Soc (chm Yorks branch), former chm Leeds Round Table; memb Law Soc; *Recreations* music, beekeeping; *Clubs* Leeds; *Style—* David Evans, Esq; Thorner Lodge, Thorner, Leeds LS14 3DE (☎ 0532 892 517); 41 Park Square, Leeds LS1 2NS (☎ 0532 433 433, fax 0532 445598, car 0860 227 telex 55376)

EVANS, HE David Wyke; s of Mervyn Evans (d 1987), and Phyllis Evans; *b* 13 March 1934; *Educ* Prince Alfred Coll Adelaide S Aust, Univ of Adelaide (BEc), Univ of Oxford (MA); *m* 3 Oct 1959, Pamela Rubina, da of Peter McKenzie Strang (d 1945); 2 s (Kym b 1961, Peter b 1967), 1 da (Nicola b 1964); *Career* Aust Dip Serv 1959-: third sec Jakarta 1962-65 (later second sec), political affrs UN Branch Dept of Foreign Affrs 1965-68, first sec UN NY 1968-70, cnsllr Belgrade 1970-72, dir orgn staffing and trg 1972-74, high cmmr Accra 1974-77 (ambass to Senegal 1974-77 and the Ivory Coast 1975-77), asst sec Info Branch 1977-79, head Europe Americas and NZ Div 1980, memb Aust Nat Observer Gp to Zimbabwe Elections 1981, ambass Moscow and Mongolia 1981-84, high cmmr Kuala Lumpur 1984-87, dep high cmmr London 1987-90, high cmmr New Delhi 1990-; Freeman City of London 1987; *Style—* HE Mr David W Evans; Australian High Commission, New Delhi, India (☎ 601 336)

EVANS, David Wyn; s of Gareth Norman Evans, of 3 Clwyd Ave, Cwmbach, Aberdare, Mid Glamorgan, S Wales, and Wendy Maureen Evans; *b* 1 Nov 1965; *Educ* Aberdare Boys GS, Univ Coll Swansea (BSc), Univ Coll Oxford (Dip Social Studies, Rugby blue); *m* 7 July 1990, Roberta King-Evans, da of Stuart King; *Career* Rugby Union fly-half and centre Cardiff RFC and Wales (8 caps); clubs: UC Swansea RFC (capt), Cardiff RFC (debut 1984, capt 1990-), Oxford Univ RFC (toured Fiji, Aust, NZ, USA), Barbarians RFC, Public Sch Wanderers RFC, Welsh Academicals RFC, Crayshaws RFC; rep: Welsh Univs (capt), Welsh Students (capt, 12 caps), Br Students, Glamorgan (capt), Wales U15, Wales U18 Schs, Wales U21, Wales U23 (capt), Wales B (debut 1989, tour Canada); Wales: debut v France 1989; Chartered Trust plc; *Recreations* guitar, learning to speak Welsh, golf, football and all sports; *Style—* David Evans, Esq; Cardiff RFC, Westgate St, Cardiff, South Glamorgan (☎ 0222 383546)

EVANS, Prof (William) Desmond; s of Bryn Gwyn Evans, and Evelyn Evans (d 1974); *b* 7 March 1940; *Educ* Ystalyfera GS, Univ of Swansea (BSc), Univ of Oxford (DPhil); *m* 26 Aug 1966, Mari, da of Murray Richards (d 1960); 2 s (Dyfed b 1969, Owain b 1973); *Career* Univ Coll Cardiff: lectr 1964-73, sr lectr 1983-75, reader 1975-77, prof 1977-; London Maths Soc: memb 1964, editorial advsr 1977-86, ed Proceedings 1986-, memb Cncl 1989-; *Publications* Spectral Theory and Differential Equations (with D E Edmunds, 1987), over 60 articles on differential equations in academic jls; *Recreations* squash, tennis, music; *Style—* Prof Desmond Evans; Sch of Mathematics, Univ of Wales Coll of Cardiff, Senghennydd Rd, Cardiff CF2 4AG (☎ 0222 874206, fax 0222 371921, telex 4998635)

EVANS, Hon Edward Broke; VRD; yr s of 1 Baron Mountevans (d 1958), and his 2 wife Elsa, *née* Andvord (d 1963); *b* 21 Aug 1924; *Educ* Wellington; *m* 15 July 1947, Elaine Elisabeth, da of late Capt (S) William Wilson Cove, RN (ret), of The Clock House, Bodenham, Wilts; 2 s, 1 da; *Career* Cdr (E) RNR (ret), employed ICI Ltd; *Style—* The Hon Edward Evans, VRD; 15 York Mansions, Prince of Wales Drive, London SW11 4DN

EVANS, Lady; Elizabeth; da of William Jaffray, of Aberdeen; *m* 8 Sept 1945, Sir (Sidney) Harold Evans, 1 and last Bt, CMG, OBE (d 1983); 1 da, and 1 s decd; *Style—* Lady Evans; 1 Kipling Court, St Aubyns Mead, Rottingdean, Sussex

EVANS, Prof (David) Ellis; yr s of David Evans (d 1948), and Sarah Jane, *née* Lewis; *b* 23 Sept 1930; *Educ* Llandeilo GS, UCW Aberystwyth, Univ Coll of Swansea, Jesus Coll Oxford; *m* 1957, Sheila Mary, er da of David Thomas Jeremy, of Swansea, Wales; 2 da; *Career* former lectr, reader and prof of Welsh language and literature Univ Coll Swansea, Jesus prof of Celtic Univ of Oxford and fell of Jesus Coll 1978-; Univ Coll Swansea: hon fell 1985-, hon prof Dept of Welsh 1990-; *Recreations* music, walking; *Style—* Prof Ellis Evans; Jesus College, Oxford (☎ 0865 279700/279739)

EVANS, Ena Winifred; da of Frank Evans (d 1986), of Farndon, Cheshire, and Leonora, *née* Lewis; *b* 19 June 1938; *Educ* The Queen's Sch Chester, Royal Holloway Coll Univ of London (BSc), Hughes Hall Cambridge (Cert Ed); *Career* Girls' Div Bolton Sch 1961-65, Bath HS GPDST 1965-72 (head of maths and second mistress 1970-72), dep head Friends' Sch Saffron Walden 1972-77, headmistress King Edward VI HS for Girls Birmingham 1977-; pres: Girls' Sch Assoc 1987-88, W Midland Branch of Mathematical Assoc 1980-82; memb: Central Birmingham DHA 1988-90, Cncl Univ of Aston; govr: Kingswood Sch Bath, Bluecoat Sch Birmingham, St James's and The Abbey Sch Malvern; memb: SHA 1977, GSA 1977; Maths Assoc 1961; FRSA 1986; *Recreations* music; *Clubs* Univ Women's; *Style—* Miss Ena Evans; King Edward VI High School for Girls, Edgbaston Park Rd, Birmingham B15 2UB (☎ 021 472 1834, fax 021 472 0221)

EVANS, Very Rev (Thomas) Eric; s of Eric John Rhys Evans and Florence May Rogers; *b* 1 Feb 1928; *Educ* St David's Coll, St Catherines's Coll Oxford; *m* 1957, Linda Kathleen, *née* Budge; 2 da; *Career* ordained Canterbury Cathedral: deacon 1954, priest 1955; curate St John Margate 1954-58, first dir Bournemouth Samaritans and diocesan youth chaplain Dio of Gloucester 1962-69, canon missioner Gloucester Cathedral 1969-75, archdeacon Cheltenham 1975-88, dean St Paul's 1988-; memb Bd of Govrs Church Cmmrs (Assets Ctee) 1978-88, dir Ecclesiastical Insur Office 1978-, chm Cncl for Care of Churches 1981-88, memb Standing Ctee of Gen Synod 1981-88, chm Glos Assoc of Mental Health 1983-85, govr Cheltenham Ladies' Coll 1983-, chm Glos Diocesan Advsy Cmmn 1984-88; dean: Order of the Br Empire, Order of St Michael and St George; chaplain OStJ; chaplain to the Guild of Freemen of the City of London; *Recreations* travel (especially Middle East); *Clubs* Carlton, City Livery, The Downhill Only (Wengen, Switzerland); *Style—* The Very Rev the Dean of St Paul's; The Deanery, 9 Amen Court, London EC4M 7BU (☎ 071 236 2827)

EVANS, His Hon Judge Fabyan Peter Leaf; s of Peter Fabyan Evans, and Catherine Elise Evans; *b* 10 May 1943; *Educ* Clifton; *m* 12 Sept 1967, Karen Myrtle, da of Lionel Joachim Balfour; 2 s (Nigel Henley Fabyan b 26 April 1971, Alexander Peter Sommerville b 21 Feb 1976), 1 da (Jessica Ann b 30 May 1973); *Career* called to the Bar Inner Temple 1969, rec 1985, judge South Eastern Circuit 1988; *Recreations* sailing, singing; *Clubs* Brooks's; *Style—* His Hon Judge Fabyan Evans

EVANS, Frederick Anthony; CVO (1973); s of Herbert Anthony Evans, and Pauline, *née* Allen; *b* 17 Nov 1907; *Educ* Charterhouse, Corpus Christi Coll Cambridge (MA); *m* 1934, Nancy, da of H Meakin; 2 s (Peter, Richard), 1 da (Suzanne); *Career* HM Colonial Serv 1935-57, colonial sec and actg govr Bahamas 1947-51, perm sec Ghana 1951-57; gen sec Duke of Edinburgh's award 1959-72; *Books* (nom de plume Deric) The State Apartments at Buckingham Palace - a Souvenir (1985); *Style—* Frederick Evans, Esq, CVO; Bellsfield, Odiham, Hants

EVANS, Garth; *Educ* Slade Sch of Art, UCL (Dip Fine Art), Manchester Regnl Coll of Art, Manchester Jr Coll of Art; *Career* artist and sculptor; solo exhibitions: Rowan Gallery London 1962, 1964, 1966, 1968, 1969, 1972, 1974, 1976, 1978, 1980, Sch of Art and Design Gallery Sheffield 1971, Ferens Art Gallery Hull 1971, Faculty of Art and Design Gallery Leeds Poly 1971, Oriel Gallery of the Welsh Arts Cncl Cardiff 1976, Mount Molyoke Coll Art Museum S Hadley Mass 1980, Robert Elkon Gallery NY 1983, Tibor de Nagy Gallery NY 1984, HF Manes Gallery NY 1984, John Davis Gallery Akron Ohio 1986, Garth Evans Sculptures and Drawings 1979-87 (Yale Center for Br Art New Haven Conneticut) 1988, Charles Cowles Gallery NY 1988, Compass Rose Gallery Chicago 1989, Hill Gallery Birmingham Michigan 1990; gp exhibitions incl: John Moore's Exhibition (Liverpool) 1960, Reliefs Collages and Drawings (V & A) 1967, Drawings (Museum of London Art NY) 1969, British Sculpture '72 (Royal Acad London) 1972, The Condition of Sculpture (Hayward Gallery London) 1975, David Leuerett Garth Evans and Dicter Rot (Tate Gallery London) 1978, Sculpture Now 1 (Gallery Wintersburger Cologne) 1983, Three Sculptors (Wolff Gallery NY) 1984, Quest-Drawings by Faculty (NY Studio Sch) 1989, Before Sculpture British Sculptors Drawings (NY Studio Sch) 1990, Evans Saunders Tribe Tucker Turnbull (Phillips Staib Gallery NY) 1990, Newer Sculpture (Charles Cowles Gallery NY) 1990; visiting lectr: Central Sch of Art London 1960-65, Camberwell Sch of Art London 1960-69, St Martin's Sch of Art London 1965-79, Chelsea Sch of Art London 1978-79, Yale Sch of Art Yale Univ 1983, 1985 and 1986; visiting prof Minneapolis Coll of Art and Design 1973; external examiner: Ulster Coll The NI Poly Belfast 1974-78, Maidstone Coll of Art Kent 1977-79, Nat Coll of Art and Design Dublin Ireland 1978; visiting tutor Slade Sch of Fine Art UCL 1970-81, Goldsmiths Coll London 1978-81; visiting artist: Sculpture Dept RCA London 1970-81, Mount Molyoke Coll S Hadley Mass 1979-81, Manchester Poly 1978-83, NY Studio Sch 1988-; assoc lectr in sculpture Camberwell Sch of Art London 1971-83, lectr Faculty of Sculpture Br Sch at Rome 1978-83; memb: Fine Art Advsy Panel S Glamorgan Inst of Higher Educn 1977-79, Fine Arts Award Policy Ctee Arts Cncl of GB 1977-79, Fine Art Bd Photography Bd CNAA 1976-79, Ctee for Art and Design CNAA 1976-79; work in numerous pub collections; several pub cmmns; *Awards* Newcastle Cruddas Park Sculpture Competition 1961, Gulbenkian Purchase award 1964, Arts Cncl of GB Sabbatical award 1966, BSC fellowship 1969, Oxford Gallery purchase prize 1972, Welsh Arts Cncl purchase prize 1974, Arts Cncl of GB maj award 1975, Gtr London Arts Assoc bursary 1978, Arts Cncl of GB film bursary 1979, Br Cncl exhibitions abroad grant 1979, Mount Holyoke Coll faculty award 1980, residency Yaddo Saratoga Springs NY 1982, John Simon Guggenheim Meml Fndn fellowship 1986; pubns incl: Some Steel 1970, A Question of Feeling (contrib, 1973), The Student Book (contrib, 1976), Nineteen Assignments Student Responses (1979); *Style—* Garth Evans, Esq; 106 North 6th St, Brooklyn, NY 11211, USA

EVANS, Geoffrey Clifford; s of Ralph Clifford Evans (d 1967), of Carisbrooke, Isle of Wight, and Florence Grace, *née* Grimshaw (d 1973); *b* 18 Sept 1921; *Educ* King James I Sch Newport IOW; *m* 24 Sept 1949, (Mina Betty) June, da of Bertram Downer (d 1953), of Freshwater, IOW; 1 da (Caroline b 1955); *Career* regnl dir Lloyds Bank 1982-84 (jt gen mangr 1975-81); dir: C E Heath plc 1982-87, Hunting Group plc 1981-89, Trade Indemnity plc 1982-90, Greyhound Bank plc 1982-, Pitman plc 1982-85; FCIB 1975; *Recreations* golf, sailing, gardening, painting; *Style—* Geoffrey Evans, Esq; Lymore Gate, Lymington Road, Milford-on-Sea SO41 0QN (☎ 0590 42044)

EVANS, George Harold; s of George John Evans (d 1988), of London, and May, *née* Frazer; *b* 20 Oct 1920; *Educ* Quinton Sch, King's Coll London (BSc), Imperial Coll London (DIC); *m* 14 March 1946, Hazel Evelyn, da of Frederick Charles Brett (d 1958), of London; 1 s (Michael Andrew b 1948), 1 da (Lesley Ann b 1953); *Career* WW11 Flying Offr RAF 1939-45; sr engr Holst & Co Ltd 1948-58, sr ptnr Alan Marshall & Ptnrs 1958-82; Freeman Worshipful Co of Paviors; FICOB 1939, FIStructE 1950; *Recreations* golf, swimming, bridge; *Clubs* RAC; *Style—* George Evans, Esq; 7 Broom Park, Teddington, Middx TW11 9RN (☎ 081 977 5591)

EVANS, Sir Geraint Llewellyn; CBE (1959); s of William John Evans; *b* 16 Feb 1922; *Educ* Guildhall Sch of Music and Drama; *m* 1948, Brenda Evans Davies; 2 s; *Career* opera singer, ret; princ baritone Covent Garden; appearances at: Covent Garden, Glyndebourne, Vienna Staatsoper, La Scala, The Metropolitan, San Francisco, Lyric Chicago, Salzburg, Edinburgh Festival, Paris Opéra, Colon Buenos Aires, Berlin, Warsaw, Welsh Nat Opera, Scottish Opera; Sir Charles Santley Meml award 1963, Harriet Cohen Int Museum award 1967, Fidelio medal Int Assoc Opera Dirs 1980, San Francisco Opera medal 1980; dir Harlech TV; patron Churchill Theatre Bromley; memb: Gorsedd of Bards Royal Nat Eisteddfod of Wales, Royal Soc of Musicians 1981; vice pres: Kidney Res Unit for Wales Fndn, Hon Soc of Cymmrodorion; memb Worshipful Co Musicians, Freeman City of London 1984; fell: Univ Coll Cardiff, Jesus Coll Oxford 1979, Trinity Coll London 1987, Univ Coll London 1987, Univ Coll Aberystwyth 1987, Univ Coll Swansea 1990; FGSM, FRNCM, FRCM, FRSA; Hon DMus: Wales 1965, Leicester 1969, London 1982, Coll of Nat Academic awards 1982, Oxford 1985; Hon RAM 1969; OStJ; kt 1969; *Books* Sir Geraint Evans: a Knight at the Opera (jtly with Noel Goodwin, 1984); *Style—* Sir Geraint Evans, CBE; Trelawney, Vulcan Place, Aberaeron, Dyfed SA46 OBD, Wales

EVANS, Huw Prideaux; s of Richard Hubert Evans (d 1963), and Kathleen Annie, *née* Collins; *b* 21 Aug 1941; *Educ* Cardiff HS, King's Coll Cambridge (MA), LSE (MSc); *m* 1 April 1966, Anne, da of Prof Percival Thomas Bray (d 1988), of Cyncoed, Cardiff; 2 s (Richard b 1969, Lewis b 1971); *Career* dep sec HM Treasy Overseas Fin Gp 1989 (Econ Assessment Gp 1980-86); *Style—* Huw P Evans, Esq; HM Treasury, Parliament St, London (☎ 071 270 4380)

EVANS, Iain Richard; *b* 17 May 1951; *Educ* Univ of Bristol (BSc), Harvard Business Sch (MBA); *Career* sr accountant Arthur Young McClelland Moores & Co 1975-76 (joined 1972); Bain & Co: conslt 1978-80, mangr 1980-82, ptnr 1982-83; non-exec dir: Welsh Water plc 1989-, Welsh Development International 1989-; chm The LEK Partnership 1991- (fndr ptnr 1983-) ; FCA 1981 (ACA 1975); *Recreations* golf, fishing, tennis; *Style—* Iain Evans, Esq; The LEK Partnership, The Adelphi, 1-11 John Adam St, London WC2N 6BW (☎ 071 930 1244, fax 071 839 3790, telex 8950994)

EVANS, James; s of Rex Powis Evans, and Louise Evans; *b* 27 Nov 1932; *Educ* Aldenham, St Catharine's Coll Cambridge (MA); *m* 1961, Jette Holmboe; 2 da; *Career* md and chief exec Int Thomson Orgn plc 1985-; dir: Reuters Hldgs plc 1984-, The Press Assoc Ltd 1983-; *Style—* James Evans, Esq; First Floor, The Quadrangle, PO Box 4YG, 180 Wardour Street, London W1A (☎ 071 437 9787, telex 261349)

EVANS, Capt James; RD (1975), JP (1975), DL (1978); s of Thomas Evans (d 1966), and Hilda Margaret, *née* Atkinson (d 1976); *b* 9 May 1933; *Educ* Merchiston Castle Sch, Univ of Newcastle (BSc); *m* 12 July 1958, Patricia Alexana (Pat), da of Harry Kerr (d 1973); 1 s (Ian b 1963), 2 da (Lynn b 1961, Gwen b 1967); *Career* Nat Serv RNR 1956-58, Sub Lt 1956, Lt 1962, Lt Cdr 1966, Cdr 1971, Capt 1978, Hon ADC 1979-80, ret 1980; apprenticeship: Wm Weatherhead & Sons 1950-52, Swan Hunter and Whigham Richardson 1952-56; engr Yarrow-Admiralty Res Dept 1958-63, nuclear engrg certificate 1960, engr UK Atomic Energy Authy 1963-68, md Eyemouth Boat Building Co Ltd 1968-90, chm Fishing Boat Builders Assoc 1979-90; Nuclear Engrg Soc Silver Medal Award for a paper on Features of Interest in Small Pressurised

Water Reactors 1963, author of East Coast Fishing Boat Building (1990) a tech paper of NE Coast Inst of Engrs and Shipbuilders; pres Eyemouth Rotary Club 1980-81, chm Berwickshire Dist Co Cncl 1980-, chm SCUA Local Govt Advsy Ctee 1987-90; Freeman of Berwick-upon-Tweed; memb: Court of Freemen of Eng and Wales, Court of Deans of Guilds of Scotland; CEng, FRINA, MIMechE; *Clubs* Naval; *Style—* Capt James Evans, RD, JP, DL; Makore, Northburn View, Eyemouth, Berwickshire TD14 5BG (☎ 08907 50701); Dundee House, Harbour Rd, Eyemouth, Berwickshire TD14 5DQ (☎ 08907 50231)

EVANS, Hon Jane Lucy Cynlais; da of Baron Evans of Claughton, JP, DL (Life Peer), *qv*; *b* 3 Feb 1968; *Educ* Birkenhead HS GPDST, Nottingham Univ (BA); *Career* admin sec Gruber Levinson & Franks, chartered accountants; memb: Friends of the Earth, League Against Cruel Sports; *Recreations* general interst in the arts, riding, tennis, squash, skiing, travel; *Clubs* Oxton Cricket, Birkenhead Squash Racquets; *Style—* The Hon Jane Evans; c/o Gruber, Levinson & Franks, Chartered Accountants, 46 Rodney Street, Liverpool L1 (☎ 051 709 3255)

EVANS, Hon Jeffrey Richard; s of 2 Baron Mountevans (d 1974), and hp of bro, 3 Baron; *b* 13 May 1948; *Educ* Nautical Coll Pangbourne, Pembroke Coll Cambridge; *m* 1972, Hon Juliet, *qv*, da of 2 Baron Moran, KCMG; 2 s (Alexander b 1975, Julian b 1977); *Career* shipbroker; dir H Clarkson & Co; Liveryman Worshipful Co of Shipwrights; *Recreations* cross-country skiing, fishing, reading; *Style—* The Hon Jeffrey Evans

EVANS, John; MP (Lab) St Helens North 1983-; s of James Evans (d 1937), and Margaret, *née* Robson (d 1987); *b* 19 Oct 1930; *Educ* Jarrow Central Sch; *m* 1959, Joan, da of Thomas Slater; 2 s, 1 da; *Career* former marine fitter and engr, memb Hebburn UDC 1962-74 (chm 1972-73, ldr 1969-74), memb S Tyneside Met Dist Cncl 1973-74, MP (Lab) Newton Feb 1974-1983, memb Euro Parl 1975-79 (chm Regnl Policy and Tport Ctee 1976-79), asst govt whip 1979, PPS to Rt Hon Michael Foot as ldr of oppn 1980-1983, NEC 1982-, oppn front bench spokesman Employment 1983-87; *Style—* John Evans, Esq, MP; House of Commons, London SW1

EVANS, John Alexander Llewellyn; s of Alan Lile Llewellyn Evans (d 1982), and Charlotte Mary, *née* Alexander (d 1989); *b* 30 Nov 1942; *Educ* Rugby, Univ of Southampton (BSc); *m* 19 March 1983, (Carol) Ann, da of John Cornelius Richard Ferris (d 1988); *Career* CAP Ltd 1976-80, Bos Software Ltd 1981-84, dir Vamp Health 1985-; Liveryman Worshipful Co of Cutlers; CEng; *Recreations* fishing; *Clubs* Hurlingham; *Style—* John Evans, Esq; 16 Langthorne St, London SW6 6JY (☎ 071 385 9809); Pool Cottage, Newcastle, Monmouth, Gwent; Vamp Health, 39 East Hill, London SW18 (☎ 081 871 2866)

EVANS, John Alfred Eaton; s of John Eaton Evans (d 1961), of Oakfield Grove, Clifton, Bristol, and Millicent Jane, *née* Righton (d 1987); *b* 30 July 1933; *Educ* Bristol GS, Worcester Coll Oxford (MA, Rugby first XV, half blue Rugby Fives); *m* 9 Aug 1958, Vyvyan Margaret, da of (Arthur) Henry Mainstone, of Bishopsworth, Bristol; 2 s (Stephen John Eaton b 1961, Hugh Jeffrey Eaton b 1963), 1 da (Susan Beverly Louise Eaton b 1965); *Career* Lt Nat Serv and AER RAOC 1952-58; asst master and house tutor: Old House Blundells 1958-63, Sch House Rugby 1963-73 (and housemaster Killbracken 1973-81); classics tutor and housemaster Phillips Acad Mass USA 1968-69, headmaster Brentwood Sch 1981-; author of various articles on community serv in educn for HMC magazine (Conference); memb: Brentwood Music Soc 1981-, CMS Selection 1983-, Admty Interview Bd 1987-, Army Scholarship Bd 1990-; AMMA 1958, JACT 1970, FRSA 1983; *Recreations* rugger, rugby fives, cricket, walking, reading, composing, piano, singing; *Clubs* East India, Vincent's (Oxford), Oxford Union, Cryptics CC, Jesters; *Style—* John Evans, Esq; Roden House, 4 Shenfield Rd, Brentwood, Essex CM15 8AA (☎ 0277 228036); Brentwood School, Ingrave Rd, Brentwood, Essex CM15 8AS (☎ 0277 212271, fax 0277 260218)

EVANS, Dr (Noel) John Bebbington; CB (1980); s of William John Evans, and Gladys Ellen, *née* Bebbington; *b* 26 Dec 1933; *Educ* Hymers Coll Hull, Christ's Coll Cambridge (MA, MB BChir), Univ of London (DPH); *m* 1, 1960 (m dis), Elizabeth Mary Garbutt; 2 s (David, Hugh), 1 da (Sarah); m 2, 1974, Eileen Jane, *née* McMullan; *Career* called to the Bar Gray's Inn 1965; dep CMO DHSS 1977-83, dep sec DHSS 1977-84, proprietor John Evans Photographic Grosmont, conslt in pub health and health service mgmnt; chm: Nat Biological Standards Bd, UK Transplant Serv; FFPHM, FRCP; *Style—* Dr John Evans, CB; Athelstan, Grosmont, Abergavenny, Gwent NP7 8LW (☎ 0981 240616)

EVANS, His Hon Judge John Field; QC (1972); 2 s of John David Evans (d 1950), of Llandaff, Cardiff, and Lucy May, *née* Field (d 1975); *b* 27 Sept 1928; *Educ* Cardiff HS, Exeter Coll Oxford (MA); *Career* RAF 1947-49, pilot offr 1948; called to the Bar Inner Temple 1953; dep chm Worcs QS 1964-71, rec Crown Ct 1972-78, circuit judge Midland and Oxford 1978-; *Recreations* golf; *Clubs* Vincent's (Oxford), Royal St David's Golf; *Style—* His Hon Judge Evans, QC; 1 Fountain Court, Birmingham B4 6DR; Dudley Crown Court, Dudley, West Midlands

EVANS, Prof (Henry) John; s of David Evans, DCM (d 1963), and Gladys May, *née* Jones; *b* 24 Dec 1930; *Educ* Llanelli GS, UCW Aberystwyth (BSc, PhD); *m* 1, 1 June 1957, Gwenda Rosalind, *née* Thomas (d 1974); 4 s (Paul b 16 Dec 1958, Hugh b 1 April 1960, John b 28 Dec 1961, Owen b 24 July 1963); m 2, 9 June 1976, Dr Roslyn Rose, da of Dr Leigh Angell, of Canberra, Aust; *Career* Res Scientist MRC Radiobiological Res Unit Harwell 1955-64, prof genetics Univ of Aberdeen 1964-69, dir MRC Human Genetics Unit Edinburgh 1969-; hon prof Univ of Edinburgh 1970; FRSE 1968, FIBiol 1980, FRCPEd 1989; *Books* Human Radiation Cytogenetics (1967), Mutagen-Induced Chromosome Damage in Man (1978); *Recreations* golf, music; *Clubs* Royal Cwlth, New; *Style—* Prof John Evans, FRSE; 45 Lauder Rd, Edinburgh EH9 1UE (☎ 031 667 2437); MRC Human Genetics Unit, Western Gen Hosp, Edinburgh (☎ 031 332 2471, fax 031 343 2620)

EVANS, John Noel Gleave; s of James Gleave Evans (d 1963), of Malaya, and Irene, *née* Schofield (d 1989); *b* 9 Dec 1934; *Educ* Cranbrook Sch Kent, St Thomas' Hosp London (MB BS, DLO); *m* 23 July 1960, Elizabeth Violet, da of Rev Cuthbert Edward Guy Glascodine (d 1980); 1 s (Mark b 1966), 3 da (Philippa Donald b 1962, Charlotte Reid b 1963, Kate b 1971); *Career* SSC RAMC 1960-63, cmmn TA 1964-76, Maj RAMC (V); conslt ENT surgn: St Thomas' Hosp London 1971, Hosp for Sick Children London 1972; hon conslt ENT surgn: Queen Elizabeth Hosp Woolwich 1982, King Edward VII Hosp for Offrs 1988; hon conslt in otolaryngology to the Army 1989-; hon sec Br Assoc of Otolaryngologists 1980-88, hon treas Br Academic Conf in Otolaryngology 1984, ENT rep Euro Union of Med Specialists 1985; Freeman City of London 1979, elected Liveryman Worshipful Soc of Apothecaries of London 1979; FRCS 1965 (Edinburgh 1987), memb RSM 1972 (Cncl laryngology section 1975, vice pres 1985-86); corresponding memb American Laryngology Assoc 1984, int memb American Soc of Paediatric Otolaryngology 1989; *Books* Paediatric Otolaryngology Vol 6 Scott-Brown's Otolaryngology (1987); *Recreations* foreign travel, windsurfing; *Clubs* RSM; *Style—* John Evans, Esq; 55 Harley St, London W1N 1DD (☎ 071 580 1481)

EVANS, (Norman) John; s of Norman Harrison Evans, and late Mrs Evans; *b* 21 March 1935; *Educ* Rydal Sch North Wales, Univ of Birmingham; *m* 20 June 1959, Sylvia, da of late Arnold Sydney Blanckensee; 1 s (David John b 30 April 1960), 1 da (Carolyn Bridget b 6 Dec 1964); *Career* admitted slr 1958-; clerk of the peace Walsall Met Borough 1965-71, NP; memb: Walsall Law Assoc 1958- (past pres), Law Soc 1958-; hon sec of charitable orgn; *Recreations* hunting; *Clubs* Meynell and South Staffs Hunt; *Style—* John Evans, Esq; St Pauls Chambers, 6-8 Hatherton Rd, Walsall WS1 1XS (☎ 0922 720333, fax 0922 720623)

EVANS, Lt-Col John Roberts; TD (1954), DL (1973); s of David James Haydn Evans (d 1961); *b* 16 Jan 1917; *Educ* Llandovery Coll, Univ of Exeter; *m* 1945, Sheila Rita, da of Richard Ball (d 1940); 1 s, 1 da; *Career* served WWII HAC and RA (India and Far East), Welch Regt (TA) 1947-66, Lt-Col 6 (Glam) Bn Welch Regt 1963-66; admitted slr 1952; pres Cardiff and Dist Law Soc 1981-82 (former vice pres); hon slr Welsh Rugby Union, govr and hon slr Welsh Sports Aid Fndn, chm Tstees Llandovery Coll, memb Ct of Govrs Univ Coll Cardiff; *Recreations* rugby football, music and fishing; *Clubs* Army and Navy, Cardiff and County; *Style—* Lt-Col John Evans, TD, DL; Greenbanks, Highfields, Llandaff, Cardiff, S Glam (☎ 0222 562480)

EVANS, John Russell; s of Henry Claude Evans, of Hamilton, Scotland; *b* 2 Aug 1945; *Educ* King James I GS Bishop Auckland, City Univ London (BSc); *m* (m dis); 1 s (Jonathan), 1 da (Nicola); *Career* apprentice Rolls Royce 1960-70, Ford 1970-72, General Motors 1972-77, gen mangr Butec Electrics (BL) 1977-78; md: Park Bros 1978-79, Bonser Engineering 1980-85; mfrg dir: Lansing Henley 1979-81 (md 1981-85), Data Magnetics 1985-87; md: Renold Automotive 1988-90, Hamworthy Engineering 1990-; CEng, FIProdE; *Recreations* flying, rugby, sailing, squash; *Style—* John Evans, Esq; Hamworthy Engineering Ltd, Fleet Corner, Poole, Dorset (☎ 0202 665566)

EVANS, John Stanley; QPM (1990); s of William Stanley Evans (d 1970), and Doris, *née* Wooldridge; *b* 6 Aug 1943; *Educ* Wade Deacon GS, Univ of Liverpool (LLB); *m* 25 Sept 1965, Beryl, da of Albert Smith (d 1976); 1 s (Mark 1967), 1 da (Lindsey 1971); *Career* Liverpool City then Merseyside Police 1960-80, asst chief constable Gtr Manchester Police 1980-84, dep chief constable Surrey Constabulary 1984-88, chief constable Devon & Cornwall Constabulary 1989-; sec Police Athletic Assoc 1989-, memb several ctees of Assoc Chief Police Offrs incl: Gen Purposes (chm), Complaints and Discipline (chm), Public Order; FBIM 1980; *Recreations* most sports (ran London Marathon in 1988 and 1989), service and charitable activities; *Style—* John S Evans, Esq, QPM; c/o Devon and Cornwall Constabulary, Police Headquarters, Middlemoor, Exeter, Devon EX2 7HQ ☎ 0392 52101)

EVANS, John Walter; OBE (1988), JP (Staffordshire 1978-); s of Walter Evans (d 1957), of Birmingham, and Florence Beatrice, *née* Morton-Tooze (d 1978); *b* 10 July 1928; *Educ* George Dixon GS, Univ of Birmingham (BSc); *m* 18 Dec 1954, Barbara Anne Evans, da of Harry Atkins (d 1974), of Staffordshire; *Career* National Coal Board: chief mining engr Staffs Area 1972-74 (colliery gen mangr 1956-67, prodn mangr 1967-70, dep chief mining engr 1970-72), chief mining engr Western Area 1974-80; area dir Western Area Br Coal 1984-88 (dep area dir 1980-84), consulting mining engr 1988-; memb Royal Soc of St George, vice pres Staffs Soc; Freeman City of London 1984, memb Worshipful Co of Engrs 1984; FGS 1953, FIMinE 1972, FIMEMME 1986, FRSA 1987, FEng 1988; *Recreations* music, travel; *Clubs* City Livery; *Style—* John Evans, Esq, OBE, JP; Aincourt, 127 Allport Street, Cannock, Staffs WS11 1JZ (☎ 0543 504959)

EVANS, Hon Mrs (Juliet); *née* Wilson; only da of 2 Baron Moran, KCMG; *b* 29 Sept 1950; *Educ* St Mary's Sch Calne, Newnham Coll Cambridge; *m* 1972, Hon Jeffrey Richard de Corban Evans *qv*; 2 s (Alexander, Julian); *Style—* The Hon Mrs Evans

EVANS, (William) Kenneth; s of Judge William Hugh Evans, ICS (d 1969), of Bournemouth, and Gladys Gertrude, *née* Williamson (d 1975); *b* 19 July 1925; *Educ* CCC Oxford (MA); *m* 11 Dec 1954, Lorna Maureen, da of Capt Basil Woodd Cahusac (d POW Far East); 1 s (Christopher b 1955), 1 da (Jennifer-Ann b 1964); *Career* enlisted RE 1943, trg OTS Kirkee India 1944-45, 2 Lt RE Lahore India 1945, Capt 854 Bridge Co Burma 1946, Adj to CRE Maymyo Burma 1946-47, demob 1947; local purchase buyer Uganda Co Kampala 1950-52, produce buying asst Dar Es Salaam and Kampala 1952-54, buyer Pirelli Ltd 1954-56, Peat Marwick Mitchell & Co London 1956-60; Commercial Union Group: joined 1960, taxation mangr 1968, gen mangr 1974, dir 1980 (main bd and 25 subsid cos), ret 1985; chm: Reffet Ltd (insur indust consortium) 1981, Cogent Ltd (technol co) 1982-84; chm Taxation Ctee Br Insur Assoc 1973-80; former memb Taxation Ctees: CBI, Life Offices Assoc, IOD, Business and Indust Ctee OECD; former memb: Cncl Inst of Fiscal Studies, UK Ctee Int Fiscal Assoc; cncllr: Met Borough of Hampstead 1959-62, London Borough of Camden 1964-71 (chm Public Bldgs Ctee, chm Building Works and Servs Ctee); ACA 1960, FCA 1966; *Books* Tax Consequences of Changes in Foreign Exchange Rates (1972), The Effects of Losses in One Country On the Income Tax Treatment in Other Countries of an Enterprise or of Associated Companies Engaged in International Activities (UK Reports to Congress of the Int Fiscal Assoc, 1979); *Clubs* Carlton, IOD; *Style—* Kenneth Evans, Esq; Reffet Ltd, St Helens, 1 Undershaft, London EC3 P3DQ (☎ 071 283 7500 ext 2851, fax 071 283 7500 ext 2420, telex 887626)

EVANS, Kevin Paul; s of Eric Evans, of Calverton, Nottingham, and Eileen, *née* Ludlam; *b* 10 Sept 1963; *Educ* Colonel Frank Seely Sch Calverton, Arnold & Carlton Coll of Further Educn; *m* 19 March 1988, Sandra, da of George Rowlinson; *Career* professional cricketer Nottinghamshire CCC, debut v Cambridge Univ Trent Bridge 1984, awarded county cap Sept 1990; *Recreations* football, tennis, DIY, gardening; *Style—* Kevin Evans, Esq; Nottinghamshire CCC, Trent Bridge, Nottingham NG2 6AG (☎ 0602 821525)

EVANS, Laurie; s of Hugh Evans, of Weston, Avon, and Greta, *née* Bryden (d 1989); *b* 10 July 1955; *Educ* Royal HS Edinburgh, Newcastle Poly, Bournemouth and Poole Coll of Art (DipAD); *m* March 1982, Lesley, da of Stanley Richardson, of Edinburgh; 2 s (James Ewan b 30 May 1983, Calum Thomas b 21 Sept 1986); *Career* photographer; Arts in Fife, freelance reportage photographer for Rock and Roll press (NME, Melody Maker), asst to Bryce Attwell, proprietor Laurie Evans Photographer 1982- (specialising in food and still life); clients incl: Boots, Sainsbury's, Nestlé, John West, Tescos; magazines incl: Good Housekeeping, Homes & Gardens; winner various awards incl: Silver award Assoc of Photographers 1986, 3 Clio awards USA 1986 1988 and 1989, Award of Excllence Communication Arts Magazine, Silver award D&ADA 1990; columnist Image Magazine, contrib to over 30 cookery books; memb Assoc of Photographers (memb Cncl 1989, 1990, 1991); *Recreations* very keen sailor, blues & jazz guitar; *Style—* Laurie Evans, Esq; Laurie Evans Photography, 3rd Floor, 30-31 Great Sutton St, London EC1V 0DX (☎ 071 251 5383, fax 071 253 7082)

EVANS, Leslie Douglas; s of Leslie Edward Evans, of St Albans, and Violet Rosina, *née* Rogerson; *b* 24 June 1945; *Educ* St Albans GS for Boys, St Albans Sch of Art, Leeds Coll of Art (DipAD), Hornsey Coll of Art (Art Teachers' Certificate); *m* 4 Sept 1965, Fionnuala Boyd, *qv*, da of Joseph Douglas Allen Boyd; 1 s (Jack Luis b 12 Sept 1969), 1 da (Ruby Rose b 2 Dec 1971); *Career* artist; began working with Fionnuala Boyd 1968, Bi-Centennial fell USA 1977-78; artist in residence: Milton Keynes Devpt Corp 1982-84, Brunei Rainforest Project 1991-92; solo exhibitions (with Boyd): Angela Flowers Gallery 1972, 1974, 1977, 1979, 1980, 1982, 1984, 1986, 1988, Park Square Gallery Leeds 1972, Boyd and Evans 1970-75 (Turnpike Gallery, Leigh) 1976, Fendrick Gallery Washington DC 1978, Graves Art Gallery Sheffield 1979, Spectro Arts Workshop Newcastle 1980, Ton Peek Utrecht 1981, A Decade of Paintings

(Milton Keynes Exhibition Gallery) 1982-83, Drumcroon Art Centre Wigan 1985, Bird (Flowers East, London) 1990, English Paintings (Brendan Walter Gallery, Santa Monica) 1990, Angela Flowers (Ireland) 1990, Flowers East London 1991; gp exhibitions incl: Postcards (Angela Flowers Gallery) 1970, British Drawing 1952-72 (Angela Flowers Gallery) 1972, British Realist Show (Ikon Gallery) 1976, Aspects of Realism (Rothmans of Pall Mall, Canada) 1976-78, The Real British (Fischer Fine Art) 1981, Black and White Show (Angela Flowers Gallery) 1985, Sixteen (Angela Flowers Gallery) 1986, State of the Nation (Herbert Gallery, Coventry) 1987, Contemporary Portraits (Flowers East) 1988, The Thatcher Years (Flowers East) 1989, Picturing People: British Figurative Art since 1945 (touring exhibition Far East) 1989-90, Art '90 London (Business Design Centre) 1990; work in public collections of: Arts Cncl of GB, Br Cncl, Museum of Modern Art NY, Sheffield City Art Gallery, Wolverhampton City Art Gallery, Leeds City Art Gallery, Contemporary Art Soc Leicester Educn Authy, Manchester City Art Gallery, Unilever plc, Tate Gallery, Williamson Art Gallery, Borough of Milton Keynes; *Awards* prizewinner Bradford Print Biennale, first prize 6 Festival Int de la Peinture Cagnes-sur-Mer; *Recreations* squash, films, friends, music, hill-walking; *Style—* Leslie Evans; Boyd and Evans, Flowers East, 199-205 Richmond Rd, London E8 3NJ (☎ 081 985 3333, fax 081 985 0067)

EVANS, Rt Rev (Edward) Lewis; s of Rev Edward Foley Evans (d 1933), and Mary, *née* Walker; *b* 11 Dec 1904; *Educ* St Anselm's Croydon, Tonbridge Sch, Bishop's Coll Cheshunt, Univ of London (external, BD, MTh); *m* 1967, Vera Lydia (d 1981), da of John Percival Groome; *Career* ordained: deacon 1937, priest 1938; curate St Mary's Prittlewell Chelmsford, warden St Peter's Coll Jamaica 1940, rector Kingston Parish Church Jamaica 1949-52, rector Woodford-Craigton Jamaica 1952-57, suffragan bishop of Kingston Jamaica 1957-60, bishop of Barbados 1960-71, ret 1971; *Style—* The Rt Rev Lewis Evans; No 1 Bungalow, Terry's Cross, Brighton Rd, Henfield, West Sussex BN5 95X (☎ 0273 493334)

EVANS, Hon Liesel Morwenna; o da of Thomas Charles Evans (d 1985), and Baroness Blackstone, *qv*; *b* 17 Sept 1966; *Educ* Campden Sch for Girls, Bristol Univ; *Recreations* drama, socialising; *Style—* The Hon Liesel Evans; 2 Gower St, London WC1

EVANS, Lionel James Carlyon; OBE (1959); s of Lionel Lewis Carlyon Evans (d 1949), of Bucks, and Margaret Etheldreda Mary Gore Browne (d 1978); *b* 12 July 1916; *Educ* Bradfield, Wye Coll, Univ of London (Dip Ag); *m* 1942, Beryl Eulalie, da of Thomas Eyre McKenzie (d 1973), of Barbados; 1 s (Robin b 1944), 2 da (Margaret b 1947, Janet b 1950); *Career* sr lectr Imperial Coll of Tropical Agric Trinidad 1939-50, agric advsr Colonial Devpt Corp 1950-61; dir: Agric Dept The World Bank Washington DC USA 1961-73, Booker Agric Int Ltd 1975-88; chm Booker Farming Ltd 1979-; *Style—* L J C Evans, Esq, OBE; Little Acre,, Alderpark Meadow,, Long Marston,, Tring, Hertfordshire HP23 4RB (☎ 0296 668 237)

EVANS, Hon Lucinda Mary Deirdre; did not assume husband's surname on marriage; da of 2 Baron Mountevans (d 1974), and Deirdre, Lady Mountevans; *b* 8 Jan 1951; *Educ* Queen's Gate Sch London; *m* 19 July 1980, John Edward Hooper, journalist, o s of W J Hooper, of Wimbledon; *Career* journalist with Daily Telegraph; *Recreations* reading about Antarctic exploration; *Style—* The Hon Lucinda Evans; c/o The Daily Telegraph, South Quay Plaza, 181 Marsh Wall, London E14

EVANS, (Ieuan) Lynn; s of Rev Thomas John Evans (d 1973), of Ealing Green, London, and Jenny, *née* Lloyd-Williams (d 1958); *b* 15 July 1927; *Educ* Bradford GS, Haverfordwest GS, St Marys Hosp Med Sch (MB BS); *m* 6 June 1956, Menna, da of Rev Evan James (d 1966), of Porthcawl; 1 s (Rowland b 1961), 1 da (Siân b 1963); *Career* Nat Serv jr surgical specialist RAMC Queen Alexandra's Mil Hosp 1951-53; conslt surgn: Lewisham & St John's Hosp 1965-87, Guys Hosp 1982-84; surgical tutor Guys Hosp Med Sch 1970-87; hon conslt surgn: St Lukes Hosp for the Clergy 1983-87, Royal Soc of Musicians of GB; memb Cncl: Assoc of Surgns of GB & Ireland, Section of Surgery RSM, Med Soc of London, Harveian Soc; pres W Kent Medico-Chirurgical Soc; elder Utd Reformed Church; Freeman: Worshipful Soc of Apothecaries of London, City of London 1975; FRCS 1954; *Recreations* skiing, gardening, travel; *Style—* Lynn Evans, Esq; 34 Birchwood Rd, Petts Wood, Orpington, Kent

EVANS, Mark; s of Rev Clifford Evans (d 1968), of Cardiff, and Mary, *née* Jones; *b* 21 March 1946; *Educ* Christ Coll Brecon, King's Coll London (LLB); *m* 25 Sept 1971, Dr Barbara Lesley Skew, da of Harrows Arthur Skew, of Puerto Rico, Gran Canaria; 1 s (John Clifford b 30 March 1974), 1 da (Claire Elizabeth b 1 April 1976); *Career* called to the Bar Gray's Inn 1977, currently head of chambers; *Style—* Mark Evans, Esq; Glanmire House, 6 Cotham Rd, Bristol BS6 6DR (☎ 0272 739080); St Johns Clambers, Small St, Bristol BS1 1DW (☎ 0272 213456, fax 294821)

EVANS, Mark Singleton; s of Capt Arthur Singleton Evans, RA (d 1954), of Torquay, and Constance Mary, *née* Jenkins (d 1980); *b* 27 Oct 1933; *Educ* Winchester, New Coll Oxford (MA); *m* 15 Dec 1962, Belinda Jane, da of Sir Kenelm Cayley, 10 Bt (d 1967); 2 s, 1 da; *Career* Nat Serv 2 Lt The Royal Dragoons 1952-54; pres: Scarborough Cons Assoc 1981, Kensington Cons Assoc 1989 (chm 1986-89); ptnr Laing & Cruickshank 1964; dir: Mercantile House Holdings 1987, Credit Lyonnais Capital Markets 1987; *Clubs* White's, Swinley Forest Golf, Ganton Golf; *Style—* Mark Evans, Esq; 6 Argyll Rd, London W8 7DB (☎ 071 937 1182); Manor House, Brompton-by-Sawdon, nr Scarborough, North Yorkshire (☎ 0723 85233); Laing & Cruickshank, Broadwalk House, Appold St, London EC2A 2DA (☎ 071 588 4000)

EVANS, Lady (Mary); *née* Darby; *m* 1937, Prof Sir David Gwynne Evans, CBE (d 1984); 1 s, 1 da; *Style—* Lady Evans; 4 Craig Wen, Rhos-on-Sea, Clwyd LL28 4TS

EVANS, Prof Michael Charles Whitmore; s of Allen Whitmore Evans, of London, and Doris, *née* Smith; *b* 24 Sept 1940; *Educ* King Edwards Sch Birmingham, Univ of Sheffield (BSc, PhD); *m* 28 Dec 1963, Christine Stella, da of John Marshall (d 1983); 2 s (Peter Whitmore b 1967, Nicholas John b 1969); *Career* assoc specialist Dept of Cell Physiology Univ of California Berkeley 1964-66, lectr in botany King's Coll London 1966-73, prof in plant chemistry UCL 1982- (reader 1973-82); contrib to numerous papers in scientific jls; chm Plant Sci and Microbiology Sub Ctee 1987-90 (memb 1985-90); memb: Ctee Biological Sci Ctee, SERCC 1987-90; *Recreations* birdwatching, gardening; *Style—* Prof Michael Evans; Dept of Biology, Darwin Building, University College London, Gower St, London WC1E 6BT (☎ 071 380 7312, fax 071 380 7026)

EVANS, Michael Murray; s of Harold Fisher Evans (d 1983), of Wigan, Lancs, and Constance, *née* Shannon (d 1984); *b* 6 July 1942; *Educ* Hesketh Fletcher Secdy Sch Atherton Manchester; *Career* National Provincial Bank Ltd 1958-62, journalist Iliffe Press 1962-68, fndr and md Murray Evans Assocs PR Conslts (now Westminster Communications Group) 1968- (jt md 1989-), dir PR Conslts Assoc 1979-89; MIPR 1973; *Recreations* motorcycling, motoring, reading, computing, travel; *Clubs* RAC; *Style—* Michael Evans, Esq; Westminster Communications Group Ltd, 7 Buckingham Gate, London SW1E 6JS (☎ 071 630 5454, fax 071 630 5767)

EVANS, Michael Stephen James; s of William Henry Reginald Evans, of Seaford, Sussex, and Beatrix Catherine, *née* Mottram; *b* 5 Jan 1948; *Educ* Christ's Hospital, QMC London (BA); *m* 1971, Robyn Nicola, da of Samuel John Wilson Coles; 3 s (Samuel b 29 Nov 1974, Christopher b 6 July 1978, James b 1 July 1980); *Career* news ed Express & Independent Loughton Essex 1969-70 (reporter E London Office 1968); Daily Express: reporter Action Line consumer column 1970-72, gen news reporter 1972-77, home affairs corr 1977-82, def and dip corr 1982-86; def corr The Times 1987- (Whitehall corr 1986-87); vice pres and acting pres Dip and Cwlth Writers Assoc 1985-86; *Books* A Crack in the Dam (1978), False Arrest (1979), Great Disasters (1981), South Africa (1987), The Gulf Crisis (1988); *Recreations* cricket, tennis, golf, playing piano; *Style—* Michael Evans, Esq; The Times, 1 Pennington St, London E1 9XN (☎ 071 782 5921, fax 071 488 3242)

EVANS, Ven Patrick Alexander Sidney; *b* 28 Jan 1943; *Educ* Clifton Coll Bristol, Lincoln Theol Coll; *m* 1969, Jane; 2 s, 1 da; *Career* curate: Holy Trinity Lyonsdown Barnet 1973-76, Royston 1976-78; vicar: Gt Gaddesden 1978-82, Tenterden 1982-89; rural dean West Charing 1988-89, archdeacon Maidstone 1989-, dir of ordinands Diocese of Canterbury 1989-; Hon Canon Canterbury Cathedral 1989; *Style—* The Ven the Archdeacon of Kent; Archdeacon's House, Charing, Ashford, Kent TN27 0LU

EVANS, Col Peter Benwell; s of Harold Evans (d 1988), and Vera Mary, *née* Benwell (d 1989); *b* 11 Sept 1934; *Educ* Eastbourne Coll, RMA Sandhurst, Cambridge Univ (MA); *m* 11 May 1957, Rachel (Ray), da of Leonard Walter, of 37 Haddon Way, Carlyon Bay, St Austell, Cornwall; 2 s (Simon b 1959, Timothy b 1962), 2 da (Jacqueline b 1958, Catharine b 1961); *Career* joined Army 1953, cmmnd 1957, Capt Tport Regt BAOR 1960-65, Capt Op 55 Air Despatch Sqdn RCT Singapore and Borneo 1965-66, staff course RMC Shrivenham 1967, Maj RAF Staff Coll Andover 1968, staff offr Miny of Technol 1969-71, offr i/c 55 Air Despatch Sqdn RCT 1971-73, Army liaison offr RAF Strike Cmd 1973-75, Lt-Col NI 1975, cdr 3 Armd Divnl Regt RCT 1976-78, GSOI staff chief scientist Army MOD 1978-80, instr on loan Ghana Armed Force Staff Coll 1980-83, Army Sch of Mech Tport 1983-84, Col 1984, def advsr 1984-87, team ldr of mil study RMCS Shrivenham 1987-88, ret 1988; md 1989-: Strider Mgmnt Conslts, Strider Def Servs; MBIM 1980, MCIT 1985; *Recreations* fishing, swimming, skiing; *Style—* Col Peter Evans; The Strider Group of Companies, 59/50 Hawley Square, Margate, Kent CT9 1NY (☎ 0843 299058, fax 0843 291983)

EVANS, Peter Michael; s of Michael Evans (d 1976), of Chesterfield, and Fiona Mary, *née* Cassidy; *b* 21 Sept 1952; *Educ* Uppingham, Univ of Oxford (MA); *m* 1975 (m dis 1989), Mary-Ann, da of George Vere Howell; 1 s (Simon Michael b 9 May 1980), 1 da (Eloise Mary b 21 Sept 1981); *Career* IMI plc 1975-80 (personnel trainee, graduate recruitment offr, export mktg exec), regnl mangr West Africa Wellcome plc 1980-83, int personnel exec Booker plc 1983-85, MSL International (formerly Hay-MSL) 1985- (conslt, regnl dir, dir); MIPM 1985, MInstD 1988; *Style—* Peter Evans, Esq; Tanelorn, Lower Rd, Cookham, Berks SL6 9HW (☎ 06285 20767); MSL International, 32 Aybrook St, London W1M 3JL (☎ 071 487 5000, fax 071 224 2350)

EVANS, Lt-Col Richard; MC (1944); s of Robert Henry Evans, MBE (d 1960), of Eyton Old Hall, Leominster, and Phyllis Eleanor, *née* Eden (d 1982); *b* 15 Jan 1920; *Educ* Stowe, Worcester Coll Oxford; *m* 22 May 1985, Marian Elizabeth Magee, da of Maj-Gen Brian Cuff, CB (d 1970), of Fleetham House, Kirkby Fleetham, Northallerton, Yorks; 1 s (Richard Jonathan b April 1966); *Career* cmmnd KSLI 1940, served N Africa (1 Army), Italy and Palestine, Adj 4 KSLI (TA) 1947-51, Hong Kong 1951, Korea 1952 (wounded), Kenya 1956-58, cmd KSLI 1960-63, ret 1963; magistrate N Herefordshire 1965-90; American Bronze Star 1945; *Recreations* field sports; *Style—* Lt-Col Richard Evans, MC; The Mead House, Eyton, Leominster, Hereford HR6 0AQ (☎ 0568 2109)

EVANS, Prof Richard John; s of Ieuan Trefor Evans, and Evelyn, *née* Jones; *b* 29 Sept 1947; *Educ* Jesus Coll Oxford (MA), St Antony's Coll Oxford (DPhil); *m* 2 March 1976, Elín Hjaltadóttir, da of Hjalti Arnason; step da (Sigridur Jónsdóttir b 1964); *Career* lectr history Univ of Stirling 1972-76, prof european history UEA 1983-89 (lectr 1976-83), prof history Birkbeck Coll Univ of London 1989-; visiting assoc prof european history Columbia Univ NY 1980; Litt D UEA 1990; Wolfson Literary Award for History 1988, William H Welch Medal of the American Assoc for the History of Med 1989; *Books* The Feminist Movement in Germany 1894-1933 (1976), The Feminists (1977), Society and Politics in Wilhelmine Germany (ed, 1978), Sozialdemokratie und Frauenemanzipation im Deutschen Kaiserreich (1979), The Germany Family (ed with W R Lee, 1981), The German Working Class (ed, 1982), The German Peasantry (ed with W R Lee, 1986), Rethinking German History (1987), Death in Hamburg (1987), Comrades and Sisters (1987), The German Unemployed (ed with D Geary, 1987), The German Underworld (ed, 1988), Kneipengesprache im Kaiserreich (1989), In Hitler's Shadow (1989), Proletarians and Politics (1990); *Recreations* music (piano), gardening; *Style—* Prof Richard Evans; Department of History, Birkbeck College, University of London, Malet Street, London WC1E 7HX (☎ 01 631 6283)

EVANS, Sir Richard Mark; KCMG (1984, CMG 1978), KCVO (1986); s of Edward Walter Evans, CMG (d 1985), and Anna Margaret, *née* Young (d 1976); *b* 15 April 1928; *Educ* Repton, Magdalen Coll Oxford (BA); *m* 1973, Rosemary Grania Glen Birkett; 2 s; *Career* Dip Serv; served London, Peking, Berne, London; head of Near Eastern and subsequently Far Eastern Dept FCO 1970-74, commercial cnsllr Stockholm 1975-77, min (econ) Paris 1977-79, dep under sec of state FO 1982-84 (previously asst under sec), ambass Peking 1984-88; sr res fell Wolfson Coll Oxford; memb: Int Bd of Advice, ANZ Banking Group; *Style—* Sir Richard Evans, KCMG, KCVO; Sevenhampton House, Sevenhampton, Highworth, Wiltshire SN6 7QA

EVANS, Lt-Col Richard Seaton; s of Frederick Anthony Evans, CVO, of Bells Field, South Ridge, Odiham, Hants, and Nancy, *née* Meakin; *b* 6 Jan 1940; *Educ* Charterhouse, RMA Sandhurst, Staff Coll Camberley, US Armed Forces Staff Coll; *m* 8 Dec 1962, Elizabeth Inez, da of William Lascelles (d 1973); 2 da (Vanessa b 29 Aug 1965, Candida b 27 Sept 1969); *Career* cmmnd 2 Lt RTR 1960 (promoted Lt-Col 1979), cmdg offr 3 RTR 1981-83; served: Royal Scots Greys, 14/20 Hussars; army aviator; saw serv: BAOR, Middle East, NI; ret 1984; dep dir sales mktg Alvis Ltd Coventry 1985-88, fndr and chm The Watch Security Ltd Warwick 1985-, mil conslt Alvis Ltd 1988-; dep patron Lord Leycester Hosp; memb: RTR Assoc, RUSI 1984; FBIM 1988; *Recreations* skiing, gardening, writing, bridge; *Clubs* Cavalry and Guards; *Style—* Lt-Col Richard Evans; Yew Tree Farmhouse, Avon Dassett, Leamington Spa, Warks CV33 0AY (☎ 0295 89 764); The Watch Security, 9 The Market Place, Warwick CV34 4SA (☎ 0926 493460, fax 0926 494826, car 0860 731273)

EVANS, Robert; CBE (1987); s of Gwilym Evans, and Florence May Evans; *b* 28 May 1927; *Educ* Old Swan Coll Liverpool, City Tech Liverpool, Blackburn Tech; *m* 1950, Lilian May, *née* Ward; 1 s (David b 1954), 1 da (Vikki b 1959); *Career* mechanical engr 1943-50, gas exec 1950-56, exec Burmah Oil 1956-62, dir of engrg Southern Gas 1970-72, dir of ops Gas Cncl and Br Gas Corp 1972-75, dep chm N Thames Gas 1975-77, chm E Midlands Region 1977-82; Br Gas Corp: md 1982-83, chief exec 1983-89, memb Bd 1983-; chm Br Gas plc 1989- (chief exec 1986-); pres Inst of Gas Engrs 1981; Freeman: City of London 1976, Worshipful Co of Engrs 1984 (Liveryman 1985); CEng, CBIM, FIGA (hon), FInstE, FIMechE; *Recreations* reading, DIY, golf; *Style—* Robert Evans, Esq, CBE; Br Gas plc, Rivermill House, 152 Grosvenor Rd, London SW1V 3JL

EVANS, Robert George; s of George Cecil Evans, of Northampton, and Francis Ennis, *née* Townsend; *b* 15 Nov 1947; *Educ* Northampton GS, Univ of Newcastle (LLB), LSE (LLM); *m* 3 March 1973, Judith, da of Thomas Edward Bartlett (d 1976);

2 s (Michael Robert, Peter David); *Career* slr; ptnr Cockburn & Evans Spennymoor, sr lectr in law Newcastle upon Tyne Poly; memb Law Soc 1975; *Recreations* cricket, cycling, fell walking; *Style*— Robert Evans, Esq; 1 The Bridle Path, Howden-le-Wear, Crook, Co Durham (☎ 0388 762 008); 53 Parkwood Precinct, Spennymoor, Co Durham DL16 6AB (☎ 0388 815 317)

EVANS, Robert John Weston; s of Thomas Frederic Evans, of Cheltenham, and Margery, *née* Weston; *b* 7 Oct 1943; *Educ* Dean Cross Sch Cheltenham, Jesus Coll Cambridge (BA, MA, PhD); *m* 10 May 1969, Catherine (Kati), da of Ferenc Róbert (d 1972), of Budapest; 1 s (David b 1973), 1 da (Margaret b 1979); *Career* res fell Brasenose Coll Oxford 1968-, reader Univ of Oxford 1990- (lectr 1969-90), jt ed English Historical Review 1986-; chm Cumnor and Dist Hist Soc; FBA 1984; *Books* Rudolf II and his World (1984), The Making of the Habsburg Monarchy (1984); *Style*— Robert Evans, Esq; Brasenose College, Oxford OX1 4AJ (☎ 0865 277 890)

EVANS, (David) Roderick; QC (1989); s of Thomas James Evans, of 3 Pine Crescent, Morriston, Swansea, and Dorothy, *née* Carpenter; *b* 22 Oct 1946; *Educ* Bishop Gore GS Swansea, UCL (LLB, LLM); *m* 6 Nov 1971, Kathryn Rebecca, da of Leonard Thomas Lewis, of 6 Mount Crescent, Morriston, Swansea; 3 s (Ioan b 1972, Gwion b 1974, Gruffudd b 1978), 1 da (Saran b 1976); *Career* called to the Bar Gray's Inn 1970; recorder of the Crown Ct attached to the Wales and Chester circuit 1987-; *Style*— Roderick Evans, Esq, QC; Angel Chambers, 94 Walter Rd, Swansea SA1 5QA (☎ 0792 464 623)

EVANS, Roderick Michael; s of Michael White Evans, of Monaco, and Helga Ingeborg, *née* Schneider; *b* 19 April 1962; *Educ* Millfield; *Career* dir of numerous companies incl: Astra House Ltd, Furnival Estates Ltd, Garpool Ltd, Mulgate Investmts Ltd, Studfair Ltd, Lichfield Securities Ltd, Speylands Ltd, Evans Universal Ltd, Roando Holdings Ltd, Rowite Properties Ltd; *Recreations* motorcycling, shooting, flying; *Clubs* RAC, Royal Yorkshire YC; *Style*— Roderick Evans, Esq; Evans of Leeds plc, Millshaw, Ring Road Beeston, Leeds 11 (☎ 0532 711 888)

EVANS, Roger; s of Eric Evans (d 1947), of Bristol, and Celia Mavis, *née* Roe; *b* 28 Oct 1945; *Educ* Lord Wandsworth Coll; *m* Julia Margaret, da of Arthur Horace Moore Household; 1 s (Rupert Alexander b 14 June 1981), 1 da (Rebecca Grace b 14 June 1981); *Career* management trainee NHS 1966-68, admin Taunton and Somerset Hosp 1968-70, asst gp sec Northwick Park Hosp Harrow 1970-74, asst dist admin Hammersmith Health Dist 1974-82, dep admin Wandsworth Health Authy 1982-85, gen mangr St George's Hosp 1985-; memb Inst of Health Serv Mangrs 1971; *Books* Commissioning Hospitals (1974); *Recreations* cricket, rugby union, fine arts, 18th century music, genealogy, Victorian novels; *Clubs* Glos Co Cricket, Wasps Rugby FC; *Style*— Roger Evans, Esq; 36 Pepys Rd, Wimbledon, London SW20 8PF (☎ 081 879 0729); St George's Hospital, Blackshaw Rd, London SW17 (☎ 081 784 2565)

EVANS, Roger Kenneth; s of Gerald Raymond Evans, and Dr Annie Margaret Evans; *b* 18 March 1947; *Educ* Bristol GS, Trinity Hall Cambridge (MA); *m* 6 Oct 1973, (Doris) June, da of James Rodgers, of Co Down, NI; 2 s (Edward Arthur, Henry William); *Career* called to the Bar Middle Temple (ad eundum Inner Temple) 1970, in practice MO Circuit; Parly candidate (C): Warley West Oct 1974 and 1979, Ynŷs Mŏn (Anglesey) 1987; prospective Parly candidate (C) Monmouth 1990-; chm Cambridge Univ Cons Assoc 1969, City of London Cons Lawyers into Town and Country Planning Acts; pres: Cambridge Georgian Gp 1969, Cambridge Union 1970; memb Exec Ctee Friends of Friendless Churches 1983-; Freeman City of London 1976; *Recreations* architectural history; *Clubs* Carlton, Coningsby (chm 1976-77, treas 1983-87); *Style*— Roger Evans, Esq; 2 Harcourt Buildings, Temple, London EC4Y 9DB (☎ 071 353 6961, fax 071 353 6968, telex 269871 MONREF G, 74 NFL 3053, Telecom Gold NFL 3053); Harcourt Chambers, Churchill House, 3 St Aldates' Courtyard, 38 St Aldates', Oxford OX1 1BA (☎ 0865 791 559, fax 0865 791 585)

EVANS, Roy Lyon; s of David Lewis Evans, of Pontarduulais, West Glam (d 1937), and Sarah, *née* Lyon (d 1960); *b* 13 Aug 1931; *Educ* Gowerton GS; *m* 17 Sept 1960, Brenda Yvonne, da of William George Jones (d 1972), of Gorseinon, West Glam; 1 s (Ian b 1967), 2 da (Julie b 1963, Lisa b 1973); *Career* Nat Serv RAF 1949-51; operator tin plate strip mill 1948-49 and 1951-64; gen sec Iron & Steel Trades Confedn 1985- (organiser 1964-73, asst gen sec 1973-85); chm TUC Steel Ctee 1985; memb: NEC Lab Pty 1981-84, Euro Metalworkers Fedn, TUC Gen Cncl 1985-, ECSC Consultative Ctee 1985- (pres 1986-88), Bd BSC Industries Ltd; pres Industrial Orthopaedic Soc 1986-; *Style*— Roy L Evans, Esq; 26 Crecy Gdns, Redbourn, St Albans, Herts (☎ 058 285 2174); ISTC, Swinton House, 324 Gray's Inn Rd, London WC1 (☎ 017 837 6691)

EVANS, Russell Wilmot; MC (1945); s of late William Henry Evans, and Ethel Williams, *née* Wilmot; *b* 4 Nov 1922; *Educ* King Edward's Sch Birmingham, Univ of Birmingham (LLB); *m* 1956, Pamela Muriel, *née* Hayward (d 1989); 2 s, 1 da; *Career* chm Rank Organisation 1981-83 (dep chm 1981, gp md 1975); dir: Rank Xerox Ltd 1973-83, Southern Television 1974-83, Fuji Xerox Ltd 1976-83; chm: Butlin's Ltd 1975-82, Rank City Wall Ltd 1975-83; *Recreations* tennis, golf, photography; *Clubs* English Speaking Union, Roehampton; *Style*— Russell Evans, Esq, MC; Walnut Tree, Roehampton Gate, London SW15 (☎ 081 876 2433)

EVANS, Hon Sarah Louise Cynlais; da of Baron Evans of Claughton JP, DL (Life Peer), *qv*; *b* 11 July 1966; *Educ* Birkenhead HS GPDST, Univ of Liverpool (BA), Coll of St Paul and St Mary Cheltenham (postgraduate certificate in educn); *Career* infant teacher 1990-; *Recreations* literature, tennis, skiing; *Clubs* Oxton Cricket; *Style*— The Hon Sarah Evans

EVANS, Stephen Graham; s of William Campbell Evans, OBE, of Bradley Green, Redditch, Worcs, and Sarah Annie, *née* Duckworth; *b* 20 May 1944; *Educ* Northampton Town and Co GS, W Bromwich GS, Hall Green Tech Coll Birmingham, S Birmingham Tech Coll; *m* 11 May 1968, Gillian Kathleen, da of John Skidmore; *Career* engr and sr engr Cooper MacDonald 1970-78, sr engr and assoc Peel and Fowler 1979-85 (ptnr 1985-); FIStrucE (memb Cncl, former chm Midland Co Branch), CEng, memb Assoc of Consulting Engrs 1986; *Recreations* sport, music, the arts, travel; *Style*— Stephen Evans, Esq; Peel and Fowler, Griffin House, Ludgate Hill, Birmingham B3 1DW (☎ 021 236 7207, fax 021 236 6918)

EVANS, Stuart John; s of John Redshaw Evans, and Mabel Elizabeth, *née* Brown (d 1974); *b* 31 Dec 1947; *Educ* Royal GS Newcastle upon Tyne, Univ of Leeds (LLB); *m* 2 Jan 1971, Margaret Elizabeth, da of Edgar John Evans (d 1966); 2 s (John Daniel b 1976, Thomas b 1977), 1 da (Elizabeth b 1983); *Career* articled clerk Stanley Brent & Co 1970-72, asst slr Slaughter & May 1972-79, ptnr Simmons & Simmons 1981- (asst slr 1979-80); reader St Stephens Church Canonbury; Freeman City of London Slrs Co; *Books* A Practitioner's Guide to the Stock Exchange Yellow Book (contrib 1989); *Recreations* squash, pictures; *Style*— Stuart Evans, Esq; Simmons & Simmons, 14 Dominion St, London EC2M 2RJ (☎ 071 628 2020, fax 071 588 4129, telex 888562 Simmon G)

EVANS, Dr Susan; da of Maj Heinz Fuld, of Llanarmon-Yn-Ial, Clwyd, and Jean Rosemary Downing, *née* Wilson (d 1965); *b* 17 July 1940; *Educ* Huyton Coll Nr Liverpool, Univ of Liverpool (MB ChB, MD); *m* 5 Feb 1966, Christopher Charles Evans, s of Robert Percy Evans (d 1974); 1 s (Matthew b 1973), 2 da (Joanne b 1971, Sophie b 1975); *Career* lectr dept of dermatology Univ of Liverpool 1968-80, conslt dermatologist Liverpool AHA and Mersey RHA 1980-; hon vice pres N Womens Lacrosse Assoc; vice pres: Liverpool Med Inst, Sports Ctee Br Lung Fndn; govr Huyton Coll; memb Br Assoc Dermatologists; *Recreations* lacrosse, skiing, choral singing; *Style*— Dr Susan Evans; Lagom, Glendyke Rd, Liverpool L18 6JR (☎ 051 724 5386); Whiston Hospital, Prescot, Merseyside (☎ 051 426 1600)

EVANS, Dr Trevor John; o s of Evan Alban (John) Evans, of Market Bosworth, Leics, and Margaret Alice, *née* Hilton; *b* 14 Feb 1947; *Educ* King's Sch Rochester, UCL (BSc, PhD); *m* 1973, Margaret Elizabeth, da of Felix Whitham, of Anlaby, Hull; 3 s (Thomas b 1979, Owen b 1984, Jacob b 1988), 1 da (Jessica b 1981); *Career* chem engr; gen sec Inst of Chem Engrs 1976-, jt sec-general Euro Fedn of Chem Engrg, former bd memb of Cncl of Sci and Technol Insts, memb Exec Ctee Cwlth Engrs Cncl; CEng, FIChemE, FBIM; *Recreations* home renovation, travel; *Style*— Dr T J Evans; The Bakery Cottage, 2 Rectory Lane, Market Bosworth, nr Nuneaton, Warwicks CV13 0LS (☎ 0455 290480); Geo E Davis Bldg, 165-171 Rlwy Terrace, Rugby, Warwickshire CV21 3HQ (☎ 0788 578214)

EVANS, Trevor Mills; s of William Arthur Evans (d 1966), of Swansea, and Alma, *née* Mills (d 1945); *b* 28 Sept 1924; *Educ* Swansea GS; *m* 4 Oct 1952, Margaret, da of Evan James Jones (d 1986), of Narberth, Pembrokeshire; 3 s (Eifrion Mills b 1954, Adrian Mills b 1962, Mills Meirion b 1966), 1 da (Susan Alma b 1957); *Career* slr in private practice, HM coroner for S Powys; ACIS, ATII; *Recreations* dogs, sports interests, photography; *Clubs* Kennel; *Style*— Trevor M Evans, Esq; Plasnewydd, Broadway, Builth Wells, Powys LD2 3DB; Sydney G Thomas & Co, West End House, West St, Builth Wells, Powys LD2 3AH

EVANS, Sir (William) Vincent John; GCMG (1976, KCMG 1970, CMG 1959), MBE (1945), QC (1973); s of Charles Herbert Evans (d 1978), and Elizabeth, *née* Jenkins (d 1965); *b* 20 Oct 1915; *Educ* Merchant Taylors', Wadham Coll Oxford (BA, BCL, MA); *m* 4 Jan 1947, Joan Mary, da of Angus Bryant Symons (d 1964), of London; 1 s (David b 1950), 2 da (Marion b 1948, Jane b 1952); *Career* WWII Lt-Col GB and N Africa; called to the Bar Lincoln's Inn 1939 (hon bencher 1983); asst legal advsr FO 1947-54, legal cnsllr UK Perm Mission to UN NYC 1954-59, dep legal advsr FO 1960-68, legal advsr FCO 1968-75; chm: Bryant Symons & Co 1964-85, Euro Ctee on Legal Co-operation; memb Cncl of Europe 1969-71, UK rep Cncl of Europe Steering Ctee on Human Rights 1976-80 (chm 1979-80); memb: Human Rights Ctee (set up under Int Covenant on Civil and Political Rights) 1976-84, Perm Ct of Arbitration 1987-; judge of Euro Ct of Human Rights 1980-; hon fell Wadham Coll Oxford 1981, Hon DUniv Essex 1986; *Recreations* gardening; *Clubs* Athenaeum; *Style*— Sir Vincent Evans, GCMG, MBE, QC; 2 Hare Court, Temple, London EC4 (☎ 071 583 1770); 4 Bedford Road, Moor Park, Northwood, Middx (☎ 09274 24085)

EVANS, William Anthony Lloyd (Bill); *b* 4 Feb 1924; *Educ* Aberdare Co Sch, Univ of Birmingham, Imperial Coll London (MSc, PhD); *m* 1949, Kathleen Evans, OBE, JP; 1 s (Sqdn Ldr CPA Evans b 1954); *Career* athletics administrator; Cardiff Amateur Athletics Club: hon sec 1969-74, chm 1974-75, pres 1983-85; hon sec Welsh Amateur Athletics Assoc 1974-, chm Br Amateur Athletics Bd 1980-84 (memb Cncl 1974-); Amateur Athletics Assoc: memb Gen Ctee 1974-, chm Sub Ctee on Amateur Status in Athletics 1980, chm Working Pty writing constitution for a Br Athletics Fedn 1988, chm 1989-; memb Welsh Sports Cncl 1984-90 (memb Devpt Ctee 1981-84); chm: Ctee of Advsrs Welsh Sports Aid Fndn 1983-, Centre Ctee 1984-87, SE Wales Advsy Ctee 1987-90, Welsh Athletics Cncl 1987-89; hon sec Athletics Assoc of Wales 1989-; sr lectr in zoology and dean of sci UC Cardiff 1979-82, chief examiner in biology and zoology Welsh Jt Educn Ctee 1964-72, former memb Academic Bd and various Ctees Univ of Wales, former pres Cardiff Scientific Soc; Award of Honour for outstanding service to Welsh Amateur Athletics Assoc 1988; *Recreations* athletics; *Style*— Bill Evans, Esq; Winterbourne, 8 Greenway Close, Llandough, Penarth, South Glamorgan CF6 1LZ (☎ 0222 708102)

EVANS, William Emrys; CBE (1981); s of Richard Evans (d 1965), of Bwlch-y-Pentre, Foel, Llangadfan, Welshpool, Powys, and Mary Elizabeth Evans (d 1956); *b* 4 April 1924; *Educ* Llanfair Caereinion Co Sch; *m* 26 May 1946, Mair, da of Evan Thomas (d 1953); 1 da (Ceridwen Eleri); *Career* WWII RN 1942-46 (despatches 1944); Midland Bank Ltd 1941-84: asst gen mangr 1967-72, regnl dir South Wales 1972-74, regnl dir Wales 1974-76, sr regnl dir Wales 1976-84; dir: Align-Rite Ltd 1984-, Module 2 Ltd 1988-89, Nat Welsh Omnibus Service Ltd 1988-; chm: CBI Wales 1979-81, Cncl Univ Coll of Wales Swansea 1982-, Welsh Ctee for Economic and Industl Affairs 1982-, Midland Bank Advsy Cncl for Wales 1984-, Wishing Well Appeal in Wales 1987-89, Barnardos Centenary in Wales Appeal 1987-88, Menter a Busnes 1988-, Welsh Sports Aid Fndn 1988-; vice chm Executive Secondment Ltd 1984-90; pres: Royal Nat Eisteddfod of Wales 1980-83, Welsh Congregational Church 1988-90; vice pres: Royal Welsh Agric Soc 1972-, Tenovus Cancer Res Unit 1990-, Kidney Res Unit for Wales Fndn 1980-; dir: Devpt Corpn for Wales 1974-78, Wales Industl Devpt Advsy Bd, Devpt Bd for Rural Wales 1976-89 (chm Fin and Mktg Ctee); treas: Welsh Congregational Church 1975-87, Mansfield Coll Oxford 1977-88; tstee: Catherine and Lady Grace James Fndn 1973-, John and Rhys Thomas James Fndn 1973-, Llandovery Coll 1980-, Mansfield Coll Oxford 1988-; memb: Ct and Cncl Univ Coll Swansea 1972-, Cncl for the Welsh Language 1972-76, Ct and Cncl Univ of Wales 1973-, Prince of Wales Ctee 1975-87; High Sheriff Co of S Glamorgan 1985-86; Hon LLD Univ of Wales 1983; FCIB; *Recreations* golf, gardening, music; *Clubs* Cardiff and County; *Style*— W Emrys Evans, Esq, CBE; Maesglas, Pen-y-turnpike, Dinas Powis, S Glamorgan CF6 4HH (☎ 0222 512 985)

EVANS, Hon Mrs (Winifred); *née* Gormley; da of Baron Gormley, OBE; *b* 1940; *m* 1960, Arthur Evans; *Style*— The Hon Mrs Evans; c/o The Rt Hon the Lord Gormley, OBE, 1 Springfield Grove, Sunbury-on-Thames, Surrey

EVANS, Rev (Charles) Wyndham; s of William Lloyd Evans, of Brookside Cottage, Corwen, and Ada Henrietta, *née* Wright; *b* 16 Oct 1928; *Educ* Bala Church in Wales Sch, Bala GS, Univ Coll of N Wales (BA), St Catherines Coll Oxford (BA, MA), St Stephens House Oxford; *m* 2 Aug 1961, Sheila Huw, da of Hugh Jones, JP, MBE (d 1975), of Fern Bank, Llanfairfechan, Gwynedd; 1 s (Johnathan b 1966), 1 da (Helen b 1965); *Career* ordained: deacon 1952, priest 1953; curate Denbigh 1952-55, chaplain and housemaster Llandovery Coll 1958-67, chaplain and sr lectr in educn Trinity Coll Carmarthen 1967-79, vicar Llanrhaeadr YC 1979-, chaplain Ruthin Sch 1979-, rural dean Denbigh 1984-; tstee St Mary's Tst, memb Welsh Nat Religious Educn Centre Bangor; *Books* Bible Families (1965); *Style*— The Rev Wyndham Evans; The Vicarage, Llanrhaeadr, Denbigh, Clwyd LL16 4NN; Parciau, 12 The Close, Llanfairfechan, Gwynedd, (☎ 074 578 250)

EVANS, (John) Wynford; s of Gwilym Everton Evans, of Llanelli (d 1968), and Margaret Mary Elfreda, *née* Jones (d 1982); *b* 3 Nov 1934; *Educ* Llanelli GS, St John's Coll Cambridge (MA); *m* 20 April 1957, Sigrun, da of Gerhard Brethfeld; 3 s (Mark, Chris, Tim); *Career* dep chm London Electricity 1977-84, chm S Wales Electricity 1984-; dir Nat Garden Festival Wales 1987-88, Welsh Nat Opera 1988-, memb Welsh Language Bd 1988-89, dep chm Prince of Wales Ctee 1989-; *Recreations* fly-fishing, cross-country skiing, golf; *Clubs* Fly-fishers, Cardiff & County, City Livery, London Welsh; *Style*— Wynford Evans, Esq; South Wales Electricity, St Mellons, Cardiff CF3 9XW

EVANS-BEVAN, David Gawain; s and h of Sir Martyn Evans-Bevan, 2 Bt; *b* 16 Sept 1961; *m* 7 Nov 1987, Philippa Alice, yst da of Patrick Sweeney, of East Moors, Helmsley, N Yorks; 1 da (Alice Laura b 14 Oct 1989); *Style*— David Evans-Bevan, Esq

EVANS-BEVAN, Sir Martyn Evan; 2 Bt (UK 1958); s of Sir David Martyn Evans-Bevan, 1 Bt (d 1973); *b* 1 April 1932; *Educ* Uppingham; *m* 12 Oct 1957, Jennifer Jane Marion, da of Robert Hugh Stevens, of Lady Arbour, Eardisley, Herefords; 4 s; *Heir* s, David Evans-Bevan, *qv*; *Career* High Sheriff of Breconshire 1967-68, Freeman of City of London, Liveryman Worshipful Co of Farmers; company dir; *Clubs* Carlton; *Style*— Sir Martyn Evans-Bevan, Bt; Felin-Newydd, Llande Falle, Brecon, Powys

EVANS-FREKE, Hon John Anthony; 2 s of 11 Baron Carbery, *qv*; *b* 9 May 1949; *Educ* Downside, RAC Cirencester; *m* 1972, Veronica Jane, yst da of Maj Eric Williams, of House of Lynturk, Alford, Aberdeenshire; 2 s (James Eric b 1976, Charles William Anthony b 1981), 1 da (Flora Mary b 1979); *Career* Cluttons Chartered Surveyors 1975-84 (ptnr 1980-), ptnr Humberts Chartered Surveyors 1984-88, head agent to Northumberland Estates 1988-; FRICS; *Style*— The Hon John Evans-Freke; Abbeylands House, Alnwick, Northumberland; Estates Office, Alnwick Castle, Northumberland (☎ 0665 510777)

EVANS-FREKE, Hon Michael Peter; s and h of 11 Baron Carbery; *b* 11 Oct 1942; *Educ* Downside, Christ Church Oxford (MA), Strathclyde Univ (MBA); *m* 9 Sept 1967, Claudia Janet Elizabeth, o da of late Capt Percy Lionel Cecil Gurney, of Little Chart, Penshurst, Kent; 1 s (Dominic Ralfe Cecil b 1969), 3 da (Richenda Clare b 1971, Isabel Lucy b 1973, Anna-Louise b 1979); *Style*— The Hon Michael Evans-Freke; Sandpit House, Toothill, Romsey, Hants

EVANS-FREKE, Hon Stephen Ralfe; s of 11 Baron Carbery; *b* 2 March 1952; *Educ* Downside, Trinity Coll Cambridge (BA); *m* 1990, Valerie Beattie Johnson, e da of Russell Beattie of Stonington, Connecticut, USA; *Career* sr vice pres Blythe Eastman PaineWebber Inc (USA), former pres PaineWebber Devpt Corpn (USA), former dir PaineWebber Inc (USA) (a maj US fin servs firm); dir: Telesoft AB (Sweden), Centocor Devpt Corpn (USA), Amgen Devpt Corpn, Tocor Inc (USA); chm and chief exec offr Virtual World Entertainments Inc, chm Selectide Corp (USA); *Clubs* Brooks'; *Style*— The Hon Stephen Evans-Freke; Norfolk, Connecticut 06058, USA; 18 East 82nd St, New York, NY 10028, USA; Wool Mountain Ranch, Alderpoint, California, USA

EVANS LOMBE, Capt Peter Michael; s of Maj John Michael Evans Lombe, MC (d 1938), and Patricia Routledge, *née* Gibson; *b* 5 June 1933; *Educ* Wellington Coll, RMA Sandhurst; *m* 1964, Vera-Alexandra, da of Laurens Rijnhart Boissevain (d 1986), of Monte Carlo; 2 s (James Nicholas b 1967, Charles Patrick Laurens b 1971); *Career* Army 1951-60, cmmnd 3 Carabiniers Prince of Wales Dragon Gds 1953, 15/19 Kings Royal Hussars 1954, resigned 1960; ptnr and memb Stock Exchange; Kitcat and Aitken Stockbrokers 1960-83, dir Hambros Bank 1983; Liveryman Worsipful Co of Skinners; *Recreations* fishing, shooting, sailing, golf; *Clubs* Swinley Forest Golf, Royal West Norfolk GC; *Style*— Capt Peter Evans Lombe; 10 Child's St, London SW5 9RY (☎ 071 370 5381); Roydon Lodge, Roydon, nr King's Lynn, Norfolk (☎ 0485 600 215); Hambros Bank Ltd, 41 Tower Hill EC3 (☎ 071 480 5000)

EVANS-LOMBE, Edward Christopher; QC (1978); only s of Vice Adm Sir Edward Evans-Lombe, KCB, JP, DL (himself gs of Rev Henry Lombe, who took the name Lombe *vice* Evans 1862 under the terms of the will of his great-uncle, Sir John Lombe, 1 Bt. Sir John was bro of Mary, the Rev Henry's mother, who m Thomas Browne Evans). The surname of the Admiral's f, Alexander, became Evans Lombe following the marriage of his f with a cousin, Louisa Evans; *b* 10 April 1937; *Educ* Eton, Trinity Coll Cambridge; *m* 1964, Frances Marilyn, er da of Robert Ewen Mackenzie, of Lincoln; 1 s, 3 da; *Career* served Royal Norfolk Regt 1955-57, 2 Lt; barr Inner Temple 1963, standing counsel to Dept of Trade in Bankruptcy Matters 1971, rec SE Circuit 1982-; chm Agric Land Tbnl SE Area 1983; master of bench Inner Temple 1985; *Style*— Edward Evans-Lombe, Esq, QC; 4 Stone Buildings, Lincolns Inn WC2 A3XT (☎ 071 242 5524); Marlingford Hall, nr Norwich (☎ 0603 880319)

EVANS OF CLAUGHTON, Baron (Life Peer UK 1978), of Claughton, Merseyside; (David Thomas) Gruffydd Evans; JP, DL (Merseyside); s of Maj John Cynlais Evans and Nellie Euronwy Evans; *b* 9 Feb 1928; *Educ* Birkenhead Sch, Friars Sch Bangor, Liverpool Univ (LLB); *m* 1956, Moira Elizabeth, da of late James Rankin; 1 s (Hon David Robert Cynlais b 1964), 3 da (Hon Elizabeth Ann Cynlais (Hon Mrs Johnson) b 1957, Hon Sarah Louise Cynlais b 1966, Hon Jane Lucy Cynlais b 1968); *Career* slr 1952, pres Lib Party 1977-78 (chm 1965-68), Lib spokesman on Local Govt and Housing in House of Lords, chm Gen Election Ctee 1979 and 1983, chm Marcher Sound Ltd (independent local radio for Wrexham/Chester), dir Granada TV, pres Nat Assoc of Wharehouse Keepers 1983-88; govr Birkenhead Sch 1985-; *Recreations* golf, watching Welsh rugby and Liverpool Football Club; *Clubs* Nat Liberal, Wirral Golf, Oxton Cricket (pres), Birkenhead Squash Racquets, MCC; *Style*— The Rt Hon Lord Evans of Claughton, JP, DL; House of Lords, London SW1 (☎ 071 219 3121)

EVARISTI, Marcella Silvia; da of Louis Evaristi, and Marcella, *née* Visocchi; *b* 19 July 1953; *Educ* Notre Dame HS, Univ of Glasgow (MA); *m* 28 Jan 1982, (John) Michael Boyd, s of Dr John Truesdale Boyd; 1 s (Daniel b 25 Nov 1988), 1 da (Gabriella (twin) b 1988); *Career* playwright, plays incl: Dorothy and The Bitch 1976, Scotia's Darlings 1978, Hard to Get 1980, Wedding Belles and Green Grasses 1981, Eve Set the Balls of Corruption Rolling 1982 (BBC Play for Today and winner of Pye Award for best writer new to TV 1982), Commedia 1982 (nominated Evening Standard Award best play by newcomer 1982), Checking Out 1984, There's Something About A Convent Girl (1991); radio plays incl: The Works 1985, The Hat 1988, Terrestrial Extras 1985; playwright in residence: Univ of St Andrews 1979-80, Univ of Glasgow 1984-85, Univ of Strathclyde 1984-85; fell in creative writing Univ of Sheffield 1982-84; *Books* contrib: Delighting the Heart: a Notebook of Women Writers (1989), Plays without Wires (1989); *Style*— Marcella Evaristi

EVE, Martin Weston; s of Thomas Eve (d 1951), and Enid, *née* Orange (d 1961); *b* 22 June 1924; *Educ* Bryanston, Univ of Cambridge (MA); *m* 1, 19 June 1949 (m dis 1979), Betty; 2 s (Christopher b 1951, William b 1957), 1 da (Catherine b 1955); m 2, 1982, Patricia; *Career* Lt RNVR 1942-46; fndr Merlin Press 1956; memb Nat Ctee Euro Nuclear Disarmament 1980-; *Books* Old Gaffers Tale; *Recreations* sailing; *Style*— Martin Eve, Esq; Merlin Press Ltd, 10 Malden Rd, London NW5 (☎ 071 267 3399)

EVE, Robin Anthony; s of late Frederick Latymer Eve; *b* 20 April 1934; *Educ* City of London Freemens Sch; *m* 1953, Anne Augusta, *née* Mead; 2 s, 2 da; *Career* dir Midland Bank Industl Finances Ltd, common councilman Corp of London Ward of Cheap 1980; FCIS, FCCA, AJII, MIMC; *Recreations* sailing (yacht Contessa 32 'Picardy II'), music, fishing; *Clubs* City Livery, City Livery Yacht; *Style*— Robin Eve, Esq; 36 Poultry, EC2 (☎ 071 638 8861)

EVE, Trevor John; s of Stewart Frederick Eve, of Staffordshire, and Elsie, *née* Hamer; *b* 1 July 1951; *Educ* Bromsgrove Sch Worcs, Kingston Art Coll, RADA; *m* 1 March 1980, Sharon Patricia Maughan, da of Francis Maughan, of Rotary Court, Hampton, Surrey; 1 s ((James Jonathan) Jack b 23 Sept 1985), 1 da (Alice b 6 Feb 1982); *Career* actor; film: Hindle Wakes 1976, Dracula, A Wreath of Roses, The Corsican Brothers, A Knight's Tale; tv: Shoestring (best actor) 1980, Jamaica Inn, A Sense of Guilt 1990, Parnell and the Englishwoman 1991; theatre: Children of a Lesser God (best actor) 1981, High Society, Royal Nat Theatre 1989; memb Ctee Br Deaf Assoc; *Recreations* painting, tennis; *Clubs* Queen's, Hurlingham, St James's; *Style*— Trevor Eve, Esq; Secretary to T Eve, 36 Kensington Park Gdns, London W11 (☎ 071 229 7955, fax 071 221 7185)

EVE, William Raymond Cedric; s of John Harvey Sutcliff Eve, JP, DL, of Kingswood, Surrey, and Yvonne Audrey, *née* Alabaster; *b* 26 Oct 1944; *Educ* Tonbridge; *m* 12 Oct 1973, Susan Margaret, da of Dermot Whelan, of Epsom, Surrey; 2 s (Andrew Michael Patrick b 1971, Charles William Harvey b 1978), 1 da (Juliette Amanda b 1979); *Career* chm VISI systems Ltd, dir Carter-Parratt Ltd the Holding Co 1973- (VISI systems are the leading suppliers of micro-computer systems based on IBM to the motor trade in the UK); *Recreations* squash, tennis, golf, cricket, bridge; *Clubs* RAC, South Hatch Racing, Brockham Conservative Assoc (treas); *Style*— William R C Eve, Esq; Mowillands, Reigate Road, Betchworth, Surrey (☎ 0737 784 2176); VISI systems Ltd, VISI system House, Kimpton Road, Sutton, Surrey (☎ 081 644 4355, fax 081 644 0532, car 0836 272)

EVELEIGH, Hon Mrs (Deborah Gay Le Messurier); da of Baron Wolfenden, CBE (d 1985), and Eileen Le Messurier, *née* Spilsbury; *b* 14 Nov 1943; *m* 1966, Francis Michael James Eveleigh, s of Prof Francis Hedley Arthur Eveleigh; 1 s (Daniel b 1972), 1 da (Christian b 1971); *Style*— Hon Mrs Eveleigh; Madeley Green, Billesley Lane, Avechurch, Worcestershire

EVELEIGH, Rt Hon Sir Edward Walter Eveleigh; PC (1977), ERD; s of Walter William Eveleigh (d 1952), and Daisy Emily Eveleigh (d 1989); *b* 8 Oct 1917; *Educ* Peter Symonds Sch, BNC Oxford (MA); *m* 1, 1940, Vilma Bodnar; m 2, 1953, Patricia Helen Margaret (d 1990), da of Marcel Bury; 2 s (and 1 s decd); *Career* cmmnd RA (SR) 1936, served WWII (despatches), Maj; barr Lincoln's Inn 1945, QC 1961, rec Burton-upon-Trent 1961-64, rec Gloucester 1964-68, bencher Lincoln's Inn 1968, judge High Court of Justice (Queen's Bench) 1968-77, presiding judge SE Circuit 1971-76, Lord Justice of Appeal 1977-85; memb Royal Cmmn on Criminal Procedure 1978-80; pres: Br-German Jurists' Assoc 1974-85, Bar Musical Soc 1980-89; chm Statute Law Soc 1985-90, treas Lincoln's Inn; kt 1968; *Clubs* Garrick; *Style*— The Rt Hon Sir Edward Eveleigh, ERD; Royal Courts of Justice, Strand, London WC2

EVELEIGH, Hon Mrs (Victoria Morina); *née* Butler; da of 28 Baron Dunboyne, and Anne Marie, *née* Mallet; *b* 19 Dec 1959; *Educ* Benenden, Univ of St Andrews (BSc), Wye Coll Univ of London (MSc); *m* 27 Sept 1986, Christopher Eveleigh; 1 s (George Jethro b 1987), 1 da (Sarah b 1990); *Career* self employed in farm tourism, working on family farm; *Recreations* horse riding, painting, campanology; *Style*— The Hon Mrs Eveleigh; West Ilkerton Farm, Lynton, North Devon EX35 6QA (☎ 0598 52310)

EVELEIGH-ROSS DE MOLEYNS, Hon Mrs Francis; Olivia Phoebe; da of Capt Percy Neave Leathers, of Robertsbridge, E Sussex; *m* 1, 25 March 1950, Lord John Conyngham (d 31 May 1963), s of 6 Marquess Conyngham; m 2, 4 Aug 1963, as his 4 w, Hon Francis Alexander Innys Eveleigh-Ross-de-Moleyns (d 29 April 1964), s of 6th Baron Ventry; *Style*— The Hon Mrs Francis Eveleigh-Ross de Moleyns; 317 The Water Gdns, Hyde Park, London W2 2DQ

EVELYN, John Patrick Michael Hugh; DL (Surrey 1983); s of Maj Peter Evelyn, Grenadier Gds (presumed d of wounds 1943, ggs through his paternal grandmother of Rev George Chichester, bro of 1 Baron O'Neill and hence of the oldest traceable family in Europe, the O'Neills, of the Irish Royal House of Tara); *b* 16 Oct 1939; *Educ* Eton; *m* 1, 1965 (m dis 1974), Jennifer Browne; 1 s; m 2, 1974, Anne, da of Richard Lindsell, DFC, of Northwood House, Sharpthorne, Sussex; 2 s; *Career* farmer; High Sheriff Surrey 1982-83, ccnclr Surrey; *Recreations* winter and field sports, Italian 19th century opera; *Clubs* Boodle's; *Style*— J Patrick Evelyn, Esq, DL; The Estate Office, Wotton, Dorking, Surrey

EVELYN, (John) Michael; CB (1976); s of Edward Ernest Evelyn, ISO (d 1950), and Kate Rosa, *née* Underwood (d 1954); *b* 2 June 1916; *Educ* Charterhouse, ChCh Oxford (MA); *Career* WWII 1939-46 Oxfordshire and Buckinghamshire LI, demobbed temp Maj; called to the Bar 1939; asst dir Public Prosecutions Dept 1969-76 (joined 1969), author of over 40 crime novels since 1954 under the pseudonym Michael Underwood; *Recreations* reading, listening to music; *Clubs* Garrick, Detection; *Style*— Michael Evelyn, Esq, CB; 100 Ashdown, Eaton Rd, Hove, E Sussex BN3 3AR (☎ 0273 776104)

EVENNETT, David Anthony; MP (C) Erith and Crayford 1983-; s of Norman Thomas Evennett, and Irene Evennett; *b* 3 June 1949; *Educ* Buckhurst Hill Co HS for Boys, LSE (MSc); *m* 1975, Marilyn Anne, da of Ronald Stanley Smith; 2 s (Mark, Thomas); *Career* sch teacher 1972-74; Lloyds': broker 1974-81, memb 1976-, dir Underwriting Agency 1982-; memb Redbridge Borough Cncl 1974-78, contested (C) Hackney S and Shoreditch 1979; memb Select Ctee of Educn Sci and the Arts 1986-; *Recreations* family, reading novels and biographies, cinema, going to theatre; *Clubs* Carlton, Priory (Belvedere); *Style*— David Evennett, Esq, MP; House of Commons, London SW1

EVENS, Mark David; s of Ronald Clarence Evens, of Hawridge Common, Nr Chesham, Bucks and Rita Laura, *née* Meeks; *b* 13 Dec 1953; *Educ* Dr Challoners GS Amersham, Exeter Coll Oxford (exhibitioner, BA, MA); *m* 17 Sept 1977, Alison, da of George William Brown; 1 s (David Anthony b 17 June 1984), 1 da (Heather Frances b 6 May 1987); *Career* articled clerk Arthur Young McClelland Moores & Co 1975, qualified CA 1978, ptnr Arthur Young 1985 (mangr 1981), nat dir Information Systems Audit Ernst & Young (following merger) 1989-; FCA 1988 (ACA 1978); *Recreations* squash, running, brewing; *Style*— Mark Evens, Esq; Ernst & Young, Becket House, 1 Lambeth Palace Rd, London SE1 7EU (☎ 071 931 3027, fax 071 928 1345)

EVERALL, Mark Andrew; s of John Dudley Everall, of 122 Harley St, London, and Pamela, *née* Odone; *b* 30 June 1950; *Educ* Ampleforth, Lincoln Coll Oxford (MA); *m* 16 Dec 1978, (Elizabeth) Anne, da of Thomas Hugh Richard Perkins; *Career* called to the Bar Inner Temple 1975, W Circuit; *Style*— Mark Everall, Esq; 1 Mitre Court Buildings, Temple, London EC4 (☎ 071 353 0434)

EVERARD; *see*: Welby-Everard

EVERARD, Richard Anthony Spencer; s of Maj Richard Peter Michael Spencer (d 1990), of Rotherby Grange, Melton Mowbray, Leicestershire, and Betty Ione, formerly Lady Newton Butler (d 1989); *b* 31 March 1954; *Educ* Eton, RMA Sandhurst; *m* 9 May 1981, Caroline Anne, da of Reginald J Tower Hill, of Holfield Grange, Coggeshall, Essex; 1 s (Julian b 1989), 1 da (Charlotte b 1985); *Career* Royal Horse Guards 1 Dragoons (Blues and Royals) 1973-77; cmmnd 1973, Lt 1975; trainee Courage, Bass, Everards Brewery 1977-80; dir: Anglesey Road Devpts Ltd 1982, John Sarson and Son Ltd 1983-; Everards Brewery Ltd: dir 1983-, vice chm 1985-, chm 1987-; memb: IOD Leicestershire Branch Ctee, Army Benevolent Fund Leicestershire Branch Ctee; Dip in company direction of IOD; *Recreations* shooting, skiing, cricket, flying helicopters, motorcycling, golf; *Clubs* Eton Ramblers, Butterflies, Cavalry & Guards, Helicopter of GB, Leicestershire Golf; *Style*— Richard Everard, Esq; East Farndon Hall, Market Harborough, Leicestershire LE16 9SE (☎ 0858 66671); Everards Brewery Ltd, Castle Acres, Narborough, Leicester LE9 5BY (☎ 0533 630900, fax 0533 827270, telex 342863)

EVERARD, Sir Robin Charles; 4 Bt (UK 1911); s of Lt-Col Sir Nugent Henry

Everard, 3 Bt (d 1984), and Frances Audrey, *née* Jesson (d 1975); *b* 5 Oct 1939; *Educ* Harrow, Sandhurst; *m* 28 Sept 1963, Ariel Ingrid, elder da of Col Peter Cleasby-Thompson, MBE, MC (d 1981), of Blackhill House, Little Cressingham, Norfolk; 1 s (Henry Peter Charles b 1970), 2 da (Catherine Mary b 1964, Victoria Frances b 1966); *Heir* s, Henry Peter Charles b 6 Aug 1970; *Career* three year cmmn Duke of Wellington's Regt; md P Murray-Jones Ltd 1961-75, mgmnt conslt 1975-; *Style—* Sir Robin Everard, Bt; Church Farm, Shelton, Long Stratton, Norwich NR15 2SB

EVERARD, Simon; TD (1967), DL (Leics 1984); s of Charles Miskin Everard (d 1953), and Monica Mary Barford (d 1970), of Werrington Hall, Peterborough; *b* 30 Oct 1928; *Educ* Uppingham, Clare Coll Cambridge; *m* 1955, Joceline Margaret, da of Francis Jaime Wormold Holt (d 1985), of Seaview, IOW; 3 s (Nicholas b 1956, Mark b 1958, James b 1962), 1 da (Serena b 1967); *Career* Capt Leics and Derbys Yeo TA; pres Ellis & Everard plc (industl chemical distributor) 1990- (chm 1980-90), vice chm Leicester Bldg Soc 1982- (Alliance and Leicester Bldg Soc 1984-); *Recreations* shooting, gardening, tennis; *Clubs* Cavalry & Guards; *Style—* Simon Everard, Esq, TD, DL; c/o Ellis & Everard plc, 46 Peckover Street, Bradford, West Yorkshire BD1 5BD

EVERED, Dr David Charles; s of Thomas Charles Evered (d 1959), of Bannatyne, Furzefield Road, Beaconsfield, Bucks, and Enid Christian, *née* Frost; *b* 21 Jan 1940; *Educ* Cranleigh Sch, Middx Hosp Med Sch Univ of London (BSc, MB BS, MD); *m* 6 June 1964, Anne Elizabeth Massey (Kit), da of John Massey Lings (d 1944), of Bolton, Lancashire; 1 s (Alexander b 1975), 2 da (Elizabeth b 1966, Susanna b 1969); *Career* second sec MRC 1988-, formerly dir City Fndn 1978-88, conslt physician Royal Victoria Infirmary Newcastle upon Tyne; memb: Assoc of Med Res Charities Ctee 1980-84 (vice chm 1987-88), St George's Hosp Med Sch Cncl 1983- (Fin Ctee 1984-), Fndn Louis Jeanet de Médecine Geneva 1984- (vice pres Sch Ctee 1 memb: Zoological Soc of London (Cncl 1985-89), Scientists Inst for Public Info New York, MRS Advsy Ctee 1985-; Freeman City of London 1983, Liveryman Worshipful Soc of Apothecaries; FRCP, FRSM Med, FZS, FInstBiol; *Books* Diseases of the Thyroid (1976), Atlas of Endocrinology (with R Hall 1979, 2 edn 1990), Collaboration in Medical Research in Europe (with M O'Connor, 1981); *Recreations* tennis, sailing, reading, history; *Style—* Dr David Evered; Medical Research Council, 20 Park Crescent, London W1N 4AL (☎ 071 636 5422, fax 071 436 6179)

EVEREST, Dr David Anthony; s of George Charles Everest (d 1957), of Kenton, Middx, and Ada Bertha, *née* Wheddon (d 1950); *b* 18 Sept 1926; *Educ* Lower Sch of John Lyon Harrow, UCL (BSc, PhD); *m* 31 March 1956, Audrey Pauline, da of Reginald Holford Sheldrick, of Herts; 3 s (Peter Lindsey b 1958, Michael David b 1960, Richard Martin b 1966); *Career* environmental scientist, sr res assoc CEED (UK Centre for Econ and Environmental Devpt), res fell Dept of Environmental Sciences Univ of East Anglia, ed Energy and Environment, energy conservation and res in materials and metrology Dept of Trade and Indust 1977-79 (superintendent of div: Inorganic and Metallic Structure 1970-75, Chemical Standards 1975-77), chief scientific offr environmental pollution DOE 1979-86, The Nat Physical Laboratory; memb Bd Hydraulics Res Ltd 1982-86; FInstD; *Publications include* The Chemistry of Beryllium, Elsevier (1964); chapter on beryllium in "Comprehensive Inorganic Chemistry" (1972), The Greenhouse Effect: Issues for Policy Makers (1988), The Provision of Expert Advice to Government on Environmental Matters: The Role of Advisory Committees (1990); numerous papers and patents in inorganic chemistry, materials science, thermal plasmas energy conservation and the environment; *Recreations* walking; *Style—* Dr David Everest; Talland, Chorleywood Road, Chorleywood, Herts WD3 4ER (☎ 0923 773253); Gazebo Cottage, High St, Porlock, Somerset TA24 8PS (☎ 0643 862393)

EVEREST, Richard Anthony; s of Cecil Carlyle Everest (d 1974), of Barton-on-Sea, and Dorothy Helen, *née* Soldan; *b* 26 April 1938; *Educ* Highgate Sch, ChCh Oxford (MA); *m* 9 August 1969, Brenda Anne, da of Frederick John Ralph, of Westdene, Brighton; 2 s (Timothy b 1971, Philip b 1974); *Career* RCS 1966-68; accountant; articled clerk Pridie Brewster and Gold 1962-66, audit sr Black Geoghegan and Till 1966-70, asst mangr Layton-Bennett Billingham and Co 1970-74, audit gp mangr Josolyne Layton-Bennett and Co 1974-79, princ mangr Arthur Young McClelland Moores and Co 1979-82, dir and sec Henry G Nicholson (Underwriting) Ltd (Lloyd's membs' agents) 1986-, dir Bell Nicholson Henderson Ltd (Lloyd's reinsurance brokers) 1987- (gp chief accountant 1982-); underwriting memb Lloyd's 1986-; churchwarden Christ Church Barnet 1975-79, govr Foulds JMI Sch 1984-85, hon treas Friends of Herts County Youth Band 1987-; Freeman City of London 1959, Master Worshipful Co of Cutlers 1990 (Freeman 1959); ACA 1966, FCA 1976; *Recreations* swimming, jogging; *Style—* Richard Everest, Esq; 2 Palfrey Close, St Albans, Herts AL3 5RE (☎ 0727 835550); Bell Nicholson Henderson Limited, 12-14 Folgate St, London E1 6BX (☎ 071 377 1800, tlx 883516, fax 071 377 9430)

EVERETT, Maj Anthony Michael; s of Cyril Frederick Cunningham Everett (d 1941), laterly of Hinton House, Hinton St Michael, New Forest, Hampshire, and Marcella, *née* Lawless (d 1957); *b* 25 Nov 1921; *Educ* Stonyhurst Coll, Staff Coll Camberley; *m* 7 May 1955, Sara, da of Vice Adm Sir Hector MacLean, KBE, CB, DSC; 2 s (Simon b 12 May 1956, Rupert b 29 May 1959); *Career* WWII serv: cmmnd Wiltshire Regt 1939 (became Duke of Edinburgh's Royal Regt Berkshire and Wiltshire 1957), active serv with 1 Bn Wiltshire Regt Burma, GSO2 (ops), Tactical HQ 15 Corps Burma 1944-45, Bde Maj 13 Br Inf Bde BLA Germany 1945-46; regtl and staff appts 1946-62 (dep COS Combat Intelligence HQ NATO Copenhagen, chief instr tactics RMA Sandhurst), ret 1962; conslt Laurie Milbank & Co (stockbrokers) 1981-83 (ptnr 1962-81, sr ptnr 1975-81), fin advsr and conslt to various tsts and orgns 1984-; tstee: Duke of Edinburgh's Royal Regt (Berks & Wilts), The Wardrobe Bldg Salisbury Cathederal Close, Wilts Regt Museum; Wilts St John Ambulance; memb Stock Exchange 1964; *Recreations* travel, photography, bloodstock and racing, art and architectural drawings; *Clubs* Turf; *Style—* Maj Anthony Everett; Enford Grange, Enford nr Pewsey, Wiltshire; 32 Stanhope Gdns, London SW7; La Casa, Amnaby Cheeuh, Djemaa El Moknaa, Tangier, Moracco Windsor House, 50 Victoria St, London SW1 (☎ 0980 70475, fax 071 0980 70872); (☎ 071 799 2233, 071 373 4388, fax 071 799 1321, telex 883356 CALCOM G)

EVERETT, Bernard Jonathan; s of Arnold Edwin Everett, of Adderbury, Oxon, and Helene May, *née* Heine; *b* 17 Sept 1943; *Educ* Kings College Sch Wimbledon, Lincoln Coll Oxford (BA); *m* 1 Oct 1970, (Maria) Olinda, *née* Goncalves de Albuquerque, da of Raul Correia de Albuquerque, of Faro, Portugal; 2 s (Christopher b 1980, Edward b 1981), 2 da (Caroline b 1974, Diana b 1976 d 1979); *Career* Dip Serv 1966-: third (later second) sec Lisbon 1967-71, consul Luanda 1975, first sec and head of chancery Lusaka 1978-80, consul (commercial) Rio de Janeiro 1980-83, asst head Information Dept FCO 1983-84, head Sub Saharan Africa Branch DTI 1984-87, ambassador Guatemala 1987-90; *Recreations* reading, the performing arts, walking, numismatics; *Style—* Bernard Everett, Esq; Foreign and Commonwealth Office, London SW1

EVERETT, Christopher Harris Doyle; CBE (1988); s of late Alan Doyle Everett, MBE (d 1987), of Leatherhead, Surrey, and Annabel Dorothy Joan (Nancy), *née* Harris; *b* 20 June 1933; *Educ* Winchester, New Coll Oxford (exhibitioner, BA); *m* 6 Aug 1955, Hilary Anne (Billy), da of Maj Raymond Gildea Robertson, DSO (two bars) (d 1954), of Ashtead and Farnham; 2 s (Charles b 7 May 1959, Nicholas b 31 May 1962), 2 da (Victoria b 30 Jan 1958, Alexandra b 2 Dec 1965); *Career* Nat Serv 2 Lt 1Bn Grenadier Gds Windsor and London; HM Dip Serv: ME Centre for Arab Studies Lebanon 1957-59, Br Embassy Beirut 1959-61, Personnel Dept FO 1962-63, private sec to Ambass (later Chancery) HM Embassy Washington 1963-67, planning staff FCO 1967-70; headmaster: Workshop Coll 1970-75, Tonbridge Sch 1975-89; DG Daiwa Anglo-Japanese Foundation 1990-; JP: Nottinghamshire 1972-75, Kent 1976-89; chm HMC 1986; Hon FCP 1988; *Recreations* walking, current affairs; *Style—* Christopher Everett, Esq, CBE; Dainwa Anglo-Japanese Foundation, 5 King William St, London EC4N 7AX (☎ 071 548 8302, fax 071 548 8303)

EVERETT, Martin Thomas; s of Dr Thomas Everett (d 1975), and Ingeborg Maria, *née* Vogt; *b* 24 Sept 1939; *Educ* Bryanston; *m* 14 Sept 1963, Susan Mary, da of John Peter Sworder, MC, TD (d 1987); 2 s (Oliver b 2 July 1965, George b 8 Sept 1967), 1 da (Daisy b 14 May 1975); *Career* Nat Serv 2 Lt 9/12 Royal Lancers 1959-61; Mayor Sworder and Co Ltd Wine Shippers: joined 1962, dir 1967, jt md 1974, md 1980; tstee St Olaves Southwark Church Act of 1918; Freeman City of London, Liverman Worshipful Co of Glass Sellers and Glaziers; memb Inst of Masters of Wine 1968; *Recreations* gardening, walking; *Style—* Martin Everett, Esq; Sydenham, London SE26 (☎ 081 778 2569); Mayor Sworder & Co Ltd, 21 Duke St Hill, London SE1 2SW (☎ 071 407 5111, fax 071 378 1804, telex 8954102 MAYOR SWORDER)

EVERETT, Oliver William; LVO (1980); s of Walter George Charles Everett, MC, DSO (d 1979), of Streete Ct, Victoria Drive, Bognor Regis, and Gertrude Florence Rothwell, *née* Hellicar ; *b* 28 Feb 1943; *Educ* Felsted Sch Essex, Western Res Acad Ohio USA, Christs Coll Cambridge (MA), Fletcher Sch of Law & Diplomacy Tufts Univ Mass USA (MA), LSE; *m* 28 Aug 1965, Theffania, da of Lt Robert Vesey Stoney (d 1944), of Rosturk Castle, Co Mayo, Ireland; 2 s (Toby b 1979, William b 1982), 2 da (Kathleen b 1966, Grania b 1969); *Career* Dip Serv: first sec Br High Cmmn New Delhi 1969-73, first sec FCO 1973-78, asst private sec to HRH The Prince of Wales 1978-80, head Chancery Br Embassy Madrid 1980-81, private sec to HRH The Princess of Wales and comptroller to TRH The Prince and Princess of Wales 1981-83, asst librarian Windsor Castle 1984, librarian and asst Keeper of the Queen's archives Windsor Castle 1985-; *Recreations* skiing, rackets, real tennis; *Clubs* Ski Club of GB; *Style—* Oliver Everett, Esq, LVO; Garden House, Windsor Castle, Berks SL4 1NG (☎ 0753 868 286); The East Wing, Kirtlington Pk, Oxon OX5 3JN (☎ 0869 505 89); The Royal Library, Windsor Castle, Berks SL4 1NJ (☎ 0753 868 286, fax 0753 854 910)

EVERETT, Peter; s of Henry Everett (d 1984), of Edinburgh, and Kathleen Isabel, *née* Cuddeford (d 1961); *b* 24 Sept 1931; *Educ* George Watson's Boys Coll Edinburgh, Univ of Edinburgh; *m* 1 Oct 1955, Annette Patricia, da of George Edward Hyde (d 1988), of London; 3 s (David b 1959, Michael b 1962, John b 1964), 1 da (Judith Anne b 1957); *Career* Nat Serv RE 1953-55, 2 Lt 1954; Shell International Petroleum Co 1955-89: trainee engr The Hague 1955, petroleum engr Indonesia 1957-61, prodn engr Brunei 1963-64 (petroleum engr 1961-63), chief petroleum engr Trinidad 1968-70 (sr prodn engr 1964-68), exploration and prodn economist Projects and Agreements Dept The Hag 1970, chief petroleum engr Brunei 1970-72, gen ops mangr Nigeria 1977-79 (petroleum engr mangr 1972-76, div man western div 1976-77), md Brunei 1979-84; md: Shell UK Ltd 1984-89, Shell UK Exploration and Prodn 1984-89; memb: Cncl UK Offshore Operators Assoc, Dept of Energy's Offshore Energy Bd; Advsy bd memb Petroleum Engrg Depts: Heriot Watt Univ, Imperial Coll London; dir: Forth Ports Authy 1990, Scottish Hydro Electric plc 1990-; chm of Bd Pict Petroleum plc 1990-; MBIM 1985; Seri Paduka Mahkota (Brunei) 1984; *Recreations* golf,squash; *Clubs* Watsonian, Wimbledon Park, Royal Wimbledon; *Style—* Peter Everett, Esq; 12 Newstead Way, Wimbledon, London SW19 5HS (☎ 081 944 7397)

EVERETT, Thomas Henry Kemp; s of Thomas Kemp Everett (d 1934), of Bristol, and Katharine Ida, *née* Woodward (d 1972); *b* 28 Jan 1932; *Educ* Queen Elizabeth's Hosp Bristol, Univ of Bristol (LLB) 1957; *m* 1954, June, da of Edward Howard Bryce Partridge (d 1972), of Bristol; 3 s (Rupert Charles Kemp b 1961, Richard Jolyon Kemp b 1965, Robert Edward Kemp b 1968); *Career* special cmmr of Income Tax 1983-; admitted slr 1960, ptnr Meade-King & Co 1963-83; clerk to gen cmmr 1965-83; chm: Service 9 1972-75, Bristol Cncl of Voluntary Service 1975-80, St Christopher's Young Persons' Residential Tst 1976-83; vice chm Govrs of Queen Elizabeth's Hosp 1980-, memb Governing Cncl of St Christophers Sch 1983-89, hon treas and vice chm Rowberrow PCC, memb Axbridge Deanery Synod; *Recreations* music, reading, walking, gardening; *Style—* Thomas Everett, Esq; Dolebury Cottage, Dolberrow, Churchill, Bristol BS19 5NS; 5th Floor, Turnstile House, 98 High Holborn, London WC1V 6LQ (☎ 071 831 5253)

EVERITT, Michael Boswell; JP (1971); s of Ernest Skelton Everitt, JP, of North Place, Lincoln, and Mary Gertrude, *née* Boswell; *b* 13 Dec 1933; *Educ* Gresham's Sch, Leicester Sch of Architecture (Dip Arch); *m* 18 Sept 1965, Bridgid Mary, da of Harold Thomas Ransley, of Little Abington, Cambridge; 2 s (Richard b 18 Feb 1971, William b 6 Feb 1973), 1 da (Mary b 30 Dec 1967); *Career* Nat Serv, served 1 Bn The Sherwood Foresters, Malaya 1958-59, cmmnd 2 Lt 1958; Sir Hugh Casson Neville Conder and Ptnrs 1959-61, ptnr Feilden & Mawson Architects 1966 (joined 1961); pres Norfolk & Norwich Art Circle, chm Norfolk Art in Architecture Gp; memb RIBA 1961, ACIArb 1975, FRSA 1990; *Recreations* the visual arts; *Clubs* Strangers, Norwich; *Style—* Michael Everitt, Esq, JP; 113 St Leonards Rd, Norwich NR1 4JF (☎ 0603 621020); Feilden & Mawson, Ferry Rd, Norwich NR1 1SU (☎ 0603 629571, fax 0603 633569)

EVERITT, Prof (William) Norrie; s of Charles Ernest Everitt (d 1979), of Birmingham and Sidmouth, and Elizabeth Cloudsley, *née* Ross; *b* 10 June 1924; *Educ* Kings Norton GS Birmingham, Univ of Birmingham, Univ of Oxford; *m* 25 July 1953, Katharine Elizabeth, da of Rev Dr Arthur John Howison Gibson (d 1967), of Edinburgh; 2 s (Charles Kingston b 7 Jan 1956, Timothy Fraser b 25 March 1958); *Career* midshipman and Sub Lt RNVR 1944-47; princ lectr in mathematics RMCS 1954-63; Baxter prof of mathematics: Univ of St Andrews 1963-67, Univ of Dundee 1967-82; emeritus prof Univ of Birmingham (Mason prof of mathematics 1982-89), visiting prof Univ of Surrey 1986-; author of numerous pubns in mathematical periodicals; memb: Br Nat Ctee for Mathematics 1972-78, Cncl and Academic Advsy Cncl Univ of Birmingham 1973-, Cncl London Mathematical Soc 1957-; memb Cncl and pres Edinburgh Mathematical Soc 1963-, memb Cncl and vice pres RSE 1966-; awarded Mathematics medal Union of Czech Mathematicians and Physicists Prague 1990; memb: Royal Soc of Sciences Sweden 1973, Acad of Letters Sci and Arts Palermo Italy 1978; FIMA 1965, FRSE 1966; *Recreations* music, walking, Parson Woodforde Soc; *Style—* Prof Norrie Everitt, FRSE; 103 Oakfield Rd, Selly Park, Birmingham B29 7HW (☎ 021 471 2437); Dept of Mathematics, University of Birmingham, PO Box 363, Birmingham B15 2TT (☎ 021 414 6601)

EVERITT, William Howard; s of Howard George Everitt (d 1978); *b* 27 Feb 1940; *Educ* Brentwood Sch, Univ of Leeds (BSc); *m* 1963, Anthea Cecilia, da of late William Nield; 2 children; *Career* dir: AE plc 1978-86, T&N plc 1987-89; md Automotive T&N plc 1989-; FEng; *Recreations* golf, squash; *Style—* William Everitt, Esq; Horley House, Hornton Lane, Horley, nr Banbury, Oxon (☎ 029 573 603)

EVERS, (Frank) Michael; s of Frank Anthony Evers, of 19 Norton Rd, Stourbridge, W Mids, and Ida Rosemary, *née* Watson; *b* 2 Aug 1937; *Educ* Rugby; *m* 21 Dec 1968 (m dis 1981), Elaine, *née* Priestly; 2 s (Richard 31 Jan 1971, Andrew b 21 May 1972); *Career* slr 1961, dep coroner N Worcs 1966-, clerk to Stourbridge Cmmrs of Income Tax 1966- (Warley Cmmrs 1972-); pres Dudley Law Soc; memb Stourbridge Rotary club 1980-, chm Claverley CC 1984-87, govr Redhill Sch Stourbridge 1988; memb Law Soc 1961-; *Recreations* cricket, squash, walking, gardening; *Style—* Michael Evers, Esq; 19 Norton Rd, Stourbridge, W Mids (☎ 0384 396 417); 1 Worcester St, Stourbridge W Mids (☎ 0384 378 821, fax 0384 378 898)

EVERS, Peter Lawson; s of John Henry Evers (d 1982), and Evelyn Jessica, *née* Hill; *b* 4 Jan 1938; *Educ* King Edward VI GS; *m* 5 Oct 1963, Margaret Elaine, da of William Edwin Homer; 2 s (Jonathan b 21 March 1971, Philip Alexander (twin) b 21 March 1971), 2 da (Elaine Louise b 14 Sept 1965, Alison Jane b 4 June 1967); *Career* press offr J Lucas Industries 1965-67 (pres and publicity asst 1959-67), publicity mangr Fafnir Bearing Co Ltd 1967-68, gp press offr John Thompson Group 1968-71, conslt John Fowler Public Relations 1971-72, ptnr and co fndr Edson Evers Public Relations 1972-, dir and chief exec Edson Evers Communications Ltd 1980-, UK dir PR Organisation International Ltd 1973- (former pres); BAIE newspaper award winner in: 1985, 1988, 1989, 1990; MIPR 1969, memb BAIE 1974, FRHS 1980; *Recreations* golf, tennis, gardening; *Clubs* Brocton Hall Golf, Lichfield Friary Tennis; *Style—* Peter Evers, Esq; Edson Evers & Associates, Priory House, Friars Terrace, Stafford ST17 4AG (☎ 0785 55146, fax 0785 211518, car 0836 504278)

EVERSFIELD, Col John Claude; ERD (1967), TD (1979); s of Philip Claude Eversfield (d 1966), and Gladys Irene (d 1990), *née* Cottle; *b* 9 Dec 1932; *Educ* Norwich Sch; *m* 6 Sept 1958, Beryl Irene, da of Stanley Wymer (d 1940); 1 s (Geoffrey b 23 April 1964); *Career* Nat Serv 2 Lt RCS 1951, AER and TA Royal Signals 1953-86, cmd 31 Signal Regt TA 1973-75, Col TA 1976-86, ADC TA 1980-84; Nat Assistance Bd 1953-67 (exec offr 1953-), DHSS 1967-88 (princ 1971-), Dept of Social Security 1988- (asst sec 1989-); civil def community advsr Buckinghamshire CC; vice pres: Middx Yeo Regtl Assoc, memb First Div Assoc; *Recreations* foreign travel, walking, theatre; *Clubs* Civil Serv; *Style—* Col John Eversfield, ERD, TD; Dept of Social Security, Euston Tower, 286 Euston Rd, London NW1 3DN (☎ 071 388 1188 ext 3220, fax 071 387 2873)

EVERSHED, Ralph Jocelyn; s of Norman William Evershed (d 1983), and Jocelyn Slade, *née* Lyons; *b* 16 Nov 1944; *Educ* St Albans Boys GS, Univ of Strathclyde (BA); *m* 6 Sept 1968, Carol Ann, da of Jerry Esmond Cullum (d 1987); 3 s (Timothy b 1973, David b 1974, John b 1982), 2 da (Ruth b 1977, Susannah b 1980); *Career* md Verulam Properties Ltd 1981; chm: J E Properties Hldgs Ltd 1987, Eversheds Gp Ltd 1987 (md 1974-75, dir 1975-81, dir Evershed Estates Ltd 1982-87); dir Woodsilk Properties Ltd 1988, memb Bd Inter Varsity Press 1988; MIOP, FInstD; *Style—* Ralph Evershed, Esq; Eversheds Ltd, Alma Rd, St Albans, Herts AL1 3AS (☎ 0727 54652, fax 0727 43908, car 0836 599244)

EVERSON, Sir Frederick Charles; KCMG (1968, CMG 1956); s of Frederick Percival Everson (d 1946); *b* 6 Sept 1910; *Educ* Tottenham Co Sch, London Univ; *m* 1937, Linda Mary (d 1984), da of Samuel Clark; 3 s (eldest of whom d 1984), 1 da; *Career* entered Foreign Serv 1934, ambass to El Salvador 1956-60, commercial counsellor Stockholm 1960-63, min (econ) Paris 1963-68; *Style—* Sir Frederick Everson, KCMG; 8 Gainsborough Court, College Rd, Dulwich, London SE21 7LT (☎ 081 693 8125)

EVERSON, John Andrew; s of Harold Leslie Everson (d 1976), of Surrey, and Florence Jane, *née* Stone (d 1982); *b* 26 Oct 1933; *Educ* Tiffin Boys Sch Kingston upon Thames, Christ's Coll Cambridge (MA), King's Coll London (PGCE); *m* 1961, Gilda, da of Osborne Ramsden (d 1956), of Manchester; 2 s (Simon John b 1965, Benedict David b 1967); *Career* 2 Lt RA 1952-54; schoolmaster: Haberdashers' Sch Elstree 1958-65, City of London Sch 1965-68; HM inspr of schs: HMI 1968-78, staff inspr 1978-81, chief inspr for secdy educn 1981-89, chief inspr for teacher educn 1990-; sch cncl chief offr of examination unit 1971-76, seconded to Peat Marwick McLintoch 1989-90; *Recreations* opera, chess, walking; *Clubs* Athenaeum; *Style—* John Everson, Esq; Dept of Education and Science, Elizabeth House, York Rd, London SE1 7PH

EVERSON, Noel Williams; s of Mervyn Cyril George Everson (d 1981), and Beryl Irene, *née* Williams; *b* 8 Dec 1944; *Educ* W Monmouth Sch, Middx Hosp Med Sch (MB BS), Univ of London (MS); *m* 1, 1969 (m dis 1982), Caroline Juliet Adams; 2 da (Juliet Claire b 1971, Katherine Frances Vivien b 1974); m 2, 27 June 1987, Elizabeth Mary, da of Donald Sellen; 1 da (Francesca Victoria Louise b 1990); *Career* conslt surgn Leicester Royal Infirmary 1981-; memb: Br Assoc of Paediatric Surgns, Assoc of Surgns; FRSM, FRCS 1972; *Recreations* fly-fishing; *Style—* Noel Everson, Esq; 6 Meadowcourt Rd, Oadby, Leicester, Leicestershire LE2 2PB (☎ 0533 712512); The Leicester Royal Infirmary, Leicester, Leicestershire (☎ 0533 541414)

EVERY, Sir Henry John Michael; 13 Bt (E 1641); o s of Sir John Simon Every, 12 Bt (d 1988), and his 2 w Janet Marion, *née* Page; *b* 6 April 1947; *Educ* Malvern; *m* 1974, Susan Mary, da of Kenneth Beaton, JP; 3 s; *Heir* s, Edward James Henry Every b 3 July 1975; *Career* CA, ptnr BDO Binder Hamlyn; head Birmingham Audit Dept, memb Ctee Birmingham and W Midlands Dist Soc of CAs (chm Dist Trg Bd), parish cncllr; FCA 1970; *Style—* Sir Henry Every, Bt; Cothay, 26 Fish Pond Lane, Egginton, nr Derby DE6 6HJ; The Rotunda, 150 New Street, Birmingham B2 4PD (☎ 021 643 5544)

EVERY, Dowager Lady; Janet Marion; *née* Page; 2 da of John Page, of Blakeney, Norfolk; *m* 1, 1934 (m dis 1942), John Kenrick Maw; 1 s (John Mowbray Trentham b 1936), 1 da (Anne Bridget b 1935); m 2, 1943, as his 2 w, Sir John Simon Every, 12 Bt (d 1988); 1 s (Sir Henry John Michael, 13 Bt), 2 da (Celia Jane b 1944, Juliet Frances b 1945); *Style—* The Dowager Lady Every; Wycroft, Egginton, nr Derby DE6 6HJ (☎ 028 373 2245)

EVES, David Charles Thomas; s of Harold Thomas Eves (d 1967), and Violet, *née* Edwards (d 1972); *b* 10 Jan 1942; *Educ* King's Sch Rochester, Univ of Durham (BA); *m* 1 Aug 1964, Valerie Ann, da of George Alexander Carter, of Pinner, Middx; 1 da (Catherine Alice b 1969); *Career* HM chief inspr of factories 1985-88, dep dir gen Health and Safety Exec 1989-, dep sec Employment Dept Gp; *Recreations* sailing, walking, painting, golf, gardening, reading; *Style—* David Eves, Esq; Health and Safety Executive, Baynards House, Chepstow Place, London (☎ 071 243 6450)

EVETTS, Hon Mrs (Susan Katharine Lucy); da of 1 and last Baron Ismay (d 1965), and Laura Kathleen, *née* Clegg; *b* 29 May 1922; *m* 1 28 April 1942 (m dis 1946), Maj Neville Ewart Hyde Chance, o s of William Hyde Chance; 1 da; m 2, 16 Dec 1949, Lt-Col Michael John Evetts, MC, RHF, o s of Lt-Gen Sir John Fullerton Evetts, CB, CBE, MC; 2 s; *Style—* The Hon Mrs Evetts; Wormington Grange, Broadway, Worcs

EVISON, Lady Beatrix Dora; *née* Alexander; JP; da of 1 and last Earl Alexander of Hillsborough (d 1965), and Esther Ellen, *née* Chapple, CBE (d 1969); *b* 7 May 1909; *Educ* London Univ; *m* 26 Sept 1936, William Bernard Evison, s of Henry Evison, of Scunthorpe, Lincs; 1 s, 1 da; *Style—* Lady Beatrix Evison; 101 Old Park Ave, Enfield, Middx EN2 6PN

EWAN, Gordon Francis David; s of Albert Francis Ewan, of Herts, and Rosemary, *née* Orchard (d 1988); *b* 9 Oct 1938; *Educ* St Audreys Hatfield, Poly of N London (DipArch); *m* 28 Nov 1959, Anne Freda, da of Norman McCard (d 1985), of Herts; 2 s (Simon b 1960, Mark b 1964), 1 da (Lesley b 1961); *Career* architect; sr dir Vincent and Gorbing Architects and Planners 1982-; RIBA; *Recreations* golf, fine wines, Rotary Int; *Style—* Gordon Ewan, Esq; 5 Long Ridge, Aston, Stevenage, Herts SG2 7EW (☎ 0438 88296); Vincent and Gorbing Ltd, Sterling Court, Norton Rd, Stevenage, Herts SG1 2JY (☎ 0438 316331, fax 0438 722035)

EWAN, Pamela Wilson; s of Norman Wilson Ewan, of 14 Applecourt, Newton Road, Cambridge, and Frances Patterson, *née* Sellars (d 1984); *b* 22 Sept 1945; *Educ* Forfar Acad, Royal Free Hosp Sch of Med (MB BS, DObstRCOG, FRCP); *m* 15 Sept 1979, Prof (David) Keith Peters, s of Lionel Herbert Peters; 2 s (James b 1980, William b 1989), 1 da (Hannah b 1982); *Career* sr lectr in clinical immunology and dir Allergy Clinic St Mary's Hosp 1980-88, clinical scientist MRC and hon conslt clinical immunologist Addenbrookes Hosp 1988-, dir of med studies Clare Hall Cambridge 1988-, assoc lectr Univ of Cambridge 1988-; hon sec RCP Ctee in Clinical Immunology, memb Cncl Br Soc for Allergy and Clinical Immunology memb Ctee Euro Acad of Allergy and Clinical Immunology; memb Assoc of Physicians 1986, FRCP 1986; memb: BSACI, BSI, MRS; *publications* author of various chapters and papers in med books and scientific jls; *Style—* Ms Pamela Ewan; 7 Chaucer Rd, Cambridge CB2 2EB; MRC Centre, Hills Rd, Cambridge CB2 2QH (☎ 0223 402422, fax 0223 213556)

EWANS, Sir Martin Kenneth; KCMG (1987, CMG 1980); s of John Ewans; *b* 14 Nov 1928; *Educ* St Paul's, Corpus Christi Coll Cambridge (MA); *m* 1953, Mary Tooke; 1 s, 1 da; *Career* head E African Dept FCO 1973-78, min New Delhi 1978-82; high cmmr: Zimbabwe 1983-85, Nigeria 1986-88, dir The Casalee Gp SA; *Publications* Bharatpur: Bird Paradise (1988); *Recreations* ornithology; *Clubs* Norfolk; *Style—* Sir Martin Ewans, KCMG; The Barn, Old Hall Farm, South Walsham, Norfolk, NR13 6DS

EWARD, Paul Anthony; s of Rev Harvey Kennedy Eward (d 1969), and Delphine Eugenie Louise, *née* Pain; *b* 22 Dec 1942; *Educ* Radley; *m* 6 Sept 1966, Dene Kathleen, da of Geoffrey Louis Bartrip, of Ross-on-Wye; 2 da (Sarah b 1969, Lucy b 1971); *Career* admitted slr 1967; ptnr: Leslie J Slade & Co Newent, Orme Dykes & Yates Ledbury; chm Newent Business & Professional Assoc 1981-83, sec PCC Ross-on-Wye 1972-88, lay co chm Ross and Archenfield Deanery Synod 1988- (hon treas (1980-88); Hereford Diocesan Synod: memb Bd of Fin, Revenue Ctee, Vacancy in See Ctee 1985, Patronage Ctee 1988-, memb Ctee Gloucestershire & Wiltshire Law Soc 1990-; *Clubs* Gloucester Model Railway, EM Gauge Soc, Ross on Wye Cons; *Style—* Paul Eward, Esq; Oakleigh, Gloucester Rd, Ross-on-Wye, Herefordshire HR9 5NA (☎ 0989 63845); Leslie J Slade & Co, 5 Broad St, Newent, Glos GL18 1AX (☎ 0531 820281)

EWART, David John; s of John Henry Ewart (d 1976); *b* 30 April 1936; *Educ* Harrow; *m* 1973, Janet Law; 4 children; *Career* former dep chm Guinness Mahon and dir Guinness Peat to Nov 1981; former dir Linfood Hldgs to Sept 1981; chm RHP Gp plc 1979-; exec dir Morgan Grenfell Corporate Finance Dept 1981-85; gp fin dir Morgan Grenfell 1985-; dir: Pirelli, Talbot Designs; Majedie Investmts plc; FCA; *Recreations* hunting, shooting, sailing; *Clubs* Boodle's; *Style—* David Ewart, Esq; The Old Rectory, Stoke Lyne, Oxfordshire OX6 9RU; c/o Morgan Grenfell & Co, 23 Great Winchester St, London EC2 (☎ 071 588 4545)

EWART, Gavin Buchanan; s of George Arthur Ewart (d 1942), of London, and Dorothy Hannah, *née* Turner (d 1979); *b* 4 Feb 1916; *Educ* Wellington, Christ's Coll Cambridge (BA, MA); *m* 24 March 1956, Margaret Adelaide (Margo), da of Selwyn George Bennett, MC (d 1950), of New Malden; 1 s (Julian Robert b 4 July 1958), 1 da (June Susan b 21 Oct 1956); *Career* E Surreys 1940-41, OCTU 1941, RA 1941-46, LAA and AAOR, Capt 1946; salesman Contemporary Lithographs 1938-39, ed Editions Poetry London 1946, Br Cncl 1946-52, SH Benson Ltd 1952-57, various advertising agencies incl J Walter Thompson 1966-71, freelance writer 1971-; memb: Poetry Soc, Soc of Authors, Int PEN; *Books incl*: Poems and Songs (1939), Londoners (1964), Pleasures of the Flesh (1966), The Deceptive Grin of the Gravel Porters (1968), The Gavin Ewart Show (1971), Be My Guest (1975), No Fool Like An Old Fool (1976), Or Where a Young Penguin Lies Screaming (1978), The Collected Ewart 1933-80 (1980), The Penguin Book of Light Verse (ed, 1980), The New Ewart (1982), Other People's Cherihews (ed, 1983), The Ewart Quarto (1984), The Young Pobble's Guide to his Toes (1985), The Learned Hippopotamus (1986), The Complete Little Ones (1986), Late Pickings (1987), Penultimate Poems (1989), Collected Poems 1960-90 (1990), Caterpillar Stew (1990); in the USA: Selected Poems 1983-88, The Gavin Ewart Show (1986); *Recreations* reading, listening to music; *Style—* Gavin Ewart, Esq; 57 Kenilworth Court, Lower Richmond Rd, London SW15 1EN (☎ 081 788 7071)

EWART, Sir (William) Ivan Cecil; 6 Bt (UK 1887) of Glenmachan, Strandtown, Co Down and of Glenbank, Belfast, Co Antrim; DSC (1945), JP; s of late Maj William Basil Ewart, gs of 1 Bt; suc kinsman, Sir Talbot Ewart, 5 Bt, 1959; *b* 18 July 1919; *Educ* Radley; *m* 21 July 1948, Pauline Chevallier (d 1964), da of late Wing Cdr Raphael Chevallier Preston, OBE, AFC, JP; 1 s, 2 da; *Heir* s William Michael Ewart; *Career* Lt RNVR WWII 1939-45, Coastal Forces (POW Germany); chm: William Ewart and Son Ltd 1968-73, Ewart New Northern Ltd 1973-77; E Africa rep Royal Cwlth Soc for the Blind 1977-84; admin Ngora Freda Carr Hosp Ngora Uganda (Association of Surgeons of East Africa) 1984-89; pres NI C of C and Indust 1974, Belfast Harbour Cmmr 1968-77; High Sheriff Co Antrim 1976; *Clubs* Naval, Ulster Reform, Nairobi; *Style—* Sir Ivan Ewart, Bt, DSC, JP; Hill House, Hillsborough, Co Down, Northern Ireland BT26 6AE (☎ 0846 683000); PO Box 30171, Nairobi, Kenya (☎ 010 254 2 725726)

EWART, John Walter Douglas; s of Maxwell Douglas Ewart; *b* 27 Jan 1924; *Educ* Beaumont Coll Old Windsor Berks; *m* 1946, Joan Valerie, *née* Hoghton; 1 da (Lavinia Anne (Mrs C G Perry) b 1947); *Career* Lt Royal Horse Gds 1942-46; md Paterson Ewart Group Ltd 1958-70; Carclo Engineering Group plc: md 1973-, chm 1982-; memb Northants CC 1970-; High Sheriff Northants 1977-78; *Recreations* hunting, sailing; *Clubs* Cavalry and Guard's, Royal London Yacht; *Style—* John Ewart, Esq; Astrop, Banbury, Oxfordshire (☎ 0295 811 210)

EWART, William Michael; s and h of Sir Ivan Ewart, 6 Bt; *b* 10 June 1953; *Style—* William Ewart, Esq; Kelsey Hall, Great Steeping, Spilsby, Lincolnshire PE23 5PY

EWART-BIGGS, Baroness (Life Peer UK 1981), of Ellis Green, Co Essex; (Felicity) Jane; da of Major Basil Fitzherbert Randall (d 1930), and Rena May Randall; *b* 22 Aug 1929; *Educ* Downe House Newbury; *m* 1960, Christopher Thomas Ewart-Biggs, CMG, OBE (assassinated 1976, ambass to Dublin), s of Henry Ewart-Biggs (d 1957); 1 s (Hon Robin Thomas Fitzherbert b 1963), 2 da (Hon Henrietta b 1961, Hon Kate b 1967); *Career* sits as Lab Peer in House of Lords; opposition whip and front bench spokesman on: home affrs, overseas devpt, consumer affrs; active on matters relating to children and young people; freelance journalist, broadcaster and lectr; *Books* memoirs: Pay, Pack and Follow (1984), Lady in the Lords (1988); *Recreations* travel, discussion, foreign affrs; *Style—* The Rt Hon Lady Ewart-Biggs; 31 Radnor Walk, London SW3 4BP

EWBANK, Hon Mr Justice; Hon Sir Anthony Bruce; s of Rev Harold Ewbank, Rector of Windermere, and Gwendolen, *née* Bruce; *b* 30 July 1925; *Educ* St John's Sch Leatherhead, Trinity Coll Cambridge (MA); *m* 1958, Moya, da of Peter McGinn; 4 s, 1 da; *Career* RNVR 1945-47 and 1951-56; schoolmaster 1947-53, called to the Bar

Gray's Inn 1954; jr counsel to the Treasy in probate matters 1969, QC 1972, rec Crown Ct 1975-80, bencher Gray's Inn 1980, judge of the High Ct of Justice Family Div 1980-; chm Family Law Bar Assoc 1978-80; kt 1980; *Style—* Hon Mr Justice Ewbank; Royal Courts of Justice, Strand, London WC2

EWIN; *see*: Floyd Ewin

EWING, Harry; MP (Lab) Falkirk East 1983-; s of William Ewing; *b* 20 Jan 1931; *Educ* Beath HS Cowdenbeath; *m* 1954, Margaret Greenhill; 1 s, 1 da; *Career* memb PO Workers' Union; contested (Lab) Fife E 1970; MP (Lab) Stirling Falkirk & Grangemouth 1974-83, sec Scottish Parly Lab Gp 1972-74, parly under sec Scottish Off 1974-79, sr vice chm Trade Union Gp of Labour MPs 1979-; oppn front bench spokesman: Scottish Affrs 1981-83, Trade and Industry 1983-; specialist on Health Service matters; *Style—* Harry Ewing, Esq, MP; 16 Robertson Ave, Leven, Fife (☎ 0333 26123)

EWING, Kenneth Hugh Robert; s of Hugh Wands Ewing (d 1945), of Northwood, Middx, and Agnes Jack, *née* McCance (d 1968); *b* 5 Jan 1927; *Educ* Merchant Taylors Sch Herts, St John's Coll Oxford (MA); *Career* writer and broadcaster BBC Euro Serv 1950-52; gen mangr Connaught Theatre Worthing 1952-59, md Fraser and Dunlop Scripts Ltd 1959-, jt chm Peters Fraser and Dunlop Gp 1988; currently dir: Kenlyn Enterprises Ltd, Oliver Moon Ltd; memb Personal Mangrs Assoc; *Recreations* flying (PPL), theatre, dog-walking; *Clubs* Garrick; *Style—* Kenneth Ewing, Esq; 2 Crescent Grove, London SW4; 44 Sussex Sq, Brighton, W Sussex; Peters Fraser and Dunlop Group, The Chambers, Chelsea Harbour, London SW10 (071 376 7676, fax 071 352 7356, telex 28965 SCRIPT G)

EWING, Margaret Anne; MP (SNP) Moray 1987-; da of John McAdam (d 1984), of Biggar, and Margaret Jamieson Cuthbert, *née* Lamb; *b* 1 Sept 1945; *Educ* Univ of Glasgow (MA), Univ of Strathclyde (BA); *m* 1, 1968 (m dis 1980), Donald Bain; m 2, 30 Nov 1983, Fergus Stewart, s of Stewart Martin Ewing, of Glasgow; *Career* asst Eng and mathematics teacher Our Lady's High Cumbernauld 1968-71 princ teacher of remedial educn St Modans High Stirling 1971-74; MP (SNP) East Dunbartonshire 1974-79; freelance journalist 1979-81; coordinator W of Scot CSS Scheme 1981-87, SNP Parliamentary Leader 1988- (contested Strathkelvin and Bearsden; *Style—* Mrs Margaret Ewing, MP; Burns Cottage, Tulloch's Brae, Lossiemouth, Moray IV31 6QY (☎ 034381 3218); House of Commons, London SW1A 0AA (☎ 071 219 3494, fax 071 219 6716)

EWING, Winifred Margaret; MEP (SNP) Highlands and Islands 1979-; da of George Woodburn, and Christina Bell, *née* Anderson; *b* 10 July 1929; *Educ* Queen's Park Sr Secdy Sch, Univ of Glasgow (MA, LLB); *m* 1956, Stewart Martin Ewing; 2 s, 1 da; *Career* MP: (Scot Nat Pty) Hamilton 1967-70, (SNP) Moray and Nairn Feb 1974-79; memb Euro Parl 1975-; vice pres Rainbow Alliance 1989, pres Scot Nat Pty 1987-; *Style—* Mrs Winifred Ewing, MEP; Goodwill, Miltonduff, Elgin, Scotland

EXETER, Archdeacon of; *see*: Richards, Ven John

EXETER, 69 Bishop of (cr 1050) 1985-; Rt Rev (Geoffrey) Hewlett Thompson; patron of 121 livings and of two alternately with the Crown, the Precentorship, Chancellorship, Subdeanery, 4 Canonries and 29 Prebends in his Cathedral, and the Archdeaconries of Exeter, Totnes, Barnstaple and Plymouth; this see, created 1050, consists of Devon (except seven parishes) and one parish in Somerset; s of Lt-Col Ralph Reakes Thompson, MC (late RAMC, d 1960), and Eanswythe Frances, *née* Donaldson; *b* 14 Aug 1929; *Educ* Aldenham, Trinity Hall Cambridge (MA); *m* 29 Sept 1954, Elizabeth Joy, da of Col Geoffrey Fausitt Taylor, MBE (late IMS, d 1982); 2 s (Andrew b 1957, Benjamin b 1963), 2 da (Mary Clare b 1955, Louise b 1961); *Career* 2 Lt Royal West Kents 1948-49; curate St Matthew Northampton 1954-59; vicar: St Augustine Wisbech 1959-66, St Saviour Folkestone 1966-74; bishop of Willesden 1974-85; took seat in House of Lords 1990; *Clubs* United Oxford and Cambridge; *Style—* The Rt Rev the Bishop of Exeter; The Palace, Exeter EX1 1HY (☎ 0392 72362)

EXETER, 8 Marquess of (UK 1801; a previous Marquessate of Exeter was enjoyed by Henry Courtenay, Earl of Devon and gs of Edward IV, 1525-39); William Michael Anthony Cecil; also Baron Burghley (E 1571) and Earl of Exeter (E 1605; the de Reviers Earls of Devon, who enjoyed that title 1141-1262, were sometimes called Earls of Exeter), Hereditary Grand Almoner, and Lord Paramount of the Soke of Peterborough; s of 7 Marquess of Exeter (d 1988) (14 in descent from the Lord Burghley who was Elizabeth's I chief minister), and his 1 w Edith Lilian (d 1954), o da of Aurel Csanady de Telegd, of Budapest, Hungary; *b* 1 Sept 1935; *Educ* Eton; *m* 1967, Nancy Rose, da of Lloyd Arthur Meeker; 1 s, 1 da (Lady Angela Kathleen, b 1975); *Heir* s, Lord Burghley, *qv*; *Career* businessman and lecturer; *Books* The Rising Tide of Change (1986), Living at the Heart if Creation (1990); *Style—* The Most Hon the Marquess of Exeter; PO Box 8, 100 Mile House, Br Columbia VOK 2EO, Canada

EXMOUTH, Maria Luisa, Viscountess; Maria Luisa; also Marquesa de Olias (Sp cr 1652 of Philip IV); da of Luis de Urquijo, Marquøes de Amurrio, of Madrid, by his w Marquesa de Zarreal; *m* 1, Don Gonzalo Alvarez-Builla y Alvera (decd); m 2, 2 Jan 1938, 9 Viscount Exmouth (d 1970); 2 s (including 10 Viscount), 2 da; *Style—* The Rt Hon Maria Luisa, Viscountess Exmouth; c/o Lloyds Bank, High St, Exeter, Devon

EXMOUTH, 10 Viscount (UK 1816); Sir Paul Edward Pellew; 10 Bt (GB 1796); also Baron Exmouth (UK 1814); patron of one living; s of 9 Viscount (d 1970) and Maria Luisa, Marquesa de Olias (Sp cr of 1625), da of late Luis de Urquijo, Marques de Amurrio, of Madrid; *b* 8 Oct 1940; *Educ* Downside; *m* 1, 10 Dec 1964 (m dis 1974), Maria Krystina, o da of late Don Recaredo de Garay y Garay, of Madrid; 1 da (Hon Patricia b 1966); m 2, 1975, Rosemary Frances, da of Francis Harold Scoones, MRCS, LRCP, JP, and formerly w of Earl of Burford (now 14 Duke of St Albans, *qv*); 2 s (Hon Edward, Hon Alexander b (twin) 30 Oct 1978); *Heir* s, Hon Edward Francis Pellew b 30 Oct 1978; *Career* sits as Conservative Peer in House of Lords; memb IOD; *Style—* The Rt Hon Viscount Exmouth; Canonteign, nr Exeter, Devon EX6 7RH (☎ 0647 52666)

EXTON, Clive Jack Montague; s of Jack Ernest Brooks (d 1970), of Islington, London, and Marie, *née* Rolfe (d 1984): name changed by deed poll; *b* 11 April 1930; *Educ* Christ's Hosp; *m* 1, 1951 (m dis 1957), Patricia Fletcher, *née* Ferguson (d 1983); 2 da (Frances (Mrs N Morgan), *née* Brooks b 1952, Sarah Brooks b 1954); m 2, 30 Aug 1957, Margaret Josephine (Mara); 1 s (Saul b 1965), 2 da (Antigone b 1961, Plaxy b 1964); *Career* Nat Serv 1948-50; actor 1951-59, writer 1959-; films: Night Must Fall, Isadora (with Melvyn Bragg), 10 Rillington Place, Entertaining Mr Sloane; tv plays: No Fixed Abode 1959, Where I Live 1960, I'll Have You to Remember 1961, Hold My Hand Soldier 1961, The Trial of Doctor Fancy 1963, The Big Eat 1963, Land of My Dreams 1964, The Bone Yard 1965, The Close Prisoner 1965, The Boundary (with Tom Stoppard); tv series': Agatha Christie's Poirot 1989-91, Jeeves and Wooster 1990; tv dramatizations of works by authors incl: Agatha Christie, Jean Cocteau, Daphne Du Maurier, Graham Greene, Somerset Maugham, Ruth Rendell, Georges Simenon, H G Wells, P G Wodehouse; theatre prodn: Have You Any Dirty Washing Mother Dear 1969; *Style—* Clive Exton, Esq; 3 Blenheim Cottages, Church Cres, Hackney, London E9 7DH; c/o A D Peters, 5th Floor, The Chambers, Chelsea Harbour, London SW10 (☎ 071 376 7676)

EXTON, Rodney Noel; JP (Surrey 1968); s of Maj Noel Exton (d 1969), and Winifred *née* Stokes (d 1963); *b* 28 Dec 1927; *Educ* Clifton Coll, Lincoln Coll Oxford (MA), CCC Cambridge (PGCE); *m* 1961, Pamela Beresford, da of Alan Hardie, of Rose Bay, Sydney, NSW (d 1947), and wid of Ian Menzies Sinclair, of Glen Innes, NSW; 2 step s (Andrew, Colin), 2 step da (Virginia, Jane); *Career* Royal Hampshire Regt 1946-48; Hampshire cricketer 1946; asst master Eton 1951-52, asst master (later housemaster) Mill Hill Sch 1952-63, Int Res Fund Scholarship to USA 1952, New South Wales State Educn Dept 1959-60, headmaster Reed's Sch Cobham 1964-77; md Exton Hotels Co Ltd 1966-80; ESU/HMC Page scholar to USA 1971; memb: Nat Working Pty on Disadvantaged Children 1972, Br Atlantic Educn Ctee 1974-, GAP Cncl of Mgmnt 1978-; dir: Independent Schools Careers Orgn (ISCO) 1978-88, Vocational Guidance Assoc 1989-90; dep chm Johansens Hotel Guides 1990-; pres Flycatchers CC 1989-; *Publications* Industrial Cadets (1972); *Recreations* guitar; *Clubs* MCC, Inst of Directors, Royal Mid-Surrey Golf, Vincent's (Oxford); *Style—* Rodney Exton, Esq, JP; 85 Mount Ararat, Richmond, Surrey TW10 6PL (☎ 081 940 0305)

EYKYN, Dr Susannah Jane; (Viscountess Dilhorne); da of late Cdr W C Eykyn, RN; *Educ* Sherborne Sch for Girls, St Thomas's Hosp Med Sch (MB BS 1962, MRCP, FRCPath); *m* 1, 12 June 1962 (m dis 1980), Colin Gilchrist; 1 s (Mark b 1 June 1966), 1 da (Virginia b 18 Aug 1963); m 2, 17 Dec 1981, 2 Viscount Dilhorne, *qv*; *Career* sr lectr and hon conslt in clinical microbiology St Thomas's Hosp 19 reader and hon conslt 1982-; author of numerous papers on bacterial infection and antibiotics; memb res and Med Advsy Ctee Cystic Fibrosis Research Tst 1985-90; *Recreations* skiing, mountain walking, riding, opera; *Style—* Dr Susannah Eykyn; 164 Ebury Street, London SW1W 8UP; Dept of Microbiology, St Thomas Hospital, London SE1 7EH

EYLES, Peter George; s of George Henry Eyles, MBE, of Surrey, and Louise Cleeves; *b* 22 April 1946; *m* 1975 (m dis) Fallulah Jane, da of Sir Maxwell Joseph (d 1983); 1 s (Kieren b 1978), 1 da (Marelka b 1980); *Career* former gp md Norfolk Capital Group plc; former chm: Norfolk Capital Hotels, Norfolk Capital Inns, Norfolk Capital Securities, Celebrated Country Hotels, Norfolk Capital Developments, St James Club Ltd; chm and chief exec Pavilion Leisure plc; *Recreations* work, shooting, skiing; *Clubs* St James; *Style—* Peter Eyles, Esq; Princes House, 36-40 Jermyn St, London SW1Y 6DT (☎ 071 439 2785)

EYNON, (Richard) Mark; s of Capt Melville Victor Eynon, of The Cedars, Lodge Road, Caerleon, Gwent, and Phyllis Bertha, *née* Aitken-Smith, MBE, JP; *b* 9 Nov 1953; *Educ* Monmouth, Univ of Manchester (BSc), Manchester Business Sch (MBA); *m* 18 Oct 1980, Susan Elspeth, da of Dr J T D Allen, of 5 Linden Ave, Liverpool; *Career* vice pres Bank of America 1982-86; dir: London Int Fin Futures Exchange 1984-, Warburg Securities 1986-; *Recreations* rugby, cricket; *Style—* Mark Eynon, Esq; Warburg Securities, 1 Finsbury Avenue, London EC2M 2PA (☎ 0628 26829, 071 382 4477)

EYRE, Dr Brian Leonard; s of Leonard Georg Eyre (d 1988), and Mabel, *née* Rumsey (d 1984); *b* 29 Nov 1933; *Educ* Greenford GS, Univ of Surrey (BSc, DSC); *m* 5 June 1965, Elizabeth Caroline, da of Arthur Rackham (d 1954); 2 s (Peter John b 5 March 1966, Stephen Andrew b 22 Oct 1967); *Career* res offr GEGB 1959-62, prof of materials sci Univ of Liverpool 1979-84; UKAEA: various posts 1972-79, dir of fuel and engrg 1984-87, bd memb 1987-, dep chm 1989, chief exec 1990-; author over 100 scientific papers, jt ed Jl of Nuclear Materials; memb: Inst of Metals, Inst of Physics; FRSA; *Recreations* walking, reading; *Style—* Dr Brian Eyre; AEA Technology, Corporate Headquarters, 11 Charles II St, London SW1Y 4QP (☎ 071 389 6565, fax 071 389 6741, telex 22565 A)

EYRE, Hon Mrs (Edith Joy Marion); *née* Best; o da of 7 Baron Wynford (d 1943), and his 1 wife Evelyn Mary Aylmer, *née* May (d 1929); *b* 14 Aug 1915; *m* 3 April 1937, Cdr Walpole John Eyre, RN (ret) (d 1987), s of Rev George Frederick Eyre, MA, of West Hill, Lyme Regis, Dorset; 1 s, 1 da, and 1 adopted da; *Style—* The Hon Mrs Eyre; Sadborow, Myll, Thorncombe, Chard, Somerset

EYRE, Sir Graham Newman; QC (1970); s of Cdr Newman Eyre, RNVR (d 1970); *b* 9 Jan 1931; *Educ* Marlborough, Trinity Coll Cambridge (MA, LLB); *m* 1954, Jean Dalrymple, da of late A D Walker; 1 s, 3 da; *Career* barr 1954, bencher Middle Temple, rec Crown Ct 1975-; memb Lincoln's Inn, Head of Chambers 1981; inspr Airport Inquiries (held at Quendon and Heathrow) 1981-83, Eyre Report on Airports submitted Nov 1984; kt 1988; *Clubs* Athenaeum; *Style—* Sir Graham Eyre, QC; Walberton House, Walberton, W Sussex (☎ 0243 551205); Chambers, 8 New Square, Lincoln's Inn, London WC2 (☎ 071 242 4987)

EYRE, Maj-Gen Sir James Ainsworth Campden Gabriel; KCVO (1986, CVO 1978), CBE (1980, OBE 1975); 2 s of Edward Joseph Eyre (d 1962), by his w, Hon Dorothy Elizabeth Anne Pelline, *née* Lyon-Dalberg-Acton, *qv*, 2 da of 2 Baron Acton; *b* 2 Nov 1930; *Educ* Harvard (BA, LLB); *m* 1967, Monica Ruth Esther, da of Michael Joseph Smyth (d 1964), of Harley Street, London; 1 s (James b 1969), 1 da (Annabelle b 1970); *Career* RHG 1955 and RHG/D 1969; sec Chiefs of Staff Ctee MOD 1980-82, dir Def Prog Staff 1982-83; GOC London Dist and Maj-Gen Commanding Household Div 1983-86; dir Westminster Associates International Ltd 1989-; *Recreations* shooting, racing; *Clubs* Turf; *Style—* Maj-Gen Sir James Eyre, KCVO, CBE; Somerville House, East Garston, Berks RG16 7EY

EYRE, Maj John Vickers; JP (Gloucestershire 1987); s of Nevill Cathcart Eyre (d 1971), of Bristol, and Maud Evelyn, *née* Truscott, now Mrs Wallace; *b* 30 April 1936; *Educ* Winchester; *m* 19 Oct 1974, Sarah Margaret Aline, da of Maj Geoffrey Beresford (Tim) Heywood MBE, DL, of North Farm, Edgeworth, Glos; 1 s (Charles b 8 Jan 1980), 1 da (Georgina b 1 Jan 1977); *Career* RA 1954-59, RHA 1959-62, Capt 14/20 Kings Hussars 1962 (Cyprus Emergency 1963-64), Gen Staff 4 div 1966-67, Maj 1968, Army Staff Coll 1969, Gen Staff 1970-71, N Ireland Emergency 1972, ret 1973, Royal Gloucestershire Hussars TA 1980-83; asst to chm Savoy Hotel plc 1973-75, administrator Brian Colquhoun and Ptnrs Consltg Engrs 1975-79, proprietor Haresfield Gdn Centre 1981-86, md George Truscott Ltd 1986- (dir 1969-86); chm Haresfield Parish Cncl 1990-, chm of govrs Haresfield Sch 1989-; dist cmmr Berkeley Hunt Pony Club 1986-, memb Ctee Berkeley Hunt 1988-; *Recreations* country pursuits; *Style—* Maj John Eyre, JP; Cromwell House, Haresfield, Stonehouse, Glos (☎ 0452 720 410); George Truscott Ltd, College Court, Glos (☎ 0452 524914)

EYRE, (Ethel) Mary; da of Cdr Charles Harding Drage (d 1983), and Enid Margaret, *née* Lomer; *b* 10 Sept 1931; *Educ* Elmhurst Ballet Sch, Rambert Sch, Royal Ballet Sch; *m* 1, 8 April 1958, Roderick Andrew (Rory) Fraser (d 1964), s of Maj the Hon Alastair Fraser, DSO (d 1949), of Moniack; 3 s (Anthony b 1959, Archibald b 1960, Thomas b 1964), 1 da (Eleanor b 1961); m 2, 7 July 1969, Edward (Ned) Eyre, s of Edward Eyre; 1 s (Robert b 1971), 3 da (Mathilda b 1970, Virginia b 1974, Constance b 1976); *Career* ballet dancer; Sadler's Wells Theatre Ballet 1948-50, Sadlers Wells Ballet (later the Royal Ballet) 1950-58, soloist 1953, sr soloist 1956-58; govr: Royal Ballet Sch 1984, Royal Ballet Co 1986; FISTD 1988; *Recreations* gardening, opera; *Clubs* Farmers; *Style—* Mrs Edward Eyre; The Field House, Great Durnford, Salisbury, Wilts SP4 6AY (☎ 0722 73 523); Royal Ballet School, White Lodge, Richmond Park, Surrey

EYRE, Hon Mrs ((Dorothy Elizabeth Anne) Pelline); *née* Lyon-Dalberg-Acton; 2 da of 2 Baron Acton (d 1924); *b* 25 June 1906; *m* 6 June 1928, Edward Joseph Eyre (d 6 Oct 1962), s of Edward Eyre, of New York and London; 5 s (including James

Ainsworth Campden Gabriel, *qv*), 2 da; *Style—* The Hon Mrs Eyre; 18 Petersham House, Harrington Rd, London SW7

EYRE, Sir Reginald Edwin; s of Edwin Eyre, of Birmingham; *b* 28 May 1924; *Educ* King Edward's Camp Hill Sch Birmingham, Emmanuel Coll Cambridge; *m* 1978, Anne Clements; 1 da; *Career* served WWII, RNVR, Midshipman and Sub-Lt; slr 1950; sr ptnr Eyre & Co; contested (C) Birmingham Northfield 1959; chm: W Midlands Area Cons Political Centre 1960-63, Nat Advsy Ctee 1964-66; MP (C) Birmingham Hall Green 1965-87; oppn whip 1966-70, Lord Cmmr Treasury 1970, comptroller of HM Household 1970-72, Parly under sec, Environment (Housing and Construction) 1972-74, vice chm Conservative Party, responsible for Urban Areas 1974-79, PUSS Trade 1979-82, Tport 1982-83; chm: Birmingham Heartlands Ltd (East Birmingham Urban Devpt Agency 1987-, Birmingham Cable Ltd 1988; vice chm cmmn for the New Towns 1988-; kt 1984; *Publications* Hope for our Towns and Cities (1977); *Clubs* Carlton; *Style—* Sir Reginald Eyre; 1041 Stratford Rd, Birmingham B28 8AS; 45 Aylesford St, London SW1

EYRE, Richard Hastings Charles; s of Richard Galfrious Hastings Giles, of Dorset, and Minna Mary Jessica Royds; maternal gf was antarctic explorer - Scott's 1st Lt; *b* 28 March 1943; *Educ* Sherborne, Cambridge Univ (BA); *m* 1973, Susan Elizabeth Birtwistle; 1 da (Lucy b 1974); *Career* theatre and film dir; assoc dir Lyceum Theatre Edinburgh 1968-71, dir Nottingham Playhouse 1973-78, prodr Play For Today BBC TV 1978-80, dir Nat Theatre 1988- (assoc dir 1980-86); films: The Ploughman's Lunch (Evening Standard Award for Best Film 1 Loose Connections (1983), Laughterhouse (TV Prize Venice Film Festival 1984); TV films: The Imitation Game, Pasmore (1980), Country (1981), The Insurance Man (1986, Tokyo Prize), Past Caring (1986), V (1988), Tumbledown (winner Italia RAI Prize 1988, BAFTA Award 1988), SWET Dir of the Year 1982, Standard Best Dir 1982, STV Awards for Best Production: 1969, 1970, 1971; *Style—* Richard Eyre; Royal National Theatre, South Bank, London SE1 9PX (☎ 071 928 2033)

EYRE, Very Rev Richard Montague Stephens; s of Montague Henry Eyre (d 1974), and Ethel Mary, *née* Raw (d 1975); memb of Derbys branch of Eyre family; *b* 16 May 1929; *Educ* Charterhouse, Oriel Coll Oxford (MA); *m* 28 Dec 1963, Anne Mary, da of Canon G B Bentley, of 5 The Cloisters, Windsor Castle; 2 da (Chantal b 1966, Henrietta b 1972); *Career* asst curate St Mark Portsea 1956-59, tutor and chaplain Chichester Theol Coll 1959-62, chaplain Eastbourne Coll 1962-65; vicar: Arundel with Tortington and South Stoke 1965-73, Good Shepherd Brighton 1973-75; archdeacon of Chichester 1975-80, treas Chichester Cathedral 1978-81, dean of Exeter 1981-; *Recreations* golf, travel, wine, music; *Clubs* United Oxford and Cambridge Univ; *Style—* The Very Rev the Dean of Exeter; The Deanery, Exeter EX1 1HT (☎ 0392 72697)

EYRE, Stephen John Arthur; s of Leslie James Eyre, of Solihull, and Joyce Mary, *née* Whitehouse; *b* 17 Oct 1957; *Educ* Solihull Sch, New Coll Oxford (MA, BCL); *m* 1 July 1989, Margaret Lynn, da of William John Goodman, of Coalville; *Career* called to the Bar Inner Temple 1981; lectr in law New Coll Oxford 1980-84; memb Solihull Met Borough Cncl 1983-; Parly candidate (C): Birmingham (Hodge Hill) 1987, prospective Strangford 1990; *Recreations* reading, theatre, bridge; *Style—* Stephen Eyre, Esq; 1 Fountain Court, Steelhouse Lane, Birmingham B4 6DR (☎ 021 236 5721)

EYSENCK, Prof Hans Jürgen; s of Eduard Auton Eysenck (d 1972), and Ruth, *née* Werner (d 1986); *b* 4 March 1916; *Educ* Bismarck Gymnasium Berlin, Friedrich Wilhelm Real-Gymnasium Berlin, Univ of London (BA, PhD, DSc); *m* 1, 1942 (m dis 1950), Margaret Davies; 1 s (Michael b 1944); m 2, 30 Sept 1950, Sybil Bianca Guiletta, da of Max Rostal, OBE, of Berne, Switzerland; 3 s (Gary b 1953, Kevin b 1959, Darrin b 1966), 1 da (Connie b 1957); *Career* res psychologist Mill Hill Emergency Hosp 1942-49; Univ of London: reader in psychology 1949-55, prof 1955-83, emeritus prof 1983-; visiting prof: Univ of Pennsylvania 1949-50, Univ of Calif Berkeley 1955; pres Int Soc for Study of Individual Differences 1983-85; Distinguished Sci award American Psychologist Assoc 1988; fell: Br Psychological Soc, American Psychologcal Assoc, German Psychological Assoc; *Books* Dimensions of Personality (1947), Sense and Nonsense in Psychology (1958), Behaviour Therapy and Neurosis (ed, 1960), Smoking Health & Personality (1965), The Structure of Human Personality (1970), Handbook of Abnormal Psychology (ed, 1973), The Future of Psychiatry (1975), You and Neurosis (1977), The Psychology of Sex (with G D Wilson, 1979), Decline and Fall of the Freudian Empire (1985), Suggestion and Suggestibility (jt ed, 1989), Rebel with a Cause (autobiography, 1990); *Recreations* tennis, squash; *Style—* Prof Hans Eysenck; 10 Dorchester Drive, London SE24 (☎ 071 733 8129); Inst of Psychology, Denmark Hill, London SE5

EYSENCK, Prof Michael William; s of Hans Jürgen Eysenck, of London, and Margaret Malcolm, *née* Davies (d 1986); *b* 8 Feb 1944; *Educ* Dulwich, UCL (BA, Rosa Morison Prize for outstanding arts graduate); *m* 22 March 1975, (Mary) Christine, da of Waldemar Kabyn, of London; 1 s (William James Thomas b 1983), 2 da (Fleur Davina Ruth b 1979, Juliet Margaret Maria Alexandra b 1985); *Career* reader in psychology Birkbeck Coll London 1981-87 (lectr 1965-80), prof of psychology and head of Dept Royal Holloway and Bedford Coll Univ of London 1987-; chm Cognitive Psychology Section Br Psychological Soc 1982-87, memb Advsy Bd Euro Jl of Cognitive Psychology; MBPsS 1965; *Books* Human Memory: Theory, Research and Individual Differences (1977), Mindwatching (with H J Eysenck, 1981), Attention and Arousal: Cognition and Performance (1982), A Handbook of Cognitive Psychology (1984), Personality and Individual Differences (with H J Eysenck, 1985), Memory: A Cognitive Approach (with G Cohen and M E Levoi, 1986), Student Learning: Research in Education and Cognitive Psychology (with J T E Richardson and D W Piper, 1987), Mindwatching: Why We Behave the Way We Do (1989), Happiness: Facts and Myths (1990), Cognitive Psychology: An International Review (1990), Cognitive Psychology: A Student's Handbook (with M T Keane, 1990), Blackwell's Dictionary of Cognitive Psychology (1990); *Recreations* tennis, travel, walking, golf; *Style—* Prof Michael Eysenck; Royal Holloway and Bedford New College, University of London, Department of Psychology, Egham Hill, Egham, Surrey TW20 0EX (☎ 0784 443530, fax 0784 437520)

EYSTON, Lady Anne Priscilla; *née* Maitland; 2 da of Viscount Maitland (ka in N Africa 1943), o s of 15 Earl of Lauderdale, (d 1953); granted the rank and precedence of an Earl's da 1953; *b* 4 May 1940; *m* 6 Feb 1968, John Joseph Eyston, *qv*, 1 s, 2 da; *Style—* The Lady Anne Eyston; Mapledurham House, Reading, (☎ 0734 723350)

EYSTON, John Joseph; s of Capt Thomas More Eyston (d 1940 of wounds received in action in Belgium); ggs of Charles Eyston, whose w, Agnes, was of the Blount family, of Mapledurham House), and Lady Agnes Savile, *qv*, da of 6 Earl of Mexborough; younger bro of Thomas More Eyston, *qv*; *b* 27 April 1934; *Educ* Ampleforth, Trinity Coll Cambridge; *m* 6 Feb 1968, Lady Anne Maitland, *qv*; 1 s, 2 da; *Career* chm South Oxfordshire District Cncl 1986-88; High Sheriff designate of Oxfordshire; *Style—* J J Eyston, Esq; Mapledurham House, Nr Reading, Oxfordshire RG4 7TR (☎ 0734 723350)

EYSTON, Thomas More; Lord of the Manor of Arches, Abbey Manor and Catmore; s of Thomas More Eyston, JP, and Lady Agnes Savile, da of 6 Earl of Mexborough; bro of John Eyston, of Mapledurham, *qv*; *b* 24 Dec 1931; *Educ* Ampleforth, Trinity Coll Cambridge (BA); *Style—* T M Eyston, Esq; Hendred House, East Hendred, Wantage, Oxon, OX12 8JZ (☎ 0235 833 203)

EYTON, Anthony John Plowden; s of Capt John Seymour Eyton (d 1979), of Old Meadows, Silchester, nr Reading, and Phyllis Annie, *née* Tyser (d 1929); *b* 17 May 1923; *Educ* Canford, Univ of Reading, Camberwell Sch of Art (NDD); *m* 20 Aug 1960, (Frances) Mary; 3 da (Jane Elizabeth Phyllis, Clare Alice, Sarah Mary); *Career* served Army 1942-47; artist; Abbey Maj Scholarship 1951-53, John Moores prizewinner Liverpool 1972, first prize second Br Int Drawing Biennale 1975, retrospective S London Art Gallery 1980, Charles Woolaston award Royal Acad 1981; exhibitions: Browse and Darby 1975 (1978, 1981, 1985, 1987, 1990), Imp War Museum Hong Kong 1983, Austin/Desmond Fine Art 1990; teacher Royal Acad Schs; RA 1986 (ARA 1976), RWS 1987; memb: NEAC, RWA; hon memb Pastel Soc, fell Worshipful Co of Grocers 1973; ROI; *Recreations* gardening; *Clubs* Arts; *Style—* Anthony Eyton, Esq

EZEKIEL, David Richard Simon; s of Victor David Oscar Ezekiel (d 1976), and Sarah Ethel Ezekiel (d 1963); *b* 27 Sept 1930; *Educ* St John's Sch Leatherhead Surrey; *m* 27 Oct 1960, Carolyn Joan, da of Kenneth Gordon Gale, of South Devon; 2 s (Marcus b 1962, William b 1964); *Career* Nat Serv RAF (FO) 1953-55; qualified FCA, Moore Stephens 1948-53, and 1953-57; co sec Controls & Communications Ltd 1961-69; fin dir Celestion Industries plc 1969-90 (dir associated cos incl: Slix Ltd 1978-90, Truvox Engrg Co Ltd 1968-90, Wood Bastow Hldgs plc 1978-90, Celestion Int Ltd); memb Ct Worshipful Co of Needlemakers; FCA, FCT; *Recreations* music, bridge, sailing, watching sport - particularly rugby; *Clubs* Lansdowne, Little Ship, Chichester Yacht; *Style—* David R S Ezekiel, Esq; 47 Leigh Hill Road, Cobham, Surrey KT11 2HU (☎ 0932 868220)

EZRA, Baron (Life Peer UK 1982), of Horsham in the Co of West Sussex; Derek Ezra; MBE (1945); s of late David and Lillie Ezra; *b* 23 Feb 1919; *Educ* Monmouth Sch, Magdalene Coll Cambridge (MA); *m* 1950, Julia Elizabeth, da of Thomas Wilkins, of Portsmouth, Hants; *Career* army serv 1939-47; memb UK Delgn to Euro Coal and Steel Community 1952-56; Nat Coal Bd: joined 1947, regnl sales mangr 1958-60, dir gen Marketi memb Bd 1965-67, dep chm 1967-71, chm 1971-82; chm Br Iron & Steel Consumers' Cncl 1983-87; dir: Redland plc 1982-89, Sankey Building Supplies, Associated Heat Servs Ltd, Br Fuel Co; chm: Br Inst of Mgmnt 1976-78, Energy and Technical Services Group Ltd 1990-; conslt on industl matters to Morgan Grenfell 1982-87; pres: Coal Indust Soc 1981-86, Inst of Trading Standards Admin 1987-; kt 1974; *Style—* The Rt Hon Lord Ezra, MBE; House of Lords, Westminster, London SW1

EZZAMEL, Prof Mahmoud Azmy; s of Mahmoud Mahmoud Ezzamel (d 1975), of Egypt, and Fatima, *née* El-Shirbini; *b* 24 Oct 1942; *Educ* Univ of Alexandria (BCom, MCom), Univ of Southampton (PhD); *m* 31 March 1979, Ann, da of Herbert Edgar Jackman, of Coventry; 1 s (Adam b 29 March 1983), 2 da (Nadia b 29 Jan 1985, Samia b 6 July 1988); *Career* lectr and sr lectr Univ of Southampton 1975-88, Ernst & Young prof of accounting Univ Coll Wales Aberystwyth 1988-90, Price Waterhouse prof of accounting and fin UMIST 1990; *Books* Advanced Management Accounting: An Organisational Emphasis (1987); *Recreations* volley-ball, tennis; *Clubs* UCW Aberystwyth, Aberystwyth Tennis; *Style—* Prof Mahmoud Ezzamel; The Manchester School of Management, UMIST, PO Box 88, Manchester M60 1QD (☎ 061 200 3455, fax 061 200 3505, telex 6660 94)

F

FABER, Lady (Ann) Caroline; *née* Macmillan; da of 1 Earl of Stockton (d 1986); *b* 1923; *m* 1944, Julian Tufnell Faber; 4 s, 1 da; *Style*— The Lady Caroline Faber; Fisher's Gate, Withyham, Hartfield, E Sussex TN7 4BB (☎ 0892 770 246)

FABER, Hon Mrs (Diana Catriona); *née* Howard; da of 3 Baron Strathcona and Mount Royal (d 1959), and Hon Diana Evelyn, *née* Loder (d 1985), da of 1 Baron Wakehurst; *b* 13 March 1935; *m* 7 June 1956, Michael Leslie Ogilvie Faber, er s of George Valdemar Faber (d 1958); 2 s, 2 da (twins); *Style*— The Hon Mrs Faber; The Combe, Glynde, Lewes, Sussex BN8 6RP (☎ 0273 858402)

FABER, Sir Richard Stanley; KCVO (1980), CMG (1977); er s of Sir Geoffrey Cust Faber (d 1961), and Enid Eleanor, da of Sir Henry Erle Richards, KCSI, KC; bro of Thomas Erle Faber, *qv*; *b* 6 Dec 1924; *Educ* Westminster, ChCh Oxford (MA); *Career* served RNVR 1943-46; entered HM Dip Serv 1950; served: Baghdad, Paris, Abidjan, Washington; cnsllr: The Hague 1969-73, Cairo 1973-75; asst under sec of state FCO 1975-77, ambass Algiers 1977-81, ret; *Books* Beaconsfield and Bolingbroke (1961), The Vision and the Need: Late Victorian Imperialist Aims (1966), Proper Stations: Class in Victorian Fiction (1971), French and English (1975), The Brave Courtier (Sir William Temple) (1983), High Road to England (1985), Young England (1987); *Clubs* Travellers'; *Style*— Sir Richard Faber, KCVO, CMG

FABER, Thomas Erle; yr s of Sir Geoffrey Cust Faber (d 1961); bro of Sir Richard Faber, KCVO, CMG, *qv*; *b* 25 April 1927; *Educ* Oundle, Trinity Coll Cambridge (MA, PhD); *m* 1, 1959, Penelope Morton (d 1983); 2 s (Matthew b 1963, Tobias b 1965), 2 da (Henrietta b 1961, Polly b 1971); m 2, 1986, Elisabeth van Houts; 1 s (Benjamin b 1988), 1 da (Sophie b 1986); *Career* Fell Corpus Christi Coll Cambridge 1953-, lectr in physics Univ of Cambridge 1959-; chm Geoffrey Faber Holdings Ltd 1977- (dir 1969-); *Recreations* shooting, fishing, walking; *Style*— Thomas Faber, Esq; The Old Vicarage, Thompson's Lane, Cambridge (☎ 0223 356685)

FABER, Thomas Henry; s of Capt F S Faber (d 1954), of Ampfield House, Romsey, Hants, and Amy, *née* Purcell-Gilpin (d 1957); *b* 5 Nov 1922; *Educ* Ampleforth, ChCh Oxford; *m* 28 July 1951, Jennifer Mary, da of A E L Hill, OBE, DL (d 1986), of Twyford Lodge, Twyford, Winchester, Hants; 1 s (Robin H G Faber b 1955), 2 da (Caroline (Mrs Faber-Zini) b 1952, Juliet (Mrs Moore) b 1959); *Career* WWII Capt Grendier Gds; served: N Africa, Italy (wounded 1944), Palestine, Egypt; chartered surveyor; ptnr James Harris Winchester (sr ptnr 1980); dir: Strong & Co 1967-73, Whitbread Wessex 1973-81; chm Hants branch CLA 1976-79; ARICS 1950, FRICS 1956; *Recreations* hunting, shooting; *Style*— Thomas Faber, Esq; The Drove, West Tytherley, Salisbury, Wilts (☎ 0794 40 378); Messrs James Harris, Jewry Chambers, Winchester, Hants (☎ 0962 841 842)

FABER, Trevor Martyn; s of Harry Faber (d 1986), of Edgbaston, Birmingham, and Millicent, *née* Waxman (d 1988); *b* 9 Oct 1946; *Educ* Clifton, Merton Coll Oxford (MA, Capt OVABC and Rowing blue); *m* 16 Aug 1985, Katrina Sally, da of George James Clay, of Harborne, Birmingham; *Career* called to the Bar Gray's Inn 1970, in practice MO circuit; memb Tanworth in Arden Assoc for the Prosecution of Felons; *Recreations* theatre, literature, sport, music, food and wine; *Clubs* Vincent's (Oxford); *Style*— Trevor Faber, Esq; Woodside House, Salter Street, Earlswood, Warwickshire B94 6BY (☎ 056 46 3499); 3 Fountain Court, Steelhouse Lane, Birmingham B4 6DR (☎ 021 236 5854, fax 021 236 7008)

FABIAN, Andrew Paul; s of Andrew Taggart Fabian (d 1990), and Edith Mary, *née* Whorwell (d 1964); nephew of Robert Honey Fabian ('Fabian of the Yard'); *b* 23 May 1930; *Educ* St Paul's, Wadham Coll Oxford (MA); *m* 1, 1957 (m dis), Elizabeth Vivienne Chapman; 1 s (Andrew b 1961), 2 da (Susan b 1958, Jill b 1960); m 2, 29 Oct 1983, Eryll Francesca, da of Ronald Sigmund Dickinson, CMG (d 1985); *Career* Nat Serv Lt Singapore Engr Regt RE 1952-54; dist offr Tanganyika 1955-64, seconded to FO as vice consul (later second sec Ruanda-Urundi) 1961-64; HM Dip Serv 1964-; served: Lusaka, Ankara, New Delhi, Islamabad, Karachi, Br high cmmr Nukúalofa; currently chief sec Grand Turk; *Recreations* chess, bird watching; *Clubs* Combined Oxford and Cambridge Univ; *Style*— Andrew Fabian, Esq; c/o FCO, King Charles St, London SW1; Goverment Secretariat, Grand Turk, Turks and Caicos Islands, British West Indies

FABLING, Hon Mrs (Fiona Faith); *née* Campbell-Gray; eld da of Maj Hon Lindsay Stuart Campbell-Gray, MC, Master of Gray (d 1945), and Doreen McClymont, *née* Tubbs (d 1948); sis of 22 Lord Gray; raised to rank of Baron's da 1950; *b* 12 Jan 1933; *m* 11 June 1955, Maj (Ronald Hugh) Desmond Fabling (d 1974), served in 14 PWO Scinde Horse (IA) then 1 Royal Dragoons, twin son of Hugh Fabling (d 1972), of Moat House, Grandborough, nr Rugby; 2 da (Victoria b 1958, Fenella b 1963); *Clubs* Sloane; *Style*— The Hon Mrs Fabling; Victoria House, Ampleforth, York YO6 4DA (☎ 043 93 330)

FACER, Roger Lawrence Lowe; s of John Ernest Facer (d 1983), of Epsom, and Phyllis, *née* Lowe (d 1979); *b* 28 June 1933; *Educ* Rugby, St John's Coll Oxford (MA); *m* 2 April 1960, Ruth Margaret, da of Herbert Mostyn Lewis, PhD (d 1985), of Gresford, Clwyd; 3 da (Sian b 1961, Lucinda b 1961, Emma b 1965); *Career* East Surrey Regt 2nd Lt 1951-53; War Office 1959, asst private sec to Sec of State 1958, Cabinet Office 1966-68, private sec to Min of State (equipment) MOD 1970, Int Inst for Strategic Studies 1972-73, cnsllr UK Delegation MBFR Vienna 1973-75, private sec to Sec of State for Def 1976-79, asst under sec of state MOD 1979-81, under sec Cabinet Office 1981-83, Rand Corp Santa Monica USA 1984, asst under sec of state MOD 1984-87, dep under sec of state MOD 1988-; *Recreations* alpine gardening, hill walking, opera; *Style*— Roger Facer, Esq; Ministry of Defence, London SW1

FACETTI, Hon Mrs (Mary Frances); *née* Crittall; yst da of 1st and last Baron Braintree (d 1961); *b* 30 Dec 1922; *Educ* Langford Grove, Maldon; *m* 21 July 1950, Germano Luigi Facetti, s of Mario Giovanni Facetti, of Milan, Italy; 1 da (Lucia Olivia Josephine b 1954); *Style*— The Hon Mrs Facetti

FACEY, Mathew George Charles; s of William Facey; *b* 11 Dec 1937; *Educ* Cardiff HS for Boys; *m* 1967, Judith Ann, *née* Davies; 1 s, 1 da; *Career* dir: Everbright Fasteners Ltd, Baestan Ltd, Gordian Everbright Tstees Ltd, Everbright Fasteners Inc USA; pres Schnitzer Alloy Products Co USA; *Recreations* music, literature; *Style*— Mathew Facey, Esq; The Beeches, 19 Park Rd, Hampton Hill, Middx (☎ 081 979 1743); Everbright Fasteners Ltd, Stainless House, 4-6 Edwin Rd, Twickenham TW1 4JN (☎ 081 891 0111, telex 933506); 220 W Jersey Street, Elizabeth, NJ 07208, USA

FAGAN, Neil John; s of Lt Cdr C H Fagan, of Bucks Horn Oak, nr Farnham, and Majorie Sadie-Jane, *née* Campbell-Bannerman; *b* 5 June 1947; *Educ* Cheam Sch Charterhouse, Univ of Southampton (LLB); *m* 21 June 1975, Catherine, da of R J Hewitt, of Hurtmore, Godalming, Surrey; 3 da (Caroline Louise b 31 Oct 1977, Felicity Clare b 1 May 1980, Emily Catherine b 20 June 1983); *Career* Lovell White Durrant (formerly Durrant Piesse, orginally Durrant Cooper and Hambling): articled clerk 1969-71, ptnr 1975; memb Worshipful Co of Slrs; memb: Law Soc, Int Bar Assoc; *Books* Contracts of Employment (1990); *Recreations* walking, gardening, swimming, family; *Style*— Neil Fagan, Esq; Little Orchard, Farm Lane, Crondall, Farnham, Surrey GU10 5QE; Lovell White Durrant, 65 Holborn Viaduct, London EC1 (☎ 071 236 0066)

FAGAN, Maj-Gen Patrick Feltrim; CB, MBE; s of Air Cdre Thomas Patrick Feltrim (Paddy) Fagan, RAF (d 1985), and Hon Isabel Mairi, *née* Arundell; *b* 8 Dec 1935; *Educ* Stonyhurst, RMA Sandhurst, UCL (MSc); *m* 29 July 1967, Veronica Eileen, da of Joseph Lorant (d 1990); 2 s (Daragh Patrick Feltrim b 1969, Rory Michael Feltrim b 1972); *Career* cmmnd RE 1955, served Gibraltar, Germany, Aden and Oman; int scientific expedition Karakoram 1961-62, UAE-Oman border survey 1964, jt servs expedition South Georgia 1964-65 (ldr surveying party which first climbed an un-named peak, now offically known as Mount Fagan), 42 Survey Engrg Regt 1965-68, Ordnance Survey 1969-73 (Maj 1969), Survey 4 MOD 1973-76 (Lt-Col 1974), cmd Tech Servs Gp 1976-79, geographic advsr HQ Allied Forces Central Europe (NATO) Netherlands 1979-83 (Col 1979), chief geographic advsr Supreme HQ Allied Powers Europe (NATO) Belgium 1983-85, dir Survey Ops MOD 1985-87 (Brig 1985), dir gen Military Survey 1987- (Maj-Gen 1987); author of numerous articles on surveying and mapping in: Geographical Journal, Photogrammetic Record, Survey Review, Chartered Surveyor, RE Journal; author articles on ski mountaineering in subject journals; memb: Nat Ctee for Photogrammetry and Remote Sensing 1987-, Cncl RICS (Land Survey) 1987-, Cncl RGS 1987- (vice pres 1990-), Ctee Royal Soc (Cartography) 1987-90, Cncl Br Schs Exploring Soc 1987-90, Advsy Bd Inst of Engrg Surveyors Univ of Nottingham 1988-, Cncl Mount Everest Fndn 1989- (dep chm 1990-); dep pres Army Rugby Union 1989-; FRGS 1966, FRICS 1981 (ARICS 1971), FBIM 1981 (MBIM 1971); *Recreations* mountain sports, orienteering, cricket, boats, photography, music; *Clubs* MCC, Alpine, Alpine Ski, Eagle Ski (pres), Geographical; *Style*— Maj-Gen Patrick Fagan, CB, MBE; c/o Lloyds Bank PLC, 7 Pall Mall, London SW1Y 5NH

FAGGE, John Christopher; s and h of Sir John Fagge, 11 Bt, *qv*; *b* 30 April 1942; *m* 13 April 1974, Evelyn Joy, *née* Golding; *Style*— John Fagge, Esq

FAGGE, Sir John William Frederick; 11 Bt (E 1660); s of William Archibald Theodore Fagge (d 1924), 4 s of 8 Bt, and Nellie, *née* Wise (d 1924); suc unc, Sir John Harry Lee Fagge, 10 Bt, 1940; *b* 25 Sept 1910; *m* 11 May 1940, Ivy Gertrude, da of William Edward Frier, of Newington, Kent; 1 s, 1 da; *Heir* s, John Christopher Fagge, *qv*; *Career* farmer; *Style*— Sir John Fagge, Bt; 26 The Mall, Faversham, Kent

FAHERTY, Colman James Bernard; s of Patrick Faherty, of London, and Elizabeth Cristina, *née* Devlin; *b* 1 Sept 1949; *Educ* St Josephs Coll, Galway; *m* 4 Oct 1969, Jacqueline Francis, da of Robert Richard Ford, of Southend-on-Sea, Essex; 2 s (Paul b 16 Jan 1975, Adam b 23 Oct 1977), 1 da (Clare b 2 Aug 1972); *Career* dir Foreign and Colonial: Unit Management Ltd 1983-, Management Ltd 1985-, Pensions Management Ltd 1986-, Nominees Ltd 1986-, Management (Jersey) Ltd 1988-; chm Circa Leisure plc 1988-89, dir SE Essex Technol Centre 1988-89; memb: Rochford DC 1986-90, IOD 1986-; *Recreations* golf, rugby, snooker; *Style*— Colman Faherty, Esq; 26 Gladstone Rd, Hockley, Essex (☎ 0702 202 844); Exchange House, Primrose St, London EC2A 2NY (☎ 071 628 8000, fax 071 628 8188, telex 886197)

FAINT, (John) Anthony Leonard; s of Thomas Leonard Faint (d 1976), and Josephine Rosey, *née* Dunkerley; *b* 24 Nov 1942; *Educ* Chigwell Sch, Magdalen Coll Oxford (BA), Fletcher Sch Medford Mass USA (MA); *m* 24 June 1978, Elizabeth Theresa, da of Walter Winter (d 1960); *Career* Min of Overseas Devpt 1965-71, 1974-80 and 1983-86; study leave Cambridge Mass 1968-69, first sec (aid) Blantyre Malawi 1971-73; head SE Asia Devpt Div Bangkok 1980-83, UK alternate exec dir IBRD/IMF Washington 1986-89; head E Asia Dept ODA London 1989-90, under sec Int Div ODA 1990-; *Recreations* music, bridge, chess, squash, tennis; *Style*— Anthony Faint, Esq; Overseas Development Administration, Eland House, Stag Place, London SW1 (☎ 071 273 3000)

FAIR, (James) Stuart; s of late James S Fair, of Perth, and Margaret, *née* McCallum; *b* 30 Sept 1930; *Educ* Perth Acad, Univ of St Andrews (MA), Univ of Edinburgh (LLB); *m* 13 July 1957, Anne Lesley, da of late Rev Neil Cameron, of Monifieth; 2 s (Andrew Nigel b 1961, Donald James Cameron b 1965), 1 da (Hilary Anne b 1963); *Career* slr: sr ptnr Thorntons WS Dundee; hon sheriff and temp sheriff; lectr in taxation and tutor in professional ethics Univ of Dundee; clerk to Cmmrs on Inland Revenue Dundee Dist; dir of private investmt tst companies; memb: Dundee Port Authy, Tayside Health Bd; chm of Dundee University Court; past pres Dundee and Tayside C of C & Indust; past chm Review Ctee Perth Prison; former memb Scot Slrs Discipline Tbnl, former cncl memb Soc of Writers to Her Majesty's Signet; pres Dundee Choral Union; tstee Caird's Travelling Scholarship Trust; *Recreations* bridge, hill walking, travel, opera-going; *Clubs* New (Edinburgh), RSA (Glasgow); *Style*— Stuart Fair, Esq; Beechgrove House, 474 Perth Rd, Dundee (☎ 0382 69783); Vicarage Court, Kensington W8; Whitehall Chambers, 11 Whitehall St, Dundee (☎ 0382 29111)

FAIRBAIRN, Dr Andrew Finlay; s of Thomas Andrew Fairbairn, of Melrose, Scotland, and Pauline Mary, *née* Tuttle; *b* 16 May 1950; *Educ* George Watsons Coll Edinburgh, Univ of Newcastle-upon-Tyne (MB BS); *m* 14 Aug 1971, Andrea Mary, da of Eric Gibson Hudson; 1 s (Timothy b 1979), 2 da (Nicola b 1975, Rebecca b 1977); *Career* lectr psychiatry Univ of Newcastle-upon-Tyne 1978-81; conslt psychiatrist: St Nicholas Hosp Newcastle 1981-88, Newcastle Gen Hosp 1989-; author 50-60 academic papers on psychiatry of old age; memb exec ctee: Newcastle Mind 1982-87, NE Alzheimers Disease Soc 1983-85; memb N Tyneside Health Authy 1988-; MRCPsych (memb cncl 1986-); *Style*— Dr Andrew Fairbairn; 3 Killiebrigs, Heddon on the Wall, Northumberland NE15 0DD (☎ 0661 852686); Brighton Clinic, Newcastle-upon-Tyne

(☎ 091 273 8811, fax 091 272 2641)

FAIRBAIRN, Sir (James) Brooke; 6 Bt (UK 1869), of Ardwick, Lancs; s of Sir William Albert Fairbairn, 5 Bt (d 1972), and Christine Renée Cotton, *née* Croft; *b* 10 Dec 1930; *Educ* Stowe; *m* 5 Nov 1960, Mary Russell, o da of late William Russell Scott; 2 s (Robert William b 1965, George Edward b 1969), 1 da (Fiona Mary b 1967); *Heir* s, Robert Fairbairn, b 1965; *Career* proprietor of J Brooke Fairbairn & Co Newmarket (furnishing fabric converters); *Style*— Sir Brooke Fairbairn, Bt; Barkway House, Bury Rd, Newmarket, Suffolk CB8 7BT (☎ 0638 662733);The Railway Station, Newmarket, Suffolk CB8 9BA (☎ 0638 665766, fax 0638 665124)

FAIRBAIRN, David; s of Ernest Hulford Fairbairn (d 1981), and Iva May Shilling (d 1968); *b* 9 Aug 1924; *Educ* Haileybury, Trinity Hall Cambridge (MA); *m* 1946, Helen Merriel de la Cour, da of Harold Lewis Collingwood (d 1983); 2 s (Michael b 1947, Christopher b 1949), 2 da (Linda b 1952, Joy b 1958); *Career* Lt RNVR 1939-45; called to the Bar Middle Temple 1949; met stipendiary magistrate 1971-89, dep circuit judge 1972, dep chm Surrey QS 1969-71; Freeman City of London 1958; *Recreations* golf, tennis, country life; *Style*— David Fairbairn, Esq; Craigdistant, Newton Stewart, Dumfries & Galloway, SW Scotland DG8 7BN

FAIRBAIRN, Hon Sir David Eric; KBE (1977), DFC (1944); s of Clive Prell Fairbairn (d 1961), of NSW, Aust, and Marjorie Rose, *née* Jowett (d 1951); *b* 3 March 1917; *Educ* Geelong GS, Jesus Coll Cambridge (MA); *m* 1945, Ruth Antill, da of late Dr Robert Affleck Robertson, of NSW; 3 da; *Career* farmer, politician, diplomat; memb House of Reps 1949-75; min for: Air 1962-64, Nat Devpt 1964-69, Educn and Sci 1971, Def 1971-72; Aust ambass to the Netherlands 1977-80; Hon Col 1981-85; *Recreations* golf, gardening; *Clubs* Melbourne, Cwlth (Canberra), Royal Canberra Golf; *Style*— The Hon Sir David Fairbairn, KBE, DFC; 18 Yarralumla Bay, 51 Musgrave St, Yarralumla, ACT 2600, Australia (☎ 2814659)

FAIRBAIRN, David Ritchie; OBE (1990); s of George Forrester Fairbairn (d 1967), and Eileen Bartlett (d 1988); *b* 4 July 1934; *Educ* Mill Hill Sch, Gonville and Caius Coll Cambridge (BA); *m* 6 Sept 1958, Hon Susan, da of Baron Hill of Luton (Life Peer, d 1989); 1 s (Charles b 1963), 2 da (Carolyn b 1960, Heather b 1965); *Career* 2 Lt RA (Korea) 1952-54; overseas market mangr Arthur Guinness Son & Co Ltd 1960, mktg Guinness Overseas Ltd 1969, md ICC Dataset Ltd 1970, mangr Retail and Distribution Sector Int Computers Ltd 1975, co dir and md James Martin Assoc UK Ltd 1985-89, md James Martin Assoc PLC 1989-; dir: The Nat Computing Centre 1980-86, Mkt EMI Medical Ltd 1976, British Standards Inst 1985; chm Automation and Information Technol Cncl 1985; has various other directorships; pres: Cambridge Union Soc 1958, Guinness Harp Corp NY 1964; vice chm Parly Info Technol Ctee 1982; memb: Focus Ctee on Standards 1982, Monopolies and Mergers Cmmn 1985, Patent Office Steering Bd 1989-; Liveryman Worshipful Co of Information Technologists 1987-; FIDpm; FBCS, FID, FRSA; *Recreations* sailing, skiing, water-skiing; *Clubs* Institute of Directors; *Style*— David Fairbairn, Esq, OBE; Oak End, 11 Oak Way, Harpenden, Herts (☎ 05827 5820); James Martin House Littleton Rd, Ashford, Middx (☎ 0784 245058, telex 928230 SMA UKG, fax 0784 243003)

FAIRBAIRN, Hon Mrs (Elizabeth Mary); *née* Mackay; da of 13 Lord Reay (d 1963); *b* 21 June 1938; *m* 29 Sept 1962 (m dis 1979), Nicholas Fairbairn, QC, MP (now Sir Nicholas Fairbairn, *qv*); 3 da (and 1 s, 1 da decd); *Career* chm: Castle Rock Housing Assoc, Friends of the Edinburgh Int Festival memb Scottish Arts Cncl; *Style*— The Hon Mrs Fairbairn

FAIRBAIRN, John Sydney; s of Capt Sydney George Fairbairn, MC, and Angela Maude, *née* Fane; *b* 15 Jan 1934; *Educ* Eton, Trinity Coll Cambridge (BA); *m* 18 March 1968, Camilla, da of Geoffrey Norman Grinling, of Belmont, Hoathly, Sussex; 1 s (John b 1969), 2 da (Rose b 1969, Flora b 1972); 2 step s, 2 step da; *Career* Nat Serv 2 Lt 17/21 Lancers 1952-54; with Monkhouse Stoneham & Co 1957-60; M&G Group plc: joined 1961, dir 1974, dep chm 1989-89; dep chm LAURTO Ltd 1986-89; hon treas and memb Cncl King's Coll London 1972-84, memb Cncl Univ of Buckingham 1987-; chm: Esme Fairbairn Charitable Tst 1988- (tstee 1965-), Unit Tst Assoc 1989- (memb Exec Ctee 1980-); tstee Wincott Fndn; Hon FKC, FCA; *Clubs* Brooks's, MCC; *Style*— John Fairbairn, Esq; Harvest Hill, Cuckfield, West Sussex

FAIRBAIRN, Robert William; s and h of Sir Brooke Fairbairn, 6 Bt; *b* 10 April 1965; *Educ* King's Sch Ely, Durham Univ (BA); *m* 10 Nov 1990, Sarah Frances Colleypriest, er da of Roger Griffin, of Malmesbury, Wilts; *Career* investmt mangr GT Mgmnt plc 1987-; *Clubs* City Univ; *Style*— Robert Fairbairn, Esq; GT Management plc, 8 Devonshire Sq, London EC2 M4YJ

FAIRBAIRN, Maj Ronald; TD; s of John Douglas Fairbairn (d 1964), and Letitia Ellen Fairbairn (d 1966); *b* 15 April 1916; *Educ* Dulwich; *m* 5 Oct 1940, Doris Edith, da of David Sydney Stevens (d 1948), of 23 Old Burlington St, London W1; *Career* cmmnd 24 London Regt (later 1/7 Queen's Royal Regt) TA 1935, Capt 1939, served France 1940, 8 Army 1942, unit attached 7 Armd Div (The Desert Rats) and promoted Maj 1942, served Alamein (severely wounded) 1942, returned UK and served non-combat units 1943, demob 1946 (disabled with partial paralysis); Bank of England: continued after war 1946-, head of accounting servs 1968, asst sec 1970; staff conslt Ctee of London Clearing Bankers and Br Bankers Assoc 1972-78, ret 1978; hon treas The Queen's (Southwark) Regtl Assoc, memb Ctee Albury and St Marthas Branch Mole Valley Cons Assoc, fndr tstee and treas Fabric Fund Tst St Michaels Church Farley Green 1984-89; tstee Queen's Royal Surrey Regt Museum (memb Working Pty for Devpt a Maintenance), govr Central Fndn Schs 1966-76; Freeman City of London 1962, memb Worshipful Co of Bakers 1962; assoc Chartered Inst of Bankers; *Recreations* sailing until recent years, music, local activities, stock market; *Style*— Maj Ronald Fairbairn, TD; Lowingfold, Farley Green, Albury, Surrey GU5 9DN (☎ 048 641 2254)

FAIRBAIRN, Hon Mrs (Susan); *née* Hill; yst da of Baron Hill of Luton, PC (Life Peer; d Aug 1989), and Marion Spencer, *née* Wallace (d 1989); *b* 27 Dec 1936; *m* 6 June 1958, David Ritchie Fairbairn, s of late George Forrester Fairbairn; 1 s, 3 da; *Style*— The Hon Mrs Fairbairn; 11 Oak Way, West Common, Harpenden, Herts

FAIRBAIRN OF FORDELL, Sir Nicholas Hardwick; QC (Scotland 1972), MP (C) Perth and Kinross 1983-; holder of territorial Barony of Fordell; s of William Ronald Dodds Fairbairn, MD (d 1966), and Mary, *née* More-Gordon of Charlton and Kinnaber (d 1951); *b* 24 Dec 1933; *Educ* Loretto, Univ of Edinburgh (MA, LLB); *m* 1, 29 Sept 1962 (m dis 1979), Hon Elizabeth Mary Mackay, da of 13 Lord Reay; 1 s (Edward Nicholas d 1965), 4 da (Charlotte Elizabeth b 22 Dec 1963, Micheline (Twin) b 22 Dec 1963 d 1964, Anna Karina b 13 May 1966, Francesca Katharine Nichola b 15 Jan 1969); m 2, 28 May 1983, Suzanne Mary, da of Col George Hilary Wheeler (d 1987); *Career* Capt RA (TA); called to Scots Bar 1957; MP (C) Kinross & Perths W Oct 1974-83; slr gen Scotland 1979-82; chm Traverse Theatre Edinburgh 1964-72, cmmr of Northern Lighthouses 1979-82, hon pres Soc Preservation Duddingston Village, tstee Nat Museum of Scotland 1987-, chm Historic Buildings Cncl Scotland 1988-; FSA (Scot); Kt Chevalier Order of Polonia Restituta 1988; KLJ, KStJ, kt 1988; *Books* A Life is too Short (1987); *Clubs* Beefsteak, Buck's, Puffin's (Edinburgh), New (Edinburgh), Carlton; *Style*— Sir Nicholas Fairbairn of Fordell, QC, MP; Fordell Castle, by Dunfermline, Fife

FAIRBAIRNS, Zoë Ann; da of John Fairbairns, and Isabel Catherine, *née* Dippie; *b* 20 Dec 1948; *Educ* St Catherine's Convent Sch Twickenham, Univ of St Andrews (MA), Coll of William and Mary Williamsburg Virginia USA (exchange scholarship); *Career* writer; works incl: Live as Family (1968), Down (1969), Benefits (1979, shortlisted for Hawthornden prize 1980, adapted for stage 1980), Stand We At Last Closing (1983), Here Today (1984, winner Fawcett book prize 1985), Daddy's Girls (1991), Tales I Tell My Mother (contrib, 1978), Despatches From the Frontiers of the Female Mind (contrib, 1985), Voices from Arts for Labour (contrib, 1985), More Tales I Tell My Mother (contrib, 1987), The Seven Deadly Sins (contrib, 1988), Finding Courage (contrib, 1989), The Seven Cardinal Virtues (contrib, 1990), Dialogue and Difference: English into the Nineties (contrib, 1989); journalist; ed Sanity 1973-74, freelance journalist 1975-82; contrib: The Guardian, TES, Times Higher Educational Supplement, The Leveller, Women's Studies International Quarterley, New African, New Scientist, New Society, New Behaviour, New Statesman, Spare Rib, Time Out; poetry ed Spare Rib 1978-82; occasional contrib 1982-: Women's Review, New Internationalist, New Statesman and New Society; fiction reviewer Everywoman 1990-, contrib Sunday Times and Independent 1991-; C Day Lewis fellowship Rutherford Sch Paddington London 1977-78; creative writing tutor: City Lit Inst London 1978-82, Holloway Prison 1978-82, Wandsworth Prison 1987, Silver Moon Women's Bookshop London 1987-1989, Morley Coll London 1988-1989; various appts London Borough of Bromley under Writers in Schs Scheme 1981-; writer in residence: Deakin Univ Geelong Victoria Aust 1983, Sunderland Poly 1983-85, Surrey CC (working in schs and Brooklands Tech Coll) 1989; *awards* Br Cncl travel grant to attend and give paper Women's Worlds: Realities and Choices Congress NY; memb Writers Guild of GB 1985; *Recreations* walking, reading; *Style*— Mrs Zoe Fairbairns; A M Heath & Co, 79 St Martins Lane, London WC2N 4AA (☎ 071 836 4271, fax 071 497 2561)

FAIRBANKS, Douglas Elton Jr; Hon KBE (1949), DSC (1944); o s of Douglas Fairbanks Sr (d 1939), and his 1 wife, Anna Beth, *née* Sully (d 1967); *b* 9 Dec 1909,New York City; *Educ* Bovée Sch, Knickerbocker Greys Mil Sch, Harvard Mil Sch, Pasadena Poly; *m* 1, 3 June 1929 (m dis 1933), Joan Crawford, the film actress (d 1977); m 2, 22 April 1939, Mary Lee (d 1988), da of Dr Giles Epling, of Bluefield, W Virginia, and formerly w of George Huntington Hartford; 3 da; *Career* theatre, cinema and television actor; prodr; company dir, writer, sculptor and painter; former vice pres Franco-Br War Relief and nat vice pres Ctee Defend America by Aiding the Allies 1939-40, former presidential envoy; Capt USNR, ret; chm: Douglas Fairbanks Ltd, Fairtel Inc (US), Boltons Trading Co Inc and dir other cos; KStJ 1950; has received a great number of foreign decorations; *Films include* Stella Dallas, The Green Hat, The Dawn Patrol, Morning Glory, Catherine The Great, Mimi (La Boheme), The Prisoner of Zenda, Gunga Din, The Corsican Brothers, Sinbad the Sailor, The Exile, State Secret (The Great Manhunt), Ghost Story, *Plays include* Young Woodley, The Jest, Romeo and Juliet, My Fair Lady, The Pleasure of His Company, The Secretary Bird, Present Laughter, Out on a Limb, Sleuth; *Style*— Douglas Fairbanks Jr, DSC; 575 Park Ave, New York, NY 10021, USA (☎ 212 838 4900; 212 207 2135); c/o Countess Benckendorf, 29-A Chalcot Rd, London NW1

FAIRBROTHER, Dr Jeremy Richard Frederick; s of Prof Fred Fairbrother (d 1983), of 8 Athol Rd, Bramhall, Stockport, and Grace, *née* Spann; *b* 4 June 1939; *Educ* Cheadle Hulme Sch, Balliol Coll Oxford (MA, DPhil), Manchester Business Sch (MBA); *m* 12 Nov 1979, Linda Alison, da of Fred Reilly, of 16 Linkside, New Malden; 1 s (Edmund b 1988), 2 da (Laura b 1983, Lucy b 1985); *Career* banker; dir Baring Bros & Co Ltd 1982; sr advsr Saudi-Arabian Monetary Agency 1979-86; *Recreations* skiing, tennis, sailing; *Style*— Dr Jeremy R F Fairbrother; 41 Sheen Rd, Richmond, Surrey TW9 1AJ; Baring Bros & Co Ltd, 8 Bishopsgate, London EC2N 4AE (☎ 071 283 8833)

FAIRBROTHER, Neil Harvey; s of Leslie Robert Fairbrother, and Barbara, *née* Wakefield; *b* 9 Sept 1963; *Educ* Lymm GS; *m* 23 Sept 1988, (Margaret) Audrey, da of Robert Stewart Paul; *Career* professional cricketer; represented Cheshire Schs under 13 and under 19; Lancashire CCC: debut as amateur 1982, professional 1983-, scored 94 not out on professional debut, awarded county cap 1985; England: represented schs under 15 and under 19, 7 Test matches (debut v Pakistan Old Trafford 1987), 11 one day Ints; wins with Lancs: Benson & Hedges Cup 1984, Refuge Cup 1988, Refuge League 1989, Benson & Hedges Cup 1990, NatWest Trophy 1990; scored 366 v Surrey at the Oval 1990: highest score by an Englishman this century, highest score at the Oval, third highest score in England, twelfth highest score in the world, second highest score by a left hander, highest score by a player batting at number four; *Style*— Neil Fairbrother, Esq; Lancashire CCC, Talbot Rd, Old Trafford, Manchester M16 (☎ 061 848 7021)

FAIRCLOTH, John Duncan Ibberson; s of John Ibberson Faircloth, of Flat 2, Oxton House, Kenton, Exeter, Devon, and Yvonne Alastair, *née* Hall; *b* 18 Nov 1942; *Educ* Haileybury and Imperial Serv Coll; *m* 23 Oct 1971, Nicola Margaret, da of Prof John Kenneth Sinclair St Joseph, of Histon Manor, Cambridge; 1 da (Clare b 1975); *Career* insur exec Excess Insur Gp; dir: Excess Insur Co 1984, Reinsur Underwriting 1987; *Recreations* golf, swimming, running, gardening, music; *Clubs* RAC, Jesters; *Style*— J D I Faircloth, Esq; 1 Southfield Gardens, Strawberry Hill, Twickenham, Middlesex (☎ 081 892 0529); Excess Insurance Co, 13 Fenchurch Avenue, London EC3 (☎ 071 626 0555)

FAIRCLOUGH, Anthony John; s of Wilfrid Fairclough (d 1975), of 290 Hamstead Road, Handsworth, Birmingham, and Lillian Anne, *née* Townsend (d 1967); *b* 30 Aug 1924; *Educ* St Philip's GS Birmingham, St Catharine's Coll Cambridge (BA, MA); *m* 3 Sept 1957, Patricia, da of Alexander Hamilton Monks (d 1967), of London; 2 s (Philip Simon b 19 Aug 1958, Andrew Joseph b 19 May 1962); *Career* researcher RAE Farnborough 1944-48; private sec to Min of State for Colonial and Cwlth Affrs Colonial Office 1948-64, head depts in Colonial Office and FCO 1964-70, transfd to DOE 1970, head of div responsible for Br new towns 1970-72, under sec i/c a number of divs responsible for various environmental affrs 1973-74, dir Central Unit on Environmental Pollution 1974-78, dir int tport UK Dept of Tport 1978-81, dir for the environment with Cmmn EC 1981-85, acting dir gen for the environment, consumer protection and nuclear safety Cmmn EC 1985-86, dep dir gen for devpt Cmmn EC 1986-89, special advsr Cmmn EC 1989-; dir: Environmental Resources Ltd UK, Groundwork Fndn UK; chm Network for Environmental Technology Transfer (NETT) Brussels; FRSA 1980, companion ICE 1990; *Recreations* reading, gardening, travelling; *Style*— Anthony Fairclough, Esq, CMG; Director, Environmental Resources Ltd, 106 Gloucester Place, London W1H 3DB (☎ 071 465 7200, fax 071 935 8355)

FAIRCLOUGH, Ian Walter; s of Walter Amedee Fairclough (d 1978), and Ella Mildred, *née* Watson (d 1970); *b* 29 May 1938; *Educ* St Andrew's Sch Eastbourne, Malvern; *m* 2 Sept 1967, Patricia Margaret Anne, da of Brig Thomas Patrick Keene (d 1979); 1 s (William b 1977), 3 da (Annabel b 1968, Celia b 1970, Katharine b 1972); *Career* Nat Serv Lt 5 Royal Inniskilling Dragoon Gds 1957-59; rep Agent for Int SOS Assistance (med repatriation serv) 1981-; dir: Fairclough Dodd & Jones (I & P) Ltd 1961-89, Ethos Candles Ltd; memb Cncl Sail Trg Assoc 1980-, govr St Andrew's Sch Eastbourne; Liveryman Worshipful Co of Girdlers (Renter Warden 1990); *Style*— Ian W Fairclough, Esq; Merrow Farm, Dunsfold, Godalming, Surrey GU8 4NX (☎ 048

649 215)

FAIRCLOUGH, Sir John Whitaker; *b* 23 Aug 1930; *Educ* Univ of Manchester (BSc); *m* Margaret Ann; 2 s, 1 da; *Career* chm IBM (UK) Laboratories Ltd, dir mfrg and devpt IBM (UK) Ltd, chief scientific advsr Cabinet Office 1986-; memb: Engrg Cncl 1982-, Govt Advsy Cncl Sci and Technol (ACOST); pres Br Computer Soc 1987; Hon DSc: Southampton 1983, Cranfield 1986, Manchester 1987, Loughborough 1990, Aston 1990; FEng, FBCS, FIEE; kt 1990; *Style—* Sir John Fairclough; The Old Blue Boar, 25 St Johns St, Winchester, Hants

FAIRCLOUGH, Mark; OBE, TD; s of Harry Fairclough (d 1966), of Warrington, and Elsie Marian Rhondda, *née* Briggs (d 1977); *b* 20 Dec 1919; *Educ* Oundle; *m* 30 April 1953, Nance Marjorie, da of Herbert Hayes (d 1946); 2 da (Belinda Ann, Philippa); *Career* served S Lancs Regt and RE (Major) in N Africa, Italy, Greece, ME; chm: Harry Fairclough Ltd, Fairmitre Ltd; *Recreations* golf, bridge; *Clubs* Warrington; *Style—* Mark Fairclough, Esq, OBE, TD; Southworth Hall, Croft, Warrington, Cheshire (☎ 092 576 3189); Harry Fairclough Ltd, Building & Civil Engineering Contractors, Howley, Warrington (☎ 0925 32214); Fairmitre Ltd, Warrington (☎ 0925 574848)

FAIRCLOUGH, Philip; OBE (1986); s of Albert Edward (d 1947), and Sarah (d 1973); *b* 17 July 1926; *Educ* Oldershaw GS; *m* 15 Sept 1951, Marjorie, da of William Holmes (d 1973); 2 da (Jane b 1952, Ann b 1954); *Career* md Castrol Ltd 1985 (dir 1970), dir Burmah Oil plc 1985; memb Worshipful Co of Coach and Harness Makers 1982; FInstPet 1975; *Style—* Philip Fairclough, Esq, OBE; Mill Ridge, Field Rise, Swindon, Wilts (☎ 0793 538594)

FAIREST, Prof Paul Brant; s of Colin Banner Fairest (d 1975), and Marjorie Rosa, *née* Crutchley; *b* 18 Jan 1940; *Educ* King Edward VII Sch Sheffield, Univ of Cambridge; *m* 1, 20 March 1965 (m dis 1987), Patricia Ann Rattee; 2 s (John Brant b 1966, David Nicholas b 1972), 1 da (Jane Alison b 1968); m 2, 15 April 1988, Hilary Christine, da of Leslie Edward Putman; *Career* lectr in law Univ of Cambridge 1969-74 (asst lectr 1964-69, fell Selwyn Coll 1964-74), prof of law Univ of Hull 1974-; chm: NE Gas Consumers Cncl 1977-86, Transport Users' Consultative Ctee NE Eng 1987; *Books* Mortgages (1975), Consumer Protection Act (1987); *Recreations* walking, music, travel; *Style—* Prof Paul Fairest; Law School, University of Hull, Hull HU6 7RX (☎ 0482 465736, telex 592592 UHMAIL G)

FAIRFAX, Hon Hugh Nigel Thomas; 2 s of 13 Lord Fairfax of Cameron (d 1964), and Sonia, *née* Gunston; *b* 29 March 1958; *m* 25 Feb 1984, Victoria Janet, elder da of Digby Sheffield Neave, of Champflour, Marly-le-Roi, France; 1 s (Alexander b 8 Feb 1986), 2 da (Laura b 1987, Marina b 1989); *Style—* The Hon Hugh Fairfax ; 4 Routh Rd, London SW18

FAIRFAX, Lady; Mary; *née* Wein; AM, OBE; o da of Kevin Wein; *Educ* Presbyterian Ladies Coll Univ of Sydney; *m* 1959, as his 3 w, Sir Warwick Oswald Fairfax (d 1987), o s of Sir James Oswald Fairfax , KBE (d 1928); *Career* Hon Consul of Monaco 1979, dir Industrial Equity Ltd 1985-; chm Australian Region Metropolitan Opera Auditions NY 1981; life governor, founder and dir Opera Foundation, Aust Founder Aust; Opera Auditions in co-op Metropolitan Opera, NY Founder Aust, Opera Scholarships to Bayreuth (Germany), La Scala (Italy), London Opera Centre (UK), founder and pres Friends of the Ballet, memb Cultural Grants Ctee of Ministry for Culture Sport and Recreation NSW, past pres Smith Family Summer Ctee, formerly an Exec of Ladies Ctee Elizabethan Theatre Trust and Red Cross; memb: Int Ctee for the Ronald Reagan Presidiential Fndn, Int Ctee US Information; founder: Julliard Scholarship Lincoln Centre NY 1977, of Lady James Fairfax Memorial prize for photography as art-portraiture for the Art Gallery of NSW, Lady James Fairfax Memorial prize for painting Australian Birds and flowers for the Royal Agricultural Soc of New South Wales; *Recreations* working, the arts, writing, poetry, sculpture, fashion, entertaining, reading, swimming, walking, travel; *Clubs* Royal Yacht Squadron (Sydney), Assoc Union (Sydney), American National (Sydney), Lansdowne (London), Metropolitan (New York); *Style—* Lady Fairfax , AM, OBE; Fairwater, 560 New South Head Road, Double Bay, NSW 2028, Australia

FAIRFAX, Hon Peregrine John Wishart; yr s of 12 Lord Fairfax of Cameron (d 1939); *b* 8 March 1925; *Educ* Eton, Trinity Coll Cambridge; *m* 5 Oct 1965, Virginia Alexandra de L'Etang, yr da of Hon Philip Leyland Kindersley; 1 s, 1 da; *Career* late Lt 12 Royal Lancers; High Sheriff Northumberland 1971; *Clubs* White's, Northern Counties (Newcastle); *Style—* The Hon Peregrine Fairfax ; Mindrum, Northumberland (☎ 089 085 246)

FAIRFAX, Hon Rupert Alexander James; MVO (1988); yst s of 13 Lord Fairfax of Cameron (d 1964) and bro of 14 Lord; *b* 21 Jan 1961; *Educ* Eton; *Career* Hanson Tst 1980-86; asst private sec to HRH The Prince of Wales 1986-88; Hanson plc 1988-89, ptnr Beech Dawson (Management Conslts) and dir Thorowgood Ltd 1990-; *Recreations* riding, skiing; *Clubs* Brooks's; *Style—* The Hon Rupert Fairfax , MVO; 165 Draycott Avenue, London SW3 (☎ 071 589 8220)

FAIRFAX-LUCY, Hon Lady (RAMSAY-) (Alice Caroline Helen); *née* Buchan; o da of 1 Baron Tweedsmuir, GCMG, GCVO, CH (d 1940); *b* 1908; *m* 29 July 1933, Maj Sir Brian Fulke (Ramsay-)Fairfax -Lucy, 5 Bt (d 1974); 1 s (Sir Edmund, 6 Bt), 1 da (Emma b 1946, m 1, 1967, James Scott, 2 da; m 2, 1982, James Louis Lambe, only s of late Adm of the Fleet Sir Charles Lambe); *Career* writes as Alice Buchan and Alice Fairfax -Lucy; *Books* A Scrap Screen (1979), Mistress of Charlecote (1983), Charlecote and the Lucys (1990); *Style—* The Hon Lady Fairfax -Lucy; 15 Sylvester Close, Burford, Oxon OX8 4RU; Charlecote Park, Warwick

FAIRFAX-LUCY, Duncan Cameron Ramsay; s of Capt Ewen Aymer Robert Ramsay-Fairfax -Lucy (d 1969), and Margaret Westall, o da of Sir John Westall King, 2 Bt; hp of kinsman, Sir Edmund Ramsay-Fairfax -Lucy, 6 Bt; *b* 18 Sept 1932; *Educ* Eton; *m* 26 Sept 1964, Janet Barclay, o da of late P A B Niven and Mrs K Niven, of Malt Cottage, Charlecote, Warwick; 1 s (Spencer Angus Ramsay b 1966), 1 da (Anna Margaret Barclay); *Career* bursar Queen's Coll Birmingham 1981-; FCA; *Clubs* Army and Navy Club; *Style—* Duncan Fairfax -Lucy, Esq; The Malt House, Charlecote, Warwick CV35 9EW

FAIRFAX-LUCY, Sir Edmund John William Hugh Ramsay-; 6 Bt (UK 1836); s of Maj Sir Brian Fulke Ramsay-Fairfax -Lucy, 5 Bt (d 1974), and Hon Alice, *née* Buchan, *qv*, da of 1 Baron Tweedsmuir, GCMG, GCVO, CH, PC; *b* 4 May 1945; *Educ* Eton, Royal Acad of Arts (Dip); *m* 1, 1974 (m dis), Sylvia, da of Graeme Ogden; m 2, 1986 (m dis), Lady Lucinda, *née* Lambton; *Heir* 1 cous, Duncan Cameron Ramsay-Fairfax -Lucy; *Career* painter; exhibits yearly at the Royal Acad 1967-; *Recreations* landscape gardening, waterworks; *Style—* Sir Edmund Ramsay-Fairfax -Lucy, Bt; Charlecote Park, Warwick

FAIRFAX OF CAMERON, 14 Lord (S 1627); Nicholas John Albert Fairfax ; s of 13 Lord (d 1964; ninth in descent from the bro of the 2 Lord who defeated Prince Rupert at Marston Moor, and unc of the 3 Lord who, as C-in-C of the Parliamentarians, was the victor at Naseby, and who hired the poet, Andrew Marvell, as a tutor for his da Mary who m another poet, the 2 Duke of Buckingham); *b* 4 Jan 1956; *Educ* Eton, Downing Coll Cambridge; *m* 24 April 1982, Annabel, er da of late Nicholas Morriss, of 36 Cambridge Rd, SW11; 2 s (Hon Edward Nicholas Thomas b 20 Sept 1984, Hon John Frederick Anthony b 27 June 1986); *Heir* s, Hon Edward Nicholas Thomas b 20 Sept 1984; *Career* sits as Con in House of Lords; barr Grays Inn 1977; *Recreations* sailing, skiing; *Clubs* Queen's; *Style—* The Rt Hon the Lord Fairfax of Cameron; 10 Orlando Road, London SW4 OLF

FAIRFAX OF CAMERON, Sonia, Lady; Sonia Helen; JP (Berks 1957); yr da of Capt Cecil Bernard Gunston, MC (d 1934; er bro of Sir Derrick Gunston, 1 Bt), and Lady Doris Gwendoline Hamilton-Temple-Blackwood (da of 2 Marquess of Dufferin and Ava); sis of Mrs G W Luttrell; *m* 17 April 1951, 13 Lord Fairfax of Cameron (d 1964); 3 s (including 14 Lord), 1 da (Hon Mrs Bell); *Career* temp lady of the bedchamber to HM The Queen 1967-71; *Style—* The Rt Hon Sonia, Lady Fairfax of Cameron, JP; The Garden House, Stanford Dingley, Reading, Berks

FAIRFIELD, Ian McLeod; CBE (1982); s of late Geoffrey Fairfield, and Inez Helen Thorneycroft Fairfield (d 1977); *b* 5 Dec 1919; *Educ* Monkton House Sch Cardiff, Manchester Coll of Technol; *m* 1941, Joyce Ethel, da of Cdr Percy Fletcher, RN (d 1965); 2 s (Clive, Julian); *Career* cmmnd RNVR Electrical Branch 1940-45; engrg trainee Callenders Cables & Construction Co Ltd (now BICC plc), area sales mangr St Helens Cable & Rubber Co 1945-51, gp chm Chemring Group plc 1985- (sales dir 1951, md 1952, dep chm, chm and gp chief exec 1980, chm 1984, chm and gp chief exec 1985); *Recreations* motor boat cruising; *Clubs* Athenaeum, Royal Naval Sailing Assoc; *Style—* Ian Fairfield, Esq, CBE; Chemring Gp plc, Alchem Works, Fratton Trading Estate, Portsmouth PO4 8SX (☎ 0705 735457, telex 86242)

FAIRGRIEVE, Sir (Thomas) Russell; CBE (1974), TD (1959), JP (Selkirkshire 1962); s of late Alexander Fairgrieve, OBE, MC, JP, of Galashiels, and Myma Margaret, *née* Crow; *b* 3 May 1924; *Educ* St Mary's Sch Melrose, Sedbergh, Scottish Coll of Textile Galashiels; *m* 7 Dec 1952, Millie, da of Alexander Mitchell; 1 s (Sandy), 3 da (Patricia, Rosemary, Marjorie); *Career* cmmnd 8 Gurkha Rifles IA 1943, Co Cdr 1/8 Gurkha Rifles 1944-46, GSO (2) (Ops) 15 Indian Corps SE Asia 1964; TA, 4 KOSB 1947-63, Maj 2 i/c; pres Scottish Cons Assoc 1965-66, memb Exec Ctee Euro Movement (Scotland) 1970-74, MP (C) W Aberdeenshire 1974-83, chm Scottish Cons Gp for Europe 1974-78, Scottish Cons whip 1975, chm Scottish Cons Party 1975-80 (vice chm 1971), Parly under sec of state Scotland 1979-81; md Laidlaw & Fairgrieve Ltd 1958-68 (dir 1953-58); dir: Dawson Int plc 1961-73, William Baird & Co plc 1975-, Hall Advertising Ltd 1981-; conslt Saatchi & Saatchi Co 1976-; chm: Scottish Woollen Spinners' Assoc, Scottish Cncl of Independent Schs; memb: Exec Ctee Scottish Cncl, Cncl Scottish Woollen Mfrs Assoc; govr: St Mary's Sch Melrose, Scottish Coll of Textiles; kt 1981; *Recreations* golf; *Clubs* Carlton, New (Edinburgh), Royal and Ancient (St Andrews); *Style—* Sir Russell Fairgrieve, CBE, TD, JP; Pankalan, Boleside, Galashiels, Selkirkshire TD1 3NX (☎ 0896 2278)

FAIRHAVEN, 3 Baron (UK 1961); Ailwyn Henry George Broughton; JP (S Cambs 1975), DL (Cambridgeshire and Isle Ely 1977); s of 2 Baron (d 1973), and Hon Diana (d 1937), da of Capt Hon Coulson Fellowes (s of 2 Baron De Ramsey, JP, DL, and Lady Rosamond Spencer-Churchill, da of 7 Duke of Marlborough, KG); *b* 16 Nov 1936; *Educ* Eton, RMA Sandhurst; *m* 23 Sept 1960, Kathleen Patricia, er da of Col James Henry Magill, OBE; 4 s (Hon James, Hon Huttleston Rupert b 1970, Hon Charles Leander b 1973, Hon Henry Robert b 1978); 2 da (Hon Diana Cara (Hon Mrs Thornton), Hon Melanie Frances (Hon Mrs Smith)); *Heir* s, Hon James Broughton b 25 May 1963; *Career* RHG 1957-71, Maj; Vice Lord-Lt Cambridgeshire 1977-85; Kt of the White Rose (Finland) 1970, CStJ 1983; *Recreations* shooting, cooking; *Clubs* Jockey (sr steward 1985-89), Turf; *Style—* The Rt Hon the Lord Fairhaven, JP, DL; Anglesey Abbey, Cambridge (☎ 0223 811746)

FAIRHOLM, David Victor; s of Albert Fairholm, of Nottingham, and Doreen Lilian, *née* Dennis; *b* 15 Aug 1945; *Educ* High Pavement GS Nottingham; *m* 25 Jan 1965, Angela Dolores, da of John Townsend Hanson, of Nottingham; 5 s (Richard b and d 1965, Thomas b 1968, Robert b 1970, Jonathan b 1976, Christopher b 1984); *Career* accountant; ptnr: Dexter and Co 1971-86, Saul Fairholm and Co 1987-; treas Rotary Club, sec Round Table 41 Club, memb MENSA; FCA; *Recreations* golf, cycling; *Clubs* Woodhall Spa Golf; *Style—* David Fairholm, Esq; Pendling, Tattershall Road, Woodhall Spa, Lincolnshire LN10 6TW (☎ 0526 52103); Saul Fairholm and Co, Chartered Accountants, Lewer House, 12 Tentercroft St, Lincoln LN5 7DB (☎ 0522 537 575, fax 0522 43506)

FAIRHURST, Harry Marshall; s of Philip Garland Fairhurst (d 1987), and Janet Meikle, *née* Marshall; *b* 18 June 1925; *Educ* Clifton, Clare Coll Cambridge (MA), Northern Poly (Dip Arch); *m* 20 June 1959, Elizabeth Mary, da of Bernard Hudson Thorp, of Cheadle, Cheshire; 1 s (Timothy b 1968), 3 da (Katharine b 1960, Rachel b 1962, Philippa b 1964); *Career* architect in private practice; architect and surveyor to Fabric of Manchester Cathedral 1970-90, cmmnd architect for English Heritage 1978- (bldgs for commerce, indust, educn, med and scientific res); Hon MA Univ of Manchester, hon fell UMIST, FRIBA; *Recreations* forestry, contemporary art, design and crafts; *Clubs* St James's (Manchester); *Style—* Harry M Fairhurst, Esq; 33 Macclesfield Road, Wilmslow, Cheshire SK9 2AF (☎ 0625 523784)

FAIRLEY, Eric Claude William; s of Robert Alexander (d 1966), of Bearsden, Glasgow, and Euphemia Mitchell, *née* Murrie (d 1979); *b* 10 Sept 1925; *Educ* Alan Glen's Sch Glasgow, Bearsden Acad, West of Scotland Agric Coll, Univ of Glasgow (MA, DipEd); *m* 2 July 1956, Stella Thurlow (d 1983), da of John William Lindley (d 1958), of Bearsden, Glasgow; 3 da (Jan Thurlow Murrie b 1958, Lois Elizabeth Mitchell b 1960, Karen Ann Mackenzie b 1963); *Career* science teacher Possil Sr Secdy Sch 1956-62; asst organiser West of Scotland Ctee for Tech Educn 1962-63, asst sec Scottish Assoc for Nat Certificates and Diplomas 1963-73, educn offr Scottish Tech Educn Cncl 1973-85, asst dir Scottish Vocational Educn Cncl 1985-87, advsr to Open Coll 1987-, chm and sec The Dullatur Assoc, chm Dullatur Community Cncl; *Recreations* hill walking, cross country skiing, photography; *Clubs* Dullatur Golf, Arlington Baths; *Style—* Eric Fairley, Esq; 11 Victoria Terrace, Dullatur Glasgow G68 0AQ (☎ 0236 724202)

FAIRLIE, James; OBE (1990); s of Maj Francis Walter Fairlie (d 1971), and Margaret Morton, *née* Wilson (d 1954); *b* 15 Dec 1924; *Educ* Glenalmond Coll Perthshire, Corpus Christie Coll; *m* 14 Oct 1955, (Joan) Catherine McKinnon, da of Dr John Ernest Morrison (d 1966), of Stirling; 1 s (Peter James Morrison b 18 Dec 1957), 1 da (Diana Margaret b 27 Oct 1956); *Career* volunteered air crew trg RAF 1943, pilot training No 4 BFTS, Arizona USA, cmmnd PO Aden 1945, Flt Lt RAFVR 103 Reserve Centre Scone Perth 1948-55; asst gen mangr Campbell Henderson Ltd Glasgow 1951-57, chm and md Glenturret Distillery Ltd Crieff Perthshire 1957-, dir and sec Cosco Ltd 1981-, advsr to Cointeau of Paris on scotch whisky prodn 1981-, author of papers on distilling and tourism; Cons Pty: Parly candidate for Stirling and Clackmannan consituency 1968, memb Central Ctee 1968-72, memb Regnl Cncl Ctee and chm Bridge of Allan branch, memb Perth and Kinross Business Support Gp 1990-; hon citizen State of Arizona USA 1982; FInstD 1966, MASMechE USA 1966; *Recreations* golf, hill-walking, flying; *Clubs* Old Glenalmond, IOD; *Style—* James Fairlie, Esq, OBE; Craig Wallace, Chalton Road, Bridge of Allan, Stirling FK9 4DX (☎ 0786 832358); Glenturret Distillery Ltd, Crieff, Perthshire PH7 4HA (☎ 076 4242 ext 1/25, fax 0764 4366)

FAIRLIE-CUNINGHAME, Sir William Henry; 16 Bt (NS 1630), of Robertland, Ayrshire; s of Sir William Fairlie-Cuninghame, 15 Bt, MC (d 1981), and Irene Alice (d

1970), da of late Henry Margrave Terry; *b* 1 Oct 1930; *m* 1972, Janet Menzies, da of late Roy Menzies Saddington; *Heir* s, William Robert Henry; *Style—* Sir William Fairlie-Cuninghame, Bt; 29A Orinoco Rd, Pymble, New South Wales 2073, Australia

FAIRLIE-CUNINGHAME, William Robert Henry; s and h of Sir William Henry Fairlie-Cuninghame, 16 Bt; *b* 19 July 1974; *Style—* William Fairlie-Cuninghame Esq; 29A Orinoco Rd, Pymble, New South Wales 2073, Australia

FAIRLIE OF MYRES, Capt David Ogilvy; MBE (1984), JP (Fife 1975), DL (Fife 1981); s of James Ogilvy Fairlie of Myres (d 1960), of Myres Castle, Auchtermuchty, Fife, and Constance Gertrude, *née* Lascelles (d 1981); *b* 1 Oct 1923; *Educ* Ampleforth, Oriel Coll Oxford; *m* 19 April 1969, Ann Constance (d 1986) da of Dermot Francis Bolger (d 1974), of Quinta Avista Navios, Funchal, Madeira; *Career* Bde Signal Offr 32 Gds Bde UK 1943, PA to Maj-Gen C M F White France and Belgium 1944, Signal Offr HQ Allied Land Forces SE Asia Ceylon and Singapore 1945, Bde Signal Offr 37 Indian Bde Java and Malaya 1946, Signal Regt Scottish Cmd Edinburgh 1947-48, Signal Regt Northern Cmd Catterick 1949-50, Bde Signal Offr 29 Inf Bde Korea 1951-52, 2 i/c Signal Sqdn SHAPE 1953, Adj 51 Highland Divnl Signal Regt 1954-56, dist cmmr Cupar Scout dist 1960-65, co cmmr Fife Scouts 1966-85, chm E Fife branch Arthritis and Rheumatics Cncl 1986-; memb Queen's Body Guard for Scotland (The Royal Co of Archers) 1964-; Knight of the Equestrian order of the Holy Sepulchre of Jerusalem (c the order in Scotland) 1988; *Books* Fairlie of that Ilk (history and genealogy of the family, 1987); *Recreations* gardening, bee keeping, photography, genealogy; *Clubs* Army and Navy, Royal Overseas, Royal and Ancient Golf; *Style—* Capt David Fairlie of Myres, MBE, JP, DL; Myres castle, Auchtermuchty, Fife KY14 7EW (☎ 0337 28350)

FAIRMAN, Dr Martin John; s of Henry Douglas Fairman, FRCS, of Bristol, and Stella Margaret, *née* Sheath; *b* 8 May 1945; *Educ* Monkton Combe Sch Bath, London Hosp Med Coll (MB BS); *m* 12 Aug 1967, Marianne Alison Louis, da of Sqdn Ldr Roland Ernest Burton, of Limousin, France; 2 s (James b 1969, Jack b 1978), 2 da (Jocelyn b 1971, Lydia b 1980); *Career* conslt physician S Lincolnshire Health Authy 1979-, hon sr lectr Med Leicester Univ 1979-, fell gastroenterology Cincinnati 1976-77; FRCP; *Recreations* golf, sailing; *Style—* Dr Martin J Fairman; Skirbeck Grange, Sibsey Rd, Boston, Lincs (☎ 0205 360743); Pilgrim Hosp, Boston, Lincs (☎ 0205 364801)

FAIRRIE, Lt-Col (Adam) Angus; s of Lt-Col Adam Grainger Fairrie, MBE (d 1956), and Elizabeth, *née* Dobie (d 1983); *b* 9 Dec 1934; *Educ* Stowe, RMA Sandhurst; *m* 16 April 1966, Elizabeth Rachel, da of Rev Archibald Selwyn Pryor (ka 1944); 1 s (Adam Hugh b 1967), 1 da (Elizabeth Margaret Emma b 1968); *Career* regular army offr; cmmnd: The Queen's Own Cameron Highlanders 1955, Queen's Own Highlanders 1961; attended Staff Coll Camberley 1966, attended Nat Def Coll 1973, cmd 1 Bn Queen's Own Highlanders 1974-77, ret 1978, Regl Sec 1978-; *Books* Cuidich 'n Righ - A History of the Queens Own Highlanders (1983), The Northern Meeting 1788-1988 (1988); *Recreations* painting, photography; *Clubs* Naval and Military; *Style—* Lt-Col Angus Fairrie; Craighill, N Kessock, Ross and Cromarty (☎ 046 373 616); RHQ Queens Own Highlanders, Cameron Barracks, Inverness (☎ 0463 224 380)

FAIRTLOUGH, Gerard Howard; CBE (1989); s of Maj-Gen Eric Victor Howard Fairtlough, DSO, MC (d 1944), and Agatha Zoë, *née* Barker; *b* 5 Sept 1930; *Educ* Marlborough, King's Coll Cambridge; *m* 1954, Elizabeth Ann, *née* Betambeau; 2 s, 2 da; *Career* Lt RA; md Shell UK Ltd 1974-78, div dir NEB 1978-80, chief exec Celltech Ltd 1980-90; chm The Coverdale Organisation plc 1984-; Hon DSc: City Univ 1987, CNAA 1990; *Recreations* walking, theatre, yoga; *Style—* Gerard Fairtlough, Esq; 5 Belmont Grove, London SE13 (☎ 081 852 8648)

FAIRWEATHER, Col Andrew Burton; OBE (1990), TD (1972); s of Andrew Fairweather (d 1960), of Edinburgh, and Marion Ramsay, *née* Ritchie; *b* 26 Feb 1931; *Educ* Royal High Sch Edinburgh, Univ of Edinburgh, Open Univ (BA); *m* 16 July 1955, Elizabeth Fairbairn, da of James Brown (d 1982), of Edinburgh; 3 s (David Andrew b 1956, Alan James b 1958, Ian Cowper b 1961); *Career* Rifle Brigade and RAEC, Royal Scots (TA), and Royal Corps of Transport (TA), CO 495 Movement Control Liasion Unit BAOR 1977-81 (Col 1981); exec offr Dept of Health for Scotland 1951-54, sec Scot Med Practices Ctee 1954-58; Rent Assessment Panel for Scotland: higher exec offr 1958, sr exec offr 1965, sec 1965-67; princ Civil Service Dept 1970, chief admin offr Civil Serv Coll 1970-72, princ Scot Economic Planning Dept 1972-74, sec Local Govt Staff and Property Cmmns 1974-77, princ Scot Devpt Dept 1977-81, princ Scot Office Central Servs 1981-82, sr princ Scot Office 1982-91, gen sec Abbeyfield Soc for Scot 1991-; MBIM 1976; *Style—* Col Andrew Fairweather, OBE, TD; 127 Silverknowes Gardens, Edinburgh EH4 5NG (☎ 031 336 4427)

FAIRWEATHER, Carlton; s of Myrtle Fairweather; *b* 22 Sept 1961; *Educ* William Penn Secdy Sch; *m* 26 June 1987, Debbie Leigh Thornton, da of Richard Stanley Watkins; *Career* professional footballer Wimbledon 1984-; semi-professional: Bromley 1980-82, Tooting & Mitcham 1982-84; FA Cup Winners medal v Liverpool 1988; FA Advanced Coaching Licence, coach to Univ of London soccer team; *Recreations* table tennis, ten-pin bowling; *Style—* Carlton Fairweather, Esq; Wimbledon FC, 49 Durnsford Rd, Wimbledon, London SW19 4HG (☎ 081 946 6311); c/o Ambrose Mendy, 212 Tower Bridge Rd, London SE1 2UP (☎ 071 378 0009, fax 071 403 1040)

FAIRWEATHER, Prof Denys Vivian Ivor; s of Albert James Ivor Fairweather (d 1935), and Gertrude Mary, *née* Forbes (d 1953); *b* 25 Oct 1927; *Educ* Forfar Acad, Websters Seminary Kirriemuir, Univ of St Andrews (MB ChB, MD); *m* 21 April 1956, (Gwendolen) Yvonne, da of John Phillips Hubbard, of Heckington, Lincs; 1 s (John b 1957), 2 da (Debbie b 1959, Sally b 1966); *Career* Sqdn Ldr med branch RAF 1950-55; registrar to Sir Dugald Baird Aberdeen 1955-59, sr lectr Univ of Newcastle upon Tyne 1959-66, vice provost med UCL 1984-87 (prof and head Dept Obstetrics and Gynaecology 1966-89, dean Faculty Clinical Sci 1982-84), head UCH and Middx Sch of Med 1988-89, vice provost UCL 1988-90, pro vice chllr med Univ of London 1989-; memb Bloomsbury Health Authy 1983-90, vice pres Br FPA 1985-, sec gen Int Fedn of Gynaecology and Obstetrics 1985-, memb Int Med Advsy Panel IPPF 1988- (former pres Euro Regnl Cncl 1974-80, former chm Mgmnt and Planning Ctee 1975-77); hon fell: American Assoc Reproductive Med 1969, UCL 1985; Freeman City of Krakow 1989; FRCOG 1967, FRSM 1968; *Books* Amniotic Fluid Research and Clinical Application (1973), Labour Ward Manual (1985); *Recreations* gardening, fishing, do-it-yourself; *Style—* Prof Denys Fairweather; pro vice chancellor for Medicine, Univ of London, Senate House, Malet Street, London WC1E 7HU (☎ 071 636 8000, 071 436 7814)

FAIRWEATHER, Dr Frank Arthur; s of Frank Fairweather (d 1970), of Norwich Norfolk, and Maud Harriet, *née* Jolly (d 1983); *b* 2 May 1928; *Educ* City of Norwich Sch, Middlesex Hosp Med Sch London (MB BS); *m* 18 July 1953, Christine Winifred, da of Frederick James Hobbs (d 1959), of Watford Hertfordshire; 2 s (Martin Frank b 7 Feb 1 1957, Howard John b 21 May 1959); *Career* Mil Serv Surgn Lt HMS President RNR 1958-61; clinical house appts Ipswich Gp of Hosps 1955-56; pathologist 1956-60: Bland Sutton Inst of Pathology, Courtauld Inst of Biochemistry Middlesex Hosp and Soho Hosp for Women; jt sr registrar in pathology Middlesex and W Middlesex Hosps 1960-62, conslt pathologist Benger Laboratories 1961-62, chief pathologist and Nuffield Fndn scholar Br Industl Biological Res Assoc and hon sr lectr RCS 1962-65, assoc res dir Wyeth Laboratories Taplow 1965-69, SMO and PMO DHSS Ctee on Safety of Medicines 1969-72; 1972-82: sr PMO DHSS and head Chemical Contamination and Environmental Pollution Div, memb EEC Scientific Ctee on Food, chm EEC Scientific Ctee on Cosmetology, memb WHO Panels on Food Safety and Environmental Pollution; conslt advsr in toxicology to DHSS 1978-81, dir DHSS Toxicological Laboratory St Bartholomews Hosp London 1978-82 (hon dir 1982-84), hon prof of toxicology Dept of Biochemistry Univ of Surrey 1978-84, hon prof of toxicology and comparative pathology Sch of Pharmacy Univ of London 1982-88, environmental safety offr Res and Engrg Div Unilever plc 1982-; examiner RCPath 1979-, chm Br Industl Biological Res Assoc Toxicology Int 1987-, chief examiner in toxicology Inst of Biology 1989-; FRCPath 1975 (MRCPath 1963), FIBiol 1972, memb Parly and Scientific Cmmn 1988, hon FFOM 1991; *Recreations* angling, gardening and water colours; *Style—* Dr Frank Fairweather; 394 London Rd, Langley, Slough, Berks SL3 7HX; Unilever House, Research Division, Blackfriars, London EC4P 4BQ (☎ 071 822 5318, fax 071 822 5881)

FAIRWEATHER, Hon Mrs (Jean Simpson); *née* Mackie; er da of Baron John-Mackie (Life Peer); *b* 2 July 1937; *m* Alexander Fairweather; *Style—* The Hon Mrs Fairweather; 31 Arbirlot Road, Arbroath, Scotland

FAIRWEATHER, Leslie Stephen; s of William Stephen Fairweather (d 1975), of Lewes, Sussex, and Ethel Mary Elizabeth, *née* Keen (d 1981); *b* 7 March 1929; *Educ* St Olave's GS, Dorking Co GS, Brighton Poly (ARIBA); *m* 26 Oct 1963, (Felicity) Anne, da of Henry Martin Williamson, MBE, of Balcombe, W Sussex; 3 s (David b 14 March 1966, Mark b 10 Oct 1968, Michael b 8 June 1971), 2 da (Ruth b 8 Sept 1964, Rachel b 11 Aug 1967); *Career* former architect London and Sussex, work incl extensions and alterations to Glyndebourne Opera House, pt/t studio master Dept of Architecture Brighton Coll of Art and private tutor, lectr and res fell Dept of Architecture Univ of Bristol 1965-67, res fell Jl Architects 1962-65; ed: Info Library for Architects 1967-69, Architects Jl 1973-84 (tech ed 1969-73); chm MBC Architectural Press and Bldg Pubns (div of Maxwell Business Communications) 1989-; contrib: Architects' Jl, Br Jl of Criminology, BBC Radio 4 A Look Inside 1986; conslt: UNSDRI Rome, res into prison design with N London Poly and Home Office; chm RIBA Cmmn on Evidence to Lord Justice Woolf's Prison Enquiry 1990, initiator and sec prison Design Study Gp, dir Land Ltd, fndr memb Land Decade Educnl Cncl, external examiner at univ and poly depts of architecture, judge and assessor of nat and int awards and competitions; memb final year design thesis juries: Architectural Assoc, Barlett Sch of Architecutre Univ of London; fndr and sec The Conslt Contractor Barrier Gp, memb Panel of Church Surveyors Diocese of Chichester, chm Balcombe Scout Gp Exec, parent govr Haywards Health Sixth Form Coll 1981-86, govr Balcombe Primary Sch 1990-; memb: Howard League for Penal Reform, Int Bldg Press, The Architecture Club, Action Aid; memb RIBA 1959 (Ashpital prizewinner 1957); *Books* contrib The English Prisons (1960), AJ Metric Handbook (1968), Prison Architecture (UN Social Defence Research Institute, 1975), Balcombe, the story of a Sussex Village (1981); *Recreations* music, writing, browsing, owl collecting; *Style—* Leslie Fairweather, Esq; MBC Architectural Press & Building Publications, 33-35 Bowling Green Lane, London EC1R ODA (☎ 071 837 1212, telex 299 049 MBC BGL G, fax 071 278 4003)

FAITH, Dr Lesley; da of Norman Faith (d 1970), of Belfast, and Estelle, *née* Sharp; *b* 30 Sept 1955; *Educ* Methodist Coll Belfast, Univ of St Andrews (BSc), Univ of Manchester (MB ChB); *m* 13 June 1987, Ashwani Kumar, s of Krishan Kumar Korpal, of Manchester; 2 da (Natassha b 1988, Nicole b 1989); *Career* conslt psychiatrist: Bermuda 1986, Sydney Aust 1986-87, Stepping Hill Hosp Stockport Cheshire 1987-; Special Interest Devpt Serv for Drug Addiction and Alcohol Abuse; MRCPsych 1984; *Recreations* travel, reading; *Style—* Dr Lesley Faith; 27 Broomfield Rd, Heaton Moor, Stockport SK4 4NB (☎ 061 432 0449); Stepping Hill Hospital, Stockport, Cheshire (☎ 061 483 1010)

FAITH, (Irene) Sheila; JP (Inner London 1978); yr da of late I Book; *b* 3 June 1928; *Educ* Central HS Newcastle, Univ of Durham (LDS); *m* 1950, Dennis Faith; *Career* dental surgn; contested (C) Newcastle Central Oct 1974, MP (C) Belper 1979-83, sec Cons Backbench Health and Social Servs Ctee 1982-83, Parly Maritime Gp 1984, MEP (C) Cumbria and Lancashire N 1984-89, Euro Parl Road Safety Report 1985-86; memb: Northumberland CC 1970-74, Newcastle City Cncl 1975-77, Select Ctee Health and Soc Servs 1979-83, Exec Ctee of Cons Med Soc 1979-84, Ctee on Unopposed Bills 1980-83, Br-American Parly Gp, Cwlth Parly Assoc, Inter-Parly Union, UN Parly Gp, Euro Movement, Euro Parl Tport Ctee and Regnl Devpt Ctee 1984-86, Euro Parl Energy Res and Technol Ctee 1987-89; vice chm: Jt Consultative Ctee on Educn for Dist of Newcastle 1973-74, Swiss Delegation; served as chm of several sch governing bodies and mangr of community JP: Northumberland 1972-74, Newcastle 1974-78; *Style—* Mrs Dennis Faith, JP; 11 Merlin House, Oak Hill Park, London NW3 7LJ (☎ 071 4353702)

FAITHFULL, Baroness (Life Peeress UK 1975), of Wolvercote, Co of Oxfordshire; Lucy Faithfull; OBE (1972); da of Lt Sydney Leigh Faithfull, RE (ka 1916), and Elizabeth Adie, *née* Algie; *b* 26 Dec 1910; *Educ* Talbot Heath Sch Bournemouth, Birmingham Univ (Social Sciences Diploma, Child Care and Family Case Work Certificates); *Career* sits as Conservative Peer in House of Lords; social worker; sub warden Birmingham Settlement 1932-35; organiser LCC Care Ctee 1935-40, evacuation welfare offr Miny of Health 1940-45, inspr Home Off (Children's Branch) 1946-58, children's offr Oxford City 1958-70, dir Social Servs Oxford City Cncl 1970-74; govr: Bessells Leigh Sch for Maladjusted Children Oxford, Caldecott Community Sch Merstham-le-Hatch Kent; pres Nat Children's Bureau; chm All Party Parly Gp Children Westminster; vice pres: British Assoc for Counselling, Nat Assoc of Voluntary Hostels; Hon MA (Oxon), Hon DLitt (Warwick); *Recreations* travel; *Style—* The Rt Hon Baroness Faithfull, OBE; 303 Woodstock Rd, Oxford OX2 7NY (☎ 0865 55389)

FALCON, Michael Gascoigne; CBE (1979), DL (Norfolk 1981); s of Michael Falcon, JP (d 1976), by his w Kathleen Isabel Frances, *née* Gascoigne (d 1985); *b* 28 Jan 1928; *Educ* Stowe, Heriot Watt Coll; *m* 1954, April Daphne Claire, *née* Lambert; 2 s (Michael b 1956, Andrew b 1958), 1 da (Claire b 1960); *Career* former head brewer and jt md E Lacon & Co Gt Yarmouth, tstee E Anglian Tstee Savings Bank 1963-75, exec dir Edgar Watts (Bungay Suffolk) 1968-73; dir: Securicor E Ltd 1969-72, Lloyds Bank (UK) Management Ltd 1979-85, Matthew Brown plc 1981-87, Greene King & Sons plc 1988-, Br Rail Anglia Regional Bd 1988-, chm: Nat Seed Devpt Orgn Ltd 1972-82, Pauls & Whites Ltd 1976-85 (dir 1973-), Lloyds Bank Eastern Counties Regional Bd 1979-91 (dir 1972), Norwich Dist Health Authy 1988-, tstee John Innes Fndn 1990; Norwich Union Insurance Group: dir 1963, vice chm 1979, chm 1981; High Sheriff of Norfolk 1979-80, High Steward Borough Gt Yarmouth 1984-, JP Norfolk 1967; Hon LLD Univ of Nottingham 1988; CStJ 1986, OStJ 1968; *Recreations* country pursuits; *Clubs* Norfolk County, Royal Norfolk and Suffolk Yacht; *Style—* Michael G Falcon, Esq, CBE, DL; Keswick Old Hall, Norwich, Norfolk NR4 6TZ (☎ 0603 54348); Kirkgate, Loweswater, Cockermouth, Cumbria (☎ 090 085 271)

FALCONBRIDGE, Brian William; s of James Henry Falconbridge, of Cromer Norfolk, and Joyce Vera Lucy Spong; *b* 1 May 1950; *Educ* Fakenham GS, Canterbury Coll of Art, Goldsmiths' Coll Sch of Art, Slade Sch of Fine Art; *m* 1970 (m dis 1989),

Elizabeth Margaret, *née* Green; 1 s (Oliver William Merton b 9 Aug 1985), 1 da (Camilla Elizabeth Vita b 9 Sept 1982); *Career* lectr: Eton 1977-81, Goldsmiths' Coll 1978-, Slade Sch of Fine Art 1979-86, Blackheath Sch of Art 1985-89; pt/t and visiting lectr 1974: Brighton Museum, Brighton Poly, Bristol Poly, Camberwell Sch of Art, Colchester Inst Sch of Art, Falmouth Sch of Art, Maidstone Coll of Art, Morley Coll, Norwich Sch of Art, Portsmouth Poly, Ravensbourne Coll of Art and Design, The Royal Acad Schs, Sainsbury Centre for the Visual Arts Univ of E Anglia; memb Visual Art Panel Eastern Arts Assoc 1983-88, selector for post of Artist in Residence Lady Lodge Arts Centre Peterborough 1983, memb Exec Ctee for Tolly Cobbold/Eastern Arts 5th Nat Exhibition 1984-86, curator and selector A Spiritual Dimension 1986-90, Academic and Mgmnt Bds Blackheath Sch of Art 1987-89; solo exhibitions: House Gallery London 1977, Angela Flowers Gallery 1983, The Minories Colchester 1984, Newcastle Poly Art Gallery 1984, Arcade Gallery Harrogate 1984, Drawing Schs Gallery Eton Coll 1984, The Fermoy Centre Art Gallery King's Lynn 1986, Artist in Residence Kings' Lynn Festival (All Saints' Church with The Fermoy Centre) 1986, Artist in Residence Gaywood Park HS King's Lynn 1987, Great St Mary's Cambridge 1989, Thumb Gallery London 1990; gp exhibitions incl: Goldsmiths' (S London Art Gallery) 1972, Royal Acad Summer exhibition 1977, 1988, 1990, Art for Today (Portsmouth Festival) 1979, Tolly Cobbold/Eastern Arts 3rd Nat Exhibition, Small is Beautiful (Angela Flowers Gallery) 1983, The Falconbridge Cross Highgate URC 1984, Art for Everywhere (Peterborough Museum and Art Gallery) 1985, A Spiritual dimension touring exhibition 1989 and 1990, LA Art Fair (Thumb Gallery) 1989, New Icons touring exhibition 1989-90, Academicians' Choice (London Contemporary Arts and the Eye Gallery Bristol) 1990, London to Atlanta (Atlanta Thumb Gallery) 1990; work in several public collections, *awards* Walter Newrath Art History award 1972, Arts Cncl minor award 1976, Eastern Arts Assoc award 1977, Tolly Cobbold E Arts regnl prize 1981, E Vincent Harris award for mural decoration 1984, prize winner 3 Int Exhibition of Miniature Art (Del Bello Gallery Toronto) 1988; *Style—* Brian Falconbridge, Esq; Thumb Gallery, 38 Lexington St, Corner of Silver Place, Soho, London W1R 3HR (☎ 071 439 7319/7343)

FALCONER, Hon Sir Douglas William Falconer; MBE (1946), QC (1967); s of William Falconer (d 1956), of South Shields; *b* 20 Sept 1914; *Educ* Westoe S Shields, Univ of Durham; *m* 1941, Joan Beryl Argent (d 1989), da of late Archibald Samuel Bishop, of Hagley, Worcs (d 1961); 1 s (Ian), 1 da (Sally); *Career* called to the Bar Middle Temple 1950, appointed to exercise appellate jurisdiction of Bd of Trade under Trade Marks Act 1970, chm Patent Bar Assoc 1971-80, bencher Middle Temple 1972; memb Senate: of Four Inns of Court 1973-74, of Four Inns of Court and Bar 1974-77; memb Standing Advsy Ctee: on Patents 1975-79, on Trade Marks 1975-79; judge of High Ct of Justice 1981-89; *Recreations* music, theatre; *Style—* Hon Sir Douglas Falconer, MBE, QC; Ridgewell House, West St, Reigate, Surrey RH2 9BZ

FALCONER, Peter Serrell; s of Thomas Falconer, FRIBA (eighth in descent from Patrick Falconer of Newton, unc of 1 Lord Falconer of Halkerton, S Lordship cr 1646, which was subsequently held by the Earls of Kintore, with the death of the tenth of whom in 1966 the Lordship became dormant; Peter is the presumed heir), and Florence Edith Falconer; *b* 7 March 1916; *Educ* Bloxham; *m* 1941, Mary, da of Rev C Hodson; 3 s, 1 da; *Career* architect; FRIBA; *Style—* Peter Falconer, Esq; St Francis, Minchinhampton, Glos (☎ 0453 882188, fax 0452 814044)

FALCONER OF HALKERTON, Lordship (S 1646); *see*: Falconer, Peter Serrell

FALDO, Nicholas Alexander (Nick); MBE (1988); s of George Arthur Faldo, of Welwyn Garden City, Herts, and Joyce, *née* Smalley; *b* 18 July 1957; *Educ* Sir Fredric Osborne Sch Welwyn Garden City; *m* 3 Jan 1986, Gillian, da of Gerald Bennett; 1 s (Matthew Alexander b 17 March 1989), 1 da (Natalie Lauren b 18 Sept 1986); *Career* professional golfer; amateur victories: Br Youths' Open 1975, English Championship 1975; tournament victories since turning professional 1976: Skol Lager 1977, Br PGA Championship 1978, 1980, 1981 and 1989, ICL Tournament SA 1979, Haig Whisky 1982, French Open 1983, 1988 and 1989, Martini Int 1983, Car Care Plan Int 1983 and 1984, Lawrence Batley Int 1983, Swiss Open 1983, Sea Pines Heritage Classic USA 1984, Spanish Open 1987, Br Open 1987 and 1990, Volvo Masters 1988, US Masters 1989 and 1990, Suntory World Match-Play 1989, England Boy's 1974, England int 1975-, with Br team 1975; memb Ryder Cup team: 1977, 1979, 1981, 1983, 1985 (winners), 1987 (winners) and 1989 (winners); memb England team Dunhill Cup (winners) 1987; rookie of the year 1977, finished top Order of Merit 1983, BBC Sports Personality of the Year 1989; *Recreations* fly-fishing, woodwork, photography; *Style—* Nick Faldo, Esq, MBE; c/o John Simpson, IMG, Pier House, Strand-on-the-Green, London W4 3NN (☎ 081 994 1444, fax 081 994 9606)

FALETAU, Inoke Fotu; 2 s of 'Akau'ola Siosateki Faletau (d 1954), and Cecelia, *née* Lyden (d 1962); *b* 24 June 1937; *Educ* St Peters Sch, Auckland GS NZ, Tonga HS, Univ of Wales, Univ of Manchester; *m* 'Evelini Ma'ata Hurrell; 3 s, 3 da; *Career* diplomat; High Cmmr for Tonga to UK 1972-82 (concurrent ambass to: W Germany, France, Luxembourg, Netherlands, Belgium, Denmark, Italy, USSR, USA); dir Mgmnt Devpt Programme Cwlth Secretariat 1983-84, dir Cwlth Fndn 1985-; hon fell Univ Coll Swansea 1990; Kt Grand Cross: Order of Merit (W Germany) 1980, Order of Merit (Luxembourg) 1982; *Clubs* Royal Over-Seas League, Royal Cwlth Soc; *Style—* Inoke Faletau, Esq; Commonwealth Foundation, Marlborough House, Pall Mall, London SW1Y 5HY (☎ 071 930 3783/4)

FALK, Brian Geoffrey; s of Lt Col Geoffrey Ferdinand Falk (d 1955), and Kathleen Falk (d 1982); *b* 8 Sept 1930; *Educ* Bryanston, Architectural Assoc (AA Dip), Havard Univ (McP); *m* 7 Nov 1959, Gunilla Elisabet, da of Haåkon Wilhelm Adenius (d 1981), of Wasa Ordren; 3 s (Benedict b 1962, Magnus b 1963, Jasper b 1967); *Career* dir: Covell Matthews & Ptnrs and Covell Matthews Partnership International 1963-82, Falk Assocs Ltd 1983-, Moxley Jenner & Partners (London) Ltd 1988-; chm Assoc Conslt Architects 1976-77, memb Haringey Borough Cncl 1968-78; Freeman of City of London 1975; RIBA 1955, MRTPI 1959, MUSA 1965, MAAK 1965, SADG 1954; *Recreations* gardening, travelling, sketching; *Style—* Brian Falk, Esq; High House, Bressingham, Diss IP22 2AP (☎ 0379 88388); High House Studio, Bressingham, Diss IP22 2AP; 1 Hobhouse Ct, Suffolk Place, London SW1Y 4HH

FALK, Fergus Antony; TD (1979); s of Leonard Solomon Falk, lately of 4A Abercorn Place, London, and Meg, *née* Cohen (d 1970); *b* 30 Aug 1941; *Educ* Uppingham, Univ of London (BSc); *m* 5 May 1973, Vivian Dundas, da of Leonard Cockburn Dundas Irvine (d 1968, Surgn-Capt RNVR) of Hove; 1 s (Sebastian b 1980), 2 da (Harriet b 1976, Annabel b 1979); *Career* Maj HAC 1961-80; dept mangr: John Lewis and Co Ltd 1959-63, C Ulysses Williams Ltd 1964-65, Touche Ross and Co 1965- (ptnr 1975); treas Islington South and Finsbury Cons Assoc 1974-76 (Radwinter Branch 1976-79); memb: Ct of Assistants HAC 1975-, Ct of Common Cncl 1984-; candidate (C) Islington Borough Elections 1974; memb Worshipful Co of CA; ACA 1969, FCA 1973; *Recreations* small children, gardening; *Clubs* HAC, MCC, Farringdon Ward, City Livery, Aldeburgh Yacht; *Style—* Fergus Falk, Esq, TD; Canfield Moat, Little Canfield, Gt Dunmow, Essex CM6 1TD (☎ 0371 872565); Hill House, 1 Little New St, London EC4A 3TR (☎ 071 936 3000, fax 071 936 2638)

FALK, Sir Roger Salis; OBE (Mil 1945); s of Lionel David Falk (d 1949), of London; *b* 22 June 1910; *Educ* Haileybury, Univ of Geneva; *m* 1938, Margaret Helen (d 1958), da of Albert Stroud (d 1946); 1 s, 2 da; *Career* served WWII Wing Cdr RAFVR 1943; md D J Keymer & Co 1945-49 (dir 1935-49, vice chm 1950); chm: P E International Ltd 1973-76, London Board Provincial Insurance Co Ltd; dir gen BETRO 1950-52, dep chm Gaming Bd of GB 1978-81, vice pres Sadlers Wells Fndn 1986- (chm 1976-86); memb: Cncl of Industl Design 1958-67, Monopolies Cmmn 1965-79, Cncl RSA 1968-74, Cncl Imperial Soc of Kts Bachelor 1979-; life govr Haileybury 1971- (memb Cncl 1978-); Hon DLitt City Univ 1984; CBIM; kt 1969; *Books* Business of Management (5 edns, 1961); *Recreations* music, writing, reading; *Clubs* Garrick, MCC; *Style—* Sir Roger Falk, OBE; 603 Beatty House, Dolphin Square, London SW1 (☎ 071 828 3752)

FALKENDER, Baroness (Life Peeress UK 1974), of West Haddon, Co Northants; Marcia Matilda Falkender; *née* Field; CBE (1970); da of Harry Field; assumed by deed poll 1974 surname Falkender in lieu of Williams; *b* 10 March 1932; *Educ* Queen Mary Coll London (BA); *m* 1955 (m dis 1960), George Edmund Charles Williams; issue by Walter Frederick Terry (d 1991); 2 s; *Career* private sec Morgan Phillips (gen sec of Labour Pty) 1955-56; private and political sec to Rt Hon Lord Wilson of Rievaulx, formerly Rt Hon Sir Harold Wilson, KG, OBE, MP; political columnist Mail on Sunday 1983-, memb Screen Advisory Cncl and Film Ctee 1976-; dir Peckham Building Soc 1986-, chm Carwasbock Productions 1989-; pres Tstees of UK Ctee of UNIFEM 1989-, lay govr Queen Mary and Westfield Coll London 1988-; *Books* Inside No 10 (1972), Perspective on Downing Street (1983); *Recreations* reading, film; *Clubs* Reform; *Style—* The Rt Hon Lady Falkender, CBE; 3 Wyndham Mews, Upper Montagu St, London W1

FALKINER, Benjamin Simon Patrick; s and h of Sir Edmond Charles Falkiner, of Herts, and Janet Iris, *née* Darby; *b* 16 Jan 1962; *Educ* Queen Elizabeth Boys' Sch Barnet; *Career* retail outlet mangr; *Recreations* rugby, cricket, music (drummer), youth work; *Clubs* Old Elizabethans Rugby Football, Old Elizabethans Cricket; *Style—* Benjamin Falkiner, Esq; 80 Crawford Rd, Hatfield, Herts (☎ 0707 266031); 50 Coleridge Rd, Crouch End (☎ 081 340 1845)

FALKINER, Sir Edmond Charles; 9 Bt (I 1778), of Annmount, Cork; s of Sir Terence Falkiner, 8 Bt (d 1987); *b* 24 June 1938; *Educ* Downside; *m* 8 Oct 1960, Janet Iris, da of Arthur Edward Bruce Darby, of The Park, Stoke Lacey, Bromyard, Herefords; 2 s (Benjamin b 1962, Matthew b 1964); *Heir* s, Benjamin Simon Patrick Falkiner, *qv*; *Career* pacifist; probation officer 1968-; *Clubs* Ronnie Scott's; *Style—* Sir Edmond Falkiner, Bt; 111 Wood St, Barnet, Herts EN5 4BX (☎ 081 440 2426)

FALKLAND, Capt the Master of; Hon (Lucius) Alexander Plantagenet Cary; s and h of 15 Viscount of Falkland, *qv*; *b* 1 Feb 1963; *Educ* Westminster, Loretto, RMA Sandhurst; *Career* Capt 2 Bn Scots Guards; *Recreations* drawing, skiing, tennis; *Clubs* Cavalry and Guards'; *Style—* Capt The Master of Falkland

FALKLAND, 15 Viscount of (S 1620); Premier Viscount of Scotland; Lucius Edward William Plantagenet Cary; also 15 Lord Cary (S 1620); s of 14 Viscount (d 1984), and his 2 w Constance Mary, *née* Berry; *b* 8 May 1935; *Educ* Wellington Coll; *m* 1, 26 April 1962 (m dis 1990), Caroline Anne, da of late Lt Cdr Gerald Butler, DSC, RN, of Astron House, Ashton Keynes, Wilts; 1 s, 2 da (Hon Samantha b 1973, Hon Lucinda b 1974) (and 1 da decd); m 2, 12 Sept 1990, Nicole Mackey; *Heir* s, Master of Falkland, *qv*; *Career* 2 Lt 8 King's Royal Irish Hussars; journalist, theatrical agent and former chief exec C T Bowring Trading (Hldgs) Ltd; memb House of Lords Select Ctee Overseas Trade 1954-85; dep whip Social and Lib Democrats House of Lords 1988-; *Recreations* golf, cinema; *Clubs* Brooks's, Sunningdale Golf; *Style—* The Rt Hon Viscount of Falkland; House of Lords, London SW1

FALKNER, Sir (Donald) Keith; s of John Charles Falkner (d 1937), and Alice Hannah, *née* Wright (d 1928); *b* 1 March 1900; *Educ* New Coll Sch, Perse Sch, RCM, private study Berlin, Vienna, Paris; *m* 1930, Christabel Margaret (d 1990), o da of Thomas Fletcher Fullard (d 1911); 2 da (Julia b 1936, Philippa b 1938); *Career* served WWI Sub Lt RNAS 1917-1919, served WWII Sqdn Ldr RAFVR 1940-45; asst lay vicar St Paul's Cathedral 1922-26; professional singer 1923-40 (lead in three Warner Bros musicals 1936-37: Mayfair Mel, The Singing Cop, Thistledown); music offr Br Cncl Italy 1946-50; prof of music Cornell Univ NY USA 1950-60, dir RCM 1960-74; jt artistic dir King's Lynn Festival 1981-83; ed Voice (with 24 contributors) 1983; Hon DMus (Oxon); ARCM, FRCM; Royal Humane Soc Medal for Life Saving at Sea 1918-19; kt 1967; *Recreations* present: golf, gardening; *Clubs* Athenaeum, MCC, Free Foresters, RAC, Norfolk County; *Style—* Sir Keith Falkner; Low Cottages, Ilketshall St Margaret, Bungay, Suffolk (☎ 0986 2573)

FALKNER, (Frederic Sherard) Neil; s of Francis Sherard Melville Falkner (d 1972), of Louth, Lincs, and Doris Mary, *née* Matthews; *b* 28 Aug 1927; *Educ* Northampton Sch, Lincoln Coll Oxford (MA), Oberlin Coll Ohio USA (MA); *m* 27 June 1951, Maria Luisa, da of Max Aub (d 1974), of Mexico City; 1 s (Martin b 1959), 2 da (Elaine b 1954, Lynne b 1956); *Career* mktg exec Procter & Gamble 1951-56, mktg mangr Mars 1956-61, chief exec Cheesebrough-Ponds 1961-66, ran own mfrg business 1966-77, chm and chief exec Development Capital Group 1977-89, dir Lazard Bros 1985-89, chm and chief exec FMS Partners 1989-; Liveryman Worshipful Co of Painter-Stainers 1971; *Recreations* music, medieval history; *Clubs* East India, City Livery; *Style—* Neil Falkner, Esq; 10 Emmanuel Road, Cambridge CB1 1JW (☎ 0223 461750)

FALKUS, Christopher Hugh; s of Hugh Edward Lance Falkus, *qv*, of Ravenglass, Cumbria, and Doris Marjorie Falkus (d 1980); *b* 13 Jan 1940; *Educ* St Boniface's Coll Plymouth, Univ Coll London (BA); *m* 1, 1965 (m dis 1976), (Ann) Margaret Mathias; 1 s (Justin b 21 Oct 1967), 1 da (Sarah b 9 Dec 1971); m 2, 28 May 1977, Gila Ann, da of Brig Francis Curtis, of Cambridge; 1 s Thomas (b 22 Feb 1981), 1 da (Helen b 28 Feb 1979); *Career* publisher; md Weidenfeld & Nicolson Ltd 1970-79, chm Methuen General 1980-88, publishing dir Weidenfeld & Nicolson 1989-; *Books* The Life and Times of Charles II (1971); *Recreations* watching cricket; *Clubs* Garrick, MCC; *Style—* Christopher Falkus, Esq; 89 Portland Rd, London W11 (☎ 071 229 2683); 91 Clapham High St, London SW4 (☎ 071 622 9933, fax 071 627 3361, telex 918066)

FALKUS, Hugh Edward Lance; s of James Everest Falkus (d 1959), and Alice, *née* Musgrove (d 1962); *b* 15 May 1917; *Educ* The East Anglian Sch Culford; *m* ; 2 s (Christopher, *qv*, Malcolm); *Career* former RAF fighter pilot; writer and film dir; films incl: Shark Island, Drake's England, Signals for Survival, The Gull Watchers, The Beachcombers, The Sign Readers, The Tender Trap, Portrait of a Happy Man, Highland Story, Animal War Animal Peace, Salmo the Leaper; film awards: Italia Prize, American Blue Ribbon, Royal Geographical Soc, Cherry Kearton Medal and Award; currently teaches game fishing and spey casting; *Books* Sea Trout Fishing, Salmon Fishing, Freshwater Fishing, Successful Angling, The Stolen Years, Nature Detective, Master of Cape Horn, Sydney Cove to Duntroon, Signals for Survival; *Recreations* fishing, shooting, sailing, oil painting; *Style—* Hugh Falkus, Esq; Cragg Cottage, Ravenglass, Cumbria CA18 1RT (☎ 0229 717247)

FALL, His Excellency Brian James Proetel; CMG (1984); s of John William Fall and Edith Juliet, *née* Proetel; *b* 13 Dec 1937; *Educ* St Paul's Sch, Magdalen Coll Oxford, Univ of Michigan Law Sch; *m* 1962, Delmar Alexandra Roos; 3 da; *Career* joined HM Dip Serv 1962, served in FO UN Dept 1963, Moscow 1965, Geneva 1968, Civil Serv Coll 1970, E Euro and Soviet Dept and Western Orgs Dept FO 1971, New York 1975, Harvard Univ Center for Int Affrs 1976, cnsllr Moscow 1977-79; head of

Energy, Sci and Space Dept FCO 1979-80; head of E Euro and Soviet Dept FCO 1980-81, princ private sec to Sec of State for Foreign and Cwlth Affrs 1981-84; dir private office, sec gen NATO 1984-86, asst under sec (Def) FCO 1986-88, min Washington 1988-89, high cmmr Ottawa 1989-; *Style*— His Excellency Mr Brian Fall, CMG; c/o Foreign & Commonwealth Office, King Charles St, London SW1

FALLA, Paul Stephen; s of late Brig Norris Stephen Falla, CMG, DSO, of Wellington, New Zealand, and Audrey Frances, *née* Stock; *b* 25 Oct 1913; *Educ* Wellington, Christ's Coll NZ, Balliol Coll Oxford; *m* 1958, Elizabeth Mary, *née* Shearer; 1 da; *Career* HM Foreign Service 1936-67, cnsllr (FO, FCO) 1950-67 (dep dir of Res 1958-67); editor Oxford English-Russian Dictionary published 1984; Scott Moncrieff Prize for translation from French 1972 and 1981, Schlegel-Tieck Prize for translation from German 1983; translated about 45 books from various languages on politics, history, art; FIL, fell Inst of Translation and Interpreting; *Recreations* reading (history, politics, philosophy, belles-lettres), studying languages; *Clubs* Travellers'; *Style*— P S Falla, Esq; 63 Freelands Rd, Bromley, Kent BR1 3HZ (☎ 081 460 4995)

FALLE, Sir Samuel (Sam); KCMG (1979, CMG 1964), KCVO (1972), DSC (1945); s of Theodore de Carteret Falle (d 1966), of Ickenham, Middx, and Hilda Falle (d 1979); *b* 19 Feb 1919; *Educ* Victoria Coll Jersey; *m* 1945, Merete, da of Paul Rosen, of Fredensborg, Denmark; 1 s, 3 da; *Career* RN 1937-48; FO 1948, Shiraz and Tehran 1949-52, Beirut 1952-55, Baghdad 1957-61, consul-gen Gothenburg 1961-63, head of UN Dept FO 1963; dep high cmmr: Kuala Lumpur Malaysia 1967, Aden 1967; ambass to Kuwait 1969-70, Br high cmmr in Singapore 1970-74, ambass to Sweden 1974-77, Br high cmmr to Nigeria 1977-78, ret; delegate Cmmn of the Euro Communities Algeria 1979-82, conslt chm of the Euro Communities Zambia 1983; *Recreations* swimming, skiing, languages; *Style*— Sir Sam Falle, KCMG, KCVO, DSC; Slattna, 57030 Mariannelund, Sweden

FALLER, John Benson; s of Albert Faller (d 1967), and Eileen, *née* Couche (d 1976); *b* 26 Sept 1921; *Educ* Downside, Jesus Coll Cambridge (MA); *m* 1947, Mary, da of Sir Joseph Sheridan (d 1964, former Chief Justice Kenya and pres Court of Appeal for E Africa); 1 s (decd), 2 da (Juliet b 1948 (m T L Hunter-Tilney, o s of Dame Guinevere Tilney, DBE, and stepson of Sir John Tilney), Clare b 1952 (m S M Copeman, s of late Vice Adm Sir Nicholas Copeman, KBE, CB, DSC, and Lady Copeman); *Career* served WWII Lt Coldstream Gds, N Africa and Italy (wounded 1944); formerly chm Henry W Peabody Grain Ltd and its subsid; *Recreations* shooting; *Clubs* Boodle's, MCC; *Style*— J B Faller, Esq; Benton House, Worplesdon Hill, nr Woking, Surrey GU22 0QU

FALLON, Ivan Gregory; s of Padraic Joseph Fallon (d 1974), and Dorothea, *née* Maher (d 1985); *b* 26 June 1944; *Educ* St Peter's Coll Wexford, Trinity Coll Dublin (BBS); *m* 14 Jan 1967, Susan Mary, da of Dr Robert Francis Lurring, of Kidderminster; 1 s (Padraic Robert b 1974), 2 da (Tania Helen b 1967, Lara Catherine b 1970); *Career* Irish Times 1964-66, Thomson Provincial Newspapers 1966-67, Daily Mirror 1967-68, Sunday Telegraph 1968-84, city ed Sunday Telegraph 1979-84, dep ed Sunday Times 1984-; govr Univ of Buckingham; tstee: Project Tst 1984, Generation Tst, Guy's; pres Trinity Coll Dublin Business Alumni London Chapter; FRSA 1989; *Books* DeLorean: The Rise and Fall of a Dream Maker (with James Srodes, 1983), Takeovers (with James Srodes, 1987), The Brothers: The Rise of Saatchi and Saatchi (1988); *Recreations* squash, tennis; *Clubs* Beefsteak, RAC; *Style*— Ivan Fallon, Esq; The Sunday Times, 1 Pennington St, Wapping, London (☎ 071 782 5000)

FALLON, (James) Jim; s of Thomas Fallon (d 1987), of Cambuslang, and Elizabeth, *née* Gormley (d 1986); *b* 24 March 1950; *Educ* Holy Cross HS Hamilton, Glasgow Royal Infirmary Sch of Physiotherapy; *m* 4 June 1976, Marilyn, da of William Weir; 1 s (Steven b 8 May 1979), 1 da (Gemma b 4 Jan 1983); *Career* professional football coach and physiotherapist; Clydebank FC: player 1968-86, 620 League appearances, Div 2 Championship medal 1976, Spring Cup runners-up medal 1975-76, coach 1986-, coached team to Scottish Cup semi-final 1990; Scotland: schoolboy caps 1966-68, semi-professional caps 1979-82; physiotherapist 1974-; MCSP 1974; *Recreations* reading, swimming; *Style*— Jim Fallon, Esq; 16 Thorndene, Eldelslie, Renfrewshire PA5 9DA (☎ 0505 25524); Clydebank FC, New Kilbowie Park, Clydebank (☎ 041 952 2887/2800)

FALLON, Michael Cathel; MP (C) Darlington 1983-; s of Martin Fallon, OBE, and Hazel Fallon; *b* 14 May 1952; *Educ* Univ of St Andrews (MA); *m* 1986, Wendy Elizabeth, da of Peter Payne, of Holme-on-Spalding Moor, Yorkshire: 2 s (Peter, Timothy Bernard Michael b 1990); *Career* lectr, advsr to Rt Hon Lord Carrington 1975-77, EEC desk offr CRD 1977-79, PPS to Rt Hon Cecil Parkinson, MP, sec of state for energy 1987-88, asst govt whip 1988-90, Parliamentary Under Sec Dept of Educn and Science 1990-; *Style*— Michael Fallon, Esq, MP; House of Commons, London SW1

FALLON, Padraic Matthew; s of Padraic Fallon (d 1974), and Dorothea, *née* Maher (d 1985); *b* 21 Sept 1946; *Educ* St Peter's Coll Wexford, Blackrock Coll Co Dublin, Trinity Coll Dublin (BA); *m* 8 April 1972, Gillian Elizabeth, da of Graham Hellyer, of Drewton Manor, South Cave, N Humberside; 1 s (Jolyon b 1975), 3 da (Nicola b 1977, Harriet b 1980, Annabel (twin) b 1980); *Career* fin reporter: Thomson City Office London 1969-70, Daily Mirror 1970-72; City pages Daily Mail 1972-74, seconded as managing ed ME Money Beirut 1974, ed Euromoney Magazine 1974-86; Euromoney Publications PLC (formerly Euromoney Publications Ltd): dir 1975, dep md 1982, md 1985, chief exec 1989; non-exec dir: Assoc Newspapers Holdings Ltd (formerly Assoc Newspapers Holdings plc), Allied Irish Banks plc, Harmsworth Media Ltd; pres Latin American Financial Publications Inc, memb Creditanstalt Advsy Bd; *Recreations* fishing, shooting, tennis; *Clubs* Kildare Street and Univ (overseas memb); *Style*— Padraic Fallon, Esq; 20 Lower Addison Gardens, London W14 8BQ (☎ 071 602 1253); Euromoney Publications PLC, Nestor House, Playhouse Yard, London EC4V 5EX (☎ 071 779 8888/8556, fax 071 236 6937)

FALLOWELL, Duncan Richard; s of Thomas Edgar Fallowell, of Crowthorne, Berkshire, and La Croix Valmer, France, and Celia, *née* Waller; *b* 26 Sept 1948; *Educ* Palmer's Sch, St Paul's, Magdalen Coll Oxford; *Career* author; *Books* Drug Tales (1979), April Ashley's Odyssey (1982), Satyrday (1986), The Underbelly (1987), To Noto (1989); *Style*— Duncan Fallowell, Esq; 44 Leamington Rd Villas, London W11

FALLOWFIELD, Richard Gordon; s of Capt Walter Herman Gordon Fallowfield, RN (d 1954), and Elizabeth Burnett, *née* Baker (d 1956); *b* 25 Jan 1935; *Educ* Marlborough; *m* 21 Sept 1963, Elfrida Charlotte, da of Sir Timothy Calvert Eden, 8 Bt (d 1963); 2 s (Timothy Gordon b 1965, Nicholas John b 1967), 1 da (Laura Louise b 1974); *Career* Capt Argyll and Sutherland Highlanders 1952-54; dir: Young and Rubicam Inc 1973-80, McCann Erickson Ltd 1980-84; dep chm Grandfield Rork Collins 1985-; memb IPA; *Recreations* squash, tennis, walking, reading biographies; *Style*— Richard Fallowfield, Esq; 78 West Side, Clapham Common, London SW4 9AY (☎ 071 228 4428); Prestige House, 14-18 Holborn, London EC1 (☎ 071 242 2002)

FALLSIDE, Prof Frank; s of William Thomas Fallside (d 1979), of Edinburgh, and Daisy Helen Kinnear Madden Fallside (d 1981); no other known bearers of the name Fallside; *b* 2 Jan 1932; *Educ* George Heriot's Sch Edinburgh, Univ of Edinburgh (BSc), Univ of Wales (PhD), Univ of Cambridge (MA); *m* 8 March 1958, Maureen Helen, da of Matthew Michael Couttie (d 1969), of Tir-Nam-Oig, Portland, Victoria, Aust; 2 s (David b 1958, Hamish b 1967), 1 da (Helen b 1973); *Career* Univ of Cambridge: prof of info engrg 1983, head of Info Engrg Div 1988; fell Trinity Hall 1962; *Recreations* sailing, maritime history; *Style*— Prof Frank Fallside; 37 Earl St, Cambridge (☎ 0223 353966); Cambridge University, Engineering Dept, Trumpington St, Cambridge (☎ 0223 332752)

FALMOUTH, 9 Viscount (GB 1720); George Hugh Boscawen; also 26 Baron Le Despencer (E 1264) and Baron Boscawen-Rose (GB 1720); patron of five livings; 2 s of 8 Viscount (d 1962), and Mary Margaret Desirée, Viscountess Falmouth (d 1985); *b* 31 Oct 1919; *Educ* Eton, Trinity Coll Cambridge; *m* 9 May 1953, (Beryl) Elizabeth Price, er da of Arthur Harold Browne, of Spring Field, W Peckham, Kent; 4 s (Hon Evelyn b 1955, Hon Nicholas b 1957, Hon Charles b 1958, Hon Vere b 1964); *Heir* s, Hon Evelyn Boscawen b 1955; *Career* served WWII, Italy (despatches, wounded), Capt Coldstream Gds; Lord Lt of Cornwall 1977- (DL 1968); Master Clockmakers Co 1986; *Clubs* Athenaeum, Army and Navy; *Style*— The Rt Hon Viscount Falmouth; Tregothnan, Truro, Cornwall

FANCOURT, Dr Graham John; s of Leonard Frank Fancourt (d 1982), of Gidea Park, Essex, and Iris, *née* Anscombe; *b* 23 Feb 1953; *Educ* Brentwood Sch, Univ of London (MB BS); *m* 22 July 1978, Julie Valerie, da of Leslie Thomas, of Brentwood, Essex; *Career* conslt physician: Leicester Gen Hosp, Glenficlogen, Loughborough Gen Hospital, Groby Rd Hosp, Coalville Community Hosp; clinical tutor Univ of Leicester; pubns on respiratory med and physiology of ageing; memb BMA, MRCS 1977, MRCP 1980; *Style*— Dr Graham Fancourt; Leicester General Hosp, Gwendolen Rd, Leicester LE5 4PW (☎ 0533 490490)

FANE, Hon Mrs Mountjoy; Agatha Isabel; da of Lt-Col Arthur Acland-Hood-Reynardson, OBE (2 s of Sir Alexander Fuller-Acland-Hood, 3 Bt); *b* 3 Oct 1903; *m* 29 April 1926, Lt-Col Hon Mountjoy John Charles Wedderburn Fane, TD (d 1963), s of 13 Earl of Westmorland; 1 s, 1 da; *Style*— The Hon Mrs Mountjoy Fane; The Thatched House, Teigh, Oakham, Leics

FANE, Hon Harry St Clair; 2 s of 15 Earl of Westmorland; *b* 19 March 1953; *Educ* Harrow; *m* 6 Jan 1984, Tessa, da of Capt Michael Philip Forsyth-Forrest; 1 s (Sam Michael David b 1989), 1 da (Sophie Jane b 1987); *Career* page of honour to HM The Queen 1966-68; *Style*— The Hon Harry Fane

FANE, Hon Julian Charles; s of 14 Earl of Westmorland (d 1948), and Diana (d 1983), da of 4 and last Baron Ribblesdale (d 1925); *b* 25 May 1927; *Educ* Harrow; *m* 1976, Gillian, yr da of John Kidston Swire and sis of Sir John and Sir Adrian Swire of the Far East trading empire; *Career* author of many books incl: Morning, Best Friends and Hope Cottage; FRSL 1974; *Style*— The Hon Julian Fane; Rotten Row House, Lewes, E Sussex BN7 1TN

FANE, Julian Francis; JP (Lincs 1978); s of Lt Francis Fane, RN (4 in descent from Hon Henry Fane, MP, 2 s of 8 Earl of Westmorland); *b* 2 Oct 1938; *Educ* Marlborough, Emmanuel Coll Cambridge (MA 1966); *m* 5 June 1965, (Mary) Julia, da of Michael William Allday, of the Shrubbery, Hartlebury, Worcs; 1 s, 1 da; *Career* farmer; High Sheriff Lincs 1981; *Style*— Julian Fane, Esq, JP; Fulbeck Manor, Grantham, Lincs

FANE, Col Julian Patrick; MC (1940, and bar 1945); o s of Col Cecil Fane, CMG, DSO (d 1960), by his wife, Gladys Dorothy, *née* MacGeorge (d 1983); *b* 17 Feb 1921; *Educ* Stowe, RMA Sandhurst; *m* 1, 27 April 1949, Lady Ann Mary Lowther (d 23 Aug 1956), da of Anthony Edward, Viscount Lowther, s of 6 Earl of Lonsdale; 1 s, 1 da; m 2, 1959, Diana Ewart, da of Ivan Hill; 1 s, 1 da; *Career* 2 Lt Gloucestershire Regt 1939, served WWII 2 Bn, GHQ Liaison Regt and Staff (despatches), 12 Royal Lancers 1946, Life Gds 1960, ret 1969; former dir: Samuel Montagu & Co, Orion Bank Ltd; ret; Croix de Guerre 1943; *Recreations* shooting, gardening; *Style*— Col Julian Fane, MC; Winterley House, Inkpen Road, Kintbury, Berks (☎ 04884 357)

FANE, Vere John Alexander; s of John Lionel Richards Fane (d 1945; whose gf Robert was 7 s of Hon Henry Fane, 2 s of 8 Earl of Westmorland), and Barbara, da of Falconer Wallace of Candacraig; *b* 21 April 1935; *Educ* Eton, Trinity Coll Cambridge; *m* 30 May 1964, Tessa Helen Murray, o da of John Murray Prain, DSO, OBE, DL, and Helen, *née* Skene; 1 s (Rupert b 1967), 1 da (Miranda b 1968); *Career* former Lt Coldstream Gds; previously chm Wallace Brothers & Co (Hldgs); dep chm D A L Gp plc; *Recreations* shooting, adventure; *Clubs* White's, Pratt's, Leander, Royal and Ancient, Swinley; *Style*— Vere Fane, Esq; 7 Cavendish Sq, London W1

FANE GLADWIN, Col Peter Francis; OBE (1954, MBE 1951); s of Ralph Hamilton Fane Gladwin, Scots Gd (ka 1914), and Isabelle Mary, *née* Douglas-Dick later Mrs Fletcher (d 1956); *b* 27 Feb 1915; *Educ* Ampleforth, RMC Sandhurst; *Career* cmmnd Scots Gds 1935, served W Desert 1941 (wounded), cmd 1 Bn Scots Gds 1951, Col 1959, ret 1963; Highland TA Assoc 1963-81; memb Queens Bodyguard for Scotland Royal Co of Archers (non active list); Cadet Cmdt Argyll and Bute 1963-79, chm W Loch Fyne Community Cncl 1970-76, memb Children's Panel Argyll and Bute, pres SSAFA Argyll and Bute, gen cmmr of income tax 1974; fell Royal Cwlth Soc, FSA Scotland, memb Cncl for Scottish Archaeology; memb High Order of St Sebastianus of Schutzenbund of Germany; *Books* archaeological papers: Excavations on the Line of the Roman Wall in Hadrian's Camp Carlisle (1980), The Solar Alignment at Brainport Bay Minard Argyll (1985); *Clubs* New (Edinburgh); *Style*— Col Peter Fane Gladwin, OBE; Braigh Varr, Minard, Argyll, Scotland PA32 (☎ 0546 86217)

FANE TREFUSIS, Hon Charles Patrick Rolle; s and h of 22 Baron Clinton; *b* 21 March 1962; *Style*— Hon Charles Fane Trefusis

FANNER, His Hon Judge Peter Duncan; s of Robert William Hodges Fanner (d 1945), slr, of Sheffield, and Doris Kitty, *née* Whiffin (d 1981); *b* 29 May 1926; *Educ* Pangbourne Coll; *m* 23 April 1949, Sheila Eveline, da of George England, of Bromley (d 1946); 1 s (Roger b 1953), 1 da (Elizabeth b 1957); *Career* pilot Fleet Air Arm, Lt (A) RNVR; admitted slr 1951, dep clerk to the Justices Gore div 1952-56, clerk to Justices Bath 1956-72, memb Cncl of Justices Clerks Soc 1966-72, assessor memb Departmental Ctee on Liquor Licensing 1971-72, Met Stipendiary Magistrate 1972-86, dep circuit judge 1974-80, rec Crown Ct 1980-86; *Style*— His Honour Judge Fanner; Bristol Crown Court

FANNIN, Thomas Francis; s of Robert Fannin (d 1972), of Lambeg, Co Antrim, N Ireland, and Jean, *née* Morrison (d 1978); *b* 16 Aug 1938; *Educ* Ballymena Acad, FRCS Edin, Queen's University Belfast (MB BCh, MD); *m* 4 Aug 1964, Joy, da of James D Black, of 33 Harmony Hill, Lisburn, N Ireland; 3 s (David b 1968, Mark b 1970, Richard b 1974), 1 da (Ru b 1967); *Career* conslt neurosurgeon: Hallamshire, Sheffield 1977-79, Royal Victoria Hosp Belfast 1979-; SBNS; memb: Ulster Med Soc, Irish Neurological Assoc; *Recreations* walking, foreign travel, music; *Style*— Thomas Fannin, Esq; Dept of Neurosurgery, Royal Victoria Hospital, Belfast, N Ireland BT12 6BA (☎ 0232 240503)

FANSHAWE, Lady Beatrix Lilian Ethel; *née* Cadogan; er da of 6 Earl Cadogan, CBE (d 1933); *b* 12 May 1912; *m* 1, 22 Jan 1931 (m dis 1941), (Henry Peregrine) Rennie Hoare (d 1981), of Gasper House, Stourton, Warminster, Wilts, er s of Henry Hoare, of Ellisfield, Hants; 1 s, 1 da; m 2, 22 Aug 1942, Col Edward Leighton Fanshawe (d 1982), eldest s of Lt-Gen Sir Edward Arthur Fanshawe, KCB (d 1952), of Rathmore, Naas, Co Kildare; 2 da; *Style*— Lady Beatrix Fanshawe; 174 Cranmer Court, Sloane Ave, London SW3 3HF

FANSHAWE, Hon Mrs (Maura Clare); *née* Evans-Freke; er da of 11 Baron Carbery, *qv*; *b* 13 Sept 1946; *m* 10 Sept 1966, Richard Henry William Fanshawe, o s of Capt Peter Evelyn Fanshawe, CBE, RN; 1 da (Louisa Mary Constance b 1987); *Career* admin asst Royal Coll of Music 1987; Hon RCM 1986; *Style—* The Hon Mrs Fanshawe; 30 Bark Place, London W2 4AT

FANSHAWE, Peter Douglas; DFC; s of Brig George Hew Fanshawe, CBE (d 1974), and Mary Holme, *née* Wiggin (d 1969); *b* 28 Feb 1930; *Educ* Ampleforth, RMA Sandhurst; *m* 18 June 1955, Clemency Mary Marcia, da of Lt-Col Rudolph Philip Elwes, OBE, MC (d 1962); 3 s (John b 1956, Damian b 1959, Anthony b 1964), 1 da (Susanna b 1961); *Career* enlisted 1948, cmmnd the Queens Bays, 2 Dragoon Gds 1950, seconded 1 RTR, served Korean War 1952-53, attached USAF 1953; Distinguished Flying Cross and Air Medal (USA); dir UMECO Hldgs Gp 1969-77, fndr dir James Yorke Hldgs 1976-; *Recreations* gardening, photography, conservation; *Style—* Peter Fanshawe, Esq, DFC; Welltown Manor, Boscastle, Cornwall PL35 0DY (☎ 08405 242); James Yorke Holdings Ltd, Yorke House, Corpus Street, Cheltenham, Gloucestershire GL52 6XH (☎ 0242 584224, fax 0242 222445, telex 43269 ROMPAC G)

FANSHAWE OF RICHMOND, Baron (Life Peer UK 1983), of South Cerney, Co Glos; Sir Anthony Henry Fanshawe Royle; KCMG (1974); er s of Sir Lancelot Carrington Royle, KBE (d 1978), and Barbara Rachel, *née* Haldin (d 1977); *b* 27 March 1927; *Educ* Harrow, RMA Sandhurst; *m* 1957, Shirley, da of John Ramsay Worthington (d 1953); 2 da (Hon Susannah Caroline Fanshawe b 1960, Hon Lucinda Katherine Fanshawe b 1962); *Career* served with Life Gds in Germany, Egypt, Palestine and Transjordan 1945-48, 21 SAS Regt (TA) 1948-51; MP (C) Richmond (Surrey) 1959-83, PPS to: under-sec of state for the Colonies 1960, sec of state for Air 1960-62, min of Aviation 1962-64; memb Assembly Cncl of Europe and WEU 1965-67, oppn whip 1967-70, Parly under-sec of state 1970-74, vice chm Cons Party Orgn and chm Cons Int Off 1979-84; awarded Most Esteemed Family Order of Brunei (1st class); *Clubs* Pratt's, White's, Brooks's; *Style—* The Rt Hon Lord Fanshawe of Richmond, KCMG; House of Lords, London SW1

FANTONI, Barry Ernest; s of late Peter Nello Secondo Fantoni, of 74 Dumbarton Ct, London SW2, and Sarah Catherine, *née* Deverell; *b* 28 Feb 1940; *Educ* Archbishop Temple Sch, Camberwell Sch of Arts & Crafts; *m* 1972, Teresa Frances, da of Col Charles James Reidy, OBE, of 52 Carlyle Rd, Egbaston, Birmingham; *Career* writer, artist, musician and broadcaster; memb Ed Staff Private Eye 1963; cartoonist: The Listener 1968, Times Diary 1983; dir: Barry Fantoni Merchandising Co Ltd 1985, Snartz 1989; *Clubs* Chelsea Arts, Stocks; *Style—* Barry Fantoni, Esq; Abner Stein, 10 Roland Gardens, London SW7 3PH

FARAJ, Mohammed; s of Faiq Faraj, of Baghadad, Iraq, and Hassiba Amin (d 1978); *b* 21 July 1947; *Educ* Coll of Engrg Univ of Baghdad Iraq (BSc), Inst of Planning Studies Univ of Nottingham (MA); *Career* architect; conslt firm Iraq 1968-70, James Cubitt & Ptnrs London 1973-80, conslt Design Works London 1980-; memb: ARCUK, RIBA 1982, RTPI 1984; *Recreations* tennis, keep fit, photography; *Style—* Mohammed Faraj, Esq; Designworks, 84 Cheviot Gardens, London NW2 1QA

FARAM, Hon Mrs (Felicity Lilla); *née* Wallace; o da of Baroness Dudley *qv*, and Guy Raymond Hill Wallace (d 1967); *b* 14 Feb 1944; *m* 29 July 1967, Philip Neil Faram, eldest s of Ewart Faram, of Penkhull, Stoke-on-Trent; 3 s; *Style—* The Hon Mrs Faram; Heath Hill, Queenhill, Upton-on-Severn, Worcs

FARARA, Katharine Georgia (Kate); da of Christopher John Farara, of Guildford, Surrey, and Alison Mary, *née* Duguid; *b* 19 Nov 1962; *Educ* Queen Elizabeth II Silver Jubilee Sch, Woking Sixth Form Coll, Newnham Coll Cambridge (BA); partner, Richard Michael Bruges, s of Maj Michael Bruges; *Career* J Walter Thompson: joined as graduate trainee 1984, appointed to assoc bd, youngest bd appointment 1989, currently dir i/c various accounts; memb Gen Mgmnt Ctee Nat Advertising Benevolent Soc; *Recreations* riding, playing flute and piano, travelling, contemporary literature; *Style—* Miss Kate Farara; J Walter Thompson Co Ltd, 40 Berkeley Square, London W1X 6AD (☎ 071 499 4040, fax 071 493 8432/8418)

FARBEY, Harry Alexander; s of Charles Solomon Farbey (d 1974), and Rose, *née* Schlesserman (d 1060); *b* 7 Sept 1921; *Educ* Orange Hill Sch Edgware; *m* 22 Dec 1948, Phyllis, da of Hyman Temkin (d 1950); 2 s (Roger Anthony b 25 April 1953, David Samuel b 1 July 1955); *Career* served WWII, RAF 1942-46; dir C S Farbey (London) Ltd mfrg silversmiths 1938-76, gen sec Trades Advsy Cncl of Br Jewry 1979- (ed of Trades Advsy Cncl Bulletin), gen sec assoc of Jewish Ex-servicemen and Women 1988-; OStJ 1966; Mayor Southgate Borough Cncl 1964-65 (memb 1958-65), pres Bowes Park Div St John Ambulance Brigade, treas Southgate Branch Cncl of Christians and Jews, chm Monash Branch Royal Br Legion, vice chm Govrs Southgate Coll; Freeman City of London 1980; *Recreations* stamp collecting, walking, antique sliver; *Style—* Harry A Farbey, Esq; 20 Pellipar Close, Palmers Green, London N13 4AG (☎ 081 886 8229), Ajex House, East Bank, London N16 5RT (☎ 081 800 2844)

FARINGDON, 3 Baron (UK 1916); Sir Charles Michael Henderson; 3 Bt (UK 1902); s of Lt-Col Hon Michael Thomas Henderson (16/5 Lancers, d 1953), 2 gs of 1 Baron; suc unc 1977; *b* 3 July 1937; *Educ* Eton, Trinity Coll Cambridge (BA 1961); *m* 30 June 1959, Sarah Caroline, o da of Maj John Marjoribanks Eskdale Askew and Lady Susan Askew, *qv*; 3 s (Hon James b 1961, Hon Thomas b 1966, Hon Angus b 1969), 1 da (Hon Susannah b 1963); *Heir* s, Hon James Henderson; *Career* ptnr Cazenove & Co 1968-, chm Witan Investment plc 1980-; chm Bd of Govrs Royal Marsden Hosp 1980-85, hon treas Nat Art Collections Fund 1985-; *Style—* The Rt Hon the Lord Faringdon; Barnsley Park, Cirencester, Glos; Buscot Park, Faringdon, Oxon

FARIS, John Brian; s of William James Faris (d 1964), and Ivy Agnes, *née* Wheeler (d 1935); *b* 11 May 1934; *Educ* Eastbourne GS; *m* 20 June 1970, Patricia Millicent, *née* Bolongaro; 1 s (James Robert b 5 July 1972), 1 da (Alexandra Clare b 27 Aug 1974); *Career* Nat Serv RAEC 1952-54; chartered accountant Deloitte Plender Griffiths & Co 1960-73 (articled clerk 1954-60), ptnr Deloitte & Co 1973-, currently tech ptnr Coopers & Lybrand Deloitte; pt/t lectr in accounting NW Poly London 1961-64; ICAEW: frequent lectr 1968-, memb Tech Ctee 1986-90, chm Working Pty of Accounting Standards Ctee (reviewing SSAPIO) 1989-90; tstee King James's Charity; FCA (ACA 1960); *Recreations* talking and reading; *Style—* John Faris, Esq; 18 Tolmers Ave, Cuffley, Hertfordshire EN6 4QA (☎ 0707 873580); Coopers & Lybrand Deloitte, 128 Queen Victoria St, London EC4P 4JX (☎ 071 583 5000)

FARLEY, Prof Martyn Graham; s of Herbert Booth Farley (d 1985), of Bristol, and Hilda Gertrude, *née* Hendey (d 1963); *b* 27 Oct 1924; *Educ* Bristol Aeroplane Tech Coll, Merchant Venturers Tech Coll; *m* 20 March 1948, Freda, da of Fred Laugharne (d 1958), of Coventry; 2 s (Robin Laugharne b 1949 d 1984, Simon Laugharne b 1952), 1 da (Jane Elizabeth b 1958); *Career* Engine Div Bristol Aeroplane Co 1939-55: design apprentice, devpt engr, sr gas turbine designer; Bristol Siddeley Engines 1955-65: asst chief devpt engr, asst chief mechanical engr, chief devpt engr, chief engr (design and devpt); Rolls Royce Ltd 1965-75: chief engr, gen works mangr, mfrg and prodn dir, HQ exec to Vice Chm; RMCS and Cranfield Inst of Technol: prof of mgmnt sci 1975-85, vice chm Sch of Mgmnt and Mathematics 1984-, emeritus prof 1986-; chm: RC Ltd 1985-89, Br Management Data Foundation Ltd 1979-; dir: World Tech Ventures Ltd 1984-87, Aeronautical Trusts Ltd 1975-84 (chm 1984-88), Harwell Computer Power Ltd 1986-; memb Advsy Cncl RNEC 1988-; memb Ct: Univ of Loughborough 1977-89, Cranfield Inst 1977-, Brunel Univ 1977-80, Univ of Bath 1983-; pres: RAES 1983-84, CGIA Assoc 1984-, IProdE 1984-85; vice pres IIM 1979-; memb sr awards ctee CGLI 1979, hon memb C & G Cncl; hon fell: COLI 1990, American IIM, American Soc Mfrg Engrs (elected charter fell 1986), Aust IIM, Indian IProdE; hon CGIA; Freeman City of London, Liveryman Worshipful Co of Coachmakers and Harness Makers; CEng, FRAeS, FIProdE, FIMechE, FIIM, CBIM, MAIAA; *Recreations* gardening, walking, watching rowing and rugby; *Clubs* Athenaeum, Shrivenham, Ariel Rowing; *Style—* Prof Martyn Farley

FARLEY, Maryrose Christine; *née* Bateman; da of Cdr G A Bateman, RN, and M R Bateman, *née* Carruthers; *b* 16 March 1935; *Educ* The Abbey Malvern Wells Worcs, St Anne's Coll Oxford (MA); *Career* asst English mistress: Westonbirt Sch 1957-60, Ashford Sch Kent 1960-61, Lady Eleanor Holles Sch Middx 1961-64; head of English dept: Westonbirt Sch 1964-69, Brighton and Hove HS 1969-71; headmistress: Berkhamsted Sch for Girls 1971-80, Perse Sch for Girls 1980-89; *Recreations* theatre, opera, crosswords; *Style—* Mrs Maryrose Farley; Yerdley House, Long Compton, Shipston on Stour, Warwicks CV36 5LH (☎ 060 884 231)

FARMAN, Ian Glencairn Crisp; s of Stuart C Farman, of Chichester, W Sussex, and Joan G, *née* Wallace; *b* 27 Oct 1947; *Educ* Rugby, Univ of Southampton (LLB); *m* Susan Margaret; 4 da (Anna b 1975, Jenny b 1977, Christina b 1982, Isabel b 1984); *Career* Leslie & Goodwin 1970-72; dir: MPA Ltd 1972-84, William M Mercer Fraser Ltd 1984-; slr of The Supreme Court 1975-; *Recreations* sailing, tennis, wine; *Style—* Ian Farman, Esq; William M Mercer Fraser Ltd, Telford House, 14 Tothill St, London SW1H 9NB (☎ 071 222 9121, fax 071 222 6140)

FARMBROUGH, Stuart Charles Yalden; JP (1969); s of Charles Luton Farmbrough (d 1973), and Ida Mabel, *née* French (d 1976); *b* 24 July 1923; *Educ* Bedford Sch, Coll of Estate Mgmnt; *m* 28 Oct 1957, Jean Patricia, da of Godfrey Osborn Luton (d 1988); 2 s (Simon b 1959, James b 1961); *Career* Lt RE 1942-47, Madras Sappers and Miners IA 1945-47; self employed chartered surveyor Luton 1958-85; High Sheriff Beds 1984-85, dep Lt Beds 1989; pres Luton Dunstable and Dist C of C and Indust 1977, co cmmr St John Ambulance Beds 1987-90; FRICS 1952; *Recreations* country life, beagling; *Style—* Stuart Farmbrough, Esq, JP; Lee Cross, High St, Pavenham, Bedford MK43 7PD (☎ 02302 2403)

FARMER, Dr (Edwin) Bruce; s of Edwin Bruce Farmer, and Doris, *née* Darby; *b* 18 Sept 1936; *Educ* King Edward's Birmingham, Univ of Birmingham (BSc, PhD); *m* 1962, Beryl Ann, da of late William Alfred Griffiths, of Birmingham; 1 s (Andrew b 1967), 1 da (Amanda b 1969); *Career* dir and gen mangr Brico Metals 1967-69; md: Brico Engrg 1970-76 (tech dir 1969-70), Wellworthy Ltd 1976-81; dir: The Morgan Crucible Co plc 1981-83 (gp md 1983-), Morganite Aust Pty Ltd; CBIM, FRSA; *Recreations* squash, cricket, music; *Style—* Dr Bruce Farmer; Weston House, Bracken Close, Wonersh, Surrey GU5 0QS (☎ 0483 898182); The Morgan Crucible Co plc, Chariott House, Victoria St, Windsor, Berks SL4 1EP (☎ 0753 850331, telex 849025, fax 0753 850872)

FARMER, David William Horace; VRD (1969); s of Horace Edwin Farmer, OBE (d 1979), and Marion, *née* Blain; *b* 19 Oct 1935; *Educ* Tonbridge, St John's Coll Cambridge (MA); *m* 7 May 1988, Johanna Joy, da of Sir Peter Seligman, of Lymington, Hants; *Career* Lt RM 1954-56, RM res (Capt) 1956-69; admitted slr 1962; private practice Slaughter and May 1962-66, exec dir Roan Selection Trust (later AMAX) Group of Cos 1966-76; gp sec Lonrho Ltd 1976-79, dir Standard Chartered Merchant Bank (now Chartered West LB) 1984- (joined 1979); *Recreations* travel; *Style—* David Farmer, Esq, VRD; 29A Warwick Square, London SW1V 2AD (☎ 071 834 3541); 33-36 Gracechurch St, London EC3V 0AX (☎ 071 220 8492)

FARMER, Sir (Lovedin) George Thomas; s of Lovedin George Farmer (d 1952), of Droitwich Spa; *b* 13 May 1908; *Educ* Oxford HS, JDipMA; *m* 1, 1938, Editha Mary (d 1980), da of late F W Fisher, of Worcs; m 2, 1980, Muriel Gwendoline Mercer, *née* Pinfold; *Career* chm Rover Co Ltd 1963-73, dep chm Br Leyland Ltd 1970-73, chm Zenith Carburetter Co Ltd 1973-77, dir Rea Bros (IOM) Ltd 1976-88; pres: Birmingham C of C 1960-61, Soc of Manufacturers and Traders 1962-64 (dep pres 1964-65, chm Exec 1968-72), Loft Theatre; past memb ECGD (Bd of Trade); govr, chm Fin Ctee and chm Exec Cncl of Royal Shakespeare Theatre 1955-75; pro-chllr Univ of Birmingham 1966-75; Hon LLD Birmingham 1975; FCA; kt 1968; *Recreations* theatre, golf, fishing; *Clubs* Royal and Ancient; *Style—* Sir George Farmer; Longridge, The Chase, Ballakillowey, Colby, Isle of Man (☎ 0624 832603)

FARMER, Michael Keith; s of Frederick Charles Farmer, of London, and Winifred Nora, *née* Hartigan; *b* 5 April 1942; *Educ* Highgate Sch, Spöehrerschule Calw W Germany; *m* 1970 (m dis 1987); 2 da (Sonja b 1972, Ingrid b 1974); *Career* jt md: Interwood Ltd, H & F Investments Ltd, Stafford Engrg Co Ltd; chm Woodworking Machinery Suppliers Assoc 1988-; MInstD 1964; *Recreations* classical music, opera, walking; *Style—* Michael Farmer, Esq; 26 Orchard Mead, Finchley Rd, London NW11 8DJ (☎ 01 209 1747); Interwood Ltd, Stafford Ave, Hornchurch, Essex RM11 2ER (☎ 04024 52591, fax 04024 57813, telex 896801)

FARMER, Penelope Jane; da of Hugh Robert Macdonald Farmer, of Yping, Midhurst, Sussex, and Penelope Frances, *née* Boothby (d 1963); *b* 14 June 1939; *Educ* private sch, St Anne's Coll Oxford (MA), Bedford Coll London (Dip in Sociology); *m* 1, 1962 (m dis), Michael John Mockridge; m 2, 1982, Simon David Shorvon, s of Dr H Shorvon; 1 s (Thomas Michael Louis b 4 Dec 1965), 1 da (Clare Penelope b 2 April 1964); *Career* author; children's novels: The Summer Birds (1963), Emma in Winter (1965), Charlotte Sometimes (1969), Castle of Bone (1972), Year King (1976), Thicker Than Water (1989); adult novels: Standing in the Shadow (1984), Eve: Her Story (1985), Away From Home (1987), Glasshouses (1988); runner-up Carnegie prize 1963; memb: Soc of Authors, PEN; *Recreations* walking, listening to music, reading; *Style—* Ms Penelope Farmer; c/o Deborah Owen Ltd, 78 Narrow St, London E14 8BP (☎ 071 987 5119)

FARMER, Prof Richard Donald Trafford; s of Hereward Anderton Farmer (d 1987), and Kate Elizabeth Farmer (d 1986); *b* 14 Sept 1941; *Educ* Ashville Coll Harrogate, King's Coll London (MB BS), Univ of Leiden (PhD); *m* 20 Nov 1965, Teresa, da of Kenneth Roland Rimer, of Beckenham, Kent; 2 s (Dominic Michael Trafford b 5 Sept 1966, Christopher Kenneth Trafford b 24 June 1968); *Career* lectr Univ of Birmingham 1971-74, sr lectr Westminster Med Sch 1974-84, Boerhaave prof Univ of Leiden 1985, sr lectr Charing Cross and Westminster Med Sch 1986, prof community med Univ of London 1986-; MRCS 1963, LRCP 1965, MRCGP 1968, MFCM 1979; *Books* The Suicide Syndrome (1979), Lecture Notes on Epidemiology and Community Medicine (1977, 1983), Epidemiology of Diseases (1982); *Style—* Prof Richard Farmer; Sandtiles, 55 Leith Hill Rd, Cobham, Surrey (☎ 0932 62561); Westminster Hosp, London SW1 (☎ 01 746 8000)

FARMER, Thomas; CBE (1990); s of John Farmer, and Margaret, *née* Mackie; *b* 10 July 1940; *Educ* Holy Cross Acad Edinburgh; *m* 10 Sept 1966, Anne Drury, da of James Scott; 1 s (John Philip b 14 June 1968), 1 da (Sally Anne b 4 July 1967); *Career* sales rep 1961-64, fndr Tyre and Accessory Supplies 1964-68, dir Albany Tyre Serv 1968-70, fndr md Kwik-Fit Holdgs Ltd 1971-84, chm chief exec Kwik-Fit Hldgs plc 1984-; *Recreations* swimming, tennis, skiing; *Style—* Thomas Farmer, Esq, CBE;

Kwik-Fit Holdings plc, 27 Corstorphine Rd, Edinburgh (☎ 031 337 9200, fax 031 337 0062, telex 727625)

FARMILOE, Timothy Miles; s of Miles Damer Bligh Farmiloe (d 1983), and Cynthia Joyce, *née* Holt (d 1990); *b* 22 Feb 1935; *Educ* Winchester, New College Oxford (MA); *Career* academic publishing dir Macmillan 1965- (ed 1957-65); *Style—* Timothy Farmiloe, Esq; The Macmillan Press Ltd, Stockton House, 1 Melbourne Place, London WC2B 4LF (☎ 071 836 6633, fax 071 379 4980, telex 914690)

FARNCOMBE, Charles Frederick; CBE (1977); s of Harold Farncombe (d 1963), of London, and Eleanor Mary, *née* Driver (d 1965); *b* 29 July 1919; *Educ* Univ of London (BSc), Royal Sch Church Music, RAM (LRAM); *m* 20 May 1963, Sally Mae, da of Hugh Edgar Felps, MD (d 1976), of Riverside, California, USA; 1 da (Eleanor b 8 May 1967); *Career* REME 1942-47 (Capt 21 Army Gp 1943); civil engr John Mowlem & Co 1940-42; musical dir: Handel Opera Soc 1955-85, Royal Court Theatre Drottningholm Sweden 1970-79; chief conductor Annual Handel Festival Badisches Staats Theater Karlsruhe W Germany 1979-; musical dir: London Chamber Opera 1984-, Malcolm Sargent Festival Choir 1986-; Hon Dr Music: Columbus Univ Ohio 1959, Yankton Coll S Dakota 1959, City Univ 1988; AMICE 1945, FRAM 1963, hon fell Swedish Acad Music 1972, Gold Medal Drottningholm Sweden 1971, Kt Cdr Order of North Star 1982; *Recreations* cottage on Offa's Dyke; *Style—* Charles Farncombe, Esq, CBE; Royal Bank of Scotland, Columbia House, 69 Aldwych, London WC2B 4JJ

FARNCOMBE, Hon Mrs (Jenefer Anne); *née* Lawson; da of 5 Baron Burnham, *qv*; *b* 17 Dec 1949; *Educ* The Downs Seaford, Heathfield Sch Ascot, Guildhall Sch of Music and Drama (AGSM), Inchbald Sch of Design; *m* 20 April 1985, Andrew Farncombe, s of G F Farncombe, of Ipswich, Suffolk; 1 s (Frederick Alexander Edward b 1987), 1 da (Joanna Abigail b 1990); *Career* formerly specialist drama teacher; now kitchen designer (own co: Jenefer Lawson); *Recreations* sailing, diving; *Clubs* Island Sailing, Br Sub-Aqua; *Style—* The Hon Mrs Farncombe; c/o Lloyds Bank plc, The Broadway, Wycombe End, Beaconsfield, Bucks

FARNDALE, Gen Sir Martin Baker; KCB (1983, CB 1980); s of late Alfred Farndale, of Leyburn, N Yorks, and Margaret Louise, *née* Baker; *b* 6 Jan 1929,Alberta, Canada; *Educ* Yorebridge Sch Yorks, RMA Sandhurst; *m* 1955, Margaret Anne, da of late Percy Robert Buckingham; 1 s; *Career* RA 1948, 1 Regt RHA 1949-54 (Egypt and Germany 1951-54), HQ 7 Armd Div Germany 1955-56, Staff Coll 1959, HQ 17 Gurkha Div Malaya 1960-62, Mil Ops War Office 1962-64, cmd Chestnut Troop 1 Regt RHA South Arabia 1964-66, instr Staff Coll 1966-69, cmd 1 Regt RHA 1969-71, (UK, NI, Germany); sec def policy staff MOD 1971-73, Cdr 7 Armd Bde Germany 1973-75, dir PR (Army) MOD 1975-78, dir Mil Ops MOD 1978-80, GOC 2 Armd Div BAOR 1980-83, cmd 1 Br Corps 1983-85, C in C BAOR and Cmd Northern Army Gp Germany 1985-87, ret Jan 1988; Col Cmdt RA 1982-, Col Cmdt AAC 1980-88, Hon Col 3 Bn Yorks Volunteers 1983-89, Hon Col 1 Regt RHA 1984-89, Master Gunner St James' Park 1988-, Col Cmdt RHA 1988-; pres 2 Div Dinner Club 1983-; sr def advsr: Short Bros 1988-, Touche Ross 1988-; vice pres Royal Patriotic Fund, chm Royal United Services Inst; chm Royal Artillery Historical Affairs ctee; *Books* History of Royal Artillery France 1914-18 (1987), History of Royal Artillery, The Forgotten Fronts 1914-18 (1988); *Recreations* gardening, military history; *Clubs* E India, Sports, Public Schs, Devonshire; *Style—* Gen Sir Martin Farndale, KCB; c/o Lloyds Bank, 6 Pall Mall, London SW1

FARNELL, Graeme; s of Wilson Elliot Farnell, of Nottingham, and Mary Montgomerie Wishart, *née* Crichton (d 1987); *b* 11 July 1947; *Educ* Loughborough GS, Univ of Edinburgh (MA), London Film Sch; *m* 19 July 1969, Jennifer Gerda, da of William Holroyd Huddlestone, of Nottingham; 1 s (Paul b 1983); *Career* asst keeper Museum of E Anglian Life Stowmarket 1973-76, curator Inverness Museum and Art Gallery 1976-79, dir Scot Museums Cncl 1979-86, dir gen Museums Assoc 1986-89, dir Museum Devpt Co 1989-; FMA, MBIM, FS (Scot); *Recreations* Baroque opera; *Style—* Graeme Farnell, Esq; 8 Faraday Dr, Shenley Lodge, Milton Keynes MK5 7DA (☎ 0908 660 629); Museum Development Co, Premier Suites, Exchange House, 494 Midsummer Boulevard, Central Milton Keynes MK9 2EA (☎ 0908 690880, fax 0908 370013)

FARNHAM, 12 Baron (I 1756); Sir Barry Owen Somerset Maxwell; 14 Bt (NS 1627); s of Hon Somerset Arthur Maxwell, MP (died of wounds received in action 1942); suc gf 1957; *b* 7 July 1931; *Educ* Eton, Harvard Univ; *m* 19 Jan 1959, Diana Marion, er da of Nigel Eric Murray Gunnis; 2 da (adopted); *Heir* bro, Hon Simon Kenlis Maxwell; *Career* dir Brown Shipley & Co (merchant bankers) 1959-; chm: Brown Shipley Hldgs plc 1976-, Avon Rubber plc 1978-, Provident Mutual Life Assurance Association 1989-; deputy grand master United Grand Lodge of England 1989-; *Clubs* Boodle's, Kildare Street and Univ (Dublin), City of London; *Style—* The Rt Hon Lord Farnham; 11 Earl's Court Gardens, London SW5 0TD; Farnham, Co Cavan; Founders Court, Lothbury, London EC2R 7HE

FARNHAM, (Edward) George Adrian; DL (1984 Leics); er s of John Adrian George Farnham (d 1930), of 36 Earls Court Square, London, and Lilian Edith, *née* Powell; descended from Thomas Farnham, of the Nether Hall, Quorndon, living 16 cent (*see* Burke's Landed Gentry, 1952 edn); *b* 20 July 1927; *Educ* Harrow, RMA Sandhurst; *m* 20 Aug 1948, Barbara Elizabeth, eldest da of Charles Mathers (d 1976), of Holly Lodge, Rothley, Leics; 3 s (John, Charles, Matthew), 1 da (Georgina); *Career* cmmnd Gordon Highlanders 1946, Bde Intelligence Offr 153 Highland Bde BAOR 1947-48; cncllr Leics CC 1958-84 (chm 1977-80), High Sheriff of Leics 1986; chm Leics Health Authy 1986-90, pres E Midlands Heraldry Soc; *Recreations* art, history, architecture, conservation; *Style—* George Farnham, Esq; Quorn Hse, Quorn, Loughborough (☎ 0509 412502); Leicestershire Health Authority, Princess Rd West, Leicester (☎ 0533 559777)

FARNSWORTH, Jonathan Bower; s of William Farnsworth (d 1964); *b* 9 Dec 1929; *Educ* Oundle; *m* 14 Nov 1953, Ann Isobel; 3 s (Anthony b 1955, Adam b 1956, Rupert b 1961), 1 da (Joanna b 1959); *Career* chartered surveyor; *Style—* Jonathan Farnsworth, Esq; The Old Rectory, Thorpe Achurch, Oundle, Peterborough PE8 5SL

FARQUHAR, David Michael; s of Col Noel Percival Farquhar, and Patricia Mary, *née* Giblin; *b* 29 March 1941; *Educ* Edinburgh Acad, Scotch Coll Melbourne Aust; *m* 6 April 1972, Juliette Diana Galer, da of Konrad Maximillian Hellman (d 1979); 1 s (James b 29 April 1980), 1 da (Rebecca b 4 March 1975); *Career* PR mangr F & T Industs Aust 1963-66, dir Lonsdale Hands Info 1967-71, PR and advtg mangr Toyota 1972-77, corporate and PR mangr Nissan 1977-78, md Juliette Hellman Ltd 1979-; memb PR Inst of Aust 1964; *Recreations* sailing, golf, motor cars; *Clubs* West Sussex Golf, Sea View Yacht; *Style—* David Farquhar, Esq; Media House, Petworth, West Sussex, (☎ 0798 43737, car 0836 282896, fax 0798 43391)

FARQUHAR, Gordon Ferguson; s of George Frederick Farquhar (d 1967), and Minnie Margaret, *née* Smith (d 1977); *b* 20 April 1933; *Educ* Hutcheson's GS, Univ of Glasgow (BSc), Imperial Coll London (DIC); *m* 24 July 1957, Jill Elizabeth, da of John David Banner, of Uddingston, nr Glasgow; 1 s (Michael Frank Banner b 1964), 2 da (Shirley Elizabeth b 1959, Fiona Ann b 1962); *Career* Nat Serv Sgt RE 1956-58 mainly as lectr/demonstrator RMC Shrivenham; asst Design and Devpt Dept Atomic Power Div GEC 1958-59, sr agent Monier Construction Co Nigeria 1959-61; W A Fairhurst & Ptnrs consulting civil and structural engrs: sr engr 1962-66, ptnr 1967-86, managing ptnr 1986-89, sr ptnr 1989-; responsible for major civil and structural projects on motorways and bldgs; IStructE Oscar Faber medal 1971; former pres Stepps Lawn Tennis Club 1963-66, CEng, FICE, FIStructE, FIHT, MConsE; *Recreations* golf; *Clubs* Royal Scottish Auto, Kilmacolm Golf; *Style—* Gordon Farquhar, Esq; 2 Hatfield Court, Kilmacolm, Renfrewshire PA13 4LY (☎ 050 587 2245); W A Fairhurst Ptnrs, 11 Woodside Terrace, Glasgow G3 7XQ (☎ 041 332 8754)

FARQUHAR, Sir Michael FitzRoy Henry; 7 Bt (GB 1796); s of Lt-Col Sir Peter Walter Farquhar, 6 Bt, DSO, OBE (d 1986), and Elizabeth Evelyn, *née* Hurt (d 1983); *b* 29 June 1938; *Educ* Eton, RAC Cirencester; *m* 29 June 1963, Veronica Geraldine, er da of Patrick Rowan Hornidge, of Helford Passage, nr Falmouth, Cornwall; 2 s (Charles Walter FitzRoy b 21 Feb 1964, Edward Peter Henry b 6 Dec 1966); *Heir* s, Charles Walter FitzRoy Farquhar b 21 Feb 1964; *Recreations* fishing, shooting, gardening; *Clubs* White's; *Style—* Sir Michael Farquhar, Bt; Manor Farm, West Kington, Chippenham, Wilts SN14 7JG (☎ 0249 782671)

FARQUHAR, Peter Guy Powlett; s of Guy Farquhar (d 1962), and Daphne Mary Christian, *née* Henry (d 1983); *b* 13 Feb 1936; *Educ* Eton; *m* 1, 1961, Rosemary Anne Eaton, da of Eaton Hammond, of Wroxham, Norfolk; 2 s (Richard Charles b 7 April 1962, James Edward b 6 Dec 1963); m 2, Carolyn, da of D Graham Robertson, of Sydney, Aust; 2 s (George Peter b 29 Feb 1980, Hugh Graham b 7 June 1984), 2 da (Jane Elizabeth b 12 Dec 1982 d 1983, Alice Rose Jane b 17 Nov 1987); *Career* asst PR offr H J Heinz Company 1959-66, md Hill & Knowlton UK Ltd 1969-79 (sr exec 1967-69), fndr/dir Ludbrook Ltd 1979-, md Fleishman-Hillard Europe Ltd 1987-, chm Fleishman-Hillard UK Ltd 1987-; MIPR, memb Int PR Assoc; *Recreations* Cartophily; *Clubs* MCC; *Style—* Peter Farquhar, Esq; Fleishman-Hillard Europe Ltd, 25 Wellington St, London WC2E 7DA (☎ 071 306 9000, fax 071 497 0096)

FARQUHAR, William John; s of John Catto Farquhar (d 1953), of Maud, Aberdeenshire, and Mary, *née* Whyte (d 1974); *b* 29 May 1935; *Educ* Peterhead Acad, Univ of Aberdeen (MA), Univ of Manchester (DSA); *m* 24 Feb 1962, Isabel Henderson, da of Rev Dr William Morgan Robertson Rusk (d 1965), of Aberdeen; 4 s (Callum, Tor, Gavin, Barry); *Career* admin trainee NHS 1958-61, hosp sec Whitehaven 1961-64, dep gp sec W Cumberland 1964-66, regnl staff offr SERHB Edinburgh 1966-69, dep sec Eastern RHB Dundee 1969-74, dist admin Lothian 1974-85, sec Planning Cncl Scottish Health Serv 1985-89, dir Planning Unit SHHD 1987-, sec Advsy Cncl Scottish Health Serv 1989-, elder Colinton Parish Church; memb: Chaplaincy Ctee Church of Scotland, Exec Ctee Cross Roads Edinburgh; FHSM 1963; *Recreations* walking, gardening, philately; *Style—* William Farquhar, Esq; Craigengar, 7 Harelaw Rd, Colinton, Edinburgh EH13 0DR (☎ 031 441 2169); St Andrew's House, Edinburgh EH1 3DE (☎ 031 244 2750)

FARQUHARSON, Capt Colin Andrew; JP (Aberdeenshire 1969), DL (1966); s of late Norman Donald Farquharson, of Whitehouse, Alford, Aberdeenshire; *b* 9 Aug 1923; *Educ* Rugby; *m* 1, 1948, Jean Sybil Mary (d 1985), da of late Brig-Gen John George Harry Hamilton, DSO, JP, DL, of Skene House, Aberdeenshire; 2 da (1 decd) (*see* Master of Arbuthnott); m 2, 1987, Clodagh, JP, DL, 2 da of late Sir Kenneth Murray JP, DL, of Geanies, Ross-shire and widow of Major Ian Houldsworth, DL, of Dallas Morayshire; 3 step s, 2 step da (*see* Earl of Haddo); *Career* Capt Grenadier Gds 1942-48; chartered surveyor (land agent); dir MacRobert Farms (Douneside) Ltd 1971-87; memb Royal Cornhill and Assoc Hosps Bd of Mgmnt 1962-74, chm Gordon Dist Local Health Cncl 1975-81, memb Grampian Area Health Bd 1981-89; memb Royal Co of Archers (Queen's Body Guard for Scotland); Vice Lord Lt for Aberdeenshire 1983-87; Lord Lt of Aberdeenshire 1987: FRICS; *Recreations* shooting, fishing; *Clubs* Royal Northern, Univ (both Aberdeen); MCC; *Style—* Capt Colin Farquharson of Whitehouse, JP; Whitehouse, Alford, Aberdeenshire AB3 8DP (☎ 0336 2503); Estate Off, Mains of Haddo, Haddo House, Aberdeen AB4 0ER (☎ 06515 664)

FARQUHARSON, Rt Hon Lord Justice; Rt Hon Sir Donald Henry; yr s of Charles Anderson Farquharson (d 1929), of Logie Coldstone, Aberdeenshire, and Florence Ellen, *née* Fox; *b* 26 Feb 1928; *Educ* Royal Commercial Travellers Schs, Keble Coll Oxford; *m* 1960, Helen Mary, er da of late Cdr H M Simpson, RN (ret), of Abbots Brow, Kirkby Lonsdale, Westmorland; 3 s, 1 da (decd); *Career* called to the Bar Inner Temple 1952, dep chm Essex QS 1970-72, QC 1972, rec of Crown Cts 1972-81, legal assessor GMC and Gen Dental Cncl 1978-81, bencher Inner Temple 1979, High Ct judge (Queen's Bench) 1981-89, Fresiding judge SE circuit 1985-88, Lord Justice of Appeal 1989; kt 1981; *Recreations* opera going; *Style—* The Rt Hon Lord Justice Farquharson; Royal Courts of Justice, Strand, London WC2A 2LL (☎ 071 936 6000)

FARQUHARSON, Sir James Robbie; KBE (1960, CBE 1948, OBE 1944); s of Frank Farquharson, of Cortachy, Angus, and Agnes Jane, *née* Robbie; *b* 1 Nov 1903; *Educ* Royal Tech Coll Glasgow, Univ of Glasgow (BSc); *m* 1933, Agnes Binny, da of James Graham, of Kirriemuir, Angus; 2 s; *Career* chief engr Tanganyika Railways 1941-45 (gen mangr 1945-48), chief engr and dep gen mangr E African Railways 1948-52; gen mangr: Sudan Railways 1952-57, E African Railways 1957-61; asst crown agent and engr-in-chief Crown Agents for Overseas Govts and Admins 1961-65, chm Millbank Technical Services Ordnance Ltd 1973-75; fell Scottish Cncl Devpt and Indust 1986; farmer; *Style—* Sir James Farquharson, KBE; Kinclune, by Kirriemuir, Angus, Scotland (☎ 0575 74710)

FARQUHARSON, Robert Alexander (Robin); CMG (1975); s of Capt J P Farquharson, DSO, OBE, RN (d 1960), of Homington Manor, Salisbury, and Phyllis Ruth, *née* Prescott-Decie (d 1969); *b* 26 May 1925; *Educ* Harrow, King's Coll Cambridge (MA); *m* 4 Feb 1955, Joan Elizabeth, da of Sir Ivo Mallet, GBE, KCMG (d 1988) 3 s (John James b 1956, William b 1961, d 1984, Edward b 1962), 1 da (Charlotte b 1959); *Career* Sub Lt RNVR 1943-46; Dip Serv (formerly Foreign Serv): third sec Moscow 1950, second sec FO 1952, first sec Bonn 1955 (Panama 1958, Paris 1960), FO 1964, cnsllr and dir of Trade Devpt SA 1967, min Madrid 1971, consul gen San Francisco 1973, ambass Yugoslavia 1977; econ advsr Davy McKee Int 1980; chm local Parish Cncl, lay co-chm Deanery and Diocesan Synods; Lord of the Manor of Bockleton; *Recreations* country; *Clubs* Naval and Military, Flyfishers'; *Style—* R A Farquharson, Esq, CMG; Tollard Royal, Salisbury SP5 5PS (☎ 0725 516 278)

FARQUHARSON OF FINZEAN, Angus Durie Miller; DL; s of Dr Hugo Durie Newton Miller (d 1984), and Elsie Miller, *née* Duthie; *b* 27 March 1935; *Educ* Trinity Coll Glenalmond, Downing Coll Cambridge (MA); *m* 1 July 1961, Alison Mary, da of William Marshall Farquharson-Lang, CBE; 2 s (Donald b 1963, Andrew b 1969), 1 da (Jean b 1962); *Career* chartered surveyor; factor Finzean Estate; memb Cncl Scottish Landowners Fedn 1980-88, memb Regnl Advsy Ctee Forestry Cmmn E Scotland 1980-84 and N Conservancy 1985-; memb: Red Deer Cmmn 1986-, Nature Conservancy Cncl Ctee for Scotland 1986-; pres Deeside Field Club, memb: Church of Scotland Judicial Cttee, Presbytery of Kincardine/Deeside; dir Lathallan Sch; vice Lord Lt of Aberdeenshire 1987-; FRICS; *Recreations* shooting, fishing, gardening, nature conservation; *Clubs* New (Edinburgh); *Style—* Angus Farquharson of Finzean, DL; Finzean House, Finzean, Aberdeenshire AB3 5ED (☎ 033045 229)

FARR, Dr Dennis Larry Ashwell; CBE (1991); s of Arthur William Farr (d 1961), and Helen Eva, *née* Ashwell; *b* 3 April 1929; *Educ* Luton GS, Univ of London,

Courtauld Inst of Art; *m* 1959, Diana (author), da of Capt H J Pullein-Thompson, MC; 1 s, 1 da; *Career* asst keeper Tate Gallery 1954-64, curator Paul Mellon Collection Washington DC 1965-66, sr lectr and dep keeper Univ Art Collections Univ of Glasgow 1967-69, dir Birmingham City Museums Art Gallery 1969-80, memb UK Exec Bd Int Cncl of Museums 1976-84, dir Courtauld Inst Galleries Univ of London 1980-; tstee Birmingham City Museums Art Gallery Appeal Fund 1980, chm Assoc of Art Historians 1983-86 (memb Exec Ctee 1981), memb Comité International d'Histoire de l'Art 1983-; JP Birmingham 1977-80; Hon DLitt Birmingham; FRSA, FMA; *Publications* William Etty (1958), Tate Gallery Modern British School Catalogue (2 vols, with Mary Chamot and Martin Butlin, 1964), English Art 1870-1940 (1978), Impressionist and Post-Impressionist Paintings from the Courtauld Collections (with William Bradford, 1984), The Northern Landscape (with William Bradford, 1986), Impressionist and Post Impressionist Masters: The Courtauld Collections (with John House and others, 1987), 100 Masterpieces from The Courtauld Collections (ed and contrib, 1987), Lynn Chadwick: Sculptor A Complete Catalogue (with Eva Chadwick, 1990); *Recreations* reading, riding, music, foreign travel; *Clubs* Athenaeum, Inst of Contemporary Arts; *Style—* Dr Dennis Farr, CBE; 35 Esmond Rd, Bedford Park, Chiswick, London W4 1JG (☎ 081 995 6400)

FARR, Diana; da of Capt Harold James Pullein-Thompson, MC (d 1957), and Joanna Maxwell, *née* Cannan; *b* 1 Oct 1930; *Educ* Wychwood Sch Oxford; *m* 6 June 1959, Dennis Larry Ashwell Farr, s of Arthur William Farr; 1 s (Benedict Edward b 7 March 1963), 1 da (Joanna Helen b 6 July 1964); *Career* professional author 1946-; dir Grove Riding Schs Peppard and Oxford 1946-52, PA to literary agent Rosica Colin 1952-54, memb Public Lending Right Ctee 1960-64, fndr memb Children's Writers Gp 1963-65, hon sec Save the Mere Campaign 1970-73; memb: Soc Authors, International PEN; *Books* as Diana Pullein-Thompson books incl: I Wanted a Pony (1946), The Boy and The Donkey (1958), Cassidy In Danger (1979), Dear Pup, Letters To A Young Dog (1988); as Diana Farr: Gilbert Cannan, A Georgian Prodigy (1978), Five at 10: Prime Ministers' Consorts Since 1957 (1985), Choosing (1988); *Recreations* walking, cinema, travel; *Style—* Mrs Dennis Farr; 35 Esmond Rd, Bedford Park, Chiswick, London W4 1JG (☎ 081 995 6400)

FARR, Jennifer Margaret; da of Charles Percival Holliday, of Nottingham, and Vera Margaret Emily, *née* Burchell; *b* 20 July 1933; *Educ* Nottingham Girls' HS, Middx Hosp, Royal Victoria Infirmary Newcastle upon Tyne; *m* 28 July 1956, Sydney Hordern Farr (d 1981), s of Col Sydney Farr, MC, JP, DL (d 1967), of Nottingham; 2 s (Timothy b 1957, Charles b 1961), 1 da (Rosemary b 1959); *Career* physiotherapist 1954-56; chm Nottingham and Dist NSPCC; JP 1979-89; *Recreations* golf, tennis, gardening, music; *Clubs* Notts Golf; *Style—* Mrs Jennifer Farr; Lanesmeet, Epperstone, Notts NG14 6AU

FARR, Sir John Arnold; MP (C) Harborough 1959-; 2 and er survg s of Capt John Farr, JP (d 1951) of Worksop Manor, Notts, and Margaret Anne, *née* Heath; *b* 25 Sept 1922; *Educ* Harrow; *m* 26 Aug 1960, Susan Ann, yr da of Sir Leonard John Milburn, 3 Bt (d 1957); 2 s (Jonathan b 1962, George b 1967); *Career* RN 1940-46, demob Lt-Cdr RNVR; memb of Lloyd's, landowner; dir Home Brewery Co Ltd 1950-55, pres Worksop Boys' Club 1951-55, contested (C) Ilkeston 1955, sec Cons Agric Ctee 1970-74 (vice chm 1979-84), memb UK Delgn to WEU and Cncl of Europe 1973-78, vice chm Cons NI Ctee 1974-78; chm: Anglo-Irish Parly Gp 1977-80, Br Korea Parly Gp 1980-89, Br Zimbabwe Parly Gp 1980-89; memb Select Ctee on Standing Orders 1981-, sec All Pty Conservation Ctee, chm All Pty Knitwear Group; kt 1984; *Clubs* Boodle's, MCC; *Style—* Sir John Farr, MP; 11 Vincent Square, London SW1; Shortwood House, Lamport, Northampton (☎ 060 128 260)

FARR, Richard Peter; s of Peter James Farr (d 1987), and Josephine Farr; *b* 8 July 1954; *Educ* Bedford Sch, Ecole de Commerce Neuchatel, Univ of Reading (BSc); *m* 1979, Susan Jane, *née* Fairburn; *Career* surveyor Knight Frank and Rutley 1977-80, sr surveyor Richard Ellis 1980-83, assoc dir Greycoat Group plc 1983-88, chief exec New Cavendish Estates plc 1988-90, chief exec Park Square Developments 1990-; ARICS; *Recreations* skiing, vintage Bentleys, sailing; *Clubs* Naval and Military, RAC; *Style—* Richard Farr, Esq; Park Square, Development, 10 Bruton St, London W1X 7AG (☎ 071 495 4664, fax 071 629 4732)

FARR, Prof Robert MacLaughlin (Rob); s of Robert James Farr (d 1984), of Clooneen, Marino, Holywood, Co Down, NI, and Henrietta Williamson, *née* MacLaughlin (d 1973); *b* 10 Dec 1935; *Educ* Sullivan Upper Sch Holywood, The Queen's Univ Belfast (BA, MA), Trinity Coll Dublin (Divinity Testimonium), Univ of London (PhD); *m* 3 Sept 1966, Ann-Marie, da of Henry James Wood (d 1964), of The Hundred House, Udimore, nr Rye, Sussex; 1 s (Angus b 10 May 1971), 1 da (Fiona b 2 Nov 1973); *Career* asst lectr Queen's Univ Belfast 1962-64, res offr science 4 (RAF) MOD London 1964-66, lectr social psychology UCL 1966-79, proj psychology Univ of Glasgow 1979-83, proj social psychology LSE 1983-; govr NE London Poly 1975-79; memb: Psychology Bd Cncl Nat Academic Awards 1980-84, Sr Scholars Ctee Fulbright Cmmn 1984-; pres Br Psychological Soc 1985-86 (hon gen sec 1970-75), chm Library Ctee Br Library Political and Econ Sci 1987-, memb Br Nat Ctee Psychological Sci 1988-; fell Br Psychological Soc, Chartered Occupational Psychologist 1988-; *Books* Social Representations (ed with S Moscovici, 1984 and 1989); guest ed special issues: British Journal of Social Psychology on The History of Social Psychology (1983), Journal for the Theory of Social Behaviour on Social Representations (1987); *Recreations* walking, reading; *Style—* Prof Rob Farr; Brownings Down, Warren Rd, Guildford, Surrey GU1 2HQ (☎ 0493 571700); Dept of Social Psychology, LSE, Houghton St, The Aldwych, London WC2A 2AE (☎ 01 405 7687, telex 24655 GLPES G)

FARR, Suzanne Elizabeth; da of Tom Priday Farr, JP, of Worcestershire, and Anne Farr, *née* Thomas; *b* 14 Aug 1936; *Educ* The Alice Ottley Sch, Bedford Coll of Physical Educn, Lady Margaret Hall Oxford (MA, MSc); *Career* house mistress Wycombe Abbey 1963-75, head mistress Downe House 1978-89; govr The Alice Ottley Sch 1990-; memb English Lacrosse Team 1963-67, Girls Schs Assoc; *Recreations* gardening, showing & breeding Irish Setters; *Clubs* Lansdowne, Kennel; *Style—* Miss Suzanne E Farr; Garraway House, How Caple, Herefordshire HR1 4SS (☎ 098 986253)

FARRANCE, Roger Arthur; CBE; s of Ernest Thomas Farrance (d 1985), and Alexandra Hilda May, *née* Finch (d 1989); *b* 10 Nov 1933; *Educ* Trinity Sch of John Whitgift, LSE (BSc); *m* 8 Dec 1956, Kathleen Sheila, da of Henry Stephen Owen (d 1974); 1 da (Denise Lesley b 1957); *Career* HM inspr of factories Manchester, Doncaster and Walsall 1956-64, asst sec W of England Engrg Employers' Assoc Bristol 1964-67, industl rels and personnel mangr Foster Wheeler John Brown Boilers Ltd 1967-68, dep dir Coventry and Dist Engrg Employers Assoc and Coventry Mgmnt Trg Centre 1968-75; Electricity Cncl: dep industl rels advsr 1975-76, industl rels advsr 1976-79, full time memb 1979-89, dep chm 1988-90; chief exec Electricity Association 1990-, pres elect Inst of Personnel Mgmnt 1990-91; memb Cncl: ACAS 1983-89, CBI 1983-; OStJ; CIEE, FIBM, FIPM; Liveryman Worshipful Co of Basketmakers; *Clubs* RAC; *Style—* Roger Farrance, Esq, CBE; 4 Southridge Place, The Downs, Wimbledon, London SW20 8JQ (☎ 081 946 9650); The Electricity Association, 30 Millbank, London SW1P 4RD (☎ 071 834 2333, fax : 071 834 6453)

FARRANT, Malcolm George; s of Andrew Cecil Farrant, (d 1956), of Roskrow, Penryn, Cornwall, and Winifred Mary, *née* Fox, (1974); *b* 1 July 1937; *Educ* Eton; *m* 1, 1963 (m dis 1965), Dorothy, da of Robert Farrow (d 1972), of Melbourne, Australia; m 2 (m dis 1987), Angela Margery Smith-Bosanquet, *née* Moore, da of John Edward Hugh Moore (d 1957); 2 s (Henry Malcolm b 22 Jan 1970, Oliver Jasper b 28 March 1974); *Career* Nat Serv, Duke of Cornwall's LI served Jamaica and Germany 1956-57; memb Stock Exhange London 1954-55 and 1957-59; property developer and estate agent Perth Aust 1963-73, property devloper Bath England 1973-, local dir Gold Estates of Australia (1903) Ltd 1970-82 (local chm 1970-73); chm and md Moore Farrant Ltd 1987-; *Recreations* fishing, golf, model making; *Clubs* Lansdowne, Bath Golf; *Style—* Malcolm Farrant, Esq; 4 Charlotte St, Bath, Avon BA1 2NE (☎ 0225 332047, fax 442960, car 0860 220026)

FARRAR, Austin Packard; s of Capt Alfred Farrar (d 1916), and Edith Celia, *née* Packard (d 1960); *b* 21 Feb 1913; *Educ* Imp Serv Coll Windsor; *Career* tech offr Amiralty Dept of Torpedoes and Mining 1941-46; tech mangr Sussex Yacht Works Ltd 1939-41, md Woolverstone Shipyard Ltd 1946-62, memb Br Olympic Yachting Team 1948, dir: Seahorse Sails 1955-70, Austin Farrar Sails Ltd 1970-82; Austin Farrar & Ptnrs conslts 1980-, editorial conslt Ship and Boat; memb various Ctees: YRU, RYA, Soc for Nautical Res (currently vice pres); co-chm Small Craft Ctee RINA (awarded Small Craft Gp medal 1988), vice pres Amateur Yacht Res Soc; FRINA 1970 (memb 1945); *Recreations* sailing, marine archaeology; *Clubs* Royal Ocean Racing, Royal Harwich Yacht; *Style—* Austin Farrar, Esq; Orchard House, Stutton, Ipswich, Suffolk 1P9 2RY (☎ 0473 328236)

FARRAR, David James; s of James Farrar (d 1980), of Rawdon, Yorks, and Jessie, *née* Naylor; *b* 3 July 1942; *Educ* Leeds GS, St Thomas's Hos Med Sch (MB BS, MS, FRCS); *m* 25 Jan 1969, Pamela Anne, da of Albert Sydney Allberry, MC, of Epsom, Surrey; 1 s (Nicholas b 19 Nov 1976), 1 da (Charlotte b 18 April 1970); *Career* conslt urological surgn Selly Oak Hosp Birmingham 1978, hon clinical lectr Univ of Birmingham 1978; memb: Br Assoc Urological Surgns, Int Continence Soc, Royal Soc of Medicine; *Recreations* golf, sports history; *Style—* David Farrar, Esq; 36 Mirfield Rd, Solihull, West Midlands B91 1JD (☎ 021 705 1710); 38 Harborne Road, Edgbaston, Birmingham (☎ 021 454 1390); Selly Oak Hospital, Raddlebarn Road, Birmingham B29 6JD

FARRAR, Rex Gordon; LVO (1975); s of John Percival Farrar, and Ethel Florence, *née* Leader; *b* 22 Aug 1925; *Educ* Latymer's Sch Edmonton, Univ of London (BA); *m* 1, 1955, Mary Katharine Shutts (d 1977); 1 s; m 2, 1978, Masako Ikeda, 1 s, 1 da; *Career* served RN 1944-47; FO 1947-85, vice consul New Orleans 1953, first sec Jakarta 1963 (second sec 1960); first sec: Commercial Caracas 1964, head of Chancery and Consul San Salvador 1968, first sec Commercial Tokyo 1971, head Chancery and Consul Rangoon 1978-80; consul-gen at Osaka 1980-85, ret; regnl dir (Tokyo) then conslt to The De La Rue Co plc 1985-; *Style—* Rex Farrar, Esq, LVO; 07-15 Nishi Azabu 3 Chome, Minato-Ku 106, Tokyo, Japan

FARRAR-HOCKLEY, Gen Sir Anthony Heritage; GBE (1981, MBE 1957), KCB (1977), DSO (1953, and bar 1964), MC (1944); s of Arthur Farrar-Hockley; *b* 8 April 1924; *Educ* Exeter Sch; *m* 1945, Margaret Bernadette Wells (d 1981); 2 s (and 1 s decd); m 2 1983, Linda Wood; *Career* Glos and Parachute Regt WW II; served: Med, Europe, Palestine, Korea 1950-53, later Cyprus, Port Said, Jordan, Aden; chief instr RMA Sandhurst 1959-61, princ staff offr to Dir Borneo Ops 1965-66, Cdr 16 Parachute Bde 1966-68, def fellowship Exeter Coll Oxford (BLitt) 1968-70, dir PR Army 1970, Cdr Land Forces NI 1970-71, GOC 4 Div 1971-73, dir Combat Devpt Army 1974-77, Lt-Gen 1977, GOC SE Dist 1977-79, Gen 1979, C-in-C Allied Forces N Europe 1979-82, ret 1983; def conslt and historian; cabinet office historian for Br part in Korean War, ADC Gen to HM The Queen 1981-83, Col Cmdt Para Regt 1977-83, Col The Gloucestershire Regt 1978-84; memb: steering ctee for Defence Begins at Home 1983-, Cncl Outward Bound 1983-; *Publications* The Edge of the Sword (1954), The Commander (ed 1957), The Somme (1964), Death of an Army (1968), Airborne Carpet (1969), War in the Desert (1969), General Student (1973), Goughie; The Life of General Sir Hubert Gough (1975), Opening Rounds (1988), British Part in the Korean War, Vol 1: A Distant Obligation (1990); *Style—* Gen Sir Anthony Farrar-Hockley, GBE, KCB, DSO, MC; Pye Barn, Moulsford, Oxon

FARRELL, Charles; MC (1945); s of Gerald William Farrell (d 1919); *b* 10 Feb 1919; *Educ* Ampleforth, Ch Ch Oxford (MA); *m* 1949, Lady Katharine, *qv*; 1 s, 3 da; *Career* Maj Scots Gds NW Europe 1944-45 (despatches); Foreign Serv: joined 1947, 2 sec Cmmr Gens Office Singapore 1949-51, first sec Br Embassy Brussels 1955-57, resigned 1957; md Br Sidac Ltd 1960-71, chm Sidex Ltd (jt co with ICI Ltd) 1966-71, memb Trade and Policy Ctee CBI 1970-74, chm Montagu Fine Art Ltd 1972-79, dir Christie's Publications Ltd 1972-85, chm CCA Publications plc 1985-89, dir HTV plc 1989-; memb: Oxon Health Authy 1981-85, Oxon CC 1981-87; FRSA 1989; *Clubs* White's, Beefsteak; *Style—* Charles Farrell, Esq, MC; Cuttmill House, Watlington, Oxon OX9 5BA (☎ 049 161 2327); Harlech Fine Art Holdings Ltd, 14 Dover St, London W1 (☎ 071 355 3094)

FARRELL, Hon Mrs (Clodagh Mary); *née* Morris; yr da of 2 Baron Morris (d 1975), and Jean Beatrice, *née* Maitland-Makgill-Crichton (d 1989, having m 2, Baron Salmon (Life Peer), *qv*); *b* 8 Nov 1936; *Educ* St Mary's Ascot and New Hall Chelmsford; *m* 2 May 1964, Thomas Hugh Francis Farrell, TD, DL, *qv*; 1 s, 1 da; *Style—* The Hon Mrs Farrell; 20 New Walk, Beverley, North Humberside (☎ 0482 869367)

FARRELL, James Aloysius; Sheriff; s of James Stoddart Farrell, and Harriet Louise, *née* McDonnell; *b* 14 May 1943; *Educ* St Aloysius Coll, Univ of Glasgow (MA), Univ of Dundee (LLB); *m* 2 Dec 1967, Jacqueline, da of Barnett Harvey Allen (d 1967); 2 da (Suzanne b 7 April 1970, Claire Louise b 16 Oct 1973); *Career* admitted to Faculty of Advocates 1974, advocate depute 1979-83; Sheriff: Glasgow and Strahkelvin 1984-85, Dumfries and Galloway 1985-86, Lothian and Borders at Edinburgh 1986-; *Recreations* sailing, cycling, hill walking; *Style—* Sheriff Farrell

FARRELL, Lady Katharine Mary Veronica; *née* Paget; yst da of 6 Marquess of Anglesey, GCVO (d 1947), and Lady Marjorie Manners (d 1946), eldest da of 8 Duke of Rutland; twin sis of 7 Marquess; *b* 8 Oct 1922; *m* 1, 16 April 1941 (m dis 1948), Lt-Col Jocelyn Eustace Gurney, DSO, MC (d 1973), Welsh Gds, 2 s of Sir Eustace Gurney, of Walsingham Abbey, Norfolk; 1 da; m 2, 21 Jan 1949, Charles Farrell, MC, *qv*; 1 s, 3 da; *Style—* The Lady Katharine Farrell; Cuttmill House, Watlington, Oxon OX9 5BA (☎ 049 161 2327)

FARRELL, Terry; OBE (1978); s of Thomas Farrell, and Molly, *née* Maguire; *b* 12 May 1938; *Educ* St Cuthberts GS, Univ of Newcastle Sch of Architecture (B Arch), Univ of Pennsylvania Sch of Fine Arts (M Arch, Master of City Planning); *m* 1, 1960, Angela Rosemarie Mallam; 2 da; m 2, 1973, Susan Hilary Aplin; 2 s, 1 da; *Career* Planning Dept: Camden New Jersey USA, Colin Buchanan & Partners 1964-65; fndr ptnr Farrell Grimshaw Partnership 1965-80; exec chm and dir: Terry Farrell Partnership Ltd 1980-88, Terry Farrell & Co Ltd 1988-; teaching positions: Univ of Cambridge, Univ Coll London, Architectural Assoc London, Univ of Strathclyde Glasgow, Univ of Sheffield, Univ of Pennsylvania; English Heritage: cmmr, memb London Advsy Ctee, memb Historic Areas Advsy Ctee ; former memb: RIBA Clients Advsy Bd, RIBA Visiting Bd, RIBA Awards Panel; past pres Urban Design Gp, architectural assessor for Financial Times Architectural Awards 1983, external examiner RCA; representative projects: Galleries for Craft Cncl, TV AM Breakfast TV headquarters and studios London, HQ Henley Regatta, Charing Cross devpt complex London, Edinburgh int fin and conf centre; numerous lectures in UK and abroad; MCP, ARIBA 1963, memb RTPI 1970, FCSD, FSIAD 1981; *Publications* Monograph (1984); articles in: Architectural Review, Architects' Journal, L'Architecture d'Aujourd'hui, Domus, Progressive Architecture, Baven und Wohnen, Abitare, Cree, Architectural Record, Interiors, British Architecture, RIBA Journal, Architectural Design, Architecture and Urbanism Arkitektur DK, Decorative Arts (USSR), Architecture of the Soviet Union; *Style*— Terry Farrell, Esq, OBE

FARRELL, Thomas Hugh Francis; TD (1969), DL (E Riding Yorks 1971, Humberside 1974); s of Hugh Farrell (d 1959); *b* 3 Feb 1930; *Educ* Ampleforth, Univ Coll Hull, (LLB London); *m* 2 May 1964, Hon Clodagh Mary, *qv*; 1 s, 1 da; *Career* slr 1952; cmmnd The Queen's Bays 1953-55, Lt-Col cmdg Prince of Wales's Own Yorkshire Territorials 1967-69; Sheriff of Hull 1960-61; chm: Hull Cons Fedn 1963-68, Beverley Civic Soc 1970-74; treas Univ of Hull 1976-1980, chm Cncl Hull Univ 1980-; Hon LLD (Hull) 1983; *Clubs* Cavalry and Guards'; *Style*— Thomas Farrell, Esq, TD, DL; 20 New Walk, Beverley, North Humberside (☎ Hull 0482 869367); Wilberforce Court, High Street, Hull (☎ 0482 23239)

FARREN, Graham Richard; s of Dennis Henry Saunders Farren (d 1985), and Doris Margaret, *née* Francis; *b* 19 Jan 1947; *Educ* Hemel Hempstead GS, Churchill Coll Cambridge (MA); *m* 12 April 1975, Bridget Mary, da of late William Hardisty; 1 s (Richard), 1 da (Frances); *Career* Bacon Woodrow & De Souza 1973-77, ptnr Bacon & Woodrow 1977- (joined 1969); Freeman: City of London, Worshipful Co of Actuaries; FIA 1972, ASA 1974, APMI 1980; *Recreations* gardening, travelling, photography; *Style*— Graham Farren, Esq; Beltrees, Park Rd, Stoke Poges, Bucks SL2 4PA (☎ 0753 224 84); Bacon & Woodrow, Ivy Hse, 107 St Peters St, St Albans, Herts AL1 3EW (☎ 0727 555 66, fax 0727 410 77)

FARREN, Peter Stefan; *b* 16 Oct 1944; *Educ* Mill Hill Sch, Université de Grenoble, Kings Coll London (LLB); *m* 21 July 1973, Victoria Anne; 1 s (Ben b 11 April 1978), 2 da (Amy b 4 March 1980, Jessica b 30 Aug 1984); *Career* admitted slr 1969, William Brandt Son and Co Ltd 1973-76, Linklaters and Paines 1967-73 and 1976-; memb Worshipful Co of Solicitors 1979, Freeman City of London 1979; memb Law Soc 1969; *Recreations* flying, golf, squash; *Clubs* Hadley Wood Golf; *Style*— Peter Farren, Esq; Linklaters and Paines, Barrington House, 59-67 Gresham St, London EC2 (☎ 071 606 7080)

FARRER, Hon Anne Lucy; 3 da (only da by 2 w) of 2 Baron Farrer (d 1940) (title ext 1964); *b* 12 July 1908; *Educ* Downe House; *Career* MCSP; *Style*— The Hon Anne Farrer; Newby Cote, Clapham, via Lancaster, Lancs (☎ 046 85 204)

FARRER, His Hon Judge Brian Ainsworth; QC (1978); s of Albert Ainsworth Farrer (d 1966), and Gertrude, *née* Hall (d 1985); *b* 7 April 1930; *Educ* King's Coll Taunton, UCL (LLB); *m* 1960, Gwendoline Valerie, JP, da of William Waddoup (d 1986), of Lichfield; 2 s, 1 da; *Career* called to the Bar Gray's Inn 1957, Midlands and Oxford Circuit 1958-85, rec Crown Ct 1974-85, circuit judge 1985-; *Recreations* golf, bridge, chess; *Clubs* Aberdovey Golf; *Style*— His Hon Judge Brian Farrer, QC; Shutt Cross House, Aldridge, W Mids (☎ 0922 53602); Ardudwy Cottage, Ty Ardudwy, Aberdovey, Gwynedd (☎ 065 472 397)

FARRER, (Arthur) Mark; s of Maj Hugh Frederick Francis Farrer, TD (d 1952), of Essex, and Elizabeth Mary; *b* 25 March 1941; *Educ* Eton; *m* 28 Oct 1969, Zara Jane, da of Donald Thesiger, of Essex; 1 da (Lucy Frances b 6 Aug 1971); *Career* ptnr Farrer & Co 1968-; non-exec dep chm: Essex Water Co 1985-, East Anglian Water Co 1990-; non-exec dir: Assoc of Lloyd's Members 1986-, Lyonnaise (UK) Ltd 1988-; non-exec memb Cncl Lloyds of London 1987-; Liveryman Worshipful Co of Fishmongers; memb Law Soc; *Books* various technical publications; *Recreations* gardening, salmon fishing, the steam railway; *Clubs* Brooks', Essex; *Style*— Mark Farrer, Esq; Farrer & Co, 66 Lincolns Inn Fields, London WC2 (☎ 071 242 2022, fax 071 831 9748, telex 24318)

FARRER, Sir (Charles) Matthew; KCVO (1983, CVO 1973); s of Sir (Walter) Leslie Farrer, KCVO (d 1984), and Hon Lady (Marjorie Laura) Farrer (d 1981), da of 1 Viscount Hanworth, KBE, PC; *b* 3 Dec 1929; *Educ* Bryanston, Balliol Coll Oxford; *m* 1962, Johanna Creszentia Maria Dorothea, da of Prof Hans-Herman Bennhold, of Tübingen, Germany; 1 s, 1 da; *Career* slr 1956; ptnr Messrs Farrer & Co 1959-; private slr to HM The Queen 1965-; tstee Br Museum 1989-, cmmr Royal Commission on Hist Manuscripts 1991-; *Style*— Sir Matthew Farrer, KCVO; 6 Priory Ave, Bedford Park, London W4; Messrs Farrer & Co, 66 Lincoln's Inn Fields, London WC2A 3LH (☎ 01 242 2022)

FARRER, (John) Philip William; s of William Oliver Farrer, of Popmoor, Fernhurst, Haslemere, Surrey, and Margery Hope Farrer (d 1976); *b* 12 March 1958; *Educ* Eton, Sandhurst; *m* 19 July 1986, Maria Jane Margaret, da of Cuthbert Peter Ronald Bowlby, of Liphook, Hants; 2 da (Beatrice Hope b 27 July 1987, Katherine Isabella Caroline b 17 March 1989); *Career* 2 Bn Coldstream Gds 1978-82; Grievson Grant & Co 1982-84, UBS Phillips & Drew 1985, SBC Stockbroking 1986-89, Merrill Lynch International 1989-; memb Stock Exchange; *Recreations* skiing, golf, tennis; *Style*— Philip Farrer, Esq; 25 Killieser Ave, London SW2 4NX (☎ 081 671 5792); Merrill Lynch International, Ropemaker Place, 25 Ropemaker St, London EC2Y 9LY (☎ 071 867 3993, fax 071 867 2901, telex 8811047)

FARRER, Trevor Maurice; CBE (1991); s of William Maurice Farrer, and Dorothy Joyce Farrer; *b* 21 Dec 1931; *Educ* The Knoll Sch Woburn Sands, Dauntsey's Sch Devizes; *m* 2 April 1960 (m dis 1986), Eileen Mary; 2 s (Stewart William b March 1961, Noel Ecroyd b 25 Dec 1963), 1 da (Xanthe Rachel (twin) b 25 Dec 1963); *Career* Nat Serv KORR 1950-52; farmer 1952-82; memb Cncl NFU 1965-74 (co chm 1970-73); memb: Agric Land Tbnl 1974-, Cons Nat Union Exec 1988-90, S Westmorland RDC 1963-66, Lancs River Authy and NW Water Authy 1966-84, Cumbria CC 1977-89; memb Cncl Westmorland Cons 1963-, memb NW Area Cons Exec 1981-; Freeman City of London 1986; *Recreations* music, travel, politics; *Clubs* Farmers; *Style*— Trevor Farrer, Esq, CBE; Whitbarrow Stables, Grange over Sands, Cumbria LA11 6SL (☎ 0448 52235)

FARRER, William Oliver; s of John Oliver Farrer, MC (d 1942); *b* 23 June 1926; *Educ* Eton, Balliol Coll Oxford; *m* 1, 1955, Margery Hope (d 1976), da of William Yates (d 1931); 2 s, 1 da; m 2, 1979, Hazel Mary, da of Robert Clark Taylor (d 1963); *Career* Lt Coldstream Gds; slr; ptnr Farrer & Co 1955 (sr ptnr 1976); *Recreations* golf, music; *Clubs* Brooks's, MCC, Royal and Ancient; *Style*— William Farrer Esq; Popmoor, Fernhurst, Haslemere, Surrey (☎ 0428 642564)

FARRER-BROWN, Leslie; CBE (1960); s of late Sydney Brown, and Annie, *née* Brearley (d 1944); *b* 2 April 1904; *Educ* Southgate Secondary Sch, LSE (BSc); *m* 8 Dec 1928, Doris Evelyn (d 1986), da of Herbert Jamieson (d 1910); 2 s (Malcolm Jamieson b 15 July 1930, Geoffrey b 26 May 1934); *Career* asst registrar LSE 1927-28, admin staff Univ of London 1928-36, called to the Bar Gray's Inn 1932, sec Central Midwives Bd 1936-45, seconded to Miny of Health 1941-44, sec Interdepartmental Ctee on Med Schs 1942-44, sec to First Dir Nuffield Fndn 1944-64, tstee Nuffield Provincial Hosp Tst 1955-67, pres Sussex and Surrey Rent Assessment Panel 1965-76, chm Alliance Building Soc 1975-81 (dir 1969-85); JP: Middx 1947-65, Sussex 1966-81; chm Highgate Juvenile Ct 1952-61, Malta Med Servs Ctee 1956, Rhodesia Med Sch Ctee 1956-57, Nat Cncl Soc Serv 1960-73, Highgate Magistrates Ct 1961-65, Inst of Child Health Univ of London 1966-76; UK govr Cwlth Fndn 1966-89, memb Cncl and pro chllr Univ of Sussex 1976-80; chm: Overseas Visual Aid Ctee 1958-70, Centre for Educnl TV Overseas 1962-70, Ctee on R & D in Modern Languages 1964-70, Vol Ctee on Overseas Aid and Devpt 1965-76, Centre for Info on Language Teaching 1966-72; Hon LLD: Univ of Birmingham, Univ of Witwatersrand, Univ of Sussex; Hon DSc Univ of Keele; *Recreations* travel, painting; *Clubs* Athenaeum; *Style*— Leslie Farrer-Brown, Esq, CBE; 3 Kennet Court, Woosehill, Wokingham, Berkshire RG11 9BD

FARRER-BROWN, Malcolm Jamieson; s of Leslie Farrer-Brown, CBE, of 3 Kennet Court, Wooshill, Wokingham, Berks, and Doris Evelyn, *née* Jamieson (d 1986); *b* 15 July 1930; *m* 2 Jan 1960, Heather Josephine, da of Roy Gale (d 1983); 1 s (Robert Jamieson b 17 Dec 1969), 1 da (Catherine Gale b 17 July 1965); *Career* Nat Serv 2 Lt The Border Regt 1949-50; slr; Freshfields: articled clerk to Sir Charles Whishaw 1951-55, asst slr 1955-58; Richards Butler: asst slr 1958-61, ptnr 1961-91; gen mangr Guildhall String Ensemble; Liveryman: Worshipful Co of Slr's, Worshipful Co of Musician's; memb Law Soc, hon treas and sec The City Law Club; *Recreations* music, gardening, travel; *Clubs* City Law, Justinian; *Style*— Malcolm Farrer-Brown, Esq; 111 Defoe House, Barbican, London EC2Y 8DN (☎ 071 638 1725, fax 071 382 9179)

FARRINGTON, David; s of Ellis Farrington, of Dickley Wood, Ashford Rd, Harrietsham, Kent, and Pauline Eleanor Miles, *née* Toyne; *b* 2 Dec 1948; *Educ* Balshaw's GS Leyland Lancs, UCL (LLB); *Career* called to the Bar Middle Temple 1972; in practice and tenant Chambers of Louis Blom-cooper, QC, Goldsmith Buildings Temple EC4 1973-76, dep head of chambers of R Slowe, Esq, 4 Kings Bench Walk Temple EC4 1976-85, head of chambers 2 Garden Court Temple EC4 1985-91; *Books* Know Your Rights (ed, 1976), Law for the Consumer (ed, 1978), A Practical Guide to the Criminal Justice Act 1988 (jtly); *Recreations* theatre, films, ballet, tennis; *Style*— David Farrington, Esq

FARRINGTON, Col Sir Henry Francis Colden; 7 Bt (UK 1818); s of Sir Henry Anthony Farrington, 6 Bt (d 1944); *b* 25 April 1914; *Educ* Haileybury; *m* 22 March 1947, Anne, eldest da of late Maj William Albert Gillam, DSO, Border Regt; 1 s, 1 da (Susan Maria b 1949); *Heir* s, Henry William Farrington (*qv*); *Career* 2 Lt RA 1936, Maj 1942, ret 1960, Hon Col 1966; *Style*— Col Sir Henry Farrington, Bt; Higher Ford, Wiveliscombe, Taunton, Somerset TA4 2RL (☎ 0984 23219)

FARRINGTON, Henry William; s and h of Col Sir Henry Farrington, 7 Bt, *qv*; *b* 27 March 1951; *Educ* Haileybury, RAC Cirencester; *m* 1979, Diana Donne, da of Albert Geoffrey Broughton, of North Petherton, Somerset, 2 s (Henry John Albert b 1985, Charles George Donne b 1988); *Career* ARICS; farmer; landowner; *Style*— Henry Farrington Esq; Castle, Wiveliscombe, Taunton, Somerset TA4 2TJ (☎ 0984 23606)

FARRINGTON, Robin Neville; MC; s of Wyndham Brookes Farrington (d 1970), and Violet Muriel Neville (d 1981); *b* 1 July 1928; *Educ* Rugby, Magdalene Coll Cambridge (BA); *m* 6 Dec 1957, Suzanne Mary, *née* Holman; 3 s (Neville Leigh b 4 Dec 1958, Jonathan Piers b 13 May 1961, Rupert James b 31 Aug 1962); *Career* Nat Serv 1946-48, awarded Belt of Honour Eaton Hall OCTU, cmmnd Rifle Bde, served 2 KRRC Palestine; Matthews Wrightson 1952-58, Whitbread and Co 1958-88, chm Whitbread Investment Co PLC 1988-; Liveryman Worshipful Co of Grocers; *Recreations* skiing, sailing, travel, music, gardening; *Style*— Robin Farrington, Esq, MC; Whitbread Investment Company plc, Brewery, Chiswell St, London EC1Y 4SD (☎ 071 606 4455)

FARRINGTON, (William) Trevor; s of William Raymond Farrington, and Millicent, *née* Johnson; *b* 26 May 1941; *Educ* King's Coll Hosp Med Sch Univ of London (MB BS, LRCP); *Career* currently consIt otolaryngologist Dept of Otolaryngology Univ of Manchester and consIt head and neck surgn Christie Hosp and Holt Radiological Inst Manchester; memb Cncl Br Assoc of Otolaryngologists, examiner RCS; memb RSM, MRCS, FRCS; *Recreations* country pursuits; *Clubs* St James's (Manchester), East India; *Style*— Trevor Farrington, Esq; Sandilands Farm, Crowley, Northwich, Cheshire CW9 6NX (☎ 208 056585 208); Elm House, 2 Mauldeth Road, Withington, Manchester M20 9ND (☎ 061 434 9715)

FARROR, Shelagh Ann (Mrs Nicholas Jones); da of Robert Maitland Farror, of Maidenhead, Berks, and Rosemary Beatrice, *née* Croft (d 1975); *b* 25 March 1947; *Educ* St Michael's Sch Limpsfield, St Anne's Coll Oxford (BA, MA); *m* 25 Sept 1976, Nicholas Graham Jones, s of Albert Jones; 1 s (Benjamin Nicholas b 5 Aug 1986); *Career* called to the Bar Middle Temple 1970, family law practice; memb Family Law Bar Assoc; *Recreations* sailing, walking, reading, golf; *Clubs* Bar Yacht, Frensham Pond Sailing; *Style*— Miss Shelagh Farror; 3 Hare Court, Temple, London EC4 (☎ 071 353 7561)

FARROW, Douglas Henry; s of Henry George Nicholas Farrow (d 1961), and Elizabeth Margery, *née* Melish (d 1959); *b* 28 Oct 1924; *Educ* Harrow, RADA (LRAM, LGSM); *m* 1, 12 June 1951 (m dis 1957), (Maria) Margrit, da of Charles Hildebrand, of Basel; m 2, 29 Aug 1959 (m dis 1964), Belle Pomeroy, *née* Goldberg ;1 da (Victoria Elizabeth b 13 June 1960); m 3, 6 Nov 1971, Marie Lucette Mireille, da of Pierre Lucien Docourneau; 2 s (Paul Henri b 15 Jan 1975, Sebastian Guy b 17 July 1978); *Career* ptnr Allsop & Co Soho Square, ret 1963; md: Kinghill Group 1963-74, Hill Group 1974-81, Medalcrest Ltd 1981-; Freeman City of London, Liveryman Worshipful Co of Paviors 1964; FSVA; *Recreations* gardening, antique collecting, cruising; *Clubs* City Livery; *Style*— Douglas Farrow, Esq; Wickham Green Farm, Newbury, Berkshire RG16 8HL (☎ 0488 38255), Medalcrest Ltd, Charnham House, 29/30 Charnham St, Hungerford, Berkshire RG17 OEJ (☎ 0488 684157, car 0860 201418)

FARROW, Kenneth John; s of Wing Cdr Cyril Arthur Farrow of Harpenden, and Phyllis Mary, *née* Driver; *b* 31 Aug 1942; *Educ* Culford Sch Bury St Edmunds, Pembroke Coll Oxford (MA, BCL); *m* 15 April 1972, Jennifer Ann, da of late Ronald Lusby; 1 s (Robert b 1978), 1 da (Catherine b 1973); *Career* called to the Bar Gray's Inn 1966, chambers of Charles Sparrow QC 1967-, asst recorder 1985-, memb Legal Aid Bd 1988-; *Style*— Kenneth Farrow, Esq; 13 Old Square, Lincolns Inn, London WC2A 3UA (☎ 071 2426105, telex 262207 ACT10, fax 071 4054

FARROW, Nigel Alexander Emery; s of Arthur Hemsworth Farrow, of Bentley, Hants, and Estelle Frances, *née* Emery; *b* 24 March 1939; *Educ* Cheltenham, Queens' Coll Cambridge (MA); *m* 2 Dec 1961, Susan, da of Thomas Bertram Daltry (d 1974); 3 da (Miranda b 1965, Sarah b 1967, Imogen b 1970); *Career* publisher; ed Business Mgmnt 1964-67; chm: Xerox Publishing Group Ltd 1972-82, Ginn & Co Ltd 1972-78, University Microfilms Ltd 1972-82; dir and chm: Gower Publishing Group Ltd, Ashgate Publishing Ltd, Dartmouth Publishing Co Ltd, Edward Elgar Publishing Ltd, Information Publications International Ltd, Information Publications, PTE Ltd Singapore; pres Cheltonian Soc 1988-, memb Cheltenham Coll Cncl, tstee New Ashgate Gallery; FRSA; *Books* Gower Handbook of Management (ed), The English Library (ed); author of numerous articles on business and management; *Recreations* reading books, looking at pictures; *Style*— Nigel Farrow, Esq; Dipenhall Gate, Dippenhall, Farnham, Surrey; 19 Whitehall, 9-11 Bloomsbury Square, London; Gower House, Croft Road, Aldershot, Hants

FARROW, Victoria Elizabeth (Mrs Nicholas Elton); *née* Farrow; da of Douglas Henry Farrow, and Belle, *née* Goldberg; *b* 13 June 1960; *Educ* Francis Holland Sch, Chelsea Sch of Art (BA); *m* 7 Dec 1985, Nicholas George Stephen Elton, s of Paul Elton; *Career* mktg mangr J Trevor & Sons 1985-, mktg conslt Allsop & Co 1987-90, currently md Victoria Farrow Publicity; *Recreations* freelance journalism, design; *Style*— Miss Victoria Farrow; 45 Burnaby Street, London SW10 OPW; 58 Grosvenor Street, London WIX ODD (☎ 071 629 8151, fax 01 499 5555, car 0860 251 468)

FARRY, James; s of James Farry (d 1972), and Helen Carlin; *b* 1 July 1954; *Educ* Queen's Park Senior Secdy, Hunter HS, Claremont HS; *m* 17 June 1978, Elaine Margaret, da of William Alexander Campbell McInnes, of Glasgow; 1 s (Ewan b 31 July 1984), 1 da (Alyson b 18 March 1982); *Career* sec The Scottish Football League 1979-89, chief exec The Scottish Football Assoc 1990 (admin asst 1972-77, asst sec 1977-79, sec elect 1989); *Recreations* football spectating, fishing, reading; *Clubs* Royal Scottish Automobile, Cambuslang RFC; *Style*— James Farry, Esq; The Scottish Football Association Ltd, 6 Park Gardens, Glasgow G3 7YF (☎ 041 332 6372, fax 041 3327559, telex 778904)

FARSTAD, Jan-Arne; s of Petter N Farstad (d 1982), of Aalesund, Norway, and Klara, *née* Bjoerhovde; *b* 9 Sept 1950; *Educ* Jacksonville State Univ USA (BS), Univ of California Berkeley USA (MBA); *m* 9 Sept 1977, Marie-France, da of Edouard Durand (d 1966), of Rio de Janeiro, Brazil; 1 da (Anne-Christine b 29 June 1980); *Career* vice pres Wells Fargo Bank 1975-83, sr vice pres Bank of Montreal 1983-87, md Royal Trust Bank 1988-; *Recreations* golf, skiing, classical music; *Clubs* RAC, Overseas Bankers Club; *Style*— Jan-Arne Farstad, Esq; Royal Trust Bank, Royal Trust House, 48-50 Cannon St, London EC4N 6LD (☎ 071 236 6044, fax 071 248 0828, telex 8952879)

FARTHING, (Richard) Bruce Crosby; s of Col Herbert Hadfield Farthing, RA (d 1978), and Marjorie Cora, *née* Fisher (d 1981); *b* 9 Feb 1926; *Educ* Alleyn's Sch, St Catharine's Coll Cambridge (BA, MA); *m* 1, 14 Feb 1959 (m dis 1986), (Anne) Brenda, da of Capt Thomas Williams (d 1961); 1 s (Richard Crosby b 24 July 1962), 1 da (Anne Crosby b 30 Nov 1959); m 2, 6 Nov 1986, Moira Jess Roupell, da of Lt-Col Curties, RA (d 1970); *Career* joined RA 1944, RA OCTU 1945-46, sr under offr 1946, served various field regts and 7 RHA in Europe, Egypt and Palestine 1946-47, demobbed as Lt 1948; called to the Bar Inner Temple 1954; govt legal serv 1954-59; Chamber of Shipping of the UK: legal advsr 1959, asst gen mangr 1966; sec Ctee of Euro Shipowners 1967-74, sec Ctee of Euro Nat Shipowners Assocs 1967-74, sec gen Cncl of Euro and Japanese Nat Shipowners Assoc (CENSA) 1974- 76, dir gen Cncl of Br Shipping 1976-80 (dep dir 1980-83); Rapporteur Sea Tport Cmmn Int C of C 1976-, conslt to ICC on maritime affrs 1983-, conslt dir Int Assoc of Dry Cargo and Shipowners 1983-; memb ct of common cncl Corpn of London (Ward of Aldgate) 1982-, pres Aldgate Ward Club 1985 (vice pres 1984); govr: City of London Sch 1983- (vice chm Bd of Govrs 1988, chm 1990), SOAS 1985; chm reception ctee for state banquet to King of Norway 1988, tstee Nautical Museums Tst 1983-; Freeman City of London 1978, Liveryman Worshipful Co of Shipwrights 1982 (Freeman 1978); FBIM 1983; Cdr Royal Norwegian Order of Merit 1988; *Books* Aspinalls Maritime Law Cases (ed vol 20, 1961), International Shipping: an introduction to the Policies Politics and Institutions of the Maritime World (1987); *Recreations* sailing, gardening, music; *Clubs* Royal Ocean Racing, MCC, Incogniti Cricket, Rye Golf; *Style*— Bruce Farthing, Esq; Snaylham House, Icklesham, East Sussex TN36 4AJ (☎ 0424 812 983, fax 0424 814746); 44 St Georges Dr, London SW1 4BT (☎ 071 834 1211); Fifth Floor, 39 Dover St, London W1X 3RB (☎ 071 629 7079, fax 071 493 7865)

FARTHING, Ramon; s of Clifford Ramon George Farthing (d 1983), and Patricia Carter, of 64 Rosebank, Parkeston Rd, Harwich, Essex; *b* 9 Feb 1961; *Educ* Sir Anthony Deane Secdy Sch, Colchester Inst of Higher Educn; *m* Karen Elaine, da of John Arundel; 1 s (Kai Ramon b 6 Dec 1990); *Career* apprentice under Chris Oakley at The Pier Restaurant 1978-80, commis chef under Sam Chalmers at Le Talbooth Restaurant Dedham Essex 1980-83, personal chef to Lord and Lady Spencer Althrop House Northamptonshire 1983-84, second chef to Chris Oakes The Castle Hotel Taunton 1984-86, first head chef Calcot Manor Gloucestershire 1986-; *awards* entries in Egon Ronay and The Good Food Guide, Michelin Star Rating 1986, 1 AA Rosette for cooking 1987, Ackermann Guide Clover Leaf 1990; *Recreations* music, reading cookery books; *Clubs* Caterer Acorn; *Style*— Ramon Farthing, Esq; 8 Cherrytree Close, Nailsworth, Gloucestershire GL6 0DX (☎ 0453838 4655); Calcot Ventures, Calcot Manor Hotel, nr Tetbury, Gloucestershire GL8 8YJ (☎ 0666 890391, fax 0666 890394)

FARTHING, Stephen Frederick Godfrey; s of Dennis Jack Farthing (d 1985), of London, and Joan Margaret, *née* Godfrey; *b* 16 Sept 1950; *Educ* St Martins Sch of Art, Royal Coll of Art, Br Sch Rome (Abbey Major scholar); *m* Joan Elizabeth, *née* Jackson; 1 da (Constance Beatrice); *Career* lectr in painting Canterbury Coll of Art 1977-79, tutor in painting Royal Coll of Art 1979-85, head of Dept of Fine Art W Surrey Coll of Art and Design Farnham 1987-88 (head of painting 1985-87), artist in residence Hayward Gallery 1989; selected one man exhibitions: Town and Country (Edward Totah Gallery London) 1986, New Ashgate Gallery Farnham 1987, Edward Totah Gallery London 1987, Mute Accomplices (Museum of Modern Art Oxford (touring) 1988, Stephen Farthing and the Leonardo Exhibition (Queen Elizabeth Hall London) 1989, Stephen Farthing at the Paco Imperial Rio De Janeiro, National Museum of Art Montevideo Uruguay, Museo de Monterray Mexico 1990, Museo de Gil Mexico 1990; selected exhibitions: Advent Calendar Gallery North Lancashire 1989-90, Now for the Future (Haywood Gallery London) 1990, RA Summer Exhibiton 1990, Heritage Exhibition Cornerhouse Manchester (touring) 1990; collections incl: Leicester City Museum, Nat Museum of Wales, Bradford Art Galleries and Museums, Government Art Collection Fund, Br Cncl; elected Ruskin master and professorial fell of St Edmund Hall Oxford; *Recreations* photography, travel; *Style*— Stephen Farthing, Esq; Ruskin School of Drawing, Oxford University, The High St, Oxford OX1 4BG (☎ 0865 276940)

FARTHING, Thomas William; OBE (1983); s of late Thomas Farthing; *b* 19 Dec 1927; *Educ* Middlesbrough HS, Jesus Coll Cambridge (MA, PhD); *m* (m dis); 1 s, 1 da; *Career* metallurgist; IMI Res 1951-58, Beryllium project mangr IMI 1958-62, res mangr Traditional Metals IMI 1962-64, Euro res dir Int Copper Res Assoc 1964-66; md: Wolverhampton Metal Ltd 1966-74, IMI Titanium 1974-, additional responsibility for corporate res and devpt 1983-; cncl memb: The Inst of Metals, SBAC; chm SBAC Materials Gp Ctee, treas and cncl memb BNF Metals Technol Centre Wantage; memb DTI Aviation Ctee, DTI Metals and Minerals Ctee; FEng; *Recreations* walking, reading, music, gardening; *Style*— Thomas Farthing, Esq, OBE; c/o IMI Titanium Ltd, PO Box 704, Birmingham B6 7UR (☎ 021 356 1155, telex 336771)

FARWELL, Mrs Arthur Barbara; *née* Baroness Barbara Korff; da of Baron Serge Alexandrovitch Korff, of Russia; *b* 31 Jan 1911; *m* 1, 1941, Hon Edward Wriothesley Curzon Russell, OBE (d 1982, sometime managing ed Morning Post), 3 s of 2 Baron Ampthill; 2 da (Diana b 1943, Margaret Angela b 1946); m 2, 1988, Arthur Farwell; *Style*— Mrs Arthur Farwell; Tall Pines, 308 Hearthstone Ridge, Landrum, S Carolina 29356-9602, USA (☎ 803 457 4689); Pony's Point, Iona, CB1, Nova Scotia, (BOA 1LO) Canada (☎ 902 622 2766)

FASHANU, John; s of Patrick Fashanu, of Nigeria, and Pearl Gopaul; *b* 18 Sept 1962; *Educ* Attleborough Secdy Sch Norfolk; 1 da (Amal b 21 April 1989); *Career* professional footballer; jr player: Peterborough Utd, Cambridge Utd, Norwich City: signed professional 1979, debut v Derby County 1982, 7 league appearances; 1 league appearance on loan Crystal Palace 1983, 36 league appearances Lincoln City 1983-84, 50 league appearances Millwall 1984-86, over 160 league appearances Wimbledon 1986-; 2 full England caps 1989; FA Cup winners medal Wimbledon 1988, Charity Shield medal Wimbledon 1988; former county champion Norfolk; md: Fash Enterprises, Admiral Nigeria Ltd, Blue Orchid; dir Kiss FM; Lions Youth for int community work, Business Fedn award Lloyds Bank 1990, black men and women in media award World Sports Corp 1990, citation from pres UN Maj-Gen Joe Garba; *Recreations* my businesses, tennis; *Style*— John Fashanu, Esq; Admiral Nigeria Limited, Gayfere House, 22/23 Gayfere St, Westminster, London SW19 3HP (☎ 071 222 8161, fax 071 799 1457)

FATCHETT, Derek John; MP (Lab) Leeds Central 1983-; s of Herbert and Irene Fatchett; *b* 8 Aug 1945; *Educ* Lincoln Sch, Birmingham Univ, LSE; *m* 1969, Anita Bridgens, *née* Oakes; 2 s; *Career* university lecturer, cncllr Wakefield Met Boro; *Style*— Derek Fatchett Esq, MP; House of Commons, London SW1

FATHERS, Antony; *b* 27 June 1931; *Educ* Charterhouse, Oxford Univ (MA); *m* 21 July 1962, Elizabeth Margaret, da of Frederick Brewer (d 1963), late Mayor of Oxford; 1 s (Richard b 1967, d 1979), 1 da (Victoria b 1970); *Career* md Czech & Speake 1984-; FID; *Recreations* squash, opera, gardening; *Clubs* IOD; *Style*— Antony Fathers, Esq; 613 Upper Richmond Road, West Richmond, Surrey; Czech & Speake, 39 Jermyn St, London (☎ 081 980 4567)

FATHERS, Michael Allen; s of Walter Armstrong Fathers, of Takapuna, New Zealand, and Joyce Alice, *née* Barwell (d 1975); *b* 7 July 1941; *Educ* King's Coll Auckland NZ, Victoria Univ Wellington NZ (BA); *m* 8 January 1972, Angela Lemoine, *née* Denman; 1 s (Thomas Benjamin b 31 July 1976), 1 da (Alexandra Frankie b 21 Sept 1974); *Career* journalist; NZ Press Assoc 1966-69; Reuters London office: 1970-71, 1976-78, 1984-85; foreign corr Reuters: Vietnam 1972-73, Tanzania 1974-75, Pakistan 1979-81, Thailand 1981-83, E Africa 1986; Asia ed The Independent 1986-89, foreign specialist writer The Independent on Sunday 1989-; *Books* Tiananmen; The Rape of Peking (with Andrew Higgins, 1989); *Style*— Michael Fathers, Esq; The Independent on Sunday, 40 City Rd, London EC1Y 2DB (☎ 071 253 1222, fax 071 415 1333)

FATTORINI, Joseph; MBE (1945), TD; s of Edward Joseph Fattorini (d 1950), of Bradford, and Lilian Mary, *née* Harrop (d 1956); *b* 8 Nov 1912; *Educ* Stonyhurst; *m* 5 June 1941, Mary, da of Maj Edward Joseph Collingwood; 2 s (Peter b 2 May 1942, Edward b 25 Sept 1943), 1 da (Jane (Mrs de Halpert) b 14 Nov 1948); *Career* 2 Lt West Yorks Regt TA 1938, WWII 1939-45 Maj 2 i/c 601 Regt RA (West Yorks) TA; Empire Stores (Bradford) Ltd: md 1945-65, chm 1965-72, vice chm 1972-75; chm Yorks and Lancs Investmt Trust Ltd until 1975; vice chm and dir: Arbuthnot Securities (CL) Ltd, Assoc Investmt Tsts 1975-85; chm Singer & Friedlander (CI) Ltd; non-exec dir: Colonnade Reinsurance Ltd, Guernsey Catholic Nat Mutual Ltd (Guernsey); chm: St Bedes GS Bradford until 1973, Cardinal Hinsley and St Margaret Clitheroe GS until 1975, Leeds Area Health Authy Teaching 1973-75; memb: Leeds Regnl Hosp Bd (chm fin and geriatrics) 1952-67, Bradford Borough Mgmnt Ctee 1948-51, Guernsey Soc for Cancer Relief, Ct Univ of Leeds; govr Leeds Utd Teaching Hosp 1966-74, pres Stonyhurst Old Boys Assoc 1974; JP (City of Bradford 1955-75); FBIM, FRSA; KSG 1963, Knight of the Holy Sepulchre 1963; *Recreations* golf, skiing; *Clubs* Utd Guernsey, Royal Channel Islands Yacht; *Style*— Joseph Fattorini, Esq, MBE, TD; Saumarez Lodge, The Queens Rd, St Peter Port, Guernsey (☎ 0481 229 11)

FAUCONBERG AND CONYERS, Baronies of (E 1283 and 1509); *see*: Miller, Lady Diana and Lycett, Lady Wendy

FAULDER, Carolyn Mary; *née* Calburn; da of Charles Clement Calburn (d 1977) (*see* Burke's Landed Gentry 18th Edn, vol.3), and Maria Clemencia, *née* Echeverria (d 1969); *b* 13 Feb 1934; *Educ* Convent of the Holy Child Jesus St Leonards on Sea, Bedford Coll, Univ of London (BA); *m* 2 June 1956, (m dis 1989), John Sewell Faulder, s of Ronald Sewell Faulder (d 1983); 1 s (Dominic b 1958), 2 da (Sarah b 1957, Clemencia b 1961); *Career* journalist, author and lectr; *Books incl* Treat Yourself to Sex, The Women's Cancer Book, Whose Body is it?; *Recreations* the company of friends; *Style*— Ms Carolyn Faulder; 25 Belsize Park Gardens, London NW3 4JH (☎ 071 722 5557)

FAULDER, John Sewell; s of Ronald Sewell Faulder (d 1975), and Ruth, *née* Huggins (d 1972); *b* 16 Jan 1930; *Educ* Marlborough, Ch Ch Oxford (MA), IMEDE Lausanne (Dip); *m* 2 June 1956 (m dis 1989), Carolyn Mary, da of Charles Clement Calburn (d 1977); 1 s (Dominic b 1958), 2 da (Sarah b 1957, Clemencia b 1961); *Career* Nat Serv 2 Lt Royal Dragoons 1951-53, Capt Inns of Court HQ 56 (London) Armoured Div TA 1953-62; controller Crosse & Blackwell The Nestlé Co Ltd 1958-69, Henry Anbacher Ltd 1970-71, dir Chaterhouse Devpt and chm subsidiaries Charterhouse Gp plc 1971-82, dir Sandell Perkin's plc 1975-88, chm Electrothermal Engrg Ltd and dir B T Basford Ltd 1982-; Freeman City of London, Master Worshipful Co of Builders Merchants 1986; FInstBM 1986; *Recreations* shooting, painting; *Clubs* Bucks, Hurlingham; *Style*— John Faulder, Esq; 27 Marloes Road, London W8 6LG (☎ 071 2447663)

FAULDS, Andrew Matthew William; MP (Lab) Warley E 1974-; s of Rev Matthew Faulds and Doris Faulds; *b* 1 March 1923; *Educ* George Watson's Coll Edinburgh, King Edward VI GS Louth, Daniel Stewart's Sch Edinburgh, Stirling HS, Univ of Glasgow; *m* 1945, Bunty Whitfield; 1 da; *Career* actor; formerly with Shakespeare Meml Co Stratford, also TV, radio and films; MP (Lab) Smethwick 1966-74; PPS to Min of State for Aviation Miny of Technol 1967-68, PMG 1968-69; oppn front bench spokesman arts 1970-73 and 1979-82 (sacked for opposing official Labour policy on Falklands crisis); chm: Parly Assoc Euro-Arab Cooperation UK branch 1974-, All-Party Heritage Gp, Br Delegation to Cncl of Europe and WEU 1975-80 and 1987-, Exec Ctee IPU Br Section 1983-; *Style*— Andrew Faulds, Esq, MP; 14 Albemarle St, London W1 (☎ 071 499 7589)

FAULDS, Ian Craig; s of Basil Craig Faulds, of Bromsgrove, and Paula, *née* Klausner; *b* 4 July 1948; *Educ* Rossall, Univ of Durham (BA, Cert Ed); *m* 20 July 1974, Clare, da of Albert Wiliam Harper (d 1979); 2 s (Matthew b 1977,William b 1984); *Career* asst master King William's Coll IOM 1971-74, dir Shearwater Press Ltd 1975-80, ed The Manxman 1976-78, md Trafalgar Press Ltd 1982-; ed: The Peel City Guardian 1986-, The Ramsey Chronicle 1987-, Manx Life 1988-; chm Peel Chamber of Trade 1986-88; *Recreations* antiques, gardening, walking; *Style*— Ian Faulds Esq; The Lynague, German, Isle of Man, (☎ 0624 842045); 14 Douglas St, Peel, Isle of Man, (☎ 0624 843882 - 0624 843882)

FAULKNER, Amanda Jane; da of Richard George Butler Faulkner (d 1976), and Gillian Mary Josephine Hopkinson, *née* Park; *b* 5 Dec 1953; *Educ* St Anthony's Leweston, Canford Sch, Bournemouth Coll of Art, Ravensbourne Coll of Art, Chelsea Sch of Art; *Career* artist; solo exhibitions incl: Woodlands Art Gallery Blackheath London 1983, Angela Flowers Gallery 1985-1986, Big Woman (Metropole Arts Centre Folkestone) 1987, Seven Deadly Sins and Recent Drawings and Prints (Flowers East

Gallery London) 1988, Breaking Water (Drumcroon Arts and Educn Centre Wigan) 1989, Flowers East London 1990; gp exhibitions incl: The Print Show (Angela Flowers Gallery London) 1983; What's New in the Arts Council Collection (touring) 1984, Double Elephant (Concourse Gallery Barbican London) 1985, The Print Show - Woodcuts and Linocuts (Angela Flowers Gallery London 1985, Identity/Desire - Representing the Body (Scot Arts Cncl touring) 1986, On a Plate (Serpentine Gallery London) 1987, Print Biennale of Liège (Musée d'Art Moderne Belgium) 1987, Mother and Child (Lefevre Gallery London) 1988, Ljubljana Print Biennale (Yugoslavia) 1989, More Artists Against Apartheid (Canon Collins) 1989, Angela Flowers Gallery 1990 (Barbican Concourse Gallery London) 1989, Flowers at Moos (Gallery Moos NY) 1990; work in various public collections, selector for various awards; appointed princ lectr in printmaking Sch of Fine Art, Chelsea Coll of Art and Design London 1991; *Clubs* Chelsea Arts; *Style—* Ms Amanda Faulkner; Flowers East, c/o 199-205 Richmond Rd, London E3 3NJ (☎ 081 985 3333)

FAULKNER, Hon (Lucy) Claire; da of Baron Faulkner of Downpatrick (Life Peer, d 1977); *b* 1954; *Educ* Hillcourt Dublin, Moreton Hall Shropshire, Univ of Edinburgh; *Career* Br Tourist Authy 1979-84; started own business Project Planning (conference and exhibition organiser) 1984; *Recreations* eventing, hunting; *Style—* The Hon Claire Faulkner; The Gate Lodge, Spa Road, Ballynahinch, Co Down, Northern Ireland

FAULKNER, Hon (Brian) David Alexander; s of Baron Faulkner of Downpatrick (Life Peer, d 1977); *b* 1951; *Educ* Glenalmond Coll, Perthshire, Aberdeen Univ (MA); *m* 28 Aug 1982, (Belinda) Gail, eldest da of James Elliott Wilson, OBE, DL, of White Lodge, Boardmills, Co Down; 2 s, 1 da; *Career* haulage contractor; *Recreations* hunting, sailing; *Style—* The Hon David Faulkner; Highlands, Seaforde, Downpatrick, Co Down, NI

FAULKNER, David Andrew Vincent; s of John Andrew Gordon Faulkner, and Maureen Anne, *née* Shardlow; *b* 10 Sept 1962; *Educ* Brune Park Sch Gosport, Highbury Tech Coll Cosham; *m* 10 Aug 1985, Jane Margaret, da of Alan Gordon Salmons; 1 s (Simon David b 7 July 1990); *Career* hockey player; over 400 appearances Havant 1978-, 50 appearances Guildford 1982-84; 125 England caps (capt 1990-), 77 GB caps (capt 1990-); major int appearances: Euro Cup Amsterdam 1983 and Moscow 1987 (Silver medal), World Cup London 1986 (Silver medal) and Lahore 1990, Olympics Seoul 1988 (Gold medal), Champion's Trophies 1984-90 (Bronze medal Karachi 1984, Silver medal Aust 1985); 12 appearances Jr Euro Cup Barcelona 1980, 7 appearances Jr Indoor Euro Cup Vienna 1981; Player of the Year: Poundstretcher Nat League 1988-89, Hockey Writers 1989; Marconi Space & Defence Systems 1979-84, Thame Components Ltd 1984-86, ECMS Computers Ltd 1986-88, gen mangr Promotions Div Hargreaves Sports Ltd 1988-; *Recreations* squash, music, history; *Style—* David Faulkner, Esq; Havant Hockey Club, Havant Park, Havant, Hampshire (☎ 0705 482497)

FAULKNER, David Edwart Riley; CB (1985); s of Harold Ewart Faulkner (d 1968), of Manchester and London, and Mabel, *née* Riley (d 1960); *b* 23 Oct 1934; *Educ* Manchester GS, Merchant Taylors', St John's Coll Oxford (MA); *m* 16 Sept 1961, Sheila Jean, da of James Stevenson (d 1985), of Buckinghamshire; 1 s (Martin b 1962), 1 da (Rosemary b 1965); *Career* Nat Serv RA and Intelligence Corps, 2 Lt 1957-59; Home Office: asst princ 1959, princ 1963, asst sec 1969, private sec to the Home Sec 1969, Prison Dept 1970, Police Dept 1975, asst under sec of state 1976 (seconded to the Cabinet Office 1978-79 dir of operational policy Prison Dept 1980, dep under sec of state Criminal and Res and Statistical Depts 1982, princ Establishment Offr 1990; memb: United Nations Ctee on Crime Prevention and Control, Advsy Bd of Helsinki Inst for Crime Prevention and Control; *Style—* David Faulkner, Esq, CB; Home Office, 50 Queen Anne's Gate, London SW1 (☎ 071 273 3000)

FAULKNER, Hon Mrs (Deborah Jane); o da of 2 Baron MacAndrew (d 1989); *b* 1956; *Educ* Tudor Hall, Wykham Park Banbury, Winkfield; *m* 1979, Maj Mark William Bingham Faulkner, 5 Royal Inniskilling Dragoon Gds; 2 s (James William MacAndrew b 1983, Alexander Charles MacAndrew b 1987); *Recreations* riding, skiing, tennis, bridge; *Style—* The Hon Mrs Faulkner; c/o Officers' Mess, 5 Royal Inniskilling Dragoon Gds, BFPO 16

FAULKNER, Prof Douglas; s of Vincent Faulkner (d 1976), of Eastbourne, and Florence Emily, *née* Weller (d 1985); *b* 29 Dec 1929; *Educ* Royal Dockyard Col Devonport (Naval Constructor Cadetship and Whitworth scholar), RNE and RN Colls, MIT Cambridge Mass (PhD); *m* 1 (m dis); 3 da (Wendy Ruth b 1956, Karelia Ann b 1958, Alison Claire b 1960); m 2, 11 Aug 1987, Isobel Parker, *née* Campbell; *Career* asst constructor (sea service, aircraft carrier structural design, prodn engrg) 1954-59, naval constructor and structural res (structural design of HMSM Dreadnought) 1959-63, asst prof RNC Greenwich 1963-68, constructor cdr Washington 1968-70, defence fell MIT Boston 1970-71, chief constructor Bath and Box Girder Bridge Enquiry 1971-73, head Dept of Naval Architecture and Ocean Engineering Glasgow 1973-, dean of engrg Glasgow 1978-81, conslt Conoco Inc Houston 1981-83, dir Veritec Limited 1985-88, visiting prof VPI Blacksburg Virginia 1986-87, ed Journal of Marine Structures 1987-; advsr Merison Box Girder Bridge Enquiry 1972; memb: American Ship Structures Ctee 1968-71, Defence Scientific Advsy Cncl Ctees 1975-86, DEn Advsy Gps on Offshore Structures 1976-81; UK rep Int Ship and Offshore Structures Congress 1976-85, chm Conoco-ABS Tension Leg Platform Design Ctee 1981-83, memb Bd of Govrs BMT Quality Assessors Ltd; memb: Whitworth Soc 1950, Soc Noval Architects and Marine Engs 1969; FRINA 1971, FIStructE 1972, FEng 1981; *Books* Integrity of Offshore Structures (ed 1981, 1987 and 1990); *Recreations* hill walking, chess; *Style—* Prof Douglas Faulkner; 57 Bellshaugh Place, Glasgow G12 0PF (☎ 041 357 1748); Department of Naval Architecture and Ocean Engineering, University of Glasgow, Glasgow G12 8QQ (☎ 041 330 4303, fax 041 330 5917, telex 777070 UNIGLA)

FAULKNER, Sir Eric Odin; MBE (1945), TD; s of Sir Alfred Edward Faulkner, CB, CBE (d 1963), and Edith Florence, *née* Nicoll; *b* 21 April 1914; *Educ* Bradfield, CCC Cambridge (hon fell); *m* 1939, Joan Mary, da of Lt-Col F A M Webster; 1 s, 1 da; *Career* WWII Lt-Col RA; banker; dir: Hudson's Bay Co 1950-70, Vickers plc 1957-79; chm: Union Discount Co 1959-70 (dir 1949-70), Glyn Mills & Co 1963-68, Lloyds Bank Ltd 1968-77; dir and dep chm Fin for Indust 1977-80, advsy dir Unilever plc 1979-84; chm Industl Soc 1973-76, pres Br Bankers Assoc 1979-83; warden Bradfield Coll 1965-83; kt 1974; *Recreations* fishing (formerly cricket and associaton football (CUAFC XI 1935)); *Style—* Sir Eric Faulkner, MBE, TD; Farriers Field, Sevenoaks Rd, Ightham, Kent TN15 9AA

FAULKNER, Hugh Branston; OBE (1980); s of Frank Faulkner (d 1964), and Ethel, *née* Branston (d 1968); *b* 8 June 1916; *Educ* Lutterworth GS; *m* 1954, Anne Carlton, *née* Milner; 1 s (Anthony), 1 da (Jane); *Career* admin asst City of Leicester Educn Ctee 1936-46, organising sec Fellowship of Reconciliation 1946-54, christian peace delegate USSR 1952, lectr in int affrs USA 1953; hon dir Voluntary and Christian Serv 1954-79 (tstee), dir Help the Aged (fndr memb) 1961-83, del and speaker UN World Assembly on Ageing Vienna 1982, dir Asthma Res Cncl 1983-88; charity conslt 1988-; tstee: Voluntary and Christian Serv, World in Need Tst, Lester Tst; hon advsr Elderly Accomodation Counsel, memb Exec Ctee Cncl for Music in Hosps 1983-; FCIS; *Recreations* music, gardening; *Clubs* Nat Liberal; *Style—* Hugh Faulkner, Esq, OBE; Longfield, 4 One Tree Lane, Beaconsfield, Bucks HP9 2BU (☎ 0494 674 769)

FAULKNER, Cdr Hugh Douglas Younger; LVO (1991); s of Rear Adm Hugh Webb Faulkner, CB, CBE, DSO, DL (d 1969), and Olave Mary, *née* Younger (d 1989); *b* 17 May 1931; *Educ* West Downs Winchester, RNC Dartmouth; *m* 28 July 1956, Fiona Naomi, da of Brig Dominick Andrew Sydney Browne, CBE (d 1981), of Breaghwy, Castlebar, Co Mayo; 2 s (Christopher Gerald b 15 Aug 1958, Anthony Dominick Hugh b 5 April 1961); *Career* HMS Liverpool 1949-50, HMS Sheffield 1952-54, HMS Hornet (CO MTB Dark Antagonist) 1954-56, HMS Mercury (signal offr qualifying course) 1957-58, staff of C-in-C Home Fleet (FCA) 1959-60, HMS Mercury 1961-62, staff of SNO W Indies 1962-64, staff course RNC Greenwich 1964, HMS Mercury 1965-66, MOD 1967-70, Cdr HMS Mercury 1970-72, 2 i/c HMS Collingwood 1973-75, staff of C in C Naval Home Cmd 1975-78, ret 1978; sec Royal Warrant Holders Assoc 1979-; *Recreations* shooting, fishing, golf; *Clubs* Army and Navy; *Style—* Cdr Hugh Faulkner, LVO; Currie Lee Crichton, Nr Parkhead, Midlothian EH37 5XB (☎ 0875 320563), 95 Cambridge St, London SW1V 4PY (☎ 071 821 6334)

FAULKNER, John Richard Hayward; s of Capt Richard Hayward Ollerton (d 1943), and Lilian Elizabeth, *née* Carrigan; *b* 29 May 1941; *Educ* Archbishop Holgate's Sch, Keble Coll Oxford (BA); *m* 1970, Janet Gill, da of Alfred George Herbert Cummings; 2 da (Abigail b 1976, Emma b 1984), 2 step da (Zoe b 1963, Amanda b 1966); *Career* worked with several theatre cos incl: Meadow Players, Century Theatre, Prospect Theatre Co (fndr memb), Cambridge Theatre Co, Sixty-Nine Theatre Co 1964-72; drama dir: Scottish Arts Cncl 1972-76, Arts Cncl of GB 1976-83; assoc prodr and later head of artistic planning Nat Theatre 1983-88; theatre and mgmnt conslt 1988-; gen mangr Entertainment Corpn, UK rep American-Anglo-Soviet Theatre Initiative 1988-; non-exec dir: Galactic Smallholdings Ltd, Minotaur Films, The Arts for Nature Ltd; govr Arts Educnl Schs; chm: TNC/Writers Agreement Ctee, Assoc of Br Theatre Technicians; memb TMA Commercial Prodrs' Ctee; *Recreations* intricacies and wildernesses; *Style—* John Faulkner, Esq; 33 Hadley Gardens, Chiswick, London W4 4NU (☎ 081 995 3041)

FAULKNER, John Selway; s of Joseph Robert Faulkner, of Witts Cottage, Arlington Green, Bibury, Cirencester, Glos, and Rosalind Violet, *née* Selway; *b* 30 May 1933; *Educ* Univ Coll Sch, Coll of Estate Mgmnt London Univ; *m* 22 June 1963, Patricia Ann, da of Alfred Richard Harrold; 1 s (Julian Miles b 2 Dec 1971); *Career* cmmnd RA 1956, 3 Div HQ Staff 1956-57; chartered surveyor; with Folkard & Hayward 1959-66, equity ptnr Keith Cardale Groves 1972- (joined 1967-); vice pres Execs Assoc of GB 1986- (chm 1985-86); Freeman City of London 1984, Worshipful Co of Farriers 1985; FRICS 1974; *Recreations* national hunt racing, rugby union, cricket, music; *Style—* John Faulkner, Esq; 65 Sheringham Queensmead, St John's Wood Park, London NW8 6RB (☎ 071 586 1205); 22 Grosvenor Square, Mayfair, London W1X 9LF (☎ 071 629 6604, fax 071 495 0150, car 0836 661 0568, telex 27839)

FAULKNER, Hon (James) Michael Sewell; s of Baron Faulkner of Downpatrick (Life Peer, d 1977), and Lady Faulkner; *b* 1956; *Educ* Glenalmond Coll, Univ of Aberdeen (LLB); *m* 1990, Miss Lynn, *née* McGregor; *Career* business; *Style—* The Hon Michael Faulkner; Quilchena, Fosseway, Kinross-shire

FAULKNER, Richard Oliver; s of Harold Ewart Faulkner (d 1968), and Mabel, *née* Riley (d 1960); *b* 22 March 1946; *Educ* Merchant Taylors', Worcester Coll Oxford (MA); *m* 5 July 1968, Susan, da of Donald James Heyes (d 1978); 2 da (Julia b 1969, Tamsin b 1970); *Career* communications advsr: Railway Trade Unions 1976-77, Bd BR 1977-, British Gas plc 1980-, TSB Group plc 1987-, Interparly Union 1987-90, CAA 1988-, The Bishop at Lambeth 1990; vice chm Transport 2000 Ltd, jt md Westminster Communications Group Ltd 1988-; Parly candidate (Lab): Devizes 1970 and Feb 1974, Monmouth Oct 1974, Huddersfield 1979; memb Merton Borough Cncl 1971-78, communications advsr to oppn ldr gen election 1987, co fndr Parly jl The House Magazine; Football Tst: fndr tstee 1979-83, sec 1983-86, dep chm 1986-90, first dep chm 1990-; memb Sports Cncl 1986-88, chm Womens FA 1988-; MIPR 1977; *Recreations* collecting Lloyd George memorabilia, tinplate trains, watching association football, travelling by railway; *Clubs* Reform; *Style—* Richard Faulkner, Esq; 7 Buckingham Gate, London SW1E 6JS (☎ 071 630 5454, fax 071 630 5767)

FAULKNER OF DOWNPATRICK, Baroness; Lucy Barbara Ethel; CBE; da of William John Harkness Forsythe (d 1960), of Bangor, and Jane Ethel, *née* , Sewell; *b* 1 July 1925; *Educ* Trinity Coll Dublin; *m* 1951, Baron Faulkner of Downpatrick (Life Peer d 1977); 2 s, 1 da; *Career* nat govr BBC NI 1978-85; chm Bdcasting Cncl NI 1981-85; co dir; former journalist Belfast Telegraph; genealogist; tstee Ulster Hist Fndn 1980-, govr Belfast Linen Hall Library, 1983-; memb NI Tourist Bd 1985-; chm NI Advsy Bd Salvation Army; *Recreations* hunting, dressage, gardening, book collecting; *Clubs* Royal Over-Seas League; *Style—* The Rt Hon Lady Faulkner of Downpatrick, CBE; Toberdoney, Seaforde, Downpatrick, Co Down, NI (☎ 039 687 712)

FAULKS, Edward Peter Lawless; s of Judge Peter Faulks, MC, of Downs Cottage, Boxford, Berks, and Pamela, *née* Lawless; *b* 19 Aug 1950; *Educ* Wellington, Jesus Coll Oxford (MA); *m* 1990, Catherine Frances Turner; *Career* called to the Bar Middle Temple 1973, in practices Midland and Oxford Circuit; *Recreations* cricket; *Clubs* Garrick; *Style—* Edward Faulks, Esq; 61 Artesian Road, London W2 (☎ 071 727 7823); 6 King's Bench Walk, Temple, London EC4 (☎ 071 353 9901)

FAULKS, Esmond James; s of Sir Neville Major Ginner Faulks, MBE, TD (d 1985), and Bridget Marigold, *née* Bodley (d 1962); *b* 11 June 1946; *Educ* Uppingham, Sidney Sussex Coll Cambridge (MA); *m* 12 Sept 1972, Pamela Margaret, da of William Arthur Ives, of Almora, Rockcliffe, Kircudbright; 1 s (Sam b 17 Oct 1973), 1 da (Nicola b 6 March 1976); *Career* barr; rec of the Crown Court 1987; *Recreations* country pursuits; *Style—* Esmond Faulks, Esq; Chesterwood, Haydon Bridge, Northumberland (☎ 0434 84 329); 33 Broad Chare, Newcastle upon Tyne (☎ 091 2320541)

FAULKS, His Hon Peter Ronald; MC (1943); s of late Maj James Faulks, of Reigate Heath, Surrey, and A M, *née* Ginner; *b* 24 Dec 1917; *Educ* Tonbridge, Sidney Sussex Coll Cambridge; *m* 1949, Pamela Brenda, da of late Philip Henry (Peter) Lawless; 2 s; *Career* slr 1949-80, rec of the Crown Court 1972-80, dep chm Agric Land Tbnl (SE England) 1972-80, circuit judge 1980-90; *Recreations* country life; *Clubs* MCC, Farmers'; *Style—* His Hon Peter Faulks, MC; Downs Cottage, Boxford, Newbury, Berks (☎ 048 838 382)

FAULL, David Wenlock; s of Eldred Faull (d 1964), of Newquay, Cornwall, and Mary Jessie, *née* Wenlock (d 1982); *b* 25 Feb 1929; *Educ* Taunton Sch; *Career* admitted slr 1954; registrar and legal sec Diocese of: Chelmsford 1963-88, Southwark 1963, St Albans 1963-78, London 1963; legal sec to Bishop of Rochester 1963, chapter clerk St Paul's Cathedral; sr ptnr Winckworth & Pemberton; chm Ecclesiastical Law Assoc, treas Ecclesiastical Law Soc, former memb Paddington Church Housing Assoc, memb Nobody's Friends; considerable involvement in charitable housing and law relating to the nursing profession; FRSA; *Recreations* walking, theatre; *Clubs* Athenaeum; *Style—* David Faull, Esq; c/o Winckwork & Pemberton, 35 Great Peter Street, Westminster, London SW1P 2LR (☎ 071 222 7381, fax 071 222 1614, car 0860 823 212, telex 895 5719)

FAULL, Dr Margaret Lindsay; da of Norman Augustus Faull (d 1956), of Sydney, Australia, and Myra Beryl, *née* Smith; *b* 4 April 1946; *Educ* Fort St Girls HS, Univ of

Sydney (BA), Univ of Macquarie (MA), Univ of Leeds (PhD); *Career* secdy sch teacher NSW Dept of Educn 1970-71, dep Co archaeologist W Yorks CC 1984-85 (field archaeologist 1975-84), project mangr Thwaite Mills Industl Museum 1985-86, dir Yorkshire Mining Museum Caphouse Colliery 1986-; ed Soc for Landscape Studies 1979-86, chm Yorkshire and Humberside Cncl for Br Archaeology 1982-84, sec Thwaite Mills Soc 1986-; MIFA 1983, MILAM 1986, Assoc Inst of Mining Engrs 1988; *Books* Domesday Book: Yorkshire Chichester (jt ed, 1986); *Recreations* collecting African carvings, opera, cricket; *Style*— Dr Margaret Faull; 39 Eldon Terrace, Leeds Road, Wakefield, West Yorks WF1 3JW (☎ 0924 379690), Yorkshire Mining Museum, Caphouse Colliery, New Rd, Overton, Wakefield, W Yorkshire WF4 4RH (☎ 0924 848806, fax 0924 840694)

FAURE, Eric Simon Noel; s of Henry Martin Frederick Faure (d 1937), and Anna Elizabeth Van Der Graf; *b* 25 Dec 1913; *Educ* Rugby, Ecole d'Commerce Neuchâtel Switzerland, UC Oxford; *m* 25 June 1941, Irene, da of Edward Battes (d 1933); 2 s (Andrew b 1948, John (twin) b 1948), 1 da (Caroline b 1949); *Career* Sqdn Ldr RAF, posted to Air Miny 1942, seconded as air advsr Bletchley Park 1942-46; dir HMF Faure & Co 1937-, chm Faure Fairclough Ltd 1977; jt pres United Oilseeds Marketing until 1987; memb of Baltic Exchange (as princ 1937-), pres Baltic Golfing Soc 1972-87; semi ret but still active in arbitration and ctees concerning vegetable seeds and oils; Liveryman Worshipful Co of Skinners 1943-; *Recreations* golf, bridge; *Clubs* Rye and Thorpeness Golf; *Style*— Eric S N Faure, Esq; 15 Pishiobury Drive, Sawbridgeworth, Herts; Federation of Oils Seeds and Fats Associations (☎ 071 283 5511)

FAURE, Monsieur Hubert Rene Joseph; s of Frederic Faure (d 1978), and Jacqueline, *née* de Vendegies d'Hust (d 1957); *b* 5 Sept 1919; *Educ* Ecole Libre Sciences Politiques, Sorbonne Paris; *m* m 1948 (m dis 1957), Elizabeth de Cuevas; m 2, 1973, Genevieve Polonceau; 1 s (Adrien b 15 Jan 1975); *Career* attaché French Embassy Bogota Columbia 1947, mangr Ateliers Metallurgiques St Urbain 1949; pres: Ascinter-Otis 1961-72, Otis Europe Paris 1969-; Otis Elevator Company: pres and chief operating offr NYC 1975-77, chief exec 1977-79, chm, pres and chief exec 1979-81, chm and chief exec 1981-86; dir: Société Imetal until 1981, Grands Magasins Jones until 1979, United Technologies Corporation until 1987 (sr exec vice pres 1981-86), Danone Swiss Re (US), Sotheby's, N M Rothschild (London), Rothschild Espana; Rothschild Italia; chm: Supervisory Bd Rothschild & Associes Banque; memb Volvo Int Advsy Bd (1989-90); memb Conseil Economique et Social 1963 and 1964; chev French Legion of Honour; *Clubs* Nouveau Cercle, Brook (NYC); *Style*— Hubert Faure, Esq; Albany, Piccadilly, London W1 (☎ 071 439 4039); La Bruyere, Auvillars, 14340 Cambremer, France (☎ 010 33 3165 0980) NM Rothschild & Sons Ltd, New Court, St Swithin's Lane, London EC4 (☎ 071 280 5000)

FAURE WALKER, Henry John (Harry); s of Lt-Col Henry William Faure Walker (d 1990), and Elizabeth Alice Catherine, *née* Fordham; *b* 25 July 1940; *Educ* Eton, Trinity Coll Cambridge (BA); *m* 5 Nov 1966, Elizabeth, da of Maj William Boyd Kennedy Shaw, OBE, of Elford, Staffordshire; 2 s (William b 1970, Henry b 1972), 1 da (Alice b 1968); *Career* regnl dir Barclays Bank plc (Cambridge Region), dir H W Faure Walker Farms Ltd 1969-; *Recreations* field sports, garden; *Style*— Harry Faure Walker, Esq; c/o Barclays Bank plc, Cambridge Regional Office, Cambridge

FAURE WALKER, Hon Mrs ((Angela) Mary); *née* Chaloner; da of 2 Baron Gisborough, TD, JP; *b* 5 April 1925; *m* 27 Nov 1946 (m dis 1973), as his 1 wife, Roderick Edward Faure Walker *qv*; 2 s (Rupert, *qv*, James b 1948, m Vivian Knight), 1 da (Camilla b 1953, m Timothy Coghlan, and d 1981); *Style*— The Hon Mrs Faure Walker; Geranium Cottage, Ditchling, Sussex

FAURE WALKER, Rupert Roderick; er s of Maj Roderick Edward Faure Walker, *qv* and his 1 w, Hon Mrs Faure Walker, *qv*; *b* 9 Sept 1947; *Educ* Eton, Univ of Bristol (BSc); *m* 1975, Sally Anne Vivienne, da of Lt Cdr Francis John Sidebotham, RN; 1 s (Nicholas b 1978), 2 da (Julia b 1980, Joanna b 1984); *Career* dir Samuel Montagu 1982-; FCA; *Style*— Rupert Faure Walker, Esq; Abbotswood, Wickham Bishops, Essex CM8 3EA; c/o Samuel Montagu & Co Ltd, Lower Thames St, London EC3 (☎ 071 260 9000)

FAUSSET, Robin John; *b* 6 Jan 1925; *Educ* Haileybury, Magdalene Coll Cambridge (MA); *m* 10 July 1965, Sarah Elizabeth, da of Hamilton Walters (d 1983); 2 s (Rupert b 1966, Adam b 1968); *Career* cmmnd II Cavalry IA 1946, transfd 17/21 Lancers 1947; serv: Syria, Lebanon, Egypt, India, Palestine; copywriter Masius & Ferguson 1951, sales promotion mangr Readers Digest (Canada) 1954, account dir Ogilvy & Mather 1955-68, md Mathers & Streets 1969; chm and chief exec: Mathers & Bensons 1971-78, Foster Turner & Benson 1977-78; farmer 1979-; cncl memb Devonshire Assoc 1983-84, chm Devon Gardens Tst 1990; *Books* The Creation of the Gardens at Castle Hill; *Recreations* writing, sheep, garden design, architecture; *Style*— Robin Fausset, Esq; Pyne Farm, Black Dog, Crediton, Devon (☎ 0884 860695)

FAUX, (James) Christopher; s of Dr Francis Reginald Faux (d 1974), of Bolton, Lancs, and Alison Mungo, *née* Park (d 1981); *b* 11 March 1940; *Educ* Fettes, Univ of Liverpool (MRCS, LRCP), Univ of Glasgow (FRCS); *m* 29 July 1967, Patricia Anne Lyon, da of Hugh Lyon Denson, of Chester; 1 s (James), 2 da (Rachel, Charlotte); *Career* Liverpool Scottish TA 1960-65; conslt orthopaedic Surgn Preston Health Authy 1977-; memb: Arthritis and Rheumatism Cncl, Charnley Low Friction Soc, Liverpool Orthopaedic Circle; memb: BMA, Liverpool Med Inst; FBOA; *Recreations* boating, rugby; *Style*— Christopher Faux, Esq; Shepherds Hill, Claughton on Brock, Preston, Lancs PR3 0PD (☎ 0995 40510); 7 Moor Park Ave, Preston, Lancs PR1 6AS (☎ 0772 204710)

FAVELL, Anthony Rowland; MP (C) Stockport 1983-; s of Arnold Rowland Favell, and Hildegard Wilhelmene Marie, *née* Weerpas; *b* 29 May 1939; *Educ* St Bees Cumbria, Univ of Sheffield; *m* 1966, Susan Rosemary, *née* Taylor; 1 s, 1 da; *Career* slr Parly candidate (c) Bolsover 1979; PPS to Rt Hon John Major, MP (then Chllr of the Exchequer) 1989-90; *Style*— Anthony Favell Esq, MP; House of Commons, London SW1

FAWCETT, Howard Antony; s of Frederick Albert Fawcett (d 1988), of Oxford, and May, *née* Smith (d 1986); *b* 8 July 1941; *Educ* Oxford GS, Oxford Sch of Architecture; *m* 27 Dec 1975, Jane, da of Patrick Bernard Brittain, of Chalfont St Peter, Bucks; 2 da (Claire Jane b 1977, Zoe Natalie b 1980); *Career* architect; sr ptnr Howard Fawcett & Ptnrs 1977-; chm: Gt Missenden Cncl 1984-86, Bucks Soc of Architects 1977-79; RIBA 1970; *Recreations* boating; *Clubs* Rotary Int, Grimms Hill Lawn Tennis Assoc; *Style*— Howard Fawcett, Esq; Brackenrigg, Moat Lane, Prestwood, Great Missenden, Bucks (☎ 02406 3600); Howard Fawcett & Partners, Chartered Architects, Chandos House, Back St, Wendover, Bucks (☎ 0296 625995, fax 0296 622817)

FAWCETT, Sir James Edmund Sandford; DSC (1942), QC (1984); s of Rev Joseph Fawcett (d 1942), and Edith Annie, *née* Scattergood (d 1942); *b* 16 April 1913; *Educ* Rugby, New Coll Oxford; *m* 7 Aug 1937, (Frances) Beatrice, 2 da of late Dr Elias Avery Lowe; 1 s (Edmund b 1946), 4 da (Sarah b 1939, Charlotte b 1942, Philippa b 1950, Sophia b 1957); *Career* WWII served RN; barr 1937-39 and 1950-55, asst legal advsr to FO 1945-50, gen counsel IMF 1955-60, dir of studies Royal Inst of Int Affairs 1969-73, pres Euro Cmmn of Human Rights 1972-78 (memb 1962-84), prof of int law King's Coll London 1976-80 (emeritus prof 1980), memb Inst of Int Law 1973-, chm Br Inst 1977-81; kt 1984; *Style*— Sir James Fawcett, DSC, QC; 20 Murray St, 80 Banbury Rd, Oxford

FAWCETT, Robert; MBE (1945), TD (1946); s of late Percival Charles Fawcett, and Evelyn Fawcett, of Hatten, Sevenoaks, Kent; *b* 16 June 1917; *Educ* Rugby, Trinity Coll Oxford; *m* 1939, Esmé Boileau, da of Lt-Col Nevill George Boileau Henderson, DSO; 1 s, 1 da (and 1 child decd); *Career* Lt-Col RA, served UK and NW Europe; ptnr Messrs Jackson Taylor Abernethy & Co 1948-1976; co dir: Andrew Weir & Co Ltd, Utd Baltic Corpn Ltd, Spink & Son Ltd 1977-84; ret 1984; gen cmmr of Income Taxes 1984-; former chm: Investmt Ctee Merchant Navy Offrs Pension Fund, Ensign Trust plc, Merchant Navy Investment Management Ltd; dep chm CDFC Trust plc; def chm Kent and E Sussex Regnl Ctee Nat Tst, memb Cncl Romney Marsh Historic Churches Tst, churchwarden St Peter and St Paul Appledore; FCA; *Recreations* reading, travelling; *Clubs* MCC; *Style*— Robert Fawcett, Esq, MBE, TD; Vine House, Appledore, Ashford, Kent TN26 2BU (☎ 023 383 260)

FAWCUS, Maj-Gen Graham Ben; s of Col Geoffrey Arthur Ross Fawcus, OBE (d 1972), of 39 St Catherine's Rd, Hayling Island, Hants, and Helen Sybil Graham, *née* Stronach; *b* 17 Dec 1937; *Educ* Wycliffe Coll Stonehouse Glos, RMA Sandhurst, King's Coll Cambridge (BA, MA); *m* 23 July 1966, Diana Valerie, da of Dr Patrick John Spencer-Phillips, of Levells Hall, Bildeston, Suffolk; 2 s (Jeremy b 1967, Caspian b 1969), 1 da (Abigail b 1972); *Career* cmmnd RE 1958, 2 Lt (later Lt) troop cmd 33 Ind Fd Sqdn RE Cyprus 1959-60, Lt (later Capt) troop cmd 25 Corps Engr Regt BAOR 1963-65, GSO3 (Ops) HQ 19 Inf Bde Borneo and UK (Colchester) 1965-68, Adj 35 Corps Engr Regt 1968, Capt (later Maj) RMCS Shrivenham and Staff Coll Camberley 1969-70, Maj GS02 (W) MG0 Sec 3 MOD 1971-72, OC 39 FD Sqdn RE BAOR 1973-75, DAAG AG7 MOD 1975-76, Lt-Col GSO1 (DS) Staff Coll Camberley 1977-78, CO 25 Engr Regt BAOR 1978-81, Col Cabinet Off 1981, Brig Cmdt RSME 1982-83, ACOS HQ 1 (Br) Corps BAOR 1984-85, Maj-Gen Chief Jt Servs Liaison Orgn 1986-89, Maj-Gen Cos Live Oak Shape 1989-91; *Recreations* skiing, tennis, wind surfing, furniture restoring, bird watching, Scottish Dancing; *Style*— Maj-Gen G B Fawcus; c/o Lloyds Bank Ltd, Cox's & King's Branch, 6 Pall Mall, London SW1Y 5NH; Chief of Staff, Live Oak Shape BFPO 26 (☎ 01032 6544 2600)

FAWCUS, Sir (Robert) Peter; KBE (1964), CMG (1960); s of Arthur Francis Fawcus, OBE (d 1950), of Claygate, Surrey; *b* 30 Sept 1915; *Educ* Charterhouse, Clare Coll Cambridge; *m* 1943, Isabel Constance, da of late Simon Ethelston; 1 s, 1 da; *Career* served WWII, Lt Cdr RNVR; barr 1941; Overseas Civil Serv: admin Basutoland 1946-54, govt sec Bechuanaland Protectorate 1954-59, resident cmmr 1959-63, Queen's cmmr 1963-65, ret; *Recreations* gardening; *Clubs* Royal Cwlth Soc; *Style*— Sir Peter Fawcus, KBE, CMG; Dochart House, Killin, Perthshire (☎ 056 72 225)

FAWCUS, Prof Robert; s of Percival William Henry Fawcus (d 1984), of Harrow, Middlesex, and Helena, *née* Smith (d 1979); *b* 12 Dec 1936; *Educ* Acton Co GS, Kingdon Ward Sch of Speech Therapy, Birkbeck Coll Univ of London (BSc), Guy's Hosp Med Sch; *m* 21 Jan 1961, Margaret Ailsa, da of Leslie Charles Bingham Penwill, CBE; 1 s (Kemble Daniel b 9 Mar 1968), 2 da (Jennifer Mary b 18 Aug 1964, Nadia b 8 Oct 1966); *Career* Nat Serv RAF 1955-57; tutor Kingdon Ward Sch of Speech Therapy 1960-62, speech therapist Middx Hosp 1960-68, dir of studies Kingdon Ward Sch 1962-70, sr speech therapist Guy's Hosp 1968-80, course dir human communication Guy's Hosp Med Sch 1970-82, sr lectr Sch for the Study of Human Communication 1970-82, prof and head of dept CCS City Univ 1982-; memb: Advsy Ctee on Telecommunications for Elderly and Disabled People, Biological Engrg Soc, Br Psychological Soc; tstee: Kingdon Ward Speech Therapy Tst, Computer Aid for Disabled People, Int Soc for Augmentative and Alternative Communication UK (exec vice pres Int Soc; fell Coll of Speech Therapists 1972 (memb, licentiate 1960); *Books* contrib: Language Disability in Children, Voice Disorders and their Management, Assistive Communication Aids, Handbook of Dentistry; *Recreations* cooking and eating, music, theatre, gardening; *Clubs* Friends of Greenwich Theatre; *Style*— Prof Robert Fawcus; Department of Clinical Communication Studies, City University, Northampton Square, London EC1 V0HB (☎ 071 253 4399)

FAWCUS, His Hon Judge Simon James David; s of Gp Capt Ernest Augustus Fawcus (d 1966), and Joan Shaw (Jill), *née* Stokes; *b* 12 July 1938; *Educ* Aldenham, Trinity Hall Cambridge (BA, MA); *m* 12 March 1966, Joan Mary, da of William John Oliphant, of Morgans Farm, Drayton Beauchamp, nr Aylesbury, Bucks; 1 s (Adrian John Oliphant b 10 April 1974), 4 da (Juliet Jane b 11 March 1970, Meriel Ann b 13 Dec 1972, Madeline Clare b 22 Sept 1975, Annabel Barbara (twin) b 22 Sept 1975); *Career* called to the Bar Gray's Inn 1961, N circuit 1962-85, rec of Crown Ct 1981-85, circuit judge 1985-; memb Ctee of Cncl of Circuit Judges 1985-; *Recreations* tennis, rackets, golf, music, bridge; *Clubs* MCC, Manchester Tennis and Racquet; *Style*— His Hon Judge Fawcus; Rosehill, Brook Lane, Alderley Edge, Cheshire; Courts of Justice, Crown Sq, Manchester

FAWKE, Pamela; OBE (1981); da of Laurence Drader (d 1963), of Lyndon, Leics, and Mabel Blanche, *née* Kidner (d 1987); *b* 14 May 1919; *Educ* Hamilton House Tunbridge Wells; *m* 3 May 1947, Leslie Arthur Fawke (d 1982), s of Arthur Fawke (d 1945); 2 s (William Laurence b 1948, Richard Arthur Leslie b 1950); *Career* 2 Offr WRNS 1941-47; chm Rudgwick Brickworks 1982- (dir 1978-82); chm SE Ctee Cons Women 1970-80; *Style*— Mrs Pamela Fawke, OBE; The Cottage, The Common, Cranleigh, Surrey GU6 8SJ; Rudgwick Brickworks, Lynwick St, Rudgwick, W Sussex (fax 0483 72 3357)

FAWKES, Sir Randol Francis; s of Edward Ronald Fawkes and Mildred, *née* McKinney; *b* 20 March 1924; *Educ* in the Bahamas; *m* 1951, Jacqueline *née* Bethel; 3 s, 1 da; *Career* attorney-at-law Bahamas 1948-; MHA for Progressive Lib Party 1956, fndr and pres Bahamas Fedn of Labour, fndr People's Penny Savings Bank 1951; kt 1977; *Style*— Sir Randol Fawkes; PO Box N 7625, John F Kennedy Drive, Nassau, NP, Bahamas

FAWSSETT, Robert Seymour; s of Capt Arthur Charles Fawssett, DSO, RN (d 1961), of Lindfield, Sussex, and Sybil Frieda, *née* Salaman (d 1977); *b* 4 May 1931; *Educ* Bradfield, Pembroke Coll Cambridge (BA); *m* 17 May 1958, Philippa Karen, da of George Philip Fox, MBE (d 1970), of Glasshouses, nr Harrogate, Yorks; 1 s (Edward b 1962), 2 da (Nicola b 1961, Katherine b 1965); *Career* Nat Serv 2 Lt RA 1950-51, TA 1951-58, ret Actg Capt RA; admitted slr 1957, sr ptnr Biddle & Co 1976- (ptnr 1958-); memb Lowtonian Soc 1977; *Recreations* gardening, tennis, opera; *Clubs* Naval, City Univ; *Style*— Robert Fawssett, Esq; Biddle & Co, 1 Gresham St, London EC2V 7BU (☎ 071 606 9301, fax 071 606 3305, telex 888197)

FAY, Charles Stewart; s of His Hon Edgar Stewart Fay, QC, *qv*, of 13 Egbert St, London NW1 and Knox End, Ashdon, Essex, and Kathleen Margaret, *née* Buell (d 1970); *b* 16 May 1931; *Educ* Bradfield Coll, Lincoln Coll Oxford (BA, MA); *m* 1, 16 July 1955, (Ann) Patricia Fay, OBE (d 1979), da of Lawrence Moore (d 1973) of Harrogate, Yorks; 2 da (Caroline b 1957, Rachel b 1959); m 2, 24 March 1984, Audrey Augusta, da of Percy Joseph Semon (d 1963); *Career* Nat Serv RE 1950-51; called to the Bar Inner Temple 1955; memb: Western circuit 1955-, Plymouth Legal Aid Ctee 1958-68; pt/t lectr in town planning law Dept of Town Planning Univ of London 1965-67, inspr holding Okehampton By-Pass Inquiry 1979-80; memb: Local

Govt and Planning Bar Assoc, Parly Bar Mess, Soc of Cons Lawyers; memb: Amersham RDC 1961-64, Chenies Parish Cncl 1986- (vice chm 1989-); chm Chenies Estate Res Assoc 1987-; *Books* Hill's Town and Country Planning Acts (jt ed, 5 edn 1967); *Clubs* Royal Ocean Racing, Hampshire (Winchester); *Style*— Charles Fay, Esq; Roughwood Cottage, Chalfont Lane, Chorleywood, Herts WD3 5PP (☎ 0923 285410); 2 Mitre Court Buildings, The Temple, London EC4Y 7BX (☎ 071 5831380, fax 071 3537772, telex 28916)

FAY, His Hon Edgar Stewart; QC (1956); s of Sir Sam Fay (d 1953), of Romsey, Hants, and Beatrice Charlotte Scamell (d 1957); *b* 8 Oct 1908; *Educ* Courtenay Lodge Sch, McGill Univ (BA), Pembroke Coll Cambridge (MA); *m* 1, Kathleen Margaret, eld da of Charles Hewitt Buell, of Montreal, Quebec, and Brockville, Ontario; 3 s (Charles, Peter, William); m 2, Jenny Julie Marie Henriette (d 1990), yr da of Dr William Roosegaarde Bisschop (d 1945), of Lincoln's Inn London; 1 s (Francis); *Career* called to the Bar Inner Temple 1932, master of the bench Inner Temple 1962, practised at common law and Parly Bars 1932-71; rec of Andover 1956-61, Bournemouth 1961-64, Plymouth 1964-71; dep chm Hants Quarter Sessions 1960-71, official ref of the Supreme Ct and Circuit Judge 1971-80; memb: Bar Cncl 1955-59 and 1966-70, Senate of Four Inns of Court 1970-72, Compton Ctee on NI 1971; chm Inquiry into Munich Air Disaster 1960 and 1969, Inquiry into Crown Agents 1975-77; FCIArb 1981; *Books* Life of Mr Justice Swift (1939), Official Referee's Business (1983, 2 edn 1988); *Style*— His Hon Judge Fay, QC; Knox End, Ashdon, Saffron Walden, Essex (☎ 079 984 275)

FAYRER, Sir John Lang Macpherson; 4 Bt (UK 1896); s of Lt-Cdr Sir Joseph Herbert Spens, 3 Bt, DSC, RNVR (d 1976), and Helen Diana Scott, *née* Lang (d 1961); *b* 18 Oct 1944; *Educ* Edinburgh Acad, Univ of Strathclyde; *Heir* none; *Career* memb HCIMA; chief catering officer 1973-77; hotel night mangr 1977-80; clerical offr Univ of Edinburgh 1980-90; insurance broker 1989-; *Recreations* reading, walking, riding; *Style*— Sir John Fayrer, Bt; Overhailes, Haddington, E Lothian (☎ 062 086 0444); 9 Westfield St, Edinburgh 11; Insurance Advisory Centre, Edinburgh (☎ 031 225 8660)

FAZAKERLEY, (Andrew) Neil; s of George Fazakerley of Denmead, Portsmouth, and Muriel Boyd Fazakerley (d 1968); *b* 22 March 1950; *Educ* Abergele GS, Manchester Poly (BA); *m* 25 Sept 1976, Vibeke, da of Lt-Col Jens Christian Axel Eric Lunn (d 1959), of Copenhagen; 3 s (Sam b 1979, Jack b 1980, Pip b 1987); *Career* creative dir and bd dir: Davidson Pearce Ltd 1982-87, Boase Massimi Pollitt Ltd 1987-88; memb D & ADA; *Style*— Neil Fazakerley, Esq; Hope Cottage, 42 Nelson Rd, Harrow on the Hill, Middx HA1 3ET (☎ 081 864 0309); BMP Davidson Pearce Ltd, 12 Bishops Bridge Rd, London WC2 6AA (☎ 071 258 3979)

FAZEY, Ian Hamilton; OBE (1990); s of Albert Ronald Fazey (d 1959), of Birmingham, and Alice, *née* Livingston (d 1987); *b* 9 Aug 1942; *Educ* Kings Norton GS Birmingham, Univ of Aston (BSc); *m* 1966, Dr Cindy Sylvia Joyce Fazey, da of Horace Joseph Brookes; *Career* asst engr W Midlands Gas Bd 1964-65; The Birmingham Post: gen reporter 1965-66, educn and sci corr 1966-68, asst business ed 1968-69; Liverpool Daily Post: chief feature writer April-Dec 1969, features ed Jan-Nov 1970, chief sub ed 1970-71; dep ed Liverpool Echo 1972-74, md Wirral Newspapers 1974-76, gen mangr Liverpool Daily Post & Echo 1977-80, freelance journalist 1980-, retained contrib Financial Times 1981-86; dir: Saxon Forlags Stockholm 1985-87 (non-exec), Data TV 1988-; northern corr Financial Times 1986-; Glaxo award (sci writing) 1967, commended Provincial Journalist of the Year 1967; FBIM 1977; *Books* Waterloo FC, 1882-1982, The How to of Small Business (1985), The Pathfinder: The Origins of the Enterprise Agency in Britain (1987); *Recreations* rugby union, visiting museums and galleries, lurchers, cooking and eating, opera, books; *Clubs* Waterloo Football (Rugby Union), British Field Sports Soc, National Trust; *Style*— Ian Hamilton Fazey, Esq, OBE; 8 Beach Lawn, Waterloo, Liverpool L22 8QA (☎ 051 928 3441, fax 051 949 0067); Financial Times, Alexandra Buildings, Queen St, Manchester M2 5LF (☎ 061 834 9381)

FEARN, Alan d'Arcy; s of Charles Henry Fearn, MM (d 1982), and Gladys Lily, *née* d'Arcy Jones (d 1983); *b* 24 July 1924; *Educ* Bury GS, Terra Nova Sch Southport, Shrewsbury, Guys Hosp Dental Sch; *m* 1, 1947, (m dis 1966), Kathleen, da of Frank Humphries (d 1955); 2 da (Gail b 1947, Cheryl b 1950); m 2, 19 Aug 1966, Doreen Barbara, da of Walter Milne (d 1989), of Rochdale; *Career* RAF Air Gunner Sgt 1942-46; dental surgn, elected memb Gen Dental Cncl 1962- (longest serving elected memb); pres Br Dental Assoc 1986-87; Parly candidate (C): Ashton under Lyne 1970, Accrington 1974, Middleton & Prestwich 1974, Ashton under Lyne 1979, Rochdale 1983; generalist Tameside and Glossop AHA 1976-85 dep ldr Tameside MBC 1978-79; sr steward Nat Greyhound Racing Club 1988- (steward 1974-); *Recreations* greyhound racing, gardening, theatre; *Clubs* Naval and Military London, The Royal Soc of Medicine London; *Style*— Alan Fearn, Esq; Tall Trees, Bentmeadows, Rochdale OL12 6LF (☎ 0706 45276)

FEARN, (Charles) Barry d'Arcy; s of Charles Henry Fearn (d 1982), and Gladys Lily, *née* d'Arcy Jones (d 1983); *b* 4 March 1934; *Educ* Shrewsbury, Gonville and Caius Coll Cambridge (MA, MB BChir), St Mary's Hosp Univ of London; *m* 21 April 1962, Gay Barbara Ann, da of Capt Edward Smythe (d 1940); 1 s (Giles b 1964), 3 da (Alexandra b 1967, Victoria b 1971, Jocasta b 1973); *Career* Nat Serv Capt RAMC, MO Royal Irish Fusiliers 1960, Capt RAMC (V) TAVR Regtl Surgn Kent and Co of London Yeo 1966, Maj RAMC (V) TA Regtl MO 71 YEO Signal Regt 1981; sr lectr and hon conslt orthopaedic surgn Khartoum Univ of Sudan 1969-70, sr registrar Nuffield Orthopaedic Centre Oxford 1970-72; conslt orthopaedic surgn 1972-: Royal Sussex Co Hosp Brighton, Cuckfield Hosp W Sussex; memb: Hove Civic Soc, Haywards Heath Amenity Soc; Freeman City of London, Liveryman Worshipful Soc of Apothecaries; memb RSM, FRCS 1967, FRCSEd 1967; memb Société Internationale de Chirurgie Ortopaedique et Traumatologie 1982; *Recreations* rowing coaching, opera, the theatre, territorial army, racing; *Clubs* Leander; *Style*— Barry Fearn, Esq; Colwell House, Haywards Heath, West Sussex

FEARN, Brian Leslie; s of Leslie Fearn, of Stonycroft, Stevenage, and Eileen Lily, *née* Keeley (d 1966); *b* 5 April 1954; *Educ* Hitchin Boys' Grammar; *m* separated; *Career* information technology strategist, corporate structure conslt; ACMA, JDipMA; *Recreations* DIY, swimming, piano, golf; *Style*— Brian L Fearn, Esq; 49 St Botolphs Rd, Sevenoaks, Kent TN13 3AG; PA Consulting Group, 123 Buckingham Palace Rd, London SW1

FEARN, Ronnie; OBE (1985), MP (Lib Democrat) Southport 1987; s of James Fearn (d 1972), of 201 Meols Cop Rd, Southport, and Martha Ellen, *née* Hodge; *b* 6 Feb 1931; *Educ* King George V GS Southport; *m* 11 June 1955, Joyce Edna, da of John Dugan (d 1945), of 51 Salisbury St, Southport; 1 s (Martin John b 1962), 1 da (Susan Lynn b 1959); *Career* Nat Serv RN; sr asst bank mangr Royal Bank of Scotland plc 1947-87; pres Southport and Waterloo Athletic Club; FCIB; *Recreations* badminton, athletics, drama, politics; *Clubs* Nat Lib; *Style*— Ronnie Fearn, Esq, OBE, MP; Norcliffe, 56 Norwood Ave, Southport (☎ 0704 28577); House of Commons, London SW1A 0AA

FEARNLEY, Ian James; s of Dr Charles Fearnley, of Torrivieja, Spain, and Grace Muriel, *née* Askhan; *b* 4 April 1959; *Educ* Stockport GS, Stockport Coll of Technol, Field Park Coll (HND); *Career* Media Solutions Ltd 1983-88, Market Communications 1988-; memb Bd of Govrs Stockport Coll of Technol 1980; memb Inst of Sales Promotion 1990; *Recreations* badminton, football, cricket, softball; *Style*— Ian Fearnley, Esq; Marketplace Communications, 7 Holyrood St, London SE1 2EL (☎ 071 403 8993, fax 071 403 8896/7)

FEARNLEY, Stella Marie; da of Sydney Yates, of Barrow on Soar, Leics, and Mary, *née* Prime; *b* 22 Jan 1946; *Educ* Astley GS, Univ of Leeds (BA); *m* 15 Sept 1973, Paul Douglas Fearnley, s of Raymond Fairfax Fearnley (d 1986); 2 da (Helen Mary b 31 Oct 1977, Rachel Florence b 12 Sept 1981); *Career* VSO 1968-69, Govt of Singapore 1969-70, Careers Res and Advsy Centre 1970-73; articled clerk Price Waterhouse 1970-73, Grant Thornton 1973-86 (audit sr rising to tech mangr) sr lectr Bournemouth Poly 1986-90 (asst to dir 1988-89), Grant Thornton lectr in accounting Univ of Southampton 1990; dep pres Southern Soc of Accountants, vice chm Student Educn Advsy Gp ICEAW; FCA 1978; *Recreations* music, swimming, fell walking; *Style*— Mrs Stella Fearnley; Department of Accounting and Management Science, University of Southampton, Southampton SO9 5WH (☎ 0509 595000)

FEARON, Daniel; s of Henry Bridges Fearon, of Maidenhead, Berks, and Alethea, *née* McKenna; *b* 14 Oct 1944; *Educ* Canford; *m* 20 Feb 1971, Karen Dawn, da of Clifford M Wark, of Toronto, Canada; 1 s (James Adrian b 1978), 1 da (Letitia Jane b 1981); *Career* Sotheby & Co 1963-69, Parke Bernet NY 1969-70, Spink & Son 1970-86; md Glendining & Co 1986- (joined 1986); memb Br Numismatic Soc 1960 (memb Cncl 1986); memb Worshipful Co of Drapers 1970; FRNS 1968; *Books* Catalogue of British Commemorative Medals (1984), Victorian Souvenir Medals (1986); *Clubs* Savage; *Style*— Daniel Fearon, Esq; Glendining & Co, 101 New Bond St, London W1Y 9LG (☎ 071 493 2445, fax 071 491 9181, telex 298855 BLEN G)

FEATES, Dr Frank S; s of Stanley James Feates, and Dorothy Jenny, *née* Oxford (d 1986); *b* 21 Feb 1932; *Educ* Poole GS Dorset, John Ruskin Sch Croydon, Birkbeck Coll London (BSc, PhD); *m* Gwenda Grace, da of Henry Victor Goodchild (d 1963); 1 s (Nigel Graham b 1959), 3 da (Lynda Jacqueline b 1958, Karen Frances b 1964, Ann Gwenda b 1967); *Career* chemist Wellcome Research Fndn Kent 1949-52, res scientist's 1952-56 (Chester Beatty Res Inst, University of London), UK Atomic Energy Authy Oxford 1956-65; visiting scientist Argonne Nat Lab Univ of Chicago 1965-67; AERE Hanwell mangr1967-78: Hazardous Materials Serv, Nat Chem Emergency Centre, Environmental Safety Gp; chief radio chem inspr Dept of Environment 1978-87, dir HM Inspectorate of Pollution 1989-90 (chief inspr 1987-90), visiting prof of environmental engrg UMIST; FRIC 1972, chartered chemist 1974; *Books* Handbook of Hazardous Material Spills (1982); *Recreations* cycling, walking, travelling; *Style*— Dr Frank Feates, Esq; The Kilns, Beggarsbush Hill, Benson, Wallingford, Oxon OX10 6PL (☎ 0491 39276); HM Inspectorate of Pollution, Dept of the Environment, Romney House, 43 Marsham St, London SW1 3PY (☎ 071 276 8080, fax 071 276 8800, car 0860 562753)

FEATHER, Baroness; Alice Helena; da of John Fernyhough; *m* 1930, Baron Feather (Life Peer, d 1976); 1 s (Hon Harry Alexander, 1 *qv*), 1 da (Hon Patricia Margaret (Hon Mrs Palmer) b 1934); *Career* JP, ret 1978; Red Cross worker; memb WRVS; *Style*— The Rt Hon Lady Feather; Mill House, Sudborough, Kettering, Northants NN14 3BX (☎ 08012 3763)

FEATHER, Hon Harry Alexander; s of Baron Feather (Life Peer, d 1976), and Alice Helena, *née* Fernyhough, *qv*; *b* 3 Aug 1938; *m* 1972, Patricia Lesley, JP, da of Gilbert Victor Green; 2 da (Victoria, Jessica); *Career* master mariner; nat staff offr The Iron and Steel Trades Confedn; *Style*— The Hon Harry Feather; The Mill, Sudborough, Kettering, Northants NN14 3BX; The Iron and Steel Trades Confederation, Swinton House, 324 Gray's Inn Rd, London WC1X 8DD

FEATHER, Prof John Pliny; s of Harold Renton Feather (d 1968), and Ethel May, *née* Barrett (d 1966); *b* 20 Dec 1947; *Educ* Heath Sch Halifax , Queen's Coll Oxford (Hastings scholar, BLitt, MA), Univ of Cambridge (MA), Univ of Loughborough (PhD); *m* 10 July 1971, Sarah, da of Rev Arthur Winnington Rees, of Cardiff; *Career* ed Scolar Press 1970-71, asst librarian Bodleian Library Oxford 1972-79, fell Darwin Coll Cambridge 1977-78, Munby fell in bibliography Univ of Cambridge 1977-78; Univ of Loughborough: lectr 1979-84, sr lectr 1984-87, prof of library and info studies 1987-89, head of Dept of Library and Info Studies 1989-; pres Oxford Bibliographical Soc, memb numerous nat and int professional ctees; *Books* A Dictionary of Book History (1986), The Provincial Book Trade in Eighteenth-Century England (1986), English Book Prospectuses: An Illustrated History (1988), A History of British Publishing (1988), Preservation and the Management of Library Collections (1991); *Recreations* cookery, photography; *Clubs* Savage; *Style*— Prof John Feather; Department of Library and Information Studies, Loughborough University, Leics LE11 3TU (☎ 0509 223050, fax 0509 223053)

FEATHERBY, William Alan; s of Joseph Alan Featherby, of Cranleigh, Surrey, and Patricia Annie, *née* Davies; *b* 16 May 1956; *Educ* Haileybury, Trinity Coll Oxford (LLB); *m* 12 April 1980, Clare Francis, da of Ian Richard Posgate, of Henley-on-Thames, Oxon; 2 s (Francis b 1982, George b 1986), 2 da (Victoria b 1985, Elizabeth b 1988); *Career* called to the Bar Middle Temple 1978; currently in private practice SE circuit; *Recreations* reading, gardening; *Clubs* Carlton, Royal Motor Yacht; *Style*— William Featherby, Esq; Mansel House, Mansel Rd, Wimbledon, London SW19 4AA; 12 King's Bench Walk, Temple, London EC4Y 7EL (☎ 071 583 0811, fax 071 583 7228)

FEAVER, William Andrew; s of Douglas Russell Feaver, and Katherine Muriel Rose, *née* Stubbs (d 1987); *b* 1 Dec 1942; *Educ* St Albans Sch, Nottingham HS, Keble Coll Oxford; *m* 1, 1964-85, Anne Victoria Turton; m 2, 1985, Andrea Gillian Lester Rose; 6 c (Jane b 14 Oct 1964, Emily b 27 April 1966, Jessica b 20 Aug 1969, Silas b 1 Oct 1970, Dorothy b 11 May 1985, Alice b 21 Oct 1986); *Career* South Stanley Boys' Modern Sch Co Durham 1964-65, Royal GS Newcastle upon Tyne 1965-71, Univ of Newcastle (James Knott fell) 1971-73; art critic: Newcastle Jl 1968-73, London Magazine 1970-74, Art International 1970-74, Listener 1971-75, Sunday Times Magazine 1972-75, Vogue 1972-, Financial Times 1974-75, Art News 1974-, The Observer 1975-, various other pubns, radio and TV; exhibition organizer, work incl: George Cruikshank (V&A) 1974, Thirties (Hayward Gallery 1979), Peter Moores Liverpool exhibitions 1984 and 1986; memb Art Panel Arts Cncl 1974-78; Critic of the Year Nat Press awards 1983 (commended 1986); *Books* The Art of John Martin (1975), Masters of Caricature (1980), Pitman Painters (1988); *Recreations* painting; *Style*— William Feaver, Esq; The Observer, Chelsea Bridge House, Queenstown Rd, London SW; Rogers Coleridge and White (Agent)

FEDDEN, (Adye) Mary; da of Harry Vincent Fedden (d 1936), of Bristol, and Ida Margaret, *née* Prichard (d 1972); *b* 14 Aug 1915; *Educ* Badminton Sch Bristol, Slade Sch of Art; *m* 20 March 1951, Julian Otto Trevelyan (d 1988), s of Robert Calverley Trevelyan (d 1951), of Leith Hill, Surrey; *Career* tutor painting RCA 1956-64, art teacher Yehudi Menuhin Music Sch 1964-74, exhibitions London and prov art galleries; work displayed: city galleries America, Germany, Sweden, Russia and Australia; work in collections of the Queen at Windsor Castle and The Crown Prince of Jordan, murals Charing Cross and Colindale Hosps; pres Royal W of England Acad 1983-88; *Recreations* reading; *Style*— Ms Mary Fedden; Durham Wharf, Hammersmith Terrace,

London W6 9TS (☎ 081 748 2749)

FEDER, Ami; s of Joseph Feder (d 1985), and Nicha, *née* Dornstein; *b* 17 Feb 1937; *Educ* Hebrew Univ of Jerusalem Tel-Aviv (LLB); *m* 26 March 1970, Frances Annabel, da of late Michael August; 1 s (Ian b 1974), 1 da (Shelley b 1972); *Career* Israeli Army 1956-58; called to the Bar Inner Temple 1965, SE Circuit, advocate practising at the Israeli Bar; memb Hon Soc Inner Temple; *Recreations* sport, music, theatre; *Style*— Ami Feder, Esq; 118 King Henry's Rd, London NW3 3SN (☎ 071 586 4339); Chambers: Lamb Building, Temple, London EC4Y 7AS (☎ 071 353 0774, fax 071 353 0535); Office: 9 Malchei Israel Square, Tel-Aviv 64163 (☎ 03 5243381, fax 03 5243387)

FEELY, Terence John; s of Edward John Feely (d 1961), of Liverpool, and Mary Maude, *née* Glancy; *b* 20 July 1935; *Educ* St Francis Xavier Jesuit Coll Woolton Lancs, Univ of Liverpool (BA); *m* 15 Aug 1959, Elizabeth, da of Alphonsus William Adams (d 1963), of Southampton; *Career* has written theatre plays, films, television and books; plays: Shout For Life (1963), Don't Let Summer Come (1965), Adam's Apple (1967), Who Killed Santa Claus ? (1972), Murder in Mind (1982), The Team (1985); creator of TV series: Callan (with James Mitchell), Arthur of The Britons (Writers' Guild Award), Affairs of The Heart (New York Literary Circle Award), Number Ten, The Gentle Touch, Cats' Eyes, Eureka (1989); films: Hazard of Hearts, The Lady and the Highwayman, A Ghost in Monte Carlo, Dangerous Love (1990); memb: Cncl of PDSA, Cncl of The Writers' Guild, Ctee 1900 Club; *Books* Rich Little Poor Girl (1981), Limelight (1984), Number 10 (1982); *Recreations* travel, shooting, boxing (spectator), Shakespearian research; *Clubs* Garrick, Carlton; *Style*— Terence Feely, Esq; c/o Douglas Rae Management, 28 Charing Cross Road, London WC2H ODB

FEENY, Anne Dudley; da of Robert Dudley Best (d 1984), and Beryl Gladys, *née* Smith (d 1939); *b* 14 July 1920; *Educ* Bedales, Univ of Neuchatel, Birmingham Coll of Art; *m* 7 Feb 1948, Peter Joseph Feeny, *qv*, s of Gerard Feeny (d 1972); 1 s (William b 17 Feb 1951), 3 da (Mary Anne (Mrs Tooke) b 15 Nov 1945, Katy (Mrs Burness) b 26 Dec 1953, Frances Xavier Feeny-Sohiez b 30 Nov 1959); *Career* WAAF, section offr Photographic Interpretation 1941-46; dir Best & Lloyd Ltd; memb Arthritic and Rheumatism Cncl for Res; *Clubs* RAF; *Style*— Mrs Anne Feeny; 2 Greening Drive, Edgbaston, Birmingham B15 2XA (☎ 021 454 4002); Ran de Mar, Puerto, Andraitx, Mallorca (☎ 010 34 71 671 285)

FEENY, Peter Joseph; DL (W Midlands 1975); s of Gerard Feeny (d 1966); *b* 19 March 1916; *Educ* Stonyhurst; *m* 1948, Anne Dudley, *née* Best, *qv*; 4 c; *Career* Maj WWII; hon consul for Thailand 1960-90, pres Birmingham Consular Assoc 1969-70; memb Stock Exchange 1952-89; Hon LLD; *Recreations* travel; *Clubs* All England Lawn Tennis; *Style*— Peter Feeny, Esq, DL; 2 Greening Drive, Edgbaston, Birmingham B15 2XA (☎ 021 454 4002); Smith Keen Cutler, Exchange Buildings, Stephenson Place, Birmingham B2 4NN (☎ 021 643 9977)

FEESEY, Mervyn Thomas; s of William Feesey (d 1926), of Bourne End, Bucks, and Grace Miriam, *née* Gilmore (d 1988); *b* 8 March 1926; *Educ* Queen Elizabeth Sch, Crediton and Barnstaple GS; *m* 1 Dec 1947, Doreen Esme, da of Edward James Norman (d 1989); 3 s (David Charles b 18 March 1949, John Graeme b 22 Nov 1954, James Andrew b 4 Dec 1955), 3 da (Susan Elizabeth b 22 Dec 1950, Jane Lavinia b 1 July 1953, Elizabeth Anne b 18 June 1958); *Career* RAF 1942-47; architect; Charles Ware & Sons 1942 and 1947-54; Oliver & Dyer Architects and Surveyors (later Dyer Feesey Wickham): joined 1954, ptnr 1964, princ 1974; memb Ctee: Exeter branch RIBA, NCCPG Nat Plants Collection and Devon Br Nat Cncl Conservation of Plants and Gardens, Exeter Br Alpine Garden Soc, NCCPG Nat Plants Collection Devon Gdns Tst, Men of Trees; co organiser Nat Gdns Scheme Devon, chm Barnstaple Conservation Advsy Ctee, memb Assoc Ancient Monuments Soc; memb RIBA, FIArB; *Books* Ornamental Grasses and Bamboos - Wisley Handbook (1983); *Recreations* horticulture, cricket, badminton; *Style*— Mervyn Feesey, Esq; Woodside, Higher Raleigh Rd, Barnstaple, N Devon EX31 4JA (☎ 0271 43095); Dyer Feesey, Wickham, 24 Castle St, Barnstaple, N Devon, (fax 0271 74334, car 0836 537877)

FEGGETTER, Jeremy George Weightman; TD (1986); s of George Y Feggetter, of Newcastle Upon Tyne, and Doris, *née* Weightman; *b* 5 May 1943; *Educ* Harrow, Univ of Newcastle upon Tyne (MB BS); *Career* sr res assoc Dept of Surgery Univ of Newcastle upon Tyne 1972-74, sr urological registrar Newcastle Gen Hosp 1975-76, sr surgical registrar Royal Victoria Infirmary Newcastle upon Tyne 1 (house offr 1966-67, demonstrator in anatomy 1967-68, SHO 1968-69, registrar 1969-72), RSO St Pauls Hosp London 1978-79, conslt urologist Freeman Hosp and Ashington Hosp 1979-; FRCS, OStJ 1990; *Recreations* aviation, travel; *Clubs* RSM; *Style*— Jeremy Feggetter, Esq, TD; Dept of Urology, Ashington Hospital, Ashington, Northumberland (☎ 0670 812541 ext 2076)

FEHR, Basil Henry Frank; CBE (1979); s of Frank Emil Fehr, CBE (d 1948), and Jane Poulter (d 1961); *b* 11 July 1912; *Educ* Rugby, Ecole de Commerce Neuchatel Switzerland; *m* 1, 1936 (m dis 1951), Jane Marner, *née* Tallent; 2 s (Richard, James), 1 da (Ann); m 2, 1951 (m dis 1974), Greta Constance, *née* Bremner; 1 da (Olinda); m 3, 1974, Anne Norma, *née* Cadman; 1 da (Amanda); *Career* served WWII HAC, later instr Gunnery Sch of Anti-Aircraft RA, ret Maj; joined family firm Frank Fehr & Co 1934 (ptnr 1936), governing dir (later chm) Frank Fehr & Co Ltd London 1948, pres (later chm) Fehr Bros (Manufactures) Inc NY 1949; chm: Cocoa Assoc of London 1952, London Commodity Exchange 1954, London Oil and Tallow Trades Assoc 1955, Copra Assoc London 1957, Inc Oilseed Assoc 1958, United Assocs Ltd 1959, Colyer Fehr Pty Ltd Sydney 1984; elected to Baltic Exchange 1936, dir Baltic Mercantile and Shipping Exchange 1963-69 and 1970- (vice chm 1973-75, chm 1975-77); landowner; jurat of liberty of Romney Marsh 1979; *Recreations* sports, farming; *Clubs* City Livery (Aldgate Ward), MCC, RAC, West Kent CC, Littlestone Golf, Little Ship; *Style*— Basil Fehr, Esq, CBE; Slodden Farm, Dymchurch, Romney Marsh, Kent (☎ 0303 872 241); Frank Fehr & Co Ltd, Prince Rupert House, 64 Queen St, London EC4 (☎ 071 248 5066)

FEILDEN, Sir Bernard Melchior; CBE (1976, OBE 1969); s of Maj Robert Humphrey Feilden, MC, RHA (d 1925), of BC, Canada, and Olive, *née* Binyon (d 1971); *b* 11 Sept 1919; *Educ* Bedford Sch, Architectural Assoc (AADip); *m* 1949, Ruth Mildred, da of Robert John Bainbridge, of Apple Tree Farm, Gt Plumstead, Norfolk; 2 s (Henry, Francis), 2 da (Harriet, Mary); *Career* architect to Norwich Cathedral 1962-77; surveyor to: York Minster 1965-77, St Paul's Cathedral 1969-77; conslt architect to UEA 1968-77; dir: ICCROM 1977-81 (emeritus 1983); kt 1985; *Books* The Wonder of York Minster (1976), Introduction to Conservation (1979), Conservation of Historic Buildings (1982), Between Two Earthquakes; *Recreations* sketching, chess, sailing; *Clubs* Norfolk (Norwich); *Style*— Sir Bernard Feilden, CBE; Stiffkey Old Hall, Wells next the Sea, Norfolk NR23 1QJ (☎ 0328 830585, fax 0263 741098)

FEILDEN, Henry Rudyard; s and h of Sir Henry Feilden, 6th Bt, and Lady (Ethel May) Feilden, *née* Atkinson; *b* 26 Sept 1951; *Educ* Kent Coll Canterbury, Univ of Bristol, (BVSC); *m* 1982, Anne, da of William Frank Bonner Shepperd (d 1985); 1 s (William Henry b 5 April 1983); *Career* veterinary surgn in small animal and equine practice 1975-84; Tuckett Gray and Partners Aylesbury Bucks 1976-78, Fraser and Smith Binfield Berks 1978-83, L A Gould Rossendale Lancs 1983-84, currently veterinary advsr Duphar Veterinary Ltd Southampton 1984-; MRCVS; *Recreations* gardening, DIY, fine wine, antiques, good company; *Clubs* Old Canterburians; *Style*— Henry Feilden, Esq; 30 Manor Close, Wickham, Fareham, Hants PO17 5BZ (☎ 0329 832805); Duphar Veterinary Ltd, Solvay House, Flanders Rd, Hedge End, Southampton SO3 4QH (☎ 0489 781711)

FEILDEN, Sir Henry Wemyss; 6 Bt (UK 1846), of Feniscowles, Lancashire; s of Col Wemyss Feilden, CMG (3 s of Sir William Feilden, 3 Bt, JP); suc 1 cous, Sir William Feilden, 5 Bt, MC, 1976; *b* 1 Dec 1916; *Educ* Canford Sch, King's Coll London; *m* 25 Aug 1943, Ethel May, da of late John Atkinson, of Annfield Plain, Co Durham; 1 s (Henry Rudyard Feilden b 26 Sept 1951), 2 da (Mrs Graham Donald b 1944, Mrs William Stokoe b 1947); *Heir* s, Henry Rudyard Feilden, *qv*; *Career* served in RE WWII; civil servant (ret); *Recreations* gardening, watching cricket; *Clubs* MCC; *Style*— Sir Henry Feilden, Bt; Little Dene, Heathfield Rd, Burwash, Etchingham, E Sussex TN19 7HN (☎ 0435 882205)

FEILDEN, Lady; Mary Joyce; only da of Sir John Frecheville Ramsden, 6th Bt, DL, and sis of Maj Sir William Pennington-Ramsden, 7th Bt; *b* 12 Nov 1907; *m* 1929, Maj-Gen Sir Randle Guy Feilden, KCVO, CB, CBE, DL, sometime sr steward of the Jockey Club, High Sheriff Oxon, and VQMG (d 1981); 2 s (Randle Joseph b 1931, *see also* Lady Caroline Gosling; Andrew James b 1941) and 1 s decd; *Style*— Lady Feilden; 3 Kingston House South, SW7 (☎ 071 589 7135); Cot Farm, Minster Lovell, Oxon OX8 5RS

FEILDEN, Dr (Geoffrey Bertram) Robert; CBE (1966); s of Maj Robert Humphrey Feilden, MC, RHA (d 1925), of Canada, and Olive, *née* Binyon (d 1971); *b* 20 Feb 1917; *Educ* Bedford Sch, King's Coll Cambridge (BA, MA); *m* 1, 1945, Elizabeth Ann, da of Rev J P Gorton (d 1952); 1 s (Richard b 1950), 2 da (Jane b 1948, Fiona b 1953); m 2, 1972, Elizabeth Diana, da of P C Lloyd (d 1961); *Career* chartered mechanical engr Lever Bros and Unilever Ltd 1939-40, Power Jets Ltd 1940-46; Ruston & Hornsby Ltd 1946-59: chief engr 1950, engrg dir 1954; md Hawker Siddeley Brush Turbines and dir Hawker Siddeley Industries 1959-61, gp technical dir Davy Ashmore Ltd and dir of princ operating cos 196 dir gen Br Standards Inst 1970-81 (dep dir gen 1968-70), non-exec dir Avery's Ltd 1974-79, sr ptnr Feilden Associates Ltd 1981-, non-exec dir Plint & Ptnrs Ltd 1982-; Hon DTech Loughborough Univ 1970, Hon DSc Queen's Univ Belfast 1971; jt winner MacRobert Award for Engineering Innovation 1983; FRS 1959, FEng 1976, Sr FRCA 1986; *Recreations* sailing, skiing, photography; *Clubs* Athenaeum; *Style*— Dr Robert Feilden, CBE, FRS; Feilden Associates Ltd, Verlands, Painswick, Glos GL6 6XP (☎ 0452 812112, fax 0452 812912, telex 437244 CMINT

FEILDING, Viscount; Alexander Stephen Rudolph Feilding; s and h of 11 Earl of Denbigh and Desmond; *b* 4 Nov 1970; *Style*— Viscount Feilding

FEILDING, Hon Henry Anthony; MC; yst s of Lt-Col Rudolph Edmund Aloysius, Viscount Feilding, CMG, DSO (d 1937, eld s of 9 Earl of Denbigh, who *d* 1939); *b* 27 Feb 1924; *Educ* Ampleforth, King's Coll Cambridge (MA); *m* 2 Aug 1950, Dunia Maureen, yr da of late Gordon Spencer, MD, of Putley, nr Ledbury, Herefordshire; 1 s (Jasper b 1953), 1 da (Penelope b 1954); *Career* late Capt Coldstream Gds, High Sheriff of Warwicks 1978, land agent; FRICS; *Style*— The Hon Henry Feilding, MC; The Manor House, Pailton, nr Rugby

FEILDING, Hon Hugh Richard; 4 s of Lt-Col Rudolph Edmund Aloysius, Viscount Feilding, CMG, DSO (d 1937, eld s of 9 Earl of Denbigh, who d 1939); *b* 15 July 1920; *Educ* Ampleforth; *m* 28 March 1944, Sheila Katharine, o da of Brig Charles Arthur Bolton, CBE; 1 s (John b 1945); *Career* Sqdn Ldr RAFVR (despatches); co dir in Mauritius and UK, dir Country Landowners Assoc; FCA; *Recreations* fishing, shooting; *Clubs* RAF; *Style*— The Hon Hugh Feilding; Home Farm, Bainton, Driffield, N Humberside YO25 9NJ

FEILDING, Hon Mrs Basil; Rosemary; da of late Cdr (Frederick) Neville Eardley-Wilmot, RN (d 1956), and Dorothy, *née* Little (d 1959); sis of Sir John Eardley-Wilmot, 5 Bt; *b* 17 July 1920; *m* 14 Sept 1939, Capt Hon Basil Egerton Feilding (d 1970), bro of 10 Earl of Denbigh; 3 s (Peter b 1941, Giles b 1950, Crispin b 1960), 2 da (Jennifer (Mrs Crawley) b 1947, Imelda (Mrs Piers Rendell) b 1958); *Style*— Hon Mrs Basil Feilding; The Park Cottage, Monks Kirby, Rugby, Warwicks

FEINBERG, Peter Eric; s of Leon Feinberg (d 1976), of Bradford, and May, *née* Frais (d 1969); *b* 26 Oct 1949; *Educ* Bradford GS, UCL (LLB); *m* 13 Aug 1988, Tina, da of James Flannery, of Leeds; *Career* barr Inner Temple 1972, SE Circuit, asst rec; *Recreations* music, opera, squash; *Style*— Peter Feinberg, Esq; 1 Crown Office Row, Temple, London EC4 (☎ 071 583 3724, fax 071 353 3923)

FELD, Robert Philip; s of Alfred Feld, and Lily, *née* Green; *b* 3 Jan 1953; *Educ* Brighton & Hove Sussex GS, Imperial Coll of Sci and Technol; *m* 6 March 1987, Tara Louise, da of Edward Scannell; 1 s (Daniel Mark Joseph b 1988); *Career* md Resort Hotels plc; chm Brighton Regency Round Table, non-exec dir Guide Dogs for the Blind Assoc Recreational Servs Ltd; Freeman City of London, Liveryman Worshipful Co of Loriners; MHCIMA, FInstD, MCFA; *Recreations* private pilot, yachting; *Clubs* Carlton, City Livery, Sussex Motor Yacht; *Style*— Robert Feld, Esq; Resort Hotels plc, Resort House, Clifton Mews, Clifton Hill, Brighton BN1 3HR (☎ 0273 207671, fax 0273 729552, telex 877247 RESORT G)

FELDMAN, Anthony; *b* 27 Nov 1953; *Educ* St Stithians, Architectural Assoc London (AADip); *Career* head Dept of Interior Design American Coll in London, princ Anthony Feldman Architects; RIBA, memb Architectural Assoc; *Recreations* composing music; *Clubs* Athenaeum; *Style*— Anthony Feldman, Esq; 61A South Audley Street, Mayfair, London W1

FELDMAN, Sir Basil Samuel; s of Philip Feldman, and Tilly Feldman; *b* 23 Sept 1926; *Educ* Grocers' Sch; *m* 1952, Gita, da of Albert Julius (d 1964); 2 s, 1 da; *Career* chm: Marlet Servs Gp Ltd 1973-81, Salport Ltd 1980-85, Watchpost Ltd 1983-; Cons Pty: Gtr London area Nat Union of Cons and Unionist Assocs: dep chm 1975-78, chm 1978-81, pres 1981-85, vice pres 1985-; author of several party booklets and pamphlets; memb Exec Ctee Nat Union 1975-, jt chm Cons Pty's Impact 80s Campaign 1982-; memb: Policy Gp for London 1975-81 and 1984-, Nat Campaign Ctee 1976 and 1978, Advsy Ctee on Policy 1981-, Ctee for London 1984-; vice pres Gtr London Young Cons 1975-77; pres: Richmond and Barnes Cons Assoc 1976-84, Hornsey Cons Assoc 1978-82; patron Hampstead Cons Assoc 1981-86, contested GLC elections Richmond 1973; memb: GLC Housing Mgmnt Ctee 1973-77, GLC Arts Ctee 1976-81; chm Nat Union of Cons Pty 1985-86 (vice chm 1982-85, vice pres 1986-); dir Young Entrepreneurs Fund 1985-, memb Free Enterprise Loan Soc 1977-84; chm: Better Made in Britain Campaign 1983-, The Quality Mark 1987, Shopping Hours Reform Cncl 1988-; membre consultatif Institutional Internat de Promotion et de Prestige Geneva (affiliated to UNESCO) 1978-; memb: Post Office Users Nat Cncl 1978-81, English Tourist Bd 1986-; chm: Clothing EDC (NEDO) 1978-85, maker/user working party (NEDO) 1988-89; FRSA 1987; kt 1982; *Books* Some Thoughts on Jobs Creation (for NEDO, 1984), Constituency Campaigning- a guide for conservative party workers; *Recreations* travel, golf, tennis, theatre, opera; *Clubs* Carlton; *Style*— Sir Basil Feldman; c/o Nat Union of Conservative & Unionist Associations, 32 Smith Sq, London SW1 (☎ 071 222 9000)

FELDMAN, Dr Geoffrey Vivian; s of Leonard Feldman (d 1963), and Fanny, *née*

Messer (d 1962); *b* 3 April 1920; *Educ* Manchester GS, Univ of Manchester (MB ChB), London (DCH, MRCP (Edinburgh)); *m* 18 Sept 1963, (Doris) Anne, da of William Hall Walton (d 1975); *Career* Capt RAMC 1945-47; house physician Manchester Royal Infirmary 1945, house physician and registrar Royal Manchester Childrens Hosp 1947-49, lectr Dept of Child Health Univ of Manchester 1953-84 (res asst and asst lectr 1949-53); hon conslt paediatrician St Mary's Hosp Manchester and Royal Manchester Childrens Hosp 1961-63, conslt paediatrician S Manchester Health Authy 1963-84; memb Br Paediatric Assoc, Neonatal Soc, Manchester Med Soc; FRCP 1968, FRCPE, BMA; *Recreations* fishing, gardening, painting; *Style*— Dr Geoffrey V Feldman

FELDMAN, Dr Keith Stuart; s of Reuben Feldman, of London, and Karola, *née* Landau (d 1977); *b* 29 July 1943; *Educ* Christ's Coll Finchley, Imp Coll of Sci and Technol (BSc, PhD); *m* 8 July 1971, Teresa Ann, da of Simon Wallace, of Elstree, Herts; 1 s (Alexander b 15 Dec 1981), 1 da (Cordelia b 15 May 1979); *Career* fndr Inter-Bond Services Ltd 1969-81, sr exec Datastream International Ltd 1979-81, dir Carr Kitcat & Aitken Ltd (formerly Galloway & Pearson) 1981-; FIA 1976, memb Int Stock Exchange 1984; *publications* The Zilch in General Relativity (1965), Dispersion Theory Calculations for Nucleon-Nucleon Scattering (1965), A Model to Explain Investment Trust Prices and Discounts (1977), The Gilt Edged Market Reformulated (1977), AIBD Yield Book (1979); *Recreations* chess, skiing; *Clubs* Argonauts; *Style*— Dr Keith Feldman; Skybreak, The Warren, Radlett, Hertfordshire WD7 7DU (☎ 0923 853777), Carr Kitcat & Aitken Ltd, 1 London Bridge, London SE1 9TJ (☎ 071 3787050, fax 071 4030755, telex 8956121)

FELDMAN, Maurice Avrom; s of Lewis Feldman (d 1963), of Cardiff, and Leah, *née* Voloshen (d 1942); *b* 7 Aug 1927; *Educ* Cardiff HS for Boys, Univ of Bristol (MB ChB); *m* 22 Feb 1959, Vera, da of Armand Cohen (d 1973), of Bristol; 1 s (Adam b 1964), 1 da (Leah b 1960); *Career* Nat Serv RAMC Capt served in Singapore and Malaya 1953-55 (Malaya medal 1955), AER 1955-58; conslt surgn Dudley Rd Hosp Birmingham 1967-, sr clinical lectr in surgery at Birmingham Med Sch 1975-; contrib to professional papers in various med and surgical jls; memb: Vascular Surgical Soc, W Midlands Surgical Soc, NHS conslts Assoc, Assoc for Victims of Med Accidents; FRCSEd, FRCS; *Recreations* walking, gardening, toy making; *Style*— Maurice Feldman, Esq; 90 Knightlow Road, Harborne, Birmingham B17 8QA (☎ 021 4293357), Dudley Rd Hospital, Birmingham B18 7QH

FELDMAN, Dr Michael Morris; s of Louis Feldman (d 1975), and Shura Miller (d 1981); *b* 3 Dec 1989; *Educ* King Edward VII Sch Johannesberg, UCL (BA), UCH Univ of London (MPhil); *m* 7 July 1960, Wendy Bankes, da of Arthur Gerald Bankes Morgan (d 1975); 1 s (Matthew Richard Bankes b 1969), 2 da (Melanie Jane Bankes b 1960, Susan Rose b 1964); *Career* house officer UCH 1966, conslt psychotherapist Bethlem Royal and Maudsley Hosp 1975- (registrar 1969-72) sr lectr Inst of Psychiatry 1982- (lectr 1974-75), training analyst Inst of Psycho-Analysis 1983 (assoc member 1975, full member 1981); MRCP, FRCPsych; *Books* Psychic Equilibrium and Psychic Change: Selected Papers of Betty Joseph (co-ed, 1989),The Oedipus Complex Today: Clinical Implications (jtly, 1989); *Recreations* gardening, music, photography, inland waterways; *Style*— Dr Michael Feldman; Psycotherapy Unit, Maudsley Hosp, Denmark Hill, London SE5 8AZ (☎ 071 703 6333); 32 Southwood Ave, London N6 5RZ

FELDWICK, Paul; s of Cyril Eric Feldwick, of Abergavenny, Gwent, and Ruby Marian, *née* Frances; *b* 25 April 1952; *Educ* Monmouth Sch, Trinity Coll Oxford (MA); *m* 9 May 1981, Karen Millicent, da of David Rolf Thesen; 3 s (Oliver Paul b 5 June 1985, Hereward David b 2 Aug 1987, Gregory William b 20 Feb 1989); *Career* Boase Massimi Pollitt: account planner 1974-86, dep head of planning 1986-88, head of planning 1988-; chm: Assoc of Qualitative Res Practitioners 1986-87, Account Planning Gp 1990-; convenor of judges IPA Advertising Effectiveness Awards 1988-90; FIPA; full memb Market Res Soc; *Books* Advertising Works 5 (ed, 1990), Advertising Works 6 (ed, 1991); *Recreations* music, countrywide, cooking, books; *Style*— Paul Feldwick, Esq; BMP DDB Needham, 12 Bishops Bridge Rd, London W2 (☎ 071 258 3979)

FELL, Alison; da of Andrew Fell (d 1970), and Doris Johnstone; *b* 4 June 1944; *Educ* Kinloch Rannoch Sch, Lochmaben Sch, Lockerbie Acad, Dumfries Acad, Edinburgh Coll of Art (Dip Sculpture, post-Dip Scholarship and Travelling Scholarship); *m* 1964 (m dis 1966), Roger, s of Ronald Coleman; 1 s (Ivan b 1967); *Career* poet and novelist; co-fndr: The Welfare State Theatre Leeds 1969, The Women's Street Theatre Gp; journalist: Ink, Oz, Time Out; memb Spare Rib Editorial Collective 1975-79 latterly fictioned, C Day Lewis fell (writer in residence) London Borough of Brent 1978, writer in residence London Borough of Walthamstow 1981-82, tutor at writing workshops in Arts Centres across UK, writer in action SE Arts Kent 1985, tutor Arvon Fndn 1985-, writer in residence NSW Inst of Technol 1986, has read work at various arts venues throughout UK; awarded Alice Hunt Bartlett prize (Nat Poetry Soc) for first collections 1985; memb Greater London Arts Lit Panel 1984-86; *Publications* Hard Feelings (ed, 1979), The Grey Dancer (1981), Every Move You Make (1984), Truth, Dare or Promise (contrib 1985), The Bad Box (1987), Close Company-Stories of Mothers and Daughters (contrib, 1988), The Seven Deadly Sins (ed and contrib, 1988), The Shining Mountain (1987, 2 edn 1988), Sex and the City (contrib 1989) The Seven Cardinal Virtues (ed and contrib 1990); *Poetry* Kisses for Mayakovsky 1984, The Crystal Owl (1988); Poetry in anthologies: Licking The Bed Clean (1978), Bread and Roses (1979), One Foot on the Mountain (1979) Smile Smile Smile Smile (1980), Angels of Fire, Apples and Snakes, The New British Poetry, Is That The New Moon?; publications in various magazines; *Style*— Ms Alison Fell; c/o Tony Peake, Peake Associates, 18 Grafton Crescent, London NW1 8SL (☎ 071 485 6392, fax 071 267 4241)

FELL, Sir Anthony; s of Cdr David Mark Fell, RN; *b* 18 May 1914; *Educ* Bedford Sch and in NZ; *m* 1938, June Warwick; 1 s, 1 da; *Career* contested (C): Brigg 1948, Hammersmith S 1949 and 1950; MP (C): Yarmouth 1951-66 (resigned party whip 1956 in protest at withdrawal from Suez), Yarmouth 1970-83; kt 1981; *Style*— Sir Anthony Fell; 11 Denny St, London SE11 4UX (☎ 071 735 9021)

FELL, David; CB (1990); s of Ernest Fell (d 1964), of Belfast, NI, and Jessie, *née* McCreedy (d 1981); *b* 20 Jan 1943; *Educ* Royal Belfast Academical Inst, Queen's Univ Belfast (BSc); *m* 22 July 1967, Sandra Jesse, da of Hubert Moore (d 1982), of Co Fermanagh, NI; 1 s (Nicholas b 1976), 1 da (Victoria b 1972); *Career* sales mangr Rank Hovis McDougall 1965-66, teacher Belfast Model Sch 1966-67, res assoc Queen's Univ Belfast 1967-69; NI civil serv: asst princ Miny of Agric 1969-72, princ Miny of Commerce 1972-77, under sec Dept of Commerce 1981-82 (asst sec 1977-81), dep chief exec Industl Devpt Bd for NI 1982-84, perm sec Dept of Econ Devpt 1984-91; head N I Civil Serv and 2 perm under-sec of state N I Office 1991-; CBIM; *Recreations* golf, rugby, listening to and playing music; *Clubs* Belfast Old Instonians; *Style*— David Fell, Esq, CB; Department of Economic Development, Netherleigh, Massey Ave, Belfast BT4 2JP (☎ 0232 763244)

FELL, John Arnold; s of Charles Arthur Fell, of James House, 2 Sandy Lodge Way, Northwood, Middx, and Susannah, *née* Arnold (d 1978); *b* 31 Aug 1928; *Educ* Merchant Taylor's, Pembroke Coll Oxford (MA); *m* 10 Aug 1963, Janet Eva, da of Irvine Charles Parr, of Greenhollow, Lower Broadoak Rd, West Hill, Ottery St Mary, Devon; 2 da (Ruth Anne b 19 June 1966, Rachel Elizabeth b 18 May 1968); *Career* admitted slr 1955; articled clerk Kimbers 1952-56; asst slr: Conquest Clare & Binns 1956-58, Hatchett Jones & Co 1958-63; ptnr Wilde Sapte 1964- (asst slr 1963-64); dir: Portman Family Settled Estates Ltd, Portman Burtley Estate Co, Moor Park (1958) Ltd, Seymour Street Nominees Ltd; former chm: Broad St Ward Club, Queenhithe Ward Club (common councilman Corp of London 1982-); chm Tstees of Truro Fund; tstee: Royal Acad of Arts, Housing Assoc Charitable Tst, Lord Mayor's 800th Anniversary Awards Tst; dep chm of the bd of govrs City of London Sch, donation govr of Christ's Hosp; Freeman City of London 1980, Liveryman Worshipful Co of Gardeners 1982; *Recreations* walking, gardening, youth work with Crusaders; *Clubs* Old Merchant Taylor's Soc Guildhall, City Livery; *Style*— John Fell, Esq; Dellfield, 43 Sandy Lodge Lane, Moor Park, Northwood, Middx HA6 2HX (☎ 092 74 26508); Queensbridge House, 60 Upper Thames St, London EC4V 3BD (☎ 071 236 3050, fax 071 236 9624, telex 887793)

FELLOWES, Hon Andrew Edward; s of 3 Baron De Ramsey, KBE, TD; *b* 24 March 1950; *m* 1974, Anne Mary, da of Roy Tweedy, of Mungle, North Star, NSW, Australia; 1 s, 2 da; *Career* agriculture; *Recreations* motor racing; *Clubs* Pratt's; *Style*— Hon Andrew Fellowes; Bodsey House, Ramsey, Huntingdon, Cambridgeshire

FELLOWES, Hon (John) David Coulson; s of late Capt Hon Coulson Churchill Fellowes (eld s of 2 Baron De Ramsey) and half-bro of 3 Baron; *b* 1 May 1915; *Educ* Eton, Univ Coll Oxford (BA); *m* 1, 31 May 1946 (m dis 1962), Louise (d 1975), yr da of Lt Sir James Henry Domville, 5 Bt, RN, and formerly w of Leslie Alexander Mackay; 1 s (Peter b 1948), 1 da (Jacqueline b 1955); m 2, 4 April 1963, Joan Lynette (d 1965), o da of Edgar G Rees, of Llanelly, and formerly w of Richard Dewar Neame; m 3, 1977, Mervyn, da of late Reinold de Toll, and former w of Peter Sherwood; *Career* WWII Lt Rifle Bde, wounded POW Colditz (despatches); *Style*— Hon David Fellowes; Flat 3, 117 Elgin Crescent, London W11

FELLOWES, David Lyon; s of Brig Reginald William Lyon Fellowes (d 1982), of Cladich, and Dulcie Margaret Blessing Hurt, *née* Peel (d 1957); *b* 16 May 1931; *Educ* Winchester; *m* 13 Oct 1955, Elizabeth Mary, da of Maj-Gen Errol Arthur Edwin Tremlett, CB, TD (d 1982), of Devon; 1 s (Mark b 1967), 1 da (Emma b 1965); *Career* farming; *Style*— David Fellowes, Esq; Inistrynich, Dalmally, Argyll PA33 1BQ (☎ 08382256)

FELLOWES, Lady (Cynthia) Jane; da (by 1 m) of 8 Earl Spencer, LVO, JP, DL, *qv*; sis of HRH The Princess of Wales (*see* Royal Family); *b* 11 Feb 1957; *Educ* West Heath; *m* 20 April 1978, Sir Robert Fellowes, KCB, KCVO, *qv*; 1 s, 2 da; *Style*— The Lady Jane Fellowes

FELLOWES, Hon John Ailwyn; s and h of 3 Baron De Ramsey, KBE; *b* 27 Feb 1942; *Educ* Winchester; *m* 1, 1973 (m dis 1983), Phyllida Mary, da of Philip Athelstan Forsyth; 1 s (Freddie John b 1978); m 2, 1984, Alison Mary, da of Archibald Birkmyre, *qv*; 1 s (Charles Henry b 1986), 1 da (Daisy b 1988); *Career* farmer; dep chm Cambridge Water Co, dep pres CLA; *Recreations* fishing; *Clubs* Boodles; *Style*— Hon John Fellowes; Abbey Hse, 6 Church Green, Ramsey, Huntingdon, Cambs PE17 1DW

FELLOWES, Julian Alexander; s of Peregrine Edward Launcelot Fellowes, of Chipping Campden, and Olwen Mary, *née* Stuart-Jones (d 1980); forebears include Sir John Fellowes, sub-govr of South Sea Bubble, and naval hero Sir Thomas Fellowes; b 17 Aug 1949; *b* 17 Aug 1949; *Educ* Ampleforth, Magdalene Coll Cambridge (BA, MA); *m* 28 April 1990, Emma, da of Hon Charles Kitchener, ggniece of 1 Earl Kitchener of Khartoum; 1 s (b 1991); *Career* actor, prodr; West End appearances incl: Joking Apart (Globe), Present Laughter (Vaudeville), Futurists (Nat Theatre); Film and TV appearances incl: Baby (Walt Disney), Fellow Traveller (BFI), Goldeneye (Anglia), Swallows and Amazons (BBC), Knights of God (TVS), Sophia and Constance (BBC), The Greater Good (BBC); co-prodns as dir of Lionhead incl: Married Man (with LWT), Little Sir Nicholas (with BBC); *Recreations* history, building; *Style*— Julian Fellowes, Esq; 15 Moore St, London SW3

FELLOWES, Lady Maureen Thérèse Josephine; *née* Noel; o da of 4 Earl of Gainsborough (d 1927), and Alice Mary, *née* Eyre; *b* 7 March 1917; *m* 1, 18 Feb 1944, 15 Baron Dormer (d 1975); 2 da (Hon Mrs Glennie, Hon Mrs Bird); m 2, 22 July 1982, Peregrine Edward Launcelot Fellowes (who m 1935, as his first w, Olwen Stuart-Jones (d 1980), by whom he has 4 s); *Style*— Lady Maureen Fellowes; The Court, Chipping Campden, Gloucestershire GL55 6JQ (☎ 0386 840 201)

FELLOWES, Peregrine Edward Launcelot; s of Henry Shirley Morant Fellowes (d 1915), of Hurstborn Priors, Hants, and Georgiana Maria Hulton, *née* Wrightson, (d 1956); *b* 8 July 1912; *Educ* Ampleforth, UCL (BSc); *m* 1, 27 July 1935, Olwen Mary (d 1980), da of James Stuart-Jones, CBE (d 1948), of Welwyn, Herts; 4 s (Nicholas b 1937, David b 1944, Roderick b 1946, Julian b 1949); m 2, 22 July 1982, Lady Maureen Thérèse Josephine, *née* Noel, da of 4 Earl of Gainsborough (d 1927), of Exton Park, Oakham; *Career* Mil Serv 1940-44, Capt Sudan Ethiopia and E Africa; civil engr 1933-40, HM Foreign Serv 1946-53, co-ordinator of trade rels Shell International 1967-69 (joined 1913), conslt to Ford Foundation 1969-73, dir Lionhead Productions 1980-; memb Br Cncl of Churches 1969-87; Kt of Hon and Devotion SMO Malta; *Recreations* religion and politics; *Clubs* Athenaeum; *Style*— Peregrine Fellowes, Esq; The Court, Chipping Campden, Gloucestershire GL55 6JQ (☎ 0386 840201)

FELLOWES, Robert; s of Lt-Col Percy Ailwyn Fellowes, MBE (d 1964), of Kings Sombourne, Hants, and Joyce Madelaine, *née* Fordham (d 1976); *b* 30 June 1931; *Educ* Charterhouse, RAC Cirencester; *m* 26 Aug 1961, Sarah Ann, da of John White (d 1961), of Fyfield, Glos; 2 s (Nicholas John Ailwyn b 23 Feb 1964, James Robert William b 3 July 1966); *Career* RHA 1949-51; agent to the Jockey Club 1964-; tstee: Stable Lads Welfare Tst, New Astley Club, Nat Horse Racing Museum; pres Links Golf Club Newmarket, co cncllr 1981-85; FRICS; *Recreations* golf, tennis, shooting, fishing, racing; *Style*— Robert Fellowes, Esq; Portland Lodge, Newmarket, Suffolk CB8 0NQ (☎ 0638 662252); Jockey Club Office, Newmarket (☎ 0638 665122, fax 0638 662490, car ☎ 0860 528865)

FELLOWES, Rt Hon Sir Robert; KCB (1991, CB 1987), KCVO (1989, LVO 1982), PC (1990); s of Sir William Albemarle Fellowes, KCVO (d 1986), agent to HM at Sandringham 1936-64, and Jane Charlotte (d 1986), da of Brig-Gen Algernon Francis Holford Ferguson; bro of Thomas Fellowes, *qv*; *b* 11 Dec 1941; *Educ* Eton; *m* 20 April 1978, Lady (Cynthia) Jane Spencer, da of 8 Earl Spencer; 1 s (Alexander Robert b 1983), 2 da (Laura Jane b 1980, Eleanor Ruth b 1985); *Career* Lt Scots Guards 1960-63; dir Allen Harvey & Ross (discount brokers and bankers) 1968-77, private sec to HM The Queen 1990- (asst private sec 1977-86, dep private sec 1986-90); *Recreations* watching cricket, shooting, golf; *Clubs* White's, Pratt's, MCC; *Style*— Rt Hon Sir Robert Fellowes, KCB, KCVO

FELLOWES, Thomas William; s of Sir William Albemarle Fellowes, KCVO, DL (d 1986), and Jane Charlotte, *née* Ferguson (d 1986); bro of Sir Robert Fellowes, KCVO, CB, PC, *qv*; *b* 3 Nov 1945; *Educ* Eton; *m* 1, 1968, Caroline Moira (m dis 1972), da of Capt D J R Ker; m 2, 1975, Rosamund Isobelle, da of Bernard Van Cutsem (d 1975), and Lady Margaret Fortescue; 2 da (Catherine b 1977, Mary b 1978); *Career* dir Gerrard and Nat Disc Co Ltd 1973; dep chm Gerrard & Nat Hldgs plc and subsidiary cos 1989; govr Queen Elizabeth Fndn for the Disabled; *Recreations* shooting, fishing;

Clubs Whites, Pratts, Overseas Bankers; *Style—* Thomas Fellowes; The Old Rectory, Barking, Ipswich, Suffolk IP6 8HH (☎ 0449 720734); c/o Gerrard & National Holdings, 33 Lombard St, London EC3V 9BQ

FELLOWS, Derek Edward; s of Edward Frederick Fellows (d 1986), of Sussex, and Gladys Marguerite, *née* Parker (d 1989); *b* 23 Oct 1927; *Educ* Mercers Sch; *m* 1948, Mary, da of William George Watkins (d 1977), of Surrey; 2 da (Angela b 1954, Nicola b 1959); *Career* memb Occupational Pensions Bd 1974-78; actuary: Prudential Assurance Co Ltd 1981-88, Prudential Corporation plc 1985-88 (dir); vice pres Inst of Actuaries 1980-82, dir Securities and Investmts Bd 1989-; fell Pensions Mgmnt Inst, FIA; *Recreations* music, gardening, bridge, travel; *Clubs* Actuary's, Gallio; *Style—* Derek Fellows, Esq; 20 Fairbourne, Cobham, Surrey KT11 2BT (☎ 0932 65488)

FELLOWS, Derrick Charles; s of Charles Arthur Fellows (d 1988), and Peggy Irene, *née* Keeley (d 1989); *b* 28 Dec 1954; *Educ* Edmonton Co GS; *Career* area trg advsr Distributive Ind Trg Bd 1977-82, sole proprietor Consultancy and Trg Servs 1982-; FBSC 1978, FCI 1978, MABE 1978, ACIS 1979, FIPM 1980, FYD 1980, FSCA 1981, MITD 1981, FFA 1986; *Recreations* skiing, flying; *Clubs* Mensa; *Style—* Derrick Fellows, Esq; 63 Wynndale Road, Woodford, London E18 1DY (☎ 081 5044639)

FELLOWS, Susannah Fitch; da of Donald Emory Fellows, of London, and Suzanne Knight, *née* Phillips; *b* 7 Oct 1956; *Educ* USA, Holland Park Comp London, Kingsway Coll London, LAMDA; partner, Teddy Kempner; *Career* actress; theatre incl: Evita (Prince Edward) 1978-79, RSC London season 1979-80 (Once In A Lifetime and The Greeks at the Aldwych), Me and My Girl (Adelphi) 1985-86, Lend Me A Tenor (Globe) 1986-87, Aspects of Love (Sydmonton Festival '88 Prince of Wales) 1989-90, Chess (Manchester Opera House) 1990; TV incl: Separate Tables, Dempsey and Makepeace, Exiles (BBC Play of the Month); radio incl: Summer Lightning and Pigs Have Wings (PG Wodehouse serialisations), Farewell My Lovely, Songs from the Shows, featured various plays; concert Some Enchanted Evening with LSO (Barbican Hall); organised and participated in many charity events and concerts for: Terence Higgins Tst and other AIDS charities, Children in Need, The Variety Club, Stage for Age; *Recreations* mosaic artwork, antiques, travelling, gardening, currently writing a book on performing in musical theatre; *Style—* Miss Susannah Fellows; Barry Burnett Organisation Ltd, Suite 42-43 Grafton House, 2-3 Golden Square, London W1 (☎ 071 437 7048)

FELLS, Prof Ian; s of Dr Henry Alexander Fells, MBE (d 1975), of Sheffield, and Clarice, *née* Rowell; *b* 5 Sept 1932; *Educ* King Edward VII Sch Sheffield, Trinity Coll Cambridge (MA, PhD); *m* 17 Aug 1957, Hazel Denton, da of Donald Murgatroyd Scott, of Sheffield; 4 s (Nicholas Scott b 1959, Jonathan Wynne b 1961, Alastair Rowell b 1963, Crispin Denton b 1966); *Career* cmmnd RCS 1951, Chief Wireless Offr Br Troops in Austria 1952; lectr and dir of studies Dept of Fuel Technol and Chem Engrg Univ of Sheffield 1958-62, reader in fuel sci Univ of Durham 1962-75, prof of enery conversion Univ of Newcastle upon Tyne 1975- (public orator 1971-74), exec David Davies Inst of Int Affairs 1975-, pres Inst of Energy 1978-79; memb: Sci Consultative Gp BBC 1976-81, Electricity Supply Res Cncl 1979-89, Cncl for Nat Academic Awards 1988-; Hatfield Meml medal & prize 1974, Beilby Meml medal & prize 1976, Sir Charles Parsons Meml medal & prize 1988; involved with various TV series incl Young Scientist of the Year, The Great Egg Race, Earth Year 2050, Take Nobody's Word for It, Tomorrow Tonight; tstee Northern Sinfonia Orch; FEng 1979, FInstE, FRSC, FIChemE; *Books* Energy for the Future (1973, 2 edn 1986); *Recreations* sailing, guitar, energy conversation; *Clubs* Naval and Military; *Style—* Prof Ian Fells; 29 Rectory Terrace, Newcastle upon Tyne NE3 1YB (☎ 091 285 5343); Dept of Chemical & Process Engineering, University of Newcastle upon Tyne NE1 7RU (☎ 091 222 7276)

FELTHAM, Mark Andrew; s of Leonard William Feltham, of Putney, London SW15, and Patricia Louise, *née* Malcolm; *b* 26 June 1963; *Educ* Tiffin Boys Sch Kingston; *m* 22 Sept 1990, Debra Elizabeth, da of Walter Osborn; *Career* professional cricketer; Surrey CCC: joined 1983-, Young Player of the Year 1984, county cap 1990; MCC Young Professionals 1981 and 1982, represented England schools at under 15 and under 19 levels; business interests in vehicle security company; *Recreations* music, American politics; *Style—* Mark Feltham, Esq; Surrey CCC, The Fosters Oval, Kennington, London SE11 (☎ 071 582 6660)

FELTON, Ralph; s of Robert Forrester Felton (d 1947), of The Rest, Colnbrook, Buckinghamshire, and Maude Isobel, *née* Gray (d 1956); *b* 28 April 1911; *Educ* Kings Coll Sch Wimbledon; *m* 1, 1 May 1939 (m dis), Elizabeth; m 2, 27 June 1969, Mabel Clara, da of Frederick Charles Lodge, of Brighton; *Career* wireless instr 1 Bn Bovington RTC; conslt dir (former dir) Felton & Sons Ltd; former chm: Vintry & Dowgate Ward Club, City of London Retail Traders Assoc; Freeman City of London, Liveryman Worshipful Co Fruiterers 1957; *Recreations* golf; *Clubs* City Livery, Little Ship SC; *Style—* Ralph Felton, Esq; 63A Thorneyhedge Rd, Chiswick, London W4 5SB (☎ 081 995 5935)

FELTON, Timothy John Fowler; s of Maj William Fowler Felton, RAMC, and Felicity Anne Hamilton, *née* Hervey; *b* 8 March 1954; *Educ* Brighton Coll, Univ of Leeds (LLB), Seale Hayne Coll (Dip Farm Mgmnt); *m* 18 Sept 1982, Sarah Elizabeth, da of Peter Norman Whitley, of Leighland House, Leighland, Somerset; 2 da (Emily b 21 July 1985, Chloë b 17 June 1987); *Career* called to the Barr Middle Temple Trinity 1977; share farmer Gogwell Share Farm 1984-91, lectr Seale-Hayne Coll Poly of the SW, memb Stoke Hill Beagles, Liveryman Worshipful Co of Carpenters 1975; *Recreations* running, hill walking; *Clubs* Tiverton Harriers Athletic; *Style—* Timothy Felton, Esq

FELTWELL, Ray Parker; s of Henry Augustus Feltwell (d 1966), of Forest Row, Sussex, and Flora, *née* MacDonald Stewart (d 1977); *b* 13 July 1915; *Educ* Plumpton Coll, Harper Adam's Agric Coll Newport Salop (Nat Dip of Poultry Husbandry); *m* 27 Jan 1940, Edna Mary, da of Robert William Edmonds (d 1955), of Croydon; 2 s (Robert Leslie b 1944, John Edmonds b 1948); *Career* WWII 1939-43, Capt RASC served Guards Armd Div (invalided 1943); poultry advsy offr Miny of Agric 1938-56, poultry devpt mangr Vitamin Ltd (later Beechams), dir assoc cos (inc: Norfolk Newlay Ltd, Mainline Eggs Ltd, Nicholas Italiano SPA) 1956-70, int agric conslt 1970-; memb: Br Govt Delegation to World Poultry Congress (Australia 1962, USSR 1966), chm Poultry Indust Conf Ltd 1965-70; former chm Br Eggs Assoc, past vice chm Br Chicken Assoc; winner Poultry Assoc of GB award 1969; Freeman City of London 1954, Liveryman Worshipful Co of Poulterers 1955; *Books* Small Scale Poultry Keeping (1980, 1987), Practical Poultry Feeding (co-author, 1978), Turkey Farming (1953, 1963), Turkeys (1959), Intensive Methods of Poultry Farming (1953, 1958); *Recreations* riding, travel; *Clubs* Farmers, Whitehall Court; *Style—* Ray Feltwell, Esq

FENBY, Dr Eric William; OBE (1962); s of Herbert Henry Fenby (d 1954), of Scarborough, and Ada, *née* Brown (d 1974); *b* 22 April 1906; *Educ* Municipal Sch Scarborough, articled pupil to A C Keeton (BMus, FRCO); *m* 22 July 1944, Rowena Clara Teresa, da of Rev Percy Marshall (d 1950), of Scarborough; 1 s (Roger Delius), 1 da (Ruth b 1949); *Career* amanuensis to Frederick Delius 1928-34: A Song of Summer for orchestra, Songs of Farewell; composer film score Jamacia Inn 1939, prof of composition RAM 1964-77, numerous lectrs on Delius and his music 1935-82; memb: Composers' Guild of GB, Soc of Authors; hon memb Royal Philharmonic Soc; Hon DMus Jacksonville Univ Florida 1978; Hon DLitt: Univ of Bradford 1978, Univ of Warwick 1978; *Books* Delius As I Knew Him (1936), Menuhin's House of Music (1969), Delius (1971); *Style—* Dr Eric Fenby, OBE; 1 Raincliffe Ct, Stepney Rd, Scarborough, North Yorks (☎ 0723 372 988)

FENBY, Jonathan Theodore Starmer; s of Charles Fenby (d 1974), and June, *née* Head; *b* 11 Nov 1942; *Educ* King Edward's Sch Birmingham, Westminster, New Coll Oxford (BA); *m* 1 July 1967, Renée; 1 s (Alexander b 1972), 1 da (Sara b 1970); *Career* corr bureau chief Reuters and ed Reuters World Serv 1963-77, corr The Economist France and West Germany 1982-86, home ed and asst ed The Independent 1986-88, dep ed the Guardian 1988-, dir the Guardian 1990-; *Books* The Fall of the House of Beaverbrook (1979), Piracy and the Public (1983), The International News Services (1986); *Style—* Jonathan Fenby, Esq; c/o The Guardian, 119 Farringdon Rd, London EC1 (☎ 071 278 2332)

FENDALL, Prof (Neville) Rex Edwards; s of Francis Alan Fendall (d 1967), and Ruby, *née* Matthews (d 1975); *b* 9 July 1917; *Educ* Wallingbrook Devon, UCL and UCH (BSc, MB BS, MD, MRCS, LRCP), London Sch of Tropical Med and Hygiene (DPH); FFCM, FFPHM; *m* 11 July 1942, Margaret Doreen, da of William Beynon (d 1917), of Pontadawe, S Wales; *Career* Overseas Med Serv 1944-64: Nigeria, Malaya, Singapore, Br Mil Admin Malaya 1945-46, Kenya 1948-64; Rockefeller Fndn NYC: travelling fell 1963, dir med servs 1962-64; regnl dir Population Cncl 1967-71, Middlemass Hunt prof of tropical community health Liverpool Sch of Tropical Med 1971-81, emeritus prof Univ of Liverpool 1982-, visiting prof of public health Boston Univ USA 1982-, adjunct prof of community health sciences Univ of Calgary Canada 1983-, visiting lectr Harvard Univ 1965-71; memb Panel of Experts WHO 1957-, conslt SE Asia WHO 1960, memb UK UNSCAT Delgn 1963; conslt to: S Pacific Cmmn 1963, World Bank (investmt survey E Africa) 1970, UNFPA (family planning prog) Arab Repub of Egypt 1972, ODA to Pakistan Govt (rural health care) 1974-76, UNFPA to Pakistan Govt (manpower devpt) 1974-, Imperial Social Servs Iran (long term health planning) 1972-74, Int Devpt Res Cncl Canada (trg of health auxiliary teachers Nigeria, Malawi, Iran) 1973-75; lead speaker Cwlth Mins of Health Conf Colombo 1974, conslt in health planning Mauritius Govt 1975, memb Econ Devpt Advsy Panel WHO Ochocerciasis 1976-77, UK project mangr CENTO (low cost rural health care) 1976-79, Cwlth Fndn travelling fell S Pacific 1976, Cwlth Secretariat conslt health manpower Bangladesh 1976, UNFPA conslt (manpower devpt) Bangladesh 1978, Br Cncl conslt health manpower Bangladesh 1976 and 1987, India - Br Univ collaboration scheme ODA 1978-; memb: UK Delgn WHO/UNICEF (primary health care ALMA ATA) 1978, Exec Bd Cwlth Human Ecology Cncl, USA Nat Cncl for Int Health (fndr memb) 1974-85; conslt: WHO (health and manpower devpt) Maldives 1984, Project Hope USA (primary health care planning for displaced persons) El Salvador 1986; attended Cwlth Min of Health Conf (community approaches to health promotion and disease prevention) Aust 1989; conslt and advsr to numerous nat and int orgns and especially developing countries since 1961; Gold medal Migrendra Med Tst Nepal 1983; memb: Cwlth Human Ecology Cncl, Soc of Public Health, Soc of Social Med, American Public Health Assoc; BMA 1942, FFCM 1972; *Books* Auxiliaries in Health Care (1972), Use of Paramedicals for Primary Health Care in the Commonwealth (with J H Paxman and F M Shattock, 1979), contrib various health and population articles to specialists pubns; *Recreations* travel, gardening; *Clubs* Royal Cwlth Soc, Athenaeum (Liverpool); *Style—* Prof Rex Fendall; Berwyn, North Close, Bromborough, Wirral L62 2BU (☎ 051 334 2193); The Coach House, Mill St, Ludlow, S Shropshire SY8 1BB

FENDER, Peter Robert Keevhey; s of late Wing Cdr Percy George Herbert Fender, DL, of Horsham, Surrey, and Ruth Marian, *née* Clapham (d 1937); *b* 15 Aug 1927; *Educ* Haileybury, Clare Coll Cambridge; *m* 1, 9 May 1959, Bridgit Judith, da of Roderick Nelson Guy, of Sidmouth Devon; 1 s (Guy Robert Keevney), 1 da (Georgina Elizabeth Clare); m 2, 21 July 1984, Katharine Josephine, da of David Bevil Tregoning (d 1985), of Sunningdale, Berks; *Career* RE TEES 1945-48, RAFVR 1949-54; with Br Iron & Steel Fedn 1948-49, Herbert Fender & Co Ltd 1952-72, Peter Fender (Free Vintner) 1972-80, London Wine Exchange Ltd 1972-85, P&K Fender Amway 1985-, gp dir L'Arome (UK) Ltd 1990-; Freeman: City of London 1948, Worshipful Co of Vintners 1948; *Recreations* gliding, sailing, touring; *Clubs* Horsham; *Style—* Peter Fender, Esq; 27 Marlborough Road, St Leonards, Exeter, Devon (☎ 0392 71445)

FENHALLS, Richard Dorian; s of Roydon Myers and Maureen Fenhalls; *b* 14 July 1943; *Educ* Hilton Coll Univ of Natal (BA), Christ's Coll Cambridge (MA, LLM); *m* 1967, Angela Sarah, *née* Allen; 1 s, 1 da; *Career* Goodricke & Son, Attorney SA 1969-70, Citibank 1970-72; sr vice pres: Marine Midland Bank 1972-77, American Express Bank 1977-81, dep chm and chief exec Guinness Mahon & Co Ltd 1981-85; chm Henry Ansbacher & Co Ltd, gp chief exec Henry Ansbacher Holdings plc 1985-; *Recreations* sailing, skiing; *Clubs* Royal Ocean Racing, Royal Southern Yacht (Hamble), Royal Thames Yacht, Ski Club of Great Britain, Campden Hill Lawn Tennis; *Style—* R D Fenhalls, Esq; 15 St James's Gardens, London W11 4RE; Henry Ansbacher & Co Ltd, 1 Mitre Sq, London EC3A 5AN (☎ 071 283 2500, telex 884580 & 886738)

FENN, His Excellency Sir Nicholas M; KCMG (1989, CMG 1980); s of Rev Prof J Eric Fenn, of Worcs, and Kathleen M, *née* Harrison; *b* 19 Feb 1936; *Educ* Downs Sch, Kingswood Sch, Peterhouse Cambridge (MA); *m* 1959, Susan Clare, da of Rev Dr G L Russel, of Dorset; 2 s (Robert b 1962, Charles b 1963), 1 da (Julia b 1974); *Career* Flying Offr RAF 1954-56; Burmese studies SOAS 1959-60 , vice-consul Mandalay Burma 1960-61; third sec Br Embassy Rangoon Burma 1961-63; asst private sec to four successive Secs of State for Foreign and Cw Affrs 1963-67; first sec and head of Chancery Br Interests Section Swiss Embassy Al Algeria 1967-69; first sec for public affrs UK Mission to the UN 1969-72; dep head successively of Sci and Technol Dept and Energy Dept FCO 19 counsellor head of Chancery and consul-gen Br Embassy Peking 1975-77 RCDS 1978; head of News Dept FCO, spokesman of the FCO and press sec successively to Lord Carrington a Francis Pym 1979-82 (press Sec to Lord Soames, last Governor of S Rhodesia now Zimbabwe 1979-80); HM Ambassador: Rangoon Burma 1982-86, Dublin Republic of Ireland 1986-; *Recreations* sailing; *Clubs* Utd Oxford & Cambridge Univ, Hibernian Utd Servs (Dublin); *Style—* His Excellency Sir Nicholas Fenn, KCMG, British Embassy, 33 Merrion Rd, Dublin 4, Republic of Ireland (☎ 0001 695211)

FENN-SMITH, Clive Antony Kemp; s of Gurth Kemp Fenn-Smith, MRCVS, of 2 Otter Road, Poole, Dorset, and Mary Esmée, da of Malcolm Watson (d 1977); *b* 13 March 1933; *Educ* Charterhouse, Cambridge Univ (MA); *m* 29 April 1961, Jane Hester, da of Rt Rev Edward Barry Henderson (d 1986), formerly Bishop of Bath and Wells; 2 s (Oliver b 1965, Edward b 1974), 1 da (Emma b 1962); *Career* late 4/7 Royal Dragoon Gds, Lt 1952; slr: Messrs Letcher & Son Ringwood 1958-64, M & G Gp Ltd 1968-80 (md 1977); dir: Barclays Bank Tst Co Ltd 1984-, Barclays Fin Services Ltd 1986-, Investment Managment Regulatory Organisation Ltd 1986, Investors Compensation Scheme Ltd 1988-, Pearl Gp plc 1989-, Premier Portfolio Gp plc 1989-; *Recreations* sailing, gardening; *Clubs* Calvalry and Guards; *Style—* Clive A K Fenn-Smith, Esq; 23 West End Terrace, Winchester, Hampshire SO22 5EN (☎ 0962 54351)

FENNELL, Hon Mr Justice; Hon Sir (John) Desmond Augustine; OBE (1982); s of Dr Augustine Joseph Fennell (d 1980), of Lincoln, and Maureen Eleanor, *née* Kidney; *b* 17 Sept 1933; *Educ* Ampleforth, Corpus Christi Coll Cambridge (MA); *m* Feb 1966, Susan Primrose, da of John Marshall Trusted (d 1979); 1 s (Simon b 1969), 2 da (Alexandra b 1967, Charlotte b 1972); *Career* Lt Grenadier Gds 1956-58; called to the Bar Inner Temple 1959, dep chm Beds Quarter Sessions 1971-72, rec Crown Ct 1972-90, QC 1974, ldr Midland and Oxford circuit 1983-88, master of the Bench Inner Temple 1983-, judge of the Court of Appeal Jersey and Court of Appeal Guernsey 1984-90, justice of The Queen's Bench Div of the High Court 1990-; memb Gen Cncl of the Bar 1984 (vice chm 1988, chm 1989, memb Senate 1983), inspr King's Cross Underground Fire Investigation 1987-88 (produced 1988), chm WARA (formed to oppose siting of third London airport in Bucks) and 1979-90, vice chm Wessex Area Cons 1978-80, pres Bucks Div Cons Assoc 1983-89 (chm 1976-79); *Clubs* Boodle's, Pilgrims; *Style—* The Hon Mr Justice Fennell, OBE; Royal Courts of Justice, Strand, London WC2A 2LL

FENNELL, Hon Mrs (Sarah Elizabeth Jane); *née* Hawke; da of 10 Baron Hawke; *b* 10 Nov 1935; *Educ* Tudor Hall; *m* 5 Oct 1957, John Norris Fennell, er s of late Col Harold Percival Fennell, of Hove, East Sussex; 1 s (Adrian Martin Alexander b 1963), 1 da (Olivia Louise b 1961); *Career* security service, charity work; memb County Distressed Gentlefolks Aid Assoc Ctee; *Recreations* art and craft pursuits, flower arrangement/decoration; *Clubs* Sloane; *Style—* The Hon Mrs Fennell; 31 Summers St, Lostwithiel, Cornwall PL22 ODH (☎ 0208 873150)

FENNEMORE, Roger Arnold; s of Joseph Percy Fennemore (d 1983), of Paulerspury, Northants, and Dorothy, *née* Francis (d 1985); *b* 14 April 1943; *Educ* Bedford Sch, Coll of Law; *m* 21 Sept 1968, Susan Mary, da of Dr Alastiar Marshall , of Aspley Heath, Beds; 3 da (Katie b 1971, Juliet b 1972, Lucinda b 1977); *Career* first sr ptnr Fennemores Milton Keynes 1984; chief exec Butlers Wharf Ltd 1984-; Capt Woburn Golf & Country Club 1985; pres Milton Keynes Rotary Club 1981; Liveryman Co of Coopers; *Recreations* golf, politics, gardening; *Clubs* Woburn Golf, Oriental, Bedford Rugby FC; *Style—* Roger A Fennemore, Esq; Yew Tree Farm, Sherington, Bucks; Butlers Wharf Ltd, Shad Thames, London SE1 2NP

FENNER, John Ronald; s of Louis Finkel, and Claire Lubkin (d 1975); *b* 7 Dec 1935; *Educ* Brunswick Sch Haywards Heath Sussex, Tonbridge, UCL (LLB); *m* 24 March 1963, Gillian Adelaide, da of Stanley Joshua Simmons; 2 s (Robert Matthew b 19 June 1965, Adam Edward b 28 Feb 1972), 1 da (Harriet Jane b 25 May 1967, d 1971); *Career* served articles Zeffertt Heard & Morley Lawson 1956-59, ptnr Lionel Leighton & Co 1962-70; Berwin Leighton: fndr ptnr 1970, managing ptnr 1980-84, chm 1984-90, sr ptnr 1990; chm: Nat Cncl for Soviet Jewry, chm of appeal Nightingale House Home for Aged Jews; memb: Worshipful Co of Fletchers, City of London Slrs Co; Freeman City of London; *Awards* City of London Slrs Co Grotius prize; memb: Law Soc 1959-, Southwestern Legal Fndn (USA) 1985, Int Bar Assoc 1985; *Recreations* tennis, skiing, opera, politics; *Clubs* City of London, Carlton, RAC; *Style—* John Fenner, Esq; Berwin Leighton, Adelaide House, London Bridge, London EC4R 9HA (☎ 071 623 3144 fax 071 623 4416)

FENNER, Dame Peggy Edith; DBE (1986), MP (Cons Medway 1983-); *b* 12 Nov 1922; *Educ* LCC Sch Brockley, Ide Hill Sevenoaks; *m* 1940, Bernard S Fenner, s of F W Fenner, of Sevenoaks, Kent; 1 da; *Career* chm Sevenoaks UDC 1962 & 1963 (memb 1957-71), vice pres UDCs Assoc 1971, Parly candidate (Cons) Newcastle-under-Lyme 1966, MP (Cons) Rochester and Chatham 1970-74 and 1979-83, Parly sec MAAF 1972-74 and 1981-86, govt co chm Womens Nat Cmmn 1983-; memb: Br delgn to Euro Parl 1974, Cncl of Europe 1987, Western Euro Union (Def) 1987 Select Ctee Membs' Interests; *Style—* Dame Peggy Fenner, DBE, MP; 12 Star Hill, Rochester, Kent (☎ 0634 42124)

FENNESSY, Sir Edward; CBE (1957, OBE Mil 1944); s of Edward Patrick Fennessy (d 1955), of London, and Eleanor, *née* Arkwright (d 1942); *b* 17 Jan 1912; *Educ* West Ham GS, Queen Mary's College London (BSc); *m* 1, 1937, Marion (d 1983), da of late Albert Edwin Banks, of Sheffield; 1 s, 1 da; m 2, 1984, Leonora Patricia, wid of Trevor Birkett; *Career* WWII 60 Gp RAF; md: Decca Radar 1950-65, Plessey Electronics 1965-69, PO Telecommunications 1969-77; dep chm: PO 1975-77, Muirhead to 1982, LKB Instruments Ltd 1978-87; chm: Biochrom 1978-87, Br Medical Data Systems Ltd 1981-; Hon Doctorate Univ of Surrey; FIEE, FRIN; kt 1975; *Recreations* gardening, sailing; *Clubs* RAF, Island Sailing; *Style—* Sir Edward Fennessy, CBE; Northbrook, Littleford Lane, Shamley Green, Guildford, Surrey (☎ 0483 892444)

FENNEY, Roger Johnson; CBE (1973, MBE 1945); s of James Henry Fenney (d 1952), of St Helens, and Annie Sarah Fenney; *b* 11 Sept 1916; *Educ* Cowley GS, Univ of Manchester; *m* 1942, Dorothy Porteus (d 1989); 2 da; *Career* Maj Field Artillery, N Africa, Italian Campaigns (despatches); sec Statutory Bd 1947-80, first Nuffield fellow for health affrs USA 1968, field dir Int Jt Study Gp (Accra, Yaounde, Nairobi, Dakar, San José, Bogota) 1972-76, chm Tstees of Charing Cross Hosp 1980-88; *Style—* Roger Fenney, Esq, CBE; 11 Gilray House, Gloucester Terrace, London W2 3DF (☎ 071 262 8313)

FENTON, Prof Alexander; CBE (1986); s of Alexander Fenton (d 1960), and Annie Stirling Stronach; *b* 26 June 1929; *Educ* Turriff Acad, Univ of Aberdeen (MA), Univ of Cambridge (BA), Univ of Edinburgh (DLitt); *m* 1956, Evelyn Elizabeth, *née* Hunter; 2 da; *Career* sr asst ed Scottish National Dictionary 1955-59, Nat Museum of Antiquities of Scot: asst keeper 1959-75, dep keeper 1975-78, dir 1978-85; res dir Nat Museums of Scot 1985-89, dir Euro Ethnological Res Centre; Hon DLitt Univ of Aberdeen 1989; chair of Scottish Ethnology and dir School of Scottish Studies Univ of Edinburgh 1990; author; *Books incl*: The Various Names of Shetland, Scottish Country Life, The Island Blackhouse, The Northern Isles: Orkney and Shetland, The Rural Architecture of Scotland, The Shape of the Past (2 vol), Wirds an' Wark 'e Seasons Roon', Country Life in Scotland, The Turra' Coo; *Recreations* languages; *Clubs* New (Edinburgh); *Style—* Prof Alexander Fenton, CBE; 132 Blackford Ave, Edinburgh EH9 3HH (☎ 031 667 5456)

FENTON, Charles Miller; OBE (1982), JP; s of Sir William Charles Fenton, MC, JP (d 1976), of Fieldhead, Cleckheaton, W Yorks, and Margaret, *née* Hirst; *b* 24 Feb 1931; *Educ* Uppingham, Univ of Leeds (Dip Textile Industs); *m* 1963, Shirley Jane, da of George Arthur Windsor (d 1982), of Priestley Green, Halifax , W Yorks; 1 s, 1 da; *Career* chm Fenton Hldgs Ltd, exec dir BBA Gp plc, non-exec chm British Mohair Hldgs plc, non-exec dir Barr & Wallace Arnold Tst plc; High Sheriff W Yorks 1981; FTI, CBIM; *Recreations* gardening, fishing; *Clubs* Carlton; *Style—* Charles Fenton, Esq, OBE, JP; Priestley Green, Norwood Green, Halifax , W Yorks (☎ 0422 202373)

FENTON, Rev Christopher Miles Tempest; s of Dr Victor Norman Fenton (d 1983), of Farnham, Surrey, and Doril, *née* Trewartha-James (d 1966), of Itchenor, W Sussex; descended from Sir Geoffrey Fenton, Princ Sec of State in Ireland for Elizabeth I; *b* 24 Jan 1928; *Educ* Bradfield, Queens' Coll Cambridge (BA, LLB, MA); *m* 1964, Elizabeth Christine, da of Robert Sutherland Macadie (d 1957), of Kington, Herefordshire; 2 s (Jonathan b 1968, Daniel b 1971); *Career* RAEC, Sergeant BAOR 1946-48; asst curate Welling Parish Church 1954-57, chaplain Malsis Sch W Yorks 1957-63, asst curate Bishop Hannington Church Hove 1963-65, vicar Christ Church Ramsgate 1965-71, priest-in-charge St Albans Mottingham 1971-73; Westminster Pastoral Fndn London: staff psychotherapist 1971-72, supervisor and head of Dept of Gp Studies 1972-83; in private practice as an analytical psychotherapist; conslt: Assoc for Pastoral Care and Counselling, Cambridgeshire Consultancy in Counselling; memb Gp Analytic Soc, founding memb Inst of Psychotherapy and Counselling, ed St Anne's Centre Ledbury Herefordshire 1984-, ed Foundation 1983-89; *Recreations* design and typography, literature, walking, food and wine; *Clubs* East India and Sports; *Style—* The Rev Christopher Fenton; Under Down, Ledbury, Herefs HR8 2JE (☎ 0531 2669)

FENTON, Derek Risian; MVO (1977), MBE (1973); s of Arthur Fenton (d 1954), and Gladys, *née* Donaldson (d 1968); *b* 20 July 1921; *Educ* Clark's Coll; *m* 1943, Iris May, da of Sidney Francis Rendle Diamond (d 1958); 1 s, 1 da; *Career* SBA RN 1940-42; Outra Betting & Rubber Ltd 1935-50, md Heston Codan Rubber Ltd 1978-86 (memb 1950-86); cdr London (Prince of Wales dist) St John Ambulance 1983- (vol memb 1935-); Freeman City of London 1977, Liveryman Worshipful Soc of Apothecaries 1984-; KStJ 1975; *Recreations* St John Ambulance and grandchildren; *Clubs* Directors, St John House; *Style—* Derek Fenton, Esq, MVO, MBE; 11 Links Rd, West Acton, London W3 0ER (☎ 081 993 4353); office: Edwina Mountbatten House, 63 York St, London W1H 1PS (☎ 071 258 3456)

FENTON, Dr Eamon Joseph Francis; s of Michael Maurice Fenton (d 1960), of 11 Oxman Town Mall, Birr, Co Offaly, Ireland, and Kathleen Frances, (MA), *née* Sutton (d 1989); *b* 27 March 1938; *Educ* Clongowes Wood Coll Co Kildare Ireland, Univ Coll Dublin (MB, BCh, BAO); *m* 1, 8 July 1964 (m dis 1974), Catherine Gemma, da of Joseph Keappock (d 1963), of Navan, Co Meath; 2 s (Peter Michael b 1965, Keith Andrew b 1968), 1 da (Ruth Catherine b 1974); m 2, 4 Jan 1982, Cynthia Margaret, da of Philip Clarence Hill, OBE, of 49 The Park, St Albans, Herts; *Career* registrar psychiatry Cane Hill Hosp Coulsden Surrey 1966-69, prin-gen med practice Streatham 1969-75, sr registrar psychiatry St George's Hosp Tooting 1975-80 (jtly with Holloway Sanatorium Virginia Water Surrey), conslt psychiatrist NW RHA 1980-; memb: Nat Tst, Wildfowl Tst, RSPB, Edgworth Conservation Soc; diplomate RCPI 1975; memb: RCPsych 1975, Manchester Medico-Legal Soc 1981, BMA; *Recreations* cricket, music, theatre, photography, walking; *Style—* Dr Eamon Fenton; 177 Bolton Rd, Edgworth, Lancs BL7 0AF (☎ 0204 390765); Bolton District Gen Hosp, Farnworth, Gtr Manchester BL4 0JR (☎ 0204 22444)

FENTON, Ernest John; s of Forbes Duncan Campbell Fenton (d 1970), of Angus, Scotland, and Janet Burnfield, *née* Easson (d 1978); *b* 14 Oct 1938; *Educ* Harris Acad Scot; *m* 2 March 1965, Ann Ishbel, da of Robert Ramsay; 1 s (Forbes b 1965), 2 da (Joanna b 1969, Elizabeth b 1976); *Career* CA, ptnr W Greenwell & Co Stockbrokers 1968-81, dir Greenwell Montagu & Co 1986-87; chief exec: Greenwell Montagu Stockbrokers 1988-, Smith Keen Cutler Ltd 1988-; ASIA; *Recreations* shooting, curling; *Style—* Ernest Fenton, Esq; Dundale Farm, Tunbridge Wells, Kent (☎ 089 282 2175); 406 Seddon House, The Barbican, London; 114 Old Broad St, London EC2P 2HY (☎ 071 588 8817)

FENTON, Hon Mrs (Geraldine Jane); *née* Milner; er da of 2 Baron Milner of Leeds; *b* 24 Nov 1954; *m* 1978, Mark Anthony Fenton; 1 s (Harry b 1982); *Style—* The Hon Mrs Fenton; 5 Crofton Terrace, Shadwell, Leeds LS17 8LD

FENTON, John Hirst; s of Col Sir William C Fenton, MC (d 1976), of Fieldhead, Cleckheaton, W Yorks, and Lady Margaret, *née* Hirst (d 1972); *b* 6 July 1928; *Educ* Uppingham, RMA Sandhurst; *m* 1, 23 June 1956 (m dis 1981), Juanita, da of Hadleigh Seaborne (d 1962), of Knowle, West Midlands; 2 s (William b 29 Sept 1957, Marcus b 25 March 1966), 1 da (Suzanne (twin) b 29 Sept 1957); m 2, 29 May 1981, Shirley, da of Aston Hayes Mayhall (d 1975), of Alvanley, Cheshire; *Career* RAC 1946-47, Sandhurst 1947-48, RTR 1948-53, served Germany and Korea, ret Capt 1953; BBA Gp plc 1953-70, dir and flying instr Yorks Flying Servs 1970-; represented GB in two Aviation World Champs; chm Spen Valley Civic Soc; Freeman City of London, Upper Freeman Guild of Air Pilots and Air Navigators; *Recreations* fishing, vintage motor cycles; *Style—* John Fenton, Esq; Fieldhead, Cleckheaton, W Yorks BD19 3UE; Knight Air Ltd, Leeds/Bradford Airport, Leeds LS19 7TU (☎ 0532 503 840)

FENTON, Lawrence Stanley; s of Charles Fenton (d 1974), of London, and Jochebed, *née* Leboff; *b* 3 Sept 1930; *Educ* The Kilburn GS; *m* 7 Oct 1956, Susan Fay, da of Bertram Barnet Defries (d 1985), of London; 1 s (David b 1965), 2 da (Alison b 1958, Danielle b 1961); *Career* chartered accountant; articled clerk F Rowland & Co 1947-52, sr Touche Ross 1952-54, mangr W A Browne & Co 1954-56; ptnr: Lawrence Fenton Masters & Co 1956-69, Stoy Hayward 1969-87; business and fin conslt 1988-, various non-exec directorships 1988-; former county treas Boy Scouts Assoc, hon treas of various nat charities; FCA 1952; *Books* Hotel Accounts and Their Audit (1978, 1989), Charities and Voluntary Organisations, The Honorary Treasurer (1980); *Recreations* painting, golf, swimming, scuba diving, underwater photography, music, skiing; *Clubs* Grims Dyke Golf, Hartsbourne Golf & Country, RAC; *Style—* Lawrence Fenton, Esq

FENTON, Maria Elizabeth Josephine; *née* Neuman; da of Karol Kurt Neuman, of Surrey, and Betty Joan, *née* Hine; *b* 9 May 1956; *Educ* St Mary's Providence Convent, Kingston Poly, Coll of Law Guildford (BA); *m* 14 Nov 1981 (m dis 1990), William James Timothy Fenton, s of Wing Cdr William James Ferguson Fenton (ret), of Surrey; *Career* admitted slr of the Supreme Ct 1980, principle sole practicioner; memb: Law Soc, Sussex Law Soc; *Clubs* Network; *Style—* Ms Maria Fenton; 13 Sceptre, Towergate, London Rd, Brighton BN1 6UF

FENTON, Thomas James; s of Capt James Edmund Fenton, OBE (d 1959), and Margaret Dorothea, *née* Cripps (d 1979); *b* 28 July 1948; *Educ* Elstree Sch, Bradfield Coll Berks; *m* 1 April 1978, Deborah Clare, da of Arthur John Medcalf, of Harwell, Oxon; 2 da (Olivia b 1979, Georgina b 1981); *Career* memb Gloucester Cathedral Choir; fndr memb Friends of Highnam Church, cncl memb Friends of Gloucester Cathedral, advsr to Exec Ctee of Cncl For The Care of Churches; Lord of Manor of Highnam (suc Highnam Ct 1966) Linton and Over, Patron of Living of Highnam; tstee Ely Stained Glass Museum; *Recreations* music, architecture; *Style—* Thomas Fenton, Esq; The Old Rectory, Highnam, Glos GL2 8DG (☎ 0452 412341)

FENTON, Dr Thomas William; s of Thomas William Fenton (d 1986), and Anne Elizabeth, *née* Pearson (d 1961); *b* 31 Aug 1931; *Educ* Gateshead GS, Univ of Edinburgh (MB, ChB, DPM); *m* 19 Aug 1956, Wilma Favill Mackay; 1 s (Andrew Mackay b 25 Oct 1964), 2 da (Rachel Catherine b 26 Aug 1961, Laura Morrison b 24 July 1967); *Career* registrar in psychiatry Hollyway Sanatorium Virginia Water Surrey 1959-62, sr registrar in psychiatry United Birmingham Hosp 1962-65, conslt psychiatrist Hollymoor Hosp Birmingham and E Birmingham Hosp 1965-, med dir Hollymoor Hosp Birmingham 1970-; FRCPsych 1984; *Recreations* concerts, ballet, opera, wargaming, walking; *Style—* Dr T W Fenton; Hollymoor Hospital, Northfield, Birmingham (☎ 021 4757421)

FENTON, Tom; s of Thomas Fenton and Anne Mary, *née* Palethorpe; *b* 29 Aug 1933; *Educ* Barnsley GS, Nat Coal Bd (Colliery Mangr's Cert); *m* 1963, Dorothy Anne, *née* Race; 1 s (Charles b 1964), 1 da (Joanne b 1966); *Career* md Huwood (mining equipment mfrs subsidiary of Babcock Int) 1981-; former md Becorit (GB); dir Br Coal Int; pres (int) Assoc of Br Mining Equipment Companies 1983-; cncl memb Instn of Mining Engrs (chm Conference Ctee 1983); fellow Inst Mining Electrical and Mining Mechanical Engrs 1983-; memb NEDO Mining Machinery Sector Working Pty; CEng;

Recreations golf, fishing, shooting; *Clubs* Inst of Directors; *Style—* Tom Fenton, Esq; Glebe House, Kirkwhelpington, Northumberland NE19 2RS (☎ 0830 40305); Huwood Ltd, Team Valley, Gateshead, Tyne and Wear NE11 0LP (☎ 0632 878888, telex HUWOOD G 53368)

FENTON-JONES, Michael Langford; s of Charles Langford Fenton-Jones (d 1946), of Kent, and Rita Beryl Violet, *née* Webster; *b* 1 June 1930; *Educ* Cranbrook Sch Kent; *m* 1956, Gillian Mary, da of Elford Charles Pimble (d 1985), of Surrey; 3 s (Richard b 1959, Jonathan b 1960, David b 1963); *Career* property advsr: DOE 1979-81, BA plc 1983-; chm: Commercial Union Properties Ltd 1982-, Central Station Properties Ltd 1983-, Midland Hotel & Conf Centre 1984-; memb Fin Inst Gp, Prov Insurance plc 1982-; chm of Int Christian C of C (UK) 1986-; tstee: The Carpenters Tst, The Durleston Tst; *Recreations* golf, swimming, reading; *Clubs* National (at Carlton); *Style—* Michael Fenton-Jones, Esq; Eastlea, Felix Lane, Shepperton, Middx; TW17 8NN (☎ 0932 227228); British Airways, Trident House, Heathrow Airport, London, Hounslow TW6 2JA (☎ 081 562 0185)

FENWICK, (John) Andrew; s of John James Fenwick, of London, and Muriel Gillian, *née* Hodnett; *b* 8 Oct 1959; *Educ* Eton, Univ of Exeter (BA); *Career* accountant Deloitte Haskins & Sells 1985-86 (articled clerk 1982-84), fin PR Broad St Assocs London 1986-87, fin dir and fin PR dir Brunswick Public Relations Ltd 1987-; Freeman: Worshipful Co of Mercers 1990, City of London 1990; ACA 1985; *Recreations* travel, bridge, agriculture, horticulture; *Style—* Andrew Fenwick, Esq; Brunswick Public Relations Ltd, 15 Lincoln's Inn Fields, London WC2A 3ED (☎ 071 404 5959, fax 071 831 2823)

FENWICK, Maj Charles Xtafer Sebastian; LVO (1977); s of David Fenwick (d 1982); *b* 7 April 1946; *Educ* Ampleforth; *Career* Maj, Regt Offr Grenadier Guards 1965-78, tutor to Sheik Maktoum Bin Rashid Al Maktoum of Dubai 1968-69, equerry to HRH The Duke of Edinburgh 1975-77; dir: By Pass Nurseries Ltd 1978-, By Pass Nurseries (Seeds) Ltd 1978-; chm Int Garden Centre Assoc (Br Gp) Ltd 1984-; md The Chelsea Gardener 1984-; *Clubs* Turf; *Style—* Maj Charles Fenwick, LVO; Barhams Manor, Higham, nr Stoke by Nayland, Suffolk (☎ 0206 37231); 125 Sydney Street, Chelsea, London SW3; Bypass Nurseries Ltd, Ipswich Rd, Colchester, Essex

FENWICK, Very Rev Jeffery Robert; s of Stanley Robert Fenwick, of West Clandon, Surrey, and Dorothy Evelyn, *née* Jeffery; *b* 8 April 1930; *Educ* Torquay and Selhurst GS, Pembroke Coll Cambridge (MA); *m* 12 April 1955, Pamela Frances, da of Rev Canon Leonard Galley (d 1979), of St Margarets, Foulsham, Norfolk; 1 s (Jeffery Francis b 1958), 2 da (Alison b 1956, Clare b 1960); *Career* priest: Dio of Liverpool 1955-58, Mashonaland 1958-75; examining chaplain to Bishops of Mashonaland 1966-75, rector Salisbury E Rhodesia and archdeacon of Charter 1970-75, dean and archdeacon of Bulawayo 1975-78, canon of Worcester 1978-88, dean of Guernsey and rector St Peter Port 1989-, canon of Winchester 1989-; memb: Cncl USPG 1978-, Gen Synod 1989-91; chm: Cathedrals France Conf 1984-87 (memb 1978-88), Cathedrals Libraries Conf 1987-88 (memb 1978-88), govrs Elizabeth Coll Guernsey 1989-; govr King's Sch Worcester 1979-88; *Books* A Pattern of History (1970), Chosen People (1971); *Recreations* walking, painting, gardening, music; *Style—* The Very Rev the Dean of Guernsey; The Deanery, Guernsey, CI (☎ 0481 20036, fax 0481 713915)

FENWICK, John James; DL (Tyne and Wear 1986); s of James Frederick Trevor Fenwick (d 1979), and Elizabeth Vere, *née* Meldrum; *b* 9 Aug 1932; *Educ* Rugby, Pembroke Coll Cambridge (MA); *m* 27 April 1957, (Muriel) Gillian, da of George Robert Hodnett (d 1978); 3 s (Andrew b 8 Oct 1959, Adam b 20 Oct 1960, Hugo b 29 Dec 1964); *Career* md Fenwick Ltd 1972-82 (dep chm 1972-79, chm 1979-), regnl dir Lloyds Bank plc 1982-86; dir Northern Rock Bldg Soc 1984-; tstee Civic Tst (North East) 1979-; govr Royal GS Newcastle upon Tyne 1975- (chm 1987-); memb Worshipful Co of Mercers 1981; *Recreations* travel, theatre, shooting; *Clubs* Garrick, MCC; *Style—* J J Fenwick, Esq, DL; 27 St Dionis Rd, London SW6 4UQ; 35 Osborne Road, Newcastle-upon-Tyne NE2 2AH

FENWICK, Maj Justin Francis Quintus; s of David Fenwick (d 1982), of Barhams Manor, Higham, nr Colchester, Suffolk, and Maita Gwladys Joan, *née* Powys-Keck; *b* 11 Sept 1949; *Educ* Ampleforth, Clare Coll Cambridge (MA); *m* 21 June 1975, Marcia Mary, da of Archibald Dunn (d 1977), of Overbury Hall, Layham, Hadleigh, Suffolk; 1 s (Hubert George Francis b 3 Aug 1990), 3 da (Corisande Mary b 1983, Rosamond Xanthe b 1985, Madeleine Isobel b 1988); *Career* Grenadier Gds 1968-81: Maj and Adj 2 Bn 1977-79, Extra Equerry to HRH Duke of Edinburgh 1979-81; barr Temple 1981; dir By Pass Nurseries Ltd 1982-; chm Soc of Chelsea Res Assoc 1988-; *Recreations* shooting, reading, wine; *Clubs* Garrick, Travellers; *Style—* Maj Justin Fenwick; Geldeston Hall, Geldeston, Norfolk; 17 Lennox Gardens, London SW3 (☎ 071 581 1533); 2 Crown Office Row, The Temple, London, EC4 (☎ 071 583 8155)

FENWICK, Leonard Raymond; s of Leo Stanislaws Fenwick (d 1983), of Newcastle upon Tyne, and Hilda May, *née* Downey (d 1989); *b* 10 Aug 1947; *Educ* West Jesmond and John Harlay Schs Newcastle upon Tyne; *m* 1969, Jacqueline; 1 da (Kate b 1982); *Career* NHS: joined 1965, various posts in health serv mgmnt in NE Eng and Humbs 1966-74, admin then gen mangr Freeman Hosp since 1975, chief exec Freeman Gp of Hosps NHS Tst 1990; cncllr Tyne and Wear CC 1981-86; Freeman City of Newcastle upon Tyne, memb Worshipful Co of Shipwrights 1968, chm Stewards Ctee of Incorporated Cos and Ct of Guild of City of Newcastle upon Tyne; memb Inst of Health Servs Mgmnt 1972; *Style—* Leonard Fenwick, Esq; The Freeman Group of Hospitals, High Heaton, Newcastle upon Tyne NE7 7DN (☎ 091 2843111, fax 091 213 1968

FENWICK, Mark Anthony; s of John Fenwick, of South Audley St, London, and Sheila E M, *née* Edwards; *b* 11 May 1948; *Educ* Millfield Sch, Univ of Business Studies Switzerland; *m* 9 Nov 1972, Margaret Kathleen, da of Col Frederick Roger Hue-Williams (d 1987), of Newbury, Berks; 1 s (Leon b 26 Sept 1980), 1 da (Mia b 14 April 1978); *Career* dir EG Mgmnt Ltd 1971-77; mangr: Roxy Music 1972-83, King Crimson 1972-85; md EG Records Ltd 1977-88, chm EG Music Gp Ltd 1980-, dir Fenwick Ltd 1978-, dep chm Yeoman Security Gp plc 1986-, chm Old Chelsea Gp plc 1986-, dir Ricemans (Hldgs) Ltd 1986-, chm Fenwick of Bond St 1988-, dir Natural Nutrition Co plc 1989, ptnr Athol & Co Ltd 1989-; *Recreations* shooting, music, reading; *Style—* Mark Fenwick, Esq; Athol & Co, 63A Kings Rd, London SW3 4NT (☎ 071 730 2162, fax 071 730 1330)

FENWICK, Dr Peter Brooke Cadogan; s of Anthony Fenwick (d 1954), of Kenya, and Betty, *née* Darling (d 1983); *b* 25 May 1935; *Educ* Stowe, Trinity Coll Cambridge (MB BChir), St Thomas Hosp, Univ of London (DPM), FRC Psych; *m* 18 May 1963, Elizabeth Isobel, da of Harry Nicholas Roberts (d 1985), of Bracewell, Yorkshire; 1 s (Tristram Nicholas Cadogan b 2 Nov 1967), 2 da (Annabel Sarah Cadogan b 9 March 1964, Natasha Jane Cadogan b 13 Nov 1965); *Career* sr lectr Institute of Psychiatry Univ of London 1972-, hon conslt research neurophysiologist Broadmoors Hosp 1973-; conslt neurophysiologist: Westminster Hosp 1974-77, St Thomas's Hosp 1974-89, Radcliffe Infirmary 1989-; conslt neuropsychiatrist Maudsley Hosp 1977-; numerous articles on: epilepsy, neurophysiology, violence, automatic behaviour; *Recreations* flying, music, hill walking, trout fishing; *Style—* Dr Peter Fenwick; The Maudsley Hospital, Denmark Hill, London SE5 8AZ (☎ 071 703 6333)

FENWICK, Lady Sophia Anne; *née* Crichton-Stuart; er da of 6 Marquess of Bute; *b* 27 Feb 1956; *m* 1, 1979 (m dis 1988), Jimmy Bain, musician; 1 da (Samantha Isabella b 1981); m 2, 3 March 1990, Alexius J B Fenwick, s of Benedict Fenwick, of Sholebrook, Towcester, Northants; *Style—* The Lady Sophia Fenwick; 24 Fernhurst Rd, London SW6

FENWICK, Thomas Richard Featherstone; s of Edwin Arthur Featherstone Fenwick (d 1978), of Foresters Lodge, Wolsingham, Co Durham, and Marjorie Newton, *née* Weeks (d 1989); *b* 11 Dec 1926; *Educ* Charterhouse, Jesus Coll Cambridge; *m* 27 April 1957, Sarah Mary, da of Thomas Alexander Page (d 1970); 3 s, 1 s decd, 1 da; *Career* RA 1945; landowner, farmer, forester; JP Co Durham 1966-79, High Sheriff Co Palatine of Durham 1975-76; *Recreations* shooting; *Clubs* Farmers; *Style—* Thomas Fenwick, Esq; Bishop Oak, Wolsingham, Bishop Auckland, Co Durham DL13 3LT (☎ 0388 527 435)

FENWICK, Trevor James; s of Leslie Fenwick, of London, and Mabel Alice, *née* Lee; *b* 28 Feb 1954; *Educ* Highgate Sch, Univ of Essex (BA); *m* Jane Seton Hindley; 2 s (James 1987, Edward 1989); *Career* md Euromonitor plc 1988-(dir 1980-); MCIM 1979; *Style—* Trevor Fenwick, Esq; 99 Richmond Avenue, London N1 0CT (☎ 071 607 4757), Euromonitor plc, 87-88 Turnmill St, London EC1M 5QU (☎ 071 251 8024, telex 21120 (2281), fax 071 608 3149)

FENWICKE-CLENNELL, (Geoffrey Thomas) Warren; s of Lt-Col Geoffrey Edward Fenwicke-Clennell (d 1963), of Claydon, Oxon, and Barbara Enid, *née* Jolliffe (d 1977); *b* 15 Jan 1928; *Educ* Winchester, RMA Sandhurst; *m* 1 June 1957, Caroline Ann, da of Maj Sir Charles Douglas Blackett, 9 Bt (d 1968), of Northumberland; 2 s (Nicholas b 1959, Luke Thomas b 1961), 1 da (Katherine Mary b 1963); *Career* Capt 11 Hussars PAO resigned 1958; sales mangr Taplows 1962-64, prodn mangr/dir IDV/WA Gilbey 1964-69, CE Murphy's Brewery Cork 1969-71, dir Watney-Mann 1971-76, md Truman Ltd 1976-81, commercial dir Watney-Mann & Truman Brewers 1981-82 (dir 1976-82); comptroller The Earl of Harewood 1984-; dir: Harewood Property Co, Harewood House Tst Ltd, Diaceteon Property Ltd; *Recreations* country sports, gundogs, poultry; *Clubs* Cavalry and Gds; *Style—* Warren Fenwicke-Clennell, Esq; Kirk Hammerton House, York (☎ 0423 331016); 8 Donne Place, London SW3 (☎ 071 584 2350); Estate Office, Harewood, Leeds (☎ 0532 886331)

FERENS, (Charles) Richard; s of John Leslie Ferens (d 1987), of Harrogate, and Joan, *née* Mannington; *b* 23 Dec 1936; *Educ* Trinity Hall Cambridge (MA); *m* 17 Sept 1960, Penelope Jane, da of Lt-Col Stuart Dewes Hayward (d 1983), of Suffolk; 3 da (Emma b 1962, Caroline b 1963, Sophie b 1965); *Career* Lt E Yorks Regt 1955-57; hon sec Land Agency and Agric Div RICS 1977-80 (chm E Anglian Branch dir Royal Show 1982-87, vice pres Royal Agric Soc of England, chm Lincs Branch Br Food and Farming 1989; arbitrator to Lord Chllr; conslt surveyor to Strutt and Parker, agric mortgage corporation valuer, memb Min of Tport's Landscape Advsy Ctee; *Recreations* shooting, fishing, gardening; *Clubs* Farmers, Anglo Belgian; *Style—* Richard Ferens, Esq; Casthorpe Lodge, Barrowby, Grantham, Lincs (☎ 0476 63559)

FERENS, Sir Thomas Robinson; CBE (1952); s of John Johnson Till Ferens, of Hull (d 1957), and Marion, *née* Runton; *b* 4 Jan 1903; *Educ* Rydal, Univ of Leeds (BSc); *m* 1 Sept 1934, Jessie (d 1982), da of late P G Sanderson, of Hull and Scarborough; 1 da, 1 step da (dec); 2 da; *Career* engr; md Shipham & Co Ltd, George Clark & Son (Hull) Ltd, dir Newman Hender Ltd, ret 1970; kt 1957; *Recreations* fly-fishing; *Style—* Sir Thomas Ferens, CBE; Sunderlandwick House, Driffield, Humberside (☎ 0377 42323)

FERGUS, John Graham; s of Leslie Fraser Fergus (d 1987), of Glasgow, and Barbara Ireland, *née* Pringle; *b* 2 July 1933; *Educ* Glasgow HS, Glasgow Acad, Kings Park Sch Glasgow; *m* 1958, Helen Davidson, da of Andrew Davidson McLay (d 1982); 2 s (Alasdair b 1965, Colin b 1967), 1 da (Linda b 1972); *Career* Nat Serv PO RAF, serv UK; CA; md Scottish Lowland Holdings Ltd and Subsidiaries 1974-82; dir Arbuckle Smith & Co Ltd 1972-74, md Castlegreen Warehousing Co Ltd 1966-72, chm: Scottish Tanning Industries Ltd 1982-; dir: Barr and Wray Ltd 1982-, AA Bros Ltd 1987-, Thomas Auld & Son Ltd 1988-; pres Br Leather Confedn Ltd 1990- (memb Cncl 1986-); *Recreations* garden, golf, curling, church affairs, City of Glasgow; *Clubs* RSAC; *Style—* John G Fergus, Esq; Carleith, Kilmacolm, Renfrewshire PA13 4AS (☎ 050 587 2520); Scottish Tanning Industries Ltd, Bridge of Weir, Renfrewshire (☎ 050 561 2953, telex 778057, fax 050 561 4964)

FERGUSON; *see*: Johnson-Ferguson

FERGUSON, Alexander Chapman; OBE; s of Alexander Beaton Ferguson (d 1979), and Elizabeth, *née* Hardy (d 1986); *b* 31 Dec 1941; *Educ* Govan High Sr Secdy Sch; *m* 12 March 1966, Catherine Russell, da of Hugh Holding (d 1952); 3 s (Mark b 18 Sept 1968, Jason b 9 Feb 1972, Darren b (twin) 9 Feb 1972); *Career* professional footballer: Queen's Park Rangers 1958-60, St Johnstone 1960-64, Dumfermline Athletic 1964-67, Glasgow Rangers 1967-69, Falkirk FC 1969-73, Ayr Utd 1973-74, two Scot League caps; mangr: E Stirling 1974, St Mirren 1974-78, Aberdeen FC 1978-86 (Euro Cup winners 1983, Super Cup winners 1983, Premier Div champions 1980, 82, 84, four times Scot FA cup winners, League Cup winners 1985), Scot Nat Team 1985-86 (asst mangr under Jock Stein 1985-86), Manchester Utd FC 1986- (FA Cup winners 1990); Mangr of The Year 1983-85; *Books* A Light in the North (1985); *Recreations* golf, snooker; *Style—* Alexander Ferguson, Esq, OBE; Manchester Utd FC, Old Trafford, Manchester M16 0RA (☎ 061 872 1661, fax 061 873 7210, telex 666564 UNITED G)

FERGUSON, Andrew John Duncan; s of James Duncan Ferguson (d 1980), of Heath Drive, Sutton, Surrey, and Kathleen Ann, *née* Kemp (d 1986); *b* 9 June 1940; *Educ* Epsom Coll, St John's Coll Cambridge (MA); *m* 25 March 1967, Elizabeth Mary, da of Cdr Leslie Edward Wright (d 1988), of 4 Glebe Way, Wisborough Green, W Sussex; 1 s (Ian Duncan b 5 April 1968), 3 da (Joanna Elizabeth b 12 Nov 1970, Kate Juliet b 30 Aug 1979, Gillian Mary b 1 Jan 1983); *Career* with Andrew W Barr & Co 1962-64, Standard Industrial Group 1964-67, Johnston Group plc 1967-87 (chief exec 1978-87); chm Duncan Group plc 1987-; Freeman City of London, Liveryman Worshipful Co of Coachmakers and Coach Harness Makers 1965 FCA 1963; *Recreations* sailing, squash; *Clubs* RAC, Caledonian; *Style—* Andrew Ferguson, Esq; Mundys Hill, Shere Road, Ewhurst, Surrey GU6 7PQ (☎ 0483 277237); Duncan Gp plc, High St, Ripley, Surrey GU23 6AY (☎ 0483 211 379, fax 0483 211 382, car 0836 756140)

FERGUSON, Anne Adams; da of Norman G D Ferguson, of NI, and Margaret, *née* Adams; *b* 10 May 1960; *Educ* Princess Gardens Sch Belfast, Univ of Reading (BSc), London Business Sch; *Career* prodn asst Grosvenor Press 1981-82, prodn mangr The Magazine 1982; Management Today: ed asst 1982-83, prodn ed 1983-86, assoc ed 1986-87, sr ed 1987-89; mgmnt ed The Independent on Sunday 1990-; *Style—* Ms Anne Ferguson; The Independent on Sunday, Newspaper Publishing, 40 City Rd, London EC1Y 2DB (☎ 071 253 1222)

FERGUSON, Christopher Mark; s of Maj Michael Frederick George Ferguson (d 1982), and Josephine Manners, *née* Ackland (d 1987); *b* 29 Nov 1957; *Educ* Sherborne; *m* 1 May 1982, Jacqueline, da of William Alexander Kirkwood, of 15 Witham Close, Stamford, Lincs; 1 s (Robert b 1985), 2 da (Lucy b 1987, Alice b 1989); *Career* called to the Bar Middle Temple 1979; memb Middle Temple 1975-; *Recreations* various sports, music, theatre; *Style—* Christopher Ferguson, Esq; 7 The Glen, Westbury Park, Bristol BS6 7JH (☎ 0272 732283); Assize Court Chambers, 14 Small St, Bristol BS1 1DE (☎ 0272 264587, fax 0272 226835)

FERGUSON, Cdre (Robert) Duncan; s of Lt-Col Robert Hunter Ferguson, ED (d 1966), of Glenlair, Knockvennie, Castle Douglas, Kirkcudbrightshire, and Jane Cooper, *née* Baxter; *b* 2 May 1940; *Educ* Fettes, Univ of London (BSc), Nato Defense Coll; *m* 2 Sept 1967, Henrietta MacDonald, da of Maj John Dunlop Williamson (KAR, ka Abyssinia 1942); 1 s (Angus b 1971), 2 da (Samantha b 1969, Emily b 1979); *Career* joined RN 1958, Weapon Engr Offr HMS Brighton 1965-67, Polaris Exec 1967-70, RNEC Maradon 1970-73, Weapon Engr Offr HMS Arrow 1974-77, Naval Sec 1977-78 Cdr 1977, BRNC Dartmouth 1978-80; Weapon Engr Offr: 4 Frigate Sqdn 1980-82 (despatches 1982), Dep Fleet Weapon Engr 1982-84; Capt 1983, Def advsr Wellington, Suva, Nuku' Alofa 1984-87, Flag Offr Scotland and NI as project co-ordinator Pitreavie Devpt Pr 1987-90, Asst COS (CIS) Div AFSOUTH 1990-, Cdre 1990; chm RN Winter Sports Assoc 1988-90; FMIEE 1990 (MIEE 1978); *Recreations* offshore sailing, skiing, golf, fishing, shooting; *Clubs* Lansdowne, RN Sailing Assoc, RN Winter Sports Assoc; *Style*— Cdre Duncan Ferguson, RN; Braeside, Gatehouse of Fleet, Castle Douglas, Kirkcudbrightshire (☎ 05574 536)

FERGUSON, George Robin Paget; s of Robert Spencer Ferguson, MVO, of Manningford Bruce House, Pewsey, Wilts, and Eve Mary, *née* Paget; *b* 22 March 1947; *Educ* Wellington , Univ of Bristol (BA, B Arch); *m* 24 May 1969, (Aymée) Lavinia, da of Sir John Clerk, 10 Bt, of Penicuik House, Midlothian; 1 s (John b 1974), 2 da (Alice b 1971, Corinna b 1979); *Career* architect; fndr practice 1973, ptnr Ferguson Mann 1979-87 (md 1988-), fndr and dir Acanthus Associated Architectural Practices Ltd 1986-, chm Coteval Ltd 1988-; memb Ct Univ of Bristol, tstee Bristol Exploratory, memb Cncl for Preservation of Ancient Bristol, memb Ctee Bristol Civic Soc, pres Bristol West Liberal Democrats; Bristol City cncllr (Lib) 1973-79, Party candidate (Alliance) Bristol West 1983-87; MRIBA 1972; *Books* Races Against Time (1983); *Recreations* writing, broadcasting, travel, photography, sketching; *Style*— George Ferguson, Esq; Ferguson Mann Architects/Acanthus Bristol, Royal Colonnade, 18 Great George St, Bristol BS1 5RH (☎ 0272 273140, fax 0272 225027)

FERGUSON, Brig (John) Gordon Goddard De Poulton; OBE (1984); s of Dr Stanley Fisher Ferguson, of 92 Linden Lea, Finchfield, Wolverhampton, W Mids, and Johanna Margaret McDougall, *née* Gordon (d 1952); *b* 5 March 1943; *Educ* Downside, RMA Sandhurst, Staff Coll Camberley, NATO Def Coll Rome; *m* 5 Jan 1968, Celia Mary, da of Cdr Claudius Alexander Herdman, DL, RN, of Braewood, Sion Mills, Strabane, Co Tyrone; 2 s (Edward Alexander De Poulton b 1978, Rory James De Poulton b 1980), 2 da (Clare Joanna De Poulton b 1968, Lucy Adelia De Poulton b 1970); *Career* cmmnd Queen's Dragoon Gds 1962, helicopter pilot 1967-71, MA Cincnorth 1977-79, dir staff Army Staff Coll Camberley 1980-82, CO The Queen's Dragoon Gds 1982-85, Cdr Br Forces Lebanon 1983, ACOS G3 HQ 1 Br Corps 1985-87, chief policy SHAPE 1988-90, head Reinforcement cell HQ NATO 1990; FBIM 1989; *Recreations* fishing, cross country skiing, opera, ballet, int affairs and politics; *Clubs* Army & Navy; *Style*— Brig Gordon Ferguson, OBE; c/o UK MILREP, HQ NATO, BFPO 49 (☎ 010 322 728 4140, fax 010 322 728 4117)

FERGUSON, Dr Howard; s of Stanley Ferguson, of Belfast, NI, and Frances, *née* Carr; *b* 21 Oct 1908; *Educ* Westminster, RCM; *Career* composer pianist and musicologist; compositions incl: Violin Sonatas 1 and 2 (1933 & 1949), Two Ballads (1934), Partita (1937), Piano Concerto (1952), Discovery Song-Cycle (1952), Amore Langueo (1956), The Dream of the Rood (1959); edns of music incl complete keyboard works of: Purcell (1963), Dagincour (1969), Croft (1974), Schubert (1978); asst organizer daily war-time Nat Gallery Concerts 1939-46; DMus Queens Univ Belfast 1959; *Books* Keyboard Interpretation (1975); *Recreations* reading, cooking; *Style*— Dr Howard Ferguson; 51 Barton Road, Cambridge CB3 9LG (☎ 0223 359206)

FERGUSON, James Gordon Dickson; s of Col James Dickson Ferguson, OBE, ERD, DL (d 1979), of Aghaderg Glebe, Loughbrickland, Banbridge, Co Down, and Jean, *née* Gordon; *b* 12 Nov 1947; *Educ* Cargilfield Sch Edinburgh, Winchester Coll, Trinity Coll Dublin (BA); *m* 20 June 1970, Nicola Hilland, da of Walter G H Stewart, of Lausanne, Switzerland; 2 s (Jim, William), 1 da (Jessica); *Career* chm Stewart Ivory & Co Ltd (formerly Stewart Fund Managers Ltd) 1989 (joined 1970, dir 1974-), dep chm Association of Investment Trust Cos 1984-86; dir: Value & Income Trust plc, Olim Convertible Trust plc; *Recreations* country pursuits; *Clubs* New; *Style*— James Ferguson, Esq; 25 Heriot Row, Edinburgh, EH3 6EN; Aghaderg Glebe, Loughbrickland, Banbridge, Co Down; Stewart Ivory & Co Ltd, 45 Charlotte Square, Edinburgh EH2 4HW (☎ 031 226 3271, fax 031 226 5120, telex 72500

FERGUSON, Col James Henderson; s of John Ferguson (d 1953), and Esther Isobel (d 1981); *b* 26 July 1928; *Educ* Dunoon GS, NATO Defence Coll Camberley, Staff Coll Rome; *m* 16 Nov 1957; 1 s (John Stuart b 20 Feb 1960), 2 da (Catherine Mary Esther b 6 Sept 1958, Jennifer Mary Anne b 1 Aug 1964); *Career* dir Salmon and Trout Assoc 1985-, memb Salmon Advsy Ctee; *Recreations* golf, skiing, fishing; *Clubs* Army and Navy, Rye Golf; *Style*— Col James Ferguson; Salmon and Trout Association, Fishmongers Hall, London Bridge, London (☎ 071 283 5838, fax 071 429 1389)

FERGUSON, Jeremy John; s of Archibald John Lindo Ferguson (d 1975), of Great Missenden, Bucks, and Ann Meryl, *née* Thomas; *b* 12 Nov 1935; *Educ* Stowe; *m* 19 July 1958, Joesphine Mary, da of Arthur William John Hitchcock (d 1969), of Coombe Vale, Sandymere Road, Northam, Bideford, Devon; 1 s (Paul b 1962), 1 da (Elizabeth b 1966); *Career* ptnr: Seldon Ward & Nuttall 1960-74, Jeremy Ferguson & Co 1974-, Chanters Barnstaple 1986-; dep coroner N Devon 1964-74, memb N Devon Manufacturers Assoc, hon slr (memb and past pres) Bideford C of C, fndr and sec Bideford Devpt Project, pres Law Soc Motor Club, memb Legal Aid Area Ctee; *Recreations* motor racing, video photography; *Style*— Jeremy Ferguson, Esq; Langleys, 25 Bay View Rd, Northam, Bideford, Devon EX39 1BH (☎ 0237 474855); 17 The Quay, Bideford, North Devon EX39 2EN (☎ 0237 478751, fax 0237 470893); Bridge Chambers, Barnstaple, North Devon EX31 1HF (☎ 0271 42268)

FERGUSON, John; s of late Maj William George Ferguson, and Grace Ferguson; *b* 28 Sept 1940; *Educ* Cumnock Acad, Univ of Tennessee; *m* 25 Oct 1967, Margaret Janet, da of late William Anderson; 2 s (Ross William George b 31 May 1970, Sean Gray b 6 July 1972); *Career* gen mangr Holiday Inns 1971-82, dist dir Holiday Inns UK 1982-86; shareholder: Liverpool FC, Tranmere FC; Freeman Ports of Canada 1981; Pride award Univ of Olive Branch Mississippi; HCIMA; *Recreations* watching sports, keep fit; *Clubs* Liverpool Football; *Style*— John Ferguson, Esq; The Orchard, Aigburgh, Liverpool L17 6BT (☎ 051 494 0235); 9 Miller Road, Ayr, Ayrshire (☎ 0292 283017); John Weir Ave, Cumnock, Ayrshire (☎ 0290 22480); Churchills Tithebarn Street, Liverpool L2 2PB; Eagle Hotel, Paradise Street, Liverpool L1; Vale Automation, Aintree Ind Estate, Liverpool (☎ 051 227 3877, car 0836 605426)

FERGUSON, Kenneth Gordon; OBE (1990), JP (1988); s of James Ferguson, of 27 Hawkcraig Rd, Aberdour, Fife, and Blanche Stockdale, *née* MacDonald; *b* 17 Feb 1944; *Educ* Leith Acad, Heriot Watt Univ, Napier Coll; *m* da of Hugh MacTaggart Love, of Greenacres, Milltimber, Aberdeen; 2 da (Amanda b 11 Aug 1971, Rebecca b 19 June 1975); *Career* chartered quantity surveyor; trainee Robert TB Gilray 1962-67; asst: Boyden and Cockrane 1967-69, City of Edinburgh Architects Dept 1969-71, Todd and Ledson 1972-79; sr ptnr Ferguson and Partners 1979-; vice pres SCUA 1985-87, memb Edinburgh DC 1977-; FRICS 1969; *Clubs* Scottish Arts; *Style*— Kenneth Ferguson, Esq, OBE, JP; Glebeside, 2 Pentland Avenue, Edinburgh EH13 0HZ (☎ 031 441 3046); 14 Broughton St, Lane, Edinburgh EH1 3LY (☎ 031 557 8988)

FERGUSON, Prof Mark William James; s of James Ferguson, of Marple Bridge, Cheshire, and Elanor Gwendoline, *née* McCoubrey; *b* 11 Oct 1955; *Educ* Coleraine Academical Inst, Queen's Univ Belfast (BSc, BDS, PhD); *m* 22 June 1984, Janice Elizabeth, da of David Forsythe, of Carrickfergus, NI; 1 da (Fleur Marcia b 9 Sept 1987); *Career* Winston Churchill fell 1978, lectr in anatomy Queens Univ Belfast 1979-84, prof of basic dental sci and head Dept of Cell and Structural Biol Univ of Manchester 1984-; winner Colyer prize RSM 1980, Alan J Davis Achievement award American Dental Assoc 1981, Conway medal Royal Acad of Med in Ireland 1985, Darwin lectr Br Assoc for the Advancement of Sci 1987, distinguished scientist award Int Assoc for Dental Res Washington 1988, President's medal Br Assoc of Oral and Maxillofacial Surgeons 1990, John Tomes prize RCS 1990, hon fell RCS (Ireland) 1990; SERC Br rep to NATO, vice chm for sci IUCN SSC Crocodile Gp Geneva, memb Scientific Advsy Ctee on Research into Ageing MRC, launched Oral and Dental Res Tst; author of over 100 papers and books on: palate devpt, alligators and crocodiles, sex determination; *Books* The Structure, Development & Evolution of Reptiles (1984), Crocodiles & Alligators an Illustrated Encyclopaedic Survey by International Experts (1989), Cleft Lip & Palate: Long Term Results & Future Prospects (1990), Egg Incubation, It's Effects on Embryonic Development in Birds & Reptiles (1990); *Recreations* scientific research, biology, travel, wildlife, reading, antiques; *Style*— Prof Mark Ferguson; Department of Cell & Structural Biology, University of Manchester, Coupland 3 Bldg, Manchester M13 9PL (☎ 061 2756775, fax 061 2756776)

FERGUSON, Nicholas Eustace Haddon; s of Capt Derek Ferguson, of Craigard, Tighnabruaich, Argyll, and Betsy, *née* Eustace; *b* 14 Oct 1948; *Educ* Winchester Coll, Univ of Edinburgh (BSc Ordinary, First-Class Econs), Harvard Business Sch (MBA, Baker scholar); *m* 18 Dec 1976, Margaret Jane Dura, da of Robert Collin, of Wheatsheaf House, Hook Norton, Oxon; 2 s (Alexander b 1978, Thomas b 1985), 1 da (Cornelia b 1979); *Career* banker; UK dirships: chm Schroder Ventures, J Henry Schroder Wagg and Co Ltd, Schroder Ventures Ltd, Int Students Club (C of E) Ltd; overseas dir: Singapore Int Merchant Bankers Ltd, Schroder Real Estate Investment Inc, Schroder Venture Mangrs (Guernsey) Ltd, Schroder Securities (Japan) Ltd, Schroder PTV Ptnrs KK; *Recreations* sailing, skiing; *Clubs* Brooks's; *Style*— Nicholas Ferguson, Esq; 18 Queensdale Rd, London W11 4QB (☎ 071 229 0503); 120 Cheapside, London EC2V 6DS (☎ 071 382 6896, telex 885029, fax 071 382 6878)

FERGUSON, Richard; QC (NI 1973, UK 1986); s of Wesley Ferguson (d 1973), of Enniskillen, and Edith, *née* Hewitt; *b* 22 Aug 1935; *Educ* Methodist Coll, Queens Univ Belfast (LLB), Trinity Coll Dublin (BA); *m* 1 (m dis), Janet, da of Irvine MaGowen, CB (d 1978), of Mount Norris, Co Armagh; 3 s (Richard b 1964, William b 1966, James b 1968), 1 da (Kathrine b 1962); *m* 2, Roma Felicity, da of J A Whelan, of Antrim Rd, Belfast; 1 s (Patrick b 1987); *Career* Lt Royal Irish Fus TA 1958-61; called to the Bar Gray's Inn 1956, sr counsel Rep of Ireland 1983; chm Mental Health Review Tbnl (NI), govr Methodist Coll, chm Mountain Trg Bd, memb Irish Sports Cncl, MP S Antrim 1986-88; FRGS; *Recreations* swimming, hill walking; *Clubs* Kildare St (Dublin); *Style*— Richard Ferguson, Esq, QC; Sandhill House, Derrygonnelly, Fermanagh, NI; 84 Buckingham Rd, London N1; 1 Crown Office Row, Temple, London EC4 (☎ 071 583 3724, fax 071 353 3923)

FERGUSON, Dr Roger; s of Capt Alan Hudspeth Ferguson (d 1967), and Betty Fielding, *née* Willatt; *b* 23 Aug 1946; *Educ* City Sch Lincoln, Univ of Birmingham (MB ChB, MD); *m* 12 Jan 1974, Ruth Elizabeth, da of Prof Harold Spencer, of Willaston, Cheshire; 3 da (Sarah Helen b 1975, Jean Alison b 1976, Fiona Jane b 1978); *Career* med registrar Worcester Royal Infirmary 1970-73, res registrar Birmingham Gen Hosp 1973-75, sr med registrar Nottingham Gen Hosp and Derby Royal Infirmary 1975-79, conslt physician and gastroenterologist Arrowe Park Hosp Wirral 1979-; memb: Midland Gastroenterological Soc, Northern Gastroenterological Soc, Br Soc of Gastroenterology; former chm Wirral Wine Soc; FRCP 1987 (MRCP 1972); *Books* Text Book of Gastroenterology (contrib, 1990); *Recreations* swimming, golf, music, reading; *Style*— Dr Roger Ferguson; 89 Bidston Rd, Oxton, Birkenhead, Wirral, Merseyside L43 6TS (☎ 051 652 3722); Arrowe Park Hospital, Arrowe Park Rd, Upton, Wirral L4G 5LM (☎ 051 678 5111)

FERGUSON, William James; DL (Aberdeen); s of William Adam Fergsuon (d 1955), and Violet, *née* Wiseman; *b* 3 April 1933; *Educ* Turriff Acad, N of Scotland Coll of Agric; *m* 27 June 1961, Carroll Isobella, da of Robert Shaw McDonald Milne, of Kincardineshire; 1 s (William b 27 April 1962), 3 da (Kim b 29 May 1963, Nicola b 17 Aug 1965, Emma b 5 Aug 1968); *Career* 1 Bn Gordon Highlanders 1952-54; farmer 1954-, vice chm Aberdeen and Dist Milk Mktg Bd 1984-; chm: N of Scotland Coll of Agric 1988-, Advsy Ctee BBC Scottish Rural and Agric Affrs 1985-88; vice chm: Scottish Agric Colls, Rowet Res Inst; memb Scottish Co Life Museums Tst Ltd; *Recreations* golf, skiing, field sports; *Style*— William Ferguson, Esq, DL; Rothiebrisbane, Fyvie, Turriff, Aberdeenshire (☎ 06516 213)

FERGUSON DAVIE, Sir Antony Francis; 6 Bt (E 1641, revived UK 1847 in favour of Gen Henry Ferguson, who m Frances sis of Sir John Davie, 9 Bt, and who assumed by Royal Licence the additional surname and arms of Davie); s of Rev Sir (Arthur) Patrick Ferguson Davie, 5 Bt, TD (d 1988); *b* 23 March 1952; *Educ* Stanbridge Earls Sch, Birkbeck Coll London; *Style*— Sir Antony Ferguson Davie, Bt

FERGUSON DAVIE, Lady; Iris Dawn; *née* Cable-Buller; o da of Capt Michael Francis Buller, of Devon, and Hon Dawn Weston, da of 1 and last Baron Cable; *b* 7 March 1929; *m* 8 Dec 1949, Rev Sir (Arthur) Patrick Ferguson Davie, 5 Bt (d 1988); 1 s (Sir Antony, 6 Bt, *qv*); *Style*— Lady Ferguson Davie; Skalatos House, Girne, Mersin 10, Turkey

FERGUSON-SMITH, Prof Malcolm Andrew; s of Dr John Ferguson-Smith (d 1978), of Strathay, Perthshire, and Ethel May, *née* Thorne; *b* 5 Sept 1931; *Educ* Stowe, Univ of Glasgow (MB ChB); *m* 11 July 1960, Marie Eve, da of Stanislaw Franciszek Gzowski (d 1981), of Baltimore, USA; 1 s (John b 1970), 3 da (Anne b 1961, Nicola b 1965, Julia b 1976); *Career* prof of med genetics Univ of Glasgow 1973-87, dir West of Scot Regnl Genetics Serv 1973-87, ed in chief Prenatal Diagnosis 1980-, prof of pathology Univ of Cambridge 1987-, dir E Anglian Regnl Genetics Serv 1987-, fell of Peterhouse Cambridge 1987-, Makdougall-Brisbane prize Royal Soc of Edinburgh 1988; memb Neurology Bd MRC 1974-76, vice pres Genetical Soc 1978-81, pres Clinical Genetics Soc 1979-81, memb Cncl RC Path 1983-86, pres Perm Ctee Int Congress of Human Genetics 1986-, fndr memb Exec Ctee of Human Genome Orgn 1988-, WHO advsr in human genetics 1988-, memb Cell Bd MRC 1989-; FRSE 1978, FRS 1983, foreign memb Polish Acad of Sci 1988; *Books* Early Parental Diagnosis (1983), Essential Medical Genetics (1987); *Recreations* sailing, swimming, fishing; *Style*— Prof Malcolm Ferguson-Smith; 16 Rustat Rd, Cambridge CB1 3QT (☎ 0223 246277); Dept of Pathology, University of Cambridge, Tennis Court Rd, Cambridge CB2 3QP (☎ 0223 333691, fax 0223 333346, telex 81240 C)

FERGUSSON, Adam Dugdale; yr s of Sir James Fergusson, 8 Bt, of Kilkerran (d 1973), and bro of Sir Charles, 9 Bt; *b* 10 July 1932; *Educ* Eton, Trinity Coll Cambridge (BA); *m* 11 Dec 1965, (Elizabeth Catherine) Penelope, eldest da of Thomas Peter Hughes, of Furneaux Pelham Hall, Buntingford, Herts; 2 s (James b 1966, Marcus 1972), 2 da (Petra b 1968, Lucy b 1970); *Career* politician, author and journalist;

Glasgow Herald 1956-60 (ldr writer, diplomatic correspondent), Statist 1961-67 (foreign ed 1964-67); Times feature writer 1967-77; MEP (Con) W Strathclyde 1979-84; political affrs spokesman for Euro Democratic Gp 1979-82, vice-pres Political Affrs Ctee Euro Parl 1982-84, special advsr European affairs FCO 1985-89; conslt European affairs 1989-; *Books* Roman Go Home (1969), The Lost Embassy (1970), The Sack of Bath (1973), When Money Dies (1975); *Clubs* Brooks's; *Style*— Adam Fergusson, Esq; 15 Warwick Gardens, London W14 (☎ 071 603 7900)

FERGUSSON, Sir Ewen Alastair John; KCMG (1987); s of Sir Ewen MacGregor Field Fergusson (d 1974), and Winifred Evelyn Fergusson; *b* 28 Oct 1932; *Educ* Rugby, Oriel Coll Oxford (MA); *m* 19 Dec 1959, Sara Carolyn, da of late Brig-Gen Lord Esmé Gordon-Lennox KCVO, CMG, DSO; 1 s (Ewen b 30 Nov 1965), 2 da (Anna b 15 June 1961, Iona b 7 May 1967); *Career* 2 Lt 60 Rifles KRRC 1954-56; Dip Serv 1956, asst private sec MOD 1957-59, Br Embassy Addis Ababa 1960, FO 1963, Br Trade Devpt Office NYC 1967, cnsllr and head of Chancery Office UK Perm Rep to Euro Communities, 1 private sec to Foreign and Cwlth Sec 1975-78, asst under sec state FCO 1978-82, ambass SA 1982-84, dep under sec state FCO 1984-87, ambass France 1987-; govr Rugby 1985-, hon fell Oriel Coll Oxford 1987; *Clubs* RAC, Jockey (Paris), Cercle de l'Union Interalliée (Paris); *Style*— Sir Ewen Fergusson, KCMG; c/o Foreign and Commonwealth Office, London SW1A 2AH

FERGUSSON, Hon George Duncan Raukawa; s of Baron Ballantrae (Life Peer), KT, GCMG, GCVO, DSO, OBE (d 1980), 3 s of Sir Charles Fergusson, 7 Bt, of Kilkerran, by his w Laura Margaret Grenfell (d 1979) (*see* Peerage Baron Grenfell 1976); *b* 30 Sept 1955; *Educ* Hereworth Sch NZ, Eton, Magdalen Coll Oxford (BA); *m* 10 Jan 1981, Margaret Sheila, da of Michael John Wookey, of Camberley, Surrey; 1 s (Alexander b 1984), 2 da (Laura b 1982, Alice b 1986); *Career* civil servant 1978- (Home Civil Serv 1978-90), first sec Br Embassy Dublin 1988- (transferred to Dip Serv 1990); *Style*— The Hon George Fergusson; c/o Foreign and Commonwealth Office, King Charles St, London SW1

FERGUSSON, Ian Lewis Campbell; s of John Douglas Fergusson (d 1978), of 82 Portland Place, London W1, and Alice Aleyn, *née* Maartewsz (d 1968); *b* 11 April 1942; *Educ* Rugby, Univ of Cambridge (MA, MB BChir); *m* 16 Dec 1972, Marylin Susan, da of Lt-Col Guy Philip Arthur Shelley, OBE (d 1988), of Turleigh Wiltshire; 1 s (Jamie b 4 Sept 1974), 3 da (Katie b 28 April 1976, Sally b 20 Feb 1980, Molly b 25 July 1982); *Career* RNR Lt-Cdr and surgn (ret 1980); conslt obstetrician and gynaecologist St Thomas' Hosp 1979, conslt gynaecologist Chelsea Hosp for Women 1980-89, sr civilian gynaecologist to the RN 1982-, hon gynaecologist to St Lukes Hosp for the Clergy; jt chm St Thomas' Hosp Baby Fund; Freeman: City of London, Worshipful Co of Apothecaries; FRCS 1971, FRCSEd 1971, memb BMA; *Books* Records and Curiosities in Obstetrics and Gynaecology (1980); *Recreations* fishing, water colour painting; *Clubs* Army and Navy, MCC, West Surrey Golf; *Style*— Ian Fergusson, Esq; 112 Fentiman Rd, London SW8 1QA (☎ 071 735 3867); 10 Upper Wimpole St, London W1 (☎ 071 935 8273)

FERGUSSON, (Frederick) James; s of Frederick Peter Fergusson, of Yalding, Kent, and Oenone Barbara, *née* Wicks; *b* 28 March 1943; *Educ* Haileybury, ISC, Univ Coll Oxford (BA); *m* 11 Nov 1966, Diane Frances (Sophie), da of Leslie Eric Duncan Darley (d 1986), of Rochester, Kent, 2 s (William b 1975, Edward b 1984), 2 da (Polly b 1973, Isobel b 1982); *Career* James Capel and Co: joined 1969, ptnr 1976, dir 1984, dep chm 1987; *Recreations* skiing, tennis, music, reading; *Style*— James Fergusson, Esq; James Capel and Co, 6 Bevis Marks, London EC3A 7JQ (☎ 071 621 0011, fax 071 621, telex 888866 JC LDN G)

FERGUSSON, William Gordon; s of Capt John Gordon Fergusson, of Sandy Brow, Tarporley, Cheshire, and Marielou, *née* Gaggero (d 1988); *Educ* Ampleforth; *Career* 9/12 Royal Lancers (Prince of Wales) 1978-81, ret as Lt; dir Walter Judd Ltd (practitioners in fin advtg and PR) 1989-90 (joined 1982), ret; currently manages family estate at Sandy Brow; MIPA 1987; *Recreations* skiing, golf, shooting; *Style*— William Fergusson, Esq

FERGUSSON-CUNINGHAME OF CAPRINGTON, Capt Robert Wallace; DL (Ayrshire 1960); 17 of Caprington; Lord of the Barony of Caprington; er s of Lt-Col William Wallace Smith Cuninghame, DSO (d 1959), of Caprington, and Ella Cutlar Fergusson (d 1928), 20 of Craigdarroch, Dumfries; *b* 4 Aug 1919; *Educ* Eton, RMC; *m* 1958, Rosemary Elisabeth Euing, er da of Brig Alastair W E Crawford, of Auchentroig, Buchlyvie, Stirling; 1 s; *Career* 2 Lt Scots Gds 1939, served WW II; Capt RARO 1949; memb Queen's Body Gd for Scotland (Royal Co of Archers) 1948-; *Clubs* Turf, Pratt's, New (Edinburgh); *Style*— Capt Robert Fergusson-Cuninghame, DL; Caprington Castle, Kilmarnock, Ayrshire (☎ 0563 26157)

FERMONT, Dr David Calvin; s of David Andre Fermont, of Esher, Surrey, and Edith Mary, *née* Kew; *b* 31 Oct 1946; *Educ* Cheltenham, Middx Hosp Med Sch (MB, BS); *m* 28 Sept 1974, Linda Jane, da of Maj Geoffrey Noel Marks, of Hove, Sussex; 1 s (James Alexander b 29 July 1983), 1 da (Sara Louise b 7 June 1980); *Career* conslt oncologist Clinical Oncology Centre Mount Vernon Hosp, Northwick Park and Barnet General Hosps 1983-; tstee Barnet Cancer Care Appeal, chm Hillingdon Health Authy District Med Ctee, memb Hillingdon DHA Mgmnt Bd, med exec dir Mount Vernon Hosp Tst; FRCS (Eng), FRSM, FRCR, memb Br Inst Radiology; *Books* numerous med pubns; *Recreations* cricket; *Style*— Dr David Fermont; Great Sarratt Hall Cottage, Sarratt, Herts WD3 4PD; Centre for Clinical Oncology, Mount Vernon Hospital, Northwood, Middlesex HA6 2RN (☎ 0895 78231, fax 0923 835803)

FERMOR, Patrick Michael Leigh; DSO (1944), OBE (mil 1943); s of Sir Lewis Leigh Fermor, OBE, FRS (d 1954), and Muriel Eileen, da of Charles Taaffe Ambler (d 1972); *b* 11 Feb 1915; *m* 1968, Hon Joan Elizabeth, da of 1 Viscount Monsell, PC, GBE; *Career* WWII, enlisted Irish Guards 1939, 2 Lt I Corps 1940, Lt Br mil mission to Greece, liaison offr Greek forces in Albania, campaigns of Greece and Crete, Maj and SOE German occupied Crete 1942-44, team Cdr Allied Airborne Reconnaissance Force N Germany; dep dir Br Inst Athens until 1946; author; books: The Travellers Tree (Heineman Fndn prize for literature 1950, Kemsley prize 1951); translated Colete, Chance Aquaintances (1952), A Time to Keep Silence (1953), The Violins of St Jacques (1953), Mani (1958, Duff Cooper Meml prize, Book Soc's choice), translated George Psychoundakis's The Cretan Runner (1955), Roumeli (1966), A Time of Gifts (1977, WH Smith & Son literary award 1978), Between the Woods and the Water (1986, Thomas Cook travel book award 1986, int PEN/Time Life Silver Pen award 1986); hon citizen: Herakleion Crete 1947, Gytheion Laconia 1966, Kardamyli Messenia 1967; Hon DLitt Univ of Kent, visiting memb Acad of Athens, Gold medal Municipality of Athens; *Recreations* travel, reading; *Clubs* Travellers', White's, Pratt's, BeefSteak, Special Forces, Puffins (Edinburgh); *Style*— Patrick Fermor, Esq, DSO, OBE; c/o Messrs John Murray Ltd, 50 Albermarle St, London W1

FERMOR-HESKETH, Hon John; s of 2 Baron Hesketh (d 1955); *b* 15 March 1953; *Educ* Ampleforth; *m* 1, 2 Dec 1980 (m dis), Anna, o da of Hamish Wallace, of Old Corrimony, Glen Urquhart, Inverness; m 2, 14 July 1986, Helena Marian, o da of Robert Hunt, of Petropolis, Brazil; 1 da (Alice Mary Louisa b 5 March 1987); *Clubs* White's; *Style*— The Hon John Fermor-Hesketh

FERMOR-HESKETH, Hon Robert; s of 2 Baron Hesketh (d 1955); *b* 1 Nov 1951; *Educ* Ampleforth; *m* 10 Oct 1979, Jeanne, da of Patrick McDowell and Violette Duvenois; 1 s (Blaise b 1987); *Style*— The Hon Robert Fermor-Hesketh

FERMOY, Lady; Lavinia Frances Elizabeth; *née* Pitman; o da of late Capt John Pitman (d 1943), of Foxley House, Malmesbury, Wilts, and Elizabeth Cattanach, *née* Donaldson; *b* 18 April 1941; *m* 22 June 1964, 5 Baron Fermoy (d 1984), 2 s (6 Baron, *qv*, Hon Edmund Hugh Burke b 1972), 1 da (Hon Frances Caroline Burke (Hon Mrs Stanley) b 1965); *Style*— The Rt Hon the Lady Fermoy; Axford House, nr Marlborough, Wilts

FERMOY, 6 Baron (I 1856); (Patrick) Maurice Burke Roche; s of 5 Baron Fermoy (d 1984), and Lady (Lavinia) Fermoy, *qv*, *née* Pitman; bro of Hon Hugh Roche, *qv*, and Hon Frances Roche; *b* 11 Oct 1967; *Educ* Eton, RMA Sandhurst; *Heir* bro, Hon (Edmund) Hugh Burke Roche b 5 Feb 1972; *Career* page of honour to HM Queen Elizabeth The Queen Mother 1982-85, The Blues and Royals 1987-; *Clubs* Cavalry and Guards'; *Style*— The Rt Hon the Lord Fermoy; Axford House, Marlborough, Wilts

FERN, Dan; s of George Fern (d 1967), of Gainsborough, and Gwen Fern (d 1981); *b* 1 July 1945; *Educ* Queen Elizabeth GS Gainsborough, Manchester Coll of Art and Design, RCA; *m* 1969, Kate Fern; 1 s (Hugo b 1985), 2 da (Zoë b 1976, Ella b 1979); *Career* illustrator; prof of illustration RCA 1989- (head of illustration 1986); solo exhibitions: Print and Collage Constructions (Curwen Gallery London) 1982, Collage, Print and Type Constructions (Curwen Gallery) 1985, recent work (Entrepotdok Amsterdam) 1986; gp exhibitions incl: Art/Work (Nat Theatre) 1979, Homage to Herge (Joan Miro Fndn Barcelona) 1984, Art Meets Science (Smiths Gallery London) 1988, Image and Object (Nat Museum of Modern Art, Kyoto, Japan) 1990, Permanent Collection Victoria and Albert Museum; freelance illustration work incl: Sunday Times Magazine, Radio Times, New Scientist, Penguin Books, Pan Books, J Walter Thompson, Young and Rubicam, Conran Design, Michael Peters Group, Pentagram, Thames Television, Assoc of Illustrators, The Royal Court Theatre, Royal Acad London; lectr and speaker various conferences and workshops; head Educn Ctee Assoc of Illustrators 1977-79, memb various jury panels; twice winner of both Gold & Silver D & ADA awards; FRCA, FCSD, FRSA; *Books* Works with Paper (1990); *Recreations* opera, mountaineering, collecting (books, stamps, printed ephemera); *Style*— Dan Fern, Esq; 58 Muswell Rd, London N10 2BE (☎ 081 883 5604); Illustration, Royal College of Art, Kensington Gore, London SW7 (☎ 071 584 5020, fax 071 225 1487)

FERNANDO, Oswald Nihal; s of Cyril Philip Neri Fernando, and Louise, *née* Edline; *b* 22 Oct 1934; *Educ* Ceylon (MB BS); *m* 8 April 1961, (Susan Dulcie) Tallulah, da of Dr Charles Talbot; 3 s (Dr Hiran Chrishantha b 16 Jan 1962, Rohan Prashantha b 1 April 1963, Bimbi Shiran b 28 Feb 1967); *Career* conslt surgn Royal Free Hosp 1976- (res fell in renal transplantation 1969-70, lectr in surgery 1971-76); hon sr lectr Royal Free Hosp Sch of Med 1976-; hon conslt surgn 1976-: Hosp of St John and St Elizabeth, Hosp for Sick Children Gt Ormond St; memb: Br Transplant Soc, RSM, Br Assoc of Urological Surgns; FRCS, FRCSEd; *Recreations* swimming, squash; *Style*— Oswald N Fernando, Esq; Renal Transplant Unit, Royal Free Hospital, Pond St, London NW3 2QG (☎ 071 794 0500, car 0860 323 002)

FERNEYHOUGH, Prof Brian John Peter; s of Frederick George Ferneyhough (d 1982), and Emily May, *née* Hopwood; *b* 16 Jan 1943; *Educ* Birmingham Sch of Music, Royal Acad of Music, Royal Conservatory Amsterdam, Musikakademie Basel; *m* 19 May 1990, Stephanie Jan, *née* Hurtik; *Career* prof of composition Musikhochschule Freiburg Germany 1973-86, leader composition master class Civica Scuola di Musica di Milano 1984-87, composition teacher Royal Conservatory of The Hague Netherlands 1986-87, composition lectr Darmstadt Summer Sch 1976-, prof of music Univ of Calif at San Diego 1987-; memb: Jury Gaudeamus Int Composition Competition 1984 (Netherlands), Int Jury for World Music Days of Int Soc for Contemporary Music (Finland 1978, Hong Kong 1989); ARAM 1990; Chev dans L'Ordre des Arts et des Lettres Paris 1984, Koussevitsky prize 1978; compositions incl: Sonatas for String Quartet 1967, Transit 1975, Time and Motion Studies I-III 1974-77, La Terre est un Homme 1979, Carceri d'Invenzione 1981-86, La Chute d'Icare 1988, Fourth String Quartet 1990; *Recreations* reading, wine, cats; *Style*— Prof Brian Ferneyhough; Music B-0326, University of Calif at San Diego, La Jolla, CA 92093-0326 (☎ 619 534 3230, fax 619 534 8502)

FERNIE, Prof Eric Campbell; s of Sidney Robert Fernie (d 1988), of Johannesburg, SA, and Catherine Reid, *née* Forrest (d 1959); *b* 9 June 1939; *Educ* Marist Brothers Coll Johannesburg, Univ of Witwatersrand (BA); *m* 28 Nov 1964, (Margaret) Lorraine, da of John Henry French, of Norfolk; 1 s (Ivan b 1969), 2 da (Lyndall b 1965, Jessica b 1969); *Career* sr lectr Univ of East Anglia 1974-84, dean Faculty of Arts Univ of Edinburgh 1989- (Watson Gordon prof of fine art 1984-); chm Ancient Monuments Bd Scotland; memb: Res Awards Ctee Leverhulme Tst, Br Acad Corpus of Romanesque Sculpture Ctee; fell Soc of Antiquaries London; *Books* The Communar and Pitancer Rolls of Norwich Cathedral Priory (1972), The Architecture of the Anglo Saxons (1983); *Style*— Prof Eric Fernie; 17 Buckingham Terrace, Edinburgh EH4 3AD (☎ 031 332 6858); University of Edinburgh, Faculty of Arts Office, David Hume Tower, George Square, Edinburgh EH8 9JX (☎ 031 6671011 ext 6208, fax 031 6682252, tele 727442 UNIVED G)

FEROZE; *see*: Moolan-Feroze

FEROZE, Sir Rustam; s of Dr Jehangir Moolan-Feroze (d 1962), and Diana Lester; *b* 4 Aug 1920; *Educ* Sutton Valence, Univ of London (MB BS, MD); *m* 1947, Margaret, da of Harry Dowsett (d 1975); 3 s, 1 da; *Career* Surgn Lt RNVR Atlantic and Far E 1943-46; conslt obstetrician Queen Charlotte's Hosp London 1952-73, conslt gynaecologist Chelsea Hosp for Women 1952-73, conslt obstetrician and gynaecologist KCH London 1952-85, dean Inst of Obstetrics and Gynaecology Univ of London 1954-67; now ret; contrib to med books 1981-84; pres RCOG 1981-84, currently hon pres Euro Assoc of Gynaecologists and Obstetricians (first pres 1985-88); FRCS, FRCOG; kt 1983; *Recreations* swimming, gardening; *Clubs* RAC; *Style*— Sir Rustam Feroze; 21 Kenwood Drive, Beckenham, Kent BR3 2QX (☎ 081 650 2972)

FERRANTI; *see*: de Ferranti

FERRARS, Elizabeth (Mrs Morna Brown); da of Peter Clouston MacTaggart (d 1922), of Bexley, Kent, and Marie, *née* Ferrars (d 1964); *b* 6 Sept 1907; *Educ* Bedales Sch, Univ of London (Dip Journalism); *m* 1940, Robert Brown, s of Thomas William Brown; *Career* author of 63 detective novels 1940- incl: Give a Corpse a Bad Name, I Said The Fly, Murder Among Friends, A Legal Fiction, Murders Anonymous, Frog In The Throat, Sleep of the Unjust, Smoke Without Fire, Last Will and Testament; awarded Silver Dagger by CWA; memb: CWA, Detection Club; *Recreations* cooking; *Style*— Ms Elizabeth Ferars; 5 Treble House Terrace, London Rd, Blewbury, Didcot, Oxfordshire OX11 9NZ (☎ 0235 850 415); David Higham Associates Ltd, 5-8 Lower John St, Golden Square, London W1R 4HA

FERRERS, 13 Earl (GB 1711); Sir Robert Washington Shirley; 19 Bt (E 1611), PC (1982), DL (Norfolk 1983); also Viscount Tamworth (GB 1711); s of 12 Earl Ferrers (d 1954, 17 in descent from Sir Hugh Shirley, Grand Falconer to Henry IV and victim of mistaken identity at the Battle of Shrewsbury through being accoutred as the King; 16 in descent from Sir Ralph Shirley, one of the principal commanders at Agincourt; 9 in descent from Dorothy, da of Elizabeth I's, favourite Essex, through whom Lord Ferrers descends from Edward III, hence the quartering of the arms of Fr and Eng on the Shirley escutcheon; 5 in descent from Hon Walter Shirley, yr bro of 4 Earl, the last Lord to be tried for homicide by his Peers; *b* 8 June 1929; *Educ* Winchester, Magdalene Coll Cambridge (MA); *m* 21 July 1951, Annabel Mary, da of Brig William Greenwood Carr, CVO, DSO, JP, DL (d 1982), of Ditchingham Hall, Norfolk; 2 s (Viscount Tamworth b 1952, Hon Andrew b 1965), 3 da (Lady Angela Ellis b 1954, Lady Sallyanne b 1957, Lady Selina Chenevière b 1958); *Heir* s, Viscount Tamworth; *Career* sits as (C) Peer in the House of Lords; served Coldstream Gds, Lt, Malaya; chm S Norfolk Cons Assoc 1953-65 (pres 1971-); lord-in-waiting and govt whip Lords 1962-64 and 1971-74, oppn whip Lords 1964-67, jt-dep ldr oppn Lords 1976-79, parly sec Agric Fish and Food 1974, min state Agric Fish and Food 1979-83, dep ldr Lords 1979-83 and 1988-, min state Home Office 1988-; memb: Cncl Food from Britain 1985-88, Armitage Ctee on Political Activities of Civil Servants 1976, Central Bd TSB 1977-79; tstee: E Anglian TSB 1957-75 (vice-chm 1971-75), TSB of E England 1975-79 (chm 1977-79), Central TSB Ltd 1978-79, TSB Trustcard 1978-79; dir: Economic Forestry Gp plc 1985-88, Norwich Union Insurance Gp 1975-79 and 1983-88, Chatham Historic Dockyard Tst 1984-88, Governing Body of Rothamstead Agric Station 1984-88; pres (Eastern Counties Region) MENCAP 1979-88; chm British Agric Export Cncl 1984-88; High Steward Norwich Cathedral 1979-; chm Royal Cmmn on Historical Monuments (England) 1984-88; fell Winchester Coll 1988; *Recreations* shooting, music, travel; *Clubs* Beefsteak; *Style*— The Rt Hon the Earl Ferrers, PC, DL; Ditchingham Hall, Bungay, Suffolk (☎ 050 844 250)

FERRERS-WALKER, Thomas Weaving; s of Thomas Ferrers (d 1970), and Undine Ferrers, *née* Weaving (d 1962); *b* 24 Sept 1925; *Educ* Bradfield; *m* 1, 1948, late Pamela Mary Beer; 2 s (Richard b 1949, John b 1952); m 2, 1956, Shirley, wid of Edward Kenneth Dunlop, and da of Herbert Cordingley (d 1950); 1 s (Edward b 1961), 1 da (Undine b 1965); *Career* WWII served RNVR combined ops Europe and Pacific 1942-46; RNVSR 1947-65, Lieut RNR 1965-71; chm and chief exec Thomas Walker plc 1971-; tstee: Shakespeare Birthplace Tst 1985- (Exec Ctee 1986-), RN Museum 1987-; pres Stratford-on-Avon Nat Tst Assoc 1985-, vice pres Solihull Nat Tst Centre 1980-, patron of the living of Baddesley Clinton, achieved transfer at Baddesley Clinton to Nat Tst 1980, memb Regnl Ctee Historic Houses Assoc Heart of England Region 1975-88; memb Cncl Order of St John for the County of W Midlands 1974- (OStJ 1985); *Recreations* gardening, photography for recording purposes, historical and naval research and preservation, conservation of historic and natural landscape and buildings; *Style*— T W Ferrers-Walker, Esq; Westfield, 30 Fiery Hill Rd, Barnt Green, Worcestershire B45 8LG (☎ 021 445 1785); 39 St Paul's Square, Birmingham B3 1QY (☎ 021 236 5565, telex 338836, fax 021 236 6275)

FERRIER, Maj Alan Gray; TD (1974, Bar 1980), DL (Caithness 1984); s of Robert Millar Ferrier (d 1958) of Glasgow, and Constance Mary, *née* Shand (d 1976); *b* 23 May 1939; *Educ* Hillhead High Sch Glasgow, Univ of Strathclyde; *m* 19 June 1965, Jean da of late Fred Bramhill; 1 s (Alastair), 1 da (Diane); *Career* Univ of Glasgow OTC 1959, 71(S) Engr Regt 1968, 251 HLD Vols 1973 (Co Cdr 1976), 236 Field Sqdn ADR (V) 1985-90 (Sqdn Cdr 1986); Unilever Sales 1961-62, Norwich Union Insur Gp 1962; chm: Royal Br Legion Scot Wick Branch, Earl Haig Wick Branch; vice chm Northern Ctee Highland TAVRA; memb Insur Inst 1962; *Recreations* fishing; *Clubs* The Caithness; *Style*— Maj Alan Ferrier, TD, DL; Fitchins, 81 Willow Bank, Wick, Caithness KW1 4PE (☎ 0955 3178); Norwich Union Insurance Group, 11 Back Bridle St, Wick, Caithness KW1 4AH (☎ 0955 2985)

FERRIER, Maj (Richard) Anthony Plowden Gournay; s of Capt Richard Gournay Ferrier (d 1984), of Hemsby Hall, Hemsby, Norfolk, and Doris Esperanza Rosemary Chichele, *née* Plowden (d 1966); *b* 13 Jan 1920; *Educ* Old Buckenham Hall, Radley, RMC Sandhurst, Staff Coll Camberley; *m* 1, 15 Oct 1946 (m dis 1975), Eelin Ailsa, da of William Archibald Campbell (d 1944), of Boroughbridge, Yorks; 2 s (Richard b 1948, Michael b 1949); m 2, 8 July 1977, Peta Ann, da of Gp Capt David Christie, CBE, AFC, of Sheringham, Norfolk; *Career* cmmnd Royal Norfolk Regt 1939, served India and Far East 1939-45, POW 1942-45, Adj Royal Norfolk Regt 1946-47, General Staff HQ 7 Armd Div 1947-49, Chief Instr Rhine Army Trg Centre 1949-50, Parachute Regt ME 1952-53, DAAG HQ 16 Airborne Div 1953-55, Royal Norfolk Regt Cyprus 1955-57, GHQ UK Land Forces GSO 11 (Plans) 1957-59, ret 1960; regnl sec and chief exec Country Landowners Assoc E Anglia 1964-85; area pres and memb Cncl St John Ambulance Bde Norfolk 1960-70, Cdr Bn Norfolk Army Cadet Force 1963-66, Co Trg Offr Norfolk Army Cadet Force, 1966-69, pres Central Norfolk Far East POW Assoc 1967-; CStJ 1970; *Recreations* shooting, golf, sailing, ornithology; *Clubs* Naval and Military, Norfolk Co; *Style*— Maj Anthony Ferrier; Meadow House, Stow Bedon, Attleborough, Norfolk NR17 1BZ (☎ 095 383 498)

FERRIER, Prof Robert Patton; s of William McFarlane Ferrier (d 1963), and Gwendoline Melita, *née* Edward (d 1976); *b* 4 Jan 1934; *Educ* Glebelands Sch, Morgan Acad, Univ of St Andrews (BSc, PhD) Univ of Cambridge (MA); *m* 2 Sept 1961, Valerie Jane, da of Samuel George Duncan (d 1986); 2 s (Hamish b 1965, Alan b 1969), 1 da (Elizabeth b 1967); *Career* sci offr UKAERE Harwell 1959-61, res assoc Mass Inst of Technol USA 1961-62, asst dir of res Cavendish Lab Univ of Camb 1966-73 (sr asst 1962-66), guest scientist IBM Res Div San Jose Calif USA 1972-73, prof of nat philosophy Univ of Glasgow 1973-; memb: of local Episcopal Church, Various Ctees of Sci and Engrg Res Cncl 1970-85 (former chm); FInstP 1964, FRSE 1977; *Recreations* tennis, gardening, reading crime novels; *Style*— Prof Robert Ferrier; Glencoe, 31 Thorn Road, Bearsden, Glasgow G61 4BS (☎ 041 942 3592); Department of Physics and Astronomy, The University, Glasgow G12 8QQ (☎ 041 330 5388, 041 339 8855, fax 041 334 9029, telex 777070 UNIGLA)

FERRIER, Baron (Life Peer UK 1958), of Culter, Co Lanark; Victor Ferrier Noel-Paton; ED (1945), DL (Lanarks 1960); s of Frederick Waller Ferrier Noel-Paton (d 1914), of Edinburgh, dir-gen Commercial Intelligence to Govt of India, and Ethel Margaret, *née* Alt (d 1963); *b* 29 Jan 1900; *Educ* Edinburgh Acad; *m* 9 March 1932, Joane Mary (d 1984), er da of Sir Gilbert Wiles, KCIE, CSI (d 1961); 1 s (Hon Ranald b 1938), 3 da (Hon Lady Fergusson, Hon Mrs Laird, Hon Mrs Hacking); *Career* Maj (ret) Bombay Light Horse Aux Force India and IA Reserve of Offrs 19 KGVO Lancers, Hon ADC to Govr of Bombay; East India merchant and industrialist; formerly MLC Bombay, former dir Imperial Bank of India (among other directorships), pres Bombay Chamber of Commerce; past chm: Fedn of Electricity Undertakings of India, Indian Road and Tport Devpt Assoc Bombay, Edinburgh Pharmaceutical Industries; memb Queen's Body Gd for Scotland (Royal Co of Archers); dep speaker & chm of Ctees House of Lords 1970-73; *Recreations* field sports; *Clubs* New (Edinburgh), Cavalry and Guards', Beefsteak; *Style*— The Rt Hon the Lord Ferrier, ED, DL; Kilkerran, Maybole, Ayrshire KA19 7SJ (☎ 065 54 515)

FERRIS, Neil Jeremy; s of Oscar Ferris, and Benita, *née* Lewis; *b* 5 April 1955; *Educ* Brighton Hove and Sussex GS; *m* 25 Jan 1980, Jill Denise, da of William Charles Anderson , of London; 1 s (Daniel Mark); *Career* jr PR Dept EMI Records 1974; PR Dept: NEMS Records 1976, CBS Records 1977; formed The Ferret Plugging Co 1980 representing: UB40, Erasure, Depeche Mode, Spandau Ballet, XTC, Bros, S-Express, Howard Jones among others; produced tv special about Erasure for BBC 2 1988, and a documentary on Depeche Mode for BBC TV 1989; speaker on various subjects relating to the music indust and the media; *Recreations* photography, power-boats, antiques (early oak furniture); *Style*— Neil Ferris, Esq; Ferret and Spanner PR, 76 Stanley Gardens, London W3 7BL (☎ 081 746 1818, fax 081 746 1011, car 0836 211045)

FERRIS, Paul Fredrick; s of Frederick Morgan Ferris (d 1965), and Olga, *née* Boulton; *b* 15 Feb 1929; *Educ* Swansea GS; *m* 1953, Gloria; 1 s (Jonathan b 1955), 1 da (Virginia Ann b 1960); *Career* journalist and author; S Wales Evening Post 1949-52, Woman's Own 1953, Observer foreign news serv 1953-54; *Books* incl: The City (1960), The House of Northcliffe (1971), The Detective (1976), Dylan Thomas (1977), Talk to Me About England (1979), Children of Dust (1988), Sir Huge. The Life of Huw Wheldon (1990); *Style*— Paul Ferris, Esq; c/o Curtis Brown Ltd, 162-168 Regent St, London W1 5TB

FERRO, Gabriele; s of Pietro Ferro (composer); *Career* conductor; concert debut Italy 1971, has conducted leading Italian orchestras incl La Scala Milan; opera debut conducting Mercandante's il Bravo Rome Opera 1977; other opera engagements incl: Tancredi, Seniramide, La Bottaglia di Legnano, La Cenerentola (all with Rome Opera), La Fenice, Parsifal, Die Ferna Klang (world premiere), Faustsezen, La Cenarentola (Stuttgart Opera), Judas Maccabaeus' (Bavarian State Opera, Munich), La Cenerentola and L'Italiana in Algeri (Chicago Lyric Opera), il Barbiere di Siviglia (debut with Royal Opera 1985), L'Elisir d'Amore (Royal Opera), Ermione, Armide, Iphigénie en Aulide; has worked with many leading orchestras incl the Cleveland Orchestra, the BBC Symphony Orchestra (Br debut Zemlinsky's Lyrische Sinfonie 1979); festival appearances incl: Athens, Baalbeck, Munich, Venice and Maggio Musicale Florence; repertoire incl: Britten, Boulez, Nono, Stockhausen and Benio; *Style*— Gabriele Ferro, Esq; c/o The Royal Opera House, Covent Garden, London WC2E 9DD (☎ 071 240 1200, telex 27988)

FERRY, Alexander; MBE (1978); s of Alexander Ferry (d 1932), and Susan Cavan Ferry (d 1987); *b* 14 Feb 1931; *Educ* St Patrick's Sr Secdy Sch Dunbartonshire Scot; *m* 15 Feb 1958, Mary, da of late Patrick M'Alaney; 2 s (Alexander b 1958 d 1977, Andrew b 1966), 2 da (Carlann b 1960, Mary b 1962); *Career* Nat Serv RAF 1952-54; engr 1951-64; trade union offr AEU 1964-78, gen sec Confedn of Shipbldg and Engrg Unions 1978-; active in Br Lab Pty, bd memb Harland Wolff Belfast 1984-, memb MMC 1986-; *Recreations* golf, reading, crosswords; *Style*— Alexander Ferry, Esq, MBE; 190 Brampton Rd, Bexley Heath, Kent DA7 4YS (☎ 081 303 5338); 140/142 Walworth Rd, London SE17 (☎ 071 703 2215, fax 071 252 7397)

FERRY, Bryan; s of Frederick Charles Ferry (d 1984), and Mary Ann, *née* Armstrong (d 1991); *b* 26 Sept 1945; *Educ* Washington GS, Univ of Newcastle; *m* 26 June 1982, Lucy Margaret Mary, da of Patrick Helmore; 4 s (Charles b 1 Nov 1982, Isaac b 16 May 1985, Tara b 6 Jan 1990, Merlin b 5 Dec 1990); *Career* Vocalist and fndr memb Roxy Music 1971-, solo recording artist; recordings with Roxy Music: Roxy Music (1972), For Your Pleasure (1973), Stranded (1973), Country Life (1974), Siren (1975), Viva (1976), Manifesto (1979), Flesh & Blood (1980), Avalon (1982), The High Road (1983), Streetlife (1986); solo recordings: These Foolish Things (1983), Another Time Another Place (1974), Let's Stick Together (1976), In Your Mind (1977), The Bride Stripped Bare (1978), Boys and Girls (1985), Bête Noir (1987); *Style*— Bryan Ferry, Esq; c/o Virgin Records, Kensal House, Harrow Road, London W10

FERSHT, Prof Alan Roy; s of Philip Joseph Fersht (d 1970), and Betty, *née* Mattleson; *b* 21 April 1943; *Educ* Sir George Monoux GS, Gonville & Caius Coll Cambridge (MA, PhD); *m* 14 Oct 1966, Marilyn, da of Montague Persell (d 1975); 1 s (Philip b 1972), 1 da (Naomi b 1970); *Career* memb scientific staff MRC Laboratory of Molecular Biology Cambridge 1969-77, Wolfson res prof Royal Soc and prof of chemistry Imperial Coll 1978-, Herchel Smith prof of organic chemistry Univ of Cambridge 1988-, dir Cambridge Interdisciplinary Res Centre for Protein Engrg 1989; memb: EMBO 1980, Academia Europaea 1989; FRS 1983, FRSC 1986, hon foreign memb American Acad of Arts and Sciences 1988; *Books* Enzyme Structure and Mechanism (1978, 1985); *Recreations* chess, horology; *Style*— Prof Alan Fersht; 2 Barrow Close, Cambridge CB2 2AT (☎ 0223 352 963); University Chemical Laboratory, Lensfield Rd, Cambridge CB2 1EW (☎ 0223 336 341, fax 0223 336 445)

FETHERSTON-DILKE, Capt Charles Beaumont; JP (Warwicks 1969-); s of Dr Beaumont (Albany) Fetherston-Dilke, MBE (d 1968), of Maxstoke Castle, Warwickshire, and (Phoebe) Stella, *née* Bedford (d 1968); *b* 4 April 1921; *Educ* RN Coll Dartmouth; *m* 12 May 1943, Pauline, da of Maj Horatio Stanley-Williams, DSO (d 1936), of Ebbw Lodge, Irthlingborough; 1 s (Michael b 1948), 1 da (Anne b 1945); *Career* RN 1935-68; WWII served: Home Fleet, Med, Battle of the Atlantic; torpedo and anti submarine specialist, served Korean War 1952-54, Cdr 1955, Danish Naval Staff 1955-57, ops offr S Atlantic and S America Station 1960-61, Capt 1961, naval dep to UK Nat Mil Rep SHAPE 1962-64; cmd: HMS Maidstone, HMS Adamant, HMS Forth; cmd HMS St Vincent 1964-66, def policy staff MOD 1966-68, ret 1968; pres Cncl Kingsley Sch Leamington Spa, govr Lady Katherine Leveson Hosp, govr (chm) Coleshill GS Endowment Fndn, pres T S Stirling Sea Cadet Unit Birmingham, chm Warwicks CLA 1984-87, chm Warwick CC 1978-80 (memb 1970-81); High Sheriff Warwicks 1974, Vice-Lord Lt Warwicks 1990 (DL 1974); SBStJ; *Recreations* country pursuits; *Clubs* Army and Navy; *Style*— Capt Charles Fetherston-Dilke, RN, JP; Keeper's Cottage, Maxstoke, Coleshill, Birmingham B46 2QA (☎ 0675 465100)

FETHERSTON-DILKE, Michael Charles; s of Capt Charles Beaumont Fetherston-Dilke, JP, DL, *qv*, and Pauline *née* Stanley-Williams; *b* 30 Dec 1948; *Educ* Rugby, Univ of Bristol (BSc); *m* 25 June 1983, Rosemary Ann, da of Michael Telfair Keith (d 1966), of Hoe Hall, Dereham, Norfolk; 2 s (George b 1985, Edward b 1986), 1 da (Sarah b 1989); *Career* Peat Marwick Mitchell London, Nat Enterprise Bd 1978-79, BET plc Industrial Holding Co 1980-, various subsidiary co directorships, exec dir United Transport International plc; FCA; *Recreations* archery, photography, country pursuits; *Clubs* Boodle's, MCC; *Style*— Michael Fetherston-Dilke, Esq; Maxstoke Castle, Coleshill, Warks B46 2RD (☎ 0675 467676); United Transport International plc, Stratton House, Piccadilly, London W1X 6DD (☎ 071 491 2633)

FETHERSTON-DILKE, Lt Cdr (John) Timothy; CBE (1986); y s of Dr Beaumont Albany Fetherston-Dilke, MBE (d 1968), of Warks, and Phoebe Stella, *née* Bedford (d 1968); family resident at Maxstoke Castle since 1598; *b* 4 Feb 1926; *Educ* RNC Dartmouth; *m* 1, 1956 (m dis), Idonea, da of Sir Hugh Chance, CBE, DL (d 1981), of Worcs; 1 s (Timothy b 1958), 1 da (Miranda b 1956); m 2, 1966, Olivia, da of Dr E C Turton (d 1983), of Hants; 1 s (Edmund b 1969), 1 da (Natalia b 1967); *Career* RN 1939-59: sea serv during WWII and Korean War; ret 1959 Lt Cdr; patent agency 1959-65, HM Coastguard Serv 1966-86 (HM Chief Coastguard 1978-86), int marine conslt 1986-; *Recreations* gardening, carpentry, archery, music; *Style*— Lt Cdr Timothy Fetherston-Dilke, CBE; 85 Christchurch Rd, Winchester, Hants SO23 9QY (☎ 0962 868661)

FEUCHTWANGER, Antonia Mary (Mrs Simon Cox); da of Dr Edgar Joseph Feuchtwanger, of Highfield House, Dean, Sparsholt, nr Winchester, Hampshire, and Primrose Mary, *née* Essame; *b* 12 Nov 1963; *Educ* St Swithun's Sch Winchester, Jesus Coll Cambridge (exhibitioner, MA, Gray prize for Latin Reading, Fencing half blue); *m* 24 June 1989, Simon Cox, s of Prof Antony Dawson Cox; *Career* graduate trainee Morgan Grenfell 1985-87, corporate fin analyst C J Lawrence Morgan Grenfell

Inc (New York) 1987-89, banking corr Daily Telegraph 1989- (city reporter 1989); *Style—* Ms Antonia Feuchtwanger; The Daily Telegraph City Office, Salters' Hall, 4 Fore St, London EC2Y 5DT (☎ 071 538 6909, fax 071 628 0343)

FEVERSHAM, Countess of; Lady Anne Dorothy; *née* Wood; OBE (1979, MBE 1950); da of 1 Earl of Halifax ; *b* 31 July 1910; *m* 9 May 1936, 3 and last Earl of Feversham (d 1963) the Barony devolving to his kinsman *qv*; 1 da (Lady Clarissa Collin); *Career* MFH Sinnington; co organiser WRVS N Yorks; JP Ryedale N Yorks; *Books* Strange Stories of the Chase; *Style—* The Rt Hon the Countess of Feversham, OBE; Bransdale Lodge, Fadmoor, Kirbymoorside, N Yorks (☎ 0751 31500)

FEVERSHAM, 6 Baron (UK 1826; the full designation is 'Feversham of Duncombe Park'); Charles Antony Peter Duncombe; s of Col Antony John Duncombe-Anderson, TD (d 1949; gggs of 1 Baron Feversham), and Gloranna Georgina Valerie, *née* McNalty (d 1989); suc to Barony of kinsman, 3 Earl of Feversham and Viscount Helmsley (which titles became extinct 1963); *b* 3 Jan 1945; *Educ* Eton; *m* 1, 12 Sept 1966, Shannon (d 1976), da of late Sir Thomas Foy, CSI, CIE; 2 s (Hon Jasper b 1968, Hon Jake b 1972), 1 da (Hon Melissa b 1973); m 2, 6 Oct 1979, Pauline, da of John Aldridge, of Newark, Notts; 1 s (Hon Patrick b 1981); *Heir* s; *Career* journalist and author; chm: Yorks Arts Assoc 1969-80, Standing Ctee of Regional Arts Assocs 1969-76, Tstees Yorks Sculpture Park 1982-; co pres Arvon Foundation 1976-86; pres: Yorks Parish Cncls Assoc 1977-, Yorks Arts Assoc 1986-, Nat Assoc Local Cncls 1986-; *Books* A Wolf in Tooth (1967), Great Yachts (1970); *Style—* The Rt Hon the Lord Feversham; Duncombe Park, Helmsley, York YO6 5EB (☎ 0439 70217)

FEWTRELL, Nicholas Austin; s of Austin Alexander Fewtrell, of 3 Bryn Clwyd, Abergele, Wales, and Marjorie Edna, *née* Kimberlin; *b* 1 July 1955; *Educ* Bramcote Hills GS, Queen Mary's Coll Univ of London (LLB); *m* 26 Nov 1983, Mahshid, da of Kazem Pouladdej, of 999 Badakhshan Ave, Tehran, Iran; 1 da (Stephanie Roxanne b 6 June 1989); *Career* called to the Bar Inner Temple 1977; memb The Honourable Soc of the Inner Temple 1975; *Recreations* golf, football, squash, travel; *Clubs* The St James's (Manchester); *Style—* Nicholas Fewtrell, Esq; 6 Green Pastures, Heaton Mersey, Stockport, Cheshire (☎ 061 431 9520); 5 John Dalton St, Manchester M2 6ET (☎ 061 834 6875, fax 061 834 8557)

FFOLKES, Sir Robert Francis Alexander; 7 Bt (GB 1774); s of Sir (Edward John) Patrick Boschetti Ffolkes, 6 Bt (d 1960); *b* 2 Dec 1943; *Educ* Stowe, Ch Ch Oxford; *Career* involved with Save The Children Fund 1974-; *Clubs* Turf; *Style—* Sir Robert Ffolkes, Bt; Coastguard House, Morston, Holt, Norfolk

FFOOKS, Roger Cambridge; s of Edward Cambridge Ffooks (d 1965), and Eileen Catharine, *née* Gordon (d 1988); *b* 3 Oct 1924; *Educ* Edinburgh Acad, Univ of Durham (BSc); *m* 1, 28 July 1951 (m dis 1988), Gillian Melville, da of Lt-Col B R Turner, DSO, of Tittlesfold Farm Cottage, Billingshurst, Sussex; 2 s (Anthony b 11 Dec 1952, Adrian b 27 May 1955), 1 da (Stephanie (Mrs Trafford) b 24 Dec 1963); m 2, 9 Sept 1988, Barbara Joyce; *Career* tech dir conch methane servs Shell Int Marine 1973-76 (joined 1946), ind consit naval architect 1976-; memb: Br Tech Ctee, American Bureau of Shipping 1970-89; rep Br Maritime League (W Dorset), chm Local Resident's Assoc; FRINA; *Books* Natural Gas by Sea: The Development of a New Technology (1979), Gas Carriers (ed, 1984); *Recreations* books, boating, music; *Style—* Roger Ffooks, Esq; Priors Dean, Long Lane, Bothenhampton, Bridport, Dorset DT6 4BX (☎ 0308 23122)

FFORDE, Lady Jean Sybil Violet; *née* Graham; DL (Ayr and Arran); yr da of 6 Duke of Montrose, KT, CB, CVO, VD, LLD (d 1954); *b* 7 Nov 1920; *m* 8 Oct 1947 (m dis 1957), Col John Patrick Ilbert Fforde, yr s of Maj Charles Annesley Lilbraham Ford; 1 s (Charles b 1948); *Style—* The Lady Jean Fforde, DL; Strabane, Brodick, Isle of Arran KA27 8DD (☎ 0770 2276)

FFOWCS WILLIAMS, Prof John Eirwyn; s of Rev Abel Ffowcs Williams (d 1989), and Elizabeth, *née* Davies; *b* 25 May 1935; *Educ* Friends' Sch Gt Ayton, Derby Tech Coll, Univ of Southampton (BSc, PhD), Univ of Cambridge (MA, ScD); *m* 10 Oct 1959, Anne Beatrice, da of Percy Cecil Mason (d 1984); 2 s (Aled Ceiriog b 1969, Gareth Idris b 1980), 1 da (Awena Lynn b 1966); *Career* Rolls Royce prof of applied mathematics Imperial Coll London 1969-72 Rank prof of engrg Univ of Cambridge 1972-, dir Vickers Ship and Engineering plc 1988-; FEng; *Recreations* friends and cigars; *Clubs* Athenaeum, Danish; *Style—* Prof John Ffowcs Williams; Emmanuel College, Cambridge (☎ 0223 332629)

FFRENCH, 8 Baron (I 1758); Sir Robuck John Peter Charles Mario; also Bt (I 1779); s of 7 Baron ffrench (d 1986), and Katherine Sonia, da of late Maj Digby Coddington Cayley; *b* 14 March 1956; *m* 20 June 1987, Dörthe Marie-Louise Schauer-Lixfeld, da of Capt Wilhelm Schauer, of Zürich, Switzerland, and Mrs Marie-Louise Schauer-Lixfeld, of Attymon House, Co Galway; *Style—* The Rt Hon Lord ffrench; Castle ffrench, Ballinasloe, Co Galway, Ireland

FFRENCH BLAKE, Lady Caroline Anne de Vere; *née* Beauclerk; da (by 2 m) of 13 Duke of St Albans, OBE (d 1988); *b* 19 July 1951; *Educ* Fritham House, Queen's Gate Sch, Open Univ (BA); *m* 1970 (m dis 1986), Neil St John ffrench Blake, *qv*; 2 da (Clare Eleanor de Vere b 1972, Kate Juliana de Vere b 1977); *Style—* The Lady Caroline ffrench Blake; Barn House, Midgham, Reading, Berks RG7 5UG

FFRENCH BLAKE, Neil St John; s of Lt-Col Robert Lifford Valentine ffrench Blake, DSO, of Lodden Lower Farm, Spencer's Wood, Reading, Berks, and Grania Bryde, *née* Curran; *b* 4 Nov 1940; *Educ* Eton; *m* 1970 (m dis 1986), Lady Caroline de Vere Beauclerk, *qv*, da of 13 Duke of St Albans by his 2 w; 2 da; *Career* BBC producer 1963-69, md Network Broadcasting Ltd 1969-73, programme controller Thames Valley Bdcasting Ltd 1975-80; advsr: MOD (London) 1982, SID Mindef (Singapore) 1983-86, US Govt (Bangkok) 1987-91; communications conslt and author, ret 1991; *Recreations* skiing, golf; *Clubs* Brooks's; *Style—* Neil Ffrench Blake, Esq; 560/286 Dindaeng Rd, Samsannai Payatai, Bangkok 10400, Thailand (☎ 01066 2455815); 504 Arc en Ciel, Vallandry, Bourg St Maurice, 73700 France

FFRENCH BLAKE, Col Robert John William; s of Lt-Col Desmond O'Brien Evelyn Ffrench Blake (d 1943), of Hants, and Elizabeth Iris Hogg, *née* Cardale; *b* 21 June 1940; *Educ* Eton, RMA Sandhurst; *m* 21 Sept 1976, Ilynne Sabina Mary, da of Michael Charles Eyston, of Oxon; 3 da (Nicola b 1977, Alice b 1980, Emily b 1983); *Career* 13/18 Royal Hussars (QMO): cmmnd 1960, CO 1981-83, Col 1990-; asst mil attaché Washington DC 1985-88, ret 1989; chief exec Guards Polo Club 1989-, memb HM Body Guard of The Hon Corps of Gentlemen at Arms 1990-; *Recreations* farming, shooting, riding, travel; *Clubs* Cavalry and Gds; *Style—* Col Robert J W ffrench Blake; c/o Hoares Bank, 37 Fleet Street, London EC4P 4DQ; c/o Guards Polo Club, Smith's Lawn, Windsor Great Park, Englefield Green, Egham, Surrey TW20 0HP (☎ 0784 434212/3)

FFRENCH-FUCHS, Hon (Rose Sofia Iris Mary); er da of 7 Baron ffrench (d 1986); *b* 27 Jan 1957; *m* April 1989, Albert Fuchs, o s of late Albert Alois Fuchs, of Pöcking, Bavaria; *Style—* The Hon Mrs ffrench-Fuchs; 1 Küffner Strasse, Regensburg 8400, Germany

FFYTCHE, Timothy John; s of Louis E S ffytche (d 1987), of Wilbraham Place, London, and Margaret Law; *b* 11 Sept 1936; *Educ* Lancing, King's Coll London, St Georges Hosp (MB BS, DO); *m* 13 May 1961, Bärbl, da of Günther Fischer, of W Germany; 2 s (Dominic b 1962, Mattias b 1965); *Career* conslt ophthalmic surgeon: St Thomas's Hosp London, Moorfields Hosp, King Edward VII Hosp London, Hosp for Tropical Diseases; surgeon oculist to Royal Household; author of articles and papers on retinal disease and ocular leprosy; FRCS; *Recreations* fishing, occasional cricket; *Style—* Timothy ffytche, Esq; 1 Wellington Square, London SW3 4NJ; 149 Harley Street, London W1N 2DE

FICKLING, Benjamin William; CBE (1973); s of late Robert Marshall Fickling, and Florence, *née* Newson; *b* 14 July 1909; *Educ* Framlingham Coll, St George's Hosp, Royal Dental Hosp; *m* 1942, Shirley Dona, er da of late Albert Latimer Walker; 2 s, 1 da; *Career* dental surgn: Royal Dental Hosp of London 1935-74, St George's Hosp 1936-74; oral surgn to Dept of Dental and Oral Surgery Mount Vernon Hosp (formerly Hill End Hosp) 1941-74, dean Faculty of Dental Surgery RCS 1968-71; dir: Medical Sickness Annuity & Life Assur Soc 1967-86, Perm Insur Soc and Medical Sickness Fin Corp; MGDS, MRCS, FRCS, FDS; *Books* Injuries of the Jaws and Face (jtly, 1940); *Recreations* travel, gardening; *Clubs* Ski Club of GB; *Style—* Benjamin Fickling, Esq, CBE; 29 Maxwell Road, Northwood, Middx (☎ 092 74 22035)

FIDGEN, Roger Stewart; s of Eric Frank Fidgen, and Vera, *née* Clark; *b* 14 May 1946; *Educ* Sherborne; *m* 1, 10 Nov 1971 (m dis 1988), Sarah Dorothy, da of William Nevill Dashwood Lang (d 1988); 2 s (Patrick b 1973, Robert b 1976), 1 da (Joanna b 1979); m 2, 20 May 1988, Jennifer Godesen, da of Stanley Angold; *Career* Sub Lt RNR 1969-72; chartered quantity surveyor; ptnr Gardiner and Theobald 1975-, non exec dir Winglaw Gp 1988-; Liveryman: Worshipful Co of Barbers 1973, Worshipful Co of Chartered Surveyors 1980; FRICS; *Recreations* fishing, shooting, sailing, skiing; *Clubs* Royal Thames Yacht, Flyfishers; *Style—* Roger Fidgen, Esq; Wield House Farm, Wield, Alresford, Hants (☎ 0420 64292); 49 Bedford Sq, London WC1B 3EB (☎ 071 637 2468)

FIDLER, Brian Harvey; s of Philip Fidler, of Manchester, and Esther, *née* Levy; *b* 19 Oct 1938; *Educ* Manchester GS, Manchester Univ (LLB); *m* 12 Aug 1962, Wendy, da of Abraham Gouldman; 1 s (Benjamin Philip b 1970), 2 da (Sarah Jane b 1964, Ruth Yvette b 1966); *Career* chief accountant Pressed Steel Fisher Coventry 1967-70 (fin accountant Cowley 1962-67), gp mgmnt accountant Amey Roadstone plc 1970-73, chief fin exec Northern Foods plc 1974-85, gp fin dir Christian Salvesen plc 1985-; *Style—* Brian Fidler, Esq; Broompark, Liberton Dr, Edinburgh EH16 6TH (☎ 031 666 1346); 24 Langford Green, Camberwell, London SE5; Christian Salvesen plc, 50 East Fettes Ave, Edinburgh EH4 1EQ (☎ 031 552 7101, fax 031 552 5809, telex 72222)

FIDLER, Ian Douglas Field; s of Reginald Douglas Field Fidler (d 1944), and Lillian Dorothy, *née* Gregor-Pearse (d 1988); *b* 17 April 1927; *Educ* St Georges Putney Hill, Surbiton GS; *m* 25 Oct 1958, Elizabeth Jean, da of Maj James Morton, RA (d 1977); 4 da (Caroline Elizabeth b 8 May 1962, Alexandra Louise b 31 Oct 1964, Charlotte Anne b 22 Dec 1965, Henrietta Mary Sirkka b 18 Oct 1973); *Career* RM 1943-47, 42 Commando, 3 Commando Bde, Substantive Lt; trainee Albert E Reed Co Ltd 1947; asst mangr: London Paper Mills Ltd 1947-54, Empire Papers Mills Ltd 1954-56; sales dir Reed Paper and Bd Sales Ltd 1958-68 (formerly tech mangr 1956-58), dep md Lamco Paper Sales 1976-86 (formerly sales dir 1968-75), chm Hunt and Broadhurst Ltd 1983-86, md Lamco Servs Ltd 1987-; memb Stationers Social Soc, past pres Paper Agents Assoc, tstee Lamco Pension Fund Mgmnt; Freeman City of London 1982, Liveryman of Worshipful Co of Stationers and Newspapermakers; Knight First Class of the Order of the Lion of Finland 1986; *Recreations* golf, gardening, walking dogs; *Clubs* Burhill Golf, Norwegian, RAC; *Style—* Ian Fidler, Esq; Brackens, Heathdown Rd, Pyrford, Surrey GU22 (☎ 0932 349603); Norfolk Hse, 31 St James's Sq, London SW1Y 4JJ (☎ 071 895 0077, fax 071 895 0039, car 0836 223 688, telex 8950107)

FIDLER, Peter John Michael; s of Dr Harry Fidler, of Bramhall, nr Stockport, Cheshire, and Lilian, *née* Kahn; *b* 16 March 1942; *Educ* Bradford GS, St John's Coll Oxford (MA); *m* 19 July 1984, Barbara Julia Gottlieb, da of Harold Pinto, of Wembley, Middx; 1 s (David Robert b 1985), 1 step s (Richard Charles b 1979), 2 step da (Clare Rachel b 1973, Katherine Anna b 1977); *Career* admitted slr 1967; articled clerk Peacock Fisher & Finch (now Field Fisher & Waterhouse & Martineau) 1964-67, Coward Chance 1967-72, DJ Freeman & Co 1972-84, Stephenson Harwood 1984-; rep GB at Croquet 1974; memb: City of London Solicitors Co, Law Soc, City of London Law Soc; *Books* Sheldon's Practice and Law of Banking (now Sheldon and Fidler's, asst ed 1972, ed 1982); *Recreations* music, theatre; *Style—* Peter Fidler, Esq; 237 West Heath Rd, London NW3 7UB (☎ 081 455 2247); Stephenson Harwood, One St Paul's Churchyard, London EC4M 8SH (☎ 071 329 4422, fax 071 606 0822, telex 886789)

FIELD, Alan Frank; s of Frank William Field, of Holme Pierrepoint, Notts, and May Field; *b* 26 Sept 1937; *Educ* Trent Bridge; *m* 1970, Olga Ann, da of Charles Keightley (d 1972), of Leics; *Career* creative dir and chm Garratt Baulcombe Ltd 1972-87, dir Foote Cone & Belding Ltd 1984-87; *Recreations* music, fly fishing, illustration, cooking; *Style—* Alan Field, Esq

FIELD, Brig Anne; CB (1980); da of Capt Harold Derwent and Annie Helena, *née* Hodgson; *b* 4 April 1926; *Educ* Keswick Sch, St George's Harpenden, LSE; *Career* joined ATS 1947, cmmnd 1948; WRAC 1949-: Lt-Col 1968, Col 1971, Brig 1977-82, Dep Controller Cmdt 1984-; Hon ADC to HM The Queen 1977-82; regional dir Lloyds Bank plc London Regions 1982-91; Freeman City of London 1981, Liveryman Worshipful Co of Spectacle Makers 1990; *Style—* Brig Anne Field, CB; c/o Lloyds Bank plc, 6 Pall Mall, London SW1Y 5NH

FIELD, Arnold; OBE (1965); s of Wilfred Field (d 1933); *b* 19 May 1917; *Educ* Sutton Coldfield Royal Sch, Erdington C of E Sch, Birmingham Tech Coll; *m* 1943, Kathleen Dulcie, da of Albert Bennett (d 1930); 1 s, 1 da; *Career* served RAF WWII, Sqdn Ldr Coastal Cmd and Air Miny Special Duty List 1940-46; air traffic control offr 1946-61, divnl air traffic control offr 1961-65, supt London Air Traffic Control Centre 1965-71, dir Civil Air Traffic Ops 1971-74, dir gen Nat Air Traffic Serv 1974-77; aviation conslt and technical journalist 1977-; memb aviation/space writers assoc; gp ed: International Defence Newsletter, Law Enforcement Industry Digest; dir ITX (UK) Ltd 1987; *Books* The Control of Air Traffic (1980), International Air Traffic Control Management of the World's Airspace (1985), International Directory of Military Simulation and Training Aids (1988); *Recreations* vintage motor cars, flying; *Clubs* Bentley Drivers'; *Style—* Arnold Field, Esq, OBE; Footprints, Stoke Wood, Stoke Poges, Bucks SL2 4AU (☎ 0753 64 2710)

FIELD, Barry John Anthony; TD (1984); MP (Cons Isle of Wight 1987-); s of Edward Ernest Field, of Crawley, Sussex, and Marguerite Eugenie, *née* Bateman (d 1979); *b* 4 July 1946; *Educ* Collingwood Boys Sch, Mitcham GS, Bembridge Sch, Victoria Street Coll; *m* 11 Oct 1969, Jacqueline Anne, da of Cdr Alfred Edward Joseph Miller, RN, of Emsworth, Hants; 1 s (Jason b 1977), 1 da (Penny b 1978); *Career* dir: Gt Southern Cemetery and Crematoria Co Ltd 1969-86, J D Field and Sons 1981-; cncllr Horsham Dist Cncl 1983-86 (vice chm Housing Ctee 1984-85), memb IOW CC 1986-; *Recreations* sailing, skiing, theatre; *Clubs* Island Sailing; *Style—* Barry Field, Esq, TD, MP; Medina Lodge, 25 Birmingham Rd, Cowes, Isle of Wight PO31 7BH; House of Commons (☎ 071 219 3453, office 0983 522645)

FIELD, Derek Harold; s of Harold Field (d 1945), of Lion House, Chichester, Sussex, and Edith Muriel, *née* Harrison (d 1980); *b* 26 March 1923; *Educ* Marlborough, St John's Coll Cambridge (MA); *m* 3 July 1948, (Catherine) Rosemary, da of Leonard Howson Jones (d 1968), of Beechcliffe, Trentham, Staffs; 4 s (Christopher b 1951, Godfrey b 1953, Stephen b 1956, Mark b 1960); *Career* WWII Capt REME, served Palestine 1943-47; Dorman Long & Co: engr and designer 1947-48, engr i/c Vila Franca Bridge over River Tagus 1949-51; Shelton Iron Steel & Coal Co (subsid of John Summers & Sons Ltd): structural engr 1953-62, works mangr 1963, dir 1964, gen mangr 1968-78; dir: N Staffs C of C & Indust 1980-84, Tableware Distributors Assoc 1984; dep chm W Midlands Regn TSB Eng & Wales 1985-89; High Sheriff of Staffs 1989-90; MICE (1956), CEng; *Recreations* tennis, fell walking, country pursuits, philately, reading; *Clubs* Army & Navy; *Style*— Derek Field, Esq; The Dairy House, Trentham Park, Stoke-on-Trent, Staffs ST4 8AE (☎ 0782 657 908); Commerce House, Festival Park, Stoke-on-Trent, Staffs ST1 5BE (☎ 0782 202 222, fax 0782 202 448, telex 36250 CHAMCOM G)

FIELD, Frank; MP (Lab) Birkenhead 1979-; s of late Walter Field, and Annie Field; *b* 16 July 1942; *Educ* St Clement Danes GS, Univ of Hull; *Career* former lobbyist, memb TGWU, cncllr Hounslow 1964-68, Parly candidate (Lab) S Bucks 1966; dir Child Poverty Action Gp 1969-79, dir and fndr Low Pay Unit 1974-80, Oppn spokesman on educn 1979-81, Parly conslt to Civil and Public Servs Assoc, front bench Oppn spokesman health and social security 1983-, chm Select Ctee on Social Servs 1987-; *Books* Unequal Britain (1974); Inequality In Britain: Freedom, Welfare and The State (1981); Poverty and Politics (1982); The Minimum Wage: Its Potential And Dangers (1984); Freedom And Wealth In A Socialist Future (1987), The Politics of Paradise (1987); Losing Out: The Emergence of Britain's Underclass (1989); co author To Him Who Hath: A Study of Poverty And Taxation (1976); ed: 20th Century State Education (co-ed, 1971), Black Britons (co-ed, 1971), Low Pay (1973), Are Low Wages Inevitable? (1976), Education And The Urban Crisis (1976); The Conscript Army: A Study of Britain's Unemployed (1976); The Wealth Report (1979, 2 edn 1983); Policies Against Low Pay: An International Perspective (1984); *Style*— Frank Field, Esq, MP; House of Commons, London SW1

FIELD, Guy; s of Norman Field (d 1985), and Marie-Therese Leonie Henriette, *née* Bouchet; *b* 28 Dec 1926; *Educ* Lycee Condorcet Paris France, Wallasey GS Wirral Cheshire; *m* 23 May 1953, Dorothy Evelyn, da of John Reginald Blakely (d 1959); 1 s (Alastair b 1961), 1 da (Sonya b 1958); *Career* RM 1945-47; exec dir Samuel Montagu & Co Ltd 1954-77, dir Derby & Co Ltd 1977-82, sr vice pres Morgan Guaranty Trust Co of NY London 1982-88, vice chm London Bullion Market Assoc 1987-88; chm Buckland Branch Cons Assoc, Freeman City of London 1983, Liveryman Worshipful Co of Fan Makers; *Recreations* gardening, walking, music, opera, photography, philately; *Style*— Guy Field, Esq; Little Perrow, Old Rd, Buckland, Betchworth, Surrey RH3 7DY (☎ 073784 3227)

FIELD, Dr Ian Trevor; s of Major George Edward Field, MBE and Bertha Cecilia, *née* Davies; *b* 31 Oct 1933; *Educ* Shri Shivaji Sch Poona, Bournemouth Sch, Royal Sch of Military Engrg, Guy's Hosp Med Sch London (MB BS); *m* 14 May 1960, Christine Mary Field, JP, da of Roland Reginald Osman; 3 s (Hugh Michael b 1962, Giles Edmund b 1964, Clive Robert b 1965), 1 da (Clare b and d 1961); *Career* Nat Serv RE 1952-54; house posts 1960-62, in gen practice 1962-64 (asst then princ), BMA 1964-75 (asst sec then under sec), sr princ med offr/under sec DHSS 1978-85 (sr med offr 1975-78), chief med and health services advsr ODA of FCO 1978-83, sec BMA 1989- (dep sec 1985-89); memb: Cncl Liverpool Sch of Tropical Med 1979-83, Bd of Mgmnt London Sch of Hygiene & Tropical Med 1979-83, Cncl RVC London 1982-88, Upper Norwood Cncl of Churches 1970- (chm 1984-89), Southwark RC Diocesan Ecumenical Cmmn for SE London 1984-, Camberwell Deanery Pastoral Cncl 1986-; Freeman City of London, memb Ct of Assts Worshipful Soc of Apothecaries 1986- (Liveryman 1971); FFPHM 1979 (memb 1975), FFOM 1991; *Recreations* opera, military history, watching rugby & cricket; *Clubs* Athenaeum; *Style*— Dr Ian Field; BMA House, Tavistock Square, London WC1H 9JP (☎ 071 387 4499, fax 071 383 6400)

FIELD, John Arthur; s of Lt-Col Arthur William Henry Field, MBE (d 1980), of Bromley, Kent, and Rebecca Annie Rose, *née* Bolt (d 1986); *b* 28 Feb 1932; *Educ* Bromley GS, Keble Coll Oxford (BA,MA), Univ of London (BSc, PGCE, Ac Dip Ed); *m* 11 May 1955, Heather Mavis, da of Eric Douglas Liddiard (d 1986), of Enfield, Middx; 3 s (Andrew b 1962, Richard b 1963, Martin b 1968), 1 da (Alison b 1965); *Career* asst master: City of Norwich Sch 1956-59, Dauntsey's Sch 1959-64; head of Sci Dept Dover GS 1964-68; headmaster: Springhead Sch Northfleet 1969-81, Wombwell Hall Sch Northfleet 1977-81, Northfleet GS 1981-88; co inspr of secdy educn Kent 1988-; lay reader at Fawkham and Hartley, dir of reader trg Rochester Dio, dep co cmmr Scout Movement Kent, fndr chm Gravesham Town Twinning Assoc 1981-85; memb: SHA, Assoc for Sci Educn, Botanical Soc of Br Isles, Br Biological Soc, Freshwater Biological Assoc; FIBiol 1979; *Recreations* foreign travel, railways, choral music; *Style*— John Field, Esq; Kent County Council, New Rd, Gravesend, Kent DA11 0AT

FIELD, (Edward) John; CMG (1991); s of Lt-Col Arthur Field, OBE, MC, TD, of 4 Fox Hill, Northam, nr Bideford, N Devon, and Dorothy Agnes, *née* Strouts (d 1943); *b* 11 June 1936; *Educ* Highgate, Corpus Christi Coll Oxford (MA), Univ of Virginia (ESU scholar); *m* 16 July 1960, Irene du Pont (Renny), da of Colgate Whitehead Darden Jr (d 1981), former Govr of Virginia; 1 s (Edward du Pont Darden b 12 July 1968), 1 da (Dorothy Agnes Justine b 24 March 1964); *Career* Nat Serv 2 Lt RA then Intelligence Corps 1954-56; Courtaulds Ltd 1960-63; FCO: Br Embassy Tokyo 1963-68, American Dept London 1968-70, 1 sec (cultural) Br Embassy Moscow 1970-72, 1 sec (commercial) Br Embassy Tokyo 1973-76; asst head: South Asian Dept 1976-77, exports to Japan Unit DTI London 1977-79; cnllr Br Embassy Seoul 1980-83; Centre for Int Affrs Harvard Univ 1983-84; cncllr (economic and social) UK Mission to UN New York 1984-87; min Tokyo 1988-; *Recreations* tennis, golf; *Clubs* Tokyo; *Style*— John Field, Esq; British Embassy, Chiyoda-Ku, Tokyo 102, Japan (☎ 03 265 5511, fax 03 265 5580)

FIELD, Malcolm David; s of Maj Stanley Herbert Raynor Field (d 1970), of Link Cottage, Selsey, Sussex, and Constance Frances, *née* Watson; *b* 25 Aug 1937; *Educ* Highgate Sch, London Business Sch; *m* 1, 1963 (m dis 1970), Jane, da of James Barrie, of 11 South Grove House, Highgate Village; m 2, 1974 (m dis 1982), Anne Carolyn, *née* Churchill; 1 da (Joanna Clare b 1974); *Career* 2 Lt WG 1956-58; dir WH Smith & Son Ltd 1970; WH Smith & Son Holdings Ltd: dir 1974, wholesale md 1978, retail md 1978, gp md 1982; chm WH Smith Group (USA) Inc 1988; NAAFI (non-exec): dir 1973, dep chm 1985, chm 1986; non-exec dir MEPC plc 1988; CBIM 1988; *Recreations* tennis, cricket, golf, collecting water colours, civil aviation; *Clubs* Garrick, MCC, Vanderbilt; *Style*— Malcolm Field, Esq; 47 Cadogan Gdns, London SW3 (☎ 071 581 2576); Strand House, 7 Holbein Place, London SW1 (☎ 071 730 1200, fax 730 1200 ext 5563, telex 887777)

FIELD, Marshall Hayward; CBE (1985); s of Maj Harold Hayward Field (d 1973), and Hilda Maud, *née* Siggers (d 1983); *b* 19 April 1930; *Educ* Dulwich; *m* 9 July 1960, Barbara Evelyn, da of Douglas Richard Harris (d 1950); 2 da (Alexandra b 1962, Katherine b 1964); *Career* Nat Serv Intelligence Corps 1955-57, serv Cyprus; Phoenix Assurance: joined 1958, actuary 1964, gen mangr and actuary 1972-85, dir 1980-85; chm Life Offices Assoc 1983-85, memb Fowler Enquiry into Provision for Retirement 1984, conslt Securities and Investments Board 1985-86, conslt ptnr to Bacon Woodrow 1986-; non-exec dir: TSB Trust Co 1985-89, TSB Group plc 1990- (memb TSB Group Insurance and Investment Services Board 1989-); chm Dulwich Estates 1988-90 (memb Bd 1973); govr: Dulwich Coll 1987-, James Allen's Girls Sch 1981-; memb Dulwich Picture Gallery Ctee 1985-; Freeman City of London 1980, Liveryman Worshipful Co of Actuaries 1984 (Court asst 1989); FIA 1957 (memb Cncl 1966, hon sec 1975-77, vice pres 1979-82, pres 1986-88); *Recreations* theatre, art generally; *Style*— Marshall Field, Esq, CBE; 35 Woodhall Drive, London SE21 7HJ (☎ 081 693 1704); Bembridge IOW; Bacon & Woodrow, St Olaf House, London Bridge, London SE1 2PE (☎ 071 357 7171)

FIELD, Philip Sidney; TD; s of Sidney Field (d 1943), of 17 Motspur Park, New Malden, and Edith Mary, *née* Duggin (d 1958); *b* 19 Jan 1917; *Educ* Dulwich, Univ of Oxford (BA); *Career* enlisted TA 1938, Actg Maj TARO, ret 1967; clerk Cargo Superintendents (London) Ltd 1936-39, cost accountant second asst sec Aplin & Barrett Gp 1946-52, in practice as accountant 1952-; managing tstee many local charities 1954-; controller of Civil Def Corps Evesham Dist 1959 (until disbanding), church treas 1960- (warden 1960-71), serv on Mgmnt Ctee Evesham Co of Sea Cadets 1962-66, memb Royal Utd Services Inst 1965-78, area supt St John Ambulance Bde 1958-74; vice pres: Broadway CC, Broadway FC; clerk Broadway Parish Cncl 1989; OStJ 1974; *Recreations* music, carpentry; *Clubs* St John House; *Style*— P S Field, Esq, TD; Little Hill, Evesham Rd, Broadway, Worcs WR12 7DG (☎ 0386 852 405)

FIELD, Richard Alan; QC (1987); s of Robert Henry Field, and Ivy May, *née* Dicketts; *b* 17 April 1947; *Educ* Ottershaw Sch, Univ of Bristol (LLB), LSE (LLM); *m* 31 Aug 1968, Lynne, da of Ismay Hauskind; 2 s (Matthew Ismay b 15 Feb 1978, Thomas Richard b 26 Nov 1988), 2 da (Rachel Eva b 3 June 1974, Beatrice Jasmine b 17 June 1981); *Career* asst prof Faculty of Law Univ BC 1969-71, lectr Hong Kong Univ 1971-73, assoc prof Faculty of Law McGill Univ Montreal Canada 1973-77, called to the Bar Inner Temple 1977; memb Honourable Soc of The Inner Temple; *Recreations* opera, theatre, cricket, rugby football (as a spectator); *Clubs* Reform, Roehampton; *Style*— Richard Field, Esq, QC; 11 King's Bench Walk, Temple, London EC4Y 7EQ (☎ 071 583 0610, telex 884620 BARLEX, fax 071 583 9123/3690)

FIELD, Richard David; OBE (1987); s of Lt-Col G W H Field, of Lancaster, and Pepita Mary; *b* 7 April 1945; *Educ* Malvern; *m* 15 July 1967, Shirley Philippa (Pippa), da of F P Mountford (d 1968), of Sheffield; 2 da (Catherine b 1969, Elizabeth b 1971); *Career* CA 1968; chief accountant Bridon Wire 1973-75 (fin dir 1975-78); Manchester Business Sch 1978; Bamford Business Servs conslt 1978- (dir 1980-); chm: Dyson Refractories Ltd 1980-87, govrs Queen Margarets Sch Escrick York, Young Enterprise Sheffield, Bamford Business Servs Ltd, J & J Dyson plc; memb: Nat Cncl (Sheffield pres) C of C, Cncl (exec memb, fin ctee chm) Industl Soc, Indust Matters (Sheffield ctee chm), RSA Indust Refactories Assoc of GB, Careers Advsy Bd Univ of Sheffield, Cncl St Williams Fndn York; chm Sheffield Trg and Enterprise Cncl (TEC), pres Sheffield Centre for Science & Technol; FCA, CBIM, FITD, FRSA; *Recreations* martial arts (black belt in ju-jitsu 2 Dan), walking, reading, collecting glass; *Style*— Richard D Field, Esq; 134 Townhead Road, Dore, Sheffield S17 3AQ; J & J Dyson plc, 381 Fulwood Rd, Sheffield S10 3GB (☎ 0742 303921, fax 308583)

FIELD, Robin Shaun; s of Harold Ivor Field (d 1988), of Highworth, Wilts, and Margaret Gleaves, *née* Doyle; *b* 10 May 1938; *Educ* Cheltenham, Corpus Christi Coll Cambridge (MA); *m* 23 July 1960, Wendy, da of Joseph Addison Brace (d 1963); 2 s (Mark b 28 Dec 1961, Michael b 9 Dec 1964), 1 da (Alison b 3 Nov 1973); *Career* Shell Int Petroleum Co 1960-66, mgmnt servs mangr John Waddington Ltd 1967-69, commercial dir (later dir and gen mangr) Plastona (John Waddington) 1969-76, ptnr Touche Ross Management Conslts 1980- (joined 1976), fndr Health Group 1983 (health care, defence and defence industs); CEng, MIProdE, FCMA, FSS; *Recreations* squash, sailing, skiing, opera, gardening; *Clubs* Wig and Pen; *Style*— Robin Field, Esq; Touche Ross Management Consultants, Hill House, Little New St, London EC4A 3TR (☎ 071 936 3000)

FIELD, Roy William; s of William Laurie Field, and Cicely May, *née* Holland; *b* 19 Aug 1934; *Educ* Eton Coll Choir Sch, Buckingham Coll Harrow; *m* 13 Sept 1958, Patricia Ann, da of William Muston; 2 s (Timothy William b 1961, Peter Michael b 1962), 1 da (Alison Louise b 1965); *Career* GAOC 1952-54, NCO Austria; Br Film Indust 1952-, Rank Organisation 1956-71; md: Field Films Ltd 1971-, Optical Film Effects Ltd 1981-; Hollywood Oscar for achievement in Visual Effects Superman the Movie, Br Acad award Sir Michael Balcon award for outstanding achievement in Br Cinema Superman, nomination for BAFTA award Visual Effects Dark Crystal, nomination for BAFTA award Visual Effects Labyrinth; Br soc of Cameramen, FRKSTS; memb: Guild of Br Camera Technicians, Br Acad of Film and TV Arts; *Style*— Roy Field, Esq; Redroof Cottage, Templewood Lane, Farnham Common, Bucks S22 3HA (☎ 02814 4156); Optical Film Effects Ltd, Pinewood Studios, Iver Heath Bucks SLO0 ONH (☎ 0753 655486, fax 0753 656844, telex 847505 PINEW G)

FIELD-FISHER, Thomas Gilbert; TD (1949), QC (1969); s of Caryl Hillyard Field-Fisher (d 1953), of Torquay, Devon, and Dora Kate, *née* Purvis (d 1946); *b* 16 May 1915; *Educ* King's Sch Bruton, Peterhouse Cambridge (BA, MA); *m* 8 Sept 1945, Ebba, da of Max Larsen, of Linwood, Utah, USA; *Career* QVR KRRC WWII 1939-47, BEF 1940 (POW, despatches), Maj i/c War Crimes Dept DJAG CMF (Italy) 1945-47; called to the Bar Middle Temple 1942 (bencher 1976); joined Western Circuit 1947, rec of the Crown Ct 1972-86; memb Bar Cncl 1962-66, chm Maria Colwell Inquiry 1973-74; dep chm: SW Agric Claims Tbnl 1962-82, Cornwall QS 1967-72; vice chm London Cncl of Social Serv 1966-79, vice pres London Vol Serv Cncl 1979-, memb Home Office Ctee on Animal Experiments 1980-87 (memb Animal Pro Ctee 1987-89), chm Dogs' Home Battersea 1982-, chm and fndr Assoc of Br Dogs' Homes 1985-, pres Cornwall Magistrates Assoc 1985-; *Books* Animals and the Law (1964), Rent Regulation and Control (1967), contribs to Halsbury's Laws of England (3 and 4 edns) and other lega; *Recreations* dogs, collecting watercolours, gardening, lawn tennis; *Clubs* Hurlingham, Int Lawn Tennis of GB; *Style*— Thomas Field-Fisher Esq, TD, QC; 38 Hurlingham Court, London SW6 3UW (☎ 071 736 4627); 2 Kings Bench Walk, Temple, London EC4Y 7DE (☎ 071 353 1746)

FIELD-JOHNSON, Nicholas Anthony; s of Henry Anthony Field-Johnson (d 1988), and Magdalena, *née* von Everett (d 1971); *b* 28 March 1951; *Educ* Harrow, Univ of Oxford (BA, MA, treas Oxford Union Soc), Harvard Business Sch; *m* Sarah Katherine, *née* Landale; 3 s (Anthony Russell b Oct 1984, Ben Sebastian b May 1986, Oliver Nicholas b Dec 1988); *Career* corporate banker Citibank NA London 1974-78, investmt advsr Atlantic Richfield Co Los Angeles Calif 1979-82, gen mangr World Trade Bank Los Angeles 1983-85, head of MA Dresdner Bank AG London 1986-90, dir NM Rothschild & Sons Ltd 1990-; *Recreations* fishing, sailing, shooting, tennis, food and bridge; *Clubs* Carlton, Annabel's; *Style*— Nicholas Field-Johnson, Esq; 7 Kildare Gardens, London W2 5JS (☎ 071 229 2265); NM Rothschild & Sons, New Court, St Swithin's Lane, London EC4P 4DU (☎ 071 280 5000, fax 071 283 4276, car 0836 229152)

FIELDEN, (John) Anthony Haigh; s of Lt-Col John Haigh Fielden, TD, of 1 Willow Crescent, Broughton Gifford, Melksham, Wilts, and late Jean, *née* Turnbull; *b* 18 March 1937; *Educ* Rossall, Keble Coll Oxford (MA); *m* 29 Sept 1962, Deryl Anne, da of Arthur Leonard Collinson, of 16 Hampton Grove, Bury, Lancs; 1 s (Nicholas b 30 May 1964), 1 da (Tiffany b 23 Nov 1965); *Career* admitted slr 1961; ptnr: Emerson & Fielden 1962-68, Whitworths 1968-70; sr ptnr: Leak Almond & Parkinson 1985-87 (ptnr 1970-85), Cobbett Leak Almond 1987-; clerk to tstees Manchester Guardian Soc Charitable Tst, memb Bd of Mgmnt Wood St Mission; memb Law Soc; *Recreations* cricket, squash, rackets, real tennis; *Clubs* MCC, Manchester Tennis and Racquet; *Style*— Anthony Fielden, Esq; Rosehill, Rostherne, Knutsford, Cheshire WA16 6RT (☎ 0565 830 430); The Old Manor House, Westington, Chipping Campden, Glos; Cobbett Leak Almond, Ship Canal Hse, King St, Manchester M2 4WB (☎ 061 833 3333, fax 061 833 3030)

FIELDEN, Dr Christa Maria; *née* Peix; da of Ludwig Robert Peix (d 1974), and Margaret Freer-Hewish, *née* von Neumann; *b* 28 June 1943; *Educ* Hamps Co HS for Girls, Univ of London (BSc, MSc, PhD); *m* 29 Jan 1964 (m dis 1983), Christopher James Fielden; 2 s (James b 15 July 1966, William b 4 Oct 1968, d 1989); *Career* with Civil Serv 1970-74, head computer Dept CNAA 1974-75, called to the Bar Lincoln's Inn 1982, in practice SE Circuit; FSS 1982; *Recreations* skiing, psychology; *Style*— Dr Christa Fielden; 9 Woburn Ct, Bernard St, London WC2 (☎ 071 837 8752); 12 Old Square, Lincoln's Inn, London WC2 (☎ 071 242 4289, fax 071 831 6736)

FIELDEN, Christopher Thomas; s of Wilfred Fielden, of Nottingham (d 1968), and Nellie, *née* Shaw; *b* 22 Nov 1942; *Educ* Nottingham HS, Downing Coll Cambridge (MA, LLB); *m* 30 March 1964, Pauline Mary, da of Joseph Frederick Hoult, of Nottingham (d 1982); 2 s (Henry b 1964, Timothy b 1968); *Career* slr 1967; dir: Gallaher Ltd 1987- (gp legal advsr 1972), Gallaher Tobacco Ltd 1986, Forbuoys plc 1984, Whyte & Mackay Distillers Ltd 1990; memb: Ctee Tilford Bach Soc, Law Soc 1967; *Recreations* golf; *Style*— Christopher Fielden, Esq; Evergreens, Elstead Rd, Tilford, Farnham, Surrey GU10 2AJ (☎ 02518 2407); Gallaher Ltd, Members Hill, Brooklands Rd, Weybridge, Surrey KT13 0QU (☎ 0932 859777, fax 0932 857829)

FIELDEN, Mark; s of Cyril Lupton Fielden (d 1985), and Annie Mary Gladys, *née* Air (d 1979); *b* 17 Oct 1934; *Educ* Mill Hill Sch, Worcester Coll Oxford (MA); *m* 20 June 1959, Margaret Helen; 4 s (Roger b 1962, Gavin b 1965, Nicholas and Philip b 1970); *Career* Nat Serv RA; chartered accountant 1961, ptnr Bland Fielden & Co Colchester 1961-65; chief accountant Sundour Fabrics 1966-69; md Firth Carpets Ltd 1983- (fin dir 1969-83), dir Readicut Int plc 1984-; *Recreations* reading and walking; *Style*— Mark Fielden, Esq; The Moorings, 47 Station Road, Baildon, Shipley, W Yorks BD17 6HS (☎ Bradford 586477); Firth Carpets Ltd, Clifton Mills, Brighouse, W Yorks (☎ 0484 713371)

FIELDHOUSE, Adm of the Fleet Baron (Life Peer UK 1990), of Gosport in the County of Hampshire; Sir John David Elliott Fieldhouse; GCB (1982, KCB 1980), GBE (1982); s of Sir Harold Fieldhouse, KBE, CB; *b* 12 Feb 1928; *Educ* RNC Dartmouth (DSc); *m* 1953, Margaret Ellen, da of late David Dorrington Cull; 1 s (Hon Mark Elliott James b 8 July 1955), 2 da (Hon Amanda Elaine b 12 April 1959, Hon Sarah Lucinda b 15 Nov 1962); *Career* RN 1941; cmd HMS: Acheron, Tiptoe, Walrus, Dreadnought, Hermes, Diomede; dir Naval Warfare MOD 1973-74, Flag Offr Second Flotilla 1974-76, Flag Offr Submarines 1976-78, Controller of Navy 1979-81, Admiral 1981, C-in-C Fleet, Allied C-in-C Channel and C-in-C Eastern Atlantic Area 1981-82, in overall command during Falklands Islands op 1982, First Sea Lord and Chief of Naval Staff, First and Princ Naval ADC to HM The Queen 1982-85, Adm of the Fleet 1985; Chief of the Def Staff 1985-88; conslt Vosper Thornycroft (UK) Ltd 1990-, external dir DESC Ltd 1990-; *Recreations* sailing; *Clubs* Royal Yacht Sqdn, Army and Navy; *Style*— Admiral of the Fleet the Rt Hon Lord Fieldhouse, GCB, GBE; Ministry of Defence, Main Building, Whitehall, London SW1A 2HB (☎ 071 218 6190)

FIELDHOUSE, (James) Richard; s of Sir Harold Fieldhouse, KBE, CB, of Dormy House, Sunningdale, Surrey, and Lady Mabel Elaine, *née* Elliot; *b* 4 May 1933; *Educ* Merchant Taylors', Guy's (BDS, LDS, Golf Purple), RCS (Dip in Orthodontics); *m* 1957, Lily Guillemina, da of late Carlos Augusto Lopez; 2 da (Laura Catherine b 23 Oct 1958, Katherine Anne Clare b 9 Sept 1961); *Career* short serv cmmn surgn Lt (D) RN in Malta HMS Rampura and Ausonia 1957-61; gen dental practice Epsom Surrey 1962-72, lectr in children's dentistry Royal Dental Hosp of London 1972-75; specialist orthodontic practice: High Wycombe Bucks 1975-, Cavendish Square London 1975-87, Harley St London 1987-; Liveryman Worshipful Co of Clockmakers, Freeman City of London; memb: BDA, Br Assoc of Orthodontics, Br Soc for the Study of Orthodontics; *Recreations* tennis, golf, bridge, gardening, and friends; *Clubs* West Hill Golf (Surrey, hon life memb); *Style*— Richard Fieldhouse, Esq; 77 Harley St, London W1N 1HD (☎ 071 935 8837)

FIELDING, Claude Eric; s of Frederick Fischl (d 1943), and Elisabeth, *née* Medola (d 1937); *b* 29 June 1926; *Educ* King's Sch Canterbury; *m* 8 Feb 1953, Olga Rachel, da of Dr Jacob Michael Raphael (d 1972); 2 da (Rachel b 1956, Jenny b 1959); *Career* slr; clerk Stephens and Scown Solicitors St Austell 1941-43, managing clerk in articles Crawley & de Reya London 1943-50, admitted slr 1950; ptnr Crawley & de Reya (film, entertainment and media law) 1950-78, head entertainments and communications Law Dept Bartletts de Reya 1978-88 (Michon de Reya 1988-); hon clerk Oxshott Heath Conservators 1971-; Liveryman Worshipful Co of Solicitors 1960; memb: Law Soc 1950, Int Bar Assoc 1976; Commendatore Republic of Italy; *Recreations* sailing, skiing; *Clubs* Bosham Sailing, Downhill Only, Royal Over-Seas League; *Style*— Claude Fielding, Esq; Windfalls, 29 Prince's Drive, Oxshott, Surrey KT22 0UL (☎ 037284 292); 125 High Holborn, London WC1V 6QP (☎ 071 405 3711, fax 071 404 5982, telex 21455 M

FIELDING, Hon Mrs (Daphne Winifred Louise); da of 4 Baron Vivian, DSO (d 1940); *b* 11 July 1904; *m* 1, 27 Oct 1926 (m dis 1953), 6 Marquess of Bath, *qv*; 2 s (Viscount Weymouth, Lord Christopher Thynne, *qqv*) and 2 s decd, 1 da (Duchess of Beaufort, *qv*); m 2, 11 July 1953 (m dis 1978), Major Alexander Wallace Fielding, DSO, s of Alexander Lumsden Wallace (d 1966), of Kirkcaldy; *Career* writer; *Books* Mercury Presides (autobiography), The Nearest Way Home (autobiography), The Duchess of Jermyn Street (biography of Rosa Lewis), Emerald and Nancy (biography of Emerald and Nancy Cunard), The Rainbow Picnic (biography of Iris Tree), The Face on the Sphinx (biography of Gladys Deacon, Duchess of Marlborough), The Adonis Garden (fiction); *Style*— The Hon Mrs Fielding; Old Laundry, Badminton, Avon GL9 1DD

FIELDING, Leonard John; s of Leonard Francis Fielding (d 1946), of Smethwick Sandwell, and Lilian, *née* Kimberley; *b* 29 June 1931; *Educ* Smethwick Jr Tech Sch, Chance Tech Coll (HND); *m* 1, 4 April 1953, Jeanne Mary Allen (decd); 1 s (Adrian John b 6 Oct 1972), 2 da (Helen Louise b 18 Aug 1968, Hilary Jane b 14 March 1970); m 2, 27 Dec 1988, Jean Margaret (formerly Mrs Wharton), da of Frank Ridgeway; *Career* development engr: MOS 1953-56, Birmid Foundries 1956-65; prodn dir Birmal Div of Birmid Foundries 1965-79, tech dir Worcester Parsons 1979-; chm Br Standard Tech Sub Ctee For Hardware Products; memb: several Br Standard Tech Ctees, Tech Ctee Assoc of Br Hardware Mfrs, Euro Fedn Assocs of Lock and Building Hardware Mfrs, CEN Tech Ctee Working Gp (convenor Task Gp); maj projects incl adjustable hinges and espagnolette locking systems; winner Design award (for espagnolette handle) 1990; CEng, MIProd E 1953; *Style*— Leonard Fielding, Esq; 'Woodlea', 5 Sutton Lodge, Blossomfield Road, Solihull B91 1NB (☎ 021 705 1800); Worcester Parsons, Lifford Lane, Kings Norton, Birmingham B30 3JR (☎ 021 459 2421)

FIELDING, Sir Leslie; KCMG (1988); o s of Percy Archer Fielding (d 1963), and Margaret, *née* Calder Horry; *b* 29 July 1932; *Educ* Queen Elizabeth's Sch Barnet, Emmanuel Coll Cambridge (MA), SOAS London, St Antony's Coll Oxford (MA); *m* 1978, Dr Sally Patricia Joyce Fielding, da of late Robert Stanley Thomas Stibbs Harvey; 1 s, 1 da; *Career* Foreign Serv 1956, Tehran 1957-60, FO 1960-64, chargé d'affaires Phnom Penh 1964-66, Paris 1966-70, FCO 1970-73; transferred to European Cmmn in Brussels 1973-, head of delgn Cmmn of Euro Communities in Japan 1978-82, dir gen for external rels Euro Cmmn in Brussels 1982-87; vice chllr Univ of Sussex 1987-, memb High Cncl Euro Univ Inst Florence 1988-, hon fell Emmanuel Coll Cambridge; memb House of Laity of the General Synod of the C of E 1990-; Knight Cdr: Order of the White Rose Order of St Agatha of San Mariono 1987, of Finland 1987, Silver Order of Merit Austria 1989; FRSA; *Recreations* living in the country; *Clubs* Travellers'; *Style*— Sir Leslie Fielding, KCMG; Vice Chancellor, University of Sussex, Falmer, Brighton, Sussex BN1 9RH

FIELDING, Michael; s of Maurice Frisch (d 1982), and Ides, *née* Kessler; *b* 27 March 1946; *Educ* Hackney Downs GS, Univ of Sheffield (LLB); 1, Sept 1968, Sandra Estelle, da of Sidney Shulman, of London; 2 s (Jeremy Richard b 1972, Nicholas James b 1975); *Career* slr; ptnr Brecher & Co, chm Palmerston Holdings plc 1987; memb Law Soc; *Recreations* tennis, travel, reading, work; *Clubs* Harry's Bar, Annabel's; *Style*— Michael Fielding, Esq; Regents Park, London NW1; 78 Brook St, London W1 (☎ 071 493 5141, fax 071 493 6255, telex 263486)

FIELDING, Richard Walter; s of Walter Harrison, MBE (d 1988), of Burnleigh, Ashley Common Rd, New Milton, Hants, and Marjorie Octavia Adair, *née* Roberts; *b* 9 July 1933; *Educ* Clifton; *m* 1, 27 April 1961, Felicity Ann (d 1981), da of the late Dr V D Jones; 1 s (Timothy b 1965), 3 da (Vanessa b 1962, Anabel b 1968, Lucinda (twin) b 1968); m 2, 1983, Jacqueline Winifred Digby, *née* Hussey; *Career* Nat Serv Lt RE 1951-53; broker rising to dir Bland Welch & Co Ltd 1954-68, dir and md C E Heath & Co Ltd 1968-75, fndr chm and chief exec offr Fielding and Ptnrs 1975-86; CE Heath plc: chief exec 1986, chm & chief exec offr 1987-90, chm 1990-; *Style*— Richard Fielding, Esq; C E Heath plc, Cuthbert Heath House, 150 Minories, London EC3N 1NR (☎ 071 488 2488)

FIELDS, Gordon Ivan (Gifi); s of Gordon Ivan Fields, of LA, USA, and Dr Nancy Davidson Gayer; *b* 29 June 1951; *Educ* Shrewsbury, William Ellis Sch London; *m* Catherine, da of Fredrick Henry Aldham; 1 s (Jacob Harry Samual b 29 March 1987), 1 da (Elisha b 26 Jan 1986); *Career* memb staff: International Times 1967-68, UFO Club 1967-68, Middle Earth Club 1968-69; travelled to Afghanistan 1969-70; fashion entrepreneur: Trotsky International Ragfreak Clothing Co 1970-71, Gingernut Clothing Co 1971-75, Snob Shops 1983-87, Coppernob Group 1976-; designs sold throughout the world since 1970; retailers incl: Harvey Nichols, Harrods, Bloomingdales, Henri Bendels, I Magnum, Galeries La Fayette, Karstadt, J C Pennys, Sears Group, Burton Group, BHS; reg contrib Fashion Weekly and Retail Week magazines; fndr first retail and mfrg Co USSR (instigator jt venture with Leningrad State Bank, Nevski Zori Lilia Co-op); trade and indust advsr Lab Pty on clothing and textiles (memb Pty); reg conf speaker; fndr memb Br Fashion Cncl; nominee Br Fashion Awards 1990; FCIM 1989; *Recreations* golf, wine; *Clubs* Coombe Hill Golf Kingston Surrey; *Style*— Gifi Fields, Esq; Coppernob Group, 95 Gt Portland St, London W1 (☎ 071 436 3600, fax 071 637 3232)

FIELDS, Terence (Terry); MP (Lab) Liverpool Broadgreen 1983-; s of late Frank Fields; *b* 8 March 1937; *m* 1962, Maureen Mongan; 2 s, 2 da; *Career* fireman, former memb NW Regnl Exec Ctee Lab Pty; *Style*— Terry Fields Esq, MP; House of Commons, London SW1A 0AA (☎ 071 219 6342; home: 051 521 6413)

FIELDSEND, John Charles Rowell; s of Charles Edward Fieldsend, MC (d 1962), of Polegate, Sussex, and Phyllis Mary, *née* Brucesmith (d 1963); *b* 13 Sept 1921; *Educ* Michaelhouse Natal, Rhodes Univ Coll Grahamstown SA (BA, LLB); *m* 4 Dec 1945, Muriel, da of Oswald Gedling (d 1959), of Ripon, Yorks; 1 s (Peter Charles Rowell b 1949), 1 da (Catherine Margaret Ann b 1953); *Career* Lt RA 1941-45; pres Special Income Tax Ct Fedn Rhodesia and Nyasaland 1958-63, judge High Ct S Rhodesia 1963 (advocate 1947-63, QC 1959) resigned 1968; sec Law Cmmn England and Wales 1979-80 (asst slr 1968-79); chief justice: Zimbabwe 1980-83, Turks Caicos Is 1985-87; pres Ct of Appeal: Gibralta 1991 (memb 1986), St Helena 1987, Falklands 1987, Antarctic Dependencies 1987; Br Indian Ocean Territory 1988; *Style*— John Fieldsend, Esq; Great Dewes, Ardingly, W Sussex RH17 6UP (☎ 0444 892343)

FIENNES *see also*: Twisleton-Wykeham-Fiennes

FIENNES, Oliver William; *see*: Twistleton-Wykeham-Fiennes, Very Rev the Hon Oliver William

FIENNES, Ralph Nathanial; s of Mark Fiennes, of 29 Therapia Rd, London, and Jennifer, *née* Lash; *b* 22 Dec 1962; *Educ* St Kieran's Coll Kilkenny Ireland, Bishop Wordsworth Sch Salisbury, Chelsea Sch of Art, RADA (Kendal award, Forbes-Robertson award, Emile Littler award); *Career* actor; appearances incl at The Open Air Theatre 1985: Twelfth Night, A Midsummer Night's Dream, Ring Round The Moon; Theatre Clwyd: Night and Day, See How They Run; The Oldham Coliseum 1986: The Mann Sez, Don Quixote, Cloud Nine; The Open Air Theatre 1986: Romeo in Romeo & Juliet, Lysander in A Midsummer Night's Dream; Nat Theatre 1987-88: Six Characters in Search of an Author, Fathers and Sons, Ting Tang Mike; RSC 1988-91: Henry VI in The Plantagenets, Claudio in Much Ado about Nothing, Lewis the Dauphin in King John, Bert Jefferson in The Man Who Came to Dinner, Grant in Playing with Trains, Troilus in Troilus and Cressida, Edmund in King Lear, Beronne in Love's Labours Lost; memb Br Actors' Equity Assoc; *Recreations* reading, swimming, music; *Style*— Ralph Fiennes, Esq; c/o Larry Dalzell Associates, Suite 12, 17 Broad Court, London WC2B 5QN (☎ 071 379 0875)

FIENNES, Hon Richard Ingel; s and h of 21 Baron Saye and Sele; *b* 19 Aug 1959; *Style*— The Hon Richard Fiennes; Broughton Castle, Banbury, Oxon

FIENNES-CLINTON, Hon Edward Gordon; o s and h of 18 Earl of Lincoln, *qv*; *b* 7 Feb 1943; *m* 1970, Julia, da of William Howson, of 10 Waltham Rd, Armadale, Perth, W Australia; 2 s (Robert Edward b 1972, William Roy b 1980), 1 da (Marian Dawn b 1973); *Style*— The Hon Edward Fiennes-Clinton; 6 Jasminum Place, Carcoola Estate, Pinjarra, W Australia 6208, Australia

FIFE, Eugene Vawter (Gene); s of Clark E Fife, and Margaret Ellen, *née* Morton; *b* 23 Sept 1940; *Educ* Virginia Poly Inst (BS), Univ of Southern California (MBA); *m* 1, 4 June 1966, Susan Schucker (d 1981); 1 s (David b 1971), 1 da (Amy b 1974); m 2, 16 June 1984, Anne, da of Waldo Leisy; 1 s (Alexander b 1985), 1 da (Elizabeth b 1988); *Career* Lt US Air Force 1962-65; assoc Blyth & Co Inc 1968-70, Goldman Sachs & Co NY, Los Angeles and San Francisco 1970-76, chm and md Goldman Sachs Int Ltd 1986-; *Clubs* Union (NY); *Style*— Gene Fife, Esq; Goldman Sachs International Ltd, 8-10 New Fetter Lane, London EC4A 1DB (☎ 071 489 2000, fax 071 489 5431, telex 887902)

FIFE, 3 Duke of (UK 1900); James George Alexander Bannerman Carnegie; also Earl of Macduff (UK 1900), Lord Carnegie, Master of Southesk, Master of Carnegie, Master of Kinnaird and Leuchars; o s of 11 Earl of Southesk, *qv*, and his 1 w HH Princess Maud Alexandra Victoria Georgina Bertha (d 1945; granted title of Princess, style of Highness, and special precedence immediately after all members of Royal Family bearing style of Royal Highness 1905), 2 da of 1 Duke of Fife and HRH Princess Louise (The Princess Royal), eldest da of HM King Edward VII; suc his maternal aunt, HRH Princess Arthur of Connaught, Duchess of Fife 1959; *b* 23 Sept 1929; *Educ* Gordonstoun, Royal Agric Coll Cirencester; *m* 11 Sept 1956 (m dis 1966), Hon Caroline Cecily Dewar, da of 3 Baron Forteviot (she m 2 Gen Sir Richard Worsley, *qv*); 1 s (Earl of Macduff b 1961), 1 da (Lady Alexandra b 1959); *Heir* s; *Career* served in Malaya Campaign Scots Guards 1948-50; landowner, farmer; Freeman City of London 1954, Sr Liveryman of Clothworkers' Co 1954; pres Amateur Boxing Assoc 1959-73, vice patron 1973; vice patron of Braemar Royal Highland Soc; vice pres British Olympic Assoc; *Clubs* Turf; *Style*— His Grace the Duke of Fife; Elsick House, Stonehaven, Kincardineshire AB3 2NT, Scotland

FIFOOT, (Erik) Richard Sidney; MC (1945); s of Cecil Herbert Stuart Fifoot (d 1975), and Hjördis Baars, *née* Erikson; *b* 14 June 1925; *Educ* Berkhamstead Sch, Univ of Oxford (BA, MA), Univ of London (Dip in Librarianship); *m* 2 Sept 1949, Jean Meriel, da of late Lt-Col Stuart Thain, MC, of Wells, Somerset; 2 da (Susannah b 1959, Jane b 1961); *Career* Lt Coldstream Gds 1943-46; sub librarian Univ of Leeds 1952-58, dep librarian Univ of Nottingham 1958-60, librarian Univ of Edinburgh 1960-79, Bodleys librarian Univ of Oxford 1979-81, fndr and dir Three Rivers Books Ltd 1981-; chm Standing Ctee of Nat and Univ Libraries, memb Exec Bd Int Fedn of Library Assocs and Instns; *Recreations* reading, village life; *Style*— Richard Fifoot, Esq, MC; Castle View, Bridge Street, Bampton, Oxfordshire OX8 2HA (☎ 0993 850479)

FIGG, Sir Leonard Clifford William; KCMG (1981, CMG 1974); s of Sir Clifford Figg (d 1947), of Gt Missenden, Bucks, and Eileen Maud, *née* Crabb (d 1968); *b* 17 Aug 1923; *Educ* Charterhouse, Trinity Coll Oxford; *m* 1955, Jane, eldest da of late Judge Harold Brown; 3 s; *Career* Dip Serv 1947: consul gen and min Milan 1973-77, asst under sec of state 1977-80, ambass to Republic of Ireland 1980-83; vice chm Br Red Cross Soc 1983-88; pres: Aylesbury Divnl Cons Assoc 1985-, Bucks Assoc of Youth Clubs 1987-; Chiltern Soc 1990-; chm Bucks Farming & Wildlife Advsy Gp 1990-; *Clubs* Brooks's; *Style*— Sir Leonard Figg, KCMG; Court Field House, Little Hampden, Great Missenden, Bucks

FIGGESS, Sir John George; KBE (1969, OBE 1949), CMG (1960); eldest s of Percival Watts Figgess, and Leonora, *née* McCanlis; *b* 15 Nov 1909; *Educ* Whitgift Sch; *m* 1948, Alette, da of Dr P J A Idenburg, of The Hague; 2 da; *Career* cmmnd Intelligence Corps 1939, Japanese linguist, liaison offr with C-in-C Eastern Fleet WWII (India, Burma), Maj 1942, Temp Lt-Col 1943, Temp Col 1956; Mil Attaché Tokyo 1956-61, cnsllr (info) Br Embassy Tokyo 1961-68, cmmr gen for Britain at EXPO 70 Osaka 1968-70, dir Christie Manson and Woods Ltd 1973-82; *Style*— Sir John Figgess, KBE, CMG; The Manor House, Burghfield, Berks

FIGGINS, Hon Mrs (Sarah Rachel Jane); *née* Kay-Shuttleworth; da of 4 Baron Shuttleworth (d 1975); *b* 18 July 1950; *Educ* Southover Manor, City and Guilds Art Sch; *m* 1, 1970 (m dis 1984), Richard Francis Foster, 2 s of William Robert Brudenell Foster, *qv*; 1 s, 2 da; m 2, 20 Dec 1988, Peter R Figgins; 1 s (Tom b 27 Sept 1990); *Style*— The Hon Mrs Figgins; Flat 15, 16 Pembridge Square, London W2 4EH

FIGGIS, Anthony St John Howard; s of R R Figgis (d 1984), and Philippa Maria, *née* Young (d 1988); *b* 12 Oct 1940; *Educ* Rugby, King's Coll Cambridge; *m* 6 June 1964, Miriam Ellen (Mayella), da of Dr F C Hardt (d 1954); 2 s (Benedict b 1968, Oliver b 1972), 1 da (Sophie b 1966); *Career* HM Dip Serv: joined 1962, Belgrade 1963-65 and 1982-85, Bahrain 1968-70, Madrid 1971-74 and 1979-82, Bonn 1988-89; dir res and analysis FCO 1989-; *Recreations* fly fishing, tennis, music (piano); *Clubs* Roehampton; *Style*— Anthony Figgis, Esq; Foreign & Commonwealth Office, King Charles Street, London SW1A 2AH (☎ 071 210 6199)

FIGGIS, Dermot Samuel Johnstone; s of Terence Samuel Ernest Figgis, of Heath Drive, Potters Bar, Herts, and Irene Elizabeth, *née* Arnold; *b* 31 Dec 1933; *Educ* Uppingham; *m* 24 Sept 1960, Penelope Jane, da of Leslie Harris East, OBE, of Chaffcombe House, Chard, Somerset; 2 s (Andrew b 1962, Matthew b 1970), 1 da (Charlotte b 1965); *Career* chm and md S Figgis & Co Ltd; *Recreations* gardening, tennis, country pursuits, sailing; *Clubs* MCC; *Style*— Dermot S J Figgis, Esq; The Limes, Essendon, Hatfield, Herts (☎ 07072 61400); 53-54 Aldgate High St, London EC3 (☎ 071 488 4511)

FIGURES, Sir Colin Frederick; KCMG (1983, CMG 1978), OBE (1969); s of Frederick and Muriel Figures; *b* 1 July 1925; *Educ* King Edward's Sch Birmingham, Pembroke Coll Cambridge (MA); *m* 1956, Pamela Ann Timmis; 1 s, 2 da; *Career* FO 1951; first sec Vienna 1966, FCO 1969-85, dep sec Cabinet Office 1985-89; *Style*— Sir Colin Figures, KCMG, OBE; c/o Cabinet Office, 70 Whitehall, London SW1

FILBY, Ven William Charles Leonard; s of William Richard Filby (d 1946), of Middx, and Dorothy, *née* Evans (d 1980); *b* 21 Jan 1933; *Educ* Ashford Co Sch Middx, London Univ (BA); *m* 1958, Marion Erica, da of Prof T W Hutchinson, of Birmingham; 4 s (Jonathan b 1959, Andrew b 1961, Christopher b 1963, William b 1968), 1 da (Rebecca b 1966); *Career* archdeacon of Horsham 1983-; vicar of: Holy Trinity Richmond 1965-71, Bishop Hannington Hove 1971-79; rector of Broadwater 1979-83, rural dean of Worthin 1980-83; chm: Redcliffe Missionary Trainl Coll 1970, Diocesan Stewardship Ctee 1983-, Sussex Churches Bdcasting Ctee 1984-; govr: St Mary's Hall Brighton 1984-, W Sussex Inst of High Educn 1985-; memb Keswick Convention Cncl 1973-; bishop's advsr for Hosp Chaplains 1986-; *Recreations* sport, music; *Style*— The Ven the Archdeacon of Horsham; The Archdeaconry, Itchingfield, Horsham, N Sussex RH13 7NX

FILER, Denis Edwin; TD (1962, bar 1974); s of Edwin Francis Filer (d 1951), of Manchester, and Sarah Ann, *née* Stannard (d 1984); *b* 19 May 1932; *Educ* Manchester Central GS, Univ of Manchester (BSc), Open Univ (BA); *m* 17 Aug 1957, Pamela, da of Sam Armitage, of Manchester; 1 s (Nigel John Denis b 1967), 2 da (Fiona Anne b 1962, Katharine Helen b 1964); *Career* Nat Serv 2 Lt REME served BAOR 1953-55; TA serv culminating: Lt-Col ADEME 1970-75, Col 1975-78, Hon Col REME(V) West 1978-87; ICI: project mangr and maintenance engineer (Holland, Grangemouth and Hillhouse) 1955-73, asst works mangr Wilton Works 1973-76, engrg mangr Welwyn 1976-78, engrg and prodn dir Welwyn 1978-81, dir of engrg 1981-88; non-exec dir: Electra Corporate Ventures Ltd 1989-, Adwest Group plc 1991-; DG The Engrg Cncl 1988- (formerly memb Cncl); memb Gen Ctee Lloyd's Register 1988-; FEng, FIMechE, FIChemE; *Recreations* squash; *Clubs* Wilton Castle Club, Army and Navy; *Style*— Denis E Filer, Esq, TD; Brambles, Watton Green, Watton-at-Stone, Hertford SG14 3RB (☎ 0920 830207); The Engineering Council, 10 Maltravers St, London WC2R 3ER (☎ 071 240 7891)

FILER, Michael Harold; s of Louis Horace Filer, of Bournemouth, Dorset, and Raie, *née* Behrman (d 1978); *b* 11 Aug 1939; *Educ* Clifton, Inst of Taxation (ATII); *m* 5 Dec 1965, Anne Brenda, da of Peter Packer; 1 s (Samuel b 1978), 3 da (Lucy b 1967, Katy b 1970, Sadie b 1981); *Career* CA 1963; currently sr ptnr Filer, Knapper & Co; memb Bournemouth CC 1969-79 and 1983-87; Mayor of Bournemouth 1984-85; memb numerous charitable ctees; FCA; *Recreations* cricket (played in 1957 Clifton Coll Cricket Team at Lords, player mangr UK Cricket Team in Maccabiah Games Israel 1974), tennis; *Style*— Michael H Filer, Esq; 8 Boscombe Cliff Rd, Bournemouth, Dorset BH5 1JL (☎ 0202 396 302); Filer Knapper & Co, Chartered Accountants, 10 Bridge St, Christchurch, Dorset BH23 1EF (☎ 0202 483 341, fax 0202 483 550)

FILKIN, David Shenstone; s of Brian Shenstone Filkin, of Birmingham, and Lilian Winifred, *née* Franklin; *b* 22 Nov 1942; *Educ* King Edward's Sch Birmingham, Univ Coll Oxford (BA); *m* 31 Aug 1968, Angela Elizabeth, da of Federick Callam (d 1970), of Woking, Surrey; 3 s (Neil b 1973, Jonathan b 1975, Matthew b 1978); *Career* BBC TV: prodr Man Alive 1964-79, exec prodr Holiday 74 1974, devisr and ed Brass Tacks 1978, ed Tomorrow World 1979-84, ed QED 1984-, devisr and ed Body Matters 1985-90; pres BBC RFC 1979-86, memb Surrey Met RF Referees Soc; *Books* Tomorrow's World Today (1982), Bodymatters (1987); *Recreations* rugby union football coaching and refereeing, sea angling, wine tasting; *Clubs* BBC RFC, Bisley and Dist Sea Anglers, The Wine Soc; *Style*— David Filkin, Esq; 29 Bloomfield Rd, Kingston upon Thames, Surrey TK1 2SF (☎ 081 549 3204); BBC TV, Kensington House, Room 4075, Richmond Way, London W14 0AX (☎ 081 895 6052/6068, fax 081 743 0640, telex 265781)

FILKIN, Elizabeth Jill; da of John Tompkins, and Frances Trollope; *b* 24 Nov 1940; *Educ* Univ of Birmingham (BSocSci), Brunel Univ; *m* 1974, David Goeffrey Nigel Filkin; 3 da; *Career* organiser Sparkbrook Association Birmingham 1961-64, res fell Anglo-Israel Association London and Israel 1964, lectr and researcher Univ of Birmingham 1964-68, lectr National Institute for Social Work London 1968-71 (also community worker North Southwark), community work services offr London Borough of Brent Social Services Dept 1971-75, lectr in social studies Univ of Liverpool 1975-83, chief exec National Association CAB 1983-88, dir Community Services London Docklands Development Corporation 1988-; memb: BBC Advsy Cncl, Advertising Standards Authy, Econ and Social Res Cncl; *Books* The New Villagers (1969), What Community Worker Needs to Know (1974), Community Work & Caring for Children (1979), Caring for Children (1979), Women and Children First (1984); *Recreations* swimming, walking; *Style*— Elizabeth Filkin; 20 Circus Street, London SE10 8SN; London Docklands Development Corp, Thames Quay, 191 Marsh Wall, London E14 9TJ (☎ 071 512 3000, fax 071 512 0777)

FILLING, Roy Paul; OBE (1988); s of William Arthur Filling (d 1960), of Egham, Surrey, and Alice May, *née* Field (d 1925); *b* 18 May 1924; *Educ* Ashford Secdy Sch Middx; *m* 19 July 1945, Audrey Margaret, da of Fred Wilfred Highland (d 1972), of Staines, Middx; 1 da (Ann Linda); *Career* air crew navigator RAFVR 1943-47; trainee accountant Mackay Industrial Equipment Feltham Middx 1948-54, fin dir Isaac Walton & Co Ltd London 1954-66, chm and md Wellsway Garage Ltd Bath 1966-77, counselling advsr Dept of Employment Business Devpt Service & Small Firms Service 1977-, chm Corintech Ltd Salisbury & Fordingbridge 1986-87; FIBC 1990 (currently pres), memb Assoc of the Freeman of England 1990; Freeman City of London 1989; *Recreations* travel, swimming, model aircraft; *Clubs* Mansion House (Poole), Luncheon; *Style*— Roy Filling, Esq, OBE; 4 Kestrel Court, Highfield Road, Ringwood, Hampshire BH24 1QT (☎ 0425 470 600)

FINAN, John Charles; *b* 2 May 1938; *m* Denise Mary; 3 c; *Career* Pearl Assurance; joined as insurance agent 1959, various field mgmnt and head office mgmnt appts until 1987, directorships 1987-88 (Pearl Assurance plc, Pearl Assurance Unit Funds Ltd, Pearl Assurance Marketing Services Ltd, Pearl Trust Managers Ltd, Pearl Assurance Unit Linked Pensions Ltd), rep on Home Service Ctee Assoc of Br Insurers; chief exec and dep chm NEL Britannia (insurance arm of INVESCO MIM plc - formerly Britannia Arrow) 1989-, dir numerous subsid cos; former dir (at INVESCO MIM) until 1990: MIM Britannia Unit Trust Managers Ltd, MIM Ltd; NEL acquired by UNUM Corporation 1990; former chm UK and Rep of Ireland Advsy Ctee LIMRA International, fndr chm Euro Educn Ctee LIMRA; *Style*— John Finan, Esq; Isomer Cottage, The Warren, Caversham, nr Reading, Berks RG4 7TG (☎ 0734 497901); NEL Britannia, Milton Court, Dorking, Surrey RH4 3LZ (☎ 0306 887766, fax 0306 884880, car 0836 663761)

FINBOW, Roger John; s of Frederick Walter Finbow, of Sudbourne, Woodbridge, Suffolk, and Olivia Francis, *née* Smith; *b* 13 May 1952; *Educ* Woodbridge Sch Suffolk, Mansfield Coll Oxford (MA); *m* 23 May 1984, Janina Fiona (Nina), da of John Doull of Shorne, Kent; 3 da (Romy b 1985, Georgina b 1987, Isobel b 1989); *Career* Ashurst Morris Crisp London: articled clerk 1975-77, asst 1977-83 (Paris 1978-79), assoc 1983-75, ptnr 1985-; former pres Old Woodbridgian Soc, memb Cncl Mansfield Coll (memb Appeal Ctee), pres Mansfield Assoc, chm Business Sub Gp; *Recreations* cars, collecting model cars, badminton, football spectating, ballet; *Clubs* Ipswich Town FC; *Style*— Roger Finbow, Esq; Yew Tree House, Higham, Colchester, Essex CO7 6LN (☎ 020 637 378); Broadwalk House, 5 Appold St, London EC2A 2HA (☎ 071 638 1111, fax 071 972 7990, telex 887067)

FINCASTLE, Viscount Malcolm Kenneth Murray; er s and h of 11 Earl of Dunmore' and Margaret Joy, *née* Cousins (d 1976); *b* 17 Sept 1946; *Educ* Queechy HS, Launceston Schools' Bd 'A' certificate; *m* 1970, Joy Anne, da of A Partridge (d 1987), of Launceston, Tasmania; 1 s (Leigh b 1977), 1 da (Elisa b 1980) (both adopted); *Career* electrical tech offr, civil aviation authy, licenced aircraft maintenance engr; patron Scottish Australian Heritage Cncl's Annual Sydney Scottish Week; *Recreations* flying, astronomy; *Clubs* Soaring of Tasmania; *Style*— Viscount Fincastle; PO Box 100E, E Devonport, Tas 7310, Australia

FINCH, Martin Anthony; s of Francis James William Finch, and Margaret Helen, *née* Simmons (d 1967); *b* 24 Feb 1938; *Educ* Tech Sch Kent, Art Sch Kent (NDD); *Career* Nat Serv 1958-60; jr visualiser Smees Advertising 1960-61, graphic designer ICT (now ICL) 1961-63; publicity mangr: A B Dick Co 1963-64, Letraset 1964-68; dir Matthew Finch Associates Ltd 1968-; MCIM 1967, FCSD 1971, FInstD 1975; *Recreations* antiquarian books (speciality cookery), fine arts, painting, ceramics; *Style*— Martin Finch, Esq; Fernwood House, High St, Farningham, Kent DA4 ODT (☎ 0322 862140); Matthew Finch Group Incorporating, Matthew Finch Design Consultants Ltd, 17 High St, Swanley, Kent BR8 8AE (☎ 0322 669333, fax 0322 614157)

FINCH, Michael James; s of Reginald James Finch, of Chadwell Heath, Essex, and Florence Anne, *née* Selby; *b* 6 July 1957; *Educ* Redbridge Tech Coll, Ravensbourne Coll of Art (BA), RCA (MA, Wigginsteape award, Milner Kite award); partner, Emily, da of Martin Russell; *Career* painter; one man shows: Peterborough City Museum and Art Gallery 1983, Groucho Club 1987 and 1988, Pomeroy Purdy Gallery 1990 (curator since 1988), included in various gp shows; paintings in collections: Peterborough City, Unilever, Burston, County NatWest, BDO Binder Hamlyn; Unilever award 1985, Burston award 1985; *Recreations* jazz; *Clubs* Groucho; *Style*— Michael Finch, Esq; 68c Chetwynd Rd, London NW5 1DE (☎ 071 267 7742), Pomeroy Purdy Gallery, Jacob Street Film Studios, Mill St, London SE1 2BA (☎ 071 237 6062, fax 071 252 0118)

FINCH, Nigel Lucius Graeme; s of Harold George Graeme, and Elizabeth, *née* Turner; *b* 1 Aug 1949; *Educ* Ravensbourne Boys Sch, Univ of Sussex (BA, Dip Ed); *Career* ed Arena BBC TV 1985-; dir: Chelsea Hotel, Raspberry Ripple, Your Honor I Object; Freedom New Orleans USA 1988; *Recreations* listing, I list therefore I am;

Style— Nigel Finch, Esq; The Bishopric, 80 Culverden Road, London SW12 (☎ 081 673 0896)

FINCH, Peter John; s of Richard Stuart Finch (d 1981), of Essex, and Charlotte Betsy, *née* Finch; *b* 17 April 1948; *Educ* Plaistow GS, City of London Poly; *m* 1, 1967, Angela Ruth, da of George Herbert Harold Watkins (d 1982); m 2, 1986, Carol Joyce, da of Douglas Arthur Wilson (d 1985), of Kent; 1 s (James Douglas b 19 Nov 1989); *Career* dir: M & G Life Assurance Co Ltd 1979-, M & G Pensions and Annuity Co Ltd 1979-; pres Insurance Inst of Chelmsford 1980-81; *Recreations* sailing, squash; *Clubs* Royal Corinthian Yacht; *Style*— Peter Finch, Esq; 17 Barnmead Way, Burnham-on-Crouch, Essex CM0 8QD (☎ 0621 784309); M & G Life, M & G House, Victoria Rd, Chelmsford CM1 1FB (☎ 0245 266266, fax 0245 267789)

FINCH, Robert Gerard; s of Brig J R G Finch, OBE, of 7 Newton Hall, Great Dunmow, Essex, and Patricia Hope, *née* Ferrar; *b* 20 Aug 1944; *Educ* Felsted; *m* Patricia Ann; 2 da (Alexandra b 8 May 1975, Isabel b 8 June 1978); *Career* articled clerk Monro Pennefather & Co 1963-68, ptnr Linklaters & Paines 1974- (slr Property Dept 1969-); Blundell Memorial lectr; Freeman City of London, Liveryman City of London Slrs Co; memb Law Soc 1969; *Recreations* sailing, hill walking, skiing, ski mountaineering; *Clubs* West Mersea Yacht, Alpine Ski, Ski Club of Great Britain; *Style*— Robert Finch, Esq; Mitre House, 160 Aldersgate St, London EC1; Linklaters & Paines, Barrington House, 59-67 Gresham St, London EC2 (☎ 071 606 7080, fax 071 600 2885)

FINCH, Stephen Clark; OBE (1989); s of Frank Finch (d 1955), of Haywards Heath, and Doris, *née* Lloyd (d 1958); *b* 7 March 1929; *Educ* Ardingly, RMCS, Sch of Signals; *m* 26 April 1975, Sarah Rosemary Ann, da of Admiral Sir Anthony Templer Frederick Griffith Griffin, GCB, *qv*, of Bosham; 2 da (Clare b 1977, Alice b 1980); *Career* cmmnd Royal Signals 1948, Korea 1951-52, RMCS 1953-56, Instr Sch of Signals 1956-59, Troop Cdr BAOR 1959-62, seconded Miny of Aviation 1962-64, Sqdn Cdr BAOR 1964-66, Staff Offr BAOR 1966-68, ret as Maj 1968; asst coordinator info systems BP 1984-89 (mangr Communications div 1968-71, gp communications mangr 1971-81, sr advsr regulatory affairs 1981-84), ind conslt in info tech 1989-, chm Telecommunications Mangrs Assoc 1981-84 (memb 1968-, memb exec ctee 1971-), chm Int Telecommunications Users Gp 1987-89 (memb Cncl 1981-); memb: MMC 1985-, Sec of State's Advsy Panel on Licensing Value Added Network Servs 1982-87, City of London Deanery Synod 1981-, London Area Synod 1989-; Freeman City of London 1975; FInstAM (memb Cncl 1981-84, medallist 1985), FBIM; *Recreations* sailing, skiing, swimming, music; *Clubs* National; *Style*— Stephen Finch, Esq, OBE; 97 Englefield Rd, Canonbury, London N1 3LJ

FINCH HATTON, Hon Robin Heneage; 2 s of 15 (and 10) Earl of Winchilsea and Nottingham; *b* 1 Nov 1939; *Educ* Gordonstoun; *m* 7 Sept 1962, Molly Iona, da of the late Col Palgrave Dawson Turner Powell, MBE, TD; 2 s (Christopher b 1966, Rupert b 1968), 1 da (Louisa b 1971, Nicola b 1964, d 1967); *Style*— The Hon Robin Finch Hatton; Town House Farmhouse, Clemsfold, Horsham, Sussex

FINCH-KNIGHTLEY, Hon Anthony Heneage; JP (Huntingdon); s of 10 Earl of Aylesford (d 1958); *b* 27 April 1920; *Educ* Oundle; *m* 12 June 1948, Susan Mary, o da of Maj-Gen Geoffrey Woodroffe Palmer, CB, CBE; 2 da (Minette b 1950, Joanna b 1954); *Career* Lt and temp Capt Black Watch, served ME 1939-46 (despatches); formerly with ICI; dep chm Huntingdon Bench; pres Huntingdon Cons; *Recreations* shooting, fishing, archery; *Clubs* The Bean; *Style*— The Hon Anthony Finch-Knightley, JP; Broomleigh House, Brampton, Huntingdon, Cambs (☎ 0480 453163)

FINDLAY, Brig (William Francis) Allan; OBE (1973); s of James Arthur Findlay (d 1966), of London, and Gladys Anna, *née* Ker (d 1971); *b* 30 Nov 1929; *Educ* Eagle House Sch, Wellington Coll, RMA Sandhurst; *m* 21 April 1956, Bridget Gay, da of Air Vice Marshal Augustus Henry Orlebar, CBE, AFC (d 1943), of Sandy, Beds; 2 s (Giles b 1959, Oliver b 1962); *Career* CO Queen's Own Yeo 1971-73, Brig 1977, Col 5 Royal Inniskilling Dragoon Gds 1981-86, ADC to HM The Queen 1982; mktg exec MEL Defence Electronics 1982-89; memb Chichester DHA 1989-; master Catterick Beagles 1955-56; *Recreations* gardening, field sports; *Clubs* Cavalry and Guards'; *Style*— Brig Allan Findlay, OBE; Upmeadow Lodge, Graffham, Petworth, West Sussex (☎ 079 86 236)

FINDLAY, Donald Russell; QC (1988); s of James Findlay (d 1980), of Edinburgh, and Mabel, *née* Muirhead (d 1985); *b* 17 March 1951; *Educ* Harris Acad Dundee, Univ of Dundee (LLB); *m* 28 Aug 1982, Jennifer Edith, *née* Borrowman; *Career* lectr in law Heriot Watt Univ Edinburgh 1975-76, advocate 1975-; vice chm North Cunninghame Cons and Unionist Assoc, prospective Parly candidate North Cunninghame; memb: Lothian Health Bd 1987, Faculty of Advocates 1975; *Recreations* Glasgow Rangers FC, Egyptology, The Middle East, wine, American football, Sumo; *Clubs* Caledonian, Edinburgh, Royal Burgess Golfing Soc, Glasgow Rangers Premier; *Style*— Donald R Findlay, Esq, QC; 26 Barnton Park Crescent, Edinburgh EH4 6EP (☎ 031 336 3734); Advocates Library, Parliament House, Edinburgh EH1 1RF (☎ 031 226 2881, fax 031 225 3642, car 086 749, telex 727856 FACADV 9)

FINDLAY, Gordon Francis George; s of Francis Gordon Findlay (d 1975), of Edinburgh, and Muriel Arras Maitland; *b* 9 Feb 1950; *Educ* George Watson's Coll Edinburgh, Univ of Edinburgh (BSc, MB ChB); *m* 5 April 1975, Andrea May, da of Lt Ewart Leslie Cooper, of Buxted, Surrey; 1 s (Iain b 5 Jan 1978), 2 da (Claire b 10 Oct 1980, Emma b 27 Dec 1985); *Career* conslt neurosurgn with special interest in spinal disease Walton Hosp Liverpool 1983-; extensive pubns in jls and textbooks on spinal disease; memb Br Soc of Neurosurgns; fndr: memb Br Cevical Spine Soc, memb Euro Spine Soc, Liverpool Spine Course; FRCS 1978; *Recreations* family, golf, music; *Style*— Gordon Findlay, Esq; Croftwood, Croft Drive East, Caldy, Wirral L48 1LT (☎ 051 625 2403); Walton Hosp, Conslt Neurosurgn, Dept of Neurosciences, Rice Lane, Liverpool L9 1AR (☎ 051 525 3611)

FINDLAY, Martin Charles; s of Cdr Noel Charles Mansfeldt Findlay, RN (d 1976), of Court Lodge, Hastingleigh, Kent, and Lady Mary Cecilia, da of 7 Earl Dartmouth, GCVO, JP, DL; *b* 27 June 1935; *Educ* Marlborough, St John's Coll Cambridge (MA); *m* 26 May 1966, Davina Margaret da of Sir Thomas Dundas Bt, MBE (d 1970), of The Old Rectory, Slaugham, Sussex; 2 s (Mark b 1967, Adam b 1969); *Career* Nat Serv 2 Lt Royal Dragoons 1953-55; Whitbread & Co: personnel dir 1976-86, vice chm 1982-; non-exec dir Provident Mutual Life Assurance Assoc 1989; chm Business in the Community, memb Cncl London Educn Business Partnership; Freeman: City of London 1986, Worshipful Co of Brewers; MInstD, FRSA 1988; *Recreations* country pursuits which lead to peace; *Style*— Martin Findlay, Esq; Ledburn Manor, Leighton Buzzards, Bedfordshire (☎ 0525 373110); Whitbread & Co, Chiswell St, London EC1 (☎ 071 606 4455)

FINDLAY, Lady Mary Cecilia; *née* Legge; eldest da of 7 Earl of Dartmouth, GCVO (d 1958); *b* 27 Oct 1906; *m* 17 Oct 1929, Cdr Noel Charles Mansfeldt Findlay, RN (d 1976), s of Sir Mansfeldt de Cardonnel Findlay, GBE, KCMG, CB; 2 s (Jonathan b 1933, Martin b 1935), 1 da (Mrs J Debenham b 1930); *Style*— The Lady Mary Findlay; 2 South Close, The Precincts, Canterbury, Kent CT1 2EJ

FINDLAY, Paul Hudson Douglas; s of Prof John Niemeyer Findlay (d 1987), and Aileen May, *née* Davidson; *b* 26 Sept 1943; *Educ* Univ Coll Sch London, Balliol Coll Oxford (BA), London Opera Centre; *m* 9 Sept 1966, Francoise Christiane, da of Albert Victor Willmott (d 1987); 1 s (Anthony b 4 May 1968), 1 da (Lucy b 4 June 1972); *Career* prodn and tech mangr New Opera Co 1967, dir London Sinfonietta 1967-, stage mangr Glyndebourne Touring Opera and English Opera Gp 1968, chm Opera 80 1987, opera dir Royal Opera House Covent Garden 1987- (asst dir 1976-87, PA to Gen Dir 1972-76, asst press offr 1968-72); Cavaliere Ufficiale Del 'Ordine Al Merito Della Repubblica Italiana; *Recreations* tennis, gardening, walking; *Style*— Paul Findlay, Esq; Royal Opera House, Covent Garden, London WC2 (☎ 071 240 1200, telex 27988 COVGAR G)

FINE, Anne; da of Brian Laker (d 1989), and Mary Baker; *b* 7 Dec 1947; *Educ* Northampton HS for Girls, Univ of Warwick (BA); *m* 3 Aug 1968, Kit Fine, s of Maurice Fine; 2 da (Ione b 3 Aug 1971, Cordelia b 26 Feb 1975); *Career* writer; children's books incl: The Summer House Loon (1978), The Other Darker Ned (1979), The Stone Menagerie (1980), Round Behind the Icehouse (1981), The Granny Project (1983), Scaredy-Cat (1985), Anneli the Art Hater (1986), Madame Doubtfire (1987), Crummy Mummy and Me (1988), A Pack of Liars (1988), Stranger Danger? (1989), The Country Pancake (1989), A Sudden Puff of Glittering Smoke (1989), Goggle-Eyes (1989), Bill's New Frock (1989), Only a Show (1990), A Sudden Swirl of Icy Wind (1990); books for adults: The Killjoy (1986), Taking the Devil's Advice (1990); *Awards* Scot Arts Cncl book award 1986, Smarties award 1990, Guardian Children's Fiction award 1990, Carnegie medal 1990; memb Soc of Authors; *Recreations* walking, reading; *Style*— Mrs Anne Fine; c/o Murray Pollinger, 222 Old Brompton Rd, London SW5 0BZ (☎ 071 373 4711, fax 071 373 3775)

FINE, Dr Jeffrey Howard; s of Nathan Fine, of 52 Baron's Court Rd, Penylan, Cardiff, and Rebecca, *née* Levi; *b* 5 Oct 1955; *Educ* The Howardian HS Cardiff, Bart's Med Coll; *partner*, Kirsty Elizabeth, da of Adolf Knul; 1 s (Alexander David b 27 June 1990); *Career* professioral registrar Acad Unit of Psychiatry Royal Free Hosp London 1981, registrar Psychological Med Nat Hosp for Nervous Disease London 1982-83, MO Home Office 1981-89, gen med practice London 1985, Euro neuroendocrine advsr ELI Lilly Pharmaceuticals Co 1986-87, private med psychiatric practice 1987-; completed London marathon 1983; freedom and key Kansas City Missouri USA 1976; MRPsych 1984, FRSM 1987; memb: BMA 1980, Euro Assoc and Int Coll of Neuropsychopharmacology, Br Assoc of Neuropsychiatry 1988, Assoc Independent Drs 1989; *publication:* author of papers on depression, light and obesity (Jl of Affective Disorder, 1987); *Recreations* jazz, tennis, sailing, classic cars, painting, architecture; *Clubs* Ronnie Scott's, West Heath Lawn Tennis; *Style*— Dr Jeffrey Fine; 68 Harley St, London W1N 1AE (☎ 071 935 3980, fax 071 636 6262)

FINER, Alexander; s of Sir Morris Finer (d 1974), of London, and Lady Finer, *née* Edith Rubner; *b* 12 March 1947; *Educ* Mill Hill Sch, LSE (LLB), Univ of California Berkeley (LLM); *m* 13 Sept 1974, Linda Anne, da of John Barnard, of California; *Career* journalist; Sunday Times 1970-78, Evening Standard 1978-79, Illustrated London News 1982-88, Daily Telegraph 1988-90 (asst ed special projects); ed Esquire 1990-; *Books* Deepwater (1983); *Clubs* Zanzibar; *Style*— Alexander Finer, Esq; Esquire, 72 Broadwick St, London W1V 2BP (☎ 071 439 5453, fax 071 437 6886)

FINER, Dr Nicholas; s of Sir Morris Finer (d 1974), and Lady Edith, *née* Rubner; *b* 24 Dec 1949; *Educ* The Hall Sch Hampstead, Mill Hill Sch, UCL (BSc, MB BS); *m* 1 May 1974, Susan, da of Prof Charles Dent, CBE (d 1975); 3 da (Emily b 30 Nov 1976, Sarah b 2 Aug 1978, Louise (twin) b 2 Aug 1978); *Career* conslt physician Luton and Dunstable Hosp 1988-; hon conslt physician Guy's Hosp, hon lectr United Med and Dental Schs of Guy's and St Thomas' Hosp 1988 (lectr 1981-88); ctee memb Assoc for The Study of Obesity, assoc ed Drugs and Therapeutics Bulletin; MRCP 1977; *Books* contrib: Health Consequences of Obesity (1988), Progress in Sweeteners (1989); *Style*— Dr Nicholas Finer

FINESTEIN, His Hon Judge; Israel; QC (1970); yst s of Jeremiah Finestein (d 1957), of Hull, Yorks; *b* 29 April 1921; *Educ* Kingston HS Hull, Trinity College Cambridge (MA); *m* 1946, Marion Phyllis, er da of Simon Oster, of Hendon, Middx; *Career* formerly major scholar and prizeman of Trinity Coll Cambridge; memb Cncl of Utd Synagogue, pres Cncl of Jewish Historical Soc of England; barr Lincoln's Inn 1953, a circuit judge 1972-; author; *Books* Short History of the Jews of England, Sir George Jessel; *Style*— His Hon Judge Finestein, QC; 18 Buttermere Court, Boundary Rd, London NW8

FINGALL, Countess of; Clair Hilda Plunkett; *née* Salmon; MBE; da of late Henry Robert Salmon, of Ballarat, Victoria, Australia; *b* 2 Feb 1903; *m* 1, Frank Richardson (decd), of Geelong, Victoria, Australia; m 2, 4 May 1966, as his 2 w, 12 Earl of Fingall (d 5 March 1984, when title became extinct); *Clubs* RACV (Melbourne), Geelong; *Style*— The Rt Hon the Countess of Fingall; 13 Lockwood St, Point Lonsdale, Victoria 3225, Australia

FINGLAND, Sir Stanley James Gunn; KCMG (1979, CMG 1966); s of Samuel Gunn Fingland (d 1969), of Edinburgh, and Agnes Christina, *née* Watson; *b* 19 Dec 1919; *Educ* Royal HS Edinburgh; *m* 1946, Nell, da of late Charles Lister; 1 s, 1 da; *Career* Maj RS (despatches Italy) 1939-47; Dip Serv; dep high cmmr Port of Spain 1962, Salisbury Rhodesia 1964, high cmmr Freetown 1966-69, asst under sec of state FO 1969-71, ambass Havana 1972-75, high cmmr Nairobi and Br rep to the UN Environmental Prog and to UN Habitat HQ in Nairobi 1975-79; *Recreations* fishing; *Style*— Sir Stanley Fingland, KCMG

FINGLETON, David Melvin; s of Lawrence Arthur Fingleton, and Norma Phillips, *née* Spiro; *b* 2 Sept 1941; *Educ* Stowe Sch, UC Oxford (MA); *m* 1975, Clare, yr da of Ian Colvin (d 1975); *Career* barr 1965-80; met stipendiary magistrate 1980; music critic Daily Express, stage design corr Arts Review; *Books* Kiri (biography of Dame Kiri Te Kanawa, 1982); *Recreations* music, travel; *Clubs* Garrick, MCC; *Style*— David Fingleton, Esq; Wells Street Magistrates Court, Wells Street, London W1A 3AE (☎ 071 825 2343)

FINGRET, Peter; s of Iser Fingret (d 1975), and Irene, *née* Jacobs (d 1979); *b* 13 Sept 1934; *Educ* Leeds Modern Sch, Univ of Leeds (LLB), Open Univ (BA); *m* 1, 11 Dec 1960 (m dis), June Gertrude; 1 s (Andrew b 1963), 1 da (Kathryn b 1966); m 2, 14 March 1980, Ann Lilian Mary; *Career* slr 1960-82; stipendiary magistrate: County of Humberside 1982-85, metropolitan 1985-; rec Crown Court 1987-; *Recreations* golf, music; *Clubs* Reform, RSM; *Style*— Peter Fingret, Esq; Dairy Cottage, Richmond, TW10 7DB (☎ 071 703 0909); 6 Herring House, Holy Island, Northumbria

FINIGAN, John Patrick; s of John Joseph Finigan, of Sale, Cheshire, and Mary Matilda Finigan (d 1983); *b* 12 Nov 1949; *Educ* Ushaw Coll Univ of Durham, St Bede's Coll Manchester, Cncl of Legal Educn London, Univ of Manchester, Harvard Law Sch; *m* 6 Dec 1976, Elizabeth, da of Joseph Liew, of Bandar Seri Begawan, Brunei; 1 s (Damien b 1980), 1 da (Emily Jane b 1982); *Career* slr; Standard Chartered Bank 1967-78, National Bank of Abu Dhabi 1978-82; gen mangr The National Bank of Kuwait SAK 1982-; memb Hon Soc of Lincoln's Inn; FRSA, AIB 1970, ACIS 1973, FCIB 1980; *Recreations* tennis, squash, music, literature; *Clubs* Oriental, Overseas Bankers'; *Style*— John Finigan, Esq; Barton Hse, Middle Barton, Oxon; Deloraine, Newton Ferrers, Devon; The National Bank of Kuwait, 13 George St, London W1H 5PB (☎ 071 224 2277, fax 071 224 2101, telex 892348)

FINK, Graham Michael; s of Horace Bertram Fink, of Oxford, and Margaret May, *née* Betts; *b* 7 Sept 1959; *Educ* Wood Green Comp Sch Oxford, Banbury Sch of Art,

Univ of Reading; *Career* creative advtg exec; French Gold Abbott 1980-81, Collett Dickenson Pearce 1981-87, head of art WCRS 1987, gp head Saatchi & Saatchi 1987-90, dep creative dir Gold Greenless Trott 1990-; winner various awards for: Hamlet, Land Rover, Benson & Hedges, Metropolitan Police, British Airways and Silk Cut; judge Campaign Poster awards 1991-; memb: Creative Circle, D & ADA; *Style*— Graham Fink, Esq; Gold Greenlees Trott, 82 Dean St, London W1V 5AB

FINKELSTEIN, Prof Ludwik; OBE (1990); s of Adolf Finkelstein (d 1950), of London, and Amelia, *née* Diamanstein (d 1980); *b* 6 Dec 1929; *Educ* Univ of London (BSc, MSc), City Univ (DSc); *m* 1957, Mirjam Emma, da of Dr Alfred Wiener (d 1964), of London; 2 s (Anthony b 1959, Daniel b 1962), 1 da (Tamara b 1967); *Career* scientist Instrument Branch Mining Res Estab NCB 1952-59, Northampton Coll London and City Univ 1959-: prof of instrument and control engrg, dean Sch of Electrical Engrg and Applied Physics, head Dept of Physics, head Dept of Systems Sci, dir Measurement and Instrumentation Centre, dean Sch of Engrg; Queen's Silver Jubilee Medal 1977; Liveryman Worshipful Co Scientific Instrument Makers; FEng 1986, FIEE, FInstMC (Sir Harold Hartley Silver medal 1981), CPhys, FInstP; *Recreations* books, conversation, Jewish studies; *Style*— Prof Ludwik Finkelstein, OBE; 9 Cheyne Walk, Hendon, London NW4 3QH (☎ 081 202 6966); City University, Northampton Square, London EC1V 0HB (☎ 071 253 4399 ext 4400, fax 071 250 0837)

FINLAY, Sir David Ronald James Bell; 2 Bt (UK 1964), of Epping, Co Essex; s of Sir Graeme Finlay, 1 Bt, ERD (d 1987); *b* 16 Nov 1963; *Educ* Marlborough, Univ of Grenoble, Univ of Bristol; *Career* trainee chartered accountant KPMG Peat Marwick McLintock; *Style*— Sir David Finlay, Bt; The Garden Flat, 106 Chesterton Rd, London W10 6EP

FINLAY, (Robert) Derek; s of William Templeton Finlay (d 1972), and Phyllis, *née* Jefferies (d 1948); *b* 16 May 1932; *Educ* Kingston GS, Emmanuel Coll Cambridge (BA, MA); *m* 1956, Una Ann, da of late David Smith Grant; 2 s (Rory, James), 1 da (Fiona); *Career* Lt Gordon Highlanders Malaya 1950-52, Capt Gordon Highlanders TA 1952-61; Mobil Oil Co UK 1955-61, assoc McKinsey & Co Inc 1961-67 (princ 1967-71, dir 1971-79), md H J Heinz Co Ltd 1979-81, sr vice pres corp devpt and chief fin offr World HQ H J Heinz Co Pittsburgh Pa USA 1981-; *Recreations* tennis, rowing, music, theatre; *Clubs* Highland Brigade, Leander, Allegheny Country, Duquesne, Annabel's; *Style*— Derek Finlay, Esq; Backbone Rd, Sewickley Heights, Pennsylvania 15143, USA (☎ 412 741 4763); World Headquarters, H J Heinz Co, PO Box 57, Pittsburgh, Pa 15230, USA (☎ 412 456 5707)

FINLAY, Fiona D M B; da of Sir Graeme Bell Finlay, Bt (d 1987), and June Evangeline, *née* Drake; *b* 7 Feb 1956; *Educ* Univ of Leicester (BA), Univ of Cardiff (Dip Theatre Arts); *Career* asst dir Haymarket Theatre Leicester 1980-81, asst to dir Royal Court Theatre (Young People's Theatre Scheme) Sloane Square 1980-81, asst dir Gateway Theatre Chester 1981-82, asst to dirs of new writing and clasical repertoire Nat Theatre S Bank 1982-85, drama prodr BBC 1988- (drama script ed 1985-88); *Recreations* opera, reading, restaurants, friends; *Style*— Miss Fiona Finlay; BBC TV, Drama Films and Drama Series, Wood Lane, Shepherds Bush Green, London W12 (☎ 081 743 8000, fax 081 749 7520)

FINLAY, Lady; June Evangeline; *née* Drake; da of Col Francis Collingwood Drake, OBE, MC, DL (d 1976), 10 Royal Hussars; *m* 22 May 1953, Sir Graeme Finlay, 1 Bt, ERD (d 1987); 1 s (Sir David Finlay, 2 Bt), 2 da; *Style*— Lady Finlay; 45 Artesian Rd, London W2 5DB (☎ 071 229 6886)

FINLAY, Ronald Adrian (Ron); s of Harry Finlay, of London NW3, and Tess, *née* Matz; *b* 4 Dec 1956; *Educ* Univ Coll Sch London, St John's Coll Cambridge (BA, MA); *Career* Br Market Res Bureau 1979-81, Merrill Lynch 1982-83, dir Valin Pollen Ltd 1986- (joined 1983), sec SDP Hendon S 1984-85; assoc memb Market Res Soc 1980; *Recreations* squash, bridge, hill-walking; *Style*— Ron Finlay, Esq; 24B Belsize Grove, London NW3 4TR (☎ 071 586 8716); Valin Pollen Ltd, 18, Grosvenor Gardens, London SW1W ODH (☎ 071 730 3456, fax 071 730 7445, telex 296846 BIZCOM G)

FINLAY-MAXWELL, Dr David Campbell; s of Luke Greenwood Maxwell (d 1937), and Lillias Maule Finlay (d 1955); *b* 2 March 1923; *Educ* St Paul's, Heriot-Watt Univ Edinburgh (CEng, MIEE), Univ of Leeds (PhD); *m* 1954, Constance Shirley, da of James Douglas Hood, CBE (d 1981); 1 s (Douglas), 1 da (Carol); *Career* Maj Royal Signals SOE Operations 1939-45, served in Europe, India and Malaysia; dir and chm John Gladstone & Co Ltd and John Gladstone & Co (Engrg) 1948-89 (dir and pres 1989-); chm: Manpower Working Party NEDO 1970-73, Wool Industs Research Assoc 1974-77, Textile Research Cncl 1977-82, Wool Textile EDC 1977-79; cncllr and dir Br Textile Cncl 1977-84; UK rep Consultative Ctee for R & D Brussels 1979-84; memb: Cncl Textile Inst 1972-74 (granted fellowship), Textile Industry Advsy Ctee, Leeds Univ Cncl 1974- (hon lectr), Soc of Dyers & Colourists 1950- (granted fellowship), Scientific Devpt Sub Ctee, CBI Science & Research Ctee 1980-87; dir The Wool Fndn (IWS) 1985-, pres Comitextil Sci and Res Ctee Brussels 1979-85, EEC reviewer Esprit prog 1986-, dir and vice chm Sound Recording Bd of Dirs RNIB; hon organizer UK Technical Volunteer Helpers for Blind 1947-; MIEE, CEng, FTI, FSDC; *Recreations* radio propagation, satellite tracking; *Clubs* RSAC, Special Forces; *Style*— Dr David Finlay-Maxwell; Folly Hall House, Cross Lane, Kirkburton, Huddersfield HD8 0ST; John Gladstone & Co Ltd, Wellington Mills, Huddersfield HD3 3HJ (☎ 0484 653437, fax 0484 647321, telex 51442)

FINLAYSON, Dr Niall Diarmid Campbell; s of Dr Duncan Ian Campbell Finlayson, of Edinburgh, and Helen Rita, *née* Blackney; *b* 21 April 1939; *Educ* Loretto, Univ of Edinburgh (BSc, MB ChB, PhD); *m* 12 Aug 1972, Dale Kristin, da of Dr Richmond Karl Anderson, of Chapel Hill, North Carolina, USA; 1 s (Iain b 1977), 1 da (Catriona b 1973); *Career* asst prof of med Cornell Univ Med Coll NY 1970-72, conslt physician Royal Infirmary Edinburgh 1973-, hon sr lectr in med Univ of Edinburgh Med Sch 1973-; memb: American Assoc for the Study of Liver Diseases, BMA, Br Soc of Gastroenterology; FRCP, FRCP (Ed); *Books* Diseases of the Gastro Intestinal Tract and Liver (jtly, 2 edn 1989); *Recreations* music; *Style*— Dr Niall Finlayson; 10 Queen's Crescent, Edinburgh EH9 2AZ (☎ 031 6673969); Gastrointestinal and Liver Service, Royal Infirmary, Lauriston Place, Edinburgh EH3 9YW (☎ 031 229 2477 ext 4648)

FINLEY, Michael John; s of Walter Finley (d 1940), and Grace Marie Butler, *née* Sykes; *b* 22 Sept 1932; *Educ* King Edward VII Sch Sheffield; *m* 19 March 1955, Sheila Elizabeth, da of late Harold Cole, of Osbournby, Lincs; 4 s (Nicholas b 1955, Andrew b 1959, Jonathan b 1967, Robert b 1968); *Career* ed Sheffield Telegraph 1964-69, gen mangr and dir Kent Messenger Group 1979-82 (editorial dir 1969- 79), exec dir Periodical Publishers Assoc 1982-88, dir Fedn Int de la Presse Periodique 1989-; memb Advsy Cncl BBC 1975-80, govr Int Press Fndn 1988-; chm Kent IOD 1980-82, govr Cranbrook Sch 1977-; *Books* Advertising And The Community (contrib, 1969); *Recreations* tennis, golf, snooker, watching rugby, walking; *Style*— Michael Finley, Esq; Sorrento, Staplehurst, Kent; Fipp, Press Foundation House, 5 St Matthew St, London SW1 2JT (☎ 071 873 8158)

FINLINSON, Alastair John; s of Malcolm Everard Finlinson (d 1960), of Brayfield House, Olney, Bucks, and Violet Marion, *née* Leventhorpe (d 1983); *b* 25 Feb 1929; *Educ* Radley, RMA Sandhurst; *m* 19 Jan 1980, Anne Elizabeth, da of Norman Stanley Holland (d 1945), of Saxbys Cowden, Kent; *Career* dist agent Lord Falmouth's Tregothnan Estates 1955-58, asst land cmmr MAFF Somerset 1958-59, asst area agent Cornwall and SW Devon Nat Tst 1959-66, agent W Somerset Nat Tst 1966-71, regnl dir Severn Region Nat Tst 1971-87; ministerial appointee Exmoor Nat Park Ctee 1989; FRICS; *Recreations* gardening, walking, music, conservation; *Style*— Alastair Finlinson, Esq

FINN, Dr (Reginald) Anthony; s of Reginald Lloyd Finn (d 1983), and Alison Beatrix Stuart, *née* Tegner; *b* 31 Oct 1960; *Educ* Harrow, Univ of Edinburgh (BSc), Univ of Cambridge (PhD); *m* Emma Susan Conyngham, da of Wing Cdr Frank William Breeze (d 1977); 1 s (Harry Lloyd Guthrie b 24 April 1989), 1 da (India Rose b 22 Feb 1988); *Career* computer programmer BOC Datasolve 1979, chm Selcar 1981-86 (dir 1979-81), devpt engr Ferranti Int 1983-85, res tutor Univ of Cambridge 1985-89, self-employed res 1989-91; res scientist DSTO/SRL (Australian Dept of Defense) 1991-; int fencer Scotland 1979-81; MIMechE, MRIN; *Recreations* golf, bridge, opera; *Clubs* Lansdowne; *Style*— Dr Anthony Finn; c/o Pattinson, Wells House, Skelton Wood End, Penrith, Cumbria CA11 9UB (☎ 08534 306)

FINN, Hugh Roderick; CBE (1974), DL (Kent 1979); s of George William Finn; *b* 12 April 1911; *Educ* Haileybury; *m* 1954, Muriel Enid (Mel), da of Walter Dale; 2 s; *Career* farmer and co dir; chm: Stonegatefarmers Ltd, Kent Salads Ltd, SSP Ltd; chm: Kent Agric Exec Ctee 1954-68, BBC Agric Advsy Ctee, Gen Advsy Ctee BBC 1966-75, Miny of Agric Regnl Advsy Ctee 1974-80, ARC Hops Tech Ctee 1976-86; memb Lord Chllrs Advsy Ctee (Kent) 1976-86; memb Cncl Protection Rural England 1954-85 (chm Kent Branch 1981-); govr Wye Coll 1948-88 (chm Estates Panel 1954-85); FRZS, FRAgS; *Clubs* Athenaeum; *Style*— Hugh Finn, Esq, CBE, DL; Nackington Farmhouse, Canterbury, Kent CT4 7AD (home ☎ 0227 463 169, office: 0227 763 100)

FINN, Johanna Elizabeth (Mrs Nicholas Siddle); da of Bartholomew Anthony Finn, of London, and Anna Maria, *née* Kreuth; *b* 30 Aug 1951; *Educ* Convent of the Sacred Heart London, UCL (BSc); *m* Sept 1978, Nicholas Charles Siddle, s of Stephen Geoffrey Siddle; 2 s (Benedict Daniel b 20 Jan 1982, Leo Dominic b 1 Oct 1984), 1 da (Chloe Anneliese b 22 June 1990); *Career* King's Coll Hosp London 1972-73, nat admin trainee NHS Nat Training Scheme SE Thames RHA 1973-75, asst admin Northwick Park Hosp Harrow Middx 1975-77, dep sector admin Withington Hosp S Manchester 1977-79, sector admin W Middx Univ Hosp Isleworth 1979-82, unit admin St Mary's Hosp Paddington 1982-85, acting dep dist admin Paddington & North Kensington Health Authy London 1985-86; unit gen mangr: Mile End Hosp and Bethnal Green Hosp Tower Hamlets London 1986-89, Community & Priority Services Tower Hamlets London 1989-90; acting chief exec The Royal London and Assoc Community Services NHS Trust 1990-; govr: Tower Hamlets Coll of Further Educn 1990-, The Princess Alexandra & Newham Coll of Nursing 1990-; assoc memb Inst of Health Service Mangrs 1975; *Recreations* eating, theatre, opera, reading, skiing; *Clubs* October, Hospital Discussion Group; *Style*— Miss Johanna Finn; The Royal London Hospital (Mile End), Bancroft Rd, London E1 4DG (☎ 071 377 7801)

FINN, John Wilson; s of Edwin Finn (d 1968), and Frances Evelyn, *née* Moody (d 1975); *b* 4 Feb 1916; *Educ* Westminster; *m* 24 Aug 1940, Mildred Mary, da of George Edward Bermingham (d 1966); 1 s (Martin Anthony b 1942), 1 da (Susan Mary b 1944); *Career* joined TA 1939, served WW II Maj RA 1939-45; qualified CA 1938; co sec De la Rue Co Ltd 1974-78 (joined 1958); FCA; *Recreations* construction of miniature antique furniture, beagling, opera; *Style*— John Finn, Esq; Pond Oast, Frittenden, Kent TN17 2BE (☎ 058 080 431); Lloyds Bank, High St, Cranbrook, Kent

FINN, Paul Howard; s of Thomas Finn (d 1982), of Heaton, Bradford, West Yorkshire, and Mary, *née* Heathcroft; *b* 10 July 1939; *Educ* St Bede's GS Heaton Bradford; *m* 3 Oct 1964, Jill, da of John France; 3 s (James Alexander b 14 Aug 1969, Robert Adam b 2 March 1972, Charles Edward b 26 March 1974); *Career* articled clerk Clifford Long & Son Bradford 1959-63, qualified chartered accountant 1963, Trevelyan & Co Leeds 1965, Chalmers Impey & Co 1981 (following merger), nat dir Corp Reconstruction and Insolvency Servs Hodgson Impey 1989 (merged 1985), Kidsons Impey 1990 (following merger), md Jamie Group 1970-78; FCA 1974 (ACA 1964), FFB 1974, memb Insolvency Practitioners Assoc; *Books* Insolvency in Business - How to Avoid It: How to Deal With It (1988, 1990); *Recreations* swimming, music, golf; *Clubs* Wig & Pen; *Style*— Paul Finn, Esq; Tong Hall, Tong Village, West Yorkshire LS1 2QH; Kidsons Impey, Chartered Accountants, 41 Park Cross Street, Leeds LS1 2QH (☎ 0532 422666, fax 0532 422038)

FINNEY, His Hon Judge Jarlath John; s of Victor Harold Finney (d 1970), (Lib MP for Hexham 1923-24, subsequently sec gen Lloyd George's Cncl of Action for Peace and Reconstruction) of Dorking, Surrey, and Aileen Rose Finney, *née* Gallagher; *b* 1 July 1930; *Educ* Wimbledon Coll; *m* 27 April 1957, Daisy Emöke, da of Dr Matyas Veszy, formerly of Budapest (d 1959); 2 s (Mark b 1960, Gavin b 1963), 2 da (Patricia b 1958, Victoria b 1965); *Career* Nat Serv 1953-55, 2 Lt 8 RTR 1953-55 (Lt 1955); called to the Bar Gray's Inn 1953; rec of the Crown Ct 1980-86, circuit judge 1986; *Books* Gaming, Lotteries, Fundraising and The Law (1982), Sales Promotion Law (jtly, 1988); *Recreations* books, wild flowers, walking in the country; *Clubs* Wig and Pen; *Style*— His Hon Judge Finney; c/o Ground Floor, 1 Essex Court, Temple, London EC4Y 9AR

FINNEY, Malcolm James; s of Alfred James Finney (d 1983), and Audrey, *née* Saynor; *b* 19 March 1948; *Educ* Univ of Hull, Univ of Sheffield and Univ of Bradford (MSc, BSc); *m* (sep); 2 s (Matthew b 1977, Nicholas b 1980); *Career* Spear and Jackson Int 1970-72, Duncan C Fraser and Co 1972-73, J Henry Schroder Wagg and Co Ltd 1973-76, J F Chown and Co Ltd 1976-79, Grant Thornton 1979-89, Malcolm J Finney & Ptnrs 1989-; MBIM 1975, AFIMA 1972; *Books* Captive Insurance Cos: Tax Strategy 1979, Business Tax Handbook 1978, Companies Operating Overseas and Tax Strategy 1983; Captives: A Tax Analysis, Tolleys International Tax Planning; *Recreations* photography, cars, cycling, reading; *Style*— Malcolm Finney, Esq; 1 The Slype, Gustard Wood, Wheathampstead, Herts AL4 8RY

FINNIS, Prof John Mitchell; s of Maurice Meredith Steriker Finnis, of Adelaide, and Margaret McKellar, *née* Stewart; *b* 28 July 1940; *Educ* St Peter's Coll, St Mark's Coll Adelaide (LLB), Univ of Oxford (DPhil); *m* 20 June 1964, Marie Carmel, *née* McNally; 3 s (John-Paul b 1967, Jerome b 1977, Edmund b 1984), 3 da (Rachel b 1965, Catherine b 1971, Maria b 1974); *Career* assoc in law Univ of California Berkeley 1965-66; Univ of Oxford: fell and praelector in jurisprudence Univ Coll 1966-, Rhodes reader in laws of Br Cwlth and US 1972-89, prof of law and legal philosophy 1989-; prof and head Law Dept Univ of Malawi 1976-78; called to the Bar Gray's Inn 1970, special advsr to Foreign Affrs Ctee of House of Commons on the role of UK Parliament in Canadian Constitution 1980-82; memb Int Theological Cmmn Vatican 1986-; *Books* Natural Law and Natural Rights (1980), Fundamentals of Ethics (1983), Nuclear Deterrence, Morality and Realism (1987), Commonwealth and Dependencies Halsbury's Laws of England (vol 6 1971, 1990); *Style*— Prof John Finnis; 12 Staverton Rd, Oxford OX2 6XJ; University College, Oxford OX1 4BH (☎ 0865 276602); 12 Gray's Inn Sq, London WC1R 5JP (☎ 071 405 8654)

FINSBERG, Sir Geoffrey; MBE (1959), JP (Inner London 1962), MP (C) Hampstead and Highgate 1983-; o s of Montefiore Finsberg, MC (d 1972), and May, *née*

Grossman (d 1979); *b* 13 June 1926; *Educ* City of London Sch; *m* 1, 1969, Pamela Benbow (d 1989), da of Roland Benbow Hill (d 1973); 1 step s; m 2, Jan 1990, Yvonne Elizabeth, *née* Wright; 2 step s; *Career* memb: Hampstead Borough Cncl 1949-65, Camden Borough Cncl 1964-74; dir London and SE TSB 1963-75, industl relations advsr Gt Universal Stores 1968-79 and 1983-, dep chm SE Regnl Bd TSB 1986-89; memb: Cncl CBI 1968-79, POUNC 1970-77; former nat chm Young Cons, chm Gr London Cons local govt ctees; MP (Cons) Hampstead 1970-1983, vice chm Cons Party Orgn 1975-79 and 1984-87, opposition spokesman Gr London 1974-79; Parly under sec: Environment 1979-81, DHSS 1981-83; memb: Parly Assembly of the Cncl of Europe 1983- (delgn ldr 1987-), Western Euro Union; Freeman City of London; holder of Cdr's Cross 1 Class Order of Merit of the Austrian Republic, Grosse Goldene Ehrenzeichen für Verdienste um die Republik Österreich verliehen; Encomienda de la Expresada Orden de Isabel la Catolica of Spain; kt 1984; *Recreations* bridge; *Clubs* Royal Over-Seas League; *Style*— Sir Geoffrey Finsberg, MBE, JP, MP; 80 Westbere Rd, London NW2 3RU (☎ 071 435 5320)

FINTRIE, Lord; James Alexander Norman Graham; s of Marquess of Graham; *b* 16 Aug 1973; *Educ* Belhaven Hill, Eton; *Style*— Lord Fintrie; Auchmar, Drymen, Glasgow

FIREMAN, Bruce Anthony; s of Michael Fireman; *b* 14 Feb 1944; *Educ* Kilburn GS, Jesus Coll Cambridge; *m* 1968, Barbara, *née* Mollett; *Career* slr 1970, merchant banker, chm Fireman Rose Ltd 1986-; dir: Newspaper Publishing plc (The Independent) 1986-, D G Durham Group plc 1988-; *Style*— Bruce Fireman, Esq; c/o Fireman Rose Ltd, 39 Botolph Lane, London EC3R 8DE (☎ 071 929 4001); 19 Southwood Hall, London N6 (☎ 071 444 7125)

FIRMAN, Clive Edward; s of John Edward Firman (d 1984), of Rustington, Sussex, and Rosaline Mary, *née* Smith; *b* 22 May 1951; *Educ* Cranleigh Sch Surrey, Univ of London (BA); *m* 1974, Wendy, da of John Gill Burrell; 1 s (Duncan Mark Edward b 4 Jan 1981), 1 da (Carolyn Mary b 16 Oct 1982); *Career* NHS: trainee admin 1973-74, personnel mangr Harrow Health Authy 1974-76, admin St George's Hosp London 1976-78, dep sector admin rising to sector admin Waltham Forest 1979-81, admin Tooting Bec Hosp 1981-86, gen mangr All Saints' Hosp Birmingham 1986-; memb Inst of Health Serv Mgmnt 1976, MIPM 1978, MBIM 1986; *Recreations* sch governance, badminton, swimming, weight-training, mainly family; *Style*— Clive Firman, Esq; All Saints' Hospital, Lodge Rd, Birmingham B18 5SD (☎ 021 523 5151)

FIRMIN, David; s of Eric Henry, of 2 Bay Walk, Aldwick Bay, W Sussex, and Margaret Freda, *née* Hales; *b* 20 Sept 1937; *Educ* The Leys Sch Cambridge, Brixton Sch of Bldg; *m* 20 Sept 1979, Zara Synolda, da of Maj John Atholl Duncan, MC (d 1983) and Hon (Doreen) Synolda, *née* Butler, da 27 (17) Baron Donboyne, of Sloane St, SW1; 2 s (Philip Duncan b 1981, Robert Charles b 1985), 1 da (Zoe Charlotte b 1980); *Career* sr ptnr Sidney Kaye Firmin Partnership 1968-; ARIBA 1965, FRIBA 1970; *Recreations* golf; *Clubs* Carlton, New Zealand Golf (Surrey); *Style*— David Firmin, Esq; 11 Westmoreland Place, London SW1V 4AA (☎ 071 834 2520); SKF Architects, Thavies Inn House, 5 Holborn Circus, London EC1 (☎ 071 583 8811)

FIRMSTON-WILLIAMS, Peter; CBE (1987, OBE 1979); s of Geoffrey Firmston-Williams (d 1964), and Muriel Firmston-Williams; *b* 30 Aug 1918; *Educ* Harrow; *m* 1945, Margaret, da of Wilfred Butters Beaulah (d 1967); 1 s, 1 da; *Career* Capt (mil) N Africa, Low Countries and Germany; md: Cooper and Co's Stores Ltd 1958-62, Key Markets Ltd 1962-71, Asda Stores Ltd 1971-81; dir: Assoc Dairies Ltd 1973-81, BAT Stores 1981-82; dep chm Woolworth Hldgs 1982-; chm: Covent Garden Market Authy 1982-, Retail Consortium 1984-, Flowers and Plants Assoc 1985-; *Recreations* golf, water skiing, wind surfing; *Style*— Peter Firmston-Williams, Esq, CBE; Oak House, 12 Pembroke Road, Moor Park, Northwood, Middx

FIRNBERG, David; s of Leopold Bernard Firnberg (d 1984), and Karin Lubof Ernestine, *née* Kellgren; *b* 1 May 1930; *Educ* Merchant Taylors'; *m* 1957, Sylvia Elizabeth, da of William C du Cros; 1 s (Jonathan b 1969), 3 da (Nichola b 1960, Sarah b 1961, Virginia b 1965); *Career* dir Nat Computing Centre 1975-80; chm: The Networking Centre Ltd 1985-, Easys Ltd 1989-; pres: Assoc of Project Mangrs 1979-84, Br Computer Soc 1983-84; memb Cncl Parly IT Ctee; chm: IT Support for Disabled People Project, UK Cncl for Computing Devpt; Freeman City of London; FID, FBCS, FIIS; *Books* Cassell's Spelling Dictionary; Computers, Management and Information; *Recreations* writing; *Clubs* Wig and Pen; *Style*— David Firnberg, Esq; The Great House, Tring, Herts HP23 6NX; Albas, 11360 Durban-Corbieres, France

FIRTH, Geoffrey Shipston; s of Harold Firth (d 1959), of Halifax , and Gladys, *née* Shipston (d 1961); *b* 27 Jan 1934; *Educ* Silcoates Sch Wakefield; *m* 16 April 1960, Patricia Anne, da of Thomas Henry Mines (d 1984), of Hove; 2 da (Pamela Anne b 1961, Angela Mary b 1963); *Career* RAPC 1952-54; md James Royston Co Ltd 1959-80 (co sec 1956-59), dir Hawkins & Tipson Ltd 1969-82, md Smith Wires Ltd 1982-; chm: Wire and Wire Rope Indust Trg Assoc, Young Enterprise Area Bd (calderdale); memb Rotary Club Halifax Calder; Master Worshipful Co of Tinplate Worker alias Wire Workers 1988-89 (memb 1965); memb IOD 1960; *Recreations* golf, walking, photography; *Clubs* City Livery; *Style*— Geoffrey Firth, Esq; Fourways, Hammerstone Leach Lane, Elland, West Yorkshire HX5 0QW (☎ 0422 372077); Smith Wires Ltd, Charlestown Rd, Halifax , West Yorks HX3 6AB (☎ 0422 341211, telex 51188 SMITH G)

FIRTH, Rt Rev Peter James; *see*: Malmesbury, Bishop of

FIRTH, Prof Sir Raymond William; s of Wesley Hugh Bourne Firth (d 1977), and Marie Elizabeth Jane, *née* Cartmill (d 1962); *b* 25 March 1901; *Educ* Auckland GS NZ, Auckland Univ Coll (MA), LSE (PhD); *m* 1936, Rosemary, da of Sir Gilbert Upcott, KCB (d 1967); 1 s; *Career* lectr and acting prof of anthropology Univ of Sydney 1930-32, lectr in anthropology LSE 1933-35 (reader 1936-44), prof of anthropology Univ of London 1944-68 (now emeritus), visiting prof various USA univs, research in Tikopia Solomon Islands and Kelantan Malaysia; author of numerous pubns on anthropological subjects; life pres Assoc Social Anthropologists; Hon degrees: Oslo, Michigan, Exeter, E Anglia, Br Columbia, Chicago, Australian NU, Auckland, Cracow, London; hon fell LSE 1970; FBA; kt 1973; *Recreations* Romanesque painting and sculpture, early music; *Clubs* Athenaeum; *Style*— Prof Sir Raymond Firth; 33 Southwood Ave, London N6 (☎ 081 348 0768)

FISCH, Ian (Isadore); s of Solomon Fisch (d 1985), of Leeds, and Rebecca, *née* Swift; *b* 28 Dec 1924; *Educ* Nether Edge GS Sheffield, Univ of Sheffield (LLB); *m* 2 March 1952, Phyllis Miriam, da of Leon Elgrod (d 1983); 1 s (Nigel Ian b 1959), 3 da (Suzanne Joy b 1953, Juliet Diane b 1955, Alison Jane b 1963); *Career* slr; chm: Arncliffe Holdings plc, Dewsbury Social Servs Appeal Tbnl, Driving Standards Agency Tbnl; pres NSPCC Leeds Childrens Centre Appeal; former pres: Leeds Lodge B'nai B'rith, Street Lane Gardens Synagogue; memb Ctee Home Farm Trust; former chm: Children's Aid Soc (Leeds), Leeds Friends of Bar-Ilan Univ; fndr The Isadore Fisch Charitable Fndn; Lord of the Manor of Sutton Holland; memb Law Soc and Leeds Law Soc; *Recreations* swimming, skiing, tennis, reading; *Clubs* RAC; *Style*— Ian Fisch, Esq; Appartment 30, The Moorings, Harrogate Road, Leeds LS17 8EN (☎ 0532 683775); 114 Monarch Court, Lyttelton Road, London NW2; Follifoot Hall, Follifoot Ridge, Pannal Road, Harrogate, N Yorkshire HG3 1RU (☎ 0423 879988, fax 0423 873495, car 0860 620989)

FISCHEL, John Roy; s of late Roy Fischel, MC; *b* 2 Sept 1924; *Educ* Cheltenham and RN; *m* 1952, Anita, da of late Capt Maximilian Despard, DSC, RN; 2 s, 3 da; *Career* commodity merchant; L M Fischel & Co Ltd: dir 1960-, chm 1966-, non-exec dir 1984-90; Baltic Mercantile & Shipping Exchange 1975-80; underwriting memb Lloyd's; *Recreations* shooting; *Clubs* Castaways, RCC, RNSA, MCC, Kent CCC; *Style*— John Fischel, Esq; The Mount, Shoreham, nr Sevenoaks, Kent (☎ 095 92 2071)

FISH, Anthony William (Tony); s of George Fish (d 1952), of Weybridge, Surrey, and Edith Eliza, *née* Donaldson; *b* 16 April 1951; *Educ* Kingston GS Kingston Surrey; *m* 23 Nov 1974 (m dis 1987), Suzanne Hobley; 2 da (Jo b 1975, Sarah b 1983); *Career* BBC Radio: radio presenter London 1975-81, radio trainer local radio trg unit 1981-83, prog organiser York 1983-88, station mangr Newcastle 1988-; govr Newcastle Free Festival; memb Radio Acad; *Recreations* cycling; *Style*— Tony Fish, Esq; BBC Radio Newcastle, Broadcasting Centre, Barrack Rd, Fenham, Newcastle upon Tyne NE99 1RN (☎ 091 232 4141)

FISH, Prof Francis (Frank); OBE (1989); s of William Fish (d 1980), of Houghton-le-Spring, Tyne and Wear, an Phyllis Fish, *née* Griffiths (d 1983); *b* 20 April 1924; *Educ* Houghton-Le-Spring GS, Sunderland Tech Coll (BPharm, external London Univ), Univ of Glasgow (PhD); *m* 10 Aug 1949, Hilda Mary, da of James Percy Brown (d 1980), of Houghton-le-Spring; 2 s (David James, Andrew William); *Career* Univ of Strathclyde (formerly The Royal Coll of Sci and Tech Glasgow) asst lectr and lectr 1946-62, sr lectr 1962-69, reader in pharmacognosy and forensic sci 1969-76, prof and head Forensic Sci Unit 1976-78, dean Sch of Pharmaceutical Sci 1977-78 (vice dean 1974-77); Univ of London: dean Sch of Pharmacy 1978-88, prof pharmacy 1988, emeritus prof 1989-; author of res papers in pharmaceutical and forensic jls; memb: Chemistry Pharmacy and Standards Sub Ctee of Ctee on Safety of The Br Pharmacopoeia Cmmn, Ctee on Review of Medicines; chm Post Qualification Educn Bd for Health Serv Pharmacists in Scotl former: memb UGC Med Sub Ctee, chm UGC panel on studies allied to medicine, memb Ctee on Safety of Meds, memb Nuffield Fndn Ctee of Inquiry into Pharmacy, vice chm DHSS Standing Pharmaceutical Advsy Ctee, vice pres Cncl of Forensic Sci Soc; FRPharmS 1946; *Recreations* gardening, golf, wine-making; *Clubs* Crieff Golf; *Style*— Prof Frank Fish, OBE; Trollheim, Connaught Terrace, Crieff, Perthshire

FISH, George Marshall; JP; s of George Frederick Fish (d 1940), of Hamilton House, and Dorothy, *née* Creswell (d 1984); *b* 26 June 1928; *Educ* Sedbergh; *m* 9 Feb 1952, Josephine Lilian, da of Joseph Sydney Plant Lowater; 3 s (William, James, Charles); *Career* Capt RA 1946-48, Capt S Notts Hussars, 350 Heavy Regt RA (TA) 1948-52; chartered builder; currently vice chm Notts Magistrates Cts Ctee (chm Bldgs and Boundaries Sub Ctee), dep chm Nottingham PSD, chm and tstee Nottingham Bldg Fndn; FCIOB, FFB; *Recreations* cricket, walking, golf, gardening; *Style*— George Fish, Esq, JP; The Manor House, Old Main Rd, Bulcote, Notts NG14 5GU (☎ 0602 313159); Great Freeman St, Nottingham

FISH, William Francis (Frank); s of William Francis Fish, of Lancs, and Marie, *née* Williams (d 1942); *b* 26 Feb 1940; *Educ* St Josephs Coll Darjeeling, Xaverian Coll, Univ of Manchester (LLB); *m* 6 Jan 1967, Mary Rosetta Hughes, da of Dr Peter Esmond Gosgrove, of NI; 1 s (Kevin b 1969), 3 da (Paula b 1968, Anne-Marie b 1971, Helen b 1980); *Career* slr; pt/t lectr in law Univ of Manchester; sometime dep dist registrar of the High Court and Dep County Court Registrar 1974-76; sometime asst dep coroner of the High Peak Derbys 1978; memb area ctee No 10 Legal Aid Area; *Books* Butterworth's Family Law Service (ed); *Recreations* walking, swimming, angling, gardening; *Style*— Frank Fish, Esq; Mount Delphi, 11 Melia Close, Rawtenstall, Rossendale, Lancashire (☎ 0706 220 487); 61 Mosley Street, Manchester M2 3HZ (☎ 051 236 0321)

FISHBURN, J Dudley; s of late Eskdale Fishburn and Mrs Peter Murray-Lee; *b* 8 June 1946; *Educ* Eton, Harvard; *m* 1981, Victoria, da of Sir Jack Boles and step da of Lady Anne Boles (da of 12 Earl Waldegrave); 2 da (Alice b 1982, Honor b 1984); *Career* exec ed The Economist; (Cons) candidate IOW 1979; pres Harvard Club of London; tstee Open Univ Foundation; treas Br American Arts Assoc; dir Aidcom Int plc; *Clubs* Harvard (NY), Brooks's; *Style*— J Dudley Fishburn Esq; 16 West Halkin St, London SW1 (☎ 071 235 1184); The Old Rectory, Englefield, Berkshire (☎ 0734 302497)

FISHER, (Jervis) Andrew; s of John George Fisher, of Birmingham, and Joyce, *née* Horton; *b* 23 Oct 1955; *Educ* Malvern, Univ of London (LLB); *m* 3 April 1982, Catherine Maura, da of Peter Phillimore Swatman, of Gwynedd; 1 s (Alexander b 1984), 1 da (Lara b 1986); *Career* barr; *Style*— Andrew Fisher, Esq; The Ark, Noah's Green, Feckenham, Worcs; Coleridge Chambers, Citadel, 190 Corporation St, Birmingham B4 6QD (☎ 021 233 3303, fax 021 236 6966)

FISHER, Hon Mrs (Audrey Joan); *née* Vernon; 3 da of 5 Baron Lyveden (d 1973); *b* 1922; *m* 1, 14 Nov 1940 (m dis), Russell Parker; 3 s, 1 da; m 2, 17 Nov 1983, Maurice Fisher; *Style*— The Hon Mrs Fisher

FISHER, Hon Benjamin Vavasseur; s (by 1 m) of 3 Baron Fisher; *b* 21 Sept 1958; *m* 31 Aug 1985, Pamela M, o da of A Cooper, of Tolcarne, Rough Close, Staffs; 1 s (Peter Vavasseur b 13 Oct 1986), 1 da (Rose Kathleen b 31 Oct 1988); *Style*— Hon Benjamin Fisher

FISHER, Charles Murray; s of Kenneth John Fisher, of Cheltenham, and Beryl Dorothy, *née* Pearman; *b* 24 Dec 1949; *Educ* Cheltenham Coll, St Edmund Hall Oxford, Harvard Business Sch; *m* 29 Sept 1984, Denise Ellen, *née* Williams; 2 da (Louisa Dora b 13 Dec 1985, Jasmine Diana b 24 June 1987); *Career* int trainee Petrofina SA in Bussels and Paris 1971-76; dir Sandfords Ltd 1976-80 (md 1980-84); dir Sharpe & Fisher plc 1980-84 (chief exec 1985-89, chm 1989-), non-exec dir South-Western Electricity plc 1990-; chm Cheltenham Arts Festivals Ltd 1990; Freeman of City of London, Liveryman Worshipful Co of Builders Merchants; *Recreations* tennis, travel, reading; *Clubs* MCC, Turf, Annabel's; *Style*— Charles Fisher, Esq; Hampnett Lodge, Hampnett, Glos GL54 3NN (☎ 0451 60596); Sharpe & Fisher plc, Gloucester Road, Cheltenham, Glos (☎ 0242 224833)

FISHER, Dudley Henry; CBE (1990); s of Arthur Fisher (d 1926), and Mary Eliza, *née* Greenacre (d 1965); *b* 22 Aug 1922; *Educ* City of Norwich Sch; *m* 1, 1946, Barbara Lilian Sexton (d 1984); 1 s (Christopher), 2 da (Pamela, Angela); m 2, 1985, Jean Mary Livingstone, da of late Dr and Mrs R B Miller of Stafford House, Cowbridge, S Glam; *Career* Flt Lt RAF 1941-46; chm Wales Region British Gas Corporation 1974-87 (fin dir 1968-70, dep chm 1970-74); memb: Audit Cmmn for Local Authorities in Eng and Wales 1983-88, Bdcasting Cncl for Wales 1985-90, Cncl Univ of Wales Coll of Cardiff 1988-; chm: CBI Cncl for Wales 1987-89 (memb 1974-77), Admin Ctee WEC 1986-89; hon treas Br Nat Ctee World Energy Conference 1977-89, nat tstee Help the Aged Charity 1987-, govr United World Coll of the Atlantic 1987-; High Sheriff South Glamorgan 1988-89; *Recreations* golf, music, reading; *Clubs* Cardiff & County; *Style*— Dudley Fisher, Esq, CBE; Norwood Edge, 8 Cyncoed Ave, Cardiff CF2 6SU (☎ 0222 757958)

FISHER, Hon Geoffrey Robert Chevallier; 5 s of Baron Fisher of Lambeth, GCVO, PC (Life Peer, d 1972), formerly 99 Archbishop of Canterbury, and Rosamond Chevallier, *née* Forman (d 1986); *b* 4 April 1926; *Educ* Repton, Emmanuel Coll Cambridge (BA, MB BChir); *m* 20 May 1961, Jill Audrey, eldest da of James Henry

Cooper, of New Malden, Surrey; 2 s, 1 da; *Career* Surgn Lt RN (Emergency Res); DObstRCOG 1952; *Style*— The Hon Robert Fisher; 3 Wendover Drive, New Malden, Surrey

FISHER, Geoffrey Wilson O'Neill; OBE (Mil 1943), DFC (1941 and Bar 1943); s of Rev Walter Francis O'Neill Fisher (d 1955), and Elizabeth Gladys, *née* Wilson (d 1959); *b* 10 July 1921; *Educ* HMS Worcester, RAF Staff Coll, Joint Services Staff Coll; *m* 1, 1945, Kathleen Helliwell, *née* Forester Parker (d 1960); m 2, 12 July 1961, Olive Mary, da of Arthur Dunwell (d 1960), of Otley, Yorks; 3 s (Simon b 1962, Michael b 1964, Paul b 1966); *Career* Wing Cdr RAF 1939-61, active serv in 149 and 101 Sqdns Bomber Cmd as Pilot and Flt Cdr; cmd: 207 Sqdn B29 (Washington) 1952-53, 139 Jamaica Sqdn (Canberra) 1958-59; ret 1961; co dir 1970-73; farmer; *Recreations* history, biography, sailing; *Clubs* RAFYC and Cruising Assoc; *Style*— Geoffrey Fisher, Esq, OBE, DFC; Cotswold, Jack Straw's Lane, Headington, Oxford OX3 0DW (☎ 0865 62033)

FISHER, Gerald (Gerry); s of Oliver Charles Fisher (d 1980), and Margaret, *née* Eyles (d 1978); *b* 23 June 1926; *Educ* Bishopshalt Sch Hillingdon Middx, Watford Tech Sch; *m* 20 Jan 1951, Jean Aline, da of late John Hawkins; 1 s (Cary Adam); *Career* RN 1943-46; draughtsman De Havilland Aircraft Co 1943, clapper loader Alliance Films 1946, asst cameraman Br Lion 1949, camera operator on 18 films mostly with Jack Hildyard 1957-67, first film as cinematographer Accident 1967, cinematographer on 50 films including 8 with Joseph Losey, notably The Go-Between and Don Giovanni; memb: Br Soc Cinematographers 1967, BAFTA 1975; *Style*— Gerry Fisher, Esq; Pebble Cottage, River Bank, Hurstfield Rd, W Molesey, Surrey KT8 9QX (☎ 081 979 5498)

FISHER, Hon Sir Henry Arthur Pears; el s of Most Rev and Rt Hon Baron Fisher of Lambeth, GCVO, PC (d 1972), formerly 99 Archbishop of Canterbury, and Rosamond (d 1986), da of Rev Arthur Forman; br Hon Humphrey Fisher, Hon Robert Fisher and Hon Temple Fisher *qqqv*; *b* 20 Jan 1918; *Educ* Marlborough, Ch Ch Oxford; *m* 18 Dec 1948, Felicity, da of late Eric Sutton, of Cheyne Place, Chelsea; 1 s (Thomas Henry Sutton b 1958), 3 da (Emma b 1949, Lucy b 1951, Francesca b 1955); *Career* served WW II Leics Regt & at Staff Coll Quetta, also as Staff Offr (GSO 14th Army 1945, rank of Hon Lt-Col 1946); chm Appeal Ctee of Panel on Take-overs & Mergers 1981-86; pres Wolfson Coll Oxford 1975-85, fellow (emeritus 1976-) All Souls 1946-73 (sub-warden 1965-67), memb Cncl Marlborough Coll 1965-82 (chm 1977-81), chm Governing Body Imperial Coll 1974-88, tstee Pilgrim Tst (chm 1979-83 and 1989-); barr 1947, QC 1960, recorder Canterbury 1962-68, High Ct Judge (Queen's Bench) 1968-70, chm Gen Cncl Bar 1966-68 (vice-chm 1965-66, memb 1959-63 & 1964-68); vice pres Senate of Inns of Court 1966-68 & of Bar Assoc for Commerce Finance & Industry 1973-; chm various ctees of inquiry (most recently (1979-80) into self-regulation at Lloyd's); chm Jt Lib/Soc Democrat Cmmn on Constitutional Reform; former memb Cncl on Tbnls and Law Reform Ctee; memb BBC Programmes Complaints Cmmn 1972-79; kt 1968; *Style*— The Hon Sir Henry Fisher; c/o Wolfson College, Oxford (☎ 0865 274100)

FISHER, Hon Humphrey Richmond; 4 s of Baron Fisher of Lambeth GCVO, PC (*d* 1972, Life Peer); br Hon Sir Henry and Hon Geoffrey Fisher *qv*; *b* 21 Aug 1923; *Educ* Repton; *m* 22 July 1959, Diana Beresford (writer for the Australian magazine *Woman's Day*), o da of C Beresford Davis; *Career* Lt RA, film technician and producer 1946-54, exec producer BBC TV 1954-64, rep Australia and NZ 1964-67 and head of science and features BBC TV 1967-69, dir of TV features Australian Broadcasting Cmmn 1969-; *Style*— The Hon Humphrey Fisher; 32 South St, Edgecliff, NSW 2027, Australia

FISHER, Lady Jane Angela; da of George Cecil Paulet (d 1961), and sis of 18 Marquess of Winchester, *qv*; *b* 15 Nov 1939; *m* 1972, Christopher John Fisher; *Career* raised to rank of Marquess's da 1970; *Style*— The Lady Jane Fisher

FISHER, (Michael Laurens) Jeremy; s of Edwin Fisher, of Barleys, Offham, Lewes (d 1947), and Theodora Cecilia (d 1976); *b* 13 Feb 1929; *Educ* Eton, ChCh Oxford (MA); *m* 1958, Susan, da of Capt Richard Lovatt, OBE, RN (d 1941); 2 s (Nicholas, James); *Career* ptnr Colegrave & Co 1961-75, conslt Grenfell & Colegrave 1986-87 ptnr 1975-86; memb Cncl: Stock Exchange 1976-86 (memb 1960-89), memb Cncls Membership and Quotations Ctees 1987 and 1988; *Style*— Jeremy Fisher, Esq; 21 Flood St, London SW3

FISHER, John Adrian; s of Henry William Fisher (d 1986), and Bessie, *née* Clymer; *b* 8 July 1943; *Educ* Ross-on-Wye GS Herefs, Aston Univ (BSc); *m* 28 Jan 1966, Julie Anne, da of Cyril Joseph Smith (d 1971); 2 da (Karen b 1966, Claire b 1972); *Career* md: Chance Pilkington Group plc 1987, Change Pilkington Ltd 1984-87 (marketing dir 1980-), Chance Pilkington 1987- (chm and dir various subsidiaries 1980-87); former pres Colnyn Bay Lions; *Recreations* wine, food; *Style*— John Fisher, Esq; Carreg-y-Bryn, Llanfair Rd, Abergele, Clwyd (☎ 0745 824565); Change Pilkington Ltd, Glascoed Rd, St Aspah Clwyd (☎ 0745 583301, fax 0745 584913)

FISHER, Prof John Robert; s of John Robert Fisher, of 31 Anzac Ave, Barrow-in-Furness, Cumbria, and Eleanor, *née* Parker; *b* 6 Jan 1943; *Educ* Barrow GS, UCL (BA, MPhil), Univ of Liverpool (PhD); *m* 1 Aug 1966, (Elizabeth) Ann, da of Stephen Gerard Postlethwaite, of 36 Carlton Ave, Barrow-in-Furness; 3 s (David John b 27 Sept 1967, Nicholas Stephen b 10 Dec 1970, Martin Joseph b 27 Aug 1973); *Career* Univ of Liverpool: lectr 1966-75, sr lectr 1975-81, dir Inst of Latin American Studies 1983-, dean Faculty of Arts 1986-, prof 1987; chm Soc of Latin American Studies 1986-88; FRHistS 1975; *Books* Government and Society in Colonial Peru (1970), Silver Mines and Silver Miners in Colonial Peru (1976), Commercial Relations between Spain and Spanish America 1778-1797 (1985); *Recreations* theatre, music, walking, gardening, travel; *Style*— Prof John Fisher; 27 Stapleton Ave, Greasby, Wirral L49 2QT (☎ 051 677 9091); University of Liverpool, PO Box 147, Liverpool L69 3BY (☎ 051 794 3078, fax 051 708 6502, telex 627095 G)

FISHER, 3 Baron (UK 1909); John Vavasseur Fisher; DSC (1944), JP (Norfolk 1970); s of 2 Baron (d 1955, himself s of Adm of the Fleet, 1 Baron (Sir John) Fisher, GCB, OM, GCVO); *b* 24 July 1921; *Educ* Stowe, Trinity Coll Cambridge; *m* 1, 25 July 1949 (m dis 1969), Elizabeth Ann Penelope, yr da of late Maj Herbert P Holt, MC; 2 s (Hon Patrick *qv*, Hon Benjamin b 1958), 2 da (Hon Frances b 1951, Hon Bridget b 1956); m 2, 1970, Hon Rosamund Anne, da of 12 Baron Clifford of Chudleigh and formerly w of Geoffrey Forrester Fairbairn (*see* Fisher, Baroness); *Heir* s; *Career* sometime Lt RNVR WWII; dir Kilverstone Latin American Zoo 1973; memb: Eastern Gas Bd 1961-70, E Anglian Economic Planning Cncl 1972; DL Norfolk 1968-82; *Style*— The Rt Hon the Lord Fisher, DSC, JP; Kilverstone Hall, Thetford, Norfolk (☎ 0842 2222)

FISHER, Jonathan Simon; s of Aubrey Fisher; *b* 24 Feb 1958; *Educ* St Dunstan's Coll, N London Poly (BA), St Catharines Coll Cambridge (LLB); *m* 21 Dec 1980, Paula Yvonne, da of Rev Louis Goldberg (d 1988); 2 s (Benjamin b 1984, David b 1990), 1 da (Hannah b 1986); *Career* called to the Bar Gray's Inn 1980 ad eundem Inner Temple 1985; visiting fell City Univ, UK case corr Jl of Int Banking Law; memb: Justice, Selden Soc, The Maccabaens; *Style*— Jonathan Fisher, Esq; 5 King's Bench Walk, Temple, London EC4 (☎ 071 353 4713, fax 071 353 5459)

FISHER, Lady Karen Jean; *née* Carnegie; da of 13 Earl of Northesk; *b* 22 Dec 1951; *Educ* Queen's Coll London; *m* 1977, Hon Patrick Vavasseur Fisher, *qv*; 2 s (John b 1979, Benjamin b 1986), 3 da (Juliet b 1978, Penelope b 1982, Suzannah b 1984); *Career* dir Macrae Farms Ltd 1981-; memb for Risby Ward on St Edmundsbury Borough Cncl 1989-; chm Appeals for Suffolk Red Cross 1989-; memb Bd of Govrs Riddlesworth Hall Sch Norfolk; *Style*— The Lady Karen Fisher; Highwayman's Vineyard, Heath Barn Farm, Risby, Bury St Edmunds, Suffolk

FISHER, Keith Plunket; s of Francis St George Fisher (d 1990), of Cragg, and Patricia, *née* Lyon (d 1955); *b* 28 Oct 1935; *Educ* Harrow; *m* 1 (m dis), Anne, da of Percy Collingwood Charleton; 1 s (Kiwa b 1956); m 2, 1986, Julia, da of Derek Pattinson; 2 s (Jeremy b 1987 d 1987, Alexander b 1989); *Career* partner Overton Shirley & Barry 1981-; landowner Higham Estate 1990-; *Style*— Keith Fisher, Esq; Cragg, Cockermouth, Cumbria (☎ 07687 76277); 30 Stephendale Rd, London (☎ 071 248 0355)

FISHER, Kenneth John; s of Stanley Joseph Fisher (d 1983), of High Beckside, Dalton-in-Furness, Cumbria, and Gertrude Isabel, *née* Riddi (d 1980); *b* 26 June 1927; *Educ* Uppingham, St John's Coll Cambridge (MA, LLM); *m* 8 May 1954, Mary Florence, da of William Isaac Towers, JP (d 1971), of The Croft, Abbey Road, Barrow-in-Furness, Cumbria; 1 s ((Stephen) John b 6 Oct 1957), 1 da (Anne Rosemary (Mrs Biggar) b 24 April 1956); *Career* Sub Lt RNVR 1945-48; slr 1953; sr ptnr Kendall & Fisher ; chm: Agric Land Tbnl (Northern Area), Supplementary Benefit Appeal Tbnl, Med Servs Ctee for Cumbria, govrs of Chetwynd Sch, Dalton and Dist Recreational Charity Tst ; memb: Cumbria Family Health Servs Authy, Area Ctee, The Law Soc; past pres: N Lonsdale Law Assoc, N Lonsdale Lowick and Cartmel Agric Soc; pres Barrow-in-Furness Branch Royal Soc of St George; life govr Imperial Cancer Research Fund; chm Govrs of Chetwynde Sch, life memb Lancs RFC; FRC; *Recreations* rugby, cricket, skiing, gardening; *Clubs* Hawks, Cambridge LX, Uppingham Rovers, Cambridge Union; *Style*— Kenneth J Fisher, Esq; Glenside House, Springfield Rd, Ulverston, Cumbria LA12 OEJ (☎ 0229 53437); 68 Market St, Dalton-in-Furness, Cumbria LA15 8AD (☎ 0229 62126, fax 0229 62083)

FISHER, Margery Lilian Edith; da of Sir Henry Samuel Edwin Turner (d 1978), and Edith Emily Rose (d 1948); *b* 21 March 1913; *Educ* Amberley House Sch New Zealand, Somerville Coll Oxford (MA, BLitt); *m* 1936, James Maxwell McConnell Fisher (d 1970), s of Kenneth Fisher (d 1945); 2 s (Edmund, Adam), 3 da (Selina, Anstice, Clemency); *Career* freelance writer; *Books* Intent upon Reading (1961), Matters of Fact, Who's Who in Children's Books (1975), The Bright Face of Danger (1986); sole writer ed and publisher of Growing Point (bi-monthly journal of reviews of books for children and young people); *Recreations* music, gardening; *Style*— Mrs Margery Fisher; Ashton Manor, Northampton NN7 2JL (☎ 0604 862277)

FISHER, Mark; MP (Lab) Stoke-on-Trent Central 1983-; s of Sir Nigel Thomas Loveridge Fisher, MC, *qv*, by his 1 w, Lady Gloria Vaughan, da of 7 Earl of Lisburne; *b* 29 Oct 1944; *Educ* Eton, Trinity Coll Cambridge; *m* 1971, Ghilly (Mrs Ingrid Hunt), da of late James Hoyle Geach; 2 s, 2 da; *Career* former principal Tattenhall Educn Centre; former documentary writer and film producer; contested (Lab) Leek 1979; memb: Staffs CC 1981-85, Treasy and Civil Service Select Ctee 1983-86, BBC Gen Advsy Cncl 1987-, Cncl Policy Studies Inst 1989-; dep pro-chllr Univ of Keele 1989-; opposition whip 1985-86, shadow min for Arts and Media 1987-; *Books* City Centres, City Cultures (1988); *Style*— Mark Fisher, Esq, MP; House of Commons, London SW1A 0AA

FISHER, Max Henry (Fredy); s of Dr Friedrich Fischer (d 1971), of Locarno, and Sophia Baks (d 1965); *b* 30 May 1922; *Educ* Fichte Gymnasium Berlin, Rendcomb Coll, Lincoln Coll Oxford (MA); *m* 1952, Rosemary Margaret, da of Dr Leslie Algernon Ivan Maxwell (d 1964), of Melbourne; 2 s (Stephen, Andrew), 1 da (Caroline); *Career* ed Financial Times 1973-80; dir: S G Warburg & Co Ltd 1981-, Commercial Union Assurance Co plc 1981-, Booker plc 1981-; govr LSE 1980-; *Recreations* music; *Clubs* RAC; *Style*— Fredy Fisher; 16 Somerset Sq, Addison Rd, W14 8EE; 2 Finsbury Ave, EC2M 2PR

FISHER, Sir Nigel Thomas Loveridge; MC (1945); s of Cdr Sir Thomas Fisher, KBE, RN, by his w Aimée Constance (who m 1926, subsequent to Sir Thomas's death (1925), and as his 1 w, Sir Geoffrey Shakespeare, 1 Bt, PC); through his mother Sir Nigel is half-bro of Sir William Shakespeare, 2 Bt, *qv*; Sir Nigel is also 3 cous twice removed of late Lord Fisher of Lambeth; *b* 14 July 1913; *Educ* Eton, Trinity Coll Cambridge (MA); *m* 1, 1935 (m dis 1952), Lady Gloria Vaughan, da of 7 Earl of Lisburne; 1 s (Mark Nigel Thomas Vaughan, MP, *qv*), 1 da (Amanda Gloria Morvyth Vaughan b 1939); m 2, 1956, as her 2 husb, Patricia, only da of Lt-Col Sir Walter Smiles, CIE, DSO, DL, MP; *Career* volunteered Welsh Gds 1939, Capt 1940, Maj 1944, served Hook of Holland and Boulogne 1940 (despatches), NW Europe 1944-45, wounded; Parly candidate (Cons) Chislehurst 1945; MP (Cons): Hitchin 1950-55, Surbiton 1955-74, Kingston-upon-Thames, Surbiton 1974-83; PPS to: Min of Food 1951-54, Home Sec 1954-57; Parly under sec for: Colonies 1962-63, Cwlth Rels and Colonies 1963-64; oppn spokesman Cwlth Affrs 1964-66; vice pres Bldgs Socs Assoc, dep chm Cwlth Parly Assoc 1979-83; kt 1974; *Books* Ian Macleod (1973), The Tory Leaders (1977), Harold Macmillan (1982); *Clubs* MCC, Boodles; *Style*— Sir Nigel Fisher, MC; 45 Exeter House, Putney Heath, London SW15 (☎ 081 788 6103)

FISHER, Hon Patrick Vavasseur; s (by 1 m) and h of 3 Baron Fisher; *b* 14 June 1953; *m* 1977, Lady Karen Jean Carnegie, *qv*, da of 13 Earl of Northesk; 2 s (John, Benjamin), 3 da (Juliet, Penelope, Suzannah); *Style*— The Hon Patrick Fisher; Highwayman's Vineyard, Heath Barn Farm, Risby, Bury St Edmunds, Suffolk

FISHER, Hon Richard Temple (Tim); 6 and yst s of Most Rev and Rt Hon Baron Fisher of Lambeth, GCVO, PC (Life Peer) (d 1972), and Rosamond Chevallier, *née* Forman (d 1986); *b* 26 Jan 1930; *Educ* St Edward's Sch Oxford, King's Coll Cambridge (choral scholar, MA); *m* 17 May 1969, Clare Margaret, da of J Lewen Le Fanu; 1 s (Paul b 1970), 1 da (Rosamond b 1973); *Career* Hon Maj TA Gen List late 16/5 Queen's Royal Lancers; asst master and housemaster Repton 1953-69, headmaster Bilton Grange Prep Sch 1969-; dir Bilton Grange Shop Ltd; dir (govr) Leicester HS for Girls; dir (memb of cncl) Inc Assoc of Prep Schs (vice chm 1986, chm 1987); *Recreations* skiing, sailing, music, drama, travel; *Style*— The Hon Tim Fisher; Bilton Grange, Dunchurch, Rugby (☎ 0788 810958, business 0788 810217)

FISHER, (Francis George) Robson; s of John Henry Fisher (d 1941), and Hannah Clayton Fisher (d 1969); *b* 9 April 1921; *Educ* Liverpool Coll, Univ of Oxford; *m* 1965, Sheila Vernon, o da of late David Dunsire; 1 s; *Career* schoolmaster; housemaster and head of English Kingswood Sch Bath 1950-59, headmaster Bryanston Sch 1959-74, chief master and headmaster of the Schs of King Edward VI Birmingham 1974-82; dep sec Headmasters' Conference 1982-86; *Recreations* music, sailing, reading, gardening; *Style*— Robson Fisher, Esq; Craig Cottage, Lower St, Dittisham, S Devon TQ6 0HY

FISHER, Dr Ronald Albert; JP; s of Albert Edward Fisher (d 1963), and Hannah Jackson, *née* Byrom (d 1986); *b* 3 June 1917; *Educ* Heversham Sch Cumbria, Downing Coll Cambridge (MA), Middx Hosp London; *m* 23 Feb 1952, Gwyneth Ena, da of Harold Arthur Mackinnon (d 1983); 2 da (Deborah Anne b 22 March 1956, Teresa b 2 Dec 1963); *Career* Surgn Lt RNVR 1943-46, convoy duties 1943-45 (Western Approaches, Russia, Gibraltar), landing in Java and MO Port Souabaya 1945-46; Bournemouth and E Dorset Gp of Hosps: conslt anaesthetist and admin 1953-73, memb Hosp Mgmnt Ctee 1960-71, chm med Exec Ctee 1965-71 (memb Med Advsy Ctee to Wessex Regnl Health Bd), dir postgrad educn 1963-67; fndr then conslt physician to the Macmillan Unit at Christchurch Hosp Dorset (pioneering hospice care in the NHS) 1974-82, started first home - care serv (McMillan Serv) in the NHS 1975, started first day-care unit in the NHS 1977; chm Select Ctee of Experts on Problems Relating to Death Cncl of Europe Strasbourg 1977-80, opened new hospice Riverside Hosp Columbus Ohio and gave first Libby Bradford Meml Lecture 1989, hon conslt in continuing cancer care and tstee Cancer Relief; chm bd of dirs Palace Ct Theatre Bournemouth; formerly: chm Bournemouth Little Theatre Club, dir LM Theatres Ltd; President's medal Cancer Relief; MRCS, LRCP, FFARCS; memb: BMA, Nat Soc for Cancer Relief; *Books* Palliative Care for People with Cancer (ed, 1991); *Recreations* philosophy, theatre, literature, family; *Style—* Dr Ronald Fisher, JP; Waders, 6 Lagoon Rd, Lilliput, Poole, Dorset BH14 8JT (☎ 0202 708 867)

FISHER, Baroness; Hon Rosamund Anne; *née* Clifford; da of 12 Baron Clifford of Chudleigh (d 1964); *b* 22 May 1924; *Educ* St Mary's Convent Ascot; *m* 1, 21 July 1945 (m dis 1965), Geoffrey Forrester Fairbairn (decd); 2 s (James b 1950, Charles b 1956), 1 da (Katrina b 1947); m 2, 1970, 3 Baron Fisher, DSC, *qv*; *Career* zoo dir and author; *Style—* The Rt Hon Lady Fisher; Kilverstone Hall, Thetford, Norfolk; Marklye, Rushlake Green, Heathfield, Sussex

FISHER, Roy; s of Walter Fisher (d 1959) of Birmingham, and Emma, *née* Jones (d 1965); *b* 11 June 1930; *m* 1, 1953 (m dis 1987), Barbara, da of Harold Davenport Venables; 2 s (Joel b 1957, Benjamin b 1963); m 2, 1987, Joyce, da of Arthur Holliday; *Career* lectr rising to sr lectr in Eng Dudley Coll of Educn 1958-63, head of Dept of Eng and Drama Bordesley Coll of Educn Birmingham 1963-71, lectr rising to sr lectr Univ of Keele 1971-82; freelance writer, broadcaster and jazz pianist 1982-; books: City (1961), The Ship's Orchestra (1966), Collected Poems 1968 (1968), Matrix (1971), The Cut Pages (1971), The Thing About Joe Sullivan (1978), Poems 1955-80 (1980), A Furnace (1986), Poems 1955-87 (1988); Andrew Kolus poetry prize 1969, Cholmondeley award 1980; memb: Musicians' Union 1957-, Soc of Authors 1980-; *Style—* Roy Fisher

FISHER-HOCH, Hon Mrs (Nesta Donne); *née* Philipps; TD (1947), DL (Carmarthenshire); da of late 1 Baron Kylsant; *b* 20 Nov 1903; *m* 1, 17 Sept 1921, 10 Earl of Coventry (ka 1940); 1 s, 2 da; m 2, 17 Jan 1953, Maj Terrance Vincent Fisher-Hoch, RA (d 1978), s of John Henry Fisher-Hoch, of Basle, Switzerland; *Career* chief cdr ATS 1939-45; *Style—* Hon Mrs Fisher-Hoch, TD, DL; Plâs Llanstephan, Carmarthen, Dyfed, Wales SA33 5JP

FISHER OF CAMDEN, Baroness; Millie; da of Isaac Gluckstein; *m* 1930, Baron Fisher of Camden (Life Peer, d 1979); 1 da; *Style—* The Rt Hon Lady Fisher of Camden; 48 Viceroy Ct, Prince Albert Rd, NW8

FISHER OF REDNAL, Baroness (Life Peeress UK 1974), of Rednal in the City of Birmingham; Doris Mary Gertrude Fisher; JP (Birmingham 1961); da of late Frederick James Satchwell, BEM; *b* 13 Sept 1919; *Educ* Tinker's Farm Girls' Sch, Fircroft Coll, Bournville Day Continuation Coll; *m* 1939, Joseph Fisher (d 1978); 2 da (Hon Pauline Mary (Hon Mrs Platt) b 1940, Hon Veronica Mary (Hon Mrs Pickering) b 1945); *Career* sits as Labour peer in House of Lords; joined Lab Pty 1945, memb Birmingham City Cncl 1952-74, MP (Lab) Birmingham (Ladywood) 1970-74, MEP 1975-79; hon alderman Birmingham 1974, memb Warrington New Town Dvpt Corpn 1974-81; memb Gen Medical Cncl 1974-79, govr Hunters Hill Sch Bromsgrove 1988; vice-pres: Assoc of Municipal Authorities, Assoc of District Cncls, Guardian Birmingham Assay Office 1982-89, Inst of Trading Standards Admin 1988, Hallmarking Cncl 1989-; pres Birmingham Royal Institution for the Blind 1983-; *Style—* The Rt Hon Lady Fisher of Rednal, JP; 60 Jacoby Place, Priory Road, Birmingham B5 7UW

FISHLOCK, Dr David Jocelyn; OBE (1983); s of William Charles Fishlock (d 1958), of Bath, and late Dorothy Mary Fishlock; *b* 9 Aug 1932; *Educ* City of Bath Boys' Sch (now Beechen Cliff Sch), Bristol Coll of Tech (now Univ of Bath); *m* 21 Dec 1959, Mary Millicent, *née* Cosgrove; 1 s (William David b 12 June 1960); *Career* assoc ed McGraw-Hill Publishing Co 1959-62, technol ed New Scientist 1962-67, science ed Financial Times 1967-; Hon DLitt Royal Univ of Salford 1982; FIBiol 1988, companion Inst of Energy 1987; *Books* author and ed of twelve books incl: The Business of Science (1975), Biotechnology - Strategies for Life (with Elizabeth Antebi, 1987); *Clubs* Athenaeum; *Style—* Dr David Fishlock, OBE; Traveller's Joy, Copse Lane, Jordans, Bucks HP9 2TA (☎ 02407 3242); Financial Times, 1 Southwark Bridge, London SE1 9HL (☎ 071 873 3000)

FISHMAN, Prof William Jack; *b* 1 April 1921; *Educ* Central Fndn GS for Boys London, LSE (BSc Econ), Univ of London (DSc Econ); *m* 1 June 1947, Doris; 2 s (Barrie Paul b 26 June 1948, Michael Ian b 8 March 1953); *Career* Home Serv and Far East Br Army 1940-46; princ Tower Hamlets Coll of Further Educn 1954-69; visiting prof: Columbia Univ NY 1967, Univ of Wisconsin Madison 1969-70; Action Tst Major Res Fell in Histroy 1970-72, prof QMC London 1986 (Barnet Shine sr res fell 1972); conslt and participant BBC radio and TV and ITV progs relating to the East End (US and W German TV), local res conslt Public Policy Res Unit Queen Mary and Westfield Coll 1987, govr Raines Fndn Sch, academic advsr Museum of Labour History, tstee East End Jewish Museum; *Books* The Insurrectionist (1970), East End Jewish Radicals (1975), The Streets of East London (1979), East End 1988 (1988); *Recreations* travel, reading and conducting local history tours; *Style—* Prof William Fishman; 42 Willowcourt Avenue, Kenton, Harrow, Middlesex (☎ 081 9075166), Dept of Political Studies, Queen Mary and Westfield College, Mile End Rd, London E1 (☎ 071 9755555)

FISHWICK, Avril; DL (Gtr Manchester 1982); da of Frank Platt Hindley (d 1966), and Charlotte Winifred, *née* Young (d 1940); *b* 30 March 1924; *Educ* Woodfield Sch, Wigan HS for Girls, Univ of Liverpool (LLB, LLM); *m* 4 Feb 1950, Thomas William Fishwick, s of William Fishwick, of Rainford; 2 da (Lizbeth Joanna b 1951, Hilary Alean b 1953); *Career* FO Bletchley Park 1942-45; admitted slr 1949; ptnr Frank Platt & Fishwick 1958-; High Sheriff Gtr Manchester 1983-84, Vice Lord Lt Gtr Manchester 1988-; memb Wigan and Leigh Hosp Mgmnt Ctee 1960-73, chm Wigan AHA 1973-82, hon memb Soroptimist Int, pres Wigan branch RSPCA 1974-, dir N Advsy Bd Nat West Bank 1984-; memb: Ct of Univ of Manchester 1984-, Appeals Ctee Prince of Wales Youth Business Tst; pres Wigan Little Theatre 1985-, countryside cmmn rep Groundwork Tst, chm: Tidy Britain Enterprises Co Ltd; memb: Bd Groundwork Trading Co Ltd, Wigan Groundwork Tst; memb Law Soc; *Recreations* countryside, natural history; *Style—* Mrs Avril Fishwick, DL; Haighlands, Haigh Country Park, Haigh, Wigan (☎ 0942 831 291); Victoria Buildings, King Street, Wigan (☎ 0942 43281, fax 0942 495 522)

FISHWICK, Lady Mary Louise; *née* Northcote; da of 4 Earl of Iddesleigh; *b* 14 April 1959; *Educ* St Mary's Convent Shaftesbury Dorset; *m* 12 Sept 1981, Maj Simon Nicholas Fishwick, 13/18 Royal Hussars (Queen Mary's Own), yr s of Clifford Fishwick, of Salisbury House, Monmouth St, Topsham, Devon; 2 s (James Nicholas b 1983, Hugh Simon b 1984, d 1987), 1 da (Lucy Mary b 1988); *Style—* Lady Mary Fishwick; Lower Woodrow, Brampford Speke, nr Exeter, Devon EX5 5DY

FISK, David John; s of late John Howard Fisk, and Rebecca Elizabeth, *née* Haynes; *b* 9 Jan 1947; *Educ* Stationers' Company's Sch Hornsey, St John's Coll Cambridge (BA, MA, ScD), Univ of Manchester (PhD); *m* 1972, Anne Thoday; 1 s, 1 da; *Career* DOE; Building Res Estab 1972, higher sci offr 1972-73, sr sci offr 1973-75, princ sci offr 1975-78, sr princ sci offr and head Mechanical and Electrical Engrg Div 1978-84, asst sec Central Directorate of Environmental Protection 1984-87, dep chief scientist 1987-88, under sec and chief scientist 1988-; visiting prof Univ of Liverpool 1988-; FCIBSE 1983; *Books* Thermal Control of Buildings (1981); author of numerous papers on building science, systems theory and economics; *Style—* David Fisk, Esq; Department of the Environment, 43 Marsham St, London SW1

FISK, Dr Peter Geoffrey; s of Sydney Harold Fisk (d 1990), and Mrs Fisk, *née* Gawan (d 1981); *b* 4 Feb 1945; *Educ* Queen Elizabeth Coll, London Hosp Med Coll (BSc, MB BS); *m* 20 Oct 1973, Ann Prentice, da of Graeme Smith (d 1979); 1 s (Christopher Jeffrey b 1 Aug 1979), 1 da (Emily Mary b 6 Oct 1976); *Career* registrar St Thomas' Hosp 1976-79, sr registrar and hon lectr Middx Hosp 1979-83, conslt in genitourinary med 1983-; memb: Assurance Med Soc, MSSCD, memb BMA, MRCP 1980; *Books* Pocket Guide to Cystitis (1982), Learning Genitourinary medicine and HIV disease through MCA (1990); *Recreations* squash, rugby; *Style—* Dr Peter Fisk; 6 Holt Drive, Kirby Muxloe, Leicester LE9 9EX (☎ 0533 386057), Department of Genitourinary Medicine, Leicester Royal Infirmary, Leicester (☎ 0533 541414)

FISKE, Hon Giles Geoffrey; s (by 1 m) of late Baron Fiske (Life Peer, d 1975); *b* 1935; *Style—* The Hon Giles Fiske

FISON, Sir (Richard) Guy; 4 Bt (UK 1905), DSC (1944); s of Capt Sir (William) Guy Fison, 3 Bt, MC (d 1964); *b* 9 Jan 1917; *Educ* Eton, New Coll Oxford; *m* 28 Feb 1952, Elyn (d 1987), da of Mogens Hartmann, of Bordeaux, and formerly wife of Count Renaud Doria; 1 s, 1 da; *Heir* s, Charles William Fison; *Career* Lt RNVR; served: Atlantic, N Sea, Channel; chm Fine Vintage Wines plc, non-exec dir Whitehead Mann 1982-84, former chm Saccone and Speed Int (dir 1952-83); pres Wine and Spirit Assoc of GB 1976-77, Master Vintners' Co 1983-84 (Upper Warden 1982-83); chm Wine Devpt Bd 1982-83, dir Wine Standards Bd 1984-87, Master of Wine 1954; *Clubs* MCC; *Style—* Sir Guy Fison, Bt, DSC; Medwins, Odiham, Hants RG25 1NE (☎ 0256 704075)

FISTOULARI, Anatole; s of Gregor Fistoulari (conductor, pianist, composer, d 1842), and Sophie Fistoulari (d 1965); *b* 20 Aug 1907; *m* 1, 1943 (m dis 1956), Anna, da of Gustav Mahler, the composer (d 1911); 1 da (Marina b 1943); m 2, 1957, Mary Elizabeth, da of James Lockhart (d 1943), of Edinburgh; *Career* princ conductor London Philharmonic Orchestra 1943-44, princ conductor and musical dir London Int Orchestra 1946; hon dir Madrid Sinfonica; *Recreations* reading; *Style—* Anatole Fistoulari, Esq; 65 Redington Road, Hampstead, London NW3

FITCH, Adrian Hill; s of Brian Hill Fitch, of Grayleigh, St Huberts Lane, Gerrards Cross, Bucks, and Susan Margeret, *née* Edwards; *b* 2 March 1959; *Educ* Merchant Taylors; *Career* money broker Tullett & Tokyo Forex International Ltd, dir London & Westminster Property Co Ltd 1980-; registered rep Securities Assoc; *Recreations* squash, shooting, wind surfing, classic car collecting; *Clubs* Cannons Sports, MG Owners, Jaguar Drivers; *Style—* Adrian H Fitch, Esq; 1 Elystan Walk, Cloudesley Rd, Islington, London N1 (☎ 071 833 1806); Tullett & Tokyo Forex International Ltd, Cable House, New Broad St, London EC2 (☎ 071 895 0300)

FITCH, Brian Hill; s of Stanley Hill Fitch (d 1961), of Hampstead, and Marjorie Winifred, *née* Browne; *b* 19 May 1930; *Educ* Haileybury; *m* 1955, Susan Margaret, da of Rex Edwards, LDS (d 1935), of Scarborough; 1 s, 1 da; *Career* Lloyd's Insur broker 1950-65, md The London & Westminster Property Co Ltd 1965- (dir 1956-), chm Caledonian Municipal Investments Ltd 1970-80, chm and md The London & Westminster (Sterling Brokers) Ltd 1972-80, licensed dealer in securities 1974-87, md London Fin Agency Ltd 1980-, underwriting memb Lloyd's 1982-; *Recreations* curio and antique collector, vintage motor cars, shooting, swimming; *Clubs* IOD (fell), Rolls Royce Enthusiasts, Royal Agric Soc of England, Br Assoc for Shooting and Conservation; *Style—* Brian Fitch Esq; Grayleigh, St Hubert's Lane, Gerrards Cross, Bucks (☎ 0753 884702, fax 0753 888302); Cheviot Court, Broadstairs, Kent (☎ 0843 63293)

FITCH, Colin Digby Thomas; s of Thomas Charles Fitch, of Hayling Is, Hampshire, and Grace Leila Fitch; *b* 2 Jan 1934; *Educ* St Paul's, St Catharine's Coll Cambridge (MA, LLM); *m* 15 Dec 1956, Wendy Ann, da of Edward Davis (d 1961); 4 s (Alaric 1959, Quentin b 1960, Joshua b 1971, Felix b 1972), 1 da (Cressida b 1964); *Career* Nat Serv 1951-53, cmmnd into The Queens Own Royal W Kent Regt TA 1953-58; called to the Bar Inner Temple 1970, ptnr Rowe and Pitman 1968-76, md Wardley ME Ltd 1976-80, ptnr Grieveson Grant and Co 1980-86, dir Kleinwort Benson Securities Ltd 1986-; memb Stock Exchange 1968, FCIS 1970, FRSA 1987; *Clubs* Brooks's; *Style—* Colin Fitch, Esq; The Coach House, Royston, Hertfordshire (☎ 0763 242 072); Bouyou, Mayrinhac-Lentour, Gramat Lot, France; 20 Fenchurch St, London EC3 (☎ 071 623 8000, telex 8873480)

FITCH, (John) Derek; s of John Dowson Fitch (d 1979), and Nora Fitch (d 1984); *b* 22 Sept 1937; *Educ* Rutherford GS Newcastle upon Tyne, Univ of Durham (BA); *m* 22 June 1963, Maureen Rose; 1 s (John Stephen b 1968); *Career* dir: Hill Samuel Registrars 1979, Devpt Planning Ltd 1982, Hill Samuel & Co 1985, Hill Samuel Life Assurance Co 1987, Hill Samuel Investment Services Group 1989 (dir 1987); Universal Credit Ltd 1979, Hill Samuel Personal Finance 1987; *Recreations* golf, swimming (ex British record holder); *Style—* Derek Fitch, Esq; Douglas Cottage, Coombe End, Kingston, Surrey KT2 7DQ (☎ 081 942 8009); NLA Tower, 12-16 Addiscombe Rd, Croydon CR9 6BP (☎ 081 686 4355)

FITCH, Douglas Bernard Stocker; s of William Kenneth Fitch (d 1970), and Hilda Alice, *née* Barrington (d 1953); *b* 16 April 1927; *Educ* St Albans Sch, Abbey Gateway St Albans, RAC Cirencester; *m* 1952, Joyce Vera, da of Arthur Robert Griffiths-Cirencester (d 1941), of Glos; 3 s (Christopher b 1958, Simon b 1961, Adrian b 1964); *Career* RE (Germany, Belgium, Netherlands) 1944-48; chartered surveyor, under sec, dir land and water serv MAFF 1980-87 (ret); RICS: memb Gen Cncl 1980-86, pres Land Agency and Agric Divnl Cncl 1985-86, memb standing conf marine resources 1985-91; memb govr the RAC 1986-; prof rural planning and natural resources mgmnt Euro Faculty for Land Use 1988; FRICS, FAAV, MRAC; *Clubs* Farmers, Civil Service; *Style—* Douglas Fitch, Esq; 71 Oasthouse Crescent, Hale, Farnham, Surrey GU9 0NP (☎ 0252 716742)

FITCH, Adm Sir Richard George Alison; KCB (1985); s of Instr Capt Edward William Fitch, RN (d 1953), and Agnes Jamieson, *née* Alison (d 1979); *b* 2 June 1929; *Educ* RNC Dartmouth (13 year-old entry); *m* 1969, Kathleen Marie-Louise, da of Robert Igert (d 1984), of Biarritz, France; 1 s (Richard b 1972); *Career* cmd HMS Hermes 1976-78, Dir Naval Warfare (MOD) 1978-80, Naval Sec 1980-83, Flag Offr 3 Flotilla and Cdr Anti-Submarine Gp Two 1983-85, Chief of Naval Personnel, Second Sea Lord and Admiral, Pres RNC Greenwich 1986-88; ret 1988; Liveryman Worshipful Co of Coachmakers and Coach Harness Makers; CBIM; *Recreations* boating, gardening, following sport, the family; *Clubs* Royal Yacht Sqdn, RN Sailing Assoc; *Style—* Adm Sir Richard Fitch, KCB; West Hay, 32 Sea Lane, Middleton-on-Sea, West Sussex (☎ 0243 58 2361)

FITCH, Rodney Arthur; CBE (1990); s of Arthur Francis Fitch (d 1982), of Wilts, and Ivy Fitch; *b* 19 Aug 1938; *Educ* Willesdon Poly, Sch of Architecture, Central Sch of

Arts & Crafts, Hornsey Sch of Art; *m* 28 Aug 1965, Janet Elizabeth, da of Sir Walter Stansfield, CBE, QPM (d 1984); 1 s (Edward b 18 Aug 1978), 4 da (Polly Jane b 27 May 1967, Emily Kate b 18 June 1968, Louisa Claire b 7 Nov 1971, Tessa Grace b 29 Oct 1974); *Career* Nat Serv pay corps RA 1958-60; trainee designer Hickman Ltd 1956-58, Charles Kenrick Assoc 1960-62, Conran Design Gp Ltd 1962-69, CDG (design conslts) Ltd 1969-71, fndr Fitch-RS plc (formerly Fitch & Co) 1971-; memb Design Cncl 1988-, dep chm ct of govrs London Inst 1989-, CSD (formerly SIAD) pres 1988-90 (vice pres 1982-86, hon treas 1984-87), former pres Designers & Arts Directors Assoc 1983; FRSA 1976; *Recreations* cricket, tennis, opera, theatre, family; *Style—* Rodney Fitch, Esq, CBE; Fitch RS plc, Porters South, 4 Crinan St, London N1 9UE (☎ 071 278 7200)

FITCHEW, Geoffrey Edward; s of Stanley Edward Fitchew (d 1976), and Elizabeth, *née* Scott (d 1971); *b* 22 Dec 1939; *Educ* Uppingham, Magdalen Coll Oxford (MA), LSE (MSc); *m* 17 Sept 1966, Mary Theresa, da of Dr Joseph Patrick Spillane (d 1989); 2 s (William Owain b 1971, Benedict Wyndham b 1975); *Career* asst princ HM Treasy 1964, private sec to Perm Sec Dept of Economic Affairs 1966-67; H M Treasy: private sec to Econ Sec 1967-68, asst sec 1975, cnsllr (econ and fin) UK Perm Representation to EC 1978-80, under sec (Euro Communities Gp) 1983-85, under sec (Int Fin Gp) 1985-86; dir gen DGXV (Fin Instn and Co Law) EC Cmmn 1986-; *Recreations* tennis, golf, reading, theatre; *Clubs* Castle, Welembeek-Oppem (Brussels); *Style—* Geoffrey Fitchew, Esq; Directorate-General XV, The Commission of the European Communities, Room 98/2nd Floor, 100 Ave De Cortenbergh, 1010 Brussels, Belgium (☎ 235 3719, fax 235 6500, telex 2187 COMEU B)

FITT, Baron (Life Peer UK 1983), of Bell's Hill, Co Down; Gerard Fitt; s of George Patrick and Mary Ann Fitt; *b* 9 April 1926; *Educ* Christian Brothers Sch Belfast; *m* 1947, Susan Gertrude, *née* Doherty; 5 da (and 1 da decd); *Career* merchant seaman 1941-53; cllr Belfast Corp (alderman) 1958-61; MP (Eire Lab) NI for Dock Div of Belfast 1962-72; MP (Repub Lab) Belfast W 1966; dep chief exec NI Exec 1974; fndr and ldr Social Democratic and Lab Pty NI, MP (SDLP) 1970-79, MP (Socialist) Belfast W 1979-83; *Style—* The Rt Hon Lord Fitt; House of Lords, London SW1A 0PW

FITTER, Richard Sidney Richmond; s of Sidney H Fitter (d 1962), of Banstead, Surrey, and Dorothy Isacke, *née* Pound (d 1926); *b* 1 March 1913; *Educ* Eastbourne Coll, LSE (BSc); *m* 19 April 1938, Alice Mary Stewart (Maisie), da of Dr R Stewart Park (d 1945), of Huddersfield, Yorks; 2 s (Julian Richmond b 1944, Alastair Hugh b 1948), 1 da (Jenny Elizabeth (Mrs Graham) b 1942); *Career* RAF Ops Res Section Coastal Cmd 1942-45; res staff: PEP 1936-40, Mass Observation 1940-42; sec Wild Life Conservation Special Ctee, Miny of Town & Country Planning 1945-46, asst ed The Countryman 1946-59, open air corr The Observer 1958-66, dir Intelligence Unit Cncl for Nature 1959-63; Fauna Preservation Soc: hon sec 1964-81, vice chm 1981-84, chm 1984-87, vice pres 1987-; Berks Bucks & Oxon Naturalists Tst 1959- (hon sec, vice chm, chm, pres), memb Survival Serv Cmmn Int Union for Conservation of Nature 1963- (chm Steering Ctee 1975-88), tstee and memb Cncl World Wildlife Fund UK 1977-85; memb: Cncl RSPB, Royal Soc for Nature Conservation; sci FZS; *Books* London's Natural History (1945), Wildlife for Man (1986), Field Guide to the Countryside in Winter (with Alastair Fitter, 1988), and 28 other books on wildlife mainly field guides on birds and wild flowers; *Recreations* bird watching, botanising, reading; *Clubs* Athenaeum; *Style—* Richard Fitter, Esq; Drifts, Chinnor Hill, Oxford OX9 4BS (☎ 0844 51223)

FITTON, Lady Eileen Cecil Theo; *née* Paulet; yr da of Capt Charles Standish Paulet, MVO (d 1953), and Lillian Jane Charlotte, *née* Fosbery; sis of 17 Marquess of Winchester (d 1968); raised to rank of Marquess's da 1970; *b* 1916; *m* 1, H Martin (d 1947); 2 children; m 2, 1949, Joseph Fitton; 6 children; *Style—* The Lady Eileen Fitton; 1610E 11th Ave, Vancouver 12, BC, Canada

FITTON BROWN, Prof Anthony David; s of Capt Walter Ernest Brown (d 1963), of Bangor, and Katharine, *née* Fitton (d 1966); *b* 15 Aug 1925; *Educ* Malvern, King's Coll Cambridge; *m* 19 Sept 1953, Daphne Mary, da of Edward Charles Cooper; 2 s (Simon b 22 Oct 1954, Edmund b 5 Oct 1962), 1 da (Rebecca 14 Aug 1957); *Career* admin offr Foreign Office 1943-45 (assigned to GCHQ); lectr in classics Univ Coll of N Wales Bangor 1949-63, fell and dir of studies in classics CCC Cambridge 1963-69, prof of classics Univ of Leicester 1969-87 (emeritus prof 1987); lay canon Leicester Cathedral 1980; *Books* Greek Plays as First Productions (1970); *Recreations* walking, cycling; *Style—* Prof Anthony Fitton Brown; 2 Sackville Gardens, Leicester LE2 3TH (☎ 0533 703486); Univ of Leicester, University Rd, Leicester LE1 7RH

FITZ CLARENCE, Lady Georgina; da of 7 Earl of Munster by his 2 w; *b* 1966; *Career* civil servant; memb Nat Tst; *Clubs* squash, badminton; *Style—* The Lady Georgina Fitz Clarence; Park View, Hollies Court, Weybridge, Surrey

FITZALAN HOWARD, Lord Gerald Bernard; yr s of 17 Duke of Norfolk, KG, CB, CBE, MC; *b* 13 June 1962; *Educ* Ampleforth; *m* 1 Dec 1990, Emma Georgina Edgerton, da of Dr Desmond James Cecil Roberts (d 1988); *Career* dir Greystoke Automotive Ltd; *Recreations* motor racing, skiing, shooting; *Style—* The Lord Gerald Fitzalan Howard; 27 Redcliffe Mews, London SW10 9JT; Carlton Towers, Goole, North Humberside DN14 9LZ; Greystoke Automotive Ltd, Witch Hazel Plantation, Tylney Hall, Rotherwick, Basingstoke, Hants RG27 9AY (☎ 0256 766137)

FITZALAN HOWARD, Lord Mark; 4 and yst s of 3 Baron Howard of Glossop, MBE (d 1972), and Baroness Beaumont, OBE (d 1971); bro of 17 Duke of Norfolk, KG, GCVO, CB, CBE, MC; *b* 28 March 1934; *Educ* Ampleforth; *m* 17 Nov 1961, Jacynth Rosemary, o da of Sir Martin Alexander Lindsay of Dowhill, 1 Bt, CBE, DSO; 2 da (Amelia b 1963, Eliza b 1964, m 1987 Timothy Bell); *Career* late Coldstream Gds; chm Assoc of Investmt Tst Cos 1981-83; dir Robert Fleming Holdings Ltd 1971-, non-exec dir BET plc 1983-, dir Nat Mutual Life Assurance Soc; *Style—* The Lord Mark Fitzalan Howard; 13 Campden Hill Square, London W8 7LB (☎ 071 727 0996)

FITZALAN HOWARD, Lord Martin; JP (N Riding of Yorks 1966), DL (N Yorks 1982); 3 s of 3 Baron Howard of Glossop, MBE (d 1972), and Baroness Beaumont, OBE; bro of 17 Duke of Norfolk, KG, GCVO, CB, CBE, MC; *b* 22 Oct 1922; *Educ* Ampleforth, Trinity Coll Cambridge; *m* 5 Oct 1948, Bridget Anne, da of late Lt-Col Arnold Ramsay Keppel (fourth in descent from Hon Frederick Keppel, sometime Bp of Exeter and 4 s of 2 Earl of Albemarle, KG, KB); 1 s, 4 da; *Career* served WWII (wounded), Palestine 1945-46, Capt Gren Gds; High Sheriff N Yorks 1979-80; *Style—* Lord Martin Fitzalan Howard, JP, DL; 3/E Whittingstall Rd, SW6 (☎ 071 736 0520); Brockfield Hall, Warthill, York (☎ 0904 489298)

FITZALAN HOWARD, Maj-Gen Lord Michael; GCVO (1981, KCVO 1971, MVO 4 Class 1952), CB (1968), CBE (1962, MBE 1949), MC (1944), DL (Wilts 1974); 2 s of 3 Baron Howard of Glossop, MBE, and Baroness Beaumont, OBE (Barony called out of abeyance in her favour 1896); bro of 17 Duke of Norfolk, KG, GCVO, CB, CBE, MC; granted rank of Duke's s 1975; *b* 22 Oct 1916; *Educ* Ampleforth, Trinity Coll Cambridge (MA); *m* 1, 4 March 1946, Jean Marion (d 1947), da of Sir Hew Hamilton-Dalrymple, 9 Bt; 1 da ; m 2, 20 April 1950, Jane Margaret, yr da of Capt William Particle Meade Newman; 4 s, 1 da; *Career* served WWII, Scots Gds, Europe and Palestine, subsequently Malaya, GOC London Dist and Maj-Gen cmdg Household Div 1968-71, Marshal Dip Corps 1972-82; Col Life Gds 1979-, Gold Stick to HM The Queen 1979-; pres cncl TAVR Assocs 1981- (chm 1973-81); Freeman City of London 1985; kt SMO Malta; *Clubs* Pratt's, Buck's; *Style—* Maj-Gen Lord Michael Fitzalan Howard, GCVO, CB, CBE, MC, DL; Fovant House, Fovant, Salisbury, Wilts (☎ 072 270 617)

FITZGEORGE-BALFOUR, Sir (Robert George) Victor; KCB (1968, CB 1965), CBE (1945), DSO (1950), MC (1939), DL (W Sussex 1977); o s of Robert Shekleton Balfour (d 1942), of Stirling, and (Mabel) Iris, *née* FitzGeorge (d 1976), who m subsequently (as his 2 w) Prince Vladimir Emmanuelovitch Galitzine (*see* Prince George Galitzine); Iris was da of Col George William Adolphus FitzGeorge (d 1907), Royal Welch Fusiliers, who was in his turn s of HRH Prince George, 2 Duke of Cambridge (whose f was 7 s of King George III); *b* 15 Sept 1913; *Educ* Eton, King's Coll Cambridge; *m* 4 Dec 1943, Mary Diana, er da of Adm Arthur Henry Christian, CB, MVO, descended from an ancient family of Manx landowners; 1 s (Robin b 1951), 1 da (Diana b 1946); *Career* served Coldstream Gds 1934-73 in M East, NW Europe (WW II), later Dir Mil Ops MOD, Sr Army Instructor IDC, Vice CGS 1968-70, UK Mil Rep NATO 1971-73; Col Cmdt HAC 1976-84; former chm Nat Fund for Res into Crippling Diseases 1975-89; *Clubs* Army and Navy; *Style—* Gen Sir Victor FitzGeorge-Balfour, KCB, CBE, DSO, MC, DL; The Old Rectory, W Chiltington, W Sussex (☎ 0798 812255)

FITZGERALD, Adrian James Andrew Denis; s and h of Sir George FitzGerald, 5 Bt, MC, 23 Knight of Kerry, *qv*; *b* 24 June 1940; *Educ* Harrow; *Career* hotelier; cncllr Royal Borough of Kensington and Chelsea 1974- (mayor 1984-85); dep ldr London Fire and Civil Def Authy 1989-90, chm Anglo Polish Soc 1989- vice chm London chapter Irish Georgian Soc 1990-; *Clubs* Pratt's; *Style—* Adrian FitzGerald, Esq; 16 Clareville St, London SW7; Lackaneask, Valentia Island, Co Kerry

FITZGERALD, Brian John; s of John Fitzgerald, of Glasgow, and Margaret, *née* McCaffrey; *b* 17 Sept 1946; *Educ* Salesian Coll Farnborough Hants, Univ of Glasgow (BSc); *m* 1969, Maren Lina, da of Capt George Hunter (d 1972), of Glasgow; 2 s (Michael b 1973, Philip b 1977); *Career* civil engr; dir: John Laing Construction Ltd, John Laing Developments Ltd, Norcity plc, Norhomes plc, Manchester Village Homes plc, Norcity II plc; CEng, FICE; *Recreations* squash; *Style—* Brian Fitzgerald, Esq; John Laing Construction Ltd, Page St, London NW7 2ER (☎ 081 906 5585, fax 081 906 5522)

FITZGERALD, Christopher Francis; s of Lt Cdr Michael Francis FitzGerald, RN, of Hove, E Sussex, and Anne Lise, *née* Winther; *b* 17 Nov 1945; *Educ* Downside, Lincoln Coll Oxford (MA); *m* 1, 1968 (m dis 1984); 1 s (Matthew b 1973), 2 da (Francesca b 1975, Julia b 1978); m 2, 31 Oct 1986, Jill, da of Dr Douglas Gordon Freshwater, of Upton-on-Severn, Worcs; 2 step da (Joanna b 1978, Victoria b 1979); *Career* admitted slr 1971; ptnr Slaughter and May 1976 (exec ptnr fin 1986-90, head of banking 1990-); *Recreations* travelling, music, reading; *Style—* Christopher FitzGerald, Esq; 21 Palace Gardens Terr, London W8 4SA; 35 Basinghall St, London EC2V 5DB

FITZGERALD, Rev Daniel Patrick; s of late Sir John Fitzgerald, 2 Bt and hp of bro, Rev (Sir) Edward Fitzgerald (3 Bt); *b* 28 June 1916; *Style—* The Rev Daniel Fitzgerald

FITZGERALD, Desmond John Villiers; *see*: Glin, Knight of

FITZGERALD, Dr Frank; CBE (1989); s of George Arthur Fitzgerald (d 1970), and Sarah Ann Brook (d 1974); *b* 11 Nov 1929; *Educ* Barnsley Holgate GS, Univ of Sheffield (BSc (Tech), PhD); *m* 25 Aug 1956, Dorothy Eileen, da of Frederic David Unwin (decd); 2 s, 1 da; *Career* scientific offr Rocket Propulsion Dept Royal Aircraft Estab Westcott Bucks 1955-58, lectr Birmingham Coll of Advanced Technol 1958-60; United Steel Cos (later British Steel Corp, now British Steel plc) 1960-: head Fuel and Furnace Res Section 1965-70, process res mangr Special Steels Div 1970-72, head Corporate Advanced Process Laboratory 1972-77, dir res and devpt 1977-81, chm BSC (overseas servs) Ltd 1981-89, md tech 1981-, dir British Steel 1986-, chm British Steel Stainless 1989-; chm Tech Ctee Int Iron and Steel Inst 1987-90, memb Advsy Cncl on Res Devpt Dept of Energy 1990; Hadfield medal (Iron and Steel Inst) 1972, Melchett medal (Inst of Energy) 1988, Frank Scott Russell meml lecture (Refractories Assoc) 1983, Hatfield meml lecture (Univ of Sheffield) 1990; FEng 1977, FIChemE, FInstE; *Recreations* music, rock climbing, mountaineering; *Clubs* Alpine, Climbers'; *Style—* Dr Frank Fitzgerald, CBE; British Steel plc, Technical Headquarters, Swinden House, Moorgate, Rotherham, S Yorkshire S60 3AR (☎ 0709 820166, fax 0709 825337)

FITZGERALD, Garret; s of Desmond FitzGerald (min external affrs Irish Free State 1922-27, min Def 1927-32) and Mabel, *née* McConnell; *b* 9 Feb 1926; *Educ* St Brigid's Sch Bray, Colaiste na Rinne Waterford, Belvedere Coll Dublin, Univ Coll Dublin & King's Inns Dublin; *m* 1947, Joan, da of late Charles O'Farrell; 2 s, 1 da; *Career* called to the Bar 1946, res and schedules mangr Aer Lingus 1947-58; Rockefeller res asst Trinity Coll Dublin 1958-59, lectr in Political Econ Univ Coll Dublin 1959-73; memb: Seanad Eireann 1965-69, Dail Eireann for Dublin SE 1969-, TD; min Foreign Affrs 1973-77, ldr and pres Fine Gael 1977-87; Taoiseach (meaning chieftain; title used by Irish PMs) of Eire 1981-82, 1982-87; pres: Cncl of Mins of EEC Jan-June 1975, Euro Cncl July-Dec 1984, Irish Cncl of Euro Mvmnt 1977-81, 1982; formerly vice pres Euro People's Pty Euro Parly; formerly Irish corr: BBC, Financial Times, Economist and other overseas papers; formerly econ corr Irish Times, md Economist Intelligence Unit of I; dir: Guinness Peat Aviation, International Institute for Economic Development, Trade Development Institute, Comer International, Corporate Finance Group; memb: Royal Irish Acad, Senate National University of Ireland, Action Ctee for Europe; Euro vice chm Trilateral Cmmn; Hon LLD: NY, St Louis, St Mary's Univ Halifax Canada, Univ of Keele, Boston Coll Mass, Univ of Oxford; *Publications* State-Sponsored Bodies (1959), Planning in Ireland (1968), Towards a New Ireland (1972), Unequal Partners (UNCTAD 1979), Estimates for Baronies of Minimum Level of Irish Speaking amongst Successive Decennial Cohorts 1771-1781 to 1861-1871 (1984); *Style—* Garret FitzGerald, Esq; Leinster House, Kildare St, Dublin 2, Ireland

FITZGERALD, James Gerard; s of John Fitzgerald (d 1974), and Josephine, *née* Murphy (d 1952); *b* 22 May 1935; *m* 1; 1 s (Timothy John b 1962), 1 da (Lisa Siobhan b 1964); m 2, 22 March 1978, Jane Latta, da of A C Leggat, of Lindsaylands, Biggar, Lanarks; 1 da (Kirsty Isobel b 1985); *Career* racehorse trainer; major races won include: Tote Cheltenham Cup, Power Gold Cup, Vincent O'Brien Irish Gold Cup, Arkle Challenge Trophy Cheltenham, Princess of Wales's Stakes Newmarket, Hennessy Cognac Gold Cup, Tote-Ebor Handicap, Tote Cesarewitch (twice), NBA Northumberland Plate, Sun Alliance Chase Cheltenham, Timeform Chase Haydock (twice), Philip Cornes Saddle of Gold Final Newbury, WM Hill Scottish Nat Ayr (twice), SGB Chase Ascot, Hermitage Chase Newbury, Coral Golden Hurdle Final Cheltenham, Victor Chandler Handicap Chase Ascot; best horses trained include: Androma, Brave Fellow, Bucko, Canny Danny, Danish Flight, Fairy King, Fair Kitty, Forgive N' Forget, Galway Blaze, Kayudee, Tickite Boo, Treasure Hunter, Sapience, Meikleour, Trainglot; *Recreations* shooting; *Style—* James Fitzgerald, Esq; Norton Grange, Norton, Malton, N Yorkshire YO17 (☎ 0653 692718, fax 0653 600214)

FITZGERALD, Lord John; 2 s of 8 Duke of Leinster by his 2 w Anne, yr da of late Lt-Col Philip Eustace Smith, MC; *b* 3 March 1952; *Educ* Millfield, RMA Sandhurst; *m* 11 Dec 1982, Barbara, eldest da of late Andreas Zindel, of St Moritz, Switzerland; 1 s (Edward b 27 Oct 1988), 1 da (Hermione b 11 Oct 1985); *Career* Capt 5 Royal

Inniskilling Dragoon Gds; racehorse trainer (Graham Place, Newmarket); *Recreations* shooting, fishing; *Clubs* Turf, Naval and Military; *Style—* The Lord John FitzGerald; Graham Lodge, Newmarket, Suffolk CB8 OWE (☎ 0638 669879)

FITZGERALD, Michael Frederick Clive; QC (1980); s of late Sir William James FitzGerald MC, QC, and late Erica Critchley, *née* Clarke; *b* 9 June 1936; *Educ* Downside, Christ's Coll Cambridge (MA); *m* 15 Feb 1966, Virginia Grace, da of Col William Sturmy Cave, DSO, TD (d 1953); 1 s (Hamilton b 14 March 1971), 3 da (Emma Grace b 2 Feb 1967, Charlot Grace b 7 June 1968, Harriet Grace b 4 Aug 1969); *Career* 2 Lt 9 Queens Royal Lancers 1954-56, called to the Bar Middle Temple 1961, Master of the Bench 1987; *Recreations* opera, fishing, shooting; *Clubs* Athenaeum, Special Forces; *Style—* Michael FitzGerald, Esq, QC; 2 Mitre Court Buildings, Temple, London EC4 (☎ 071 583 1380, fax 071 353 7772)

FITZGERALD, Michael John; s of Albert William Fitzgerald (d 1980), of Dynerth, Heather Lane, West Chiltington, and Florence Margaret Fitzgerald, *née* Stannard (d 1981); *b* 14 May 1935; *Educ* Caterham Sch; *m* 9 June 1962, Judith-Ann, da of Dr A C Boyle of The Barn, Iping; 2 s (Alistair b 1964, Malcolm b 1966), 1 da (Aimee-Louise b 1970); *Career* CA, vice pres Occidental Int Oil Inc 1987, vice pres and gen mangr Occidental Int (Libya) Inc 1985; dir: Occidental Petroleum (Caledonia) Ltd, Langham Publishing Ltd, Arundale Sch Tst; *Recreations* golf, gardening opera; *Clubs* West Sussex G; *Style—* Michael J Fitzgerald, Esq; Fir Tops, Grove Lane, West Chiltington, Sussex (☎ 07983 2258); 16 Palace St, London SW1 (☎ 071 828 5600)

FITZGERALD, Niall William Arthur; s of William FitzGerald (d 1972), and Doreen, *née* Chambers; *b* 13 Sept 1945; *Educ* St Munchins Coll Limerick, Univ Coll Dublin (MCom); *m* 2 March 1970, Monica Mary, da of John Cusack (d 1985); 2 s (Colin b 30 Jan 1976, Aaron b 24 March 1982), 1 da (Tara b 5 Dec 1973); *Career* N American commerical memb Unilever plc 1978-80 (overseas commercial offr 1976-78), md Unilver SA 1982-85 (fin dir 1980-82), dir Unilever NV & Unilever plc 1987- (gp treas 1985-86); memb: Ctee on Indust and Fin NEDC, Accounting Standards Review Ctee; FCT 1986; *Recreations* opera, running, golf, and an active family; *Clubs* RAC; *Style—* Niall W A FitzGerald, Esq; Unilever, Blackfriars, London EC4P 4BQ (☎ 01 822 6328)

FITZGERALD, Penelope Mary; *née* Knox; da of Edmund Valpy George Knox (poet and ed of Punch, d 1971), and Christina Frances, *née* Hicks (d 1934); *b* 17 Dec 1916; *Educ* Wycombe Abbey, Somerville Coll Oxford (BA 1938); *m* 15 Aug 1942, Desmond John Lyon Fitzgerald, MC, s of Thomas Fitzgerald (d 1960); 1 s ((Edmund) Valpy b 1947), 2 da (Christina Rose b 1950, Maria b 1953); *Career* writer; biography: Edward Burne-Jones (1975), The Knox Brothers (1977), Charlotte Mew and her Friends (1984, Br Acad Mary Rose Crawshay award); fiction: The Bookshop (1978), Offshore (1979, Booker McConnell award for fiction), At Freddies (1982), Innocence (1986), The Beginning of Spring (1988); FRSL 1989; *Style—* Mrs Penelope Fitzgerald; c/o Collins Publishers, 8 Grafton St, London W1X 3LA

FITZGERALD, Peter Gilbert; s of P H FitzGerald, and Hilda Elizabeth, *née* Clark; *b* 13 Feb 1946; *Educ* Harvey GS Folkestone; *m* 5 Dec 1970, Elizabeth Thora, da of F L Harris (d 1970), of Cornwall; 1 s (Timothy b 24 Oct 1973); *Career* CA; dir Valor Vanguard Ltd 1965-66, md FitzGerald Lighting Ltd 1980- (dir 1973-80); dir Bodmin & Wenford Railway plc 1985-; FCA 1972; *Recreations* cycling, walking, model railways; *Style—* Peter G FitzGerald, Esq; FitzGerald Lighting Ltd, Normandy Way, Bodmin, Cornwall (☎ 0208 75611, fax 0208 74893)

FITZGERALD, Dr Richard; s of Dr Patrick Fitzgerald, of Model Farm Rd, Cork, Eire, and Mary, *née* O'Donnell; *b* 14 May 1955; *Educ* Christian Brothers' Coll Cork Eire, Univ Coll NUI (MB BCh, BAO); *Career* house offr Cork Regnl Hosp 1979-81, registrar then sr registrar West Midlands Radiology Trg Scheme Birmingham 1981-86, conslt radiologist to Wolverhampton Hosps 1986-; FRCR 1985, memb BIR; *Recreations* swimming, hillwalking, cinema; *Clubs* Shifnal Squash and Swimming; *Style—* Dr Richard Fitzgerald; 10 Wyke Way, Idsall Green, Shifnal, Shropshire TF11 8SF (☎ 0952 461729); X-Ray Department, New Cross Hospital, Wolverhampton WV10 0QP (☎ 0902 732255)

FITZGERALD, Lady Rosemary Ann; *née* FitzGerald; da of 8 Duke of Leinster by his 1 w Joane, da of late Maj Arthur MacMurrough Kavanagh, MC; *b* 4 Aug 1939; *Educ* Lady Margaret Hall Oxford; *m* 9 Feb 1963 (m dis 1967), Mark Killigrew Wait, o s of Peter Lothian Killigrew Wait, of 10 Pembroke Square, W8; reverted to maiden name; *Career* botanist; *Style—* The Lady Rosemary FitzGerald; Beggars Roost, Lilstock, nr Bridgwater, Somerset TA5 1SU

FITZGERALD, Dr William Knight; CBE (1981), JP (1958), DL (1974); eldest s of John Alexander Fitzgerald (d 1963), of Brunton, Fife, and Janet, *née* Knight (d 1938); *b* 19 March 1909; *Educ* Robertson Acad SA; *m* 1, 1938, Elizabeth (d 1980), da of Alexander Grant; 3 s (Alexander, John, William); m 2, 1984, Margaret Eleanor, da of George Baird Bell (d 1965); *Career* co dir (ret); local govt Dundee City Treas 1967-70, Lord Provost of Dundee 1970-73, dep convener Tayside Regnl Cncl 1974-77 (convener 1977-86); former chm Tay Road Bridge Bd (ret 1986); pres Dundee Bn Boys' Bde; ex-pres COSLA; *Recreations* gardening, walking; *Clubs* Univ of Dundee; *Style—* Dr W K Fitzgerald, CBE, JP, DL; 1 Roxburgh Terrace, Dundee DD2 1NZ (☎ 0382 68475)

FITZGIBBON, Louis Theobald Dillon; Comte Dillon in France; s of Lt Cdr Robert Francis Dillon FitzGibbon, RN (d 1954), and Kathleen Clare, *née* Atcheson (d 1950); *b* 6 Jan 1925; *Educ* St Augustine's Abbey Sch Ramsgate, RNC Dartmouth, Univ of London Sch of Eastern European and Slavonic Studies (for Nav Polish Interpreters' Course); *m* 1, 1950 (m dis 1962), Josephine Miriam Maud Webb; m 2, 15 Aug 1962, Madeleine Sally Hayward-Surry (d 1980); 1 s (James b 7 Nov 1963), 2 da (Simone b 16 Nov 1962, Michèle b 24 April 1965); m 3, 12 Sept 1980, Joan Elizabeth Jevons; *Career* Midshipman RN 1942, Sub Lt 1944, Lt 1946, Lt Cdr (ret) 1954; dir De Leon Properties Ltd 1954-72; hon sec Jt Ctee for Preservation of Historic Portsmouth 1959-61; slrs articled clerk 1960-63; Anglo-Polish Conf Warsaw 1963; PA to Rt Hon Duncan Sandys, MP (later Lord Duncan-Sandys) 1967-68; gen sec Br Cncl for Aid to Refugees 1968-72; UN Mission to S Sudan 1972-73; dir of a med charity 1974-76; exec offr Nat Assoc for Freedom 1977-78; gen sec of a trade assoc 1978-80; memb several missions to: Somalia 1978-85, Sudan and Egypt 1982, Sudan, German Parly, Euro Parly (1984, UN 1984, 1986, 1987, 1988, 1989); author of reports and contribs to int and nat jls; memb: RIIA 1982 and 1988, Anglo-Somali Soc; won first Airey Neave Meml scholarship 1981; hon sec Katyn Meml Fund 1971-77; area pres St John Ambulance Bde (Hants East) 1974-76; SMOM: Kt of Honour and Devotion 1972, Officer of Merit 1985; Polish Gold Cross of Merit 1969; Order of Polonia Restituta (Polish govt in exile): Offr 1971, Cdr 1972, Kt Cdr 1976; Katyn Meml medal Bronze (USA) 1977, Laureate van de Arbeid (Netherlands) 1982, Officer Order of Merit (Germany) 1990; hon sec Br Horn of Africa Cncl 1984-; *Books* Katyn - A Crime without Parallel (1971), The Katyn Cover-up (1972), Unpitied and Unknown (1975), Katyn - Triumph of Evil (Ireland 1975), The Katyn Memorial (1976), Katyn Massacre (paper 1977, 3rd edn 1989) Katyn (USA 1979), Katyn (in German 1979), The Betrayal of the Somalis (1982), Straits and Strategic Waterways in the Red Sea (1984), Ethiopia Hijacks the Hijack (1985), The Evaded Duty (1985); *Recreations* travel, politics, writing, reading, history, languages, refugee problems, Horn of Africa affairs, Islamic matters; 8 Portland Place, Brighton BN2 1DG (☎ 0273 685661)

FITZHARRIS, Viscount; James Carleton Harris; s and h of 6 Earl of Malmesbury; *b* 19 June 1946; *Educ* Eton, Queen's Coll Univ of St Andrews (MA); *m* 14 June 1969, Sally Ann, da of Sir Richard Newton Rycroft, 7 Bt; 3 s (Hon James, Hon Edward b 1972, Hon Guy b 1975), 2 da (Hon Frances b 1979, Hon Daisy b 1981); *Heir* s, Hon James Hugh Carleton Harris b 29 April 1970; *Style—* Viscount FitzHarris; Greywell Hill, Greywell, Basingstoke, Hampshire RG25 1DB (☎ 0256 702107)

FITZHERBERT, Giles Eden; CMG (1985); er s of Capt Henry Charles Hugh FitzHerbert, and Sheelah, *née* Murphy; *b* 8 March 1935; *Educ* Ampleforth, ChCh Oxford; *m* 1, 1962, Margaret (d 1986), da of Evelyn Waugh, the novelist; 2 s, 3 da; m 2, 1988, Alexandra, *née* Eyre; 1 s; fought Fermanagh and S Tyrone in Lib interest 1964; *Career* 2 Lt 8 King's Royal Irish Hussars; formerly with Vickers da Costa & Co; Dip Serv: first sec Rome 1968-71, cnsllr Kuwait 1975-77 and Nicosia 1977-78, head Euro Community Dept (External) FCO 1978-81, sabbatical year 1982, inspr 1983, min Rome 1983-87; ambass Caracas 1988-; *Clubs* Beefsteak, Kildare St Univ (Dublin); *Style—* Giles FitzHerbert, Esq, CMG; Cove House, Cove, Tiverton, Devon

FITZHERBERT, Nicholas John; s of Cuthbert Fitzherbert (d 1986), and Barbara, *née* Scrope (d 1975); *b* 3 Nov 1933; *Educ* Ampleforth; *m* 26 March 1968, Countess Teréz Szapáry, da of Count Gyula Szapáry (d 1985); 1 s (Henry Laszlo b 1972), 1 da (Elizabeth Magdolna b 1970); *Career* Coldstream Gds BAOR 1952-54; Lloyds broker 1954-58, Leonard Wadsworth 1958-60, Kleinwort Benson Ltd 1960-77, devpt dir Ketson plc 1985-90, Nicholas Fitzherbert Assoc 1990-; *Books* The History of Robert Fleming Holdings 1845-1982, Sir Alexander Kleinwort and Herman Kleinworth and their bank; *Clubs* Cavalry and Guards; *Style—* Nicholas Fitzherbert, Esq

FITZHERBERT, Hon Philip Basil; 3 s of 14 Baron Stafford (d 1986); *b* 7 Oct 1962; *Educ* Ampleforth Coll; *Career* sporting agents; *Recreations* shooting, cricket, golf, snooker, darts, reading, photography, beer tasting; *Clubs* I Zingari, MCC, Free Foresters, Staffordshire Gentlemen, Old Amplefordians; *Style—* The Hon Philip Fitzherbert; c/o Rt Hon Lord Stafford, Swynnerton Park, Stone, Staffordshire

FITZHERBERT, Sir Richard Ranulph; 9 Bt (GB 1784), of Tissington, Derbyshire; o s of Rev David Henry FitzHerbert, MC (d 1976), and Charmian Hyacinthe, da of late Samuel Ranulph Allsopp, CBE, DL; suc his uncle, Sir John Richard Frederick FitzHerbert, 8 Bt 1989; *b* 2 Nov 1963; *Educ* Eton; *Heir* kinsman, Arthur William FitzHerbert, b 2 Sept 1922; *Clubs* Bachelor's, Flappers; *Style—* Sir Richard FitzHerbert, Bt; Tissington Hall, Ashbourne, Derbyshire DE6 1RA

FITZHERBERT, Hon Thomas Alastair; 2 s of 14 Baron Stafford (d 1986); *b* 9 Aug 1955; *Educ* Ampleforth; *m* 8 May 1982, Deborah S, yr da of late P A Beak and Mrs B S A Westley, of The Coach House, Englefield Green; 1 s (Rory b 27 Sept 1989), 2 da (Tamara Frances b 1986, Purdita Aileen b 1987); *Career* marketing; *Style—* The Hon Thomas Fitzherbert; 72 Foxbourne Rd, London SW17

FITZHERBERT-BROCKHOLES, Francis Joseph; eldest s of Michael John Fitzherbert-Brockholes, *qv*; *b* 18 Sept 1951; *Educ* Oratory Sch, Corpus Christi Coll Oxford (BA, MA); *m* 7 May 1983, Jennifer, da of Geoffrey George Watts, of Grassdale, Wandering, W Aust; 2 s (Thomas Antony b 8 Nov 1985, George Frederick b 1 March 1988), 1 da (Susannah Louise b 23 Feb 1984); *Career* called to the Bar 1975, admitted New York Bar 1978; in chambers, Manchester 1976-77; assoc: Cadwalader Wickersham & Taft 1977-78, White & Case 1978-85 (ptnr 1985-); *Style—* Francis Fitzherbert-Brockholes, Esq; Bailiff's Cottage, Claughton-on-Brock, nr Garstang, Lancs PR3 OPN; White & Case, 66 Gresham St, London EC2V 7LB (☎ 071 726 6361, fax 071 726 8558, telex 884757)

FITZHERBERT-BROCKHOLES, Michael John; OBE (1989), JP (Lancashire 1960), DL (1975); s of John William Fitzherbert-Brockholes, CBE, MC, JP, DL (d 1963), sometime Privy Chamberlain of Sword and Cape to Pope Pius XI, and Hon Eileen French, da of 4 Baron de Freyne; the Brockholes have been seated at Claughton since the 14 century and the estate passed through female descent to the Hesketh in 1751 and from them to the Fitzherberts in 1783, when William Fitzherbert assumed the additional surname and arms of Brockholes (*see* Burke's Landed Gentry, 18 edn, vol II, 1969); *b* 12 June 1920; *Educ* Oratory Sch, New Coll Oxford; *m* 28 Sept 1950, Mary Edith, da of Capt Charles Joseph Henry O'Hara Moore, CVO, MC, late Irish Guards (d 1965), of Mooresfort, Co Tipperary, by his w Lady Dorothie Feilding, da of 9 Earl of Denbigh, GCVO; 4 s (Francis Joseph b 18 Sept 1951, *qv*, Antony John b 23 Nov 1952, Simon Peter b 15 March 1955, William Andrew Charles b 1 Dec 1958); *Career* Maj Scots Gds (Italy and N W Europe) 1940-46; memb Lancashire CC 1967-89 (chm Education Ctee 1977-81); Vice Lord-Lieut Lancs 1977-; Kt of St Gregory 1978, OStJ; *Recreations* gardening; *Style—* Michael Fitzherbert-Brockholes, Esq, OBE, JP, DL; Claughton Hall, Garstang, nr Preston, Lancashire (☎ 0995 40286)

FITZPATRICK, Christopher Hugh Eugene; s of Hugh Joseph Fitzpatrick (d 1979) of Cleator Moor, Cumbria, and Monica Alice, *née* Piper; *b* 5 Oct 1940; *Educ* Priory Sch Bishops Waltham; *m* 3 April 1971, Margaret Anne, da of John Thomas Bell (d 1974), of Florence Rd, Sanderstead, Surrey; 3 da (Clare Marie b 1972, Charlotte Ellen b 1974, Victoria Jane b 1979); *Career* md: Transtar Ltd 1976-81, Victor Products plc 1984-88 (dep md 1981-84); gp md dir Scholes Gp plc, chm Wylex Ltd; dir: PDL-Wylex SDN Malaysia, ABB-Wylex Sales Ltd; *Recreations* motoring, caravanning, golf; *Clubs* Ponteland Lions, Catenians, Caravan; *Style—* Christopher Fitzpatrick, Esq; 35 Bow Green Rd, Bowdon, Cheshire WA14 3LF (☎ 061 928 6247); Sharston Rd, Wythenshawe, Manchester M22 4RA

FITZPATRICK, (Gen) Sir (Geoffrey Richard) Desmond; GCB (1971, KCB 1965, CB 1961), DSO (1945), MBE (1942), MC (1940); o s of Brig-Gen Sir (Ernest) Richard Fitzpatrick, CBE, DSO (d 1949), and Georgina Ethel, *née* Robison; *b* 14 Dec 1912; *Educ* Eton, RMC Sandhurst; *m* 22 April 1944, Mary Sara, o da of Sir Charles Campbell, 12 Bt, of Auchinbreck (d 1948); 1 s (Brian), 1 da (Sara); *Career* Royal Dragoons 1932, served Palestine 1938-40 (MC), Middle E, Italy, NW Europe 1941-45 (despatches, DSO, MBE), Brevet Lt-Col 1951, Col 1953, ADC to HM the Queen 1959, Asst Chief of Def Staff (Maj-Gen) 1959-61, Dir of Mil Ops, WO 1962-63, COS BAOR 1964-65, GOCIC NI Cmd 1965-66, Lt-Gen 1965, Vice CGS 1966-68, C in C BAOR and Cdr NAG 1968-70, Gen 1968, Dep Supreme Cdr Allied Forces Europe 1970-74; Lt-Govr and Cin C Jersey 1974-79; Dep Col Blues and Royals 1969-74, Col 1979-, Gold Stick to the Queen 1979-; Col Cmdt RAC 1971-74; *Recreations* sailing, shooting; *Clubs* RYS, Cavalry and Guards; *Style—* Sir Desmond Fitzpatrick, GCB, DSO, MBE, MC; Belmont, Otley, Ispwich, Suffolk IP6 9PF (☎ 0473 890 206)

FITZPATRICK, James Bernard; CBE (1983), DL (1985), JP (1977); s of Bernard Arthur Fitzpatrick (d 1963), and Jessie Emma, *née* Blunt; *b* 21 April 1930; *Educ* Bootle GS, Univ of London (LLB); *m* 2 Sept 1965, Rosemary, da of Capt Edward Burling Clark, RD, RNR, of Glust Hendre, N Wales; 1 s (Simon b 1967), 1 da (Susan b 1970); *Career* chm: Mersey Docks and Harbour Co 1984-87 (md 1977-84), Liverpool Health Authy 1986-91, Royal Liverpool Univ Hosp Tst 1991-; dir Plan Investment plc 1984-; *Recreations* fell walking, gardening; *Clubs* Oriental, Pilgrims, Racquet (Liverpool); *Style—* James Fitzpatrick Esq, CBE, DL, JP; 57 Hilbre Road, West Kirby, Wirral L48 3HB (☎ 051 625 9612); Royal Liverpool Hospital, Prescot Street, Liverpool L7 8XP (☎ 051 706 2000)

FITZPATRICK, Air Marshal Sir John Bernard; KBE (1984), CB (1982); s of Joseph Fitzpatrick, and Bridget Fitzpatrick; *b* 15 Dec 1929; *Educ* St Patrick's Sch

Dungannon, RAF App Sch Halton, RAF Coll Cranwell; *m* 1954, Gwendoline Mary, da of Edwin Abbott; 2 s, 1 da; *Career* RAF offr: SASO HQ Strike Cmd 1980-83, Air Marshal 1983, AOC No 18 Gp 1983-86; *Recreations* reading, DIY; *Clubs* RAF; *Style—* Air Marshal Sir John Fitzpatrick, KBE, CB; c/o Lloyd's Bank Ltd, 23 Market Place, Fakenham, Norfolk NR21 9BT

FITZPATRICK, (Francis) Michael John; s of Francis Latimer FitzPatrick (d 1982), of E Bergholt, Suffolk, and Kathleen Margaret, *née* Gray; *b* 14 July 1938; *Educ* Brentwood Sch; *m* 4 April 1964, Patricia Hilbery, da of Sir George Frederick Chaplin, CBE, DL, JP (d 1975), of Great Warley, Essex; 1 s (Richard b 1965), 1 da (Kathryn b 1967); *Career* chartered surveyor, ptnr Messrs Hilbery Chaplin; Freeman City of London, Liveryman Worshipful Co of Chartered Surveyors; FRICS; *Recreations* music, travel, gardening; *Clubs* Royal Over-Seas League; *Style—* Michael FitzPatrick, Esq; Wood House, Stratford St Mary, Suffolk CO7 6LU (☎ 0206 322266); 4 Eastern Rd, Romford, Essex (☎ 0708 745000)

FITZPATRICK, Nicholas David; s of Prof Reginald Jack Fitzpatrick, of Norwoods, Rectory Lane, Heswall, Wirral, Merseyside, and Ruth, *née* Holmes; *b* 23 Jan 1947; *Educ* Bristol GS, Nottingham Univ (BA); *m* 23 Aug 1969, (Patricia) Jill, da of Peter Conway Brotherton; 1 s (Daniel b 12 Jan 1976), 1 da (Paula b 14 Dec 1973); *Career* trainee analyst Friends Provident 1969-72, equity mangr Abbey Life 1972-76, equity mangr then investmt mangr BR Pension Fund 1976-86, ptnr and investmt specialist Bacon & Woodrow 1986-; ASIA 1972, FIA 1974; *Recreations* teenage rugby, woodwork; *Style—* Nicholas Fitzpatrick, Esq; 9 Grovelands Rd, Purley, Surrey (☎ 081 668 2412); Bacon & Woodrow, St Olafs House, London Bridge City, London SE1 2PE (☎ 071 357 7171)

FITZPATRICK, Roger; s of Charles Fitzpatrick, and Mary; *b* 8 May 1944; *Educ* Leeds Central HS; *m* 23 June 1976, Patricia Norma, da of Leonard Boniface; 1 s (Nicholas Mark), 1 da (Leanne); *Career* chm & md Ashfield Gp Ltd; dir: Instagraphic Ltd, Instagraphic Prods Ltd, Ashfield International Ltd, Instagraphic Computer Systems; FInstD; *Recreations* business; *Clubs* IOD; *Style—* Roger Fitzpatrick, Esq; work: (☎ 0532 589893, fax 0532 580720, telex 557266)

FITZROY, Lord Charles Patrick Hugh; yr s of 11 Duke of Grafton, KG; *b* 7 Jan 1957; *Educ* Eton, Magdalene Coll Cambridge (BA); *m* 16 July 1988, Diana, da of Hubert Miller-Stirling, of Cape Town, SA; *Style—* The Lord Charles FitzRoy; Euston Hall, Thetford, Norfolk

FITZROY, Hon Edward Anthony Charles; o surviving s and h of 6 Baron Southampton, *qv*; *b* 8 July 1955; *Educ* Gresham's Sch Holt, RAC Cirencester; *m* 1978, Rachel Caroline Vincent, 2 da of Peter John Curnow Millett, of West Underdown, Drewsteignton, Devon; 1 s (Charles Edward Millett b 18 Jan 1983), 3 da (Fiona Joan Margaret b Nov 1979, Sarah Barbara Sibell b April 1981, Julia Rachel Caroline b Nov 1984); *Style—* The Hon Edward FitzRoy; Venn Farm, Morchard Bishop, Crediton, Devon EX17 6SQ

FITZROY, Lord Edward Anthony Charles; DL (Norfolk 1986); s of 10 Duke of Grafton (d 1970), and his 2 wife Lucy Eleanor, *née* Barnes (d 1943); *b* 26 Aug 1928; *Educ* Eton, RMA Sandhurst; *m* 26 April 1956, Veronica Mary, da of Maj Robert Francis Ruttledge, MC, of Doon, Newcastle Greystones, Co Wicklow; 1 s (Michael b 1958), 2 da (Joanna b 1957, Shauna b 1963); *Career* joined Coldstream Gds 1948, Capt 1954, ret 1955; chm Ross Poultry Ltd 1969-75, chm and md Imperial Foods International Technical Services 1975-82; dir: Imperial Foods Ltd 1969-82, Ross Breeders Ltd, Ross Poultry (NZ) Ltd 1982-, Ross Breeders Peninsular Spain 1984-; chm Caledonian Cartridge Co 1987-; High Sheriff of Norfolk 1987; memb: Cncl Norfolk Naturalists Tst, Lloyd's; *Recreations* shooting, stalking, gardening, travel; *Clubs* Pratt's, Norfolk; *Style—* The Lord Edward FitzRoy, DL; Norton House, Norwich, Norfolk NR14 6RY (☎ 050 846 303); 40 Eland Rd, Battersea, London SW11 (☎ 071 585 2526); office 61-65 Rose Lane, Norwich (☎ 0603 612415, telex 97237)

FITZROY NEWDEGATE, Hon James; s and h of 3 Viscount Daventry, JP, DL; *b* 27 July 1960; *Style—* The Hon James Fitzroy Newdegate

FITZSIMMONS, Rt Hon William Kennedy; PC (NI) 1965, JP (Belfast 1951); *b* 31 Jan 1909; *Educ* Skegoniell Nat Sch, Belfast Jr Tech Sch; *m* 1935, May Elizabeth Lynd; 2 da; *Career* resigned 1985; memb Royal Soc of Health until 1985-, chm Belfast City and Dist Water Commissioners 1954-55 (member 1948-57), pres Duncairn (Belfast) Unionist Assoc; NI Parl MP Duncairn 1956-72; Parly sec: Miny of Commerce 1961-65, Miny of Home Affrs 1963-64; Devpt Miny 1964-65; min of: Educn 1965-66 and 1968-69, Devpt 1966-68, Health and Soc Servs 1969-72; *Style—* The Rt Hon William K Fitzsimmons, JP; 16 Cleaver Court, Cleaver Ave, Malone Road, Belfast BT9 5JA

FITZSIMONS, (Patrick) Anthony; *b* 16 March 1946; *Educ* St Phillips GS Birmingham, LSE (BSc); *m* 1967 (m dis 1985), Carolann; 2 s; *Career* Rank Xerox: Aust 1972-75, Southern Europe 1975-76, Middle East 1976-79, regnl control dir London 1979-81; md Host Gp Grand Metropolitan 1983-85 (dir Fin Systems and Strategy Brewing and Retail Div 1981-83), md personal banking Citibank London 1985-89; *Recreations* squash, polo, antiques, music; *Style—* P Anthony FitzSimons, Esq; Bristol & West Building Society, PO Box 27, Broad Quay, Bristol BS99 7AX (☎ 0272 294271, fax 0272 211632)

FITZWALTER, 21 Baron (E 1295); (Fitzwalter) Brook Plumptre; JP (Kent 1949); s of George Beresford Plumptre (d 1934), yr bro of 20 Baron (d 1932, but the present Lord FitzWalter was not summoned to Parl till 1953); Lord FitzWalter is eleventh in descent from Frances, w of Sir Thomas Mildmay and half sis of 3 Earl of Sussex (whose 2 w Frances, da of Sir William Sydney, of Penshurst, left £5,000 to establish a Cambridge Coll to be called 'Sydney Sussex'); Frances was twelfth in descent from Robert FitzWalter, the leading enforcer among the Barons of Magna Carta; by his w (and 1st cousin) Mary Augusta, *née* Plumptre (d 1953); *b* 15 Jan 1914; *Educ* Diocesan Coll Cape Town, Jesus Coll Cambridge; *m* 29 Sept 1951, Margaret Melesina, 3 da of Herbert William Deedes, JP (d 1966), and sis of William Deedes, sometime ed of the Daily Telegraph; 5 s (Julian, Henry, George, William, Francis); *Heir* s, Hon Julian Plumptre; *Career* served WWII Capt; landowner and farmer (2,500 acres); *Recreations* shooting, gardening; *Style—* The Rt Hon the Lord FitzWalter; Goodnestone Park, Canterbury, Kent CT3 1PL (☎ 0304 840218)

FITZWALTER, Raymond Alan; s of Robert Fitzwalter, of 28 Maudsley St, Bury, Lancashire, and Lucy Fitzwalter; *b* 21 Feb 1944; *Educ* Derby Sch, LSE (BScEcon); *m* 6 Aug 1966, Mary, da of Richard Towman, DSC (d 1989), of 22 Prestbury Close, Bury, Lancashire; 2 s (Stephen b 1968, Matthew b 1970), 1 da (Kathryn b 1974); *Career* reporter Telegraph and Argus Bradford 1965 (dep news ed 1968), CPU scholar to Pakistan 1968, Young Reporter of the Year IPC Awards 1969 (commended 1967); World in Action Granada TV: joined 1970, prodr and dir 1975, ed 1976, exec prodr 1986; head current affrs Granada TV 1989- (commissioning exec news and current affrs 1987); BAFTA award best factual series for World in Action 1987, RTS awards to World in Action 1981, 1983 and 1985; *Books* Web of Corruption: The Story of John Poulson and T Dan Smith (with David Taylor, 1981); *Recreations* chess, naval history, a garden; *Style—* Raymond Fitzwalter, Esq; Granada Television, Quay Street, Manchester M60 9EA (☎ 061 832 7211, fax 061 953 0286)

FITZWILLIAMS, Richard Braithwaite Lloyd; s of Maj Robert Campbell Lloyd Fitzwilliams, TD, and Natalie Jura Stratford, *née* Mardall (d 1965); the family has three registered Royal Descents from Ethelred II (Ethelred the Unready), Edward I (through the Howards) and Henry (Lord Percy) Hotspur, all through Richard Fitzwilliam's ggg grandmother Jane Maria, da and co-heir of Adm Richard Brathwaite; *b* 14 Oct 1949; *Educ* Univ of Cape Town (BA); *m* 16 Nov 1981, Gillian, da of Frederick William Savill, of Blaby, Leicestershire; *Career* worked on project for Shadow Min of Educn United Party SA 1972, Europa Publications London 1972-, ed Int Who's Who 1975-; memb Bow Gp; *Books* contrib numerous political articles and film reviews to SA newspapers; *Recreations* entertaining, cinema, shooting, travel; *Style—* Richard Fitzwilliams, Esq; 84 North End Rd, London NW11 7SY (☎ 081 455 7393); Europa Publications Ltd, 18 Bedford Square, London WC1B 3JN (☎ 071 580 8236, 071 636 1664, telex 21540 EUROPA G)

FLACK, Mervyn Charles; s of Maj Henry George Flack (d 1978), and Marjorie, *née* Lofthouse; *b* 30 June 1942; *Educ* Raynes Park Co GS, Northampton Coll of Advanced Technol; *m* 5 Oct 1963, Margaret Elizabeth, da of George Robert Cumnock (d 1983); 1 s (James b 3 Nov 1969), 1 da (Emma b 2 Oct 1975); *Career* asst statistician Gillette Industs Ltd 1962-67, co statistician Marplan Ltd 1967-69, chief statistician Attwood Statistics Ltd 1969-70, dir Opinion Research Centre 1971-79, dep md Louis Harris International 1978-79 (res dir 1973-78); chm: City Research Associated Ltd 1980-, Strategic Marketing Consultancy Ltd 1989-, City Res Gp plc 1990-; FSS 1963, FIS 1978 (MIS 1964); *Recreations* flying; *Style—* Mervyn Flack, Esq; Crossrigg, Pondfield Road, Kenley, Surrey; Surrey City Research Group plc, Lector Court, 151-153 Farringdon Rd, London EC1R 3AD (☎ 071 833 1681, fax 071 278 5981)

FLAGG, Rt Rev John William Hawkins (Bill); s of Wilfred John Flagg (d 1974), and Emily, *née* Hawkins (d 1989); *b* 16 April 1929; *Educ* Wolsey Hall, All Nations Christian Coll, Clifton Theological Coll; *m* 4 May 1954, Marjorie, da of Norman Lund (d 1968); 2 s (Andrew, Timothy), 4 da (Richenda, Rachel, Rosalind, Patricia); *Career* agric missionary in Southern Chile 1951-58, anglican chaplain and mission supt Paraguay 1959-64, archdeacon Northern Argentina 1964-69; bishop of: Paraguay and Northern Argentina 1969-73, Peru 1977 (asst 1973-77); asst bishop: Chile and Bolivia 1973-77, Liverpool 1978-86; vicar St Cyprians' with Christ Church 1978-85, priest i/c Christ Church Waterloo 1985-86, gen sec S American Missionary Soc 1986-, hon asst bishop Rochester 1986-; presiding bishop Anglican Cncl of S America 1974-77; memb: Anglican Consultative Cncl 1974-79, S Atlantic Cncl 1984-, Mission Issues and Strategy Gp (Anglican Cmmn) 1988-; *Recreations* walking, chess; *Style—* The Rt Rev Bill Flagg; 55 Liptraps Lane, Tunbridge Wells, Kent TN2 3BU (☎ 0892 20431); The South American Missionary Society, Allen Gardiner House, Pembury Rd, Tunbridge Wells, Kent TN2 3QU (☎ 0892 38647, 0892 38648, fax 0892 25797)

FLANAGAN, Mary; da of Martin James Flanagan (d 1981), and Mary, *née* Nesbitt (d 1977); *b* 20 May 1943; *Educ* Brandeis Univ Waltham Mass (BA); *Career* writer; began writing 1979; works to date: Bad Girls (1984), Trust (1987), Rose Reason (1991); critic for: Sunday Times, Evening Standard, New Statesman, Observer; reviewer for Kaleidoscope (Radio 4); memb: Soc of Authors 1986, Authors Guild (USA) 1986, PEN (Eng and American) 1990; *Recreations* gardening, music; *Style—* Ms Mary Flanagan

FLANAGAN, Prof Terence Patrick (Terry); OBE (1987); s of Thomas Flanagan (d 1933), of Dudley, Worcs, and Harriet Selina, *née* Beard (d 1978); *b* 25 Sept 1924; *Educ* St Josephs Sch Dudley, Queen Mary's Coll (BSc, MSc); *m* 1, 9 July 1949 (m dis 1980), Marian Margaret, da of Horace Riddleston (d 1954), of Chesterfield, Derbys; 3 da (Helen (Mrs Russell) b 6 Feb 1955, Jane b 19 Jan 1957, Margaret b 19 Sept 1959); m 2, 31 Jan 1981, Sheila Mary, da of John Wallace McDonald, of Bromley, Kent; *Career* Flt Sgt RAF Aircrew 1943-47; electronics designer Marconi Instruments 1950-57; SIRA Ltd: head Nucleonics Dept 1957-63, head Indust Measurement Div 1963-74, exec dir 1974-79, md 1979-87; conslt UKAEA 1964-88, indust conslt 1987-; non-exec dir: Ometron Ltd (chm 1981-87), SIRA Safety Services Ltd 1987-; ed Measurement and Control Series 1987-; visiting prof City Univ London; memb Metrology & Standards Requirements Bd DTI 1980-87, chm Sch of Engrg Advsy Ctee City Univ 1980-, pres Inst of Measurement and Control 1983, govr Ravensbourne Coll of Design & Communication 1984-88, lectr Kent Area Understanding Industry Campaign, treas Tenterden Residents Assoc, chm Bromley NSPCC Centenary Ctee 1990-91; Freeman City of London 1982, Liveryman Worshipful Co of Scientific Instrument Makers 1982; Hon DSc City Univ 1990; FIEE, FInstP, FInstMC; *Recreations* cricket, music, DIY, local affairs; *Clubs* 54; *Style—* Prof Terry Flanagan, OBE; 11 Eastgate Rd, Tenterden, Kent (☎ 0580 64070); 19 Foxleas Ct, Spencer Rd, Bromley, Kent (☎ 081 464 4436)

FLANDERS, Dennis; s of Bernard Charles Flanders (d 1964), musician, of Woodford, London E18, and Jessie Marguerite, *née* Sandell (d 1964), artist; *b* 2 July 1915; *Educ* Merchant Taylors', various art schools; *m* 1952, Dalma Joan Darnley, da of Jack Darnley Taylor (d 1949); 1 s (Julian b 1956), 1 da (Alison b 1953); *Career* Staff Sergeant RE 1942-46; artist drawings of Britain, particularly elaborate architectural compositions - townscapes and landscapes in black and white and water-colour; series of drawings in Yorkshire Post, Birmingham Post, Sunday Times, Illustrated London News; occupied last 50 yrs in proclaiming the superior beauties of the landscapes and townscapes of England, Wales, Scotland and Ireland in more than 3000 drawings and water colours, 224 of which (half in colour and half in black and white) are reproduced in a book (*see below*); RBA 1970, ARWS 1970, RWS 1976; *Books* Dennis Flanders' Britannia (1984); *Recreations* travel; *Clubs* Art Workers' Guild (Master 1975); *Style—* Dennis Flanders Esq; 51 Gt Ormond St, London WC1N 3HZ (☎ 071 405 9317); Baker's Cross House, Cranbrook, Kent TN17 3AQ (☎ 0580 712018)

FLANNERY, Martin Henry; MP (Lab) Sheffield Hillsborough 1974-; s of Martin Flannery, of Sheffield; *b* 2 March 1918; *Educ* De La Salle GS, Sheffield Teacher Trg Coll; *m* 1949, Blanche Mary; 1 s, 2 da; *Career* head teacher Middle Sch 1969-74 (dep head 1965-69), exec memb NUT 1969-1974, sponsored by MSF, former sec PLP Chile Gp, chm Tribune Gp 1980-82, chm PLP N Ireland Ctee, memb Select Ctee on Educn Sci and Arts 1981-; conslt to NUT; *Recreations* music, lit, rambling; *Style—* Martin Flannery, Esq, MP; 53 Linaker Rd, Sheffield (☎ 0742 334911)

FLATHER, Gary Denis; QC (1984); s of Denis Gerald Flather, of Sheffield, and Joan Ada, *née* Walker; *b* 4 Oct 1937; *Educ* Oundle, Pembroke Coll Oxford; *m* Shreela, da of Aftab Rai; *Career* 2 Lt 1 Bn York and Lancaster Regt 1958-58, Hallamshire Bn TA 1958-61; called to the Bar 1962, asst Parly boundary cmmr 1982-, memb Panel of Chm ILEA Parly Disciplinary Tbnl 1974-90, asst rec 1983-86 (rec 1986-), inspr DTI for enquiries under Fin Servs Act 1987-88, chm Police Disciplinary Appeal Tbnl 1987-, legal memb Mental Health Review Tbnl 1987-; legal assessor: GMC 1987-, Gen Dental Cncl 1987-; chm Statutory Ctee Royal Pharmaceutical Soc of GB 1990-; escort to Mayor Royal Borough of Windsor and Maidenhead 1986-87, vice pres Community Cncl for Berkshire 1987-; pres Maidenhead Rotary 1990-; *Recreations* travel, music, coping with Multiple Sclerosis; *Clubs* Oriental; *Style—* Gary Flather, Esq, QC; Lamb Building, Temple, London EC4Y 7AS (☎ 071 353 6701, fax 071 353 4686, car 0860 8758

FLATHER, Baroness (Life Peer UK 1990), of Windsor and Maidenhead in the Royal County of Berkshire; Shreela Flather; JP (1971); da of Rai Bahadur Aftab Rai (d 1972),of New Delhi, and Kristina (d 1989); *Educ* UCL (LLB); *m* Gary Flather, QC; 2 s (Paul Marcus); *Career* infant teacher ILEA 1965-67; teacher of English as foreign language: Altwood Comp Sch Maidenhead 1968-74, Broadmoor Hosp 1974-78;

currently cncllr Royal Borough Windsor and Maidenhead, UK del to Econ and Soc Ctee EC (until 1990), pres Cambs Chilterns and Thames Rent Assessment Panel, vice pres Building Socs Assoc; vice chm and fndr memb Maidenhead Community Rels Cncl, vice chm Maidenhead Volunteer Centre, sec and organiser Maidenhead Ladies' Asian Club 1968-78, fndr New Star Boys' Club for Asian boys, fndr summer sch project for Asian children in Maidenhead, vice chm and memb management Ctee CAB, vice chm Estates and Amenities and Leisure Ctees Royal Borough of Windsor and Maidenhead, sec Windsor and Maidenhead Cons Gp, exec ctee memb Anglo-Asian Cons Soc, Thames and Chilterns Tourist Bd, memb Dist Youth and Community Ctee, community rels advsr Berks Girl Guides, race rels tutor sr police offrs' courses, govr Slough Coll of Higher Educn 1983-89; memb: Berks FPC, Spoore Marry and Rixman Fndn, Poole's Charity, Ring's Charity; dir Daytime TV Ltd; memb: Lord Chllr's legal Aid Advsy Ctee 1958-88, Broadmoor Hosp Bd, BBC South and East Regnl Advsy Ctee, W Met Conciliation Ctee of Race Rels Bd 1973-78, Bd of Visitors Holloway Prison, Police Complaints Bd 1982-85, Swann Ctee (inquiry into educn of children from ethnic minority gps) 1979-85, HRH Duke of Edinburgh's Ctee of Inquiry into Br Housing 1984-85, Commission for Racial Equality 1980-86; Mayor Royal Borough of Windsor and Maidenhead 1986-87 (Dep Mayor 1985-86); memb: Social Security Advsy Ctee 1987-90, Servite Houses Ctee of Management, Nat Union Exec Ctee Cons Pty, Cons Women's Nat Ctee, exec ctees of Br sections Int Unions of Local Authys, LWT Programme Advsy Bd, Hillingdon Hosp Tst, Thames Valley Training and Enterprise Cncl; pres Broadmoor League of Friends; vice pres Assoc of District Cncls; chm Maidenhead Community Consultative Cncl; vice chm: Police Consultative Ctee, The Refugee Cncl; tstee Berks Community Tst; *Recreations* travel, cinema; *Clubs* Oriental; *Style—* The Rt Hon Lady Flather, JP; Triveni, Ascot Rd, Maidenhead SL6 2HT

FLATT, Kate; da of John Clifford Flatt, of London, and Joy Ashmore, *née* Thompson; *b* 12 Jan 1949; *Educ* Francis Bacon GS St Albans, Royal Ballet Sch, London Sch of Contemporary Dance; *m* 20 May 1980, Timothy John Lamford, s of Capt Randolph Morris Lamford, of Watford, Herts; 1 s (Oliver William b 1985), 1 da (Chloe Maria b 1980); *Career* choreographer; productions incl: WNO Eugene Oneg 19880, The Bartered Bride 1982, Merry Widow 1984; Royal Opera: Los Angeles Olympic Arts Festival and TV Turandot 1984; Fidelio 1986, Guillaume Tell 1990, Les Misérables 1985; *Style—* Ms Kate Flatt

FLAVELL, Geoffrey; s of William Alfred Flavell, JP, of Dunedin, New Zealand (d 1953); *b* 23 Feb 1913; *Educ* Waitaki and Otago HS, Univ of Otago, St Bartholomew's Hosp London; *m* 1943, Joan Margaret, o da of late Sydney Ewart Adams, of Hawkwell, Essex; *Career* served RAF 1942-46, OC Surgery Divs Cairo Carthage Algiers; advsr in surgery, Mediterranean and ME Cmd, Wing Cdr, ret 1958; former conslt cardio-thoracic surgn to Hosps: NE Thames Regnl Health Authy, Royal Masonic Hosp, LCC and British Legion Hosp; hon conslt cardio-thoracic surgn: The Royal London Hosp (former head Dept Cardio-Vascular and Thoracic Surgery), Chelmsford Gp Hosps, Harlow and Epping Gp, Whipps Cross Hosp 1978-; travelling lectr for Br Cncl ME and Far East 1961, advsr in surgery Govt of Qatar; chm Advsy Ctee on Cardiothoracic Surgery RHA 1970-78; FRCS, FRCP; *Books* Introduction to Chest Surgery (1957), The Oesophagus (1963), Chest Diseases (1963), Scientific Foundations of Surgery (1974); *Recreations* architecture, art, history, wine and food; *Clubs* Bath and County, RAF; *Style—* Geoffrey Flavell, Esq; 9 Camden Crescent, Bath BA1 5HY (☎ 0225 444 903)

FLAVELLE, Sir (Joseph) David Ellsworth; 3 Bt (UK 1917); s of Sir (Joseph) Ellsworth Flavelle, 2 Bt (d 1977), and Muriel, *née* McEachren (d 1982); *b* 9 Nov 1921; *m* 1 Sept 1942, Muriel Barbara, da of David Reginald Morton; 3 da; *Heir* none; *Career* Lt Cdr (t) RCNVR, ret; *Clubs* Albany, Canadian, Empire (all Toronto); *Style—* Sir David Flavelle, Bt; 1420 Watersedge Rd, Clarkson, Ontario L5J 1A4, Canada

FLAXEN, David William; s of William Henry Flaxen (d 1963), of Tyldesley, and Beatrice, *née* Laidlow (d 1984); *b* 20 April 1941; *Educ* Manchester GS, BNC Oxford (MA), UCL (DipStat); *m* 22 Feb 1969, Eleanor Marie, da of Stewart Ferguson Eaton (d 1975), of Andover, Massachusetts; 2 da (Sophia b 1970, Clare b 1974); *Career* statistician; Miny of Lab 1967-71, UN advsr Swaziland 1971-72, Dept of Employment 1973-76, Inland Revenue 1977-81, asst dir Central Statistical Office 1983-89 (1964-67, 1976-77, 1981-83), dir of statistics Dept of Tport 1989-; *Recreations* bridge, wine, books, music, cooking; *Style—* David Flaxen, Esq; 65 Corringham Rd, London NW11 7BS (☎ 081 458 5451); Dept of Transport, Romney House, 43 Marsham St, London SW1P 3PY (☎ 071 276 8030)

FLAXMAN, Charles; s of William Henry Flaxman, and Amy, *née* Williams; *b* 12 April 1926; *Educ* Owen's Sch London; *m* 7 April 1947, (Muriel) Jane, *née* Colbear; 2 s (Roger b 1951, Jeremy b 1954), 1 da (Sara b 1953); *Career* Nat Serv 1944-48, cmmnd Royal Fusiliers 1945 (Capt 1947); worked for various Lloyd's Brokers 1942-61, underwriter Frank Barber & Ors Lloyds 1982-86 (dep underwriter 1962-81), ptnr Morgan Fentiman & Barber Lloyds 1982-, conslt Bowring Professional Indemnity Fund Ltd 1987-90, tech dir Solicitosr Indemnity Fund Ltd 1987-; memb Saffron Walden Town Cncl 1979-87; memb Worshipful Co of Insurers 1984; ACII 1952; *Recreations* music, walking, reading, work; *Style—* Charles Flaxman, Esq; Birbecks, Redgate Lane, Sewards End, Saffron Walden, Essex (☎ 0799 27364)

FLAXMAN, Edward Wasley (Ted); s of Edward George Flaxman of Forest Lodge, The Common, Southwold, Suffolk, and Ellen Ashton *née* Youngman; *b* 7 April 1928; *Educ* Culford Sch, Imperial Coll, (BSc 1952, DIC 1957); *m* 2 Apr 1955, Joan Edwina, da of the late Edwin John Knight, 2 s (Peter Edward b 1959, John Wesley, b 1962) 1 da (Penelope Ann, b 1957); *Career* Nat Serv 2 Lt RE 1947-49; FICE chm Int Soc for Trenchless Technology, fell Fellowship of Engrg, pntr Binnie and Partners 1973 (assoc 1968- 72, res engr 1958-60, joined 1952; *Recreations* bird watching, genealogy; *Style—* Ted Flaxman Esq; The Coach House, Capenor, Coopers Hill Road, Nutfield, Surrey RH1 4HS (☎ 0737 823454, fax 0737 822165); Binnie and Partners, Grosvenor House, 69 London Road, Redhill, Surrey RH1 1LQ (☎ 0737 774155, fax 0737 772767)

FLECHA DE LIMA, His Excellency Ambassador Paulo-Tarso; s of Sebastiao Dayrell de Lima, and Maria de Lourdes Flecha de Lima; *b* 8 July 1933; *Educ* Law Sch Univ of Brazil Rio de Janeiro; *m* Lúcia, *née* Martins; 3 s (Paulo, Joao Pedro, Luiz Antonio), 2 da (Isabel, Beatriz); *Career* with Brazilian dip serv 1955; memb Presidential staff 1956-59, head of Govr's Office (of then State of Guanabara 1960), sec Brazilian Embassy Rome 1961-62, dep rep Permanent Delgn of Brazil to the Latin American Free Trade Assoc Montevideo 1962-66, dep consul gen and head of Trade Promotion Sector Brazilian Consulate General NY 1969-71; Miny of External Relations: dir Latin American Free Trade Div 1966-68, head of Trade Promotion Dept 1971-84, under sec gen for econ and commercial affairs 1984, sec gen for external relations 1985, ambass special mission for negotiations with the USA (on econ and commercial matters of bilateral interest) 1986; special rep Brazilian Govt for trade negotiations 1986, ambass extraordinary and plenipotentiary to the Ct of St James 1990-; prestigious nat and foreign decorations incl: Order of Rio Branco (Grand Cross) Brazil, Mil Order of Christ (Grand Cross), Order of Prince Henry of Portugal (Grand Cross), Order of Merit (Grand Cross) Portugal, Nat Order of San Martin the Liberator (Grand Cross), Order of Merit of the Argentine Republic (Grand Cross) Argentina, Order of the Maltese Merit of the Sovereign and Mil Order of Malta (Grand Cross), Order of Sun of the Republic (Grand Cross) Peru, Order of the Liberator (Grand Cross), Order of Generalissimo Francisco Miranda (Grand Cross) Venezuela, Order of the Aztec Eagle of Mexico (Grand Cross), Ataualpa Order of Merit (Grand Cross) Ecuador, Order of Merit (Grand Cross) Chile, Alauite Order (Grand Cross) Morocco, Order of Isabel the Catholic (Grand Cross) Spain, Nat Order of Merit (Grand Cross) Paraguay, Nat Order of the Condor of the Andes (Grand Cross) Bolivia, Order of the Sacred Treasure (knight cdr), Japan, Nat Order of Merit (knight cdr), France, Legion of Honour of the French Republic (knight cdr), Order of Merit of the Federal Republic of Germany (knight cdr); *Style—* His Excellency Senhor Paulo-Tarso Flecha de Lima; Brazilian Ambassador, Brazilian Embassy, 32 Green St, London W1Y 4AT (☎ 071 499 0877)

FLECK, Prof Adam; s of Adam Fleck (d 1981), of Glasgow, Scotland, and Beatrice Ada Stirton, *née* Goldie; *b* 19 Oct 1932; *Educ* Hillhead HS, Allan Glens Sch Glasgow, Univ of Glasgow (BSc, MB ChB, PhD); *m* 12 July 1960, Elizabeth, da of Alexander MacLean, of Glasgow; 1 s (Adam b 1962), 2 da (Barbara Anne b 1965, Isabel Beatrice b 1968); *Career* conslt biochemist Glasgow Royal Infirmary 1966-74, sr lectr in pathological biochemistry Univ of Glasgow 1974-79 (lectr 1961-65), hon conslt W Infirmary Glasgow 1974-79; prof of chemical pathology Charing Cross and Westminster Med Sch 1979-, hon conslt chem pathologist Charing Cross and Westminster Hosps; memb Cncl Assoc of Clinical Biochemists, chm Joint Examining Bd For The Mastership In Clinical Biochemistry (1988-91); Burgess of the City of Glasgow, memb of the Incorporation of Bakers of Glasgow 1988; FRSC 1971, FRSEd 1973, FRCPath 1979, FRCP 1979, FRSM 1980, FIBIOL 1988; *Recreations* sport; *Clubs* Roehampton; *Style—* Prof Adam Fleck; Dept of Chemical Pathology, Charing Cross & Westminster Med Sch, St Dunstans Rd, London W6 8RF (☎ 071 846 7075, fax 071 846 7007)

FLECK, Richard John Hugo; s of Peter Hugo Fleck (d 1975), and Fiona Charis Elizabeth, *née* Miller; *b* 30 March 1949; *Educ* Marlborough, Univ of Southampton (LLB); *m* 1983, Mary, da of Wing Cdr Frederick Thomas Gardiner, DFC; 1 s (Peter Frederick Hugo b 5 March 1990), 1 da (Sara Katherine Victoria b 10 May 1987); *Career* ptnr Herbert Smith 1980- (joined 1971); memb Auditing Practices Ctee 1986-; Freeman City of London, Liveryman Tallow Chandlers Co; memb Law Soc; *Recreations* sailing, real tennis, golf, rackets; *Clubs* MCC, Royal Ocean Racing, City Law, Jesters, Itchenor Sailing, Petworth House Tennis; *Style—* Richard Fleck, Esq; Slinfold Manor, Slinfold, nr Horsham, Sussex (☎ 0403 790978); Herbert Smith, Exchange House, Primrose St, London EC2A 2HS (☎ 071 374 8000, fax 071 496 0043)

FLECKER, James William; s of Henry Lael Oswald, CBE (d 1958), and Mary Patricia, *née* Hessey; *b* 15 Aug 1939; *Educ* Marlborough, Brasenose Coll Oxford (BA); *m* 22 July 1967, Mary Rose, da of Noel Jeremy Firth, of Sandal, Yorks; 3 da (Rachel b 1969, Lara b 1970, Brontë b 1974); *Career* asst master: Sydney GS NSW 1962-63, Latymer Upper Sch Hammersmith 1964-67; housemaster Marlborough 1975-80 (asst master 1967-80), headmaster Ardingly 1980-; *Recreations* hockey, flute playing, writing children's operas; *Style—* James Flecker, Esq; Headmaster's House, Ardingly Coll, Haywards Heath, W Sussex RH17 6SQ (☎ 0444 892330)

FLEET, Kenneth George; s of Frederick Major Fleet, and Elizabeth Doris, *née* Brassey; *b* 12 Sept 1929; *Educ* Calday Grange GS Cheshire, LSE (BSc); *m* 1953, Alice Brenda, da of Capt H R Wilkinson, RD; 3 s (Ian b 1957, Malcolm b 1959, Graham b 1964), 1 da (Elizabeth b 1962); *Career* Jl of Commerce Liverpool 1950-52; Sunday Times 1955-56, dep city ed Birmingham Post 1956-58, dep fin ed the Guardian 1958-63; city ed: Sunday Telegraph 1963-66, Daily Telegraph 1966-67 (dep city ed 1963); ed business news Sunday Times 1977-78, city ed Sunday Express 1978-82, city ed i/c Express Newspapers plc 1982-83, exec ed (fin & indust) The Times 1983-87; dir Young Vic 1976-83, chm Chichester Festival Theatre 1985- (dir 1984), govr LSE 1989; Wincott Award 1974; *Recreations* theatre, books, sport; *Clubs* MCC, Lord's Taverners, Piltdown Golf; *Style—* Kenneth Fleet, Esq; Chetwynd House, 24 St Swithin's Lane, London EC4N 8AE

FLEET, Dr Stephen George; s of George Fleet (d 1976), of Lewes, Sussex, and Elsie Fleet; *b* 20 Sept 1936; *Educ* Brentwood Sch, Lewes County GS, St John's Coll Cambridge (MA, PhD); *Career* registrary Univ of Cambridge 1983-, univ lectr in mineralogy at Cambridge 1967-83, bursar Downing Coll 1974-83 (pres 1983-85, vice master 1985-88); chm: Bd of Examinations 1974-83, Bursars' Ctee 1980-83; tstee of Fndn of Edward Storey 1977-; memb: Cncl of Senate Univ of Cambridge 1975-82, Fin Bd Univ of Cambridge 1979-83, Ctee of Mgmnt of Charities Property Unit Tst 1983-88, Fin Ctee of Int Union of Crystallography 1987-; tstee Mineralogical Soc of GB 1977-87, treas Cambridge Cwlth Tst 1983-; fell: Fitzwilliam House Cambridge 1963-66, Downing Coll 1973-; fndn fell Fitzwilliam Coll 1966-73; pres: Fitzwilliam Soc 1977, Downing Assoc 1991; FInstP; *Recreations* books, music, history of Sussex; *Clubs* Athenaeum, Royal Over-seas League; *Style—* Dr Stephen Fleet; Downing College, Cambridge CB2 1DQ (☎ 0223 334843); University Registry, Old Schools, Cambridge (☎ 0223 332294)

FLEETING, Jim; s of Robert Fleeting, and Elsie, *née* Taylor; *b* 8 April 1955; *Educ* St Mary's Irvine, St Michael's Acad Kilwinning; *m* Irene, da of Patrick Walker; 1 s (Barry b 24 June 1984), 2 da (Gemma b 24 Jan 1978, Julie b 18 Dec 1980); *Career* professional football manager; player: Norwich City 1975-78, Tampa Bay Rowdies 1978, Ayr Utd 1978-82, Clyde 1984-85; asst mangr Airdrieonians 1985-87; mangr: Stirling Albion 1988, Kilmarnock 1988-; *Recreations* family; *Style—* Jim Fleeting, Esq; Kilmarnock FC, Rugby Rd, Kilmarnock, Ayrshire (☎ 0563 25184, fax 0563 22181)

FLEETWOOD, Susan Maureen; da of John Joseph Kells Fleetwood, of St Andrews, Scotland, and Bridget Maureen, *née* Brereton; *b* 21 Sept 1944; *Educ* sixteen schs incl Convent of the Nativity Sittingbourne Kent, RADA (Bancroft Gold medal); *Career* actress; toured Arizona USA 1964 roles incl: Rosalind in As You Like It and Lady Macbeth in Macbeth; fndr memb Liverpool Everyman 1965-67; roles incl: Lady Percy in Henry IV, Gwendolen in The Importance of Being Earnest, Alison in Look Back in Anger, Liz in Fando and Liz, Margaret in The Great God Brown, chorus leader in Murder in The Cathedral, The Woman in The Four Seasons, Lady Macbeth in Macbeth; RSC 1967-91 roles incl: Regan in King Lear, Marina and Thaisa in Pericles, Julia in The Two Gentlemen of Verona, Portia in The Merchant of Venice, Katharine in The Taming of the Shrew, Princess of France in Love's Labours Lost (also US tour), Rosalind in As You Like It, Beatrice in Much Ado About Nothing, Madame Arkadina in The Seagull; NT 1976-89 roles incl: Pegeen Mike in Playboy of the Western World, Ophelia in Hamlet, Jo in Watch it Come Down, Zenocrate in Tamburlaine The Great, Nora in Plough and The Stars, Clare in Lavender Blue, Ismene in The Woman, Vanya in The Cherry Orchard, wife in La Ronde, June Taylor in Way Upstream, Titania in A Midsummer Nights Dream, Laura in The Father; films incl: Clash of the Titans, Heat and Dust, Young Sherlock Holmes, The Sacrifice, White Mischief, Dream Demons, The Krays; TV serials incl: Eustace and Hilda, The Good Soldier, Strangers and Brothers, Murder of a Moderate Man, Summer's Lease; TV plays incl: Watercress Girl, Don't be Silly, Dangerous Corner, Flying in the Branches; numerous radio plays; hon assoc memb RSC 1988 (assoc memb 1980-88); *Recreations* listening to music, going to the theatre, travelling, doing everything I can't do when working; *Clubs* Zanzibar; *Style—* Ms Susan Fleetwood; Duncan Heath, Paramount

House, 162 Wardour St, London W1V 3AT (☎ 071 439 1471)

FLEGG, Michael Robert; s of the late Robert William Flegg, and Eileen, *née* Blanshard; *b* 10 March 1938; *Educ* Preston Manor County GS, Open Univ (BA); *m* 1, 3 Sept 1960, Ann Wendy (d 1990), da of Elwyn Pryce Williams, of 28A Sheen Rd, Richmond, Surrey; m 2, 17 Nov 1990, Margaret Joan, da of late Cyril William Herbert Pitcher; *Career* admitted slr 1960; chm Tstees Kidney Res Aid Fund; memb 41 Club, former memb Round Table; memb: Law Soc, Legal Assoc of RTPI; *Recreations* photography, cinematography; *Style—* Michael Flegg, Esq; Seymour House, 11 and 13 Mount Ephraim Road, Tunbridge Wells, Kent TN1 1EN (☎ 0892 515121, fax 0892 544878)

FLEISCHMANN, Laureen Ann Rose; da of Jack Isadore Rose, of Spain, and Zena, *née* Gordon; *b* 6 Dec 1948; *Educ* Orange Hill Girls GS, Univ of London (LLB); *m* 7 June 1970, Robert Henry Fleischmann, s of Otto Fleischmann (d 1983); 1 s (Edward Ross b 31 Jan 1982), 1 da (Leonie Joslyn Rose b 8 Dec 1984); *Career* called to the Bar Inner Temple 1978; chm Women Lawyers Ctee; memb: Criminal Bar Assoc, Family Bar Assoc; *Recreations* reading, swimming, entertaining; *Style—* Mrs Laureen Fleischmann; 3 Kings Bench Walk, Temple, London EC4 (☎ 071 353 2416, fax 071 353 2941)

FLEMING, Lady (Francesca Georgina) Caroline; *née* Acheson; er da of 6 Earl of Gosford (d 1966), and his 1 wife Francesca Augusta Maria, *née* Cagiati; *b* 23 April 1940; *m* 15 Sept 1967, David Wallace Fleming, s of Wallace Fleming, of Santa Barbara, Calif, USA; 1 s (Alexander b 1968); *Style—* The Lady Caroline Fleming; 1045 5th Ave, New York 10028, NY, USA

FLEMING, Christopher Michael; 2 s of Capt Michael Valentine Fleming (d 1940), and Letitia Blanche (later Mrs James Currie Thomson), da of Hon Malcolm Algernon Borthwick (granted rank of a Baron's son 1913), s of Sir Thomas Borthwick, 1 Bt; *b* 8 May 1937; *Educ* Eton; *m* 1975, Judith Marion, da of Col Godfrey Jeans, of Broadchalke, Salisbury, Wilts ; 2 da; *Career* dir Thomas Borthwick plc; *Recreations* shooting, fishing, racing; *Clubs* Turf; *Style—* Christopher Fleming, Esq; Briff Farm, Bucklebury Common, nr Reading, Berks RG7 6SS (☎ 0635 63814)

FLEMING, Ven David; s of John Frederick Fleming, BEM (d 1976), of Norfolk, and Emma Fleming; *b* 8 June 1937; *Educ* Hunstanton Co Primary, King Edward VII GS Kings Lynn, Kelham Theol Coll; *m* 1966, Elizabeth Anne Marguerite, da of Bernard Bayleys Hughes (d 1947), of Birmingham; 3 s (Christopher b 1967, Nicholas b 1968, Matthew b 1972), 1 da (Fiona b 1970); *Career* curate of St Margaret Walton on the Hill 1963-67, chaplain HM Gaynes Hall, vicar Great Staughton 1968-76, rural dean of St Neots 1972-76, vicar Whittlesey 1976-85, rural dean March 1977-82, hon canon Ely Cathedral 1982-, archdeacon of Wisbech 1984-, vicar of Wisbech St Mary 1985-88; *Recreations* television, tennis, extolling Hunstanton; *Clubs* Whittlesey Rotary; *Style—* The Venerable the Archdeacon of Wisbech; 20 Barton Rd, Ely, Cambs CB7 4DE (☎ 0353 663 632)

FLEMING, Hon Mrs (Dorothy Charmian); *née* Hermon-Hodge; 3 da of 2 Baron Wyfold, DSO, MVO (d 1942), by Dorothy, *née* Fleming, aunt of Peter and Ian, the writers; *b* 4 Jan 1913; *m* 12 May 1938, her 1 cous, Maj Richard Evelyn Fleming, MC, 3 son of late Maj Valentine Fleming, DSO, MP, and yr bro of Peter and Ian; 5 s (two of whom m sisters, daughters of Sir Hereward Wake, 14 Bt), 3 da; *Style—* The Hon Mrs Fleming; Leygore Manor, Northleach, Glos (☎ 60234)

FLEMING, Dr Ian; s of John Fleming (d 1939), of Glasgow, and Catherine, *née* McLean (d 1970); *b* 19 Nov 1906; *Educ* Hyndland Sch Glasgow, Glasgow Sch of Art, Jordanhill Trg Coll Glasgow; *m* 27 April 1943, Catherine Margaret, da of Walter John Weetch (d 1948); 1 s (Alisdair Ian b 4 Dec 1949), 2 da (Elspeth Jane b 15 Oct 1944, Fiona Margaret b 10 Oct 1947); *Career* WWII serv, Police War Res Glasgow Police F Div 1940-43, cmmn into Army, 2 Lt Pioneer Corps 1943-46, serv Normandy, Holland and Germany, 30 Corps Capt 1945; sr lectr Glasgow Sch of Art 1946-48 (asst lectr 1931-41), warden Patrick Allen and Fraser Art Coll Hospitalfield Arbroath 1948-54, head Gray's Sch of Art RGIT Aberdeen 1954-72; chm: Peacock Printmakers Workshop Aberdeen 1972-85, Cyrenians Workshop 1985-; artworks in many public galleries in Britain, France, Norway and private collections in America, Canada, Germany, South Africa; Hon LLD Univ of Aberdeen 1984; memb RSW 1947, ARSA 1956; memb: RSA, Royal W of Eng Acad 1975, Royal Glasgow Inst of Fine Arts 1984; *Recreations* art only (being as good an artist as I can be); *Style—* Dr Ian Fleming; 15 Fonthill Rd, Aberdeen AB1 2UN (☎ 0224 580680)

FLEMING, Rear Adm Sir John; KBE (1960), DSC (1944); s of James Fleming, of Jarrow, Co Durham; *b* 2 May 1904; *Educ* County Sch Jarrow, St John's Coll Cambridge; *m* 1930, Jean Law, da of James Stuart Gillitt, of S Shields, Co Durham; *Career* RN 1925, Instr Cdr 1939, served at Admty (Naval Weather Service) 1939-42, Fleet Instr and Fleet Meteorological Offr on Staff of C-in-C Home Fleet 1942-44, Fleet Meteorological Offr to Allied Naval Cdr Expeditionary Force 1944-45, Asst Dir Naval Weather Serv 1945-47, Dep Dir 1947-49, Instr Capt 1950, Fleet Instr and Meteorological Offr on Staff of C-in-C Home Fleet 1950-51, Cmd Instr Offr on staff of C-in-C The Nore 1951-52, on staff of Dir Naval Educn Serv 1952-56, Instr Rear Adm 1956, Dir Naval Educn Serv 1956-60, ret; *Style—* Rear Adm Sir John Fleming, KBE, DSC; Mullion Cottage, Tanners Lane, Haslemere, Surrey (☎ 0428 2412)

FLEMING, John Grierson; s of Richard Grierson Fleming of Riseholme, Lincoln (d 1966), and Mildred Mary, *née* Birkett (d 1984); *b* 2 Feb 1926; *Educ* Lincoln Sch Lincoln, Trinity Coll Cambridge (BA, MA, LLB, LLM); *m* 29 Aug 1953, Margaret, da of John Edward Rayner, of Lincoln (d 1960); 1 s (Alistair b 1958), 2 da (Amanda b 1955, Nicola b 1961); *Career* RA short course Univ of Edinburgh 1944-45, primary trg corps trg OCTU 1945-46, cmmnd RA 1946, ADC to GOC 5AA Gp 1946-48, (Capt 1947); articled clerk Johnson Jecks and Landons 1950-52, admitted slr 1953 (first in order of merit Law Soc final exam); awarded Scott scholarship, Clements Inn, Maurice Nordon, City of London Slrs Co Grotius, and John Mackerell prizes, asst slr Reynolds Parry Jones and Crawford 1953-54, ptnr Evill and Coleman 1955-58 (asst slr 1954-55); admin ptnr Stephenson Harwood 1983- (head of Commercial Dept 1973-83, ptnr 1959-, joined 1958); Club Capt Beaconsfield CC 1979- (hon sec 1962-79); Freeman Worshipful Co of: Gardeners (former clerk), Slrs; craftsmen Gardeners of Glasgow; *Recreations* cricket, golf, gardening, travel, maps, watercolours; *Clubs* Western (Glasgow), Gresham, ROL, MCC; *Style—* John G Fleming, Esq; Quantocks, 73 Burkes Road, Beaconsfield, Bucks, HP9 1PP (☎ 0494 674 264); Stephenson Harwood, One St Paul's Churchyard, London, EC4M 8SH (☎ 071 329 4422, fax 071 606 0822, telex 886 789)

FLEMING, John Marley; s of David A Fleming, of Methuen, Massachusetts USA, and Mary L, *née* Marley; *b* 4 April 1930; *Educ* Harvard (BA), Harvard Sch of Business Admin (MBA); *m* 1961, Jeanne Claire, da of Edward Retelle, of Lawrence, Massachusetts; 1 s, 2 da; *Career* served Lt USN; chm and chief exec Vauxhall Motors 1982-; *Recreations* skiing, sailing, golf; *Clubs* Harpenden Golf, Harvard (London); *Style—* John Fleming Esq; Barnards, Oakhurst Ave, Harpenden, Herts AL5 2ND; c/o Vauxhall Motors plc, Kimpton Rd, Luton, Beds (☎ 0582 21122)

FLEMING, Robert Atholl; s of Atholl Fleming, MBE (d 1972), and Phyllis Wallace, *née* Best (d 1983); *b* 19 July 1933; *Educ* Cranbrook Sch, Sydney; *m* 15 Sept 1982, Marion Heather, da of Maurice Leigh (d 1969); *Career* TV documentary prodr, dir and writer; md ARGO Prodns Ltd; Freeman City of London; JP (1983-84); *Clubs* Garrick, MCC, Royal Sydney Golf; *Style—* Robert Fleming, Esq; 5 South Villas, Camden Square, London NW1 9BS (☎ 071 267 3316)

FLEMING, (Ronald) Stewart; s of Norman Fleming, and Laurena Fleming; *b* 14 Aug 1943; *Educ* Wallesey GS, Horace Mann Sch NY, Emmanuel Coll Cambridge; *m* Jennifer Mary, da of Gordon McQuie; 2 s (Sam Jonathan b 8 Feb 1973, Joshua James b 17 Nov 1975); *Career* journalist; Bootle Times 1963-65, Prudential Assurance 1965-68, The Guardian 1968-74; Financial Times: joined 1974, NY corr 1976-80, Frankfurt corr 1980-83, US economics corr Washington 1983-86, US ed Washington 1986-89, fin ed 1989-; *Recreations* reading, swimming; *Style—* Stewart Fleming, Esq; Financial News Editor, The Financial Times, 1 Southwark Bridge, London SE1 9HL (☎ 071 873 4171, fax 071 873 3074)

FLEMING, (Dr) Thomas Kelman (Tom); OBE (1980); s of Rev Peter Fleming (d 1939); *b* 29 June 1927; *Educ* Daniel Stewart's Coll Edinburgh; *Career* actor, writer, prodr, broadcaster; co-fndr Edinburgh Gateway Co 1953-65, RSC 1962-64, fndr and dir Royal Lyceum Theatre Co 1965-66, govr Scottish Theatre Tst 1980-82, dir Scottish Theatre Company 1982-87; Edinburgh Festival prodns of: Moliere, Aristophanes, Sir David Lyndsay, Sidney Goodsir Smith; The Thrie Estaites STC Warsaw 1986 (Roman Szydlowski award); films incl: King Lear, Mary Queen of Scots, Meetings with Remarkable Men; numerous TV plays incl: title role Jesus of Nazareth, Henry IV (parts 1 & 2), Weir of Hermiston, Reith; over 2000 broadcasts since 1944; BBC Radio commentator (royal events) 1950-; BBC TV commentator on over 250 national and state occasions incl: Silver Wedding 1972, Princess Anne's Wedding 1973, Prince of Wales's Wedding 1981, State visits to USA and Japan, Silver Jubilee 1977, The Queen Mother's 80th Birthday Celebrations 1980, The Queen's 60th Birthday 1986, Queen's Birthday Parade 1970-88, Cenotaph Service of Remembrance 1961 and 1965-88, Installations of Archibishop of Canterbury 1975 and 1980, two Papal Inaugurations 1978, funerals of Duke of Gloucester, Duke of Windsor, Montgomery of Alamein, Mountbatten of Burma, King Frederick of Denmark, Marshal Tito, Princess Grace, King Olav, Cardinal Heenan, Pope John Paul I; DUniv Heriot-Watt 1984; FRSAMD 1986; *Books* So That Was Spring (poems), Miracle at Midnight (play), Voices Out of the Air, BBC Book of Memories (contrib); *Recreations* hill walking, music; *Clubs* Royal Cwlth Soc, Scottish Arts (Hon), Royal Scottish Pipers' Soc (Hon); *Style—* Tom Fleming, Esq, OBE; 56 Murrayfield Gardens, Edinburgh; Tomfarclas, Ballindalloch, Banffshire

FLEMING-GALE, Roger Adrian; s of Frederick Henry Gale, of 7 Corwell Lane, Hillingdon, Middlesex, and Beatrice Ada, *née* Lee; *b* 20 March 1946; *Educ* Southall GS, Univ of Newcastle (BA, BArch); *m* Jan 1970 (m dis 1988), Patricia Anne, da of William Thurlow; 2 s (Hamilton Elliot b 16 Sept 1970, Jacob Thomas Henry b 28 Feb 1979), 2 da (Jessica Mary Elizabeth b 6 Oct 1976, Sophie Emily Rose (twin) b 28 Feb 1979); *Career* architect; Pring White & Partners 1971-72, Richard Turley Associates 1972-73, Champman Taylor Partners 1973-76, Coxon Associates 1976-85, McColl 1985-89 (latterly divnl dir), divnl dir Retail Div Fitch RS 1989-; memb ARCUK; *Style—* Roger Fleming-Gale, Esq; Fitch RS, Porters South, 4 Crinan Street, London N1 9UE (☎ 071 278 7200, fax 071 465 6473)

FLEMINGTON, Roger; s of Walter Harold Flemington (d 1977), of Market Drayton, Shrops, and Mary Elizabeth Julia, *née* Stone (d 1985); *b* 7 May 1932; *Educ* Nantwich and Acton GS; *m* 3 Sept 1955, Doreen Helen (d 1990), da of Claude George Smyter (d 1968), of London; *Career* Nat Serv RAF 1950-52; Nat West Bank Gp 1948-: md The Diners Club Ltd 1975-77, sr int exec 1978-79, chief int exec Asia, Australasia and Africa 1979-81, asst gen mangr Int Banking Div 1981-84, dir Westminster Ltd 1984-, gen mangr Premises Div 1984-86, gen mangr Domestic Banking Div 1986-88, chief exec UK fin serv 1989-90, dep gp chief exec 1990-; dir: Coutts & Co 1986-, Nat West Bank plc 1988-, Lombard North Central plc 1989-; dep chm Chartered Inst of Bankers 1990- (memb Cncl 1986-); memb: Br Bankers Assoc Exec Ctee 1989-, CBI City Advsy Gp 1990-; tstee Ind Broadcasting Telethon Tst 1989; Freeman City of London 1979, Liveryman Worshipful Co of Woolmen; FCIB 1986, FRSA; *Recreations* music, fly-fishing, country pursuits, antiques, travel, reading; *Clubs* MCC, Over-Seas Bankers; *Style—* Roger Flemington, Esq; Larkrise, Rectory Lane, Buckland, Betchworth, Surrey (☎ 0737 844522); National Westminster Bank plc, 41 Lothbury, London EC2P 2BP (☎ 071 726 1266)

FLEMMING, John Stanton; s of Sir Gilbert Nicolson Flemming, KCB (d 1981), and Virginia, *née* Coit; *b* 6 Feb 1941; *Educ* Rugby, Trinity Coll Oxford, Nuffield Coll Oxford (BA); *m* 1963, Jean Elizabeth, da of George Briggs (d 1982); 3 s (Edward b 1968, Thomas b 1970, William b 1973), 1 da (Rebecca b 1966); *Career* economist; offical fell and bursar Nuffield Coll Oxford 1965-80, ed Economic Journal 1976-80; chief advsr Bank of England 1980-83, econ advsr to the Govr Bank of England 1983-, exec dir Bank of England 1988-91, chief economist Euro Bank of Reconstruction and Devpt; memb Cncl and Exec Ctee Royal Econ Soc 1980-, memb Advsy Bd on Res Cncls 1986-91; *Clubs* Reform; *Style—* John Flemming, Esq; European Bank of Reconstruction and Devpt, Level 7, 6 Broadgate, London EC1 (☎ 071 496 0060)

FLEMMING, Lady; Virginia; da of Stanton Coit, PhD, of London; *m* 1935, Sir Gilbert Flemming, KCB (d 1981), sometime Permanent Sec Miny of Educ, s of Percy Flemming, FRCS, of London; 2 s, 2 da; *Style—* Lady Flemming; G3 Burton Lodge, Portinscale Rd, London SW15 (☎ 081 874 9375)

FLEMONS, Kenneth John; s of Sidney Flemons (d 1968), of Eastbourne, and Amy Elizabeth, *née* Davies (d 1972); *b* 27 Jan 1924; *Educ* All Saints Sch, Bloxham & Cathedral Sch Shanghai, Northampton Engrg Coll London (now City Univ); *m* 19 March 1955, Margaret Joan Ogilvy (d 1990) da of Sydney Duncan Mai 1961), of Purley; 1 s (Gordon b 4 July 1959), 1 da (Rosemary (Mrs C Bayford) b 18 March 1957); *Career* interned by Japanese in Lunghwa Camp Shanghai (as civilian) 1941-45; chartered civil engr; Taylor Woodrow Construction 1949-53, Air Miny works directorate 1953-55, Sir Frederick Snow & Ptnrs 1955-88 (assoc 1964-88, conslt 1988-); hon fell Inst of Water and Environmental Mgmnt (memb Cncl 1987-88); CEng, FICE, Hon FIPHE (memb Cncl 1979-87, pres 1986-87); *Recreations* walking, lawn bowls, gardening; *Clubs* Royal Overseas League; *Style—* Kenneth Flemons, Esq; Belgrove, 45 Rose Bushes, Epsom Downs, Surrey KT17 3NT (☎ 0737 354 821)

FLESCH, Michael Charles; QC (1983); s of Carl Franz Flesch, and Ruth, *née* Seligsohn (d 1987); *b* 11 March 1940; *Educ* Gordonstoun, UCL (LLB, 1st XV rugby, 1st VI tennis); *m* 2 Aug 1962, Gail, *née* Schrire; 1 s (Daniel b 1976), 1 da (Dina b 1973); *Career* called to the Bar Gray's Inn 1963 (Lord Justice Halker sr scholarship), Bigelow teaching fell Univ of Chicago 1963-64, pt/t lectr in revenue law UCL 1965-82, practice at Revenue Bar 1966-, chm Taxation and Retirement Benefits Ctee of Bar Cncl 1985-; govr Gordonstoun Sch 1976-; *Recreations* all forms of sport; *Clubs* Arsenal FC, Middx CCC, Brondesbury Lawn Tennis and Cricket; *Style—* Michael Flesch, Esq, QC; Gray's Inn Chambers, Gray's Inn, London WC1R 5JA (☎ 071 242 2642, fax 071 831 9017)

FLESHER, Peter Stewart; s of William Owen Flesher (d 1981), of Shelf, Halifax , and Edith Alice, *née* Asquith (d 1969); *b* 20 Nov 1942; *Educ* Hipperholme GS; *m* Carol Lesley, da of Lesley Taylor; 1 s (David Gregory b 2 May 1976), 1 da (Adele Suzanne b 15 March 1974); *Career* Williamson Butterfield Roberts (now Grant Thornton):

articled clerk 1958-64, qualified chartered accountant 1964, audit and tax 1964-73, fndr ptnr i/c insolvency Leeds/Bradford 1974, ptnr i/c NE Regn insolvency, memb Insolvency Panel, managing ptnr Bradford Office 1988-90; memb Cncl: Insolvency Practitioners Assoc 1989- (chm Ethics Ctee 1989-), Soc of Practitioners of Insolvency 1990-; FCA 1977 (ACA 1964), FIPA 1983, MICM 1980; *Recreations* cricket, golf, watching rugby & soccer, music, travel, reading; *Clubs* Bradford, Shipley Golf, Shelf Cricket; *Style*— Peter Flesher, Esq; Grant Thornton, St Johns Centre, 110 Albion Street, Leeds LS2 8LA (☎ 0532 455514, fax 0532 465055, car 0860 659429)

FLETCHER, Adrian James; s of Col Michael J R Fletcher, MBE, of Folkestone, Kent, and Marguerite, *née* Sproule; *b* 16 Dec 1943; *Educ* Sir Roger Manwood's Sch Sandwich Kent, Imperial Coll Univ of London (BSc, MSc, DIC); *m* 20 April 1974, Carolyn Lennox, da of Arthur E Davis (d 1975), of Sydney, Aust; 2 s (James E b 1975, Nicholas A L b 1980), 1 da (Emily C b 1978); *Career* head business policy courses Graduate Business Sch Univ of NSW Aust 1972-75, exec ctee memb and mangr corporate devpt Glass Containers Ltd Sydney 1975-79, princ Adrian Fletcher & Assocs 1979-, chm Petroleum Securities Group 1981-, dir Morganite Aust Pty Ltd 1981-, exec ctee memb and gen mangr fin planning Westpac Banking Corp Sydney 1983-87 (chief mangr 1980-83), gen mangr global investmt banking Westpac Banking Corp London 1987-89; ARCS, memb Inst of Dirs of Aust, ARCS, FAIM; *Recreations* music, reading; *Clubs* Australian (Sydney), Union (Sydney), Royal Sydney Yacht Squadron; *Style*— Adrian Fletcher, Esq; 9 The Vale, Chelsea, London SW3 6AG (fax : 071 351 1378)

FLETCHER, Alan Gerard; s of Bernard Fletcher, and Dorothy, *née* Murphy; *b* 27 Sept 1931; *Educ* Christ's Hosp Sch, Central Sch of Arts and Crafts, RCA, Sch of Architecture & Design Yale Univ (MFA); *m* 5 July 1956, Paola Biagi; 1 da (Raffaella b 1961); *Career* designer Fortune Magazine NY 1958-59, freelance practice London 1959-62; ptnr: Fletcher Forbes Gill 1962-65, Crosby Fletcher Forbes 1965-72, Pentagram Design 1972-; pres Designers & Art Dirs Assoc 1973, int pres Alliance Graphique Int 1982-85; Awards: Royal Designer for Indust RSA 1972, One Show Gold award NY 1974, Gold award 1974 and President's award Designers and Art Dirs Assoc London 1977, medal Soc of Industl Artists and Designers 1982; FSIAD 1964, ARCA; memb: AGI, RDI; sr fell RCA 1989; *Books* Graphic Design: Visual Comparisons (with Colin Forbes and Bob Gill, 1963), Was Ich Sah (1967), A Sign Systems Manual (with Theo Crosby and Colin Forbes, 1970), Identity Kits: A Pictorial Survey of Visual Arts (with Germans Facetti, 1971); with Pentagram ptnrs: Pentagram: The Work of Five Designers (1972), Living by Design (1978), Ideas on Design (1986); *Style*— Alan Fletcher, Esq; Pentagram, 11 Needham Rd, London W11 2RP (☎ 071 229 3477, fax 071 727 9932, telex 8952000 PENTA G)

FLETCHER, Alfred William (Willie); s of Lt-Col Geoffrey Littledale Fletcher, JP (d 1945), of Glan Aber, Abergele, Clwyd, N Wales, and Lilian Steuart, *née* Gladstone (d 1960); *b* 30 Jan 1909; *Educ* Eton; *m* 21 Feb 1940, Olive Daphne, da of Maj James Gardiner, OBE, JP (d 1971), of Tanners Pool, Lymm, Cheshire; 1 s (Guy b 21 Nov 1944), 1 da (Joseene b 7 Aug 1942); *Career* Civil Air Guard 1939, LDV and Cheshire Home Guard 1940, Flt Lt RAFVR at the Air Miny 1940-46, Cheshire Co SO in the Civil Def 1953-68; memb Liverpool Stock Exchange 1934-49, chm G F Hunt Ltd 1949-56, chm and md Moreton Engrg Co Ltd 1956-76, chm Carlton Masonic Hall Ltd; Liverpool Trustee Savings Bank: mangr 1946, tstee 1957, dep chm 1955-67, chm 1957-59; Trustee Savings Bank Assoc: NW Area dep chm 1961-62, chm 1963-64; memb: Nat Rifle Assoc, Altcar Rifle Club; exec ctee memb WABGI 1953-65, pres Dee Wildfowlers Club 1956-74, Cdr TBS Club 1975-76, chm Leighton and Parkgate Mens Cons Branch 1948-67, church official; MRSH; *Recreations* shooting, fishing, sailing; *Clubs* Carlton, Athenaeum (Liverpool); *Style*— Willie Fletcher, Esq; Perdituft, Brook Lane, Parkgate, South Wirral, Cheshire L64 6TP (☎ 051 336 1276)

FLETCHER, Andrew Fitzroy Stephen; s of (Maj) Fitzroy Fletcher, of Lodge House, Ansford, Castle Cary, Somerset, and Brygid, *née* Mahon; *b* 20 Dec 1957; *Educ* Eton, Magdalene Coll Cambridge (MA); *m* 1 Sept 1984, Felicia, da of Maj John Philip Pagan Taylor (d 1986), of Egland House, nr Honiton, Devon; 2 s (Thomas b 1987, James b 1989); *Career* 2 Lt Welsh Gds 1976; practising Barrister (Inner Temple, 1980); Freeman City of London 1986; *Recreations* travel, fishing, reading; *Clubs* Boodle's; *Style*— Andrew Fletcher, Esq; 4 Pump Ct, Temple, London EC4 (☎ 071 353 2656)

FLETCHER, Prof Anthony John; s of John Molyneux Fletcher (d 1986), and Delle, *née* Chenevix-Trench; *b* 24 April 1941; *Educ* Wellington, Merton Coll Oxford (BA); *m* 29 July 1967, Tresna Dawn, da of Charles Henry Railton Russell; 2 s (Crispin b 1970, Dickon b 1972); *Career* history teacher Kings Coll Sch Wimbledon 1964-67, reader (formerly lectr and sr lectr) Dept of History Univ of Sheffield; FRHistS; *Books* Tudor Rebellions (1967), A County Community in Peace and War: Sussex 1600-1660 (1975), The Outbreak of the English Civil War (1981), Reform in the Provinces (1986); *Recreations* theatre, music, opera, walking, gardening; *Style*— Prof Anthony Fletcher; 2 Blue Coat Court, Durham DH1 1WS; Dept of History, Univ of Durham, Durham DH1 3EX (☎ 091 374 2010)

FLETCHER, Dr Archibald Peter; s of Walter Archibald Fletcher (d 1970), and Dorothy Mabel Fletcher; *b* 24 Dec 1930; *Educ* Kingswood Sch Bath, London Hosp Med Coll, UCL, St Mary's Hosp Med Sch; *m* 1972, Patricia Elizabeth Samson, *née* Marr; 3 s, 2 da; *Career* sr lectr in chemical pathology St Mary's Hosp London 1967-70, head of biochemistry American Nat Red Cross 1970-73, princ med offr and med assessor to Ctee on Safety of Medicines 1977-, chief scientific offr and sr princ med offr DHSS 1978, res physicican Upjohn Int 1978-80, sr med offr DHSS; ptnr Documenta Biomedica, med dir IMS International, dir PMS International Ltd; *Publications* numerous papers in scientific and med jls on: glycoproteins, physical chemistry, metabolism of blood cells, safety evaluation of new drugs; *Recreations* gardening, cooking; *Clubs* Wig and Pen, Royal Society of Medicine; *Style*— Dr Archibald Fletcher; Hall Corner Cottage, Little Maplestead, Halstead, Essex (☎ 0787 475465)

FLETCHER, Audrey Littledale; da of Lt-Col Geoffrey Littledale Fletcher, JP (d 1945), and Lilian Steuart, *née* Gladstone (d 1960); *b* 14 Jan 1910; *Career* awarded: The Distinguished War Serv Cert 1946, Queen's Voluntary Serv Medal and 9 Bars, War Serv Medal, hon life memb BRCS 1943-, chm local branch Cons Assoc 1937-39, asst co cmmr GG Assoc, asst co VAD controller 1940-45, co dir BRCS 1945-50, staff offr special ctees BRCS Nat HQ London 1950-72, patrol offr War Orgn Red Cross and St John 1940-56, VAD cdr N Cmd Catterick Mil Hosp, JP Co Denbigh 1945-80; SSStJ 1962-; *Clubs* Ladies Carlton, VAD Ladies; *Style*— Miss Audrey Fletcher

FLETCHER, Prof Charles Montague; CBE (1952); s of Sir Walter Morley Fletcher, KBE, CB, FRS (d 1933), and Mary (Maisie) Frances, *née* Cropper (d 1972); *b* 5 June 1911; *Educ* Eton, Trinity Coll Cambridge, St Bartholomew's Hosp Med Sch (MD); *m* 24 Oct 1941, Hon Louisa Mary Sylvia Seely, da of 1 Baron Mottistone; 1 s (Mark Walter b 1942), 2 da (Susanna Mary b 1945, Caroline Anne b 1949); *Career* Michael Foster res student Trinity Coll 1934-36, Nuffield Res student Oxford 1940-42; asst physician EMS 1943-44, Goulstonian lectr 1947, dir MRC Pneumoconiosis Res Unit 1945-52; Hammersmith Hosp: physician, 1952-76 prof clinical epidemiology 1973-76 (reader 1960-73, sr lectr 1952-60), sec MRC Ctee on Bronchitis Res 1954-76, vice pres RCP 1975 (memb Cncl 1959-62), sec Ctee on Smoking and Health 1961-71; WHO conslt: Pulmonary Heart Disease 1960, Chronic Bronchitis 1962, Smoking and Health 1970; vice chm Health Educn Cncl 1967, pres Action on Smoking and Health (ASH) 1979- (chm 1971-76); appeared on many TV med progs incl: Matters of Medicine 1952, Hurt Mind 1955, Your Life in Their Hands 1958-65, Television Doctor 1969-70; Editorial Bd Jl Med Educn 1975-; vice pres Coll of Health 1983-; memb: Central Health Services Cncl and Standing Med Adv Ctee 1966-76, British Diabetic Assoc (chm Education Section 1973-78), Governing Body Inst of Med Ethic 1973-77, Asthma Res Cncl 1968-; (SOC memb Exec and Med Advsy Ctee 1979); Rock Carling fell Nuffield Provincial Hosps Fund 1973; *Books* Communication in Medicine (1973), Natural History of Chronic Bronchitis and Emphysema (1976), Talking and Listening to Patients (1989); many papers on: First Use Penicillin (1941), Dust Diseases on Lungs (1946-55), Bronchitis and Emphysema (1953-76); *Recreations* gardening, music, bee keeping; *Clubs* Brooks's; *Style*— Prof Charles Fletcher, CBE; 24 West Square, London SE11 4SN (☎ 071 735 8753); 2 Coastguard Cottages, Newtown, Newport, Isle of Wight PO30 4PA (☎ 0983 78321)

FLETCHER, Rev Hon David Clare Molyneux; s of late Baron Fletcher, PC (Life Peer); *b* 15 May 1932; *Educ* Repton, Worcester Coll Oxford (MA); *m* 1970, Susan Charlotte, da of late Alan Stockdale Langford, of Jersey; 2 children; *Career* ordained 1958, curate of St Mary's Islington 1958, Scripture Union staff worker 1962, rector of St Ebbe's Oxford 1986; *Style*— Rev the Hon David Fletcher; St Ebbe's Rectory, 2 Roger Bacon Lane, Oxford OX1 1QE

FLETCHER, Geoffrey; MBE (1944), TD (1947), JP (Kent 1965), DL (1979); s of Brig Harold Fletcher, OBE, TD, JP (d 1964); *b* 27 April 1920; *Educ* Repton; *m* 1947, Cynthia Diana Howard, da of David Howard Lloyd (d 1966), of Newmarket; 2 s, 2 da; *Career* Maj BEF 1940 and 1944; engr; chm Drake & Fletcher Ltd; FIAgrE; *Recreations* golf, bridge, gardening; *Clubs* Farmers', Royal St Georges Golf; *Style*— Geoffrey Fletcher, Esq, MBE, TD, JP, DL; Thornham Friars, Pilgrims Way, Thurnham, Kent; Drake & Fletcher, Parkwood, Sutton Rd, Maidstone, Kent (☎ 0622 55531)

FLETCHER, Giles; s of Thomas Simons Fletcher (d 1985; nephew of 1 Earl Attlee, KG, OM, CH, PC), of Nunton Cottage, Nunton, Salisbury, and Janet, *née* Bigg (d 1987); *b* 12 Aug 1936; *Educ* Marlborough; *m* 18 Jan 1964, Jennifer Marion Edith, da of Sir Eric Cecil Heygate Salmon, MC, DL (d 1946), of The Vale House, Old Church St, London SW3, and sis of Rev Anthony James Heygate Salmon, *qv*; 2 s (James b 1965, Timothy b 1974), 1 da (Alice b 1967); *Career* Fletcher and Partners: ptnr 1964-76, senior ptnr 1977-; govr Godolphin Sch, treas Southern Cathedrals Festival, tstee Charitable Tsts; churchwarden; FCA 1961; *Recreations* hill walking, English and French Cathedrals and Churches; *Style*— Giles Fletcher, Esq; Apple Tree House, Middle Woodford, Salisbury SP4 6NG (☎ 0722 733 29); c/o Fletcher and Partners, Crown Chambers, Bridge St, Salisbury SP1 2LZ (☎ 0722 327801, fax 0722 32839)

FLETCHER, Ian Macmillan; WS; s of John Malcolm Fletcher, JP, of Gourock, Scotland, and Jane Ann Cochran Fletcher (d 1980); *b* 16 Feb 1948; *Educ* Greenock Acad, Univ of Glasgow (LLB); *m* 15 Jan 1977, Jennifer Margaret, da of Capt John Brown William Daly, MN (d 1972), of Glasgow; 1 s (Richard John Malcolm b 13 Jan 1980), 2 da (Elizabeth Jane b 4 Aug 1978, Eleanor Kathleen b 21 Aug 1985); *Career* admitted slr: Scotland 1971, England 1978; asst slr Richards Butler 1977-79; ptnr: MacRoberts 1980-87, Richards Butler 1987-; authorised insolvency practitioner; co sec Chilton Bros Ltd, memb Cncl Insolvency Lawyers Assoc Ltd; memb: Law Soc, Law Soc of Scotland, Soc WS, Int Bar Assoc (memb Ctee J Section on Business Law), Soc of Scottish Lawyers London (pres); LTCL, LRAM, ARCO, MInstD, MIPA; *Books* The Law and Practice of Receivership in Scotland (jtly, 1987); *Recreations* music, golf, swimming; *Clubs* Caledonian, Western (Glasgow); *Style*— Ian Fletcher, Esq, WS; Beaufort House, 15 St Botolph St, London EC3A 7EE (☎ 071 247 6555, fax 071 247 5091, telex 949494 RBLAW)

FLETCHER, Prof James Pearse; s of Harold Stanton Fletcher (d 1985), of Clifton, Bristol, and Bessie Florence, *née* Pearse (d 1976); *b* 25 Oct 1928; *Educ* King's Coll Taunton, Univ of Bristol (BDS); *m* 8 Sept 1962, Judith Mary, da of John Abbott (d 1982), of The Hall, Caerleon, Gwent; 1 s (Anthony b 1963), 1 da (Suzanne b 1967); *Career* Nat Serv RADC 1953-55, Lt, Capt; NHS Hosp appts and private practice 1952-57, conslt sr lectr in dental med Univ of Bristol 1963-80 (lectr in dental surgery 1959, lectr in dental med 1959-63), emeritus prof and sr fell Univ of Liverpool 1990- (lectr in paradontal diseases 1957-58, prof of dental surgery 1980-82, Louis Cohen prof of dental surgery 1982-90); pres Br Soc of Periodontology 1981-82 (vice pres 1980-81, 1982-83); chm: Mersey Region Hosps Gp BDA 1986-87, Post Grad Advsy Panel for Hosp Dental Surgery Mersey Regn 1989-90; memb: Liverpool Health Authy 1981-87, Cncl Br Soc for Oral Med 1982-85, BDA, Int Assoc for Dental Res, Br Soc for Dental Res, Br Soc for Oral Pathology, Br Soc for Oral Med, Int Assoc of Oral Pathologists, Liverpool Odontological Soc; Liverpool Medical Inst; alternate advsr Mersey region RCS Faculty of Dental Surgery 1981-87; FRSM, LDSRCS, FDSRCS (Eng); *Books* Human Disease for Dental Students (jtly, 1981), Elementi di Patologia Generale e di Patologia Umana (Medica e Chirurgica) Per Studenti di odontoiatria (jtly, 1983); *Recreations* music, watercolour painting, photography; *Style*— Prof James Fletcher; School of Dentistry, Pembroke Place, PO Box 147, Liverpool L69 3BX (☎ 051 706 5267, fax 051 709 0724, telex 627095 UNILPLG)

FLETCHER, John Duncan; s of Joseph Fletcher, of Farnham, nr Knaresborough, N Yorks; *b* 20 Oct 1942; *Educ* Leeds GS, St Catherine's Coll Oxford, Harvard Business Sch (MBA); *m* 1967, Gloria; 1 s; *Career* former chief exec Oriel Foods; dir Assoc Dairies Gp plc, md Asda Foods 1981-; *Recreations* golf, walking; *Clubs* RAC, Pannal Golf; *Style*— John Fletcher, Esq; c/o Asda, Asda House, Britannia Rd, Morley, Leeds LS27 0BT (☎ 0532 539141); The Priory, Follifoot, Harrogate, N Yorks HG3 1DT (☎ 0423 871537)

FLETCHER, Dr (Timothy) John; s of George Spencer Fletcher (d 1981), of Silsden, W Yorks, and Pattie Margaret, *née* Beaver; *b* 12 Sept 1946; *Educ* The Leys Sch Cambridge, Univ of Glasgow (BVMS), Magdalene Coll Cambridge (PhD); *m* 8 July 1972, Nichola Rosemary, da of Hubert Henry Ormerod Chalk (d 1981); 2 da (Stella b 1978, Martha b 1979); *Career* fndr first Br deer farm 1973, dir Br Deer Producers Soc Ltd 1983; chm Br Deer Farmers' Assoc 1982-84, pres Veterinary Deer Soc, dir Scot Deer Centre 1987-90; Reediehill Deer Farm awarded The Queen's award for Export Achievement 1990; *Recreations* food, wine, travel, collecting deer literature and ephemera, gardening; *Clubs* The Farmers Club; *Style*— Dr John Fletcher; Reediehill Farm, Auchtermuchty, Fife KY14 7HS (☎ 0337 28369, fax 0337 27001, telex 72165G)

FLETCHER, John W S; *Educ* Uppingham, Teeside Poly (H Dip in Civil and Structural Engrg); *m* 1964, Jacqueline; 2 s, 2 da; *Career* Cleveland Bridge and Engineering Company (acquired by Cementation 1968, pt of Trafalgar 1970): joined as trainee civil engr, dir 1968-75, md 1975-82, divnl md 1982; currently mktg and business devpt dir Trafalgar House plc (and dir various subsid Cos), md Trafalgar House Corporate Development Ltd; dir: John Brown plc, The Cunard Steam-Ship Co plc, Conwy Barrage Co Ltd, Parclose Ltd, Poole Power Co Ltd, Scott Lithgow Ltd, EuroRoute Construction Ltd, Anglo Japanese Construction Ltd, City of London Heliport Ltd, Dartford River Crossing Ltd, Eurorail Ltd, Tunesure Ltd, Cleveland Bridge &

Engineering Middle East (Private) Ltd, British Rail Engineering Ltd; AICE; *Recreations* sailing; *Style—* John Fletcher, Esq; Trafalgar House plc, 1 Berkeley St, London W1A 1BY (☎ 071 499 9020, fax 071 493 5484, telex 921341, private line 071 491 1495)

FLETCHER, Prof John Walter James; s of Roy Arthur Walter Fletcher, MBE, of Sherborne, Dorset, and Eileen Alice, *née* Beane; *b* 23 June 1937; *Educ* Yeovil Sch Somerset, Trinity Coll Cambridge (BA, MA), Univ of Toulouse (MPhil, PhD); *m* 14 Sept 1961, Beryl Sibley, da of William Stanley Connop (d 1963), of Beckenham, Kent; 2 s (Hilary b 1976, Edmund b 1978), 1 da (Harriet b 1972); *Career* lectr in English Univ of Toulouse 1961-64, lectr in French Univ of Durham 1964-66, prof French studies Univ of E Anglia 1989- (French lectr 1966-68, reader French 1968-69, prof comparative lit 1969-89, pro vice chllr 1974-79; memb: Soc of Authors, Translators Assoc; *Books* The Novels of Samuel Beckett (1964), Claude Simon and Fiction Now (1975), Novel and Reader (1980); *Recreations* listening to Eighteenth Century music; *Style—* Prof John Fletcher; Sch of Modern Languages and European History, Univ of E Anglia, Norwich, Norfolk NR4 7TJ (☎ 0603 56161, fax 0603 58553, telex 975197)

FLETCHER, Rev the Hon Jonathan James Molyneux; s of Baron Fletcher, PC (Life Peer); *b* 22 Sept 1942; *Educ* Dragon Sch, Repton, Hertford Coll Oxford; *Career* ordained: deacon 1968, priest 1969; curate: Christ Church Cockfosters 1968-72, Holy Sepulchre Church Cambridge 1972-76, St Helen's Bishopsgate 1976-81; incumbent Emmanuel Wimbledon 1982-; *Style—* The Rev the Hon Jonathan Fletcher; Emmanuel Parsonage, 8 Sheep Walk Mews, Ridgway, Wimbledon, London SW19 4QL (☎ 081 946 4728)

FLETCHER, Kenneth William Ian; s of William Walter Fletcher (d 1982), and Minnie Ena, *née* Day (d 1982); *b* 17 Sept 1927; *Educ* Coopers' Company's Sch; *m* 23 July 1949, Alice Harriett, da of James George Fewtrell (d 1978); 1 s (Martin Andrew b 1954), 1 da (Susan Carol b 1950); *Career* Nat Serv signalman RCS 1947-49; Pearl Assurance Co Ltd 1949-81, chm and pres The Monarch Insurance Co of Ohio 1981-85, gen mangr Pearl Assurance plc 1987-90 (asst gen mangr 1986-87); pres First New York Syndicate Corp 1986-90, dir Hallmark Insurance Co Ltd 1987-; FCII 1959; *Style—* Kenneth Fletcher, Esq; Brimley Lodge, Megg Lane, Chipperfield, Kings Langley, Herts WD4 9JN (☎ 0923 260883), Hallmark Insurance Co Ltd, Portsoken House, Minories, London EC3N 1EE (☎ 071 480 7221, fax 071 702 4944)

FLETCHER, Sir Leslie; DSC (1945); s of Ernest Fletcher (d 1960), and Lily Fletcher; *b* 14 Oct 1922; *Educ* Nether Edge Secdy Sch Sheffield; *m* 1947, Audrey Faviell, da of William Faviell Jackson (d 1972); 1 s, 1 da; *Career* Nat Serv WWII, Lt (A) RNVR, Europe and Far East, Fleet Air Arm 1942-46; Rolls Royce Ltd 1938-39, Nat Provincial Bank 1939-42 and 1946-47 (articled clerk 1947), dir J Henry Schroder Wagg & Co Ltd 1955-71, Glynwed International plc 1966-86 (chm 1971-86), dep chm Standard Chartered plc 1972-89, chm Standard Chartered Merchant Bank Ltd 1983-89, RMC Group plc 1983-, The Rank Organisation plc 1984-, chm Westland plc 1988-; *Recreations* golf, gardening, photography; *Clubs* MCC, RAC, Brooks's, R and A; *Style—* Sir Leslie Fletcher, DSC

FLETCHER, Hon Mrs (Louisa Mary Sylvia); *née* Seely; yst da of 1 Baron Mottistone, CB, CMG, DSO, TD (d 1947), and his 1 wife Emily Florence, *née* Crichton (d 1913); *b* 9 Aug 1913; *m* 24 Oct 1941, Prof Charles Montague Fletcher, CBE, s of Sir Walter Morley Fletcher, KBE, CB, FRS (d 1933); 1 s, 2 da; *Style—* The Hon Mrs Fletcher; 24 West Sq, London SE11 4SN (☎ 071 735 8753)

FLETCHER, Mandie Elizabeth; da of Sqdn-Ldr C W Fletcher (ret), of Homefield, Lodsworth, Midhurst, Sussex, and Shirley, *née* Hull; *b* 27 Dec 1954; *Educ* Guildford HS Surrey; *Career* prodr/dir: The Fainthearted Feminist 1985 (ACE award winner best comedy dir), Blackadder II 1988 (ACE award winner best comedy series), Blackadder III 1988 (BAFTA award winner best comedy series), Shalom Joan Collins 1989, various commercials; *Recreations* cycling; *Style—* Miss Mandie Fletcher; 34 Inglethorpe St, London SW6 6NT (☎ 071 385 5465)

FLETCHER, Cmdt Marjorie Helen Kelsey; CBE (1988); da of Norman Farler Fletcher, and Marie Amelie, *née* Adams; *b* 21 Sept 1932; *Educ* Avondale HS, Sutton Coldfield HS for Girls; *Career* slr's clerk 1948-53; WRNS: Telegraphist 1953, Third Offr 1956, Second Offr 1960, First Offr 1969, Chief Offr 1976; NDC 1979, directing staff RN Staff Coll 1980-81, psc 1981, Supt 1981, Int Mil Staff NATO HQ 1981-84, asst dir Naval Staff Duties 1984-85, Cmdt 1986, dir WRNS 1986-88; ADC to HM the Queen 1986-88; CBIM 1987; *Books* The WRNS; *Recreations* reading, collecting pictures, needlework, painting, natural and English history; *Style—* Cmdt Marjorie Fletcher, CBE

FLETCHER, Martin Anthony; s of Anthony Travers Nethersole Fletcher, of Brandeston, Suffolk, and Nancy Evelyn, *née* Scott; *b* 7 July 1956; *Educ* Uppingham, Univ of Edinburgh, Univ of Pennsylvania (MA); *m* 10 Jan 1981, Katy Jane, *née* Beney; 1 s (Barnaby Martin b 12 April 1986), 2 da (Hannah Catherine b 2 June 1984, Imogen Nancy b 26 April 1989); *Career* journalist; North Herts Gazette 1980-82, Daily Telegraph 1982-83, Washington corr The Times 1989- (lobby corr 1986-89); *Books* The Good Caff Guide (1980); *Recreations* tennis, squash, skiing, children; *Style—* Martin Fletcher, Esq; 3252 Juniper Lane, Falls Church, VA 22044, USA (☎ 703 534 2953); The Times of London, 1333 H St NW, Suite 440, Washington DC 20005 (☎ 0101 202 3477659)

FLETCHER, Michael Granville; s of (Henry) Granville Fletcher, of London, and (Dorothy) Lesley Fletcher; *b* 10 Oct 1945; *Educ* Clayesmore Sch, Univ of Keele (BA); *m* 28 Aug 1981, Terezia Laura Fernandes (Tess), da of Max Calais; 1 s (Benjamin Granville Fletcher b 18 May 1987), 1 da (Emily Alexandra Fletcher b 9 May 1989); *Career* Mktg Dept Organics Div ICI 1969-74, MIL Investments Ltd 1974-77, memb Bd Dundonian plc 1976, managing ptnr Seyski 1977-81, dir then md Planned Savings Ltd/Dominion Financial Management Ltd 1981-86; dir Johnson Fry plc 1987-; md Johnson Fry Finanical Services Ltd 1987-, chm Johnson Fry Asset Managers plc 1990-; *Recreations* fishing, bridge; *Style—* Michael Fletcher, Esq; Johnson Fry Asset Managers plc, Dorland House, 20 Regent St, London SW1Y 4PZ (☎ 071 321 0220, fax 071 437 4844)

FLETCHER, Nathan; CBE (1984); s of Nathan Fletcher (d 1937), of York, and Mary Hannah Maria, *née* Gledhill (d 1980); *b* 8 Aug 1920; *Educ* Welbeck Boys Sch Castleford, Whitwood Technical Coll Yorks; *m* 1946, Iris Hilda, da of Richard Jackson (d 1961), of Cheshire; 1 da (Lesley b 1950); *Career* chm Kadek Press Ltd 1968-; memb Taylor Woodrow Exec Bd 1972-; dir Taylor Woodrow plc 1974-; vice pres of Small Business Bureau 1982-; pres Ealing North C Assoc 1985; vice pres (life) Tug of War Assoc 1987 (pres 1985-86); *Recreations* reading, music; *Style—* Nathan Fletcher, CBE; Whitwood, 7 Oak Tree Drive, Englefield Green, Surrey (☎ Egham 37489); Taylor Woodrow plc, 345 Ruislip Rd, Southall, Middlesex (☎ 081 578 2366, telex 24428, fax 081 575 4701)

FLETCHER, Brig (Bolton) Neil Littledale; CBE (1976); s of Maj Bolton Littledale Fletcher (d 1943), and Vera Marguerite, *née* Edmondson (d 1977), who later m Lt-Col David Ritchie, OBE, MC (d 1974); *b* 19 Aug 1923; *Educ* Stowe; *m* 30 July 1947, Mary Elizabeth, formerly w of Maj Dennis William Seddon-Brown (ka 1944), and da of Col John Hugh Lovett Poë, DSO, DL (d 1974); 1 da (Elizabeth Caroline Anne b 1950), 1 step s (Jonathan Lovett Seddon-Brown b May 1943); *Career* cmmnd KSLI 1943, cmd Depot KSLI 1959-60, DS Staff Coll Camberley 1960-63, cmd 1 KSLI in UK Singapore and Malaysia 1965-67, Army's author 1968-69, Col GS Hong Kong 1970-71, cmd 2 Inf Bde 1973-75, dep constable Dover Castle 1973-75; ret 1978; ADC to HM The Queen 1976-78; *Recreations* shooting, golf; *Clubs* Army and Navy; *Style—* Brig Neil Fletcher, CBE; Old Vicarage, Shipton Bellinger, Tidworth, Hants SP9 7UG

FLETCHER, (Peter) Neil; s of Alan Fletcher, of Thurnby, Leicester, and Ruth Fletcher (d 1961); *b* 5 May 1944; *Educ* Wyggeston Boys' GS Leicester, City of Leeds Coll of Educn, London Univ (BA); *m* 9 Sept 1967, Margaret Mary, da of Anthony Gerald Monaghan (d 1967); 2 s (Ben b 25 May 1971, Sam b 18 July 1974); *Career* teacher Leeds 1966-68; lectr in further educn: Leeds 1969-70, Harrow 1970-73, Merton 1973-76; princ admin offr NALGO 1976-91; dep leader Camden Cncl 1982-84 (memb 1978-86); ILEA: memb 1979-90, chm Further and Higher Educn sub ctee 1981-87, leader 1987-90; chm: Assoc of Metropolitan Authorities Educn Ctee 1987-90 (memb 1981-90), Cncl of Local Educn Authorities 1987-90; govr: London Inst 1985-91, LSE 1990-91; FRSA 1989; hon fell Coll of Preceptors 1990; *Recreations* cooking, walking, cricket, football; *Style—* Neil Fletcher, Esq; 13 Ravenshaw Street, London NW6 1NP (☎ 071 435 5306); NALGO Headquarters, 1 Mabledon Place, London WC1H 9AJ (☎ 071 388 2366, 071 387 6692)

FLETCHER, Paul Thomas; CBE (1959); s of Stephen Baldwin Fletcher (d 1971), of Maidstone, and Jessie Carrie, *née* Rumsby (d 1963); *b* 30 Sept 1912; *Educ* Nicholson Inst Isle of Lewis, Maidstone GS, Medway Tech Coll (BSc); *m* 12 April 1941, Mary Elizabeth, da of Percy Howard King (d 1936), of Maidstone; 3 s (John b 1947, David b 1949, Peter b 1952); *Career* chartered engrg; chief engr Miny of Works 1951-54 (joined 1939), engrg dir UKAEA Industrial Group 1954-61, dir United Power Co 1961-65, md GEC Process Engineering Ltd 1965-70, dep chm Atomic Power Construction Ltd 1976-80 (md 1970-75), conslt 1980-; dep pres Br Standards Inst 1981-89 (chm 1979-81), hon fell IMechE 1989 (pres 1975-76); FEng; FICE; FIMechE, FIEE; *Recreations* motoring, photography; *Style—* Paul T Fletcher, Esq, CBE

FLETCHER, Air Chief Marshal Sir Peter Carteret; KCB (1968), OBE (1944), DFC (1942), AFC (1952); s of Frederick Wheeler Trevor Fletcher (d 1964), of Norton, S Rhodesia, and Dora, *née* Clulee; *b* 7 Oct 1916; *Educ* St George's Coll S Rhodesia, Rhodes Univ; *m* 1940, (Marjorie) Isobel, da of Gilbert Percival Kotzé (d 1953), of Grahamstown, SA; 2 da (Anne, Elizabeth); *Career* transferred from S Rhodesian Air Force to RAF 1941, CO 135 Fighter Sqdn and 258 Fighter Sqdn 1940-42, CO 25 Elementary Flying Training Sch 1942-43, directing staff of RAF Staff Coll 1943-44, of Jt Services Staff Coll 1945-46, and IDC 1956-57, CO RAF Abingdon 1958-60, dir Operational Requirements (B) Air Miny 1961-63, Air Cdre 1961, Air Vice-Marshal 1964, Asst Chief of Air Staff (Policy and Planning) 1964-66, AOC 38 Gp, Transport Cmd 1966-67, Air Marshal 1967, Vice-Chief of Air Staff 1967-70, Controller of Aircraft, Miny of Aviation Supply 1970, Air Systems Controller Def Procurement Exec 1971-73; dir: Hawker Siddeley Aviation Ltd 1974-77, Corporate Strategy and Planning, Br Aerospace 1977-82, Airbus Industry Supervisory Bd 1979-82, ret Br Aerospace 1982; aerospace conslt 1983-; FRAeS 1986; *Recreations* books, travel; *Clubs* RAF; *Style—* Air Chief Marshal Sir Peter Fletcher, KCB, OBE, DFC, AFC; 85A Campden Hill Court, Holland St, Kensington, London W8 7HW (☎ 071 937 1982)

FLETCHER, Philip John; s of Alan Philip Fletcher, QC, of Royston Herts, and Annette Grace, *née* Wright; *b* 2 May 1946; *Educ* Marlborough, Trinity Coll Oxford (MA); *m* 12 Feb 1977, Margaret Anne, da of J E Boys, of Witley, Surrey; 2 da (Helen b 1978 d 1989, Sarah b 1982); *Career* teacher VSO 1967-68; DOE 1968- (formerly MPBW): asst princ 1968, W Midlands Regnl Office 1973-76, private sec to Perm Sec 1978, asst sec Private Sector Housebuilding 1980, local govt expenditure 1982-85, under sec Fin 1986-90, land use planning 1990-; lay reader St Michael's Stockwell; *Style—* Philip Fletcher, Esq; Department of the Environment, 2 Marsham St, London SW1P 3EB (☎ 071 276 3854)

FLETCHER, Piers Michael William; s of Col Michael James Rex Fletcher, MBE, of Folkestone, Kent, and Mary Anita, *née* Williams; *b* 10 Aug 1956; *Educ* Wellington Coll, Christ Church Oxford (MA); *m* 8 Aug 1986, Paula Harvey Anne, da of Brig John Levey, of Burghfield Common, Hampshire; *Career* 2 Lt 6 QEO Gurkha Rifles 1975; dir: GNI Ltd 1984, Baltic Futures Exchange 1988-; *Recreations* polo, cooking, photography; *Style—* Piers Fletcher, Esq; 46 Lessar Ave, London SW4 9HQ (☎ 081 673 8508); GNI Ltd, Colechurch House, 1 London Bridge Walk, London SE1 2SX (☎ 071 378 7171, car 0860 834174)

FLETCHER, (Leopold) Raymond; s of Leopold Raymond Fletcher, of Ruddington, Notts; *b* 3 Dec 1921; *Educ* overseas, Humboldt Univ Berlin; *m* 1, 1947, Johanna Klara Elisabeth (d 1973), da of Karl Ising, of Berlin; m 2, 1977, Dr Catherine Elliott, widow of Jasper Fenn; *Career* served WWII Indian Army Ordnance Corps and Intelligence BAOR; journalist (columnist with The Times); MP (Lab) Ilkeston 1964-83; former leader UK Delegn to WEU and Cncl of Europe (where was ldr Socialist Gp) and vice pres Consultative Assembly; fndr Airship Assoc 1970; *Style—* Raymond Fletcher, Esq; 23 Ilkeston Rd, Heanor, Derbyshire DE7 7DT (☎ 0773 712682)

FLETCHER, Dr Robin Anthony; OBE (1984), DSC (1944); s of Maj P C Fletcher, MC, TD (d 1961), of Hinton Priory, Hinton Charterhouse, Bath, and Edith Maud, *née* Okell, JP (d 1978); *b* 30 May 1922; *Educ* Marlborough, Trinity Coll Oxford (MA, DPhil); *m* 9 Dec 1950, Jinny May; 2 s (Clive b 1951, Denys b 1954); *Career* WWII: ordinary seaman RN HMS Gambia 1941-42, Sub Lt (later Lt) RNVR 1943-46 (Levant Schooner Flotilla Med, minesweeping trawlers UK); Univ of Oxford: lectr Modern Greek 1949-79, domestic bursar Trinity Coll 1950-74, sr proctor 1966-67, memb Hebdomedal Cncl 1967-74; sec Rhodes Tst and warden Rhodes House 1980-89, tstee Oxford Preservation Tst; former memb Bd Govrs: Kelly Coll Cheltenham Coll, Marlborough Coll, Radley Coll, Sherborne Sch; bronze medallist GB hockey team Olympic Games 1952, hockey player for England 1949-55, pres Hockey Assoc 1972-83; *Books* Kostes Palamas (1984); *Recreations* golf, listening to music; *Clubs* Naval, Vincent's; *Style—* Dr Robin Fletcher, OBE, DSC; Binglea, Quoyloo, Stromness, Orkney KW16 3LU (☎ 085 684 532)

FLETCHER, Prof Roger; s of Harry Fletcher (d 1942), and Alice, *née* Emms; *b* 29 Jan 1939; *Educ* Huddersfield Coll, Univ of Cambridge (MA), Univ of Leeds (PhD); *m* 23 Sept 1963, Mary Marjorie, da of Charlie Taylor (d 1970), of 28 Leyland Rd, Harrogate; 2 da (Jane Elizabeth b 17 Nov 1968, Sarah Anne b 13 Sept 1970); *Career* lectr Univ of Leeds 1963-69, princ scientific offr Aere Harwell 1969-73, prof Univ of Dundee 1984- (sr lectr and reader 1973-84); FIMA, FRSE; *Books* Practical Methods of Optimization Vol I (1980), Vol 2 (1981); *Recreations* hillwalking, bridge; *Style—* Prof Roger Fletcher; Dept of Mathematics and Computer Science, University of Dundee, Dundee DD1 4HN (☎ 0382 23181, telex 76293)

FLETCHER, Dr Ronald Frank; s of Capt Roland Fletcher, OBE (d 1973), and Lizzie May, *née* Furniss (d 1970); *b* 30 Jan 1927; *Educ* Kind Edward VI HS Birmingham, Univ of Birmingham (BSc, MB ChB, PhD, MD); *m* 22 April 1954, June Margaret, da of Ephraim Preston Astill (d 1971); 3 s (Martin b 12 May 1956, Preston b 29 Dec 1958, Stephen b 29 March 1962); *Career* Nat Serv Capt RAMC 1952-54; sr house offr Metabolic Res Unit E Birmingham Hosp 1954-59, Eli Lilly res fell Sinai and Johns Hopkins Hosps Baltimore USA 1959-60, conslt physician Dudley Rd Hosp Birmingham 1965-, sr clinical lectr Univ of Birmingham 1965- (lectr in med 1960-65); vice chm W

Birmingham Health Authy; FRCP 1972; *Books* Lecture Notes on Endocrinology (1967, 1978, 1982 and 1987); *Recreations* mountaineering, travel; *Clubs* Midland Assoc of Mountaineers, Birmingham Med Res Expeditionary Soc; *Style*— Dr Ronald Fletcher; 11 St Mary's Rd, Harborne, Birmingham B17 0EY (☎ 021 427 4043); Dudley Rd Hospital, Dudley Rd, Birmingham B18 7QH (☎ 021 554 3801)

FLETCHER, Stuart David; s of Brough Fletcher, and Norma Hilda, *née* Taylor; *b* 8 June 1964; *Educ* Rastrick HS; *m* 4 Oct 1986, Katharine Anne, da of Joseph McEvoy; 1 s (Craig Stuart b 26 June 1989); *Career* professional cricketer Yorkshire CCC: debut 1983, awarded county cap 1988, best bowling 8 for 58 v Essex 1988; represented: Rastrick CC under 17, Yorks Fedn under 19, N of England under 19; Benson & Hedges Cup Winner's medal 1987; formerly: coach builder Reliance Garage, builder Conroy & Booth, cricket coach Canberra; *Recreations* watching Leeds Utd FC, golf, snooker; *Style*— Stuart Fletcher, Esq; Yorkshire County Cricket Club, Headingley, Leeds LS6 3BU (☎ 0532 787394)

FLETCHER, Tracy Dain; s of Barrie Dain Fletcher (d 1989), of Birmingham, and Betty, *née* Daniels (d 1977); *b* 11 March 1960; *Educ* Hodge Hill Comp Sch, Matthew Bolton Tech Coll (HNC); *m* 24 Aug 1989, Gaynor Maria, da of Morris James Highfield; *Career* draughtsman Newman Tonks Hardware 1978-86, project design engr Worcester Parsons 1987-; winner Br Design Cncl award 1990; three separate patents in his name on behalf of Worcester Parsons; *Style*— Tracy Fletcher, Esq; 3 Cearl Court, 67A Shirley Rd, Acocks Green, Birmingham B27 7NB (☎ 021 708 0865); Worcester Parsons, Lifford Lane, Kings Norton, Birmingham B30 3JR (☎ 021 459 2421, fax 021 459 6405)

FLETCHER, Wilfred Leslie; CBE (1977); s of Frederick Smith Fletcher, OBE (d 1970), of Marton, Cleveland, and Isabella, *née* Litler (d 1967); *b* 25 July 1913; *Educ* Rossall Sch, Univ of Durham; *m* 20 May 1939, (Margaret) Joan, da of John Coates Hird (d 1947), of Yarm; 1 s (John b 1940), 1 da (Penelope b 1942, d 1975); *Career* dir: Teeside Bridge Engineering Co Ltd 1945-70 (md 1950-70), British Structural Steel Co 1956-67, Dorman Long (Steel) Ltd 1959-67, Dorman Long (Africa) Ltd 1959-67, Dorman Long (Nigeria) 1962-67, Redpath Dorman Long Ltd 1967-73, BSC Works Group 1969-71, BSC Constructional E Div 1971-73; md Dorman Long (Bridge Engineering) Ltd 1962-67; pres: Cleveland Sci Inst 1969-70, Br Constructional Steelwork Assoc 1972-75; govr Teesside Poly 1963-72, chm NSG Engrg Employers Fedn 1964-67; Rear Cdre Salcombe YC 1978-81, chm Salcombe and Kingsbridge Estuary Assoc 1989-90, memb Salcombe Harbour Ctee of S Hams DC; MICE 1939, FIStructE 1959, CEng 1970; *Recreations* yachting, beekeeping, philately; *Clubs* Salcombe Yacht; *Style*— Wilfred Fletcher, Esq, CBE; Whitehorses, Salcombe, Devon (☎ 054 884 2652); Waterfoot Lodge, Pooley Bridge, Cumbria

FLETCHER, Winston; s of Albert Fletcher (d 1963), of London, and Bessie, *née* Miller (d 1955); *b* 15 July 1937; *Educ* Westminster City Sch, St John's Coll Cambridge (MA); *m* 14 June 1963, Jean, da of Alfred Brownston (d 1968), of Bristol; 1 s (Mathew b 5 Nov 1970), 1 da (Amelia b 1 Jan 1966); *Career* dir Sharps Advertising 1964-69 (joined as trainee 1959), md MCR Advertising 1970; Fletcher Shelton Delaney: fndr 1974, md 1974-81, chm 1981-83; chm and chief exec Ted Bates UK 1983-85; chm: Delaney Fletcher Delaney 1985-89, Delaney Fletcher Slaymaker Delaney and Bozell 1989-; advertising conslt SDP, regular author for nat business and advertising trade pres; memb Cncl Advertising Standard Authy; FIPA (pres 1989-), FRSA; *Books* The Admakers (1972), Teach Yourself Advertising (1978), Meetings, Meetings (1983), Commercial Breaks (1984), Superefficency (1986), The Manipulators (1988), Creative People (1990); *Recreations* reading, writing, arithmetic; *Clubs* Reform, Royal Institution, Annabels, Thirty, Mosimanns; *Style*— Winston Fletcher, Esq; Souldern Mill, Bicester, Oxon (☎ 0869 345 497); 12 Bourdon St, Berkeley Sq, London W1 (☎ 071 629 4844)

FLETCHER-COOKE, Sir Charles; QC (1958); yr s of Capt Charles Arthur Fletcher-Cooke (d 1924), and Gwendolen May Fletcher-Cooke; bro of Sir John Fletcher-Cooke, CMG, *qv*; *b* 1914; *Educ* Malvern, Peterhouse Cambridge; *m* 1959 (m dis 1967), Diana Mary Margaret Westcott, yr da of Capt Edward Westcott King, RA, and formerly wife of 3 Baron Avebury; *Career* barrister 1938, contested East Dorset Div (Lab) 1945, later resigned from Labour Party, MP (C) Darwen 1951-83, jt parly under-sec of state Home Office 1961-63, MEP 1977-79; Dato of the Kingdom of Brunei 1978; kt 1981; *Clubs* Garrick, Pratt's; *Style*— Sir Charles Fletcher-Cooke, QC; The Red House, Clifton Hampden, Oxon OX14 3EW (☎ 086730 7754)

FLETCHER-COOKE, Sir John; CMG (1952); er s of Capt Charles Arthur Fletcher-Cooke (d 1924), and Gwendolen May, *née* Bradford; *b* 8 Aug 1911; *Educ* Malvern, Université de Paris, St Edmund Hall Oxford; *m* 1, 8 Aug 1935 (m dis 1949), (Margaret) Louise, da of James Paterson Brander, of Edinburgh; 1 s (Charles Louis Brander b 1947); m 2, 10 Sept 1949 (m dis 1971), Alice Elizabeth, da of Dr Russell Forest Egner, of Washington, DC, USA; 1 s (Richard Mark Forest b 1951), 1 da Anne Gillian b 1953); m 3, 1977, Marie-Louise, da of Roger Jonchim Ducasson, French Colonial Service (d 1947), and wid of Louis, Viconte Fournier de la Barrer; *Career* Colonial Office 1936-42 and 1946, POW Japan 1942-45, under-sec to Govt of Palestine 1946-48, colonial sec and occasional actg govr Cyprus 1951-55, occasional actg govr Tanganyika 1959-61, stood for (C) Luton 1963, MP (C) Southampton Test 1964-66, author; kt 1962; *Recreations* writing, building dry Cotswold stone walls; *Clubs* Travellers', Royal Commonwealth Soc; *Style*— Sir John Fletcher-Cooke, CMG; c/o Lloyds Bank Ltd, Finsbury Circus Branch, 3 Broad St Pla, EC2

FLETCHER ROGERS, David Geoffrey; s of Murray Rowland Fletcher Rogers, of Flat 10, Mount View Rd, London N4, and Dorothy Lilian, *née* Bardsley (d 1950); *b* 20 May 1927; *Educ* St Edward's Sch Oxford; *m* 28 Sept 1972, Helen Susan, da of Peter Alexander Stewart, of 5 Windsor Lodge, Windsor Rd, Ansdell, Lytham St Annes; 2 s (Anthony, Jonathan) 1 da (Karen Elizabeth); *Career* cmmnd RNVR HMS Conway; called to the Bar Grays Inn; mangr Legal Dept Monotype Corp 1957-65; legal advsr: NRDC 1965-69, Dunlop Co Ltd (Dunlop Ltd) 1969-85; advsr to and dir of various cos 1985-; chm local Cons Assoc, first chm Anti Counterfeiting Gp; memb: Inst of Patent Agents, Licensing Exec Soc; *Books* Butterworths Encyclopaedia of Forms and Precedents vols 16 and 16a (princ contrib chapter on patents and designs), Pre-action Discovery; *Recreations* sailing (cruising), enjoying pleasant company; *Clubs* Army and Navy, Conway Cruising Assoc; *Style*— David Fletcher Rogers, Esq; Conway House, Furlong Lane, Totternhoe, Dunstable, Beds LU6 1QR (☎ 0582 472 300); AWD Ltd, Boscombe Rd, Dunstable, Bedfordshire (☎ 0582 472 244)

FLETCHER-VANE; *see*: Vane

FLETT, David John; s of Alec Flett, DFC, QPM, of Acle, Norfolk, and Catherine May, *née* Read; *b* 13 Dec 1946; *Educ* Colfes GS; *m* 11 May 1974, Susan Hilda Georgina, da of Sidney Rimmington (d 1972); 1 s (Jonathon Alexander b 2 May 1980), 1 da (Claire Susannah b 24 April 1977); *Career* RBT Bradford Ltd 1963-64, active underwriter Syndicate 250 Lloyds 1983- (jr underwriting asst 1964-83); dir: RBT Bradford Holdings Ltd 1983, Wren Underwriting Agencies Ltd 1987; ACII 1971; *Recreations* fishing, metal detecting; *Style*— David Flett, Esq; Wren Underwriting Agencies Ltd, Minster House, Arthur St, London EC4R 9AB (☎ 071 623 3050)

FLEURY, Noel Wilfred; s of Gerald Wilfred Fleury (d 1949), and Claire Maud Fleury; *b* 1 Dec 1908; *Educ* Central Sch of Arts and Crafts (NDD); *m* 4 Feb 1961, Helen Amy, da of James McLean; 1 s (Simon Marc b 31 Jan 1964), 1 da (Samantha b 28 May 1965); *Career* chief designer Bakelite Xylonite Ltd 1966-70; Bissell Appliances Ltd: design dir 1970-84, md 1984-88, sr vice pres 1988-; winner Plastics Design prize 1966 and 1969, Duke of Edinburgh Design prize; outside assessor for the Design Cncl; memb: Bursary Ctee RSA, Design Ctee Plastics Inst, Selection Ctee Design Cncl; Freeman Worshipful Co of Horners; FCSD; *Recreations* golf; *Clubs* Old Ford Manor Golf; *Style*— Noel Fleury, Esq; Bissell Appliances Ltd, 2 Jubilee Ave, Highams Park Ind Est, Highams Park, London E4 9HN (☎ 081 531 7241)

FLEW, Prof Antony Garrard Newton; o s of Rev Dr R Newton Flew (d 1962); *b* 11 Feb 1923; *Educ* Kingswood Sch Bath, St John's Oxford Oxford; *m* 1952, Annis Ruth Harty, da of Col Frank Siegfred Vernon Donnison; 2 da; *Career* prof of philosophy: Univ of Keele 1954-71, Calgary Univ 1972-73, Univ of Reading 1973-82, York Univ Toronto 1983-85; fndr memb Cncl of Freedom Assoc, dir Academic Cncl Adam Smith Inst Educn Gp of the Centre for Policy Studies until 1990; *Books incl*: Hume's Philosophy of Belief (1961), God and Philosophy (1967), Crime or Disease (1973), Sociology, Equality and Education (1976), The Presumption of Atheism (1976), A Rational Animal (1978), The Politics of Procrustes (1981), Darwinian Evolution (1984), Thinking about Social Thinking (1985), David Hume: Philosopher of Moral Science (1986), The Logic of Mortality (1987), Power to the Parents (1987); *Recreations* walking, house maintenance; *Style*— Prof Antony Flew; 26 Alexandra Rd, Reading, Berks RG1 5PD (☎ 0734 61848)

FLICK, (Michael) Tony; s of Maj Samuel Godfrey Flick, of The Laurels, Saxmundham, Suffolk, and Madge, *née* Brownlow; gggf established auctioneering business in 1833 (William H Brown Ltd, now trading as Flick & Son), presentation of clock in Saxmundham Church Tower in his memory ca 1880 by his family; *b* 15 May 1935; *Educ* Eversley Sch Southwold, Dover Coll, RAC Cirencester (Dip); *Career* 2 Lt Suffolk Regt, seconded Somaliland Scouts Br Somaliland (acting Capt for 7 months); chartered surveyor; divnl area dir William H Brown, dir Suffolk Agricultural Assoc; farmer; FRICS, FAAV, MRAC; *Recreations* shooting, gardening; *Style*— Tony Flick, Esq; Westering Middleton, Saxmundham, Suffolk IP17 3NY (☎ 0728 73 382); Ashford House, Saxmundham, Suffolk (☎ 0728 603232)

FLIGHT, Howard Emerson; s of Bernard Thomas Flight, of Devon, and Doris Mildred Emerson, *née* Parker; *b* 16 June 1948; *Educ* Brentwood Essex, Magdalene Coll Cambridge (MA), Univ of Michigan Business Sch (MBA); *m* 1973, Christabel Diana Beatrice, da of Christopher Paget Norbury (d 1975), of Worcestershire; 1 s (Thomas b 1978), 3 da (Catherine b 1975, Josephine b 1986, Mary Anne b 1988); *Career* jt md Guinness Flight Global Asset Mgmnt (formerly Invest div of Guinness Mahon); dir: Guinness Flight Int Fund Ltd, Guinness Flight Global Strategy Fund Ltd; memb Lloyds; C Party Candidate Bermondsey and Southwark both elections 1974, C Parly candidate approved list; govr Brentwood Sch, tstee The Elgar Fndn, memb Planning Ctee Magdalene Coll Cambridge; *Books* All You Need to Know About Exchange Rates (jtly, 1988); *Recreations* skiing, classical music, fruit farming; *Clubs* Carlton, Winchester House; *Style*— Howard Flight, Esq; 6 Ruvigny Gardens, Putney, London SW15 (☎ 081 789 0923); The Norrest, Leigh Sinton, Worcestershire; Guinness Flight Global Asset Management Ltd, 32 St Mary at Hill, London EC3 (☎ 071 626 9333)

FLINDALL, Jacqueline; JP (Oxford and Salisbury Bench 1982); da of Henry Flindall (d 1940), and Lilian, *née* Evans (d 1940), brought up by unc Alfred Thomas Evans, OBE, late Chief Constable of Pembrokeshire; *b* 12 Oct 1932; *Educ* St David's Sch Ashford, Middlesex; *Career* SRN Univ Coll Hosp; SCM: St Lukes Hosp Guildford, Watford Maternity Hosp; asst matron Wexham Park Hosp 1957-63, dep supt of Nursing Prince of Wales Hosp 1964-66; chief nursing offr: Northwick Park Hosp 1969- 73, Oxfordshire Health Authy 1973-83; regnl nursing offr Wessex RHA 1985-; assoc conslt PA Mgmnt Conslts; pres UCH Nurses League; hon FRCN 1983; *Recreations* painting; *Style*— Miss Jacqueline Flindall, JP; 4 Mill Lane, Romsey, Hants SO51 8EU (☎ 0794 513 926)

FLINN, Donal Patrick; s of Hugo Victor Flinn (d 1943); *b* 8 Nov 1923; *Educ* Christian Brothers Coll Cork, Univ Coll Cork (BComm); *m* 1954, Heather Mary, da of Fred W Cole (d 1979); 2 s (Hugo, Richard b 1958), 1 da (Jennifer b 1961); *Career* chm: Barclays Bank plc (Irish Branch), Barclays Bank Ireland Ltd, De La Rue Smurfit Ltd; dir: Fitzwilton Ltd, Abbey Life Assurance Co (Ireland) Ltd; memb Bd and pres US C of C in Ireland; FICA (pres 1976-77); *Recreations* golf, tennis, fishing; *Clubs* Portmarnock Golf, Fitzwilliam Lawn Tennis, Royal St George Yacht; *Style*— Donal Flinn, Esq; 44 Orwell Park, Rathgar, Dublin 6, Eire; Hurricane Lodge, Glenbeigh, Co Kerry (☎ 010 35366 68255)

FLINN, Dr Roger Martin; Percy Leonard Flinn (d 1978), of Manchester, and Edith Amy Isaac; *b* 30 Oct 1934; *Educ* Manchester GS, Univ of Manchester (MB ChB), Univ of Birmingham (MSc); *m* 27 Aug 1960, Hazel Spark, da of Thomas Roydon Spark, of Leicester; 2 s (Graham b 1965, Neil b 1969), 1 da (Marian b 1967); *Career* Nat Serv 1960-62; dir Centre for Computer Studies Univ of Birmingham 1971- (lectr in anatomy 1963-70, sr lectr 1970-78); int parachute judge, chief judge World Cup 1989 1990, 1991; med advsr Br Parachute Assoc; fell Zoological Soc 1965, MBCS 1970; *Recreations* sport, rugby football, parachuting; *Style*— Dr Roger Flinn; 35 Medcroft Ave, Birmingham B20 1NB (☎ 021 554 9582); Centre for Computer Studies, Medical School, University of Birmingham (☎ 021 472 1311, fax 021 414 4036)

FLINT, Prof Anthony Patrick Fielding; *b* 31 Aug 1943; *m* 1967, Chan Mun Kwun; 2 s; *Career* res fell Depts of Physiology and Obstetrics and Gynaecology Univ of Western Ontario 1969-72, sr res biochemist Dept of Obstetrics and Gynaecology Welsh Nat Sch of Med 1972-73, lectr Nuffield Dept of Obstetrics and Gynaecology Univ of Oxford 1973-77; AFRC: sr scientific offr 1977-79, princ scientific offr 1979-85, sr princ scientific offr 1985-87, visiting scientist 1987-; dir Inst of Zoology Univ of London 1987-, dir of sci Zoological Soc 1987-; visiting prof: Dept of Biology Univ Coll London 1989-, Biosphere Scis Div King's Coll London 1989-; special prof of molecular biology Dept of Physiology and Environmental Sci Univ of Nottingham Sch of Agriculture 1987-; memb numerous ctees and ed bds; author of over 240 publications in scientific journals; medal Soc for Endocrinology 1985, medal of Polish Physiological Soc 1990; memb: Endocrine Soc (US) 1988, Assoc of Researchers in Med and Sci 1987, Physiological Soc 1979, Blair-Bell Res Soc 1974, Soc for the Study of Fertility 1973, Soc for Endocrinology 1973, Biochemical Soc 1967; FInstBiol 1982; *Clubs* Athenaeum, Zoological; *Style*— Prof Anthony Flint; Institute of Zoology, Regent's Park, London NW1 4RY (☎ 071 722 3333)

FLINT, Christopher Gardiner; s of George Elmslie Flint (d 1973), and Mary Turner (d 1966); *b* 2 Jan 1922; *Educ* Edinburgh Acad, Edinburgh Univ (BSc); *m* 8 April 1942, Kathlyn Ellen, da of Frederick George Vallance, Mus Doc (d 1960), USA; 1 s (Christopher b 1947), 1 da (Kathlyn Robin b 1943); *Career* Military Serv Maj REME (despatches) Burma and Indo China 1940-46; chm James Fleming & Co Ltd 1983-89; dir: Fleming Howden Ltd 1967-85, George Dunbar (1928) Ltd 1967-85; Pres Edinburgh Chamber of Commerce and Manufactures 1987-88; dir: Chamber Devpts Ltd 1985-, William Hunters Fund 1985-, John Wilson Bequest 1987-, Edinburgh's Capital Ltd 1985-; vice-pres (Fin) Edinburgh C of C and Mfrs 1984-; gen cmmr of Income Tax 1983-; memb of Court The Co of Merchants of The City of Edinburgh

1971-74; vice-convenor Daniel Stewart's and Melville Coll 1972-74; *Recreations* golf, fishing, gardening; *Clubs* New (Edinburgh), Royal Burgess Golfing Society; *Style—* Christopher G Flint, Esq; EAS Sarachan, Strathlachlan, Argyll (☎ 036 986 636); 14 Almond Court East, 5 Braehead Park, Barnton, Edinburgh (☎ 031 339 4169)

FLINT, Prof Colin David; s of Oswald George Flint (d 1981), of London, and Maud Elisabeth, *née* Hayes; *b* 3 May 1943; *Educ* Leyton HS, Imperial Coll London (BSc, DIC, PhD, DSc); *m* 3 Aug 1968, Florence Edna, da of Charles Cowin (d 1969), of Isle of Man; 2 s (Richard Charles b 6 March 1972, Peter David b 25 July 1974); *Career* NATO Postdoctoral Fell Univ of Copenhagen Denmark 1967-69, prof of chemistry Birkbeck Coll London 1981- (lectr 1969-76, reader chemical spectroscopy 1976-81, head of dept 1979-86); visiting prof: Univ of Virginia USA 1982, Univ of Chile 1985 and 1987, Tech Univ of Graz Austria 1986 and 1989, Univ of Copenhagen 1988; author of about 120 pubns in learned jls; ARCS, FRSC, CChem; *Books* Vibronic Processes in Inorganic Chemistry (ed, 1989); *Recreations* swimming, travel; *Style—* Prof Colin Flint; 34 Woolhampton Way, Chigwell Row, Essex IG7 4QH; Laser Laboratory, Birkbeck College, Gordon House, 29 Gordon Square, London WC1H 0PP (☎ 071 380 7466, 071 380 7467, fax 071 380 7464)

FLINT, Gillian Margaret (Julie); da of Percy Sydney George (Pip) Flint, of Sevenoaks, and Joyce Marjorie Peggy, *née* Papworth; *b* 1 Jan 1948; *Educ* Talbot Heath Sch Bournemouth, Girton Coll Cambridge (BA); *Career* Rome corr Assoc Press 1974-76, Middle East corr United Press Int 1982-84 (Madrid corr 1976-81); radio corr Beirut ABC News 1983-89; corr: Beirut Guardian 1985-89, Beirut Observer 1986-; runner up Foreign Radio Reporter of the Year Overseas Press Club of America 1984, Foreign Reporter of the Year What the Papers Say 1988; *Books* Tearing Down the Curtain (1990); *Recreations* swimming, reading, tennis; *Style—* Ms Julie Flint; Observer, Chelsea Bridge House, Queenstown Rd, London SW8 4NN (☎ 071 627 0700, fax 071 627 5570, telex 888963)

FLINT, Michael Frederick; s of Gp Capt Frederick Nelson La Farque Flint (d 1972), and Nell Dixon, *née* Smith (d 1965); *b* 7 May 1932; *Educ* St Peters Sch York, Kingswood Sch Bath, Law Soc Sch of Law; *m* 1, 6 Nov 1965 (m dis 1984), Susan Kate Rhodes; 2 s (Jonathon Frederick Rest b 22 Jan 1958, Anthony Michael Rest b 30 Oct 1962), 1 da (Sarah Rest b 19 Feb 1960); m 2, 6 April 1984, Phyllida Margaret Edwyn, da of Dr Trevor Hughes, of Ruthin, Clwyd; *Career* ptnr Denton Hall and Burgin 1961-66 (asst slr 1956-60), vice-pres Paramount Pictures Corpn 1967-70, chm London Screen Enterprises 1970-72, chm Denton Hall Burgin and Warrens 1988- (ptnr 1972-), exec prodr Glastonbury Fyare, Can I Help You?; FSA 1965, vice-pres Br Archaeological Assoc 1988, fndr memb Cncl of Common Law Inst of Intellectual Property Ltd; *Books* A User's Guide to Copyright (1979), Television by Satellite: Legal Aspects (1987), Intellectual Property: The New Law (jtly, 1989); *Recreations* tennis, skiing, painting; *Clubs* Savile, Hurlingham; *Style—* Michael Flint, Esq; 62 Onslow Gardens, London SW7 3QD; Five Chancery Lane, Clifford's Inn, London EC4A 1BU (☎ 071 242 1212, telex 263567 BURGIN G, fax 071 404 0087, car 08607 23826)

FLINT, Hon Mrs (Pamela Margaret); *née* Lee; only child of Baron Lee of Newton, PC (Life Peer) (d 1984); *b* 19 Sept 1945; *Educ* Newton-le-Willows GS; *m* 1965, Rodney Owen Flint, s of Edwin Arnold Flint; 3 s (Mark b 1965, Jason b 1966, Daniel b 1970); *Style—* The Hon Mrs Flint; The Willows, Church Drive, Newton-le-Willows, Merseyside WA12 9SR (☎ 09252 6970); Keyspools Ltd, Mono Lodge, Bridge St, Golborne, Warrington WA3 3QA (☎ 0942 712566, telex 67228)

FLOCKHART, (David) Ross; s of Very Rev D J Flockhart (d 1965), and Jean Isobel, *née* Ingram (d 1955); *b* 20 March 1927; *Educ* Knox GS, Sydney Univ NSW (BA), Univ of Edinburgh (BD); *m* 1 March 1951, Pamela Ellison, da of Ellison Macartney (d 1956); 3 s (David b 1952, Andrew b 1955, Patrick b 1961), 2 da (Carola b 1965, Fiona decd); *Career* minister Church of Scotland; chaplain to overseas students Edinburgh 1955-58, minister Northfield Aberdeen 1958-63, warden Carberry Tower 1963-66, lectr and sr lectr Moray House Coll of Educn 1966-72; dir Scottish Cncl for Voluntary Orgnisations 1972-; *Recreations* beekeeping, sailing; *Clubs* New (Edinburgh); *Style—* Ross Flockhart, Esq; Longwood, Humbie, East Lothian EH36 5PN (☎ 087 533 208); Scottish Cncl for Voluntary Organisations, 19 Claremont Crescent, Edinburgh EH7 4QD

FLOOD, David Andrew; s of Frederick Joseph Alfred Flood, of Selsey, W Sussex, and June Kathleen, *née* Alexander; *b* 10 Nov 1955; *Educ* Royal GS Guildford, St John's Coll Oxford (MA), Clare Coll Cambridge (PGCE); *m* 26 June 1976, Alayne Priscilla, da of Maurice Ewart Nicholas, of Farnborough, Hants; 2 s (Christopher Nicholas b 1982, Joshua Samuel b 1986), 2 da (Olivia Kathryn b 1979, Annalisa Harriet b 1989); *Career* asst organist Canterbury Cathedral 1978-86, music master King's Sch Canterbury 1978-86; organist and master of choristers: Lincoln Cathedral 1986-88, Canterbury Cathedral 1988-; organist for enthronement of Archbishop Runcie 1980, organist for visit of Pope John Paul II 1982; asst dir Canterbury Choral Soc 1978-85, fndr and dir Canterbury Cantata Choir 1985-86; musical dir: Lincoln Choral Soc 1986-88, Canterbury Music Club 1984-86 and 1988-, for enthronement of Archbishop Carey; hon sr memb Darwin Coll Univ of Kent; FRCO 1976 (chm 1975); *Recreations* travel, motoring, DIY; *Style—* David Flood, Esq; 6 The Precincts, Canterbury, Kent CT1 2EE (☎ 0227 765 219, office 0227 762 862, fax 0227 762

FLOOD, Prof John Edward; OBE (1986); s of Sydney Edward Flood (d 1983), of London, and Elsie Gladys Flood (d 1967); *b* 2 June 1925; *Educ* City of London Sch, QMC London (BSc, PhD, DSc); *m* 23 April 1949, Phyllis Mary, da of John Charles Groocock (d 1978), of Worthing; 2 s (Nicholas John b 20 Oct 1951, Stephen Charles b 25 May 1954); *Career* experimental offr Admiralty Signals Estab 1944-46, devpt engr Standard Telephones and Cables Ltd 1946-47, exec engr PO Res Station 1947-52, chief engr advanced devpt laboratories Telecommunications Div Assoc Electrical Industries Ltd 1952-65; Aston Univ: prof of electrical engrg 1965-, head dept 1967-81 and 1983-89, dean of Faculty Engrg 1971-74, sr pro vice chancellor 1981-83; chm: IEE Professional Gp on Telecommunications Systems & Networks 1974-77, Univs Ctee on Integrated Sandwich Courses 1981-82, Br Standards ctee on Telecommunications 1981-, S Midland Centre IEE 1967-68; memb MMC 1985-; memb Cncl Selly Oak Colls 1966-85, pres Birmingham Electrical Club 1989-90; Freeman City of London 1957, Liveryman Worshipful Co of Engrs 1984; FIEE 1959, FInstP 1987; *Books* Telecommunication Networks (1975); *Recreations* swimming, writing, winemaking; *Clubs* Royal Over-Seas League; *Style—* Prof John Flood, OBE; 60 Widney Manor Rd, Solihull, West Midlands B91 3JQ (☎ 021 705 3604); Aston University, Aston Triangle, Birmingham, B4 7ET (☎ 021 359 3611, fax 021 359 7358, telex 336 997)

FLOOD, Michael Donovan (Mik); s of Gp Capt Donovan John Flood, DFC, AFC, of Brampton, Huntingdon, Cambs, and Vivien Ruth, *née* Allison; *b* 7 May 1949; *Educ* St Georges Coll Weybridge Surrey, LLangefni County Sch Anglesey Wales; *m* 1975 (m dis 1989), Julie, da of Paul Ward; 1 da (Amy Louise b 8 April 1976); partner, Judy Preece; *Career* fndr and artistic dir Chapter Arts Centre Cardiff 1970-81, devpt dir Baltimore Theater Project USA 1981-82, administrator Pip Simmons Theatre Group 1982-83, freelance prodr and conslt 1983-85; dir: Watermans Arts Centre Brentford, Inst of Contemporary Arts 1990-; prodr: Woyzeck (open air prodn with Pip Simmons Theatre Group) 1976, Deadwood (open air prodn with Lumiere & Son Theatre Group, Time Out award winner) 1986, Offshore Rig (open air prodn with Bow Gameian Ensemble) 1987; awarded HRH Queen Elizabeth II Silver Jubilee medal for outstanding services to the arts and community in Wales 1977; dir Pip Simmons Theatre Group Ltd 1977-81, co-fndr Nat Assoc of Arts Centres 1976; memb: West Midlands Arts Assoc Assesment Ctee 1976-, Welsh Arts Cncl Film Ctee 1976-80, S E Wales Arts Assoc Exec Ctee 1980-81; *Recreations* sailing, icthyology; *Style—* Mik Flood, Esq; Institute of Contemporary Arts, The Mall, London SW1Y 5AH (☎ 071 930 0493, fax 071 873 0051)

FLORENCE, Prof Alexander Taylor; s of Alexander Charles Gerrard Florence (d 1985), and Margaret, *née* Taylor; *b* 9 Sept 1940; *Educ* Queen's Park Sch Glasgow, Univ of Glasgow (BSc, PhD), Royal Coll of Sci and Technol, Univ of Strathclyde (DSc); *m* 6 June 1964, Elizabeth Catherine, da of James McRae (d 1969); 2 s (Graham b 1966, Alastair b 1969), 1 da (Gillian b 1972); *Career* prof of pharmacy Univ of Strathclyde 1976-88 (lectr in pharmaceutical chemistry 1966-72, sr lectr 1972-76), dean Sch of Pharmacy Univ of London 1989-; various pubns; memb Ctee on Safety of Meds (chm Sub Ctee on Chemistry Pharmacy and Standards), vice-chm Standing Pharmaceutical Advsy Ctee; FRSC 1977, FRSE 1987, FRPharmS 1987, FRSA 1989; *Books* Solubilization by Surface Active Agents (with P H Elworthy and C B Macfarlane, 1968), Surfactant Systems (with D Attwood, 1981), Physicochemical Principles of Pharmacy (with D Attwood, 1988); *Recreations* music, painting, writing; *Style—* Prof Alexander Florence; 29 Torrington Square, London WC1E 7JL (☎ 071 637 2695); Ardencaple, Mochrum Rd, Glasgow G43 2QE (☎ 041 637 9705); The School of Pharmacy, University of London, 29-39 Brunswick Square, London WC1N 1AX (☎ 071 753 5800, fax 071 278 0622)

FLOREY, Hon Charles du Vé; s of late Baron Florey, OM, FRS, MD (Life Peer, d 1968), and his 1 w Mary Ethel, *née* Reed (d 1966); *b* 11 Sept 1934; *Educ* Rugby, Univ of Cambridge (MD), Yale Univ (MPH); *m* 14 April 1966, Susan Jill, da of Cecil Hopkins, of Tuttle Hill, Nuneaton, Warwicks; 1 s, 1 da; *Career* prof Dept of Epidemiology and Public Health Ninewells Hosp and Medical Sch; FFCM; FRCPE; *Style—* The Hon Charles Florey; Ninewells Hospital and Medical Sch, Dundee DD1 9SY (☎ 0382 60111)

FLOREY, Baroness; Hon Margaret Augusta; *née* Fremantle; 2 da of 3 Baron Cottesloe, CB, VD, TD (d 1956) and Florence, *née* Tapling (d 1956); sis of 4 Baron Cottesloe; *b* 2 Dec 1904; *Educ* Oxford Univ (MA, DM 1950); *m* 1, 9 April 1930 (m dis 1946), Denys Arthur Jennings, BM, BCh, o s of A E Jennings, of Budleigh Salterton, Devon; m 2, 6 June 1967, as his 2 w, Baron Florey, OM, FRS (d 21 Feb 1968; scientist who pioneered the use of penicillin); *Career* lecturer Oxford Univ (Pathology) 1945-72, research fellow of LMH Oxford 1952-72; *Books* Antibiotics (contrib, 1949); contrib to scientific journals 1939-67; *Style—* The Rt Hon Lady Florey; 4 Elsfield Rd, Old Marston, Oxford

FLOUD, Jean Esther; CBE; da of Ernest Walter McDonald (d 1957), and Annie Louisa, *née* Watson (d 1958); *b* 3 Nov 1915; *Educ* LSE (BSc Econ); *m* 2 April 1938, Peter Castle Floud, CBE (d 1960), s of late Sir Francis Floud, KCB, KCIS, KCMG; 1 s (Andrew Thomas b 27 Nov 1948, d 1981), 2 da (Frances Ellen (Mrs Little) b 11 May 1952, Esther Mary (Mrs Bagenal) b 27 Dec 1955); *Career* asst dir of educn City of Oxford 1940-46; teacher of sociology: Univ of London, LSE and Inst of Educn 1947-62; hon fell: LSE 1972, Nuffield Coll 1983 (official fell 1963-72), Darwin Coll Cambridge 1986; memb: Franks Cmmn of Inquiry into the Univ of Oxford 1964-66, Univ Grants Ctee 1969-74, Social Sci Res Cncl 1970-73, Exec Ctee PEP 1975-77, Advsy Bd for the Res Council's 1976-81, Cncl Policy Studies Inst 1979-83; Hon LittD Univ of Leeds 1973, Hon D Litt City Univ 1978; *Books* Social Class and Equal Opportunity (with A A Halsey and F M Martin, 1956), Dangerousness and Criminal Justice (with Warren Young, 1981); *Style—* Mrs Jean Floud, CBE; White Lodge, Osler Rd, Old Headington, Oxford OX3 9BJ (☎ 0865 62317); Nuffield College, Oxford

FLOUD, Prof Roderick Castle; s of Bernard Francis Castle Floud (d 1967), and Ailsa, *née* Craig (d 1967); *b* 1 April 1942; *Educ* Brentwood Sch, Wadham Coll Oxford (BA, MA), Nuffield Coll Oxford (DPhil); *m* 6 Aug 1964, Cynthia Anne, da of Col Leslie Harold Smith, OBE, of Leicester; 2 da (Lydia b 1969, Sarah b 1971); *Career* lectr in econ history: UCL 1966-69, Univ of Cambridge 1969-75; fell and tutor Emmanuel Coll Cambridge 1969-75, prof of modern history Birkbeck Coll London 1975-88, visiting prof Univ of Stanford 1980-81, provost and prof City of London Poly 1988-; FRHistS 1980; *Books* An Introduction to Quantitative Methods for Historians (1973, 1979), Essays in Quantitative Economic History (ed, 1974), The British Machine Tool Industry 1850-1914 (1976), The Economic History of Britain since 1700 (co-ed, 1981), The Power of the Past: Essays in Honour of Eric Hobsbaw (co-ed, 1984), Height Health and History: Nutritional Status in the United Kingdom 1750-1980 (with K Wachter and A Gregory, 1990); numerous articles and reviews incl Words, not Numbers: John Harold Clapham - Historians in their Times (History Today, 1989); *Recreations* walking, skiing, theatre; *Clubs* Athenaeum; *Style—* Prof Roderick Floud; 21 Savernake Rd, London NW3 2JT (☎ 071 267 2197); City of London Poly, 117-119 Houndsditch, London EC3A 7BU (☎ 071 283 1030, fax 071 623 2858)

FLOWER, Hon Anthony John Warburton; yr s of 10 Viscount Ashbrook, KCVO, MBE, *qv*; *b* 6 June 1938; *Educ* Eton; *m* 1970, Bridget Karen, yr da of J Duncan; 1 da (Alexandra Jane b 1972); *Style—* The Hon Anthony Flower; Prouts Farm, Hawkley, Liss, Hampshire

FLOWER, Dr Antony John Frank (Tony); s of Frank Robert Edward Flower (d 1977), of Clyst Hydon, Devon, and Dorothy Elizabeth, *née* Williams; *b* 2 Feb 1951; *Educ* Chipping Sodbury GS, Univ of Exeter (BA, MA), Univ of Leicester (PhD); *Career* graphic designer 1973-76, first gen sec Tawney Soc 1982-88, co-ordinator Argo Venture 1984-; fndr memb SDP 1981, memb Cncl for Soc Democracy; dir: Res Inst for Econ and Social Affrs 1982-, Argo Tst 1986-, Healthline Health Info Serv 1986-88, Health Info Tst 1987-88 (tstee 1988-), Centre for Educ Choice 1988-, Environmental Concern Centre in Euro 1990-; GAIA: memb Cncl, ed Tawney Journal 1982-88; assoc Open Coll of the Arts 1988-, co-fndr and managing ed Samizdat magazine 1988-; tstee Mutual Aid Centre 1990-; assoc: Redesign Ltd 1989-, Nicholas Lacey Jobst and Ptnrs (architects) 1989-, Inst for Pub Policy Res 1989-; *Books* Starting to Write (with Graham Mort, 1990), The Alternative (with Ben Pimlott and Anthony Wright, 1990); *Recreations* boats, making and restoring musical instruments; *Style—* Dr Tony Flower; 18 Victoria Park Square, London E2 9PF (☎ 081 980 6263)

FLOWER, Dr Christopher Dennis Robin; s of William Grosvenor Flower (d 1942), and Molly, *née* Jacobs; *b* 3 Aug 1939; *Educ* Royal Masonic Sch, King's Coll Cambridge, St Bartholomew's Hosp (MA, MB BChir); *m* 21 Jan 1963, Diana Mary, da of Charles Patrick Crane (d 1988); 1 s (Paul b 1966), 1 da (Emma b 1968); *Career* house physician St Bartholomews Hosp 1964, resident Toronto Western Hosp 1968, conslt radiologist Addenbrookes Hosp Cambridge 1973-, ed Clinical Radiology 1987-90, warden Royal Coll Radiologists 1990-; co-author books and articles on radiology and thoracic med; FRCR, FRCP (Canada); *Recreations* travel, golf, ornithology; *Style—* Dr Christopher Flower; Addenbrookes Hosp, Hills Rd, Cambridge CB2 2QQ (☎ 0223 216203)

FLOWER, Lady Gloria Regina Malet; *née* Vaughan; eldest da of 7 Earl of Lisburne (d 1965), and Maria Isabel Regina Aspasia, *née* de Bittencourt (d 1944); *b* 1916; *m* 1, 7

June 1935 (m dis 1952), Sir Nigel Thomas Loveridge Fisher, MC, s of late Cdr Sir Thomas Fisher, KBE, RN; 1 s, 1 da; m 2, 10 June 1952, Ronald Philip Flower, OBE, o s of late Philip Arthur Flower; 1 s; *Style—* The Lady Gloria Flower; Manor Farm Cottage, Weston Patrick, nr Basingstoke, Hants

FLOWER, Johannes Graham (Johnny); s of Graham Warner Flower, of 88 Yelvertoft Rd, Kingsthorpe, Northampton, and Huberta, *née* Jannsens; *b* 9 Dec 1964; *Educ* Moulton Upper Sch Northampton; *partner*: Elaine Susan Redley, da of Roy Norman Nicholls; 1 s (Keiran Johannes b 2 Aug 1989); *Career* professional footballer; Sheffield Utd FC 1989-, on loan to Aldershot 1991; previous clubs as amateur: Brixworth, Spratton, Corby Town 1985-89; winner various player of the year awards; former: engr, civil engr, dustman, postman; *Recreations* all sport, music, computers; *Style—* Johnny Flower, Esq; Sheffield United FC, Bramall Lane, Sheffield (☎ 0742 738955)

FLOWER, Keith David; s of Frank Leslie Flower (d 1976), of 20 St Ursula Grove, Pinner, Middx, and Catherine Elizabeth, *née* Millo (d 1981); *b* 20 Jan 1945; *Educ* Merchant Taylors; *m* 11 May 1973, Jennifer, da of Edward Arthur Howick; 1 da (Melanie b 1976); *Career* admitted slr 1969; HJ Heinz Ltd 1970-73, John Laing Properties Ltd 1973-76, sr ptnr Keith Flower & Co 1976-; memb Rotary Club Pinner; memb Law Soc; *Clubs* Sloane, Durrants; *Style—* Keith Flower, Esq; Lane End, Sandy Lodge Rd, Moor Park, Rickmansworth, Herts WD3 1LJ; 25/27 Pinner Green, Pinner, Middx HA5 2AF (☎ 081 868 1277, fax 081 868 1356, car 0836 281 058, telex 8951947 FLOWER G)

FLOWER, Hon Michael Llowarch Warburton; JP (Cheshire 1983), DL (Cheshire 1982); s and h of 10 Viscount Ashbrook, KCVO, MBE; *b* 9 Dec 1935; *Educ* Eton, Worcester Coll Oxford (MA); *m* 8 May 1971, Zoë Mary, da of Francis Henry Arnold Engleheart, of The Priory, Stoke-by-Nayland, Suffolk (d 1963); 2 s (Rowland b 1975, Harry b 1977), 1 da (Eleanor b 1973); *Career* 2 Lt Gren Gds 1955; landowner; admitted slr 1963, ptnr Farrer & Co 1966-76, ptnr March Pearson & Skelton Manchester 1986-; chm Taxation Sub Ctee 1984-86; *Recreations* gardening, shooting; *Clubs* Brooks's, St James's (Manchester); *Style—* The Hon Michael Flower, JP, DL; The Old Parsonage, Arley Green, Northwich, Cheshire CW9 6LZ (☎ 056 585 277); 41 Spring Gardens, Manchester M2 2BB (☎ 061 832 7290)

FLOWERDEW, Anthony David John (Tony); s of Lt-Col George Douglas Hugh Flowerdew, MBE, of 3 Lovelace Rd, Oxford, and Sheila Mary, *née* Bishop; *b* 7 Nov 1935; *Educ* Eton, Univ of Cambridge (MA); *m* 1, 25 July 1959, Elizabeth Marjorie Jennifer (Jenny) (d 1978), da of Prof Norman Bache Lewis (d 1988); 1 s (Dan b 1964), 1 da (Lucy b 1961); m 2, 26 May 1979, Lesley Jean, *née* Murdoch; *Career* Field Investigation Gp NCB 1957-61, Operational Res Dept Richard Thomas & Baldwin Ltd 1961-66, sr planner GLC 1966-68, dep dir of res Cmmn of Third London Airport 1968-70, sr lectr in urban econs LSE 1971-77, prof of mgmnt sci Univ of Kent 1978-89, md Marcial Echenique & Ptnrs 1989- (ptnr 1977-85, chm 1985-89); former: memb Cncl ORS, memb Air Transport Users Ctee; *Style—* Tony Flowerdew, Esq

FLOWERS, Angela Mary; da of Charles Geoffrey Holland (d 1974), of Ashford, Kent, and Olive Alexandra, *née* Stiby (d 1987); *b* 19 Dec 1932; *Educ* Westonbirt Sch Glos, Wychwood Sch Oxford, Webber Douglas Sch of Singing & Dramatic Art (Dip); *m* 1, 1952 (m dis 1973) Adrian Flowers; 3 s (Adam b 1953, Matthew b 1956, Daniel b 1959), 1 da (Francesca b 1965); *partner* Robert Heller; 1 da (Rachel Pearl b 1973); *Career* worked in stage, film and advtg until 1967, fndr Angela Flowers Gallery Lisle St 1970 (Portland Mews W1 1971-78, Tottenham Mews W1 1978-88, Richmond Rd E8 1988-), promotes encourages and shows the work of young and emerging artists; memb: Bd Nat Youth Jazz Orchestra 1988, Exec Ctee Soc of London Art Dealers 1990; *Recreations* singing; *Style—* Mrs Angela Flowers; Flowers East, 199-205 Richmond Road, London E8 3NJ (☎ 081 985 3333, fax 081 985 0067)

FLOWERS, Baron (Life Peer UK 1979); Brian Hilton Flowers; o s of late Rev Harold Joseph Flowers, of Swansea; *b* 13 Sept 1924; *Educ* Bishop Gore GS Swansea, Gonville and Caius Coll Cambridge, Univ of Birmingham; *m* 1951, Mary Frances, er da of Sir Leonard Frederick Behrens, CBE (d 1978); 2 step s; *Career* physicist; head Theoretical Physics Div AERE Harwell 1952-58, prof of theoretical physics Univ of Manchester 1958-61, Langworthy prof of physics Univ of Manchester 1961-72, rector Imperial Coll of Sci and Technol 1973-85; chm: SRC 1967-73, Royal Cmmn on Environmental Pollution 1973-76, Standing Cmmn on Energy and Environment 1978-81; managing tstee Nuffield Fndn 1982- (chm 1987-); chm Ctee of Vice Chllrs and Princs 1983-85; vice chllr Univ of London 1985-90; awarded: Rutherford medal and prize IPPS 1968, Glazebrook medal IPPS 1987, Chalmers medal Sweden 1980; FInstP 1961, Hon FCGI 1975, Hon MRIA 1976, Hon FIEE 1975; Hon MA (Oxon) 1956; Hon DSc: Sussex 1968, Wales 1972, Manchester 1973, Leicester 1973, Liverpool 1974, Bristol 1982, Oxford 1986; Hon DEng: Nova Scotia 1983, NUI 1990; sr fellow RCA 1983; Offr de la Légion d'Honneur 1981; Hon ScD (Dublin); Hon LLD (Dundee), Hon LLD (Glasgow) 1987; FRS; kt 1969; *Style—* The Rt Hon Lord Flowers, FRS; 53 Athenaeum Road, London N20 9AL (☎ 081 446 5993)

FLOWERS, John; s of John Alfred Flowers (d 1990), and Irene, *née* Jordon; *b* 1 April 1940; *Educ* Hymers Coll Hull; *m* Patricia, da of Joseph Griffin; 1 s (Andrew John), 1 da (Alison Kay); *Career* articled clerk Smailes Holtby & Gray Hull 1955-61, qualified chartered accountant 1961, ptnr John A Flowers & Co Hull 1964-69 (joined 1961), sr mangr Lovewell Blake & Co Gt Yarmouth 1969-74; ptnr: Hemming Graham & Co Lincoln, Hemming Graham & Lawrence Scunthorpe, Hemming Graham & Poole Norwich 1974-80; sr ptnr Neville Russell E Midlands 1981-; ACA 1961, ATII 1961; *Recreations* boating, travel, golf; *Clubs* Lincolnshire Agric Soc; *Style—* John Flowers, Esq; Neville Russell, Aquis House, Clasketgate, Lincoln (☎ 0522 543051, fax 0522 543073)

FLOWERS, Lady Mary Joy; *née* Abney-Hastings; da of Countess of Loudoun, *qv*, and (3 husb) Peter Abney-Hastings; *b* 18 March 1957; *Educ* Leicester Univ (BA, MA); *m* 11 Sept 1982, David John Flowers; 1 da (Clare Hannah Flowers b 1987); *Style—* The Lady Mary Flowers

FLOWERS, Matthew Dominic; s of Adrian John Flowers, of 147 Talgarth Rd, London, and Angela Mary, *née* Holland; *b* 8 Oct 1956; *Educ* William Ellis GS; *m* 17 Feb 1985, Lindy, da of Arthur James Wesley-Smith; 1 s (Patrick b 30 Jan 1987); *Career* asst Angela Flowers Gallery 1975-78, mangr and keyboard player for pop group Sore Throat 1975-81, played in various other bands including Blue Zoo (Cry Boy Cry Top Twenty hit 1982, led to two appearances on Top of the Pops) 1981-83; Angela Flowers Gallery (became a plc 1989): pt/t asst 1981-83, mangr 1983-88, md 1988-; memb: Cncl Mgmnt of Art Servs Grants 1987, Organising Ctee of London Art Fair 1989, Bradford Print Biennale Ctee 1989, Cncl of Mgmnt Byam Shaw Sch of Art 1990; *Recreations* play football for Central YMCA; *Clubs* Chelsea Arts; *Style—* Matthew Flowers, Esq; Flowers East, 199-205 Richmond Road, Hackney, London E8 3NJ (☎ 081 985 3333, fax 081 985 0067)

FLOWERS, Timothy David (Tim); s of Kenneth Alfred Flowers, of 12 Ash Drive, Kenilworth, Warwicks, and Mary Bryan, *née* Garlick; *b* 3 Feb 1967; *Educ* Abbey Hall Secdy Sch; *m* 11 June 1988, Jane Louise, da of Brian Alan Everett; 1 da (Emma Jane b 24 Dec 1989); *Career* professional footballer; 63 league appearances Wolverhampton Wanderers (debut v Sheffield Utd) 1984-86, over 100 appearances Southampton 1986-, 7 appearances on loan Swindon Town 1987; England: 3 youth caps v Scotland (twice) and Yugoslavia, 3 under 21 caps (v Morocco, France, W Germany) 1987-88; Player of the Year Wolverhampton Wanderers 1984, Young Player of the Year Midland Sportswriters 1984, Away Player of the Year Southampton 1990; *Recreations* fishing, music, walking; *Style—* Tim Flowers, Esq; Southampton Football Club, The Dell, Milton Rd, Southampton, Hampshire (☎ 0703 220505)

FLOYD, David Henry Cecil; s and h of Sir Giles Floyd, 7 Bt; *b* 2 April 1956; *Educ* Eton; *m* 20 June 1981, Caroline Ann, da of John Henry Beckly, of Manor Farm, Bowerchalke, Wilts; 2 da (Suzanna b 1983, Claire b 1986); *Career* Lt 15/19 The King's Royal Hussars; merchant banker ACA 1982; *Clubs* Cavalry & Guards; *Style—* David Floyd, Esq; Tinwell Manor, Stamford, Lincs

FLOYD, Sir Giles Henry Charles; 7 Bt (UK 1816); s of Lt-Col Sir John Duckett Floyd, 6 Bt, TD (d 1975); *b* 27 Feb 1932; *Educ* Eton; *m* 1, 23 Nov 1954 (m dis 1978), Lady Gillian Moyra Katherine Cecil, da of 6 Marquess of Exeter, KCMG; 2 s; m 2, 1985, Mrs Judy Sophia Lane, er da of William Leonard Tregoning, CBE, of Landue Launceston, Cornwall; *Heir* s David Henry Cecil Floyd; *Career* farmer; dir Burghley Estate Farms 1958-, High Sheriff of Rutland 1968; *Recreations* fishing; *Clubs* Turf, Farmers'; *Style—* Sir Giles Floyd, Bt; Tinwell Manor, Stamford, Lincs (☎ 0780 62676)

FLOYD, John Anthony; s of Lt-Col Arthur Bowen Floyd, DSO, OBE (d 1965, himself grandson of Major-General Sir Henry Floyd, 2 Bt), and Iris Clare, *née* Belding; *b* 12 May 1923; *Educ* Eton; *m* 5 Oct 1948, Margaret Louise, o da of late Major Hugo Rosselli, of Worlington Old Hall, Suffolk; 2 da (Elizabeth b 1951, Caroline b 1953); *Career* served WW II in KRRC; chm: Christie Manson & Woods Ltd 1974-85, Christie's International plc 1976-88; *Clubs* Boodle's, White's, MCC; *Style—* John Floyd, Esq; Ecchinswell House, Newbury, Berkshire (☎ 0635 298237)

FLOYD, Peter Joseph; s of Arthur Floyd, CBE (d 1978), and Nora Floyd, *née* Poulton (d 1978); *b* 2 Dec 1928; *Educ* Charterhouse, Balliol Coll Oxford (BA, MA); *m* 29 July 1972, Madeline Edna Clare, da of Charles Samuel Lincoln Whiteley, of Wantage, Oxon; *Career* admitted slr 1954; dep clerk Devon CC 1971-73, co sec Oxon CC 1973, co slr Oxon CC 1980-, clerk Oxon Magistrates Cts Ctee 1974-, Probation Ctee 1974-, sec Oxon Ld-Lt's Advsy Ctee 1976-, chm Soc of County Secs 1985-86; ret 1989; *Recreations* inactivity, reading; *Clubs* Sloane; *Style—* Peter J Floyd, Esq; The Stables, East Hanney, Wantage, Oxon OX12 0JJ (☎ 023 587 240)

FLOYD, Richard Eaglesfield; s of Harold Bailey Floyd, of Purley, Surrey, and (Edith) Margeret, *née* Griffith (d 1954); *b* 9 June 1938; *Educ* Dean Close Sch Cheltenham; *m* 16 June 1973 (m dis 1984), Caroline, da of Maurice Clement Jones (d 1957); 1 da (Emilia Margaret b 1974); *Career* articled clerk Fincham Vallance & Co 1956-61 (sr clerk 1961-62 and 1964-65), insolvency admin Cork Gully 1965-70, ptnr Floyd Nash & Co (later styled Floyd Harris) 1971 (held appointments as admin receiver, administrator, liquidator and tstee); author of many articles on insolvency matter in specialised jls; memb: Assoc Européenne des Practiciens des Procédures Collectives, Ed Advsy Bd of Insolvency Law Practice; Freeman City of London 1985; *Books* with I S Grier: Administration, Voluntary Liquidation and Receivership (2 edn, 1987), Personal Insolvency - A Practical Guide (1987), Company Administration Orders and Voluntary Arrangements (1988); *Publications* author of many articles on insolvency matter in specialised journals; memb Editorial Advsy Bd of Insolvency Law & Practise; *Recreations* writing, lecturing, mountain walking; *Style—* Richard Floyd, Esq; 9 Beaufort Rd, Kingston-upon-Thames, Surrey KT1 2TH (☎ 081 546 5833); Floyd Harris, 44-46 Fleet St, London EC4Y 1BN (☎ 071 583 7108, fax 071 583 2921)

FLOYD EWIN, Sir David Ernest Thomas; LVO (1954), OBE (1965); 7 s of Frederick P Ewin (d 1929), and Ellen, *née* Floyd, of Blackheath; *b* 17 Feb 1911; *Educ* Eltham, MA (Lambeth); *m* 1948, Marion Irene, da of William Robert Lewis, of Paignton, S Devon; 1 da; *Career* NP; lay admin St Paul's Cathedral 1939-43, registrar and receiver 1944-78, conslt to the Dean and Chapter 1978-; chm: Tubular Edgington Group plc 1978-, memb of Ct Common Cncl for Ward of Castle Baynard (dep 1972-), vice pres Castle Baynard Ward Club (chm 1962 and 1988); chm Corpn of London Gresham Ctee 1975-76; memb Lord Mayor and Sheriffs Ctee 1976, 1978 (chm 1988); Ct of Assts Hon Irish Soc 1976-79; surrogate for Province of Canterbury; tstee: City Parochial Fndn 1967- (chm Pensions Ctee 1978-), St Paul's Cathedral Tst 1978-, Temple Bar Tst 1979-, City of London Endowment Tst for St Paul's Cathedral (dep chm 1982-), Allchurches Tst; hon dir Br Humane Assoc; govr: Sons of the Clergy Corpn (memb Ct), St Gabriel's Coll Camberwell 1946-72; past Master Worshipful Co of Scriveners, Liveryman Worshipful Co of Wax Chandlers, Freeman City of London, sr past Master Guild of Freemen of City of London; gold staff offr at Coronation of HM 1953; KStJ 1970 (OStJ 1965); kt 1974; *Books* A Pictorial History of St Paul's Cathedral (1970), The Splendour of St Paul's (1973); *Recreations* tennis, fishing, gardening; *Clubs* City Livery, Guildhall; *Style—* Sir David Floyd Ewin, LVO, OBE; Silver Springs, Stoke Gabriel, South Devon (☎ 080 428 264); Chapter House, St Paul's Churchyard, London EC4M 8AD (☎ 071 248 2705); St Augustine's House, 4 New Change, London EC4M 9AB (☎ 071 248 0683)

FLOYER, Prof Michael Antony; s of Cdr William Antony Floyer, RN, Chev Legion of Honour (d 1943), of Inglewood, Camberley, Surrey, and Alice Rosalie, *née* Whitehead (d 1979); *b* 28 April 1920; *Educ* Sherborne, Trinity Hall Cambridge (MB, ChB, MD), The London Hosp Med Coll; *m* 8 June 1946, Lily Louise Frances, da of H P Burns (d 1940); 2 s (David b 1947, Christopher b 1951), 1 da (Jennifer b 1948); *Career* Sqdn Ldr RAF 1946-48, med specialist RAF Hosps at Karachi and Cawnpore; London Hosp Med Coll 1948-86: lectr 1948, sr lectr 1951, asst dir of Med Unit 1953, reader 1967, prof of medicine 1974, dean 1982, fell 1988-; The London Hosp: hon conslt physician 1958-86, conslt i/c Emergency and Accident Dept 1976-86, conslt physician 1986-, locum consultant 1987; seconded as prof of med to Nairobi Univ 1973-75; sec Med Res Soc 1962-67 (memb 1949-), memb Tower Hamlets Dist Health Authy 1982-86; pres and treas The London Hosp Clubs Union, pres RFC; memb: Climbing and Backpacking Club, History Soc; MD 1952, FRCP 1963; *Recreations* wild things and wild places, music, rugby football; *Style—* Prof Michael Floyer; Duke's Cottage, Willingale, Ongar, Essex CM5 OSW (☎ 0277 86270); Medical Unit, The London Hosp Med Coll, London E1 2AD (☎ 071 377 7602)

FLYNN, Prof Frederick Valentine; eldest s of Frederick Walter Flynn (d 1957), of London, and Jane Laing, *née* Valentine; *b* 6 Oct 1924; *Educ* UCL, UCH Med Sch London (MB BS, MD); *m* 24 Sept 1955, (Catherine) Ann, o da of Dr Robert Walter Warrick (d 1950), of Blackheath, London; 1 s (David b 6 Nov 1956), 1 da (Frances b 25 Feb 1959); *Career* prof of chemical pathology Univ Coll Sch of Med 1970-89, conslt chemical pathologist to UCH London 1960-89, civil conslt in chemical pathology to RN 1978-; FRCP, FRCPath; *Recreations* photography, carpentry, gardening; *Style—* Prof Frederick Flynn; 20 Oakleigh Ave, Whetstone, London N20 9JH (☎ 081 445 0882)

FLYNN, John Gerrard; s of Thomas Flynn (d 1985), of Glasgow, and Mary Chisholm (d 1963); *b* 23 April 1937; *Educ* Univ of Glasgow (MA); *m* 10 Aug 1973, Drina Anne Coates, da of Lt Herbert Percival Coates (d 1971), of Montevideo, Uruguay; 1 s (Andrew b 1984), 1 da (Alexandra b 1985); *Career* FO: joined 1965, second sec Lusaka 1966, first sec FCO 1968, asst dir gen Canning House 1970, head of Chancery Montevideo 1971, FO 1976, chargé d'affaires Luanda 1978, head of Chancery Brasilia 1979, cnsllr (economic and commercial) Madrid 1982, high cmmr Mbabane 1987-90,

HM ambass Luanda 1990; *Recreations* walking, golf; *Clubs* Travellers; *Style—* John Flynn, Esq; c/o Foreign and Commonwealth Office (LUANDAE), King Charles St, London SW1A 2AH

FLYNN, Dr Patricia Josephine; da of Michael Joseph Flynn, of 35 Nutley Lane, Dublin, and Mary Josephine, *née* O'Dwyer; *b* 1 April 1947; *Educ* Convent of the Sacred Heart Dublin, Univ Coll Dublin (MB BCh, BAO, DCH, DObst, DA FFARCSI, FCAnaes); *m* 26 Sept 1987, Anthony William Goode, s of William Henry Goode, of 57 Beachcroft Ave, Tynemouth, Northumberland; *Career* sr lectr in anaesthesia London Hosp Med Coll 1982-; sec gen Br Acad Forensic Scis; memb: Assoc of Anaesthetists of GB and Ireland, Anaesthetic Res Soc, Euro Acad of Anaesthesiology, RSM, BMA; *Recreations* antiquarian books, art, music; *Style—* Dr Patricia Flynn; Anaesthetics Unit, The London Hospital Medical College, Whitechapel, London E1 2AD (☎ 071 377 7119)

FLYNN, Paul Phillip; MP (Lab) Newport West 1987-; s of James Flynn (d 1939), and Kathleen Rosien, *née* Williams (d 1988); *b* 9 Feb 1935; *Educ* St Illtyd's Coll Cardiff, Univ Coll Cardiff; *m* 1, 6 Feb 1962, Ann Patricia; 1 s (James Patrick b 1965), 1 da (Rachel Sarah b 1963 d 1979); m 2, 31 Jan 1985, Lynne Samantha; *Career* chemist in steel indust 1955-81; since worked in local radio and as research asst to Euro MP Llewellyn Smith; Labour Pty: front bench spokesman Welsh Affairs May 1988-, front bench spokesman Social Security Nov 1988-; *Clubs* Ringland Labour, Pill Labour; *Style—* Paul Flynn, Esq, MP; House of Commons, London SW1A 0AA (☎ 071 219 3468)

FLYTE, Ellis Ashley; da of Thomas Hynd Flyte, and Anne Margaret Paterson Little Duncan; *Educ* The Mary Erskine Sch for Young Ladies Edinburgh, London Coll of Fashion (Dip in Art and Fashion Design); *Career* fashion and costume designer, bunny girl Dorchester Hotel; costumes: RSC, Royal Opera House, Thames TV; designed costumes for films incl: Dark Crystal, Out of Africa, Labyrinth, The Tall Guy; fndr Ellis Flyte Fashion Design Showroom London 1984; ACTT, NATTKE; *Recreations* travel, photography, film, dance, jacuzzis, music, art, dressing up; *Clubs* Le Petit Opportune Paris, Chelsea Arts, The Ritz Casino; *Style—* Ms Ellis Flyte; 18 Parliament Hill, Hampstead, London, NW3 (☎ 071 267 9653); Camden, London, NW1 0ND (☎ 071 267 9653)

FOAKES, Prof Reginald Anthony; s of William Warren Foakes, and Frances, *née* Poate; *b* 18 Oct 1923; *Educ* West Bromwich GS, Univ of Birmingham (MA, PhD); *m* 1951, Barbara (d 1988), da of Harry Garratt, OBE; 2 s, 2 da; *Career* sr lectr in English Univ of Durham 1963-64 (lectr 1954-62), Cwlth Fund (Harkness) fell Yale Univ 1955-56; Univ of Kent at Canterbury: prof of English lit 1964-82, dean Faculty of Humanities 1974-77, currently emeritus prof of Eng and American lit; visiting prof: Univ of Colum bia Toronto 1960-62, Univ of Calif Santa Babara 1968-69, UCLA 1981; prof of English UCLA 1983; *Books* Shakespeare's King Henry VIII (ed 1957), Henslowe's Diary (ed with R T Rickert, 1961), Coleridge on Shakespeare (1971) Marston and Tourneur (ed, 1978) Illustrations of the English Stage 1980-1642 (1985), Coleridge's Lectures 1808-1819, On Literature (ed 2 Vols, 1987); *Style—* Prof Reginald Foakes; Department of English, University of California at Los Angeles, 405 Hilgard Avenue, Los Angeles, Calif 90024, USA

FOALE, Air Commodore Colin Henry; s of William Henry Foale (d 1979), of Galmpton, Devon, and Frances Margaret, *née* Muse (d 1969); *b* 10 June 1930; *Educ* Wolverton GS, RAF Coll Cranwell, RAF Staff Coll Bracknell, Jt Servs Staff Coll Latimer, RCDS Belgrave Sq; *m* 19 Sept 1954, Mary Katherine, da of Prof Samuel Bannister Harding (d 1925), of Minneapolis, USA; 2 s (Michael b 6 Jan 1957, Christopher b 13 March 1958, d 1979), 1 da (Susan b 2 May 1962); *Career* pilot 13 photo recce sqdn (Meteor) Kabrit Egypt 1952-53, Flt Cdr 32 Fighter Sqdn (Vampire), Deversoir Egypt 1953-54, RAF Flying Coll Manby (fighter instr Hunters) 1954-57, instr in selection techniques Offr Selection Centre RAF Hornchurch 1958-60, Sqdn Cdr 73 light Bomber Sqdn Akrotiri Cyprus 1960-63, organiser Biggin Hill Battle of Br display 1963, chm Cockpit Ctee TSR2 MOD (PE) 1965, Wing Cdr Air Plans HQ RAF Germany 1965-68, Sqdn Cdr 39 photo recce sqdn (Canberras) Luqa Malta 1969-71, Gp Capt SO flying MOD (PE) 1971-74, station cdr RAF Luqa Malta 1974-76, dir RAF PR 1977-79, ret at own request 1979; aviation advsr Yorks TV Drama 1979-80, trg advsr to Chm Cons Pty Central Office 1980-81, pilot to Ctee for Aerial Photography Univ of Cambridge 1981-90; memb: Nat Tst, Woodland Tst, RSPB, RYA, St Catharine's Coll Cambridge 1981; hon memb Univ Air Sqdn Cambridge 1981, dining memb Selwyn Coll Cambridge 1981, fndr memb RAF Historical Soc 1986; Cormorant 1969, RCDS 1977, RUSI 1980, FBIM 1980, FIWM 1981; *Recreations* flying, sailing, travel, theatre, music, writing; *Clubs* RAF; *Style—* Air Cdre Colin H Foale; 37 Pretoria Rd, Cambridge CB4 1HD (☎ 0223 352684); St Catharine's College, University of Cambridge

FOALE, Lady Emma Cecile; *née* Gordon; er da of 6 Marquess of Aberdeen and Temair, *qv*; *b* 26 May 1953; *m* 6 Sept 1980, Dr Rodney Foale, eldest s of Maurice Spencer Foale, of Melbourne, Australia; 2 s (Archie Alexander b 17 Sept 1984, Jamie b 1 April 1986); *Style—* The Lady Emma Foale

FOALE, Graham Douglas Kenneth; JP (1981); s of Hubert Douglas Foale (d 1985), of Essex, and Lilian Kate, *née* Tolchard (d 1985); *b* 27 May 1938; *Educ* Clifton; *m* 30 May 1964, Jean Barbara, da of Frederick Kershaw Sunderland (d 1949), of Sunderland; 2 s (Robin b 1967, Matthew b 1969); *Career* ptnr Bishop Fleming CAs Plymouth 1969-; memb S W Regnl Ind Devpt Bd 1977-83; chm: Plymouth Round Table 1974-75; Cornwall & Plymouth Branch of CAs 1979-80; memb: Small Practitioners' Ctee, Inst of CAs 1982-86; FCA; *Recreations* walking, toy collecting; *Style—* Graham D K Foale, JP; 8 Blue Haze Close, Plymbridge Road, Glenholt, Plymouth PL6 7HR (☎ 0752 695188); 2 Marlborough Rd, North Hill, Plymouth PL4 8LP (☎ 0752 262611)

FOALE, Dr Rodney Alan; s of Maurice Spencer Foale, of Melbourne, Australia, and Lyle Gwendolin, *née* Wallace; *b* 11 Sept 1946; *Educ* Scotch Coll Melbourne, Univ of Melbourne Med Sch; *m* 1980, Lady Emma Gordon, *qv*, da of the Marquis of Aberdeen, Tamar and Fife; 2 s (Archie Alexander b 17 Sept 1984, Jamie Alexander b 1 April 1986); *Career* St Vincent's Hosp Univ of Melbourne 1972-73, med offr Austrialian Himalayan Expdn through Indonesia India and Kashmir 1974-75, registrar Nat Heart Hosp 1975-79, clinical res fell Harvard Univ and MIT, Massachusetts Gen Hosp 1980-82, sr registrar in cardiology Hammersmith Hosp 1982-85, conslt cardiologist St Mary's Hosp 1985-; hon sr lectr Hammersmith Hosp 1985-, recognised teacher Univ of London 1985-; MRCP 1976, FACC 1986; *Recreations* various outdoor and indoor sporting pursuits; *Style—* Dr Rodney Foale; 66 Harley St, London W1N 1AE (☎ 071 323 4687, fax 071 631 5341)

FOCKE, Paul Everard Justus; QC (1982); s of Frederick Justus Focke (d 1959), and Muriel Focke; *b* 14 May 1937; *Educ* Downside, Exeter Coll Oxford, Trinity Coll Dublin; *m* 13 Dec 1973, Lady Tana Focke, da of 6 Earl of Caledon (decd); 2 da (Diana Natasha b 1974, Victoria Justine b 1976); *Career* Nat Serv 1955-57; Capt Cheshire Yeo TA 1957-65; called to the Bar: Gray's Inn 1964, NZ 1982; QC NSW 1984; recorder; *Recreations* travelling, aeroplanes; *Clubs* Turf, Beefsteak, Pratt's, Cavalry and Guards'; *Style—* Paul Focke, Esq, QC; 7 Cheyne Walk, London SW3 5QZ (☎ 071 351 0299); 1 Mitre Court Buildings, Temple, London EC4Y 7BS (☎ 071 353 0434, fax 071 353 3988, car 0836 215504)

FOCKE, Lady Tana Marie; *née* Alexander; da of 6 Earl of Caledon (d 1980), by 1 w, Ghislaine, o da of Cornelius Willem Dresselhuys; *b* 2 March 1945; *m* 1973, Paul Everard Justus Focke, QC, s of Frederick Justus Focke; 2 da; *Style—* The Lady Tana Focke; 7 Cheyne Walk, London SW3

FODEN, Edwin Peter; s of Edwin Richard Foden (d 1950), and Mary, *née* Cooke; *b* 24 Feb 1930; *Educ* Rossall, N Staffs Tech Coll; *m* 1957, Judith, da of James Harding Baxter, of Nantwich, Cheshire; 3 s; *Career* Lt REME (UK and Germany); chm and chief exec ERF (Hldgs) plc; chm: ERF Ltd (family firm), ERF S Africa (Pty) Ltd, vice pres: SMMT 1971-83, Inst of Motor Industry 1981-; pres Congleton Cons Assoc; FRSA, FIMI; *Recreations* golf, shooting, motor racing; *Clubs* REME Officers', Annabel's; *Style—* Edwin Foden, Esq; Oak Farm, The Heath, Sandbach, Cheshire (☎ 0270 762732); ERF Ltd, Sun Works, Sandbach, Cheshire (☎ 0270 763223, fax 0270 766068, telex 36152)

FOGDEN, Michael Ernest George (Mike); s of George Charles Arthur Fogden (d 1970), of Worthing, Sussex, and Margaret May Fogden; *b* 30 May 1936; *Educ* Worthing HS Sussex, Lycee du Garcons Le Mans France; *m* 1 June 1957, (Rose) Ann, da of James Arthur Diamond (d 1983), of Morpeth, Northumberland; 3 s, 1 da; *Career* Nat Serv RAF 1956-58; Miny of Social Security 1959-67, private sec of state for Social Services 1968-70, DHSS 1971-82, Dept of Employment 1982-87; chief exec British Employment Service 1987-; chm: First Division Assoc 1979-82, Royal Inst of Public Admin (London); *Recreations* music, gardening, snooker; *Clubs* Royal Commonwealth; *Style—* Mike Fogden, Esq; St Vincent House, 30 Orange St, London WC2H 7HT (☎ 071 389 1497, fax 071 389 1520)

FOGEL, Steven Anthony; s of Joseph Gerald Fogel, JP, and Benita Rose Fogel; *b* 16 Oct 1951; *Educ* Carmel Coll, King's Coll London (LLB, LLM); *m* 21 Jan 1977, Joan Selma, da of Curtis Holder (d 1973); 1 da (Frances Leah), 2 s (George Curtis, Jonathan Raphael); *Career* admitted slr 1976; ptnr Titmuss Sainer & Webb; memb: Jt Ctee on commercial leases, Ed Bd Jl of Property Finance, Br Cncl of Shopping Centres, Br Cncl of Offices, Anglo American Real Property Inst; Freeman: City of London, Worshipful Co of Slrs; memb: Law Soc, RICS; *Books* Rent Reviews (1986); *Recreations* cycling, jazz, gardening, skiing, writing; *Style—* Steven Fogel, Esq; 2 Serjeants' Inn, London EC4Y 1LT (☎ 071 583 5353, fax 071 353 3683/2830)

FOGELMAN, Dr Ignac; s of Richard Fogelman (d 1975), and Ruth, *née* Tyras; *b* 4 Sept 1948; *Educ* HS of Glasgow, Univ of Glasgow (BSc, MB ChB, MD); *m* 18 March 1974, Coral Niman, da of Harvey Norton (d 1980); 1 s (Richard b 1982), 1 da (Gayle b 1974); *Career* dir Osteoporosis Screening and Res Unit Guy's Hosp 1988- (conslt physician 1983-, dir Nuclear Med Dept 1988-); memb Cncl Nat Osteoporosis Soc, external examiner in MSc nuclear med Univ of Glasgow, memb Int Skeletal Soc 1988; FRCP 1987; *Books* Bone Scanning in Clinical Practice (1987), An Atlas of Clinical Nuclear Medicine (with M Maisey, 1988), An Atlas of Planar and Spect Bone Scans (with D Collier, 1988); *Recreations* bridge, theatre, opera, music, tennis, books; *Style—* Dr Ignac Fogelman; Dept of Nuclear Medicine, Guy's Hosp, St Thomas St, London SE1 9RT (☎ 071 955 4593, fax 071 955 4657)

FOGELMAN, Kenneth Robert; s of Joseph Alfred Fogelman (d 1987) and Vera May *née* Corrie; *b* 24 Jan 1945; *Educ* Ifield GS Crawley Sussex, Univ of Keele (BA); *m* 26 Aug 1967, Audrey Elaine, da of Angus Corkan, of Douglas IOM; *Career* secdy maths teacher 1966-67, res offr Sch to Univ Res Unit Nat Fndn for Educnl Res 1969-72 (res asst section for mathematical and conceptual studies 1967-69), asst dir Nat Children's Bureau 1981-85 (princ res offr 1972-81), dep dir Social Statistics Res Unit City Univ 1985-88, prof of educn Univ of Leicester 1987-; fndr memb: Br Educnl Res Assoc, Soc Res Assoc; memb Assoc of Child Psychiatrists (chm of the Leicester Gp); FBPsS 1988; *Books* Piagetian Tests for the Primary School (1970), Leaving the Sixth Form (1972), Britain's Sixteen Year Olds (1976) Growing Up in Great Britain (1983) Putting Children First (ed with I Vallender, 1988); *Recreations* badminton, music, travel, photography; *Style—* Ken Fogelman, Esq; 30 South View, Letchworth, Herts; 4 Stonehill Court, Great Glen, Leicester; School of Education, University of Leicester, 21 University Rd, Leicester LE1 7RF (☎ 0533 522522, fax 0533 522200

FOGG, Prof Gordon Elliott (Tony); CBE (1983); s of Rev Leslie Charles Fogg (d 1951), of Ranmoor, Sheffield, and Doris Mary, *née* Elliott (d 1976); *b* 26 April 1919; *Educ* Dulwich, Queen Mary Coll London (BSc), St John's Coll Cambridge (PhD, ScD); *m* 7 July 1945, Elizabeth Beryl, da of Rev Thomas Llechid Jones (d 1946), of Old Colwyn, Clwyd; 1 s (Timothy b 1951), 1 da (Helen b 1947); *Career* seaweed survey of Br Isles Miny of Supply 1942, plant physiologist Pest Control Ltd Cambridge 1943-45; Dept of Botany UCL 1945-60: asst lectr, lectr, reader; prof botany Westfield Coll Univ of London 1960-71, prof marine biology Univ Coll of N Wales 1971-85, prof emeritus marine biology Univ of Wales 1985-; govr Marine Biol Assoc 1973-, pres section K Br Assoc 1973 (biological gen sec 1967-72), chm Cncl Freshwater Biological Assoc 1974-85, pres Inst Biology 1976-77, tstee Br Museum (Natural History) 1976-85, memb Royal Cmmn Environmental Pollution 1979-85, tstee Royal Botanic Gdns Kew 1983-89; Hon LLD Univ of Dundee 1974; FIBiol 1960, FRS 1965; *Books* The Metabolism of Algae (1953), The Growth of Plants (1963), Photosynthesis (1968), The Bluegreen Algae (with WDP Stewart, P Fay and AE Walsby, 1973), Algal Cultures and Phytoplankton Ecology (with B Thake, 1987), The Explorations of Antarctica (with D Smith, 1990); *Recreations* walking, antarctic history, listening to music; *Clubs* Athenaeum; *Style—* Prof Tony Fogg, CBE, FRS; Bodolben, Llandegfan, Anglesey, Gwynedd LL59 5TA (☎ 0248 712 916); Sch of Ocean Sciences, Marine Science Laboratories, Menai Bridge, Anglesey, Gwynedd LL59 5EY (☎ 0248 351 151)

FOGGIN, Erica; da of Wilhelm Myers Foggin, CBE (d 1986), of London, and Lotte Lina, *née* Breitmeyer; *b* 24 Sept 1957; *Educ* Francis Holland Sch, Westminster, Somerville Coll Oxford (MA); *Career* called to the Bar Middle Temple 1980; *Recreations* flying, scuba diving, skiing, riding; *Style—* Miss Erica Foggin; 11 Kings Bench Walk, Temple, EC4 (☎ 071 353 2484, fax 353 1261)

FOLEY, 8 Baron (GB 1776); Adrian Gerald Foley; s of 7 Baron Foley (d 1927), and Minoru, *née* Greenstone (d 1968); *b* 9 Aug 1923; *m* 1, 23 Dec 1958 (m dis 1971), Patricia, da of Joseph Zoellner III, of Pasadena, California, and formerly w of Minor de Uribe Meek; 1 s, 1 da (Hon Alexandra Mary, *qv*); m 2, 1972, Ghislaine, da of Cornelius Willem Dresselhuys, of Long Island, USA and formerly w of (1) Maj Denis James Alexander, later 6 Earl of Caledon, and (2) 4 Baron Ashcombe, *qv*; *Heir* s, Hon Thomas Henry Foley; *Career* composer and pianist; *Clubs* White's; *Style—* The Rt Hon Lord Foley; c/o Marbella Club, Marbella, Malaga, Spain

FOLEY, Hon Alexandra Mary; *née* Foley; resumed her maiden name; da (by 1 m) of 8 Baron Foley; *b* 3 April 1960; *m* 25 July 1987 (m dis 1989), (Somerset) Carlo de Chair, s of Capt Somerset Struben de Chair, and his 2 w, June, *née* Appleton; *Career* arms and armour cataloguer Sotheby's; *Style—* The Hon Alexandra Foley; 36 Rosary Gardens, London SW7

FOLEY, Graham Gregory; s of Theodore Gregory Foley (d 1940), and Florence Cassan, *née* Page (d 1967); *b* 13 June 1923; *Educ* Wade Deacon GS Widnes, Queen Elizabeth GS Wakefield, King Edward's GS Aston Birmingham, King's Coll London, St John's Coll Durham (BA, Dip Theology); *m* 14 June 1944, Florence, da of late Charles Frederick Redman; 2 s (Mark Gregory b 1954, Simon John b 1957), 2 da (Alison Moyra b 1948, Sheelagh Mary b 1951); *Career* ordained priest 1951, curate of

Holy Trinity South Shore Blackpool 1950-54, vicar of St Luke Blackburn 1954-60, dir of educn Diocese of Durham 1960-71, rector of Brancepeth Co Durham 1960-71, vicar of Leeds 1971-82, chaplain to HM The Queen 1977-82, bishop of Reading 1982-89, assistant bishop Diocese of York 1989-; ret hon canon: Durham Cathedral 1965-71, Ripon Cathedral 1971-82; *Books* Religion in Approved Schools (1965); *Recreations* walking on the moors, reading detective stories, watching other people mow lawns; *Clubs* Royal Commonwealth; *Style*— The Right Rev Graham Foley; Ramsey Cottage, 3 Poplar Avenue, Kirkbymoorside, York YO6 6ES (☎ 0751 32439)

FOLEY, Hugh Smith; s of John Walker Foley (d 1970), and Mary Hogg, *née* Smith; *b* 9 April 1939; *Educ* Dalkeith HS; *m* 7 Sept 1966, Isobel King, da of James Halliday (d 1970); 2 s (Mark b 31 May 1970, Paul b 28 Jan 1974); *Career* Nat Serv RAF 1959-61; student actuary Standard Life Assurance Co 1956-59, entered Scot Ct Serv (Ct of Session Branch) 1962, asst clerk of session 1962-71, depute clerk of session 1972-80, seconded to Sheriff Ct Edinburgh 1980-81, princ sheriff clerk depute Glasgow 1981-82, sheriff clerk Linlithgow 1982, dep princ clerk of session 1982-86, sr dep princ clerk 1986-89, princ clerk of session and justiciary 1989-; *Recreations* walking, reading, listening to music; *Style*— Hugh Foley, Esq; Supreme Courts, Parliament House, Edinburgh EH1 1RQ (☎ 031 225 2595, fax 031 220 6773)

FOLEY, Johanna Mary (Jo); da of John Andrew Foley, of Leamington Spa, Warwickshire, and Elizabeth Monica, *née* Savage; *b* 8 Dec 1945; *Educ* St Joseph's Convent Kenilworth, Univ of Manchester (BA); *Career* woman's ed Walsall Observer 1968, reporter Birmingham Post 1970; Eng teacher: Monwick Secdy Mod Sch Colchester, More House Sch London 1972-73; launched and ed Successful Slimming Magazine 1976, sr asst ed Woman's Own 1978 (dep beauty ed 1973), woman's ed The Sun 1980, ed Woman 1982, exec ed (features) The Times 1984-85, managing ed Daily Mirror 1985-86; ed: Observer Magazine 1986-88, Options Magazine 1988-; Ed of Year, Br Soc Magazine Eds 1983; memb Gen Advsy Ctee BBC 1984-88; *Style*— Miss Jo Foley; Options Magazine, Kings Reach Tower, Stamford St, London SE1 9LS (☎ 071 261 5000)

FOLEY, Maj-Gen John Paul; MC (1976), OBE (1979); s of Maj Henry Thomas Hamilton Foley, MBE (d 1959), of Stoke Edith, Hereford, and Helen Constance Margaret, *née* Pearson (d 1985); *b* 22 April 1939; *Educ* Bradfield Coll (Mons OCS), Army Staff Coll; *m* 3 June 1972, Ann Rosamund, da of Maj John William Humphries; 2 da (Annabel b 11 July 1973, Joanna b 8 May 1976); *Career* Royal Green Jackets: Lt 1959-60, Capt 1961-69; Maj RMCS 1970-71; Cmdg Offr 3 bn 1978-80; Brigade Maj, 51 Inf Bde Hong Kong 1974-76; Camberley: army staff course 1972-74, Lt Col dir staff 1976-78; Cmdt jr dir Staff Coll Warminster 1981-82; Brig: arms dir MOD 1983-85, student RCDS 1986; chief Br mission to Soviet forces Berlin 1987-89; Maj gen central staffs MOD 1989-; memb Worshipful Co of Skinners 1965-72, Liveryman Worshipful Co of Skinners 1972-; *Recreations* tennis, walking, shooting, reading; *Clubs* Boodles; *Style*— Maj-Gen John Foley; Ministry of Defence, Main Building, Whitehall, London SW1A 2HB

FOLEY, Sheila; da of Leslie Crossley (d 1970), of Hebden Bridge, W Yorkshire, and Agnes, *née* Mitchell (d 1976); *b* 5 July 1944; *Educ* Calder HS Mytholmroyd, Mabel Fletcher Tech Coll Liverpool; *m* 5 March 1966 (m dis), John Kevin Foley, s of Robert Foley; 1 s (Sean Michael b 16 Feb 1968), 1 da (Siobhain Clare b 25 Jan 1967); *Career* registered mental nurse St John's Hosp Lincoln 1974-78, registered general nurse Luton Dunstable Hosp 1978-84, nurse mangr Charing Cross Hosp London 1984-85, dir of nursing servs West Lambeth Health Authy 1985-86; unit gen mangr and chief nurse advsr: Mental Health Unit 1986-89, Priority Care Servs 1989-; gen sec Psychiatric Nurses Assoc 1986; memb: Health Advsy Serv 1986-, Wirral Health Authy 1987-90, Rampton Review Team 1989; memb Royal Coll of Nursing 1971; *Recreations* walking, reading; *Style*— Mrs Sheila Foley; Longfield, 16 Crossley Crescent, Hoole, Chester CH2 3EZ (☎ 0244 342857); Chester Health Authority, Countess of Chester Hospital, Liverpool Rd, Chester (☎ 0244 364224)

FOLEY, Hon Thomas Henry; s (by 1 m) and h of 8 Baron Foley; *b* 1 April 1961; *Style*— The Hon Thomas Foley

FOLJAMBE, (George) Michael Thornhagh; s of Capt Robert Francis Thornhagh Foljambe, MC, RA (d 1987), and Zaida Nell, *née* Priestman (d 1985); *b* 28 May 1934; *Educ* Eton, Magdalene Coll Cambridge (BA); *Career* Nat Serv, 2 Lt 15/19 Hussars; pres Notts Branch CLA 1986-; FLAS 1966-70, FRICS 1970; Bledisloe Gold medal (RASE) 1983; *Recreations* riding, shooting, fishing; *Style*— Michael Foljambe, Esq; Mill Farm, Osberton, Worksop, Notts (☎ 0909 472206); Estate Office, Osberton (☎ 0909 472206)

FOLKESTONE, Viscount; William Pleydell-Bouverie; s (by 1 m) and h of 8 Earl of Radnor; *b* 5 Jan 1955; *Educ* Harrow, RAC Cirencester; *Style*— Viscount Folkestone; Round House, Charlton All Saints, Wilts (☎ 0722 330 295)

FOLKMAN, Peter John; s of Eric Folkman; *b* 30 Aug 1945; *Educ* Univ of Oxford (BA), Wharton (MBA); *m* 25 July 1969, Judith Lella, da of Sir Hugh Weeks; 3 s (Michael Philip b 1972, David Thomas b 1975, James Peter b 1980); *Career* Burroughs Machines Ltd 1967-70, Rank Xerox Ltd 1971-73, 3i plc 1973-88 (dir 1986-88); md North of England Ventures Ltd 1989-; dir: Salford Univ Hldgs plc, Royal Exchange Teatre Co; skiing: Br Trg Team 1962-64, Univ of Oxford Team 1968-69; *Recreations* skiing, squash; *Clubs* St James (Manchester), Ski Club of GB; *Style*— Peter Folkman, Esq; 6 Oakfield Rd, Manchester M20 0XA (☎ 061 434 5489); North of England Ventures Ltd, Cheshire House, Booth St, Manchester M2 4AN (☎ 061 236 6600, fax 061 236 6650)

FOLL, John; s of Wallace Arthur Foll (d 1945), of Bucks, and Ethel Emmeline Oakley (d 1960); *b* 29 April 1923; *Educ* Berkhamsted Sch; *m* 7 July 1952 (m dis 1979), Chica, da of John Douglas Lea (d 1963), of Warwickshire; 4 s (Stephen b 1955, Charles b 1960, Guy b 1963, Ian b 1965), 1 da (Caroline b 1956, d 1958); *Career* Flt Lt Navigator 3 Gp Bomber Cmd RAF 1942-46; ptnr Brown & Merry 1965-86; FRICS; *Recreations* yachting; *Clubs* Aldeburgh Yacht; *Style*— John Foll, Esq; Park House, The Avenue, Aspley Guise, Milton Keynes MK17 8HH

FOLLETT, Lady; Helen Alison; da of Alexander Wilson, of Herne Bay, and Ellen Coote, *née* Cranfield; *b* 8 Jan 1907; *Educ* Castelnau Coll; *m* 1932, Sir David Follett (d 1982), sometime dir Science Museum; 3 s decd; *Career* clerical staff Bank of England 1926-32; *Recreations* conservation and animal welfare; *Style*— Lady Follett; 3 Elm Bank Gardens, Barnes, London SW13 0NU (☎ 081 876 8302)

FOLLETT, James; s of late James Follett, and Yvonne, *née* Mills; *b* 27 July 1939; *m* 13 Aug 1960, Christine Marie, *née* Panichelli; 1 s (Richard b 2 Aug 1966), 1 da (Joanna Samatha b 16 Nov 1968); *Career* writer; trained as marine engr, worked as tech dir MOD, fulltime writer 1976-; wrote first radio play for BBC in 1973, novels: The Doomsday Ultimatum (1976, 2 edn 1991), Crown Court (1977), Ice (1979), Churchill's Gold (1980), Earthsearch (1981), Tiptoe Boys (1982, filmed as Who Dares Wins), Earthsearch II: Deathship (1982), Dominator (1984), Swift (1985), Mirage (1988), U-700 (1989), A Cage of Eagles (1990), Torus (1990); numerous plays and drama documentaries for BBC Radio 4; tv incl episodes for: Crown Court, Blake's Seven, The Squad, Today and Tomorrow, BBC Children's TV; designer of computer games; *Recreations* Radio 'Ham' (Callsign Gilxp), collecting boring postcards; *Style*— James Follett, Esq; Schehallien, Woodside Rd, Chiddingfold, Godalming, Surrey GU8 4QR (☎ 0428 682975, fax 0428 685397); c/o Jacqui Lyons, Marjacq Scripts Ltd, 32 Cumberland Mansions, Nutford Place, London W1H 5ZB (☎ 071 724 0565, fax 071 723 3405)

FOLLETT, Kenneth Martin (Ken); s of Martin Dunsford Follett, of Yatton, Somerset, and Lavinia Cynthia, *née* Evans; *b* 5 June 1949; *Educ* Harrow Weald GS, Poole Tech Coll, UCL (BA); *m* 1, 5 Jan 1968 (m dis 1985), Mary Emma Ruth, da of Horace Henry Elson (d 1988), of Kinson Bournemouth; 1 s (Emanuele b 13 July 1968), 1 da (Marie-Claire b 11 May 1973); m 2, 8 Nov 1985 (Daphne) Barbara, *née* Hubbard; *Career* journalist: S Wales Echo 1970-73, London Evening News 1973-74; dep md Everest Books 1976-77 (ed dir 1974-76); author 1977-; memb: Chelsea Lab Party, Arts for Lab, Liberty, Amnesty, American Cncl on Civil Liberties; memb: Authors Guild USA 1979, Soc of Authors 1989; *Books* Eye of the Needle (1978), Triple (1979), The Key to Rebecca (1980), The Man from St Petersburg (1982), On Wings of Eagles (1983), Lie Down With Lions (1986), The Pillars of the Earth (1989); *Recreations* bass guitarist of Kevin Small and the Trousers; *Clubs* Groucho; *Style*— Ken Follett, Esq; PO Box 708, London SW10 0DH

FOLLETT, Martin John; s of Claude Michael Trevor Follett, of Cornwall, and Maria Lyn, *née* Warne; *b* 14 Nov 1949; *Educ* Marlborough Coll, Sidney Sussex Coll, Cambridge (MA); *m* 12 Aug 1977, Orla Josephine; 2 s (Michael b 1978, James b 1985), 1 da (Sarah b 1980); *Career* slr; ptnr with Coodes; registrar of the diocese of Truro; dir Mount Edgcumbe Hospice Ltd; *Recreations* sailing; *Style*— Martin J Follett, Esq; Ingestre, Agar Road, Truro TR1 1JU (☎ 0872 73542); Coodes, 2 Princes Street, Truro TR1 2EZ

FOLLOWS, Lady; Mary Elizabeth; *née* Milner; *m* 1938, Sir Denis Follows, CBE (d 1983, chm Br Olympic Assoc); 2 da; *Style*— Lady Follows; 116b Barrowgate Rd, Chiswick, London W4 (☎ 071 994 5782)

FOLWELL, Nicholas David; s of Alfred Thomas Folwell (d 1975), and Irmgard Seefeld, of Market Drayton; *b* 11 July 1953; *Educ* Spring Grove GS, Middx Royal Acad of Music, London Opera Centre; *m* 31 Jan 1981, Anne-Marie, da of George Ives; 1 s (Alexander Thomas b 22 July 1981), 1 step s (Adrian Marshal Matheson-Bruce b 15 Aug 1974); *Career* opera singer; joined Welsh Nat Opera 1978, first professional role The Bosun in Billy Budd 1978; later roles incl: Marchese in La Traviata 1979, Melot in Triston Und Isolde 1979, Ottone in The Coronation of Poppea 1980, Figaro in The Marriage of Figaro 1981, Melitone in La Forza del Destino 1981, Leporello in Don Giovanni 1982, Klingsor in Parsifal 1983, Pizarro in Fidelio 1983, Alberich in Rheingold 1983, Schaunard in La Boheme 1984 Alberich in Siegfied 1985, Beckmesser in The Mastersingers of Nuremberg (Opera North) 1985, Alberich in Götterdämmerung (WNO) 1985 Leporello in Don Giovanni (Opera North) 1986, The Four Villians in The Tales of Hoffmann (Scottish Opera) 1986, Tonio in Pagliacci (ENO) 1986, Alberich in Der Ring (WNO at Covent Garden) 1986, Figaro in The Marriage of Figaro (WNO) 1987, The Poacher in The Cunning Little Vixen (WNO) 1987, Father in The Seven Deadly Sins (Royal Festival Hall) 1988, Figaro in The Marriage of Figaro (Scottish Opera) 1987, Papageno in The Magic Flute (ENO) 1988, Marullo in Rigoletto (Frankfurt Opera) 1988, Alberich in Rheingold (Scottish Opera) 1989, Koroviev in Der Meister und Margarita (World Premier, The Paris Opera 1989), Creon and The Messenger in Oedipus Rex (Scottish Opera) 1990, Melitone in La Forza del Destino (Scottish Opera) 1990 The Poacher in The Cunning Little Vixen (Royal Opera) 1990, Pizarro in Fidelio (Glyndebourne) 1990, Figaro in Le Nozze di Figaro (Opera Zuid Holland) 1991: also numerous classical concerts in UK and abroad: recordings: Melot in Tristan und Isolde, Jailer in Tosca, Klingsor in Parsifal, Christmas Eve by Rimsky-Korsakov, Vakula The Smith by Tchaikovsky The Poacher in Cunning Little Vixen the Haushoffmeister in Der Zwerg; ARAM; *Recreations* golf; *Style*— Nicholas Folwell, Esq; Allied Artists Agency, 42 Montpelier Square, London SW7 1J7 (☎ 071 589 6243)

FONE, Michael; s of Lawrence Fone, of Chippenfield, Herts, and late Mabel Edith Fone; *b* 21 Feb 1933; *Educ* Hemel Hempstead GS, QMC London; *Career* md Rea Bros Ltd 1972-88 (dir 1969-72), dir Jupiter Tarbutt Merlin Ltd 1988-; hon treas and dir St Peter's Res Tst 1975-; *Recreations* gardening, the arts; *Clubs* Garrick; *Style*— Michael Fone, Esq; 29 Huguenot House, 19 Oxendon St, London SW1Y 4EH (☎ 071 839 3978); Marshfield Chippenham, Wilts SN14 8NU; Jupiter Tarbutt Merlin Ltd, Knightsbridge House, 197 Knightsbridge, London SW7 1RB (☎ 071 581 8015)

FONSECA, Jose Maria; da of Amador Francis Gabriel Fonseca (d 1984), of Abergavenny, Gwent, and Kathleen, *née* Jones; *b* 9 Jan 1944; *Educ* Sacred Heart Convent Highgate, Ursuline Convent San Sebastian Spain, Ursuline Convent St Pol de Leon Brittany, St Godric's Secretarial Coll Hampstead; *m* 1, 1975 (m dis 1982); m 2, 1985, Dick Kries; *Career* secretary, waitress, mangr of boutique, worked in model agency English Boy 1966-68, fndr Models One 1968-; *Style*— Mrs Jose Fonseca; Models One, Omega House, 471-473 Kings Road, London SW10 (☎ 071 351 1195, 071 351 6033, fax 071 376 5821)

FONSECA, Julian Francis Amador; s of Amador John Gabriel Fonseca (d 1984), and Mary Kathleen, *née* Jones; *b* 20 April 1951; *Educ* Prior Park Coll Bath, Reading Univ, Coll of Law; *m* 27 Aug 1977, Clarissa Julia, da of Harry Kerr Aitken; 1 s (Louis Charles Amador b 1984), 3 da (Emma Ruth Mary b 1980, Amy Frances Ann b 1982, Isabel b 1985); *Career* slr, ptnr Fonseca & Co at Ebbw Vale Abergavenny and Newport, Rutland Properties of Brecon; pt/t chm Social Security Appeal Tbnl; *Recreations* tennis, walking; *Style*— Julian F A Fonseca, Esq; White House Farm, Llanvetherine, Abergavenny, Gwent (☎ 0873 863 02); County Buildings, Market Street, Ebbw Vale, Gwent

FOOKES, Dame Janet Evelyn; DBE (1989), MP (Cons) Plymouth Drake 1974-; da of Lewis Aylmer Fookes (d 1978), and Evelyn Margery, *née* Holmes; *b* 21 Feb 1936; *Educ* Hastings and St Leonards Ladies' Coll, Hastings HS for Girls, Royal Holloway Coll Univ of London (BA); *Career* teacher 1958-70, chm Educn Ctee Hastings County Borough Cncl 1967-70 (memb 1960-61 an 1963-70), MP (C) Merton and Morden 1970-74, sometime chm Educn, Arts and Home Office Sub-Ctee of former Expenditure Ctee, former sec Parly Animal Welfare Gp; memb: Speaker's Panel of Chairmen, Select Ctee on Home Affrs 1984-, Cwlth War Graves Cmmn 1987-; vice chm All Pty Mental Health Gp, fell Indust and Parl Tst; memb Cncl: RSPCA (chm 1979-81), Stonham Housing Assoc; SSAFA; *Recreations* keep-fit exercises, theatre, gardening; *Clubs* Royal Over-Seas League; *Style*— Dame Janet Fookes, DBE; House of Commons, London SW1A 0AA

FOOKS, John Anthony; JP; s of William John Fooks; *b* 24 Aug 1933; *Educ* Shrewsbury, Trinity Coll Univ of Cambridge; *m* 1959, (Maureen) Heather, da of Percival Charles Jones, sometime High Sheriff of Gwent; 3 s, 1 da; *Career* chm Cardiff & Provincial Properties plc 1980-, Fooks Property Co Ltd, E Surrey Water Co; dir: Garnar Booth plc, Pittard Garnar plc, The Bradford Porperty Tst plc, The Sutton Dist Water Co; gen cmmr Inland Revenue; memb Lloyd's 1975; Freeman City of London 1976, Liveryman Worshipful Co of Broderers; FCA; *Recreations* golf, shooting, music, bridge; *Clubs* Cardiff and Co, Rye Golf, Golf Match United, Oxford and Cambridge Univ, MCC, Lloyd's Yacht; *Style*— John Fooks, Esq, JP; 52 Trinity Church Sq, London SE1; Woodgate House, Beckley, Rye, Sussex TN31 6HU

FOORD, Derek Fergus Richard; *b* 19 Aug 1931; *m* 1; 1 s (John b 1965), 1 da (Rachel b 1963); m 2, 1985, Kate; 2 step da (Vanessa b 1968, Sandra b 1971); *Career*

fin dir Stag Furniture Holdings PLC 1990-, chm Jaycee Furniture Ltd; FCA; *Recreations* fell walking, dinghy sailing; *Style*— Derek Foord Esq; Low Paddock Barn, Shelton Newark, Notts NG23 5JQ (☎ 0949 51107); Stag Furniture Holdings PLC, Maydn Rd, Nottingham NG5 1DU (☎ 0602 605007)

FOOT, Hon Benjamin Arthur; 3 and yst s of Baron Caradon, GCMG, KCVO, OBE, PC (Life Peer, d 1990), and Florence Sylvia, *née* Tod (d 1985); *b* 19 Aug 1949; *Educ* Leighton Park Sch, Univ Coll Swansea; *m* 18 April 1981, Sally Jane, o da of Maj Mark Francis Swain Rudkin, MC (d 1953); 1 s (Alexander Mark Isaac b 1986), 1 da (Joanna Dingle b 1983); *Career* Save The Children Fund: dep dir Karamoja Uganda 1980-82, field dir, Pakistan 1982-84, field dir Nepal 1985, Somalia 1986-88, regnl advsr E Africa 1988-; *Style*— The Hon Benjamin Foot; Save the Children Fund, PO Box 67253, Nairobi, Kenya

FOOT, Baron (Life Peer UK 1967), of Buckland Monachorum, Co Devon; John Mackintosh Foot; 3 s of Rt Hon Isaac Foot, PC (d 1960), and his 1 w Eva, *née* Mackintosh (d 1946); bro of Lord Caradon (d 1990) and Michael Foot, former ldr of Lab Pty; *b* 17 Feb 1909; *Educ* Bembridge Sch, Balliol Coll Oxford (BA); *m* 25 June 1936, Anne Bailey, da of Dr Clifford Bailey Farr, of Bryn Mawr, Pa, USA; 1 s (Hon John Winslow b 1939), 1 da (Hon Katherine Elliott (Hon Mrs Illingworth) b 1937); *Career* Maj RASC WWII; slr 1934 (sr ptnr Foot & Bowden of Plymouth), chm UK Immigrants Advsy Serv 1970-78; Lib candidate: Basingstoke 1934 and 1935, Bodmin 1945 and 1950; pres Dartmoor Preservation Assoc 1976-; chm Cncl of Justice 1983-89; *Recreations* Royal Western Yacht; *Style*— The Rt Hon Lord Foot; Yew Tree, Crapstone, Yelverton, Devon (☎ 0822 853417)

FOOT, Hon John Winslow; s of Baron Foot (Life Peer); *b* 23 Oct 1939; *Educ* Sidcot Sch, Philadelphia Coll of Art USA; *Style*— The Hon John Foot; Yew Tree, Crapstone, Yelverton, Devon

FOOT, Michael David Kenneth Willoughby; s of Kenneth Willoughby Foot (d 1980), and Ruth Joan, *née* Cornah; *b* 16 Dec 1946; *Educ* Latymer Upper Sch, Pembroke Coll Cambridge (BA, MA), Yale Univ USA (MA); *m* 16 Dec 1972, Michele Annette Cynthia, da of Michael Stanley Macdonald, of Kingsgate, Kent; 1 s (Anthony b 5 June 1978), 2 da (Helen b 28 Oct 1980, Joanna b 22 July 1985); *Career* Bank of England 1969-: mangr Gilt-Edged Div 1981, mangr Money Market Div 1983, head Foreign Exchange Div 1988-90, head Euro Div 1990-; UK alternate dir to IMF 1985-87; AIB 1973; *Recreations* church singing, chess, youth work, soccer referee; *Style*— Michael Foot, Esq; Bank of England, Threadneedle St, London EC2R 8AU (☎ 071 601 4123 fax 071 601 4822, telex 885001)

FOOT, Rt Hon Michael Mackintosh; PC (1974), MP (Lab) Blaenau Gwent 1983-; 4 s of Rt Hon Isaac Foot, PC (d 1960), MP (Lib) for Bodmin 1922-24 and 1929-35, pres Lib Party Orgn 1947, and 1 w Eva, *née* Mackintosh (d 1946); bro of Lord Caradon (d 1990) and Lord Foot; *b* 23 July 1913; *Educ* Forres Sch, Leighton Park, Wadham Coll Oxford; *m* 21 Oct 1949, Jill, *née* Craigie, former w of Jeffrey Dell; *Career* pres Oxford Union 1933; contested (Lab) Monmouthshire 1935; MP (Lab): Devonport (now Rt Hon David Owen's constituency) 1945-55, (contested Devonport 1959), Ebbw Vale 1960-1983; ed Tribune 1948-52 and 1955-60 and md 1945-74 (actg ed Evening Standard 1942, later book critic; wrote column for Daily Herald 1944-64); oppn spokesman on Power and Steel Industries 1970-71, shadow ldr of House 1971-72, spokesman EEC Affairs 1972-74, sec of state Employment 1974-76, lord pres of Cncl and leader House of Commons 1976-79, succeeded Rt Hon James Callaghan as ldr of Oppn 1980-Oct 1983, received Freedom of City of Plymouth 1982, Freedom of Borough of Blaenau Gwent 1983; hon fellow Wadham Coll; *Books* Guilty Men (with Frank Owen and Peter Howard) (1940), Armistice 1918-39 (1940), Trial of Mussolini (1943), Brendan and Beverley (1944), Still at Large (1950), Full Speed Ahead (1950), Guilty Men (with Mervyn Jones, 1957), The Pen and the Sword (1957), Parliament in Danger (1959), Aneurin Bevan Vol I 1897-1945 (1962), Vol II 1945-60 (1973), Debts of Honour (1980), Another Heart and Other Pulses (1984), Politics of Paradise (1988); *Style*— The Rt Hon Michael Foot, MP; House of Commons, London SW1A 0AA

FOOT, Michael Richard Daniell; s of Richard Cunningham Foot (d 1979), of Clareville Beach, NSW, and Nina, *née* Raymond (d 1980); *b* 14 Dec 1919; *Educ* Winchester, New Coll Oxford (MA, BLitt), Univ of Manchester (MA); *m* 1, Philippa Ruth, da of William Sydney Bence Bosanquet, DSO; m 2, Elizabeth Mary, da of Thomas Irvine King; 1 s (Richard Jeffery b 1963), 1 da (Sarah Rosamund Irvine (Mrs G M K Schrecker) b 1961); m 3, Mirjam Michaela, da of Prof Carl Paul Maria Romme; *Career* WWII RA rose to rank of Maj (dispatches twice); taught at Univ of Oxford 1947-59, prof of modern history Univ of Manchester 1967-73, dep warden European Discussion Centre 1973-75; historian; pubns: Gladstone and Liberalism (with J L Hammond, 1952), British Foreign Policy since 1898 (1956), Men in Uniform (1961), SOE in France (1966), The Gladstone Diaries (volumes I and II, ed, 1968, volumes III and IV ed with H C G Matthew, 1974), War and Society (ed, 1973), Resistance (1976), Six Faces of Courage (1978), MI9 Escape and Evasion 1939-45 (with JM Langley, 1979), SOE: an outline history (1 edn 1984, 2 edn 1990), Holland at War against Hitler (1990), Art and War (1990); Croix de Guerre 1945, offr Order of Orange-Nassau 1990; memb: Royal Hist Soc 1958, Soc of Authors 1960; *Recreations* reading; *Clubs* Savile, Special Forces; *Style*— M R D Foot, Esq; 45 Countess Rd, London NW5 2XH; agent: Michael Sissons, Messrs Peters, Fraser & Dunlop, 5th Floor The Chambers, Chelsea Harbour, Lots Rd, London SW10 0XF (☎ 071 376 7676, fax 071 352 7356)

FOOT, Hon Oliver Isaac; 2 s of Baron Caradon, GCMG, KCVO, OBE, PC (Life Peer, d 1990), and Florence Sylvia, *née* Tod (d 1985); *b* 19 Sept 1946; *Educ* Leighton Park Sch, RAC Cirencester, Goddard Coll Vermont USA; *m* 1967 (m dis 1975), Nancy Foot; 1 s (Jesse Isaac b 1973), 1 da (Mary Rachel b 1971); *Style*— The Hon Oliver Foot; 16 Cedar Avenue, Locust Valley, NY 11560, USA

FOOT, Hon Paul Mackintosh; eldest s of Baron Caradon, GCMG, KCVO, OBE, PC (Life Peer, d 1990), and Florence Sylvia, *née* Tod (d 1985); *b* 8 Nov 1937; *Educ* Univ Coll Oxford; *m* 23 June 1962 (m dis 1970), Monica, da of Dr Robert P Beckinsale; 2 s (John Mackintosh b 1964, Matthew Isaac b 1966); m 2, 27 July 1971, Roseanne, da of Robert Harvey; 1 s (Tom b 1979); *Career* journalist; *Books* Immigration and Race in British Politics (1965), The Politics of Harold Wilson (1968), The Rise of Enoch Powell (1969), Who Killed Hanratty ? (1971), Why You Should Be a Socialist (1977), Red Shelley (1981), The Helen Smith Story (1983), Murder at the Farm: Who Killed Carl Bridgewater ? (1986), Who Framed Colin Wallace ? (1989); *Style*— The Hon Paul Foot; Daily Mirror, Holborn Circus, London EC1

FOOTE, Andrew Veitch; s of Dr William Foote (d 1970), of Kirkcaldy, and Janet Anderson, *née* Cameron (d 1989); *b* 7 Jan 1929; *Educ* Dunfermline HS, Univ of Edinburgh (MB ChB, ChM); *m* 5 May 1954, Patricia Cynthia, da of Col Harry Canning (d 1953), of Lahore, India; 1 da (Kaetrin b 1965); *Career* Nat Serv RAF 1952-54; cardiac res fell UCLA 1959-60, sr lectr in surgery Univ of Aberdeen 1965-75, conslt cardio-thoracic surgn Royal Infirmary Aberdeen 1975-; FRCSEd 1956; memb: SCTS, EACTS; *Recreations* golf, billiards, chess; *Style*— Andrew Foote, Esq; Edgehill Cottage, Culter House Rd, Milltimber AB1 0EN (☎ 0224 732368); Cardio-thoracic Unit, Royal Infirmary, Aberdeen AB9 2ZB (☎ 0224 681818)

FOOTTIT, Ven Anthony Charles; s of Percival Frederick Foottit (d 1961), and Mildred, *née* Norris (d 1977); *b* 28 June 1935; *Educ* Lancing, King's Coll Cambridge (MA); *m* 10 Dec 1977, Rosamund Mary Alyson, da of Robert James Buxton (d 1968); 1 s (James b 1978), 2 da (Caroline b 1980, Georgina b 1983); *Career* asst curate Wymondham Abbey 1981, team vicar Blakeney Gp 1964, team rector Camelot Parishes 1971, rural dean Cary 1979, St Hugh's missioner Lincolnshire 1981, archdeacon 1987-; *Recreations* gardening, botany, conservation; *Style*— The Ven the Archdeacon of Lynn; Ivy House, Whitwell Street, Reepham, Norwich NR10 4RA (☎ 0603 870340)

FOPP, Dr Michael Anton; s of Sqdn-Ldr Desmond Fopp, AFC, AE, and Edna Meryl, *née* Dodd; *b* 28 Oct 1947; *Educ* Reading Blue Coat Sch, Met Police Coll, Met Police Trg Estab, City Univ (MA, PhD); *m* 5 Oct 1968, Rosemary Ann, da of V G Hodgetts, of Ashford, Kent; 1 s (Christopher Michael b 5 April 1973); *Career* Met Police Cadet Corps 1964-66, Constable 1966-69, Met Police Mounted Branch 1969-79, ret due to injury on duty; keeper Battle of Britain Museum 1982-85 (dep keeper 1979-81), co sec Hendon Museums Trading Co Ltd 1981-85, visiting lectr City Univ 1984-; dir: London Tport Museum 1985-87, RAF Museum 1988-; chm London Tport Flying Club, vice pres Friends of RAF Museum, London Underground Railway Soc; Freeman City of London 1980, Guild of Air Pilots and Navigators 1987; FBIM 1990 (MBIM 1980); *Books* The Battle of Britain Museum (1981), The Bomber Command Museum (1982), Washington File (1983), The Royal Air Force Museum (1984), RAF Museum Children's Activity Book (ed, 1985); *Recreations* flying light aircraft, chinese cookery, walking, writing; *Clubs* RAF; *Style*— Dr Michael A Fopp; Royal Air Force Museum, Hendon, London NW9 5LL (☎ 081 205 2266)

FORBES; *see*: Stuart-Forbes

FORBES, The Hon Sir Alastair Granville; s of Granville Forbes (d 1943), and Constance Margaret, *née* Davis; *b* 3 Jan 1908; *Educ* Blundell's, Clare Coll Cambridge; *m* 11 Jan 1936, Constance Irene Mary, da of late Capt Charles Everard Hughes White, DSO, DSC, RN; 2 da (Anne Margaret b 1936, Elizabeth Mary b 1938); *Career* called to the Bar Gray's Inn 1932; HM Colonial Serv 1936, HM Overseas Judiciary 1956, puisne judge Kenya 1956, justice of appeal Ct of Appeal for Eastern Africa 1957 (vice pres of the Ct 1958), federal justice Federal Supreme Ct of Rhodesia and Nyasaland 1963; pres Cts of Appeal: Seychelles, St Helena, Falkland Is, Br Antarctic Territories 1965-88, Gibraltar 1970-83 and Br Indian Ocean Territory 1986-88; pres Pensions Appeal Tbnl for England and Wales 1973-80; kt 1960; *Recreations* gardening, fishing; *Clubs* Royal Cwlth Soc; *Style*— The Hon Sir Alastair Forbes; Badgers Holt, Church Lane, Sturminster Newton, Dorset DT10 1DH

FORBES, Anthony David Arnold William; s of Lt-Col David Walter Arthur William Forbes, MC, Coldstream Guards (ka 1943), and Diana Mary, *née* Henderson (who m 2, 6 Marquess of Exeter; he d 1981, she d 1982); *b* 15 Jan 1938; *Educ* Eton; *m* 1, 14 June 1962 (m dis 1973), Virginia June, yr da of Sir Leonard Ropner, 1 Bt, MC, TD (d 1977); 1 s (Jonathan David b 1964), 1 da (Susanna Jane b 1966); m 2, 1973, Belinda Mary, da of Sir Hardman Earle, 5 Bt (d 1979); *Career* Lt Coldstream Gds 1956-59; memb Stock Exchange 1965, jt sr ptnr Cazenove & Co (Stockbrokers); chm: Hosp and Homes of St Giles, Wellesley House Educnl Tst; govr: Cobham Hall, Royal Choral Soc; *Recreations* music, shooting, gardening; *Style*— Anthony Forbes, Esq; 16 Halsey St, London SW3 (☎ 071 584 4749); Cazenove & Co, 12 Tokenhouse Yard, London EC2R 7AN (☎ 071 588 2828, telex 886758)

FORBES, Maj Anthony David Knox; s of Lt-Col William John Herbert Forbes of Rothiemay, DSO, *qv*, and Diana Burrel de Ker, *née* Knox; *b* 20 March 1944; *Educ* Eton, RMA Sandhurst; *m* 1985, Reidun, *née* Setane, of Norway; 1 s (Iain Aigin Setane b 20 April 1990); *Career* Maj Scots Gds; *Recreations* ski mountaineering, cycling, sailing; *Clubs* RHYC; *Style*— Maj Anthony Forbes, yr of Rothiemay; c/o RHQ Scots Guards, Wellington Barracks, Birdcage Walk, London SW1E 6HQ

FORBES, Archibald Peter Sturrock; CBE (1960); s of Alexander Menzies Forbes (d 1970), and Elizabeth Lilian, *née* Campbell (d 1960); *b* 5 May 1913; *Educ* George Heriot's Sch Edinburgh, Univ of Edinburgh (BSc), Univ of Cambridge (Dip Agric); *m* 10 June 1939, Mary, da of Capt Robert William Manning (d 1936); 1 s (Maj Alexander Robert Menzies b 23 April 1940), 1 da (Heather Mary Menzies (Mrs Loxton) b 20 March 1942); *Career* Colonial Serv: agric offr 1937, chief agric offr Nyasaland 1953 (sr agric offr 1946), perm sec Miny of Agric and Co-op Devpt Tanganyika 1960 (dep dir of agric 1954, dir of agric 1958); consultancy work in Africa and Asia 1963-78: World Bank, Food and Agric Orgn, UN, Nordic Bd (Finland, Norway, Sweden, Denmark), engrg and tech firms in natural resources field; Oxfam 1963-85: tstee, memb Admin Ctee, chm Ctee Dealing with East; memb and chm PPC Bledington 1976-89; *Recreations* rugby, cricket, tennis, gardening; *Style*— Archibald Forbes, Esq, CBE; The Chesnuts, The Green, Bledington, Oxford OX7 6XQ (☎ 0608 658308)

FORBES, Bernard Norman Sefton; s of Gerald Sefton (d 1937), and Emily Rose, *née* Wischhusen (d 1964); *b* 8 April 1929; *Educ* Norwood Orphanage, Hackney Tech Coll, Swinton Coll; *m* 1, 15 Oct 1949 (m dis 1968), Hazel Helen, da of George Davies, of Anglesey; 1 s (Philip b 1954), 1 da (Hazel b 1950); m 2, 1973; 1 step da (Maxine b 1968); *Career* Nat Serv RAF WO/DF Air Sea Rescue 1947-49; divnl dir BSA Motor Cycles 1968-71, dir of personnel Dawson & Barfos 1971-73, md Aish & Co 1985-86, dir of business devpt Hortsmann Group 1986-89 (gp exec 1973-75), chm Management Effectiveness Ltd 1989-; non-exec dir: Apex New Enterprises Ltd, Hortsmann Timers & Controls, Notedale Ltd, Aish & Co, Hortsmann Gauge & Metrology; town councillor Solihull 1953-55, pres Bath C-of-C 1981, dir Dorset Employers' Network, involved with various industl, advsy and charitable ctees; FIPM, FITO, FInstD; *Recreations* after dinner speaking, literature, writing, various charities; *Style*— Bernard Forbes, Esq; Fairfield Lodge, Blandford, Dorset DT11 7HL (☎ 0258 451768)

FORBES, Bryan; *b* 22 July 1926; *Educ* Westham Secdy Sch, RADA; *m* 1958, Nanette Newman *qv* ; 2 da (one of whom, Sarah, m Sir John Leon, 4 Bt, *qv*); *Career* actor 1948-60, formed Beaver Films with Sir Richard Attenborough 1959, writer, dir and prodr of numerous films incl: The League of Gentlemen, Only Two Can Play, Whistle down the Wind 1961, The L Shaped Room 1962, Seance on a Wet Afternoon 1963, King Rat 1964, The Wrong Box 1967, The Madwoman of Chaillot 1968, The Raging Moon 1970, The Tales of Beatrix Potter 1971, The Stepford Wives 1974, The Slipper and the Rose 1975, International Velvet 1978, The Sunday Lovers 1980, Better Late than Never 1981, The Naked Face 1983; dir and prodr for tv incl: Edith Evans I Caught Acting Like the Measles (Yorkshire TV) 1973, Elton John Goodbye Norma Jean and other Things (ATV) 1973, Jessie (BBC) 1980, The Endless Game 1988; theatre dir incl: Macbeth (Old Vic) 1980, Killing Jessica (Savoy) 1986, The Living Room 1987; acted in: December Flower (Granada) 1984, First Among Equals (Granada) 1986; winner of: Br Academy Award 1960, writers Guild Award (twice), numerous int awards; md and head of prodn ABPC Studios 1969-71, md and chief exec EMI-MGM Elstree Studios 1970-71, dir Capital Radio Ltd 1973-; memb: BBC Gen Advsy Cncl 1966-69, BBC Schs Cncl 1971-73; pres: Beatrix Potter Soc 1982-, Nat Youth Theatre 1984-, Writers Guild of GB; Hon Doctorate of Literature London 1987; *Books* Truth Lies Sleeping (1950), The Distant Laughter (1972), Notes for a Life (1974), The Slipper and the Rose (1976), Ned's Girl (biog of Dame Edith Evans 1977), International Velvet (1978), Familiar Strangers (1979), That Despicable Race (1980), The Rewrite Man (1983), The Endless Game (1986), A Song At Twilight (1989);

Recreations running a bookshop, reading, photography, landscape, gardening; *Style*— Bryan Forbes, Esq; Bryan Forbes Ltd, c/o The Bookshop, Virginia Water, Surrey

FORBES, Prof Charles Douglas; s of John Forbes (d 1985), and Annie Robertson, *née* Stuart (d 1982); *b* 9 Oct 1938; *Educ* HS of Glasgow, Univ of Glasgow (MB ChB, MD, DSc); *m* 6 March 1965, Janette MacDonald, da of Ewan Robertson (d 1980); 2 s (John Stuart b 20 Dec 1967, Donald Alexander Ewan b 20 Sept 1971); *Career* lectr med Univ of E Africa Nairobi 1965-66, Fullbright fell American Heart Assoc 1968-70, sr lectr then reader in med Univ of Glasgow 1972-86 (lectr therapeutics 1962-65), prof in med Univ of Dundee 1986-; specialist books on blood coagulation and thrombosis; FRCPG 1974, FRCPE 1976, FRCP 1978, FRSA 1990; *Recreations* gardening, walking; *Style*— Prof Charles Forbes; East Chattan, 108 Hepburn Gdns, St Andrews, Fife KY16 9LT (☎ 0334 72428); Dept of Med, Ninewells Hosp and Med Sch, Dundee DD1 9SY (☎ 0382 60111, fax 0382 60675)

FORBES, Derek Francis Kemball; s of Flt Lt Francis William Forbes (d 1972), of E Finchley, and Vera Maud Rosalind Forbes; *b* 2 Feb 1943; *Educ* City of London Sch, Law Soc Sch of Law; *m* 1 Aug 1972, Carol Ann, da of Colin Robert Knight (d 1985), of Highgate, London; *Career* sr assoc Abbey Life 1971-79 (advertising mangr 1968-71), sr branch mangr Crown Life 1979-84, asst head of sales Sun Alliance 1984-88, agency mangr Sun Life 1988; Life Insur Assoc: chm Nat Ctee of Mangrs Forum 1984-87 (hon sec 1985, treas 1986, elected to nat exec 1984-87); Freeman City of London 1964, Liveryman Worshipful Co of Gold and Silver Wyre Drawers; memb Million Dollar Round Table 1976; fell Life Insur Assoc 1971; *Books* The Save and Prosper Book of Money (jtly 1968); *Style*— Derek Forbes, Esq; 22 Cherry Tree Rd, East Finchley, London N2 9QL (☎ 071 883 2985); Sun Life Unit Services, 10-12 Ely Place, London EC1 (☎ 071 242 2905)

FORBES, Donald James; s of Andrew Forbes (d 1960), of Hythe, Southampton, and Amy Forbes (d 1969); *b* 6 Feb 1921; *Educ* Oundle, Clare Coll Cambridge (MA), Santander Univ (Dip); *m* 21 Dec 1945, Patricia Muriel, da of Percival Douglas Yeo (d 1966); 2 s (Ian b 1947, Anthony b 1949), 1 da (Elizabeth b 1961); *Career* Sandhurst 1941, cmmnd Scots Gds 1941, Signals Offr 1942; 1 Bn Scots Gds: Signals Offr, Platoon Cdr, 2 i/c C Coy, Co Cdr HQ Coy served in N Africa and Italy 1943-46; asst master Dulwich Coll 1946-55; headmaster: Dauntsey's Sch West Lavington Wilts 1956-69, Merchiston Castle Sch Edinburgh 1969-81; capt Univ of Cambridge Rugby Fives 1941, cricket MCC 1957-76; chief invigilator ICA Scotland, pres Edinburgh Chamber Orchestra, sec Wengen Reunion Curling Club; *Recreations* golf, curling; *Clubs* Hon Co Edinburgh Golfers Muirfield, Edinburgh, Wengen & Forest Hills; *Style*— Donald Forbes, Esq; 33 Coates Gardens, Edinburgh EH12 5LG (☎ 031 346 0844); Breachacha (New) Castle, Isle of Coll, Argyllshire

FORBES, Very Rev Graham John Thomson; s of John Thomson Forbes (d 1986), of Edinburgh, and Doris, *née* Smith; *b* 10 June 1951; *Educ* George Heriots Sch Edinburgh, Univ of Aberdeen (MA), Univ of Edinburgh (BD), Edinburgh Theol Coll; *m* 25 Aug 1973, Jane, da of John Tennant Miller, of Edinburgh; 3 s (Duncan, Andrew, Hamish); *Career* curate Old St Paul's Edinburgh 1976-82; provost: St Ninian's Cathedral Perth 1982-90, St Mary's Cathedral Edinburgh 1990-; non-exec dir Radio Tay, chm Radio Tay Charity Auction 1986-90, fndr Canongate Youth Project Edinburgh, pres Lothian Assoc of Youth Clubs 1986-; memb: Scottish Community Educn Cncl 1981-87, Children's Panel Advsy Ctee Tayside 1986-90, Parole Bd 1990-; *Recreations* discovering dry rot, fly-fishing, running, visiting Russia; *Style*— The Very Rev the Provost of St Mary's Cathedral Edinburgh; 8 Lansdowne Crescent, Edinburgh EH12 5EQ (☎ 031 225 2978); St Mary's Cathedral, Palmerston Place, Edinburgh EH12 5AW (☎ 031 225 6293)

FORBES, Maj Sir Hamish Stewart; 7 Bt (UK 1823) of Newe and Edinglassie, MBE (Mil 1945), MC; s of late Lt-Col James Stewart Forbes (d 1957, gs of 3 Bt), and Féridah Frances, da of Hugh Lewis Taylor; suc cousin, Col Sir John Stewart Forbes, 6 Bt, DSO, JP, DL (d 1984); *b* 15 Feb 1916; *Educ* Eton, Lawrenceville, USA (Abbott scholarship), SOAS London; *m* 1, 2 June 1945 (m dis 1981), Jacynthe Elizabeth Mary, o da of late Eric Gordon Underwood; 1 s, 3 da; m 2, 1981, Mary Christine, MBE, da of late Ernest William Rigby; *Heir* s, James Thomas Stewart Forbes, b 28 May 1957, *qv*; *Career* Maj (ret) WG, served WWII (POW) France, Germany, Turkey; KJStJ 1983; patron Lonach Highland and Friendly Society; hon dir Br Humane Assoc, Inc Soc The Church Lads' and Girls' Bde; *Recreations* shooting, sculpture; *Clubs* Turf, Chelsea Arts, Pilgrims, Royal Asian Soc; *Style*— Maj Sir Hamish Forbes, Bt, MBE, MC; Brughs, Strathdon, Aberdeenshire AB36 8UT (☎ 09756 51431)

FORBES, James; s of Maj Donald Forbes (d 1963), of Edinburgh, and Rona Ritchie, *née* Yeats (d 1963); *b* 2 Jan 1923; *Educ* Christ's Hosp, Offrs Trg Sch Bangalore S India; *m* 14 Aug 1948, Alison Mary Fletcher, da of Maj George K Moffat (d 1979), of Dunblane, Perthshire; 2 s (Lindsay b 11 Oct 1953, Moray b 29 June 1962); *Career* WWII cmmnd 15 Punjab Regt 1942, transfd to IAOC qualifying as Inspecting Ordnance Offr, CO (Capt) Mobile Ammunition Inspection Unit 1943-44, Maj DADOS Amm GHQ (1) 1945-46, released as Hon Maj 1947; Peat Marwick Mitchell 1952-58; Schweppes plc 1958-69: ops res mangr 1960-63, gp chief accountant and dir of subsid cos 1963-69; gp fin dir Cadbury Schweppes 1970-78 (fin advsr on formation 1969-70); non-exec dir: British Transport Hotels 1978-83, British Rail Investments 1980-84, Steetley plc 1984-89, Compass Hotels Ltd 1984-, Lautro Ltd 1986-90; vice chm Tate & Lyle 1980-84 (sr exec dir 1978-80, chm Pension Fund 1978-85); Forestry cmmr 1982-88, tres and chm Cncl of Almoners Christs Hosp 1987- (chm Resources Ctee 1985-87); Freeman Worshipful Co of Accountants in England and Wales; FCA 1966 (memb Cncl 1971-88, treas 1984-86), memb Highland Soc of London; *Recreations* golf; *Clubs* Caledonian; *Style*— James Forbes, Esq; Lower Ridge, Courts Mount Rd, Haslemere, Surrey GU27 2PP (☎ 0428 652461); Great Eastern Hotel, Liverpool St, London EC2M 7QN (☎ 071 626 6647)

FORBES, James Duncan Mallen; VRD; s of James Alexander Forbes (d 1986), and Marjorie Beckley, *née* Mallen (d 1978); *b* 19 Dec 1926; *Educ* City of London Sch; *m* 1960, June, da of Harry De Behr Acheson-Gray (d 1952); 1 s (Patrick), 1 da (Susan); *Career* Sub Lt RNVR 1944-47; dir: Booker Line Ltd 1960-84 (md 1969-83, chm 1983-84), Clarkson Booker 1965-66, Booker Bros (Liverpool) Ltd 1966-84 (chm 1982-84), Liverpool Maritime Terminals Ltd 1972-84, London Steamship Owners Mutual Insur Assoc 1978-84, Coe Metcalf Shipping Ltd 1983-84, N American fishing Insur Mutual Assoc Ltd 1987-90; chm Such & Schosley Ltd 1974-84; memb: Merchant Navy Trg Bd 1974-76, Port of Preston Advsy Bd 1977-79, NW Econ Planning Cncl 1978-79; chm: W India Assoc of Liverpool 1967-71, Liverpool Steamship Owners Assoc 1977-78, Merseyside C of C 1980-82; vice chm Merseyside Residuary Body 1985-90; *Style*— James Forbes, Esq, VRD; 30 Boundary Rd, West Kirby, Wirral, Merseyside L48 1LF (☎ 051 625 5598)

FORBES, James Thomas Stewart; s and h of Sir Hamish Stewart Forbes, 7 Bt, MBE, MC; *b* 28 May 1957; *Educ* Eton, Univ of Bristol (BA); *m* 1986, Kerry Lynne, o da of Rev Lee Toms, of Sacramento, Calif, USA; 2 da (Theodora Christine b 23 Jan 1989, Katherine Elizabeth b 16 Nov 1990); *Career* proprietor Spats Catering Co (film location and party catering), Forbes Mount Veeder Vineyards Napa Valley Calif; *Clubs* Pratt's; *Style*— James Forbes, Esq; The Cottage, Hambleden, nr Henley-on-Thames, Oxon RG9 6RT (☎ 0491 575 914); 47 Kendal St, London W2 (☎ 0836 201 216)

FORBES, Hon Mrs John; Joan; 3 da of A Edward Smith, of Sherlockstown House Sallins, Co Kildare; *m* 23 Jan 1947, Hon John Forbes (d 1982), yr s of 8 Earl of Granard (d 1948), and bro of 9 Earl, *qv*; 1 s (Peter A E H Forbes, *qv*), 3 da; *Style*— Hon Mrs John Forbes c/o Mrs R J G Dillon-Mahon, Stockham Farm, Dulverton, Somerset TA22 9DW

FORBES, Vice Adm Sir John Morrison; KCB (1978); s of Lt-Col Robert Hogg Forbes, OBE (d 1976), and Gladys M, *née* Pollock; *b* 16 Aug 1925; *Educ* RNC Dartmouth; *m* 1950, Joyce Newenham, da of late Addison Perrit Hadden, of Ireland; 2 s, 2 da; *Career* 2 i/c and Operational Cdr Royal Malaysian Navy 1966-68, directorate of Naval Plans 1969-71, Capt HMS Triumph 1971-72, Capt RNC Dartmouth 1972-74, naval sec 1974-76, Vice Adm 1977, flag offr Plymouth 1977-79, Cdr Central Sub Area Eastern Atlantic and Cdr Plymouth Sub Area Channel 1977-79; chm Civil Serv Cmmrs Interview Panel 1980-; Naval ADC to HM The Queen 1974; awarded Kesatria Manku Negara 1968; *Recreations* country pursuits; *Clubs* Army & Navy, RNSA; *Style*— Vice Adm Sir John Forbes, KCB; c/o Nat Westminster Bank, Waterlooville, Portsmouth, Hants

FORBES, Hon Jonathan Andrew; 2 s of 23 Lord Forbes, KBE; *b* 20 Aug 1947; *Educ* Eton; *m* 10 Jan 1981, Hon Nicola Frances, da of 10 Baron Hawke, *qv*; 1 s (James Frederick Nicholas b 1987), 2 da (Camilla Rose b 1983, Annabella Jane b 1985); *Career* Capt Gren Gds; md Profile Security Services Ltd; *Style*— The Hon Jonathan Forbes; Tullynessle House, Alford, Aberdeenshire AB3 8QR (☎ 09755 62509)

FORBES, Master of; Hon Malcolm Nigel Forbes; s and h of 23 Lord Forbes, KBE, *qv*; *b* 6 May 1946; *Educ* Eton, Univ of Aberdeen; *m* 1, 30 Jan 1969 (m dis 1982), Carole Jennifer Andrée, da of Norman Stanley Whitehead (d 1981), of Aberdeen; 1 s (Neil Malcolm Ross b 10 March 1970), 1 da (Joanne Carole b 23 April 1972); m 2, 15 Feb 1988, Mrs Jennifer Mary Gribbon, da of Ian Peter Whittington, of Tunbridge Wells, Kent; *Heir* s, Neil Malcolm Ross Forbes b 1970; *Career* dir Instock Disposables Ltd; farmer and landowner; sec Donside Ball; *Recreations* skiing, cricket, croquet; *Clubs* Royal Northern & Univ (Aberdeen), Eton Ramblers, XL Club; *Style*— The Master of Forbes; Castle Forbes, Alford, Aberdeenshire AB33 8BL (☎ 09755 62574)

FORBES, Muriel Rose; CBE (1963); da of John Henry Cheeseright; *b* 20 April 1894; *Educ* Gateshead GS, Southlands Teacher Trg Coll; *m* 1923, Charles Gilbert Forbes (d 1957); 2 da; *Career* memb: Willesden Borough Cncl 1936-47, Middlesex CC 1934-65; JP County of Middx 1946; memb GLC 1964-67 (vice chm 1964-66); chm: St Charles Gp Hosp Mgmnt Ctee 1968-69, Paddington Gp Hosp Mgmnt Ctee 1963-68, Central Middx Hosp 1948-63; DTech Brunel Univ 1966; *Style*— Ms Muriel Forbes, CBE; 9 Rosemary Road, Halesowen, West Midlands B63 1BN (☎ 021 550 2866)

FORBES, 22 Lord (Premier S Lordship before July 1445); Nigel Ivan Forbes; KBE (1960), JP (Aberdeenshire 1955), DL (1958); s of 21 Lord Forbes (d 1953), and Lady Mabel Anson (d 1972), da of 3 Earl of Lichfield; *b* 19 Feb 1918; *Educ* Harrow, RMC Sandhurst; *m* 23 May 1942, Hon Rosemary Katharine Hamilton-Russell, da of 9 Viscount Boyne; 2 s, 1 da; *Heir* s, Master of Forbes, *qv*; *Career* served WWII, France and Belgium (wounded), N Africa, Sicily, NW Europe Adjt Grenadier Gds, Staff Coll 1945-46, mil asst high cmmr Palestine 1947-48, Maj Grenadier Gds; representative peer for Scotland 1955-63; pres Royal Highland and Agric Soc for Scot 1958-59; memb Inter-Parly Union Delgn to: Denmark 1956, Hungary 1965, Ethiopia 1971; memb Cwlth Parly Assoc Delgn to: Canada 1961, Pakistan 1962; min of state Scottish Office 1958-59; chm Don Dist River Bd 1961-73; bd memb: Scottish Nature Conservancy 1961-67, Aberdeen Milk Mktg Bd 1962-72; memb Sports Cncl for Scot 1966-71; dep chm Tennant Caledonian Breweries Ltd 1964-74, chm Rolawn Ltd 1975-; dir: Blenheim Travel Ltd 1981-88, Grampian TV 1960-88; pres Scottish Scouts Assoc 1970-88, chm Scottish Branch Nat Playing Fields Assoc 1965-80; farmer and landowner; *Recreations* wildlife, conservation, travel; *Clubs* Army and Navy; *Style*— The Rt Hon the Lord Forbes, KBE, JP, DL; Balforbes, Alford, Aberdeenshire AB33 8DR (☎ 09755 62516, office 09755 62574)

FORBES, Prof Sebastian; s of Dr Watson Forbes, and Mary Henderson, *née* Hunt; *b* 22 May 1941; *Educ* Univ Coll Sch Hampstead, RAM, Univ of Cambridge (MA, MusD); *m* 1, 29 June 1968 (m dis 1977), Hilary Taylor; 2 da (Joanna b 1971, Emily b 1974); m 2, 24 Sept 1983 Tessa Mary, da of John Brady (d 1967); 1 s (Alistair b 1984), 1 da (Nicola b 1986); *Career* prodr BBC (sound) 1964-67; lectr: Univ Coll of N Wales Bangor 1968-72, Univ of Surrey 1972- (prof of music 1981-); conductor Horniman Singers 1981-90; compositions incl: String Quartet no 1 (Radcliffe Award 1969), Essay for Clarinet and Orchestra (1970), Death's Dominion (1971), Symphony in Two Movements (1972); Sinfonias: 1 (1967, rev 1989), 2 (1978), 3 (1990); Sonata for 21 (1975), Voices of Autumn, 8 Japanese Tanka for choir and piano (1975), Sonata for 8 (1978), Violin Fantasy no 2 (1979), Evening Canticles (Aedis Christi 1 (1980), Aedis Christi 2 (1984), String Quartet no 3 (1981), Sonata for 17 (1987); memb: Performing Right Soc, Assoc of Professional Composers, Composers Guild of GB; LRAM, ARCM, ARCO, ARAM; *Style*— Prof Sebastian Forbes; 32 Wykeham Road, Guildford, Surrey GU1 2SE (☎ 0483 571806); Department of Music, University of Surrey, Guildford, Surrey GU2 5XH (☎ 0483 509317)

FORBES ADAM, Sir Christopher Eric; 3 Bt (UK 1917), of Hankelow Court, Co Chester; s of Eric Forbes Adam, CMG (2 s of Sir Frank Forbes Adam, 1 Bt, CB, CIE, JP, DL), by his w Agatha, widow of Sidney Spooner and eldest da of Reginald Walter Macan, sometime Master Univ Coll, Oxford; suc unc, Gen Sir Ronald Forbes Adam, 2 Bt, GCB, DSO, OBE, 1982; *b* 12 Feb 1920; *Educ* Abinger Hill Sch Surrey, privately; *m* 17 Sept 1957, Patricia Anne Wreford, yr da of John Neville Wreford Brown, of Maltings, Abberton, Colchester, Essex; 1 adopted da (Sarah Anne (Mrs Allen) b 1960); *Heir* 1 cous, Rev (Stephen) Timothy Beilby Forbes Adam, *qv*; *Career* sometime journalist with *Yorkshire Post*; *Style*— Sir Christopher Forbes Adam, Bt; 46 Rawlings St, London SW3

FORBES ADAM, Nigel Colin; JP (1960); s of Colin Forbes Adam, CSI, DL (d 1982, 3 s of Sir Frank Forbes Adam, 1 Bt, CB, CIE, JP, DL), and Hon Mrs (Irene Constance) Forbes Adam, *née* Lawley (d 1976), da of 3 Baron Wenlock, PC, GCSI, GCIE, KCB; bro of Rev Timothy, *qv*; *b* 7 Dec 1930; *Educ* Eton, King's Coll Cambridge (BA); *m* 1954 (m dis 1987), Teresa Hermione Idena, o da of Cdr David Lambert Robertson, RN (d 1979); 4 s; m 2, 1987, Malise, formerly w of David Ropner, *qv*, and da of late Col Armitage, MC, TD, of Newburgh House, Coxwold, Yorks; *Heir* s Charles David Forbes Adam; *Career* landowner and farmer; High Sheriff N Yorks 1976; chm Yorks Region Nat Tst 1985-; *Recreations* tennis, shooting, gardening; *Clubs* Brooks's; *Style*— Nigel Forbes Adam, Esq, JP; Skipwith Hall, Selby, Yorks (☎ 0757 288434)

FORBES ADAM, Rev (Stephen) Timothy Beilby; er s of Colin Gurdon Forbes Adam, CSI, JP, DL (d 1982, 3 s of Sir Frank Forbes Adam, 1 Bt, CB, CIE, JP, DL), by his w Hon Mrs (Irene Constance) Forbes Adam (d 1976), bro of Nigel Forbes Adam, *qv*; hp to 1 cous, Sir Christopher Forbes Adam, 3 Bt; *b* 19 Nov 1923; *Educ* Eton, Balliol Coll Oxford, RADA, Chichester Theol Coll; *m* 28 Sept 1954, Penelope, da of George Campbell Munday, MC, of Leverington Hall, Wisbech, Cambs; 4 da; *Career* served Rifle Bde 1942-47 in France and Far East; ordained 1962, rector of Barton-in-Fabis with Thrumpton, Southwell, Notts 1964-70, priest-in-charge: Southstoke 1974-84, Bath & Wells 1984-; non-stipendiary priest Tadmaston UB Dio of

Oxford; *Style—* Rev Timothy Forbes Adam; 1 Bakers Lane, Tadmaston, Banbury, Oxon OX15 5SS (☎ 0295 8305)

FORBES ADAM, Hon Mrs (Vivien Elisabeth); *née* Mosley; da of Sir Oswald Mosley, 6 Bt (d 1986), of Temple de la Gloire, 91400 Orsay, France, and Lady Cynthia (d 1933), da of 1 Marquess Curzon of Kedleston; raised to the rank of a daughter of a Baroness 1967; *Educ* Francis Holland Sch, Owlstone Croft Cambridge; *m* 15 Jan 1949, Desmond Francis Forbes Adam (d 1958), s of Colin Forbes Adam, CSI (d 1982), of Skipwith Hall, Selby, Yorks; 1 s (Rupert b 1957), 2 da (Cynthia (Mrs Chaddock) b 1950, Arabella b 1952); *Style—* The Hon Mrs Forbes Adam; 11 Mulberry Walk, London SW3 6DZ (☎ 071 352 3107)

FORBES-BELL, Barry Russell; s of Frederick George Bell (d 1963), and Hilda Marion, *née* Stanfield (d 1971); *b* 9 April 1941; *Educ* Univ of Leeds (LLB); *m* 1, Sept 1966 (m dis 1971), Margaret, *née* Rutherford; 1 s (Russell James Bell, (now Goater) b 1969); m 2, 4 April 1971 (m dis 1990), Penelope Beryl, da of John Forbes, of Saltburn, Cleveland; 2 s (Christian b 1974, Philip b 1979), 3 da (Charlotte b 1971, Eleanor b 1976, Olivia b 1983); *Career* slr; former hon sec Harrogate Law Soc; former professional footballer with Charlton Athletic and Millwall F 1957-60; MBIM; *Recreations* sport, theatre, amateur dramatics, travel, music; *Style—* Barry Forbes-Bell, Esq; Tiree, New Lane, Nun Monkton, York YO5 8EP; Osborne House, 20 Victoria Ave, Harrogate HG1 5QY (☎ 0423 523 011, 0423 711 327, fax 0423 507775); High St, Pateley Bridge, N Yorks

FORBES-LEITH OF FYVIE, Sir Andrew George; 3 Bt (UK 1923); s of Sir (Robert) Ian Algernon Forbes-Leith of Fyvie, 2 Bt, KT, MBE (d 1973), and Ruth Avis, *née* Barnett (d 1973); *b* 20 Oct 1929; *Educ* Eton; *m* 1962, Jane Kate (d 1969), da of late David McCall-McCowan, of Dalwhat, Moniaive, Dumfries; 2 s, 2 da; *Heir* s, George Ian David Forbes-Leith b 26 May 1967; *Style—* Sir Andrew Forbes-Leith of Fyvie, Bt; Dunachton, Kingussie, Inverness-shire (☎ 054 04 226)

FORBES-LEITH, George Ian David; s and h of Sir Andrew George Forbes-Leith of Fyvie, 3 Bt; *b* 26 May 1967; *Style—* George Forbes-Leith Esq; Estate Office, Fyvie, Turriff, Aberdeenshire (☎ 065 16 246)

FORBES-MICHIE, Capt Stanley Allan; s of Allan Black Wyness Michie (d 1958), and Isobel Joan Forbes Michie (d 1944); *b* 23 Feb 1934; *Educ* Bankhead Acad Aberdeen; *m* 1959, Marjorie, da of Joseph Elliott Robson (d 1986); 1 da (Susan Elizabeth b 1968); *Career* former Capt RA, served Egypt, Malta, Cyprus, BAOR; chief probation offr Sunderland Tyne and Wear 1973-81; John Goschen Meml Prize 1951, hon sec SSAFA S Tynside 1961-80, memb Heraldry Soc of Scot 1981, received grant of arms from Lord Lyon 1981; Cdr with Star Order Polonia Restituta 1984; memb Heraldry Soc of Scotland; *Books* Poems of a Probation Officer (1978); *Recreations* heraldry, poetry, tapestry, genealogy; *Style—* Capt Stanley Forbes-Michie; Marstan, St John's Terrace, East Boldon, Tyne and Wear NE36 0LL (☎ 091 5362142)

FORBES OF CRAIGIEVAR, Hon Sir Ewan; 11 Bt (NS 1630), of Craigievar, Aberdeenshire, JP (Aberdeenshire 1969); s of late 18 Lord Sempill; suc to Btcy only of bro, 19 Lord Sempill, AFC, 1965; *b* 6 Sept 1912; *Educ* Munich, Aberdeen Univ (MB, ChB); *m* 10 Oct 1953, Isobel, da of late Alec Mitchell, of Glenrinnes, Banffshire; *Heir* kinsman, John Alexander Cumnock Forbes-Sempill; *Career* Senior Casualty Officer, Aberdeen Royal Infirmary; *Books* The Aul' Days (1984); *Recreations* shooting, fishing, highland dancing; *Style—* Hon Sir Ewan Forbes of Craigievar, Bt, JP; Brux, Alford, Aberdeenshire (☎ 097 55 223)

FORBES OF ROTHIEMAY, Lt-Col William John Herbert; DSO (1945); Representor of the House of Forbes of Rothiemay, formerly of Dunira, by Comrie, Perthshire; descendant of John Forbes, of Newe (6 in descent from Sir William Forbes, 1 of Kynaldy and Pitsligo 1419-46 and bro of Sir Alexander, who was cr 1 Lord Forbes, a Barony which is now extinct); s of Cdr William Stronach Forbes, OBE, RN (d 1949), and Helen, da of George Herbert Strutt, of Kingairloch, Argyll; *b* 25 Sept 1912; *Educ* Downe House; *m* 1941, Diana Burrell de Ker, only child of late William Barr Knox, of Ryefield House, Dalry, Ayrshire; 2 s (and 1 s decd), 1 da; *Heir* s, Anthony Forbes, *qv* yr of Rothiemay; *Career* Argyll and Sutherland Highlanders, served NW Frontier, India 1934-39 (medal and clasp), served WWII NW Europe (despatches), instr Staff Colls Haifa and Camberley, GSO Mil Intelligence War Off, invalided out of Services 1949; farming in Norfolk and Perthshire until 1978 (breeder of Supreme Ayrshire Champion Royal Shows 1955/56); *Recreations* stalking, shooting, fishing, gardening; *Clubs* New, Army and Navy, Royal Highland Yacht; *Style—* Lt-Col William Forbes of Rothiemay, DSO; Pound House, Sopworth, nr Chippenham, Wilts SN14 6PT

FORBES-ROBERTSON, Cdr Kenneth Hugh; s of Col James Forbes-Robertson, VC, DSO, MC, DL (d 1955), and Hilda Forster, ARRC (d 1986); *b* 12 Sept 1933; *Educ* Rugby, Britannia RNC; *m* 25 July 1959, Elspeth Janet, da of Marvin Arundel Puttock (d 1970), of Lancing, Sussex; 3 da (Fiona b 1960, Kirsten b 1962, Grania Helen b 1966); *Career* RN; cmmnd HMS Yarnton 1965, HMS Russell 1967, HMS Londonderry 1973, HMS Kent 1981-83, served in submarines and various other ships on the Home, E Indies and Far East Stations, ret Cdr 1983; *Recreations* fishing, shooting; *Clubs* Farmers, IOD; *Style—* Cdr Kenneth Forbes-Robertson; West Barn, Soberton, Hampshire (☎ 0489 877563)

FORBES-SEMPILL, Hon Janet Cecilia; da of late Lord Sempill (19 in line), by 2 w, Cecilia, *née* Dunbar-Kilburn; half-sis of Lady Sempill, *qv*; *b* 4 May 1942; *Educ* Colchester Coll of Art; *Career* artist; *Style—* The Hon Janet Forbes-Sempill

FORBES-SEMPILL, John Alexander Cumnock; JP; s (by 3 m) of late Rear Adm Hon Arthur Lionel Ochoncar Forbes-Sempill, s of 17 Lord Sempill; hp of kinsman, Hon Sir Ewan Forbes of Craigievar, 11 Bt, JP; *b* 29 Aug 1927; *Educ* Stowe; *m* 1, 26 June 1956 (m dis 1963), Penelope Margaret Ann, da of Arthur Gordon Grey-Pennington; m 2, 1966, Jane Carolyn, da of C Gordon Evans, of Portpatrick, Wigtownshire; *Career* Capt Seaforth Highlanders; memb: Scottish Cncl, Br Show Jumping Assoc; *Clubs* Naval and Military, RSAC; *Style—* John Forbes-Sempill, Esq, JP; Auchendoon House, Newton Stewart, Wigtownshire DG8 6AN

FORBES TURNER, Rev Timothy John; CF; s of Maj Henry John Richard Turner, of Whitstable, Kent, and Hazel Forbes, *née* Burnett; *b* 10 Jan 1946; *Educ* Canterbury Tech HS for Boys, Pontifical Beda Coll Rome; *Career* clerk in Holy Orders at present serving Chaplain to H M Forces (Army); *Recreations* work with the RLSS, country pursuits; *Style—* The Rev Timothy Forbes Turner, CF; Ford Rise, Birches Nook, Stocksfield, Northumberland NE43 7JP (☎ 0661 843261)

FORD; *see*: St Clair-Ford

FORD, Rev Adam; s of Rev John Ford, and Jean Beattie, *née* Winstanley; *b* 15 Sept 1940; *Educ* Minehead GS, King's Coll London (BD, AKC), Univ of Lancaster (MA); *m* 2 Aug 1969, Veronica Rosemary Lucia, da of David Cecil Wynter Verey (Capt Royal Fus, d 1984), of Barnsley House, Cirencester, Glos; 2 s (Nathaniel b 1972, Joshua b 1977), 2 da (Imogen b 1970, Natasha b 1973); *Career* asst Ecumenical Inst of World Cncl of Churches Geneva 1964, curate Cirencester Parish Church Glos 1965-69, vicar Hebden Bridge W Yorks 1969-76, chaplain St Paul's Girls' Sch London 1976- (head Lower Sch 1986-), regular contrib to Prayer for the Day BBC Radio 4 1978-, priest in ordinary to HM The Queen Chapel Royal 1984-90; author of several articles in The Times and science jls on the relationship between science and religion, Star Gazers Guide to the Night Sky (audio guide to astronomy, 1982), Whose World? (6 video progs for TV, 1988) FRAS 1960; *Books* Spaceship Earth (1981), Weather Watch (1982), Universe: God, Man and Science (1986), The Cuckoo Plant (1991); *Recreations* astronomy, dry stone walling, field walking; *Style—* The Rev Adam Ford; 55 Bolingbroke Rd, Hammersmith, London W14 0AH (☎ 071 602 5902); Saintbridge Cottage, Barnsley, Cirencester, Glos (☎ 0285 74 246); St Paul's Girls' School, Brook Green, London W6 (☎ 071 603 2288)

FORD, Prof Alec George; s of George Thomas Ford (d 1958), of Leicester, and Alice Ann, *née* Agar (d 1954); *b* 22 June 1926; *Educ* Wyggeston Sch Leicester, Wadham Coll Oxford (BA, MA, DPhil); *m* 1, 17 Sept 1952, Peggy (d 1972), da of John Peck (d 1955), of Coventry; 2 s (Mark b 1955, Alan b 1958), 1 da (Sara b 1953); m 2, 28 May 1983, Angela, da of E Needham, of Gerrards Cross; *Career* Sgt RA WWII 1944-47; sr lectr in econ Univ of Leicester 1963-65 (lectr 1953-63), pro vice chllr Univ of Warwick 1977-89 (reader in econ 1965, prof of econ 1970-89, emeritus prof of econ 1989); memb: Royal Econ Soc, Econ Hist Soc; Hon DLitt Warwick 1990; *Books* The Gold Standard 1880-1914: Britain and Argentina (1962), Planning and Growth in Rich and Poor Countries (ed, 1965), Income Spending and the Price Level (1971); *Recreations* photography, steam railways, church architecture; *Style—* Prof Alec Ford; 26 Church Hill, Leamington Spa, Warwickshire CV32 5AY (☎ 0926 426596); Dept of Economics, University of Warwick, Coventry CV4 7AL (☎ 0203 523523)

FORD, Sir Andrew Russell; 3 Bt (UK 1929); s of Sir Henry Russell Ford, 2 Bt, TD, JP (d 1989); *b* 29 June 1943; *Educ* Winchester, New Coll Oxford; *m* 8 Aug 1968, Penelope Anne, o da of Harold Edmund Relph, of West Kirby, Wirral; 2 s (Toby Russell b 1973, David Andrew b 1984), 1 da (Julia Mary b 1970); *Heir* s, Toby Russell Ford b 11 Jan 1973; *Style—* Sir Andrew Ford, Bt; 20 Coniston Road, Chippenham, Wilts

FORD, (John) Anthony; s of Frank Everatt Ford, of Banstead, Surrey, and Dorothy Mary, *née* Hearn; *b* 28 April 1938; *Educ* Epsom Coll, St Edmunds Hall Oxford; *m* 1, 1963 (m dis), Caroline Rosemary Wharrad; 1 da (Joanna); m 2, 1984 Sandra Edith Williams; *Career* dir: Arts Services Grants 1974-79, Crafts Cncl 1988- (joined 1979); vice pres for Europe World Crafts Cncl 1987-; memb: Working Party Calouste Gulbenkian Tst Craft Initiative 1985-89, Visual Arts Advsy Ctee The British Cncl 1988-, Fabric Ctee Rochester Cathedral 1989-, Court RCA 1989-; FRSA 1989; *Style—* Anthony Ford, Esq; Crafts Council, 12 Waterloo Place, London SW1Y 4AT (☎ 071 930 4811, fax 071 321 0427)

FORD, Benjamin Thomas (Ben); DL (W Yorks 1982-); s of Benjamin Charles Ford (d 1947), and Mary Ethel, *née* Moorton; *b* 1 April 1925; *Educ* Rowan Road Central Sch Surrey; *m* 30 Dec 1950, Vera Ada, da of Flt-Lt Henry Fancett (d 1973); 2 s (Tony b 1952, Ivan b 1961); 1 da (Paula b 1956); *Career* Petty Offr air fitter electrics RN Fleet Air Arm 1943-47; convener of shop stewards The Marconi Co 1955-64; cnllr Clacton UDC 1959-62, alderman Essex CC 1959-65, MP Bradford North 1964-83; chm: Br Gp Interparly Union 1977-79, Accommodation and Admin Select Ctee 1979-83, All Party Wool Textile Ctee 1979-83; memb Firearms Consultative Ctee Home Office 1989-, main bd memb and chm Central & Southern Regn Ctees Bradford and Northern Housing Assoc; JP 1963-67, chm English Shooting Cncl, vice pres and memb Cncl NRA, vice pres Br Assoc for Shooting and Conservation; pres: Yorkshire Regn MENCAP, Bradford Civic Soc; Freeman City of London 1979, Liveryman Worshipful Co of Gunmakers 1979; Hon FAIA; Grand Offr Order of the Southern Cross Brazil; *Recreations* family, shooting, politics, music, gardening; *Clubs* RAC, Idle Working Men's; *Style—* Ben T Ford, Esq, DL; 9 Wynmore Crescent, Bramhope, Leeds (☎ 0532 675054); Bradford & Northern Housing Association, Butterfield House, Otley Rd, Shipley, W Yorks BD17 7HF (☎ 0274 588840, fax 0274 531023)

FORD, Sir (Richard) Brinsley; CBE (1978); eld s of Capt Richard Ford (d 1940), and Rosamund Isabel (d 1911), da of Sir John Ramsden, 5 Bt (and gggda of Richard Brinsley Sheridan, the orator and dramatist); ggs of Richard Ford, author of Handbook for Spain; *b* 10 June 1908; *Educ* Eton, Trinity Coll Oxford; *m* 1937, Joan Mary, da of Capt Geoffrey Vyvyan, Royal Welch Fus (ka 1914); 2 s (Francis, Augustine), 1 da (Marianne); *Career* joined TA 1939; served for one year as Troop Sgt Maj RA, cmmnd 1941, and transferred to Intelligence Corps, Maj (1945); memb: Nat Art-Collections Fund 1927-, Exec Ctee 1960-88, (vice chm 1974-75, chm 1975-78); tstee: Nat Gallery 1954-61, Watts Gallery, Compton 1955- (chm 1974-84); sec of Soc of Dilettanti 1972-88, jt hon advsr on paintings to the Nat Tst 1980, hon fell RA 1981, companion NEAC 1983, chm Nat Tst Fndn for Art Ctee 1986-90, pres Walpole Soc 1986-; contrib to Burlington Magazine and Apollo; Hon LLD (EXON) 1990; FSA 1973; owner Ford Collection of Richard Wilsons; Belgian Order of Leopold II (1945), US Bronze Star (1946), Médaille d'Argent de la Reconaissance, Francaise (1947), Order of Isabel la Catolica of Spain (First Class A 1986); kt 1984 (for services to the arts); *Publications* The Drawings of Richard Wilson (1951); *Clubs* Brooks's; *Style—* Sir Brinsley Ford, CBE, FSA; 14 Wyndham Place, Bryanston Square, London W1H 1AQ (☎ 071 723 0826)

FORD, Hon Mrs (Caroline Jane); *née* Nelson; er da of 2 Baron Nelson of Stafford; *b* 11 Jan 1942; *m* 2 April 1964, Michael John Henry Ford, *qv*; 2 s (James, Andrew), 1 da (Annabel); *Style—* The Hon Mrs Ford; Lower Moorhayne Farm, Yarcombe, nr Honiton, Devon EX14 9BE (☎ 040 486284)

FORD, Colin John; s of John William Ford, of London, and Hélène Martha, *née* Jones; *b* 13 May 1934; *Educ* Enfield GS, Univ Coll Oxford (MA); *m* 1, 12 Aug 1961 (m dis 1980), Margaret Elizabeth, da of Ernest Cordwell; 1 s (Richard John b 22 Nov 1970), 1 da (Clare Michaela Elizabeth b 5 Dec 1972); m 2, 7 Sept 1984, Susan Joan Frances Grayson; 1 s (Thomas Grayson b 29 May 1985); *Career* mangr and prodr Kidderminster Playhouse 1958-60, gen mangr Western Theatre Ballet 1960-62, visiting lectr in English and drama California State Univ at Long Beach UCLA 1962-64, dep curator Nat Film Archive 1965-72, organiser Thirtieth Anniversary Congress of Int Fedn of Film Archive London 1968, dir Cinema City exhibition 1970, prog dir London Shakespeare Film Festival 1972, keeper of film and photography Nat Portrait Gallery 1972-81, head Nat Museum of Photography, Film and TV 1982-; film: Masks and Faces 1966 (BBC TV version Omnibus 1968); Hon MA Univ of Bradford 1989; *Books* An Early Victorian Album (with Roy Strong, 1974, 2 edn 1977), The Cameron Collection (1975), Happy and Glorious: Six Reigns of Royal Photography (ed, 1977), Rediscovering Mrs Cameron (1979), People in Camera (1979), A Hundred Years Ago (with Brian Harrison, 1983), Portraits (Gallery World of Photography, 1983), Oxford Companion to Film (princ contrib), André Kértesz: The Manchester Collection (contrib, 1984), The Story of Popular Photography (ed, 1989); *Recreations* travel, music, small boats; *Style—* Colin Ford, Esq; National Museum of Photography, Film and Television, Prince's View, Bradford, W Yorkshire BD5 0TR (☎ 0274 727 488, fax 0274 723 155)

FORD, David Moxon; s of James Ford (d 1975), of St Annes on Sea, Lancs, and Annie, *née* Hunt (d 1987); *b* 20 Oct 1937; *Educ* King Edward VII Sch Lytham; *m* (m dis 1981); 2 s (Richard b 24 Aug 1965, Patrick b 2 Aug 1968); *Career* chief exec and sec Billiards and Snooker Control Cncl 1987- (former devt offr 1977-87), nat coaching dir Billiards and Snooker Fndn; contrib numerous pubns; sec: Int Billiards and Snooker Fedn, Euro Billiards and Snooker Assoc; sec and dir World Snooker Promotions Ltd;

AIB 1973, MSAE 1988; *Recreations* all sports (as spectator now); *Style—* David Ford, Esq; 1 West Park Gardens, West Park Road, Roundhay, Leeds LS8 2HD (☎ 0532 668383); The Billiards and Snooker Control Council, 92 Kirkstall Rd, Leeds LS3 1LT (☎ 0532 440586, fax 0532 468418)

FORD, Hon Mrs Diana Elizabeth; *née* Maxwell; da of Cdr (John) David Maxwell, RN, *qv*, and 27 Baroness de Ros (d 1983); sister of 28 Baron de Ros, *qv*; *b* 6 June 1957; *Educ* Godstowe Sch High Wycombe, Hillcourt Sch Dunlaoghaire; *m* 1, 1976 (m dis 1978), Jonathan Watkins; m 2, 1978 (m dis 1981), Don Richard Bell; m 3, 1987, Eric Ford; 1 da (Neesha b 10 May 1988); *Style—* The Hon Mrs Ford

FORD, Sir Edward William Spencer; KCB (1967, CB 1952), KCVO (1957, MVO 1949), ERD (1987), DL; s of Very Rev Lionel George Bridges Justice Ford, Dean of York (d 1932), and Mary Catherine, *née* Talbot; bro of Neville M Ford, *qv*; *b* 24 July 1910; *Educ* Eton, New Coll Oxford; *m* 1 Dec 1949, Hon Virginia, *qv*, da of 1 and last Baron Brand; 2 s; *Career* WWII Lt-Col Grenadier Gds; called to the Bar 1937, in practice 1937-39; asst private sec to HM King George VI 1946-52 and to HM The Queen 1952-67 (extra equerry 1955-); dir: Eydon Hall Estates Ltd 1963-83, London Life Assoc Ltd 1970-83; sec Pilgrim Tst 1967-75, sec and registrar Order of Merit 1975-; High Sheriff Northants 1970; OStJ 1976; hon fell New Coll Oxford 1982; memb Ct of Assts Worshipful Co of Goldsmiths 1970- (Prime Warden 1979); *Clubs* White's, MCC, Beefsteak; *Style—* Sir Edward Ford, KCB, KCVO, ERD, DL; Canal House, 23 Blomfield Rd, London W9 1AD (☎ 071 286 0028)

FORD, Air Marshal Sir Geoffrey Harold; KBE (1979), CB (1974); s of Harold Alfred Ford (d 1961), of Lewes; *b* 6 Aug 1923; *Educ* Lewes GS, Univ of Bristol; *m* 1951, Valerie, da of late Douglas Hart Finn, of Salisbury; 2 s; *Career* served RAF WWII, cmmnd (Tech Branch) 1942, air offr Engrg Strike Cmd 1973-76, DG Engrg and Supply 1976-78, chief engr 1978-81; dir Metals Soc 1981-84, sec Inst of Metals 1985-88; FEng; *Clubs* RAF; *Style—* Air Marshal Sir Geoffrey Ford, KBE, CB; c/o Barclays Bank plc, The Old Bank, Lewes, E Sussex

FORD, (James) Glyn; MEP (Lab) Gtr Manchester East 1984-; s of Ernest Benjamin Ford (d 1990), of Glos, and Matilda Alberta James (d 1986); *b* 28 Jan 1950; *Educ* Marling Sch Stroud, Univ of Reading (BSc), UCL, (MSc); *m* 1973, Hazel Nancy, da of Hedley John (d 1969), of Guernsey; 1 da (Elise Jane b 1981); *Career* undergraduate apprentice BAC 1967-68, course tutor in oceanography Open Univ 1976-78, teaching asst UMIST 1977-78; res fell: Univ of Sussex 1978-79, Univ of Manchester 1976-79; lectr Univ of Manchester 1979-80, sr res fell Prog of Policy Res in Engrg Sci and Technol 1980-84, hon visiting res fell Univ of Tokyo 1984- (visiting prof 1983); Parly candidate (Lab) Hazel Grove Gen Election 1987, chm Ctee of Inquiry into Growth of Racism and Fascism in Europe for Euro Parl 1984-86, vice chm Security and Disarmament Sub Ctee of Euro Parl 1987-89, rapporteur Ford Report Ctee of Inquiry into Racism and Xenophobia 1990 ldr Br labour gp of MEPs 1989-, vice chm Socialist Gp Euro Parl 1989-; *Publications* The Future of Ocean Technology (1987), author of various articles in jls of sci and technol; *Style—* Glyn Ford, Esq, MEP; 46 Stamford Rd, Mossley, Lancs OL5 OBE (☎ 04578 36276, fax 04578 34927)

FORD, Harold Frank; yr s of Sir Patrick Johnston Ford, 1 Bt (d 1945), and Jessie Hamilton, *née* Field (d 1962); *b* 17 May 1915; *Educ* Winchester, Univ Coll Oxford, Univ of Edinburgh; *m* 29 July 1948, Lucy Mary, da of late Sheriff John Rudolph Wardlaw Burnet, KC; 1 s, 3 da; *Career* Capt WWII Lothians and Border Yeo, POW; Maj Home Guard; advocate 1945; legal advsr to UNRRA and IRO (Germany) 1947; sheriff substitute Forfar 1951-71, sheriff Perth 1971-80; *Recreations* gardening, golf; *Clubs* New (Edinburgh), Hon Co Edinburgh Golfers, Royal Perth Golfing Soc; *Style—* Harold Ford, Esq; Millhill, Meikleour, Perthshire PH2 6EF (☎ 073-871 311)

FORD, Prof Sir Hugh; s of Arthur Ford (d 1969), of Welwyn Garden City, Herts, and Constance Ford; *b* 16 July 1913; *Educ* Northampton Sch, Imperial Coll London (DSc, PhD); *m* 1942, Wynyard Scholfield; 2 da; *Career* res engr ICI 1939-42, chief engr Br Iron & Steel Fedn 1942-48; Imperial Coll London: prof of applied mechanics (formerly reader) 1948-65, prof of mechanical engrg and head of dept 1965-78, pro rector 1978-80, prof of mechanical engrg 1969-82, currently emeritus prof; memb Agric Res Cncl 1976-81, pres Inst of Mechanical Engrs 1976-77; chm: Engrs Bd SERC 1970-74, Sir Hugh Ford & Assocs Ltd 1982- (formerly of Ford & Dain Ptnrs Ltd); dir: Air Liquide UK, International Dynamics Ltd 1982- (formerly RD Projects Ltd); vice pres Fellowship of Engrg 1981-84; pres: Welding Inst 1983-85 Inst of Metals 1985-87; fell Imperial Coll 1983; Hon Doctorate Univ of Sheffield 1984; Hon DSc: Univ of Salford, Queen's Univ Belfast, Aston Univ, Univ of Bath, Univ of Sussex; James Watt Int Gold medal 1985; FRS 1967, FEng, Hon MASME, FCGI, FICE, Hon FIMechE, Hon FIChemE, FIM; kt 1975; *Recreations* gardening, music, model engineering; *Clubs* Athenaeum; *Style—* Prof Sir Hugh Ford, FRS; 18 Shrewsbury House, Cheyne Walk, London SW3; Shamley Cottage, Shamley Green, Surrey

FORD, James Allan; CB (1978), MC (1946); 2 s of Douglas Ford (d 1948), and Margaret Duncan, *née* Allan; *b* 10 June 1920; *Educ* Royal HS Edinburgh, Univ of Edinburgh; *m* 1948, Isobel, *née* Dunnett; 1 s, 1 da; *Career* WWII Capt 2 Bn The Royal Scots Hong Kong; civil servant: registrar gen for Scotland 1966-69, princ estab offr SO 1969-79, ret 1979; tstee Nat Library of Scotland 1981-; novelist; *Books* The Brave White Flag (1961), Season of Escape (1963, Frederick Niven Award 1965), A Statue for a Public Place (1965), A Judge of Men (1968, Scottish Arts Cncl Award 1968), The Mouth of Truth (1971); *Recreations* trout fishing; *Clubs* Scottish Arts, Royal Scots; *Style—* James Ford, Esq, CB, MC; 29 Lady Rd, Edinburgh, EH16 5PA (☎ 031 667 4489)

FORD, Sir John Archibald; KCMG (1977, CMG 1967), MC (1945); s of Ronald Mylne Ford (d 1963), of Newcastle-under-Lyme, Staffs, and Margaret Jesse Coghill (d 1977); *b* 19 Feb 1922; *Educ* Sedbergh, Oriel Coll Oxford; *m* 1956, Emaline, da of Mahlon Burnette (d 1989), of Leesville, Virginia, USA; 2 da; *Career* served WWII as Maj RA Field Regt; HM Dip Serv ret 1981: consul gen NY, DG Br Trade Devpt in USA 1971-75, Br ambassador Jakarta 1975-78, high cmmr Ottawa 1978-81; lay admin Guildford Cathedral 1982-84; chm: Voluntary and Christian Service 1985-88, Aids Care Educn and Trg 1989-; *Books* Honest to Christ (1988); *Recreations* walking, writing, sailing; *Clubs* Farmers, RHS; *Style—* Sir John Ford, KCMG, MC; Loquats, Guildown, Guildford, Surrey

FORD, Lt Cdr John Worthington; s of William Ernest Ford (d 1961), of Bradford on Tone, Somerset, and Agnes Mary, *née* Worthington (d 1979); *b* 8 Sept 1932; *Educ* RNC Dartmouth; *m* 7 June 1968, Anne, da of Maj Harold Vandeleur Phelps, of Priors Marston, Warwickshire; 1 s (Nicholas Worthington b 1973); *Career* RN 1950-65: serv HM submarines UK and abroad 1954-62, Flag Lt to Flag Offr Scot and NI 1963-65, ret Lt Cdr; Clerk of the Course: Wolverhampton Racecourse 1972, Stratford Racecourse 1974, Uttoxeter Racecourse 1974-88; cdr and co cmmr St John Ambulance Northamptonshire 1974-79; OStJ 1978; *Recreations* hunting; *Style—* Lt Cdr John Ford; The Gables, Everdon, Daventry, Northamptonshire NN11 6BL (☎ 032 736 221)

FORD, Leslie John; s of Sidney George Frederick Ford (d 1971), and Doris Irene, *née* Davies; *b* 16 March 1936; *Educ* Sir Walter St John Sch, Univ of London (BSc); *m* 24 Sept 1960, Janet Loraine, da of Max Gilbert Frost (d 1972); 1 s (Samuel b 1964), 1 da (Madeleine b 1966); *Career* chem engr with ICI plc 1959-86 (consult chem engr 1986-), co-ordinator for the Sci and Engrg Res Cncl prog in particulate technol 1984-; vice chm: Hitchin UDC 1974-75, Bd of Dirs IFPRI 1979-85; pres Int Fine Particle Res Inst Inc 1985-; CEng, FIChemE, ACMA; *Recreations* squash, badminton, politics; *Clubs* Naval; *Style—* Leslie Ford, Esq; 2 High View, Helsby, Cheshire WA6 9LP (☎ 09282 3886); G1, Waterloo Centre, Waterloo Rd, Widnes, Cheshire WA8 0PR (☎ 051 420 1850, fax 051 424 1495)

FORD, Dowager Lady; Mary Elizabeth (Molly); *née* Wright; yst da of Godfrey FitzHerbert Wright, JP (d 1947), of Whiddon, Bovey Tracey, Devon, and Maud Frances Bateman, *née* Wright; *m* 8 Aug 1936, Sir Henry Russell Ford, 2 Bt, TD, JP (d 1989); 1 s (Sir Andrew Russell, 3 Bt), 3 da (Jill Dorothy b 1937, Alison Patricia (Mrs Robert M Cowe) b 1946, Belinda Christine (Mrs Graeme P C McWilliam) b 1951); *Style—* The Dowager Lady Ford; 1 Broadgait Green, Gullane, East Lothian EH31 2BQ (☎ 0620 842214)

FORD, Michael John Henry; s of late Lt-Col Mortimer Noel Ford, TD, DL, and Miriam Margaret Ford; *b* 23 May 1936; *Educ* Harrow; *m* 2 April 1964, Hon Caroline Jane, *qv*, da of 2 Baron Nelson of Stafford; 2 s (James, Andrew), 1 da (Annabel); *Career* 2 Lt KAR also Devonshire Regt; dir estate agents firm; memb Cncl of Sail Trg Assoc, pres West of England Deaf Sch, regnl sec Game Conservancy Devon; Freeman Worshipful Co of Gunmakers; Kenya Medal 1956; *Recreations* sailing, shooting, fishing; *Clubs* Royal Ocean Racing; *Style—* Michael Ford, Esq; Lower Moorhayne Farm, Yarcombe, nr Honiton, Devon EX14 9BE (☎ 040 486 284)

FORD, (John) Peter; CBE (1969); s of late Ernest Ford, of Westminster, and Muriel Ford; *b* 20 Feb 1912; *Educ* Wrekin Coll, Gonville and Caius Coll Cambridge; *m* 1939, Phoebe Seys, da of Herbert McGregor Wood, of Hampstead; 1 s, 2 da; *Career* md: Brush Export, Assoc Brit Oil Engines Export Ltd 1949-58, Coventry Climax International Ltd 1958-63; dir Plessey Overseas Ltd 1963-70, chm Inst of Export 1954-56 and 1965-67, vice pres London C of C 1972-; chm: Brit Shippers Cncl 1972-75, md International Jt Ventures Ltd 1974-, Metra Martech Ltd 1988-; Master Worshipful Co of Ironmongers 1981; *Recreations* athletics (Cambridge Univ and Int teams); *Clubs* United Oxford & Cambridge, City Livery, MCC, Hawks (Cambridge), Royal Wimbledon Golf; *Style—* Peter Ford, Esq, CBE; 40 Fairacres, Roehampton Lane, London SW15 (☎ 081 876 2146, office: 081 563 0666)

FORD, Richard James Cameron; s of Bernard Thomas Ford (d 1967), of Little Estcotts, Burbage, Wilts, and Eveline Saumarez Ford (d 1952); *b* 1 Feb 1938; *Educ* Marlborough; *m* 27 Sept 1975, Mary Elizabeth, da of James Arthur Keevil; 3 s (James Richard Keevil b 26 July 1976, Charles John Cameron b 26 July 1978, William Bernard Saumarez b 29 May 1980); *Career* admitted slr 1961, ptnr Ford and Ford 1965, sr ptnr Ford Gunnigham and Co 1970-; dir: Ramsbury Building Society 1984-86, West of England Building Society 1986-89, Regency and West of England Building Society 1989-90, Portman Building Society 1990-; tstee Glos and Wilts Law Soc 1983-(pres 1982-83); memb Salisbury Diocesan Synod 1985-, lay chm Pewsey Synod 1987-; memb: Wyvern Hosp Mgmnt Ctee 1967-70, Swindon Hon Mgmnt Ctee 1970-74, Wiltshire Area Health Authy 1974-82; vice chm Swindon Health Authy 1982-87; memb Law Soc; *Recreations* riding, sailing; *Clubs* Royal Solent Yacht; *Style—* Richard Ford, Esq; Little Estcotts, Burbage, Wilts SN8 3AG; Kingsbury House, Marlborough, Wilts (☎ 0672 52265)

FORD, Gen Sir Robert Cyril; GCB (1981, KCB 1977, CB 1973), CBE (1971, MBE 1958); s of John Stranger Ford (d 1970), and Gladys Ford (d 1986), of Yealmpton, Devon; *b* 29 Dec 1923; *Educ* Musgrave's Coll; *m* 1949, Jean Claudia, da of Gp Capt Claude Luther Pendlebury, MC, TD (d 1961), of Yelverton; 1 s; *Career* served WWII 4/7 Royal Dragoon Gds NW Europe (despatches), Egypt and Palestine 1947-48 (despatches); instr Mons OCS 1949-50, trg offr Scottish Horse (TA) 1952-54, Staff Coll Camberley 1955, GSO2 Mil Ops WO 1956-57, GSO1 to Adm of Fleet Earl Mountbatten 1964-65, CO 4/7 Royal Dragoons 1966-67, Cdr 7 Armd Bde 1968-69, Princ Staff Offr to CDS 1970-71, Maj-Gen 1971, Cdr Land Forces NI 1971-73, Cmdt RMA Sandhurst 1973-76, Lt-Gen 1976, Mil Sec MOD 1976-78, General 1978, Adj-Gen 1978-81 and ADC Gen to HM The Queen 1980-81, ret 1981; Col Cmdt RAC 1980-82 and SAS 1980-85, Col 4/7 Royal Dragoon Gds 1984-88; govr: Royal Hosp Chelsea 1981-87, Corps of Commissionaires 1981-; chm: Army Benevolent Fund 1981-87 (pres 1986-), Royal Cambridge Home for Soldiers' Widows 1981-87; nat pres Forces Help and Lord Roberts Workshops 1981-, cmmr Cwlth War Graves Cmmn 1981-88 (vice chm 1989-); CBIM; *Recreations* tennis, cricket, war studies; *Clubs* Cavalry & Guards, MCC; *Style—* Gen Sir Robert Ford, GCB, CBE; c/o National Westminster Bank, 45 Park St, Camberley, Surrey GU15 3PA

FORD, Robert Webster; CBE (1982); s of Robert Ford, and Beatrice, *née* Webster; *b* 27 March 1923; *Educ* Alleyne's Sch; *m* 2 June 1956, Monica Florence, da of Ernest George Tebbett; 2 s (Martin b 1957, Giles b 1964); *Career* WWII RAF 1939-45; radio offr 1945; Br Mission Lhasa Tibet, Political Agency Sikkin and Bhutan, Tibetan Govt Serv, political prisoner communist China 1950-55, freelance writer and broadcaster Tibetan and Chinese affrs 1955-56; HM Dip Serv 1956-83: Saigon 1957-58, Djakarta 1959, Washington 1960-62, FO 1962-67, Tangier 1967-70, Luanda 1970-74, Bordeaux 1974-78, Gothenburg 1978-80, Geneva 1980-83; memb Cncl Tibet Soc; FRGS 1956, FRComs 1956; *Books* Captured in Tibet (1956, 2 edn 1990); *Recreations* skiing, gardening, travelling; *Style—* Robert Ford, Esq, CBE; Cedar Garth, Latimer Rd, Monken Hadley, Barnet, Herts EN5 5NU

FORD, Roland Ernest (Bob); s of Leslie Ernest Ford (d 1966), of Little Kimble, Bucks, and Una Winifred, *née* Farley (d 1971); *b* 16 Aug 1926; *Educ* Hendon GS London, Imp Coll of Sci and Technol London, LSE (BSc); *m* 26 Aug 1950, Barbara Maie Jessie, da of Percy Charles William Carter (d 1970), of Edgware, Middx; 2 da (Susan (Mrs Fairlamb), Judith (Mrs Illingworth)); *Career* Nat Serv RAF NI and Burma 1945-48; gen mangr and dir Elliott Automation Gp 1965-68 (project mangr 1951-58, div mangr 1958-63, asst gen mangr 1963-65), md Negretti and Zambia (Aviation) Ltd 1969-73, chm and chief exec Negretti and Zambia plc 1975-81 (dep gp chm 1973-75), mgmnt conslt 1981-; treas Little Compton PCC, chm Little Compton Parish Cncl, memb Action Ctee S Warwickshire Combined Parishes; FInst D, ARCS; *Recreations* music, reading; *Clubs* Inst of Dirs Pall Mall; *Style—* Bob Ford, Esq; Wray House, Little Compton, Moreton-in-Marsh, Gloucestershire GL56 0SF (☎ 060 874 217)

FORD, Stephen Paul; s of Gerald Ford (d 1978), of Docks in Cardiff, and Joan, *née* James; *b* 15 Aug 1965; partner, Jayne, da of Terry McDonnell; 1 s (Luke b 8 March 1988); *Career* Rugby Union wing threequarter Cardiff RFC and Wales (7 caps); clubs: Glamorgan Wanderers RFC, Rumney RFC, Cardiff RFC 1988- (70 appearances); rep: Wales B (debut v Canada 1989, scored 7 tries in 47-0 defeat v Saskatchewan setting a Welsh record); Wales: debut v Ireland 1990; *Recreations* football; *Style—* Stephen Ford, Esq; 3 Chester Close, St Mellons, Cardiff (☎ 0222 790112); Cardiff RFC, Cardiff Arms Park, Westgate St, Cardiff, South Glamorgan

FORD, Dr Sydney John; s of Sidney James Ford (d 1983), of West Huntspill, Burnham-on-Sea, Somerset; *b* 23 Aug 1936; *Educ* Bishop Gore Sch Swansea, Univ of Wales (BSC, PhD, Dip in Math Statistics); *m* 1, 1960 (m dis 1990), Beryl, da of Albert G Owen; 2 s; m 2, 1990, Morag, da of Finlay J Munro; *Career* chm: Aluminium Corpn, British Alcan Ltd (dep md until 1985); md (dep md to 1982) The British Aluminium Co 1982-85; dir Williams Holdings 1985; *Recreations* rugby referee and coach; *Style—* Dr S John Ford; Christian Salvesen plc, Rödingsmarkt 9, 2000 Hamburg 11, Germany

FORD, Timothy Graham; s of John Hamilton Ford (d 1974), of Charleston, Cornwall, and Dorothy Joyce Ford; *b* 27 Jan 1945; *Educ* Bancrofts Sch Woodford Green Essex, Coll of Law Lancaster Gate; *m* 4 March 1972, Marian Evelyn, da of Charles Frederick Bernard Hayward, MBE, of 2 Orchard Close, Mersham, nr Ashford, Kent; 2 s (Paul b 1973, Simon b 1977); *Career* Inns of Ct and City Yeo 1965-67, cmmd RCS TA 1967, 36 Eastern Signal Regt V; admitted slr 1969, ptnr Park Nelson slrs 1971-, dir Guy's and Lewisham NHS Tst, gen sec Nat Pawnbrokers Assoc 1988-, contrib to professional press, particularly in architectural press on business and planning law matters; Parly candidate Alliance Greenwich constituency Gen Election 1983; memb: Industrial Tribunal; Freeman: City of London 1978, City of London Slrs Co, Liveryman Worshipful Co of Painter Stainers; memb: Law Soc 1969, IOD 1987; *Books* practice manual on procedures under the Consumer Credit Act 1974 for Lending Insts; *Recreations* golf, fly fishing, cricket, music, reading Charles Dickens; *Clubs* Royal Blackheath Golf, East India, MCC, City Livery; *Style*— Timothy Ford, Esq; The Pavilion, Manorbrook, Blackheath, London SE3 9AW (☎ 081 318 9817); 1 Bell Yard, London WC2A 2JP (☎ 071 404 4191, fax 071 405 4266)

FORD, Hon Lady (Virginia); *née* Brand; er da of 1 and last Baron Brand, CMG (d 1963), by his wife, Phyllis (d 1937), sis of the celebrated Lady Astor, both das of Chiswell Dabney Langhorne, of Greenwood, Va, USA; *b* 31 Aug 1918; *m* 1, 9 Dec 1939, John Metcalfe Polk (d 1948), s of Frank Polk, of USA; 2 s; m 2, 1 Dec 1949, Sir Edward William Spencer Ford, KCB, KCVO, ERD, *qv*; 2 s; *Style*— The Hon Lady Ford; Canal House, 23 Blomfield Rd, London W9 1AD (☎ 071 286 0028)

FORD DAVIES, Oliver Robert; s of Robert Cyril Davies (d 1974), of Ealing W5, and Cicely Mary, *née* Ford (d 1990); *b* 12 Aug 1939; *Educ* King's Canterbury, Merton Coll Oxford (DPhil, pres OUDS); *m* Jenifer Armitage, da of Edward Armitage; 1 da (Miranda Katherine b 1975); *Career* lectr in history Univ of Edinburgh 1964-66; actor; seasons at: Birmingham, Cambridge, Leicester, Oxford, Nottingham; played Bishop Talacryn in Hadrian VII (Mermaid, Haymarket) 1968-69, Tonight at Eight (Hampstead, Fortune) 1971-72, Mary Rose 1972 and 1975-87; 25 prodns with RSC incl: Henry IV, Henry V, Henry VI, Henry VIII, As You Like It, Coriolanus, Love's Labours Lost, The Greeks, Troilus and Cressida, The Love Girl and The Innocent, The Forest, Measure for Measure, Waste (also Lyric 1985), The Danton Affair, Principia Scriptoriae, Merry Wives of Windsor; Royal Nat Theatre 1988-: The Shaughraun, Hamlet, Lionel Espy in Racing Demon (Olivier award Actor of the Year), The Shape of the Table; recent TV incl: Cause Célèbre, A Taste for Death, Death of a Son, A Very British Coup, Inspector Morse, The Police, The War That Never Ends; films incl: Luther, Defence of the Realm, Scandal, Paper Mask; has written plays produced by: Orange Tree Theatre, ATV, BBC Radio; *publications* co author God Keep Lead out of Me - Shakespeare on War and Peace 1985; *Recreations* music, history, carpentry; *Style*— Oliver Ford Davies, Esq; CDA, Appt 9, 47 Courtfield Rd, SW7 4DB (☎ 071 370 0708)

FORD-HUTCHINSON, Sally Mary Ann (Mrs Anthony Yeshin); da of Peter William Scott Ford-Hutchinson (d 1961), and Giuseppina Adele, *née* Leva; *b* 20 Aug 1950; *Educ* Holy Trinity Convent Kent, Bristol Poly (HND, Dip in Mktg); *m* 2 June 1977, Anthony David Yeshin; 2 s (Mark b 26 Dec 1979, Paul b 31 May 1983); *Career* res exec Leo Burnett Advertising Agency 1972-74, Benton & Bowles 1974-77; res mangr H J Heinz Ltd 1977-79, head Res Dept Wasey Campbell Ewald 1979-83, memb Planning Dept Grandfield Rork Collins 1983-86, dir head Planning Dept and memb Mgmnt Ctee DMB & B 1986-; winner commendation IPA Advtg Effectivenes award; memb MRS, assoc MInstM; *Recreations* opera, walking in the country, reading, playing games with my children; *Style*— Ms Sally Ford-Hutchinson; D'Arcy Masius Benton & Bowles, 2 St James's Square, London SW1Y 4JN (☎ 071 839 3422)

FORDE, Lady Anthea Geraldine; *née* Lowry-Corry; er da of 7 Earl Belmore, JP, DL (d 1960); *b* 16 Feb 1942; *m* 24 April 1965, Patrick Mathew Desmond Forde, JP, DL, s of late Lt-Col Desmond Charles Forde, DL, of Seaforde, Co Down; 3 s, 1 da; *Style*— The Lady Anthea Forde; Seaforde, Co Down, N Ireland (☎ 039 687 225)

FORDE, Dr Harold McDonald; s of William McDonald Forde (d 1978), of Bridgetown, Barbados, and Gertrude, *née* Williams (d 1920); *b* 10 Jan 1916; *Educ* Harrison Coll Barbados, Univ Coll Hosp London (MD); *m* 1949, Alice Elaine, da of William Leslie, of Belize City; 1 s (William d 1987), 2 da (Stella, Ann); *Career* MO Govt of Belize 1947-52, lectr in med Univ of WI 1952-57, conslt physician Miny of Health Govt of Barbados 1957-84, sr lectr in med Univ of WI 1967-78, memb Privy Cncl Barbados 1980-85, high cmmr for Barbados to UK 1984-86; conslt physician in private practice 1986-;former ambass to: Norway, Sweden, Denmark, Finland, Iceland, Holy See; memb: NY Academic Sciences, Lions Clubs Int (life memb and past dist govr); FRCP (Edinburgh), Hon FACP, DPH, DTM & H (London); *Recreations* cricket, soccer, bridge; *Clubs* Surrey Co Cricket; *Style*— Dr Harold Forde; Bethesda Medical Centre, Black Rock, St Michael, Barbados, W1 (☎ home 809 424 9580, office 809 436 5862)

FORDER, Hon Mrs (Elizabeth Sarah); *née* David; yr da of Baroness David (Life Peer), and Richard William David, CBE; *b* 1947; *Educ* Badminton Sch, Central Sch of Speech and Drama; *m* 1, 1966 (m dis 1977), Martin Anthony Potter; 2 da; m 2, 1979, John Forder; 1 da; *Career* photojournalist; *Books* Open Fell Hidden Dale (1985), Faces of Lakeland (1987), Hill Shepherd (1989), Tales From The Fell (1991); *Style*— The Hon Mrs Forder; The Photo Gallery, Dent, Cumbria LA10 5QL

FORDER, Kenneth John; s of James A Forder (d 1973), and Elizabeth, *née* Hammond (d 1952); *b* 11 June 1925; *Educ* West Cliff Sch, Hertford Coll Oxford (MA); *m* 1948, Dorothy Margot, da of Nelson Burles; 2 da (Jane, Lamorna); *Career* RAF Flt Lt Aircrew 1943-47; called to the Bar Gray's Inn, colonial magistrate 1951-63, registrar of the Architects Registration Cncl of the UK 1977-90; *Recreations* tennis; *Clubs* Hurlingham; *Style*— Kenneth Forder, Esq; Napier Cottage, Napier Ave, London SW6 3NJ (☎ 071 736 3958)

FORDHAM, Cecil Frank Alan (Dick); s of Joseph Anthony Quinton Fordham (d 1955), of London N12, and Sarah Louisa, *née* Waite (d 1979); *b* 3 Sept 1921; *Educ* Christ Coll Finchley, Central Navigation Sch RAF; *m* 18 Dec 1948, Eileen Joyce, da of Thomas Charles Higby (d 1966), of Mottingham; 1 s (Nigel b 1951), 1 da (Susan b 1952); *Career* RAF 1942-46, Flt Lt Europe; co sec: Foodtech Ltd 1958-86, Multivac Packaging Systems Ltd; *Recreations* bellringing; *Style*— Dick Fordham, Esq; 11 Vicarage Close, Northa, Potters Bar, Herts EN6 4NY (☎ 0707 59929)

FORDHAM, John Anthony; s of Lt Cdr J H Fordham, CBE (d 1967), and Ebba Fordham; *b* 11 June 1948; *Educ* Gresham's Sch Holt Norfolk; *m* 25 June 1974, Lynda Patricia, da of Bernard Green, of Weston-Super-Mare; 2 s (Michael b 28 Dec 1979, Timothy b 3 Aug 1983); *Career* with Bowater Corpn Ltd 1973-81, head of mergers and acquisitions Hill Samuel Bank Ltd 1986-90 (joined 1981, dir 1985), sr exec dir and head of mergers and acquisitions Lloyds Merchant Bank Limited 1990-; *Recreations* squash, running, golf, gardening; *Clubs* Royal Wimbledon Golf, Rye Golf, The Jesters, The Escorts; *Style*— John Fordham, Esq; Sandgate, 81 Thurleigh Road, London SW12 8TY (☎ 081 675 7950); Lloyds Merchant Bank Limited, 48 Chiswell Street, London EC1Y 4XX (☎ 071 522 5000)

FORDHAM, John Michael; s of John William Fordham, and Kathleen Mary; *b* 15 Dec 1948; *Educ* Dulwich, Gonville and Caius Coll Cambridge (MA); *m* 28 Oct 1972, Sarah Anne, da of Denis Victor Burt; 1 s (Benjamin John b 1979), 1 da (Rebecca Kate b 1977); *Career* slr: admitted slr 1974, ptnr Stephenson Harwood 1979-; Liveryman Worshipful Co Solicitors, memb Law Soc; *Recreations* cricket (player), abstract art, jazz, twentieth century literature, pasta and chianti (consumer); *Style*— John Fordham, Esq; High Trees, 31 Shirley Avenue, South Cheam, Surrey SM2 7QS (☎ 02 642 1517); Stephenson Harwood, One St Paul's Churchyard, London EC2M 8SH (☎ 071 329 4422, fax 071 6060822, telex 886789 SHSPC G)

FORDHAM, Hon Mrs (June Jane Coupar); *née* Barrie; er da of 1 and last Baron Abertay, KBE (d 1940), and Ethel, *née* Broom (d 1983); *b* 27 Feb 1928; *m* 1, 19 April 1952 (m dis 1977), Brig Alan Norman Breitmeyer, Grenadier Guards, o s of late Louis Cecil Breitmeyer, of Snape Hill, Rickinghall, Suffolk; 1 s, 1 da; m 2, 1977, Christopher Jeremy King Fordham, FRICS; *Style*— The Hon Mrs Fordham; Odsey Park, Ashwell, Herts (☎ 046 274 2237)

FORDY, (George) Malcolm; s of George Laurence Fordy (d 1970), and Louise *née* Birdsall; *b* 27 Aug 1934; *Educ* Durham Sch; *m* 7 June 1957, Pauline da of William Stanley Thompson, of Thirsk Rd, Northallerton, North Yorks; 1 s (Nicholas b 1960), 2 da (Susan b 1958, Sarah b 1965); *Career* chm and chief exec: FT Construction Group (George Fordy & Sons Ltd/Walter Thompson (Contractors) Ltd), Fordy Holdings; chm BEC Pension Tstee Ltd; pres Nat Fedn Bldg Trades Employers 1982-83, memb Bd Construction Indust Trg Bd, chm Vocational Trg Cmmn of the Fedn de L'Industrie Européene de la Construction, dir Guild of Business Travel Agents Ltd; FCIOB 1978, FBIM 1978; *Recreations* the countryside, travel; *Clubs* Cleveland (Middlesbrough); *Style*— Malcolm Fordy, Esq; High Farm House, Ingleby Greenhow, Great Ayton, North Yorks TS9 6RG; Construction House, Northallerton, North Yorks DL7 8ED (☎ 0609 780 700, fax 0609 777 236, telex 58376 FORDYS G)

FORDYCE, (John) Alistair; s of Thomas Fordyce (d 1935), and Marion Fordyce, *née* Broadley (d 1970); *b* 14 May 1921; *Educ* Merchant Taylors' Sch; *m* 7 Oct 1950, Hazel Ethel Robertson Stone; 2 s (Stuart Alistair b 1951, Andrew Murray b 1955), 1 da (Elspeth Lindsay Mary b 1960); *Career* CA; ptnr Fordyce Curry & Co, dir various private cos; sec Butchers & Drovers Charitable Inst; Liveryman Worshipful Co of Butchers; *Recreations* choral music, gardening, golf; *Clubs* MCC; *Style*— J Alistair Fordyce, Esq; 61 West Smithfield, London EC1 (☎ 071 606 5711)

FORECAST, Trevor Cecil; s of Cecil Arthur Forecast (d 1989), of St Albans, Herts, and Daisy Edith, *née* Lovell; *Educ* St Albans Sch; *m* 29 June 1963, Christine Kay, da of Keith Lionel Stephens (d 1978); 2 da (Katie Jane b 1967, Emma Kay b 1969); *Career* RAF 1956-58; mktg mangr Polymer Corpn (UK) Ltd 1968-72; md and proprietor: Crown Hotel Downham Market Ltd 1972-82, Congham Hall Country House Hotel Kings Lynn Norfolk 1982-; dir Norfolk & Waveney TEC, dir Pride of Britain Ltd 1988-, former pres Kings Lynn Hotels & Catering Assoc, chm BHRCA Eastern Regn, memb BHRCA Nat Cncl, memb ctee West Norfolk Tourism Forum, former pres Downham Market Chamber of Trade, fndr pres Downham Market RC, pres Grimston CC; MIPE 1955, CEng 1956, MInstM 1968; *Recreations* shooting; *Clubs* Old Albanian, IOD; *Style*— Trevor Forecast, Esq; Congham Hall, Country House Hotel & Restaurant, Grimston, Kings Lynn, Norfolk PE32 1AH (☎ 0485 600 250, fax 0485 601191, telex 81508 CHOTEL)

FOREIGN, Peter John Chandos; s and h of Sir Peter Van Notten Pole, 5 Bt; *b* 27 April 1952; *m* 1973, Suzanne Norah, da of Harold Raymond Hughes; 2 s (Michael b 1980, Andrew b 1986), 1 da (Naomi b 1983); *Style*— Peter Pole, Esq; 41 Webster St, Nedlands 6009, W Australia

FOREMAN, Keith; OBE (1986); s of John Foreman (d 1977), of Kettering, Northants, and Phyllis, *née* Barker (d 1982); *b* 19 May 1935; *Educ* Kettering GS, Univ of Durham (BA, MEd), Univ of Cambridge (PGCE); *m* 5 Jan 1957, Ruth Mary, da of Haydn Lawrence Sail (d 1972), of Kettering; 1 s (Paul b 1967), 2 da (Helen b 1964, Anne b 1966); *Career* warden Comberton Village Coll Cambridge 1969-86, princ Burleigh Community Coll Loughborough 1986-, memb Sch Mgmnt Task Force DES 1988-; memb Trinity Methodist Church Lougborough; FRSA 1983; *Recreations* sailing, walking; *Style*— Keith Foreman, Esq, OBE; 5 De Verdun Avenue, Belton, Loughborough, Leics LE12 9TY (☎ 0530 222 832); Burleigh Community Coll, Loughborough, Leics (☎ 0509 268 996)

FOREMAN, Michael; s of Walter Foreman (d 1938), of Lowestoft, Suffolk, and Gladys, *née* Goddard (d 1982); *b* 21 March 1938; *Educ* Notley Road Secdy Modern, Lowestoft Sch of Art, RCA (USA scholar, MA, Silver medal); *m* 22 Dec 1980, Louise Amanda, da of Basil Gordon Phillips; 3 s (Mark b 1961, Ben b 1982, Jack b 1986); *Career* illustrator; former: art dir Playboy, King and Ambit magazines, prodr animated films in Scandinavia and for BBC; writer and illustrator of over 100 books (incl children's and travel books), reg contrib American and Euro magazines, held exhibitions Euro, America and Japan; awards: Aigle d'Argent at Festival International du Livre France 1972, Francis Williams prize V & A Museum and Nat Book League 1972 and 1977, graphic prize Bologna, Kurt Maschler award, Kate Greenaway medal 1982 and 1989, children's book award 1984; memb: AGI 1972, RDI 1986, hon fell RCA 1989; *Clubs* Chelsea Arts; *Style*— Michael Foreman, Esq

FOREMAN, Sir Philip Frank; CBE (1972), DL (Belfast 1975); s of late Frank and Mary Foreman; *b* 16 March 1923; *Educ* Soham GS, Loughborough Coll; *m* 1971, Margaret, da of John Petrie Cooke, of Belfast; 1 s; *Career* with RN Scientific Serv 1943-58; chm chief exec and md Short Brothers Ltd (aerospace mfrs) 1983-88 (joined 1958, md 1967); dir: Renaissance Hldgs plc, Simon Engrg plc, Ricardo International plc; chm: BSI 1988-, Progressive Building Soc; conslt Foreman Assoc; Freeman City of London; Hon FRAeS, Hon DSc, Hon DTech; FEng, FIMechE, FIProdE, FRSA, CBIM; kt 1981; *Style*— Sir Philip Foreman, CBE, DL; Ashtree House, 26 Ballymenoch Rd, Holywood, Co Down BT18 0HH (☎ 02317 5767)

FOREMAN-PECK, Prof James Stanley; s of John Foreman-Peck (d 1984), and Muriel Joan Foreman-Peck; *b* 19 June 1948; *Educ* Alleyns Sch, Univ of Essex (BA), LSE (MSc, PhD); *m* 22 June 1968, Lorraine, da of Walter Alexander McGimpsey; 1 s (Alexander b 1978), 1 da (Eleanor b 1985); *Career* economist Electricity Cncl 1971-72, lectr in econs Thames Poly 1972-79, visiting lectr Univ of Reading 1974-75, lectr in econs Univ of Newcastle Upon Tyne 1979-88, visiting assoc prof Univ of California 1981-82, prof of econ history Univ of Hull 1988-, visiting fell Dept of Econs Univ of Warwick 1989; memb: Amnesty Int, Nat Tst; cncllr London Borough Greenwich 1978-79; memb: Royal Econ Soc, Econ History Soc; *Books* A History of the World Economy: International Economic Relations since 1850 (1983), European Telecommunications Organisations (ed, 1988), New Perspectives on the Later Victorian Economy (ed, 1990); *Recreations* squash, sailing, literature, piano; *Style*— Prof James Foreman-Peck; 8 Church Lane, Withernwick, Humberside HU11 4TX (☎ 0964 527045); School of Economic and European Studies, University of Hull, Hull HU6 7RX (☎ 0482 466331, fax 0482 466205)

FORESTER, 8 Baron (UK 1821); (George Cecil) Brooke Weld-Forester; s of 7 Baron Forester (d 1977), and Marie Louise Priscilla (d 1988), da of Col Sir Herbert Perrott, 6 and last Bt, CH, CB; *b* 20 Feb 1938; *Educ* Eton, RAC Cirencester; *m* 14 Jan 1967, Hon (Elizabeth) Catherine Lyttelton, 2 da of 10 Viscount Cobham, KG, GCMG, GCVO, TD, PC; 1 s (Hon George b 1975), 3 da (Hon Selina b 1968, Hon Alice b 1969, Hon Alexandra b 1973); *Heir* s, Hon (Charles Richard) George Forester b 8 July 1975; *Career* Patron of 3 livings; this nobleman has in his possession a licence of the time of Henry VIII, giving to John Forester of Watling St, Co Salop, the privilege of wearing his hat in the Royal presence; *Style*— The Rt Hon Lord Forester; Willey Park, Broseley, Shropshire (☎ 0952 882146); (☎ 071 589 8543)

FORESTER, Baroness; Hon (Elizabeth) Catherine; *née* Lyttelton; 2 da of 10 Viscount Cobham, KG, GCMG, GCVO, TD, PC (d 1977); *b* 7 Feb 1946; *m* 14 Jan 1967, 8 Baron Forester, *qv*; *Style*— The Rt Hon Lady Forester; Willey Park, Broseley, Shropshire TF12 5JJ (☎ 0952 882146)

FORESTIER-WALKER, Alan David; s of Urbain Evelyn Forestier-Walker, 2 s of Ivor Augustus Forestier-Walker (5 s of 2 Bt); hp of cous, Sir Michael Forestier-Walker, 6 Bt; *b* 29 Aug 1944; *Educ* Prior Park Coll Bath; *m* 7 Nov 1969, Adela Judith, da of Simon Philip Davis, of Hampstead; 1 s 2 da; *Career* Lt-Col 7 Duke of Edinburgh's Own Gurkha Rifles; *Style*— Lt-Col Alan Forestier-Walker; Whitegates, Sandhill Lane, Longbridge Deverill, Warminster, Wilts BA12 7DW (☎ 0985 40477)

FORESTIER-WALKER, Maj (George) Clive; s of Edmund Annesley Forestier-Walker, of Broombank, Aldeburgh, Suffolk (gggs of Sir George Walker, 1 Bt, GCB), by his w Bridget, da of Cdr Sir Geoffrey Hughes-Onslow, KBE, DSC, JP, DL, RN (kin to the Earls of Onslow), and Hon Eileen, da of 4 Baron Crofton; *b* 17 April 1946; *Educ* Wellington; *m* 8 April 1970, (Ruth) Christian, yst da of John Gurney, *qv*, of Walsingham Abbey, Norfolk; 4 da (Camilla b 1973, Susanna b 1976, Liza b 1980, Mary b 1983); *Career* Maj Coldstream Gds; stockbroker; *Recreations* shooting, skiing, sailing (yacht 'Casalamy'); *Clubs* Cavalry & Guards, Royal Yacht Squadron; *Style*— Maj Clive Forestier-Walker; Plum Tree Cottage, North Heath, Chieveley, Newbury, Berks RG16 8UD (☎ 0635 248 673)

FORESTIER-WALKER, Sir Michael Leolin; 6 Bt (UK 1835); s of Lt-Col Alan Ivor Forestier-Walker, MBE, 7 Gurkha Rifles (ka Malaya 1954, s of Ivor Forestier-Walker, 5 s of 2 Bt) and Margaret Joan, da of Maj Henry Bennet Marcoolyn, MBE; suc kinsman, Sir Clive Radzivill Forestier-Walker, 5 Bt, 1983; *b* 24 April 1949; *Educ* Wellington, Royal Holloway Coll London (BA); *m* 16 July 1988, Elizabeth, da of Joseph Hedley, of Bellingham, Northumberland; 1 da (Chloë b 15 Jan 1990); *Heir* cous, Alan David Forestier-Walker, b 29 Aug 1944; *Career* teacher Feltonfleet Sch Cobham; *Recreations* sailing, electronics, computing; *Style*— Sir Michael Forestier-Walker, Bt; Bibury, 116 Hogshill Lane, Cobham, Surrey

FORFAR, Dr (John) Colin; s of Prof J O Forfar, MC, of 110 Ravelston Dykes, Edinburgh, and Isobel Mary Langlands, *née* Fernback; *b* 22 Nov 1951; *Educ* Edinburgh Acad, Univ of Edinburgh (BSc, MD, PhD), Univ of Oxford (MA); *m* (m dis), 1 da (Katriana Louise b 1981); *Career* reader in cardiovascular med Univ of Oxford 1985-86, physician and conslt cardiologist Oxford RHA 1986-; author of numerous med pubns; memb: Br Cardiac Soc (former local sec), MRS, Oxford Med Soc; FRCPE 1987; *Recreations* walking, squash; *Style*— Dr Colin Forfar; 6 Church Rd, Ickford, Aylesbury, Bucks HP18 9HZ (☎ 0844 339626); Dept of Cardiology, John Radcliffe Hospital, Oxford OX3 9DU (☎ 0865 220326)

FORMAN, Sir (John) Denis; OBE (1956); s of Rev Adam Forman, CBE (d 1977), of Dumcrieff, Moffatt, Scot, and Flora, *née* Smith; *b* 13 Oct 1917; *Educ* Loretto, Pembroke Coll Cambridge; *m* 1, 1948, Helen Blondel de Moulpied (d 1987); 2 s; m 2, 1990, Moni Cameron; *Career* Lt-Col (OSDEF Battle Sch, N Africa, Italy); chief prodn offr COI Films 1947; chm: Bd Govt's Br Film Inst 1971-73 (dir 1948-55), Granada TV 1974-87 (dir 1955-87), Novello and Co 1971-88, dep chm Granada Gp 1984-90 (memb 1964-); Royal Opera House: dir 1980, dep chm 1984, chm Opera Bd 1988; memb Cncl Royal Northern Coll of Music 1977; Hon doctorate: Univ of Stirling 1982, Univ of Essex 1986; Hon LLD: Manchester 1983, Lancaster 1989, Keele 1990; kt 1976; *Recreations* music; *Clubs* Garrick, Savile; *Style*— Sir Denis Forman, OBE; The Mill House, Howe St, Chelmsford, Essex CM3 1BG; Granada Group Ltd, 36 Golden Sq, London W1P 4AH (☎ 071 734 8080)

FORMAN, (Francis) Nigel; MP (Cons) Carshalton and Wallington 1983-; s of late Brig J F R Forman; *b* 25 March 1943; *Educ* Shrewsbury, New College Oxford, Coll of Europe Bruges, Harvard Univ, Univ of Sussex; *Career* former asst dir CRD, Parly candidate (C) Coventry NE Feb 1974, MP (C) Sutton Carshalton 1976-83; memb Select Ctee on Sci and Technol 1976-79; sec Cons ctees: Educn 1976-79, Energy 1977-79; PPS to Douglas Hurd as Min of State FCO 1979-1983, vice chm Cons Fin Ctee 1983-87, PPS to the Chllr of the Exchequer Nigel Lawson 1987-89; memb: Foreig Affairs Select Ctee 1990-, Exec 1922 Ctee 1990-; chm GB-East Europe Centre 1990-; *Style*— Nigel Forman, Esq, MP; House of Commons, London SW1A 0AA

FORMAN, Roy; s of Edwin Leslie Forman (d 1988), and Wilhelmina Mowbray, *née* Donkin (d 1964); *b* 28 Dec 1931; *Educ* Nunthorpe GS, Univ of Nottingham (BA); *m* 24 July 1954, Mary, da of Kenneth Francis Nelson (d 1961); 3 s (Ian b 1957, Nicholas b 1960, Simon b 1962), 1 da (Sally b 1964); *Career* Flying Offr RAF 1953-56; commercial dir S Wales Electricity Bd 1972-76, commercial advsr The Electricity Cncl 1976-80; Private Patients Plan Ltd: gen mangr mktg and sales 1980-81, mktg dir 1981-85, md and chief exec 1985-; memb Cncl and chm Kent Branch IOD 1982-85, chm Tunbridge Wells CAB 1988-, chm Private Med Insur Ctee Assoc of Br Insurers; *Recreations* music, walking; *Style*— Roy Forman, Esq; Private Patients Plan Ltd, PPP House, Tunbridge Wells, Kent TN1 2PL (☎ 0892 512345, fax 0892 511578, telex 95525 PPP UK G, car 0860 798415)

FORMARTINE, Viscount; George Ian Alastair; s and h of Earl of Haddo, *qv* (himself s and h of 6 Marquess of Aberdeen and Temair, *qv*), and Joanna Clodagh, da of late Maj Ian George Henry Houldsworth; *b* 4 May 1983; *Style*— Viscount Formartine

FORMBY, Roger Myles; s of Myles Landseer Formby, CBE, of Storrington, W Sussex, and his 1 w, Dorothy Hussey, *née* Essex (d 1991); *b* 15 March 1938; *Educ* Winchester, Univ of Oxford (BA); *m* 15 Sept 1962, (Alice) Jane, da of Herbert Victor Woof (d 1950), of Bedford; 2 da (Kate b 1965, Emily b 1967); *Career* Nat Serv 2 Lt Oxford and Bucks LI 1957; admitted slr 1965; managing ptnr Macfarlanes 1987- (ptnr 1967-, head of property 1970-8; *Recreations* golf, skiing, travel; *Clubs* City of London; *Style*— Roger M Formby, Esq; 10 Norwich St, London EC4A 1BD (☎ 071 831 9222, fax 071 831 9607, telex 296381)

FORRES, 4 Baron (UK 1922); Sir Alastair Stephen Grant Williamson; 4 Bt (UK 1909); s of 3 Baron Forres (d 1978), by his 1 w, Gillian Ann Maclean, *née* Grant; *b* 16 May 1946; *Educ* Eton; *m* 2 May 1969, Margaret Ann, da of late George John Mallam, of Mullumbimby, NSW; 2 s (Hon George, Hon Guthrie b 1975); *Heir* s, Hon George Archibald Mallam Williamson b 16 Aug 1972; *Career* chm Agriscot Pty Ltd; dir Jaga Trading Pty Ltd; Australian rep Tattersalls; *Clubs* Australian Jockey, Tattersalls (Sydney), Sydney Turf; *Style*— The Rt Hon the Lord Forres; c/o Clark Oliver Solicitors, Brothobank House, Arbroath, Angus DD11 1NJ

FORREST, Prof (William) George Grieve; s of William Downie Forrest, of 19b East Heath Rd, London, and Christina (Ina) Mitchell, *née* Grieve; *b* 24 Sept 1925; *Educ* LCC Merton Pk, UCS Hampstead, New Coll Oxford (MA); *m* 14 July 1956, Margaret Elizabeth Mary, da of Frederick Drummond Hall (d 1955); 2 da (Catherine b 1957, Alison b 1959); *Career* served RAF 1943-47, Actg Corp; fell Wadham Coll 1951-76, fell New Coll Oxford 1976-; visiting prof: Toronto 1961, Yale 1968; Wykeham prof of ancient hist Univ of Oxford 1976-, visiting fell Br Sch of Athens 1986; Univ memb Oxford City 1962-65; *Books* Emergence of Greek Democracy (1966), History of Sparta (1968); *Recreations* socialism; *Style*— Prof George Forrest; 9 Fyfield Rd, Oxford, Oxon OX2 6QE (☎ 0865 56187); New Coll, Oxford OX1 3BN (☎ 0865 248451)

FORREST, John Orchover; *b* 4 May 1918; *Educ* Centl Fndn Sch, Univ of London, Guy's Hosp Dental Sch; *m* 1944, Irene, *née* Leanse; 2 s; *Career* sr hosp dental offr Guy's Hosp 1961-68, hon lect Guy's Dental Hosp 1969-71; Gibbs Prize Scholar 1968; pres: Br Periodontal Soc 1964, Br Endodontic Soc 1966, Metropolitan Branch Br Dental Assoc 1977, Euro Dental Soc 1983-85; Int Coll Dentists: UK regent 1980-86, vice pres 1989, pres Euro Section 1989-90, int pres elect 1990; *Books* Preventive Dentistry (1981), A Guide to Successful Dental Practice (1984), The Good Teeth Guide (2 ed, 1985), A Handbook for Dental Hygienists (2 ed, 1985); *Recreations* photography, writing, collecting snuff bottles and rejection slips; *Clubs* RAF; *Style*— John Forrest, Esq; 74 Lawn Rd, Hampstead, London NW3 2XB (☎ 071 722 8589); c/o Coutts & Co, 16 Cavendish Sq, London W1

FORREST, Dr John Richard; s of Prof John Samuel Forrest, and Ivy May Ellen, *née* Olding; *b* 21 April 1943; *Educ* King's Coll Sch Wimbledon, Sidney Sussex Coll Univ of Cambridge (BA, MA), Keble Coll Univ of Oxford (DPhil); *m* 8 Sept 1973, Jane Patricia Robey, da of John Robey Leech, of Little Hockham Hall, Great Hockham, Norfolk; 2 s (Nicholas John b 1975, Alexander Iain b 1980), 1 da (Katharine Elizabeth b 1977); *Career* UCL: lectr 1970-79, reader 1979-82, prof 1982-84; tech dir Marconi Defence Systems Ltd, dir of engrg IBA 1986-90, exec chm National Transcommunications Ltd 1991-; FIEE 1980, FEng 1985, FRSA 1987, FRTS 1990, Hon FBKSTS 1990; Chevalier dans l'Ordre des Arts et des Lettres 1990; *Recreations* theatre, music, reading, walking; *Style*— Dr John Forrest; Hilfield Farm House, Hilfield Lane, Aldenham, Watford, Herts WD2 8DD (☎ 081 950 1820); National Transcommunications Ltd, Crawley Court, Winchester, Hants SO21 2QA (☎ 0962 822 455, fax 0962 822 434, car 0836 213 634, telex 477211)

FORREST, Michael William; s of William Edward Forrest (d 1969), of St Clement, Jersey, CI, and Kathleen Honor, *née* Foxall (d 1985); *Educ* Victoria Coll Jersey CI; *m* 25 July 1973, Linda Mary, da of William Giles, of Manchester; 2 s (Richard b 1975, Thomas b 1979), 1 da (Laura b 1981); *Career* sr ptnr Robson Rhodes Jersey CI, chm The Langtry House Gp of Cos; memb: Jersey Race and Hunt Club, Jersey Motor Cycle and Light Car Club, Riding Club; memb IOD, FCA, FCCA, ACIArb; *Recreations* hunting, riding, skiing; *Clubs* Old Victorians Assoc, IOD; *Style*— Michael Forrest, Esq; La Sergente, St Mary, Jersey, CI (☎ 0534 838 24); Les Chevrons, Les Diablerets, Vaud, Switzerland; Langtry House, La Motte St, St Helier, Jersey, CI (☎ 0534 739 21, fax 0534 246 68, car 0860 740 240, telex 4192069 FIDES G)

FORREST, Nigel; s of Wing Cdr Gerald Vere Forrest, of Sydney New South Wales, Aust, and Elizabeth, *née* Burnett; *b* 12 Sept 1946; *Educ* Harrow, Oriel Coll Oxford (MA), INSEAD (MBA); *m* 22 Nov 1980, Julia Mary, da of Philip Nash (d 1970), of Dorking, Surrey; 1 s (Dominic b 18 April 1982), 1 da (Harriet b 9 Feb 1984); *Career* commercial technol sales mangr Rolls Royce Ltd 1972 (graduate trainee 1969), mangr Lazard Bros & Co Ltd 1978 (exec 1973), dep md Nomura International plc 1989 (assoc md 1986, exec dir 1983, mangr 1981); chm Fundraising Ctee Highbury Roundhouse 1978-81; *Publication* The Channel Tunnel - Before The Decision (1973); *Style*— Nigel Forrest, Esq; Nomura Int plc, 1 St Martin's-le-Grand, London EC1A 4NP (☎ 071 320 2292, fax 071 236 7711)

FORREST, Prof Sir (Andrew) Patrick McEwen; s of Rev Andrew James Forrest BD (d 1962), and Isabella, *née* Pearson (d 1962); *b* 25 March 1923; *Educ* Dundee HS, Univ of St Andrews (BSc, MB ChB, ChM, MD); *m* 1, 1955, Margaret Beryl (d 1961), da of Capt Frederick Hall, MBE; 1 s (Andrew David b 27 Sept 1961), 1 da (Susan Catriona b 9 May 1959); m 2, 1964, Margaret Anne, da of Harold E Steward (d 1980); 1 da (Anne Elizabeth); *Career* Surgn Lt RNVR 1946-48; civilian conslt to RN (surgery res) 1977-88; prof of surgery Welsh Nat Sch of Med 1962-71, regius prof of clinical surgery Univ of Edinburgh 1971-88 (prof emeritus 1989-); visiting scientist Nat Institutes of Health (Bethesda) 1989-90; memb: MRC 1976-80, Advsy Bd for Res Cncls 1982-85, Cncl RCSEd 1974-84; chief scientist Scottish Home and Health Dept (pt/t) 1981-87; pres: Surgical Res Soc 1974-76, Assoc of Surgns GB and I 1988-89; FRSE; Hon DSc: Univ of Wales, Chinese Univ of Hong Kong; Hon LLD Univ of Dundee; Hon FACS, FRACS, FRCSCan; Hon FIBiol; Lister medal RCSEng 1987, Gold medal Netherlands Assoc of Surgeons 1988, McKenzie-Davidson Medal Br Inst Radio 1 1988; *Books* Prognostic Factors in Breast Cancer (jt ed 1968), Principles and Practice of Surgery (jtly 1985, 1990), Breast Cancer: The Decision to Screen (1990); *Recreations* golf, sailing; *Clubs* New (Edinburgh); *Style*— Sir Patrick Forrest, FRSE; 19 St Thomas Road, Edinburgh EH9 2LR (☎ 031 667 3203)

FORREST, Paul Esme Acton; s of Richard Acton Forrest, of Ashcott, Somerset, and Lucille Muriel, *née* Knott; *b* 1 Jan 1943; *Educ* Dr Morgans GS Bridgwater, Univ of Southampton; *m* 29 April 1967, Josephine Anne, da of Gp Capt John Enfield Kirk, OBE, of Winscombe, Avon; 2 s (Richard b 1975, James b 1977), 1 da (Charlotte b 1980); *Career* admitted slr 1971, called to the Bar Gray's Inn 1979-; dep HM coroner County of Avon 1989 (asst dep coroner 1981); memb Coroners Soc; *Recreations* golf, fishing, jazz; *Clubs* Burnham and Berrow Golf, Weston-Super-Mare Golf, Bristol Savages, Bristol Commercial Rooms, Bridgwater County; *Style*— Paul Forrest, Esq; Rowington, Winscombe, Avon BS25 1NA; All Saints' Chambers, Holbeck House, 9-11 Broad St, Bristol BS1 2HP

FORREST, Dr (Alexander) Robert Walker; s of Alexander Muir Forrest, of Boston, Lincolnshire, and Rose Ellen, *née* Ringham (d 1976); *b* 5 July 1947; *Educ* Stamford Sch, Univ of Edinburgh (BSc, MB ChB); *m* Teresa Anne, da of Albert E Booth, of Sheffield; 2 s (Michael b 1981, David b 1984); *Career* conslt chem pathologist Royal Hallamshire Hosp 1981-, hon lectr in forensic toxicology Univ of Sheffield 1985- (clinical lectr in human metabolism and clinical biochemistry 1981-), asst dep coroner S Yorks West 1989-; gp med offr S Yorks branch BRCS; MRPath 1980, FRSC 1985 FRCPE 1989; *Recreations* computers, books; *Style*— Dr Robert Forrest; 10 Oakbrook Ct, 411 Fulwood Road, Sheffield S10 3GF (☎ 0742 302768); Royal Hallamshire Hospital, Sheffield S10 2JF (☎ 0742 766222)

FORREST, Prof (Archibald) Robin; s of Samuel Forrest (d 1982), of Edinburgh, Scotland, and Agnes Dollar, *née* Robin; *b* 13 May 1943; *Educ* Daniel Stewart's Coll Edinburgh, Univ of Edinburgh (BSc), Trinity Coll Cambridge (PhD); *m* 7 April 1973, Rosemary Ann, da of Ralph Kenneth Foster (d 1983), of Grantham, Lincs; 1 s (Matthew b 1975), 1 da (Susanna b 1977); *Career* asst res dir Computer Laboratory Cambridge Univ 1971-74 (tech offr Engrg Dept 1968-71); visiting prof: Syracuse Univ NY 1971-72, Univ of Utah, 1979; visiting expert Beijing Inst Aeronautics and Astronautics 1979, prof of computing sci UEA 1980- (reader in computing studies 1974-80), visiting scientist Xerox Palo Alto Res Centre 1982-83; FBCS, FIMA 1978; *Recreations* collecting wine, reading maps; *Style*— Prof Robin Forrest; 3 Highlands, Folgate Lane, Old Costessey, Norwich, Norfolk NR8 5EA (☎ 0603 742315); University of East Anglia, School of Information Systems, University Plain, Norwich, Norfolk NR4 7TJ (☎ 0603 592605, 0603 507720)

FORREST, Rear Adm Sir Ronald Stephen; KCVO (1975), JP (Honiton 1978) DL (Devon 1985); s of Dr Stephen Forrest (d 1957), of Edinburgh, and Maud M McKinstry; *b* 11 Jan 1923; *Educ* Belhaven Hill, RNC Dartmouth; *m* 1, 1947, Patricia (d 1966), da of Dr E N Russell, of Alexandria, Egypt; 2 s, 1 da; m 2, 1967, June, wid of Lt G Perks, RN, and da of L W Weaver (d 1945), of Budleigh Salterton; 1 step s, 1 step da; *Career* RN: serv at sea 1940-72, dir Seamen Offrs Appts 1968, CO HMS London 1970, Def Serv sec 1972-75, Rear Adm 1972; co cmmr St John Ambulance Bde Devon 1976-81, cdr St John Ambulance Devon 1981-87, pres Devon Cs Agric Assoc 1990; KStJ; *Clubs* Naval, Army & Navy; *Style*— Rear Adm Sir Ronald Forrest, KCVO, JP, DL; Higher Seavington, Stockland, Honiton, Devon EX14 9DE

FORRESTER, Rev Prof Duncan Baillie; s of William Roxburgh Forrester, MC, and Isobel Margaret Stewart, *née* McColl; *b* 10 Nov 1933; *Educ* Madras Coll St Andrews, Univ of St Andrews (MA), Univ of Chicago, Univ of Edinburgh (BD), Univ of Sussex (DPhil); *m* 9 June 1964, Rev Margaret Rae, da of William R McDonald; 1 s (Donald McColl b 1966), 1 da (Catriona McAskill b 1968); *Career* pt/t asst in politics Univ of Edinburgh 1957-58, asst minister Hillside Church Edinburgh and leader St James Mission 1960-61, Church of Scotland missionary, lectr and then prof of politics Madras Christian Coll Tambaram S India 1962-70; ordained presbyter Church of S India 1962; pt/t lectr in politics Univ of Edinburgh 1966-67, chaplain and lectr in politics Univ of Sussex 1970-78, prof of christian ethics and practical theol Univ of Edinburgh 1978-, princ New Coll Univ of Edinburgh 1986-; chm Edinburgh Cncl of Social Serv 1983-86; memb: World Cncl of Churches Faith and Order Cmmn 1983-, Policy Ctee Scottish Cncl of Voluntary orgns 1986-89; dir Centre for Theology and Public Issues 1984-; *Books* Caste & Christianity (1980), Encounter with God (co-author, 1983), Studies in the History of Worship in Scotland (co-ed, 1984), Christianity and the Future of Welfare (1985), Theology and Politics (1988), Just Sharing (co-author, 1988), Beliefs, Values and Policies (1989), Worship Now Book II (co-ed, 1989), Theology and Practice (1990); *Recreations* hill walking, reading, listening to music; *Style*— The Rev Prof Duncan Forrester; 25 Kingsburgh Road, Edinburgh EH12 6DZ (☎ 031 337 5646); University of Edinburgh, New College, The Mound, Edinburgh EH1 2LU (☎ 031 225 8400)

FORRESTER, Ian Stewart; QC (1988); s of Alexander Roxburgh Forrester (d 1976), of Glasgow, and Elizabeth Richardson, *née* Stewart (d 1947); *b* 13 Jan 1945; *Educ* Kelvinside Acad Glasgow, Univ of Glasgow (MA, LLB), Tulane Univ of Louisiana New Orleans (MCL); *m* 7 March 1981, Sandra Anne Thérèse, da of M C Keegan, of Jefferson, Louisiana, USA; 2 s (Alexander Stewart Daigle b 24 Sept 1982, James Roxburgh b 29 May 1985); *Career* with Maclay Murray & Spens 1968-69, Davis Polk & Wardwell 1969-72 (admitted Faculty of Advocates Scots Bar 1972), Cleary Gottlieb Steen & Hamilton 1972-81 (admitted Bar State of NY 1977), estab ind chambers Brussels (with Christopher Norall) 1981 (now known as Forrester Norall & Sutton), practising before Euro Cmmn and Court; chm: Br Cons Assoc in Belgium 1982-86, Euro Trade Law Assoc 1987-; hon visiting prof of law Univ of Glasgow 1991-; memb: UK Assoc for Euro Law, American Bar Assoc, The Stair Soc; *Publications* The German Civil Code (1975), The German Commercial Code (1979), author of numerous articles and chapters on EEC law and policy in The Oxford Yearbook of European Law, International Antitrust Law, The European Law Review, The Common Market Law Review; *Recreations* politics, wine, cooking, restoring old houses; *Clubs* Athenaeum, International Château Sainte-Anne (Brussels), Royal Yacht of Belgium; *Style*— Ian Forrester, Esq, QC; 73 Square Marie-Louise, 1040 Brussels, Belgium; 36 Rue Joseph II, 1040 Brussels, Belgium (☎ 010 32 219 16 20, fax 010 32 219 16 26, telex 23190)

FORRESTER, Prof Peter Garnett; CBE (1981); s of Arthur Forrester (d 1949), of Cheshire, and Emma, *née* Garnett (d 1962); *b* 7 June 1917; *Educ* Manchester GS, Univ of Manchester (BSc, MSc); *m* 1942, Marjorie Hewitt, da of Robert Berks (d 1940), of Staffs; 2 da (Patricia b 1945, Claire b 1954); *Career* metallurgist; Royal Aircraft Estab Farnborough, Tin Research Inst; chief metallurgist Glacier Metal Co 1948-63; conslt John Tyzack & Ptnrs 1963-66; dir Cranfield Sch of Mgmnt 1967-82; Cranfield Inst of Technol: prof of industl mgmnt 1966-82, pro-vice chllr, emeritus prof 1983-; dir: Jackson Taylor Int Gp Ltd 1984-88, Faculties Partnership Ltd; Hon DSc Cranfield 1983; Burnham Medal 1979; FIM, CBIM, FRSA; *Recreations* research, writing, gardening, walking, sailing; *Style*— Prof Peter Forrester, CBE; Strawberry Hole Cottage, Ewhurst Lane, Northiam, nr Rye, E Sussex TN31 6HJ (☎ 079 74 2255)

FORRESTER-PATON, His Hon Douglas Shaw; QC (1965); s of Alexander Forrester-Paton, JP (d 1954), and Hon Mary Emma Louise Shaw (d 1974), da of 1 Baron Craigmyle (d 1937); *b* 22 June 1921; *Educ* Gresham's, Queen's Coll Oxford (BA); *m* 1948, Agnete, da of late Hr Ingenior Holger Tuxen, of Denmark; 1 s (Thomas), 2 da (Kirsten, Elspeth); *Career* Sqdn Ldr RAFVR; called to the Bar Middle Temple 1947, rec of Middlesbrough 1963-68, rec of Teesside 1968-70, co ct judge 1970-71, circuit judge 1972-86; *Recreations* gardening, walking; *Style*— His Hon Douglas Forrester-Paton, QC; 24 Kirkby Lane, Gt Broughton, Middlesbrough (☎ 0642 712301)

FORSHALL, Isabella Louise; da of Peter Hyde Forshall (d 1980), of Tentworth, Midhurst, Sussex, and Constance Mary Diana, *née* Bremner; *b* 9 May 1956; *Educ* Chichester HS, Newnham Coll Cambridge (BA); *Career* called to the Bar Gray's Inn 1982; *Clubs* Haldane Soc of Socialist Lawyers; *Style*— Ms Isabella Forshall; Doughty St Chambers, 11 Doughty St, London WC1N 2PG (☎ 071 404 1313)

FORSTER, Alan Roger; s of Harold Edgar Forster (d 1979), and Annie Dorothy, *née* Wenham; *b* 27 Oct 1933; *Educ* Eastbourne GS; *m* 1, 1956, Diana, da of Herbert Raymond Love; 1 s (Paul b 1957), 1 da (Emma b 1966); m 2, 1979, Valerie, da of James Fisk; *Career* chm Booker Overseas Trading Ltd, Bookers Sugar Co Ltd memb exec cncl of West India Ctee; *Recreations* horse racing, watching cricket; *Clubs* MCC; *Style*— Alan R Forster, Esq; Little Ridge, Chislehurst Rd, Chislehurst, Kent (☎ 081 467 1094, 081 467 3684); 66 Mark Lane, London EC3R 7BT (telex 8952713, fax 071 481 8763)

FORSTER, Sir Archibald William; s of William Henry Forster (d 1955), and Matilda (d 1969); *b* 11 Feb 1928; *Educ* Tottenham GS, Univ of Birmingham (BSc); *m* 1954, Betty Margaret, da of Edgar Norman Channing (d 1984); 3 da (Nicola b 1959, Jacqueline b 1961, Amanda b 1967); *Career* RAF (FO) 1949-51; chm Esso Pension Trust 1980-, chief exec Esso Petroleum Co Ltd 1980-, exec memb Bd Lloyds Register of Shipping 1981-; chm and chief exec: Esso UK plc 1983-, Esso Exploration and Prodn UK Ltd 1983-; non-exec memb Bd: Midland Bank 1986-, Rover Group plc 1986-88; FEng; kt 1987; *Recreations* sailing; *Clubs* Royal Southampton Yacht; *Style*— Sir Archibald Forster; Esso House, Victoria St, London SW1E 5JW (☎ 071 245 3294, telex 24942, fax 071 245 3154)

FORSTER, Rev Bennet Fermor; s of Lt-Gen Alfred Leonard Forster, CB, DSO (d 1963), and Gladys Maud Godfrey-Faussett; *b* 27 May 1921; *Educ* Lancing, BNC (MA); *m* 31 March 1951, Anthea Monica, da of Raymond Walter Beall (d 1949); 1 s (Keith b 1953), 1 da (Clare b 1954); *Career* Maj Royal Marine 1940-46, ME, Far E, Normandy; vicar St Cuthbert Copnor Portsmouth 1957-65, chaplain Bedford Sch 1965-72, sr teacher Newnham Sch Bedford 1972-78, vicar Hawkley and Froxfield Hants 1978-; *Recreations* walking, tennis; *Clubs* RM Assoc; *Style*— The Rev Bennet Forster; Flat 2, Holywell House, Holywell Rd, Malvern Wells, Worcs WR14 4LF (☎ 06845 72170)

FORSTER, Donald; CBE; s of Bernard Forster (d 1983), and Rose, *née* Deutsch (d 1975); *b* 18 Dec 1920; *Educ* Manchester GS; *m* 1942, Muriel Steinman; 1 s (Steven), 2 da (Susan, Vanessa); *Career* served Pilot Fl Lt RAF 1940-45; md B Forster & Co Ltd Textile Manufacturers 1946-81 (chm 1981-85); memb Bd Skelmersdale Devpt Corpn; chm: Warrington Runcorn Devpt Corpn 1981-85, Merseyside Devpt Corpn 1984-87; *Recreations* golf, music, art; *Clubs* Dunham Forest, Whitefield; *Style*— Donald Forster, Esq, CBE; 6 The Dell, South Downs Rd, Hale, Altrincham, Cheshire WA14 3HU (☎ 061 926 9145)

FORSTER, His Hon Donald Murray; s of John Cameron Forster (d 1970), and Maisie Constance, *née* Nicoll (d 1990); Tom Forster led the English Jacobites to defeat at Preston in 1715; Nicolls were a Skye clan - Nicolson; *b* 18 June 1929; *Educ* Wrekin Coll Shropshire, St Edmund Hall Oxford; *Career* circuit judge 1984-90, assigned to N circuit; *Recreations* sport; *Clubs* Liverpool Ramblers FC, Liverpool Racquet, Mersey Bowmen Tennis; *Style*— His Hon Donald Forster; Milton Hall Nursing Home, Brampton, Cumbria CA8 1JA

FORSTER, John Henry Knight; s of Henry Knight Forster, MBE, of Salcombe, Devon, and Margaret Rutherford, *née* Metcalf; *b* 14 Feb 1941; *Educ* Dean Close Sch Cheltenham; *m* 1, 1965 (m dis 1985), Hilary; 1 s (Gregory), 2 da (Heidi, Hayley); m 2, 1986, Carol Ann, *née* Lamond; *Career* dir: Hart Ventures plc, Color Steels Ltd, Elvetham Hall Ltd, Hadley Garages Ltd, Kaye Enterprises Ltd, Pegasus Holdings Ltd, Kaye Office Supplies Ltd, Industrial Modernisation Ltd, Pool & Sons (Hartley Wintney) Ltd; FCA, FCT; *Recreations* country pursuits; *Style*— John Forster, Esq; The Bothy, Ellisfield, Hampshire RG 25 2QE (☎ 025683 265); Hart House, Hartley Wintney, Hampshire RG27 8PE (☎ 025126 3811)

FORSTER, Margaret; da of Arthur Gordon Forster, and Lilian, *née* Hind; *b* 25 May 1938; *Educ* Somerville Coll Oxford; *m* 1960, (Edward) Hunter Davies, *qv*; 1 s, 2 da; *Career* author; *Books incl* Georgy Girl (1965); *Style*— Miss Margaret Forster; 11 Boscastle Rd, London NW5

FORSTER, Neil Milward; s of Norman Milward Forster and Olive Christina, *née* Cockrell; bro of Sir Oliver Forster *qv*; *b* 29 May 1927; *Educ* Hurstpierpoint, Pembroke Coll Cambridge (BA); *m* 1954, Barbara Elizabeth Smith; 1s, 2 da; *Career* dir Brit and Cwlth Shipping Co plc 1982-; *Style*— Neil Forster, Esq; c/o British & Commonwealth Shipping Co plc, Queens House, 64/65 St James's Street, London SW1 (☎ 071 493 2682); 18 Carlton Rd, Ealinng, London W5

FORSTER, Norvela F; *b* 1931; *Educ* South Wilts GS Salisbury, Univ of London (BSc); *m* 1981, Michael Jones, s of Norman Jones; *Career* fndr chm and md IAL Conslts Ltd consultancy co; MEP (EDG) Birmingham S 1979-84; past memb: Hampstead Borough Cncl, Cncl Bow Gp; memb Cncl Mgmnt Consults Assoc; *Clubs* Royal Ocean Racing, Royal Mid-Surrey Golf; *Style*— Miss Norvela Forster; c/o IAL Consultants Ltd, 14 Buckingham Palace Rd, London SW1W 0QP (☎ 071 828 5036); 6 Regency House, Regency St, London SW1

FORSTER, Sir Oliver Grantham; KCMG (1983, CMG 1976), LVO (1961); 2 s of Norman Milward Forster, and Olive Christina, *née* Cockrell; bro of Neil Milward Forster, *qv*; *b* 2 Sept 1925; *Educ* Hurstpierpoint, King's Coll Cambridge; *m* 1953; 2 da; *Career* Cwlth Rels Office 1951, 1 sec 1959, min Br High Cmmn New Delhi 1975, asst under sec of state, and dep chief clerk FCO 1975-79, ambass Pakistan 1979-84; *Style*— Sir Oliver Forster, KCMG, LVO; The White House, 71 Raglan Road, Reigate, Surrey

FORSTER, Robert Anthony; s of Capt Henry Knight Forster, MBE, of Fernbank, Coronation Rd, Salcombe, S Devon, and Margaret Rutherford, *née* Metcalf; *b* 26 July 1945; *Educ* Llandaff Cathedral Sch Llandaff, Dean Close Sch Cheltenham; *m* 12 Sept 1970, Christine Elizabeth, da of Frederick William Milward, of 3 St Michael's Rd, Llandaff, Cardiff; 1 da (Annabel b 16 May 1973); *Career* accountant 1952-74: EM Manufacturing Co Ltd, Western Mail & Echo Ltd, Standard Telephone & Cables Ltd, Aeroquip UK Ltd; md Biomet Ltd 1974-; former pres Cardiff C of C; memb ctee: IOD Wales Div (former sec), CIMA S Wales Branch (former sec, chm, pres); FCMA 1973, FInstD 1977; *Recreations* travel, gardening, fine arts; *Style*— Robert Forster, Esq; 7 Duffryn Crescent, Peterston Super Ely, South Glamorgan CF5 6NF (☎ 0446 760162); BIOMET Ltd, Waterton Industrial Estate, Bridgend, South Glamorgan CF31 3YN (☎ 0656 655221, fax 0656 645454, telex

FORSYTH, Alastair Elliott; s of Maj Henry Russell Forsyth (d 1941), and Marie Elaine, *née* Greensmith (d 1958); *b* 23 Oct 1932; *Educ* Christ's Hosp, Keble Coll Oxford (MA); *m* 21 July 1973, Margaret Christine, da of Maj Royston Ivor Vallance, of Lark Rise, Weasenham St Peter, nr King's Lynn Norfolk; 4 s (Angus b 1963, Jamie b 1966, Alexander b 1975, John b 1978); 1 da (Arethusa b 1980); *Career* banker; dir J Henry Schroder Wagg & Co Ltd 1982-; *Recreations* Colombian and Venezuelan history; *Clubs* Annabels; *Style*— Alastair Forsyth, Esq; The Old Rectory, Foulsham, Norfolk NR20 5SF; J Henry Schroder Wagg & Co Ltd, 120 Cheapside, London EC2V 6DS (☎ 071 382 6000)

FORSYTH, Dr Angela; da of James Robert Forsyth, of The Cliff, Malmesbury, Wilts, and Mary, *née* Fennell; *b* 5 Feb 1945; *Educ* St Anne's Convent GS Southampton, Univ of Glasgow (MB ChB); *m* 24 June 1975, Robert Andrew Marshall, s of Andrew Gardner Marshall, of Upper Hazelhurst, Haugh of Urr Rd, Dalbeattie, Kirkudbrightshire; 1 s (Alasdair b July 1980), 2 da (Jane b June 1977, Ruth b Dec 1982); *Career* conslt dermatologist Gtr Glasgow Health Bd 1979, hon clinical lectr Univ of Glasgow 1980; author of pubns on methods of measurement of skin reactions by instruments; memb Ctee Br Contact Dermatitis Gp; FRCPG 1985; *Recreations* music, gardening, cooking, needlework; *Style*— Dr Angela Forsyth; Contact Dermatitis Unit, Belvidere Hospital, London Rd, Glasgow G31 4PG (☎ 041 554 1855)

FORSYTH, Gordon Scott; s of George Stirling Forsyth (d 1982), of Rutherglen, Scotland, and Betty Agnes, *née* Scott; *b* 20 April 1926; *Educ* Glasgow HS, Univ of Glasgow (MA); *m* 6 March 1954, Nancy Scott, da of John Molesworth Reid (d 1971), of Hale, Cheshire; 1 s (Andrew b 1969), 1 da (Fiona b 1966); *Career* Mil Serv 1945-48, Lt The Highland LI; CA; chief accountant The BP Co plc 1974-81; dir: BP Petroleum Development Ltd 1976-86, BP Oil Development Ltd 1976-86; fin dir BP Exploration Co Ltd 1981-86; hon treas Inst of Petroleum 1985-; *Recreations* golf, walking; *Clubs* Royal Overseas League, Langley Park Golf; *Style*— Gordon Forsyth, Esq; 89 Barnfield Wood Rd, Beckenham, Kent; The Institute of Petroleum, 61 New Cavendish St, London W1M 8AR (☎ 071 636 1004, telex 264380)

FORSYTH, James Law; s of Richard Forsyth (d 1970), of Glasgow, and Jessie, *née* Law (d 1967); *b* 5 March 1913; *Educ* HS of Glasgow, The Glasgow Art Sch (Dip); *m* 1, 1938 (m dis 1945), Helen Stewart; 2 s (Antony b 1940, Richard b 1948); m 2, 5 Aug 1955, Dorothy Louise Tibble; *Career* Nat Serv WWII 1940-46: trained Scots Gds Chelsea, cmmnd 2 Monmouthshire Regt S Wales Borderers, Capt Signals Inf (serv Normandy, NW Euro Theatre), Adj Italy (decorated for gallantry 1946); artist, exhibitions 1934-35, designer GPO film unit 1936-40, illustrator Basic Eng Project 1936-40, Sussex annual exhibitions 1981-90; playwright, active serv and writing 1940-46; poetry incl: Poetry in Wartime (1942), The War Poets (1945); collections of poems: on the Sussex days- On Such A Day As This 1989, From Time to Time (1990); in residence Old Vic 1946-48; stage plays incl: The Medicine Man 1950, Heloise 1951, The Other Heart 1952, The Pier 1958, Trog 1959, Emmanuel 1960, Dear Wormwood 1965, If My Wings Heal 1966, Lobsterback 1975; TV plays incl: The

English Boy 1969, Four Triumphant 1969, The Last Journey 1972, The Old Man's Mountain 1972; radio plays incl: The Bronze Horse 1948, Christophe 1958, Every Pebble on the Beach 1962, When the Snow Lay Round About 1978, Fifteen Strings of Cash 1979, The Threshing Floor 1982; visiting prof of drama: Howard 1962, Tufts Univ 1963, Florida State Univ 1964; memb: Exec Ctee League of Dramatists 1950-75, Theatres Advsy Cncl 1962-67; dir Tufts in London, overseas drama programme Tufts Univ Mass 1967-71; artistic dir Forsyth's Barn Theatre Sussex 1971-83; awarded Civil List Pension for Servs to Lit 1984; memb Soc of Authors (1946-); Bronze Cross Netherlands 1946; *Recreations* walking, gardening, music, reading; *Style—* James Forsyth, Esq; Grainloft, Ansty, West Sussex RH17 5AG (☎ 0444 413 345)

FORSYTH, John Howard; s of George Howard Forsyth, MBE, (d 1980), of Cartmel, Cumbria, and Marjorie Christine, *née* Cook; *b* 23 Aug 1945; *Educ* Oundle, St Johns Coll Cambridge; *m* 19 Sept 1968, Barbara, da of Major C G G Cook of Ockbrook, Derbyshire; 2 s (Mark b 1977, James b 1980), 1 da (Alicia b 1975); *Career* merchant banker; chief economist Morgan Grenfell & Co Ltd 1973; gp dir: Morgan Grenfell & Co Ltd 1988- (dir 1979-88); memb of Cncl Royal Inst of Int Affair 1983-; *Recreations* books, country pursuits; *Clubs* City of London; *Style—* John Forsyth, Esq; 38 Well Walk, London NW3 (☎ 071 794 3523); 23 Great Winchester St, London EC2 (☎ 071 588 4545)

FORSYTH, Michael Bruce; MP (C) Stirling 1983-; s of John Tawse Forsyth and Mary Watson; *b* 16 Oct 1954; *Educ* Arbroath HS, Univ of St Andrews (MA); *m* 1977, Susan Jane, da of John Bryan Clough; 1 s, 2 da; *Career* nat chm Fedn of Cons Students 1976; memb Westminster City Cncl 1978-83; PPS Foreign Sec 1986-June 1987; Parly under-sec of State at the Scottish Office June 1987-90, chm Scottish Cons Pty 1989-90, Scottish Office 1990-; *Recreations* mountaineering, photography, astronomy; *Style—* Michael Forsyth, Esq, MP; House of Commons, London SW1

FORSYTH, Michael Eric; s of Thomas Michael Forsyth, of Earlswood, West Midlands, and Patricia Ann, *née* Bulmer; *b* 20 March 1966; *Educ* Woodrush HS Birmingham; *m* 2 July 1988, Veronica Mary, da of Michael Charles Moss; 1 s (Samuel Michael b 19 Oct 1989); *Career* professional footballer; 33 appearances West Bromwich Albion 1983-86, over 200 appearances Derby County 1986-; England caps: 8 youth 1982-84, 1 under 21 v Switzerland 1988, 1 B 1990; player of the year Derby County 1987-88; *Recreations* golf, snooker; *Style—* Michael Forsyth, Esq; Derby County FC, Baseball Ground, Shaftesbury Crescent, Derby DE3 8NB (☎ 0332 40105)

FORSYTH, Dr Michael Graham de Jong; s of Eric Forsyth, of Wallasey, Merseyside, and Lucy Rebecca, *née* de Jong; *b* 26 Nov 1951; *Educ* Univ of Liverpool Sch of Architecture (BA, BArch), British School at Rome, Univ of Bristol (PhD); *m* 18 Sept 1987, Vera, da of Nicos Papaxanthou, of Nicosia, Cyprus; 1 s (James b 28 Sept 1983), 2 da (Antonia b 18 Dec 1985, Henrietta b 18 March 1988); *Career* ptnr architectural practice Toronto Canada, res fell Univ of Bristol 1984-90 (lectr 1979-84), dir Plato Consortium Ltd Bath 1985-, ptnr Forsyth Architects Bath 1987-; awarded: Rome Scholarship in Architectre 1975, nineteenth annual ASCAP Deems Taylor award for books on music; many articles reviews and radio bdcasts; memb: Selection Board British School at Rome Renovations Ctee Bath Preservation Tst, Exec Ctee Friends of Bristol Art Gallery; hon sec Soc of Rome Scholars; RIBA 1979, ARCUK 1979; *Books* Buildings for Music: The Architect, the Musician, and the Listener from the Seventeenth Century to the Present Day (1985), Auditoria: Designing for the Performing Arts (1987); *Style—* Dr Michael Forsyth; 26 Great Pulteney St, Bath, BA2 4BU

FORSYTH, Timothy William; *Educ* Architectural Assoc Sch of Architecture (AA Dip); *Career* architect; private practice West End and Richmond (specialist in office schemes and housing); D Y Davies Associates: joined 1979, ptnr 1980-, dir DY Davies plc, md D Y Davies International, chm various cos within D Y Davies Gp; exhibited Royal Acad Summer Exhibition; MRIBA: former chm S E Region and Kingston upon Thames branch, memb Cncl, memb Overseas Affairs Ctee; awards incl: DOE (for design in housing), Civic Trust, Richmond Soc, Civic awards (Richmond and North Herts); *Style—* Timothy Forsyth, Esq; D Y Davies plc, 36 Paradise Road, Richmond, Surrey TW9 1SE (☎ 081 948 5544, fax 081 948 5525)

FORSYTH-JOHNSON, Bruce Joseph; s of John Frederick Forsyth-Johnson, (d 1961), and Florence Ada Forsyth-Johnson (d 1957); *b* 22 Feb 1928; *Educ* Latimer Sch Edmonton; *m* 1, 1951, Olivia, da of Calvert, of NI; 3 da (Debbie b 1955, Julie b 1958, Laura b 1964); m 2, 24 Dec 1973, Anthea, da of Bernard Redfern, of Torquay; 2 da (Charlotte b 1976, Louisa b 1977); m 3, 15 Jan 1983, Wilnelia, da of Enrique Merced, of Puerto Rico; 1 s (Jonathan Joseph b 1986); *Career* theatre: Little Me original British prod 1964, Travelling Music Show 1978, One Man show, Winter Garden NY 1979, Huntington Hartford Los Angeles 1979, London Palladium; numerous extensive tours: UK, NZ, Aust; film: Star 1968, Can Heironymous Merkin Ever Forgive Mercy Humppe and Find True Happiness 1969, Bedknobs and Broomsticks 1971, The Seven Deadly Sins 1971, Pavlova 1984, TV: Sunday Night at the London Palladium 1958-63, Piccadilly Spectaculars, Bruce Forsyth Show ATV, The Generation Game BBC 1971-77 (seven series), Bruces Big Night LWT 1978, Play Your Cards Right 1980-87 (ten series), Slingers Day Thames 1985-86, Hollywood or Bust 1984, You Bet! LWT 1987-89; numerous specials incl: Bring on the Girls Thames 1976, Bruce and More Girls Thames 1977, Bruce Meets the Girls; The Forsyth Follies; Sammy and Bruce (with Sammy Davis Jr): The Entertainers (with Rita Moreno), The Muppet Show, The Mating Season, The Canterville Ghost; awards: Daily Mirror National TV Award 1961, Variety Club Showbusiness Personality of the Year 1975, The Sun TV Personality of the Year (twice) 1976 and 1977, TV Times Favourite TV Personality (male; three times 1975, 1976, 1977) TV Times Favourite Game Show Host 1984; *Recreations* golf, tennis; *Clubs* Tramp, Crockfords; *Style—* Bruce Forsyth-Johnson, Esq; Bruce Forsyth Enterprises Ltd, Straidarran, Wentworth Dr, Virginia Water, Surrey GU25 4NY (☎ 09904 4056)

FORSYTH OF THAT ILK, Alistair Charles William; JP (Angus); Chief of the Name and Clan of Forsyth, Baron of Ethie (territorial); s of Capt Charles Forsyth of Strathendry, FCA (d 1981), and Ella Millicent Hopkins (d 1983); *b* 7 Dec 1929; *Educ* St Paul's Sch; *m* 1958, Ann OStJ, da of Col Percy Arthur Hughes, IA (d 1950); 4 s; *Career* cmmnd The Queen's Bays (2 Dragoon Gds) 1948-50; commodity broker 1950-68, dir and chm Caledonian Produce (Holdings) Ltd and Subsidiaries 1968- cncllr Angus DC, convenor Industl Devpt Ctee, memb Highland TAVRA, memb Montrose Harbour Trust 1990-; CStJ; *Recreations* hill walking, Scottish antiquities; *Clubs* Cavalry and Guards', New (Edinburgh); *Style—* Alistair Forsyth of that Ilk, JP; Ethie Castle, by Arbroath, Angus

FORSYTHE, Clifford James; MP (OUP) South Antrim 1983-; *b* 1929; *Career* former professional footballer Linfield and Derry City, plumbing and heating contractor, Mayor of Newtonabbey 1982-83, memb NI Assembly 1982-86, vice-chm Health & Social Servs Ctee, memb Environment Ctee, Party spokesman Tport, Communications and Local Govt; fell Indust and Parly Tst, pres NI section of Inst of Plumbing, chm Chest, Heart and Stroke Assoc Glengormley branch; *Style—* Clifford Forsythe Esq, MP; House of Commons, London SW1 (☎ 071 219 4144); constituency office: 19 Fountain St, Antrim BT41 4BG (☎ 08494 60776)

FORSYTHE, Dr (John) Malcolm; s of Dr John Walter Joseph Forsythe (d 1988), and Dr Charlotte Constance Forsythe, *née* Beatty (d 1981); *b* 11 July 1936; *Educ* Repton, Guy's Hosp Med Sch London Univ (BSc, MB BS, MRCS, DObstRCOG), Univ of N Carolina, London Sch Hygiene and Tropical Med, Univ of London (MSc); *m* 1, 28 Oct 1961 (m dis 1984), Delia Kathleen, da of late Dr J K Moore; 1 s (Marcus John Malcolm b 30 Sept 1965), 3 da (Suzanne Delia b 9 July 1962, Nicola Kathleen (twin) b 9 July 1962, Sarah Louise b 16 May 1969); m 2, 27 Jan 1985, Patricia Mary Murden, *née* Barnes; *Career* house surgn Guy's Hosp 1961-62, house offr Farnborough 1962, house physician Lewisham 1962-63, GP Beckenham 1963-65, MO Birmingham Regnl Hosp Bd 1965-68, princ asst sr admin med offr SE Met RHB 1973-74 (dep 1972-73), area MO Kent area Health Authy 1974-78; regnl MO SE Thames RHA 1978-84 (dir of planning 1983, regnl MO and dir of public health and service devpt 1989-); pt/t: memb Bd Public Health Laboratory Serv 1985-, dir Inst of Public Health 1990-; FRSM, FFCM FRCP; *Recreations* tennis, ornithology; *Clubs* RSM, RSA; *Style—* Dr Malcolm Forsythe; Kapalua, 5 Ryders, Langton Green, Tunbridge Wells, Kent TN3 ODX (☎ 0892 863852); South East Thames Regional Health Authority, Thrift House, Collington Avenue, East Sussex TN39 3NQ (☎ 0424 730073, fax 0424 730249); Institute of Public Health (☎ 0892 535352)

FORTE, Baron (Life Peer UK 1982), of Ripley, Co Surrey; Sir Charles Forte; s of Rocco (Giovanni) Forte, of Monforte, Casalattico, Italy; *b* 26 Nov 1908; *Educ* Alloa Acad, Dumfries Coll, Mamiani Rome; *m* 1943, Irene Mary, da of Giovanni and Olga Chierico, of Venice; 1 s, 5 da (Hon Olga (Hon Mrs Polizzi di Sorrentino), Hon Marie Louise (Hon Mrs Burness), Hon Irene (Hon Mrs Danilovich), Hon Giancarla (Hon Mrs Alen-Buckley), Hon Portia b 7 Feb 1964); *Career* chm Trusthouse Forte Ltd (started as milk bar in Regent Street 1935); hon consul-gen for San Marino; FRSA, FBIM; kt 1970; *Books* Forte (autobiography); *Recreations* music, fencing, golf, fishing, shooting; *Clubs* Carlton, Caledonian, Royal Thames Yacht; *Style—* The Rt Hon Lord Forte; 166 High Holborn, London WC1V 6TT

FORTE, Hon Rocco John Vincent; o s of Baron Forte (Life Peer), *qv*; *b* 18 Jan 1945; *Educ* Downside, Pembroke Coll Oxford (MA); *m* 15 Feb 1986, Aliai, da of Prof Giovanni Ricci, of Rome; 2 da (Lydia Irene b 1987, Irene Alisea b 1988); *Career* chief exec Trusthouse Forte plc; memb: Br Tourist Authy, Grand Cncl Hotel & Catering Benevolent Assoc; vice-pres Cwlth Games Cncl; memb Worshipful Co of Bakers; FMICA, ACA; Cavaliere Ufficiale of Order of Merit of the Italian Republic 1988; *Recreations* golf, fishing, shooting, running; *Clubs* Garrick, Turf; *Style—* The Hon Rocco Forte; 166 High Holborn, London WC1V 6TT (☎ 071 836 7744, fax 071 240 9993, telex 264678 THF PLC)

FORTE DELLE MANDRIOLE, Marchese (Marquis of Mandriole, creation of the Republic of San Marino 1963, AD, and in year 1663 of the Republic) Olimpio; Grand Cordon of the Order of Polonia Restituta, Grand Cross Ordre of Merit Legion de Honor de la Republica de Cuba, Grand Croix de l'Ordre de l'Encouragement Public Français, Medaille d'Honneur d'Or de Sociéte d'Encouragement au Progress, Kt Cdr Ordre du Merite Francais D'Outre Mer, Kt Cdr Royal Order of St Sava, Kt Sov Mil Order of Malta, Kt Cdr Italian Republic, Kt Grand Offr Holy Sepulchure of Jerusalem, Kt Order St Gregory the Great, Grand Offr Royal Crown of Yugoslavia; s of Francesco Forte (d 1940) and Maria Ciaraldi, original founder of family: Angelo Forte di Lecce who was granted the title of Baron by Charles VIII, King of France, on 1st April 1485, in Naples. Giovanni Forte was among the first fifty people to be made a Kt of Justice of the Order of Constantine St George 19 March 1834; *b* 8 March 1918,Casalattico Frosinone, Italy; *Educ* in Casalattico; *m* 1948, Iolanda Dese (b in Scotland), da of Silviano Forte (d 1956); 1 s (Francesco Pietro, m 1984, Rosalin Good; 1 s, Gino Olimpio b 1985), 1 da (Sandra Francesca Maria); *Heir* s, *see above*; *Career* 1940-46 Italian Army, memb Allied Resistance Force Underground Movement First Lt Italian Army 1945, Lt-Col Allied Resistance Forces IMOS 1947, DSC, IMOS (first class), Monte Cassino Cross, War Cross of the Royal Yugoslav Army 1941-45 and Sword of Honour, Military Cross Virtuti Military (silver), Commemorative War Medal Dwight D Eisenhower 1939-45, Commemorative War Medal Gen George Patton 1944-45, Certificate of Gratitude from Field Marshal Alexander 1939-45, Grand Cross of the Fed of Partisan 1939-45, Euro Cross, DDL, Nat Univ of Canada 1947; present day, financier, Institute des Relations Diplomatiques: Ordre du Merite Diplomatique; Medaille D'or of Association Nationale Franco-Britannique, Etoile du Mérite Franco-Allié (of Union of Mérite Franco Alliés) 1939-45; landowner and dir of various cos; *Recreations* golf; *Style—* Marchese Forte delle Mandriole; Montforte, Cassalattico, Frosinone, Italy; Balsorano, 207 Cooden Drive, Bexhill-on-Sea, E Sussex (☎ 04243 5306)

FORTESCUE, (John) Adrian; LVO (1972); s of Trevor Victor Norman Fortescue, CBE, and Margery Stratford Fortescue; *b* 16 June 1941; *Educ* Uppingham, King's Coll Cambridge (BA), LSE (Dip in Business Admin); *m* 1 (m dis 1988), Jillian, *née* Valpy; 1 s (James b 1966); m 2, 26 May 1989, Marie, *née* Wolfcarius; *Career* HM Dip Serv 1964-; Lebanon 1964-65, Amman Jordan 1966-68, Paris 1968-72, Brussels 1973-75, Washington 1979-81, FCO London 1976-79 and 1981-82, Budapest 1983-84, seconded to Euro Cmmn Brussels 1985-; Ordre du Mérite France 1972; *Style—* Adrian Fortescue, Esq; 44 Avenue Beau-Séjour, 1180 Brussels, Belgium (☎ 010 322 374 3810); Commission of the European Communities, 200 Rue De La Loi, 1049 Brussels, Belgium (☎ 010 322 235 5727)

FORTESCUE, Lady Margaret; eldest da of 5 Earl Fortescue, KG, PC, CB, OBE, MC (d 1958), and Hon Margaret Helen Beaumont, CBE (d 1958), eldest da of 1 Viscount Allendale; *b* 13 Dec 1923; *m* 30 July 1948 (m dis 1968), Bernard van Cutsem (d 1975), s of late Henry Harcourt van Cutsem; 2 da (*see* Earl of Arran); *Career* resumed surname Fortescue 1966; *Style—* The Lady Margaret Fortescue; The Garden House, Filleigh, Barnstaple, N Devon (☎ 05986 402)

FORTESCUE, Hon Martin Denzil; yr s of 6 Earl Fortescue, MC, TD (d 1977), and his 1 wife Marjorie Ellinor, OBE, *née* Trotter (d 1964); *b* 5 Jan 1924; *Educ* Eton; *m* 23 April 1954, Prudence Louisa, yr da of Sir Charles Samuel Rowley, 6 Bt, TD; 2 s, 2 da; *Career* Lt RN (Emergency List); FRICS; *Style—* The Hon Martin Fortescue; Wincombe Park, Shaftesbury, Dorset

FORTESCUE, 7 Earl (GB 1789); Richard Archibald Fortescue; JP (Oxon 1964); also Baron Fortescue (GB 1746), Viscount Ebrington (GB 1789); s of 6 Earl, MC, TD (d 1977), by his 1 w Marjorie, OBE; *b* 14 April 1922; *Educ* Eton, Christ Church Oxford; *m* 1, 24 Oct 1949, Penelope Jane (d 28 May 1959), yr da of late Robert Evelyn Henderson, by his w Beatrice, da of Sir William Clerke, 11 Bt; 1 s, 1 da; m 2, 3 March 1961, Margaret Anne, da of Charles Michael Stratton; 2 da; m 3, 5 Jan 1989, Carolyn Mary, eld da of Clement Hill, by his w Violet, da of Charles Phillimore; *Heir* s, Viscount Ebrington; *Career* sits as Cons in House of Lords; late Capt Coldstream Gds; *Clubs* White's; *Style—* The Rt Hon Earl Fortescue, JP; House of Lords SW1

FORTESCUE, Lady Sarah Jane; da (by 2 m) of 7 Earl Fortescue; *b* 16 Aug 1963; *Style—* The Lady Sarah Fortescue

FORTESCUE, Hon Seymour Henry; s of 6 Earl Fortescue, MC, TD (d 1977), and his 2 w Hon Sybil Mary (d 1985), da of 3rd Viscount Hardinge (d 1985); *b* 28 May 1942; *Educ* Eton, Trinity Coll Cambridge, London Graduate Sch of Business Studies; *m* 1, 25 July 1966 (m dis 1990), Julia, o da of Sir John Arthur Pilcher GCMG (d 1990); 1 s (James Adrian b 1978), 1 da (Marissa Clare b 1973 m 2, 23 Aug 1990, Jennifer

Ann Simon; *Career* chief exec Barclaycard July 1982-85; dir: UK retail servs Barclays Bank plc 1987- (gen mangr 1985-87), Mercantile Gp PLC, EftPos UK Ltd; ct memb Worshipful Co of Grocers; *Style—* Hon Seymour Fortescue; 30 Holland Park Gdns, London W14 8EA (☎ 071 371 1173)

FORTEVIOT, 3 Baron (UK 1917); Sir Henry Evelyn Alexander Dewar; 3 Bt (UK 1907), MBE (Mil 1943), DL (Perth 1961); s (by 2 m) of 1 Baron (d 1929), suc half-bro 1947; *b* 23 Feb 1906; *Educ* Eton, St John's Oxford; *m* 25 April 1933, Cynthia Monica (d 1986), da of late Piers Cecil Le Gendre Starkie and his w Cicely , 2 da of Sir James de Hoghton, 11 Bt; 2 s, 2 da; *Heir* s, Hon John James Evelyn Dewar; *Career* chm John Dewar & Sons Ltd 1954-76, late dir Buchanan-Dewar Ltd and Distillers Co; *Clubs* Brook's; *Style—* The Rt Hon Lord Forteviot, MBE, DL; Dupplin Castle, Perth, Perthshire PH2 0PY

FORTH, Eric; MP (C) Mid-Worcs 1983-, MEP (EDG) Birmingham North 1979-84; s of William Forth, and Aileen Forth; *b* 9 Sept 1944; *Educ* Jordanhill Coll Sch Glasgow, Univ of Glasgow; *m* 1967, Linda St Clair; 2 da; *Career* memb Brentwood UDC 1968-72, contested (C) Barking Feb and Oct 1974, chm EDG Backbench Ctee 1979-83, chm Euro Affrs Backbench Ctee House of Commons 1986-87 (vice chm 1983-86), PPS to min of State Dep of Educn and Sci 1986-87; Parly under-sec of state: for indust and consumer affrs DTI 1988-90, Dept of Employment 1990-; *Clubs* Carlton; *Style—* Eric Forth, Esq, MP; House of Commons, London SW1

FORTIN, Richard Chalmers Gordon; s of Gordon Chalmers Fortin, of Lavenham, Suffolk, and Nancy Avant, *née* Chivers (d 1969); *b* 12 April 1941; *Educ* Wellington, CCC Oxford (Trevelyan scholarship); *m* 12 July 1969, Jane Elizabeth, da of C L Copeland; 3 da (Abigail Sarah Jane b 16 Feb 1973, Elizabeth Ruth Alice b 1 May 1975, Katharine Mary Anne b 6 May 1977); *Career* Lever Brothers Limited 1964-72, London Sloan fellowship 1972-73, asst dir Morgan Grenfell & Co Limited 1973-79, head of corp fin Lloyds Bank International Limited 1979-85, md Lloyds Merchant Bank Limited 1985-; tstee Royal Armories; *Recreations* sailing, cricket, walking, beekeeping, theatre; *Clubs* MCC, Vincents' (Oxford); *Style—* Richard Fortin, Esq; Lloyds Merchant Bank Limited, 48 Chiswell St, London EC1Y 4XX (☎ 071 522 5000)

FORTUNE, Lt-Col (John) Bruce; MC (1943); s of Maj Gen Sir Victor Morven Fortune, KBE, CB, DSO (d 1949), of Bengairn, Castle Douglas, Scot, and Eleanor Steel (d 1971); *b* 19 July 1921; *Educ* Winchester; *m* 23 Oct 1945, Susan Mary, da of Charles James Mackie (d 1934), of Aberdeen; 2 s (David Victor b 1946, John Philip b 1955), 1 da (Angela Morven b 1949); *Career* Lt Col Black Watch cmmnd 1941, wounded N Africa 1943, ADC to HE the Viceroy and Govr Gen of India 1943-45, DAMS HQ Allied Forces Netherlands E Indies 1945-46; Staff Coll 1953, Staff and RD 1954-60, instr RMA Sandhurst 1960-62, cmd 6/7 Bn The Black Watch 1962-65, AA and QMG 51 Highland Div 1965-68, GSOI Supreme HQ Allied Powers Europe 1968-71; ret; landowner, farmer, forester; memb: Scot Landowners Fedn, Timber Growers UK Ltd, Game Conservancy; *Recreations* all countryside pursuits, music; *Clubs* MCC; *Style—* Lt-Col Bruce Fortune, MC; Bengairn, Auchencairn, Castle Douglas, Kirkcudbrightshire DG7 1QN (☎ 055 664 209)

FORTUNE, Ernest Forrester; MBE; s of Ernest George Fortune (d 1962), of Buchlyvie, Stirlingshire, and Sophia Farley Kennedy (d 1934); *b* 29 May 1911; *Educ* Glasgow Acad, Uppingham; *m* 1948, Dorothy Frances, da of Sir Thomas Dunlop, 3 Bt, (d 1963), of Helensburgh, Dumbartonshire; 1 s (George Dunlop b 1953), 1 da (Susan Elizabeth b 1949); *Career* Maj RA, N Africa 1942, Italy 1943, Normandy and NW Europe 1944-46; paper maker 1928; formerly: pres Fife Kinross and Clackmannon Charitable Soc 1948, chm Edinburgh Branch Action Research for the Crippled Child 1968-75; Deacon Incorporation of Bakers Glasgow 1960, Craftsman, Incorporation of Hammermen Glasgow, memb Merchants House Glasgow; CStJ 1978 (Sec priory of Scotland of the Order of St John of Jerusalem 1973-77); *Recreations* golf, walking, painting, gardening; *Clubs* Elie Golf House; *Style—* E F Fortune, Esq, MBE, TD; Allanton, 31 South St, Elie, Fife KY9 1DN (☎ 0333 330 352)

FORTY, Prof (Arthur) John; s of Alfred Louis Forty (d 1947), and Elizabeth, *née* East (d 1938); *b* 4 Nov 1928; *Educ* Univ of Bristol (BSc, PhD, DSc); *m* 8 Aug 1950, (Alicia) Blanche Hart, da of William Gough (d 1943); 1 s (Jonathan b 1957); *Career* Short Serv Cmmn RAF 1953-56; sr scientist TI Res Laboratories 1956-58, lectr in physics Univ of Bristol 1958-65; Univ of Warwick 1965 -86: a prof of physics, head Physics Dept, pro-vice chllr; princ and vice chllr Univ of Stirling 1986-; author of various pubns in learned jls; memb and vice chm UGC 1982-86; chm: Computer Bd Univs and Res Cncls 1988-, Jt Policy Ctee for Advanced Res Computing 1988-; Hon LLD Univ of St Andrews 1989; FRSE 1988, FRSA 1989; *Recreations* sailing, gardening; *Clubs* Caledonian; *Style—* Prof John Forty; Principal's House, 1 Airthrey Castle Yard, University of Stirling, Stirling FK9 4LA (☎ 0786 73171)

FORWELL, Dr George Dick; s of Harold Cecil Forwell (d 1955), and Isabella L Christie; *b* 6 July 1928; *Educ* George Watson's Coll, Univ of Edinburgh (MB ChB, PhD); *m* 1957, Catherine Forsyth Campbell, *née* Cousland; 2 da; *Career* lectr Dept of Public Health & Social Med, asst dean Faculty of Med Univ of Edinburgh 1959-63, sr admin med offr Eastern Regnl Hospital Bd 1963-67, princ med offr Scot Home & Health Dept 1967-73, chief admin offr and dir of Public Health Greater Glasgow Health Bd visiting prof Univ of Glasgow; QHP 1980-83; memb GMC 1984-89; *Recreations* running; *Clubs* RAF; *Style—* Dr George Forwell; 60 Whittinghame Drive, Glasgow (☎ 041 334 7122)

FORWOOD, Sir Dudley Richard; 3 Bt (UK 1895), of The Priory, Gateacre, Childwall, Co Palatine of Lancaster; s of Lt-Col Sir Dudley Baines Forwood, 2 Bt, CMG (d 1961), and Norah Isabel, *née* Lockett (d 1961); gs of Rt Hon Sir Arthur Bower Forwood, 1 Bt, Lord Mayor of Liverpool, Privy Cncllr, MP; *b* 6 June 1912; *Educ* Stowe; *m* 1, 27 May 1952, Mary Gwendoline, da of Basil Foster (she m 1, Inigo Brassey Freeman-Thomas, Viscount Ratendone (later 2 Marquess of Willingdon); m 2, Frederick Robert Cullingford; m 3, Brig Donald Croft-Wilcock); 1 adopted s (Rodney Simon Dudley); *Heir* cous, Peter Noel Forwood; *Career* Scots Guards (Capt); hon attaché British Legation Vienna 1934-37; equerry to HRH the Duke of Windsor 1937-39; underwriting memb of Lloyd's; master New Forest Buckhounds 1957-65; vice pres Royal Agric Soc of England (hon dir 1972-77); chm: New Forest Agric Soc 1964-82 (pres 1983-), New Forest Consultative Panel 1970-82, Crufts Dog Show 1970-87; official verderer New Forest 1974-82; vice pres The Kennel Club; chm British Deer Soc 1984-87; *Recreations* hunting, wildlife conservation; *Style—* Sir Dudley Forwood, Bt; Uppacott, Bagnum, nr Ringwood, Hants BH24 3BZ (☎ 0425 471480); 43 Addison Rd, London W14 (☎ 071 603 3620)

FORWOOD, Margaret; da of Christopher Warren Forwood (d 1975), and Mona Blanche, *née* Williams (d 1978); *b* 25 March 1943; *Educ* Oswestry Girls' HS Shropshire, Univ of Manchester; *Career* reporter Wolverhampton Express & Star 1964-70, tv ed and critic The Sun 1970-84; tv columnist: The People 1984-89, Daily Express 1989-; chm Bdcasting Press Guild 1981-83; *Style—* Miss Margaret Forwood; East Sheen, London SW

FORWOOD, Nicholas James; QC (1987); s of Lt-Col Harry Forwood, RA, of Cobham, Surrey, and Wendy, *née* French-Smith; *b* 22 June 1948; *Educ* Stowe, St Johns Coll Cambridge (BA, MA); *m* 4 Dec 1971, Sally Diane, da of His Hon Judge Basil Gerrard, of Knutsford, Cheshire; 3 da (Victoria b 1974, Genevra b 1976, Suzanna b 1979), 1 s (Thomas b 1990); *Career* called to the Bar Middle Temple 1970, called to the Irish Bar 1982; *Recreations* golf, opera, skiing, sailing, shooting; *Clubs* United Oxford and Cambridge, SCGB; *Style—* Nicholas Forwood, Esq, QC; 11 Avenue Juliette, 1180, Brussels, Belguim (☎ 02 3752542); 15-19 Devereux Ct, Temple, London EC4 (☎ 071 583 0777)

FORWOOD, Peter Noel; s (by 2 m) of Arthur Noel Forwood (d 1959), 3 s of 1 Bt; hp of cousin, Sir Dudley Richard Forwood, 3 Bt; *b* 15 Oct 1925; *Educ* Radley; *m* 1950, Roy, da of James Murphy, MBE, FRCS, LRCP, of Horsham, Sussex; 6 da; *Career* Welsh Gds WW II; *Style—* Peter Forwood, Esq; Newhouse Farm, Shillinglee, Chiddingfold, Surrey

FORWOOD, William Grantham Lewis; s of Philip Lockton Forwood (d 1976), of Bucks, and Barbara Muriel Lewis, *née* Richards (d 1982); *b* 3 Aug 1927; *Educ* Kings Coll Choir Sch Cambridge, Eton, Clare Coll Cambridge (MA, LLM); *m* 22 Dec 1951, Joyce Barbara Addenbrooke, da of Lt-Col Gordon Spencer Marston, DSO, MC, of Bucks; 4 s (Kemeys b 1954, Edward b 1959, Richard b 1961, Henry b 1963), 2 da (Philippa b 1957, Felicia b 1966); *Career* cmmnd Royal Welch Fus 1947; admitted slr 1954, legal & fin conslt; dir: Sedgwick Dineen Gp Ltd 1976-, Applied Chemical Ireland Ltd 1983-; *Recreations* shooting, rough gardening, book collecting; *Clubs* Kildare Street Univ (Dublin); *Style—* William G L Forwood, Esq; Woodstock, Newtownmountkennedy, Co Wicklow (☎ 0001 874151); 30 Upper Pembroke Street, Dublin 2 (☎ 0001 765881, telex 93238, fax 0001 613409)

FOSS, Prof Brian Malzard; s of Rev Francis S Foss (d 1978), and Ann Eliza, *née* Malzard (d 1950); *b* 25 Oct 1921; *Educ* Emmanuel Coll Cambridge (MA), Univ of Oxford (Dip Psychology, MA); *Career* experimental offr Army Op Res Gp, Mil Op Res Unit 1942-46; jr lectr Univ of Oxford 1948-51, lectr Birkbeck Coll 1951-64; Univ of London: prof educnl psychology 1964-65, prof psychology 1968-87; ed: New Horizons in Psychology 1966, Determinants of Infant Behaviour 1961-69; pres: Br Psychology Soc 1974, Section J Br Assoc for the Advancement of Sci 1974; *Style—* Prof Brian Foss; 180 Latymer Court, London W6 7JQ

FOSS, Hon Mrs (Janet Mary Penrose); *née* Lewis; yr da of 1 & last Baron Brecon (d 1976); *b* 2 Oct 1944; *Educ* Cheltenham Ladies Coll; *m* 1969, Christopher John Foss, er s of K J Foss, of Greenwood, Torquay; 2 da; *Style—* The Hon Mrs Foss; 3 Sterling St, Montpelier Sq, London SW7

FOSS, Kate; *née* Arden; da of George Arden (d 1958), and May Elizabeth Arden (d 1959); *b* 17 May 1925; *Educ* Northampton HS, Whitelands Coll; *m* 1951, Robert Foss, s of Laurence Foss (d 1957); 1 s (Jonathan b 1959); *Career* chm: Insur Ombudsman Bureau 1985-, chm Direct Mail Servs Standards Bd 1989- (memb 1983-); memb: Cncl Licensed Conveyancers 1985-88, Standing Ctee Licenced Conveyancing 1985-88, Data Protection Tribunal 1986-, Nat Consumer Cncl 1981-84; *Recreations* golf; *Style—* Mrs Kate Foss; Merston, 61 Back Lane, Knapton, York (☎ 0904 782549); Insurance Ombudsman Bureau, 31 Southampton Row, London

FOSTER, (David) Alan; s of Wilfred John Foster (d 1971), of Esher, Surrey, and Edith Mary, *née* Rowling (d 1990); *b* 13 April 1935; *Educ* Oundle, ChCh Oxford; *m* 17 Sept 1960, Jacqueline Marie, da of Charles Edward Fredrick Stowell (d 1976), of Langstone, Hants; 2 s (Mark b 1961, Richard b 1962), 2 da (Nicola b 1964, Susannah b 1971); *Career* cmmnd RA 1953-55; ptnr DeZoete & Gorton (later DeZoete & Bevan) 1963, dep chm Barclays DeZoete Wedd Investment Mgmnt Ltd 1986-88; Freeman City of London 1959, Sr Warden Worshipful Co of Needlemakers 1990 (Freeman 1959, Memb Ct 1982); FPMI 1988 (APMI 1976); *Recreations* sailing; *Clubs* City of London, RAC; *Style—* Alan Foster, Esq; Torrington, 10 Fairmile Lane, Cobham, Surrey KT11 2DJ (☎ 0932 64249)

FOSTER, Andrew Gerard; s of Sydney Edward Lancelot Foster, MC (d 1963), of The Shieling, Oak Hill, Wethersfield, Braintree, Essex, and Elsa Glyn, *née* Barnett (d 1979); *b* 9 Aug 1936; *Educ* Braintree Co HS, Univ of Nottingham (LLB); *m* 1, 21 March 1962, da of John Adams (d 1943), of Stour House, Sudbury, Suffolk; 1 s (Roland b 1965), 2 da (Ann b 1963, Jane b 1967); m 2, 7 Aug 1980, (Shirley) Jennifer, da of Joseph Harold Davies, of Tudor Cot, Styal, Cheshire; *Career* slr 1961, sr ptnr Steed & Steed 1985, Notary Public 1979; memb Law Soc; *Recreations* rugby union football, rowing, fell walking; *Style—* Andrew Foster, Esq; 6 Gainsborough St, Sudbury, Suffolk CO10 6ET (☎ 0787 73387, fax 0787 880287)

FOSTER, Anthony; s of Rufus Foster (d 1971), of Gravesend, Kent, and Margery Beatrice, *née* Dace (d 1978); *b* 11 April 1926; *Educ* private; piano: Anne Collins, Arthur Tracy Robson; organ: John Cook, John Webster; orchestration: Richard Arnell, Dr Gordon Jacob, CBE; LRAM, ARCO; *m* 26 July 1952, Barbara, da of Capt Frederick William Humphreys (d 1967), of Gravesend; 1 da (Charlotte b 1958); *Career* composer published compositions incl: Slow Waltz and Calypso (instrumental, 1968), Dona Nobis Pacem (vocal and instrumental, 1973), Jonah and the Whale (vocal and instrumental, 1974), The St Richard Evening Service (vocal, 1981), Christ The Lord is Risen Again (Easter Carol, 1982), A Child is Born (vocal, 1983), Jubilate Deo (for organ, 1985), Three Sketches for Guitar (1989), Classical Suite (for organ, 1990); incidental music for BBC prodns: Monty Python's Flying Circus (1970), The Wizard of Oz (1970); hon vice pres Brighton Schs Music and Drama Assoc 1977-; memb: Composer's Guild of GB 1961, Performing Rights Soc 1982; *Recreations* cinematography; *Clubs* Composers' Guild; *Style—* Anthony Foster, Esq; 1 Cawley Road, Chichester, West Sussex PO19 1UZ (☎ 0243 780134)

FOSTER, Brendan; MBE (1976); s of Francis Foster, and Margaret Foster; *b* 12 Jan 1948; *Educ* St Joseph's GS Co Durham, Univ of Sussex (BSc), Carnegie Coll Leeds (DipEd); *m* 1972, Susan Margaret, da of Kenneth Frank Alston, of Clacton, Essex; 1 s (Paul b 1977), 1 da (Catherine b 1979); *Career* sch teacher St Joseph's GS Hebburn 1970-74, recreation mangr Gateshead Metropolitan Borough Cncl 1974-81, chm Nike (UK) Ltd 1981-87 (md Nike Europe), md Nova International Ltd 1987-; Cwlth Games medals include: Bronze 1500 m 1970, Silver 5000 m 1974, Silver 5000 m 1978, Gold 10000 m 1978; Euro Games medals include: Bronze 1500 m 1971, Gold 5000 m 1974; Olympic Games Bronze medal 10000 m 1976; World record holder: 2 miles 1973, 3000 m 1974; UK record holder: 10000 m 1978, 1500 m, 3000 m, 2 miles, 5000 m; *Style—* Brendan Foster, Esq, MBE; Whitegates, 31 Meadowfield Rd, Stocksfield, Northumberland NE43 7PY

FOSTER, Brian Joseph; s of Joseph Robert Foster, of Letchworth Garden City, Herts, and Mabel, *née* Picton (d 1957); *b* 28 Sept 1925; *Educ* Letchworth GS, London Hosp Med Coll Univ of London (MB BS, DPM); *m* 25 Aug 1950, Elizabeth Joan, da of Arthur Charlton (d 1954), of Newcastle Upon Tyne; 1 s (Timothy Huw b 12 May 1950), 2 da (Christine Gwynneth (Mrs Schmidhaüsler) b 17 July 1851, Vanessa Jane (Mrs Paminger) b 3 Aug 1954); *Career* Nat Serv Capt RAMC 1950-52, area psychiatrist Northern Cmd; GP 1952-, special interest in community psychiatry; local med conslt: BP Oil and Shell Oil 1960, Texaco Oil Co 1982; hosp practitioner in psychogeriatric med Moorgreen Hosp 1964-, hon teacher primary med care Univ of Southampton, fndr memb and current med conslt Bitterne and Woolston Rotary Club Housing Soc for the Elderly; sec Southampton Flower Fund Homes, pres Bitterne and Woolston Rotary Club 1970-71; MRCS 1949, LRCP 1949, MRCGP, memb BMA; *Recreations* gardening, antiques, walking, foreign travel (Europe and Middle East); *Clubs* Royal Southern Yacht (Hamble); *Style—* Dr Brian Foster; Landor House, 59 St

Cross Rd, Winchester SO23 9RE; Blackthorn Surgery, Netley Abbey, Southampton (☎ 0703 4539720)

FOSTER, Charles Arthur; ERD (1969); s of Arthur William Foster (d 1974), and Alice Katherine Mabel, *née* Browne; *b* 25 June 1926; *Educ* Blundell's, St Thomas's Hosp Med Sch (MB BS, LRCP); *m* 1, 18 Dec 1948 (m dis 1963), Elizabeth Darby, da of late Alec Draper; 2 s (Richard Charles Darby b 6 Jan 1951, Simon John Darby b 22 April 1957); m 2, 9 March 1963, Virginia Caroline (Juniper) Delap; 1 da (Tiffany Victoria b 18 Nov 1966); *Career* conslt anaesthetist: St Thomas's Hosp London 1958-86, Royal Masonic Hosp 1970-86; hon sec Snape Hist Tst, church warden St Mary Magdalene Sternfield; Freeman City of London, Liveryman Worshipful Co Barbers 1980; FCA; *Books* An Introduction to Anaesthetics (1966), Anaesthesia for Operating Theatre Technicians (jtly, 1968); *Recreations* bird watching, archaeology; *Style*— Dr Charles Foster, ERD; Glebe Farm, Sternfield, nr Saxmundham, Suffolk IP17 1ND (☎ 0728 60 2579)

FOSTER, Sir Christopher David; s of Capt George Cecil Foster (d 1978), and Phyllis Joan, *née* Mappin (d 1964); *b* 30 Oct 1930; *Educ* Merchant Taylor's, King's Coll Cambridge (MA); *m* 26 July 1958, Kay Sheridan, da of Hubert Percy Bullock (d 1987), of Horsehay, Shropshire; 2 s (Oliver Drummond b 1960, Sebastian Luke b 1968), 3 da (Henrietta Sheridan Jane b 1959, Cressida Imogen Dakeyne b 1963, Melissa Catherine Mappin b 1964); *Career* RAOC 1949, cmmd 1 Bn The Seaforth Highlanders Malaya 1949-50, 1 Bn The London Scottish TA 1950-53, General Service Medal Malaya 1950; res fellowship 1954-64: Univ of Pennsylvania, King's Coll Cambridge, Univ of Manchester, Jesus Coll Oxford; official fell and tutor in econs Jesus Coll Oxford 1964-66, dir gen of econ planning Miny of Tport 1966-69, visiting prof of econs and urban studies 1969-70, visiting fell Dept of City Planning Univ of California Berkeley 1970; LSE: head of Centre for Urban Econs 1970-75, prof of econs and urban studies 1975-78, visiting prof of econs 1978-79; dir Centre for Environmental Studies 1976-78; Coopers and Lybrand: head of Econs and Pub Policy Div 1978-84, head of business devpt 1984-85, memb Mgmnt Ctee and MCS Mgmnt Ctee (econs practice ldr) 1988; commercial advsr to the Bd British Telecom 1986-88; memb Smead Ctee on Road Pricing 1962-63, pt/t econ advr to DOE 1974-77, chm Ctee of Inquiry on Roads Goods Licensing 1978-79, memb Ctee of Inquiry into Civil Serv Pay 1981-82, memb Audit Cmmn 1983-88, econ assessor Sizewell B Inquiry 1982-86; memb: ESRC 1985-89, London Docklands Devpt Cmmn 1987-; chm NEDO Construction Industry Sector Group; *Books* The Transport Problem (1963), Politics, Finance and the Role of Economics (1972), Local Government Finance (with R Jackson and M Perlman, 1980); *Recreations* opera, theatre; *Clubs* Reform, RAC; *Style*— Sir Christopher Foster; 6 Holland Park Avenue, London W11 (☎ 071 727 4757); Coopers and Lybrand, Plumtree Court, London EC4A 4HT (☎ 071 822 4795, telex 887470)

FOSTER, Christopher Kenneth; s of Kenneth John Foster, of Sunningdale, and Christina Dorothy, *née* Clark; *b* 5 Nov 1949; *Educ* Harrow HS; *Career* chm and dir Springwood Books Ltd 1975-, dir Chase Corp plc 1985-88; Lord of the Manor Little Hale; *Recreations* golf, music, art; *Clubs* Wentworth Golf; *Style*— Christopher Foster, Esq; Springwood House, The Avenue, Ascot, Berks SL5 7LR (☎ 0990 28 753); 130 Park Lane, London W1 (☎ 071 495 8686)

FOSTER, Christopher Norman; s of Maj-Gen Norman Leslie Foster, CB, DSO, *qv*; *b* 30 Dec 1946; *Educ* Westminster; *m* 1981, Anthea Jane, da of Geoffrey Tait Sammons; 2 s (Nicholas b 1983, Piers b 1986); *Career* Cooper Bros & Co 1965-73, Weatherbys 1973-90; dep chief exec Jockey Club 1990 (keeper of the Match Book 1983-), govr Westminster Sch Soc 1990-, memb Cncl 1972-; FCA; *Recreations* racing, shooting, fishing, gardening; *Clubs* MCC; *Style*— Christopher Foster, Esq; 29 Homefield Rd, Chiswick, London W4 2LW (☎ 081 995 9309); 42 Portman Square, London W1 (☎ 071 486 4921)

FOSTER, David Carrick; s of Ernest John Thomas Carrick Foster (d 1949), and Evelyn Claire Hilda Hunter, *née* Lynes (d 1985); *b* 9 Oct 1936; *Educ* Repton, Leeds Univ (LLB); *m* 27 July 1963, Joan Margaret, da of Lt-Col Ronald Reginald Waugh, OBE, ED (d 1977); 1 s (Daniel b 1973), 2 da (Sarah b 1965, Clair b 1967); *Career* slr 1960, sr ptnr Watson Burton Newcastle 1981 (ptnr 1966-); memb Law Soc; *Recreations* playing the piano and harpsichord; *Style*— David Foster, Esq; 12 Castleton Close, Jesmond, Newcastle upon Tyne, NE2 2HF (☎ 091 281 0859), Watson Burton, 20 Collingwood St, Newcastle upon Tyne NE1 1LB (☎ 091 232 3101, fax 091 232 0532, telex 53529 WATSON G)

FOSTER, David Kenneth Dudley; s of Kenneth Dudley Foster, MBE (d 1972), and Amy Margaret, *née* Walduck (d 1970); *b* 20 April 1931; *Educ* Charterhouse, Pembroke Coll Cambridge; *m* 1 Aug 1962, Hon Susan Elizabeth, *qv*, 2 da of 2 Viscount Bridgeman, KBE, CB, DSO, MC; 3 s (Robert b 1966, Edward b 1967, Simon b 1969); *Career* Accountancy Management Services Ltd; *Recreations* skiing, chess; *Style*— David Foster, Esq; Beech House, Shifnal, Shropshire (☎ 0952 460261)

FOSTER, Derek; MP (Lab) Bishop Auckland 1979-; s of Joseph Foster (d 1959), and Ethel, *née* Ragg (d 1982); *b* 25 June 1937; *Educ* Bede GS Sunderland, St Catherine's Coll Oxford; *m* 1972, (Florence) Anne, da of Thomas Bulmer, of Sunderland; *Career* youth and community worker 1970-73, further educn organiser 1973-74, asst dir of educn Sunderland Cncl 1974-79, chm N of England Devpt Cncl 1974-76, memb Tyne & Wear CC and Sunderland Borough Cncl; additional oppn spokesman Social Security 1982, oppn whip 1982, PPS to Neil Kinnock 1983-85; oppn chief whip 1985-; vice chm Youthaid 1979-85; *Recreations* brass bands, male voice choirs; *Style*— Derek Foster, Esq, MP; 3 Linburn, Rickleton, Washington, Tyne and Wear (☎ 091 417580)

FOSTER, (John) Francis Harold; DSO (1945), OBE (1944), TD (and 3 bars), DL (Sussex 1968); s of Capt William Thomas Benjamin Foster (d 1945), and Lilian Frances, *née* Lea (d 1975); *b* 6 Feb 1904; *Educ* St Leonards Sch Seaford, Uckfield GS; *m* 1, 1930, Dorothy Christian, *née* Brooke (d 1962); m 2, 1963, Gwendolene Rebecca, *née* Funnell; 2 step da; *Career* cmmnd RE TA 1924, Maj 1936, WWII BEF 1940 (despatches), CRE Corps Troops CRE 1 Div 1942-45 (despatches), Substantive Col 1950, Hon Col RE 44 Div 1950-67, Cmdt Sussex ACF 1960-69; chartered architect, private practice at Seaford 1933-73; memb RIBA; *Clubs* Sussex; *Style*— Col Francis Foster, DSO, OBE, TD, DL; Wildbees, 11 Kings Ride, Seaford, E Sussex BN25 2LN (☎ 0323 895526)

FOSTER, Giles Henry; s of Stanley William Foster (d 1986), and Gladys Maude, *née* Moon; *b* 30 June 1948; *Educ* Monkton Combe Sch, Univ of York (BA), RCA (MA); *m* 28 Sept 1974, Nicole Anne, da of Alan Coates, of London; 2 s (George b 1982, William b 1987); *Career* film and TV dir; TV films incl: The Lilac Bus, Monster Maker, Northanger Abbey, Hotel du Lac (BAFTA Award), Silas Marner (BAFTA nomination), Dutch Girls, The Aerodrome, Last Summers Child, The Obelisk, and five scripts by Alan Bennett (incl Talking Heads: A Lady of Letters BAFTA nomination); cinema films: Devices and Desires (Grierson award), Consuming Passions, Tree of Hands; *Clubs* Grouchos; *Style*— Giles Foster, Esq; c/o Anthony Jones, Peters Fraser and Dunlop, 5th Floor, The Chambers, Chelsea Harbour, Lots Rd, London SW10 OXF (☎ 071 376 7676)

FOSTER, Hon Mrs (Gillian Rosemary); o da of 22 Lord Forbes, KBE, *qv*; *b* 3 April 1949; *Educ* St Mary's Sch Wantage; *m* 26 March 1969, Alexander Neil Foster, o s of Lt-Col (Brevet Col) Neil Phipps Foster, DL; 1 s (Michael Alexander b 1 March 1973), 1 da (Lucia Katharine b 12 Feb 1970); *Style*— The Hon Mrs Foster; Church Farmhouse, Blakesley, Towcester, Northants (☎ 0327 860364); 25 Bury Walk, London SW3 (☎ 071 589 7678)

FOSTER, Jerome; s of Cecil William Foster, of East Sheen, London, and Rosaleen, *née* Game (d 1988); *b* 3 Aug 1936; *Educ* Wellington, Univ of Grenoble; *m* 27 May 1961, Joanna, da of Michael Mead, OBE; 1 s (Hugo b 1969), 1 da (Kate b 1972); *Career* Nat Serv 2 Lt Oxfordshire & Bucks LI (now 1 Green Jackets) 1954-56; advertisement mangr Benn Bothers Ltd 1957-61, mangr TLS Times Newspapers Ltd 1961-67, dir Euro Offices Benn Group 1967-72, dir Continuing Educn INSEAD 1972-79, assoc dean for exec educn Carnegie-Mellon Univ Pittsburgh 1979-82; assoc dean: Templeton Coll Oxford 1982-84, exec educn INSEAD 1984-87; chief exec Ambrosetti Europe (mgmnt conslts) 1987-89, dean exec educn London Business Sch 1990-; FRSA; *Recreations* family, Europe, singing, sailing; *Style*— Jerome Foster, Esq; 43 Bainton Rd, Oxford OX2 7AG (☎ 0865 514 400); London Business School, Sussex Place, Regent's Park, London NW1 4SA (☎ 071 262 5050, fax 071 724 7875)

FOSTER, Joanna; *née* Mead; da of Michael Mead, of Winterbourne, Bristol, and Lesley Mead; *b* 5 May 1939; *Educ* Benenden Sch Kent, Grenoble Univ France (Dip); *m* 1961, Jerome Foster, s of Cecil William Foster; 1 s (Hugo b 1969), 1 da (Kate b 1972); *Career* sec Vogue magazine's press attaché INSEAD Fontainebleau France 1975-79, dir of educn corp servs Western Psychiatric Inst and Clinic Univ of Pittsburgh USA 1980-82, head Youth Trg Industl Soc London 1983-85, head Pepperell Unit Industl Soc 1985-88, chair Equal Opportunities Cmmn 1988-; hon fell St Hilda's Coll Oxford; *Recreations* family, food, friends; *Style*— Mrs Joanna Foster; 43 Bainton Rd, Oxford OX2 7AG; Equal Opportunities Commission, Overseas House, Quay St, Manchester M3 3HN (☎ 061 833 9244)

FOSTER, John; CBE (1985); s of David Little Foster (d 1985), of Lochside House, Castle Douglas, Kircudbrightshire, and Isabella, *née* Livingston, JP (d 1979); *b* 13 Aug 1920; *Educ* Whitehill Sch Glasgow, Royal Tech Coll Glasgow; *m* 10 June 1950, Daphne, da of Charles Frederick Househam (d 1965); 1 s (Alasdair Graham b 4 June 1954), 1 da (Caroline Mary b 10 May 1957); *Career* WWII staff Air Miny 1940-45; surveyor in private practice 1937-40, asst planning offr Kirkcudbright CC 1945-47, planning offr Holland CC 1948-52; dir: Peak Nat Park Bd 1954-68 (dep planning offr 1952-54), Countryside Cmmn for Scot 1968-85; pt/t conslt in countryside and recreation 1985-; hon vice pres Countrywide Holidays Assoc, vice pres Ramblers Assoc (Scot), memb Cncl RICS; memb: Cmmn on Nat Parks, Int Union for the Conservation of Nature; hon fell Royal Scot Geographical Soc; ARICS 1943, FRTPI 1946, MRIBA 1950, FRICS 1954, ARIAS 1968; *Recreations* hillwalking, swimming, philately, reading, travel; *Clubs* Cwlth; *Style*— John Foster, Esq, CBE; Birchover, Ferntower Rd, Crieff, Perthshire PH7 3DH (☎ 0764 2336)

FOSTER, Dr John Barnes; s of Richard Rogerson Foster (d 1973), of Newcastle upon Tyne, and Maude, *née* Barnes (d 1987); *b* 26 June 1930; *Educ* Royal GS, Univ of Durham (MB BS, MD); *m* 17 June 1959, Jennifer, da of Thomas Allan Waters (d 1986), of Newcastle upon Tyne; 2 s (Dr Jonathan Charles Foster b 1964, James b 1966), 1 da (Sally Anne b 1962); *Career* Nat Serv Surgn Lt Cdr: RNR 1955-57, RNVR 1957-63; reader in neurology Univ of Newcastle upon Tyne sr conslt neurologist Regnl Neurological Center, currently conslt neurologist Northern RHA; memb: Assoc Br Neurologists, American Neurological Assoc; memb: RSM, Assoc of Physicians of GB and Ireland; FRCP 1979; *Books* Syringomyelia (1973), Progress in Clinical Medicine (1984); *Recreations* golf, skiing, music; *Clubs* Royal and Ancient Golf (St Andrews), Northumberland Golf, Vilamoura Golf (Portugal); *Style*— Dr John B Foster; 4 Lindisfarne Rd, Newcastle upon Tyne NE2 2HE (☎ 091 2811717); Newcastle General Hospital, Westgate Rd, Newcastle upon Tyne (☎ 091 2738811)

FOSTER, Sir John Gregory; 3 Bt (UK 1930); o s of Sir Thomas Saxby Gregory Foster, 2 Bt (d 1957), and Beryl, *née* Ireland; *b* 26 Feb 1927; *Educ* Michaelhouse Coll Natal, Witwatersrand Univ (MB, BCh); *m* 24 Nov 1956, Jean Millicent, eldest da of late Elwin Watts, of Germiston, S Africa; 1 s, 3 da; *Heir* s, Saxby Gregory Foster; *Career* MRCP Edinburgh 1955, med registrar 1955-56, med offr 1957, physician 1961; FRCP Edinburgh 1984; *Style*— Sir John Foster, Bt; 7 Caledon Street, PO Box 1325, George 6530, Cape Province, S Africa (☎ 010 27 441 3251)

FOSTER, John Leonard William; s of Herbert Frederick Brudenell Foster, JP, TD, of Park House, Drumoak, Kincardineshire, and Christine Leonard *née* Lucas Tooth; *b* 20 July 1948; *Educ* Stambridge Earls, Univ of Aberdeen (HSDA); *m* 1 March 1973, Clarinda Anna, da of Maj Bruce William Cottrell (d 1985); 2 s (William Francis Edward b 8 Aug 1976, Edward John Frederick b 25 June 1983), 1 da (Alice Clarinda Edith b 18 Oct 1978); *Career* farming and forestry; chm: Kameruka Estates Ltd 1976-, Drumoak Investments Ltd 1978-, Faskally Investmts Ltd 1978-, Drumoig Ltd 1987-, dir John Foster & Son plc 1982-87; organiser: Ecurie Ecosse Historic Motor Show, St Andrews Horse Trails; *Recreations* motor racing, fishing, shooting, skiing, sailing; *Clubs* Royal Northern (Aberdeen); *Style*— John Foster, Esq; Craigie, Leuchars, St Andrews, Fife

FOSTER, John Stewart; s of Dr Donald Stewart Foster, of Kenilworth, Warwickshire, and Rosemary Margaret Kate, *née* Weber; *b* 16 June 1947; *Educ* The King's Sch Canterbury, Univ of Lancaster (BA); *m* 14 Nov 1969, Alethea Valentine Mary, da of Prof Roberto Weiss (d 1969), of Henley on Thames, Oxfordshire; 2 s (Julien b 1971, William b 1973); *Career* reporter then sr reporter and specialist feature writer Coventry Evening Telegraph 1969-74 (special award winner Midlands Journalist the Year Competition 1974); BBC: regnl journalist TV Birmingham 1974-78, Parly journalist Radio News 1978-82, TV reporter and radio and TV presenter of assorted progs on current Scotland 1982-85, home affrs corr TV Scotland 1985, chief Parly journalist Corporate News 1985-88, chief Parly corr News and Current Affrs 1988-89, chief Parly corr and Parly ed regnl TV News and Current Affrs 1989-; memb House of Commons Press Gallery Ctee 1989; *Recreations* skiing, video-photography, bridge; *Clubs* Belle Toute (Lancaster); *Style*— John Stewart Foster, Esq

FOSTER, Jonathan Rowe; QC (1989); s of Donald Foster (d 1980), and Hilda Eaton, *née* Rowe; *b* 20 July 1947; *Educ* Oundle, Keble Coll Oxford; *m* 18 March 1978, Sarah; 4 s (Thomas b 1980, Henry b 1982, Edward b 1986, Charles b 1989); *Career* called to the Bar Gray's Inn 1970, rec Crown Ct 1988-; govr Ryley's Sch; *Recreations* children, golf, bridge; *Clubs* St James Manchester, Hale Golf, Bowdon Lawn Tennis; *Style*— Jonathan Foster, Esq, QC; 18 St John Street, Manchester (☎ 061 834 0843)

FOSTER, Murray Egerton; s of Maurice Foster, OBE, of Grindleford, Derbyshire, and Mary, *née* Davies; *b* 17 Dec 1946; *Educ* Carliol Carlisle, Welsh Nat Sch of Med (BDS, MB BCh, MScD); *m* 13 July 1974, Margaret Elizabeth, da of Glynmore Jones, of Chester; 2 s (Lawrence b 1981, Richard b 1983), 1 da (Catherine b 1984); *Career* sr registrar St Georges Hosp and St Thomas' Hosp 1977-80, conslt in oral maxillo-facial NW Regnl and postgrad tutor Univ of Ma sec Tameside BMA; memb: RSM, BMA, BDA, Cncl BAOMS; FDS, FFD, FRCSEd; *Books* Dental, Oral and Maxillo-facial Surgery (jtly, 1986); *Recreations* walking, photography; *Clubs* Pillar, Oral Surgery (sec); *Style*— Murray Foster; 9 Townscliffe Lane, Mellor, Stockport SK6 5AW (☎ 061 427 3833); 2 St John St, Manchester (☎ 061 835 1149)

FOSTER, Neil William Derick; s of William Robert Brudenell Foster, *qv*, and Jean Leslie, *née* Urquhart (d 1986); *b* 13 March 1943; *Educ* Harrow, Aix en Provence

Univ; *m* 2 Sept 1989, Anthea Caroline, da of Ian Gibson Macpherson, MC, of The Old Hall, Blofield, Norwich, Norfolk; *Career* underwriting memb Lloyds 1971-, dir John Foster & Sons plc 1975-; dir and chm former: Norfolk Churches Tst 1976-, Norfolk Marketing Ltd 1985-; memb Ctee HHA East Anglia, vice chm CLA Norfolk, chm East Anglia Div Royal Forestry Soc; past chm: The Game Conservancy Norfolk, East Anglia regn Timber Growers UK Ltd; Liveryman Worshipful Co of Clothworkers 1965; *Recreations* shooting, forestry, gardening; *Clubs* Boodles, Norfolk; *Style*— Neil Foster, Esq; Lexham Hall, King's Lynn, Norfolk PE32 2QJ (☎ 0328 701 341); The Estate Office, Lexham Hall, King's Lynn, Norfolk PE32 2QJ (☎ 0328 701 288, fax 0328 700 053)

FOSTER, Nigel Pearson; s of Gordon Pearson Foster (d 1985), of Wilmslow, Cheshire, and Margaret Elizabeth, *née* Bettison (d 1989); *b* 18 Feb 1952; *Educ* Oswestry Sch Shropshire; *m* 20 May 1988, Mary Elizabeth, da of Edward Bangs; 1 da (Elizabeth Margaret b 9 June 1990); *Career* Rowlinson-Broughton 1969-72, Clough Howard Richards Manchester 1972-74, prodn asst Royds Manchester 1974-76, account exec The Advertising and Marketing Organisation 1976-79, TV prodr Wasey Campbell Ewald 1980-82 (account exec 1979-80), TV prodr Foote Cone Belding 1982-84; Head of TV: KMP 1984-86, J Walter Thompson 1989- (TV prodr 1986-89); MIPA; *Style*— Nigel Foster, Esq; J Walter Thompson Ltd, 40 Berkeley Square, London W1X 6AD (☎ 071 499 4040)

FOSTER, Sir Norman Robert; s of Robert Foster (d 1976), of Manchester, and Lilian, *née* Smith (d 1971); *b* 1 June 1935; *Educ* Univ of Manchester Sch of Art (Dip Arch 1961, Cert TP), Yale Univ Sch of Architecture; *m* 18 Aug 1964, Wendy Ann (d 1989), da of late Reginald George Lewis Cheesman; 4 s (Tib b 1965, Cal b 1967, Steve b 1967, Jay b 1986); *Career* Nat Serv RAF 1953-55; architect; fndr Foster Assocs 1967; winner of int competitions 1979-89 for projects incl: Hong Kong and Shanghai Bank, BBC Radio Centre, Nat German Athletics Centre Frankfurt, Stansted Airport Terminal, Telecommunications Tower Barcelona, Bilbao Metro System, King's Cross Masterplan; conslt architect Univ of East Anglia 1978-87; teacher 1967-77: London Poly, Bath Acad of Arts, Univ of Pennsylvania, Architectural Assoc; numerous awards incl: Royal Gold Medal for Architecture 1983, Civic Tst Award 1984, RIBA Awards 1969, 72, 77, 78, 81, RS Reynolds Award 1976, 1979 & 1986, Fin Times Industl Architecture Award 1967, 1970, 1971, 1974, 1981, Premio Compasso d'Oro Award 1987, Ambrose Congreve Award 1980, Kunstpreis Berlin Award 1989, Structural Steel Award 1972, 1980, 1984, 1986, International Prize for Architecture 1976, 1980, Br Tourist Bd Award 1979; tv documentaries incl BBC Omnibus 1981 and Anglia Enterprise 1983, featured in int publications and jls; exhibitions of work held in: London, New York, Paris, Tokyo, Berlin, Madrid, Barcelona, Milan, Florence; work in permanent collection of Museum of Modern Art New York; vice-pres AA 1974 (memb Cncl 1973), memb RIBA Visiting Bd of Educn 1971 (external examiner 1971-73); Hon LittD East Anglia 1980, Hon DSc Bath 1986; memb RIBA 1965, FCSD 1985, ARA 1983, RDI 1988, hon memb Bund Deutscher Architekten 1983, hon fell American Inst of Architects 1980; kt 1990; *Books* The Work of Foster Associates (1978), Norman Foster, Buildings and Projects, Vols 2 and 3 (1989); *Recreations* flying, skiing, running; *Style*— Sir Norman Foster; Foster Associates, Riverside Three, Albert Wharf, 22 Hester Road, London SW11 4AN (☎ 071 738 0455, fax 071 738 1107)

FOSTER, Peter George; s of Thomas Alfred Foster (d 1945), and Eileen Agnes, *née* Moore (d 1980); *b* 1 Oct 1936; *Educ* Merchant Taylor's, CCC Oxford (MA, hon memb Greyhound RFC); *m* 26 Oct 1968, Hilary Anne Foster, da of Thomas Frederick Barton; 2 da (Katrina Jane b 27 June 1969, Jessica Sophie b 4 March 1971); *Career* Baileys Shaw-Gillett: asst slr (formerly articled clerk) 1963, ptnr 1964, sr ptnr 1988-; pres Legalliance Europe; Freeman City of London 1976; memb Law Soc 1964; *Recreations* walking, music, watching sport, archaeology; *Style*— Peter Foster, Esq; Baileys Shaw & Gillett, 17 Queen Square, London WC1N 3RH (☎ 071 837 5455, fax 071 837 0071)

FOSTER, (John) Peter; OBE (1990); s of Francis Edward Foster (d 1953), of Newe Strathdon, and Evelyn Marjorie Forbes (d 1953); *b* 2 May 1919; *Educ* Eton, Trinity Hall Cambridge (MA); *m* 1944, Margaret Elizabeth, da of George John Skipper (d 1948); 1 s (Edward Philip John b 1949), 1 da (Elizabeth Anne b 1946); *Career* cmmnd RE 1941, served Norfolk Div, joined Gds Armd Div 1943, served France and Germany, Capt (SORE2) 30 Corps 1945, discharged 1946; architect; Marshall Sisson: joined 1948, later ptnr, sole ptnr 1971; ptnr with John Peters of Vine Press Hemingford Grey 1957-63; surveyor: Royal Acad of Arts 1965-80, fabric of Westminster Abbey 1973-88; memb: Tech Panel Soc of Protection of Ancient Bldgs 1976, Historic Bldgs Cncl for Eng 1977-84, Advsy Bd Redundant Churches 1979-91; pres Surveyors Club 1980, govr Suttons Hosp Charterhouse 1982, memb Exec Ctee Georgian Gp 1983, tstee Art Workers Guild 1985 (memb 1971, master 1980), chm Cathedral Architects Assoc 1987-90, chm Fabric Ctee Canterbury Cathedral 1990 (memb 1987-), Surveyor Emeritus Westminster Abbey 1989; ARIBA 1949, fell Soc of Antiquaries 1973, memb Fabric Ctee Ely 1990-; Commander brother OStJ 1988; *Recreations* painting, shooting, books; *Clubs* Athenaeum; *Style*— Peter Foster, Esq, OBE; Harcourt, Hemingford Grey, Huntingdon, Cambs PE18 9BJ (☎ 0480 61101)

FOSTER, Peter Martin; CMG (1975); s of Capt Frederick Arthur Peace Foster, RN (d 1948), and Marjorie Kathleen, *née* Sandford (d 1988); *b* 25 May 1924; *Educ* Sherborne, Corpus Christi Coll Cambridge; *m* 1947, Angela Hope, *née* Cross; 1 s, 1 da; *Career* WWII Maj Royal Horse Gds; HM Dip Serv 1948, HM Embassy Vienna 1948-52, FO 1952-54, Warsaw 1954-56, FO 1956-59, S Africa 1959-61, FO 1961-64, Bonn 1964-66, dep high cmmr Kampala 1966-68, Imperial Def Coll 1969, cnsllr Tel Aviv 1970-72, head of Central and S Africa Dept FCO 1972-74, ambass and UK perm rep to Cncl of Europe Strasbourg 1974-78, ambass GDR 1978-81, ret 1981; dir Cncl for Arms Control 1984-86; chm Int Soc Serv (GB) 1985-90; *Style*— Peter Foster, Esq, CMG; Rew Cottage, Abinger Common, Dorking, Surrey (☎ 0306 730114)

FOSTER, Peter Walter; CBE (1983, OBE 1959), MC (1943), TD (1947), DL (Gtr London 1967); s of Harold Foster, of London; *b* 8 Dec 1919; *Educ* Oundle, Imperial Coll; *m* 1949, Anne, da of Arthur Thomas Sturgess, of London; 2 s, 2 da; *Career* served TA 1939-61 (Col); chartered electrical engr; dir William White and Co (Switchgear) Ltd; *Style*— P W Foster, Esq, CBE, MC, TD, DL; 27 Peckarman's Wood, London SE26 6RY

FOSTER, Prof Peter William; s of Percy William Foster (d 1966), and Florence Harriet, *née* Bedford (d 1976); *b* 6 Dec 1930; *Educ* UCL (BSc, PhD); *m* 16 Aug 1952, Elizabeth, da of Walter Goldstern, of Altrincham; 2 s (Anthony P b 1958, Andrew P b 1960), 2 da (Frances M b 1956, Theresa K b 1962); *Career* tech offr Nobel Div ICI 1954-57, assoc prof Univ of Nebraska 1957-58, res chemist E I du Pont de Nemours Inc 1958-63, mangr Du Pont International SA Geneva 1963-66, md and dir Heathcoat Yarns and Fibres and John Heathcoat 1966-82, chm Steam Storage Co Ltd 1975-, md Universal Carbon Fibres Ltd 1982-85, prof Dept Textiles UMIST 1986-; memb: Textile Inst, Chem Soc; FTI, FRSA; *Recreations* chess, theatre; *Clubs* Rotary; *Style*— Prof Peter Foster; Dept of Textiles, UMIST, PO Box 88, Sackville St, Manchester M60 1QD (☎ 061 200 4142, fax 061 228 7040, telex 666094)

FOSTER, Richard Anthony; s of Eric Kenneth Foster (d 1945), of Bournemouth, and Sylvia Renee, *née* France, (now Mrs Westerman); *b* 3 Oct 1941; *Educ* Kingswood Sch, LSE (BSc), Univ of Manchester (MA); *m* 31 Aug 1964, Mary Browning, da of Arthur Leslie James, OBE (d 1990) of Saltburn, Cleveland; 2 s (James b 28 May 1970, William b 27 1973), 1 da (Polly b 12 Aug 1979); *Career* student asst Leicester Museum 1964-66, museum asst Bowes Museum 1967-68, keeper i/c Durham LI Museum and Arts Centre 1968-70; dir: Oxford City and Co Museum 1970-78, Oxfordshire Co Museums 1974-, Merseyside Co Museums 1978-86, Nat Museums and Galleries on Merseyside 1986-, Merseyside Tourism Bd; memb: Bd NW Museums and Art Galleries Serv, Bd Inst of Popular Music Univ of Liverpool; chm Boat Museum Ellesmere Port, advsr Fabric Ctee Liverpool Cathedral; FSA 1976, FMA 1980; *Recreations* sailing, watching football; *Style*— Richard Foster, Esq; National Museums and Galleries on Merseyside, Liverpool Museum, William Brown St, Liverpool, L3 8EN (☎ 051 207 0001, fax 051 207 3759)

FOSTER, Sir Robert Sidney; GCMG (1970, KCMG 1964, CMG 1961), KCVO (1970); s of late Sidney Charles Foster, and late Jessie Edith, *née* Fry; *b* 11 Aug 1913; *Educ* Eastbourne Coll, Peterhouse Cambridge; *m* 1947, Margaret, da of Joseph Charles Walker; *Career* Serv 2 Bn N Rhodesian Regt (Africa and Madagascar) 1940-43; entered Colonial Serv N Rhodesia 1936, sr dist offr 1953, prov cmmr 1957, sec to Min of Native Affairs 1960, chief sec Nyasaland 1961-63, dep govr 1963-64, high cmmr for Western Pacific 1964-68, govr and C-in-C Fiji 1968-70, govr-gen Fiji 1970-73; Offr Légion d'Honneur, KStJ 1968; *Clubs* Leander (Henley on Thames), Royal Over-seas League; *Style*— Sir Robert Foster, GCMG, KCVO; Kenwood, 16 Ardnave Cres, Southampton (☎ 0703 769412)

FOSTER, Rosalind Mary (Mrs R M Englehart); da of Ludovic Anthony Foster (d 1990), of Greatham Manor, Pulborough Sussex, and Pamela Margaret, *née* Wilberforce; *b* 7 Aug 1947; *Educ* Cranborne Chase Sch Tisbury Wiltshire, Lady Margaret Hall Oxford (BA); *m* 2 Jan 1971, Robert Michael Englehart, QC, s of Gustav Axel Englehart 1969), of London; 1 s (Oliver b 1982), 2 da (Alice b 1976, Lucinda b 1978); *Career* called to the Bar Middle Temple 1969, rec Crown Ct 1987-; *Recreations* music, theatre, travel; *Style*— Miss Rosalind Foster; 2 Temple Gardens, The Temple, London EC47 9AY (☎ 071 583 6041)

FOSTER, Roy William John; s of Francis Edwin Foster, of Hawkchurch, Axminster, Devon, and Marjorie Florence Mary, *née* Chapman (d 1944); *b* 25 May 1930; *Educ* Rutlish Sch Merton; *m* 6 Sept 1957, Christine Margaret, da of Albert Victor Toler (d 1972); 2 s (Nicholas Charles Roy b 23 April 1960, d 1969, Richard James b 25 March 1964); *Career* Nat Serv RAF 1953-54, cmmnd PO 1953; qualified CA 1955; ptnr Coopers & Lybrand Deloitte 1960-90; memb Cncl CBI; Freeman City of London; Liveryman: Worshipful Co of Painter Stainers, Worshipful Co of CAs; ATII 1964, FCA 1965; *Recreations* rugby, cricket watching, music, theatre, food and wines; *Clubs* RAC, HAC, MCC, City Livery; *Style*— Roy Foster, Esq; Cuddington, 28 Downs Side, Cheam, Surrey SM2 7EQ (tel and fax : 081 770 1698)

FOSTER, Saxby Gregory; s and h of Sir John Gregory Foster, 3 Bt; *b* 3 Sept 1957; *Style*— Saxby Gregory Esq

FOSTER, Hon Mrs (Susan Elizabeth); *née* Bridgeman; 2 da of 2 Viscount Bridgeman, KBE, CB, DSO, MC; *b* 19 Oct 1935; *m* 1 Aug 1962, David K D Foster, *qv*; 3 s; *Career* former lady-in-waiting to Lady May Abel Smith, when Lady May's husband was govr of Queensland 1958-60; *Style*— The Hon Mrs Foster; Beech House, Shifnal, Shropshire (☎ 0952 460261)

FOSTER, William Robert Brudenell; s of Col Herbert Anderton Foster (d 1930), of Faskally, Pitlochry and Frances Edith Agnes, *née* Brudenell-Bruce (d 1976); *b* 14 April 1911; *Educ* Wellington, CCC Oxford (MA); *m* 1942, Jean Leslie (d 1986), da of Leslie Urquhart, of Brasted Place, Kent; 3 s (Neil b 1943, Richard b 1945, Charles b 1955), 1 da (Melanie (Mrs Boyle) b 1948); *Career* Capt 6 Black Watch RHR, (TA) invalided 1940, Col 30 Middx HG; called to the Bar Inner Temple 1936, dir and chm John Foster & Son Ltd 1939-76, dir and vice chm Enfield Rolling Mills Ltd 1941-76; dir: MIM Hldgs, Mount Isa Mines Ltd 1955-78; dir and chm St Piran Mining Ltd 1943-76, dir and vice chm London Brick Co 1970-82; hon vice pres Br Field Sports Soc; High Sheriff Norfolk 1969-70, High Steward's Ctee Norwich Cathedral 1970-80; Liveryman Worshipful Co of Cloth Workers (Master 1976-77); FRSA; *Recreations* field sports, art, travel; *Clubs* Carlton, Norfolk; *Style*— William Foster, Esq; Church Farm, East Lexham, King's Lynn, Norfolk PE32 2QJ (☎ 0328 701239)

FOSTER-SUTTON, Sir Stafford William Powell; KBE (1957, OBE 1945), CMG 1948, QC (1938 Jamaica, 1948 Fedn of Malaya); s of G W Foster-Sutton; *b* 24 Dec 1898; *Educ* St Mary Magdalen Sch; *m* 1919, Linda Dorothy, da of John Humber Allwood, OBE, of Enfield, St Anne, Jamaica; 1 da (and 1 s decd); *Career* served WW I and in Army to 1926, also in RFC and RAF; called to the Bar Gray's Inn 1926, solicitor-gen Jamaica 1936, attorney-gen Cyprus 1940, Col Cmdg Cyprus Volunteer Force and inspr Cyprus Forces WW II; attorney-gen Kenya 1944-48, actg govr Kenya 1947, attorney-gen Malaya 1948-50, actg high cmmr Aug-Dec 1950, chief justice Fedn Malaya 1950-51, pres W African Court Appeal 1951-55, chief Justice Fedn Nigeria 1955-58 (actg govr-gen 1957); pres Pensions Appeal Tbnl for England and Wales 1958-72; chm: Zanzibar Cmmn of Inquiry 1961, Kenya Regional and Electoral Cmmns 1962-, Malta Referendum Observers 1964-; master Tallow Chandlers' Co 1981, (dep master 1982-83); kt 1951; *Style*— Sir Stafford Foster-Sutton, KBE, CMG, QC; 7 London Rd, Saffron Walden, Essex

FOSTER-THOMPSON, Dr Foster; s of F Foster Thompson (d 1965), of Sunderland, Co Durham, and Maude Ann, *née* Quenet; *b* 18 June 1929; *Educ* Durham Sch, Univ of Durham (MB BS); *m* 1, (m dis 1972), Shirley Margaret Creighton, *née* Nuttal; m 2, Sonja Fredrikke, da of Olav Poppe; 1 s (Andrew Iain Thompson), 1 da (Abigail Margaret Sargent); *Career* Intelligence Corps 1946-48, Capt RAMC (TA) 1954-57; conslt physician 1964-; md: John Thompson & Sons Ltd Sunderland 1968-70, Air Commuter Ltd 1970-72; chm Coventry Airport Users Assoc 1970; aviation med examiner: CAA 1970-, Dept of Transportation Federal Aviation Admin of USA 1988-; owner Newlands Nursing Home 1972-89; hon treas Hosp Conslts Specialists Assoc 1987-; MRCP 1964, memb Br Nuclear Med Soc 1989; *Recreations* aviation, golf; *Style*— Dr Foster Foster-Thompson; 1 Clarendon Crescent, Leamington Spa, Warwickshire CV32 5NR (☎ 0926 335487); Walsgrave General Hospital, Dept of Medicine, Clifford Bridge Rd, Coventry CV2 2DX (☎ 0203 602020)

FOTHERGILL, Michael John; s of Frederick Samuel Abraham Fothergill, of Pembridge, Herefordshire, and Ethel Irene, *née* Frappell; *b* 23 March 1945; *Educ* Latymer Upper Sch, Jesus Coll Cambridge (MA); *m* 28 Aug 1970, Christina Anne, da of Maj Charles Frederick Bushell, OBE, of Milton Keynes; 2 s (Alexander b 1974, Julian b 1979); *Career* founded M J Fothergill Assocs 1973, now chm and md Fothergill & Co Ltd, consulting civil and structural engrs; maj projects incl Euro HQ for Air Products Hersham, Jamaican High Cmmn London, Livery Hall of Founders' Co, Theatre Wycombe Abbey Girls' Sch; tstee Berrite Tst 1980 (managing tstee 1988), md Berrite Ltd 1990; dir: Richmond Computer Services 1977, Rivercourt Insurance Ltd 1989; chm Thames Amateur Rowing Cncl 1978, 1979, 1980; chm Nat Rowing Championships of GB 1981, 1982; chm Amateur Rowing Assoc 1982, 1983; int umpire (FISA); tstee Jesus Coll Cambridge BC Tst; CEng, FICE, MIStructE, MConsE; *Recreations* family, rowing, skiing; *Clubs* London Rowing, Leander; *Style*— Michael Fothergill, Esq; 14 Bolton Rd, Chiswick, London, W4 3TB (☎ 081 994 1010);

Fothergill & Co Ltd, 62 Hill St, Richmond, Surrey TW9 1TW (☎ 081 948 4165, fax 081 948 5105)

FOUCAR, Antony Emile; s of Emile Charles Victor Foucar (d 1963), of Devon, and Mabel Emma, *née* Harris (d 1956); *b* 3 Aug 1926; *m* 1959, Anne, da of Arthur Otway Gosden (d 1950), of Sussex; 2 s (Adam b 1960, James b 1961), 1 da (Charlotte b 1964); *Career* called to the Bar Middle Temple 1950; chm: River & Mercantile Trust plc 1985, F & C Pacific Investment Trust plc 1985; *Clubs* Oriental, Royal Wimbledon Golf; *Style*— Antony Foucar, Esq; Greystock, 5 Peek Crescent, London SW19 5ER (☎ 081 9468973, fax 081 944 0853)

FOULDS, Gordon Lang; s of William Foulds (d 1987), of Paisley, and Elizabeth Young, *née* Lang (d 1988); *b* 7 May 1937; *Educ* Paisley GS; *m* 29 Aug 1959, Margaret Mortimer, da of William Crawford (d 1947); 1 s (Paul b 1961), 1 da (Natalie b 1970); *Career* W Lang Jr & Co Ltd (later W Lang Paisley Ltd): dir 1965-67, md 1967-85; dir Brownlee plc 1985-87, mangr Sinclair Lang Ltd 1990- (dir 1987-90); dir St Mirren Football Club 1977-81, pres Rotary Club Paisley 1986-87 (memb); FInstD; *Recreations* golf, bowls; *Clubs* Whitecraigs Golf, Whitecraigs Bowling; *Style*— Gordon Foulds, Esq; 7 Broomcroft Rd, Little Broom, Newton Mearns, Glasgow G77 5ER (☎ 041 639 1539); Earls Rd, Grangemouth, Stirlingshire FK3 8UU (☎ 0324 482 778, fax 0324 665397, telex 778464); 102 New Sneddon St, Paisley, Renfrewshire PA3 2BH (☎ 041 889 8826, fax 041 889 5541, telex 778950, car 0860 413113)

FOULDS, Roy; s of Franklin Foulds (d 1964), of Long Eaton, and Agnes, *née* Merriman; *b* 30 Jan 1947; *Educ* Nottingham HS for Boys; *m* 2 Aug 1969, Christine, da of late Rev Ronald E Thorne; 1 s (Simon b 2 May 1972), 1 da (Rachel b 19 Aug 1975); *Career* Barclays Bank plc: joined 1963, accountant Gallowtree Gate Leicester 1973-75, office mangr Loughborough 1975-78, asst mangr Carlisle 1978-80, mangr Business Advsy Service 1980-81, mangr Old Market Square Nottingham 1981-82; admin St John's Coll Nottingham 1982-89, gen sec Fin Div Methodist Church 1989-; chm Methodist Ministers' Housing Soc; sec: Central Fin Bd Methodist Church, Methodist Ministers' Retirement Fund; govr Kingswood Sch Bath, memb various Methodist bds and ctees; ACIB 1969; *Recreations* music, theatre, reading, collecting; *Style*— Roy Foulds, Esq; The Methodist Church Division of Finance, 1 Central Buildings, Westminster, London SW1H 9NH (☎ 071 222 8010, fax 071 930 5355)

FOULDS, Prof Wallace Stewart; CBE (1988); s of James Foulds (d 1977), of Renfrewshire, and Nellie Margach, *née* Stewart; *b* 26 April 1924; *Educ* Geo Watson's Coll Edinburgh, Paisley GS, Univ of Glasgow (MB ChB, MD, ChM); *m* 20 Dec 1947, Margaret Holmes, da of Albert Daniel Walls (d 1952), of Ealing; 1 s (Iain Stewart b 1950), 2 da (Margaret Elizabeth (Mrs Rudd) b 1951, Alison Sutherland (Mrs Tambling) b 1958); *Career* RAF Med Branch 1947-49; house surgn to Sir Charles Illingworth Glasgow 1946-47, res surgn Moorfields Eye Hosp London 1950-52, sr registrar UCH 1953-58, res fell and hon sr lectr Inst of Ophthalmology 1953-64, conslt ophthalmologist Addenbrooke's Hosp Cambridge 1958-64, hon lectr Univ of Cambridge 1960-64, prof of ophthalmology Univ of Glasgow 1964-89, conslt ophthalmologist Gtr Glasgow Health Bd 1964-89; hon memb: NZ Ophthalmological Soc, Egyptian Opthalmological Soc, Portuguese Ophthamological Soc; memb and pres: Coll of Ophthalmologists, Ophthalmological Soc UK, Faculty of Ophthalmologists, Jules Gonin Soc (vice pres); memb: Assoc Eye Research, American Macula Soc, Oxford Ophthalmological Congress; FCOphth (current pres), FRCS (England and Glasgow), FRACO; *Books* pubns relating to ophthalmology; *Recreations* sailing, gardening, natural history; *Clubs* Royal Scot Automobile; *Style*— Prof Wallace Foulds, CBE; 68 Dowanside Rd, Glasgow G12 9DL; Ross Hall AMI Hosp, 221 Crookston Rd, Glasgow G52 3NQ; The Glasgow Nuffield Hosp, Beaconsfield Rd, Glasgow G12 0PJ (☎ 041 810 3151, 041 334 9441, fax 041 882 7439, 041 337 1088)

FOULIS; *see*: Liston-Foulis

FOULIS, Sir Iain Primrose Liston; 13 Bt (NS 1634), Bt of Colinton (1634), and Bt of Ravelston (1661, But For The Attainder); s of Lt-Col James Alastair Liston Foulis (d 1942, s of Lt-Col Archibald Primrose Liston-Foulis (ka 1917), 4 s of 9 Bt), by his w Kathleen, da of Lt-Col John Moran and Countess Olga de la Hogue, yr da of Marquis De La Hogue (Isle of Mauritius); suc kinsman, Sir Archibald Charles Liston-Foulis, 12 Bt (d 1961); Sir James Foulis, 2 Bt, was actively engaged in the wars of Scotland after the death of Charles I and was knighted during his f's lifetime; distant cous of Sir Archibald Primrose Bt of Ravelston who took arms and name of Primrose; fought with Hussars at Culloden, beheaded at Carlisle 1746, Title of Ravelston and Estates forfeited; *b* 9 Aug 1937; *Educ* Hodder, St Mary's Hall, Stonyhurst, Cannington Farm Inst Bridgewater; *Career* Nat Serv Argyll and Sutherland Highlanders 1957-59, Cyprus 1958; language tutor Madrid 1959-61 and 1966-; trainee exec Bank of London and S America 1962, Bank of London and Montreal Ltd Bahamas, Guatemala and Nicaragua 1963-65, sales Toronto Canada 1966; landowner 1962-; *Recreations* mountain walking, country pursuits (hunting wild boar), swimming, camping, travelling, car racing and rallies, looking across the plains of Castille to the mountains; *Clubs* RACE, Friends of the Castles, Friends of the St James' Way (all in Spain); *Style*— Sir Iain Foulis, Bt; Residencial Cuzco, Calle Soledad 11, Portal 5-2-C, San Agustin de Guadalix, 28750 Madrid, Spain (☎ 010 34 91 8418978)

FOULKES, George; JP (Edinburgh 1975), MP (Lab) Carrick, Cumnock and Doon Valley 1983-; s of late George Foulkes, and Jessie M A W Foulkes; *b* 21 Jan 1942; *Educ* Keith GS, Haberdashers' Aske's, Univ of Edinburgh; *m* 1970, Elizabeth Anna, da of William Hope; 2 s, 1 da; *Career* pres Univ of Edinburgh Students Rep Cncl 1963-64, Scottish Union of Students 1965-67, rector's assessor at Univ of Edinburgh; dir: Enterprise Youth 1968-73, Age Concern Scotland 1973-79; cncllr and bailie Edinburgh City Cncl 1970-75, chm Lothian Region Educn Ctee 1974-79, cncllr Lothian Regnl Cncl 1975-79; chm: Educn Ctee Convention of Scot Local Authys 1976-79, Scottish Adult Literacy Agency 1977-79; MP (Lab) S Ayrshire 1979-, memb Commons Select Ctee on Foreign Affrs, jt chm Commons All-Party Pensioners' Ctee; front bench oppn spokesman: Euro and Community Affrs 1983-85, Foreign Affrs 1985-; memb: Exec Cwlth Parly Assoc (UK), Inter Parly Union (GB); *Recreations* boating, supporting Heart of Midlothian FC; *Clubs* Edinburgh Univ Staff; *Style*— George Foulkes, Esq, JP, MP; 8 Southpark Rd, Ayr, Scotland (☎ 0292 265776); House of Commons, London SW1A 0AA

FOULKES, Sir Nigel (Gordon); s of Louis Augustine Foulkes and Winifred Foulkes; *b* 29 Aug 1919; *Educ* Gresham's, Balliol Coll Oxford (MA); *m* ; 1 s, 1 da; m 2, 1948, Elisabeth, da of Ewart B Walker, of Toronto; *Career* WWII Sqdn Ldr RAF; formerly with: H P Bulmer, P E Management Group, International Nickel, Rank Xerox (dep md 1964-67, md 1967-70); dir: Charterhouse Group 1972-83, Bekaert Group 1973-85, Stone-Platt Industries 1975-80; chm: Brtish Airports Authy 1972-77, CAA 1977-82, Equity Capital for Industry 1983-86 (vice-chm 1982-83), ECI Managment Jersey 1986-, ECI International Management Ltd 1987-, Equity Capital Trustee Ltd 1983-90; CBIM; kt 1980; *Clubs* RAF; *Style*— Sir Nigel Foulkes; ECI Ventures, Brettenham House, Lancaster Place, London WC2E 7EN (☎ 071 606 1000)

FOULKES, Prof (Albert) Peter; s of Henry Foulkes, of Yorks, and Edith Cavell, *née* O'Mara (d 1989); *b* 17 Oct 1936; *Educ* Univ of Sheffield (BA), Univ of Cologne, Univ of Tulane (PhD); *m* 1959, (Barbara) Joy, da of William Joseph French (d 1981); 2 da (Imogen b 21 May 1960, Juliet b 26 Nov 1961); *Career* prof Univ of Stanford California 1965-75, prof of German Univ of Wales 1977-; Alexander Von Humboldt fell 1972; Inst of Linguists: memb Cncl 1982-89, chm Examinations Bd 1985-, tstee 1986-; FIL 1982; *Books* The Reluctant Pessimist, Franz Kafka (1967), The Search for Literary Meaning (1975), Literature and Propaganda (1983); *Recreations* gardening, rambling, theatre, conjuring, photography; *Style*— Prof Peter Foulkes; Clara, Prades, 66500 France (☎ 010 33 6896 4288); School of European Studies, University of Wales, PO Box 908, Cardiff (☎ 0222 874 232)

FOUNTAIN, Eric Dudley; OBE (1986); s of William Arthur Fountain (d 1957), of Markyate, Herts, and Lily Eva, *née* Severn; *b* 15 March 1929; *m* 18 May 1957, Yvonne Ruby, da of Edward Blacknell (d 1967); 2 s (Roderic Mark, Gregory Richard), 1 da (Lynn Janette); *Career* chm: Inst of Motor Indust, Becenta (Beds and Chiltern Enterprise Agency), Indust Matters for E Anglia, Luton Int Airport, Gibbs & Dandy plc, Luton Initative Ltd; pres Luton Industl Coll, area pres St John Ambulance, pres Luton Beds and Dist C of C, vice chm Bedfordshire TEC; High Sheriff Elect Bedfordshire; FIMI, FInstD; *Recreations* golf, football, tennis; *Style*— Eric Fountain, Esq, OBE; 41 Church Rd, Westoning, Bedfordshire MK45 5LP (☎ 0525 712352)

FOUNTAIN, Malcolm Gordon; s of Gordon Arthur Fountain (d 1988), and Evelyn Marie, *née* Mannion; *b* 31 July 1947; *Educ* Brockington HS Enderby Leicestershire; *m* 1, 30 Nov 1968 (m dis 1976), Linda Susan, da of Robert Wood (d 1986), of 31 Middlesex Rd, Aylestone, Leics; 1 s (Mark Edward b 1973), 1 da (Sarah Louise b 1971); m 2, 30 June 1990, Jane Elizabeth *née* Starling; *Career* sr ptnr Fountain Greeting Cards 1978-; memb Leics Aero Club Ltd; *Recreations* flying; *Style*— Malcolm Fountain, Esq; Sunny Dykes, 36 Knights End Rd, Great Bowden, Market Harborough, Leics LE16 7EY (☎ 0858 66365); Fountain (Greeting Cards), 92 Freemans Common Rd, Leicester LE2 7SQ (☎ 0533 546804, fax 0533 471576, car 0860 319892)

FOURCIN, Prof Adrian John; *b* 30 Aug 1927; *Career* prof UCL 1977- (sr scientific offr 1960, reader in experimental phonetics 1966); *Style*— Prof Adrian Fourcin; University College London, London WC1E 6BT (☎ 071 387 1055, fax 071 380 7408)

FOURIE, Johan; s of Johan Fourie, of Cape Town, SA, and Isabella Johanna, *née* Prins; *b* 3 March 1949; *Educ* Rhodes Univ Grahamstown SA (BA); *m* 1 (m dis 1982), Anne Persida Hay; m 2, 16 Dec 1988, Lynne Anne, da of Morris Hannah Pixley, of Bellingham, USA; 1 da (Lily b 2 Aug 1990); *Career* client serv dir Lintas Advertising Johannesburg SA 1978-79, dir Lintas London 1980-82, ptnr and dir FCB Partnership Johannesburg SA 1983-86, dir Publicis London 1986-89, dir and mgmnt supervisor DMB&B 1989-90, chief exec Yellowhammer Advertising Ltd 1990-; memb: Progressive Party Youth Movement 1973-75, Inkatha 1976-77, Detainees Parents Support Ctee 1984-86; memb Inst of Mktg Mgmnt; *Publications* author of various SA newspaper articles on apartheid and detentions (1984-86), Aids and the Implications for Advertisers (Marketing Week, 1987); *TV film documentary* Witness to Apartheid (contrib 1986); *Recreations* tennis, long distance running, reading, cinema, theatre, opera; *Clubs* Vanderbilt Racquet, Holland Park Lawn Tennis, LRRC, Nat Film Theatre; *Style*— Johan Fourie, Esq; Yellowhammer Advertising Limited, 76 Oxford St, London W1A 1DT (☎ 071 436 5000, fax 071 436 4630, telex 8953837)

FOURMAN, Prof Michael Paul; s of Prof Lucien Paul Rollings Fourman (d 1968), of Leeds, and Dr Julia Mary, *née* Hunton (d 1981); *b* 12 Sept 1950; *Educ* Allerton Grange Sch Leeds, Univ of Bristol (BSc), Univ of Oxford (MSc, DPhil); *m* 12 Nov 1982, Jennifer Robin, da of Hector Grainger Head (d 1970), of Sydney, Aust; 1 s (Maximillian b 1987), 1 da (Paula b 1984); *Career* jr res fell Wolfson Coll Oxford 1974-78, JF Ritt asst prof mathematics Columbia Univ NY 1976-82; Dept of Electrical and Electronic Engrg Brunel Univ: res fell 1983-86, Hirst reader in integrated circuit design 1986, prof of formal systems 1986-88; prof computer systems Univ of Edinburgh 1988-; *Recreations* cooking, sailing; *Style*— Prof Michael Fourman; Department of Computer Science, University of Edinburgh, James Clerk Maxwell Building, The King's Buildings, Edinburgh EH9 3JZ (☎ 031 650 5197, fax 031 667 7209)

FOWDEN, Sir Leslie; s of Herbert Fowden, and Amy D Fowden; *b* 13 Oct 1925; *Educ* UCL (PhD); *m* 1949, Margaret Oakes; 1 s, 1 da; *Career* UCL: lectr in plant chemistry 1950-55, reader 1956-64, prof 1964-73, dean Faculty of Sci 1970-73; dir: Rothamsted Experimental Station 1973-86, AFRC Inst of Arable Crops Res 1986-88; chm Agric Vet Advsy Ctee Br Cncl 1987; memb: Cncl Royal Soc 1970-72, Scientific Advsy Panel Royal Botanic Gardens Kew 1977- (Bd of Tstees 1983-); FRS; kt 1982; *Style*— Sir Leslie Fowden; 31 Southdown Rd, Harpenden, Herts

FOWKE, Sir David Frederick Gustavus; 5 Bt (UK 1814), of Lowesby, Leicestershire; s of late Lt-Col Gerrard Fowke, 2 s of 3 Bt; suc unc, Sir Frederick Fowke, 4 Bt (d 1987); *b* 28 Aug 1950; *Style*— Sir David Fowke, Bt

FOWLE, (William) Michael Thomas; s of William Thomas Fowle (d 1968), of Salisbury, and Nancy, *née* Williams (d 1971); *b* 8 Jan 1940; *Educ* Rugby, Clare Coll Cambridge (MA); *m* (m dis); 1 da (Emma), 1 s (John); *Career* KPMG Peat Marwick McLintock: ptnr 1976-, memb Bd 1982, sr UK banking and fin ptnr 1986-90, chm UK Planning Ctee 1989, chm KPMG Banking & Finance Group 1989, sr UK audit ptnr 1990; FCA (ACA 1965); *Recreations* collecting; *Clubs* City of London Club; *Style*— Michael Fowle, Esq; KPMG Peat Marwick McLintoch, 1 Puddle Dock, London EC3V 4PD (☎ 071 236 8000)

FOWLER, Prof Alastair David Shaw; s of David Fowler (d 1939), and Maggie, *née* Shaw (d 1978); *b* 17 Aug 1930; *Educ* Queens Park Sch Glasgow, Univ of Glasgow, Univ of Edinburgh (MA), Pembroke Coll Oxford (MA), Queen's Coll Oxford (DPhil, DLitt); *m* 23 Dec 1950, Jenny Catherine, da of Ian James Simpson (d 1981), of Giffnock House, Helensburgh; 1 s (David b 1960), 1 da (Alison b 1954); *Career* jr res fell Queen's Coll Oxford 1955-59, visiting instr Univ of Indiana 1957-58, lectr Univ Coll Swansea 1959-61, fell and tutor of Eng lit BNC Oxford 1962-71; visiting prof: Univ of Columbia 1964, Univ of Virginia 1969, 1979 and 1985-; Regius prof of rhetoric and Eng lit Univ of Edinburgh 1972-84, visiting fell Cncl of Humanities Univ of Princeton 1974, fell of humanities Res Centre Canberra 1980, visiting fell All Souls Coll Oxford 1984, univ fell Univ of Edinburgh 1984-87, memb Inst Advanced Study Princeton 1966 and 1980; external assessor Open Univ 1972-77; advsy ed: New Literary History, English Literary Renaissance, Spenser Encyclopaedia, Word and Image, Swansea Review, The Seventeenth Century, Connotations Translation and Literature; memb: Harrap Academic Advsy Ctee 1983-89, Scottish Arts Cncl 1972-74, Nat Printed Books Panel 1977-79; FBA 1974, AUT 1971-84; memb: Carlyle Soc (hon vice pres 1972), Eng Union Edinburgh (pres 1972), Renaissance Soc, Renaissance Eng Text Soc, Soc Emblem Studies, Spenser Soc, Bibliographical Soc Virginia; *Books* Spenser and the Numbers of Time (1964), The Poems of John Milton (with John Carey, 1968), Triumphal forms (1970), Conceitful Thought (1975), Catacomb Suburb (1976), From the Domain of Arnheim (1982), Kinds of Literature (1982), A History of English Literature (1987); *Recreations* swimming; *Clubs* United Oxford and Cambridge, Scottish Arts; *Style*— Prof Alastair Fowler; Dept of English Literature, Univ of Edinburgh, George Square, Edinburgh EH8 9JX (☎ 031 667 1011 ext 6259, 031 667 7681); Dept of English, University of Virginia, Wilson Hall, Charlottesville, va 22903, USA (☎ 804 924 7105, 804 979 9119)

FOWLER, Christopher Gordon; s of Gordon Fowler, of Cardiff, Wales, and Elizabeth

Aled, *née* Biggs; *b* 19 March 1950; *Educ* King Alfred's GS Wantage, Middx Hosp Med Sch, Univ of London (BSc, MB BS); *m* 15 Dec 1973, Clare Juliet, da of Peter Amyas Wright, of Horton-on-Studley, Oxon; 1 s (William b 9 Aug 1980), 1 da (Alice b 28 June 1977); *Career* sr lectr in urology London Hosp Med Sch 1988- (lectr 1982), conslt urologist The London Hosp and Newham Health Dist 1988-; author of articles and chapters on fibreoscopy, laser surgery and uro-neurology; MRCP, FRCS (Urol); *Recreations* horse riding, jogging, family; *Clubs* Y; *Style*— Christopher Fowler, Esq; Department of Urology, The Royal London Hospital, London E1 1BB (☎ 071 377 7327)

FOWLER, Dr Clare Juliet; da of Peter Wright, of Oxford, and Dr Jean Crum; *b* 1 July 1950; *Educ* Wycombe Abbey Sch, Middx Hosp Med Sch; *m* 15 Dec 1973, Christopher Gordon Fowler; 1 s (William Gordon Peter b 9 Aug 1980), 1 da (Alice Clare b 28 June 1977); *Career* sr registrar in clinical neurophysiology Middx Hosp and Nat Hosp 1984-86; conslt in clinical neurophysiology: Bart's 1987-89, Middx and UCH 1987-; conslt in uro-neurology Nat Hosp 1987-, hon conslt Eastman Dental Hosp 1988-; memb Cncl EEG Soc 1987, hon sec Clinical Automatic Res Soc 1986-89, memb RSM; *Style*— Dr Clare Fowler; 27 Lime Grove, London W12 8EE; Dept of Uro-Neurology, The National Hospital, Queen Square, London WC1N 3BG (☎ 071 837 3611)

FOWLER, Gerald Teasdale; s of James A Fowler (d 1964), of Long Buckby, Northants, and Alfreda, *née* Teasdale; *b* 1 Jan 1935; *Educ* Northampton GS, Lincoln Coll Oxford, Univ of Frankfurt-am-Main (BA, MA); *m* 1982, Lorna Fowler, da of William Lloyd (d 1983), of Ribbleton, Preston; 1 s (Julian Giles); *Career* pt/t lectr Pembroke Coll Oxford 1958-59, lectr Hertford and Lincoln Coll Oxford 1959-65; asst dir Huddersfield Poly 1970-72, prof of educnl studies Open Univ 1972-74, prof assoc Dept of Govt Brunel Univ 1977-80, dep dir Preston Poly 1980-81; rector NE London Poly 1982-, vice chm Ctee of Dirs of Polytechnics 1986-88 (chm 1988-90); pres: Comparative Educn in Euro Soc 1980, Assoc of Business Execs 1979-81; memb: Oxford City Cncl 1960-64, Wrekin DC (ldr) 1973-77, Shropshire CC 1979-84, The Wrekin 1966-70 and 1974-79; jt Parly sec to: Min of Technol 1967-69, Min of State DES Oct 1969-June 1970, March-Oct 1974 and Jan-Sept 1976; UK rep PCCU Cncl of Europe 1986-, Erasmus Advsy Ctee EC 1990-; FBIM 1984, FRSA 1985, FABAC 1986, HonFABE 1981; *Books* Education In Britain & Ireland (1973), Decision-Making In British Education Systems (ed 1974), Development in Recurrent & Lifelong Education (ed 1987); author of numerous educnl articles and Open Univ Units; *Clubs* Reform; *Style*— Prof Gerald Fowler; Polytechnic of East London, Romford Road, London E15 4LZ (☎ 081 590 7722, fax 081 519 3740)

FOWLER, Godfrey Heath; OBE; s of Donald Heath Fowler (d 1985), of Wolverley, Worcs, and Dorothy, *née* Bealey (d 1987); *b* 1 Oct 1931; *Educ* Sebright Sch, University Coll Oxford (MA, BM BCh); *m* 15 Sept 1962, Sissel, da of Arnfred Vidnes (d 1983), of Oslo, Norway; 2 s (Jeremy Kristen b 1964, Adrian Dag b 1965); *Career* GP Oxford 1959-, professorial fell Balliol Coll and reader in gen practice Univ of Oxford 1978-; *Books* Preventive Medicine in General Practice (1983), Essentials of Preventive Medicine (1984); *Recreations* skiing, mountaineering, photography; *Style*— Dr Godfrey Fowler, OBE; Orchard House, Squitchey Lane, Oxford OX2 7LD (☎ 0865 58331); 19 Beaumont St, Oxford (☎ 0865 240501)

FOWLER, Ian; s of Norman William Frederick Fowler, OBE, QPM, of Herne Bay, Kent, and late Alice May, *née* Wakelin; *b* 20 Sept 1932; *Educ* The King's Sch Canterbury, St Edmund Hall Oxford (MA); *m* 3 April 1961, Gillian Cecily Fowler, JP, da of late Desmond Allchin; 2 s (Aidan Lewis b 12 May 1966, Edmund Ian Carloss b 18 March 1970), 1 da (Sarah May b 1964); *Career* Nat Serv 2 Lt (Lt TA) 2 Bn The Green Howards 1951-53; called to the Bar Gray's Inn 1957; princ chief clerk and clerk to Ctee of Magistrates Inner London Magistrates' Courts Serv 1979- (joined 1959); cncllr: Herne Bay UDC 1961-74, Canterbury City Cncl 1974-83; Mayor of Canterbury 1976-77; Court memb Univ of Kent 1976-; *Recreations* reading; *Style*— Ian Fowler, Esq; 6 Dence Park, Herne Bay, Kent (☎ 0227 375530); ILMCS, 3rd Floor, North West Wing, Bush House, Aldwych WC2 (☎ 071 836 9331, fax 071 379 6694)

FOWLER, Lady Jennifer Evelyn; *née* Chichester; da of 7 Marquess of Donegall; *b* 3 April 1949; *m* 1971, John Robert Henry Fowler; 2 s (Robert Henry b 22 Sept 1975, Charles James b 9 Oct 1977); *Style*— The Lady Jennifer Fowler; Rahinston, Summerhill, Co Meath

FOWLER, Jennifer Joan; da of Russell Aubrey Fowler (d 1971), and Lucy, *née* Tobitt; *b* 14 April 1939; *Educ* Bunbury HS, Univ of W Aust (BA, BMus, DipEd); *m* 18 Dec 1971, John Bruce, s of Maj Frederick Paterson (d 1983); 2 s (Martin b 1973, Adrian b 1976); *Career* composer; major works: Hours of the Day (for 4 singers, 2 oboes and 2 clarinets, 1968), Ravelation (for string quintet 1971), Veni Sancte Spiritus (for 12 solo singers, 1971), Chant with Garlands (for orchestra, 1974), Voice of the Shades (for soprano, oboe, violin, 1977), Tell Out My Soul (for soprano, cello, piano, 1980), When David Heard (for choir and piano, 1982), Echoes from an Antique land (for ensemble, 1983), Lament (for baroque oboe, viol, 1988), And Ever Shall Be (for mezzo and ensemble, 1989); int prizes: Acad of the Arts Berlin, Radcliffe award of GB, Gedok prize Mannheim; memb: Composers Guild of GB, Women in Music, EMAS, SPNM, Fellowship of Aust Composers; *Recreations* literature, gardening; *Style*— Ms Jennifer Fowler; 21 Deodar Road, Putney, London SW15 2NP

FOWLER, John; s of Jack Fowler, of Porlock, Somerset, and Ida Annie, *née* Odgen; *b* 3 Oct 1947; *Educ* Bury GS, Southampton Univ (BA); *m* 17 Feb 1979, Lesley Margaret, da of Melvyn Samuel Jeffries (d 1984), of Fulham; *Career* dir res and planning: United Biscuits Ltd 1967-74, Cadbury Schweppes 1974-78, McCann Erickson Advertising 1978-85, Burson-Marsteller 1985-; memb Market Res Soc; *Recreations* reading, eating, drinking, driving, France; *Clubs* Chelsea Arts; *Style*— John Fowler, Esq; 77 Santos Rd, London SW18 (☎ 081 870 9245); Burson Marsteller, 24-28 Bloomsbury Way, London WC1A 2PX (☎ 071 831 6262, fax 071 430 1033, telex 267531)

FOWLER, Keith Harrison; s of late Lancelot Harrison Fowler; *b* 20 May 1934; *Educ* Aldenham; *m* 1961, Vicki Belinda, *née* Pertwee; 3 c; *Career* Lt Army Suez Canal; exec chm Edman Communications Group plc 1977-88, chief exec Cresta Corporate Services Ltd 1988-89, dir Cresta Holdings Ltd 1988-89, dir KLP Group plc 1990-; memb Cncl Nat Advertising Benevolent Soc 1978-, govr Winchester House Sch 1968-, dir Pertwee Holdings 1982-; ACIS; *Recreations* riding, crested china, classic cars, pictures; *Clubs* Arts, Solus; *Style*— Keith Fowler, Esq; Little Hundridge Farm, Little Hundridge Lane, Great Missenden, Bucks (☎ 024 06 2034); KLP Group plc, No 1 Craven Hill, London W2 3EN (☎ 071 723 4388)

FOWLER, Lionel Albert; s of Alan Jack Fowler (d 1976), of 17 The Terrace, Finchfield, Wolverhampton, and Violet Florence Fowler; *b* 23 May 1952; *m* 10 May 1975, (Margaret) Mary, da of George Griffin (d 1985); 1 s (James Alexanda Lionel b 23 May 1983), 1 da (Suzanne Louise b 28 May 1981); *Career* buyer Alcan Metal Centres 1968-74, salesman RTZ Metal Stockholders 1974-86 (full bd memb 1983), md Skipper Gp 1990- (sales and mktg dir 1987-90); memb IOD 1988; *Recreations* golf; *Clubs* Brocton Hall Golf; *Style*— Lionel Fowler, Esq; Skipper Group, Skipper House, Metroplex Business Centre, Broadway, Salford, Manchester M5 2UY (☎ 061 848 7801, car 0860 832832, home 078 571 4023)

FOWLER, Maurice Anthony; s of Benjamin Arthur Fowler (d 1975), of Broadstairs, Kent, and Dorothy Fowler (d 1970); *b* 17 July 1937; *Educ* Whitgift Sch Croydon; *m* 9 Sept 1961, Evelyn Jessica, da of Joseph Sidney Currell (d 1961), of Croydon, Surrey; 1 s (Russell b 1967), 1 da (Louise b 1964); *Career* CA Hartley Fowler 1971-; memb London Borough of Croydon, treas Croydon C of C, govr Whitgift Fndn; Freeman City of London, Liveryman Worshipful Co of Carmen; FCA 1961, FCIArb 1965; *Recreations* politics, sport, bridge; *Clubs* City Livery; *Style*— Maurice Fowler, Esq; 240 London Rd, Mitcham, Surrey CR4 3TY (☎ 081 646 4522, fax 081 640 3540, car 0836 6

FOWLER, Rt Hon Sir (Peter) Norman; PC (1979), MP (C) Sutton Coldfield Feb 1974-; s of N F Fowler (d 1964), of Chelmsford, and Katherine Fowler; *b* 2 Feb 1938; *Educ* King Edward VI Sch Chelmsford, Trinity Hall Cambridge; *m* 1, 1968 (m dis 1976), Linda Christmas; m 2, 1979, Fiona Poole, da of John Donald; 2 da (Kate Genevieve b Nov 1981, Isobel Geraldine b July 1984); *Career* with The Times 1961-70 (special corr 1962-66, home affrs 1966-70), memb Editorial Bd Crossbow 1962-69; MP (C) Nottingham S 1970-74; pps NI Office 1972-74, oppn spokesman Home Affrs 1974-75; chief oppn spokesman: Social Servs 1975-76, Tport 1976-79; min Tport 1979-81; sec of state: Tport Jan-Sept 1981, Social Servs 1981-87, Employment 1987-90; *Style*— The Rt Hon Sir Norman Fowler, MP; House of Commons, London SW1A 0AA

FOWLER, Prof Peter Howard; s of Prof Sir Ralph Howard Fowler, OBE (d 1944), and Eileen, *née* Rutherford (d 1930); *b* 27 Feb 1923; *Educ* Winchester, Univ of Bristol (BSc, DSc); *m* 23 July 1949, Rosemary Hempson, da of Rear-Adm (E) George Herbert Hempson Brown, CBE, RN (d 1977); 3 da (Mary b 1950, Anne b 1952, Susan b 1962); *Career* FO RAF 1942-46; Univ of Bristol: asst lectr 1948-50, lectr 1950-59, res fell in physics 1959-63, reader 1963-64, Royal Soc res prof 1964-88; private conslt on uses of nuclear radiation in indust and radiation protection 1988-; Royal Soc Rutherford Meml lectr 1971, Royal Soc Hughes Medal 1974; memb: various sci and engrg res cncl bds in astronomy and space areas 1971-88, Meteorological Ctee 1983-; FRS 1964, FRAS 1962, FRMetS 1983; *Books* The Study of Elementary Particles by the Photographic Method (with CF Powell and DH Perkins, 1959), Solid State Nuclear Track Detectors (with VM Clapham, 1981), Forty Years of Particle Physics (with B Foster, 1988); *Recreations* gardening, meteorology; *Clubs* Royal Soc Dining; *Style*— Prof Peter Fowler, FRS; HH Wills Physics Laboratory, Royal Fort, Tyndall Ave, Bristol BS8 1TL (☎ 0272 303 030 ext 3702, fax 0272 732 657, telex 0272 445938)

FOWLER, Richard Nicholas; QC (1989); s of Ronald Hugh Fowler (d 1971), and Winifred Mary, *née* Hull; *b* 12 Oct 1946; *Educ* Bedford Sch, Brasenose Coll Oxford (BA); *Career* called to the Bar Middle Temple 1969; Liveryman Worshipful Co of Goldsmiths 1989 (Freeman 1980); *Recreations* walking, opera, dogs; *Style*— Richard Fowler, Esq, QC; 93 Cheyne Walk, London SW10 0DQ (☎ 071 352 4966); 4 Raymond Buildings, Gray's Inn, London WC1R 5BP (☎ 071 405 7211, fax 071 405 2084); 28 Rue de Toulouse, 1040 Brussels

FOWLER, Ronald Frederick; CBE (1950); s of Charles Frederick Fowler (d 1942), and Amy Beatrice, *née* Hollyoak (d 1976); *b* 21 April 1910; *Educ* Bancroft's Sch, LSE (BCom), Univ of Lille, Univ of Brussels; *m* 17 April 1937, Brenda Kathleen, da of Henry William Smith (d 1970); *Career* asst and lectr in commerce LSE 1932-40, Cabinet Office and Central Statistical Office 1940-50, dir of statistics and under sec Miny of Labour 1950-68, dir statistical res DOE 1968-72; statistics conslt: Statistics Canada Ottawa 1971-72, Prices Cmmn 1973-77; hon treas RSS 1950-60, memb Advsy Ctee Retail Prices Index 1956-86; *Books* The Depreciation of Capital (1934), The Duration of Unemployment (1968), Some Problems of Index Number Construction (1970), Further Problems of Index Number Construction (1973) author of numerous articles in Br and American learned jls; *Clubs* Reform; *Style*— R F Fowler, Esq, CBE; 10 Silverdale Rd, Petts Wood, Orpington, Kent

FOWLER, Dr Timothy John; s of Eric Fowler (d 1978), of Crowborough, E Sussex, and Agatha Clare, *née* Turner (d 1985); *b* 10 Dec 1937; *Educ* Downside, Oriel Coll Oxford (BA, MA, BM BCh, DM, MRCP), Bart's; *m* 6 Sept 1975, Sheila Barbara, da of Harrison Parkin (d 1977); 1 s (Thomas Gregory b 3 July 1979), 2 da (Clare Judith b 10 Nov 1976, Emma Jane b 23 Feb 1978); *Career* house physician St Bartholomew's Hosp, registrar in neurology Queen Elizabeth Hosp Birmingham, registrar and sr registrar in neurology Nat Hosp for Nervous Diseases, sr registrar in neurology St Mary's Hosp London; conslt neurologist 1974-: The Brook Hosp London, West Hill Hosp and Joyce Green Hosps Dartford, Kent and Sussex Hosp, Tunbridge Wells Hosp, Pembury Hosp; memb Assoc of Br Neurologists; FRCP 1979; *Books* Guide for House Physicians in the Neurological Unit (1982), Neurology (jtly, 1985), Headache (ed, 1987), Clinical Neurology (jtly, 1990); *Style*— Dr Timothy Fowler; The Brook Hospital, Shooters Hill Rd, Woolwich SE18 4LW

FOWLES, Prof Gerald Wilfred Albert; s of Albert Edward Fowles, of Woodmancote, Dursley, Glos, and Winifred Maud, *née* Bloodworth (d 1974); *b* 9 Oct 1925; *Educ* Dursley GS, Univ of Bristol (BSc, PhD, DSc); *m* 30 Dec 1950, Joyce Ellen, da of George Tocknell (d 1978); 1 s (Andrew Mark b 30 Nov 1959), 1 da (Kathryn Sarah b 21 Jan 1963); *Career* Private Army 1944-45 (invalided out); lectr (later sr lectr, then reader) Univ of Southampton 1952-65, prof chemistry Univ of Reading 1966- (head dept 1966-74 and 1981-, dean Faculty of Sci 1969-72 and 1984-87, dep vice chllr 1979-83); memb: Br Ctee Chemical Educn, American Chemical Soc 1964, American Soc Enology and Viticulture 1980; FRSC (MRSC 1946); *Books* Valency and Molecular Structure (1956), Straightforward Winemaking (1975), Straightforward Liqueur Making (1979), Must (1982), Valency Without Tears (1989); *Recreations* enology, pewter collecting, sketching; *Style*— Prof Gerald Fowles; 61 Church Rd, Woodley, Reading, Berks RG5 4PT (☎ 0734 691518); Dept of Chemistry, Univ of Reading, Whiteknights, Reading, Berks (☎ 0734 875123, fax 0734 314404, telex 847813)

FOWLES, John; OBE (1986), JP (1972); s of Harold Fowles (d 1983), and Helen Fowles (d 1983); *b* 28 June 1932; *Educ* Reading Collegiate Sch, Harvard Business Course; *m* 22 April 1961, Diana Mary, da of Victor Urrey Oldland; 2 s (Charles b 1962, James b 1964), 1 da (Jayne b 1963); *Career* RAF Tech Trg Cmd, Fighter Cmd 90 Gp 1949-53; chm Gowring Group (joined 1953); CBI: memb Southern Regn Cncl 1979-89 (chm 1983-85, vice chm 1981-83), memb Nat Cncl, (chm's Ctee and Pres Ctee 1981-86); dir: Newbury Racecourse plc 1983, Southern Advsy Bd National Westminster PLC 1990; chm Berkshire Indust Year 1986; HM gen cmmr for Inland Revenue 1981-; Freeman City of London; *Recreations* fishing, shooting, golf; *Clubs* MCC, Guild of Freemen, City Livery; *Style*— John Fowles, Esq, OBE, JP; Burghclere Manor, Near Newbury, Berkshire; Gowrings Ltd, 18-21 Church Gate, Thatcham, Berkshire (☎ 0635 64464)

FOWLIE, Dr Hector Chalmers; OBE (1989); s of Hector McIntosh Fowlie (d 1954), and Agnes Blue, *née* Turner (d 1966); *b* 21 June 1929; *Educ* Harris Acad Dundee, Univ of St Andrews (MB ChB); *m* Christina Napier Morrison, da of Peter Walker (d 1967); 2 s (Stephen b 1956, Peter b 1962), 1 da (Kay b 1958); *Career* psychiatrist; formerly physician supt Royal Dundee Liff and Strathmartine Hosps Dundee, conslt psychiatrist Tayside Health Bd Dundee; vice chm: Mental Welfare Cmmn for Scotland, Parole Bd for Scotland; govr Dundee Inst of Technol, chm Dundee Assoc of Mental Health; *Style*— Dr Hector Fowlie, OBE; 21 Clepington Road, Dundee (☎ 0382 41926)

FOX; *see*: Scott Fox

FOX, Dr Alan Martin; s of Sidney Nathan Fox (d 1987), and Clarice, *née* Solov; *b* 5

July 1938; *Educ* Bancrofts Sch Woodford, Queen Mary Coll London (BSc, PhD, Pres of Union); *m* 20 June 1965, Sheila Naomi, da of Lazarus Pollard, of Bournemouth; 1 s (James Henry Paul b 1974), 2 da (Victoria Charlotte b 1968, Louise Rachel b 1971); *Career* Miny of Aviation and Technol 1963-72 (private sec to John Stonehouse MP and Julian Snow MP 1965-67), First Sec of Aviation and Def Br Embassy Paris 1973-75; MOD: operational analysis studies Fin of Def Nuclear Weapons Prog 1975-78, RCDS 1979, fin control of RAF Material Requirements 1980-84, Def Intelligence Staff 1984-88, asst under-sec (ordnance) 1988-; *Style—* Dr Alan Fox; Room 2210 Main Building, Ministry of Defence, Main Building, Horseguards Avenue, London SW1 (☎ 071 218 7315)

FOX, Allan Spencer; s of Joseph Bower Fox (d 1964), of Bradford, and Florence Mary, *née* Farrow (d 1986); *b* 3 Feb 1932; *Educ* Bradford GS, Univ of Sheffield (BA, DipEd); *m* 15 Aug 1959, Margaret Seddon, da of Reginald Charles Eveleigh (d 1933), of Reading; 2 da (Susan b 1962, Carolyn b 1967); *Career* Flying Offr RAF (Educn Branch) 1955-58; asst master: Excelsior Sch Kingston Jamaica 1958-62, Bedford Lower Sch Bedford Sch 1962-67; headmaster jr sch: Daniel Stewarts' Coll Edinburgh 1967-74, Daniel Stewarts' and Melville Coll Edinburgh 1974-77; master Highgate Jr Sch 1977-; Capt Univ of Sheffield CC 1953 and 1955, memb Mgmnt Ctee Highgate Literary and Scientific Inst 1984-86, tstee The Whipple Tst 1984-; FRGS 1960; *Recreations* hill walking, gardening, painting; *Style—* Allan Fox, Esq; Cholmeley House, 3 Bishopswood Rd, Highgate, London N6 (☎ 081 340 9193)

FOX, Christopher Jonathan; s of Richard Glanfield Fox, of Penlea, Freshwater Lane, St Mawes, Truro, Cornwall, and Ella Tweed, *née* Bingley; *b* 2 June 1948; *Educ* LSE (BSc); *m* 26 June 1982, Susan Agnes Bridget, da of John Charles McNicol (d 1971), of Maidenhead, Berks; *Career* CA, former jt treas and chm Fin and Admin Bd Lib Pty, ldr SLD Gp Guildford Borough Cncl, contested (Lib) Guildford Feb and Oct 1974; Liveryman Worshipful Co of Weavers; *Recreations* reading, history, politics, genealogy; *Clubs* Guildford Cncl Sports and Social; *Style—* Christopher Fox, Esq; 173 Worplesdon Rd, Guildford, Surrey GU2 6XD (☎ 0483 31739)

FOX, David John; s of Frederick Oswald Fox (d 1966), and Beatrice, *née* Roberts-Clarke (d 1988); *b* 13 March 1935; *m* Norma Kathleen, da of (Ernest) Norman Parkes (d 1973); 1 s (Tavis John b 15 March 1975); *Career* Grenadier Gds 1953-56; legal exec; memb: Dorset CC 1975- (chm Public Protection Ctee 1980-), Christchurch Borough Cncl 1983- (Mayor 1987-88); chm Assoc CCs Fire and Emergency Planning Ctee; area sec Cons Club Advsy Ctee; *Recreations* genealogy; *Style—* David Fox, Esq; 1 Canberra Rd, Christchurch, Dorset BH23 2HL (☎ 0202 482 787); 194 Seabourne Rd, West Southbourne, Bournemouth (☎ 0202 423 232, fax 0202 417 047)

FOX, Edward Charles Morice; eld s of late Maj Robin Fox, RA, of Sussex, and Angela Muriel Darita, *née* Worthington; *b* 13 April 1937; *Educ* Harrow; *m* 1958 (m dis), Tracy Reed, da of Anthony Pelissier, of Sussex; 1 da (Lucy Arabella b 1950); partner since 1972, Joanna David, *qv*; 1 s (Frederick Samson Robert Morice b 5 April 1989), 1 da (Emilia Rose Elizabeth b 31 July 1974); *Career* late Coldstream Gds, 2 Lt Loyal N Lancs Regt; stage screen and TV actor 1958-; *Recreations* music, gardening; *Clubs* Garrick, Savile; *Style—* Edward Fox, Esq

FOX, Freddie Frank; OBE (1977); s of Ing Arnost Fuchs (d in holocaust 1944/5), of Prague, and Alice Fuchs (d in holocaust 1944/5); *b* 6 July 1919; *Educ* Tech Coll Prague; *m* 11 May 1944, Gertrude, da of Leopold Preiss (d in holocaust 1943/4), of Zilina, Czechoslovakia; 1 s (John b 1946), 1 da (Vivienne (Mrs Erdos) b 1949); *Career* md: Record Food Products Ltd 1947-64, Record Bakery Equipment Co Ltd 1947-, Pasta Foods Co Ltd (RHM) 1964-81 (and chm); currently chm: Adv Holdings Co Ltd, Javin Property Co (London) Ltd; memb Sci and Technol Bd MAFF, chm Bakery Equipment Mfrs Soc 1960-63, cncl and exec memb Food Mfrg Fedn 1958-80, chm External Rels Ctee FMF 1970-74, pres UNAFPA (Union of Pasta Mfrs in EEC) 1977-78, treas Hammerson Meml Home for the Elderly Hampstead 1980-88, memb Inst of Br Engrs 1958; Freeman: City of London 1968, Worshipful Co of Bakers 1968; *Recreations* golf, skiing, theatre; *Style—* Freddie Fox, Esq, OBE; Unit 2, Verulam Industl Estate, London Rd, St Albans, Herts AL1 1JF (☎ 0727 43136, fax 0727 39018)

FOX, Frederick Donald; s of Lesley James Fox (d 1950), of Urana, NSW, Aust, and Ruby Mansfield, *née* Elliott (d 1965); *b* 2 April 1931; *Educ* St Josephs Convent Sch Jerilderie NSW Aust; *Career* milliner, started in business 1962, currently designer for the Royal Family; pres Millinery Trades Benevolent Assoc; granted Royal Warrant to HM The Queen 1974; Freeman City of London 1989, Liveryman Worshipful Co of Feltmakers 1989; *Recreations* gardening, photography; *Style—* Frederick Fox, Esq; 47 Adams Row, Grosvenor St, London W1; Model Hats, 87-91 New Bond St, London W1Y 9LA (☎ 071 629 5705, 5706, fax 071 629 3048)

FOX, George Frew; *b* 18 Nov 1913; *Educ* Grove Acad Broughty Ferry Dundee; *m* 27 Sept 1941, Violet Jane; 2 da (Caroline Jane b 1944, Valerie Elizabeth b 1948); *Career* Lance Corpl RASC 1940-42, Capt RAPC 1942-46; sr dir Dundee United FC (chm 1962-70 and 1984-89), former treas Scot Football Assoc (currently life memb); life memb and former capt Carnoustie Golf Club, life memb and former sec Broughty Golf Club, life memb Tayside Athletic Club, hon pres Caroustie Panmure FC, hon vice pres Broughty Opera; FICAS; *Recreations* golf; *Clubs* Carnoustie Golf, Broughty Golf (Monifieth), Carnoustie Caledonia Golf; *Style—* George Fox, Esq; 17 Lochty Street, Carnoustie, Dundee DD7 6EE (☎ 0241 52181); Tannadice Park, Dundee (☎ 0382 833166)

FOX, Lady; Hazel Mary; da of John Matthew Blackwood Stuart, CIE (d 1941), and Joan Daria, *née* Elliot Taylor; *b* 22 Oct 1928; *Educ* Roedean, Somerville Coll Oxford (MA); *m* 5 June 1954, Rt Hon Sir Michael John Fox, s of Michael Fox (d 1926); 3 s (Matthew b 1957, Patrick b 1958, Charles b 1968), 1 da (Jane b 1962); *Career* called to the Bar 1950, practising 1950-54, lectr in jurisprudence Somerville Coll Oxford 1951-58, lectr Cncl of Legal Educn 1962-76; chm: London Rent Assessment Panel 1977-, London Leasehold Valuation Tbnl 1981-; dir Br Inst of International and Comparative Law 1982-89, gen ed Int and Comparative Law Quarterly 1987-, memb Home Office Departmental Ctee on Jury Serv 1953-65, chm Tower Hamlets Juvenile Ct 1968-76; JP London 1956-77; additional Bencher Lincoln's Inn 1989; *Books* International Arbitration (with J L Simpson 1959), International Economic Law and Developing States (ed 1988), Joint Development of Offshore Oil and Gas (ed 1989); *Style—* Lady Fox; British Institute of International and Comparative Law, Charles Clore House, 17 Russell Square, London WC1B 5DR (☎ 071 636 5802)

FOX, James; s of Maj Robin Fox, MC (d 1971), of Cuckfield, Sussex, and Angela Fox; *b* 19 May 1939; *Educ* 15 Sept 1973, Mary Elizabeth, da of Maj Allan Piper, of Wadhurst, Sussex; 4 s (Thomas b 1975, Robin b 1976, Laurence b 1978, Jack b 1985), 1 da (Lydia b 1979); *Career* actor; The Servant 1963, King Rat 1964, Thoroughly Modern Millie 1966, Performance 1969, A Passage to India 1984, The Russia House 1990; *Books* Comeback An Actors Direction (1983); *Recreations* tennis, windsurfing; *Style—* James Fox, Esq; 49 Murray Road, Wimbledon SW19 4PF; c/o Michael Whitehall, 125 Gloucester Rd, London SW7 4TE (☎ 071 244 8466)

FOX, James Ewart; s of Ewart Lyndall Fox (d 1963), and Gwendoline Rose Hann (d 1988); *b* 30 Sept 1941; *Educ* Wellington, Royal West of England Acad, Univ of Bristol (BArch, DipArch); *m* 18 Dec 1976, Bridget Ann, da of Maj Basil Frank Jones, of Chilton Cantelo, Somerset; 1 s (Sebastian James b 1985), 2 da (Charlotte Ann b 1978, Melanie Sarah b 1981); *Career* princ architect 1964-; underwriting memb Lloyd's of London 1978-; ARIBA 1964; *Recreations* salmon fishing, pheasant/partridge shooting, tennis, skiing, flying, golf; *Clubs* Conservative, Lloyd's of London, Flying; *Style—* James E Fox, Esq; Highfield, Leweston, Sherborne, Dorset; 55 The Park, Yeovil, Somerset BA20 1DF (☎ 0935 20831)

FOX, James George; s of George Romney Fox (d 1968), of Trewardreva Constantine, Falmouth, Cornwall, and Barbara Muriel, *née* Twite; *b* 14 May 1943; *Educ* Eton, Univ of Newcastle upon Tyne (BA), Univ of Pennsylvania (MBA); *m* 4 May 1974, Rebecca Jane, da of Charles Wright, of Canyon, Texas; 2 s (Francis b 1977, Romney b 1981), 2 da (Rachel b 1975, Sarah b 1979); *Career* dir: Hill Samuel Investmt Mgmnt 1968-78, Warburg Investmt Mgmnt 1982-85; chm Falmouth Hotel plc 1981-, md Morgan Grenfell Tst Mangrs 1985-; *Recreations* sailing; *Clubs* Athenaeum, Penn; *Style—* James Fox, Esq; Trewardreva, Constantine, Falmouth, Cornwall (☎ 0326 40207); 57 St Andrewes House, Barbican, London EC2 (☎ 071 638 9103); 20 Finsbury Circus, London EC2M 1NB (☎ 071 256 7500)

FOX, Dr (Anthony) John; s of Fred Frank Fox, OBE, and Gertrude, *née* Preis; *b* 25 April 1946; *Educ* Dauntseys Sch, UCL (BSc), Imperial Coll London (PhD, DIC); *m* 9 Sept 1971, Annemarie, da of Ladislas Revesz, of Frankfurt; 1 s (Sebastian Stefan b 3 Dec 1982), 2 da (Simone Nikki b 11 Oct 1973, Zoe Valerie b 31 Jan 1977); *Career* statistician: Health and Safety Exec, Office of Population Censuses and Surveys (OPCS); prof of social statistics City Univ, chief med statistician OPCS; FSS 1970; *Books* Socio-Demographic Mortality Differentials (1982), Health Inequalities in European Countries (1989); *Recreations* tennis, bridge, family; *Clubs* RSM; *Style—* Dr John Fox; 46 Redington Road, London NW3; Office of Population Censuses and Surveys, St Catherine's House, Kingsway, London WC2 (☎ 242 0262 ext 2167)

FOX, Capt John Rupert Anselm; s of Sqdn Ldr John Arnold Fox, MBE (d 1984), of Worcestershire, and Eleanor Margaret, *née* Green (d 1986), (gs of William Owen design and architect for Port Sunlight for 1 Lord Leverhulme); *b* 10 Dec 1935; *Educ* Stonyhurst; *m* 10 Oct 1965, Isabel June Mary Jermy Fox, da of H E Le Bailli Quintin Jermy Gwyn, former Grand Chancellor Sov and Mil Order of Malta; 5 s (Oliver b 1967, d 1986, Benjamin b 1969, Justin b 1970, Quintin b 1972, Anthony b 1980), 1 da (Eleanor b 1966); *Career* 2 Lt RASC BAOR 1955-56, Capt Cheshire Yeo 1958-65; admitted slr 1960; ptnr Whatley Weston & Fox (Worcester, Malvern, Hereford) 1963-76, NP 1965, Under Sheriff City of Worcester 1964-76, ptnr John Fox Slrs 1978-; tstee Order of Malta Homes; kt of Magisterial Grace; Sov of Mil Order of Malta 1975-, Offr of Merit, Pro Merite Melitensi; *Recreations* interior decoration, gardening, picture collector, water colourist; *Clubs* Travellers'; *Style—* Capt John Fox; Condicup Farm, Willersey Rd, Badsey, Worcestershire (☎ 0386 830327)

FOX, The (O'Sionnaigh); John William Fox; s of James George Fox (d 1957), of Gypsum, Tempsey, NSW, and Ethel, *née* Laidlaw; suc his kinsman, Nial Arthur Hubert Fox, The Fox, as Chief of his Name 1959; *b* 22 Aug 1916; *m* 1939, Margaret Frances Wilson; 4 s, 1 da; *Heir* s, Douglas John Fox b 23 Aug 1942; *Style—* The Fox; Koorlong, Vic 3501, Australia

FOX, Kim Michael; s of Lt-Col Michael Allen Fox (d 1980), of Edinburgh, and Veronica Venetia Fox, *née* Sweeney; *b* 17 June 1948; *Educ* Fort Augustus Abbey Sch, Univ of St Andrews (MB ChB, MD); *m* Eleanor Elizabeth, da of James Downs; 1 s (Michael James b 6 March 1978); *Career* currently conslt cardiologist at Nat Heart Hosp; ed and author of textbooks in cardiology, assoc ed British Heart Journal; memb Fin and Gen Purposes Ctee Br Heart Fndn (former memb Cncl and chm Editorial Ctee); MRCP, FRCP 1988, fell Euro Soc of Cardiology; *Books* Diseases of the Heart (ed 1988), Wolfe Atlases of Cardiology; *Clubs* Roehampton; *Style—* Dr Kim Fox; 13 Lower Common South, Putney, London SW15; National Heart Hospital, Westmoreland St, London W1 (☎ 071 486 4433); 34 Devonshire Place, London W1 (☎ 071 486 4433)

FOX, Dr Levi; OBE (1964), DL (1967 Warwickshire); s of John William Fox (d 1952), of Coleorton, Leics, and Julia Sophia, *née* Stinson (d 1938); *b* 28 Aug 1914; *Educ* Ashby de La Zouch Boys' GS, Oriel Coll Oxford (MA), Univ of Manchester; *m* 1938, Jane Richards; 1 s, 2 da; *Career* dir and sec: Incorporated Tst, Shakespeare Birthplace Tst 1945-89 (dir emeritus 1990); author of books on Shakespeare Stratford-upon-Avon and Warwickshire; dep chm Int Shakespeare Assoc; Hon LHD George Washington Univ, Hon DLitt Birmingham Univ; medallist New York Univ; FSA, FRHistS, FRSL; *Books* Coventry's Heritage (1945), The Borough Town of Stratford-upon-Avon (1953), Shakespeare's England (1972), A Country Grammar School (1967), In Honour of Shakespeare (1972), Stratford-upon-Avon: an appreciation (1976); *Recreations* country life, gardening; *Style—* Dr Levi Fox, OBE, DL, FSA; Silver Birches, 27 Welcombe Rd, Stratford-upon-Avon, Warwickshire CV37 6UJ (☎ 0789 292648); The Shakespeare Centre, Stratford-upon-Avon, Warwickshire (☎ 0789 204016)

FOX, Sir (John) Marcus; MBE (1963), MP (C) Shipley 1970-; s of late Alfred Hirst Fox; *b* 11 June 1927; *Educ* Wheelwright GS Dewsbury; *m* 1954, Ann, da of F W J Tindall; 1 s, 1 da; *Career* served Duke of Wellington's Regt and The Green Howards 1945-48; memb Dewsbury Borough Cncl 1957-65; contested (C): Dewsbury 1959, Huddersfield W 1966; memb Race Relations and Immigration Select Ctee 1970-72, asst govt whip 1972-73, Lord Cmmr of the Treasy 1973-74; oppn front bench spokesman: Environment 1974, Housing 1974-75, Tport 1975-76; vice-chm Cons Pty (responsible for candidates) 1976-79, under-sec state DOE 1979-81, memb Select Ctee on Members' Salaries 1981-82, vice-chm 1922 Ctee 1983-, chm Ctee of Selection 1984-; nat chm Assoc of Cons Clubs 1988-; kt 1986; *Style—* Sir Marcus Fox, MBE, MP; House of Commons, London SW1A 0AA

FOX, Michael Anthony; JP (1988); s of Gregory Henry Fox (d 1967), of Manchester, and Betty Lilian, *née* Solomon; *b* 10 Feb 1947; *Educ* Manchester Central GS, Univ of Manchester (BSc); *m* 4 Sept 1977, Miriam, da of Robert Werner (d 1972); 3 s (Henry Robert b 18 Dec 1978, Jonathan Daniel b 24 Nov 1980, Nicholas Leon b 24 May 1983); *Career* optometrist, JP Manchester Bench, memb Lloyds 1987; FBCO 1972; *Recreations* squash, tennis, opera, music, overseas travel; *Clubs* Dunham Forest Golf; *Style—* Michael Fox, Esq, JP; The Old Spinney, 1 Bruntwood Lane, Cheadle, Cheshire SK8 1HS (☎ 061 428 5585); 124 Wilmslow Rd, Handforth, Cheshire (☎ 0625 527991)

FOX, Lord Justice; Rt Hon Sir Michael John; PC (1981), QC (1968); s of Michael Fox; *b* 8 Oct 1921; *Educ* Drayton Manor Sch Hanwell, Magdalen Coll Oxford; *m* 1954, Hazel Mary (formerly fellow Somerville Oxford, dir Br Inst Int & Comparative Law 1982-), da of John Matthew Blackwood Stuart, CIE; 3 s, 1 da; *Career* served Admty 1942-45; called to the Bar Lincoln's Inn 1949, judge High Ct (Chancery) 1975-81, Lord Justice of Appeal 1981-; kt 1975; *Style—* The Rt Hon Lord Justice Fox; Royal Courts of Justice, Strand WC2 (☎ 071 405 7641)

FOX, Michael Pease; s of Julian Pease Fox (d 1979), of Pennant, Wellington, Somerset, and Marjorie Ellis, *née* Gibbins (d 1981); *b* 21 Aug 1921; *Educ* Leighton Park Sch Reading, Corpus Christi Coll Cambridge (MA); *m* 24 July 1948, Yvonne Hotham, da of Joel Hotham Cadbury (d 1946), of King's Norton, Birmingham; 2 s (Julian b 1949, Roger b 1953), 2 da (Jeanie b 1951, Diana b 1955); *Career* Friends Ambulance Unit China Convoy 1942-46; main bd dir Friends Provident Life Office 1967-; Fox Bros & Co Ltd: joined 1948, dir 1952, vice chm 1964, chm and md 1968-;

chm and md William Bliss & Son 1968-; memb Wool Textile EDC 1965-69, chm Public Health Cncl RDC 1966-69, assoc memb ATI 1966, pres Rotary Club Wellington 1967, chm W of Eng Wool Textile Assoc 1968- (chm Jt Industl Cncl 1968-); *Recreations* sailing, gardening, mountain walking; *Style*— Michael Fox, Esq; Legglands, Wellington, Somerset TA21 9NU (☎ 0823 66 2119); Fox Bros & Co Ltd, Tonedale, Wellington, Somerset (☎ 0823 66 2271, fax 0823 66 6963, telex 46158)

FOX, Miles; s of Victor Fox (d 1950), and Marie Fox (d 1988); *b* 22 Feb 1927; *Educ* Univ of Manchester (MB ChB, MD, ChM); *m* Valerie Jean; 5 da (Helena b 1957, Mary Jane b 1959, Candida b 1965, Emily Susan b 1978, Anna Victoria (twin) b 1978); *Career* MRC res fell in transplantation Dept of Surgery Univ of Edinburgh 1959-60; sr registrar in urology: St Peter's Hosp London 1959-60, Gen Infirmary and St James' Hosp Leeds 1962-66; conslt urological surgn Sheffield Health Authy 1966-, hon clinical teacher Univ of Sheffield 1966-, surgical res fell in tranplantation Harvard Med Sch and Peter Bent Brigham Hosp Boston USA 1966, dir Renal Transplant Unit Royal Hallamshire Hosp Sheffield 1970-83, Hunterian prof RCS 1976, Br Cncl travelling fell Turkey 1977; memb: Br Assoc of Urological Surgns, Int Soc of Urology, Br Transplantation Soc, Int Transplantation Soc, Finnish Med Soc, Br Microsurgical Soc; FRCS 1955; *Books* numerous pubns incl: Prostatectomy in Patients of 70 years and Over (1980), Renal Transplantation with Multiple Arteries (1979); *Recreations* skiing, stamp collecting, walking, classical music, gardening, computers; *Clubs* Sheffield Doctors; *Style*— Miles Fox, Esq; 54 Stumperlowe Crescent Road, Sheffield S10 3PR; 27 Wilkinson St, Sheffield S10 2GD (☎ 0742 723711); Royal Hallamshire Hospital, Glossop Rd, Sheffield S10 2JF (☎ 0742 766222)

FOX, Sir (Henry) Murray; GBE (1974); s of Sidney Joseph Fox (d 1962), of London, and Molly Button; *b* 7 June 1912; *Educ* Malvern, Emmanuel Coll Cambridge; *m* 1941, Helen Isabella Margaret (d 1986), da of late J B Crichton; 1 s, 2 da; *Career* Alderman Ward of Bread St 1966-82, Sheriff City of London 1971-72, Lord Mayor of London 1974-75, one of HM Lts City of London 1976-82; pres City & Metropolitan Building Soc, chm Trehaven Holdings Ltd; dir: Municipal Mutual Insurance Ltd, Toye Kenning & Spencer Ltd 1976-; Order of Rising Sun and Sacred Treasure (Japan) 1971, Order of Stor (Afghanistan) 1971, Order of Orange (Netherlands) 1972; *Style*— Sir Murray Fox, GBE; 7 Aldford St, London W1Y 5PQ (☎ 071 408 2454)

FOX, Neil; MBE (1983); s of Thomas Fox (d 1986), of Sharlston, West Yorks, and Stella, *née* Schofield; *b* 4 May 1939; *Educ* Sharlston Sch West Yorks; *m* 3 June 1961, Molly, da of Hubert Bentley; 1 s (Jonathan Neil b 20 March 1965), 1 da (Amanda Jayne b 16 Feb 1963); *Career* former rugby league player; capt Yorkshire Schs 1954, 574 appearances Wakefield Trinity 1956-74 (professional debut aged 16); various clubs 1974-79: 70 appearances Bradford Northern, 59 appearances Hull Kingston Rovers, 13 appearances York, 23 appearances Bramley, 21 appearances Huddersfield, last professional match Aug 1979; 17 Yorkshire Co caps, 29 GB caps; holder of various records with Wakefield Trinity: most goals in a match 12, most goals in a season 183, most goals in a career 1836, most points in a match 33, most points in a career 4,488; world record points scorer 6,220 between 1956-79; Lance Todd Trophy winner v Huddersfield 1962, entered Rugby League Hall of Fame 1989; former: apprentice fitter NCB, fitter CEGB, proprietor chain of betting shops; jt proprietor: two retail sports shops, mail order sportswear company; *Style*— Neil Fox, Esq, MBE

FOX, Norman Alfred; s of Rupert Alfred Fox (d 1972), of Whitstable, and Evelyn Clare, *née* Earle; *b* 28 April 1942; *Educ* Sir William Nottidge Sch Whitstable, Canterbury Tech Coll; *m* 3 Oct 1964, Gillian, da of late Archie Lawrance, MBE; 2 da (Anneliese b 14 Aug 1969, Melanie b 5 June 1971); *Career* apprentice Whitsable Times and Kentish Observer 1959-62, chief reporter Mitcham News 1962-63, dep sports ed Kentish Times 1963, sub ed and writer World Sports Magazine 1963-66; The Times 1966-89: sub ed and reporter 1966-76, football corr 1976-80, athletics and gen sports corr 1980-82, sports ed 1982-86, dep managing ed 1986-89 (covered: Cwlth Games 1970 and 1974, Olympic Games 1972, 1976 and 1980, World Cup 1978 and 1982); sports corr The Independent On Sunday (covered World Cup 1990); memb Sports Writers Assoc; *Books* World Cup '82; *Recreations* walking, golf, motorcycling; *Style*— Norman Fox, Esq; The Independent On Sunday, 40 City Rd, London EC1Y 2DH (☎ 071 253 1222, fax 071 415 1333)

FOX, Paul Joseph; s of Joseph Bower Fox, of Bramhope, Yorkshire, and Kathleen Barbara, *née* Cambden (d 1988); *b* 8 Dec 1941; *Educ* Mill Hill, Wadham Coll Oxford (MA); *m* 22 Sept 1967, Judith Mary, da of Norman Robson, OBE (d 1969); 2 s (James b 23 June 1970, Alexander b 25 June 1973), 1 da (Louise b 30 Oct 1968); *Career* chief accountant Munich Reinsurance Co UK branches 1976-; former chm Folkestone 41 Club, hon treas Clc Tennis Club; Freeman: City of London, Worshipful Co of Chartered Accountants; FCA 1966, FCII 1974, CI 1989; *Recreations* tennis, philately, skiing and bridge; *Clubs* New Folkestone Soc; *Style*— Paul Fox, Esq; Munich Reinsurance Company, UK Life Branch, 154 Fenchurch Street, London EC3M 6JJ (☎ 071 626 2566, telex 886845 MRLDNG, fax 071 626 4036)

FOX, Peter Gerald; s of Thomas Fox (d 1985), and Stella, *née* Schofield; *Educ* Wakefield Jr Tech Coll; *m* 30 Nov 1957, Joan Margaret, da of late Arthur Nicholson; 2 da (Karen Beverley b 19 Sept 1958, Susan Elizabeth b 30 Nov 1961; *Career* professional rugby league coach; player: Yorks Schs 1948, Featherstone Rovers 1953-56, Batley 1956-62 and 1964-67, Hull Kingston Rovers 1962-64, Wakefield Trinity 1967 (ret through injury); coach: Featherstone Rovers 1971-74 and 1987-, Wakefield Trinity 1974-76, Bramley 1976-77, Bradford Northern 1977-85, Leeds 1985-86, England 1977 (v Wales and France), GB 1978 (3 Tests v Aust), Yorkshire 1985- (unbeaten); honours as coach incl: Challenge Cup winners Featherstone Rovers 1973 (runners up 1974), promotion to Div 1 Bramley 1977 and Featherstone Rovers 1988, Premiership Cup winners Bradford Northern 1978 (runners up 1979 and 1980), Yorkshire Cup winners Bradford Northern 1979 (various runners up), Div 1 champions Bradford Northern 1980 and 1981, John Player Cup winners Bradford Northern 1980, Div 2 Premiership Cup runners up Featherstone Rovers 1988; Bradford Northern first team to retain Div 1 title 1981; rugby league coach of the year 1980; draughtsman British Jeffrey Diamond Wakefield 1953-59 (apprentice engr 1948-53), design draughtsman Yorkshire Imperial metals Leeds 1960-77, trg and safety offr IMI Yorkshire Alloys Leeds 1977-; *Recreations* rugby, golf, boxing, most other sports; *Style*— Peter Fox, Esq; 7 Woodlands, East Ardsley, nr Wakefield, West Yorkshire WF3 2JG (☎ 0924 824314); c/o Featherstone Rovers RLFC, Post Office Road, Featherstone, West Yorkshire (☎ 0997 702386, fax 0532 534075)

FOX, Philip Hamilton; DL (1977); s of Maj Cuthbert Lloyd Fox MC (d 1972), of Glendurgan, Mawnan Smith, Falmouth, and Moyra Florence, *née* Sulivan (d 1988); family business G C Fox & Co established 1762 in Falmouth previously in Fowey about 1646, still an operating partnership; *b* 11 March 1922; *Educ* Harrow, Magdalene Coll Cambridge; *m* 1948, Rona, da of late Kenneth D Briggs; 3 s (Robert, Charles, William); *Career* Lt Northern Europe 1944-45, High Sheriff of Cornwall 1973-74; chm Fed Cncl of UK and Irish Co Membs of Inst of Chartered Shipbrokers 1985-87; travel agent; dir: Shipping Services (Falmouth) Ltd, Falmouth Syndicate Ltd; FICS, MInstTT; orders: Orange Nassau (Netherlands), Vasa (SW), Polar Star (SW), Olaf (Norway), Merit (Norway), Danneborg (Danish); *Recreations* sailing (aux sloop 'Quaker Girl'), gardening; *Clubs* Royal Cruising, Royal Ocean Racing, Royal Cornwall Yacht; *Style*— Philip Fox, Esq, DL; Stable Court, Mawnan Smith, Falmouth, Cornwall TR11 5JZ (☎ 0326 311300, telex 45-237, fax 0326 317913)

FOX, Raymond Charles Hayne; s of Henry James Fox (d 1949), of Muswell Hill, and Dora Lilian, *née* Welch (d 1929); *b* 10 July 1914; *Educ* City of London Sch, King's Coll London (LLB); *m* 1, 26 July 1947, Dorothea Cunliffe (d 1974), da of Ernest Hamilton Sharp, OBE, KC (d 1922), of Surrey and Hong Kong; m 2, 11 Oct 1975, Geraldine Mary Brett, da of Capt Thomas Gerald Cahill, MC (d 1969), of Kingsgate, Kent; *Career* WWII RMC 1939-40, Royal Welch Fusiliers 1940-46 served Normandy to Hamburg (Capt 1944); Town Clerk's Dept City of London 1934-39 and 1946-76 (asst Town Clerk 1973-76), involved in Barbican devpt 1960-76; dir: Tally-Ho Estates Ltd 1948-, Wimbledon Guild of Social Welfare; Freeman City of London 1935, Liveryman Worshipful Co of Cutlers 1936; Offr Order de Mayo al Merito Argentine Republic 1961, Knight Official, Order of African Redemption Republic of Liberia 1962, Chevalier of L'Ordre de la Valeur Camerounaise 1963, Offr of the Nat Order of Niger 1969; *Recreations* reading, gardening, music, walking, shooting; *Style*— Raymond Fox, Esq; 1 Wilberforce Way, Wimbledon, London SW19 4TH (☎ 081 946 3362)

FOX, Richard John; s of Dennis William Fox (d 1956), of Bristol, and Winifred Joan Fox; *b* 23 Dec 1943; *Educ* Cotham GS, Bristol, UCW Cardiff (BSc); *m* Sandra Wynne, 2 c (Mark Douglas b 1970, Helen Victoria b 1971); *Career* Grace Darbyshire & Todd Bristol 1965-71 (articled clerk 1965-68), Coopers & Lybrand 1971-78, ptnr Neville Russell 1982-87 (joined 1978), ptnr KPMG Peat Marwick McLintock 1989 (joined 1987); pres Guildford Dist C of C 1991-, memb Bd Surrey Trg and Enterprise Cncl 1990-, fndr memb Guildford Chamber Choir; ACA 1968; *Books* Tolleys Charities Manual (1986); *Recreations* trekking, music especially choral, the countryside, reading, badminton; *Clubs* Wentworth; *Style*— Richard J Fox, Esq; KPMG Peat Marwick McLintock, Chartered Accountants, Eastgate Court, Guildford, Surrey GU1 3AE (☎ 0483 303000, fax 0483 68732)

FOX, Richard Munro; MBE (1986); s of Roger Henry Fox, of Finsbury Park, London, and Jennifer Jean Munro, *née* Betten; *b* 5 June 1960; *Educ* St Albans Grammar Verulam Sch, Univ of Birmingham (BA); *m* 30 Sept 1990, Myriam da of Victor Jerusalmi, of Marseilles; *Career* World canoe slalom champion: 1981, 1983, 1985, 1989; winner Europa Cup: 1982, 1984, 1986, 1988; winner World Cup 1988 and 1989, 7 times Br champion; appointed Sports Cncl 1988; Freeman City of Wausau Wisconsin USA 1988; *Recreations* skiing, travel; *Clubs* Nottingham Kayak; *Style*— Richard Fox, Esq, MBE; 16 Melford Hall Drive, West Bridgford, Nottingham NG2 7SP

FOX, Prof Robert; s of Donald Fox (d 1972), and Audrey Hilda, *née* Ramsell; *b* 7 Oct 1938; *Educ* Doncaster GS, Oriel Coll Oxford (BA, MA, DPhil); *m* 20 May 1964, Catherine Mary Lilian, da of Dr Edmund Roper Power (d 1990); 3 da (Tessa b 1967, Emily b 1969, Hannah b 1972); *Career* asst master Tonbridge 1961-63, Clifford Norton res fell The Queen's Coll Oxford 1965-66, prof of history of sci Univ of Lancaster 1988 (lectr 1966-72, sr lectr 1972-75, reader 1975-87), dir Centre de Recherche en Histoire des Sciences et des Techniques Cité des Sciences et de l'Industrie Paris 1986-88, asst dir Sci Museum 1988, prof of history of sci and fell Linacre Coll Oxford 1988-; pres Br Soc History of Sci 1980-82, first vice pres Div of History of Sci Int Union the History and Philosophy of Sci 1989-; FRHistS 1974, FSA 1989; *Books* The Caloric Theory of Cases from Lavoisier to Regnault (1971), Sadi Carnot Réflexions sur La Puissance Motrice du Feu (1978, 1986 and 1988), The Organization of Science and Technology in France 1808-1914 (ed with G Weisz, 1980); *Clubs* Athenaeum; *Style*— Prof Robert Fox, FSA; Modern History Faculty, Broad St, Oxford OX1 3BD (☎ 0865 277254)

FOX, Robert Michael John; s of Robin Fox (d 1971), of Cuckfield, Sussex, and Angela Muriel Darita, *née* Worthington; *b* 25 March 1952; *Educ* Harrow; *m* 26 Feb 1974 (m dis 1990), Celestia, *née* Sporborg; 1 s (Sam Henry b 24 June 1978), 2 da (Chloe Victoria b 24 May 1976, Louisa Mary b 18 July 1983); m 2, 16 Dec 1990, Natasha Jane, *née* Richardson; *Career* prodr; actor When Did You Last See My Mother? (Royal Court Theatre) 1970, asst dir Royal Court Theatre 1971-73, PA to Michael White (Michael White Ltd) 1973-80, fndr Robert Fox Ltd 1980-; prodns incl: Goose Pimples 1981, Anyone for Denis?, Another Country 1982 (exec prodr of film), Crystal Clear, The Seagull, Torch Song Trilogy, Interpreters, Orphans, J J Farr, Chess, Lettice & Lovage, Anything Goes, A Madhouse in Goa, Burn This; winner: Evening Standard Drama Desk award for Best Comedy Goose Pimples 1981, Laurence Olivier award for Best Play Another Country 1982, Evening Standard Drama Desk award for Best Comedy Lettice & Lovage 1988; *Recreations* tennis; *Clubs* Bucks; *Style*— Robert Fox, Esq; Robert Fox Ltd, 6 Beauchamp Place, London SW3 (☎ 071 584 6855, fax 071 225 1658)

FOX, Robert Trench; s of Waldo Trench Fox (d 1953), of Penjerrick, Falmouth, Cornwall; *b* 1 Jan 1937; *Educ* Winchester, Univ Coll Oxford (BA); *m* 1962, Lindsay Garrett, da of Sir Donald Forsyth Anderson (d 1973); 2 s, 2 da; *Career* dir Kleinwort Benson Ltd 1972-85, vice chm Kleinwort Benson Group 1986-; *Recreations* shooting, walking, sailing; *Clubs* Brooks's; *Style*— Robert Fox, Esq; Kleinwort Benson Ltd, 20 Fenchurch St, London EC3P 3DB (071 623 8000); Cheriton House, Cheriton, Alresford, Hants (☎ 096 2771 230)

FOX, Ronald David; s of Walter Fox (d 1985), of London, and Eva, *née* Covo; *b* 27 Sept 1946; *Educ* Mercers Sch, City of London Sch, Lincoln Coll Oxford (MA); *m* 11 Feb 1973, Sonya Claudine, da of Shalom Birshan; 1 s (Michael b 31 Jan 1979), 1 da (Susan b 8 July 1976); *Career* admitted slr 1972; ptnr Oppenheimers 1974-88 (joined as articled clerk 1969, chm Practice Devpt Ctee 1983-85); ptnr Denton Hall 1988-89, sr ptnr Fox Williams 1989-; nominated Star of Year 2000 by Legal Business Magazine 1990, Distinguished Serv award City of London Slr's Co 1989; Freeman Worshipful Co of Slrs 1984; hon slr Br-Israel C of C 1989 (memb Exec Ctee 1988), memb Br-German Jurists Assoc 1979-; Law Soc: co-opted memb of Completion Cheque Scheme Working Pty 1981-82, memb Standing Ctee on Co Law 1985-89, appointed Cncl Membership Ctee 1990; City of London Law Soc: memb Problems of Practice Sub Ctee 1985-, liaison offr Oppenheimers 1986-88, chm Working Pty (preparing evidence of City Slrs to Lady Marre's Ctee on the future of the legal profession) 1986, coordinator Survey on City Slrs' Attitudes to Multi-Disciplinary Practices 1987 (co-opted memb Ctee 1988, elected memb of Ctee 1988); chm Working Party (preparing the response of City Slrs to the Govt Green Paper on the Work and Organisation of the Legal Profession) 1989 (dep chm Ctee 1989), chm Working Party (Professional Indemnity Insurance) 1990; *Books* Legal Aspects of Doing Business in the United Kingdom (1984), Due Diligence, Disclosures and Warranties in Corporate Acquistion Practice - the United Kingdom (1988), International Business Transactions-Service Agreements for Multinational Corporate Executives in the United Kingdom (1988), Payments on Termination of Employment (1 edn 1981, 2 edn 1984, 3 edn 1990), Legal Aspects of Doing Business in England & Wales (1990); *Recreations* opera, theatre, cinema, swimming, skin diving, and scuba diving, motoring and other forms of transport, management studies; *Style*— Ronald Fox, Esq; Fox Williams, City Gate House, 39-45 Finsbury Square, London EC2A 1UU (☎ 071 628 2000, fax 071 628 2100, car 0836 238436)

FOX, Stephen Howard; s of Louis Fox, and Augusta Fox; *b* 8 Oct 1948; *Educ* Manchester GS, Coll of Law; *Career* admitted slr 1973, sr ptnr Betesh Fox & Co slrs, dir Fox Bros (warehousemen) Ltd, md Van Daele Chocolatier Ltd; *Recreations* writing;

Style— Stephen Fox, Esq; 17 Ralli Ct, West Riverside, Manchester M3 5FT (☎ 061 832 6131)

FOX, Hon Mrs; (Virginia Sarah); yr da of Baron Carr of Hadley (Life Peer); *b* 1957; *m* 1984, Michael Frederick Fox; 1 da (Alice Kate b 15 March 1989); *Style*— Hon Mrs Fox

FOX, William; JP (Cumbria); s of Philip Henry Fox, JP (d 1937), of High House, St Bees, and Hilda Mary, *née* Brinton (d 1969); *b* 13 Jan 1922; *Educ* St Bees Sch, Univ of Oxford (MA); *m* 28 Jan 1948, (Lillian) Esme, da of Maj L B Hogarth, OBE (d 1966), of Whitehaven; 1 s (Anthony b 29 Nov 1948), 2 da (Prudence b 31 July 1951, Joanna b 2 April 1960); *Career* Capt 18 Royal Garhwal Rifles IA 1942-46, Malayan CS 1946-58; bursar St Bees Sch 1958-83; chm and memb numerous local orgns incl Cumbria Probation Ctee; *Recreations* golf, skiing, windsurfing, fell walking; *Style*— William Fox, Esq, JP; High House, St Bees, Cumbria CA27 0BZ (☎ 0946 822 228)

FOX, William; s of Thomas Fox, and Doris, *née* Jones; *b* 6 Jan 1928; *Educ* Queen Elizabeth's GS; *m* 17 Feb 1953, Marjorie, da of Frank Hindle; 1 s (Michael Thomas Ian), 3 da (Christine, Elaine, Claire); *Career* enlisted Ballykinlar 1946, Nat Serv RA transfd E Lancs Regt Lance Corp 1947, paid corp 1947, demob 1948 as small arms instr; chm Wholesale Potato Co 1968-88 (merchant 1943-), rep Nat Fedn of Fruit and Potato Trades Ware Potato Imports Advsy Ctee and Potato Mktg Bd Jt Consultative Ctee, md Fox Commercial Vehicles Ltd (Renault-Dodge main dealers for NE Lancs), chm Blackburn Rovers FC 1982- (bd memb 1976, vice chm 1979); pres Football league 1989 (2 div rep in restructuring negotiations 1985, 2 div memb Football League Management Ctee 1986); memb FA (memb Exec Ctee and cnllr); *Recreations* football only; *Clubs* Blackburn Rovers FC; *Style*— William Fox, Esq; Treetop, Billinge End Road, Blackburn, Lancs BB2 6PT (☎ 0254 679786); Blackburn Rovers plc, Ewood Park, Blackburn, Lancashire (☎ 0254 55432, fax 0254 671042)

FOX, Winifred Marjorie (Mrs Eustace Gray Debros); da of Frederick Charles Fox (d 1968), and Charlotte Marion Ogborn; *b* 31 March 1915; *Educ* Streatham County Sch, St Hugh's Coll Oxford; *m* 1953, Eustace Gray Debros, formerly Eustacius Debrowski (d 1954); 1 da; *Career* entered Home Civil Serv, Unemployment Assistance Bd 1937, War Cabinet Office 1942, Miny of Town and Country Planning (later Housing and Local Govt) 1943, res chm Civil Serv Selection Bd 1971-72, under sec DOE (Planning) 1972-77; *Recreations* reading, listening to music; *Style*— Mrs Eustace Gray Debros; (☎ 0280 702100)

FOX-ANDREWS, James Roland Blake; QC (1968); step s of Norman Roy Fox-Andrews, QC (d 1971), and s of Mary Gammell, *née* Stuart (d 1973); *b* 24 March 1922; *Educ* Stowe, Pembroke Coll Cambridge; *m* 1950, Angela Bridget, da of Brig Charles Swift, OBE, MC; 2 s (Mark b 1952, Piers b 1954); *Career* called to the Bar Gray's Inn 1949, rec of Winchester 1971-72, (rec 1972-85, hon rec 1972-), ldr W Circuit 1982-84, circuit judge assigned to official referee work 1985; bencher Gray's Inn 1974; dep chm Devon GS 1969-71; *Style*— James Fox-Andrews, Esq, QC; 20 Cheyne Gardens, London SW3

FOX-ANDREWS, (Jonathan) Mark Piers; s of Judge James Fox-Andrews, QC, and Bridget Fox-Andrews, JP, *née* Swift; *b* 7 May 1952; *Educ* Eton, Trinity Hall Cambridge (BA, MA); *m* 22 Sept 1984, Rosemary Anne, da of Dennis Jenks; 1 s (Maximillian George b 28 March 1987), 1 da (Florence Rose b 14 July 1989); *Career* Drexel Burnham Lambert: trader 1977-80, mangr Singapore Office 1980-83, mangr Sydney Office 1984, md (Futures Ltd) London Office 1984-90; *Style*— J M P Fox-Andrews, Esq; 20 St Dunstans Hill, London EC3R 8HY (☎ 071 621 0156)

FOX BASSETT, Nigel; s of Thomas Fox Bassett (d 1960), of London, and Catherine Adriana, *née* Wiffen (d 1960); *b* 1 Nov 1929; *Educ* Taunton Sch, Trinity Coll Cambridge (MA); *m* 9 Sept 1961, Patricia Anne, da of Stanley William Lambourne (d 1986), of E Horsley, Surrey; 1 s (Jonathan b 30 July 1966), 1 da (Emma (Mrs Lines) b 19 Jan 1964); *Career* Nat Serv 2Lt RA 1949-50 (served Canal Zone Egypt with Mauritian Gds) Capt 264 (7 London) Field Regt RA TA 1950-60; admitted slr 1956, sr ptnr Clifford Chance (formerly Coward Chance) 1990- (articled clerk 1953, ptnr 1960); chm Exec Ctee Br Inst of Int and Comparative Law 1986- (memb Cncl 1977); memb Cncl: Int Assoc for the Protection of Industl Property (Br Gp) 1984-89, Int Law Assoc (Br Branch) 1974-86; chm Ctee Int Regulation of Fin Markets 1989-, memb UK Govt Know How Fund Banking and Fin Mission to Poland 1989-, chm Intellectual Property Sub Ctee City of London Slrs Co 1982-87 (memb Sub Ctee 1969-87), memb Ctee Business Section IBA (Anti Tst, Patents and Trademarks, Securities Ctees) 1969-; memb: Law Soc Euro Gp 1969-, American Bar Assoc (Futures Regulation Ctee) 1979-, Assoc Europeenne d'Etudes Juridiques et Fiscales (UK memb) 1969-; memb Cncl Taunton Sch, hon legal advsr to Partially Sighted Soc; memb: Glyndebourne Festival Opera Soc and Kent Opera, The Pilgrims of GB 1988-; vice pres Dulwich Hockey Club, chm Old Tauntonians Sports Club until 1989; Freeman Worshipful Co of Slrs 1960; memb Law Soc; *Books* English Sections of: Branches and Subsidiaries in the European Common Market (1976), Business Law in Europe (1982 and 1990); *Recreations* shooting, beagling, cricket, art, opera; *Clubs* Garrick, City of London, MCC, Seaview Yacht; *Style*— Nigel Fox Bassett, Esq; Clifford Chance, Blackfriars House, 19 New Bridge St, London EC4V 6BY (☎ 071 353 0211, fax 071 956 0114, telex 887847)

FOX-LEDGER, David Harold; s of Rev Harold Stanley Fox (d 1944), and Robina Mary, *née* Burns (d 1955); *b* 13 Jan 1939; *Educ* Sir Roger Manwood's Sch Sandwich; *m* 4 Feb 1968, Barbara Ann, da of John Stones; 2 da (Mary Jane b 1968, Susan Virginia b 1969); *Career* asst advsr High Cmmn Aden 1964-67, personal advsr to Ruler of Fujairah 1968-73, dir Hollowcore Systems 1974-86 (chm 1979), chm Dince Hill (Holdings) 1974-; numerous articles on Middle Eastern affrs; Freeman Worshipful Co of Gunmakers; FIL 1964; *Books* Shifting Sands (1983); *Recreations* country pursuits; *Clubs* East India; *Style*— David Fox-Ledger, Esq; Cator Court, Widecombe in the Moor, Devon TQ13 7UA (☎ 036 42 324); 29B Lexham Gds, London W8 (☎ 071 373 0804); Dince Hill (Holdings) Ltd, Manor Mill, South Brent, Devon TQ10 9TD (☎ 036 47 2779, telex 929010, fax 036 47 2801); 51 Abingdon Rd, London W8 (☎ 071 376 0796)

FOX-ROBINSON, Robert Andrew; Lancing, Trinity Coll Dublin (MA); s of Wilfred Henry Fox-Robinson, of London, and Jane Mary, *née* Home; *b* 11 Dec 1940; *m* 7 Oct 1972, Anne Thornton, da of Humphrey Challis (d 1958), of Essex; 3 s (Richard Charles b 14 Oct 1973, John Edward b 2 Feb 1976, William Robert b 23 March 1979); *Career* TAVR IV HAC London Gunner B Battery 1966-69; slr Supreme Ct 1970-88, dir of various co's; tstee Boothby Hall Tst Lincs 1968-84; former memb: Ely Diocesan Synod former memb Linton Deanery Synod; memb: Law Soc, Westminster C of C; *Recreations* squash, sailing and chess; *Clubs* Oriental; *Style*— Robert Fox-Robinson, Esq; 307 Grays Inn Rd, London WC1X 8DY (☎ 071 833 4099/8222, fax 071 833 8319)

FOX-STRANGWAYS, Hon Raymond George; 2 s of 8 Earl of Ilchester (d 1970), and hp of bro, 9 Earl; *b* 11 Nov 1921; *Educ* Exeter Sch, Seale Hayne Agric Coll; *m* 15 Nov 1941, Margaret Vera, da of late James Force, of North Surrey, BC, Canada; 2 s; *Career* served RAF WWII; Civil Serv 1949-76, ret; *Recreations* walking, riding, ornithology; *Style*— The Hon Raymond Fox-Strangways; Cherry Orchard Yews, Trull, Taunton, Somerset TA3 7LF (☎ 0823 282879)

FOXALL, Colin; s of Alfred George Foxall, of Chatham, Kent, and Ethel Margaret, *née* Hall; *b* 6 Feb 1947; *Educ* Gillingham GS; *m* 2 Feb 1980, Diana Gail, da of John Edward Bewick; 2 s (Ian b 1981, Neil b 1984); *Career* Dept of Trade 1974-75, under sec ECGD 1986 (joined 1966, asst sec 1982), gp dir ECGD Insur Servs; MIEx, MICM; *Recreations* clay pigeon shooting; *Style*— Colin Foxall, Esq; ECGD, Crown Building, Cathays Park, Cardiff (☎ 0222 82 4664, fax 0222 82 4003, telex 0222 497305/497

FOXALL, Prof Gordon Robert; s of Gordon William Foxall (d 1978), of Birmingham, and Marion, *née* Radford; *b* 16 July 1949; *Educ* Holly Lodge Sch Worcs, Univ of Salford (BSc, MSc), Univ of Birmingham (PhD), Univ of Strathclyde (PhD); *m* 26 June 1971, Jean, da of William Morris, of Birmingham; 1 da (Helen b 1977); *Career* Univ of Newcastle upon Tyne 1972-79, Univ of Birmingham 1980-83; reader Cranfield Inst of Technol 1983-86; prof: Univ of Strathclyde 1987-90, Univ of Birmingham 1990-; AFBPsS 1987, C Psychol 1988; *Books* Consumer Behaviour (1980), Marketing Behaviour (1981), Consumer Choice (1983) , Corporate Innovation (1984), Strategic Marketing Management (1986), Consumer Psychology (1989); *Recreations* reading, walking; *Style*— Prof Gordon Foxall; 4 Ridgewood Drive, Four Oaks, Sutton Coldfield, B75 6TR; University of Birmingham, Department of Commerce, Edgbaston, Birmingham B15 2TT (☎ 021 414 3344)

FOXELL, Clive Arthur Peirson; CBE; s of Arthur Turner Foxell (d 1955), and Lillian, *née* Ellerman (d 1979); *b* 27 Feb 1930; *Educ* Harrow HS, Univ of London (BSc); *m* 1956, Shirley Ann Patey, da of Idwal Morris; 1 da (Elizabeth); *Career* mangr GEC Semiconductor Labs 1968, md GEC Semiconductors Ltd 1971; dep dir: of res PO 1975, PO Procurement Exec 1978-79; dir: of purchasing PO 1980, of procurement BT (chief exec 1983-85), BT Systems Ltd 1982-89, chm: Fulcrum Communications Ltd 1985-86, Phonepoint Ltd 1989-; memb Bd BT 1986-89; author of numerous articles and papers on electronics; memb: Bulgin Premium IERE 1964, Cncl IEE 1975-78 and 1982-85 and 1987- (vice chm Electronics Div 1980-81, dep chm 1982-83, chm 1983-84), Engrg Bd SRC 1977-80, ACARD Working Pty on Info Tech 1981, DTI CS Ctee 1985-88, Cncl SERC 1986-90; Liveryman Worshipful Co of Engrs; FEng, FIEE, FInstP, FIPS; *Books* Low Noise Microwave Amplifiers (1968); *Recreations* photography, railways; *Style*— Clive Foxell, Esq, CBE; 4 Meades Lane, Chesham, Bucks (☎ 0494 785737); British Telecom, BT Centre, 81 Newgate St, London EC1A 7AJ

FOXLEY-NORRIS, Air Chief Marshal Sir Christopher Neil; GCB (1973, KCB 1968, CB 1966), DSO (1945), OBE (1956); s of Maj John Perceval Foxley-Norris, Cheshire Regt (d 1922), and Dorothy Brabant Smith; *b* 16 March 1917; *Educ* Winchester, Trinity Coll Oxford, Middle Temple; *m* 1948, Joan Lovell, da of Maj Percy H Hughes (d 1953), of Crondall, Hants; *Career* Air Chief Marshal 1970, chief of personnel and logistics MOD 1971-74, ret; chm General Portfolio Life Insurance Co; chm: Battle of Britain Fighter Assoc 1978-, Gardening for the Disabled Tst 1980-, Ex-RAF and Dependants Severely Disabled Holiday Tst 1984-; chm emeritus Leonard Cheshire Fndn 1982- (chm 1974-82), vice pres RUSI; CBIM; *Recreations* golf, cricket, writing, bridge; *Clubs* RAF, Huntercombe Golf; *Style*— Air Chief Marshal Sir Christopher Foxley-Norris, GCB,DSO,OBE; Tumble Wood, Northend Common, Henley-on-Thames, Oxon (☎ 049 163 457)

FOXWELL, Lady Edith Sybil; *née* Lambart; o child of Capt Hon Lionel John Olive Lambart, DSO, RN (ka 1940, 2 s of late 9 Earl of Cavan; bro of 10 and 11 Earl), and Adelaide Douglas, *née* Randolph; raised to the rank of an Earl's da 1947; *b* 11 June 1918; *m* 28 Feb 1940 (m dis 1975), Maj Ivan Cottam Foxwell, *qv*, 2 da (Zia b 1940, Atalanta Edith b 1956); *Career* public relations conslt; *Recreations* travelling, swimming, charitable activities; *Clubs* Polo (Windsor and Cirencester); *Style*— The Lady Edith Foxwell; c/o National Westminster Bank, 1 Grosvenor Gardens, London SW1W 0BG

FOXWELL, Ivan Cottam; er s of Lt-Col Herbert Somerton Foxwell (d on active serv 1943); *b* 22 Feb 1914; *Educ* Stubbington House, Wellington, RMC Sandhurst; *m* 28 Feb 1940 (m dis 1975), Lady Edith, *qv*; 2 da (Zia (Mrs David Kruger) b 1940, Atalanta b 1956, m Prince Stefano Massimo, *qv*); *Career* substantive Maj Royal Norfolk Regt, served BEF France 1940, France and Germany 1944-45; film prodr and screenwriter 1947-; prodns incl: No Room At the Inn, Guilt Is My Shadow, Stefan Zweig's Twenty Four Hours of A Woman's Life, The Intruder, The Colditz Story, Manuela, A Touch of Larceny, Tiara Tahiti, The Quiller Memorandum, Evelyn Waugh's Decline and Fall; *Recreations* reading, writing, swimming; *Clubs* Buck's, Pratt's; *Style*— Ivan Foxwell, Esq; c/o Baker Tilly, Clement House, 99 Aldwych, London WC2 4JY

FOXWELL, Rupert Edward Theodore; s of Peter Cottam Foxwell, of Farnham, Surrey, and Marika, *née* Soutzos, of London; *b* 24 Nov 1954; *Educ* Radley, Magdalene Coll Cambridge (MA); *m* 5 May 1979, Penelope, da of Brig Sir Nicholas Somerville, of Greywell, Hants; 3 s (Jonathan b 1980, Mark b 1982, Edward b 1986); *Career* slr Allen & Overy 1979; dir Barclays de Zoete Wedd 1983-86, md Euro Investmt Banking Div Prudential-Bache London 1986-88, currently dep md UBS Phillips & Drew; tstee First Challenge Tst; memb Law Soc 1979; *Recreations* shooting, driving; *Style*— Rupert Foxwell, Esq; UBS Phillips & Drew, Broadgate, 100 Liverpool St, London EC2 (☎ 071 901 3333)

FOXWOOD, Capt Philip Anthony; o s of Maj Prince Ibrahim Fazil, RA (d 1978; naturalized Br subject 1920; of Franco-Turkish descent; gs of Prince Mustapha Fazil, leading Ottoman cabinet minister who d 1875 - *see* Burke's Royal Families of the World), and his 1 w Kate (d 1973), o da of Calvin Amory Stevens, of New York; *b* 5 Sept 1935,Upper Woodford; *Educ* Harrow, RMA Sandhurst; *m* 12 July 1971, (Rose) Mary, o da of Clifford Mansel Reece, QC (d 1973); 1 s (Hugo b 1973); *Career* Coldstream Gds 1954-66; served Cyprus (Gds Para Co) and Aden (wounded); individual memb: Royal Assoc for Disability and Rehabilitation (RADAR) 1977-, Friends of Navarino; Oxon War Pensions Ctee 1986-90, Beds, Bucks, Herts and Oxon War Pensions Ctee 1991-, hon treas W Oxon Cons Assoc 1985-; *Recreations* gardening, genealogy; *Clubs* Pratt's, Tent XII; *Style*— Capt Philip Foxwood; Ann's Cottage, Ramsden, Oxford OX7 3AZ (☎ 0993 868592)

FOYLE, Christina Agnes Lilian; da of William Alfred Foyle (d 1963), and Christina Tulloch (d 1976); *b* 30 Jan 1911; *Educ* Aux Villas Unspunnen, Interlaken Switzerland; *m* 1938, Ronald Frederick Batty; *Career* began Foyle's Literary Luncheons, where distinguished writers and artists meet the reading public, 1930; memb Ctee Univ of Essex, memb Cncl Royal Soc of Arts 1963-69 (chm E Anglican Region 1978); landowner (1000 acres); *Recreations* book collecting, reading; *Style*— Miss Christina Foyle; Beeleigh Abbey, Maldon, Essex; Foyles, Charing Cross Rd, London WC2

FOYLE, (William Richard) Christopher; s of (William) Richard Foyle (d 1957), and Alice, da of Eugen Kun, of Vienna; the Foyles are an ancient W Country family (*see* Burke's Landed Gentry, 18 Edn, vol 3); *b* 20 Jan 1943; *Educ* Radley; *m* 27 July 1983, Catherine Mary, da of Rev David William Forrester Jelleyman, of Melbourn, Cambs; 3 da (Charlotte b 1984, Annabel b 1985, Christine b 1987); *Career* trained in publishing and bookselling in London, Tübingen, Berlin, Helsinki and Paris; mangr W & G Foyle Ltd 1965-72, ptnr Emson & Dudley and dir Emson & Dudley Securities Ltd 1972-78, proprietor Christopher Foyle Aviation (Leasing) Co 1977-; md: Air Foyle Ltd 1978-, Air Foyle Executive Ltd 1988-, Air Foyle Handling Ltd 1989-; memb: Air Tport Ctee of Gen Aviation Mfrs and Traders Assoc 1986-, Small Business Ctee Aviation Trg Assoc 1987-; *Recreations* travel, skiing, flying, reading non-fiction, wine and food; *Clubs* White's; *Style*— Christopher Foyle, Esq; c/o Lloyds Bank plc, 16 St James's St, London SW1A 1EY; Air Foyle Ltd, Halcyon House, Luton Airport, Luton, Beds LU2 9LU (☎ 0582 419792, telex 825538 AFOYLE G, fax 0582 400958)

FOYLE, Grace Joan; da of Frederick Joseph Hayball (d 1948), of Ottery St Mary, Devon, and Alice Harriette, *née* Bonfield; *b* 9 April 1918; *Educ* King's Sch Ottery St Mary, Inchbold Sch of Design (Dip Fine Arts); *m* 25 July 1942, Gilbert Eric Foyle (d 1975), s of Gilbert Samuel Foyle (d 1971), of Eastbourne; 1 s (Roger John b 1944), 1 da (Angela Fenella b 1956); *Career* pres Foyle's Educational Ltd 1988- (dir 1973-88); cncllr Worthing Borough Cncl 1966-72; chm Friends of Worthing Museum 1972-74; *Recreations* tennis, gardening, local organisations, charity work; *Clubs* West Worthing Tennis, Parrot; *Style*— Mrs Grace J Foyle; Dukes Cottage, The Street, Patching, W Sussex (☎ 090 674 275); Foyle's Educational Ltd, Feldon House, Victoria Way, Burgess Hill, W Sussex (☎ 04446 2797)

FOYLE, John Ernest; s of Gilbert Samuel Foyle (d 1971), of Eastbourne (founder of W & G Foyle Ltd, booksellers, 1903), and Ethel, *née* Cook (d 1981); *b* 9 Oct 1920; *Educ* Christ's Coll Finchley; *m* 29 March 1952, Margaret Patricia, da of William White, of Haywards Heath; 2 s (Lance b 14 Aug 1954, Robert b 2 May 1958), 1 da (Deborah b 16 May 1961); *Career* served RE 1940-46 as Lt in Africa and Italy; dir: Foyle's Educnl Ltd 1947-, Unifoyle Ltd 1977-, Croom Helm Publishers 1972-78; govr Gilbert Foyle Educnl Tst; *Recreations* fishing, bowls, travel; *Clubs* IOD, Royal Cwlth; *Style*— John Foyle, Esq; Feldon House, Victoria Way, Burgesshill, W Sussex (☎ 04446 2797)

FOYLE, John Lewis; s of Roland Bernard Foyle, of Portsmouth, Hants, and Rose Vera, *née* Taylor; *b* 7 June 1948; *Educ* Portsmouth Northern GS, St John's Coll Cambridge (MA); *m* 19 Feb 1972, Patricia Mary, da of John Victor Ketteringham (d 1986), of Ruthin, Clwyd; 3 s (James b 1972, Thomas d 1978, William b 1980); *Career* co sec: Inflation Accounting Steering Gp 1976-78, Jt Exchanges Ctee 1982-, ECOFEX 1988-; md ops London Int Fin Futures Exchange, dir Assoc Futures Brokers and Dealers 1985-; FCA 1973; *Recreations* sport, music; *Style*— John Foyle, Esq; Brookmead, Moat Farm Chase, Chipping Hill, Witham, Essex CM8 2DE; LIFFE, Royal Exchange, London EC3V 3PJ (☎ 071 623 0444, fax 071 588 3624)

FOZARD, Dr John William; OBE (1981); s of John Fozard (d 1958), and Eleanor, *née* Paulkit (d 1948); *b* 16 Jan 1928; *Educ* Univ of London (BSc), Coll of Aeronautics (MSc), Cranfield Inst of Technol; *m* 1, 1951 (m dis 1985), Mary, da of late RSM Charles Burley Ward, VC; 2 s; *m* 2, 1985, Gloria Ditmars Stanchfield, wid of Alan Roberts, of Alexandria, Virginia, USA; *Career* chief designer Harrier 1963-78, exec dir Hawker Siddeley Aviation 1971-78, mktg dir Kingston-Brough Div Br Aerospace 1978-84, divnl dir Special Projects Mil Aircraft Div Br Aerospace 1984-89 (ret 1989); Gold medal London Soc of Engrs 1972, Br Silver medal for Aeronautics 1972; Hon DSc Strathclyde 1983; fell of UK Fellowship of Engrg 1984, fell of Royal Soc of London 1987; pres RAes 1986-87; CEng, FRAeS, FIMechE, FAIAA, FRSA; James Clayton prize Instn of Mech Engrs 1983, The Mullard award (with RS Hooper) Royal Soc 1983, Lindbergh prof of aerospace history Smithsonian Instn Nat Air & Space Museum Washington DC USA for 1988; visiting prof in aircraft design Univ of Michigan at Ann Arbor 1989; *Books* many papers in specialist aeronautical jls and tech press 1958-; Sydney Camm and the Hurricane: perspectives on the Master Fighter Designer (ed, 1991); *Recreations* music, engineering history; *Style*— Dr John Fozard, OBE; 306 N Columbus St, Alexandria, VA 22314, USA (☎ 703 549 5142); Smithsonian Institution, National Air and Space Museum, Washington DC, 20560, USA (☎ 202 357 2515)

FRACKOWIAK, Dr Richard Stanislaus Joseph; s of Capt Joseph Frackowiak, of London, and Wanda, *née* Majewska; *b* 26 March 1950; *Educ* Latymer Upper Sch, Peterhouse Cambridge (MB BChir, MA, MD); *m* 17 Feb 1972, Christine Jeanne Françoise, da of Lt Louis Thepot, of St Cloud, France; 1 s (Matthew), 2 da (Stephanie, Annabelle); *Career* hon conslt and sr lectr Hammersmith Hosp and Nat Hosp for Nervous Diseases 1984, asst dir MRC Cyclotron Unit 1988 (clinical scientist 1984), head of Neurology Unit Dept of Med Hammersmith Hosp 1988, sr lectr Nat Hosp and Inst of Neurology London 1989 (consIt 1988); dir Int Soc for Cerebral Blood Flow and Metabolism, corresponding memb American Neurological Assoc; FRCP 1987; *Recreations* tennis, travel, pulp fiction; *Clubs* Hurlingham; *Style*— Dr Richard Frackowiak; MRC Cyclotron Unit, Hammersmith Hospital, 150 Ducane Rd, London W12 0HS (☎ 081 740 3172, fax 081 743 3987)

FRAENKEL, Peter Maurice; s of Ernest Fraenkel, and Luise, *née* Tessmann; *b* 5 July 1915; *Educ* Battersea Poly, Imperial Coll London (BSc); *m* 1946, Hilda Muriel, da of William Norman; 2 da; *Career* sr ptnr Peter Fraenkel & Ptnrs (consulting engrs), dir British Maritime Technology Ltd; chm: Peter Fraenkel BMT Ltd, Peter Fraenkel Group; Queen's award for Export 1982; FEng, FICE, FIStructE; *Clubs* Athenaeum; *Style*— P M Fraenkel, Esq; Tuition House, 27-37 St George's Rd, Wimbledon, London SW19 3EU (☎ 081 879 0335)

FRAKER, Ford McKinstry; s of Harrison Shedd Fraker, and Marjorie Tomlinson Fraker (d 1987); *b* 15 July 1948; *Educ* Phillips Acad Andover Mass USA, Harvard (BA); *m* 24 Dec 1984, Linda Margaret, da of T Hanson; 2 s (Jonathan b 2 May 1987, Charles b 29 Jan 1990), 1 da (Antonia b 21 Jan 1986); *Career* vice pres and regnl mangr Chemical Bank (NY) Bahrain Arabian Gulf 1977-79; Saudi International Bank London: mangr Middle East 1979-82, asst gen mangr, head of gen banking 1982-85, head of credit 1985-90, head of client devpt and mktg 1990-; dir Saudi International Bank Nassau 1987-90; *Recreations* tennis, art, travel; *Clubs* Nantucket Yacht, RAC, Overseas Bankers, Owl, Vanderbilt Racquet; *Style*— Ford M Fraker, Esq; 51 Clarendon Rd, London W11 (☎ 071 727 2567); 12 Mt Vernon St, Nantucket, Mass 02554

FRAKES, Ronald Alfred; s of Alfred Henry Frakes (d 1946), of London, and Edith Amelia, *née* Marsden (d 1981); *b* 2 June 1928; *m* 27 May 1950, (Joan) Heather, da of John Austen Chamberlain (d 1977), of London; 2 da (Janet b 1958, Alison b 1960); *Career* wireless operator served Malaya (SEAC) RAF 1946-48; freelance heraldic artist 1972-; numerous commissions incl painting Arms of Queen Elizabeth I and Queen Elizabeth II plus heraldic symbols of England, Scotland, Ireland and Wales in the border of a Royal Charter presented to the Painter-Stainers in 1981; memb: Richard III Soc, Heraldry Soc; Freeman: City of London 1972, Worshipful Co of Painter-Stainers 1972 (Liveryman 1981); FRSA 1981; *Recreations* study of medieval history; *Clubs* Queenhithe Ward; *Style*— Ronald Frakes, Esq; 77 Highfield Rd, Woodford Green, Essex IG8 8JB (☎ 081 504 6717)

FRAME, Sir Alistair Gilchrist; s of Alexander Frame, and Mary, *née* Fraser; *b* 3 April 1929; *Educ* Univ of Glasgow (BSc), Univ of Cambridge; *m* 1953, Sheila, *née* Mathieson; 1 da; *Career* dir Britoil 1982, chm RTZ Corp 1985- (dir 1973-85), former dir Plessey plc; chm: Davy Corp plc 1990-, Wellcome plc; non-exec dir Eurotunnel; former memb Engrg Cncl, memb NEB, dir Reactor and Res Gps UKAEA; FEng; kt 1981; *Style*— Sir Alistair Frame; 6 St James's Square, London SW1Y 4LD

FRAME, Frank Riddell; *b* 15 Feb 1930; *Educ* Hamilton Acad, Univ of Glasgow (MA, LLB); *m* 1958, Maureen, *née* Milligan; 1 s, 1 da; *Career* North of Scotland Hydro-Electric Board 1955-60, UKAEA 1960-68, The Weir Group plc 1968-76 (dir 1971-76); The Hong Kong and Shanghai Banking Corporation Limited: joined as gp legal advsr 1977, exec dir 1985, ret as dep chm 1990, currently advsr to the board; chm: South China Morning Post Limited 1981-87, Far Eastern Economic Review Limited 1981-87; dir: Marine Midland Banks Inc 1986-90, Swire Pacific Limited 1986-90, The British Bank of the Middle East 1986-90, Securities and Futures Cmmn Hong Kong 1989-90; JP Hong Kong 1985; *Publications* The Law Relating to Nuclear Energy (with Prof Harry Street); *Clubs* The Hong Kong, Shek Country (Hong Kong); *Style*— Frank Frame, Esq; The Hongkong and Shanghai Banking Corporation Ltd, 99 Bishopsgate, London EC2P 2LA (☎ 071 638 2300)

FRAME, Roger Campbell Crosbie; s of Andrew Crosbie Frame, of Giffnock, Glasgow, and Jessie Caldwell, *née* Campbell; *b* 7 June 1949; *Educ* Glasgow Acad; *m* 10 Sept 1973, Angela Maria, da of Louis Evaristi, of Giffnock, Glasgow; 2 s (Nicholas Roger b 1976, Mark Christopher b 1980), 1 da (Lauren Charlotte b 1988); *Career* CA; sr ptnr Frame & Co; dir: Camos Ltd, Frame & Co Management Services Ltd; treas Glasgow Gp of Artists 1983-89; sec: Glasgow Eastern Merchants and Tradesman Soc, Royal Scottish Soc of Painters in Watercolour (RSW) 1986-;, chm James Custator Wards Fund (Univ of Glasgow) 1984-, offr Incorporation of Weavers of Glasgow; Freeman: City of Glasgow, City of London; *Recreations* clay pigeon shooting, art; *Clubs* Glasgow Art; *Style*— Roger C C Frame, Esq; Dunglass, 56 Manse Rd, Bearsden, Glasgow G61 3PN; Frame & Co Chartered Accountants, 29 Waterloo St, Glasgow G2 6BZ (☎ 041 226 3838)

FRAME, Ronald William Sutherland; s of Alexander D Frame, and Isobel D Frame; *b* 23 May 1953; *Educ* The High Sch of Glasgow, Univ of Glasgow (MA, Foulis scholarship, Bradley medal), Jesus Coll Oxford (BLitt); *Career* writer 1981-; two TV plays and many short stories on radio; novels and short story collections: Winter Journey (1984, 3 Sony radio award nominations 1985), Watching Mrs Gordon (1985), A Long Weekend with Marcel Proust (1986), Sandmouth People (1987), A Woman of Judah (1987), Paris: A Television Play (1987), Penelope's Hat (1989), Bluette (1990), Underwood and After (1991); *awards* Betty Trask prize (jt winner) 1984, Samuel Beckett prize 1986, TV Industs Panel Most Promising Writer New to TV 1986; *Recreations* swimming, walking; *Style*— Ronald Frame, Esq; A P Watt Ltd, 20 John St, London WC1N 2DR (☎ 071 405 6774, fax 071 831 2154)

FRANCE, Sir Arnold William; GCB (1972, KCB 1965, CB 1957); s of William Ernest France (d 1939), of Knutsford, Cheshire and Southport, Lancs; *b* 20 April 1911; *Educ* Bishop's Stortford Coll; *m* 1940, Frances Margaret Linton, da of Dr Charles John Linton Palmer (d 1926), of Gosport; 4 da (*see* J N B Penny); *Career* served WWII Capt ME; civil servant; HM Treasy 1945-63, perm sec Miny of Health 1964-68 (civil servant 1963-68), chm Bd Inland Revenue 1968-73, ret; *Recreations* reading; *Clubs* Reform; *Style*— Sir Arnold France, GCB; Thornton Cottage, Lingfield, Surrey (☎ 0364 832278)

FRANCE, Rev Dr Richard Thomas; s of Edgar France, of Haslemere, Surrey, and Doris Woosnam, *née* Morgan (d 1984); *b* 2 April 1938; *Educ* Bradford GS, Balliol Coll Oxford (MA), Univ of London (BD), Univ of Bristol (PhD); *m* 30 July 1965, Barbara, da of Ernest Wilding (d 1972), of Stockport, Cheshire; 1 s (David Martyn b 22 May 1968), 1 da (Susan Janet b 10 Jan 1971); *Career* lectr Univ of Ife Nigeria 1969-73, sr lectr Univ of Ahmadu Bello Zaria Nigeria 1976-77, warden Tyndale House Cambridge 1978-81 (librarian 1973-76), vice princ London Bible Coll 1981-88, princ Wycliffe Hall Oxford 1989-; SNTS 1977; *Books* Jesus and the Old Testament (1971), Gospel Perspectives Vols 1-3 (ed, 1980-83), The Gospel of Matthew (1985), The Evidence for Jesus (1986), Jesus the Radical (1989), Matthew: Evangelist and Teacher (1989), Divine Government (1990); *Recreations* wild life, travel, mountain walking, theatre; *Style*— Rev Dr Richard France; Wycliffe Hall, 54 Banbury Rd, Oxford OX2 6PW (☎ 0865 274205)

FRANCIES, Duncan; s of Joseph Standish Noel Francies (d 1988), and Jeanne Zoe, *née* Dordan-Pyke; *b* 5 June 1945; *Educ* Sutton Valence; *m* 24 June 1983, Patricia Mary, da of Samuel Field, of Brisbane, Aust; 1 s (Edward), 1 da (Olivia); *Career* admitted slr 1968; ptnr Richards Butler; Freeman: Worshipful Co of Slrs 1976, City of London 1978; memb: Law Soc 1963, Slrs Benevolent Assoc 1976; *Recreations* gardening, swimming; *Clubs* Wig and Pen; *Style*— Duncan Francies, Esq; Beaufort House, 15 St Botolph St, London EC3A 7EE (☎ 071 247 6555, telex 9494 94 RBLAW, fax 071 247 5091)

FRANCIS, Andrew James; s of Frank Sidney Francis, DFC (d 1971), of Ashtead Park, Ashtead, Surrey, and Ann, *née* Velody; *b* 1 Nov 1953; *Educ* City of London Freeman's Sch, Univ of Oxford (BA); *m* 18 Dec 1982, Victoria Louise, da of Francis Henry Gillum-Webb (d 1972), of Weybridge, Surrey; 2 da (Amelia Rose Louise, Alexandria Lucy Olivia); *Career* called to the Bar Lincoln's Inn 1977, in practice at Chancery Bar 1979-; motoring corr Law Soc's Gazette, chm Alton Line User's Assoc; Kennedy and Tancred scholar; memb Hon Soc Lincoln's Inn; *Recreations* walking, commuting, motoring; *Style*— Andrew Francis, Esq; 28 Frensham Road, Lower Bourne, Farnham, Surrey; 11 New Square, Lincoln's Inn, London WC2 (☎ 071 831 0081, fax 071 405 2560)

FRANCIS, Clare Mary; MBE (1978); da of Owen Francis, CB, and Joan St Leger, *née* Norman; *b* 17 April 1946; *Educ* Royal Ballet Sch, UCL (BSc); *m* 1977 (m dis 1985), Jacques Robert Redon; 1 s (Thomas Robert Jean b 1978); *Career* transatlantic singlehanded crossing 1973, first woman home Observer Singlehanded Transatlantic Race and holder women's record 1976, first woman skipper Whitbread Round The World Race 1977-78; hon fell: UCL 1979, UMIST 1981; *Books* non-fiction: Come Hell or High Water (1977), Come Wind or Weather (1978), The Commanding Sea (1981), Night Sky (1983), Red Crystal (1985), Wolf Winter (1987); *Recreations* opera, theatre; *Style*— Miss Clare Francis, MBE

FRANCIS, Clive; s of Raymond Francis (d 1987), of Brighton, and Margaret, *née* Towner; *b* 26 June 1946; *Educ* Ratton Secdy Modern Sch Sussex, RADA; *m* May 1989, Natalie, da of Martin Ogle, OBE; 1 da (Lucinda b Dec 1989); *Career* actor; West End appearances incl: The Servant of Two Masters, Three, The Mating Game, Bloomsbury, The Return of A J Raffles, The Rear Column, The School for Scandal, Benefactors, The Importance of Being Earnest, Single Spies, What the Butler Saw, A Small Family Business and Tis Pity She's A Whore (Nat Theatre); 'Tis Pity She's A Whore, What The Butler Saw (Wyndhams Theatre); Chichester Festival Theatre performances incl: Monsieur Perichon's Travels, The Circle, Look After Lulu, many TV appearances incl: Poldark, Entertaining Mr Sloane, As You Like It, Masda, The Critic, A Married Man, The Far Pavilions, Yes Prime Minister, Oedipus, Adventures of Sherlock Holmes, After The War, The Rear Column, Quartermain's Terms, Old Flames, The Piglet Files; caricaturist 1983-; five solo exhibitions; designer various theatre posters and book covers; *Books* Laughlines (1989); *Recreations* walking, exploring England, twentieth century first editions; *Clubs* Garrick; *Style*— Clive Francis, Esq; Ken McReddie, 91 Regent St, London W1R 7TB

FRANCIS, Ven Edward Reginald; s of Alfred John Francis (d 1978), of 43 Monins Rd, Dover, Kent, and Elsie Hilda, *née* Hiscock; *b* 31 Jan 1929; *Educ* Monmouth, Dover GS, Rochester Theol Coll; *m* 21 Oct 1950, Joyce Noreen, da of George James Atkins (d 1935); 3 s (Paul, Nigel, Jonathan); *Career* ordained 1961, chaplain Training Ship Arethusa and asst curate All Saints' Frindsbury Rochester 1961-64, vicar St

William's Chatham 1964-73, vicar and rural dean Rochester 1973-79, archdeacon of Bromley 1979-; memb Gen Synod 1981-90, jt chm Canterbury and Rochester Diocesan Cncl for Social Responsibility 1983-88; ACII 1958; *Recreations* ornithology, walking, rugby football, poetry; *Style—* The Ven the Archdeacon of Bromley

FRANCIS, Gp Capt Geoffrey; DSO (1941), DFC (1940); s of F S Francis (d 1950), and Lillian, *née* Drake; *b* 13 Jan 1907; *Educ* Wellington, RAF Cadet Coll Cranwell; *m* 1, 6 June 1936 (m dis 1947), Patience Elinor, da of Lt-Col Sir Thomas Salt, DSO (d 1946); 1 da (Jessica b 1 Jan 1942); m 2, 4 March 1949, Joan Millicent Kirkland Vavasour, da of Arthur John Robb (d 1956); 1 s (Andrew b 29 Nov 1951), 3 da (Rosemary b 14 July 1950, Jilly b 12 March 1955, Miranda b 4 June 1957); *Career* 202 Flying Boat Sqdn Malta 1928, i/c Station Flt Malta 1930, PA to C-in-C Coast Cmd Lee-on-Solent 1932, 20l flying Boat Sqdn Calshot 1933-34, HQ Coastal Cmd Lee-on-Solent 1935-36, HQ Far East Cmd Singapore 1936, 230 Flying Boat Sqdn Singapore 1938, Ceylon 1939, i/c Alexandria 1940-41 (despatches 1940), 201 Gp temp i/c Alexandria 1941, No 4 (C) Operational Trg Unit, i/c Invergordon 1941-42 (despatches 1942), HQ Coastal Cmd Air Staff 1943, attached C-in-C US Pacific Fleet 1943; HQ SE Asia Cmd: Planning Staff Delhi 1944, Air Cmd, Air Staff Delhi 1944; RAF Station Kogalla i/c Ceylon 1944-45, RAF Station Seletar i/c Singpore 1945, Air Miny 1946, HQ 38 Gp Sr Offr Admin 1947, RAF Station i/c Netheravon 1948, RAF Station i/c Bassingbourn 1949, resigned cmmn 1951; farmer Sussex 1951-56; owned and operated Sandwich Boatyard Kent 1956-70; athletics; runner up for Victor Ludorum Cranwell, broke Cranwell record for 120 yard Hurdles 1926; sailed from Hong Kong to Singapore 1938, fndr memb RAF YC; Freeman City of London 1928, memb Worshipful Co of Cordwainers 1927; Greek Flying Cross 1946; *Recreations* yachting; *Clubs* Royal Cruising (life memb), RAF Yacht, Royal Lymington Yacht (fndr memb); *Style—* Gp-Capt Geoffrey Francis, DSO, DFC; 28 Stanley Rd, Lymington, Hants SO41 9SG (☎ 0590 674616)

FRANCIS, George Carwardine; s of Guy Lancelot Brereton Francis (d 1962); *b* 15 April 1929; *Educ* Malvern; *m* 1960, Barbara Peggy, da of John Francis Brooke (d 1977), of W Chiltington; 2 da; *Career* admitted slr 1956; md The Chepstow Racecourse plc 1963-, vice chm Racecourse Assoc Ltd 1986-; *Recreations* cricket, racquets, real tennis, squash, shooting; *Clubs* MCC, Free Foresters, I Zingari; *Style—* George Francis, Esq; East Cliff, Chepstow, Gwent NP6 7PT (☎ 0291 622 072)

FRANCIS, Gerald Charles James (Gerry); s of Royston Albert Francis, and Pauline Elsie Francis; *b* 6 Dec 1951; *Educ* Stavely Secdy Modern Sch Chiswick; *Career* professional footballer manager; player Queens Park Rangers 1968-79 and 1981-82: debut v Liverpool as apprentice 1968, 352 appearances, 65 goals; other clubs as player: 66 appearances Crystal Palace 1979-81 (9 goals), 54 appearances Coventry City 1982-83 (2 goals), 7 appearances Swansea City 1984-85, 5 appearances Portsmouth 1985; Exeter City 1983-84: player-mangr, 31 appearances, 3 goals; Bristol Rovers 1985-: 39 appearances, 1 goal, mangr 1987-; England: 6 under 23 caps (capt 1973-75), 12 full caps (capt 1975-76), 3 goals; honours as players Queens Park rangers: promotion to Div 1 1972-73, runners up League Championship 1976; honours as mangr Bristol Rovers: Div 3 Championship 1990, runners up Leyland Daf Cup 1990; Barclays Div 3 mangr of the year 1990, mangr of the month March 1988 and March 1990; *Recreations* racing pigeons, squash, Winston Churchill; *Style—* Gerry Francis, Esq; Bristol Rovers FC, 199 Two Mile Hill Rd, Kingswood, Bristol BS15 1AZ (☎ 0272 352508)

FRANCIS, Prof Hazel; da of Harry Wright (d 1961), of Brownhills, Staffs, and Ethel Vera, *née* Bedson (d 1965); *b* 12 April 1929; *Educ* Queen Mary's HS for Girls Walsall, Girton Coll Cambridge (MA), Univ of Leeds (MA, PhD); *m* 23 May 1953, Dr Huw Wesley Stephen Francis, s of Rev Matthew Francis (d 1954), of Walsall; 2 s (Andrew Martin b 1958, Jonathan Mark b 1962), 3 da (Susan Margaret b 1954, Keren Mary b 1956, Hilary Ann b 1960); *Career* teacher Handsworth GS for Girls Birmingham 1950-53; lectr and sr lectr Sch of Educn Univ of Leeds 1973-78 (p/t lectr Dept of Psychology 1969-73), pro-dir Inst of Educn Univ of London 1985- (prof of educnl psychology 1978-); author of numerous articles in relevant scientific jls; FBPsS 1980 (memb Cncl 1979-85); memb: Br Educnl Res Assoc, Univs Cncl for the Educn of Teachers 1978-; chartered psychologist 1988; *Books* include: Language in Childhood (1975), Language in Teaching and Learning (1977), Learning to Read-Literate Behaviour and Orthographic Knowledge (1982), Minds of Their Own (1984), Learning to Teach: Psychology in Teacher Training (ed, 1985), The British Journal of Educational Psychology (ed, 1985); *Recreations* mountain walking, swimming, tennis; *Style—* Prof Hazel Francis; Institute of Education, University of London, 20 Bedford Way, London WC1H 0AL (☎ 071 636 1500)

FRANCIS, Jennifer (Jenni); da of Winston Harry Gordon Francis, and Clytie Jeanne Francis; *b* 13 July 1959; *Educ* St Augustine's C of E, City of London Univ (Dip CAM, PR); *Career* mktg mgmnt Brook Street Bureau 1978-83, PR exec Cannons Sports Club London 1983-86, md and chief exec offr Networking PR 1986-, Black Business Woman of the Year 1989; memb Mgmnt Cncl Women's Enterprise Devpt Agency, Mktg Ctee Ind Theatre Cncl; MIPR, MInstD; *Recreations* squash, weightlifting, church, concerts, reading; *Style—* Miss Jenni Francis; 25 Milton Avenue, Highgate, London N6 5QF; Networking PR Ltd, Canalot Prodn Studios, 222 Kensal Rd, London W10 5BN (☎ 081 968 3757, fax 081 960 1452)

FRANCIS, Capt John Lionel; OBE (1988), DL (Dyfed 1971); s of Maj John Francis, DSO, TD, DL (d 1960); *b* 4 July 1921; *Educ* Cheltenham, RAC Cirencester; *m* 1947, Susan Mary Macleod (d 1986), da of Arthur Macleod Clarke (d 1932), and gda of Ven A F Clarke, Archdeacon of Lancaster; 2 da (Sophie Patricia Marguerite (Mrs Boggis-Rolfe), Judith Joanna Mary (Mrs Bromley-Davenport)); *Career* served WWII as Capt 17/21 Lancers in N Africa, Sicily and Italy (wounded twice), Capt Reserve; High Sheriff of Carmarthenshire 1969; pres: Carmarthen Cons Assoc (chm 1973-77), Mid-West Wales Cons Cncl (chm 1983-85); vice pres Carmarthen & Cardigan Country Landowners Assoc (chm 1957-60), chm Carmarthen Journal Co; OStJ 1977; FRICS; *Clubs* Cavalry and Guards'; *Style—* Capt John Francis, OBE, DL; Llwynhelig, Llandeilo, Dyfed SA19 6AZ (☎ 0558 822 302)

FRANCIS, Dr John Michael; s of William Winston Francis (d 1939), of Haverfordwest, Pembrokeshire, and Beryl Margaret, *née* Savage; *b* 1 May 1939; *Educ* Gowerton Co GS, RCS, Imperial Coll London (BSc, PhD, DIC); *m* 14 Sept 1963, Eileen, da of Hugh Foster Sykes (d 1977), of Hutton Mount, Shenfield, Essex; 2 da (Sarah Katherine b 1966, Rachel Victoria b 1968); *Career* res offr R & D Dept CEGB, first dir Soc Religion and Technol Project Church of Scot 1970-74, sr res fell in energy studies Heriot-Watt Univ 1974-76, asst sec Scot Office 1981- (princ 1976-80); chief exec Nature Conservancy Cncl for Scot 1991- (formerly known as (Scot) Nature Conservancy Cncl, memb Advsy Ctee 1974-76, dir 1984-91); visiting fell Inst for Advanced Studies in the Humanities Univ of Edinburgh; contribs to numerous professional and scientific jls; conslt (science, technol and social ethics) World Cncl of Churches Geneva 1971-83; chm: Ctee on Society Religion and Technol Church of Scot 1980-, Edinburgh Forum 1986-; memb: Oil Devpt Cncl for Scot 1973-76, Ind Cmmn on Tport 1974, Cncl Nat Tst for Scot 1984-, St Giles Cathedral Edinburgh; assoc memb Scot Inst of Human Rels; ARCS, FRIC 1969; *Books* Scotland in Turmoil (1973), Changing Directions (jtly, 1974), The Future as an Academic Discipline (jtly, 1975), Facing up to Nuclear Power (1976), The Future of Scotland (jtly, 1977); *Recreations* ecumenical travels, hill walking, theatre; *Style—* Dr John Francis; 49 Gilmour Rd, Newington, Edinburgh EH16 5NU (☎ 031 667 3996); Headquarters, Nature Conservancy Council for Scotland, 12 Hope Terrace, Edinburgh EH9 2AS (☎ 031 447 4784)

FRANCIS, John Stuart; s of Jack Edward Evelyn Francis (d 1980), of Taunton, and Mary June, *née* Ball; *b* 13 Feb 1950; *Educ* Churchers Coll Hants, Kingston Poly (BA); *Career* designer; Property Services Agency 1972, Michael Aukett Associates 1974, Chester Jones Ltd 1973 (pt of Colefax & Fowler); DEGW Partnership (now Ltd): joined DEGW Partnership 1980, first interior design ptnr 1982, appointed Main Bd 1988, head of interiors 1988; design projects incl: PSA offices 1973, retail projects for the Burton Group 1974-74, Landis GYR factory 1976, IBM (Chiswick offices 1977, Winchester offices 1986), Rolls Royce headquarters 1979, Christies Auctioneers 1981-84 (NY, London, Amsterdam), Sturge Holdings headquarters 1985, Lloyds of London 1987/90, Freshfields headquarters 1989/90; memb: CSD, Art and Architecture; *Recreations* tennis, books, art; *Clubs* Groucho; *Style—* John Francis, Esq; 76 Palace Road, London SW2 3JX (☎ 081 674 4846); DEGW Ltd, 8 Crinan St, London N1 9SQ (☎ 071 239 7777, fax 071 278 3618/3713)

FRANCIS, Kevin Michael Derek; s of Raymond Colinston Francis, of Small Health, Birmingham, and Agnes Theresa, *née* Shoy; *b* 6 Dec 1967; *Educ* Waverley GS Birmingham; partner, Sharon Joan Harrison; 1 da (Stacey Jayne Francis); *Career* professional footballer Derby County 1989-, over 25 appearances; formerly semi-professional footballer and successively: trainee draughtsman, asst to civil engr, doorman, army reservist, postman, security guard and delivery driver; *Recreations* music, reading, driving; *Style—* Kevin Francis, Esq; Derby County FC, Baseball Ground, Shaftesbury Crescent, Derby DE3 8NB (☎ 0332 40105)

FRANCIS, Mark Robert; s of Cecil Francis, and Lilian Louisa, *née* Richards; *b* 6 Sept 1962; *Educ* Scabo HS Newtownards, Regent House GS Newtownards, St Martin's Sch of Art (BA), Chelsea Sch of Art (MA); *Career* artist; exhibitions incl: Summer Show (Tom Coldwell Gallery Dublin) 1983, New Contemporaries (The Mall Gallery London) 1983, Stowells Trophy (Royal Acad London) 1984, Summer Gp Show (Tom Caldwell Gallery Belfast) 1984, Another View of Ireland (Irish Artists in London) 1985, Athena Int Awards (Mall Galleries London) 1985, Riverside Open (Riverside Studios London) 1985, 4 New Painters (Paton Gallery London) 1986, ILEA Class of 86 (Royal Festival Hall London) 1986, On The Wall Gallery Belfast 1986, Contemporary Art Soc Market (Smith's Gallery London) 1987, 1989, Art '89 (Business Centre London) 1989, Christie's New Contemporaries (RCA London) 1989, 5 Abstract Painters (Thumb Gallery London) 1989, 4th Int Contemporary Art Fair LA, USA (Thumb Gallery) 1989, Four Painters (New Acad Gallery London) 1990, Art '90 London (Thumb Gallery) 1990, Bonhams Contemporary Auction (London) 1990, London to Atlanta (Atlanta, USA) 1990, 5th Int Contemporary Art Fair LA, USA (Thumb Gallery) 1990, solo exhibition (Thumb Gallery London) 1990; work in collections: Unilever plc, British Credit Trust Co, (Hammersmith and Fulham), Heytesbury Holdings Ltd, Arthur Anderson and Co Ltd, Leicester Educn Authy, Chelmsford Borough Cncl, Metropolitan Museum NY, Stanhope PLC; *Style—* Mark Francis, Esq; 196 Claydon, Deacon Way, London SE17 1UG (☎ 071 703 3914); Paragon Centre, Searles Rd, London SE1; (Business) Thumb Gallery, 38 Lexington St, London W1R 3HR (Gallery, tel 071 439 7343)

FRANCIS, His Hon Judge (William) Norman; s of Llewellyn Francis (d 1953), of Llanishen, Cardiff, and Margaret Ceridwen, *née* Davies (d 1963); *b* 19 March 1921; *Educ* Bradfield, Lincoln Coll Oxford (BCL, MA); *m* 16 May 1951, Anthea Constance, da of James Leslie Kerry (d 1951), of Llanishen, Cardiff; 1 s (Stephen b 1952), 1 da (Nicola (Mrs Thomas) b 1955); *Career* serv WWII Lt RA Europe 1941-45; called to the Bar Gray's Inn 1946; dep chm Brecknock QS 1962-71, judge County Court 1969 (converted to circuit judge 1972); cncllr Diocese of Llandaff 1979; *Recreations* walking; *Clubs* Cardiff Athletic; *Style—* His Hon Judge Norman Francis; 2 The Woodlands, Lisvane, Cardiff CF4 5SW (☎ 0222 753070)

FRANCIS, Richard Mark; s of Ralph Lawrence Francis, of Oakham, Leicestershire, and Eileen Nellie, *née* Jenkins; *b* 20 Nov 1947; *Educ* Oakham Sch Rutland, Selwyn Coll Cambridge (BA), Courtauld Inst of Art (MA); *m* 7 Oct 1976, Tamar Janine Helen, da of Donald Beazley Burkhill (d 1972); 1 da (Jasmine Helen b 1979); *Career* Walker Art Gallery Liverpool 1971-72, exhibition offr Arts Cncl of GB 1973-80, asst keeper of mod collection The Tate Gallery 1980-86, curator Tate Gallery Liverpool 1986-90; memb CNAA Examination pool; *Books* Jasper Johns (1984); *Recreations* riding, buying books; *Style—* Richard Francis, Esq; 64 Hungerford Rd, London N7 9LP (☎ 071 609 1022)

FRANCIS, Richard Maurice; s of Hugh Elvet Francis, QC (d 1986), and Emma Frances Wienholt, *née* Bowen; *b* 28 June 1946; *Educ* Mill Hill, Univ of Durham (BA); *Career* called to the Bar Gray's Inn 1974, practising barr Wales and Chester Circuit 1976-; elder United Reformed Church; chm: Wales Aid to Poland 1982-, Cardiff 2000 1985; dep chm and sec Cardiff Building Preservation Tst 1984-; RIIA 1972, memb Criminal Bar Assoc 1978; Golden Cross of the Polish Republic 1985; *Books* The British Withdrawal from the Baghdad Railway Project (1973), A History of Oakley Park Church (1976); *Recreations* church work, conservation, reading quality newspapers, listening to BBC Radios 3 and 4; *Clubs* Cardiff and Co; *Style—* Richard Francis, Esq; 34 Park Place, Cardiff, South Glamorgan CF1 3TN (☎ 0222 382731, fax 0222 222542, telex 5 CARDIFF 2)

FRANCIS, Sir Richard Trevor Langford; KCMG; s of Eric Roland Francis, and Esther Joy, *née* Todd; *b* 10 March 1934; *Educ* Uppingham, Univ Coll Oxford (MA); *m* 1, 1958 (m dis), Beate Ohlhagen; 2 s; m 2, 1974, Elizabeth Penelope Anne Fairfax Crone; 2 s; *Career* joined BBC 1958; former asst ed Panorama and 24 Hours; headed Euro Broadcasting Union coverage of: US presidential elections 1968 and 1972, Apollo missions 1969-72; asst head Current Affrs TV 1971-73, controller BBC NI 1973-77, dir News and Current Affrs BBC 1977-82, dep chm Visnews 1979-82, md BBC Radio 1982-86; vice chm Br Exec IPI 1982-86, DG Br Cncl 1987-; *Recreations* offshore sailing, photography, the children; *Clubs* Reform; *Style—* Sir Richard Francis, KCMG; The British Council, 10 Spring Gardens, London SW1A 2BN (☎ 071 389 4879)

FRANCIS, Rita Winifred; da of James Stone (d 1962), of Manchester, and Winifred, *née* Myatt; *b* 10 Dec 1947; *Educ* Alderman Newtons GS for Girls; *m* 7 Jan 1967 (m dis 1983), Graham Francis; 1 s (Scott James b 4 June 1968), 1 da (Keely b 26 March 1970); *Career* dir: Ensign Computers plc 1985, Ensign Systems Ltd 1986, T F Services Ltd 1986, Ensign Computer Holdings plc 1986-, T F Group of Cos 1988-; *Style—* Mrs Rita Francis; The Lodge, Stanhope Gdns, Wigston, Leics; Ensign House, Vaughan Way, Leicester LE1 4SG (☎ 0533 532 555, fax 0533 536 834, car 0860 387 510)

FRANCIS, Stewart; s of Elgar Francis Thompson, of Rudgwick, Sussex, and Cathleen Winifred, *née* Allwood; *b* 7 March 1951; *Educ* Warlingham Co Sch; *m* 16 May 1970, Stephanie Jane, da of Richard Stanley Butler, of Sanderstead, Surrey; 2 s (Matthew b 20 Dec 1973, Nicholas Peter b 7 Feb 1978); *Career* freelance disc-jockey 1968-72, presenter LBC 1973-75, dep prog controller Pennine Radio 1975-79, md Hereward Radio plc 1984-87 (prog controller 1980-83), md Mid Anglia Radio plc 1988-, dir

Kettering and Corby Broadcasting 1989-; dir Assoc of Ind Radio Contractors (chm 1991-), chm AIRC mktg ctee; tstee: Hereward Radio, CNFM Appeal for the Blind; *Recreations* cricket, football; *Style*— Stewart Francis, Esq; Mid Anglia Radio plc, Queensgate Centre, Peterborough PE1 1XJ (☎ 0773 46225, fax 0733 42714, car 0860 37 9937)

FRANCIS-JONES, Capt Ronald Carew (Jake); s of Lt-Col Ronald Francis-Jones (d 1949), and Muriel Constance, *née* James; *b* 18 Nov 1937; *Educ* Downside, Britannia RN Coll Dartmouth; *m* 19 Oct 1963, Diana, da of John Stapleton le Poer Trench, of Nairobi, Kenya; 2 s (Jamie b 1965, Maxwell b 1970); *Career* trg HMS Leopard 1958-60, Lt 1960, asst sec HMS Centaur 1960-62, Lt's course RNC Greenwich 1962, Flag Lt to C in C S Atlantic and S America Station 1963-65, supply charge course 1965, sec ops/trg CINC Far East Staff 1965-68, Lt Cdr 1968, supply offr HMS Ajax 1968-89, offr's trg offr RN Supply Sch 1969-72, sec to Asst Chief of Fleet Support MOD 1972-74, dep supply offr HMS Hermes 1974-75, Cdr 1975, sec to Flag Offr 2 Flotilla 1975-77, sec to Flag Offr Submarines 1977-79; supply offr: HMS Blake 1979-80, HMS Hermes 1980-81; base supply offr Portsmouth 1981-83, exec offr HMS Excellent 1983-84, Capt 1984, sec to C in C Fleet 1984-87, Chief SO (Personnel) staff of Flag Offr Naval Air Cmd 1987-89, Chief SO (Naval Bases) staff of C in C Naval Home Cmd 1989-; *Recreations* shooting, photography, country pursuits, genealogy; *Style*— Capt Jake Francis-Jones, RN; Staff of Commander in Chief, Naval Home Command, HM Naval Base, Portsmouth

FRANCKE, John Valdemar Gordon; s of Frederick Francke (d 1955), of 263 Sheen Lane, London SW14, and Helen, *née* Craven (d 1970); gs of Max Francke (b 1867) holder of the Order of the Red Eagle (Prussia); *b* 1933; *Educ* Harrow, St Catharine's Coll Cambridge; *m* 1, 23 March 1957, Joan Deirdre, da of Sydney Bolster (d 1979); 1 da (Caroline b 1958); m 2, 29 June 1968, Elizabeth Ann, da of John Geoffrey Lax Lovell (d 1965), of Haywards Heath; 1 s (Giles b 1973), 2 da (Alison b 1969, Angela b 1975); *Career* Offr Cadet 15/19 Hussars 1953; Selection Tst Ltd 1955-57, Hawker Aircraft Ltd 1957-59, Vickers Armstrong (Aircraft) Ltd 1959-60, Handley Page Ltd 1960-70, Science Museum 1970, BUA, Br Caledonian 1971-87, fndr own company JF Aircraft 1987-; *Style*— John Francke, Esq; Glengarriff, Stone Quarry Rd, Chelwood Gate, Haywards Heath, Sussex RH17 7LS

FRANCOME, John; MBE (1986); s of Norman John Francome, and Lillian Maud Francome; *b* 13 Dec 1952; *Educ* Park Sr HS Swindon; *m* 1976, Miriam, da of Andrew Stringer, of London; *Career* champion jockey seven times, 1138 wins (Nat Hunt Record); racehorse trainer; *Books* Born Lucky (autobiography, 1985), Eavesdropper (1986), Riding High (1987), Declared Dead (1988), Bloodstock (1989); *Recreations* tennis, music; *Style*— John Francome, Esq, MBE; Trabbs Farm, Lambourn, Berks

FRANK, Dr Andrew Oliver; s of Ernest Oliver Frank, of Haywards Heath, Sussex, and Doris Helen, *née* McBean (d 1985); *b* 4 Sept 1944; *Educ* Kingswood Sch Bath, Middx Hosp Med Sch (MB BS); *m* 23 June 1973, Cynthia Mary, da of James Siviter, of Lugwardine, Hereford; 1 s (Anthony b 1979), 2 da (Christina b 1982, Julia b 1986); *Career* lectr in med Univ of Malaya 1974-76, sr registrar in med rheumatology and rehabilitation Salisbury Health Dist 1977-80, conslt physician in rehabilitation and rheumatology Northwick Park Hosp and Clinical Res Centre Harrow 1980-; fndr and hon sec Med Disability Soc 1984-87; memb: Disability Ctee RCP 1979-87, Arthritis and Rheumatism Cncl, Royal Nat Inst Blind, RSM; MRCP 1971, FRCP 1990; *Books* Disabling Diseases: Physical, Environmental and Psychosocial Management (with G P Maguire, 1989); *Recreations* family, music; *Style*— Dr Andrew Frank; Dept of Rehabilitation, Northwick Park Hospital, Watford Rd, Harrow, Middlesex HA1 3UJ (☎ 081 869 2102)

FRANK, Sir (Robert) Andrew; 4 Bt (UK 1920), of Withyham, Sussex; s (by 2 m) of Sir Robert John Frank, 3 Bt (d 1987), and his 2 w Margaret Joyce, *née* Truesdale; *b* 16 May 1964; *Educ* Ludgrove, Eton; *m* 23 June 1990, Zoë Alia, eld da of S A Hasan, and P Hasan, *née* Davidson; *Heir* none; *Career* actor, prodr; *Recreations* theatre, travel; *Style*— Sir Andrew Frank, Bt; Wood Edge Cottage, Under-the-Wood, Bisham, Marlow, Bucks (☎ 06284 752 98)

FRANK, Sir (Frederick) Charles; OBE (1946); eld s of Frederick Frank (d 1971), and Medora Frank; *b* 6 March 1911; *Educ* Thetford GS, Ipswich Sch, Lincoln Coll Oxford; *m* 1940, Maia Maita, yst da of Prof Boris Michaelovich Asché (d 1943); 1 c (d at birth); *Career* scientist; Air Scientific Intelligence 1940-46; Bristol Univ Dept of Physics 1946-76: prof 1954, head of dept 1969-76; vice pres Royal Soc 1967-69, Royal Medallist 1979; FRS; kt 1977; *Recreations* gardening; *Clubs* Athenaeum; *Style*— Sir Charles Frank, OBE; Orchard Cottage, Grove Rd, Coombe Dingle, Bristol BS9 2RL (☎ 0272 681708)

FRANK, David Thomas; s of Thomas Frank (d 1984), of Robertsford, Shrewsbury, and Margaret McCrea, *née* Cowan; *b* 29 April 1954; *Educ* Shrewsbury, Bristol Univ (LLB); *m* 10 July 1982, Diane Lillian, da of Stephen Nash Abbott, of Farnham Common, Bucks; 1 s (Charles b 1988), 1 da (Lucinda b 1986); *Career* admitted slr 1979; ptnr Slaughter and May 1986- (asst slr 1979-86); *Recreations* lawn tennis, golf; *Style*— David Frank, Esq; Slaughter and May, 35 Basinghall St, London EC2V 5DB (☎ 071 600 1200, fax 071 726 0038, telex 883486)

FRANK, Sir Douglas George Horace; QC (1964); s of late George Maurice Frank, of Osterley, and Agnes Winifred Frank; *b* 16 April 1916; *Educ* City of London Sch and privately; *m* 1, 1939, Margaret Clara, da of Alfred William Shaw, OBE; 1 s, 2 da; m 2, 1963, Sheila Frances, da of late Cdre Lawrence King Beauchamp, RN, and widow of Jack Eric Jones; 2 da; m 3, 1979, Audrey, yr da of Charles Leslie Thomas, of Neath, Glamorgan; *Career* served Lt RA 1939-43; called to the Bar Gray's Inn 1946, bencher 1970, dep judge of the High Ct 1975-89; memb ctee for Public Participation in Planning 1968, pres Lands Tbnl 1973-88, hon pres Anglo-American Real Property Inst 1980-89; one time dep boundary cmmr for England and Wales; kt 1976; *Style*— Sir Douglas Frank, QC; 1 Verulam Buildings, London WC1 (☎ 071 242 5949); La Mayne Longue Haute, Sauveterre-La-Lemance, 47500 Fumel, France (☎ 010 335 406 898)

FRANKEL, Michele Shauna; da of Denis Frankel (d 1972), of London, and Sheila Joyce, *née* Jacobs (d 1989); *b* 11 May 1954; *Educ* Queens Coll Harley St, Queenswood Hertfordshire, St Clares Hall Oxford, Davies Tutorial Coll, Dartington Coll of Arts (Totnes Dip in Drama), Rolle Coll Exmouth (Teachers Certificate); *m* 1 July 1989, Guthrie Campbell Barrett, s of Dudley Barrett; *Career* theatre dir; actress: Lament for 3 (Women New Cycle Theatre NY) 1978, The Dream and Swans (Oval House) 1979, The Warp (ICA Edinburgh Festival) 1979, Minnie Kabini (St Marks Theatre NY) 1981; co-devised: Who are the Guinea Pigs (and performed) 1977, Nuts 1979; devised and directed: Radiation Anonymous (New Cycle Theatre NY) 1979, Is Denis Really the Menace? (toured England, Europe, Sweden and NY, filmed for Swedish TV) 1978, Love and Danger (New Cycle Theatre and West Beth Theatre NY) 1979-80, Radiation Anonymous 2 (toured streets of London) 1980, Familiar Stories (Oval House) 1982; asst dir: Comic Pictures 1982, And All Things Nice 1982, Special Powers 1983, Wonderful Town (Leonard Bernstein's Musical) 1986; dir: Limbo Tales (Gate Theatre 1982 and 1983, Channel 4, Alter Image 1983, Not The Not The RSC Festival Stratford 1989), These Foolish Things (Old Red Lion Theatre) 1983, Offshore Island (prodr, written by Marghanita Laski) 1983, Bag (Battersea Arts Centre and tour of England) 1983, Scream and Dream Again (Man in the Moon Theatre) 1984, John (Hardcorps Theatre Co London and Traverse Theatre) 1985, Video Wicked (Half Moon YPT Theatre) 1985, Ellen (Riverside Studios) 1985, Heart of Five (Soho Poly Theatre) 1985; co-dir My Mother (with Michael Eaton Bloomsbury Theatre) 1984, assoc dir The Complete Berk 1985, co-ordinator for Supotco London Fashion Week 1984, observer Directors Guild 1983, short arts cncl bursary attachment Watford Palace Theatre 1986, dir The Women Writer's Workshop 1987-, staff dir Royal National Theatre 1988-89 (prodns Magic Olympical Games and The Misanthrope), workshop leader Royal National Theatre WH Smith Interact Programme 1988-, drama worker Southbank Saturday Morning Programme 1988-; memb: Directors Guild 1984, Equity 1988; *Recreations* travel, languages, gardening, writing; *Style*— Ms Michele Frankel; 91 Chevening Rd, Queens Park, London NW6 6DA; Barrett and James, 8 South Molton St, London W1 (fax 071 491 0820)

FRANKEL, Dr Richard John; s of Oscar Irving Frankel, QC (d 1987), of Sydney, Aust, and Marie Clare, *née* Leon; *b* 24 May 1940; *Educ* St Stithians Sch Johannesburg, Univ of Witwatersrand (MB, BCh); *m* 8 May 1968, Merula Jane, da of Ronald Montagu Simon (d 1971); 1 s (Benjamin Stephen Montagu b 1974), 3 da (Sarah Rebecca b 1969, Georgina Kate b 1971, Hannah Jessica b 1978); *Career* clinical lectr London Hosp 1967-71, sr registrar St Georges Hosp 1972-77, conslt physician Frimley Park Hosp 1977- (chm Med Advsy Ctee 1983-87); FRCP, FRSM; *Recreations* tennis, gardening, skiing, travel; *Style*— Dr Richard Frankel; The Priory, Howard's Lane, Holybourne, Alton, Hants GU34 4HH (☎ 0420 83326); Frimley Park Hosp, Portsmouth Rd, Frimley, Camberley, Surrey GU16 5UJ (☎ 0276 692777)

FRANKEL, William; CBE (1971); s of Isaac Frankel (d 1963), of London, and Anna, *née* Lecker (d 1946); *b* 3 Feb 1917; *Educ* Poly Secdy Sch Regent St London, Univ of London (LLB); *m* 1, 1939 (m dis 1972), Gertrude Freda, da of Louis Reed, of London; 1 s (John), 1 da (Anne); m 2, 1973, Mrs Claire Neuman, da of Herold J Schwab, of Birmingham, Alabama, USA; *Career* barr; currently dir Jewish Chronicle (ed 1958-77); chm: Social Security Appeal Tbnl 1977-89, Mental Health Review Tbnl 1978-89; special advsr to The Times 1977-81, London corr Statesman (Calcutta and Delhi), ed Survey of Jewish Affairs (annual); *Books* Israel Observed: an anatomy of the State (1981); *Clubs* Athenaeum, MCC; *Style*— William Frankel, Esq, CBE; 30 Montagu Sq, London W1H 1RJ

FRANKISH, (John) Keith; s of Fred Skelton Frankish (d 1985), and Mary, *née* Ellerby (d 1983); *b* 1 Aug 1927; *Educ* Humberside Fndn Sch Cleethorpes; *m* 2 April 1955, Mary Hilda, da of Charles William Brunton (d 1970); 2 s (Simon Charles b 1961, John Antony b 1964), 1 da (Susan Mary b 1957); *Career* slr; employed by Vauxhall Motors for nearly 30 years, finally as sec and gen counsel all Gen Motors Corpns UK operations 1981-87; dir to A C Spark Plug Overseas, Delco Products Overseas and many other G M Assoc Cos 1982-87, ret 1987; chm Legal Ctee MMT 1985-87, pres Luton Bedford and Dist Chamber of Commerce & Industry 1980-81, currently vol counsellor and legal advsr Bedfordshire Community Enterprise Assoc, memb Nat Cncl Assoc of Br Chambers of Commerce; *Recreations* ornithology, travel; *Style*— Keith Frankish, Esq; Garden Cottage, Cobbet Lane, Flitton, Bedford MK45 5DX (☎ 0525 60562)

FRANKLAND, Dr Alfred William (Bill); s of Rev H Frankland (d 1960), of Scotby, Carlisle, and Rose, *née* West (d 1947); *b* 19 March 1912; *Educ* St Bees Sch, Oxford Univ (MA, DM, BCh); *m* 27 May 1941, Pauline Margaret Wrench, da of Rowland Bower Jackson (d 1972); 1 s (Andrew William b 1956), 3 da (Penelope Jane b 1946, Jenifer Rosemary b 1949, Hilary Fern b 1951); *Career* WWII serv: Lt (later Capt) RAMC 1939-46 (Far East); conslt physician (allergy) St Mary's Hosp; hon sec Asthma Res Cncl 1959; church sidesman; Liveryman Worshipful Co of Drapers 1959; memb RSM; *Books* Allergies Questions and Answers (with Doris Rapp, 1980), numerous articles on aerobiology and related allergic diseases; *Recreations* medicine, gardening, foreign travel; *Style*— Dr Bill Frankland; 46 Devonshire Close, London W1N 1LN (☎ 071 6371994); 139 Harley St, London W1N 1DJ (☎ 071 935 5421)

FRANKLAND, Hon Mrs (Barbara Mary); *née* Frankland; da of Baroness Zouche (17 holder of the title), and Sir Frederick Frankland, 10 Bt; aunt of 18 Baron Zouche; *b* 1906; *m* 1, 6 July 1926 (m dis 1937), Brig (now Sir) Otho Prior-Palmer, DSO (d 1986); 1 s (decd), 1 da (Diana de Marco b 1929); m 2, 5 July 1937 (m dis 1943), 5 Earl of Normanton (d 1967); m 3, 4 Feb 1944 (m dis 1962), Peter Lucas; resumed name of Frankland by deed poll 1958; *Style*— The Hon Mrs Frankland; Ridge House, Stockland, Honiton, Devon (☎ 040 483 325)

FRANKLAND, Christopher John (Chris); s of Leonard Frankland (d 1958), and Kathleen Mary, *née* Burningham; *b* 7 Nov 1942; *Educ* Forest Sch London; *m* 18 June 1966, Eve Marie, da of Lt Cdr Victor J Chown, of Feniton, Devon; 1 s (Philip Thomas b 16 Aug 1969), 2 da (Angela Tara (twin) b 16 Aug 1969, Gail Marie b 4 Dec 1972); *Career* chartered accountant; articled clerk Hereward Scott Davies & Co 1959-65; Ernst & Young: joined Bristol office 1966, mangr 1968, transfered to London office 1972, ptnr 1978, currently audit ptnr Japan Business Group; Freeman City of London 1980, Liveryman Worshipful Co of Needlemakers; FCA; *Recreations* hill and beach walking; *Style*— Chris Frankland, Esq; 29 Montalt Rd, Woodford Green, Essex IG8 9RS (☎ 081 504 2106); 14c Cliff Parade, Hunstanton, Norfolk PE36 6DP (☎ 0485 534531); Ernst & Young, Rolls House, Fetter Lane, London EC4A 1NL (☎ 071 928 2000)

FRANKLAND, (Frederick) Mark; s of The Hon Roger Nathaniel Frankland (d 1989), and Elizabeth Cecil, *née* Sanday (d 1968); *b* 19 April 1934; *Educ* Charterhouse, Pembroke Coll Cambridge (BA), Brown Univ USA; *Career* FO 1958-59, dep ed Time & Tide 1960-61; The Observer: Moscow corr 1962-64, Indochina corr (also for The Economist) 1967-73, Toyko corr 1973-75, Washington corr 1975-78, Moscow corr 1982-85, East Euro corr 1987-90; winner David Holden award (Br Press Awards) 1984 and 1986; memb Soc of Authors; *Books* Khrushchev (1966), The Mother-of-Pearl Men (1985), Richard Robertovich (1987), The Sixth Continent (1987), The Patriot's Revolution (1990); *Recreations* travel; *Style*— Mark Frankland, Esq; 38 Redcliffe Rd, London SW10 9NJ (☎ 071 352 3205); The Observer, Chelsea Bridge House, Queenstown Rd, London SW8 4NN (☎ 071 627 0700)

FRANKLAND, Dr (Anthony) Noble; CB (1983), CBE (1976), DFC (1944); s of Edward Percy Frankland (d 1958), of Needlehouse, Ravenstonedale, Westmorland, and Maud, *née* Metcalfe-Gibson (d 1979); *b* 4 July 1922; *Educ* Sedbergh, Trinity Coll Oxford (open scholar, MA, DPhil); *m* 1, 28 Feb 1944, Diana Madeline Forvargue (d 1981), da of George Victor Tavernor (k 1928); 1 s (Arnold Edward Roger b 1951), 1 da (Linda Helga Elizabeth (Mrs Michael O'Hanlon) b 1953); m 2, 7 May 1982, Sarah Katharine, da of His Hon the late Sir David Davies, QC; *Career* RAF: joined 1941, navigator Bomber cmd 1943-45, Flt Lt 1945; narrator Air Hist Branch Air Miny 1948-51, official mil historian Cabinet Office 1951-60; dep dir of studies RIIA 1956-60, dir IMP War Museum 1960-82 (Duxford 1976-82, HMS Belfast 1978-82); Rockefeller fell 1953, Lees Knowles lectr Trinity Coll Cambridge 1963, hist advsr Thames TV Series The World at War 1971-74; vice chm Br Nat Ctee of Int Ctee for the Study of WWII 1976-82; memb: Cncl Morley Coll 1962-66, HMS Belfast Tst 1971-78 (vice chm 1972-78), HMS Belfast Bd 1978-82; *Books* Crown of Tragedy, Nicholas II (1960), The Strategic Air Offensive Against Germany 1939-45 (4 Volumes with Sir Charles Webster, 1961), The Bombing Offensive Against Germany, Outlines and Perspectives

(1965), Bomber Offensive, The Devastation of Europe (1970), Prince Henry, Duke of Gloucester (1980), The Politics and Strategy of the Second World War (jt ed series, 1974-), Decisive Battles of the Twentieth Century, Land, Sea and Air (jt ed, 1976), The Encyclopedia of Twentieth Century Warfare (gen ed, 1989); *Style—* Dr Noble Frankland, CB, CBE, DFC; Thames House, Eynsham, Oxford OX8 1DA (☎ 0865 881 327)

FRANKLAND, Timothy Cecil; s of Hon Roger Nathaniel Frankland (d 1989, yr s of Mary Cecil, Baroness Zouche), and his 1 w Elizabeth Cecil, *née* Sanday (d 1968); *b* 4 Oct 1931; *Educ* Charterhouse; *m* 4 Sept 1957 (m dis 1968), Lynette, da of Lt Cdr Ian Hope Dundas; 3 s; *Career* Lt 15/19 Hussars 1950-52; Binder Hamlyn & Co CAs 1952-67; dir: Hill Samuel & Co 1967-, Newman Tonks Gp; chm: James Neill Holdings, Jarris Porter Group plc; FCA 1957; *Clubs* MCC, Berkshire; *Style—* Timothy Frankland, Esq; Hill Samuel & Co, 100 Wood St, London EC2 (☎ 071 628 8011)

FRANKLAND MOORE, Dr Elizabeth; OBE (1963, MBE 1950); da of Henry Thomas Guy (d 1915), and Eda Sarah, *née* Bangerter (d 1964); *b* 10 Dec 1901; *Educ* privately in London and Switzerland; *m* 1, 17 Nov 1927 (m dis), Harold Bellet Miller; m 2, 1949, Maj Charles Frankland Moore, OBE; *Career* WWII Civil Def 1939-45, ret WVS 1962; res asst to Mr Lloyd George for Cncl of Action 1937-38, political sec to Eleanor Rathbone, MP 1938-42, hon chief exec and organiser Spanish Relief Ctee 1939, organising sec Br United Aid to China 1942, hon sec Int Family Planning Assoc 1934, tstee Basque Children and After Care Tst 1942; currently: chm and tstee Sino-Br Fellowship Tst, hon dir Nat Appeal BLESMA, co fndr and dir Nat Star Centre Disabled Youth, memb cncl Distressed Gentlefolk Aid Assoc, co fndr and memb cncl Prospect Hall Selly Oak Birmingham, vice pres Youth Clubs UK United; Freeman City of London 1984, Liveryman Worshipful Co Bakers 1984; hon LLD Univ of Hong Kong 1974; Brilliant Star of China 1946; *Recreations* music, golf, bridge; *Clubs* Special Forces, Hurlingham (hon memb), Royal Mid-Surrey Golf; *Style—* Dr Elizabeth Frankland Moore, OBE; Bede House, Manor Fields, London SW15 3LT

FRANKLIN, Daniel John (Dan); s of Michael Howard Franklin, of Much Hadham, Herts, and Suzanne Mary, *née* Cooper; *b* 2 May 1949; *Educ* Bradford Coll, UEA (BA); *m* 29 June 1985, Lucy, da of Michael Hughes-Hallett, Barton-on-the-Heath Glos; *Career* ed dir William Heinemann 1987, publisher Secker & Warburg 1988; *Style—* Dan Franklin, Esq; Secker & Warburg, Michelin House, 81 Fulham Rd, London SW3 6RB (☎ 071 581 9393, fax 071 589 8421)

FRANKLIN, Sir Eric Alexander; CBE (1952); s of William John Franklin (d 1942), and Sarah, *née* Hutton (d 1958); *b* 3 July 1910; *Educ* English Sch Maymyo Burma, Emmanuel Coll Cambridge; *m* 1936, Joyce Stella, da of late George Oakes Lucas, of Cambridge; *Career* Indian Civil Service 1935, dist and sessions judge Arakan 1941-42, dep sec to Govt Burma 1942-45, registrar High Court Rangoon 1946-48, dep sec to Govt Pakistan 1949-52, estab offr 1953-56, estab sec 1956-57, chm Sudan Govt Terms of Service Cmmn 1958-59, UN admin advsr to Jordanian Govt 1960-63, sr admin advsr to Nepalese Govt 1964-67; chm Cambridgeshire Soc for the Blind 1969-74 (vice pres 1974-); Star of Jordan 1963; kt 1954; *Recreations* walking in alpine valleys, gardening; *Style—* Sir Eric Franklin, CBE; 18 Cavendish Avenue, Cambridge CB1 4US (☎ 0223 248661)

FRANKLIN, George Henry; s of George Edward Franklin (d 1975), and Annie Franklin; *b* 15 June 1923; *Educ* Hastings GS, Hastings Sch of Art, Architectural Assoc Sch of Architecture (AADip), Sch of Planning and Res for Regnl Devpt London (SPDip); *m* 1950, Sylvia Daisy, *née* Allen; 3 s, 1 da; *Career* WWII Capt RE, served Europe Parachute Sqdn RE; SE Asia, Bengal Sappers and Miners Royal Indian Engrs; architect planner Finchley Borough Cncl 1952-54, architect Christian Med Coll Punjab India 1954-57; physical planning advsr: Republic of Indonesia 1958-62, Govt of Malaysia 1963-64; Overseas Devpt Admin FCO 1966-83, conslt third world planning and devpt, hon prof Dept of Town Planning UWIST 1982-88, sr advsr Devpt Planning Unit UCL, memb Int Advsy Bd Centre for Devpt and Environmental Planning Oxford Poly, chm overseas sch Town and Country Summer Sch 1970-75; Cwlth Assoc of Planners: memb Exec Ctee 1970-80, pres 1980-84, hon sec 1984-88; memb Exec Ctee Cwlth Human Ecology Cncl 1970-; memb Editorial Bd: Third World Planning Review 1979-, Cities 1983-; memb: World Service Ctee United Bible Socs 1968-77, Warminster Cncl of Churches; chm Warminster and Westbury Family Support Serv, coordinator Christian Aid Warminster Dist; ARIBA, assoc Indian Inst of Architects, FRTPI, assoc Inst of Town Planners India, FRSA; *Recreations* Bible Society, church, third world and environmental interests and activities, fly fishing; *Clubs* Royal Cwlth Soc, Victory Services; *Style—* George Franklin, Esq; The Manse, Sutton Veny, Warminster, Wiltshire BA12 7AW (☎ 0985 400 72)

FRANKLIN, Dr Ian Maxwell; s of Edwin William Franklin, of London, and Elizabeth Joyce, *née* Kessler; *b* 6 Sept 1949; *Educ* Owen's Boys Sch Islington London, Univ of Leeds (BSc, MB ChB), UCH Med Sch (PhD); *m* 19 July 1975, Anne Christine, da of Harry Norman Bush, of Leeds; 1 s (Matthew Charles Maxwell b 1988); *Career* MRC res fell UCH Med Sch 1977-80, sr registrar haematology UCH and Hosp for Sick Children Gt Ormond St 1980-82, conslt haematologist Queen Elizabeth Hosp Birmingham 1982-, dir of haematology Central Birmingham Health Authy 1989-; FRCP 1990 (MRCP 1977); *Recreations* windsurfing, cycling; *Clubs* Barnt Green Sailing; *Style—* Dr Ian Franklin; Department of Haematology, Queen Elizabeth Hospital, Birmingham B15 2TH (☎ 021 472 1311 ext 3837)

FRANKLIN, Hon Mrs (Joan Edith); *née* Eden; JP (Essex 1966); er da of 7 Baron Auckland, MBE (d 1955), and Dorothy Ida, *née* Harvey (d 1964); *b* 31 Jan 1920; *Educ* North Foreland Lodge, Chelsea Art Sch; *m* 1, 6 Sept 1941, Rev Alfred Lisinea Pond (d 21 July 1947), s of late Chaloner Pond; 2 da (Rosemary b 1942, Sally b 1945); m 2, 31 Aug 1948, Rev Arthur Harrington Franklin, MBE, TD, er s of late Maj Percival Charles Franklin; 2 da (Elizabeth b 1949, Caroline b 1952); *Career* ATS 1939-41; chm: Chelmsford Bench 1987-90, govrs of Chelmsford Co HS for Girls 1978-89; *Recreations* gardening; *Style—* The Hon Mrs Franklin, JP; Hea Corner, Mill Rd, Felsted, Dunmow, Essex CM6 3HQ (☎ 0371 820519)

FRANKLIN, John Andrew; s of Bernard Franklin (d 1979); *b* 21 Nov 1943; *Educ* Rugby, Pembroke Coll Cambridge (MA); *m* 1976, Elizabeth Anthea, da of Samuel John Noel Bartley, of Constantine Bay, Cornwall; 2 s; *Career* slr Slaughter and May 1968-72, dir Morgan Grenfell & Co Ltd 1979- (joined 1972), chm First Mortgage Securities Ltd 1987-; govr Utd World Coll of the Atlantic; *Recreations* skiing, sailing, wine, golf, shooting; *Clubs* Boodle's, Royal Harwich Yacht, Hurlingham, HAC, The Leash, (New York); *Style—* John Franklin Esq; Morgan Grenfell & Co Ltd, 23 Great Winchester St, London EC2P 2AX (☎ 071 588 4545)

FRANKLIN, Sir Michael David Milroy; KCB (1983, CB 1979), CMG (1972); s of Milroy Llewellyn Capon Franklin, of Trowbridge; *b* 24 Aug 1927; *Educ* Taunton Sch, Peterhouse Cambridge; *m* 1951, Dorothy Joan, da of James Stuart Fraser, of Wallasey, Cheshire; 2 s, 1 da; *Career* joined MAFF 1950, UK delgn to OEEC (now OECD) 1959-61, private sec to Min 1961-64, under sec MAFF 1968-73; dep dir gen to Directorate-Gen of Agric EEC 1973-77, dep sec to Head Euro Secretariat Cabinet Office 1977-82; perm under sec Dept of Trade 1982-83, perm sec MAFF 1983-87; dir Barclays plc 1988-; memb Cncl Henley Mgmnt Coll, memb Int Policy Cncl on Agric and Trade, memb Cncl RIIA, pres W India Ctee; *Clubs* Oxford and Cambridge; *Style—* Sir Michael Franklin, KCB, CMG; 15 Galley Lane, Barnet, Herts EN5 4AR

FRANKLIN, Dr Owen Geoffrey; s of Cyril M E Franklin (d 1989), of London, and Miriam, *née* Israels; *Educ* Stanstead Coll Canada, Bryanston, Trinity Coll Cambridge (BA), UCH (MB BChir, DObst RCOG); *m* 1964, Sonja, da of Mirko Cacija; 2 s (Sasha b 1965, Fedja b 1967); *Career* GP Kilburn 1961-90; sculptor 1990-; collector of contempory painting and sculpture; memb: BMA 1957, ICA; patron of new art Tate Gallery 1982-; *Recreations* painting, sculpture, sports, music; *Clubs* Highgate Golf; *Style—* Dr Owen Franklin, Esq

FRANKLIN, Peter; s of William Sydney Franklin (d 1987), of Winchester, Hants, and Mary Elizabeth, *née* Todd; *b* 11 May 1952; *Educ* Peter Symonds' Sch Winchester, UCL (LLB); *m* 1976, Susan Ann, da of John Goslett Edwards; 3 s (Daniel Thomas b 19 March 1982, Nicholas Stephen b 14 June 1984, Edward Mark b 12 Feb 1987); *Career* sr auditor Thomas McLintock 1973-77, fin controller BFI Line 1977-79, treasy mangr FMI Ltd 1979-81, mangr of int control Salomon Brothers International 1981-84, asst vice pres Bache Securities (UK) Ltd 1984-86, dir of capital market operations County Natwest 1986-89, dir of fin and admin REA Brothers Ltd 1989-; FRSA 1990, FCA 1981 (ACA 1978); *Recreations* cinema, music, a great fondness for all sports; *Style—* Peter Franklin, Esq; 34 Minchenden Crescent, Southgate, London N14 7EL (☎ 081 882 9204); Rea Brothers Ltd, Aldermans House, Aldermans Walk, London EC2M 3XR (☎ 071 623 1155, fax 071 623 2694)

FRANKLIN, Prof Raoul Norman; s of Norman George Franklin, JP (d 1977), of Auckland, NZ, and Thelma Brinley, *née* Davis; *b* 3 June 1935; *Educ* Howick DHS NZ, Auckland GS NZ, Auckland Univ (BE, BSc, ME, MSc), Univ of Oxford (DPhil, MA, DSc); *m* 29 July 1961, Faith, da of Lt-Col Harold Thomson Carew Ivens (d 1951), of Beaconsfield; 2 s (Robert b 1965, Nicholas b 1967); *Career* Capt NZ Def Scientific Corps 1957-63, sr res fell RMCS Shrivenham 1961-63, lectr in engrg sci Univ of Oxford 1966-78, vice-chllr The City Univ 1978-; dir: City Technol Ltd 1978-, OTEC Ltd 1988-; vice chm Gen Bd of Faculties Univ of Oxford 1971-74; memb: Hebdomadal Cncl 1971-74 and 1976-78, Cncl Gresham Coll 1981, Sci Bd SERC 1982-85, London Pension Fund Authy 1989-; hon fell Keble Coll Oxford 1980- (fell 1963-78); govr Ashridge Mgmnt Coll 1987-; Liveryman Worshipful Co of Curriers; FEng 1990; *Books* Plasma Phenomena in Ionized Gas (1976), Physical Kinetics (ed 1981), Interaction of Intense Electromagnetic Fields with Plasma (1981); *Recreations* walking, gardening, tennis; *Clubs* Athenaeum; *Style—* Prof Raoul Franklin; 20 Myddelton Square, London EC1R 1YE; The City University, Northampton Square, London EC1V 0HB (☎ 071 253 4399 ext 3000, fax 071 250 0837)

FRANKLIN, Richard Harrington; CBE (1973); s of late Percival Charles Franklin, of Twickenham, and late Winifred Eliza Mary; *b* 3 April 1906; *Educ* Merchant Taylors', Univ of London (MB BS); *m* 5 Oct 1933, Helen Margaret (d 1987), da of Sir Henry Dixon Kimber (d 1950), of Maidenhead; 2 s (Richard b 15 Jan 1936, Peter b 28 Feb 1948, d 1984); *Career* WWII surgn EMS 1940-45; hon visiting surgn Royal Postgrad Med Sch, emeritus conslt surgn Kingston and Longrove Gp Hosps, hon conslt surgn Royal Star and Garter Home 1957-85 (govr 1969-85), conslt surgn emeritus to RN; RCS: Hunterian prof 1947, Bradshaw lectr 1973, Hunterian orator 1977, memb Ct of Examiners 1956-66; examiner in surgery Univ of Cambridge 1958-69, visiting prof Univ of California 1972; life govr Imperial Cancer Res Fund 1975 (memb Cncl 1967-82, vice chm 1975-79); memb Med Soc of London, hon memb Hellenic Surgns Soc; Freeman: City of London 1950, Worshipful Soc Co of Apothecaries FRSM (pres surgns 1969-70), FRCS (vice pres 1974-76); fell: Assoc of Surgns of GB and Ireland, Br Assoc of Paediatric Surgeons; *Books* Surgery of the Oesophagus (1952); *Recreations* sailing, gardening; *Clubs* Aldeburgh Yacht, Ranelagh Sailing; *Style—* Richard Franklin, Esq, CBE; The Stern Walk, Crespigny Rd, Aldeburgh, Suffolk IP15 5EZ (☎ 072 845 2600)

FRANKLIN, Stephen Roy; s of Prof George Henry Franklin, of Wilts, and Sylvia Daisy, *née* Allen; *b* 10 Dec 1954; *Educ* St Lawrence Coll Ramsgate; *m* 7 Dec 1985, Amanda Patricia, da of Keith Clegg, of St Albans, Herts; 3 da (Hannah b 1986, Sophie b 1987, Emma b 1989; *Career* CA; sr ptnr Franklin Chartered Accountants; FCA; *Recreations* hockey, squash, fishing; *Clubs* RAC; *Style—* Stephen R Franklin, Esq; Locksley Hall, North Somercotes, nr Louth, Lincs (☎ 050785 305); Suite 210, The Chambers, Chelsea Harbour, London SW10 OXF (☎ 071 823 3888, fax 071 823 3046, car 0836 371659)

FRANKLIN, Rt Rev William Alfred; OBE (1965); s of George Amos Franklin (d 1956), and Mary Ann Catherine, *née* Scott (d 1980); *b* 16 July 1916; *Educ* Church Sch in London, Kelham Theol Coll Nottingham; *m* 1945, Winifred Agnes, *née* Jarvis; 1 s, 1 da; *Career* ordained: deacon 1940, priest 1941; curate: St John Bethnal Green 1940-43, St John's Palmers Green 1943-45; asst chaplain St Saviour's Anglican Church Buenos Aires 1945-48, rector Holy Trinity Lomas De Zamora Buenos Aires 1948-58, rector canon and sub dean St Andrew's Santiago Chile 1958-65, rector St Alban's Anglican Church Bogota and archdeacon of Colombia (Episcopal church of USA) 1965-71, consecrated Lord bishop of Colombia 1972, resigned 1978; full-time asst bishop Diocese Peterborough and hon canon Peterborough Cathedral 1978-86; hon canon emeritus of Peterborough Cathedral 1987, hon asst bishop of Canterbury 1985-; *Recreations* fishing, writing, study of Church growth; *Style—* The Rt Rev William Franklin, OBE; Flat 26C, The Beach, Walmer, nr Deal, Kent CT14 7HJ

FRANKLIN, William John; DL (Mid Glamorgan 1989-); s of William Thomas Franklin (d 1958), and Edith Hannah Franklin (d 1954); *b* 8 March 1927; *Educ* Monkton House Sch Cardiff; *m* 1951, Sally, da of David Roderick Davies (d 1967); 1 da (Ann Elizabeth b 1952); *Career* chief exec Powell Duffryn plc 1976-85, dep chm Chartered Tst plc 1986-; chm: Powell Duffryn Wagon Ltd 1986-89, Howells Motors Ltd 1986-89; treas Univ Coll of Swansea 1989- (dep treas 1988-89); FCA; *Recreations* Royal Porthcawl Golf; *Style—* John Franklin, Esq, DL; 80 South Road, Porthcawl, Mid Glam CF36 3DA (☎ 0656 715194)

FRANKLYN, William Leo; s of Leo Franklyn (d 1975), of London, and Mary Victoria, *née* Rigby; *b* 22 Sept 1925; *Educ* Wesley Coll Melbourne, Haileybury Coll Melbourne, Leas House Sch London; *m* 1969, Susanna Jane, da of Edmund Jupp (d 1943), of Hong Kong; 3 da (Sabina, Francesca, Melissa); *Career* actor; films incl: The Snorkel, The Flesh is Weak, Danger Within, Fury at Smuggler's Bay, Pit of Darkness, The Legend of Young Dick Turpin, The Intelligence Men, Cul-de-Sac, The Satanic Rites of Dracula; BBC TV serials: The Makepeace Story, No Wreath for the General, No Cloak, No Dagger; ITV TV series: Top Secret, What's On Next, Paradise Island, Masterspy, The Steam Video Company, GBH; London theatre incl: The Tunnel of Love, There's a Girl in my Soup, Deathtrap, Dead Ringer, A Touch of Danger, Noel Coward in Two Keys, The Man Most Likely To, The Greenhouse Effect; TV film series incl: The Scarlet Pimpernel, Charlie Chan, The Avengers, The Saracens, Troubleshooters, Public Eye; theatre dir incl: There's a Girl in my Soup, Tunnel of Love, Subway in the Sky, Later Leonardo, That's No Lady (re-titled The Bedwinner), Castle in the Air, Rope, Same Time Next Year; *Recreations* cricket, squash, tennis, Italy; *Clubs* MCC, Hurlingham; *Style—* William Franklyn, Esq; Hobsons Personal Management, Burlington House, 64 Chiswick High Rd, London W4 1SY

FRANKS, Anthony Kenric Stapleton; s of Maurice Kenric Franks (d 1955); *b* 13 June 1928; *Educ* Nautical Coll Pangbourne; *m* 1960, Sarah Georgina Cochrane, *née*

Watson; 3 s; *Career* md Phicom plc (previously Plantation Holdings Ltd) 1971-84 (chm and chief exec 1984-86), chm Beck Electronics Ltd 1986-; chm Royal Hosp and Home Putney 1988-, dep treas RNLI 1989-; *Recreations* shooting, sailing; *Clubs* Boodle's, Royal Yacht Sqdn; *Style*— Anthony Franks, Esq; Becketts Grove, Matfield, Tonbridge, Kent TN12 7LH (☎ 089 272 2175)

FRANKS, Sir Arthur Temple (Dick); KCMG (1979, CMG 1967); s of late Arthur Franks, of Hove, Sussex; *b* 13 July 1920; *Educ* Rugby, Queen's Coll Oxford; *m* 1945, Rachel Marianne, da of Rev A E S Ward, of Thame, Oxon; 1 s, 2 da; *Career* serv WWII (despatches); entered Foreign Serv 1949, Br ME Office 1952, Tehran 1953, Bonn 1962, FCO 1966-81, ret; *Clubs* Travellers', Army and Navy, Aldeburgh Golf; *Style*— Sir Dick Franks, KCMG; Roefield, Alde Lane, Aldeburgh, Suffolk

FRANKS, Cecil Simon; MP (C) Barrow Furness 1983-; *b* 1 July 1935; *Educ* Manchester GS, Manchester Univ; *Career* solicitor, ldr of (C) Gp Manchester City Cncl; *Style*— Cecil Franks Esq, MP; House of Commons, London SW1

FRANKS, His Hon Judge; Desmond Gerald Fergus; s of late Frederick Franks, MC; *b* 24 Jan 1928; *Educ* Cathedral Choir Sch Canterbury, Manchester GS, UCL; *m* 1952, Margaret Leigh, da of late Clarence Daniel; 1 da; *Career* called to the Bar Middle Temple 1952, in practice N Circuit, asst rec Salford 1966, dep rec Salford 1971, rec of Crown Ct 1972, circuit judge 1972-, pres SW Pennine Magistates Assoc, liaison judge to Oldham Magistrates; *Recreations* music, photography; *Style*— His Hon Judge Franks; 4 Beathwaite Drive, Bramhall, Cheshire

FRANKS, John Alexander; s of Morris Franks, JP, and Jennie, *née* Alexander; *b* 10 Dec 1928; *Educ* Shaftesbury GS, Univ Coll London (LLB), Inst of Advanced Legal Studies (LLM); *m* 1, 1952, Golda Yacha (d 1976), da of Michael Lawrence (d 1950); 2 s (Michael b 1954, Gerald b 1958), 1 da (Jane b 1961); m 2, 1983, Sheila, da of William J J Clark (d 1969); 1 da (Sara b 1954); *Career* slr (1952); chm: Sunlight Service Group 1974- (merged Godfrey Davis Group plc 1987), Disciplinary Ctee of Architects Registration Cncl 1981-88, Appeal Ctee of Nat House Builders' Registration Cncl; memb Cncl Law Soc 1974-; FCIArb; *Books* Company Directors and the Law (edn 1986); *Recreations* collecting Vanity Fair caricatures and English Cottage Glass; *Clubs* City Livery, United Wards, Royal Automobile; *Style*— John Franks, Esq; Chethams, 84 Baker St, London W1M 1DL (☎ 071 935 7360, fax 071 935 4068, telex 24932 JETAMS)

FRANKS, Lynne Joanne (Mrs Paul Howie); da of Leslie Samuel Franks, and Angela, *née* Herman; *b* 16 Jan 1949; *Educ* Minchenden GS Southgate; *m* 16 Dec 1972, Paul Leonard Howie, *qv*; 1 s (Joshua b 21 Feb 1974), 1 da (Jessica b 22 Jan 1976); *Career* secretary Petticoat magazine 1965-67, asst ed Freemans mail order staff newspaper 1967-69, estab Lynne Franks PR 1971; *Style*— Miss Lynne Franks; Lynne Franks PR, 6-10 Frederick Close, Stanhope Place, London W2

FRANKS, Michael John Alan; s of Jacob Franks, MD (d 1976); *b* 6 May 1928; *Educ* Epsom Coll, Merton Coll Oxford (MA); *m* 1, 3 Nov 1962 (m dis 1978), Anne, yr da of Sir David George Home, 13 Bt; 2 da (Lucinda b 1964, Miranda b 1966); m 2, 1980, Nicola Stewart, da of Col George Harcourt Stewart Balmain (d 1962); *Career* called to the Bar Gray's Inn 1953, in practice Chancery Bar 1953-59; Royal Dutch Shell 1959-69, dir Beaverbrook Newspapers 1969-73; chm: Clyde Paper Co 1971-76, Schwarzkopf UK 1981-86, Innsite Hotel Services 1987-90, Silicon Bridge 1989-; dep chm Goodhead Group plc 1985-; non-exec dir: Select Appointments plc 1987-, Direct Entertainment 1989-, Unipower Vehicles 1988-; *Recreations* sailing, skiing, travel; *Clubs* Royal Thames Yacht; *Style*— Michael Franks, Esq; Field House, Mapledurwell, Basingstoke, Hants RG25 2LU (☎ 0256 464861)

FRANKS, Baron (Life Peer UK 1962), of Headington, Co Oxford; Sir Oliver Shewell Franks; OM (1977), GCMG (1952), KCB (1946), KCVO (1986), CBE (1942), PC (1949), DL (Oxon 1978); s of Rev Robert Sleightholme Franks (d 1964), of Leppington, Winscombe, Somerset, and Katharine, *née* Shewell; *b* 16 Feb 1905; *Educ* Bristol GS, Queen's Coll Oxford (BA, MA); *m* 3 July 1931, Barbara Mary (d 1987), da of Herbert George Tanner, JP, of Llanfuist, Clifton Down, Bristol; 2 da (Hon Caroline Lesley (Hon Mrs Dinwiddy) b 1939, Hon Alison Elizabeth (Hon Mrs Wright) b 1945); *Career* prof of moral philosophy Univ of Glasgow 1937-45, Miny of Supply 1939-46 (perm sec 1945-46), provost Queen's Coll Oxford 1946-48, chm Marshall Plan Negotiations (Paris) 1947, ambass to USA 1948-52, dir Lloyds Bank 1953-75 (chm 1954-62), provost Worcester Coll Oxford 1962-76, chllr Univ of E Anglia 1965-84; chm: Wellcome Trust 1965-82, Ctee on Official Secrets Act (Section 2) 1971-72, Ctee on Ministerial Memoirs 1976, Political Honours Scrutiny Ctee 1976-86, Ctee of PCs on the Falklands Invasion 1982-83; lord warden of the Stannaries and dep chm of the Cncl of the Duchy of Cornwall 1983-85 (memb Cncl Duchy of Cornwall 1966-85); FBA; *Style*— The Rt Hon Lord Franks, OM, GCMG, KCB, CBE, PC, DL; Blackhall Farm, Garford Rd, Oxford OX2 6VY (☎ 0865 511286)

FRANKS, Stephen George; s of Geofrey Raymond Francis (d 1988), and Jean Margaret, *née* Macgree; *b* 18 Sept 1955; *Educ* De-Burgh Sch Epsom; *m* Sarah, da of Tony Bagnal Smith; 2 s (Archie b 4 Oct 1986, Henry b 14 Sept 1989); *Career* designer Lock and Petersen 1979-82, sr designer Tayburn London 1982-83, Landsdown Euro 1983-84; ptnr and design dir Coley Porter Bell 1984-; memb Design and Advertising 1980-; *Style*— Stephen Franks, Esq; Coley Porter Bell, 4 Flitcroft St, London WC2 (☎ 071 379 4355, fax 071 734 7345)

FRANSMAN, Laurens Francois (Laurie); s of Henri Albert Fransman, of Johannesburg, SA, and Stanmore, London, and Hannah Lena, *née* Bernstein; *b* 4 July 1956; *Educ* King David HS, Linksfield Johannesburg South Africa, Univ of Leeds (LLB); *m* 7 Aug 1977 (m dis 1985), Claire Frances, da of Prof Colin Howard Ludlow Goodman (d 1990), of Mill Hill, London; 1 s (Piers b 1980); *Career* barr, author, lectr, broadcaster and advsr; called to the Bar Middle Temple 1979, immigration barr Tower Hamlets Law Centre 1981, assoc with Allen E-Kaye PC NY 1983, barr-at-law 2 Garden Ct Temple 1987-; UK contrib ed Immigration Law and Practice Reporter NY 1985, editorial bd Immigration and Nationality Law and Practice 1987, conslt in Nationality Law to Halsbury's Laws of England (4 edn) 1991; numerous lectures in UK, USA, Hong Kong; numerous radio and TV broadcasts in UK 1982-; fndr Immigration Law Practioners Assoc 1983 (chm, memb Exec Ctee); *Books* British Nationality Law and the 1981 Act (1982), Tribunals Practice and Procedure (jtly, 1985), Immigration Emergency Procedures (jtly, 1986), Fransman's British Nationality Law (1989); *Recreations* guitar playing, history, geology, food, music, theatre; *Style*— Laurie Fransman, Esq; 2 Garden Court, Temple, London EC4Y 9VL (☎ 071 353 1633, fax 071 353 4621)

FRAPPELL, Charles Edward; s of Charles Joseph Frappell (d 1972), and Kate Lilian, *née* Smith (d 1969); *b* 26 April 1919; *Educ* Plaistow Municipal Secdy Sch, Univ of London; *m* 25 March 1945, Violet Eileen, da of Richard Edward Batcheler (d 1950), of Rainham, Essex; 3 da (Carole Eileen b 15 Oct 1946, Susan Ellen b 26 Sept 1948, Hazel Elizabeth b 24 Aug 1957); *Career* 54 (EA) Divnl Signals TA 1939, 4 Divnl Signals 1939, Intelligence Corps Ciphers ATT 4 Div 1941, No 3 Intelligence Sch WO 1942, HQ E Africa Cmd-ATT HQ Eastern Fleet Mombasa (Ciphers) 1942, Fortress HQ Diego Suarez Madagascar (Ciphers), HQ 11 (E African) Div (Ciphers) Kenya, serv Ceylon, Burma and India 1943-44, returned UK 1945, demobbed 1946; trainee Grieveson Grant & Co Stockbrokers London 1935 (mangr 1946-58); W Greenwell & Co: joined 1959, ptnr 1961, ptnr i/c gilt edged securities 1965, ret 1985; memb London and SE Bd Bradford & Bingley Building Society 1985-90; common councilman ward of Bread Street City of London (memb Ct 1973), chm Spitalfields Market Ctee 1977-80, fndr memb City of London Branch IOD; Freeman City of London 1973, Liveryman Worshipful Co of Gold and Silver Wyre Drawers 1973; memb Stock Exchange 1961, FInstD 1968, FBIM 1978; *Recreations* golf, puzzles, conversation, travelling; *Clubs* RAC, City Livery, Guildhall; *Style*— Charles Frappell, Esq; White Oaks, Forest Road, Burley, Ringwood, Hants BH24 4DE

FRASE, (Anthony) Richard Grenville; s of Flt Lt Sanislaw Frase (d 1957), and Joy, *née* Thompson; *b* 8 July 1954; *Educ* Repton, Trinity Coll Cambridge (MA); *m* 26 May 1990, Sarah-Louise, da of John Gregor Walker, of Milford, Surrey; *Career* 2nd Lt TAVR 1976-78; admitted slr 1981, asst slr Allen & Overy 1981-83 (articled clerk 1978-80), ptnr Denton Hall Burgin & Warrens 1988 (asst slr 1983-87); seconded to Association of Futures Brokers and Dealers Ltd and The Securities and Futures Association Limited 1989-91; memb: City of London Slrs Co, Int Bar Assoc, Law Soc; *Publications* The Gt Guide to World Equity Markets (contrib, 1991), author of various articles on fin servs law; *Recreations* financial history, travel, art, literature; *Clubs* United Oxford and Cambridge Univ, Wig and Pen, Cavalry and Guards'; *Style*— Richard Frase, Esq; Denton Hall Burgin & Warrens, 5 Chancery Lane, Clifford's Inn, London EC4 (☎ 071 242 1212)

FRASER, Alasdair Campbell; *b* 5 Oct 1930; *Educ* St Mary's Hosp Med Sch London (MB BS, MRCS, LRCP); *m* Ann Elaine; 4 c; *Career* dir of clinical studies St Mary's Hosp Med Sch 1973-78; currently: conslt obstetrican and gynaecologist St Mary's Hosp and Samaritan Hosp for Women London, hon conslt St Lukes Nursing Home for the Clergy London, regnl advsr in maternal deaths Dept of Health, med advsr Family Div High Ct of Justice; examiner: final MB examination to Univs of London Manchester Liverpool and Glasgow, Diploma and membership to RCOG; memb: Bd of Govrs St Mary's Hosp 1971, Fellowship Selection Ctee RCOG; pres Section of Obstetrics RSM 1991-92, chm and memb numerous hosp and med sch ctees; FRCOG; *Books* Handbook for Obstetric House Officers (with Miss M Anderson, 1968), author of numerous articles in med jls; *Style*— Alasdair Fraser, Esq; 100 Harley St, London W1N 1AF

FRASER, Alasdair MacLeod; QC (1989); s of Rev Dr Donald Fraser, and Ellen Hart McAllister (d 1986); *b* 29 Sept 1946; *Educ* Sullivan Upper Sch, Trinity Coll Dublin (BA, LLB), Queen's Univ Belfast (Dip in Laws); *m* 8 Aug 1975, Margaret Mary, da of Dr Brian Patrick Glancy; 2 s (Andrew Ian b 1979, James Michael b 1986), 1 da (Katy Margaret b 1983); *Career* called to the Bar NI 1970; Dept of Dir of Public Prosecutions NI: court prosecutor 1973, asst dir 1974, sr asst dir 1982, dep dir 1988, dir 1989-; *Style*— Alasdair Fraser, Esq, QC; Royal Courts of Justice, Belfast, NI BT1 3NX (☎ 0232 235111)

FRASER, Hon (Alexander) Andrew Macdonell; o s of Baron Fraser of Tullybelton, PC (Life Peer; d 1989); *b* 1946; *m* 28 April 1982 (m dis), Sarah J, da of Henry Jones, of Kitsbury Orchard, Oddington, Moreton-in-Marsh, Glos; 1 s (b 1984); *Style*— The Hon Andrew Fraser; 16 Lord North St, London SW1

FRASER, Hon Andrew Roy Matthew; s of 17 Lord Lovat, DSO, MC, TD; *b* 24 Feb 1952; *Educ* Ampleforth, Magdalen Coll Oxford; *m* 10 Sept 1979, Lady Charlotte Anne Greville, only da of 8 Earl of Warwick; 2 da (Daisy b 1985, Laura b 1987); *Career* dir: China Trading Int, Cordle & Co; memb Queen's Bodyguard for Scotland (The Royal Co of Archers); Col-in-Chief 78 Fraser Highlanders; sec gen Br Assoc of Knights of Malta; *Clubs* White's, Pratt's; *Style*— The Hon Andrew Fraser; 1 Petyt Place, London SW3 5DJ; 5 Radnor Walk, London SW3 4BP (☎ 071 351 0223, fax 071 351 7902)

FRASER, Sir Angus McKay; KCB (1985, CB 1981), TD (1965); s of late Thomas Douglas Fraser; *b* 10 March 1928; *Educ* Falkirk HS, Univ of Glasgow, Bordeaux Univ; *m* 1955 (m dis 1968), Margaret Neilson; 1 s, 1 da; *Career* RA 1950-52; 44 Para Bde (TA) 1953-66; Customs and Excise 1952-61, 1965-73, 1976-80, 1983-87 (dep chm 1978, chm Bd 1983-87); Treasy 1961-64; CSD 1973-76, 1980-83 (first cmmr 1981-83); govt advsr on efficiency in public serv 1988-; *Clubs* Reform, Royal Over-Seas League, Caledonian, Norfolk (Norwich); *Style*— Sir Angus Fraser, KCB, TD; 84 Ennerdale Rd, Kew, Richmond, Surrey TW9 2DL (☎ 081 940 9913)

FRASER, Angus Robert Charles; s of Donald Fraser, and Irene, *née* Tonge; *b* 8 Aug 1965; *Educ* Gayton HS Harrow, Orange Hill Senior HS; *Career* professional cricketer; Middlesex CCC 1984-, awarded county cap 1988; England début 1989; England: 11 Test matches 1989-90, 24 one-day Ints, memb tour Aust and NZ 1990-91; honours with Middlesex: County Championship 1985 and 1990, Nat West Trophy 1988, Benson & Hedges Cup 1986, Nixdorp Computers Middlesex Player of the Year 1988 and 1989; qualified cricket coach; *Recreations* golf, watching Liverpool FC and rugby internationals, anything in sport but racing; *Style*— Angus Fraser, Esq; c/o Middlesex CCC, Lord's Cricket Ground, London NW8 8QN (☎ 071 289 1300)

FRASER, Hon Ann Lewis; o da of 1 Baron Fraser of Allander (d 1966), and Baroness Fraser of Allander, *née* Hutcheon Lewis; bro disclaimed his peerage for Life 1966, Sir Hugh Fraser 2 Bt (d 1987 when extinct); *b* 5 April 1932; *Educ* Westbourne Sch Glasgow; *Career* tstee Hugh Fraser Fndn; *Style*— The Hon Ann Fraser

FRASER, Air Commodore Anthony Walkinshaw; s of Robert Walkinshaw Fraser (d 1956), and Evelyn Elisabeth, *née* Watts (d 1955); *b* 15 March 1934; *Educ* Stowe; *m* 1955(m dis 1990), Angela Mary Graham, da of George Richard Shaw (d 1983), of Darlington, Co Durham; 1 s (Robert), 3 da (Amanda, Antonia, Alexandra); m 2, Grania Eleanor Ruth, da of Ean Stewart-Smith, MBE, of Stanley Hall, Halstead, Essex; *Career* RAF Pilot, Instr and Staff Offr, Air Cdre 1977, Cmdt Central Flying Sch, ret 1979; ADC to HM The Queen 1977-79; dir Soc of Motor Mfrs & Traders Ltd 1980-88, pres Organisation Internationale des Constructeurs d'Automobiles 1983-87, Goddard Kay Rogers (Northern) Ltd 1988-89, dir Nissan UK Ltd 1989-; *Recreations* golf, shooting, fishing, languages; *Clubs* Boodle's, RAF, Sunningdale; *Style*— Air Cdre Anthony Fraser; 31 Grove End Rd, London NW8 9LY; Nissan House, Columbia Drive, Worthing, W Sussex BN13 3HD (☎ 0903 68561)

FRASER, Lady Antonia; *née* Pakenham; da of 7 Earl of Longford, PC, and Lady Longford, the biographer of Queen Victoria and the Duke of Wellington; *b* 27 Aug 1932; *Educ* Dragon Sch Oxford, St Mary's Convent Ascot, LMH Oxford; *m* 1, 25 Sept 1956 (m dis 1977), Rt Hon Sir Hugh Fraser, MBE, PC, MP (d 1984), s of 16 Lord Lovat; 3 s (Benjamin b 1961, Damian b 1964, Orlando b 1967), 3 da (Rebecca (Mrs Edward Fitzgerald) b 1957, Flora (Mrs Robert Powell-Jones) b 1958, Natasha b 1963); m 2, 1980, Harold Pinter, CBE, *qv*; *Career* writer: books incl: Mary Queen of Scots (James Tait Black Memorial Prize 1969), Cromwell our chief of Men (1973), James I & VI of England and Scotland (1974), Kings and Queens of England (ed, 1975), King Charles II (1979), The Weaker Vessel (Wolfson History Award 1984), Boadicea's Chariot: The Warrior Queens (1988), Quiet as a Nun (1977), Cool Repentance (1980), The Wild Island (1978), Oxford Blood (1985), Your Royal Hostage (1987), A Splash of Red (1981, basis TV series Jemima Shore 1983), Jemima Shore's First Case (1986), The Cavalier Case (1990); chm: Soc of Authors 1974-75, Crimewriters' Assoc 1985-86; pres English PEN 1988-89; *Recreations* gardening, swimming; *Style*— The Lady Antonia Fraser; Curtis Brown, 167 Regent Street W1

FRASER, Dr (Robert) Ashley; s of Robert James Alexander Fraser, of Aberdeen, and

Mary Ewen, *née* Chalmers; *b* 7 Jan 1948; *Educ* Robert Gordon's Coll Aberdeen, Univ of Aberdeen (MB ChB, PhD); *m* 16 April 1977, Susan Mary, da of Andrew David Monteath, OBE, TD, of Edinburgh; 2 s (Jamie b 1982, David b 1986), 1 da (Anna b 1979); *Career* lectr in pathology Univ of Aberdeen 1973-85, hon sr registrar Aberdeen Royal Infirmary 1981-85, conslt pathologist Royal Shrewsbury Hosp 1985-; treas Shropshire Div BMA, treas and post grad tutor Shrewsbury Med Inst; memb Rotary Club; MRCPath 1984; *Recreations* skiing, keep fit, computing, wines; *Style—* Dr Ashley Fraser; Kinder, 10 Port Hill Rd, Shrewsbury, Shropshire SY3 8SE (☎ 0743 343130); Department of Pathology, Royal Shrewsbury Hospital (North), Mytton Oak Rd, Shrewsbury, Shropshire (☎ 0743 231122 ext 3545)

FRASER, Sir Basil Malcolm; 2 Bt (UK 1921); s of Sir (John) Malcolm Fraser, 1 Bt, GBE (d 1949), and Irene, *née* Brightman; *b* 2 Jan 1920; *Educ* Eton, Queens' Coll Cambridge; *Heir* none; *Career* Capt RE WW II, Madras Sappers and Miners (despatches); *Style—* Sir Basil Fraser, Bt; 175 Beach St, Deal, Kent

FRASER, Sir Bruce Donald; KCB (1961, CB 1956); s of Maj-Gen Sir Theodore Fraser, KCB, CSI, CMG (d 1953), and Constance Ruth, *née* Stevenson (d 1918); *b* 18 Nov 1910; *Educ* Bedford Sch, Trinity Coll Cambridge (MA); *m* 12 May 1939, Audrey (d 1982), da of Lt-Col Evan Leigh Croslegh (d 1942); 1 s (decd), 1 da (decd); *Career* entered Civil Service Scot Office 1933, transferred Treasy 1936; perm sec Miny of Health 1960-64, jt perm under sec of state DES 1964-65, perm sec Miny of Land and Natural Resources 1965-66, comptroller and auditor gen Exchequer and Audit Dept 1966-71; *Books* The Complete Plain Words by Sir Ernest Gowers (revised edn, 1973); *Style—* Sir Bruce Fraser, KCB; Jonathan, St Dogmael's, Cardigan, Dyfed SA43 3LF (☎ 0239 612387)

FRASER, Bruce William; s of Douglas Edward Fraser, of Tayport, and Isobel, *née* Cockburn; *b* 21 Oct 1947; *Educ* Madras Coll St Andrews, Royal Scot Acad of Music, Guildhall Sch of Music (DRSAM); *m* 20 Sept 1969, Patricia Martha; 2 da (Lynn b 4 Feb 1971, Aileen b 15 June 1974); *Career* Scot Opera Orch 1971-79, first pubn Suite for 4 Trombones 1978, numerous cmmns for both amateur and professional gps, prizewinner Worshipful Co of Musicians Competition 1984, world prizewinner Corciano Int Competition 1985, fndr Lomond Music; memb: Ctee BASBWE, Fife Sinfonia Ctee; conductor: Levenmouth Concert Band, Buckhaven Brass Band, Anstruther Philharmonic Soc; memb: Composers Guild of GB, Scot Soc of Composers; PRS, MCPS; *Recreations* swimming, walking; *Style—* Bruce Fraser, Esq; Heston Bank, 32 Bankton Park, Kingskettle, Fife KY7 7PY (☎ 0337 30974)

FRASER, Sir (James) Campbell; s of Alexander Ross Fraser, and Annie McGregor Fraser; *b* 2 May 1923; *Educ* Univ of Glasgow, McMaster Univ Hamilton Canada, Dundee Sch of Economics; *m* 1950, Maria Harvey, *née* McLaren; 2 da; *Career* pres CBI 1982-84 (former chm CBI Industrial Policy Ctee); chm: Dunlop Holdings 1978-83, Scottish TV 1975-; non-exec dir: BP, BAT Industries, Bridgewater Paper Co, Tandem Computers, Alexander Proudfoot; tstee The Economist 1978-; memb NEDC 1982-84; pres Soc of Business Economists 1972-84; former visiting prof Univ of Stirling; FRSE, CBIM, FPRI, Hon LLD Strathclyde, Hon DUniv Stirling Del (Bishops); kt 1978; *Style—* Sir Campbell Fraser; 114 St Martins Lane, London WC2N 4AZ

FRASER, Sir Charles Annand; KCVO (1989, CVO 1985, LVO 1968), DL (1985), WS (1956); s of Very Rev Dr John Annand Fraser, MBE, TD (d 1985), and Leila, *née* Campbell, of 4-3 Gillsland Rd Edinburgh (d 1989); *b* 16 Oct 1928; *Educ* Hamilton Acad Lanarkshire, Univ of Edinburgh (MA, LLB); *m* 1957, Ann, da of William Francis Scott-Kerr (d 1974), of Sunlaws Roxburghshire; 4 s (Simon, Ian, James, Robert); *Career* WS; purse bearer to Lord High Cmmr to Gen Assembly of Church of Scot 1969-87; dir: Ettrick Nominees Ltd 1968-, Signetics (UK) Ltd 1969-, W&J Burness Trustee Ltd 1971, Br Assets Tst 1972-, Scot Widows Fund and Life Assur Soc 1976; vice chm United Biscuits Holdings Ltd 1977; dir: Scot TV plc 1979-, Solsgirth Investmt Tst co Ltd 1981-89, Scottish Widows Unit Funds Ltd 1981, Walter Alexander plc 1981, Grosvenor Developments Ltd 1981, Selective Assets Trust plc 1981-, Scot Business in the Community 1982-, Adam and Co plc 1983-, The Patrons of the Nat Galleries of Scot 1984-, The John Muir Tst 1984-, Anglo-Scot Investmt Tst plc 1984-; tstee Scot Civic Tst 1978-; memb Cncl Law Soc of Scotland 1966-72, memb Ct Heriot-Watt Univ 1972; *Clubs* New (Edinburgh), Caledonian (London); *Style—* Sir Charles Fraser, KCVO, DL, WS; Shepherd House, Inveresk, Midlothian (☎ 031 665 2570); Wester Dalvoult, Boat of Garten, Inverness-shire (☎ 047 983 343); W & J Burness, 16 Hope St, Charlotte Sq, Edinburgh EH2 4DD (☎ 031 226 2561, fax 031 225 2964, telex 724

FRASER, Lady Charlotte Anne; *née* Greville; da of 8 Earl of Warwick, and Sarah (now Mrs H Thomson Jones), da of Alfred Chester Beatty, the financier; *b* 6 June 1958; *Educ* Heathfield; *m* 10 Sept 1979, Hon Andrew Roy Matthew Fraser, *qv*, 4 s of 17 Lord Lovat; 2 da; *Style—* The Lady Charlotte Fraser; 1 Petyt Place, London SW3 5DJ

FRASER, Colin Gall; TD (1966), GSM (with Malaya Clasp) 1953; s of Douglas Fraser (d 1978), and Annie Louise (Nancy), *née* Gall; *b* 18 Feb 1934; *Educ* Cottesmore Sch, Aldenham, Trinity Hall Cambridge (MA); *m* 14 Dec 1963, Gabrielle Genista (Gay), da of Brig-General Sir Eric Edward Boketon Holt-Wilson, CMG, DSO (d 1950); 1 s (Andrew b 1967), 1 da (Fiona b 1964); *Career* rifleman RB 1952, Nat Serv Queen's Own Royal W Kent Regt 1953; served as subaltern: 1 Bn Malaya 1953-54, BAOR 1954; served in 4/5 Bn (TA) 1954-68, ret as Maj; admitted slr 1960, ptnr Joynson-Hicks 1964 (articled clerk 1957-60), ptnr and jt head Commercial Dept Taylor Joynson Garett 1989, speaker at seminars, contrib articles on copyright; dep to under sheriff of Surrey 1966-79, chm Dorking Gp Home Sub Ctee Surrey Fedn Housing Assoc 1980-, tstee Cottesmore Sch Old Boys Educn Tst 1981-; chm: Dorking Cncl of Churches (first lay chm) 1981-84, Dorking Christian Centre Mgmnt Policy Ctee 1985-; memb Br Literary and Artistic Copyright Assoc, assoc Queen Mary Coll London; *Recreations* golf, cricket and (formerly) hockey and reading history; *Clubs* United Oxford and Cambridge; *Style—* Colin Fraser, Esq, TD; High Trees, South Drive, Dorking, Surrey RH5 4AG (☎ 0306 883423); 180 Fleet St, London EC4A 2NT; 10 Maltravers St, London WC2R 3BS (☎ 071 836 8456, fax 071 379 7196)

FRASER, David James; s of Charles Smith Fraser, and Jesse Fraser; *b* 1 July 1952; *Educ* Peterhead Acad, Univ of Aberdeen (MA); *m* 15 July 1974, Margaret Anne, da of Dr James Naughton; 1 s (Keith James b 12 Sept 1982); *Career* nat mgmnt trainee Scottish Health Service 1975-77;; Lethian Health Board: hosp admin 1977-84, unit admin 1984-86, unit gen mangr 1986-; memb Inst of Health Serv Mgmnt 1978, MIPM 1982; *Recreations* photography; *Style—* David Fraser, Esq; 4 St Catherines Place, Edinburgh EH9 1NU (☎ 031 667 3667); Lothian Health Board, Royal Edinburgh Hospital, Morningside Place, Edinburgh EH10 5HF (☎ 031 447 2011)

FRASER, Gen Sir David William; GCB (1980, KCB 1973), OBE (1962), DL (Hants, 1982); er s of Brig Hon William Fraser, DSO, MC (d 1964, yst s of 18 Lord Saltoun), and Pamela Cynthia, *née* Maude (d 1975); *b* 30 Dec 1920; *Educ* Eton, Ch Ch Oxford; *m* 1, 26 Sept 1947 (m dis 1952), Anne, yr da of Brig Edward William Sturgis Balfour, CVO, DSO, OBE, MC; 1 da (Antonia Isabella b 1949); m 2, 11 Oct 1957, Julia Frances, yr da of Maj Cyril James Oldridge de la Hey; 2 s (Alexander James b 1960, Simon b 1963), 2 da (Arabella b 1958, Lucy b 1965); *Career* WWII cmmnd Grenadier Gds 1941; served: UK and NW Europe 1939-45, Malaya 1948, Egypt 1952-54, Cyprus 1958, British Cameroons 1961, Borneo 1965; NATO Brussels 1975-77, GOC 4 Div 1969-71, ACDS 1971-73, vice CGS 1973-75, Br mil rep to NATO 1975-77, Cmdt RCDS 1977-80, ADC Gen to HM The Queen 1977-80, Col The Royal Hampshire Regt 1981-87; pres Soc for Army Historical Res 1980-; chm Treloar Tst and Governing Body Lord Mayor Treloar Coll 1982-; *Books* Alanbrooke (1982), And We Shall Shock Them (1983), The Christian Watt Papers (1983), August 1988 (1983), A Kiss for the Enemy (1985), The Killing Times (1986), The Dragon's Teeth (1987), The Seizure (1988), A Candle for Judas (1989), In Good Company (1990), Adam Hardrow (1990); *Recreations* shooting; *Clubs* Turf, Pratt's; *Style—* Gen Sir David Fraser, GCB, OBE, DL; Vallenders, Isington, Alton, Hants (☎ 0420 23166)

FRASER, Donald David (Don); s of David Sydney Fraser (d 1975) of Broadstairs, Kent, and Ellen Louise, *née* Grogan (d 1957); *b* 4 June 1941; *Educ* Holy Trinity Sch Broadstairs Kent, St Georges Sch Ramsgate Kent (awarded 1st year top place prize by Archbishop of Canterbury in July 1953 for Academic Achievement); *m* 1, 23 July 1960 (m dis 1970), Jennifer Carol, da of Sidney Palmer; 2 da (Rebecca Jane b 11 Aug 1961, Deborah Ann b 11 Oct 1962); m 2, 11 Sept 1971 (m dis 1982) Anne, da of Kenneth William Whyatt; 1 s (Mark Simon Lovat b 2 March 1972); *Career* internationally recognised induslt photographer; apprentice Industl/Advtg Photography Debt of Sunbeam Photos Thanet 1957-60; photographer Valerie Lilley Studios Surbiton 1960, implant photographer Carrier Engineering London 1961; sr photographer Kingston Photographic Ltd 1963, fndr dir Academy Studios Ltd Surrey 1964 (md 1965-), fndr Academy Design Ltd and Academy Communications Gp 1976 (chm 1977-); many awards incl: Industl Photographer of The Year FT 1971 and 1974, Export trophy FT 1972, Best Monochrome Industl Photograph FT 1973, Fame award Norway 1989, many Ilford awards; FBIPP 1974 (nat pres 1982-83), FRPS 1974, Fell Master Photographers Assoc 1964; *Style—* Don Fraser, Esq; Academy Communications Group Ltd, Academy House, Unit 6 Capital Place, Stafford Rd, Croydon CR0 4TU (☎ 081 667 0307, fax 081 666 0273, car 0860 368506)

FRASER, Donald Hamilton; s of Donald Fraser (d 1964), and Dorothy Christiana, *née* Lang (d 1973); *b* 30 July 1929; *Educ* Maidenhead GS, St Martins Sch of Art London, Paris (French Govt Scholarship); *m* 6 July 1954, Judith, da of Francis William Wentworth-Sheilds (d 1969); 1 da (Catherine Jane b 1955); *Career* artist; tutor RCA 1958-83, more than sixty one-man exhibitions in Br, Euro, Japan and North America; work in public collections include: Boston Museum of Fine Arts, Albright-Knox Gallery Buffalo, Carnegie Inst Pittsburgh, Yale Univ Art Gallery, City Art Museum St Louis, Wadsworth Atheneum Hartford, Desert Art Museum Palm Springs, Smithsonian Inst Washington DC, Nat Gallery Canada, Nat Gallery Victoria Melbourne, many corp collections and Br galleries, Arts Cncl, Govt Art collection; designed Cwlth issue postage stamps 1983; vice pres: Artists' Gen Benevolent Inst 1981- (chm 1981-86), Royal Overseas League 1986-; cmmr Royal Fine Art Cmmn 1986-; hon fell RCA; RA 1985 (ARA 1975); *Books* Gauguin's Vision after the Sermon (1969), Dancers (1989); *Clubs* Arts; *Style—* Donald Hamilton Fraser, Esq; c/o Royal Academy of Arts, Burlington House, Piccadilly, London W1V ODS

FRASER, Hon Mrs (Elizabeth Penelope); *née* Methuen; o da of 5 Baron Methuen (d 1975); *b* 4 July 1928; *Educ* Downe House Newbury; *m* 8 Dec 1956, Malcolm Henry Alastair Fraser, er s of (Hugh) Alastair Hamilton Fraser, JP, of Mill Place, Stanton Drew, Somerset; 2 da (Elizabeth b 1957, Anne b 1961); *Career* past county pres Somerset YFC; SW Area Pres YFC 1987-90, nat dep pres NFYFC 1988-; area pres St John's Ambulance; vice chm Bath and Dist ESU Branch, memb Nat Ctee for England and Wales ESU; *Recreations* travel, the arts; *Clubs* ESU Dartmouth Ho, The GB-China Centre; *Style—* The Hon Mrs Fraser; Grey Gables, Pilton, Shepton Mallet, Somerset BA4 4DB (☎ 074 989 370)

FRASER, Dr Ewan John Stanley; s of Maj I M Fraser MC (d 1988), of Chipstead, Surrey, and Mary Stanley (d 1964); *b* 15 May 1947; *Educ* Eton, Christ Church Oxford (MA, DPhil); *Career* investmt analyst James Capel and Co (Stockbrokers) 1975 - (sr exec 1985); memb (Cons) Oxford City Cncl 1969-70 and 1971-72; memb Int Stock Exchange 1984; *Recreations* fly fishing, cricket, reading, ballet; *Style—* Dr Ewan Fraser; 80 Hadley Highstone, Barnet, Herts EN5 4PY (☎ 081 440 5386); PO Box 551, 6 Bevis Marks, London EC3A 7JQ (☎ 071 621 0011, fax 071 621 0496, telex 888866)

FRASER, George MacDonald; s of William Fraser, of Carlisle, and Anne Struth, *née* Donaldson; *b* 2 April 1925; *Educ* Carlisle GS, Glasgow Acad; *m* 1949, Kathleen Margarette, da of George Hetherington, of Carlisle; 2 s (Simon, Nicholas), 1 da (Caroline); *Career* served Br Army 1943-47, infantryman Border Regt Burma, Lt Gordon Highlanders; journalist 1947-69, dep ed Glasgow Herald; author; *Books* the Flashman novels and various other books; *film screenplays include* The Three Musketeers (1973), The Four Musketeers (1974), Octopussy (1983), Casanova (1987), The Return of the Musketeers (1989); *Recreations* writing, history, talking to wife; *Style—* George Fraser, Esq; Baldrine, Isle of Man

FRASER, Helen Jean Sutherland; da of George Sutherland Fraser (d 1980), and Eileen Lucy, *née* Andrew; *b* 8 June 1949; *Educ* Collegiate Girls' Sch Leics, St Anne's Coll Oxford (MA); *m* 16 April 1982, Grant James McIntyre, s of Atholl McIntyre, of Cornwa, 2 da (Blanche b 1980, Marina b 1983); *Career* ed dir William Collins 1977-87, publisher William Heinemann 1987-; *Style—* Miss Helen Fraser; William Heinemann, Michelin House, 81 Fulham Rd, London SW3 6RB ☎ 071 581 9393, fax 071 589 8437

FRASER, Iain Michael; er s (and h) of Prof Sir James Fraser, 2 Bt, and Lady Fraser, *née* Maureen Reay; *b* 27 June 1951; *Educ* Trinity Coll Glenalmond, Edinburgh Univ (BSc); *m* 30 Jan 1982, Sherylle Ann, da of Keith Gillespie, of Wellington, NZ; 1 s (Benjamin b 1986), 1 da (Joanna b 1983); *Career* Shipping co mangr; mktg mangr American President Lines Hong Kong; *Style—* Iain Fraser, Esq; 16B Barnton Court, Canton Rd, Hong Kong

FRASER, Brig Sir Ian; DSO (1944), OBE (1941), DL (Belfast 1955); s of Robert Moore Fraser, MD, of Knock, Belfast, and Margaret Boal, *née* Ferguson; *Educ* Royal Belfast Academical Inst, Queen's Univ Belfast; *m* 2 Sept 1931, Eleanor Margaret, da of Marcus Adolphus Mitchell, of Quarry House, Belfast; 1 s, 1 da; *Career* served WWII RAMC: W Africa, N Africa, France, India; Brig 1945; Hon Col: No 4 Field Ambulance 1948-71, 204 Gen Hosp TA 1961-71; sr surgn Royal Victoria Hosp Belfast and Royal Belfast Hosp for Children 1955-66; currently conslt surgn; surgn in ordinary to the Govr of NI, hon conslt Surgn to the Army in NI; chm Police Authy RUC 1970-76; Hon DSc: Oxon, New Univ of Ulster; FRSE, FRCS, FRCSI, FACS; GCStJ 1974, Ordre de la Couronne Belgium 1963, Ordre des Palmes Académiques France 1964, Order of Orange Nassau 1969, Chevalier de la Légion d'Honneur (France) 1981, Kt Cdr Commandery of Ards (Ulster); kt 1963; *Style—* Brig Sir Ian Fraser, DSO, OBE, DL, FRSE; 19 Upper Malone Rd, Belfast, N Ireland (☎ 0232 668235)

FRASER, Lt Cdr Ian Edward; VC (1945), DSC (1943), RD (and Bar 1948), JP (Wirral 1957); s of Sydney Fraser (d 1976), of Bourne End, Bucks; *b* 18 Dec 1920; *Educ* Royal GS High Wycombe, HMS Conway; *m* 1943, Melba Estelle, da of late Stanley Hughes; 4 s, 2 da; *Career* Lt Cdr RNR Atlantic, Pacific, N Africa, N Sea; dir Star Offshore Services Ltd 1975-82, chm Nordive (W Africa) Ltd; md: North Sea Diving Services Ltd 1965-77, Universal Divers Ltd 1946-90; younger brethren Trinity House 1980; *Books* Frogman VC (1952); *Recreations* golf, model ships; *Clubs* Hoylake

Sailing, New Brighton Rugby, Leasowe Golf (first capt 1975); *Style*— Lt Cdr Ian Fraser, VC, DSC, RD, JP; Sigyn, 1 Lyndhurst Rd, Wallasey, Merseyside L45 6AX

FRASER, Sir Ian James; CBE (1972), MC (1945); s of Hon Alastair Thomas Joseph Fraser, DSO, Lovat Scouts (d 1949, s of 13 Lord Lovat), and Lady Sibyl, *née* Grimston (d 1968), da of 3 Earl of Verulam; *b* 7 Aug 1923; *Educ* Ampleforth, Magdalen Coll Oxford; *m* 25 Oct 1958, (Evelyn Elizabeth) Anne (d 1984), yr da of Maj Alastair Edward George Grant, DSO, 9 Lancers, of Nutcombe Manor, Clayhanger, Tiverton; 2 s, 2 da; *Career* Lt Scots Gds WWII (despatches); former Reuter corr; dir S G Warburg & Co 1959-69, DG City Panel on Take-overs and Mergers; dir: Davy International, BOC International 1972-73, S Pearson & Son, Pearson Longman, EMI; chm Rolls Royce Motors 1971-80, Datastream 1976-77, Lazard Bros 1980-85; dep chm: Vickers 1980-, TSB Gp plc 1985-; chm Accepting Houses Ctee 1981-85; FRSA, CBIM; Kt of Honour and Devotion, SMOM 1971; kt 1986; *Style*— Sir Ian Fraser, CBE, MC; South Haddon, Skilgate, Taunton, Somerset TA4 2DR (☎ 03983 31247); Lazard Brothers, 21 Moorfields, London EC2P 2HT (☎ 071 588 2721)

FRASER, Prof Sir James David; 2 Bt (UK 1943), of Tain, Co Ross; o s of Sir John Fraser, 1 Bt, KCVO, MC (d 1947), and Agnes Govane, *née* Herald (d 1983); *b* 19 July 1924; *Educ* Edinburgh Acad, Magdalen Coll Oxford, Univ of Edinburgh (MB ChB, ChM); *m* 16 Sept 1950, Edith Maureen, da of late Rev John Reay, MC; 2 s; *Heir* s, Iain Fraser; *Career* late Maj RAMC, served Far East 1949-51; sr lectr in clinical surgery Univ of Edinburgh and hon conslt surgn Royal Infirmary 1963-70, prof of surgery Univ of Southampton 1970-80, hon conslt surgn Univ of Southampton Hosp Gp 1970-80, postgrad dean Univ of Edinburgh Med Sch 1981-89; pres RCS Edinburgh 1982-85; *Recreations* golf, gardening; *Style*— Prof Sir James Fraser, Bt; 2 Lennox St, Edinburgh (☎ 031 332 3205)

FRASER, James Edward; CB (1990); s of Dr James Fowler Fraser, TD (d 1979), of Aberdeen, and Dr Kathleen Nevill Blomfield (d 1974); *b* 16 Dec 1931; *Educ* Aberdeen GS, Univ of Aberdeen (MA), Christ's Coll Cambridge (BA); *m* 10 Oct 1959, Patricia Louise, da of John Henry Stewart (d 1970), of Perth; 2 s (Paul Anthony b 1960, Mark Edward b 1962); *Career* Capt RA HQ Tel-el-Kebir Garrison 1954-55; civil servant; private sec to Permanent Under Sec Scot Office 1960-62, Parly under sec Scot Office 1962-; Cabinet Office 1964-66, HM Treasy 1966-68, under sec Scot Office Local Govt Fin Gp 1976-81, Scot Home & Health Dept 1981-; pres Scot Hellenic Soc of Edinburgh and Eastern Scotland 1987-; FSA (Scot); *Recreations* reading, music, walking, Greece (ancient and modern); *Clubs* Scottish Arts (Edinburgh); *Style*— J Edward Fraser, Esq, CB; c/o St Andrews House, Edinburgh EH1 3DE (☎ 031 244 2131)

FRASER, Hon Mrs (Jane Bronwen); *née* Short; only da of Baron Glenamara, CH, PC (Life Baron), *qv*; *b* 1945; *m* 1970, James Weir Fraser; issue; *Style*— The Hon Mrs Fraser; 62 Martis Ave, New Jersey 07446, USA

FRASER, John Denis; MP (Lab) Norwood 1966-; s of Archibald Fraser (d 1976), and Frances, *née* Benedict; *b* 30 June 1934; *Educ* Sloane GS Chelsea, Loughborough Co-Op Coll, Law Soc Sch of Law; *m* 1960, Ann, da of George Oswald Hathaway; 2 s (Mark b 26 July 1961, Andrew John Fitzgerald b 5 Aug 1964), 1 da (Sarah Ann b 22 July 1962); *Career* aank official 1950-52; Sgt RAEC 1952-54; admitted slr 1960; ptnr (now sr ptnr) Lewis Silkin; Lambeth Borough Cncllr 1962-68; unsuccessfully contested Norwood 1964, PPS to Barbara Castle, MP as Employment and Productivity Sec 1968-70, oppn front bench spokesman Home Affrs 1972-74, parly under sec Employment 1974-76, min state Dept of Prices and Consumer Protection 1976-79; front bench oppn spokesman: trade prices and consumer protection 1979-83, housing and construction 1983-87; Shadow Law Officer 1987-; memb Law Soc 1960; *Recreations* walking, music, football; *Style*— John Fraser, Esq, MP; House of Commons, London SW1A 0AA (☎ 071 219 5128)

FRASER, John Stewart; s of Donald Stewart Fraser, of Seacliff Park, Adelaide, Aust; *b* 18 July 1931; *m* 1955, Diane Louise, da of late William Frederick Witt; 3 children; *Career* mktg mangr Ilford (Aust) Party Ltd 1968-73, head of mktg Ilford 1973-78, md and chief exec Ilford Ltd 1978-84, md CIBA-GEIGY (plastics and additives) 1982-84; chm: The Clayton Aniline Co, CIBA-GEIGY Chemicals Ltd; CIBA-GEIGY PLC: gp md 1984-87, gp md and chief exec 1987-90, chm and chief exec 1990-; *Recreations* tennis; *Style*— John Fraser, Esq; CIBA-GEIGY PLC, Hulley Rd, Macclesfield, Cheshire SK10 2NX (☎ 0625 421933, fax 0625 619637, telex 667336); Carters Farm, High Wych, Sawbridgeworth, Bishop's Stortford, Herts CM21 0LB (☎ 0279 725619)

FRASER, June (Mrs Allen Cull); da of Donald Stuart Denholm Fraser (d 1986), of Dorset, and Myrtle Josephine, *née* Ward; *b* 30 Aug 1930; *Educ* Talbot Heath Sch Bournemouth, Beckenham Coll of Art, RCA; *m* 7 Oct 1963, Allen Hans Cull, s of Ernest Albert Cull, of Burridge, Southampton, Hants; 1 da (Zoë Gail b 27 July 1970); *Career* dir Design Res Unit 1968 (ptnr 1963), head of graphic design John Lewis Partnership 1980-84, head of the Industl Design Div The Design Cncl 1984-88, own design practice 1988; former pres Chartered Soc of Designers 1983-85, memb Ct RCA 1986; govr: Kent Inst, Bournemouth & Poole Coll of Art, Talbot Heath Sch; memb Bd ICSID 1987-, ARCA 1957, memb CSD (pres 1983-85), MInstP 1968; *Recreations* travel, horticulture, design, tennis, piano, films, theatre; *Style*— Miss June Fraser; 5 Combemartin Rd, London SW18 5PP (☎ 081 788 2353, fax 081 877 1173)

FRASER, Kenneth John Alexander; s of Jack Sears Fraser, and Marjorie Winifred, *née* Savery; *b* 22 Sept 1929; *Educ* Thames Valley GS, LSE (BSc); *m* 1953, Kathleen Grace, da of Herbert Bramwell Booth; 2 s (Neil, Alexander), 1 da (Julie); *Career* joined: Erwin Wasey & Co Ltd 1953, Lintas Ltd 1958; md Res Bureau Ltd 1962, head of Mktg Analysis and Evalutation Gp Unilever 1965, head of Mktg Div Unilever 1976; memb: Consumer Protection Advsy Ctee, Dept of Prices and Consumer Protection 1975; chm: CBI Mktg and Consumer Affairs Ctee 1977, Int Chamber of Commerce Mktg Cmmn 1978-; secondment to NEDO as industl dir 1979-81; head of external affairs Unilever; *Clubs* Royal Cwlth, Wig and Pen; *Style*— Kenneth Fraser, Esq; 14 Coombe Lane, West Kingston, Surrey KT2 7BX; Unilever House, Blackfriars (☎ 071 822 5971)

FRASER, Hon Kim Maurice; 2 s of 17th Lord Lovat, DSO, MC, TD; *b* 4 Jan 1946; *Educ* Ampleforth; *m* 1975, Joanna Katherine, da of Maj Geoffrey Edward Ford North, MC; 3 s (Tom Thomas Oswald Mungo (Tom) b 1976, Joe, Max b 1981); *Career* Lt Scots Gds; *Style*— The Hon Kim Fraser; c/o Beaufort Castle, Beauly, Inverness-shire

FRASER, Hon Mrs George; Margaret Elizabeth; 2 da of Reginald Barnes, of St Ermin's, Westminster; *m* 1934, as his 2 w, Rear Adm Hon George Fraser, DSO, RN (d 1970), 2 s of 18 Lord Saltoun; 2 s; *Style*— Hon Mrs Fraser

FRASER, Nicholas Andrew; s of W Lionel Fraser, CMG (d 1965), of London and Cynthia Elizabeth, *née* Walter, OBE; *b* 2 March 1935; *Educ* Eton, King's Coll Cambridge (MA); *m* 1, 1964 (m dis 1979), Jill, da of Roy Butterfield (d 1985), of Yorkshire; 1 s (Tom b 1968), 2 da (Kate b 1960, Emily b 1966); m 2, 1981, Charlotte Ann, da of John Warren-Davis, of Dyfed, Wales; *Career* Helbert Wagg & Co Ltd 1957-62, Doubleday Inc and William Heineman 1963-65, Bank of London & S America 1965-67; James Capel & Co 1967-: head of institutional equity sales 1977, head of investmt mgmnt 1983-, dir 1986; Liveryman Worshipful Co of Fishmongers; *Style*— Nicholas Fraser, Esq; James Capel House, 6 Bevis Marks, London, EC3A 7JQ (☎ 071 626 0566, fax 071 283 3189, telex 888866)

FRASER, Air Marshal Rev Sir (Henry) Paterson; KBE (1961, CBE 1945), CB (1953), AFC (1937); s of late Harry Paterson Fraser, MBE (d 1956), of Johannesburg, and Edith May, *née* Coxhead; *b* 15 July 1907; *Educ* St Andrew's Coll Grahamstown S Africa, Pembroke Coll Cambridge (MA); *m* 1933, Avis Gertrude, da of Hugh Charles Haswell, of Johannesburg (d 1962); 2 s; *Career* joined RAF 1929, directorate War Organization 1938-40, CO Experimental Flying Section (Royal Aircraft Estab) 1940-42, Gp Capt 1941, memb RAF element Combined Chiefs of Staff Washington 1942, dep AOA 2 TAF 1944, Air Cdre cmdg Aircraft and Armament Experimental Estab 1945, SASO Fighter Cmd 1952-54, Air Vice-Marshal 1953, COS AAFCE (actg Air Marshal) 1954-56, AOC 12 Gp Fighter Command 1956-58, Air Marshal 1959, dir RAF Exercise Planning 1959, UK rep on Perm Military Deputies Gp Central Treaty Orgn Ankara 1960-62, Inspr-Gen RAF 1962-64, ret; concrete conslt (former technologist with Readymix (IOM) Ltd); ordained Dec 1977; CEng, FRAeS; *Style*— Air Marshal Rev Sir Paterson Fraser, KBE, CB, AFC; 803 King's Court, Ramsey, Isle of Man (☎ 0624 813069)

FRASER, Hon Patricia Lydia; eldest da (by 1 m) of Sir Hugh Fraser, 2 Bt (2 Baron Fraser of Allander, who disclaimed his peerage for life 1966, d 1987 when title became extinct); *b* 20 Jan 1963; *Style*— The Hon Patricia Fraser

FRASER, (Rowland) Roley Lovat; s of William Lovat Fraser, CBE (d 1968), of Parkfield House, by Perth, and Belle, *née* Ballantyne (d 1952); *b* 11 March 1931; *Educ* Merchiston Castle Sch; *m* 22 May 1954, Lilian Mary, da of Sir Frederick Archibald Bell (d 1972), of Chapelbank, Auchterarter; 2 s (Simon b 1957, Mark b 1958), 2 da (Sarah Jane b 1960, Nina b 1962); *Career* Lt Royal Scots Fus 1950, Capt Scottish Horse 1955; United Auctions (Scotland) Ltd: dir 1962, chm 1982-; chm: Fraser Tennant Ltd 1970-, UA Properties Ltd, UA Forestry Ltd, Holiday Cottages (Scotland) Ltd; chm Perth Beef Breeds Assoc 1984-, vice-chm Scotch Quality Beef and Lamb Assoc 1984; fell Inst of Auctioneers in Scotland 1966- (pres 1981-82); *Recreations* vintage cars; *Clubs* Bentley Drivers; *Style*— R L Fraser, Esq; Parkfield House, By Perth, Scotland (☎ 0738 51745); Perth Agricultural Centre, East Huntingtower, Perth PH1 3JJ (☎ 0738 26183)

FRASER, Shena Eleanor; da of Robert Dick Fraser (d 1936), of 4 Snowdon Place, Stirling, Scotland, and Eleanor Sarah, *née* Hanson (d 1952); *b* 26 May 1910; *Educ* Queen Margaret's Sch Scarborough, RCM (ARCM piano and violin); *m* 19 Jan 1935, Laurence Beale Neame (d 1970), s of Harry Sidney Neame, of Alfred House, Faversham, Kent; 3 s (Colin b 1936, Stuart b 1945, Roderick b 1946), 1 da (Tessa b 1940); *Career* composer; works incl: Carillon, To Him Give Praise, Child of Bliss, Full Fathom Five, Sonatina for Flute/piano, also many part songs and instrumental pieces; pres Faversham Music Club, hon memb Talbot-Lampson Sch for Conductors; memb: Performing Right Soc, Br Fedn of Music Festivals, Inc Soc of Musicians, Composers' Guild of GB; *Books* Sing at Sight (1986), More Singing at Sight (1989), Listen! (1989); *Recreations* walking, reading; *Clubs* University Women's; *Style*— Miss Shena Fraser

FRASER, Veronica Mary; da of Archibald Fraser (d 1966), of London, and Eleanor Fairfield, *née* Chinn (d 1976); *b* 19 April 1933; *Educ* Richmond County Sch for Girls, St Hugh's Coll Oxford (MA); *Career* headmistress Godolphin Sch Salisbury 1968-80, diocesan dir of educn Worcester Diocese 1985-; chm Diocesan Dirs 1990-91 (vice chm 1984-); memb: SHA 1968; *Recreations* choral singing, painting, bargello; *Style*— Miss Veronica Fraser; The Old Palace, Deansway, Worcester WR1 2JE (☎ 0905 20537)

FRASER, William Hamilton; s of William Hamilton Fraser (d 1978), of Scotland, and Agnes Pender, *née* Pate; *b* 20 Feb 1938; *Educ* Hamilton Acad Scotland, Strathclyde Univ Glasgow (BSc metallurgy); *m* 1968, Evelyn Christine, da of Richard Henry Chapman (d 1954), of London; 2 s (Mark William b 1969, John Richard b 1972), 1 da (Lauren Eve b 1972); *Career* md Foster Wheeler Offshore Ltd 1973-78, dir and vice pres McDermott Marine Engrg 1978-85, chm and chief exec Humpreys & Glasgow Ltd 1985-; CEng; *Recreations* tennis, skiing, swimming, shooting, local politics; *Clubs* Caledonian, Les Ambassadeurs, Oil Industries; *Style*— William Hamilton Fraser, Esq; Humphreys & Glasgow Ltd, Chestergate House, 253 Vauxhall Bridge Road, London SW1V 1HD (071 828 1234)

FRASER, Prof William Irvine; s of Duncan Fraser (d 1979), and Muriel, *née* Macrae (d 1977); *b* 3 Feb 1940; *Educ* Greenock Acad, Univ of Glasgow (MB ChB, MD, DPM); *m* 1 Oct 1964, Joyce Carrol, da of Douglas Gilchrist (d 1978); 2 s (Ewen Duncan b 31 May 1966, Alan Douglas b 1 Sept 1968); *Career* physician supt and dir Fife Mental Handicap Servs 1974-78, hon sr lectr Psychology Univ of St Andrews 1973-89, pt/t sr lectr Univ of Edinburgh 1974-89, conslt psychiatrist Royal Edinburgh Hosp 1978-79, ed Journal of Mental Deficiency Research 1982-, cncl memb Int Assoc for the Scientific Study of Mental Deficiency 1982-88, prof of mental handicap Univ of Wales Coll of Med 1988-; Burden Neurological Inst prize medallist for res into mental handicap 1989; memb: Gen Projects Ctee Mental Health Fndn 1981-87, Med Advsy Panel to Royal Soc for Mentally Handicapped Children and Adults 1982-; FRCPsych 1978; *Books* Communicating with Normal and Retarded Children (with R Grieve, 1981), Care of the Mentally Handicapped (with A Green R McGillray, 1990); *Recreations* sailing; *Clubs* RSM; *Style*— Prof William Fraser; 146 Wenallt Rd, Rhiwbina, Cardiff CF4 6TQ (☎ 0222 628644); Academic Unit, Ely Hospital, Cardiff (☎ 0222 562323)

FRASER, Sir William Kerr; GCB (1984, KCB 1979, CB 1978); s of late Alexander Macmillan Fraser, and Rachel, *née* Kerr; *b* 18 March 1929; *Educ* Eastwood Sch, Glasgow Univ (MA, LLB); *m* 1956, Marion Anne, *née* Forbes; 3 s, 1 da; *Career* joined Scot Home Dept 1955, perm under sec of state Scot Office 1978-88 (dep sec 1975-78); princ and vice chllr Univ of Glasgow 1988-; Hon LLD Univ of Glasgow; FRSE; *Clubs* New (Edinburgh); *Style*— Sir William Fraser, GCB, FRSE; Principal's Lodging, The University Glasgow G12 8QG (☎ 031 339 8855)

FRASER OF ALLANDER, Baroness; Kate Hutcheon; *née* Lewis; da of Sir Andrew Jopp Williams Lewis, LLD (d 1952), and Anne, *née* Walker (d 1940); *b* 2 April 1910; *Educ* St Margaret's Aberdeen, La Casita Lausanne; *m* 2 April 1931, 1 Baron Fraser of Allander (d 6 Nov 1966); 1 s (Sir Hugh Fraser, 2 Bt - he disclaimed his Peerage and d 1987), 1 da (Hon Ann Fraser); *Career* tstee Hugh Fraser Fndn; Hon LLD Aberdeen Univ 1984; *Style*— The Rt Hon the Lady Fraser of Allander; Allander Lodge, 39 Craigmillar Avenue, Milngavie, Glasgow G62 8AX

FRASER OF CARMYLLIE, Baron (Life Peer UK 1989), of Carmyllie in the District of Angus; Peter Lovat Fraser; PC (1989), QC (Scot 1982); s of Rev George Robson Fraser, and Helen Jean, *née* Meiklejohn; *b* 29 May 1945; *Educ* Loretto, Gonville and Caius Coll Cambridge, Univ of Edinburgh; *m* 1969, Fiona Macdonald Mair; 1 s, 2 da; *Career* advocate (Scotland) 1969-; lectr constitutional law Heriot-Watt Univ 1972-74; standing jr counsel (Scotland) to FCO 1979; contested (C) Aberdeen North Oct 1974; MP (C): Angus South 1979-83, Angus East 1983-87; PPS to George Younger (sec state Scotland) 1981-82, slr gen for Scotland 1982-89, Lord Advocate 1989-; Hon Bencher of Lincoln's Inn 1989; *Style*— The Rt Hon Lord Fraser of Carmyllie, PC, QC; Slade House, Carmyllie by Arbroath, Angus (☎ 024 16 215)

FRASER OF KILMORACK, Baron (Life Peer UK 1974), of Rubislaw in Co of City of Aberdeen; Sir (Richard) Michael; CBE (1955, MBE (Mil 1945)); yr s of Dr Thomas Fraser, CBE, DSO, TD, DL (d 1951), and Maria-Theresia, *née* Kayser (d

1965); *b* 28 Oct 1915; *Educ* Fettes Coll, King's Coll Cambridge (BA, MA); *m* 1944, Elizabeth Chloë, da of Brig Cyril Alexander Fraser Drummond, OBE (d 1979); 1 s (Angus b 1945) (and 1 s Hugo b 1949 d 1970); *Career* served WWII RA, Lt-Col, GSO1 1945; Cons Res Dept: joined 1946, head of Home Affrs Section 1950-51, dir 1951-64, chm 1970-74; dep chm Cons Pty Advsy Ctee on Policy 1970-75 (sec 1951-64), sec to Cons Leader's Consultative Ctee 1964-70 and 1974-75, dep chm Cons Pty Orgn 1964-75; dir: Glaxo Holdings plc 1975-85, Glaxo Group Ltd 1975-85, Whiteaway Laidlaw Bank Ltd 1981-, Glaxo Enterprises Inc (USA) 1983-85, Glaxo Trustees Ltd 1975-86; kt 1962; *Clubs* Brooks's, Carlton, St Stephens Constitutional (hon), Coningsby (hon pres); *Style—* The Rt Hon Lord Fraser of Kilmorack, CBE; 18 Drayton Ct, Drayton Gdns, London SW10 9RH (☎ 071 370 1543)

FRASER OF TULLYBELTON, Baroness; (Mary Ursula) Cynthia Gwendolen; o da of Lt-Col Ian H Macdonell, DSO, late HLI, of Connel, Argyllshire; *m* 1943, Baron Fraser of Tullybelton, PC (Life Peer; d 1989); 1 s (Hon (Alexander) Andrew Macdonell Fraser, *qv*); *Style—* The Lady Fraser of Tullybelton

FRATER, Alexander Russell; s of Dr Alexander Smail Frater (d 1972), and Lorna Rosie, *née* Fray (d 1986); *b* 3 Jan 1937; *Educ* Scotch Coll Melbourne, Univ of Melbourne, Univ of Durham, Univ of Perugia; *m* 1963, Marlis, da of Erwin Pfund; 1 s (Alexander John b 1969), 1 da (Tania Elisabeth b 1964); *Career* asst ed Punch 1963-66, retained writer The New Yorker 1964-68, staff writer Daily Telegraph Magazine 1979-84, asst ed Radio Times 1977-79; Observer: asst ed magazine 1979-84, dep ed magazine 1984-86, chief travel corr 1986-; tv presenter: The Last African Flying Boat (BBC) 1990, Monsoon (BBC) 1991; 2 commendations Br Press Awards 1982 and 1989; *Books* Stopping-Train Britain (1983), Great Rivers Of The World (ed; 1984), Beyond The Blue Horizon (1986), Chasing The Monsoon (1990); *Recreations* walking; *Style—* Alexander Frater, Esq; The Observer, Chelsea Bridge House, Queenstown Rd, London SW8 4NN (☎ 071 627 0700, fax 071 627 5570)

FRATINI, Gina Georgina Carolin Eve; da of The hon Somerset Butler, CIE (d 1960), and Barbara, *née* Jackom-Hood (d 1978); *b* 22 Sept 1931; *Educ* in Canada, Burma, India and UK, Royal Coll of Art (Dip Fashion); *m* 1, 1954 (m dis), David Goldberg, s of David Goldberg; m 2, 1960 (m dis 1964), Renato Fratini, s of Fernucio Fratini, of Rome; m 3, 1966 (m dis 1985), Jimmy Logan; *Career* fashion and theatre designer, involved in various art colls, communities and lectures; *Recreations* gardening, horse racing; *Style—* Mrs Gina Fratini; Wandle Rd, London SW17; Church Cottage, Wilts

FRAY, Prof Derek John; s of Arthur Joseph Fray, of 39 Thornton Road, London SW12, and Doris Lilian Wilson (d 1981); *b* 26 Dec 1939; *Educ* Emanuel Sch, Imperial Coll Univ of London (BSc Eng, ARSM, PhD, DIC, state scholar, royal scholar), Univ of Cambridge (MA); *m* 14 Aug 1965, Mirella Christine Kathleen, da of Leslie Honey, of 21 Claygate Lane, Thames Ditton, Surrey; 1 s (Shelton Lanning b 1972), 1 da (Justine Chloe b 1975); *Career* asst prof of metallurgy MIT Cambridge Mass USA 1965-68, gp ldr Res Dept Imperial Smelting Corp Ltd Avonmouth Bristol 1968-71, univ lectr Dept of Materials Sci and Metallurgy Univ of Cambridge 1971-90; Fitzwilliam Coll Cambridge: fell 1972-90, librarian 1973-74, tutorial and estates bursar 1974-86, bursar 1986-88; prof of mineral engrg Univ of Leeds 1991-; *Awards* Matthey prize 1967, AIME Extractive Metallurgy Technol award 1980, Sir George Beilby medal 1981, Nuffield SERC visiting fellowship 1981, Bd of Review AIME 1985, Kroll medal and prize Inst of Metals 1987, MIM 1966, FIMM 1988 (memb Organizing Ctee for: extraction metallurgy 1981-85, and 1987, pyrometallurgy 1987; memb Editorial Bd), FEng 1989, memb AIME; *Books* Worked Examples in Mass and Heat Transfer in Materials Technology (1983), author of over 100 papers and 30 published patents; *Recreations* sailing, reading; *Style—* Prof Derek Fray; 157 Shelford Rd, Trumpington, Cambridge CB2 2ND (☎ 0223 841680); Department of Mining and Mineral Engineering, The University of Leeds, Leeds LS2 9JT (☎ 0532 332 081, fax 0532 332032, 556473 UNILDS)

FRAYLING, Prof Christopher John; s of Maj Arthur Frederick Frayling, and Barbara Kathleen, *née* Imhof; *b* 25 Dec 1946; *Educ* Repton, Churchill Coll Cambridge (scholar, MA, PhD); *m* 1981, Helen Ann Snowdon; *Career* lectr in history Univ of Exeter 1971-72, film archivist Imperial War Museum 1972-73, lectr in history of ideas Univ of Bath 1973-79, prof of cultural history and head of dept RCA 1979-; tstee: Victoria & Albert Museum 1983-, Holburne of Menstrie Museum Bath 1983-; govr Br Film Inst 1982-86 (chm Educn Ctee BFI 1983-86); memb Crafts Cncl 1982-85; Arts Council of GB: memb Photography Panel 1983-85 chm Arts Projects Ctee 1985-88, chm Visual Arts Panel 1987- (del 1983-87), memb Cncl 1987-; chm: Crafts Study Centre Bath 1981-, Free Form Arts Trust 1984-89; memb Nat Advsy Body Working Party on Higher Educn in the Arts 1985-88; *Books* Napoleon Wrote Fiction (1972), The Vampyre - Lord Ruthven to Count Dracula (ed, 1977), Spaghetti Westerns Cowboys and Europeans, from Karl May to Sergio Leone (1981), The Royal College of Art: one hundred and fifty years of art and design (1987); numerous articles in learned and rather less learned journals on aspects of Euro and American Cultural history; *Recreations* finding time; *Style—* Prof Christopher Frayling; Faculty of Humanities, Royal College of Art, Kensington Gore, London SW7 (☎ 071 584 5020)

FRAYLING, Rev Canon Nicholas Arthur; s of Arthur Frederick Frayling, OBE, and Barbara Kathleen, *née* Imhof; *b* 29 Feb 1944; *Educ* Repton, Univ of Exeter (BA), Cuddesdon Coll Oxford; *Career* mgmnt trg retail trade 1962-64, temp probation offr (prison welfare) Inner London Probation and After-care Serv 1965-66 (pt/t 1966-71), ordained Southwark Cathedral 1971, asst curate St John's Peckham 1971-74, vicar All Saints Tooting Graveney 1974-83, canon residentiary and precentor Liverpool Cathedral 1983-87, rector of Liverpool 1987-; chaplain: Huyton Coll 1987-, St Paul's Eye Hosp Liverpool 1987-90; hon canon Liverpool Cathedral 1989-, chm Diocesan Advsy Ctee for Care of Churches 1980-83; memb Worshipful Co of Skinners 1980-; *Recreations* music, friends; *Clubs* Cwlth Tst, Athenaeum (Liverpool); Lyceum, Artists, Liverpool Racquet; *Style—* The Rev Canon Nicholas Frayling; 25 Princes Park Mansions, Sefton Park Road, Liverpool L8 3SA (☎ 051 727 4692); Liverpool Parish Church, Old Churchyard, Liverpool L2 8TZ (☎ 051 236 5287)

FRAYN, Michael; s of late Thomas Allen Frayn, and late Violet Alice, *née* Lawson; *b* 8 Sept 1933; *Educ* Kingston GS, Emmanuel Coll Cambridge; *m* 1960 (m dis 1989), Gillian, *née* Palmer; 3 da; *Career* author and playwright; columnist: The Guardian 1959-62 (reporter 1957-59), Observer 1962-68; stage plays: The Two of Us 1970, The Sandboy 1971, Alphabetical Order 1975, Donkeys' Years 1976, Clouds 1976, Balmoral 1978 (new version Liberty Hall 1980), Make and Break 1980, Noises Off 1982, Benefactors 1984, Look Look 1990; tv plays and films incl: Jamie, On a Flying Visit 1968, Birthday 1969, First and Last 1989; tv documentaries incl: Second City Reports 1964, Beyond a Joke 1972, Making Faces (series) 1975, One Pair of Eyes 1968, Laurence Sterne Lived Here 1973, Imagine a City Called Berlin 1975, Vienna: The Mask of Gold 1977, Three Streets in the Country 1979, The Long Straight (Great Railway Journeys of the World) 1980, Jerusalem 1984; translations of plays incl: The Cherry Orchard, Three Sisters, The Seagull, Uncle Vanya, Wild Honey, The Fruits of Enlightment (Tolstoy), Exchange (Trifonov), Number One (Anouilh); The Sneeze (adaption of Chekhov Short Stories); script for feature film Clockwise 1985; recipient of numerous drama awards; hon fell Emmanuel Coll Cambridge 1985; *Books novels* incl: The Tin Men (1965), The Russian Interpreter (1966), Towards the End of the Morning (1967), A Very Private Life (1968), Sweet Dreams (1973), The Trick of It (1989), *non-fiction* incl: Constructions (philosophy, 1974), several volumes of collected writings and translations; *Style—* Michael Frayn, Esq; c/o Elaine Green Ltd, 31 Newington Gdns, London N16 9PU

FRAZER, Christopher Mark; s of Michael Leslie Frazer, of 7 The Green, Twickenham, Middx, and Pamela Mary, *née* Stoakes; *b* 17 June 1960; *Educ* King's Coll Sch Wimbledon, St John's Coll Cambridge (Exhibitioner, Macaulay scholar, McMahon law student, MA, LLM, College prizeman); *m* 20 May 1989, Victoria Margaret, da of John Peter Hess, of Chorlton Hall, Chorlton-by-Backford, Chester; *Career* called to the Bar Middle Temple 1983, ad eundem Inner Temple; practises on Midland and Oxford, Western and Wales and Chester circuits; Gen Cncl of the Bar of Eng: memb 1989, memb Fees and Legal Aid Ctee, memb Public Affrs Ctee, memb Bar Ctee, vice chm Bar Conf 1990 and 1991; chm Young Barristers' Ctee 1991; vice chm and treas Twickenham Cons Assoc 1985-89, common councilman Corporation of London 1986- (memb City of London Police Ctee), prospective Parly candidate (C) Peckham, chm and fndr Cons Young Lawyers 1984, sec Soc of Cons Lawyers 1988-89; dir and tstee Law Aid Tst; memb: Br Atlantic Ctee, Peace Through NATO; patron and ctee memb Richmond Music Festival; fell: Ancient Monuments Soc, Friends of Friendless Churches; Freeman City of London 1986; *Books* Thoughts for a Third Term (1987); *Recreations* dinghy sailing, music, architecture and heritage; *Clubs* Guildhall, West Wittering Sailing; *Style—* Christopher Frazer, Esq; 2 Harcourt Buildings, Temple, London EC4Y 9DB (☎ 071 353 6961, fax 071 353 6968)

FRAZER, Ian William; s of William George Frazer (d 1982), of Hutton, Essex, and Grace Marjorie, *née* Willis (d 1979); *b* 26 Jan 1933; *Educ* Framlingham Coll; *m* 3 March 1964, Priscilla, da of Capt John Daniell (ka 1943), of Kimpton, Herts; 3 da (Annabel b 30 May 1965, Katharine b 14 Nov 1966, Henrietta b 5 March 1970); *Career* Nat Serv cmmnd The Queen's Bays (2 Dragoon Gds) 1955-57; Army Emergency Reserve 1957-64, ret Lt 1 Queen's Dragoon Gds; qualified CA 1955, sr ptnr (formerly ptnr) Littlejohn Frazer (formerly Frazer Whiting & Co) 1971-; govr: Morpeth Sch Tower Hamlets 1967-, St Mary's Sch Wantage 1984-; cncl memb Chelsea Soc 1972-; FCA 1955; *Recreations* music, reading, shooting, skiing; *Clubs* Cavalry and Guards', City of London; *Style—* Ian Frazer, Esq; 6 Edith Terrace, Chelsea, London SW10 0TQ (☎ 071 352 3310); Irish Hill Cottage, Hamstead Marshall, Newbury, Berks RG15 0JB; Littlejohn Frazer, 2 Canary Wharf, London E14 9SY(☎ 071 987 5030)

FRAZER, Lady Juliet Clare; *née* Chichester; yr da of 7 Marquess of Donegall; *b* 2 Nov 1954; *m* 1983, Andrew David Frazer, yr s of J W Frazer, of Hillmount, Cullybackey, Co Antrim; 1 s (William John Andrew b 1985), 1 da (Mary Emma (twin) b 1985); *Style—* The Lady Juliet Frazer; Nether Hazelfield, Castle Douglas, Scotland

FRAZER, Oliver Haldane; s of Wilson Ray Frazer, OBE (d 1963), and Grace Haldane, *née* Robbs (d 1966); *b* 13 July 1913; *Educ* Dulwich, Coopers Hill Trg Coll; *m* 18 Feb 1950, Dorothy Adeline, da of Kingsley Newman, MM (d 1965); *Career* WWII Staff Sgt Glider Pilot Regt, served D-Day and Arnhem; ret teacher of biology and gen sci, lectr, broadcaster and author, conservation conslt and advsr, voluntary bat warden Nature Conservancy Cncl, pres IOW Natural History and Archaeological Soc 1960-63 (vice pres 1963-), author and presenter of What's in a Habitat? (series of 12 educnl radio broadcasts with supporting slides and info pack for schs) BBC Radio Solent 1974; contrib AA Leisure Guide to the IOW (1988), The Island Within (ed R Sawyer, 1990); *Books* Amphibians (with J F D Frazer, 1973), The Natural History of The Isle of Wight (1990); *Recreations* natural history, photography; *Style—* Oliver Frazer, Esq; Mottistone Mill, Brighstone, Newport, IOW PO30 4AW (☎ 0983 740318)

FREARS, Stephen Arthur; s of Dr Russell E Frears (d 1977), of Nottingham, and Ruth M Frears (d 1971); *b* 20 June 1941; *Educ* Gresham's, Trinity Coll Cambridge (BA); *m* 1967 (m dis 1973), Mary K, *née* Wilmers; 2 s (Sam b 1972, William b 1973); partner, Anne Rothenstein; 1 s (Francis Frears b 1983), 1 da (Lola Frears b 1985); *Career* film dir; *Films* Gumshoe (1971), Bloody Kids (1980), The Hit (1984), My Beautiful Launderette (1985), Prick up Your Ears (1986), Sammy and Rosie Get Laid (1987), Dangerous Liaisons (1988), The Grifters (1989); *Style—* Stephen Frears, Esq; c/o Casarotto Company, 62 Wardour St, London W1 (☎ 071 287 4450, fax 071 287 9128)

FREDERICK, Sir Charles Boscawen; 10 Bt (GB 1723), of Burwood House, Surrey, JP (Bucks); s of Lt-Col Sir Edward Boscawen Frederick, 9 Bt, CVO (d 1956), and Edith Katherine (Kathleen) Cortlandt, *née* Mulloy (d 1970); *b* 11 April 1919; *Educ* Eton; *m* 8 Oct 1949, Rosemary, er da of late Lt-Col Robert John Halkett Badde MC; 2 s, 2 da; *Heir* s Christopher St John Frederick; *Career* Maj (ret) Grenadier Gds; memb London Stock Exchange 1954-62, gen cmmr Income Tax 1966-, memb Stock Exchange Cncl 1973-75, chm Provincial Unit of Stock Exchange 1973-75; *Recreations* woodwork, fishing; *Style—* Sir Charles Frederick Bt, JP; Virginia Cottage, Stoke Trister, Wincanton, Somerset BA9 9PQ

FREDERICK, Christopher St John; s and h of Sir Charles Frederick, 10 Bt; *b* 28 June 1950; *Style—* Christopher Frederick, Esq

FREDJOHN, Dennis; MBE (1990); s of late Maurice Fredjohn; *b* 22 Feb 1925; *Educ* Westminster City Sch, St John's Coll Cambridge; *m* 1947, Pamela Jill, *née* Samms; 1 s, 2 da; *Career* Flying Offr RAF served WWII, Lt RN; exec dir Rio Tinto Zinc 1970-73, dir Arbuthnot Latham Hldgs 1973-76, md Alusuisse (UK) Ltd 1976-80, dir BPB Industs plc 1980-, chm Capital Ventures Ltd 1981-, dir London Wall Hldgs 1986-; memb: Doctors' and Dentists' Review Body 1989-, Cncl Lloyd's of London 1982-84; *Recreations* squash, farming, bridge; *Style—* Dennis Fredjohn, Esq, MBE; Fairfields, Redmarley, Glos GL19 3JU (☎ 053 1650477)

FREEBORN, David Michael; s of Herbert Aubury Freeborn (d 1976), of Whetstone, London, and May Beatrice, *née* Inwards; *b* 15 May 1950; *Educ* Christ Church Secondary Sch London, Tottenham Tech Coll, St Albans Coll of Further Educn; *m* 25 Feb 1983, Janis, da of Roy James Lambert, of Maidstone; 1 da (Claire b 27 June 1983); *Career* chief exec J A Elliott (Holdings) Ltd 1988 (dir 1982); J A Elliott Ltd: md 1983, dir 1979, chm 1988; J A Elliott (Leyford) Ltd: md 1980, dir 1978, chm 1988; chm: J A Elliott (Developments) Ltd 1988 (dir 1980), chm J A Elliott (New Homes) Ltd 1988 (dir 1985), J A Elliott (Projects) Ltd 1988 (dir 1980), J A Elliott (Plant) Ltd 1988; (dir 1988), dir Seedbed Centres Ltd 1985, non-exec dir Land & Urban plc 1986, dir Fedn Industl Assocs 1987, chm J A Elliot (Northern) Ltd 1988 (dir 1988), dir Regional & City plc 1990; MCIOB 1972, FRICS 1983, IOD; *Recreations* golf; *Clubs* RAC; *Style—* David M Freeborn, Esq; c/o J A Elliott (Holdings) Ltd, 133 Stansted Rd, Bishops Stortford, Herts CM23 2AN (☎ 0279 755 962, fax 0279 655504, telex 818853 JAE G)

FREEDLAND, Michael Rodney; s of David Freedland, and Lily, *née* Mindel; *b* 18 Dec 1934; *Educ* Luton GS; *m* 3 July 1960, Sara, da of Abram Hockerman; 1 s (Jonathan Saul b 1967), 2 da (Fiona Anne b 1963, Daniela Ruth b 1964); *Career* journalist for local newspapers, Daily Sketch; freelance journalist 1961-; contrib: The Times, Economist, Spectator; broadcaster 1971-; progs incl: You don't have to be Jewish, The Jewish World; *Books* 28 books including studies of: Al Jolson (1971), Irving Berlin (1973), Fred Astaire (1976), Gregory Peck (1979), The Warner Brothers

DEBRETT'S PERSONALITIES OF TODAY

Darcey Bussell

PHOTOGRAPH: ANTHONY CRICKMAY

John Eliot Gardiner

PHOTOGRAPH: RICHARD HOLT

Paul Gascoigne

PHOTOGRAPH: ACTION IMAGES

DEBRETT'S PERSONALITIES OF TODAY

Stephen Glover

Michael Grade

Sir Ralph Halpern

(1982), Danny Kaye (1987), Leonard Bernstein (1987), Jane Fonda (1988), Dustin Hoffman (1989), Kenneth Williams (1990); *Recreations* reading, being with my wife and family; *Style—* Michael Freedland, Esq; Bays Hill Lodge, Barnet Lane, Elstree, Herts WD6 3QU (☎ 081 953 3000)

FREEDMAN, Cyril Winston; s of Sydney Freedman (d 1951), and Irene Rosalind, *née* Anekstein; *b* 31 Aug 1945; *Educ* Brighton Coll, Brighton Coll of Art and Design (Dip Graphic Art and Design); *m* 25 March 1970, Christine Mary, da of Cecil Shipman, of Swanwick, Derbys; 1 s (Mark b 1973), 1 da (Anna b 1977); *Career* chm: CWF Advertising Ltd 1971-74, Halls Homes and Gardens 1978-80 (md 1977-78, dir 1974-81); dir Pentos plc and subsidiaries 1979-81, chm Serco Ryan Ltd 1982-87, chief exec WBH Group Ltd (subsidiary of Lopex plc) 1985-88, dir Armour Automotive Products Group (subsidiary of Armour Trust plc 1985-; chm: Deeko plc 1988-90 (dir 1986-90), Hennell Holdings Ltd 1988-; dir Alan Patricof Associates Ltd 1988-; MCIM; *Recreations* painting, collecting fine art; *Style—* Cyril Freedman, Esq; Alan Patricof Associates Ltd, 24 Upper Brook St, London W1 (☎ 071 872 6300)

FREEDMAN, Ivor Stuart Douglas Andrew; s of Mordka (Mick) Freedman (d 1980), of 21 Glebe Crescent, Hendon, London, and Rita, *née* Isaacs; *b* 18 July 1947; *Educ* Hendon County GS; *m* 15 Oct 1972, Linda, da of Samuel Tischler, of 41 Greenacres, Finchley, London; 1 s (Michael James b 15 Sept 1980), 1 da (Emma Jane b 26 March 1975); *Career* chm: WIMTA Credit Bureau 1976-83, Western International Wholesale Fruit 1977- 82, Jt Mgmnt Ctee Hounslow Borough 1978-81, H Freedman Ltd 1980-83, Fruita-Plan (UK) Ltd 1980-, Gammalodge Ltd 1983-87, London Market Corporation 1987-, ISI International Holdings 1987-, Moordale Enterprises Ltd 1987-; memb: Cons Pty, Variety Club of GB 1970-82, Fruit Importers Assoc 1975-82; *Recreations* tennis, football, cricket, snooker, stamp collecting, general music; *Style—* Ivor Freedman, Esq; LMC House, 74-76 Cheshire Street, London E2 6EH (☎ 071 739 9900, fax 071 739 9400, car 0836 284213, car answerphone 0836 862420, telex 297073 COPRA G)

FREEDMAN, Prof Lawrence David; s of Lt Cdr Julius Freedman, RN (d 1987), and Myra, *née* Robinson; *b* 7 Dec 1948; *Educ* Whitley Bay GS, Univ of Manchester (BA), Univ of York (BPhil), Univ of Oxford (PhD); *m* 1974, Judith Anne, da of Harry Hill; 1 s (Samuel b 1981), 1 da (Ruth b 1984); *Career* teaching asst dept of politics Univ of York 1971-72; res (prize) fell Nuffield Coll Oxford 1974-75; lectr in politics (pt/t) Balliol Coll Oxford 1975; res assoc Int Inst for Strategic Studies 1975-76; res fell on British Foreign Policy Royal Inst of Int Affairs 1976-78; head of policy studies Royal Inst of Int Affairs 1978-82; prof of war studies King's Coll London 1982-; columnist Independent 1987-; specialist advsr House of Commons Defence Ctee 1980-; memb: Current Affairs Advsy Gp Channel 4 1986-87, govt and law ctee Economic and Social Res Cncl 1982-87, cncl Int Inst for Strategic Studies 1984-; editorial bds: Futures, Foreign Policy, Int Security, Political Quarterly, Intelligence and National Security; *Books* US Intelligence and the Soviet Strategic Threat (1977, reprinted with new foreword 1986), Britain and Nuclear Weapons (1980), The Evolution of Nuclear Strategy (1981, 2nd edn 1989), The Atlas of Global Strategy (1985), The Price of Peace: Living with the Nuclear Dilemma (1986), Britain and the Falklands War (1988), The Troubled Alliance: Atlantic Relations in the 1980s (ed 1983), Nuclear War and Nuclear Peace (jtly 1983, 2nd edn 1988), US Nuclear Strategy: A Reader (co-ed 1989), Military Power in Europe: Essays in Memory of Jonathan Alford (ed 1990), Signals of War: The Falklands Conflict of 1982 (jtly, 1990); *Recreations* political cartoons, tennis; *Style—* Prof Lawrence Freedman; Department of War Studies, King's College, London, The Strand, London WC2R 2LS (☎ 071 873 2193, fax 071 873 2026)

FREEDMAN, Lawrence Samuel; s of Alexander Freedman (d 1989), and Marjorie, *née* Harris; *b* 18 July 1954; *Educ* St Mary's Hosp Med Sch London (MB BS); *m* 6 Jan 1979, Nicola Lesley, da of Lesley Owen Swain (d 1986); 3 s (Adam b 1980, Guy b 1986, Sam b 1989) 1 da (Lindsay b 1982); *Career* conslt traumatic and orthopaedic surgn 1988-; memb: Br Orthopaedic Assoc, Hong Kong Orthopaedic Assoc, Br Scollosis Soc, RSM; FRCS; *Recreations* travel, photography; *Style—* Lawrence Freedman, Esq; Clementine Churchill Hosp, Harrow on the Hill, Middx (☎ 081 422 3464)

FREEDMAN, Michael John; s of Joseph Leopold Freedman, of London, and Rosa Annie, *née* Bosman (d 1987); *b* 4 July 1946; *Educ* Clifton, Christ's Coll Cambridge; *m* 1973, Pamela Dawn, da of late Cyril Kay; 1 s (Jonathan Leonard b 13 April 1979), 1 da (Natalie Kay b 31 Jan 1976); *Career* mktg mangr Royal Angus Hotels 1965-69; mktg dir: Securadet Ltd 1969-72, Paul Kaye Studio Ltd 1972-; chm Cover Girl International Ltd 1990-; memb Cncl BIPP 1989-; FBIPP, fell Master Photographers Assoc; *Recreations* squash, swimming, reading, walking; *Style—* Michael Freedman, Esq; Paul Kaye Studio Ltd, 20 Park Rd, London NW1 4SH (☎ 071 723 2444, fax 071 262 5966)

FREELAND, James Gourlay; s of James Gourlay Freeland, of Surrey, and Jessie McRobie, *née* Brown; *b* 3 Aug 1936; *Educ* Haileybury & ISC, Trinity Hall Cambridge (MA); *m* 27 May 1961, Diana, da of Bryce Graham Dewsbury (d 1971); 1 s (Jeremy b 1963), 2 da (Joanna b 1965, Stephanie b 1971); *Career* Nat Serv RM Malta 1955-57; shipbroker; dir: H Clarkson & Co Ltd London 1970-, Clarkson Res Studies Ltd London 1986-, Distribution Consulting Servs Inc Dallas USA 1986-; underwriting memb Lloyd's 1985-; Liveryman Worshipful Co of Shipwrights 1963- (Asst to Ct 1984-); *Recreations* golf, shooting; *Clubs* MCC, Jesters; *Style—* James G Freeland, Esq; 122 Rivermead Court, Ranelagh Gardens, London SW6 3SD (☎ 071 736 1511; Grenna House, Chilson, Oxford OX7 3HU (☎ 060 876 349); H Clarkson & Co Ltd, 12 Camomile St, London EC3A 7BP (☎ 071 283 9020)

FREELAND, Sir John Redvers; KCMG (1984, CMG 1973), QC (1987); o s of Clarence Redvers Freeland, and Freda, *née* Walker; *b* 16 July 1927; *Educ* Stowe, Corpus Christie Coll Cambridge; *m* 1952, Sarah Mary, er da of late Sidney Pascoe Hayward, QC; 1 s (Nicholas b 1956), 1 da (Petra b 1959); *Career* RN 1945 and 1948-51; called to the Bar Lincoln's Inn 1952, bencher 1985, asst legal advsr FO 1954-63 and 1965-67, legal advsr HM Embassy Bonn 1963-65, legal cnsllr FCO 1967-70 and 1973-76, cnsllr (legal advsr) UK Mission to UN NY 1970-73, second legal advsr FCO 1976-84, legal advsr 1984-87; judge Arbitral Tbnl and Mixed Cmmn for the Agreement on German External Debts 1988-; memb US-Chile Int Cmmn of Investigation 1989-; *Clubs* Travellers'; *Style—* Sir John Freeland, KCMG, QC

FREELAND, Rowan Charles Bayfield; s of Col Paul Rowan Bayfield Freeland, of Lacock, Wilts, and Susanna Brigitta Elizabeth, *née* Burch; *b* 13 Dec 1956; *Educ* Wellington, St Catherine's Coll Oxford (BA); *m* 12 Dec 1987, Davina Alexandra Claire, da of Maj Dennis Edward Salisbury (d 1964); 1 da (Marigold Claire Salisbury b 31 Oct 1990); *Career* admitted slr 1982; ptnr Simmons & Simmons 1988-; sec The Haydn-Mozart Soc 1984-, memb LES 1989; *Recreations* opera, gardening, reading; *Style—* Rowan Freeland, Esq; 14 Dominion St, London EC2M 2RJ (☎ 071 628 2020, fax 071 588 4129, tlx 888562)

FREELING, Nicolas; *b* 3 March 1927; *Educ* some scraps of education in too many schools England, Ireland and France; *m* 1954, Cornelia; 4 s, 1 da; *Career* Nat Serv RAF 1947-49; various jobs in kitchens, hotels and restaurants throughout Europe 1950-62; writer 1960; *Books* incl: Love in Amsterdam (1961), Because of the Cats (1963), Gun before Butter (1963), Valparaise (1964), Double Barrel (1964), Criminal Conversation (1965), The King of the Rainy Country (1966), The Dresden Green (1966), Strike out Where Not Applicable (1967), This is the Castle (1968), Tsing-Boum (1969), Kitchen Book (1970), Over the High Side (1971), Cook Book (1972), A Long Silence (1972), Dressing of Diamond (1974), What Are the Bungles Blowing For (1975), Lake Isle 1976), Gadget (1977), The Night Lords (1978), The Widow (1979), Castang's City (1980), One Damned Things After Another (1981), Wolfnight (1982), The Back of the North Wind (1983), No Part in Your Death (1984), A City Solitary (1985), Cold Iron (1986), Lady Macbeth (1988), Not as far as Velma (1989), Sandcastles (1989), Those in Peril (1990), The Flanders Sky (1991); *Recreations* environment, gardening, treeplanting; *Style—* Nicolas Freeling, Esq; Grandfontaine, 67130 Schirmeck, France

FREEMAN, Brig Alfred Francis; MC (1940); s of Henry Alfred Freeman (d 1975), and Murielle Theodora, *née* Cameron-Stuart (d 1975); *b* 24 March 1916; *Educ* Imperial Serv Coll Windsor, RMA Woolwich; *m* 6 April 1944, Dorothy Peart, da of Capt Ivo Peart Robinson (d 1950); 2 s (Francis b 1948, Nigel b 1953), 2 da (Susan b 1950, Judith b 1957); *Career* cmmnd Royal Signals 1936, Sch of Signals Catterick 1936-37, 3 Divnl Signals Bulford 1937-39, Signal Offr 7 Gds Bde 1939, SO3 to Chief Signal Offr 2 Corps France 1939-40, SO2 to Chief Signal Offr 6 Corps NI 1940-41, Staff Coll Camberley 1941-42, SO2 WO Signals 1 1942-44, 2 i/c (later cmd) 8 Corps Signals 1944, cmd 1 Corps Signals 1944-45, SO1 to Signal Offr in Chief SE Asia Cmd Ceylon 1945, SO1 to Chief Signal Offr Malaya 1946-47, Instr RMA Sandhurst 1947-49, long telecommunications course Catterick 1949-50, SO2 Signals Div Allied Land Forces Central Europe 1951-53, 2 i/c Cwlth Signal Regt Korea 1953-54, Instr and SO1 planning wing Sch of Signals Catterick 1954-59, Cdr 54 Divnl Signal Regt TA 1959-60, Cdr Royal Signals Singapore 1960-62, Col GS Signals 1 MOD 1963-65, Chief Signal Offr Northern Cmd 1965-68, ret 1968; membership recruitment offr Oxon and N Cotswold Royal Agric Soc of Eng 1969-80, chm Brailes branch Royal Br Legion, former chm and pres Annual Brailes Show, life govr Three Counties Agric Soc; *Recreations* gardening; *Clubs* Army & Navy; *Style—* Brig Alfred Freeman, MC

FREEMAN, Andrew Lawrence D; s of Richard D Freeman, and Diana L, *née* Cranwell; *b* 4 March 1963; *Educ* Balliol Coll Oxford (BA Hons), Merton Coll Oxford (sr scholar); *m* Hazel Mary, *née* Mills; *Career* asst ed Global Investor Euromoney Publications 1988 (staff writer 1987); Financial Times: stockmarket reporter 1988, Euromarket reporter 1989, Lex Column 1990-; *Books* Managing Global Portfolios (co-ed C Stoakes, 1989), The Armoire de Fer and the French Revolution (1990); *Style—* Andrew Freeman, Esq; Financial Times, Number One, Southwark Bridge, London SE1 9HL

FREEMAN, Catherine; da of Harold Dove (d 1966), and Eileen, *née* Carroll (d 1982); *b* 10 Aug 1931; *Educ* Convent of the Assumption, St Anne's Coll Oxford (BA, MA); *m* 1, 1958 (m dis 1961), Charles Wheeler; *m* 2, 1962 (m dis 1976), Rt Hon John Freeman; 2 s (Matthew b 1961, Tom b 1963), 1 da (Lucy b 1966); *Career* prodr and dir BBC 1954-58 (joined as trainee prodr 1954); Thames Television: joined as sr prodr 1976, ed daytime programmes, originator and series prodr Citizen 2000 1976-82, controller of documentaries, features and religion 1982-86, controller of features and religion 1986-89; fndr dir Dove Productions 1989-, dir One World Broadcasting Trust 1990-; memb Devlin Ctee on Identification Procedures 1974-76, dir ICA 1983-, memb: Lit Panel Arts Cncl 1981-84, Broadcasting, Film and Video Panel Arts Cncl 1986-88; *Style—* Mrs Catherine Freeman; 2 Chalcot Crescent, London NW1 8YD (☎ 071 586 0448); Dove Productions, 93 Ashmill St, London NW1 6RA (☎ 071 262 0063, fax 071 724 1233)

FREEMAN, Colin James; s of Albert Ernest Freeman, of Streatham, London, and Ivy Kathleen, *née* James; *b* 8 Aug 1940; *Educ* Bec GS; *m* 25 Jan 1964, Margaret Anne, da of Capt Robert Robinson (d 1983); 2 s (James b 30 Oct 1968, David b 22 March 1972); *Career* TAVR, RAMC, Lt RARO 1980; LWT: mangr of drama 1968-69, head of prog fin 1971, controller of prog fin and resources 1984, controller of transmission fin 1989; *Recreations* walking, travelling and reading; *Style—* Colin Freeman, Esq; London Weekend Television, South Bank Television Centre, Upper Ground, London SE1 9LT (☎ 071 261 3262, fax 071 928 0396)

FREEMAN, David Alexander; s of John Freeman (d 1963), of Hampstead, and Betty, *née* Morris (d 1970); *b* 13 May 1928; *Educ* Univ Coll Sch London, Sorbonne, Univ of St Andrews (MA); *m* 4 Sept 1956, Margaret Joan (Meg), da of Lt-Col Sir Geoffrey Stewart Tomkinson, OBE, MC (d 1963), of Kidderminster, Worcs; 1 s (Charles Geoffrey John b 1963), 2 da (Victoria Frances Margaret b 1960, Alexandra Jane b 1969); *Career* air raid messenger Sch Boy Civil Def Hampstead 1942-44; md: Spa Brushes Ltd Chesham 1954-62, Freeman Dawson & Co Ltd 1965-83, Guarantee Protection Tst 1983-; Parly candidate (Lib) E Fife 1950; memb Cncl Br Wood Preserving Assoc; *Books* Choosing The Right School (1983); *Recreations* chatting, trombone, biking; *Clubs* The Lansdowne, Nat Lib, Leander; *Style—* David Freeman, Esq; Stoneleigh, Naphill, Bucks HP14 4QX; The Guarantee Protection Trust, PO Box 77, High Wycombe HP11 1BW (☎ 0494 447 049)

FREEMAN, David Charles; s of Howard Wilfred Freeman, of Sydney, and Ruth Adair, *née* Nott; *b* 1 May 1962; *Educ* Sydney GS, Sydney Univ (BA); *m* 1 May 1985, Marie Louise, da of (Francis) John Angel (d 1968), of Pinnaroo, Australia; 1 da (Catherine Elinor b 13 May 1989); *Career* fndr and dir: Opera Factory Zurich 1973-76, Opera Factory Zuirch 1976-, Opera Factory London 1981-; assoc artist ENO 1981-; prodns incl: Punch and Judy Birtwistle (OFL) 1981, Orfeo Monteverdi (ENO) 1981, The Mask of Orpheus (Birtwistle ENO) 1986, Cosi Fan Tutte (OFL) 1986, Akhnaten Glass (Houton NY and London), Goethes Faust I and II (Lyric Hammersmith) 1988; TV prodns incl: Punch and Judy Birtwistle (C4 TV) 1982, Cosi Fan Tutte (C4 TV) 1989; Chevalier dans L'Ordre des Arts et Lettres France 1985; *Style—* David Freeman, Esq; Opera Factory London Sinfonietta, Kingston Polytechnic, Kingston Hill, Kingston upon Thames, Surrey KT2 7LB (☎ 071 549 5747, telex 269654 AMC GDR G)

FREEMAN, David John; s of Meyer Henry Freeman (d 1984), of London, and Rebecca, *née* Lubinsky (d 1980); *b* 25 Feb 1928; *Educ* Christ's Coll Finchley; *m* 19 March 1950, Iris Margaret, da of Cyril Henry Alberge (d 1980), of London; 2 s (Michael Ian b 1951, Peter Geoffrey b 1955), 1 da (Jill Barbara b 1953); *Career* Army Lt 1946-48; admitted slr 1952; fndr and sr ptnr DJ Freeman & Co 1952-; Dept of Trade inspr into affairs of AEG Telefunken (UK) Ltd and Credit Collections Ltd 1977; govr Royal Shakespeare Theatre 1979-; memb Law Soc; *Recreations* reading, theatre, gardening; *Clubs* Reform, Huntercombe Golf; *Style—* David J Freeman, Esq; 6 Hyde Park Gardens, London W2 (☎ 071 262 0895); Old Greenfield House, Christmas Common, Watlington, Oxon; 43 Fetter Lane, London EC4A 1NA (☎ 071 583 4055, fax 071 353 7377, telex 894579)

FREEMAN, Dr Ernest Allan; s of William Freeman, and Margaret Freeman; *b* 16 Jan 1932; *Educ* Sunderland Poly, King's Coll Univ of Durham (BSc, PhD), Univ of Oxford (MA), Univ of Newcastle-upon-tyne (DSc); *m* 1987, Mary Jane; 2 da; *Career* The Sunderland forge and Engineering Co Ltd 1948-55, The English Electric Company 1957-58, Feranti Ltd Edinburgh 1958-59, research dir in applied electronics for Sunderland Tech Coll 1959-61, head Dept of Control Engineering Sunderland Poly 1965-72, dir Low Cost Automation Centre 1967, fell and tutor in engrg St Edmunds Hall Oxford 1972-76, rector Sunderland Poly 1976-80, dir Trent Poly 1981-83;

consultancy and secondment to numerous cos; referee to IEE and American IEE for papers submitted for pubn; former memb: Ctee of IEE for Control Theory, CNAA Systems and Instrumentation Bd, Electronics Divnl Bd of IEE London Ctee, Advsy Ctee to Dept of Mathematics and Statistics Thames Poly, Br Cncl Ctee for Academic Interchange with Europe, Control Theory Centre Advsy Bd Univ of Warwick, Science Bd of Science and Engrg Res Cncl, Cncl Inter Univs and Polys Cncl Higher Educn Overseas; vice chm: N Eastern Centre Ctee of IEE for Electronic and Control, Sci Res Cncl Ctee for Control Engrg (memb Educn Panel, chm Inter- Univ Inst of Engrg Control Panel); Ctee Dirs of Polys (memb, chm Advsy Ctee on Computing, Acad Affairs Ctee, memb Technician Educn Liason Gp, memb Fin and Planning Ctee); external examiner various Univ and Polys; FIEE 1968, FIMA 1969, FRSA 1980; *publications* many contribs to the Proceeding IEE and other Scientific Jls; *Recreations* photography, swimming, browsing around antiques; *Style—* Dr Ernest Freeman; 12 Rolfe Place, Headington, Oxford OX3 0DS

FREEMAN, Frederick Clement; s of (Clement) Sidney Freeman (d 1985), and Margaret, *née* Yorke (d 1947); *b* 14 March 1921; *Educ* Repton; *m* 20 July 1946, Yvonne, da of John Pye Bibby; 2 s (Andrew b 1950, Richard b 1953), 1 da (Hazel b 1947); *Career* Maj King's (Liverpool) Regt and Para Regt, served Burma (Chindits); chm and md Freemans (Liverpool) Ltd and subsid cos 1948-; chm and hon dir: United Way (registered charity) 1972-, United Tsts (registered charity) 1987-; bd memb Interphil (int philanthropy) 1975-85; *Publications* The SUVOC Application (1983) (SUVOC is the Soc of United Voluntary Orgns within Community); FBIM, JP (ret); *Recreations* charitable work, gardening, golf; *Clubs* Army and Navy, Athenaeum (Liverpool); *Style—* Frederick Freeman, Esq; Broughshane, Croft Drive West, Caldy, Wirral, Merseyside L48 2JQ (☎ 051 625 8306); PO Box 14, 8 Nelson Rd, Edge Hill, Liverpool L69 7AA (☎ 051 709 8252)

FREEMAN, Gillian; da of Jack Freeman (d 1981), of London and Henley on Thames, and Freda, *née* Davids; *b* 5 Dec 1929; *Educ* Francis Holland, Lynton House Maidenhead, Univ of Reading (BA); *m* 12 Sept 1955, Edward Thorpe, s of Ronald Thorpe (d 1985), of Hythe, Hants; 2 da (Harriet Amelia b 1957, Matilda Helen Rachel b 1960); *Career* author; plays incl: Pursuit (NT 1969), Mayerling-Scenario (Royal Ballet 1978); films incl: The Leather Boys (1963), That Cold Day in the Park (1969), Day After the Fair (1987); *Books* 12 novels incl: The Liberty Man (1955), The Leather Boys (1961), The Marriage Machine (1975), An Easter Egg Hunt (1981), Termination Rock (1989); non fiction incl: The Undergrowth of Literature (1967), The Schoolgirl Ethic: The Life and Work of Angela Brazil (1976); *Style—* Ms Gillian Freeman; c/o Rochelle Stevens & Co, 2 Terretts Place, Upper St, N1 1QZ

FREEMAN, Prof Hugh Lionel; s of the late Bernard Freeman, and Dora Doris, *née* Kahn; *b* 4 Aug 1929; *Educ* Altrincham GS, St John's Coll Oxford (DM, MA); *m* 1957, (Sally) Joan, da of Philip Casket; 3 s, 1 da; *Career* Capt RAMC 1956-58; house surgn Manchester Royal Infirmary 1955, registrar Bethlem Royal and Maudsley Hosps 1958-60, sr registrar Littlemore Hosp Oxford 1960-61; conslt psychiatrist Salford Royal Hosp 1961-70; hon conslt: Salford Health Authy, Univ of Manchester Sch of Med 1988-; WHO conslt: Grenada 1970, Chile 1978, Philippines 1979, Bangladesh 1981, Greece 1985; rapporteur: WHO Conf on Mental Health Servs Trieste 1984, WHO Ruanda 1985, Cncl of Europe Conf on Health in Cities 1985; ed Br Jl of Psychiatry 1983- (asst ed 1978-83); lectr worldwide; vice chm MIND 1983-87; visiting fell Green Coll Oxford; memb: Mercian Regnl Ctee Nat Tst, Mental Health Cmmn 1983, Mental Health Review Tbnls, City of Manchester Bldgs Panel, memb Home Sec's Ctee on Fear of Crime 1989; vice chm Manchester Heritage Tst; hon memb: Chilean Soc of Psychiatry Neurology and Neurosurgery, Egyptian Psychiatric Assoc, Polish Psychiatric Assoc; hon prof Univ of Salford; Freeman City of London, Liveryman Worshipful Soc of Apothecaries; FRCPsych, FFCM; *Publications*: Trends in Mental Health Services (1963), New Aspects of the Mental Health Service (jt ed, 1968), Mental Health Services in Europe (1985), Mental Health and the Environment (ed, 1985), Dangerousness (jt ed, 1982); *Recreations* architecture, travel, music; *Clubs* United Oxford & Cambridge, Whitefriars; *Style—* Prof Hugh Freeman; 21 Montagu Square, London W1H 1RE (☎ 071 486 2604); British Journal of Psychiatry, 17 Belgrave Square, London SW1X 8PG (☎ 071 235 8857, fax 071 245 1231)

FREEMAN, (Edgar) James Albert; MC (1945); s of Horace Freeman (d 1954), of London, and Beatrice Mary, *née* Craddock (d 1946); *b* 31 Dec 1917; *Educ* Westminster, Trinity Coll Cambridge (MA); *m* 15 May 1948, Shirley Lake (d 1988), da of William Henry Whatmough (d 1963), of Streatham; 1 s (Peter b 1 March 1951), 2 da (Catherine b 22 Sept 1955, Ruth b 12 Feb 1958); *Career* Suffolk Regt 1939, 2 Lt The Durham Light Infantry 1940-44 (Maj 1944); served: UK, India, Burma; called to the Bar Lincoln's Inn 1947; Chancery Bar 1947-72, vice pres Value Added Tax Tribunals 1972-90, regnl chm of Industl Tbnls 1984-90 (chm 1975-84); *Recreations* sailing, cycling; *Clubs* Royal Cruising, Bar Yacht; *Style—* James Freeman, Esq, MC; 45 Nightingale Avenue, Cambridge CB1 4SG

FREEMAN, Sir James Robin; 3 Bt (UK 1945), of Murtle, Co Aberdeen; s of Sir Keith Freeman, 2 Bt (d 1981), and Patricia, Lady Freeman, *qv*; *b* 21 July 1955; *Heir* none; *Style—* Sir James Freeman, Bt; c/o Midland Bank, 151 Hoe St, Walthamstow, E17

FREEMAN, Rt Hon John; MBE (1943), PC (1966); eldest s of Horace Freeman, barrister-at-law (d 1954); *b* 19 Feb 1915; *Educ* Westminster, BNC Oxford; *m* 1, 1938 (m dis 1948), Elizabeth Allen, *née* Johnston; m 2, 1948, Margaret Ista Mabel, *née* Kerr (d 1957); 1 adopted da; m 3, 1962 (m dis 1976), Catherine, da of Harold Dove and formerly wife of Charles Wheeler; 2 s, 1 da; m 4, 1976, Judith, *née* Mitchell; 2 da; *Career* served WWII; MP (Lab) Watford Div of Herts 1945-50, Borough of Watford 1950-55; New Statesman: asst ed 1951-58, dep ed 1958-60, ed 1961-65; Br high cmmr in India 1965-68, ambass in Washington 1969-71; chm: LWT 1971-84, Ind TV News 1976-81, LWT (Hldgs) 1976-84, Hutchinson Ltd 1978-83, Page & Moy (Hldgs) 1979-84; winner of Royal Television Soc Gold Medal 1981 (for distinguished service to the broadcasting industry); visiting prof of int rels UCLA hon fell Brasenose Coll Oxford, vice pres Royal Television Soc 1975-84; Hon LLD Univ of S Carolina; *Style—* The Rt Hon John Freeman, MBE; Barclay's Bank, 58 Southampton Row, London WC1B 4AT

FREEMAN, John Frederick; s of Albert George Freeman (d 1985), of Salisbury, and Catherine Sarah, *née* Crowe (d 1977); *b* 11 Dec 1937; *Educ* Bishop Wordsworth Sch Salisbury, Univ of Durham (BA); *m* 12 Aug 1960, Betty, *née* Wolstencroft (d 1960); 1 s (Ivan Xenon b 25 May 1965); *Career* teacher with Stockport LEA 1965-, chief moderator for Eng NW Region Examining Bd 1982-87 (moderator 1978-82), Info Tech Dept and Educnl Admin Software Devpt N Area Coll 1987-; *Books* Creative Writing (1965), Xenona (plays, 1968); *Recreations* travel; *Style—* John Freeman, Esq; 42 Ravenoak Rd, Davenport, Stockport SK2 7BQ (☎ 061 483 4903); North Area Sixth Form College, Buckingham Rd, Heaton Moor, Stockport SK4 4RA (☎ 061 442 7494)

FREEMAN, Matthew Philip George; s of Philip Edmund Freeman, of Great Yarmouth, Norfolk, and Thelma Doreen, *née* Pike (d 1962); *b* 13 March 1953; *Educ* Great Yarmouth GS, RCM London (GRSM, ARCM), Univ of London; *Career* musical dir: theatre, recording, tv; memb Worshipful Co of Musicians 1977; *Style—* Matthew Freeman, Esq; Leighton House, Glade Rd, Marlow, Bucks

FREEMAN, Michael Alexander Reykers; s of Donald George Freeman (d 1937), of Gatton Manon, Ockley, Surrey, and Florence Julia, *née* Elms (d 1962); *b* 17 Nov 1931; *Educ* Stowe, Corpus Christi Coll Cambridge (BA, MB BCh), London Hosp Med Coll; *m* 1, 1951 (m dis), Elizabeth Jean; 1 s (Jonathan b 29 May 1954), 1 da (Julianne b 5 June 1952); m 2, 1959 (m dis), Janet Edith; 1 s (Dominic b 3 April 1965), 1 da (Emma b 18 May 1962); m 3, 26 Sept 1968, Patricia, da of Leslie Gill (d 1976), of Bristol; 1 s (James b 14 April 1971 d 1971), 1 da (Clare b 31 Dec 1972); *Career* clinical trg in med surgery and orthopaedic surgery London Hosp, Westminster Hosp and Middx Hosp; awarded Copeman Medal, Robert Jones Gold Medal, co-fndr and dir Biomechanics Unit Dept of Med Engrg Imperial Coll 1966-79, sr lectr orthopaedic surgery London Hosp Med Coll 1968-, conslt orthopaedic surgn London Hosp 1968-, co-dir Bone and Joint Res Unit London Hosp Med Coll 1975; pres Br Hip Soc, past pres Int Hip Soc; past memb: bd of govrs London Hosp, Clinical Res Bd MRC; memb: Cncl Br Orthopaedic Assoc (currently vice pres), Advsy Ctee Health Unit Inst of Econ Affrs; Yeoman Worshipful Co of Apothecaries; AAOS, BOA, RSM, BES, ORS, IHS, SICOT, FRCS; *Books* Adult Articular Cartilage (ed, 1973), The Scientific Basis of Joint Replacemnet (ed with S A V Swanson, 1977), Arthritis of the Knee (ed, 1980), Osteoarthritis in the Young Adult Hip (ed with D Reynolds, 1984); *Clubs* Athenaeum; *Style—* Michael Freeman, Esq; 79 Albert St, London NW1 (☎ 071 387 0817); 149 Harley St, London W1 (☎ 071 935 4444 ext 4004, fax 071 935 4771)

FREEMAN, Prof Michael David Alan; s of Raphael Freeman, of London, and Florence, *née* Wax; *b* 25 Nov 1943; *Educ* Hasmonean GS Hendon, UCL (LLB, LLM); *m* 23 July 1967, Vivien Ruth, da of Sidney Brook, of Leeds; 1 s (Jeremy Simon Richard b 1973), 1 da (Hilary Rachel b 1971); *Career* called to the Bar Gray's Inn 1969; lectr in law: E London Coll of Commerce 1965-66, Univ of Leeds 1967-69 (asst lectr 1966-67); reader in law UCL 1979-84 (lectr 1964-79), ed Annual Survey of Family Law 1983-, prof of English law Univ of London (tenable at UCL) 1984-, dir of trg Nicholson Graham and Jones 1989-; govr S Hampstead HS; *Books* incl: Introduction To Jurisprudence (1 edn 1972, 3 edn 1985), The Children Act 1975 (1976), Violence In The Home (1979), Cohabitation Outside Marriage (1983), The Rights and Wrongs of Children (1983), Essays In Family Law (1986), Dealing With Domestic Violence (1987), Medicine Ethics And The Law (1988); *Recreations* opera, theatre, cricket, literature; *Clubs* Middlesex CCC; *Style—* Prof Michael Freeman; Bentham House, Endsleigh Gdns, London WC1 (☎ 071 387 7050)

FREEMAN, Prof Neil Chappell; s of Claude Chappell Freeman, and Annie, *née* Wilkinson; *b* 28 April 1933; *Educ* Kendal GS, Univ of Manchester; *m* 31 Dec 1955, Gwyneth Christine, da of Frederick W Eyres; 1 s (Mervyn Paul b 24 Dec 1964), 3 da (Kirsteen Joy Kim b 25 Sept 1959, Tanya Helen b 11 June 1961, Miriam Wendy Wynne b 21 Feb 1963); *Career* sr scientific offr Nat Physical Lab Teddington 1955-62, reader in aerodynamics Imperial Coll London 1963-69, emeritus prof of applied mathematics Univ of Newcastle 1989- (prof 1969-89); fell Inst of Mathematics and its Applications 1964; *Style—* Prof Neil Freeman; 29 Avondale Rd, Darras Hall, Ponteland, Newcastle upon Tyne NE20 9NA (☎ 0661 24195); Department of Mathematics and Statistics, University of Newcastle, Newcastle upon Tyne NE1 7RU (☎ 091 222 6000)

FREEMAN, Lady; Patricia Denison; *née* Thomas; yr da of late Charles W Thomas, of Sandown, IOW; *m* 21 Dec 1946, Sir (John) Keith Noël Freeman, 2 Bt (d 5 June 1981); 1 s (Sir James, 3 Bt), 1 da and 1 s decd; *Style—* Lady Freeman; c/o Royal Bank of Scotland, 32 St Giles, Oxford OX1 3ND

FREEMAN, Dr Paul Illife; s of late John Percy Freeman, and Hilda Freeman; *Educ* Univ of Manchester (BSc, PhD); *m* 1959, Enid Ivy May Freeman; 1 s, 1 da; *Career* post doctoral fell Nat Res Cncl of Canada 1959-61, res sci Dupont De Nemours Co Ltd USA 1961-64; princ sci offr Nat Physical Laboratory 1970-74 (sr sci offr 1964-70), exec offr Res Requirements Bds Dept of Indust 1973-77; dir: Computor Aided Design Centre 1977-83, Nat Engrg Laboratory 1980-83, Central Computor and Telecommunications Agency HM Treasy 1983-88; controller and chief exec HM Stationery Office and The Queen's printer of acts of Parliament 1989-; author of various scientific papers; memb: Advsy Cncl Civil Serv Coll 1983-, Bd Nat Computor Centre 1983-88; visiting prof Univ of Strathclyde 1981-86; *Recreations* reading, walking, gardening; *Style—* Dr Paul Freeman

FREEMAN, Peter Asaph; s of Reverend Albert Charles Freeman, MM (d 1976), of Wick Cottage, Ashley, Market Drayton, and Winifred Wilma, *née* Wilson (d 1989); *b* 24 Jan 1925; *Educ* Christ's Coll Cambridge (MA), St Bartholomew's Hosp London (MB); *m* 3 April 1959, Daphne Nicholson, da of Capt Harold Drew, CBE, DSO (d 1987), of Sinniness, Old Barracks, Auchenmalg, Glenluce; 3 da (Lindsay Anne b 1960 d 1966, Elizabeth Mary b 31 Dec 1964, Victoria Alice b 11 Nov 1966); *Career* Robert Jones and Agnes Hunt Hosp Oswestry 1954-57, Western Infirmary Glasgow 1957-61, hon lectr in orthopaedics Mass Gen Hosp Harvard Univ Boston USA 1959-61, conslt orthopaedic surgn Bon Secours Hosp Glasgow 1961-; examiner for RCPS Glas, memb Med Appeals Tbnl Glasgow; memb:Br Orthopaedics Assoc 1958, BMA 1960; FRCPS Glas 1980; *Recreations* game fishing, stalking, military history; *Clubs* Royal Scottish Automobile; *Style—* Peter Freeman; Sinniness Old Barracks, Auchenmalg, Newton Stewart, Wigtownshire DG8 0JX (☎ 058 15 274); Bon Secours Hosp, 36 Mansion House Rd, Glasgow G41 3DW (☎ 041 632 9231)

FREEMAN, Sir Ralph; CVO (1964), CBE (1952, MBE (mil 1945); s of Sir Ralph Freeman (d 1950), and Mary, *née* Lines (d 1958); *b* 3 Feb 1911; *Educ* Uppingham, Worcester Coll Oxford (BA, MA); *m* 19 May 1939, Joan Elizabeth, da of Col John George Rose, DSO, VD (d 1973), of Wynberg, Cape Town, South Africa; 2 s (Anthony b 29 March 1946, Hugh b 16 Feb 1949), 1 da (Elizabeth b 10 May 1942); *Career* temp Maj RE 1939-45, Admiralty and other war work, served RE 1943-45 at Experimental Bridging Estab, later seconded as bridging advsr to CE 21 Army Gp HQ NW Europe campaign, Col Engr and Tport Staff Corps RE (TA), Col Cmdg 1969-74, ret 1976; chartered engr; construction engr: Dorman Long & Co (S Africa, Rhodesia and Denmark) 1932-36 and 1937-39, Braithwaite & Co 1936-37; Freeman Fox and Ptnrs: on staff 1939-43 and 1946, ptnr 1947-79, sr ptnr 1963-79, conslt 1979-88; pres Inst Civil Engrs 1966-67, chm ACE 1974-75, pres Welding Inst 1974-76; consltg engr Sandringham Estate 1949-76, memb Royal Fine Art Cmmn 1968-85; hon fell Worcester Coll Oxford 1980, Hon Doctorate Univ Surrey, Hon MConsE, Hon MIRoyE, Hon FIMechE, hon fell Zimbabwe Inst of Engrs, memb Emeritus Smeatonian Soc, FEng, FICE, FWeldI, FRSA, FASCE; kt (4th class) Order of Orange Nassau 1945; kt 1970; *Recreations* carpentry, metal work, writing letters; *Clubs* Army and Navy, Leander; *Style—* Sir Ralph Freeman, CVO, CBE; Ballards Shaw, Ballards Lane, Limpsfield, Oxted, Surrey RH8 0SN (☎ 0883 723284)

FREEMAN, Prof Raymond (Ray); s of Albert Freeman (d 1940), and Hilda Frances, *née* Bush (d 1983); *b* 6 Jan 1932; *Educ* Nottingham HS, Lincoln Coll Oxford (MA, DPhil, DSc); *m* 19 April 1958, Anne-Marie Catherine, da of Philippe Périnet-Marquet (d 1969); 2 s (Jean-Marc b 1964, Lawrence b 1969), 3 da (Dominique b 1959, Anne b 1960, Louise b 1962); *Career* engr Centre D'Études Nucléaires de Saclay France 1957-59, sr sci offr Nat Physical Laboratory Teddington Middx 1959-63, mangr Nuclear Magnetic Resonance Res Varian Assoc Palo Alto California 1963-73; Univ of Oxford: lectr in physical chemistry 1973-87, fell Magdalen Coll 1973-87, Aldrichian praelector in chemistry 1982-87; Univ of Cambridge: John Humphrey Plummer prof of magnetic resonance 1987-, fell Jesus Coll 1987-; FRS 1979; *Books* A Handbook of Nuclear Magnetic Resonance (1987); *Style—* Prof Ray Freeman, FRS; 29 Bentley Rd, Cambridge CB2 2AW (☎ 0223 323958); Dept of Physical Chemistry, Univ of Cambridge, Lensfied Rd, Cambridge CB2 1EP (☎ 0223 336450)

FREEMAN, Richard Dempsey; *b* 27 June 1943; *Educ* Kingston-upon-Hull GS, Univ of Leicester (BSc); *Career* mathematics teacher Dartington Hall Sch 1964-66, head of the advsy serv Advsy Centre for Educn 1966-72, exec dir Nat Ext Coll 1976-87 (educnl dir 1972-76), courses dir Open Coll 1987-; memb: Educn Ctee NFWI, Managing Design Ctee CNAA, Flexible Learning Ctee BTEC, Starnet Satelite Project Ctee Plymouth Poly; external examiner for open learning Dundee Coll; *Books* How to Study Effectively (1972), Structured Basic (1984), Beyond Basic (1984), Step by Step Basic (1985); *Recreations* music and gardening; *Style—* Richard Freeman, Esq; The Open College, 101 Wigmore St, London W1A 9AA (☎ 071 935 8088, fax 071 935 0415)

FREEMAN, Roger John; s of Lt Cdr Harold Cecil Freeman, MBE, VRD (d 1984), of Much Hadham, Herts, and Jacqueline Mary Freeman; *b* 21 June 1944; *Educ* Wellington, Exeter Univ (BA), Wharton Sch Univ of Pennsylvania (MBA); *m* 12 May 1971, Kitty, da of Juan Carlos Yegros (d 1966), of Asuncion, Paraguay; 2 s (Jonathan b 1981, Christopher b 1989); *Career* Bank of London and S America 1968-72, Harris Tst 1974-79, Libra Bank 1979-90 (gen mangr 1985-90), dir Morgan Grenfell & Co Ltd 1990-; *Recreations* sport; *Clubs* MCC; *Style—* Roger Freeman, Esq; 11 Grove Terrace, London NW5 (☎ 071 485 2685); Morgan Grenfell & Co Ltd, 23 Winchester St, London EC2P 2AX (☎ 071 826 7905, fax 071 826 7900, telex 8953511 MG LDN G)

FREEMAN, Roger Norman; MP (C) Kettering 1983-; s of Norman and Marjorie Freeman; *b* 27 May 1942; *Educ* Whitgift Sch, Balliol Coll Oxford (MA); *m* 1969, Jennifer Margaret, *née* Watson; 1 s, 1 da; *Career* pres Oxford Univ Cons Assoc 1964, md Bow Publications 1968 (former memb Cncl and treas Bow Group), Parly candidate (C) Don Valley 1979; FCA 1978; merchant bank dir; md Lehman Brothers 1972- (joined Lehman Bros (US merchant bank) 1969, first Englishman invited to join US ptnrship); non-exec dir: Martini & Rossi Ltd, McCormick International Investments Ltd; fndr memb Hundred Gp of UK CA Fin Dirs; Parly under sec of state: Armed Forces MOD 1986-88, Dept of Health 1988-90, min for state Dept of Tport 1990-; *Publications include* Pensions Policy, Professional Practice, A Fair Deal for Water; *Recreations* sailing, shooting; *Clubs* City of London, Carlton, Kennel; *Style—* Roger Freeman, Esq, MP; House of Commons, London SW1A 0AA (☎ 071 219 6436)

FREEMAN, Roland John Michael; JP (1972); s of Cornelius Alexander Freeman (d 1972), of London, and Marjorie Dolores Kathleen Freeman (d 1974); *b* 7 May 1927; *Educ* Chippenham GS, St Joseph's Coll Beulah Hill, LSE; *m* 18 Dec 1976, Marian, da of John Kilroy, of Rugby; *Career* sch master 1947-53, Cons Res Dept 1958-59, dir London Municipal Soc 1959-61, campaign mangr Aims of Indust 1961-65; md: PR (Indust) Ltd 1965-69, Welbeck City Ltd 1969-76, Roland Freeman Ltd 1976-; dir LWT Ltd 1981-89, memb LWT Prog Advsy Bd 1989-; Wandsworth Borough Cncl: memb 1949-65, ldr and fin chm; govr LSE 1961-85; GLC: memb and fin chm 1967-70, memb 1975-81; Parly candidate: (Cons) Nuneaton 1974, (SDP/Alliance) Tonbridge and Malling 1983; memb Alliance Central Ctee Gen Election 1987; joined Labour Pty 1990, Liveryman Worshipful Co of Tallow Chandlers 1970; FCIS 1962, MIPR 1986; *Books* Becoming a Councillor (2 edn, 1975); *Recreations* music (piano, organ), mountain walking, gardening; *Clubs* Reform, Royal Overseas League; *Style—* Roland Freeman, Esq, JP; 14 Northridge, Northiam, East Sussex, TN31 6PG (☎ 0797 252290)

FREEMAN, Simon David; s of Alfred Freeman (d 1976), of Hove, Sussex, and Doris Freeman; *b* 16 Aug 1952; *Educ* Hove GS for Boys Sussex, Worcester Coll Oxford (BA); *Career* graduate training scheme Mirror Group Plymouth 1974-76, reporter Evening Standard London 1976-79, Sunday Times 1979-89 (rep, co ed (Insight), special writer, foreign corr), chief foreign corr Sunday Correspondent 1989-90, news ed The European London 1990-; NCTJ proficiency certificate; runner up: IOJ Young Journalist of the Year 1975, commended Reporter of the Year Br Press Awards 1980; commended Argos Press Awards 1982; memb NUJ; *Style—* Simon Freeman, Esq; The European, Orbit House, 5 New Fetter Lane, London EC4 (☎ 071 822 2002, fax 071 377 4773)

FREEMAN, Lady Winefride Alice; *née* Fitzalan-Howard; yst da of 15 Duke of Norfolk, KG, PC, CVO (d 1917), and his 2 wife Gwendolen Mary, Lady Herries of Terregles (d 1945); *b* 31 Oct 1914; *m* 7 May 1943, Lt-Col John Edward Broke Freeman (d 1986), s of late Sir Philip Horace Freeman, KCVO, KBE; 1 s, 2 da; *Career* JP Suffolk, pres Suffolk Red Cross 1972-84, ret; *Style—* The Lady Winefride Freeman; St Catherine's Cottage, Hook Lane, Aldingbourne, West Sussex

FREEMAN-ATTWOOD, Major (Harold) Warren; s of Maj-Gen Harold Augustus Freeman-Attwood, DSO, OBE, MC (d 1963), and Jessie (d 1958), da of Hon William Carson Job, of Newfoundland, and Liverpool; the family claims descent from the ancient Worcestershire house of Attwood of Park Attwood, Wolverly and Perdiswell (*see* Burke's Landed Gentry, 18 Edn, vol 3); *b* 20 Sept 1923; *Educ* Marlborough, RMC Sandhurst; *m* 1, 9 July 1947 (m dis 1960), Elizabeth, da of Lt-Col Roger Mostyn-Owen, DSO, JP (d 1947); 1 s (Julian b 1953), 1 da (Rosamond b 1951); m 2, 15 Oct 1960, Mrs Marigold Diana Sneyd Wedderburn, da of Edward Mark Philips, OBE (d 1937); 1 s (Jonathan b 1961); *Career* cmmnd Grenadier Gds 1942, served WW II in N Africa, Italy and Austria (despatches); psc 1952; DAA and QMG 32 Guards Bde 1953-54, Regtl Adj Grenadier Gds 1957-59, 2 i/c 3 Bn Grenadier Gds 1959-60; ret 1960; memb: London Stock Exchange 1962-85, Baltic Exchange 1969-85; *Recreations* music, fine woodwork; *Style—* Major Warren Freeman-Attwood; West Flexford, Wanborough, Guildford, Surrey (☎ 0483 810 884)

FREEMAN-GRENVILLE, Dr Greville Stewart Parker; s of Ernest Charles Freeman (d 1936), of Shipton-under-Wychwood Oxon, and Agnes Mary Gibson, *née* Parker (d 1966); surname changed from Freeman to Freeman-Grenville by Decree of the Lord Lyon King of Arms 1950; *b* 29 June 1918; *Educ* Eastbourne Coll, Worcester Coll Oxford, (BA, BLitt, MA, DPhil); *m* 29 Aug 1950, Beatrice Mary Grenville, Lady Kinloss, da of Rev the Hon Luis Francis Chandos Temple Morgan-Grenville, Master of Kinloss (d 1944); 1 s (Bevil David Stewart Chandos, Master of Kinloss b 1953), 2 da (Teresa Mary Nugent b 1957, Hester Josephine Anne b 1960); *Career* WWII Capt Royal Berks Regt, Personnel Selection Staff 1939-46; HM Overseas Civil Service Tanganyika 1951-60; educnl advsr Aden Protectorate 1961-64; sr res fell: Univ of Ghana 1964-66, Univ of York 1966-69; hon fell Univ of York 1969-, prof of history State Univ of NY 1969-74; author and writer; memb: Br Acad Ctee on Fontes Historiae Africanae 1972-, Cncl of the Hakluyt Soc 1986-90; contrib to: Encyclopaedia Britannica, Encyclopaedia of Islam, various journals; Papal Cross Pro Ecclesia et Pontifice 1984, Kt of the Holy Sepulchre 1982 fell Royal Numismatic Soc 1956, FSA 1961, FRAS 1966; *Books* The Medieval History of the Coast of Tanganyika (1962), The East African Coast: Select Documents (1962), The Muslim and Christian Calendars (1963), Chronology of African History (1973), Chronology of World History (1976), Modern Atlas of African History (1976), The Queen's Lineage: from AD 495 to HM The Queen Elizabeth II (1977) Atlas of British History (1977), The Mombasa Rising of 1631 (1980), The Beauty of Jerusalem (second edn 1988), The Beauty of Rome (1988), The Swahili Coast 2nd to 19th Centuries (1988), A New Atlas of African History (1991); *Recreations* travel, gardening; *Clubs* Royal Cwlth Soc; *Style—* Dr G S P Freeman-Grenville, FSA; North View House, Sheriff Hutton, York YO6 1PT (☎ 034 77 447)

FREEMAN-GRENVILLE, Hon Teresa Mary Nugent; er da of Lady Kinloss and Greville Stewart Parker Freeman-Grenville; *b* 20 July 1957; *Style—* The Hon Teresa Freeman-Grenville; North View House, Sheriff Hutton, York

FREEMAN-THOMAS, Hon Mrs (Moyra); *née* Marjoribanks; da of 3 and last Baron Tweedmouth (d 1935); *b* 1902; *m* 1, 12 June 1923, Lt-Col Reginald Francis Heyworth, of 1 Royal Dragoons (ka 1941); 1 s, 1 da; m 2, 5 Nov 1943, Maj Reginald Brodrick Freeman-Thomas, KOYLI; *Style—* The Hon Mrs Freeman-Thomas; Kingswall House, nr Malmesbury, Wilts (☎ 0666 822338)

FREEMANTLE, Brig Andrew; MBE (1982); s of Lt-Col Arthur Freemantle, and Peggy Frances, *née* Wood; *b* 26 Sept 1944; *Educ* Framlingham Coll Suffolk, Royal Mil Coll of Sci; *m* 10 June 1972, Patricia Mary, da of Brig J H Thompson, of the White House, 16 Shaftesbury Rd, Wilton; 4 da (Victoria b 1974, Lucy b 1976, Emily b 1979, Gemma b 1983); *Career* cmmnd Royal Hampshire Regt 1965; served: Germany, Malaya, Borneo 1965-69; Royal Aust Regt and Aust SAS Regt (served Aust and S Vietnam) 1969-72; Royal Hampshire Regt: served Hong Kong, UK, NI 1972-76; Staff Coll Camberley 1978, DS at Staff Coll 1983-84, CO 1 Bn Royal Hampshire Regt Berlin and UK 1985-87 (despatches 1987), Cdr 19 Inf Bde 1987-89; ret 1990; dir Scot Ambulance Serv; memb: MENSA 1989, RCDS 1990; FBIM 1989; *Recreations* running, cooking, field sports; *Clubs* Special Forces; *Style—* Brig Andrew Freemantle, MBE; National Headquarters, The Scottish Ambulance Service, Clifton House, Clifton Place, Glasgow (☎ 041 332 3115)

FREEMANTLE, Brian Harry; s of Harold Freemantle, and Violet, *née* Street; *b* 10 June 1936; *Educ* Bitterne Park Secdy Modern Sch Bitterne Park Southampton; *m* 1956, Maureen Hazel, *née* Tipney; 3 da (Emma b 2 Aug 1973, Victoria b 13 June 1975, Charlotte b 13 July 1978); *Career* reporter: New Milton Advertiser 1953-58, Bristol Evening World 1958, London Evening News 1959-61; reporter and asst foreign ed Daily Express 1961-68; foreign ed: Daily Sketch 1969-71, Daily Mail 1971-75; author; non fiction incl: KGB, CIA, The Fix (int drug trade), The Steal (industl espionage); novels incl: The Factory, The Bearpit, The Run Around, The Kremlin Kiss, The Man Who Wanted Tomorrow, 9 books in The Charlie Muffin series; nominee Mystery Writers of America Edgar Allan Poe award 1985; *Recreations* reading, driving; *Clubs* Lord's Taverner's; *Style—* Brian Freemantle, Esq; 4 Great Minster St, Winchester, Hampshire SO23 9HA (☎ 0962 861212); Jonathan Clowes Ltd, 10 Iron Bridge House, Bridge Approach, London NW1 8BD (☎ 071 722 7674, fax 071 722 7677)

FREEMONT, Dr Anthony John; s of Walter Freemont (d 1972), of Ealing, London, and Sarah, *née* Burnett; *b* 27 March 1953; *Educ* Latymer Upper Sch Hammersmith, St Thomas' Hosp Med Sch (BSc, MB BS, MD); *m* 4 Dec 1976, Susan Elspeth, da of David Brierley Murray, of Blackburn, Lancs; 1 da (Katherine Sarah b 1981); *Career* sr lectr in osteoarticular pathology Univ of Manchester 1987-; FRCPE 1990, MRCPath 1986; *Recreations* fell walking, sailing; *Style—* Dr Anthony Freemont; 26 Cecil Ave, Sale, Cheshire M33 5BQ (☎ 061 973 1869); Division of Connective Tissue Pathology, University of Manchester, Stopford Building, Oxford Rd, Manchester M13 9PT (☎ 061 275 5269)

FREER, (Joan Marian) Penelope (Mrs Terence Fuller); da of Frederick George Sinderby Freer, of Bromley, Kent, and Doris Florence, *née* Wynne; *b* 6 Feb 1950; *Educ* Bromley HS for Girls, Lady Margaret Hall Oxford (exhibitioner, BA, MA); *m* 1975, Terence Ronald Fuller, s of Cecil Ronald Fuller; 1 s (Timothy b 17 Dec 1980), 1 da (Emily b 17 July 1983); *Career* articled clerk Lee & Pembertons 1971-73, asst slr Nabarro Nathanson 1973-75, ptnr Freshfields 1979- (asst slr 1975-79); memb The City of London Slrs Co; memb Law Soc; *Clubs* Reform; *Style—* Ms Penelope Freer; Freshfields, Whitefriars, 65 Fleet St, London EC4Y 1HT (☎ 071 936 4000, fax 071 248 3487/8/9)

FREER, Air Chief Marshal Sir Robert William George; GBE (1981, CBE 1966), KCB (1977); s of William Freer (d 1979), of Stretton, Cirencester, Glos, and Margaret Jane, *née* Clements (d 1957); *b* 1 Sept 1923; *Educ* Gosport GS; *m* 1950, Margaret Tinkler, 2 da of late John William Elkington, of Ruskington Manor, nr Sleaford, Lincs; 1 s (Adrian), 1 da (Anna); *Career* Queen's Commendation 1955; cmd 92 Fighter Sqdn 1955-57, station cdr RAF Seletar 1963-66, Air ADC to HM The Queen 1969-71, dep cmdt RAF Staff Coll 1969-71, SASO HQ Near East Air Force 1971-72, AOC 11 Gp 1972-75, dir gen orgn MOD Air 1975, AOC 18 Gp 1975-78, dep C-in-C RAF Strike Cmd 1979-80, Air Chief Marshal, cmdt RCDS 1980-82, ret; dir: Rediffusion 1982-88, Rediffusion Simulation Ltd 1985-88, British Manufacture and Research Co Ltd 1984-88, Pilatus Britten-Norman 1988-; chm: BM Pension Tstees Ltd 1985-88; CBIM, FRSA; *Recreations* tennis, golf; *Clubs* RAF, Hankley Common Golf, All England Lawn Tennis; *Style—* Air Chief Marshal Sir Robert Freer, GBE, KCB; c/o Lloyds Bank, 75 Castle St, Farnham, Surrey; Pilatus Britten-Norman Ltd, Bembridge, IOW (☎ 0983 872 511)

FREESON, Rt Hon Reginald Yarnitz; PC (1976); *b* 24 Feb 1926; *Educ* Jewish Orphanage W Norwood; *m* (m dis); 1 s, 1 da; *Career* served in Army 1944-47; journalist 1948-64; memb: Willesden Cncl 1952-68 (chm 1958-65), Brent Cncl 1952-68 (1964-65); MP (Lab) Willesden E and Brent E 1964-87, PPS to Min Transport 1964-67; Parly sec: Miny Power 1967-69, Miny Housing and Local Govt 1969-7; oppn front bench spokesman Housing, Construction and Urban Affairs 1970-74, min of Housing and Construction (responsible for inner cities, planning, land and local govt) 1974-79, oppn front bench spokesman Social Security 1979-80; memb: Select Ctee on the Environment 1980-83 (chm 1982-83), Cncl of Europe Parly Assembly 1983-87, Western Euro Assembly 1983-87; memb: Jewish Welfare Bd 1971-74 (memb Exec 1973-74), Housing Centre Tst 1987-, Nat Cncl for Civil Liberties, Int Voluntary Service, UNA Int Serv; fndr chm Willesden/Brent Community Rels Cncl and Cncl of Voluntary Service 1959; fndr memb: War on Want, CND; fndr ed Searchlight (against facism and anti-semitism) 1964-66; dir J B G Housing Soc 1982-83, fndr Reg Freeson & Associates (Urban Renewal Conslts) 1986-, chm Poale Zion 1981-85 (political sec 1987-), ed Jewish Vanguard 1988-; memb: Co-operative Party 1958, Fabian Soc 1958, Poale Zion-Labour Party 1964, Lab Party 1964; *Recreations* gardening, reading, theatre, music, country walking; *Style—* The Rt Hon Reginald Freeson; 159 Chevening Rd, London NW6 6DZ

FREESTON, Hon Mrs (Anne Boswall); *née* Jackson; er da of Baron Jackson of Burnley (Life Peer, d 1970), and Mary Elizabeth, *née* Boswall; *b* 9 Oct 1939; *Educ* Sutton HS, Froebel Educational Inst Roehampton (Teachers Dip); *m* 18 March 1967, David Garner Freeston, s of Charles Garner Freeston (d 1969), of Stonewall, Philpots Lane, Hildenborough, Kent; 2 children; *Career* teacher 1961-65, secretary 1980-; *Recreations* painting, cooking, conservation, German; *Style—* The Hon Mrs Freeston; Hazel Cottage, North Heath, Chieveley, Newbury, Berks (☎ (0635 248 654)

FREETH, Denzil Kingson; s of late Walter Kingson Freeth, and Alice Vera Freeth; *b* 10 July 1924; *Educ* Sherborne, Trinity Hall Cambridge; *Career* Flying Offr RAF; pres Union Soc Cambridge 1949, chm Cambridge Union Cons Assoc 1949, MP (Cons)

Basingstoke 1955-64, Parly sec to Min for Sci 1961-63; memb London Stock Exchange 1964-90; churchwarden All Saints Margaret Street London W1 1977-; *Recreations* good food, wine, conversation; *Clubs* Carlton, Pitt (Cambridge); *Style—* Denzil Freeth Esq; 3 Brasenose House, 35 Kensington High St, London W8 (☎ 071 937 8685)

FREETHY, Norman Derek; s of Arthur Thomas Freethy (d 1961), and Helen Maud, *née* Cook (d 1977); *b* 23 Feb 1923; *Educ* Pinner Co Sch; *m* 1, 1958; 2 s (Simon Julian b 1964, Conrad Stephen Mark b 1971), 1 da (Nicola b 1962); m 2, 1985, Alison Lesley Vaughan, da of William Arthur Sparke (d 1978); 1 da (Sophie Dawn Vaughan b 1987); *Career* qualified actuary 1957; sr ptnr Hymans Robertson & Co Consulting Actuaries; frequent writer and speaker on pensions and investmt matters; dir: City of London Computer Services Ltd, Coulter Pension Tstees; Liveryman Worshipful Co of Actuaries; FIA; *Recreations* music, gardening, golf; *Clubs* RAC, City Livery, Addington Golf; *Style—* Norman Freethy, Esq; Overcombe, 87 Harvestbank Rd, West Wickham, Kent; Hymans Robertson & Co Consulting Actuaries, 190 Fleet St, London EC4A 2AH (☎ 071 831 9561, fax 071 831 6800, telex 881 3786)

FREIDMAN, Bernard Marcus; s of Mayer Freidman (d 1945), of Chichele Mansions, London, and Rosie, *née* Lipman (d 1945); *b* 18 Sept 1913; *Educ* private; *m* 31 March 1946, Hilda Phyllis, da of Ernest Solk (d 1944), of Teignmouth Rd, London NW2; 2 da (Susan Elaine (Mrs Stoney) b 1947, Anne Michelle (Mrs Curran) b 1951); *Career* WWII 1940-46, RAOC Donnington Base Depot 1940, Egypt and Palestine 1940-43, ME Army Personnel Selection Unit 1943-45, Germany control cmmn 1945-46, rank of War Substansive Sgt; works mangr Rotorohms 1929-35; mangr and tech exec Marks and Spencer plc 1935- (except war years), post war took control of all store devpts and design of all bldg and equipment incl eight foot hot cathode fluorescent light tube, ret 1977; chm Embassy Ct Lessees Assoc 1985-; Freeman: City of London, Worshipful Co of Plumbers 1955; *Style—* Bernard M Freidman, Esq; 84 Embassy Court, Kings Road, Brighton, BN1 2PY, E Sussex (☎ 0273 726182)

FREMANTLE, Hon Christopher Evelyn; 4 s of 3 Baron Cottesloe (d 1956); *b* 17 Dec 1906; *Educ* Eton, Balliol Oxford; *m* 12 Nov 1930, Anne Marie Huth, da of late Rt Hon Frederick Huth Jackson; 3 s; *Style—* The Hon Christopher Fremantle; 252 East 78th St, New York, NY 10021, USA

FREMANTLE, Hon Elizabeth Cecilia Jane; da of 4 Baron Cottesloe, GBE, TD, and his 2 w, Gloria Jean Irene Dunn; *b* 28 Aug 1962; *Educ* Heathfield; *Career* fashion editor Vogue (UK) 1989-; *Style—* The Hon Elizabeth Fremantle; c/o Vogue, Vogue House, 1 Hanover Square, London W1R OAD (☎ 071 499 9080, fax 071 493 1345)

FREMANTLE, Cdr the Hon John Tapling; JP (Bucks 1984); s and h of Lt-Col 4 Baron Cottesloe, GBE, DL, *qv*; *b* 22 Jan 1927; *Educ* Eton; *m* 26 April 1958, Elizabeth Ann, er da of Lt-Col Henry Shelley Barker, DSO (d 1970), of Rugby; 1 s (Tom), 2 da (Betsy, Fanny); *Career* joined RN 1945, Lt 1949, Lt Cdr 1957, Cdr 1962, ret 1966; chm: Bucks County Show 1977-82, Oxon-Bucks Div Royal Forestry Soc 1981-83; pres Bucks Branch CLA (chm 1976-79); vice pres: Hosp Saving Assoc, BASC (previously WAGBI); memb Cncl Royal Agric Soc of England 1974-; Radcliffe Tstee; govr Stowe Sch 1983-89; High Sheriff of Bucks 1969-70, Lord Lieut 1984-; KStJ (1984); *Recreations* shooting, stalking, crosswords; *Clubs* Travellers', RN and Royal Albert (Portsmouth); *Style—* Cdr the Hon John Fremantle, JP, RN (ret); The Old House, Swanbourne, Milton Keynes, Bucks MK17 0SH (☎ 029 672 263); The Estate Office, Home Farm, Swanbourne, Milton Keynes, Bucks MK17 0SW (☎ 029 672 256)

FREMANTLE, Hon Katharine Dorothy Honor; yr da of 3 Baron Cottesloe (d 1956); *b* 23 May 1919; *Educ* Girton Coll Cambridge; *Career* PhD London 1956; *Style—* The Hon Katharine Fremantle; Dennenlaan 48, Hollandsche Rading, Netherlands

FRENCH, Dr Cecil Charles John; s of late Ernest French, of Harlow, Essex, and late Edith Hannah, *née* Norris; *b* 16 April 1926; *Educ* Newport Essex Sch, King's Coll London (MSc, DSc), Columbia Univ NY; *m* 1, 14 July 1956, (Olive) Joyce (d 1969), da of late Arthur James Edwards, of Lancing, Sussex; 2 da (Alison b 1957, Hilary b 1961); m 2, 23 Oct 1971, Shirley Frances, da of late Montague Charles Outten, of Colchester, Essex; 1 s (Matthew b 1975), 1 da (Elizabeth b 1973); *Career* Ricardo Consulting Engineers Ltd 1952-90: dir 1969, vice chm 1982; chm G Cussons Ltd 1985-87, gp tech dir Ricardo International plc 1990-; visiting prof in mechanical engr King's Coll 1983-89; author of numerous papers on internal combustion engrg; pres: IMechE 1988-89 (vice pres 1982-86, dep pres 1986-88), Int Cncl on Combustion Engines (CIMAC) 1983; Freeman of City of London 1986, Liveryman of Worshipful Co of Engrs 1986; FEng, FIMechE, FBIM, MASME, MSAE; *Recreations* folk dancing, photography; *Clubs* Shoreham and Southwick Rotary; *Style—* Dr Cecil French; 303 Upper Shoreham Rd, Shoreham-by-Sea, W Sussex BN43 5QA (☎ 0273 452050); Ricardo International plc, Brunswick House, Upper York St, Bristol BS2 8QB (☎ 0272 232162, fax 0272 428349, telex 449107)

FRENCH, Hon (Fulke) Charles Arthur John; s (by 1 m) of 7 Baron De Freyne; *b* 21 April 1957; *Educ* Downside, RAC Cirencester (DipAg), Poly of the South Bank London (BA); *m* 12 April 1986, Julia Mary, o da of Dr James H Wellard, PhD, FLA, FRGS, of Hampstead, London; 1 s (Alexander James Charles b 22 Sept 1988); *Career* planning and devpt conslt; FRGS, MRAC; *Recreations* sailing, tennis, photography, literature, travel; *Style—* The Hon Charles French; 26 Oakhill Rd, London SW15 2QR

FRENCH, (Edward Frank) Christopher; s of Frank Charles French, of W Malling, Kent, and Mary, *née* Parish; *b* 28 July 1950; *Educ* Roan GS for Boys; *m* 29 March 1969, Rita Margaret, da of Brian Stewart; 1 s (James b 1983), 1 da (Sally b 1977); *Career* Nationwide Bldg Soc: trainee mangr 1971, branch mangr 1978, sec 1985; asst gen mangr Nationwide Anglia Bldg Soc 1988, gen mangr 1990; chm: Nationwide Bldg Soc Staff Assoc 1983-85, Fedn of Bldg Soc Staff Assocs 1984-85; FCBSI 1978, DMS 1985; *Recreations* music, horticulture; *Style—* Christopher French, Esq; Nationwide Anglia Building Society, Princes St, Swindon, Wilts SN1 2HQ (☎ 0793 510340, fax 0793 510400)

FRENCH, Hon Mr Justice; Hon Sir Christopher James Saunders; s of Rev Reginald French, MC (d 1961, hon chaplain to HM The Queen and to the late King George VI), and Gertrude Emily Mary, *née* Haworth; *b* 14 Oct 1925; *Educ* Denstone Coll (scholar), Brasenose Coll Oxford (scholar); *m* 1957, Philippa, da of Philip Godfrey Price, of Abergavenny, Monmouthshire; 1 s, 1 da; *Career* called to the Bar Inner Temple 1950, QC 1966, dep chm Bucks QS 1966-71, rec Coventry 1971, rec and hon rec Coventry 1972-79, high court judge (family) 1979-82, Queen's Bench Div 1982-, presiding judge S Eastern Circuit 1982-86; memb Lord Chllr's Advsy Ctee on Trg Magistrates 1974-80; kt 1979; contrib Agency in Halsbury's Laws of England (4th edn); *Recreations* walking, music, painting; *Clubs* Garrick; *Style—* The Hon Mr Justice French; Royal Courts of Justice, Strand, London WC2

FRENCH, David; s of Capt Godfrey Alexander French, CBE, RN (d 1988), of Stoke Abbott, Dorset, and Margaret Annis, *née* Best; *b* 20 June 1947; *Educ* Sherborne, St Johns Coll Durham (BA); *m* 3 Aug 1974, Sarah Anne, da of Rt Rev Henry David Halsey, former Bishop of Carlisle; 3 s (Thomas b 1978, Alexander b 1980, William b 1983); *Career* with Nat Cncl of Social Serv 1971-74, head Social Servs Dept RNID 1974-78, dir of serv C of E Childrens Soc 1978-87, dir RELATE Nat Marriage Guidance Cncl 1987-; Liveryman Worshipful Co of Glaziers 1990; MIPM, MRSM; *Recreations* children; *Style—* David French, Esq; 21 Prospect Rd, St Albans, Herts AL1 2AT; RELATE Marriage Guidance, Herbert Gray College, Little Church Street, Rugby CV21 3AP (☎ 0788 573241)

FRENCH, Douglas Charles; MP (C) Gloucester 1987-; s of Frederick Emil French, of Surrey, and late Charlotte Vera, *née* Russell; *b* 20 March 1944; *Educ* Glyn GS Epsom, St Catharine's Coll Cambridge (MA), Inns of Court Sch of Law; *m* 1978, Sue, da of late Philip Arthur Phillips; 2 s (Paul b 1982, David b 1985), 1 da (Louise b 1983); *Career* dir PW Merkle Ltd 1972-87 (exec 1966-71), called to the Bar Inner Temple 1975, Parly candidate Sheffield Attercliffe 1979, md Westminster & City Programmes 1979-87, special advsr to Chllr of Exchequer 1982-83 (asst to Rt Hon Sir Geoffrey Howe QC, MP 1976-79); PPS to the Min of State: FCO 1988-89, ODA 1989-90; chm Bow Group 1978-79; *Recreations* skiing, gardening, squash; *Clubs* RAC, Coningsby; *Style—* Douglas French, Esq, MP; House of Commons, London SW1A 0AA (☎ 01 219 4564)

FRENCH, Prof Edward Alexander; s of Edward Francis French (d 1967), and Clara French (d 1982); *b* 17 Oct 1935; *Educ* Bemrose Sch Derby, LSE (BSc (Econ), LLB, PhD); *m* 11 Aug 1967, Lillias Margaret, da of Walter Riddoch (d 1972); 3 s (Daniel b 1974, Gregory b 1976, Steven b 1979); *Career* Nat Serv RAF 1955-57; called to the Bar Lincoln's Inn; audit examiner Dist Audit Serv 1955-59, princ (former asst princ) Home Civil Serv GPO 1963-67, lectr in accounting LSE 1967-77, prof and head of Dept of Accounting and Fin Control Univ Coll Cardif 1977-87, prof Univ of Wales Coll of Cardiff 1987-; pres S Wales Soc of Certified Accountants 1982-83, memb Nat Cncl Chartered Soc of Certified Accountants 1983-86; FCCA, FRSA; *Recreations* golf, swimming, reading; *Clubs* Radyr Golf; *Style—* Prof Edward French; 112 Pencisely Rd, Llandaff, Cardiff CF5 1DQ (☎ 0222 562599); University of Wales College of Cardiff, Aberconway Building, Colum Drive, Cardiff CF1 3EU (☎ 0222 874000 ext 5740, fax 0222 874419)

FRENCH, Jeremy Godfrey; s of Capt Godfrey Alexander French, CBE (d 1988), and Mary Neville, *née* Gilhespy (d 1965); *b* 26 May 1930; *Educ* Sherborne, RMA Sandhurst; *m* 1, 11 Aug 1954, Ann Mary, *née* Rowland; 1 da (Caroline Mary Hudson b 1957); m 2, 1963, June Mary Prescott, da of Aidan Arnold Wallis, of Ashdown House, Forest Row, Sussex; 1 step s (Cdr J A Prescott), 1 step da (Mrs N A Mièville); *Career* The Duke of Cornwall's Light Infantry, Capt 1950-62; joined Shell Mex and BP Ltd 1962, regnl mangr Shell UK Oil 1978-80, mangr public affairs Shell UK Oil 1980-82; *Recreations* gardening, music, woodwork; *Clubs* Army and Navy; *Style—* Jeremy French, Esq; Jasmine Lodge, School Lane, Stoke Poges, Bucks (☎ 0753 662484)

FRENCH, Hon Mrs Hubert; Mary Frances; da of Charles Hasslacher, of 3 Kensington Park Gdns, London; *m* 19 Jan 1937, Hon Hubert John French (d 7 Dec 1961), 8 s of 4 Baron de Freyne (d 1918); 2 s, 2 da; *Style—* The Hon Mrs Hubert French; Stychfield, Stychens Lane, Bletchingley, Redhill, Surrey

FRENCH, Peter Reginald; RD (1965); s of Rev Reginald French, MC, QHC (d 1961), and Gertrude Emily Mary, *née* Haworth (d 1968); *b* 22 July 1921; *Educ* Rugby, St Thomas' Hosp Univ of London; *m* 29 March 1958, (Norna Elizabeth) Ann, da of Capt David Norman Drybrough (d 1925); 2 s (James b 1965, Michael b 1966); *Career* Surgn Lt RNVR 1945-47, Naval Hosp Hong Kong 1945-46, Naval Res HMS President London, Surgn Lt Cdr RNR, ret 1966; orthopaedic surgn: St George's Hosp London 1961-86, Royal Masonic Hosp London 1963-88; private orthopaedic practice London 1961-; Freeman City of London, Liveryman Worshipful Soc of Apothecaries; FRCS 1952, FRSM, fell Br Orthopaedic Assoc; *Books* contributions to numerous surgical books and jls; *Recreations* golf, swimming, fishing, gardening; *Clubs* Garrick, Hurlingham, Naval, Berkshire Golf, Royal Wimbledon, Royal Clinque Ports; *Style—* Peter French, Esq, RD; 1 Hurlingham Gardens, London SW6 3PL (☎ 071 736 3547)

FRENCH, Philip Neville; s of John Wakefield French (d 1971), and Bessie, *née* Funston (d 1978); *b* 28 Aug 1933; *Educ* Merchant Taylor Sch Liverpool, Bristol GS, Exeter Coll Oxford (BA), Indiana Univ; *m* 31 Dec 1957, Kersti Elisabet, da of Dr Mauritz Molin, of Karlstad, Sweden; 3 s (Sean, Patrick, Karl); *Career* Nat Serv cmmnd 2 Lt Duke of Cornwall's Light Inf, seconded to The Parachute Regt 1952-54; drama critic New Statesman 1957-58, film critic London Magazine 1957-58; BBC: prodr N American Serv 1959-61, sr prodr talks and documentaries 1961-90; film critic The Observer 1978-; reg contrib: Sight and Sound, The Times Literary Supplement, Financial Times, Encounter, Movie, 20th Century; *Books* Age of Austerity 1945-51 (jt ed, 1963), The Novelist As Innovator (ed, 1965), The Movie Moguls (1969), Westerns (1974), Three Honest Men: Edmund Wilson, Lionel Trilling, F R Leavis (1981), The Third Dimension (ed, 1983); *Style—* Philip French, Esq; 62 Dartmouth Park Rd, London NW5 1SN (☎ 071 485 1711); Kärne 65590, Karlstad, Sweden

FRENCH, Ralph John; OBE; s of Alfred William French (d 1965), and Flora Regan (d 1972); *b* 22 June 1935; *Educ* Haberdashers' Aske's, Waldschulheim Breuer Aachen, Coll of Law London, Inns at Ct Sch of Law, Manchester Business Sch, Ashridge Coll Bucks; *m* 1, 1964 (m dis 1982); m 2, 1982, Rosemary Joan (Rosie), da of John Frederick Wearing (d 1974); 1 s (Rupert John Wolfe b 6 Nov 1967), 2 da (Charlotte Elizabeth b 25 Jan 1966, Juliette Louise b 22 July 1970), 2 step da; *Career* Royal Welch Fusiliers 2 Lt 1954-56, HMOCS 1957-62; called to the Bar Lincoln's Inn 1964; ICI: asst sec Plastics Div 1965-71, div sec and business res mangr Plastics Div 1971-75, head East Euro Dept Corp HQ 1975-85, dir East Euro Rels and ICI (Export) 1985-89; memb Bar Assoc for Fin Commerce and Indust 1965-, E Euro Trade Cncl BOTB 1980-89; chm: Welwyn Garden City YMCA 1967-75 (fndr memb 1965), BSCC 1980-89 (memb Cncl 1975), ldr first and second Br Trade Missons to Mongolia 1987 and 1988; Freeman City of London 1972, Freeman and Liveryman Worshipful Co of Masons 1972; 1300th Anniversary of Fndn of Bulgarian State medal 1981 (for servs Bulgaria), NY 1988 (for services to export); *Recreations* climbing, sailing, water sports, wine; *Clubs* Athenaeum; *Style—* Ralph French, Esq, OBE; 30 Addison Grove, London W4 1ER (☎ 081 995 7959)

FRENCH, Richard Martin; s of Gordon Harcourt-French (d 1985), of Cape Town, South Africa, and Charlotte Marianne, *née* Martin (d 1986); *b* 4 Oct 1939; *Educ* King Edward VII Sch Johannesburg South Africa; *m* Diana Gay, da of Philip Bates Robinson; 4 da (Jemima-Jane b 18 Nov 1965, Lucinda Joanne b 28 July 1966, Pollyanna Charlotte b 18 Sept 1968, Olivia Rose b 18 Nov 1980); *Career* dir KMP Partnership 1970, md French Gold Abbott 1970-76; chm: FCO 1977-89, Young & Rubicam London 1990-; *Style—* Richard French, Esq; Young & Rubicam Ltd, Greater London House, Hampstead Rd, London NW1 7QP (☎ 071 387 9366, fax 071 380 6570, car 0836 225 545)

FRENCH, Lady Rosemary; *née* Mackay; da of 2 Earl of Inchape (d 1939); *b* 5 Nov 1936; *m* 19 Jan 1957, Francis Martin French, s of late Francis Holroyd French; 1 s (decd), 3 da; *Style—* The Lady Rosemary French; Little Offley, Hitchin, Herts

FREND, Rev Prof William Hugh Clifford; TD (clasp); s of Rev Edwin George Clifford Frend (d 1937), of Tyneham Rectory, Dorset, and Edith Bacon (d 1966); *b* 11 Jan 1916; *Educ* Haileybury, Keble Coll Oxford (BA, DPhil, MA, DD), Univ of Cambridge (BD), Berlin Univ, Sorbonne; *m* 2 June 1951, Mary Grace, da of E A Crook (d 1984); 1 s (Simon William Clifford b 1957), 1 da (Sarah Anne b 1952); *Career* WWII asst princ WO 1940-41, Cabinet Offices 1941-42, PWE Intelligence Offr 1942-45, mil govt Austria 1945-46, 2 Lt S Queens Regt TA 1947; TA 10 Bde; 131 Bde; liaison offr vol serv Cambridge 1962-67; full time memb Ed Bd German Foreign Miny Project 1947-51, res fell Univ of Nottingham 1951-52, asst lectr then lectr in church history and doctrine Univ of Cambridge 1954-69, dir of studies in archaeology and anthropology Gonville and Caius Coll Cambridge 1961-69 (Bye fell 1952-54, asst lectr then lectr in church history and doctrine 1954-69, fell of Gonville and Caius 1956), dean of divinity Univ of Glasgow 1972-75 (prof of ecclesiastical history 1969-84); visiting prof: Univ of SA 1976, John Carroll Univ Ohio 1981; sr fell Dunbarton Oaks 1984; deacon 1982, ordained as priest 1983, non stipendiary minister St Mary's Aberfoyle 1983-84, priest i/c Barnwell Benefice 1984-90; chm AUT Scotland 1976-78, pres Cmmn International d'Histoire Ecclesiastie Comparée 1980-83; Hon DD Edinburgh 1974; FSA 1952, FRHistSoc 1954, FRSE 1979, FBA 1983; Gold Cross of Merit with Swords Polish govt in exile 1950; *Books* Martyrdom and Persecution in the Early Church (1965), Religion Popular and Unpopular in the Early Christian Centuries (1976), Rise of the Monophlysite Movement (1979), Town and Country in the Early Christian Centuries (1980), Rise of Christianity (1984), The Donatist Church (3 edn, 1985), The Early Church (4 edn, 1985), Saints and Sinners in the Early Church (3 edn 1987), Archaeology and History in the Study of Early Christianity (1988); *Recreations* romano-british archaeology; *Clubs* Authors; *Style—* Rev Prof William Frend, TD, FRSE, FSA; The Clerks Cottage, Little Wilbraham, Cambridge CB1 5LB (☎ 0223 811731)

FRERE, James Arnold; s of late Maj John Geoffrey Frere, of Rhodesia, and late Violet Ivy, *née* Sparks, who m 2 The Hon (Rothwell) Charles Wentworth Willoughby; *b* 20 April 1920; *Educ* Eton, Architectural Assoc Sch of Architecture, Trinity Coll Cambridge; *Career* Lt Intelligence Corps 1944-47; Bluemantle Pursuivant of Arms 1948-56, Chester Herald of Arms 1956-60, Officer of the Supreme Court of Judicature 1966-69, Clairvaux King of Arms Supreme Mil Order of the Temple of Jerusalem 1981- (Solemnium Rituum Magister 1982-), Rey De Armas y Cronista de Perpignan to HRH Don Roberto II 1987-89 (life Rey de Armas y Cronista de Paternò 1989, Hereditary Gentleman of the Bedchamber 1989-), Mountjoy King of Arms and Sr Judge-at-Arms Int Coll of Arms of the Noblesse 1982- (Supreme Herald-Marshal Depute 1986-), pres Royal Coll of Arms of Aragon 1987-89, King of Arms Royal Aragonese Order of St George and the Double Crown 1990-; memb: Cncl of the Surrey Archaeological Soc 1949-53, 1954-58 and 1959-63, Cncl Harleian Soc 1950-66, Cncl Museum of Costume 1953-63 (vice pres), Liveryman currently Sr Liveryman) Worshipful Co of Scriveners 1950-; Academico de Merito de la Clase de Historia summa cum laude of the Real Aula Mallorquesa 1986; FSA 1950, FRGS; Grand Cross with Collar Supreme Mil Order of the Temple of Jerusalem 1981, Grand Cross Professed Mil Order of St Agatha of Paternò 1986, Grand Cross Order of the Royal Balearic Crown 1987, Knight of Justice Aragonese Province of Our Lady of Montessa 1988, Gold Cross of Merit of Poland, Commander's Cross Polonia Restituta; *Books* The British Monarchy at Home (1961), Now...The Duchesses (1963); *Recreations* walking, music, archaeology, painting, heraldry, genealogy, visiting historic houses, travel; *Clubs* City Livery; *Style—* James A Frere, Esq, FSA; c/o Society of Antiquaries, Burlington House, Piccadilly, London W1

FRERE, Richard Burchmore; s of Harold Arthur Frere (d 1945), of Maryfield, Inverness, and formerly of Roydon Hall, Diss, Norfolk, and Finningham, Suffolk (both of which he sold 1934), and Mary Elvira Carter, *née* Harrison; the Frere family can be traced back to John Frere, of Sweffling, Suffolk, living in the reign of Henry III; Finningham was in their possession from the 17 century and Roydon Hall was purchased by Shepherd Frere in 1766 (*see* Burke's Landed Gentry, 18 edn, vol II, 1969); *b* 8 June 1922; *Educ* Inverness Acad, privately; *m* 8 Sept 1943, Joan, da of Arthur Pareezer, formerly of Hove, Sussex; 1 s (Richard Tudor b 28 Nov 1947), 2 da (Heather Stephanie b 20 Feb 1945, Jane Gwendoline b 2 Dec 1959); *Career* served rising to rank of full Corpl; WWII with RAF Motor Tport 1941-45; memb: Soc of Authors, Woodland Tst, John Muir Tst; *Books* Thoughts of a Mountaineer (1952), Maxwell's Ghost (1976), Beyond the Highland Line (1984), Loch Ness (1988), In Sympathy Austere (1989); contributor: to Scots Magazine, Scotsman, Scottish Field, Discover Scotland, Dictionary of National Biography; *Recreations* hill walking, rock climbing, gardening, DIY; *Style—* Richard Frere, Esq; Drumbuie House, Drumnadrochit, Inverness-shire (☎ 04562 210)

FRERE, Rear Adm Richard Tobias (Toby); s of Alexander Stewart Frere, CBE (d 1984), and Patricia, *née* Wallace; *b* 4 June 1938; *Educ* Eton, Britannia Royal Naval Coll; *m* 27 July 1968, Jane, da of Sir Kenneth Barraclough; 2 da (Susannah b 1971, Kate b 1974); *Career* Nat Serv 1955-56, cmmnd RN 1958, served Canada and Aust 1960-66; cmd submarines: HMS Andrew 1968, HMS Odin 1971, HMS Revenge 1978; cmd frigate HMS Brazen 1984; RCDS 1982, currently DG Gen Fleet Support; Freeman City of London 1970, Liveryman Grocers Co 1989; FBIM; *Recreations* sailing, walking; *Clubs* Garrick, MCC; *Style—* Rear Adm Toby Frere; Ministry of Defence, Main Building, Whitehall, London SW1 (☎ 071 218 9000)

FRESHWATER, Timothy George (Tim); s of George John Freshwater (d 1986), and Rosalie, *née* MacLauchlan (d 1987); *b* 21 Oct 1944; *Educ* Eastbourne Coll, Emmanuel Coll Cambridge (MA, LLB); *m* Judy, *née* Lam; *Career* Slaughter and May: joined 1967, ptnr 1975, seconded to Hong Kong office 1979-85, ptnr London (corp fin) 1985-; pres Law Soc Hong Kong 1984-85, co-chm Jt Working Party on China of Law Soc and the Bar, memb Japan Ctee Br Invisibles; *Books* The Practitioner's Guide to the City Code on Take-Overs and Mergers (contrib); *Style—* Tim Freshwater; Slaughter and May, 35 Basinghall St, London EC2V 5DB (☎ 071 600 1200, fax 071 726 0038)

FRESNES; *see*: de Fresnes

FRETER, Michael Charles Franklin; s of Leslie Charles Freter, of 1 The Browns, Sidmouth, Devon, and Myra, *née* Wilkinson; *b* 29 Oct 1947; *Educ* Whitgift Sch, St Edmund Hall Oxford (BA); *m* 2 June 1979, Jan, da of Brian Wilson, of Ealing, London; *Career* sr brand mangr Elida Gibbs Ltd 1970-76, account dir BBDO Advertising Ltd 1976-78, exec dir McCann-Erickson Advertising Ltd 1988- (joined 1978, dir 1980-); *Style—* Michael Freter, Esq; 17 Beaufort Close, Lynden Gate, Putney Heath, London SW15; McCann-Erickson Ltd, 36 Howland St, London W1

FRETWELL, Sir (Major) John (Emsley); GCMG (1987, KCMG 1982, CMG 1975); s of Francis Thomas Fretwell, of Chesterfield; *b* 15 June 1930; *Educ* Chesterfield GS, Univ of Lausanne, King's Coll Cambridge; *m* 1959, Mary Ellen Eugenie, da of Frederick Charles Dubois; 1 s, 1 da; *Career* Army 1948-50; joined FO 1953, served Hong Kong and Peking, first sec Moscow 1959-62, FO 1962-67, first sec (commercial) Washington 1967-70, cnsllr (commercial) Warsaw 1971-73, head EID 1973-76, asst under sec FCO 1976-79, min Washington 1980-81, ambass France 1982-87, political dir FCO 1987-90; memb Cncl of Lloyd's 1991-; *Style—* Sir John Fretwell, GCMG

FREUD, Sir Clement Raphael; s of Ernst L Freud (d 1970), and Lucie, *née* Brasch (d 1989); bro of Lucian Freud, *qv* (gs of Prof Sigmund Freud); *b* 24 April 1924; *Educ* Dartington Hall, St Paul's; *m* Sept 1950, June Beatrice (Jill), 2 da of H W Flewett; 2 s (Dominic Martin b 11 Nov 1958, Matthew Rupert b 2 Nov 1963), 2 da (Nicola Mary b 24 Oct 1951, Emma Vallencey b 25 Jan 1962); *Career* Royal Ulster Rifles 1942-47, liaison off Int Mil Tribunal Nüremberg 1946-47; writer, broadcaster, rector Dundee Univ 1974-80, MP (Lib) Isle of Ely 1973-1983, sponsor Official Info Bill 1978-79; MP (Lib) NE Cambridgeshire 1983-87; Master Open Univ 1989; kt 1987; *Books* Grimble (1968), Grimble at Christmas (1973), Freud on Food (1978), Book of Hangovers (1981), Below the Belt (1983), No-One Else Has Complained (1988); *Clubs* MCC, Br Rail Staff Assoc, March, Groucho's; *Style—* Sir Clement Freud; 22 Wimpole St, London W1 (☎ 071 580 2222)

FREUD, Lucian; CH (1983); s of Ernst L Freud (d 1970), and Lucie, *née* Brasch (d 1989); bro of Sir Clement Freud, *qv*; *b* 8 Dec 1922; *Educ* Central Sch of Art, E Anglian Sch of Painting and Drawing; *m* 1, 1948 (m dis 1952), Kathleen Garman, da of Jacob Epstein; 2 da; m 2, 1953 (m dis 1957), Lady Caroline Maureen Blackwood, da of 4 Marquess of Dufferin and Ava (*see* Lowell, Lady Caroline); *Career* ordinary seaman SS Baltrover 1942; painter; teacher Slade Sch of Art 1948-58; visiting asst Norwich Sch of Art 1964-65; exhibitions: Lefevre Gallery 1944 and 1946, London Gallery 1947 and 1948, British Cncl and Galerie René Drouin Paris 1948, Hanover Gallery 1950 and 1952, British Cncl and Vancouver Art Coll 1951, British Cncl Venice Biennale 1954, Marlborough Fine Art 1958, 1963 and 1968, Anthony d'Offay 1972, 1978 and 1982, first retrospective (Hayward Gallery, then Bristol, Birmingham and Leeds) 1974, Nishimura Gallery Tokyo 1979, Thomas Agnew & Sons 1983, second retrospective (British Cncl, Hirshhorn Museum and Sculpture Garden, Smithsonian Inst Washington DC Sept-Nov 1987, Musée National d'Art Moderne Paris 1987-88, Hayward Gallery Feb-April 1988, Neue Nationalgalerie Berlin May-June 1988, Scottish Nat Gallery of Modern Art Edinburgh July-Oct 1988), works on paper retrospective exhibition (Ashmolean Museum Oxford May-June 1988, The Fruitmarket Gallery Edinburgh June-July 1988, Ferens Art Gallery Hull July-Aug 1988, Walker Art Gallery Liverpool Sept-Oct 1988, Royal Albert Memorial Museum Exeter Oct-Nov 1988, The Fine Arts Museum of San Francisco USA 1988, Minneapolis Inst of Art USA March-April 1989, Brooke Alexander Gallery NY May- July 1989, Cleveland Museum of Art July-Sept 1989); works in public collections: Tate Gallery, Nat Portrait Gallery, V & A Museum, Arts Cncl of GB, British Museum, British Cncl, DoE, Cecil Higgins Museum Bedford, Fitzwilliam Museum Cambridge, Nat Museum of Wales Cardiff, Scottish Nat Gallery of Modern Art Edinburgh, Hartlepool Art Gallery, Walker Art Gallery Liverpool, Univ of Liverpool, City Art Coll and Whitworth Gallery Manchester, Ashmolean Museum of Art Oxford, Harris Museum and Art Gallery Preston, Rochdale Art Gallery, Southampton Art Gallery, Queensland Art Gallery Brisbane, Art Gallery of S Australia Adelaide, Art Gallery of Western Australia Perth, Musée Nationale d'Art Moderne Pompidou Centre Paris, The Art Inst of Chicago, Beaverbrook Fndn Fredericton, Museum of Modern Art NY, Cleveland Museum of Art Ohio, Museum of Art Carnegie Inst Pittsburgh, Achenbaach Fndn for Graphic Arts ande Fine Arts Museum San Francisco, The Saint Louis Art Museum, Hirshhorn Museum and Sculpture Garden, Smithsonian Inst Washington DC; hon memb American Acad and Inst of Arts and Letters 1988; *Style—* Lucian Freud, Esq, CH; c/o James Kirkman Ltd, 46 Brompton Square, London SW3 2AF (☎ 071 589 4328, fax 071 823 7102)

FREW, Dr Iain David Owen; s of Hugh Wallace Owen Frew (d 1965), of Giffnock, Renfrewshire, and Annie Blanche Elizabeth, *née* Keillor (d 1975); *b* 1 June 1936; *Educ* Hutcheson's Boys GS, Univ of Glasgow (MB ChB, MD); *m* 13 Oct 1962, Wilma Croll, da of William Arthur, MBE (d 1983); 2 s (Colin b 1968, Alastair b 1970), 2 da (Elaine b 1965, Linda b 1967); *Career* house offr Glasgow Royal Infirmary 1959-60; Dept of Pathology: Glasgow Victoria Infirmary 1960-65, Newcastle Gen Hosp 1965-67; Dept of Haematology Good Hope Hosp Sutton Coldfield 1967-; co organiser: Inter Regnl Quality Assurance Scheme (B 12, Folate) 1978-, W Mids Regnl Quality Assur Scheme (haematology) 1978-; chm W Mids Regn Working Pty for Devpt of Blood Bank Computer System 1981-89; memb various nat and W Mids ctees of United Reformed Church; *Books* A Chronology of the Electric Railways of Great Britain and Ireland (1979); *Recreations* a study of the history of urban transport throughout the world; *Style—* Dr Iain Frew; Department of Haematology, Good Hope Hospital, Sutton Coldfield, West Mids (☎ 021 378 2211); Department of Pathology, Little Aston Hospital, Sutton Coldfield, W Mids

FREWER, Richard John Barrett; s of Dr Edward George Frewer (d 1972), and Bridget Audrey Christina Pennefather, *née* Ford, of Etwall, Derbys; *b* 24 Jan 1942; *Educ* Shrewsbury, Gonville and Caius Coll Cambridge (MA), AA (Dip Arch); *m* 19 July 1969, Carolyn Mary, da of Thomas Arthur Butler (d 1969); 1 da (Emelye b 1971); *Career* architect, Arup Assocs 1966- (ptnr 1977); major works incl: Sir Thomas White Bldg, St John's Coll Oxford (with Sir Philip Dowson), Theatre Royal Glasgow, Liverpool Gardon Festival Hall, Baburgh DC Offs Suffolk, Stockley Park Arena Heathrow; prof of architecture Univ of Bath; pt/t professional tenor soloist, Bach Specialist, Lieder and Oratorio repertoire; memb: Cncl RSCM, RIBA Educn Bd, Bursary Jury RSA; RIBA, FRSA; *Recreations* painting, music; *Style—* Prof Richard Frewer; Avebury Cottage, High St, Fulbourn, Cambs; Arup Associates, 2-4 Dean St, London W11 (☎ 071 734 8494, fax 071 439 1457); Dept of Architecture and Building Engineering, University of Bath, Claverton Down, Bath BA2 7AY

FREWIN, Dr Tom; s of Noel Frewin, and Sylvia Maud, *née* Lindsey, of Kent; *b* 9 Dec 1946; *Educ* Borden GS, Univ of Bristol (MB ChB); *m* 12 Dec 1970, Susan Elizabeth, da of Anthony George Williams, of Gwent; 2 s (Charles b 1971, Hugo b 1980), 2 da (Joanna b 1973, Alice b 1976); *Career* med practitioner; *Style—* Dr Tom Frewin; 13 Mortimer Rd, Clifton, Bristol BS8 4EY (☎ 0272 736407); 52 Clifton Down Rd, Clifton, Bristol BS8 4AH (☎ 0272 732178)

FREYBERG, 2 Baron (UK 1951); Col Paul Richard Freyberg; OBE (Mil 1965), MC (1945); s of 1 Baron Freyberg, VC, GCMG, KCB, KBE, DSO and 3 bars (d 1963), and Barbara, GBE (d 1973), da of Sir Herbert Jekyll, KCMG, niece of Getrude Jekyll and widow of Hon Francis Walter Stafford MacLaren, MP, s of 1 Baron Aberconway, KC; *b* 27 May 1923; *Educ* Eton; *m* 23 July 1960, Ivry Perronelle Katharine, o da of late Cyril Harrower Guild, of Aspall Hall, nr Debenham, Suffolk; 1 s, 3 da; *Heir* s, Hon Valerian Bernard Freyberg b 15 Dec 1970; *Career* Col late Grenadier Gds; with New Zealand Expeditionary Force 1940-42, with Grenadier Gds 1942-45, AAG HQ London Dist 1962-65, cmd HAC Inf Bn 1965-68, on Defence Policy Staff MOD 1968-71, dir Volunteers Territorials and Cadets 1971-75, Col Gen Staff 1975-78; *Books* Bernard Freyberg VC (1991); *Style—* Col the Rt Hon Lord Freyberg, OBE, MC; Munstead House, Godalming, Surrey (☎ 0483 146004)

FREYD, Michael; s of Cecil Freyd (d 1971), and Joan, *née* Woodhead (d 1960); *b* 5 June 1948; *Educ* Burnage GS Manchester, Univ of Hull (BSc); *m* 21 March 1971, Marilyn Sharon (Lyn), da of Ivor Paul Levinson (d 1960); 1 s (Mark b 29 Aug 1979), 2 da (Danielle b 14 June 1972, Elana b 7 May 1976); *Career* UBS Phillips & Drew (formerly Phillips & Drew) 1969-: ptnr 1980, currently dir (appointed to Option Ctee 1986); memb: United Synagogue Investmt Ctee, Soc of Investmt Analysts; *Recreations* golf, skiing, bridge, chess; *Style—* Michael Freyd, Esq; UBS Phillips & Drew, 100 Liverpool St, London EC2M 2RH (☎ 071 901 3333)

FRICKER, Alan Derek; s of late Norman Fricker, OBE; *b* 20 June 1924; *Educ* Charterhouse, Trinity Coll Oxford; *m* 1950, Margaret Mary, *née* Snelgrove; 2 s, 4 da; *Career* called to the Bar 1949; ret; dir Cawoods Solid Fuels Ltd; *Recreations* sailing, fishing, walking; *Clubs* Naval, New (Cheltenham); *Style—* A D Fricker, Esq; The Cottage, Mill St, Prestbury, Cheltenham, Glos (☎ 0242 244 555)

FRICKER, Colin Frank; s of Frank Charles Fricker (d 1989), and Hilda Emily, *née* Ingle (d 1955); *b* 9 April 1936; *Educ* Dulwich, Univ of London (LLB); *m* 20 June 1964, Elizabeth Ann Brooke, da of John Douglas Skinner, of Eastleigh, Hants; 2 s (Henry b and d 1975, Robert), 1 da (Annabel); *Career* Nat Serv RAF 1954-56; asst dir C E

Heath Home Ltd 1968-70, dir Assoc of Br Launderers & Cleaners 1979-84, ldr employers' side of Laundry Wages Cncl 1979-84, dir gen Br Direct Mktg Assoc 1985-; memb Cncl CBI 1979-84; Freeman: City of London, Worshipful Co of Launderers 1979; FCII 1960; *Recreations* cricket, rugby, genealogy; *Clubs* MCC; *Style—* Colin Fricker, Esq; c/o BDMA, 35 Grosvenor Gardens, London SW1W OBS (☎ 071 630 7322, fax 071 828 7125, telex 8951182

FRICKER, (Anthony) Nigel; QC (1977); s of late Dr William Shapland Fricker, and Margaret, *née* Skinner; *b* 7 July 1937; *Educ* King's Sch Chester, Univ of Liverpool (LLB); *m* 1960, Marilynn Ann, da of August L Martin, of Pennsylvania, USA; 1 s (Joseph b 1969), 2 da (Deborah b 1962, Susan b 1964); *Career* barr; prosecuting counsel to DHSS Wales and Chester Circuit (North) 1975-77, rec Crown Court 1975-84, asst cmmr Boundary Cmmn Wales 1981-84; circuit judge Yorks 1984-; author of articles in legal jls; *Books* Family Courts: Emergency Remedies and Procedures (gen ed and jt author, 1990); articles in Civil Justice Quarterly and 2nd Family Law periodical; *Clubs* Yorkshire (York); *Style—* His Honour Judge Fricker, QC; 6 Park Square, Leeds LS1 2LW (☎ 0532 459763)

FRICKERS, Gordon Stuart Allen; s of Capt Alan Frickers (d 1988), and Winnifred Anne Frickers; *b* 25 May 1949; *Educ* Broomham, South Bromley Coll, Maidstone Coll of Art, Medway Coll of Art (Dip Visual Communications), Falmouth Tech Coll; *m* m 26 Nov 1983, Patricia Eileen, da of George Winterburn, of Brentwood, Old Swan, Liverpool; 1 s (Aaron b 9 June 1987), 1 da (Hannah b 24 Aug 1985); *Career* photographer advertising and press 1971-74, md SE Boatbuilders Ltd 1975-79; artist and painter (marine/aviation); assignments incl: Virgin Atlantic Challenge II for Richard Branson 1986, The Schooner Vagrant for Peter de Savery 1987, America's Cup Challenge for Blue Arrow 1988, Sumaili for Robin Knox Johnston 1989, Royal Soc for Nature Conservation, BT (Marine) Ltd, Robin Knox-Johnston, Peter De Savaray, Richard Branson, The Clipper Ship Cutty Sark, The Brig Maria Asumpta, The Nat Tst, Blue Arrow America's Cup Challenge, Imperial Tobacco (won award), Royal Plymouth Corinthian Yacht Club; work displayed at Buckingham Palace 1989, first ltd edn published The Times of London 1989; reg contribs to magazines; memb: Nat Scorpion Assoc 1973-79, Soc Nautical Res, World Ship Soc, Nat Maritime Historical Soc of USA, Steamship Historical Soc of USA, WWF; *Recreations* sailing, travel, historical research (marine); *Clubs* Royal Plymouth Corinthian Yacht; *Style—* Gordon Frickers, Esq; Lakeside Studio, 94 Radford Park Rd, Plymstock, Devon PL9 9DX (☎ 0752 403344)

FRIDD, Nicholas Timothy; s of Norman Sidney Fridd, of Withenfield, West Quantoxhead, Somerset, and Beryl Rosamond, *née* Phillips; *b* 21 Sept 1953; *Educ* Wells Blue Sch, ChCh Oxford (MA); *m* 14 Sept 1985, Fiona Bridgnell, da of Keir Mackessack-Leitch, of Chart House, Bloxham, Oxon; 1 s (John Bridgnell b 2 Nov 1989), 1 da (Charlotte Mary b 11 Jan 1988); *Career* called to the Bar Inner Temple 1975; *Books* Basic Practice in Courts and Tribunals (1989); *Recreations* carpentry, walking disused railways; *Style—* Nicholas Fridd, Esq; 105 Netheravon Rd South, Chiswick, London W4 2PZ (☎ 081 994 2307/9227); Bell Yard Chambers, 16 Bell Yard, London WC2A 2JR (☎ 071 306 9292, fax 071 404 5143)

FRIEBE, John Percy; s of Charles Friebe (d 1962); *b* 9 May 1931; *Educ* Glasgow HS, Univ of Glasgow; *m* 1966, Laura Mary, da of Archibald Fleming (d 1961); *Career* mktg dir: Smith and MacLaurin Ltd 1958-64, Millard Brothers Ltd 1964-70; gp md Stoddard Holdings plc 1970-83, md Carpets International (UK) 1984-85 (mktg dir 1983-84); dir: Carpets International plc 1984-86, John Crowther Group plc 1985-86; chm Kuninklijke Vereenigde Tapijtfabrieken NV 1989-90; Fleming Friebe Assoc; vice chm Intersport GB Ltd 1986; MICAS, FICMA; *Recreations* golf, gardening; *Style—* John P Friebe, Esq; Hunters Heights, Uphampton, Ombersley, Worcs (☎ 0905 620 854)

FRIEDBERGER, Maj-Gen John Peter William; CB (1991), CBE (1986, MBE 1975); s of Brig John Cameron Friedberger, DSO (d 1971), and Phyllis, *née* Daniels (d 1971); *b* 27 May 1937; *Educ* Wellington, Sandhurst; *m* 13 Aug 1966, Joanna Mary, da of Andrew Thorne, ERD; 1 s (Richard b 1973), 2 da (Rosanna b 1967, Lucinda b 1970); *Career* cmmnd 10 Royal Hussars (PWO) 1956; served: Jordan, Germany, S Arabia; seconded Northern Frontier Regt Sultan's Armed Forces Oman 1961-63, RMCS Science 1968, Aust Army Staff Coll 1969, MOD 1970-72, Brig Major 8 Brig 1973-75, CO Royal Hussars (PWO) 1975-78, Royal Coll of Def Studies 1978-79, seconded cdr Royal Brunei Armed Forces 1982-86, administrator Sovereign Base Areas and cdr Br Forces Cyprus 1988-90; DPKT (Brunei) 1984; *Recreations* travel; *Clubs* Cavalry and Guards'; *Style—* Maj-Gen John Friedberger, CB, CBE

FRIEDMAN, David Peter; QC (1990); s of Wilfred Emanuel Freidman (d 1973), and Rosa, *née* Lees (d 1972); *b* 1 June 1944; *Educ* Tiffin Boy's Sch, Lincoln Coll Oxford (BCL, MA); *m* 29 Oct 1972, Sara Geraldine, da of Dr Sidney Linton; *Career* called to the Bar 1968; *Recreations* good food (cooked by others), reading, computer programming; *Clubs* Landsdowne; *Style—* David P Friedman, Esq, QC; 3 Paper Buildings, Temple, London EC4Y 7EU (☎ 071 583 1183, fax 071 583 2037)

FRIEND, Bernard Ernest; CBE (1986); s of Richard Friend (d 1972), and Ada Florence Friend (d 1952); *b* 18 May 1924; *Educ* Dover GS; *m* 1951, Pamela Florence, da of Frederick Henry Amor Alcester; 1 s (Nigel Andrew b 1963), 2 da (Gillian Diana b 1952, Penelope Elaine b 1955); *Career* Flying Offr RAF 1943-47; CA; dir Br Aerospace plc 1977-89; non-exec dir: Iron Trades Gp 1981, SD-Scicon plc, Ballast Nedam BV, Bellest Nedan Construction Ltd; chm: Brooke Engineering Holdings plc, Grahams Rintoul Investment Trust; memb Cncl Br Assoc for Advancement of Sci; FCA; *Recreations* cricket; *Clubs* RAF, RAC, MCC; *Style—* Bernard Friend, Esq, CBE; 27 Archer House, Vicarage Crescent, London SW11 3LF

FRIEND, Carol Anne; da of Leslie George Friend, of London, and Ida Margaret, *née* Earl; *b* 11 Sept 1949; *Educ* Tiffins Girls GS Kingston upon Thames, St Johns Coll of Further Educn Manchester (HND, DipCAM); *Career* dir Wyndham Public Relations 1977-80, md Pielle and Co Ltd 1980-; chm Orbit Cromwell Housing Assoc 1984-86, govr CAM Fndn 1985-, pres The Inst of Public Relations 1986, memb PO Users Nat Cncl 1987-90; chm London W End PO and Telecommunications Advsy Ctees 1987-; tstee PR Educn Tst (chm Educn and Trg Ctee) 1989-, memb CBI London Region Cncl 1990-; FIPR 1987; *Style—* Miss Carol Friend; Pielle and Company Limited, Museum House, Museum St, London WC1A 1JT (☎ 071 323 1587, fax 071 631 0029)

FRIEND, Lionel; s of Norman Alfred Child Friend, of Kingston upon Thames, Surrey, and Moya Lilian, *née* Dicks; *b* 13 March 1945; *Educ* Royal GS High Wycombe, RCM, London Opera Centre; *m* 1969, Jane, da of Norman Edward Hyland; 1 s (Toby Thomas b 1984), 2 da (Clea Deborah b 1972, Corinne Jane b 1977); *Career* conductor WNO 1969-72, Glyndebourne Festival and Touring Opera 1969-72; 2 kapellmeister Staatstheater Kassel Germany 1972-75; staff conductor ENO 1976-89; music dir: Nexus Opera 1981-, New Sussex Opera 1989-; guest conductor: Philharmonia, City of Birmingham Symphony Orch, BBC Symphony Orch, Orchestre National de France, Nouvel Orchestre Philharmonique, Austrian Radio Symphony Orch, Swedish Radio Symphony Orch, Hungarian State Symphony Orch, Budapest Symphony Orch, Scot Chamber Orch, London Sinfonietta, Nash Ensemble, and other orchs and ensembles abroad; recordings incl: The World's Winter(Payne), Songs (Bliss), Le Bal Masqué, Chansons de Bilitis, The Great Journey (Matthews), Variations Symphony 1 (Milner), Symphony 3 (Brian), L'histoire du Soldat, Sinfonietta (Durkó), Sonata (Soaster); *Recreations* reading, theatre; *Style—* Lionel Friend, Esq; 136 Rosendale Road, London SE21 8LG (☎ 081 761 7845); Allied Artists, 42 Montpelier Square, London SW7 1SZ (☎ 071 589 6243, fax 071 581 5269)

FRIEND, Martyn Patrick; s of Philip Wyndham Friend (d 1987), and Eileen Marion Adams, *née* Erskine; *b* 23 Nov 1942; *Educ* Steyning GS, Hertford Coll Oxford (BA); *m* 1968 (m dis 1980), Nicole June, *née* Hamilton-Fletcher; 2 da (Cassandra Maria b 28 May 1973, Emily Alice Louisa b 24 Nov 1977); *Career* freelance TV and film director; ITV and BBC: researcher and writer 1964, formerly floor manager prodn mangr and asst dir; dir BBC 1973-76 (incl Onedin Line, Softly Softly), freelance TV video and film dir 1976-; film credits incl: The Voyage of Charles Darwin 1978, Sweet Nothings 1980, Fair Stood The Wind for France 1981, Shackleton 1987, Anna of the Five Towns 1984, The Daughter in Law 1985, The Daily Woman 1985, All Passion Spent 1986, 4.50 from Paddington 1987, Summer's Lease 1989, Survival of the Fittest 1990; TV credits incl: first episode of Bergerac 1980, first episode of Campion 1988; winner: BAFTA award 1978, RTS award 1986; twice BAFTA nominee; memb: BAFTA 1980, Dirs Guild of GB 1987; *Recreations* theatre, film, walking, photography, music, travelling; *Style—* Martyn Friend, Esq; c/o Peters Fraser & Dunlop, The Chambers, Chelsea Harbour, Lots Road, London SW10 OXF (☎ 071 376 7676, fax 071 352 7356)

FRIEND, Peter Henry; s of Henry Eugene Friend, and Anne, *née* Richards; *b* 1 Oct 1950; *Educ* Colfe's GS; *m* 8 Nov 1980, Christine Megan, da of William Herbert Hames, of London; 2 da (Aimi Christina b 29 June 1981, Lucy Amanda b 16 Oct 1982); *Career* CA; audit mangr Hill Vellacott 1969-74, controller of ops and fin Salomon Bros Int Ltd 1974-78, mangr ops Salomon Bros New York 1979-80, vice pres ops planning and control Merrill Lynch Int Co 1980-83, exec dir ops Goldman Sachs Int Ltd 1983-; dir: Goldman Sachs Government Securities (UK) Ltd, Goldman Sachs Equity Securities (UK) Ltd; FCA; *Style—* Peter H Friend, Esq

FRIEND, Dame Phyllis Muriel; DBE (1980, CBE 1972); da of Richard Edward Friend; *b* 28 Sept 1922; *Educ* Herts & Essex HS Bishop's Stortford, London Hosp (SRN), Royal Coll Nursing (RNT); *Career* dep matron St George's Hosp 1956-59; chief nursing offr: London Hosp 1969-72 (matron 1961-68, dep matron 1959-61), DHSS 1972-82; *Style—* Dame Phyllis Friend, DBE; Barnmead, Start Hill, Bishop's Stortford, Herts (☎ 0279 654873)

FRIER, Dr Brian Murray; s of William Murray Frier, of Edinburgh, and Christina Roper, *née* Anderson; *b* 28 July 1947; *Educ* George Heriot's Sch Edinburgh, Univ of Edinburgh (BSc, MB ChB, MD); *m* 25 Oct 1985, Isobel Margaret, da of Dr Henry Donald Wilson, of Edinburgh; 1 da (Emily Margaret b 15 Nov 1989); *Career* jr med appts Edinburgh 1972-74, med registrar Dundee 1974-76, res fell in diabetes and metabolism Cornell Univ NY 1976-77, sr med registrar Edinburgh 1978-82; conslt physician: W Infirmary and Gartnavel Gen Hosp Glasgow 1982-87, Royal Infirmary Edinburgh 1987-; author of numerous papers on diabetes and hypoglycaemia; memb: Br Diabetic Assoc (RD Lawrence lectr 1986), Assoc of Physicians GB and I, Scot Soc of Physicians; FRCPE 1984, FRCP (Glasgow) 1986; govr George Heriot's Tst Edinburgh; *Recreations* history (ancient and modern), appreciation of the arts; *Style—* Dr Brian M Frier; 100 Morningside Drive, Edinburgh EH10 5NT (☎ 031 447 1653); Royal Infirmary of Edinburgh, Lauriston Place, Edinburgh EH3 9YW (☎ 031 229 2477)

FRIER, (Gavin Austin) Garry; s of Gavin Walter Rae Frier (d 1985), and Isabel Fraser, *née* Austin (d 1981); *b* 18 May 1953; *Educ* Hutchesons' Boys Glasgow, Univ of Strathclyde (BA); *m* 1978, Jane Carolyn, da of John Keith Burton, of Glasgow; 1 s (Stuart Austin b 1981); *Career* CA; dir County Bank Ltd (renamed Co Natwest Ltd) 1985-87, currently fin dir Ferrum Hldgs plc; memb Scot Inst of CAs 1978; *Recreations* tennis, shooting, photography; *Clubs* Western (Glasgow); *Style—* Garry Frier, Esq; Old Carpenters, Dares Lane, Ewshot, nr Farnham, Surrey GU10 5BS (☎ 0252 850 401); Ferrum Holdings plc, Brettenham House, Lancaster Place, London WC2E 7EN (☎ 071 379 5190)

FRIGGENS, William Godfrey; *b* 18 Aug 1926; *Educ* UCL (BSc); *m* 1, 1946, Betty Eileen Swinnerton (decd); 2 s; m 2, 1981, Janet Patricia Gunn; 1 da; *Career* dir: Manufacturers Equipment Co Ltd 1960-68, J H Fenner & Co Ltd 1962-68, Mastabar Mining Equipment Co 1962-68, Pioneer Laura NV (Holland) 1964-68, Rapistan Lande NV (Holland) 1964-71, Fenner GmbH 1964-68, J H Fenner & Co Holdings Ltd 1965-68, Pioneer Oilsealing & Moulding Co Ltd 1962-71, F Pratt Engineering Corporation plc 1969-84, Pratt Burnerd International Ltd 1969-84, Crawford Collets Ltd 1969-84, Pratt Woodworth Ltd 1970-84, Precor Investments Ltd 1970-84, Precor VB 1979-84, Jiltward Ltd 1981-84, Trojan Structures Ltd 1983-84, Prenco Products Ltd 1984-, Prenco Dairy Products Ltd 1984, Engrg Ind Trg Bd 1985-88; CEng, MIEE, FIMechE; *Recreations* swimming, tennis, reading, music; *Style—* William Friggens, Esq; Trevelyan, 17 Greenhill Rd, Farnham, Surrey GU9 8JP

FRINK, Dame Elisabeth Jean; DBE (1982, CBE 1969); *b* 14 Nov 1930; *Educ* Convent of the Holy Family Exmouth, Guildford Sch of Art, Chelsea Sch of Art; *m* 1, 1955 (m dis 1963), Michel Jammet; 1 s; m 2, 1968 (m dis 1974), Edward Pool, MC; m 3, 1974, Alexander Csáky; *Career* RA 1977 (ARA 1971); sculptor; tstee British Museum 1975-90, memb Royal Fine Art Cmmn 1976-81; Hon Doctorate: Univ of Surrey 1977, Univ of Manchester 1990; Hon DUniv: Open Univ 1983, Cambridge 1988, Exeter 1988; Hon DLitt Warwick 1983; awarded Doctorate RCA 1982; Hon Doctorate: Oxford 1989, Keele 1989; *Style—* Dame Elisabeth Frink, DBE; Woolland, Blandford, Dorset

FRISBY, Simon Rollo; s of Lt-Col Lionel Claud Frisby, DSO, MC (d 1936), of Farleigh Valoynes, Farleigh Wallop, Basingstoke, Hants, and Angela Beryl, *née* Hoare; *b* 23 Oct 1933; *Educ* Ludgrove Sch, Eton; *m* 29 Sept 1959, (Sara) Belinda, da of Capt William Herbert Fox (ka 1940), of Adbury Park, Newbury, Berks; 1 s (Richard b 1961), 2 da (Angela (Mrs Wolrige Gordon) b 1963, Caroline (Mrs Henson) (twin) b 1963); *Career* Lt short serv cmmn Coldstream Guards 1952-56; C Hoare & Co Bankers 1956-57, ptnr: David A Bevan Simpson & Co 1968 (joined 1957), De Zoete & Bevan 1970-86, Barclays de Zoete Wedd 1986-90; memb London Stock Exchange 1963; *Recreations* fishing, gardening; *Clubs* Cavalry and Guards', MCC, Worplesdon Golf; *Style—* Simon Frisby, Esq; Bramley Grange, Bramley, Basingstoke, Hants RG26 5DJ (☎ 0256 881245); 59 Rosaville Rd, London SW6 (☎ 071 381 0918)

FRISBY, Terence Peter Michael; s of William Alfred Frisby (d 1967), of Borough Green, Kent, and Kathleen Campbell Day, *née* Caseley; *b* 28 Nov 1932; *Educ* Dartford GS, Central Sch of Speech Trg and Dramatic Art; *m* 28 Aug 1963 (m dis 1971), Christine, da of Luigi Vecchione; 1 s (Dominic b 9 Sept 1969); *Career* playwright, actor, dir, prodr (over 200 acting and directing roles in theatre, TV, film, West End and rep for over 32 years); most notable prodn Woza Albert (Criterion) 1983-84; published plays: The Subtopians (1964), There's A Girl In My Soup (1967, filmed 1971 starring Peter Sellers and Goldie Hawn, winner Writers' Guild of GB award for Best Br Comedy 1971), The Bandwagon (1970), It's All Right If I Do It (1977), Seaside Postcard (1978); radio play Just Remember Two Things: It's Not Fair And Don't Be Late (1989, winner Giles Couper award); many TV plays incl: Blackmail, Guilty, Don't Forget The Basics; two TV series: Lucky Feller (LWT 1976), That's Love (TVS 1988-90); acting roles in theatre incl: A Christmas Carol (1978), Rookery Nook (1979), The Real Inspector Hound (1983-84), The Entertainer (1984), Hay Fever (1985), Once A Catholic (1986); TV roles incl: Two Townsmen, When The Boys Come Out

To Play, The Brothers, A Strike Out of Time; memb: Writers' Guild of GB, Equity; *Style*— Terence Frisby, Esq

FRISCHMANN, Wilem William; CBE; s of Lajos Frischmann (d 1944), of Hungary, and Nelly Frischmann (d 1945); *Educ* Hammersmith Coll of Art and Building, Imperial Coll of Sci and Technol (DIC), City Univ of London (PhD); *m* 1 Sept 1957, Sylvia, da of Maurice Elvey (d 1980), of Glasgow; 1 s (Richard Sandor), 1 da (Justine Elinor); *Career* CJ Pell & Partners 1956-68 (ptr 1961-68), sr ptnr Pell Frischmann & Ptnrs 1968-, chm Pell Frischmann Group 1984-; FEng, FCGI, FIStructE, MConsE, MASCE; MSISdeFr; *Recreations* tennis, swimming, skiing; *Clubs* Arts; *Style*— Dr Wilem Frischmann, CBE; Haversham Grange, Haversham Close, Twickenham TW1 2JP; 5 Manchester Square, London W1A 1AU (☎ 071 486 3661, fax 071 487 4153, telex 21536 Consec G)

FRITH, John William Gabriel; s of Canon Herbert Charles Frith (d 1953), of Chichester, and Nora Frith, *née* Gabain (d 1974); *b* 25 March 1925; *Educ* Marlborough, Magdalene Coll Cambridge; *m* 21 June 1952, Cherry Jill, da of Frank Anthony Dorset Challoner, of Blackheath (d 1954); 2 s (Simon b 1955, Michael b 1957), 1 da (Gillian b 1953); *Career* Lt RNVR 1943-47; CA; fin dir C J Clark Ltd 1963-85, memb Cncl Inst Chartered Accountants 1966-74; tstee Wells Cathedral Preservation Tst, treas Friends Wells Cathedral; chm: Somerset Health Authy 1977-82, St Margarets Hospice Somerset, Malvern Girls Coll; *Recreations* walking, gardening; *Style*— John W G Frith, Esq; 35 New Street, Wells BA5 2LE (☎ 0749 73221); 5 Market Place, Wells BA5 2RF (☎ 0749 74241)

FRITH, Stanley William; s of Reuben Stanley Frith, and Isabella Evelyn, *née* Bilke; *b* 15 July 1943; *Educ* Southern Methodist Univ (MBA); *m* 17 June 1972, Gillian Anne, da of Lt-Col W W Bailey; 2 s (Jason Anthony b 22 March 1976, Rory Nicholas b 8 Jan 1981); *Career* accountant 1964-66, chief accountant GS Int SA Tripoli Libya 1966-70, fin controller GSI (Singapore) Pte 1970-73, gp fin controller Texas Instruments Dallas USA 1973-78, personnel dir Texas Instruments (UK) Ltd 1978-81, euro personnel dir Texas Instruments HQ Nice France 1981-85, gp personnel dir House of Fraser plc 1985-91; patron Christian Childrens Fund; memb Chartered Inst of Secs and Admins; *Books* The Expatriate Dilemma (1978), A Step in the Right Direction (1981); *Style*— Stanley Frith, Esq

FRIZZELL, Colin Frazer; s of Thomas Norman Frizzell (d 1976), of Grosvenor House Hotel, London, and Susanna Alice Clogh, *nèe* Boyd (d 1979); *b* 8 April 1939; *Educ* Oundle; *m* 9 June 1962, Anna Georgina, da of Thomas Stewart-Johnstone (d 1986); 2 da (Nicola b 1963, Sarah b 1965); *Career* Lt Royal Fusiliers 1958-59; chm The Frizzell Group Ltd (with the Gp 1957-); Insur Brokers and Fin Servs and at Lloyds; *Recreations* fly-fishing, golf, music; *Clubs* Royal and Ancient Golf (St Andrews); *Style*— Colin Frizzell, Esq; Chuffs House, Holyport, Maidenhead, Berkshire SL6 2NA (☎ 0628 20827); Frizzell House, 14-22 Elder St, London E1 6DF (☎ 071 247 6595, telex 8811077, fax 071 377 9114, car 0836 340333)

FRODSHAM, Anthony Freer; CBE (1978); s of George William Frodsham (d 1929), and (Constance) Violet, *née* Neild (d 1949); descendant of Charles Frodsham (1810-71), the London clockmaker; *b* 8 Sept 1919; *Educ* Ecole Lacordaire Paris, Faraday House Engrg Coll London (DFH); *m* 1953, Patricia Myfanwy, da of Cdr A H Wynne-Edwards, DSC, RN (d 1971); 2 s (Simon, David); *Career* Lt (E) RN 1940-46, served in China, E Indies and Med (despatches); mgmnt conslt, chartered engr and co dir; chief exec P-E Consulting Gp 1963-72; dir: Tace plc 1973-75, UDT Industs Ltd 1973-75, F Pratt Engineering Corp 1982-85, Greyfriars Ltd 1984-87; conducted study for MOD on the provision of Engr Offrs for the Armed Forces 1983; dir gen Engrg Employers' Fedn 1975-82, ind chm Int Compressed Air and Allied Machinery Ctee 1977-, vice chm Br Export Fin Advsy Cncl 1982-87; chm: Mgmnt Conslts Assoc 1968-70, Machine Tools EDC 1973-79, Advsy Ctee Euro Business Inst 1982-; pres: Inst of Mgmnt Conslts 1966-68, Inst of Linguists 1986-89; memb: Engrg Indust Trg Bd 1975-79, CBI Employment Policy Ctee 1975-82, CBI Grand Cncl 1975-82, CBI President's Ctee 1979-82; gen cmmnr of taxes 1975-, underwriting memb Lloyds 1977-, chm Cncl Euro Business Sch 1983-, memb Advsy Cncl Royal Naval Engrg Coll 1988-, DTI Enterprise cnsllr 1988-; *Clubs* Carlton, RAC; *Style*— Anthony Frodsham, Esq, CBE; 36 Fairacres, Roehampton Lane, London SW15 5LX (☎ 081 878 9551)

FROGGATT, Sir Peter; s of Albert Victor Froggatt (d 1964), of Belfast, and Edith, *née* Curran (d 1949); *b* 12 June 1928; *Educ* Royal Belfast Acad Inst, Trinity Coll Dublin (MB, MA, MD, LLD), Queen's Univ Belfast (DPH, PhD); *m* 1958, Norma Alexandra Irene, da of Robert Alexander Cochrane (d 1976), of Belfast; 4 s (Mark b 1961, Richard b 1964, Ian b 1968, Keith b 1970); *Career* medical conslt 1963-86; Queen's Univ Belfast: prof of epidemiology 1968-76, dean Sch of Med 1971-76, vice-chllr and pres 1976-86; non-exec dir Allied Irish Banks plc; FRCP (1979), FFCM, FRCP (Ire), FFCM (Ire), FFOM (Ire), DSc (hc NUI), FRCS (Ire, hc), MRIA, CBIM; kt 1985; *Recreations* golf, music, travel; *Clubs* Royal Commonwealth Soc; *Style*— Sir Peter Froggatt; c/o Allied Irish Banks plc, 2 Royal Avenue, Belfast 1 (☎ 0232 246 559)

FROOD, Alan Campbell; CBE; s of James Campbell Frood, MC (d 1964), and Margaret Helena Frood (d 1969); *b* 15 May 1926; *Educ* Cranleigh Sch, Peterhouse Cambridge (BA); *m* 1960, Patricia Ann, da of Frederick Wynn Cotterel; 2 s, 2 da; *Career* RN 1944-47, Sub Lt RNVR; Bank of England 1949, Colonial Admin Servs 1952, Bankers' Tst Co 1962, dir Bankers' Trust Int; Crown Agents: gen mangr banking dept 1975, md 1978-88, crown agent 1980, ret 1988; *Recreations* gardening; *Clubs* Royal Cwlth Soc; *Style*— Alan Frood, Esq; West Orchard, Holmbush Lane, Henfield, W Sussex BN5 9TJ

FROSSARD, Sir Charles Keith; s of Rev Edward Louis Frossard, CBE (d 1968), formerly Dean of Guernsey, and Margery Smith, *née* Latta (d 1958); *b* 18 Feb 1922; *Educ* Elizabeth Coll Guernsey, Univ of Caen (Bachelier en Droit); *m* 10 April 1950, Elizabeth Marguerite, da of John Edmund Leopold Martel, OBE (d 1973), of Grange Court, Guernsey; 2 da (Marguerite, Jeanne); *Career* WWII: enlisted Gordon Highlanders 1940, cmmnd IA 1941, Capt 17 Dogra Regt, seconded Tochi Scouts and Chitral Scouts, NW Frontier India 1942-46; called to the Bar Gray's Inn 1949, advocate of the Royal Ct of Guernsey 1949; People's Dep States of Guernsey 1958, conseiller States of Guernsey 1967, slr gen 1969, attorney gen 1973, dep bailiff 1977, bailiff of Guernsey 1982; Docteur de L'Universite (Honoris Causa) Caen 1990, ACIArb; KGStJ 1987; Médaille de Vermeil Ville de Paris 1984; kt 1983; *Recreations* golf; *Clubs* Naval and Military; *Style*— Sir Charles Frossard; Les Lierres, Rohais, St Peter Port, Guernsey, Channel Islands (☎ 0481 22076); The Bailiff's Chambers, Royal Court House, Guernsey, Channel Islands (☎ 0481 26161)

FROST, Alan John; s of Edward George Frost (d 1981), and Ellen Lucy *née* Jamieson (d 1979); *b* 6 Oct 1944; *Educ* Stratford Co GS, Univ of Manchester (BSc); *m* 15 Dec 1973, Valerie Jean, da of Francis David Bennett; 2 s (Christopher, Patrick); *Career* asst gen mangr (investmts): London & Manchester Assurance Group plc 1980-84, Sun Life Assurance Society plc 1984-86; investmt dir Abbey Life Group 1986-89; md Abbey Life Assurance Co Ltd 1989-; Freeman City of London 1986, Liveryman Worshipful Co of Actuaries 1986, FIA 1970; *Books* A General Introduction to Institutional Investment (with D P Hager, 1986), Debt Securities (with D P Hager, 1990); *Recreations* reading, music, genealogy; *Clubs* East India; *Style*— Alan Frost, Esq; Rondels, 20 Little Forest Rd, Bournemouth, Dorset BN4 9NW; Abbey Life House, PO Box 33, 80 Holdenhurst Rd,Bournemouth, Dorset BN8 8AL (☎ 0202 407278, fax 0202 296816, telex 41310)

FROST, Albert Edward; CBE (1983); s of Charles Albert Frost (d 1953), and Minnie Frost; *b* 7 March 1914; *Educ* Oulton Sch Liverpool, London Univ; *m* 1942, Eugénie Maud Barlow; *Career* barrister Middle Temple; HM inspr of taxes 1937-49, dep head taxation ICI Ltd 1949-57, dep treasurer 1957-60, treasurer 1960-68, finance dir 1968-76; dir: Marks & Spencer 1976-, S G Warburg 1976-83, BL Ltd 1977-80, British Airways 1976-80, British Steel Corp 1980-83, Remploy Ltd (chm 1983-), Guinness Mahon & Co Ltd (chm 1984-), Guinness Mahon Hldgs Ltd 1984-, The Guinness Peat Gp plc 1984-; memb: Panel on Take-overs and Mergers, Cncl United Med Schs of Guy's and St Thomas' Hosps (and chm Fin Ctee), Cncl and Fin Ctee Morley Coll London to 1983; dir Youth Music Ltd, chm Robert Mayer Trust for Youth and Music 1981-, dir City Arts Trust Ltd 1982-, chm London Soc of Chamber Music 1983-; memb: Royal Academy of Arts Appeal Ctee, Cncl British United Industrialists, Advsy Cncl Assoc for Business Sponsorship of the Arts, Orgn Ctee Carl Flesch Int Violin Competition London, Exec Ctee for Dvpt Appeal Royal Opera House, Arts Cncl of GB 1982-83; *Recreations* violinist, swimming, athletics, walking, arts generally; *Clubs* RAC; *Style*— Albert Frost, Esq, CBE; Guinness Mahon & Co Ltd, 32 St Mary Axe Hill, London EC3 (☎ 071 623 9333)

FROST, David Paradine; OBE (1970); s of Rev Wilfred John Paradine Frost (d 1967), of Tenterden, Kent, and Monna Evelyn, *née* Aldrich; *b* 7 April 1939; *Educ* Gillingham GS, Wellingborough GS, Gonville and Caius Coll Cambridge (MA); *m* 1, 1981 (m dis 1982), Lynne Frederick, widow of Peter Sellers; m 2, 19 March 1983, Lady Carina Mary Anne Gabrielle, da of 17 Duke of Norfolk, KG, GCVO, CB, CBE, MC, *qv*; 3 s (Miles Paradine b 1984, Wilfred Paradine b 1985, George Paradine b 1987); *Career* television presenter, producer, author; BBC television programmes include: That Was The Week That Was 1962-63, A Degree of Frost 1963 and 1973, Not So Much a Programme More a Way of Life 1964-65, The Frost Report 1966-67, Frost Over England 1967, Frost Over America 1970, Frost's Weekly 1973, The Frost Interview 1974, We British 1975-76, Forty Years of Television 1976, The Frost Programme 1977, The Guinness Book of Records Hall of Fame 1986, 1987, 1988; ITV series and programmes include: The Frost Programme 1966-67 and 1967-68, Frost on Friday 1968-69 and 1969-70, The Sir Harold Wilson Interviews 1976, The Nixon Interviews 1976-77, The President and Mrs Bush Talking With David Frost 1989; produced films: The Rise and Rise of Michael Rimmer 1970, Charley-One-Eye 1972, Leadbelly 1974, The Slipper and the Rose 1975, James A Michener's Dynasty 1975, The Ordeal of Patty Hearst 1978, The Remarkable Mrs Sanger 1979; chm and chief exec The David Paradine Gp of Cos 1966-; jt fndr London Weekend Television; jt fndr and dir TV-AM plc 1981-; memb Cncl Birthright 1989-; Freeman of Louisville (Kentucky, USA) 1971; Hon LLB Emerson Coll Boston Mass USA 1970; *Recreations* cricket, soccer, tennis, food, wine; *Clubs* MCC, Mark's, Annabel's, Harry's Bar, Mosimann's; *Style*— David Frost, Esq, OBE; The David Paradine Gp of Cos, 115-123 Bayham St, Greenland Place, London NW1 OAG (☎ 071 482 2898, fax 071 482 0871, telex 27613 TALKING)

FROST, Derek Norton; s of John Norton Frost, of Little Garde, Crowborough Rd, Nutley, E Sussex, and Elizabeth, *née* Gibson; *b* 24 April 1952; *Educ* Tonbridge; *partner* (since 1978), Jeremy Gordon Norman, *qv*; *Career* designer; trained under David Hicks; dir of interior design Mary Fox Linton Ltd; formed own co Derek Frost Design Ltd 1984; int practice specialising in interior design/furniture design; projects include: Heaven Discotheque, The Kobler Centre, many residential installations; solo exhibition of furniture Leighton House 1988; ISID; *Recreations* gardening, music, contemporary arts, craft, scuba diving; *Style*— Derek Frost, Esq; Moreton Yard, London SW1V 2NT; 2 Needsore, Warren Lane, Beaulieu, Hants; Derek Frost Design Ltd, 5 Moreton Terrace Mews North, London SW1V 2NT (☎ 071 828 6270, fax 071 976 5059)

FROST, James Douglas (Jim); s of Richard George Frost, and Glynn Valirie, *née* Middlemass; *b* 31 July 1958; *Educ* Ashburton Secdy Sch; *m* 29 July 1986, Nicola, da of Tony Horby; 2 s (Daniel George b 24 Sept 1987, Hadden James b 19 July 1990); *Career* professional jockey; first ride as amateur 1972, turned professional 1982, ridden over 300 winners; major wins: Grand National 1989 (Little Polvier), Breeder's Cup Steeplechase 1990 (Morely Street), Sandeman Hurdle and Supreme Novice Hurdle (Forest Sun) Cheltenham Festival 1990, Bishop Cleve Hurdle 1991 (Crystal Spirit); youngest rider to win a 3 mile steeplechase aged 13; farmer; *Recreations* skiing, playing with the kids; *Style*— Jim Frost, Esq; Hawson Court, Buckfastleigh, South Devon TQ11 0HP (☎ 036 44 2267)

FROST, James John; s of Maj David Richard Frost, MC, TD, of Bencewell Orchard, Keston Mark, Kent, and Leta Mary, *née* Ridley, MBE; *b* 27 Oct 1958; *Educ* Haileybury, Univ of Birmingham (BA), Universite D'Aix-Marseille; *Career* mgmnt trainee WK Webster & Co Int Underwriters' Agents 1981-84 (seconded Roger Houghton Recoveries Ltd Hong Kong 1983-84), reinsurance treaty broker CT Bowring & Co Ltd 1984-, memb Lloyds 1986-; Freeman City of London 1983, Liveryman Worshipful Co of Shipwrights 1984; *Recreations* tennis, squash, theatre, cookery, classic cars; *Style*— James Frost, Esq; 44 Musard Rd, Fulham, London W6 8NW (☎ 071 385 8668); C T Bowring & Co Ltd, The Bowring Bldg, Tower Place, London EC3 (☎ 071 357 1000, fax 071 929 2705, telex 882191)

FROST, (Cecil) John William; s of Benjamin John Frost (d 1963), and Gladys, *née* Raynes (d 1979); *b* 27 May 1942; *Educ* Royal Liberty GS; *m* 1 Sept 1962, Janice Rhoda, da of Herbert Cook (d 1971); 2 s (Stephen John, Jeremy William); *Career* md Cater Allen Ltd 1977-, dir Cater Allen Holdings plc 1983-; hon sec Lombard Assoc London; FCIB 1965; *Recreations* sailing, opera, jazz; *Style*— John Frost, Esq; Redwalls, Friars Close, Shenfield, Brentwood, Essex CM15 8HX; Cater Allen Ltd, 20 Birchin Lane, London EC3V 9DJ (☎ 071 623 2070)

FROST, Hon Mrs (Marygold); *née* Mills; da of 3 Baron Hillingdon (d 1952); *b* 19 Oct 1924; *m* 1948, Kenneth Frost; 2 s, 4 da; *Style*— The Hon Mrs Frost

FROST, Michael Eric; s of Donald Jack Frost, MBE, and Marion Cecily, *née* Lines; *b* 26 Aug 1934; *Educ* Ipswich Sch; *m* 6 Sept 1967, Elsie Jean, da of Walter Whitehead; *Career* photographer; studio mangr Desmond Groves Ltd London and Wilmslow 1963-66, fndr The Michael Frost Studio York 1966, lectr on portraiture and wedding photography in Britain and abroad at professional photographic seminars; memb Qualifications Bd BIPP; awards: BIPP Wedding Photographer of the Year 1977, BIPP Portrait Photographer of the Year 1978 and 1981, Kodak Gold award for Portraiture 1985, 1988 and 1989; FBIPP, FRPS, FRSA, fell The Master Photographers' Assoc, memb Professional Photographers of America; *Books* Saleable Portraits - The Style and Technique (1989); *Recreations* travel, music, art; *Style*— Michael Frost, Esq; Chantry House, Lloyd Close, Heslington, York YO1 5EU; The Michael Frost Studio, The Shambles, York YO1 2LZ (☎ 0904 623895)

FROST, Patrick Edward; s of Richard Edward Frost (d 1980), of Kingsley Green, Surrey, and Audrey Kate, *née* Jenkins (d 1986); *b* 22 Nov 1948; *Educ* Midhurst GS, Guildford Coll (HND); *m* 19 Feb 1977, Susan Anne, da of Col Leonard Bindon Arrowsmith Thacker; *Career* area surveyor Marshall-Andrew Construction 1974-81, chief surveyor C J Sims Ltd 1981-84, chm and md Patrick Frost Associates Ltd 1985-;

Freeman: City of London 1982, Worshipful Co of Carmen 1983; memb Royal Soc of St George (City of London Branch), assoc Chartered Inst of Building; *Recreations* sailing, shooting, golf, antiques restoration; *Clubs* City Livery; *Style—* Patrick Frost, Esq; Furnace Ct, Haslemere, Surrey GU27 2EJ (☎ 0428 652255)

FROST, Hon Raymond; s of Baroness Gaitskell (d 1989) by her 1 husb, David Frost; *b* 6 May 1924; *Educ* Oundle, Worcester Coll Oxford; *m* 6 Sept 1958, June Virginia Johnston Gonzalez, da of Eduardo Rodriguez del Rey, of Cienfuegos, Cuba; 1 s, 1 da; *Career* dir Econ Devpt Inst at World Bank Washington DC; *Style—* Hon Raymond Frost; 2917 Q Street NW, Washington DC 20007, USA

FROST, Ronald Edwin; s of Charles Henry Frost, and Doris, *née* Foggin; *b* 19 March 1936; *m* 19 Sept 1959, Beryl, da of Leonard Ward (d 1964), of Windsor; 1 s (Stephen Charles b 1962), 2 da (Jane Samantha b 1965, Louise Karen b 1966); *Career* chm and chief exec Hays Group Ltd 1986-89, exec chm Hays plc 1989-; dir: HWC Superannuation Trust Ltd 1983-, Hays Commercial Services Ltd 1983, Hays Holdings Ltd 1985, Hays Farms (Hursley) Ltd 1986, Hays Personnel Services Ltd 1986, Hays Contract Distribution Ltd 1986, Farmbridge Finance Ltd 1986, Hays Chemical Distribution Ltd 1988, Hays Specialist Distribution Ltd 1989, Hays Specialist Holdings Ltd 1989; *Recreations* game shooting, sailing; *Clubs* RAC, Royal Thames Yacht, IOD; *Style—* Ronald Frost, Esq; Shamley Wood, Shamley Green, nr Guildford, Surrey GU5 0SP (☎ 0483 893338); Hays plc, Hays House, Millmead, Guildford, Surrey GU2 5HJ (☎ 0483 302203, fax 0483 300388, car 0836 222159)

FROST, Hon Sir (Thomas) Sydney; QC (1961); s of late Thomas Frost; *b* 13 Feb 1916; *Educ* Univ of Melbourne (LLM); *m* 1943, Dorothy Gertrude, *née* Kelly; 2 s, 1 da; *Career* called to the Bar 1945, judge of the County Court of Victoria 1964, judge of Supreme Court of Papua New Guinea 1964-75, chief justice of Independent State of Papua New Guinea 1975-78; chm: Aust Govt Inquiry into Whales and Whaling 1978, Royal Cmmn Inquiry into Housing Cmmn Land Purchases and Valuation Matters 1979-81; memb Bd of Accident Inquiry into Aircraft Crash at Sydney Airport Feb 1980; pres Med Serv Review Tbnl 1979-85; kt 1975; *Recreations* golf; *Clubs* Australian (Melbourne), Royal Melbourne Golf; *Style—* The Hon Sir Sydney Frost, QC; Park Tower, 201 Spring St, Melbourne, Victoria 3000, Australia (☎ 010 61 3 662 3239)

FROST, Terence Ernest Manitou (Terry); *b* 13 Oct 1915; *Educ* Central Sch Leamington Spa, Camberwell Sch of Art; *m* 11 Aug 1945, Kathleen May, *née* Frost; 5 s (Adrian Dudley b 14 July 1947, Anthony b 4 May 1951, Matthew James b 24 Sept 1954, Stephen George b 28 Dec 1955, Simon Arnold b 13 Feb 1958), 1 da (Mary Charlotte Kate b 9 June 1961); *Career* WWII Serv 1939-45, conscripted Army, served France and Palestine, transferred Commandos 1941, served Sudan, Abyssinia, Egypt and Crete, POW Poland then Bavaria 1941-45; formerly employed in non-artistic professions 1930-39; artist; visiting lectr Bath Acad of Art Corsham 1952-54, Gregory fell in painting Univ of Leeds 1954-56; pt/t teacher: Leeds Coll of Art 1956-67, Coventry Sch of Art 1963-64; fell in painting Univ of Newcastle 1965, prof emeritus Univ of Reading 1981- (pt/t then full time lectr Dept of Fine Art 1964-70, reader 1970-77, prof of painting 1977-81); solo exhibitions incl: Leamington Public Library 1944, Leicester Galleries London 1952, 1956 and 1958, Waddington Galleries 1959-80, Bertha Schaeffer Gallery NY 1960 and 1962, Retrospective Exhibition (Laing Gallery Newcastle upon Tyne and tour to York, Hull and Bradford, San Francisco, Santa Barbara and San Joes Art Galleries) 1964, Museum of Modern Art Oxford 1969, Arnolfini Gallery Bristol 1972, Retrospective Exhibition (Serpentine Gallery London) 1977, New Art Centre London 1981, Terry Frost - Painting in the 1980's (Univ of Reading and tour to Lincoln, Ayre, Plymouth and Newlyn) 1987-88, The Belgrave Gallery London and Austin Desmond Fine Art London 1989; works in public collections incl: Aberdeen Art Gallery, Art Gallery of South Aust Adelaide, Arts Cncl of GB, Birmingham City Art Gallery, Bristol City Art Gallery, Christchurch Art Gallery NZ, Contemporary Art Soc London, Dept of Environment, Fitzwilliam Museum Cambridge, Univ of Glasgow, Nat Gallery of Canada Ottowa, Nat Gallery of NSW Sydney, Nat Portrait Gallery, Scot Nat Gallery of Modern Art Edinbrugh, Tate Gallery, Tel Aviv Museum, Ulster Museum Belfast, V & A; Hon LLD CNAA 1978; hon fell RCA 1990; *Clubs* Chelsea Arts; *Style—* Terry Frost, Esq; Gernick Field Studio, Tredavoe Lane, Newlyn, Penzance (☎ 0736 65902)

FROSTICK, Raymond Charles; DL (Norfolk 1979); s of Harry Frostick, of Hoveton, Norfolk (d 1965), and Ethel Marion, *née* Preston (d 1983); *b* 18 May 1931; *Educ* Norwich Sch, CCC Cambridge (MA, LLM); *m* 27 July 1957, (Rosemary) Claire, da of Sir George Harold Banwell, of Lincoln (d 1982); 2 s (Richard b 1960, Andrew b 1963), 2 da (Marion b 1958, Elizabeth b 1961); *Career* Nat Serv RAF 1949-51; admitted slr 1957, dir R G Carter (Holdings) Ltd 1975-, vice chm East Anglian Radio plc 1987- (dir 1984-); chm: Partnership Bd Daynes Hill & Perks 1988- (ptnr 1962-), Radio Broadland Ltd 1990-; dir Suffolk Group Radio plc 1990-; Univ of East Anglia: memb Cncl 1972-, treas 1985-90, pro chllr and chm Cncl 1990-; chm: Norfolk AHA 1978-82, Norwich Health Authy 1982-85; pres Norwich and Norfolk C of C and Indust 1985-88; cllr: Norwich City Cncl 1966-79, Norfolk CC 1973-85 (chm 1983-84); Lord Mayor of Norwich 1976-77, vice pres Nat Exec RELATE Nat Marriage Guidance 1990- (chm 1986-90); memb Law Soc 1957, FRSA 1985; *Books* The Dutch Connection: Some Norfolk Maps and Their Makers (1988); *Recreations* cartography, travel; *Clubs* Royal Cwlth Soc; *Style—* Raymond Frostick, Esq, DL; 425 Unthank Rd, Norwich, Norfolk NR4 7QB (☎ 0603 52337); Daynes Hill & Perks, Holland Court, The Close, Norwich, Norfolk NR1 4DX (☎ 0603 611 212, fax 0603 610 535, telex 97197)

FROWEN, Prof Stephen Francis; s of Adolf Frowein (d 1964), and Anna, *née* Bauer (d 1968); *b* 22 May 1923; *Educ* Univs of Cologne, Wuerzburg, Bonn and London (BSc, MSc); *m* 21 March 1949, Irina, da of Dr Sam Minskers; 1 s (Michael b 17 Jan 1950 d 1989), 1 da (Tatiana b 20 Sept 1955); *Career* ed The Bankers' Magazine (now Banking World) 1954-60, econ advsr Indust and Commercial Fin Corp 1960-61, res offr NIESR and Soc Res 1961-62; sr lectr: Thames Poly 1962-67, Univ of Surrey 1967-87; prof of econ Univ of Frankfurt 1987, Bundesbank prof of monetary econs Free Univ of Berlin 1987-88; *Books* numerous jl articles and editing of conf transactions in the field of monetary econs; hon research fell UCL 1989-; books ed: Economic Issues (with H C Hillmann, 1957), Monetary Policy and Economic Activity in West Germany (jtly, 1977), A Framework of International Banking (1979), Controlling Industrial Economies (1983), Business, Time and Thought: Selected Papers of GLS Shackle (1988), Unknowledge and Choice in Economics (1990), Monetary Policy and Financial Innovations in Five Industrial Countries: The UK, USA, Germany, France and Japan (1991); *Recreations* numismatics, painting, music, reading; *Clubs* Reform; *Style—* Prof Stephen Francis Frowen; 40 Gurney Drive, London N2 0DE (☎ 081 458 0159)

FROY, Prof Martin; s of late William Alan Froy, and Helen Elizabeth, *née* Spencer; *b* 9 Feb 1926; *Educ* St Paul's, Magdalen Coll Cambridge, Slade Sch of Fine Art, Univ of London (Dip Fine Art), Univ of Leeds; *Career* teacher: engraving Slade Sch of Fine Art 1952-55, Bath Acad of Art 1954-65 (latterly head of fine art); head Painting Sch Chelsea Sch of Art 1965-72, prof of Fine Art Univ of Reading; Gregory fell in painting Univ of Leeds 1951-54; commission mosaic decoration Belgrade Theatre Coventry 1957-58; public collections: Tate Gallery London, Museum of Modern Art New York, Museum of Art Santa Barbara, Chicago Art Inst, The Arts Council of GB, Contemporary Art Society, Royal W of England Acad, Univ of Leeds, Univ Coll London, The Slade Collection, City Art Galleries (Bristol, Carlisle, Leeds, Reading, Southampton, Wakefield); solo exhibitions: Hanover Gallery London 1952 and 1969, Univ of Leeds 1953, Wakefield City Art Gallery 1953, Belgrade Theatre Coventry 1958, Leicester Galleries London 1961, Royal W England Acad Bristol 1964, Univ of Sussex 1968, Alforni Gallery Bristol 1970, Park Square Gallery Leeds 1970, Seven Paintings (City Art Gallery Bristol) 1972, Univ of Reading 1979, New Ashgate Gallery Farnham 1979, Arts Cncl Serpentine Gallery London 1983; group exhibitions incl: Int Abstract Artist (Riverside Museum New York, ICA London) 1950, Figures in Their Setting (Tate Gallery London, Beaux Arts Gallery London) 1953, Br Painting and Sculpture (Whitechapel Gallery London) 1954, Le Congres pour la Liberte de la Culture Rome Paris Brussels 1955, Pittsburgh Int 1955, Six Young Painters (Arts Cncl touring the UK) 1956, ICA Gregory Memorial (Bradford City Art Gallery) 1960, Corsham Painters and Sculptors (Arts Cncl touring UK) 1965, Three Painters (Bath Festival) 1970, Park Square Gallery Leeds and The Ruskin Sch Univ of Oxford 1978, Newcastle Connection (Newcastle Poly) 1980, Six Painters (Unvi of Reading Art Gallery) 1984, Homage to Herbert Read (Canterbury Coll) 1984, Public Property (Reading Museum and Art Gallery) 1987, Corsham a Celebration (Victoria Art Gallery Bath and touring); memb: Fine Art Panel Nat Cncl for Dips in Art and Design 1962-71, Nat Cncl for Dips in Art and Design 1969-71, Panel of Advisors Cwlth Scholarships Cmmn 1974-78, Standing Conf Univ Entrance Cncl Museum of Modern Art Oxford 1974-79, Cncl Nat Tst 1976-79, Faculty of Painting British Sch Rome 1978-81, Consortium for Art Design and Architecture Hants 1983-86, Bd Studies in Fine Art Univ of London, Ctee for Slade Sch Univ Coll London 1966; tstee: Nat Gallery 1972-79, Tate Gallery 1975-79; Leverhulme Res award 1963, Sabbatical award Arts Council of GB 1965; *Style—* Prof Martin Froy; Department of Fine Art, University of Reading, Earley Gate, Reading, Berkshire RG1 5AQ

FROY, Robert Anthony Douglas; s of Hienz Louis Froy (d 1981), and Giezela Anna, *née* Salomon; *b* 23 Aug 1936; *Educ* Clarks Coll; *m* 8 July 1960, (Diana) Wendy, da of Maj Clifford Anderson Likeman (d 1980); 2 s (Stephen b 4 April 1963, Nicholas b 21 Feb 1965); *Career* md: Montagu Loebl Stanley 1969-87, Lloyds Bank Stockbrokers 1987-, dir Lloyds Merchant Bank Ltd 1990-; non-exec dir: The Otford Group, Hanover Property Unit Trust; dep chm Chambers & Remington Ltd Stockbrokers, chm Sennocke Services Ltd; memb Int Stock Exchange, chm govrs Sevenoaks Sch; Freeman City of London, Liveryman Worshipful Co of Pattenmakers; AMSIA; *Recreations* sport, walking, gardening; *Clubs* City of London; *Style—* Robert Froy, Esq; 171 Defoe House, Barbican, London EC2Y 8DN (☎ 071 628 0083); Lloyds Bank Stockbrokers Ltd, 48 Chiswell St, London EC1Y 4XX (☎ 071 522 5000, fax 071 522 5563, telex 888301)

FRY, Dr Anthony Harold; s of Henry Fry (d 1976), and Marjorie, *née* Davies; *b* 9 Nov 1942; *Educ* Highgate Sch, King's Coll Hosp (MB BS, LRCP, MRCS, MPhil, DPM); *m* 16 Nov 1974, Lynda Mary, da of Leslie Reginald Devenish, of Sussex; 3 s (Alexander b 4 June 1976, Nick b 28 April 1978, Robert b 6 Aug 1980); *Career* conslt psychiatrist; recognised teacher psychiatry United Med Sch of Guy's and St Thomas' Univ of London, sr conslt physician psychological med Guy's Hosp 1977-90; med dir: Stress Mgmnt Unit London Bridge Hosp 1988, Out Patient Servs Charter Nightingale Hosp 1990; MRCPsych 1972, memb BMA 1980; *Books* Safe Space (1987); *Recreations* travel, squash, walking, poetry; *Clubs* RAC; *Style—* Dr Anthony Fry; 129 Hemingford Rd, Barnsbury, Islington, London N1 1BZ (☎ 071 609 0000); Suite 207, London Bridge Hospital, 27 Tooley St, London SE1 (☎ 071 607 3937, 071 258 3828, 927026 LBHOSP G)

FRY, Anthony Michael; s of Denis Seymour Fry, of Worthing, Sussex, and Trixie, *née* Barter; *b* 20 June 1955; *Educ* Stonyhurst, Univ of Florence, Magdalen Coll Oxford (BA, Atkinson prize, treas Oxford Union Soc); *m* 27 July 1985, Anne Elizabeth, da of Harry Birrell; *Career* N M Rothschild & Sons Ltd: joined 1977, mangr International Pacific Corporation Melbourne Australia (renamed Rothschild Australia 1983) 1980-85, exec dir 1985-; vice chm British Lung Fndn, memb Guild of Bonnetmakers Glasgow; *Recreations* opera, theatre, cricket; *Clubs* Carlton, Australian, Armadillos CC, Incogniti CC, The Blake; *Style—* Anthony Fry, Esq; N M Rothschild & Sons Ltd, New Court, St Swithins Lane, London EC4 (☎ 071 280 5000, fax 071 283 4276)

FRY, Christopher; *b* 18 Dec 1907; *Career* dramatist; actor Citizen House Bath 1927, teacher Hazelwood Prep Sch Limpsfield Surrey 1928-31; dir: Tunbridge Wells Repertory Players 1932-35, Oxford Repertory Players 1940 and 1944-46; staff dramatist Arts Theatre London 1947 (dir 1945); plays: A Phoenix Too Frequent (Mercury) 1946 and (St Georges) 1983, The Lady's Not for Burning (Arts) 1948 (and Globe 1949, Chichester 1972), The Firstborn (Edinburgh Festival) 1948, Thor with Angels (Canterbury Festival) 1948, Venus Observed (St James's 1950, The Boy with a Cart (Lyric) 1950, Ring Round the Moon (trans from French of Jean Anouilh, Globe) 1950, A Sleep of Prisoners (St Thomas's Regent St) 1951, The Dark is Light Enough (Aldwych) 1954, The Lark (trans form French of Jean Anouilh, Lyric) 1955, Tiger at the Gates (trans from French of Jean Giraudoux, Apollo) 1955, Duel of Angels (trans from Pour Lucrece of Jean Giraudoux, Apollo) 1958, Curtmantle (RSC) 1962, Judith (trans from Giraudoux, Her Majesty's) 1962, A Yard of Sun (National) 1970, Peer Gynt (trans, Chichester) 1970, Cyrano de Bergerac (trans, Chichester) 1975, One More Thing or Caedmon Construed (Chelmsford Cathedral) 1986; TV: The Brontës of Haworth (four plays) 1973, Sister Dora 1977, The Best of Enemies 1977; film commentary for The Queen is Crowned (Coronation film, 1953); film scripts: (participation) Ben Hur, The Bible, The Beggars Opera, Barabbas; publications: The Boy with a Cart 1939, The First Born 1946, A Phoenix too Frequent 1946, The Lady's Not for Burning 1949, Thor with Angels 1949, Venus Observed 1950, A Sleep of Prisoners 1951, The Dark is Light Enough 1954, The Lark (trans) 1955, Tiger at the Gates 1955, Duel of Angels (trans) 1958, Curtmantle (1961, Heinemann award RSL), Judith (trans) 1962, A Yard of Sun 1970, Peer Gynt (trans) 1970, Cyrano de Bergerac (trans) 1975, Can You Find Me: a family history 1978; Queen's Gold medal for poetry 1962; Hon DLitt Lambeth 1988; FRSL; *Clubs* Garrick; *Style—* Christopher Fry; The Toft, East Dean, Chichester, West Sussex

FRY, Dr John; CBE (1988, OBE 1978); s of Dr Ansel Fry (d 1972), and Barbara, *née* Minton (d 1979); *b* 16 June 1922; *Educ* Whitgift Middle Sch, Univ of London, Guy's Hosp Med Sch (MD); *m* 1, 2 April 1944, Joan Lilian (d 1989), da of James Sabel (d 1941); 1 s (James b 26 Feb 1946), 1 da (Dimity Jane (Mrs Dawson) b 28 May 1947) m 2, 10 Sept 1989, Gertrude Albertine, da of Emil Schwer (d 1954); *Career* GP 1947-; memb Cncl RCGP 1957-90, governing tstee Nuffield Provincial Hosp Tst 1957-91, memb GMC Cncl 1970-91, Jephcott prof Univ of Oxford 1981-82; conslt and advsr WHO 1962-91, conslt ed Update 1968-91, civilian conslt in Gen Practice to the Br Army 1967-87; Queen Elizabeth the Queen Mother fell and lectr 1988; FRCS, FRCGP, Hon FRSM 1989; memb: BMA 1944, RSM 1946, RCGP 1952; *Books* Medicine in Three Societies (1969), Common Dilemmas in Family Medicine (1983), Common Diseases (4 edn, 1984), Disease Data Book (1986), Primary Health Care: 2000 (1986), General Practice and Primary Health Care 1940s-1980s (1988); *Recreations* reading, writing, running; *Style—* Dr John Fry, CBE; 3 Kings Court, Kelsey Park Avenue, Beckenham, Kent BR3 2TT (☎ 081 650 5414); 138 Croydon

Rd, Beckenham, Kent BR3 4DG (☎ 081 650 0568)

FRY, John Marshall; s of Montague Philip Fry, and Margery Maud, *née* Marshall; *b* 3 March 1936; *Educ* Tonbridge, Trinity Hall Cambridge (MA); *m* 12 Aug 1967, Diana Margaret, da of John Wybert Nowell Clark; 2 da (Amanda b 1969, Susannah b 1971); *Career* Royal Dragoons 1954-56; mgmnt trainee Marshall Ltd Cambridge 1959-61; Abbey National Building Society: mangr personnel and trg 1965-72, divnl mangr 1972-79, gen mangr 1979, dir 1984, dir and gen mangr gp servs 1988; gp servs dir Abbey National plc 1989-; pres Chartered Bldg Socs Inst 1986-87 (memb Cncl 1979); chm govrs St Mary's Sch Gerrards Cross, govr Queenswood Sch Herts; FCIS 1972; *Recreations* gardening, equestrian activities; *Clubs* Cavalry and Guards'; *Style*— John Fry, Esq; Clonmel, Flaunden, nr Hemel Hempstead, Herts HP3 0PP (☎ 0442 832 204); Abbey House, Baker St, London NW1 6XL (☎ 071 486 5555, fax 071 486 555 ext 24230, telex 266103 ABBNAT G)

FRY, Jonathan Michael; s of Stephen Fry (d 1979), of London, and Gladys Yvonne, *née* Blunt; *b* 9 Aug 1937; *Educ* Repton, Trinity Coll Oxford (MA); *m* 21 Feb 1970, Caroline Mary, da of Col Vincent Ashforth Blundell Dunkerly, DSO, JP (d 1968); 4 da (Lucy b 1971, Camilla b 1973, Victoria b 1977, Sophie b 1979); *Career* account exec Pritchard Wood & Ptnrs 1961-65, account supervisor Norman Craig & Kummel 1965-66, engagement mangr McKinsey & Co 1966-72, dir and chief exec Foods Div Unigate Ltd 1972-77, md Burmah Control plc 1990 (joined 1978-); chm: Woodborough Cons Assoc 1976-83, Beechingstoke Parish Cncl 1978-, St Francis Sch Pewsey 1984-; *Recreations* cricket, skiing, archaeology; *Clubs* MCC, Vincents (Oxford); *Style*— Jonathan Fry, Esq; Beechingstoke Manor, Pewsey, Wilts; Burmah Control plc, Burmah Control House, Piper's Way, Swindon, Wilts (☎ 0793 512 712, fax 0793 513 419, car 0836 230 387)

FRY, Kenneth George; s of Harry Fry (d 1967), and Irene Maud, *née* Clarke (d 1984); *b* 30 Nov 1922; *Educ* Royal Latin Sch, Open Univ (BA); *m* 2 April 1949, Gladys Alice Fry (d 1989); *Career* Colonial Office 1947-60, Dept of Tech Cooperation 1960-64, Inter-Univ Cncl for Higher Educn Overseas 1972-75, Miny of Overseas Devpt 1975-79 (and 1964-72), FCO Overseas Devpt Admin 1979-82; Phoenix House: bd memb 1983-, vice chm 1985-; memb various local church and residents assocs; *Recreations* opera, ballet, walking; *Style*— Kenneth Fry, Esq; Phoenix House, 47-49 Borough High St, London SE1 1NB (☎ 071 407 2789, fax 071 407 6007)

FRY, Dr Lionel; s of Dr Ancel Fry (d 1972), and Barbara, *née* Mintzman (d 1979); *b* 19 March 1933; *Educ* King's Coll London (BSc, MD, BS); *m* 27 Nov 1955, Minné, da of Dr Jack Sidney Zidel; 1 s (Michael b 1959), 2 da (Tessa Joanne b 1961, Kathrine b 1963); *Career* conslt dermatologist St Mary's Hosp London; author: Dermatology - An Illustrated Guide, Immunological Aspects of Skin Disease; *Recreations* tennis, walking, music, theatre; *Style*— Dr Lionel Fry; 16 Caroline Place, London W2 4AN (☎ 071 229 7790); St Mary's Hosp, London W2 1NY; 96 Harley St, London W1 (☎ 071 935 2421)

FRY, Dame Margaret Louise; da of Richard Reed Dawe, of Tavistock, and Ruth Dora, *née* Every (d 1968); *b* 10 March 1931; *Educ* Tavistock GS; *m* 11 April 1955, (Walter William) John Fry, s of Walter William Fry (d 1972), of Launceston; 3 s (Jeremy b 24 March 1957, Patrick b 17 March 1960, Robert b 12 May 1966); *Career* former Devon hockey player; memb: Cons Party 1947-, Transport Users' Consultative Ctee, Nat Union of Cons and Unionist Assocs, S W Regnl Health Authy, local church cncl; chm: Western Area Women's Advsy Ctee 1978-81 (former memb and vice chm 1975-78), Cons Women's Advsy Ctee 1984-87 (vice chm 1981-82), Torridge and W Devon Cons Assoc, Nat Union of Conservative and Unionist Assocs 1990-91 (vice chm 1987-90); former memb: Tavistock Cons Assoc, Tavistock Young Cons, Nat Fedn of Young Farmers Clubs; *Recreations* farming and conservation, sport; *Style*— Dame Margaret Fry, DBE; Thorne Farm, Launceston, Cornwall PL15 9SN (☎ 0566 84308)

FRY, Nicholas Rodney Lowther; s of Rodney William Lowther Fry, of Derby, and Mary Winifred Rosalind, *née* Ellis; *b* 28 April 1947; *Educ* Malvern, Christ's Coll Cambridge (MA); *m* 1972, Christine Sarah, da of Edmund De Chazal Rogers (d 1967), of London; 1 s (Jonathan b 1976), 2 da (Emma b 1974, Lucy b 1981); *Career* merchant banker; dir S G Warburg & Co Ltd 1983-; FICA; *Recreations* music, gardening, recreational sport; *Style*— Nicholas Fry, Esq; 38 Lyford Rd, London SW18 3LS (☎ 081 874 7608); S G Warburg & Co Ltd, 2 Finsbury Ave, London EC2M 2PA (☎ 071 860 1090, telex 920301, fax 071 860 0901)

FRY, Peter Derek; MP (C) Wellingborough 1969-; s of Harry Walter Fry, of High Wycombe, Bucks, and late Edith Fry; *b* 26 May 1931; *Educ* Royal GS High Wycombe, Worcester Coll Oxford (MA); *m* 1, 1958 (m dis 1982), Edna, da of John Roberts, of Liverpool; 1 s, 1 da; m 2, 1982, Helen Claire Mitchell, da of late James Gregson; *Career* memb Bucks CC 1961-67, insur broker 1963-, London area political educn offr CCO 1961-63; contested (C): Nottingham N 1964, Willesden E 1966; memb Transport Select Ctee 1979-, chm Political Research & Communications International Ltd 1982-87, dir Countryside Political Communications Ltd 1987-; vice pres British Yugoslav Soc; *Clubs* RAC; *Style*— Peter Fry, Esq, MP; House of Commons, London SW1

FRY, Stephen John; s of Alan John Fry, ARCS (Lieut REME), of Booton, Norfolk, and Marianne Eve, *née* Newman; *b* 24 Aug 1957; *Educ* Uppingham, Queens' Coll Cambridge (MA); *Career* actor and writer; appeared with Cambridge Footlights in revue The Cellar Tapes at Edinburgh Festival 1981 (Perrier Award); plays: Latin (Scotsman Fringe First award 1980 and Lyric Hammersmith 1983), Forty Years On (Chichester Festival and Queen's Theatre London) 1984, The Common Pursuit (Phoenix Theatre London) 1988; TV series: Alfresco 1982-84, The Young Ones 1983, Happy Families 1984, Saturday Night Live 1986-87, A Bit of Fry and Laurie 1987 and 1989, Blackadder's Christmas Carol 1988, Blackadder Goes Forth 1989; radio: Loose Ends 1986-87, Whose Line Is It Anyway? 1987, Saturday Night Fry 1987; weekly column in the Listener, re-wrote script for musical Me and My Girl 1984 (London, Broadway, Sydney); patron: Studio 3 (arts for young people), Freeze (nuclear disarmament charity); memb: Amnesty Int, Comic Relief; *Recreations* chess, computing, dining out, light alcoholic refreshments; *Clubs* Oxford and Cambridge, Chelsea Arts, Groucho, Freds, Zanzibar; *Style*— Stephen Fry, Esq; c/o Noel Gay Artists, 24 Denmark St, London WC2 8NJ (☎ 081 836 3941)

FRYDENSON, Henry; s of Samuel Frydenson, and Barbara Frydenson; *b* 9 Nov 1954; *Educ* Hasmonean GS for Boys, UCL (LLB); *m* Aug 1980, Sarah, da of Samuel Reiffer; 5 s (Alan, Jonathan, Martin, Sheldon, Andrew), 1 da (Deborah); *Career* admitted slr 1981; ptnr Paisner and Co 1984- (joined 1979); Freeman City of London 1984; *Recreations* swimming, climbing, football, cricket, first aid; *Style*— Henry Frydenson, Esq; Paisner & Co, Bouverie House, 154 Fleet St, London EC4A 2DQ (☎ 071 353 0299, fax 071 583 8621, telex 263189 pailex g)

FRYE, Eric; s of William Barnard Frye (d 1949); *b* 15 March 1923; *Educ* Tom Hood Coll, SE Essex Tech Coll; *m* 1947, Doreen Joan, da of Edward Thomas Day (d 1958); 2 s (Roger, Richard); *Career* Warrant Offr, air observer Europe, POW Japan 1941-45; sr exec Ford Motor Co 1964; dir: Staveley Industries 1964-67, The Plessey Co plc 1969-78 (dep chief exec 1976-78), H Brammer plc 1978-87, Deborah Services plc 1979-86; chm and chief exec Arcotronics Holding BV 1982-86; FCA 1952, CBIM; *Recreations* golf, travel, bridge, carpentry; *Style*— Eric Frye, Esq; Little Orchard, 209 Cooden Sea Rd, Cooden, Bexhill-on-Sea, E Sussex TN39 4TR (☎ 04243 3995); Casa Doric, Quinta do Paraiso, Praia do Carvoeiro, Algarve, Portugal

FRYER, John Albert; CBE (1970); s of George Albert Fryer, RN; *b* 17 Jan 1925; *Educ* Portsmouth Northern Secdy Sch, Southern Coll of Art Winchester, Camborne Sch of Mines, Univ Coll London, Univ of Southampton; *m* 1, 1960, Brenda Sheila (d 1984), da of Reginald Charles Frederick Baugh, of Cardiff; 1 s; m 2, 1986, Audrey Jean, da of Eric Gilbert Wells, of Hove; *Career* Lt RE, FARELF; Colonial Survey Serv N Borneo 1948, dir lands and surveys Sabah Malaysia 1966-70; transportation res offr GLC 1970-86; ARICS 1960; *Recreations* genealogy; *Clubs* MENSA; *Style*— John Fryer, Esq, CBE; New Orchard, 6 Meadowlands, Havant, Hants

FRYER, John Beresford; s of Reginald Arthur Fryer (d 1966), and Joyce Edith Fryer (d 1986); *b* 18 Feb 1945; *Educ* Chigwell Sch Essex; *m* 3 April 1971, Jennifer Margaret Glew; 2 da (Polly Jane b 12 Dec 1976, Sally Ann b 31 March 1980); *Career* sub-ed and reporter: local newspapers in East London and Essex 1963-67, Daily Sketch 1967-68, London Evening Standard 1968-69; labour corr then labour ed Sunday Times 1969-82, industl corr (formerly labour corr) BBC TV News 1982-; regular contribs to all TV news progs incl the Money Programme and Newsnight; *Recreations* tennis, watching West Ham United FC; *Clubs* Grays, Buckhurst Hill Lawn Tennis (Essex); *Style*— John Fryer, Esq; BBC TV News, BBC Television Centre, Wood Lane, London W12 (☎ 081 837 7485)

FRYER, Noel; s of John Fryer (d 1985), of Alsager, Cheshire, and Norah, *née* Leeson; *b* 15 Dec 1943; *Educ* Repton; *m* Anne Katherine, da of John William Walton; 1 s (James Christian Walton b 26 July 1976); *Career* articled clerk Peat Marwick Mitchell 1961-66, self employed chartered accountant 1966-89, exec ptnr Pannell Kerr Forster 1989-; hon treas Rotary Int 1990- (dist govr 1986-87); memb Br Soc Commerce, ACA 1966; *Recreations* shooting, fishing, farming; *Clubs* East India, Lancashire CCC; *Style*— Noel Fryer, Esq; Little Moss Farm, Oakhanger, nr Crewe, Cheshire (☎ 0270 874012); Pannell Kerr Forster, St Georges Chambers, Merrial Street, Newcastle-under-Lyme, Staffordshire ST5 2BG (☎ 0782 632111, fax 0782 711202, car 0836 529463)

FRYER SPEDDING, John Henry Fryer; OBE, DL; s of Lt-Col James Eustace Spedding, OBE (d 1969), of Windebrowe, Keswick, Cumbria, and Mary Catherine, *née* Fryer; *b* 23 Jan 1937; *Educ* Harrow, Trinity Coll Cambridge (MA); *m* 15 Aug 1968, Clare Caroline, da of Ven Walter Frederick Ewbank, of 7 Castle Court, Carlisle, Cumbria; 2 s (James b 1970, Jack b 1972); *Career* Royal Green Jackets 1958-68; serv: Germany, Cyprus, Borneo; ret Maj 1968; DLI (TA) 1969-78, CO 7 Bn LI (TA) 1976-78, ret Lt-Col 1978; called to the Bar Gray's Inn 1970, practising Newcastle upon Tyne; tstee: Wordsworth Tst, Calvert Tst for Disabled People; vice pres Tennyson Soc; *Recreations* forestry, beekeeping; *Style*— John Fryer-Spedding, Esq, OBE, DL; Mirehouse, Keswick, Cumbria CA12 4QE (☎ 07687 72287); Trinity Chambers, 12 Trinity Chare, Quayside, Newcastle NE1 3DF (☎ 091 232 1927, fax 091 232 7975)

FRYERS, (Charles) Geoffrey; s of Charles Ronald Fryers, of Bradley, W Yorks, and Margaret, *née* Mattock; *b* 4 June 1950; *Educ* Ermysteds GS Skipton; *m* 25 Sept 1971, Elizabeth Anne, da of Fred Hird Hodgson, of Bradley, W Yorks; 1 s (Paul b 1975), 1 da (Rachel b 1973); *Career* dir and co sec: Merrit & Fryers Ltd 1975-, Nicholas Smiths Garages Ltd 1981-, E Midgley & Co (Builders Merchants) Ltd 1976-; capt Bradford League Side Keighley CC 1972, capt Lancashire League Side Colne CC 1984 and 1985; apptd Nat Cricket Assoc Coach 1987; *Recreations* cricket player, snooker player, football spectator and lover of all sports; *Clubs* Colne Cricket; *Style*— Geoffrey Fryers, Esq; Harden Clough Farm, Skipton Old Road, Colne, Lancashire BB8 7ER (☎ 0282 843777); Merritt & Fryers Ltd, Firth Street Works, Skipton, N Yorks BD23 2PX

FUCHS, Sir Vivian (Ernest); s of Ernest Fuchs (d 1957), of Heatherdene, Tilford, Surrey, and Annie Violet, *née* Watson; *b* 11 Feb 1908; *Educ* Brighton Coll, St John's Coll Cambridge (MA, PhD); *m* 1933, Joyce, 2 da of John Alexander Connell (d 1914), of Langley, Putney; 1 s (Peter), 2 da (Rosalind (decd), Hilary); *Career* Maj served W Africa and NW Europe; geologist; expeditions include: Greenland 1929, E Africa 1930-31, 1934 and 1937-38; field cdr Falkland Islands Dependencies Survey 1947-50, dir FIDS Scientific Bureau 1950-55, dir Br Antarctic Survey 1958-73, leader Commonwealth Trans-Antarctic Expedition 1955-58; pres: Int Glaciological Soc 1963-66, British Assoc for the Advancement of Science 1972, Royal Geographical Soc 1981-83; author; FRS; kt 1958; *Books* Crossing of Antarctica (1958), Antarctic Adventure (1959), Forces of Nature (ed, 1977), Of Ice and Men (1982), A Time to Speak (1990); *Recreations* sailing, gardening; *Clubs* Athenaeum; *Style*— Sir Vivian Fuchs, FRS; 106 Barton Rd, Cambridge CB3 9LH (☎ 0223 359238)

FUGARD, Maj-Gen Michael Teape; CB (1990); s of Rev Theodore Charles William Cooper Teape Fugard (d 1984), rural dean of Malton, Yorks, and Lilian Rhodes, *née* Freeman Baker (d 1954); *b* 27 March 1933; *Educ* Sherborne; *m* 22 Dec 1961, Theresia, da of Anton Hollensteiner (d 1952), of Leiben, Lower Austria; 2 s (Robert b 1963, William b 1970), 2 da (Alison b 1962, Berenice b 1966); *Career* admitted slr 1957; cmmnd Army Legal Servs (now Army Legal Corps) 1958, Maj CO Army Legal Aid FARELF 1960-64, Lt-Col asst dir BAOR 1971, Col Legal Staff HQUKLF 1979-82, Brig cdr Army Legal Gp UK 1983-86, dir of Army Legal Servs 1986-90, Maj-Gen; memb Law Soc's Salaries Slr's Ctee 1973-78, asst rec 1986-, chm UK Gp Int Soc for Military Law of War 1988-90; hon legal advsr Kingston upon Thames CAB 1965-66, govr Royal Sch Bath 1984-, memb Spire Appeal Ctee Salisbury Cathedral 1985-86, chm govrs Leadenhall Sch Salisbury 1988-, adjudicator Immigration Appeals 1990-, memb Lord Chllr's Panel of Ind Insprs 1990-; *Recreations* walking preferably with a dog, reading, coarse gardening; *Clubs* Lansdowne; *Style*— Maj-Gen Michael Fugard, CB; c/o Immigration Appeals, Thanet House, 23 Strand, London WC2R 1DA

FUGE, Dr (Charles) Alistair; s of Dr (Charles Arthur) Ian Fuge (d 1975), of High Wycombe, Buckinghamshire, and Melene Lloyd, *née* Liddell; *b* 14 Nov 1933; *Educ* Shrewsbury Sch, St John's Coll Oxford, Bart's (BA, BM BCh); *m* 31 March 1962, Susan (Sue), da of Maj Royston Boulter, of Liphook, Hampshire; 2 s (Charles b 1966, Christopher b 1968), 1 da (Sarah b 1964); *Career* RAF MO: Christmas Island 1961, HQ Allied Air Forces Fontainebleau 1961-63; ret Sqdn Ldr; conslt anaesthetist Bath District Health Authy 1970-; memb Cncl History of Anaesthesia Soc; Wessex Regnl Res Essay prize 1967; FC Anaes 1967; *Books* Number Nine Bedford Square; A Connection with Mesmerism in Anaesthesia (1988); *Recreations* skiing, photography, making things out of bits of bent wire; *Style*— Dr Alistair Fuge; The Bath Clinic, Claverton Down Rd, Combe Down, Bath (☎ 0225 835555, fax 0225 835900)

FULCHER, Derick Harold; DSC (1944); s of Percy Frederick Fulcher (d 1951), of London, and Gertrude Lilian, *née* Robinson (d 1971); *b* 4 Nov 1917; *Educ* St Olave's GS; *m* 2 Dec 1943, (Florence Ellen) May, da of John Barr Anderson (d 1956), of Glasgow; 1 s (Derick John b 19 Aug 1945), 1 da (Moira Joy b 12 Dec 1949); *Career* RN 1940-46, Lt RNVR; asst accountant War Office 1936, princ Miny of Nat Insur 1950-56 (asst princ 1947-50), princ HM Treasy 1957-59, asst sec Miny of Social Security 1959, asst under sec of state DHSS 1969-70, admin Staff Coll Henley 1952, interviewer Civil Serv Cmmn 1971-79, chm Supplementary Benefit Appeals Tribunals 1971-75, head of UK res project in W Euro into social security provision for disablement 1971-72, res conslt Office of Manpower Econs 1972-73; chm: NATO Mgmnt Survey Ctee 1970-71, Cncl of Euro Mgmnt Survey Ctee 1971-72; conslt on Mgmnt Servs to Govt of Indonesia 1973; conslt on Social Security to: Govt of Trinidad and Tobago 1967-69, ILO 1973-80, EEC Statistical Office 1974, Govt of Thailand 1978-79 and 1981; fell Inst for Euro Health Servs Res Leuven Univ Belgium 1974; *Books* Medical Care Systems (1974), Social Security for the Unemployed (1976); *Recreations* photography, travel; *Clubs* Civil Service; *Style*— Derick Fulcher, Esq, DSC; 100 Downs Rd, Coulsdon, Surrey CR5 1AF (☎ 0737 554231)

FULFORD, Francis Christopher; s of Lt-Col Francis Edgar Anthony Fulford (d 1969), and Joan Shirley, *née* Blackman, who m 2, 1979, Sir John Carew Pole, 12 Bt (*qv*); Fulfords have been seated at Fulford, Devon, since *temp* Richard I; *b* 31 Aug 1952; *Educ* Milton Abbey; *Career* memb Lloyd's; dir Hargreaves Reiss and Quinn Ltd (Lloyds Brokers); landowner (3000 acres); Liveryman Fishmongers Co; *Recreations* shooting, territorial army, books, trees; *Clubs* Turf; *Style*— Francis Fulford Esq; Great Fulford, Dunsford, nr Exeter, Devon (☎ 064 724 205); 10 Crispin St, London E1 (☎ 071 247 8133)

FULFORD, Robert Ian; s of (Howard) Bruce Fulford, of Ramparts Farm, Bakers Lane, Colchester, Essex, and Mary Elizabeth, *née* Frost; *b* 26 Aug 1969; *Educ* Colchester Royal GS, St Aidan's Coll Durham; *Career* croquet player; memb Colchester Croquet Club, competitive debut 1986; achievements incl: Br under 19 champion 1986 and 1987, Br mens champion 1990, Br Open doubles champion (with C Clarke) 1990, world champion 1990, runner up Br Open and NZ Open 1990; 4 GB Test matches: USA 1989 and 1990, Aust 1990, NZ 1990; *Recreations* bridge, chess, snooker, most other sports and games; *Style*— Robert Fulford, Esq; Ramparts Farm, Bakers Lane, Colchester, Essex CO4 5RB (☎ 0206 852635)

FULHAM, Bishop of 1985-; Rt Rev (Charles) John Klyberg; s of Charles Augustine Klyberg (Capt MN, 1975), and Ivy Lilian, *née* Waddington (d 1978); *b* 29 July 1931; *Educ* Eastbourne Coll, Lincoln Theol Coll; *Career* 2 Lt 1 Bn The Buffs 1952-53; asst estates mangr Cluttons 1953-57; curate St John's E Dulwich 1960-63, rector Fort Jameson Zambia 1963-67, vicar Christ Church and St Stephen Battersea 1967-77, dean Lusaka Cathedral Zambia and rector of parish 1977-85 (vicar gen 1978-85), chm Church Property Devpt Gp 1978-85, dean emeritus 1985; UK commissary for Anglican Church in Zambia 1985-89; archdeacon of Charing Cross 1989-; ARICS; *Recreations* reading, music, travel; *Clubs* Athenaeum; *Style*— The Rt Rev the Bishop of Fulham; 4 Cambridge Place, London W8 5PB

FULLARD, Hon Mrs (Glenys); *née* Macdonald; da of 1 Baron Macdonald of Gwaenysgor, KCMG, PC (d 1966), and Mary, *née* Lewis (d 1967); *b* 1923; *m* 1949, Robert Fullard, BSc, yst s of Herbert Fullard (d 1958), of Werneth, Lancs; 2 da; *Career* JP Lancs; *Style*— The Hon Mrs Fullard; 2 Thornley Lane, Grotton, Oldham

FULLENWIDER, Fran; da of Dale Fullenwider (d 1975), and Kelsey La Verrier-Stuart Fullenwider (d 1963); *b* 16 Nov 1945; *Educ* Univ of Maryland (BA), NY Univ (Graduate Study in Film, TV and Radio), RADA (Stage Mgmnt Diploma); *Career* actress, starring in romantic film comedies in Italy 1976-, dir Pilgrim Prodns 1987-; *Recreations* writing, interior decoration, food; *Clubs* Groucho; *Style*— Miss Fran Fullenwider; c/o Miss Susan James, Personal Management, 22 Westbeer Rd, London NW2 (☎ 071 794 1286)

FULLER, Anthony Gerard Fleetwood; CBE (1990); 2 s of Maj Sir Gerard Fuller, 2 Bt, JP (d 1981), and his 1 w, Lady Fiona Pratt (later Countess of Normanton, d 1985), yr da of 4 Marquess Camden; *b* 4 June 1940; *Educ* Eton; *m* 19 Nov 1964, Julia Mary, er da of Lt-Col Eric Astley Cooper-Key, MBE, MC; 1 s (William Gerard Fleetwood b 13 July 1968), 1 da (Camilla Fleetwood b 16 Feb 1966); *Career* Lt Life Gds 1959-62; Lloyd's underwriter; Fuller Smith & Turner plc (brewers): dir 1967-, md 1978-, md and chm 1982-; Freeman, Liveryman and past Master Brewers' Co; chm Brewers Soc 1986-89; *Recreations* shooting, gardening; *Style*— Anthony Fuller, Esq, CBE; Griffin Brewery, Chiswick, London W4 2QB (☎ 071 994 2162); Little Chalfield Manor, Melksham, Wilts SN12 8NN (☎ 022 16 5934)

FULLER, Charles Christopher Fleetwood; JP; s of Lt Col CHF Fuller, TD (d 1976), of Jaggards, Corsham, Wilts, and Beatrice Susan, *née* Hambro (d 1977); *b* 24 June 1945; *Educ* Winchester; *m* 9 March 1984, Bryony Jane, *née* Kup; 1 s (George b 3 April 1985), 1 da (Claire b 16 July 1987); *Career* 5 Royal Inniskilling Dragoon Gds 1964-67, Royal Wiltshire Yeo 1970-74; *Clubs* Pratt's; *Style*— Charles Fuller, Esq, JP; Jaggards, Corsham, Wilts

FULLER, David William; s of Edward William Jack Fuller (d 1969), of Suffolk, and Alice Marjorie, *née* Budd (d 1956); *b* 27 May 1935; *Educ* Forest Sch; *m* 25 Jan 1969, Sheila Mary, da of Erst Ellis (d 1952); 1 s (Julian b 1971), 1 da (Katharine b 1972); *Career* Nat Serv with RN; marine broker Lloyds 1956-58, Arthur Ackermann & Son Ltd 1958- (dir 1965, jt md 1985); Master Worshipful of Co Tylers & Bricklayers 1988-89; *Clubs* Arts; *Style*— David W Fuller, Esq; Barnards Bridge, Duton Hill, nr Dunmow, Essex (☎ 037 184 255); 33 New Bond St, London W1 (☎ 071 493 3288)

FULLER, Hon Mrs (Geraldine Anne); *née* FitzRoy; o da of 6 Baron Southampton, *qv*; *b* 31 Dec 1951; *m* 1976, Richard G Fuller; 2 s (Joshua FitzRoy b 1978, Oliver b 1981), 1 da (Victoria b 1983); *Style*— The Hon Mrs Fuller; Strete House, Strete, Whimple, nr Exeter, Devon

FULLER, Sir John William Fleetwood; 3 Bt (UK 1910), of Neston Park, Corsham, Wiltshire; s of Maj Sir (John) Gerard Henry Fleetwood Fuller, 2 Bt (d 1981), by his 1 w, Lady Fiona Pratt, yr da of 4 Marquess Camden; *b* 18 Dec 1936; *Educ* Bradfield; *m* 9 Jan 1968, Lorna Marian, o da of F Richard Kemp-Potter, of Findon, Sussex; 3 s (James, Andrew William Fleetwood b 1972, Edward Richard Fleetwood b 1977); *Heir* s, James Henry Fleetwood Fuller b 1 Nov 1970; *Career* Maj (ret) Life Gds; *Style*— Sir John Fuller, Bt; Neston Park, Corsham, Wilts SN13 9TG (☎ 0225 810211)

FULLER, Keith; s of Charles Fuller (d 1964), of Cheam, Surrey, and Marie, *née* Varndell (d 1968); *b* 27 Oct 1932; *Educ* Epsom Coll, Univ of London (BSc); *m* 1973, Patricia, da of F Bernard Humphreys; 2 da (Rowena b 6 Dec 1975, Cassandra b 1 Oct 1977); *Career* Mullard (now Philips) Res Labs 1956-81, gp tech dir Racal-Decca 1981-85, md Philips Res Labs 1985-; chm Electronics Div IEE 1989-90; FIEE 1975 (AMIEE 1956), FEng 1987; *Recreations* cars, music, photography; *Clubs* Aston Martin Owners; *Style*— Keith Fuller, Esq; Philips Res Labs, Cross Oak Lane, Redhill, Surrey RH1 5HA (☎ 0293 785544, fax 0293 776495)

FULLER, Martin Elliott; *b* 9 Feb 1943; *Educ* Mid-Warwickshire Coll of Art, Hornsey Coll of Art; *Career* awarded Guggenheim-McKingley scholarship (American Art Workshop, Italy) 1964, worked in Italy and America, now London; one-man exhibitions incl: Arnolfini Gallery (Bath) 1968, Midland Art Centre (Birmingham) 1968, Centaur Gallery (Bath) 1969, Bristol Art Gallery 1970, Arnolfini Gallery (Bristol) 1971, Bear Lane Gallery (Oxford) 1971, Camden Art Centre (London) 1971, Bear Lane Gallery (Oxford) 1973, Festival Gallery (Bath) 1973, Grabowski Gallery (London) 1973, Thumb Gallery (Bath) 1976 and 1979, Oxford Gallery 1983, RZA Galerie (Dusseldorf) 1983, Austin Desmond Fine Art 1985, On The Wall Gallery (Belfast) 1987, Hendriks Gallery (Dublin) 1987, Austin Desmond Fine Art 1990; commissioned New Mexico (USA) Feb-Oct 1990; *Clubs* Chelsea Arts, Colony Room, Groucho; *Style*— Martin Fuller, Esq; c/o The Chelsea Arts Club, 143 Old Church Street, London SW3 6EB

FULLER, Mary, Lady; (Katherine) Mary; da of Douglas Leigh Spence, (d 1965), of Melksham, Wilts; *b* 26 Dec 1918; *m* 1, E H Leventon (decd); 1 s decd, 1 da; m 2, 21 Oct 1966, as his 3 w, Maj Sir Gerard Fuller, 2 Bt, JP, Maj Life Gds (d 1981); *Style*— Mary, Lady Fuller; Bay Tree Cottage, Chapel Lane, Neston, Corsham, Wilts SN13 9TD (☎ Hawthorn 0225 810497); Balmore, Cannich, by Beauly, Invernes-shire (☎ 045 65 262)

FULLER, Michael John; s of Thomas Frederick Fuller, of Great Bookham, and Irene Emily, *née* Pope; *b* 20 July 1932; *Educ* Wallington GS; *m* 26 March 1955 (m dis 1989), (Maureen) Rita, da of Frederick Slade; 2 s (Nicholas b 1960, Richard b 1962), 2 da (Laura b 1966, Jacqueline (twin) b 1966); *Career* Midland Bank plc: various positions 1948-77, gp public affairs advsr 1977-79, regnl dir Southampton 1979-81, gen mangr 1981-83, gen mangr business devpt 1983-85, UK ops dir 1985-87, dep chief exec UK banking sector 1987-89, chief exec UK banking sector 1989-; FCIB; *Recreations* reading, travelling, rough golf; *Style*— Michael Fuller, Esq; Midland Bank plc, 47 Cannon St, London EC4M 5SQ (☎ 071 260 7947)

FULLER, Paul Malcolm; s of John Taylor Fuller, of Billericay, Essex; *b* 4 Nov 1946; *Educ* Southend HS for Boys; *m* 1969, Jenifer Mary Elizabeth, da of Percy Beere (d 1955); 1 s, 2 da; *Career* accountant; memb Inst of Dirs; fin dir: Lacrinoid Products Ltd 1973-78, TKM Foods Ltd 1978-83, Touche Ross 1983- (consulting ptnr Touche Ross 1987); *Recreations* walking, the arts; *Style*— Paul Fuller, Esq; Pen-Y-Bryn House, 1 Buckingham Rd, Hockley, Essex SS5 4UE

FULLER, Roy Broadbent; CBE (1970); s of Leopold Charles Fuller (d 1920), of Oldham, and Nellie, *née* Broadbent (d 1949); *b* 11 Feb 1912; *Educ* privately; *m* 1936, Kate (Kathleen), da of Henry North Smith; 1 s (John Leopold b 1937); *Career* ordinary seaman RN 1941-42, leading radar mechanic 1942-43, Petty Offr radar mechanic 1943-44, Lt RNVR 1944-46; asst slr private practice 1934-38; Woolwich Equitable Building Soc: asst slr 1938-58, slr 1958-69, dir 1969-87; prof of poetry Univ of Oxford 1968-73, govr BBC 1972-79; *Books* many books of verse, novels, autobiography and criticism; *Clubs* Athenaeum; *Style*— Roy Fuller, Esq, CBE; 37 Langton Way, London SE3 7TY (☎ 081 858 2334)

FULLER, Simon William John; s of Rowland William Bevis Fuller, of 14 Byron Court, Ham Common, Richmond, and Madeline, *née* Bailey (d 1963); *b* 27 Nov 1943; *Educ* Wellington, Emmanuel Coll Cambridge (BA); *m* 15 Sept 1984, Eleanor Mary, da of Peter Breedon, of Crondal Rd, Crookham Village, Hants; 2 s (Edward William b 5 Sept 1986, James Francis b 13 June 1988); *Career* HM Dip Serv 1968-; FCO 1968, third sec Br High Cmmn Singapore 1969-71, second sec Br Embassy Kinshasa 1971-73; first sec: Cabinet Office 1973-77, UK Mission to UN NY 1977-80, FCO 1980-84; counsellor and dep head Personnel Ops Dept 1984-86, dep head Mission Br Embassy Tel Aviv 1986-90, head of Near East and N Africa Dept FCO 1990-; *Recreations* cricket, golf; *Clubs* United Oxford and Cambridge Univ, MCC; *Style*— Simon Fuller, Esq; 27 Carlisle Mansions, Carlisle Place, London SW1P 1EZ (☎ 071 828 6494); Foreign and Commonwealth Office, King Charles St, London SW1 (☎ 071 270 3000)

FULLER, Prof Watson; s of Edward Fuller (d 1983), of Haslingden, Lancashire, and Alice, *née* Worrall; *b* 25 Feb 1935; *Educ* Haslingden GS, King's Coll London (BSc, PhD); *m* 9 Sept 1961, Shirley Ann, da of Cedric Pollack (d 1934), of London; 1 s (Laurence b 17 Dec 1965), 1 da (Catherine b 13 Nov 1967); *Career* scientific staff MRC 1960-63, reader in biophysics King's Coll London 1967-73 (lectr 1963-67), prof of physics Univ of Keele 1973- (dep vice chllr 1980-83, 1984-5, 1988-); FInstP 1974; *Style*— Prof Watson Fuller; Oaklands, 50 Station Rd, Keele, Staffs ST5 5AH (☎ 0782 627220); Dept of Physics, University of Keele, Staffs ST5 5BG (☎ 0782 621111, telex 36113 UNKLIB G, fax 0782 711093)

FULLER-ACLAND-HOOD, Dr Hon Mrs John; Phyllis Lily Frances; o da of Dr Denys Bouhier Imbert Hallett (d 1969); *b* 14 Oct 1915; *Educ* Cheltenham Ladies' Coll, UCL, Univ Coll Hosp London; *m* 1 June 1939, Hon (Arthur) John Palmer Fuller-Acland-Hood (d 2 Nov 1964), yr s of 1 Baron St Audries (d 1917), and Hon Mildred Rose Eveleigh de Moleyns (d 1949), da of 4 Baron Ventry; 3 da (Elizabeth Perian (Lady Gass), Mary Mildred (Mrs Blackaby), Sylvia (Mrs Ray)); *Career* Fl Lt RAF Med Serv 1942-43; registered med practitioner house surgn Univ Coll Hosp 1940-41, Govt Health Serv Singapore 1952-53, psychiatrist Mendip Hosp Wells 1964-79; *Recreations* gardening, bridge; *Clubs* New Cavendish; *Style*— Dr the Hon Mrs John Acland-Hood; Wootton House, nr Glastonbury, Somerset BA6 8TX (☎ 0458 42348)

FULLER-ACLAND-HOOD, Sir (Alexander) William; 8 Bt (UK 1806), of Hartington, Co Derby, and 6 Bt (UK 1809), of St Audries, Co Somerset; in remainder to Irish Barony of Bridport; naturalised an American citizen 1926; s of late William Fuller-Acland-Hood (d 1933), 5 s of 3 Bt (cr 1809); suc cous, 2 Baron St Audries (also 7 and 5 Bt) 1971, and Elizabeth, *née* Kirkpatrick (d 1966); gggf commanded Mars in famous battle between Mars and Hercules and died at moment of victory 21 April 1796; *b* 5 March 1901; *Educ* Wellington, RMA Woolwich (Lieut RE), Univ of California (BSMA); *m* 1925, Mary Violet, da of late Augustus Edward Jessup, of Philadelphia, USA (d 1925); 1 da (Elisabeth), 1 s (John d 1947); *Heir* none; *Career* formerly Lt RE; prof Los Angeles City Coll, ret; *Books* (co-author with Mary V Hood) Nature and the Camper, Wildflowers of Yosemite and their Story; *Recreations* photography; *Style*— Sir William Acland-Hood, Bt; SR2 Box 577, 29 Palms, Calif 92277, USA (☎ 714 3679345)

FULLERTON, Edward; s of Thomas Henry Fullerton (d 1924), and Mary Dickson (d 1987); *b* 27 April 1921; *Educ* St Mary's Catholic Sch Grimsby; *m* 10 July 1943, Irene Ivy, da of Harry Whiteley (d 1954), of Hull, N Humberside; 1 da (Margaret Ivy b 1949); *Career* design engnr, fndr md and chm Turbo Tools (Hull) Ltd 1957-, fndr chm Trinity Graphics Ltd 1970-, fndr and chm Fullerton Patents Ltd 1989; memb: Inst of Patentees and Inventors, Nat Geographic Soc, RAF Assoc (life), American Biographical Inst Res Assoc; FInstD; *Recreations* pencil drawings, water colour painting, computer programming; *Style*— Edward Fullerton, Esq; 177 Westella Rd, Westella, Hull, N Humberside HU10 7RP (☎ 0482 659212; Turbo Tools (Hull) Ltd, 1 Gillett St, Hull, N Humberside (☎ 0482 25651, telex 597626, car 0860 363731)

FULLERTON, Fiona Elizabeth; da of Brig B V H Fullerton, CBE, ADC, RAPC, and Pamela Fullerton, *née* Crook; *b* 10 Oct 1956; *Educ* Elmhurst Ballet Sch; *m* (m dis 1982), Simon MacCorkindale *qv*; *Career* actress; films incl: Run Wild, Run Free (1968), Nicholas and Alexandra (1970, as Anastasia), Alice's Adventures in Wonderland (1972, title role), The Human Factor (1979), The Ibiza Connection (1984), A View to a Kill (1984), A Girl Called Henry (1990); stage incl: Cinderella (1976-77, title role), I am A Camera (1979, as Sally Bowles), The Beggar's Opera (1980, as Polly Peachum), Gypsy (1981, as Gypsy Rose Lee), The Boyfriend (1982), Camelot (1982-83, as Queen Guinevere), The Royal Baccarat Scandal (1988-89, Theatre Royal Haymarket); TV incl: Angels (1975-76), Gaugin, The Savage (1979), Leo Tolstoy: A Question of Faith (1979), Shaka Zulu (1985), Hold the Dream (1986), The Charmer (1986), Hazard of Hearts (1987), The Life of Hemingway (1988), A Taste for Death (1988), A Ghost in Monte Carlo (1989), Secret Life of Ian Fleming (1989), To Be The Best (1990); dir Savoy Theatre Ltd; *Style*— Miss Fiona Fullerton; c/o Jean Diamond, London Mgmnt, 235 Regent St, London W1

FULLERTON, John Charles Mark; s of Capt John Robert Rankin Fullerton (d 1966), by his 2 wife Evelyn Mary (d 1960), 2 da of Sir Alfred Molyneux Palmer, 3 Bt; *b* 21 Dec 1924; *Educ* Eton; *m* 1, 1955, Pamela Blanche Gwynedd (d 1982), da of Robert Crespigny Gwynedd Vivian (d 1984), of Jersey; 2 s (John, David), 1 da (Carolin); m 2, 1984, Philippa Nancy Le Marchant, *née* Denby; *Career* Staff Capt 60 Rifles KRRC; advertising exec; md Ogilvy & Mather Ltd Hong Kong 1978-79 (dir 1967), chm Assoc of Accredited Advertising Agents (Hong Kong) 1979; MIPA; *Novels incl* If Chance is a

Stranger, Beloved Enemy, The Man Who Spoke Dog; *Recreations* writing, sailing (aux sloop 'Myschief'); *Style—* John Fullerton, Esq; The Old Estate House, Heytesbury, Warminster, Wiltshire BA12 0HQ (☎ 0985 40727); 25 St George's Court, 87 St George's Drive, London SW1V 4DB (☎ 071 828 5275)

FULLERTON, William Hugh; CMG (1990); s of Maj Arthur Hugh Theodore Francis Fullerton, RAMC (d 1950), and Mary, *née* Parker; *b* 11 Feb 1939; *Educ* Cheltenham, Queens' Coll Cambridge (MA); *m* 1968, Arlene, da of late Dr J Jacobowitz; 1 da (Elizabeth b 1970); *Career* Shell Int Petroleum Co Uganda 1963-65; joined FO 1965, MECAS Lebanon 1965-66; info offr Jedda 1966-67, UK Mission to UN (NYC) 1967, FCO 1968-70; head of Chancery: Kingston Jamaica 1970-73, Ankara 1973-77; FCO 1977-80, cnsllr (econ and commercial) 1980-83, consul gen Islamabad 1981-83, HM ambassador Mogadishu 1983-87, on loan to MOD London 1987-88, govr of the Falkland Islands 1988, high cmmr British Antarctic Territory 1988-89, cmmr South Georgia and South Sandwich Islands 1988; *Recreations* travelling in remote areas, sailing, reading, walking; *Clubs* Travellers'; *Style—* William Fullerton, Esq, CMG; c/o FCO, King Charles St, London SW1

FULLWOOD, Keith Saxon; s of Percy Fullwood; *b* 9 May 1928; *Educ* HS Sheffield; *m* 1962, Rosemary Anne, *née* Law; 2 s; *Career* chartered sec, accountant John Brown Gp 1954-60, gp chief accountant Bestwood Gp 1960-62, gp sec Sprite Gp 1962-67; dir: Autopack Ltd, Scientific & Educnl Aids Ltd 1967-82; chm Wayfeed 1983-87 (mgmnt conslt 1983-), exec dir Falcon Packaging Ltd 1987-; Freeman City of London, Liveryman Scriveners Co and Chartered Secs Co; FCIS, FBIM; *Style—* Keith Fullwood, Esq; Shazam, Upper St, Defford, Worcs (☎ 0386 750241, office 0386 45925)

FULTHORPE, Jonathan Mark; s of Henry Joseph Fulthorpe, and Betty May, *née* Forshew; *b* 21 March 1949; *Educ* Sir Joseph Williamson's Mathmatical Sch Rochester, UCL (LLB), Univ of London (LLM); *m* 1, 1973 (m dis 1978), Clare Elizabeth, *née* Stephenson; m 2, 1979, Carol Margaret, da of late Stanley Gordon Greenfield, of Brantford, Ontario, Canada; 1 s (James Mark Charles b 1981), 3 step da (Sarah Lynne b 1970, Jennifer Anne b 1972, Alison Claire b 1975); *Career* called to the Bar Inner Temple 1970, practising Western circuit 1973-; FRGS 1972-; *Recreations* watching cricket and soccer; the study of geography, travel to rare places; *Clubs* Hampshire (Winchester), Hampshire CCC, Bentham; *Style—* Jonathan Fulthorpe, Esq; 16 Abbotts Way, Southampton, Hants SO2 1QT (☎ 0703 584 879); 17 Carlton Crescent, Southampton SO1 2ES (☎ 0703 636 036, fax 0703 223 877); 3 Paper Buildings, Temple, London EC4 (☎ 071 583 8055, fax 071 353 6271)

FULTON, Robert Andrew; s of Rev Robert Morton Fulton, of Isle of Bute, Scotland, and Janet White, *née* Mackenzie; *b* 6 Feb 1944; *Educ* Rothesay Acad, Univ of Glasgow (MA, LLB); *m* 29 Aug 1970, Patricia Mary Crowley; 2 s (Daniel Robert b 8 Oct 1972, Edward Patrick b 8 Sept 1974), 1 da (Joanna Mary b 9 May 1979); *Career* HM Dip Serv; third sec FCO 1968, third then second sec Saigon 1968-72; first sec: Rome 1973-77, E Berlin 1978-81, FCO 1981-84; cnsllr: Oslo 1984-87, FCO 1987-88, UK Mission to UN NY; *Recreations* golf, national hunt racing, reading, cinema; *Style—* R A Fulton, Esq

FUMMI, Lady (Cynthia) Anne; *née* Lindsay; da of late 27 Earl of Crawford and 10 of Balcarres, KT, PC, and Constance, da of Sir Henry Carstairs Pelly, MP, 3 Bt; *b* 21 June 1904; *m* 1, 12 Nov 1931, Per Erik Folke Arnander (d 26 Feb 1933), first sec Swedish Legation Rome; 1 s; m 2, 2 April 1934, Giovanni Fummi (d 1970), s of Pietro Fummi; 1 da; *Style—* The Lady Anne Fummi

FUNG, Hon Sir Kenneth Ping-fan; CBE (1965, OBE 1958), JP (Hong Kong 1952); yr s of Fung Ping-shan, JP; *b* 28 May 1911; *Educ* Govt Vernacular Sch, Sch of Chinese Studies Hong Kong Univ; *m* 1933, Ivy, Shiu-Han, OBE, JP, da of late Kan Tong-Po, JP; 4 s, 1 da; *Career* unofficial memb Urban Cncl 1951-60, unofficial MLC 1959-65, MEC 1962-72; chm Fung Ping Fan & Co; dir (chief mangr ret) The Bank of East Asia Ltd Hong Kong; life memb Court of Univ of Hong Kong; cmdr St John Ambulance Bde (first Chinese to serve) 1953-58, KStJ 1958; Order of the Sacred Treasure (Japan) 1969; kt 1971; *Style—* Hon Sir Kenneth Fung, CBE, JP; home: 14 South Bay Rd, Hong Kong (☎ 92514); office: Fung Ping Fan & Co Ltd, 2705-2715 Connaught Centre, Hong Kong (☎ 220311)

FUNG-ON, Eton Gregory; s of Leslie Rupert Fung-On, of Kent, and Avis Christabel, *née* Woon-Shing; *b* 14 Oct 1947; *Educ* Beckenham and Penge GS; *m* 3 July 1971, Patricia Helen, da of Frederick Ernest Dodd, of Sussex; 2 s (Richard b 1973, Neil b 1974); *Career* CA, mgmnt conslt; various sr fin and mgmnt positions public, commercial, industl orgns 1966-86; fin and investmt advsr Ficci Investments Ltd 1986-; FCA; *Recreations* church activities, gardening, sports; *Style—* Eton G Fung-On, Esq; 412 Upper Shoreham Rd, Shoreham-by-sea, W Sussex BN4 5NE (☎ 0273 462656); Ficci Investments Ltd, 13th Floor, Bowater House, 1 Edinburgh Gate, London SW1X 7LT (☎ 071 589 9600)

FUNNELL, Barry Oliver Bevan; OBE (1969), JP (E Sussex 1974); s of Hubert John Funnell (d 1957), of Sussex, and Kathleen Doris, *née* Bevan (d 1942); *b* 29 Sept 1924; *Educ* Preston Coll Brighton, Montpellier Coll; *m* 1942, Pamela Margery Maud, da of Frederick Joseph Harding (d 1971); *Career* chm and md: Bevan Funnell Ltd, John Lawrence & Co (Dover) Ltd, A K Verity Ltd, Shard Stebbing Ltd, H & A G Alexander Ltd, Reprodux Inc North Carolina USA, Bevan SA; former chm BFM Exports Ltd; Mayor of Hove 1960-61; *Recreations* yachting; *Clubs* IOD; *Style—* Barry Funnell, Esq, OBE, JP; Innisfree, Cuckmere Rd, Seaford, Sussex; Le Beaupre, Sark, Channel Islands; Reprodux House, Norton Road, Newhaven, Sussex (☎ 0273 513762)

FUNSHINE, Geoffrey Nicholas Christopher Peter; s of Leonard Funshine (d 1976); *b* 16 Nov 1936; *Educ* Shrewsbury; *m* 1962, Barbara Joan, *née* Foxcroft; 1 s, 2 da; *Career* chm The Grand Theatre Tst Ltd 1981-, md BPB Corpn 1976, dir The 525 Co and subsidiaries 1959; *Recreations* pleasure, ice skating, squash, travel; *Clubs* Cambridge Union, Primrose, Fylde Conservative, Travellers and Explorers; *Style—* Geoffrey Funshine, Esq; Grosvenor House, Grosvenor Rd, Poulton-le-Fylde

FURBER, (Robert) John; s of Frank Robert Furber, of 8 Pond Rd, Blackheath, London, and Anne Wilson, *née* McArthur; *b* 13 Oct 1949; *Educ* Westminster, Gonville and Caius Coll Cambridge (MA); *m* 16 April 1977, (Amanda) Cherry, da of Frederick Colbran Burgoyne Varney, OBE, of 21 Lock Chase, Blackheath, London; 1 s (Thomas b 1980), 2 da (Sophia b 1983, Olivia b 1989); *Career* called to the Bar Inner Temple 1973; *Books* jt ed: Halsbury's Laws of England (Landlord and Tenant) (1981), Hill and Redman's Law of Landlord and Tenant (1988); *Recreations* wine, literature, music, cricket; *Clubs* Buck's, Beefsteak; *Style—* John Furber, Esq; 52 Southbrook Rd, Lee, London SE12 (☎ 081 852 5770); 2 Paper Buildings, Temple, London EC4 (☎ 071 353 5835)

FURLONG, Monica; da of Alfred Gordon Furlong (d 1972), of Co Cork, and Bessie Winifred Esther, *née* Simpson (d 1985); *b* 17 Jan 1930; *Educ* Harrow Co Girls Sch, UCL; *m* 12 Aug 1953 (m dis 1977), William John Knights; 1 s (Alexander William b 1961), 1 da (Charlotte Ann b 1957); *Career* Daily Mail 1961-68, prodr BBC 1974-78; moderator Movement for the Ordination of Women 1982-85, co fndr St Hilda Community 1987; DD Gen Theol Seminary NY 1986; *Books* With Love To The Church (1964), Travelling In (1974), The Cat's Eye (1976), Merton (1980), Cousins (1983), Genuine Fake (1986), Thérèse of Lisieux (1987), Wise Child (1987), A Year and a Day (1990); *Clubs* Soc of Authors; *Style—* Mrs Monica Furlong; c/o Anthony Sheil Associates, 43 Doughty St, London WC1

FURMSTON, (Bentley) Edwin; s of Rev Edward Bentley Furmston (d 1959), and Mary, *née* Bennett (d 1983); *b* 7 Oct 1931; *Educ* Nelson Sch Wigton, Univ of Manchester (BSc); *m* 1957, Margaret, da of Thomas Jackson (d 1970); 2 s (Michael, Robin), 1 da (Susan); *Career* surveyor; Directorate of Overseas Surveys Colonial Office: surveyor 1953, princ surveyor 1967, asst dir 1971; dep dir Ordnance Survey 1974; dir and survey advsr: Miny for Overseas Devpt, Directorate of Overseas Surveys 1980, DOS merged with Ordnance Survey 1984; dir Overseas Surveys Ordnance Survey 1984-89; *Recreations* gardening, mountain walking; *Style—* Edwin Furmston Esq; The Orchards, Carters Clay Rd, Newtown, Romsey SO51 0GL

FURMSTON, Prof Michael Philip; s of Joseph Philip Furmston (d 1987), of Chipstead, Surrey, and Phyllis, *née* Clowes; *b* 1 May 1933; *Educ* Wellington, Exeter Coll Oxford (BA, BCL, MA), Univ of Birmingham (LLM); *m* 26 Sept 1964, Ashley Sandra Maria, da of Edward Cope, of The Spinney, Appleton Rd, Cumnor, Oxon; 3 s (Simon b 1977, Thomas b 1981, Timothy b 1983), 7 da (Rebecca b 1967, Rachel b 1969, Charlotte b 1971, Clare b 1973, Alexandra b 1975, Antonia b 1978, Olivia b 1979); *Career* Nat Serv RA 1951-53, cmmnd 2 Lt 1952, TA serv 1953-78 (Maj 1966); lectr in law Univ of Birmingham 1957-62 and Queens Univ Belfast 1962-63, fell Lincoln Coll Oxford and lectr in law 1964-78, pro vice chllr Univ of Bristol 1986-89 (prof of law 1978-, dean faculty of law 1980-84); bencher Gray's Inn 1989; Freeman Worshipful Co of Arbitrators; *Books* Cheshire Fifoot and Furmston's Law of Contract (ed 8 to 11 edn, 1972-86), A Building Contract Casebook (with V Powell-Smith, 1984, 2 edn 1990), The Law of Tort: Policies and Trends in Liability for Damage to Property and Economic Loss (ed, 1986), You and the Law (ed with V Powell-Smith, 1987), Sale of Goods (1990); *Recreations* chess (rep British team in second correspondence olympiads), dogs, Austin A35s, watching cricket; *Clubs* Reform, Naval and Military; *Style—* Prof Michael Furmston, TD; The Old Post Office, Shipham, Winscombe, Avon BS25 1TQ (☎ 093484 2253); Faculty of Law, University of Bristol, Wills Memorial Building, Queens Rd, Bristol BS8 1RJ (☎ 0272 303373, fax 0272 251870)

FURNEAUX, Paul; s of James Furneaux, of 11 Ashley Rd, Aberdeen, and Nora Mavis, *née* Davidson; *b* 2 March 1962; *Educ* Aberdeen GS, Edinburgh Coll of Art (BA, postgrad Dip); *Career* self employed artist; solo exhibitions: Todd Gallery 1989 and 1991, Compass Gallery Glasgow 1989, Gordonstoun Sch Scotland 1990, Yamaquchi City Japan; numerous gp exhibitions incl: RSA Student Show 1985, 1986 and 1987, Edinburgh Scene (City Art Centre) 1986, Christmas Show Mercury Gallery 1986, Christmas Show Compass Gallery 1986, New Generation (Compass Gallery, Edinburgh) 1987, On a Small Scale (Open Eye Gallery) 1987, New Works (Backroom Gallery) 1987, The Chosen Few (Open Eye Gallery, Edinburgh)1988, Figure form and Fantasy (Todd Gallery, London) 1988, Prints from the Four Colleges (Printmakers Workshop, Edinburgh) 1988, Dozen Full of Talent (Kingfisher Gallery, Edinburgh) 1989, Royal Scottish Acad Annual show 1989 and 1990, Idylls of 89 (Todd Gallery, London) 1989, Christmas Exhibition (Compass Gallery, Edinburgh) 1989, Aberdeen Against the Poll Tax (Arts Centre) 1989, Aberdeen Artists Annual Sho 1990, Surrealist Tendencies in Contemporary Scottish Art (Open Circle Gallery, Glasgow) 1990, Peacock Printmakers Members Annual Christmas Show (Artspace, Aberdeen) 1990; works in the collections of: City Art Centre Edinbugh, Jean F Watson Bequest Purchase, Aberdeen Art Gallery, Heriot-Watt Univ, Edinburgh Coll of Art, Royal Scottish Acad, BBC Scotland; awards: Royal Scottish Acad Keith prize 1986, Edinburgh DC Spring Fling first prize for painting 1986, Young Scottish Artist of the Year 1987, Clason-Harie Bursary for Postgrad Exhibition 1987, Print prize 1987, Largo award Edinburgh Coll of Art, Sunday Times Scotland Mayfest award for visual art 1989, Royal Over-Seas League prize winner 1989, Alister E Salveson Art scholar 1990; *Style—* Paul Furneaux, Esq; 11 Ashley Road, Aberdeen, Scotland AB1 6RU (☎ 0224 5858432); Jenny Todd, Todd Gallery, 326 Portobello Road, London W10 5RU (☎ 081 960 6209)

FURNELL, Dr James Rupert Gawayne; s of Percy Gawayne Furnell (d 1986), of London, and Margaret Katherine Aslett, *née* Wray (d 1979); *b* 20 Feb 1946; *Educ* Leighton Park Soc of Friends Sch Reading, Univ of Aberdeen (MA), Univ of Glasgow (DCP), Univ of Stirling (PhD), Univ of Dundee (LLB, Dip LP); *m* 14 Sept 1974, Lesley Anne, da of John Ross, of Glasgow; 1 s (Alistair b 1976), 1 da (Rachael b 1978); *Career* clinical psychologist Royal Hosp for Sick Children Glasgow 1970-72, conslt clinical psychologist (child health) Forth Valley Health Bd 1980- (sr clinical psychologist 1972-80), memb Forth Valley Health Bd 1984-87; memb Nat Consultative Ctee in Professions Allied to Med 1984-87, chm Div of Clinical Psychology Br Psychological Soc 1988-89; hon fell Univ of Edinburgh 1987-; FBPsS; *Recreations* flying, cross country skiing; *Clubs* Gleneagles; *Style—* Dr James Furnell; Glensherup House, Glendevon, Perthshire (☎ 025981 234); Dept of Child Clinical Psychology, Stirling Royal Infirmary, 1 Randolph Rd, Stirling (☎ 0786 73151)

FURNELL, Stephen George; s of George Edward Furnell (d 1971), of Kettering, Northants, and Norah Delia, *née* Barritt; *b* 30 June 1945; *Educ* Kettering GS, Cambridgeshire HS, Leicester Poly (Dip); *m* 12 Feb 1972, Maxine, da of Harry Smith (d 1989), of Edmonton, London; 2 s (Thomas b 1972, Henery b 1982); *Career* Architects Dept Leicester CC 1967, ptnr TP Bennett 1987 (joined 1969); memb Concrete Soc, ARIBA 1970, MCSD 1987, FRSA 1987; *Recreations* cricket, badminton, photography; *Clubs* Surrey CCC; *Style—* Stephen George; TP Bennett Partnership, 262 High Holborn, London WC1V 7DU (☎ 071 405 9277, fax 071 405 3568)

FURNESS, Alan Edwin; s of Edwin Furness (d 1985), and Marion *née* Senton (d 1988); *b* 6 June 1937; *Educ* Eltham Coll, Jesus Coll Cambridge (BA, MA); *m* 27 Nov 1971, (Aline) Elizabeth Janine, da of Cdr R Barrett, RN (d 1972); 2 s (Roderick b 1972, Christian b 1975); *Career* CRO 1961, private sec to Parly Under Sec of State, CRO (Duke of Devonshire) 1961-62, third then second sec Br High Cmmn New Delhi 1962-66, DSAO 1966-69; first sec: UK Delegation to Euro Communities Brussels 1967-72, Br Embassy Dakar 1972-75; FCO 1975-78; cnsllr Br Embassy: Jakarta 1978-81, Warsaw 1982-85; head of S Pacific Dept FCO 1985-89, Br dep high cmmr Bombay 1989-; *Clubs* United Oxford and Cambridge Univ; *Style—* Alan Furness, Esq; Foreign and Commonwealth Office, King Charles St, London, SW1A 2AH (☎ 071 270 3000)

FURNESS, Michael Fitzroy Roberts; s and h of Sir Stephen Furness, 3 Bt, and Mary, *née* Cann; *b* 12 Oct 1962; *Educ* Sedbergh, Askham Bryan Coll of Agric and Hort (HND); *Career* farmer, pig husbandry; *Recreations* rugby, shooting, travelling, contemplation, music; *Style—* Michael Furness Esq; Stanhow Farm, Great Langton, Northallerton, North Yorks (☎ 0609 748614)

FURNESS, Michael John; s of Stanley Charles Furness, of Eastbourne, E Sussex, and Gladys Violet Furness; *b* 20 March 1941; *Educ* Rutlish Sch, Royal Dental Hosp and St George's Hosp Univ of London (MB BS, BDS); *m* 23 Sept 1972, Mary Elizabeth, da of Rev William Clifford Smallman (d 1980), of Sheffield; 3 da (Cordelia b 1973, Nadine b 1976, Eleanor b 1977); *Career* house surgn oral surgery St George's Hosp London 1964, house physician Whittington Hosp London 1970; house surgn ENT surgery Charing Cross Hosp 1971, clinical asst head and neck surgery Royal Marsden Hosp London 1972-75, private dental practitioner 1972-; pres Coll Union at Univ of

London; Freeman City of London 1983, Liveryman Worshipful Soc of Apothecaries 1978; FRSA 1979; *Recreations* fishing, shooting, antiques, swimming; *Clubs* Athenaeum, MCC; *Style*— Dr Michael Furness; 31 Wilton Place, London SW1 (☎ 071 235 3824); Clifton House, Clifton Hill, Winchester, Hants; Tyddyn Bach, Cwm Cynfal, Ffestiniog, Gwynedd

FURNESS, Prof Raymond Stephen; s of Albert Victor Furness (d 1965), of Hatfield, Herts, and Margaret Anne, *née* O'Neil (d 1977); *b* 25 Oct 1933; *Educ* Univ of Wales(BA, MA), Univ of Munich, Univ of Berlin, Univ of Manchester (PhD); *m* 28 Aug 1965, Janice Clare, da of Norman Frank Fairey, of 5 Driffold, Sutton Coldfield, W Midlands; 1 s (Rupert William b 1967), 2 da (Cordelia Jane b 1969, Rosalind Lydia b 1974); *Career* Artillery and Intelligence Corps 1955-57; Univ of Manchester: lectr, sr lectr, reader 1959-84; prof Univ of St Andrews; *Books* Expressionism (1973), A Literary History of Germany 1890-1945 (1978), Wagner and Literature (1982); *Recreations* old horror films; *Style*— Prof Raymond Furness; The Dirdale, Boarhills, Fife KY16 8PP (☎ 0334 88469); The University, St Andrews, Fife KY16 9PH (☎ 0334 76161)

FURNESS, Lt-Col Simon John; s of Sir Christopher Furness, 2 Bt (d 1974), of Netherbyres, Eyemouth, Berwickshire, and Violet Flower Chipchase, *née* Roberts (d 1988); *b* 18 Aug 1936; *Educ* Charterhouse, RMA Sandhurst; *Career* cmmnd Durham LI 1956, cmd 5 Bn 1976-78, ret Lt-Col 1978; Dep Col Durham LI 1989-; memb Exec Ctee Nat Tst for Scotland (chm Gardens Ctee); Vice Lord Lieut Berwickshire 1990 (DL 1984); *Recreations* gardening, field sports; *Clubs* Army and Navy; *Style*— Lt-Col Simon Furness; Netherbyres, Eyemouth, Berwickshire TD14 5SE (☎ 08907 50337)

FURNESS, Sir Stephen Roberts; 3 Bt (UK 1913), of Tunstall Grange, W Hartlepool; s of Sir Christopher Furness, 2 Bt (d 1974, 2 cous of 2 Viscount Furness), and Violet Flower Chipchase, *née* Roberts; *b* 10 Oct 1933; *Educ* Charterhouse; *m* 6 April 1961, Mary, er da of Jack Fitzroy Cann, of Newland, Cullompton, Devon; 1 s, 1 da; *Heir* s, Michael Fitzroy Roberts Furness; *Career* late Lt RN, ret 1962; farmer and sporting artist (as Robin Furness); jt MFH Bedale Foxhounds 1979-87; *Recreations* hunting, racing, looking at paintings; *Style*— Sir Stephen Furness, Bt; Otterington Hall, Northallerton, North Yorkshire DL7 9HW (☎ 0609 772061)

FURNISS, Air Vice-Marshal Peter; DFC (1944), TD (1964); s of John Furniss (d 1930), and Mary Furniss; *b* 16 July 1919; *Educ* Sedbergh; *m* 1954, Denise Andrée Gisèle, da of Charles Cotet, of S France; 1 s, 2 da; *Career* cmmnd Liverpool Scottish TA, Queens Own Cameron Highlanders 1939, seconded to RAF 1942, served in med theatre of ops, cmd 73 Fighter Sqdn, demob 1946; admitted slr 1948, cmmnd in Legal Branch RAF 1950, dir Legal Servs HQ Air Forces M East, Aden 1961-63, HQ Far E AF Singapore 1969-71, HQ RAF Germany 1973-74, dir Legal Servs RAF 1978-82 (dep 1975-78); pres: Maidstone Branch RAFA, 40 (F) Maidstone Sqdn ATC; *Recreations* country pursuits; *Clubs* RAF; *Style*— Air Vice-Marshal Peter Furniss, DFC, TD; 18 Sevington Park, Loose, Maidstone, Kent (☎ 0622 744620)

FURNIVAL, John Stephen; s of Thomas Bourne Furnival (d 1967), and Phyllis Elizabeth, *née* Corke (d 1983); *b* 13 Aug 1939; *Educ* Kimbolton Sch, Mander Coll Bedford, Coll of Estate Mgmnt; *m* 1, June 1961 (m dis 1981), Susan Marilyn, *née* Everett; 1 s (John Everett b 8 Oct 1971), 2 da (Clare Susan b 11 Jan 1962, Victoria Merrie Louise b 31 March 1964); m 2, 17 July 1981, Patricia Mary, da of William Geoffrey Herbert (d 1988); 1 step s (Roger Smith b 9 Oct 1963); *Career* patrol offr BSA Police 1958-60; agric farm mangr and dir 1960-64, ptnr gen practice estate agency 1964-69; property and projects mangr UK Hertz International 1969-71, estates mangr Granada TV Rental 1971-80, property dir The Oliver Group plc 1988- (estates mangr 1980-81, property dir 1981-), md Castle Acres Developments Ltd 1988-; dir: Hiltons Footwear Ltd, Timpson Shoes Ltd, William Timpson Ltd, Brick Studio & Manufacturing Ltd, Timpson Shops Ltd, Photo Shop plc, Frame Express plc, Frame It Ltd; pres Property Mangrs Assoc 1983-85, 1986-87, 1989-90; memb Real Estates Ctee Br Retailers Assoc 1985, dir Br Cncl of Shopping Centres 1987-89, memb Cncl The Land Inst 1987, memb Charter Soc Coll of Estate Mgmnt 1988; chm of govrs Walnuts Special Sch for Handicapped Children Milton Keynes 1978-80, tstee Leics Autistic Soc 1990; memb: IOD, RSPB, Nat Autistic Soc, Ctee Nat Autistic Care & Training Appeal, Ctee Mid Counties Autistic Soc; FASI, FLandInst, FFB 1971, ACIArb 1982, FBIM 1984, FRSA 1987, FIAVI 1989; *Recreations* country pursuits, conservation; *Clubs* Farmers; *Style*— John S Furnival, Esq; 4 Warrington Drive, The Spinney, Groby, Leicester LE6 0YS (☎ 0533 879986); The Oliver Group plc, Grove Way, Castle Acres, Narborough, Leicester LE9 5BZ (☎ 0533 630 444, fax 0533 630014, telex 341270)

FURNIVAL JONES, Sir (Edward) Martin; CBE (1957); s of Edward Furnival Jones (d 1946); *b* 7 May 1912; *Educ* Highgate Sch, Gonville and Caius Coll Cambridge (MA); *m* 1955, Elizabeth Margaret, da of Bartholomew Snowball, AMIEE; 1 da; *Career* served WWII GSO SHAEF and War Office (despatches); slr 1937; attached to MOD; chm Bd Frensham Heights 1973-76 (pres 1977); kt 1967; *Style*— Sir Martin Furnival Jones, CBE

FURNIVALL, Barony of (E 1295); *see*: Hon Rosamond Dent, Hon Mrs Bence

FURSDON, (Edward) David; o s of Maj-Gen (Francis William) Edward Fursdon, CB, MBE, *qv*, and Joan Rosemary, *née* Worssam; succeeded uncle as owner of 700 year old Fursdon family estate in Devon 1981; Lord of the Manors of Cadbury and South Zeal, Devon; c/o Stags, 21 Southernhay West, Exeter (☎ 0392 55202); *b* 20 Dec 1952; *Educ* Sherborne, St John's Coll Oxford (BA, MA); *m* 7 Oct 1978, Catriona Margaret, da of Geoffrey Crichton McCreath, of Berwick-upon-Tweed; 3 s (Oliver b 1980, Thomas b 1982, Charles b 1986); *Career* short serv limited cmmn as 2 Lt 6 QEO Gurkha Rifles 1972; assoc ptnr Stags auctioneers 1988-; govr Blundell's Sch 1984-; ARICS 1988, FAAV 1988; *Recreations* sport; *Clubs* MCC; *Style*— David Fursdon, Esq; Fursdon, Cadbury, Exeter, Devon; c/o Stags, 19 Bampton St, Tiverton, Devon (☎ 0884 256331)

FURSDON, Maj-Gen (Francis William) Edward; CB (1980), MBE (1958), KStJ (1980); s of George Ellsworth Sydenham Fursdon (d 1936), and Aline Lucinda, *née* Gastrell (d 1982); family resident at Fursdon in Devon since 1251; *b* 10 May 1925; *Educ* Westminster, Aberdeen (MLitt), Leiden (DLitt); *m* 1950 Joan Rosemary, da of Charles Archie Worssam, OBE (d 1971); 1 s ((Edward) David, *qv*), 1 da (Sabina b 1956); *Career* RE 1942; Cmd 25 Engr Regt BAOR 1967-69; AA & QMG HQ Land Forces Gulf 1970-71, Dep Cmd and COS Land Forces Gulf 1971, Col Qtg HQ BAOR 1972-73; dir: Def Policy MOD (Euro and NATO) 1974-77, MOD Mil Asst Off 1977-80; advsr to Rhodesian Govr and sr Br offr Zimbabwe 1980; ret Maj-Gen 1980; def and mil corr Daily Telegraph 1980-86; dir of Ceremonies Order of St John 1980-, ind def conslt, author and freelance corr 1986-; Freeman City of London; *Books* Grains of Sand (1971), There are no Frontiers (1973), The European Defence Community - a History (1980), Falklands Aftermath (1988); *Recreations* travel, writing, gardening; *Clubs* Special Forces, St John House; *Style*— Maj-Gen Edward Fursdon, CB, MBE; c/o The National Westminster Bank, 1 St James's Square, London SW1Y 4JX

FYFE, Brig Alastair Ian Hayward; s of Archibald Graham Fyfe (d 1979), of Misterton, Somerset, and Alison Amy, *née* Hayward (d 1982); *b* 21 Oct 1937; *Educ* Lancing, RMA Sandhurst, Staff Coll Camberley; *m* 15 Aug 1964, Deirdre Bettina, da of Air Cdre James Maitland Nicholso Pike, CB, DSO, DFC, of Watlington, Oxford; 1 s (Andrew b 31 Aug 1967), 1 da (Nicola b 22 June 1966); *Career* cmmnd Duke of Cornwalls LI 1958, cmd 1 Bn LI 1980-82 (Adj 1968-69), mil attaché Moscow 1988-91, hon ADC to HM The Queen 1989; memb Nat Tst; *Recreations* music, walking, cricket; *Clubs* Army and Navy; *Style*— Brig Alastair Fyfe

FYFE, Maria; MP (Lab) Maryhill 1987-; da of James O'Neill (d 1972), and Margaret, *née* Lacey (d 1980); *b* 25 Nov 1938; *Educ* Notre Dame High Glasgow, Univ of Strathclyde (BA); *m* 4 April 1964, James Jospeh Fyfe (d 1986), s of James Fyfe (d 1974); 2 s (Stephen James b 1965, Christopher Paul b 1966); *Career* lectr 1976-87; memb: Glasgow Dist Cncl 1980-87, CND, Anti-Apartheid, Campaign for Scottish Assembly; *Recreations* reading, walking, cooking, eating, dancing; *Style*— Ms Maria Fyfe, MP; c/o House of Commons, London SW1A 0AA (☎ 071 219 4430/6819); Constituency Office, 1508 Maryhill Rd, Glasgow G20 (☎ 041 945 1495)

FYFFE, Maj Laurence Ronald Kington; MC (1943 and bar 1944), JP (Aberdeenshire 1963), DL (Aberdeenshire 1973); s of Bishop Rolleston Sterritt Fyffe (d 1964), of Church Cottage, Lindfield, Sussex, and Annis Kathleen, *née* Hardy (d 1963); *b* 27 Feb 1920; *Educ* Eton, New Coll Oxford (MA); *m* 6 Dec 1952, Cynthia Phyllis Juliet, da of Stephen Devey Smith Farmer (d 1958), of The White House, Aston Munslow, Shropshire; 2 s (Richard b 1956, David b 1956), 1 da (Cassandra b 1954); *Career* cmmnd RB 1941: 7 Bn, 8 Army Africa and Italy 1942-45, Capt 1943, Maj 1944; HM Colonial Serv Western regn Nigeria 1951-57, ptnr Corsindae Home Farms Aberdeenshire 1957-88; memb: Aberdeenshire CC 1961-74, Grampion Regnl Cncl 1974-78; *Recreations* cricket, football, rough shooting, music; *Style*— Maj Laurence Fyffe, MC, JP, DL; Little Sauchen of Corsindae, by Inverurie, Aberdeenshire AB51 7QR (☎ 03303 236)

FYSHE, (Robert) Alexander Dennis; s of Alexander Gordon Fyshe, of Hurstans, Sollershope, Hereford, and Gwendoline Joan, *née* Dennis; *b* 15 Nov 1938; *Educ* Sherborne; *m* 29 April 1965, (Angel) Margaret, da of Lt-Col Geoffrey Babington (d 1956), of Easter Ross, Comrie, nr Crieff, Perthshire; 1 s (Henry b 21 Dec 1975); *Career* Nat Serv 2 Lt KSLI 1957-59; md Artscope International Insurance Services Ltd 1979; dir: Seascope Insurance Holdings Ltd 1984, APS International Ltd 1988, APS Insurance Brokers Inc 1988, Leslie and Godwin Ltd 1989; memb Lloyds 1964; *Recreations* shooting, classic Italian cars; *Clubs* Boodle's, City of London; *Style*— Alexander Fyshe, Esq; St Peter's Square, London

FYSON, (Richard) Oliver; MBE; s of Richard Wallace Fyson (d 1965); *b* 9 Sept 1924; *Educ* Soham GS Cambs, Loughborough Coll; *m* 1, 27 March 1947, Mary, da of Walter Ivett; 1 s (Kim b 27 Dec 1950), 1 da (Rosemary (Mrs Borland) b 9 Aug 1954); m 2, 11 July 1988, Hilary Jane, *née* Clark; *Career* mechanical engr: Blackstone Diesels Stamford 1940, Bristol Aeroplane Co 1946, Fyson And Son Ltd 1948-90; former pres: Mechanical Handling Engineers Assoc, Fédération Européene De la Manutention; FIMechE; *Style*— Oliver Fyson, Esq, MBE; The Orchard, Soham, Ely, Cambs CB7 5JA (☎ 0353 720325)

G

GABATHULER, Prof Erwin; s of Hans Gabathuler (d 1972), of NI, and Anne Lena Gabathuler, *née* Graham (d 1970); *b* 16 Nov 1933; *Educ* Queen's Univ of Belfast (BSc, MSc), Univ of Glasgow (PhD); *m* 27 July 1962, Susan Dorothy, da of Charles Powell Jones (d 1988), of Essex; 2 s (John b 1966, David b 1970), 1 da (Helen b 1964); *Career* res fell Cornell Univ USA 1961-64, gp leader in res for SERC, Daresbury Laboratory UK 1964-74; CERN: visiting scientist Geneva 1974-77, head Experimental Physics Div 1978-80 dir of Res; head of Physics Dept Univ of Liverpool 1986- (prof of physics 1983-); author of various articles in res jls; chm Particle Physics Ctee SERC 1985-88; memb: Extended Scientific Cncl of Desy Hamburg W Germany, CNRS (IN2P3), France, Euro Physical Soc; Doctoris Honoris Causa Uppsala Univ of Sweden 1982; CPhys, FInstP, FRS 1990; *Recreations* swimming, walking; *Style—* Prof Erwin Gabathuler, FRS; 3 Danebank Rd, Lymm, Cheshire; Physics Dept, Oliver Lodge Laboratory, Oxford St, University of Liverpool, PO Box 147, Liverpool L69 3BX (☎ 051 7943350, fax 051 7943444, telex 627095 UNIPL G)

GABITASS, (William) Michael; s of William Gabitass (d 1979), of Plymouth, and Nellie Margaret, *née* Chaffe (d 1978); *b* 20 Nov 1938; *Educ* LSE (BSc); *m* 8 Aug 1959, Dianne, da of Prof Ray Linsley (d 1990); 1 s (Michael Linsley b 1 April 1961), 1 da (Christine Anne b 8 Dec 1963); *Career* Bank of America: graduate mgmt trainee (Bank of America NT & SA) San Francisco 1959, London 1963-67 and 1970-72, Birmingham 1967-70; asst dir NM Rothschild 1972-74, vice pres and mangr (Paris branch) Bank of America 1978-81 (vice pres London 1974-76, md Bankamerica Factors Ltd 1976-78), md banking Swiss Bank Corporation (London Branch) 1981-; Freeman City of London 1983, memb Worshipful Co of Farriers 1985; chm Lombard Assoc 1990-91, FCIB 1985-; *Recreations* cooking; *Clubs* City, RAC; *Style—* Michael Gabitass, Esq; Swiss Bank Corporation, Swiss Bank House, 1 High Timber St, London EC4V 3SB (☎ 071 711 4401, fax 071 975 1354)

GABRIEL, Christopher Waithman; s of Christopher Parton Gabriel, OBE (d 1974), of Suffolk, and Rosemary, *née* Waithman; *b* 28 Feb 1941; *Educ* Charterhouse; *m* 20 May 1981, Diana Lesley Sharman, da of Everard Lesley Campion Gwilt (d 1976), of Surrey; 1 da (Lucinda Rose b 1984); *Career* md Christopher Gabriel Ltd 1979-; memb Exec Ctee: Nat Panel Products Assoc, Agents Section of Timber Trade Fedn; Liveryman Worshipful Co of Goldsmiths'; *Recreations* sailing, shooting, tennis; *Clubs* Royal Ocean Racing, Royal Southampton Yacht; *Style—* Christopher W Gabriel, Esq; Binley Cottage, Binley, nr Andover, Hants SP11 6HA (☎ 0264 738261); Christopher Gabriel Ltd, 21 Swan St, Kingsclere, Newbury, Berks RG15 8PP (☎ 0635 297705, fax 0635 297034, telex 846525 ANGEL G)

GABRIEL, David Charles; s of Richard Trevor Gabriel, of Lansdowne House, St Julian St, Tenby, Dyfed, and Beatrice Anne Victoria, *née* Foulger; *b* 29 July 1950; *Educ* Hereford Cathedral Sch, Univ of Bristol (BVSc); *m* 11 Nov 1989, Elizabeth Jane, da of Ernest Walter Chapman; *Career* veterinary surgn; mixed practise with emphasis on equine and farm work, currently with Brook and Murphy Vet Surgns Leamington Spa Warks; Atherstone Hunt Supporter; MRCVS (1973); *Recreations* skiing, boardsailing, squash, equestrian activities, surfing, books; *Clubs* Ski Club of GB; *Style—* David Gabriel, Esq; 8 Barwell Rd, Kirkby Mallory, Leics LE9 7QA (☎ 0455 845793); Brook and Murphy Veterinary Surgns, 52 Clarendon St, Leamington Spa, Warks

GABRIELCZYK, Ryszard January; s of Józef Gabrielczyk (d 1981), of Poland, and Helena, *née* Sykut (d 1931); *b* 19 Sept 1927; *Educ* State Sch Poland, Brixton Coll (HND); *m* 28 Aug 1949, Barbara Zofia, da of Lt Jozef Sadowski, Polish Army (d 1981), of London; 3 s (Jorge Jozef b 7 March 1952, Marek Ryszard b 25 July 1955, Jacek Robert b 15 Dec 1959); *Career* Polish Army under Br Cmd 1942-47 Palestine, Br Army 1947-49; structural engr Felix Samuely Consulting Engineers 1954-56; Taylor Whalley & Spyra: sr structural engr 1957-60, ptnr 1961-67, managing ptnr 1968-88; various projects incl: Univ of Leeds, Richmond Terrace Devpt Whitehall; memb Ctee Polish Benevolent Fund UK, pres Polish Educn Soc UK; CEng, FIStructE, FINuce, MConsE, MFrSCE; Polish Order of Merit 1967, Order of Polonia Restituta 1974, Order of St Sylvester (Knight) Vatican 1978, KSS; *Recreations* gardening, bee keeping; *Clubs* RAC; *Style—* Ryszard Gabrielczyk, Esq; 33 Alexandra Grove, Finchley, London N12 8HE (☎ 081 445 4352); 3 Dufferin Ave, Barbican, London EC1Y 8PQ (☎ 071 253 2626, fax 071 253 2767)

GADD, (John) Staffan; s of late John Gadd, and Ulla, *née* Olivecrona; *b* 30 Sept 1934, Stockholm; *Educ* Stockholm Sch of Economics (MBA); *m* 1958, Margaretha, da of Gösta Löfborg; 1 s, 1 da; m 2, 1990, Kay McGreeghan; *Career* sec Confedn of Swedish Industs 1958-61; Skandinaviska Banken 1961-69 (London rep 1964-67); Scandinavian Bank Ltd: dep md 1969-71, in London 1969-80, chief exec and md 1971-80; chm and chief exec Samuel Montagu & Co 1982-84 (chief exec 1980-84), chm Montagu & Co AB Stockholm 1982-85, dir Guyerzeller Zurmont Bank AG Switzerland 1983-84; chm: Saga Securities Ltd 1985-, J S Gadd & Co Ltd; *Recreations* skiing, shooting; *Style—* Staffan Gadd, Esq; Locks Manor, Hurstpierpoint, Sussex; Office: J S Gadd & Co Ltd, 45 Bloomsbury Square, London WC1A 2RA (☎ 071 242 5544)

GADDUM, Anthony Henry; s of Peter William Gaddum (d 1986), of Beech Tree House, Mobberley, Cheshire, and Josephine Margaret Ferguson Wynne, *née* Roberts (d 1983); *b* 16 Feb 1939; *Educ* Rugby, Univ of Grenoble; *m* 7 June 1968, Hilda, da of Rev James McIntosh Scott; 3 s (Toby b 1971, Giles b 1973, Benedict b 1975); *Career* Nat Serv 2 Lt 13/18 Royal Hussars 1959-61; dir Br Crepe Ltd 1976, chm H T Gaddum & Co Ltd 1984 (dir 1964); articles on silk and genealogy; nat delegate Int Silk Assoc, vice chm Silk Assoc, delegate to the Euro Commission for the Promotion of Silk, chm Clarkes & Marshalls Charity Manchester; *Recreations* genealogy, gardening, fishing; *Clubs* Institute of Directors; *Style—* Anthony Gaddum, Esq; Lane Ends House, Sutton Lane Ends, nr Macclesfield, Cheshire (☎ 02605 2456); c/o H T Gaddum & Co Ltd, 3 Jordangate, Macclesfield, Cheshire (☎ 0625 27666, fax 0625 511331, telex 667139)

GADSBY, (Gordon) Neville; CB (1972); s of William George Gadsby (d 1978), and Margaret Sarah Gadsby; *b* 29 Jan 1914; *Educ* King Edward VI Sch Stratford upon Avon, Univ of Birmingham (BSc, DipEd, Cadbury prize); *m* 1938, Jeanne, *née* Harris; 2 s, 1 da; *Career* dir: Army Operational Res Estab 1961-64, Biological and Chemical Def MOD 1965-67; dep chief scientist (Army) MOD 1967-68, dir Chemical Def Estab 1968-72, min and head of Def Res and Devpt Staff Br Embassy Washington 1972-75; gp ldr The MITRE Corporation USA 1976-80, conslt NUS Corporation USA 1980-; Cchem, FRSC; *Recreations* oil painting; *Style—* G Neville Gadsby, Esq, CB; Ruan House, Cliff Rd, Sidmouth, Devon EX10 8JN (☎ 0395 577842)

GADSDEN, Sir Peter Drury Haggerston; GBE (1979), AC (1988); er s of Rev Basil Claude Gadsden, ACT, ThL (d 1958), of Whitney-on-Wye, Hereford, and Mabel Florence, *née* Drury (d 1964); *b* 28 June 1929; *Educ* Wrekin Coll, Jesus Coll Cambridge (MA); *m* 16 April 1955, Belinda Ann de Marie, eld da of Capt Sir (Hugh) Carnaby de Marie Haggerston, 11 Bt (d 1971); 4 da (Juliet Mary (Mrs Cartwright) b 4 March 1956, Caroline Mabel (Mrs Simpson) b 4 Aug 1957, Clare Louise (Mrs McWhirter) b 29 June 1960, Elizabeth Ann b 28 Feb 1962); *Career* served as 2 Lt King's Shropshire LI 1948-49; Alderman City of London 1971-, Lord Mayor 1979-80; dir: Ellingham Estate Ltd 1974-, Clothworkers' Fndn 1978-, Williams Jacks 1984-; chm Private Patients Plan plc 1984-; mineral mktg conslt, memb London Metal Exchange; pres: Nat Assoc of Charcoal Mfrs 1970-, Metropolitan Soc for Blind; tstee Chichester Festival Theatre, chm The Britain-Australia Bicentennial Ctee Tst 1984-, chm The Britain-Australia soc 1989-, pt/t memb Crown Agents for Overseas Govts and Admin, also Crown Agents' Hldg & Realisation Bd 1981-; Fndr Master Worshipful Co of Engineers; vice pres Robert Jones and Agnes Hunt Orthopaedic Hosp, pres Ironbridge Gorge Museum Devpt Trust; Liveryman Worshipful Co of Clothworkers' (Sr Warden 1982-83, Master 1989-90); Hon Liveryman: Worshipful Co of Plaisterers', Worshipful Co of Marketers; Hon Freeman Worshipful Co of Actuaries'; memb Guild of Freemen (Master 1984); Master Guild of World Traders in London 1987; Hon DSc City Univ 1980; FInstM 1976, CEng 1979, FEng 1980, FIMM 1979; KStJ (1980, OStJ 1977); Officier de l'Etoile Equatoriale de la Republique Gabonaise 1970; *Recreations* farming, forestry, shooting, fishing, sailing, walking, photography, skiing; *Clubs* City Livery, City of London, Guildhall, Royal London Yacht, Pilgrims; *Style—* Sir Peter Gadsden, GBE, AC; 606 Gilbert House, Barbican, London EC2Y 8BD (☎ 071 638 9968)

GADSDEN, Peter John; s of Lt-Col George Edward Graham Gadsden, DSO, OBE, TD (d 1981), and Doris Lillian, *née* Benson; *b* 28 May 1929; *Educ* Eton, Worcester Coll Oxford (MA); *m* 19 Dec 1953, Yvonne, da of Issa Khalil Shousha (d 1964); 3 s (Paul Martin b 1954, Mark b 1956, James Michael b 1964 d 1983), 2 da (Mary Anne b 1958, Jane Christine b 1963); *Career* slr; clerk Stroud RDC 1965-73, superintendent registrar 1965-91; vice chm Stroud Building Society, chm Co of the Proprietors of the Stroudwater Navigation, former memb Ctee Glos and Wilts Inc Law Soc, dep asst coroner 1965-68; *Recreations* travel, sailing, reading; *Clubs* Leander; *Style—* Peter Gadsden, Esq; Bournestream, Wotton-under-Edge, Glos GL12 7PA (☎ 0453 842202); 4/7 Rowcroft, Stroud, Glos GL5 3BJ (☎ 04536 3381, fax 04536 71997)

GAFFNEY, Maj Edward Fane Travers; s of Capt Edward Desmond Gaffney (d 1940), and Irene Mary, *née* Travers; *b* 7 Jan 1937; *Educ* Cheltenham, RMC Sandhurst; *m* 10 June 1961, Fiona Esmé Gildroy, da of George Richard Shaw (d 1983); 3 s (Edward William b 1962, Richard Desmond Travers b 1963, Adrian Toby George Hannaford b 1972), 1 da (Miranda Mary b 1967); *Career* 1 Bn Welsh Gds 1957-68, Maj BAOR 1961-66, Aden 1966-67; admitted slr 1976; Dep Under Sheriff of Durham & Cleveland 1982, Jt Under Sheriff of Durham and Cleveland 1989; *Recreations* tennis, squash, shooting, fishing; *Style—* Maj Edward F T Gaffney; Crossbank Hill, Hurworth-on-Tees, Darlington DL2 2JB (☎ 0325 720537); 64 Stanhope Rd, Darlington DL3 7SE (☎ 0325 466 545)

GAFFNEY, Thomas Francis; s of Thomas F Gaffney (d 1954), and Margaret, *née* Carroll; *b* 2 April 1932; *Educ* St John's Univ NY (BA), St John's Law Sch, American Inst of Foreign Trade Phoenix Arizona; *m* 30 Oct 1954, Carmen, da of Benito Vega Luna, of Bucaramanga, Colombia; 2 s (Thomas b 30 Dec 1957, Peter b 21 Sept 1968), 1 da (Elisa b 14 Jan 1960); *Career* Chase Manhattan Bank NY 1954-87, seconded to several Latin-American Banks (incl period as chief exec Banco Continental Lima) 1962-72, chief exec Libra Bank plc London 1972-84, pres Chase Investment Bank London 1984-87, chief exec and md West LB UK Ltd 1988-; author numerous articles on econ and fin matters in professional magazines; registered rep Securities Assoc; *Recreations* art appreciation, music, theatre; *Clubs* Mark's, Ends of the Earth, Oriental; *Style—* Thomas Gaffney, Esq; Marvells, Five Ashes, Mayfield, East Sussex TN20 6NL (☎ 0435 873030); West LB UK Ltd, 51 Moorgate, London EC2R 6AE (☎ 071 638 6141, fax 071 628 1843, telex 887984/5)

GAFFORD, Geoffrey; s of Laurence Charles Gafford, of 56 Holmesdale Rd, Brundall, Norwich, Norfolk, and Mary Barbara, *née* Hawkes; *b* 13 July 1951; *Educ* Nobel Sch Stevenage; *m* 19 Aug 1978, Amanda Carolyn, da of Ernest Henry Brett Smith, of 15 Southwood Rd, Cookham, Berks; 1 s (James Alexander Geoffrey b 1985), 1 da (Philippa Mary b 1983); *Career* admitted slr 1979, currently ptnr with Cole & Cole; hon sec Chipping Norton and Dist Abbeyfield Soc, govr St Mary's Sch Chipping Norton; clerk Over Norton Parish Cncl; memb Law Soc; *Recreations* reading, music, walking; *Clubs* Regent; *Style—* Geoffrey Gafford, Esq; 56 The Leys, Chipping Norton, Oxon OX7 5HH (☎ 0608 641284); 2 New Street, Chipping Norton, Oxon OX7 5LJ (☎ 0608 643051, fax 0608 641019)

GAGE, Sir Berkeley Everard Foley; KCMG (1955, CMG 1949); s of Brig-Gen Moreton Foley Gage, DSO (d 1953), and his 1 wife Anne Massie, *née* Strong (d 1915); *b* 27 Feb 1904; *Educ* Eton, Trinity Coll Cambridge; *m* 1, 15 Jan 1931 (m dis 1954), Hedwig Maria Gertrud Eva (who m 2, 1954, as his 3 wife, HH Prince Rostislav Alexandrovich of Russia, who d 1978), da of Carl von Chapuis, of Liegnitz, Silesia; 2 s; m 2, 4 Oct 1954, Mrs Lillian Riggs Miller, da of late Vladimir Vukmirovich, sometime Yugoslav Consul-Gen in Chicago; *Career* joined Dipl Serv 1928, consul gen Chicago 1950-54, ambass to Thailand 1954-57, ambass to Peru 1958-63; memb: Cncl for Volunteers Overseas 1964-66, Br Nat Export Cncl 1964-66 (chm Latin American Ctee); chm Anglo-Peruvian Soc 1969-71, Grand Cross Order of the Sun (Peru) 1964; *Clubs* Beefsteak, Buck's, Tavern (Chicago); *Style—* Sir Berkeley Gage, KCMG; 24 Ovington Gdns, London SW3 1LE (☎ 071 589 0361)

GAGE, Viscountess; Diana; 4 da of Col Rt Hon Lord Richard Cavendish, CB, CMG (bro of 9 Duke of Devonshire, KG, GCMG, GCVO, PC, JP, DL), and Lady Moyra Beauclerk, da of 10 Duke of St Albans; *b* 15 Sept 1909; *m* 1, 21 March 1935 (m dis 1937), as his 1 w, Robert (Bob) Boothby, MP (later Baron Boothby, KBE, who d

1986); m 2, 7 July 1942, Lt-Col Hon Ian Douglas Campbell-Gray (d 1946), 3 s of Henry Craig-Campbell and Lady Gray (holder of the Scottish Lordship in her own right and gm of 22 Lord Gray); m 3, 1971, as his 2 w, 6 Viscount Gage, KCVO (d 1982); *Style*— The Rt Hon Viscountess Gage; Hole of Ellen, Cark-in-Cartmel, Grange-over-Sands, Cumbria

GAGE, Lady Diana Adrienne; *née* Beatty; el da of 2 Earl Beatty, DSC (d 1972); *b* 13 Sept 1952; *Educ* St Paul's Girls' Sch, London; *m* 1974, Hon (Henry) Nicolas Gage, yr s of 6 Viscount Gage, KCVO (d 1982); 2 s; *Style*— Lady Diana Gage; The Cottage, Charwelton, Daventry, Northants (☎ 0327 205)

GAGE, 7 Viscount; Sir George John St Clere Gage; 14 Bt (E 1622); also Baron Gage of Castlebar (I 1720) and Baron Gage of High Meadow (GB 1790, title in House of Lords); er s of 6 Viscount Gage, KCVO (d 1982) and Viscountess Gage, *qv*; *b* 8 July 1932; *Educ* Eton; *m* 1971 (m dis 1975), Valerie Ann, da of Joseph E Dutch, of Horam, Sussex; *Heir* bro, Hon (Henry) Nicholas Gage; *Style*— The Rt Hon the Viscount Gage; Firle Place, Lewes, Sussex BN8 6LP

GAGE, Kevin William; s of Gerald William Gage, of Weybridge, Surrey, and Freda Gage; *b* 21 April 1964; *Educ* St Paul's Sch Weybridge; *m* 13 June 1988, Tina Elizabeth; 2 s (Daniel Kevin b 12 April 1985, Oliver William b 6 Aug 1987); *Career* professional footballer; Wimbledon 1981-87: apprentice then professional, 195 appearances, 18 goals; Aston Villa 1987-, over 130 appearances, 5 England youth caps; Div 4 Championship Wimbledon 1983; *Style*— Kevin Gage, Esq; Aston Villa FC, Villa Park, Trinity Rd, Birmingham B6 6HE (☎ 021 327 6604)

GAGE, Hon (Henry) Nicolas; yr s of 6 Viscount Gage, KCVO; hp to bro, 7 Viscount; *b* 9 April 1934; *Educ* Eton, Ch Ch Oxford; *m* 1974, Lady Diana Adrienne Beatty, da of 2 Earl Beatty; 2 s (Henry William b 1975, David Benedict b 1977); *Career* 2 Lt Coldstream Gds 1953; *Style*— Hon Nicholas Gage; The Cottage, Charwelton, Rugby, Warwickshire (☎ 0327 205) 205)

GAGE, Quentin Henry Moreton; s of Brig-Gen Moreton Foley Gage, DSO, DL (d 1953), and Frances, *née* Lippitt (d 1955); *b* 22 Aug 1920; *Educ* Eton, Ch Ch Oxford; *m* 16 April 1949, Hazel, da of Col George Archibald Swinton Home, DSO, OBE (d 1961); 1 s (Jonathan Moreton b 26 March 1954), 1 da (Deborah Pamela b 31 March 1950); *Career* Grenadier Gds 1940-46, T/Maj, Capt served Tunisia, Italy, Palestine (wounded Anzio 1944); insur broker: East, Central and S Africa, USA, UK; *Style*— Quentin Gage, Esq; Pelham Cottage, Church Lane, Hellingly, Sussex BN27 4 HA (☎ 0323 843902)

GAGE, William Marcus; QC (1982); s of His Honour Conolly Hugh Gage (d 1984), ret circuit judge, and Elinor Nancy, *née* Martyn; *b* 22 April 1938; *Educ* Repton, Sidney Sussex Coll Cambridge (MA); *m* 16 June 1962, Penelope Mary, da of Lt-Col James Jocelyn Douglas Groves, MC (d 1985); 3 s (Marcus b 1964, Timothy b 1966, Hugh b 1970); *Career* Nat Serv 1956-58, 2 Lt Irish Gds; called to the Bar 1963, chllr Diocese of Coventry 1980-, rec 1985-, memb Criminal Injuries Compensation Bd 1987-; *Recreations* shooting, fishing, travel; *Clubs* Beefsteak; *Style*— William Gage, Esq, QC; Evershaw House, Biddlesden, Brackley, Northants; 2 Harcourt Bldgs, Temple, London SC4Y 9DB (☎ 071 583 9020)

GAGGERO, Charles Germain; OBE (1970), JP; s of Charles Gaggero, OBE, JP (d 1987), and Eugenie, *née* Rugeroni (d 1981); *b* 28 May 1930; *Educ* Downside, Magdalene Coll Cambridge (MA); *m* July 1957, Jean, da of Col John Lawrance; 3 da (Katherine b 26 April 1958, Susan b 10 March 1960, Alexandra b 31 Aug 1963); *Career* cmmnd Gilbraltar Defence Force 1957; dep chm Saccone & Speed (Gib) Ltd (and subsid cos), md Amalgamated Builders' Merchants Ltd (and subsid cos), dir Hambros Bank (Gib) Ltd; hon consul gen Greece 1967, doyen of Consular Corps Gibraltar; chm: John Mackintosh Tst, John Mackintosh Educnl Tst, Pyrmont Tst, Gibraltar Tport Assoc 1962-68, Gibraltar Museum 1965-68, St John Cncl for Gibraltar 1966-77; dir C of C 1953-62; pres: Societa Dante Alighieri (formerly Lottery Ctee) 1956-75, Social Welfare Ctee 1960-68, Econ Advsy Ctee 1963-66, Prison Bd 1964-68, Bd of Mgment Med & Health Servs 1965-68, Bd of Visitors St Joseph's Hosp 1965-68, Labour Planning and Productivity Ctee 1966-68, ; knight OStJ (LS medal), knight Order Star of Italian Solidarity (Italy), Knight Order of St Gregory the Great (Holy See), Knight of Magistral Grace SMO of Malta (Br Assoc), Knight of Merit Constantinian Order of St George Officer of Merit SMO of Malta; Freeman: City of London (1990), Worshipful Co of Builders Merchants (1990); *Recreations* numismatics; *Clubs* Utd Oxford & Cambridge Univs, Royal Gibraltar Yacht; *Style*— Charles Gaggero, Esq, OBE, JP; 4 College Lane, Gibraltar (☎ 010 350 77410); Saccone & Speed (Gibraltar) Ltd, 35 Devils Tower Rd, Gibraltar (☎ 010 350 74600, fax 010 350 78367)

GAGGERO, John George; OBE (1981), JP (1972); s of Sir George Gaggero, OBE, JP (d 1978), of Gibraltar, and Mabel, *née* Andrews-Speed (d 1986); *b* 3 March 1934; *Educ* Downside; *m* 1961, Valerie, da of John Malin, OBE, JP, of Gibraltar; 2 s, 2 da; *Career* Lt 12 Royal Lancers Malaya; hon consul for Denmark 1964-, dep chm Bland Gp (includes Gibraltar Airways, Rock Hotel, and Cadogan Travel) 1970-86, chm M H Bland & Co Ltd 1986-; MRINA; Knight of the Royal Order of the Dannebrog; *Recreations* boating; *Clubs* Cavalry and Guards, Royal Gibraltar Yacht; *Style*— John Gaggero, Esq, OBE, JP; 15 Bayside Rd, Gibraltar (☎ 77274); Cloister Building, Gibraltar (☎ 72735)

GAGGERO, Joseph James; CBE (1989); s of Sir George Gaggero, OBE, JP, and Lady Mabel, *née* Andrews-Speed; *Educ* Downside; *m* Nov 1958, Marilys Healing: 1 s (James b 1 Aug 1959), 1 da (Rosanne b 27 Dec 1960); *Career* chm and md of Bland Group of Companies (incl GB Airways, Gibraltar Airways, Rock Hotel, Bland Travel, Cadogan Travel, House of Bellingham, Bland America Inc and assoc cos); dir: Hovertravel and Gibline, Gibraltar Trust Bank (Credit Suisse); hon consul gen for Sweden in Gibraltar, dir Gibraltar C of C 1951-56, head Gibraltar Govt Tourist Dept 1955-59, memb Cncl of Br Travel Assoc 1958-69; chm: Hotel Assoc 1986-90 (1962-75, 1978), Gibraltar Shipping Assoc 1970-79; pres: Gibraltar Rotarians 1973-74, Gibraltar Branch for Maritime League 1983-84; chm Gibraltar Soc for Handicapped Children, Gibraltar Branch of Royal Life Saving Soc; Order of North Star (Sweden), Knight of the Holy Sepulchre (Vatican); *Recreations* painting; *Clubs* Travellers, Royal Gibraltar Yacht; *Style*— Joseph Gaggero, Esq, CBE; Cloister Building, Gibraltar (☎ 78456, fax 76189, telex 2118)

GAHAN, Lt-Col Gerald Patrick; s of Revell Patrick Gahan, of Abbotsbury, Dorset, and Mary Bannerman McKenzie, *née* McLean (d 1954); *b* 30 April 1933; *Educ* George Watson's Coll Edinburgh, RMA Sandhurst; *m* 11 May 1957, Jean Mary, da of Brig Andrew McGregor Stewart (d 1967); 1 s (Paul b 1962), 2 da (Susan b 1958, Caroline b 1960); *Career* Army Offr RA 1953-84, Lt-Col; served in: Cyprus, NI, Aden, Trucial Oman, BAOR, UK; civil servant 1984-90; *Recreations* music, drama, field sports; *Clubs* Lansdowne; *Style*— Lt-Col Gerald Gahan; c/o Royal Bank of Scotland, 14 Minster St, Salisbury, Wilts SP1 1TP

GAILEY, (John Lowry Dunseath) Pat; OBE (1983); s of John Taylor Gailey (d 1953), of Holywood, Co Down, NI, and Mary Lilian, *née* Dunseath (d 1988): original family name Buchanan changed to Gaylea and subsequently Gailey when family arrived in NI around 1740 from Scotland; *b* 13 Sept 1926; *Educ* Portora Royal Sch Enniskillen NI, Univ of Edinburgh; *m* 1, 1952, Lilian (d 1987), da of Howard Donaldson (d 1957), of Belfast, NI; 2 s (Andrew, John); m 2, 1988, Winifred, da of Francis Bisset (d 1970); *Career* Nat Serv RNVR 1944-47, Sub-Lt Minesweepers, 4 MS Flotilla Home Waters and Norway; md Giddings & Lewis-Fraser Ltd 1977-89 (ret), currently in practice as industl conslt; pres Machine Tool Trades Assoc 1981-83, vice pres CECIMO 1983; *Recreations* golf, gardening, classical music; *Clubs* Naval & Military; *Style*— Pat Gailey, Esq, OBE; 30 Albany Rd, Westferry, Dundee, Angus, Scotland (☎ 0382 75947); Giddings & Lewis Ltd, Wellgate Works, Arbroath, Angus (☎ 0241 73811)

GAINFORD, 3 Baron (UK 1917); Joseph Edward Pease; s of 2 Baron Gainford, TD (d 1971), by Veronica, Baroness Gainford, *qv*; *b* 25 Dec 1921; *Educ* Eton, Gordonstoun; *m* 21 March 1953, Margaret Theophila Radcliffe, da of Henry Edmund Guide Tyndale (d 1948), of Winchester Coll, and Ruth Isabel Walcott, da of Alexander Radcliffe, of Bag Park, S Devon; 2 da; *Heir* bro, Hon George Pease; *Career* serv WWII as Sgt RAF; with Hunting Aerosurveys Ltd 1947, Directorate of Colonial Surveys 1951, Soil Mechanics Ltd 1953, LCC 1958, GLC 1965, UK delegate to UN 1973; memb Coll Guardians Nat Shrine of Our Lady of Walsingham 1979-; memb Plaisterers' Co 1976; FRGS, MSST; *Clubs* MCC, Pathfinder; *Style*— The Rt Hon the Lord Gainford; 1 Dedmere Court, Marlow, Bucks SL7 1PL (☎ 0628 484679)

GAINFORD, The Dowager Lady; Veronica Margaret; o da of Sir George John William Noble, 2 Bt (d 1937), and Mary Ethel, *née* Walker-Waters; *b* 3 March 1900; *m* 3 Feb 1921, 2 Baron Gainford (d 1971); 3 s; *Style*— The Rt Hon the Dowager Lady Gainford; Taigh na Seanamhair, Tayvallich, Argyll

GAINSBOROUGH, 5 Earl of (UK 1841); Sir Anthony Gerard Edward Noel; 7 Bt (GB 1781), JP (Leics 1974, formerly Rutland 1957); also Baron Barham (UK 1805), Viscount Campden and Baron Noel (both UK 1841); patron of two livings (but being a Roman Catholic cannot present); s of 4 Earl of Gainsborough, OBE, TD, JP (d 1927), sometime Private Chamberlain to Popes Benedict XV and Pius XI; *b* 24 Oct 1923; *Educ* Worth Sussex, Georgetown Maryland USA; *m* 23 July 1947, Mary, er da of Hon John Joseph Stourton, TD, of Miniature Hall, Wadhurst, 2 s of (24) Baron Mowbray, (25 Baron) Segrave, and (21 Baron) Stourton; 4 s, 3 da (and 1 da decd); *Heir* s, Viscount Campden; *Career* vice pres Caravan Club; chm Rutland CC 1970-73, pres Assoc of Dist Cncls 1974-80; Bailiff Grand Cross SMO Malta (pres Br Assoc 1968-74); Hon FICE, KStJ; *Clubs* Brooks's, Bembridge Sailing, Pratts, Royal Yacht Squadron; *Style*— The Rt Hon the Earl of Gainsborough, JP; Horn House, Exton Park, Oakham, Leics LE15 7QU

GAINSBOROUGH, George Fotheringham; CBE (1973); s of Rev William Anthony Gainsborough (d 1972), and Alice Edith, *née* Fennell (d 1941); *b* 28 May 1915; *Educ* Christ's Hosp, King's Coll London (BSc, PhD); *m* 28 April 1937, Gwendoline (d 1976), da of John Berry (d 1944); 2 s (Michael b 1938, John b 1942); *Career* called to the Bar Gray's Inn; scientific staff Nat Physical Laboratory 1938-46, radio physicist Br Cwlth Scientific Office Washington DC 1944-45, admin civil servant Minys of Supply and Aviation 1946-62, Imperial Def Coll 1960, sec Inst of Electrical Engrs 1962-80, dir of external relations Int Electrotechnical Cmmn 1980-83; author of papers on proceedings of Inst of Electrical Engrs; *Clubs* Athenaeum; *Style*— George Gainsborough, Esq, CBE; 19 Glenmore House, Richmond Hill, Richmond, Surrey TW10 6BQ (☎ 081 940 8515); Moncorbon, 41360 Savigny-sur-Braye, France (☎ 54 23 99 25)

GAINSFORD, Ian Derek; s of Rabbi Dr Morris Ginsberg (d 1969), and Anne Freda, *née* Aucken (d 1950); *b* 24 June 1930; *Educ* Thames Valley GS, King's Coll London (BDS, LDS, FDS, MGDS RCSEng), Toronto Univ (DDS); *m* 13 June 1957, Carmel, da of Dr Lionel Bertram Liebster; 1 s (Jeremy Charles b 1961), 2 da (Ann Marietta b 1959, Deborah Jane b 1965); *Career* jr staff King's Coll Hosp 1955-57, lectr (later sr lectr) London Hosp Med Coll 1957-70; King's Coll Hosp Med Sch 1970: sr lectr (hon consIt) Conservative Dentistry Dept, dep dean of dental studies 1973-77, dean of dental studies 1977-87, dean of med and dentistry 1988-; memb Univ of London Ctees: Senate, Academic Cncl, Standing Ctee in Med; FKC 1984; hon memb American Dental Assoc; FICD, FACD; *Books* Silver Amalgam in Clinical Practise; *Recreations* canal cruising, theatre; *Clubs* Carlton, Athenaeum; *Style*— Ian Gainsford, Esq; 31 York Terrace East, London NW1 4PT (☎ 071 935 8659); 16 Sloane Square, London SW1; School of Medicine and Dentistry, King's College London, Bessemer Road, London SE5 9PJ (☎ 071 326 3000)

GAIR, Alan Graham; s of Sydney Gair (d 1968), and Margaret Evelyn, *née* Graham (d 1975); *b* 12 Nov 1930; *Educ* Ashville Coll Harrogate Yorks, Univ of Manchester (MBA), Univ of Leeds (MBA); *m* 1, 28 March 1957 (m dis 1984), Marion Edith, *née* Farson; 1 s (Crispin Robert William b 1966), 2 da (Camilla Jane b 1962, Miranda Kate b 1963); m 2, Francine Gaye, *née* Hutchins, of USA; 2 s (Justin b 1985 (decd), Alexander Thomas William b 1988); *Career* Nat Serv RAF; The Distillers Co, Lewis's, Selfridges; exec dir Royds (Manchester) Ltd (advertising agency) 1987- (dir 1973-); md until 1990: McCann Business Devpt, McCann Public Relations, McCann Recruitment and Corporate Communications; chm TFBI Int Advertising Consits; govr Cheadle Hulme Sch, memb Results (non pty political lobby gp for third world); FBIM, MInstM, FIIM; *Recreations* fencing (foil), AFA coach; *Style*— Alan G Gair, Esq; TFBI, Endon Hall West, Oak Lane, Kerridge, Cheshire SK10 5AL (☎ 0625 574 147)

GAIRY, Rt Hon Sir Eric Matthew; PC (1977); s of Douglas Gairy, of St Andrew's, Grenada; *b* 18 Feb 1922; *Educ* St Andrew's RC Sch; *m* 1949, Cynthia Clyne; 2 da; *Career* PM and min of external affairs Grenada 1974-79, Premier (before independence) 1967-74; kt 1977; *Style*— The Rt Hon Sir Eric Gairy

GAISFORD, Ven John Scott; s of Joseph Gaisford, and Margaret Thompson, *née* Scott; *b* 7 Oct 1934; *Educ* Burnage GS, Univ of Durham (BA, MA, Dip Theol); *m* 6 Oct 1962, Gillian, da of Francis Murdo Maclean; 1 s (Giles Gregory John b 6 July 1972), 1 da (Sophia Elizabeth Eve b 9 July 1970); *Career* Sr Aircraftsman RAF 1953-55; asst curate: St Hilda Audenshaw 1960-62, Bramhall 1962-65; vicar St Andrew Crewe 1965-86, rural dean Nantwich 1974-85, archdeacon of Macclesfield 1986-; memb: Gen Synod 1975-, C of E Pensions Bd 1982-; hon Canon Chester Cathedral 1980-86; church cmmr 1986-; *Recreations* fell walking, caravanning; *Clubs* Victory Services; *Style*— The Ven the Archdeacon of Macclesfield; 2 Lovat Drive, Knutsford, Cheshire WA16 8NS (☎ 0565 634456)

GAISFORD, Philip David; s of late (George) David Gaisford, and Vera Elizabeth, *née* Webb; *b* 15 Sept 1942; *Educ* Chigwell Sch, Univ of Southampton (LLB); *m* 27 Aug 1984, Petra, da of Walter Hammer, of Inzlingen, Germany; 2 da (Julia b 1 Nov 1988, Victoria (twin) b 1 Nov 1988); *Career* called to the Bar Gray's Inn 1969, practices SE Circuit; *Style*— Philip Gaisford, Esq; 1 Carlisle Mansions, Carlisle Place, London SW1; 3 Serjeants Inn, London EC4Y 1BQ (☎ 071 353 5537, fax 071 353 0425)

GAISMAN, Jonathan Nicholas Crispin; o s of Peter Gaisman, of Kirdford, W Sussex; *b* 10 Aug 1956; *Educ* Eton, Worcester Coll Oxford (BCL, MA); *m* 24 April 1982, Teresa Mignon (Tessa), MBE (1991), eldest da of Sir John Jardine Paterson, of Norton Bavant, Wilts; 1 s (Nicholas b 1989), 2 da (Clementine b 1986, Imogen b 1987); *Career* called to the Bar Inner Temple 1979; memb Ctee Old Etonian Assoc 1982; Freeman Worshipful Co of Grocers; *Recreations* the arts, travel, country pursuits; *Clubs* I Zingari, Brooks's; *Style*— Jonathan Gaisman, Esq; 32 Grafton Square, London SW4 (☎ 071 622 6485); Cobley House, Woodyates, Salisbury, Wilts (☎ 0725 52214); 7 King's Bench Walk, Temple, London EC4 (☎ 071 583 0404)

GAIT, (Robert) Charles Campbell; s of Robert William Gait (d 1986), of Pembroke, and Jean, *née* Campbell (d 1981); *b* 16 July 1955; *Educ* Pembroke GS, Jesus Coll Cambridge (MA); *m* 9 Sept 1978, Anne Rose, da of Edward Nicholson, of Pembroke; 3 s (Michael Huw b 30 Sept 1984, Jonathan Edward b 25 June 1986, Nicholas Matthew b 27 July 1988); *Career* admitted slr 1980; ptnr McKenna & Co 1985 (articled clerk 1978-80), specialising in property devpt work; memb: Law Soc, Westminster Law Soc; *Recreations* rugby football (Oloepsomian RFC as player and London Welsh RFC as supporter), enthuisiastic but incompetent skier; *Style*— Charles Gait, Esq; Inversk House, 1 Aldwych, London WC2R 0HF (☎ 071 836 2442, telex 27251, fax 071 379 3059)

GALASKO, Prof Charles Samuel Bernard; s of David Isaac Galasko (d 1951), and Rose, *née* Shames; *b* 29 June 1939; *Educ* King Edward VII Sch Johannesburg, Univ of Johannesburg (MB BCh, ChM); *m* 29 Oct 1967, Carol Freyda, da of Michael Lapinsky; 1 s (Gavin b 1972), 1 da (Deborah b 1970); *Career* med trg Johannesburg Gen Hosp 1963-66, lectr Univ of Witwatersrand 1964-66; registrar: Hammersmith Hosp 1967-69, Royal Postgrad Med Sch 1967-69; sr registrar Radcliffe Infirmary and Nuffield Orthopaedic Centre Oxford 1970-73; conslt orthopaedic surgn Hammersmith Hosp 1973-76 (former dir orthopaedic surgery), asst dir Division of Surgery Royal Postgrad Med Sch 1973-76 (former dir orthopaedic surgery), prof orthopaedic surgery Univ of Manchester 1976-, hon conslt orthopaedic surgn Salford Health Authy 1976-; contrib over 150 published articles; temp advsr World Health Authy 1981, pres SIROT 1990- (memb Exec Ctee 1981-, Prog Ctee 1981-84, prog chm 1984-87, Chm Membership Ctee 1987-90), chm Award Ctee SICOT 1987, treas Int Assoc Olympic Med Offrs 1988-; chm Assoc Prof Orthopaedic Surgery 1983-86, vice pres Section of Oncology RSM 1987 (memb Cncl 1980-87); memb: Cncl Br Orthopaedic Assoc 1988-, Med Sub Ctee BOA 1988-, Panel External Assessors for Conslt Appts RCS; fndr memb: Int Orthopaedic Res Soc, Metastatis Res Soc, S African Surgical Res Soc; Hon MSc Univ of Manchester 1980; memb: Rhino Club, BMA, Br Orthopaedic Res Soc; fell Br Orthopaedic Assoc, FRSM, FRCS (London), FRCS (Edin); *Books* Radionuclide Scintigraphy in Orthopaedics (jt ed, 1984), Principles of Fracture Management (ed, 1984), Skeletal Metastases (1986), Neuromuscular Problems in Orthopaedics (ed, 1987), Recent Developments in Orthopaedic Surgery (jt ed, 1987), Current Trends in Orthopaedic Surgery (jt ed, 1988), Imaging Techniques in Orthopaedics (jt ed, 1989); *Recreations* sport, music, theatre; *Style*— Prof Charles Galasko; Dept of Orthopaedic Surgery, Clinical Sciences Building, Hope Hospital, Eccles Old Rd, Salford M6 8HD (☎ 061 789 7373)

GALATOPOULOS, Stelios Emille; s of John Galatopoulos (d 1978), of Nicosia, Cyprus and Athens, and Maria, *née* Stylianaki (d 1948); *b* 2 Aug 1932; *Educ* The English Sch Nicosia, Univ of Southampton (BSc); *Career* civil and structural engr; designer: T C Jones 1954-55, Kellogg Int Corp 1956-60; designer and head of Civil and Structural Dept Tripe and Wakeham (chartered architects) London and Cyprus for Akrotiri Strategic Base 1960-66, freelance engr 1967-72, designer Pell Frischmann 1972-75, freelance engr 1975-, lectr; opera and music critic-journalist: Music and Musicians, Records and Recordings, Lirica nel Mondo (Italy), Opera, Musical America; broadcaster: BBC, CBC (Cyprus), America; memb Soc of Authors 1971-, vice pres Opera Italiana 1985; *Books* Callas La Divina (1966), Italian Opera (1971), Callas Prima Donna Assoluta (1976); *Recreations* opera, theatre, ballet, concerts, tennis, swimming, skiing; *Style*— Stelios Galatopoulos, Esq; Flat 2, 38 Shalstone Road, London SW14 7HR (☎ 081 8789731)

GALBRAITH, Hon David Muir Galloway; 5 but 3 surviving s of 1 Baron Strathclyde, PC, JP (d 1985); *b* 8 March 1928; *Educ* Wellington, RAC Cirencester; *m* 5 Aug 1967, Marion Bingham, o da of Maj Bruce Bingham Kennedy, TD, of Doonholm, Ayr; 1 s, 3 da; *Career* chartered land agent, chartered surveyor; *Recreations* country pursuits; *Style*— Hon David Galbraith; Burnbrae Lodge, Mauchline, Ayrshire (☎ 0290 50210)

GALBRAITH, (James) Donald; s of James Alexander Galbraith (d 1972), and Anne Gibb, *née* Selbie; *b* 26 April 1943; *Educ* Robert Gordons Coll, Univ of Aberdeen (MA, MLitt); *m* 11 June 1983, Frances Jennifer, da of James Bonnar Shaw, of Loch Rd, Edinburgh; *Career* 2 Lt Highland Vols 1972, Capt 3 and SI Highland 1982; Scottish Record Office: res asst 1972, asst keeper 1976, curator of historical records 1984; *Books* St Machars Cathedral-The Celtic Antecedants (1982), Caldendar of Documents Relating to Scotland (1986); *Recreations* hillwalking, skiing, manuscript illumination; *Style*— Donald Galbraith, Esq; Scottish Record Office, HM General Register House, Edinburgh EH1 3YY (☎ 031 5566585)

GALBRAITH, Hon Heather Margaret Anne Galloway; yr da of 1 Baron Strathclyde (d 1985); *b* 27 Feb 1930; *Style*— Hon Heather Galbraith; Barskimming, Mauchline, Ayrshire

GALBRAITH, Hon Ida Jean Galloway; er da of 1 Baron Strathclyde (d 1985); *b* 21 Jan 1922; *Educ* Queen Ethelburga's Sch; *Career* served WW II as 3 Offr WRNS; *Recreations* riding, gardening, wildlife, country pursuits; *Style*— Hon Ida Galbraith; Barskimming, Mauchline, Ayrshire

GALBRAITH, Hon James Muir Galloway; CBE (1984); 3 but eldest surviving s of 1 Baron Strathclyde, PC, JP (d 1985); *b* 27 Sept 1920; *Educ* RNC Dartmouth, ChCh Oxford, RAC Cirencester; *m* 27 Sept 1945, Anne, er da of late Maj Kenneth Paget, of Old Rectory House, Itchen Abbas, Hants; 3 s, 1 da; *Career* served with RN WW II (wounded); dir Buccleuch Estates Ltd; chm: Timber Groves UK 1980-86, Forestry Indust Ctee GB 1987-90, Scottish Forestry Tst 1990-; JP Inverness-shire 1953-54; FRICS; *Clubs* Army & Navy, New (Edinburgh); *Style*— Hon James Galbraith, CBE; Rawflat, Ancrum, Roxburghshire (☎ 083 53 302)

GALBRAITH, Hon Norman Dunlop Galloway; 4 but 2 surviving s of 1 Baron Strathclyde, PC, JP (d 1985); *b* 24 Jan 1925; *Educ* Wellington; *m* 9 Sept 1950, Susan Patricia, er da of Cdr Jan Herbert Farquharson Kent, RN, of La Coupe, St Martin, Jersey; 1 s, 2 da; *Career* served WW II, Sub-Lt RNVR, HMS Malaya 1943, HMS Undine 1943-46, Normandy Landing 1944, Br Pacific Fleet 1944-46; dir Ben Line Steamers Ltd 1968-86; farmer; *Recreations* farming, country pursuits; *Clubs* New (Edinburgh); *Style*— The Hon Norman Galbraith; Over Newton, by Haddington, East Lothian (☎ 062 081 470)

GALE, Capt Douglas William; s of William Charles Gale (d 1980), and Helen Sophia Watt (d 1985); *b* 16 Sept 1935; *Educ* Wandsworth GS, Harrow Sch of Art, Sch of Military Survey RE, London Coll of Printing; *m* 7 May 1962 (m dis 1982), Donna Marion, da of John Herbert de Kewer Williams (d 1974), of Oxford; 2 step s (Nicholas Gregory Harding b 1951, Mark Cedric Harding b 1955); *Career* RE: land surveyor, joined Corps 1956, cmmnd and served 42 Survey Engr Regt Cyprus, 22 Litho Sqdn Sch of Mil, 13 Field Survey Sqdn Aden, Print Troop Cdr Sch of Mil Survey UK, Tech Adj 42 Survey Engr Regt; ret RARO 1972; estab De Kewer Gale Bldg Co 1975 (specialising in renovation of timber frame bldgs) won Suffolk Assoc of Architects Craftmanship award Best New House 1984; *Recreations* shooting, sailing, skiing; *Clubs* Inst of Royal Engrs, Inst of Printing, Br Cartographic Soc, Suffolk Preservation Soc; *Style*— Capt Douglas W Gale; Tailors Green Cottage, Tailors Green, Bacton, Stowmarket Suffolk IP14 4LL (☎ 0449 781227)

GALE, Dr Edwin Albert Merwood; s of Dr (George) Edwin Gale, of 23 St Helen's Court, St Helen's Parade, Southsea, Hants, and Carole, *née* Waldron; *b* 21 March 1945; *Educ* Sevenoaks Sch, Univ of Cambridge (MA, MB BChir); *m* 26 June 1982, Lone Anita Brogaard, da of Jens Christian Pedersen; 1 s (John b 1986), 2 da (Emily b 1982, Rebecca b 1984); *Career* sr lectr med 1984-, hon conslt physician, currently head Dept Diabetes and Metabolism St Bartholomews Hosp, dir Barts-Oxford Family Study of Childhood Diabetes; memb: Br Diabetic Assoc, American Diabetic Assoc, Euro Assoc for Study of Diabetes; FRCP (1987); *Books* Diabetes: Clinical Management (with R B Tattersall, 1989); *Recreations* collecting fossils; *Style*— Dr Edwin Gale; 76 Linthorpe Rd, Stamford Hill, London N16 5RF (☎ 081 802 6061); Dept of Diabetes and Metabolism, St Bartholomew's Hosp, London EC1 (☎ 071 606 2032)

GALE, Hon George Alexander; CC (1977), QC (KC 1944); s of Robert Henry Gale (d 1950), and Elma Gertrude Gale; *b* 24 June 1906; *Educ* Prince of Wales HS, Vancouver BC, Toronto Univ (BA), Osgoode Hall Law Sch Toronto; *m* 1934, Hilda Georgina, da of William Arthur Daly (d 1943); 3 s; *Career* barrister; Supreme Ct of Ontario 1946, Ct of Appeal for Ontario 1963, chief justice of the High Ct of Justice 1964, chief justice of Ontario 1967-76; vice chm Ontario Law Reform Cmmn 1977-81; hon pres: Lawyers Club 1970, Ontario Curling Assoc 1978; *Recreations* golf; *Clubs* York, University, Chippewa; *Style*— The Hon George Gale, CC, QC; 7700 Bayview Ave, Thornhill, Ontario, Canada (☎ 416 881 0252)

GALE, (Thomas Henry) John; OBE (1986); s of Frank Haith Gale (1970), and Martha Edith Gale; *b* 2 Aug 1929; *Educ* Christ's Hosp, Webber Douglas Sch of Drama; *m* 24 Nov 1950, Liselotte Ann, da of Ian Dennis Wratten, CBE (d 1988); 2 s (Timothy Simon b 1956, Matthew Ian b 1959); *Career* 2 Lt RASC 1948; former actor; dir: Gale Enterprises Ltd 1960-, John Gale Productions Ltd 1960-, West End Managers Ltd 1972/89, Lisden Productions Ltd 1975-82, Chichester Festival Theatre 1985-89 (exec prodr 1983-84); prodr and co prodr more than eighty plays around the world incl: Candida 1960, On The Brighter Side 1961, Boeing-Boeing, Devil May Care 1963, Windfall 1963, Where Angels Fear to Tread 1963, The Wings of the Dove 1963, Amber for Anna 1964, Present Laughter 1964 and 1981, Maigret and the Lady 1965, The Platinum Cat 1965, The Sacred Flame 1966, An Evening With GBS 1966, A Woman of No Importance 1967, The Secretary Bird 1968, Dear Charles 1968, Highly Confidential 1969, The Young Churchill 1969, The Lionel Touch 1969, Abelard and Heloise 1970, No Sex Please - We're British 1971 (the longest running comedy in Br theatre history), Lloyd George Knew My Father 1972, The Mating Game 1972, Parents Day 1972, At the End of the Day 1973, Birds of Paradise 1974, A Touch of Spring 1975, Separate Tables 1977, The Kingfisher 1977, Sextet 1977, Cause Celebre 1977, Shut Your Eyes and Think of England 1977, Can You Hear Me At The Back? 1979, Middle Age Spread 1979, Private Lives 1980, A Personal Affair 1982; pres Soc West End Theatre 1972-75, govr and almoner Christ's Hosp 1976-, chm Theatres Nat Ctee 1979-85, memb Amicable Soc Blues 1981-; Liveryman Worshipful Co Gold and Silver Wyredrawers 1974-; *Recreations* travel, rugby; *Clubs* Garrick and Greenroom, London Welsh RF; *Style*— John Gale, Esq, OBE; 1 East Dean Hill, East Dean, nr Chichester, W Sussex PO 18OJA (☎ 0243 63407)

GALE, Michael; QC (1979); s of Joseph and Blossom Gale; *b* 12 Aug 1932; *Educ* Cheltenham GS, Grocers Sch, King's Coll Cambridge; *m* 1963, Joanna Stephanie Bloom; 1 s, 2 d; *Career* Royal Fus 1956-58, called to the Bar Middle Temple 1968; rec Crown Court 1977-, bencher; memb Gen Cncl of the Bar; *Recreations* arts, country pursuits; *Clubs* United Oxford & Cambridge, MCC; *Style*— Michael Gale, Esq, QC; 6 Pump Court, Temple EC4 (☎ 071 353 7242)

GALE, Roger James; MP (C) North Thanet 1983-; s of Richard Byrne Gale, and Phyllis Mary, *née* Rowell (d 1948); *b* 20 Aug 1943; *Educ* Hardye's Sch Dorchester, Guildhall Sch of Music and Drama; *m* 1, 1964 (m dis 1967), Wendy Dawn Bowman; m 2, 1971 (m dis), Susan Sampson; 1 da (Misty); m 3, 1980, Suzy Gabrielle, da of Thomas Leopold Marks (d 1972); 2 s (Jasper, Thomas); *Career* formerly: reporter BBC Radio, prodr BBC Radio 4 Today Show, dir BBC Children's TV, prodr and dir Thames Children's TV, editor Teenage Unit Thames; Parly candidate (C) Birmingham Northfield (by-election) 1982; *Recreations* swimming, sailing; *Clubs* Garrick; *Style*— Roger Gale, Esq, MP; House of Commons, London SW1A 0AA (☎ 071 219 4021)

GALGANI, Franco; s of Piero Galgani, of Leghorn and Vilia Galgani; *b* 28 March 1949; *Educ* Saffi Secdy Sch Florence Italy, Florence Hotel Sch Florence (Nat Dip), Open Univ UK (BA); *m* 1, 1967 (m dis 1977), Mary Ellen, *née* McElhone; 3 s (Lorenzo b 1968, Riccardo b 1969, Giancarlo b 1971); m 2, 1981, Lynne, *née* MacDonald; 1 da (Daniela b 1983); *Career* restaurateur; industl trg 1963-68: Alberg Ristorante L'Elba nr Grosseto Italy, Grand Hotel Florence, Hotel Iselba Island of Elba, Hotel de la Plage St Raphael France, Hotel Baglioni Florence, Grand Hotel Florence, George Hotel Keswick Eng, Hotel Parco Rimini Italy; food and beverage supervisory and mgmnt appts 1968-76: Granville Restaurant Glasgow, MacDonald Hotel (Thistle) Giffnock Glasgow, Stuart Hotel (Thistle) and Bruce Hotel (Swallow) E Kilbride Strathclyde; mangr and ptnr Balcary Bay Hotel Scot 1976-82; gen mangr: Buchanan Arms Hotel Loch Lomond Scot 1982-85, Stakis Dunkeld House Perthshire Scot 1985-86, Marine Highland Hotel Troon Ayrshire Scot 1986-; memb: Bd of Dirs Ayrshire Tourist Bd, Cncl Ayr Coll of Further Educn; gp ldr Ayrshire Local Business Educn Partnership; *Awards* Master Innholders award 1989, Scottish Highland Hotels Group Mangr of the Year 1990: FHCIMA 1989; *Recreations* travel, theatre and classical music, outdoor pursuits with family; *Clubs* Glasgow Art; *Style*— Franco Galgani, Esq; Marine Highland Hotel, Troon, Ayrshire KA10 6HE (☎ 0292 314444, fax 0292 316922)

GALITZINE, Prince (Russian kniaz, cr 1408 confirmed 1798) George; name also spelt Golitsyn, Gallitzinn, etc; 2 s of Prince Vladimir Emanuelovitch Galitzine (d 1954), by his 1 w Countess Catherine von Carlow (d 1940); product of the morganatic m between Natalia, *née* Wonlarsky, cr Countess von Carlow, and HH Duke Georg Alexander of Mecklenburg-Strelitz; the latter's maternal gf was yst s of Tsar Paul I of Russia, while through his mother's mother Georg was fifth in descent from HRH Princess Augusta, sis of George III; hence Prince George Galitzine is sixth cous once removed of HM The Queen); *b* 3 May 1916; *Educ* Lancing, St Paul's, BNC Oxford (MA); *m* 1, 11 Sept 1943 (m dis 1954), Baroness Anne-Marie von Slatin, da of Maj-Gen (Baron) Sir Rudolf von Slatin Pasha, GCVO, KCMG, CB (d 1928); 2 s (Alexander b 1945, George b 1946), 1 da (Caroline b 1944); m 2, 5 May 1963, Jean, da of Frederick Dawnay; 1 da (Katya b 1964); *Career* formerly Maj Welsh Gds; company dir; Royal Humane Soc Med 1936; *Recreations* travel, photography, skiing; *Style*— Prince George Galitzine; Mulberry Cottage, Brown Candover, Alresford, Hants; 75 Eaton Sq, London SW1W 9AW (☎ 071 235 3113)

GALL, Henderson Alexander (Sandy); CBE (1988); s of Henderson Gall (d 1963), of Banchory, Scotland, and Jean, *née* Begg (d 1970); *b* 1 Oct 1927; *Educ* Glenalmond Perthshire, Univ of Aberdeen (MA); *m* 11 Aug 1958, Eleanor Mary Patricia Anne, da of Michael Joseph Smyth (d 1964), of London; 1 s (Alexander Patrick Henderson b 17 June 1960), 3 da (Fiona Deirdre b 7 May 1959, Carlotta Maire Jean b 2 Nov 1961, Michaela Monica b 27 March 1965); *Career* Corp RAF 1945-48; foreign corr Reuters 1953-63: Berlin, Nairobi, Suez, Geneva, Budapest, Johannesburg, Congo; ITN 1963-: roving reporter, maker of seven TV documentaries; rector Univ of Aberdeen 1978-81; Sitara-i-Pakistan 1985, Lawrence of Arabia Medal RSAA 1987; Hon LLD Univ of Aberdeen 1981; *Books* Gold Scoop (1977), Chasing the Dragon (1981), Don't Worry

About the Money Now (1983), Behind Russian Lines, an Afghan Journal (1983), Afghanistan: Agony of a Nation (1986), Salang (1989); *Recreations* golf, Cresta Run; *Clubs* Turf, Special Forces, Rye Golf, Royal St Georges Golf; *Style*— Sandy Gall, Esq, CBE; Doubleton Oast Hse, Penshurst, Kent TN11 8JA; ITN, 200 Gray's Inn Rd, London WC1X 8XZ (☎ 071 833 3000, home fax 0892 870 871)

GALL, Maurice Henry Willis; s of Douglas Crisp Gall (d 1984), of Nutley, Sussex, and Grace Florence, *née* Willis (d 1972); *b* 15 June 1926; *Educ* King's Canterbury, Cheltenham, Univ of Cambridge (MA); *m* 1, 1954 (m dis 1966), Ghyslaine Monique Danielle; 3 da (Chantal b 25 May 1955, Odile b 1 Oct 1958, Alice b 1 Aug 1963); m 2, 16 Aug 1967, Pamela Margaret Alice, da of Sir Guthrie Thomas Russell, KCSI, KCIE (d 1966), of Glasgow; *Career* RNVR 1944-47 (Sub Lt 1945) minesweeping Far East and Home Waters; dir H Tinsley & Co Ltd 1959-67, md Precision Varionics Ltd 1968-; Freeman Worshipful Co of Girdlers 1956 (Master 1986), Master Worshipful Co of Scientific Instrument Makers 1984; FIEE, FInstP; *Recreations* ocean racing, sailing; *Clubs* RNSA, RNVR Offrs Assoc; *Style*— Maurice Gall, Esq

GALLACHER, Bernard; s of Bernard Gallacher Sr, of Bathgate, Scotland, and Matilda Gallacher; *b* 9 Feb 1949; *Educ* St Marys Acad Bathgate Scotland; *m* Lesley; 1 s (Jamie b 22 May 1977), 2 da (Kirsty Jane b 20 Jan 1976, Laura Kate b 28 June 1987); *Career* professional golfer; club professional Wentworth 1975-; amateur: boys int 1965 and 1966, full int 1967, Scot Open Amateur Stroke Play Champion 1967; professional wins: Schweppes PGA 1969, Westward Ho Wills Open 1969, Martini Int 1971 and 1982, Young Professionals 1973, Carrolls Int 1974, Dunlop Masters 1974 and 1975, Spanish Open 1977, French Open 1979, Tournament Players 1980, Manchester Open 1981, Jersey Open 1982 and 1984; Ryder Cup: memb team 1969, 1971, 1973, 1975, 1977, 1979, 1981, 1983, capt 1991; Hennessy Cognac Cup 1974, 1978, 1982, 1984, World Cup 1969, 1971, 1974, 1982, 1983, Scot Professional Champion 1971, 1973, 1974, 1977, 1984; rookie of the year 1968, Harry Vardon Trophy winner 1969; *Recreations* reading, walking dogs, keeping fit; *Style*— Bernard Gallacher, Esq; Professional Shop, Wentworth Club, Virginia Water, Surrey GU25 4LS (☎ 0344 843353, fax 0344 842122)

GALLACHER, John; s of John Gallacher (d 1983), of Garrowhill, Glasgow, and Catherine, *née* Crilly; *b* 16 July 1931; *Educ* Our Lady's HS Motherwell; *m* 8 Feb 1956, Eileen Agnes, da of John McGuire (d 1965); 1 s (John Kevin b 1964); *Career* RAF Nat Serv 1950-52; superintendent Kenya Police 1953-65, advsr to Miny of Interior Libyan Govt 1965-67, cnsllr HM Dip Serv 1967-85, gp security advsr Gallaher Ltd 1985; *Recreations* golf, travel, reading; *Clubs* Royal Overseas League; *Style*— John Gallacher, Esq; 1 Clive Rd, Strawberry Vale, Twickenham, Middx TW1 4SQ; Gallaher Limited, Weybridge, Surrey

GALLAGHER, Jock James Young; s of Joseph Gallagher (d 1938), and Margaret, *née* Young (d 1984); *b* 31 March 1938; *Educ* Greenock HS; *m* 31 Dec 1971, Sheenagh Glenn, da of Richard Jones (d 1958); *Career* journalist various newspapers 1958-66; BBC: news prodr 1966-70, head network radio 1980-89 (ed 1970-80), head special projects 1989-90; dir: Broadstaff, News Fact Ltd, Assoc Br Eds; chm Georgina Van Etzdorf Ltd, artistic advsr D'Art Design Ltd, md Broadvision; govr RASE, former pres Radio and TV Industs Club (Midlands), pres Wyre Forest SLD, dir Bewdley Festival; memb: Inst of Journalists, Radio Acad; *Books* History of the Archers (1975), Portrait of A Lady (1980), The Life And Death of Doris Archer (1981), To The Victor The Spoil (1986), Borchester Echoes (1988); *Recreations* golf, reading, politics; *Clubs* Chelsea Arts, Edgbaston Golf; *Style*— Jock Gallagher, Esq; Rock House, Bewdley, Worcs DY12 1BY (☎ 0299 403110); Broadvision, 49 Frederick Road, Birmingham (☎ 021 455 7949)

GALLAGHER, Hon Mrs (Kristin); er da of Baron Wynne-Jones (Life Peer) (d 1982); *b* 1931; *Educ* Cheltenham Ladies' Coll, Somerville Coll Oxford (MA, BSc); *m* 1956, Dr Charles Joseph Gallagher (d 1964); children; *Style*— The Hon Mrs Gallagher

GALLAGHER, Patrick Joseph; DFC (1943); s of Patrick Gallagher and Mary Berndine, *née* Donnellan; *b* 15 April 1921; *Educ* Prior Park Bath; *m* 1950, Veronica Frances Bateman (d 1981); 1 s; *Career* md Patrick Gallagher Associates 1979-; *Style*— Patrick Gallagher, Esq, DFC; 12 Parsons Green, London SW6

GALLAGHER, Patrick Joseph David; s of Matthew Gallagher, of Cashel, Co Sligo; *b* 28 Feb 1909; *Educ* Trinity Coll Dublin, Temple Univ Philadelphia USA; *m* 1944, Mary, da of Joseph Gleason, of Philadelphia; 3 s, 2 da; *Career* chm Abbey Ltd Dublin 1977-; dir Abbey Homesteads Ltd London and Cyprus; *Recreations* golf, football; *Clubs* Kildare Street Univ; *Style*— Patrick Gallagher, Esq; Liskilleen, Shankill, Dublin, Eire (☎ 01 852426)

GALLAGHER, (Arthur) Robin; s of James Albert Gallagher, (d 1965), of York, and Winifred Mary, *née* Dill; *b* 7 April 1941; *Educ* St Bedes Coll Manchester; *m* 1 July 1969, (Irene) Denise, da of James Rothwell, Ambleside; 2 da (Kirsten b 8 March 1974, Kate b 1 Dec 1977); *Career* Lt RNR 1960-66; Touche Ross and Co Manchester and Leeds 1966-74, Ladyship Int Gp 1974-80, Whitecroft plc 1980-81, Antler Property Corp plc 1981-88, md Wellholme Ltd 1988; FCA; *Recreations* tennis, riding; *Style*— Robin Gallagher, Esq; 12 Churchfields Rd, Brighouse, W Yorks HD6 1DH (☎ 0484 400740, fax 0484 400540, car 0860 342303)

GALLAGHER, Sister Maire Teresa; OBE; da of Owen Gallagher (d 1952), of Glasgow, and Annie, *née* McVeigh; *b* 27 May 1933; *Educ* Notre Dame HS Glasgow (MA), Notre Dame Coll of Educn Glasgow (DCE); *Career* memb Sisters of Notre Dame de Namur 1959-, princ teacher of History Notre Dame HS Glasgow 1965-72, lectr in secondary educn Notre Dame Coll Glasgow 1972-74, headteacher Notre Dame HS Dumbarton 1974-87, Sister Superior Convent of Notre Dame Dumbarton 1987-; memb: Consultative Ctee on the Curriculum 1976-, Ctee of Enquiry into Salary and Conditions of Service of Teachers 1986-; chm: Ctee on Secondary Educn 1983-87, Consultative Ctee 1987-88, Scottish Consultative Cncl on the Curriculum 1988-; fell Scottish Vocational Educn Cncl 1989; *Recreations* reading, birdwatching; *Style*— Sister Maire Teresa Gallagher, OBE, SND; Convent of Notre Dame, Cardross Road, Dumbarton, Scotland G82 4JH (☎ 0389 62361)

GALLAGHER, Stephen; *b* 13 Oct 1954; *Career* writer; res Documentaries Dept Yorkshire TV, Presentation Dept Granada TV 1975, freelance writer 1980-; novels incl: Chimera (1982), Follower (1984), Valley of Lights (1987), Oktober (1988), Down River (1989), Rain (1990), The Boat House (1991); radio plays incl: The Last Rose of Summer 1977, Hunter's Moon 1978, The Babylon Run 1979, A Resistance to Pressure 1980, The Kingston File 1987, By The River, Fontainbleau 1988, The Horn 1989; tv: Warriors' Gate (BBC) 1981, Terminus (BBC) 1984, Moving Targets (BBC) 1988, Chimera (Zenith/Anglia) 1991; writings also incl short fiction and criticism; *Style*— Stephen Gallagher, Esq; New English Library, Hodder & Stoughton Ltd, 47 Bedford Square, London WC1B 3DP

GALLAHER, Dr (Alfred) Trevor; s of George Gallaher (d 1936), and Maud, *née* Thomas (d 1975); *Educ* Canterbury Coll NZ, Balliol Coll Oxford (BA, MA, PhD); *m* 10 June 1944, Ailsa Jean (d 1988), da of William Robert Crompton (d 1973); 2 s (Nigel b 5 April 1950, Brendan b 8 Dec 1954), 2 da (Ailsa Durelle b 14 Nov 1946, Marissa b 7 May 1957); *Career* RNZAF 1941-46, Sqdn Ldr RAF 1947-57; lawyer Zimbabwe 1958-69, Civil Aeronautics Bd Washington DC 1970-72; aviation advsr: Saudi Arabia 1972-73, Guatamala 1973-74; asst gen counsel IATA Geneva 1975-76, legal advsr Libya Int Civil Aviation Orgn Tripoli 1977-88, mentor Columbia Pacific Univ USA 1979-; FRMetS 1945, ARAeS 1945, ACAC 1950, MIAA 1950, ABAC 1955; *Recreations* flying, tennis, windsurfing, golf, travel; *Clubs* Naval and Military, Picadilly, Leander, Vincents, Stewards; *Style*— Dr Trevor Gallaher; 43 Sunderland Avenue, Oxford OX2 8DT (☎ 0865 58681)

GALLAND, Robert Brian; s of Raymond Harry Galland, and Olywyn Lilian Gladys, *née* Aston; *b* 26 Dec 1947; *Educ* Halesowen GS Univ of Manchester (MB ChB, MD); *m* 21 May 1977, Janet Carmichael, da of Edward Yates (d 1982); 3 da (Emma Louise b 30 March 1979, Joanne Laura b 20 June 1980, Rebecca Jamie b 26 Dec 1985); *Career* conslt surgn Royal Berkshire Hosp Reading 1988-; author of pubns on: vascular surgery, gastroenterology, surgical infection; FRCS 1976; *Books* Radiation Enteritis (ed with J Spencer, 1990); *Recreations* reading; *Style*— Robert Galland, Esq; Little Orchard, Gardner's Lane, Upper Basildon, Berks RG8 8NN (☎ 0496 671852); Department of Surgery, Royal Berkshire Hospital, London Rd, Reading, Berks (☎ 0734 87511)

GALLETLY, Prof Gerard Duncan; s of John Edward Galletly (d 1972), and Marian, *née* Musker (d 1973); *b* 17 March 1928; *Educ* Bootle GS, Univ of Liverpool (BEng, MEng, DEng), MIT Cambridge USA (SM, ScD); *m* 17 Oct 1953, Marjorie, da of Leonard Archer (d 1973); 1 da (Diana b 1974); *Career* airfield construction serv RAF 1947-49, Flying Offr Germany; head Plates and Shells Section David Taylor Model Basin US Navy Washington DC 1952-55, specialist structural mechanics Shell Devpt Co Emeryville California 1955-61, asst dir Advanced Materials R & D Laboratory Pratt & Whitney Aircraft North Haven Connecticut 1961-64, prof (now Alexander Elder prof 1987-) of applied mechanics Univ of Liverpool 1964- (dean engrg 1980-83); author 100 tech papers in various journals; memb Tech Ctees Br Standards Inst, govr Birkenhead HS for Girls (GPDST); FICE 1976, FIMechE 1977, FEng 1989, Eur Ing 1989; *Recreations* sport, music; *Clubs* RAF; *Style*— Prof Gerard Galletly; Dept of Mechanical Engineering, The University, PO Box 147, Liverpool, Merseyside L69 3BX (☎ 051 794 4827, fax 051 794 4848, telex 627095)

GALLEWAY, William Henry; s of Major Harold Galleway, JP (d 1963), and Marjorie, *née* Frankland; *b* 30 July 1931; *Educ* Whitby GS, Univ of Leeds (BCom); *Career* articled to M Wasley Chapman 1949; ptnr: Carlill Burkinshaw Ferguson 1963-, Hodgson Impey (formerly Hodgson Harris) 1970, Price Waterhouse 1990-; pres Humberside and Dist Soc CA's 1982-83; memb Cncl ICEAW 1982; memb Worshipful Co of CAs 1988; FCA 1966 (ACA 1955); *Recreations* antique collecting, philately; *Clubs* Landsdowne; *Style*— William H Galleway, Esq; 26 Argyle Road, Whitby, N Yorks, (☎ 0947 602280); Queen Victoria House, Guildhall Road, Hull, HU1 1HH (☎ 0482 224111, fax 0482 27479, telex 597641F)

GALLEY, Dr Robert Albert Ernest; s of John Atkinson Galley (d 1971), of Hayling Island, and Jane Alice, *née* James (d 1970); *b* 23 Oct 1909; *Educ* Colfe's GS, Sir John Cass Coll, Imperial Coll London (BSc, DIC, PhD); *m* 1, 29 July 1933, (Elsie) Marjorie (d 1985), da of late John Stannix Walton, of London; 1 s (John b 1936), 2 da (Gillian b 1939, Susan b 1944); m 2, 27 April 1988, Ann Louise, da of Wing Cdr John Henry Dale (d 1946); *Career* res chemist Wool Industs Res Assoc 1932-34, chemist War Dept 1934-37, lectr in Chemistry Dept Sir John Cass Coll 1937-39, sr experimental offr Miny of Supply 1939-46 (princ experimental offr 1945-46), sr princ sci offr Agric Res Cncl 1946-50 (sec Interdepartmental Insecticides Ctees), various short term consultancies WHO and FAO 1948-72, Office of the Lord Pres of the Cncl (memb Advsy Cncl's Sci Policy and Natural Resources Ctee) 1950-52; dir: Tropical Prods Inst Colonial Off 1953-60, Woodstock Agric Res Centre Shell Res Ltd 1960-69; memb 1970-82: Bredgar Parish Cncl, Bredgar Village Hall Ctee, Bredgar Village Fete Ctee; ARSC 1930, FRSC; *Recreations* bowls, gardening, foreign travel; *Style*— Dr Robert Galley; 10 Riverside Ct, River Reach, Teddington, Middx TW11 9QN (☎ 081 943 1884); ATICO 7 Bloque 7, Javea Park, Javea, Alicante, Spain

GALLEY, Roy; s of Kenneth Haslam Galley, and Letitia Mary, *née* Chapman; *b* 8 Dec 1947; *Educ* King Edward VII GS Sheffield, Worcester Coll Oxford; *m* 1976, Helen Margaret Butcher; 1 s, 1 da; *Career* PO mangr; contested (C) Dewsbury 1979, MP (C) Halifax 1983-87; memb Social Services Select Ctee 1983-87, sec Cons Backbench Health Ctee 1983-87; memb Calderdale Met Borough Cncl 1980-83, chm Kingston and Esher Health Authy 1989-; *Style*— Roy Galley, Esq

GALLIANO, John Charles; s of John Joseph Galliano, of London, and Anita, *née* Guillen; *b* 28 Nov 1960; *Educ* Wilsons GS, St Martins Sch of Art; *Career* fashion designer; collections incl: Spring/Summer collections 1985, 1986, 1988, 1989/90, 1990 and 1991, Autumn/Winter collections 1985, 1986, 1987/88, 1988/89, 1989/90, 1990/91 and 1991; worked on Courtelle project 1985, first Br designer ever to show collection in Paris at The Louvre during Paris Fashion Week 1990, introduced Galliano's Girl 1991; awards: a John Galliano design is picked as Dress of the Year to be put on permanent display in The Museum of Costume in Bath 1987, Designer of the Year award (Br Cncl) 1987, nominated for Cristobel Balenciaga award (Spain) 1988, guest designer for Courtelle Fabric awards 1988; Freeman Beverley Hills; *Style*— John Galliano, Esq

GALLIE, Thomas Holmes (Tom); TD; s of Henry Holmes Gallie (d 1947), of Glasgow, Rangoon and Tunbridge Wells, and Marion Evelyn, *née* Morphew (d 1970); *b* 1 Sept 1917; *Educ* Edinburgh Acad, Fettes; *m* 21 Aug 1943, Doreen Yvonne Lily (Dee), da of George Charles Sydney Pike (d 1967), of London; 2 da (Rosemary b 1944, Josephine b 1949); *Career* WWII Bde Maj 69 HAA Regt RA TA UK and India; Metals Div ICI 1936-75: overseas dir 1961, later md Copper Div and Gen Mangr Mktg and Overseas; dir Irish Metal Industs 1963-75; cncl memb Br Non-Ferrous Metals Fedn, Br del to Int Wrought Copper Cncl (pres 1973-75); chm Birmingham Marriage Guidance Cncl 1969-77; memb: Stratford-on-Avon DC 1976- (chm 1982-83), S Warwicks Community Health Cncl 1976-79; tstee Brandwood Tst; gen cmmr for income tax 1974-, JP Birmingham 1971-87; *Recreations* gardening, bridge, family; *Clubs* Special Forces; *Style*— Tom Gallie, Esq, TD; Greenacres, Vicarage Hill, Tanworth in Arden, Warwicks B94 5EA (☎ 05644 2550)

GALLIERS-PRATT, Rupert Anthony; s of Anthony Malcolm Galliers-Pratt, CBE, and Angela, 2 da of Sir Charles Cayzer, 3 Bt; *b* 9 April 1951; *Educ* Eton; *m* 1973, Alexandra Mary, da of Maj Hugh Rose; 2 s (George b 1979, Frederick b 1980), 2 da (Isabella b 1985, Alexandra b 1988); *Career* chm Harvey & Thompson plc 1983- (dir 1982-); *Clubs* White's, Turf; *Style*— Rupert Galliers-Pratt, Esq; Mawley Hall, Cleobury Mortimer, Worcs (☎ 0299 270711)

GALLIFORD, Peter; OBE (1981); s of T J Galliford; *b* 21 Oct 1928; *Educ* King Edward VI Sch Nuneaton; *m* 1963, Rona, *née* Pearson; 3 s; *Career* fndr dir Galliford & Sons Ltd, md Galliford Group of Cos 1952-73, chm Galliford plc (Wolvey Leics) 1973-; chm Fedn of Civil Engrg Contractors 1978 (currently pres and chm Fin Ctee); pres: Construction Indust Res and Info Assoc, Fedn of Int Euro Construction; dir Birmingham Heartlands Ltd (urban renewal agency), non-exec dir Rugby NHS Tst; memb: Warwicks CC 1964-70, Severn Trent Water Authy 1973-76, Civil Engrg Ctee NEDO 1978-84; vice pres Warwicks Rural Community Cncl; *Style*— Peter Galliford, Esq, OBE; Hunters Gap, Ashlawn Rd, Rugby CV22 5QE (☎ 0788 543835)

GALLIGAN, Prof Denis James; s of John Felix Galligan (d 1973), and Muriel Maud, *née* Johnson; *b* 4 June 1947; *Educ* Downlands Coll Toowoomba Aust, Univ of

Queensland (B of Law), Univ of Oxford (MA, B of Civil Law); *m* 20 June 1972, Martha Louise, da of Alfred Luigi Martinuzzi, of Innisfail, Queensland, Aust; 1 s (Finbar John b 10 Sept 1977), 1 da (Francesca Louise b 22 Feb 1975); *Career* lectr Faculty of Law UCL 1974-76, pt/t lectr Magdalen Coll Oxford 1975, fell Jesus Coll Oxford and CUF lectr Univ of Oxford 1976-81, sr lectr Faculty of Law Univ of Melbourne 1982-84, dean of the Faculty of Law Univ of Southampton 1987- (prof 1985); pres UK Assoc for Legal and Social Philosophy 1989-, memb Howard League for Penal Reform; barrister of the Supreme Ct Queensland; *Books* Essays in Legal Theory (1984), Law, Rights and the Welfare State (1986), Discretionary Powers: A Legal Study of Official Discretion (1986); *Recreations* reading, gardening; *Style*— Prof Denis Galligan; The Rosery, Beckley, Oxford OX3 9UU (☎ 086735 281); Faculty of Law, The University, Southampton SO9 5NH (☎ 0703 593414, fax 0703 593024)

GALLIMORE, Michael; s of John Gallimore, of Surbiton, Surrey, and Rita Ida Doreen, *née* Clarke; *b* 8 March 1958; *Educ* Kingston GS, St Catharine's Coll Cambridge (MA, capt Hockey Club, Hockey Blue); *m* 29 July 1983, Jane Frances, da of Alfred Aspinall, of Southport, Merseyside; 1 s (William Mark b 1990); *Career* admitted slr 1983, ptnr Lovell White Durrant 1988-; England Hockey Int; memb: Law Soc 1983, City of London Slrs Co 1983; *Recreations* golf, hockey, theatre, skiing; *Clubs* Porters Park Golf, Ladykillers Hockey, Hawks; *Style*— Michael Gallimore, Esq; 21 Holborn Viaduct, London EC1A 2DY (☎ 071 236 0066, telex 887122, fax 071 248 4212)

GALLINER, Peter; s of Dr Moritz Galliner and Hedwig Isaac; *b* 19 Sept 1920; *Educ* Berlin and London; *m* 1, 1948, Edith Marguerite Goldschmidt; 1 da; m 2, 1990, Helga Stenschke; *Career* Reuters 1942-45, foreign mangr Financial Times 1945-61, chm and md Ullstein Publishing Group (Berlin) 1961-64, vice chm and md British Printing Corporation Publishing Group 1967-70, int publishing conslt 1965-67 and 1970-75; chm Peter Galliner Associates 1970-; dir International Press Institute 1975-; Federal Cross of Merit (first class, FGR), Ecomienda Orden de Isabel la Catolica (Spain), Knight Cdr's Cross (Badge and Star) Order of Merit (FRG); *Recreations* music, reading; *Style*— Peter Galliner, Esq; 27 Walsingham, St John's Wood Park, London NW8 6RH (☎ 071 722 5502); Untere Zäune 15, Zürich 8001, Switzerland (☎ 01 251 8664)

GALLON, Col Anthony William; s of John Walter (d 1971), and Alice Maud Ellen Gallon (d 1957); *b* 10 July 1929; *Educ* King Edward VI Sch Totnes, RMA Sandhurst psc, jssc; *m* 17 Dec 1953, Muriel, da of Victor Oliver Baldwin (d 1985); 3 s (Robin b 1955, Peter b 1958, Martin b 1961); *Career* served Regular Army 1947-78; asst mil attaché Khartoum 1962-65, Regt Cdr 1966, Col Logistics HQ BOAR; business mangr The American Sch London 1978-81, bursar Sherborne Sch 1981-89; *Recreations* fishing, shooting, gardening; *Clubs* MCC; *Style*— Col Anthony W Gallon; Orchard Barn, Colebrook Lane, Cullompton, Devon EX15 1PD (☎ 0884 38579)

GALLOWAY, David Richard; s of John Campbell Galloway (d 1963), and Kathleen Adelaide, *née* Herbert; *b* 5 Nov 1931; *Educ* Blackrock Coll Dublin, Lincoln Coll Oxford (MA); *m* 18 May 1963, Ann Penelope Clare, da of William John Clare Gaskell (d 1965), of Kent; 1 s (James b 1969), 2 da (Lucinda b 1964, Natasha b 1967); *Career* writer and fin conslt; dep city ed Sunday Telegraph 1964-67, res ptnr Spencer Thornton (stockbroker) 1967-77, money columnist ('David Hume') Harpers & Queen 1970-, conslt GT Management (fund mangrs) 1977-, chm Imagine (computer graphics) 1985-; memb ctees E Ashford Rural Tst; *Books* The Public Prodigals (1976), Outbid (as 'David Hume', 1984); *Recreations* theatre, opera, concert going, gardening, swimming, skiing, croquet; *Clubs* Garrick; *Style*— David R Galloway, Esq; c/o Coutts & Co, 188 Fleet St, London EC4A 2HT

GALLOWAY, George; MP (Lab) Glasgow Hillhead 1987-; s of George Galloway, of Dundee, and Sheila Reilly; *b* 16 Aug 1954; *Educ* Harris Acad; *m* 1979, Elaine, da of James Fyffe, of Dundee; 1 da (Lucy b 1982); *Career* labourer jute & flax indust 1973, prodn worker Michelin Tyres 1973, organiser Dundee Lab Pty 1977, dir War on Want 1983; *Recreations* sport, films, music; *Style*— George Galloway, MP; House of Commons, London SW1

GALLOWAY, Bishop of (RC) 1981-; Rt Rev Maurice Taylor; s of Maurice Taylor (d 1967), of Hamilton, and Lucy, *née* McLaughlin (d 1975); *b* 5 May 1926; *Educ* Our Lady's HS Motherwell, Pontifical Scots Coll Rome, Pontifical Gregorian Univ Rome (DTheol); *Career* Nat Serv RAMC 1944-47, served in UK, India, Egypt; lectr in theol St Peter's Coll Cardross Scotland 1960-65 (lectr in philosphy 1955-60), rector Royal Scots Coll Valladolid Spain 1965-74, parish priest Our Lady of Lourdes East Kilbride 1974-81; episcopal sec Bishops' Conf, vice pres Catholic Inst for Int Rels London; *Books* The Scots College in Spain (1971); *Style*— The Rt Rev the Bishop of Galloway, DD; Candida Casa, 8 Corsehill Rd, Ayr, KA7 2ST (☎ 0292 266750)

GALLOWAY, Nicholas Robert; s of Norman Patrick Robert Galloway, and Eileen, *née* Thompson; *b* 12 May 1935; *Educ* Shrewsbury, Univ of Cambridge, Univ of Edinburgh (BA, MB ChB, DO, MD); *m* 28 July 1962, Jennifer, *née* Shell; 2 s (Peter b 10 March 1969, James b 15 Jan 1978), 1 da (Sarah b 15 Oct 1967); *Career* house surgn Western Gen Hosp Edinburgh 1959-60, sr registrar Moorfields Eye Hosp 1963-65, conslt ophthalmic surgn and clinical teacher Nottingham Univ Hosp 1967-; master Ophthalmological Congress 1988-90, memb Bd Int Soc for Clinical Electrophysiology of Vision; FRCS, FRCOpth; memb: BMA, Johnian Soc; *Books* Ophthalmic Electrodiagnosis (1981), Common Eye Diseases and their Management (1985), Ophthalmology (1988); *Recreations* gardening, photography; *Clubs* Royal Soc of Med; *Style*— Nicholas Galloway, Esq; Queens Medical Centre, Clifton Boulevard, Nottingham NG7 2UH

GALLOWAY, Rev Dr Peter John; JP (City of London 1989); Henry John Galloway (d 1986), and Mary Selina, *née* Beshaw; *b* 19 July 1954; *Educ* Westminster City School, Univ of London (BA, PhD); *Career* ordained: deacon 1983, priest 1984; curate: St John's Wood London 1983-86, St Giles-in-the-Fields London 1986-90; priest-in-charge at Emmanuel of West Hampstead London 1990-; fndn govr Soho Parish Sch 1989-, chm govrs Emmanuel Sch 1990-, tstee Grant Maintained Schs Tst 1990-; St John Ambulance: asst DG 1985-, chm Nat Publications Ctee 1988-, memb Nat Schs Ctee 1989-; memb Royal Society of Literature 1988; FRSA 1988; OStJ (1986); *Books* The Order of St Patrick 1783-1983 (1983), Henry F B Mackay (1983), Good and Faithful Servants (1988); *Recreations* reading, writing, travel; *Clubs* Athenaeum; *Style*— The Rev Dr Peter Galloway, JP; The Vicarage, Lyncroft Gardens, London, NW6 1JU (☎ 071 435 1911)

GALLOWAY, 13 Earl of (S 1623); Sir Randolph Keith Reginald Stewart; 12 Bt (of Corsewell S 1627 and 10 Bt of Burray S 1687); also Lord Garlies (S 1607) and Baron Stewart of Garlies (GB 1796); s of 12 Earl of Galloway, JP (d 1978); *b* 14 Oct 1928; *Educ* Harrow; *m* 1975, Mrs May Lily Budge, yst da of late Andrew Miller, of Duns, Berwickshire; *Heir* kinsman, Andrew Stewart; *Style*— The Rt Hon the Earl of Galloway

GALLWEY; *see*: Frankland-Payne-Gallwey

GALPERN, Baron (Life Peer UK 1979), of Shettleston in the District of the City of Glasgow; Myer Galpern; JP (City of Glasgow), DL (Co of City of Glasgow 1962); s of Maurice Galpern (d 1939); *b* 1903; *Educ* Hutcheson's Boys' GS, Glasgow Univ; *m* 1940, Alice Campbell, JP, da of late Thomas Stewart; 1 s (Hon Maurice Lionel b 1945), 1 da (Hon Virginia (Hon Mrs Stewart) b 1941); *Career* Lord-Lt Co of City of Glasgow 1958-59, Lord Provost Glasgow 1958-60; MP (Lab) Glasgow Shettleston 1959-79, first dep chm Ways & Means 1974-79; kt 1960; *Style*— Rt Hon Lord Galpern, JP, DL; House of Lords, London SW1A 0AA

GALPIN, Rodney Desmond; s of Sir Albert James Galpin, KCVO, CBE (d 1984), and Vera Alice, *née* Tiller (d 1980); *b* 5 Feb 1932; *Educ* Haileybury, Imperial Serv Coll; *m* 1956, Sylvia, da of Godfrey Craven (d 1981); 1 s (Paul), 1 da (Fenella); *Career* exec dir Bank of Eng 1984-88, chm Standard Chartered plc 1988-; OStJ; *Style*— Rodney Galpin, Esq; Standard Chartered plc, 1 Aldermanbury Square, London EC2V 7SB (☎ 071 280 7001)

GALSWORTHY, Anthony Charles; CMG (1985); s of Sir Arthur Norman Galsworthy, KCMG (d 1986), and Margaret Agnes, *née* Hiscocks (d 1973); *b* 20 Dec 1944; *Educ* St Pauls, Corpus Christi Coll Cambridge (BA, MA); *m* 30 May 1970, Jan, da of Dr A W Dawson-Grove; 1 s (Andrew b 1974), 1 da (Carolyn b 1975); *Career* Dip Serv; Far East Dept FCO 1966-67, language student Hong Kong 1967-69, third sec (later second sec) Peking 1970-72, Rhodesia Dept FCO 1972-74, private sec Min of State 1974-77, first sec Rome 1977-81, first sec (later cnsllr and head of Chancery) Peking 1982-84, head Hong Kong Dept FCO 1984-86, princ private sec to Sec of State Foreign and Cwlth Affrs 1986-88; visiting res fell Royal Inst of Int Affrs 1988-89; sr Br rep Sino-Br Jt Liason Gp on Hong Kong 1989-; Order of the Lion of Finland 1975, Order of Adolph of Nassau Luxembourg 1976; *Recreations* ornithology, wildlife; *Clubs* Oxford and Cambridge; *Style*— Anthony Galsworthy, Esq, CMG; FCO, King Charles St, London SW1A 2AH

GALSWORTHY, Elizabeth; da of Thomas William Firman (d 1976), and Annie, *née* Ryan (d 1963); *b* 15 Sept 1938; *Educ* Jarrow GS Tyne and Wear, Notts Co Teacher Trg Coll; *m* 20 July 1963, John Galsworthy, s of William Galsworthy (d 1967); 1 s (Michael John b 17 Nov 1966); *Career* physical educn teacher: Frederick Bird SM Sch 1959-64, Stoke Park GS 1964-66; head Sch of Recreation and Leisure Coventry Tech Coll 1971-; netball player England Netball Int 1963-66, Warwicks Co netball coach 1975-87, England coach 1987-91, BANC-Dextrosol Coach of the Year England 1988; pres Coventry Sch Netball Assoc; *Books* Netball: The Skills of the Game (1990); *Recreations* tennis; *Clubs* Greyfriars Netball (Coventry), Beechwood Tennis (Coventry); *Style*— Mrs Elizabeth Galsworthy; Coventry Technical College, Butts, Coventry (☎ 0203 257221)

GALSWORTHY, Sir John Edgar; KCVO (1975), CMG (1968); s of Capt Arthur Galsworthy (d 1957), and Violet Gertrude, *née* Harrison (d 1964); bro of Sir Arthur Norman Galsworthy (d 1986); *b* 19 June 1919; *Educ* Emanuel Sch, Corpus Christi Coll Cambridge; *m* 1942, Jennifer Ruth, da of George Horace Johnstone, OBE; 1 s, 3 da; *Career* served in HM Forces 1939-41; entered FO 1941; first sec: Athens 1951, Bangkok 1958-61; cnsllr Brussels (UK Delegation to EEC) 1962-64; econ cncllr: Bonn 1964-67, Paris 1967-69; Min for Euro Econ Affrs Paris 1970-71, ambass Mexico 1972-77, ret; UK observer to El Salvador elections March 1982; *Style*— Sir John Galsworthy, KCVO, CMG; Lanzeague, St Just in Roseland, Truro, Cornwall TR2 5JD

GALSWORTHY, (Arthur) Michael Johnstone; s of Sir John Galsworthy, KCVO, CMG, of Lanzeague, St Just-in-Roseland, Truro, Cornwall, and Jennifer Ruth, *née* Johnstone; *b* 10 April 1944; *Educ* Radley, Univ of St Andrews (MA); *m* 20 June 1972, Charlotte Helena Prudence (d 1989), da of Col S M Roberts (d 1958), of Soranks Manor, Fairseat, Kent; 1 s (Stamford Timothy John b 20 May 1976), 2 da (Olivia Victoria Jane b 4 Aug 1974, Susannah Catherine Rose b 14 Nov 1979); *Career* mangr market res (Europe) International Harvester Corp (UK) 1967-69, planning dir English China Clays International PLC 1977-81 (regnl sales dir 1970-77), md Hawkins Wright Assocs 1981-86, dir Woodard Corp 1983-87; chm: Trewithen Estates Management Co 1985-, Probus Estate Co 1985-; regnl dir Barclays Bank 1987-; chm Cornwall County Playing Fields Assoc 1978-, memb Prince's Cncl 1985-, dir Cncl for Small Industs in Rural Areas 1985-88, tstee Nat Agric Centre Rural Tst 1986-, devpt cmmr 1988-; chm Cornwall Rural Housing Assoc 1986-; fell Zoological Soc of London; Freeman: City of London, Worshipful Co of Goldsmiths; *Recreations* gardening, fishing, shooting; *Clubs* Brooks's, Farmers'; *Style*— Michael Galsworthy, Esq; Trewithen, Grampound Road, nr Truro, Cornwall; Trewithen Estates Management Company, 1 Lemon Villas, Truro, Cornwall (☎ 0872 74646)

GALT, Hon Mrs (Catriona Mary); *née* Morrison; da (by 1 m) of 2 Viscount Dunrossil; *b* 10 July 1952; *Educ* Cheltenham Ladies' Coll; *m* 1973, John James Galt; 2 s, 1 da; *Style*— The Hon Mrs Galt; 64 Templeton St, Sandy Hill, Ottawa, Ontario K1N 6X3, Canada

GALTON, Prof David Jeremy; s of Maj Ernest Manuel Galton, and Cecilia, *née* Leyburn; *b* 2 May 1937; *Educ* Highgate School, Univ of London (MD, MSc); *m* 11 April 1967, (Gywnne) Merle; 1 s ((James) Seth b 1970), 1 da (Clare Judith b 1968); *Career* conslt physician St Bartholomew's Hosp 1971-, conslt physician i/c Moorfields Eye Hosp 1974-, prof Univ of London 1987-; chm Clinical Science 1979-81, sec Euro Atherosclerosis Soc; memb: Med Res Soc 1971, Assoc Physicians UK 1975, RSM; *Books* The Human Adipose Cell (1971), Molecular Genetics of Common Metabolic Disease (1985); *Recreations* skiing, sailing, music; *Style*— Prof David Galton; St Bartholomew's Hosp, West Smithfield, London EC1 (☎ 071 601 8432, fax 071 601 7656)

GALTON, Prof Maurice James; s of James Galton (d 1948), and Olive, *née* Prendergast (d 1987); *b* 31 May 1937; *Educ* Salesian Coll Oxford, Univ of Durham (BSc), Univ of Newcastle (MSc), Univ of Leeds (MEd); *m* 19 March 1960, Pamela Jean, da of Rev Canon Albert John Bennitt (d 1985); 3 s (Simon b 1960, Giles b 1963, Matthew b 1964), 3 da (Philippa b 1968, Bridget b 1969, Su b 1977); *Career* asst master St Pauls Sch 1960-65, instr Univ of Leeds 1965-70, prof Univ of Leicester 1982- (lectr 1970-82); Parly cand (Lib) Bosworth 1974-75; conslt Cncl of Europe Primary Project 1982-88, memb Primary Ctee Nat Curriculum Cncl (NCC) 1988-; memb Leicester Theatre Tst 1975-81; FRSA 1986; *Books* Inside The Primary Classroom (1980), Moving From The Primary Classroom (1984), Primary Teaching (1988), Handbook of European Primary Education (1989); *Recreations* golf, cricket, walking, theatre; *Style*— Prof Maurice Galton; Brookside House, Main St, Tilton on the Hill, Leics LE7 9RF (☎ 053 754 268); Sch of Educn, 21 Univ Rd, Leics LE1 7RF (☎ 0533 523 680)

GALTON, Raymond Percy; s of Herbert Galton, and Christina Galton; *b* 17 July 1930; *Educ* Garth Sch Morden; *m* 1956, Tonia Phillips; 1 s, 2 da; *Career* scriptwriter and author; television scripts (with Alan Simpson, *qv*): Hancock's Half Hour (1956-61), Citizen James (1961), BBC Comedy Playhouse, Steptoe and Son (1962-74), Galton and Simpson Comedy (1969), Milligan's Wake, Frankie Howerd, Clochemerle (1971), Casanova (1973), Dawson's Weekly (1975), The Galton and Simpson Playhouse (1976-77); Room at the Bottom (with John Antrobus); films (with Alan Simpson): The Rebel (1960), The Bargee (1963), The Wrong Arm of the Law (1964), The Spy with the Cold Nose (1966), Loot (1970), Steptoe and Son (1971), Steptoe and Son Ride Again (1973), Den Siste Fleksnes (Norway, 1974), Camping (Denmark, 1990); theatre (with Alan Simpson): Way Out In Piccadilly (1966-67), The Wind in the Sassafras Trees (1968), Albert och Herbert (Sweden, 1981), When Did You Last See Your Trousers (with John Antrobus, 1987-88); radio (with Alan Simpson): Hancock's Half Hour (1954-59), The Frankie Howerd Show, Back with Braden, Steptoe and Son (1966-73); awards: John Logie Baird for outstanding contribution to TV, Writers Guild

Award (twice), The Guild of TV Producers and Directors 1959 Merit Awards Scriptwriters of the Year, Best TV Comedy Series (Steptoe and Son, Screenwriters Guild) 1962/3/4/5, Best Comedy Series (Steptoe and Son, Dutch TV) 1966, Best Comedy Screenplay (Steptoe and Son, Screenwriters Guild) 1972; *Books* Hancock (1961), Steptoe and Son (1963), The Reunion and Other Plays (1966), Hancock Scripts (1974), The Best of Hancock (1986), Hancock - The Classic Years (1987), The Best of Steptoe and Son (1988); *Works include* Hancock's Half Hour (1963), Steptoe & Son (1974); *Style*— Raymond Galton, Esq; The Ivy House, Hampton Court, Middx (☎ 081 977 1236)

GALVIN, Guglielmo Patrizio; s of William Jospeh Galvin (d 1976), and Rosina, *née* Gabriele; *b* 15 March 1939; *Educ* St Michael's Sch Dublin, Bolton St Tech Coll Dublin, City of Westminster Coll London; *m* 18 July 170, Patricia , da of John Dennis Reardon; 1 s (Liam b 20 Dec 1972), 1 da (Roisin Amy b 15 Oct 1974); *Career* professional photographer: photographic colour printer, pt/t lectr London Coll of Printing, freelance photographer for Sunday Times, Observer and numerous other pubns; *Style*— Guglielmo Galvin, Esq; 26 Curzon Road, Muswell Hill, London N10 2RA (☎ 081 883 6131)

GALVIN, Patrick Derek Thomas; s of Maj Thomas Derek Galvin (d 1952), and Teresa Christina, *née* Innes; *b* 20 March 1939; *Educ* Downside, Christ's Coll Cambridge (BA); *m* 23 Jan 1982, (Hilda) Juliana Mary, da of Conrad Marshall Swan, CVO, York Herald of Arms, *qv*; 5 s (Thomas b 23 Jan 1984, Edward b 9 June 1985, Nicholas b 3 Dec 1986, Alexander b 8 Sept 1988, Frederick b 5 March 1990), 1 da (Elizabeth b 12 Nov 1982); *Career* investmt analyst Equity and Law Life 1960-62, property ed Investors Chronicle 1963-68, assoc Rowe Rudd and Co 1971 (joined 1968), memb London Stock Exchange 1971, ptnr de Zoete & Bevan 1982, dir Barclays de Zoete Wedd Int Equities 1986-; AMSIA 1970 (memb Cncl 1979-84, treas 1982-83); *Recreations* gardening, wine, opera, skiing, sailing, travel; *Clubs* Royal Harwich Yacht; *Style*— Patrick Galvin, Esq; Longwood House, Nayland, nr Colchester, Essex (☎ 0206 262 482); Barclays De Zoete Wedd, Ebbgate House, 2 Swan Lane, London EC4R 3TS (☎ 071 623 2323, fax 071 975 1193, telex 8953239)

GALWAY, 12 Viscount (I 1727); George Rupert Monckton-Arundell; CD; also Baron Killard (I 1727); s of Philip Marmaduke Monckton (d 1965), and Lavender, *née* O'Hara; suc 1 cous once removed, 11 Viscount, 1980; *b* 13 Oct 1922; *Educ* Victoria Coll; *m* 1944, Fiona Margaret, da of Capt W de P Taylor (d 1979), of Sooke, Br Columbia; 1 s, 3 da; *Heir* s, Hon (John) Philip Monckton; *Career* Lt-Cdr RCN, WWII; stockbroker, ret; *Recreations* painting, 'birding', golfing, travelling; *Style*— The Rt Hon the Viscount Galway, CD; 583 Berkshire Drive, London, Ontario N6J 3S3, Canada

GALWAY, James; OBE (1977); s of James Galway; *b* 8 Dec 1939; *Educ* RCM, Guildhall Sch of Music, Conservatoire National Supérieur de Musique (Paris); *m* 1; 1 s; m 2; 1 s, 2 da (twin); m 3, 1984, Jeanne Cinnante; *Career* flute-player; princ flute: London Symphony Orch 1966, Royal Philharmonic Orch 1967-69, Berlin Philharmonic Orch 1969-75; solo career 1975-; Hon MA Open Univ 1979; Hon DMus: Queen's Univ Belfast 1979, New England Conservatory of Music 1980; *Publications* Flute (Yehudi Menuhin Music Guide Series, 1982), James Galway - An Autobiography (1978); *Recreations* music, swimming, walking, theatre, films, TV, chess, backgammon, talking to people; *Style*— James Galway, Esq, OBE; c/o Helene Kern, IMG Artists, Media House, 3 Burlington Lane, London W4 2TH (☎ 081 747 9977, fax 081 747 9131, telex 291009 McMARK G)

GAMBACCINI, Paul Matthew; s of Mario Matthew Gambaccini, of Westport, Connecticut, and Dorothy, *née* Kiedrick; *b* 2 April 1949; *Educ* Staples HS, Dartmouth Coll (BA), Univ Coll Oxford (MA); *Career* disc jockey and music journalist; Rolling Stone Magazine 1970-77, Radio One 1973-86, Kaleidescope Radio Four 1976-, ILR 1986-88, Capital Radio 1988-, TV-am 1983-; TV incl: Omnibus (BBC 1), Pebble Mill at One (BBC 1), Summer Festivals (BBC 2), The Other Side of the Tracks (C4) 1983-85; fundraiser Amnesty International; *Books* Guinness Book of British Hit Singles (co-ed 8 edns), Guinness Book of British Hit Albums (co-ed 4 edns), Radio Boy (1986), Top 100 Albums (1987); *Recreations* Regents Park softball club, gym, squash, films, theatre, music, comic books; *Clubs* RAC, United Oxford and Cambridge Univ; *Style*— Paul Gambaccini, Esq; 196 Shaftesbury Ave, London WC2 (☎ 071 240 7345)

GAMBLE, Sir David Hugh Norman; 6 Bt (UK 1897), of Windlehurst, St Helens, Co Palatine of Lancs; s of Sir David Gamble, 5 Bt (d 1984), and Dawn Adrienne, da of late David Hugh Gittins, (Pilot Offr RAF); *b* 1 July 1966; *Style*— Sir David Gamble, Bt; c/o Keinton House, Keinton Mandeville, Somerton, Somerset

GAMBLE, David Martin; s of Rev Alfred Edward Gamble, of Scotland, and Yvonne, *née* Cornforth (d 1973); *b* 10 March 1953; *Educ* Soham Village Coll, Ealing Sch of Photography; *m* 21 Feb 1981, Pantip, da of Montri Vipatasilan, of Thailand; *Career* photographer Observer Magazine 1984-; other magazines incl: Independent, Telegraph, NY Life, NY Fortune, NY Face, Time, Paris Match, World of Interiors, Town and Country; photographic subjects incl: Margaret Thatcher, Dali Lama, Capt Mark Phillips, Nigel Lawson, Lord Caernarvon, Sir George Solti, Alastair Cooke, Edward Heath; exhibitions incl: Arles 1987 (jtly), Assoc of Fashion, Advtg and Eds Photographers' Gallery 1987, Kodak Euro Exhibition 1988; winner Kodak Grande Prix Euro Award France 1987; film documentary Faces 1989; memb of Assoc Fashion Advtg Editorial Photographers; *Recreations* watching cricket, jazz, photography; *Style*— David Gamble, Esq

GAMBLING, Prof William Alexander (Alex); s of late George Alexander Gambling, of Port Talbot, and late Muriel Clara, *née* Bray; *b* 11 Oct 1926; *Educ* Port Talbot Co GS, Univ of Bristol (BSc, DSc), Univ of Liverpool (PhD); *m* 25 July 1952, Margaret, da of the late Wilfred Alan Pooley; 1 s (Paul b 1956), 2 da (Alison b 1960, Vivien b 1962); *Career* lectr Univ of Liverpool 1950-55, NRC fell Univ of Br Columbia 1955-57; Univ of Southampton: lectr and reader 1957-64, head Dept of Electronics 1974-79, dean of engrg 1972-75, prof of electronics 1964-89, dir Optoelectronics Res Centre 1989-; visiting prof: Univ of Colorado 1966-67, Bhabha Atomic Res Centre India 1970, Univ of Osaka Japan 1977, Univ of Cape Town SA 1979; memb: Nat Electronics Cncl 1977-78 and 1984-, Engrg Cncl 1983-88, Engrg Indust Trg Bd 1985-88; chm Cmmn Int Union of Radio Sci 1984-87; dir: York Ltd, York Technology Ltd 1980-; author of several books and over 200 res papers on optical fibres, quantum electronics, microwave engrg and plasma physics; Selby fell Aust Acad of Sci 1982, foreign memb Polish Acad of Sci 1985; hon prof Huazhong Univ and Beijing Univ, hon dir Beijing Optical Fibre Res Lab; Hon DSc Eurotech Res Univ Calif; Freeman City of London, Liveryman Worshipful Co of Engrs; Hon FIEE 1983, FEng 1979, FRS 1983, FRSA 1979; *Recreations* music, travel, walking; *Style*— Prof Alex Gambling, FRS; Optoelectronics Research Centre, University of Southampton, Southampton SO9 5NH (☎ 0703 593373, fax 0703 671391)

GAMBON, Michael John; CBE (1990); s of Edward Gambon, and Mary Gambon; *b* 19 Oct 1940; *Educ* St Aloysius Sch for Boys London; *m* 1962, Anne Miller; *Career* actor; formerly engr apprentice; first stage appearance Edwards/Mac Liammair Dublin 1962, Nat Theatre, Old Vic 1963-67, RSC Aldwych 1970-72; London Theatre Critics Award Best Actor for Galileo Nat Theatre 1980, RSC 1982-83, numerous TV and film appearances; *Recreations* flying, gun collecting, clock making; *Style*— Michael Gambon, Esq, CBE; c/o Larry Dazell Associates, 126 Kennington Park Road SE11 4DJ

GAMES, Abram; OBE; s of Joseph Games, and Sarah Games; *b* 29 July 1914; *Educ* Grocer's Company Sch; *m* 1945, Marianne, *née* Salfeld; 1 s, 2 da; *Career* served Army Infantry 1940-41; graphic designer; Fleet Street Studio 1932-36, freelance designer 1936-40, poster designer War Office 1941-46 (first official poster designer, over 100 posters), freelance 1946-, lectr Royal Coll of Art 1946-53; cmmns incl: Festival of Br Emblem 1948, BBC Television emblem 1953, British Intl posters designer Queen's Award to Indust 1966; solo exhibitions: Stockholm, Brussels, Jerusalem, Tel Aviv, Sao Paulo, Rio de Janeiro, Belo Horizonte, New York, Chicago, London, UK Touring 1990-91; represented GB at Museum of Modern Art Four European Poster Designers 1953; works in collections incl: V & A Museum, Imperial War Museum, Museum of Modern Art, Australian Nat Gallery; author Over My Shoulder (1960), inventor and holder of many process and mechanical patents; RDI 1959, design medal Soc of Industl Artists and Designers 1960, RSA Silver medal 1962; *Recreations* painting, walking, carpentry; *Style*— Abram Games, Esq, OBE; 41 The Vale, London NW11 8SE (☎ 081 458 2811)

GAMES, Prof David Edgar; s of Alfred William Games (d 1956), and Frances Elizabeth Bell, *née* Evans; *b* 7 April 1938; *Educ* Lewis Sch Pengam, King's Coll London (BSc, PhD), Univ of Wales (DSc); *m* 28 Dec 1961, Marguerite Patricia, da of John Lee, of 21 Enville Rd, Newport, Gwent; 2 s (Gwilym John b 1971, Evan William b 1972); *Career* Univ of Wales Coll of Cardiff 1965-89: lectr in chem, sr lectr, reader, personal chair; prof of mass spectrometry and dir of Mass Spectrometry Res Unit Univ Coll of Swansea 1989-; FRSC, CChem; *Recreations* swimming, walking; *Style*— Prof David Games; Mass Spectrometry Research Unit, Department of Chemistry, University College of Swansea, Singleton Park, Swansea SA2 8PP (☎ 0792 295298, telex 48358, fax 0792 295717)

GAMESTER, Lady Jane Margaret; *née* Annesley; eld da of 10 Earl of Annesley; *b* 15 June 1948; *Educ* Marist Convent Sunninghill, Croydon Coll of Art; *m* 1966, Vernon Hugh Gamester, o s of Edward Arthur Gamester, of The Retreat, 23 Wendover Rd, Staines, Middx; 1 s (Carl b 1970), 2 da (Colette b 1967, Juliet b 1969); *Style*— Lady Jane Gamester; The Retreat, 23 Wendover Road, Staines, Middlesex

GAMMAGE, Anthony Marshall (Tony); s of Thomas Marshall Gammage (d 1986), of Deal, Kent, and Cicely May, *née* Coates (d 1980); *b* 22 Aug 1934; *Educ* Dover Coll; *m* 25 July 1959, Janet, da of Dr John Colin Dixon Carothers, of Havant, Hants; 3 s (Derek b 1963, Mark b 1965, Thomas b 1967); *Career* dir and sec French Kier Hldgs plc 1973-86; dir: Beazer plc 1986, Dunton Gp plc 1986-; conslt Fitzpatrick plc 1986-, dir Jarvis plc 1987-; asst dist cmmr Essex Co Scout Assoc; Freeman City of London 1973; FCA 1957, ACMA 1962; *Recreations* sailing, genealogy; *Style*— Tony Gammage, Esq; 57 Great Eastern St, London EC2A 3QD (☎ 071 7298020, fax 071 7393560)

GAMMELL, James Gilbert Sydney; MBE (1944); eld s of Lt-Gen Sir James Andrew Harcourt Gammell, KCB, DSO, MC (d 1975), of Alrick, Glenisla, Angus, and Gertrude, *née* Don (d 1960); *b* 4 March 1920; *Educ* Winchester; *m* 1944, Susan Patricia, yr da of late Edward Bowring Toms, of Melbury Ct, London W8, and Harbour Light, Sandbanks, Dorset; 5 s, 1 da; *Career* CA 1949; chm Cairn Energy plc; dir: Standard Life Assurance Co 1954-90, Bank of Scotland 1969-90; *Style*— James Gammell, Esq, MBE; Foxhall, Kirkliston, W Lothian, (☎ 031 333 3275); Cairn Energy plc, 61 Dublin St, Edinburgh EH3 6NL (☎ 031 557 2299, fax 031 557 2220)

GAMMIE, Gordon Edward; CB (1981), QC (1989); eld s of late Dr Alexander Edward Gammie, and Ethel Mary, *née* Miller; *b* 9 Feb 1922; *Educ* St Paul's, Queen's Coll Oxford (MA); *m* 1949, Joyce, da of late Arthur Arnold Rust; 2 s (David, Peter); *Career* WWII Capt 1 Bn Argyll and Sutherlands Highlanders served Western Desert and Italy; under sec Cabinet Office 1975-77, dep slr Treasy 1977-79, legal advsr and slr to MAFF 1979-83, counsel to the Speaker (Euro legislation) 1983; *Recreations* tennis, music; *Clubs* Athenaeum; *Style*— Gordon Gammie, Esq, CB, QC; 52 Sutton Lane, Banstead, Surrey SM7 3RB (☎ 0737 355287); House of Commons, London SW1A 0AA (☎ 071 219 5561)

GAMMIE, Malcolm James; s of Maj James Ian Gammie, MC (d 1987), of Bickley, Kent, and Florence Mary, *née* Wiggs; *b* 18 Feb 1951; *Educ* Edge Grove Sch Alderham, Merchant Taylors'; Sidney Sussex Coll Cambridge (MA); *m* 21 Dec 1974, Rosalind Anne, da of William James Rowe, of Bromley, Kent; 1 s (Christopher James b 18 May 1981), 3 da (Helen Victoria b 10 Feb 1979, Isabel Margaret Ruth b 19 Feb 1985, Catharine Alice Louise b 17 Feb 1988); *Career* Linklater & Paines: articled clerk 1973-75, asst slr Tax Dept 1975-78, slr Tax Dept 1985-87, ptnr 1987-; dep head of Tax Dept Confedn of Br Indust 1978-79; dir: Nat Tax Office Thomson McLintock & Co 1979-84, Nat Tax Servs KMG Thomson McLintock 1984-85; ed Law and Tax Review 1982-88, contrib to Financial Times on tax matters 1983-87; sr visiting fell Centre for Commercial Law Studies Queen Mary and Westfield Coll London; memb: Ed Bd Law and Tax Review, Taxation Ctee IOD, Law Soc's Corp Tax Sub-Ctee, Br Branch Ctee Int Fiscal Assoc, Cncl of LCCI 1989-, City of London Slrs Co; sec, memb Exec Ctee, memb Cncl and chm Capital Taxes Working Pty Inst of Fiscal Studies; chm: Administrative Ctee Inst of Taxation 1987-88 (memb Cncl 1983-), Taxation Ctee London C of C and Indust 1989- (memb 1976-); sec and memb Cncl Assoc of Taxation Technicians 1989-; *Books* Taxation Publishing (1980), Tax on Company Reorganisations (with Susan Ball, 1980), Tax Strategy for Companies (1981), Stock Relief (with D Williams, 1981), Tax Focus on Interest and Discounts (with D Williams, 1983), Tax Strategy for Directors, Executives and Employees (1983), Land Taxation (1985), Whiteman on Capital Gains Tax (with P Whiteman, QC and Mark Herbert, 1988); contrib to: Simon's Taxes, Butterworths Income Tax Service, Strategic Tax Planning; *Recreations* playing recorder, church architecture, jogging; *Style*— Malcolm Gammie, Esq; Linklaters & Paines, Barrington House, 59-67 Gresham St, London EC2V 7JA (☎ 071 606 7080, fax 071 606 5113, tlx 884349 888167)

GAMMIE, Robert Christie; JP (1986); s of William Christie Gammie (d 1946), and Ivy, *née* Turner (d 1988); *b* 26 Oct 1932; *Educ* St Joseph's Coll Ipswich, Mid-Essex Sch of Architecture, Thames Poly; *m* 23 Aug 1962, Alice Elizabeth Julia, da of William Pain 1 s (Blaise William Christie b 19 Feb 1967), 1 da (Bridget Lucy b 7 Sept 1965); *Career* Nat Serv Cmmnd RPC 1955-57; architect; Lewis Solomon Kaye & Partners 1957-62, R Seifert & Partners 1962-; memb Bd of Visitors Chelmsford Prison 1980-; memb RIBA 1972; *Recreations* rugby, cricket, squash; *Clubs* Chelmsford Rugby Football, The Chelmsford; *Style*— Robert Gammie, Esq, JP; Hookers, 25 Priory Farm Rd, Nounsley, Essex CM3 2NJ (☎ 0245 381497); Seifert Ltd, 164 Shaftesbury Ave, London WC2H 8HZ (☎ 071 242 1644, fax 071 379 0099)

GAMMIE, William Forbes Petrie; DL (W Sussex 1988); s of Robert Petrie Gammie, OBE (d 1990), of Bishop's Stortford, and Margaret Marr, *née* Forbes (d 1971); *b* 1 Dec 1926; *Educ* Bishop's Stortford Coll, Univ Coll Oxford (BM BCh, MA), London Hosp Med Coll; *m* 13 May 1955, (Elsa) Verena, da of Max Muller (d 1969), of Zurich; 1 s (Walter b 1956), 2 da (Susan b 1957, d 1960, Catherine b 1961); *Career* Nat Serv Flt Lt med branch RAF 1952-54; conslt surgn: Royal W Sussex Hosp Chichester 1964-, King Edward VII Hosp Midhurst 1969-; memb: W Sussex Area Health Authy 1977-83, Chichester Dist Health Authy 1982-87, Med Appeals Tbnl 1988-; Freeman City of London, Liveryman Worshipful Soc of Apothecaries 1962; FRCS 1956; *Recreations* walking, gardening; *Style*— William Gammie, Esq, DL; Field Place, Church Lane, Clymping, Littlehampton, West Sussex BN17 5RR; 24 West St, Chichester,

West Sussex PO19 1QP (☎ 0243 789 630)

GAMMON, Philip Greenway; s of Stanley Arthur John Gammon (d 1979), of Chippenham, Wilts, and Phyllis Joyce, *née* Paul; *b* 17 May 1940; *Educ* Chippenham GS, RAM (scholar), Badische Müsikhochschule Karlsruhe Germany; *m* 1963, Floretta, da of Konstantin Volovinis; 2 s (Paul Christopher b 1968, Anthony John b 1970); *Career* pianist; dep piano teacher RAM and RSAM 1964, pianist Royal Ballet Covent Garden 1964-68, princ pianist Ballet For All 1968-71, Royal Ballet 1971-; major solo performances with Royal Ballet incl: The Four Temperaments 1973, Elite Syncopations 1974, A Month in the Country 1976, La Fin Du Jour 1979, Rhapsody 1980, Return to the Strange Land 1984, Rubies 1989, Winter Dreams, 1991; solo pianist and conductor London Contemporary Dance 1979; toured many countries incl: Brazil, USSR, Aust and China; solo pianist: concert for the 50th Anniversary of the Royal Ballet with the Royal Liverpool Philharmonic Orchestra (Philharmonic Hall Liverpool) 1981, gala performance celebrating 100 years of Performing Arts (Metropolitan Opera House NY) 1984, meml serv for Sir Frederick Ashton Westminster Abbey 1988; debut solo pianist Royal Festival Hall and Barbican Hall 1984; credits in conducting incl: Coppelia Ballet for All (debut, Theatre on the Green Richmond) 1970, Royal Ballet Touring Company 1976, Sleeping Beauty Royal Ballet (debut Royal Opera House) 1978, Royal Ballet Sch performances (Royal Opera House) 1987, 1989 and 1990; recent conducting assignments with Royal Ballet incl: Ondine 1989, The Planets 1990, The Prince of the Pagodas 1990; first orchestral arrangement of La Chatte metamorphosée en femme by Offenbach (Staatsoper Vienna, Royal Opera House Covent Garden) 1985, arrangement of MacMillan's Winter Dreams by Tchaikovsky 1991; recordings incl: Elite Syncopations for Continental Record Distributors, A Month in the Country for EMI Int Classical Div; awarded: Assoc Bd Gold medal Grade 8 1954, Recital Diploma 1960, Walter MacFarren Gold medal 1961, Karlsruhe Culture prize 1962, Performer's Dip Badische Musik-Hochschule Karlsruhe 1963; ARCM 1968; *Recreations* walking, reading, holidaying in Greece; *Style—* Philip Gammon, Esq; 19 Downs Avenue, Pinner, Middlesex HA5 5AQ (☎ 081 866 3260)

GAMON, Hugh Wynell; CBE (1979), MC (1944); s of His Hon Judge Hugh Reece Percival Gamon (d 1953), of The Lodge, Acomb, York, and Eleanor Margaret Gamon, *née* Lloyd, of Hartford House, Hartley Wintney, Hants; *b* 31 March 1921; *Educ* St Edward's Sch Oxford, Exeter Coll Oxford (MA); *m* 17 Dec 1949, June Elizabeth, da of William Temple (d 1986), of Underriver, Sevenoaks, Kent; 1 s (Charles b 1956), 3 da (Mary-Anne b 1952, Sarah b 1954, Jane b 1959); *Career* WWII 1940-46, Maj 1 Div Signals; served: N Africa, Italy, Palestine; slr and Parly agent; sr ptnr Sherwood & Co 1972; HM Govt Agent 1970; *Recreations* gardening, motoring; *Clubs* St Stephens and Constitutional, Westminster; *Style—* Hugh W Gamon, CBE, MC; Black Charles, Underriver, Sevenoaks, Kent TN15 0RY (☎ 0732 833036); Messrs Sherwood & Co, Queen Annes Chambers, 3 Dean Farrar St, Westminster SW1H 9LG (☎ 01 222 0441)

GANDER, Dr Derek Reginald; s of Owen Douglas Gander (d 1965), of Farringleys, Shortlands, Kent, and Annie Neil (d 1985); *b* 20 Sept 1928; *Educ* Cathedral Sch Shanghai China, prisoner Japanese camp 1942-45, Worcester GS, Middx Hosp Med Sch Univ of London (MB BS, DPM, Inorganic Chemistry prize, Walter Butcher prize); *m* 1, 1955, Phyllis Marian (d 1974), da of Joseph C Williams; 1 s (Timothy Paul b 7 July 1960), 3 da (Alison Jane b 22 Sept 1957, Sarah Elizabeth b 23 July 1962, Jill Fiona b 2 July 1964); m 2, 1979, Barbara Ann, da of Thomas L Hewitt; 1 da (Kate Eliza b 6 Feb 1981); *Career* Middx Hosp: house physician 1953, house surgn 1954, casualty offr 1955; house surgn Queen Alexandra Hosp for Children Brighton 1955, asst in gen practice London 1956, med registrar Mt Vernon Hosp 1956-59, registrar Bethlehem Royal and Maudsley Hosp 1959-62, chief asst Dept Psychological Med St Thomas Hosp 1962-66, sr conslt psychiatrist Queen Elizabeth II Hosp 1966-87 (sec then vice chm, then chm Med Staff Ctee and memb E Dist Med Ctee), jtly set-up Drug Addiction Clinic 1968, Br Postgrad Med Fedn tutor in psychiatry with jt responsibility for Postgrad Centre Queen Elizabeth II Hosp (lectr to student mid-wives), lectr N W Thames Royal Health Authy, psychiatric conslt Hertfordshire Marriage Guidance Counselling Serv; MRCP 1959 (memb Educn Sub Ctee and clinical tutor), FRCPsych 1977 (MRCPsych 1971, memb RCPsych Visiting Accreditation Teams); *Recreations* travel, swimming, shooting, gardening; *Style—* Dr Derek Gander; 8 St Peters Close, St Albans, Herts AL1 3ES (☎ 0727 50584); 138 Harley St, London W1N 1AH (071 935 0554)

GANDHI, Ramesh Govindlal; s of Govindlal Jivanlal Gandhi (d 1973), of Ahmedabad, India, and Kamladevi Shah (d 1987); *b* 2 Sept 1935; *Educ* B J Med Coll Gujarat Univ India (MB BS); *m* 1, 1961 (m dis 1975); 1 s (Mayur Ramesh b 7 May 1966); m 2, 16 July 1975, Frances May, da of Francis Mark Fletcher, of Barnsley, S Yorks; 2 s (Neil Ramesh b 28 June 1978, Mark Ramesh b 18 Feb 1980); *Career* registrar in cardio-thoracic surgery: Killingbeck Hosp Leeds 1969-72, Leeds Gen Infirmary 1972-74; sr registrar in cardio-thoracic surgery Univ Hosp of Wales Cariff and Llandough Hosp Penarth 1974-78, conslt cardio-thoracic surgn 1978-; vice pres Overseas Dirs Assoc UK Ltd, pres Br Heart Fndn Wyre Ctee, vice chm Blackpool Musical Festival, divnl surgn St John Ambulance Brigade Poulton-le-Fylde; memb Manchester Med Assoc; hon fell Int Coll of Angiology USA 1988; memb: Soc of Cardio-thoracic Surgns of UK and I, Hosp Specialist Conslt Assoc; FRCSEd 1973, FRCS 1974, fell Overseas Dirs Assoc in the UK Ltd 1988; *Recreations* listening to music, swimming, bridge playing; *Style—* Ramesh Gandhi, Esq; April Cottage, Hardhorn, Poulton-Le-Fylde, Blackpool FY6 8DJ (☎ 0253 899075); Victoria Hospital, Whinney Heys Rd, Blackpool, Lancashire FY3 8NR (☎ 0253 303668)

GANDON, Christopher Martin; s of Norman Gandon, of Chiddingstone Hoath, nr Penshurst, Kent, and Sadie, *née* Evans; *b* 13 Nov 1945; *Educ* Penarth Co GS, Leamington Coll for Boys; *m* 6 July 1974, Christine Margaret, da of Harry Wharton; 2 s (Simon William b 10 Dec 1975, Nicholas Robert b 10 Oct 1977), 1 da (Joanna Elizabeth Edith b 19 Oct 1980); *Career* articled clerk Leech Peirson Evans & Co Coventry; CA Whinney Murray (now Ernst & Young) 1970, Rowland & Co 1971; ptnr Rowland Nevill (upon merger of Rowland & Co and Nevill Hovey Gardiner) 1975- (firm now known as Moores Rowland following merger with Edward Moore & Sons); Freeman City of Coventry 1969; FCA 1979 (ACA 1969); *Recreations* sailing, rugby football, squash, gardening, DIY; *Clubs* Wig & Pen, Sevenoaks RFC; *Style—* Christopher Gandon, Esq; Moores Rowland, 7 St Botolph's Rd, Sevenoaks, Kent TN13 3AJ (☎ 0732 460808)

GANE, Barrie Charles; CMG (1988), OBE (1978); s of Charles Ernest Gane, and Margaret, *née* Price; *b* 19 Sept 1935; *Educ* King Edward's Sch Birmingham, CCC Cambridge (MA); *m* 1, (m dis 1974); 2 da (Christine Anne b 1963, Nicola Vanessa b 1966); m 2, 5 July 1974, Jennifer Anne, da of Lt Cdr George Pitt; *Career* Nat Serv RN 1955-57, Sub Lt RNVR; FO 1960, third sec Vientiane 1961-63, seconded staff HM Govr Sarawak 1963, second sec Kuching 1963-66, FO 1966, first sec Kampala 1967-70, FCO 1976, on loan to HQ Br Forces Hong Kong 1977-82, FCO 1982-; *Recreations* reading, walking; *Style—* Barrie Gane, Esq, CMG, OBE; c/o Foreign & Commonwealth Office, King Charles St, London SW1

GANE, Denis; s of Granville Gane (d 1970), of Pontypool, and Elizabeth, *née* Buckley; *b* 6 July 1939; *Educ* Jones W Monmouth GS, Univ of Wales (MSc); *m* 5 June 1965, Joyce, da of Percival Rosser, of Pontypool; *Career* Nat Serv RCS 1960-62; news ed Western Mail Cardiff 1974-88, news and features ed Wales on Sunday Cardiff 1989-; *Style—* Denis Gane, Esq; 26 Llandegveth Close, Croesyceiliog, Cwmbran, Gwent NP44 2PE (☎ 06333 4339); Thomson House, Cardiff CF1 1WR (☎ 0222 342530)

GANE, Michael; s of Rudolf E Gane, and Helen Gane; *b* 29 July 1927; *Educ* Colyton GS, Univ of Edinburgh, Univ of London, Univ of Oxford; *m* 1954, Madge Stewart Taylor; 1 da; *Career* dir England Nature Conservancy Cncl 1974-81; int conslt on economic forestry and environmental matters 1982-; *Style—* Michael Gane, Esq; 1 Ridgeway Close, Sidbury, Sidmouth, Devon EX10 0SW (☎ 039 57 510)

GANELLIN, Prof (Charon) Robin; s of Leon Ganellin (d 1969), and Beila, *née* Cluer (d 1972); *b* 25 Jan 1934; *Educ* Harrow Co GS, QMC London (BSc, PhD), Univ of London (DSc); *m* 27 Dec 1956, Tamara, da of Jacob Greene (d 1988); 1 s (Mark b 1963), 1 da (Nicole b 1960); *Career* res chemist Smith Kline & French Labs Ltd 1958-59, res assoc MIT 1960, vice pres Smith Kline & French Research Ltd 1984-86 (vice pres res 1980-84, dir 1978-86, head of chemistry 1962-78, medicinal chemist 1961-62); Smith Kline & French prof of medicinal chemistry UCL 1986-, dir Upjohn Euro Discovery Unit UCL 1987-; Hon Prof Univ of Kent 1979-, Prix Charles Mentzer 1978; Royal Soc of Chemistry: Medicinal Chemistry medal 1977, Tilden medal 1982; chm Soc for Drug Res 1985-87; Div of Medicinal Chemistry award American Chemical Soc 1980, Soc Chemistry Indust Messel Medal 1988, Soc for Drug Res award for Drug Discovery 1989, USA Nat Inventors Hall of Fame 1990; FRSC 1968, FRS 1986; *Books* Pharmacology of Histamine Receptors (1982), Frontiers in Histamine Research (1985); *Recreations* music, sailing, walking; *Style—* Prof Robin Ganellin, FRS; Department of Chemistry, University College London, 20 Gordon St, London WC1H 0AJ (☎ 071 387 7050)

GANILAU, Ratu Sir Penaia Kanatabatu; GCMG (1983, CMG 1968), KCVO (1982, CVO 1970), KBE (1974, OBE 1960), DSO (1956), ED (1974); s of late Ratu Epeli Gavidi Ganilau; *Educ* Queen Victoria Memorial Sch Fiji, Wadham Coll Oxford; *m* 1, 1949, Adi Laisa Delaisomosomo (decd), da of Livai Yavaca; 5 s, 2 da; m 2, 1975, Adi Davila Vunivalu (decd); *Career* Fiji Mil Forces 1940-46; entered Colonial Admin Serv 1947, dist offr 1948-53; memb of cmmn on Fijian Post Primary Educn 1953; Fiji Mil Forces 1953-56, Lt-Col 1956; Fijian economic devpt offr and Roko Tui Cakaudrove 1956, tour mangr and Govt rep Fiji Rugby Football tour of NZ 1957, dep sec for Fijian Affrs 1961, ldr of Govt Business and min Home Affrs, lands and mineral resources 1970, min Communications, Works and Tourism 1972, memb Cncl of Mins, official MLC; chm: Fijian Affrs Bd, Fijian Devpt Fund Bd, Native Land Trust Bd, Great Cncl of Chiefs; dep PM and min Fijian Affrs and Rural Devpt 1973-83, govr-gen Fiji and C-in-C of Mil Forces 1983-88; Pres and C-in-C of Mil Forces 1988-; Hon Col 2 Bn (TA) Fiji Inf Regt 1973; *Recreations* rugby; *Clubs* Defence, Suva, Fiji; *Style—* Ratu Sir Penaia Ganilau, GCMG, KCVO, KBE, DSO, ED; Government House, Suva, Fiji (☎ Suva 314244)

GANS-LARTEY, Joseph Kojo; s of Charles Botway Lartey (d 1977), of Ghana, and Felicia Adoley, *née* Gans-Boye; *b* 28 Aug 1951; *Educ* Presbyterian Secdy Sch X'Borg Accra Ghana, Croydon Coll Surrey (HNC), Ealing Coll of Higher Educn (LLB), LSE (LLM); *m* 28 Oct 1978, Rosmarie, da of Harold Ramrattan (d 1987), of Trinidad and Tobago; 1 da (Josephine Annmarie Laatele b 11 Sept 1985), 1 s (Charles Andrew b 10 April 1990); *Career* sr enrolled psychiatric nurse 1978-82 (trainee 1974-76, enrolled 1976-78), sr legal asst RAC 1985-86, crown prosecutor 1986-, sr crown prosecutor 1989-, princ crown prosecutor 1990-; voluntary legal advsr Croydon Community Rels Cncl; memb: Hon Soc of Lincoln's Inn 1983, Bar of Trinidad and Tobago 1984; *Recreations* tennis, reading, writing, parenting; *Style—* Joseph Gans-Lartey, Esq; 10 Willow Wood Crescent, Selhurst, London WE25 5PZ (☎ 081 684 8058); Crown Prosecution Service, The Cooperage, 8 Gainsford St, London EC1 2NG (☎ 071 962 2652)

GANZONI, Hon (Mary) Jill; DL (Suffolk 1988); only da of 1 Baron Belstead (d 1958); *b* 27 March 1931; *Educ* Crofton Grange Sch, Eastbourne Sch of Domestic Economy; *Career* memb Gen Synod of Church of England 1970-, church cmmr 1978-; *Recreations* bridge; *Style—* The Hon Jill Ganzoni, DL; Rivendell, Spring Meadow, Playford, nr Ipswich (☎ 0473 624662)

GAON, Dr Solomon; s of Isaac Gaon, and Rachael Gaon; *b* 15 Dec 1912; *Educ* Jesuit Secdy Sch Travnik Yugoslavia, Jewish Teachers' Seminary Sarajevo, Jews Coll London Univ; *m* 1944, Regina Hassan; 1 s, 1 da; *Career* Haham (Chief Rabbi) Assoc of Sephardi Congregations 1977-80; Haham of Communities affiliated to World Sephardi Fedn in the Diaspora 1978-; *Style—* Dr Solomon Gaon; 25 Ashworth Rd, London W9 (☎ 071 289 1575)

GARBER, Hon Mrs (Fiona); *née* Spring Rice; 3 and yst da of 6 Baron Monteagle of Brandon; *b* 10 April 1957; *m* 26 March 1982, Andrew Louis Garber, yst s of S Garber, of St John's Wood; 2 da (Rose Anne b 13 July 1985, Eliza Kate b 8 Aug 1987); *Style—* Hon Mrs Garber; 6 Amies St, London SW11

GARBUTT, Nicholas Martin Antony; s of Anthony Joseph Garbutt, of Manchester, and Norah, *née* Payne; *b* 21 June 1959; *Educ* Xaverian Coll Manchester, Oriel Coll Oxford (BA, Judo half blue); *m* 3 Sept 1988, Frances, da of Francis Burscough, of Preston; *Career* journalist; reporter: Ashton-under-Lyme Reporter 1980-83, Chester Evening Leader 1983-84, Telegraph and Argus Bradford 1984; mgmnt trainee Liverpool Echo 1987-88 (reporter 1984-87), news ed Daily Post Liverpool 1988-89, asst ed Sunday Tribune Dublin 1989-90, ed The Irish News Belfast 1990-; *Recreations* study of Irish History and Culture, martial arts; *Style—* Nicholas Garbutt, Esq; The Irish News, 113-117 Donegall St, Belfast BT1 2GE (☎ 0232 322226, fax 0232 231282)

GARCIA, Russell Simon; s of Julie Ann, *née* Carter; *b* 20 June 1970; *Educ* City of Portsmouth Boys Sch, Portsmouth Coll of Art; *Career* hockey player; yst GB capped player 17, under 21 Silver medalist Euro Cup 1988, Gold medallist 5 Nation Tournament Malaysia 1988, yst Gold medallist Seoul Olympics 1988; memb: Hockey Assoc 1988, GB Men's Hockey Bd 1988; *Recreations* hockey; *Clubs* Havant Hockey, Fareham Indoor Hockey; *Style—* Russell Garcia, Esq; 9 Sandhurst Ct, Victoria Grove, Southsea, Hants (☎ 0705 815 577)

GARDAM, Jane Mary; da of William Pearson (d 1988), of Coatham, N Yorkshire, and Kathleen Mary, *née* Helm (d 1988); *b* 11 July 1928; *Educ* Saltburn HS for Girls, Bedford Coll London; *m* 20 April 1954, David Hill Gardam, QC, s of Harry Hill Gardam; 2 s (Tim b 1956, Thomas b 1965), 1 da (Catharine b 1958); *Career* novelist; travelling librarian Red Cross Hospital Libraries 1951, sub ed Weldon's Ladies Jl 1952, asst literary ed Time and Tide 1952-54; memb Ctee: NSPCC, PEN; FRSL 1973; novels: A Long Way from Verona (1971), The Summer After (1973), Bilgerwater (1977), God on the Rocks (1978), The Hollow Land (1981, Whitbread Award), Bridget and William (1981), Horse (1982), Kit (1983), Crusoe's Daughter (1985), Kit in Boots (1986), Swan (1987), Through The Doll's House Door (1987); short stories: A Fair Few Days (1971), Black Faces, White Faces (1975, David Highams Award, Winifred Holtby Award), The Sidmouth Letters (1980), The Pangs of Love (1983, Katherine Mansfield Award 1984), Showing The Flag (1989), The Queen of the Tambourine (1991); *Recreations* botanical; *Clubs* Arts, PEN, University Women's; *Style—* Mrs Jane Gardam; Haven House, Sandwich, Kent (☎ office 0304 612680)

GARDAM, Susan Rosemary; *née* Martin; da of Louis Thomas Martin, of Milford-on-

Sea, Hants, and Margaret Hilda, *née* Hinder; *b* 18 July 1953; *Educ* St Albans HS for Girls, LSE, Guildford Coll of Law (LLB); *m* 15 June 1985, Robert Alan Gardam, s of Gerald Frederick Gardam (d 1985), of Potters Bar, Herts; 2 s (Paul Robert b 1981, Ian Thomas b 1982), 1 da (Victoria Margaret b 1986); *Career* slr; private practice; *Recreations* sailing, riding, antiques, travel, swimming; *Clubs* Royal Lymington Yacht, Careys Manor Carat; *Style*— Mrs Susan R Gardam; Haywood House, Sway Rd, Brockenhurst, Hants (☎ 0590 23810); Martins, The New House, 32 Brookley Road, Brockenhurst (☎ 0590 23252)

GARDAM, Timothy David; s of David Hill Gardam, QC, of Sandwich, and Jane, *née* Pearson; *b* 14 Jan 1956; *Educ* Westminster, Gonville and Caius Coll Cambridge (BA); *m* Kim Scott, da of Capt Gordon Walwyn, RN, CVO, of Warblington; *Career* BBC: trainee 1977, prodr Newsnight 1979-82, exec prodr Timewatch 1982-85 and Bookmark 1984-85, output ed Newsnight 1985-86, dep ed Gen Election 1987, ed Panorama 1987-; *Recreations* gardening, ruins; *Style*— Timothy Gardam, Esq; 28 School Rd, Kidlington, Oxford; BBC TV, Wood Lane, London W12 (☎ 081 576 1957)

GARDEN, Dr (David) Graeme; s of Robert Symon Garden (d 1982), of Preston, Lancs, and Janet Anne, *née* McHardy; *b* 18 Feb 1943; *Educ* Repton, Emmanuel Coll Cambridge (BA), King's Coll Hosp (MB BChir); *m* 1, 16 March 1968 (m dis 1981), (Mary) Elizabeth, da of Clive Wheatley Grice (d 1979); 1 s (John b 9 June 1975), 1 da (Sally b 2 April 1971); m 2, 12 Feb 1983, Emma, da of John David Valentine Williams; 1 s (Thomas b 2 Dec 1984); *Career* actor and writer; writer and performer: I'm Sorry I'll Read That Again (radio), I'm Sorry I Haven't A Clue (radio), The Goodies (TV); writer with Bill Oddie TV: Dr In The House, Dr At Large, The Astronauts; presenter Bodymatters BBC TV; theatre: Nat Theatre, Royal Ct, Royal Exchange Manchester, Cambridge Theatre Co; author The Magic Olympical Games Nat Theatre, writer and dir trg films Video Arts; *Books* The Seventh Man (1981), The Skylighters (1987); *Recreations* TV, fishing; *Style*— Dr Graeme Garden

GARDEN, (Olivier) James; s of James Garden, OBE, of Broompark, 15 Cleghorn Rd, Lanark, and Marguerite Marie Jeanne, *née* Vourc'h; *b* 13 Nov 1953; *Educ* Lanark GS, Univ of Edinburgh (BSc, MB ChB, MD); *m* 15 July 1977, Amanda Gillian, da of Austin Merrills, OBE, of Clyde House, Kirkfieldbank, Lanark; 1 s (Stephen James b 21 July 1988); *Career* lectr in surgery Univ Dept of Surgery Glasgow Royal Infirmary 1985-88, chef de clinique Unit de Chrurgie Hepatobiliare Hopital Paul Brousse Villejuif France 1986-87, sr lectr in surgery and hon conslt surgn Univ Dept of Surgery Royal Infirmary Edinburgh 1988-; FRCS 1981; *Recreations* golf, skiing; *Style*— James Garden, Esq; University Department of Surgery, The Royal Infirmary, Edinburgh EH3 9YW (☎ 031 229 2477 ext 2275, fax 031 228 2661)

GARDEN, Air Vice-Marshall Timothy; s of Joseph Garden (d 1979), and Winifred Mary, *née* Mayes; *b* 23 April 1944; *Educ* Worcester Cathedral King's Sch, St Catherine's Coll Oxford (MA), Magdalene Coll Cambridge (MPhil); *m* 13 Nov 1965, Susan Elizabeth, da of Henry George Button, of Cambridge; 2 da (Alexandra b 1970, Antonia b 1971); *Career* RAF: joined 1963, pilot 1967-71, flying instr 1972-75; Army Staff Coll 1976, staff offr MOD 1977-79; OC 50 Sqdn 1979-81, dir def studies 1982-85; station cdr RAF Odiham 1985-87, asst dir Def Progs 1987-88, dir Air Force Staff Duties MOD 1988-90; Asst Chief of the Air Staff MOD 1991-; memb Cncl RUSI 1984-87; memb: IISS, Cncl for Arms Control; govr King's Sch Worcester; *Books* Can Deterrence Last? (1984), The Technology Trap (1989); *Recreations* writing, bridge, photography, computing, electronics; *Clubs* RAF; *Style*— Air Vice-Mashall Timothy Garden; MOD, Room 6243, Main Bldg, Whitehall, London SW1A 2HB (☎ 071 218 6316)

GARDHOUSE, Ian Robert; s of Robert Gardhouse (d 1976), of Newcastle upon Tyne, and Mildred Roper, *née* Dorward (d 1984); *b* 5 Sept 1945; *Educ* Royal GS Newcastle upon Tyne, Univ of Bristol (BA); *m* 24 Aug 1967, Kathleen; 2 da (Lisa b 3 April 1971, Chloë b 7 March 1973); *Career* actor, milkman, teacher, lectr; BBC: Newcastle 1970-76, London 1976; sr prodr BBC; work incl: Start the Week, Midweek, Stop the Week, Russell Harty's Musical Encounters, Funny You Should Sing That, Rollercoaster, Loose Ends (award winner); *Style*— Ian Gardhouse, Esq; BBC, Broadcasting House, Portland Place, London W1A 1AA (☎ 071 927 5074, fax 071 436 2771)

GARDINER, Dr Austen James Sutherland; s of James Martin Gardiner, CBE, of The Firs, Dalmunzie Road, Aberdeen, and Nellie Wallace, *née* Sutherland (d 1979); *b* 27 Jan 1934; *Educ* Aberdeen GS Strathallan, Univ of Aberdeen (MA, ChB, MD); *m* 27 July 1961, Ruth, da of Leslie Duncan, of Costorphine, Edinburgh; 2 s (Nicholas b 1962, Peter b 1966), 1 da (Julia b 1964); *Career* sr registrar internal med Royal Infirmary Aberdeen 1968, res fell Dept of Med McGill Univ of Montreal 1967-69, conslt physician (specializing in respiratory disease) and postgrad tutor Monklands Hosp Lanarkshire 1975-; author of numerouse pubns on respiratory physiology and respiratory disease; MRCP 1966, FRCP (Ed) 1978, FRCP (Glasgow) 1979; *Recreations* reading, classical music, golf, fishing, shooting; *Clubs* Dunblane, Gleneagles; *Style*— Dr Austen Gardiner; Farringford, St Margaret's Drive, Dunblane, Perthshire (☎ 0786 822124); Medical Unit, Monklands Hosp, Airdrie, Lanarkshire (☎ 0236 69344)

GARDINER, David Alfred William; s of Neil William Gardiner (d 1973), of Burghfield Common, Berks; *b* 11 April 1935; *Educ* Winchester, Imperial Coll London, Harvard Business Sch; *m* 1963, Carolyn Georgina, da of Thomas Humphrey Naylor (d 1966), of Ashton, Chester; 2 s (James b 1965, Andrew b 1971), 1 da (Georgina b 1968); *Career* Lt Grenadier Gds 1953-55; dir Huntley & Palmers Ltd and assoc companies 1961-83; farmer and landowner; High Sheriff of Berkshire 1988-89; chm Berks CLA 1989; *Recreations* field sports; *Style*— David Gardiner, Esq; The Old Rectory, Lilley, Newbury, Berks RG16 0HH (☎ 048 82 227)

GARDINER, (John) Duncan (Broderick); s of Frederick Keith Gardiner, JP (d 1989), and Ruth, *née* Dixon (d 1985); *b* 12 Jan 1937; *Educ* St Edward's Sch Oxford; *m* 1965, Geraldine Mallen; 1 s, 1 da; *Career* author and broadcaster; ed Western Mail 1974-81; *Style*— Duncan Gardiner, Esq; 145 Pencisely Rd, Llandaff, Cardiff (☎ 0222 563636)

GARDINER, Gavin Thomas; s of George Gardiner (d 1965), of Wellington, NZ, and Constance Gardiner; *b* 1 Oct 1941; *Educ* Wellington Coll Wellington NZ, Univ of Otago NZ, St Bartholomew's Hosp London; *Career* sr registrar oral surgery: Royal Dental Hosp, St George's Hosp, Royal Surrey Co Hosp Guildford; conslt oral and Maxillo Facial surgn 1979-: Mt Vernon Hosp, Hillingdon Hosp, Northwick Park Hosp; fell: RSM, Br Assoc Oral and Maxillofacial Surgns; *Recreations* golf; *Style*— Gavin Gardiner, Esq; Clementine Church Hosp, Sudbury Hill, Harrow, Middx (☎ 081 422 3464)

GARDINER, Sir George Arthur; MP (C) Reigate 1974-; s of Stanley Gardiner (d 1958), of Maldon, Essex, and Emma Gardiner (d 1987); *b* 3 March 1935; *Educ* Harvey GS Folkestone, Balliol Coll Oxford; *m* 1, 1961 (m dis 1980), Juliet Wells; 2 s, 1 da; m 2, 1980, Helen, *née* Hackett; *Career* dep political corr The Sunday Times 1966-70, chief political corr Thomson Regional Newspapers 1964-74; contested (C) Coventry S 1970; ed Cons News 1972-79, memb Exec 1922 Ctee, vice chm Cons Foreign Affrs Ctee; memb: Home Affrs and Race Rels Select Ctee, Immigration Sub Ctee 1979-82; chm Cons Euro Affrs Ctee 1980-87 (former sec 1976-79, vice chm 1979-80); kt 1990; *Books* The Changing Life of London (1972), Margaret Thatcher, from Childhood to Leadership (1975); *Recreations* cooking, gardening; *Style*— Sir George Gardiner, MP; House of Commons, London SW1A 0AA

GARDINER, Guy Clavell Inge; CBE (1960); s of Charles Herbert Inge Gardiner (d 1922), and Rufa Flora Clavell, *née* Hore (d 1975); *b* 18 July 1916; *Educ* Westminster; *m* 9 Sept 1939, Louise Mabelle (Jane), da of Walter Clerk Randolph Rose (d 1938); 3 s (Michael b 12 March 1942, Colin b 25 Sept 1943, David b 13 March 1945); *Career* De Havilland Aircraft Co Ltd: aeronautical tech sch 1936-38, designer undercarriage and hydraulics (Mosquito) 1938-43; De Havilland Propellor Co Ltd: chief designer 1945-47, chief engr 1947-52, tech dir and chief engr 1952-59, chief exec (Blue Streak) 1959-61; tech dir (guided weapons) Hawker Siddeley Aviation 1961-63; Hawker Siddeley Dynamics: dir and gen mangr 1963-67, md 1967-71, conslt 1971; Freeman Worshipful Co of Coach and Coach Harness Makers 1971; FRAeS 1956, FIMechE 1955; *Recreations* shooting, golf, sailing; *Clubs* Naval and Military; *Style*— Guy Gardiner, Esq, CBE; Heron Cottage, Heronsgate, Rickmansworth, Herts (☎ 0923 282584)

GARDINER, Dame Helen Louisa; DBE (1961, CBE 1952) MVO (1937); yst da of late Henry Gardiner, of Bristol; *b* 24 April 1901; *Educ* Clifton HS; *Career* formerly in Private Sec's Office Buckingham Palace (chief clerk 1946-61); *Recreations* reading, gardening; *Style*— Dame Helen Gardiner, DBE, MVO; Lostwithiel, Cornwall

GARDINER, Ian David; s of Maj David Gardiner, MC (d 1939), and Dorothea, *née* Caswell (d 1985); *b* 14 April 1928; *Educ* Harlow Coll, Univ of London (BSc); *m* 12 Aug 1950, Dorothy Anderson, da of Frank Arnold Onians (d 1985); 2 s (David b 1954, Andrew b 1969), 2 da (Elizabeth b 1951, Anne b 1958); *Career* TA RE 1972, Col 1984; The Eng Electric Co 1948-70: mangr Bombay 1957, mangr Calcutta 1959, mangr Victoria Aust 1960-65, commercial mangr Diesel Div 1965-70; BR Engrg Ltd 1970-81: commercial dir 1970-73, engrg dir 1973-76, md 1976-81; dir of engrg BR 1981-85; memb Cncl City Univ 1982- (chm Convocation 1978-81), memb of Cncl and chm Prodn Ctee CBI 1980-84, memb of Bd BSI 1982-84, vice pres IMechE 1984-90; Freeman City of London 1982, Liveryman Worshipful Co of Engrs 1984; FIMechE 1970, FIEE 1971, FRSA 1975, FEng 1982; *Recreations* gardening, swimming, fishing, choral singing; *Style*— Ian Gardiner, Esq; Cottesloe, 8 Barrs Ave, New Milton, Hants BH25 5HJ (☎ 0425 638039)

GARDINER, John Eliot; CBE (1990); s of Rolf Gardiner, and Marabel, *née* Hodgkin; *b* 20 April 1943; *Educ* Bryanston, King's Coll Cambridge (MA), King's Coll London; *m* 1981, Elizabeth Suzanne, *née* Wilcock; 3 da; *Career* conductor; studied with Nadia Boulanger in Paris 1966-68, fndr and artistic dir Monteverdi Choir, Monteverdi Orchestra and English Baroque Soloists; youngest conductor Henry Wood Promenade concert Royal Albert Hall 1968; debut: Sadler's Wells Opera London Coliseum 1969, Royal Festival Hall 1972, Royal Opera House 1973; English Baroque Soloist 1978; guest conductor with orchestras in: Paris, Brussels, Geneva, Frankfurt, Dresden, Leipzig, London; US debuts: Dallas Symphony 1981, San Francisco Symphony 1982, Carnegie Hall NY 1988; Euro music festivals incl: Aix-en-Provence, Aldeburgh, Bath, Berlin, Edinburgh, Flanders, Holland, City of London; revived works of Purcell, Handel and Rameau (world premiere stage of opera Les Boréades in Aix-en-Provence 1982); princ conductor CBC Vancouver Orchestra 1980-83; Opéra de Lyon: fndr 1983, musical dir 1983-88, chef fondateur 1988-; artistic dir: Göttingen Handel Festival 1981-90, Veneto Music Festival 1986; has made over 100 records: Grand Prix du Disque 1978, 1979 and 1980, Prix Caecilia 1982, 1983 and 1985; awards: Edison award 1982, 1986, 1987 and 1988, Arturo Toscanini Music Critics award 1985 and 1986, IRCA prize Helsinki 1987, Deutscher Schallplatten preis 1986, Nat Acad of Recording Arts and Sciences nominations 1986, 1987 and 1989; Hon DUniv Lumière de Lyon 1987; Officier Ordre des Arts et des Lettres 1988; *Recreations* forestry, organic farming; *Style*— John Eliot Gardiner, Esq, CBE; Gore Farm, Ashmore, Salisbury, Wilts; 7 Pleydell Avenue, London W6

GARDINER, Prof John Macdonald; s of Kenneth Macdonald Gardiner (d 1977), of Swansea, and Alice Marjorie, *née* Taylor (d 1975); *b* 15 Sept 1941; *Educ* Wycliffe Coll Stonehouse Glos, Goldsmiths Coll London (BSc), Birkbeck Coll London (PhD); *Career* City Univ London: lectr 1972, sr lectr 1978, reader 1981, prof of psychology 1986-; consulting ed: Journal of Experimental Psychology, Learning Memory and Cognition 1985-; memb: Experimental Psychology Soc, Euro Soc for Cognitive Psychology, Psychonomic Soc; fell Br Psychological Soc; *Recreations* travel, walking, lunch; *Style*— Prof John Gardiner; Memory and Cognition Research Group, City University, Northampton Square, London EC1V 0HB (☎ 071 253 4399, fax 071 490 7204)

GARDINER, Baroness; Muriel; *née* Baker; da of Charles Baker; *m* 1 (m dis), Sydney Box; 1 da (Leonora); m 2, 1970, Baron Gardiner, PC, CH (Life Peer, d 1990); 1 step da (Hon Carol Gardiner, *qv*); *Style*— The Rt Hon the Lady Gardiner; Mote End, Nan Clark's Lane, Mill Hill, London NW7

GARDINER, Patrick Lancaster; s of Clive Gardiner (d 1960), and Lilian, *née* Lancaster (d 1973); *b* 17 March 1922; *Educ* Westminster, Christ Church Oxford (MA); *m* 7 July 1955, (Kathleen) Susan, da of Herbert Booth (d 1984); 2 da (Josephine b 1956, Vanessa b 1960); *Career* Army 1942-45: Lt 1943, Capt 1945, serv N Africa and Italy; visiting prof Columbia Univ NY 1955, fell and tutor in philosophy Magdalen Coll Oxford 1958-89 (lectr in philosophy Wadham Coll 1949-52, fell in philosophy St Anthony's Coll 1952-58), FBA 1985, emeritus fell Magdalen Coll Oxford 1989-; *Books* The Nature of Historical Explanation (1952), Schopenhauer (1963), Kierkegaard (1988); ed: Theories of History (1959), Nineteenth-Century Philosophy (1969), The Philosophy of History (1974); *Style*— Patrick Gardiner, Esq; The Dower House, Wytham, Oxford (☎ 0865 242205); Magdalen Coll, Oxford (☎ 0865 276000)

GARDINER, Hon Mrs (Susanna Catherine Crawshay); er da of Baron Greenwood of Rossendale, PC (Life Peer, d 1982); *b* 1943; *m* 1970, Christopher Gardiner; 1 s (Thomas Keir b 1982), 1 da (Anna Kathryn b 1980); *Style*— The Hon Mrs Gardiner; 1 Oak Tree House, Redington Gardens, London NW3 7RY (☎ 071 435 4383)

GARDINER, Victor Alec; OBE (1977); *b* 9 Aug 1929; *Educ* Whitgift and City and Guilds Schs; *m* ; 1s, 2 da; *Career* dir and gen mangr London Weekend TV 1971-, dir London Weekend TV (Hldgs) Ltd and London Weekend Services Ltd 1976-; chm Dynamic Technol Ltd and Standard Music Ltd 1972-; *Style*— Victor Gardiner, Esq, OBE; The Gables, Sulhamstead, Reading, Berks

GARDINER, William Griffiths; s of James Gardiner (d 1962), of Glasgow, and Muriel, *née* Griffiths; *b* 8 March 1938; *Educ* Glasgow HS; *m* 7 July 1967, Una, da of David Anderson (d 1945); 2 s (David b 1969, Ian b 1971); *Career* CA 1960, co sec Stenhouse Hldgs plc 1970-84, head fin investmt small business div Scottish Devpt Agency 1984-87, fin dir Glasgow Investmt Mangrs Ltd 1987-; *Recreations* golf, curling, music; *Clubs* Glasgow HS, Glasgow Golf; *Style*— William Gardiner, Esq; 5 Ardoch Rd, Bearsden, Glasgow (☎ 041 942 7338); Glasgow Investment Managers Ltd, 29 St Vincent Place, Glasgow G1 2DR (☎ 041 226 4585, fax 041 226 3632, telex 779503)

GARDNER; *see*: Bruce-Gardner

GARDNER, (David) Alistair; s of David Dalgleish Gardner (d 1978), of Inverness, Scotland, and Sarah Jane, *née* McColl (d 1931); *b* 10 Oct 1930; *Educ* Fettes, Scottish Hotel Sch Ross Hall Glasgow (Dip Hotel Mgmnt); *m* 12 Oct 1955, Sheila Maree, da of George Alexander Stewart (d 1969), of Jersey, CI; 1 da (Carol b 7 Oct 1962); *Career* Nat Serv RAF 1949-50; owner and dir various hotels and restaurants 1954-87, freelance broadcaster BBC 1958-80; chm: Moray Firth Radio Ltd 1980-, Tourism Servs Scotland Ltd (trading as Hi-Line) 1985-; memb Sutherland C C, co fndr Inverness Hosps Broadcasting Serv; farmer: pres Inverness and Highland Regn Licensed Trade Assoc, sen baillie Dernoch Town Cncl; *Recreations* travel, broadcasting, golf, photography, swimming; *Clubs* Inverness Golf, Royal Dornoch Golf; *Style*— Alistair Gardner, Esq; Altyre, 10 Abertarff Rd, Inverness IV2 3NW (☎ 0463 230684); Moray Firth Radio, PO Box 271, Inverness IV3 65F (☎ 0463 224433, fax 0463 243224, telex 75643); Hi-Line House, Station Rd, Dingwall, Ross Shire IV15 9JE (☎ 0349 62022, fax 0349 64044, telex 75137)

GARDNER, Brenda Ann Ellen; da of Michael Sweedish, of Canada, and Flora, *née* Gibb; *b* 1 June 1947; *Educ* Univ of Saskatchewan (BA), Washington Univ; *m* 1968, (James) Douglas Gardner (d 1986), s of James Gardner (d 1966); *Career* teacher USA and UK 1968-72, asst ed Penguin Books 1972-77; ed: W H Allen 1977-79, ELJ Arnold 1979-81, Evans 1981-83; md and chairperson Piccadilly Press 1983-; chairperson Children's Book Circle 1981-82; *Recreations* reading, aerobics, swimming, tennis, theatre, films; *Clubs* Groucho; *Style*— Mrs Brenda Gardner; 5 Castle Road, London NW1 8PR (☎ 071 267 4492, fax 071 267 4493, telex 295441)

GARDNER, Brian Patrick; s of T C Gardner, CBE, of Hill Court, Station Rd, Whittlesford, Cambs, and B T Gardner; *b* 17 June 1948; *Educ* St George's Coll Harare Zimbabwe, Beaumont Coll Old Windsor, Oxford Univ (BA, MA, BM BCh); *m* 18 Oct 1980, Stephanie Catherine Mary, da of Dr Faller (d 1980); 2 s (Paul b 1983, Martin b 1988), 3 da (Catherine b 1982, Laura b 1984, Annabelle b 1989); *Career* various jr med posts 1974-79, registrar in neurosurgery Royal Victoria Hosp Belfast 1980-82, sr registrar in spinal injuries Mersey Regnl Spinal Cord Injuries Centre Southport 1982-85, conslt surgn in spinal injuries Nat Spinal Injuries Centre 1985-; memb BMA; MRCP 1978, FRCS 1980; *Recreations* tennis, squash; *Style*— Brian Gardner, Esq; 2 Northumberland Ave, Aylesbury, Bucks, HP21 7HG (☎ 0296 23420); National Spinal Injuries Centre, Stoke Mandeville Hosp, Aylesbury, Bucks HP21 8AL (☎ 0296 84111, fax 0296 82906)

GARDNER, Cecil John; *b* 11 June 1912; *m* 1936, Marjorie Isobel; 2 da (Pamela, Diana); *Career* Gardners Transformers Ltd (Queen's Award for Export 1980); founded business as Gardners Radio 1928, incorp 1934, name changed to Gardners Transformers 1962, now chm; *Recreations* sailing; *Clubs* Royal Solent Yaccht, Royal Lymington Yacht, Christchurch Sailing; *Style*— Cecil Gardner, Esq; Willow Close, Bridge Street, Christchurch, Dorset BH23 1DY (☎ 0202 482827); Gardners Transformers Ltd, Christchurch, Dorset BH23 3PN (☎ 0202 482284, telex 41276 GRSXCH G)

GARDNER, Dr David Alan; s of John Lawrence Gardner, of Hadley Wood, Herts, and Alice Winifred, *née* Cattermole; *b* 29 April 1938; *Educ* Minchenden Sch Southgate, Univ of Leeds; *m* 17 Sept 1966, Gillian Ann, da of Capt Edmund Patrick Flowers, of Bangor, N Wales; 3 s (Leon b 1977, Oliver b 1980, Joshua b 1985), 4 da (Philippa b 1967, Amanda b 1969, Samantha b 1971, Jemima b 1974); *Career* registrar Guy's Hosp London 1968-70, conslt pathologist Kensington Chelsea and Westminster Hosp 1973-74, conslt pathologist UCH 1974- (sr registrar 1971-73, sr lectr 1974-); chm: S Camden Pathology Ctee, NE Thames Regnl Biochemistry Ctee; memb NE Thames Regnl Scientific Ctee; FRCPath 1084 (MRCPath 1971), MRCS, LRCP; *Recreations* British campaign medals, memeber baptist historical soc; *Style*— Dr David Gardner; 18 Jennings Road, St Albans, Herts AL1 4NT (☎ 0727 62019); Dept of Chemical Pathology, Windeyer Building, Cleveland St, London W1P 6DB (☎ 071 636 8333, fax 071 380 9469)

GARDNER, Cdr Derek George Montague; VRD; s of Alfred Charles Gardner (d 1952), and Florence Mary, *née* Johnson (d 1955); *b* 13 Feb 1914; *Educ* Oundle; *m* 14 July 1951, Mary, da of Joseph Harry Dalton; 1 s (Charles Henry Penn b 11 May 1954), 1 da (Angela Mary b 2 June 1952); *Career* Midshipman RNVR (Clyde Div) 1934, mobilised HMS Proserpine 1939, HM (trawler) Ocean Fisher 1939-41, HMS Osprey 1941, HMS Broke (despatches 1942), HMS Highlander 1942-43, Lt Cdr Staff of C-in-C Western Approaches HMS Eaglet 1943-45, Cdr Asst CSO to Flag Offr Ceylon HMS Lanka 1945-46, Cdr RNVR 1946, ret 1947; chartered civil engr Miny of Works Kenya HMOCS 1947-63, regnl engr Kenya 1953-63, ret HMOCS 1963; elected memb RSMA 1966; works in: Nat Maritime Museums Greenwich and Bermuda, RNC Dartmouth; one man shows Polak Gallery London: 1972, 1975, 1979, 1982, 1987, 1990; hon vice pres for life RSMA; lay vice patron of the Missions to Seamen 1983; RSMA, CEng, FICE; *Clubs* Naval; *Style*— Cdr Derek Gardner, VRD; High Thatch, Corfe Mullen, Wimborne, Dorset BH21 3HJ (☎ 0202 693211)

GARDNER, Douglas Frank; s of Lt Ernest Frank Gardner, of 32 Bramshill Gardens, London NW5, and the late Mary, *née* Chattington; *b* 20 Dec 1943; *Educ* Woolverstone Hall, Coll of Estate Mgmnt, Univ of London (BSc); *m* 5 Sept 1978, Adèle, da of Major Charles Macmillan Alexander, of Broome Cottage, The Drive, Angmering-on-Sea, Sussex; 1 s (Mark b 1972), 2 da (Teresa b 1971, Amy b 1979); *Career* chief exec properties div Tarmac plc 1976-83, md Brixton Estate plc 1983-; chm: Estates Improvement Ltd, Brixton Investments Ltd; dir Brixton France SA; *Recreations* tennis; *Style*— Douglas Gardner, Esq; 2 Woodstock Rd, Bedford Park, Chiswick, London W4 (☎ 081 994 0152); Brixton Estate plc, 22/24 Ely Place, London EC1 (☎ 071 242 6898, fax 071 405 1630, telex 22838)

GARDNER, Sir Edward Lucas; QC (1960); s of late Edward Walker Gardner, of Fulwood, Preston, Lancs; *b* 10 May 1912; *Educ* Hutton GS; *m* 1, 1950 (m dis 1962), Noreen Margaret, da of late John Collins, of Moseley, Birmingham; 1 s, 1 da; m 2, 1963, Joan Elizabeth, da of late B B Belcher, of Bedford; 1 s, 1 da; *Career* served WWII Cdr RNVR; former journalist; called to the Bar Gray's Inn 1947; dep chm QS: E Kent 1961-71, Kent 1962-71, Essex 1968-71; rec bencher Gray's Inn 1968, Crown Ct 1972-85; Soc of Cons Lawyers: chm 1975-85, vice-pres 1985-, chm Exec Ctee 1969-75; contested (C) Erith & Crayford 1955; MP (C): Billericay 1959-66, South Fylde 1970-1987; PPS to Attorney-Gen 1962-63, cmmr Cwlth War Graves Cmmn 1971-87; govr Thomas Coram Fndn for Children 1962-, steward British Boxing Bd Control 1975-84; kt 1982; *Clubs* Pratt's, Garrick; *Style*— Sir Edward Gardner, QC; Sparrows, Hatfield Broad Oak, Bishop's Stortford, Herts CM22 7HN (☎ 027970 265)

GARDNER, (Ralph Roland) Gay; s of Ralph Rodland Gardner, The Old Hall, Malpas, Cheshire, SY14 8NG, and Mima Elaine, *née* Forrester (d 1976); *b* 9 Aug 1934; *Educ* Eton; *m* 15 Oct 1966, Susan Blakeley, da of Cdr Vincent Russell, RN (d 1983); 1 s (Charles b 1968), 2 da (Louise b 1966, Chloë b 1973); *Career* cmmnd Scots Gds Nat Serv; md Smith St Aubuyn and Co Ltd, UK treas and dir Kleinwort Benson Ltd, exec dir Mees and Hope Securities Hldgs, dir Univ Life Assur Soc; *Style*— Gay Gardner, Esq; Leamington Hastings Manor, Rugby, CV23 8DY; Mees and Hope Securities 95 Gresham St, London, EC2V 7NA (☎ 071 600 9331, fax 071 606 1404, telex 946003)

GARDNER, Hon Joanna; yst da of Baroness Gardner of Parkes, *qv*; *b* 14 Nov 1964; *Educ* Univ of Essex (BA), Coll of Law Chancery Lane London; *Career* slr McKenna & Co 1991- (formerly articled clerk); *Style*— The Hon Joanna Gardner; McKenna & Co, Mitre House, 160 Aldersgate St, London EC1A 4DD

GARDNER, (Arthur) John; s of Harold John Gardner (d 1967), of Shipham, Somerset, and Lily Mary, *née* White (d 1985); *b* 19 Oct 1930; *Educ* Huish GS Taunton, London Univ (LLB); *m* 16 May 1953, Patricia Beatrice Mary, da of James Hooper (d 1954), of Ilminster, Somerset; 3 da (Rosemary b 1958, Caroline b 1963, Joanne b 1965); *Career* slr; memb Cheddar PC 1970- (chm 1973 and 1985); former: chm Somerset CCC, pres Somerset Law Soc; *Recreations* philately, cricket; *Style*— John Gardner, Esq; Staddles, Station Road, Cheddar, Somerset (☎ 0834 742261); Gardner Jackson, Roley House, Church St, Cheddar, Somerset (☎ 0934 743321)

GARDNER, John Linton; CBE (1976); s of Capt Alfred Linton Gardner, RAMC (ka 1918), of Ilfracombe, and Muriel, *née* Pullein-Thompson; *b* 2 March 1917; *Educ* Wellington, Exeter Coll Oxford; *m* 1955, Jane Margaret Mary, da of late Nigel James Abercrombie, of Ringmer, Lewes, E Sussex; 1 s, 2 da; *Career* composer; chief music master Repton 1939-40, on music staff Royal Opera House 1946-52, prof of harmony and composition RAM 1956-86; dir of music: St Paul's Girls' Sch 1962-75, Morley Coll 1965-69; dep chm Performing Rights Soc 1983-88; *Compositions incl* the opera The Moon and Sixpence, three symphonies, three string quartets, concertos for piano, trumpet and organ, many large scale choral works; *Recreations* tesseraphily; *Style*— John Gardner, Esq, CBE; 20 Firswood Ave, Ewell, Epsom, Surrey KT19 0PR

GARDNER, (David) Maitland; MBE (1945), TD; s of John James Maitland Gardner (d 1945), of Culdees Castle, Muthill, Perthshire, and Margaret, *née* Thomson (d 1953); *b* 3 April 1914; *Educ* Charterhouse, Clare Coll Cambridge (MA); *m* 5 Oct 1946, Barbara Helen, da of David John Wauchope Dundas (d 1938), of Woodhouselee, Milton Bridge, Midlothian; 1 s (Colin b 1960), 2 da (Jane b 1947, Margaret b 1949); *Career* cmmnd 2 Lt RA (TA) 1937, Staff Capt 1939, served GSO2 N Africa and Italy (despatches 1943), DAQMG Br Army Staff France 1944, transferred TARO (hon rank of Maj) 1945; A Gardner & Son Ltd (family furniture mfrs and retailers estab Glasgow 1832): dir 1938-46, md 1946-83, chm 1946-85; commercial farming interests in Perthshire 1953-90; rep Scot House Furnishers' Fedn on Trade Wages Cncl 1950-54 (pres 1951-54), hon pres Scot Furniture Trades Benevolent Assoc 1957- (pres 1954-55), chm Kinross & W Perthshire Cons Assoc 1960-65 (vice chm 1951-60); pres: Strathearn Agric Soc 1961-64, Perth and Kinross Cons Assoc 1983-89; elder Church of Scot 1950-, deacon of the Incorporation of Hammermen of Glasgow 1964-65; *Recreations* golf, curling, shooting; *Clubs* Western (Glasgow), Royal & Ancient Golf of St Andrews; *Style*— D Maitland Gardner, MBE, TD; Culdees Castle, Muthill, Crieff, Perthshire PH5 2BA (☎ 0764 81 280)

GARDNER, Capt Nicolas Charles Eric; s of Maj Laurie Gardner (d 1969), and Erica Sylva Margareta Herta, *née* Steinmann (d 1976); *b* 23 July 1946; *Educ* Eton, Keble Coll Oxford (MA); *m* 3 Oct 1974, Roseanne Serena, da of Charles Douglas Neville Walker, MM, of 58 Rue Singer, 75016 Paris; *Career* cmmnd Irish Gds 1966, Capt 1971, ADC to C-in-C UKLF 1972-74, ret 1974; ptnr: Town & Country Estate Agents 1975-83, Somerley Crayfish 1984-; Queen's Messenger 1987-; Liveryman Worshipful Co of Drapers 1983; *Recreations* shooting, gardening; *Style*— Capt Nicolas Gardner; Breamore Cottage, Breamore, Fordingbridge, Hampshire SP6 2DB (☎ 0725 22 265); Foreign & Commonwealth Office, King Charles St, London SW1

GARDNER, Peter Louis; s of Jack Louis Gardner (d 1976), and Joan Miriam, *née* Stokvis; *b* 22 June 1949; *Educ* NW Kent Coll of Technol (Dip); *m* 30 Sept 1972, Maureen Elizabeth, da of William George Collis (d 1977); 2 s (Adam b 5 Aug 1977, Neil b 24 May 1979), 1 da (Charlotte b 21 Feb 1984); *Career* architectural conslt Newman Tonks plc 1972-75, sales mangr G & S Allgood Ltd (architectural ironmongers) 1975-78; sale dir: DA Thomas Ltd 1978-88 (sales mangr), Hewi UK Ltd; gp sales dir D A Thomas Group plc; pres Guild of Architectural Ironmongers 1987-88; parent govr: Pickhurst Infants' Sch, Pickhurst Jr Sch; memb: Inst Architectural Ironmongers (chm 1984-85), IAM; *Recreations* golf, driving; *Clubs* Langley Park Golf (memb Ctee); *Style*— Peter Gardner, Esq; Beaver Construction Supplies Ltd, Unit B2 Ullswater Crescent, Coulsdon, Surrey (☎ 081 668 0731, fax 081 668 5319)

GARDNER, Prof Richard Lavenham; s of Allan Constant Gardner (d 1943), of Beare Green, Surrey, and Eileen May Alexander, *née* Gardner (d 1961); *b* 10 June 1943; *Educ* St John's Leatherhead, St Catharine's Coll Cambridge (BSc); *m* 14 Dec 1968, Wendy Joy, da of Charles Hampton Trevelyan Cresswell (d 1989), of Cobham Surrey; 1 s (Matthew Thomas b 18 April 1985); *Career* res asst the Physiological Laboratory Univ of Cambridge 1969-73, lectr in Dept of Zoology Univ of Oxford 1973-77, student of ChCh Oxford 1974-, Henry Dale res prof Royal Soc 1978-, hon dir Developmental Biology Unit Imperial Cancer Res Fund 1985-; memb Academia Europaea 1989; FRS 1979; *Recreations* sailing, painting, ornithology, gardening; *Style*— Prof Richard Gardner, FRS; Imperial Cancer Research Fund, Developmental Biology Unit, Dept of Zoology, S Parks Rd, Oxford OX1 3PS (☎ 0865 59977, fax 0865 310432)

GARDNER, Hon Sarah Louise; er da of Baroness Gardner of Parkes, *qv*; *b* 3 March 1960; *Educ* City of London Sch for Girls; *Career* gp administrator to Gp Account Dir Saatchi & Saatchi Garland Compton Ltd 1979-85; PA to MD C F Anderson & Son Ltd 1986-89, PA to Ops Mangr Prince's Youth Business Trust 1989-; govr St Edward's RC Primary Sch London 1984-89; memb: Self-Help Panel Thames Television Tst 1985, N Westminster Lay Visitors' Panel (Home Office appt) 1987-; advsr Young Leaders' London NW County Girl Guides Assoc 1987-; memb Mgmnt Ctee Nat Youth Bureau (Sec of State Dept of Educn and Science appt) 1989-; *Recreations* theatre, ballet, tapestry, cooking, entertaining; *Style*— The Hon Sarah Gardner; 3 Northwick Close, London NW8 8JG

GARDNER, Trevelyan Codrington; CBE (1960); s of Lt Cdr Thomas Gardner, DSC, RN (d 1928); *b* 3 Aug 1917; *Educ* Taunton's Sch, Queen's Coll Oxford (MA); *m* 1944, Briege Theresa, da of Patrick Feehan, of Castle Carra, Dundalk; 2 s, 3 da; *Career* Maj Royal Hampshire Regt 1939-45, serv Italy; Colonial Serv 1946-64, sec for fin N Rhodesia 1958-60, min of fin N Rhodesia 1960-64; treas Univ of Cambridge until 1983 (emeritus 1983-); admin: American Friends of Cambridge Univ 1983-87, Friends of the Oxford and Cambridge Boat Race 1988-; tstee Cambridge Cwlth Tst; memb: Stonyhurst Charitable Tst, Cambridge Union Soc; emeritus fell Wolfson Coll Cambridge; hon fell: Robinson Coll Cambridge, Darwin Coll Cambridge; *Recreations* golf, gardening; *Clubs* Army and Navy, Gog Magog Golf; *Style*— Trevelyan Gardner, Esq, CBE; Hill Court, Station Rd, Whittlesford, Cambridge (☎ 0223 832483); Friends of the Oxford and Cambridge Boat Race, Pitt Building, Trumpington St, Cambridge CB2 1RP (☎ 0223 311201)

GARDNER, Dr William Norman; s of Norman Charles Gardner (d 1979), of Sydney, NSW, Australia, and Ngaire Jean, *née* Dawson; *b* 24 Jan 1943; *Educ* Penrith HS NSW Australia, Sydney Univ (MB, BS), Univ of Oxford (DPhil); *m* 1, 1971 (m dis 1974), Lydia, *née* Sinclair; m 2, 1981, Jane Elizabeth, da of Alan Maurice Stainer, of 2 St Mary's Close, Kidlington, Oxon; 3 s (Timothy b 1981, Nicholas b 1985, Joseph b 1988); *Career* med house appts Sydney and Royal Adelaide Hosps 1966-68, sr house appt Brompton, London Chest and Westminster Hosps 1969-71, MRC res offr Dept Physiology (then Nuffield Inst) Oxford 1971-80 (memb Wolfson Coll until 1983), sr lectr and hon conslt physician King's Coll Sch med 1987- (lectr med Dept Thoracic Med 1981-87; author of various articles on respiratory and foetal physiology and respiratory med; MRCP 1971, memb Br Thoracic Soc 1981; *Recreations* windsurfing, jazz piano; *Style*— Dr William Gardner; Dept of Thoracic Medicine, King's Coll Sch of Med and Dentistry, Bessemer Rd, London SE5 9PJ (☎ 01 3263165, fax 02 326 3589

GARDNER OF PARKES, Baroness (Life Peer UK 1981), of Southgate, Greater London, and of Parkes in the State of New South Wales and Commonwealth

of Australia; (Rachel) Trixie Anne Gardner; JP (N Westminster Inner London 1971); da of Hon (John Joseph) Gregory McGirr (d 1949; MLA, NSW State Govt), and Rachel, *née* Miller; *b* 17 July 1927; *Educ* Monte Sant Angelo Coll N Sydney, Sydney Univ (BDS); *m* 1956, Kevin Anthony Gardner (Lord Mayor of Westminster 1987-88), s of George Gardner, of Sydney, Australia; 3 da (Hon Sarah Louise b 1960, Hon Rachel Trixie (Hon Mrs Pope) b 1961, Hon Joanna Mary b 1964); *Career* dental surgeon; memb: Westminster City Cncl 1968-78, GLC Havering 1970-73, Enfield-Southgate 1977-; Parly candidate (C): Blackburn 1970, N Cornwall 1974; govr National Heart Hosp 1974-90, memb Industrial Tbnl Panel for London 1974-, British chm European Union of Women 1978-82, national women's vice chm Cons Party 1978-82, UK rep on UN Status of Women Cmmn 1982-88, memb LEB 1984-90; dir: Gateway Building Society 1987-88, Woolwich Building Society 1988-; vice pres: Bldg Socs Assoc 1985-90, Nat House Building Cncl 1990-; vice chm NE Thames RHA 1990-, UK chm Plan International; *Recreations* gardening, cooking, travel, historic buildings, family life; *Style*— The Rt Hon Baroness Gardner of Parkes; House of Lords, London SW1 OPW

GARDNER-THORPE, Dr Christopher; s of Col Sir Ronald Gardner-Thorpe, GBE, TD, JP, *qv*, and Hazel, *née* Dees; *b* 22 Aug 1941; *Educ* St Philip's Sch London, Beaumont Coll Old Windsor Berks, St Thomas' Hosp Med Sch London (MB BS), Univ of London (MD); *m* 1 April 1967 (m dis 1988), Sheelah, da of Dr Edward Irvine, of Exeter; 2 s (Damian, James), 3 da (Catherine, Anne, Helen); *Career* registrar in neurology: Wessex Neurological Centre Southampton Gen Hosp 1967-69, Gen Infirmary Leeds 1969-71, Special Centre for Epilepsy Bootham Park Hosp York 1969-71; sr registrar in neurology Newcastle Gen Hosp and Royal Victoria Infirmary Newcastle upon Tyne 1971-74, conslt neurologist SW Regnl Health Authy (duties Exeter and N Devon) 1974-, hon tutor in neurology Post Grad Med Sch Univ of Exeter 1983-; ed various books and papers on epilepsy and other neurological topics; memb Int League Against Epilepsy 1969-, fndr memb and hon tres SW Eng Neurosciences Assoc 1981, fndr memb S Eng Neurosciences Assoc; memb: Harveian Soc 1966-, SW Physicians Club 1974-, Devon and Exeter Med Soc 1974- (hon asst sec 1978-81, hon sec 1981-85, hon reporting sec 1989-), Advsy Ctee Northcott Devon Med Fndn; fndr hon med advsr Devon Sports Assoc for the Disabled 1976-, memb Northumbrian Pipers Soc 1976-; Order O St J 1980, HM Lieut City of London 1981; Freeman City of London 1978, Liveryman Worshipful Co of Barbers 1980; FRSM 1968, FRCP 1985; *Books* James Parkinson 1755-1824 (1987); *Recreations* music, travel, reading, photography, sailing, gardening; *Clubs* Starcross Yacht; *Style*— Dr Christopher Gardner-Thorpe; The Coach House, 1A College Rd, Exeter EX1 1TE (☎ 0392 433 941)

GARDNER-THORPE, Sir Ronald Laurence; GBE (1980), TD (1950 and 3 bars), JP (Inner London 1965, City of London 1969); s of Joseph Alfred Gardner, of Ulverston, Lancs, and Hannah Thorpe, *née* Coulthurst; *b* 13 May 1917; *Educ* St John's De La Salle Coll Southsea Hants, Univ of Padua; *m* 1938, Hazel Mary St George, Dame of Magistral Grace SMO Malta, da of Adrian Bernard Dees, of Northumberland; 1 s (Christopher); *Career* 2 Lt Heavy Regt TA Hants (1939, Capt 1939, Maj 1940, Lt-Col 1944, Col 1960), serv Europe, Med, USA, cmd 5 Bn The Buffs 1956-60; fin memb Kent TA 1954-65; govr: St John's Coll Hants 1963 (dep chm of Govrs 1976), St Joseph's Coll London 1966-76; memb Governing Body Assoc Pub Schs 1963, alderman of the Ward of Bishopgate 1972; tstee: Utd Westminster Fndn 1975, The Buffs Royal East Kent Regt Museum 1976, Rowland Hill Benevolent Fund 1978, Morden Coll 1980, Mental Health Fndn 1981, Royal Fndn of Grey Coat Hosp 1982, Duke of Edinburgh's Award; vice pres BRCS 1978; pres: SSAFA Central London 1982, Friends of the Hosp of St John and St Elizabeth 1982, 25th Anniversary Appeal of the Duke of Edinburgh's Award; chllr City Univ 1980, chm Distressed Gentlefolk's Aid Assoc, memb Cncl Magistrates Assoc, hon memb World Trade Centre; Sheriff City of London 1978, Admiral Port of London 1980, Lord Mayor of London 1980-81, HM Lt for City of London 1980; hon citizen: Kansas City, Baltimore, Norfolk Virginia, Cusco Peru, State of Arizona; memb Ct: Worshipful Co of Painter-Stainers, Worshipful Co of Builders Merchants; Lloyd's underwriter 1979; Hon DCL City Univ 1980, Hon DH Lewis Univ Chicago 1981; KStJ 1980 (OStJ 1979), Knight SMOM 1982, KASG, Knight Cdr Royal Order of the Danneborg (Denmark) 1960, Knight Cdr Order of the Infante Henrique (Portugal) 1978, Knight Cdr Order of Gorka Dakshina Bahu (Nepal) 1980, Knight Cdr Order of King Abdul Aziz (Saudi Arabia) 1981; *Clubs* Bishopsgate Ward, City Livery, Utd Wards, Royal Soc of St George, The Belfry, Variety (vice pres), Anglo-Danish Soc (memb); *Style*— Sir Ronald Gardner-Thorpe, GBE, TD, JP; 8 Cadogan Square, London SW1X 0JU

GAREL-JONES, (William Armand Thomas) Tristan; MP (C) Watford 1979-; s of Bernard Garel-Jones, of Madrid, and Meriel, *née* Williams; *b* 28 Feb 1941; *Educ* King's Sch Canterbury; *m* 1966, Catalina, da of Mariano Garrigues, of Madrid; 4 s, 1 da; *Career* PPS to Barney Hayhoe 1981-82, asst whip 1982-83, lord cmmr to the Treasy 1983-86; HM Household: vice chamberlain 1986-87, comptroller 1987-89, treas (dep chief whip) 1989-90; min of state FCO 1990-; *Recreations* collecting books; *Clubs* Beefsteak, Carlton, Club de Campo Madrid; *Style*— Tristan Garel-Jones, Esq, MP; House of Commons, London SW1A 0AA

GARFIELD, John Samuel; s of Montagu Garfield (d 1976), of Hove, and Marguerite, *née* Elman (d 1983); *b* 13 Feb 1930; *Educ* Bradfield Coll, Emmanuel Coll Cambridge (MA, MB MChir); *m* 6 Oct 1962, Agnes Clara Teleki, da of Count Joseh Teleki de Szék (d 1985), of Pomaz, Hungary; 3 da (Stephanie b 1963, Johanna Francoise b 1965, Marie-Claire b 1969); *Career* jt specialist med RAMC 1956-58, conslt neurosurgn 1968, clinical teacher neurosurgery Univ of Southampton, numerous pubns on neurosurgical topics; pres Soc of Br Neurological Surgns vice pres and chm Cases Ctee Med Def Union, former chm Wessex Regnl Med Advsy Ctee; FRCS 1961, FRCP 1971; *Publications* The Fallen (photography, 1990); *Clubs* Athenaeum; *Style*— John Garfield, Esq; Wessex Neurological Centre, Southampton General Hosp, Shirley, Southampton SO9 4XY (☎ 0703 777222)

GARFIELD, Leon; s of David Kalman Garfield (d 1951), of London, and Rose, *née* Blaustein (d 1964); *b* 14 July 1921; *Educ* Brighton GS; *m* 23 Oct 1948, Vivien, da of John Foster Alcock, OBE (d 1980); 1 da (Jane Angela b 1964); *Career* RAMC 1941-45; hosp biochemist until 1966; author; winner of: Guardian Award 1967, Carnegie Medal 1970, Whitbread Literary Award 1980, Prix de la Fondation de France 1984, Golden Phoenix (US), Swedish Golden Cat Award, Silver Griffel Award (Holland, twice); FRSL 1985; *Books* Jack Holborn (1964), Devil in The Fog (1966), Smith (1967), Black Jack (1968), The Boy and The Monkey (1968), Mr Corbett's Ghost (1969), The Drummer Boy (1970), The Strange Affair of Adelaide Harris (1971), The Ghost Downstairs (1972), Child O' War (1972), The Sound of Coaches (1974), The Prisoners of September (1975), The Pleasure Garden (1976), The House of Hanover (1976), The Confidence Man (1978), Bostock and Harris (1969), The Apprentices (1976-79), John Diamond (1980), The Mystery of Edwin Drood (by Dickens completed by Garfield in 1980), The House of Cards (1982), Guilt and Gingerbread (1984), Shakespeare Stories (1985), The December Rose (1986), The Empty Sleeve (1988), Blewcoat Boy (1988); with Edward Blishen: The God Beneath The Sea (1970), and The Golden Shadow (1973); Picture Books: Fair's Fair (1981), King Nimrod's Tower (1982), The Writing on The Wall (1983), The King in The Garden (1984), The Wedding Ghost (1985); *Recreations* collecting Staffordshire China; *Clubs* Pen; *Style*— Leon Garfield, Esq; c/o John Johnson (Authors' Agent) Ltd, Clerkenwell House, 45/47 Clerkenwell Green, London EC1R 0HT (☎ 071 251 0125)

GARFIELD, Lewis Aubrey; s of John Garfield (d 1975), and Celia Garfield; *b* 11 June 1934; *Educ* Secondary Modern; *m* 28 April 1972, Agnes Maria, da of Prof John Morrison, of Great Shelford, Cambs; 1 s (Neill David b 1977), 1 da (Emma Rose b 1980); *Career* chm: Garfield Lewis Ltd and subsidiaries, Aluminium Stockholders Assoc; *Recreations* hunting, racing, tennis; *Clubs* Reform, Lansdowne; *Style*— Lewis A Garfield, Esq; The Hall, Thorpe Mandeville, Northamptonshire; PO Box 21, Banbury, Oxon (☎ 0295 710001, telex 837501, fax 0295 712201)

GARFIELD, Simon Frank; s of Herbert Sidney Garfield (d 1973), and Hella Helene, *née* Meyer (d 1979); *b* 19 March 1960; *Educ* UCS Hampstead, LSE (BSc Econ); *m* 1987, Diane, da of Rubin Samuels; 2 c; *Career* sub ed Radio Times 1981, scriptwriter radio documentaries BBC 1981-82, writer Time Out magazine 1982-88 (ed 1988-89), news feature writer Independent on Sunday newspaper 1990-; winner: Guardian/NUS Student Journalist of the Year 1981, Br Soc of Magazine Editors' Ed of the Year (Time Out) 1989; *Books* Expensive Habits: The Dark Side of the Music Industry (1986); *Recreations* painting, music, poker, cricket; *Clubs* Two Brydges Place; *Style*— Simon Garfield, Esq; Independent on Sunday, 3rd Floor, 40 City Rd, London EC1Y 2DB (☎ 071 415 1316, fax 071 415 1333)

GARFIT, Thomas Noel Cheney; s of Edward Christopher Cheney Garfit (d 1982), of Louth, Lincolnshire, and Dorothy Marguerite, *née* Morris (d 1978); *b* 27 Feb 1925; *Educ* Bryanston, Trinity Coll Cambridge (BA); *m* 3 May 1958, Elizabeth Mary, da of Lt-Col John Wilton Watts (d 1984), of Warminster, Wilts; 2 da (Frances Jane b 1962, Emma Anne b 1965); *Career* RA 1944-47 (cmmnd 1945); HMOCS N Rhodesia 1950-66, dist offr and private sec to the Govr 1956-57; Oil & Chemical Plant Constructors' Assoc 1966- (dir 1975-); *Clubs* Royal Cwlth Soc; *Style*— Thomas N C Garfit, Esq; Meadows Court, Fir Tree Close, Esher, Surrey KT10 9DS (☎ 0372 66061); 87 Regent St, London W1R 7HF (☎ 071 734 5246)

GARFITT, His Hon Judge Alan; s of Rush Garfitt, and Florence Garfitt; *b* 20 Dec 1920; *Educ* King Edward VII GS King's Lynn, Metropolitan Coll, Inns of Court Sch of Law (LLB); *m* 1, 1941, Muriel Ada Jaggers; 1 s, 1 da; m 2, 1973, Ivie Maud Hudson; m 3, 1978, Rosemary Lazell; 1 s, 1 da; *Career* barrister Lincoln's Inn 1948, circuit judge 1977-, judge Cambridge County Court and Wisbech Crown Court 1978-; memb Assoc of British Riding Schs 1960- (pres 1977-, fell 1989); hon fell Faculty of Law Univ of Cambridge 1978; *Style*— His Hon Judge Garfitt; Leap House, Barcham Rd, Soham, Ely, Cambs

GARGETTE, Simon Rupert John; s of J H Gargette, and Heather Patricia Jacques, *née* Grierson; *b* 15 Oct 1960; *Educ* Plymouth Southway, Plymouth Coll of Art, Watford Coll of Advertising; *Career* advertising copywriter 1979-80, photographer 1980-86; film dir: Shell Industry Gold 1986, BR Industry Gold 1988; creative dir Coats Viyella, commercials dir Matthews and Gargette (formerly Matthews and Humphries) 1989; memb: Age Concern, ACTT; *Clubs* ICA; *Style*— Simon Gargette, Esq; Mathews and Gargette, 60/66 Wardour St, W1V 3HP (☎ 071 439 0036/9, fax 071 7345973)

GARLAND, Nicholas Withycombe; s of Thomas Ownsworth Garland, and Margaret, *née* Withycombe; *b* 1 Sept 1935; *Educ* Rongotai Coll NZ, Slade Sch Fine Art; *m* 1, 1964 (m dis 1968), Harriet Crittall; m 2, 19 Dec 1969, Caroline Beatrice, da of Sir Peter Medawar; 3 s (Timothy William b 1957, Alexander Medawar b 1970, Theodore Nicholas b 1972), 1 da (Emily b 1964); *Career* political cartoonist: Daily Telegraph 1966-1986, The Independent 1986-; *Style*— Nicholas Garland, Esq; 27 Heath Hurst Rd, London NW3 2RU (☎ 071 435 3808); The Independent, 40 City Rd, London EC1 (☎ 071 253 1222)

GARLAND, Patrick; s of Capt Ewart Garland, DFC, RFC (d 1985), of Brockenhurst Hants, and Rosalind (d 1984), da of Herbert Granville Fell; *b* 10 April 1935; *Educ* St Mary's Coll Southampton, St Edmund Hall Oxford (MA); *m* 1980, Alexandra Bastedo; *Career* artistic dir Festival Theatre Chichester 1981-85; prodr: Fanfare for Europe at Covent Garden 1975, Fanfare for Elizabeth (for HM the Queen's 60 birthday) 1986, Celebration of a Broadcaster Westminster Abbey 1987, cantata The Plague and the Moonflower for Inter-Parly Union St Paul's Cathedral; interviews on television: Laurence Olivier 1987, Rex Harrison 1987; dir: Brief Lives, Forty Years On, Billy, Snow Goose (film), The Doll's House (film), The Secret of Sherlock Holmes (Wyndhams Theatre) 1989; organised Thanksgiving Serv for Lord Olivier (with Dean of Westminster) at Westminster Abbey 1989; *Books* Wings of the Morning (1988); *Recreations* idling in Corsica; *Clubs* Garrick; *Style*— Patrick Garland, Esq

GARLAND, Hon Mr Justice; Sir Patrick Neville; s of Frank Neville Garland (d 1984), and Marjorie, *née* Lewis (d 1972); *b* 22 July 1929; *Educ* Uppingham, Sidney Sussex Coll Cambridge (MA, LLM); *m* 1955, Jane Elizabeth, da of Harold John Bird, JP (d 1970), of Troston, Suffolk; 2 s, 1 da; *Career* called to the Bar Middle Temple 1953; asst rec Norwich 1971, rec Crown Court 1972, QC 1972, bencher Middle Temple 1979, dep High Ct judge 1981, High Ct judge Queen's Bench 1985; pres: Official Referees' Bar Assoc 1982-85, Central Cncl of Probation Ctees 1986-; vice chm Parole Bd 1989-90 (memb 1988-90); presiding judge S Eastern circuit 1989-; kt 1985; *Recreations* gardening, shooting, industl archaeology; *Clubs* Cumberland Lawn Tennis, Norfolk; *Style*— Hon Sir Patrick Garland; c/o Royal Courts of Justice, Strand, London WC2A 2LL

GARLAND, Dr Peter Bryan; s of Frederick George Garland (d 1978), and Molly Kate, *née* Jones; *b* 31 Jan 1934; *Educ* Hardye's Sch Dorchester, Downing Coll Cambridge (Athletics blue), Kings Coll Hosp London (MA, MB BChir, PhD); *m* 7 Feb 1959, Ann, da of Arthur Apseley Bathurst (d 1951); 1 s (James b 1964), 2 da (Joanna b 1961, Clare b 1962); *Career* reader in biochemistry Univ of Bristol 1967-70 (lectr 1964-68), prof of biochemistry Univ of Dundee 1970-84, visiting fell Aust Nat Univ Canberra 1983, princ scientist and head of biosciences Unilever Res Colworth House Laboratory 1984-87, dir of res Amersham Int 1987-89, chief exec Inst of Cancer Res London 1989-; author of numerous original articles on biochemistry and biophysics; visiting prof Johnson Res Fndn Philadelphia 1967-69, memb MRC 1980-84 (chm Cell Biology Disorders Bd 1980-82), memb Scientific Ctee Cancer Res Campaign 1985-, chm Cancer Res Campaign Technol Ltd 1988-; Colworth Medal of the Biochemical Society 1970; FRSE 1977, memb EMBO 1981; *Recreations* sport, skiing, windsurfing, sailing, theatre; *Clubs* Athenaeum, Bosham Sailing; *Style*— Dr Peter B Garland; 17A Onlsow Gardens, London SW7 (☎ 071 352 8133)

GARLAND, Hon Sir (Ransley) Victor; KBE (1981); s of Idris Victor Garland; *b* 5 May 1934; *Educ* Hale Sch, W Aust Univ (BA); *m* 1960, Lynette May Jamieson; 2 s, 1 da; *Career* memb House Reps (Lib) for Curtin W Aust 1969-81, Aust Min Supply 1971-72, opposition chief whip 1974-75, chm Expenditure Ctee 1975-77; min: Special Trade Rep 1977-79, Business and Consumer Affrs 1979-81; Aust high cmmr London 1981-83; dir: Prudential Corp plc 1984-, TR Far East Tst 1984, Throgmorton Tst 1985, Berkeley Funding Ltd 1985, Lefington Securities Ltd 1989; dep chm South Bank Bd, Royal Cwlth Soc for the Blind; FCA; *Clubs* White's, Weld (Australia); *Style*— Hon Sir Victor Garland, KBE; Wilton Place, Knightsbridge, London SW1

GARLAND, William John Harley; s of Patrick John Garland, of Pitmarston Court, Moseley, Birmingham, and Ruth, *née* Massey; *b* 14 Jan 1942; *Educ* Bloxham Sch, Univ of Aston (BSc); *m* 1 Oct 1966, Carol Ann, da of Eric Arley Whitehouse (d 1982), of Birmingham Rd, Dudley, W Midlands; 2 s (Simon b 1968, Edward b 1972), 1 da (Catherine b 1978); *Career* chm and co-fndr Anglo-Holt Group Inc 1969; former pres BEC Birmingham, memb Cncl Birmingham Chamber of Indust and Commerce; MICE 1971; *Recreations* the English countryside, model steam railways, antiques; *Style—* William Garland, Esq; Parkdale, 594 Warwick Rd, Solihull B91 1AD (☎ 021 705 4062); Anglo-Holt Group Ltd, 150 Birmingham Rd, W Bromwich, W Midlands B70 6QT (☎ 021 525 6717, fax 021 553 4701)

GARLICK, Sir John; KCB (1976, CB 1973); s of late Charles Garlick; *b* 17 May 1921; *Educ* Westcliff HS Essex, Univ of London (BSc); *m* 1945, Frances Esther, da of late Edward Stanley Munday; 3 da; *Career* entered Miny of Tport 1948, private sec to Ernest Marples 1959-60, second perm sec Cabinet Off 1974-77, perm sec Dept Environment 1978-81, dir Abbey National Building Soc 1981-; memb London Docklands Devpt Corpn 1981-, chm Alcohol Concern 1986-; *Style—* Sir John Garlick, KCB; 16 Astons Rd, Moor Park, Northwood, Middx (☎ 09274 24628)

GARLICK, Dr Kenneth John; s of David Ernest Garlick (d 1947), of Glastonbury, and Annie, *née* Hallifax (d 1962); *b* 1 Oct 1916; *Educ* Elmhurst GS, Balliol Coll Oxford (MA), Courtauld Inst of Art, Univ of London, Univ of Birmingham (PhD); *Career* WWII RAF Signals, served UK, N Africa, Italy, demob Flt-Lt 1946; lectr art history and librarian Bath Acad of Art 1946-48, Fine Art Dept Br Cncl London 1948, asst keeper City Art Gallery Birmingham 1948-50, sr lectr Barber Inst of Fine Arts Univ of Birmingham 1950-68, keeper of Western Art Ashmolean Museum Oxford Univ 1968-84, fell Balliol Coll Oxford 1968-84 (emeritus fell 1984-); govr Royal Shakespeare Theatre Stratford Upon Avon, memb Ctee Oxford Preservation Tst, memb Cncl Friends of Ashmolean; FMA, FSA, FRSA; *Books* Sir Thomas Lawrence (1954), Lawrence Catalogue Raisonné (1964), The Farington Diary Vol I-IV (ed with Angus MacIntyre, 1977-78), Sir Thomas Lawrence (catalogue of paintings, 1989); *Recreations* travel in France and Italy, music; *Clubs* Reform; *Style—* Dr Kenneth Garlick, FSA; 39 Hawkswell House, Hawkswell Gdns, Oxford OX2 7EX (☎ 0865 53731)

GARLING, Dr David John Haldane (Ben); s of Leslie Ernest Garling, and Frances Margaret, *née* Hannah; *b* 26 July 1937; *Educ* Highgate Sch, St John's Coll Cambridge (BA, MA, PhD, ScD); *m* 30 Aug 1963, Anthea Mary Eileen (Ann), da of George Richard Septimus Dixon, MBE (d 1983); 2 s (Hugh b 1969, Owen b 1974), 1 da (Julia b 1972); *Career* Nat Serv RA 1955-57; fell St John's Coll Cambridge 1963- (tutor 1971-78, pres 1987-), lectr Cambridge Univ 1964-78 (asst lectr 1963-64), head Dept Pure Maths and Mathematical Statistics Cambridge Univ 1984- (reader mathematical analysis 1978-); memb: Maths Ctee SERC 1981-84, London Mathematical Soc 1963- (memb Cncl 1984-87), Cambridge Philosophical Soc 1963-; *Books* Galois Theory (1986); *Style—* Dr Ben Garling; St John's College, Cambridge (☎ 0223 338600, fax 0223 338762)

GARMOYLE, Hon Hugh Sebastian Frederick Cairns; s and h of Viscount Garmoyle and gs of 5 Earl Cairns; *b* 26 March 1965; *Educ* Eton; *Style—* Lord Garmoyle

GARNELL, Lady Caroline Louise; *née* Bridgeman; yr da of 6 Earl of Bradford (d 1981); *b* 18 April 1952; *Educ* Benenden; *m* 1974, Brian Martin Garnell; 2 s (Thomas, Benedict), 1 da (Tara); *Style—* The Lady Caroline Garnell; 16 Holland Park Avenue, London W11 3QU

GARNER, Alan; s of Colin Garner (d 1983), of Cheshire, and Marjorie, *née* Greenwood Stuart; *b* 17 Oct 1934; *Educ* Manchester GS, Magdalen Coll Oxford; *m* 1, 1956, Ann, da of Harry Cook (d 1976), of Oxford; 1 s (Adam), 2 da (Ellen, Katharine); m 2, 1972, Griselda, da of Paul Greaves (d 1986), of St Petersburg, Russia; 1 s (Joseph b 1973), 1 da (Elizabeth b 1975); *Career* Mil Serv Lt RA; author; *plays*: Holly from the Bongs (1965), Lamaload (1978), Lurga Lom (1980), To Kill a King (1980), Sally Water (1982), The Keeper (1983); *dance drama*: The Green Mist (1970); *libretti*: The Bellybag (1971), Potter Thompson (1972); *films*: The Owl Service (1969), Red Shift (1978), Places and Things (1978), Images (1981, First Prize Chicago Int Film Festival); *Books* The Weirdstone of Brisingamen (1960), The Moon of Gomrath (1963), Elidor (1965), Holly from the Bongs (1966), The Old Man of Mow (1967), The Owl Service (1967, Library Assoc Carnegie Medal 1967, Guardian Award 1968), The Hamish Hamilton Book of Goblins (1969), Red Shift (1973), The Breadhorse (1975), The Guizer (1975), The Stone Book (1976), Tom Fobble's Day (1977), Granny Reardun (1977), The Aimer Gate (1978), Fairy Tales of Gold (1979), The Lad of the Gad (1980), A Book of British Fairy Tales (1984), A Bag of Moonshine (1986); *Recreations* work; *Clubs* The Portico Library; *Style—* Alan Garner, Esq; Blackden, Holmes Chapel, Cheshire CW4 8BY

GARNER, Anthony James; s of Lt Cdr Frederick Ernest Garner, DSC, RN (d 1976), of Carysfort, Malford Grove, Snaresbrook, Essex, and Sunshine, The Parade, Birchington-on-Sea, Kent, and Gertrude Eleanor, *née* Penwarden (d 1988); *b* 2 May 1925; *Educ* Uppingham, Hertford Coll Oxford (MA); *m* 16 April 1955, Catherine, da of William Talbot (d 1926), of Ramsgate; 2 s (Anthony Frederick John b 1956, William Talbot b 1970), 3 da (Elizabeth Catherine b 1957, Julia Nonie (Mrs Bouverat) b 1962, Mary Ann Frances (Mrs Richardson) b 1966); *Career* WWII volunteered RNVR 1943; Ordinary Seaman: HMS Ganges 1943, HMS Dauntless 1944, HMS King Alfred 1944; Midshipman 1944, Temp Actg Sub Lt 1944, HMS Woolston 1945; articled clerk Reid Sharman & Co 1947-51, admitted slr 1951, Freshfields 1951-53, Wray Smith Paterson & Co 1954, legal asst to Official Slr the Church Cmmrs 1954, conveyancing slr ICI plc 1957-81; dir: Levancroft Ltd 1978-, Iverna Covat Freehold Co Ltd 1989-; underwriting memb Lloyds 1964-; hon slr 625 Sqdn RAF Assoc; memb numerous orgns and socs incl: Uppingham Assoc and School Soc, Chelsea Cons Assoc, Huguenot Soc, CLA, Friends of Bodleian; Freeman City of London, Memb Worshipful Co of Loriners; friend Soc of St John The Evangelist; memb Law Soc 1951; *Recreations* bibliophile, gardening, swimming, music; *Clubs* Boodle's Hurlingham, St Stephen's Constitutional, Royal Temple YC, City Livery, Canning (Oxford); *Style—* Anthony Garner, Esq; 7 Iverna Ct, Kensington, London W8 6TY (☎ 071 937 1313), The Manor House, Great Mongeham, Deal, Kent CT14 9LR

GARNER, Sir Anthony Stuart; s of Edward Henry Garner, MC (d 1953), and Dorothy May Garner (d 1985); *b* 28 Jan 1927; *Educ* Liverpool Coll; *m* 1967, Shirley, da of William Henry Taylor (d 1963), of East Grinstead; 2 s; *Career* Grenadier Gds 1945-48; Cons agent Halifax 1951-56, nat organising sec of Young Cons Movement 1956-61; agent CCO: London area 1961-64, Western area 1964-66, NW area 1966-76; dir of orgn CCO 1976-88, Parly conslt 1988-; dir: Anglo Soviet Devpt Corp Ltd, Carroll Anglo American Corp Inc; life govr Liverpool Coll, memb Ctee Royal Liverpool Sch for the Blind; kt 1984; *Recreations* boating, theatre; *Clubs* Carlton, St Stephen's; *Style—* Sir Anthony Garner; 1 Blomfield Rd, London W9 (☎ 071 286 5972)

GARNER, Hon Christopher John Saville; s of Baron Garner, GCMG (d 1983; Life Peer); *b* 28 Feb 1939; *Educ* Highgate, Jesus Coll Cambridge; *m* 6 April 1962, Janet Mary, o da of Maj Harold Vaughan Rees, of Winnersham, Wokingham, Berks; 1 s; *Career* British Council officer 1963-71, asst rep Freetown Sierra Leone 1964-67, Staff Recruitment Dept British Council London 1967-70, asst rep Athens Greece 1970-71; lectr College of Technology Bournemouth 1971; *Style—* Hon Christopher Garner

GARNER, Frederick Leonard; s of Leonard Frank Garner (d 1968), and Florence Emily Garner; *b* 7 April 1920; *Educ* Sutton Co Sch; *m* 1953, Giovanna Maria, da of Pietro Anzani (d 1975), of Milan, Italy; *Career* pres Pearl Assurance Co: dir 1971-75, dep chm 1975-77, chm 1977-83, pres 1983-87; pres Pearl Group plc 1986-89; *Clubs* RAC; *Style—* Frederick Garner, Esq; 98 Tudor Ave, Worcester Park, Surrey KT4 8TU (☎ 081 337 3313)

GARNER, Hon Joseph Jonathan; s of Baron Garner, GCMG (d 1983, Life Peer); *b* 29 Dec 1940; *Educ* Highgate, Jesus Coll Cambridge; *m* 3 May 1969, Brigitte, da of Louis Pittet, of Sens, France; 1 s; *Style—* The Hon Joseph Garner; 44 Holmewood Rd, SW2

GARNER, His Hon Judge Michael Scott; s of William Garner (d 1968), of Huddersfield, and Doris Mary, *née* Scott (d 1958); *b* 10 April 1939; *Educ* Huddersfield Coll, Univ of Manchester (LLB); *m* 1, 30 July 1964, Sheila Margaret (d 1981), da of Edward Frederick Garland (d 1972); 1 s (John William Scott b 1968), 1 da (Caroline Louise b 1966); m 2, 12 Aug 1982, Margaret Anne, da of Philip Senior (d 1985); *Career* admitted slr 1965; asst rec 1978-85, rec 1985-88, circuit judge 1988-; pres Huddersfield Inc Law Soc 1985-86; *Recreations* motoring, walking, watching opera; *Style—* His Hon Judge Michael Garner; c/o Circuit Administrator, West Riding House, Albion St, Leeds

GARNER, Peter Frederick; s of Lt Cdr Frederick Ernest Garner, DSC, RN, and Gertrude Eleanor, *née* Penwarden; *b* 24 Feb 1936; *Educ* Uppingham; *m* 14 Oct 1961, (Elizabeth) Wendy, da of Benjamin John Jones, of Lampeter, Dyfed; 2 s (Robert Charles b 1964, Julian Peter b 1966); *Career* dir E Garner & Co clothing manufacture 1957-75, business devpt conslt Minet Insurance brokers 1975-89, funding conslt Shaftesbury Soc and other Christian projects 1990-; occasional speaker on Christian standards in the world of work; Anglican churchman; Freeman City of London, Liveryman Worshipful Co of Loriners; *Recreations* golf, sailing, conversation, gardening; *Style—* Peter F Garner, Esq; Flat 3, Kemble House, Broad Street, Hereford HR4 9AR (☎ 0432 342647)

GARNER, Stephen; s of Arthur Garner (d 1964), of Pedley Hill, Adlington, nr Macclesfield, Cheshire, and Madeline, *née* Turner; *b* 4 April 1901; *Educ* Ryleys Sch Cheshire, Univ of Liverpool (BARCH, MCD); *Career* Nat Serv RN 1949-50, Serv HMS Illustrious; architect, formed Garner Preston & Strebel 1960; awards: Dumbarton central area redevpt (first prize), town square and riverfront Dumbarton (civic tst), St Peter's Church Dumbarton (RIBA); ctee memb Housing Partnership Ltd, memb Richmond Soc; *Recreations* travel, water colour painting, poetry & music; *Style—* Stephen Garner, Esq; 1A Limpsfield Ave, Wimbledon, London SW19 6DL (☎ 081 788 6477); Garner, Preston & Strebel, 14 The Green, Richmond, Surrey 1PX (☎ 081 940 8244, fax 081 948 0367)

GARNER-CLARKE, Hon Mrs; Caroline Patricia; *née* Bagot; da of 9 Baron Bagot, and Patricia Muriel, *née* Moore-Boyle; *b* 6 May 1942; *m* 1962 (m dis 1985), Hugh Alexander James Cameron-Rose; 1 s (Hugh b 1962), 1 da (Georgina b 1968); m 2, 1991, Peter Garner-Clarke of Edenbridge, Kent; *Recreations* cookery, sailing, shooting; *Style—* The Hon Mrs P Garner-Clarke; c/o Silvermans, 11 High Street, Barnet, Herts

GARNETT, Hon Mrs (Anne Jeanetta Essex); *née* Cholmondeley; yr da of 4 Baron Delamere (d 1979); *b* 2 Sept 1927; *m* 30 Nov 1951, Conrad Peter Almeric Garnett, s of Dr Donald Goddard Garnett (d 1988), of Maresfield, E Sussex; 1 s (and 1 s decd 1981); *Style—* The Hon Mrs Garnett; Burnside House, Easter Balgedie, Tayside, Scotland KY13 7HQ (☎ 0592 84578)

GARNETT, Hon Mrs (Dariel); *née* Rawlinson; 2 da of Baron Rawlinson of Ewell, QC, by his 1 w; *b* 1943; *m* 1965, Harry Garnett; 2 da; *Style—* Hon Mrs Garnett; 32 Northumberland Place, London W2

GARNETT, Gerald Archer; s of Leslie Pearson Garnett (d 1985), of Westcliff-on-sea, Essex, and Betty Gladys, *née* Archer; *b* 1 March 1937; *Educ* Framlingham Coll Suffolk, INSEAD Fountainbleau; *m* 24 Feb 1973, Sheila Mary, da of Col David Bruce Ronald, CBE, of West Byfleet, Surrey; 1 s (Rupert b 13 Feb 1978), 1 da (Clare b 20 May 1980); *Career* RAF 1955-57; sec Ranks Hovis McDougall plc 1979 - (asst sec 1971-79); Freeman City of London, Liveryman Worshipful Co of Armourers and Brasiers; FCIS; *Recreations* gardening, squash, tennis; *Clubs* Naval and Military; *Style—* Gerald Garnett, Esq; Southbury Farmhouse, Ruscombe, Berks (☎ 0734 340132); Ranks Hovis McDougall plc, RHM Centre, Windsor, Berks (☎ 0753 857123, fax 0753 846537, telex 847314)

GARNETT, (William) John Poulton Maxwell; CBE (1970); s of Dr (James Clerk) Maxwell Garnett, CBE (d 1958), and Margaret Lucy Poulton; *b* 6 Aug 1921; *Educ* Rugby, Kent Sch (USA), Trinity Coll Cambridge; *m* 1, 1943 (m dis), Barbara, da of Dr Rex Rutherford-Smith; 2 s, 2 da (*see* Bottomley, Virginia, MP); m 2, 3 April 1985, Julia Cleverdon, *qv*; 2 da (Charity b 1982, Victoria b 1987); *Career* with ICI 1947-62, former dep chm UNA; dir: Spencer Stuart and Assocs Mgmnt Conslts (chm 1979-81), Industl Soc 1962-86; chm West Lambeth Health Authy 1986-90; *Style—* John Garnett, Esq, CBE; 3 Carlton House Terrace, London SW1

GARNETT, Nicholas Ian; s of Thomas Cyril Garnett (d 1988), and Anne, *née* Evans (d 1988); *b* 25 May 1950; *Educ* Hanson GS Bradford, Pembroke Coll Cambridge (MA); *Career* trainee Thomson Regional Newspapers (Evening Post, Reading) 1972-77; Financial Times: labour reporter 1977-81, northern corr 1981-86, engrg corr 1986-90, Minding Your Own Business Column Weekend Financial Times 1990-; *Style—* Nicholas Garnett, Esq; 29 Moreton Terrace, Pimlico, London SW1V 2NS (☎ 071 834 5855); Financial Times, No 1 Southwark Bridge, London SE1 (☎ 071 873 3000 ext 4057)

GARNETT, Hon Mrs (Sylvia Jane); er da of Baron Swann (Life Peer, d 1990), and Teresa Ann, *née* Gleadowe; *b* 1 April 1947; *Educ* St Andrews Univ (BSc); *m* 1970, Christopher William Maxwell Garnett; 1 s (Simon), 2 da (Lucy, Emma); *Style—* The Hon Mrs Garnett; 40 Caledonia Place, Clifton, Bristol 8

GARNHAM, Caroline Xania; da of Edward Hatch (d 1981), of Guildford, and Elisabeth Houtman; *b* 10 Oct 1955; *Educ* George Abbott Sch for Girls Guildford, Univ of Exeter (BSc); *m* 30 Dec 1977 (m dis 1984), Hugh Laurence, s of Jack Garnham; *Career* tax ptnr Taylor Joynson Garrett; writer: Saturday Financial Times (family and fin page), International Magazine; speaker personal tax int fin seminars; memb Law Soc; *Recreations* hunting, skiing, reading; *Style—* Ms Caroline Garnham; 2 Pelican Wharf, Wapping Wall, Wapping, London E1 1AA (☎ 071 702 2599); 4 Paradise Row, Hampnett, Gloucestershire (☎ 0451 60278); Taylor Joynson Garrett, 10 Maltravers St, London WC2R 3BS (☎ 071 836 8456, fax 071 379 7196, telex 268014 DHICKS G)

GARNHAM, Dr John Claude; s of Percy Cyril Claude Garnham, CMG, of Southernwood, Farnham Common, Bucks, and Esther Long, *née* Price; *b* 7 May 1932; *Educ* Merchant Taylor's, Univ of Paris (Dip de CF), Univ of London (MB BS), Med Coll of St Barts Hosp London; *m* 11 Dec 1954, Frances Joan, da of Frank Kirkup (d 1951); 3 s (Timothy Claude b 1956, Frank Jasper b 1959, Simon Philip b 1960), 1 da (Francesca b 1971); *Career* med practice 1957-65, clinical res 1965-, vice pres med affrs Abbott Laboratories USA 1970-71, private med practice 1980-; chm Chiltern Int Ltd Barbican Med plc, med dir Haventern Laboratories Ltd, dir Cardiac Res Wexham

Park Hosp Slough; Freeman City of London, memb Ct Worshipful Co of Farriers; fell Amercian Soc of Clinical Pharmacology & Therapeutics; memb: BMA, Br Soc of Pharmacology MRCS, LRCP, FRSM, FRSTM&H, FFPM RCP 1989; *Recreations* fishing, clay pigeon shooting, bridge, golf, tennis, riding; *Clubs* Guards Polo, City Livery; *Style*— Dr John Garnham; Kynance, Manor Rd, Penn, Bucks HP10 8JB (☎ 0494 812 177); Barbican Medical plc, 3 White Lyon Ct, Barbican, London EC1 (☎ 071 588 3146)

GARNHAM, Michael Anthony (Mike); s of Robert Arthur Garnham, of Perth, W Aust, and Pauline Anne, *née* Shears; *b* 20 Aug 1960; *Educ* Camberwell GS Melbourne Aust, Scotch Coll Perth Aust, Park Sch Barnstaple, N Devon Sixth Form Coll, UEA; *m* 15 Sept 1984, Lorraine; 2 da (Laura Clare b 3 Nov 1988, Eleanor Louise b 22 Oct 1990); *Career* professional cricketer; minor cos Devon CCC 1975-76, Gloucestershire CCC 1979-80, Leicestershire CCC 1980-85 and 1988, retired from first class cricket for 3 years and played for Cambridgeshire CCC 1986-88 (also Minor Cos), Essex CCC 1989-, awarded county cap 1990; England schs tour India 1978-79, Young England tour Aust 1979; achievements incl: scored winning runs Benson & Hedges Cup final Leics 1985, Young Wicketkeeper of the Year 1979, Man of the Match Cambs v Warwicks Nat West Trophy 1988; former proprietor wicketkeeping gloves mfrs, exhibition of furniture 1991; *Recreations* making reproduction antique pine furniture, renovating buildings, squash, environmental issues; memb: WWF, Friends of the Earth, Alternative Technology Assoc, Essex Wildlife Tst; *Style*— Mike Garnham, Esq; c/o Essex County Cricket Club, County Ground, New Writtle St, Chelmsford CM2 OPG (☎ 0245 252420)

GARNHAM, Roy Richard; s of Alfred Joseph Garnham (d 1990), and Elizabeth Louise, *née* Stannard (d 1986); *b* 7 July 1938; *Educ* Parmiters GS London; *m* 10 Feb 1962, Sylvia, da of Joseph Derwent, of Oliver Rd, Shenfield, Essex; 3 s (Ian Roy Cuckow b 8 Aug 1966, Matthew Richard b 5 Nov 1968, Peter Joseph b 9 June 1971); *Career* princ foreign exchange dealer Bank of London & S America London 1955-73, exec dir London & Continental Bankers London 1973-77; gen mangr: Euro Arab Bank Bahrain 1977-80, DG Bank London 1980-; non-exec dir Product Fin Ltd 1985-89, md London Continental Bankers 1989; memb: Overseas Bankers Club, Forex Club of London, Lombard Assoc, Foreign Banks Assoc; *Recreations* gardening, golf; *Clubs* Warley Park Golf; *Style*— Roy Garnham, Esq; Wellmead, Fryerning La, Ingatestone, Essex (☎ 0277 353 705); DG Bank, 10 Aldersgate, London, EC1A 4XX (☎ 071 726 6791, telex 886647)

GARNIER, Edward Henry; s of William d'Arcy Garnier (Col RA, d 1989), and Hon Mrs Garnier (*née* Hon Lavender Hyacinth de Grey), *qv*; *b* 26 Oct 1952; *Educ* Wellington, Jesus Coll Oxford (BA, MA); *m* 17 April 1982, Anna Caroline, da of Michael James Mellows (d 1974), of Belton House, Rutland; 2 s (George b 1986, James William b 1991), 1 da (Eleanor b 1983); *Career* called to the Bar Middle Temple 1976; vice pres Hemsworth Cons Assoc, contested: Wandsworth Borough Cncl by-election 1984, Tooting ILEA election 1986, Hemsworth W Yorks gen election 1987; govr Graveney Sch Tooting, prospective Parly candidate (Cons) Harborough Leics; *Books* contrib Halsbury's Laws of England (4 edn); *Recreations* cricket, shooting, opera; *Clubs* Carlton, United and Cecil; *Style*— Edward Garnier, Esq; 70 Streathbourne Rd, London SW17 (☎ 081 767 4961); Chambers, 1 Brick Ct, Temple, London EC4Y 9BY (☎ 071 353 8845, fax 071 583 9144)

GARNIER, Maj Edward Hethersett Charles; MC (1942); s of Edward Thomas Garnier (d 1924), and Dorothy Maude, *née* Hemsworth (d 1962); *b* 7 March 1920; *Educ* Eton, RMC Sandhurst; *m* 4 July 1946, Alice Mary, da of Charles Henry Hale Monro (d 1966); 2 s (Edward b 1948, Simon b 1950); *Career* cmmnd The Rifle Bde 1939, A/Maj 1942, Sub/Maj 1952, 1 Bn The Rifle Bde served UK, M East, Italy 1939-44 (despatches 1941 and 1943); instr 165 OTU 1944, Staff Coll (psc) 1944-45, BM 184 Inf Bde 1945, DAQMG Br troops Siam 1945-47, DAA and QMG 56 Armd Div 1949-51, DAA and QMG 29 Bde Korea 1953-54, MA to C-in-C FARELF 1956-57, DAA and QMG 20 Armd Bde 1959-61; fruit farmer 1968-90; chm and vice chm Shropham Parish Cncl 1970-, churchwarden Shropham Church 1968-, patron 5 livings, patronage bd for 8 livings, chm Hockham and Wretham Br Legion 1976-, memb Breckland DC 1970-78, area pres St John Ambulance Bde 1980-84 (area cmmr 1972-80), gen cmmr Income Tax 1976-; OStJ; *Recreations* shooting, gardening; *Clubs* Army and Navy, I Zingari, Free Foresters; *Style*— Maj Edward Garnier, MC; Shropham House, Attleborough, Norfolk (☎ 095 382 241)

GARNIER, Rear Adm Sir John; KCVO (1990, LVO 1965), CBE (1982); s of Rev Thomas Vernon Garnier (d 1939), and Helen Davis, *née* Stenhouse, of Stour View, The Bridge, Sturminster Newton, Dorset; *b* 10 March 1934; *Educ* Berkhamsted Sch, Britannia Royal Naval Coll; *m* 31 Dec 1966, Joanna Jane (Dodie), da of Alan Cadbury, of Haffield, Ledbury, Herefordshire; 2 s (Thomas b 1968, William b 1970), 1 da (Louisa b 1972); *Career* joined RN 1950, served in HMY Britannia 1956-57, HMS Tyne 1956, qualified navigation specialist 1959, Naval Equerry to HM The Queen 1962-65, cmd HMS Dundas 1968-69, Directorate of Naval Ops and Trade 1969-71, cmd HMS Minerva 1972-73, Def Policy Staff 1973-75, exec offr HMS Intrepid 1976, Asst Dir Naval Manpower Planning 1976-78, RCDS 1979, cmd HMS London 1980-81, Dir Naval Ops and Trade 1982-84, Cdre Amphibious Warfare 1985, Flag Offr Royal Yachts 1985-90, Extra Equerry to HM The Queen 1988; Younger Bro of Trinity House 1974, govr Sherborne Sch for Girls 1985-; Freeman City of London 1982; FIL 1965; *Recreations* sailing, gardening, opera, golf, stalking, computers; *Style*— Rear Adm Sir John Garnier, KCVO, CBE; The Old Rectory, Pulham, Dorchester, Dorset DT2 7EA

GARNIER, Hon Mrs (Lavender Hyacinth); *née* de Grey; el da of Lt-Col 8 Baron Walsingham, DSO, OBE, JP, DL (d 1965), and Hyacinth Lambart, *née* Bouwens (d 1968); *b* 14 Oct 1923; *m* 9 April 1946, Col William d'Arcy Garnier, RA (d 1989), yst s of Brig Alan Parry Garnier, CB, MBE, MC (whose paternal gf was Very Rev Thomas Garnier, fell of All Souls and successively dean of Lincoln and of Ripon, while the Brig's paternal grandmother was Lady Caroline Keppel, yst da of 4 Earl of Albemarle; the Dean was eighth in descent from Guillemin Garnier, of Joussecourt in the Champagne area of France and Seigneur du Tron, who flourished in sixteenth century); 3 s, 1 da; *Career* served WWII First Aid Nursing Yeo N Africa, Italy, India, Ceylon; *Style*— Hon Mrs Garnier; College Farm, Thompson, Thetford, Norfolk (☎ 095 383 318)

GARNIER, Thomas Stenhouse (Tom); s of Rev Thomas Vernon Garnier, OBE (d 1939), and Helen, *née* Stenhouse (later Mrs Davis); *b* 26 Oct 1932; *Educ* Berkhamsted Sch, Trinity Coll Oxford (MA), London Business Sch; *m* 11 Feb 1961, Heather Colquhoun, da of James Grant (d 1981); 2 s (Edward b 20 May 1966, James b 27 March 1981), 2 da (Rachel b 20 May 1968, Elisabeth b 7 Dec 1977); *Career* Kalamazoo plc: asst overseas sales mangr 1956-63, asst to md 1963-66, personnel divnl mangr 1966-68, dir i/c personnel and printing 1968-72, dir i/c sales and personnel 1972-74, dep md 1974-77, gp md 1977-87, gp chm 1985-89; chm: Kalamazoo Finance Ltd 1978-89, MBM Systems & Equipment Ltd Hong Kong 1982-89, K3 Software Services Ltd 1984-87, Alfred Gilbert & Sons Ltd 1984-86; administrateur Société Anonyme des Etablissements Kalamazoo 1974-86; dir: Birmingham Chamber Training Ltd 1987-, Kalamazoo (NZ) Ltd 1987-89; Birmingham Chamber of Indust & Commerce: memb Educn and Trg Ctee 1973-, ctee chm 1979-85, memb Working Pty on Industl Democracy 1977, memb Cncl 1980-, memb Gen Purposes Ctee 1981-, memb Mgmnt Ctee 1987-, vice pres 1987-89, chm Overseas Trade Policy Ctee 1987-89, pres 1989; Br Inst of Mgmnt: memb Working Pty on Indust Educn and Mgmnt 1976-77, memb Mgmnt Devpt Servs and Educn Ctee 1978-89, memb Cncl 1979-85, memb New Business Panel 1982-83, memb West Midlands Regnl Bd 1982-; tstee Middlemore Homes 1968-89, memb Bd Mgmnt Res Groups 1977-, memb West Midlands Economic Planning Cncl 1978-79, memb Bd Co-Operative Devpt Agency 1981-, memb West Midland Regnl Cncl CBI 1983-89; tstee RALI Fndn 1985-, chm Midlands Area Employer Advsy Cncl APEX Tst 1989, memb Bd Birmingham Trg and Enterprise Cncl 1989; CBIM 1982; *Recreations* languages, bridge, reading, riding, swimming; *Style*— Tom Garnier, Esq; 53 Gratton Rd, Cheltenham, Glos GL50 2BZ (☎ 0242 525126); Kalamazoo plc, Northfield, Birmingham B32 2RW (☎ 021 411 2345, fax 021 476 4293, telex 336700)

GARNSWORTHY, Baroness; Sue; da of Harold Taylor; *m* 1, Michael Farley; m 2, 1973, as his 2 w, Baron Garnsworthy, OBE (d 1974); 1 s (Hon Charles Edyvean b 1974); *Style*— The Rt Hon the Lady Garnsworthy; Little Dormers, Smithy Lane, Lower Kingswood, Tadworth, Surrey

GARRAN, Sir (Isham) Peter; KCMG (1961, CMG 1954); s of Sir Robert Randolph Garran, GCMG, QC (d 1956), and Hilda, *née* Robson (d 1936); *b* 15 Jan 1910; *Educ* Melbourne GS, Trinity Coll Melbourne (BA); *m* 1935, Mary Elisabeth, da of Sir Richard Rawdon Stawell, KBE (d 1935); 2 s, 1 da; *Career* Dip Serv 1934-70; Chief Political Div Control Cmmn Germany 1947-50, inspr Foreign Serv Estabs 1952-54, min (commercial) Br Embassy Washington 1954-60, ambass to Mexico 1960-64, ambass to the Netherlands 1964-70 (ret); dir: Lend Lease Corpn 1970-78, UK Branch AMP Soc 1970-82; chm: Quality Assur Cncl Br Standards Inst 1971-82, Securicor Nederland BV 1976-82; *Recreations* gardening; *Style*— Sir Peter Garran, KCMG; The Coach House, Collingbeams, Donhead St Mary, Shaftesbury, Dorset SP7 9DX (☎ 0747 828108)

GARRATT, Colin Dennis; s of Sqdn Ldr Dennis Herbert Garratt, of 1 Shepherd's Way, Uppingham, Leics, and Margaret Alice, *née* Clarke; *b* 16 April 1940; *Educ* Mill Hill Leicester; *m* 1, 1975 (m dis 1982), Stephanie Ann, da of Edwin Aliston Brick; m 2, Margaret Elizabeth, *née* Grzyb; 1 s (James Daniel b 2 Aug 1987); *Career* author; vice pres Br Overseas Railways Historical Tst; *Books* Symphony in Steam 1970, Twlight of Steam 1972, Masterpieces in Steam 1973, Steam Safari 1974, The Last of Steam 1976, Iron Dinosaurs 1976, Veterans in Steam 1979, Steam Locomotives of the World 1979, A Popular Guide to Preserved Steam Railways of Britain 1979, Taking Photographs 1979, Taking Photographs 1980, Colin Garratt's World of Steam 1981, Railway Photographer 1982, Preserved Steam Locomotives of Britain 1982, British Steam Lives 1984, Last Days of British Steam Railways 1985, Around the World in Search of Steam 1987, Steam Trains of the World 1979, Ironhorse 1987, British Steam Nostalgia 1987, China's Railways 1988, Steam Trains-A World Portrait 1989, Steam Trains-An American Portrait 1989; *Recreations* ornithology, politics, music, art, the appreciation of fine cigars; *Style*— Colin Garratt, Esq; The Square, Newton Harcourt, Leicester LE8 0FQ (☎ 053 7592068)

GARRATT, Stephen Kearsley; s of Maj George Herbert Garratt (d 1961), of Heron Bridge, Chester, and Aime Mary, *née* Norman (d 1960); *b* 17 May 1916; *Educ* Shrewsbury; *m* 17 Nov 1951, Felicity Ann De Laune, da of Capt Antony Percival Williams; 1 s (Jonathan), 2 da (Charlotte, Victoria); *Career* WWII serv: Middx Regt 1939, cmmnd 2 Lt Royal Berks Reg 1940, volunteered for RWAFF 1940, serv Sierra Leone Regt and Staff Capt Gen Woolner's HQ 1940-43, GSO3 to 21 Army Gp 1 Corps HQ (D Day planning staff) 1943-44, GSO3 Liason Offr 1 Corps 1944 (D Day until after Battle of Arnhem), Staff Coll Camberley 1944, magistrate in Mil Cts Legal Section of Mil Govt Berlin Dec 1944-45, demobbed with rank of Maj 1945; admitted slr 1939, official Slrs Office Royal Cts of Justice 1946, with Shell Int (China, Sri Lanka, Nigeria, London) 1947-61, PR advsr to Railways Bd 1961-66, PR sec to Law Soc 1966-69; currently ind art dealer specialising in pictures; memb London Diocesan Cncl; memb Law Soc 1939-89; *Recreations* polo, skiing; *Clubs* Garrick, Rhinefield Polo; *Style*— Stephen Garratt, Esq; 60 Addison Rd, London W14 (☎ 071 603 0681); Old Stagbury, Furzley, Bramshaw, Hants (☎ 0794 22298)

GARRATT, Timothy George; s of George Herbert Garratt (d 1976), of Chichester, Sussex, and Hylda Joyce, *née* Spalton (d 1958); *b* 7 Sept 1942; *Educ* Stowe; *m* 24 April 1965, Vanessa Ann, da of Charles Albert Wright (d 1980), of Chichester, Sussex; 2 s (Alastair b 1969, James b 1973); *Career* chartered surveyor; ptnr Rendells Auctioneers Valuers & Estate Agents S Devon 1976-; memb: Gen Cncl RICS 1969-73, Ctee Western Counties Agric Valuers Assoc (memb Agric Div Ctee Devon and Cornwall Branch); chm Devon and Cornwall Branch RICS 1989-90, pres: Chagford and Dist Lions Club 1984-85, Lions Club Int Zone (chm 1985-86); FAAV 1968, FRICS 1975; *Recreations* farming, sporting shooting, gardening; *Clubs* Lions Int, RICS 1913; *Style*— Timothy Garratt, Esq; Baileys Hey, Chagford, Devon TQ13 8AW (☎ 06473 3396); Rock House, Chagford, Devon TQ13 8AX

GARRET, Richard Anthony (Tony); CBE (1986); s of Charles Victor Garrett (d 1945), and Blanche, *née* Michell (d 1968); *b* 4 July 1918; *Educ* Kings Sch Worcester; *m* 5 Jan 1946, Marie Louise, da of Rear Adm Robin Campsie Dalglish (d 1937); 1 s (Rupert Charles Anthony b 8 July 1961), 2 da (Anne b 8 Jan 1947, Amanda b 2 Feb 1955); *Career* Royal Gloucs Hussars TA 1938, RMC Sandhurst 1940, WWII 22 Dragoons 1941-46; chm and md Imperial Tobacco ltd 1971-79 (joined 1936), dep chm HTV Group plc 1976-83, dir Standard Commercial Corporation USA 1981-; chm NABC 1980-87, tstee Glynebourne Arts Tst 1976-88; Freeman Worshipful Co of Tobacco Pipe Makers; CBIM, FID; *Recreations* golf, gardening, music; *Clubs* Naval & Military, MCC; *Style*— Tony Garrett, Esq, CBE; Marlwood Grange, Thornbury, Bristol BS12 2JB (☎ 0454 412630)

GARRETT, Anthony David (Tony); s of Sir William Garrett (d 1977), of Eastbourne, Sussex, and Lady Marion, *née* Houghton (d 1967); *b* 26 Aug 1928; *Educ* Ellesmere Coll, Clare Coll Cambridge (MA); *m* 17 May 1952, Monica, da of Richard V Harris (d 1976), of Sidmouth, Devon; 3 s (Nicholas b 1954, David b 1959, Mark b 1962), 1 da (Jennifer b 1956); *Career* Nat Serv 4 Queens Own Hussars 1946-8; md Proctor & Gamble UK & Italy 1969-73, vice pres int The Procter & Gamble Co 1973-82; bd memb The Post Office 1983-87, dep master and chief exec The Royal Mint 1988-; *Recreations* golf, bridge, chess, sailing, mountain walking, gardening; *Clubs* Utd Oxford & Cambridge; *Style*— Tony Garrett, Esq; Cammock House, Goldsmith Ave, Crowborough, E Sussex TN6 1RH

GARRETT, Colin Noël; s of Ernest Leslie Garrett, of Southwold, Suffolk, and Eileen Gladys, *née* May; *b* 3 June 1942; *Educ* Leighton Park Sch Reading, Kings Coll Cambridge (BA, MA), Univ de Nancy France; *m* 16 Sept 1967, Sarah Hamilton, da of Maj Geoffry Clemow Smith, MBE, of Cambridge; 2 da (Marion b 17 Dec 1971, Jill b 21 Feb 1974); *Career* articled clerk and asst slr Waterhouse & Co 1965-67, asst slr Few & Kester Cambridge 1968-69, co sec and slr AMOCO (UK) Ltd 1969-71, legal advsr Shell Int Petroleum Co London 1971-77, attorney Scallop Corporation NY 1977-79, legal advsr Shell London 1979-81, gp slr 3i Group plc London 1981-; memb Law Soc 1967, ABA 1977, NY Bar 1978; FBIM 1986; *Recreations* music, violin-making; *Clubs* Law Soc; *Style*— Colin Garrett, Esq; 17 North Rd, Berkhamsted, Herts HP4

3DX (☎ 0442 866 694); 91 Waterloo Rd, London SE1 8XP (☎ 071 928 3131, fax 071 928 0058, telex 917844)

GARRETT, Dr Daniel James (Dan); s of Harold Sinclair (d 1941), of Rochester, and Jenny, *née* Garrett; *b* 29 April 1941; *Educ* The Judd Sch Tonbridge, Fitzwilliam Coll Cambridge (BA), Univ of Hull (PhD); *m* 1 s (Reuben b 1974), 2 da (Tess b 1968, Leoni b 1971); *Career* head of drama Furzedown Coll 1972-75, chief prodr BBC Radio 1975-; memb: CND, Gauge O Guild; *Books* Drama Workshop Plays (4 vols, 1984), Family Frictions (1987), Girls (1988), Taking Issue (1988), Kids' Oz (with Warrill Grindrod, 1988), World in View: Australia (with Warrill Grindrod, 1989), World in View: Scandinavia (1990), World in View: Germany (with Charlotte Drews-Bernstein, 1990); *Recreations* gardening, model railways, railway history; *Clubs* Lewisham Labour; *Style—* Dr Dan Garrett; BBC (Schools Children's and Young People's Radio), Broadcasting House, London W1A 1AA (☎ 071 9275105, fax 071 6368226)

GARRETT, (William) Edward; MP (Lab) Wallsend 1964-; s of John Garrett, of Prudhoe-on-Tyne, Northumberland, and Frances, *née* Barwise; *b* 21 March 1920; *Educ* LSE; *m* 1, 1946, Beatrice (d 1976), da of John Kelly, of Prudhoe; 1 s; m 2, 1980, Noel Stephanie Ann Johnson; *Career* engr; memb AEU 1935, formerly with ICI; Parly candidate (Lab): Hexham 1955, Doncaster 1959; memb: Northumberland CC 1956, Expenditure Ctee House Commons 1971-79; Parly advsr: Machine Tool Trade Assoc 1973-, BAT Industries plc; memb Cncl of Europe 1979-; *Style—* Edward Garrett, Esq, MP; House of Commons, London SW1

GARRETT, Dr Geoffrey; s of James Garrett (d 1955), of Stockport, and Annie, *née* Dicken (d 1978); *b* 28 Feb 1927; *Educ* Manchester GS, Univ of Manchester (MD, MB ChB); *m* 2 Nov 1955, Marjorie May, da of Thomas Crook, of Bolton; 1 s (Michael b 8 Oct 1960), 1 da (Carolyn (Mrs Radcliff) b 17 Nov 1957); *Career* Nat Serv Lt (later Capt) RAMC 1953-55, Maj RAMC (TA) 1955-60; jr hosp posts Manchester 1955-60, conslt pathologist Oldham 1960-, pathologist Home Office 1968-; former pres Manchester Medico-Legal Soc; memb: BMA 1950, Br Assoc Forensic Med 1969, MRCPath 1961; *Recreations* golf; *Clubs* Lostock Park (Bolton); *Style—* Dr Geoffrey Garrett; Ash Fell, 306 Leigh Rd, Worsley, Manchester M28 4LH (☎ 061 790 3505); Royal Oldham Hospital, Oldham, Lancs OL1 2JH (☎ 061 665 3550)

GARRETT, Godfrey John; OBE (1982); s of Thomas Garrett (d 1978), and May Louisa, *née* Botten; *b* 24 July 1937; *Educ* Dulwich, Sidney Sussex Coll Cambridge (MA); *m* 23 March 1963, Elisabeth Margaret, *née* Hall; 4 s (Mark b 1964, Edward b 1967, William b 1968, Richard b 1970), 1 da (Anna b 1974); *Career* FO: joined 1961, third sec Kinshasa (formerly Leopoldville) 1963-65, second sec Prague 1965-68, first sec Buenos Aires 1971-73, first sec (later cnsllr) Stockholm 1981-83, cnsllr Bonn 1983-88, cnsllr E Berlin 1990, cnsllr Prague 1990; *Recreations* skiing, mountain walking, gardening, languages, photography; *Style—* Godfrey J Garrett, Esq, OBE; White Cottage, Henley, Haslemere, Surrey GU27 3HQ (☎ 0428 652172)

GARRETT, Maj Gen Henry Edmund Melvill Lennox; CBE (1975); s of John Edmund Garrett (d 1978), and Mary, *née* Jamieson; *b* 31 Jan 1924; *Educ* Wellington, Clare Coll Cambridge (MA); *m* 1973, Rachel Ann; 1 step s (Richard Beadon b 1961), 1 step da (Sarah Beadon b 1961); *Career* cmmnd 1944, Staff Coll 1956, US Armed Forces Staff Coll 1960, OC 7 Field Sqdn 1960, CO 35 Engr Regt 1965, Col GS, MOD 1968, Cdr 12 Engr Bde 1969, RCDS 1972, COS NI 1972, Maj Gen i/c admin UKLF 1975, Vice Adj Gen 1976, dir Army Security 1978-89; chm: Royal Engineers Assoc 1989, Forces Help Soc and Lord Roberts Workshop 1991; *Recreations* walking, riding; *Clubs* Army and Navy; *Style—* Maj Gen Lennox Garrett; c/o National Westminster Bank, 1 Market St, Bradford, W Yorks

GARRETT, John Francis; s of Dr George (d 1970), of Liverpool, and Louise Mary, *née* Harrison; *b* 1 Feb 1945; *Educ* Ampleforth, Liverpool Coll of Building, Harvard Business Sch (AMP); *m* Sept 1966, Patricia Margaret, da of John M Pinnington, of Scorton, Lancs; 1 s (Patrick b 1968), 3 da (Joanne b 1967, Kimberley b 1971, Jenni b 1974); *Career* md Gillette Australia 1980, regnl dir Gillette Australia N Zealand Pacific Basin 1983, pres Gillette Personal Care Europe 1986, non-exec dir Harrison and Jones 1985-; dir: Gillette Industries Ltd 1986-, Gillette Personal Care UK Ltd 1986-; *Recreations* rugby, cricket, golf, shooting; *Clubs* Stoke Poges Golf, Peninsula CGC (Aust), Harvard; *Style—* John Garrett, Esq; Gillette Industries Ltd, Great West Rd, Isleworth, Middx TW7 5NP (☎ 081 847 7475, fax 081 568 9357)

GARRETT, John Laurence; MP (Lab) Norwich South 1987-; s of Laurence Garrett, and Rosina Garrett; *b* 8 Sept 1931; *Educ* Sir George Monoux GS London, Univ of Oxford, UCLA Business Sch; *m* 1959, Wendy Ady; 2 da; *Career* former: lab offr in chem indust, head of market res in car indust, pub serv mgmnt conslt; dir int mgmnt consultancy practice; MP (Lab) Norwich South 1974-83, (contested 1983); PPS to: Civil Serv Min 1974, Social Security Min 1977-79; oppn spokesman: Treasy 1979-80, Energy 1987, Indust 1988- (1980-83); *Style—* John Garrett, Esq, MP

GARRETT, Prof John Raymond; s of Charles Raymond Garrett, MM (d 1976), of Winchester, and Irene Lily, *née* Rogers (d 1978); *b* 28 March 1928; *Educ* Peter Symonds Sch, King's Coll Hosp Dental Sch (LDS, RCS), King's Coll (BSc), King's Coll Hosp Med Sch (MB BS, PhD); *m* 28 April 1958, Daphne Anne, da of Edwin Owen Parr (d 1953); 1 s (Malcolm b 1964), 1 da (Claire b 1963); *Career* RADC Lt 1950-51, Capt 1951-52, Nat Serv active parachutist in Airbourne Servs in 23 Para Field Ambulance; res fell Nuffield 1961-64, sr lectr pathology King's Coll Hosp Med Sch 1964-, prof and head of Dept of Oral Pathology King's Coll Hosp Dental Sch 1971 (reader 1968) research into Secretary mechanisms; pres Int Fedn of Soc of Histochemistry and Cytochemistry, former pres Royal Microscopical Soc; Freeman City of London 1971, memb Worshipful Soc of Apothecaries; Hon MD Univ of Lund 1985; MRCPath 1965, FRCPath 1977; *Books* Histochemistry of Secretory Processes (1976); *Recreations* med history; *Style—* Prof John Garrett; 15 Deepdene Rd, London SE5 8EG (☎ 071 274 6488); The Rayne Inst, King's Coll Med Dental Sch, 123 Coadharbour Lane, London SE5 9NU (☎ 071 326 3019)

GARRETT, Nicholas Young; s of Geoffrey Elmer Garrett (d 1988), of 13 New Cavendish St, W1, and Josephine Honor Franklin, *née* Bishop (d 1988); *b* 5 June 1936; *Educ* Sherborne, Worcester Coll Oxford (MA); *Career* Nat Serv 2 Lt RA 1954-56 2 Lt RA; slr 1962, sr ptnr Ingledew Brown Bennison and Garrett 1974-88, conslt with Holmes Hardingham 1989-; *Recreations* reading, opera, television; *Clubs* Garrick; *Style—* Nicholas Garrett, Esq; 22-23 Great Tower St, London EC3 (☎ 071 283 0222)

GARRETT, Stephen James; s of James Leslie Michael Peter Garrett, of Sussex, and Margot, *née* Fleischner; *b* 16 April 1957; *Educ* Westminster, Merton Coll Oxford; *m* 22 June 1989, Layla Alla, da of Feodor Andreyev, of Tashkent, USSR; *Career* Granada TV Manchester 1978-81, BBC TV 1982-83; Channel Four: prodr Baby, Baby 1984, prodr and dir Redbrick 1985-86, prodr and dir with David Robinson Keeping Love Alive 1987, Commissioning ed youth progs 1988; *Recreations* tennis, photography, learning Russian; *Style—* Stephen Garrett, Esq; Channel 4 TV, 60 Charlotte St, London W1 (☎ 071 631 4444, fax 071 580 2618)

GARRETT, Terence; CMG (1990), CBE (1967); s of Percy Herbert Garrett (d 1972), and Gladys Annie, *née* Budd (d 1972); *b* 27 Sept 1929; *Educ* Alleyn's Sch, Gonville and Caius Coll Cambridge (MA); *m* 1960, Grace Elizabeth Bridgeman, yr da of Rev Basil Kelly Braund (d 1981); 2 s (Andrew b 1960, Charles b 1963) 3 da (Bridget b 1966, Katharine b 1969, Ruth (twin) b 1969); *Career* instr Lt RN 1952-55; lectr Ewell County Tech Coll 1955-56, sr lectr RMC of Sci Shrivenham 1957-62, Programmes Analysis Unit Miny of Technol 1967-70, scientific cnsllr Br Embassy Moscow 1970-74 (1962-66), Int Technol Collaboration Unit Dept of Trade 1974-76, sec to Bd Govrs and Gen Conf IAEA Vienna 1976-78, sci and tech cnsllr Br Embassy Bonn 1978-82; dep chief scientific offr Res and Technol Policy Div DTI 1982-87, sci & tech cnsllr Br Embassy Moscow 1987-91; *Recreations* squash, travel; *Style—* Terence Garrett, Esq, CMG, CBE; Lime Tree Farmhouse, Chilton, Didcot, Oxon OX11 0SW

GARRETT, Terence John; s of Thomas Edwin Garrett (d 1978), of Rayleigh, Essex, and May Lilian, *née* King (d 1990); *b* 6 March 1950; *Educ* Sweyne GS, Clarks Coll, City of London Poly; *m* Susan Hilda, da of George Alfred Richmond; 2 s (Matthew Lee b 25 March 1975, David James 22 November 1984); 1 da (Michelle Louise b 14 July 1970); *Career* journalist; Financial Times 1969-86 (company news ed 1978-86), Independent 1986-87; dir Streets Communications Ltd 1988-; *Style—* Terence Garrett, Esq; Streets Communications Ltd, 18 Red Lion Court, Fleet St, London EC4A 3HT (☎ 071 353 1090, fax 071 583 0661, mobile 0860 501907, pager 081 840 7000 quote 486 9210)

GARRETT, Thomas John; s of Thomas John Garrett, of Belfast (d 1977), and Violet, *née* Dudgeon (d 1982); *b* 13 Sept 1927; *Educ* Royal Belfast Academical Inst, Queen's Univ Belfast (BA), Heidelberg Univ; *m* 9 August 1958, Sheenah Agnew, da of Grey Marshall (d 1960), of Drymen, Dumbartonshire, Scot; 1 da (Catrione b 1960); *Career* asst master: Royal Belfast Academical Inst 1951-54, Nottingham HS for Boys 1954-56; house master Campbell Coll Belfast 1956-73, headmaster Portora Royal Sch Enniskillen, princ Royal Belfast Academical Inst 1978-90; *Books* Modern German Humour (1969), Two Hundred Years at the Top (1977); *Recreations* hill-walking, angling, broadcasting; *Clubs* East India, Devonshire, Sports and Public Schools; *Style—* Thomas Garrett, Esq; Carnbeg, 44 Dunmoire Rd, Spa, Ballynahinch, Co Down BT24 8PR (☎ 0238 562399)

GARRETT, Hon Mrs (Valda Jean); *née* Vernon; 2 da of 5 Baron Lyveden (d 1973), and his 1 wife Ruby, *née* Shandley (d 1932); *b* 11 July 1918; *m* 10 July 1937, Basil George Garrett; 1 s, 3 da; *Style—* Hon Mrs Garrett; 18 Tarikaka St, Ngaio, New Zealand

GARRICK, Ronald; s of Thomas Garrick and Anne, *née* MacKay; *b* 21 Aug 1940; *Educ* Royal Coll of Science and Technology Glasgow, Glasgow Univ; *m* 1965, Janet Elizabeth Taylor Lind; 2 s, 1 da; *Career* md: Weir Pumps Ltd, md Weir Gp 1982-; *Style—* Ronald Garrick, Esq; c/o Weir Pumps Ltd, 149 Newlands Rd, Glasgow 44 (☎ 041 637 7141)

GARROD, Lt-Gen Sir (John) Martin Carruthers; KCB (1988), OBE (1980); s of late Rev William Francis Garrod, and late Isobel Agnes, *née* Carruthers; *b* 29 May 1935; *Educ* Sherborne; *m* 1963, Gillian Mary, da of Lt-Col Robert Granville Parks-Smith, RM (ka 1942); 2 da (Catherine, Fenella); *Career* Lt-Gen RM, cdr 3 Commando Bde RM 1983-84 (despatches NI 1974); ADC to HM The Queen 1983-84, COS to Cmdt Gen RM 1984-87, Cmdt Gen RM 1987-90; *Recreations* portrait photography; *Clubs* East India; *Style—* Lt-Gen Sir Martin Garrod, KCB, OBE; c/o Lloyds Bank, Petersfield, Hants

GARROD, Norman John; s of Frank Albert Garrod (d 1965); *b* 10 July 1924; *Educ* Alleyns Sch Dulwich; *m* 1945, Beryl Portia Betty, *née* Bastow; 2 children; *Career* served WWII, Fl-Lt RAF, UK, Middle East, Far East; master printer; chm: Garrod Ltd 1952-, Printers Charitable Corporaation 1981; vice pres Variety Club of Great Britain (chief barker 1984); *Recreations* dogs, fishing; *Clubs* Garrick, RAF, Fly Fishers; *Style—* Norman Garrod, Esq; Great Common, Big Common Lane, Bletchingley, Surrey RH1 4QE (☎ 0883 743375); Garrod Properties Ltd, 201 Linen Hall, 162-168 Regents St, London W1R 5TB (☎ 071 287 5010)

GARRY, Brendan Laurence; s of Dr Patrick Thomas Garry (d 1952), of Liverpool, and Eileen Mary, *née* Enright (d 1982); *b* 22 Sept 1934; *Educ* Stonyhurst, Univ of Liverpool (LLB); *Career* admitted slr 1959; currently sr ptnr Messrs Witham Weld; memb Law Soc 1959; *Recreations* The Nat Tst, British Art Medal Soc, Nat Art Collections Fund, Mozart; *Clubs* MCC; *Style—* Brendan Garry, Esq; Moreton House, Holly Walk, London NW3 6RA (☎ 071 794 5023); Witham Weld, 70 St George's Square, London SW1V 3RD (☎ 071 821 8211, fax 071 630 6484, telex 8952193 WITHAM G)

GARSIDE, Gill; da of Roy Garside, of Huddersfield, West Yorkshire, and Mavis, *née* Holdsworth; *b* 23 March 1954; *Educ* Greenhead HS Huddersfield, Univ of Liverpool (BSc); *Career* ed asst: Heyden Publishing 1976, Good Housekeeping Magazine 1977-79, press offr Tesco Stores 1979-81; account exec: VandenBurg Associates PR 1981-83, Leslie Bishop Company PR 1983-84; sr account exec then memb Bd of Dirs Darwall Smith Associates Ltd PR Consultancy 1984-; memb: Mktg Soc 1988, IOD; *Recreations* horse riding, cycling, swimming, walking, cinema; *Style—* Ms Gill Garside; Darwall Smith Associates Ltd, Smoke House Yard, 44/46 St John St, London EC1M 4DT (☎ 071 490 1100, fax 071 253 0342, car 0831 382809)

GARSIDE, (Pamela) Jane; JP; da of Ronald Whitwam, and Nellie Whitwam; *b* 20 Aug 1936; *Educ* Royds Hall GS Huddersfield, Yorkshire Training Coll of Housecraft, Leeds Inst of Educn (Dip in Teaching); *m* 6 Sept 1958, Adrian Fielding Garside; 2 s (Simon Paul Fielding b 3 August 1960, Jonathan Adrian Fielding b 20 Aug 1963), 1 da (Rachel Jane b 29 Nov 1965); *Career* The Girl Guides Association: county cmmr W Yorkshire South 1977-83, chief cmmr NE England 1984-89, chief cmmr UK and Cwlth 1990-; teacher of home economics Deighton Secdy Sch 1957-58, dir Highfield Funeral Services Ltd 1964- (co sec 1959-); *Recreations* reading, gardening, music; *Style—* Mrs Jane Garside, JP; The Girl Guides Association, 17-19 Buckingham Palace Rd, London SW1W 0PT (☎ 071 834 6242, fax 071 828 8317)

GARSIDE, Roger Ramsay; s of Capt Frederick Rodney Garside, CBE, RN, and Margaret Ada Beatrice, *née* Ramsay; *b* 29 March 1938; *Educ* Eton, Clare Coll Cambridge (MA), Sloan Sch of Mgmnt (MIT, MSc); *m* 11 Oct 1969, Evelyne Madeleine Pierrette, da of André René Émile Guérin (d 1982); 3 da (Juliette b 1972, Alice b 1974, Rebecca b 1978); *Career* Nat Serv cmmnd offr 1/6 Queen Elizabeth's Own Gurkha Rifles; Dip Serv 1962-71: London, Rangoon, Hong Kong, Peking; World Bank Washington 1972-74; Dip Serv 1975-87: London, Peking, Paris; Int Stock Exchange London 1987-90, dir public affrs and advsr int relations, chm Garside Millar Associates Ltd securities markets conslts 1990-; *Books* Coming Alive: China After Mao (1981); *Recreations* tennis, riding; *Clubs* Reform; *Style—* Roger Garside, Esq; 36 Groveway, London SW9 0AR (☎ 071 582 1577); Int Stock Exchange, Old Broad St, London EC2N 1HP (☎ 071 588 2355, fax 071 256 8972)

GARSON, Cdre Robin William; CBE (1975); s of Peter James Garson (d 1922), and Ada Frances, *née* Newton (d 1965); *b* 13 Nov 1921; *Educ* SOAS (Japanese interpreter); *m* 1946, Joy Ligertwood Taylor, *née* Hickman; 1 s (Simon), 1 da (Nicola); *Career* entered RN 1937, served WWII 1939-45; HM Ships: Resolution, Nigeria, Cyclops; HM Submarines: Seawolf, H33, Spark; CO HM submarines 1945-54: Universal, Uther, Seraph, Saga, Sanguine, Springer, Thule, Astute; Chief Staff Offr Intelligence Far East 1966-68, Sr Polaris UK Rep Washington 1969-71, Capt 1 Submarine Sqdn 1971-73, Cdre HMS Drake 1973-75; ADC to HM The Queen 1974; advsr to AMA on Arts and Recreation 1976-85, memb Library Advsy Cncl (Eng) 1977-81, dir of Leisure Services London Borough of Hillingdon 1975-85, advsr Sports

Cncl 1979-85; *Recreations* golf, skiing, tennis; *Clubs* Moor Park, Army & Navy, Hunstanton Golf; *Style*— Cdre Robin Garson, CBE; Gateways, Hamilton Rd West, Old Hunstanton, Norfolk, PE36 6JB

GARSTON, Clive Richard; s of Henry Leslie Garston (d 1978), of Manchester, and Sheila Esther, *née* Cohen; *b* 25 April 1945; *Educ* Manchester GS, Univ of Leeds (LLB), Coll of Law; *m* 25 Feb 1973, Racheline Raymonde, da of Jacques Sultan; 1 s (Nicholas Nathan b 15 July 1974), 1 da (Louise Anne b 22 May 1978); *Career* slr; Hall Brydon Manchester: articled clerk 1966-68, asst slr 1968-71, ptnr 1971-78; sr ptnr Halliwell Landau Manchester 1989- (ptnr 1978-89), non-exec dir The Inter Care Group plc 1990-, memb Law Soc 1968; *Recreations* swimming, skiing, watching Manchester United and Lancashire County Cricket; *Clubs* Lancashire CC, St James's, IOD; *Style*— Clive R Garston, Esq; Sandy Ridge, Bollinway, Hale, Cheshire WA15 0NZ (☎ 061 904 9822); Halliwell Landau, St James's Court, Brown St, Manchester M2 2JF (☎ 061 835 3003, fax 061 835 2994, car 0860 254574)

GARSTON, Eric Michael; s of Dr Maurice Kopelowitz (d 1971), of Newcastle upon Tyne, and Mabel, *née* Garston (d 1949); *b* 23 May 1931; *Educ* Malvern, Univ of Durham (LLB); *m* 20 Nov 1960 (m dis 1976), Jill Rosemary, da of Jack Kleeman (d 1983), of Regents Park, London NW1; 1 s (Jeremy b 1963), 1 da (Annabel b 1966); *Career* slr; sr ptnr Reynolds Porter Chamberlain 1988-; Exec Ctee Anglo Austrian Soc, memb Ctee legal gp Friends of Hebrew Univ, chm Bd of Tstees The World Resource Fndn; non-exec dir numerous private companies (incl chm Tetra Pak Finance SA and Tetra Pak Holdings SA, both of Switzerland); Liveryman Worshipful Co of Glaziers 1986; memb Law Soc 1954, Int Bar Assoc 1966; *Recreations* swimming, walking, theatre; *Clubs* MCC, RAC; *Style*— Michael Garston, Esq; 97 Abbotsbury Rd, Holland Park, London W14 8EP (☎ 071 603 2903) Chichester House, 278-282 High Holborn, London WC1V 7HA (☎ 071 242 2877, fax 071 242 1431)

GARTHWAITE, (William) Mark Charles; s and h of Sir William Garthwaite, 2 Bt, DSC, and Patricia Beatrice Eden Allen, *née* Neate; *b* 4 Nov 1946; *Educ* Gordonstoun, Univ of Pennsylvania (BSc); *m* 1979, Victoria Lisette, da of Gen Sir Harry Tuzo, GCB, OBE, MC, and former wife of Robert Hohler; 1 s (William b 1982), 2 da (Rosie b 1980, Jemima b 1984); *Career* md Seascope Insurance Serv (Marine insur broker) 1979; *Recreations* yachting, trekking, skiing; *Clubs* Turf; *Style*— Mark Garthwaite, Esq; The Old Vicarage, 12 Foxmore Street, London SW11 4PL (☎ 071 488 3288)

GARTHWAITE, Hon Mrs (Waveney Mancroft); *née* Samuel; er da of 1 Baron Mancroft (d 1942); *b* 25 Feb 1916; *m* 1 Dec 1950, Anthony William Garthwaite (d 1972), 2 s of Sir William Garthwaite, 1 Bt (d 1956); 1 s (Nicholas Anthony William Mancroft b 1952); m 2, 1982, Caroline, da of Thomas Willbourne, of Peterborough; *Style*— The Hon Mrs Garthwaite; 98 Bickenhall Mansions, W1

GARTHWAITE, Sir William Francis Cuthbert; 2 Bt (UK 1919), DSC (1941 and Bar 1942); s of Sir William Garthwaite, 1 Bt (d 1956), and his 1 w, Francesca Margherita, *née* Parfett; *b* 3 Jan 1906; *Educ* Bradfield, Hertford Coll Oxford; *m* 1, 23 July 1931 (m dis 1937), Hon Dorothy, o da of 1 Baron Duveen; m 2, 27 June 1945 (m dis 1952), Patricia Beatrice Eden, er da of late Cdr Charles Eden Neate, RN; 1 s; m 3, 4 April 1957 (m dis), Patricia Merriel, o da of Sir Philip d'Ambrumenil; 3 s (inc twins), 1 da (decd); *Heir* s, William Mark Charles Garthwaite; *Career* Lt Cdr (A) RNR, RN Pilot and with RAF WWII (despatches thrice); underwriter and broker at Lloyds 1927-; Parly candidate (Cons): Hemsworth 1931, Isle of Ely 1935, Wolverhampton 1945; *Recreations* flying, golf, skiing; *Clubs* Portland, Naval, Royal Thames Yacht, Jockey (Paris), Royal Navy Sailing Assoc; *Style*— Sir William Garthwaite, Bt, DSC; Matfield House, Matfield, Kent TN12 7JT (☎ 089 272 2454)

GARTON, Dr (George) Alan; s of William Edgar Garton, DCM, (d 1966), and Frances Mary Elizabeth, *née* Atkinson (d 1967); *b* 4 June 1922; *Educ* Scarborough HS, Univ of Liverpool (BSc, PhD, DSc); *m* 21 Aug 1951, Gladys Frances, da of Francis James Davison (d 1978), of Glasgow; 2 da (Dr Alison Frances b 7 Sept 1952, Dr Fiona Mary b 19 May 1955); *Career* war serv in Miny of Supply; Johnston res and teaching fell Univ of Liverpool 1949-50, dep dir Rowett Res Inst 1968-83 (biochemist 1950-63, Head Lipid Biochemistry Dept 1963-83), hon res assoc Rowett Res Inst 1984-, hon res fell Univ of Aberdeen 1987-; visiting prof biochemistry Univ of North Carolina 1967, memb Cncl Br Nutrition Fndn 1982-, pres Int Conferences on Biochemistry of Lipids 1982-89, chm Br Nat Ctee for Nutritional and Food Sciences 1985-87; FRSE 1966, FRS 1978; SBStJ 1986; *Books* contributor to several multi author books on ruminant physiology and lipid biochemistry; *Recreations* gardening, golf, philately, foreign travel; *Clubs* Farmers', Deeside Golf; *Style*— Dr Alan Garton, FRS, FRSE; Ellerburn, 1 St Devenick Crescent, Cults, Aberdeen AB1 9LL (☎ 0224 867012)

GARTON, Hon Mrs (Annabel Jocelyne); da of 2 and last Viscount Hudson (d 1963); *b* 11 Aug 1952; *m* 9 Feb 1970, (Anthony) Juan Garton, eldest s of Anthony Charles Garton (d 1982); 1 s, 3 da; *Style*— Hon Mrs Garton; 8 Moncorvo Close, London SW7

GARTON, Charles Herbert Stanley; MBE (1949); s of Arthur Stanley Garton (d 1948), of Danesfield, Medmenham, Marlow, Bucks, and Mona, *née* Macaulay (d 1986); *b* 5 Feb 1920; *Educ* Eton, Magdalen Coll Oxford; *m* 14 April 1948, Sheelagh Mary Georgiana, da of Thomas Harrison Greene, OBE (d 1963); 3 da (Georgiana b 12 Aug 1949, Jane b 19 July 1951, Anne (twin) b 19 July 1951); *Career* FO 1940-54, farmer 1954-; *Recreations* shooting, fishing, stalking; *Clubs* Leander; *Style*— Charles Garton, Esq, MBE; Wadeford House, Wadeford, Chard, Somerset (☎ 046 06 3222)

GARTON, Hon Mrs (Ines Monica); *née* Wilson; twin da of 4 Baron Nunburnholme; *b* 13 Feb 1963; *m* 1 Oct 1988, Anthony Richard Leslie Garton, yst s of Anthony Charles Garton (d 1982); *Style*— The Hon Mrs Garton; 23 Sutherland Street, London SW1

GARTON, John Leslie; CBE (1974, MBE 1946); er s of Charles Leslie Garton (d 1940), and Madeline Laurence; *b* 1 April 1916; *Educ* Eton, Magdalen Coll Oxford (MA); *m* 1939, Elizabeth Frances, da of Sir Walter Erskine Crum, OBE (d 1923); 1 s (and 2 s decd); *Career* Maj TA 1938-51; chm: Coca-Cola Bottling Co (Oxford) Ltd 1951-65, Coca-Cola Western Bottlers Ltd 1966-71; Thames Conservator 1970-74; High Sheriff Bucks 1977; pres OUBC 1939, chm Henley Royal Regatta 1966-77 (pres 1978-); pres: Amateur Rowing Assoc 1969-77 (hon life vice pres 1978-), Leander Club 1980-83 (capt 1946, chm 1958-59); chm World Rowing Championships 1975, Fin and Gen Purposes Ctee Br Olympic Assoc 1969-77; *Recreations* shooting, fishing, supporting the sport of rowing; *Clubs* Leander; *Style*— John L Garton, Esq, CBE; Mill Green House, Church St, Wargrave, Berks RG10 8EP (☎ 0734 402944)

GARTON, Lady Lucy Catherine Mary; *née* Primrose; er da of 7 Earl of Rosebery, DL; *b* 24 Dec 1955; *Educ* Benenden; *m* 1976, (Anthony Gavin) Charles Garton, s of Anthony Charles Garton (d 1982), of Hyde Park Gdns; 1 s (James Anthony Leo b 1986), 1 da (Camilla Mary Eva b 1982), and 1 child decd; *Style*— Lady Lucy Garton; 9 North Terrace, Alexander Sq, London SW3 2BA (071 589 8338)

GARTON ASH, Timothy John; s of John Garton Ash, and Lorna Garton Ash; *b* 12 July 1955; *Educ* Sherborne, Exeter Coll Oxford (BA), St Antony's Coll Oxford (MA); *m* 1982, Danuta; 2 s (Thomas b 1984, Alexander b 1986); *Career* editorial writer on central euro affr The Times 1984-86, foreign ed The Spectator 1984-90, regular contrib to The Independent and New York Reviews of Books; fell: Woodrow Wilson Int Center for Scholars Washington 1986-87, St Antony's Coll Oxford 1990-; Commentator of the Year in Granada TV What the Papers Say awards 1990; *Books* Und Willst Du Nicht Mein Bruder Sein... Die DDR heute (1981), We The People (1990), The Polish Revolution: Solidarity (2 edn 1991, Somerset Maugham award 1984), The Uses of Adversity (2 edn 1991, David Watt memorial prize 1989, Prix Européen de l'Essai 1989); *Recreations* literature, architecture, travel; *Clubs* Institut für die Wissenschaten vom Menschen (Vienna); *Style*— Timothy Garton Ash, Esq; St Antony's College, Oxford OX2 6JF

GARTON JONES, Lt-Col John; MBE (1953); s of William John Garton Jones (d 1947), of Lucknow, United Provinces, India, and Mavis Noreen, *née* Mauger (d 1986); *b* 19 Sept 1930; *Educ* Bedford Sch; *m* 1, 29 Dec 1960, Mary (d 1983), da of Lt-Col Edward Roger Nanny-Wynn, DL (d 1982), of Llanfendigaid, Tywyn, Gwynedd; 2 s (William b 1961, Charles b 1970), 1 da (Edwina b 1964); m 2, 22 July 1989, Eldrydd Anne Main, da of Mr and Mrs J E M Dugdale, of Lower Cefnperfa, Co Kerry Powys; *Career* Nat Serv joined Army 1949, Eaton Hall OCS 1950, cmmn serv with Jamaica Bn 1950-51, regular cmmn Depot Royal Norfolk Regt 1951-54, 1 Bn Royal Norfolk Regt serv in Cyprus BAOR Berlin 1954-60, HQ Mid East Cmd Aden 1960-62, 4 Bn Royal Norfolk Regt 1963-65, on loan to Malaysian Government in Barawak 1965-66, 4 Royal Anglian Regt serv Malta and Eng 1967-69, MOD 1969-71, Depot The Queens Div 1971-73, HQ NI 1973-75, HQ Wales 1975-80, HQ Western Dist 1980-82, ret 1982; bursar Outward Bound Tst Sch Aberdovey 1982-84, freelance journalist (nat and provincial pubns); memb: Ctee of Shrewsbury Theatre Guild, Shrewsbury Sch Community Choir, Shrewsbury Arts and Drama Assoc; *Recreations* journalism, photography, singing, golf, tennis, skiing; *Clubs* Army and Navy; *Style*— Lt-Col John Garton Jones, MBE

GARTSIDE, Edmund Travis; TD (1968); s of Col J B Gartside, DSO, MC, TD, DL, JP (d 1964), of Crimble Cottage, Bamford, Rochdale, and Cora Maude, *née* Baker; *b* 11 Nov 1933; *Educ* Winchester, Trinity Coll Cambridge (MA); *m* 1, 29 Aug 1959 (m dis 1982), Margaret Claire, *née* Nicholls; 1 s (Michael Travis b 1961), 1 da (Vanessa Perry Anne (Mrs Anderson) b 1962); m 2, 5 May 1983, Valerie Cox, da of Cyril Vowels, of Prospect Cottage, Marine Parade, Instow, N Devon; *Career* Nat Serv 2 Lt RE and Lancs Fusiliers 1952-54; TA: Lancs Fusiliers (Maj) 1954-67, E Lancs Regt 1967-68; chm and md Shiloh plc (formerly Shiloh Spinners Ltd) 1966- (mgmnt trainee 1957, dir 1960, gen mangr Roy Mill 1961-65, dep chm 1963-66, md 1965), chm Amberguard Ltd 1977-; dir Oldham & Dist Textile Employers' Assoc 1965- (pres 1971-75), memb Central Ctee Br Textile Employers' Assoc 1969-89 (pres 1976-78); pres: Eurocoton 1985-87, Cncl of Br Cotton Textiles 1989-; memb Ct Univ of Manchester 1979-, govr Manchester GS 1984-; CBIM, FIOD; *Clubs* Army & Navy; *Style*— Edmund Gartside, Esq, TD; Shiloh plc, Holdenfold, Royton, Oldham, Lancs OL2 5ET (☎ 061 624 8161, fax 061 627 3840, telex 667558)

GARVAGH, 5 Baron (UK 1818); (Alexander Leopold Ivor) George Canning; s of 4 Baron Garvagh (d 1956) by his 2 w, Gladys Dora May (d 1982), da of William Bayley Parker, of Edgbaston, and widow of Lt-Col D M Dimmer, VC; *b* 6 Oct 1920; *Educ* Eton, Christ Church Oxford; *m* 1, 12 July 1947 (m dis 1973), Edith Christine, da of Jack H Cooper, of Worplesdon, Surrey; 1 s, 2 da; m 2, 1974, Cynthia Valerie Mary, da of Eric Ernest Falk Pretty, CMG, of Kingswood, Surrey; *Heir* s, Hon Spencer George Stratford de Redcliffe Canning; *Career* served Indian Army WW II in Burma (despatches); accredited rep trade and industry Cayman Islands 1981-, memb Court Worshipful Co of Painter and Stainers; MBIM, FInstD, MIEx; *Style*— The Rt Hon the Lord Garvagh; Apartado 289, 03724 Moraira, Alicante, Spain

GARVEY, Sir Ronald Herbert; KCMG (1950, CMG 1947), KCVO (1953), MBE (1940); s of Rev Herbert Richard Garvey (d 1955), and Alice M Lofthouse; *b* 4 July 1903; *Educ* Trent Coll, Emmanuel Coll Cambridge; *m* 30 Oct 1934, Patricia Dorothy Edge, da of Dr Victor William Tighe McGusty, CMG, OBE; 1 s (Richard b 1935), 3 da (Grania b 1939, Lavinia b 1946, Julia b 1947); *Career* entered Colonial Serv 1926, W Pacific High Cmmn, actg govr Windward Is BWI 1946-48, govr and C-in-C Br Honduras 1948-52, govr and C-in-C Fiji, govr Pitcairn Is, consul gen Western Pacific, sr cmmr for UK in S Pacific Cmmn 1952-58, Lt Govr Isle of Man 1959-66; dir Garveys (London) SA 1966-82; memb E Anglian Tourist Bd; KStJ 1954; *Books* Gentleman Pauper; Happy Days in the Isle of Man; *Recreations* golf, gardening, eating, drinking Garvey sherry, writing; *Clubs* Royal Cwlth Soc; *Style*— Sir Ronald Garvey, KCMG, KCVO, MBE; The Priory, Wrentham, Beccles, Suffolk (☎ 0502 75274); Gilmooka House, 57-61 Mortimer St, London W1N 7TD

GARVIN, Michael John Moore; s of Stephen Garvin, MBE, of Sussex, and Gilda Constance, *née* Moore (d 1955); *b* 12 Sept 1943; *Educ* Rugby; *m* 22 Sept 1976, Bridget, da of Thomas A Tolhurst (d 1969); 2 s (Patrick b 1978, Fergus b 1983), 1 da (Melissa b 1981); *Career* CA 1966; dir: Barclay Securities 1972-73, Hampton Areas 1973-79, Trident Television 1979-83, Condé Nast 1983-; *Clubs* Travellers', Oriental, Hurlingham; *Style*— Michael Garvin, Esq; 46 Guildford Road, London SW8 2BV; Witney Street, Burford, Oxon; The Conde Nast Publications Ltd, Vogue House, Hanover Square, London W1R 0AD

GASCOIGNE, Hon Mrs ((Elizabeth) Ann); *née* Harcourt; eldest da of 2 and last Viscount Harcourt, KCMG, OBE (d 1979), by his 1 w Hon (Maud) Elizabeth Grosvenor (da of 4 Baron Ebury); *b* 17 Feb 1932; *m* 19 Jan 1954, Crispin Gascoigne, o s of Maj-Gen Sir Julian Alvery Gascoigne, KCMG, KCVO, CB, DSO, *qv*; 1 s, 2 da; *Style*— The Hon Mrs Gascoigne; The Manor House, Stanton Harcourt, Oxon

GASCOIGNE, (Arthur) Bamber; s of Derick (Ernest Frederick) Orby Gascoigne, TD (of the old Yorks family dating back to the 14 century, and gggs of Gen Isaac Gascoigne, whose er bro's da Frances was the Gascoigne heiress who m 2 Marquess of Salisbury, whence also the Salisbury family name of Gascoyne-Cecil) and Hon Mary (Midi) Louisa Hermione O'Neill, sis of 3 Baron O'Neill (through which connection Mr Gascoigne belongs to one of the oldest traceable lineages in Europe, the O'Neills of the Irish Royal House of Tara, records of which date from AD 360); nephew of Sir Julian Alvery Gascoigne, *qv*; *b* 24 Jan 1935; *Educ* Eton, Magdalene Coll Cambridge; *m* 1965, Christina Mary, da of late Alfred Henry Ditchburn, CBE; *Career* publisher; proprietor of St Helena Press; author and TV presenter, notably of University Challenge and The Christians; FRSL; *Style*— Bamber Gascoigne, Esq; St Helena Terrace, Richmond, Surrey

GASCOIGNE, Crispin; s of Maj-Gen Sir Julian Gascoigne, KCMG, KCVO, CB, DSO (d 1990), of Sanders, Stokefleming, Dartmouth, Devon, and Joyce Alfreda, *née* Newman (d 1981); *b* 10 Oct 1929; *Educ* Eton, RMA Sandhurst; *m* 19 Jan 1954, Hon (Elizabeth) Ann, da of 2 Viscount Harcourt, KCMG, OBE (d 1979), of The Manor House, Stanton, Harcourt, Oxon; 1 s (William Harcourt Crispin b 1955), 2 da (Elizabeth Laura b 1958, Mary Ann b 1960); *Career* Grenadier Gds 1949-54; Morgan Grenfell & Co Ltd 1956-66, ptnr Panmure Gordon 1966-80; memb Stock Exchange Cncl 1973-80; chm Exec Ctee Oundle Schs 1987-; High Sheriff Oxon 1990-91; Memb Ct Worshipful Co of Grocers (Master 1974); *Recreations* gardening, fishing, shooting; *Style*— Crispin Gascoigne, Esq; The Manor House, Stanton Harcourt, Oxford

GASCOIGNE, Paul John; s of John Gascoigne, and Carol, *née* Harold; *b* 27 May 1967; *Educ* Brighton Avenue Jr HS, Heathfield Sr Sch; *Career* professional footballer; Newcastle Utd 1985-88: apprentice then professional, 106 appearances, 22 goals; transferred for £2m to Tottenham Hotspur 1988; England: 13 under 21 caps, 18 full caps, played in World Cup Italy 1990; *Recreations* football, fishing, tennis, swimming, table tennis, badminton, tenpin bowling, golf; *Style*— Paul Gascoigne, Esq; c/o Arram

Berlyn Gardner, 37-41 Mortimer St, London W1N 7RJ (☎ 071 636 5511, fax 071 636 2189)

GASCOYNE, David Emery; s of Leslie Noel Gascoyne (d 1968), and Winifred Isobel Emery Gascoyne (d 1970); *b* 10 Oct 1916; *Educ* Salisbury Cathedral Choir Sch, Regent St Poly Secdy Sch; *m* 17 May 1975, Mrs (Lorna) Judith Lewis, da of Capt Guy Tyler, MC (d 1966), of Upper Redpits, Marlow, Bucks; 4 stepchildren; *Career* writer and poet; FRSL 1951; *Books* A Short Survey of Surrealism (1936), Holderlin's Madness (1938), Poems 1937-42 (1943, illustrated by Graham Sutherland), A Vagrant and Other Poems (1950), Night Thoughts (1956), Collected Poems (1965), Paris Journal 1937-39 (1978), Journal 1936-37 (1980), Journal de Paris and D'Ailleurs (1984), Collected Poems (1988); *Style—* David Gascoyne, Esq

GASCOYNE-CECIL; *see*: Cecil

GASELEE, Nicholas Auriol Digby Charles (Nick); s of Lt-Col Auriol Stephen Gaselee, OBE (d 1987), of Tonbridge; *b* 30 Jan 1939; *Educ* Charterhouse; *m* 1966, Judith Mary, da of Dr Gilmer; 1 s (James b 1968), 1 da (Sarah, *qv*); *Career* Life Gds 1958-63; racing trainer to HRH The Prince of Wales; *Recreations* coursing; *Clubs* Turf; *Style—* Nick Gaselee, Esq; Saxon Cottage, Upper Lambourn, Berks (☎ 0488 71503)

GASELEE, Sarah Jane; da of Nick Gaselee, *qv*; *b* 2 June 1970; *Educ* Southover Manor Lewes, Hatherop Castle Cirencester, Clenord, France, Beechlawn Oxford; *Career* bridesmaid to Lady Diana Spencer at her marriage to HRH The Prince of Wales 1981, shop assistant in Harvey Nicholls; *Style—* Miss Sarah Jane Gaselee; Saxon Cottage, Upper Lambourn, Berks (☎ 0488 71503)

GASH, Michael Alfred; s of Benjamin Thomas Gash (d 1969), of Solihull, and Brenda Aileen, *née* Crockett; *b* 24 Oct 1943; *Educ* Sharmans Cross HS for Boys; *m* 24 Oct 1967, Sandra Ruth, da of Albert Ernest Wright (d 1977), of Kidderminster; 1 da (Kate b 1 April 1972); *Career* CA 1967; articled Cox & Furse Birmingham 1962-67, sr supervisor and mangr Coopers & Lybrand London 1967-72, ptnr Kidsons Impey Birmingham 1974- (mangr 1972-74); memb Rotary Club of Edgbaston Convention; FCA 1967, ATII 1970; *Recreations* golf, reading, theatre, cooking; *Clubs* The Edgbaston Priory, Harborne Golf; *Style—* Michael Gash, Esq; Charnwood, 54 Richmond Hill Rd, Edgbaston, Birmingham B15 3RZ (☎ 021 455 8440); Kidsons Impey Chartered Accountants Ltd, Bank House, 8 Cherry St, Birmingham B2 5AD (☎ 021 631 2631, fax 021 631 2632, telex 338973)

GASH, Prof Norman; CBE (1988); s of Frederick Gash, MM, and Kate, *née* Hunt; *b* 16 Jan 1912; *Educ* Reading Sch, St Johns Coll, Oxford (MA, MLitt); *m* 1 Aug 1935, (Ivy) Dorothy, da of Edward Whitehorn, of Reading, Berks; 2 da (Harriet b 3 March 1944, Sarah b 30 Jan 1946); *Career* Army 1940-46, Maj GS 1945; prof of mod history Univ of Leeds 1953-55, Hinkley visiting prof John Hopkins Univ 1962, Fords lectr Univ of Oxford 1963-64, dean Faculty of Arts Univ of St Andrews 1978-80 (lectr St Salvators Coll 1946-53, prof of history 1955-70, vice princ 1967-71), Sir John Neale lectr UCL 1981 (asst lectr 1936-40), Swinton lectr 1989; hon fell St Johns Coll Oxford 1987; D Litt: Univ of Strathclyde 1984, Univ of St Andrews 1985, Univ of Southampton 1988; FRHistS 1953, FBA 1963, FRSL 1973, FRSE 1977; *Books* Politics in the Age of Peel (1953), Mr Secretary Peel (1961), Reaction and Reconstruction in English Politics 1832-1852 (1965), Sir Robert Peel (1972), Aristocracy and People 1815-1865 (1979), Lord Liverpool (1984), Pillars of Government (1986); *Recreations* gardening, swimming; *Style—* Prof Norman Gash, CBE; Old Gatehouse, Portway, Langport, Somerset TA10 0NQ (☎ 0458 250334)

GASK, Mrs Daphne Irvine Prideaux; OBE (1976); da of Capt Roger Prideaux Selby (d 1975), and Elizabeth May, *née* Stirling (d 1958); *Educ* St Trinnean's Edinburgh, Chateau Brillamont Lausanne Switzerland, Open Univ (BA); *m* 31 July 1945, Dr John Gask, s of George Ernest Gask, CMG, DSO (d 1951); 1 s (Anthony b 1947), 1 da (Zebee b 1959); *Career* WWII third offr WRNs 1940-45; magistrate: Shrops 1952-80, Inner London 1982-86; asst sec Int Assoc of Juvenile and Family Ct Magistrates 1974-86; memb: Royal Cmmn on Criminal Procedure 1978-81, NACRO Cncl 1982-, Def for Children Int UK Exec Ctee 1986-, Shrops CC 1964-76; chm St Peter's Housing Plymouth, Cab Cornwall; Melo Mattos Medal Brazil 1986; *Recreations* photography, travel; *Clubs* Univ Women's; *Style—* Mrs Daphne Gask, OBE; 5 The Old School House, Garrett St, Cowsand, Cornwall PL10 1PD (☎ 0752 822 136)

GASKELL, (Richard) Carl; s of (Henry) Brian Gaskell (d 1982), and Doris Winnifred, *née* Taylor; *b* 23 March 1948; *Educ* Gateway Sch Leicester, Univ of Newcastle upon Tyne (LLB); *m* 29 Dec 1973, Margaret Annette, da of Stanley Walter Humber; 1 s (Philip b 1975), 3 da (Victoria b 1976, Elizabeth b 1979, Gillian b 1983); *Career* called to Bar Lincoln's Inn 1971, MO circuit, asst rec Crown Ct 1989-; chm Desford Branch Bosworth Cons Assoc; *Style—* Carl Gaskell, Esq; Nova Rustica, Church Lane, Desford, Leicestershire LE9 9GD (☎ 0455 822717); 2 New St, Leicester LE1 5NA (☎ 0533 625 906, fax 0533 512 023)

GASKELL, Dr Colin Simister; CBE (1987); s of James Gaskell (d 1987), of Dukinfield, Cheshire, and Carrie, *née* Simister (d 1968); *b* 19 May 1937; *Educ* Manchester GS, Univ of Manchester (BSc), St Edmund Hall Oxford (DPhil); *m* Aug 1961, Jill, da of A Travers Haward (d 1980), of Torquay, Devon; 1 s (John b 1970), 1 da (Sarah b 1974); *Career* tech dir Herbert Controls 1971-74, md Marconi Instruments Ltd 1979-90 (dir 1977-79), gp md The 600 Group PLC 1990-, dir St Albans Enterprise Agency; FEng, FIElectE (vice pres), FIEE (memb Fin Ctee and INSPEC Bd), FBIM, FRSA; *Recreations* reading, theatre, walking; *Style—* Dr Colin Gaskell, CBE; Marconi Instruments Ltd, St Albans, Herts AL4 OJN (☎ 05827 59292)

GASKELL, (John) Philip Wellesley; s of John Wellesly Gaskell, and Olive Elizabeth, *née* Baker; *b* 6 Jan 1926; *Educ* Dragon Sch Oxford, Oundle, King's Coll Cambridge (MA, PhD, LiHD); *m* 1, 1948 (m dis) Margaret, da of late H S Bennett; 2 s, 1 da; m 2, 1984 (m dis) Annette Ursula Beighton; *Career* served WWII; Lance-Bombadier RA 1943-47 (BLA 1944-46); King's Coll Cambridge: fell 1953-60, dean 1954-56, tutor 1956-58; head of English Dept and librarian Oundle Sch 1960-62; Glasgow Univ: keeper of Special Collection of Universtiy Library 1962-66, warden Maclay Hall 1962-64 and Wolfson Hall 1964-66; Sanders reader in Bibliography Cambridge Univ 1978-79, pt/t prof of literature CIT 1983-88; *Books* The First Editions of William Mason (1951), Caught (1960), A Bibliography of The Foulis Press (1964, revised edn 1986), The Library of Trinity College Cambridge (with R Dobson, 1971), From Writer to Reader (1978), The Orthotypographia of Heronymus Hornschurch (ed and translator with P Bradford, 1972); *Style—* Philip Gaskell, Esq; Trinity College, Cambridge CB2 1TQ

GASKELL, Sir Richard Kennedy Harvey; s of Dr Kenneth Harvey Gaskell (d 1990), of 18 Downleaze, Bristol, and Jean Winsome, *née* Beaven; *b* 17 Sept 1936; *Educ* Marlborough; *m* Oct 1965, Judith (Judy), da of Roy Douglas Poland (d 1963), of Hedgerley, Bucks; 1 s (Simon Poland Harvey b 1966), 1 da (Susanna Jane b 1968); *Career* admitted slr 1960; articled to Burges Salmon Bristol 1955-60, asst slr Tuckett Williams and Kew (later Tucketts) 1960-63, ptnr Tucketts 1963-85, sr ptnr Lawrence Tucketts Bristol 1989 (ptnr 1985-89); legal advsr The Laura Ashley Fndn 1988- (tstee 1990-); memb: Crown Ct Rules Ctee 1977-83, Lord Justice Watkins Working Pty on the Criminal Trials 1981-83, Lord Chllr's Efficiency Cmmn 1986-88 and 1989-, Marre Ctee on Future of Legal Profession 1986-88; Law Soc: nat chm Young Slrs Gp of Law Soc 1964-65, memb Cncl 1969-; chm: Contentious Business Ctee 1979-82, Advocacy Trg Team 1974-87; dir Law Soc Tstees 1974- (chm 1982-); Law Servs Ltd 1987-89: dep vice pres 1986-87, vice pres 1987-88, pres 1988-89; memb: Bristol Law Soc 1965-, pres 1978-79, Som Law Soc; pres Assoc of S Western Law Socs 1980-81, memb Security Service Tribunal 1989-; Wild Fowl and Wetlands Tst: memb Cncl 1980-, memb Exec Ctee 1982-88, chm 1983-87; memb Mgmnt Ctee Bristol 5 Boys Club 1960-66, hon cases sec Bristol branch NSPCC 1966-76, memb Ct Univ of Bristol 1973- (convocation 1989-), memb Cncl: Bristol Zoo 1988-, SS GB Project 1990- (also Exec Ctee); tstee Clearwater 1990-; Hon LLD Univ of Bristol 1989, Hon LLM Bristol Poly 1989; kt 1989; *Style—* Sir Richard Gaskell; Shannon Court, Corn Street, Bristol BS99 7JZ (☎ 0272 294861)

GASKELL, William Peter; CBE (1964, MBE 1953); s of late William Gaskell, late headmaster Lawrence Royal Mil Sch Sanawar, India; *b* 9 June 1914; *Educ* Dragon Sch Oxford, Blundell's, Sch of Metaliferous Mining Camborne; *Career* Capt Royal W Africa Frontier Force; mining engr Colonial Serv 1937-64 (chief inspr of mines Nigeria 1952-64); lectr Sch of Mgmnt and Business Studies Brooklands Coll Weybridge 1965-74; *Recreations* badminton, music, motoring, travel; *Clubs* Royal Commonwealth Soc; *Style—* W Peter Gaskell, Esq, CBE; 3 Cove Row, Weymouth, Dorset DT4 8TT (☎ 0305 774067)

GASKIN, Catherine Majella Sinclair; da of James Gaskin (d 1980), and Mary Harrington (d 1952); *b* 2 April 1929; *Educ* Holy Cross Coll Aust; *m* 1955, Sol Cornberg, s of Joseph Cornberg (d 1928); *Career* author; *Books* This Other Eden (1946), With Every Year (1947), Dust in Sunlight (1950), All Else is Folly (1951), Daughter of the House (1952), Sara Dane (1955), Blake's Reach (1958), Corporation Wife (1960), I Know My Love (1962), The Tilsit Inheritance (1963), The File On Devlin (1965), Edge of Glass (1967), Fiona (1970), A Falcon For A Queen (1972), The Property of A Gentleman (1974), The Lynmara Legacy (1975), The Summer of The Spanish Woman (1977), Family Affairs (1980), Promises (1982), The Ambassador's Women (1985), The Charmed Circle (1988); *Recreations* music, reading; *Style—* Miss Catherine Gaskin; White Rigg, E Ballaterson, Maughold, IOM (☎ 0624 812145)

GASKIN, James Joseph; s of James Joseph Gaskin (d 1979), of Berks, and Caroline, *née* Myers (d 1988); *b* 23 April 1945; *Educ* Wembley Co GS; *m* 26 Oct 1968, Linda, da of Thomas William Arundel, of Middx; 1 s (Matthew b 1972), 1 da (Sarah b 1974); *Career* dir 1976-84: Hull Blyth & Co Ltd, Oakwool Gp Ltd, Seatronics (UK) Ltd, Wm Jacks (UK) Ltd, Suttons Gp Ltd; fin dir: Ocean Cory Investmt 1979-80, Ocean Cory Energy 1980-82; md Repcon (UK and Ireland) Ltd 1982-84, dir of external servs FIMBRA; memb Securities Indust Exec Liaison Ctee; *Recreations* riding, classical music; *Style—* James Gaskin, Esq; 21 Sandiland Crescent, Hayes, Bromley, Kent BR2 7DP (☎ 081 462 4156); Fimbra, Hertsmere House, Hertsmere Rd, London E14 9RW (☎ 071 538 8860)

GASKIN, Prof John Charles Addison; s of Harry James Gaskin, of Mixbury, Oxfordshire, and Evelyn Mary Addison Gaskin, *née* Taylor; *b* 4 April 1936; *Educ* City of Oxford Sch, Univ of Oxford (MA, BLitt); *m* 20 May 1972, Diana Katherine, da of Maurice Dobbin (d 1969); 1 s (Rupert John Addison b 1974), 1 da (Suzette Jane Addison b 1975); *Career* Royal Bank of Scotland 1959-61, prof of philosophy Trinity Coll Dublin 1983- (previously jr dean and lectr); FTCD; *Books* incl: Hume's Philosophy of Religion (1978, 1988), The Quest for Eternity (1984), varieties of Unbelief (1989); *Recreations* riding, writing ghost stories, shooting, gardening, walking; *Clubs* Kildare St and University (Dublin); *Style—* Prof John C A Gaskin; Trinity College Dublin, Dublin 2, Irish Republic (☎ 0001 772941); Crook Crossing, Netherwitton, Northumberland

GASKIN, Malcolm Graeme Charles; s of Charles Augustus Gaskin (d 1981), of Blyth, Northumberland, and Jean, *née* Denton; *b* 27 Feb 1951; *Educ* Blyth GS, Manchester Poly, Sch of Art and Design; *m* Deborah Ann, da of Michael Loftus, of Osterley, Middx; 2 s (Jack Alexander b 1983, Lewis Ross (twin) b 1983), 1 da (Francesca Vita b 1985); *Career* art dir Leo Burnett 1973-77, creative dir TBWA 1977-81, creative dir Woollams Moira Gaskin O'Malley 1987-, inventor of Eau in Perrier; advertising awards for Lego, Land Rover, CIGA, Nursing Recruitment, AIDS; memb: Design and Art Direction, Creative Circle, AIDS Drugs and Alcohol Assoc; ctee memb Fulham Palace Allotments Assoc; memb Design and Art Dirs Assoc 1975; *Books* Design and Art Direction (1975); *Recreations* gardening, angling, hiking, art; *Clubs* Zanzibar; *Style—* Malcolm Gaskin, Esq; 33 Clonmel Road, Fulham, London SW6; Woollams Moira Gaskins O'Malley, Portland House, 12-13 Greek St, London W1 (☎ 071 494 0770, fax 071 734 6684)

GASKIN, Prof Maxwell; DFC (1944, Bar 1945); s of Albert Gaskin (d 1960), and Beatrice Ada, *née* Boughey (d 1967); *b* 18 Nov 1921; *Educ* Quarry Bank Sch, Univ of Liverpool (BA, MA); *m* 24 July 1952, Brenda Patricia Rachel, da of Rev William Dale Stewart (d 1954), of Crieff, Perthshire; 1 s (Richard b 1960), 3 da (Rosemary b 1953, Hilary b 1957, Fiona b 1962); *Career* WWII Flt Engr RAF Bomber Cmd 1941-46, 161 Sqdn, 7 (PFF) Sqdn; sr lectr (formerly lectr) in econ Univ of Glasgow 1951-65; prof emeritus political economy Univ of Aberdeen 1985- (Jaffrey prof political economy 1965-85); chm Bd of Mgmnt Foresterhill & Assoc Hosps 1972-74, memb Scottish Agric Wages Bd 1972-90, chm: Retail Bespoke Tailoring Wages Cncl 1978-, Section F Br Assoc 1978-79; memb: Civil Engrg EDC 1978-84, Royal Econ Soc 1951, Scot Econ Soc 1951 (pres 1981-84); *Books* Scottish Banking (1965), North East Scotland: A Survey of its Development Potential (jtly 1969), The Economic Impact of North Sea Oil on Scotland (jtly 1978), The Political Economy of Tolerable Survival (jtly 1981); *Recreations* music, gardening; *Style—* Prof Maxwell Gaskin, DFC; Westfield, Ancrum, Roxburghshire TD8 6XA (☎ 08353 237)

GASS, Lady; Elizabeth Periam; *née* Acland-Hood; da of Hon (Arthur) John Palmer Fuller-Acland-Hood (d 1964; s of 1 Baron St Audries, Barony extinct 1971); *b* 2 March 1940; *Educ* Cheltenham Ladies' Coll, Girton Coll Cambridge (MA); *m* 1975, Sir Michael David Irving Gass, KCMG (d 1983, sometime HM Overseas Civil Serv in W Africa, colonial sec Hong Kong, high cmmr for W Pacific, British high cmmr for New Hebrides); *Career* memb Somerset County Cncl 1985-, chm Exmoor National Park Ctee 1989-; *Style—* Lady Gass; Fairfield, Stogursey, Bridgwater, Somerset (☎ 0278 732251)

GASSON, Andrew Peter; s of Sidney Samuel and Elsie Gasson; *b* 18 July 1943; *Educ* Dulwich Coll PS, Henry Thornton GS, City Univ; *Career* in private practice (specalising in contact lenses) 1972-; pres Contact Lens Soc 1974-75; examiner: Spectacle Makers Co, Br Coll of Optometrists 1975-84, memb: Cncl Br Contact Lens Assoc 1986, Contact Lens Ctee of BSI 1980-82; lectr numerous sci meetings; sec Wilkie Collins Soc 1981-; Freeman City of London, Liveryman Worshipful Co of Spectacle Makers; FBOA, FSMC, FBCO, DCLP,GFell Amer Acad of Optometry; ARPS; *Recreations* antiquarian books, travel, photography, cricket, motoring; *Clubs* MCC, RSM; *Style—* Andrew Gasson, Esq; 6 De Walden St, London W1M 7PH (☎ 01 224 5959)

GATEHOUSE, Graham Gould; s of George Gatehouse (d 1953), of West Coker, Somerset, and Gwendoline Maud, *née* Gould; *b* 17 July 1935; *Educ* Crewkerne Sch Somerset, Univ of Exeter, LSE, Univ of Birmingham; *m* 31 Jan 1960, Gillian Margaret, da of Dr Norman Wade Newell (d 1964); 2 s (Mark b 1960, John b 1963), 1 da (Jane b 1962); *Career* served RA 1954-56, subaltern; social worker Somerset CC 1957-67, dep co welfare offr Worcestershire CC 1967-70, asst dir social servs Norfolk CC 1970-73, dep dir social servs W Sussex CC 1973-81, dir social servs Surrey CC 1981-; advsr to Social Servs Ctees ACC, Dept of Sociology Advsry Bd Univ of Surrey; ADSS 1981, BASW 1969, FRSA 1987; *Recreations* music, rugby, theatre, cricket; *Style*— Graham Gatehouse, Esq; Surrey County Council, Social Services Dept, 7 Penrhyn Rd, Kingston upon Thames KT1 2DS (☎ 081 541 9600, fax 081 541 9654)

GATEHOUSE, Hon Mr Justice; Sir Robert Alexander Gatehouse; s of Maj-Gen Alexander Hugh Gatehouse, DSO, MC (d 1964), and Helen Grace, *née* Williams (d 1969); *b* 30 Jan 1924; *Educ* Wellington Coll, Trinity Hall Cambridge (BA); *m* 1, Oct 1950, Henrietta, da of Air Vice-Marshal Sir Oliver Swann (d 1948); m 2, 18 Aug 1966, Pamela Riley, da of late Frederick Fawcett; *Career* WWII 1939-45, cmmnd Royal Dragoons, 1944 N West Europe; called to the Bar Lincoln's Inn 1950; QC 1969, High Court Judge (Queen's Bench Div) 1985; govr Wellington Coll 1970; kt 1985; *Recreations* golf; *Style*— The Hon Mr Justice Gatehouse; Royal Courts of Justice, Strand, London WC2A 2LL

GATENBY, Ian Cheyne; s of Lt-Col William Gatenby (d 1971), of Esher, Surrey, and Frances Alice, *née* Davies (d 1982); *b* 30 June 1942; *Educ* RGS Newcastle-upon-Tyne, Exeter Coll Oxford (MA); *m* Jan 1973 (m dis 1989); 1 s (Piers b 5 Aug 1975), 1 da (Catherine b 9 April 1977); *Career* admitted slr 1968, assoc ptnr Lovell White & King 1973-77 (previously articled clerk 1966 and asst slr), McKenna & Co 1975- (ptnr 1977-, currently head planning and rating gp); former co-ed Law Soc Gazette business issues, ed property section Kluwer-Harrap on business law, author numerous articles on planning and rating; memb Law Soc 1988; *Recreations* skiing, sailing, English national opera, gardening; *Clubs* Ski of GB, Ranelagh Sailing; *Style*— Ian Gatenby, Esq; 51 Lewin Road, East Sheen, London SW14 8DR (☎ 081 8781325); McKenna & Co, Mitre House, 160 Aldersgate St, London EC1A 4DD (☎ 071 606 9000)

GATENBY, John Keirl; s of Walter Edmund Gatenby, of Hartlepool, Cleveland, and Mary, *née* Keirl; *b* 26 April 1950; *Educ* Hartlepool GS, Trinity Hall Cambridge (MA, LLM); *m* 20 Sept 1975, (Thelma) Eunice, da of George Edmund Holmes, of The Hyde, London NW9; 2 da (Amy b 1980, Joanna b 1982); *Career* admitted slr 1975; slr Linklaters & Paines 1975-82 (articled clerk 1973-75), admitted slr and barrister NZ 1980, head Litigation Dept Withers 1983-84, ptnr Addleshaw Sons & Latham 1985- (assoc 1984-85); occasional speaker civil procedure and arbitration law; elder Poynton Baptist Church; memb: Nat Tst, RSPB, Hallé Concerts Soc; memb: ACI Arb 1983, Law Soc, Manchester Law Soc, London Slrs Litigation Assoc, Int Bar Assoc; MICM 1990; *Books* Notes on Discovery and Inspection of Documents 2 edn (1975), Recovery of Money (4 edn 1976, 7 edn 1989); *Recreations* music (play piano, organ, clarinet), gardening, photography, computers and walking the dog; *Style*— John Gatenby, Esq; Addleshaw Sons & Latham, Dennis House, Marsden St, Manchester M2 1JD (☎ 061 832 5994, fax 061 832 2250, telex 668886)

GATES, Malcolm Gilbert; s of Douglas Gilbert Gates (d 1953); *b* 6 March 1940; *Educ* Wallington Sch Surrey, Southampton Univ; *m* 1963, Valerie Diane, da of Harold William Hudson; 3 children; *Career* vice pres (international) Royal Trust Toronto; md: Royal Trust Bank (Jersey) Ltd, Royal Trust Co Canada (CI) Ltd; dir: Royal Trust International Fund Mgmnt, International Investment Trust; MInstD; *Recreations* golf, sailing; *Clubs* City of London, Victoria, Royal Commonwealth; *Style*— Malcolm Gates, Esq; Royal Trust, PO Box 7500, Station A, Toronto, Ontario, Canada

GATES, Martin Douglas Clift; s of Douglas Hansford Ellis Gates (d 1980), and Lily Madeline, *née* Pook; *b* 30 March 1934; *Educ* Epsom Coll; *m* 26 Sept 1964, Margaret Florence, da of William Albert George Smith; 2 s (Richard b 4 May 1966, Andrew b 5 March 1968); *Career* Nat Serv RAF 1955-57; articled clerk EC Brown & Batts 1951-55 and 1958-59, qualified chartered accountant 1960; audit sr: Finnie Ross Welch & co 1961-64, Peat Marwick Cassleton Elliott & Co Nigeria 1965-66, Woolley & Waldron 1966-68; ptnr: Woolley & Waldron 1969-77, Whinney Murray & Co 1977-79, Ernst & Whinney 1979-89, Ernst & Young 1989- (all following mergers); FCA (ACA 1960); *Recreations* golf, politics, gardening; *Style*— Martin Gates, Esq; Ernst & Young, Wessex House, 19 Threefield Lane, Southampton SO1 1TW (☎ 0703 230230, fax 0703 227409)

GATH, Dr Ann Mary Gethin; da of Sqdn Ldr Henry Gethin Lewis (d 1986), of Penárth, Glamorgan, and Gwendolen Joan, *née* David (d 1989); *b* 4 July 1934; *Educ* Westonbirt Sch, St Hugh's Coll Oxford (DM, MA), St Thomas's Hosp (BM, BCH); *m* 3 Dec 1960 (m dis 1978), Dennis Hanson; 1 s (Alexander b 1964), 2 da (Charlotte (Mrs Miller) b 1962, Victoria (Mrs Echlin) b 1963); *Career* conslt psychiatrist Borocourt Hosp Oxfordshire 1976-79, conslt child and adolescent psychiatrist W Suffolk Hosp 1980-87, conslt in the psychiatry of mental handicap in childhood and adolescence Maudsley and Bethlem Royal Hosps 1987-; registrar of the RCP 1988-, chm Assoc for Child Psychology and Psychiatry; MRCPsych 1972, FRCPsych; *Books* Down's Syndrome and the Family - The Early Years (1978); *Recreations* carriage driving, Connemara ponies, opera; *Style*— Dr Ann Gath; Hilda Lewis House, Bethlem Royal Hospital, 579 Wickham Rd, Shirley, Croydon CR0 8DR (☎ 081 777 6611)

GATHERCOLE, Ven John Robert; s of Robert Gathercole (d 1976), of Turvey, Bedfordshire, and Winifred Mary, *née* Price (d 1982); *b* 23 April 1937; *Educ* Judd Sch Tonbridge, Fitzwilliam Coll Cambridge (BA, MA), Ridley Hall Theol Coll; *m* 6 July 1963, (Joan) Claire, da of Eric Horton London, MBE, of Bexhill-on-Sea; 1 s (Andrew John b 1967), 1 da (Katharine Claire (Kate) b 1965); *Career* curate: St Nicholas Durham City 1962-66, St Bartholomew's Croxdale 1966-70; social and industl advsr to Bishop of Durham 1967-70, industl chaplain Redditch, Diocese of Worcester 1970-87, rural dean Bromsgrove 1978-85, hon canon Worcester Cathedral 1980-, team ldr Worcestershire industl Mission 1985-, archdeacon of Dudley 1987-; memb Industl Mission Assoc, sec The Malvern Conf 1991; *Recreations* vintage cars, motor sport, music; *Clubs* The Vintage Sports Car; *Style*— The Ven The Archdeacon of Dudley; Diocese of Worcester, The Old Palace, Deansway, Worcester WR1 2JE (☎ 0905 773301, fax 0905 612302)

GATHERCOLE, Richard Benjamin David; s of Evan Frederick James Gathercole, and Kathleen Mary, *née* Burrows; *b* 28 Sept 1956; *Educ* Salesian Coll, Univ of Leicester (BSc), UCL (MSc); *Career* dir and head Govt Sales Hoare Govett Ltd 1981-88, dir UK Govt Sales Credit Suisse First Boston 1988-; *Recreations* rugby, racing, ballet; *Style*— Richard Gathercole, Esq; 13 Landgrove Rd, Wimbledon SW19 7LL; Ludham House, Wells-next-the-Sea, Norfolk NR23 1E7 (☎ 081 947 2260); 2A Great Titchfield St, London W1 (☎ 071 322 4000)

GATHORNE-HARDY, Hon Hugh; s of 4 Earl of Cranbrook (d 1978), and his 2 w, Fidelity (*see* Dowager Countess of Cranbrook); *b* 30 Dec 1941; *Educ* Eton, Corpus Christi Coll Cambridge; *m* 1971, Caroline Elisabeth, da of William Nigel Ritchie (gs of 1 Baron Ritchie of Dundee) and Baroness Sibylla, da of late Baron von Hirschberg, of Murnau, Bavaria; 2 s, 2 da; *Career* timber merchant; *Style*— The Hon Hugh Gathorne-Hardy; The Hall Farm, Great Glemham, Saxmundham, Suffolk (☎ 072 878 420)

GATHORNE-HARDY, Hon Mrs Antony; Mary Catherine; da of Bernard Joseph Smartt (d 1963); *b* 26 March 1917; *Educ* Varndean Sch for Girls, Brighton Teachers Trg Coll; *m* 1974, as his 2 w, Surgn Cdr Hon Antony Gathorne Gathorne-Hardy, RN (d 1976), s of 3 Earl of Cranbrook (d 1911), and Lady Dorothy Montagu Boyle, da of 7 Earl of Glasgow; *Recreations* painting, golf; *Clubs* Richmond Art Soc; *Style*— The Hon Mrs Antony Gathorne-Hardy; 21 Cranebrook, Manor Rd, Twickenham, Middx TW2 5DJ (☎ 081 894 1174)

GATLEY, Dr Malcolm Stanley; *b* 3 June 1933; *Educ* Univ of Liverpool (MB, ChB), MRCS, LRCP, RCP (DLO, DIH); *m* 1, 10 July 1959, Marcia (d 1975); 1 s (Stephen b 22 Sept 1959), 1 da (Denise b 18 Dec 1962); m 2, 9 Sept 1976, Clelia; *Career* conslt occupational physician N Manchester Health Authy and NW RHA 1983-; fndr memb: Assoc NHS Occupational Physicians, Conslt Occupational Physicians NHS; memb BMA, FFOM 1985 (assoc 1977, memb 1982); *Recreations* music, skiing, European languages, travel; *Style*— Dr Malcolm Gatley; 125 Manchester Rd, Wilmslow, Cheshire SK9 2JN (☎ 0625 524760); N Manchester Gen Hosp, Occupational Health Dept, Delaunays Rd, Manchester M8 6RB (☎ 061 795 7199); 16 St John St, Manchester M3 4EA (☎ 061 835 1144)

GATTY, Trevor Thomas; OBE (1974); s of Thomas Alfred Gatty (d 1959), of Looe, Cornwall, and Lilian, *née* Wood (d 1980); *b* 8 June 1930; *Educ* King Edward's Sch Birmingham, Univ of London; *m* 1, 21 April 1956 (m dis 1983), Jemima Silver, da of Thomas Bowman; 2 s (Timothy James b 1957, Nicholas Trevor b 1959), 1 da (Jane Margaret (Mrs Clay) b 1960); m 2, 18 March 1989, Myrna, da of Albert Saturn; 1 step s (Daniel Scott Rodriguez), 1 step da (Michael-Amy Rodriguez (Mrs Sterry)); *Career* Army 1948-50, 2 Lt Royal Warwickshire Regt, TA 1950-54, Lt Royal Fusiliers; HM Dip Serv 1950-85, vice consul Leopoldville, first sec Bangkok; commercial consul: San Francisco, Zurich; cnsllr 1977, head Migration and Visa Dept FCO, dip serv inspr FCO, consul gen Atlanta 1981-85; conslt Pragma International (Paris and Washington); pres MGT; *Recreations* reading, the arts, English springer spaniels, physical fitness, railway history; *Style*— Trevor Gatty, Esq, OBE; 4026 Land O'Lakes Drive, Atlanta, Georgia, USA, 30342 (☎ 0101 404 264 9033); MGT International, PO Box 550328, Atlanta, Georgia, USA 30355 (☎ 0101 404 264 9033, fax 0101 404 256 2602)

GATWARD, (Anthony) James; s of George James Gatward (d 1964), and Lillian Georgina, *née* Strutton; *b* 4 March 1938; *Educ* George Gascoigne Sch Walthamstow, SW Essex Tech Coll and Sch of Art; *m* 1969, Isobel Anne Stuart, da of Ian Stuart Black, of Devon; 3 da; *Career* entered TV indust 1957; freelance drama prodr/dir: Canada and USA 1959-65, BBC and most ITV cos 1966-70; ptnr in prodn co (exec prodr and dir numerous int drama co-prodns in UK, Ceylon, Aust and Germany) 1970-78; dir: Southstar, Scottish and Global TV 1971-78, Independent Television Publications Ltd 1982-88, Oracle Teletext Ltd 1982-88, Solent Cablevision Ltd 1983-, Channel 4 TV Co 1984-89, Independent Television News Ltd 1986-, Super Channel Limited 1986-88, ITV Super Channel Limited 1986-89; dep chm and chief exec TVS Television 1984-, chm TVS Production 1984-, pres Telso Communications Inc 1987-; chm: Telso Communications Limited 1987-, Telso Overseas Ltd 1987-, Midem Organisation SA 1987-89; chm and chief exec TVS North American Holdings Inc 1988-, chm MTM Entertainment Inc 1989-; instigator and leader preparation of application for South and SE England ITV franchise 1979-80 (awarded Dec 1980); memb Cncl Operation Raleigh; govr South of England Agric Soc; *Recreations* farming, sailing, music; *Clubs* Reform, Royal Thames Yacht; *Style*— James Gatward, Esq; TVS Entertainment plc, Television Centre, Southampton SO9 5HZ (☎ 0703 634211)

GAU, John Glen Mackay; CBE (1989); s of Cullis William Gau (d 1944), and Nan, *née* Munro; *b* 25 March 1940; *Educ* Haileybury and ISC, Trinity Hall Cambridge (BA), Univ of Wisconsin USA; *m* 2 Sept 1966, Susan, da of John William Tebbs (d 1976); 2 s (William Merlin b 17 Aug 1972, Christopher Wilkie b 1 July 1978); *Career* BBC TV: prodr current affairs 1966-72, dep ed Midweek 1973-74, ed Nationwide 1975-78, head of current affairs 1978-81; independent and chief exec John Gau Productions 1981-88, dep chief exec and dir progs British Satellite Broadcasting 1988-90, jt chief exec John Gau Productions 1991-; chm: Ind Prog Prodrs Assoc 1984-86, RTS 1986-89; dir Channel 4 Bd 1985-88; fell RTS 1985; *Books* Soldiers (with John Keegan and Dr Richard Holmes, 1985); *Style*— John Gau, Esq, CBE; John Gau Productions, Burston House, 1 Burston Rd, London SW15 6AR (☎ 081 788 8811)

GAUDRY, Roger; *b* 15 Dec 1913; *Educ* Laval Univ (BA, BSc, DSc), Univ of Oxford (Rhodes scholar); *m* 1941, Madeleine Vallée; 2 s, 3 da; *Career* rector Univ of Montreal 1965-75, chm UN Univ 1974-76, pres Int Assoc of Univs 1975-80; chm Sci Cncl of Canada 1972-75; CC (1968); FRSC; *Style*— Roger Gaudry, Esq; 445 Beverley Ave, Mount Royal, Montreal, Quebec, Canada (☎ home 514 342 4759; office 514 343 7761)

GAULD, Alastair William Mitchell; s of William Mitchell Gauld (d 1950), of Rocquaine, Woking, Surrey, and Freda Caroline, *née* Condrup (d 1961); *b* 26 Sept 1914; *Educ* Roy GS Guildford, Oriel Coll Oxford (MA, Dip Econ); *m* 29 Nov 1947, Cynthia Rowena, da of Thomas Steel Downie, OBE (d 1931), of Chenar, Woking; 1 s (Andrew b 1955), 1 da (Fiona b 1949); *Career* WWII served Argyll and Sutherland Highlanders 1941-46 (demobbed as Major); Scottish Amicable Life Assurance Society 1937-40, Gresham Life Assurance Society 1946-70; chm: Old Woking branch Woking Cons Assoc 1951-54, Wood St branch Guildford Cons Assoc 1970-75; chief steward Wimbledon LT Championship 1973-, pres Puttenham Garden Club 1987-; Freeman City of London 1957, Liveryman Worshipful Co of Farriers 1963; *Recreations* gardening, golf, reading; *Clubs* The All England Lawn Tennis; *Style*— A W M Gauld, Esq; Pilgrims Way Cottage, The Heath, Puttenham, Guildford, Surrey GU3 1AL (☎ 0483 810288)

GAULT, David Hamilton; s of Leslie Hamilton Gault, and Iris Hilda Gordon Young; *b* 9 April 1928; *Educ* Fettes; *m* 1950, Felicity Jane Gribble; 3 s, 2 da; *Career* exec·chm Gallic Mgmnt 1974-; *Recreations* gardening, walking; *Clubs* Boodle's, City of London; *Style*— David Gault, Esq; Telegraph House, N Marden, Chichester, W Sussex (☎ 073 085 206, office 01 628 4851)

GAULTER, Andrew Martin; s of Derek Vivian Gaulter, of Chorleywood, Herts, and Edith Irene, *née* Shackleton; *b* 4 April 1951; *Educ* Merchant Taylors', Peterhouse Cambridge (exhibitioner, BA); *m* 30 Sept 1978, Susan Jane Wright; 2 da; *Career* articled clerk Messrs Beachcrofts London, admitted slr 1976; co sec: J Henry Schroder Wagg & Co Ltd 1990- (joined 1976), Schroders plc (holding co of Schroder Group) 1990-; memb: Law Soc, Law Soc Commerce and Industry Gp; *Recreations* golf; *Style*— Andrew Gaulter, Esq; Schroders plc, 120 Cheapside, London EC2V 6DS (☎ 071 382 6329, fax 071 382 3977)

GAULTER, Derek Vivian; CBE (1978); s of Jack Rudolf Gaulter, MC (d 1967), of Newport House, Clarence Ave, Cleveleys, nr Blackpool, and Muriel, *née* Westworth (d 1982); *b* 10 Dec 1924; *Educ* Denstone Coll, Peterhouse Cambridge; *m* 1 Jan 1949, Edith Irene, da of Frederick Norman Shackleton (d 1964), of 10 St Edmumds Ave, Hunstanton, Norfolk; 1 s (Andrew b 1951), 3 da (Briony b 1953, Catherine b 1959, Deborah b 1964); *Career* Sub Lt RNVR 1943-46 (serv MTBs in N Sea and minesweepers in Far East); called to the Bar Gray's Inn 1949, practising Common Law bar (Manchester) 1955-56; Fedn of Civil Engrg Contractors: legal sec, gen sec, dep DG, DG 1967; chm Construction Indust Trg Bd 1985-; former memb Cncl and President's Ctee CBI; former memb Civil Engrg Econ Devpt Ctee; companion of The Inst of Civil Engrs 1983; *Recreations* golf, gardening, travel, photography; *Clubs* IOD; *Style*— Derek Gaulter, Esq, CBE; Construction Industry Training Board, 24-30 West Smithfield, London EC1A 9JA (☎ 071 489 1662, fax 071 236 2875)

GAUME, Bernard Jean; s of Marie Henri Robert (d 1974), of Diou Allier, France, and Eugenie Francoise, *née* Prunier (d 1974); *b* 14 Oct 1934; *Educ* College Amede Gasquet Clermont Ferrand, Chambre des Metiers du Loiret France (Certificat de Compagnon); *m* 20 Dec 1963, Daphne Elizabeth, da of Frederick Arthur Perry; 1 s (Jean-Pierre Louis b 26 March 1963), 1 da (Helene Elizabeth b 1 May 1963); *Career* chef; apprentice under Marconet Louis Hotel de l'Allier Moulins France 1951-53, chef poissonier The Savoy Hotel London 1959-60, sous chef Hotel de l'Abbaye Talloires June-Oct 1960, chef de cuisine Restaurant Meunier Autun 1960-61; chef saucier: Les Bergues Geneva 1961-62, Gleneagles Hotel Perthshire March-Sept 1962, Americana of New York 1962-63, Regency Hotel New York March-Oct 1963; sous chef Hotel Intercontinental Geneva 1964-65; exec chef: Hotel Intercontinental Dublin 1965-68, Hyatt Carlton Tower London 1968-; Maitrise Escoffier 1972, Maitre Cuisinier de France 1982; Medaille des Operations de Securite et de l'Ordre en AFN Chevalier du Merite Agricole; memb: Mutuelle des Cuisiniers de France, Academie Culinaire de France; *Recreations* fishing; *Style—* Bernard Gaume, Esq; Hyatt Carlton Tower Hotel, Cadogan Place, London SW1X 9PY (☎ 071 245 6570)

GAUNT, Lawrence Michael; s of Robert Gaunt (d 1972), of London, and Lily, *née* Phillips; *b* 2 Oct 1934; *Educ* Ilford Co HS, The London Hosp (BDS, LDS, Harold Final prize Clinical Dental Surgery); *m* 31 March 1957, Ruth Margarette, da of late William Trackman; 3 s (Colin Murry b 25 Sept 1959, Peter Tony b 6 Nov 1961, David Ramon b 26 April 1964); *Career* house surgn The London Hosp 1957, in gen dental practice 1958-70, registrar Guy's Hosp 1960, in private practice Harley St 1970-, ptnr Lawrence Antiques (Victorian & Georgian jewellery) computer software specialist LMG Randon Data; memb RCS; *Recreations* bridge, computing; *Clubs* Dyrham Park Golf, New Amersham Bridge; *Style—* Lawrence Gaunt, Esq; 92 Harley St, London W1 (☎ 071 935 4392, 071 486 9359, car 0831 528701)

GAUNTLETT, John Wilson; s of Reginald Wilson Gauntlett (d 1916), and Kate Susanna, *née* Gibbs (d 1974); *b* 11 Jan 1914; *Educ* Christ's Hosp; *m* 29 July 1948, Alice Betty Magee, *née* Deane; 1 step s (Sean b 1943), 1 step da (Mary b 1941); *Career* WWII RA, Maj 1939-46; slr 1936, ptnr Linklater & Paines 1951, ret 1978; dep chm: RMC Gp plc, Malcolm Sargent Cancer Fund for Children 1987; *Recreations* carpentry, reading; *Style—* John W Gauntlett, Esq; Church House, Church St, Ticehurst, E Sussex TN5 7ES (☎ 0580 200281); RMC Group plc, 32 Chesham Place, London SW1X 8HB (☎ 071 235 0711)

GAUNTLETT, Malcolm Victor; s of Michael Errington Gauntlett (d 1971), and Adele Sylvia Dolores, *née* Montgomerie; *b* 20 May 1942; *Educ* St Marylebone GS; *m* 22 Oct 1966, Jean, da of James Brazier, of Burwarton, Shropshire; 3 s (Michael b 1971, Mark b 1981, Richard b 1982), 1 da (Sarah b 1969); *Career* exec chm Aston Martin Lagonda Ltd 1981-; chm: Aston Martin Lagonda Group Ltd 1984-, Proteus Petroleum Ltd; *Recreations* motor racing, aviation; *Clubs* Carlton, Cavalry and Guards', RAC, MCC; *Style—* Victor Gauntlett, Esq; 37 Chesham Place, SW1; Aston Martin Lagonda Ltd, Tickford St, Newport Pagnell, Bucks (☎ 0908 610620, telex 892341, fax 0908 613708)

GAUSSEN, Hon Mrs (Diana Bridget); da of Hon Robert Godfrey de Bohun Devereux (d 1934; only s of 17 Viscount Hereford); raised to the rank of a Viscount's da 1953; *b* 25 March 1931; *m* 16 Oct 1967, Col Samuel Charles Casamajor Gaussen, Welsh Gds, o surv s of late James Archibald Casamajor Gaussen, of Pegglesworth, Glos; 1 s, 1 da; *Style—* The Hon Mrs Gaussen; Nutbeam, Duntisbourne Leer, Cirencester, Glos GL7 7AS

GAUTREY, Peter; CMG (1972), CVO (1961), DK (Brunei) 1972; s of Robert Harry Gautrey (d 1961), of Surrey, and Hilda Morris (d 1972); *b* 17 Sept 1918; *Educ* Abbotsholme Sch Derbyshire; *m* 1947, Marguerite Etta, da of Horace Ewart Uncles (d 1963); 1 s (Christopher b 1948), 1 da (Sarah Jennifer b 1951); *Career* WWII Army Capt 1939-46; Home Office 1936, CRO 1948; first sec: Br Embassy Dublin 1950-53, New Delhi 1955-57; cnsllr New Delhi 1960-63, dep high cmmr Bombay 1963-65, Corps of Dip Serv Inspr 1965-68; high cmmr: Swaziland 1968-72, Brunei 1972-75, Guyana (concurrently ambass Surinam) 1975-78; *Recreations* walking, music; *Style—* Peter Gautrey, CMG, CVO; 24 Fort Rd, Guildford, Surrey GU1 3TE (☎ 0483 68407)

GAUVAIN, Col Anthony de Putron (Tony); s of Roland de Putron Gauvain, (ka Singapore 1943), and Marcelle Iris Clisson (now Mrs Hugo), *née* Mitchell; *b* 11 Jan 1941; *Educ* Wellington, RMA Sandhurst; *m* 9 Dec 1967, Avril, da of Brig Pat Hancock (d 1987), of Aynho: 2 da (Claire b 1973, Bonamy b 1975); *Career* cmmnd Cheshire Regt 1961, Trucial Oman Scouts 1966, Staff Coll 1972, Cmd 1 Bn Cheshire Regt 1981 (despatches 1983), MA to CDS Oman 1984, DACOS G2 Int HQ BAOR 1987-, Dacos G3 Ops HQUKLF 1991; *Recreations* tennis, water and snow skiing, sailing, amateur dramatics; *Clubs* Army and Navy; *Style—* Col Tony Gauvain; c/o Lloyds Bank plc, 7 Pall Mall, London SW1Y 5NH

GAVIN, Maj-Gen James Merricks Lewis; CB (1967), CBE (1963, OBE 1953); s of Joseph Merricks Gavin (d 1945), of Antofagasta, Chile, and Frances Edith, *née* Lewis (d 1955); *b* 28 July 1911; *Educ* Uppingham, Univ of Cambridge (MA); *m* 1942, Barbara Anne Elizabeth, da of Gp Capt Charles Geoffrey Murray, CBE (d 1962), of Hayling Island, Hants; 1 s (Angus), 2 da (Lindy, Janine); *Career* cmmnd 2 Lt RE 1931; served WWII: Far East, ME, Italy, France, also post-war in USA, Germany and France, Maj-Gen at SHAPE 1964-67; memb Everest Expedition 1936; *Recreations* yachting (Corruna), skiing, climbing; *Clubs* Royal Yacht Sqdn, Royal Cruising, Alpine; *Style—* Maj-Gen James Gavin, CB, CBE; Slathurst Farm, Milland, Liphook, Hants

GAWKRODGER, Dr David John; s of Walter Robert Gawkrodger, of Keynsham, Bristol, and Elma Jean, *née* Chalmers; *b* 14 Nov 1953; *Educ* King Edward's Sch Bath, Univ of Birmingham (MB ChB, MD); *Career* house physician and surgn Queen Elizabeth Hosp Birmingham 1976-77, med sr house offr and registrar N Staffordshire Hosp Centre Stoke-on- Trent 1977-81, registrar and sr registrar dermatology Royal Infirmary Edinburgh 1981-85, lectr in dermatology Univ of Edinburgh 1985-88, conslt dermatologist Royal Hallamshire Hosp Sheffield, clinical lectr dermatology Univ of Sheffield 1988-; hon sec Dowling club 1987-88, referee Med Res Cncl NZ, memb: MRCP (collegiate memb London and Edinburgh Colls), Br Assoc of Dermatologists; *Books* Skin Disorders in the Elderly (contrib, 1988), Immunology (contrib, 2 edn, 1989); *Recreations* painting, drawing; *Style—* Dr David Gawkrodger; Brook Cottage, Back Lane, Sheffield S17 4HP (☎ 0742 364226); Dept of Dermatology, Royal Hallamshire Hosp, Glossop Rd, Sheffield S10 2JF (☎ 0742 766222)

GAWLER, Dr Jeffrey; *b* 17 July 1945; *Educ* St Olave's GS London, Med Coll St Bartholomews Hosp Univ of London (MB BS); *m* 19 Dec 1970, Janet Mary; 1 s (Robert b 12 March 1973), 3 da (Ruth b 23 Sept 1975, Susan b 4 April 1978, Sarah b 6 Oct 1980); *Career* conslt i/c and dir Dept of Neurology St Bartholomew's Hosp 1988- (conslt neurologist 1976-); memb: BMA, Assoc Br Neurologists; FRCP; *Books* Neurology and Computed Tomography; *Recreations* literature, oenology; *Style—* Dr Jeffrey Gawler; 109 Harley St, London W1N 1DG (☎ 071 935 7505); St Bartholomews Hospital, London EC1A 7BE (☎ 071 601 7664)

GAWLEY, Dr Thomas Henry; s of Thomas Henry Gawley (d 1933), and Mary Withers, *née* Wilson (d 1978); *b* 5 Oct 1928; *Educ* Boys' Model Sch Belfast, Queen's Univ Belfast (MD); *m* 5 Oct 1949, Ethel Florence, da of James Bell Thompson (d 1969); 1 da (Ethel b 28 Jan 1951); *Career* Supt Qua Iboe Mission Hosp Nigeria 1965-70, res fell Royal Victoria Hosp 1972-74; Belfast City Hosp: chm Div of Annesthetists 1982-83, chm med Exec Ctee 1983-90; first chm of unit mgmnt gp 1984-87, unit clinician 1978-90, gen mangr 1990-; church elder and sec Calvary Baptist Church Belfast; FFARCS; *Style—* Dr Thomas Gawley; 165 Lower Braniel Road, Belfast, Northern Ireland BT5 7NN (☎ 0232 798726), Belfast City Hosp, Lisburn Rd, Belfast 9, Northern Ireland (☎ 0232 329241)

GAY, Barrie; s of Walter Lionel Gay (d 1970), and Florence Emily, *née* Upson (d 1983); *b* 9 Sept 1938; *Educ* Peter Symonds Sch Winchester; *m* 15 Oct 1966, Sylvia Ann, da of Charles Allen Parsons (d 1978); 1 s (James b 1969), 1 da (Catherine b 1971); *Career* CA; sr ptnr Weeks Green Southampton 1979-; FCA; *Style—* Barrie Gay, Esq; 9 The Abbey, Romsey, Hampshire SO51 8EN (☎ 0794 523413); College Keep, 4-12 Terminus Terrace, Southampton SO1 1XJ (☎ 0703 632023)

GAY, Bramwell Clifford (Bram); s of Clifford Gay, of Wolverhampton, and Effield, *née* Brown; *b* 19 Sept 1930; *Educ* Porth County Sch, Birmingham Sch of Music, Guildhall Sch of Music; *m* 9 Jan 1954, Margaret Ivy, da of late Augustus Bywater; 3 s (Peter John Noel b 1956, David b 1957, Jonathan Michael b 1958); *Career* served Scots Guards 1949-53; princ trumpet: City of Birmingham Symphony Orch 1953-60, Halle Orch 1960-69, Royal Opera House Covent Garden 1969-74; orch dir Royal Opera House 1974-; fndr: CBSO Brass Ensemble, Halle Brass Ensemble, Granada Brass Band Festival 1971-87; ed Brass Music (Novello & Co) 1967- LRAM 1950; *Recreations* music, boating; *Style—* Bram Gay, Esq; Royal Opera House, Covent Garden, London WC2 (☎ 071 240 1200)

GAY, Lt-Col Geoffrey Charles Lytton; s of Charles Millne Gay (d 1952), and Ida (d 1978), er da of Sir Henry Lytton (famous Savoyard); *b* 14 March 1914; *Educ* St Paul's; *m* 6 Sept 1947, Dorothy Ann, da of Maj Eric Rickman; 1 s (Charles), 2 da (Vivien, Louise (Mrs Fox)); *Career* WWII 1939-45, Durham LI BEF 1940, Staff Coll Camberley, Lt-Col COSIND Dist India; Knight Frank and Rutley: joined 1929, ptnr 1952, sr ptnr 1969-75, conslt 1975-85; chm and vice pres Westminster C of C; KStJ; memb Worshipful Co of Broderers; FRICS, FSVA, FRSA, FRGS, LRPS; Chevalier de l'Ordre de l'Economie Nationale 1960, Vermeille Medal of Paris 1975; *Recreations* photography, fishing, music, theatre; *Clubs* Carlton, Flyfishers', MCC; *Style—* Lt-Col Geoffrey Gay; Castle View, 122 Newland, Sherborne, Dorset DT9 3DT (☎ 0935 816676)

GAY, Rear Adm George Wilsmore; CB (1969), MBE (1946), DSC (1943), JP (1970 Plymouth); s of George Murch Gay, Engr Cdr RN (d 1933), and Olive Trounsell, *née* Allen (d 1971); *b* 2 Oct 1913; *Educ* Eastmans Sch Southsea, The Nautical Coll Pangbourne, RN Engrg Coll Keyham; *m* 15 Feb 1941, Nancy Agnes, da of Robert John Hinton Clark, MBE (d 1976), of 29 Whiteford Rd, Mannamead, Plymouth, Devon; 2 s (John b 1943, Paul b 1945), 1 da (Jane b 1948); *Career* RN 1930-69; WWII submarines, Cdr 1947, Capt 1958; CO HMS Sultan 1960-3; Chief Staff Offr material to Flag Offr Submarines 1963-66; Rear Adm 1967; dir gen Naval Trg 1967-69; ret 1969; FIMechEng; *Recreations* fishing, gardening; *Clubs* Army and Navy; *Style—* Rear Adm George Gay, CB, MBE, DSC, JP; 29 Whiteford Rd, Mannamead, Plymouth, Devon PL3 5LU (☎ 0752 664486)

GAY, John Edward; s of Edward John Clement Gay (d 1980) Florence Ellen, *née* Coombs; *b* 5 May 1934; *Educ* Bishop Wordsworth Sch Salisbury; *m* 15 Sept 1962, Sharon, da of Fred Duke, of Bromley, Kent; 1 s (Richard James Clement b 1967), 3 da (Katherine (Mrs Harrison) b 1963, Mary Lousie (Mrs Navey) b 1964, Margaret Elizabeth b 1969); *Career* Nat Serv 1957-59: 2 Lt Loyal NL Regt, active serv Malaya, HK, GSM with Malaya bar; articled clerk Fawcett Brown & Pinnegar Salisbury 1951-56, personal asst to Tax Ptnr Champness & Co 1959-62; ptnr: Dawson & Gordon 1966-78 (mangr 1962-66), Miles Dawson & Co (following merger) 1978-81; sr ptnr Spicer & Oppenheim International (following merger) 1987-90 (managing ptnr 1981-87), sr ptnr Touche Ross & Co 1990-; ICAEW: chm Bournemouth students 1967-68, chm Bournemouth Local Membs Gp 1972-73 (sec 1968-71), careers advsr Bournemouth CA 1971-79, memb SOSCA Soc Ctee 1971-81 (pres 1979-80), hon auditor Bournemouth Private Hotel & Guest House Assoc 1965-, pres Rotary Club Bournemouth 1990-91; St Saviour's Church Ilford: hon treas 1973-80, warden 1980-86, vice chm 1988-; FCA 1968 (ACA 1957); *Recreations* computers, books, crosswords, music, opera, glass etching, oil painting, sailing, walking, discovering France; *Clubs* Bournemouth Speakers (hon treas 1968), Bournemouth Constitutional, Rotary (Bournemouth), Fishheads (memb ctee 1975-), 3/4d Luncheon; *Style—* John Gay, Esq; Sandown, 76 Durrington Rd, Bournemouth, Dorset BH7 6PZ (☎ 0202 428474); Touch Ross & Co, Richmond Point, 43 Richmond Hill, Bournemouth BH2 6LR (☎ 0202 291655, fax 0202 553551)

GAYA, Dr Harold; s of Ralph Gaya, of 23 Beechlands Ave, Netherlee, Glasgow, and Anne, *née* Salamon (d 1964); *b* 15 Oct 1940; *Educ* Glasgow HS, Univ of Glasgow (MB ChB); *m* 1 June 1969, Celia, da of Ronald Mark Jeffries (d 1964); 3 s (Andrew b 1970, David b 1972, Richard b 1974); *Career* lectr in microbiology St Bartholomew's Hosp Med Coll London 1968-71, conslt bacteriologist and lectr Royal Post Grad Med Sch Hammersmith Hosp London 1971-74, reader in bacteriology Wright-Fleming Inst St Mary's Hosp Med Sch and hon conslt bacteriologist St Marys Hosp 1974-80, conslt microbiologist Royal Brompton Nat and Lung Heart Hosps, hon sr lectr Nat Heart and Lung Inst 1980-, conslt microbiologist The London Clinic 1983-; treas Int Anti-Microbial Therapy Co-op Gp of the Euro Orgn for Res and Treatment of Cancer 1987- (fndr chm 1973-78, co-ordinating sec and treas 1978-87); author of numerous pubns on prevention and treatment of infection; FRSM 1969, corresponding fel of Infectious Diseases Soc of America 1983; MRCPath 1970, FRCPath 1982; *Recreations* bridge, travel, music, photography; *Clubs* Royal Soc Med; *Style—* Dr Harold Gaya; 10 Mowbray Rd, Edgware, Middx HA8 8JQ; Royal Brompton National Heart and Lung Hospital, Sydney Street, London SW3 6NP (☎ 071 351 8440, fax 071 351 8443)

GAYMER, Janet Marion; da of Ronald Frank Craddock, of Nuneaton, Warwickshire, and Marion Clara, *née* Stringer (d 1988); *b* 11 July 1947; *Educ* Nuneaton HS for Girls, St Hilda's Coll Oxford (MA), LSE (LLM); *m* 4 Sept 1971, John Michael Gaymer, s of Kenneth John Gaymer, of Gt Bookham, Surrey; 2 da (Helen b 1977, Natalie b 1979); *Career* admitted slr 1973; ptnr and head Employment and Immigration Law Dept Simmons & Simmons 1977-; memb Employment Law Ctee Law Soc 1987, chm Employment Law Sub Ctee City of London Law Soc 1987, memb Ed Advsy Bd Sweet & Maxwell's Encyclopedia of Lab Rels 1987, memb Justice Ctee Industl Tbnls 1987; Freeman Worshipful Co of Slrs 1977; affiliate IPM, memb Law Soc; *Recreations* learning to play the flute, riding, swimming, theatre, music; *Style—* Mrs Janet Gaymer; Simmons & Simmons, 14 Dominion St, London EC2M 2RJ (☎ 071 628 2020, fax 071 588 4129, 071 588 9418, telex 888562 SIMMON G)

GAYMER, Vivien Murray; *née* Gall; da of Dr Louis Adrian Murray Gall (d 1973), of Spalding, Lincs and Patricia Violet, *née* Boothby, JP (d 1989); *Educ* Felixstowe Coll, English Speaking Union scholar at Northfield Sch Mass USA, Univ of Sheffield (LLB); *m* 12 Aug 1978, Keith Edward (Sam) Gaymer, s of Ernest Edward Gaymer; 1 step da (Victoria b 1961); *Career* called to the Bar Middle Temple 1971; counsel Mobil Oil London and NY 1975-84, head of legal affrs Enterprise Oil plc 1984-; tstee Petroleum and Mineral Law Educn Tst; memb: Editorial Bd Oil and Gas Law and Taxation Review, Editorial Advsy Bd International Co and Commercial Law Reviews; *Recreations* cooking and eating; *Style—* Mrs Vivien Gaymer; 5 Strand, London WC2N

5HU (☎ 071 930 1212, fax 071 930 0321, telex 8950611 EPRISE G)

GAYTON, Alan William; JP (Leicester 1963); s of Frank Gayton (d 1961), of Leicester, and Susannah Edith Anne Drackley (d 1975); *b* 21 June 1923; *Educ* Wyggeston GS Leicester, LSE, Sandhurst; *m* 1, Dec 1948 (m dis), Jean Urquhart; 1 s (John Charles b 1956), 1 da (Susan Mary b 1953); m 2, Feb 1974, Jean Frances, da of Frank Kelly (d 1976), of Leicester; *Career* WWII served N Africa and Italy Capt 17/21 Lancers; dir Gayton Advtg Ltd Leicester, chm Leicester City Bench 1987; FIPA; *Recreations* golf, theatre; *Style*— Alan W Gayton, Esq, JP; Old Boot Cottage, Main St, Houghton-on-the-Hill, Leics (☎ 0533 414 131)

GAZDAR, Prof Gerald James Michael; s of John Gazdar (d 1966), of Hatfield, and Kathleen, *née* Cooper; *b* 24 Feb 1950; *Educ* Heath Mount Sch, Bradfield Coll, UEA (BA), Univ of Reading (MA, PhD); *Career* dean of sch of cognitive and computing sciences Univ of Sussex 1988- (lectr in linguistics 1975-80, reader in linguistics 1980-84, reader in AI and linguistics 1984-85, prof of computational linguistics 1985-), fell Center for Advanced Study in the Behavioural Sciences Stanford 1984-85; memb: ACL, ASL, LAGB, AAAI, ACM; FBA 1988; *Books* Pragmatics (1979), Order, Concord and Constituency (with Klein and Pullum, 1983), Generalized Phrase Structure Grammar (1985), New Horizons in Linguistics II (with Lyons, Coates and Deuchar, 1987), Natural Language Processing in the 1980's (with Franz, Osborne, Evans, 1987), Natural Language Processing in Prolog/Lisp/Pop-11 (with Mellish, 1989); *Style*— Prof Gerald Gazdar; School of Cognitive and Computing Sciences, University of Sussex, Brighton BN1 9QH (☎ 0273 678029, telex 877159 RR Hove UNISEX)

GAZE, Mark Nicholas; s of John Owen Gaze (d 1987), and May Susan, *née* Skelton; *b* 6 Feb 1958; *Educ* Med Coll of St Bartholomew's Hosp Univ of London (MB BS); *m* 22 June 1987, Dr Janet Ann Wilson, da of Dr Henry Donald Wilson; *Career* house surgn Southend Hosp Essex 1981-82, house physician St Bartholemews Hosp London 1982; sr house offr in med: Severalls Hosp Colchester 1983, St Mary's Hosp Portsmouth 1983-85; registrar in radiation oncology Royal Infirmary and Western Gen Hosp Edinburgh 1985-87; lectr in radiation oncology: Univ of Edinburgh 1987-89, Univ of Glasgow 1989-; chm Collegiate Membs Ctee RCPE 1989- (memb Cncl 1988-); MRCP 1984, FRCR 1988; *Style*— Dr Mark Gaze; Docharn, 9 Blackford Ave, Edinburgh EH12 2PJ (☎ 031 667 2917); Beatson Oncology Centre Research Laboratories, Alexander Stone Building, Beatson Institute for Cancer Research, Garscube Estate, Bearsden, Glasgow

GAZE, Dr (Raymond) Michael; s of William Mercer Gaze (d 1959), of Blue Mills, Wickham Bishops, Essex, and Kathleen Grace, *née* Bowhill (d 1974); *b* 22 June 1927; *Educ* Sch of Med of the Royal Colls Edinburgh, Univ of Oxford (BA, DPhil); *m* 20 March 1957, Robinetta Mary, da of Prof Roger Noel Armfelt (d 1955), of Woodlea, Shadwell Lane, Leeds; 1 s (Julian Mercer b 1959), 2 da (Harriet Carlin b 1958, Hannah Mary (twin) b 1959); *Career* MO RAMC 1953-55; house physician Chelmsford and Essex Hosp 1949, lectr in physiology Univ of Edinburgh 1955-62, Alan Johnston Lawrence and Moseley res fell of the Royal Soc 1962-66, reader in physiology Univ of Edinburgh 1966-70, head Div of Developmental Biology Nat Inst Med Res London 1970-83, head MRC Neural Devpt and Regeneration Gp Dept of Zoology Univ of Edinburgh 1984-; FRSE 1964, FRS 1972; *Books* The Formation of Nerve Connections (1970); author of numerous scientific papers; *Recreations* hill walking, drawing, music; *Style*— Dr Michael Gaze, FRSE, FRS; Institute of Cell, Animal and Population Biology, Ashworth Laboratory, West Mains Rd, Edinburgh EH9 3JT

GAZE, Nigel Raymond; s of Raymond Ernest Gaze, of Knutsford Cheshire, and Beatrice Maud, *née* Caswell; *b* 11 Feb 1943; *Educ* Prescot GS, Univ of Liverpool (MB ChB), Univ of London (BMus); *m* 6 Aug 1966, Heather Winifred, da of Ronald Douglas Richardson, of Oakley House, Leeswood, Mold, Clwyd; 3 s (Richard b 8 April 1972, Thomas b 27 Aug 1974, Harry b 29 March 1985), 3 da (Julia b 4 Aug 1967, Celia b 23 March 1970, Mary b 7 Jan 1979); *Career* conslt plastic surgn Royal Preston and Blackpool Victoria Hosps 1980-; contrib various articles on med subjects in jls; organist, accompanist and composer: conductor Elizabeth Singers, accompanied Hutton GS Chamber Choir on the record And My Heart Shall Be There, accompanist Preston County Hall Singers, assoc organist Preston Parish Church, several published compositions for organ and choir; memb: Victorian Soc, Preston Select Vestry, CPRE, Nat Tst, Cncl Br Assoc of Aesthetic Plastic Surgns; memb: BMA, Br Assoc Plastic Surgns; FRCS, FRCSEd, FRCO, FTCL, FVCM, LRAM; *Books* Year Book of Plastic Surgery (contrib, 1981); *Recreations* collecting books and interesting junk, architecture, DIY; *Style*— Nigel Gaze, Esq; Priory House, 35 Priory Lane, Penwortham, Preston, Lancs PR1 0AR (☎ 0772 743821); Senior Consultant Plastic Surgeon, Royal Preston Hospital, Sharoe Green Lane, Fulwood, Preston, Lancs (☎ 0772 716565); Fulwood Hall Hospital, Midgery Lane, Fulwood, Preston PR2 5SX

GAZI, Dr Thrity Framroze; da of Framroze Edulji Gazi (d 1959), and Allan, *née* Turner (d 1988); *b* 6 Aug 1939; *Educ* Univ of Bombay (MB BS, DGO), Univ of London (DA); *Career* conslt anaesthetist Maastricht Holland 1974-76, assoc specialist Law Hosp Carluke Lanarks 1985- (locum conslt 1976-85); MPS, memb BMA; *Recreations* gardening, photography; *Style*— Dr Thrity Gazi; Law Hospital, Carluke, Lanarkshire ML8 5ER (☎ 0698 351100)

GAZZARD, Dr Brian George; s of Edward George Gazzard, and Elizabeth, *née* Hill; *b* 4 April 1946; *Educ* Cambridge Univ (MA, MD); *m* 21 June 1969, Joanna Alice, da of Thomas Benson Keeler; 3 s (Simon, Nicholas, Luke); *Career* sr registrar: Liver Unit KCH 1974-76, St Bartholomew's Hosp 1976-78; conslt physician and AIDS co-ordinator Westminster and St Stephen's Hosps 1978-; memb various ctees organising res and fin for AIDS patients; FRCP; *Books* Peptic Ulcer (1988), Gastroenterological Manifestations of AIDS, Clinics in Gastroenterology (1988); *Recreations* gardening; *Style*— Dr Brian Gazzard; Old Blew House, Dulwich Common, London SE21 (☎ 071 693 1151); 138, Harley St, London W1 (☎ 071 828 9811, fax 081 834 4240, telex 919263 VHAG)

GAZZARD, Roy James Albert; s of James Henry Gazzard, MBE (d 1976), of New Milton, Hants, and Ada Gwendoline, *née* Willis (d 1973); *b* 19 July 1923; *Educ* Stationers' Company's Sch Hornsey Middx, Architectural Assoc Sch of Architecture (Dip), Sch of Planning & Res for Regnl Devpt (Dip); *m* 6 Jan 1947, (Muriel) Joy, da of Frederick William Morgan (d 1952), of Higher Odcombe, Somerset; 2 s (Paul b and d 1948, Mark b 1953), 2 da (Sarah (twin) b 1953, Naomi b 1958); *Career* cmmnd Middx Regt 1942, Glider Pilot Regt 1943, Support Capt HQ 6 Airlanding Bde 6 Airborne Div 1944, demobbed Maj 1947; govt town planner Uganda 1949-54 (devpt plans for Jinja 1954), staff architect Barclays Bank 1953-60, chief architect planner Peterlee New Town Devpt Corp 1960-62; dir: devpt Northumberland CC 1962-70, postgrad studies urban geography and planning Univ of Durham 1970-76, under sec DOE 1976-79, dir centre for Middle Eastern and Islamic studies Univ of Durham 1984; advsr: Sultanate of Oman 1973, Republic of Vanuatu 1989, Republic of Seychelles 1990; memb Sec of State's Working Party preparing UK evidence for UN conf on the environment 1972, chief professional advsr Sec of State's Environmental Bd 1976-79; chm Northern region RIBA 1970, vice chm BBC NE Advsy Cncl 1970-73, govr Sunderland Poly 1972-76, memb Cncl Northern Arts 1970-76, chm BBC Radio Newcastle Advsy Cncl 1980-83, tstee City of Durham Tst 1970-91; Liveryman Worshipful Co of Stationers 1970 (Renter Warden 1985-86); hon fell Centre for Middle Eastern and Islamic Studies Univ of Durham 1988; FRTPI 1957, FRIBA 1967; *Books* Durham: Portrait of a Cathedral City (1983); *Recreations* independent travel in remote locations, esp Arabia, dry stone walling, castles and castle towns; *Clubs* City Livery; *Style*— Roy Gazzard, Esq; 13 Dunelm Court, South Street, Durham City DH1 4QX (☎ 091 386 4067)

GEAR, William; s of Porteous Gordon Gear (d 1965), of Fife, Scotland, and Janet, *née* Inglis (d 1955); *b* 2 Aug 1915; *Educ* Edinburgh Coll of Art, Univ of Edinburgh, Academie Fernand Leger Paris; *m* 7 July 1949, Charlotte, da of Moses Chertok (d 1962), of New York; 2 s (David Alexander b 1949, Robert Gordon b 1951); *Career* RCS, Middle East, Italy, Germany 1940-47, cmmnd 1941, staff off MFA and A control cmmn for Germany 1946-47; painter; head of fine art Birmingham Coll of Art and Poly 1964-75; worked in Paris 1947-50, Arts Cncl Purchase prize Festival of Britain 1951, David Cargill award 1967, Lorne Fellowship 1976; one-man exhibitions incl: London Gimpel Fils Gall 1948-, S London Art Gall (retrospective) 1954, Edinburgh Fest 1966, Arts Cncl N Ireland 1969, Scottish Arts Cncl (retrospective) 1969, Univ of Sussex 1975, RBSA Birmingham (retrospective) 1976, Talbot Rice Art Centre, Univ of Edinburgh and Ikon Gallery 1982, Spacex Gallery Exeter 1983, Kirkcaldy Art Gallery 1985, Netherbow Art Centre 1985, Cobra Malmo 1986, Redfern GAllery London 1987, Taipeh 1987, Stockholm 1987, Odense Denmark 1988, Galerie 1900-2000 Paris 1988, Karl & Faber Munich 1989, Gabriele von Loeper Hamburg 1989, Kunsthandel Leeman Amsterdam 1990, Redfern Gallery London 1990; works in permanent collections incl: Tate Gallery, Arts Cncl, Contemp Art Soc, Scottish Nat Gallery of Modern Art, Scottish Arts Cncl, V & A Museum, Laing Art Gallery, Inst of Contemp Art Lima, Towner Gallery Eastbourne, Nat Gallery of Aust, Br Museum, Nat Gallery of Canada, Musée d'Art Moderne Liège; memb: Cncl NCDAD, Fine Art Ctee CNAA; RBSA 1966; *Recreations* travel, music, sport; *Style*— William Gear, Esq; 46 George Road, Birmingham B15 1PL (☎ 021 454 1602)

GEAREY, John Marchant; s of Reginald George Gearey (d 1973), of St Albans, and Dorothy May, *née* Townsend (d 1982); *b* 27 March 1938; *Educ* St Albans Sch; *m* 11 Feb 1961, Margaret Isobel, da of Ronald George Reek; 3 s (Michael b 5 Dec 1961, David b 7 Oct 1964, Ian b 27 Feb 1967), 1 da (Carolyn b 26 June 1963); *Career* CA; articled clerk Hartleys Wilkins & Flew 1955, ptnr Peat Marwick Uganda 1964-67 (mangr 1962-64); Mann Judd: joined 1967, ptnr 1969, ptnr in charge Midlands practice 1969-79 (now Touche Ross, following merger 1979), memb Mgmnt Bd 1975-79, memb Policy Bd 1978-79, chm Computer Steering Ctee 1978-79, internal auditor 1983-84, regnl mktg ptnr 1984-87, ptnr in charge Midland region mgmnt consultancy practice 1986-88 (seconded as dir of fin Cerestar SA/NV Brussels 1988-89); author of various professional books; memb of Cncl Birmingham Chamber of Indust and Commerce 1986-; FCA 1972 (ACA 1961); *Recreations* church treasurer, travelling, walking, music, light opera, grandchildren; *Clubs* Birmingham; *Style*— John M Gearey, Esq; The Manor House, Hadzor, Droitwich, Worcs WR9 7DR (☎ 0905 772588); Touche Ross & Co, Kensington House, 136 Suffolk St Queensway, Birmingham B1 1LL (☎ 021 631 2288, fax 021 631 4512)

GEARING, Eric Gerard; s of Bertrand John Gearing (d 1969), of Wallasey, and Winifred Anastasia, *née* Smith (d 1964); *b* 21 Sept 1922; *Educ* private, Liverpool Collegiate Sch, Univ of Liverpool (LLB); *m* 7 Nov 1959, Pauline Mary, da of Charles Ebo (d 1964), of Crosby; 1 da (Maria Winefride b 1971); *Career* Army 1941-45, Lt (actg Capt) wounded N Africa; slr Gearing and Wilde; pt/t chm Social Security Appeal Tbnl, former Borough Cncllr and Parly candidate (Cons); pres: Wallasey Civic Soc (ex chm), Wallasey Operatic Soc (ex chm), Wallasey YMCA, The Rotary Club of Wallasey; former pres and life vice pres Wallasey Cons Assoc (vice chm and treas), chm Wallasey Soc for Mentally Handicapped, life govr Cancer Res Fund, Co Borough Cncllr; *Recreations* amateur drama & operatics, politics, painting, photography, theatre, spectator sports, music; *Clubs* Rotary, Catenians, YMCA; *Style*— Eric G Gearing, Esq; Tarsus, 6 Gorsehill Rd, Wallasey, Wirral (☎ 051 639 5802); 110 Wallasey Rd, Wallasey, Wirral (☎ 051 638 2113, fax 051 658 8688, telex 628761 BUTEL G)

GEARING, Graham David; s of Jack Gearing (d 1974), and Clara Elizabeth, *née* Patterson; *b* 17 Oct 1943; *Educ* East Ham GS; *m* 25 April 1981, Kathleen Elizabeth, da of Patrick Cardinall Mason Sedgwick, CMG (d 1985); 1 s (Patrick b 1985), 1 da (Nicola b 1982); *Career* md G D Gearing Electronics Ltd 1975-; *Recreations* power boating, mountaineering; *Style*— Graham Gearing, Esq; Tarskavaig, Sleat, Isle of Skye, Scotland IV46 8SA (☎ 047 15 263)

GEARING, Ian Martin; s of Jack Gearing (d 1974), and Clara Elizabeth, *née* Patterson (now Mrs Walker); *b* 23 Sept 1950; *Educ* East Ham GS, Thames Poly (BA); *m* 24 Aug 1974, Liselotte, da of Herr Konrad Roder, of Bayreuth, West Germany; 1 s (David Alexander b 14 Oct 1980), 1 da (Andrea Elizabeth b 31 July 1982); *Career* advertising exec J Walter Thomson Advtg Agency Frankfurt W Germany 1973-74, mktg mangr Bunzl Paper Subsidiary London 1974-76 (gen mangr Antwerp 1976-79), mktg mgmnt Utd Rum Merchants International Ltd London 1980-87, pres and md Tia Maria International London; vice pres Camberley Rugby FC; MInstM; *Recreations* sport and music; *Style*— Ian Gearing, Esq; Tia Maria International Ltd, Heritage House, 21 Inner Park Rd, London SW19 6ED (☎ 081 788 4400, fax 081 788 4323, telex 919396 HIWALKG)

GEARY, Michael John; s of John Geary (d 1980), of Hemel Hempstead, Herts, and Joyce Nellie, *née* Lee; *b* 18 June 1950; *Educ* Apsley GS Hemel Hempstead, Worcester Coll Oxford (BA, MA); *m* 4 Jan 1975, Susan Mary, da of Henry Spilman Wood (d 1989), of Turweston, Northants; 2 s (John b and d 1979, Malcolm b 1980), 1 da (Hazel b 1982); *Career* exec engr PO Telecommunications (now Br Telecom) 1971-74, controller Industrial and Commercial Finance Corporation Ltd (now 3i plc) 1974-79, investmt exec Charterhouse Development Ltd 1979-82, md Munford White plc 1982-85; dir: Tunstall Development Ltd 1985-86, Prudential Venture Managers Ltd 1986-; *Recreations* sailing, skiing; *Clubs* Royal Southern Yacht, Ski (GB); *Style*— Michael Geary, Esq; Audrey House, Ely Place, London EC1N 2NH (☎ 071 831 7747)

GEAVES, Fiona Jane; da of Robert William Geaves (d 1974), and Janet Hillary; *b* 6 Dec 1967; *Educ* Brockworth Comprehensive Sch; *Career* represented England at squash at U16, U19 and sr level, team memb of U19 Squash World Jr Open Winners 1985, British Open U23 Champion 1989, World Ranking 12 British 6; Nat Eng Squash Squad; *Style*— Miss Fiona Geaves; Riverside Sports & Leisure Club, St Oswald's Rd, Gloucester (☎ 0452 413214)

GEBBETT, Stephen Henry; s of Albert Gebbett, of Hundon, Suffolk, and Elsie Mary, *née* Kettle; *b* 24 Jan 1949; *Educ* Raynes Park CGS, Univ of Wales (BSc); *m* 22 Dec 1973, Linda Margaret; 1 s (Timothy Giles b 5 Oct 1976), 1 da (Kimberley Sarah b 13 May 1981); *Career* graduate trainee and assoc dir F J Lyons PR Consultancy 1970-76; Charles Barker Lyons 1976-: assoc dir 1976-79, dir 1979-86, md 1986-88, chief exec 1988-; MIPR 1976; *Recreations* squash, gardening, humour; *Style*— Stephen Gebbett, Esq; Charles Barker Lyons, 30 Farringdon St, London EC4A 4EA (☎ 071 634 1014)

GÈBLER, Carlo Ernest; s of Ernest Gèbler, of Oakley, Co Dublin, and Edna, *née* O'Brien; *b* 21 Aug 1954; *Educ* Bedales Sch, Univ of York (BA), Nat Film and TV Sch; *Career* author, script writer, film dir; pubns: The Eleventh Summer (1985), August In July (1986), Work and Play (1987), Driving through Cuba: An East-West Journey

(1988), The TV Genie (1989), Malachy and his Family (1990), Life of a Drum (1991); reviews, articles, short stories, travel pieces for: Cosmopolitan, Departures, Discount Traveller, Fiction Magazine, Harpers and Queen, Image, Irish Independent, Irish Press, Irish Times, Literary Reviews, London Evening Standard, Mail on Sunday, Sunday Independent, Sunday Press, Sunday Tribune, Telegraph; contrib to short story collections: Travellers Tales, London Tales, 20 under 35, Winter's Tales 6; writer and dir films: Croagh Patrick (1977), The Beneficiary (1979), Over Here (1980), Rating Notman (1981), Country & Irish (1982), Two Lives: A Portrait of Francis Stuart (1985), George Barker (1987), August in July (writer, 1990); memb Aosdana (Eire) 1990; *Recreations* walking, travelling; *Style—* Carlo Gébler, Esq; c/o Antony Harwood, Curtis Brown, 162-168 Regent St, London W1R 5TB (☎ 071 872 0331, fax 071 872 0332)

GEDDES, Hon David Campbell; TD; s of 1 Baron Geddes, GCMG, KCB, PC (d 1954); *b* 11 March 1917; *Educ* Stowe, Gonville and Caius Coll Cambridge, UCL (PhD); *m* 31 Dec 1948, Gerda, da of State Cncllr Gerdt Meyer Bruun, of Bergen, Norway (d 1945); 2 da (Jane, Harriet); *Career* joined RA 1938, served 1939-45 on staff, Maj 1943; dir Jardine Matheson Hongkong 1953-58 and assoc cos; civil servant FCO 1959-65, (princ overseas devpt admin 1969-77); *Clubs* Brooks's; *Style—* Dr the Hon David Geddes, TD; Clayfield, Etchingham, East Sussex TN19 7QJ

GEDDES, Enid, Baroness; Enid Mary; *née* Butler; o da of late Clarance Howell Butler, of Shanghai and Tenterden, Kent; *m* 26 Jan 1931, 2 Baron Geddes (d 1975); 2 s (3 Baron and 1 s decd), 1 da (Hon Mrs van Koetsveld); *Style—* The Rt Hon Enid, Lady Geddes; 12 Courtenay Place, Lymington, Hants (☎ 0590 73333)

GEDDES, 3 Baron (UK 1942), of Rolvenden; Euan Michael Ross Geddes; s of 2 Baron, KBE (d 1975), and Enid, *née* Butler; *b* 3 Sept 1937; *Educ* Rugby, Gonville and Caius Coll Cambridge (MA), Harvard Business Sch; *m* 7 May 1966, Gillian, yr da of late William Arthur Butler, of Henley-on-Thames; 1 s (James b 1969), 1 da (Clair b 1967); *Heir* s, Hon James George Neil Geddes; *Career* Lt Cdr RNR (ret); chm: Geddes & Co Ltd 1985-, Dawson Strange Photography Ltd 1988-, Parasol Portrait Photography Ltd 1988-; dep chm: Faber Prest Holdings plc 1987-; dir: Barchester Shipping Ltd 1984-, John Broadwood & Sons Ltd 1986-, City Harbour Hotel Ltd 1987-, Eurospa (Chelsea) Ltd 1987-, Harbour Inns Ltd 1988-, Stewart Consultants & Offshore Technology Services Ltd 1986-, British Rail (Southern) 1990-, Regional Airports Ltd 1990-; *Recreations* golf, skiing, bridge, gardening; *Clubs* Brooks's, Aldeburgh Golf, Hong Kong, Royal Hong Kong Golf; *Style—* The Rt Hon the Lord Geddes; The Manor House, Long Sutton, Basingstoke, Hants RG25 1ST (☎ 0256 862105, fax 0256 862029)

GEDDES, Ford Irvine; MBE (Mil 1943); s of Irvine Campbell Geddes (d 1962, bro of 1 Baron Geddes), and Dorothy Jefford, *née* Fowler; *b* 17 Jan 1913; *Educ* Loretto, Gonville and Caius Coll Cambridge; *m* 8 Dec 1945, Barbara Gertrude Vere, o da of Charles Fitzmaurice Parry Okeden, JP; 1 s (David), 4 da (Jennian (Mrs Nicholas Montagu), Merryn (Mrs Michael Lloyd), Fiona (Mrs Colin Goodwille), Ailie (Mrs Adrian Collins)); *Career* dir Anderson Green & Co Ltd 1947-68, The Equitable Life Assurance Soc 1955-76 (pres 1963-71), The Peninsular & Oriental Steam Navigation Co 1960-72 (chm 1971-72); memb London Advsy Bd Bank of New South Wales 1950-81; *Clubs* City of London, Union (Sydney); *Style—* Ford Geddes, Esq, MBE; 18 Gordon Place, London W8 4JD

GEDDES, Keith Irvine; DFC; s of Irvine Campbell Geddes (d 1962), and Dorothy Jefford, *née* Fowler (d 1976); *b* 25 Oct 1918; *Educ* Loretto, Gonville and Caius Coll Cambridge (BA, rugby football blue); *m* 1, 1946 (m dis 1967), Marion Olive, da of late Sir John Stirling; 2 s (Rorie b 1948, Angus b 1954), 2 da (Rona b 1947, Shian b 1951); m 2, 1968, Anne Mary, da of Richard Pullen; 1 s (Marcus b 1975), 2 da (Katherin b 1970, Serena b 1973); *Career* cmmnd RAFVR 1939, 604 Fighter Sqdn 1940-41, staff HQ Fighter Cmd 1943-45 (demobilised 1945 rank of Sqdn Ldr); dir Anderson Green & Co Ltd 1950-62, fndr memb and dir Economic Forestry Gp 1959-87, memb Lloyd's 1961; Capt 1944-47: Scotland Ruby Football XV, RAF RFC, London Scottish RFC; *Recreations* shooting; *Clubs* City of London; *Style—* Keith I Geddes, Esq, DFC; Westbrook House, Upwey, Weymouth, Dorset (☎ 0305 812929, 036982 284)

GEDDES, Philip Clinton; s of David Geddes, and Audrey Clinton, *née* Phillips; *b* 26 Aug 1947; *Educ* Sherborne, Queens' Coll Cambridge; *m* 27 Oct 1984, Selina Valerie, da of Capt Derek Head, RNR; 2 s (David b 1985, James b 1989); *Career* gen trainee BBC 1970, prodr BBC features 1973-80, exec prodr TVS and head of sci and indust progs 1981-88; currently writer and conslt to business; *Books* In the Mouth of the Dragon (1981), Inside the Bank of England (1988); *Recreations* cricket; *Clubs* Ooty; *Style—* Philip Geddes, Esq; Manor Farm, Upper Wield, Alresford, Hants (☎ 0420 62361)

GEDDES, Sir (Anthony) Reay Mackay; KBE (1968, OBE 1943); s of Rt Hon Sir Eric Campbell Geddes, GCB, GBE (bro of 1 Baron Geddes, d 1937), and Ada Gwendolen, *née* Stokes (d 1945); *b* 7 May 1912; *Educ* Rugby, Magdalene Coll Cambridge; *m* 14 April 1938, Imogen, da of Capt Hay Matthey; 2 s (Duncan, Piers), 3 da (Alison, Lindsay, Candida); *Career* chm Dunlop Holdings 1968-78, dep chm Midland Bank 1978-83 (dir 1967-83); dir: Shell Transport of Trading 1968-82, Rank Organization 1975-84; pres The Abbeyfield Soc 1985-89, chm Charities Aid Fndn, 1985-90; tstee Nat Cncl for Voluntary Organizations, Overseas Devpt Inst; govr Volunteer Centre UK; *Style—* Sir Reay Geddes, KBE; 49 Eaton Place, London, SW1X 8DE (☎ 071 235 5179)

GEDDES TAYLOR, Hon Mrs (Pamela Margaret); has used name of Geddes Taylor since 1960; o da of Baron Geddes of Epsom, CBE (Life Peer, d 1983), and Julia, *née* Burke; *b* 27 Sept 1925; *m* 11 Oct 1957 (m dis 1966), Louis Patrick Taylor, s of Louis Herbert Taylor, of Cambridge; *Career* Coll lect; ret; *Recreations* bridge, wine making; *Style—* Hon Mrs Geddes Taylor; North Cottage, Pump Lane, Framfield, Sussex TN22 5RQ (☎ 082 584 512)

GEDDIS, (Andrew) David Roberston; s of Andrew Geddis (d 1975), and Jean Baikie, *née* Gunn (d 1976); *b* 13 Oct 1915; *Educ* Merchiston Castle Sch Edinburgh; *m* 3 Dec 1955, Enid Joan Millicent (d 1979), da of George Edward Lambert Houghton (d 1961); 1 da (Jean b 1959); *Career* Maj 2 King Edward VII's Own Gurkha Rifles, Western Desert, Italy, Greece (despatches); vice chm Bombay Exchange Banks Assoc 1940-66, fell Indian Inst of Bankers and memb Cncl 1960-66; memb: Mgmnt Ctee Labour Secretariat of Banks in Indian (chm 1965-66), Gen Ctee Bombay C of C 1963-66, Mgmnt Ctee UK Citizen's Assoc Bombay Branch 1961-66 (chm 1965-66); vice pres and memb Cncl Central Admin of The UK Citizen's Assoc in India 1965-66, asst gen mangr National Grindlays Bank London 1967-69 (gen mangr 1970-72), ret 1973; *Recreations* golf, travel; *Clubs* Overseas Bankers (London); *Style—* David Geddis, Esq; c/o Grindlays Bank plc, 13 St James Square, London SW1Y 4LF

GEDYE, Robin Eric Bernard; s of George Eric Rowe Gedye (d 1971), and Alice, *née* Mehler; *b* 17 Aug 1949; *Educ* Clifton Coll, Portsmouth Poly (BA), Univ of Cardiff; *m* 20 July 1985, Rowena Elizabeth, da of Stephen Hugh Sharp; 1 da (Melita Alice Rachel b 1 Nov 1989); *Career* journalist; Reuters (corr Vienna for 18 months) 1974-79, Daily Telegraph: joined 1979, Warsaw corr 1980, Eastern Europe corr 1982 and 1985, Moscow corr 1985, German corr 1989; *Recreations* dry fly-fishing, skiing, fast cars; *Style—* Robin Gedye, Esq; Daily Telegraph, ZR19 Pressehaus 1, Heussallee 2-10, Bonn 53, Germany (☎ 010 49 228 215 631)

GEE, Anthony Francis (Tony); s of Frank Gee, of Hazel Grove, Cheshire (d 1959), and Hilda May, *née* McHaffie (d 1942); *b* 16 Feb 1934; *Educ* Malvern, Selwyn Coll Cambridge (MA); *m* 1, 26 Dec 1958 (m dis 1979), Patricia Ann (Pat), da of Sqn Ldr Harry Millington, of Lower Withington, Cheshire; 1 s (Timothy b 1962), 1 da (Sally b 1961); m 2, 30 March 1984, Patricia Louise Rudham (Patti), da of George Simmons, of Sutton, Surrey; *Career* dir Tony Gee Chapelle Hong Kong 1982-; conslt: Tony Gee & Quandel Atlanta USA 1986- (fndr 1982), Tony Gee & Partners 1988- (fndr 1974); FICE 1959, FIStructE 1962, FIMechE 1975, MConsE 1978; *Books* Civil Engineering Reference Book (jtly, 1961); *Recreations* golf, bridge; *Clubs* Walton Heath Golf, Cherokee T and C C (Atlanta USA); *Style—* Tony Gee, Esq; Atlanta, Arbour Close, The Mount, Fetcham, Leatherhead, Surrey KT22 9DZ (☎ 0372 376 787); 290 Halah Circle, Sandy Springs, Atlanta, Georgia 30328, USA (☎ 0101 404 250 0515); Tony Gee and Partners, TGP House, 45-47 High St, Cobham, Surrey KT11 3DP (☎ 0932 868277, fax 0932 866003)

GEE, David William; s of William George Gee (d 1975), and Gladys Elizabeth Gee; *b* 4 Dec 1930; *Educ* Univ of Birmingham (BSc); *m* 31 August 1957, Margaret, da of James Harvey Rowson (d 1949), of Lancashire; 2 s (Steven William b 1962, Martin Philip James b 1965), 1 da (Janet Elizabeth Sara b 1960); *Career* Royal Navy Instr Lt 1942-55; chartered patent agent, Euro patent attorney; dir Trade Marks Patents Designs Fedn 1977-86, jt fndr Anti-Counterfeiting Group 1974; vice-pres: North Warwickshire Small Business Bureau, North Warwickshire Constituency Cons Assoc; chm North Warwickshire Ctee Br Horse Soc 1980-90, regnl chm & Horse Soc 1990-; fndr and prop: David W Gee Patent and Trade Mark Agents, Gee Computer Services; *Recreations* riding, golf; *Style—* David W Gee, Esq; Farmhouse Court, Marston, W Midlands B76 0DU (☎ 0675 470621, fax 0675 470202)

GEE, Prof Geoffrey; CBE (1958); s of Thomas Gee (d 1962), of Overdale Rd, New Mills, Derby, and Mary Ann Gee; *b* 6 June 1910; *Educ* New Mills Sch, Univ of Manchester, Univ of Cambridge; *m* 1934, Marion, da of late Fred Bowden, of New Mills; 1 s, 2 da; *Career* dir of res Br Rubber Prodrs Res Assoc 1947-53, prof of chem Univ of Manchester 1953-77 (with periods of appointment as pro vice chllr), now emeritus prof; Hon DSc Univ of Manchester 1983; FRS; *Recreations* theology, Methodist Church; *Clubs* Royal Society; *Style—* Prof Geoffrey Gee, CBE, FRS; 8 Holmfield Drive, Cheadle Hume, Cheshire (☎ 061 485 3713)

GEE, Ian Ernest; s of William Alan Gee (d 1986), of Cheltenham Gloucestershire, and Anne Mary Duncan, *née* Walton (d 1987); *b* 19 Oct 1936; *Educ* The Manchester GS, Manchester Coll of Science and Technol; *m* 1964, Anne Rosemary, *née* Thorpe; 2 s (Nicholas Ian b 10 March 1969, Andrew Nigel b 11 July 1975); *Career* Nat Serv photographer RAF 1957-59, indust/photographer AV Roe & Co Ltd 1959-60, commercial photographer and colour printer Stagshead Studios Manchester 1960-63, self employed indust photographer then specialist portrait photographer in exec portraits of authors, artists and politicians 1963-, currently lectr on professional techniques for Fuji Photo Film Company; co-fndr The Guild of Wedding Photographers 1988, author of various articles in specialist photographic press; winner of numerous awards incl: Photographic Craftsman award (Professional Photographers of America) 1988, BIPP President's award 1988, BIPP Brides' Choice Album award Wedding Photographer of the Year 1990; BIPP: memb Admissions and Qualifications Panel 1975-, memb Cncl 1976-88, pres 1980-81; memb Professional Photographers of America 1961, FBIPP 1974 (MBIPP 1957); *Recreations* cricket, theatre, reading political biography, walking; *Clubs* RPS; *Style—* Ian Gee, Esq; 54 The Downs, Altrincham, Cheshire WA14 2QJ (☎ 061 928 3716, fax 061 927 9037)

GEE, Prof Kenneth Philip; s of Philip Gee (d 1984), of Bramhall, and Nancy, *née* Green; *b* 27 Dec 1946; *Educ* Cheadle Hulme Sch, Univ of Bristol (BSc), Univ of Manchester (PhD); *m* 31 July 1971, Hilary, da of Gerald James Carmichael (d 1989), of Sale; 1 da (Freya b 9 Oct 1973); *Career* lectr Dept of Mgmnt Sciences UMIST 1972-74, sr lectr Dept of Accounting and Fin Univ of Lancaster 1974-79, prof of accountancy Univ of Salford 1979-; vice chm British Accounting Assoc 1990; *Books* Management Control and Information (1973), Management Planning and Control in Inflation (1977), Advanced Management Accounting Problems (1986); *Recreations* reading; *Style—* Prof Kenneth Gee; 50 Broad Rd, Sale, Cheshire M33 2BN (☎ 061 973 4034); Dept of Business and Management Studies, University of Salford, Salford M5 4WT (☎ 061 745 5000, fax 061 745 5999, telex 668680 (Sulib))

GEE, Dr Maggie Mary; da of Victor Gee, of Holt, Norfolk, and Aileen, *née* Church; *b* 2 Nov 1948; *Educ* Horsham HS for Girls Sussex, Somerville Coll Oxford (major open scholar, BA, MA, BLitt), Wolverhampton Poly (PhD); *m* 1983, Nicholas Rankin; 1 da (Rosa b 1986); *Career* writer 1982-; published works: Dying In Other Words (1981), The Burning Book (1983), Light Years (1985), Grace (1987), Where are the Snows (1991); judge Booker Prize 1989; Hawthornden fell Univ of E Anglia 1989 (writing fell 1982), hon visiting fell Univ of Sussex 1986-, memb Soc of Authors; *Recreations* playing with daughter, visual arts, walking, swimming; *Style—* Dr Maggie Gee; Anne McDermid Curtis Brown, 162-168 Regent St, London W1R 5TB (☎ 071 872 0331, fax 071 872 0332)

GEE, Ronald Davenport; s of Fred Davenport Gee (d 1975); *b* 16 May 1925; *Educ* Manchester GS, Balliol Coll Oxford; *m* 1950, Marianne, da of Prof Paul Kalbeck, of Vienna (d 1949); 2 da; *Career* Lt RNVR (Fleet Air Arm) 1942-45, served Pacific, Torpedo Dive Bomber Sqdns; company director; chm London Gold Futures Market 1983- (vice chm 1982); dir Metal Market & Exchange Co; *Recreations* opera, golf; *Clubs* Sunningdale, Vincent's; *Style—* Ronald Gee, Esq; BICC Cables Ltd, PO Box 5, 21 Bloomsbury St, London WC1B 3QN (☎ 071 637 1300, telex 62881 BICC G)

GEE, Steven Mark; s of Dr Sidney Gee, of 42 Chester Close North, Regent's Park, London NW1, and Dr Hilda *née* Elman; *b* 24 Aug 1953; *Educ* Tonbridge, Brasenose Coll Oxford (MA); *Career* barr Middle Temple; in commercial practice, standing jr counsel in export credit guarantee matters DTI; MCC Sporting memb London Maritime Arbitrators Assoc; *Books* The Law and Practice of Mareva Injunctions (1987); *Recreations* marathon running; *Clubs* Serpentine Running; *Style—* Steven Gee, Esq; 38 Eaton Terrace, London, SW1 (☎ 071 823 4660), 4 Essex Court, Temple, London, EC4 (☎ 071 583 9191, fax 353 3421)

GEERING, Kenneth Redman; s of Walter Redman Geering (d 1937), of Wootton Manor, Charing, Kent, and Edith Amelia, *née* Giles (d 1960); *b* 26 Jan 1910; *Educ* Bedford Sch; *m* 6 June 1934, Mary Pauline, da of William Davis (d 1937), of Ashford, Kent; 1 s (Christopher b 1937 d 1976); *Career* Aux Fire Serv Ashford Cmdt 1942, Nat Fire Serv Column Offr E Kent 1943; chm Ashford Chamber of Trade 1952-53; chm Office Machinery Ltd 1964-70, chm Business Machines (SE) Ltd 1974-79, Geerings of Ashford Ltd 1938-; co fndr Ashford Children's Day 1949; pres: Ashford Cattle Show 1974, Typewriter Trades Fedn of GB and Ireland 1955-56, Ashford Cricket Club 1973-78; chm Assoc of Imperial Typewriter Agents 1963-64; pres: Town Div St John Ambulance Bde 1947-59, Ashford GC 1973-90, Wengen Curling Club 1986-87, Ashford Rotary Club 1946; Paul Harris fell 1985, cncllr Ashford Urban Dist Cncl 1939-49 (chm 1947); *Recreations* curling, golf, cricket; *Clubs* MCC, Paternosters; *Style—* Kenneth Geering, Esq; Wootton Manor, Charing, Kent TN27 0DU (☎ 0233 71 2310); Cobbs Wood House, Chart Rd, Ashford, Kent TN23 1EP (☎ 0233 33366, telex 965009, fax

39404)

GEERING, Michael William; s of John George William Geering, of London, and Winifred, *née* Green; *b* 5 Aug 1944; *Educ* Stationers' Company's Sch, Univ of Southampton (BSc); *m* 19 Sept 1970, Jean Mavis, da of Samuel Frederick George Fletcher, of Cardiff; 1 s (Jonathan b 3 July 1974), 1 da (Nicola b 4 Aug 1972); *Career* CA 1965; articled clerk Binder Hamlyn 1965-68, trainee analyst Laing & Cruickshank Stockbrokers 1968-69, audit sr Ernst & Whinney 1969-72; James Capel & Co 1973-: investmt analyst, head UK Equity res 1985-, memb bd 1987-, dir for UK equity div 1987-; FCA; *Recreations* golf, swimming, tennis, horse racing; *Clubs* Gnomes; *Style*— Michael Geering, Esq; Lion Hill, West Rd, St George's Hill, Weybridge, Surrey KT13 OLZ; James Capel & Co, James Capel House, PO Box 551, 6 Bevis Marks, London EC3A 7JQ (☎ 071 621 0011, fax 071 621 0496, telex 888866)

GEFFERS, Maj Iain George Huntly; s of Col Frederick William Geffers (d 1980), of Berks, and Mildred Maud Sumner (d 1979); *b* 27 Jan 1932; *Educ* Haileybury, RMA Sandhurst; *m* 8 Nov 1958, Johanna Jane Frances, da of Francis Raymond George Nason Sherrard (d 1974); 2 da (Georgina b 1960, Fiona b 1961); *Career* cmmnd 2 Lt 12 Lancers 1952 (served Malaya, Korea, Cyprus), ret Maj 1968; conservation of paintings 1968-; memb: Assoc of Br Picture Restorers, Int Inst for Conservation, UK Govt Conservation Register; *Recreations* hunting; *Clubs* Cavalry and Guards'; *Style*— Maj Iain Geffers; The Manor House, Piddletrenthide, Dorchester, Dorset DT2 7QX (☎ 03004 203)

GELBER, David; s of Edward Gelber (d 1970), of Toronto, and Anna, *née* David (d 1974); *b* 10 Nov 1947; *Educ* Whittinghame Coll Brighton, Hebrew Univ Jerusalem (BSc), Univ of London (MSc); *m* 1, 1969 (m dis 1979), Laura Beare; 1 s (Jeremy Edward b 1973), 1 da (Amy b 1975); m 2, 1982, Vivienne, da of Harry Cohen, of Weybridge; *Career* Morgan Guaranty Tst 1975-76, vice pres Citibank/Citicorp 1976-85, md (head global SWAPS and Foreign Exchange options) Chemical Bank 1985-89, gen mangr (head SWAPS and options) Hong Kong Bank 1989-; *Recreations* tennis, squash; *Clubs* RAC Cumberland Lt; *Style*— David Gelber, Esq; 6 Clorane Gardens, London NW3 7PR (☎ 071 794 1352); Chemical Bank, 180 Strand, London WC2R 1ET (☎ 071 380 8366), fax 071 380 5948, car 0836 202187

GELBER, The Lady Henrietta Mary; *née* Spencer-Churchill; da of 11 Duke of Marlborough, by his 1 w, Susan Mary, *née* Hornby (now Mrs John Gough, *qv*); *b* 7 Oct 1958; *Educ* St Mary's Wantage, Inchbald Sch of Design; *m* 14 March 1980 (m dis 1989), Nathan Gelber, s of Aba Gelber; 2 s (David b 1981, Maximilian b 1985); *Career* interior decorator; dir: Woodstock Designs, Spencer-Churchill Designs Ltd; *Style*— Lady Henrietta Gelber; 3 Parthenia Road, London SW6 4BD (☎ 071 384 1657); Woodstock Designs, 7 High St, Woodstock, Oxon OX7 9XX; 55 Hollywood Rd, London SW10 9HX

GELDARD, Robin John; s of Cyril John Geldard (d 1984), of Thornton Dene, South Glam, and Gertrude Nellie Lawrence (d 1971); *b* 9 Aug 1935; *Educ* Aldenham, Coll of Law; *m* 4 Sept 1965, Susan Elizabeth, da of Sir Martin Llewellyn Edwards (d 1987), of Pentwyn Farm, Lisvane, nr Cardiff; 2 s (Bruce b 1967, Michael b 1972), 1 da (Anna b 1972); *Career* recruit RM 1958, Mons Offr Cadet Sch, cmmnd RM 1959, 2 Lt Commando Trg Unit, RM rugby team 1958-60; slr and ptnr Edwards Geldard 1962, asst registrar 1980-85; dir: Thames Valley Lift Co Ltd 1987-90, The Biglis Co Ltd 1980-, Highfield Holiday Park Ltd 1979-90, Hendre Gritstone Ltd 1980-87, Hadley Wholesale Suppliers Ltd 1980-; pres Cardiff Incorporated C of C and Indust 1987-89, vice pres Cardiff Incorporated Law Soc 1987-88 (pres 1988-89), pres Federated Welsh C of C 1988- (vice pres 1987-88), memb cncl Nat Cncl of the Assoc Br C of C, memb Lloyd's 1986; *Recreations* sailing, flyfishing, music, photography; *Clubs* Naval, Cardiff and Co, Royal Porthcawl Golf; *Style*— Robin Geldard, Esq; Llanquian Farm, Aberthin, nr Cowbridge, South Glam CF7 7HB (☎ 0446 772484); 16 St Andrew's Crescent, Cardiff CF1 3RD (☎ 0222 238239)

GELDER, Prof Michael Graham; s of Philip Graham Gelder (d 1972), and Alice Margaret, *née* Graham (d 1985); *b* 2 July 1929; *Educ* Bradford GS, Queen's Coll Oxford, Univ Coll Hosp Med Sch; *m* 21 Aug 1954, Margaret Constance, da of Lt-Col John William Smith Anderson (d 1984); 1 s (Colin b 31 May 1960), 2 da (Fiona b 31 May 1960), 2 da (Fiona b 12 Jan 1963, Nicola b 9 May 1964); *Career* Capt RAMC 1955-57; sr house physician Univ Coll Hosp 1957 (house physician 1955), registrar Bethlem Royal and Maudsley Hosps 1958-61, MRC fell in clinical res 1962-63; Inst of Psychiatry: lectr 1964-65, sr lectr 1965-67, vice dean 1967-68; prof of psychiatry Univ of Oxford 1969-, fell Merton Coll Oxford 1969-, hon conslt Oxfordshire Health Authy 1969-; chm Neurosciences Bd MRC 1978-79 (memb 1976-78), vice pres RC Psych 1982-84; FRCP 1970, FRCPsych 1973; *Books* Psychological Aspects of Medical Practice (ed 1973), Agoraphobia: Nature and Treatment (jtly 1981), Oxford Textbook of Psychiatry (jtly 1983, 2 edn 1989); *Recreations* real tennis, reading, photography; *Clubs* Athenaeum; *Style*— Prof Michael Gelder; University Dept of Psychiatry, Warneford Hospital, Oxford; Merton College, Oxford

GELL, Peter Donald Marriott; s of Harold Marriot Gell, MC, of Chipping Campden, Glos; *b* 17 March 1929; *Educ* Sherborne, Worcester Coll Oxford (MA); *m* 1960, Jean, da of Lt-Col David Livingstone Graham, of Crowborough; 1 s, 3 da; *Career* dir Bunzl plc, chm Bucks FHSA; FCA, FCIS; *Recreations* music, field sports; *Style*— Peter Gell, Esq; Shearings, Witheridge Lane, Penn, Bucks (☎ 049 481 3243)

GELLES, Dr Edward; s of Dr David Gelles (d 1964), of Vienna, Austria, and Regina, *née* Griffel (d 1954); *b* 24 Nov 1927; *Educ* Haberdashers' Aske's, Balliol Coll Oxford (MA, DPhil); *Career* post-doctoral res fell, res assoc and lectr in physical chemistry various univs 1950-60; numerous pubns in scientific jls; author, lectr, and conslt on antiques and fine arts; numerous pubns in collectors' magazines; *Books* Nursery Furniture (1982); *Recreations* historical studies, theatre; *Clubs* Oxford and Cambridge; *Style*— Dr Edward Gelles; 3 Hyde Park Crescent, London W2 2PW (☎ 071 724 8722)

GELLHORN, Hon Mrs (Olive Shirley); 3 da of 1 Baron Layton, CH, CBE (d 1966), and Eleanor Dorothea, *née* Osmaston (d 1959); *b* 18 Dec 1918; *m* 18 May 1943, Peter Gellhorn, *qv*, s of late Dr Alfred Gellhorn; 2 s, 2 da; *Style*— The Hon Mrs Gellhorn; 33 Leinster Ave, London SW14 7JW

GELLHORN, Peter; s of Dr Alfred Gellhorn (d 1972), and Else Agathe, *née* Fischer (d 1950); *b* 24 Oct 1912; *Educ* Schiller Real Gymnasium Charlottenburg, Univ of Berlin, Berlin Acad of Music (passed with distinction final exams as pianist 1932 and conductor 1934); *m* 18 May 1943, Olive Shirley, 3 da of 1 Baron Layton of Danehill, CH, (d 1966); 2 s (Martin b 1945, Philip b 1951), 2 da (Mary b 1959, Barbara b 1960); *Career* musical dir Toynbee Hall London 1935-39, asst conductor Sadler's Wells Opera 1941-43, indust war serv 1943-45, conductor Royal Carl Rosa Opera 1945-46, conductor and head music staff Royal Opera House Covent Garden 1946-53, conductor and chorus master Glyndebourne Festival Opera 1945-61, dir BBC chorus (incl conducting Promenade Concerts) 1961-72, rejoined Glyndebourne 1974-75, co fndr and musical dir Opera Barga Italy 1967-69; conductor: The Elizabethan Singers 1976-80, Morley Coll Opera Gp 1973-79, Barnes Choir 1973-; on opera sch staff RCM 1980-88, prof Guildhall Sch of Music and Drama 1981-, lectr and adjudicator GB and overseas; compositions incl: music for the silhouette and puppet films of Lotte Reiniger, Aucassin and Nicolette (Festival of London 1972); Royal Philharmonic Soc, ISM; *Recreations* swimming, walking, going to plays; *Style*— Peter Gellhorn, Esq; 33 Leinster Ave, East Sheen, London SW14 7JW (☎ 081 876 3949)

GELLING, Robert Raisbeck (Robin); s of Douglas Raisbeck Gelling, of Millersdale, Derbyshire, and Marjorie Nicklin, *née* Roberts (d 1977); *b* 29 Nov 1930; *Educ* Bishop Vesey's GS Sutton Coldfield; *m* 29 July 1961, Shelagh Mary, da of Arthur Kenneth Hannah (d 1979), of Sutton Coldfield; 3 da (Susan b 1962, Sarah b 1964, Louise b 1966); *Career* Nat Serv 1954-56, Intelligence Corps Cyprus; CA; ptnr Wenham Major; *Recreations* golf, gardening, travel; *Clubs* Little Aston, Blackwell, Sutton Coldfield, Birmingham; *Style*— Robin Gelling, Esq; 4 Oaklands Road, Four Oaks, Sutton Coldfield, W Midlands B74 2TB (☎ 021 308 1298); 89 Cornwall Street, Birmingham B3 3BY (☎ 021 236 1866, fax 021 200 1389)

GELLNER, Ernest André; s of Rudolf Gellner (d 1987), and Anna, *née* Fantl (d 1954); *b* 9 Dec 1925; *Educ* Balliol Coll Oxford (MA), Univ of London (PhD); *m* 23 Sept 1954, Susan, da of Curteis Norwood Ryan, CB, CMG, DSO, MC (d 1969); 2 s (David b 18 Nov 1957, Benjamin b 3 July 1963), 2 da (Sarah b 8 March 1959, Deborah 10 Feb 1961); *Career* WWII Private Czechoslovak Armoured Bde BLA 1944-45; LSE 1949-84 (prof 1962-), William Wyse prof of soc anthropology Cambridge 1984-, professorial fell King's Coll Cambridge 1984-; hon fell LSE 1986, Hon DSc Bristol 1986, Hon DLitt Queen's Univ Belfast 1989; FBA 1974; hon foreign memb American Acad of Arts and Scis 1988, memb Academia Europaea 1989; *Books* Words and Things (1959), Thought and Change (1964), Saints of the Atlas (1969), Contemporary Thought and Politics (1974), The Devil in Modern Philosophy (1974), Legitimation of Belief (1975), Spectacles and Predicaments (1979), Muslim Society (1981), Nations and Nationalism (1983), The Psychoanalytic Movement (1985), Culture, Identity and Politics (1987), State and Society in Soviet Thought (1988), Plough, Sword and Book (1988); *Clubs* Reform; *Style*— Prof Ernest Gellner; 9 Clarendon St, Cambridge CB1 1JU (☎ 0223 66 155); Department of Social Anthropology Univ of Cambridge, Free School Lane, Cambridge CB2 3RF (☎ 0223 334 599)

GEMMELL, Gavin John Norman; s of Maj Gilbert Anderson Sloan Gemmell, of Gullane, E Lothian, and Dorothy Maud, *née* Mackay; *b* 7 Sept 1941; *Educ* George Watson's Coll; *m* 18 March 1967, Kathleen Fiona (Kate), da of Alexander Drysdale, of Edinburgh; 1 s (John Gilbert b 9 Sept 1971), 2 da (Alison Fiona b 28 Aug 1969, Lynsey Jane b 4 April 1975); *Career* CA 1964; apprentice John M Geoghegan 1959; Baillie Gifford & Co: investmt trainee 1964, ptnr 1967, ptnr i/c pension fund clients 1973, sr ptnr 1989; chm: Baillie Gifford Overseas Ltd 1983, Toyo Trust Baillie Gifford Ltd 1990; dir: Scottish Widows Fund & Life Assurance Society 1984, Baillie Gifford Shin Nippon plc 1985; memb Business Ctee Scot Episcopal Church 1982, pres Watsonian Squash Rackets Club 1986-89, capt Watsonian Golf Club 1988; chm AITC Tax Ctee 1980-88; *Recreations* golf, squash, travel; *Clubs* Gullane Golf, Watsonian Golf; *Style*— Gavin Gemmell, Esq; 14 Midmar Gardens, Edinburgh EH10 6DZ (☎ 031 447 8135); Baillie Gifford & Co, 10 Glenfinlas St, Edinburgh EH3 6YY (☎ 031 225 2581, fax 031 225 2358, telex 72310 BGCO G)

GEMMELL, James Henry Fife; s of James Walter Shanks Gemmell (d 1962), and Vera McKenzie, *née* Scott (d 1990); *b* 17 May 1943; *Educ* Dunfermline HS, Univ of Edinburgh; *m* 27 Dec 1972, (Catherine) Morna Davidson, da of John Wilson Gammie, of Elgin, Morayshire; 2 da (Caroline b 1974, Catriona b 1976); *Career* CA 1965; ptnr: Fryer Whitehill and Co 1975-82, Clark Whitehill (on merger of Fryer Whitehill and Co and Clark Pixley) 1982-; vice chm Kenneth Leventha 1990-, chm Bradford Career Mgmnt Ltd 1990-; memb: Disciplinary Ctee Insur Brokers Registration Cncl 1985, Cncl ICAS 1988 (chm Fin and Gen Purposes Ctee 1990, Eng and Wales Area Ctee 1989-); *Books* RICS Accounts Rules (1978), Insurance Brokers Accounts and Business Requirement Rules (1979), How to Value Stock (1983); *Recreations* gardening; *Style*— James Gemmell, Esq; Clark Whitehill, 25 New St Sq, London EC4A 3LN (☎ 071 353 1577, fax 071 583 1720, telex 887422)

GEMMILL, (Alexander) David; s of William Gemmill (d 1961), and Kathleen Gertrude Stoney, *née* Archer; *b* 11 April 1941; *Educ* Univ of Oxford (MA); *m* 30 Sept 1967, Jacqueline Gaye, da of Denis Benjamin Conoley (d 1969); 1 s (Mark William), 1 da (Lucy); *Career* Nat Serv, 2Lt Rhodesia 1965-67; Lazard Bros and Co Ltd 1967-85 (md 1983-85), dep chief exec Chartered WestLB Ltd 1986-; *Recreations* tennis, gardening, bee keeping; *Clubs* Brooks's; *Style*— David Gemmill, Esq; Chartered WestLB Ltd, 33-36 Gracechurch St, London EC3V 0AX (☎ 071 623 8711, telex 884689 SCBMER G, fax 071 626 1610, car 0860 387135)

GEMMILL, Scot; s of Archie Gemmill (the football coach), of Allestree, Derby, and Elizabeth Travers, *née* Maitland; *b* 2 Jan 1971; *Educ* Ecclesbourne Comp Sch Duffield Derbyshire; *Career* professional footballer; Nottingham Forest: YTS apprentice April 1988- Jan 1990, professional Jan 1990-; Young Player of the Year award Sept 1990; *Recreations* music, golf, tennis; *Style*— Scot Gemmill, Esq; Nottingham Forest FC, City Ground, West Bridgford, Nottingham NG2 5FJ (☎ 0602 822202)

GEMS, Iris Pamela (Pam); da of Jim Price (d 1930), of Christchurch, Dorset, and Elsa Mabel Annetts (d 1989); *Educ* Christchurch Priory Sch, Brockenhurst GS, Univ of Manchester; *m* Sept 1949, Keith Leopold Gems, s of Leopold Frederick Gems; 2 s (Jonathan b 1952, David b 1960), 2 da (Sara b 1954, Elizabeth (Lalla) b 1965); *Career* playwright; author of: Dusa, Fish, Stas and Vi (1976), Queen Christina (1977), Piaf (1978) Franz into April (1978), The Treat (1979), Pasionaria (1981), Camille (1985), The Danton Affair (1986); novels: Mrs Frampton (1989), Bon Voyage, Mrs Frampton (1990); memb: Writers Guild, Dramatists Guild (US); *Recreations* gardening; *Style*— Mrs Pam Gems; Sebastian Born, c/o James Sharkey, 15 Golden Square, London W1

GENNARD, Prof John; s of Arthur Gennard (d 1962), of Manchester, and Vera Edith, *née* Stone (d 1980); *b* 26 April 1944; *Educ* Univ of Sheffield (BA), Univ of Manchester (MA); *m* 8 May 1976, Florence Anne, da of Daniel Russell (d 1973), of Iver Heath; 1 s (John Cooper), 1 da (Julie Anne); *Career* lectr LSE 1970-81 (res offr 1968-70), prof of industl rels Univ of Strathclyde 1981-, dean Strathclyde Business Sch 1987-; memb: Panel of Arbitrators ACAS, Educn Ctee IPM; fell IPM; *Books* The Reluctant Militants (1972), Financing Strikers (1977), Closed Shop in British Industry (1983), A History of the National Graphical Association (1990); *Recreations* football, politics, food and drink; *Clubs* Carluke Rotary; *Style*— Prof John Gennard; 4 South Avenue, Carluke, Lanarkshire ML8 5TW (☎ 0555 51361), Strathclyde Business School, Sir William Duncan Building, 130 Rottenrow, Glasgow G4 0GE (☎ 041 5524400 ext 4030, fax 041 522, telex UNSLIB 77472)

GENT, (John) David Wright; s of Pilot Offr Reginald Philip Gent, RAFVR (d 1942), and Stella Eve Wright (d 1988); *b* 25 April 1935; *Educ* Lancing; *m* 19 Aug 1970, Anne Elaine, da of John Leslie Hanson (d 1988), of Ilkley, Yorks; *Career* admitted slr 1959; dep dir SMMT 1971-80 (legal advsr 1961-63, asst sec 1964, sec 1965-70), gen mangr Lucas Service UK Ltd 1980-82, gp PR mangr Lucas Industries plc 1982-83; dir Rd Fedn 1983-85, DG Retail Motor Indust Fedn (formerly Motor Agents Assoc) 1985-; chm: MAA Pensions Ltd, GPA Holdings Ltd 1985-; memb Rd Tport Indust Trg Bd 1985-; Freeman City of London 1985, Liveryman Worshipful Co of Coach Makers and Coach Harness Makers 1985; FIHT (1984), FIMI (1985); *Recreations* farming, gardening; *Clubs* RAC; *Style*— David W Gent, Esq; 44 Ursula St, London SW11 3DW (☎ 071 228 8126); 219 High St, Henley-in-Arden, Warwickshire B95 5BG (☎ 05642 3922); Retail Motor Industry Federation, 201 Great Portland St, London W1N 6AB (☎ 071 580 9122, fax 071 580 6376)

DEBRETT'S PERSONALITIES OF TODAY

PHOTOGRAPH: THE PRESS ASSOCIATION LTD

Sarah Hogg

Sir Peter Holmes

Nicholas Hytner

DEBRETT'S PERSONALITIES OF TODAY

Kazuo Ishiguro

PHOTOGRAPH: NIGEL PARRY PHOTOGRAPHY

Elton John

Ronald Jones

GENT, Marcus James; OBE (1974); s of Sir (Gerard) Edward James Gent, KCMG, DSO, OBE, MC (d 1948), and Gwendolen Mary, *née* Wyeth; *b* 5 Feb 1925; *Educ* Malvern, Trinity Coll Oxford; *m* 1952, Marian Elizabeth, da of Lancelot Newling Rawes (d 1976); 4 da; *Career* barr 1950; dir: The Guthrie Corpn plc (rubber and palm oil gp) 1970- (chm 1979-81); Phoenix Assurance Co 1979-85; *Style*— Marcus Gent, Esq, OBE; c/o The Guthrie Corporation plc, 6 Devonshire Square, London EC2

GENTLE, Mary; da of George William Gentle, of Dorset, and late Amy Mary, *née* Champion; *Educ* Bournemouth Poly (BA), Goldsmith's Coll London (MA); *Career* author; *Books* A Hawk in Silver (1977), Golden Witchbreed (1983), Ancient Light (1987), Scholars and Soldiers (1989), Rats and Gargoyles (1990), The Architecture of Desire (1991); *Recreations* sword fighting, live role-play games; *Style*— Ms Mary Gentle; Maggie Noach Literary Agency, 21 Redan St, London W14 0AB

GENTLEMAN, David William; s of Tom Gentleman (d 1966), and Winifred Murgatroyd (d 1966); *b* 11 March 1930; *Educ* Hertford GS, St Albans Sch of Art, Royal Coll of Art; *m* 1, 1953 (m dis 1966), Rosalind Dease; 1 da (Fenella); m 2, 1968, Susan, da of George Ewart Evans (d 1988), of Brooke, Norfolk; 1 s (Tom), 2 da (Sarah, Amelia); *Career* painter and designer; work incl: watercolours (landscapes, buildings and people), lithography, wood engraving, book illustration; Eleanor Cross platform mural designs for Charing Cross Underground 1979; posters and postage stamps; *Books* David Gentleman's Britain (1982), David Gentleman's London (1985), A Special Relationship (1987), David Gentleman's Coastline (1988), David Gentleman's Paris (1991); *Style*— David Gentleman, Esq; 25 Gloucester Crescent, London NW1 7DL (☎ 071 485 8824)

GENTRY, Maj-Gen Sir William George; KBE (1957, CBE 1947, OBE 1941), CB (1954), DSO (1942 and bar 1945); s of Maj Frederick Charles Gentry, MBE, and Eliza Amy Gentry; *b* 20 Feb 1899; *Educ* Wellington Coll NZ, Royal Mil Coll of Aust; *m* 1926, Alexandra Nina, da of Charles Robert Caverhill (d 1951); 1 s (Steven), 1 da (Sally); *Career* regular soldier GSO1 2 NZ Div 1941-42, Cdr 6 NZ Inf Bde 1942-43, 9 NZ Inf Bde 1945, Adj Gen NZ Army 1949-52, CGS NZ Army 1952-55, served Greece, Crete, Western Desert, Libya, Italy; *Recreations* walking; *Style*— Maj-Gen Sir William Gentry, KBE, CB, DSO; 52 Kings Crescent, Lower Hutt, NZ (☎ 010 64 660208)

GEORGALA, Prof Douglas Lindley; CBE; s of John Michael Georgala (d 1966), and Izetta Iris, *née* Smith; *b* 2 Feb 1934; *Educ* S African Coll Sch, Univ of Stellenbosch (BSc), Univ of Aberdeen (PhD); *m* 18 Dec 1959, Eulalia Catherina, da of George Philip Lochner (d 1962); 1 s (David b 12 May 1963), 1 da (Jeanette b 5 March 1961); *Career* res microbiologist Fishing Res Inst Univ of Cape Town SA 1957-60, tech memb Unilever Coordination 1973-77, head Unilever Res Colworth Laboratory 1977-86 (res microbiologist and div mangr 1960-72), industrial conslt DTI 1987-88; dir of food res Inst of Food Res AFRC 1988-; memb: Food Advsy Ctee, Advsy Ctee on Microbiological Safety of Food 1991; FIFST 1988; *Recreations* gardening, music, cycling; *Style*— Prof Douglas Georgala, CBE; AFRC Institute of Food Research, Shinfield, Berks RG2 9AT (☎ 0734 884530, fax 0734 884764)

GEORGE, Rear Adm Anthony Sanderson; CB (1983); s of Sandys Parker, and Winifred Marie George; *b* 8 Nov 1928; *Educ* RNC Dartmouth, RN Engrg Coll Manadon; *m* 1953, Mary Veronica Frances Bell; 2 da; *Career* Captain 1972 (served aboard HMS Nelson), Rear Adm 1981; dir Dockyard Production & Support 1981-82, chief exec Royal Dockyards 1983-; *Style*— Rear Adm Anthony George, CB; c/o Dockyard Dept, Ministry of Defence, Whitehall, SW1

GEORGE, Sir Arthur Thomas; AO (1987); s of Thomas George; *b* 17 Jan 1915; *Educ* Sydney Boys' HS, Slrs' Admission Bd Course; *m* 1939, Renée, da of Anthony Freeleagus; 1 da; *Career* slr and co dir; chm and md The Sir Arthur George Family Trust Group; dir: Thomas Nationwide Transport Ltd 1973-, Australian Solenoid Holdings Ltd, G & P Hotels Ltd; chm Assoc Classical Archaelogy Sydney Univ 1966- (endowed chair of classic archaelogy, hon fell 1985); pres Aust Soccer Fedn 1969-88, hon pres Ctee Oceania Football Confedn, exec memb FIFA, chm and govr the Arthur T George Fndn Ltd 1972-; fell Confedn Aust Sport 1985; Queen's Silver Jubilee Medal, Elizabethan Medal, Gold Cross Order of Phoenix (Greece), Grand Cdr and Keeper Cross of Mt Athos Greek Orthodox Church; kt 1972; *Recreations* swimming, theatre; *Clubs* American Nat; *Style*— Sir Arthur George, AO; 1 Little Queen's Lane, Vaucluse, NSW 2030, Australia (☎ 371 4030)

GEORGE, Brian Victor; s of Victor George, of 3 Cortmerren, 64 Westcliffe Road Bournemouth, and Agnes Amelia, *née* Sweet; *b* 5 Feb 1936; *Educ* Southall GS, Southall Tech Coll, Brunel Coll of Advanced Tech (now Brunel Univ) (BTech); *m* 19 May 1962, Joan Valerie, da of John Keith Bingham; 2 s (Graham Michael b 2 Dec 1965, David Brian b 10 April 1968); *Career* welding and sheet metal worker APV (Aust) Pty Ltd 1952-54, trade and student apprentice D Napier & Sons Ltd 1954-60; NPC (W) Ltd Whetstone: engr 1960-63, section leader 1963-66, office head Boilers and Gas Circuits 1966-69, asst chief engr Mech Plant 1969-70, asst chief engr Future Systems 1970-75, chief engr Mech Plant & Systems Dept 1975-76, mangr Fast Reactors 1976-77, engr mangr designate PWR; head Nuclear Plant Design Branch CEGB GD & CD 1979-81, dir PWR CEGB CD & CD 1981-89, project and tech dir Project Mgmnt Bd PWR 1984-89, chief exec PWR Project Gp Nuclear Electric plc 1989-; FEng, FIMechE, Hon FINucE; *Recreations* golf, bowls, DIY; *Style*— Brian George, Esq; 22 Monica Drive, Pittville, Cheltenham, Gloucestershire GL50 4NQ (☎ 0242 510762); PWR Project Group, Nuclear Electric plc, Booths Hall, Chelford Rd, Knutsford, Cheshire WA16 8QG

GEORGE, Bruce Thomas; MP (Lab) Walsall South 1974-; s of Edgar Lewis George, of Mountain Ash, Glam; *b* 1 June 1942; *Educ* Mountain Ash GS; Univ Coll of Wales Swansea and Univ of Warwick; *Career* asst lectr politics Glamorgan Coll of Technol 1964-66, lectr in politics Manchester Poly 1968-70, contested (Lab) Southport 1970, sr lectr politics Birmingham Poly and part-time tutor Open Univ 1971-74, memb Select Ctee on Defence 1979-; *Recreations* football; *Style*— Bruce George, Esq, MP; 42 Wood End Road, Walsall, W Midlands (☎ 0922 27898)

GEORGE, (William Norman) Bruce; s of Norman Macdonald George (d 1922), and Isobella Elizabeth Dunn (d 1964); *b* 3 Dec 1915; *Educ* Liverpool Univ Sch of Architecture (B Arch), Sch of Planning and Res for Regnl Devpt; *Career* WWII Lt RA 1940-46 (POW Malaya); architect; formerly sr ptnr: George/Trew/Dunn/Beckles Willson/Bowes; ret 1984; served: Practice Ctee and Panel of Arbitrators RIBA, CNAA; princ buildings: The Guards' Chapel 1963, Wellington Barracks London 1984, Huddersfield Royal Infirmary 1966, Aberdeen Royal Infirmary 1967 and 1976; other works at: King's Coll Hosp London, King's Coll Hosp Med Sch, Halifax Gen Hosp, New Cross Hosp Wolverhampton; ARIBA, AMTPI; *Books* The Architect in Practice; *Recreations* sculpture, portrait painting, music, cricket; *Style*— Bruce George, Esq; 1 Copley Dene, Wilderness Rd, Chislehurst, Kent (☎ 081 467 5809)

GEORGE, Prof Charles Frederick; s of William Hubert George (d 1957), and Evelyn Margaret, *née* Pryce, of Lymington, Hants; *b* 3 April 1941; *Educ* Oundle, Univ of Birmingham (BSc, MB, ChB, MD); *m* 17 May 1969 (m dis 1973), Rosemary, da of late Edward Moore, JP; *Career* med registrar: Birmingham Gen Hosp 1968-69, Hammersmith Hosp London 1969-71; tutor in med and clinical pharmacology Royal Postgraduate Med Sch London 1971-73; Univ of Southampton: sr lectr in med 1974-75, prof of clinical pharmacology 1975-, dean of med 1986-90; memb GMC; chm: Jt Formulary Ctee of Br Nat Formulary; hon fell Faculty of Pharmaceutical Med RCP 1989; FRCP 1978; *Books* Topics in Clinical Pharmacology (1978), Presystemic Drug Metabolism (with Renwick & Shand, 1982); *Recreations* windsurfing; *Style*— Prof Charles George; 15 Westgate St, Southampton SO1 OAY (☎ 0703 229100); Clinical Pharmacology Group, University of Southampton, Medical & Biological Sciences Building, Bassett Crescent East, Southampton SO9 3TU, (☎ 0703 594263, fax 0703 671778, telex 47661 SOTONU G)

GEORGE, Edward Alan John; s of Alan, and Olive Elizabeth George; *b* 11 Sept 1938; *Educ* Dulwich, Emmanuel Coll Cambridge (BA, MA); *m* 1962, Clarice Vanessa, *née* Williams; 1 s, 2 da; *Career* Bank of England 1962-: seconded to Bank for Int Settlements and later to Int Monetary Fund 1972-74, dep chief cashier 1977-80, asst dir Gilt-Edged Div 1980-82, exec dir 1982-90, dep govr 1990-; *Style*— E A J George, Esq; c/o Bank of England, Threadneedle St, London EC2R 8AH (☎ 071 601 4444)

GEORGE, Hywel; CMG (1967), OBE (1963); s of Rev William Morris George (d 1970), of Llys Hywel, Llanfairfechan, and Catherine Margaret, *née* Lloyd (d 1984); *b* 10 May 1924; *Educ* Llanelli GS, UC of Wales Aberystwyth (BA), SOAS, Pembroke Coll Cambridge (MA); *m* 1955, Edith, da of Karl Pirchl (d 1959), of Offensee, Austria; 3 da (Carol, Tamara, Frances); *Career* mil serv RAF Flying Offr 1942-46; colonial admin serv N Borneo 1949-63, resident Tawau Malaysia 1963-66, admin St Vincent 1967-69, govr St Vincent 1969-70, admin Br Virgin Islands 1971; fell and bursar Churchill Coll Cambridge 1972-90 (fell 1971-); CStJ 1968, PDK (Malaysia) 1964, JMN (Malaysia) 1966; *Recreations* walking, watching rugby; *Style*— Hywel George, Esq, CMG, OBE; Churchill Coll, Cambridge

GEORGE, Jill Findlay; da of Ronald Francis George (d 1987), and Joan Findlay, *née* Brooks (d 1987); *b* 12 Sept 1954; *Educ* St Margaret's Sch Bushey, Univ of Florence, Sheffield Coll of Art (BA); *Career* PR Dept V&A Museum 1972-74, antique shop N Devon 1976-77; Thumb Gallery: joined 1978, dir 1981, co dir 1983, sole owner and dir 1986, changed name of gallery to Jill George Gallery 1991; represented Herts in jr tennis; memb Ctee Art Business Design Centre 1989-92; *Recreations* theatre going, films, music, tennis, classic car shows, croquet; *Clubs* Groucho, Chelsea Arts; *Style*— Ms Jill George; 7 West Common Way, Harpenden, Herts (☎ 0582 460383); 16 Gillingham Rd, London NW2 (☎ 081 450 1867); Jill George Gallery, 38 Lexington St, Soho, London W1R 3HR (☎ 071 439 7343/7319, fax 071 287 0478)

GEORGE, John Charles Grossmith; er s of Col Edward Harry George, OBE, WS (d 1957), and Rosa Mary, Papal Medal Benemerenti (d 1988), da of George Grossmith, OStJ, Chev de la Legion d'Honneur, Gold Cross of the Order of the Redeemer, Cross Pro Ecclesia et Pontefice; *b* 15 Dec 1930; *Educ* Ampleforth; *m* 1972, Margaret Mary Maria Mercedes (late sec to Garter King of Arms), Dame of Honour and Devotion SMO Malta, Offr of Order Pro Merito Melitense, da of Maj Edric Humphrey Weld, TD, JP (d 1969), and Maria Mercedes, da of Henry Scrope, of Danby; *Career* Lt Hertfordshire Yeo (RA, TA); College of Arms 1963-72, Earl Marshal's liaison offr with Churchill family for State Funeral of Sir Winston Churchill 1965, Green Staff Offr Investiture of HRH The Prince of Wales 1969, Kintyre Pursuivant of Arms 1986-, Garioch Pursuivant of Arms 1976-86; memb Cncl: The Heraldry Soc 1976-84, The Heraldry Soc of Scotland 1986-89; co-designer Royal Wedding Stamp (Crown Agents Issue 1981), vice pres BBC Mastermind Club 1979-81; FSA (Scot) 1975, FHS 1983; Freedom of Loudon County of Virginia USA 1968; Kt of Obedience SMO Malta 1975, Kt of Grace and Devotion 1971, dir of ceremonies British Assoc SMOM 1976-80, Cdr of Order Pro Merito Melitense 1983, Offr 1980; *Books* The Puffin Book of Flags; *Recreations* nineteenth century English operetta, musical comedy, hagiography, watching sport principally racing, rugby and golf; *Clubs* New (Edinburgh); *Style*— J C G George, Esq, FSA; 115 Henderson Row, Edinburgh EH3 5BB (☎ 031 557 1605); Court of the Lord Lyon, HM New Register House, Edinburgh EH1 3YT (☎ 031 556 7255)

GEORGE, Prof Kenneth Desmond; s of Horace Avory George (d 1962), of Craig-Cefn-Parc, nr Swansea, and Dorothy Margaret, *née* Hughes; *b* 11 Jan 1937; *Educ* Ystalyfera GS, Univ Coll of Wales Aberystwyth; *m* 18 July 1959, Elizabeth Vida, *née* Harries; 2 s (Alun Michael b 30 Nov 1962, David Keith b 16 Feb 1964), 1 da (Alison Elizabeth b 5 March 1969); *Career* lectr in econs: Univ of WA 1960-63, Univ Coll N Wales 1963-64; Univ of Cambridge: res fell Dept of Applied Econs 1964-66, lectr in econs 1966-73, fell Sidney Sussex Coll 1965-73; prof of econs and head dept: Univ Coll Cardiff 1973-88, Univ Coll Swansea 1988-; pt/t memb MMC 1978-86; memb Cncl Royal Econ Soc 1987-; *Books* The Allocation of Resources (with J Shorey, 1978), Industrial Organization (with C Joll, 1981), The Welsh Economy (ed with Dr L Mainwaring, 1988); *Recreations* walking, photography, music; *Style*— Prof Kenneth George; Dept of Econs, Univ Coll Swansea, Singleton Park, Swansea (☎ 0792 295168, fax 0792 295618, telex 48358)

GEORGE, Llewellyn Norman Havard; s of late Cdr Benjamin William George, DSO, RNR, and late Annie Jane George; *b* 13 Nov 1925; *Educ* Cardiff HS, Fishguard GS; *m* 30 Aug 1950, Mary Patricia Morgan, da of late David Morgan Davies, of Fishguard; 1 da (Sarah b 1957); *Career* slr; HM Coroner 1965-80, rec Wales and Chester circuit 1980-; pres: West Wales Law Soc 1973-74, Pembs Law Soc 1982-3; chm (no5) S Wales Law Soc Legal Aid Ctee 1979, chm Agric Land Tbnl Wales 1990- (dep chm 1985-90); *Recreations* golf, reading, chess; *Clubs* Newport Pembs Golf, Pembs County; *Style*— Llewellyn George, Esq; Four Winds, Tower Hill, Fishguard, Dyfed (☎ 0348 873894); Goodwick House Chambers, West St, Fishguard (☎ 0348 873691)

GEORGE, Michael; s of John James George (d 1964), of Thorpe St, Andrew, Norwich, Norfolk, and Elizabeth, *née* Holmes; *b* 10 Aug 1950; *Educ* King's Coll Cambridge Choir Sch, Oakham Sch, RCM; *m* 15 July 1972, Julie Elizabeth Kennard (soprano), da of Stanley Kennard; 1 s (Nicholas James Stanley b 19 Aug 1980), 2 da (Lucy Elizabeth Sullivan b 27 May 1975, Emilie Jane b 1 Aug 1978); *Career* bass baritone; ranges from twelfth century to present day; has appeared at all maj festivals throughout Britain incl The Proms 1990 (4 separate concerts performing Bach, Janacek, Arvo Part and Renaissance music), The Three Choirs Festival and elswhere with City of Birmingham Symphony, Scot Chamber and BBC Symphony Orchs; performed abroad 1990: Messiah (Italy, Spain, Poland and France), Mozart's Requiem (with Trevor Pinnock, Ottawa), Handel (California and Boston), Haydn's Creation (under Hogwood, Holland, Germany and Italy) *Recordings* incl: Carmina Burana (4 vols), Acis and Galatea, Haydn's Creation, Beethoven's Ninth Symphony, Missa Solemnis (with Hanover Band), Handel's Messiah, St John Passion (with The Sixteen), Handel's Joshua, Stravinsky's Le Rossignol (with BBCSO), Holst's At the Boar's Head (under David Atherton); *Recreations* tennis, golf, food; *Clubs* Riverside, Concert Golfing; *Style*— Michael George, Esq; Lies Askonas Ltd, 186 Drury Lane, London WC2B 5RY (☎ 071 405 1808, fax 071 2421831)

GEORGE, Nicholas; s of Wallace Yewdall Evelyn George and Joy Isabel Gilbert, *née* Hickey; *b* 1 Feb 1954; *Educ* Radley; *Career* articled clerk Edward Moore & Sons 1973-77, Joseph Sebag & Co 1977-79, Rowe & Pitman; dir: WI Carr Sons & Co 1981-86, BZW Securities 1986-, Drayton Asia Trust plc 1989-; FCA 1978, ASIA 1980; *Recreations* shooting, fishing, travelling; *Style*— Nicholas George, Esq; 7 Shalcomb St, London SW10 (☎ 071 352 5660); BZW, Ebbgate House, Swan Lane, London EC4 (☎ 071 623 2323)

GEORGE, Patrick Herbert; s of Alfred Herbert George, of Croix de Guerre (avec Palme), and Nora, *née* Richards; *b* 28 July 1923; *Educ* Bryanston, Edinburgh Coll of Art (scholar), Camberwell Sch of Art; *m* 1, July 1953 (m dis 1980), June, da of Dr A Griffith; m 2, 1981, Susan Jean Elizabeth, *née* Ward; 4 da (Kate, Victoria, Alice, Nancy); *Career* artist; RNVR 1942-46; lectr: Slade Sch UCL 1949-58 and 1961-82, Nigerian Coll of Art Zaria 1959-60; Univ of London: reader, prof 1983-86, Slade prof 1986-89, emeritus prof 1989-; numerous exhibitions incl: One Man Exhibition Gainsboroughs House Sudbury 1975, Retrospective Serpentine Gallery London 1980; dealer Browse & Darby; works in numerous public collections in GB and USA; memb: Arts Cncl of GB, Eastern Arts, Gainsboroughs House, Nat Cncl for Dips in Art and Design; *Style—* Patrick George, Esq; 33 Moreton Terrace, London SW1V 2NS (☎ 071 828 3302); Grandfather's, Great Saxham, Bury St Edmunds, Suffolk IP29 5JR (☎ 0284 810 997)

GEORGE, Peter Michael Christol; s of Col Edward Henry George, OBE, WS (d 1957), and Rosa Mary, *née* Grossmith (d 1988); bro of John Charles Grossmith George, *qv* and Timothy David George; *b* 12 Jan 1935; *Educ* Ampleforth; *m* 14 Aug 1971, Denise Dowding, da of Maj Charles Davenport, RM (d 1951); 6 s (Jamie b 1972, Charles b 1974, Columba b 1975, Kentigern (twin) b 1975, Gervase b 1980, Tom b 1984), 1 da (Talitha b 1978); *Career* Nat Serv cmmnd 2Lt RA; admitted slr 1962, ptnr Charles Russell 1964-; memb Law Soc; *Recreations* reading, chess, bridge, music; *Style—* Peter George, Esq; Hydeacre Worthy Rd, Winchester; Hale Court, New Square, Lincoln's Inn, London WC2 (☎ 071 242 1031, fax 071 430 0388, telex 23521 LAWER G)

GEORGE, Philip William; s of Capt Rex George (d 1986), of Melbourne, Aust, and Marie Cecil, *née* Soutar; *b* 15 Aug 1951; *Educ* Chigwell Sch Essex, Magdalene Coll Cambridge (MA); *m* 10 July 1982, Lorraine, da of Dennis James Whiting (d 1985); 2 s (Thomas b 1984, Samuel b 1987); *Career* admitted slr 1975; Beachcrofts of Chancery Lane 1973-75, asst slr Smith Morton & Long (Colchester, Halstead, Clacton-on-Sea) 1975-76 (ptnr 1976-89), ptnr Birkett Westhorp & Long (Colchester, Clacton, Felixstowe, Framlingham, Halstead, Ipswich, London) 1989-; Cricket: Essex second eleven 1970-72, Essex League 1975-87, memb South Woodford CC 1965-, memb Colchester and East Essex CC 1980-; memb Colchester Round Table (chm 1987-88); memb Law Soc 1976; *Recreations* cricket, squash; *Clubs* MCC, Colchester Garrison Offrs, Gentlemen of Essex Cricket; *Style—* Philip George, Esq; Birkett, Westhorp & Long, Essex House, 42 Crouch St, Colchester, Essex C03 3HH

GEORGE, Phyllis Ann; da of Cecil Oswald George (d 1974), of Essex House, Thame, Oxon, and Ann Kate, *née* Wells (d 1958); *b* 18 Feb 1925; *Educ* City of London Sch for Girls, Royal Free Hosp Sch of Med (MB BS, LRCP); *Career* jr appts 1949-60: Royal Free Hosp, Central Middx Hosp, Gt Ormond St Hosp for Sick Children; residency and special fellowship Memorial Hosp NY 1957-59, conslt surgn Royal Free Hosp 1961-87; RCS 1979-: memb Cncl 1979-, vice pres 1988-; memb Ct of Examiners 1982-88, chm 1988, life memb: RSPB, Nat Tst, Eng Heritage; memb Cncl Assoc of Surgns of GB and Ireland 1976-79, pres Surgery Section RSM 1984-85; Freeman City of London 1983, Liveryman Worshipful Soc of Apothecaries 1988; MRCS, FRCS, fell Royal Statistical Soc; *Books* Carcinoma of the Liver, Biliary Tract and Pancreas (jtly, 1983); *Recreations* travel, archaeology, woodland conservation (owner of a 26 acre wood); *Style—* Miss Phyllis George; 9B Rosslyn Hill, London NW3 5UL; Royal College of Surgeons, 35-43 Lincoln's Inn Fields, London WC2A 3PN (☎ 071 405 3474, telex 936573 RCSENG, fax 071 831 9438)

GEORGE, Rowland David; DSO (1944), OBE (1943); s of John Ellis George (d 1935), of Combe Park, Bath, and Mary Louisa, *née* Fear; *b* 15 Jan 1905; *Educ* Wycliffe Coll, Lincoln Coll Oxford (MA); *m* 22 April 1933, Hon Sylvia Beatrice, *née* Norton, da of 1 Baron Rathcreedan (d 1930); 3 s (Kester William Norton b 21 July 1934, Ryan Cecil Norton b 11 Oct 1936, Sebastian Piers Norton b 23 Feb 1947 d 16 July 1951), 1 da (Eiluned Mary Norton (Mrs Patrick Alan Crozier-Cole) b 11 Feb 1940); *Career* RAFVR 1939-45, in Equipment Branch, Wing-Cdr 1943, RAuxAF 1948-51, CO 3619 (Co of Suffolk) Fighter Control Unit, Fighter Cmd, RAuxAF Res 1951-; chm Bath Cncl of Social Serv 1960-75; *Recreations* rowing (Olympic Gold medallist 1932); *Style—* Rowland George, Esq, DSO, OBE; Pythouse, Tisbury, Wilts SP3 6PB (☎ 0747 870841)

GEORGE, Susan Melody; da of Norman Alfred George, of Wraysbury, Berks, and Eileen, *née* Percival; *b* 26 July 1950; *Educ* Corona Acad; *m* 1984, Simon MacCorkindale, *qv*; *Career* actress; films include: Billion Dollar Brain 1965, The Sorcerers 1966, The Strange Affair 1967, Eye Witness 1969, Fright 1970, Straw Dogs 1971, Dirty Mary, Crazy Larry 1972, Dr Jekyll and Mr Hyde 1972, Mandingo 1973, Tiger Shark 1975, Tomorrow Never Comes 1977, Venom 1980, A Texas Legend 1980, Enter The Ninja 1981, The House Where Evil Dwells 1982, The Jigsaw Man 1984, Czech Mate 1985, The White Stallion 1986; dir AMY International Productions; exec prodr: Stealing Heaven 1988-89, White Roses 1988-89; Valentino award for best actress, Virgin Islands Film Festival award for best actress; *Books* Songs to Bedroom Walls (1987); *Clubs* St James's; *Style—* Ms Susan George; c/o Roz Chatto, Chatto & Linnett, Prince of Wales Theatre, Coventry Street, London W1V 7FE

GEORGE, Terence Paul; s of Harold Dennis George (d 1988), and Olive Maud, *née* Swann; *b* 1 June 1948; *Educ* Gt Yarmouth GS, Churchill Coll Cambridge (BA, MA); *m* 15 July 1972, Diana, da of Prof Edward O'Farrell Walsh (d 1972), of Hong Kong; 2 s (Richard b 1976, William b 1984), 1 da (Joanna b 1979); *Career* engr Sir Alexander Gibb & Ptnrs 1971-74, coordinator Severn Trent Water Authy 1974-79, conslt PA Mgmnt Conslts 1979-82; HTV Ltd: tech controller 1982-, dir of engrg 1987-; dir HTV Gp 1988-, md Intecom Ltd 1988-; dir ITEC Ltd; MICE 1974, AMIMC 1982; *Recreations* swimming, tennis, hill walking; *Style—* Terence George, Esq; The Television Centre, Culverhouse Cross, Cardiff (☎ 0222 590300, fax 0222 596163)

GEORGE, Timothy David; s of Col Edward Harry George, OBE, WS (d 1957), and Rosa Mary, *née* Grossmith (d 1988); bro of John Charles Grossmith George and Peter Michael Christol George, *qv*; *b* 28 May 1933; *Educ* Ampleforth; *Career* Lt Scots Guards 1953; md Radnor Estates Ltd, memb Lloyd's Insur; Knight Constantinian Order of St George, Green Staff Offr at Investiture of HRH Prince of Wales at Caernarvon 1969; *Recreations* opera, painting, fishing; *Style—* Timothy George, Esq; 2 Putney Common, London SW15 (☎ 081 788 1508)

GEORGE, Timothy John Burr; s of Brigadier John Burr George (d 1990), and Margaret Brenda, *née* Harrison (d 1989); *b* 14 July 1937; *Educ* Aldenham Sch, Christ's Coll Cambridge (BA, scholar); *m* 21 July 1962, Richenda Mary, da of late Alan Read; 1 s (Andrew John Timothy b 1963), 2 da (Rebecca Caroline Ann b 1965, Natasha Mary Ann (twin) b 1965); *Career* mil serv 2 Lt RA 1956-58; dip serv: entered FCO 1961, third sec Hong Kong 1962-63, second sec Peking 1963-66, second then first sec FCO 1966-68, first sec (econ) New Delhi 1969-72, asst political advsr Hong Kong 1972-74, first sec FCO 1974-78, cnsllr and head of chancery Peking 1978-80, res assoc Int Inst for Strategic Studies London 1980-81, cnsllr UK Perm Delgn to OECD Paris 1982-86, head Repub of Ireland Dept FCO 1986-90, ambass Kathmandu 1990-; *Books* Security in Southern Asia (co author 1984); *Style—* Timothy George, Esq; c/o Foreign and Commonwealth Office, King Charles St, London SW1A 2AH

GEORGE, Dr William Richard Philip; s of William George (d 1967), and Anita Williams (d 1943); *b* 20 Oct 1912; *Educ* Friars Sch Bangor Gwynedd, Wrekin Coll, Wellington; *m* 19 Dec 1953, Margarete, da of Leonhard Bogner (d 1956), of Nurnberg; 1 s (Philip b 1956), 3 da (Anita b 1959, Elizabeth b 1961, Gwen b 1966); *Career* slr 1934, pt/t clerk to Justices Barmouth 1948-75, dep circuit judge 1975-80; co cncllr rep Criccieth Ward Gwynedd CC 1967- (chm Cncl 1982-83, currently chm Gen Purposes Ctee), memb ACC 1989, vice chm Assembly of Welsh Counties 1989-91; chm Criccieth Meml Hall Ctee, sec Criccieth Welsh Baptist Church 1958-; winner Poetry Crown-Royal Nat Eisteddfod of Wales 1974; Archdderwydd Cymru (Archdruid of Wales) 1990-; Hon DLitt Univ of Wales 1988; memb Law Soc; *Books* 5 vols Welsh verse (1947, 1969, 1974, 1979, 1989), The Making of Lloyd George (1976), Lloyd George: Backbencher (1983), Gyfaill Hoff (the letters of Welsh Patagonian authoress Eluned Morgan, ed 1982); *Recreations* golf and (formerly) boating; *Clubs* Criccieth; *Style—* Dr William George; Garthcelyn, Criccieth, Gwynedd (☎ 76652 2625); 103 High St, Porthmadog, Gwynedd (☎ 76651 2011, 76651 2474, fax 076651 4363)

GEORGHIADES, Elikkos; s of Andreas Elias Georghiades, and Phani, *née* Kamberis; *b* 21 June 1951; *Educ* The Eng Sch Nicosia, Univ of London (LLB); *m* 25 April 1986, Marilyn, da of Donald Cecil Woodwards; *Career* exec offr New Scotland Yard 1970-72; called to the Bar Middle Temple 1975, currently dep head of chambers of M Wolkind in Grays Inn; professional graphologist using the pseudonym James Woodward, lectr in graphology; analysed several notorious murderers incl: Dennis Neilson, Charles Manson and Christie; cases published in Murder Casebook; parliamentary candidate for Lib Pty 1979, left pty 1983; memb: Lab Pty, Br Graphology Soc; *Style—* Elikkos Georghiades, Esq; PO Box 310, London SE20 7RA (☎ 081 659 9072); 12 South Square, Gray's Inn, London WC1 (☎ 071 242 1052)

GERAGHTY, Billy; s of William Thomas Geraghty, of Galway, and Catherine Lansbury; *b* 12 March 1963; *Educ* Woodroffe Sch Lyme Regis, East 15 Acting Sch; *Career* actor; stage prodns incl: Road, Midnight Hour (Bolton Octagon Theatre) 1987, Buddy Holly in The Buddy Holly Story (Victoria Palace Theatre) 1990-91, Lie of the Mind (Royal Court), How I got to Spain (one man show, Foundry) 1984-85, Gentleman Jim (Nottingham Playhouse) 1983-84; TV incl: The Ritz, Hard Cases, Split Enz, Aufwiedersehen Pet, Chancer 1990-91; films incl: Wilt 1989, Closing Ranks; *Recreations* football, baseball, swimming, athletics, cycling, rally cross, hang gliding, scuba diving, playing drums, guitar and singing in a number of bands; *Style—* Billy Geraghty, Esq; Fraser & Dunlop, 503 The Chambers, Chelsea Harbour, London SW10 0XF (☎ 071 352 7356)

GERAGHTY, Lady; Lilian Irene; *née* Travis; da of late Frederick Glover Travis, of Chessington, Surrey; *m* 1946, Sir William Geraghty, KCB (d 1977); *Style—* Lady Geraghty; 29 Park Lane, Cheam Village, Surrey SM3 8BN (☎ 081 643 4552)

GERARD, Anthony Robert Hugo; s of Maj Rupert Gerard, MBE (d 1978, great nephew of 2 Baron); hp to 2 cous once removed, 4 Baron Gerard; *b* 3 Dec 1949; *Educ* Harvard; *m* 1976, Kathleen, eldest da of Dr Bernard Ryan, of New York; 2 s (Rupert Bernard Charles b 17 Dec 1981, John Frederick William b 1986); *Style—* Anthony Gerard, Esq; 120 E 79th Street, New York, NY 10021, USA

GERARD, Hon Heloise Katherine Marie; 3 da of of 3 Baron Gerard (d 1953); *b* 21 June 1911; *Career* a nun; *Style—* The Hon Heloise Gerard; Blakesware, Ware, Herts (☎ 0920 3665)

GERARD, 4 Baron (UK 1876); Sir Robert William Alwyn Frederick Gerard; 16 Bt (E 1611); s of 3 Baron, MC (d 1953), by his cous Mary, da of Sir Martin Gosselin, GCVO, KCMG, CB, and Hon Katharine Gerard (2 da of 1 Baron); *b* 23 May 1918; *Educ* Ampleforth; *Heir* 2 cous once removed, Anthony Gerard; *Recreations* nature study, poetry writing; *Style—* The Rt Hon the Lord Gerard; Parkwood House, Blakesware, Ware, Herts (☎ 0920 463665)

GERARD LEIGH, Col William Henry; CVO (1983), CBE (1981); s of Lt-Col J C Gerard Leigh (d 1965), of Thorpe Satchville Hall, Melton Mowbray, Leics, and Helen, *née* Goudy (d 1964); *b* 5 Aug 1915; *Educ* Eton, Univ of Cambridge; *m* 29 Oct 1946, (Nancy) Jean, da of Wing Cdr Sir Norman Leslie 8 Bt, CMG, CBE (d 1937); 2 s (John b 24 Jan 1949, David b 28 Aug 1958), 2 da (Carolyn (Mrs Charles Benson) b 12 Nov 1947, Camilla (Mrs Hugh Seymour) b 4 July 1952); *Career* LG: joined 1937, served ME Italy and Germany 1939-45, Lt-Col Cmdg 1953-56, Col Cmdg Household Cavalry and Silver Stick in Waiting to HM The Queen 1956-59, Gentleman Usher to HM The Queen 1967-85; chm Nat Cncl YMCA,S 1974-81; *Clubs* Whites; *Style—* Col W H Gerard Leigh, CVO, CBE; Hayes, East Woodhay, Newbury, Berks (☎ 048 84228); 15 Eaton Mansions, London SW1 (☎ 071 730 5900)

GERHARD, Dr (Derek James) Jeremy; CB (1986); s of Frederick James Gerhard (d 1983), of Banstead, Surrey, and Lily Muriel, *née* Hubbard (d 1984); *b* 16 Dec 1927; *Educ* Highgate, Fitzwilliam Coll Cambridge (MA), Univ of Reading (PhD); *m* 5 April 1952, Dr Sheila Decima, da of Dr Gerald Kempster Cooper, (d 1979); 3 s (Timothy b 1955, Mark b 1961, Christopher b 1965), 2 da (Jane b 1957, Julia b 1963); *Career* civil servant 1951-88; Air Miny, Dept of Scientific and Industl Res, Br Embassy in Washington, BOT, DTI; dep master and comptroller (chief exec) Royal Mint 1978-88, business conslt 1988-; hon fell Fitzwilliam Coll Cambridge; *Recreations* woodwork, gardening; *Style—* Dr Jeremy Gerhard, CB; Little Dowding, Walton Heath, Surrey KT20 7TJ (☎ 0737 813045)

GERKEN, Vice Adm Sir Robert William Frank; KCB (1986), CBE (1975); s of Francis Sydney Gerken, and Gladys Gerken; *b* 11 June 1932; *Educ* Chigwell Sch, RNCs Dartmouth and Greenwich; *m* 1, 1966, Christine Stephenson (d 1981); 2 da (Charlotte b 1967, Victoria b 1970); m 2, 1983, Mrs Ann Fermor, widow of Graham Fermor, née Blythe; *Career* Capt of the Fleet (C-in-C Fleet's Staff at Northwood Middx) 1978-81, Rear Adm and Flag Offr 2 Flotilla 1981-83, dir gen Naval Manpower and Trg 1983-84, Vice Adm 1984-87, Flag Offr Plymouth and Port Adm Devonport, placed on Retired List April 1987; dir Corps of Commissionaries Management Ltd; chm Marine Studies Faculty Cncl Polytechnic SW; govr Chigwell Sch, pres Port of Plymouth Lifeboat (RNLI), chm of tstees China Fleet Club (UK) 1987; *Recreations* tennis, moor walking; *Clubs* Army & Navy, Royal Western YC of England; *Style—* Vice Adm Sir Robert Gerken, KCB, CBE; Faunstone Cottage, Shaugh Prior, Plymouth, Devon PL7 5EW (☎ 075 539 445)

GERLACHE; *see*: de Gerlache de Gomery

GERMAIN, (Dennis) Richard; s of Capt Dennis George Alfred Germain (d 1956), and Catherine Emily Violet, *née* Tickner; *b* 26 Dec 1945; *Educ* Mayfield Coll; *m* 7 Sept 1968, (Jadwiga) Anne Teresa, da of Zygfryd Nowinski (d 1988); 1 s (Richard b 1973), 1 da (Suzanne b 1976); *Career* called to the Bar Inner Temple 1968; memb Criminal Bar Assoc; *Recreations* skiing, cricket, photography, philately; *Style—* Richard Germain, Esq; Oak Lodge, Hill Waye, Gerrards Cross, Bucks SL9 8BH (☎ 0753 885775); 4 Brick Court, Temple, London EC4Y 9AD (☎ 071 583 8455, fax 071 353 1699)

GERMAN, (Frank) Clifford; s of Reginald Frank German, of Northampton, and Jessie, *née* Henson; *b* 13 March 1934; *Educ* Northampton GS, St John's Coll Cambridge (open exhibitioner, BA, pres C U Liberal Club); *m* 1967, Muriel Mary Norton, da of Stanislaus Norton; 2 c (Catherine Victoria b 1970, Richard George b 1972); *Career* Nat Serv RN 1952-54, Lt RNVR; teaching fell Univ of Michigan Ann Arbor 1957-58, lectr in geography Wayne State Univ Detroit 1958-61, Financial Times 1961-63, The Times

1963-66; Daily Telegraph: joined 1966, fin correspondent 1968-86, dep city ed 1972-76, assoc city ed 1976-86; city ed: Today 1986-87, The Scotsman 1987-; FRGS 1959; Geography of the Soviet Union (with JP Cole, 1961), Guide to Mortgage Finance (1988); *Recreations* cricket, old cars; *Clubs* MCC; *Style—* Clifford German, Esq; 25 Rollscourt Ave, London SE24 0EA (☎ 071 274 7126); The Scotsman, Pemberton House, East Harding St, London EC4 (☎ 071 353 9051)

GERMAN, Lady; Dorothy; *née* Sparks; da of Richard Sparks; *m* 1931, Sir Ronald Ernest German, KCB, CMG (d 1983, dir-gen Post Office 1960-66); *Style—* Lady German; Flat 1, 8A Grassington Rd, Eastbourne, E Sussex BN20 7BU

GEROSA, Peter Norman; s of Enrico Cecil Gerosa (d 1944), and Olive Doris Minnie, *née* Harry (d 1931); *b* 1 Nov 1928; *Educ* Whitgift Sch, Birkbeck Coll London (BA); *m* 1955, Dorothy Eleanor, da of Newton Cunningham Griffin; 2 da (Susan, Catherine); *Career* Civil Serv 1945-82; served in: FO, Home Office, Customs & Excise, Dept of Tport; under sec DOE 1972-82; sec Tree Cncl 1983-91, vice pres ROSPA 1984-, chm Nat Automobile Safety Belt Assoc 1986-; *Recreations* languages, numismatics, singing, enjoying architecture and the countryside; *Style—* Peter Gerosa, Esq; 17 Friths Drive, Reigate Surrey RH2 0DS (☎ 0737 243771)

GERRARD, His Hon Basil Harding; s of Lawrence Allen Gerrard (d 1955), of Lancs, and Mary, *née* Harding (d 1972); *b* 10 July 1919; *Educ* Bryanston Sch, Univ of Cambridge (BA); *m* 1948, Sheila Mary Patricia, da of C J Coggins (d 1972), and widow of Walter Dring, DSO, DFC (ka 1945); 1 s (Christopher Michael b 1962), 2 da (Sally Diane b 1949, Anne Rosemary b 1950), 1 step da (Susan Dring); *Career* RNVR (MTBs) 1942-44; asst to naval attaché Washington DC 1945; barr 1947; recorder Barrow-in-Furness 1969-70; circuit judge 1970 (ret 1982); memb Parole Bd England, Wales 1974-76; chm Selcare Tst 1971-78 (vice pres 1978-), Registered Homes Tribunal 1983-89; *Recreations* golf, gardening, croquet; *Clubs* Knutsford Golf, Bowdon Croquet (Cheshire); *Style—* His Hon Basil Gerrard; North Wood, Toft Rd, Knutsford

GERRARD, The Ven David Keith Robin; s of Eric Henry Gerrard, and Doris Jane, *née* Dance; *b* 15 June 1939; *Educ* Royal GS Guildford, St Edmund Hall Oxford (BA); *m* 12 Oct 1963, Jennifer Mary, da of John Stell Hartley (d 1981); 2 s (Stephen John b 1967, Jacob b 1972), 2 da (Ruth b 1965, Rachel b 1969); *Career* ordained: deacon 1963, priest 1964; curate: St Olave Woodberry Down 1963-66, St Mary Primrose Hill 1966-69; vicar: St Paul Lorrimore Square 1969-79, St Andrew and St Mark Surbiton 1979-89; rural dean Kingston 1983-88, hon canon Southwark Cathedral 1985, Archdeacon of Wandsworth 1989-; *Books* Urban Ghetto (1976); *Recreations* family, Yorkshire, embroidery, Proust; *Style—* The Ven The Archdeacon of Wandsworth; 68 North Side, Wandsworth Common, London SW18 2QX (☎ 081 574 5766); Kingston Episcopal Area Office, Whitelands College, West Hill, London SW15 3SN (☎ 081 780 2308)

GERRARD, David Lester; *b* 13 Dec 1942; *Educ* King Edward VI Sch Birmingham, Birmingham Coll of Art; *m* 6 April 1974, Catherine Robin; 2 da (Sophia Elizabeth b 22 March 1978, Charlotte Mary b 16 Oct 1980); *Career* designer Cox of Watford Ltd 1964-66, industl designer Robert Matthew Johnson-Marshall & Partners Edinburgh 1967-72, visiting lectr Edinburgh Coll of Art 1969-72 and 1980, designer Scottish Hosp Centre 1972-74, prod design expert Pakistan Design Inst Karachi 1974-76, external assessor Nat Coll of Art Lahore Pakistan 1976, visiting design lectr Dept of Architecture Nova Scotia Tech Coll Halifax 1977, princ Gerrard & Medd 1977-, internal assessor Design Sch Glasgow Sch of Art 1991 (visiting lectr 1978-90); designer of domestic and contract furniture; products incl: med electronic prods for various clients 1977-91, interior of Glasgow Royal Concert Hall 1990; chm Scottish Region CSD 1986-88, vice pres CSD 1990- (hon sec 1988-90); *awards* Scottish Designer of the Year 1980, Civic Trust award (for Distillers House interiors) 1985, Oscar for a domestic sink design for Carron Phoenix, Bureau du Syndicat National des Architectes d'Interieur Paris 1990; assoc Soc of Typographic Designers 1969, FCSD 1978; *Recreations* gardening, skiing, travelling, worrying; *Style—* David Gerrard, Esq; Gerrard and Medd, Quadrant, 17 Bernard St, Edinburgh EH6 6PW (☎ 031 555 0670, fax 031 554 1850)

GERRARD, Peter Noël; s of Sir Denis Gerrard (d 1965), of Fulbourn, Cambs, and Lady (Hilda Goodwin) Cantley, *née* Jones; *b* 19 May 1930; *Educ* Rugby, ChCh Oxford (MA); *m* 15 June 1957, Prudence, da of Herbert Lipson-Ward (d 1937), of Shanghai; 1 s (Hugo b 1963), 2 da (Phyllida b 1958, Deborah b 1960); *Career* Nat Serv 2 Lt XII Royal Lancers Malaya; admitted slr 1959, sr ptnr Lovell White & King 1980-88 (ptnr 1960-80), sr ptnr Lovell White Durrant 1988-91; memb: Bd of Banking Supervision 1990-, City Capital Markets Ctee 1974-91, Cncl of St George's Hosp Med Sch 1982-, Bd of Inst of Advanced Legal Studies 1985-, Cncl of the Law Soc 1972-82; *Recreations* walking, music; *Clubs* Athenaeum; *Style—* Peter Gerrard, Esq; Pightle Cottage, Ashdon, Saffron Walden, Essex CB10 2HG (☎ 079 984 374); 40 Canonbury Park North, London N1 2JT (☎ 071 354 0481); 65 Holborn Viaduct, London EC1A 2DY (☎ 071 236 0066, fax 071 248 4212, telex 887122 LWD G)

GERRARD, Ronald Tilbrook; s of Henry Thomas Gerrard and Edith Elizabeth, *née* Tilbrook; *b* 23 April 1918; *Educ* Imperial Coll of Sci and Technol, London Univ; *m* 1950, Cecilia Margaret Bremner; 3 s, 1 da; *Career* sr ptnr Binnie and Ptnrs consulting engrs 1974-; *Style—* Ronald Gerrard, Esq; 6 Ashdown Rd, Epsom, Surrey (☎ 037 27 24834)

GERRARD-WRIGHT, Maj-Gen Richard Eustace John; CB (1985), CBE (1977), OBE (1971), MBE (1965); s of Rev R L Gerrard-Wright; *b* 9 May 1930; *Educ* Christ's Hosp, RMA Sandhurst; *m* 1960, Susan Kathleen Young; 2 s, 2 da; *Career* Dep Col Royal Anglian Regt 1975-80, Col Cmdt The Queen's Div 1981-84, GOC Eastern Dist 1980-82, Dir TA & Cadets MOD 1982-85; *Style—* Maj-Gen R E J Gerrard-Wright, CB, CBE; Welney House, Welney, Wisbech, Cambs

GERSON, Mark; *b* 3 Oct 1921; *Educ* Central Foundation Sch for Boys, Regent St Poly; *m* 1949, Renée, *née* Cohen; 2 da (Ruth b 1950, Jane b 1953); *Career* RAF 1941-46; wireless operator - mechanic; apprenticeship London Advertising Studio 1937-39, taught photography under EVT Scheme Paris 1946, proprietor own studio 1947-87, freelance 1987-; exhibitions: in conjunction with Kodak, World Book Fair 1964, NBL 1970, Fox Talbot Museum 1981, Writers Observed, 1983, 1984; FBIPP; *Recreations* theatre, films; *Style—* Mark Gerson, Esq; 3 Regal Lane, Regents Park Rd, London NW1 7TH (☎ business 071 286 5894, home 071 267 9246)

GERSON, Michael Joseph; s of Maj John Leslie Gerson, TD (d 1980), and Jeanne Ida, *née* Marx (d 1981); *b* 2 Nov 1937; *Educ* Gresham's Sch Holt; *m* 28 Oct 1962, Shirley Esther, da of Alfred Simons; 3 s (Anthony, Peter, Simon); *Career* RNVR 1952-58; chm Michael Gerson Ltd 1980- (md 1961-80), chm Inst of Furniture Warehousing and Removal Indust, pres Fedn Int Brussels 1982-83, govr Barnet Coll; Freeman City of London 1984, Liveryman Worshipful Co of Carmen 1984; MCIT, FInstFF, FWRI; *Recreations* sailing; *Clubs* City Livery; *Style—* Michael Gerson, Esq; Downland Close, Whetstone, London N20 9LB (☎ 081 446 1300, fax 081 446 5088, telex 23965)

GERSTENBERG, Frank Eric; s of Eric Gerstenberg (d 1982), and Janie, *née* Thomas (d 1989); *b* 23 Feb 1941; *Educ* Glenalmond Coll Perthshire, Clare Coll Cambridge (MA), London Inst of Educn (PGCE); *m* 30 July 1966, Valerie Myra, da of Dr Peter Desmond MacLelland, of Little Rosings, Farley Lane, Westerham, Kent; 1 s (Neil John b 1968), 2 da (Anna Myra b 1971, Wendy Jane b 1971); *Career* asst master Kelly Coll Devon 1963-67, housemaster and head of history Millfield Sch Somerset 1967-74, headmaster Owestry Sch Shropshire 1974-85, princ George Watson's Coll Edinburgh 1985-; memb: Headmasters Conf 1985, Secdy Heads Assoc 1974; *Recreations* golf, skiing, travel; *Clubs* New (Edinburgh); *Style—* Frank Gerstenberg, Esq; George Watson's College, Colinton Rd, Edinburgh EH10 5EG (☎ 031 447 7931, fax 031 452 8594)

GERVAISE-BRAZIER, Colin Peter; s of Reginald Ernest Gervaise-Brazier (d 1957), and Joan Otto Bridie, *née* Babbe; *b* 5 April 1943; *Educ* Elizabeth Coll Guernsey; *m* 1971, Lynne Elizabeth, da of James Wilson, of Ikeringill; 1 s (James b 1976), 1 da (Alexandra b 1980); m 2, 1989, Joanna Dorothy, da of James Lepp; 1 da (Samantha-Joanna b 1990), 2 step s (Jonothan b 1979, Jack b 1985), 1 step da (Georgina b 1976); *Career* represented Guernsey at football, cricket, swimming, water polo, athletics, basketball; powerboat Br class I Champion (offshire) 1984; dir: Theodore Allen & Co Ltd, A Brown & Sons plc, Accorde Holdings Ltd, OCS Bureau Ltd, Rock Gardens Group plc; *Clubs* Lord Taverners, Guernsey Yacht, Royal Yachting Assoc UKOBA; *Style—* Colin Peter Gervaise-Brazier, Esq; La Trappe, Berget, Ruette De La Generotte, Câtel, Guernsey, Channel Islands; 16A Cornet St, St Peter Pont, Guernsey (☎ 0481 20622, telex 4191623, fax 0481 712482)

GERVASE-WILLIAMS, Kenneth; s of George Herbert Williams (d 1978), and Edith Esther, *née* Shipway (d 1980); *b* 25 Feb 1929; *Educ* Brockenhurst Co GS Hampshire; *m* 1, 13 July 1960 (m dis 1981), Shirley Elizabeth, da of HW Barritt, OBE (d 1967); 2 s (Christopher b 26 Feb 1961, Anthony b 26 Feb 1963); m 2, 18 March 1982, Gillian, da of Dr James Burns, CBE, GM; *Career* RAF 1947-49; quantity surveyor 1949-63, md Gervase Instruments Ltd 1964-88 (devpt of G ILFLO Primary Flow Sensor), pres Gervase Metering Inc USA 1987, chm Gervase Instruments Ltd 1988-; Freeman: City of London, Worshipful Co of Blacksmiths; FIOD 1987, MISA 1988; *Recreations* golf, tennis; *Clubs* City Livery, West Hill Golf Surrey; *Style—* Kenneth Gervase-Williams, Esq; Gervase Instruments Limited, Britannia Works, Cranleigh, Surrey GU6 8ND (☎ 0483 275 566, fax 0483 271 923, telex 859 473)

GESTETNER, David; s of Sigmund Gestetner (d 1956), of 12 Charles St, W1, and Henny Gestetner; er bro of Jonathan Gestetner, *qv*; *b* 1 June 1937; *Educ* Midhurst GS, Bryanston, Univ Coll Oxford (MA); *m* 16 Oct 1961, Alice Floretta, er da of Oliver Robert Marne Sebag-Montefiore, TD, of Halstead, Essex; *Career* pres Gestetner Holdings; *Recreations* sailing, tennis; *Style—* David Gestetner, Esq; 66 Chiltern St, London W1M 2AP (☎ 071 465 1011)

GESTETNER, Jonathan; s of Sigmund Gestetner (d 1956), of 12 Charles St, W1, and Henny Gestetner; yr bro of David Gestetner, *qv*; *b* 11 March 1940; *Educ* Bryanston, MIT (BSc); *m* 1968, Jacqueline Margaret Strasmore; *Career* Gestetner Holdings plc: jt chm 1972-87, jt pres 1987-88; dir: DRS USA 1987-89, Klein Associates USA 1987-90; chm Marlborough Rare Books 1990-; *Style—* Jonathan Gestetner, Esq

GETHIN, Fara, Lady; Fara; *née* Bartlett; yst da of late Joseph Henry Bartlett, of Garrick's Villa, Hampton, Middx; *m* 8 May 1946, Lt-Col Sir Richard Patrick St Lawrence Gethin, 9 Bt (d 1988); 1 s, 4 da; *Career* former 2 Offr WRNS; *Style—* Lady Gethin; Flat 28, The Maltings, Tewkesbury, Glos GL20 5NN

GETHIN, Maj Sir Richard Joseph St Lawrence; 10 Bt (I 1665), of Gethinsgrott, Cork; s of Lt-Col Sir Richard Patrick St Lawrence Gethin, 9 Bt (d 1988), and Fara, *née* Bartlett; *b* 29 Sept 1949; *Educ* Oratory, RMA Sandhurst, RMC Shrivenham (BSc), Cranfield Inst of Technol (MSc); *m* 1974, Jacqueline Torfrida, da of Cdr David Cox; 3 da; *Heir* uncle, Lt-Col William Allan Tristram Gethin, MC, RA b 13 Oct 1913; *Career* serv HM Forces, Maj, N Ireland, Germany and UK; MCIT; *Recreations* tennis, carpentry; *Style—* Maj Sir Richard Gethin, Bt; Greystones, 16 Coxwell Rd, Faringdon, Oxon (☎ 0367 21003)

GETHIN-JONES, Richard Llewellyn; s of Rev James Gethin-Jones, MC (d 1971), and Gwendoline Margaret, *née* Lewis (d 1942); *b* 6 June 1935; *Educ* Haileybury; *m* 8 Oct 1964, Rosemary Jennifer, da of William Arthur Hicklin (d 1969); 2 da (Amanda b 1966, Kate b 1968); *Career* Nat Serv Welsh Gds 1955-58; ptnr Ernst Whinney 1975-83; dir: Lime Street Underwriting Agencies Ltd 1983-, Kingsley Gethin-Jones and Assocs 1983-; FCA 1971; *Recreations* sailing, skiing, tennis, theatre; *Clubs* City of London; *Style—* Richard Gethin-Jones, Esq; 48 Queen's Gate Gardens, London SW7 5ND (☎ 071 584 6949); Fleur de Lys House, London EC3A 7BD (☎ 071 626 8331, fax 071 626 3943)

GETHING, Brian Constantine Peter; s of Lt-Col Burton William Eills Gething, of 5 Royal Northumberland Fus (d 1936), and Lady Donatia Faith Mary, *née* Wentworth-Fitzwilliam, 3 da of 7 Earl Fitzwilliam, KCVO, CBE, DSO; *b* 11 June 1926; *Educ* RNC Dartmouth; *m* 6 Jan 1954, (Ann) Sigrid (d 1991), da of Sir John Musker, of Shadwell Park, Thetford, Norfolk; 1 s (William b 1959), 1 da (Caroline b 1957); *Career* served RN 1943-52, Lt 1948, ADC to HE Govr of Trinidad and Tobago 1950-52; dir: Hurst Park Club Syndicate Ltd 1957-63, British Bloodstock Agency plc 1964-; underwriting memb of Lloyd's; *Recreations* shooting; *Clubs* White's, Pratt's, MCC, Jockey Club Rooms (Newmarket); *Style—* Brian Gething, Esq; British Bloodstock Agency plc, Queensberry House, High Street, Newmarket, Suffolk CB8 9BD (☎ 0638 665021)

GETHING, Air Cdre Richard Templeton; CB (1960), OBE (1945), AFC (1939); s of George A Gething, of Wilmslow, Cheshire; b (Aug 1911); *b* 1911,Aug; *Educ* Malvern, Sydney Sussex Cambridge; *m* 1940, Margaret Helen, da of Sir Herbert William Gepp (d 1954), of Melbourne, Vic, Australia; 1 s, 1 da; *Style—* Air Cdre Richard Gething, CB, OBE, AFC; Garden Hill, Kangaroo Ground, Vic 3097, Australia

GETTY, John Paul; Hon KBE (1986); s of J Paul Getty (d 1976), of Sutton Place, Guildford, and Helen Ann, *née* Rork (d 1988); *b* 7 Sept 1932; *Educ* Univ of San Francisco; *m* 1, Jan 1956 (m dis), Gail, da of Judge George Harris, of California; 2 s (Paul b 1956, Mark b 1960), 2 da (Aileen b 1959, Ariadne b 1962); m 2, 1967, Talitha Dina, da of Willem Pol, painter; 1 s (Tara b 1968); *Career* served US Army Korea 1952-53; md Getty Oil Italiana 1959-68; *Recreations* bibliophilia, early gramophone recordings, films, watching cricket; *Clubs* MCC, Pratt's; *Style—* John Paul Getty II, Esq, KBE

GEWANTER, Henry Leonard; s of Sidney Martin Lester Gewanter, of North Carolina, USA, and Louise Davida, *née* Pearlman; *b* 4 Jan 1954; *Educ* Bronx HS of Sci NY City, Univ of Lausanne Switzerland, King's Coll Cambridge (BA, MA); *Career* National Westminster Bank plc: Domestic Banking Div Foreign Dept Head Office 1978-79, International Banking Div Corporate Financial Services 1979-82, Business Devpt Div Advertising Dept 1983-86, tutor Investmt Revision Course NatWest Training Centre 1983-87; dep head PR County NatWest Ltd 1986-88, dir First Corporate Communications Ltd 1988-; lectr 1987- (Hammersmith and West London Coll, City of London Poly, Chartered Inst of Bankers (asst examiner in investmt)); Real Estate Bd Examination NY State 1977; memb: ACIB 1982, Assoc for Consumer Research, Consultancy Panel of the Assoc of Banking Teachers 1982, Inst of PR City & Financial Group, Royal Soc for the Encouragement of Arts Manufactures and Commerce 1985; MIPR 1989; *Recreations* collecting comic books and ancient Roman coins; *Style—* Henry L Gewanter, Esq; First Corporate Communications Ltd, Drury House, 34-43 Russell Street, London WC2B 5HA (☎ 071 497 8892, fax 071 753 8406)

GHAFFAR, Dr (Abu Jafar Muhammad) Abdul; s of Abdul Maabud (d 1988), of

Dhara, Bangladesh, and Shaheda Begum; *b* 1 March 1936; *Educ* Calcutta Univ, Dhaka Univ (MB, BS), Univ of Glasgow (DCH); *m* 19 March 1967, Khurshid Ara, da of Bashirul Islam (d 1971), of Dhara, Bangladesh; 2 s (Arif b 19 Feb 1968, Atiq (twin) b 19 Feb 1968), 2 da (Ayesha b 16 Feb 1973, Sonia Asia b 2 Sept 1975); *Career* conslt physician in geriatrics 1977-; practising: acupuncture NHS 1980-, homeopathy 1983-; chm Jamiatul Muslimeen Warrington 1977-, memb World Sufi Cncl; memb: BMA, Br Geriatric Soc, Br Med Acupuncture Soc, Br Faculty of Homeopathy; MRCP 1971; *Recreations* gardening; *Style*— Dr Abdul Ghaffar; 49 Denbury Ave, Stockton Heath, Warrington WA4 2BW; Warrington District General Hospital, Lovely Lane, Warrington, Gtr Manchester WA5 1QG

GHAFFARI, Dr Kamran; s of Mir Jalil Ghaffari, of Milan, Italy, and Aschraf Ghaffari; *b* 17 July 1948; *Educ* King's Sch Ely, Univ of Milan (MD); *m* 9 Nov 1986, Farnaz, da of Mir Jafar Ghaffari-Tabrizi; *Career* sr registry lectr in psychiatry St Thomas's Hosp 1984-86, locum conslt psychiatrist West Middx Univ Hosp 1986-87, md and conslt psychiatrist Psychiatric and Psychological Conslt Servs Ltd 1987-; assoc memb: Br Psychoanalytic Soc, Assoc Psychoanalytic Psychotherapy in the NHS; conslt in charge Eating Disorders Unit Huntercombe Manor 1991-; conslt in charge In-Patient Psychotherapy Unit Charter Clinic Chelsea 1991-; MRCPsych; *Recreations* theatre, bridge, chess, computer sciences; *Style*— Dr Kamran Ghaffari; 14 Devonshire Place, London W1N 1PB (☎ 071 935 0640)

GHANI, Gus; s of Amin Ghani, of Portugal, and Nahid Ghani; *b* 29 June 1954; *Educ* Stowe, Univ of Newcastle (BDS), Univ of London Inst of Dental Surgery, Eastman Dental Hosp (MSc); *m* 1980 (m dis 1985), Katherine, da of Peter Lavle; 1 da (Maryam b 1980); *Career* house offr oral surgery Kingston Hosp 1977-78, gen dental practice London 1978-79; sr house offr: oral Surgery Whipps Cross Hosp 1978, paediatric dentistry Leeds Dental Hosp 1979, Restorative Dept Eastman Dental Hosp 1979-83; gen dental practice: Leatherhead 1982-85, ptnr Hampton 1985-, Harley St 1989-; BDA 1977-89, Br Endodontic Soc 1979-, Br Soc For Restorative Dentistry 1979-83; *Recreations* golf, skiing, swimming, travel; *Clubs* Lansdowne; *Style*— Gus Ghani, Esq; 130 Harley St, London W1 (☎ 071 935 8538)

GHILÈS, Francis Christopher; s of Marcel Francois Ghiles, of Grenoble, France, and Margaret Esme Hyman; *b* 13 Nov 1944; *Educ* Lycée Francois de Londres, Lycée Champollion Grenoble, Institut d'Etudes Politiques Grenoble France, Univ of Keele (MA), St Antony's Coll Oxford (BLitt); *Career* journalist; worked for M Pierre Mendes France MP; reporter: City Press 1974-76, Euromoney 1976-77, The Financial Times 1977- (Euromarket 1977-82, N Africa corr 1982-); freelance assignments for: Le Monde, Liberation, Int Herald Tribune, The Times, Middle East International, TLS, Institutional Investor, Christian Science Monitor, BBC, CBC, Voice of America, El Pais, Nihon Kezai Shimbun; lectures given numerous location UK and overseas; *Recreations* skiing, travelling, cooking; *Style*— Francis Ghilès, Esq; 43A Glenmore Rd, London NW3 4DA (☎ 071 586 5622)

GHODSE, Prof Abdol-Hamid (Hamid); s of Abdol Rahim Ghodse, of Iran, and Batool, *née* Daneshmand; *b* 30 April 1938; *Educ* Univ of Iran (MD), Univ of London (PhD, DPM); *m* 30 June 1973, Barbara, da Capt of William Bailin, of Tring; 2 s (Amir-Hossein b 1975, Ali-Reza b 1979), 1 da (Nassrin b 1977); *Career* Lt Iranian Health Corps 1965; conslt St George's and St Thomas' Hosp 1978-87, prof of psychiatry addictive behaviour St George's Med Sch 1987-, dir SW Thames Regnl Drug Problem Team, hon sec Soc Study Addiction; pres: Wandsworth Alchohol Gp, Assoc Prevention of Addiction; memb Expert Advsy Panel WHO; MRCP 1988, FRCPsych 1985 (MRCPsych 1980); *Books* about 100 pubns incl: Misuse of Drugs (with P Bucknell, 1986), Psychoactive Drugs: Improving Prescribing Practices (1988), Drugs and Addictive Behaviour: A Guide to Treatment (1989); *Recreations* cycling, reading; *Clubs* Athenaeum; *Style*— Prof Hamid Ghodse; St George's Medical School, Cranmer Terrace, London SW17 ORE (☎ 081 672 9516)

GHOSH, Dr Chandra; da of Prof Bhupendranath Ghosh (d 1988), and Dr Sati Ghosh; *b* 15 June 1944; *Educ* St Johns Diocesan Girls HS, Univ of Calcutta (MB BS), Univ of London (DPM); *m* 22 May 1983, Dr Norman Alexander Hindson, s of John Savage Hindson; *Career* sr house offr, registrar and sr registrar Univ of Liverpool, conslt psychiatrist Broadmoor Special Hosp 1988- (Park Lane Special Hosp 1977-87); memb: NW Mental Health Assoc, Trans-Cultural Soc; MRCPsych; *Style*— Dr Chandra Ghosh; Broadmoor Hospital, Crowthorne, Berks RG11 7EG (☎ 0344 773111)

GHOSH, Dr Mrinal Kanti; s of Dr Jitendra Nath Ghosh (d 1981), of India, and Lalita, *née* Ghosh (d 1947); *b* 17 Jan 1938; *Educ* Calcutta Univ India (MB BS), Delhi Univ India (DTCD); *m* 12 Dec 1963, (Chitralekha) Roma, da of Sudhir Chandra Konar, of Burdwan, W Bengal, India; 1 s (Neil b 6 Aug 1973), 1 da (Mita b 23 Nov 1966); *Career* sr house offr geriatric med and neurology 1972-74, asst physician Amersham Gen Hosp Bucks 1974-76, conslt physician geriatric med Rotherham DHA 1976-, clinical tutor Rotherham Postgrad, med educn Rotherham Dist Gen Hosp 1985-, conslt and tutor undergrad and postgrad students Rotherham Dist Gen Hosp Univ of Sheffield; vice chm GP Vocational Trg Scheme Rotherham; memb: Advsy Sub Ctee Geriatric Med Trent RHA, registrar Sub Ctee Trent regn; Rotherham Dist Gen Hosp: memb Nurses Educn Ctee, memb Ethical Ctee, memb Library Liaison Ctee; MRCP, FRCPG 1987, FRCP 1988; *Recreations* sporting activities; *Style*— Dr Mrinal Ghosh; 79 Woodfoot Rd, Moorgate, Rotherham, S Yorks S60 3EH (☎ 0709 363770); Badsley Moor Lane Hosp, Rotherham, S Yorks S65 2QL (☎ 0709 820000 ext 2452)

GIARDELLI, (Vincent Charles) Arthur; MBE (1973); s of Vincent Ausonio Elvezio Giardelli (d 1953), of Broadway Mansion, Laugharne, Dyfed, and Annie Alice Sophia, *née* Lutman (d 1972); *b* 11 April 1911; *Educ* Hertford Coll Oxford (BA, MA); *m* 1, 10 April 1937 (d 1980), Phillis Evelyn, da of Lt Cdr John Berry; 1 s (Lawrence b 1942), 1 da (Judith b 1940); m 2, 21 May 1976, Beryl Mary, da of George Trotter (d 1952), of Havelock Rd, Croyden, Surrey; *Career* Aireman 1939-45, tutor then sr tutor Univ Coll of Wales Aberystwyth 1958-78, artist attached to Grosvenor Gallery London 1962-; one man exhibitions incl: Nat Library Wales 1963, Manchester Coll of Art 1964, Welsh Arts Cncl 1975, Univ of Wales 1977 and 1978, Gallerie Convergence Nantes 1980, Grosvenor Gallery 1987; collections incl: Nat Library Wales, Nat Museum Wales, Gallery Modern Art Dublin, Arts Cncl of GB, Welsh Arts Cncl, Museé des Beaux Arts Nantes, Nat Gallery Slovakia, Nat Gallery Prague, Tate Gallery; winner of Br Cncl award 1979, chm 56 Gp Wales 1958-91, nat chm Assoc of Tutors in Adult Educn 1964-67, memb Calouste Gulbenkian Enquiry into economic situation of visual artist 1977, hon fell Univ Coll Wales 1979-85; memb Artists and Designers Wales; Silver medal Czechoslovak Soc for Int Rels 1985; *Books* Up with the Lark (1939), The Delight of Painting (1976), The Grosvenor Gallery 1960-71 (1988); *Recreations* viola, foreign travel; *Style*— Arthur Giardelli, Esq, MBE; The Golden Plover, Warren, Pembroke, Dyfed SA71 5HR (☎ 0646 661 201)

GIBB, Prof (Arthur) Allan; O B E (1987); s of Arthur Gibb (d 1975), and Hilda, *née* Coleman (d 1977); *b* 20 Nov 1939; *Educ* Monkwearmouth GS Sunderland, Univ of Manchester (BA), Univ of Durham (PhD); *m* 12 Aug 1961, Joan, da of Eric Waterhouse (d 1964); 1 s (Stephen b 21 Sept 1962), 1 da (Jennie b 23 March 1965); *Career* res assoc and conslt Economist Intelligence Unit 1961-65, res fell Univ of Durham 1965-70, mangr Craven Bros 1970-71, dir small business centre Durham Univ Business Sch 1971-; chm Steering Gp, memb UK Enterprise and mgmnt Assoc; *Recreations* fell walking, tennis, watching football, travel; *Style*— Prof Allan Gibb, OBE; Kendonville, Crossgate Peth, Nevilles Cross, Durham (☎ 091 386406) Durham Univ Business Sch, Mill Hill Lane, Durham DH1 3LB (☎ 091 3742234, fax 374 3748, telex 537351 DURUBG)

GIBB, Andrew (McArthur); s of William Gibb (d 1983), and Ruth Margaret, *née* Railton; *b* 8 Sept 1927; *Educ* Sedbergh, Univ of Cambridge (MA); *m* 6 Sept 1956, Olga Mary, da of Leonard Marlborough Morris (d 1977); 3 da (Rosalind Emily (Mrs Nicholas Morrill) b 1958, Fiona Margaret (Mrs Christopher Rees) b 1959, Vanessa Grace b 1964); *Career* served FAA and RN; called to the Bar Middle Temple 1957; dep circuit judge 1972-76, rec of the Crown Ct 1976-79; chm Ctee of Enquiry into Fire at Wensley Lodge Old Peoples Home 1978 and other non-public enquiries; *Recreations* music, reading, watching golf, cricket; *Clubs* MCC, LCCC; *Style*— Andrew Gibb, Esq; 263 Colne Road, Sough, Earby, via Colne, Lancs BB8 6SY; Steele & Son, Solicitors, Castlegate, Clitheroe, Lancs, BB7 1AZ (☎ 0200 27431)

GIBB, Frances Rebecca; da of Matthew Gibb, of Islington, London, and Bettina Mary, *née* Dawson; *b* 24 Feb 1951; *Educ* St Margaret's Sch Bushey Herts, Univ of East Anglia Norwich (BA); *m* 5 Aug 1978, Joseph Cahill, s of Col E J Cahill; 3 s (Thomas b 3 Aug 1983, James b 19 April 1985, Patrick b 8 April 1989); *Career* reporter; news res asst Visnews 1973, trainee reporter Times Higher Education Supplement 1974-78, art sales corr Daily Telegraph 1978-80, legal affairs corr The Times 1982- (reporter 1980-82); memb Bd of Govrs Rosemead Prep Sch; *Style*— Ms Frances Gibb; The Times, 1 Pennington St, London E1 9XN (☎ 071 782 5931)

GIBB, Sir Francis Ross (Frank); CBE (1982); s of Robert Gibb (d 1932) and Violet Mary Gibb; *b* 29 June 1927; *Educ* Loughborough Coll (BSc); *m* 1950, Wendy Marjorie, da of Bernard Fowler (d 1957); 1 s, 2 da; *Career* dir Taylor Woodrow Int 1969-85; chm: Taywood Santa Fe 1975-85, chm and chief exec Taylor Woodrow plc 1985-89 (jt md 1979-85, jt dep chm 1983-85), pres Taylor Woodrow Construction Ltd 1985- (chm 1978-85, jt md 1979-84); non-exec dir: Babcock Int Gp plc 1990-, Steetley plc 1990-, Nuclear Electric 1990-; pres Fedn of Civil Engrg Contractors 1984-87 (vice chm 1978-79, chm 1979-80, vice pres 1980-84); dir: Holiday Pay Scheme 1980-83, Tstees Benefits Scheme 1980-83, Bldg and Civil Engrg Tstees 1980-83; chm: Agreement Bd 1980-82, Nat Nuclear Corp 1981-88; dir Br Nuclear Assocs 1980-88; memb: CBI Cncl, Governing Body London Business Sch 1985-89; vice pres Inst Civil Engrs 1988-90; Hon DTech 1989, Hon FCGI, FICE; kt 1987; *Recreations* ornithology, gardening, walking, music; *Clubs* Arts; *Style*— Sir Frank Gibb, CBE; Taylor Woodrow Construction Ltd, 345 Ruislip Rd, Southall, Middx (☎ 081 575 4373, telex 24428)

GIBB, James Robertson; RD (1983); s of David Craig Gibb (d 1971), and Mina, *née* Speirs (d 1980); *b* 19 April 1934; *Educ* Paisley GS, Univ of Glasgow (MA); *m* 21 March 1973, Elizabeth Milford, da of James Herries Henderson; 1 s (Donald James Hepburn), 1 da (Audrey Hepburn); *Career* investmt mangr Scottish Amicable Life Assurance Society 1962-67 (apprentice actuary 1956-62), dir Speirs & Jeffrey Ltd 1967-; Lt Col RNR (ret), FFA 1962; *Recreations* yachting, curling, skiing; *Clubs* Mudhook Yacht, R Gourock Yacht, Scottish Ski, Partick Cricket; *Style*— James Gibb, Esq; Speirs & Jeffrey Ltd, 36 Renfield St, Glasgow G2 1NA (☎ 041 248 4311, fax 041 221 4764)

GIBB, Walter Frame; DSO (1945), DFC (1943); s of Robert Gibb, and Mary Florence, *née* Davies; *b* 26 March 1919; *Educ* St Peter's Weston-super-Mare, Clifton; *m* 26 Feb 1944, (Pauline) Sylvia, da of Edward Baines Reed (d 1972); 3 da (Philippa Jane b 1947, Alison Mary b 1950, Anne Charlotte b 1956); *Career* RAFVR 1940, Night Fighter Mosquitos 264, 6O5, 515, 239 Sqdns, Wing Cdr 1944, CO 239 Sqdn, Wing Cdr Flying TFU 1945, RAF Defford, demobbed 1946; Bristol Aeroplane Co: apprentice Engine Div 1937-40, war service until 1946, test pilot, chief test pilot 1956; achieved World Altitude Record in Olympus Canberra WD 952 1953 (63, 668 feet) and 1955 (65, 890 feet), flew Brabazon and Britannia Aircraft; sales and service mangr British Aircraft Corporation (now British Aerospace plc) 1961, chm and md British Aerospace Australia Ltd 1978, ret 1984; JP Bristol 1974; *Recreations* sailing, swimming; *Clubs* RAF, Royal Sydney Yacht Sqdn, Thornbury Sailing; *Style*— Walter Gibb, Esq, DSO, DFC; Merlin Haven Lodge, 21 Merlin Haven, Wotton-under-Edge, Glos GL12 7BA (☎ 0453 844 889)

GIBB, William (Bill) Elphinstone; s of George Gibb and Jessie, *née* Reid, of Brae Neuk, New Pitsligo, Aberdeenshire; *b* 23 Jan 1943; *Educ* Fraserburgh Acad Scotland, St Martin's Sch of Art (Dip AD), Royal Coll of Art (DesRCA); *Career* couturier; Vogue Designer of the Year 1970, chm Glenclair Ltd; works are included in following museum collections: Bath, V & A, Leeds, Royal Ontario (Canada), National Museum of Antiques Edinburgh; fell Soc of Industl Artists and Designers 1975; *Recreations* travel, history of costume research, illustration; *Clubs* The Gardens, Ritz Casino, The Saddle Room, Legends, Hippodrome, Chelsea Arts; *Style*— Bill Gibb, Esq; 38 Drayton Court, Drayton Gdns, London SW10; 12 Queensdale Rd, Holland Park, London W11 (☎ 071 727 4994)

GIBBENS, Barnaby John (Barney); OBE (1989); s of Dr Gerald Hartley Gibbens (d 1989), of Sidmouth, Devon, and Deirdre Mary, *née* Wolfe (d 1972); *b* 17 April 1935; *Educ* Winchester; *m* 1, 30 June 1960 (m dis 1990), Sally Mary, da of Geoffrey Harland Stephenson (d 1970), of Guildford; 1 s (Nicolas b 1974), 2 da (Penelope b 1962, Virginia b 1967); m 2, 26 Feb 1990, Kristina, da of Romulo de Zabala (d 1961); *Career* fndr CAP Gp (later SEMA Gp) 1962; pres Computing Servs Assoc 1975; chm: Computing Servs Industry Trg Cncl 1984-, Info Technol Industry Lead Body 1987-; dir Nat Computing Centre 1987-, memb Nat Cncl for Vocational Qualifications, chm Tstees Skin Treatment and Research Tst 1990-; Freeman City of London 1987; fndr master Co of Info Technologists 1987; FBCS 1970, FCA 1972; *Recreations* golf, real tennis, photography, gardening; *Style*— Barney Gibbens, Esq, OBE; 12 Kings Rd, Wimbledon, London SW19 8QN (☎ 081 542 3878); SEMA Group plc, 22 Long Acre, London WC2E 9LY (☎ 071 379 4711, fax 071 839 4221, telex 263498)

GIBBERD, Dr (Frederick) Brian; s of Dr George Frederick Gibberd, CBE (d 1976), and Margaret Erica, *née* Taffs (d 1976); *b* 7 July 1931; *Educ* Aldenham, Univ of Cambridge (BA, MB BChir, MD), Westminster Med Sch; *m* 3 Sept 1960, Margaret Clare, da of David James Sidey (d 1939); 4 da (Ruth b 1962, Judith b 1965, Lucy b 1966, Penelope b 1968); *Career* conslt physician Westminster Hosp London 1965-; memb Cncl RSM 1972 and 1975-79, chm Standing Ctee of Membs RCP 1970-72 (examiner 1973-); chm Med Ctee: Westminster Hosp 1983-85, Riverside DHA 1985-87 (conslt memb 1987); memb Cncl RCP 1989- (censor 1990-); hon librarian RSM 1975-79 (pres Clinical Section 1972-74); Liveryman Worshipful Soc of Apothecaries 1968-, (memb Ct 1986-); FRCP 1972; *Style*— Dr Brian Gibberd; 7A Alleyn Park, London SE21 8AU (☎ 081 670 2197); Westminster Hospital, London SW1 (☎ 071 828 9811)

GIBBERD, Lady; Patricia; *née* Spielman; *b* 17 Oct 1926; *m* 1, - Fox-Edwards; m 2, 1972, as his 2 w, Sir Frederick Gibberd, CBE, RA, FRIBA, FRTPI, FILA (d 1984, architect of Liverpool Met Cathedral, Inter-Continental Hotel London, London Airport Terminal Buildings and Chapel); *Career* memb: Crafts Cncl, Eastern Arts Assoc, Harlow Art Tst, Yorkshire Sculpture Park, Kettles Yard; *Style*— Lady Gibberd; Marsh Lane, Harlow, Essex CM17 0NA

GIBBINGS, Hon Lady (Louise Barbara); *née* Lambert; o da of 2 Viscount Lambert,

TD (d 1989); *b* 29 March 1944; *m* 1975, as his 2 wife, Sir Peter Walter Gibbings, KBE, *qv*; 1 s; *Style—* The Hon Lady Gibbings

GIBBINGS, Sir Peter Walter; KBE (1989); s of Walter White Gibbings (d 1963), of London, and Margaret Russell, *née* Torrance (d 1963); *b* 25 March 1929; *Educ* Rugby, Wadham Coll Oxford (MA); *m* 1, Sept 1953 (m dis 1974), Elspeth Felicia, da of Cedric Macintosh; 2 da (Sarah b 1957, Jane b 1959); m 2, March 1975, Hon Louise Barbara Lambert, da of 2 Viscount Lambert; 1 s (Dominic b 1976); *Career* 2 Lt 9 Queen's Royal Lancers 1951-52, Capt Northants Yeomanry (TA); called to the Bar Middle Temple 1953, dep legal advsr Trinidad Oil Co Ltd 1955-56, Associated Newspapers Ltd 1956-60, The Observer 1960-67 (dep mangr and dir 1964-67), md Guardian Newspapers Ltd 1967-73, chm Guardian and Manchester Evening News 1973-88 (dir 1967-73); Anglia TV Gp plc: dir 1981, dep chm 1986-88-; Reuters Holdings plc 1984-88, chm Press Association Ltd 1986-87 (dir 1983-88), The Economist 1987-; memb Press Cncl 1970-74 pres CPU 1989-; *Recreations* tennis, skiing; *Style—* Sir Peter Gibbings, KBE; Anglia Television Gp plc, Anglia House, Norwich NR1 3JG (☎ 0603 615151, fax 0603 631032, car 0836 222181)

GIBBINS, Dr Frederick Johnson; s of Frederick Johnson Gibbins, of Aldridge, W Midlands, and Jennie Gillespie, *née* Liddle; *b* 20 July 1936; *Educ* Gosforth GS, Univ of St Andrews (MB ChB); *m* 15 July 1961, Brenda Margaret, da of Christian Agner Nielson (d 1970), of Newcastle upon Tyne; 2 s (Frederick b 1962, Andrew b 1964), 1 da (Fiona b 1969); *Career* conslt physician and geriatrician N Tees Health Dist 1967-, memb N Tees Dist Health Authy 1984-, non-exec dir St Andrews Homes 1987-; clinical examiner MRCP UK, memb Policy and PR Ctee Br Geriatrics Soc; pres Rotary Club Sedgefield; memb: BMA, BGS (former chm No 1 Regn); FRCPE; scientific papers incl: Blood Transfusion in the Elderly (1966), Haematological problems in the Older Patient (1975), Anaphylactic reaction to Vitamin B12 (with V N UgWu, 1981), Routine Chest Radiology in the Elderly (1985), Chest Pain in the Elderly (1986), The Future of the Long Stay Geriatric Patient (1989); *Recreations* duplicate bridge, pres Rotary Club of Sedgefield; *Style—* Dr Frederick Gibbins; Hamilton Lodge, W Park Lane, Sedgefield, Stockton-on-Tees, Cleveland TS21 2BA (☎ 0740 20488); N Tees Gen Hosp, Hardwick, Stockton-on-Tees, Cleveland TS21 2BA (☎ 0642 672122)

GIBBINS, Michael Edward Stanley; s of Stanley Stuart Gibbins (d 1986), and Mary Ellen, *née* Emin (d 1984); *b* 9 April 1943; *Educ* Marlborough, Sorbonne (Alliance Française); *m* 1, 16 Oct 1970, Sarah Francis Miller-Logan; 1 da (Bryony Mary Scilla b 8 March 1975); m 2, Britt Adrian; *Career* KPMG Peat Marwick McLintock: articled clerk 1962-66, qualified chartered accountant 1966, ptnr i/c Tehran Office Iran 1976-79, ptnr London 1979-, ptnr i/c External Debt Advsy Serv 1979- (advsr to Poland, Romania, Yugoslavia, Morocco, Ivory Coast, Sudan, Zambia, Nigeria on external debt), head E Europe Practice Gp 1990-; FCA (ACA 1966); *Recreations* water-skiing, squash, tennis; *Clubs* RAC; *Style—* Michael Gibbins, Esq; KPMG Peat Marwick McLintock, 1 Puddle Dock, Blackfriars, London EC4V 3PD (☎ 071 236 8000, fax 071 248 6552)

GIBBON, (William) Arthur; s of William Henry Gibbon (d 1967), of Hale-Barns, Cheshire, and Evelyn, *née* Burrows (d 1956); *b* 9 April 1921; *Educ* Altrincham GS, Univ of Manchester Hons Sch of Architecture (MA, BA); *m* 22 July 1944, Judith Eleanor, da of Arthur Lough (d 1975), of Keynsham, Somerset; 2 s (Christopher b 1945, Nicholas b 1964), 1 da (Catherine b 1950); *Career* architect; Cruickshank & Seward: ptnr 1958, sr ptnr 1968-86; conslt architect 1986-; works incl: power stations in Eng, Mexico and Argentina, Ashby Building Queen's Univ of Belfast, Renold Building UMIST, Library Extension Emmanuel Coll Cambridge, Arts Building Univ of Manchester, Manchester Business Sch, NW Water Authy Head Office Warrington, Royal London Assurance Co Head Office Colchester; awards incl: Truscon Travelling Scholarship 1954, RIBA medal 1955, RIBA Rose Shipman student 1956, Annual medal Reinforced Concrete Assoc 1958; memb: RIBA Cncl 1964-68, Architects Registration Cncl 1964-68; pres Manchester Soc of Architects 1965-67; hon fell UMIST 1976; FRIBA 1967; *Recreations* music, walking, reading Thomas Hardy, English art, family; *Clubs* The Athenaeum; *Style—* Arthur Gibbon, Esq; 132 The Close, Salisbury, Wilts SP1 2EY (☎ 0722 330522); Cruickshank & Seward, Royal London House, Deansgate, Manchester M3 3WP (☎ 061 832 6161, fax 061 832 0820)

GIBBON, Gen Sir John Houghton; GCB (1977, KCB 1972, CB 1970), OBE (1945, MBE 1944); er s of Brig John Houghton Gibbon, DSO (d 1960), of The Manor House, Little Stretton, Salop, and Jessie Willoughby, *née* Campbell; *b* 21 Sept 1917; *Educ* Eton, Trinity Coll Cambridge; *m* 1951, Brigid Rosamund, da of Dr David Armitage Bannerman, OBE, of London; 1 s; *Career* cmmnd RA 1939, served France, Western Desert, Sicily and Europe WWII, 6 Airborne Div Palestine 1945-47, instr and chief instr RMA Sandhurst 1947-51, AQMG WO 1955-58, Co Field Regt 1959-60, Bde Cdr Cyprus 1962, Dir Def Plans MOD 1962-65, Maj-Gen 1966, Sec Chiefs of Staff Ctee and Dir Def Ops Staff MOD 1966-68, DASD (Army) 1969-71, Lt-Gen 1971, Vice-Chief of Def Staff 1971-74, Gen 1974, Master Gen of the Ordnance 1974-77, ADC Gen to HM the Queen 1976-77, Col Cmdt RA 1972-82; *Recreations* fishing, shooting, rowing; *Clubs* Naval and Military, Leander; *Style—* Gen Sir John Gibbon, GCB, OBE; Beech House, Northbrook Close, Winchester, Hants SO23 8JR (☎ 0962 866 155)

GIBBON, Maggie; da of Peter Lewin Gibbon, of Le Bourg, Taillecavat, 33580 Monségur, France, and Alice Louise, *née* Hall; *b* 6 July 1949; *Educ* Fareham Girls' GS Fareham Hants, Univ of Essex (BA); *Career* advertisement sales exec on Radio Times for BBC Publications 1974-76, media planning exec with two advertising agencies (BBDO and CDP) 1976-80, advertisement sales exec The Observer 1980-81, memb Launch Team (advertising sales) on World of Interiors Magazine then Tatler for Condé Nast Publications 1980-84, advertisement mangr then publisher Over 21 Magazine 1984-88, publisher New Woman Magazine 1988-; *Style—* Miss Maggie Gibbon; Murdoch Magazines, Fanum House, 48 Leicester Square, London WC2H 7FB (☎ 071 930 9300, fax 071 976 1964)

GIBBON, His Hon Judge Michael; QC (1974); s of Frank Oswald Gibbon (d 1959), of Ty-Draw Rd, Cardiff, and Jenny Muriel, *née* Leake (d 1958); *b* 15 Sept 1930; *Educ* Brightlands, Charterhouse, Pembroke Coll Oxford (MA); *m* 15 Feb 1956, Malveen Elliot, da of Capt John Elliot Seager, MC, DL, JP, OStJ (d 1955); 2 s (Nigel Elliot b 1958, David Frank b 1960), 1 da (Juliet Rebecca b 1963); *Career* RA 1949-50, Lt TA 1950-58; called to Bar 1954, rec Crown Ct 1972-79, circuit judge 1979; chm Advsy Ctee to Home Sec 1972, Local Govt Boundary Cmmn for Wales 1978-79 (dep chm 1974-79); memb Parole Bd for England and Wales 1986-88; hon recorder of the City of Cardiff 1986-; *Recreations* music, golf; *Clubs* Cardiff and County, Royal Porthcawl Golf; *Style—* His Hon Judge Gibbon, QC; Newport (Gwent) Crown Court, Civic Centre, Newport, Gwent (☎ 0633 66211)

GIBBON, Ronald Bryan; s of Robert Robinson Gibbon (d 1967), and Ethel Winifred Gibbon (d 1978); *b* 23 Sept 1928; *Educ* Kings Coll Durham (BSc); *m* 19 April 1958, Brenda Eunice, da of Sidney Walter Nicholls; 2 s (David Keith Christopher b 6 July 1960, Andrew Neil Michael b 3 Oct 1962); *Career* graduate apprentice CA Parsons 1952-54, AERE 1954-56, head Materials Technology International Research and Development Co 1957-66; Gas Council: design advsr Engineering Research Centre 1966-68, quality control engr then engrg servs mangr HQ 1968-75; British Gas: central controller Prodn and Supply Div 1975-87, HQ dir construction 1987-90, dir The National Transmission System 1990-; chm Bd QUASCO; dir: Port Greenwich Ltd, Methane Services Ltd; memb UK Offshore Operators Assoc 1980- (chm Engrg and Devpt Ctee 1984-87); awarded H Jones medal 1987; MInstM 1963, FIQA 1969, FIGasE 1970, FEng 1988; *Recreations* wine tasting, gardening, church work; *Style—* Ronald Gibbon, Esq, OBE; Suoluno, Curls Lane, Maidenhead, Berks SL6 2QF (☎ 0628 23017); British Gas, Rivermill House, 152 Grosvenor Rd, London SW1V 3JL (☎ 071 821 1444)

GIBBON-WILLIAMS, Andrew; s of Ivor James Williams (d 1990), of Barry, S Glamorgan, and Grace Mary, *née* Thomas; *b* 6 March 1954; *Educ* Barry Boys' GS, Edinburgh Coll of Art Univ of Edinburgh (Huntly-MacDonald Sinclair Travelling scholarship, MA); *Career* artist and art critic; solo exhibitions 369 Gallery Edinburgh 1979, 1980, 1982 and 1986; group exhibitions incl: Scottish Painters (Chenil Gallery, London) 1978, The Royal Scottish Academy 1980, Scottish Painting (Watts Gallery, Phoenix, Arizona) 1981, Best of 369 (St Andrews Festival) 1983, The Scottish Expression: 1983 (Freidus Ordover Gallery, NY) 1983, Peintres Contemporains Ecossais (Galerie Peinture Fraiche, Paris) 1983, New Directions - British Art (Puck Bldg, NYC) 1983, Chicago Int Art Exposition 1983-89, Int Contemporary Art Fair (London) 1984, Contemporary Scottish Art (Clare Hall, Cambridge) 1984, Scottish Painting (Linda Durham Gallery, Sante Fe) 1985, Scottish Art Since 1900 (Scottish Nat Gallery of Modern Art, Edinburgh and The Barbican Gallery, London 1989-90; work in public collections incl: The Scottish Arts Cncl Dundee Art Gallery, IBM UK Ltd, Philips Petroleum, Scottish Nat Gallery of Modern Art, City of Edinburgh Public collection, The Warwick Arts Tst collection, L&M Moneybrokers Ltd, NatWest Bank, The McDonald Corporation (USA); art critic The Sunday Times Scotland 1988-, regnl art critic The Times 1988-, regular contrib to BBC Arts progs; winner: Young Artist bursary Scottish Arts Cncl 1982, Warwick Arts Tst Artist award 1989; *Books* The Scottish School (1991); *Recreations* travel, music; *Clubs* Chelsea Arts, Scottish Arts; *Style—* Andrew Gibbon-Williams, Esq; 18 Frederick St, Edinburgh EH2 2HB (☎ 031 225 2082)

GIBBONS, Christopher Adney Walter; s of Adney Walter Gibbons (d 1941), of London, and Lady Taylor, *née* Constance Ada Shotter (d 1989); *b* 14 May 1930; *Educ* Charterhouse, Trinity Coll Cambridge; *m* 1, Jan 1953 (m dis 1964), Gillian Elizabeth Sugden Temperley; 1 da (Virginia b 10 March 1954); m 2, Sept 1964, Charlotte Sophia, da of Sir George Bull Bt (d 1986); 2 da (Jemima b 31 Aug 1965, Loveday b 8 Nov 1967); *Career* 2 Lt Grenadier Gds 1949-50; called to the Bar Middle Temple 1954, practised at Bar 1954-60, slr 1961, asst slr Linklater and Paines 1961-66, ptnr Stephenson Harwood 1966-; non-exec dir: The Throgmorton Tst plc, The New Throgmorton Tst plc, The Throgmorton Dual Tst plc, TT Fin plc 1986-, The Fifth Throgmorton Co plc 1988-; City of London Slrs Co: dep chm Professional Business Ctee 1982-84 (memb 1976-84), chm Banking Law Sub-Ctee 1980-84, memb Co Law Sub Ctee 1968-86; memb Law Soc Standing Ctee on Co Law 1978-, leader Accounting Matters Gp 1987, cnclr Hammersmith Met Borough 1968-71 (vice chm Fin Ctee); memb Mgmnt Ctee: Hammersmith Cncl of Community Rels 1968-74, Fulham Legal Advice Centre 1968-74, Shepherds Bush Housing Assoc 1968-80; Freeman City of London 1978, Liveryman City of London Slrs Co; memb Law Soc; *Recreations* racing, walking; *Style—* Christopher Gibbons, Esq; 1 St Paul's Churchyard, London EC4M 8SH (☎ 071 329 4422, fax 071 606 0822, telex 886789 SHSPC G)

GIBBONS, Christopher Peter; s of William Frederick Gibbons, of Holmes Chapel, Cheshire, and Hazel Doreen, *née* Flint; *b* 10 March 1949; *Educ* Manchester GS, Keble and Wolfson Coll Oxford (MA, DPhil, BM BCh, MCh); *m* 4 July 1970, Ann Lawrence, da of George Robert White Dalgleish; 3 da (Kate b 1975, Rachel b 1978, Susannah b 1982); *Career* surgical registrar Univ Hosp of Wales 1979-82, surgical registrar Royal Hallamshire Hosp Sheffield 1982-83, clinical res fell Univ of Sheffield 1984-85, sr surgical registrar Cardiff and Swansea 1985-89, conslt gen surgn Morriston Hosp Swansea 1989-, pubns on aspects of physiology and surgery; FRCS 1980; memb: BMA, Br Transplantation Soc 1975, Assoc of Surgns 1978; *Style—* Christopher Gibbons, Esq; Morriston Hosp, Swansea (☎ 0792 702222)

GIBBONS, Hon Sir (John) David; KBE (1985), JP (Bermuda 1974); s of Edmund Graham Gibbons, CBE (d 1972), and Winifred Gladys Gibbons, MBE, *née* Robinson (d 1972), of Palm Grove, Devonshire, Bermuda; *b* 15 June 1927; *Educ* Saltus GS Bermuda, Hotchkiss Sch Connecticut USA, Harvard Univ (BA); *m* 1958, Lully, da of Johannes Jorgen Lorentzen, of Oslo; 3 s (William, John, James), 1 da by former marriage (Edith); *Career* MP (Utd Bermuda Pty) 1972-75, min health and social servs 1974-75, min fin 1975-84 (post held concurrently with premiership), premier of Bermuda 1977-82; chm: Bermuda Monetary Authy 1984-86, Bank of N T Butterfield & Son Ltd 1986-; *Recreations* tennis, golf, skiing, swimming; *Clubs* Lyford Cay (Bahamas), Royal Bermuda Yacht, Royal Hamilton Dinghy, Mid Ocean, Riddells Bay, Harvard (New York); *Style—* Hon Sir David Gibbons, KBE, JP; Leeward, 5 Leeside Drive, Point Shares, Pembroke, Bermuda HM 05 (☎ 809 29 5 2396); Apartment 7A 3 East 71 St, NY 10021, USA; 29 Montpelier Walk, London SW7 1JF; Bank of N T Butterfield & Son Ltd, Hamilton, Bermuda (☎ 809 295 8154)

GIBBONS, David Paul; *née* Baynes; s of Geoffrey Albert Gibbons, of Milton Keynes, and Lorna June, *née* Howard; *b* 20 Nov 1957; *Educ* Weymouth GS, Bristol Univ (BSc); *Career* CA; Arthur Andersen & Co (articles) 1979-82, investmt analyst electronics James Capel & Co 1982-; ACA 1981; *Recreations* windsurfing, skiing; *Style—* David Gibbons, Esq; 48 Clapham Manor St, London SW4 6DZ (☎ 071 627 4652); James Capel & Co, 6 Bevis Marks, London EC3A 7JQ (☎ 071 621 0011)

GIBBONS, Dr John Ernest; s of John Howard Gibbons (d 1979), and Lilian Alice, *née* Shale (d 1982); *b* 20 April 1940; *Educ* Oldbury GS, Birmingham Sch of Architecture (Dip Arch, Dip TP), Univ of Edinburgh (PhD); *m* 3 Nov 1962, Patricia, da of Eric John Mitchell, of Albany, WA; 1 s (Mark b 16 March 1963), 2 da (Carey b 20 May 1964, Ruth b 29 July 1967); *Career* lectr: Aston Univ 1964-66, Univ of Edinburgh 1969-72; Scot Devpt Dept: princ architect 1972-74 and 1976-78, superintending architect 1978-82; res scientist CSIRO Melbourne Aust 1975; SO: dep dir bldg directorate 1982-84, dir of bldg 1984-, chief architect 1984-; memb: Cncl Edinburgh Architectural Assoc 1977-80, Cncl Royal Incorporation of Architects in Scot 1977-80, Cncl Architects Registration Cncl of UK 1984-, Design Cncl 1984-88; RIBA 1964, ARIAS 1967, FSA (Scot) 1984, FRSA 1987; *Style—* Dr John Gibbons; Crichton Ho, Pathhead, Midlothian EH37 5UX (☎ 0875 320 085); Scottish Office, New St Andrews House, Edinburgh EH1 3SZ (☎ 031 244 4149)

GIBBONS, John Robert Pelham; MBE (1970), TD (1968); s of Leonard Norman Gibbons (d 1948), of Solihull, Warwickshire, and Gladys Elizabeth, *née* Smith (d 1989); *b* 26 Nov 1926; *Educ* Moseley GS, Pates Sch Cheltenham, Univ of Leeds (MB ChB); *m* 7 Nov 1952, (Elizabeth) Marie-Jeanne Morwenna, da of Maj Philip Brookes, TD, of Kirkstall House, Kirkstall, Leeds, Yorks; 4 s (Robert b 1954, Maxime b 1958, Paul b 1966, Charles b 1967), 2 da (Anne-Marie b 1956, Marie-Lucie b 1960); *Career* Lt Royal Warwickshire Regt, Maj Parachute Regt; conslt Royal Free Hosp London 1976, conslt surgn Royal Victoria Hosp Belfast 1977, Hunterian prof RCS 1984, hon consulting surgn Military Wing Musgave Park Hosp Belfast, conslt thoracic surgn Cambridge Military Hosp Aldershot 1989-; memb: Forces Help Soc, Lord Roberts Workshops, Br Legion, Parachute Regt Assoc; FRCS 1960, FRCSEd, FRSCI 1988; *Recreations* watching rugby football; *Clubs* Ulster Reform; *Style—* John Gibbons, Esq,

MBE, TD; 35 Palace Rd, Hampton Court, East Molesey, Surrey KT8 9DJ (☎ 081 783 1401); 23 Hawthornden Drive, Belfast, Co Antrim BT4 2HG; Royal Victoria Hospital, Belfast BT12 6BA (☎ 0232 240503, fax 0232 040899); Cambridge Military Hospital, Aldershot, Hampshire

GIBBONS, Ven Kenneth Harry; s of Harry Gibbons (d 1968), and Phyllis, *née* Priday (d 1963); *b* 24 Dec 1931; *Educ* Blackpool GS, Chesterfield GS, Univ of Manchester (BSc), Cuddesdon Coll Oxford; *m* 2 June 1962, Margaret Ann, da of Bertie Tomlinson (d 1962), of Billinghay, Lincoln; 2 s (David Austen b 1963, Andrew Kenneth b 1964); *Career* RAF 1952-54; ordained 1956, asst curate of Fleetwood 1956-60, sec Student Christian Movement in Schs 1960-62, sr curate St Martin-in-the-Fields Westminster 1962-65; vicar: St Edward New Addington 1965-70, St Mary's Portsea 1970-81, Weeton 1981-85, St Michaels-on-Wyre 1985-; hon canon 1974 (rural dean 1973-79), acting chaplain to the Forces at Weeton Barracks 1981-85, archdeacon of Lancaster 1981-, diocesan dir of Ordination Candidates 1982-90; *Recreations* gardening, cinema; *Clubs* Reform; *Style—* The Ven the Archdeacon of Lancaster; The Vicarage, Hall Lane, St Michael's-on-Wyre, nr Preston, Lancs PR3 0TQ (☎ 099 58 242)

GIBBONS, (Ronald) Peter; s of Lt Arthur James Gibbons (d 1935), of Bombay, and Mary Christina, *née* Kiernan; *b* 7 Nov 1929; *Educ* Abbey Sch Fort Augustus, Univ of Glasgow (MA), Balliol Coll Oxford (BA); *m* 2 Dec 1957 (m dis 1980), Jill Rosemary, da of Arthur Holden Lowe (d 1958), of Kensington, London; 1 s (Nicholas b 1960), 4 da (Caroline b 1958, Lucy b 1961, Julia b 1963, Mary Jane b 1967); *Career* Slrs Office Inland Revenue, called to the Bar Gray's Inn 1958, chm Social Security Appeal Tbnl Central London 1981-; head of Chambers 1988-; contrib reference books on revenue law; *Recreations* swimming; *Style—* Peter Gibbons, Esq; 136-9 Temple Chambers, Temple Ave, London EC4Y OBB

GIBBONS, Robert Frank; s of Robert Rex Maynard Gibbons (d 1986), of Lawers House, Comrie, Perthshire, and Maria Carmella, *née* Difelice (d 1976); *b* 19 March 1937; *Educ* Downside, Coll of Law; *m* 14 May 1964, Rita Ann; 3 s (Nigel b 1965, Charles b 1966, Edward b 1972), 1 da (Amelia b 1969); *Career* slr 1962, sr ptnr Fox & Gibbons; memb Law Soc; *Recreations* shooting, fishing, carriage driving; *Style—* Robert Gibbons, Esq; 67 Eccleston Sq, London SW1 (☎ 071 439 8271); Lawers, Comrie, Perthshire PH6 2LT; 2 Old Burlington St, London W1X 2QA (☎ 071 439 8271, fax 071 734 8843, telex 267108 GIBLAW G)

GIBBONS, Sir William Edward Doran; 9 Bt (GB 1752), of Stanwell Place, Middlesex; JP (Portsmouth 1990); s of Sir John Edward Gibbons, 8 Bt (d 1982), and Mersa Wentworth, *née* Foster; *b* 13 Jan 1948; *Educ* Pangbourne Sch, RNC Dartmouth, Univ of Bristol; *m* 1972, Patricia Geraldine Archer, da of Roland Archer Howse; 1 s, 1 da; *Heir* s, Charles William Edwin Gibbons b 28 Jan 1983; *Career* mangr Harwich Sealink UK Ltd 1985-87, gen mangr Isle of Wight Services Sealink UK Ltd 1987-90, tport and mgmnt conslt 1990-, chm Manningtree Parish Cncl 1985-87, non-exec memb IOW Dist Health Authy 1990; *Style—* Sir William Gibbons, Bt, JP; 5 Yarborough Road, Southsea, Hants

GIBBS, Maj Andrew Antony; MBE (1945), TD (1945); s of Ven Hon Kenneth Francis Gibbs (d 1935, 5 s of 1 Baron Aldenham), Archdeacon of St Albans, and Mabel Alice, *née* Barnett (d 1953); *b* 31 March 1914; *Educ* Winchester, ChCh Oxford (MA); *m* 9 May 1947, Elizabeth Joan, wid of Capt Peter George William Savile Foljambe (ka 1944), and da of Maj Eric Charles Montagu Flint, DSO (d 1962); 2 s; *Career* served WWII, Maj Herts Regt; dir: Barclays Bank 1962-84, Barclays UK Mgmnt Ltd 1971-79, Barclays Insur Servs Co Ltd 1970-75, York Waterworks Co 1969-89; memb: York Minster Fund (memb High Steward's Ctee) 1967-89, York Diocesan Bd of Fin 1964-85; chm Dean & Chapter of York Fin Ctee 1969-; hon life memb BRCS; fell of the Midland Div of Woodard Corp 1959-84 (hon fell 1985), chm of Sch Cncl Worksop Coll 1962-84, govr St Edward's Sch Oxford 1948-88; *Recreations* shooting; *Clubs* Travellers', Pratt's, MCC; *Style—* Maj Andrew Gibbs, MBE, TD; Kilvington Hall, Thirsk, N Yorkshire YO7 2NS (☎ 0845 537213)

GIBBS, Antony Richard; s of Dr Antony James Gibbs, of Mercers Cottage, The Common, Cranleigh, Surrey, and Helen Margaret, *née* Leuchars; *b* 25 May 1939; *Educ* Bradfield, Byam Shaw Sch of Drawing & Painting (scholar), Kingston Sch of Art (NDD); *m* Sept 1965, Mary Jane (Janey), da of Frank Day; 1 s (Rupert Nicolas Anthony b 28 April 1968), 1 da (Emily Jo b 26 July 1970); *Career* formerly: designer David Ogle Associates, prod designer STC Consumer Product Div, chief stylist Radfords (Coachbuilders) Ltd, assoc TEE Design; dir Murdoch & Gibbs 1975-80; Hop Studios 1980- (fndr ptnr, co sec, dir); awarded: Design Cncl award for outstanding design 1977, BIO Industrial Design award Yugoslavia 1977; memb: Design Cncl, Design Cncl Awards Ctee, Bursaries Judging Panel RSA; moderator BA Assessment Panel Central Sch of Art; *Books* Industrial Design in Engineering (jtly); FCSD, FRSA; *Recreations* music compositions; *Style—* Antony Gibbs, Esq; 6 Tarleton Gardens, Forest Hill, London SE23 3XN (☎ 081 699 4610); Hop Studios Limited, 2 Jamaica Road, London SE1 2BX (☎ 071 252 0808, fax 071 237 7199)

GIBBS, Capt Beresford Norman (Bobby); DL (1990); s of The Rev Canon John Stanley Gibbs, MC (d 1952), of Didmarton House, Badminton Avon, and Mary Rosamond, *née* McCorquodale (d 1966); *b* 27 Feb 1925; *Educ* Hawtreys Sch Westgate on Sea, Eton, RAC; *m* 22 Aug 1956, (Mary) Jane, da of William Arthur Norman Thatcher (d 1965), of The Grove, Ovor Worton, Middle Barton, Oxon; 2 s (Jack b 1957, David b 1965), 2 da (Cecily (Mrs Illingworth) b 1960, Alice (Mrs Kerr) b 1963); *Career* Nat Serv Capt RHG 1943-47, RHG RARO 1950-75 (The Blues and Royals 1969-); in gen Practice as land agent; GC Laws of Westcote Barton Oxon 1952-58, own account managing properties 1958- incl: Gloucestershire, Wilts, Oxon, Staffs, Eire; High Sheriff Wilts 1989-90; memb: Land Agents Soc 1957, Malmesbury DC 1958-64, Oaksey Parish Cncl 1961-66; church warden Oaksey 1968-88, vice chm CPRE N Wilts Gr 1979-, chm Oaksey CC 1985; MRAC, FRICS 1958; *Recreations* lawn tennis, history, cricket, genealogy, forestry; *Clubs* Mary Le Bone Cricket; *Style—* Capt Bobby Gibbs, DL; Flintham House, Oaksey, Malmesbury, Wilts SN16 9SA (☎ 0666 7282)

GIBBS, Bryan Somerset Andrew; s of Somerset Bryan Gibbs (Capt Welsh Gds), of Witcham House, Witcham, Cambs, and Elspeth Oriana Elisabeth, *née* Russi; *b* 30 Nov 1950; *Educ* Ampleforth; *m* 12 Oct 1974, Suzette Elizabeth, da of Maj Ronald John Stephens, of Southrepps, Norfolk; 3 da (Lucy b 1981, Gemma b 1983, Alice b 1987); *Career* audit mangr (formerly articled clerk) Coopers & Lybrand 1969-78, gp chief accountant (latterly gp fin controller) Phicom plc (formerly Plantation Hldgs Ltd) 1978-86; Corporate Communications plc (formerly City Commercial Communications plc): fin dir 1986-89, gp fin dir 1989-; FCA; *Recreations* golf, tennis, table tennis, chess, old house restoration; *Clubs* Royal Worlington & Newmarket Golf, City of London; *Style—* Bryan Gibbs, Esq; Dalnyveed, Bakers Lane, Barley, Royston, Herts SG8 8HJ (☎ 076384 504); Corporate Communuications plc, Bell Court House, 11 Blomfield Street, London EC2M 7AY (☎ 071 588 6050, fax 071 638 3398, car tel 0836 233717, telex 883502 CCC G)

GIBBS, Christopher Henry; 5 and yst s of Hon Sir Geoffrey Cokayne Gibbs, KCMG (d 1975; 2 s of 1 Baron Hunsdon of Hunsdon, 4 s of 1 Baron Aldenham, JP), and Helen Margaret Gibbs, CBE, JP, *née* Leslie (d 1979); *b* 29 July 1938; *Educ* Eton, Stanbridge, Université de Poitiers; *Career* art dealer; dir: Christopher Gibbs Ltd, Faversham Oyster Fishery Co; tstee: Edward James Fndn, J Paul Getty Jr Charitable Tst, J Paul Getty Jr Endowment Inst (Nat Gallery), Serpentine Gallery; memb Oxford Diocesan Ctee for the Care of Churches; *Recreations* antiquarian pursuits, gardening; *Clubs* Beefsteak; *Style—* Christopher Gibbs, Esq; Manor House, Clifton Hampden, Abingdon, Oxon; L6 Albany, Piccadilly; Christopher Gibbs Ltd 8 Vigo St, London W1 (☎ 071 439 4557)

GIBBS, David Charles Leslie; eldest s of Hon Sir Geoffrey Cokayne Gibbs, KCMG (d 1975; 2 s of 1 Baron Hunsdon of Hunsdon, JP, himself 4 s of 1 Baron Aldenham, JP), and Helen Margaret, CBE, JP, *née* Leslie; *b* 15 Aug 1927; *Educ* Eton, ChCh Oxford; *m* 20 March 1965, (Charmian) Fleur, da of Dalzell Pulteney Mein, of Toolang, Coleraine, Victoria, Aust; 2 s, 2 da; *Career* Antony Gibbs Group in Eng and Aust 1949-80, (dir Antony Gibbs & Sons, chm Gibbs Bright & Co); chm: C T Bowring Reinsurance Australia Pty Ltd 1981-, Marsh & McLennan Pty Ltd and predecessors 1981-87, B G J Holdings Ltd 1982-86, Folkestone Ltd 1983 (dir 1976-), ANZ Executors & Trustee Co Ltd 1990- (dir 1985-); dir: Australia & NZ Banking Group 1979-91, John Swire & Sons Pty Ltd 1983-, Parbury Henty Holdings 1984-, Marsh and McLennan 1987-89, Victoria State Opera Co Ltd 1985-; pres: World Wide Fund for Nature Aust 1988- (memb Cncl 1983-), Victoria State Opera Fndn 1986- (memb Cncl 1982-); memb Cncl: Museum of Victoria 1979-85, Victoria Cncl, Aust Bicentennial Authy 1984-88; *Recreations* fishing, opera, ornithology, farming, old master drawings; *Clubs* White's, Pratt's, Flyfishers, Melbourne, Australian (Melbourne), Australia (Sydney) Queensland; *Style—* David Gibbs, Esq; 21 William St, S Yarra, Melbourne, Vic 3141, Australia

GIBBS, David Evelyn; s of Brig Lancelot Merivale Gibbs, CVO, DSO, MC (and Bar) (d 1966), and Hon Marjory Florence, *née* Maxwell (d 1939), da of 11 Baron Farnham, DSO; *b* 22 March 1931; *Educ* Eton; *m* 6 June 1959, Phyllida Lovaine , da of Col Piers Standish Plowden, OBE (d 1990) of East Wing, Somborne Park, Kings Somborne, Hants; 2 s (Giles b 6 Nov 1962, Crispin b 14 Dec 1966), 1 da (Quenelda); *Career* cmmnd Lt Coldstream Gds 1949-51, served UK and Tripoli; Gold Staff Offr Westminster Abbey at Coronation of HM The Queen 1953; ptnr Norris Oakley Richardson & Glover (formerly Capel Cure Myers until incorp 1975); memb London Stock Exchange; *Recreations* shooting, tennis, underwater diving, gardening; *Clubs* Pratt's; *Style—* David Gibbs, Esq; The Clock House, Sparsholt, Winchester, Hants SO21 2LX (☎ 0962 72 461)

GIBBS, David Phillip; s of William Charles Gibbs (d 1961); *b* 6 May 1941; *Educ* Cranleigh Sch; *m* 1, 1964 (m dis 1981), Gillian; 2 s, 1 da; m 2, 1982, Vanessa Susan Jane; *Career* dir Hambros Bank Ltd 1973-; *Recreations* golf, gardening; *Style—* David Gibbs, Esq; Hill Farm House, Slaugham Lane, Plummers Plain, Sussex; Hambros Bank, 41 Tower Hill, London (☎ 071 480 5000)

GIBBS, Dr Denis Dunbar; s of The Very Rev Michael McCausland Gibbs (d 1962), and Edith Marjorie, *née* Ward (d 1968); *b* 19 July 1927; *Educ* Diocesan Coll Cape Town, Univ of Cape Town, Keble Coll Oxford (BA, BM BCh, DM), St Mary's Hosp Med Sch; *m* 11 April 1953, Rachel Elizabeth, da of Geoffrey Bernard Youard, MBE (d 1987); 1 s (Nicholas Mark b 1954), 1 da (Sarah Mary b 1956); *Career* Flt Lt RAF med branch 1955-57; house physician: St Mary's Hosp, Radcliffe Infirmary, Hammersmith Hosp 1953-55; registrar and sr registrar The London Hosp 1958-62, res fell Boston City Hosp and Mass Meml Hosp 1963; conslt physician: Good Hope Gen Hosp Sutton Coldfield and North Birmingham 1964-73, The London Hospital 1974; CMO Provident Life 1976, memb Med Appeal Tribunals 1989, FRCP 1973, FRSM; *Books* Exfoliative cytology of the Stomach (1968), Emblems, Tokens and Tickets of the London Hospital (1985); *Recreations* books, photography, walking, medical history; *Clubs* Athenaeum; *Style—* Dr Denis Gibbs; 21 Albion Square, London E8 4ES (☎ 071 249 8211); 152 Harley St, London W1N 1HH (☎ 071 935 8868)

GIBBS, Hon Mrs (Elizabeth Beatrice); *née* Baring; yr da of 1 Baron Howick of Glendale, KG, GCMG, KCVO (d 1973); *b* 10 Jan 1940; *m* 15 Jan 1962, Capt Nicholas Albany Gibbs, 9 Royal Lancers (d 1984), yr s of Capt Lionel Cyril Gibbs (d 1940); 1 s (Andrew b 1966), 2 da (Mary b 1964, Eliza b 1968); *Style—* Hon Mrs Gibbs; c/o Rt Hon Lord Howick of Glandale Howick, Alnwick, Northumberland; Drayton House, East Meon, Hants

GIBBS, Hon Sir Eustace Hubert Beilby; KCVO (1986), CMG (1982); 4 s of 1 Baron Wraxall, TD, PC, JP, DL (d 1931), yr s by his 2 w (Hon Ursula Mary Lawley, OBE, er da of 6 and last Baron Wenlock); hp to bro, 2 Baron; *b* 3 July 1929; *Educ* Eton, Ch Ch Oxford; *m* 23 Oct 1957, Veronica, o da of Sydney Keith Scott, of Reydon Grove Farm, Southwold; 3 s (Hubert b 1958, Andrew b 1965, Jonathan b 1969), 2 da (Miranda b 1961, Alexandra b 1971); *Career* entered Foreign Serv 1954, ret 1986; HM The Queen's Vice-Marshal of the Dip Corps 1982-86; RCDS 1974-75, served Bangkok, Rio de Janeiro, Berlin, Caracas, Vienna & Paris, ret 1986; *Recreations* music, golf; *Clubs* Pratt's, Beefsteak; *Style—* Hon Sir Eustace Gibbs, KCVO, CMG; Coddenham House, Coddenham, Ipswich, Suffolk (☎ 044 979 332)

GIBBS, Air Marshal Sir Gerald Ernest; KBE (1954, CBE 1945), CIE (1946), MC (1918, and two bars 1918); s of Ernest William Cecil Gibbs (d 1933), and Fanny Wilmina Gibbs (d 1944); *b* 3 Sept 1896; *m* 1938, Margaret Jean, da of Henry Hulatt Bradshaw (d 1962); 1 s (John), 1 da (Pamela); *Career* served WWI 7 Wilts Regt and RFC, transferred RAF 1918, cmd 47 Sqdn Sudan and RAF Kenya 1935-36, SASO 11 Fighter Gp 1940-41 (Battle of Britain), dir Overseas Ops 1942-43, SASO 3 TAF Air Cmd SE Asia 1944, chief air staff offr HQ Supreme Allied Cmd SE Asia 1945-46, SASO Tport Cmd 1946-48, head serv advsrs to UK Delgn at UNO NY and chm UK Membs of Mil Staff Ctee UN 1948-51, CAS and C-in-C IAF 1951-54; Air Cdre 1940, Air Vice-Marshal 1944, Air Marshal 1951, ret 1954; Legion of Honour, Croix de Guerre 1918; *Books* Survivor's Story (1956); *Recreations* golf, sailing, skiing; *Clubs* RAF, Royal Wimbledon Golf, Trevose Golf, Seaford Golf (E Blatchington); *Style—* Air Marshal Sir Gerald Gibbs, KBE, CIE, MC; Lone Oak, 170 Coombe Lane West, Kingston upon Thames, Surrey KT2 7DE

GIBBS, Rt Hon Sir Harry Talbot; GCMG (1981), AC (1987), KBE (1970), PC (1972); s of Harry Victor Gibbs (d 1969), of Ipswich, Queensland, and Flora Macdonald Gibbs (d 1972); *b* 7 Feb 1917; *Educ* Ipswich GS, Queensland Univ; *m* 1944, Muriel Ruth, da of Hugh Hector Harold Dunn (d 1970), of Maryborough, Queensland; 1 s, 3 da; *Career* QC 1957; barr Queensland 1939, justice High Court Australia 1970, chief justice Australia 1981-87; *see Debrett's Handbook of Australia and New Zealand for further details*; *Recreations* tennis, theatre; *Clubs* Australian (Sydney), Queensland (Brisbane); *Style—* The Rt Hon Sir Harry Gibbs, GCMG, AC, KBE, PC; 30 Lodge Rd, Cremorne 2090, Australia (☎ 909 1844)

GIBBS, Lady Hilaria Agnes; *née* Edgcumbe; eld da of 6 Earl of Mount Edgcumbe, TD, DL (d 1965), and Lilian Agnes, *née* Arkwright (d 1964); *b* 16 Jan 1908; *m* 17 Oct 1933, Lt-Col Denis Lucius Alban Gibbs, DSO (d 27 April 1984), 3 s of Rev Canon Reginald Gibbs (d 1940) and gs of Rev John Gibbs, yr bro of 1 Baron Aldenham; 4 da (Jillianne, Margaret, Rosamund, Penelope); *Career* former pres: Tavistock Branch Red Cross, Plymouth League of Pity; *Style—* Lady Hilaria Gibbs; Aldenham, Deer Park Lane, Tavistock, Devon (☎ 0822 2731)

GIBBS, Jeremy Herbert; s of Rt Hon Sir Humphrey Gibbs, GCVO, KCMG, OBE (d 1990, 3 s of 1 Baron Hunsdon of Hunsdon), and Dame Molly Gibbs, DBE; *b* 26 May

1935; *Educ* Bishops Sch Cape Town, Christ Church Oxford (MA); *m* 8 April 1958, Alison Douglas, da of Col Douglas McCrone Martin, of Dunchattan, Troon, Ayrshire; 4 da; *Career* insur broker; govr: St Mary's Sch Wantage, London House for Overseas Students; *Recreations* fishing; *Clubs* Bulawayo (Zimbabwe); *Style*— Jeremy Gibbs, Esq; Upper Kennards, Leigh, Kent TN11 8RE (☎ 0732 832160; office: 0732 771818)

GIBBS, Rt Rev John; s of late Arthur Edgar Gibbs, of Bournemouth; *b* 15 March 1917; *Educ* Univ of London, Univ of Bristol, Western Coll Bristol, Lincoln Theological Coll; *m* 1943, G Marion, da of late W J Bishop, of Poole, Dorset; 1 s, 1 da; *Career* SW sec Student Christian Movement 1949-51, study sec and ed Student Movement 1951-55, ordained 1955, curate St Luke Brislington Bristol 1955-57, chaplain and lectr Coll of St Matthias Bristol 1957-64, princ of Keswick Hall Norwich 1964-73; examining chaplain to: Bishop of Norwich 1968-73, hon canon of Norwich cathedral 1968-73, Bishop of Bradwell 1973-76, Bishop of Coventry 1976-85; *Style*— The Rt Rev John Gibbs; Farthingloe, Southfield, Minchinhampton, Stroud, Glos GL6 9DY (☎ 0453 886211)

GIBBS, Julian Herbert; 3 s of Hon Sir Geoffrey Cokayne Gibbs, KCMG (2 s of 1 Baron Hunsdon of Hunsdon, JP, himself 4 s of 1 Baron Aldenham, JP), and Helen Margaret, CBE, *née* Leslie (d 1977); *b* 26 Nov 1932; *Educ* Eton; *Career* 2 Lt KRRC 1951-53, Lt Queen's Westminsters (TA) 1953-56; with Antony Gibbs & Sons Ltd (merchant bankers) 1953-74; chm Antony Gibbs Personal Fin Planning Ltd, Julian Gibbs Associates Ltd 1975-82, First Market Intelligence Ltd 1983-; dir Mencap Unit Tst, former vice chm London Fedn of Boys' Clubs, former chm P M Club; former memb ctee: Distressed Gentlefolks' Assoc, Queen's Inst of Dist Nursing; Freeman City of London, Liveryman Worshipful Co of Grocers 1961; FCII (vice pres); *Books* Living with Inflation, a Simple Guide to Lump Sum Investment; *Recreations* travel, theatre, opera, France; *Clubs* Carlton, Beefsteak, Pratt's, MCC; *Style*— Julian Gibbs, Esq; 35A Colville Terrace, London W11 (☎ 071 221 8034); 824 Johnson Lane, Key West, Florida, USA; First Market Intelligence Ltd, 56A Rochester Row, London SW1P 1JU (☎ 071 834 9192, fax 071 630 0194)

GIBBS, Hon Mrs ((Sarah) Marcia); *née* Kimball; er da of Baron Kimball (Life Peer); *b* 8 Feb 1958; *m* 1982, David Alexander Somerset Gibbs, 2 s of Lt-Col Patrick Somerset Gibbs, MBE, of Hazeley House, Hartley Witney, Hampshire; 1 s (James Patrick b 1983), 2 da (Emily Rose b 1985, (Alexandra) Harriet b 1989); *Style*— Hon Mrs Gibbs; Kentmere House, Castor, Peterborough PE5 7BY

GIBBS, Maj Martin Antony; JP (Wilts 1966), DL (1977); s of Col William Otter Gibbs, JP, DL (d 1960), of Barrow Court, Barrow Gurney, Somerset, and Janet Blanche Gibbs (d 1974), his cous and sis of 1 Baron Wraxall; *b* 12 March 1916; *Educ* Eton, Sandhurst; *m* 17 Jan 1947, Elsie Margaret Mary, er da of Sir Hew Hamilton-Dalrymple, 9 Bt, of North Berwick; 1 s (Antony), 5 da (Blanche, Bridget, Cecily, Katharine, Julian); *Career* Maj Coldstream Gds, regular soldier joined 1 Bn Coldstream Gds 1936, 3 Bn 1939; WWII serv: Palestine, Egypt, Western Desert (Long Range Desert Gp); 2 Bn 1947, Malaya 1948-50; ret 1952; now opens house and garden to the public; *Recreations* horticulture, dendrology, travel; *Clubs* Pratt's; *Style*— Maj Martin Gibbs, JP, DL; Sheldon Manor, Chippenham, Wilts (☎ 0249 653120)

GIBBS, Col Martin St John Valentine (Tim); CB (1958), DSO (1942), TD, JP (Glos 1965); s of Maj Guy Melvil Gibbs, TD, of Cirencester (yr bro of William Otter Gibbs, *see* Gibbs, Martin Antony), and Margaret, da of Henry St John (gs of Hon Ferdinand St John, 2 s of 3 Viscount Bolingbroke and (4) St John by his 2 w Isabella Baroness Hompesch) by his w Maud (da of Hon Pascoe Glyn, sometime MP E Dorset and 5 s of 1 Baron Wolverton); *b* 14 Feb 1917; *Educ* Eton; *m* 1947, Mary Margaret, er da of Lt-Col Philip Mitford (seventh in descent from Humphrey Mitford, whose yr bro John was ancestor of the Barons Redesdale) by his w Alice, yst da of Sir John Fowler, 2 Bt, and widow of Capt Michael Wills, MC; 2 da, 3 step s; *Career* 2 Lt Royal Wilts Yeo 1937, Maj 1942, Lt-Col 1951, Bt-Col 1955, Col 1958, Ld-Lt for Glos 1978-; Hon Col Royal Wilts Yeomanry Sqdn TAVR 1972, Col Cmdt Yeomanry RAC 1975-82; High Sheriff Glos 1958; *Recreations* country pursuits; *Clubs* Cavalry and Guards, MCC; *Style*— Col Martin Gibbs, CB, DSO, TD, JP; Ewen Manor, Ewen, Cirencester, Glos GL7 6BS (☎ 0285 770206)

GIBBS, Michael John; s of Harold Percy Gibbs (d 1980), of Solihull, and Alice, *née* Groom (d 1974); *b* 8 April 1931; *Educ* Solihull Sch, Univ of Bristol (BA); *m* 22 June 1957, Pamela Jessie, da of Jesse Pane, of Bristol; 1 s (Alexander b 22 April 1964); *Career* sec Leicester Permanent Building Society 1968-71; Gateway Building Society: asst gen mangr 1971-75, dep chief exec 1975-81, md 1981-88; exec vice chm Woolwich Building Society 1988-91; dir: Woolwich Building Society 1988-, Woolwich Life Assurance Company Ltd 1990-, Woolwich (Guernsey) Ltd 1990-; chm: Woolwich Property Services Ltd 1991-, Woolwich Financial Advisory Services Ltd 1991-; chm Met Assoc of Bldg Socs 1984-85, cncl memb Bldg Socs Assoc 1982-88; CBIM; *Recreations* golf, cricket, horse racing; *Clubs* MCC, British Sportsmens, Lords Taverners; *Style*— Michael Gibbs, Esq; Woolwich Building Society, Gateway House, Worthing, Sussex (☎ 0903 68 555)

GIBBS, Dame Molly Peel; *née* Nelson; DBE (1969); (The Hon Lady Gibbs); 2 da of John Peel Nelson, of Bulawayo; *b* 13 July 1912; *Educ* Girls' HS Barnato Park Johannesburg; *m* 17 Jan 1934, Rt Hon Sir Humphrey Vicary Gibbs, GCVO, KCMG, OBE (d 1990), 3 s of 1 Baron Hunsdon of Hunsdon; 5 s (*see* Jeremy Herbert Gibbs); *Style*— Dame Molly Gibbs, DBE; 22 Dornie Rd, Borrowdale, Harare, Zimbabwe

GIBBS, HE Mr Oswald Moxley; CMG (1976); s of Michael Gibbs (d 1958), of Moliniere, St George's, Grenada, W Indies, and Mary Emelda, *née* Cobb (d 1963); *b* 15 Oct 1927; *Educ* Happy Hill RC, St George's Sr Boys RC, Grenada Boys Secdy Sch, City of London Coll (BSc); *m* 8 Oct 1955, Dearest Agatha (d 1989), da of Sendall Mitchell (d 1969), of Grand Anse, Grenada, W Indies; 1 s (Dr Kenyatta b 1957), 2 da (Beatrice b 1960, Patricia b 1963); 1 adopted s (Marius b 1949); *Career* economist and diplomat; trade sec and cmmr Eastern Caribbean Mission London 1965-75, high cmmr for Grenada London 1974-78, conslt to Centre for Industl Devpt Brussels 1979-81, high cmmr for Grenada (London 1984-90, ambass to EEC 1985-90, ambass to Belgium 1987-90), head of Grenada's Delgn to Cwlth Heads of Govt Meeting Kuala Lumpur 1989-; memb Cwlth Human Ecology Cncl 1990- (advsr devpt and trade); Queen's Silver Jubilee Medal 1977; *Recreations* gardening, photography, DIY; *Style*— HE Mr Oswald M Gibbs, CMG; Woodside Green, South Norwood, London SE25 5HU

GIBBS, Rachel Elizabeth; JP (Inner London 1977); da of Lt-Col Geoffrey Bernard Youard, MBE (d 1987), of Gwernowddy Old Farmhouse, Llandrinio, Llanymynech, Powys, and Hon Rosaline Joan, *née* Atkin (d 1973); *b* 26 Feb 1930; *Educ* Benenden Sch Kent, St Paul's Girls Sch London; *m* 11 April 1953, Denis Dunbar Gibbs, s of Very Rev Michael McCausland Gibbs, Dean of Chester (d 1962); 1 s (Nicholas b 1954), 1 da (Sarah b 1956); *Career* Lib Pty Orgn 1949-65; sec to: Arthur Holt MP (Bolton West), Alasdair Mackenzie MP (Ross and Cromarty), Sir Russell Johnston MP (Inverness-shire); Lib Pty Res Dept (4 yrs); memb: Ctee of Inquiry into UK prison serv 1979, Bd of Visitors HM Prison Swinfon Hall 1970-76 (chm 1975-76), Bd of Visitors HM Prison Pentonville 1977-83 (chm 1981-83), Parole Bd 1987-89; fndr memb: Lichfield Marriage Guidance Cncl, Lichfield CAB, Lichfield Adventure Playground Assoc 1965-76; memb: Ctee Friends of Christchurch Spitalfields 1979-82, Ctee Prisons and Penal Concerns Gp (Diocese of London and Southwark 1984-), Prison Serv Chaplaincy Advsy Gp 1991-; chm Albion Square Res Assoc 1988-91; JP Lichfield 1971-76; *Books* Pedigree of the Family of Gibbs of Pytte in the Parish of Clyst St George (ed 4 edn, 1981); *Recreations* gardening, china mending, family history, lurchers, carpentery; *Style*— Mrs Rachel Gibbs, JP; 21 Albion Square, London E8 4ES (☎ 071 249 8211)

GIBBS, Richard John Hedley; QC (1984); s of Brian Conaway Gibbs (d 1946), Asst Dist Cmmr Colonial Admin Serv, and Mabel Joan, *née* Gatford; *b* 2 Sept 1941; *Educ* Oundle, Trinity Hall Cambridge (MA); *m* 26 June 1965, Janet, da of Francis Herbert Whittall, of Reigate, Surrey; 1 s (Christopher b 1979), 3 da (Sarah b 1966, Susannah b 1966, Julia b 1971); *Career* barr Inner Temple 1965; rec of the Crown Ct 1981; chm Birmingham Friendship Housing Assoc 1987; *Style*— Richard Gibbs, Esq, QC; 4 King's Bench Walk, Temple, London EC4Y 7DL (☎ 071 353 3581); 1 Fountain Court, Steelhouse Lane, Birmingham B4 6DR (☎ 021 236 5721)

GIBBS, Roger Geoffrey; 4 s of Hon Sir Geoffrey Gibbs, KCMG (2 s of 1 Baron Hunsdon of Hunsdon, JP, who himself was 4 s of 1 Baron Aldenham) and Hon Lady Gibbs, CBE, JP, *qv*; *b* 13 Oct 1934; *Educ* Eton, Millfield; *Career* chm The Wellcome Trust 1989-; dir: Gerrard and National Holdings plc 1989- (chm 1975-89), Howard de Walden Estates Ltd 1989-, The Colville Estate Ltd 1989-; memb Cncl Royal Nat Pension Fund for Nurses 1975-, dir Arsenal FC 1980-, govr The London Clinic Ltd 1983-, special tstee Guy's Hosp 1985-, memb Cncl Imperial Cancer Res Fund 1989-; *Recreations* sport; *Clubs* Pratt's, Swinley; *Style*— Roger Gibbs, Esq; 23 Tregunter Rd, London SW10 9LS (☎ 071 370 3465); The Wellcome Trust, 1 Park Square West, London NW1 4LJ (☎ 071 486 4902)

GIBBS, Field Marshal Sir Roland Christopher; GCB (1976, KCB 1972), CBE (1968), DSO (1945), MC (1943), JP; yr s of Maj Guy Melvil Gibbs, TD (d 1959), of Parkleaze, Ewen, Cirencester, and Margaret, *née* St John (d 1964); bro of Col Martin Gibbs, CB, DSO, TD, *qv*, Lord-Lt Glos; *b* 22 June 1921; *Educ* Eton, Sandhurst; *m* 1955, Davina, da of Lt-Col Eion Merry, MC (d 1966), of Lucknam Park, Chippenham, and Jean (da of Hon Arthur Crichton, 3 s of 4 Earl of Erne, KP, PC, sometime MP Enniskillen); 2 s, 1 da; *Career* served WWII: N Africa, Italy, NW Europe, 2 Lt 60 Rifles 1940; Lt-Col 1960, Brig 1963, cmd 16 Parachute Bde 1963-66, COS Middle East Cmd 1966, IDC 1968, Cdr Br Forces Gulf 1969, Maj-Gen 1969, Lt-Gen 1971, GOC1 (Br) Corps 1971-74, GOC-in-C UKLF 1974, Gen 1974, Chief of Gen Staff 1976-79, ADC Gen to HM The Queen 1976-79, Field Marshal; Col Cmdt: 2 Bn Royal Green Jackets 1971-78, Parachute Regt 1973-77; Lord-Lt Wilts 1989- (Vice Lord-Lt 1982-89, DL 1980-82); constable HM Tower of London 1985-90; *Recreations* out door recreations, painting; *Clubs* Turf, Cavalry & Guards'; *Style*— Field Marshal Sir Roland Gibbs, GCB ,CBE, DSO, MC, JP; Patney Rectory, Devizes, Wilts (☎ 038 084 733)

GIBBS, Lady Sarah; *née* Bingham; yr da of 6 Earl of Lucan, MC (d 1964); *b* 5 Sept 1936; *Educ* Badminton Sch Bristol; *m* 17 June 1958, Rev William Gilbert Gibbs, yr s of late Col Ralph Crawley Boevey Gibbs, of Little Gaddesden, Herts; 1 s, 3 da; *Career* magistrate for Daventry 1987; *Style*— Lady Sarah Gibbs; The Vicarage, Guilsborough, Northampton

GIBBS, Somerset Bryan; s of Maj Bryan Northam Gibbs, MBE; *b* 16 Jan 1926; *Educ* Eton; *m* 1950, Elspeth, da of Maj F Russi, MC; 3 s, 1 da; *Career* memb Stock Exchange 1952-77, chm Capel-Cure Myers 1975-77; chm Directorship Appointments Ltd 1977-; dir: Rotaflex plc, Moray Firth Maltings Ltd, Equity Consort Investmt Tst plc, New Ct Tst plc; *Recreations* golf, sailing, photography; *Clubs* Boodle's, Royal Worlington & Newmarket Golf, Royal London Yacht; *Style*— Somerset B Gibbs, Esq; 62 Oakwood Court, London W14 (☎ 071 602 2633); Withcam House, Headley's Lane, Witcham, Ely, Cambs CB6 2LH (☎ 0353 778212); Directorship Appointments Ltd, 66 Great Cumberland Place, London W1H 8BP (☎ 071 402 3233)

GIBBS, Stephen; CBE (1981); s of Arthur Edwin Gibbs, and Anne Gibbs; *b* 12 Feb 1920; *Educ* Oldbury GS, Birmingham Univ; *m* 1941, Louise Pattison; 1 s, 1 da; *Career* chm Turner & Newall plc (plastics and chemicals); fellow Plastics and Rubber Inst; *Style*— Stephen Gibbs, Esq, CBE; Turner & Newall plc, 20 St Mary's Parsonage, Manchester M3 3NL (☎ 061 833 9272, telex 669281)

GIBBS, Stephen Cokayne; 2 s of Hon Sir Geoffrey Gibbs, KCMG (d 1975, 2 s of 1 Baron Hunsdon of Hunsdon, JP, himself 4 s of 1 Baron Aldenham, JP), and Hon Lady Gibbs, CBE, JP, *qv*; *b* 18 July 1929; *Educ* Eton; *m* 1972, Lavinia Winifred, 2 da of Sir Edmund Bacon, 13 Bt, KG, KBE, TD (d 1982); 2 s, 1 da; *Career* 2 Lt KRRC, Maj QVR (TA) 1960-63 and Royal Greenjackets; dir: Charles Barker plc 1962-87, Vaux Group plc 1971-; *Recreations* shooting, gardening; *Clubs* White's, Pratt's; *Style*— Stephen Gibbs, Esq; Dougarie, Isle of Arran KA27 8EB (☎ 077 084 229)

GIBBS, Lady; Sylvia Madeleine; *née* Knight; da of late Henry Knight, of Buenos Aires, Argentina; *m* 1944, Sir Frank Stannard Gibbs, KBE, CMG (d 1983, ambass to The Philippines 1954-55); 1 s, 1 da; *Style*— Lady Gibbs; El Rincón, High St, Old Woking, Surrey (☎ 0483 70147)

GIBBS, Lady Virginia; *née* Rous; da of 5 Earl of Stradbroke (d 1983), and Hon Mrs Keith Rous, *qv*; *b* 13 June 1954; *m* 1974, Antony William Hew Gibbs, s of Maj Martin Antony Gibbs, Coldstream Gds, and Elsie, da of Sir Hew Clifford Hamilton-Dalrymple, 9 Bt; 2 s (Abram b 1976, William b 1986), 4 da (Mary b 1975, Emily-Anna b 1978, Elizabeth Rose b 1979, Margaret Blanche b 1988); *Style*— The Lady Virginia Gibbs; The Home Farm, Barrow Gurney, nr Bristol

GIBBS-SMITH, Lavinia Marie; *née* Snelling; da of George Edward Snelling (d 1961), and Maisie Binder (d 1961); descendant of Thomas Snelling whose collection of coins and medals founded the numismatic collection in Br Museum; *b* 20 Dec 1946; *Educ* Hollington Park Sch, St Leonards, Guildhall Sch of Music, Univ of Cologne (Musikhochschule); *m* 24 Jan 1974, Charles Harvard Gibbs-Smith, s of Dr E G Gibbs; *Career* prof de Luth Centre d'Etude de Musique Baroque Beziers France 1983-; flute accompanist to soloists; festival organiser Le Petit Festival des Baux en Provence; dir Les Bons Vins Occitans; hon memb Int Lyceum; *Recreations* gardening, walking, skiing, reading; *Clubs* IOD; *Style*— Lavinia Gibbs-Smith; c/o Messeurs Coutts & Co, 1 Cadegau Place, SW1

GIBRALTAR IN EUROPE, Bishop of, 1980-; Rt Rev John Richard Satterthwaite; diocese of Gibraltar in Europe created 1980; s of William Satterthwaite, and Clara Elisabeth Satterthwaite; *b* 17 Nov 1925; *Educ* Univ of Leeds (BA), Community of the Resurrection Mirfield; *Career* history master St Luke's Sch Haifa 1946-48; curate: St Barnabas Carlisle 1950-53, St Aidan Carlisle 1953-54, St Michael Paternoster Royal London 1955-59 (curate-in-charge 1959-65); gen sec C of E Cncl on Foreign Relations 1959-70 (asst gen sec 1955-9), gen sec Archbishop's Cmmn on Roman Catholic Relations 1965-70, vicar St Dunstan in the West 1959-70, bishop suffragan of Fulham 1970, bishop of Gibraltar 1970 (known as bishop of Fulham and Gibraltar until creation of new diocese 1980), canon of Canterbury 1963-70, canon of the Old Catholic Cathedral Utrecht 1968-; ChStJ 1972; *Clubs* Athenaeum; *Style*— The Rt Rev the Lord Bishop of Gibraltar in Europe; 5A Gregory Place, London W8 4NG (☎ 071 937 2796)

GIBSON, Sir Alexander Drummond; CBE (1967); s of James McClure Gibson (d 1946), and Wilhelmina, *née* Williams; *b* 11 Feb 1926; *Educ* Dalziel HS Motherwell, Univ of Glasgow, RCM Mozarteum Salzburg, Accademia Chigiano Siena; *m* 1959, Ann Veronica, *née* Waggett; 3 s (James b 1959, Philip b 1962, John b 1965), 1 da (Claire b

1968); *Career* orchestral conductor: princ conductor and musical dir Royal Scot Nat Orchestra 1959-84 (guest conductor), fndr and artistic dir Scot Opera 1962-85 (music dir 1985-87), princ guest conductor Houston Symphony Orch 1981-83; Arnold Bax medal for Conducting 1959, Distinguished Musician of the Year award ISM 1976, Sibelius medal 1978, Br Music Year Book Musician of the Year 1980; OStJ 1975, hon pres of the Royal Scot Nat Orch 1985-; founder and conductor Laureate Scottish Opera 1987-; FRSE, FRSA; kt 1977; *Recreations* music, reading; *Clubs* Garrick, Oriental; *Style—* Sir Alexander Gibson, CBE, FRSE; 15 Cleveden Gardens, Glasgow G12 (☎ 041 339 6668)

GIBSON, Andrew Norman; s of (Norman) Alan Stuart Gibson, of Taunton, Somerset, and Oliven, *née* Hughes; *b* 27 July 1951; *Educ* Monkton Combe Sch Bath, Queen's Coll Oxford (MA); *Career* admitted slr 1979; ptnr Foot & Bowden 1984- (asst slr 1979-84); chm Plymouth branch Slrs Civil Litigation Assoc, memb SW Legal Aid Area Ctee; memb Law Soc 1979; *Recreations* golf, cricket; *Clubs* Yelverton Golf, St Mellion Golf, Saints Cricket; *Style—* Andrew Gibson, Esq; Foot & Bowden Slrs, 70-76 North Hill, Plymouth PL4 8HH (☎ 0752 663416, fax 0752 671802, telex 45223)

GIBSON, Anne; da of Harry Tasker (d 1967), of Lincolnshire, and Jessie, *née* Roberts; *b* 10 Dec 1940; *Educ* Caistor GS, Chelmsford Coll of Further Educn, Univ of Essex (BA); *m* 1, 1962 (m dis 1985), John Donald Gibson; 1 da (Rebecca Bridgid b 1964); m 2, 8 Oct 1988, John Bartell, s of Henry Bartell (d 1983), of Liverpool; *Career* full-time organiser Lab Pty (Saffron Walden) 1965-70, researcher House Magazine (jl of Houses of Parliament) 1975-77, Party candidate (Lab) Bury St Edmunds 1979, asst/asst sec and dep head Orgn and Industl Rels Dept TUC (with special responsibility for equal rights area of work) 1977-87, nat offr MSF (with special responsibility for voluntary sector and equal rights section) 1987-; memb: Gen Cncl TUC 1989-, Lab Pty NEC Women's Ctee 1990-, Lab Pty Euro Trg Gp; chm: Nat Jt Ctee of Working Women's Orgns, Mary MacArthur Tst; *Books* author numerous TUC and MSF Equal Opportunities Booklets incl latest Charter of Equal Opportunities For 1990s (1990), Disability and Employer - A Trade union Guide (1989), Lesbian and Gay Rights in Employment (1990), Recruitment of Women Workers (1990); *Recreations* reading, theatre, knitting, embroidery; *Style—* Ms Anne Gibson; M S F, Park House 64/66 Wandsworth Common, North Side, London SW18 2SH (☎ 081 871 2100, fax 081 877 1160)

GIBSON, Anthony Gair; TD (1971); s of Wilfrid Humble Gibson, of Linnel Hill, Hexham, Northumberland, and Joan Margaret, *née* Gair; *b* 10 Nov 1937; *Educ* Ampleforth, Lincoln Coll Oxford (BA); *m* 23 July 1966, (Jennifer) Bryony, da of Maj Timothy Basil Ellis, of Trinity Hall, Bungay; 4 s (Benjamin Timothy b 7 Jan 1968, Toby James b 12 Sept 1969, Richard Gair (twin) b 12 Sept 1969, Anthony Daniel b 30 April 1975); *Career* Kings Dragoon Gds 1956-58 (despatches), Northumberland Hussars & Queens Own Yeo 1958-77; admitted slr 1965; memb Slrs Disciplinary Tbnl 1980-, pres Newcastle upon Tyne Incorp Law Soc 1989-90; dir Hexham Steeplechase Co Ltd, sec Haydon point-to-point 1962-88; memb Law Soc; *Recreations* shooting, fishing, forestry; *Clubs* Cavalry & Guard's, Northern Counties; *Style—* Anthony G Gibson, Esq, TD; Newbiggin, Hexham (☎ 0434 602 649); Barclays Bank Chambers, Denton Burn, Newcastle-upon-Tyne (☎ 091 274 1241, fax 091 274 2164)

GIBSON, Cdr Bryan Donald; s of Donald Gibson (d 1983), of Barnston, Wirral, Cheshire, and Inez Margaret, *née* Lawrence (d 1983); *b* 21 Jan 1937; *Educ* Birkenhead Park HS Victoria, Univ of Manchester (BSc, MSc); *m* 1 Jan 1966, (Frances) Mary, da of Reginald Herbert Greenhalgh (d 1982), of Swinton, Lancashire; 1 s (James b 1968), 1 da (Helen b 1970); *Career* cmmnd RN 1962, lectr RN Engrg Coll 1963-66; served: HMS Bulwark 1967, HMS Sultan (Nuclear Propulsion Sch) 1968-70; sr lectr Dept of Nuclear Sci and Technol RNC Greenwich 1970-72, head of materials technol RN Engrg Coll Manadon Plymouth 1973-78, ret 1978; academic sec Chartered Assoc of Certified Accountants 1978-82, sec Inst of Metallurgists 1982-84, dep sec Inst of Metals 1985-; former ctee memb: CNAA, RSA, Engrg Cncl, CSTI; vice pres Inst Nuclear Engrs 1976-78; Freeman City of London 1984, Liveryman Worshipful Co of Engrs 1984 (Clerk 1986-); hon memb CGLI; FIM 1975, CEng 1977; *Recreations* gardening, DIY; *Clubs* Anglo Belgian, City Livery; *Style—* Cdr Bryan Gibson, RN; Kiln Bank, Bodle St Green, nr Hailsham, E Sussex BN27 4UA (☎ 0323 833 554); 1 Carlton House Terrace, London SW1Y 5DB (☎ 071 839 4071, 071 839 3097, fax 071 839 1702, telex 8814813)

GIBSON, Carl; adoptive s of Ernest Gibson (d 1972), of Batley, and Phyllis Gibson Sr (d 1977); *b* 23 April 1963; *m* 11 Aug 1984, Elizabeth, da of George Henry Stenton; 4 s (Lee b 11 Nov 1985, Luke b 9 Sept 1987, Jake b 15 Nov 1988, Joel b 8 Sept 1990); *Career* rugby league player; Batley 1981-85, Leeds 1986-, represented Yorkshire Co (5 winner's medals v Lancashire); GB: 10 full caps, tour Aust and NZ 1988, tour Papua New Guinea and NZ 1990, 3 Tests v Aust 1990; represented Yorks schoolboys at rugby union, holder various schs athletics awards; *Recreations* snooker, cricket; *Style—* Carl Gibson, Esq; c/o Leeds RLFC

GIBSON, Christopher Allen Wood; s of Sir Ralph Brian Gibson, of London, and Ann Chapman, *née* Reuther; *b* 5 July 1953; *Educ* St Paul's, BNC Oxford (BA); *m* 4 Aug 1984, Alarys Mary Calvert, da of David Eaton, of Emsworth, Hants; 2 da (Harriet b 10 Dec 1984, Julia b 24 May 1987); *Career* called to the Bar Middle Temple 1976; memb Hon Soc of Middle Temple; *Recreations* sailing, motorcycles, photography, reading; *Clubs* Vincents, Emsworth Sailing, BSA Owners; *Style—* Christopher Gibson, Esq; 2 Crown Office Row, Temple, London EC4Y 7HJ (☎ 071 583 8155, fax 071 583 1205)

GIBSON, Rev Christopher Herbert; CP; s and h of Sir Christopher Gibson, 3 Bt, *qv*; *b* 17 July 1948; *Career* ordained priest 1975; *Style—* Rev Christopher Gibson, CP; Holy Cross, Buenos Aires, Argentina

GIBSON, Sir Christopher Herbert; 3 Bt (UK 1931); s of Sir Christopher Herbert Gibson, 2 Bt (d 1962); *b* 2 Feb 1921; *Educ* St George's Coll Argentina; *m* 16 Aug 1941, Lilian Lake, da of late Dr George Byron Young, of Colchester, Essex; 1 s, 3 da; *Heir* s, Rev Christopher Gibson, CP; *Career* mangr: Leach's Argentine Estates 1946-51, of Encyclopaedia Britannica 1952-55; design draughtsman Babcox & Wilcox USA 1956-57, tea plantation mangr then ranch mangr Liebig's Extract of Meat Co 1958-64, bldg inspector Indust Kaiser Argentina 1964-68, mangr and part owner Lakanto Poultry Farms 1969-76; *Style—* Sir Christopher Gibson, Bt

GIBSON, Hon Clive Patrick; 2 s of Baron Gibson (Life Peer), and Elizabeth, da of Hon Clive Pearson (2 s of 1 Viscount Cowdray, GCVO, PC, DL), and Hon Alicia Knatchbull-Hugessen, da of 1 Baron Brabourne; *b* 24 Jan 1948; *Educ* Eton, Magdalen Coll Oxford (BA); *m* 1974, Anne Marie Jeanne, da of late Comte Jacques de Chauvigny de Blot; 1 s (Patrick Clive b 1975), 1 da (Beatrice Dione Elizabeth b 1978); *Career* Cmmn of the Euro Communities 1973-74, Pearson Gp 1974-83; dir: Château Latour (chm), Pearson Longman 1979-82, Financial Times 1978-83, The Economist 1978-83, Penguin Books 1978-82, Longman Gp 1978-82, J Rothschild Group 1985-; *Recreations* music, shooting, skiing; *Clubs* Brooks's; *Style—* The Hon Clive Gibson; 15 St James's Place, London SW1A 1NW

GIBSON, Craigie Alexander; s of Cdr James Brown Gibson, RNR (d 1984), of Stenhousemuir, Stirlingshire, and Cora Jessie, *née* Craigie; *b* 19 Sept 1927; *Educ* Falkirk HS, Univ of Edinburgh (BSc); *m* 26 Nov 1955, Margaret Louise, da of Albert Frederick De Villiers Richter (d 1967), of Shanghani, Rhodesia; 2 da (Kate b 1962, Sandra b 1965); *Career* Navigators Yeoman RN 1945-48; exploration geologist Anglo American Corp 1952-57; Rio Tinto Rhodesia Ltd: exploration geologist 1957-60, mine mangr 1960-67, exec dir 1967-76, md 1976-78; md: Rossing Uranium Ltd 1978-82, RTZ Metals Ltd 1982-83; chm Rossing Fndn 1979-82, mining dir Rio Tinto Zinc Corp 1983-87, dir Rossing Uranium Ltd (dep chm), Rio Tinto Zimbabwe Ltd; pres Chamber of Mines: Rhodesia 1976-78, SW Africa and Namibia 1981-82; FGS 1952, FIMM 1983; *Recreations* geology, snooker; *Clubs* RAC, Harare, Windhoek; *Style—* Craigie Gibson, Esq; Maple Hse, Copyhold Lane, Cuckfield, Sussex RH17 5EB (☎ 0444 452107); 6 St James's Square, London SW17 4LD

GIBSON, David; s of Frank Edward Gibson (d 1973), of Retford, Notts, and Nora Jessie, *née* Gurnhill (d 1989); *b* 8 Sept 1939; *Educ* King Edward VI GS Retford; *m* 6 Sept 1963, Roberta Alexandra, da of James Henry McMaster (d 1963), of Newtownabbey, Co Antrim; 1 s (Peter), 2 da (Catherine, Sarah); *Career* exec offr: GPO 1958-63, MAFF 1963-68; various posts Belfast City Cncl 1968-72; princ offr Dept of Commerce 1973-81; Dept Econ Devpt: dir Accounting Servs 1982-85, asst sec 1985-87, under sec 1987-; memb and pres Chartered Assoc Certified Accountants Irish Regional 1982-83, FCCA 1969; *Recreations* reading, music, walking; *Style—* David Gibson, Esq; Department of Economic Development, Netherleigh, Massey Ave, Belfast BT4 2JP (☎ 0232 763244, fax 761430, telex 747152)

GIBSON, Rev Sir David Ackroyd; 4 Bt (UK 1926); s of Sir Ackroyd Herbert Gibson, Bt (d 1975); *b* 18 July 1922; *Educ* Cathedral GS Wells, Warfleet Trg Coll Dartmouth, Greenwich Coll, Oscott Coll; *Career* Lt RNVR 1939-46: N Sea and N Atlantic 1940-41, Med 1941-43, Indian and Pacific Oceans 1944-45; Roman Catholic priest: Plymouth 1956-60, Weymouth 1960-66; fndr Societas Navigatorum Catholica (Catholic Mariner's YC) 1958; Capt RA chaplain: Germany 1967-69, NI 1969-70; RC priest: Helston 1971-75, Liskeard 1975-85; *Books* A Series of Circles (autobiog); *Recreations* sail cruising, history of marine shipwrighting, English and Roman law, producing the perfect English marmalade; *Clubs* Societas Navigatorum Catholica; *Style—* The Rev Sir David Gibson, Bt; The Reens, Ross Rd, Killarney, Co Kerry, Republic of Ireland

GIBSON, David Frank; s of Reginald James Gibson, of Warrington, Cheshire, and Emily, *née* Tanner; *b* 4 Dec 1946; *Educ* Boteler GS Warrington, UCL (BSc, Dip Arch); *m* 2 Sept 1969, Mary, da of John Greaves, of Warrington, Cheshire; 1 s (Timothy Edward Phillip b 1984), 1 da (Helen Emily Mary b 1988); *Career* architectural asst James Stirling and Ptnr 1968-70, assoc Colin St John Wilson and Ptnrs 1978-79 (architect 1971-79), studio tutor Bartlett Sch of Architecture 1979-88, Julian Harrap Architects 1981-84, assoc Alex Gordon and Ptnrs 1985-87 (architect 1979-80), princ David Gibson Architects 1987-; memb RIBA 1979; *Recreations* architecture, flying; *Clubs* Reform; *Style—* David Gibson, Esq; 22 St George's Ave, London N7 0HD (☎ 071 607 8193); 131 Upper St, London N1 1QP (☎ 071 226 2207, fax 071 226 6920)

GIBSON, David Horsburgh; s of George Paterson Gibson (d 1977), of Pencaitland, East Lothian, and Marguerite Gladys Mary Gibson, MBE, *née* Primrose (d 1955); *b* 25 June 1937; *Educ* Gordonstoun; *m* 30 June 1962, (Elizabeth) Christine, da of Foster Neville Woodward, CBE (d 1985); 2 s (Jonathan b 1963, Duncan b 1966), 1 da (Juliette b 1969); *Career* Nat Serv RN 1956-58: Home and Med fleets Suez campaign 1956; CA; Mollins Machine Co Ltd 1966-71, commercial dir Penelectro Int Ltd 1971-81, dir King Taudevin & Gregson Ltd 1978-81, jt md Hargreaves Reiss & Quinn Ltd 1981-83, dir fin and admin Henderson Admin Gp plc 1983-; memb Royal Br Legion; Freeman City of London, memb Worshipful Co Distillers; MICAS 1963, FBIM 1980; *Recreations* golf, skiing, music, gardening; *Clubs* City of London, Sloane; *Style—* David Gibson, Esq; Paprills Farmhouse, East Hanningfield, Essex CM3 5BW (☎ 0245 400 294); Henderson Administration Gp plc, 3 Finsbury Ave, London EC2M 2PA (☎ 01 638 5757, fax 01 377 5742, telex 884616)

GIBSON, David Reginald Ernest; s of Reginald Gibson (d 1970), of Northallerton, and Betty, *née* Hewitt (d 1963); *b* 9 May 1945; *Educ* HS for Boys Scarborough Yorkshire, Northern Poly; *m* 3 Oct 1970, Marion Elaine, da of William Alexander McLeish, of 3 Abbotsford Grove, Darwick, Melrose, Roxburghshire; 2 da (Julia Amanda b 20 Sept 1972, Rowena Anne b 27 Oct 1975); *Career* chief architect Loughborough Recreation Planning Conslts 1971-79, dir Consarc partnership 1979-84, ptnr The Gibson Hamilton Partnership 1984-89; pres Leicestershire and Rutland Soc of Architects 1987-89 (chm Enviroment Ctee 1979-84) memb Ctee Loughborough Civic Tst 1989-; memb RIBA 1971-89, FRSA; *Recreations* walking, fishing, reading, travel; *Style—* David Gibson, Esq; Unit 19 Loughborough Technology Centre, Epinal Way, Loughborough, Leicestershire LE11 OQE (☎ 0509 610510, fax 0509 610481)

GIBSON, Hon (William) David; OBE (1944), TD; s of Hon Edward Gibson (d 1928), and gs of 1 Baron Ashbourne; bro of 3 Baron Ashbourne, CB, DSO, JP; raised to rank of Baron's s 1943; *b* 22 March 1914; *Educ* Sherborne, Trinity Coll Cambridge (MA); *m* 6 Jan 1947, Sabina, da of late Dr Ernst Landsberg, of Cape Town; 3 da (Celia b 1948, Monica b 1951, Philippa b 1953); *Career* served army WWII (France, N Africa, Italy), Col; second master Clifton Coll 1966-74 (housemaster 1948-65), memb of Council of World Disarmament Campaign 1985-88; *Recreations* sailing, skiing, bridge; *Style—* Hon David Gibson, OBE, TD; Buckley Cottage, Batson, Salcombe, Devon (☎ 054 884 3143)

GIBSON, Maj (William) David; s of George Cock Gibson, OBE (d 1989), of Landwade Hall, Exning, Newmarket, Suffolk, and Angela Madelaine, *née* Llewellin-Evans; *b* 26 Feb 1925; *Educ* Harrow, Trinity Coll Cambridge; *m* 1, 16 Jan 1959, Charlotte Henrietta (d 1973), da of Norman Selwyn Pryor, JP, DL (d 1982), of Manuden House, Bishops Stortford, Herts; 3 s (Martin, George, Edward), 1 da (Anna); m 2, 1975, Jane Marion, da of Brig Ladas L Hassell, DSO, MC (d 1963); *Career* serv Welsh Guards 1944-57 (Palestine 1947, Egypt 1953-56, Maj); dir: W J Tatem Ltd 1957 (chm 1970-), Atlantic Shipping & Trading Co Ltd 1957 (chm 1970-77), West of England Ship Owners Mutual Protection & Indemnity Assoc London 1959-86 (Luxembourg 1970-83), Int Shipowners Investmt Co 1970-83 (chm 1977-83); chm: Tatem Industries plc 1990- (dir), Components and Products Ltd 1990- (dir); Nat Hunt Ctee steward 1963-66 (sr steward 1966), dep sr steward Jockey Club 1969-71; memb: Tattersalls Ctee 1963-69 (chm 1967-69), Farriers Registration Cncl; master Worshipful Co of Farriers 1979; *Recreations* racing, sailing (Klaxton), shooting; *Clubs* Jockey, Royal Yacht Squadron, Royal Thames Yacht, Cavalry and Guard's; *Style—* Maj David Gibson; Bishopswood Grange, nr Ross on Wye, Herefordshire HR9 5QX (☎ 0594 60444)

GIBSON, Sir Donald Evelyn Edward; CBE (1951); s of Prof Arnold Hartley Gibson (d 1959), of Beech House, Alderley Edge, Manchester, and Amy, *née* Quarmby; *b* 11 Oct 1908; *Educ* Manchester GS, Univ of Manchester (MA); *m* 1, 19 Oct 1935, Winifred Mary (d 1977), da of Dr Sinclair McGowan, of Oldham, Lancs; 3 s, 1 da; m 2, 1978, Mrs Grace Haines; 2 step s; *Career* RA (TA) Western Cmd 1938-40; Building Res Station 1935-37, dep county architect Isle of Ely 1937-39, city architect and planning offr Coventry 1939-55, co architect Nottingham 1955-58, dir gen of works WO 1958-62, dir gen of res and devpt Miny of Public Building and Works 1962-67, Hoffman Wood prof of architecture Univ of Leeds 1967-68, controller gen Miny of Public Building and Works 1967-69; currently conslt; pres RIBA 1964-65; Hon DCL

Univ of Durham; FRIBA, FRTPI; kt 1962; *Style—* Sir Donald Gibson, CBE; Bryn Castell, Llanddona, Beaumaris, Gwynedd LL58 8TR (☎ 0248 810399)

GIBSON, Lt-Col Edgar Matheson; MBE (1986), TD (1975), DL (1976); s of James Edgar Gibson (d 1976); *b* 1 Nov 1934; *Educ* Kirkwall GS, Gray's Coll of Art; *m* 1960, Jean, *née* McCarrick; 2 s, 2 da; *Career* Lt-Col, Nat Serv 1958-60, TA & TAVR Lovat Scouts 1961-, Cadet Cmdt Orkney 1979-86, JSLO Orkney 1980-85; asst headmaster Kirkwall GS until 1990; ind artist 1990-; Hon Col Orkney Lovat Scouts ACF 1986; chm: St Magnus Cathedral Fair 1982-, Northern Area Highland TA&VR Assoc 1987; *Recreations* BA playing, whisky tasting; *Clubs* Highland Brigade; *Style—* Lt-Col Edgar M Gibson, MBE, TD, DL; Transcona, New Scapa Rd, Kirkwall, Orkney (☎ 0856 2849)

GIBSON, Hon Mrs (Frances Phoebe); *née* Phillimore; granted 1949, title, rank and precedence of a Baron's da, which would have been her's had her f survived to succeed to title of Baron Phillimore; da of Capt Hon Anthony Francis Phillimore (ka 1940, s and h of 2 Baron Phillimore), of Coppid Hall, Henley-on-Thames, Oxon, and Anne Julia, *née* Pereira; *Educ* St Mary's Convent Ascot; *m* 1, 11 Feb 1961, Colin John Francis Lindsay-MacDougall of Lunga, o s of Maj John Stewart Lindsay-MacDougall, of Lunga, DSO, MC, Argyll and Sutherland Highlanders; 3 s, 2 da; *m* 2, 8 Nov 1980, Joseph Peter Gibson, s of Charles Gibson, of Kelty Hill, Kelty, Fife; *Style—* The Hon Mrs Gibson; Quinta das Madres, Ulgueira, Colras, 2710 Sintra, Portugal (☎ 010 351 1 929 0956)

GIBSON, Hon Hugh Marcus Thornely; eldest s of Baron Gibson (Life Peer), *qv*; *b* 23 June 1946; *Educ* Eton, Magdalen Coll Oxford (BA); *m* 31 March 1967, Hon Frances Towneley, da of Hon Anthony Strachey (d 1955); 1s (Jasper Tallentyre b 1975), 2 da (Effie Dione b 1970, Amelia Mary b 1973); *Career* md Royal Crown Derby and Minton, dir Royal Doulton Ltd; *Recreations* Nat Tst, book collecting, wine, fishing; *Style—* Hon Hugh Gibson; The Fold, Parwich, Ashbourne, Derbys

GIBSON, Ian Robert; s of John Wilfred Gibson (d 1971), of Bridlington, and Eileen Margaret, *née* Pudsey (d 1965); *b* 19 Aug 1948; *Educ* St Peter's York, The Queens Coll Oxford (BA); *m* 9 Sept 1972, Valerie Ann, da of Capt Frederick Alfred Armitage, MBE, GM, SGM (d 1968); 1 s (Edward b 1984), 2 da (Alison b 1975, Anna b 1978); *Career* admitted slr 1972; ptnr Frere Cholmeley 1978-; memb Law Soc; *Recreations* music, walking; *Style—* Ian Gibson, Esq; Parkgate, Aldwickbury, Harpenden, Herts AL5 1AB; 28 Lincoln's Inn Fields, London WC2A 3HH (☎ 071 405 7878, fax 071 405 9056, telex 27623)

GIBSON, Rev Prof John Clark Love; s of Rev Herbert Booth Gibson (d 1968) of Manse of Whifflet, Coatbridge, Lanarkshire, and Margaret Harvey, *née* Marshall (d 1975); *b* 28 May 1930; *Educ* Coatbridge HS, Univ of Glasgow (MA, BD), Magdalen College Oxford (DPhil); *m* 25 Dec 1956, Agnes Gilmour, da of Robert Russell, of Bellshill, Lanarkshire; 4 s (Ian b 1957, Robin b 1961, Peter b 1964, Guy b 1965), 1 da (Jane (Mrs Weatherly) b 1960); *Career* min of New Machar Aberdeenshire 1959-62; Univ of Edinburgh: lectr in Hebrew and Semitic languages 1962-73, reader 1973-87, prof of Hebrew and Old Testament studies 1987-; *Books* Textbook of Hebrew and Moabite Inscriptions (1971), Textbook of Aramaic Inscriptions (1975), Canaanite Myths and Legends (1978), Genesis: Daily Study Bible (2 vols 1981 and 1982), Textbook of Phoenician Inscriptions (1982), Reader's Digest Family Guide to the Bible (ed, 1984), The Motherhood of God (contrib, 1984), Job: Daily Study Bible (1985), The Bible in Scottish Life and Literature (contrib, 1988), Ascribe to the Lord: In Memory of Peter C Craigie (contrib, 1988); *Recreations* scottish literature, spy novels, golf; *Style—* Rev Prof John Gibson; 10 South Morton Street, Edinburgh EH15 2NB (☎ 031 669 3635); Faculty of Divinity, University of Edinburgh, New College, Mound Place, Edinburgh EH1 2LX (☎ 031 225 8400)

GIBSON, Dr John Dudley; s of Stanley Charles Gibson, of 33 Gt Pultney St, Bath, Avon, and Ella Prudence, *née* Blackmore; *b* 18 July 1946; *Educ* Calne Bentley GS, (BSC, MB BS, MRCP, MD); *m* 23 June 1979, Eva, da of Dr Karl Joseph Höfinger, of Sindelburg 32, 3313 Wallsee, Austria; 2 s (Karl Clement b 8 March 1980, Marc Benedict b 27 May 1983), 1 da (Emma Prudence b 25 Nov 1981); *Career* conslt neurologist to Plymouth Gen hosps 1981-; chm governing body Wembury Co Primary Sch; *Recreations* organist, musician, gardening; *Style—* Dr John Gibson; Thorn House, Wembury, Devon PL9 0EQ (☎ 0752 862494) Dept of Neurology, Level 11, Derriford Hospital, Plymouth, Devon PL6 8DH (☎ 0752 792618)

GIBSON, John King; s of Eric King Gibson (d 1982), and Ada Wills, *née* Danson (d 1982); *b* 23 July 1939; *Educ* Liverpool Inst HS for Boys, Univ of Leeds, Farnborough Coll of Technol; *m* 18 Dec 1965, Mari, da of Hovanes Postalian (d 1943); 1 s (Berdge King b 11 Jan 1968), 1 da (Miranda Jane b 22 March 1973); *Career* Nat Serv RAF 1959-61; entered Meteorological Office MOD 1961, asst experimental offr Civil Serv 1962; forecaster: Liverpool Airport 1966-70, Nicosia Airport Cyprus 1963-66; data processing meteorological office Bracknell 1970-76, Euro Centre for Medium-Range Weather Forecasts 1976-90; memb cmmn for basic systems' working gp on data mgmnt World Meteorological Orgn; FRMetS 1975, AFIMA 1982; *Recreations* musical appreciation, mountain walking; *Style—* John Gibson, Esq; 14 Hawkins Close, Bracknell, Berks RG12 6RF (☎ 0344 489254); European Centre for Medium-Range Weather Forecasts, Shinfield Park, Reading RG2 9AX (☎ 0734 499400, fax 0734 869450, telex 847908 ECMWF G)

GIBSON, Dr John Robin; s of Norman John Gibson (d 1983), and Marie Louise Elizabeth, *née* Edwards; *b* 16 Dec 1949; *Educ* Eastwood HS Glasgow, Univ of Glasgow (MB ChB, MRCP); *Career* hosp MO Bulawayo Zimbabwe 1974-77, med registrar Glasgow 1977, hon conslt dermatologist London Hosp 1983-89 (hon dermatology registrar and sr registrar 1978-82), head Dermatology Section Wellcome Res Labs Beckenham 1978-89, exec dir clinical res Bristol-Myers Squibb Co (dir 1989-); author multiple book chapters and papers on: dermatology, therapeutics, pharmacology, allergy; Freeman City of London 1987, Liveryman Worshipful Soc Apothecaries 1988 (Yeoman 1982); memb: BMA, BAD, ESDR, SPS; FRCPG 1987, FRSM; *Recreations* guitar playing, song writing, bridge, squash; *Style—* Dr John Gibson; 21 St Catherine's Court, Buffalo, New York 14222, USA (☎ 716 882 3882); 9 Cabo Del Sol, Denia, Alicante, Spain; Bristol-Myers Squibb Co, Pharmaceutical Research Institute, 100 Forest Ave, Buffalo, New York 14213, USA (☎ 716 887 3428)

GIBSON, John Sibbald; s of John MacDonald Frame Gibson, MBE (d 1965), of Giffnock, Glasgow, and Marion Watson, *née* Sibbald (d 1955); *b* 1 May 1923; *Educ* Paisley GS, Univ of Glasgow; *m* 4 Sept 1948, Moira Helen, da of David Ogilvie Gillespie (d 1961), of Lanarkshire; 1 s (David John Armstrong b 1954), 1 da (Elizabeth Marion (Mrs Halliday) b 1951); *Career* army 1941-46, cmmnd 2 Lt 1943, served 1 Commando 1943-45 (Lt then Capt, India and Burma); Scot Office: asst princ 1947, asst private sec to Sec of State for Scot 1950, private sec to Permanent Under Sec of State 1952, princ 1953, sec Highlands and Islands Advsy Panel 1955-61, asst sec 1962, under sec 1973-83, re-employed to write centenary history and to organise exhibition in Edinburgh 1984-85; memb: Agric Res Cncl 1979-83, Cncl Scottish History Soc, Cncl Saltire Soc 1985-90; *Books* Ships of the '45 (1967), Deacon Brodie (1977), The Thistle and the Crown (1985), Playing The Scottish Card (1988), The Jacobite Threat (with Dr B P Lenman, 1991); *Recreations* historical research, walking dogs; *Clubs* Scottish Arts (Edinburgh); *Style—* John Gibson, Esq; 28 Cramond Gardens, Edinburgh EH4 6PU (☎ 031 336 2931)

GIBSON, Dr Joseph; CBE (1980); s of George Gibson (ka 1918), and Mary Ann Scott, *née* Mordy (d 1980); *b* 10 May 1916; *Educ* Washington GS; King's Coll now Univ of Newcastle upon Tyne (MSc, PhD), Univ of Durham; *m* 22 Dec 1944, Lily McFarlane, da of late David McCutcheon Brown; 1 s (David McFarlane b 1950), 1 da (Carole Ann b 1954); *Career* res Northern Coke Res Lab 1938-46, head Chemistry Dept Sunderland Tech Coll 1948-55, lectr Univ of Durham 1948-55, chief scientist Northumberland and Yorkshire Divisions NCB 1956-64, dir Coal Res Establishment 1968-75, dir Coal Utilisation Res 1975-77; NCB (responsible for sci) 1977-81: coal sci advsr 1981-83, dir several NCB Cos 1977-81; author of many articles on coal utilisation and conversion; pres Institute of Fuel 1975-76, pres BCURA 1977-81 (chm 1972-77); meml lectures: Cadman 1980 and 1982, Prof Moore 1981; coal sci lectr and medal 1977, carbonization sci medal 1979; Hon DCL Univ of Newcastle 1981; Hon FIChemE 1977, FEng 1979; *Publications* jtly: Carbonisation of Coal (1971), Coal and Modern Coal Processing (1979), Coal Utilisation: Technology, Economics and Policy (1981); *Recreations* bridge, gardening; *Style—* Dr Joseph Gibson, CBE; 31 Charlton Close, Charlton Kings, Cheltenham, Glos GL53 8DH (☎ 0242 517832)

GIBSON, Lt-Col Kenneth Charles Robert; TD (1968), DL (Avon 1986); s of Charles Robert Gibson (d 1974), and Jane Boyd Young, *née* Aitken (d 1978); *b* 16 Sept 1935; *Educ* Monkton Combe Sch Bath, Clare Coll Cambridge (MA, LLM); *m* 10 June 1964, Jill Seaton, da of Douglas Campbell Connor (d 1964); 3 s (Douglas b 1966, James b 1970, Mark b 1971), 1 da (Elizabeth b 1967); *Career* Nat Serv 5 Bn Kings African Rifles Kenya 1954-56, Somerset LI (TA) 1956-71, CO 6 Bn LI (vol) 1971-74, hon Col Avon ACF 1987-; admitted slr 1962, sr ptnr Wansbroughs 1985-, pres Bristol Law Soc 1984-85; reader Diocese of Bristol; *Style—* Lt-Col Kenneth Gibson, TD, DL; Rosewell, Bitton, Bristol BS15 6LJ (☎ 0272 322 122); Wansbroughs, 103 Temple St, Bristol BS99 7UD (☎ 0272 268 981, fax 0272 291 582)

GIBSON, Col Leonard Young; CBE (1961, MBE 1940), TD (1947, clasp and 3 bars 1961), DL (Northumberland 1971); s of William McLure Gibson (d 1959), of The Grove, Gosforth, Northumberland, and Wilhelmina Mitchell, *née* Young (d 1930); *b* 4 Dec 1911; *Educ* Royal GS Newcastle upon Tyne, Paris, Germany; *m* 1949, Pauline Mary, da of Newsam Cawcutt Anthony, of Newcastle upon Tyne; 1 s, 1 da; *Career* CSM RGS Newcastle upon Tyne OTC 1928-29, TA 1931-61, 2 Lt, Lt, then Capt The Elswick Battery, 72 (N) Fd Regt RA TA, Staff Coll Camberley 1939, tsc Bde Maj RA 50 (N) Div, rearguard Dunkirk 1940 (despatches) BMRA 43 (W), Div, GSO2 SE Army 1941-1942, GSO2 Directing Staff, Staff Coll Camberley 1942-43, psc GSO1 Ops Eastern Cmd 1943-44; 2-in-C 107 led Regt S Notts Hussars RHA; TA: France, Belgium, Holland, Germany 1944-45 (despatches, French Croix de Guerre Gold Star); GSO1 Mil Govt Westphalia Germany 1945, Bty Cmd The Elswick Bty 272 (N) Fd Regt TA 1947-51, 2-in-C, CO 272 (N) Fd Regt RA TA 1956-58, Dep Cdr RA 50 (N) Div TA 1959-61, Col TA; memb Northumberland TA and AF Assoc 1958-68, pres Master's Harriers and Beagles Assoc 1968, master Newcastle and District Beagles 1946-83 (elected pres 1983); *Recreations* beagling, breeding hounds and horses; *Style—* Col Leonard Gibson, CBE, TD, DL; Simonburn Cottage, Humshaugh, Hexham, Northumberland (☎ 0434 681 402)

GIBSON, Capt Michael Bradford; s of Lt-Col B T Gibson; *b* 20 March 1929; *Educ* Taunton Sch, Sandhurst, Sidney Sussex Coll Cambridge; *m* 1953, Mary Helen Elizabeth Legg; 2 s; *Career* md Racquet Sports Int 1976-; *Style—* Capt Michael Gibson; Courtyard House, Warnham, Horsham, Sussex (☎ 0403 65589)

GIBSON, Baron (Life Peer UK 1975), of Penn's Rocks, Co of East Sussex; (Richard) Patrick Tallentyre Gibson; o s of Thornely Carbutt Gibson (d 1969), of 2 Kensington Gate, and late Elizabeth Anne Augusta, *née* Coit; *b* 5 Feb 1916; *Educ* Eton, Magdalen Coll Oxford (MA, hon fell 1977); *m* 14 July 1945, (Elisabeth) Dione, 3 da of Hon (Bernard) Clive Pearson (d 1965; 2 s of 1 Viscount Cowdray), and Hon Alicia Knatchbull-Hugessen, da of 1 Baron Brabourne; 4 s (Hon Hugh Marcus Thornely b 1946, Hon Clive Patrick b 1948, Hon William Knatchbull b 1951, Hon Piers Nathaniel b 1956); *Career* served WWII, Middx Yeo, Maj (POW 1941-43); sits as Ind Peer in House of Lords; chm S Pearson & Son 1978-83, Financial Times 1957-78 (chm 1975-77), dir Economist Newspaper Ltd 1957-78; chm: Arts Cncl of GB 1972-77, Nat Tst 1977-86; tstee Glyndebourne Festival Opera 1965-72 and 1977-87, memb Bd Royal Opera House 1977-87, treas Univ of Sussex 1983-87; Hon DLitt Reading 1980, Hon DUniv Sussex 1988; *Clubs* Brooks's, Garrick; *Style—* The Rt Hon Lord Gibson; 4 Swan Walk, SW3 (☎ 071 351 0344); Penn's Rocks, Groombridge, Sussex (☎ 0892 864 244)

GIBSON, Paul Alexander; s of Wing Cdr L P Gibson (d 1954), and Betty, *née* Peveler; *b* 11 Oct 1941; *Educ* Kingswood Sch Bath, Kings Coll London, Canterbury Sch of Architecture, Regent Street Poly Sch of Architecture; *m* 29 Aug 1969, Julia Rosemary, da of Leslie Atkinson; *Career* architect; Farrell Grimshaw Partnership 1968-69, lectr N Dakota State Univ USA 1969-70, Foster Associates 1970-72, private practice Sidell Gibson Partnership 1973-; major projects incl: MEPC office buildings Frankfurt 1974, master plans Univ of Arack Iran and housing at Kermanshaw Iran 1976, 15 varied housing schemes English Courtyard Assoc 1976-91, office buildings and housing Frankfurt 1991; winner major architectural competition for Grand Buildings Trafalgar Square 1987; memb RIBA 1969; *Recreations* painting, music; *Style—* Paul Gibson, Esq; Sidell Gibson Partnership, Fitzroy Yard, Fitzroy Rd, London NW1 8TP (☎ 071 722 5009, fax 071 722 0083)

GIBSON, Rear Adm Peter Cecil; CB (1968); 2 s of Alexander Horace Cecil Gibson (d 1968), and Phyllis Zéline, *née* Baume (d 1948); *b* 31 May 1913; *Educ* Ealing Priory; *m* 1938, Phyllis Anna Mary, da of Norman Haliburton Hume (d 1936); 2 s, 1 da; *Career* entered RN 1931; service mainly marine and aeronautical engrg, maintenance test flying, staff and Admty aviation appts; dir engr offr's appts 1961-63, dep controller aircraft (RN) Ministries Aviation and Technol 1966-69, ret RN 1969; business mgmnt conslt 1973-; *Recreations* bridge, fly-fishing; *Clubs* Army & Navy; *Style—* Rear Adm Peter Gibson, CB

GIBSON, Gp Capt Peter Hurst; MBE (1959); s of Stanley Silvers Gibson (d 1955), of Leeds, and Florence Muriel, *née* Blackie (d 1971); *b* 10 Dec 1930; *Educ* Leeds Modern Sch, Univ of Leeds (BA, MA); *m* 19 June 1965, June Carlisle, da of Capt Albert Brierley (d 1944), of Tideswell; 1 da (Caroline Spirett b 1966); *Career* RAF 1955; served: Germany, Singapore, Huntingdon, Wilts MOD; ret Gp Capt 1977; Bilston Coll 1977-80, princ Aylesbury Coll 1980-90, professional conslt 1990-; hon memb City Guilds Inst; FBIM 1980, FRSA 1982; *Recreations* theatre, music, cooking, gardening; *Style—* Gp Capt Peter Gibson, MBE; Fairlands Terrick, Aylesbury, Bucks HO22 5XL (☎ 0296 61 2591)

GIBSON, Hon Mr Justice; Hon Sir Peter Leslie Gibson; s of Harold Leslie Gibson, and Martha Lucy, *née* Diercking; *b* 10 June 1934; *Educ* Malvern, Worcester Coll Oxford; *m* 1968, Katharine Mary Beatrice Hadow; 2 s, 1 da; *Career* called to the Bar Inner Temple 1960, Treasy counsel (Chancery) 1972-81, bencher Lincoln's Inn, High Ct judge (Chancery) 1981-, judge of Employment Appeal Tbnl 1984-86; chm Law Cmmn 1990-; kt 1981; *Style—* Hon Mr Justice Peter Gibson; Royal Courts of Justice, Strand, London WC2A 2LL (☎ 071 405 7641)

GIBSON, Hon Piers Nathaniel; 4 and yst s of Baron Gibson (Life Peer), *qv*; *b* 15 March 1956; *Educ* Eton, Magdalen Coll Oxford (BA); *m* 19 Oct 1981, Melanie Jane Stella, er da of Jack Walters, OBE, of La Torre, Gavirate, Varese, Italy; 1 s (Harry Maximilian b 1988), 1 da (Lucy b 1986); *Career* entrepreneur; *Recreations* music, skiing; *Clubs* Annabel's; *Style—* The Hon Piers Gibson

GIBSON, Prof Robert Donald Davidson; s of Nicol Aitken Gibson (d 1976), of 4 Westmorland Rd, London, and Ann, *née* Campbell (d 1977); *b* 21 Aug 1927; *Educ* Leyton Co HS, Kings Coll London (BA), Magdalene Coll Cambridge (PhD), Ecole Normale Supérieure Paris; *m* 21 Dec 1953, Sheila Elaine, da of Bertie Goldsworthy (d 1983), of 83 Sandford St, Exeter; 3 s (Ian b 1956, Graham b 1958, Robin b 1962); *Career* served RAF 1948-50, Flying Offr Educn Branch; asst lectr Univ of St Andrews 1954-55; lectr: Queens Coll Dundee 1955-58, Univ of Aberdeen 1958-61; prof of French: Queens Univ Belfast, Univ of Kent 1965-; master Rutherford Coll Univ of Kent 1985-90; govr: Nonington Coll 1966-85, Eversley Coll 1967-74, Sittingbourne Coll 1968-76; memb Soc for French Studies; *Books* The Quest of Alain - Fournier (1953), Modern French Poets on Poetry (1961), Le Grand Meaulnes by Alain-Fournier (1 edn 1968), The Land Without a Name (1975), Annals of Ashdon (1988), Studies in French Fiction (ed 1988); *Recreations* writing, reading, walking; *Style—* Prof Robert Gibson; 7 Sunnymead, Tyler Hill, Canterbury, Kent (☎ 0227 472373); Rutherford Coll, The Univ of Kent, Canterbury, Kent (☎ 0227 764000)

GIBSON, Prof Robert Edward; s of Edward Robert Ward (d 1941), of Felpham, W Sussex, and Ellen Constance Mack (d 1931), adopted s of John Gibson, and Mary, *née* Mack; *b* 12 May 1926; *Educ* Emanuel Sch, Battersea Poly, Imperial Coll (BSc, PhD, DSc); *m* 10 Oct 1950, Elizabeth Jocelyn (d 1986), da of Donald Edward Bideleux; 2 s (Alastair Robert b 10 Oct 1952, Jonathan Edward b 21 June 1963), 1 da (Caroline Lucy b 1 April 1957); *Career* Royal Aircraft Establishment Farnborough 1945-46, res student then asst Imperial Coll 1948-53, sr scientific offr Building Research Station 1953-56, lectr then reader in Civil Engrg Analysis Imperial Coll 1956-65, King's Coll London 1965-83 (reader in civil engrg, prof of engrg sci), Cwlth visiting prof Univ of Sydney 1969-70, Rankine lectr British Geotechnical Soc 1974, sr princ and dir Golder Associates 1974-, industl fell Wolfson Coll Oxford 1983-85, adjoint prof Univ of Colorado Boulder 1987-; *Books* Via Vector to Tensor (with W G Bickley, 1962); *Recreations* travel, listening to music especially Bach's Cantatas and all Mozart; *Clubs* Athenaeum; *Style—* Prof Robert Gibson; Golder Associates (UK) Ltd, 54 Moorbridge Rd, Maidenhead, Berks SL6 8BN (☎ 0628 771731, fax 0628 770699)

GIBSON, Robert Myles; ERD (1973), TD (1980); s of Robert Gibson (d 1976), of Port Patrick and Oban, and Mary Elizabeth, *née* Harvey; *b* 6 May 1927; *Educ* Kilmarnock Acad, Univ of Glasgow, McGill Univ (MD, MSc); *m* 4 Aug 1962, Ena Edith Christina, da of Dr Christian Balfour Fotheringham Millar (d 1965), of Newport, Gwent; 1 s (Alastair b 1967), 1 da (Stroma b 1965); *Career* RCAMC 1950-51, Lt-Col RAMC 1951-53, RAMC TA 1953-58, hon conslt neurosurgn to Army and BAOR 1960-; conslt neurosurgn Gen Infirmary Leeds 1959-, author of papers on surgery and neurosurgery; memb: BMA Cncl 1969-80, GMC, Cncl RCSEd (vice pres 1983-86); convenor Intercollegiate Bd (UK) of Neurosurgery, vice chm Med Protection Soc, chm Med Protection Europe; chief med advsr to Football League and FA, hon sec Mil Surgical Soc; Freeman City of London, Liveryman Worshipful Co of Apothecaries; fell Int Coll of Surgns; memb: RSM, Soc Br Neurological Surgns; FRCS, FRCSEd; CStJ 1970; *Books* Health Service Financing (jointly, 1972); *Recreations* golf, railways, railway travel; *Clubs* Atheneum; *Style—* R Myles Gibson, Esq, ERD, TD; 35 Park Lane, Leeds (☎ 0532 661998); Department of Neurosurgery, General Infirmary, Leeds LS1 3EX (☎ 0532 32799); 10 Harley St, London W1 (☎ 071 580 4280)

GIBSON, Rosemary (Rose); da of Donald Bruce Cameron (d 1987), of London, and Ruth Margaret, *née* Watson; *b* 16 Feb 1961; *Educ* Lady Margaret GS, Wadham Coll Oxford (BA, MA); *m* 31 July 1987, James Ernest Gibson, s of Joseph David Gibson, CBE; *Career* news reporter and feature writer City of London Recorder 1982-84, account exec Communications Arc Ltd (subsid of General Advertising Ltd) 1984-85; Chambers Cox PR Ltd: sr account exec 1985-86, account dir 1986-89, dir 1989-; awarded Daily Express Young Sportswriter of the Year 1978; *Recreations* theatre, cinema, music, golf, short story writing, cookery, appreciating good wine, literature, travel; *Clubs* The Lady Taveners; *Style—* Ms Rose Gibson; Chambers Cox PR Ltd, 7/8 Rathbone Place, London W1P 1DE (☎ 071 631 5414, fax 071 580 7719)

GIBSON, Roy; s of Robert Gibson, OBE (d 1984), of Belfast, and Mary Gibson, of Belfast; *b* 10 Sept 1933; *Educ* Royal Belfast Acad Inst, Queens Univ Belfast (MB BCh, BAO); *m* 5 July 1962, Elizabeth Deirdre, da of William Jordan Addis (d 1981), of Belfast; 2 da (Lesley Deirdre b 1966, Jennifer Maxine b 1970); *Career* Royal Victoria Hosp Belfast: house surgn, registrar, conslt ENT surgn; clinical fellowship in otolarngology Washington Univ St Louis Missouri USA 1965-66; memb BMA: Central Ctee for Hosp Med Servs 1980-85, Cncl BMA 1983-85; chm (ex officio memb) Area Med Advsy Ctee: E Health Bd NI 1986-, Med Advsy Ctee E Health and Soc Servs Bd; memb Central Med Advsy Ctee Dept of Health NI; FRCSEd 1962, FRCS 1964; *Recreations* watching rugby football and cricket, golf, gardening, reading; *Clubs* Instonians, RSM; *Style—* Roy Gibson, Esq; 12 Harberton Drive, Belfast BT9 6PF (☎ 0232 665418); Consulting Rooms, 13 Ulsterville Avenue, Belfast (☎ 667741)

GIBSON, Ven Terence Allen; s of Fred William Allen Gibson, of Boston, Lincs, and Joan Hazel, *née* Bishop; *b* 23 Oct 1937; *Educ* Boston GS, Jesus Coll Cambridge (MA), Cuddesdon Coll Oxford; *Career* curate St Chad Kirkby Liverpool 1963-66, warden Centre 63 C of E Youth Centre and vicar for Youth Work 1966-75, rector of Kirkby Liverpool 1975-84, rural dean Walton Liverpool 1979-84; archdeacon of: Suffolk 1984-87, Ipswich 1987-; *Style—* The Ven The Archdeacon of Ipswich; 99 Valley Rd, Ipswich, Suffolk IP1 4NF (☎ 0473 250333)

GIBSON, Terence Bradley (Terry); s of Terence Michael Gibson, of Woodford Green, Essex, and Doris Marie Betty, *née* Gorst; *b* 23 Dec 1962; *Educ* Highmans Park Sch; *m* 10 July 1982, Paula, da of Frank Leslie James Reed; 1 s (Joshua Terence b 16 Feb 1989), 1 da (Chloë Paula b 19 Oct 1985); *Career* professional footballer; Tottenham Hotspur 1979-83, Coventry City 1983-86, Manchester Utd 1986-87, Wimbledon 1987-; England caps: schoolboy 1977, youth 1979-81 (scored winning goal UEFA Youth Championship final v Poland 1980); FA Cup winners Wimbledon 1988; finalist 100m English Schs Athletics Championship 1977; *Recreations* golf, american football, cinema; *Style—* Terry Gibson, Esq; Wimbledon FC, Durnsford Rd, Wimbledon, London SW19 (☎ 081 946 6311)

GIBSON, Thomas Herbert; s of Clement Herbert Gibson (d 1976), of England and Argentina, and Marjorie Julia *née* Anderson (d 1982); *b* 12 April 1943; *Educ* Eton; *m* 1966, Anthea Fiona Catherine, da of late Lt-Col G A Palmer, RE; 3 s (Miles Cosmo Archdale b 1968, Sebastian Thomas Maximilian b 1972, Benjamin Hugh George b 1973); *Career* fndr chm Thomas Gibson Fine Art Ltd 1969-; memb Soc of London Art Dealers (memb Exec Ctee 1987-89); *Recreations* tennis; *Clubs* Hurlingham, RAC, Vanderbilt Racquet; *Style—* Thomas Gibson, Esq; Thomas Gibson Fine Art Limited, 44 Old Bond St, London W1X 3AF (☎ 071 499 8572)

GIBSON, Hon William Knatchbull; 3 s of Baron Gibson, *qv*, and Elizabeth Dione, da of Hon Clive Pearson; *b* 26 Aug 1951; *Educ* Eton, Magdalen Coll Oxford (BA); *m* 1988, Lori Frances, o da of Herbert Mintz, of Miami, Florida, USA; 1 s (Matthew Charles b 6 Dec 1990); *Career* newspaper mangr with Westminster Press (industl rels specialist 1976-82), Sloan fell London Grad Sch of Business Studies 1983, dir of admin Financial Times 1984-86, publisher of Financial Times magazines 1986-89, md Financial Times Business Information 1989-; *Recreations* opera, shooting, skiing; *Clubs* Garrick; *Style—* The Hon William Gibson; 11 Paultons Sq, London SW3 5AP; Financial Times, 1 Southwark Bridge, London SE1 0HZ

GIBSON PHILLIPS, Hon Mrs (Margaret Askew Alexander); da of 2 Baron Harmsworth; *b* 31 Oct 1928; *m* 1, Wendell Holmes McCulloch; 2 s (Kevin Desmond b 25 Jan 1950, Dan Eric b 17 Sept 1951); m 2, 1960, Frank Gibson Phillips, s of late Henry Gibson Phillips, of Windmill Hill, Alton, Hants; *Style—* The Hon Mrs Gibson Phillips

GIBSON-WATT, Baron (Life Peer UK 1979), of The Wye, in the District of Radnor; (James) David Gibson-Watt; MC (1943 and 2 bars), PC (1974), DL (formerly Radnorshire 1968, now Powys); s of Maj James Miller Gibson-Watt, JP, DL (d 1929; ggs of James Watt the engineer and inventor of the steam engine), and Marjorie Adela, *née* Ricardo, MBE (gggda of David Ricardo, the political economist); *b* 11 Sept 1918; *Educ* Eton, Trinity Coll Cambridge (BA); *m* 10 Jan 1942, Diana, 2 da of Sir Charles Hambro, KBE, MC (d 1963); 3 s (Jamie b 1943 d 1946, Hon Julian David b 13 June 1946, Hon Robin (*qv*) b 25 March 1949), 2 da (Hon Claerwen (Hon Mrs Green) b 20 Oct 1952, Hon Sian Diana b 1 April 1962); *Career* served WWII Welsh Gds (North African and Italian campaigns); Parly candidate Brecon and Radnor 1950 and 1951, MP (C) Hereford 1956-74, lord cmmr of the Treasury 1959-61, min of state Welsh Office 1970-74; memb Historic Bldgs Cncl Wales 1975-79, a forestry cmmr 1976-86; chm: Cncl of Royal Welsh Agric Soc 1978-, Cncl on Tribunals 1980-86; FRAgs; JP until 1988; *Clubs* Boodle's, Pratt's; *Style—* The Rt Hon Lord Gibson-Watt, MC, PC, DL; Doldowlod, Llandrindod Wells, Powys LD1 6HF (☎ 059 789 208)

GIBSON-WATT, Hon Robin; 3 and yst s of Baron Gibson-Watt, MC, PC, JP, DL, *qv*; *b* 25 March 1949; *Educ* Eton; *m* 1971, Marcia Susan, da of Sir Roger Hugh Cary, 2 Bt; 3 s (Anthony David b 1975, Edward Ricardo b 1978, Guy Charles b 1982), 1 da (Phoebe Charlotte b 1980); *Career* High Sheriff Powys 1981; *Style—* The Hon Robin Gibson-Watt; Gelli Garn, Llanyre, Llandrindod Wells, Powys

GIBSON-WATT, Hon Sian Diana; yst da of Baron Gibson-Watt, PC, MC, DL; *b* 1 April 1962; *Style—* The Hon Sian Gibson-Watt

GIBSON-CRAIG-CARMICHAEL, Sir David Peter William; 15 Bt of Keirhill (NS 1702) and 8 Bt of Riccarton (UK 1831); s of Sir (Archibald Henry) William Gibson-Craig-Carmichael, 14 and 7 Bt (d 1969), and Rosemary Anita, *née* Crew (d 1979); *b* 21 July 1946; *Educ* Queen's Univ Kingston Canada (BSc); *m* 1973, Patricia, da of Marcos Skarnic, of Santiago, Chile; 1 s, 1 da; *Heir* s, Peter William Gibson-Craig-Carmichael b 29 Dec 1975; *Style—* Sir David Gibson-Craig-Carmichael, Bt

GIBSON-CRAIG-CARMICHAEL, Emily, Lady; Emily Ellen; o da of Henry Rummell, of Falkland Islands; *m* 2 Sept 1914, Sir Eardley Gibson-Craig-Carmichael, 13 and 6 Bt (d 24 Feb 1939); 1 s (14 and 7 Bt, decd), 2 da; *Style—* Emily, Lady Gibson-Craig-Carmichael

GIDDINGS, Air Marshal Sir (Kenneth Charles) Michael; KCB (1975), OBE (1953), DFC (1945, AFC 1950, and bar 1955); s of Charles Giddings, and Grace, *née* Gregory; *b* 27 Aug 1920; *Educ* Ealing Co Sch, UCL; *m* 1946, Elizabeth, da of Joseph McConnell; 2 s, 2 da; *Career* test pilot; Dep Chief Def Staff Op Requirements 1973-76; ind panel inspr DOE 1978-, dir National Counties Building Society 1982-85; *Recreations* golf, gardening, music; *Clubs* RAF; *Style—* Air Marshal Sir Michael Giddings, KCB, OBE, DFC; 159 Long Lane, Tilehurst, Reading, Berks (☎ 0734 23012)

GIDDINGS, Robert; *Educ* Univ of Bristol (BA, M Litt, DipEd), Univ of Keele (PhD); *Career* sr English master Ryefields and St Nicholas Sch 1962-63; lectr: WEA South and West 1962-64, Extra Mural Dept Univ of Bristol 1963-65, English and Liberal Studies Yeovil Tech Coll 1963-64, English and communication studies City of Bath Coll of Further Educn 1964-82, researcher Educn Systems Ltd Bristol 1966-67, assoc tutor Sch of Educn Univ of Bath 1971-79, course tutor The Open Univ 1971-79, Fulbright Exchange prof St Louis Community Coll Flonssant Valley 1975-76; author and journalist 1961- (contrib New Statesman, New Society, The Listener, Radio Times, The Guardian, Sunday Times, Radio Academy Journal, various radio and television progs); researcher and writer: The Late Show, The Clive James Unit, various radio and television progs; radio and television scriptwriter and broadcaster 1966- (contrib Woman's Hour, Home for the Day, Does He Take Sugar? Pebble Mill at One); radio columnist Tribune 1977-85, media columnist Music and Musicians 1980-84, professional attachment TVS Southampton 1987-88; currently sr lectr Dept of Communication and Media Bournemouth Poly Dorset; Books incl: The Tradition of Smollett (1967), British Social and Political History (1967), You Should See Me in Pyjamas (autobiog, 1981), Mark Twain - A Sumptuous Variety (1987), The Changing World of Charles Dickens, JRR Tolkien - This Far Land, Who Was Really Who in Fiction (with Alan Bold), The War Poets 1914-1918 (1988), Screening the Novel, Literature and Imperialism 1990, Echoes of War (1991); *Style—* Robert Giddings, Esq; Dept of Communication and Media, Bournemouth Polytechnic, Poole, Dorset BH12 5BB (☎ 0202 595240); c/o Sheila Watson, Authors Agents, 12 Edgert St, London NW1 8LJ (☎ 071 722 9514)

GIDDINS, Alan Clifford Bence; s of Dr Alan Grey Giddins, of Blacknest Hall, Grand Ave, Worthing, Sussex, and Dr Esther Anne, *née* Bence; *b* 25 Aug 1965; *Educ* Eton, Belmont Hill Sch USA, Univ of Durham (BA); *Career* CA; public schs singles and doubles rackets finalist, Br Univs doubles rackets finalist; rep English and Welsh Univs Athletics Union lawn tennis; *Recreations* lawn tennis, rackets, real tennis, golf; *Clubs* Lansdowne, Queens; *Style—* Alan Giddins, Esq; Blacknest Hall, Grand Ave, Worthing, Sussex BN11 5AG (☎ 0903 202965); 2 Barnfield Place, Westferry Rd, Isle of Dogs, London (☎ 071 515 7209); KPMG Peat Marwick McLintock, 1 Puddle Dock, London EC2 (☎ 071 236 8000)

GIDDINS, Anthony David Chaffey (Pip); s of Dudley Dyster Chaffey Giddins (d 1979), of Mymms Hall, Hert, and Irene Dorothy, *née* Lock; *b* 19 July 1951; *Educ* Univ of Leicester (LLB); *m* 22 April 1978, Anne Patricia, da of Kenneth Raymond Coward, of Northbourne, Bournemouth; 1 s (David Robert Chaffey b 22 March 1980), 1 da (Fiona Victoria b 3 April 1979), 1 step s (Mark Andrew); *Career* admitted slr 1976; lectr law Coll of Law 1976-77, Bowmakers Ltd 1977-83, head legal servs Br Credit Tst Ltd 1983-85, Warner Goodman & Streat and Trethowans 1985-88, ptnr Lester Aldrigde 1988-, visiting lectr Dorset Inst Higher Educn 1988-; memb examination bd Fin Houses Assoc 1979-; *Style—* Pip Giddins, Esq; 28 Harrier Drive, Wimborne, Dorset, BH21 1XE (☎ 0202 841723) Lester Aldridge, Vandale House, Post Office Rd, Bournemouth BH1 1BT (☎ 0202 21426, fax 0202 290725)

GIDLOW-JACKSON, Charles Michael; s of Lt-Col Roger Myles Gidlow-Jackson, DSO (d 1945), of Glos, and Norah, *née* Ramsay (d 1982); *b* 12 Sept 1944; *Educ* Eton Coll, Ch Ch Oxford; *m* 30 March 1968, Nuala Wynne, da of Patrick Griffin, of Oxfordshire; 1 s (Mark b 1972), 1 da (Ratia b 1970); *Career* dir of sales York Ltd 1986-; *Recreations* travel, shooting; *Clubs* Naval and Military; *Style—* Charles M Gidlow-Jackson, Esq; 84 Exeter St, Salisbury, Wilts SP1 2SE (☎ 0722 339 213)

GIDMAN, Richard Hippsley; s of Towers Halcott Gidman (d 1963), and Phyllis Mary, *née* Hippsley, MBE (d 1979); *b* 15 June 1928; *Educ* Nottingham HS, RAF Coll Cranwell; *m* 15 March 1952, Mary Elizabeth Whiteway, da of Lt-Col Cyril Harry Sands (d 1941); 2 s (Simon b 1953, Alastair b 1954); *Career* RAF pilot (gen duties), Sqdn Ldr Bomber Cmd and MEAF 1946-60; mgmnt conslt 1970-87, vice pres Towers Perrin Forster & Crosby 1970-83; *Recreations* gardening, cooking; *Clubs* RAF; *Style—* Richard H Gidman, Esq; Frieth Court, Little Frieth, nr Henley on Thames, Oxon RG9 6NU (☎ 0494 881080)

GIDNEY, Norman; CBE; s of George Gidney (d 1953), of Birmingham, and Abia (d 1969); *b* 26 Dec 1931; *Educ* Billesley Secdy Modern Birmingham; *m* 1957, Carol Ann, da of Alfred Mole (d 1957), of Birmingham; 3 s (Simon Mark b 1961, Daniel George b 1969, Jonathan Alfred (twin) b 1969), 1 da (Rachel Elizabeth b 1963); *Career* Mil Police Italy, Austria; chm: Warwick Industries Ltd, Industrial Holding Co; regnl chm Prince of Wales Business Tst; *Recreations* tennis, squash, horse-riding, reading, philosophy & theology; *Style—* Norman Gidney, CBE; Haven Pastures, Henley-in-Arden, Solihull B95 5QS (☎ 05642 792734/793289); Gidney Securities Ltd, 66 High Street, Henley-in-Arden B95 5BX (☎ 0564 793232, telex 339358, fax 0564 279 2743)

GIDWANEY, Dhanraj Chatamal Teckchand Hassasingh; s of Dewan Chatamal Teckchand Hassasingh Gidwaney (d 1974), of Giddubhandar, and Mohini, *née* Jhagiani; *b* 3 Dec 1949; *Educ* Delhi Univ (BSc); *m* 1 (m dis 1979), Nagina; m 2, 26 June 1987, Tina, da of Felix Bernard Manley, of Chandigarh, India; *Career* CA; chm and md Accountancy Tutors Ltd 1983; ACA 1981; *Recreations* cricket, tennis, polo; *Style—* Dhandraj Gidwaney, Esq; Accountancy Tutors Ltd, 6 Avonmouth St, London SE1 (☎ 071 403 3767, fax 071 378 7153)

GIEDROYĆ, Michal Graham Dowmont (Miko); s of Michal Jan Henryk Giedroyć, of Oxford, and Rosemary Virginia Anna, *née* Cumpston; *b* 5 May 1959; *Educ* Ampleforth Coll York, New Coll Oxford (BA); *m* 1 Nov 1986, Dorothee Ulrike Alexandra, da of Dr Ernst Friedrich Jung, of Bonn; *Career* Investmt Div J Henry Schroder Wagg and Co Ltd 1980-83, vice pres Schroder Captital Management Inc 1984-85, dir Warburg Securities 1985-; *Recreations* jazz piano; *Style—* Miko Giedroyć, Esq; Warburg Securities, 1 Finsbury Ave, London EC2M 2PA (☎ 071 382 4677, fax 071 382 4800)

GIELGUD, Sir (Arthur) John; CH (1977); s of Frank Gielgud, stockbroker (d 1949), and Kate Terry Lewis (d 1958, niece of Dame Ellen Terry 1847-1928); *b* 14 April 1904; *Educ* Westminster, Lady Benson Sch of Drama, RADA; *Career* actor, stage dir and prodr; stage debut Old Vic 1921 as the herald in Henry V, suc Noel Coward as Nicky Lancaster in The Vortex 1925 and as Lewis Dodd in The Constant Nymph 1927, Richard II in Richard of Bordeaux 1932, alternated Mercutio and Romeo with Laurence Olivier in Romeo and Juliet 1935 (also dir); appeared in Hamlet 1930, 1934, 1936, 1939, 1944, 1945, 1946 (over 500 appearances in this role); Ernest Worthing in The Importance of Being Earnest 1930, 1939, 1942; Prospero in The Tempest 1930, 1940, 1957, 1974; King Lear 1931, 1950, 1955; dir: The Heiress 1949, The Lady's Not For Burning 1949, The Cherry Orchard 1954, The Chalk Garden 1956, Hamlet (starring Richard Burton) USA 1964, Private Lives 1972, The Constant Wife 1973, The Gay Lord Quex 1975; played Oedipus in Seneca's Oedipus 1968, Headmaster in 40 Years On 1968, Home 1970, No Man's Land 1975, Julius Caesar 1977, Volpone 1977, Half-Life 1977, The Best of Friends 1988; TV performances incl: Brideshead Revisited 1981, Inside the Third Reich 1983, Neck 1983, The Scarlet and the Black 1983, Time After Time 1985, Marco Polo 1986, Oedipus the King 1986, The Canterville Ghost 1987, Quartermaine's Terms 1987, War & Remembrance 1988, Summers Lease 1989; films incl: Richard III 1955, Chimes at Midnight 1966, Oh, What a Lovely War! 1968, Murder on the Orient Express 1974, Providence 1977, The Elephant Man 1979, Arthur 1982 (Oscar for Best Supporting Actor), Wagner 1983, Plenty 1985, The Shooting Party 1985, Leave All Fair 1987, The Whistle Blower 1987, Arthur on the Rocks 1988, Getting Things Right 1988, Loser Takes All 1988; Special Award for services to theatre Lawrence Olivier Awards 1985; Hon LLD St Andrew's 1950, Hon DLitt Oxon 1953, Hon DLitt London 1977, Companion Légion d'Honneur 1960; kt 1953; *Books* Early Stages (1938), Stage Directions (1963), Distinguished Company (1972), An Actor and His Time (autobiog 1979), Backward Glances (1989); *Recreations* music, painting; *Clubs* Garrick, Arts, Players (New York); *Style—* Sir John Gielgud, CH; South Pavilion, Wotton Underwood, Aylesbury, Bucks

GIELGUD, Maina Julia Gordon; da of Lewis Evelyn Gielgud (d 1953), and Elisabeth Sutton (author and actress under name of Zita Gordon); niece of Sir John Gielgud; *b* 14 Jan 1945; *Educ* BEPC France; *Career* ballerina with Cuevas Co and Roland Petit Co to 1963; Grand Ballet Classique de France 1963-67; principal ballerina: Béjart Co 1967-71, Berlin 1971, London Festival Ballet 1972-76, Sadler's Wells Ballet 1976-78; freelance ballerina and guest artist 1978-82, rehearsal dir London City Ballet 1982, artistic dir Australian Ballet 1983-; creations and choreographies: Steps Notes and Squeaks (London) 1978, Petit Pas et Crac (Paris) 1979, Ghosties and Ghoulies (London City Ballet) 1982, The Sleeping Beauty (Australian Ballet) 1984, Giselle (Australian Ballet) 1986; *Style—* Miss Maina Gielgud; 2 Kavanagh St, S Melbourne 3205, Australia (☎ 03 649 8600, fax 03 614 7081); Stirling Court, 3 Marshall St, London W1 (☎ 071 73 6612)

GIFFARD, Adam Edward; o s and h of 3 Earl of Halsbury (but does not use courtesy title Viscount Tiverton); *b* 3 June 1934; *Educ* Stowe, Jesus Cambridge; *m* 1, 1 Aug 1963, Ellen, da of late Brynjolf Hovde, and formerly w of Matthew Huxley; m 2, 1976, Joanna Elizabeth, da of Frederick Harry Cole; 2 da (Sarah b 1976, Emma b 1978); *Career* late 2 Lt Seaforth Highlanders; *Style—* Adam Giffard, Esq; PO Box 13, North Branch, New York 12766, USA

GIFFARD, Peter Richard de Longueville; DL (1984); s of Thomas Giffard, MBE, JP, DL (d 1971), and Angela, da of Sir William Trollope, 10 Bt; is sr male rep of the Giffards of Chillington, one of the few English families to be able to trace their ancestry from pre-Conquest times, who flourished in Normandy in the tenth century, came over with William the Conqueror, are mentioned in Domesday and have held Chillington since 1178; bro of Baroness Airey of Abingdon; *see also* Bellew, Hon Patrick; *b* 20 May 1921; *Educ* Eton, ChCh Oxford; *m* 1949, Mary Roana, da of Ronald Gandar Dower (d 1963), of Old Park, Warninglid, Sussex; 1 s, 1 da; *Career* called to the Bar 1947; dir S Staffs Waterworks Co 1974, pres CLA 1983-85, chm Mercia Region Nat Trust 1979-89; pres: Staffordshire Soc 1979, European Landowners Orgn 1985-87; FRSA 1987; *Recreations* shooting, tree planting; *Clubs* Army & Navy, Boodle's, MCC; *Style—* Peter Giffard, Esq, DL; Chillington Hall, Codsall Wood, Wolverhampton (☎ 0902 850236)

GIFFARD, Sir (Charles) Sydney Rycroft; KCMG (1984, CMG 1976); s of Walter Giffard, JP (d 1970), of Gypsy Furlong, Lockeridge, Wilts, and Minna, *née* Cotton (d 1966); *b* 30 Oct 1926; *m* 1, 1951 (m dis 1976), Wendy, *née* Vidal; 1 s (Bererger b 1959), 1 da (Theresa b 1960); m 2, 1976, Hazel Roberts, OBE; *Career* joined Foreign Serv 1951; HM Ambass: Berne 1980-82, Tokyo 1984-86; *Style—* Sir Sydney Giffard, KCMG; Winkelbury House, Berwick St John, nr Shaftesbury, Dorset SP7 0EY

GIFFIN, Michael; s of John Metcalfe Giffin (d 1984); *b* 2 May 1935; *Educ* Sevenoaks Sch; *m* 1963, Jane Agnes, da of Col Howard Watson Wright (d 1974); 2 s, 1 da; *Career* md: St Olaf Bonding Co Ltd 1974-81, Hays Commercial Services Ltd 1985-89; chm: Hays Business Services Ltd 1981-89, Britdoc Ltd 1981-89; FCA; *Recreations* sailing; *Clubs* RAC, Medway Yacht; *Style—* Michael Giffin, Esq; Tussocks, 19 Burntwood Rd, Sevenoaks, Kent TN13 1PS (☎ 0732 451536)

GIFFORD, 6 Baron (UK 1824); Anthony Maurice Gifford; QC (1982); s of 5 Baron Gifford (d 1961), and (Ellice) Margaret, *née* Allen (d 1990); *b* 1 May 1940; *Educ* Winchester, King's Coll Cambridge; *m* 1, 22 March 1965 (m dis 1988), Katherine Ann, da of Max Mundy, of 52 Hornton St, Kensington; 1 s, 1 da (Hon Polly Anna b 1969); m 2, 24 Sept 1988, Elean Roslyn, da of Bishop David Thomas, of Kingston, Jamaica; *Heir* s, Hon Thomas Adam Gifford b 1 Dec 1967; *Career* sits as Lab Peer in Lords; barr 1962; chm: Ctee for Freedom Mozambique, Angola and Guiné 1968-75, N Kensington Law Centre 1974-77, Legal Action Gp 1978-81, Mozambique Angola Ctee 1984; vice-chm British Defence and Aid Fund 1985; chm: Broadwater Farm Inquiry 1986, Liverpool 8 Inquiry 1989; attorney at law Jamaica 1990; *Books* Where the Justice (1986); *Style—* The Lord Gifford, QC; 8 Kings Bench Walk, Temple, London EC4 (☎ 071 353 7851)

GIFFORD, Rev Prof Douglas John; TD; s of George Lawrence Gifford (d 1957), of Santiago de Chile, and Augusta Luisa, *née* Hammont (d 1965); *b* 21 July 1924; *Educ* Park Lodge Sch France, Wycliffe Coll, Queen's Coll Oxford (MA, BLitt); *m* 6 Sept 1947, Hazel Mary, da of Stanley Earnest Collingwood (d 1972), of Bristol; 4 s (Malcolm b 1948, Hugh b and d 1954, Roger b 1955, David b 1957), 1 da (Frances b 1950); *Career* War and Army Serv 1943-47, Intelligence Corps Normandy Landings 1944, TA Cameron Highlanders, cmd St Andrews OTC 1960-67, ret with rank of Lt-Col 1967; lectr Univ of St Andrews 1950 (sr lectr 1962, prof 1975-89); fndr Centre for Latin American Linguistic Studies 1968 (dir 1968-88); ordained: deacon 1980, priest 1981; univ chaplain Univ of St Andrews 1981-89, parish priest Argentina 1989-90; dir Renaissance Gp 1955-89, pres Assoc of Hispanists of GB and Ireland 1972-75, FSA 1986; France and Germany Star 1939-45, War Medal, Victory Medal; *Books* Textos Lingüísticos del Medioevo Espanol (with F Hodcroft, 2 edn 1966), A Study of Washing Habits in 4 Latin American Areas (1973), A Study of Foodlore in 4 Latin American Areas (1976), Carnival and Coca Leaf (with P Hoggarth, 1976), Gods Warriors and Spirits (1983); *Recreations* squash, music, golf; *Clubs* Athenaeum; *Style—* The Rev Prof Douglas Gifford, TD, FSA; 3 Balfour Place, St Andrews, Fife KY16 9RQ (☎ 0334 72742); Dept of Spanish, The University of St Andrews, Fif KY16 9AJ (☎ 0334 76161)

GIFFORD, Joshua Thomas (Josh); MBE (1989); s of Thomas H Gifford (d 1968), and Dinah Florence, *née* Newman (d 1981); *b* 3 Aug 1941; *Educ* Huntingdon C of E Sch, Eaglehurst Coll Northampton; *m* 1969, Althea Meryl, da of George Roger Smith; 1 s (Nicholas b 1971), 1 da (Kristina b 1970); *Career* national hunt trainer; flat racing jockey 1951-58; first ride for Mr Beechner at Newmarket 1951, 56 winners Sam Armstrong's stable 1952-58, winner HM the Queen's Ten Bells 1956; nat hunt jockey 1958-70; 700 winners Capt Ryan Price's stable, champion jockey 1962, 1963, 1967, 1968; nat hunt trainer 1970-; over 1175 winners incl: Grand Nat 1981 (Aldaniti), Hennessey Cognac Gold Cup, Whitbread Gold Cup, Tote Gold Trophy, SGB Chase Ascot, Black and White Whiskey; *Recreations* golf, shooting, cricket; *Clubs* Findon CC, Lords Taverners; *Style—* Josh Gifford, Esq, MBE; The Downs, Findon, West Sussex (☎ 0903 872226)

GIFFORD, Prof Paul Peerless-Denis; s of David Arthur Gifford, of 25 Grove Walk, Norwich, and Vera Rosina, *née* Palmer; *Educ* King Edward VI Norwich, Univ of Cambridge (MA), Univ of Toulouse (Lès, Dr 3 Cycle, Dés L); *m* 20 Sept 1969, (Irma) Cynthia Mary, da of Lt-Col AFS Warwick (d 1961); 1 s (Gregory b 27 May 1979), 2 da (Fiona b 20 Sept 1972, Joanne b 8 May 1975); *Career* Buchanan Chair of French Univ of St Andrews 1987; *Books* Valery - Le Dialogue des Choses Divines (1989); *Recreations* sailing, skiing, golf, tennis; *Style—* Prof Paul Gifford; 51 Radernie Place, St Andrews, Fife KY16 8QR (☎ 0334 77243); Buchanan Building, Department of French, Univ of St Andrews, St Andrews, Fife

GIFFORD, Zerbanoo; da of Bailey Irani, and Kitty Mazda; *b* 11 May 1950; *Educ* Roedean, Open Univ, Watford Coll of Technol, London Sch of Journalism; *m* 14 Sept 1973, Richard David Gifford, s of David Arthur Gifford, of Norwich; 2 s (Mark Mazda b 28 Aug 1975, Alexander Justice (Wags) b 27 Feb 1979); *Career* Lib cncllr Harrow 1982-86; Parly candidate (Lib Alliance): Hertsmere 1983, Harrow East 1987; chm: Lib Pty Community Rels Panel 1985, Cmmn into Ethnic Involvement 1986); memb Status of Women Cmmn 1987, fndr tstee The Urban Tst, co-chair Univ of Warwick Centre for Res Asian, Migration (1989), community affairs advsr to leader of Lib Democrats; ed Libas magazine, coloumnist Lib Democrat News; runner-up Special Interest Magazine Ed of the Year 1988; memb Advsy Cncl The Prince's Youth Business Tst; Freeman City of Lincoln Nebraska, Nehru Centenary Award from Non-Resident Indians Assoc 1989; Asian City Club Annual Award 1990; *Books* The Golden Thread (1990); *Recreations* collecting antique embroidery, dancing, sleeping next to phone; *Style—* Mrs Zerbanoo Gifford; Herga House, London Rd, Harrow on the Hill, Middlesex HA1 3JJ (☎ 081 422 8556)

GIGGALL, Rt Rev (George) Kenneth; OBE (1960); s of Arthur William Giggall (d 1959), and Matilda Hannah, *née* Granlese (d 1964); *b* 15 April 1914; *Educ* Manchester Central HS, Univ of Manchester (BA), St Chad's Coll Univ of Durham (Dip Theol); *Career* ordained deacon 1939, priest 1940; curate: St Alban's Cheetwood 1939-41, St Elisabeth's Reddish 1941-45; chaplain RNVR and RN: HMS Braganza 1945, 34 Amphibious Support Regt RM 1945-46, Sch of Combined Ops Fremington 1946-47, HMS Norfolk 1947-49, Ocean 1949- 50, Flotilla Cmd Med and HMS Phoenicia 1950-52, HMS Campania for Operation Hurricane 1952, BRNC Dartmouth 1952-53, HMS Centaur 1953-56, Ceylon 1956-58, Fisgard 1958-60, Royal Arthur and lectr RAF Chaplains' Sch 1960-63, HMS Eagle 1963-65, Drake 1965-69; QHC 1967-, dean of Gibraltar and officiating chaplain HMS Rooke and to Flag Offr Gibraltar 1969-73, Bishop St Helena 1973-79, consecrated St Saviours Church E London, Cape Province, RSA, chaplain San Remo with Bordighera 1979-81, Aux Bishop Diocese of Gibraltar (subsequently Europe) 1979-81, Asst Bishop Diocese of Blackburn 1982-; *Recreations* music; *Clubs* Commonwealth Soc, Sion Coll, Exiles (Ascension Island); *Style—* The Rt Rev Kenneth Giggall, OBE; Fosbrooke House, Clifton Drive, Lytham St Annes FY8 5RQ (☎ 0253 735 683)

GIGNOUX, Peter Alan; s of Frederick Evelyn Gignoux, Jr (d 1968); *b* 17 June 1945; *Educ* St Albans Sch, The Gunnery Sch, Boston Univ, Columbia Univ; *m* 26 Jan 1984, Katherine Elizabeth Phillips; *Career* London fndr and mangr Int Energy Desk; sr vice pres Shearson Lehman Brothers Inc; *Recreations* shooting, travelling, yacht cruising; *Clubs* Buck's, Mark's, Hurlingham, St Anthony (New York); *Style—* Peter Gignoux, Esq; 22 Woodfall St, Chelsea, London SW3 (☎ 071 730 4132); Shearson Lehman Brothers Inc, 1 Broadgate, London EC2M 7HA (☎ 071 601 0011)

GILBART-DENHAM, Lt-Col Seymour Vivian; s of Maj Vivian Vandeleur (d 1940), and Diana Mary, *née* Beaumont (d 1983); *b* 10 Oct 1939; *m* 1 April 1976, Patricia Caroline, da of Lt-Col Granville Brooking, of E Sussex; 2 da (Sophie b 1977, Georgina b 1980); *Career* cmmnd Life Gds 1960 (Adjutant 1965-67), cmd Household Cavalry Regt 1986-87, Crown Equerry 1987; *Recreations* riding, shooting, fishing, skiing; *Clubs* Cavalry and Guards; *Style—* Lt-Col Seymour Gilbart-Denham; The Royal Mews, Buckingham Palace, London SW1W 0QH (☎ 071 930 4832)

GILBART-SMITH, (Oliver) Denham; s of Oliver Brian Gilbart-Smith (d 1988), and Doris Florence, *née* Martin-Harvey; *b* 24 May 1947; *Educ* St Columbas Coll nr Dublin

Eire; *m* 1 Nov 1975, Lesley Anne, da of Michael Gordon Evans, of Devon; 3 s (Matthew b 1981, Luke b 1983, Adam b 1987), 1 da (Ruth b 1980); *Career* ptnr Geo H Fryer & Co Lloyd's Brokers 1968-71, Bryant and Shaw Lloyds Brokers 1971-74, self employed insur broker assoc with F Bolton & Co and Frizzell Gp 1974-86, md F Bolton & Co Marine Ltd 1987, fin conslt Cornerstone Investmt and Devpt 1990-; Freeman: City of London, Worshipful Co of Poulters; memb of Lloyds 1968-; *Recreations* swimming, travel; *Style—* Denham Gilbart-Smith, Esq; The Stables, Job's Lane, Cookham Dean, Berks; 103 Mallon Dene, Rustington, Sussex; Victoria House, Victoria Rd, Marlow, Bucks (☎ 0628 424014, fax 0628 890667)

GILBERT, David Richard; TD (and 3 clasps); s of Ernest Stanley Gilbert (d 1984), and Agnes Ena, *née* Doxey; *b* 10 Aug 1932; *Educ* Edward VI GS Retford, Sidney Sussex Coll Cambridge (MA, LLM); *m* 24 Sept 1960, Mary, da of late Wilfred Eden; 1 s (Christopher b 17 Jan 1963), 1 da (Catherine b 15 June 1965); *Career* Nat Serv cmmnd Intelligence Corps 1955, currently Lt-Col Intelligence Corps (TA), attached to COS' Secretariat MOD; called to the Bar Middle Temple 1957; ICI 1957-61, currently gp sec, memb Gp Exec and dir various admin subsid cos Hawker Siddeley Gp (joined 1961-); JP Maidenhead bench 1973-80, tstee E Berks Postgrad Med Tst, chm local recreational tst; memb Bar Assoc 1957, BACFI; *Recreations* golf, reading, opera; *Clubs* Royal Automobile; *Style—* David Gilbert, Esq, TD; Hawker Siddeley Group plc, 18 St James's Square, London SW1Y 4LJ (☎ 071 930 6177, fax 071 627 7597, telex 919011 HAWSID G)

GILBERT, Dennis; s of Gordon S Gilbert (d 1973), and Beatrice Maskell-Hall (d 1968); *b* 7 Jan 1922; *Educ* Lewisham Sch, SW Essex Tech Coll, St Martins Sch of Art (NDD); *m* 14 July 1949 (m dis 1976), Joan, da of Harold Musker, OBE, MC (d 1974); 3 s (Hugh b 1952, Michael b 1957, Joseph b 1963), 1 da (Mary b 1965); *Career* WWII Warrant Offr and Navigator 1942-46; lectr (visiting): Hammersmith Coll of Art 1950-65, Wimbledon Coll of Art 1954-60, Kingston Coll of Art 1958-65; lectr Hammersmith Coll of Art 1965-75, sr lectr Chelsea Sch of Art 1975-84; exhibitions incl: RA, Paris Salon, Royal Festival Hall, Royal Soc of Portrait Painters (annually 1959-81), Contemporary Portrait Soc, Royal Soc of Br Artists, Royal Inst of Oil Painters, New English Art Club (annually 1959-), Nat Soc of Painters (annually 1957-), Chelsea Art Soc, Ben Uri Gallery, Browse and Darby Gallery, Chenil Gallery, Redfern Gallery, Wildenstein Gallery, W H Patterson Fine Art, Phoenix Gallery, Southwell Brown Gallery; memb: New English Art Club, Soc of Landscape Painters, Comtemporary Portrait Soc (chm 1984-86), Nat Soc of Painters, Nine Elms Gp of Artists; *Clubs* Arts, Chelsea Arts; *Style—* Dennis Gilbert, Esq; Top Studio, 11 Edith Grove, London SW10 0JZ (☎ 071 352 9476)

GILBERT, Lt-Col Ernle Reginald Forester; s of Capt Humphrey Gilbert, of Bishopstone House, Bishopstone, Hereford; *b* 1 June 1921; *Educ* Marlborough, Staff Coll Camberley; *m* 1946, Helene Maria Margarete, da of Prof Dr Hans Reiter, of Graz, Austria; 1 da (Sybella); *Career* Reg Army Offr 1940-61, served N Africa, Italy, Greece, Palestine, Malaya; merchant banker; consultant: Save and Prosper 1966-70, Keyser Ullmann 1971-75; High Sheriff Herefordshire 1973-74; vice pres Herefordshire and Radnorshire Nature Trust; *Recreations* cricket, natural history, shooting, fishing; *Clubs* Army & Navy; *Style—* Lt-Col Ernle Gilbert; Bishopstone House, Bishopstone, Hereford HR4 7JG (☎ 098 122 277)

GILBERT, Dr Fiona Jane; da of Dr John Knight Davidson, OBE, of Glasgow, and Edith Elizabeth, *née* McKelvie; *b* 1 May 1956; *Educ* Hutchesons' Girls GS, Univ of Glasgow (MB ChB), Univ of Aberdeen (DMRD); *m* 4 June 1982, Martin James Gilbert, s of James Robert Gilbert, of Aberdeen; 1 s (Jamie b 1986), 1 da (Mhairi b 1989); *Career* conslt radiologist 1988-, dir NE Scotland Breast Screening Service; memb BMA 1978, MRCP 1981, FRCR 1986; *Recreations* sailing, skiing, squash, theatre, classical music; *Style—* Dr Fiona Gilbert; Balgranach, 269 North Deeside Rd, Milltimber, Aberdeen AB1 0HD (☎ 0224 733231); Department of Radiology, Aberdeen Royal Infirmary, Foresterhill, Aberdeen (☎ 0224 681818)

GILBERT, Francis Humphrey Shubrick; s of Cdr Walter Raleigh Gilbert (d 1977), of Compton Castle, S Devon, and Joan Mary Boileau, *née* Willock; *b* 25 Jan 1946; *Educ* Stowe, Trinity Coll Dublin (MA); *m* 19 April 1975, Sarah Marian, da of Col Douglas Kaye, DSO, DL of Brinkley Hall, nr Newmarket, Suffolk; 1 s (Raleigh b 28 Oct 1982), 2 da (Emma b 11 Nov 1976, Rosella b 15 Feb 1979); *Career* called to the Bar Lincoln's Inn 1970, asst rec; memb Devon CC 1977-85; *Recreations* sailing, shooting; *Clubs* Royal Yacht Sqdn, Royal Torbay Yacht; *Style—* Francis Gilbert, Esq; Dunley House, nr Bovey Tracey, South Devon TQ13 9PW (☎ 0626 833934); 15 Southernhay West, Exeter EX1 1PJ (☎ 0392 79751)

GILBERT, Maj-Gen Glyn Charles Anglim; CB (1974), MC (1944); s of C G G Gilbert, OBE, MC, and Marjory Helen Gilbert, MBE, of Bermuda; *b* 1920; *Educ* Eastbourne Coll, RMC Sandhurst; *m* 1943, Heather Mary, wid of Pilot Offr A E Jackson, DFM, and da of late F Green; 3 s, 1 da; *Career* served: NW Europe 1944-45, Palestine 1945-47, Cyprus 1951, Egypt 1951, Malaya 1955-56, Cyprus 1958-59, IDC 1966, Maj-Gen 1970, cmd 44 Para Bde Gp 1963-65, cmd Sch of Infantry 1967-70, GOC 3 Div 1970-72; cmd Jt Warfare Establishment 1972-74, ret 1974; dir: Riverside Holidays 1974-80, Fitness for Industry Ltd 1980-; chm The Airborne Initiative Holdings Ltd 1990; *Recreations* following the sun; *Clubs* Army & Navy, Royal Bermuda Yacht; *Style—* Maj-Gen Glyn Gilbert, CB, MC; c/o Lloyds Bank, Warminster, Wilts

GILBERT, Ian Grant; s of Capt Alexander Grant Gilbert, DCM (d 1943), and Marion Patrick, *née* Cruickshank (d 1963); *b* 18 June 1925; *Educ* Fordyce Acad Banffshire Scot, Royal HS of Edinburgh, Univ of Edinburgh (MA); *m* 1 July 1960, Heather Margaret, da of Rev Francis Cantlie Donald (d 1974), of Lumphanan, Scot; *Career* WWII 1943-47, RA; seconded to Indian Artillery (Capt): 10 Indian Field Regt 1944-45, Sch of Artillery Deolali India 1946-47; entered Home CS as asst princ Miny of Nat Insur 1950, private sec to Perm Sec (Sir Geoffrey S King, KCB) 1953, private sec to Parly Sec (Rt Hon Ernest Marples, MP) 1955, princ Miny of Pensions and Nat Insur 1956, princ HM Treas 1962-66, asst sec Miny of Soc Sec (later DHSS) 1966-, under sec Int Rels Div DHSS 1979-85, memb UK delegation to World Health Assembly Geneva 1979-84, clerk and advsr Select Ctee on Euro Legislation House of Commons 1987-90; session clerk Crown Ct Church of Scot Covent Gdn 1975-80, Church of Scot memb Churches Main Ctee 1986-; *Recreations* keeping half an acre, choral singing, local history; *Clubs* Royal Cwlth Soc London; *Style—* Ian Gilbert, Esq; Wellpark, Moorside, Sturminster Newton, Dorset DT10 1HJ (☎ 0258 820306)

GILBERT, (Cecil) James; s of Thomas C Gilbert (d 1959), of Edinburgh, and Mabel, (d 1945); *b* 15 May 1923; *Educ* Edinburgh Acad, Univ of Edinburgh, RADA; *m* 10 July 1951, Fiona, da of George Clyne (d 1972), Noss House, Wick, Caithness; 1 s (Colin b 3 April 1952), 2 da (Susan b 17 Nov 1953, Julia b 24 Nov 1962); *Career* composer and lyricist: Grab Me a Gondola (Lyric Theatre Shaftsbury Ave 1957), The Golden Touch (Picaddilly Theatre 1960), Good Time Johnny; prodr and dir BBC TV 1957-73; head: Comedy BBC TV 1973-77, Light Entertainment Gp BBC TV 1977-82, Comedy Thames TV 1982-88; exec prodr Thames TV 1988-; BAFTA awards 1960, 1967, 1973, winner Golden Rose Montreux and Int Emmy; *Books* Grab me a Gondola (1958); *Recreations* golf, walking, music, theatre; *Style—* James Gilbert, Esq; Thames TV, Broom Rd, Teddington, Middlx (☎ 081 977 3252)

GILBERT, Jane; da of William Richard Grice (d 1985), of Wolverhampton, and Louisa May, *née* Gibbons; *b* 18 March 1950; *Educ* Wolverhampton HS for Girls, Univ of Birmingham (BCom, Theodore Mander prize, Doris Griffiths prize); *m* 1, 1972 (dis 1976), Brian Arthur Gilbert; m 2, 27 May 1988, Brian Dennis Woods-Scawen, s of Dennis Charles Woods-Scawen; 1 step s (Tristan b 2 Dec 1978), 1 step da (Suzannah b 28 April 1977); *Career* Coopers & Lybrand Deloitte (formerly Cooper Brothers & Co, then Coopers & Lybrand): articled clerk 1971-74, seconded to Wolverhampton Met Borough Cncl 1982-83, ptnr 1983- (first female ptnr); dir Grand Theatre Wolverhampton 1982-87; Soroptimist International: memb Wolverhampton 1975-87 (pres 1983-84), memb Central Birmingham 1987-; memb Cncl Wolverhampton C of C 1982-87; *Recreations* theatre, music, literature, food; *Style—* Jane Gilbert; The Stables, Hunt Paddocks, Rouncil Lane, Kenilworth, Warwickshire CV8 1NL (☎ 0926 58225); Coopers & Lybrand Deloitte, 35 Newhall St, Birmingham B3 3DX (☎ 021 200 4000, fax 021 200 2829)

GILBERT, John Arthur; *b* 11 Aug 1932; *Educ* Kings Norton GS for Boys, Birmingham Coll of Technol (later Univ of Aston) (HNC, BSc); *m* 1, 19 Nov 1955, late Marion Audrey; 2 s (Simon Gerard b 11 April 1958, Andrew Boyd b 1 Jan 1960), 1 da (Rosamund Grace (Mrs Jackson), b 25 Feb 1964); m 2, 22 April 1983, Nicola Ann; *Career* trainee engr S Willis 1949, ptnr James-Carrington & Partners 1967-89 (assoc 1964-67); work incl: maj town redevelopment schemes, large retail stores, hosps, refurbishment of listed bldgs, developing on deep landfill sites; awarded Inst Civil Engrs George Stephenson medal for paper on maj Belfast project 1988; FICE 1961, FIStructE 1963, ACIArb 1979; *Style—* John A Gilbert, Esq; White Lodge, Bevere, Worcs WR3 7RQ (☎ 0905 51285); Gilbert Consulting, White Lodge, Bevere, Worcs WR3 7RQ (☎ 0905 755111, fax 0905 755112), and Birmingham (☎ 021 333 4036)

GILBERT, Rt Hon Dr John William; PC (1978), MP (Lab) Dudley East 1974-; *b* 5 April 1927; *Educ* Merchant Taylors', St John's Coll Oxford, New York Univ (PhD); *m* 1; 2 da; m 2, 1963, Jean Olive Ross Skinner; *Career* MP Dudley 1970-74, financial sec Treasury 1974-75, min for Transport DOE 1975-76, min state MOD 1976-79; *Style—* The Rt Hon Dr John Gilbert, MP; House of Commons, London SW1

GILBERT, Jonathan Sinclair; s of Brian Hamlyn Gilbert (d 1978), and Joan, *née* Sinclair; *b* 29 Sept 1937; *Educ* Bilton Grange Sch, Rugby; *m* 10 Aug 1962, Lene, da of Palle Palsby (d 1988); 3 s (Andrew b 12 Nov 1964, Nicholas (twin) b 12 Nov 1964, Peter b 22 July 1967); *Career* Nat Serv, Lt Kings Hussars 1955-57; bd dir Bland Payne Ltd 1968, dir Bland Payne Holdings Ltd 1978, chm Sedgwick Offshore Resources Ltd 1980, dir Sedgwick Group plc 1981-, dep chm Sedgwick Broking Services 1990-; memb Lloyds; *Recreations* golf; *Clubs* Burhill Golf, Royal St George's Golf, Lloyd's Golf, Lucifer Golfing Soc, MCC; *Style—* J S Gilbert, Esq; Nash House, 6 The Quillot, Burwood Park, Walton-on-Thames, Surrey KT12 5BY (☎ 0932 227 214); Sedwick House, The Sedgwick Centre, London E1 8DX (☎ 071 377 3153, fax 071 377 3199, telex 882 131)

GILBERT, Martin James; s of James Robert Gilbert, of Netherley House, Kincardinshire, Scotland, and Winifred, *née* Walker; *b* 13 July 1955; *Educ* Robert Gordons Coll, Univ of Aberdeen (MA, LLB); *m* 4 June 1982, Dr Fiona Jane Gilbert, da of Dr John K Davidson; 1 s (Jamie), 1 da (Mhairi); *Career* CA; Deliotte Haskins and Sells 1978-81, Brander and Cruickshank 1982-83, gp md Aberdeen Trust plc 1983-; non exec dir: Aberdeen Cable Servs Ltd, Abtrust New Thai Investment Trust plc, Abtrust Unit Trust Management Ltd, Abtrust Fund Managers Ltd, CGA plc, Abtrust Scotland Investment Co plc, Radiotrust plc; MICAS; *Recreations* golf, hockey, skiing, sailing; *Clubs* Royal Aberdeen Golf, Royal Selangor Golf, Gordonians HC; *Style—* Martin Gilbert, Esq; Balgranach, Milltimber, Aberdeen (☎ 0224 733231); Aberdeen Trust PLC, 10 Queens Terrace, Aberdeen AB9 1QJ (☎ 0224 631999)

GILBERT, Martin John; CBE (1990); s of Peter Gilbert (d 1976), of London, and Mirian, *née* Green; *b* 25 Oct 1936; *Educ* Highgate Sch, Magdalen Coll Oxford (MA), St, Antony's Coll Oxford; *m* 1, 1964 (m dis), Helen, da of Joseph Robinson, CBE; 1 da (Natalie b 1967); m 2, 1974, Susan, da of Michael Sacher; 2 s (David b 1978, Joshua b 1982); *Career* fell Merton Coll Oxford 1962-, official biographer of Sir Winston Churchill 1968-; books incl: British History Atlas (1968), American History Atlas (1968), First World War Atlas (1970), Winston S Churchill Vols 3-8 (1971-88), Sir Horace Rumbold, Portrait of a Diplomat (1973), Atlas of the Holocaust (1986), The Holocaust, The Jewish Tragedy (1986), Second World War (1989), Churchill: A Life (1991); FRSL; *Recreations* drawing maps; *Clubs* Athenaeum; *Style—* Martin Gilbert, Esq, CBE

GILBERT, Michael Francis; CBE (1980), TD (1950); s of Bernard Samuel Gilbert (d 1927), and Berwyn Minna, *née* Cuthbert (d 1966); *b* 17 July 1912; *Educ* Blundell's, Univ of London (LLB); *m* 26 July 1947, Roberta Mary, da of late Col R M W Marsden; 2 s (Richard b 1956, Gerard b 1960), 5 da (Harriett b 1948, Victoria b 1950, Olivia b 1952, Kate b 1954, Laura b 1958); *Career* WWII HAC (Maj) served N Africa, Italy 1939-45 (despatches 1943); ptnr Trower, Still & Keeling 1952-83 (slr 1947), legal advsr to Ruler of Bahrain 1960; memb: Royal Literary Fund Ctee 1964, Cncl Soc of Authors 1975; pres Luddesdown Cricket Club 1965; *Books* author of: 24 novels of detection and suspense, over 200 short stories, 4 stage plays, various critical articles; ed of 2 anthologies; *Recreations* walking; *Clubs* Garrick; *Style—* Michael Gilbert, Esq, CBE, TD; The Old Rectory, Luddesdown, Gravesend, Kent DA13 0XE (☎ 0474 814272)

GILBERT, Patrick Nigel Geoffrey; s of Geoffrey Thomas Gilbert (d 1968), of Paignton, Devon, and Gertrude Evelyn, *née* Miller (d 1949); *b* 12 May 1934; *Educ* Cranleigh Sch, Merton Coll Oxford; *Career* Nat Serv 1952-54; lectr in further educn South Berks Coll 1959-62, PA to Sir Edward Hulton 1962-64, Oxford Univ Press 1964-69, md Linguaphone Group of Westinghouse 1969-71, gen sec Soc for Promoting Christian knowledge 1971-, dir Surrey Building Society 1988-; involvement with the arts incl: steward Artists' Gen Benevolent Inst 1971-, fndr chm Nat Assoc of Local Arts Cncl 1976-80, chm Gtr London Arts Assoc 1980-84 (fndr memb 1966, exec 1968-78, initiator 1972 festivals of London, hon life memb 1978, dep chm 1979-80), chm Concord Multicultural Arts Tst 1980-89; govr Contemporary Dance Tst 1981-90 (memb Fin Ctee 1983-90), chm Dancers Resettlement Tst 1987-90, memb Bd Nat Youth Dance 1988-; vice chm St Martin-in-the-Fields Sch 1978-; governorships incl: Ellesmere Coll Shrops 1977-87 (memb Fin Ctee 1979-87), Roehampton Inst of Higher Educn 1978- (chm Audit Ctee 1989-), St Michael's Sch Petworth 1978-88, Pusey House Oxford 1985-; memb Ct City Univ 1987-; involvement with the church incl: tstee Richards Tst 1971-, memb Governing Body SPCK Aust 1977-, memb Bd SPCK USA 1983-, chm Nikaean Club 1984-, memb Governing Body SPCK NZ 1989-; tstee: All Saints Tst, Woodard Corp; memb: Appeal Ctee Br Sch of Osteopathy 1982-85, Ctee London Europe Soc 1985-, Cncl The Publishers Assoc 1990-, chm Embroideres Guild 1977-78 (hon treas 1974-77), chm tstees and hon treas The Art Workers Guild 1976-86; Freeman: City of London, City of Savannah; Liveryman Worshipful Co of Woolmen 1966 (master 1985-86); Lord of the Manor Cantley Netherhall, parish clerk All Hallows Bread Street 1981-; Hon DLitt Columbia Pacific Univ 1982; FRSA 1978, FBIM 1982, FInstD 1982; Order of St Vladimir USSR 1977; *Recreations* reading, walking, golf, enjoying the arts; *Clubs* Athenaeum (chm of exec 1985-89), City Livery, Walton Heath Golf; *Style—* Patrick Gilbert, Esq; 3 The Mount Sq, London NW3 6SU

(☎ 071 794 8807); SPCK, Holy Trinity Church, Marylebone Rd, London NW1 4DU (☎ 071 387 5282, fax 01 388 2352)

GILBERT, Paul Jonathan; s of John Bernard Gilbert, of Dordon, North Warks, and Eileen Mary, *née* Brown; *b* 24 June 1954; *Educ* Queen Elizabeth GS Tamworth Staffs, Birmingham Poly; *m* 22 March 1977, Christine Ann, da of Arthur Lacey; 3 c (Matthew John b 6 July 1982, James Paul b 4 March 1985, Catherine Ann b 8 Sept 1968); *Career* ptnr Burman & Co Chartered Accountants Birmingham 1980-87 (articled clerk 1972-77), fin dir GG (Holdings) Ltd 1987-; FCA 1983 (ACA 1977); *Recreations* golf, ten pin bowling; *Clubs* Seedy Mill Golf (Lichfield); *Style—* Paul Gilbert, Esq; G G (Holdings) Ltd, Wishbone House, Bradford St, Birmingham B12 ONS (☎ 021 773 0181, fax 021 772 6215, car 0836 784537)

GILBERT, Richard Simon; s of Nigel John Gilbert, of 2 Seafields, Emsworth, Hants, and Mair, *née* James; *b* 1 Nov 1957; *Educ* Sevenoaks Sch Kent, Falmouth Sch of Art (BA), Wimbledon Sch of Art (BA), Chelsea Sch of Art (MA), Br Sch in Rome (Abbey Major scholar in painting), Sch of the Art Inst of Chicago (Harkness fell); *Career* self-employed fine artist and pt/t teacher 1985-; solo exhibitions: Recent Work (Main Gallery Warwick Arts Trust London) 1986, Recent Work (Raab Gallery London) 1988; gp exhibitions incl: Wet Paint (Festival Gallery Bath) 1984, CAS Market (Smiths Gallery London) 1984-87 and 1990, John Moores Fourteenth Nat Exhibition (Walker Art Gallery Liverpool) 1985, Forty European Artists (Raab Gallery) 1986, Athena Arts awards (Barbican) 1987, Art for the City (Lloyds Building London) 1987, Fellowship Exhibition (Sch of Art, Inst of Chicago) 1989, The Landscape and the Cityscape (Raab Gallery London) 1990, Rome scholars 1980-90 (Gulbenkian Gallery RCA London) 1990, The Discerning Eye (Mall Gallery London) 1990; work in the collections of: Contemporary Art Soc, Victoria Art Gallery Melbourne Arthur Anderson plc, Barclays Bank plc, Business Design Centre and in private collections; Barclays Postgrad Painting award 1984; *Style—* Richard Gilbert, Esq; Acme Studios, 105 Carpenters Rd, London E15 2DU; Raab Gallery, 6 Vauxhall Bridge Rd, London SW1 2SD (☎ 071 828 2588, fax 071 976 5041)

GILBERT, Stuart William; CB (1983); s of Rodney Stuart Gilbert (d 1978), and Ella Edith, *née* Esgate; *b* 2 Aug 1926; *Educ* Maidstone GS, Emmanuel Coll Cambridge (MA); *m* 1955, Marjorie Laws, da of Stanley Aloysius Vallance (d 1975); 1 s, 1 da; *Career* served WWII Sgt RAF, India, Burma; civil servant; dep sec and dir Dept for Nat Savings 1981-86; tstee Bldg Conservation Tst 1987-, treas Bromley Branch Univ of 3 Age 1989-; *Recreations* sailing, music, electronics, painting, woodwork; *Clubs* Oxford and Cambridge, Bewl Valley Sailing; *Style—* Stuart Gilbert, Esq, CB; 3 Westmoat Close, Beckenham, Kent BR3 2BX (☎ 081 650 7213)

GILBERTSON, Arthur Geoffrey; JP (Glam 1959); s of Charles Geoffrey Gilbertson (d 1963), of Gellygron, Pontardawe; *b* 18 May 1913; *Educ* Shrewsbury; *m* 1937, Hilarie Annette, da of Hubert S Williams-Thomas, of Stourbridge; 3 da (Phebe, Ruth, Diana); *Career* md Brown Lenox & Co of Pontypridd 1949-71, dir Royal Brierley Crystal 1965-82; High Sheriff Glamorgan 1970-71; memb Western Railway Bd 1963-77, pres S Glamorgan Br Red Cross Soc 1974-81, chm Vale of Glamorgan Magistrates 1981, former hon sec Llandaff Diocesan Conference; former memb: Cncl St David's Univ Coll Lampeter, Cncl for Wales and Monmouthside 1958-67, Governing and Rep Body and Electoral Coll of The Church in Wales; CStJ; *Recreations* cricket, fishing, shooting, gardening; *Clubs* MCC; *Style—* Arthur Gilbertson, Esq, JP; Castle Cottage, Llanblethian, Cowbridge, S Glamorgan (☎ 044 677 2809)

GILBERTSON, David Stuart; s of Donald Stuart Gilbertson, and Jocelyn Mary, *née* Sim; *b* 21 Sept 1956; *Educ* Birkenhead Sch Merseyside, Trinity Hall Cambridge (MA); *Career* corr Reuters 1980-81, ed Metal Bulletin 1981-87, ed Lloyds List 1987-; NUJ; *Style—* David Gilbertson, Esq

GILBERTSON, (Cecil) Edward Mark; s of Francis Mark Gilbertson, of Ham, Hungerford, Wilts, and Elizabeth Margaret, *née* Dawson; *b* 2 June 1949; *Educ* Eton; *m* 1, May 1975 (m dis 1980), Astrid Jane, da of late Lt Col Vaughan; m 2, 3 Sept 1986, Nicola Leslie Bellairs, yr da of Maj J A B Lloyd Philipps (d 1974), of Dale Castle, Dale, Dyfed; 1 da (Georgina Charlotte Bellairs b 29 Oct 1987), 1 s (Harry Edward Bellairs b 20 Feb 1990); *Career* memb Stock Exchange 1976, dir Bell Lawrie White & Co Ltd 1990; *Recreations* cricket, shooting, squash, tennis; *Clubs* MCC, Cardiff and County, Royal Porthcawl Golf; *Style—* Edward Gilbertson, Esq; Cathedine Hill, Bwlch, Nr Brecon, Powys; Llangwarren Estate, Letterston, Dyfed SA62 5UL

GILBEY, Anthony James; s of Quintin Holland Gilbey (d 1979), of 19 Chelsea Lodge, Tite St, London SW3, and Rosemary Marguerite, *née* Hope-Vere (d 1990); *b* 2 April 1933; *Educ* Repton, Ecole des Roches, ChCh Oxford; *m* 1, 1958 (m dis 1971) Lenore, *née* Shatton; 2 s (Dennis b 1959, Paul b 1964), 1 da (Emma b 1961); m 2, 1981 (m dis 1984), Rena, *née* Ungley; m 3, 27 Sept 1984, Lady Penelope Ann Rous, da of Earl of Stradbroke (d 1983), of Henham, Wangford, Beccles, Suffolk; *Career* 2 Lt Grenadier Guards 1951; reporter Newcastle Chronicle and Newcastle Journal 1954-56, Paris correspondent Sunday Dispatch 1957-59, diarist Daily Telegraph 1959-60, Daily Sketch 1960-64 (NY correspondent 1962-64), dir Library of Imp History 1970-75, chm Gilbey Collections 1975-; *Books* Champion Racehorses (ed, 1974), Champion Racehorses (ed, 1975); *Recreations* horseracing; *Clubs* Buck's, Jockey Club Rooms, White's, MCC; *Style—* Anthony Gilbey, Esq; 13a St Loo Court, London SW3 5TJ (☎ 071 351 1072; White Lion House, Wangford, Beccles, Suffolk WR3G 8RL (☎ 050 278 464); Gilbey Collections Ltd, White Lion Court, Wangford, Beccles, Suffolk (☎ 050 278 416, fax 0986 873555)

GILBEY, Hon Anthony William; s and h of 10 Baron Vaux of Harrowden, by his 1 cous Maureen Gilbey; *b* 25 May 1940; *Educ* Ampleforth; *m* 4 July 1964, Beverley, o da of Charles Alexander Walton, of Cooden, Sussex; 2 s (Richard b 1965, Philip b 1967), 2 da (Victoria b 1969, Elizabeth b 1989); *Career* accountant, farmer; *Recreations* politics, fishing, shooting; *Style—* Hon Anthony Gilbey; Rusko, Gatehouse of Fleet, Kirkcudbrightshire

GILBEY, Sir (Walter) Derek; 3 Bt (UK 1893); s of Walter Ewart Gilbey (d 1941), and Alice Dora, *née* Sim (d 1961); suc gf, Sir (Henry) Walter Gilbey, 2 Bt, 1945; *b* 11 March 1913; *Educ* Eton; *m* 1948, Elizabeth Mary, da of Col Keith Gordon Campbell, DSO, of Standen House, Newport, Isle of Wight; 1 s, 1 da (Camilla Elizabeth b 1953); *Heir* s, (Walter) Gavin Gilbey; *Career* Lt Black Watch 1940-45; export dir W & A Gilbey Ltd to 1970; *Style—* Sir Derek Gilbey, Bt; Grovelands, Wineham, nr Henfield, West Sussex (☎ 044 482 311)

GILBEY, (Walter) Gavin; s and h of Sir Derek Gilbey, 3 Bt; *b* 14 April 1949; *Educ* Eton; *m* 1, 1980 (m dis 1984), Mary, da of late William E E Pacetti, of Florida, USA; m 2, 1984, Anna, da of Edmund Prosser, of Cheshire; *Style—* Gavin Gilbey, Esq; 8201 SW 115 Street, Miami, Fla 33156, USA

GILBEY, Mark Newman; s of Henry Newman Gilbey (d 1956; s of Newman Gilbey, JP, who was both n of Sir Walter Gilbey, 1 Bt, and great unc of 9 and 10 Barons Vaux of Harrowden), and his 1 wife Myn Beatrice, *née* Brunwin (d 1936); *b* 21 Nov 1923; *Educ* Beaumont, Trinity Coll Cambridge; *Career* Capt Gren Gds 1942-47; fndr and former chm Duncan Gilbey & Matheson Gp of Cos; hon consul of Ecuador to Morocco 1967-; *Recreations* travel, reading, antique and picture collecting; *Clubs* Boodle's, Buck's; *Style—* Mark Gilbey, Esq; Ile de Gorée, Dakar, Senegal (☎ 216966); Dar el Bab, Casbah, Tangier, Morocco (☎ 932942)

GILBEY, Hon Mary Agnes Margaret; da of Baroness Vaux of Harrowden (d 1958); *b* 13 April 1928; *Style—* Hon Mary Gilbey; Glenmore House, Orlingbury Road, Gt Harrowden, Wellingborough, Northants

GILBEY, Hon Michael Christopher; 3 s of 10 Baron Vaux of Harrowden, and Maureen, nee Gilbey (a 1 cous, da of Hugh Gilbey, yr bro of William Gilbey who m Baroness Vaux of Harrowden, m of 9 and 10 Barons); *b* 29 Dec 1949; *Educ* Ampleforth, St Andrews Univ (MA); *m* 1971, Linda, da of Arthur Sebastian Gilbey (d 1964, ggs of Sir Walter Gilbey, 1 Bt) and his 3 cous once removed; 3 s (Henry b 1973, Julian b 1975, William b 1979); *Career* chartered surveyor 1974-; dir: The Eton Wine Bar 1975-, M & W Gilbey Ltd (Wine Merchants) 1981-; *Recreations* tennis, golf, sailing; *Style—* Hon Michael Gilbey; Red Hatch, Harpsden Woods, Henley-on-Thames, Oxon RG9 4AF (☎ 0491 573202); (☎ office 0491 579104, telex 846565 GILBEY)

GILBEY, Lady Penelope Anne; *née* Rous; yr da of 4 Earl of Stradbroke (d 1983); *b* 31 July 1932; *m* 1, 19 June 1950 (m dis 1960), Cdr Ian Dudley Stewart Forbes, DSC, RN, s of late Lt-Col James Stewart Forbes (gs of late Sir Charles Forbes, 3 Bt) by his 2 w, Feridah; 1 s (Charles b 1956), 2 da (Catriona, m 1981 Michael Bradley; 1 s, 2 da; Caroline, photographer, m 1977 (m dis 1982) Katsuhisa Sakai, of Tokyo, Japan, 1 s); m 2, 15 May 1961 (m dis 1969), John Cator, s of late Col Henry Cator, MC, JP, DL, of Woodbastwick Hall, Norfolk; m 3, 27 Sept 1984, as his 3 w, Anthony James Gilbey, s of Quintin Holland Gilbey, gn of Sir Walter Gilbey, 1 Bt; *Career* dir: David Carritt Ltd (picture gallery) 1972-82, Artemis Fine Arts UK Ltd (art dealers) 1972-82, Gilbey Collections Ltd 1983-; *Style—* The Lady Penelope Gilbey; White Lion House, Wangford, Beccles, Suffolk NR34 8RL

GILBEY, Walter Anthony; MHK (Glenfaba IOM 1982-); s of Sir Henry Walter Gilbey, 2 Bt, JP (d 1945), of Portman Sq, London W1, and his 2 w Marion, *née* Robert; half-bro of Sir Derek Gilbey, 3 Bt; *b* 26 Feb 1935,as Anthony Walter, names reversed by Deed Poll 1955; *Educ* Eton; *m* 2 April 1964, Jenifer Mary, eldest da of Capt James Timothy Noël Price, of Brookfield, Ramsey, IOM, and his w, Hon Anne Younger, yr da of 2 Viscount Younger of Leckie; 1 s (Walter Anthony b 20 Jan 1966), 2 da (Caroline Anne b 2 Oct 1967, Sarah Elizabeth b 3 Nov 1969); *Career* merchant banker with Kleinwort Benson Ltd London 1954-62; fin dir Gilbeys Ltd (int distillers and vintners) 1962-72; chm: Mannin Tst Bank Ltd IOM 1972-82, Mannin Int Ltd IOM 1982-88; dir and chm Vannin Int Securities Ltd IOM 1972-, dir IOM Steam Packet Co Ltd 1976-, chm Mannin Industries Ltd IOM 1972-, dir Gilbey Farms Ltd IOM 1974-, ptnr Gilbey Grianagh Horses IOM 1978-, chm Manx Telecom Ltd 1986-; chm Cons Pty Candidate for Ealing Southall 1971-74, Civil Service Cmmn and Whitley Cncl IOM 1985-90, memb Dept of Local Govt and the Environment IOM 1987-90, chm Planning Ctee Dept of Local Govt IOM 1987-90, memb Dept of Highways Ports and Properties IOM 1990-, chm London Harness Horse Parade 1985-, chm gp of almshouses; Sr Master IOM Bloodhounds, sec Manx Horse Cncl; memb: Euro Atlantic Gp, Euro League for Econ Co-operation, Coaching Club, Br Driving Soc, Br Horse Soc, Shire Horse Soc, Masters of Drag Hounds Assoc; memb Berkshire CC 1966-74; memb Vintners' Co; *Recreations* horses, riding, driving; *Style—* Walter Gilbey, Esq, MHK; Ballacallin Mooar, Crosby, Marown, IOM (☎ 0624 851450, fax 0624 852852)

GILBEY, Hon William John; s of 10 Baron Vaux of Harrowden; *b* 24 Feb 1944; *Educ* Ampleforth; *m* 1971, Caroline Susan, da of Alan Ball, of Ramsbury, Wilts; 2 s (Thomas, James), 1 da (Charlotte); *Career* dir M & W Gilbey Ltd; *Recreations* golf, tennis, fishing, sailing, photography; *Style—* The Hon William Gilbey; The Grange, Waltham St Lawrence, Twyford, Berks RG10 0JJ

GILBODY, (Bryan) Martin; s of Thomas Gilbody (d 1985), of Norwich, and Iris Mary, *née* Bryan; *b* 5 Feb 1947; *Educ* Hawarden GS, Nottingham Coll of Educn; *m* 29 Dec 1971, Pamela Ann, da of Raphe Stuart Davies; 2 s (Oliver Bryan b 14 Dec 1976, Tristan Bryan 10 June 1980); *Career* hockey manager; player: South Nottingham Hockey Club 1969- (capt 1972-84), 162 appearances Nottinghamshire 1971-86, Midlands indoor squad 1976-84 (also capt, coach, mangr), Wales under 23 cap 1970, memb Wales sr squad 1977-78; mangr: Wales under 21 indoor 1981-89, Wales under 21 outdoor 1986-89, Wales sr indoor 1984-, Wales sr outdoor 1988-; asst teacher Alderman White Sch Nottingham 1970-74, head of modern languages Wilford Meadows Sch Nottingham 1974-87; gen mangr: EMS International Ltd 1988-90, EMS Signs Ltd 1990- (contract mangr 1987-88); *Recreations* golf, squash; *Style—* Martin Gilbody, Esq; EMS Signs Ltd, The Midway, Nottingham (☎ 0602 860860, fax 0602 860861)

GILCHRIST, Sir Andrew Graham; KCMG (1964, CMG 1956); eldest s of James Graham Gilchrist (d 1945), of Kerse, Lesmahagow, Lanarkshire; *b* 19 April 1910; *Educ* Edinburgh Acad, Exeter Coll Oxford; *m* 1946, Freda Grace (d 1987), da of Alfred George Slack (d 1947), of London; 2 s, 1 da; *Career* served Force 136 (India, Burma and Siam, despatches) 1944-46, Maj; Consular Service Siam 1933, first sec Bangkok 1946, consul-gen Stuttgart 1951-54, cnsllr Office of UK Cmmr-Gen in S E Asia 1954-56; ambass: Iceland 1956-60, Indonesia 1963-66, Republic of Ireland 1966-70; chm Highlands and Islands Devpt Bd 1970-76; *Books* Bangkok Top Secret (1970), Cod Wars and How to Lose Them (1979), The Russian Professor (1984), The Watercress File (1985), The Ultimate Hostage (1986), South of Three Pagodas (1987), Death of an Admiral (1989); *Recreations* outdoor, opera; *Clubs* Special Forces, New (Edinburgh); *Style—* Sir Andrew Gilchrist, KCMG; Arthur's Crag, Hazelbank, by Lanark ML11 9XL (☎ 055 586 263)

GILCHRIST, Archibald; s of James Gilchrist (d 1972); *b* 17 Dec 1929; *Educ* Loretto Sch, Pembroke Coll Cambridge (MA); *m* 1958, Elizabeth Jean, da of Robert Cumming Greenlees (d 1983); 2 s, 1 da; *Career* Capt Glasgow Yeomanry (TA); engr and shipbuilder, md Vosper Private Ltd Singapore 1980-, dir (non exec) Vosper plc; *Recreations* golf, reading, music; *Clubs* Hon Co of Edinburgh Golfers, Western (Glasgow); *Style—* Archibald Gilchrist, Esq; 19 Victoria Park Rd, Singapore (☎ 010 65 4662354); Vosper Private Ltd, PO Box 95 Maxwell Rd, Singapore 9001

GILCHRIST, Clive Mace; s of John Llewellyn Gilchrist (d 1984), and Ida, *née* Mace; *b* 27 Sept 1950; *Educ* LSE Univ of London (BSc); *m* 21 July 1979, Angela Rosemary, da of Roger Watson Hagger; 2 da (Philippa Jane (Pippa) b 1984, Julia Joy b 1986); *Career* stockbroker; J & A Scrimgeour & Co 1972-75, Joseph Sebag & Co 1975-78; dep dir of investmt Postel Investments Ltd 1978-87, dir Argosy Asset Management plc (formerly MN Investment Management Ltd) 1987-; Nat Assoc of Pension Funds: chm Investment ctee 1990 (vice chm 1988-90), vice chm Cncl 1990 (memb 1988-); AMSIA 1979; *Recreations* gardening, music, travel; *Style—* Clive Gilchrist, Esq; Gallinar, Pilgrims Close, Westhumble, Dorking, Surrey; 30 Finsbury Circus, London EC2M 7QQ (☎ 071 588 6000, fax 071 588 1224, telex 888607)

GILCHRIST, Graeme Elder; TD; s of Sir (James) Finlay Elder Gilchrist, OBE (d 1987), of South Cottage, Hapstead Farm, Ardingly, Sussex, and (Dorothy) Joan, *née* Narizzano (d 1986); *b* 4 Dec 1934; *Educ* Sherborne, Queens' Coll Cambridge (MA); *m* 2 April 1981, Susie Elizabeth, da of Douglas William Fenwick, of Bluebell Cottage, The Croft, Lodsworth, W Sussex; 1 s (Thomas William Elder b 1982); *Career* Lt RA 1953-55, Col HAC 1971-73, hon Col RA 1973-75; mangr Baring Bros 1963-71, md and dep chm Union Discount Co of London 1971-; Freeman of Cities of London and Glasgow; hon fell City Univ; *Recreations* tennis, golf, music; *Clubs* HAC, Brooks's, MCC; *Style—* Graeme Gilchrist, Esq, TD; 50 Holmbush Road, Putney, London SW15 3LE (☎ 081 788 1667); 39 Cornhill, London EC3V 3NV (☎ 071 623 1020)

GILCHRIST, Raymond King; DL (Northumberland); s of Robert Gilchrist (d 1981), of 6 Howick Terrace, Tweedmouth, Berwick-upon-Tweed, and Mary, *née* Ray (d 1975); *b* 7 May 1922; *Educ* Berwick-upon-Tweed Co Schs; *m* 18 Sept 1950, Olive May, da of Charles Edward Dixon (d 1974); 1 s (David Robert b 1962), 1 da (Susan King b 1957); *Career* PT Instr RAF 1942, Sgt 1943, WO 1945; gen mangr Tweedside Co-op Soc 1968, div mangr N Northumberland NE Co-op Soc 1971 (sales mangr 1976-); memb Berwick Borough Cncl 1964- (Mayor 1983-84), vice chm Northumberland CC 1984- (chm 1987-88) memb Northumberland: Health Authy, Family Practioners Tstees, Salmon Queen Ctee; pres Old Peoples Organisations, chm of First Schs; *Style—* Raymond Gilchrist, Esq, DL; 17 Highcliffe, Spittal, Berwick-upon-Tweed, Northumberland (☎ 0280 206787)

GILCHRIST, Roderick Munn Renshaw; s of Ronald Renshaw Gilchrist (d 30 June 1971), and Vera, *née* Ashworth; *b* 6 Dec 1934; *Educ* Mill Hill Sch; *m* 19 March 1959, Patricia Frances, da of late Robert Charles Durrant; 2 s (Adam Munn Renshaw b 1959, Luke Ronald Renshaw b 1965); *Career* slr of Supreme Ct of England and Wales, Cmmr for Oaths, former princ of Bennett and Gilchrist Guildford, ptnr Renshaw Gilchrist Slrs Fleetwood and Garstang; life govr Imperial Cancer Res Fund 1978, tstee and clerk to the tstees W H King Alms Houses Garstang 1982-; FSA (Scot); *Recreations* hunting (beagle hounds), heraldry, celtic mythology; *Clubs* Old Millhillians; *Style—* Roderick Gilchrist, Esq; Sion Hill, Garstang PR3 1ZB (☎ 0995 602 389); 9 St Peters Place, Fleetwood FY7 6ED (☎ 03915 3569)

GILDER, Eric George; s of David Richard Gilder (d 1971), of Westcliffe-on-Sea, and Minnie, *née* Walman (d 1974); *Educ* Henry Thornton Sch, RCM; *m* 23 Dec 1939, Jessica Lilian, da of Walter Clay (d 1946), of Hitchin, Herts; 2 da (Heather Melody b 1945, Paula June b 1949); *Career* RA 1939-45; composer; over 1000 broadcasts as: author, composer, pianist, conductor, choir master, actor; composer symphonic works and lyrics and musicals, princ of own sch of music 1959-87, author critical essays in periodicals; memb: Royal Music Soc 1965, Composers Guild 1966; *Books* Dictionary of Composers (1985); *Recreations* gardening; *Style—* Eric Gilder, Esq; 21 Fieldend, Strawberry Hill, Twickenham TW1 4TF (☎ 081 892 0742)

GILES, Prof Anthony Kent (Tony); s of Harry Giles (d 1967), of Rochester, Kent, and Eva Gertrude, *née* Kent (d 1972); *b* 30 June 1928; *Educ* Sir Joseph Williamson's Mathematical Sch Rochester, Queen's Univ of Belfast (BSc); *m* 1, 2 Jan 1954 (m dis 1985), Helen Elizabeth Margaret, da of J Charles Eaton (d 1968), of Londonderry; 1 s (John b 1960), 3 da (Ann b 1954, Amanda b 1957, Alison b 1963); m 2, 6 Aug 1987, Heather Constance, da of Frank HJ Pearce (d 1987), of Durban SA; 1 step s (Sean Hewson b 1971), 1 step da (Linda Hewson b 1975); *Career* PO personnel section RAF 1947-49; asst agric economist Univ of Bristol 1953-59; Univ of Reading: lectr 1960-70, sr lectr 1970-83, prof farm mgmnt 1983-, chm Sch Applied Mgmnt Studies 1986-, dir Farm Mgmnt Unit 1979-; chm UK Farm Business Survey Ctee 1975-; active in Samaritans 1972-82 (dir Reading Branch 1978-80); nat chm Centre Mgmnt in Agric 1987-89, pres Agric Econ Soc 1988, memb Int Soc Agric Economists 1964-67 (UK country rep 1973-87); FBIM 1989; *Books* The Farmer as Manager (1980), Agricultural Economics 1923-73, The Manager's Environment; *Recreations* watching sport (rugby and cricket), aviation, collecting books (especially early Penguins), allotment; *Clubs* Clifton Rugby Football; *Style—* Prof Tony Giles; The Cottage, 63 Northumberland Ave, Reading, Berks RG2 7PS (☎ 0734 752763); Department of Agricultural Economics and Management, University of Reading, Earley Gate, Whiteknights, Reading, Berks (☎ 0734 875123)

GILES, Brian John; s of Alfred Giles (d 1984) of Kent, and Constance, *née* Barndon; *b* 22 Sept 1941; *Educ* Westlands Sittingbourne Kent; *m* 23 Feb 1963, Shirley Jennifer; 2 da (Sarah Louise b 24 June 1965, Philippa Clare b 30 April 1969); *Career* apprentice jockey Fairlawne Racing Stables 1958-62, ed Chaseform Raceform 1963-66, equestrian corr Daily Mail 1967 (racing ed 1987-); memb Sports Writers Assoc; *Awards* Horse Trials Gp award of the Year for Servs to Sport 1990; *Books* How to Win on the Flat, Twenty-Five Years in Showjumping a Biography of David Broome, So You Think You Know About Horses, Behind The Stable Door, SR Direct Mail Book of Eventing (jtly with Alan Smith); *Recreations* golf, reading, classical music; *Style—* Brian Giles, Esq; Daily Mail, Northcliffe House, Derry St, Kensington, London W8 (☎ 071 938 6203)

GILES, Christopher Henry; s of Gp Capt Henry Giles (d 1986), and Yvonne Molly, *née* Wiseman; *b* 7 Oct 1943; *Educ* Harrow Tech Coll; *m* 12 Oct 1962, Ann Margaret, *née* Hornsby; 1 s (Henry b 1963), 1 da (Emma b 1966); *Career* licenced conveyancer financier and property developer in private practice; memb Brighton Borough Cncl 1983-90; Liveryman City of London, memb Worshipful Co of Loriners; memb FIMBRA 1988; *Clubs* Reform, Hove, Sussex Motor Yacht; *Style—* Christopher Giles, Esq; 8 Wykeham Terrace, Brighton BN1 3FF (☎ 0273 29372); 1 Sydney Street, Brighton BN1 4EN (☎ 0273 603605, fax 0273 603488)

GILES, (John) David William; s of Herbert Giles (d 1965), of Shipley, Yorkshire, and Louise, *née* Proctor (d 1947); *b* 18 Oct 1926; *Educ* Bingley GS, The Northern Theatre Sch; *Career* dir RADA under John Fernald, various regnl repertory cos, trained by BBC 1963; dir: Compact, The Newcomers, The Flying Swan in early carer; TV dir: The Forsyte Saga (BBC) 1967, Vanity Fair (BBC) 1968, Resurrection (BBC) 1969, The First Churchills (BBC) 1970, Sense And Sensibility (BBC) 1971, Thursdays Child (Granada) 1971, Diary of an Encounter (BBC) 1971, Symphonic Variations (Granada) 1971, Facade (Granada) 1971, The Strauss family (ATV) 1972, Hamlet (with Ian McKellan) 1972, Craven Arms (Granada) 1972, The Recruiting Officer (BBC) 1973, Twelfth Night (BBC) 1974, The Emigrants (BBC) 1975, When We Are Married (BBC) 1976, The Winslow Boy (BBC) 1976, Six Characters In Search of An Author (CBC) 1977, The Mayor of Casterbridge (BBC) 1977, The Wolf (CBC) 1978, Richard II (BBC) 1978, Henry IV Part I (BBC) 1979, Henry IV Part II (BBC) 1979, Henry V (BBC) 1979, On Approval (BBC) 1980, Fame is The Spur (BBC) 1981, The Barchester Chronicles (BBC, BAFTA nomination) 1982, Mansfield Park (BBC) 1983, King John (BBC) 1984-, Drummonds (LWT) 1985-, The Fools On The Hill (BBC) 1986, Hannay (BBC) 1986, The London Embassy (Thames) 1987, Forever Green (LWT) 1989, A Breath of French Air (YTV) 1990; theatre incl: Measure for Measure (Stratford Ontario) 1969, Twelfth Night (Windsor Festival) 1970, 'Tis Pity She's A Whore (Edinburgh Festival) 1972, Edward Bond's Lear (Yale Repertory Theatre) 1973, The Wood Demon (Edinburgh Festival) 1973, Gigi (West End) 1976, A Midsummer Night's Dream and The Tempest (Edinburgh Festival) 1978; dir of prodns Lyric Theatre Hammersmith 1979-; prodns incl: You Never Can Tell 1979, The Potsdam Quartet 1980, Hobsons Choice 1981, Twelfth Night (Stratford Ontario) 1985, The Young Idea (Guildford) 1988, The Waltz of The Toreadors (Shaw Festival Theatre Niagara-on-the-Lake Canada) 1990-; films: The Dance of Death (with Laurence Oliver and Geraldine McEwan) 1969, A Murder is Announced (BBC Film) 1984; memb The Directors Guild; *Recreations* cooking; *Style—* David Giles, Esq; 26 The Terrace, Barnes, London SW13 ONR (☎ 081 878 2414); c/o Elspeth Cochrane, 11/13 Orlando Rd, London SW4 OLE (☎ 071 622 0314/5)

GILES, Frank Thomas Robertson; s of Col Frank Lucas Netlam Giles, DSO, OBE, of Barn Close, Finchampstead, Berks; *b* 31 July 1919; *Educ* Wellington, BNC Oxford; *m* 29 June 1946, Lady Katharine Pamela, *qv*; 1 s (Sebastian b 1952), 2 da (Sarah b 1950, Belinda b 1958); *Career* Nat Serv WWII ADC to govr Bermuda, later WO Directorate of Mil Ops; FO 1945-46 (priv sec to Ernest Bevin); Sunday Times: dep ed 1967-81, foreign ed 1966-77, ed 1981-83 (formerly with The Times 1946-60: asst corr Paris 1947, chief corr Rome 1950-53 and Paris 1953-60); dir Times Newspapers 1981-85; memb Exec Ctee GB-USSR Assoc; govr Sevenoaks Sch, Wellington Coll 1968-89; chm Painshill Park Tst, memb Governing Body Br Inst in Florence; author; *Books* A Prince of Journalists: the life and times of de Blowitz (1962), Sundry Times, (autobiography, 1986), Forty Years On (ed, collection of essays to mark 40 anniversary Anglo-German Königswinter Conf, 1990); *Style—* Frank Giles, Esq; Bunns Cottage, Lye Green, Crowborough, E Sussex N6 1UY (☎ 089 26 3701); 42 Blomfield Rd, W9 1AH (☎ 071 286 5706)

GILES, Lady Katharine Pamela; *née* Sackville; o da of 9 Earl De La Warr, GBE, PC (d 1976), and his 1 w Diana, *née* Leigh (d 1966); *b* 4 March 1926; *m* 29 June 1946, Frank Thomas Robertson Giles, *qv*; 1 s, 2 da; *Career* JP Inner London 1966; chm North Westminster P S D; *Style—* The Lady Katharine Giles; 42 Blomfield Rd, London W9 (☎ 071 286 5706); Bunns Cottage, Lye Green, Crowborough, E Sussex

GILES, (Derryck) Peter Fitzgibbon; s of Arthur Frederick Giles, CBE (d 1960), of 21 Princes Court, Brompton Rd, Knightsbridge, London, and Gladys Adelaide, *née* Hird; *b* 17 Nov 1928; *Educ* Sherborne, Univ of Bristol (LLB); *Career* called to the Bar Gray's Inn 1954; Stewarts and Lloyds Ltd 1955-62, Charity Cmmn 1962-69 and 1974-84 (asst cmmr 1967), legal advsr Glaxo Hldgs 1970-72; sec: Crosby Hall 1973; memb: Heraldry Soc, Soc of Genealogists, Soc of Authors 1973; *Recreations* heraldry, genealogy, music, reading, pipe smoking; *Clubs* Savile; *Style—* Peter Giles, Esq; 22 Petworth Rd, Haslemere, Surrey GU27 2HR (☎ 0428 644425)

GILES, Robert William; OBE (1989); s of William George Giles (d 1968); *b* 30 Dec 1937; *Educ* Archbishop Tenisons GS, Univ of London (BSc); *m* 1961, Doreen June; 3 c; *Career* md Bovis Civil Engineering Ltd 1981-84, chm and md Farr plc 1984-90, md Amey-Farr Ltd 1990-; CEng, FICE, FCIOB, FIHT; *Recreations* golf, running; *Style—* Robert Giles, Esq, OBE; The Rockery, 25 High St, West Lavington, Wilts SN10 4HQ (☎ 038 081 3256); Amey-Farr Ltd, Bridge House, Station Rd, Westbury, Wilts (☎ 0373 864444)

GILES, Roy Curtis; s of Herbert Henry Giles (d 1988), and Dorothy Alexandra, *née* Potter; *b* 6 Dec 1932; *Educ* Queen Elizabeth Sch Barnet, Jesus Coll Cambridge (BA, MA); *m* 17 Aug 1963, Christine, da of Baron Konrad von Alten (d 1963); 2 s (Andrew Curtis b 1 July 1968, Timothy Benedict Michael b 9 June 1981), 1 da (Caroline Alexandra b 11 Dec 1965); *Career* Nat Serv 1951-53 (cmmnd RA 1951); head of modern languages Dean Close Sch 1956-60, lectr in Eng language and literature Univ of Hamburg 1960-63 (guest lectr Br Cncl), head modern languages Eton 1970-74 (asst master 1963-74), headmaster Highgate Sch 1974-89; govr: The Hall Sch Hampstead 1976-89, Channing Sch Highgate 1977-89; memb: Cncl Davies Educnl Servs (now Vernon Educnl Tst) 1975-, House of Bishops' Marriage Educn Panel, Assoc for the Apostolic Miny 1987-; Bishop of London's educnl selector ACCM; *Recreations* music, theatre, modern novels, walking, cooking; *Style—* Roy Giles, Esq; Wayfield House, Uplyme, Lyme Regis, Dorset DT7 3SA (☎ 02974 3065)

GILI, Jonathan Francesc; s of Joan Lluis Gili, and Elizabeth Helen, *née* Macpherson; *Educ* Dragon Sch, Bryanston Sch, New Coll Oxford (MA); *m* 27 July 1968, Phillida Bovill, da of Alan Reynolds Stone, CBE (d 1979); 2 s (Oliver b 1972, Orlando b 1984), 1 da (Daisy b 1974); *Career* publisher Warren Editions 1967-, film ed Overlord 1974; BBC film dir: Public School Westminster 1979, Year of the French 1982, She Married a Yank 1984, To the World's End 1985, Mixed Blessings 1988, All About Ambridge 1989, Chocolate! 1990; *Clubs* Double Crown; *Style—* Jonathan Gili, Esq; BBC Television, Kensington House, Richmond Way, London W14 OAX

GILKES, Dr Jeremy John Heming; s of Lt-Col Geoffrey Heming Gilkes, DSO, RA (d 1991), and Mary Stella, *née* Richardson; *b* 2 Dec 1939; *Educ* Charterhouse, St Bartholomew's Hosp Med Coll (MB BS), Univ of London (MD); *m* 8 July 1978, Robyn Vanessa, da of Maj Nigel Bardsley (d 1962); 2 s (Alexander, Charles), 3 step da (Emma, Sara, Katrina); *Career* conslt dermatologist: Univ Coll Hosp, Middx Hosp, King Edward VII Hosp for Offrs, St Lukes Hosp for Anglican clergy, Eastman Dental Hosp, London Foot Hosp; memb: Br Assoc Dermatologists, RSM; FRCP; *Clubs* The Hurlingham; *Style—* Dr Jeremy J H Gilkes; 115A Harley Street, London W1N 1DG

GILKISON, (Charles) Anthony; s of Capt Dugald Stewart Gilkison (ka 1914), and Janet Kate, *née* Harcourt-Vernon (d 1968); *b* 3 June 1913; *Educ* Dragon, Stowe, Prof Erlers Art Sch Munich; *m* 1, 1937; 2 da; m 2, 1972, Brita Margareta, da of Julius Andersson; *Career* serv WWII 1939-45; various jr jobs in film indust 1932-39; prodr int current affairs film series Spotlight (20th Century Fox) 1946; md Rayant Pictures Ltd; chm: Anthony Gilkison Assoc Ltd, Viscom Ltd, Viscom Prodn Ltd, A G Assocs Pty S Africa, Viscomarket Ltd; int conslt to govts and multi-nat cos on audiovisual communications; Cross of Freedom Finland 1940; *Recreations* gardening; *Style—* Anthony Gilkison, Esq; Huish Old Rectory, Merton, Okehampton, Devon EX20 3EH

GILKS, (Geoffrey) Paul; s of Geoffrey Lewis Gilks, of 110 Widney Lane, Solihull, W Midlands, and Evelyn Marie, *née* Parkinson; *b* 12 May 1954; *Educ* Tudor Grange GS, Univ Coll London (LLB); *m* 1 June 1985, Josephine Verrier, da of Capt Basil Edward Holman Elwin (d 1976), of Kingsdown, Kent; *Career* DG IX EEC Cmmn Brussels 1977, asst slr Allen & Overy 1979-85 (articled clerk 1977-79, seconded as legal advsr to Int Airports Projects MOD and Aviation Saudi Arabia 1982-83), ptnr Berwin Leighton 1987-(asst slr 1985-87); memb Nat Ctee of the Trainee Slrs' Gp 1978-79; memb: Law Soc, Slrs Euro Gp; *Recreations* yachting, squash raquets; *Style—* Paul Gilks, Esq; Adelaide House, London Bridge, London EC4R 9HA (☎ 071 623 3144, fax 071 623 4416)

GILL, Anthony Keith; s of Frederick William Gill (d 1955), of Colchester, Essex, and Ellen, *née* Davey; *b* 1 April 1930; *Educ* Colchester HS, Imperial Coll London (BSc); *m* 4 July 1953, Phyllis, da of Maurice Cook (d 1954), of Colchester; 1 s (Simon b 2 Oct 1964), 2 da (Joanna b 21 Feb 1958, Sally b 5 May 1960); *Career* REME (Nat Serv Offr) 1954-56; engrg apprenticeship Davey Paxman 1945-51, md Lucas Bryce Ltd 1965-72 (joined 1956), gen mangr Lucas CAV Ltd 1974 (dir 1967-); Lucas Industries plc: md and dir 1978, jt gp md 1980, gp md 1984, dep chm 1986, chm and chief exec 1987; non-exec dir: The Post Office 1989-, National Power 1990-; memb Engrg Cncl 1988-; pres IProdE 1986-87; memb ACOST 1986-; Fell City of Birmingham Poly 1989; Hon D Eng Univ of Birmingham 1990; FIMechE, FIProdE, FCGI 1979, FEng 1983; *Recreations* sailing, music; *Style—* Anthony Gill, Esq; Mockley Close, Gentleman's Lane, Ullenhall, nr Henley-in-Arden, Warwickshire (☎ 056 442337); Lucas Industries plc, 44-46 Park St, London W1Y 4DJ (☎ 071 493 6793, fax 071 491 0096)

GILL, Brett Richard Joseph; s of Richard Robert Gill (d 1959), of Hamble, and Dorothy, *née* Slade (now Mrs Turner); *b* 17 Oct 1942; *Educ* Blundell's; *m* 20 Nov 1965, Caroline Virginia, da of late James Herbert Bright; 1 s (William James b 15 Jan 1969), 1 da (Alice Kate b 25 April 1973); *Career* Woolley & Waldron Chartered Accountants Southampton: articled clerk 1961-65, seconded to Barton Mayhew London 1967, ptnr 1969-79; Ernst & Whinney: appointed staff ptnr following merger 1979-85, mktg ptnr 1985-88, office managing ptnr 1988-89; office managing ptnr Ernst & Young (following merger) 1989-; dir South C of C 1978-, memb Exec Ctee Hants Devpt Assoc; govr: Southampton Inst of Higher Educn, Embley Park Sch; memb Cncl Univ of Southampton; FCA 1970 (ACA 1965), ABIM 1968; *Recreations* rugby fives, sailing, archeology, skiing, walking, bicycling; *Clubs* Royal Southern Yacht, Royal Southampton Yacht, Winchester Rugby Fives, Trojans Sports; *Style*— Brett Gill, Esq; Reapers, Duke St, Micheldever, nr Winchester, Hants (☎ 0962 89 287); Ernst & Young, Wessex House, 19 Threefield Lane, Southampton SO1 1TW (☎ 0703 230230, fax 0703 227409, car 0836 774409)

GILL, Hon Mrs (Celia Mary); *née* Gore-Booth; da of Baron Gore-Booth, GCMG, KCVO (d 1984, Life Peer), and his w, Patricia Mary, da of late Montague Ellerton, of Yokohama, Japan; *b* 6 Jan 1946; *Educ* Downe House Sch, London Acad for Music and Dramatic Art, York Repertory Theatre 1967, Jacques Lecoq Sch Paris 1968-69; *m* 21 May 1983, Douglas George Gill; *Style*— Hon Mrs Gill; 29 The Vale, London SW3

GILL, Hon Mrs (Charlotte Mary Magdalen); *née* Hunt; da of Baron Hunt of Tanworth, GCB, and his 1 wife Hon Magdalen Mary Robinson (d 1971), da of 1 Baron Robinson; *b* 1947; *m* 1976, Dr Herbert Gill; 1 da (Julia Magdalen b 1980); *Style*— Hon Mrs Gill; 22230 Drums Court, Woodland Hills, California 91364, USA

GILL, Christopher J F; RD (1971), MP (C) Ludlow 1987-; s of F A Gill, and D H Gill, *née* Southan; *b* 28 Oct 1936; *Educ* Shrewsbury; *m* 2 July 1960, Patricia, da of late E V Greenway; 1 s (Charles b 1961), 2 da (Helen b 1963, Sarah b 1967); *Career* Lt Cdr RNR, ret 1979; butcher and farmer; dir F A Gill Ltd 1968; *Recreations* walking, sailing, skiing; *Style*— Christopher Gill, Esq, RD, MP; c/o House of Commons, Westminster, London SW1A 0AA

GILL, Rev Dr David Christopher; s of Alan Gill (d 1940), and Muriel, *née* Hodgson (d 1985); *b* 30 July 1938; *Educ* Bellevue GS Bradford, Univ of St Andrews (MB ChB), Salisbury Theol Coll, Univ of Nottingham (Dip Theol and Pastoral Studies); *Career* TA OTC 1956-61, RAMC 1961-66, 153 Highland Field Ambulance, Capt, RARO 1966-; house offr then sr house offr registrar 1963-66: Perth Royal Infirmary, Bridge of Earn Hosp, Kings Cross Hosp Dundee; medical supt and dist MO Mkomaindo Hosp Masasi Mtwara Region Tanzania 1966-72 (regnl leprosy offr 1967-72), registrar then sr registrar psychiatry Knawle Hosp Fareham Hants 1974-78, conslt psychiatrist Mapperley Hosp Nottingham 1978-, clinical teacher Univ of Nottingham Med Sch 1978-; ordained: deacon 1981, priest 1985; chm Collegiate Trainees Sub Ctee Royal Coll of Psychiatrists 1976-78, memb cncl Univ of St Andrews; MRCPsych 1976, FRCPsych 1986; *Recreations* sailing, theatre, opera; *Clubs* RAF Yacht, Royal Yachting Assoc, Army Sailing Assoc, The Lansdowne; *Style*— The Rev Dr David Gill; 1 Malvern Court, 29 Mapperley Road, Nottingham NG3 5AG (☎ 0602 622351); Knoydart, 2 Calligary, Ardvasar, Isle of Skye IV45 8RU; The Mandala Centre, Gregory Boulevard, Nottingham NG7 6LB (☎ 0602 606082)

GILL, Frank Maxey; 5 s of Frederick Gordon Gill, DSO, and Mary Gill; *b* 25 Sept 1919; *Educ* Marlborough, De Havilland Aeronautical Tech Sch; *m* 1, 1942, late Sheila Rosemary Gordon; 3 da; m 2, 1952 Erica Margaret Fulcher; 1 s; *Career* chm Gill and Duffus Gp Ltd 1976 (dir 1957-80, md 1969); *Style*— Frank Gill, Esq; Tile House, Reigate Heath, Reigate, Surrey

GILL, Air Vice-Marshal Harry; CB (1979), OBE (1968); s of John William Gill, of Newark, Notts, and Lucy Gill; *b* 1922,Oct; *Educ* Barnby Rd Sch, Newark Tech Coll; *m* 1951, Diana Patricia, da of Colin Wood, of Glossop; 1 da; *Career* flying duties RAF 1941-49, dir-gen Supply RAF 1976-79; *Recreations* fishing, shooting, cycling; *Clubs* RAF; *Style*— Air Vice-Marshal Harry Gill, CB, OBE; Gretton Brook, S Collingham, Notts

GILL, Maj-Gen Ian Gordon; CB (1972), OBE (1959, MBE 1949), MC (1940, and Bar 1945); s of Brig Gordon Harry Gill, CMG, DSO (d 1962), and Doris Gill; *b* 9 Nov 1919; *Educ* Repton; *m* 1963, Elizabeth Vivian (Sally), MD, MRCP (d 1990), da of A F Rohr, of London; *Career* cmmnd 4/7 Royal Dragoon Gds 1938, served BEF France 1939-40, NW Europe 1944-45 (despatches), Palestine 1946-48, Tripolitania 1950-51, cmd 4/7 Royal Dragoon Gds 1957-59, Coll Cdr RMA Sandhurst 1961-62, Cdr 7 Armoured Bde 1964-66, dep mil sec (1) MOD 1966-68, head Br Def Liaison Staff Canberra 1968-70, Asst Chief Gen Staff Operational Requirements MOD 1970-72, ret 1972; Col 4/7 Royal Dragoon Gds 1973-78; Hon Liveryman Worshipful Co of Coachmakers and Coach Harness Makers; *Recreations* equitation, skiing, squash rackets, cricket; *Clubs* Cavalry & Guards, MCC; *Style*— Maj-Gen Ian Gill, CB, OBE, MC; Cheriton House, Thorney, Peterborough, PE6 0QD (☎ 0733 270246)

GILL, Jack; CB (1984); s of Jack and Elizabeth Gill; *b* 20 Feb 1930; *Educ* Bolton Sch; *m* 1954, Alma Dorothy; 3 da (Alison b 1957, Helena b 1959, Alexandra b 1961); *Career* govt serv; under sec and princ fin offr Export Credits Guarantee Dept 1975-79, sec Monopolies and Mergers Cmmn 1979-81, dep sec and dir Industl Devpt Unit DOI 1981-83, chief exec Export Credits Guarantee Dept 1983-87; memb: BOTB 1981-87; dir Govt Rels BICC plc 1987-, advsr Northern Eng Ind plc 1987-89, British Aerospace plc 1987-89, Cncl CBI 1988- (currently chm Pub Procurement Contact Gp); *Recreations* music, chess problems; *Clubs* Overseas Bankers; *Style*— Jack Gill, Esq, CB; 9 Ridley Rd, Warlingham, Surrey CR3 9LR (☎ 088362 2688)

GILL, John Nichol; s of William Gill, MBE (d 1959), of Llandaff, Cardiff, and Jane Nichol, *née* Adamson; *b* 10 April 1930; *Educ* Boston GS, Chesterfield GS, St Edmund Hall Oxford (MA); *m* 20 Aug 1958, Ann Therese Frances, da of Charles Clifford Turner (d 1970), of Chesterfield; 1 s (Richard b 1963), 2 da (Susan (Mrs Micklethwaite) b 1960, Stephanie (Mrs Backhouse) b 1965); *Career* Nat Serv RCS 1948-49; admitted slr 1956; asst slr Stanton and Walker (Slrs) Chesterfield 1956 following articles with same firm, ptnr 1959, sr ptnr 1978; chm Chesterfield Round Table 1967-68, pres Chesterfield and N E Derbyshire Law Soc 1980-81, pt/t chm Social Security Appeal Tbnls 1988-; memb: Law Soc 1956, Cmmn for Oaths 1962; *Recreations* golf, hill walking; *Clubs* Chesterfield Golf; *Style*— John N Gill, Esq; The White House, 38 Summerfield Road, Chesterfield, Derbyshire, S40 2LJ (☎ 0246 232681); Stanton and Walker, Solicitors, 12 Soresby Street, Chesterfield S40 1JL (☎ 0246 236926, fax 0246 221321)

GILL, Kenneth Edward; s of Fred Gill, of Ryton, Tyne and Wear, and Elsie, *née* Ezard (d 1984); *b* 22 May 1932; *Educ* Harrogate GS Hartley Victoria Coll Manchester; *m* 20 April 1957, Edna, da of Harrison Hammond (d 1977); 1 s (Paul Robert b 1959), 2 da (Katharine Anne b 1961, Lynda Jane b 1964); *Career* Nat Serv RAF 1950-52; Karnataka South India: presbyter Hassan 1958-65, supt Vocational Training Centre Tumkur 1965-72, bishop of Central Diocese 1972-80; asst bishop of Newcastle 1980-; *Books* Meditations On The Holy Spirit (1979), Count Us Equal (1990); *Recreations* gardening; *Clubs* Rotary; *Style*— The Rt Rev Kenneth Gill; 83 Kenton Road, Gosforth, Newcastle upon Tyne NE3 4NL (☎ 091 2851502); Bishops House, 29 Moor Road South, Newcastle upon Tyne NE3 1PA (☎ 091 2852220)

GILL, (James) Kenneth; s of late Alfred Charles Gill and Isabel Gill; *b* 27 Sept 1920; *Educ* Highgate; *m* 1948, Anne Bridgewater; 1 s; *Career* pres Saatchi & Saatchi Co plc 1985- (chm 1976-85); FIPA; *Style*— Kenneth Gill, Esq; c/o Saatchi & Saatchi Co plc, 80 Charlotte St, W1 (☎ 071 636 5060)

GILL, Air Vice-Marshal Leonard William George; DSO (1944); s of Leonard William Gill (d 1963), and Marguerite, *née* Dutton (d 1955); *b* 31 March 1918; *Educ* UC Sch London; *m* 1, 1943 (m dis), Joan Favill; 2 s (David b 1946, James b 1958), 2 da (Rosemary b 1945, Frances b 1947); m 2, 1982, Constance Mary Cull, da of late James Henry Button; *Career* RAF: Far East 1937-42 then UK, Cmd 68 Sqdn 1945 (despatches 1941), Cmd 85 and 87 Sqdn, DS RAF Staff Coll, Station Cdr Linton on Ouse 1957-60, dir Overseas Ops 1960-62, NDC of Canada 1962-63, dir of Orgn (Estabs) 1963-66; SASO RAF Germany 1966-68, DG Manning RAF MOD 1968-73, ret; planning advsr P&O Steam Navigation Co 1973-79; vice pres RAF Assoc 1973-89, chm Merton Assocs (Conslts) Ltd, 1985- (dir 1979-85); FIPM, FBIM; *Recreations* shooting, cricket, boats, amateur woodwork; *Clubs* Phyllis Court, RAF; *Style*— Air Vice-Marshal Leonard Gill, DSO; 3 Wickham Court, 7 Ashburn Gardens, Kensington, London SW7 4DG (☎ 071 370 2716); Merton Associates (Consultants) Ltd, Merton House, 70 Grafton Way, London W1P 5LE (☎ 071 388 2051)

GILL, Malcolm Alexander; TD (1972); s of Alexander Gill (d 1972), of Cults, Aberdeenshire, and Gladys Muriel, *née* Bullock; *b* 22 March 1940; *Educ* St Edward's Sch Oxford, Univ of Aberdeen (MA); *m* 13 July 1968, Jane Quincey, da of Col William Quincey Roberts, CVO, CBE, DSO, TD (d 1981), of Newton St Loe, Bath, Avon; 2 da (Suzanna b 3 April 1970, Philippa b 18 Feb 1971); *Career* md: Thomson Publications SA (PTY) Ltd 1974-78, Standbrook Publications Ltd 1978-83, Int Thomson Publishing Ltd 1984-89, MDIS Gp 1989-; pres Int Fedn of the Periodical Press 1987-89; Liveryman Worshipful Co of Stationers and Newspaper Makers 1981; *Recreations* skiing, travel; *Clubs* Travellers, Naval and Military, City Livery; *Style*— Malcolm Gill, Esq, TD; The Dene, Hook Lane, Aldingbourne, Chichester, West Sussex PO20 6TQ (☎ 0243 543165); MDIS House, 8 Eastgate Square, Chichester, West Sussex PO19 1JN (☎ 0243 533322)

GILL, Nicholas Paul (Nick); s of George Michael Gill, of 27 Campden Hill Road, London, and Yvonne Janette, *née* Gilan; *b* 5 April 1957; *Educ* Holland Park Comp, Westminster Coll of Catering London (City and Guilds Certificates); *m* 23 July 1987, Sarah Louise Harrison; 1 s (Louis Oliver b 14 Oct 1985), 1 da (Hannah Kate b 14 March 1988); *Career* chef; commis chef: City Livery Club 1975-76, Savoy Hotel 1976-77, Waltons Restaurant 1976-77; asst pastry chef Park Lane Hotel 1977-78, asst chef Restaurant Paul Chêne Paris 1978-79, sous chef Moulin du Village Paris 1979, chef de partie Maxims Paris 1979-80, head chef Hambleton Hall Oakham Leicestershire 1980-87, conslt various London restaurants The Ackerman Guide and Marks & Spencer 1988-90, exec chef Feathers Hotel Woodstock Oxfordshire 1990-, fndr Tall Order London 1990, lectr and demonstrator La Petite Cuisine Cookery Sch Richmond; judge at annual Roux Brothers competition; *Awards* Hotel of the Year plus star (Egon Ronay Guide) 1984, Caesar award for outstanding excellence Good Hotel Guide, Country House Hotel of the Year Good Food Guide, two rosettes AA Guide, first Michelin Star 1984, first prize Mouton Chefs competition 1984, Chef Laureate to the Br Acad of Gastronomes 1986; Master Chef of GB 1986; memb Relais Chateaux 1984, assoc memb Academic Culinaire Francaise 1986-, fndr memb Country Chefs Seven 1983-86; *Books* contrib: The Last Supper, Master Chefs Cookery Book, The Observer Guide to British Cookery, Great New British Cookery, Country Cuisine, The Great Ice Cream Book, A Taste of Health; *Recreations* conjuring, juggling, kite flying; *Style*— Nick Gill, Esq

GILL, Peter; OBE (1980); s of George John Gill (d 1986), and Margaret Mary, *née* Browne (d 1966), union representative Spillers Flower Mill General Strike 1926; *b* 7 Sept 1939; *Educ* St Illtyd's Coll Cardiff; *Career* dir, dramatic author and former actor; actor 1957-65; directed his first prodn A Collier's Friday Night at the Royal Court 1965; plays directed since then incl: The Local Stigmatic 1966, Crimes of Passion 1967, The Daughter in Law 1967, The Widowing of Mrs Holroyd 1968, The Duchess of Malfi 1971, Twelfth Night 1974, As You Like It 1975, The Fool 1975; assoc artistic dir Royal Court Theatre 1970-72, dir Riverside Studios 1976- where his prodns incl: The Cherry Orchard (own version), The Changeling 1978, Measure for Measure 1979, Julius Caesar 1980; appointed assoc dir Nat Theatre 1980 where his prodns incl: Month in the Country 1981, Don Juan 1981, Major Barbara 1982, Tales from Hollywood 1983, Venice Preserv'd 1984, Fool for Love 1984, The Garden of England 1985, The Murderers 1985, Mrs Klein 1988, Juno and The Paycock 1989; dir Nat Theatre Studio 1984-90; wrote and produced: The Sleepers Den 1966 and 1969, Over Garden's Out 1969, A Provincial Life (after Chekov) 1969, Small Change 1976 and 1983, As I Lay Dying (after Faulkner) 1985, In The Blue 1985, Mean Tears 1987; his prodn of The Daughter-in-Law won first prize at the Belgrade Int Theatre Festival 1968; *Style*— Peter Gill, Esq, OBE; National Theatre, South Bank, London SE1 (☎ 071 928 2033, telex 297306 NATTRE G)

GILL, Robin Denys; s of Thomas Henry Gill (d 1931), of Hastings, NZ, and Marjorie Mary, *née* Butler; *b* 7 Oct 1927; *Educ* Dulwich, Brasenose Coll Oxford (MA); *m* 5 Oct 1951, Mary Hope (d 1986), da of John Henry Alexander (d 1953), of Harrogate, Yorks; 3 s (Stephen b 23 July 1953, Richard b 9 Sept 1955, Jonathan b 25 March 1957); *Career* sales mangr: Van der Berghs (Unilever Ltd) 1949-54, Br Int Paper Ltd 1954-59; founded Border TV Ltd (md 1960-64), md Assoc TV Corporation Ltd 1964-69; chm: ITN Ltd 1968-70, Tst Ltd 1970-; dir: Reed Paper Group Ltd 1970-75, Hewlett Packard 1975-; chm Ansvar Insurance Co Ltd 1975-, Heidelberg Instr 1984-89, Barine Hambreckt Alpine Ltd 1986-, SD Scicon plc 1988-; chm Standard Ind Tst 1970-81, former memb Bd Claremont Fan Ct Sch, memb Ctee The Royal Family Film 1968-69; memb: Nat Advsy Bd for Higher Educn, Mgmnt Education GP, Visiting Ctee of RCA, Oxford Univ Appts Ctee, NW Regnl Cncl for Higher Educn; memb bd IESTE (UK), chm Organisation and Executive The Queen's 40th Jubilee Celebration 1992, tstee The Royal Anniversary Tst 1990-; *Recreations* golf, opera, music, travel, art collecting; *Clubs* Vincents (Oxford), St Georges Hill Coll; *Style*— Robin Gill, Esq; 1970 Trust Ltd, 52 Queen Anne St, London, W1M 9LA (☎ 04865 5290)

GILL, Hon Mrs (Rosemary Eva Gorell); *née* Barnes; o da of 3 Baron Gorell, CBE, MC (d 1963); *b* 9 July 1925; *Educ* Priors Field, Masters Sch Dobbs Ferry New York, NFF Roehampton, Bedford Coll London (BA); *m* 16 July 1961, Peter Douglas Gill, s of Charles Douglas Gill, CBE; 1 s, 2 da; *Career* teacher; chm: Yorks Regnl Euro Movement 1970-74, Fawcett Soc 1976-80; memb: Ripon Diocesan Synod 1979-87, General Synod of C of E 1981-87, Oxford Diocesan Synod 1987-; SSStJ; *Recreations* reading, gardening, observing; *Style*— Hon Mrs Gill; c/o The Midland Bank plc, 34 Westgate, Ripon, N Yorks HG4 2BL

GILL, His Hon Stanley Sanderson; s of Sanderson Henry Briggs Gill, OBE (d 1966), of Snow Hill Grange, Wakefield, and Dorothy Margaret, *née* Bennett (d 1977); *b* 3 Dec 1923; *Educ* Queen Elizabeth's Sch Wakefield, Magdalene Coll Cambridge (MA); *m* 1954, Margaret Mary Patricia, da of James Grady (d 1976), of Coventry; 1 s, 2 da; *Career* Flt Lt Bomber Cmmd Europe 1941-46; called to the Bar Middle Temple 1950, in practice 1950-71; memb York Rent Assessment Ctee 1966-71, dep chm West Riding Quarter Sessions 1968-72; Co Ct judge 1971, circuit judge 1972-87, memb Co Ct Rule Ctee 1980-84; *Recreations* reading (mainly history), cooking, walking; *Style*— His Hon Stanley Gill; Arden Lodge, Thirkleby, Thirsk, N Yorks YO7 2AS

GILLAM, Gp Capt Denys Edgar; DSO (1940, and 2 bars), DFC (1940, and bar), AFC (1938), DL (W Riding Yorks 1959); s of Maj Thomas Henry Gillam (d 1946), and Doris, *née* Homfray (d 1988); *b* 18 Nov 1915; *Educ* Wrekin Coll, RAF Staff Coll; *m* 1, 1946, (Nancye) Joan (d 1986), da of late Godfrey Short, of S Africa; 1 s (Christopher James b 17 April 1952), 2 da (Marilyn b 3 May 1947, Penelope b 31 May 1948); m 2, 1987, Mrs Irene Scott; *Career* RAF 1935, Gp Capt 1944, ret 1946; md Br Furtex Ltd, chm Homfray & Co Ltd 1971, ret 1981; *Recreations* sailing, shooting, fishing; *Clubs* Royal Ocean Racing; *Style*— Gp Capt Denys Gillam, DSO, DFC, AFC, DL; The

Glebe, Brawby, Malton, N Yorks (☎ 0751 31530)

GILLAM, Patrick John; s of Cyril Bryant Gillam (d 1978), and Mary Josephine, *née* Davis; *b* 15 April 1933; *Educ* Clapham Coll, LSE (BA); *m* 23 Nov 1963, Diana, da of Dr Francis A Echlin (d 1988); 1 s (Luke b 1973), 1 da (Jane b 1970); *Career* 2 Lt RA 1954-56; FO 1956-57; various appointments in crude oil sales and oil supply BP Co 1957-68, vice pres (commercial) BP N America Inc New York 1971-74; BP Int: gen mangr Supply Dept 1974-78, dir opns 1978-80, regnl dir 1980-81; chm: BP Shipping Ltd 1981-88, BP Minerals Int 1982-, BP Coal Ltd 1986-88, BP Coal Inc 1988-, BP America Inc 1989-91, BP Oil Int 1989-, BP Nutrition 1989-; dir: BP NZ Ltd 1981-89, BP Aust Hldgs Ltd 1981-89, BP SA (Pty) Ltd 1981-89, BP Africa Ltd 1982-88, BP Exploration Co 1983-, BP Canada Inc 1989-; md The BP Co plc 1981-, non-exec dir Standard Chartered plc 1988-; memb: Ct of Govrs LSE 1989-, The Cook Soc 1983, Appeal Ctee Queen Elizabeth's Fndn for the Disabled 1984-, Appeal Ctee Imperial War Museum 1984-; chm ICC UK 1989-; Freeman City of London, Liveryman Worshipful Co of Shipwrights 1985; FRSA 1983, FInstD 1984; *Recreations* gardening, skiing, fine and decorative art; *Style—* Patrick Gillam, Esq; c/o The British Petroleum Co plc, Britannic House, 1 Finsbury Circus, London EC2M 7BA (☎ 071 496 4000, fax 071 496 4514, telex 888811)

GILLAM, Dr Peter Michael Stephen; s of Dr Geoffrey Gerard Gillam (d 1970), and Mary Frances Oldaker, *née* Davies; *b* 2 Dec 1930; *Educ* Gresham's, St Catharine's Coll Cambridge (BA), UCH (MB BChir, MD); *m* 18 Sept 1954, Anne Mary, da of Dr Louis O'Brien-Bell (d 1943); 3 s (Stephen b 24 Sept 1955, David b 27 July 1957, James b 20 March 1968), 1 da (Emma b 10 Feb 1965); *Career* Nat Serv Capt (former Lt) RAMC 1957-59, Registrar: UCH 1959-62 (house physician and house surgn 1955-57), Postgrad Med Sch Hammersmith Hosp 1962-63; sr registrar UCH and Whittington Hosp 1963-67, conslt physician Salisbury Gen Hosp 1967-; pres Wessex Physicians Club; chm: Salisbury Med Soc, Salisbury Hospice Care Tst, Salisbury Hosps Tst; FRCP; *Style—* Dr Peter Gillam; Ash Hill House, Sherfield English, Romsey, Hants (☎ 0794 884 200); Salisbury General Infirmary, Salisbury, Wilts (☎ 0722 336212)

GILLARD, David Owen; s of Robert Gillard (d 1983), of Croydon, Surrey, and Winifred, *née* Owens (d 1981); *b* 8 Feb 1947; *Educ* Tavistock Sch Croydon; *Career* arts writer and critic; scriptwriter and asst dir Assoc Br Pathé 1967-70, film and theatre critic Daily Sketch 1970-71, opera critic Daily Mail 1971- (ballet critic 1971-88), instituted Drama Preview Pages in The Listener 1982, fndr ed Friends (ENO magazine) 1983-, radio corr Radio Times 1984-91; memb: Critic's Circle 1974-, NUJ 1963-; *Books* Oh Brothers! (play, 1971), Beryl Grey: A Biography (1977); *Recreations* hill walking, collecting children's books; *Style—* David Gillard, Esq; 16 Grasmere Rd, Bromley, Kent BR1 4BA (☎ 081 464 6892)

GILLARD, Francis George (Frank); CBE (1961, OBE 1946); s of Francis Henry Gillard (d 1952), of Stockleigh Lodge, Exford, Somerset, and Emily Jane, *née* Burridge (d 1958); *b* 1 Dec 1908; *Educ* Wellington Sch Somerset, Univ of London (BSc), St Luke's Univ Coll Exeter; *Career* BBC: war corr N Africa, Italy Normandy and Berlin 1940-45, head of progs Radio and TV Bristol 1945-55, controller and S and W England 1956-62, dir later md Radio 1963-70, memb Bd of Mgmnt 1963-70; distinguished fell Corp for Public Broadcasting USA 1960-66, conslt to Public Broadcasting Interests USA 1966-; author numerous articles for pubns incl The Listener; memb Cncl Educational Fndn Visual Aids 1968-87, memb Fin Ctee Univ of Exeter 1968-86, chm Wellington Sch Somerset 1975-81 (govr 1960-); LLD Univ of Exeter 1987; FRSA 1972; *Recreations* country interests, walking, reading, music; *Clubs* Farmers'; *Style—* Frank Gillard, Esq, CBE; Trevor House, Poole, Wellington, Somerset TA21 9HN (☎ 0823 662890)

GILLARD, Isabelle; da of Prof Robert Gillard, of Univ of Wales, Cardiff, and Diana, *née* Laslett; *b* 17 Dec 1959; *Educ* Howell's Sch LLandaff, Univ of Birmingham (LLB), London Hosp; *Career* called to the Bar Middle Temple 1980, practising SE circuit; *Recreations* movies; *Style—* Miss Isabelle Gillard; 1 Crown Office Row, Temple, London EC4 (☎ 071 583 3724)

GILLBERRY, Col George Kendall; s of George Kendall Gillberry (d 1965), of Liverpool, and Muriel, *née* Evans (d 1975); *b* 14 Aug 1936; *Educ* Liverpool Inst, RMA Sandhurst; *m* 2 May 1959, Shirley, da of Richard Sedgwick McDougall, CBE (d 1982), of Stevenage, Herts; 2 da (Susan Elizabeth (Mrs Taylor) b 1959, Margaret Anne (Mrs Goodliff) b 1961); *Career* Army; 2 Lt 1956, Maj 1969, Lt-Col and Chief Planning Offr Central Ordnance Depot Bicester 1976, Cmdt and Chief Instr Petroleum Centre RAOC 1980, Col Directorate of Supply Mgmnt (Army) 1984, sr stores offr Central Ordnance Depot Bicester 1989; FInstPet 1976; *Recreations* travel, geneology; *Style—* Col George K Gillberry; Central Ordnance Depot, Bicester, Oxon OX6 0LD (☎ 0869 246534)

GILLES, Prof Dennis Cyril; s of Cyril George Gilles (d 1970), of Sidcup, Kent, and Gladys Alice Annesley, *née* Bachelor (d 1971); *b* 7 April 1925; *Educ* Chislehurst and Sidcup GS, Imperial Coll Univ of London (BSc, PhD); *m* 10 Dec 1955, Valerie Mary, da of Gerald Gardiner (d 1988), of Abbey Wood, Kent; 2 s (Christopher b 1957, Andrew b 1962), 2 da (Susan b 1960, Julia b 1969); *Career* asst lectr: Mathematics Dept Imperial Coll London 1945-47, Oceanography Dept Univ of Liverpool 1947-49; mathematician Scientific Computing Services Ltd 1949-55, res fell Computing Machine Laboratory Univ of Manchester 1955-57, prof computing sci Univ of Glagow 1966- (dir computing laboratory 1957-65); FRSE, FIMA, FBCA, FRSA; *Style—* Prof Dennis Gilles, FRSE; Ardbeg, Kilman, by Dunoon, Argyll PA23 8SE (☎ 036 984 342); University of Glasgow G12 8QQ (☎ 041 330 5391)

GILLESPIE, David Buchanan; s of William Hugh Gillespie (d 1986), of Littlehampton, Sussex, and Elizabeth, *née* Buchanan (d 1986); *b* 12 Dec 1938; *Educ* Dover Coll; *m* 1, 4 March 1967 (m dis 1976), Joanna Mary, da of Capt John Anthony Campbell Rupert, of Montreux-Territet, Switzerland; 1 s (Benjamin b 6 March 1971), 1 da (Antonia b 20 Oct 1968); m 2, 20 June 1977, Elizabeth Mary, da of Maj James Malcolm Hay of Seaton (d 1987), Edinglassie, Aberdeenshire; 1 s (Hamish b 10 Sept 1979); *Career* currently chief exec Kimpton Kitchens; FCA 1969 (ACA 1962); *Style—* David Gillespie, Esq; Snipe Cottage, Kingsley Green, Haslemere, Surrey GU27 3LT (☎ 0428 2621); Kimpton Kitchens, Fernhurst, Haslemere, Surrey GU27 3JL (☎ 0428 52043)

GILLESPIE, Prof Iain Erskine; s of John Gillespie (d 1974), of Glasgow, and Flora, *née* MacQuarie (d 1978); *b* 4 Sept 1931; *Educ* Hillhead HS, Univ of Glasgow (MB ChB, MD), Univ of Manchester (MSc); *m* 5 Sept 1957, (Mary) Muriel, *née* McIntyre; 1 s (Gordon McIntosh b 1963), 1 da (Rhona Kirstine b 1960); *Career* Nat Serv cmmnd Lt RAMC 1954, Regtl Med Offr then Capt till 1956; hon conslt Manchester Royal Infirmary 1970-, dean Faculty of Med Univ of Manchester 1983-86 (prof of surgery 1970); memb Med Sub Ctee UGC 1975-86, former office bearer Br Soc of Gastroenterology; memb: Surgical Res Soc of GB and Ireland, Assoc of Surgns of GB and Ireland, Assoc of Profs of Surgery, Sub-Ctee Hong Kong Univs and Polys Grants Ctee 1985-89, ed bds of several surgical and gastroenterological jls, North West RHA 1982-86, govr Stockport GS (formerly founding chm Parents Assoc), pres Manchester Branch Royal Scottish Dance Soc; FRCSE 1959, FRCS 1963, FRCSG 1970; *Books* Gastroenterology - An Integrated Course (ed with T J Thomson, 3 edn, 1983), Current Opinion in Gastroenterology - Stomach Duodenum (with TV Taylor, 1986, 1987, 1988); *Recreations* golf, gardening, music; *Clubs* New Golf (St Andrews); *Style—* Prof Iain E Gillespie; 27 Athol Rd, Bramhall, Cheshire SK7 1BR (☎ 061 439 2811); Univ Dept of Surgery, Manchester Royal Infirmary, Oxford Rd, Manchester M13 9WL (☎ 061 276 4033)

GILLESPIE, Prof John Spence; s of Matthew Forsyth Gillespie, and Myrtle Murie, *née* Spence; *b* 5 Sept 1926; *Educ* Dumbarton Acad, Univ of Glasgow (MB ChB, PhD); *m* 1 Sept 1956, Jemima Simpson, da of Alexander Ross; 4 s (David b 1957, Graeme b 1959, Adrian b 1963, Ian b 1964), 1 da (Ruth b 1968); *Career* Nat Serv RAMC 1949-51; Faulds fell then Sharpey scholar UCL 1955-57, Sophie Fricke res fell RS at Rockefeller Inst 1959-60, vice princ Univ of Glasgow 1983- (McCunn scholar in physiology 1952-54, lectr 1957-59, sr lectr 1961-68, prof of pharmacology 1968-); sec Physiological Soc, memb Ctee Pharmacological Soc; FRCP Glasgow, FRSE, FIBiol; *Recreations* gardening, painting; *Style—* Prof John Gillespie, FRSE; Camptower, 5 Boclair Rd, Bearsden, Glasgow G61 2AE (☎ 041 942 0318); Department of Pharmacology, Univ of Glasgow, Glasgow (☎ 041 339 8855)

GILLETT, (John) Anthony Cecil Walkey; s of Eric Walkey Gillett (d 1978), and Joan, *née* Edwards (d 1956); *b* 17 March 1927; *Educ* Malvern, Brasenose Coll Oxford (MA); *m* 18 Oct 1952, Jacqueline Eve, da of Philippe Leslie Caro Carrier, CBE (d 1975), of Ashdown House, St Anne's Hill, Lewes, Sussex; 2 s (Charles b 1954, John b 1958), 1 da (Amanda b 1961); *Career* serv as Lt RM 1945-47; Colonial Serv dist offr Somaliland Protectorate 1950-58, called to the Bar Inner Temple 1955, magistrate Aden (sometime acting chief justice, puisne judge and chief magistrate) 1958-63, Crown cnsl and asst attorney gen of Aden 1963-63, dep advocate gen Fedn of S Arabia 1963-68, temp legal asst Cncl on Tbnls (UK) 1968-70, legislative draftsman States of Guernsey 1970-83, Stipendiary Magistrate of Guernsey; author of State of Aden Law Reports (1959-60); played polo for Somaliland Protectorate and Aden; hon sec Oxford University Tennis Club (Royal Tennis); *Recreations* lawn tennis, reading; *Clubs* Royal Channel Islands Yacht, MCC, Vincents (Oxford); *Style—* Anthony Gillett, Esq; Bellieuse Farm, St Martin's, Guernsey, CI (☎ 0481 36986); The Magistrate's Chambers, Royal Court House, Guernsey, CI (☎ 0481 25277)

GILLETT, Dr (George) Bryan; s of Dr George Gillett (d 1982), of Flat 7, Heathfielde, Lyttlelton Rd, London, and Winifred Clare, *née* Bryan; *b* 23 Oct 1931; *Educ* Leighton Park Sch Reading, St Bartholomews Hosp Med Sch (MB BS); *m* 2 Sept 1961, Margaret Adeline, da of Arthur Bottoms (d 1937), of Gravenhurst, Beds; 2 da (Susan b 1967, Jane b 1970); *Career* conslt anaesthetist: St Bartholomews Hosp 1965- (sr anaesthetist 1990), Homerton Hosp 1986-; memb: BMA 1956, Assoc of Anaesthetists 1961 (DA): FFARCS; *Recreations* classical music, watching sports, photography; *Style—* Dr Bryan Gillett; 22 Kingsley Place, Highgate, London N6 5EA (☎ 081 340 1899); Department of Anaesthesia, St Bartholomew's Hospital, London EC1A 7BE (☎ 071 601 7518)

GILLETT, Charlie; s of Anthony Walter Gillett, and Mary Diana, *née* Maltby; *b* 20 Feb 1942; *Educ* Grangefield GS Stockton-on-Tees, Cambridge Univ (BA), Columbia Univ NY (MA); *m* 19 Dec 1964, Elizabeth (Buffy), da of Kenneth Chessum; 1 s (Ivan b 28 July 1970), 2 da (Suzy b 18 May 1966, Jody b 5 Sept 1968); *Career* lectr Kingsway Coll 1966-71, researcher BBC TV 1971, presenter BBC Radio London 1972-78; co-dir Oval Records & Music 1972-, presenter Capital Radio 1980-, presenter The Late Shift Channel 4 TV 1988; *Books* The Sound of the City (1970, 1983), Making Tracks (1974, 1985); *Recreations* athletics, soccer, African holidays, cinema; *Style—* Charlie Gillettt, Esq; 11 Liston Rd, London SW4 (☎ 071 622 0111); Oval Records & Music, 326 Brixton Rd, London SW9 7AA (☎ 071 326 4907)

GILLETT, Christopher John; yr s of Sir Robin Gillett, 2 Bt, GBE, RD, *qv*; *b* 16 May 1958; *Educ* Durlston Court Sch, Pangbourne Coll, King's Coll Cambridge (choral scholar, MA), RCM, Nat Opera Studio; *m* 7 Jan 1984, Julia A, yr da of late W H Holmes, of Tunbridge Wells; 1 da (Tessa Holmes b 1987); *Career* opera singer: New Saddlers Wells, Glyndebourne, Kent Opera, Covent Garden; Liveryman Worshipful Co of Musicians 1981; *Style—* Christopher Gillett, Esq; 41 Stanhope Gardens, Highgate, London N6

GILLETT, Rev David Keith; s of Norman Arthur Gillett, of Rushden, Northants, and Kathleen, *née* Pitts; *b* 25 Jan 1945; *Educ* Wellingborough GS, Univ of Leeds (BA, MPhil); *m* 3 Sept 1988, (Susan) Valerie, da of Samuel Vernon Shannon (d 1981); *Career* curate St Luke's Watford 1968-71, northern sec Pathfinders and CYFA 1971-74, lectr St John's Coll Nottingham 1974-79, co-leader Christian Renewal Centre NI 1979-82, vicar St Hugh Lewsey Luton 1982-87; memb: Gen Synod C of E 1985-88 and 1990-, C of E Evangelical Cncl, Cncl Evangelical Alliance, Cncl Reference for Anglican Renewal Ministries; *Books* How Congregations Learn (1979), A Place in the Family (co-author, 1981), The Darkness where God is (1982), Whose Hand on the Tiller (co-author, 1984); *Recreations* gardening, photography, travel; *Style—* The Rev David Gillett; 16 Ormerod Rd, Stoke Bishop, Bristol BS9 1BB (☎ 0272 682646); Trinity College, Stoke Hill, Bristol BS9 1JP (☎ 0272 682803, fax 0272 682803)

GILLETT, Nicholas Danvers Penrose; er s and h of Sir Robin Gillett, 2 Bt, GBE, RD; *b* 24 Sept 1955; *Educ* Durlston Court Sch, Pangbourne Coll, Imperial Coll London (BSc); *m* 3 Jan 1987, Haylie Brooks, eld da of Dennis Brooks, of Swansea, Glamorgan; *Career* Br Aerospace: trials engr 1977-84, product assur mangr 1984-87, project mangr 1987-89, business devpt mangr 1989-; Liveryman Worshipful Co of Coachmakers 1982; ARCS, FBIS; *Recreations* photography, sub-aqua, computing, reading, skiing, DIY; *Style—* Nicholas Gillett, Esq; 7 Downs Park East, Westbury Park, Bristol BS6 7QF

GILLETT, Sir Robin Danvers Penrose; 2 Bt (UK 1959), of Bassishaw Ward, City of London, GBE (1976), RD (1965); s of Sir Sydney Harold Gillett, 1 Bt, MC, FCA (d 1976; Lord Mayor London 1958-59), and Audrey Isabel Penrose (d 1962), da of late Capt Edgar Penrose Mark-Wardlaw; *b* 9 Nov 1925, (Lord Mayor's day); *Educ* Hill Crest Sch, Pangbourne NC; *m* 22 Sept 1950, Elizabeth Marion Grace, er da of late John Findlay, JP, of Busby House, Lanarks; 2 s (Nicholas, Christopher, *qqv*); *Heir* s, Nicholas D P Gillett; *Career* Canadian Pacific Steamships Ltd 1945-60: cadet 1943-45, master mariner 1951-57, staff cdr 1957-60; dir: Wigham Poland Home Ltd, Wigham Poland Management Services Ltd 1965-86; chm St Katherine Haven Ltd 1990-, conslt Sedgwick Insurance Brokers 1987-89; underwriting memb Lloyd's, common councilman for Ward of Bassishaw 1965-69 (Alderman 1969-), sheriff City of London 1973-74 (HM Lt 1975, Lord Mayor 1976-77); RLSS: UK pres 1979-82, dep Cwlth pres 1982-; vice chm PLA 1979-84, er brother Trinity House 1978- (yr brother 1973-78), fell and fndr memb Nautical Inst, tstee Nat Maritime Museum, pres Inst of Admin Mgmnt 1980-84; vice pres: City of London Red Cross, City of London Outward Bound Assoc; Hon Co of Master Mariners: memb 1962-, warden 1971-85, master 1979-80; Hon Cdr RNR, Hon DSc City of London Univ 1976 (chllr 1976-77); Offr Order of Leopard (Zaire) 1974, Cdr Order of Dannebrog 1974, Order of Johan Sedia Mahkota (Malaysia) 1974, Grand Cross Municipal OM (Lima) 1977, Gold medal Admin Mgmnt Soc (USA) 1983; FInstD; KStJ 1976; Gentleman Usher of the Purple Rod 1985; *Recreations* photography, sailing (yacht 'Lady Libby'); *Clubs* City Livery, Guildhall, City Livery Yacht (Adm), Royal Yacht Sqdn, Royal London Yacht (Cdre 1984-85), Guild of World Traders Yacht (Adm), hon life memb Deauville Yacht; *Style—* Robin

Gillett, Bt, GBE, RD; Elm Cottage, Biddestone, Wilts; 4 Fairholt St, London SW7 1EQ (☎ 071 589 9860)

GILLFORD, Lord; Patrick James Meade; o s and h of 7 Earl of Clanwilliam; *b* 28 Dec 1960; *m* 1989, Serena Emily, da of Lt-Col Brian Lockhart, of Maugersbury, Glos; 1 da (Hon Tamara Louise b 2 Dec 1990); *Style*— Lord Gillford

GILLHAM, Dr Anthony John; s of Leslie James Gillham; *b* 17 May 1939; *Educ* Whitgift Sch, Imperial Coll London, St Catharine's Coll Cambridge (PhD); *m* 1969, Sheila Marion, *née* Adnitt; 2 s (Charles, Richard); *Career* cmmnd Cheshire Yeomanry 1968; chemical engr, md Chemoxy International plc 1984-, chm Pentagon Chemicals Ltd; CEng; *Recreations* fishing; *Clubs* IOD; *Style*— Dr Anthony Gillham; The Grange, Chop Gate, Middlesbrough, Cleveland (☎ 043 96 351); Chemoxy International Ltd, All Saints Refinery, Cargo Fleet Rd, Middlesbrough, Cleveland TS3 6AF (☎ 0642 248555/9, telex 587185 Cemint Mbro)

GILLHAM, Paul Maurice; s of Gerald Albert Gillham, and Doris, *née* Kinsey; *b* 26 Nov 1931; *Educ* RCM, GSM (LGSM), Christ's Coll Cambridge (BA, MA); *m* 3 Sept 1960, Jane Marion, da of Sir George Pickering (d 1982); 2 s (Adam b 27 Dec 1965, Dan b 13 April 1968), 1 da (Carola b 7 July 1963); *Career* chm: Keith Prowse Group 1970-80, St Giles Properties Ltd 1980-, Patent Developments Int Ltd 1980-, Actonbarn Ltd 1983-, CP Roberts and Co plc 1985-; chm LPO Cncl 1983-87, Poststyle Ltd 1987-; *Recreations* playing cello and piano, walking; *Style*— Paul Gillham, Esq; Edmonds Farmhouse, Gomshall, Guildford, Surrey GU5 9LQ (☎ 048641 2299); CP Roberts & Co plc, Roberts House, Station Close, Potters Bar, Herts EN6 3JW (☎ 0707 52361, fax 0707 44942)

GILLIAM, Terry Vance; s of James Hall Gilliam, and Beatrice, *née* Vance; *b* 22 Nov 1940; *Educ* Occidental Coll (BA); *m* 1973, Maggie Weston; 1 s (Harry Thunder), 2 da (Amy Rainbow, Holly du Bois); *Career* assoc ed Help! magazine 1962-64, freelance illustrator 1964-65, advertising copywrier and art dir 1966-67, res cartoonist We Have Ways of Making You Laugh 1968; animator Do Not Adjust Your Set 1968-69, animator actor and co-writer Monty Python's Flying Circus 1969-74 and 1979; animator The Marty Feldman Comedy Machine 1971-72, The Do-It-Yourself Film Animation 1974; *films:* co-writer actor and animator: And Now For Something Completely Different 1971, Monty Python and The Holy Grail 1974 (also co-dir), Monty Python's Life of Brian 1979, Monty Python's Live at The Hollywood Bowl 1982, Monty Python's The Meaning of Life 1983; animator writer The Miracle of Flight 1974, co-writer dir Jabberwocky 1977, co-writer prodr dir Time Bandits 1981; co-writer dir: Brazil 1985, The Adventures of Baron Münchhausen 1989; dir The Fisher King 1990; Hon DFA: Occidental Coll 1987, RCA 1989; *Books* The Cocktail People (1967), Monty Python's Big Red Book (jtly, 1971), Monty Python's Papperbok (jtly, 1973), Monty Python and The Holy Grail (jtly, 1977), Monty Python's Life of Brian (jtly, 1979), Animations of Morality (1978), Time Bandits (jtly, 1981), Monty Python's The Meaning of Life (jtly, 1983), The Adventures of Baron Münchhausen (jtly, 1989), Monty Python's Just the Words (jtly, 1989) *Albums* Monty Python's Flying Circus (jtly, 1970), Another Monty Python Record (jtly, 1971), Monty Python's Previous Record (jtly, 1972), The Monty Python Matching Tie and Handkerchief (jtly, 1973), Monty Python Live at Drury Lane (jtly, 1974), Monty Python and the Holy Grail (jtly, 1975), Monty Python Live at City Centre (jtly, 1976), The Monty Python Instant Record Collection (jtly, 1977), Monty Python's Life of Brian (jtly, 1979), Monty Python's Contractual Obligation Album (jtly, 1980), Monty Python Live at the Hollywood Bowl (jtly, 1981), Monty Python's The Meaning of Life (jtly, 1983), Monty Python The Final Rip Off (jtly, 1987), Monty Python Sings (jtly, 1989); *Recreations* sitting extremely still for indeterminate amounts of time; *Style*— Terry Gilliam, Esq; Mayday Management, 68A Delancy St, London NW1 7RY (☎ 071 284 0242, fax 071 284 1020)

GILLIAT, John Martyn; s of George Nicholas Earle Gilliat (d 1968), and Marjorie Florence, *née* Stott (d 1968); *b* 4 Dec 1923; *Educ* William Hulme's GS Manchester, BNC Oxford, Univ of Manchester (BA); *m* 25 July 1953, Mary Patricia, da of John Wadsley Rollitt (d 1954); 1 s (Simon Timothy Francis b 1958), 1 da (Joanna Mary Frances b 1961); *Career* served RCS (Capt) India 1944-47; CA, ptnr Dearden Gilliat & Co (and successor firms) 1958-84; sole practitioner John M Gilliat 1984-88; memb: Ct Univ of Manchester 1987-, VAT Tbnl Panel Manchester 1987-; bursar Wilmslow Prep Sch 1984-, pres Manchester Soc CAs 1972-73; FCA (memb Cncl 1975-89); *Clubs* Royal Overseas League; *Style*— John Gilliat, Esq; Sycamore Cottage, Bonis Hall Lane, Butley, Macclesfield, Cheshire SK10 4LP

GILLIAT, Lt-Col Sir Martin John; GCVO (1981, KCVO 1962, CVO 1954), MBE (1946); s of Lt-Col John Babington Gilliat, DSO (d 1949), and Muriel Helen Lycette Gilliat; *b* 8 Feb 1913; *Educ* Eton, RMC; *Career* 2 Lt KRRC 1933, serv BEF WWII (despatches, POW), temp Lt-Col 1953, Dep Mil Sec to Viceroy and Govr-Gen of India 1947-48, comptroller to UK Cmmr-Gen SE Asia 1948-51, mil sec to Govr-Gen of Australia 1953-55, private sec and equerry to HM Queen Elizabeth the Queen Mother 1956-, Vice-Lt for Herts 1971- (DL 1963); memb Nat Hunt Ctee 1964; hon bencher Middle Temple 1977; Hon LLD London 1977; KStJ 1983; *Style*— Lt-Col Sir Martin Gilliat, GCVO, MBE; Appletrees, Welwyn, Herts (☎ 043 871 4675); 31A St James's Palace, London SW1 (☎ 071 930 1440)

GILLIATT, Penelope Ann Douglass Conner; da of Cyril Conner, JP (d 1981), and Mary Stephanie, *née* Douglass (now Mrs Ivan Smith); *Educ* Queen's Coll London, Bennington Coll Vermont; 1 da (Nolan Kate Conner b 25 Feb 1965); *Career* writer; former contrib: New Statesman, Spectator, Guardian, Sight and Sound, Encore, Grand Street, Encounter, London Magazine, London Review of Books, Observer (film critic 1961-65 and 1966-67, theatre critic 1965-66), New Yorker (film critic 1967-79); novels incl: One by One (1965), A State of Change (1967), The Cutting Edge (1979), Mortal Matters (1983), A Woman of Singular Occupation (1988); story collections incl: What's it like out? (1968), Come Back if it doesn't get Better, (1967), Penguin Modern Stories (contrib, 1970), Nobody's Business (1972), Splendid Lives (1978), Quotations from Other Lives (1982), They Sleep Without Dreaming (1985), 22 Stories (1986); non-fiction: Unholy Fools: film and theatre (1975), Jean Renoir: essays, conversations, reviews (1975), Jaques Tati (1977), Three Quarter Face: profiles and reflections (1980); BBC plays incl: Living on the Box, The Flight Fund (1978), In the Unlikely Event of Emergency (1979); stage plays incl: Property and Nobody's Business (1980), But When All's Said and Done (1981); libretto of Beach of Aurora (cmmnd EKO music by Tom Eastwood 1982); screenplay: Sunday Bloody Sunday (1971; best original screenplay award: NY Film Critics Circle, Nat Soc of Film Critics USA, Br Soc of Film Critics; Oscar nomination); numerous profiles for New Yorker, Sunday Telegraph, Observer; memb: Labour Pty, bd of advsy sponsors Symphony of UN 1985-; grant for creative achievement in fiction Nat Inst of Arts and Letters 1972; FRSL 1978; *Style*— Penelope Gilliatt

GILLIBRAND, Alec Lindow; OBE (1975); s of Harold Lindow Gillibrand (d 1953), of Accrington, Lancs, and May, *née* Ramsbottom (d 1983); *b* 30 March 1932; *Educ* Queen Mary's Royal GS Clitheroe; *m* 29 June 1957, Jennifer Bridget, da of Maj Jasper Cyril Holmes, MC (d 1976), of Tavistock, Devon; 1 s (Guy Nigel b 1962), 1 da (Susan Jane (Mrs Massie) b 1960); *Career* Nat Serv 1960-62; banker, served over 32 yrs overseas with British Bank of the Middle East and Hongkong and Shanghai Banking Corpn in Bahrain, Doha, Aden, Jordan, Kuwait, Abu Dhabi, Beirut, Iran, Saudi Arabia, Hong Kong and India; ret as chief exec offr India; dir British and South Asian Trade Assoc; memb Exec Ctee British Cwlth Ex-Services League; ACIB 1975; *Recreations* walking, sport, reading, Arab affairs; *Clubs* Oriental, Bombay Gymkhana, Bombay Willingdon; *Style*— Alec Gillibrand, Esq, OBE; 181A Ashley Gardens, Emery Hill St, London SW1P 1PD (☎ 071 834 5626); British and South Asian Trade Association (BASATA), Centre Point, 103 New Oxford St, London WC1A 1DU (☎ 01 379 7400, fax 071 240 1578, telex 21332)

GILLIBRAND, Sydney; CBE (1991); s of Sydney Gillibrand (d 1990), and Maud Gillibrand; *b* 2 June 1934; *Educ* Preston GS, Harris Coll Preston, Coll of Aeronautics Cranfield (MSc); *m* 15 May 1960, Angela Ellen, da of Richard Williams (d 1982); 3 s (Paul b 1964, Simon b 1965, Jonathan b 1969); *Career* English Electric: apprentice 1950, chief stress engr 1966, works mangr Preston 1974; BAC (Preston) Ltd 1974-78 (gen mangr mfrg, special dir, dir mfrg Mil Aircraft Div); British Aerospace Aircraft Group: dep md Warton Div 1981, divnl md Kington/Brough Div 1983, divnl md Weybridge Div 1984; British Aerospace plc: md Civil Aircraft Div 1986, gp dir 1987-, chm BAe (Commercial Aircraft) Ltd 1988-, chm (Mil Aircraft) Ltd 1990, chm BAe (Dynamics) Ltd 1990-, chm BAe (Consultancy) Ltd 1990-, chm BAe (Liverpool Airport) Ltd 1990-, chm BAe Inc; chm Royal Ordance plc 1990-; pres Soc of Br Aerospace Cos 1990-; FEng 1987, FRAeS 1975; *Recreations* golf; *Clubs* St James's; *Style*— Sydney Gillibrand, Esq, CBE; British Aerospace plc, 11 Strand, London WC2N 5JT (☎ 071 389 3845, fax 071 389 3953, telex 919221, car 0836 545497)

GILLIE, Dr Oliver John; s of John Calder Gillie, of Tynemouth, Northumberland, and Ann, *née* Philipson; *b* 31 Oct 1937; *Educ* Bootham Sch York, Univ of Edinburgh (BSc, PhD), Stanford; *m* 3 Dec 1969 (m dis 1988), Louise, da of Col Phillip Panton; 2 da (Lucinda Kathrine b 1970, Juliet Ann b 1972); *Career* lectr in genetics Univ of Edinburgh 1961-65, Nat Inst for Med Res Mill Hill 1965-68, IPC Magazines 1968-70, Haymarket Publishing 1970-72, med corr The Sunday Times 1972-86, med ed The Independent 1986-89 (special corr 1989-); *Books* The Sunday Times Book of Body Medicine (jtly, 1978), The Sunday Times Guide to the World's Best Food (jtly, 1981), The Sunday Times Self-Help Directory (jtly, 1982), The ABC Diet and Bodyplan (jtly, 1984); *Recreations* sailing, wind-surfing; *Clubs* RSM; *Style*— Dr Oliver Gillie; The Independent, 40 City Road, London EC1Y 2DB (☎ 071 253 1222)

GILLIES, (Maurice) Gordon; TD (1946 and bar 1952), QC 1958; s of James Brown Gillies (ka 1916, advocate in Aberdeen), and Rhoda Ledingham (d 1952); *b* 17 Oct 1916; *Educ* Aberdeen GS, Merchiston Castle, Univ of Edinburgh (MA, LLB); *m* 1954, Anne Bethea, da of Bryce McCall-Smith, OBE (d 1977), of Pencaitland, E Lothian; *Career* served RA 1939-46, Maj, France 1940, Europe 1944-46; advocate 1946, advocate dep 1953-58; sheriff of Lanarkshire at Lanark 1958-82; Sheriff Principal of South Strathclyde, Dumfries and Galloway 1982-88; *Recreations* golf, gardening; *Clubs* New (Edinburgh) Hon Co of Edinburgh Golfers; *Style*— Sheriff Principal Gordon Gillies, TD, QC; The Warren, Gullane, E Lothian EH31 2BE (☎ 0620 842857)

GILLIES, John Sydney Henry; s of Sydney Alfred Gillies, (d 1969), of London, and Lena Florence, *née* Dersley-Macer (d 1978); *b* 13 Oct 1921; *Educ* St Ignatius London; *m* 22 July 1950, Margaret Catherine, da of Hon Michael Whelton (d 1957), of Cork, Ireland; 2 s (John b 1951, Peter b 1955), 1 da (Anne b 1960); *Career* WWII RAF; MAFF 1947-54, official receivers BOT (later DTI) 1954-71, insolvency practitioner 1971-88; pres Insolvency Practitioners' Assoc 1987 (memb Cncl 1978), pres Anti Modern Packaging Soc; Freeman: City of London 1978, Worshipful Co of Chartered Secs and Administrators; FSCA, ACIS, FIPA; *Books* Insolvency Law and Practice (1988); *Recreations* sailing; *Clubs* City Livery; *Style*— John Gillies, Esq; Whitegates, Lodwick, Shoeburyness, Essex; Oceanair House, 133 Whitechapel High Street, London E1 7QG (☎ 071 377 6247, fax 071 375 1165)

GILLIES, Prof William; s of Iain Gillies (d 1989), of Oban, and Mary Kyle, *née* Cathie; *b* 15 Sept 1942; *Educ* Oban HS, Univ of Edinburgh (MA), Univ of Oxford (MA); *m* 24 June 1972, Valerie Roselyn Anna, da of Peter John Simmons, of Edinburgh; 1 s ((John) Lachlan b 1973), 2 da (Maeve b 1974, Mairi b 1982); *Career* Dublin Inst for Advanced Studies 1969-70, chair of Celtic Univ of Edinburgh 1979- (lectr 1970-79); dir: Scot Nat Dictionary Assoc Ltd 1982-, Comunn na Gaidhlig 1983-; FSAS 1975, FRSE 1990; *Books* Criticism and Prose Writings of Sorley Maclean (ed, 1985), Gaelic and Scotland (ed, 1989); *Style*— Prof William Gillies, FRSE; 67 Braid Avenue, Edinburgh EH10 6ED (☎ 031 447 2876); Univ of Edinburgh David Hume Tower, George Square, Edinburgh EH8 9JX (☎ 031 667 1011)

GILLIGAN, Timothy Joseph (Tim); ERD (1989), DL (Hertfordshire); s of Timothy Gilligan (d 1928) of Rosscommon, Eire, and Mary, *née* Greevy (d 1924); *b* 18 April 1918; *Educ* Handsworth Tech Coll Birmingham; *m* 2 Nov 1944, Hazel (Bunty), da of William Ariel Farmer; 2 s (Simon b 14 Oct 1945, Peter b 17 June 1952), 2 da (Anita b 29 June 1949 d 1952, Rosemary b 7 Apr 1957); *Career* WWII, Maj RASC serv BEF France, ME and N Africa, Germany (despatches 1944 and 1945) 1939-46; exec offr (1 sec grade) FO (German section) 1946-53; sales and mgmnt Dictaphone Co Ltd and WH Smith & Sons 1953-63; chm Pitney Bowes plc 1983- (joined 1963, chief exec 1967); chm: The Tree Cncl 1983-85, fndr chm conservation Fndn 1982-86, chm Herts Groundwork Tst 1984-89; memb Hertsmere BC 1983, CBIM 1983, FRSA 1977; *Recreations* the countryside and environment; *Style*— Tim Gilligan, Esq, ERD, DL; The White Cottage, Mimms Lane, Shenley Radlett, Herts WD7 9AP (☎ 0923 857 402); Pitney Bowes plc, The Pinnacles, Harlow, Essex CM19 5BD (☎ 0279 26731, fax 0279 34861, telex 81244)

GILLILAND, Alan Howard; s of Wilfred Howard Gilliland (d 1986), and Mary, *née* Miller; *b* 7 Jan 1949; *Educ* Bedford Sch, PCL, Architectural Assoc Sch; *m* 31 Oct 1975, Pauline, *née* Howkins; 5 s (Benjamin b 30 Jan 1976, Robert b 12 Dec 1980, Alexander b 4 Feb 1983, Oliver b 29 Jan 1985, Jack b 4 June 1988), 1 da (Emily b 24 Sept 1977); *Career* press photographer Evening Despatch Darlington 1979-86; editorial graphic artist: The Northern Echo 1986, London Daily News 1986-87; head of Graphics Dept Daily and Sunday Telegraph 1989- (joined 1987); winner: Graphic Artist of the Year Br Press awards 1988 and 1989, Linotype award for text and graphics (The Daily Telegraph) Newspaper Indust awards 1990, Silver award for breaking news informational graphic Soc of Newspaper Design US 1989-90; *Recreations* swimming, books; *Style*— Alan Gilliland, Esq; The Daily Telegraph, Peterborough Court, 181 Marsh Wall, London E14 9SR (☎ 071 538 6432, fax 071 538 3810)

GILLILAND, Elsie; da of James Lauder McCully (d 1985), of Belfast, and Mary Agnes, *née* Calvert; *b* 6 Dec 1937; *Educ* Richmond Lodge, Queen's Univ Belfast (LLB); *m* 22 July 1961, James Andrew David Gilliland, QC; 2 s (Jeremy b 1964, Jonathan b 1967); *Career* slr in private practice; memb Manchester Family Health Servs Authy; *Recreations* skiing, opera, painting; *Style*— Mrs Elsie Gilliland; The Shieling, Highfield, Prestbury, Cheshire (☎ 0625 828029); 30 Swedish Quays, London SE16 (☎ 071 232 0144); Towns Needham & Co, John Dalton House, 121 Deansgate, Manchester M3 2AR

GILLING, Lancelot Cyril Gilbert (Lance); OBE (1985); s of Gilbert Joseph Gilling (d 1949), of Somerset, and Esther Marianne Clapp (d 1969); *b* 7 March 1920; *Educ* Shebbear Coll Beaworthy Devon, Univ of Reading (BSc); *m* 1951, Brenda, da of Jack Copp (d 1974); 2 da (Jennifer b 1952, Hilary b 1955); *Career* Capt Royal Northumberland Fus 2 Bn UK, N Africa, Italy, Palestine, Greece 1940-46; warden and lectr Dorset Coll of Agric 1949-51, head Dept of Agric Writtle Coll Chelmsford Essex, princ Askham Bryan Coll of Agric and Horticulture York 1957-84, lectr Int Centre for Agric Educn Berne Switzerland 1968-76; pres: Agric Educn Assoc 1981-82 (hon memb 1987), Assoc of Agric Educn Staffs 1979-80, Yorks Agric Soc 1981-82; memb Cncl and chm F & GP Yorks Wildlife Tst 1985-, vice pres Yorks Philosophical Soc; chm: Exec Ctee Yorks Agric Soc, York Centre The Nat Tst 1989-; former memb Min of Agric Northern Regnl Panel of Advrs, conslt UNESCO and Br Cncl 1975 1976 and 1982, memb Royal Cmmn on Environmental Pollution 1985-89; FIBiol, FRAgS, CBiol; *Recreations* tennis, music (choral), conservation; *Style—* Lance Gilling, Esq, OBE; The Spinney, Brandsby, York YO6 4RQ

GILLINGHAM, Prof (Francis) John; CBE (1981, MBE 1945); s of Herbert John Gillingham (d 1958), of Elwell Lea, Upwey, Dorset and Lily Gillingham (d 1962); *b* 15 March 1916; *Educ* Hardye's Sch Dorset, Bart's, Univ of London (MB BS); *m* 30 Aug 1945, Irene Judy, da of F W Jude (d 1947), of Norfolk; 4 s (Jeremy, Timothy, Simon, Adam); *Career* house surgn Bart's 1940-41, surgn Mil Hosp (for head injuries) Oxford 1941-42, Maj RAMC (No 4 Mobile Neurosurgical Unit) 1942-45; conslt surgical neurologist Royal Infirmary & Western Gen Hosp Edinburgh 1950-80, prof of (now emeritus) surgical neurology Univ of Edinburgh 1963-80, hon conslt Bart's London 1980-, conslt neurosurgn Army in Scotland 1963-81, co chm TV Educn and Communications Grampian TV/Univ of Edinburgh, prof (now emeritus) Univ of King Saud 1983-85 (advsr MOD Saudi Arabia 1981-85), pres RCS Edinburgh 1979-82; Colles lectr (& medal) Irish Coll of Surgns 1974, Clark Fndn award 1989, Harveian Oration Edinburgh 1980, 17 Elsberg lecture NY 1967, Adlington Syme Oration Royal Aust Coll of Surgns 1981, Digby Meml lecture (and medal) Univ of Hong Kong 1982; Hon MD (Thessaloniki), Hon FRACS, Hon FCM (S Africa); Hon FRCS: Australia, Glasgow; Hon FRCSI, hon memb Royal Acad of Med (Valencia), hon pres World Fedn of Neurosurgical Socs, FRSE 1970; Medal City of Gdansk Poland 1978; Obrador Fndn medal Madrid 1990; *Publications* author of 75 papers on neurosurgical subjects and postgrad educn in learned magazines; ed 4 of books; *Recreations* gardening, sailing, photography, travel; *Clubs* New (Edinburgh), Bruntsfield Link's Golfing Soc Edinburgh, Club Nautico Javea Spain; *Style—* Prof John Gillingham, CBE; Easter Park House, Barnton Avenue, Edinburgh EH4 6JR (☎ 031 336 3528); Las Colinas, Jesus Pobre 03749, Alicante, Spain (☎ 010 34 6 75 70 62)

GILLINGHAM, Nicholas (Nick); s of Frank Joseph Gillingham, of 30 Longmeadow Rd, Walsall and Hazel Eileen, *née* Burns; *Educ* Blue Coat Comprehensive Sch; *Career* swimmer; 200 m breaststroke: Bronze medal Cwlth Games 1986, Silver medal Olympic Games 1988, Gold medal Euro Championships 1989 (Bronze medal 100 m 1989), Bronze medal 100m and 200m breaststroke Cwlth Games 1990, 200m breaststroke champion Euro Open 1990, Bronze medal 200m breaststroke World Championships 1991; world record holder: Euro Championships 1989, 200m breaststroke 1991; memb Amateur Swimming Assoc Ctee; *Recreations* photography, reading, music; *Style—* Nick Gillingham, Esq; 8 Old Langley Hall, Ox Leys Rd, Sutton Coldfield, W Midlands B75 7HP; Sports Devpt, Birmingham Sports Centre, Balsall Heath Rd, Birmingham B12 9DL (☎ 021 440 2061, fax 021 633 3496)

GILLINGS, Ronald James; s of James Oliver Gillings (d 1952), of Surrey, and Ivy Edith Gillings (d 1962); *b* 11 July 1931; *Educ* Dorking GS, Kingston on Thames Sch of Architecture; *m* Mary, da of Arthur Williams Enfield (d 1964); 2 da (Katharine b 1958, Sarah b 1964); *Career* architect; ptnr Gerald Murphy Burles Newton 1962-; chm Highbury Div Cmmrs of Inland Revenue 1982- (memb Finsbury Advsy Ctee 1986-); memb: Islington C of C 1980-82, Consultative Gp of Gtr London C of C 1982-83, Tourism Ctee London Borough of Islington 1986-; Indust Year London N Central 1986 (Indust Matters 1987-89); memb: Bd Islington Enterprise Centre, Co-op London Borough of Islington Employment & Econ Devpt Ctee 1970-; pres Islington Rotary Club 1976-77; ARIBA; *Recreations* boating, photography, building; *Style—* Ronald Gillings, Esq; The Japanese Garden, Codicote, Hitchin, Herts (☎ 0438 820430); Stanhope House, 4 Highgate High Street, London N6 (☎ 081 341 1307, fax 081 341 0851)

GILLIONS, Paul; s of William Stanley Gillions (d 1972), and Marie Lilian, *née* Crawley; *b* 15 May 1950; *Educ* St Albans GS for Boys; *m* 5 June 1976, Grace Kathleen, da of David Adam Smith; 2 da (Jennie b 1980, Laura b 1983); *Career* int PR conslt and main bd dir Burson-Marsteller Ltd 1987-, dir of issues mgmnt Burson-Marsteller Europe; *Recreations* reading; *Style—* Paul Gillions, Esq; 3 Whitehurst Ave, Hitchin, Herts (☎ 0462 455513); 24-28 Bloomsbury Way, London WC1 (☎ 071 831 6262)

GILLMAN, Gerry; s of Elias Gillman (d 1988), of Rottingdean, Sussex, and Gladys Maud, *née* Willomatt; *b* 14 April 1927; *Educ* Archbishop Tenison's GS; *m* 21 July 1951, Catherine Mary, da of Thomas Harvey (d 1966), of Birkenhead; *Career* Soc Civil Servants: asst sec 1953, gen sec 1973-85; memb Police Complaints Authy 1986-; *Clubs* MCC; *Style—* Gerry Gillman, Esq; 10 Gt George St, London SW1 (☎ 071 273 6469)

GILLMAN, Tricia; da of Dr Theodore Gillman (d 1971), of Cambridge, and Selma, *née* Cohen; *b* 9 Nov 1951; *Educ* Univ of Leeds (BA), Univ of Newcastle (MFA); *m* 1989, Alexander Ramsay, s of Frank Raymond Faber Ramsay (d 1977); 1 s (Thomas Jesmond b 3 Jan 1990); *Career* artist; teacher: 1977-83 (Newcastle Poly, Univ of Leeds, Ravensbourne Sch of Art, Lanchester Poly, Birmingham Poly, Edinburgh Sch of Art, Univ of Reading, Chelsea Sch of Art), St Martin's Sch of Art 1983-, RCA 1988-; solo exhibitions: Parkinson Gallery Leeds 1978, Sunderland Arts Centre 1982, Arnofini Gallery Bristol 1985, Benjamin Rhodes Gallery London 1985 and 1987, Laing Gallery Newcastle (touring) 1989-90; gp exhibitions incl: Northern Art Assoc Exhibition (Shipley Art Gallery and tour) 1978, St Martin's Painters (Seven Dial Gallery) 1982, Summer Show II (Serpentine Gallery) 1982, John Moores Liverpool Exhibition XIV (Walker Art Gallery) 1985, Thirty London Artists (The Royal Academy) 1985, Malaysian and British Exhibition Paintings and Prints (National Art Gallery, Kuala Lumpar, Singapore and Hong Kong) 1986, Summer Show (Royal Academy) 1987, London Group (RCA and tour) 1987; Tricia Gillman and Richard Gorman: Small Paintings (Benjamin Rhodes Gallery) 1989, Forces of Nature (Manchester City Art Gallery and tour) 1990; works in collections: Contemporary Arts Soc, Univ of Leeds, Television South West, The Stuyvesant Fndn, Stanhope Properties plc, Herbert Art Gallery Coventry; *Style—* Ms Tricia Gillman; Benjamin Rhodes Gallery, 4 New Burlington Place, London W1X 1SB (☎ 071 434 1768/9, fax 071 287 8841)

GILLMER, Michael David George; s of George Ernest Gillmer, of Pretoria, SA (d 1989), and (Adriana Margaretha) Janet, *née* Scholtz (d 1984); *b* 17 Jan 1945; *Educ* St Benedict's Sch Ealing, Kings Coll Hosp (MA, MD); *m* 17 Aug 1968, Janet Yvonne, da of Leslie Francis Davis (d 1987); 1 s (David Michael b 1978), 1 da (Charlotte Jane b 1973); *Career* clinical reader in obstetrics and gynaecology Nuffield dept Univ of Oxford 1979-84, conslt obstetrician and gynaecologist John Radcliffe Hosp Oxford 1984-; author of many publications on diabetes nutrition in pregnancy and contraception; hon memb Green Coll Oxford; memb Gynaecological Visiting Soc of GB and I, FRCOG 1984; *Books* 100 Cases For Students Of Medicine (1979), Nutrition In Pregnancy (1982); *Recreations* ice skating, photography, music; *Style—* Dr Michael Gillmer; Felstead House, 23 Banbury Rd, Oxford OX2 6NX (☎ 0865 512776)

GILLMORE, Sir David Howe; KCMG (1990, CMG 1982); s of Air Vice-Marshal Alan David Gillmore, CB, CBE, of Burnham-on-Sea, and Kathleen Victoria, *née* Morris; *b* 16 Aug 1934; *Educ* Trent Coll, King's Coll Cambridge (MA); *m* 1964, Lucile, da of Jean Morin (d 1972), of Paris; 2 s (Julian b 1967, Paul b 1970); *Career* RAF 1953-55; Reuters 1958-60, Polypapier SA 1960-65; schoolmaster ILEA 1965-69; FCO 1970-72, first sec Br Embassy Moscow 1972-75, cnsllr Br Delgn to MBFR Talks Vienna 1975-78, head of Def Dept FCO 1979-81; asst under sec of state FCD 1981-83; Br high cmmnr to Malaysia 1983-86; dep under sec of state FCO 1986-90, perm under sec of state FCO and head of HM Dip Ser designate 1991; visiting fell Harvard Univ 1990-91; *Recreations* books, music, exercise; *Style—* Sir David Gillmore, KCMG; Foreign & Commonwealth Office, King Charles St, London SW1

GILLON, John; s of William Millar Gillon, of Shotts, and Mary, *née* Wood; *b* 24 April 1949; *Educ* Wishaw HS, Univ of Edinburgh (MB ChB, MD); *m* 2 Sept 1972, Sandria Joy, da of Alexander Headridge, of Byburn, Ecclesmachan; 1 s (Andrew b 1981), 1 da (Aimée b 1978); *Career* lectr dept of med and gastro-intestinal unit Western Gen Hosp Edinburgh 1977-84, conslt Blood Transfusion Serv 1985-; also chef and cookery writer; winner Observer/Mouton-Cadet Cookery Competition 1981; MRCP; *Books* Le Menu Gastronomique (1982), Chambers Scottish Food Book (1989); *Recreations* golf, wine and food; *Style—* Dr John Gillon; 1 Queen's Bay Crescent, Edinburgh EH15 2NA (☎ 031 669 9355); Edinburgh and SE Scotland Blood Transfusion Service, Royal Infirmary, Lauriston Place, Edinburgh EH3 9HB (☎ 031 229 2585, telex 72163)

GILLOOLEY, John Edward; s of Timothy Peter Gillooley (d 1952), of Cork, and Mary Margaret, *née* Jennings; *b* 4 May 1941; *Educ* Christian Brothers Coll Cork; *m* 20 Sept 1969, Paula, da of Liam Kennedy (d 1985), of Cork; 3 s (Timothy b 1971, William b 1972, John b 1979); *Career* md McCarthy Dockrell 1971-76, exec dir Dockrell Gp 1976-85, chm and chief exec Dockrell Glass Gp 1985-, non-exec dir: Franford Servs Ltd, Rathmon Investments Ltd, Troffe Ltd, Rathsallagh House Ltd; chm: Dockrell Glass UK Ltd, Dockrell Toughened Glass Ltd; *Recreations* reading, golf; *Clubs* Hibernian United Servs Dublin, Sutton Golf (Dublin), Royal Dublin Soc; *Style—* John Gillooley, Esq; Ballymount Cross, Tallaght, Dublin 24, Ireland (☎ 0001 500155, fax 0001 500336); Unit 8, Highams Park, Industrial Estate, Jubilee Ave, London E4 9UB (☎ 081 527 1464, fax 081 527 9751)

GILLOTT, Nicholas Richard; TD (1948); s of Bernard Henry Gillott (d 1954), and Dorothy, *née* Mann (d 1965); *b* 2 Aug 1917; *Educ* Oundle; *m* 1966, Isobel Barrett, da of John Varley (d 1952), of Elmbank, Leamington Spa; *Career* Capt Royal Signals: UK, ME, Br Columbia, Germany; md Joseph Gillott & Sons Ltd 1948-72; chm Best & Lloyd Ltd 1972-74; md British Castors Ltd 1974-79, chm 1979-80; hon treas Birmingham C of Indust and C 1979-82; *Recreations* gardening, property maintenance, wine making; *Style—* Nicholas Gillott, Esq, TD; Orchard House, Mickleton Rd, Ilmington, Shipston-on-Stour, Warwicks CV36 4JQ (☎ 060 882 494)

GILLOTT, Roland Charles Graeme; s of John Arthur Gillott (d 1982), of Northwood, Middx, and Ursula Mary, *née* Bailey (d 1983); *b* 22 Aug 1947; *Educ* Haileybury; *m* 25 Oct 1975, (Bridget) Rae, da of Lesley Bentley Jones (d 1959), of Northwood; 1 s (Adrian b 20 Oct 1979), 2 da (Shanta b 21 April 1978, Lissa b 1 Jan 1981); *Career* admitted slr 1972, ptnr Radcliffes & Co 1979; memb: Amersham and Chesham Bois Churches Ctee, St Michaels & All Angels Amersham PCC; Liveryman Worshipful Co of Merchant Taylors 1979; memb Law Soc; *Recreations* walking, photography; *Clubs* MCC, RAC, City Livery; *Style—* Roland Gillott, Esq; 5 Great Coll St, Westminster, London SW1P 3SJ

GILLUM, John Reginald; s of Sidney Julius Gillum (d 1953), of Reigate, Surrey, and Dorothea, *née* Smith (d 1952); *b* 25 Jan 1928; *Educ* Winchester, King's Coll Cambridge; *m* 17 June 1953, Mary Rosalind (Mary Rose), da of Alan Frederick Graham Ayling (d 1990); 3 s (Benedict John Nevile b 1954, Thomas Alan b 1955, Christopher Andrew b 1961); *Career* Lt The Buffs 1948, served Hong Kong and Sudan, ret 1951; joined Robert Benson Lonsdale & Co Ltd (subsequently Kleinwort Benson) 1956, head of corporate fin Samuel Montagu & Co Ltd 1971, dir (corporate fin) N M Rothschild & Sons Ltd 1981-88; dir: BR (Eastern) Bd, Saxon Hawk plc 1986-, Ratners Gp plc 1986- (dep chm), Blagden Industries plc 1985, (dep chm), Ensign Trust plc 1990-; memb Disciplinary Ctee Inst of Chartered Accountants; Gen Cmmr for Taxes Hertford; memb Cncl Queen's Nursing Inst; *Recreations* golf; *Clubs* Brooks's; *Style—* John Gillum, Esq; Holwell Manor, Hatfield, Herts AL9 5RG (☎ 0707 261232); Tonman House, 63-77 Victoria St, St Albans, Herts AL1 3LR (☎ 0727 40907, fax 0727 39651)

GILMARTIN, John; *b* 5 Aug 1935; *Educ* Trinity Coll Dublin (BA, BCom); *Career* called to the Bar Lincoln's Inn 1972; *Style—* John Gilmartin, Esq; Cleves, nr Rodmell, Lewes, East Sussex BN7 3EZ (☎ 0273 477098); Cloisters, 1 Pump Court, Temple, London EC4Y 7AA (☎ 071 583 5123, fax 071 353 3383)

GILMORE, Brian Terence; s of John Henry Gilmore, of 48 Rockdale Gardens, Sevenoaks, Kent, and Edith Alice, *née* Johnson; *b* 25 May 1937; *Educ* Wolverhampton GS, ChCh Oxford (MA); *m* 17 Feb 1962, Rosalind, da of Sir Robert Fraser (d 1986); *Career* civil servant; dep sec Cabinet Office; *Recreations* walking, music, Greece; *Clubs* Athenaeum; *Style—* Brian T Gilmore, Esq; c/o Cabinet Office (OMCS), Horse Guards Rd, London SW1

GILMORE, David; s of David Gilmore, and Dora, *née* Baker; *b* 7 Dec 1945; *Educ* Alleyn's Sch; *m* 3 Sept 1978, Fiona, da of J P R Mollison; 3 s (Charles b 1982, George b 1985, Edward b 1989); *Career* artistic dir: Watermill Theatre, Nuffield Theatre Southampton; West End prodns incl: Nuts (Whitehall Theatre), Daisy Pulls it Off (Globe Theatre), Lend Me a Tenor (Globe Theatre), The Resistible Rise of Arturo Ui (Queens Theatre), Beyond Reasonable Doubt (Queens Theatre), The Hired Man (Astoria Theatre); other prodns incl: Cavalcade (Chichester Festival Theatre), Song and Dance (Sydney also Melbourne and Adelaide), Glen Garry Glenross (Brussels); memb: DGGB, TMA; *Recreations* golf, gardening; *Clubs* Garrick; *Style—* David Gilmore, Esq; 4 Wilton Crescent, Wimbledon, London SW19

GILMORE, Fiona Catherine; da of Robin (Dick) Triefus (d 1983), and Jean Margaret, *née* Herring; *b* 7 Nov 1956; *Educ* Queenswood Sch Hatfield Herts, Univ of Cambridge (MA); *m* 5 May 1979, Richard John Maurice, s of Richard Thomas Gilmore, of Maldon, Essex; 2 s (Daniel b 1986, Alexander b 1989); *Career* Ted Bates Advertising Agency London 1977-78, Benton & Bates Advertising Agency London 1978-84, md Michael Peters & Ptnrs 1987-90 (account mangr 1977, account dir 1979, devpt dir 1984, mktg dir 1985), md Lewis Moberley 1990-; speaker CBI conf 1986; memb: CBI vision 2010 Gp 1986-87, NEDO Maker User Working Pty 1988, Milk Mktg Bd 1988, Mktg Soc, GCSE Modern Language Working Pty 1989; govr Centre for Info on Language Teaching and Res 1987, chm Design Effectiveness Awards Scheme 1988-89; memb: RSA, IOD; *Recreations* family, skiing, tennis, walking, singing; *Style—* Mrs Fiona Gilmore

GILMORE, John Franklin; s of John Franklin Gilmore (d 1987), and Evelyn Maude Exum (d 1974); *b* 30 June 1927; *Educ* Univ of Florida (B Mech Eng); *m* 1950, Norma Rhea, da of Carl Leo Jones (d 1985), of Kentucky; 1 s (Mark b 1967), 2 da (Rebecca, Brenda); *Career* quartermaster USN 1944-46, USS Hornet CV-12, South Pacific, pres Unit Citation 1945; Blaw-Knox Co Oklahoma 1950-55: Stearns Catalytic Corp 1955-86, engr, project mangr, Philadelphia 1955-73, vice pres Catalytic Int London 1973-76 (pres 1976-81), vice pres marketing Philadelphia 1981-86; pres Life Science Inc Philadelphia Pennsylvania USA 1986-; registered professional engr State of Oklahoma and the Cwlth of Pennsylvania; memb: Pennsylvania Soc of Professional Engrs, Nat Soc of Professional Engrs, American Soc of Mech Engrs, founding memb American Assoc of Cost Engrs, memb American Inst of chemical engrs; Man of Merit to the Polish Petrochemia Commemorative Medal Krakow Poland 1980; Winner of Queen's Award for Export Achievement 1979; *Recreations* shooting, swimming, sailing, riding; *Clubs* Clinkers (Philadelphia), Sugar Mill Country (Florida); *Style—* John Gilmore, Esq; 398 Lakeside Road, Ardmore, Pennsylvania, USA (☎ 0101 215/896 6151 and 0101 215/896 0173, office: 1818 Market Street, Philadelphia, Pennsylvania, USA (☎ 0101 215/299 8700, telex 845192 CABLE: DAYZIM)

GILMORE, Maj Michael Maurice Allan; s of Lt-Col Edward Maurice Blunt Gilmore, DSO (d 1965), and Dorothy Hill, *née* Drury; third successive generation cmmnd into 61 Foot/Gloucestershire Regt; *b* 18 Dec 1931; *Educ* Dauntsey's Sch W Lavington, RMA Sandhurst; *m* 28 Sept 1963, Marion Patricia Studdy, da of Cecil John Edmonds, CMG, CBE (d 1979); 1 s (Edward b 1974), 2 da (Alexandra b 1967, Elizabeth b 1976); *Career* Army Offr (Glosters) 1952-69; serv: Kenya 1955-56, Aden 1956, Bahrain 1956-57, Cyprus 1957, Turkey 1958-59, Cyprus 1962-65, S Arabia 1966-67, ret as Maj; exec offr Tata Ltd London 1969-71, Maj Dubai Def Force UAE 1972-76; branch mangr: MAR Albahar Oman 1976-77, Binladen Telecommunications Co EP Saudi-Arabia 1978-80, YBA Kanoo (later regnl mangr) 1980-86; mgmnt conslt UK 1987-88, currently commercial mangr M A Maghrabi & Sons Saudi-Arabia; memb: Br Horse Soc, Inst of Linguists, Br Inst of Mgmnt; Assoc IOD; *Recreations* all equitation, skiing, beagling, shooting, singing, reading, amateur dramatics, gliding; *Clubs* Royal Aero; *Style—* Maj Michael Gilmore; The Old Forge, Pyrton, Watlington, Oxon OX9 5AP (☎ 049 161 2459)

GILMORE, Owen Jeremy Adrian (Jerry); s of Dr Owen Dermot Gilmore, of Inigo House, Highworth, Wilts, and Carmel, *née* Cantwell; *b* 27 Dec 1941; *Educ* Beaumont Coll, St Bartholomew's Hosp Med Sch (MB BS); *m* 19 Nov 1986, Hilary Ann Frances; 2 s (Hugh Inigo Jeremy b 1969, Quentin Roderick Zebedee b 1977), 4 da (Anna Benedicta Claire b 1967, Deborah Emma Frances b 1968, Katherine Laura Matilda b 1971, Natasha Olivia Polly b 1973); *Career* conslt surgn St Bartholomew's Hosp London 1976, conslt in charge Breast Unit St Bartholomew's Hosp; prizes: Begley prize RCS 1966, Moynihan Prize and Medal Assoc Surgns GB 1975, Hamilton Bailey Prize Int Coll Surgeons 1975, Hunterian Prof RCS 1976; MRCS (England), LRCP (London) 1966, FRCS (England) 1971, FRCS (Edinburgh) 1971, MS (London) 1976; *Books* Diagnosis and Treatment of Breast Disease, Diagnosis and Treatment of groin injuries in sportsmen (Gilmore's groin); *Recreations* skiing, squash, rugby football, wine and dining, travel; *Style—* Jerry Gilmore, Esq; 30 Harley St, London W1N 1AB (☎ 071 637 8820)

GILMORE, Rosalind Edith Jean; da of Sir Robert Brown Fraser, OBE (d 1984), and Betty, *née* Harris (d 1984); *b* 23 March 1937; *Educ* King Alfred Sch London, Univ Coll London (BA), Newnham Coll Cambridge (BA, MA); *m* 17 Feb 1962, Brian Terence, s of John Henry Gilmore; *Career* HM Treasy 1960-82: appointed 1960, asst princ 1960-62, asst priv sec to Chllr of Exchequer 1962-65, exec asst to econ dir International Bank for Reconstruction and Development 1966-67, princ 1968, princ private sec to Paymaster Gen 1973, princ private sec to Chllr of Duchy of Lancaster 1974, asst sec 1975, head of Fin Inst Div 1977-80 (Banking Act 1979, Credits Unions Act 1979), press sec to Chllr of Exchequer 1980-82, head of Information 1980-82; gen mangr corp planning Dunlop Ltd 1982-83, dir of mktg National Girobank 1983-86; dir fell St George's House Windsor Castle 1986-89; dir: Mercantile Group plc, Mercantile Credit Co Ltd, London and Manchester Group plc; marketing conslt FI Group PLC (Software) 1986-89; memb Fin Servs Act Tbnl 1986-89, chm Building Socs Cmmn 1991- (dep chm 1989-91); fell RSA 1985, UCL 1988; assoc fell Newnham Coll Cambridge 1986; *Recreations* music, reading, house in Greece; *Style—* Mrs Rosalind Gilmore; The Building Societies Commission, 15 Great Marlborough St, London W1V 2AX (☎ 071 494 6636)

GILMOUR, Dr Alan Breck; CVO (1990), CBE (1984); s of Andrew Gilmour, CMG (d 1988), of Edinburgh, and Nelle, *née* Twigg (d 1984); *b* 30 Aug 1928; *Educ* Clayesmore Sch, King's Coll Hosp London Univ (MB BS); *m* 8 June 1957, Elizabeth, da of late Henry Heath; 2 da; *Career* Nat Serv 1947-49; GP 1957-67, BMA Secretariat 1967-79, dir NSPCC 1979-89; former memb: Standing Med Advsy Ctee, cncl BMA, Educn Ctee RCGP; former treas ASME; chm Int Alliance on Child Abuse and Neglect 1984-; memb: Video Consultative Cncl of Br Bd of Film Classification 1985-, Health Educn Authy 1989-; chm Michael Sieff Fndn 1990- hon vice pres NSPCC 1990; Liveryman Worshipful Soc of Apothecaries 1973; LMSSA 1956, FRCGP 1974; *Books* Innocent Victims - The Question of Child Abuse (1988); *Recreations* walking, gardening, music; *Clubs* RSM, Royal Overseas League, IOD; *Style—* Dr Alan Gilmour, CVO, CBE; 106 Crock Lane, Bothenhampton, Bridport, Dorset DT6 4DH (☎ 0308 23116)

GILMOUR, Alexander Clement (Sandy); CVO (1990); s of Sir John Gilmour, 2 Bt (d 1977), and Lady Mary Gilmour, *qv*, da of 3 Duke of Abercorn; half bro of Rt Hon Sir Ian Gilmour, 3 Bt, MP, *qv*; *b* 23 Aug 1931; *Educ* Eton; *m* 1, 2 Dec 1954 (m dis 1983), Barbara Marie-Louise Constance, da of Hon Denis Gomer Berry, TD, *qv*; 2 s, 1 da; m 2, 1983, Susan Janet, eld da of late Capt Voltelin James Howard Van der Byl, BSC, RN (ret), and formerly wife of (1) Alwyn Richard Dudley Smith and (2) 2 Baron Chetwode; *Career* stockbroker; dir and head Corp Fin Dept Carr Sebag and Co 1972-82; conslt with: Grieveson Grant 1982-83, Gilmour & Associates Ltd 1983-84, Equity Financial Trust 1984-86, Tide (UK) Ltd 1986; dir London Wall Securities Ltd 1989-; dir Tate Gallery Fndn 1986-88; *Recreations* fishing, gardening, tennis skiing; *Clubs* White's, HEEG; *Style—* A C Gilmour, Esq, CVO; 1 Christopher Mews, Penzance St, London W11 4QZ (☎ 071 602 7270)

GILMOUR, Col Allan Macdonald; OBE (1961), MC (and bar 1942, 1943); s of Capt Allan Gilmour, of Rosehall, Sutherland (ka Salonica 1916), and Mary, *née* Macdonald; *b* 23 Nov 1916; *Educ* Winchester; *m* 1941, Jean, da of Capt E G Wood (d 1980), of Gollanfield, Invernessshire; 3 s, 1 da; *Career* WWII served Seaforth Highlanders ME, Sicily, Italy, NW Europe (despatches 1944); Col Queen's Own Highlanders 1944-66: served Germany, ME, UK, instr Staff Coll Pakistan, CGS Ghana; memb Highland Regnl Cncl; chm: Sutherland DC, Highland Health Bd; HM Lord Lt Sutherland 1972- (DL 1971); DSC (USA) 1945; *Recreations* fishing; *Style—* Col Allan Gilmour, OBE, MC; Invernauld, Rosehall, Sutherland (☎ 054 984204)

GILMOUR, Lady Caroline Margaret; *née* Montagu Douglas Scott; yr da of 8 Duke of Buccleuch, KT, GCVO, TD, PC (d 1973); *b* 17 Nov 1927; *m* 10 July 1951, Rt Hon Sir Ian Hedworth John Little Gilmour, 3 Bt, MP; 4 s, 1 da; *Style—* Lady Caroline Gilmour; The Ferry House, Old Isleworth, Middlesex

GILMOUR, David Jon; s of Douglas Graham Gilmour, and (Edith) Sylvia, *née* Wilson; *b* 6 March 1946; *Educ* Perse Sch for Boys, Cambridge Coll of Arts & Technol; *m* ; 4 c; *Career* musician and singer; with Pink Floyd 1968-; albums incl: Dark Side of the Moon (1973), The Wall (1979), A Momentary Lapse of Reason (1987); World Tour (200 shows) Sept 1987-July 1989; solo albums: David Gilmour (1978), About Face (1984); solo tour 1984; *Recreations* aviation, sailing, scuba, motor-racing; *Style—* David Gilmour, Esq

GILMOUR, David Robert; s and h of Rt Hon Sir Ian Gilmour, 3 Bt, MP, *qv*; *b* 14 Nov 1952; *Educ* Eton, Balliol Coll Oxford; *m* 1975, Sarah Anne, da of Michael Bradstock, of Whitefold, Clunas Nairn, Dorset; 1 s (Alexander b 1980), 3 da (Rachel b 1977, Katharine b 1984, Laura b 1985); *Career* writer; *Books* Dispossessed: The Ordeal of The Palestinians 1917-80 (1980), Lebanon: The Fractured Country (1983), The Transformation of Spain: From Franco to the Constitutional Monarchy (1985), The Last Leopard: A Life of Giuseppe di Lampedusa (1988); *Style—* David Gilmour, Esq; 21 Moray Place, Edinburgh

GILMOUR, Ewen Hamilton; s of Lt Cdr Patrick Dalrymple Gilmour (d 1988), and Lorna Mary, *née* Dore; *b* 16 Aug 1953; *Educ* Rugby, Downing Coll Cambridge; *m* 3 June 1978, Nicola, da of Maarten Van Mesdag; 3 s (James b 27 Feb 1980, Rowallan b 3 April 1982, Fergus b 4 May 1985), 1 da (Iona b 19 Jan 1990); *Career* CA; Peat Marwick McLintock 1974-80, dir Charterhouse Bank Ltd 1987- (joined 1980); FCA 1979; *Recreations* cricket, golf, gardening; *Clubs* MCC; *Style—* Ewen Gilmour, Esq; 20 Arthur Rd, London SW19 7DZ (☎ 081 947 6805); 1 Paternoster Row, St Pauls, London EC4 (☎ 071 248 4000, fax 071 248 1998)

GILMOUR, Rt Hon Sir Ian Hedworth John Little; 3 Bt (UK 1926), PC (1973), MP (C) Chesham and Amersham 1974-; s of Sir John Little Gilmour, 2 Bt (d 1977), by his 1 w; *see* Hon Mrs Gilmour, OBE, TD; half bro of Sandy Gilmour *qv*; *b* 8 July 1926; *Educ* Eton, Balliol Coll Oxford; *m* 10 July 1951, Lady Caroline Margaret Montagu Douglas Scott, da of 8 Duke of Buccleuch and Queensberry; 4 s, 1 da; *Heir* s, David Robert Gilmour; *Career* late Grenadier Gds; called to the Bar 1952; ed The Spectator 1954-59; MP Norfolk Central 1962-74, Parly under sec MOD 1970-71; min of state: Defence Procurement MOD 1971-72, Defence 1972-74; sec of state Defence 1974, chm Cons Research Dept 1974-75, Lord Privy Seal and dep foreign sec 1979-81; *Books* The Body Politic (1969), Inside Right: A Study of Conservatism (1977), Britain Can Work (1983); *Style—* The Rt Hon Sir Ian Gilmour, Bt, PC, MP; The Ferry House, Old Isleworth, Middx (☎ 081 560 6769)

GILMOUR, John; DL (Fife 1987); s and h of Col Sir John Gilmour, 3 Bt, DSO, TD, JP; *b* 15 July 1944; *Educ* Eton, Aberdeen Coll of Agric; *m* 6 May 1967, Valerie Jardine, yr da of late George Walker Russell and Mrs William Wilson, of Hilton House, Cupar; 2 s, 2 da; *Career* Capt Fife and Forfar Yeo/Scottish Horse (TA); farmer; memb Royal Co of Archers (Queen's Bodyguard for Scotland); MFH 1972-; company dir; *Recreations* riding, fishing, reading; *Clubs* New (Edinburgh); *Style—* John Gilmour, Esq, DL; Balcormo Mains, Leven, Fife (☎ 033336 229)

GILMOUR, Col Sir John Edward; 3 Bt (UK 1897), of Lundin and Montrave, Parishes of Largo and Scoonie, Co Fife, DSO (1945), TD, JP (Fife 1957); s of Col Rt Hon Sir John Gilmour, 2 Bt, GCVO, DSO, sometime MP E Renfrewshire and Glasgow Pollok (d 1940), by his 1 w, Mary (d 1919), da of Edward Lambert, of Telham Court, Sussex; *b* 24 Oct 1912; *Educ* Eton, Trinity Hall Cambridge, Dundee Sch of Econs; *m* 24 May 1941, Ursula Mabyn, da of late Frank Oliver Wills, of Cote Lodge, Westbury-on-Trym; 2 s (John, *qv*; Andrew b 1947, m Mary, adopted da of Sir Henry Campbell de la Poer Beresford-Peirse, 5 Bt (d 1972)); *Heir* s, John Gilmour; *Career* Bt-Col 1950; MP (C) E Fife 1961-79, chm Cons and Unionist Party Scot 1965-67; HM Lord-Lt Fife 1980-87 (vice Lord-Lt 1979-80, DL 1953); Lord High Cmmr to Gen Assembly of Church of Scot 1982 and 1983; Capt Royal Co of Archers (Queen's Body Guard for Scot); *Recreations* hunting, gardening, shooting; *Clubs* Royal and Ancient St Andrews, Cavalry and Guards'; *Style—* Col Sir John Gilmour, Bt, DSO, TD, JP; Montrave, Leven, Fife KY8 5NZ (☎ 0333 26159)

GILMOUR, Hon Mrs (Victoria Laura); OBE (1927), TD; da of Henry Arthur Cadogan, Viscount Chelsea (d 1908, s of 5 Earl Cadogan) and Hon Mildred, *née* Sturt, da of 1 Baron Alington; *b* 22 Oct 1901; *m* 22 July 1922 (m dis 1929), John Little Gilmour (afterwards 2 Bt, d 1977); 1 s (Rt Hon Sir Ian Gilmour, Bt, MP, *qv*) 1 da; *Career* controller ATS; acted as lady-in-waiting to HM Queen Elizabeth the Queen Mother when Duchess of York on tour of Australia and New Zealand 1927; *Style—* The Hon Mrs Gilmour, OBE, TD; Dacres, Bentworth, Alton, Hants (☎ 0420 62040)

GILMOUR, Hon Sheriff William McIntosh; s of Dr John Grey Gilmour, and Jessie Gilmour; *b* 9 March 1923; *Educ* Hillhead HS Glasgow, Cally House, Gatehouse of Fleet, Univ of Glasgow (BL); *m* 30 June 1961, Elinor, da of John Adams; *Career* early experience with legal firms in Glasgow, latterly ptnr and sr ptnr with firm in Dunbartonshire; presently conslt to legal firm in Glasgow, former dean and current hon memb of Faculty of Procurators Dumbarton; hon sheriff Dumbarton; chm Dumbartonshire Order of St John, fndr memb and past pres Clydebank Rotary, past deacon Soc of Deacons, memb Incorpn of Gardners (Glasgow Trades House), life memb Univ of Glasgow Union, holder of letter of commentation for prolonged servs to ATC by MOD; hon pres Vale of Leven (2319 Sqdn) ATC; Freeman City of Glasgow; *Recreations* formerly motor sport; *Clubs* RSAC Glasgow, Partick Burns (Glasgow), Scottish Sporting Car; *Style—* Sheriff William M Gilmour; 65 Killermont Rd, Bearsden, Glasgow (☎ 041 942 0498)

GILPIN, Adrian (formerly Adrian Charles Scrymsour Slattery); s of Peter Anthony Slattery, and Joanella Elizabeth Agnes, *née* Scrymsour-Nichol; *b* 9 Aug 1956; *Educ* Holmewood House Sussex, Ampleforth, Skinners Sch Tunbridge Wells, Guildhall Sch of Music and Drama, Inst of Dir's (Dip); *m* 26 Feb 1983, Francesca, *née* Marks; 2 da (Sophie Ella Storey b 19 May 1989, Phoebe Elizabeth Scrymsour b 16 Oct 1990); *Career* actor 1974-; work incl: rep, West End, tours, film, tv (incl Don't Wait up, Hot Metal); fndr Adrian Gilpin Assocs theatre consultancy (UK, USA, Australia, M East), gen mangr Theatre of Comedy Co Ltd 1982-84; md: Artatack (Stage) Ltd theatre prodrs 1986-, Unicorn Heritage plc 1986-89 (fndr Royal Britain Exhibition, London), Adrian Gilpin TV Ltd 1989-; work incl: Now We are Sixty (Cambridge Arts Theatre) 1986, If Winter Comes (Melbourne Australia) 1986; memb: Assoc of Ind Prodrs 1986, Ind Programme Prodrs Assoc, Tourism Soc 1988; MInstD 1987; *Style—* Adrian Gilpin, Esq; Harvey's Farm, Warninglid, W Sussex RH17 5TQ ; Castlelough, Portroe, Nenagh, Co Tipperary, Eire

GILROY, Angus Hugh; s of Donald Duff Gilroy (d 1963), and Margaret Campbell, *née* Forrester; *b* 4 Sept 1936; *Educ* Harrow; *m* 30 Sept 1967, Elizabeth Hurst, da of late Richard Lumley Hurst; 1 s (Fergus Hugh b 29 March 1969), 1 da (Margaret Cecilia b 22 Dec 1970); *Career* Nat Serv 2 Lt The Black Watch RHR 1955-57, CA 1963; Binder Hamlyn & Co: articled clerk 1958, ptnr 1972- (now BDO Binder Hamlyn); memb: Royal Co of Archers (Queen's Body Guard for Scot) 1972, Worshipful Co of Bowyers 1991; memb ICAEW 1963; *Recreations* golf, shooting, fishing; *Clubs* MCC, West Sussex Golf, Gresham; *Style—* Angus Gilroy, Esq; BDO Binder Hamlyn, 20 Old Bailey, London EC4M 7BH (☎ 071 489 9000)

GILROY, Dr Beryl Agatha; *née* Alnwick; *b* 30 Aug 1924; *Educ* Univ of London (BA), Univ of Sussex (MA), Century Univ LA California (PhD); *Career* educn conslt, counselling psychologist, ret univ lectr, author; memb Race Relations Bd 1964-69 and 1976-; *Books* In for a Penny (1978), Frangipani House (1985), Boy Sandwich (1989), Echoes and Voices (poems, 1990), A Love in Bondage (1991); *Recreations* walking, reading, needlework; *Style—* Dr Beryl Gilroy

GILROY, Darla-Jane; da of Patrick Eric Gilroy (d 1976), and Beryl Agatha, *née* Answick; *b* 9 Jan 1959; *Educ* Camden Girls Sch, Brighton Coll of Art, St Martin's Sch of Art (BA); *Career* costume design David Bowie Ashes to Ashes video 1980, first major show Olympia 1981, London designers collections 1981; major press features: Vogue, Options, Company, Cosmopolitan 1982; opened retail outlet 1983, freelance collection Topshop 1984, second retail outfit Kings Rd 1984; exhibited: Milan, New York, London 1986-; started mfrg in Hong Kong 1987, lectr St Martins Sch of Art 1987-, 30 min video of career and achievements Design Cncl 1987; *Recreations* horse riding, breeding dogs, film, travel; *Clubs* Chelsea Arts, Groucho's, Fred's; *Style*— Miss Darla-Jane Gilroy; Studio 23, Ransome's Dock, 35-37 Parkgate Road, London SW11 (☎ 071 223 9145/071 352 2095, fax 071 350 2389)

GILROY, Sandy; s of Alexander Gilroy (d 1952), and Thelma Mercy McClymont, *née* Tubbs (d 1980); *b* 22 June 1935; *Educ* Winchester; *m* 1959, Marion (d 1985), da of Maj David Brodie (d 1966), of Lethen, Nairn; *Career* 2 Lt The Black Watch (RHR); merchandise controller Br Home Stores, chm Alexander Gilroy Group Ltd, fndr Savoir Vivre (Social Contact Network); *Recreations* writing, miniatures, country pursuits; *Style*— Sandy Gilroy, Esq; Glen Shinnel, Tynron by Thornhill, Dumfriesshire DG3 4LE (☎ 08482 551); 866 Chelsea Cloisters, Sloane Avenue, London SW3 3DW (☎ 071 581 4328)

GIMBLETT, (Frederick) Gareth Robert; OBE (1989), DL (Berks, 1988); s of Dan William Davies Gimblett (d 1980), of Tonyrefail, Mid Glam, and Annie, *née* Flook (d 1977); *b* 20 Dec 1931; *Educ* Tonyrefail GS, University Coll of Wales Aberystwyth (BSc, MSc) Univ of Manchester; *m* (Moreen) Margaret, da of Charles Cornford (d 1970); 3 s (Richard b 1959, Michael 1960, Jonathan 1965); 1 da (Briony b 1966); *Career* scientific offr RAE Farnborough Hants 1955-58, hon sr res fell Brunel Univ 1989-90 (lectr in physical chemistry 1958-82, sr res fell 1982-89), freelance sci ed and writer 1989-; exec cncl memb ACC 1983-; chm: Sub-Ctee Manpower 1985-87, Berks CC 1986-89 (memb 1977-, ldr 1981-86), LAMSAC 1988-89, Care Sector Consortium 1988-, Local Govt Trg Bd 1990-; vice-chm: Local Govt Mgmnt Bd 1990-; FRSC 1989; cdr Royal Order of Merit Norway 1988; *Books* Inorganic Polymer Chemistry (1962), Introduction to Kinetics of Chemical Chain Reactions (1970); *Recreations* walking, rugby football (spectator); *Style*— Gareth Gimblett, Esq, OBE, DL; 6 Park View Drive South, Charvil, Reading, Berks RG10 9QX

GIMENA, Lady Anne-Marie Ines; *née* Ward; da (twin, by 1 m) of 4 Earl of Dudley; *b* 26 May 1955; *m* 1978, Laureano Perez-Andujar Gimena, of Madrid; *Style*— Lady Anne-Marie Gimena

GIMSON, Maj Richard Allynne Stanford; MC (1944), TD (1956); s of Harold Gimson (d 1939), of Daneway, Leiston, Suffolk, and Janet Marjorie, *née* Stanford (d 1946); *b* 12 Dec 1922; *Educ* Uppingham, Clare Coll Cambridge; *m* 12 July 1947, Elspeth Primrose, yst da of Col Sholto Stuart Ogilvie, CBE, DSO (d 1964), of Ness House, Sizewell, Suffolk; 1 s (Alexander Edward Stanford b 1951), 2 da (Wendy Louise b 1948, Caroline Ann (twin) b 1948); *Career* served WWII cmmnd RE 1941-47 in Egypt, Greece, Italy, Yugoslavia and NW Europe, Maj TA Royal Lincs Regt 1947-59; co dir: Ruston and Hornsby Ltd 1960-66, English Electric Diesels 1966-70, Davey Paxman Ltd 1966-70, Babcock and Wilcox (Operations) Ltd 1970-78, Gimson and Co Ltd 1979-87, Coastal Training Services 1984-; chm Kirton Healthcare Group Ltd 1989-; JP: Lincoln 1961-70, Essex 1970-78; chm Middle East Assoc 1978; memb: Br Overseas Trade Bd, European Trade Ctee 1970-77, Scot Cncl for Devpt Mission (China 1974, USSR 1976); *Recreations* swimming, stalking, sailing, music; *Clubs* Naval and Military, Aldeburgh Yacht; *Style*— Maj Richard Gimson, MC, TD, JP; Ness House, Sizewell, Suffolk IP16 4UB (☎ 0728 830007)

GIMSON, (George) Stanley; QC (1961); s of George William Gimson (d 1949), of Glasgow, and Mary, *née* Hogg (d 1950); *b* 6 Sept 1915; *Educ* HS of Glasgow, Univ of Glasgow (BL); *Career* RA TA 1938, cmmnd 1941, Lt 2 HAA Regt Indian Artillery Singapore 1941-, POW Changi (Singapore) and River Kwai (Thailand); called to the Scottish Bar 1949, advocate 1949; standing counsel Dept of Agric for Scotland and Forestry Cmmn 1956-61; Sheriff Princ: Aberdeen Kincardine and Banff 1972-74, Grampian Highland and Islands 1975-82; chm: Pensions Appeals Tbnls Scotland 1971-, Med Appeals Tbnls Scotland 1985-; dir Scottish National Orchestra Society Ltd 1962-80, chm RSPCC (Edinburgh) 1972-76; chm Bd of Mgmnt Edinburgh Central Hosps (memb 1960-70), vice chm Edinburgh Victoria Hosps 1970-74, tstee Nat Library of Scotland 1963-76; Hon LLD Univ of Aberdeen 1981; *Recreations* travel, forestry, sketching, history; *Clubs* Royal Northern and Univ (Aberdeen), Edinburgh Univ Staff; *Style*— Stanley Gimson, Esq, QC; 11 Royal Circus, Edinburgh EH3 6TL

GINGELL, Prof David; s of late William Joseph Simpson Gingell, and late Hazel Gertrude, *née* Kinns; *b* 13 Oct 1941; *Educ* Lyme Regis GS, Kings Coll London (BSc, PhD, DSc); *m* 1, 20 Dec 1969 (m dis 1989), Brenda Mary Jean, da of Earnest Butler, of 181 Dominion Rd, Worthing, Sussex; 1 s (Peter b 1982), 1 da (Claire b 1974); m 2, 28 April 1990, Regina Carmen Davies, da of Joao da Silva Cardoso, of R Dois de Dezembro, 22/601 Rio de Janeiro, Brazil; *Career* reader Middx Hosp Med Sch 1979-84 (lectr 1969-77), prof cell biology Univ of London 1987-; memb William Barnes Soc; memb: Br Soc Cell Biology, American Soc Cell Biology; *Books* Biophysics of the Cell Surface (1989), and over 60 published books and articles; *Recreations* painting, herology, paleontology; *Style*— Prof David Gingell; Department of Anatomy & Developmental Biology, University College & Middlesey School of Medicine, Gower St, London WC1E 6BT (☎ 071 387 7050 ext 3353, fax 071 380 7045)

GINGELL, Air Chief Marshal Sir John; GBE (1984, CBE 1973, MBE 1962), KCB (1978); eldest s of Ernest John Gingell; *b* 3 Feb 1925; *Educ* St Boniface's Coll Plymouth; *m* 1949, Prudence Mary, da of Brig Roy Frank Johnson; 2 s, 1 da; *Career* RAF 1943, Sub-Lieut RNVR Fleet Air Arm 1945-46, RAF 1951, Air Plans Staff HQ NEAF 1960-63, OC No 27 Sqdn (Vulcans) 1963-65, Defence Ops Staff MOD 1966-68, mil asst to chm Mil Ctee NATO Brussels 1968-70, AOA RAF Germany 1971-72, AOC No 23 Gp RAF 1973-75, asst chief of defence staff (Policy) MOD 1975-78, air memb for personnel 1978-80, AOC-in-C RAF support cmd 1980-81, Dep C-in-C Allied Forces Central Europe 1981-84; Gentleman Usher of the Black Rod and Sergeant at Arms House of Lords, sec Lord Great Chamberlain 1985-; Cmmnr Cwlth War Graves; hon bencher Inner Temple 1990-; *Clubs* RAF; *Style*— Air Chief Marshal Sir John Gingell, GBE, KCB; House of Lords, London SW1A 0PW

GINGELL, Maj-Gen Laurie William Albert; CB (1980), OBE (1966, MBE 1959); s of Maj William George Gingell, MBE (d 1960), and Elsie Grace Gingell (d 1989); *b* 29 Oct 1925; *Educ* Farnborough GS, Oriel Coll Oxford; *m* 2 June 1949, Nancy Margaret, da of Arthur Wadsworth (d 1967); 1 s (Richard William b 23 Aug 1961), 1 da (Sarah Louise b 15 June 1959); *Career* RTR: cmmnd 1945, cmd 1 RTR 1966-67, 7 Armd Bde 1970-71; MGA UKLF 1976-79; gen sec The Offrs Pensions Soc 1979-90, chm Victory Servs Club 1989-; Freeman City of London 1980; *Recreations* swimming, tennis; *Style*— Maj-Gen Laurie Gingell, CB, OBE

GINNINGS, Paul David; s of David John Ginnings, of Fordingbridge, Hants, and Betty Christina, *née* Ogle; *b* 22 July 1946; *Educ* Monkton Combe Sch; *m* Gillian, da of Leslie Saunders; 3 da (Alison b 8 Nov 1975, Hazel b 22 Sept 1978, Miriam b 10 Oct 1980); *Career* audit sr Norton Keen & Co 1969-72 (articled clerk 1964-69, qualified chartered accountant 1969), mangr Robson Rhodes 1972-74, Temple Gothard 1974-85 (mangr, ptnr), ptnr Touche Ross & Co 1985-; ACA 1970; *Books* Financial Management of Housing Associates - A Practical Guide (1989); *Recreations* fly-fishing, church activities, skiing; *Style*— Paul Ginnings, Esq; 96 Clarence Rd, St Albans, Herts AL1 4NQ (☎ 0727 53468); Touche Ross & Co, Hill House, 1 Little New St, London EC4A 3TR (☎ 071 936 3000, fax 071 583 8517)

GINSBORG, Michael David; s of Samuel Ginsborg (d 1986), of Gerrards Cross, Bucks, and Rose, *née* Gabe; *b* 25 April 1943; *Educ* Westminster King's Coll London, Central Sch of Art & Design (DipAD), Chelsea Sch of Art (Higher DipAD); *m* 1972, Rosamund (Robby) da of John Ducane Nelson; 2 da (Katharine Teeny b 3 Aug 1972, (Sonya) Charlotte b 2 Dec 1974); *Career* artist and educator; lectr and examiner numerous UK art schs 1969-, pt/t tutor Wimbledon Sch of Art until 1979, sessional lectr Univ of Reading, head of painting Ravensbourne Coll until 1984, head Sch of Fine Arts Birmingham Poly 1989- (course dir Masters Degree in Fine Arts 1984-89); solo exhibitions: Lisson Gallery 1969, Serpentine Gallery 1973, City Museum Bolton 1976, Acme Gallery London 1980, Benjamin Rhodes Gallery 1986 and 1989; numerous gp exhibitions incl: British Painting (Royal Acad) 1977, Recent Acquisitions (Hayward) 1978, British Art Show 1979; work in the collections of: Govt Art Collection, Br Cncl, Dept of the Environment, Arts Cncl of GB and in many other collections in UK, Europe and USA; cmmnd to paint St Charles Hospital Centenary Murals 1981 and 1982; awards incl: first prize Univ of London Painting Competition 1963, prizewinner Cleveland Drawing Biennale 1975, Visual Arts award Greater London Arts Assoc 1976, Arts Cncl Bursary 1977, Mark Rothko Meml award 1979; memb Register of Specialist Advsrs CNAA; *Style*— Michael Ginsborg, Esq; Benjamin Rhodes Gallery, 4 New Burlington Place, London W1X 1SB (☎ 071 434 1768/9, fax 071 237 8841)

GINSBURG, Dr Robert; s of Maj the Rev Alec Ginsburg, of Courtenay Gate, Kingsway, Hove, E Sussex, and Rose, *née* Nairn; *b* 15 June 1951; *Educ* Devonport HS for Boys, The London Hosp Med Coll (BSc, MB BS); *m* 10 July 1989, Dina, da of Dr Leon Kaufman, of London; *Career* sr registrar anaesthetics The Hosp for Sick Children Gt Ormond St 1984-85, research fell UCLA 1985-86, sr registrar anaesthetics The London Hosp 1986-88, conslt anaesthetist KCM and The Dulwich Gp of Hospitals 1988-; MRCS, FFARCS 1983, FRARCSI, LRCP; *Recreations* boating, licensed amateur radio; *Clubs* The Rugby (London); *Style*— Dr Robert Ginsberg; Department of Anaesthetics, King's College Hospital, Demnark Hill, London SE5 9RS (☎ 071 326 3154)

GINSBURY, Norman; s of Samuel Jacob Ginsbury (d 1904), and Rachel Cecily Schulberg (d 1929); *b* 8 Nov 1903; *Educ* Grocers' Co Sch, Univ of London (BSc); *m* 1945, Dorothy Agnes, da of William Jennings, of 54 Greenbank Ave, Plymouth, Devon; *Career* produced plays incl: Viceroy Sarah 1934 and 1935, Ibsen's Ghosts 1937 and 1958, Ibsen's An Enemy of The People 1939, Walk in The Sun 1939, Take Back Your Freedom 1940, (Take Back Your Freedom was derived from a play by Winifred Holtby called Hope of Thousands), The Forefathers 1940, Ibsen's Peer Gynt 1944, The First Gentleman 1945 and 1946, The Gambler 1946, Ibsen's A Doll's House 1946, The Happy Man 1949, The School for Rivals 1949, Portrait By Lawrence 1950, The Forefathers 1951, Ibsen's Rosmersholm 1960, Ibsen's The Pillars of Society 1961, Ibsen's John Gabriel Borkman 1960, Strindberg's The Dance of Death 1966, The Wisest Fool 1974, The Forefathers 1970; *Books* Viceroy Sarah (1935), Take Back Your Freedom (1939), The First Gentleman (1940 and 1946), Peer Gynt (1946); *Clubs* Dramatists'; *Style*— Norman Ginsbury, Esq; c/o Messrs Goodman Derrick & Co, 9-11 Fulwood Place, Gray's Inn, London WC1V 6HQ (☎ 071 404 0606)

GINTELL, Burton; *b* 11 May 1935; *Educ* City Univ of New York; *Career* md J G Turney & Son Ltd, winner of a Queen's Award for Export 1980, William Whiteley & Co, Glenforres Glenlivet Distillery Co Ltd 1978-; *Style*— Burton Gintell, Esq; Atlas House, 57a Catherine Place, SW1, (☎ 071 834 3771)

GIORDANO, Richard Vincent; KBE; s of Vincent and Cynthia Giordano; *b* 1934,March; *Educ* Harvard (BA, LLB, PhD); *m* 1956, Barbara Claire Beckett; 1 s, 2 da; *Career* former head Airco Corp, non-exec dir National Power plc 1982-, pt/t bd memb Georgia Pacific Corp, Atlanta GA 1984-, bd memb Grand Met plc 1985-, chm The BOC gp 1985- (chief exec 1979-91), non-exec dir Reuters Holdings plc 1991; *Recreations* ocean sailing, tennis; *Clubs* The Links, New York Yacht, Edgartown Yacht (Mass), Duquesne (Pittsburgh PA); *Style*— Richard Giordano, Esq, KBE; The BOC Group plc, Chertsey Rd, Windlesham, Surrey GU20 6HJ

GIOVENE, Laurence; s of Andrea Giovene, Duca Di Girasole, of Palazzo Ciervo St Agata Del Goti, BV, Italy, and Adeline Constance, *née* Schuberth; *b* 21 Nov 1936; *Educ* Solihull Sch, St Catharines Coll Cambridge (MA); *Career* barr, standing counsel to Italian Govt 1965-85, dep Circuit judge 1978, recorder 1986; contested (Cons) East-Ham North 1965, Fulham Borough cncllr 1962-64; pres CU 1960; MCIA; *Recreations* sailing, oil painting; *Clubs* Garrick, Bar Yacht; *Style*— Laurence Giovene, Esq; 2 Pump Court, Temple EC4 (☎ 071 583 2122)

GIPPS, Dr Ruth Dorothy Louisa; MBE (1981); da of Gerard Cardew Bryan Gipps (d 1956), and Hélène Bettina Johner (d 1966); *b* 20 Feb 1921; *Educ* Bexhill Sch of Music (ARCM), RCM (BMus, DMus); *m* 19 March 1942, Robert George Hugh Baker; 1 s (Lance Robert b 24 May 1947); *Career* professional solo pianist 1931-53, freelance oboist 1943, CBSO 1944-45, chorus master City of Birmingham Choir 1948-50, extramural lectr Univ of Oxford 1948-59, conductor London Repertoire Orchestra 1955-86, prof Trinity Coll London 1959-66, conductor London Chanticleer Orch 1961-, prof RCM 1967-77, conductor Heathfield Choral Soc 1990-; compositions incl: 5 symphonies, 5 concertos, choral works, chamber music; pres Hastings Festival 1956-87, chm Composers Guild of GB 1967; Hon RAM 1966; FRSA 1950, FRCM 1972; *Recreations* country things, keeping animals, Tudor architecture; *Style*— Dr Ruth Gipps, MBE; Tickerage Castle, Pound Lane, Framfield, Uckfield, East Sussex TN22 5RT (☎ 0825 890348)

GIRDWOOD, Prof Ronald Haxton; CBE (1984); s of Thomas Girdwood (d 1933), of Polwarth Grove, Edinburgh, and Mary Elizabeth, *née* Haxton (d 1952); *b* 19 March 1917; *Educ* Daniel Stewart's Coll Edinburgh, Univ of Edinburgh (MB ChB, MD, PhD); *m* 1945, Mary Elizabeth, da of Reginald Ralph Williams (d 1965), of Woodcroft, Calstock, Cornwall; 1 s (Richard), 1 da (Diana); *Career* RAMC Offr 1942-46, A/Lt-Col, served in India and Burma; Univ of Edinburgh: lectr in med 1946-51, sr lectr then reader 1951-62, prof of therapeutics and clinical pharmacology 1962-82, dean Faculty of Medicine 1975-79; conslt physician Royal Infirmary of Edinburgh 1948-82; about 300 papers in med jls particularly relating to haematology, clinical pharmacology and med history; pres: RCPEd 1982-85 (vice pres 1980-82), Univ of Edinburgh Graduates' Assoc 1991-; chm: Scot Nat Blood Transfusion Assoc 1980-, Medico Pharmaceutical Forum 1985-87; Freedom of township of Sirajgunj Bangladesh 1984; Hon FRACP, Hon FACP, FRCPEd, FRCPLond, FRCPI, FRCPath, FRSEd 1978; *Books* Malabsorption (co-ed, 1969), Textbook of Medical Treatment (1 edn 1971, 1987), Blood Disorders due to Drugs and other Agents (ed, 1973), Clinical Pharmacology (1 edn 1976, 3 edn 1984), Travels with a Stethoscope (1991); *Recreations* writing, photography, painting in oils; *Clubs* East India, Edinburgh Univ Staff; *Style*— Prof Ronald Girdwood, CBE; 2 Hermitage Drive, Edinburgh EH10 6DD (☎ 031 447 5137)

GIRI, Surgn Capt George Anand Rurik; OBE (1970); s of D V Giri (d 1958), conslt ophthalmic surgn, and Princess Marina Kossatkine-Rostoffsky (d 1979), da of Prince Feodor Kossatkine-Rostoffsky, Col Simeonovsky Guards, poet and playwright; *b* 28 April 1923; *Educ* Charterhouse, Jesus Coll Cambridge, St Bartholomew's Hosp (MA

(Hons), LMSSA (Lond), DPH, MFCM, AFOM); *m* 26 Jan 1957, Karin Francesca Dora Margaretha, da of Count Eric Audley Lewenhaupt (d 1968), and Dora Florence (d 1953, artist Dora Crockett), da of Sir James Crockett; 2 s (Michael George Rurik b 1958, Christopher Audley b 1959), 1 da (Alexandra Georgina Francesca b 1961); *Career* surgn Capt RN 1950-78, asst dir gen RN Med Service 1965-69, SE Asia Treaty Organisation 1970-72, dir Studies Inst Naval Medicine 1973-75, chief staff Offr Med Miny Defence 1975-78, asst sec BMA 1978-82; RN ski team Germany 1954, Capt RN hockey Far East 1963; *Recreations* music, arts, gardens; *Clubs* Naval and Military, Veteran Squash GB; *Style—* Surgn Capt George Giri, OBE; Can Quint, Mancor del Valle, Mallorca, Spain (☎ 50 4960)

GIRLING, Hon Mrs (Eleanor Brigit); *née* Addison; er da of 3 Viscount Addison; *b* 1938; *m* 1972, Michael Girling; *Style—* The Hon Mrs Girling; 9 Levana Close, SW19

GIRLING, Maj Gen Peter Howard; CB (1972), OBE (1961); *b* 18 May 1915; *m* 1942, Stella Muriel, da of Sydney Harcourt Hope (d 1931); 2 da (Carolyn, Susan); *Career* dir electrical and mechanical engrg (Army) 1969-72, Maj Gen; dir of operations Open Univ 1972-80; Liveryman Worshipful Co of Turners 1973, ret 1980; Hon MA Open Univ 1981; *Recreations* sailing, travelling; *Clubs* Army and Navy; *Style—* Maj Gen Peter Girling, CB, OBE; The Folly, Wicken, Milton Keynes MK19 6BH

GIROLAMI, Sir Paul; s of Peter Girolami (d 1956); *b* 25 Jan 1926; *Educ* LSE (BCom); *m* 1952, Christabel Mary Gwynne, *née* Lewis; 2 s, 1 da; *Career* Chantrey and Button CAs 1950-54, Coopers and Lybrand 1954-65; Glaxo Holdings: fin controller 1965, memb and fin dir 1968, chief exec 1980-86, dep chm 1985, chm 1985-; pres Glaxo Finanziaria SpA Italy; dir: Nippon Glaxo Ltd Japan, Glaxo-Sankyo Ltd Japan, Credito Italiano International 1990-; memb: CBI Cncl 1986-, Appeal Ctee of ICA 1987, Stock Exchange Listed Cos Advsy Ctee 1987; dir American C of C (UK) 1983, chm Senate of Bd for Chartered Accountants in Business 1989; Grande Ufficiate Ordine al Merito della Republica Italiana 1987, City and Guilds Indignia award in Technol 1988, Hon DSC Univ of Aston 1990, Accademico award Rome Acad of Med and Biological Sciences 1990; Freeman City of London 1980, memb Ct Worshipful Co of Goldsmiths 1986; hon fell LSE 1989; FCA; kt 1989; *Recreations* reading; *Style—* Sir Paul Girolami; 6 Burghley Rd, London SW19 5BH

GIROUARD, Mark; s of Richard Désiré Girouard (d 1989; s of Col Sir Percy Girouard, KCMG, DSO, sometime govr N Nigeria and British E Africa Protectorates, and Mary, da of Hon Sir Richard Solomon, GCMG, KCB, KCVO), and his 1 w, Lady Blanche, *née* de la Poer Beresford, da of 6 Marquess of Waterford, KP; *b* 7 Oct 1931; *Educ* Ampleforth, ChCh Oxford, Courtauld Inst of Art, Bartlett Sch, UCL; *m* 1970, Dorothy N Dorf; 1 da; *Career* writer and architectural historian; Slade prof of fine art Oxford 1975-76; memb: Royal Fine Art Cmmn, Royal Cmmn Hist Monuments, Hist Bldgs Advsy Ctee, Cncl Victorian Soc; Hon FRIBA; *Style—* Mark Girouard, Esq; 35 Colville Rd, London W11

GIRVAN, Martin; s of Peter Girvan, of Rochford, Essex, and Audrey June, *née* Harvey; *b* 17 April 1960; *Educ* Greensward Sch Essex, Southend Coll of Technol South-on-Sea Essex; *m* Shirley Ann, da of Cyril Angerstein; 3 c (Tanya Marie b 30 Jan 1980, Luke Martin James b 5 Nov 1987, Caragh Elissa b 3 May 1989); *Career* various posts incl leisure mgmnt and coaching Rochford Dist Cncl Essex 1981-84 and 1985-86, self employed coach and lectr 1984-85, recreation mangr Braintree and Bocking Recreation Tst 1986-89, centre mangr Sports Nationwide Ltd Riverside Ice and Leisure 1987-89, ice rink mangr Alexandra Palace and Park Tst 1989-, freelance mangr for televised events; Br and Cwlth record holder Hammer, 2 Cwlth Silver medals 1982 and 1986, LA Olympic finalist, Br Team capt 1982 and 1983; memb Inst of Leisure Amenity Mgmnt, ABIM; *Recreations* coaching, my family, music; *Clubs* Haringey; *Style—* Martin Girvan, Esq; Alexander Palace Ice Rink, Alexandra Palace, Wood Green, London N22 4AY (☎ 081 365 2121, fax 081 883 3999)

GISBOROUGH, 3 Baron (UK 1917); Thomas Richard John Long Chaloner; JP; s of 2 Baron Gisborough, TD, JP (d 1951); *b* 1 July 1927; *Educ* Eton, RAC Cirencester; *m* 26 April 1960, Shane, er da of late Sidney Arthur Newton, of Hyde Park Gate, SW7 (2 s of Sir Louis Newton, 1 Bt); 2 s; *Heir* s, Hon Thomas Peregrine Long Chaloner; *Career* served 16th/5th Lancers, Northumberland Hussars TA; sits as Cons peer in House of Lords; former Lt-Col Green Howards (TA); farmer and landowner; cncllr of North Riding and then Cleveland 1964-77; Lord Lt Cleveland 1981-; Hon Col Cleveland Cadet Force; memb Devpt Cmmn 1985-89; pres Nat Ski Fedn 1985-90; KStJ; *Recreations* gliding, bridge, piano, tennis, field sports, skiing; *Style—* The Rt Hon the Lord Gisborough, JP; 37 Bury Walk, London SW3 (☎ 071 581 0260); Gisborough House, Guisborough, Cleveland (☎ 0287 32002)

GITTINGS, (Harold) John; s of Harold William Gittings, of 6 Field Court, Oxted, Surrey, and Doris Marjorie, *née* Whiting; *b* 3 Sept 1947; *Educ* Duke of Yorks Sch Dover; *m* 22 July 1988, Andrea Mary, da of Arnold Fisher, of 13 Birdwood Close, Selsdon, Surrey; 1 step s (Jonathan Charles English b 1969), 1 step da (Tracey Andrea English b 1965); *Career* Beecham Group 1971-73, Peat Marwick Mitchell Hong Kong 1973-74, N M Rothschild & Sons 1974-81, Continental Illinois Bank 1981-82, md Target Group plc 1982-85, sr md Touche Remnant & Co 1985-90 (Societe Generale Touche Remnant); chm Hardie-Brown Hawkins Ltd, corp conslt for fin serv industs, dir various small private cos; ACIS 1972; *Recreations* entertaining, travel, gardening, theatre, cinema; *Style—* John Gittings, Esq; Jacobs Ladder, Crockham Hill, Kent TN8 6TD (☎ 0732 866267); 9/10 Pollen St, London W1R 9PH (☎ 071 499 0184, fax 071 629 8314, car 0836 572221)

GITTINGS, Robert William Victor; CBE (1970); s of Surg-Capt Frederick Claude Bromley Gittings, RN (ret) (d 1963), of Bosham, Sussex, and Dora Mary Brayshaw (d 1963): maternal ggf created Baron of the Austrian Empire; *b* 1 Feb 1911; *Educ* St Edward's Sch Oxford, Jesus Coll Cambridge (BA, MA, LittD); *m* 1, 1934 (m dis 1947), Katherine Edith Cambell; 2 s; m 2, 1949, Joan Grenville, da of Edwin Grenville Manton, of Broxbourne, Herts; 1 da; *Career* res student and fell Jesus Coll 1933-38; prodr BBC 1947-63, hon fell Jesus Coll 1979-; *Books* John Keats (1968), Young Thomas Hardy (1975), The Older Hardy (1978), Collected Poems (1976); *Style—* Robert Gittings, Esq, CBE; The Stables, East Dean, West Sussex (☎ 024 363 328)

GITTINS, Stephen Philip (Steve); s of Neville Gittins (d 1989), and Joyce, *née* Corbett; *b* 29 Aug 1959; *Educ* Phoenix Comp Sch Dawley; *m* 12 Aug 1978, Janice, da of Richard Laybourne; 1 s (Jamie b 9 Oct 1981), 1 da (Michelle b 24 Nov 1979); *Career* darts player; represents Shropshire and England; Welsh Open Championship Singles 1988, Swedish Open Championship Singles 1988, Finnish Open Championship Singles 1989, Scandinavian Open Championship Singles 1991, Swiss Open Championship Paris 1988, World Professional Darts Championship 1988-89; best world ranking place seventh 1989-90; *Recreations* swimming, keeping fit, travelling abroad, cycling, saunas, sun bathing, chess, snooker, computers, family outings; *Style—* Steve Gittins, Esq; 3 Ashbourne Close, Dawley, Telford, Shropshire TF4 2QR (☎ 0952 504017)

GITTUS, Dr John Henry; *b* 25 July 1930; *Educ* Univ of London (BSc, DSc), KTH Stockholm (DTech); *m* 23 May 1953, Rosemary Ann, da of John Geeves; 1 s (Michael John b 7 April 1954), 2 da (Sara Ann b 19 Aug 1956, Mary Ann b 8 Aug 1958); *Career* res worker Br Cast Iron Res Assoc 1951-56 (apprentice 1947-51), gp ldr Mond Nickel R & D Laboratories Birmingham 1956-60; UKAEA: res mangr Spring Fields 1960-80, head of water reactor fuel devpt 1980-81, head Atomic Energy Tech Unit Harwell 1981-82, dir of water reactor res Harwell 1981-82, dir of Safety Res Dept 1983-87, dir of communications 1987-90; dir gen Br Nuclear Forum 1990-; conslt: Argonne Nat Laboratory Chicago 1968, Oak Ridge Nat Laboratory Tennessee 1969; visiting prof: Ecole Polytechnic Federale Lusanne Switzerland 1976, Univ of Nancy 1985; Regents prof UCLA 1990-; FEng, FIMechE, FIM, FIS, memb MENSA; *Books* Uranium (1963), Creep, Viscoelasticity and Creep-Fracture in Solids (1976), Irradiation Effects in Crystalline Solids (1980); *Recreations* old motor cars; *Clubs* IOD, RSM; *Style—* Dr John Gittus; British Nuclear Forum, 22 Buckingham Gate, London SW1E 6LB (☎ 071 828 0116, 071 828 0110)

GIVEN, Andrew Ferguson; s of Edward F Given, CMG, CVO, of Lymington, and Phillida Naomi, *née* Bullwinkle; *b* 14 Nov 1947; *Educ* Charterhouse, Lincoln Coll Oxford; *m* 18 Sept 1971, Morwenna, da of Frederic Neil Ritchie, of Italy; 2 da (Davina, Catriona); *Career* asst to md Union Corp UK Ltd 1969-73, exec dir James Finlay Corporation 1974-75; Northern Telecom Ltd (Canada): various positions 1977-82, asst treas 1982-83, treas and controller Bell-Northern Research 1984-87, vice pres fin Northern Telecom Europe 1987-88; gp fin controller Plessey Group plc 1988-89, planning and fin dir Logica plc 1990-; *Recreations* sailing, photography, model building, running; *Clubs* Queen Mary Sailing; *Style—* A F Given; Nahanni Gate, Dipley, Hartley Wintney, Hampshire RG27 8JP (☎ 025126 3265); Logica plc, 68 Newman St, London W1A 4SE (☎ 071 637 9111, fax 071 637 8229, telex 27200)

GLADMAN, Ronald John; s of Ronald Arthur Gladman (d 1940), of Deptford, and Johanna Patricia Fifield, *née* O'Connor; *b* 19 Feb 1941; *Educ* St Edmund's Coll Ware, Pembroke Coll Cambridge (MA, LLB); *m* 29 July 1972, Wendy Anne Urling, da of John Harold Stenning, of Ringles Cross, Uckfield; 2 s (Anthony b 1974, Richard b 1977); *Career* admitted slr 1967, worked on Cmmn of Euro Communities 1971-74, asst sec and gp legal advsr Reuters Holdings plc 1976-; memb Law Soc; *Recreations* reading, music, walking, skiing; *Style—* Ronald Gladman, Esq; Reuters, 85 Fleet Street, London EC4P 4AJ (☎ 071 250 1122, fax 071 324 5406, telex 23222)

GLADSTONE, Charles Angus; s and h of Sir William Gladstone, 7 Bt, DL; *b* 11 April 1964; *Educ* Eton, Worcester Coll Oxford; *m* 16 April 1988, Caroline, o da of Sir Derek Thomas, KCMG, of Lower Sloane Street, London; 1 s (Jack William b 28 July 1989); *Career* music publishing, estate mgmnt; *Recreations* theatre, film, music, television, shooting, fishing; *Style—* Charles Gladstone, Esq; Glen Dye Lodge, Strachan, nr Banchory, Kincardineshire (☎ 033 045 227)

GLADSTONE, David Arthur Steuart; CMG (1988); s of Thomas Steuart Gladstone (d 1971), and Muriel Irene Heron, *née* Day; *b* 1 April 1935; *Educ* ChCh Coll Oxford (BA); *m* 29 July 1961, (Mary Elizabeth) April, da of Wing Cdr Patrick O'Brien Brunner (d 1966), of Wotton House, nr Aylesbury, Bucks; 1 s (Patrick b 1969), 1 da (Perdita b 1965); *Career* Nat Serv 2 Lt 4 RHA 1954-56; articled to Annan Dexter & Co 1959-60; FO 1960-: Arabic Language Student of Mecas Lebanon 1960-62, 3 sec political agency Bahrain 1962-63, FO 1963-65 and 1969-72, 2 later 1 sec HM Embassy Bonn 1965-69, 1 sec and head of chancery Cairo 1972-75, political advsr BMG Berlin 1976-79, head of Western Euro Dept FCO 1979-82, HM consul-gen Marseilles 1983-87, high cmmr Sri Lanka 1987-; fndr memb and chm the Barnsbury Assoc 1964-65, chm Homes for Barnsbury 1970-72, fndr memb Sinharaja Soc; *Recreations* domestic architecture, real tennis, German lit; *Style—* David Gladstone, Esq, CMG; c/o FCO, King Charles St, London SW1A 2AH

GLADSTONE, Sir (Erskine) William; 7 Bt (UK 1846), of Fasque and Balfour, Kincardineshire; JP (Clwyd 1982); s of Sir Charles Andrew Gladstone (6 Bt) (d 1968), and Isla Margaret, *née* Crum (d 1987); ggs of Rt Hon William Gladstone, PM; *b* 29 Oct 1925; *Educ* Eton, ChCh Oxford; *m* 10 Sept 1962, Rosamund Anne, yr da of Maj Robert Alexander Hambro (d 1943), of Milton Abbey, Dorset; 2 s, 1 da; *Heir* s, Charles Angus Gladstone; *Career* asst master Eton 1951-61, headmaster Lancing 1961-69, chief scout of the UK and Overseas Branches 1972-82 (ret 1982); chm: World Scout Ctee 1979-81, Representative Body of the Church in Wales 1977-, Cncl Glenalmond Coll 1982-86; DL Flintshire 1969, Clwyd 1974; HM Lord Lt of Clwyd 1985-; *Style—* Sir William Gladstone, Bt, JP, DL; Hawarden Castle, Clwyd CH5 3PB (☎ 0244 520210); Fasque, Laurencekirk, Kincardineshire (☎ 05614 341)

GLADSTONE OF CAPENOCH, Robert Hamilton; er s of John Gladstone of Capenoch, TD (d 1977), and his 2 w, Diana Rosamond Maud Fleming, *née* Hamilton; gggs of Thomas Steuart Gladstone, JP, who acquired Capenoch 1850; *b* 17 July 1953; *Educ* Eton, Magdalene Coll Cambridge (MA); *m* 16 Jan 1982, Margaret Jane, da of Brig Berenger Colborne Bradford, DSO, MBE, MC, of Kincardine, Kincardine O'Neil, Aberdeenshire; 2 s (John b 3 March 1983, Harry (twin) b 3 March 1983), 1 da (Catharine b 13 April 1986); *Career* chartered surveyor; John Sale & Partners 1974-78, Smiths-Gore 1978-; memb: Scottish Landowners' Fedn Cncl 1984-87, Timber-Growers UK South-West Scotland Ctee 1987-; vice pres Penpont Community Cncl 1986-; ARICS 1977, FRICS 1989; *Clubs* Whistle, '71; *Style—* Robert Gladstone of Capenoch; Capenoch, Penpont, Dumfrieshire (☎ 0848 30261); office, Smiths-Gore, 28 Castle St, Dumfries (☎ 0387 63066)

GLADWELL, Dennis Arthur; s of Arthur Frederick Gladwell (d 1987), and Alice May, *née* Liquorish (d 1973); *b* 20 June 1923; *Educ* Westcliff HS; *m* 1, 1945, Joyce Barbara; 3 s, 2 da; m 2, 1955, Yvonne Carey, da of Albert Huband Hall (d 1966); *Career* WWII Lieut RNVR served Home Fleet and Russian Convoy duties; banker; chief accountant Midland Bank plc 1967-72, gen mangr (gp fin) Midland Bank plc 1972-83, chm BACS Ltd 1970-81; dir: East India, Devonshire, Sports and Public Schs Clubs 1968-83; chm Wimborne, Ferndown and Blandford Citizens Advice Bureau 1987-; *Recreations* golf, gardening; *Clubs* Poole Harbour Yacht; *Style—* Dennis Gladwell, Esq; Serampore, 8 Martello Rd South, Canford Cliffs, Poole, Dorset BH13 7HH (☎ 0202 709237)

GLADWIN, Very Rev John Warren; s of Thomas Valentine Gladwin, of 22 Hallamgate Rd, Sheffield S10 5BS, and Muriel Joan, *née* Warren (d 1988); *b* 30 May 1942; *Educ* Hertford GS, Churchill Coll Cambridge (MA), St John's Coll Univ of Durham (Dip in Theology); *m* 5 Sept 1981, Lydia Elizabeth, da of William Adam (d 1966); *Career* asst curate St John the Baptist Church Kirkheaton 1967-71, tutor St John's Coll Durham 1971-77, dir Shaftesbury Project 1977-82, sec Bd for Social Responsibility, Gen Synod C of E 1982-88, provost of Sheffield Cathedral 1988-; memb Governing Body St John's Coll Durham, Bd of Church Army, South Yorks Probation Ctee, Cncl Univ of Sheffield, Gen Synod of C of E; *Books* God's People in God's World (1978), Dropping the Bomb (ed, 1983), The Good of the People (1987); *Recreations* gardening, music, theatre, supporter of Tottenham Hotspur FC; *Clubs* Tottenham Hotspur FC; *Style—* The Very Rev the Provost of Sheffield; Sheffield Cathedral, Church St, Sheffield S1 1HA (☎ 0742 753434, fax 0742 780244)

GLADWYN, 1 Baron (UK 1960); (Hubert Miles) Gladwyn Jebb; GCMG (1954, KCMG 1949, CMG 1942), GCVO (1957), CB (1947); s of Sydney Gladwyn Jebb, JP (d 1950), of Firbeck Hall, Rotherham, and his 1 wife Rose Eleanor, da of Maj-Gen Hugh Chichester, of Pilton House, Barnstaple, Devon; *b* 25 April 1900; *Educ* Eton, Magdalen Coll Oxford (First in History 1922, Beit Prize Essay); *m* 22 Jan 1929, Cynthia (d 1990), da of Sir Saxton William Armstrong Noble, 3 Bt; 1 s, 2 da (Vanessa, m 1963 Baron Thomas, of Swynnerton (*qv*), Stella, m 1959 Baron Joel de Rosnay,

Director of Research, Institut Pasteur); *Heir* s, Hon Miles Jebb; *Career* sits as Lib Peer in House of Lords; dep ldr Libs and spokesman on Foreign Affrs and Defence 1965-87; served Foreign Service 1924-60 (dep under sec of state Foreign Office 1948); first (acting) sec gen of United Nation 1947, perm rep UN 1950-54, ambass France 1954-60; created hereditary Peer before his retirement from Foreign Service; stood as Lib MEP candidate Suffolk 1979; chm Campaign for European Political Community, vice-chm European Movement, pres UK Cncl for Overseas Students Affrs, patron Cncl for Educn in the Cwlth, former pres Atlantic Treaty Assoc; author of various works and articles on de Gaulle and French foreign policy and nuclear matters; Grand Cross Legion of Honour; hon fell Magdalen Coll Oxford; Hon DCL: Oxon, Essex, Syracuse; *Books* The European Idea (1965), Halfway to 1984 (1967), Memoirs of Lord Gladwyn (1970); *Clubs* Garrick; *Style*— The Rt Hon Lord Gladwyn, GCMG, GCVO, CB; 62 Whitehall Court, London SW1 (☎ 071 930 3160); Bramfield Hall, Halesworth, Suffolk (☎ 098 684 241)

GLAISTER, Catherine Victoria Jane; *née* Blount; da of Christopher Charles Blount, of Manor Farm, Barkway, Hertfordshire, and Hon Mrs Susan Victoria, *née* Cobbold; *b* 15 Dec 1962; *Educ* Downe House Berks, St Mary's Convent Cambs; *m* 12 Nov 1988, Richard Martin Glaister, s of Thomas Stephen Glaister, of Croft Head, Kendal, Cumbria; *Career* Mktg Dept London Int Fin Futures Exchange 1982-84, ptnr Christopher Morgan & Ptnrs 1988 (mktg and PR exec 1985), dir Trimedia Communications Ltd 1988; *Recreations* eating, walking, talking; *Clubs* Scribes; *Style*— Mrs Richard Glaister; Trimedia Communications Ltd, 15 John Adam St, London WC2N 6LV (☎ 071 930 7642, fax 071 839 3579)

GLAISTER, Sqdn Ldr (John Leslie) Gerard; DFC (1942); s of Dr Joseph Scott Glaister (d 1955), and Stella Millicent, *née* Bell-Syer (d 1957); *b* 21 Dec 1915; *Educ* Taunton Sch; *m* 1, 18 Dec 1943 (m dis 1965), Ann, *née* Rees; 1 da (Juliet Ann Frances b 17 Sept 1947); m 2, 1966 (m dis 1971), Ann, *née* Macmillan; m 3, 9 Aug 1971, Joan Margaret, da of Arthur Bernard Crowther; 2 da (Morag Katherine b 17 Nov 1972, Isla Geraldine b 20 May 1977); *Career* RAF General Duties branch 1939-52; served as pilot: Battle of Britain, Western Desert, Greece, Crete; completed 105 operational flights, dep head intelligence SHAEF; trained as actor RADA, dir prodns Arts Council Co at Chesterfield; producer BBC (former dir): Dr Finlay's Casebook, The Brothers (co-devised), Colditz, The Expert (co-devised), Secret Army (co-devised), Howard's Way (co-devised); memb BAFTA; *Books* Howard's Way (1988); *Recreations* salmon and trout fishing; *Style*— Sqdn Ldr Gerard Glaister, DFC; BBC TV, Threshold House, Shepherds Bush, London W12 (☎ 081 576 7446)

GLANDINE, Viscount; Richard James; s and h of 6 Earl of Norbury; *b* 5 March 1967; *Style*— Viscount Glandine

GLANUSK, 4 Baron (UK 1899); Sir David Russell Bailey; 5 Bt (UK 1852); s of Hon Herbert Crawshay Bailey (d 1936; 4 s of 1 Baron) and Kathleen Mary (d 1948), da of Sir Shirley Harris Salt, 3 Bt; suc 1 cous, 3 Baron, 1948; *b* 19 Nov 1917; *Educ* Eton; *m* 25 Jan 1941, Lorna Dorothy, da of late Capt Ernest Courtenay Harold Andrews, MBE, RA; 1 s, 1 da; *Heir* s, Hon Christopher Russell Bailey; *Career* Lt-Cdr RN 1935-51; MEL Ltd 1954-64, Elliott Automation Ltd 1964-66, md Wandel & Goltermann (UK) Ltd 1966-81, chm W & G Ltd 1981-; Liveryman: Worshipful co of Clockmakers, Worshipful Co of Scientific Instrument Makers; *Style*— The Rt Hon Lord Glanusk; 16 Clarendon Gardens, London W9 1AY

GLANVILL-SMITH, John Seeley; s of Arthur Glanvill-Smith, MC (d 1965), of Madeira House, Littlestone, nr New Romney, Kent, and Margaret, *née* Harris (d 1930); *b* 26 June 1924; *Educ* Bishop's Stortford Coll; *m* 1, Alison Mary (d 1972), da of Charles Aldworth Gifford Campion (d 1963); 4 da (Virginia Mary b 1948, Mary b 1950, Angela Rosemary b 1955, Fiona Frances b 1958); m 2, 3 June 1978, Barbara Joan, *née* Young; *Career* WW11 1939-45, cmmnd Lt Royal Norfolk Regt 1943; chm: Glanvill Enthoven & Co Ltd 1976-80 (dep chm 1973-76, dir 1954), Jardine Glanvill 1980-82; dep chm Jardine Matheson (Insurance Brokers) 1980-82; dir: Clarkson Puckle (Insurance Brokers) 1982-87, Harris & Dixon Ltd 1987-; memb Lloyd's 1956-; pres Buckingham Branch Br Limbless Ex-Servicemen's Assoc; Freeman City of London, memb Worshipful Co of Gardeners; *Recreations* golf, gardening, cricket; *Clubs* MCC, Surrey CCC, Landsdowne, Norwegian; *Style*— John Glanvill-Smith, Esq; The Old Grange, Great Kimble, Nr Aylesbury, Buckinghamshire HP17 OXS (☎ 084 447 289); Harris & Dixon Ltd, 21 New St, London EC2 (☎ 071 623 6622)

GLANVILLE, Brian Lester; s of James Arthur Glanville (d 1960), and Florence, *née* Manches (d 1984); *b* 24 Sept 1931; *Educ* Charterhouse; *m* 1959, Elizabeth Pamela de Boer, da of Fritz Manasse (d 1961); 2 s (Mark, Toby), 2 da (Elizabeth, Josephine); *Career* novelist, journalist, playwright; football corr and sports columnist The Sunday Times 1958-, lit advsr Bodley Head 1958-62; *Books* novels include: Along The Arno, The Bankrupts, Diamond, The Olympian, A Roman Marriage, A Second Home, The Financiers, A Cry of Crickets, Kissing America; The Catacomb short story collections: A Bad Streak, The Director's Wife, The Thing He Loves, The King of Hackney Marshes, Love is Not Love; stage musical Underneath The Arches (co-author, 1982-83); *Recreations* playing football; *Clubs* Chelsea Casuals; *Style*— Brian Glanville, Esq; 160 Holland Park Avenue, London W11 4UH (☎ 071 603 6908)

GLANVILLE, John Foster; DSC (1942), VRD (1951); s of Leonard Foster Glanville (d 1975), of Cosham, Portsmouth, and Harriet Ann, *née* Drew (d 1975); *b* 1 Jan 1918; *Educ* Bradfield Coll; *m* 26 April 1952, Judith Anne (Judy), da of Martyn Dorey (d 1958), of St Sampsons, Guernsey; 1 s (Charles b 1956), 2 da (Pippa b 1954, Louise b 1959); *Career* RNVR 1938-54; served: E Indies Fleet 1939, Med Fleet HMS Eagle and HMS Formidable 1940, Mobile Naval Base Def Orgn Crete 1941, Inshore Sqdn Western Desert 1942, HMS Tracker Western Approaches N Atlantic 1943-44, HMS Arbiter Br Pacific Fleet 1945-46; slr 1947; sr ptnr Glanvilles Wells & Way 1972-82; coroner Portsmouth 1979 and SE Hants 1988-89; pres: Hants Incorporated Law Soc 1971, Southern Coroners Soc 1989-90; memb Southern Legal Aid Area Ctee 1972-80; dir: Portsmouth Water Co 1964, Slrs Benevolent Assoc 1966- (chm 1982); memb Portsmouth Diocesan Bd of Fin 1964-83; cdre: Royal Albert YC 1962-65, Emsworth SC 1971-72; cmmr Sea Scouts Portsmouth 1953-63 (and sec Solent Scout Ctee); memb Law Soc; *Recreations* sailing, music, country walking; *Clubs* Royal Ocean Racing, Royal Naval (Portsmouth); *Style*— John Glanville, Esq, DSC, VRD; Fowley Cottage, Emsworth, Hants PO10 7HH, (☎ 0243 372249)

GLANVILLE, Lt-Col Robert Cardew; OBE (Mil 1954), MC (1941), DL (Derbys 1967); s of Gerald Glanville, of St Germans Cornwall; *b* 29 Feb 1912; *Educ* Blundell's, Sandhurst; *m* 1947, Alice, da of John Allen, of Ilford; *Career* Reg Army Offr 1932-58; served WWII: E Africa and Ethiopia, Ceylon and Burma, NW Europe; Cdr Support Bn Supreme HQ Allied Powers Europe 1956-58, ret; TA sec Derbys 1958-68; *Recreations* gardening; *Clubs* Army and Navy, County (Derby); *Style*— Lt-Col Robert Glanville, OBE, MC, DL; Catchfrench, Bridge Hill, Belper, Derbys (☎ 0773 823255)

GLASBY, His Excellency (Alfred) Ian; s of Frederick William Glasby (d 1942), of Doncaster, S Yorks, and Harriet Maria, *née* Claridge (d 1974); *b* 18 Sept 1931; *Educ* Doncaster GS, LSE (BSc); *m* 19 June 1970, Veila Herma Maureen, da of Harry Smith, of Bradford on Avon, Wiltshire; 1 da (Beth b 23 June 1973); *Career* Nat Serv; Intelligence Corps BAOR 1950-52; Home Off 1953-68, FCO 1968-71, second and first commercial sec Br Embassy Washington DC 1971-76, dep high cmmr Kampala 1976, head Br Interests Section French Embassy Kampala 1976-77, first sec head of chancery and HM Consul Yaounde Cameroon 1977-81, non resident Charge d'Affaires Gabon Equatorial Guineau and Central African Empire 1977-81, asst head Consular Dept FCO London 1981-84, dep Consul Gen Sydney Aust 1984-88, HM Ambassador Brazzaville Peoples Republic of Congo 1988-91; dir: Trust Company of Australia Ltd, Truco (Australia) Europe Ltd; *Recreations* rugby, cricket, gardening; *Clubs* Austn Pioneers Sydney, NSW Rugby (Aust), Royal Cwlth Soc, Bristol RUF, Yorkshire CC; *Style*— His Excellency Ian Glasby; High Pitch, Strande Lane, Cookham, Maidenhead, Berkshire (☎ 06285 28054); Foreign and Commonwealth Office, King Charles St, London SW1A 2AH

GLASER, Dr Mark Gordon; s of Asher Alfred Glaser (d 1987), and Minnie, *née* Nasilewitz (d 1983); *b* 1 Dec 1944; *Educ* St Clement Dane's GS, Charing Cross Hosp Med Sch (MB BS); *Career* conslt in radiotherapy and oncology Charing Cross Hosp 1980-, hon conslt radiotherapist Hammersmith Hosp and Postgrad Med Sch 1980-, clinical teacher Univ of London 1981-, visiting prof Yale Univ USA 1984, conslt in jt charge Continuing Care Serv in Riverside (memb Working Party 1986); papers on cancer and radiation therapy; Univ of London memb: Senate 1981-, Military Educn Ctee 1982-84, Central Res Fund Ctee 1982-84, Collegiate Cncl 1987-89, Academic Cncl 1989-; MRCS 1971, LRCP 1971, DMRT 1975, FFR (RCSI) 1977, FRCR 1978; *Recreations* walking, collecting, philosophy, comparative religion; *Clubs* Reform; *Style*— Dr Mark Glaser; Dept of Radiotherapy and Oncology, Charing Cross Hospital, Fulham Palace Rd, London W6 8RF (☎ 081 846 1733)

GLASGOW, David George; s of Tom Glasgow, of 55 Embercourt Rd, Thames Ditton, Surrey, and Betty Madelaine, *née* Wells; *b* 18 Oct 1942; *Educ* Kings Coll Sch Wimbledon, RNC Dartmouth; *m* 5 Oct 1985, Bridget Gay Elizabeth, da of Joseph Stanley (John) Watson, MBE, QC, of The Old Dairy, Mickleham, Surrey; *Career* Lt RN; qualified naval interpreter (Italian); served: HMS Arethusa 1965-67, rotary wing pilot 1967, HMS Albion 1967-70, HMS Cleopatra 1970-72, ret 1973; clerk Burge & Co Stockbrokers 1973-74, tech dir Schlesinger Tst Mangrs Ltd 1976-79 (joined 1974); Abbey Life Gp 1979-87: investmt mktg dir, md Abbey Unit Tsts Mangrs Ltd; Kleinwort Benson Investmt Mgmnt 1987-: dir, dep chm Kleinwort Benson Unit Tsts Ltd; chm Unit Tst Customer Standards 1986-90, chm Unit Tst Assoc External Relns Ctee 1986-90, dir Insur Ombudsman Bureau 1989; hon sec Castaways Club; memb Int Stock Exchange 1987; *Recreations* sailing, music, theatre, skiing; *Clubs* Royal Ocean Racing, Royal London Yacht; *Style*— David Glasgow, Esq; Inwardleigh Cottage, Rockbourne, Hants (☎ 072 53 500); 117 The Colonnades, Porchester Square, London W2; Via Roma 157, Buggerru, Sardinia; Kleinwort Benson Investment Management Ltd, 10 Fenchurch St, London EC3M 3LB (☎ 071 956 6000, fax 071 956 7125)

GLASGOW, Capt Mark Richard; s of Richard Edwin Glasgow, of Ipswich, Suffolk, and Diana Geraldine Mary, *née* Markby; *b* 28 Jan 1949; *Educ* St Joseph's Coll Ipswich, King Edward VII Coll London; *m* 22 May 1976, Susan, da of Alfred McCarrison Russel, of Salisbury, Wiltshire; 2 s (Edward b 26 Jan 1979, Simon b 9 July 1981); *Career* served Merchant Marine 1966-76, Capt 1975, cmd James Cook 1975-76; dir Assoc Maritime Co London Ltd 1987; MRIN, FICS 1980; *Recreations* lawn tennis, Chinese painting; *Clubs* RAC, Hurlingham; *Style*— Capt Mark Glasgow; 30 Ullswater Road, Barnes, London SW13 9PN (☎ 081 748 1837); Metro House, 58 St James's St, London SW1A 1LD (☎ 071 491 2549, fax 071 408 0572, telex 947051, car 0836 224960)

GLASGOW, 10 Earl of (S 1703); Patrick Robin Archibald Boyle; also Lord Boyle (S 1699), Lord Boyle of Kelburn (S 1703), Baron Fairlie (UK 1897); s of Rear Adm 9 Earl of Glasgow, CB, DSC (d 1984), and his 1 wife Dorothea, only da of Sir Archibald Lyle, 2 Bt, now Dorothea, Viscountess Kelburn; *b* 30 July 1939; *Educ* Eton, Sorbonne; *m* 29 Nov 1975, Isabel Mary, da of George Douglas James; 1 s (Viscount of Kelburn b 1978), 1 da (Lady Alice Dorothy b 1981); *Heir* s, Viscount of Kelburn; *Career* Sub-Lt RNR 1960; known professionally as Patrick Boyle; asst dir Woodfall Films 1961-64, freelance asst dir 1965-68, TV documentary producer/dir Yorkshire Television 1968-70; freelance TV documentary producer/dir working for BBC, Yorkshire Television, ATV and Scottish Television 1971-81; created Kelburn Country Centre (park with recreational facilities) 1977; chm: Largs & Dist Tourist Bd 1987-89, Largs Viking Festival 1981-85; *Recreations* theatre, cinema, skiing; *Style*— The Rt Hon the Earl of Glasgow; Kelburn, Fairlie, Ayrshire KA29 OBE (☎ 0475 568204); Kelburn Country Centre, Fairlie, Ayrshire KA29 OBE (☎ 0475 568685)

GLASGOW, Archbishop of (RC) 1974-, and Metropolitan; Most Rev Thomas Joseph Winning; s of Thomas Winning (d 1959), and Agnes, *née* Canning (d 1954); *b* 3 June 1925; *Educ* Our Lady's HS Motherwell, Blairs Coll Aberdeen, St Peter's Coll Bearsden, Pontifical Scots Coll and Pontifical Gregorian Univ Rome (STL, DCL); *Career* ordained priest 1948; spiritual dir Pontifical Scots Coll Rome 1961-66, pres Scottish Catholic Trbnl 1970-71, aux bishop Glasgow 1971-74; pres Bishops Conf Scotland 1985; HonDD Univ of Glasgow 1983; hon fell Educl Inst of Scotland 1986, Grad Prior of the Scottish Lieutenancy of the Equestrian Order of the Holy Sepuchlre of Jerusalem 1989; *Recreations* golf; *Style*— His Grace the Archbishop of Glasgow; 40 Newlands Rd, Glasgow G43 2JD; vicariate: Curial Office, 196 Clyde St, Glasgow G1 4JY (☎ 041 226 5898, fax 041 221 1962)

GLASS, Alick; s of Harry Glass, of Edinburgh, and Bessie, *née* Shemenski; *b* 10 Aug 1936; *Educ* Royal HS Edinburgh; *m* 5 Sept 1961, Ruth Marion, da of William Wollenberg; 1 s (Richard Andrew b 8 May 1966), 1 da (Suzanne Lesley b 10 Aug 1962); *Career* md Young Glover & Co Ltd 1958-62, chm and chief exec Glass Glover Gp plc 1962-88, md Glass Assoc Ltd 1988; dir: Nat Fedn of Fruit and Potato Trades Ltd, Fresh Fruit and Vegetable Info Bureau; Worshipful Co fo Fruiterers 1979; FIFP 1980; *Recreations* oratory, travel; *Style*— Alick Glass, Esq; Glass Assoc Ltd, 12 York Gate, London NW1 4QS (☎ 081 348 7913, fax 081 341 3783)

GLASS, Anthony Trevor; QC (1986); s of Percy Glass (d 1946); *b* 6 June 1940; *Educ* Royal Masonic Sch, Lincoln Coll Oxford (MA); *m* 30 April 1966, Deborah, da of Dr William Wall, of Rocky Mount, North Carolina, USA; 1 s (James b 1969), 1 da (Emily b 1970); *Career* called to the Bar 1965; Queen's Counsel 1986, rec Crown Court 1985; *Recreations* antique collecting, music; *Style*— Anthony Glass, Esq, QC; Queen Elizabeth Building, Temple, London EC4 (☎ 071 583 5766, fax 071 353 0339)

GLASS, Martin; JP (1986); s of Harry Glass (d 1959), of Swansea, and Bella, *née* Cohen (d 1975); *b* 27 Sept 1935; *Educ* Swansea GS, UWIST (Dip Arch); *m* 12 May 1963, Norma Marcia, da of Hyman Corrick (d 1983), of Swansea; 2 da (Deborah b 1965, Judith b 1967); *Career* CA; princ of Martin Glass Chartered Architects 1960-; RIBA; *Clubs* Rotary (Swansea); *Style*— Martin Glass, Esq, JP; 6 Richmond Villas, Ffynone, Swansea, W Glamorgan SA1 6DQ (☎ 0792 472331); 101 Walter Rd, Swansea, W Glamorgan SA1 5QF (☎ 0792 464123)

GLASS, William Ian; s of William Glass of Weybridge (fndr Glass's Guide to Used Car Values, d 1949), and Evelyn Ellen Glass (d 1963); *b* 13 March 1916; *Educ* George Watson's Coll Edinburgh, Univ of Grenoble France; *m* 1, Ruthene Eveline Marcia, *née* Driver-Williams; 1 s (David Ian b 1942), 1 da (Patricia Lynn Ruthene b 1947); m 2, Irene Joyce (Jill), da of Edward Claud Maby, of Nether Cerne, Dorset (d 1967); *Career* WWII 1939-46; Maj GSO2 RA(AA) 8 Army, GSO2 (Hist) Allied Armies in Italy; CA 1938; sec William Glass Ltd and Used Motor Shows, dir Br Air Conditioners Ltd

1938-39, ptnr Tansley Witt & Co 1946-47, ptnr and dir Stevenson Jordan & Harrison 1947-67, chm William Glass Ltd (publishers Glass's Guides) 1963-65 (dir 1950-65); MBIM, MIMC, FInstD; *Recreations* sailing, skiing, rough shooting; *Clubs* Royal Lymington Yacht; *Style—* William Glass, Esq; Blazemore Farm, Royden Lane, Boldre, Lymington, Hampshire (☎ 0590 23047)

GLASSE, Lady Margaret Nicola; *née* Sinclair; 2 da of 19 Earl of Caithness, CVO, CBE, DSO, JP, DL (d 1965), and Grizel Margaret, *née* Cunningham (d 1943); *b* 11 Sept 1937; *Educ* Seymour Lodge Sch Crieff; *m* 1. 29 Aug 1959 (m dis), Capt (David) Colin Kirkwood Brown, late Gordon Highlanders, yr s of Gp Capt Hugh Mitchell Kirkwood Brown, of Croft Butts, Kingsbarns, Fife; 2 da (Nicola b 1960, Olivia b 1962); m 2, 9 July 1983, John James Maxwell Glasse, s of John Glasse, of Easton House, Corsham, Wilts; *Career* JP 1970-71; *Style—* Lady Margaret Glasse; The Old Rectory, Milton Bryan, Beds (☎ 0525 210 043)

GLASSER, Cyril; s of late Philip Glasser, and late Eva Glasser; *b* 31 Jan 1942; *Educ* Raine's Fndn GS, LSE (LLB, LLM); *Career* admitted slr 1967; Sheridans: ptnr and head of Litigation Dept, managing ptnr 1989-; Lord Chllr's Dept: special conslt Legal Aid and Advsy Ctee 1974-77, memb Working Party to Review Legal Aid Legislation 1974-77; chm Legal Aid Fin Provisions Working Party Legal Aid Advsy Ctee 1975-77, memb Soc Sci and Law Ctee SSRC 1979-83; visiting prof of law UCL 1987-; co fndr and dir Legal Action Gp 1972-74, memb Cncl of Mgmnt Inst of Judicial Admin Univ of Birmingham 1984-, tstee Legal Assistance Tst 1985-; *Style—* Cyril Glasser, Esq; 21 Holmes Rd, London NW5 3AA (☎ 071 485 7821); Sheridans, 14 Red Lion Square, London WC1R 4QL (☎ 071 404 0444, fax 071 831 1982, telex 21297)

GLASSMAN, Rosslyn Angela; da of Sidney Glassman, of Hove, Sussex, and Millicant, *née* Goldstein; *b* 13 May 1947; *Educ* Wistons Sch Brighton Sussex; *Career* theatrical historian specialising in antique engravings relating to the performing arts, also advsr to museums and archives worldwide; exhibitions incl: 14 at Royal Festival Hall, 2 at Royal Opera House, 6 at Glyndebourne Festival Opera, Royal Nat Theatre Tenth Anniversary, Royal Shakespeare Meml Theatre Stratford on Avon, The Bear Garden Museum; Shakespeare exhibitor for Chichester Festival; memb: Soc of Theatre Res, Soc of Dance Res, The Theatre Tst, American Soc of Theatre Res, Int Fedn of Theatre Res; *Style—* Miss Rosslyn Glassman; 27 Chalcot Square, London NW1 (☎ 071 586 4681); 31 Furze Croft, Hove, Sussex (☎ 0273 734180); The Witch Ball, 2 Cecil Court, St Martins Lane WC2 (☎ 071 836 2922, page 071 884 3344/A007); The Witch Ball, 48 Meeting House Lane, Brighton, Sussex (☎ 0273 26618)

GLASSON, Christopher Paul; s of Donald Trelawney Glasson; *b* 4 Jan 1941; *Educ* Latymer Upper Sch, Emmanuel Coll Cambridge; *m* 1964, Julie, *née* Gill; 2 c; *Career* chief exec Business Equipment Div Vickers plc 1981-87; dir: Roneo SA (France), Roneo Vickers Ltd (India) 1981-87; chm: Comforto Inc (USA) 1985-87, Comforto Systems (Switzerland) 1985-87; pres: Allsteel Inc 1987-, Koru Inc 1987-; dir Merchants Nat Bank 1988-; *Recreations* golf, dressage, music, philately; *Clubs* Naval and Military, Cambridge Union, MCC; *Style—* Christopher Glasson, Esq; 6N422 Woodhill Lane, St Charles, Illinois 60175, USA; (office ☎ 708 844 7201); 47 Rue des Dunes, 85680 La Gueriniere, France (☎ 51 39 85 76)

GLASSPOLE, Sir Florizel Augustus; ON (1973), GCMG (1981), GCVO (1983), CD (1970); s of late Rev Theophilus A Glasspole, and Florence, *née* Baxter; *b* 25 Sept 1909; *Educ* Wolmer's Boys' Sch, Ruskin Coll Oxford; *m* 1934, Ina Josephine Kinlocke; 1 da; *Career* accountant 1932-44, dir City Printery Ltd 1944-50, gen sec Jamaica TUC 1939-52, memb House of Representatives Jamaica 1944-73, min of Educn 1957-62 and 1972-73, ldr of House 1955-62 and 1972-73, min of Labour 1955-57, govr-gen of Jamaica 1983-; *Recreations* sports, gardening; *Style—* HE Sir Florizel Glasspole, ON, GCMG, GCVO, CD; King's House, Kingston 10, Jamaica

GLASSPOOL, Frank Harry; s of Lesley William George Glasspool (d 1936), and Isobel, *née* Highfield; *b* 14 May 1934; *Educ* Duke of York Royal Mil Sch; *m* 1, 1 April 1961 (m dis 1981), Olive, da of Charles Geddes (d 1982); 1 s (Stephen b 2 Nov 1964), 1 da (Wendy b 25 Jan 1963); m 2, 25 Feb 1984, Rosemary Esther, da of George Edward Saunders; 2 step s (Simon b 21 Dec 1963, Timothy b 7 Oct 1965), 1 step da (Juliette b 25 July 1971); *Career* sr engr Kellog Int 1961-68, sr ptnr Glasspool & Thaiss 1968-; pres Rotary Club Berkhamsted Bulbourne, chm Berkhamsted Lawn Tennis and Squash Rackets Club; CEng, FIStructE 1974, MConsE 1979; *Recreations* tennis, squash, photography; *Clubs* British Tennis Umpires Assoc, Berkhamsted Lawn Tennis & Squash Rackets, Berkhamsted Bulbourne Rotary; *Style—* Frank Glasspool, Esq; Linden House, Shootersway Lane, Berkhamsted, Hertfordshire HP4 3NW (☎ 0442 873873); Coughtry House, 112-116 Broad St, Chesham, Bucks HP5 3ED (☎ 0494 771314, fax 0494 791455)

GLATZEL, Donald Lawrence; s of William Paul Glatzel (d 1985), and Elsie Wilhelmina, *née* Flittner (d 1971); *b* 5 May 1934; *Educ* Wrekin Coll; *m* 22 Jan 1966, Linda, da of Frederick Henry Venning (d 1979); 1 s (Niall b 1970), 1 da (Kate b 1967); *Career* PO RAF regt 1954-55; chm Cope and Timmins Hldngs Ltd 1984 (asst sec 1956-64, dir 1964-71, md 1971-84), dir and alternate chm Castle Art Prodts Ltd 1974-; Master Worshipful Co of Upholders 1990 (Freeman 1972-); ACIS 1966; *Recreations* sailing, shooting; *Clubs* Royal Thames Yacht, City Livery; *Style—* Donald Glatzel, Esq; 48 Camlet Way, Hadley Wood, Barnet, Herts EN4 0NS (☎ 081 449 3702); 42 Newlyn Way, Port Solent, North Harbour, Portsmouth; Cope & Timmins Holdings Ltd, Angel Road Works, Edmonton, London NI8 3AY (☎ 081 803 6481, fax 081 884 2322, telex 299918 G)

GLAUERT, Dr Audrey Marion; da of Hermann Glauert (d 1934), of Farnborough, Hants, and Muriel, *née* Barker (d 1949); *b* 21 Dec 1925; *Educ* Perse Sch for Girls Cambridge, Bedford Coll Univ of London (BSc, MSc), Clare Hall Cambridge (MA, ScD); *Career* asst lectr physics Royal Holloway Coll London 1947-50, Sir Halley Stewart fell and memb sci staff Strangeways Res Lab Cambridge 1950-89, fell Clare Hall Cambridge 1966-; ed: Practical Methods in Electron Microscopy 1972-, Jl of Microscopy 1986-89; chm: Br Jt Ctee for Electron Microscopy 1968-72, Fifth Euro Congress on Electron Microscopy 1972; pres Royal Microscopical Soc 1970-72; JP Cambridge 1975-88; hon memb: Societe Francaise de Microscopie Electronique, Electron Microscopy Soc of America (Distinguished Scientist in Biological Sciences award 1990), FRMS; *Books* Fixation, Dehydration and Embedding of Biological Specimens (1974); *Recreations* vol work prison reform tst, gardening, sailing; *Style—* Dr Audrey Glauert; 29 Cow Lane, Fulbourn, Cambridge CB1 5HB (☎ 0223 880 463); 19 High St, Blakeney, Holt, Norfolk NR25 7NA; Clare Hall, Univ of Cambridge, Herschel Rd, Cambridge CB3 9AL

GLAZE, Michael John Carlisle (James); CMG (1988); s of Derek Glaze (d 1970), and Shirley Winifred Gardner, formerly Glaze, *née* Ramsay; *b* 15 Jan 1935; *Educ* Repton, St Catharine's Coll Cambridge (MA), Worcester Coll Oxford; *m* 1965, Mrs Rosemary Duff, da of Thomas McIntosh (d 1971), of Monifieth; 2 da (Fiona, Deirdre); *Career* HM Overseas Civil Serv Lesotho 1959-70, dep perm sec Miny of Fin; Dip Serv: Abu Dhabi 1975-78, Rabat 1978-80, consul gen Bordeaux 1980-84; ambass: Republic of Cameroon 1984-87, Luanda 1987-89, Addis Ababa 1990-; *Style—* James Glaze, Esq, CMG; British Embassy, Addis Ababa, c/o Foreign and Commonwealth Office

GLAZEBROOK, Col David; OBE (1973); s of Col Arthur Rimington Glazebrook, MC, TD, and Joan Annie Glazebrook; *b* 28 Jan 1933; *Educ* Queen Elizabeth's GS Wakefield, RMA Sandhurst; *m* 30 Aug 1975, Clara Jane (Wink), da of Maj Harry Collett Bolt, MBE; 2 da (Samantha b 1977, Emma b 1978); *Career* cmmnd RTR 1953, seconded Malaysian Armed Forces 1957-60, seconded Trucial Oman Scouts 1965-67, seconded Sultan of Oman's Armed Forces 1970-73, CO 9 Bn UDR 1975-77, instr Nat Def Coll 1977-79, def attache Khartoum Sudan 1979-81, def attache Jakarta Indonesia 1983-85, def advsr Kuala Lumpur Malaysia 1985-87, ret 1988; Omani Distinguished Serv Medal 1973; *Recreations* golf, shooting, gardening; *Style—* Col David Glazebrook, OBE; Streete Farmhouse, Hope Mansell, Ross-on-Wye, Herefordshire HR9 5TJ)

GLAZEBROOK, (Reginald) Mark; s of Reginald Field Glazebrook (d 1986), and Daisy Isabel, *née* Broad; *b* 25 June 1936; *Educ* Eton, Pembroke Coll Cambridge (MA), Slade Sch of Fine Art; *m* 1, 1965 (m dis 1969), Elizabeth Lea, *née* Claridge; 1 da (Lucy b 22 April 1966); m 2, 27 Sept 1974, Wanda Barbara, da of Ignacy Piotr Osinski, of Warsaw, Poland; 1 da (Bianca b 25 March 1975); *Career* Nat Serv 2 Lt Welsh Gds 1953-55; exhibition organiser Arts Cncl 1962-65, art critic London Magazine 1967-68, dir Whitechapel Art Gallery 1969-71, head of Modern British Dept Colnaghi & Co Ltd 1972-75, gallery dir San José Univ USA 1976-78; dir: Editions Alecto 1979-81, Albemarle Gallery 1986-; princ exhibition catalogues written and edited: Artists and Architecture of Bedford Park 1875-1900, John Armstrong (1957), David Hockney Paintings Prints Drawings 1960-70 (1970), Edward Wadsworth Paintings Drawings and Prints (1974), John Tunnard (1977), The Seven and Five Soc (1979), Unit One Spirit of the 30's (1984), Mark Twain USA 1977; FRSA 1971; *Recreations* travelling, theatre, tennis, swimming; *Clubs* Beefsteak, Lansdowne; *Style—* Mark Glazebrook, Esq; Albemarle Gallery, 18 Albemarle Street, London W1X 3HA (☎ 071 355 1880)

GLAZEBROOK, William Field; s of Reginald Field Glazebrook (d 1986), of Brynbella, St Asaph, Clwyd, and Daisy Isabel, *née* Broad; *b* 18 June 1929; *Educ* Eton, Pembroke Coll Cambridge (MA); *m* 19 Sept 1959, Sara Elizabeth, da of Lt Cdr Arthur Frederick Whalley Boumphrey, DSC, DL (d 1988), of Maesmor Hall, Corwen, Clwyd; 3 s (Charles b 19 March 1961, Jonathan b 2 April 1964, Neil b 30 Oct 1966, d 1989); *Career* 2 Lt S Wales Borderers 1948-49, Capt Cheshire Yeo TA 1952-59; admitted slr 1956, ptnr Lace Mawer Liverpool and Manchester; memb Law Soc 1956; *Recreations* tennis, golf, fishing, shooting, gardening; *Clubs* Liverpool Racquet; *Style—* William Glazebrook, Esq; Pontruffydd Hall, Bodfari, Denbigh, Clwyd LL16 4BP (☎ 074 575 322); Castle Chambers, 43 Castle St, Liverpool L2 9SU (☎ 051 236 1634, fax 051 236 2585, telex 627229)

GLAZIER, Barry Edward; s of Edward Thomas Glazier (d 1976), of San Antonio, Ibiza, Spain, and Gladys Mabel, *née* Faulkner; *b* 1 July 1941; *Educ* Hurstpierpoint, St Peter's Coll Oxford (MA); *m* 1, 5 Aug 1970 (m dis), Lesley (d 1990), da of John Richard Kirby (d 1986); 2 da (Anna b 1973, Rachael b 1976); m 2, 5 April 1984, Mrs Patricia McGregor, da of Cecil Mears (d 1977), of Wareham, Dorset; 1 da (Becky b 1985), 1 adopted step-da (Emma Sarah b 1981); *Career* slr 1966-; with Clifford Turners 1966-70, ptnr Mooring Aldridge 1971-88 (sr ptnr 1984-88), ptnr Lester Aldridge 1988-; vice-pres: Bournemouth and Dist Law Soc, Dorset Chamber of Commerce and Industy; slr to, and dir of Dorset Trg and Enterprise Cncl; memb Dorset War Pensions Ctee; memb Law Soc 1966; *Recreations* concerts, piano, theatre, bird watching, gardening; *Style—* Barry Glazier, Esq; Quarter Jack House, 11 The Cornmarket, Wimborne Minster, Dorset BH21 1JL (☎ 0202 885128); Lester Aldridge, Russell House, Oxford Road, Bournemouth, Dorset BH8 8EX (☎ 0202 786161, fax 0202 786150)

GLEAVE, Prof (Michael) Barrie; s of John Thomas Gleave (d 1959), and Mildred, *née* Darbyshire; *b* 22 July 1936; *Educ* Roundhay Sch Leeds, Univ of Hull (BA, MA, PhD), Univ of Reading (Dip Ed); *m* 21 Aug 1961, Jean, da of John Marshland (d 1965); 1 s (Jonathan b 1966), 1 da (Catherine b 1964); *Career* prof of geography: Fourth Bay Coll Univ of Sierra Leone 1972-74, Univ of Salford 1982- (chm of dept 1983); treas African Studies Assoc of UK 1980-84; memb: Inst of Br Geographers , Geographical Assoc; ASA UK; *Books* An Economic Geography of West Africa (jtly, 1971); *Clubs* Lancs CCC; *Style—* Prof Barrie Gleave; Baldwin Croft, 36 Church Road, Leyland, Preston PR5 2AA (☎ 0772 422056); Dept of Geography, University of Salford, Salford M5 4WT (☎ 061 745 5430, fax 061 745 5999, telex 668680 (SULIB))

GLEAVE, John Reginald Wallace; s of Rev Canon John Wallace Gleave (d 1979), of Cambridge, and Dorothy Littlefair, *née* Green (d 1978); *b* 6 April 1925; *Educ* Uppingham, Magdalen Coll Oxford (MA, BM BCh); *m* 6 Sept 1952, (Margaret) Anne, da of Michael Robert Newbolt (d 1956), of Chester; 3 s (Mark b 1957, Humphry b 1959, Arthur b 1964), 3 da (Frances b 1954, Charity b 1961, Emily b 1965); *Career* Nat Serv Maj RAMC OIC Army Neurosurgical Unit 1952-54; neurosurgeon; conslt neurosurgical emeritus Addenbrookes Hosp Cambs, conslt neurosurgn BUPA Hosp Cambs, lectr in neurosurgery Univ of Cambridge, fell and praelector St Edmund's Coll Cambridge, lectr and dir of med studies Magdalene Coll Cambridge; memb: OUBC 1946-48 (won boat race 1946), Leander 1948-49 (won grand 1949); FRCS 1957, FRSM 1975, SBNS 1962; *Recreations* coach to LMBC, gardening, travel; *Clubs* Vincent's, Leander, Utd Oxford and Cambridge; *Style—* John R W Gleave, Esq; Riversdale, Gt Shelford, Cambridge CB2 5LW (☎ 0223 843309); BUPA Hospital, Cambridge (☎ 0223 237474)

GLEDHILL, Andrew; s of Stanley Gledhill (d 1985), of Mirfield West Yorkshire, and Sheila, *née* Smith; *b* 16 March 1958; *Educ* Mirfield HS, New Coll Oxford (MA); *Career* Young & Rubicam: graduate trainee then mangr 1980-84, account dir (accounts incl Johnnie Walker, Kodak, Air Canada, Cadbury's Crunchie, Access) 1984-87, Bd account dir (accounts incl Rank Xerox Office Systems, TWA, United Distillers) 1987-88; Bd account dir Jenner Keating Becker Reay (accounts incl Pizzaland, Whyte & Mackay, McVities) 1988-90, Bd account dir Reay Keating Hamer 1990-; non-exec chm Orc's Nest retail chain; *Recreations* sailing, military theory, tai chi; *Clubs* Jaguar Drivers, Jaguar Enthusiasts; *Style—* Andrew Gledhill, Esq; Reay Keating Hamer, 65-66 Frith St, London W1 (☎ 071 439 2686)

GLEDHILL, Anthony John; GC (1967); s of Harold Victor Gledhill, of 60 Meon Rd, Milton, Portsmouth, Hants, and Marjorie Edith, *née* Prout; *b* 10 March 1938; *Educ* Doncaster Tech HS; *m* 3 Sept 1958, Marie Lilian, da of William Hughes, of 43 Eastry Ave, Hayes, Bromley, Kent; 1 s (Stewart b 1 Sept 1961), 1 da (Rachel b 13 Sept 1963); *Career* accounts clerk Offr's Mess RAF Bruggen Germany 1953-56; Met Police: cadet 1956-57, police constable 1957-75, detective sgt 1976-87; PO Investigation Dept 1987, md FCA Ltd 1988-, co exec Landhurst Leasing; memb Royal Br Legion Kent; *Recreations* football, carpentry; *Style—* Anthony Gledhill, Esq, GC; 98 Pickhurst Lane, Hayes, Bromley, Kent, BR2 7JD (☎ 081 462 4033); Landhurst Leasing, 6-7 Queen St, London EC4N 1SP (☎ 071 236 8702)

GLEDHILL, Keith Ainsworth; DL (Lancashire 1986); s of Norman Gledhill (d 1970), of Blackpool, and Louise, *née* Ainsworth (d 1988); *b* 28 Aug 1932; *Educ* Arnold Sch Blackpool; *m* 7 July 1956, Margaret Irene, da of Joseph Bramwell Burton (d 1970); 1 s (Ian C b 1958); *Career* jr offr MN 1950-54; Nat Serv RAF 1954-56; Norman Gledhill & Co Ltd 1956-65, Delta Metal Co Ltd 1965 (sr exec contract 1972); fndr: Gledhill Water Storage Ltd 1972, Nu-Rad Ltd 1974, Thermal Sense (Energy Conservation Systems) Ltd 1979; chm: Bd Govrs Arnold Sch Ltd, Lancs Youth Clubs Assoc, Talking Newspaper for the Blind, Blackpool and Fylde Soc for the Blind; former offr Rotary

Int, rotarian, tstee Foxton Dispensary, govr Skelton Bounty Tst; FInstD 1968; MInstP 1970; *Recreations* golf; *Clubs* Royal Lytham and St Annes Golf, Fylde RFC; *Style—* Keith Gledhill, Esq, DL; Broken Hill, 35 South Park Drive, Blackpool, Lancashire FY3 9PZ (☎ 0253 764462); Gledhill Water Storage Ltd, Sycamore Estate, Squires Gate, Blackpool, Lancashire FY4 3RL (☎ 0253 401 494, fax 0253 49 657, telex 677631)

GLEDHILL, Michael William; s of George Eric Louis Gledhill (d 1986), of Shelf, nr Halifax , W Yorks, and Sarah Jane, *née* Green (d 1979); *b* 28 Oct 1937; *Educ* Rishworth Sch Halifax ; *m* 18 Oct 1962, Margaret, da of Cyril Ira Fletcher (d 1965), of Hanson Lane, Halifax , W Yorks; 3 s (Marc b Nov 1963, Andrew b May 1966, Jonathan b June 1969); *Career* slr; ptnr Finn Gledhill & Co 1962-; Notary Public Halifax 1980; clerk: Waterhouse Charity Halifax 1965-, Tstees Abbotts Ladies Home Halifax 1967-, Wheelwright Charity (Rishworth Sch) 1985-; dir: G W Estates Ltd 1968, Michaels Estates Ltd 1970, Bellsounds Ltd 1983, Red Seal Ltd 1985, Gold Seal (Conveyancing) Ltd 1985, Halifax Incorporated Law Soc Ltd 1986, Hillodge Ltd 1987; *Recreations* golf, gardening, rugby; *Style—* Michael W Gledhill, Esq; Post Cottage, Warley Town, Warley, Halifax HX2 7RZ (☎ 0422 831890); Finn, Gledhill & Co, 1/4 Harrison Rd, Halifax HX1 2AG (☎ 0422 330000, fax 0422 342604)

GLEDHILL, Ruth; da of Rev Peter Gledhill, of Yr Hen Felin Pwllfanogl, Llanfairpg, Gwynedd, and Bridget Mary, *née* Rathbone; *b* 15 Dec 1959; *Educ* Thomas Alleyne's GS Uttoxeter, London Coll of Printing (HND); *m* 10 June 1989, John Edward Stammers; *Career* indentured Birmingham Post & Mail 1982-84, gen news reporter Daily Mail 1984-87; The Times: home news reporter 1987-90, religious affairs reporter 1990-91, religious affairs correspondent 1991-; memb NUJ; *Recreations* riding, opera; *Clubs* Reform; *Style—* Ms Ruth Gledhill; The Times, 1 Pennington St, London E1 9XN (☎ 071 782 5001, fax 071 488 3242)

GLEESON, Dermot James; s of Patrick Joseph Gleeson, of 160 Sandy Lane, Cheam, Surrey, and Margaret Mary, *née* Higgins; *b* 5 Sept 1949; *Educ* Downside, Fitzwilliam Coll Cambridge (MA); *m* 6 Sept 1980, Rosalind Mary Catherine, da of Lt-Col Charles Edward Moorhead (d 1953), of Chipping Campden, Glos; 1 s (Patrick b 1984), 1 da (Catherine b 1981); *Career* Cons Res Dept 1974-77 (asst dir 1979), Euro Cmmn (cabinet of C Tugendhat) 1977-79, EEC rep of Midland Bank Brussels 1980-82, dep chm and dep md MJ Gleeson Group PLC 1982-88 (chief exec 1988); dir Housing Corp 1990-; *Clubs* Beefsteak, RAC; *Style—* Dermot Gleeson, Esq; Hook Farm, White Hart Lane, Wood Street, Surrey GU3 3EA (☎ 0483 236210); M J Gleeson Group plc, Haredon House, London Road, North Cheam, Sutton, Surrey SM3 9BS (☎ 081 644 4321, fax 081 644 6366, car 0836 777972, telex 927762)

GLEESON, Judith Amanda Jane; *née* Coomber; da of Derek Young Coomber, of 10 Wraylands Drive, Reigate, Surrey, and Jennifer Isabel Coomber, JP, *née* Strudwick; *b* 24 Aug 1955; *Educ* Reigate Co Sch for Girls, Lady Margaret Hall Oxford (MA), Université Libre de Bruxelles (Dip in Civil and Community Law); *m* 5 Jan 1980, Donald Frank Gleeson, s of George Aubrey Gleeson (d 1957); *Career* slr; vice pres Oxford Univ Law Soc 1974-75, pres W Surrey Law Soc 1987-88, chm Surrey Assoc of Women Slrs; *Recreations* reading, study of language; *Clubs* Oxford Union; *Style—* Mrs Judith Gleeson; Hedleys, 6 Bishopsmead Parade, East Horsley, Surrey (☎ 04865 4567, fax 04865 4817)

GLEN, Sir Alexander Richard; KBE (1967, CBE 1964), DSC (1942, bar 1945); s of Richard Bartlett Glen, of Glasgow; *b* 18 April 1912; *Educ* Fettes, Balliol Coll Oxford; *m* 1947, Baroness Zora Cartuyvels de Collaert, da of Ago Bukovac, of Dubrovnik; 1 s; *Career* served RNVR 1939-59; chm H Clarkson & Co 1958-73, dir BICC 1964-70, chm Br Tourist Authy 1969-77, dep chm Br Tport Hotels 1978-83; memb: Horserace Totalisator Bd 1976-84, Historic Bldgs Cncl 1976-80; chm V & A Museum Advsy Cncl 1978-83; former: explorer (Arctic), banker in New York, bd memb BEA and Nat Ports Cncl 1964-70; Gold Medallist Royal Geographical Soc 1940, Medallist Royal Soc of Edinburgh and Swedish Geographical and Anthropological Soc 1938; *Books* Under the Pole Star (1937), Footholds against a Whirlwind (1978); *Recreations* travel; *Clubs* City of London, Explorers (NYC); *Style—* Sir Alexander Glen, KBE, DSC; The Dower House, Stanton, Glos (☎ 038 673 301)

GLEN, Eric Stanger; s of William Kerr Glen (d 1952), and Annie Pullar Glen; *b* 20 Oct 1934; *Educ* Univ of Glasgow (MB ChB); *m* 7 April 1965, Patricia Alexa Scott, da of Alexander Nicholson (d 1980), of Glasgow; 3 s (Jeremy b 26 Oct 1966, Stephen b 9 Sept 1968, Paul b 2 March 1971); *Career* ship surgn Royal Fleet Auxiliary 1962; conslt urological surgn, hon clinical lectr Univ of Glasgow; memb Examination Panel RCPS Glas, fndr past sec and hon memb Int Continence Soc, fndr and pres Urological Computing Soc, hon memb Italian Urodynamic Soc; chm: Area Med Ctee, Gtr Glasgow Health Bd Incontinence Resource Gp, Scottish Task Force on Incontinence; memb BMA; FRSM, FRCSEd 1967, FRCS Glas 1967, ALCM; *Books* Advances in Diagnostic Urology (contrib 1981), Surgical Management (1984), Female Stress Incontinence (1979); numerous papers on urodynamics, urology and computing; *Recreations* travel, computing applications, pottering about; *Style—* Eric Glen, Esq; 9 St John's Rd, Pollokshield, Glasgow G41 5RJ (☎ 041 423 0759); Walton Urological Teaching and Research Centre, Southern General Hospital, Glasgow G51 4TF (☎ 041 445 2466, fax 041 445 3670)

GLEN, (James) Hamish Robert; s of William Glen (d 1969), of Perthshire, and Irene Marjorie Stewart, *née* Sutherland; *b* 27 May 1930; *Educ* Merchiston Castle Sch Edinburgh; *m* 1956, Alison Helen Margaret, da of Robin Archibald Brown (d 1948); 3 s (Hamish b 1957, Graeme b 1959, Iain b 1961); *Career* 2 Lt RA 1955-56 served Hong Kong; CA investmt mgmnt, md The Scottish Investment Trust plc 1981, chm The Scottish Life Assurance Co 1987 (dir 1971); *Recreations* golf, fishing; *Clubs* New (Edinburgh), Hon Co of Edinburgh Golfers; *Style—* Hamish Glen, Esq; 6 Albyn Place, Edinburgh (☎ 031 225 7781)

GLENAMARA, Baron (Life Peer UK 1977), of Glenridding in Co Cumbria; Edward Watson Short; CH (1976), PC (1964); s of Charles and Mary Short, of Warcop, Westmorland; *b* 17 Dec 1912; *Educ* Bede Coll Univ of Durham (LLB); *m* 1941, Jennie, da of Thomas Sewell, of Newcastle upon Tyne; 1 s (Hon Michael Christian b 1943), 1 da (Hon Jane Bronwen (Hon Mrs Fraser) b 1945); *Career* WWII Capt DLI; sits as Labour peer in House of Lords; MP (L) Newcastle upon Tyne Central 1951-76, oppn whip (N) 1955-62, dep chief oppn whip 1962-64, govt chief whip (and Parly sec Treasy) 1964-66, Postmaster Gen 1966-68, sec of state Educn and Sci 1968-70, ldr pres Cncl and ldr Commons 1974-76, dep ldr Lab Pty 1972-76, chllr Newcastle upon Tyne Poly, pres Finchale Abbey Trg Coll for Disabled, chm Cable Wireless Ltd 1976-80; Hon DCL Durham, Hon DUniv Open Univ, Hon DLitt CNAA; *Books* The Story of the Durham Light Infantry (1944), The Infantry Instructor (1946), Education in a Changing World (1971), Birth to Five (1974), I Knew My Place (1983), Whip to Wilson (1989); *Style—* The Rt Hon Lord Glenamara, CH, PC; Glenridding, Cumbria (☎ 07684 82273); 21 Priory Gardens, Corbridge, Northumberland (☎ 043 463 2880)

GLENAPP, Viscount; (Kenneth) Peter Lyle Mackay; s and h of 3 Earl of Inchcape; *b* 23 Jan 1943; *Educ* Eton; *m* 7 June 1966, Georgina, da of Sydney Cresswell Nisbet; 1 s, 2 da (Hon Elspeth b 1972, Hon Ailsa b 1977); *Heir* s, Hon Fergus James Kenneth Mackay b 9 July 1979; *Career* 2 Lt 9/12 Royal Lancers served: Aden, Arabian Gulf, BAOR; dir: Duncan MacNeill & Co Ltd, Inchcape (UK) Ltd, Inchcape Family Investments Ltd; asst to Cts of Worshipful Cos of Grocers and Shipwrights; AIB; *Recreations* shooting, fishing, golf, farming; *Clubs* White's, Oriental, City of London; *Style—* Viscount Glenapp; Manor Farm, Clyffe Pypard, nr Swindon, Wilts; 63E Pont St, London SW1; office: Sir John Lyon House, 5 High Timber St, Upper Thames St, London EC4

GLENARTHUR, Dowager Baroness; Margaret Risk; o da of late Capt Henry James Howie, of Stairaird, Mauchline; *m* 1 Sept 1939, as his 2 w, 3 Baron Glenarthur (d 1976); 2 s (4 Baron, *qv*, Hon Matthew Richard Arthur), 1 da (Hon Mrs Vernon); *Style—* The Rt Hon the Dowager Lady Glenarthur; Stairaird, Mauchline, Ayrshire (☎ 0290 50211)

GLENARTHUR, 4 Baron (UK 1918); Sir Simon Mark Arthur; 4 Bt (UK 1903), DL (Aberdeenshire 1988); s of 3 Baron Glenarthur, OBE, DL (d 1976), by his 2 w (*see* Glenarthur, Dowager Baroness); *b* 7 Oct 1944; *Educ* Eton; *m* 12 Nov 1969, Susan, yr da of Cdr Hubert Wyndham Barry, RN, and Violet, da of Col Sir Edward Ruggles-Brise, 1 Bt; 1 s, 1 da (Hon Emily Victoria b 1975); *Heir* s, Hon Edward Alexander Arthur b 9 April 1973; *Career* sits as Cons peer in House of Lords; served Royal Hussars: cmmnd 1963, Capt 1970, Maj 1973, ret; served Royal Hussars TA 1975-80; MCIT; Capt Br Airways Helicopters Ltd 1976-82, dir Aberdeen & Texas Corporate Fin Ltd 1977-82; Govt whip (lord in waiting) 1982-83, Parly under-sec state DHSS 1983-85, Parly under-sec Home Office 1985-86; min of State: for Scotland 1986-87, FCO 1987-89; Hanson plc 1989-; conslt British Aerospace 1989-; memb Queen's Body Guard for Scotland (Royal Co of Archers); *Recreations* field sports, flying, gardening, choral singing; *Clubs* Cavalry and Guards'; *Style—* The Rt Hon the Lord Glenarthur, DL; c/o House of Lords, London SW1A 0PW (☎ 071 245 1245)

GLENCONNER, Baroness; Lady Anne (Veronica); *née* Coke; eldest da of 5 Earl of Leicester, MVO (d 1976); *b* 16 July 1932; *m* 12 April 1956, 3 Baron Glenconner; 3 s, 2 da; *Career* an extra lady-in-waiting to HRH The Princess Margaret, Countess of Snowdon 1971-; *Books* The Picnic Papers (with Susanna Johnstone, 1983); *Style—* The Rt Hon Lady Glenconner; 50 Victoria Road, London W8; The Glen, Innerleithen, Peebleshire

GLENCONNER, 3 Baron (UK 1911); Sir Colin Christopher Paget Tennant; 4 Bt (UK 1885); s of 2 Baron Glenconner (d 1983), and his 1 w, Pamela, Baroness Glenconner, *qv*; *b* 1 Dec 1926; *Educ* Eton, New Coll Oxford; *m* 12 April 1956, Lady Anne Veronica Coke (*see* Glenconner, Baroness); 3 s (Hon Charles Edward Pevensey b 1957, Hon Henry Lovell b 1960 d 1990, Hon Christopher Cary b 1967), twin da (Hon May and Hon Amy b 1970); *Heir* s, Hon Charles Tennant; *Career* Lt Irish Gds; governing dir Tennants Estate Ltd 1967-, chm Mustique Co; *Style—* The Rt Hon Lord Glenconner; The Glen, Innerleithen, Peeblesshire; 50 Victoria Rd, London W8

GLENCONNER, Elizabeth, Baroness; Elizabeth; er da of late Lt-Col Evelyn George Harcourt Powell, Grenadier Gds, of 31 Hillgate Place, London W8; *m* 25 March 1935, as his 2 w, 2 Baron Glenconner (d 1983); 1 s, 2 da; *Style—* The Rt Hon Elizabeth, Lady Glenconner; Rovinia, Liapades, Corfu, Greece

GLENCROSS, David; s of John William Glencross, of Salford, Lancs (d 1962), and Elsie May, *née* Ward (d 1987); *b* 3 March 1936; *Educ* Salford GS, Trinity Coll Cambridge (BA); *m* 1965, Elizabeth Louise, da of Jack Turner Richardson (d 1977), of Birmingham; 1 da (Juliet b 1966); *Career* BBC gen trainee various posts in radio and TV prodn 1958-70, sr programme offr 1970-76, head programme offr 1976-77, dir TV IBA 1983-90 (dep dir 1977-83), chief exec Independent TV Commission; fell Royal TV Soc; FRSA; *Recreations* music, reading, walking, idling; *Style—* David Glencross, Esq; ITC, 70 Brompton Rd, London SW3 1EY

GLENDEVON, 1 Baron (UK 1964); of Midhope, Co Linlithgow; John Adrian Hope; ERD (1988), PC (1959); yr (twin) s of 2 Marquess of Linlithgow, KG, KT, PC, GCSI, GCIE, OBE, TD (d 1952); *b* 7 April 1912; *Educ* Eton, Christ Church Oxford (MA); *m* 21 July 1948, Elizabeth Mary, o da of (William) Somerset Maugham, CH, FRSL, and former w of Col Vincent Rudolph Paravicini (d 1989); 2 s; *Heir* s, Hon Julian John Somerset Hope, *qv*; *Career* Maj Scots Gds Res; WWII 1939-45; serv: Narvik, Salerno, Anzio (despatches twice); MP (C): Midlothian N and Peebles 1945-50, Edinburgh Pentlands 1950-64; min Works 1959-62 (jt Parly under-sec Scotland 1957-59, Parly under-sec of state Cwlth Rels 1956-57 and Foreign Affrs 1954-66); chm: Royal Cwlth Soc 1963-66, Historic Bldgs Cncl England 1973-75, Geigy (UK) Ltd 1967-71; dir and dep chm Ciba-Geigy (UK) Ltd 1971-78; dir: Colonial Mutual Life Assur Soc Ltd 1952-54 and 1962-82, British Electric Traction Omnibus Serv 1947-52 and 1962-82; FRSA 1962; *Books* The Viceroy at Bay (1971); *Clubs* White's; *Style—* The Rt Hon Lord Glendevon, ERD, PC; Mount Lodge, Mount Row, St Peter Port, Guernsey, CI (☎ 0481 21516)

GLENDINING, Rev Canon Alan; LVO (1979), QHC (1979); s of Vincent Glendining (d 1964), and Frida Alice, *née* Berry (d 1974); *b* 17 March 1924; *Educ* Radley, Westcott House Cambridge; *m* 8 May 1948, Margaret Locke, da of Lt-Col Claud McKinnon Hawes, DSO (d 1973); 1 s (David b 1950), 2 da (Sarah Jane b 1955 d 1981, Frances b 1962); *Career* Foreign Office 1942-45, newspaper publisher and ed 1945-58; deacon 1960, ordained priest Lincoln 1961, curate South Ormsby Gp of Parishes 1960; rector: Raveningham Gp of Parishes 1963, Sandringham Gp of Parishes 1970; domestic chaplain to HM the Queen 1970, rural dean Heacham and Rising 1972-76, hon canon Norwich Cathedral 1977, rector Lowestoft Gp of Parishes 1979, vicar Ranworth and Woodbastwick 1985, sr chaplain to Norfolk Holiday Indust 1985-90; sec Norfolk Water Safety Assoc 1987-, chm West Norfolk Hospice Home Help 1990-, hon curate St Margaret's Kings Lynn 1990-; Queen's Jubilee Medal 1977; *Recreations* reading, writing, shooting; *Style—* The Rev Canon Alan Glendining, LVO, QHC; 7 Bellfosters, Kings Staithe Lane, Kings Lynn, Norfolk PE30 1LZ (☎ 0553 760113)

GLENDINNING, David Edward Hamilton; s of Dr David Glendinning, of The Hollows, S Rauceby, Sleaford, Lincs, and Kathleen Theresa, *née* Holmes; *b* 28 Dec 1946; *Educ* Carres GS Sleaford, UCH (BDS); *m* 1, 20 June 1971 (m dis 1974), Victoria Sorrell , da of Prof Raleigh Barcley Lucas, of Sevenoaks, Kent; m 2, 9 Oct 1976, Teresa Mary, da of Brendan James Bolger of St Albans Herts; 1 s (Andrew b 1986), 2 da (Laura b 1980, Sarah b 1982); *Career* house surgn UCH 1970, sr house offr in periodontology Royal Dental Hosp 1970-71, registrar Dental Dept St Bartholemews Hosp 1972-74, sr registrar in oral surgery Manchester 1974-78, conslt oral surgn S Lincolnshire Pilgrim Hosp Boston and Grantham and Kesteven Gen Hosp 1978-; various pubns in Br and US oral surgery press; fell BAOMS 1979, FDSRCS; *Recreations* golf, sailing, old cars, racing; *Clubs* Seaford Golf, Fakenham Raceclub; *Style—* David Glendinning, Esq; Hill House, South Rauceby, Sleaford, Lincolnshire NG34 8QQ (☎ 0529 8625); Dept of Oral Surgery, Pilgrim Hospital, Boston, Lincolnshire (☎ 0205 64801)

GLENDINNING, James Garland; OBE (1973); s of George Moffat Glendinning (d 1965), of Edinburgh, and Isabella, *née* Green (d 1951); *b* 27 April 1919; *Educ* Boroughmuir Edinburgh, Military Coll of Sci; *m* 1, 28 Aug 1943, Margaret Euphemia (decd), da of James Donald (d 1916); 1 da (Jennifer Ann b 1948 d 1986); m 2, 23 Oct 1980, Anne Ruth, da of Adalbert Horn (d 1984), of Reutlingen; *Career* WWII 1939-46 London Scottish (Gordon Highlanders) and REME (cmmnd Capt); HM inspr of taxes 1946-50; Shell Petroleum Co Ltd in London 1950-58; dir: Shell Egypt, Anglo Egyptian

Oilfields in Egypt 1959-61; gen mangr: PT Shell (Indonesia) in Borneo and East Java 1961-64, Shell Int London 1964-67; vice pres: (Japan) Shell Sekiyu KK, Shell Kosan KK 1967-72; md Japan Shell Technol KK, dir Showa Sekiyu KK 1967-72, chm Br C of C in Japan; memb Bd London Tport Exec 1972-80; chm North American Property Unit Tst 1975-80, dir The Fine Art Soc plc 1972-89; md Gestam Int Realty Ltd 1980-84, chm Masterpack Ltd 1980-, dir LE Vincent & Ptnrs Ltd 1984-; *Clubs* Caledonian, Oriental; *Style*— James Glendinning, Esq, OBE; 20 Albion Street, London W2 2AS; 162-168 Regent Street, London W1R 5TB

GLENDINNING, Prof Robert; s of James Watson Glendinning (d 1953), and Isabella Butters, *née* Smeaton (d 1954); *b* 11 Aug 1912; *Educ* Glasgow HS, Univ of Glasgow (MA); *m* 25 Sept 1941, Helena Lilian, da of John Greig Fenton (d 1953); 2 da (Aileen b 1944, Lorna b 1947); *Career* CA; various fin and accounting appts Br Tport Cmmn 1948-62, BR Bd 1962-72, conslt (mainly tport and engrg accounting and fin) 1972-, pt/t lectr in fin and mgmnt accounting Univ of Stirling, visiting prof of accounting Queen's Univ of Belfast, prof of financial mgmnt Int Mgmnt Centre Buckingham; pres Chartered Inst Mgmnt Accountants 1968-69; memb Panel of Judges 1979- (annual award for the best public co annual report and accounts given by the Int Stock Exchanges and the three British Insts of Chartered Accountants); contrib: The Accountant, Accountancy Age, Management Accounting; FCMA, FCIT, FInstD, JDipMA; *Recreations* lawn tennis; *Clubs* IOD; *Style*— Prof Robert Glendinning; 10 Copperfields, Beaconsfield, Bucks HP9 2NS (☎ 0494 674341)

GLENDINNING, Hon Victoria (Hon Mrs de Vere White); *née* Seebohm; er da of Baron Seebohm, TD (Life Peer, d 1990), and Evangeline (d 1990), da of His Hon Sir Gerald Berkeley Hurst, QC; *b* 23 April 1937; *Educ* St Mary's Wantage, Millfield, Somerville Coll Oxford (BA, MA), Univ of Southampton (Dip Social Admin); *m* 1, 6 Sept 1958 (m dis 1981), Prof (Oliver) Nigel Valentine Glendinning; 4 s; m 2, 1982, Terence de Vere White, *qv*; *Career* author and journalist; FRSL; *Books* A Suppressed Cry, Elizabeth Bowen: Portrait of a Writer, Edith Sitwell: A Unicorn among Lions, Vita, Rebecca West, Hertfordshire, The Grown Ups; *Recreations* gardening; *Style*— Ms Victoria Glendinning; c/o David Higham Associates, 5-8 Lower John St, Lower W1R 4HA

GLENDYNE, 3 Baron (UK 1922); Sir Robert Nivison; 3 Bt (UK 1914); s of 2 Baron Glendyne (d 1967); *b* 27 Oct 1926; *Educ* Harrow; *m* 25 April 1953, Elizabeth, yr da of Sir (Stephen) Cecil Armitage, CBE, JP, DL, of Hawksworth Manor, Notts; 1 s, 2 da; *Heir* s, Hon John Nivison; *Career* WWII Lt Grenadier Gds; sr ptnr R Nivison & Co (stockbrokers) 1967- 86, chm Glenfriars Unit Trust Managers Ltd 1971-; *Clubs* City of London; *Style*— The Rt Hon the Lord Glendyne; Craigeassie By Forfar, Angus DD8 3SE (☎ 0307 86249)

GLENKINGLAS, Baroness; Anne; da of Sir Neville Pearson, 2 Bt, by his 1 w, Hon Mary Angela Mond (da of 1 Baron Melchett); *b* 5 Feb 1923; *m* 11 Sept 1940, Baron Glenkinglas, PC (Life Peer, d 1984); 4 da; *Style*— The Rt Hon Lady Glenkinglas; 7 Egerton Gardens, London SW3 2BP

GLENN, Sir (Joseph Robert) Archibald; OBE (1965); s of Joseph Robert Glenn (d 1946), of Sale, Victoria, Aust, and Evelyn, *née* Lockett (d 1939); *b* 24 May 1911; *Educ* Scotch Coll Melbourne, Univ of Melbourne, Harvard, La Trobe Univ Victoria (Hon DUniv); *m* 1939, Elizabeth Mary Margaret (d 1988), da of James Schofield Balderstone (d 1954); 1 s, 3 da; *Career* professional engr and co dir; chm and md ICI Aust 1963-73, dir Bank of NSW (now Westpac Banking Corporation) 1967-84, dir ICI Ltd London 1970-75, chm IMI Aust 1970-78; chm Scotch Coll Cncl 1962-81, govr Atlantic Inst of Int Affrs 1973-78, chllr La Trobe Univ 1964-72; kt 1966; *see Debrett's Handbook of Australia and New Zealand for further details*; *Style*— Sir Archibald Glenn, OBE; 1A Woorigoleen Rd, Toorak, Vic 3142, Australia (☎ 827 6367)

GLENNIE, Evelyn Elizabeth Ann; da of Herbert Arthur Glennie, of Ellon, Aberdeenshire, and Isobel Mary, *née* Howie; *b* 19 July 1965; *Educ* Ellon Acad, Royal Acad of Music (GRSM, LRAM, James Blades prize for percussion and timpani, Hugh Fitch prize for percussion, Hilda Deane Anderson prize for orchestral playing, Queen's Commendation prize); *Career* musician (timpani and percussion); debut recital Wigmore Hall 1986; concerts with: LSO, the Philharmonia, London Sinfonietta, Northern Sinfonia, RTE Orch Dublin, Finnish Radio Symphony, Trondheim Symphony Norway, Eng Chamber Orch; composer: A Little Prayer, Giles, Light in Darkness; arranged and transcribed many pieces; numerous concerts and recitals as a soloist; guest appearances on TV and radio; recordings: Bartok-sonata for Two Pianos and Percussion (with Sir Georg Solti, Murray Perahia and David Corkhill 1987, Grammy award 1989), Vackar-Wallace Collection (1987), Sousa Marches-Wallace Collection (1988), Rhythm Song (1989), Light in Darkness (1990); several pieces composed for her by: John McLeod, Richard Rodney Bennett, Dominic Maldowney, James MacMillan, Howard Blake, Malcolm Singer, John Mayer, Edward Shipley, Ronald Stevenson, Paul Hancock, Menotti; awarded Gold medal Shell and LSO music scholarship 1984, Munster trust scholarship 1986, Leonardo de Vinci prize 1987, Young Professional All Music Musican of the Year Wavendon All Music awards 1988; voted by Jr Chamber as one of ten outstanding young people in the world 1989, Scotswoman of The Decade for the 1980's; autobiography Good Vibrations (1990); *Recreations* reading, walking, music, sport; *Style*— Ms Evelyn Glennie; Harrison/ Parrott, 12 Penzance Place, London W11 4PA (☎ 071 229 9166, fax 071 221 5042)

GLENNIE, Hon Mrs (Jane Maureen Thérèse); *née* Dormer; er da of 15 Baron Dormer (d 1975), and Lady Maureen Fellowes, *née* Noel; *b* 20 Nov 1945; *m* 1, 21 July 1966 (m dis 1978), (Henry Alistair) Samuel Sandbach; 1 s (James), 1 da (Emma); m 2, 1980, Sqdn Ldr Geoffrey E Meek, RAF (d 1984); m 3, 16 Jan 1988, Lt Cdr R N F Glennie; *Career* landowner; *Recreations* travel; *Style*— The Hon Mrs Glennie; 44 Homefield Rd, Chiswick, London W4 (☎ 081 994 4795); Church Farm Cottage, East Wittering, West Sussex (☎ 0243 673226)

GLENNIE-SMITH, Dr Keith; TD (1979); s of Frank Glennie Smith (d 1965), of Seaford, Sussex, and Ruth Janet, *née* Doxat-Pratt (d 1968); *b* 14 Jan 1927; *Educ* Lancing, St Thomas' Hosp Med Sch, Univ of London (MB BS); *m* 8 Nov 1952, Cecilia Mary, da of Dr Egerton Henry Valpy Hensley (d 1966), of Winchester; 1 s (Patrick b 1960), 3 da (Janet b 1953, Frances b 1956, Helen b 1963); *Career* Nat Serv: Capt RAMC (1 Cwlth Div), served Korea 1952; Maj RAMC cmd 356 Field Surgical Team 1962, Lt-Col RAMC/RARO 1980; conslt anaesthetist Bournemouth and Poole Dist Hosps 1962, clinical tutor Bournemouth Hosps 1972-77, dir anaesthesia serv Kainuu Prov Hosp Finland 1975, fndr and dir Med Acupuncture Dept Poole Hosp 1977 (fndr and dir Med Illustration Dept 1967); visiting prof: Bergen Univ Hosp Norway 1982, Shanghai Univ China 1982; memb HCSA 1962, Cncl of Europe fellowship 1972, Med and Scientific Network 1977; chm Southern Soc of Anaesthetistis 1980, pres Bournemouth and Poole Med Soc 1980, fndr memb and vice-chm Br Med Acupuncture Soc 1980, memb Nordic Acupuncture Soc 1980; memb BMA 1951; fell Int Coll of Acupuncture and Electro-Therapeutics 1978, FFARCS 1960; *Recreations* music (pianist and composer), photography, art; *Clubs* East Dorset Lawn Tennis and Croquet; *Style*— Dr Keith Glennie-Smith, TD; 17 Springfield Crescent, Parkstone, Poole, Dorset BH14 0LL (☎ 0202 768754); Le Rondeau, Chemin du Porteau, 85300 Soullans, France; 2 Clarendon Rd, Westbourne, Bournemouth, Dorset (☎ 0202 768754)

GLENNY, (Alexander) Keith; s of Lt-Col Clifford Roy Glenny, TD, of 28 Crosby Rd, Westcliff On Sea, Essex, and Eileen Winifred, *née* Smith (d 1974); *b* 19 July 1946; *Educ* Charterhouse, Gonville and Caius Coll Cambridge (MA, LLM); *m* 19 April 1975, Rachel Elizabeth, da of Rev A C Fryer, of Byfield House, Byfield, Northants; 2 s (Christopher b 5 Jan 1977, Matthew b 31 Oct 1986), 1 da (Anna b 24 May 1979); *Career* slr British Oxygen Co Ltd 1970-72; Hatten Asplin Channer and Glenny Barking Essex: slr 1972-74, ptnr 1974-88, sr ptnr 1988-; clerk Barking and Ilford United Charities and Barking Gen Charities, govr Barking Abbey Sch; Freeman Worshipful Co of Poulters 1978; memb Law Soc; *Clubs* Wig and Pen, City Livery; *Style*— Keith Glenny, Esq; Netherfield, Powdermill Lane, Leigh, Tonbridge, Kent TN11 8PY (☎ 0732 833 320); 4 Town Quay Wharf, Abbey Rd, Barking IG11 7BZ (☎ 081 591 4131, fax 081 591 1912)

GLENNY, (Reginald Thomas) Rex; CBE (1964); s of Walter Glenny (d 1955), of Beckenham, Kent, and Mary Elizabeth, *née* Dawes (d 1962); *b* 10 July 1914; *Educ* Alleyn's Sch Dulwich; *m* 1, 1939, Edith Hawthorne (d 1957), da of late Harry Stevenson; 1 da (Margaret, d 1950); m 2, 1960, Florence Eliza (Betty), da of Joseph Wilson (d 1956), of St Marylebone, London W1; *Career* WWII Capt TA served France 1940, cmmnd IA 1942, discharged Capt 1946; stockbroker 1948-, ptnr Charles Stanley & Co 1975-; chm: Bd of Fin London Diocese C of E 1977-, Gtr London Area Cons Assoc 1969-72; Age Concern Westminster vice pres Alexandra Rose Day; *Recreations* church and charitable work; *Clubs* MCC; *Style*— Rex Glenny Esq, CBE; 22 Clarewood Court, Seymour Place, London W1 (☎ 071 262 8217); Charles Stanley and Co, Gardenhouse, 18 Finsbury Circus, London EC2M 7BL (☎ 071 638 5717)

GLENTON, Anthony Arthur Edward; MBE (1983), TD (1974), DL (Northumberland, 1990); s of Lt-Col Eric Cecil Glenton (d 1978), of Gosforth, Newcastle, and Joan Lydia, *née* Taylor; *b* 21 March 1943; *Educ* Merchiston Castle Sch Edinburgh; *m* 8 April 1972, Caroline Ann, da of Maurice George Meade-King, of Clifton, Bristol; 1 s (Peter b 1977), 1 da (Sophie b 1974); *Career* joined TA 1961, Lt-Col 1984, cmd 101 (Northumbrian) Field Regt RA (V) 1984-86, Col 1986, dep cdr 15 Inf Bde 1986-89; ADC to HM the Queen 1987-89; TA Col North East District 1990-, dep Lt County of Northumberland 1990-; sr ptnr Ryecroft Glenton & Co CAs Newcastle upon Tyne, dir Port of Tyne Authy 1987, vice chm Newcastle Bldg Soc 1987; Freeman City of London, Liveryman Worshipful Co of Chartered Accountants England & Wales; FCA 1971; *Recreations* shooting, skiing, sailing; *Clubs* Army & Navy; *Style*— Anthony Glenton, Esq, MBE, TD, DL; Whinbank, Rothbury, Northumberland (☎ 0669 20361); 27 Portland Terrace, Jesmond, Newcastle upon Tyne NE2 1QP (☎ 091 2811292)

GLENTORAN, 2 Baron (UK 1939); Sir Daniel Stewart Thomas Bingham Dixon; 4 Bt (UK 1903), KBE (1973), PC (NI 1953); s of 1 Baron, OBE, PC, JP, DL (d 1950), and Hon Emily, *née* Bingham (da of 5 Baron Clanmorris); *b* 19 Jan 1912; *Educ* Eton, Sandhurst; *m* 20 July 1933, Lady Diana Mary, *née* Wellesley, er da of 3 Earl Cowley; 2 s (Hon Thomas b 1935, Hon Peter b 1948), 1 da (Hon Mrs Rudolph Agnew b 1937); *Career* served WWII and as regular Grenadier Gds, Lt-Col ret; Hon Col 6 Bn RUR (TA); MP (U) NI Parl Belfast Bloomfield 1950-61, min Commerce 1953-61, min NI Senate 1961-72 (speaker 1964-72); HM Lieut Belfast 1950-76, Lord Lieut 1976-85; *Style*— The Rt Hon Lord Glentoran, KBE, PC; Drumadarragh House, Doagh, Co Antrim, N Ireland (☎ Doagh 222)

GLENTWORTH, Viscount; Edmund Christopher Pery; s and h of 6 Earl of Limerick, KBE; *b* 10 Feb 1963; *Educ* Eton, New Coll Oxford, Pushkin Inst Moscow, City Univ; *m* 21 July 1990, Emily K, o da of Michael Gavin Lynam Thomas, *qv*, of Worcester; *Career* called to the Bar Middle Temple 1987; HM Dip Serv: FCO 1987-88, Ecole Nationale d'Adminstration 1988-89, Quai d'Orsay 1990-, second sec Dakar 1990-; *Recreations* skiing, travel, music; *Style*— Viscount Glentworth; FCO, King Charles St, London SW1A 2AH

GLENWRIGHT, Harry Donald; s of late Harry Glenwright, and Minnie Glenwright; *b* 25 June 1934; *Educ* Stockton-on-Tees Secdy Sch, Univ of Durham (BDS), Univ of Newcastle (MDS); *m* 29 Dec 1966, Gillian Minton, da of late Arthur Holland Thacker; 1 s (Robert b 1970), 1 da (Kate b 1973); *Career* house surgn Newcastle Dental Hosp 1957-58, Surg Lt (D) RN 1958-61, registrar Eastman Dental Hosp 1961-63, lectr in dental surgery Univ of Birmingham 1963-66, lectr in periodontics Queen's Univ of Belfast 1966-69, Br Cncl scholar Univ of Oslo 1968, Cncl of Europe scholar Aarhus and Oslo Univs 1971, Br Cncl scholar Colombo Univ 1985; Univ of Birmingham: sr lectr in periodontology 1969-, acting head Dept of Restorative Dentistry 1989-, chm Bd of Undergraduate Dental Educn 1989-; external examiner: Univ of Dublin 1978, Univ of London 1979-81, Univ of Manchester 1979-86, Univ of Belfast 1980-83, Univ of Leeds 1985-87, RCS 1988-; pres: Br Soc of Periodontology 1980-81, Section of Odontology Birmingham Med Inst 1981-82, Conslt in Restorative Dentistry Gp 1987- (memb Cncl); memb: Specialist Advsy Ctee in Restorative Dentistry 1987-, Central Ctee for Hosp Dental Servs 1988, Dental Health and Sci Ctee 1988; FDSRCS; *Recreations* gardening, reading; *Style*— Harry Glenwright, Esq; White House, Rushbrook Lane, Tanworth-in-Arden, Warwickshire B94 5HP (☎ 056 44 2578); The Dental School, St Chads Queensway, Birmingham B4 6NN (☎ 021 236 8611)

GLICHER, Julian Harvey; s of Samuel Glicher (d 1982), and Dorothy Glicher (d 1983); *b* 15 June 1948; *Educ* Haberdashers' Aske's, Ashridge Sch of Mgmnt; *m* 18 Aug 1976, Adrienne, da of Phillip Rose, of Elstree; 2 s (Toby Oliver b 1978, Nicholas David b 1980); *Career* CA; sr exec Price Waterhouse Paris 1968-72, mangr Hambros Bank 1972-77, asst dir Lloyds Merchant Bank 1977-85, ptnr and nat dir corporate fin Clark Whitehill 1987- (dir 1985); FCA 1978; *Recreations* badminton, cycling, sailing, family; *Style*— Julian H Glicher, Esq; 25 New St Sq, London EC4A 3LN (☎ 071 353 1577, fax 071 353 2803, telex 887422)

GLICK, Ian Bernard; QC (1987); s of Dr Louis Glick (d 1989), and Phyllis Esty, *née* Barnett; *b* 18 July 1948; *Educ* Bradford GS, Balliol Coll Oxford (MA, BCL); *m* 14 Dec 1986, Roxane Olivia Sarah, da of Dr R Eban; *Career* called to the Bar Inner Temple 1970; jr counsel in common law to the Crown 1985-87, standing counsel in export credit cases to DTI 1985-87; *Style*— Ian Glick, Esq, QC; 1 Essex Court, Temple, London EC4 (☎ 071 583 2000, fax 071 583 0118, telex 889109)

GLIDEWELL, Rt Hon Lord Justice; Rt Hon Sir Iain Derek Laing; PC (1985); s of Charles Norman Glidewell, and Nora Glidewell; *b* 8 June 1924; *Educ* Bromsgrove Sch, Worcester Coll Oxford; *m* 1950, Hilary, da of late Clinton D Winant; 1 s, 2 da; *Career* called to the Bar 1949, QC 1969; chm Panels for Examination Structure Plans: Worcs 1974, W Midlands 1975; rec Crown Ct 1976-80, conducted Heathrow Fourth Terminal Enquiry 1978, appeal judge IOM 1979-80, High Ct judge (Queen's Bench) 1980-85, memb Supreme Ct Rule Ctee 1980-83, presiding judge NE circuit 1982-85, chm Judicial Studies Bd 1989-; kt 1980; *Style*— The Rt Hon Sir Iain Glidewell, PC; Royal Courts of Justice, Strand, London WC2

GLIN, 29 Knight of (The Black Knight, Irish hereditary knighthood dating c 1300-30, though first authenticated use dates from 1424); Desmond John Villiers FitzGerald; s of 28 Knight of Glin (Desmond Windham Otho FitzGerald, d 1949, descended from John Fitz-Thomas FitzGerald (d 1261), father of three bros, The White Knight, The Knight of Glin and The Knight of Kerry (*qv*); *b* 13 July 1937; *Educ* Stowe, Univ of British Columbia, Harvard; *m* 1, 6 Oct 1966 (m dis 1970), Lulu

(Louise) Vava Lucia Henriette, da of Alain, Marquis de la Falaise de la Coudraye, of Paris; m 2, 12 Aug 1970, Olda Anne, o da of Thomas Willes, of Brompton Sq, London SW; 3 da; *Career* asst and dep keeper Furniture and Woodwork Dept Victoria and Albert Museum 1965-75, Irish agent Christie's 1975-; vice pres Irish Georgian Soc, chm and dir Irish Georgian Fndn, dir and past chm Historic Irish Tourist Houses Assoc, tstee Castletown Fndn; author of books and articles on Irish art and architecture; FSA; *Books* Ireland Observed (with Maurice Craig, 1975), Lost Demesnes (with Edward Malins, 1976), The Painters of Ireland (with Anne Crookshank, 1978), Vanishing Country Houses of Ireland (jtly 1988); *Recreations* art history; *Clubs* White's, Beefsteak, Kildare and Univ (Dublin); *Style*— The Knight of Glin; 52 Waterloo Rd, Dublin 4 (☎ 0001 680585, fax 0001 680271); Glin Castle, Co Limerick, Republic of Ireland (☎ 010353 34173 and 34112, fax 010353 34364)

GLOAK, Graeme Frank; CB (1980); s of Frank Gloak, MBE (d 1979), of Kent, and Lilian Phoebe; *b* 9 Nov 1921; *Educ* Brentwood; *m* 1944, Mary Beatrice, da of Stanley James Thorne (d 1953), of Essex; 2 s (Nigel (decd), Malcolm b 1951), 1 da (Karen b 1960); *Career* RN 1941-45, Lt RNVR served Atlantic, North Sea, France; admitted slr 1947; slr for Customs and Excise 1978-82; vice chm Agric Wages Ctee for Essex and Herts 1987-90, chm Agric Dwellings Housing Advsy Ctee for Essex and Herts 1984-; memb Barking and Havering: Family Practitioners Ctee 1986-90, Family Health Service Authy 1990-; *Publications* Customs and Excise Halsbury's Laws of England; *Recreations* badminton, walking, watching cricket; *Clubs* MCC, Essex CCC (Chelmsford); *Style*— Graeme Gloak, Esq, CB; Northwold, 123 Priests Lane, Shenfield, Essex (☎ 0277 212748)

GLOCK, Sir William Frederick; CBE (1964); s of William George Glock; *b* 3 May 1908; *Educ* Christ's Hosp, Gonville and Caius Coll Cambridge; *m* 1, 1944, Clemency, da of Swinburne Hale; m 2, 1952, Anne Genevieve, da of Charles Geoffroy-Dechaume; *Career* dir Summer Sch of Music: Bryanston 1948-52, Dartington Hall 1953-79; former music critic: The Observer, New Statesman; controller of music BBC 1959-72, former memb Bd Dirs Royal Opera House and Arts Cncl, dir Bath Festival 1975-84, chm London Orch Concerts Bd 1975-86; govr South Bank Bd 1986-90, hon memb RPO; ALbert Medal RSA 1971; kt 1970; *Style*— Sir William Glock, CBE; Vine House, Brightwell cum Sotwell, Wallingford, Oxon (☎ 0491 37144)

GLOIN, David Barclay; s of Barclay Arthur Gloin (d 1981), of Dulwich, and Dilys Margaret, *née* Williams; *b* 28 Feb 1946; *Educ* Alleyn's Sch Dulwich; *m* 25 July 1970, Elizabeth Mary, da of Leslie George Francis, MBE (d 1975), of Herne Hill, S London; 1 s (Peter b 1976), 1 da (Janet b 1980); *Career* slr; articled then ptnr Gaunt Foster and Hill 1964-70, legal asst then head of branch Post Office Slrs Office Conveyancing Dept 1970-82; British Telecom: div slr Slrs Office Commercial Dept 1982-87, dir Property Law Dept 1987-89, dir Litigation and Advsy Dept 1989-; memb: Law Soc, Int Bar Assoc; Freeman City of London Slrs Co 1989, Freeman City of London 1990; *Recreations* singing, reading, walking; *Style*— David B Gloin, Esq; The Solicitor's Office, British Telecommunications plc, British Telecom Centre, 81 Newgate St, London EC1A 7AJ (☎ 071 356 4820, fax 071 356 5894, 071 356 6317, telex 268413, TELECOM GOLD 73:TSY004)

GLOSSOP, (Charles Compton) Anthony; s of Col Alfred William Compton Glossop, OBE, TD (d 1980), of Chesterfield, Derbyshire, and Muriel Bradbury, *née* Robinson (d 1986); *b* 24 Nov 1941; *Educ* Eastbourne Coll, Queens' Coll Cambridge (MA); *m* 28 June 1969, Julia Margaret Anne, da of Capt William Forrester (d 1952), of Dalton-in-Furness, Cumbria; 2 da (Clare b 5 Jan 1971, Katherine b 21 Dec 1972); *Career* admitted slr 1967; asst sec Molins Ltd 1969-72, gp md St Modwen Properties plc (formerly Redman Heenan Int plc) 1982- (co sec 1972-82, dir 1976-); memb Worcester Civic Soc, Worcestershire Enterprise Agency; memb Law Soc 1967; *Recreations* walking, reading, gardening and bee-keeping; *Style*— Anthony Glossop, Esq; St Modwen Properties plc, Lynton House, 58-62 Hagley Rd, Birmingham B16 8PE (☎ 021 456 2800, fax 021 456 1829, car 0860 206694)

GLOSSOP, Peter; s of Cyril Glossop, and Violet Elizabeth Glossop; *b* 6 July 1928; *Educ* High Storrs GS Sheffield; *m* 1, 1955 (m dis 1977), Joyce Elizabeth Blackham; m 2, 1977, Michèle Yvonne Amos; 2 da; *Career* singer (baritone); guest artist: Royal Opera House (Covent Garden), La Scala (Milan), Met Opera (NY); *Style*— Peter Glossop, Esq; c/o Green Room, 8 Adam St, London WC2N 6AA

GLOUCESTER, Archdeacon of; *see*: Wagstaff, Ven Christopher John Harold

GLOUCESTER, 37 Bishop of (cr 1541) 1975-; Rt Rev John Yates; patron of 80 livings and Archdeaconries of Gloucester and Cheltenham; See (formerly part of Diocese of Worcester) founded by Henry VIII (along with Bristol, with which Gloucester was combined 1836-97); s of Frank Yates and Edith Ethel Yates, of Burslem; *b* 17 April 1925; *Educ* Battersea GS, Blackpool GS, Jesus Coll Cambridge, Lincoln Theological Coll; *m* 1954, Jean Kathleen Dover; 1 s, 2 da; *Career* served RAFVR 1943-47; took seat in House of Lords Nov 1981; curate Christ Church Southgate 1951-54, tutor and chaplain Lincoln Theological Coll 1954-59, vicar Bottesford-with-Ashby 1959-65, princ Lichfield Theological Coll 1966-72, suffragan bishop Whitby 1972-75; *Clubs* RAF; *Style*— The Rt Rev the Lord Bishop of Gloucester; Bishopscourt, Pitt St, Gloucester GL1 2BQ (☎ (0452) 24598)

GLOVER, Anthony Richard Haysom; 2 s of Arthur Herbert Glover (d 1941), and Margorie Florence Glover; *b* 29 May 1934; *Educ* Emmanuel Coll Cambridge; *m* 1960, Ann Penelope, da of John Scupham, OBE, of Harpenden, Herts; 2 s, 1 da; *Career* dep controller HMSO 1976-; *Style*— Anthony Glover, Esq; 7 Hillside Rd, Thorpe St Andrew, Norwich NR7 (☎ 33508)

GLOVER, Eric; s of William Arthur Glover (d 1965), of Liverpool, and Margaret, *née* Walker; *b* 28 June 1935; *Educ* Liverpool Inst HS, Oriel Coll Oxford (MA); *m* 1960, Adele Diane, da of Col Cecil Geoffrey Hilliard, of Harrogate; 3 s (Ian, Paul, Jason); *Career* sec gen Chartered Inst of Bankers 1982-90 (dir of studies 1968-82); *Recreations* golf, squash, tennis; *Clubs* Overseas Bankers; *Style*— Eric Glover, Esq; 12 Manor Park, Tunbridge Wells TN4 8XP (☎ 0892 31221); The Chartered Inst of Bankers, 10 Lombard St, London EC3V 9AS

GLOVER, Gen Sir James Malcolm; KCB (1981), MBE (1964); s of Maj-Gen Malcolm Glover, CB, OBE (d 1970), and Jean Ogilvie, *née* Will (d 1970); *b* 25 March 1929; *Educ* Wellington, RMA Sandhurst; *m* 1959, Janet Diones, da of Maj Hugo De Pree; 1 s (Jonathan), 1 da (Carolyn); *Career* cmmnd 1949, RHA 1950-54, instr RMA Sandhurst 1955-56, transferred to Rifle Bde 1956, Bde Maj 48 Gurkha Inf Bde 1960-62, memb Directing Staff Staff Coll 1966-68, CO 3 Bn Royal Green Jackets 1970-71, Col Gen Staff MOD 1972-73, Cdr 19 Airportable Bde 1974-75, Brig Gen Staff (Intelligence) MOD 1977-78, Cdr Land Forces NI 1979-80, Lt-Gen 1981, Dep Chief Def Staff (Intelligence) 1981-83, Vice-Chief Gen Staff MOD and memb Army Bd of Def Cncl 1983-85, C-in-C UKLF 1985-87, Col Cmdt Royal Green Jackets 1983-88, ret 1987; chm IT Security International Ltd; dir: British Petroleum plc, Airship Industries Ltd; *Recreations* shooting, mountain walking, gardening; *Clubs* Boodle's; *Style*— Gen Sir James Glover, KCB, MBE; c/o Lloyds Bank Ltd, Cox's and King's Branch, 7 Pall Mall, London SW1

GLOVER, Dr Jane Alison; da of Robert Finlay Glover, TD, of Malvern, Worcs, and Jean, *née* Muir; *b* 13 May 1949; *Educ* Monmouth Sch for Girls, St Hugh's Coll Oxford, (BA, MA, DPhil); *Career* freelance conductor; musical dir: Glyndebourne Touring Opera 1982-85, London Choral Soc 1983-; appeared with many orchs and opera cos incl: Glyndebourne Festival Opera 1982-, BBC Proms 1985-, Royal Opera House Covent Garden 1988-, Eng Nat Opera 1989; artistic dir London Mozart Players 1984-, princ conductor Huddersfield Choral Soc 1989-; regular broadcaster on TV and Radio, regular recordings; sr res fell St Hughe's Coll Oxford 1982-; govr BBC 1990-; memb Worshipful Co of Haberdashers; Hon DMus Univ of Exeter 1986, Hon DUniv Open Univ 1988, Hon DLitt Loughborough Univ of Technol 1988; RMA 1974, RSA 1988; *Books* Cavalli (1978); *Recreations* Times crossword, theatre; *Style*— Dr Jane Glover; c/o Lies Askonas Ltd, 186 Drury Lane, London WC2B 5RY (☎ 071 405 1708)

GLOVER, Gp Capt John Neville; CMG (1963), QC (Western Pacific Territories, 1961); s of John Robert Glover (d 1965), and Sybil, *née* Cureton (d 1983), of Hayes Barton, Exbourne, Devon; *b* 12 July 1913; *Educ* Tonbridge; *m* 1, 1940, Margaret Avice, da of Stanley George Burdick, MBE; 1 s; m 2, 1956, June Patricia Bruce, da of Wing Cdr Arthur Bruce Gaskell, DSC (d 1928); *Career* served RAF 1934-46; SASO 44 Gp 1943; RAF Res of Offrs 1946-59; called to the Bar 1949; legal advsr Western Pacific High Cmmn and attorney gen Br Solomon Is 1957-63, law revision cmmr and legal draftsman for various overseas territories 1967-91; *Recreations* fly fishing; *Clubs* RAF; *Style*— Group Capt John Glover, CMG, QC; Clam End, Trebullett, Launceston, Cornwall PL15 9QQ (☎ 0566 82347)

GLOVER, Julian Wyatt; s of (Claude) Gordon Glover (d 1975), of Arkesden, Essex, and Honor Ellen Morgan, *née* Wyatt; *b* 27 March 1935; *Educ* St Paul's, Alleyn's Sch Dulwich; *m* 1, 1957 (m dis 1966), Eileen June Atkins; m 2, 28 Sept 1968, Isla Jean Blair Hill; 1 s (Jamie Blair b 10 July 1969); *Career* Nat Serv 2 Lt RASC 1954-56; actor; started out as spear-carrier at Stratford-upon-Avon 1957, Aufidius in Coriolanus and Warwick in Henry VI 1977; recent theatre includes: Habias Corpus, Educating Rita, The Aspern Papers, Never The Sinner; first film Tom Jones; theatre seasons with: RSC, Prospect, The Old Vic and Nat Theatre Companies; many films incl: For Your Eyes Only, The Fourth Protocol, I Was Happy Here, Cry Freedom, Treasure Island, Indiana Jones and the Last Crusade, King Ralph; TV incl: Dombey and Son, By The Sword Divided, Wish Me Luck, Spy Trap, Cover Her Face; Liveryman Worshipful Co of Dyers 1956; *Books* Beowolf (1987); *Clubs* Garrick; *Style*— Julian Glover, Esq; c/o Jeremy Conway Ltd, 18-21 Jermyn St, London SW1Y 6HP (☎ 071 287 0077)

GLOVER, Malcolm; *b* 3 Nov 1943; *Educ* Doncaster GS, Univ of Bristol (LLB); *m* 30 March 1973, Diane Marilyn; 1 s (Matthew b 1977), 2 da (Katie b 1975, Caroline b 1983); *Career* admitted slr 1968; Wilde Sapte 1970-: slr 1970-71, ptnr 1971-88, dep sr ptnr 1988-; memb Worshipful Co of Slrs; memb Law Soc; *Recreations* tennis, theatre; *Style*— Malcolm Glover, Esq; 31 Ossulton Way, Hampstead Garden Suburb, London N2 OJY; Wilde Sapte, Queensbridge House, 60 Upper Thames St, London EC4V 3BD (☎ 071 236 3050, fax 071 236 9624, telex 887793 WILDES G)

GLOVER, (Herbert) Michael John; s of Herbert William Archibald Glover (d 1966), of Bideford, Devon and Ethel Alice, *née* Halbert; *b* 7 Sept 1943; *Educ* Belmont Coll Barnstaple, Bideford GS; *Career* articled clerk H Barrett Son & Taylor Bideford and Barnstaple, qualified CA 1968, Cooper Bros & Co Bristol 1969-70; Turquand Young & Co: joined Exeter 1970, ptnr Torquay 1977-80, ptnr Bideford 1980-89; managing ptnr Ernst & Young N Devon Practice Bideford & Barnstaple 1989-90; ptnr Glover Pearce & Ross (following mgmnt buy-out) 1990-; FCA 1979 (ACA 1968); *Recreations* birdwatching, conservation and the countryside; *Style*— Michael Glover, Esq; Glover Pearce & Ross, 27 Bridgeland St, Bideford, Devon (☎ 0237 471881, fax 0271 45112)

GLOVER, Maj-Gen Peter James; CB (1966), OBE (1948); s of George Herbert Glover, CBE (d 1955), of Sheephatch House, Tilford, Surrey, and Constance Eliza, *née* Sloane (d 1965); *b* 16 Jan 1913; *Educ* Uppingham, Emmanuel Coll Cambridge (MA); *m* 1946, Wendy, da of Henry George Fuller Archer, OBE (d 1944), of Trevone, Weybridge, Surrey; 1 s (Jeremy), 2 da (Philippa, Elizabeth); *Career* 2 Lt RA 1934, served WWII BEF France and Far East, Lt-Col 1956, Brig 1961, Cmdt Sch of Artillery Larkhill 1960-62, Maj-Gen 1962, GOC 49 Inf Div and N Midland Dist, head Br Def Supplies Liaison Staff Delhi 1963-66, dir RA 1966-69 (ret 1969), Col Cmdt RA 1970-78; *Recreations* sailing; *Clubs* Royal Western Yacht; *Style*— Maj-Gen Peter Glover, CB, OBE; Lukesland, Diptford, nr Totnes, Devon (☎ 054882 229)

GLOVER, Dr Richard Berry; s of Henry Graham Glover (d 1931), of Hove, Sussex, and Marjorie Florence, *née* Covell (d 1978); *b* 9 Dec 1928; *Educ* Charterhouse, Middx Hosp Univ of London (MB BS); *m* 24 April 1957, (Joan Elizabeth) Ann, da of C Stuart Chiesman (d 1969), of Bickley, Kent; 1 s (Mark Berry b 24 April 1959), 1 da (Sarah Jane (Mrs Tice) b 23 May 1962); *Career* Nat Serv Flt Lt Surgical Div Med Branch RAF 1954-58; house surgn and ENT house surgn Middx Hosp 1952-53, ptnr med practice Oxshott 1958-89; MO: Sandown Park Racecourse 1973, Epsom Racecourse 1978, Kempton Park Racecourse 1986, Lingfield Park 1989; MO Reed's Sch Cobham 1985-89; Liveryman Worshipful Co of Innholders 1961 (memb Ct 1989); MRCS, LRCP 1952; memb: BMA, Med Equestrian Assoc; *Recreations* sailing; *Clubs* Royal Automobile, Royal Corinthian Yacht, Royal Lymington Yacht; *Style*— Dr Richard Glover; Scermer, Manor Way, Oxshott, Surrey KT22 0HU; 5 Totland Court, Victoria Rd, Milford-on-Sea, Hants SO41 ONR (☎ 0372 843088)

GLOVER, Robert Finlay; TD (1954); s of Dr Terrot Reaveley Glover (d 1943), and Alice Emily Cornelia, *née* Few (d 1956); *b* 28 June 1917; *Educ* The Leys Sch, CCC Oxford (BA, MA); *m* 28 June 1941, Jean, da of Norman Gordon Muir (d 1962), of Lincoln; 1 s (Richard b 1952), 2 da (Catherine b 1947, Jane b 1949); *Career* Maj RA (TA) 1939-46, Staff Coll Camberley 1944; asst master Ampleforth Coll 1946-50, head of classics The King's Sch Canterbury 1950-53; headmaster: Adams' GS Newport Shropshire 1953-59, Monmouth Sch 1959-76; dep sec HMC 1977-82; fell Woodard Corp 1982-87; Liveryman Worshipful Co of Haberdashers 1976; *Books* Notes on Latin (1954), Latin for Historians (1954); *Recreations* normal; *Clubs* East India, Devonshire, Sports and Public Schs; *Style*— Robert Glover, Esq, TD; Brockhill Lodge, West Malvern Rd, The Wyche, Malvern, Worcs WR14 4EJ (☎ 0684 564 247)

GLOVER, Stephen Charles Morton; s of Prebendary John Morton Glover (d 1979), and Helen Ruth, *née* Jones (d 1984); *b* 13 Jan 1952; *Educ* Shrewsbury, Mansfield Coll Oxford (MA); *m* 1982, Celia Elizabeth, da of Peter Montague; 2 s (Edmund b 1983, Alexander b 1987); *Career* leader and feature writer Daily Telegraph 1978-85 (parliamentary sketch writer 1979-81), foreign ed The Independent 1986-89, ed The Independent on Sunday 1990, dir Newspaper Publishing plc 1986-; *Clubs* Beefsteak; *Style*— Stephen Glover, Esq; The Independent on Sunday, 40 City Road, London EC1Y 2DB (☎ 071 415 1303)

GLOVER, Timothy Mark; s of John Stafford (d 1958), and Frances Mary, *née* Hodson; *b* 22 Feb 1951; *Educ* Sir Anthony Browne's Sch Brentwood; *m* 26 June 1976, Sally Alexandra, da of Col Peter Anthony Stevens, of Chatley Lodge, Norton St Philip, Bath, Somerset; 2 da (Rebecca Kate b 15 Aug 1982, Jessica Fleur b 11 Sept 1984); *Career* dir sales and mktg Border TV plc 1984-; *Recreations* sailing, shooting, fishing, squash, music; *Clubs* IOD; *Style*— Timothy Glover, Esq

GLOVER, Hon Mr Justice; Sir Victor Joseph Patrick; *b* 5 Nov 1932; *Educ* Collège du Saint Esprit, Royal Coll Mauritius, Jesus Coll Oxford (BA); *m* M C Ginette Gauthier; 2 s; *Career* called to the Bar Middle Temple 1957, barr Mauritian Bar 1957-62, Attorney Gen Office 1962-76 (crown counsel, dist magistrate, sr crown counsel, princ crown counsel, Parly counsel), puisne judge Supreme Ct 1976-82, sr puisne judge 1982-88, chief justice 1988-; pt/t lectr Univ of Mauritius 1966-87, chm Cncl of Legal Educn 1985-88, hon prof of law Univ of Mauritius 1986, professeur invité Faculté de Droit Université d'Aix - Marseille 1986; chm: Cmmn of Enquiry on Post-Primary and Secdy Educn, Cmmn of Enquiry on Educn 1982, Study Panel on Tertiary Educn 1985, memb Tertiary Educn Ctee 1988-; pres Bd of Govrs Collège du Saint Esprit 1980-88, compiler and ed Abstract of decisions of Supreme Ct of Mauritius 1966-; *Style*— The Hon Mr Justice Glover; Supreme Court, Port Louis, Mauritius

GLOVER, William James; QC (1969); s of Henry Percy Glover, KC (d 1938), and Martha, *née* Latham (d 1971); *b* 8 May 1924; *Educ* Harrow, Pembroke Coll Cambridge (BA); *m* 28 July 1956, Rosemary Dymond, da of Wilfrid Henry John Long (d 1971); 2 s (James William b 1957, Richard Michael b 1961); *Career* joined Army 1943, cmmnd RA 1944, served Royal West African Frontier Force (West African Artillery) W Africa and Burma 1944-47; called to the Bar Inner Temple 1950, second jr counsel to Inland Revenue 1963-69, rec Crown Ct 1975-91, bencher 1977-; *Recreations* golf, photography; *Style*— William Glover, Esq, QC; Lomea Barn, Stowe-cum-Ebony, Kent TN30 7HY (☎ 0797 270773); 2 Mitre Court Buildings, Temple, London EC4Y 7BS (☎ 071 583 1380, fax 071 353 7772, car 0831 155216)

GLOVER, Dr William John; s of John Glover (d 1944), of Co Down, NI, and Margaret Elizabeth, *née* Mack (d 1985); *b* 20 May 1927; *Educ* Down HS Downpatrick, Queen's Univ Belfast (MB BCh); *m* 10 Sept 1960, Dr (Katharine) Raye Garrett, da of James Morton Garrett (d 1974), of Weybridge, Surrey; 1 s (Ian b 1962), 2 da (Jillian b 1961, Alison b 1962); *Career* Mayo Fndn fell of anaesthesiology Mayo Clinic USA 1960-61, sr conslt anaesthetist Gt Ormond St Hosp for Sick Children (vice chm Bd Govrs 1976-90); contrib to various pubns; memb and pres Assoc of Paediatric Anaesthetists of GB & I 1989-, memb Exec Ctee of Gt Ormond St Wishing Well Appeal 1985-89; memb: BMA 1950, Assoc of Anaesthetists 1956, Assoc of Paediatric Anaesthetists 1973; FRSM 1963, FFARCS; *Recreations* walking, gardening; *Style*— Dr William Glover; 62 Southway, Hampstead Garden Suburb, London NW11 6SA (☎ 081 458 1518); The Hospital for Sick Children, Great Ormond St, London WC1N 3JH (☎ 071 405 9200)

GLYN, Sir Alan; ERD, MP (C) Windsor and Maidenhead 1974-; s of John Paul Glyn (d 1938), and Margaret, *née* Johnston; *b* 26 Sept 1918; *Educ* Westminster, Gonville and Caius Coll Cambridge, Bart's, St George's Hosp; *m* 4 Jan 1962, Lady Rosula Caroline, *née* Windsor-Clive, *qv*, 3 da of 2 Earl of Plymouth, PC, and Lady Irene, *née* Charteris, da of 11 and 7 Earl of Wemyss and March; 2 da; *Career* WWII served UK 1939-42, Far East 1942-46, psc 1945, Bde Maj; re-employed as Capt (Hon Maj) Royal Horse Gds 1967, attached French Foreign Legion 1960 (by special permission of French Govt); doctor 1948, barrister 1955, co-opted memb LCC Educn Ctee 1956-58, war corr in Vietnam; MP (C): Wandsworth Clapham 1959-64, Windsor 1970-74; memb: No 1 LCC Divnl Health Ctee 1959-61, Chelsea Borough Cncl 1959-62, Inner London Med Ctee 1967-, GLC Valuation Panel 1967-; former govr of Henry Thornton and Aristotle Schs; one of the Earl Marshal's Green Staff Offrs at Investiture of HRH The Prince of Wales at Caernarvon 1969; govr Body of Br Postgrad Med Fedn London Univ 1968-81, memb Bd of Govrs Nat Heart and Chest Hosps 1982-; Freeman City of London 1961, memb Worshipful Soc of Apothecaries 1961; (with freedom fighters in Hungarian Revolution 1956) awarded Pro-Hungarian medal of SMO of Malta; kt 1990; *Publications* Witness to Vietnam (the Containment of Communism in SE Asia) (1968), Let's Think Again; *Clubs* Pratt's, Carlton, Special Services; *Style*— Sir Alan Glyn, ERD, MP; 17 Cadogan Place, London SW1X 9SA (☎ 071 235 2957); House of Commons, London SW1

GLYN, Hon Andrew John; yr s of 6 Baron Wolverton, CBE (d 1988); bro and h of 7 Baron; *b* 30 June 1943; *Educ* Eton, New Coll Oxford (MA); *m* 1, 1965 (m dis 1986), Celia Laws; 1 s (Miles John b 1966), 1 da (Lucy Abigail b 1968); m 2, 1986, Wendy Carlin; *Career* fell Corpus Christi Coll Oxford; *Style*— The Hon Andrew Glyn; 64 Hurst Street, Oxford

GLYN, Sir Anthony Geoffrey Leo Simon; 2 Bt (UK 1927); s of Sir Edward Rae Davson, 1 Bt, KCMG (d 1937), and Margot Elinor, OBE (d 1966), da of Clayton Louis Glyn, and Elinor Sutherland (the novelist Elinor Glyn); assumed by deed poll 1957 the surname of Glyn in lieu of his patronymic and the additional forename of Anthony; *b* 13 March 1922; *Educ* Eton; *m* 2 Oct 1946, Susan Eleanor, da of Lt-Col Sir Rhys Rhys Williams, 1 Bt, DSO, QC; 1 da (and 1 da decd); *Heir* bro, Christopher Michael Edward Davson; *Career* Capt Welsh Gds 1941-46; author; winner Book Soc Choice 1955 (Elinor Glyn), and 1959 (I Can Take it All); Vermeil medal City of Paris 1985; *Principal works* The Ram in the Thicket, Elinor Glyn (a biography), I Can Take It All, The Seine, The Dragon Variation, The Blood of a Britishman, The Companion Guide to Paris (1985); *Recreations* skiing, music, chess; *Clubs* Pratt's; *Style*— Sir Anthony Glyn, Bt; Marina Baie des Anges, Ducal Apt U-03, 06270 Villeneuve Loubet, Alpes Maritimes, France (☎ 93 73 67 52)

GLYN, Barbara Louvain; da of William Charles Ritchie Jardine, of Oxford; *m* 1, Gp Capt Francis Henwood, DFC; m 2, 1970, as his 2 w, Sir Richard Hamilton Glyn, 9 Bt, OBE, TD, DL (d 1980); *Clubs* Kennel; *Style*— Lady Glyn; 53 Belgravia Court, Ebury St, London SW1W 0NY (☎ 071 730 1963)

GLYN, Hilary Beaujolais; s of Maurice Glyn, of Albury Hall, Ware, and Hon Maud, *née* Grosvenor, da of 2 Baron Ebury, DL, by his w, Hon Emilie White, yr da of 1 Baron Annaly; *b* 12 Jan 1916; *Educ* Eton, New Coll Oxford; *m* 1938, Caroline, da of William Perkins Bull, QC (d 1948), of Toronto, Canada; 1 s (James b 1939), 2 da (Ann b 1941, Sarah b 1948); *Career* md Gallaher Ltd 1975-76, ret; *Recreations* gardening, shooting; *Style*— Hilary Glyn, Esq; Castle Hill Cottage, Boothby, Graffoe, Lincoln LN5 OLF (☎ 0522 810885)

GLYN, Dr John Howard; s of Sidney Glyn, and Clair Beatrice, *née* Vos; *b* 18 May 1921; *Educ* Harrow, Jesus Coll Cambridge (BA, MA), Middx Hosp Med Sch, NY Univ Med Sch; *m* 2 April 1947, Daphne Barbara, da of Hugh Robert Bayley, of Chingford; 1 s (Ian Robert Howard b 14 Feb 1951), 1 da (Gillian Clare Philippa (Mrs Readman) b 2 Sept 1954); *Career* Flt Lt RAFVR Neurosychiatric Unit Princess Mary RAF Hosp Halton 1947-49; conslt physician: Prince of Wales Hosp Tottenham 1957, St Charles Hosp London 1969, Osborne House St Dunstan; Liveryman Worshipful Soc of Apothecaries; FRCP; *Books* Cortisone Therapy (1959), A Concise History of Rheumatology and Rehabilitation; *Recreations* tennis, skiing, golf, photography; *Clubs* Hurlingham, RSM, Sonning Golf; *Style*— Dr John Glyn; 35 Sussex Sq, London W2 2PS (☎ 071 262 9187); Pool Ct, Thames St, Sonning-on-Thames (☎ 0734 693116)

GLYN, Sir Richard Lindsay; 6 Bt (1800) of Gaunt's House, Dorset, and 10 Bt (1759); s of Sir Richard Hamilton Glyn, OBE, TD, 5 and 9 Bt (d 1980), and Lyndsay Mary Baker; *b* 3 Aug 1943; *Educ* Eton; *m* 1970 (m dis 1979), Carolyn Ann, da of Roy Frank Williams (d 1979), of Pasadena, Calif, USA; 1 s, 1 da; *Heir* s, Richard Rufus Francis Glyn b 8 Jan 1971; *Career* 2 Lt Royal Hamps Regt 1962-65; Studio Orange Ltd (photography and design) 1966-71, Gaunts Estate 1972, dir Gaunt's House 1989; farmer 1976-; underwriting memb Lloyd's 1976-; co-fndr High Lea Sch 1982; *Style*— Sir Richard Glyn, Bt; Ashton Farmhouse, Stanbridge, Wimborne, Dorset (☎ 0258 840585)

GLYN, Lady Rosula Caroline; *née* Windsor-Clive; yst da of 2 Earl of Plymouth, PC (d 1943); *b* 30 April 1935; *m* 4 Jan 1962, Sir Alan Glyn, ERD, MP, *qv*; 2 da (Mary b 1963, Anne b 1964); *Career* OStJ; *Style*— Lady Rosula Glyn; 17 Cadogan Place, London SW1X 9SA

GLYN-JONES, Peter; s of Glyn Thomas Jones, of Abinger Hammer, Dorking, Surrey, and Annie, *née* Greenwood; *b* 27 April 1945; *Educ* Royal GS Guildford, Univ of Southampton (LLB), Guildford Law Sch; *m* 28 Sept 1968, Carolyn Mary, da of Joseph Frank Cox; 1 s (William Peter b 1 Dec 1972), 1 da (Annabel Roma (twin) b 2 Dec 1972); *Career* admitted slr 1969; Denton Hall & Burgin & Warrens: articled clerk 1967, ptnr 1973-, opened and ran Docklands Office 1983-89; memb RPS, LRPS, chm Docklands Business Club; memb Law Soc 1969-; *Recreations* photography, choral singing, marathon running, cycling, skiing, water skiing; *Clubs* Royal Motor Yacht (Poole); *Style*— Peter Glyn-Jones, Esq; Denton Hall Burgin & Warrens Slrs, Five Chancery Lane, Cliffords Inn, London EC4A 1BU (☎ 071 320 6172, fax 071 831 6901, car 0860 614365, portable 0860 228769)

GLYNN, (Brian) David; s of William Arthur Glynn, CBE (d 1976), and Norah Haden, *née* Mottram; *b* 30 May 1940; *Educ* Epsom Coll, Guy's Hosp Dental School (BDS, represented hockey and shooting teams), Univ of Oregon Dental Sch (Newland Pedley scholar); *m* 16 May 1964, Judith Mary, da of George Charles English, CBE; 2 da (Amanda Jayne b 18 March 1968, Nicola Louise b 17 June 1970); *Career* dental surgeon; Dept of Conservation Dentistry Guy's Hosp: pt/t registrar 1967-74, pt/t jr lectr 1974-76, pt/t sr demonstrator 1976-79; in private practice 35 Devonshire Place W1 1979- (pt/t 1967-74); chm Compudent Ltd 1984-; Federation Dentaire Internationale: conslt Scientific Programme Ctee 1989, conslt Cmmn of Dental Practice on Computer Aided Diagnostics 1990; lectr on use of computers in gen dental practice, author of numerous papers and courses on restorative dentistry, responsible for use of closed circuit TV in teaching at Guy's Hosp (prodr various films); memb: BDA, American Dental Soc of London (sec 1972-75); fell Int Coll of Dentists 1981 (gen sec Euro section 1984-); *Publications* Use of Closed Circuit TV (Medical and Biological Illustration, 1973); various papers to American Dental Soc of London; *Recreations* fly fishing, skiing, sailing, tennis, flying, twin & single engine aircraft; *Clubs* Fly Fishers; *Style*— David Glynn, Esq; Glynn Setchell and Allan, 35 Devonshire Place, London W1 1PE (☎ 071 935 3342/3, fax 071 224 0558)

GLYNN, Prof Ian Michael; s of Hyman Glynn (d 1984), and Charlotte, *née* Fluxbaum (d 1990); *b* 3 June 1928; *Educ* City of London Sch, Trinity Coll Cambridge (MA, PhD, MD), Univ Coll Hosp; *m* 9 Dec 1958, Jenifer Muriel, da of Ellis Arthur Franklin, OBE (d 1964); 1 s (Simon b 1964), 2 da (Sarah b 1959, Judith b 1961); *Career* Nat Serv Flt Lt RAF Med Branch 1956-57; house physician Centl Middx Hosp 1952-53; Univ of Cambridge: fell Trinity Coll 1955-, demonstrator in physiology 1958-63, lectr 1963-70, reader 1970-75, prof of membrane physiology 1975-86, vice master Trinity Coll 1980-86, prof of physiology 1986-; visiting prof Yale Univ Sch of Med 1969; memb: MRC 1976-80, Cncl of Royal Soc 1979-81, Agric and Food Res Cncl 1981-86; Hon MD Aarhus (Denmark) 1988; FRS 1970, FRCP 1987, hon foreign memb American Acad of Arts & Sciences 1984, hon memb American Physiological Soc 1990; *Books* The Sodium Pump (ed with C Ellory 1985), The Company of Biologists; *Style*— Prof Ian Glynn, FRS; Physiological Laboratory, Downing St, Cambridge CB2 3EG (☎ 0223 333 869, fax 0223 333 840, telex CAMSPL G)

GLYNN, Stanley Frederick Henry; *b* 5 Aug 1918; *Educ* Mercers'; *m* 1943, Mary Keith, *née* Dewdney; 2 da; *Career* served Army N Africa, Egypt, Italy, Greece; Maj; auctioneer and estate agent; Knight Frank and Rutley 1935-79, vice chm Regency Building Society 1970-87; govr BUPA 1970-87; chm: BUPA Med Fndn 1979-88, Chislehurst & Sidcup Housing Assoc; served Kent CCC for 20 years; memb Lloyd's; Freeman City of London, Liveryman Worshipful Co of Tallow Chandlers and Glass-Sellers; *Recreations* tennis, walking, gardening, cricket; *Clubs* Carlton, MCC, Farmers', Inst of Dirs; *Style*— Stanley Glynn, Esq; Rosemount, Cricket Ground Rd, Chistlehurst, Kent (☎ 081 467 5197); 21 Cliff House, Radnor Cliff, Folkestone, Kent

GLYNNE, Alan; *b* 21 May 1941; *Educ* Univ of Edinburgh (BSc, MB ChB), RCP (MRCP); *Career* registrar in cardiology Leeds Gen Infirmary 1967-69, registrar in endocrinology and gen med Univ Dept of Med Glasgow Royal Infirmary 1969-72, sr registrar in gen med Witmington Hosp and Royal Infirmary Manchester 1972-74, dir of clinical investigation and head of clinical pharmacology Lilly Research Centre UK 1974-82, hon conslt and lectr in med Guy's Hosp 1980-83, currently conslt physician, examiner RCP, pt/t conslt physician Cromwell Hosp; memb: Int Diabetes Fedn, Med and Scientific Section of Br Diabetic Assoc, The Thyroid Club, Chelsea Clinical Soc, Wellington Soc, BMA, RSM; FFPHM; *Publications* various contribs to sci jls; *Style*— Dr Alan Glynne; 97 Harley St, London W1N 1DF (☎ 071 935 5896)

GLYNNE-WALTON, Hon Mrs (Caroline Jane Grenville); *née* Morgan-Grenville; raised to the rank of a Baron's da 1947; yst da of Rev Hon Luis Chandos Francis Temple Morgan-Grenville, Master of Kinloss (d 1944), else 11 Baroness Kinloss; sis of Lady Kinloss, *qv*; *b* 21 March 1931; *Educ* privately, Ravens Croft School Eastbourne; *m* 18 Sept 1958, Gordon Glynne-Walton, FRGS, FRMetSoc, FRAS, FGS, late Duke of Wellington's Regt, s of late Thomas Henry Walton, of Batley, Yorks; 1 da (Charlotte b 1961); *Recreations* gardening, reading, walking, music; *Style*— The Hon Mrs Glynne-Walton; White Lea Grange, Batley, W Yorks

GOAD, Sir (Edward) Colin Viner; KCMG (1974); s of late Maurice George Viner Goad, of Cirencester, Glos, and Caroline, *née* Masters; *b* 21 Dec 1914; *Educ* Cirencester GS, Gonville and Caius Coll Camb (BA); *m* 1939, Joan Olive Bradley (d 1980); 1 s; *Career* under sec Min of Tport 1963, sec gen Intergovernmental Maritime Consultative Orgn 1968-74 (dep sec gen 1963-68), ret 1974; memb Advsy Bd Int Bank Washington DC 1975-, conslt Liberian Shipowners' Cncl 1976-; *Style*— Sir Colin Goad, KCMG; The Paddock, Ampney Crucis, Cirencester, Glos (☎ 028 585 353)

GOAD, Col Kevin John Watson; s of Maj Christopher Frederick Goad, of 51 Belmont Rd, Portswood, Southampton, and Mary Merton, *née* Watson; *b* 8 May 1942; *Educ* Coatham Sch, Windsor Sch, RMA Sandhurst; *m* 31 July 1965, Anne Elizabeth, da of Maj Hugh Lewis Thomas; 2 da (Claire Emma b 5 Aug 1966, Annabelle Lavinia b 1 Oct 1968); *Career* cmmnd RAOC 1962, Lt 1963, Capt 1969, Maj 1975, Lt-Col 1980, tech weapons instr RMCS 1981-82, Col 1988; served: UK, NI, Malaysia, Hong Kong, BAOR; *Books* Brassey's Battlefield Weapons Systems and Technology Volume III (with D H J Halsey, 1982); *Recreations* water colours, military history, Arsenal FC, antiques; *Style*— Col Kevin Goad; Ministry of Defence (Army), Military Secretary's Dept (Personnel Branch 9 RAOC), Govt Buildings, London Rd, Stanmore, Middx HA7 4PZ (☎ 081 958 6377 ext 3120, fax 081 958 6377 ext 3034, telex 01 958 6377 ext 3218)

GOALEN, Gerard Thomas; s of Philip Alec Goalen (d 1957), of Birkenhead, and Eleanor, *née* Hickey (d 1962); *b* 16 Dec 1918; *Educ* Douai Sch, Univ of Liverpool Sch of Architecture (BArch); *m* 29 April 1943, Maria de Lourdes (d 1991), da of Alvaro Lopes Malheiro (d 1943), of Oporto and Liverpool; 2 s (Martin b 1946, Paul b 1951); *Career* Gunner RA 1940-41 (2 Lt 1941-42), Lt RE 1942-45 (Capt 1945-46); planning offr LCC 1946-47, architect Harlow Devpt Corp 1947-55, ptnr with Frederick Gibberd 1955-65, practised alone 1965-, with son Martin 1975-81 (ret); bldgs incl: Our Lady of Fatima Harlow 1960, Good Shepherd Nottingham 1964 (RIBA award E Midlands 1966), St Mary Grantham (extension, 1966), St Gregory S Ruislip 1967, St Gabriel Upper Holloway 1967, St James Harlow 1968, St Thomas More Swiss Cottage 1969,

St Christopher Cranford 1971, Holy Trinity Leytonstone 1974, RC Chaplaincy (Fisher House) Cambridge 1976; ARIBA 1940, MRTPI 1948, FRIBA 1960; *Recreations* gardening, building crafts, swimming; *Style*— Gerard Goalen, Esq; Wren Green, School Lane, Walpole St Peter, Wisbech, Cambs PE14 7PA (☎ 0945 780349)

GOBBO, Hon Sir James Augustine; s of Antonio Gobbo and Regina, *née* Tosetto; *b* 22 March 1931; *Educ* Xavier Coll, Melbourne Univ (BA), Rhodes Scholar 1952, Magdalen Coll Oxford (MA); *m* 1957, Shirley, da of S Lewis; 2 s, 3 da; *Career* barr 1956, and lectr in Evidence Melbourne Univ 1964-68, QC 1971, Judge of Supreme Ct of Victoria 1978-; chm: Aust Refugee Cncl 1977, Victoria's 150 Advsy Panel 1984-85, Aust Bicentennary Multicultural Task Force 1982, Mercy Private Hosp 1977-87, Supervisory Ctee Children's Protection Soc 1982-, Italian Historical Soc 1980-, Task Force for the Italian Aged 1983-, Caritas Christi Hospice 1986-, Order of Malta Hospice Home Care Serv 1986-, Reference Gp into Public Library Funding 1987, Aust Cncl of Multicultural Affrs 1987-, Aust Bicentennial Multicultural Fndn 1988-; pres Sovereign Mil Order of Malta (Aust) 1987- (vice pres 1984-87), CO-AS-IT Italian Assistance Assoc 1979-84 and 1986-, Scout Assoc (Victorian Branch) 1987-; memb: Aust Population and Immigration Cncl 1975-83, Victoria Law Fndn 1972-84, Newman Coll Cncl 1970-85, RC Archdiocese Fin Advsy Cncl 1970, Mercy Maternity Hosp Bd 1972-, Sisters of Mercy Health Care Cncl 1977-, Cncl of the Order of Aust 1982-, Italo-Aust Educn Fndn 1974-, Exec Cncl of Judges 1986-89, Victorian Health Promotion Fndn 1988-, Palladio Fndn 1989-; pt/t cmmr Law Reform Cmmn of Victoria 1985-88; tstee Opera Fund (Victoria) 1983-; hon fell Aust Inst of Valuers 1985; Commendatore all'Ordine di Merito of the Republic of Italy 1973; kt of Magistral Grace Sovereign Mil Order of Malta; kt 1982; *Books* Cross on Evidence (ed Aust edn), numerous papers; *Style*— Hon Sir James Gobbo; 6 Florence Ave, Kew, Victoria 3101, Australia (☎ 03 817 1669, business ☎ 03 603 6149)

GOBERT, Gerald; s of Dr Richard Gobert (d 1954), of Meadway Court, Hampstead, and Greta, *née* Kaufman (d 1954); *b* 20 June 1925; *Educ* King Edward VI Sch, Regent St Poly; *m* 27 Aug 1960, Rosemary, da of Dr Bertram Shires (d 1943), of Welbeck St, London W1; 4 da (Julia 10 March 1961, Loretta b 16 Oct 1962, Rachel b 24 Aug 1965, Gina b 18 June 1968); *Career* fndr: Gallwey Chemical Co 1951, Protim and Gallwey 1954 (plc 1967, merger with FOSECO MINSEP 1969); chm Chemplant Stainless; inventor Protimer 1954, two Royal Warrants for Protim and Gallwey (wood preservative and timber treatment); memb Ctee for local sch's: Godstowe, St Helen's, Northwood; memb NSPCC and political ctees, active in numerous local fundraising events; Freeman City of London, Liveryman Worshipful Co of Clockmakers 1973; memb Inst Br Engrs, CEng, MIMechE, MIWSc, FFB, FInstD; *Recreations* travel, the garden, family; *Style*— Gerald Gobert, Esq; Woodchester, Knotty Green, Beaconsfield HP9 2TN; Chemplant, Rickmansworth, Herts (☎ 089582 2466/8, fax 089582 2469, telex 933969 CHEMPT G)

GOBLE, James Blackley Hague; s of Leslie Herbert Goble, CMG (d 1969), of The Pound House, Brabourne Lees, Ashford, Kent, and Lilian Miriam, *née* Cunningham; *b* 21 July 1927; *Educ* Marlborough, Corpus Christi Coll Cambridge; *m* 1, 24 Nov 1951, Barbara Mary (d 1986), da of Sir Thomas Claude Harris Lea, Bt (d 1985), of Worcs; 2 s (Timothy b 1957, Jonathan b 1961); m 2, 4 June 1988, Yvonne Patricia Jane Coke-Wallis, da of Lt-Col Cecil Stone (d 1988); *Career* Coldstream Gds 1945, Gdsman O/ Cadet Worcs Regt 1946-48, Capt; admin offr HM Overseas Civil Serv Gold Coast Ghana 1950-61; J Walter Thompson London: joined 1962, dir 1971-86, sr int vice pres 1983-86; dir: Pillar Pubns 1987- (chm 1990-), Winston Churchill Travelling Fellowships Fndn Inc USA 1988-; tstee Critical Care Trust 1989- (chm 1990-), memb Br Standards Inst Advsy Panel on Publicity 1971-84, advsy cnsllr English Speaking Union 1976-83; MIPA 1971-86; *Recreations* ornithology, shooting, building; *Style*— James Goble, Esq; Court Farm, Upton Snodsbury, Worcs WR7 4NN (☎ 0905 60 314)

GODBER, (Robert) Christopher; s of Geoffrey Chapman Godber, CBE, DL, *qv*; *b* 3 Nov 1938; *Educ* Bedford Sch, Merton Coll Oxford; *m* 1962, Frances Merryn Candy, da of Capt Ernest Howard Stanley Bretherton, MC (d 1960); 3 s, 1 da; *Career* Nat Serv Kings Shropshire LI served Kenya and Mau Mau Emergency 1956-58; Travis & Arnold plc: branch mangr Cambridge 1967-69, branch mangr Rugby 1969-73, dir 1973-88; dir: King's Lynn Wood Preservation 1973-, Sussex Timber Preservation 1975-; chm E Anglian Timber Trade Assoc 1988-90, dir Main Bd Travis Perkins plc 1988-, dir Travis Perkins Trading Co Ltd 1988-; *Recreations* sailing (yacht Minnow), shooting; *Clubs* Banbury Sailing, Leander, Royal Agric Soc of England; *Style*— Christoper Godber, Esq; Staverton Acres, Staverton, Daventry, Northamptonshire NN11 6JY (☎ 0327 71223); Travis & Perkins plc, Lodge Way House, Harlestone Rd, Northampton NN5 7UG (☎ 0604 752424, telex 311386)

GODBER, Geoffrey Chapman; CBE (1961), DL (W Sussex 1975); s of Isaac Godber (d 1957), of Willington Manor, Beds, and Bessie Maud, *née* Chapman; bro of Sir George Edward Godber, *qv*, and late Baron Godber, of Willington; *b* 22 Sept 1912; *Educ* Bedford Sch, Univ of London (LLB); *m* 1937, Norah Enid, da of Reginald John George Fletcher Finney (d 1942), of Derbys; 3 s (Christopher b 1938, *qv*, Jonathan b 1942, Peter b 1945); *Career* admitted slr 1936; clerk of CC and Lieutenancy Shropshire 1944-66 and West Sussex 1966-75; memb sundry govt ctees 1953-75 incl: Central Advsy Water Ctee 1961-70, SE Econ Planning Cncl 1969-75; chm Weald and Downland Museum 1975-82 (pres 1988-90), memb Br Waterways Bd 1975-81; dep chm: Chichester Harbour Conservancy 1975-78, Shoreham Port Authy 1976-82; *Recreations* sailing; *Clubs* Naval & Military, Sussex; *Style*— Geoffrey Godber, Esq, CBE, DL; Pricklows, Singleton, Chichester, W Sussex (☎ 024 363 238)

GODBER, Sir George Edward; GCB (1971, KCB 1962, CB 1958); s of Isaac Godber (d 1957), of Willington Manor, Beds, and Bessie Maud, *née* Chapman; bro of Geoffrey Chapman Godber, *qv*, and late Baron Godber, of Willington; *b* 4 Aug 1908; *Educ* Bedford Sch, New Coll Oxford (BA, DM), London Hosp; *m* 1935, Norma Hathorne, da of W H T N Rainey; 2 s, 1 da (and 2 s, 2 da decd); *Career* dep chief med offr Miny of Health 1950-60, QHP 1953-56, chief med offr DHSS, DES and Home Office 1960-73; chm Health Educn Cncl 1976-78; DPH; FRCP, FFCM; *Style*— Sir George Godber, GCB; 21 Almoners' Avenue, Cambridge CB1 4NZ (☎ Cambridge 0223 247 491)

GODBER, (Reginald) Peter; s of Geoffrey Chapman Godber, CBE, of Singleton, Chichester, and Norah Enid, *née* Finney; *b* 7 Sept 1945; *Educ* Bedford Sch, Wadham Coll Oxford; *m* 2 Sept 1972, Susan Mary, da of Isaac Hale; 2 s (Ben b 13 Jan 1975, Daniel b 31 Dec 1976), 1 da (Charlotte b 19 Jan 1980); *Career* admitted slr 1970; sr ptnr Court Training Services Partnership; dir of trg Law Soc, local Govt GP; memb Law Soc; *Recreations* skiing, sailing; *Style*— Peter Godber, Esq; The Old Vicarage, Rudgwick, Sussex (☎ 040372 2549); 10 Lynwick Street, Rudgwick, Horsham (☎ 0403 722549, fax 0403 723388)

GODBER, Hon Richard Thomas; s of Baron Godber, of Willington, PC, DL (Life Peer, d 1980), and Baroness Godber, of Willington, *qv* (*née* Miriam Sanders); *b* 4 June 1938; *Educ* Bedford Sch; *m* 1962, Candida Mary, da of late Albert Edward Parrish; 1 s, 2 da; *Career* Lt Royal Lincs 1956-58 (served Malaya); farmer, horticulturist; vice-pres Bucks Assoc Boys' Clubs (chm 1977-86); chm: CLA Game Fair, Stowe 1981, Bucks CLA 1987-; memb Cncl RASE 1970-, hon dir Royal Show 1987-; *Recreations* shooting, gardening; *Clubs* Farmers', Anglo-Belgian, Bedford; *Style*— Hon Richard Godber; Hall Farm, Little Linford, nr Milton Keynes, Bucks

GODBER, Hon (Andrew) Robin; yr s of Baron Godber, of Willington, PC, DL, of Willington Manor, Bedford (Life Peer, d 1980), and Baroness Godber, of Willington, *qv*; *b* 7 Sept 1943; *Educ* Bedford Sch; *m* 1969, Genevieve, da of late Kenneth Parrish, of Higham Gobion, Herts; 2 s; *Career* author, boat builder; *Recreations* sailing; *Clubs* Sandwich Bay Sailing; *Style*— Hon Robin Godber; Tan House, Tanhouse Lane, Peasmarsh, Rye, Sussex TN31 6UY

GODBER, Baroness; Violet Ethel Beatrice; JP; da of George Albert Lovesy, of Cheltenham, Glos; *m* 29 Aug 1914, 1 and last Baron Godber (d 1976); 2 da (Hon Joyce Violet (Hon Mrs Agnew) b 1917, Hon Daphne Joan (Hon Mrs Debenhom) b 1923); *Style*— The Rt Hon Lady Godber, JP; Cranesden, Mayfield, Sussex (☎ 0435 873271)

GODBER OF WILLINGTON, Baroness; Miriam; da of Haydon Sanders, of Lowestoft; *m* 1936, Baron Godber of Willington, PC (Life Peer, d 1980); 2 s (Hon Richard *qv*, Hon Robin *qv*); *Style*— The Rt Hon Lady Godber of Willington; Willington Manor, nr Bedford

GODBOLD, Brian Leslie; s of Leslie Robert Godbold (d 1970), of London, and Eileen Rosalie, *née* Hodkinson; *b* 14 July 1943; *Educ* Elmbridge Sch Cranlegh Surrey, Walthamstow Sch of Art (NDD), RCA Fashion Sch; *Career* designer Jovi NY USA 1965-67, head designer Wallis Shops UK 1967-69; head of design: Cojana UK 1970-74, Baccarat/Wetherall UK (headed team that designed BA uniform 1976) 1974-76; design exec Marks & Spencer 1976-; FRSA, FCSD, pres RCA Soc; *Recreations* antique collecting, gardening, decoration; *Clubs* Arts; *Style*— Brian Godbold, Esq; Marks and Spencer plc, 57 Baker St, London W1 (☎ 071 268 7014, fax 071 268 2625)

GODDARD, Ann Felicity; QC (1982); da of Graham Elliott Goddard (d 1973), and Margaret Louise, *née* Clark; *b* 22 Jan 1936; *Educ* Grey Coat Hosp Westminster, Univ of Birmingham (LLB), Newnham Coll Cambridge (LLM); *Career* called to the Bar 1960, recorder of the Crown Court 1979; *Recreations* travel; *Style*— Ms Ann Goddard, QC; 3 Temple Gardens, Temple, London EC4Y 9AU (☎ 071 353 3102)

GODDARD, Anthony John; s of Henry Gordon Goddard, DSO, DFC, and Nicolette Julienne Louise Arluison; *b* 27 May 1941; *Educ* The Oratory Sch Oxford, Univ of Leicester (DipArch), Univ of Illinois (MArch); *m* 1, 16 March 1968 (m dis 1987), Gretchen Drew, da of Stanley Damon (d 1985), of USA; 1 s (Sam b 1979); m 2, 4 March 1988, Annette Lesley, da of R Yates; 2 da (Harriet b 1988, Alice b 1989); *Career* architect; asst prof of architecture Univ of Illinois 1967-68, ptnr Goddard Manton Partnership London 1969- (specialising in the re-development of London's Docklands); ARIBA; *Recreations* travel, motor racing; *Style*— Anthony J Goddard, Esq; The Manor House, Newton Harcourt, Leicestershire (☎ 053 759 2986); 67 George Row, London SE16 4UH (☎ 071 237 2016, fax 071 237 7850)

GODDARD, David Rodney; MBE (1985); s of Air Marshall Sir Victor Goddard, KCB, CBE (d 1987), of Brasted, Kent, and Mildred Catherine Jane, *née* Inglis (d 1979); *b* 16 March 1927; *Educ* Bryanston, Wanganui Collegiate Sch NZ, Peterhouse Cambridge (MA); *m* 14 April 1951, Susan, da of Maj Gilbert Ashton, MC (d 1981), of Abberley, Worcester; 3 s (Stephen b 1952, Anthony b 1954, Thomas b 1958), 1 da (Tessa b 1963); *Career* Lt 44 Commando RM 1945-47; Lt Somerset LI 1952 served: Germany 1952, Malaya 1952-55, regtl depot Taunton 1955-58; KAR 1959-62, army DS with RM Offrs' Wing 1963-66, staff duties Bahrain 1966-68, ILI NI 1968, ret with rank of Maj at own request 1968; fndr Int Sailing Craft Assoc Ltd 1965, chief ldr Br Schs Exploring Soc Expdn to Arctic Norway 1965, dir Exeter Maritime Museum 1969-; *Recreations* shooting, fishing, sailing, photography; *Style*— David Goddard, Esq, MBE; The Mill, Lympstone Exmouth, Devon EX8 5HH (☎ 0392 265575); ISCA Ltd, The Haven, Exeter, Devon EX2 8DT (☎ 0392 58075)

GODDARD, Maj Douglas George; *b* 4 Nov 1920; *Educ* Roan Sch Blackheath, Brighton Tech Coll; *m* Eve; 1 s (Nigel Johnson), 1 da (Christina Lynne); *Career* reg cmmn RA; serv: Normandy landing, NW Europe Campaign, Germany, Egypt, Jordan; instr Royal Sch of Artillery, resigned 1959 (awarded BAOR C-in-C's certificate 1946); div sec Sulzer Bros Ltd 1959-64, asst sec and chief accountant Mallory Batteries Ltd 1959-64; Chartered Inst of Bldg 1964-85: sec and dir central servs, dep chief exec, controller nat project Bldg Tomorrow's Heritage 1984; Wokingham DC: cncllr rep Wargrave and Remenham 1978-, chm Recreation and Amenities Ctee 1980-83, vice chm Fin and Gen Purposes Ctee 1985 (chm 1990), vice chm Cncl 1986-88 (chm 1988-90); memb: Trusteeship Ctee Nat Info Age Centre 1987-90, Governing Body and Local Ctee Bulmershe Coll Higher Educn (1984-89), Wokingham Cancer Care Centre Appeal (chm), St Mary's PCC and Stewardship Ctee (sidesman), Ctee Wargrave Cons Branch, Ctee Wargrave Housing Assoc, Mgmnt Ctee Wargrave News (chm), Ctee Wargrave Resident's Assoc (former treas), Woodclyffe Almshouse Tstee Ctee, Southern Cncl for Sport and Recreation and Policy and Resources Ctee, Bracknell and Wokingham Jt Golf Courses Ctee (chm 1983-), Friends of Henley Festival, Friends Wokingham Choral Soc, Royal Berkshire Aviation Museum Ctee, Royal Br Legion Wargrave, Royal Soc St George, Wargrave and Shiplake Regatta, Wargrave Local Hist Soc, Henley Sea Cadet Corps (vice pres); rotarian Rotary Club Ascot 1973-79, hon sec Berks Industry Year Campaign 1986, chm Berks Indust Matters Campaign 1987; Queen's Silver Jubilee medal 1977; Liveryman (and Freeman) City of London; FCIS; *Clubs* Chatham Dining, Phyllis Court (Henley), MCC, Berkshire County Cricket, Reading Cricket and Hockey (vice pres), Sonning Golf, Wargrave Cricket (vice pres), Henley Rowing (patron); *Style*— Maj Douglas Goddard; Quinnells, 38 The Ridgeway, Wargrave, Berks RG10 8AS (☎ 0734 403647)

GODDARD, Harold Keith; QC (1979); s of Harold Goddard (d 1979), of Stockport, Cheshire, and Edith Goddard; *b* 9 July 1936; *Educ* Manchester GS, CCC Cambridge; *m* 1, 1963 (m dis), Susan Elizabeth, yr da of late Ronald Stansfield, of Wilmslow, Cheshire; 2 s; m 2, 1983, Maria Alicja, da of Czeslaw Lazuchiewicz (d 1981), of Lodz, Poland; *Career* barr 1959; recorder Crown Ct 1978-; *Style*— Harold Goddard, Esq, QC; 1 Dean's Court, Crown Square, Manchester (☎ 061 834 4097)

GODDARD, Prof John Burgess; OBE (1986); s of Burgess Goddard, of Rickmansworth, Herts, and Maud Mary, *née* Bridge (d 1970); *b* 5 Aug 1943; *Educ* Latymer Upper Sch, UCL (BA), LSE (PhD); *m* 24 Sept 1966, Janet Patricia, da of Stanley James Peddle (d 1956), of Rickmansworth, Herts; 1 s (David Jonathan b 4 May 1976), 2 da (Jane Elizabeth b 1 Dec 1970, Jennifer Ann b 7 Nov 1974); *Career* lectr LSE 1968-75, Leverhulme fell Univ of Lund Sweden 1974; Univ of Newcastle Upon Tyne: Henry Daysh prof Regnl Devpt Studies 1975-, dir Centre of Urban and Regnl Devpt Studies 1977-, head Geography Dept 1980-87, memb Senate 1981-83, memb Cncl 1983-86, memb Res Ctee 1984-89, dir Newcastle Initiative Ltd 1988-; memb: N Econ Planning Cncl 1976-79, Planning and Resources Ctee 1988-, Exec Ctee Newcastle Common Purpose 1989-; govr Newcastle Poly 1989-; memb: Port of Tyne Authy, Human Geography Ctee SSRC 1976-79, Editorial Bd Environment and Planning 1988-; ed Regional Studies 1979-84, advsr CBI Task Force on Urban Regeneration 1987-88; memb: Exec Ctee Regnl Studies Assoc 1979-84, Editorial Bd BBC Domesday Project 1985-86, Jt Ctee ESRC and Nat Sci Fndn of America on Large Scale Data Bases 1986-87; memb Econ Advsy Ctees: Newcastle City Cncl, Tyne and Wear C of C 1982-; FRGS 1988, MIBG 1966, memb Regnl Studies Assoc 1966; *Books* numerous books and pubns incl: Office Linkages and Location (1973), Office Location in Urban and Regional Development (1975), British Cities: An Analysis of Urban Change (with N A Spence, 1981), Economic Development Policies: an evaluation study of the Newcastle Metropolitan Region (with F Robinson and C Wren, 1987); *Recreations* rowing, walking; *Style—* Prof John Goddard, OBE; Woodruff, Long Rigg, Riding Mill, Northumberland NE44 6AL (☎ 0434 682355); Centre for Urban and Regional Development Studies, University of Newcastle Upon Tyne, Newcastle upon Tyne, NE1 7RU (☎ 091 222 6000, fax 091 232 9259)

GODDARD, Martyn Stanley; s of Thomas Raymond Goddard (d 1982), and Winifred Florence, *née* Eastman; *b* 9 Oct 1951; *Educ* Mandville Co Secdy Sch, Aylesbury Coll of Further Educn, Harrow Coll of Technol and Art (Dip Applied Photography); *m* Beverley Margret Ballard; 2 da (Lauren b 7 June 1985, Grace Natalie Goddard b 8 May 1990); *Career* photographer; asst to Gered Mankowitz and Denis Waugh 1975-76, freelance photographer IPC Young Magazine Group 1976-77; assignments 1977-91: Sunday Telegraph Magazine, Sunday Express Magazine, You Magazine, advtg projects (incl devpt of markets for car photography in Br and American magazines); ed and advtg work 1991-; exhibitions incl: Blondie in Camera (Mirandy Gallery) 1978, Montserrat Studio (Lincoln Centre NY) 1979, 10*6 Group (Battersea Arts Centre, Neal St Gallery) 1981, Polaroid Time Zero (tour of UK) 1981, Human Views 1977-81 (J S Gallery London) 1981, National Portraits (Nat Theatre) 1983, Faces of Our Time (Nat Theatre tour) 1985, The Car (V & A Museum) 1986; fell BIPP; *Recreations* historic rally car driving, black and white photographic diary; *Clubs* Vintage Sports Car; *Style—* Martyn Goddard, Esq; Martyn Goddard, Photography, 5 Jeffrey's Place, London NW1 9PP (☎ 0831 500477)

GODDARD, Dr Peter; s of Herbert Charles Goddard (d 1971), and Rosina Sarah, *née* Waite; *b* 3 Sept 1945; *Educ* Emanuel Sch London, Trinity Coll Cambridge (BA, MA, PhD, Mayhew prize, Rayleigh prize); *m* 24 Aug 1968, Helen Barbara, da of Francis Fraser Ross, of Alne, Yorks; 1 s (Michael b 1975), 1 da (Linda b 1973); *Career* res fell Trinity Coll Cambridge 1969-73, visiting scientist Cern Geneva Switzerland 1970-72 and 1978, lectr in applied mathematics Univ of Durham 1972-74; St John's Coll Cambridge: fell 1975-, lectr in mathematics 1975-91, tutor 1980-87, sr tutor 1983-87; Univ of Cambridge: univ asst lectr 1975-76, univ lectr 1976-89, reader in mathematical physics 1989-; visiting prof Univ of Virginia Charlottesville 1983, govr Berkhamsted Sch and Berkhamsted Sch for Girls 1985-; memb: Inst for Theoretical Physics Univ of Calif Santa Barbara 1986 and 1990, Inst for Advanced Study Princeton 1974 and 1988, London Mathematical Soc 1989; FRS 1989, FInstP 1990; *Style—* Dr Peter Goddard, FRS; Department of Applied Maths and Theoretical Physics, University of Cambridge, Cambridge CB3 9EW (☎ 0223 337883, fax 0223 337918, telex 81240); St John's College, Cambridge CB2 1TP

GODDEN, Rumer; da of late Arthur Leigh Godden, of Lydd House, Aldington, Kent, and Katherine Norah Hingley; *b* 10 Dec 1907; *Educ* Moira House Eastbourne Sussex; *m* 1, 1934, Laurence Sinclair Foster; 2 da (Jennifer, Janaki); m 2, 1949, James Haynes-Dixon, OBE (d 1973); *Career* author; chief books incl: Chinese Puzzle (1935), The Lady and The Unicorn (1937), Black Narcissus (1939), Breakfast with the Nikolides (1941), Fugue in Time (1944), The River (1946), A Candle for St Jude (1948), Kingfishers Catch Fire (1952), An Episode of Sparrows (1955), The Greengage Summer (1959), China Court (1961), The Battle of the Villa Fiorita (1963), In This House of Brede (1969), Prayers from the Ark (trans, 1962), Two Under the Indian Sun (autobiog, 1965), Swans and Turtles (1968), The Raphael Bible (1970), Shiva's Pigeons (with Jon Godden, 1979), Gulbadan (1980), The Dark Horse (1981), Thursday's Children (1984), Time To Dance: No Time to Weep (1987, autobiog Vol I), A House with Four Rooms (autobiog Vol II 1989), Indian Dust (short stories, 1989), Coromandel Sea Change (1991); *Style—* Miss Rumer Godden; Ardnacloich, Moniaive, Dumfriesshire DG3 4H2

GODDIN, Richard William; s of William Frederick Goddin (d 1967), and Audrey Joan, *née* Stearn; *b* 17 May 1943; *Educ* Perse Sch, London Poly (DMS); *m* 15 June 1985, Margaret Ann, da of Reginald Barlow (d 1957); 1 s (James b 1987); *Career* sr mangr Nat West Bank plc 1977-83, treas Lombard North Central plc 1983-86, dep treas Nat West plc 1986-87; County Nat West Ltd: exec dir 1987-88, head Money Mkts Gp Treasury 1989-; *Recreations* sailing, croquet, country life; *Style—* Richard Goddin, Esq; Belmington Close, Meldreth, Cambs SG8 6NT (☎ 0763 2600 61); Nat West Bank plc, 135 Bishopsgate, London EC2 (☎ 071 334 1430)

GODFREY, (William) Edwin Martindale; s of Ernest Martindale Godfrey (d 1974), of Chesterfield, Derbyshire, and Anna Lol Tedde, *née* Maas; *b* 20 Oct 1947; *Educ* Repton, Queens' Coll Cambridge (MA); *m* 10 Sept 1977, Helen Ann, da of Dr John Arthur Clement James, of Northfield, Birmingham; 2 s (William b 1978, Thomas b 1980), 1 da (Alice b 1983); *Career* admitted slr 1971; asst slr Norton Rose Botterell and Roche 1971-72, ptnr Simmons and Simmons 1977- (asst slr 1972-76); Int Bar Assoc: memb, vice chm Ctee on Anti Tst Law 1981-86, chm Sub Ctee on Structure and Ethics of Business Law 1990 (vice chm 1989); hon legal advsr Hertford CAB; memb Law Soc 1971; Freeman City of London Solicitors Co 1990 (member Commercial Law Sub Ctee); *Books* Joint Ventures in Butterworth's Encyclopaedia of Forms & Precedents (ed, 5 edn, 1990); *Style—* Edwin Godfrey, Esq; Simmons & Simmons, 14 Dominion Street, London EC2M 2RJ (☎ 071 628 2020, fax 071 588 4129, telex 888562)

GODFREY, Dr Gerald; s of Phillip Godfrey, of Stanmore, Middx, and Sophie, *née* Godfrey; *b* 22 Aug 1926; *Educ* Dunstable GS, Univ of Glasgow; *m* 9 April 1951, Florence, da of Leon Jaffé (d 1958), of Glasgow; 1 da (Leone b 1958); *Career* Southern Gen Hosp Glasgow (gen med, casualty surgery, psychiatry) 1951-52, civilian med offr RAF 1953-60, police med offr 1953-62, clinical asst med offr of Barking Hosp 1954-61, asst MOH Lewisham, Wandsworth and Croydon 1963-67; med referee insur cos: Prudential, Colonial, Mutual, Crusader, Forester, Pearl, Royal London, NEM Assur; GP: Dagenham and Streatham 1953-, Harley St 1966; LRCP 1951, MRCS 1951, MRGP 1960, memb BMA; *Recreations* sail board, tennis, squash, sailing, shooting; *Clubs* Kensington Rifle and Pistol, Tir Club d'Antibes; *Style—* Dr Gerald Godfrey; 86 Eaton Square, London SW1W 9AG (☎ 071 235 7676); 68 Harley St, London W1N 1AE (☎ 071 935 3980)

GODFREY, Howard Anthony; s of Emanuel Godfrey, of London, and Amy, *née* Grossman; *b* 17 Aug 1946; *Educ* William Ellis Sch, LSE (LLB); *m* 3 Sept 1972, Barbara, da of John Ellinger, of London; 2 s (Timothy b 1975, James b 1980); *Career* called to the Bar Middle Temple 1970, practicing SE Circuit 1972-, asst rec Crown Ct 1987-; *Recreations* wine and food, walking; *Style—* Howard Godfrey, Esq; The Red House, Swallowfield Rd, Arborfield Cross, Berks RG2 9JZ (☎ 0734 760 657); 3 Hare Ct, Temple, London EC4Y 7BJ (☎ 071 353 7561, fax 071 353 7741)

GODFREY, Laurence Howard; s of William Herbert Godfrey (d 1978), of 9 Cyncoed Place, Cyncoed, Cardiff, and Elizabeth, *née* Peel (d 1960); *b* 6 Dec 1935; *Educ* Llandaff Cathedral Sch, Cranleigh Sch; *m* 12 Oct 1963, Audrey Elizabeth , da of Donald Ernest Blake (d 1962), of The Chase, Llyswen Rd, Cyncoed, Cardiff; 1 s (Ian Blake b 1971), 1 da (Amanda Jane b 1973, d 1980); *Career* sr ptnr Fooks & Co 1982- (ptnr 1965-82); represented S Wales and Glamorgan at hockey, golf and cricket, sec, treas, chm and vice pres Glamorgan Co Golf Union, tstee Cardiff GC (former capt); FCA 1963; *Recreations* cricket, hockey, golf; *Style—* Laurence Godfrey, Esq; Coedllys, Sherborne Ave, Cyncoed, Cardiff (☎ 0222 751 732), 14 High St, Bargoed, M Glam (☎ 0443 834 047)

GODFREY, Hon Mrs ((Sonja) Lois); *née* Mitchison; er da of Baron Mitchison, CBE, QC (Life Peer, d 1970), and Naomi Mary Margaret (the authoress Naomi Mitchison), *née* Haldane; *Educ* Lady Margaret Hall, Oxford (BA); *m* 21 March 1959 (m dis), John Godfrey, s of Arthur Corfield Godfrey; 2 da; *Style—* The Hon Mrs Godfrey

GODFREY, Dr Malcolm Paul Weston; s of Harry Godfrey (d 1945), of London, and Rose Kaye; *b* 11 Aug 1926; *Educ* Hertford GS, Univ of London (MB BS); *m* 1955, Barbara, da of Louis Goldstein (d 1963), of London, and Brighton; 1 s (Richard), 2 da (Jennifer, Claire); *Career* dean Royal Postgraduate Med Sch Univ of London 1974-83, second sec Med Res Cncl 1983-88; *Recreations* reading, theatre, walking; *Style—* Dr Malcolm Godfrey; 17 Clifton Hill, St John's Wood, London NW8 0QE (☎ 071 624 6335)

GODFREY, Prof Michael DeWitt; s of George H Godfrey, of Munich, and Augusta, *née* DeWitt (d 1983); *b* 30 May 1937; *Educ* Deerfield Acad, California Inst Technol (BSc), LSE (PhD); *m* 1 (m dis 1971); 1 s (Kent b 28 June 1958), 1 da (Christa b 19 Oct 1960); m 2, 2 Aug 1973, Ilse, da of Dr Wilhelm Pokorny, of 138 Hohenberg, Austria; *Career* asst prof and res assoc Econometric Res Prog Princeton Univ USA 1963-68, Bell Telephone Laboratories and AT&T Corp 1968-77, dir res Sperry Univac 1977-83, head res ICL 1983-87, Schlumberger prof of engrg software Imperial Coll 1987- (reader in statistics 1969-77); *Books* An Incremental Cost Model of Message Toll Telephone Servs (with R L Breedlove, 1975), Machine-Independent Organic Software Tools (jtly, 2 edn, 1985); *Recreations* skiing; *Clubs* Athenaeum; *Style—* Prof Michael Godfrey; Dept of Computing, Imperial College of Science Technology & Medicine, 180 Queen's Gate, London SW7 2BZ (☎ 071 589 5111, fax 071 589 7127)

GODFREY, Patrick Lindesay; s of Rev Canon Frederick Godfrey (d 1984), of Swithland, Leicestershire, and Lois Mary Gladys, *née* Turner (d 1973); *b* 15 Feb 1933; *Educ* Abbotsholme Sch Derbyshire, Central Sch of Speech and Drama; *m* 20 April 1960, Amanda Galafres Patterson Walker; 1 s (Richard Lindesay b 29 April 1961), 1 da (Kate b 12 Feb 1964); *Career* Nat Serv 1951-53; actor; contract with BBC Drama Repertory Company; repertory experience: Dundee, Coventry, Richmond, Hornchurch; Royal Shakespeare Company London and Stratford 1970-81; work incl: Dr Dudakov in Summerfolk (by Gorky), Boyet in Love's Labours Lost, Ephraim Smooth in Wild Oats, Belarius in Cymbeline, Justice Shallow in Merry Wives of Windsor, Kulyghin in Three Sisters, Mr Kenwigs in Nicholas Nickleby (nine hour epic, later televised); other stage work incl: Friar Lawrence in Romeo and Juliet, Polonius in Hamlet (RSC tour and repertory in Stratford) 1989, Barbarians (Barbican Theatre); recent films incl: Heat and Dust, A Room with a View, Maurice, On The Black Hill, Clockwise, Manifesto; tv work: Do Not Disturb (BBC), The Count of Solar (BBC); *Recreations* golf, restoring Islington house and shared house in Greece; *Clubs* Stage Golfing Soc; *Style—* Patrick Godfrey, Esq; 23 Gibson Square, Islington, London N1 0RD (☎ 071 226 0743)

GODFREY, Paul; s of Peter Godfrey, of Exeter, and Valerie, *née* Drake; *b* 16 Sept 1960; *Career* dir: Perth Repertory Theatre Scotland 1983-84, Eden Court Theatre Inverness 1985-87 (estab small scale touring co), first play at NT 1990; *plays*: Inventing A New Colour (NT Studio 1987, Royal Court 1988), A Bucket of Eels (1988), Once in a While the Odd Thing Happens (Royal National Theatre 1990); Arts Cncl Trainee Directors bursary 1983, Arts Cncl Playwrights award 1989, David Harlech Meml bursary 1990; memb: Equity 1984, Director's Guild of GB 1985; *Recreations* travelling; *Style—* Paul Godfrey, Esq; Rodall, A P Watt Ltd, 20 John St, London WC1 (☎ 071 405 6774, fax 071 831 2154)

GODFREY, Dr Richard Charles; s of Thomas Charles Godfrey (d 1965), of Watford, and Joan Eva, *née* Clayton; *b* 8 Sept 1940; *Educ* Watford GS, Peterhouse Cambridge (MA), UCL (MD); *m* 8 June 1968, Jane Catherine, da of Stanley Goodman, of Reigate; 3 s (Thomas b 1970, Robin b 1974, Matthew b 1975), 1 da (Sarah b 1971); *Career* clinical sub-dean Univ of Southampton 1984-89 (lectr in med 1972-76, conslt physician 1976-), currently warden Farley Hosp; ARCO, FRCP; *Recreations* music, organ building, squash; *Style—* Dr Richard Godfrey; The Wardenry, Farley, Salisbury SP5 1AH (☎ 0722 72231); Southampton General Hospital, Southampton SO9 4KY (☎ 0703 777222)

GODFREY, Robert John; s of Capt Thomas Mason Godfrey (d 1968), of E Molesey, Surrey, and Winifred Alice, *née* Beresford (d 1980); *b* 10 Oct 1931; *Educ* Tiffin Sch; *m* 31 Aug 1957, Jean Barbara, da of Dr Robert Alexander Frazer, DSC (d 1959), of Ockham, Surrey; 3 s (Christopher b 1960, Peter b 1962, Stephen b 1964); *Career* sub ed: Morning Advertiser 1954-60, News Chronicle 1960, Daily Telegraph 1960-70 (later foreign chief sub); publisher and ed: Hayling Islander Newspaper 1973-89, Alderney Magazine 1989-; *Recreations* photography; *Style—* Robert J Godfrey, Esq; Simon's Place, Alderney, Channel Islands (☎ 0481 82 2085, fax 0481 82 2110)

GODLEY, Hon Christopher John; s and h of 3 Baron Kilbracken, DSC; *b* 1 Jan 1945; *Educ* Rugby, Univ of Reading (BSc); *m* 10 May 1969, Gillian Christine, yr da of Lt-Cdr Stuart Wilson Birse, OBE, DSC, RN (d 1981), of Alverstoke, Hants; 1 s (James b 1972), 1 da (Louisa b 1974); *Career* agriculturalist with ICI Plant Protection Div Fernhurst Haslemere 1982- (Agric Div 1968-78, Head Office London 1978-82); *Style—* Hon Christopher Godley; Four Firs, Marley Lane, Haslemere, Surrey (☎ Haslemere 642814; office: 644061)

GODLEY, Georgina Jane (Mrs Conran); da of Michael Godley, and Heather, *née* Couper; *b* 11 April 1955; *Educ* Putney HS, Thames Valley GS, Wimbledon Art Sch, Brighton Poly (BA), Chelsea Sch of Art (MA); *m* 16 April 1988, Sebastian Conran, s of Sir Terence Conran; 1 s (Samuel Orby Conran b 12 May 1989); *Career* picture restorer 1978-79, menswear designer Browns London and Paris 1979, ptnr designer Crolla London 1980-85, fndr and designer own label Georgina Godley (retail outlets from London to USA and Japan, and illustrations and articles in all maj fashion pubns); *Style—* Ms Georgina Godley; 19 All Saints Road, London W11 1HE (☎ 071 221 1906)

GODLEY, Kevin; *Career* musician, composer, film director; former memb of 10CC (records incl I'm Not In Love and The Dean and I), left in 1976 with Lol Creme to form musical and directing partnership; music videos incl: Herbie Hancock's Rock It (Music Week award for Top Music Promo 1983, Billboard Best Music Video award and Best Art Direction 1983, MTV Music Video award - Best Concept Video, Best Special Effects, Best Art Direction, Best Editing, Most Experimental Video 1984), Duran Duran's Girls on Film (Grammy award for Best Video Short 1983), Frankie Goes to Hollywood's The Power of Love and Two Tribes (VPA Monitor award for Top Music Promo and Top Directors award 1984), The Police's Synchronicity, Wrapped around Your Finger and Every Breath You Take (MTV Best Cinematography award 1984); TV Commercials incl: Wrangler Jeans 1983 (Silver Lion Cannes award, Kodak Craft award), New York and Boston Yellow Pages 1987 (Clio award Best Utilities, The One Show Gold Pencil and Bronze Pencil, Golden Lion award), Reebok, Nissan, Audi, Eveready Batteries; working solo 1989-; commercials incl: Planters Peanuts, RCA Homes Theatres, Granada TV Rentals; directed two hour music TV special One World One Voice 1990; *Style—* Kevin Godley, Esq; c/o Medialab Ltd, Chelsea Wharf, 15 Lots Rd, London SW10 0QH (☎ 071 351 5814, fax 071 351 7898)

GODLEY, Dr Margaret Joan; *b* 23 May 1953; *Educ* Univ of Liverpool (MB ChB); *Career* conslt in genitourinary med Royal Berks Hosp Reading 1986-; hon sec The Med Soc for the Study of Venereal Diseases 1989-; MRCOG 1981; *Style—* Dr

Margaret Godley; The Dept of Genitourinary Medicine, Royal Berkshire Hospital, London Rd, Reading RG1 5AN (☎ 0734 877206)

GODLEY, Lt Cdr Peter Brian; s of Brig Brian Richard Godley, CBE (d 1954), and Margaret Valiant, *née* Livingstone-Learmonth (d 1979); *b* 4 Oct 1933; *Educ* Cheltenham, RNC Dartmouth; *m* 7 Jan 1960, Jean, da of Col James Forbes Robertson, VC, DSO, MC; 1 s (John b 9 July 1962), 2 da (Sarah b 21 Dec 1960, Joanna b 25 Feb 1968); *Career* RN; submarines 1955-62, minesweepers 1963-65, RN Staff Coll 1966, first Lt HMS Minerva 1967-68, asst to Chief of Allied Staff Med 1969-70, RAF Coll Cromwell 1971-73; Charterhouse Group plc 1974-83 (md Charterhouse Pensions Ltd 1978-83); dir: Europa Investment Services Ltd 1987-88, Royal Br Legion 1988; Liveryman Worshipful Co of Coachmakers and Coach Harness Makers 1976; *Recreations* off shore sailing, walking; *Clubs* Army and Navy, Woodroffe's; *Style—* Lt Cdr P B Godley, RN; Down House, Westcott, Dorking, Surrey RH4 3JX (☎ 0306 881 555); Royal Br Legion, 48 Pall Mall, London SW1Y 5JY (☎ 071 930 8131)

GODLEY, Prof Hon Wynne Alexander Hugh; yr s of 2 Baron Kilbracken, CB, KC (d 1950), and his 1 wife Elizabeth Helen Monteith, *née* Hamilton; *b* 2 Sept 1926; *Educ* Rugby, New Coll Oxford (BA); *m* 3 Feb 1955, Kathleen Eleanora, da of Sir Jacob Epstein, KBE, and former w of the painter Lucian Freud; 1 da (Eve b 1967); *Career* former professional oboist; served Treasy 1957-70; dir: Investing in Success Equities Ltd 1970-85, Royal Opera House (Covent Gdn) 1976-86; Univ of Cambridge: dir Dept of Applied Economics 1970-85, fell Kings' Coll 1970-, actg dir of Dept 1985-87, prof of applied economics 1980-, visiting prof Alborg Univ Denmark 1987-88; *Style—* Prof Hon Wynne Godley; Jasmine House, Cavendish, Suffolk

GODMAN, Arthur; s of Arthur Andrew Godman (d 1958), of London, and Mary Adeline Newman (d 1946); *b* 10 Oct 1916; *Educ* UCL (BSc), Inst of Educn (Dip Ed); *m* 24 June 1950, Jean Barr, da of James Morton, OBE (d 1973), of Scotland; 2 s (Ian b 1951, Brian b 1953), 1 da (Diana b 1953); *Career* WWII Capt RA 1939: served France, India, Malaya (POW Far E 1946); Colonial Civil Serv Educn Dept Malaya, Hong Kong princ asst sec Miny of Educn Malaysia 1946-63; author 1963-; educn conslt Longman Gp 1966-77; hon fell Eliot Coll Univ of Kent 1978-, res fell Dept of SE Asian Studies Univ of Kent, memb Canterbury Rotary Club 1980-; CChem, MRSC, FRAS; *Books* Dictionary of Scientific Usage (with E M F Payne, 1979), Illustrated Science Dictionary (1981), Illustrated Dictionary of Chemistry (1981), Cambridge Illustrated Thesaurus of Computer Science (1984), Health Science for the Tropics (1962), Chemistry: A New Certificate Approach (with S T Bajah, 1969), Human and Social Biology (1973), Energy Supply (1991); *Recreations* bridge, reading, oriental languages; *Clubs* Royal Over-Seas League; *Style—* Arthur Godman, Esq; Sondes House, Patrixbourne, Canterbury, Kent CT4 5DD (☎ 0227 830 322); Room L47, Eliot College, Univ of Kent, Canterbury, Kent

GODMAN, Desmond Frederick Shirley; JP (Glos 1962), DL 1987; s of Lt-Col Edward Shirley Godman, OBE, of Chetcombe House, Mere, Wilts; *b* 31 Jan 1927; *Educ* Winchester, Univ of Cambridge; *m* 1954, Angela Janice, da of Rev John Corlett Rowson, of Ivy Cottage, Kirk Michael, IOM; 2 s, 2 da; *Career* vice chm Cotswold District Cncl; High Sheriff of Glos 1976; *Clubs* Farmers'; *Style—* Desmond Godman, Esq, JP, DL; The Manor House, Compton Abdale, Cheltenham, Glos GL54 4DR

GODMAN, Dr Norman Anthony; MP (Lab) Greenock and Port Glasgow 1983-; *b* 19 April 1937; *Educ* Westbourne St Boys' HS Hull, Univ of Hull (BA), Heriot Watt Univ (PhD); *m* Patricia; *Career* former shipwright and teacher; joined Lab Pty 1962, Parly candidate (Lab) Aberdeen S 1979; *Style—* Dr Norman Godman, MP; House of Commons, London SW1

GODSAL, Lady Elizabeth Cameron; *née* Stopford; 2 da of 8 Earl of Courtown, OBE, TD (d 1975), by his 1 w; *b* 10 April 1939; *m* 24 April 1962, Alan Anthony Colleton Godsal, o s of late Hugh Godsal, of Haines Hill, Twyford; 1 s (Hugh b 1965), 2 da (Lucy b 1964, Laura b 1968); *Career* chief pres St John Ambulance Bde 1990- (cmmr Berks 1983-90); High Sheriff Berks 1990-91; *Style—* Lady Elizabeth Godsal; Haines Hill, Twyford, Berks (☎ 0734 345 678); 7 Herbert Crescent, London SW1 (☎ 071 581 0937)

GODSAL, Philip Caulfeild; s of Maj Philip Hugh Godsal (d 1982), of Iscoyd Park, Whitchurch, Shropshire, and Pamela Ann Delisle, *née* Caulfeild; *b* 10 Oct 1945; *Educ* Eton; *m* 1, 29 Nov 1969 (m dis 1985), Lucinda Mary, da of Lt Cdr Percival Royston Dancy; 3 s (Philip Langley b 28 June 1971, Benjamin Rupert Wilmot b 17 June 1976, Thomas Henry b 3 Aug 1977), 1 da (Laura Sophie b 24 May 1973); m 2, 2 July 1986, Selina Baber, da of Thomas William Brooke-Smith, of Canford Cliffs; 3 step da (Zoe Christina b 1974, Lucinda Selina b 1976, Christina Juliet b 1980); *Career* farmer, land agent and chartered surveyor; formerly ptnr Savills Norwich, ptnr John German Shrewsbury 1984-; chm Historic Houses Assoc for Wales, chm N Wales Region Timber Growers UK, memb Ctee Shropshire Branch CLA, sec Shropshire Rural Housing Assoc, govr Higher Wych C of E Primary Sch, pres Iscoyd and Fenns Bank CC; FRICS; *Recreations* shooting, forestry, reading; *Clubs* MCC, Farmers', Salop; *Style—* Philip Godsal, Esq; Iscoyd Park, Whitchurch, Shropshire SY13 3AT; John German, Chartered Surveyors, 43 High St, Shrewsbury SY1 1ST (☎ 0743 231661)

GODSAL, Capt Walter Edward Browning; s of Lt-Col Philip Godsal, MC (d 1963), of Salop, and Violet Mary, *née* Browning (d 1978); *b* 3 Dec 1924; *Educ* Eton; *m* 7 Nov 1970, Pamela Ann De Lisle, da of Lt-Col Wilmot Smyth Caulfeild (d 1980), of Norfolk; 5 step children; *Career* RN 1943-79, Capt Underwater Weapons Acceptance Portland 1972-74, asst naval attaché Washington, Capt HMS Saker 1974-76, dep UK nat mil rep at SHAPE 1977-79; porcelain restorer; *Recreations* shooting, walking; *Clubs* Army & Navy; *Style—* Capt Walter Godsal; Edbrooke House, Winsford, nr Minehead, Somerset TA24 7AE (☎ 064385 239)

GODWIN, Dame (Beatrice) Anne; DBE (1962, OBE 1952); da of William Godwin (d 1932); *b* 6 July 1897; *Career* gen sec Clerical and Admin Workers' Union 1956-62, chm TUC 1961-62, govr BBC 1962-68, memb Industrial Ct 1963-69; *Recreations* talking, gardening, reading; *Style—* Dame Anne Godwin, DBE; 25 Fullbrooks Ave, Worcester Park, Surrey KT4 7PE

GODWIN, Charles Richard; s of Maj John Percival Godwin (d 1961), and Nancy, *née* Lee; *b* 23 Aug 1933; *Educ* Ardingly; *m* 19 Nov 1976, Gwendoline Janet, da of Geoffrey Thomas Le Butt, of Leicester; *Career* Lt Essex Regt and Somaliland Scouts 1953-54; CA; sr ptnr Manchester Office Price Waterhouse 1975-89; dir: Britannia Building Society 1989-, Readicut International 1989-; memb S Cumbria Health Authy 1990-; *Recreations* golf, skiing, wine, antiques; *Style—* Charles Godwin, Esq; c/o Britannia Building Society, Newton Hse, Leek, Staffs

GODWIN, Jeremy Purdon; s of Dr Eric George Godwin, of Tillington, Petworth, W Sussex, and Hannah (Nancy), *née* Rook; *b* 16 April 1943; *Educ* Epsom Coll, Lincoln Coll Oxford (MA), UCL (Dip of Archive Admin); *Career* archivist; asst archivist Northumberland 1969-71, Cumbria 1971-; reader The Diocese of Carlisle 1978-; sec (and ex chm) The Penrith Cncl of Churches; corr to: The Orcadian, Shetland Times, The Scotsman, Cumberland and Westmorland Herald; memb: Medieval Settlement Res Gp, Eng Place-Name Soc, Scottish Record Soc, Diocesan Synod of Carlisle (Bishop's Cncl); FSA (Scot) 1988; *Books* Jo Bens Description of Orkney 1529 (ed), articles in: Transactions of the Cumberland & Westmoreland, Antiquation & Archaeological Soc, Shetland Life; *Recreations* research (local history), walking, music; *Style—* Jeremy Godwin, Esq; 15 Drovers Lane, Penrith, Cumbria CA11 9EP (☎ 0768 64038); Cumbria Record Office, The Castle, Carlisle CA3 8UR (☎ 0228 23456 ext 2416)

GODWIN, Lesley; da of Richard George Hewitt (d 1982), and Kathleen, *née* Ingall (d 1970); *b* 17 June 1945; *Educ* Sydenham HS for Girls; *Career* Glyn Mills and Co 1961-63, Ofrex Ltd 1963-70, mktg devpt mangr Consumers' Association 1991- (advtg mangr 1980-88, direct mktg mangr 1988-91); Br Direct Mktg Assoc: memb 1988, memb Bd 1989, memb Membership and Mktg Ctee; *Recreations* cinema, theatre, swimming, tennis, badminton, reading, antiques, cats; *Style—* Ms Lesley Godwin; Consumers' Association, 2 Marylebone Rd, London NW1 4DX (☎ 071 486 5544, fax 071 383 5887)

GODWIN, Peter Raymond; *b* 16 May 1942; *Educ* Harrow Co Boys' GS; *m* 3 June 1967, Wendy Dorothy; 1 s (Philip b 1972), 1 da (Helen b 1969); *Career* banker; md Chartered West LB Ltd (formerly Standard Chartered Merchant Bank Ltd), chm CWB Export Fin Ltd; dir: Korea Merchant Banking Corp Seoul 1979-86, Lazard Bros & Co Ltd 1979-85, The Int Investmt Corp for Yugoslavia SA Luxembourg 1981-85, Fin Merchant Bank Ltd Lagos 1987-89; pres Anglo-Taiwan Trade Ctee; organist St Andrews Church Roxbourne Harrow; ACIB; *Style—* Peter R Godwin, Esq; 16 Newquay Crescent, Harrow, Middx HA2 9LJ (☎ 081 422 1801); 33-36 Gracechurch St, London EC3V 0AX (☎ 071 623 8711, fax 071 626 1610)

GODWIN-AUSTEN, Dr Richard Bertram; s of R Annesley Godwin-Austen, CBE (d 1977), of The Manor House, Pirbright, Surrey, and Beryl, *née* Odling; *b* 4 Oct 1935; *Educ* Charterhouse, St Thomas's Hosp (MB BS); *m* 12 Aug 1961, Jennifer Jane, da of Louis Sigismund Himely (d 1986), of Holne Brake, Bovey Tracey, Devon; 1 s (Jonathan Reade b 1962), 1 da (Alice Amelia b 1964); *Career* sr registrar Inst of Neurology Queen Sq London 1967-70, conslt neurologist Univ Hosp Nottingham 1970-; clinical teacher and chm of neurological sciences Nottingham, treas and memb Cncl Assoc of Br Neurologists, med advsr Parkinson's Disease Soc, memb Assoc of Br Neurologists; MD 1968, FRCP (London) 1976; *Books* The Parkinson's Disease Handbook (1984), Medical Aspects of Fitness to Drive (contrib, 1985), The Neurology of the Elderly (1989); *Recreations* gardening, dessert wines; *Clubs* Garrick, RSM; *Style—* Dr Richard Godwin-Austen; Papplewick Hall, Nottinghamshire NG15 8FE; Dept of Neurology, University Hosp, Queen's Med Centre, Nottingham (☎ 0602 421421)

GOEHR, Prof Alexander; s of Walter and Laelia Goehr; *b* 10 Aug 1932; *Educ* Berkhamsted, Royal Manchester Coll of Music, Paris Conservatoire; *m* 1, 1954 (m dis 1971), Audrey Baker; 3 da; m 2, 1972, Anthea Staunton; 1 s; m 3, 1982, Amira Katz; *Career* composer; prof of music and fell Trinity Hall Cambridge 1976-; *Style—* Prof Alexander Goehr; Trinity Hall, Cambridge

GOFF, Hon Mrs (Angela Estelle); *née* Kitson; 7 and yst da of 2 Baron Airedale (d 1944), and Florence, *née* Baroness von Schunk (d 1942); *b* 1905; *m* 12 Nov 1927, George Herbert Goff (d 1957), s of late George Charles Golf, of Birchington, Kent; 1 s (George b 1928), 1 da (Mrs Brian Richardson b 1932); *Style—* Hon Mrs Goff; 20 Field Way, Broad Oak, Brede, E Sussex

GOFF, Martyn; OBE (1977); s of Jacob Goff (d 1971), and Janey Goff (d 1978); *b* 7 June 1923; *Educ* Clifton; *Career* author; dir Nat Book League 1970-88; fiction reviewer: The Daily Telegraph 1975-88, Evening Standard 1988-; chm Henry Sotheron 1988-; chm: Sch Bookshop Assoc, Soc of Bookmen; chief exec Book Tst 1986-88 (formerly Nat Book League); FRSA, fell Int Inst of Arts and Letters; *Novels* The Plaster Fabric, A Season with Mammon, A Sort of Peace, The Youngest Director, The Flint Inheritance, Indecent Assault, The Liberation of Rupert Bannister, Tar and Cement; *Music* A Short Guide to Long Play, A Further Guide to Long Play, LP Collecting, Record Choice; *Miscellaneous* Victorian Surrey, The Royal Pavilion, Why Conform? (prize writing, 1989); *Recreations* picture collecting, travelling; *Clubs* Athenaeum, Savile, Groucho, Acad; *Style—* Martyn Goff, Esq, OBE; 95 Sisters Ave, London SW11 5SW (☎ 071 228 8164)

GOFF OF CHIEVELEY, Baron (Life Peer UK 1986), of Chieveley, Co Berkshire; Sir Robert Lionel Archibald Goff; PC (1982); s of Lt-Col Lionel Trevor Goff, RA (d 1953), of Queen's House, Monk Sherborne, Basingstoke, Hants, and his wife, *née* Denroche-Smith; *b* 12 Nov 1926; *Educ* Eton, New Coll Oxford (MA, DCL); *m* 1953, Sarah, er da of Capt Gerald Roger Cousins, DSC, RN, of Child Okeford, Dorset; 1 s (Hon Robert Thomas Alexander b 1966) and 1 s decd, 2 da (Hon Katharine Isobel b 1959, Hon Juliet Mary Constance b 1961); *Career* served Scots Guards 1945-48; fell and tutor Lincoln Coll Oxford 1951-55; called to the Bar Inner Temple 1951, QC 1967, rec 1974-75, bencher 1975, High Ct judge (Queen's Bench) 1975-82, judge i/c Commercial List and chm Commercial Ct Ctee 1979-81, Lord Justice of Appeal 1982-, Lord of Appeal in Ordinary 1986-; hon prof of legal ethics Univ of Birmingham 1980-81, Maccabaean lectr 1983; hon fell: Lincoln Coll Oxford 1983, New Coll Oxford 1986; chm: Cncl Legal Educn 1976-, Ct Univ of London 1986-, Br Inst of Int and Comparative Law 1986-; pres: Chartered Inst of Arbitrators 1986-, The Bentham Club 1986, The Holdsworth Club 1986-87; High Steward of Oxford 1990-; Hon DLitt City Univ; Hon LLD: Univ of Buckingham, Univ of Reading, Univ of London; FBA 1987; *Books* The Law of Restitution (with Prof Gareth Jones, 1966); *Style—* The Rt Hon Lord Goff of Chieveley, PC; House of Lords, London SW1

GOGUEN, Prof Joseph Amadee; s of Joseph Amadee Goguen (d 1988), and Helen Stratton Goguen (d 1985); *b* 28 June 1941; *Educ* Harvard (BA), Univ of California at Berkeley (MA, PhD); *m* 1, (m dis 1974), Nancy, da of Ernest Hammer (d 1985); 1 s (Healfdene b 25 Dec 1967), 1 da (Heather b 4 Jan 1963); m 2, 20 June 1981, Kathleen, da of Robert Morrow; 1 da (Alice b 29 Nov 1983); *Career* asst prof Ctee on Info Sci Univ of Chicago 1968-73, IBM postdoctoral fellowship T J Watson Res Centre 1971, prof Computer Sci Dept UCLA 1973-79, academic staff Naropa Inst Boulder Colorado 1974-78, sr visiting fell Univ of Edinburgh 1976, 1978 and 1983, memb Centre for Study of Language and Info Stanford Univ 1984-88, md Structural Semantics Palo Alto CA 1973-, sr sci staff SRI Int Menlo Park CA 1984-88 (Exceptional Achievement award 1984), prof of computing science Univ of Oxford; author of over 125 publications, articles in professional jls; ACM, AMS, MAA, MIEEE; *Books* Theory and Practice of Software Technology (ed, 1983); *Recreations* literature, music, philosophy; *Style—* Prof Joseph Goguen; Programming Research Group, Oxford University Computing Laboratory, 11 Keble Rd, Oxford OX1 3QD (☎ 0865 272567, fax 0865 273839)

GOH, Dr Beng Tin; s of Pang Chuan Goh, of Malaysia; *b* 14 May 1953; *Educ* Univ of Singapore (MB BS), Univ of London (Dip Dermatology), Soc of Aopthecaries (Dip Venereology); *m* 17 Dec 1978, Dr Tiar Nyak Sim, da of Kuan Sui Sim, of Malaysia; 2 da (Po-Siann b 18 May 1983, Po-Laine b 20 Jan 1985); *Career* registrar in genitourinary med King's Coll Hosp London 1980-81, sr registrar in genitourinary med London Hosp and Moorfields Eye Hosp London 1981-85, conslt genitourinary physician London Hosp and Moorfields Eye Hosp London 1985-; cncl memb Med Soc for the Study of Venereal Diseases; MRCP, MRCP (Ireland); *Recreations* travelling, photography; *Style—* Dr Beng Tin Goh; Ambrose King Centre, The London Hospital Whitechapel, London E1 1BB (☎ 071 377 7308); Moorfields Eye Hospital, City Rd, London EC1V 2PD

GOLD, Sir Arthur Abraham; CBE (1974); s of late Mark Gold, and Leah Gold; *b* 10

Jan 1917; *m* 1942, Marion, da of late N Godfrey; 1 s (Jonathan); *Career* former international athlete (high jumper); leader athletics team Mexico Olympics 1968, Munich 1972, Montreal 1976; hon sec Br Amateur Athletic Bd 1965-77, life vice pres 1977; pres: Counties Athletic Union, Euro Athletic Assoc; chm Cwlth Games Cncl for England 1979-, vice-chm Br Olympic Assoc, memb Sports Cncl 1980-; kt 1984; *Clubs* London Athletic, City Livery, MCC; *Style*— Sir Arthur Gold, CBE; 49 Friern Mount Drive, Whetstone, London N20 9DJ (☎ 081 445 2848)

GOLD, David Laurence; s of Michael Gold (d 1980), and Betty, *née* Levitt; *b* 1 March 1951; *Educ* Westcliff HS, LSE (LLB); *m* 27 Aug 1978, Sharon, da of Charles Levy, of Thorpe Bay, Essex; 2 s (Alexander b 23 Jan 1983, Edward b 5 Oct 1985), 1 da (Amanda b 30 March 1981); *Career* slr; admitted 1975, ptnr Herbert Smith 1983-; memb: Advsy Ctee Int Litigation Practitioners Forum, Law Soc; Freeman City of London Slrs Co; *Recreations* theatre, cinema, bridge, travel, family; *Style*— David Gold, Esq; Exchange House, Primrose St, London EC2A 2HS (☎ 071 374 8000, fax 071 496 0043, telex 886633)

GOLD, Jack; *b* 28 June 1930; *Educ* London Univ; *m* 1957, Denyse, *née* Macpherson; 2 s, 1 da; *Career* film director; ed Film Dept BBC 1955-60, dir TV and film documentaries and fiction 1960; BAFTA award: Death in the Morning 1964, World of Copperd 1968, Stockers Copper 1972; Peabody award 1974, Italia prize 1976, Int Emmy and Critics award 1976, Int Emmy 1981, jt winner Martin Luther King memorial prize 1980; Monte Carlo: Catholic award 1981, Critics award 1981, Grand Prix 1971; *stage play* The Devils Disciple; *Style*— Jack Gold, Esq; 18 Avenue Rd, N6 5DW

GOLD, Hon Mrs (Jocelyne Mary); *née* Boot; da of 2 and last Baron Trent (d 1956); *b* 6 Feb 1917; *m* 19 Nov 1947, Major Harcourt Michael Scudamore Gold, MC (d 1982), s of Sir Harcourt Gilbey Gold, OBE (d 1952); 1 s (John Angus b 1958), 1 da (Mrs Timothy Holcroft b 1950); *Style*— Hon Mrs Gold; Wheathill, Sparsholt, Winchester, Hants

GOLD, Sir Joseph; *b* 12 July 1912; *Educ* Univ of London, Harvard Univ; *m* 1939, Ruth Schechter; 1 s, 2 da; *Career* IMF: joined 1946, gen counsel and dir Legal Dept 1960-79, sr conslt 1979-; author of numerous pubns on monetary matters; kt 1980; *Style*— Sir Joseph Gold; 7020 Braeburn Place, Bethseda, Maryland 20817, USA

GOLD, Nicholas Roger; s of Rev Guy Alastair Whitmore Gold, TD, of Gt Bealings, nr Woodbridge, Suffolk, and Elizabeth Weldon, *née* Maythem, JP; *b* 11 Dec 1951; *Educ* Felsted, Univ of Kent (BA); *m* 23 April 1983, (Siena) Laura (Joy), da of Adam Sebastian, of Salcombe, Devon; 1 s (James Mortimer Fearon b 8 Oct 1987), 1 da (Siena Jane b 9 Jan 1985); *Career* CA Touche Ross & Co 1973-76, slr Freshfields 1977-86, Baring Bros & Co Ltd 1986- (dir Corp Fin Dept 1987-); ACA 1977, FCA 1982; *Recreations* sailing, the arts, stalking, travel; *Style*— Nicholas Gold, Esq; 14 Northumberland Place, London W2 5BS (☎ 071 229 4773); North Sands Cottage, Salcombe, Devon; Baring Brothers & Co Ltd, 8 Bishopsgate, London EC2 (☎ 071 280 1000, fax 071 283 2224, telex 883622)

GOLDBERG, Prof Sir Abraham; s of Julius Goldberg (d 1953), and Rachel, *née* Varinofsky; *b* 7 Dec 1923; *Educ* George Heriot's Sch Edinburgh, Univ of Edinburgh (MB ChB, MD, Gold medal for thesis), Univ of Glasgow (DSc); *m* 1957, Clarice, da of Jacob Cussin, of 130 Menock Rd, Glasgow; 3 children; *Career* Maj RAMC ME; Univ of Glasgow: Regius prof of materia medica 1970-78, Regius prof of practice of med 1978-89, emeritus prof, sr hon res fell Dept of Modern History 1989-; chm Ctee on Safety of Med 1980-86, fndr pres Faculty of Pharmaceutical Med Royal Colls of Physicians of UK 1989; Lord Provost award for public service (Glasgow) 1988; FRCP (London, Edinburgh, Glasgow), FRSE; kt 1983; *Books* co-author: Diseases of Porphyrin Metabolism (1962), Recent Advances in Haematology (1971), Disorders of Porphyrin Metabolism (1987); *Recreations* swimming, writing; *Clubs* RSM (London); *Style*— Prof Sir Abraham Goldberg, FRSE; 16 Birnam Crescent, Bearsden, Glasgow G61 2AU

GOLDBERG, David Gerard; QC; s of Arthur Goldberg (d 1982), of Plymouth, and Sylvia, *née* Stone; *b* 12 Aug 1947; *Educ* Plymouth Coll, LSE (LLB, LLM); *m* 22 Dec 1981, Alison Ninette, da of Jack V Lunzer, of London; 1 s (Arthur b 1986), 1 da (Selina b 1984); *Career* called to the Bar Lincoln's Inn 1971, in practice at Revenue Bar, case note ed British Tax Review 1975-87, author of numerous articles on taxation and company law; *Books* An Introduction to Company Law (jtly, 1987), The Law of Partnership Taxation (jtly, 1987); *Recreations* reading, letter writing, thinking, working out; *Style*— David Goldberg, Esq, QC; Gray's Inn Chambers, Gray's Inn, London WC1R 5JA (☎ 071 242 2642, fax 071 831 9017)

GOLDBERG, Ivan Jeffrey; s of Myer Goldberg (d 1945), and Florence, *née* Jacobson (d 1952); *b* 26 Dec 1930; *Educ* Queen Elizabeth's GS Blackburn; *m* 1, 14 July 1957, Audrey Githa, *née* Prepsler (d 1980); 1 s (Adam b 1964), 1 da (Sarah b 1966); m 2, 30 Sept 1990, Hilary Simone, *née* Kenway; *Career* mgmnt conslt; chm: Michael Adam Assoc Ltd, Teleconsultants (UK) Ltd; dir Manchester Camerata Ltd; visiting lectr: Manchester Business Sch, Univ of Manchester; CEng, FIMechE, MIMC; *Recreations* horse riding, music; *Clubs* Royal Overseas; *Style*— Ivan Goldberg, Esq; 50 Wilmslow Road, Cheadle, Cheshire SK8 1NF

GOLDBERG, Jonathan Jacob; s of Rabbi Dr Percy Selvin Goldberg, and Frimette, *née* Yudt; *b* 13 Nov 1947; *Educ* Manchester GS, Trinity Hall Cambridge (MA, LLB); *m* 7 Nov 1980, Alexis Jane, da of George Martin, CBE; 1 s (Saul Percy Lawrence b 22 Sept 1985), 1 da (Natasha Jane Frimette b 22 Dec 1982); *Career* called to the Bar Middle Temple 1971, practising SE Sircuit, asst rec 1987, QC 1989; memb NY State Bar 1985; *Recreations* reading, films, music; *Style*— Jonathan Goldberg, Esq, QC; 5 King's Bench Walk, Temple, London, EC4Y 7DN (☎ 071 353 4713, Fax 081 785 9345)

GOLDBERG, Dr Montague Joshua; s of Louis Goldberg (d 1943), of Johannesburg, SA, and Minnie, *née* Shippel (d 1973); *b* 5 Nov 1924; *Educ* King Edward VII Sch Johannesburg SA, Witwatersrand Univ (MB BCh, Dip Med); *m* 24 April 1960, Daphne Margaret, da of Ernest Clark, of Johannesburg, SA; 3 s (Martin, Rodney, Howard); *Career* house physician and house offr General Hosp and Bragwanath Hosp Johannesburg 1949-50, med registrar and tutorial registrar Dept of Med Johannesburg Hosp 1954-58, house physician Hammersmith Hosp 1958-59, sr registrar Dept Cardiology Middx Hosp 1959-65, conslt cardiologist Leics Regnl Cardiothoracic Unit Groby Rd Hosp 1965-89; Hon DSc Univ of Leicester 1989; FRCP 1973, FRSM; *Recreations* trout fishing, ornithology, music, fell walking; *Style*— Dr Montague Goldberg; 45 Spencefield Lane, Leicester LE5 6PT (☎ 0533 415640)

GOLDEN, Lewis Lawrence; OBE (1978), JP (1968); s of Samuel Arthur Golden (d 1951), and Julia, *née* Lee (d 1976); *b* 6 Dec 1922; *Educ* East Sheen Co Sch, Univ of Manchester; *m* 15 Jan 1953, Jacqueline Esther, da of Maurice Frances (d 1966); 2 s (David b 1954, Jonathan b 1961), 2 da (Deborah b 1957, Sara b 1959); *Career* WWII RCS 1941-46: cmmnd 2 Lt (later Lt) 1942, 8 Armd Div England 1942, 1 Airborne Div 1942-45 (serv: England, N Africa, Sicily, Italy, Holland, Norway), Capt 1944, Adj Arnhem 1944, 2 (Indian) Airborne Div India 1945-46, released Maj 1946; chief accountant and asst sec Emu Wool Industries Ltd 1949-50, Lewis Golden & Co CA's 1950-, fin dir Home Insulation Ltd Everest Double Glazing) 1965-88; beef and corn farmer 1971; currently treas: London Library, Friends of the Nat Libraries 1980-90, Friends of the Br Library 1989-90, Friends of Lambeth Palace Library 1984-90, Wiener Library Endowment Appeal 1980-90; pres Westminster Synagogue 1980-90; tstee: National Manuscripts Conservation Trust, Wiener Library Endowment Tst, Chalk Pits Museum Devpt Tst Amberley, Dove Cottage Grasmere until 1986; memb Advsy Cncl Chichester Cathedral Tst, memb Wisborough Green Parish Cncl until 1987; Freeman City of London 1980, memb Worshipful Co of CA's 1980; FCA 1951 (ACA 1947); *Books* Echoes From Arnhem (1984); *Recreations* walking, reading; *Style*— Lewis Golden, Esq, OBE, JP; Pallingham Manor Farm, Wisborough Green, Billingshurst, W Sussex RH14 OEZ

GOLDENBERG, Philip; s of Nathan Goldenberg, OBE, and Edith, *née* Dee; *b* 26 April 1946; *Educ* St Paul's, Pembroke Coll Oxford; *m* 1, 16 Aug 1969 (m dis 1975), Dinah Mary Pye; m 2, 12 Oct 1985, Lynda Anne, *née* Benjamin; 2 s (Jonathan b 1986, Benjamin b 1990), 1 da (Philippa b 1988); *Career* admitted slr 1972, asst slr with Linklaters & Paines 1972-82, ptnr S J Berwin & Co 1983 (asst slr 1982-83); sec Oxford Univ Lib Club 1966, pres Watford Lib Assoc 1980-81, vice chm Home Counties Regnl Lib Pty 1976-78 and 1980-81; memb: Lib Pty Cncl 1975-88, Nat Exec Ctee 1977-87, Candidates' Ctee 1976-85, Assembly Ctee 1985-87, Lib Democratic Federal Conference Ctee 1988-, Federal Policy Ctee 1990-; Parly candidate: (Lib) Eton and Slough 1974 (twice) and 1979, (Lib/SDP Alliance) Woking 1983 and 1987; elected Woking Borough Cncl 1984- (chm Highways Ctee 1988-90); former memb Exec Ctee Wider Share Ownership Cncl, memb Cncl Electoral Reform Soc 1978-82, memb London Regnl Cncl CBI, jt author Constitution of the Social and Lib Democrats, jt ed New Outlook 1974-77, govr Slough Coll of Higher Educn 1980-86; memb Law Soc; *Books* Fair Welfare (1968), Sharing Profits (with Sir David Steel, 1986), The Businessman's Guide to Directors' Responsibilities (1988), Guide to Company Law (3 edn, 1990), Gore-Browne on Companies (jt author); *Recreations* family, friends; *Clubs* National Liberal; *Style*— Philip Goldenberg, Esq; Toad Hall, White Rose Lane, Woking, Surrey GU22 7LB (☎ 0483 765377, fax 0483 764970); 236 Gray's Inn Rd, London WC1X 8HB (☎ 071 278 0444, fax 071 833 2860, telex 8814928 WINLAW G)

GOLDHILL, Jack Alfred; s of John Goldhill (d 1978), of London, and Sophie, *née* Hamburg (d 1973); *b* 18 Sept 1920; *Educ* Christ's Coll Finchley, Coll of Estate Mgmnt, Inst of Chartered Auctioneers; *m* 1, 1943, Aurelia (Rela) Freed (d 1966); 3 s (Michael b 1949, David b 1953, Simon b 1956); m 2, 1967, Grete Kohnstam; *Career* served WWII Royal Signals 1939-46; commercial property advsr; fndr ptnr Leighton, Goldhill Chartered Surveyors 1948-80, conslt 1980-; exhibitor of paintings Royal Acad Summer Exhibition 1983, 1988 and 1989; estab: bursaries for Royal Academy Sch students without grants 1981, The Goldhill award for Sculpture 1987; memb Assoc of Friends of the Royal Acad, The Royal Acad Schs Ctee; vice pres Jewish Care, involved (with Jewish Care) in the founding and building of the Rela Goldhill Lodge a residential centre for young physically handicapped; fell Inst of Chartered Auctioneers 1951, FRICS 1970; *Style*— Jack Goldhill, Esq

GOLDIE, Ian William; s of Donald Scott Goldie, and Eileen Muriel, *née* Shedden; *b* 6 Feb 1951; *Educ* Trinity Coll Glenalmond, Jesus Coll Cambridge (BA, MA); *m* 14 Feb 1976, Susan Kay, da of Max Clifford Moore, AM; 2 s (Stuart Douglas b 1 May 1984, Daniel Scott b 22 Oct 1987) 1 da (Emily Louise b 29 Aug 1989); *Career* Slaughter and May: articled clerk 1973-75, asst slr 1975, ptnr 1983-; memb Law Soc; *Recreations* golf; *Clubs* Royal St George's Golf, Royal Blackheath Golf, Woking Golf; *Style*— Ian Goldie, Esq; Slaughter & May, 35 Basinghall Street, London EC2V 5DV (☎ 071 600 1200, fax 071 726 0038/071 600 0289)

GOLDIE, Dr Lawrence; s of Bernard Goldie (d 1946), of Manchester, England, and Dora, *née* Sapper; *b* 8 Sept 1923; *Educ* Manchester Central GS, Univ of Manchester, Univ of Manchester Med Sch (MB ChB, MD); *m* 12 July 1949, Lilian Fay, da of Hyman Jaffa; 1 s (Boyd Stephen b 5 May 1957), 1 da (Helena Elspeth b 28 Sept 1954); *Career* serv WWII pilot RAF 1942-46; house offr in gen surgery: Park Hosp Manchester 1953, Withington Hosp Manchester 1954 (house offr in gen med 1954); sr house offr in gen psychiatry and at Geriatric Psychiatry Unit Bethlehem Royal Hosp 1955; registrar: Psychotherapy Unit (gp and individual) The Maudsley Hosp 1956, The Observation Ward (acute admissions) St Francis Hosp Dulwich London 1957, Neurosurgical Unit Guy's and Maudsley Hosps 1957, Paediatric Psychiatry Maudsley Hosp 1957; res asst in neurophysiology Dept of Clinical Neurophysiology Inst of Psychiatry 1957-61, lectr Inst of Child Health Postgrad Med Sch Hammersmith 1961-67, conslt psychiatrist Queen Mary's Hosp Carshalton Surrey 1961-74; conslt psychiatrist and conslt med psychotherapist: Inst of Laryngology and Otology Royal Nat ENT Hosp London 1966-89, The Royal Marsden Hosp 1971-89; sr lectr Inst of Obstetrics and Gynaecology The Hammersmith Hosp London 1974-89; currently: conslt med psychotherapist The Lister Hosp London, course dir and symposium organiser Psychosexual Problems Course Inst of Obstetrics and Gynaecology, dir Caring for the Bereaved and the Dying Course Br Postgrad Med Fedn, in private practice Harley Street; memb: Cncl CRUSE (orgn for care of widows and widowers) 1977-91, Euro Working Gp for Psychomatic Cancer Res 1978-; med memb Steering Gp Kent Voluntary Serv Cncls' Project on Social Care of the Gravely Ill at Home 1980-81, visiting conslt on psychiatric problems St Joseph's Hospice 1982, former med advsr Cancer Link, memb Editorial Bd Medical Tribune Gp Br Jl of Sexual Med until 1989; considerable experience as teacher and lectr, author of numerous papers in learned jls; Freeman City of London 1987, Liveryman Worshipful Soc of Apothecaries 1987, memb Guild of Freedmen of City of London 1988; *Recreations* theatre, music (jazz, classical, opera); *Clubs* RAC, The Aircrew Assoc; *Style*— Dr Lawrence Goldie; 23 Harley St, London W1N 1DA (☎ 071 636 4918/7658)

GOLDIE, William Law; MBE; s of Hugh Goldie (d 1964), of Norwood, Academy St, Coatbridge, and Agnes Pettigrew Law (d 1984); *b* 16 April 1922; *Educ* Coatbridge HS, Univ of Glasgow (BSc); *m* 2 Jun 1955, Sheila Veronica Mary, da of Jack Robertson Lamberton (d 1973), of Arden, Charlotte St, Helensburgh; 3 s (William b 1958, Andrew b 1962, Angus b 1968); *Career* volunteer res Flt Lt pilot coastal cmd RAF W Africa; engr; chm: Lamberton (Hldg) Ltd and Lamberton & Co Ltd, Lamberton Robotics Ltd, Lamberton Hydraulics Ltd, Scoforr Engrg Ltd; dir Lanarkshire Development Agency, pres Metalworking Plantmakers Fedn 1979-80; CEng, FIMechE; *Recreations* restoration of bldgs and machinery; *Clubs* Caledonian, RAF; *Style*— W L Goldie, Esq, MBE; Woodburn House, Milton of Campsie, Glasgow G65 8AN (☎ 0236 823249); Sunnyside Works, Coatbridge ML5 2DL (☎ 0236 20101, fax : 0236 29136)

GOLDIE-MORRISON, Keith Cooper; TD; s of Capt Wilfred Drury Goldie-Morrison (d 1933), and Elizabeth Gilmour Johnson, *née* McCall (d 1937); *b* 12 Nov 1920; *Educ* Wellingborough Sch, Airspeed Aeronautical Coll; *m* 12 Dec 1942, Synnöve, da of late Erling Monsen; 3 s (Duncan b 1955, Stewart b 1958, Angus b 1962), 2 da (Solveig b 1949, Karen b 1952); *Career* served Middx Yeomanry 1940-46 (despatches as Maj), Lt-Col TA 1947-59; sr ptnr: Carroll and Co 1968, Keith Bayley Rogers and Co 1968-78; elected to Cncl Stock Exchange 1984 (joined 1949), appt to Bd of Securities Assoc 1988; chm: Quality of Markets Ctee, Malaya Gp PLC, Alpine Group plc; tstee: Douglas Haig Meml Home, Housing Assoc for Offrs' Families; *Recreations* music, photography, painting, gardening; *Style*— Keith Goldie-Morrison, Esq, TD; c/o Keith Bayley Rogers Co, 93-95 Borough High St, London SE1 1NL (☎ 071 378 0657)

GOLDIN, (Jacob) Henry; *b* 21 Feb 1939; *Educ* Grey HS Port Elizabeth SA, Univ of Cape Town SA (MB ChB); *m* 8 Dec 1964, Elizabeth Ann; 1 s (Jonathan b 1965), 2 da (Diana b 1970, Rachel b 1974); *Career* conslt plastic surgn 1974-: Wordsley Hosp, E Birmingham Hosp, Good Hope Gen Hosp, Sandwell Dist Gen Hosp; consIt craniofacial surgn Childrens Hosp and Queen Elizabeth Hosp Birmingham; memb: Br Assoc of Plastic Surgns, Br Assoc of Aesthetic Plastic Surgns, Euro Soc for Craniofacial Surgery, Int Soc of Craniomaxillofacial Surgery; memb: BMA, RSM; FRCSEd; *Books* Plastic Surgery - Pocket Consultant (1987); *Recreations* travel, pottery; *Style*— Henry Goldin, Esq; The Edgbaston Nuffield Hospital, 22 Somerset Rd, Edgbaston, Birmingham B15 2QD (☎ 021 643 9167, fax 021 633 4206, car 0860 316199)

GOLDINER, Hon Mrs (Sigrid); yr da of Baron Wynne-Jones (Life Peer d 1982); *b* 1935; *m* 1962, Dr Marvin Goldiner, of Oakland, Cal, USA; *Style*— Hon Mrs Goldiner

GOLDING, Dr Anthony Mark Barrington; s of Dr Mark Golding (d 1954), of 29 Dawson Place, London W2, and Marian Rosalie, *née* Benjamin (d 1965); *b* 21 Aug 1928; *Educ* Marlborough, Cambridge Univ (MA, MB BChir), Middx Hosp Med Sch; *m* 29 Aug 1962, (Olwen) Valery, da of Reginald Francis Orlando Bridgeman, CMG, MVO (d 1968), of 105 Waxwell Lane, Pinner, Middx; 1 s (Richard b 1965), 3 da (Rosemary b 1963, Catherine b 1967, Charlotte b 1970); *Career* RAMC 1954-56 (Lt and Capt); jr specialist in ophthalmology Cambridge Mil Hosp; med offr DHSS 1968-72, princ asst sr med offr SE Met RHB 1972-74, dist community physician King's Health Dist (teaching) 1974-82; Camberwell Health Authy: dist med offr 1982-86, sr consIt in community med 1986-88, hon consIt 1988-; hon sr lectr: King's Coll Hosp Med Sch, King's Coll Sch of Med & Dentistry 1977-; ed Health and Hygiene 1988-; memb: Cncl RIPH & H 1987-, Section of Epidemiology and Community Med, RSM 1987- (pres 1990); tstee Ctee Against Drug Abuse; DO 1956, MFCM 1973, FFCM 1979, FRIPH & H 1983, MCOphth 1989, FFPHM 1989; contrib various pubns incl Public Health, The Lancet and British Medical Journal; *Recreations* walking the dogs; *Style*— Dr Anthony Golding; 12 Clifton Hill, London NW8 OQG (☎ 071 624 0504); Keepers, Byworth, nr Petworth, W Sussex

GOLDING, John; s of Peter John Golding, of Birmingham; *b* 9 March 1931; *Educ* Chester GS, London Univ, Keele Univ; *m* 1, 1958, Thelma, da of S G Gwillym, of Birmingham; 1 s; m 2, 1980, Llinos Lewis, *née* Edwards; *Career* political and Parly offr Post Office Engrg Union 1969-86; MP (Lab) Newcastle-under-Lyme 1969-86; PPS to Min State Technol 1970, oppn whip 1970-74, ld cmmr Treasy 1974, Parly under-sec Employment 1976-79; memb Labour NEC 1978-83 and chm Home Policy Ctee 1982-83; chm Select Ctee Employment 1979-82; made 11 hr 15 min speech in Commons against privatisation of Br Telecom 1983; gen sec Nat Communications Union 1986-; memb Gen Cncl TUC; govr Ruskin Coll; *Recreations* fly fishing, horseracing; *Style*— John Golding, Esq; c/o National Communications Union, Greystoke House, Brunswick Rd, Ealing, London W5

GOLDING, (Harold) John; s of Harold Samuel Golding (d 1990), and Dorothy Hamer (d 1991); *b* 10 Sept 1929; *Educ* Univ of Toronto (BA), Univ of London (MA, PhD); *Career* Courtauld Inst Univ of London 1959-81 (lectr, reader hist of art), sr tutor Painting Sch RCA 1981-86; temp appts: Power lectr Aust 1974, Slade prof of fine art Univ of Cambridge 1978-79; painter; one man exhibitions: Nishimura Gallery Tokyo 1982 and 1984, Coventry Gallery Sydney 1984, Juda Rowan Gallery London 1985, Mayor Rowan Gallery London 1988, Yale Centre for Br Art Conn 1989; gp shows: Museum of Modern Art Oxford 1971, British Painting '74 (Hayward Gallery) 1974, John Moores Exhibition (Liverpool) 1976 and 1978, British Painting 1952-77 (Royal Acad) 1977; works in pub collections incl: Tate Gallery, V & A, Museum of Modern Art NY, Nat Gallery of Aust, Fitzwilliam Museum Cambridge; exhibitions selected and organised: Léger and Purist Paris (Tate Gallery) 1970, Summer Show 2 (Serpentine Gallery) 1976, Picasso's Picassos (Hayward Gallery London) 1984, Braque Still Lifes and Interiors (Walker Gallery Liverpool and City Art Gallery Bristol 1990); pubns incl: Cubism 1907-1914 (1959, new edn 1988), Guillaume Apollinaire and the Art of the Twentieth Century (1963), Boccioni's Unique Forms of Continuity in Space (1972), Duchamp: The Bride stripped bare by her bachelors, even (1973), Ozenfant (1973), Picasso in Retrospect (ed with Roland Penrose, 1973), Matisse and Cubism (1978), Fauvism and the School Chatou (1980); *Style*— John Golding; 24 Ashchurch Park Villas, London W12 9SP (☎ 081 749 5221)

GOLDING, Llinos; MP (Lab) Newcastle-under-Lyme 1986-; da of Rt Hon Ness Edwards (d 1968, MP for Caerphilly 1939-68), and Elina Victoria (d 1988); *b* 21 March 1933; *Educ* Caerphilly Girls' GS, Cardiff Royal Infirmary Sch of Radiography; *m* 1, June 1957 (m dis 1971), John Roland Lewis; 1 s (Steven), 2 da (Caroline (Mrs Hopwood), Janet); m 2, 8 Aug 1980, John Golding *qv*; *Career* sec Newcastle Dist Trades Cncl 1976-, memb N Staffs DHA 1983-, W Midlands Whip 1987-; vice chm: PLP Ctee Home Affrs, PLP Parly Affrs, All Pty Parly Gp on Children; jt chm All Pty Parly Gp on the Homeless; match sec Lords and Commons Fly Fishing Club, memb BBC Advsy Cncl; memb: NUPE, Soc of Radiographers; *Style*— Mrs Llinos Golding, MP; House of Commons, London

GOLDING, Brig Dame (Cecilie) Monica; DBE (1958), RRC (1950, ARRC 1940); o da of Ben Johnson, and Clara, *née* Beames; *b* 6 Aug 1902; *Educ* Croydon Secdy Sch; *m* 1961, as his 2 wife, Brig the Rev Harry Golding, CBE (d 1969); *Career* Royal Surrey County Hosp Guildford 1922-25, Louise Margaret Hosp Aldershot and Queen Victoria's Inst of Dist Nursing; joined Army Nursing Servs 1925: India 1929-34, France 1939-40, ME 1940-43 and 1948-48; Southern Cmd 1943-44 and 1950-52, WO 1945-46, Eastern Cmd 1955-56, matron-in-chief and dir of Army Nursing Serv 1956-60, ret 1960; Col Cmdt Queen Alexandra's Royal Army Nursing Corps 1961-66; OStJ; *Recreations* motoring, nature study; *Style*— Brig Dame Monica Golding, DBE, RRC; 9 Sandford Court, 32 Belle Vue Rd, Southbourne, Bournemouth, Dorset BH6 3DR (☎ 0202 431608)

GOLDING, Dr Richard James Arthur; s of Arthur Bertram Golding, and Bridget Elizabeth, *née* Mahoney; *b* 13 April 1952; *Educ* Queen Elizabeth's Sch for Boys Barnet, Wadham Coll Oxford (BA, MA, DPhil); *Career* stockbroker 1976-; Simon and Coates 1976-81, ptnr Grieveson Grant and Co 1984-86 (joined 1981), Kleinwort Benson Ltd 1986-; dir: Kleinwort Benson Ltd, Kleinwort Benson Gilts; head of Structured Fin Gp Kleinwort Benson; chm Tax Ctee Gilt Edged Market Makers Assoc 1986-90; *Clubs* Utd Oxford and Cambridge Univ; *Style*— Dr Richard Golding; 20 Fenchurch St, London EC3P 3DB (☎ 071 623 8000, fax 071 623 4069)

GOLDING, Terence Edward; s of Sydney Richard Golding, and Elsie Golding; *b* 7 April 1932; *Educ* Harrow Co GS; *m* 1955, Sheila Jean, *née* Francis; 1 s, 1 da; *Career* chief exec Nat Exhibition Centre 1978, chm Exhibition Liaison Ctee 1979 and 1980; dir: Br Exhibitions Promotions Cncl 1981-83, Birmingham Convention and Visitor Bureau 1981-, Heart of England Tourist Bd 1984-, Sport Aid Promotions Ltd 1986-87, Nat Assoc of Exhibition Hall Owners 1988-, Exec Ctee Exhibition Indust Fedn 1988-, chief exec Int Convention Centre Birmingham 1989-; hon memb Cncl Birmingham Chamber of Indust and Commerce 1990-; *Style*— Terence Golding, Esq; Pinn Cottage, Pinner Hill, Pinner, Middx (☎ 081 866 2610, office 021 780 4141)

GOLDING, Terry; s of Gordon Eric Golding, of Berks, and Olive Lillian, *née* Gilbert (d 1972); *b* 23 May 1948; *Educ* Hounslow Coll, Park High, Bristol Coll of Commerce (LLB); *m* 8 March 1980, Penelope, da of Arthur Wilson (d 1975), of Gwent; 1 s (Nicholas b 1980), 1 da (Sarah-Jane b 1982), 2 step s (Jonathan b 1969, Simon b 1972); *Career* admitted slr 1975, Cartel Investmts 1978-; *Recreations* salmon and trout fishing; *Clubs* RAC; Phyllis Court; *Style*— Terry Golding, Esq; Well Place, Ipsden, Oxon OX10 6QZ (☎ 0491 680961); 10 Market Place, Henley on Thames, Oxon RG9 2AA (☎ 0491 573931/682053, fax 0491 682036)

GOLDING, William Gerald; CBE (1966); s of Alec A Golding, and Mildred A Golding; *b* 7 April 1932,Cornwall; *Educ* Marlborough GS, Brasenose Coll Oxford; *m* 1939, Ann, da of late E W Brookfield, of the Homestead, Bedford Place, Maidstone, Kent; 1 s, 1 da; *Career* served RN WWII; former actor, writer and prodr with various small theatre cos, teacher Bishop Wordsworth's Sch Salisbury until 1961, author; winner of: James Tail Black prize 1978, Booker prize 1980 (for Rites of Passage), Nobel prize for Literature 1983; CLitt 1984; FRSL 1955; kt 1988; *Books* Lord of the Flies (1954, filmed 1963), The Inheritors (1955), Free Fall (1959), The Spire (1964), The Pyramid (1967), Darkness Visible (1979), Rites of Passage (1980), A Moving Target (essays, 1982), The Paper Men (1984); *Recreations* Greek literature, riding, pianoforte; *Style*— Sir William Golding, CBE; c/o Faber & Faber, 3 Queen St, London WC1

GOLDINGAY, Rev Dr John Edgar; s of Edgar Charles Goldingay (d 1974), and Ada Irene, *née* Horton; *b* 20 June 1942; *Educ* King Edward's Sch Birmingham, Keble Coll Oxford (BA), Univ of Nottingham (PhD); *m* 28 Aug 1967, Ann Elizabeth, da of Arthur Wilson (d 1971); 2 s (Steven b 1968, Mark b 1971); *Career* ordained: deacon 1966, priest 1967; asst curate Christ Church Finchley 1966-69, princ St John's Coll Nottingham 1988- (lectr 1970-88); *Books* Approaches to Old Testament Interpretation (1981), Theological Diversity and the Authority of the Old Testament (1987), Daniel (1989); *Recreations* The Old Testament, Israel, France, rock music; *Clubs* Rock City (Nottingham); *Style*— The Rev Dr John Goldingay; 7 Peache Way, Bramcote Nottingham NG9 3DX (☎ 0602 224046); St John's College, Bramcote Nottingham NG9 3DS (☎ 0602 251114)

GOLDKORN, Geoffrey; s of David Goldkorn, and Judith, *née* Yudt; *b* 14 Jan 1945; *Educ* City of London, Jesus Coll Cambridge (MA); *m* 16 June 1978, Lindy, da of Leon Berman, of Flat 16a, 15 Grosvenor Sq, London; 1 s (Benjamin b 1980), 1 da (Gabriella b 1983); *Career* admitted slr 1970; sr ptnr Goldkorn Davies Mathias; dep district judge; memb Ctee The Br Technion Soc, tstee The Kennedy Leigh Charitable Tst; assoc memb Chartered Inst of Arbitrators; *Recreations* cycling, tennis, opera, philosophy; *Style*— Geoffrey Goldkorn, Esq; 4 Sheldon Ave, London N6 4JT (☎ 081 348 1028); 6 Coptic St, London WC1A 1NH (☎ 071 631 1811, fax 071 631 0431)

GOLDMAN, Ian John; s of Morris Lewis Goldman, of Liverpool, and Tina, *née* Kleinman; *b* 28 Jan 1948; *Educ* Liverpool Coll, LSE (LLB); *m* 9 Sept 1970, Diane Elizabeth, da of William Shipton (d 1984), of London; 3 da (Vikki b 1972, Katie b 1975, Charlotte b 1979); *Career* admitted slr 1971, princ Louis Godlove & Co 1971; dir: Commercial & Financial Investment Ltd 1972-, Goldman Investment Ltd 1972-90; currently sr ptnr Godlove Saffman; memb: Leeds Family Practitioner Ctee 1985-90, Leeds East Health Authy 1988-90, Leeds Law Soc Ctee 1988-, Nat Exec Ctee Jewish Nat Fund of GB 1981-87 (chm 1981-84), Leeds Family Health Services Authy 1990- (currently vice chm); memb Law Soc 1971-; *Clubs* The Leeds; *Style*— Ian Goldman, Esq; Russell House, 15 St Pauls St, Leeds, W Yorks LS1 2LZ (☎ 0532 433861, fax 0532 420714)

GOLDMAN, Prof John Michael; s of Dr Carl Heinz Goldman; *b* 30 Nov 1938; *Educ* Westminster, Magdalen Coll Oxford (DM); *Career* prof of leukaemia biology Royal Postgrad Med Sch, consIt physician and haematologist Hammersmith Hosp; med dir Anthony Nolan Res Centre, dir Leukaemia Res Fund Centre for Adult Leukaemia Hammersmith Hosp, ed Bone Marrow Transplantation; former pres Int Soc for Experimental Haematology, pres Euro Bone Marrow Transplant Gp; FRCP, FRCPath; *Books* Leukemia (1983); *Recreations* skiing, riding; *Style*— Prof John Goldman; Royal Postgraduate Medical School, Ducane Rd, London W12 0NN

GOLDMAN, Dr Kenneth Peter; s of Frank Goldman (d 1985), and Lily, *née* Cope; *b* 18 Jan 1928; *Educ* St Paul's, Peterhouse Cambridge (MA, MB BChir, MD); *m* 8 April 1960, Lorna Vera, da of James Stone (d 1983); 2 s (Robert James b 29 Nov 1963, Robert Alexander b 29 Nov 1968), 1 da (Helen Georgina b 15 Oct 1965); *Career* RAF 1947-49; consIt physician Dartford and Gravesham Health Authy 1969-, ed Tubercle 1978-90; memb: Br Thoracic Soc, BMA; FRCP; *Books* The Chest in Health and Disease (1970); *Recreations* gardening, theatre, snooker; *Style*— Dr Kenneth Goldman; 8 Coates Hill Rd, Bickley, Kent (☎ 081 467 0257); West Hill Hospital, Dartford, Kent

GOLDMAN, Dr Myer; s of Isaac Goldman (d 1956), of Liverpool, and Margaret, *née* Abrahams (d 1986); *b* 20 July 1928; *Educ* Liverpool Collegiate Sch, Univ of Liverpool (MB ChB, DMRD); *m* 8 June 1955, Elaine, da of Maxwell Julius Maxwell (d 1976), of Manchester; 1 s (Jonathan b 1968), 2 da (Nicola b 1963, Amanda b 1959); *Career* Actg Sqdn Ldr RAF Med Branch 1952-55; house physician Sefton Gen Hosp 1951-52, house surgn Liverpool Royal Infirmary 1952, sr house offr Royal Southern Hosp 1955-56, sr registrar in radiology (former registrar) Walton Hosp Liverpool 1957-66, consIt radiologist Mersey RHA (Fazakerley and Walton Hosps) 1966-, currently pt/t clinical lectr Dept of Radiodiagnosis Univ of Liverpool; pres Merseyside Jewish Rep Cncl; former chm: Mersey ConsIts and Specialists Ctee (memb Central Cmmn), Govrs King David Primary Sch Liverpool; past pres: Liverpool BMA, Liverpool Jewish Med Soc; fell BMA 1984, FRCR 1986; *Books* A Guide to the X-Ray Department (2 edn, 1986), A Radiographic Index (jtly, 8 edn, 1987); *Recreations* writing, travels; *Style*— Dr Myer Goldman; 36 Druids Cross Gardens, Liverpool, Merseyside L18 3ED (☎ 051 428 3392); X-Ray Department, Fazakerley Hospital, Liverpool L9 7AL (☎ 051 529 3915/3304)

GOLDMAN, Sir Samuel; KCB (1969, CB 1964); yst s of Philip Goldman (d 1958), and Sarah Goldman; *b* 10 March 1912; *Educ* Raine's Sch, LSE; *m* 1, 1933, Pearl Marre (d 1941); 1 s (Antony b 1940); m 2, 1943, Patricia Rosemary, *née* Hodges (d 1990); *Career* Bank of England 1940-47, Civil Serv 1947; Treasy: chief statistician 1948, asst sec 1952, under-sec 1960-62, third sec 1962-68, second perm sec 1968-72; exec dir Orion Bank 1972-74 (md 1974-76); chm: Henry Ansbacher Ltd and Henry Ansbacher Hldgs 1976-82, Covent Gdn Mktg Authy 1976-81; hon fell LSE; *Style*— Sir Samuel Goldman, KCB; White Gate, Church Lane, Haslemere, Surrey (☎ 0428 644889)

GOLDREIN, Iain Saville; s of Neville Clive Goldrein, of Torreno, St Andrew's Rd, Crosby, Liverpool, and Sonia Hannah Jane, *née* Sumner; *b* 10 Aug 1952; *Educ* Merchant Taylors', Pembroke Coll Cambridge; *m* 18 May 1980, Margaret Ruth, da of Josef De Haas, of 33 Chessington Court, Charter Way, Finchley, London; 1 s (Alastair Philip b 1 Oct 1982), 1 da (Alexandra Ann b 22 Feb 1985); *Career* called to the Bar Inner Temple 1975; in practice London and Northern circuit; visiting prof law (chair Civil Procedure) Nottingham Poly; memb: Middle Temple, Br Insur Law Assoc, Union Internationale des Advocats, Br Acad of Experts (BAE Register of Mediators), Int Litigation Forum; ACIArb; *Books* Personal Injury Litigation, Practice and Precedents (with Margaret R De Haas, 1985), Ship Sale and Purchase, Law and Technique (1985), Commercial Litigation, Pre-Emptive Remedies (with K H P Wilkinson, 1987), Butterworths' Personal Injury Litigation Service (with Margaret R De Haas), Pleadings: Principles and Practice (with Sir Jack Jacob, 1990), Bullen and Leake and

Jacob's Precedents of Pleadings (gen ed edn 13, 1990); *Recreations* law, new ideas, the family, riding; *Clubs* Athenaeum (Liverpool); *Style—* Iain Goldrein, Esq; 1 Harcourt Buildings, Temple, London EC4Y 9DA (☎ 071 353 0375, fax : 071 583 5816); 4 Linden Ave, Crosby, Liverpool L23 8UL (☎ 051 924 2610); 5th Floor The Corn Exchange, Fenwick St, Liverpool L2 7QS (☎ 051 227 5009, fax : 051 236 1120, car 0836 583 257); Flat 140, Clifford's Inn, Fetter Lane, London EC4

GOLDREIN, Neville Clive; s of Saville Goldrein (d 1946), of Hull, and Nina, *née* Aronoff (d 1977); *Educ* Hymers Coll Hull, Pembroke Coll Cambridge (MA); *m* 30 Oct 1949, Sonia Hannah Jane, da of Myer Sumner (d 1966), of Newcastle upon Tyne, and Rebecca Sumner; 1 s (Iain Saville b 1952), 1 da (Nadine (Mrs Simon Caplan) b 1954); *Career* served E Yorks Regt as Capt E Africa; slr Supreme Ct; memb: Crosby Borough Cncl 1957-71 (Mayor 1966-67, Dep Mayor 1967-68), Lancs CC 1965-74, NW Planning Cncl 1966-72, Cncl of Univ of Liverpool 1973-81, Merseyside CC 1973-86 (dep ldr Cons Gp 1975-77); ldr: Merseyside CC 1980-81 (vice-chm 1977-80), Cons Gp 1981-86; dir Merseyside Econ Devpt Co Ltd 1980-87, chm Crosby Constituency Cons Assoc 1986-89, memb Cncl Merseyside C of C; govr Merchant Taylors' Schs 1965-74, vice pres Crosby Mencap; chm: South Sefton St John Ambulance 1965-87, NW Cons Social Affrs Forum; *Recreations* videography, music, grandchildren; *Clubs* Athenaeum (Liverpool); *Style—* Neville C Goldrein, Esq; Torreno, St Andrew's Rd, Blundellsands, Merseyside L23 7UR (☎ 051 924 2065); Peel House, 5-7 Harrington St, Liverpool L2 9XP (☎ 051 255 0600, fax 051 255 0463)

GOLDRING, John Bernard; QC (1987); s of Joseph Goldring (d 1980), and Marianne Goldring; *b* 9 Nov 1944; *Educ* Wyggeston GS Leicester, Exeter Univ; *m* 2 Jan 1970, Wendy Margaret Lancaster, da of Ralph Lancaster Bennett (d 1980); 2 s (Jeremy b 1971, Rupert b 1974); *Career* called to Bar 1969, standing counsel to Inland Revenue 1985, rec Midland and Oxford circuit; *Recreations* gardening, skiing; *Style—* John Goldring, Esq, QC; 2 Crown Office Row, Temple, London EC4 (☎ 071 353 1365)

GOLDRING, Timothy John; s of Stephen Spencer Goldring (d 1979), and late Joan Francis Goldring; *b* 22 Jan 1930; *Educ* Christ's Hosp Horsham; *m* 6 Aug 1960, Penelope Mary (Penny), da of Bruin Milner-White (d 1976); 3 s (Colin b 18 May 1961, Simon b 8 Nov 1962, Dougal b 10 May 1966), 1 da (Helen b 18 April 1970); *Career* Sgt RAF 1948-49; prep sch master 1947-55, sales and sales mgmnt Kenwood Manufacturing Ltd 1955-63, sales mgmnt Simplex Electric Co (Tube Investments) 1963-66, mktg dir Bath Cabinet Makers & Arkana Ltd 1967-73, Times Furnishing (part of GUS) 1973-, dir owner Goldring & Assocs (sales and mktg conslts) 1977-84, mktg dir Ercol Furniture Ltd 1984-; memb Round Table 1963-70; Liveryman Worshipful Co of Furnituremakers 1974; MBIM 1970-85, MIMC 1986, MCIM 1959; *Recreations* travel, gardening; *Clubs* Harlequin Football, Ashridge Golf; *Style—* Timothy Goldring, Esq; Ercol Furniture Ltd, London Rd, High Wycombe, Bucks HP13 7AE (☎ 0494 521261, fax 0494 462 467, telex 83616)

GOLDS, Anthony Arthur; CMG (1971), LVO (1961); s of Arthur Oswald Golds (d 1934), of Macclesfield, and Florence, *née* Massey (d 1943); *b* 31 Oct 1919; *Educ* The King's Sch Macclesfield, New Coll Oxford (MA); *m* 9 Oct 1944, Suzanne MacDonald, da of Dr John Miller Young, MC (d 1947), of Glasgow; 1 s (Richard b 1947), 1 da (Laura (Mrs Russell) b 1952); *Career* aWII RAC 1939-46; Cwlth Office: joined 1948, first sec Calcutta and Delhi 1951-59 (Ankara 1957-59, Karachi 1959-61), cnsllr FCO 1962-65, ambass Cameroon Gabon and Equatorial Guinea 1970-72, high cmmr Bangladesh 1972-74; sr civilian instr RCDS 1975-76, Br dir Int C of C 1977-83; *Recreations* golf, literature; *Clubs* Dulwich and Sydenham Hill Golf; *Style—* Anthony Golds, Esq, CMG, LVO; 4 Oakfield Gardens, London SE19 1HF (☎ 081 670 7621)

GOLDSACK, Alan Raymond; QC (1990); s of Raymond Frederick Goldsack, MBE (d 1985), of Hastings, and Mildred Agnes, *née* Jones; *b* 13 June 1947; *Educ* Hastings GS, Univ of Leicester (LLB); *m* 21 Aug 1971, Christine Marion, da of Frank Leslie Clarke, MBE; 3 s (Ian b 1974, Richard b 1977, Stephen b 1980), 1 da (Tessa b 1975); *Career* called to the Bar Gray's Inn 1970; rec 1988; *Recreations* gardening, walking; *Style—* Alan Goldsack, Esq, QC; The Old Rectory, Braithwell, Rotherham (☎ 0709 812 167); 12 Paradise Sq, Sheffield (☎ 0742 738 951)

GOLDSACK, John Redman; MBE (1971); s of Bernard Frank Goldsack (d 1975), and Dorothy Owen (d 1984); *b* 15 Aug 1932; *Educ* Sutton Co GS, Wye College Univ of London (BSc), Queens' Coll Cambridge (Dip Agric), Imperial Coll of Tropical Agriculture Trinidad (DTA); *m* 11 Aug 1962, Madeleine Amelia Rowena, da of Robert Stanley Kibbler (d 1968); 2 s (Mark b 1964, Robert b 1966), 1 da (Margaret b 1968); *Career* agric offr HMOCS Kenya 1956-63, head Land Devpt Div Miny of Agric Kenya 1963-70, asst agric advsr ODA London 1970-74; sr agric advsr: BDDSA Malawi 1974-78, MEDD Jordan 1979-81, EADD Kenya 1981-83, ODA London 1983-85; dep chief natural resources advsr and princ agric advsr ODA London 1986-88, UK permanent rep to UNFAO Rome 1988-; *Recreations* golf, cricket, natural history; *Clubs* MCC, Farmers; *Style—* John R Goldsack, Esq, MBE; British Embassy, Via XX Settembre 80/9, 00187 Rome, Italy

GOLDSACK, Prof Stephen James; s of Rev Eustace Redman Goldsack (d 1975), and Jean Stirling Smith (d 1958); *b* 6 Aug 1926; *Educ* Barnard Castle Sch, Univ of Durham (BSc), Univ of Manchester (PhD); *m* 27 May 1953, Ginette, *née* Steinert, da of Edouard Steinert (d 1976); 2 s (Patrick b 1957, Christopher b 1961), 1 da (Anne b 1954); *Career* asst lectr Univ of Manchester 1949-53, res asst Univ of California Berkeley 1954, lectr Univ of Birmingham 1955-60, reader in Physics Imperial Coll of Sci Technol and Med 1960-72, prof of computing sci Imperial Coll of Sci Technol and Med London 1972- (reader in physics 1960-72); FInstP, FBCS, FIEE, CEng, CPhys; *Books* Programming Embedded Computer Systems in Ada (with V A Downes 1982), Ada for Specifications: Possibilities and Limitations (1985); *Style—* Prof Stephen Goldsack; 59 Rydens Ave, Walton on Thames, Surrey KT12 3JE (☎ 0932 220 418); Imperial Coll of Science, Technology and Medicine, Department of Computing, London SW7 2AZ (☎ 071 589 5111)

GOLDSCHEIDER, Gabriele Maria (Gaby); da of Ludwig Goldscheider (d 1973), of 33 Belsize Court, London NW3, and Blanka, *née* Geiringer (d 1985); *b* 7 March 1929; *Educ* Convent of Our Lady of Sion Acton Burnell Salop, Blunt House Oxted, Ruskin Sch of Art Oxford; *Career* writer and publisher, specialist bookseller of books by Sir Arthur Conan Doyle and books about Sherlock Holmes, fndr Sherlock Holmes Book Club of GB; articles in Antiquarian Books Monthly Review; memb Antiquarian Booksellers Assoc 1978-; *Books* Dolls (1977), Bibliography of Sir Arthur Conan Coyle (1977); *Recreations* book collecting, toy collecting, reading; *Clubs* Private Libraries Assoc, Windsor Literary Soc; *Style—* Miss Gaby Goldscheider; Deep Dene, Baring Rd, Cowes, IOW (☎ 0983 293598); 32 Hornton St, London W8 (☎ 071 937 7311); The Charles Dickens Bookshop, 65 High St, Cowes, IOW

GOLDSMID, John Michael Francis; s of Cyril Julian Goldsmid (d 1971), and Anna Emily, *née* McGillycuddy (d 1969); *b* 28 June 1922; *Educ* Eton, Univ of Oxford (BA); *m* 24 July 1954, Virginia Marguerite, da of Thomas Agnew Ansdell (d 1966); 1 s (Nicholas Julian b 1958), 1 da (Miranda (Mrs Sutton) b 1955); *Career* WWII Capt 9 Queens Royal Lancers served N Africa and Italy; farmer; *Style—* J M F Goldsmid, Esq; Copyhold Farm, Goring Heath, Oxon RG8 7RT (☎ 0734 842291)

GOLDSMITH, Alexander Kinglake (Alick); s of Maj-Gen Robert Frederick Goldsmith, CB, CBE, of Winchester, and Brenda, *née* Bartlett (d 1983); *b* 16 Jan 1938; *Educ* Sherborne, Trinity Coll Oxford (minor scholar, MA); *m* 9 Jan 1971, Deirdre Maude Adelaide, da of Harold Stafford, of Wadhurst; 1 s (Crispin Kinglake b 1976), 1 da (Lucinda Jane b 1973); *Career* Nat Serv 2 Lt Queen's Own Nigeria Regt 1957-58; HM Dip Serv 1961-90: New Delhi 1963-66, FCO 1967-70, first sec (Info) Wellington 1971-74, asst head SE Asian Dept FCO 1975-77, head of chancery Br Embassy E Berlin 1978-80, asst head Perm Sec's Dept FCO 1980-82, head Cwlth Coordination Dept FCO 1982-83, dep sec Security Hong Kong Govt 1984-85, consul-general Hamburg 1986-90; dep dir Export Group for the Constructional Industries 1990-; *Recreations* swimming, walking, family; *Clubs* RAC; *Style—* Alick Goldsmith, Esq; The Export Group for the Constructional Industries, Kingsbury House, 15-17 King St, St James's, London SW1Y 6QU (☎ 071 930 5377)

GOLDSMITH, Lady Annabel; *née* Vane-Tempest-Stewart; da of 8 Marquess of Londonderry (d 1955), and Romaine, *née* Combe (d 1951); *b* 11 June 1934; *Educ* Southover Manor Lewes; *m* 1, 10 March 1954 (m dis 1975), Marcus Oswald Hornby Lecky Birley, s of Sir Oswald Hornby Lecky Birley, MC (d 1952); 2 s (Rupert b 1955, Robin b 1958), 1 da (Mrs Julian Colchester b 1961); m 2, 1978, Sir James Michael Goldsmith, *qv*; 2 s (Zacharias b 1975, Benjamin b 1980), 1 da (Jemima Marcelle b 1974); *Style—* Lady Annabel Goldsmith; Ormeley Lodge, Ham Common, Surrey TW10 5HB (☎ 081 940 5677/8)

GOLDSMITH, Carl Stanley; s of Stanley Thomas Goldsmith (d 1956), and Ida, *née* Rawlinson (d 1965); *b* 14 Oct 1936; *Educ* King James GS, UCL (LLB); *m* 1958, Margaret Violetta, da of Stanley Olley (d 1966); 3 da (Delia, Sallie, Belinda); *Career* slr; ptnr Hill Dickinson & Co; dir: Devpt Capital Gp Ltd, Motofax Ltd, Anglo American Agric plc, Barbury Properties Ltd, Eletson Maritime Ltd, Trenchdean Ltd, W S Moody Hldgs plc; FInst D; *Clubs* MCC, XL; *Style—* Carl Goldsmith, Esq; 59 Grange Gdns, Pinner, Middx (☎ 081 866 2909); Irongate House, Dukes Place, London EC3

GOLDSMITH, Edward René David; s of Frank Benedict Hayum Goldsmith, OBE, TD (d 1967; MP (C) Stowmarket 1910-18), by his w Marcelle, *née* Mouiller (d 1985); er bro of Sir James Goldsmith, *qv*; *b* 8 Nov 1928; *Educ* Millfield, Magdalen Coll Oxford (MA); *m* 1, 1953, Gillian Marion Pretty; 1 s (Alexander), 2 da (Dido, Clio); m 2, 1981, Katherine Victoria, da of John Anthony James, CMG, of 136 Vipond Rd, Whanga Paraoa, Auckland, NZ; 1 s (Benedict); *Career* ed The Ecologist 1970-; author, ed; *Books* Can Britain Survive? (Tom Stacy 1971), A Blueprint for survival (co-ed 1972), The Stable Society (1977), The Social and Environmental Effects of Large Dams Vol I (with Nicholas Haldyard 1984); *Clubs* Travellers' (Paris); *Style—* Edward Goldsmith, Esq; Whitehay, Withiel, Bodmin, Cornwall (☎ 0208 831237); 254 Fanbours St Honoré, Paris; The Ecologist, Whitehay, Withiel, Bodmin, Cornwall

GOLDSMITH, Sir James Michael; s of Frank Benedict Hayum Goldsmith, OBE, TD (d 1967), and Marcelle, *née* Mouiller; yr bro of Edward Goldsmith, *qv*; *b* 26 Feb 1933; *Educ* Eton; *m* 1, 7 Jan 1954, Maria Isabel (d 15 May 1954), da of Don Antenor Patiño y Rodriguez (d 1982), sometime Bolivian ambass in London, and Maria Cristina, 3 Duchess of Durcal (*see* Vol I Burkes Royal Families of the World); 1 da (Isabel); m 2, Ginette Lery; 1 s, 1 da; m 3, 1978, as her 2 husband, Lady Annabel Vane Tempest Stewart (*see* Goldsmith, Lady Annabel); 2 s, 1 da; 2 step s, 1 step da; *Career* fndr: Generale Occidentale SA (France), Cavenham Ltd (UK); fndr and chm Gen Oriental (Hong Kong); *Books* Counterculture (1985, vol II 1988, vol III 1990), Pour la Revolution Permanente dans la Diversite (1986); *Clubs* Traveller's (Paris); *Style—* Sir James Goldsmith; c/o Swan House, Madeira Walk, Windsor, Berks SL4 1EU (☎ 0753 830707)

GOLDSMITH, John Stuart; CB (1984); o s of R W Goldsmith and S E Goldsmith; *b* 2 Nov 1924; *Educ* Whitgift Middle Sch, St Catharine's Coll Cambridge; *m* 1948, Brenda Goldsmith; 2 s, 1 da; *Career* Royal Signals 1943-47; WO 1948, joined MOD 1964, dir gen Def Accounts MOD 1980-84; *Style—* John Goldsmith, Esq, CB; Cobthorne House, Church Lane, Rode, Somerset (☎ 0373 830681)

GOLDSMITH, Peter Henry; QC (1987); s of Sydney Elland Goldsmith, and Myra, *née* Nurick; *b* 5 Jan 1950; *Educ* Quarry Bank HS Liverpool, Gonville and Caius Coll Cambridge (MA), UCL (LLM); *m* Joy; 3 s (James b 1978, Jonathan b 1983, Benjamin b 1985), 1 da (Charlotte b 1981); *Career* called to the Bar Gray's Inn 1972, SE circuit, jr counsel to the Crown Common Law 1985-87; *Style—* Peter Goldsmith, Esq, QC; Fountain Court, Temple, London EC4Y 9DH (☎ 071 583 3335)

GOLDSMITH, Stuart Andrew; s of Kenneth Ernest Goldsmith (d 1968), of Bournemouth, and Frances Ruby, *née* Wratten; *b* 1 April 1945; *Educ* Ashford GS, Univ of Bristol (BA); *m* 2 s, 2 da; *Career* dep chm and chief exec Fredericks Place Holdings plc 1985-89; non-exec dir: CCL Fin Gp plc 1985-, Stanley Gibbons Holdings plc 1986-87, Hallwood Group Inc 1987-; dir: Britannia Arrow Holdings plc, subsidiaries and managed investmt cos 1978-84 (investment dir 1978-81, md, fund mgmnt div 1981-84); chm and chief exec Planfactor Ltd trading as Ketton Investments 1989-; *Recreations* wine, opera, philately, trees; *Style—* Stuart Goldsmith, Esq; Winchester House, 77 London Wall, London EC2N 1DE (☎ 071 256 9706, fax 071 256 6424)

GOLDSMITH, Vivien; *Educ* Univ of Essex; *m* 1981, Neil Adam Collins; 1 da (Alice Laura b 1982); *Career* journalist; Colchester Express, Chelsea News, General Practitioner, Evening Standard 1977-82; personal fin ed: The Times 1988-89, The Independent on Sunday 1990; *Style—* Ms Vivien Goldsmith; Personal Finance Editor, The Independent on Sunday, 40 City Rd, London EC1Y 2DB (☎ 071 415 1397, fax 071 415 1333)

GOLDSMITH, Walter Kenneth; s of Lionel Goldsmith (d 1981), and Phoebe Goldsmith; *b* 19 Jan 1938; *Educ* Merchant Taylors'; *m* 1961, Rosemary Adele, da of Joseph Salter (d 1970); 2 s, 2 da; *Career* mangr Mann Judd & Co 1964; Black & Decker Ltd 1966-: dir of investmt, fin and admin Europe 1967, gen mangr 1970, md 1974, chief exec and Euro dir 1975 (Black & Decker USA 1976-79); corporate vice pres and pres Pacific Int Operation; chm: Korn Ferry Int Ltd 1984-86 (chief exec 1984-85), Leisure Devpt Ltd 1984-85, Ansoll Estates Ltd 1990-; dir: Bank Leumi (UK) Ltd 1984-, Bestobell plc 1980-85, The Lesser Gp 1983-85, BUPA Med Centre 1980-84, Pubns Ltd 1983-84, Trusthouse Forte Inc 1985-87, The Winning Streak Ltd 1985-, Reginald Watts Assocs Ltd 1987-, Spong plc 1987-89, Isys Ltd (dep chm 1987-), Pearson Paul Haworth Nolan 1989-; gp planning and marketing dir Trusthouse Forte plc 1985-87; memb: cncl Br Exec Service Overseas 1979-84, Eng Tourist Bd 1982-84, Br Tourist Authy 1984-86, BOTB for Israel 1984- (chm 1987-); tstee Israel Diaspora Tst 1982-, chm of tstees Stress Fndn 1984-89, dir gen IOD 1979-84, pres Inst of Word Processing 1983-, cncl memb Co-op Ireland 1985, treas Leo Baeck Coll 1987-, chm Food Frm Britain 1987-90, Free Enterprise Award Aims for Indust 1984; Liveryman Worshipful Co of CAs in England and Wales 1985; FCA; *Publications* The Winning Streak (with D Clutterbuck, 1984), The Winning Streak Workout Book (1985), The New Elite (with Berry Ritchie, 1987); *Recreations* music, boating, painting, property; *Clubs* Carlton; *Style—* Walter Goldsmith, Esq; c/o Isys Ltd, Hyde House, The Hyde, London NW9 9YP (☎ 081 200 8181)

GOLDSPINK, Prof Geoffrey; s of James Albert Goldspink, of 28 Dornoch Drive, James Reckitt Ave, Hull, Humberside, and Muriel, *née* Gee; *b* 2 April 1939; *Educ* Univ of Hull (BSc), Trinity Coll, Univ of Dublin (PhD, ScD); *m* 31 Dec 1960, Barbara, da of Frederick Staniforth (d 1966); 3 s (Mark Richard b 6 Jan 1962, Paul Harvey b 28 April 1964, Andrew Jeffrey b 27 Jan 1966); *Career* prof and head of zoology Univ of Hull, visiting prof Univ of Nairobi, Agassiz visiting prof Harvard Univ, prof of anatomy and cell biology Tufts New England Med Centre Boston USA; Univ of London: prof and dir of molecular and cellular biol RVC London, fndr chair of veterinary molecular and cellular biol; scientific advsr to Int Social and Moral Issues Cncl of the Salvation Army; FRSC; *Books* Growth and Differentiation of Cell in Vertebrate Tissues, Mechanics and Energetics of Animal Locomotion; *Recreations* restoration of houses of historical interest, music; *Style*— Prof Geoffrey Goldspink; 6 Marshalls Way, Wheathampstead, Herts AL4 8HY (☎ 05827 62403); Halsham House, Halsham, Humberside HU12 0DE; The Royal Veterinary College, University of London, Royal College St, London NW1 0TU (☎ 071 387 2898, fax 071 388 2342)

GOLDSPINK, Robert Andrew; s of Canon R W Goldspink, of Lowestoft, Suffolk, and Kathleen Edith, *née* Betts; *b* 8 Aug 1949; *Educ* Eltham Coll, Fitzwilliam Coll Cambridge; *m* 1 Sept 1973, Margo Diane, da of Roy Graham Dunlop, MBE (d 1989), of Cambridge; 1 s (James Elliot b 1985); *Career* articled clerk Wild Hewitson & Shaw Cambridge 1973-75, surpervisor in constitutional legal studies Fitzwilliam and Christs' Colls Cambridge 1973-75; slr: Freshfields 1975-80, Denton Hall Burgin & Warrens 1980; ptnr Denton Hall Burgin & Warrens 1981-; lectr on legal subjects 1975-; memb Cncl Int Litigation Practioners' Forum; tstee Care For St Anne's Limehouse; memb: Law Soc, London Slr's Litigation Assoc, Int Bar Assoc; *Recreations* water sports, music; *Style*— Robert Goldspink, Esq; The Old Seaman's Chapel, Nelson's Wharf, 2-4 Newell St, London E14 7HR (☎ 071 515 2545); Denton Hall Burgin & Warrens, Five Chancery Lane, London EC4A 1BU (☎ 071 242 1212, fax 071 404 0087, telex 262738/263567 BURGIN G)

GOLDSTAUB, Thomas Charles; s of Werner Fritz Goldstaub, and Beate Charlotte, *née* Muller; *b* 2 Sept 1953; *Educ* Forest Sch; *m* 4 June 1985, Jane Hilary Elizabeth, da of Gordon Heslop Procter; 1 s (Rollo Alexander b 16 April 1989), 1 da (Tabitha Sophie b 11 Dec 1985); *Career* md Fred & Warner Ltd 1983-86 (sales and mktg dir 1979-82), special projects dir Garrard & Co 1987-88, mktg dir Mappin & Webb 1989-90; Freeman City of London 1986, Liveryman Worshipful Co of Upholders 1986; *Books* What Do You Call A Kid (1985); *Recreations* sailing, skiing, classic cars; *Clubs* Royal London Yacht, Royal Motor Yacht; *Style*— Thomas Goldstaub, Esq; 2 Hannington Rd, London SW4 0NA (☎ 071 622 9634)

GOLDSTEIN, John Arthur; *b* 14 July 1937; *Educ* Kilburn GS, Coll of Law; *m* Daniele, da of Col and Mme G Ury of Paris; 1 s (decd), 1 da; *Career* admitted slr 1959; articled Sidney L Samson & Nyman 1954-59 (asst slr 1959-60); ptnr Titmuss Sainer & Webb 1960; City of London Slrs' Co; *Recreations* keen sportsman, law soc cricket, Francophile, opera, gardening, cooking; *Clubs* Wig and Pen; *Style*— John Goldstein, Esq; Titmuss Sainer & Webb, 2 Serjeants' Inn, London EC4Y 1LT (☎ 071 583 5353, fax 071 353 3683)

GOLDSTEIN, Dr Michael; s of Jacob Goldstein (d 1945), of London, and Sarah, *née* Goldberg (now Mrs Hyman); *b* 1 May 1939; *Educ* Hackney Downs GS London, Northern Poly (BSc, PhD, DSc); *m* 5 May 1962, Janet Sandra, da of Henry Arthur Skevington (d 1979), of London; 1 s (Richard b 1968); *Career* lectr (later sr lectr and princ lectr) Poly of North London (formerly Northern Poly) 1963-73; Sheffield Poly: head Dept of Chemistry 1974-83, dean of the Faculty of Science 1979-83; dir Coventry Poly 1987- (dep dir 1983-87); author of several review chapters in books 1966-77; chm Chemistry Bd CNAA 1978-84, involved with local regnl and nat sections of Royal Soc of Chemistry and with W Midlands Regnl Advsy Cncl for Further Educn; CChem, MRSC 1967, FRSC 1973; *Recreations* jogging, DIY, Coventry City FC; *Style*— Dr Michael Goldstein; Coventry Poly, Priory St, Coventry CV1 5FB (☎ 0203 838212, fax 0203 258597, telex 931210228 CP G)

GOLDSTEIN, Ronald Sidney; *b* 6 Jan 1937; *Career* fndr jt chm and md Superdrug (taken over Kingfisher plc 1987), non-exec dir Kingfisher plc 1990-; dir 1990-: Burginhall 430 Limited, Memo Stationery Superstores Limited, Volume One Bookshops Limited, Volume One Holdings Limited; also currently dir: Solo Properties Limited, Tangier Wood Properties Limited, Heath Drive Properties Limited; *Style*— Ronald Goldstein, Esq; Kingfisher plc, North West House, 119 Marylebone Rd, London NW1 5PX (☎ 071 724 7749, fax 071 724 1160, telex 267007)

GOLDSTEIN-JACKSON, Kevin Grierson; JP (Poole 1990); s of Harold Grierson Jackson, and Winifred Miriam Emily, *née* Fellows; *b* 2 Nov 1946; *Educ* Univ of Reading (BA), Univ of Southampton (MPhil); *m* 6 Sept 1975, Jenny Mei Leng, da of Ufong Ng, of Malaysia; 2 da (Sing Yu b 1981, Kimberley b 1984); *Career* Staff Rels Dept London Tport 1966, Scottish Widows Pension and Life Assur Soc 1967, programme organizer Southern TV 1970-73, asst prodr HK - TVB Hong Kong 1973, freelance writer and TV prodr 1973-75, fndr and dir Thames Valley Radio 1974-77, head film Dhofar Region TV Serv Sultanate of Oman 1975-76, asst to Head of Drama Anglia TV 1977-81; TV SW: fndr, controller and dir of programmes 1981-85, jt md 1981-82, chief exec 1982-85; dir ind TV pubns 1981-85, contrib Financial Times 1986-, dir private cos; govr Lilliput First Sch Poole; FRSA 1978, FBIM 1982, FInstD 1982, FFA 1988, FRGS 1989; *Books* incl: The Right Joke for the Right Occasion (1973), Encyclopaedia of Ridiculous Facts (1975), Experiments with Everyday Objects (1976), Dictionary of Essential Quotations (1983), Share Millions (1989); *Recreations* writing, tv, films, travel, music, walking; *Style*— Kevin Goldstein-Jackson, Esq, JP; c/o Alcazar, 18 Martello Rd, Branksome Park, Poole, Dorset BH13 7DH

GOLDSTONE, David Israel; CBE (1971), JP (Manchester 1958-), DL (1978); s of Philip Goldstone, and Bessie Goldstone; *b* 1908,Aug; *m* 1931, Belle, da of L A Franks; *Career* C of C and Indust: dir 1958-, vice pres 1968-70, pres 1970-72, emeritus dir of Indust 1978-; fndr and chm Sterling McGregor Ltd Group of Cos, fndr memb Bd NW Telecommunications 1974-84; exec memb: Queen's Jubilee Ctee for Gtr Manchester Co 1978-84, Br Ctee of Int Chambers of Commerce (ICC) 1975-84; chm Prince's Tst in Gtr Manchester Co 1979-84; vice pres: Gtr Manchester Youth Assoc, Gtr Manchester Assoc of Physically Handicapped and Able Bodied Clubs 1972-; fndr memb and vice pres NW Museum of Science and Indust 1973-, fndr memb Clothing Needy Ctee, exec memb St John's Cncl 1980-, govr Manchester Victoria Hosp, memb Miny of Pensions Nat Insur Tbnls, Wage Cncls and Br Standard Ctee; Hon MA Univ of Manchester 1979; *Style*— David Goldstone, Esq, CBE, JP, DL; Dellstar, Elm Rd, Didsbury, Manchester M20 0XD (☎ 061 445 1868)

GOLDSTONE, David Joseph; s of Solomon Goldstone, and Rebecca, *née* Degotts; *b* 21 Feb 1929; *Educ* Dynevor Swansea, LSE (LLB); *m* 21 March 1957, Cynthia, da of Walter George Easton; 1 s (Jonathan Lee b 3 Nov 1957), 2 da (Debra Ann b 24 Aug 1959, Karen Ella b 22 Oct 1964); *Career* legal practice 1955-66, chief exec Regalian Properties plc 1970-; memb: Football Assoc of Wales 1970-72, WNO 1984-; memb ct of govrs: LSE 1985-, Atlantic Coll 1987-; *Recreations* family, reading, farming, sport; *Clubs* RAC, Bath & Racquets, Riverside Raquet Centre; *Style*— David Goldstone, Esq; PO Box 4NR, 44 Grosvenor Hill, London W1A 4NR (☎ 071 493 9613, fax 071 491 0692)

GOLDTHORPE, Brian Lees; s of Gordon Goldthorpe, and Winifred Mary, *née* Lees; *b* 11 June 1933; *Educ* Wath-on-Dearne GS; *m* 18 May 1957, Mary (Molly) Commins; 1 s (Andrew b 20 May 1962), 1 da (Anne b 25 Aug 1960); *Career* Midland Bank plc: various positions 1949-77 (Barnsley, Leeds, Oxford, head office (Poultry), Cambridge, Leicester, Sheffield), gen mangr ops then gen mangr planning 1977-80, gen mangr Northern Div 1980-81, sr gen mangr and chief exec Forward Trust Group 1981-83, chief exec gp risk mgmnt 1983-86, chief exec corp banking 1986-87, dir and chief exec UK Banking Sector 1987-89; dir and dep gp chief exec Midland Group 1989-; chm: Midland Bank Pension Trust, Motability Finance Ltd (govr Motability); dir Int Commodities Clearing House Holdings; memb: Cncl CBI, Advsy Cncl Br American C of C UK; CBIM, FCIB (memb Cncl); *Recreations* music, golf; *Clubs* Overseas Bankers, Ward of Cheap; *Style*— Brian Goldthorpe, Esq; Midland Bank plc, Head Office, 27-32 Poultry, London EC2P 2BX (☎ 071 260 7355, fax 071 260 8969, car 0836 651185)

GOLDTHORPE, Dr John Harry; s of Harry Goldthorpe (d 1989), of Great Houghton, Barnsley, and Lilian Eliza; *b* 27 May 1935; *Educ* Wath-upon-Dearne GS, UCL (BA), LSE, Univ of Cambridge (MA), Univ of Oxford (MA); *m* 1963, Rhiannon Esyllt, da of late Isaac Daniel Harry; 1 s (David Daniel Harry), 1 da (Siân Elinor); *Career* lectr Faculty Econ and Politics Univ of Cambridge 1961-69 (fell King's Coll 1960-69); pres Int Sociological Assoc Ctee on Social Stratification 1982-85, memb Academia Europaea 1988, Br Acad assessor ESRC 1988-; Hon FBA 1984, Hon Fil Dr Univ of Stockholm 1990; *Books* The Affluent Worker; Industrial Attitudes and Behaviour (with David Lockwood, 1968), The Affluent Worker in the Class Structure (with David Lockwood, 1969), The Social Grading of Occupations: A New Approach and Scale (with Keith Hope, 1974), Social Mobility and Class Structure in Modern Britian (2 edn, 1987); *Recreations* lawn tennis, bird watching, computer chess; *Style*— Dr John Goldthorpe; 32 Leckford Rd, Oxford OX2 6HX (☎ 0865 56602); Nuffield College, Oxford OX1 1NF (☎ 0865 278559, fax 0865 278621)

GOLLANCZ, Livia Ruth; da of Sir Victor Gollancz (d 1967), and Ruth, *née* Lowy (d 1973); *b* 25 May 1920; *Educ* St Paul's Girls' Sch, RCM; *Career* hornplayer 1940-53; governing dir and jt md Victor Gollancz Ltd 1967-87 (chm 1983-89, consIt 1989-); ARCM; *Recreations* singing, gardening, mountain walking; *Style*— Miss Livia Gollancz; Victor Gollancz Ltd, 14 Henrietta St, London WC2 (☎ 071 836 2006)

GOLLINGS, Raymond Dennis; s of George Robert Gollings (d 1985), and Renee Mary, *née* Greaves; *b* 5 June 1943; *Educ* Bexleyheath Sch for Boys; *m* 4 Oct 1975, Anne Elizabeth, da of Raymond Lavallan Nugent, JP, of Knockbarragh Park, Rostrevor, Co Down, NI; *Career* dir: Hill Samuel Securities Ltd 1983-85, Hill Samuel Bank Ltd 1985-, Hill Samuel International Banking Corporation NY 1986-; Freeman City of London; *Recreations* golf, photography, music; *Clubs* North Down Golf; *Style*— Raymond Gollings, Esq; 36 Pickhurst Park, Bromley, Kent (☎ 081 460 8753); Hill Samuel Bank Ltd, 100 Wood St, London (☎ 071 606 1422, fax 071 606 8175, telex 888471)

GOLT, Sidney; CB (1964); s of Wolf Golt (d 1939), of W Hartlepool, and Fanny, *née* Mossman (d 1923); *b* 31 March 1910; *Educ* Portsmouth GS, ChCh Oxford (MA); *m* 1947, Jean Amy McMillan, da of Ralph Oliver (d 1978), of Lyme Regis; 2 da (Deborah, Isobel); *Career* econ conslt; sec Central Price Regulation Ctee 1945-46, ldr UK Delgn to UN Conf on Trade and Devpt New Delhi 1968, dep sec DTI 1968-70, chm Linked Life Assurance Group 1971-81, advsr on trade policy Int C of C 1978-90, dir Malmgren Golt Kingston & Co Ltd 1978-; *Recreations* travel, bridge; *Clubs* Reform; *Style*— Sidney Golt, Esq, CB; 37 Rowan Rd, London W6 7DT

GOMBRICH, Prof Sir Ernst Hans Josef; OM (1988), CBE (1966); s of Dr Karl B Gombrich (d 1950) and Prof Leonie, *née* Hock; *b* 30 March 1909; *Educ* Theresianum Akademie, Univ of Vienna (PhD); *m* 1936, Ilse, da of Gustav Heller, of Neuötting, Bohemia; 1 s (Richard Francis b 1937); *Career* Slade prof of fine art: Univ of Oxford 1950-53, Univ of Cambridge 1961-63; dir of Warburg Inst and prof of history of the classical tradition Univ of London 1959-76 (emeritus prof 1976-); *Books* Ehrenkreuz Für Wissenschaft und Kunst (1975 and 1984), Pour le Mérite (1977); FBA, FSA; kt 1972; *Style*— Prof Sir Ernst Gombrich, OM, CBE; 19 Briardale Gdns, London NW3 7PN (☎ 071 435 6639)

GOMER, Sara Louise; da of Derek Colin Gomer, of Torquay, Devon, and Elaine Barbara, *née* Slack; *b* 13 May 1964; *Educ* Torquay GS for Girls, Eastbourne Further Educn Coll; *Career* professional tennis player; memb: Wightman Cup Team 1985-, Fedn Cup Team 1987-88, Euro Cup Team 1986-88; competed in Seoul Olympics 1988, winner Plate Event Wimbledon 1987 (runner up 1988), winner Northern Californian Open 1988, National Doubles winner 1988, British Number One 1989; *Recreations* cycling, music, films; *Clubs* Riverside Tennis; *Style*— Miss Sara Gomer

GOMERSALL, Richard; s of Willie Gomersall, of Rotherham, and Mary, *née* Hardman; *b* 18 Oct 1945; *Educ* Mexborough GS; *m* 13 June 1970, Christine Mary Magdalene, da of Marian Zgoda; 1 s (Nicholas b 1975), 1 da (Vanessa b 1972); *Career* CA; ptnr Montgomery & Co Rotherham; chm: Abel Data Ltd 1986-, Poll Tax Consultancy Ltd 1988; *Recreations* lay reader C of E, property developing; *Clubs* Rotherham; *Style*— Richard Gomersall, Esq; Dale View House, 14 Wignall Ave, Wickersley, Rotherham (☎ 0709 546441); Montgomery & Co, Chartered Accountants, 55 Moorgate St, Rotherham (☎ 0709 376313, fax 0709 703026)

GOMEZ, Jill; *b* Br Guiana, Br and Spanish parents; *Educ* RAM, Guildhall Sch of Music; *Career* opera and concert singer; operatic debut with Glyndebourne Festival Opera 1969 and has since sung leading roles incl: Mélisande, Calisto and Ann Truelove in the Rake's Progress; has appeared with The Royal Opera, ENO and Scottish Opera in roles incl: Pamina, Ilia, Fiordiligi, the Countess in Figaro, Elizabeth in Elegy for Young Lovers, Tytania, Lauretta in Gianni Schicchi, Governess in The Turn of the Screw; created the role of Flora in Tippett's The Knot Garden (Covent Garden), Countess in Thea Musgrave's Voice of Ariadne (Aldeburgh) 1974, sang title role in Massenet's Thaïs (Wexford) 1974, Jenifer in The Midsummer Marriage (WNO) 1976, created title role in William Alwyn's Miss Julie for radio 1977, Tatiana in Eugene Onegin (Kent Opera) 1977, Donna Elvira in Don Giovanni (Ludwigsburg Festival) 1978, created the title role in BBC world premiere of Prokoviev's Maddalena 1979, Fiordiligi in Cosi Fan Tutte (Bordeaux) 1979, sang in premiere of the 8th Book of Madrigals (Zurich Monteverdi Festival) 1979, Violetta in Kent Opera's production of La Traviata (Edinburgh Festival) 1979, Cinna in Lucio Silla (Zurich) 1981, Governess in The Turn of the Screw (Geneva) 1981, Cleopatra in Giulio Cesare (Frankfurt) 1981, Teresa in Benvenuto Cellini, (Berlioz Festival, Lyon) 1982, Leïla in Les Pêcheurs de Perles (Scottish Opera) 1982-83, Governess in The Turn of the Screw (ENO) 1984, Helena in Glyndebourne's production of Britten's A Midsummer Night's Dream, Donna Anna in Don Giovanni (Frankfurt Opera) 1985, Amyntas in Il Re Pastore (Kent Opera) 1987, Donna Anna in Don Giovanni (Kent Opera) 1988; regular engagements incl recitals in: France, Austria, Belgium, Netherlands, Germany, Scandinavia, Switzerland, Italy, Spain, USA; festival appearances incl: Aix-en-Provence, Spoleto, Bergen, Versailles, Flanders, Netherlands, Prague, Edinburgh and BBC Promenade concerts; numerous recordings incl: Vespro della Beata Vergine 1610 (Monteverdi), Acis and Galatea (Handel), The Knot Garden (Tippett), three recital discs of French, Spanish and Mozart songs, Quatre Chansons Françaises (Britten), Trois Poèmes de Mallarmé (Ravel), Chants d'Auvergne (Canteloube), Les Illuminations (Britten), Bachianas Brasileiras No 5 (Villa Lobos), Knoxville, Summer of 1915 (Samuel Barber), Cabaret Classics with John Constable, South of the Border (...down Mexico way); *Style*— Miss Jill Gomez; 16 Milton Park, London N6 5QA

GOMM, Douglas Rubert; s of Horace Gomm (d 1962), of Canterbury, and Gladys

Carden Elizabeth, *née* Weeks; *b* 12 Jan 1937; *Educ* Simon Langton GS For Boys; *m* 22 Dec 1973, Sheila, da of Victor George Arthur Coombes; 2 s (Dominic b 1975, Russell b 1980); *Career* Nat Serv 1955-57, RAPC attached to 1 Bn KOSB; sr accountant McCabe Ford & Williams; cncllr Canterbury City Cncl 1983-, Sheriff of Canterbury 1987-88, govr Briary Co Primary Sch Herne Bay, tstee Herne Parochial Charities, hon life memb and vice pres Canterbury and Dist Table Tennis Assoc (past chm); memb: Assoc Men of Kent and Kentishmen, Nat Assoc City and Town Sheriffs England and Wales, Old Langtonian Assoc; FFA 1975; *Style*— Douglas Gomm, Esq; Hawthorns, 89A Greenhill Rd, Herne Bay, Kent CT6 7QW (☎ 0227 372 091); McCabe Ford & Williams, 41/43 William St, Herne Bay, Kent (☎ 0227 373 271)

GOMMON, Peter Nicholas; s of David Edward Gommon (d 1987), and Jean Gommon, *née* Vipond; *b* 19 Dec 1945; *Educ* Northampton GS, Univ of Liverpool (BArch), City of Birmingham Poly (DipLA); *m* 21 July 1973, Moira Joan, da of Leonard Thomas Maguire (d 1990), of 49 Grove Rd, Millhouses, Sheffield S7 26Y; 3 s (David b 28 Dec 1974, Joseph b 7 Aug 1976, d 2 Sept 1986, Edward b Oct 1978); *Career* architect; Nelson & Parker 1968-69 and 1971-72, Johnson & Wright 1972-75, Merseyside Improved Houses 1975-79, ptnr Innes Wilkin Partnership 1979, pt/t studio instructor Univ of Liverpool 1980-85; ptnr: Innes Wilkin Ainsley Gommon 1981, Ainsley Gommon Wood 1989; memb St Saviour PCC Oxton, chm Wirral Scope epilepsy support gp; memb RIBA 1975, ALI 1982; *Recreations* art, theatre, music, agriculture, sailing; *Clubs* RA Yacht; *Style*— Peter Gommon, Esq; 46 Shrewsbury Rd, Oxton, Birkenhead L43 2HZ (☎ 051 653 7204); TY Joseff, 6 Pen Y Fron, Penmon, Ynys Môn, Gwynedd; Ainsley Gommon Wood - Architects, 1 Price St, Birkenhead Merseyside L41 6JN; (☎ 051 647 5511, fax 051 666 2195); Techbase 3, Newtech Square, Deeside Industrial Estate, Clwyd CH5 2NV; 5 Dryden St, Covent Garden, London WC2

GONSALKORALE, Dr Mahendra; s of Edwin Gonsalkorale, of Sri Lanka, and Anula, *née* Jayanetti; *b* 27 May 1944; *Educ* Royal Coll Colombo Sri Lanka, Univ of Ceylon (MB BS, MD), Univ of Manchester (MSc); *m* 10 Dec 1977, Wendy Mary, da of Geoffrey Lock, of Thingwall, Wirral; 2 s (Gehan Richard b 1982, Roshan Edward b 1983); *Career* registrar in neurology Addenbrooke's Hosp Cambridge, conslt neurologist Gen Hosp Kandy Sri Lanka, sr registrar in geriatric med Withington Hosp Manchester, conslt physician Salford Health Authy 1980-; memb: mgmnt bd Adult Acute Unit Salford Health Authy (hon assoc lectr and clinical dir in geriatric medicine), Manchester Med Soc 1979, Br Geriatric Soc 1980, Int Continence Soc 1989; fndr memb Br Assoc of Continence Care; MRCP 1975; *Recreations* squash, badminton, walking, computing; *Clubs* Brooklands Hockey and Squash; *Style*— Dr Mahendra Gonsalkorale; Dept of Healthcare for the Elderly, Ladywell Hospital, Eccles New Rd, Salford M5 2AA (☎ 061 789 7373 ext 4044)

GOOCH, Brig Arthur Brian Sherlock Heywood; ADC 1989; s of Col Brian Sherlock Gooch, DSO, TD, JP (d 1968), of Tannington Hall, Woodbridge, Suffolk, and Monica Mary, *née* Heywood (d 1975); *b* 1 June 1937; *Educ* Eton; *m* 27 July 1963, Sarah, da of Lt Col John Francis George Perceval (d 1980), of Templehouse, Co Sligo; 2 da (Rowena b 1965, Katherine b 1967); *Career* cmmnd Life Gds 1956, Oman and Aden 1958-59, Adj 1960-63, instr RMA Sandhurst 1964-65, Malaysia and Hong Kong 1966-68, GS03 (Ops) HQ 4 Gds Armd Bde 1969-70, NI 1972, asst mil attaché Tehran 1973-75, CO Life Gds 1978-81, staff dir Army Staff Coll 1981-82, cmdt Jr Div Staff Coll 1982-86, cdr Royal Armd Corps Centre 1987-89, pres Regular Cmmns Bd 1989; *Recreations* field sports, gardening, food and wine; *Style*— Brig Arthur Gooch

GOOCH, Charles Albert; s of Ernest Edward Gooch; *b* 15 Sept 1938; *Educ* Coleman St Ward Sch London; *m* 1974, June Margaret, *née* Reardon; 2 da (Charlotte b 1976, Jessica b 1978); *Career* former chm Shaw & Marvin plc, chm and md Buckland Securities plc Group of cos; *Recreations* squash, football; *Style*— Charles Gooch, Esq; Buckland Securities plc, 28 Redchurch St, London E2 7DP (☎ 071 739 3604)

GOOCH, Sir (Richard) John Sherlock; 12 Bt (GB 1746), JP (Suffolk 1970); s of Sir Robert Eric Sherlock Gooch, 11 Bt, KCVO, DSO, JP, DL (d 1978), and Katharine Clervaux (d 1974), da of Maj-Gen Sir Edward Walter Clervaux Chaytor, KCMG, KCVO, CB; *b* 22 March 1930; *Educ* Eton; *Heir* bro, Maj Timothy Gooch, MBE; *Career* Capt Life Gds; *Style*— Sir John Gooch, Bt, JP; Benacre Hall, Beccles, Suffolk (☎ 0502 740333)

GOOCH, Richard Christopher Wyard; s of Rev Henry Wyard Gooch (d 1962), and Gwendolen, *née* Brutton (d 1988); *b* 9 Nov 1927; *Educ* Marlborough, Sidney Sussex Coll Cambridge (MA); *m* 23 Aug 1958, Joan Hemsley, da of John Hemsley Longrigg; 1 s (Nicholas b 12 July 1966), 3 da (Phillipa (Mrs Lark) b 21 May 1959, Belinda (Mrs Humphry) b 1 May 1961, Amanda b 20 Aug 1963); *Career* Lt RASC 1946-48; admitted slr 1954, ptnr Maslen & Maslen Bournemouth 1956-71, sr ptnr Thos Coombs and Son Dorchester 1967-90, legal advsr Dorset Relate (formerly Marriage Guidance Cncl) 1970-90; registrar Archdeaconry of Sherborne 1970-90; memb: Diocesan Synod 1958-88, Hodson Cmmn on Synodical Govt 1967-68, Archbishops Advsy Panel on Divorce Law Reform 1968-69, Salisbury Diocesan Bishop's Cncl 1973-88; clerk to Hardy's Sch Dorchester 1970-76; parish cncllr 1970-86; chm: Social Security Appeal Tbnl 1984-, Med Appeal Tbnl 1987- (dep registrar 1986-); pres Dorset Law Soc 1986, memb Law Soc 1954; *Recreations* riding, gardening, reading; *Style*— Richard Gooch, Esq; The Garden Hse, Frome Whitfield, Dorchester, Dorset (☎ 0305 268 414); Thos Coombs & Son, Savernake Hse, 42 High West St, Dorchester, Dorset, DT1 1UU (☎ 0305 262901)

GOOCH, Maj Timothy Robert Sherlock; MBE (1970); s of Sir Robert Eric Sherlock Gooch, KCVO, DSO, JP, DL, 11 Bt (d 1978), of Benacre Hall, Suffolk, and Katharine Clervaux (d 1974), da of Maj-Gen Sir Edward Walter Clervaux Chaytor, KCMG, KCVO, CB; hp of bro, Sir (Richard) John (Sherlock) Gooch, 12 Bt; *b* 7 Dec 1934; *Educ* Eton, RMA Sandhurst; *m* 17 Dec 1963, Susan Barbara Christie, da of Maj-Gen Kenneth Christie Cooper, CB, DSO, OBE (d 1981), of West End House, Donhead St Andrew, Wilts; 2 da (Lucinda b 1970, Victoria b 1974); *Career* Maj Life Gds; memb HM Body Gd of Hon Corps of Gentlemen at Arms 1986-; co dir; *Clubs* White's, Cavalry & Guards; *Style*— Maj Timothy Gooch, MBE; The Cedars, Covehithe, Wrentham, Beccles, Suffolk (☎ 050 275 266)

GOOCH, Sir Trevor Sherlock; 5 Bt (UK 1866), of Clewer Park, Berks; VRD; s of Charles Trevor Gooch (d 1963), and Hester Stratford, *née* Sherlock (d 1957); suc kinsman, Sir Robert Douglas Gooch, 4 Bt (d 1989); *b* 15 June 1915; *Educ* Charterhouse; *m* 1, 4 Dec 1956, Denys Anne (d 1976), o da of Harold Victor Venables, of Edificio la Vileta Camino Vechinal la Vileta 215, Palma, Mallorce; 1 s (Miles Peter b 1963), 4 da (Beverly Jacqueline (Mrs Amy) b 1957, Vanda Madelaine b 1958, Yvonne Daryl Roote b 1961, Rowan Claire b 1971); m 2, 1978, Jean, da of late John Joseph Wright; 1 child; *Heir* s, Miles Peter Gooch b 3 Feb 1963; *Career* Flt-Lt RAFVR; *Style*— Sir Trevor Gooch, Bt, VRD; Jardin de la Roque, Mont de la Roque, St Aubin, Jersey, CI

GOOD, Anthony Bruton Meyrick; *b* 18 April 1933; *Educ* Felsted; *m* ; 2 da; *Career* mgmnt trainee Distillers Group 1950-52, editorial asst Temple Press Ltd 1952-55, PR offr Silver City Airways (gp PR/marketing Br Aviation Servs Ltd) 1955-60, fndr and chm Good Relations Group plc 1961-89; chm: Good Relations India Ltd 1988-, Cox & Kings Ltd 1975- (joined bd 1971), Cox & Kings (India) Ltd 1988- (dir 1980), Foley Lodge Hotels plc; I M Holdings Ltd, Subaru (UK) Ltd, Frog Hollow Ltd, St James Court Hotel Ltd, Taj International Hotels, Wallis Tomlinson Ltd, fndr and chm Good Consultancy Ltd 1989-; FIPR; *Recreations* travel, reading, theatre; *Clubs* RAC; *Style*— Anthony Good, Esq; 2 Campden House Close, London W8 7NU (☎ 071 937 9737); Good Consultancy Ltd, 39 Bullingham Mansions, Kensington Church St, London W8 4BE (☎ 071 355 1770, fax 071 629 4683)

GOOD, Anthony Richard; s of Richard George Good; *b* 20 April 1930; *Educ* Univ of Reading; *m* 1956, Sallie Lorraine, da of Archibald Wilson; 2 s, 2 da; *Career* former dir Grand Metropolitan Ltd (chief exec Milk and Foods Div); chm: Express Dairy Co Ltd, Quadrant Holdings Cambridge Ltd; farmer; *Recreations* shooting, fishing; *Style*— Anthony Good, Esq; Warborough Farm, Letcombe Regis, Nr Wantage, Oxfordshire (☎ 023 57 3244)

GOOD, Charles Anthony; s of William Marsh Good (d 1953), of Dublin, and Doris Audrey, *née* Scott; *b* 18 May 1946; *Educ* Charterhouse, Univ of Kent (BSc); *m* 12 Jan 1966, Averil Ray, da of Lt Cdr Frank William Haxworth, RNVR, of Chobham, Surrey; 3 da (Charlotte b 1967, Natasha b 1968, Elinor b 1978); *Career* CA; Robson Rhodes 1968-71, S G Warburg and Co Ltd 1972-75, chm Good and Co 1976-, md J S Gadd and Co Ltd 1987-, dep md J S Gadd Holdings plc 1987-, dir Embassy Property Group plc 1986-; currently dir Citigate Communications Group Ltd and Neilson Milnes Ltd; govr Flexlands Sch 1974-89 (dep chm 1983-89); FCA 1972; *Recreations* tennis, squash, sailing, skiing; *Style*— Charles Good, Esq; Burchetts, Chobham, Surrey GU24 8SW; J S Gadd and Co Ltd, 45 Bloomsbury Sq, London WC1A 2RA (☎ 071 242 5544, fax 071 405 0077, car 0836 614 247, 0860 399544, telex 23260 ARCADY G)

GOOD, Dudley Joseph; s of Richard George Good, OBE, of Vine Cottage, Sutbbings Estate, and Gladys Gertrude Good (d 1967); *b* 17 Sept 1931; *Educ* Maidenhead GS, Univ of Reading, Guildhall Sch of Music, Int Opera Studio Zurich; *m* 4 May 1968, Janine Rosette, da of Roger Burkhard (d 1984), of Versoix, Geneva; 2 s (Richard Dudley b 1 Feb 1971, Oliver Roger b 22 March 1973), 1 da (Nathalie Sylvette b 5 Nov 1969); *Career* Nat Serv Kings Dragoon Guards; sales dir J Good & Sons Ltd 1952, head mktg Dairy Crest Div Milk Mktg Bd, dep chief exec Outspan Organisation Europe, md and chm Beacon Garden Centre 1975-88; opera singer; performed Glyndebourne 1951-52, European debut Zurich Opera House; dir Playhouse Theatre Tst Oxford; *Recreations* music, singing, opera; *Clubs* Farmers, Inst of Dirs, Royal Scottish Automobile; *Style*— Dudley Good, Esq; Stubbings House, Henley Road, Maidenhead, Berks

GOODACRE, (John) Michael Kendall; s of Kenneth Goodacre, TD, DL, of London, and Dorothy, *née* Kendall; *b* 19 Aug 1941; *Educ* Shrewsbury, Keble Coll Oxford (MA); *m* 29 July 1967, Yvonne Scott, da of John Milsom (d 1985); 2 s (William Henry Kendall b 5 Mar 1971, Edward James Scott b 2 Feb 1972); *Career* admitted slr 1969; asst slr Messrs Coffin Mew & Clover 1969-71 (ptnr 1971); memb: Bd of Visitors HM Prison Kingston (chm 1987 and 1988), Promotion of Int Gastronomy Soc Portsmouth (chm 1988-89); ctee memb Hants Inc Law Soc (chm Euro Sub Ctee), memb Law Soc; *Recreations* eating, drinking, reading, skiing, raising beef cattle; *Clubs* Royal Naval & Royal Albert Yacht (Portsmouth); *Style*— Michael Goodacre, Esq; Crofton Old Farm, Titchfield, Hants PO14 3ER (☎ 0329 43298); 17 Hampshire Terr, Portsmouth, Hants PO1 2PU (☎ 0705 812 511, fax 0705 291 847)

GOODALE, Hon Mrs (Pamela Muriel Dorine); *née* Hirst; MBE (1983); da of Harold Hugh Hirst (d 1919; s of 1 Baron Hirst, barony extinct 1943), and Carol Iris Hirst, MBE, *née* Lindon; raised to the rank of a Baron's da 1943; *b* 16 April 1918; *Educ* Luckley Wokingham; *m* 1, 29 Nov 1940 (m dis 1947), Capt Arthur George Bevington Colyer, RA (decd), o s of Dr Arthur Colyer, of Old Way House, Charing, Kent; m 2, 9 Dec 1949, Roy Edward Goodale (d 1 Aug 1969), s of late William Thomas Goodale, of Laleham-on-Thames; 1 s (Hugh b 1953); *Career* served WWII as Staff Capt ATS; dir and co sec H R Goodale Ltd; chm: Lingfield Parish Cncl 1957-69 (memb 1955-69), Godstone RDC 1969-72 (memb 1955-76); memb Tandridge Cncl 1974-75, hon Alderman Tandridge DC; *Recreations* voluntary work (political and public); *Style*— Hon Mrs Goodale, MBE; Peartrees, Dormansland, nr Lingfield, Surrey RH7 6QY (☎ 0342 832368; office: 0732 863993)

GOODALL, His Honour Anthony Charles; MC (1942), DL (Devon 1987-); s of Charles Henry Goodall (d 1968), of Manor House, Sutton Veny, Wilts, and Mary Helen, *née* Walker (d 1956); *b* 23 July 1916; *Educ* Eton, King's Coll Cambridge (BA, MA); *m* 8 April 1947, Anne Valerie, da of John Reginald Chichester (d 1968), of Lurley Manor, Tiverton, Devon; 1 s (Charles Roderick b 1948), 2 da (Clarissa Anne b 1950, Diana Mary Audrey b 1959); *Career* served WWII 1939-45, 1 Royal Dragoons in ME, Italy, France, Belgium, Holland (POW twice 1944), Capt; called to the Bar Inner Temple 1939, practised at the Bar 1946-67, judge County Ct 1968-72, circuit judge 1972-86; pres Plymouth Magistrates Assoc 1976-84, memb County Ct Rule Ctee 1978-83, jt vice pres Cncl of HM Circuit Judges 1985 (joint pres 1986), ret 1986; *Style*— His Honour Anthony Goodall, MC, DL; Mardon, Moretonhampstead, Devon (☎ 0647 40239)

GOODALL, Caroline Mary Helen; da of Capt Peter Goodall, CBE, TD, *qv*, of Wetherby, W Yorks, and Sonja Jeanne, *née* Burt; sis of Charles Peter Goodall, *qv*; *b* 22 May 1955; *Educ* Queen Ethelburga's Sch, Newnham Coll Cambridge (MA); *m* 1 Oct 1983, (Vesey) John, *qv*, s of Maj Vesey Michael Hill (d 1972); *Career* asst slr Slaughter and May 1980-84 (articled clerk 1978-80), ptnr Herbert Smith 1987- (asst slr 1984-87); memb Worshipful Co of Slrs; memb: Law Soc, London Young Slrs Gp; *Recreations* tennis, theatre, windsurfing, fell walking; *Clubs* Roehampton, Broadgate; *Style*— Miss Caroline Goodall; Exchange House, Primrose St, London EC2A 2HS (☎ 071 374 8000, fax 071 496 0043, telex 886633)

GOODALL, Charles Peter; s of Capt Peter Goodall, CBE, TD, of Springfield House, Sicklinghall Rd, Wetherby, W Yorks, and Sonja Jeanne, *née* Burt; bro of Caroline Mary Helen Goodall, *qv*; *b* 14 July 1950; *Educ* Sherborne, St Catharine's Coll Cambridge (MA, LLM); *Career* asst slr Slaughter and May 1976-82 (articled clerk 1974-76), ptnr Simmons & Simmons 1984- (asst slr 1982-84); memb Law Soc; *Recreations* squash, golf, sailing; *Clubs* RAC, Hawks, Cambridge, Royal Wimbledon Golf; *Style*— Charles Goodall, Esq; Simmons & Simmons, 14 Dominion St, London EC2M 2RJ (☎ 071 628 2020, fax 071 588 4129, telex 888562 SIMMON G)

GOODALL, Sir (Arthur) David Saunders; KCMG (1987, CMG 1979); o s of Arthur William Goodall (d 1968), of Whaley Bridge, Derbys, and Maisie Josephine, *née* Byers; *b* 9 Oct 1931; *Educ* Ampleforth, Trinity Coll Oxford (MA); *m* 1962, Morwenna, yst da of Percival George Beck Peecock (d 1972), of Goring, Sussex; 2 s, 1 da; *Career* 2 Lt 1 Bn KOYLI 1955-56: Kenya, Aden, Cyprus; HM Dip Serv: head of W Euro Dept FCO 1975-79, min Bonn 1979-82, seconded to Cabinet Office dep sec 1982-84, deputy under sec of State FCO 1984-87, Br High Cmmr to India 1987-; *Recreations* water colour painting, social and family history; *Clubs* Garrick, United Oxford and Cambridge Univ; *Style*— Sir David Goodall, KCMG; c/o Foreign and Commonwealth Office (New Delhi), London SW1A 2AH

GOODALL, Francis Richard Cruice; s of William Cruice Goodall (d 1958), of Liverpool, and Joan Mary, *née* Berrill (d 1955); *b* 4 Oct 1929; *Educ* Ampleforth, Queens' Coll Cambridge (MA), Architectural Assoc (AA Dipl); *m* 21 Jan 1978, Vivienne, da of Thomas Vyvyan More (d 1956), of E London and South Africa; *Career* Nat Serv 1948-49 cmmnd RE serv N Africa and Malta; ptnr Frederick MacManus &

Ptnrs 1963- (assoc 1958-63); memb Cncl: Architects' Registration Cncl UK 1984-, Soc of Construction Law 1988; Freeman City of London 1982, Liveryman Worshipful Co of Arbitrators 1982 (memb Ct of Assts 1987-); memb Cncl Chartered Inst of Arbitrators 1990-; memb: Soc of Construction Arbitrators 1988-, Br Acad of Experts 1989-; FRIBA, FCIArb, MBAE; *Clubs* Garrick, Travellers'; *Style—* Francis Goodall, Esq; 37 Molyneux St, Marylebone, London W1H 5HW (☎ 071 723 4701); 41 Upper Montagu St, Marylebone, London W1H 1FQ (☎ 071 262 6651, fax 071 402 0433)

GOODALL, Geoffrey Trevor; s of Thomas Henry Goodall (d 1947), of London, and Jane, *née* Bird (d 1980); *b* 15 Oct 1929; *Educ* Haberdashers' Askes's, CCC Oxford (MA); *m* 6 Sept 1952, Marion Rosemary, da of Arthur William Smith, MBE (d 1980), of London; 3 s (Ashley b 1956, Howard b 1958, Adrian b 1961), 1 da (Sally b 1967); *Career* craftsman REME 1948-50; languages teacher Haberdashers' Aske's Sch 1954-58, head of modern languages Uppingham Sch 1960-64, (teacher 1958-60); headmaster: Lord Williams's Sch Thame 1964-79, Exeter Sch Devon 1979-; ed Maignet Series for Macmillans 1965-; nat pres SHA 1982, chm SW Div HMC 1985, del Oxford Local Examination Bd 1974-; *Books* Themes Anglais Pour Toute la Grammaire (1963); *Recreations* music, theatre, sport; *Style—* Geoffrey Goodall, Esq; High Meadow, Barrack Rd, Exeter, Devon, EX2 5AB (☎ 0392 73679) Exeter School, Exeter, Devon EX2 4NS

GOODALL, Dr Janet; da of Bernard Goodall (d 1978) of Notts, and Elizabeth Ellen, *née* Schofield (d 1948); *b* 20 July 1930; *Educ* Retford Co HS for Girls, Univ of Sheffield (MB ChB); *Career* med registrar Hosp for Sick Children Gt Ormond St 1963-66, secondment to Childrens' Hosp of Philadelphia 1964-65, sr med registrar Sheffield Children's Hosp 1966-69, conslt paediatrician: Mulago Hosp Kampala Uganda 1969-72, N Staffs Hosp Centre 1973-90; author of various pubns on paediatrics especially concerning the emotional needs of children and matters of med ethics; memb: Christian Med Fellowship (chm 1985-87), Br Paediatric Assoc; FRCPE, memb RSM; *Books* Suffering in Childhood (1980), Help for the Cystic Fibrosis Family When a Patient Dies (1987); *Recreations* travel, photography, friendship; *Style—* Dr Janet Goodall; Melton, Burrington Drive, Trentham, Stoke-on-Trent, Staffs ST4 8SP

GOODALL, Robert John Rhodes; s of Maj John Francis Goodall, of Skipton, Yorks, and Dr Joyce Mary Goodall, *née* Rhodes (d 1963); *b* 5 Jan 1947; *Educ* Worksop Coll, Leeds Med Sch (MB ChB, ChM); *m* 1, 28 Dec 1968 (m dis 1980), Mary Christine, da of John Stott, of Morecambe; 2 da (Lara b 1969, Anna b 1971); m 2, 2 Nov 1984, Julia Mary, da of Fred Nicholson (d 1972); 2 s (John b 1986, Alex b 1987); *Career* tutor in surgery Hope Hosp Salford 1975-79, sr registrar in surgery Bradford Leeds 1979-85, conslt surgn Calderdale Health Authy 1985-; FRCSEd 1975, FRCS 1975; *Recreations* golf, bridge, walking; *Clubs* Halifax Golf; *Style—* Robert Goodall, Esq; Wheatstone, Skircoat Green Road, Halifax HX3 0LJ (☎ 0422 365889), Royal Halifax Infirmary, Free School Lane, Halifax (☎ 0422 357222)

GOODALL, Rodney David; s of Cecil Ernest Goodall (d 1972), of Reading, and Ellen May, *née* Farr (d 1982); *b* 30 June 1934; *Educ* Reading Sch, Oxford Sch of Architecture (DipArch); *m* 15 Aug 1964, Lesley Ann, da of Walter Leslie Chapman, of Thurloxton, Somerset; 1 s (Timothy b 1965), 1 da (Rachel b 1967); *Career* chartered architect; princ Rodney D Goodall, Frome 1968-; Civic Tst awards: EAHY award 1975, Commendation 1980 (for historic building repairs/conversion); restoration of St James' Church Trowbridge 1987-91; Somerset co cncllr 1975-80, town cncllr Frome 1971-87, Mayor of Frome 1977-79; C of E lay reader 1984-; RIBA, DCHM, FRSA; *Recreations* walking, music making, theatre, history; *Style—* Rodney D Goodall, Esq; The Gables, 28 Somerset Road, Frome, Somerset BA11 1HD (☎ 0373 62284)

GOODBAND, Philip Haydon; s of Philip Aubrey Goodband, of 61 The Ave, Camberley, Surrey, and Edith Emma Haydon, *née* Cooper; *b* 26 May 1944; *Educ* Strodes Sch Dijon France, Academie Du Champagne (MW); *m* 18 Dec 1971, Lynne Wendy, da of Brig Lindsey Jerment Aspland, OBE, of Vine Cottage, Ridgeway Rd, Dorking, Surrey; 2 s (Charles Lindsey Haydon b 19 June 1976, d 24 Nov 1976, Henry Lindsey Charles b 24 Oct 1978), 1 da (Emily Victoria b 19 Sept 1973); *Career* dir: Gilbey SA France 1972-73, Wine Devpt Bd 1980-, purchasing and quality Stowells of Chelsea 1981-86 (buyer 1973-80); chm Inst Masters of Wine 1984-85, tstee Wine and Spirit Trade Benevolent Soc 1986-89, wine buying and quality logistics Grants of St James's 1986-88, md Wine Div on Trade Grants of St James's 1988-; lectr and broadcaster in London, Paris, Milan, San Francisco; chm Redbourn Tennis Club 1975-82, judge Newdigate Horticultural Soc; Freeman of City of London 1972, Worshipful Co of Haberdashers 1972 (Clothed 1975); FBBI 1968; Compagnon du Beaujolais 1978, membre de L'Ordre St Etienne France 1981, Cavaleiro da Confraria do Vinho do Porto Portugal 1987; *Recreations* competition carriage driving, riding, tennis; *Clubs* Naval and Military, Brockham Harness, British Driving Soc; *Style—* Philip Goodband, Esq; Long Meadow, Parkgate Rd, Newdigate, Dorking, Surrey, RH5 5DX (☎ 030677 342); Grants of St James Wine Division, St Jame's House, Guildford Business Park, Guildford, Surrey GU2 5AD (☎ 0483 64861, fax 0483 506691, telex 859117)

GOODBODY, Michael Ivan Andrew; s of Llewellyn Marcus Goodbody (d 1989), see Burkes Irish Family Records, of Ardclough Lodge, Straffan, Co Kildare, Ireland, and Eileen Elizabeth, *née* Bourke; *b* 23 Jan 1942; *Educ* Kingstown Sch Dublin; *m* 9 March 1968, Susannah Elizabeth, da of Donald Guy Pearce (Capt Ayrshire Yeomanry RA, ka 1944); 1 s (Guy b 1972), 2 da (Sarah b 1970, Perry b 1976); *Career* Lt TA, 289 Parachute Battery RHA; stockbroker Smith Rice & Hill 1962-74, private client stockbroker Capel-Cure Myers 1974-88, dir Capel-Cure Myers Capital Mgmnt Ltd 1988-; memb Int Stock Exchange; *Books* The Goodbody Family of Ireland (1979); *Recreations* family history; *Style—* Michael Goodbody, Esq; The Old Rectory, Wickham St Paul's, Halstead, Essex CO9 2PJ; Capel-Cure Myers Capital Management Ltd, The Registry, Royal Mint Court, London EC3N 4EY

GOODBODY, Dr Richard Anthony; VRD; s of Clement Ridgway Goodbody (decd), and Eleanor Kate, *née* Skelton; *b* 30 Sept 1920; *Educ* Aldenham, Univ of London (MD, MB BS); *m* Honor Crawford, da of Clifford Durham Pullan (d 1939), of Hull; 1 s (Jonathan b 1945); *Career* Nat Serv Surgn Lt Cdr serv appts in destroyers RM and RN Haslar Hosp 1944-64; house surgn St Bartholomews Hosp 1943-44, war serv RNVR 1944-47, registrar in pathology Lewisham and Guys Hosp 1947-49, sr registrar Middx Hosp and Med Sch 1949-52, res fell Inst of Neurology Univ of London 1950, conslt pathologist Univ of Southampton Hosps 1952-85, conslt forenzic pathologist HM Coroners 1985- (conslt pathologist 1953-89), conslt advsr Govt of United Arab Emirates and Govt of Saudi Arabia 1978; fndr fell RCPath; memb: Cncl Assoc of Clinical Pathologists, Cncl Royal Inst of Public Health, Int Soc of Neuropathologists, Pathological Soc 1952, Neuropathological Soc; MRCS, LRCP, FRCPath 1962, FRIPH 1971; *Recreations* estate management and landscaping; *Style—* Dr Richard Goodbody; Littledene, 57 Kingsway, Chandlers Ford, Hants S05 1FH (☎ 0703 252495); Hamdown House, Romsey Rd, West Wellow, Hants (☎ 0794 22347); Little Dene, 57 Kingsway, Chandlers Ford, Hants SO5 1FH

GOODBURN, Andrew Robert; s of Robert Goodburn, of Camrose, Haverfordwest, and Peggy, *née* Barrett; *b* 5 Jan 1947; *Educ* Harrow HS, Monkton House Sch; *m* 28 June 1969, Elizabeth Ann, da of Joseph Henry Dunn; 3 s (Giles Andrew b 11 Nov 1972, Henry Robert b 18 April 1974, Benjamin Joseph b 24 June 1978), 1 da (Anne-Marie b 19 May 1980); *Career* Peat Marwick Mitchell & Co 1964-70 (articled clerk, audit sr); Bowthorpe Holdings plc 1970-81: gen mangr Hellermann Cassettes (fin controller), fin dir Hellermann Deutsch, commercial dir Bowthorpe EMP, marketing dir Hellermann Electric; ptnr (fin Consultancy London) Grant Thornton 1987-(joined as sr mgmnt conslt 1982); FCA (ACA 1969), AIMC 1983, MBAE 1990; *Recreations* tennis, travel, gardening; *Clubs* Haywards Heath RFC; *Style—* Andrew Goodburn, Esq; Deacons Hay, Beaconsfield Rd, Chelwood Gate, Sussex RH17 7LG (☎ 082 574 225); Grant Thornton, Grant Thornton House, Melton St, Euston Square, London NW1 2EP (☎ 071 383 5100, fax 071 383 4715)

GOODCHILD, David Hicks; CBE (1973); s of Harold Hicks Goodchild (d 1965), of Gunces, Gt Yeldham, Essex, and Agnes Joyce Wharton, *née* Mowbray (d 1989); *b* 3 Sept 1926; *Educ* Felsted Sch Essex; *m* 15 Dec 1954, Nicole Marie Jeanne Delamotte, da of Elie Bentolila (d 1966), of Paris; 1 s (Harold b 1958), 1 da (Sandra (Comtesse d'Abovville) b 1957); *Career* Mil Serv RA and Royal Indian Artillery 1944-48; admitted slr 1952, articles Messrs Longmores of Hertford 1948-52, asst slr Monsanto Chemicals Ltd London 1952-56, ptnr Sheridan Hickey & Goodchild Paris 1957-62, ptnr Clifford-Turner London and Paris 1962, ptnr Clifford Chance 1987-; admitted Conseil Juridique 1972; pres: Hertford Br Hosp Paris, Victoria Home Paris; hon pres Br Chamber of Commerce Paris; memb: Law Soc, Int Bar Assoc 1974 (offr); *Recreations* golf, cricket, travel; *Clubs* MCC, HAC, Cercle de L'Union Interalliée, Polo de Paris; *Style—* David Goodchild, Esq, CBE; 53 Avenue Montaigne, 75008 Paris, France (☎ 010 33 1 42 25 49 27); Manoir de La Bernerie, Cercles, 24320 Verteillac, France (☎ 010 33 53 91 13 96); 18 rue Jean Giraudoux, 75116 Paris, France (☎ 1 40 69 77 00, fax 1 50 69 77 47, telex 650 690 LEGIB)

GOODCHILD, David Lionel Napier; CMG (1986); s of Hugh Napier Goodchild (d 1981), of Norwich, and Beryl Cynthia Maud, *née* Coller (d 1969); *b* 20 July 1935; *Educ* Eton, King's Coll Cambridge (BA, MA); *Career* HM Dip Serv 1958-73 (third sec Tehran 1959-62), F O 1962-70 (second then first sec UK Delgn NATO 1964-66), dep political advsr Br Mil Govt Berlin 1970-72, dir Euro Commn Brussels 1979-86 (head of div 1973-79); *Style—* David Goodchild, Esq, CMG; Orchard House, Thorpe Morieux, Bury St Edmunds, Suffolk IP30 0NW (☎ 0284 828181)

GOODCHILD, Peter Robert Edward; s of Douglas Richard Geoffrey Goodchild, MBE (d 1989), of Angmering Village, W Sussex, and Lottie May, *née* Ager; *b* 18 Aug 1939; *Educ* Aldenham, St John's Coll Oxford (MA); *m* 1968, Penelope-Jane, da of Dr William Pointon-Dick (d 1956); 2 da (Abigail b 1971, Hannah b 1974); *Career* prodr Horizon BBC TV 1965-69 (1967, 1968, 1969 winner Soc of Film and TV Arts Mullard award for Science Broadcasting), ed Horizon BBC TV 1969-76 (1972 and 1974 winner BAFTA award for Best Factual Series, 1973 and 1975 winner Italia prize for Factual Programmes), exec prodr drama prodns 1977-80 (including Marie Curie 1977 and Oppenheimer 1980 which both won BAFTA awards for Best Series), prodr Bread or Blood 1980, head of Science and Features BBC TV 1980-84, head of plays BBC TV 1984-89, exec prodr Film Dept BBC 1989-, prodr The March 1990 (winner One World TV Premier Network award); CChem, FRSC; *Books* Shatterer of Worlds (the life of J Robert Oppenheimer, 1980); *Recreations* tennis, music; *Clubs* Groucho's; *Style—* Peter Goodchild, Esq; Brockdale House, Cricketer's Lane, Warfield, Berks (☎ 0344 882492); BBC Television Centre, Wood Lane, London W12 (☎ 081 743 8000)

GOODDEN, Benjamin Bernard Woulfe; o s of Cecil Phelips Goodden, JP (d 1969), and Hylda Maud (d 1970), da of Stephen Roland Woulfe, of Tiermaclane, Co Clare; *b* 16 July 1925; *Educ* Harrow, Trinity Coll Oxford (MA); *m* 1, 1952 (m dis 1966), Elizabeth Sarah, da of GI Woodham-Smith, by his w Cecil Woodham Smith (the authoress); 1 s, 2 da; m 2, 1973, Rose Emma Margaret, 2 da of Lt Cdr Hon Douglas David Edward Vivian, DSC, RN (d 1973, 2 s of 4 Baron Vivian), and formerly wife of James Collet Norman; 1 s; *Career* RA 1943-47; called to the Bar 1951; ptnr James Capel & Co 1957-71, dir M & G Securities Ltd 1974-; underwriting memb Lloyd's 1972-; hon treas and singing memb Bach Choir 1972-; *Recreations* cricket (watching, discussing, reading about), choral music; *Clubs* MCC; *Style—* Benjamin Goodden, Esq; Ferryside, Riverside, Twickenham, Middlesex TW1 3DN (☎ 081 892 1448)

GOODDEN, Rev John Maurice Phelips; er s of John Henry Goodden (d 1974), of Compton House, Sherborne, Dorset, and his 1 w, Valerie Mary, *née* Llewellyn-Evans (d 1959); descended from Robert Goodden (d 1764), of Bower Hinton and Martock, who purchased Compton House and the Lordship of the Manor of Over Compton and Nether Compton from George Abington in 1736 (*see* Burke's Landed Gentry, 18 edn, vol I, 1965); *b* 17 May 1934; *Educ* Salisbury Cathedral Sch, Sherborne, Trinity Coll Oxford, Sarum and Wells Theol Coll; *m* 1, 12 Oct 1957 (m dis 1974), Ann Rosemary, o child of Alec Vincent Tucker, of Stirling, Nether Compton, Dorset; 3 da (Sarah Helen b 12 Dec 1958, Victoria Ann b 13 Sept 1962, Maria Jeane b 24 May 1968); m 2, 12 Nov 1983, Mrs Madeleine Hilary Wilson; 1 step s (Jeremy), 1 step da (Lucy); *Career* ordained: deacon 1972, priest 1975; curate: Holy Trinity Weymouth 1972-74, Harlow New Town with Little Parndon 1974-78; industl chaplain and chaplain Princess Alexandra Hosp Harlow 1978-82; vicar St John Moulsham 1986-90, rector St Margaret's Chipstead Surrey and advsr to Bishop of Southwark for Rural Ministry 1990-; *Style—* The Rev John Goodden; Tandy Cottage, How Lane, Chipstead, Surrey CR5 3LP (☎ 0737 552157/553527)

GOODDEN, Robert Crane; yr s of John Henry Goodden (d 1974), of Compton House, and his 1 w, Valerie Mary, *née* Llewellyn-Evans (d 1959); bro of Rev John Maurice Phelips Goodden, *qv*; *b* 2 April 1940; *Educ* Salisbury Cathedral Choir Sch, Dauntsey's Sch; *m* 1 June 1968, Rosemary Joan Frances, da of Lt-Col Arthur Edward Bagwell Purefoy (d 1986); 2 s (John b 5 April 1973, Michael b 23 June 1976), 1 da (Sally b 11 May 1971); *Career* trainee: L Hugh Newman, The Butterfly Farm Ltd Bexley Kent 1957, Harrods Knightsbridge 1959; fndr and md Worldwide Butterflies Ltd 1960; co-fndr, tstee and vice pres Br Butterfly Conservation Soc, owner Lullingstone Silk Farm, former advsr to Govt of Papua-New Guinea on butterfly farming; memb: Mgmnt Ctee Almshouses of St John Sherborne, Sherborne Chamber Choir; FRHS; *Books* author of nine books on lepidoptera and entomology incl: Butterflies (1971), The Wonderful World of Butterflies (1973), Field Guide to the Butterflies of Britain (1978), Beningfield's Butterflies (1978); *Recreations* gardening, music, photography, walking, natural history, botany, travel, computer programming, arts and crafts; *Style—* Robert Goodden, Esq; Compton House, nr Sherborne, Dorset DT9 4QN (☎ 0935 74608)

GOODDEN, (Anthony) Roger; s of John William Henry Goodden, of Hythe, Kent, and Ina Mary, *née* Telfer; *b* 7 Dec 1940; *Educ* Ewell County Secdy Sch, Northern Poly (Dip Arch); *m* 25 Aug 1962, Barbara Maud, da of Albert Edwin Spencer; 2 da (Juliet Louise Patman b 16 April 1964, Emma Jane Homer b 2 June 1967); *Career* architectural asst: Middlesex County Cncl 1958-60, Westminster City Cncl 1960-63, The Fitzroy Robinson Partnership London 1963-68; The Fitzroy Robinson Partnership Cambridge: architect 1968-, assoc 1974, sr assoc 1977, ptnr 1984; memb Architects' Registration Cncl of UK 1969, ARIBA 1969; *Recreations* travel, art, music; *Clubs* Cambridge Business and Professional Men's Club, Univ Centre (Cambridge), County Farmers (Cambridge); *Style—* Roger Goodden, Esq; The Fitzroy Robinson Partnership, Grafton House, 64 Maids Causeway, Cambridge CB5 8DD (☎ 0223 61221, fax 0223 460285)

GOODE, Anthony William; s of William Henry Goode, of Tyemouth, and Eileen Veronica, *née* Brannan; *b* 3 Aug 1944; *Educ* Corby Sch, Univ of Newcastle Med Sch

(MB BS, MD); *m* 26 Sept 1987, Dr Patricia Josephine, da of Michael Flynn, of Nutley Lane, Downeybrook, Dublin; *Career* surgical appts Newcastle upon Tyne teaching hosps and demonstrator anatomy Univ of Newcastle upon Tyne 1968-74, various appts Univ of London teaching hosps 1975-; currently: reader in surgery Univ of London, hon conslt surgn London Hosp; numerous res programmes related to: nutrition, metabolism, endocrinology in surgery, role of microgravity res in future med and surgical devpt; princ investigator NASA; hon sec and treas Br Assoc Endocrine Surgns (fndr memb 1980), memb Ed Bd Medicine Sciences and the Law; FRCS 1972; memb: RSM 1972, Int Soc Surgery 1985, New York Acad Scis 1987; *Books* A textbook of Nutrition for Nurses (jtly, 1985); *Recreations* music especially opera, cricket, literature; *Clubs* MCC; *Style*— Anthony Goode, Esq; The Surgical Unit, The London Hospital, Whitechapel, London E1 1BB

GOODE, (Penelope) Cary Anne; da of Lt-Col Ernest Edgar Spink, DSO, MC (d 1987), and Rachel, *née* Atcherley-Wright; *b* 5 Dec 1947; *Educ* Westwing Sch; *m* 16 Oct 1987, Richard Nicholas Goode, s of Lt-Col Andrew Nicholas Goode, OBE, of The Bush House, Pilston, nr Shepton Mallet, Somerset; *Career* Royal Ascot Enclosure Off 1971, MOD 1973, mangr retail business 1978, domestic and social sec Royal Coll of Obstetricians and Gynaecology 1981-83, educn mangr Br Heart Fndn 1983-88, dir Nat Asthma Campaign 1988-90, memb ICFM 1989; *Recreations* gardening, garden design, classic cars, opera; *Style*— Mrs Cary Goode; The Manor House, Princes Risborough, Bucks (☎ 08444 3168); National Asthma Campaign, 300 Upper St, London N1 2XX (☎ 071 226 2260, fax 071 704 0740)

GOODE, Michael Andrew; s of Edwin Eardley Bentley Goode (d 1943), and Winifred Beatrice Whittaker, *née* Glenn; *b* 30 Nov 1924; *Educ* Pocklington Sch, Univ of Sheffield (LLB); *m* 30 Aug 1951, Auriel Jean, da of Charles Louis Emy (d 1961); 3 da (Nicola b 1954, Helen b 1956, Catherine b 1958); *Career* slr 1950-; pres: Sheffield Jr C of C 1959-60, Sheffield Chamber of Trade 1968-69, Sheffield and Dist Law Soc 1986-87; chm Social Security Appeal Tbnl 1987-; Hon MPhil 1986; *Recreations* fly fishing; *Clubs* Sheffield; *Style*— Michael Goode, Esq; Bridge End Cottage, Brough, Bradwell, Sheffield (☎ 0433 20015); Taylor & Emmet, 2 Norfolk Row, Sheffield (☎ 0433 766 111)

GOODE, Raymond Arthur; s of late Arthur Thomas Goode, of London, and Elsie Florence, *née* Hayes; *b* 24 April 1934; *Educ* Colindale Secdy Sch; *m* 1, 23 Aug 1956 (m dis 1976), Iris Margaret, da of Thomas Horn (d 1980); 2 da (Janette Ann b 15 July 1965, Karen Elizabeth b 4 Nov 1966); m 2, 28 Aug 1976, Yvonne, da of Philip Conway Cattrall; 2 da (Catherine b 27 Dec 1979, Helen b 23 April 1985); *Career* dir of photography; Rank Orgn Ltd Pinewood Studios 1956-61, Granada TV Ltd 1961-89; Brideshead Revisited (BAFTA nominee) 1981, Jewel in The Crown (BAFTA nominee) 1984; memb BSC; *Recreations* golf; *Clubs* New North Manchester Golf; *Style*— Raymond Goode, Esq; 4 Johnson Grove, Archer Park, Middleton, Manchester M24 4AE (☎ 061 654 8262)

GOODE, Prof Royston Miles (Roy); OBE (1972), QC (1990); s of Samuel Goode (d 1968), of Portsmouth, Hants, and Blooma, *née* Davies (d 1984); *b* 6 April 1933; *Educ* Highgate, Univ of London (LLB, LLD); *m* 18 Oct 1964, Catherine Anne, da of Jean Marcel Rueff; 1 da (Naomi b 1965); *Career* Nat Serv RASC 1955-57; admitted slr 1955, ptnr Victor Mishcon & Co 1963-71 (conslt 1971-88); Queen Mary Coll: prof of law 1971-73, Crowther prof of credit and commercial law 1973-89, dean of faculty laws and head dept 1976-80; fndr and dir Centre Commercial Law Studies 1979-89, Norton Rose prof of English law Univ of Oxford, fell St John's Coll Oxford 1990-, transferred to the Bar Inner Temple 1988; UK rep and memb governing Cncl UNIDROIT Rome 1989-; Freeman City of London; FBA 1988; *Books* Hire-Purchase Law & Practice (2 edn 1970), Proprietary Rights & Insolvency in Sales Transactions (1985, 2 edn, 1989), Commercial Law (revised, 1988), Legal Problems of Credit & Security (2 edn, 1988), Principles of Corporate Insolvency Law; *Recreations* chess, walking, browsing in bookshops; *Style*— Prof Roy Goode, Esq, OBE, QC; 42 St John St, Oxford OX1 2LH (☎ 0865 515494); St John's College, Oxford OX1 3JP (☎ 0865 277399)

GOODENOUGH, Anthony Michael; CMG (1990); s of Rear Adm Michael Grant Goodenough, DSO, CBE (d 1955), and Nancy Waterfield, *née* Slater; *b* 5 July 1941; *Educ* Wellington, New Coll Oxford (BA, MA, exhibitor); *m* 22 July 1967, Veronica Mary, da of Lt col Peter Pender-Cudlip, LVO; 2 s (Francis Nicholas b 1970, Robert Henry b 1979), 1 da (Eleanor Margaret b 1968); *Career* VSO Sarawak 1963-64; HM Dip Serv: joined 1967, second sec Br Embassy Athens 1967-70, private sec to Parly Under Sec FCO 1970-71, private sec to Min of State FCO 1971-74, first sec Br Embassy Paris 1974-77, first sec FCO 1977-80, cnsllr secondment to Cabinet Office 1980-82, head of Chancery Br Embassy Islamabad, cnsllr FCO 1986-89, Br high commissioner Ghana 1989-, ambassador to Togo 1989-; *Style*— Anthony Goodenough, Esq, CMG; Foreign & Commonwealth Office, King Charles St, London SW1A 2AH

GOODENOUGH, Frederick Roger; DL (Oxfordshire 1989); 3 (but 2 surviving) s of Sir William Macnamara Goodenough, 1 Bt (d 1951), and Dorothea Louisa (d 1987), da of Ven the Hon Kenneth Gibbs, DD, 5 s of 1 Baron Aldenham; *b* 21 Dec 1927; *Educ* Eton, Magdalene Coll Cambridge (MA), Oxford (MA); *m* 15 May 1954, Marguerite June, o da of David Forbes Mackintosh, sometime headmaster of Loretto; 1 s (David b 1955), 2 da (Annabel b 1957, Victoria b 1961); *Career* RN 1946-48; joined Barclays Bank Ltd 1950; local dir: Birmingham 1958-60, Reading 1960-69, Oxford 1969-87; dir: Barclays Bank UK Ltd 1971-87, Barclays International Ltd 1977-87, Barclays plc 1985-89, Barclays Bank plc 1979-89; advsy dir Barclays Bank Thames Valley Region 1988- 89, memb London Ctee Barclays Bank DCO 1966-71, Barclays Bank International Ltd 1971-80; sr ptnr Broadwell Manor Farm 1968-; curator Oxford Univ Chest 1974-; tstee: Nuffield Med Benefaction 1968- (chm 1987-), Nuffield Dominions Tst 1968- (chm 1987-), Nuffield Orthopaedic Tst 1978- (chm 1981-), Oxford & Dist Hosps Improvement & Devpt Fund 1968- (chm 1982-88), Oxford Preservation Tst 1980-89; govr: Shiplake Coll 1963-74 (chm 1966-70), Wellington Coll 1968-74; fell Linnean Soc (memb Cncl 1968-75, treas 1970-75); FRSA; govr London House for Overseas Graduates 1985-, tstee Radcliffe Med Fndn 1987-, supernumerary fell Wolfson Coll Oxford 1989-; High Sheriff of Oxfordshire 1987-88; *Recreations* shooting, fishing, photography, ornithology; *Clubs* Brooks's; *Style*— F R Goodenough, Esq, DL; Broadwell Manor, Lechlade, Glos GL7 3QS (☎ 036 786 326)

GOODENOUGH, Gary; s of Le Roy Goodenough (d 1960), of Rochester, Minnesota, USA, and Mary Wright, *née* Remington; *b* 1 Nov 1947; *Educ* Phillips Exeter Acad, Dartmouth Coll, Wharton Sch of Univ of Pennsylvenia (MBA); *m* 12 July 1969, Nancy Lee, da of Ellis Jensen; 1 s (Jason Edward b 1979); *Career* Saloman Brothers Inc: joined 1975, vice pres 1978, dir 1986, md 1987-; *Recreations* swimming; *Style*— Gary Goodenough, Esq; Salomon Bros Int Ltd, 111 Buckingham Palace Rd, London SW1W 0SB (☎ 071 721 3110)

GOODENOUGH, Sir Richard Edmund; 2 Bt (UK 1943); s of Sir William Macnamara Goodenough, 1 Bt (d 1951); *b* 9 June 1925; *Educ* Eton, Christ Church Oxford; *m* 22 Dec 1951, Jane Isobel, da of Harry Stuart Parnell McLernon (d 1950), of Gisborne, NZ; 1 s (William b 1954), 2 da (Rosemary b 1952, Joanna b 1958); *Career* Coldstream Gds WWII; *Style*— Sir Richard Goodenough, Bt

GOODENOUGH, William McLernon; s and h of Sir Richard Goodenough, 2 Bt; *b* 5 Aug 1954; *Educ* Stanbridge Earls; *m* 12 June 1982, Louise Elizabeth, da of Capt Michael Ortmans, LVO, RN, of 48 Bishops Rd, Fulham; 2 da (Sophie Julia b 1986, Celia Isobel b 1989); *Career* design conslt, md; *Recreations* shooting, fishing, stalking; *Style*— William Goodenough, Esq

GOODEVE, (John) Anthony; s of Cdr Sir Charles Frederick Goodeve, OBE (d 1980), of London NW11, and Janet Irene, *née* Wallace; *b* 4 Aug 1944; *Educ* Canford; *m* 2 Oct 1965, Susan Mary, da of Sydney John Tupper (d 1988), of Petts Wood, Kent; 1 da (Claire Michelle b 29 May 1982); *Career* RNR 1963-66; Shell Mktg Ltd 1964-68 (latterly sr indust asst Shell UK Oil), md Dupré Vermiculite Ltd 1978-79, gp mktg exec Wood Hall Bldg Gp Ltd 1979-80, chief exec and md Grosvenor Property & Fin Ltd 1980-, proprietor Mr Quickpix Photolabs 1985-; Freeman City of London 1969, Liveryman Worshipful Co of Salters 1969; FInstD, LRPS; *Recreations* work, swimming; *Clubs* IOD; *Style*— Anthony Goodeve, Esq; Highfields House, 4 Prospect Lane, Harpenden, Herts

GOODEVE, Lady; Janet Irene; *née* Wallace; PhD; da of Rev J M Wallace, of Winnipeg, Canada; *m* 1932, Sir Charles Frederick Goodeve, OBE (d 17 April 1980); 2 s; *Style*— Lady Goodeve; 38 Middleway, London NW11 6SG (☎ 081 455 7308)

GOODFELLOW, Mark Aubrey; s of Alfred Edward Goodfellow, of Tonbridge, Kent, and Lucy Emily Goodfellow; *b* 7 April 1931; *Educ* Preston Manor Co Sch Wembley, LSE; 10 Oct 1964, Madelyn Susan; 1 s (Adam b 1969), 1 da (Venetia b 1967); *Career* Nat Serv RAF 1949-51; Dip Serv 1951-: Br Mil Govt 1954-56, second sec Br Embassy Khartoum 1956-59, FO 1959-63, Br Embassy Yaounde Cameron 1963-66, Br trade cmmnr Hong Kong 1966-71, FCO 1971-74, Br Embassy Ankara 1974-78, HM consul Atlanta USA 1978-82, Br Embassy Washington DC (cnsllr Hong Kong commercial affrs also accreditted to Ottawa) 1982-84, cnsllr commercial Br high cmmn Lagas 1984-87, HM ambassador Libreville Gabon 1987-90; *Clubs* Travellers', (Hong Kong, Ikoyi, Lagos); *Style*— Mark Goodfellow, Esq

GOODGER, Donald; s of Charles Thomas Goodger (d 1986), and Miriam, *née* Rowe (d 1979); *b* 1 Oct 1930; *Educ* Wyggeston GS Leicester, Leicester Coll of Tech (BSc); *m* 29 Aug 1959, (Anne) Priscilla, da of Percy Dalton (d 1968); 1 s (Anthony b 1963), 1 da (Katharine b 1960); *Career* engr; Scott Wilson Kirkpatrick 1957-64; Pick Everard Keay and Gimson: engr 1964-67, assoc 1967-82, ptnr 1982-; past chm IStructE E Midlands Branch 1981-82; FICE 1975, FIStructE 1972, MConsE 1985; *Recreations* beagling, walking; *Clubs* Leicestershire; *Style*— Donald Goodger, Esq; 37 Grenfell Rd, Leicester LE2 2PA (☎ 0533 705150); Pick Everard Keay and Gimson, 7 Friar Lane, Leicester LE1 5JD (☎ 0533 513311)

GOODHARDT, Prof Gerald Joseph; s of George Goodhardt (d 1978), of London, and Miriam, *née* Simmons (d 1978); *b* 5 April 1930; *Educ* Downing Coll Cambridge (MA, DipMathStat); *m* 27 Jan 1957, Valerie Yvonne, da of Walter Goldsmith (d 1968), of Hove; 1 s (Ian b 1961), 1 da (Catherine b 1958); *Career* res dir Young & Rubicam Ltd 1958-65, dir Aske Research Ltd 1965-75, reader in mktg Thames Poly 1975-81, Sir John E Cohen prof of consumer studies City Univ Business Sch 1981-; chm Market Res Soc 1973-74, hon sec Royal Statistical Soc 1982-88, regnl cncllr for N Thames Gas Consumers Cncl 1986-; FSS 1954, MMRS 1958, FCIM 1983; *Books* The Television Audience (1975 and 1987); *Recreations* grandchildren; *Style*— Prof Gerald Goodhardt; City University Business School, Frobisher Crescent, Barbican Centre, London EC2Y 8HB (☎ 071 920 0111, fax 071 588 2756)

GOODHART, Hon Lady (Celia McClare); *née* Herbert; er da of 2 Baron Hemingford; *b* 25 July 1939; *Educ* St Michael's Sch Limpsfield, St Hilda's Coll Oxford (MA); *m* 21 May 1966, Sir William Howard Goodhart, 2 s of Prof Arthur Lehman Goodhart, KBE (hon), QC, of Whitebarn, Boars Hill, Oxford; 1 s (Benjamin b 1972), 2 da (Annabel Frances b 1967, Laura Christabel b 1970); *Career* Civil Serv (Miny of Agric and Treasy) 1960-66; history tutor 1966-81: Queen's Coll London, Westminster Tutors; selected as prospective Parly candidate (SDP) Kettering 1982, fought 1983 and 1987 Gen Elections for the SDP Liberal Alliance; memb: Data Protection Ctee 1976-78, Nat Gas Consumers Cncl (chm N Thames) 1978-81; pres London Marriage Guidance Cncl 1990-, chm Youth Clubs UK 1989-; hon fell St Hilda's Coll Oxford; Principal Queen's Coll London 1991-; *Style*— The Hon Lady Goodhart; 43 Campden Hill Square, London W8 7JR (☎ 071 221 4830)

GOODHART, Margaret, Lady; (Margaret Mary) Eileen; da of late Morgan Morgan, of Cray, Powys; *m* 19 Feb 1944, Sir John Gordon Goodhart, 3 Bt (d 1979); 1 s (Sir Robert *qv*), 1 da (Mrs John Soul b 1945); *Style*— Eileen, Lady Goodhart; Holtye, 17 Mavelstone Close, Bromley

GOODHART, Lt-Col Mark Henry; s of Harry Goodhart (d 1976), of W Thorpe, Lymington, Hants, and Mary Suzette, *née* Haworth (d 1986); *b* 2 May 1931; *Educ* Stowe; *m* 8 Feb 1964, Angela, da of Cdr Eric May, OBE, RN; 1 s (Jonathan b 24 July 1965), 1 da (Caroline b 29 April 1967); *Career* 14/20 Kings Hussars 1949-86; graduate Armed Forces Staff Coll (USA) 1973-74, GOS1 Fort Knox USA 1974-76; Cdr RAC Tactical Sch 1976-79, GSO1 Liaison 1 Dutch Corps 1979-81, Cdr Salisbury Plain Trg Area 1982-86; chm Rainbow Consits, yacht master examiner DTI RYA; Freeman City of London 1952, Liveryman Worshipful Co of Grocers 1959; *Recreations* sailing, country sports; *Clubs* Cavalry & Guards, Royal Yacht Sqdn; *Style*— Lt-Col Mark Goodhart; The Barn House, Hurstbourne Priors, Whitchurch, Hants (☎ 0256 893133)

GOODHART, Rear Adm (Hilary Charles) Nicholas; CB (1973); s of Gavin Caird Goodhart (d 1974), of Newbury, Berks, and Evelyn Winifred Alphega, *née* Mahon; ggf Jakob Emanuel Guthardt came to Eng in 1755 in Ct of George II; *b* 28 Sept 1919; *Educ* RNC Dartmouth, RN Engrg Coll Keyham; *m* 1975, Molly, da of Robert Copsey (d 1956), of Langstone, Farlington, Hants; 1 step s (Ian), 2 step da (Alyson, Fiona); *Career* Engrg Offr RN, served in Med 1941-43, Pilot 1944, Fighter Pilot Indian Ocean 1945, Test Pilot 1946, Naval Test Flying 1947-51, Br Naval Staff Washington 1952-55, Navy Staff Serv and MOD, Rear Adm 1970, ret 1973; dir: Brassey's Def Publishers Ltd, Res Engrgs Ltd, Southdown Aero Servs Ltd; competition glider pilot 1956-72, competed as memb Br team in 7 World Gliding Championships (world champion 1956, runner up 1958), competed in 9 Br Nat Championships (three times Nat Champion, three times runner up), competed in 2 US Nat Championships (winner 1955), holds Br Gliding Record of flight of 579 km to a declared goal, first UK pilot to get Int Diamond Gliding Badge, Royal Aero Club Silver medal 1956, Fedn Aeronautique Int Tissandier Diploma 1972; invented mirror deck-landing system for aircraft carriers; designed and built 42m span man-powered aircraft, led team bldg the Sigma advanced glider; memb Worshipful Co of Grocers (Master 1981); FRAeS; Legion of Merit (US) 1958; *Recreations* bee keeping, genealogy, computing; *Clubs* Army & Navy; *Style*— Rear Adm Nicholas Goodhart, CB; Church House, Uffculme, Cullompton, Devon EX15 3AX

GOODHART, Sir Philip Carter; MP (C) Beckenham 1983-; eld s of Prof Arthur Lehman Goodhart, KBE (hon), QC, FBA, and Cecily, *née* Carter; *b* 3 Nov 1925; *Educ* Hotchkiss Sch USA, Trinity Coll Cambridge; *m* 1950, Valerie Forbes, da of Clinton Winant, of NY; 3 s, 4 da; *Career* served KRRC and Para Regt 1943-47; ed staff: Daily Telegraph 1950-55, Sunday Times 1955-57; contested (C) Consett Co Durham 1950, MP (C) Bromley Beckenham 1957-1983, memb Cncl Consumers' Assoc 1959-68 and 1970-79, vice pres Consumers' Assoc 1983; jt sec 1922 Ctee 1960-79; memb: Cons Advsy Ctee on Policy 1973-79, Exec Ctee Br Cncl 1974-79; chm Parly NI Ctee 1976-79, memb Advsy Cncl on Public Records 1979; Parly under-sec of state: NI Office 1979-81, MOD 1981; chm Sulgrave Manor Bd 1982-; kt 1981; *Books* Fifty Ships That

Saved The World (1965), The 1922: The History of the 1922 Ctee (1973), Full-Hearted Consent (1975); *Pamphlets incl* Stand On Your Own Four Feet - a Study of Work Sharing and Job Splitting (1982); *Clubs* Beefsteak, Carlton, Garrick; *Style*— Sir Philip Goodhart, MP; Whitebarn, Boars Hill, Oxford (☎ 0865 735294); 27 Phillimore Gardens, London W8 7QG (☎ 071 937 0822)

GOODHART, Sir Robert Anthony Gordon; 4 Bt (UK 1911); s of Sir John Goodhart, 3 Bt, FRCGP (d 1979), and Eileen, Lady Goodhart, *qv*; *b* 15 Dec 1948; *Educ* Rugby, Univ of London, Guy's Hosp Med Sch (MB BS); *m* 1972, Kathleen Ellen, da of Rev Alexander Duncan MacRae (d 1979), of 45 Laggan Rd, Inverness; 2 s, 2 da; *Heir* s, Martin Andrew Goodhart b 9 Sept 1974; *Career* medical practitioner 1976-; MRCGP; *Recreations* cricket, sailing, music; *Style*— Sir Robert Goodhart, Bt; The Old Rectory, Netherbury, Bridport, Dorset DT6 5NB (☎ 030 888 248)

GOODHART, Sir William Howard; QC (1979); 2 s of Prof Arthur Lehman Goodhart, KBE (hon), QC (d 1978), and Cecily, *née* Carter; *b* 18 Jan 1933; *Educ* Eton, Trinity Coll Cambridge, Harvard Law Sch; *m* 21 May 1966, Hon Celia Herbert, da of 2 Baron Hemingford, qv; 1 s, 2 da; *Career* called to the Bar Lincoln's Inn 1957; kt 1989; *Style*— Sir William Goodhart, QC; 43 Campden Hill Sq, London W8 7JR Youlbury House, Boars Hill, Oxford

GOODHEW, Duncan Alexander; s of Donald Frederick Goodhew (d 1972), of Church House, Yapton, W Sussex, and Dolores Perle, *née* Venn; *b* 27 May 1957; *Educ* Millfield Sch, North Carolina State Univ USA; *m* 24 Dec 1984; *Career* swimmer; first int appearance Montreal Olympic Games 1976 (7th in 100 metres breast stroke final), capt Eng and GB Squad 1978-80; competitions: Commonwealth Games 1978 (3 Silver medals: 100 metres breast stroke, 200 metres breast stroke, 4 x 100 medley), World Championships 1978 (forth 100 metre breast stroke, third 4 x 100 medley relay), Moscow Olympic Games (first 100 metre breast stroke, sixth 200 metre breast stroke, third 4 x 100 medley relay); memb 2 and 4 man bob sleigh team Euro Championships 1981; currently dir the Barbican Health and Fitness Centre; *Style*— Duncan Goodhew, Esq; c/o Athole Still International Management, 113 Church Rd, London SE19 2PR (☎ 081 771 5271, fax 081 771 8172)

GOODHEW, Prof Peter John; s of Philip Arthur Goodhew (d 1979), and Sheila Mary, *née* Maurau; *b* 3 July 1943; *Educ* Kings Coll Sch, Univ of Birmingham (BSc, PhD, DSc); *m* 27 July 1968, Gwendoline Diane, da of Frederick Fletcher; 1 s (Robert b 1972), 1 da (Laura b 1974); *Career* prof: Univ of Surrey 1986-89 (lectr 1968, reader 1982), Dept of Materials Sci and Engrg Univ of Liverpool 1990-; chm Br Jt Ctee on Electron Microscopy; cncl memb: Inst of Metals, Fedn of Materials Insts; MInstP 1972, CEng 1978, FIM 1983, CPhys 1985; *Books* Specimen Preparation in Materials Science (1972), The Operation of The Transmission Electron Microscope (1984), Specimen Preparation for TEM of Materials 1984), Thin Foil Preparation for Electron Microscopy (1985), Electron Microscopy and Analysis (2 edn 1988), Light Element Analysis in the TEM (1988); *Recreations* running, reading; *Style*— Prof Peter Goodhew

GOODHEW, Sir Victor Henry; s of late Rudolph Goodhew, of Mannings Heath Sussex, and late Rose, *née* Pullen; *b* 30 Nov 1919; *Educ* King's Coll Sch; *m* 1, 1940 (m dis 1951), Sylvia Johnson; 1 s, 1 da; m 2, 1951 (m dis 1972), Suzanne Gordon-Burge; m 3, 1972 (m dis 1981), Eva Rittinghausen; *Career* served WWII RAF, Sqdn Ldr; memb: Westminster City Cncl 1953-59, LCC 1958-61; contested (C) Paddington N 1955, MP (C) St Albans 1959-83; PPS to: Civil Lord Admty 1962-63, Jt Parly Sec for Tport 1963-64; asst Govt whip 1970, ldr cmmr Treasy 1970-73; vice chm Cons Def Ctee 1965-70 and 1974-83; memb: Speaker's Panel of Chairmen 1975-83, Select Ctee House of Commons Servs 1978-83, House of Commons Cmmn 1979-83; jt sec 1922 Ctee 1979-83; kt 1982; *Clubs* Buck's; *Style*— Sir Victor Goodhew; The Coach House, St Leonard's Dale, Winkfield Road, Windsor, Berkshire SL4 4AQ (☎ 0753 859073, 071 235 4911)

GOODIER, Roger Banks; s of Benjamin Bancroft Goodier (d 1967), and Ada Irene Goodier (d 1986); *b* 7 Sept 1944; *Educ* Moseley Hall GS, Univ of Sheffield (LLB); *m* 20 July 1974, Denise, da of Eric Forshaw; 2 s (Benjamin b 1975, Oliver b 1978); *Career* admitted slr 1970, sr ptnr Rowley Ashworth slrs; *Recreations* soccer, rugby union, cricket; *Clubs* Wig & Pen, Twickenham CC; *Style*— Roger Goodier, Esq; 69 Popes Ave, Twickenham, Middx (☎ 081 894 1355); Rowley Ashworth, 247 The Broadway, Wimbledon, London SW19 1SE (☎ 081 543 2277, fax 081 543 0143, telex 8951693)

GOODING, Alfred Joseph; OBE (1981); s of Ivan Gooding (d 1988), of Clarmont, Parc Seymour, Penhow, Gwent, and Francis, *née* Grace (d 1984); *b* 13 March 1932; *Educ* Pontywaun GG, Crumlin Tech Coll; *m* 23 June 1956, Lavinia Florence, da of John George Lennon (d 1976), of Newport; 2 s (Russell b 17 Aug 1960, Lloyd b 20 May 1967), 1 da (Joanne b 25 June 1963); *Career* began own building business 1958, fndr chm Catnic Components Ltd 1969-83, chm Gooding Gp 1983-; pres Nat Fedn of Building Trades Employment S Wales Region 1969-70; CBI; memb Welsh Cncl 1968-88, chm Wales 1983-85 (vice chm 1982), memb Nat Cncl London; dep chm Bd of Govrs Rougemont Sch Newport; memb: Wales and Marches Postal Bd, BR Western Region Bd, Bd of Wales Sport Aid Fndn; High Sheriff of Gwent 1980-81; memb Royal Opera House Tst, pres Action Aid for Disabled Newport, FRSA; Freeman: City of London 1982, Worshipful Co of Marketors 1982; hon fell Poly of Wales 1988; FInst M 1980, FInstD, CBIM 1989, FRSA; *Recreations* shooting, veteran cars, rugby; *Clubs* Carlton, RAC; *Style*— Alfred Gooding, Esq, OBE; 27 Park Place, Cardiff CF1 3BA (☎ 0222 3090191)

GOODING, Christopher Anderson; s of Frank L Gooding, of Brighton, and Maureen Gooding; *b* 27 May 1957; *Educ* St Lawrence Coll Ramsgate, Brunel Univ (LLBV); *m* Sharon Miriam, da of Jafr Khajeh, of Cyprus; *Career* admitted slt 1981; ptnr Clyde & Co 1985- (joined 1981); memb Law Soc; *Recreations* motor racing, book collecting, squash; *Style*— Christopher Gooding, Esq; Clyde & Co, Beaufort House, Chertsey St, Guildford, Surrey GU1 4HA (☎ 0438 31161, telex 859477 CLYDE G, fax 0483 67330)

GOODING, Mel; s of Frederick Gooding (d 1990), and Kathleen, *née* Cox; *b* 3 June 1941; *Educ* Northgate GS for Boys Ipswich, Univ of Sussex (BA, MA); *m* 1967, Esther Rhiannon Coslette, da of Ceri Richards; 2 s (Francis b 1974, Thomas b 1979); *Career* lectr in English, pedagogics and communication various London colls 1966- (notably Sidney Webb Coll of Education 1972-80 and City of London Poly 1980-); contrib numerous articles to art press 1980- incl: Arts Review, Artscribe, Flash Art, Art Monthly; contrib numerous introductions and essays to exhibition catalogues 1979-; curator of exhibitions incl: Ceri Richards (Tate Gallery) with Bryan Robertson 1981, Ceri Richards Graphics (Nat Gallery of Wales and tour) 1979-80, Poetry into Art (UEA and Nat Library of Wales) 1982, F E McWilliam (Tate Gallery) 1989, Michael Rothenstein Retrospective (Stoke-on-Trent City Art Gallery and tour); author and publisher (with Bruce McLean) of seven artists' books 1985-90; *Publications incl*: Ceri Richards Graphics (1979), F E McWilliam (1989), Michael Rothenstein The Retrospective (1989), The Phenomenon of Presence Frank Auerbach (1989), The Experience of Painting (1989), Malevich A Box (with Julian Rothenstein, 1990), Bruce McLean (1990), John Hoyland (1990), William Alsop Architect (1991): memb Int Assoc of Art Critics; *Recreations* walking, birdwatching; *Style*— Mel Gooding, Esq; 62 Castelnau, Barnes, London SW13 (☎ 081 748 4434)

GOODISON, Sir Alan Clowes; KCMG (1985, CMG 1975), CVO (1980); o s of Harold Clowes Goodison, and Winifred, *née* Ludlam; *b* 20 Nov 1926; *Educ* Colfe's GS Lewisham, Trinity Coll Cambridge; *m* 1956, Anne Rosemary, o da of Edward Fitton, of Leeds; 1 s, 2 da; *Career* entered FO 1949; serv: Cairo, Tripoli, Khartoum, Lisbon, Amman, Bonn, Kuwait; head Southern European Dept FCO 1973-76, min Rome Embassy 1976-80, asst under sec of state FCO 1981-83, ambass to Irish Republic 1983-86; dir The Wates Fndn 1988-; Grande Ufficiale dell'Ordine Al Merito (Italy); *Style*— Sir Alan Goodison, KCMG, CVO; 12 Gardnor Mansions, Church Row, London NW3 6UR; The Wates Foundation, 1260 London Rd, Norbury, London SW16 4EG

GOODISON, Sir Nicholas Proctor; yr s of Edmund Harold Goodison, of Longacre, Radlett, Herts, and Eileen Mary Carrington, *née* Proctor; *b* 16 May 1934; *Educ* Marlborough, King's Coll Cambridge (BA, MA, PhD); *m* 18 June 1960, Judith Nicola, o da of Capt Robert Eustace Abel Smith (ka 1940), Grenadier Gds (*see* Burke's Landed Gentry 1967); 1 s, 2 da; *Career* chm H E Goodison & Co (later Quilter Goodison & Co, now Quilter Goodison Co Ltd) 1976-86; dir: Gen Accident Fire and Life Assurance Corporation plc 1987-, Ottoman Bank 1988-, TSB Bank plc 1989-, British Steel plc 1989-, Burlington Magazine Ltd; dep chm Ctee of London and Scottish Clearing Bankers 1989-, chm TSB Group plc 1989-; chm Int Stock Exchange 1986-88 (memb Cncl 1968-88); memb: Cncl Industl Soc, Exec Ctee Nat Art-Collections Fund 1976- (chm 1986-); dir: Eng Nat Opera 1977- (vice chm 1980-), City Arts Tst; chm Courtauld Inst of Art 1982-; pres: Antiquarian Horological Soc, Int Fedn of Stock Exchanges 1985-86; pres Furniture History Soc, keeper of furniture Fitzwilliam Museum Cambridge; govr Marlborough Coll; Hon DLitt City Univ 1985, Hon LLD Univ of Exeter 1989; CBIM, FIOD 1989, FCIB 1989 (vice chm 1989-); Hon Fell Royal Academy, Chev Legion d'Honneur 1990-; FSA, FRSA; kt 1982; *Publications* English Barometers 1680-1860 (1968, 2 edn 1977), Ormolu: The Work of Matthew Boulton (1974), author of many papers and articles on the history of furniture, clocks and barometers; *Recreations* history of furniture and decorative arts, opera, walking, fishing; *Clubs* Arts, Athenaeum, Beefsteak; *Style*— Sir Nicholas Goodison, FSA; TSB Group plc, 25 Milk Street, London EC2V 8LU (☎ 071 606 7070)

GOODLAD, Alastair Robertson; MP (C) Eddisbury 1983-; yst s of late Dr John Fordyce Robertson Goodlad, of Lincoln, and Isobel, *née* Sinclair; *b* 4 July 1943; *Educ* Marlborough, King's Coll Cambridge (MA, LLB); *m* 1968, Cecilia Barbara, 2 da of Col Richard Hurst (s of Sir Cecil Hurst, GCMG, KCB) by his w Lady Barbara, *née* Lindsay (6 da of 27 Earl of Crawford (and Earl Balcarres), KT, PC); 2 s; *Career* contested (C) Crewe 1970, MP (C) Northwich Feb 1974-83; asst govt whip 1981-82, lord cmmr Treasy 1982-84, jt vice chm Cons Pty Trade Ctee 1979- (jt hon sec 1978-), hon sec All Party Heritage Gp 1979-; memb: Select Ctee Agriculture 1979-, House of Commons Bridge Team in matches against Lords 1982-85, Parly under sec of state at Dept of Energy 1984-87; chm: NW Area Cons Membs of Parly 1987-89, All Pty Gp for Refugees 1987-89; memb Select Ctee on Televising Proceedings of the House, pres Water Companies Assoc 1989, comptroller Her Majesty's Household and sr govt whip 1989, treas of HM Household and dep chief whip 1990-; *Clubs* Brooks's; *Style*— Alastair Goodlad, Esq, MP; c/o House of Commons, London SW1A 0AA

GOODLAND, Judith Mary; da of Rolf Thornton Ferro (d 1985), and Joan, *née* O'Hanlon; *b* 26 May 1938; *Educ* Howell's Sch Denbigh, Univ of Bristol (BA), Charlotte Mason Coll (Cert Ed); *m* 4 April 1961 (m dis 1983), Alan Thomas Goodland; 1 s (William Royse b 1966), 2 da (Helen Joanna b 1963, Deborah Clare b 1965); *Career* head of Modern Lanuages Dept Cartmel Priory Sch Cumbria 1968-72; headmistress: St Georges Sch Ascot 1983-88, Wycombe Abby Sch 1989-; chm Bucks Co Expdn and Exploration Panel Duke of Edinburgh Award Scheme 1989- (expdn assessor Cumbria Panel 1979-); *Recreations* fell walking, golf, bridge; *Clubs* University Women's; *Style*— Mrs J M Goodland; Wycombe Abbey School, High Wycombe, Bucks HP11 1PE (☎ 0494 20381, fax 0494 473836)

GOODMAN, Andrew David; s of Bernard Goodman, and Heléne, *née* Greenspan (d 1984); *b* 4 June 1956; *Educ* Queen Elizabeth's Sch Barnet, Univ of Southampton (LLB); *m* 6 June 1982, Sandra Maureen, da of Charles Burney; 2 s (Adam Howard b 1986, Simon Nicholas b 1989); *Career* called to the Bar Inner Temple 1978; ACI Arb 1989; *Books* The Court Guide (1980, 1985-91 7 edn), The Bar Diary (1982, 1983, 1984), Gilbert and Sullivan At Law (1983), The Royal Courts of Justice Guide (1985), Gilbert and Sullivan's London (1988), Frank Cass Professional Journals (legal series ed, 1984-); *Recreations* travel, music, Victorian theatre; *Clubs* Wig & Pen; *Style*— Andrew Goodman, Esq; 2 Harcourt Buildings, Temple, EC4Y 9DB (☎ 071 353 1394, fax 071 353 4134)

GOODMAN, Baron (Life Peer UK 1965), of City of Westminster; Arnold Abraham Goodman; CH (1972); s of Joseph and Bertha Goodman; *b* 21 Aug 1913; *Educ* UCL, Downing Coll Cambridge (MA, LLB); *Career* slr 1936, sr ptnr Messrs Goodman Derrick & Co; serv WWII RA TA as Maj; chm: Jewish Chronicle Tst 1970-, Motability (charity helping the disabled) 1977-; pres: Theatres Advsy Cncl 1972-, Theatres Tst 1987-, ABSA 1989-; dep chm Br Cncl 1974-; Master UC Oxford 1976-86; *Style*— The Rt Hon Lord Goodman, CH; 9-11 Fulwood Place, Gray's Inn, London WC1V 6HQ (☎ 071 404 0606)

GOODMAN, Cyril Joshua; s of Paul Goodman (d 1949), and Romana, *née* Manczyk (d 1955); *b* 10 May 1915; *Educ* St Paul's Sch; *m* 16 Dec 1948, Ruth, da of Percy Perez Ernest Sabel (d 1946), of London and Burnham-on-Crouch; 5 s (Paul b 1952, Martin b 1953, Andrew b 1955, Roger b 1960, Thomas b 1961), 1 da (Sarah b 1950); *Career* WWII 1939-45: Field Security Police 1940, instr Intelligence Trg Centre Matlock 1941, cmmnd Intelligence Corps 1941; served: Cairo, Haifa, Beirut 1942; Asst Adjt Palestine Trg Depot Sarafand 1943, Bde Intelligence Offr Jewish Inf Bde Gp 1944-45, GSO3 1945 (despatches); admitted slr 1937, sr ptnr Lindo & Co 1949-70, ptnr Nicholson Graham & Jones 1971-81; memb Bd of Deputies Br Jews 1948-50; chm: Exec Cncl Assoc for Jewish Youth 1948-50, Camperdown House Tst 1978-; first chm Crouch Harbour Authy 1975-82 (memb 1975-); hon slr Royal Corinthian YC 1959-81; Freeman City of London 1947, Liveryman City of London Slrs Co; memb Law Soc 1937; *Recreations* sailing, gardening, reading, travelling; *Clubs* Royal Corinthian Yacht, Little Ship; *Style*— Cyril Goodman, Esq; Tideways, Creeksea, Burnham-on-Crouch, Essex CM0 8PL (☎ 0621 782 679)

GOODMAN, Frederick; s of Hyman Goodman (d 1924); *b* 4 Nov 1910; *Educ* Univ of London, Chelsea Poly and business schs; *m* 1974, Iris Gene; *Career* conslt accountant and dir: Brilaw Properties Ltd, Keystone Credits Ltd, RS Holdings Ltd, Headtown Ltd, Powerlistic Ltd, Upton Heath Properties Ltd, St James Court Estate (1977) Ltd; underwriting memb Lloyd's; *Recreations* charity work; *Style*— Frederick Goodman, Esq; 11 Warwick Place, London W9 2PX (☎ 071 286 0970); 29/30 Fitzroy Square, London W1 (☎ 071 388 2444)

GOODMAN, Maj-Gen John David Whitlock; CB (1987); s of Brig Eric Whitlock Goodman, DSO, MC (d 1981), and Norah Dorothy, *née* Stacpoole (d 1986); *b* 20 May 1932; *Educ* Wellington, RMA Sandhurst; *m* 21 Dec 1957, (Valerie) Ann, da of D H H McDonald (d 1974), of Tates, Burley, Ringwood, Hants; 1 s (Jeremy Peter Whitlock b 1961), 2 da (Amanda Clare b 1959, Philippa Ann (Pippa) b 1971); *Career* Army Offr; cmmnd into RA 1952; serv: Eng, NI, Germany, Aden, Hong Kong, Sudan; instr Sandhurst and Staff Colls Camberley and Khartoum, cmmd J (Sidi Rezyh) Bn RNA 1966, 26 Field Regt RA 1973 and Royal Sch of Artillery 1978, dep mil sec 1981, dir

Army Air Corps 1983, ret 1987; dir and memb Advsy Gp ML Holdings plc; Hon Regt Col 24 Field Regt RA and 3 Regt Army Air Corps, Hon Col 266 OP Bn (The Gloucestershire Volunteer Artillery) RA (Vol); Guild of Air Pilots and Air Navigators; *Recreations* the countryside, tennis; *Style*— Maj-Gen David Goodman, CB; c/o Lloyds Bank Ltd, 37 Market Place, Warminster, Wiltshire BA12 9BD

GOODMAN, Prof John Francis Bradshaw; s of Edwin Goodman (d 1979), and Amy Bradshaw, *née* Warrener (d 1989); *b* 2 Aug 1940; *Educ* Chesterfield Sch, LSE (BSc), Univ of Manchester (MSc), Univ of Nottingham (PhD); *m* 12 Aug 1967, Elizabeth Mary, da of Frederick William Towns, of Romiley, Greater Manchester; 1 s (Richard b 1972), 1 da (Clare b 1970); *Career* personnel offr Ford Motor Co 1962-64, lectr in industl econs Univ of Nottingham 1964-69, industl rels advsr NBPI 1969-70, sr lectr in industl rels Univ of Manchester 1970-74, vice princ UMIST 1979-81 (Frank Thomas Prof of Industl Rels 1975-, head of Manchester Sch of Mgmnt 1977-79, 1986-88 and 1989-): visiting prof of industl rels: Univ of WA 1981 and 1984, McMaster Univ 1985; govr Withington Girls Sch; memb: Ctee of Mgmnt Wood St Mission Manchester, Cncl Manchester Business Sch; pres: Manchester Industl Rels Soc, Br Univs Industl Rels Assoc 1983-86; memb: Cncl ACAS, Panel of Arbitrators ACAS; CIPM 1986; *Books* Shop Stewards (1973), Rule-making and Industrial Peace (1977), Ideology and Shop-floor Industrial Relations (1980), Employee Participation (1981), Employment Relations in Industrial Society (1984), Unfair Dismissal Law and Employment Practice (1985); *Recreations* squash, fell walking; *Style*— Prof John Goodman; Manchester School of Management, Umist, PO Box 88, Manchester M60 1QD (☎ 061 236 3311, fax 061 228 7040, telex 666094)

GOODMAN, Margaret Beatrice (Maggie); da of John Bertram Goodman (d 1985), and Cissie Phyllis, *née* Kay (d 1952); *b* 26 Nov 1941; *Educ* Plymouth HS for Girls, Coll of Commerce Univ of Birmingham; *m* 1988, Dr Anthony Harold Mercer Gaze, s of William Mercer Gaze; *Career* asst ed New Era Magazine 1960-62, Honey Magazine 1962-67 (sub ed, showbusiness ed, features ed, asst ed), asst ed rising to ed Petticoat magazine 1967-69, freelance feature writer 1969-71, dep ed Cosmopolitan 1971-79, fndr ed Company 1979-88, launch ed Hello 1988-91; Editors' Editor award Br Soc of Magazine Eds; memb Br Soc of Magazine Eds 1978-91 (chm 1982); *Books* Every Man Should Have One (jt author, 1971); *Recreations* sailing, socialising; *Clubs* The Groucho; *Style*— Ms Maggie Goodman; Hello Ltd, 34 New Bridge St, London EC4V 6HH (☎ 071 489 9064, fax 071 236 6072)

GOODMAN, Nathanial; s of Samuel Morris Goodman (d 1948), of London, and Sarah, *née* Feldman (d 1959); *b* 28 March 1915; *Educ* Battersea GS; *m* 7 Jan 1947, Edith, da of Samuel Glekin (d 1963), of Glasgow; 1 s (Louis Melville b 1951); *Career* VR Sargent RAF India 1943-45, England 1939-43; City Site Estates plc; chm and dir: City Site Construction Ltd, City Site South Ltd, City Site North Ltd, Baltic Chamber Ltd, Daniel Ross Ltd, James Allan & Son North Ltd, Cameron Hoxaxi Ltd, Hascasci Ltd, Mademoiselle Anne Ltd, City Site Properties Ltd, Queensbridge Estates Ltd; *Clubs* RNVR Scotland; *Style*— Nathanial Goodman, Esq; 50 Wellington St, Glasgow (☎ 041 248 2534/01 133 135)

GOODMAN, Perry; s of Cyril Goodman (d 1982), and Anne, *née* Rosen (d 1985); *b* 26 Nov 1932; *Educ* Haberdashers' Aske's, Hampstead Sch, UCL (BSc); *m* 1958, Marcia Ann, da of Samuel Morris (d 1982); 1 s (Nicholas b 1959), 1 da (Rachel b 1964); *Career* 2 Lt Royal Corps of Signals 1956; jt head Chemistry Res Laboratory, Morgan Crucible Co 1960, sr scientific offr DSIR 1964, princ scientific offr Miny of Technol 1965, cnsllr (Scientific) Br Embassy Paris 1970, head Policy and Perspectives Unit DOI 1980, head Electrical Engr Branch DTI 1987 (head Advsy Servs and Design Policy Branch 1982), dir Indust and Regions Electricity Cncl 1990; memb Inst of Ceramics, FRSA; *Recreations* walking, talking, birdwatching; *Style*— Perry Goodman, Esq; 118 Westbourne Terrace Mews, London W2 6QG (☎ 071 262 0925); 10 Maltravers St, London WC2R 3ER (☎ 071 240 7891)

GOODMAN, Richard Antony; s of Antony Marlow Goodman, of Totternhoe, Beds, and Florence, *née* Sowry; *b* 17 June 1952; *Educ* Dunstable GS, Selwyn Coll Cambidge (MA); *m* 14 April 1979, Julie, da of John Edwin Williams, of Chilham, Kent; 2 s (Thomas b 1982, William b 1986), 1 da (Charlotte b 1989); *Career* admitted slr 1976; ptnr Cameron Markby 1981-; memb Law Soc; *Recreations* music, garden, photography; *Style*— Richard Goodman, Esq

GOODMAN, Richard Thomas; s of Thomas Henry Goodman (d 1957), of Hanbury Rd, Tottenham, and Alma Florence, *née* Harben (d 1969); *b* 10 Jan 1920; *Educ* Tottenham GS, City of London Coll; *m* 1, 1940 (m dis 1960), Joan Doris Hutcherson; 1 s (Stephen b 1946), 1 da (Diane b 1948); m 2, Shelagh Marie, da of Arthur Brown (d 1969), of Arnwood Cottage, Ringwood, Hants; 2 s (James b 1963, Geoffrey b 1966); *Career* WWII 1940-45, served Cambridge Regt, seconded Intelligence Corps (POW Singapore 1942-45); dir Erwin Wasey 1949-60, md Green Shield Trading Stamps Ltd 1960-78, mktg conslt Argos Distributors 1978- (dir 1975-78); Freeman City of London 1974, Liveryman Worshipful Co of Carmen 1974; MCAM, FCIM, FBIM; *Recreations* fly fishing, golf, reading; *Style*— Richard Goodman, Esq; 3 Latchmoor Way, Gerrards Cross, Bucks SL9 8LW (☎ 0753 885 165)

GOODMAN, Vera; da of Hyman Appleberg (d 1952), of London, and Flora, *née* Krichefski (d 1964); *Educ* N London Collegiate Sch, Univ of London; *m* Maurice Paul Goodman, s of Paul Goodman (d 1949); *Career* chm Sephardi Women's Guild 1966, rep Union of Jewish Women at United Nations Assoc 1970, Cons rep Nat Cncl of Women 1974-79, vice chm Governing Bd Russell Sch Petersham Surrey 1974-82, memb Central Cncl Cons Pty 1976-79, life vice pres Richmond and Barnes Cons Women's Constituency Ctee (chm 1976-79); memb: Bd of Elders Spanish and Portuguese Jews Congregation London 1977-80 and 1990-, Cons Women's Gen Purposes Ctee GLA 1979-85; currently memb: Exec Ctee Bd of Deputies of Br Jews (chm PR Ctee 1988), Central London Cncl Cons Friends of Israel; former memb: Br Section Euro Union of Women, Exec Cons Womens Nat Ctee, Nat Cncl for Soviet Jewry, Br Cncl World Sephardi Fedn; *Recreations* walking, reading, theatre, travel; *Style*— Mrs Vera Goodman; 87 Ashburnham Rd, Ham, Richmond, Surrey TW10 7NN (☎ 081 948 1060)

GOODRICH, David; s of William Boyle Goodrich (d 1984), of Sunderland, and Florence Bosenquett, *née* Douglas (d 1984); *b* 15 April 1941; *m* 5 June 1965, Margaret, da of Andrew Robertson Riley, of Sunderland; 1 s (John b 1981), 3 da (Helen b 1968, Kathryn b 1970, Alison b 1972); *Career* constructor RCNC MOD (Navy) 1970-80, md Br Ship Res Assoc 1980-88, chief exec British Maritime Technol Ltd 1988- (former md); CEng, MBA, memb RCNC, FRINA; *Recreations* squash, walking; *Clubs* East India; *Style*— David Goodrich, Esq; Whitecroft, Hatton Hill, Windlesham, Surrey GU20 6AB; British Maritime Technology, Orlando House, 1 Waldegrave Rd, Teddington, Middlesex TW11 8LZ (☎ 081 943 5544, fax 081 943 5347, telex 263118)

GOODRICH, Rt Rev Philip Harold Ernest; *see*: Worcester, Bishop of

GOODSON, Cdre (Frederick) Brian; OBE (1982); s of Frederick Orlando Goodson (d 1955), of Belfast, NI, and Edythe, *née* Hamer (d 1978); *b* 21 May 1938; *Educ* Campbell Coll Belfast, Britannia RNC Dartmouth Devon; *m* 25 Aug 1965, Susan Mary, (Sue), da of Reginald John Firmin (d 1981), of Dartmouth, Devon; 2 s (Simon b 1970, Hugo b 1973), 2 da (Pip b 1968, Becky b 1980); *Career* RN: coastal forces and cruisers and destroyers 1958-64, Aden 1964-65, Staff Britannia RNC Dartmouth 1970-72, exchange serv US Navy 1972-74, Cdr RN 1974, Supply Offr HMS Invincible 1980-81, Fleet Supply Offr 1981-82, Capt 1982, dir naval logistic planning 1985-87, chm Eurolog Naval Gp (NATO), Cdre and Cmdg Offr HMS Centurion (Naval Pay and Manning Centre) 1987-; chm govrs St Francis Special Sch Fareham; *Recreations* offshore sailing, squash, outdoor pursuits, family, reading; *Clubs* Lansdowne, Royal Naval Sailing Assoc; *Style*— Cdre Brian Goodson, Esq, OBE; HMS Centurion, Grange Rd, Gosport, Hants

GOODSON, Sir Mark Weston Lassam; 3 Bt (UK 1922); o s of Maj Alan Richard Lassam Goodson (d 1941) 2 s 1 Bt, and Clarisse Muriel Weston, *née* Adamson; suc Sir Alfred Lassam Goodson, 2 Bt 1986; *b* 12 Dec 1925; *Educ* Radley, Jesus Coll Cambridge; *m* 4 May 1949, Barbara Mary Constantine, da of Surgn Capt Reginald Joseph McAuliffe Andrews, RN, of Crandel, Ferndown, Dorset; 1 s, 3 da (Phyllida b 1950, Hilary b 1953, Christian b 1958); *Heir* s, Alan Reginald Goodson b 15 May 1960; *Style*— Sir Mark Goodson, Bt; Kilham, Mindrum, Northumberland TD12 4QS (☎ 089 085 217)

GOODSON-WICKES, Dr Charles; MP (C) Wimbledon 1987-; s of Ian Goodson Wickes (d 1972), of Stock Harvard, Essex, and Monica Frances Goodson-Wickes; *b* 7 Nov 1945; *Educ* Charterhouse, St Bart's Hosp, Inner Temple; *m* 17 April 1974, Judith Amanda, da of the late Cdr John Hopkinson, RN (d 1978), Sutton Grange, nr Stamford, Lincs; 2 s (Edward b 1976, Henry b 1978); *Career* house physician Addenbrooke's Hosp Cambridge 1972, surgn Capt Life Gds (served BAOR, NI, Cyprus) 1973-77, Silver Stick Mo, Household Cavalry 1977, Capt RARO; specialist physician St Bart's Hosp 1977-80, conslt physician BUPA 1977-86, occupational physician; barr; med advsr: Barclays Bank, Hogg Robinson, Standard Chartered; previously med advsr: Br Alcan, McKinsey, Meat and Livestock Cmmn, (UK) Norwegian Directorate of Health; vice chm Constitutional Affrs Ctee, memb Jt Ctee Consolidation of Bills, chm Asbestos Licensing Regulations Appeals Tbnl; sec: Defence Ctee, Arts and Heritage Ctee; former memb: Med Advsy Ctee, Indust Soc, Fitness Advsy Panel, IOD; treas Dr Ian Goodson-Wickes Fund for Handicapped Children 1979-88, memb Public Affrs Ctee Br Field Sports Soc 1980-; govr Highbury Grove Sch 1977-85; *Books* The New Corruption (1984); *Recreations* hunting, shooting, real tennis, gardening, travel, history; *Clubs* Boodle's, Pratt's, MCC, Melton Hunt, Guards Saddle, Pegasus, formerly Pitt (Cambridge); *Style*— Dr Charles Goodson-Wickes, MP; Watergate House, Bulford, Wilts (☎ 0980 32344); 37 St James's Place, London SW1 (☎ 071 629 0981); 8 Devonshire Place, London W1 (☎ 071 935 5011)

GOODWILL, Geoffrey Mortimer; s of Reginald Mortimer Goodwill (d 1978), and Jane Margaret King; *b* 13 Jan 1944; *Educ* Nunthorpe GS for Boys York; *m* 23 June 1973, Anne, da of James Henry Jewitt (d 1981), of York; 2 s (Russell b 1975, Robert b 1983), 1 da (Catherine b 1977); *Career* chartered surveyor; co dir appointed memb Main Bd Mountleigh Group plc 1985; school govr; FRICS; *Style*— Geoffrey Goodwill, Esq; 17 Adel Towers Ct, Leeds LS16 8ER (☎ 0532 677594); Leigh House, Leeds LS28 7XG (☎ 0532 555555, fax 0532 555556)

GOODWIN, Chuck Gilbert; s of Charles Sargeant Goodwin, of 17 Woodsome Lodge, Weybridge, Surrey, and Jessie Mowat, *née* Cardy; *b* 12 Oct 1942; *Educ* St Nicholas GS Northwood, Hornsey Coll of Art; *m* 1966, Janet Campbell, da of Edwin Cohen; 1 da (Victoria Jane b 1968); *Career* graphic designer; worked for Michael Tucker and Ian Bradbery, fndr ptnr (with John Sorrell) Goodwin Sorrell 1972-, ptnr (with Clive Dorman) Goodwin Dorman (company renamed Lampada 1986), conslt design dir Identity until 1988; maj projects incl: Jubilee Exhibition for BP, exhibitions for Hawker Siddeley Group; lectr Inst of Mktg; FCSD; *Recreations* walking, countryside; *Style*— Chuck Goodwin, Esq; 27 Artesian Rd, London W2 5DA (☎ 071 229 6811, fax 071 792 8849)

GOODWIN, David Pryce; *b* 10 May 1936; *Educ* Tonbridge, St Mary's Med Sch Univ of London (BSc, MB BS, MS); *m* 10 Oct 1970, Sarah Jane; *Career* fell in surgery Tulane Univ New Orleans 1970-71, conslt surgn Royal Berks Hosp 1974-; author of various pubns in med jls; FRCS 1966, Hon FACS 1989; *Recreations* sailing, conjuring; *Clubs* Royal Southampton Yacht, Magic Circle (London); *Style*— David Goodwin, Esq; Royal Berkshire Hospital, Reading RG1 5AN (☎ 0734 877418)

GOODWIN, Hon Mrs (Gillian Theodora Marianne); *née* Chorley; only da of 1 Baron Chorley, QC (d 1978), and Katharine Campbell, *née* Hopkinson; *b* 5 April 1929; *Educ* Liverpool Coll for Girls, St Anne's Coll Oxford; *m* 19 Jan 1965, (Francis) Godfrey Goodwin, yr s of Robert Goodwin (d 1923), of Lisbon; 1 s (Robert b 1969); *Style*— Hon Mrs Goodwin; 29 Chalcot Square, London NW1

GOODWIN, Sir Matthew Dean; CBE (1980); s of Matthew Dean Goodwin (d 1965), of Bothwell, and Mary Gertrude, *née* Barrie (d 1965); *b* 12 Dec 1929; *Educ* Glasgow Acad; *m* 15 Sept 1955, Margaret Eileen, da of Harold Campbell Colvil (d 1959), of Bearsden; 2 da (Frances Margaret b 1957, Carol Elizabeth b 1959); *Career* Nat Serv Flying Offr RAF; CA 1952; ptnr Davidson Down McGown 1959-68; chm: Hewden Stuart plc 1978- (fin dir 1968-78), Murray Enterprise plc 1984-, Scotcare Ltd 1988-; dir: Irvine Development Corporation 1980-90, Rocep Holdings Ltd, Murray Ventures plc; dir East Park Children's Home, treas Scot Cons Pty 1984-; kt 1988; *Recreations* shooting, farming, bridge; *Clubs* Western (Glasgow); *Style*— Sir Matthew Goodwin, CBE; 87 Kelvin Court, Anniesland, Glasgow G12 OAH (☎ 041 339 7541); Hewden Stuart plc, 135 Buchanan St, Glasgow (☎ 041 221 7331, fax 041 248 5104)

GOODWIN, (Trevor) Noël; s of Arthur Daniel Goodwin (d 1937), and Blanche, *née* Stephens (d 1956); more than three generations of master mariners and seafarers; *b* 25 Dec 1927; *Educ* educated in France, Univ of London (BA); *m* 1, 1954 (m dis 1960), Gladys Marshall Clapham; m 2, 1963, Mrs Elizabeth Anne Myers, *née* Mason; 1 step s (Richard); *Career* freelance critic, writer, ed and broadcaster specializing in music and dance; asst music critic: News Chronicle 1952-54, Manchester Guardian 1954-55; music and dance critic Daily Express 1956-78, London dance critic Int Herald Tribune Paris 1978-83, exec ed Music and Musicians 1963-71, ed Royal Opera and Royal Ballet Yearbook 1978, 1979 and 1980; frequent broadcaster musical topics BBC Home and World Servs and Br Forces Broadcasting Serv (MOD) 1950-, interviewer and commentator on music and arts matters; prog annotator for: Royal Opera, Royal Ballet and other cos and major orchs; overseas news ed Opera; reg reviewer for: The Times, Dance and Dancers; memb Cncl Arts Cncl of GB 1979-81, chm Dance Advsy Panel (memb 1973-81), dep chm Music Advsy Panel (memb 1974-81); memb: Dance Advsy Panel Calouste Gulbenkian Fndn UK Branch 1972-76 (memb Fndn's Nat Enquiry into Dance Educn and Trg in Br 1980), Br Cncl's Drama and Dance Advsy Ctee 1973-89, HRH The Duke of Kent's UK Ctee for Euro Music Year 1985 (chm of its sub ctee for writers and critics 1982-84); tstee and dir Int Dance Course for Professional Choreographers and Composers 1975-; pres The Critics' Circle 1977 (memb 1958-, jt tstee and memb Cncl 1977-); *Books* London Symphony: Portrait of an Orchestra (1954), A Ballet for Scotland (1979), A Knight at the Opera (with Sir Geraint Evans, 1984), author of History of Theatre Music in Encyclopedia Britannica (15 edn, 1976) and of Dance (Europe) entries in Britannica Books of the Year (1980-), area ed and contrib The New Grove Dictionary of Music and Musicians (1981), contrib to Encyclopaedia of Opera (1976), The Dictionary of Composers (1977), Cambridge Encyclopaedia of Russia (1982), The Concise Oxford Dictionary of Ballet (2 edn, 1982), Pipes Enzylopädie des Musiktheaters (Munich, Vols 1-3 1987-89), A Portrait of the Royal Ballet (ed, 1988); *Recreations* travel; *Style*— Noël Goodwin, Esq; 76 Skeena Hill, London SW18 5PN (☎ 081 788 8794)

GOODWIN, (Francis) Norman; s of Norman Parkes Goodwin (d 1968), and Phylis Mary, *née* Hume (d 1975); *b* 30 Dec 1923; *Educ* HM Sch Ship Conway, Wye Coll London (BSc); *m* 14 June 1956, Ann Gillian (Gill), da of Roy Edward Furniss (d 1929); 1 s (Timothy b 1958), 2 da (Josephine b 1959, Hilary b 1961), 1 adopted s (Richard b 1963); *Career* RNR: Midshipman 1940, Lt 1946; serv HM Ships: Canton, Abdiel, Sheffield, King George V, Tintagel Castle, Allington Castle; served: S Atlantic Patrol, E and W Med, N Atlantic, Arctic Convoys incl JWSIB, Crete, Tobruk, N Cape, N Africa, Sicily; fishing protection staff Agric Dept N Nigeria 1953-63, Hunting Tech Servs 1963-76, Booker Agric Int 1976-79, ind agric conslt 1979-(working mainly with the Asian Devpt Bank and the Int Fund for Agric Devpt (IFAD); major projects and devpts incl: Lower Indus, Chasma Barrage Right Bank Canal, Pat Feeder Canal Rehabilitation and Nat Flood Protection Plan (Pakistan), IFAD Area Devpt Projects Bhutan, South Chad Irrigation Project, Kano River Phase II (Nigeria), Nat Cropping Plan (Iran), advsy work in connection with federal-funded irrigation devpts (Brazil); memb Tropical Agric Assoc 1986; *Recreations* motor caravanning, photography, helping out on son-in-law's farm; *Style*— Norman Goodwin, Esq; The Mount, Aston Munslow, Craven Arms, Shropshire SY7 9ER (☎ 058476 328, fax 0743 253 678, telex 8954667 VBSTLX Ref SHC)

GOODWIN, Peter Austin; CBE (1986); s of Stanley Goodwin (d 1967), of London, and Louise, *née* Skinner; *b* 12 Feb 1929; *Educ* Harrow Co Sch; *m* 1950, Audrey Vera, of John Webb (d 1969), of Surrey; 1 da (Julia b 1960); *Career* RAF 1947-49; exec offr Public Works Loan Cmmn 1950 (asst sec 1976, sec 1979), princ Civil Aviation Authy 1973-76, chm Pensions Commutation Bd 1980-84, comptroller gen Nat Debt Office 1979, dir Nat Investmt and Loans Office 1979; memb Ctee of Experts Advising on Investmt of Superannuation Fund Moneys of Euro Patent Office Munich; *Recreations* theatre, opera, ballet, country dancing, model railways; *Style*— Peter Goodwin, Esq, CBE; 87 Woodmansterne Rd, Carshalton Beeches, Surrey SM5 4JW; National Investmt & Loans Office, Royex House, Aldermanbury Square, London EC2V 7LR (☎ 071 606 7321)

GOODWIN, (Neville) Rex; s of Hubert Victor Goodwin (d 1978), of London Rd, Yaxley, Peterborough, Cambs, and Lilian Gertrude Goodwin; *b* 7 Feb 1932; *Educ* Deacons Sch Peterborough Cambs, Sch of Architecture, Leicester Coll of Art (Dip Arch); *m* 5 Sept 1957, Mary Alice, da of Cecil Capp, of 22 Earlswood Dr, Edwalton, Notts; 1 s (Mark b 22 Oct 1964), 1 da (Kate b 21 March 1961); *Career* Nat Serv RAF 1952-54; architect Notts CC 1957-61, dep chief architect Brockhouse Steel Structures 1961-65, ptnr Goodwin Warner & Assocs 1965-88, dir James McArtneu Architects, Nottingham 1988-, visiting lectr in bldg design Dept of Civil Engrg Loughborough Univ of Tecnol 1970-; vice pres Loughborough Colls Rugby Union Club; RIBA 1959; *Recreations* aviation, watching cricket and rugby; *Style*— Rex Goodwin, Esq; 9A, Hallfields, Edwalton, Nottingham (☎ 0602 234 283)

GOODWIN, Prof Richard Murphey; s of William Murphey Goodwin (d 1959), of Newcastle, Indiana, USA, and Mary Florea Goodwin (d 1956); *b* 24 Feb 1913; *Educ* Harvard Univ (BA, PhD), Univ of Cambridge (MA), Univ of Oxford (BA, BLitt); *m* 24 June 1937, Jacqueline, da of Henry Wynmalen (d 1964), of Kingswood House, Twyford, Berks; *Career* instructor then asst prof Harvard Univ 1938-50, lectr then reader Cambridge 1951-80, prof Univ of Sienna 1980-88; *Books* Elementary Economics (1970), Essays in Economic Dynamics (1982), Essays in Linear Economic Structures (1983), Essays in Nonlinear Economic Dynamics (1989), The Dynamics of a Capitalist Economy (with L Punzo, 1987); *Style*— Prof Richard Goodwin; Dorvis's, Ashdon, Essex CB10 2HP (☎ 079 984 302); La Carbonaia, Strada di Montechiaro, S Giovanni di Ceretto, 53100 Siena, Italy; Istituto di Econemia, Piazza S Francesco, 53100 Siena, Italy (☎ 010 39 577 298 652)

GOODWIN, Ronald; s of William Henry Goodwin (d 1951), and Kathleen Florence, *née* Vizor (d 1977); *b* 6 May 1927; *Educ* Keighley Tech Coll; *m* 11 Aug 1951, (Brenda) Molly Goodwin; 3 s (David, Glynn, Alan); *Career* 2 Bn Glos Regt 1945-48; CA; ptnr Benten & Co 1954-90; dir: Blyth & Pawsey Ltd 1955-86, Hire Purchase (Agric) Ltd 1965-; chm Saffron Walden Herts & Essex Building Soc; chm Royal Soc of St George Saffron Walden Branch, pres Saffron Walden Rotary Club 1968-69, memb Management Ctee and chm Uttlesford CAB, tstee and treas Mid Essex Doctors Emergency Care Scheme; FCCA 1952; *Recreations* gardening, travel; *Style*— Ronald Goodwin, Esq; Orchard Bungalow, Debden Rd, Saffron Walden, Essex CB11 4AB (☎ 0799 23 098)

GOODWIN, Ronald Alfred (Ron); s of James Goodwin (d 1952), of Ruislip, Middx, and Bessie Violet, *née* Godsland (d 1966); *b* 17 Feb 1925; *Educ* Willesden Co Sch, Pinner Co Sch; *m* 1, 3 July 1947 (m dis 1986), Ellen Gertrude, da of William Drew, of Ruislip, Middx; 1 s (Christopher Russell b 16 Sept 1951); m 2, 22 Sept 1986, Heather Elizabeth Mary, da of Harold Wesley Dunsden, of Blewbury, Berks; *Career* composer and conductor; 61 film scores incl: Battle of Britain, 633 Squadron, Frenzy, Where Eagles Dare, Those Magnificent Men in their Flying Machines; other compositions incl: The New Zealand Suite, The Drake 400 Suite, The Armada 400 Suite, The Brimpton Suite, Suite No 1 for Brass Quintette; guest conductor with many orchestras incl: Royal Philharmonic Orchestra, The Bournemouth Symphony Orchestra, The Scottish Nat Orchestra, The New Zealand Symphony Orchestra; vice pres: Br Acad of Songwriters Composers and Authors, The Stars Orgn for Spastics; cncl memb The Composers Guild of GB, bd memb Young Persons Concert Fndn; pres Worthing Youth Orchestra, vice pres The Friends of the Hants Co Youth Orchestra; Liveryman Worshipful Co of Musicians 1971; *Recreations* walking, swimming, amateur computer programming; *Style*— Ron Goodwin, Esq; Blacknest Cottage, Brimpton Common, Reading RG7 4RP

GOODWIN, Shirley Ann; da of Harold Harper Goodwin, of Burwash Surrey, and Jean Patricia, *née* Richmond; *b* 5 Oct 1947; *Educ* Royal Tunbridge Wells County GS for Girls, Univ of Surrey (Dip in Health Visiting), NE London Poly (BSc); *Career* health visitor Ealing West London 1971-83, gen sec Health Visitors' Assoc 1984- (in designate post 1983-84); part-time youth worker Ealing 1974-78, hon sec Health Visitors' Assoc 1980-83; memb: Health Educn Cncl 1981-83, Eng Nat Bd for Nursing Midwifery and Health Visiting 1983-, fndr memb Babymilk Action Coalition 1980 (lectr on health visitors' role in promoting breastfeeding, advsr Nat Childbirth Tst), teacher of relaxation classes 1974-; contributor to the nursing press 1979-, regular columnist and editorial advsr Nursing Mirror 1980-83; *Publications* articles published in Nursing Times, Self and Society, the British Medical Journal, New Generation (journal of the NCT), Health Visitor; *Style*— Miss Shirley Goodwin; 14 Fairlea Place, London W5 1SP (☎ 081 998 0125); 36 Eccleston Square, London SW1V 1PF (☎ 071 834 9523)

GOODWORTH, Simon Nicholas; s of Michael Thomas Goodworth, of 10 Manor Green, Stratford-upon-Avon, Warwickshire, and Lorna Ruth, *née* Skerret; *b* 9 Aug 1955; *Educ* Solihull Sch W Midlands, Univ of Manchester (LLB); *Career* admitted slr 1980, ptnr Theodore Goddard 1986; memb: Law Soc, City of London Young Slrs Soc; *Recreations* tennis, squash, theatre, music; *Style*— Simon Goodworth, Esq; 22 Oakhill Rd, London SW15 2QR (☎ 081 874 5431); Theodore Goddard, 150 Aldersgate St, London EC1A 4EJ (☎ 071 606 8855, fax 071 606 4390)

GOODYEAR, Andrew William Raeside; s of Capt Maxwell William Goodyear (d 1957), and Gwendolen Moyra Raeside (d 1975); *b* 26 April 1939; *Educ* Merchiston Sch; *m* 17 April 1971, Elizabeth Mary, da of George Hay Marshall, of The Thicket, Beech Ave, Worcester; *Career* teacher and co dir; md: PB Books Ltd 1969-77, OHO Enterprises 1986-; *Recreations* golf, amateur dramatics, writing; *Style*— Andrew Goodyear, Esq; The Sundial Cottage, Essen Lane, Kilsby, Rugby, Warks (☎ 0788 822454)

GOODYEAR, Clive; s of Melvin David Goodyear, of Lincoln, and Sylvia Ann, *née* Wilson; *b* 15 Jan 1961; *Educ* The City Sch Lincoln; *m* 25 June 1983, Sharon Georgina, da of Peter William Sell; 1 da (Victoria Anne b 20 Aug 1986); *Career* professional footballer; former schoolboy player Lincoln City, 99 appearances Luton Town 1978-84 (debut 1980), 125 appearances Plymouth Argyle 1984-87, Wimbledon 1987-; honours: Div 2 Championship Luton Town 1982, promotion to Div 2 Plymouth Argyle 1986, FA Cup Wimbledon 1988; *Recreations* photography, cricket; *Style*— Clive Goodyear, Esq; Wimbledon FC, Durnsford Rd, Wimbledon, London SW19 (☎ 081 946 6311)

GOOLD, George William; s and h of Sir George Goold, 7 Bt; *b* 25 March 1950; *m* 1973, Julie Anne, da of Leonard Crack, of Whyalla; 2 s (George b 1975, Jon b 1977); *Style*— George Goold, Esq; 2 Ambleside Ave, Mount Keira, NSW 2500, Australia

GOOLD, Baron (Life Peer UK 1987), of Waterfoot, in the District of Eastwood; Sir James Duncan Goold; DL (Renfrewshire 1985); s of John Goold (d 1934), and Janet Agnes, *née* Kirkland; *b* 28 May 1934; *Educ* Glasgow Acad, Inst of Chartered Accountants Scotland; *m* 1959, Sheena, da of Alexander David Paton, OBE (d 1986), of Troon, Ayrshire; 2 s (Hon Michael Kirkland b 1966, Hon James David b 1968), 1 da (Hon Anna Jane b 1972); *Career* CA 1958; pres: Scottish Building Contractors Assoc 1971, Scottish Building Employers Fedn 1977; chm CBI Scotland 1981-83, dir Mactaggart & Mickel Ltd; hon treas Scottish Cons Pty 1980-83 (chm 1983-89); dir: American Tst plc, Bio Mac Ltd, Edinburgh Oil & Gas plc, Gibson & Goold Ltd, Strathclyde Graduate Business School Ltd; dep chm of Ct Univ of Strathclyde, chm Royal Scot Nat Orchestra, vice pres Royal Highland Agric Soc of Scotland; kt 1983; *Recreations* gardening, hill walking, golf, tennis; *Clubs* Carlton, RSAC, Western (Glasgow), Royal Troon Golf; *Style*— The Rt Hon Lord Goold, DL; Sandyknowe, Waterfoot, Clarkston, Glasgow G76 8RN (☎ 041 644 2764); Mactaggart & Mickel Ltd, 126 West Regent St, Glasgow G2 (☎ 041 332 0001)

GOOLD, Niall John; s of John Goold, of 15 Craigfern Drive, Blanefield, and Sheila, *née* Hay; *b* 3 Sept 1948; *Educ* Glasgow Acad; *m* 22 March 1972, Sheena Kathleen, da of William Galt, of Wishaw; 2 s (Keith John b 22 Sept 1974, Euan Niall b 29 Nov 1976); *Career* md Gibson & Goold Ltd 1985- (dir 1972), pres Ayr Jr C of C 1977-78, memb cncl Rotary Club of Allander; Freeman: Worshipful Co of Wrights 1954, Worshipful Co of Merchants 1986; hon citzen State of Maryland USA 1976; *Recreations* music, walking, travel; *Clubs* Royal Scottish Automobile, Glasgow Academical; *Style*— Niall Goold, Esq; Dunglass View, Strathblane, Glasgow G63; 1/3 Scotland St, Glasgow G5 8LS (☎ 041 42967997, fax 041 4296066)

GOOLD, Peter Anthony; s of Ernest George Goold, of Spencer Brook, Chelford Rd, Prestbury, Cheshire, and Vera Rose, *née* Wilks; *b* 5 Oct 1943; *Educ* Shrewsbury, Univ of London (LLB); *m* 1, 6 May 1967 (m dis 1982), Angela Moira, da of Cedric Iliffe, of Woodbury Salterton, Devon; 1 s (Simon b 16 Nov 1970), 1 da (Georgina b 16 Jan 1973); m 2, 11 Feb 1982, (Valerie Elizabeth) Lorraine, da of Arnold Richard Holden, of Prestwich, Manchester; *Career* CA; Spicer & Oppenheim 1962-68, chm Whitecroft plc 1969-; dir Salford Univ Holdings plc; FCA 1967; *Recreations* mountain walking; *Style*— Peter Goold, Esq; Kingswood, Macclesfield Rd, Alderley Edge, Cheshire SK9 7BH (☎ 0625 582 725); Whitecroft plc, Water Lane, Wilmslow, Cheshire SK9 5BX (☎ 0625 524 677, fax 0625 535 821, telex 666150)

GOOLD-ADAMS, Richard John Moreton; CBE (1974); s of Sir Hamilton Goold-Adams, GCMG (d 1920, sometime govr of Queensland), formerly of Jamesbrook, Midleton, Co Cork, and Elsie, *née* Riordon, of Ontario and Montreal; *b* 24 Jan 1916; *Educ* Winchester, New Coll Oxford; *m* 1939, Deenagh (a horticultural author), da of Richard Francis Ponsonby Blennerhassett, only s of Rowland Ponsonby Blennerhassett, MP Kerry 1872-1885; *Career* Maj Italy 1945; ed staff The Economist 1947-55, dir within Guthrie Gp of Cos 1954-69; chm: Int Inst for Strategic Studies 1963-73, SS Great Britain Project 1968-82; economist, co dir, journalist, broadcaster, lectr, and author; *Books* incl: The Time of Power: a Reappraisal of John Foster Dulles, The Return of the Great Britain; *Recreations* photography; *Clubs* Travellers'; *Style*— Richard Goold-Adams, Esq, CBE; c/o National Westminster Bank, PO Box 192, 116 Fenchurch Street, London EC3M 5AN

GOOLDEN, Hon Mrs (Rosemary); *née* Lowther; er da of Maj Hon Christopher William Lowther (d 1935, er s of 1 Viscount Ullswater); raised to the rank of a Viscount's da 1950; *b* 25 Feb 1922; *m* 7 July 1945, Lt Douglas Cyril Aubrey Goolden, RNVR, s of late Cdr Cyril Goolden, DSO, RN; 2 s, 1 da; *Career* served WWII 2 Offr WRNS; *Recreations* painting, horses; *Style*— The Hon Mrs Goolden; Forge Cottage, Withyham, Hartfield, E Sussex

GOPAL-CHOWDHURY, Paul; *b* 1949; *Educ* Camberwell Sch of Art, Slade; *Career* artist; Boise Travelling Scholarship and French Govt Scholarship 1973-74; lectr: Chelsea Sch of Art 1973-74 (pt/t 1975-77), Fine Art Dept Univ of Leeds (pt/t) 1975-77, Byam Shaw Sch of Art (pt/t) 1975-77; Gregory fell Univ of Leeds 1975-77; artist-in-residence Gonville and Caius Coll Cambridge and Kettle's Yard Gallery Cambridge 1983-84; solo exhibitions: Art Gallery Newcastle Poly 1980, Arts Centre Folkestone 1980, Ian Birksted Gallery 1981 and 1984, Kettle's Yard Gallery Cambridge (and tour to Axiom Gallery Cheltenham and Oldham Art Gallery) 1984-85, Benjamin Rhodes Gallery 1986 and 1988, Quay Arts Centre IOW 1988; gp exhibitions incl: London Gp 1971, Royal Acad Summer Exhibition (1972, 1974, 1978, invited artist 1988), Royal Soc of Oil Painters 1973, John Moores Exhibition (Liverpool) 1974, Hayward Annual 1979 and 1981, Whitechapel Open (Whitechapel Gallery) 1980 and 1983, Imperial Tobacco Portrait awards (Nat Portrait Gallery) 1980 1981 and 1985, A Taste of Br Art Today (Brussels) 1981, Ian Birksted Gallery (NY) 1981; public collections: Bolton Art Gallery, Chase Manhattan Bank NY, Chelmsford and Essex Museum, Contemporary Art Soc, de Beers Ltd, Doncaster Museum and Art Gallery, Newcastle Poly; 2nd prize Imperial Tobacco Portrait Award (Nat Portrait Gallery) 1982; *publications:* articles incl: My Painting (Artscribe), Painting From Life (Hayward Annual 1979 Catalogue), Portrait of the Artist (Artist's and Illustrator's Magazine 1986), Reviving the Figurative Tradition (Landscape 1987); *Style*— Paul Gopal-Chowdhury, Esq

GORDIMER, Nadine; da of Isidore Gordimer (d 1961), of Springs, SA, and Nan, *née* Myers (d 1973); *b* 20 Nov 1923; *Educ* Convent Sch; *m* 1, 1949 (m dis 1952), Dr Gerald Gavronsky; 1 da (Oriane Taramasco b 1950); m 2, 29 Jan 1954, Reinhold Cassirer, s of Hugo Cassirer (d 1920), of Berlin; 1 s (Hugo b 1955); *Career* novelist and writer; ten novels completed incl My Son's Story, seven short story collections incl Something Out There, two non fictional works incl The Essential Gesture; vice pres Int PEN, hon memb American Acad of Arts and Sciences, hon memb American Acad and Inst of Arts and Letters, fell RSL, patron and regnl rep Congress of S African writers; holder of ten honorary degrees incl: DLitt Harvard Univ 1986, DLitt Yale Univ 1986, DLitt Columbia Univ; Officier de l'Ordre des Arts et des Lettres France 1986; *Style*— Ms Nadine Gordimer; 7 Frere Rd, Parktown West, Johannesburg, South Africa

GORDON; *see*: Smith-Gordon
GORDON; *see*: Duff-Gordon
GORDON, Sir Alexander John (Alex); CBE (1974, OBE 1967); s of John Tullis Gordon (d 1959), of Swansea, and Euphemia Baxter Borrowman, *née* Simpson (d 1942); *b* 25 Feb 1917; *Educ* Swansea GS, Welsh Sch of Architecture; *Career* Maj RE 1940-46; architect in partnership with T Alwyn Lloyd 1948-60, sr ptnr Alex Gordon & Partners 1960-82, conslt The Alex Gordon Partnership 1982-88; memb: Welsh Arts Cncl 1959-73, Design Cncl 1973-77, Bd of British Cncl 1980-87; Royal Fine Art Cmmr 1973-90; pres RIBA 1971-73; Hon LLD Univ of Wales 1972; FCSD 1975, ARICS 1987, Hon Fell ISE 1980, Hon Fell CIBSE 1975, Hon Memb BDA 1980, Soc of Mexican Architects 1972, and corresponding memb Danish Architects 1976, Hon FRAIC 1974, Hon FAIA 1974; kt 1988; *Recreations* reflecting on past skiing, visual arts; *Clubs* Arts, Cardiff and County; *Style—* Sir Alex Gordon, CBE; River Cottage, Llanblethian, nr Cowbridge, S Glam CF7 7JL (☎ 0446 773672)
GORDON, Andrew David; er adopted son of 4 Marquess of Aberdeen and Temair (d 1974); bro James Gordon, *qv*; *b* 6 March 1950; *Educ* Harrow, LSE; *m* 1982, Lucy Mary Frances, da of Canon William John Milligan, of Stockwell, London; 1 s (William David b 1988), 1 da (Rosie Kate Jessamine b 1986); *Style—* Andrew Gordon, Esq
GORDON, Anthony George; MBE (1979); s of Laurence Victor Gordon, MBE (d 1975), and Margaret Mary Gordon; *b* 21 April 1925; *Educ* The King's Sch Canterbury, Corpus Christi Coll Cambridge (BA); *m* 22 April 1966, (Mary) Sylvia, da of William Edward Levers, and Winifred Mary, *née* Levers (d 1975); 2 s (James b 25 Feb 1967, Jeremy b 8 Sept 1968); *Career* RAF pilot 1944-47; chm S American Freight Ctee 1958, dir Int Meat Trade Assoc 1975, chm Assoc of Br Meat Processors 1987, vice pres Assoc Européen du Commerce en Gros des Viandes 1987, pres Euro Union of Abattoir Operators 1990; sch govr; MInstM 1970; *Recreations* tennis, shooting, photography; *Style—* Anthony Gordon, Esq, MBE; 55 Fentiman Rd, London SW8 1LH (☎ 071 735 9861); 217 Central Markets, London EC1A 9LH (☎ 071 489 0005)
GORDON, Aubrey Abraham; s of Isaac Gordon (d 1962), of Sunderland, and Fanny, *née* Benjamin (d 1975); *b* 26 July 1925; *Educ* Bede Collegiate Boys Sch Sunderland, Univ of Durham (LLB); *m* 28 June 1949, Reeva Rebecca, da of Myer Cohen (d 1941), of Sunderland; 1 s (David Myer b 1956), 2 da (Anne b 1950, Susan b 1950); *Career* admitted slr 1947; rec of the Crown Ct 1978-; pres: Houghton le Spring Chamber of Trade 1955, Hetton le Hole Rotary Club 1967, Sunderland Law Soc 1976; chm: Houghton Round Table 1959, Sunderland Victims Support Scheme 1978-80, Sunderland Guild of Help 1984-; pres NE Joel Intract Memorial Home for Aged Jews; *Recreations* communal activities, photography, walking; *Style—* Aubrey A Gordon, Esq; 1 Acer Court, Sunderland, Tyne & Wear SR2 7EJ (☎ 091 565 8993)
GORDON, Boyd; s of David Gordon (d 1986), of Musselburgh, and Isabella, *née* Leishman; *b* 18 Sept 1926; *Educ* Musselburgh GS; *m* 26 Sept 1951, Elizabeth Mabel, da of Thomas Smith (d 1963); 2 da (Ruth b 1953, Pamela b 1955); *Career* served Royal Scots (WO 2) 1944-48; Dept of Agric & Fisheries Scotland: asst sec EEC and gen econ matters 1978-82, Fisheries sec 1982-86; conslt Scottish Fishermen's Orgn 1987-; *Recreations* golf, gardening, local church matters; *Style—* Boyd Gordon, Esq; 87 Duddingston Rd, Edinburgh (☎ 031 669 4380); Scottish Fishermen's Organisation, Braehead, Queensferry Rd, Edinburgh
GORDON, Catherine (Kate); JP (Inner Manchester 1969); da of William Alexander Keir (d 1963), of Ayr, Scotland, and Marion Watson, *née* Prentice (d 1987); *Educ* Ayr Acad, Open Univ (BA); *m* 20 Aug 1955, (Donald) Hugh McKay Gordon, s of James Bremner Gordon, of Huntly, Aberdeenshire; 1 s (Alistair Keir b 10 Sept 1956), 1 da (Marion Louise (Mrs Livingstone Jones) b 31 July 1959); *Career* Civil Serv and PA to chm of nationalised indust 1945-56; local and met dist cncllr 1969-, chm Trafford Ethical Ctee 1984-; memb: Trafford Health Authy 1976-, Trafford Cts Ctee 1972-88, Gtr Manchester Probation Ctee 1974-; chm Inner Manchester Magistrates 1985-; YWCA: nat pres and chm Bd of Govrs 1980-84, govr 1970-, del World Cncl YWCA Forces rep (BAOR and Cyprus) 1984-; memb Cncl Nat Magistrates Assoc 1985-; FRSA 1980; *Recreations* music, family, friends, fun; *Clubs* YWCA; *Style—* Mrs Hugh Gordon, JP; 3 West Lynn, Devisdale Rd, Bowdon, Cheshire WA14 2AT (☎ 061 928 6038, fax 061 941 5394, telex 668800)
GORDON, Sir Charles Addison Somerville Snowden; KCB (1981, CB 1970); s of Charles Gordon Snowden Gordon, TD (d 1961); *b* 25 July 1918; *Educ* Winchester, Balliol Coll Oxford; *m* 1943, Janet Margaret, da of late Douglas Porteous Beattie, of Dewsbury, Yorks; 1 s, 1 da; *Career* served 1939-45 Fleet Air Arm (Lt (A) RNVR); House of Commons: asst clerk 1946, sr clerk 1947, fourth clerk at the Table 1962, princ clerk of the Table Office 1967, second clerk asst 1974, clerk asst 1976, clerk of the House of Commons 1979-83; *Books* ed 20th edition Erskine May's Parliamentary Practice (1983); *Style—* Sir Charles Gordon, KCB; 279 Lonsdale Rd, Barnes, London SW13 9QB (☎ 081 748 6735)
GORDON, Colin Malcolm; s of Colin Pithie Gordon, of Cobham, Surrey, and Elsie Isabella, *née* Brown; *b* 19 May 1946; *Educ* Badingham Coll, Merrist Wood Agric Coll; *m* 1, 4 May 1968 (m dis 1987), Jill Margaret, da of John Walter Lawrence, of Fetcham, Leatherhead, Surrey; 2 s (Stuart Colin b 29 Oct 1970, Alisdair Robert b 29 Dec 1973); m 2, 30 April 1988, Sandra Dawn Gordon, da of Raymond Gordon Smith (d 1975); *Career* farmer 1963-73, agric fin specialist NW Securities Ltd 1973-76, area then regnl mangr Highland Leasing Ltd 1976-82, chief exec Humberclyde Fin Gp Ltd 1986- (sales and mktg dir 1982-86); memb IOD 1986; *Recreations* walking, rugby, golf, gardening; *Style—* Colin Gordon, Esq; Bydand, 11 Welham Road, Norton, Malton, N Yorkshire YO17 9DP (☎ 0653 600406); United House, Piccadilly, York YO1 1PQ (☎ 0904 645 411, car 0860 548 455)
GORDON, David Michael; s of Nathan Gordon, of London, and Diana, *née* MacKoffsky; *b* 12 Dec 1940; *Educ* Davenant Foundation GS; *m* 9 June 1968, Patricia Anne, da of Alfred Melamed (d 1982); 1 s (Andrew b 27 Oct 1971), 1 da (Nicola b 2 July 1974); *Career* actuary Pearl Assurance Plc 1984-(asst actuary 1975-83, dep actuary 1983-84); dir Pearl Assurance Plc 1987, Pearl Assurance (Unit Funds) Ltd 1987, Pearl Assurance (Unit Linked Pensions) Ltd 1987, Pearl Unit Trusts Ltd 1987, Pearl Group Plc 1988; non-exec dir Insur Ombudsman Bureaux 1988; memb: Ctees of the Assoc of Br Insurers, Lautro Selling Practices Ctee; FIA 1968, FSS 1970, FRSA 1990; *Recreations* reading, gardening, swimming; *Clubs* 59, Denarius; *Style—* David Gordon, Esq; Pearl Assurance Plc, (☎ 071 638 1717, fax 071 638 0412, telex 8811984 PEARL G)
GORDON, David Sorrell; s of Sholom Gordon, and Tania Gordon; *b* 11 Sept 1941; *Educ* Clifton, Balliol Coll Oxford (BA), LSE, Harvard Business Sch; *m* 1, 1963 (m dis 1969), Enid Albagli; m 2 , 1974, Maggi McCormick; 2 s; *Career* articled clerk Thompson McLintock (now part of Peat Marwick McLintock) 1965-68; The Economist: journalist 1968, financial ed 1972, dep business ed 1974-; gp chief exec The Economist Group 1981- (prodn and devpt dir 1978); dir: Financial Times 1983-, South Bank Centre 1986-, Target Group plc 1988-; govr BFI 1983-, memb Ct of Govrs LSE; FCA; *Books* Newspaper Money (jtly with Fred Hirsch, 1975); *Recreations* movies, magic lanterns; *Clubs* Garrick, Groucho, Harvard (NY); *Style—* David Gordon, Esq; Greenwood, 56 Duke's Avenue, Chiswick, London W4 2AF (☎ 081 994 3126)
GORDON, Donald; s of Nathan Gordon (d 1978), and Sylvia (Sheila), *née* Shevitz (d 1984); *b* 24 June 1930; *Educ* King Edward VII Sch Johannesburg, Univ of Witwatersrand; *m* 21 Jan 1958, Peggy, da of Max Cowan (d 1950); 2 s (Richard Michael b 1958, Graeme John b 1963), 1 da (Wendy Donna (Mrs Appelbaum)); *Career* CA, registered public accountant and auditor; chm: Charter Life Insurance Co Ltd (dir 1985), Guardian National Insurance Co Ltd (dir 1980), Guard Bank Management Corporation Ltd (dir 1969), First International Ltd (dir 1977), Liberty Asset Management Ltd (dir 1969), Liberty Holdings Ltd (dir 1968), Liberty Investors Ltd (dir 1971), Liberty Life Association of Africa Ltd (dir 1957), Trans-Atlantic Holdings plc (UK dir 1981), Capital & Counties plc 1990 (dir 1982); dir: Guardian Royal Exchange plc 1984, Guardian Royal Exchange Assur plc 1971-, S African Breweries Ltd 1982-, Standard Bank Investment Corp 1979-, Beverage and Consumer Industrial Holdings Ltd 1989-; Hon Doctorate Univ of Witwatersrand; *Recreations* tennis; *Clubs* Houghton Golf, Rand, Johannesburg Country, Plettenberg Bay Country; *Style—* Donald Gordon, Esq; Liberty Life Assoc of Africa Ltd, 4th Floor, Liberty Life Centre, 1 Ameshoff Street, Braamfontein 2017, PO Box 10499, Johannesburg 2000, S Africa; Trans-Atlantic Holdings plc, 40 Broadway, London SW1H 0BT, (☎ SA 011 408 2100, London 071 222 5496, fax SA 011 403 3171, London 071 222 5840)
GORDON, Lord Douglas Claude Alexander; Lt-Col; DSO (1945); yst s of Lt-Col (Granville Cecil) Douglas Gordon, CVO, DSO (d 1930, s of Lord Granville Armyne Gordon, 6 s of 10 Marquess of Huntly), and Violet Ida, *née* Streatfeild (d 1968); bro of 12 Marquess of Huntly; granted the rank of a Marquess's s 1937; *b* 30 July 1916; *Educ* Eton, RMC Sandhurst; *m* 1, 21 Dec 1940 (m dis 1961), Suzanne (d 1983), da of late Lt-Col Arthur Houssemayne du Boulay, DSO; 2 s (Andrew b 1942, Douglas b 1947), 1 da (Lady Robert Nairne *see* Peerage M Lansdowne b 1950); m 2, 1963, Bridget, da of late Lt-Col Gerald Bryan Ingram, TD, RA, and formerly wife of Maj Alexander Hutchison; 1 da; *Career* page of honour to HM 1930-33, Lt-Col Black Watch, memb Queen's Body Gd for Scotland (Royal Co of Archers), Palestine 1937-1940, Italy 1943-45 (DSO), Greece 1945-46, Staff Coll Haifa 1947, Egypt 1948-49, instr RMA Sandhurst 1949-52, ret 1953; *Recreations* antiques, fishing, horticulture; *Style—* Lt-Col The Lord Douglas Gordon, DSO; The Old Rectory, Stockbridge, Hants (☎ 0264 810662)
GORDON, Elvis Anthony; s of Arnold Gordon, and Elma, *née* Brown (d 1983); *b* 23 June 1958; *Educ* Bushbury Hill Senior Sch; *partner*, Karen Lesley Pryce; 2 s (Robert b 22 Sept 1981, Daniel b 22 Jan 1983), 1 da (Candice b 3 July 1987); *Career* judoist; Olympics 1984 and 1988; medal winner: Cwlth Gold 1986 and double Gold 1990, World Silver 1987, Euro Gold 1988, winner Shoriki Cup Japan (first Br judo player to win the cup); *Style—* Elvis Gordon, Esq
GORDON, Fiona Mary; da of Cdr David Leslie Gordon (d 1984), of Alicante, Spain, and Anne Josephine, *née* Haywood; *b* 2 June 1951; *Educ* Hurst Lodge Sunningdale Berks, Beechlawn Tutorial Coll Oxford; *Career* dir: Brook-Hart Advertising Ltd 1980-85, Hewland Conslts Int Ltd 1980-85, Mist Move Ltd 1985-, md First PR Ltd 1985-, dir Riverside Communications Ltd; MIPR, MIPA; *Clubs* Mortons, Zanzibar; *Style—* Miss Fiona Gordon; First Public Relations Ltd, 2 Cinnamon Row, Plantation Wharf, York Place, London SW11 3TW (☎ 071 978 5233, fax 071 924 3134, telex 27231)
GORDON, Frederick William; s of George Gordon (d 1980), and Susan, *née* McNelis (d 1973); *b* 13 June 1949; *Educ* Bletchley GS; *m* 14 Feb 1976, Barbara Ann, da of Sidney Clarke (d 1964); 1 s (Neil b 1980), 1 da (Anna b 1977); *Career* gen sales mangr Pergeot Talbot Motor Co 1985-; *Recreations* cricket; *Clubs* Bletchley Town; *Style—* Frederick W Gordon, Esq; Farihölme, Bon, Brickhill, Bucks (☎ 0908 642530); Luton Rd, Dunstable, Bedfordshire (☎ 0582 64171)
GORDON, George; s of Dr Adam Smith Gordon, RAMC (d 1951), of Ferniebank, Markinch, Fife, and Agnes Forbes, *née* Smith; *b* 4 Sept 1936; *Educ* Bell Baxter Sch Cupar Fife, Univ of Edinburgh (MB ChB); *m* 11 June 1966, Rosemary Gould, da of Rev Alexander Hutchison; 1 s (David b 4 Jan 1971), 1 da (Fiona b 27 March 1967); *Career* house surgn: Western Gen Hosp Edinburgh 1959-60, Royal Infirmary Edinburgh 1960; house physician Royal Hosp Sick Children Edinburgh 1961, sr house offr Simpson Meml Maternity Pavilion 1962, registrar Eastern Gen Hosp Edinburgh 1962-66, sr registrar Western Gen Hosp Edinburgh 1966-69, conslt obstetrician and gynaecologist Dumfries 1969-, admin conslt Alexandra Hospice Unit Dumfries; pres Edinburgh Obstetrical Soc, chm Confidential Enquiry into Maternal Deaths Scot, sec Scot Exec Ctee RCOG; fell BMA 1988; FRCS (Edin) 1967, FRCOG 1977; *Recreations* Scots literature, gardening, golf, music; *Clubs* New (Edinburgh); *Style—* George Gordon, Esq; Dumfries & Galloway Royal Infirmary, Dumfries (☎ 0387 53151)
GORDON, Sheriff Gerald Henry; QC; er s of Simon Gordon (d 1982), of Glasgow, and Rebecca, *née* Bulbin (d 1956); *b* 17 June 1929; *Educ* Queen's Park Sr Secdy Sch Glasgow, Univ of Glasgow (MA, LLB, PhD), Univ of Edinburgh (LLD); *m* 1957, Marjorie, yr da of Isaac Joseph, of Glasgow; 1 s (David), 2 da (Susan, Sarah); *Career* prof of scots law Univ of Edinburgh 1972-76; Sheriff of: South Strathclyde, Dumfries and Galloway at Hamilton 1976-77, Glasgow and Strathkelvin 1978-; *Books* Criminal Law (1 edn 1968, 2 edn 1978), Criminal Procedure (ed, 4 and 5 edn); *Recreations* Jewish studies, swimming; *Style—* Sheriff Gerald H Gordon, QC; 52 Eastwoodmains Rd, Giffnock, Glasgow G46 6QD (☎ 041 638 8614); Glasgow Sheriff Ct (☎ 041 429 8888)
GORDON, Ian; s of James Donald Gordon, of Montrose, Angus, and Winifred, *née* Thomson (d 1985); *b* 15 Aug 1957; *Educ* Biggar HS, Univ of Edinburgh (LLB); *m* 22 July 1988, (Mary) Angela Joan, da of Donald Macdonald, of Isle of Lewis; *Career* McGrigor Donald (formerly Moncrieff Warren Paterson & Co Slrs Glasgow): apprentice 1979-81, slr 1981, ptnr 1983-; memb: Law Soc of Scotland 1981, Assoc of Pension Lawyers 1986; NP 1981; *Recreations* getting out and about especially on wheels; *Style—* Ian Gordon, Esq; Hughenden, Glasgow; Pacific Ho, 70 Wellington St, Glasgow G2 6SB (☎ 041 248 6677, fax 041 221 1390, telex 778744 MGDGLWG)
GORDON, Ian; s of William Gordon (d 1984), and Elizabeth, *née* Brooks, of Carlisle; *b* 21 March 1939; *Educ* Carlisle GS; *m* 8 Sept 1962, Kathleen Verna, da of Ernest Francis Martin; 2 s (James Iain b 26 April 1968, Craig Martin b 23 Sept 1969), 1 da (Lindsay Kathryn b 6 Oct 1965); *Career* articled clerk N T O Reilly & Partners Carlisle 1956-61, qualified 1962; ptnr: Telfer & Co (formerly SW Telfer) 1963-70 (audit sr l mangr 1962-63), Winn & Co Newcastle (following merger) 1970-73, Tansley Witt & Co Newcastle 1973-80; sr ptnr BDO Binder Hamlyn (following merger) 1980- (memb Nat Partnership Ctee 1980-89); elected memb North Tyneside MBC (Cullercoats Ward) 1976-, gp spokesman on finance 1976-80, ldr Cons Gp 1982- (dep ldr 1980-82); memb Ctee: Policy and Resources, Educn, Environment, Econ Devpt and Strategic Planning, Women's Issues, Elderly, Outside Bodies; fndr memb Northern Region Cncls Assoc 1985-90 (ldr Cons Oppn Gp 1986-90); memb: Exec Ctee, Environment Panel, Euro Panel, Econ Panel, Staffing Panel, Famous Five Delgn on the North), prospective Parly candidate (C) Newcastle North 1990, chm Tynemouth & Whitley Bay Cons Assoc Exec Ctee 1988-90 (pres 1985-88); memb: N Area Exec Ctee (Cons) 1988-, Exec Ctee Nat Union 1989-90; vice chm Area Local Govt Ctee 1988- (memb 1982-), memb Nat Local Govt Ctee, fndr and chm N Tyneside Political Ctee 1986-; N Soc of Chartered Accountants: memb Exec Ctee 1971-80, chm Educ Training and Recruitment Sub Ctee, fndr memb & chm Fin Advice Scheme; memb Cmmn of the Peace City of Newcastle Upon Tyne 1981- (memb Domestic and Juvenile

Panels), fndr memb Northern Development Company, dir Cons Local Authy 1986-; dir: Tyne and Wear Development Co Ltd 1985-90, Signpost Europe Ltd 1989-, Tyne & Wear Devpt Corp 1989-; fndr tstee: Cullercoats Educ Tst, Cedarwood Tst; govr: Preston Grange Primary Sch (chm of govrs), John Spence Community HS, Cullercoats Primary Sch, West Moor Middle Sch; former govr Monkhouse Primary Sch, church warden St Hilda's Church Marden and Preston Grange 1984-88, lay vice chm Parish Church Cncl (chm Fin Ctee), lay chm Dist Church Cncl; ACA 1962; *Recreations* charitiy work; *Style*— Ian Gordon, Esq; 9 Wenlock Drive, Preston Grange, North Shields, Tyne & Wear NE29 9HD (☎ 091 2576879); BDO Binder Hamlyn, Pearl Assurance House, 7 New Bridge St, Newcastle upon Tyne NE1 8BQ (☎ 091 261 2481, fax 091 2320364, car 0860 307235)

GORDON, James Drummond; yr adopted son of 4 Marquess of Aberdeen (d 1974); bro Andrew Gordon, *qv*; *b* 11 April 1953; *Educ* Harrow; *m* 1985, Marilyn, yr da of A F Sim, of Sompting, Lancing, Sussex; *Style*— James Gordon, Esq

GORDON, James Stuart; CBE (1984); s of James Edward Gordon (d 1975), of Glasgow, and Elsie, *née* Riach (d 1984); *b* 17 May 1936; *Educ* St Aloysius' Coll, Glasgow Univ (MA); *m* 1971, Margaret Anne, da of Andrew Kirkwood Stevenson (d 1968), of Glasgow; 2 s (Michael Stevenson b 1974, Christopher James b 1976), 1 da (Sarah Jane b 1972); *Career* political ed STV 1965-73, md Radio Clyde 1973-, chm Scottish Exhibition Centre 1983-89; memb: Scottish Devpt Agency 1981-, Ct Univ of Glasgow 1984-, Ctee of Inquiry into Teachers' Pay and Conditions 1986; *Recreations* walking, genealogy, golf; *Clubs* Caledonian, New (Edinburgh), Prestwick Golf, Buchanan Castle Golf; *Style*— James S Gordon, Esq, CBE; Deil's Craig, Strathblane, Glasgow G63 9ET (☎ 0360 70604); Radio Clyde plc, Clydebank Business Park, Clydebank G81 2RX (☎ 041 941 1111, telex 779537, fax 041 952 0080)

GORDON, Rt Hon John Bowie (Peter); PC (1978); s of Dr William Patteson Pollock Gordon, CBE, and Dr Doris Clifton Gordon, OBE, *née* Jolly; *b* 24 July 1921; *Educ* St Andrew's Coll Christ Church NZ, Lincoln Coll Canterbury; *m* 1943, Dorothy Elizabeth, da of Robert Morton; 2 s, 1 da; *Career* MP (Clutha) 1960-78; min Tport, Railways, Aviation, Marine and Fisheries 1966-72, min Labour and State Servs 1975-78, ret 1978; co dir: banking, insur, tport; dep chm Nat Transitional Ctee Local Govt Reform, former cncllr Otago Univ; US Leader award 1964, Companion Queens Serv Order NZ 1989; *Books* Some Aspects of British Farming (1955); *Recreations* golf, cooking, gardening; *Clubs* Otago Officers, Tapanui Services; *Style*— The Rt Hon Peter Gordon; Tapanui, Otago, New Zealand

GORDON, John Edwin; s of Dennis Lionel Shute (d 1940); *b* 14 Dec 1939; *Educ* Tonbridge, Queens' Coll Cambridge; *m* 1968, Monica Anne, *née* Law; 1 s, 2 da; *Career* dir: Robert Fleming & Co 1974-77, Laing & Cruickshank (stockbrokers) 1978-82, Jackson Exploration Inc 1982-85; head of corporate fin: Capel-Cure Myers 1985-89, Beeson Gregory 1989-; treas Br Postgraduate Med Fedn, memb Br Waterways Bd 1987-; FCA; *Recreations* fishing; *Clubs* Boodle's, Leander; *Style*— John Gordon, Esq; 50 Castelnau, Barnes, London SW13 (☎ 081 748 1715); The Registry, Royal Mint Court, London EC3N 4EY (☎ 071 488 4040)

GORDON, John Keith; s of Prof James Edward Gordon, and Theodora Mary Carnilla, *née* Sinker; *b* 8 July 1940; *Educ* Marlborough, Trinity Coll Cambridge (BA), Yale Univ (Henry fell), LSE; *m* 14 Aug 1965, Elizabeth, da of Maj A J Shanks (d 1962); 2 s (Timothy Alan b 1971), Alexander Keith b 1973); *Career* Dip serv; entered FCO 1966, Budapest 1968-70, seconded to Civil Serv Coll 1970-72, FCO 1972-73, UK Mission Geneva 1973-74, head of Chancery and consul Yaoundè 1975-77 (concurrently) Chargé d'Affaires Gabon and Central African Repub), FCO 1977-80, cultural attaché Moscow 1980-81, office of UK Rep to EEC Brussels 1982-83, UK perm del to UNESCO Paris 1983-85, head Nuclear Energy Dept FCO 1986-88; dep and policy dir Global Environment Res Centre 1988-90; memb: several local and nat environment gps, Nat Campaign for UK Return to UNESCO, Pugwash Gp; *Publications* author of various contributions to books, periodicals on international environment policy issues; *Recreations* skiing, jogging, sailing; *Clubs* Cwlth Tst; *Style*— John Gordon, Esq; 68 Hornsey Lane, London N6 5LU; Global Environment Research Centre, Imperial College, London SW7 (☎ 071 225 1818, fax 071 225 0627)

GORDON, Marion, Lady; Marion; *née* Wright; 3 da of James B Wright, of Springfield, Neutral Bay, N Sydney, NSW; *m* 26 Sept 1928, Sir John Charles Gordon, 9 Bt (d 1982); 1 s, 1 da; *Style*— Marion, Lady Gordon; 61 Farrer Brown Ct, Nuffield Village, Castle Hill, NSW, Australia

GORDON, (George) Michael Winston; s of Winston Gordon, of Clonallon Rd, Warrenpoint, NI, and Marjorie Georgina Gordon; *b* 8 May 1937; *Educ* Queen's Univ Belfast (BSc, MSc), Univ of NSW (MSc); *m* 11 Aug 1966, Narelle Helen, da of Flt Lt Kenneth Charles Nicholl, of Sydney, NSW, Aust; 3 s (Matthew b 9 Sept 1967, Nicholas b 24 May 1969, Benjamin b 8 Feb 1976); *Career* graduate trainee Metropolitan Vickers 1958-60; design engr: Bristol Aircraft Co 1961-62, Amalgamated Wireless Australasia 1962-67; conslt: PA Management Consultants Aust, Singapore, Malaysia and NI 1967-76, Booz Allen and Hamilton Algeria 1976-77; dir: NI Devpt Agency 1977-80, American Monitor 1980-82, BIS London 1982-; MIEE (NY); *Style*— Michael Gordon, Esq; 5 Englehurst, Harpenden AL5 5SQ (☎ 0582 766374); 1/55 Queenscliff Rd, Manly, Australia; 20-22 Upper Ground, London SE1 9PN (☎ 071 633 0866, fax 071 962 6212)

GORDON, Murray Graham; s of Solomon Gordon; *b* 13 May 1922; *Educ* Collegiate Sch Liverpool, Univ of Liverpool Sch of Art; *m* 1950, Vera, *née* Denby; 2 s; *Career* Lt-Col (acting) India and Burma; chm and md Combined English Stores Group Ltd 1970-87; memb Royal Nat Theatre Devpt Cncl; Freeman City of London; *Recreations* golf, tennis, squash; *Clubs* Carlton, RAC; *Style*— Murray Gordon, Esq; Apartment 9, Cheyne House, Chelsea Embankment, London SW3 4LA (☎ 071 352 9311); Pythingdean Farmhouse, Coombelands Lane, Pythingdean, nr Pulborough, West Sussex (☎ 079 82 3654)

GORDON, Prof Peter; s of Louis Gordon (d 1969), and Anne, *née* Schultz (d 1941); *b* 4 Nov 1927; *Educ* Univ of Birmingham (DipEd), LSE (BSc, MSc), Univ of London Inst of Educn (PhD); *m* 30 March 1958, Tessa Joan, da of Bernard Leton, of Aylmer Lodge, 3 Aylmer Drive, Stanmore, Middlesex; 1 s (David Nicholas b 12 April 1965), 1 da (Pauline Amanda b 24 June 1961); *Career* RAF in England and India 1945-48; teacher primary and secdy schs 1951-65, HM inspr of schs 1965-73; Univ of London Inst of Educn: lectr 1973-76, reader 1976-82, prof of history of educn 1982-; FRHistS 1982; *Books* The Victorian School Manager (1974), The Cabinet Journal of Dudley Ryder, Viscount Sandon (with Christopher Howard, 1974), Curriculum Change in the 19th and 20th Centuries (with Denis Lawton, 1978), Games and Simulations in Action (with Alec Davidson, 1978), Theory and Practice of Curriculum Studies (1978), Philosophers as Educational Reformers (with John White, 1979), Selection for Secondary Education (1980), The Study of Education: Inaugural Lectures (1980, 1988), The Red Earl: The Papers of the Fifth Earl Spencer of Althorp 1935-1910 (1981, 1986), The Study of the Curriculum (ed 1981), A Guide to English Educational Terms (with Denis Lawton, 1984), HMI (with Denis Lawton, 1987), A Dictionary of Educationists (with R Aldrich, 1989), History of Education: the making of a Discipline (with R Szreter, 1989), Education and Policy in England in the Twentieth Century (ed 1991), Teaching the Humanities (ed 1991); *Recreations* music, architecture; *Style*— Prof Peter Gordon; Birtsmorton, 58 Waxwell Lane, Pinner, Middx HA5 3EN (☎ 081 868 7110); University of London Institute of Education, 20 Bedford Way, London WC1H OAL (☎ 071 636 1500)

GORDON, Peter David; s of Sydney Gordon (d 1984), and Sarah Gordon, *née* Paskin (d 1982); *b* 25 March 1939; *Educ* Hendon County GS, Univ of Sheffield (LLD, RCS); *m* 28 Sept (m dis 1990), Ruth, *née* Summers; 2 s (Keith Michael b 20 Aug 1969, Jonathan Andrew b 6 Aug 1971); *Career* dental surgn 1964-; house surgn Charles Lifford Dental Hosp Sheffield 1964, clinical lectr Middlesex Hosp London 1985- (pt/t dental surgn to Nursing Staff 1969-85), private gen practitioner 1970-; hon clinical conslt to: 3M 1977-79, Bayer UK 1981-; reg lectr in dental photography to postgrads; guest lectr: Asian Pacific Dental Congress Delhi 1987, Zoroastrian Dental Soc Bombay; lecture tour Bangkok, Kuala Lumpur, Singapore, Hong Kong 1988; memb BDA; *Books* Dental Photography (with P Wander, 1987); *Recreations* theatre, music, bridge, swimming; *Style*— Peter Gordon, Esq; 12 Upper Wimpole Street, London W1M 7TD (☎ 071 935 5454)

GORDON, Richard John Francis; s of John Bernard Basil Gordon, of 10 Ingelow House, Kensington Church Walk, London, and Winifred Josephine, *née* Keenan; *b* 26 Nov 1948; *Educ* St Benedicts Sch, Christ Church Oxford (MA), UCL (LLM); *m* 13 Sept 1975, Jane Belinda, da of Anthony George Lucey, of Rosedale House, Welburn, Yorks; 2 s (Edmund John Anthony b 17 June 1982, Adam Richard Cosby b 25 Oct 1985); *Career* called to the Bar Middle Temple 1972; ed Crown Office Digest 1988-, broadcasts and articles on admin law in legal periodicals and other pubns; Freeman City of London; FRGS, ACIArb; *Books* The Law Relating to Mobile Homes and Caravans (second edn, 1985), Judicial Review Law and Procedure (1985); *Recreations* modern fiction, theatre, cricket; *Style*— Richard Gordon, Esq; 24 Clonmel Rd, London SW6 5BJ (☎ 071 731 2126); 2 Harcourt Buildings, Temple, London EC4 (☎ 071 353 6961, fax 071 353 6968)

GORDON, Cdr Richard Redmond; OBE (1968), VRD (1959); s of Eric Redmond Sutton Gordon (d 1946), and Nancy Margaret, *née* Roff; *b* 1 March 1925; *Educ* Radley; *m* 4 Dec 1948, Ruth, da of Joseph Geoffrey Brooks (d 1953); 2 da (Elizabeth b 1953, Helen b 1955); *Career* War Serv 1943-46, London Div RNR 1946-68 (Cdr 1966-68); chm Jantar Nigeria Ltd 1965-71, dir and sec Cavendish Land Ltd 1968-73; pres Euro Fedn of Sea Anglers 1988-(chm 1976-88); Freeman City of London 1963, Liveryman Worshipful Co of Shipwrights 1965; FCIS 1955; *Recreations* sea angling, golf; *Clubs* Victory Servs; *Style*— Cdr Richard Gordon, OBE, VRD; 29 Alleyne Way, Elmer Sands, Bognor Regis, W Sussex PO22 6JZ (☎ 0243 584057)

GORDON, Sir Robert James; 10 Bt (NS 1706), of Afton and Earlston, Kirkcudbrightshire (but has not yet proved his succession), probably next in remainder to the Viscountcy of Kenmure and Lordship of Lochinvar (dormant since 1872); s of Sir John Charles Gordon, 9 Bt (d 1982), and Marion, Lady Gordon, *qv*; *b* 17 Aug 1932; *m* 1976, Helen Julia Weston, da of Margery Perry, of Cammeray, Sydney, NSW; *Style*— Sir Robert Gordon, Bt; Earlstoun, Guyra, NSW 2365, Australia

GORDON, Robert Wilson; MC (1944); s of late Malcolm Gordon, and Blanche Fayerweather Gordon; *b* 3 March 1915; *Educ* Harrow; *m* 1, 1946, Joan Alison (d 1965), da of Brig Arthur George Kenchington, CBE, MC (d 1966); 1 da; m 2, 1967, Diana Evelyn Venice (d 1980), eldest da of Edward Thomas Tyrwhitt-Drake, JP (d 1933), of Shardeloes, Bucks, former w of Robert Edward Ansell, and previously widow of Lt Arthur Michael William Blake, RN; *Career* dep chm Stock Exchange 1965-68, ptnr Pidgeon de Smitt (stockbrokers); *Style*— Robert Gordon Esq, MC; 41 Cadogan Square, SW1X 0HX (☎ 071 235 4496)

GORDON, Lord Roderic Armyne; MBE (1943), TD; 3 s of Lt-Col (Granville Cecil) Douglas Gordon, CVO, DSO (d 1930, s of late Lord Granville Armyne Gordon, 6 s of 10 Marquess of Huntly), and Violet Ida, *née* Streatfeild (d 1968); bro of 12 Marquess; *b* 20 Jan 1914; *Educ* Stowe; *m* 1, 7 Jan 1937 (m dis 1949), Anne, yr da of late Lt-Col Hon Sir Osbert Eustace Vesey, KCVO, CMG, CBE; 2 s; m 2, 26 Aug 1949, Joana Alexandra, 2 da of Ion Bujoiu, of Bucharest, Romania, and formerly wife of (1) Prince Serban Ghica and (2) Baron de Stuers; *Career* N Africa 1943; Major 72 (Hampshire) Anti-Aircraft Brig RA (TA); *Style*— The Lord Roderic Gordon, MBE, TD; 101 The Davenport, 1011 12th Ave SW, Calgary, Alberta, Canada

GORDON, Rt Rev (Archibald) Ronald McDonald; s of Sir Archibald McDonald Gordon, CMG (d 1974), and Dorothy Katharine (d 1959), da of Charles Silvester Horne, MP, by his w Hon Katharine Maria, elder da of 1 Baron Cozens-Hardy; *b* 19 March 1927; *Educ* Rugby, Balliol Coll Oxford, Cuddesdon Theol Coll; *Career* deacon 1952, priest 1953, curate of Stepney 1952-55, chaplain Cuddesdon Coll 1955-59, vicar of St Peter Birmingham 1959-67, residentiary canon Birmingham Cathedral 1967-71, vicar of Univ Church of St Mary the Virgin with St Cross and St Peter in the East Oxford 1971-75, bishop of Portsmouth 1975-84, took seat in House of Lords 1981 (relinquished 1984), sr memb Archbishop of Canterbury's Staff 1984-91, bishop to HM Forces 1985-90, res canon Christ Church Oxford 1991-; memb Church Assembly and Gen Synod and proctor in convocation 1965-71, chm ACCM 1976-83, select preacher Univ of Oxford 1985; *Style*— The Rt Rev Ronald Gordon; Christ Church, Oxford OX1 1DP

GORDON, Sir Sidney; CBE (1968, OBE 1965), JP (Hong Kong 1961); s of late P S Gordon, and Angusina Gordon; *b* 20 Aug 1917; *Educ* Hyndland Sch Glasgow, Univ of Glasgow; *m* 1950, Olive, da of late T A Eldon; 2 da; *Career* CA; sr ptnr Lowe Bingham & Matthews (chartered accountants) Hong Kong 1956-70, MLC Hong Kong 1962-66, MEC 1965-80, chm Sir Elly Kadoorie & Sons Ltd 1970-, dep chm China Light & Power Co; chm Univ and Poly Grants Ctee 1974-76; hon steward Royal Hong Kong Jockey Club; Hon LLD Chinese Univ of Hong Kong 1970; kt 1972; *Recreations* golf, racing; *Clubs* Oriental, Hong Kong, Royal Hong Kong Jockey (hon steward), Royal Hong Kong Golf (pres); *Style*— Sir Sidney Gordon, CBE, JP; 7 Headland Rd, Repulse Bay, Hong Kong (☎ 010 8525 8122577)

GORDON, Tanya Joan; s of Jean-Claude Gordon, of Bayswater, and Daphne Thomas, *née* Tucar (d 1976); *b* 15 Jan 1945; *Educ* Godolphin & Latymer Sch, Univ of Sussex (BA); *m* 15 Jan 1969, Mike Sarne, s of Alfred Schener; 1 s (William Gordon b 30 May 1972), 1 da (Claudia Aviva b 17 Jan 1970); *Career* model 1963-64, asst to Cultural Attaché Persian Embassy 1966-67, asst to Lit Agent Kramers 1967-68, freelance reader for Universal Film Studios 1967-68, supply teacher of history for GLC (mainly at St Martins in the Field) 1968-69, spent two years in Brazil helping husband make a film (Intimidade), working as a tour Guide for Brazil Safaris and modelling 1973-75; sales dir Entrepas Ltd 1976-78, fndr Miz (fashion business) 1978-83, fndr Ghost 1984-; fndr memb Fashion Indust Action Gp, memb Br Fashion Cncl; *Recreations* cooking, acquiring property and the obvious; *Clubs* Groucho, Campden Hill Tennis; *Style*— Ms Tanya Gordon; Ghost Ltd, The Chapel, 263 Kensal Rd, London W10 5DB (☎ 081 960 3121, fax 081 960 8374)

GORDON, Prof William Morrison; s of William Gordon (d 1967), of INverurie, and Helen Morrison (d 1977); *b* 3 March 1933; *Educ* Inverurie Acad, Robert Gordon's Coll, Univ of Aberdeen (MA, LLB, PhD); *m* 1 June 1957, Isabella Evelyn Melitta, da of George Duguid Robertson (d 1967), of Strathaven; 2 s (Malcolm b 1958, Mark b 1965), 2 da (Melitta b 1961, Elise b 1965); *Career* Nat Serv RN 1955-57; asst in jurisprudence Univ of Aberdeen 1957-60, dean Faculty of Law Univ of Glasgow

1974-76 (lectr in civil law 1960-65, sr lectr in law 1965-69, Douglas prof of civil law 1969-), senate assessor Ct Univ of Glasgow 1983-88; literary dir The Stair Soc, elder and session clerk Jordanhill Parish Church; memb Law Soc of Scotland; *Books* Studies in Transfer of Property by Traditio (1970), Scottish Land Law (1989); *Recreations* golf; *Style*— Prof William Gordon; Building, Glasgow University, Glasgow G12 8QQ (☎ 041 3398855 ext 5387, fax 041 3304900, telex 777070 UNIGLA)

GORDON-CLARK, Guy Lawrence; OBE (1983), JP (1970); s of Henry Michael Gordon-Clark (d 1976), of Wyatt House, Dorking, Surrey, and Gwendolyn Emily, *née* Marriner (d 1986); *b* 13 March 1928; *Educ* Winchester; *m* 3 Oct 1953, Pauline Guise; 2 da (Catherine b 1955, Lucinda b 1959); *Career* wine and spirit shipper; dir Matthew Clark & Sons Ltd (family firm) 1952-88; chm: J E Matther & Son Ltd, Br Wine Producers 1971-88, Wine and Spirit Assoc 1969-71 and 1981-83, West Sussex Probation Ctee 1979-85; *Recreations* gardening; *Clubs* City of London; *Style*— Guy Gordon-Clark, Esq, OBE, JP; Itchingfield House, Horsham, West Sussex (☎ 0403 790393)

GORDON CUMMING, Alastair Penrose; s and h of Sir William Gordon Cumming, 6 Bt; *b* 15 April 1954; *Style*— Alastair Gordon Cumming, Esq

GORDON CUMMING, Sir William; 6 Bt (UK 1804); s of Maj Sir Alexander Penrose Gordon Cumming, MC, 5 Bt (d 1939); *b* 19 June 1928; *Educ* Eton; *m* 1, 1953 (m dis 1972), Elisabeth, da of Maj-Gen Sir William Robert Norris Hinde, KBE, CB, DSO; 1 s, 3 da; m 2, 1972 (m dis 1976), Lady Pauline Anne, sis of 13 Earl of Seafield, and former w of James Henry Harcourt Illingworth; *Heir* s, Alexander Gordon Cumming; *Career* late Lt Royal Scots Greys; *Style*— Sir William Gordon Cumming, Bt; Altyre, Forres, Morayshire

GORDON-CUMMING, Gp Capt Alexander Roualeyn; CMG (1977), CVO (1969); s of Lt Cdr Roualeyn Geoffrey Gordon-Cumming, RN (d 1928), and Mary Violet Katharine, *née* Marter (d 1984); *b* 10 Sept 1924; *Educ* Eton; *m* 1, 1965, Beryl Joyce MacNaughton (d 1973), da of late Naughton Dunn, of Edgbaston; 1 da (Ann Penrose b 1968); m 2, 1974, (Elizabeth) Patricia (d 1983), da of Travers Robert Blackley (d 1982), of Co Cork; 1 da (Mary Elizabeth b 1975); *Career* RAF 1943-69 (ret), Gp Capt and Dep Capt of The Queen's Flight; Bd of Trade 1969-73; seconded HM Diplomatic Service 1974-78 (cnsllr Aviation and Shipping HBM Embassy Washington); Dept of Trade and Industry 1978-84; dir Invest in Britain Bureau; *Recreations* gardening; *Clubs* RAF; *Style*— Gp Capt Alexander Gordon-Cumming, CMG, CVO; Woodstock, West Way, Chichester, Sussex PO19 3PW (☎ 0243 776413)

GORDON DILL, Maj Richard Patrick Murray; s of Major John Martin Gordon Dill (d 1949), of Stream Hill, Doneraile, Co Cork, and of Ethné Charlton Murray (d 1979); *b* 24 Nov 1923; *Educ* Eton, Trinity Coll Cambridge (not completed due to war serv); *m* 1, 27 June 1959, Mary Chichester (m dis 1967), da of James Paul Mills (d 1987), of Middleburg, VA, USA; m 2, 1968, Kari Penelope, da of Grahan Hugh Sheppard MC, TD (d 1973); 1 s (Marcus Patrick Gordon b 5 March 1974); *Career* landowner/farmer; served with the 8 King's Royal Irish Hussars N Africa, Middle East, NW Europe (despatches), personal liason offr to Gen Sir Myles Depmsey (cdr 2 Army) and on staff, mil asst to Head of Standing Gp NATO Washington DC 1957-59, Maj ret (on amalgamation of regt 1959); subsequent to retirement from Army farmed, trained and bred racehorses, amateur jockey 1945-64 (Grand Mil Gold Cup 1957), local Jockey Club steward, Master of Foxhounds & Field Master (Warwickshire) 1965-75; Master of the Worshipful Co of Carpenters 1985-86; FRSA 1986; *Recreations* field sports, racing, travel, the arts; *Clubs* Cavalry & Guards; *Style*— Major Richard Gordon Dill; Idlicote House, Idlicote, nr Shipston-on-Stour, Warwicks (☎ 0608 61473); Treshnish, Salen, Argylli (☎ 096 785 642); Estate Office Idlicote House, Idlicote, Nr Shipston-on-Stour, Warwics (☎ 0608 61381)

GORDON-DUFF, Hon Mrs (Sheila Beatrice); *née* Davison; yr da of 1 Baron Broughshane, KBE (d 1953), by his 1 w; *b* 14 June 1907; *m* 1936, Gp Capt George Edward Gordon-Duff, CBE (d 1966); 1 s; *Style*— The Hon Mrs Gordon-Duff; 10 Jameson St, London W8

GORDON-DUFF, Col Thomas Robert; MC (1945), JP (Banffshire 1959); s of Capt Lachlan Gordon-Duff, DL (ka 1914, s of Thomas Duff-Gordon-Duff, CBE, JP, by his w Pauline, sis of 1 Baron Glenconner, Lady Ribblesdale and Margot Asquith and half-sis of Ladies Wakehurst, Elliot of Harwood and Crathorne (ie the children of Sir Charles Tennant, 1 Bt)); *b* 5 Oct 1911; *Educ* Eton, Sandhurst; *m* 1946, Jean, da of Leslie Moir, of Bicester; 1 s; *Career* Brevet Col TA Gordon Highlanders, POW Calais 1940, CO 5/6 Bn 1947-51; DL Banffshire 1948 (Vice Lord Lt 1961, Lord-Lt 1964), co cncllr 1949-75, convenor Banff CC 1962-71; landed proprietor; *Recreations* fishing, shooting; *Clubs* Army and Navy; *Style*— Col Thomas Gordon-Duff, MC, JP; Drummuir, Keith, Banffshire (☎ 054 281 300)

GORDON-HARRIS, William; s of William Gordon-Harris (d 1952), of Bexhill-on-Sea, and Florence May, *née* Doughty (d 1973); *b* 2 May 1918; *Educ* Bexhill GS, Coll of Estate Mgmnt; *m* 2 Nov 1946, Margot Wynn, da of John William Edwards (d 1971), of Oswestry; 1 s (John William b 15 March 1948), 2 da (Angela Margot (Mrs Chivers) b 26 April 1954, Jennifer Jane b 3 Oct 1955); *Career* RNVR Ordinary Seaman 1938, Contraband control 1939, served HMS Hood (Homefleet N Atlantic convoys, Med Malta convoys) 1940-41, cmmnd 1941, HMS Anson (Homefleet Russian convoys) 1941-44, HMS Glenoy (Combined Ops Burma and Malaya) 1944-45, demobbed as Lt 1945; Valuation Office Inland Revenue 1945-48, princ in private practice as surveyor and estate agent 1948-, chm Hastings and Dist Estate Agents Assoc 1960 (sec 1958-60), surveyor to Rent Assessment Ctee and Rent Tbnl for SE England; chm Gen Practice Div of Sussex branch RICS 1972, memb Lloyd's 1978-; Freeman City of London 1980, Liveryman Worshipful Co of Chartered Surveyors; FRICS 1948, FSVA 1958; *Recreations* sailing (holding an ocean yacht masters cert), vintage cars; *Clubs* Sussex RNVR, RNR Offrs Assoc, Bexhill Sailing, Royal Naval Sailing Assoc, HMS Hood Assoc, Capital Ships Assoc; *Style*— William Gordon-Harris, Esq; Bexhill-on-Sea, E Sussex

GORDON JONES, Air Marshal Sir Edward; KCB (1967, CB 1960), CBE (1956, OBE 1945), DSO (1941), DFC (1941); s of Lt-Col Albert Jones, DSO, MC, of Dulverton House, Widnes; *b* 31 Aug 1914; *Educ* Wade Deacon Sch, Univ of Liverpool; *m* 1938, Margery Thurston Hatfield; 2 s; *Career* Nat Serv WWII (despatches), Air Vice-Marshal 1961, AOC RAF Germany 1961-63, AOC Malta and dep C-in-C (Air) Allied Forces Mediterranean 1965-66, Air Marshal 1966, AOC-in-C NEAF and admin Sovereign Base Areas 1966-69, Cdr Br Forces Near East 1967-69, ret; Greek DFC 1941, Cdr Order of Orange Nassau 1945; *Recreations* music, opera, photography, sport; *Clubs* RAF; *Style*— Air Marshal Sir Edward Gordon Jones, KCB, CBE, DSO, DFC; 20 Marlborough Court, Grange Road, Cambridge CB3 9BQ (☎ 0223 63029)

GORDON-JONES, Lady Frances Christina; *née* Knox; yr da of 7 Earl of Ranfurly, *qv*; *b* 13 Feb 1961; *m* 1981, Henry Gordon-Jones; *Style*— The Lady Francis Gordon-Jones; The Red House, Bredfield Rd, Woodbridge, Suffolk

GORDON-JONES, Michael Philip; s of Cyril Gordon-Jones (d 1964), and Brenda Mary Blaker (d 1962); *b* 29 Aug 1926; *Educ* Haileybury; *m* 1, 1 May 1954, Jennifer (d 1979), da of Alan Bostock Baker (d 1965); 1 s (Henry b 1956), 3 da (Alison b 1955, Victoria b 1960, Diana b 1963); m 2, 16 Aug 1980, Teressa, da of Philip John Fortin (d 1985); *Career* slr; dir Edward Baker Holdings Ltd (chm 1983-86 and 1989); *Style*— Michael P Gordon-Jones, Esq; Esplanade House, 32 Kings Quay St, Harwich, Essex CO12 3ES (☎ 0255 506917); 61/65 Station Rd, Clacton on Sea, Essex (☎ 0255 421248, fax 0255 476485)

GORDON LENNOX, Maj-Gen Bernard Charles; CB (1986), MBE (1968); s of Lt-Gen Sir George Gordon Lennox (d 1988), and Nancy Brenda, da of Maj Sir Lionel Edward Hamilton Marmaduke Darell, 6 Bt, DSO; *b* 19 Sept 1932; *Educ* Eton, Sandhurst; *m* 1958, Sally-Rose, da of John Weston Warner (d 1981); 3 s (Edward b 1961, Angus b 1964, Charles b 1970); *Career* cmmnd 1 Bn Grenadier Gds 1974-75, GSO 1 RAF Staff Coll 1976-77, Brig 1977, Cdr Task Force H, Dep Cdr and COS SE Dist UKLF 1981-83, Maj-Gen 1982, Br Cmdt and GOC Br Sector Berlin 1983-85, sr Army memb RCDS 1986-87, Lt-Col Grenadier Gds 1989-; page of honour to HM The King 1946-49; dir Regions Motor Agents Assoc 1988-89; *Recreations* fishing, shooting, cricket, squash, music; *Clubs* Army and Navy, MCC; *Style*— Maj-Gen B C Gordon Lennox, CB, MBE; c/o Lloyds Bank plc, Cox's & King's Guards and Cavalery, PO Box 1190, 7 Pall Mall, London SW1Y 5NA

GORDON LENNOX, Lady Ellinor Caroline; da of 10 Duke of Richmond and (5 Duke of) Gordon, *qv*; *b* 28 July 1952; *Educ* Elmhurst Ballet Sch, De Vos Studio of Ballet, British Wheel of Yoga; *Career* yoga teacher; formerly teacher of ballet, dance therapy and modern dance; dancer with John Curry in Coventry Cathedral, solo dance in Chichester Cathedral 'Sweet Messenger'; naturalist painter (watercolour); *Recreations* T'ai Chi Chuan, poetry writing, singing; *Style*— The Lady Ellinor Gordon Lennox; Widmore Lodge, Church Lane, Ellisfield, nr Basingstoke, Hants RG25 2QR (office ☎ 0243 774107)

GORDON LENNOX, Lady Louisa Elizabeth; da of 10 Duke of Richmond and (5 Duke of) Gordon, *qv*; *b* 14 March 1967; *Educ* Bishop Luffa C of E Comprehensive Sch, Lancing, Balliol Coll Oxford (BA); *Style*— The Lady Louisa Gordon Lennox; Goodwood House, nr Chichester, W Sussex PO18 OPY (☎ 0243 774760)

GORDON LENNOX, Capt Michael Charles; s of Rear Adm Sir Alexander Henry Charles Gordon Lennox, KCVO, CB, DSO (d 1987, gs of 7 Duke of Richmond and Gordon), and Barbara, *née* Steele (d 1987); *b* 30 Sept 1938; *Educ* Eton, RNC Dartmouth; *m* 1974, Jennifer Susan, da of Capt Hon Vicary Gibbs (ka 1944); 1 s (Hamish b 1980), 2 da (Lucinda b 1975, Charlotte b 1978); *Career* COS to Flag Offr Scotland 1985-88, CSO (Reserves) 1988-89, Capt i/c Hong Kong 1990-; *Recreations* gardening, shooting, fishing, golf, cricket; *Clubs* Naval and Military, Pratt's; *Style*— Captain Michael Gordon Lennox, RN; Fishers Hill, Iping, Midhurst, W Sussex GU29 0PF (☎ 0730 813474)

GORDON LENNOX, Lord Nicholas Charles; KCMG (1986, CMG 1978), KCVO (1988, LVO 1957); yr son of 9 Duke of Richmond and (4 of) Gordon (d 1989); *b* 31 Jan 1931; *Educ* Eton, Worcester Coll Oxford; *m* 1958, Mary, o da of late Brig Hudleston Noel Hedworth Williamson, DSO, MC; 1 s, 3 da; *Career* late 2 Lt KRRC; entered HM Foreign Service 1954, ambass to Spain 1984-; a govr of BBC 1990-; Grand Cross Order of Isabel La Catolica (Spain); *Style*— The Lord Nicholas Gordon Lennox, KCMG, KCVO; c/o Foreign and Commonwealth Office, King Charles St, London SW1

GORDON OF LETTERFOURIE, George; s of Patrick Gordon Shee, 11 of Letterfourie (d 1938), and Louise Marie Caroline, *née* Van Dyck; descended from Sir James Gordon, 1 of Letterfourie, who cmd the Scots fleet 1513; officially recognised in the surname of Gordon of Letterfourie by the Lord Lyon 1949 (*see* Burke's Landed Gentry, 18 edn, vol III, 1972); *b* 14 Nov 1923; *Educ* Beaumont; *m* 23 April 1969, Joanna Mary, eldest da of Gerard Wilfrid Stanfield Bagshawe (d 1961), of Silwood Park Farm, Ascot, Berks; 3 s (Alexander b 1970, William b 1973, Oliver b 1975), 1 da (Emma b 1972); *Career* Irish Guards 1942-47, Lt 1943, Capt 1946, served Italy (Anzio) and NW Europe (wounded); *Style*— George Gordon of Letterfourie; Letterfourie, Buckie, Banffshire

GORDON-SAKER, Andrew Stephen; s of Vincent Gordon-Saker, and Gwendoline Alice, *née* Remmers; *b* 4 Oct 1958; *Educ* Stonyhurst, UEA (LLB); *m* 28 Sept 1985, Liza Helen, da of William James Marle; 1 da (Francesca b 1989); *Career* called to the Bar Middle Temple 1981, in practice 1981-; cncllr London Borough of Camden 1982-86; *Style*— Andrew Gordon-Saker, Esq; 4 King Bench Walk, Temple, London EC4Y 7DL (☎ 071 353 0478)

GORDON-SAKER, Liza Helen; da of William James Marle, of Chislehurst, Kent, and Doreen Maud, *née* Adams; *b* 30 Nov 1959; *Educ* Farringtons Sch Chislehurst, Univ of East Anglia (LLB); *m* 28 Sept 1985, Andrew Stephen Gordon-Saker, s of Vincent Gordon-Saker, of Norwich; 1 da (Francesca b 1989); *Career* called to the Bar Gray's Inn 1982; Freeman City of London 1984; *Recreations* golf; *Style*— Mrs Liza Gordon-Saker; Fenners Chambers, 3 Madingley Rd, Cambridge CB3 0EE (☎ 0223 68761)

GORDON-SMITH, Lt Cdr Peter Russell; s of Lt Cdr Russell Claude Gordon-Smith, DSC, RN (ka 1940), and Anne Cunitia Keen, *née* Morris (d 1986); *b* 12 June 1938; *Educ* Winchester, RNC Dartmouth; *m* 8 June 1963, Marion Elizabeth, da of Cdr Sydney Arthur Morehouse Else, OBE (d 1979); 2 s (Russell b 1964, David b 1968), 1 da (Louise b 1965); *Career* served RN 1956-78, ret as Lt Cdr; farmer 1975-; *Recreations* shooting, skiing, stamps, model railways; *Clubs* Naval and Military, W Sussex County; *Style*— Lt Cdr Peter Gordon-Smith; Lower Farm, Up Marden, Chichester, Sussex PO18 9LA (☎ 024359 274)

GORDON WALKER, Hon Alan Rudolf; er (twin) s of Baron Gordon-Walker, CH, PC (Life Peer, d 1980); *b* 1946; *Educ* Wellington Coll, Ch Ch Oxford (MA); *m* 1976, Louise Frances Amy, da of Gen Sir Charles Henry Pepys Harington, GCB, CBE, DSO, MC; 1 s (Thomas b 1978), 1 da (Emily b 1981); *Career* md Pan Books Ltd; *Style*— The Hon Alan Gordon-Walker; c/o The Hon Mrs Gowar, The Homestead, Cuddington, Bucks

GORDON-WALKER, Dr the Hon Ann Marguerite; has resumed her maiden name; da of Baron Gordon-Walker, CH, PC; *b* 1944; *Educ* N London Collegiate Sch, Queen's Coll Dundee, St Andrews Univ, Oxford; *m* 1968 (m dis 1983), Laurence Andrew Ball; 2 da (Jennifer b 1974, Katherine b 1976); *Style*— Dr the Hon Ann Gordon-Walker; 1230 University Bay Drive, Madison, Wisconsin 53705, USA

GORDON-WALKER, Baroness; Audrey Muriel; da of Norman Rudolf, of Jamaica; *m* 1934, Baron Gordon-Walker, CH, PC (Life Peer, d 1980); 2 s, 3 da; *Style*— Lady Gordon-Walker; 105 Frobisher House, Dolphin Square, London SW1V 3LL (☎ 071 821 8270)

GORDON-WALKER, Hon Robin Chrestien; yr (twin) s of Baron Gordon-Walker, CH, PC (Life Peer, d 1980); *b* 15 May 1946; *Educ* Wellington, UEA (BA); *m* 1, 1974 (m dis 1985), June Patricia, da of Patrick Barr, of Eversholt, Beds; 1 s, 1 da; m 2, 1987, Magally, da of Gilberto Flores, of Valencia, Venezuela; 1 s; *Career* sr info offr Dept of Employment; *Recreations* cricket, tennis, chess, rugby union; *Clubs* MCC, Surrey CCC; *Style*— The Hon Robin Gordon-Walker; 16 Hexham Road, London SE27 (☎ 081 670 5925)

GORDON-WATSON, Brig Michael; OBE (1949), MC (1938, 2 bars 1940 and 1944); s of Sir Charles Gordon-Watson, KBE, CMG, FRCS; *b* 23 Feb 1913; *Educ* Downside, Ch Ch Oxford; *m* 1942, Thalia, da of Charles Gordon; 3 s, 2 da; *Career* cmmnd Irish Gds 1934, served Palestine; WWII: Norway, N Africa, Italy, NW Europe; Lt-Col 1945, mil attaché Washington 1950-52, Lt-Col cmd Irish Gds 1953-55, Brig 1959, BGS BAOR 1959, dep cdr Aldershot Dist 1961, vice pres Regnl Cmmns Bd 1962, ret 1963;

farmer and bloodstock breeder; JP Dorset 1964 (ret); memb: Cncl SMO Malta, St John's and St Elizabeth's Hosp Management Bd, Tattersall's Ctee; *Recreations* shooting, stalking, fishing, racing; *Clubs* White's; *Style—* Brig Michael Gordon-Watson, OBE, MC; East Blagdon Farm, Cranborne, Dorset (☎ 072 54 304)

GORE; *see*: Ormsby-Gore

GORE, Lady Barbara Susan; *née* Montgomerie; er da of 16 Earl of Eglinton and Winton (d 1945); *b* 23 Aug 1909; *m* 1930, Capt Christopher Gerald Gore, Coldstream Gds (d 1954); 1 s, 1 da; *Style—* The Lady Barbara Gore; 31 Sloane Court West, London SW3 (☎ 071 730 2998)

GORE, Charles John; s of John Francis Gore, CVO, TD (d 1983, gggs of 2 Earl of Arran, KP), of Ringwood, Hants, and Lady Janet Helena, *née* Campbell (d 1982), er da of 4 Earl of Cawdor; *b* 11 June 1932; *Educ* Eton; *m* 10 June 1961, Jean, da of Maj C I Fraser, CBE (d 1963), of Kirkhill, Invernessshire; 2 s (Simon b 1965, John b 1971), 1 da (Helena b 1962); *Career* promotion and print design conslt, humorous book illustrator, writer of guide books and ephemera; *Recreations* traditional Scottish fiddle music, boats, history; *Style—* Charles J Gore, Esq; PO Box Taynuilt, Argyll PA35 1HU (☎ 08662 678)

GORE, Lady Mary Sophia; *née* Palmer; da of 3 Earl of Selborne (d 1971), and his 1 w, Hon Grace, da of 1 Viscount Ridley and Hon Mary Marjoribanks, da of 1 Baron Tweedmouth; *b* 6 Sept 1920; *m* 1, 11 Nov 1944, Maj Hon (Thomas) Anthony Edward Towneley Strachey (d 1955) (only s of 3 Baron O'Hagan), who assumed by deed poll surname of mother (Hon Frances, da of 1 Baron Strachie) and additional christian name of Towneley; 2 s (*see* 4 Baron O'Hagan and Hon Richard Strachey), 2 da (*see* Hon Mrs (F T) Gibson and Hon Jane Strachey; m 2, 1981, (Francis) St John Gore, *qv*; *Style—* Lady Mary Gore; 25 Elvaston Place, London SW7 (☎ 071 584 6994)

GORE, Michael Balfour Gruberg; s of Dr Victor Gore (d 1985), of London, and Victoria, *née* Slavouski; *b* 25 Oct 1937; *Educ* Felsted, Peterhouse Cambridge (BA); *m* 11 April 1972, Mozella, da of Geoffrey Ransom; 2 s (Benjamin b 1974, Daniel b 1977), 1 da (Camilla (twin) b 1977); *Career* Kemp Chatteris & Co 1959-64, S G Warburg & Co Ltd 1964- (dir 1969-), chm S G Warburg & Co (Jersey) Ltd 1979-87; dir: Mercury Securities plc 1984-, Mercury Int Gp plc 1985-; gp fin dir Mercury Int Gp plc (now S G Warburg Gp plc) 1986-, chm Rowe & Pitman Moneybroking Ltd 1986-, joint chm S G Warburg Gp Mgmnt Ltd 1986-; FCA, FRSA; *Style—* Michael Gore, Esq; S G Warburg Group plc, 1 Finsbury Avenue, London EC2M 2PA (☎ 071 382 4314)

GORE, Michael Edward John; *b* 20 Sept 1935; *Style—* Michael Gore, Esq; British Embassy, Monrovia, Liberia

GORE, Nigel Hugh St George; yr s of St George Richard Gore (d 1952), who was gn of 9 Bt; hp of n, Sir Richard Gore, 13 Bt; *b* 23 Dec 1922; *m* 3 Sept 1952, Beth Allison, *née* Hooper; 1 da (Seonaid Beth b 1955); *Style—* Nigel Gore, Esq; Hillhaven, Preston Road, M/S 852, Hodgsonvale, Qld 4350, Australia

GORE, Paul Annesley; CMG (1964), CVO (1961); s of Charles Henry Gore, OBE (d 1941), s of Sir Francis Gore, KCB, whose f (yr bro of 4 Earl of Arran) m Lady Augusta Ponsonby, 2 da of 4 Earl of Bessborough; hp of 9 Earl of Arran, *qv*; *b* 28 Feb 1921; *Educ* Winchester, Ch Ch Oxford (MA); *m* 1946, Gillian Mary, da of Tom Allen-Stevens (d 1941); 2 s (and 1 s decd); *Career* Capt 16/5 Lancers (N Africa, Italy) 1941-46; Colonial Admin Serv 1948-65, dep govr The Gambia 1962-65; JP: Oxford 1972-74, Suffolk 1976-84; *Recreations* sailing (yacht Mandora of Deben); *Clubs* Cruising Assoc; *Style—* Paul Gore, Esq, CMG, CVO; 1 Burkitt Rd, Woodbridge, Suffolk

GORE, Prof Peter Henry; s of (Walter) Michael Gore (d 1974), and Lotte Sophie, *née* Weisskopf (d 1982); *b* 23 Jan 1926; *Educ* Marist Brothers Coll Randwick NSW, Univ of Sydney (BSc, MSc) Imperial Coll London (PhD, DSc, DIC); *m* 25 April 1953, Irene, da of Michael John Youhotsky (d 1965); 2 da (Anya b 1956, Rosanna (Mrs Price) b 1960); *Career* res fell Univ of Sydney 1948-50, Rockefeller fell Imperial Coll London 1952-53, lectr Acton Tech Coll 1953-56, sr lectr Brunel Coll 1956-60, reader Brunel Coll of Advanced Technol 1960-66, prof chemistry Brunel Univ 1978- (lectr, reader 1966-78), visiting prof to univs in Cairo, Alexandria and Basrah 1975-79; memb RSA, CChem, FRSC 1970, FRSA 1982; *Books* Friedel-Crafts and Related Reactions (contrib, 1964); *Recreations* music, walking, study of and writing on church music, Egyptology; *Style—* Prof Peter Gore; 62 Hornton St, London W8 4NU (☎ 071 937 9918); Department of Chemistry, Brunel University, Uxbridge, Middx UB8 3PH (☎ 0895 7400, fax 0895 32806, telex 261173 G)

GORE, Sir Richard Ralph St George; 13 Bt (I 1622); s of Sir St George Ralph Gore, 12 Bt (d 1973; gn of 9 Bt); *b* 19 Nov 1954; *Educ* The King's Sch Parramatta, New England Univ, Queensland Coll of Art (Dip Art); *Heir* unc, Nigel Gore; *Career* artist; *Recreations* tennis, golf, handcrafts; *Clubs* Assoc of Illustrators, Soc of Scribes and Illuminators, Buddhist Soc; *Style—* Sir Richard Gore, Bt; c/o 14 Brodie St, Toowoomba, Qld 4350, Australia; Wycanna, Talwood, Qld, 4322 Australia

GORE, Lady; Shirley; da of of C Tabor, of Wauchope NSW; *m* 1950, Sir St George Ralph Gore, 12 Bt (d 1973); ls, 3 da; *Style—* Lady Gore; Wycanna, Talwood, Queensland 4322, Australia

GORE, (Francis) St John Corbet; CBE; s of Francis William Baldock Gore (gs of Rev William Gore, who was uncle of Sir St George Ralph Gore, 9 Bt, and gn of Lt-Gen Sir Ralph Gore, 6 Bt, who was cr Earl of Ross (1772), Viscount Bellisle (1768) and Baron Gore of Manor Gore (1764), all in the peerage of Ireland. His Lordship was C-in-C Ireland 1788 and d 1802, when his peerage honours became extinct); *b* 8 April 1921; *Educ* Wellington, Courtauld Inst of Art; *m* 1, 1951 (m dis 1976), Priscilla Margaret, da of Cecil Harmsworth King; 1 s (William b 1956), 1 da (Catharine (Mrs Richard Gayner)); m 2, 1981, Lady Mary Strachey, *see* Gore, Lady M S; *Career* late Capt Royal Northumberland Fusiliers, served WWII; Nat Tst: advsr on pictures 1956-86, historic bldgs sec 1973-81; Exec Ctee Nat Art Collections Fund 1963-; tstee: Wallace Collection 1975- 89, Nat Gallery 1986-; FSA 1979; *Recreations* sight-seeing; *Clubs* Boodle's, Brooks's, Beefsteak; *Style—* St John Gore, Esq, CBE; 25 Elvaston Place, London SW7 (☎ 071 584 6994); Grove Farm, Stoke-by-Nayland, Suffolk

GORE, Maj Toby Clements; s of Brig Adrian Clements Gore, DSO, of Horton Priory, Sellindge, Kent, and Enid Amy, *née* Cairnes; *b* 8 Dec 1927; *Educ* Eton, Sandhurst; *m* 28 July 1959, (Isolde) Marian, da of Edward Hyde Macintosh (d 1970), of Rebeg, Kirkhill, Invernesshire; 4 da (Fiona b 1960, Juliet b 1962, Tessa b 1968, Stephanie b 1969); *Career* cmmnd Rifle Brigade 1948-70; memb Stock Exchange 1973; ptnr: Roger Mortimer 1973-75, Sheppards & Chase; memb: Ctee of West Berkshire, Macmillan Cancer Care Appeal; played cricket for Army 1948-52; *Recreations* golf, fishing, shooting; *Clubs* Naval and Military; *Style—* Maj Toby Gore; Monks Alley, Binfield, Bracknell, Berks (☎ 0344 428200); 49 Smith St, London SW3

GORE-ANDREWS, Russell William; *Career* chm: More O'Ferrall Sales (UK) Ltd, More O'Ferrall Devpt (UK) Ltd; chm: More O'Ferrall plc, More O'Ferrall International Advertising Ltd, More O'Ferrall Publicité Int SA, SAGA SA, Adshel Ltd, More O'Ferrall SE Asia Ltd; dir Outdoor Advertising Assoc of GB Ltd; memb IOD; *Style—* Russell Gore-Andrews, Esq; More O'Ferrall plc, 19 Curzon St, London W1Y 8BJ (☎ 071 499 8146, telex 23602)

GORE-BOOTH, Sir Angus Josslyn; 8 Bt (I 1760), of Artarman, Sligo; s of Sir Josslyn Augustus Richard Gore-Booth, 6 Bt, JP, DL (d 1944); suc bro Sir Michael Savile Gore-Booth, 7 Bt (d 1987); *b* 25 June 1920; *Educ* Radley, Worcester Coll Oxford (BA); *m* 1948 (m dis 1954), Hon Rosemary Myra Vane, da of 10 Baron Barnard, CMG, MC (d 1964); 1 s (Josslyn b 1950), 1 da (Eirenice b 1949); *Heir* s, Josslyn Henry Robert, *qv*; *Career* Capt Irish Gds 1939-45; *Style—* Sir Angus Gore-Booth, Bt; Lissadell, Sligo, Republic of Ireland

GORE-BOOTH, Hon Christopher Hugh; yr (twin) s of Baron Gore-Booth, GCMG, KCVO (Life Peer, d 1984), and his w, Patricia Mary, da of Montague Ellerton, of Yokohama, Japan; *b* 15 May 1943; *Educ* Eton, Durham Univ; *m* 1979, Mrs Jolanta Nicholls, da of late Dr L S Bernacinski; 1 s (Oliver Lucian Ralph b 1980); *Style—* The Hon Christopher Gore-Booth; 42 Ringford Rd, SW18

GORE-BOOTH, Hon David Alwyn; CMG (1990); er (twin) s of Baron Gore-Booth, GCMG, KCVO (Life Peer, d 1984), and Patricia Mary, o da of late Montague Ellerton, of Yokohama, Japan; *b* 15 May 1943; *Educ* Eton, ChCh Oxford (MA); *m* 1, 1964 (m dis 1970), Jillian Sarah, da of James Wyatt Valpy, of Somerset West, S Africa; 1 s (Paul Wyatt Julian b 1968); m 2, 7 Oct 1977, Mary Elisabeth Janet Gambetta, da of Sir David Francis Muirhead, KCMG, CVO; 1 step s (Riccardo Gambetta b 1970); *Career* HM Dip Serv 1964-; third sec: FCO 1964, Baghdad 1966; third then second sec Lusaka 1967; second sec: FCO 1969, Tripoli 1969; second later first sec FCO 1971; first sec UK permanent representation to European Communities Brussels 1974; asst head of Fin Relations Dept FCO 1978; cnsllr (Commercial) Jeddah 1980-83, cnsllr and head of chancery UK mission to UN NY 1983-86, head of policy planning staff FCO 1987-88, asst under sec (Middle East) 1989-; *Recreations* tennis, squash, Island of Hydra (Greece); *Clubs* MCC; *Style—* The Hon David Gore-Booth, CMG; Foreign and Commonwealth Office, King Charles Street, London SW1A 2AU (☎ 071 270 2197, fax 071 270 3370)

GORE-BOOTH, Josslyn Henry Robert; s and h of Sir Angus Gore-Booth, 8 Bt, and Hon Rosemary Myra, *née* Vane, da of 10 Baron Barnard; *b* 5 Oct 1950; *Educ* Eton, Balliol Coll Oxford (BA), INSEAD (MBA); *m* 1980, Jane Mary, da of Hon Sir (James) Roualeyn (Hovell-Thurlow-) Cumming-Bruce, *qv*; 2 da (Mary b 1985, Caroline b 1987); *Career* mgmnt conslt; *Recreations* shooting, fishing, cooking; *Clubs* Brooks's, Kildare Street and Univ (Dublin); *Style—* Josslyn Gore-Booth, Esq; Hartforth, Richmond, Yorks DL10 5JR (☎ 0748 2410/2640)

GORE-BOOTH, Hon Mrs (Rosemary Myra); *née* Vane; da of 10 Baron Barnard, CMG, OBE, MC (d 1964); *b* 1921; *m* 1948 (m dis 1954), Angus Josslyn Gore-Booth; 1 s, 1 da; *Style—* The Hon Mrs Gore-Booth; The White House, Gainford, Darlington, Co Durham (☎ 0325 730386)

GORE BROWNE, Anthony Giles Spencer; s of (John) Giles Charles Gore Browne (d 1980), of Manton, Oakham, Leics, and Pamela Helen, *née* Newton; *b* 20 April 1944; *Educ* Rannoch Sch Perthshire; *m* 14 March 1970, Penelope Anne Courtenay, da of Prebendary Clarke Edward Leighton Thomson, vicar of Chelsea Old Church, London; 1 s (Edward b 1973), 1 da (Alexandra b 1975); *Career* stockbroker 1964-; Sheppards & Co 1964-65, Sheppards & Chase 1965-73, ptnr R C Greig & Co Glasgow (London Off) 1973-82, dir of dealing Greig Middleton & Co Ltd 1986- (ptnr 1982-86), dir Riverside Racquets plc 1988-; memb Int Stock Exchange; Liveryman Worshipful Co of Fishmongers 1965, Freeman City of London 1965; *Clubs* City of London, Riverside Racquets; *Style—* Anthony Gore Browne, Esq; 20 Melville Rd, Barnes, London SW13 9RJ (☎ 081 741 0701); Greig Middleton & Co Ltd, 66 Wilson St, London EC2A 2BL (☎ 071 247 0007, fax 071 377 0353, telex 887296)

GORE BROWNE, James Anthony; s of Sir Thomas Gore Browne, (d 1988), and Lady Gore Browne, *née* Loyd; *b* 26 March 1947; *Educ* Eton, Univ of Dundee (MA), Aston Univ (Dip Business Admin); *m* 16 April 1983, Jane Anne, da of Col Seton Dickson, of Field House, Symington, Ayrshire; 2 s (Freddie b 21 Jan 1987, Harold b 20 April 1988), 1 da (Marina b 19 Dec 1984); *Career* Cazenove & Co 1969-75, asst to Chm EMI Ltd 1976-79, Thames TV 1979-80, Lead Industries Group 1980-81; admitted slr 1986, set up litigation practice Leicester 1991; SDP candidate: Doncaster Central 1987, Bristol Bath Euro Elections 1989; joined Lab pty 1989; Liveryman Worshipful Co of Fishmongers; memb Law Soc; *Recreations* golf, studying portraiture; *Clubs* White's; *Style—* James Gore Browne, Esq; 38 Winsham Grove, London SW11 6NE (☎ 071 228 6816)

GORE-RANDALL, Philip Allan; s of Alec Albert Gore-Randall, of Uxbridge, and Joyce Margaret, *née* Gore; *b* 16 Dec 1952; *Educ* Merchant Taylors', Univ Coll Oxford (MA); *m* 15 Dec 1984, Alison Elizabeth, da of Harold Arthur Armstrong While, MBE, TD (d 1983); 2 s (William b 1986, Edward b 1987); *Career* ptnr Arthur Andersen & Co 1986- (joined 1975); MInstPet, FCA 1978; *Recreations* classical music, good food, travel; *Clubs* Vincents; *Style—* Philip Gore-Randall, Esq; 21 Rylett Rd, London W12 9SS (☎ 081 743 7054); The Old Forge, Windrush, nr Burford, Oxon OX8 4TT (☎ 04514 225); Arthur Andersen & Co, 1 Surrey St, London WC2R 2PS (☎ 071 836 1200, fax 071 831 1133, car 0860 380406, telex 8812711)

GORELL, 4 Baron (UK 1909); Timothy John Radcliffe Barnes; s of 3 Baron Gorell, CBE, MC, (d 1963), and (Maud) Elizabeth Furse (d 1954), eld da of Alexander Radcliffe, of Bag Park, S Devon; *b* 2 Aug 1927; *Educ* Grotow (Mass), Eton, New Coll Oxford; *m* 1954, Joan, da of John Collins, MC; 2 adopted da; *Heir* bro, Hon Ronald Barnes; *Career* late Lt Rifle Bde; called to the Bar 1951; sr exec Royal Dutch Shell Group 1959-84; various directorships; memb: House of Lords Select Ctee, EEC Sub Ctee 1987; Upper Bailiff Worshipful Co of Weavers 1977-78; *Recreations* golf, tennis, gardening, skiing; *Clubs* Roehampton Golf; *Style—* The Rt Hon the Lord Gorell; 4 Roehampton Gate, London SW15 (☎ 081 876 5522)

GORHAM, Martin Edwin; s of Clifford Edwin Gorham (d 1983), and Florence Ada, *née* Wright; *b* 18 June 1947; *Educ* Buckhurst Hill Co HS, Queen Mary Coll London (BA); *m* 1968, Jean McNaughton, da of Robert McNaughton Kerr; *Career* administrative trg NHS 1968-70; dep hosp sec: Scarborough Hosp 1970-72, Doncaster Royal Infirmary 1972-75; hosp administrator: Northern Gen Hosp Sheffield 1975-82, Lodge Moor Hosp Sheffield Jan-July 1983; head of corp planning Newcastle Health Authy 1983, unit gen mangr Norfolk and Norwich Hosps Acute Unit 1983-90, dep regnl gen mangr South West Thames Regional Health Authy 1990-; memb Inst of Health Service Mangrs; *Recreations* music, reading, gardening, travelling and the arts in general, sport (cricket); *Style—* Martin Gorham, Esq; South West Thames Regional Health Authority, 40 Eastbourne Terrace, London W2 3QH (☎ 071 262 8011 ext 4103, car 0860 524654)

GORHAM, Richard Arthur; s of Arthur Percy Gorham (d 1979), of Bristol, and Pamela Joan, *née* Burkitt; *b* 18 Feb 1942; *Educ* Clifton, Univ of Bristol (BDS); *m* 9 Jan 1969, Alison Jill, da of Kenneth Percy Wortley, of Poole, Dorset; 1 s (Andrew b 1971), 1 da (Catherine b 1974); *Career* house offr Bristol Dental Hosp 1966, gen dental practitioner Poole 1967, clinical asst Orthodontic Dept Boscombe Hosp 1982-86, regnl advsr in gen dental practice Wessex; chm: Bournemouth Section Br Dental Assoc 1977-78, Dorset Local Dental Ctee 1977-80; pres Wessex Branch Br Dental Assoc 1981-82, memb Nat Panel of Examiners for Dental Surgery Assts, lectr Bournemouth & Poole Coll of Further Educn; *Books* Dentistry in East Dorset (1986); *Recreations* gardening, philately, DIY, local heritage; *Style—* Richard Gorham, Esq; 14 Charborough Rd, Broadstone, Dorset BH18 8NE (☎ 0202 697 176); 68 Wimborne Rd, Poole, Dorset BH15 2BZ (☎ 0202 673 037)

GORICK, Robert Lionel; s of John Gorick, of Llandudno, N Wales; *b* 24 Feb 1927; *Educ* Blackburn Tech Coll; *m* 1968, Jean Audrey, da of Frank Harwood (d 1976), of Wilpshire, nr Blackburn; 3 ch; *Career* chm and md: Liquid Plastics Ltd 1963- (mfr of plastics-based waterproof coatings and fire retardant finishes, Queen's Award for Export 1982), Flexcrete Ltd, Industrial Copolymers Ltd; *Recreations* reading, horticulture, modern music, wining and dining; *Clubs* Preston Rotary, Preston Golf; *Style*— Lionel Gorick, Esq; Liquid Plastics Ltd, PO Box 7, London Rd, Preston, Lancs PR1 4AJ (☎ 0772 59781); The Stone House, Whittingham Lane, Broughton, nr Preston, Lancs (☎ 0772 864872)

GORING, Hon Lady (Caroline); *née* Thellusson; da of 8 Baron Rendlesham (by 1 w); *b* 29 April 1941; *m* 1960, Sir William Burton Nigel Goring, 13 Bt, *qv*; *Style*— The Hon Lady Goring; 25 Queen's Gate Terrace, London SW7 (☎ 071 581 8332)

GORING, Edward Yelverton Combe; s of Maj Frederick Yelverton Goring (d 1938), and bro and hp of Sir William Goring, 13 Bt; *b* 20 June 1936; *Educ* Wellington, RNC Dartmouth, RNC Greenwich; *m* 1969 (m dis 1990), Daphne Christine Seller; 2 da; *Career* Lt Cdr RN (ret); former dep sec and slr Stratford upon Avon Dist Cncl, currently borough slr Reigate and Banstead Borough Cncl; *Style*— Edward Goring, Esq

GORING, George Ernest; *b* 19 May 1938; *Educ* Cheltenham, Ecole Hoteliere Lausanne, Westminster Coll; *Career* md and proprietor The Goring Hotel and The Spa Hotel Tunbridge Wells; chm Master Innholders 1988, pres Reunion des Gastronomes 1988-90, vice pres Restaurant Servs Guild, chm London Div BHRCA, govr Westminster Coll; Hotel of the Year 1990, membre d'honneur Chefs d'Or; fell Tourism Soc, Master Innholder, FHCIMA; *Style*— George Goring, Esq; The Goring Hotel, Beeston Place, Grosvenor Gardens, London SW1W OJW (☎ 071 834 8211, fax 071 834 4393)

GORING, Lady Hersey Margaret; *née* Boyle; 2 da of 8 Earl of Glasgow, DSO, DL (d 1963), Capt RN; *b* 11 July 1914; *m* 1, 1940, Cdr Hon John Waldegrave DSC, RN (ka 1944), s of 5 and last Baron Radstock; 2 da; m 2, 1947, John Goring, CBE, TD, DL (d 1990), s of Charles Goring, JP, DL (ggs of Sir Charles Goring, 5 Bt); 2 s (Richard Harry, John James), 2 da (Corinna Jane, Anne Elizabeth); *Style*— The Lady Hersey Goring; Shirley House, Wiston, Steyning, Sussex BN4 3DD

GORING, Lesley Susan; da of Walter Edwin Goring (d 1963), and Peggy Lambert; *b* 23 March 1950; *Educ* Northfields Sch for Girls; *Career* fashion PR conslt; PA to Mangr BIBA 1965-67, press offr Mr Freedom 1967-72, Lynne Franks PR 1972-75; fndr and proprietor: Goring Public Relations 1975-, Lesley Goring Fashion Show Production 1980-; memb Designer Ctee Br Fashion Cncl; *Recreations* music, social gatherings, pets; *Style*— Ms Lesley Goring; Lesley Goring PR+Show Production, Studio 29, 44 Earlham St, Covent Garden, London WC2 (☎ 071 240 3022, fax 071 379 0863)

GORING, Marius; CBE (1991); s of Dr Charles Goring; *b* 23 May 1912; *Educ* Perse Sch Cambridge, Frankfurt Univ, Vienna Univ, Munich Univ, Paris Univ; *m* 1, 1931 (m dis), Mary Steel; 1 da; m 2, 1941, Lucie Mannheim (d 1976); m 3, 1977, Prudence FitzGerald; *Career* actor, vice pres Equity 1975-; *Style*— Marius Goring, Esq, CBE; Middle Court, The Green, Hampton Court, Surrey (☎ 081 977 4030)

GORING, Sir William Burton Nigel; 13 Bt (E 1678, with precedency of 1627), of Highden, Sussex; s of Maj Frederick Yelverton Goring (d 1938), 6 s of 11 Bt; suc unc, Sir Forster Gurney Goring, 12 Bt, 1956; the Goring family is of great antiquity in Sussex and were MPs from fifteenth to the nineteenth century; *b* 21 June 1933; *Educ* Wellington; *m* 1960, Hon Caroline Thellusson, da of 8 Baron Rendlesham (*see* Goring, Hon Lady); *Heir* bro, Edward Goring; *Career* Lt 1 Royal Sussex Regt; memb London Stock Exchange 1963, ptnr Quilter Goodison & Co 1976; *Recreations* squash; *Clubs* Hurlingham; *Style*— Sir William Goring, Bt; 16 Linver Rd, London SW6 (071 600 4177)

GORMAN, John Reginald; CVO (1961), CBE (1974), MC (1944), DL; s of Maj J K Gorman, MC (d 1980); *b* 1 Feb 1923; *Educ* Rockport, Haileybury and ISC, Portora Harvard Business Sch; *m* 1948, Norah Heather, *née* Caruth; 2 s, 2 da; *Career* Capt Irish Guards WWII; personnel dir BOAC 1963-70, vice chm and chief exec Northern Ireland Housing Exec 1979-85; dir: NI IOD, NI Airports, Nationwide Anglia Building Soc, Cooperation North; High Sheriff Co Down 1987; FCIT, MIH; *Recreations* gardening, fishing, beekeeping; *Clubs* Cavalry and Guards', Ulster Reform; *Style*— John Gorman, Esq, CVO, CBE, MC, DL; The Forge, Jericho Road, Killyleagh, Co Down, Ireland

GORMAN, William Moore (Terence); s of Capt Richard Gorman (d 1927), of Lusaka, N Rhodesia, and Sarah Crawford, *née* Moore; *b* 17 June 1923; *Educ* Mount Temple Sch Dublin, Foyle Coll Derry, Trinity Coll Dublin (BA, BA maths); *m* 29 Dec 1950, Dorinda Maud, da of Walter T Scott; *Career* RN 1943-46 (acting petty officer 1945); sr lectr in charge econometrics and social statistics Univ of Birmingham 1957 (asst lectr 1949, lectr 1951); prof econs: Univ of Oxford 1962-67, LSE 1967-79; Nuffield Coll Oxford: professorial fell 1962-67, official 1979, sr res fell 1984-90, emeritus fell 1990-; visiting prof various univs; memb Human Sciences Sub Ctee SRC 1962-66, chm Econ Study Soc 1963-66, memb Econs Ctee SSRC 1972-76; Hon DSocSc Univ of Birmingham 1973, Hon DSc (Soc Sc) Univ of Southampton 1974, Hon DEconSc Nat Univ of Ireland 1986, hon fell Trinity Coll Dublin 1990; fell Econometric Soc 1962 (Euro chm 1971-73, pres 1972), FBA 1979; hon foreign memb: American Acad Arts and Scis 1986, American Econ Assoc 1987, Acadamea Europeae 1990; *Recreations* reading talking; *Style*— Terence Gorman, Esq; 32 Victoria Rd, Oxford OX2 7QD (☎ 0865 56087); Moorfield, Fountainstown, Myrtleville, Co Cork, Repub of Ireland (☎ 021 831174)

GORMANSTON, 17 Viscount (I 1478, Premier Viscount of Ireland); Jenico Nicholas Dudley Preston; also Baron Gormanston (I 1365-70 and UK 1868, which latter sits as); s of 16 Viscount (ka 1940), and Pamela, *née* Hanly (whose mother was Lady Marjorie, *née* Feilding, da of 9 Earl of Denbigh); *b* 19 Nov 1939; *Educ* Downside; *m* 1974, Eva Landzianowska (d 1984); 2 s (Hon Jenico, Hon William b 3 May 1976); *Heir* s, Hon Jenico Francis Tara Preston b 30 April 1974; *Style*— The Rt Hon the Viscount Gormanston; 8 Dalmeny House, Thurloe Place, London SW7 2RY

GORMLEY, Antony Mark David; s of Arthur John Constantine Gormley (d 1977), of Hampstead, London, and Elspeth, *née* Brauninger; *b* 30 Aug 1950; *Educ* Ampleforth, Trinity Coll Cambridge (BA, MA), Goldsmiths Coll Univ of London (BA), Slade Sch of Fine Art UCL (Dip FA); *m* 14 June 1980, Emilyn Victoria (Vicken), da of Maj (Ian) David Parsons, of Baas Manor, Broxbourne, Herts; 2 s (Ivo b 16 March 1982, Guy b 17 June 1985), 1 da (Paloma b 20 July 1987); *Career* artist; one man exhibitions incl: Whitechapel Art Gallery 1981, Coracle Press 1983, Riverside Studios London, Chapter Cardiff 1984, Salvatore Ala Gallery NY 1985, 1986, 1987 and 1989, Stadtishes Gallerie Regensburg, Frankfurt Kuntsverein 1985, Serpentine Gallery 1987, Burnett Miller LA 1988 and 1990, Louisiana Museum Denmark 1989, Museum of Modern Art Edinburgh 1990; gp exhibitions: Objects and Sculpture ICA 1981, Br Sculpture of the 20 Century Whitechapel Art Gallery 1981, Venice Biennale 1982 and 1986, Biennale De Sao Paulo 1983, Int Survey Museum of Mod Art NY 1984, The Br Show Aust 1985, Between Object and Image Madrid 1986, Documenta 8 Kassel 1987, ROSC Dublin 88, British Art Now: A Subjective View 6 Museums in Japan 1990-91; catalogues: Salvatore Ala NY 1984, Regensburg W Germany 1985, Salvatore Ala NY 1985, Contemporary Sculpture Centre Tokyo 1988, Louisiana 1989; collections incl: Arts Cncl of GB, Tate Gallery, CAS, Br Cncl, Southampton Art Gallery, Neue Museum Kassel, Stadt Kassel, Walker Arts Centre Minneapolis, Leeds City Art Gallery; *Recreations* sailing, skiing, walking; *Style*— Antony Gormley, Esq; 13 South Villas, London NW3 9BS (☎ 071 482 7383); 153 Bellenden Rd, London SE15 5NN (☎ 071 639 1303)

GORMLEY, Baron (Life Peer UK 1982), of Ashton-in-Makerfield in Gtr Manchester; Joseph Gormley; OBE (1969); s of John Gormley, of Ireland; *b* 5 July 1917; *Educ* St Oswald's RC Sch Ashton-in-Makerfield; *m* 1937, Sarah Ellen, da of Levi Mather, of Ashton-in-Makerfield; 1 s (Hon Francis Edward b 1938), 1 da (Hon Winifred (Hon Mrs Evans) b 1940); *Career* miner 1931-, memb NEC 1957, gen sec NW Area NUM 1961, memb Labour Pty NEC 1963- (former chm Int and Orgn Ctee), pres NUM 1971-82, memb TUC Gen Cncl 1973-80; govr BBC June-July 1982; hon fell Univ of Manchester Inst of Sci and Technol; dir: Utd Racecourses, Br Investmt Tst 1978-; Cdr Cross Order of Merit (W Germany) 1981; *Books* Battered Cherub (autobiography 1982); *Style*— The Rt Hon the Lord Gormley, OBE

GORMLY, Allan Graham; s of William Gormly, and Christina Swinton Flockhart, *née* Arnot; *b* 18 Dec 1937; *Educ* Paisley GS, Univ of Glasgow; *m* 30 June 1962, Vera Margaret, da of late Alexander Grant; 1 s (Alisdair William b 10 Sept 1965), 1 da (Lynn Margaret b 15 Nov 1963); *Career* chm John Brown Engrg Ltd 1983-, gp md John Brown plc 1983-; dir: Trafalgar House plc 1986-, Trafalgar House Construction Hldgs Ltd 1986-, Royal Insurance Holdings PLC 1990-; chm Overseas Projects Bd 1988, dep chm Export Guarantees Advsy Cncl 1990; memb: Export Guarantees Advsy Cncl 1987, BOTB 1988, Top Salaries Review Body 1990; MICAS 1961; *Recreations* music, golf; *Style*— Allan Gormly, Esq; 20 Eastbourne Terrace, London W2 6LE (☎ 071 724 0801, fax 071 262 0387, telex 8950033 JBPLC G)

GORNA, Anne Christina; da of John Gorna, of Oak Bank, Hill Top, Hale, Altrincham, Ches, and Muriel Theresa Gorna; *b* 19 Feb 1937; *Educ* Loreto Convent Llandudno, Univ of Manchester (LLB), Univ of Neuchatel (Diploma Swiss and Int Law), Univ of The Sorbonne Paris (Dip in French Civilisation), Br Cncl scholar, Harmsworth scholar of the Middle Temple; *m* 6 July 1963, Ian Davies, s of Reginald Beresford Davies, of 55 Brook Lane, Timperly, Altrincham, Cheshire; 1 s (Caspar Dominick John b 11 May 1966), 1 da (Samantha Jane b 14 Jan 1964); *Career* writer, broadcaster, columnist; called to the Bar Middle Temple 1960; sr lectr Lanchester Poly 1973-79, in practice specialising in criminal, family, med negligence, media law and int law 1980-; numerous tv and radio appearances incl: BBC Issues of Law, ITV Summer Sunday Question Time 1988, Radio 4 Any Questions? 1988, BBC1 Kilroy 1989, Granada TV This Is Your Right 1989, ITV and TVS The Time The Place, BBC GLR The Saturday Debate, GLR Janice Long Show, BBC1 Great Expectations Women in Law, BBC2 Behind the Headlines; profiled in Independent and Guardian Newspapers Casebook Series for Brilliant Ideas; friend of: Tate Gallery, Royal Ct Theatre, Lyric Theatre Hammersmith, Royal Acad, Covent Gdn; book and theatre reviewer, after dinner speaker 1990, head of Castle Chambers Exeter established 1990; *Books* Company Law (1961), Leading Cases on Company Law (1961), Questions and Answers on Company Law (1961); *Recreations* swimming, dance, theatre, ballet, music, art collecting, visiting, galleries, cherishing friendships, writing, painting; *Clubs* Western Circuit, Network, 300, City Womens Network, Holmes Place Heath, V & A; *Style*— Miss Christina Gorna; 10a Kempsford Gardens, London SW5 (☎ 071 370 0434); 1 The Old Warehouse, Denver Rd, Topsham, Exter, Devon (☎ 0392 877736); 4 Paper Buildings, Temple, London EC4Y 7EX (☎ 071 353 3366); Castle Chambers, 14 Castle St, Exeter (☎ 0392 420 345); Agent Jaque Evans (☎ 071 722 4722)

GORNICK, Naomi; *Career* designer and design manager; course ldr of design mgmnt RCA; advsr: N London Poly, Middlesex Poly, Leicester Poly, Kingston Poly, various industl clients; ed Debrett's Interior Design Collection 1988 and 1989; Chartered Soc of Designers: vice pres 1986-89, fndr chm Design Mgmnt Gp 1981; initiated SIAD Design Mgmnt seminar series in 1983 and 1985 and the Design Mgmnt Conf for Indust Year 1986 (supported by the DTI 1985-); memb Steering Ctee on Design Mgmnt Courses CNAA, chm Design Selection Ctees Design Cncl, panel judge for Design Centre Awards 1989; FCSD, FRSA; *Style*— Mrs Naomi Gornick; Royal College of Art, Kensington Gore, London SW7 2EU (☎ 071 584 5020, fax 071 225 1487)

GORODICHE, Nicolas; s of Dr Jean Gorodiche, OBE, of Arles, France; *b* 21 July 1938; *Educ* Ecole Nationale Supérieure de l'Aéronautique, Ecole Personnel Naviguant d'Essais et de Réception, Harvard Business Sch; *m* 1968, Isabelle, da of Gen Henri Ziegler, MVO, OBE; 3 da; *Career* test pilot and Lt French Air Force; commercial pilot with Air Alpes, gen mangr UK and Ireland Air France 1981- (joined 1970), chm Air France Holidays; *Recreations* mountaineering, skiing, tennis, golf, music; *Clubs* Hurlingham, Royal Mid-Surrey Golf; *Style*— Nicolas Gorodiche, Esq; Air France, 69 Boston Manor Rd, Brentford, Middx TW8 9JQ (☎ 081 568 4411)

GORONWY-ROBERTS, Hon Ann Elizabeth; da of Baron Goronwy-Roberts, PC (Life Peer, d 1981); *b* 1947; *Educ* Pwlheli GS, Univ of Wales Sch of Educn (CertEd), Birbeck Coll London (BA); *Career* adult and secdy teaching; *Style*— The Hon Ann Goronwy-Roberts; 5 Okeover Manor, Clapham Common Northside, London SW4 0RH; c/o The Lady Goronwy-Roberts, Plas Newydd, Pwllheli, Gwynedd, N Wales

GORONWY-ROBERTS, Baroness; Marian; JP, DL; da of David Evans, of Aberdare; *Educ* Univ of Wales (BA); *m* 1942, Baron Goronwy-Roberts, PC (Life Peer d 1981), Min State FCO and Dep Ldr House of Lords 1975-79; 1 s, 1 da; *Career* writer and lecturer; memb Ctee Extra-Mural Studies Univ Coll Bangor N Wales; chm BBC Wales Appeals Advsy Ctee 1976-86, memb Appeals Panel Wales S4C; pres Caernarfonshire Historical Soc; chm Gwynedd Branch of Magistrates Assoc; chm The North Wales Probation Ctee until 1988; vice pres County Branch Cncl for Preservation of Rural Wales; hon fell Univ Coll Cardiff 1982; *Recreations* words and derivations, literature, music, protection of wild life; *Style*— The Rt Hon the Lady Goronwy-Roberts, JP, DL; Plâs Newydd, Pwllheli, Gwynedd

GORONWY-ROBERTS, Hon Owen Dafydd; s of Baron Goronwy-Roberts, PC (Life Peer) (d 1981); *b* 1946; *m* 1, 1979, Milana Majka Bartonova, da of Dr M M Jelinek, of London; m 2, 1987, Sharon Jennifer, da of Terence Taylor, of Duncan, BC, Canada; *Style*— The Hon Owen Goronwy-Roberts; c/o The Rt Hon Lady Goronwy-Roberts, Plas Newydd, Pwllheli, Gwynedd, N Wales

GORRINGE, Christopher John; s of Maurice Sydney William Gorringe (d 1981), of Newick, Nr Lewes, Sussex, and Hilda Joyce, *née* Walker; *b* 13 Dec 1945; *Educ* Bradfield, RAC Cirencester Glos; *m* 17 April 1976, Jennifer Mary, da of Roger Arthur Chamberlain (d 1979), of Ramsbury, Wilts; 2 da (Kim b 13 April 1978, Anna b 24 Feb 1981); *Career* asst land agent Iveagh Tstees Ltd (Guinness Family) 1968-73, chief exec The All Eng Lawn Tennis and Croquet Club Wimbledon 1983-(asst sec 1973-79, sec 1979-83); ARICS 1971; *Recreations* lawn tennis; *Clubs* The All England Lawn Tennis, The Queen's, Jesters, Int (GB), St George's Hill Lawn Tennis; *Style*— Christopher Gorringe, Esq; The All England Lawn Tennis Club, Church Road, Wimbledon, London, SW19 5AE (☎ 081 944 1066, fax 081 947 3354, telex 265180 AELTC)

GORROD, Prof John William; s of Ernest Lionel Gorrod (d 1981), of 29 Manton Ave, Hanwell, London, and Caroline Rebecca, *née* Richardson; *b* 11 Oct 1931; *Educ*

Univ of London (DSc, PhD), Chelsea Coll (Dip), Brunel CAT (HNC); *m* 3 April 1954, Doreen Mary, da of George Douglas Collins, of 114 Huntingfield Rd, Putney, London; 2 s (Simon b 5 April 1962, Nicholas b 16 July 1966), 1 da (Julia b 8 June 1959); *Career* res fell Dept of Biochemistry Univ of Bari Italy 1964, res fell Royal Cmmn for the Exhibition of 1851 1965-67, lectr in biopharmacy Chelsea Coll Univ of London 1968-80 (reader 1980-84), prof of biopharmacy Head of Chelsea Dept of Pharmacy King's Coll London 1984-89, res prof Faculty of Life Scis King's Coll London 1990- (head of Div of Health Scis 1988-); FRSC 1980, FRCPath 1984, Hon MRPharmS 1982; corresponding memb German Pharmaceutical Soc 1985, hon fell Hellenic Pharmaceutical Soc 1987; memb: Assoc for Res in Indoor Air 1989, Air Tport Uses Ctee CAA 1990; Assocs for Res in Substances of Enjoyment 1990, Cncl Indoor Air Int 1990-; *Books* Drug Metabolism in Man (1978), Drug Toxicity (1979), Testing for Toxicity (1981), Biological Oxidation of Nitrogen in Organic Molecules (1985), Biological Oxidation of Nitrogen (1978), Metabolism of Xenobiotics (1988), Development of Drugs and Modern Medicines (1986); *Recreations* badminton, running; *Clubs* Athenaeum, Hillingdon Athletic; *Style—* Prof John Gorrod; Kingsmead, 13 Park Lane, Hayes, Middx (☎ 081 561 3851); The Rest Orchard, Polstead Heath, nr Colchester, Essex; King's College London, Chelsea Department of Pharmacy, Manresa Rd, London, SW3 6LX (☎ 081 351 2488)

GORST, John Marcus; s of Maj James Marcus Gorst, of South Stack, Fornham All Saints, Bury St Edmunds, Suffolk, and Frances Gladys, *née* Espley; *b* 13 Jan 1944; *Educ* Culford Sch, Selwyn Coll Cambridge (MA); *m* June 1974 (m dis 1977), Marian, da of James Anthony Judge, of 2 Rockall Drive, Glasgow; *Career* md Drayson Property Hldgs Ltd 1971-, chm Folkard and Hayward Servs Ltd 1984-; Freeman Worshipful Co of Bakers; *Recreations* golf, shooting; *Clubs* United Oxford and Cambridge Univ; *Style—* John Gorst, Esq; 20 Crawford St, London WIH 2AR (☎ 071 935 7799, fax 071 486 6877, car 0836 273 555)

GORST, John Michael; MP (C) Hendon North 1987-; s of Derek Charles Gorst; *b* 28 June 1928; *Educ* Ardingly, Corpus Christi Coll Cambridge; *m* 1954, Noël Harington, da of Austin Walker, of E Kilbride; 5 s; *Career* fndr of Assocs 1974: Telephone Users, Local Radio; advertising and PR mangr Pye Ltd 1953-63, PR consult John Gorst and Assocs Ltd 1964-; contested (C): Chester-le-Street 1964, Bodmin 1966; MP (C): Hendon North 1970-74, Barnet 1974-1983, Hendon North 1983-; memb Select Ctee on Employment 1979-87, vice chm All Pty War Crimes Ctee 1988-90, chm Cons Back Bench Media Ctee 1988-; *Clubs* Garrick; *Style—* John Gorst, Esq, MP; House of Commons, London SW1

GORT, 8 Viscount (I 1816); Colin Leopold Prendergast Vereker; also Baron Kiltarton (I 1810); s of Cdr Leopold Vereker, RNR (gs of 4 Viscount); suc first cous once removed, 7 Viscount, 1975; *b* 21 June 1916; *Educ* Sevenoaks Sch; *m* 1946, Bettine, da of Godfrey Green, of Douglas, IOM, and formerly w of Arthur Jarand; 2 s, 1 da; *Heir* s, Hon Foley Vereker; *Career* Lt Cdr RNVR WWII (despatches), Mediterranean, Africa, Indian Ocean, Home Fleet, Atlantic, Russian Convoy; dir: Royal Bank of Scotland IOM (ret), Royal Skandia Life Assurance, Invesco MIM International Ltd, Euranov, Eurafish; memb House of Keys IOM 1966-71; JP Castletown IOM 1962-1986; *Recreations* golf, gardening, antique restoration; *Style—* The Rt Hon the Viscount Gort; Westwood, The Crofts, Castletown, IOM (☎ 0624 822545)

GORTON, Philip Murray; s of Rev John Percival Page Gorton (d 1951), and Muriel Gladys, *née* Murray; *b* 24 Nov 1928; *Educ* Bedford Sch, Coll of Estate Mgmnt London; *m* 3 July 1954, Rosalind Angela Mary, da of Lt-Col Sir James Edmond Henderson Neville, 2 Bt, MC (d 1983); 3 s (Simon b 24 Feb 1957, Mark b 25 Dec 1960, Colin b 24 Aug 1962), 1 da (Clare (Mrs Hill) b 7 Aug 1958); *Career* Civil Serv; Miny of Agric: asst land cmmr Norwich 1966, sr asst land cmmr London 1970, div surveyor Northampton 1975, supt surveyor London 1981, regnl mangr (land use and countryside) Cambridge 1984, ret 1988; RICS: memb Cncl Rural Div 1988-, memb (Rural Div) Educn and Membership Ctee 1981-88, assessor Test of Professional Competance 1984-89, assessor RAC Cirencester 1988-; Liveryman Worshipful Co of Fishmongers; FRICS; *Recreations* conservation, shooting; *Clubs* Civil Service; *Style—* Philip Gorton, Esq; The Emplins, Gamlingay, Cambridgeshire SG19 3ER (☎ 0767 50581)

GORTVAI, Peter; s of Dr William Gortvai, and Dr Elizabeth Gortvai, *née* Foldi; *b* 1 Dec 1929; *Educ* MA, MChir, MD (Cantab); *m* 28 Dec 1963, Prof Dame Rosalinde Hurley, da of William Hurley; *Career* sr registrar Nat Hosp for Nervous Diseases 1960-66; Fulbright Scholar Mass Gen Hosp (clinical and res fell 1964-65), res fell Harvard Univ 1964-65; conslt neurosurgn: NE Thames RHA 1967-, Bart's 1982-; FRCSEd 1960, FRCS 1961; *Recreations* gardening, travel; *Style—* Peter Gortvai, Esq; 2 Temple Gdns, Temple, London EC4Y 9AY (☎ 071 353 0577); St Bartholomew's Hospital, West Smithfield, London EC1A 7BE (☎ 071 601 3718)

GORTY, Peter; s of Nathan Gorty, and Bella, *née* Lancet; *b* 3 Nov 1944; *Educ* Owens Sch Islington, LSE (LLB); *m* 20 Sept 1970, Mariana; 1 s (Andrew), 1 da (Helen); *Career* articled clerk Gilbert Samuel & Co 1967-69, asst slr Withers 1969-70, ptnr specialising in banking and energy law Nabarro Nathanson 1972- (asst slr 1970-72); *Recreations* all sports, reading, theatre, architecture; *Style—* Peter Gorty, Esq; Nabarro Nathanson, 50 Stratton St, London W1X 5FL (☎ 071 493 9933, fax 071 629 7900)

GORVIN, Roger John; s of Dennis Richard Gorvin (d 1986), and Edith Mary, *née* Lockyer; *b* 16 June 1938; *Educ* Chippenham GS, Cheltenham GS, Witney GS; *m* 3 April 1961, Josephine Edwina Stamford, da of late Frederick George Hamilton Cooper; 3 da (Fiona b 1966, Alison b 1969, Kirsty b 1973); *Career* dir: Co-operative Bank plc, EftPos UK Ltd, Scottish Co-operative Soc Nominees Ltd, Unity Tst Bank plc (alternate), Fastline Credit Fin Ltd, Co-operative Bank (Insur Servs) Ltd, Cleveland Fin Ltd, First Co-operative Fin Ltd, Co-operative Bank Fin Advsrs Ltd, Co-operative Handycard Serv Ltd, FC Fin Ltd; special-at-large dir Visa International (EMEA); chm NW Business and Indust Awards; FCIB; *Recreations* cricket, gardening, photography, hi-fi; *Style—* Roger Gorvin, Esq; Rhodewood House, 140 Prestbury Road, Macclesfield, Cheshire SK10 3BN (☎ 0625 432244); Co-operative Bank plc, P O Box 200, Delf House, Southway, Skelmersdale, Lancs WN8 6NY (☎ 0695 24151, fax 0695 50699, telex 629300)

GOSCHEN, Viscountess; Alvin Moyana Lesley; yr da of late Harry England, of Durban, Natal, S Africa; *m* 18 Aug 1955, as his 2 w, 3 Viscount Goschen, KBE (d 1977); 1 s (4 Viscount, *qv*), 1 da; *Style—* The Rt Hon the Viscountess Goschen; Hilton House, Crowthorne, Berks

GOSCHEN, Edward Alexander; s and h of Sir Edward Christian Goschen, 3 Bt, DSO, and Cynthia, da of late Rt Hon Sir Alexander Cadogan, OM, GCMG, KCB; *b* 13 March 1949; *Educ* Eton; *m* 1976, Louise Annette, da of Lt-Col Ronald Chance, MC, and Lady Ava, *née* Baird (da of 1 Viscount Stonehaven and Lady (Ethel) Sidney, *née* Keith-Falconer, who was Countess of Kintore in her own right); 1 da (Charlotte, b 1982); *Style—* Edward Goschen, Esq; Pixton Stables, Dulverton, Taunton, Somerset

GOSCHEN, Sir Edward Christian; 3 Bt (UK 1916), DSO (1944); s of Sir Edward Goschen, 2 Bt (d 1933; s of Sir (William) Edward Goschen, 1 Bt, GCB, GCMG, GCVO, HM ambass in Berlin in 1914), and Countess Mary Danneskiold-Samsøe (d 1964), 7 da of 5 Count (Christian) Danneskiold-Samsøe; *b* 2 Sept 1913; *Educ* Eton, Trinity Coll Oxford; *m* 1946, Cynthia, da of Rt Hon Sir Alexander Cadogan, OM, GCMG, KCB, PC, sometime perm under sec at the FO (7 s of 5 Earl Cadogan), by his w Lady Theodosia Acheson, da of 4 Earl of Gosford; 1 s, 1 da; *Heir* s, Edward Alexander Goschen; *Career* memb Stock Exchange Cncl (dep chm 1968-71); Cwlth War Graves cmmr 1977-87; *Style—* Sir Edward Goschen, Bt, DSO; Lower Farm House, Hampstead Norreys, Newbury, Berks (☎ 0635 201270)

GOSCHEN, 4 Viscount (UK 1900); Giles John Harry Goschen; s of 3 Viscount Goschen, KBE (d 1977), and his 2 w Alvin, *née* England; *b* 16 Nov 1965; *Heir* none; *Style—* The Rt Hon the Viscount Goschen; Hilton House, Crowthorne, Berks

GOSDEN, John Harry Martin; s of John Montague Gosden (d 1967), of Sussex, and Peggie Gosden; *b* 30 March 1951; *Educ* Eastbourne Coll, Emmanuel Coll Cambridge (MA, Athletics blue); *m* 1982, Rachel Dene Serena Hood; 3 c; *Career* racehorse trainer; asst trainer: Sir Noel Murless 1974-76, Dr Vincent O'Brien 1976-77; trainer: USA 1978-88, England 1989-; achievements as trainer USA: among top ten 1982-88, leading trainer Calif meets, 8 state champions, 2 Eclipse Award winners; land devpt Caracas Venezuela 1974; Sussex Martlets schoolboy cricketer 1967-68, memb Blackheath Rugby Club 1969-70, memb Br under 23 rowing squad 1973; *Recreations* music, skiing, environmental issues; *Style—* John Gosden, Esq; Stanley House Stables, Bury Rd, Newmarket, Suffolk CB8 7DF (☎ 0638 669944, fax 0638 669922)

GOSDEN, Prof Peter Henry John Heather; s of Alfred John Gosden (d 1980), of Fittleworth, and Elizabeth Ann Gosden (d 1962); *b* 3 Aug 1927; *Educ* Midhurst GS, Emmanuel Coll Cambridge (BA, MA), Birkbeck Coll London (PhD); *m* 2 Sept 1964, Dr (Margaret) Sheila Gosden, da of Charles Alfred Hewitt (d 1974), of Hull; *Career* Nat Serv RAF 1949-51; schoolmaster 1951-60, jt ed Journal of Educational Administration and History 1968, pro vice chllr Univ of Leeds 1985-87 (lectr 1960, sr lectr 1967, reader 1971, prof 1978); chm JMB Manchester 1988-, memb Exec Univ Cncl for Educn of Teachers 1978-; FRHistS 1969, FRSA 1989; *Books* incl: The Friendly Societies in England 1815-1875 (1961), Self-Help: Voluntary Associations in Nineteenth Centry Britain (1973), Education in the Second World War: a study in policy and administration (1976), The Educational System since 1944 (1983), Education Committees (with George Cooke, 1986); *Recreations* music, gardening, walking; *Clubs* National Liberal; *Style—* Prof Peter Gosden; Orchard House, Creskeld Lane, Bramhope, Nr Leeds LS16 9ES; The University, Leeds LS2 9JT (☎ 0532 334522)

GOSFORD, 7 Earl of (I 1806); Sir Charles David Alexander John Sparrow Acheson; 13 Bt (NS 1628); also Baron Gosford (I 1776), Viscount Gosford (I 1785), Baron Worlingham (UK 1835, sits as), and Baron Acheson of Clancairny (UK 1847); s of 6 Earl of Gosford, OBE (d 1966), by his 1 w, Francesca, er da of Francesco Cagiati, of Rome; *b* 13 July 1942; *Educ* Harrow, Byam Shaw Sch of Drawing and Painting, Royal Academy Schs; *m* 1983, Lynnette Redmond; *Heir* unc, Hon Patrick Acheson; *Career* artist; one man shows: Barry Stern Exhibition Gallery, Sydney 1983 and 1986, Von Bertouch Galleries Newcastle NSW 1983 and 1986; *Style—* The Rt Hon the Earl of Gosford; c/o House of Lords, Westminster, London SW1

GOSFORD, Cynthia, Countess of; Cynthia Margaret; da of late Capt Henry Cave West, RHA; m 1, Maj James Pringle Delius, 13/18 Royal Hussars (d 1944); m 2, 1960, as his 2 w, 6 Earl of Gosford, OBE (d 1966); *Style—* The Rt Hon Cynthia, Countess of Gosford; Heath Cottage, Camberley, Surrey

GOSKIRK, (William) Ian MacDonald; CBE (1986); s of William Arthur Goskirk (d 1984), of Scotby, Carlisle, and Flora Rennie, *née* MacDonald; *b* 2 March 1932; *Educ* Carlisle GS, The Queen's Coll Oxford (MA); *m* 7 June 1969, Hope-Ann, da of John Knaizuk, of New York, USA; 1 da (Nadia Anna b 1970); *Career* Lt REME 1950-52; Shell International Petroleum 1956-74, md Anschutz Petroleum Ltd 1974-76, British National Oil Corporations 1976-85, md BNOC (Trading) Ltd 1980-82 (chief exec 1982-85), dir Coopers & Lybrand Assocs 1986-; CBIM 1984, FInstPet 1975; *Recreations* gardening; *Clubs* Athenaeum; *Style—* Ian Goskirk, Esq, CBE; c/o Coopers & Lybrand Associates Ltd, Plumtree Court, London EC4A 4HT (☎ 071 583 5000, telex 887470)

GOSLING, Allan Gladstone; s of Gladstone Gosling (d 1951), and Elizabeth, *née* Ward; *b* 4 July 1933; *Educ* Kirkham GS, Birmingham Sch of Architecture; *m* 18 March 1961, Janet Pamela, da of Ruben Gosling (d 1987); 1 s (Philip Allan b 8 May 1963), 1 da (Karen Francis b 29 April 1965); *Career* Nat Serv cmmnd 1959-61; architect: Lancs CC 1950-54, Surman Kelly & Surman 1957-59, Army Works Orgn 1961-63, Miny Housing and Local Govt 1963-72; PSA: regnl works offr N W Region 1972-76, dir Midland Region 1976-83, dir Scotland 1983-90, ops dir projects 1990-; MRIBA 1961, FRIAS 1988; *Recreations* rugby, gardening, walking, DIY; *Clubs* Civil Service; *Style—* Allan Gosling, Esq; Five Ways House, Islington Row, Birmingham B15 1SL (☎ 021 626 2001)

GOSLING, Lady Caroline Victoria; *née* Wood; er da of 2 Earl of Halifax , JP, DL; *b* 10 Sept 1937; *m* 1, 1958 (m dis 1970), Randle Joseph, eldest s of late Maj-Gen Sir Randle Feilden, KCVO, CB, CBE, DL, and Lady Feilden, *qv*; 1 s (Randle Charles Roderick b 1961), 2 da (Virginia Mary b 1959, Fiona Caroline b 1965); m 2, 1970, John V Gosling; *Style—* The Lady Caroline Gosling; The Claw, Brushford, Dulverton, Somerset (☎ 0398 23493)

GOSLING, Sir (Frederick) Donald; *b* 2 March 1929; *m* 1959, Elizabeth Shauna, *née* Ingram; 3 s; *Career* joined RN 1944, served Med HMS Leander; jt chm Nat Car Parks Ltd 1950-, chm Palmer & Harvey Ltd 1967-, dir Lovell Hldgs Ltd 1975-; memb Cncl of Mgmnt White Ensign Assoc 1970- (chm 1978-83, vice-pres 1983-); chm Selective Employment Scheme 1976-; tstee: Fleet Air Arm Museum Yeovilton 1974-, RYA Seamanship Fndn; patron Submarine Meml Appeal 1978-; chm Berkeley Square Ball Charitable Tst; kt 1976; *Style—* Sir Donald Gosling; National Car Parks Ltd, PO Box 4NH, 21 Bryanston St, Marble Arch, London W1A 4NH (☎ 071 499 7050)

GOSLING, Justin Cyril Bertrand; s of Vincent Samuel Gosling (d 1945), of Brewood, Stafford, and Dorothy Mary Catherine, *née* Smith (d 1964); *b* 26 April 1930; *Educ* Ampleforth, Wadham Coll Oxford (BPhil), St John's Coll Oxford (MA); *m* 2 Sept 1958, (Angela) Margaret, da of Brig Sir Iltyd Clayton, KBE (d 1955), of Herefordshire; 2 s (Samuel b 18 May 1961, Thomas b 2 March 1970), 2 da (Rachel b 9 Aug 1962, Elizabeth b 9 April 1966); *Career* Oxford Univ: Fereday fell St John's Coll 1955-58, lectr philosophy Wadham and Pembroke Coll 1958-60, fell in philosophy St Edmund Hall 1960-82, sr proctor 1977-78, princ St Edmund Hall 1982-; Barclay Acheson prof Macalester Coll Minnesota 1964, visiting res fell ANU Canberra 1970; *Books* Pleasure and Desire (1969), Plato (1973), Plato, Philebus (ed 1975), The Greeks on Pleasure (with CCW Taylor, 1982); Weakness of the Will (1990); *Recreations* gardening, intaglio printing, recorder music; *Clubs* United Oxford and Cambridge Univ; *Style—* Justin Gosling, Esq; The Principal's Lodgings, St Edmund Hall, Oxford OX1 4AR; Joymount, Northcourt Lane, Abingdon, Oxford OX14 1QA (☎ 0865 279000)

GOSLING, Capt (Henry) Miles; JP (Oxfordshire 1958); s of Maj George Edward Gosling, MC (d 1938), of Stratton Audley Park, Bicester, Oxon, and Helen Violet, *née* St Maur (d 1975); *b* 23 Oct 1927; *Educ* Eton; *m* 1 Oct 1963, Elizabeth Rosemary, da of Thomas Norris Browning; 3 da (Emma Lucia b 1964, Harriet Elizabeth b 1966, Laura Cathryn b 1967); *Career* cmmnd 11 Hussars (PAO) 1947-52; High Sheriff Oxfordshire 1970-71; *Recreations* country sports, racing; *Clubs* Cavalry and Guards';

Style— Captain Miles Gosling, JP; Manor Farm, Stratton Audley, Bicester, Oxon OX6 9BJ (☎ 0869 277251)

GOSLING, Paula Louise (Mrs John Hare); da of A Paul Osius (d 1986), and Sylvie, *née* Van Slembrouck (d 1986); *b* 12 Oct 1939; *Educ* Mackenzie HS, Wayne State Univ (BA); *m* 1, 1968 (m dis 1979), Christopher Gosling, s of Thomas Gosling; 2 da (Abigail Judith b 1970, Emily Elizabeth b 1972); m 2, 1981, John Anthony Hare, s of John Charles Hare; *Career* copywriter: Campbell-Ewald USA 1962-64, C Mitchell & Co London 1964-67, Pritchard-Wood London 1967-68, David Williams Ltd London 1968-70; copy conslt: C Mitchell & Co 1970-72, ATA Advertising Bristol 1977-79; crime writer 1979-; novels: A Running Duck (1978, US title Fair Game, John Creasey Meml award for Best First Crime Novel 1978, made into film for Japanese TV and into film Cobra), The Zero Trap (1979), Mind's Eye (as Ainslie Skinner 1980, US title The Harrowing), Loser's Blues (1980, US title Solo Blues), The Woman in Red (1983), Monkey Puzzle (1985, Gold Dagger award for Best Crime Novel 1986), The Wychford Murders (1987), Hoodwink (1988), Backlash (1989), Death Penalties (1991); author of numerous serials and short stories incl Mr Felix (nominated for Best Short Story MWA 1987); performing memb Murder We Write roadshow; Crime Writers' Assoc: memb Ctee 1984-90, chm 1988-89; memb: Soc of Authors, ALCS, Mensa; *Recreations* needlework, kite-flying; *Style*— Ms Paula Gosling; c/o Elaine Green Ltd, 37 Goldhawk Road, London W12 8QQ (☎ 081 749 0315, fax 081 749 0318)

GOSLING, Col Richard Bennett; OBE (1957), TD (1948), DL (Essex 1954); s of Thomas Spencer Gosling, JP (d 1946), of Dynes Hall, Halstead, Essex, and Miriam Gwendolyn Wickham, *née* Wyles (d 1952), ancestors founded Goslings Bank, 19 Fleet St, London 1650, amalgamated with Barclays Bank 1896; *b* 4 Oct 1914; *Educ* Eton, Magdalene Coll Cambridge (MA), Univ of Birmingham (Dip); *m* 1, 21 April 1950, Marie Terese (d 1976), o da of Philip Ronayne (d 1944), of Castle Redmond, Midleton, Co Cork; 1 s (Timothy Philip b 11 May, d 18 Nov 1953), 1 adopted s (Aidan Bennett b 27 Feb 1960), 1 adopted da (Francine Mary b 26 Jan 1959); m 2, 22 July 1978, Sybilla Jacoba Margaretha, da of Wilhelmus Matthias Jan Van Oyen (d 1935), of Venlo, Netherlands, and wid of Bernard Burgers, of Kasteel, Weurt, Nijmegen, Netherlands; *Career* Essex Yeomanry 1939-53, CO 1950-53, Dep CRA E Anglia Div (full col) 1953-56; professional engr; dir: PE Consulting Gp 1957-69, PE Int Ltd 1969-76, Royal Doulton Gp 1964-72, Revertex Chems Ltd 1974-84, Press Mouldings Ltd 1980-; chm: Constructors 1965-68, Hearne & Co 1966-80; dir gen Br Agric Export Cncl 1971-73; pres Univ of Essex Assoc, int steward Royal Show 1974-90; High Sheriff of Essex 1982-83; French Croix de Guerre with Gold Star 1945; CEng, MBIM 1950, FID 1967, FIMechE 1969, FIMC 1985; *Recreations* shooting, farming, country pursuits; *Clubs* Naval and Military, MCC, Beefsteak; *Style*— Col Richard Gosling, OBE, TD, DL; Canterburys Lodge, Margaretting, Essex CM4 OEE (☎ 0277 353073)

GOSLING, Prof William; s of Harold William Gosling (d 1980), of Cograve, Notts, and Aida Maisie, *née* Webb; *b* 25 Sept 1932; *Educ* Mundella Sch Nottingham, Imperial Coll London (BSc), Univ of Bath (DSc); *m* 5 July 1953, Patricia Mary, da of Charles Henry Best, of Rode, Somerset; 2 s (Richard b 1956, d 1958, Ceri b 1959), 1 da (Melanie b 1954); *Career* prof of electrical engrg Univ of Wales 1966, vice princ Univ Coll Swansea 1972, prof of electronic engrg Univ of Bath 1974; tech dir Plessey Co plc 1981- (formerly Plessey Electronic Systems Ltd) 1981-89; hon prof of communication engrg Southampton Univ 1981-89; dir elect devpts Securicor Gp 1990-, visiting prof Univ of Bath 1990-; pres: Euro Convention of Soc of Electronic Engrs 1977-78, Inst of Electronic and Radio Engrs 1979-80; Freeman City of London 1980; Liveryman Worshipful Co of: Scientific Instrument Makers 1980, Engrs 1985; Hon Fell UMIST 1987; ARCS, FIEE 1968, FInstD 1982; *Books* Design of Engineering Systems (1962), Field Effect Electronics (1971), Radio Receivers (1986); *Recreations* music, poetry; *Clubs* Athenaeum; *Style*— Prof William Gosling; White Hart Cottage, Rode, Bath (☎ 0373 830901, mobile 0860 528859)

GOSLING, William Douglas; MBE (1949), TD, DL (Essex 1952); s of William Sullivan Gosling (d 1952), and Lady Victoria Kerr, 5 da of 9 Marquess of Lothian; *b* 11 Sept 1904; *Educ* Eton, Univ of Cambridge; *m* 1935, Rosemary (d 1986), da of Hon Victor Alexander Frederick Russell, CBE (3 s of 1 Baron Ampthill); *Career* Nat Serv Maj RA (TA) ME WWII, Lt-Col cmd Essex Yeo 1951; farmer, local dir Barclays Bank; High Sheriff Essex 1958, patron of living of Farnham Essex; *Style*— William Gosling, Esq, MBE, TD, DL; Thrimley House, Farnham, Bishop's Stortford CM23 1HX

GOSS, Major (William) Raymond; s of Vernon William Goss (d 1968), of Lancs, and Mary Elizabeth, *née* Kingston (d 1983); *b* 29 Dec 1925; *Educ* King's Sch Worcester, RMCS; *m* 1, 1953 (m dis), Jocelyn Truell; 5 s (Robert b 1954, Richard b 1956, Patrick b 1957, Geoffrey b 1959, Quentin b 1961), 1 da (Laurel b 1965); m 2, 1990, Maureen Silvester; *Career* cmmnd RA 1946, served India 1946-47, active serv 45 Field Regt Korea 1950-51, instr Armour Sch RAC Centre 1966-69; dir Steam Marine Ltd; CEng, MRAeS; *Recreations* sailing, swimming, woodcarving; *Style*— Maj Raymond Goss; 22 Derwent Ave, Mill Hill, London NW7 3DZ (☎ 081 959 1999)

GOSS, Prof Richard Oliver; s of Sqdn-Ldr Leonard Arthur Goss (d 1956), and Hilda Nellie, *née* Casson (d 1986); *b* 4 Oct 1929; *Educ* Christ's Coll Finchley, HMS Worcester, King's Coll Cambridge (BA, MA, PhD); *m* 21 June 1958 (m dis 1983), Lesley Elizabeth, da of William Thomas Thurbon; 2 s (David Anthony b 1963, Stephen Peter b 1966), 1 da (Catherine Alice b 1960); *Career* MN: Cadet to Chief Offr 1947-56, Master Mariner 1956; statistics clerk and subsequently PA to gen mangr NZ Shipping Co Ltd (London) 1958-63; Civil Serv 1963-80: econ conslt on shipping ship bldg and ports, sr econ advsr on aviation shipping and marine, under sec for advice on shipping civil aviation, prices and consumer protection, wholesale prices; econ advsr Ctee of Inquiry into Shipping (Rochdale Ctee) 1967-70, prof maritime econs Univ of Wales Cardiff 1980-; fndr memb Nautical Inst (cncl memb 1972-76), ed (later ed-in-chief) Maritime Policy and Mgmnt; memb Hon Co of Master Mariners; Assoc Inst NA 1969, FNI 1977; *Books* Studies in Maritime Economics (1968), Advances in Maritime Economics (1977); *Recreations* cruising; *Clubs* Wyre Mill (Pershore, Worcs); *Style*— Prof Richard Goss; 8 Dunraven House, Westgate St, Cardiff CF1 1DL (☎ 0222 344 338); University College of Wales of Cardiff, Dept of Maritime Studies, Aberconway Building, Colum Drive, Cardiff (☎ 0222 874000, fax 0222 874478, telex 498635)

GOSSELIN, Peter John Nicholas; s of René Jean Gosselin (d 1977), and Edith May, *née* Bouchere; *b* 7 June 1944; *Educ* De Lasalle Coll, Somerset Coll of Agric (NCA); *m* 1 Oct 1977, Joan Elizabeth, da of Gordon Arthur Gaudin; *Career* formerly agric foreman and haulage contractor; fishing tackle dealer; memb: Jersey Records Ctee, Jersey Sea Fisheries Advsy Panel; chm Jersey Fedn of Sea Anglers; *Recreations* fishing, reading; *Clubs* Jersey Light Tackle Group, States Airport Social; *Style*— Peter J N Gosselin, Esq; Nouages, Neuvaine, Golf Lane, Grouville, Jersey (☎ 0534 74875)

GOSSIP, Michael Arthur John; OBE (1991); JP; s of Rev Robin Arthur John Gossip (d 1962), of Edinburgh, and Elizabeth Ann, *née* Ness; *b* 27 April 1933; *Educ* George Watson's Coll Edinburgh, Univ of Edinburgh (BL); *m* 10 Feb 1962, Margaret Helen, da of George McCall, of Lochgilphead, Argyll; 1 s (Robin b 1967), 2 da (Susan b 1963, Fiona b 1966); *Career* sr dep co clerk Dumfries CC 1960-71, co clerk Argyll CC 1972-75 (sr dep co clerk 1971-72), chief exec Argyll and Bute DC 1974-; Hon Sheriff at Dunoon; memb: Law Soc of Scot, Soc of Local Authy Chief Execs, Scot Records Advsy Ctee; FBIM 1974; *Recreations* bowls, gardening; *Style*— Michael A J Gossip, Esq, OBE, JP; Tigh-Na-Coille, Ardrishaig, Argyll PA30 8EP (☎ 0546 3454); Kilmory Castle, Lochgilphead, Argyll (☎ 0546 2127)

GOSWELL, Brian Lawrence; s of Albert George Goswell (d 1971), and Florence Emily, *née* Barnett (d 1980); *b* 26 Nov 1935; *Educ* St David's Sch High Wycombe, Univ of Durham; *m* 1961, Deirdre Gillian, da of Harold Stones, of Cadby Hall, Cadby, Leics; 2 s (Paul b 1964, Angus b 1967); *Career* dep sr ptnr Healey & Baker; chm: Healey & Baker Inc New York, Roux Restaurants Ltd, Avon City Ltd; dir Westminster Scaffolding Gp plc; memb Advsy Bd Sir Alexander Gibb & Partners; hon treas Carlton Club Political Ctee, chm Friends of Royal Soc for Nature Conservation Inc New York, fell and past pres Incorporated Soc of Valuers and Auctioneers, assoc Chartered Inst of Arbitrators; *Recreations* shooting, horse racing, cricket; *Clubs* Turf, Carlton, City of London, City Livery, United and Cecil, MCC; *Style*— Brian Goswell, Esq; 27 Austin Friars, London EC2N 2AA (☎ 071 628 4361); Pipers, Camley Park Drive, Pinkneys Green, Berks SL6 6QF (☎ 0628 30768); 555 Madison Ave, New York, NY 10022, USA (☎ 212 935 7251)

GOTCH, Jeremy Millard Butler; s of Ralph Butler Gotch (d 1979), and Eileen Madge, *née* Millard (d 1956); *b* 6 June 1934; *Educ* Berkhamsted Sch, Jesus Coll Cambridge (MA); *m* 28 Dec 1957, Janet Phyllis, da of Eric Ralph Rich (d 1961); 1 s (Christopher b 1969), 2 da (Jennifer b 1960, Sarah b 1962); *Career* RASC 1952-54 (2 Lt 1952), Maj ETSC (TA) 1989-; Shell International Petroleum Co 1957-59; Traffic Service Ltd: dir 1962, md 1968, chm 1978; md rail ops CAIB UK Ltd 1986-; first Br pres Union Internationale D'Associations de Propriétaires de Wagons Particuliers 1980-83 (memb 1969-); tstee Jesus Coll Cambridge Soc; chm: Assoc of Private Railway Wagon Owners 1980-, Friends of Dulwich Picture Gallery 1981-84, Educn and Trg Ctee Chartered Inst of Tport; govr: estates Alleyn's Coll of God's Gift 1981-, St Olave's and St Saviour's Schs; sec Dulwich Sports Club 1964-73; Freeman City of London, Liveryman Worshipful Co of Carmen (memb of Ct of Assts 1983-); Hon Dip London Coll of Advanced Tport Studies; underwriting memb Lloyd's 1974-; FCIT, FInstFF, FILDM; *Recreations* music, squash, golf; *Clubs* MCC, City Livery, RAC, Dulwich Sports, Wig & Pen; *Style*— Jeremy Gotch, Esq; CAIB UK Ltd, Duke's Court, Woking, Surrey GU21 5BH (☎ 0483 755556, fax 0483 755150, tlx 858829)

GOTELL, Walter; s of Jakob Gotell (d 1964), of Berlin, and London, and Margaret, *née* Cohn (d 1980); *b* 15 March 1924; *Educ* Seaford Coll Sussex, Leighton Park Sch Reading, Northern Poly; *m* 1, 6 Sept 1958, Yvonne (d 1974), da of Col RJT Hills (d 1968), latterly of Buenos Aires; 1 da (Carol Verity b 23 March 1960); m 2, 1975, Celeste Fitzgerald Mitchell, of New York; *Career* actor and engr; student Old Vic 1945, appeared in numerous plays incl: Adventure Story (at St James), Othello (for Ken Tynan); films incl: African Queen, Bismarck, Ice Cold in Alex, The Guns of Navarone, Road to Hong Kong, 55 Days at Peking, Black Sunday, The Boys from Brazil; played Gen Gogol in Seven James Bond films, and Chief Constable Cullen for six years in Softly, Softly; mechanical engr in 1950s, fndr own co 1970s, ret; govr Box Hill Sch Dorking Surrey; Hon Memb of the Guildhall Sch of Music and Drama (HMGSM) 1975, FIMH 1975; *Style*— Walter Gotell, Esq; 55 Carlisle Mansions, Carlisle Place, London SW1

GOTHARD, Dr Richard Sherwin; s of late Henry Alexander Sherwin Gothard, and Amy Rubina, *née* Baxter; *b* 22 May 1923; *Educ* Cranbrook; *m* 1955, late Margaret Eileen Milligan; 1 step s, 2 step da; *Career* joined RAF 1939, served 29 Sqdn, 174 Sqdn, 2 Tactical Airforce, 133 RAF/US Sqdn UK, RAFVR until 1963; ptnr Alexander Gothard and Ptnrs 1947, fndr md Adelphi Manufacturing Co; chm: RS Gothard and Co Ltd (fndr 1962), Gothard House Publications Ltd, RS Gothard Export Co Ltd, RS Gothard (S America) Resources Ltd, Int Subscriptions Ltd, GHG Info and Library Servs Co Ltd, Info Resources Ltd; sr ptnr Hythe Books and Gothard Investment Co, dir Noyes Data Corp USA, chm and chief exec Gothard House Group of Cos Ltd; pres: Fruit Culture Cncl 1982, RNLI Henley-on-Thames; Freeman City of London, Freeman Liveryman and Archivist Worshipful Co of Fruiterers (Master 1982); former fell IOD, former MInstM; memb: Assoc of Info Offrs in the Pharmaceutical Indust, Soc of Pharmaceutical Medicine, East Malling Res Assoc; *Books* Information Resources Guides Britain, Glossary of Terms Professionally and Commonly Used in Health, History of Worshipful Co of Fruiterers 1912-1975; *Recreations* sailing, engraving, gardening, writing; *Clubs* Royal Cinque Ports Yacht, MCC, RAF, City Livery, United Wards, Royal Soc of St George; *Style*— Dr Richard S Gothard; Sherwins, Park Place Farm, Remenham, Henley-on-Thames, Oxon; Gothard House, Henley-on-Thames, Oxon RG9 1AJ (☎ 0491 573602)

GOTO, John; *Educ* Berks Coll of Art, St Martin's Sch of Art (BA); *Career* artist; selected solo exhibitions: Goto Photographs 1971-81 (The Photographer's Gallery) 1981, Goto Photographs 1975-83 (PPS Galerie Gundlac Hamburg) 1983, ULUV Gallery Prague (Br Cncl Exhibition) 1983, Moravian Gallery Bruno Czechoslovakia 1983 (touring Czechoslovakia and Spain 1983-85), Sites of Passage (Fischer Fine Art, Ashmolean Museum Oxford) 1986 and 1988, Terezin (Cambridge Darkroom, John Hansard Gallery Southampton, Cornerhouse Manchester, Raab Galerie Berlin) 1988-89, The Atomic Yard (Kettle's Yard Cambridge, Raab Gallery) 1990-91; selected group exhibitions incl: Painting/Photography (Richard DeMarco Gallery) Edinburgh 1986, Next/Tomorrow (Kettle's Yard, Cambridge) 1986, Fifteen Studios (Museum of Modern Art Oxford) 1986, Romantic Visions (Camden Arts Centre) 1988, Blasphemies Ecstasies & Cries (Serpentine Gallery) 1989, Photographic Art in Britain 1945-89 (Barbican), Metamorphosis (Raab Gallery Millbank) 1989; pt/t lectr: Camberwell Sch of Art 1979-81, Poly of Central London 1979-87, Oxford Poly 1979-, Ruskin Sch of Drawing & Fine Art Univ of Oxford 1987; visiting lectr to numerous art colls since 1979; Br Cncl scholar: Paris 1977, Praque 1978; artist fell Girton Coll Univ of Cambridge 1988-89, vice chm Visual Arts Panel S Arts Assoc 1989-90; represented by Raab Galleries London and Berlin; *Books* Shotover (1984), Terezin (1988), The Atomic Yard (1990); *Style*— John Goto, Esq

GOUBET, Jean-Claude Jules André; s of Jules Sylvain Goubet (d 1965), and Olga Zelie, *née* Leroy; *b* 31 Dec 1943; *Educ* Lycee Carnot Paris, Institut National de Sciences Appliquees Lyons France; *m* 29 June 1964, Francoise Anette Monique; 2 s (Lionel Jean-Claude b 1963, Stephane Jules Aisène b 1969); *Career* Credit Lyonnais: joined 1966, trainee account mangr 1966-70, project and planning/mgmnt info 1970-74, branch mangr in Lorient Brittany 1974-77, head of corporate relations New York 1977-79, mangr Californian branches 1979, head of US credit dept New York 1980-81, md Luxembourg 1981-84, dep gen mangr UK branches 1984-87, md UK branches 1987-; vice pres French C of C in GB 1987, Conseiller du Commerce Exterior de la France 1983; *Recreations* skiing, sailing; *Clubs* Foxhills, Overseas Bankers; *Style*— Jean-Claude Goubet, Esq; 169 Oakwood Ct, London, W14 (☎ 071 602 3153); 6 Avenue Emile Zola, Paris; Credit Lyonnais, 84-94 Queen Victoria Street, London, EC4P 4LX (☎ 071 634 8000, fax 01 489 1909)

GOUDIE, Prof Andrew Shaw; s of William Cooper Goudie, and Mary Isobel, *née* Pulman; *b* 21 Aug 1945; *Educ* Dean Close Sch Cheltenham, Trinity Hall Cambridge (BA, MA, PhD); *m* 21 March 1987, Heather Ann, da of John Viles, of Chelmsford; 1 da (Amy Louise b 7 June 1988); *Career* Univ of Oxford: lectr in geography and fell Hertford Coll 1976-84, prof of geography and head of dept 1984-; vice pres RGS, hon vice pres Geographical Assoc; FRGS 1970, MIBG 1970; *Books* The Human Impact,

The Nature of the Environment, Environmental Change, Geomorphological Techniques, Duricrusts, The Warm Desert Environment, Land Shapes, Discovering Landscape in England and Wales, The Prehistory and Palaeogeography of the Great Indian Desert, Chemical Sediments in Geomorphology; *Recreations* old books, old records, gardening; *Clubs* Geographical; *Style*— Prof Andrew Goudie; School of Geography, Mansfield Rd, Oxford OX1 3TB (☎ 0865 271 921, telex 83147 VIA OR G)

GOUDIE, (Thomas) James Cooper; QC (1984); s of late William Cooper Goudie, and Mary Isobel, *née* Pulman; *b* 2 June 1942; *Educ* Dean Close Sch Cheltenham, LSE (LLB); *m* 30 Aug 1969, Mary Teresa, da of Martin Brick; 2 s (Martin b 5 July 1973, Alexander b 14 July 1977); *Career* slr 1966-70, called to the Bar Inner Temple 1970, SE Circuit 1970-, rec 1985-; fndr memb and ctee memb Admin Law Bar Assoc, memb Brent Cncl 1967-78 (latterly ldr); Parly candidate (Lab) Brent North 1974; *Style*— James Goudie, Esq, QC; 11 Kings Bench Walk, Temple EC4Y 7EQ (☎ 071 583 0610, fax 071 583 9123/3690, telex 884620 BARLEX)

GOUDIE, (James) Sandford; s of James Sandford Goudie (d 1981), of South Shields, and Sarah Elizabeth Hartley, *née* Harcus (d 1986); *b* 5 May 1935; *Educ* Harleys of South Shields; *m* 7 Feb 1961, June, da of Harry Hilton (d 1969), of South Shields; 1 s (J Sandford b 25 Nov 1965), 1 da (Janice b 28 Feb 1962); *Career* Nat Serv 15/19 QOH; jt md: Be Modern Ltd 1964, Mellinate Products Ltd 1973-78, Academy Crafts Ltd 1980; exec dir Aquarius Bathrooms Ltd 1983-88; jt md: Lister Mouldings Ltd 1983, Marcraft Ltd 1988; chm S Shields: Mentally Handicapped Parents Assoc 1975-77, Amateur Operatic Soc 1980-88; JP 1967-81; *Recreations* amateur and professional theatre; *Style*— Sandford Goudie, Esq; Villa in Menorca; Pine Lodge in Cumbria; Be Modern Ltd, Western Approach, S Shields, Tyne & Wear NE38 5DP (☎ 091 455 3571, fax 091 456 556, telex 537307 MERGER G)

GOUGH, (Charles) Brandon; s of Charles Richard Gough (d 1957), and Mary Evaline, *née* Goff; *b* 8 Oct 1937; *Educ* Douai Sch, Jesus Coll Cambridge (MA); *m* 24 June 1961, Sarah, da of Maurice Evans Smith (d 1987); 1 s (Richard b 1962) 2 da (Lucy b 1964, Katherine b 1967); *Career* Nat Serv Army 1956-58; Coopers & Lybrand Deloitte (formerly Coopers & Lybrand, previously Cooper Bros & Co): joined 1964, ptnr 1968-83, sr ptnr 1983-90, chm and jt sr ptnr 1990-; memb Exec Ctee Coopers & Lybrand International 1982- (chm 1985 and 1991-), chm Coopers & Lybrand Europe 1989; govt dir British Aerospace plc 1987-88, dir British Invisibles 1990-; chm Auditing Practices Ctee CCAB 1981-84 (memb 1976-84); memb: Accounting Standards Review (Dearing) Ctee 1987-88, Fin Reporting Cncl 1990-, Cambridge Univ Careers Serv Syndicate 1983-86, Cncl for Indust and Higher Educn 1985-; City Univ Business Sch: memb City Advsy Panel 1980- (chm 1986-), dep chm Cncl 1991 (memb 1986-), chm Fin Ctee 1988-; memb Cncl City Univ 1991-; memb: Cncl of Lloyd's 1983-86 (Lloyd's Silver Medal 1986), Governing Cncl Business in the Community 1984-88, Mgmnt Cncl GB-Sasakawa Fndn 1985-, Cncl Business in the Community 1988- (memb Nat Enterprise Team 1989-), CBI Task Force Vocational Educn and Trg 1989, CBI Educn and Trg Affrs Ctee 1990, UK Nat Ctee Japan-Euro Community Assoc 1989-, Cncl Fndn for Educn Business Ptnrships 1990-; tstee: Guildhall Sch Music and Drama Fndn 1990-, Common Purpose within our Cities 1989- (chm 1991); Freeman: City of London 1983, Worshipful Co of CAs 1983; FCA 1974 (memb Cncl 1981-84); *Recreations* music, gardening; *Style*— Brandon Gough, Esq; Long Barn, Weald, Sevenoaks, Kent TN14 6NH (☎ 0732 463714); Coopers & Lybrand Deloitte, Plumtree Court, London EC4A 4HT (☎ 071 583 5000, fax 071 822 4652, telex 887470 answerback: 887470 COLYLN G)

GOUGH, Brig Clifford Thomas William; OBE (1952, MBE 1946); s of Sgt Maj Thomas William Gough (ka the Somme 1916), and Kate (d 1989), *née* Dare; *b* 10 Sept 1911; *Educ* Mil Coll of Sci Tech Sch Woolwich; *m* 1, 27 Dec 1933, Lilian Mary (d 1981), da of John Brace (d 1931); 1 s (Terence William Brace b 6 April 1936); m 2, 15 Aug 1983, Olive Mary, da of Norman Griffith Thomas; *Career* apprentice artificer RA 1926-31, transferred to Engrg Branch RAOC 1937, WWII served Middle East 1939-43 (despatches 1941), cmmnd RAOC in the field (Alamein) 1942, transferred to REME on its formation 1942, Capt 1943, served Normandy and NW Europe 1943-45, Maj 1945, Lt Col cmd REME 7 Armd Div BAOR 1949-52, Sr Offrs Sch 1953, seconded dir of tech servs Arab Legion 1955-56, Col 1956, Admin Coll Henley 1957, cmd Trg Bde REME 1959-61, ret 1961; with Friary-Meux Ltd (brewers) 1961-65; Bass Charrington Ltd (formerly Charrington Utd Breweries): joined 1965, dir of distribution and tport 1970, ret 1974, special projects conslt 1974-78 (set up Bass Museum of Brewing 1977); co vice pres Royal Br Legion Pembrokeshire 1983-; hon organiser Royal Br Legion Poppy Appeal: Berkswich Branch Stafford 1974-78, Pembroke and Pembroke Dock Branch 1980-; pres: Pembrokeshire Branch Normandy Veterans Assoc, Pembroke Dock Volunteer Artillery; sec Pembrokeshire Branch REME Assoc; CEng, FIMechE 1960, FBIM 1961, FRSA; *Recreations* sailing, walking; *Style*— Brig Clifford Gough, OBE; Adlestrop, St Florence, Tenby, Dyfed SA70 8LJ (☎ 0834 871 200)

GOUGH, John Osborne; MBE (1984); s of Reginald Osborne Gough (d 1972); *b* 26 March 1932; *Educ* Tonbridge, Univ of Bristol (BA); *m* 1, 1958 (m dis 1983), Patricia Annette, da of Kenneth Blandford Lalonde; 2 children; m 2, 1983, Susan Mary, da of Michael Hornby and Nicolette, gda of 1 Earl of Dudley (Susan m 1, 1951 (m dis), Marquess of Blandford, now 11 Duke of Marlborough; 1 s (Marquess of Blandford, *qv*), 1 da (Lady Henrietta Gelber, *qv*); m 2, 1962, Alan Heber-Percy); *Career* chm: Kleeneze Hldgs 1987-90, CBI (SW region) 1982-84; memb Cncl RSA 1988-; *Recreations* fishing; *Style*— John Gough, Esq, MBE; Church House, Little Coxwell, Faringdon, Oxon

GOUGH, Hon Mrs (Madeline Elizabeth); da of 12 Baron Kinnaird, KT, KBE, JP, DL (d 1972), and Frances Clifton, JP, da of Thomas Clifton, of Lytham Hall, Lancs; *b* 30 Jan 1908; *m* 1929, Rt Rev Hugh Gough, CMG, OBE, TD, DD, *qv*; 1 da, *see* 4 Baron Swansea; *Style*— The Hon Mrs Gough; Forge House, Over Wallop, Stockbridge, Hants (☎ 0264 781315)

GOUGH, Malcolm H; s of Howard B Gough (d 1969), and Mildred, *née* Shoesmith; *b* 3 July 1927; *Educ* St Thomas's Hosp Med Sch (MB BS, MS); *m* 26 July 1952, (Jean) Sheila, da of Archibald Whyte (d 1979); 1 s (Ian Brinsmead b 1954), 2 da (Wendy Elizabeth b 1957, Penny Ann b 1965); *Career* short serv cmmn RAF 1953-56; sr lectr and hon conslt in surgery St Thomas's Hosp and UCH 1965-66, conslt surgn John Radcliffe Hosp Oxford 1966-; invited memb Cncl RCS, pres Assoc of Surgns of GB and Ireland 1990-91; memb BMA, FRCS 1957; *Books* Plain X-Ray Diagnosis of the Acute Abdomen (1986); *Recreations* gardening, music, sport, golf, real tennis; *Clubs* RAF; *Style*— Malcolm Gough, Esq; John Radcliffe Hospital, Headington, Oxford OX3 9DU (☎ 0865 220936)

GOUGH, 5 Viscount (UK 1849); Sir Shane Hugh Maryon Gough; 5 Bt (UK 1842); also Baron Gough of Chinkangfoo and of Maharajpore and the Sutlej (UK 1846); s of 4 Viscount Gough, MC, JP, DL (d 1951, ggs of Field Marshal 1 Viscount, KP, GCB, GCSI, PC, whose full title was Viscount Gough of Goojerat in the Punjaub and of the City of Limerick. His brilliant exploits in the two Sikh Wars resulted in the annexation of the Punjab to British India), by his w Margaretta Elizabeth, da of Sir Spencer Maryon-Wilson, 11 Bt; *b* 26 Aug 1941; *Educ* Winchester; *Career* late Lt Irish Gds; stockbroker with Laurence Keen Ltd; dir: West End office Royal Insurance Group (UK) plc, Mastiff Electronic System Ltd, Barwick Consultancy and Associate Cos, Corporate Capital Ltd; memb Royal Co of Archers (Queen's Body Guard for Scotland); tstee: Gardners Tst for the Blind, Schizophrenia Res Tst; memb Exec Cncl RNIB; *Clubs* White's, Pratt's; *Style*— The Rt Hon the Viscount Gough; Keppoch Estate Office, Strathpeffer, Rosshire IV14 9AD (☎ 0997 21224); 17 Stanhope Gardens, London SW7 5RQ; Laurence Keen Ltd, 49/51 Bow Lane, Cheapside, London EC4M 9LX (☎ 071 489 9493)

GOUGH, Thomas Hugh John; s of Cecil Ernest Freeman Gough, CMG, of Witham, Essex, and Gwendolen Lily Miriam, *née* Longman; *b* 7 June 1947; *Educ* King's Sch Rochester, N Western Poly (Dip Bus); *m* 2 Aug 1969, Beryl Ann Gough; 1 s (Michael b 26 Aug 1973), 1 da (Catie b 2 March 1976); *Career* musical dir Tower Theatre 1967-69, Kent Youth Orchestra (double bass) 1968, Hammersmith Philharmonic Orchestra (double bass) 1969-71, Newgate Singers (bass) 1970-72; dir Longmans Ltd Florists 1974-, chm Interflora District One 1982-84; Keyboard player with Vertically Horizontal 1986-, chm Governing body Parkhill Infant and Jr Schs; sec St Laurence PCC 1986-90, judging coordinator and memb Ctee London in Bloom 1988 (Judge, 1982-), tstee Romanian Children's Aid; Freeman City of London 1974, Liveryman Worshipful Co of Gardeners 1976 (Ct of Assistants 1990; judge Flowers in the City Campaign); *Books* How to Care for Palms and Ferns (1983), How to Care for Flowering Houseplants (1983), How to Care for More Flowering Houseplants (1983); *Recreations* music, cooking, gardening, active Christian; *Clubs* L'Ordre Mondial Des Gourmets Degustateurs; *Style*— Thomas Gough, Esq; 59-60 Holborn Viaduct, London EC1N 2FD (☎ 071 248 2828, fax 071 236 7491, telex 883497 FLOWER G)

GOULD, Bryan Charles; MP (Lab) Dagenham 1983-; s of Charles Terence Gould, of Hamilton, NZ; *b* 11 Feb 1939; *Educ* Univ of Auckland, Balliol Coll Oxford; *m* 1967, Gillian Anne Harrigan; 1 s, 1 da; *Career* FO 1964-66, 2 sec Br Embassy Brussels 1966-68, fell Worcester Coll Oxford 1968-74, MP (Lab) Southampton Test Oct 1974-79 (contested same Feb 1974), PPS to Sec of State: Trade 1975-76, Environment 1976-77; former memb Select Ctee on Euro Legislation, TV journalist, oppn front bench spokesman Trade and Indust Nov 1983-, memb Shadow Cabinet 1986, campaign coordinator 1987; shadow sec of state: Trade and Industry 1987, Enviroment 1989-; *Recreations* food, wine, walking, gardening; *Style*— Bryan Gould, Esq, MP; House of Commons, London SW1

GOULD, Cecil Hilton Monk; s of Lt Cdr Rupert Thomas Gould (d 1948), of Ashtead, and Muriel Hilda, *née* Estall (d 1979); *b* 24 May 1918; *Educ* Westminster; *Career* WWII RAF VR : Pilot Offr 1940, Flying Offr 1941, Flt Lt 1942, Sqdn Ldr 1945; Nat Gallery: asst keeper 1946, dep keeper 1961, keeper and dep dir 1973-78; FRSA; *Books* Introduction to Italian Renaissance Painting (1957), Trophy of Conquest (1965), Leonardo da Vinci (1975), Correggio (1976), Bernini in France (1981); *Recreations* music, travel; *Clubs* Reform; *Style*— Cecil Gould, Esq; Jubilee House, Thorncombe, Chard, Somerset (☎ 046 030 530)

GOULD, Edward John Humphrey; JP (Essex 1989); s of Roland Akehurst Gould, of London, and Winifred Ruth Lee, *née* Dixon; *b* 31 Oct 1943; *Educ* St Edwards Oxford, St Edmund Hall Oxford (BA, MA, DipEd); *m* 4 April 1970, Jennifer Jane, da of Ian Hunter Lamb of Edinburgh; 2 da (Karen Penelope b 1971, Nicola Mary b 1973); *Career* Harrow Sch: joined 1967, asst master head of Geography Dept 1974-79, housemaster 1979-83; headmaster Felsted Sch 1983-; memb: Ind Schs Curriculum Ctee 1985- (chm 1990-), Common Entrance Bd 1988-, Ct of Univ of Essex 1985-, Br Atlantic Educn Ctee 1987-89; chm ISIS East 1989-; govr : Heathfield Sch, Ascot & Orwell Park Sch Ipswich; Oxford rugby blue 1963-66 and swimming half blue 1965; rep GB rowing 1967; FRGS; *Recreations* music, sailing; *Clubs* East India, Devonshire Sports and Public Schools, Vincents (Oxford); *Style*— Edward Gould, Esq, JP; Headmasters House, Felsted School, Dunmow, Essex (☎ 0371 820258)

GOULD, Maj-Gen John Charles; CB (1975); s of Alfred George Webb Gould (ka 1917), and Hilda, *née* Bewsey (d 1971); *b* 27 April 1915; *Educ* Brighton Hove and Sussex GS; *m* 1941, Mollie, da of Alan James Bannister (d 1963); 1 s (Robert), 1 da (Elizabeth); *Career* paymaster-in-chief and inspr of Army Pay Services 1972-75, ret 1975; *Recreations* golf; *Clubs* Lansdowne, Piltdown Golf; *Style*— Maj-Gen J C Gould, CB; Squirrels Wood, Ringles Cross, nr Uckfield, E Sussex TN22 1HB (☎ 0825 764592)

GOULD, Jonathan; s of Cedric Gould (d 1956), of London, and Joan Wilson, *née* Spiers (d 1983); *b* 1 April 1952; *Educ* Hurstpierpoint Coll, Univ of Bristol (LLB); *Career* Allen & Overy 1974-: articled 1974-76, asst slr 1976-81, ptnr 1982-, res ptnr Hong Kong 1988-; memb City of London Slrs Co; memb: Law Soc, Law Soc of Hong Kong; *Style*— Jonathan Gould, Esq; 44 Halsey St, London SW3 2PT; 23A Century Tower, 1 Tregunter Path, Hong Kong (☎ 8400208); Allen & Overy, 9 Cheapside, London EC2V 6AD (☎ 071 248 9898, fax 071 236 2192, telex 8812801); Allen & Overy, 9th Floor, Three Exchange Sq, Hong Kong (☎ 8401282, fax 8400515, telex 68757)

GOULD, Kenneth; CBE (1973), TD; s of Capt William Charles Gould (d 1929), and Ethel Edna, *née* Board; *b* 5 Feb 1919; *Educ* Manchester GS, Victoria Univ Manchester (LLB); *m* 1946, Kathleen Ann, da of Dr Thomas O'Connell (d 1975); 1 s, 1 da; *Career* Lt-Col RA (TA), served Pacific, Burma; slr 1947; advocate and slr Singapore and Malaya 1948; chm and md Borneo Berhad/Inchcape Berhad 1966-73, chm Singapore Int C of C 1971-73; govr London Sch Oriental & African Studies; dir: Inchcape plc 1971-81, Norwich Union Insurance Group, Goal Petroleum plc; *Recreations* shooting, golf, cricket; *Clubs* Oriental (chm), City of London, MCC, Singapore Cricket, Royal Island Country (Singapore), Tanglin (Singapore); *Style*— Kenneth Gould, Esq, CBE, TD; Tithe Barn, Courts Mount Rd, Haslemere, Surrey GU27 2PP (☎ 0428 642879)

GOULD, Leonard Arthur; s of Arthur Leonard Gould (d 1981), of Gatley, Cheshire, and Mary, *née* O'Neill (d 1975); *b* 3 Feb 1948; *Educ* St Patrick's RC Secdy Coatbridge; *m* 4 Aug 1969, Sandra, da of Neil Keegans; 1 s (Leonard Anthony b 19 April 1973), 2 da (Claire Louise b 14 June 1971, Jennifer Alexsandra b 23 July 1975); *Career* Scottish Daily Express: ed asst 1966, feature writer and sub ed 1967, news sub ed 1969-71, asst chief sub 1971-73, chief sub 1973-74; Daily Express: dep night ed Manchester 1974-81, asst night ed London 1981, dep sports ed Manchester 1982; exec ed Today 1986-88 (sports ed 1985), asst ed Daily Mail 1988- (dep sports ed 1988); *Recreations* horse racing, reading, all sports, enjoying the talents of my family; *Clubs* Scribes West Int; *Style*— Leonard Gould, Esq; Associated Newspapers Ltd, Northcliffe House, London W8 5TT (☎ 071 938 6113/071 938 6200, direct 071 938 2874)

GOULD, Michael John Rodney; s of Capt Edward Russell Gould (d 1980), and Nancy Olivia Marion, *née* Johnson (d 1983); *b* 4 Feb 1930; *Educ* Summerfields Oxford, Wellington; *m* 1, 1951 (m dis 1968), Delia, da of Maj WE Johns (d 1960); 1 s (Nicholas b 18 April 1958); m 2, 25 Jan 1969, Valerie Mary, da of Maurice St John-Perry (d 1987); 2 s (Philip b 16 Dec 1970, Christopher b 16 Jan 1973); *Career* dir: BICC 1947-62, BICC (Export) Ltd 1957-62, Nat Standard Co Ltd 1962-75; chm Michael Gould & Co Ltd 1980-, dir Biselex Engrg Ltd 1983-; chm: Med Equipment Co Ltd (Jersey) 1975-, Kentredder Ltd 1975-79; dir: Eurowire Ltd (Jersey) 1983-, Callon Electric Ltd (Jersey) 1987-, Bejex Electrical (Jersey) 1985-, Echo Industl & Consltg Servs Ltd

(Jersey) 1985-, Carola Corp NV 1984-, Eurocables & Engrg (overseas) Co Ltd (Jersey) 1988-, Techno Steel Wire & Engrg Ltd (Jersey) 1989-, Transelectric (Europe) Ltd (Jersey) 1989-, Bellscan Ltd 1989, Communication & Power Eng Ltd 1990-, Flexair Ltd 1991-; *Recreations* bibliophilism; *Style*— Michael Gould, Esq; The Oaks, St John, Jersey (☎ 0534 61142); PO Box 364 Jersey (☎ 0534 62320, fax 0534 64129, telex 4192113)

GOULD, Michael Philip; s of John Gould (d 1989), of Clayhall, Ilford, Essex, and Amelia, *née* Cohen (d 1983); *b* 29 Jan 1947; *Educ* SW Essex Tech Coll; *m* 29 Aug 1971, Linda, da of Philip Keen, of Loughton, Essex; 2 da (Rosemary Julia b 1974, Jennifer Karen b 1977); *Career* CA;sr ptnr Haslers; dir: Kaymere Ltd 1978, Veryshield Ltd 1978, Brontree Ltd 1982, Scopeprop Ltd 1982, Tametree Properties Ltd 1982; ATII, FCA; *Recreations* amateur pianist, music generally, theatre, good food, skiing, travel; *Clubs* Local Sports and Recreation Centre; *Style*— Michael P Gould, Esq; Laurels, Park Hill, Upper Park, Loughton, Essex IG10 4ES (☎ 081 508 1586); Johnston House, 8 Johnston Rd, Woodford Green, IG8 0XA (☎ 081 504 3344, car 0860 321837)

GOULD, Peter; s of Rupert Gould, and Vera Alberta Louise Gould; *b* 28 March 1945; *Educ* Priory Sch, Manchester Univ (LLB); *m* 2 Sept 1978, Diana Elizabeth, da of Allan Humphreys Hart; 2 da (Stephanie b 1981, Rosalind b 1983); *Career* slr; sr ptnr Gould Fowler & Co; clerk to govrs Priory Sch 1973-80; *Recreations* squash, reading, charitable activities; *Clubs* Rotary; *Style*— Peter Gould, Esq; Upton, Lyth Hill, Shrewsbury SY3 0BS (☎ 0743 874792); The Mill House, 139 Abbey Foregate, Shrewsbury SY2 6AP (☎ 0743 235161)

GOULD, (John) Roger Beresford; s of John Cecil Beresford Gould, (d 1978), and Dorothy, *née* Entwistle; *b* 1 Jan 1940; *Educ* Bolton Sch, Merton Coll Oxford (MA); *m* 21 Sept 1968, Catherine Celia, da of William Tetlow Faulkner; 1 s (Richard b 1973), 1 da (Diana b 1970); *Career* dep chm Seton Healthcare Group plc 1984- (co sec 1972-, fin dir 1974-80, dep md 1980-84); BIM: chm Manchester branch 1983-85, memb Nat Cncl 1984-90, chm NW Area 1985-87, chm Nat Branch Policy Ctee 1987-90; methodist local Preacher; FCA 1966, CBIM 1989 (MBIM 1971); *Recreations* squash, swimming, skiing, golf; *Style*— Roger Gould, Esq; Seton Healthcare Group plc, Tubiton House, Oldham, Lancs OL1 3HS (☎ 061 652 2222)

GOULD, Sidney; s of Jack Gould, of Birnbeck Court, Temple Fortune, and Rachel Gould, *née* Mintz (d 1950); *b* 1 Feb 1932; *Educ* Hinkley GS, Univ of Cambridge (MA); *m* 13 June 1956, Jean, da of Simon Diamond, of Northways, Swiss Cottage; 3 s (Lawrence Jonathon b 1959, Simon Hilary b 1961, Matthew Stephen b 1971); *Career* fin dir SPD Group 1969-84; dir: Tibbett & Britte International Ltd, Tibbett & Britte (NI) Ltd, RDC Properties Ltd, Retail Consolidation Services Ltd, Dartford Securities Ltd; vice chm corp fin and strategy Tibbett & Britte Group plc 1984-; *Recreations* golf, bridge; *Style*— Sidney Gould, Esq; 39 Pebworth Rd, Harrow, Middx HA1 3UD (☎ 081 422 6898); Tibbett & Britte Group plc, 101-145 Great Cambridge Rd, Enfield EN1 1TL (☎ 081 367 9955, fax 081 366 7042, telex 23501)

GOULD, Lady Sylvia Davina; *née* Brudenell-Bruce; da of 8 Marquess of Ailesbury; *b* 19 June 1954; *Educ* Lawnside, Redlynch Park; *m* 1987, Peter M Gould, yst s of late R C L Gould, of Grouville, Jersey; *Style*— The Lady Sylvia Gould; Springtide, La Pulente, St Brelade, Jersey, CI

GOULD, Dr Terry Ronald; s of Sir Ronald Gould (d 1986), of Worthing, Sussex, and Nellie Denning, *née* Fish (d 1979); *b* 11 March 1934; *Educ* Culford Sch Bury St Edmunds, Kings Coll London, St Georges Hosp Med Sch (MB BS, DA, DObst, LRCP); *m* 18 June 1960, Shirley Anne, da of Robert Arthur Philip Bunce (d 1987), of Bournemouth; 2 s (Simon Mark b 1962, Nicholas James b 1965), 2 da (Caroline Emma b 1961, Sarah Kathryn b 1970); *Career* Nat Serv Lt surgn RN 1960-63; conslt anaesthetist: Royal Dental Hosp 1968-80, Atkinson Morley's Hosp 1968; St Georges Hosp London: conslt anaesthetist 1968-, chm Med Advsy Ctee 1967-79, hon archivist 1987-, chm Med Advsy Ctee 1976-79, hon archivist 1987-; hon conslt anaesthetist St Lukes Nursing Home for Clergy 1968-; Wandsworth Health Authy: chm Dist Med Exec Ctee 1980-83 (memb 1983-85), unit gen mangr Continuing Care Unit 1985-; memb: Cncl Trinity Hospice Clapham, Mgmnt Ctee Wandsworth Homes Assoc, History of Anaesthesia Soc, Assoc of Anaesthetists; memb BMA, DObstRCOG, MRCS, FFARCS; *Recreations* gardening, reading, art, history; *Style*— Dr Terry Gould; St Georges Hospital, Blackshaw Rd, Tooting, London SW17 0QT (☎ 081 6721255)

GOULDING, Hon Mrs (Caroline Laurence Patricia); *née* Cavendish; da of 7 Baron Waterpark; *b* 3 March 1952; *Educ* French Lycée London, St Annes Oxford; *m* 1979, (Richard Michael) George Goulding; 1 s (Rory b 1983), 1 da (Laura b 1986); *Career* slr; *Recreations* antiques, travel, reading, skiing; *Style*— The Hon Mrs Goulding

GOULDING, Sir (Ernest) Irvine; s of Dr Ernest Goulding (d 1938); *b* 1 May 1910; *Educ* Merchant Taylors', St Catharine's Coll Cambridge (MA, hon fell 1971-); *m* 1935, Gladys Ethel (d 1981), da of Rear Adm Marrack Sennett (d 1935); 1 s (Marrack Irvine, *qv*), 1 da; *Career* served as Instr Offr (Lt Cmdr) RN 1931-36, 1939-45; called to the Bar Inner Temple 1936, QC 1961, bencher Lincoln's Inn 1966- (treas 1983), judge of High Court (Chancery Div) 1971-85; *Clubs* Travellers'; *Style*— Sir Irvine Goulding; Penshurst, Wych Hill Way, Woking GU22 0AE (☎ 0483 761012)

GOULDING, Jeremy Wynne Ruthven; s of Denis Arthur Goulding (d 1979), of Nottingham, and Doreen Daphne, *née* Phizackerley; *b* 29 Aug 1950; *Educ* The Becket Sch Nottingham, Magdalen Coll Oxford (MA); *m* 24 Aug 1974, Isobel Mary, da of Arnold Samuel Fisher, of Worcester; 2 s (Richard b 1979, Paul b 1988), 2 da (Laura b 1983, Vanessa b 1988); *Career* asst master Abingdon Sch 1974-78, asst master Shrewsbury Sch 1978-89 (housemaster Oldham Hall 1983-89), headmaster Prior Park Coll 1989-; memb: Oxford Soc, HMC; *Recreations* hillwalking, reading, cooking; *Style*— Jeremy Goulding, Esq; Kent House, Ralph Allen Drive, Bath, Avon BA2 5BJ (☎ 0225 835353), Prior Park College, Bath Avon (☎ 0225 835353)

GOULDING, Sir (William) Lingard Walter; 4 Bt (UK 1904), of Millicent, Clane, co Kildare, and Roebuck Hill, Dundrum, co Dublin; er s of Sir Basil Goulding, 3 Bt (d 1982), and Hon Lady Goulding, *qv*. Sir Lingard is tenth in descent from William Goulding, who arrived in Ireland as a member of Oliver Cromwell's army; *b* 11 July 1940; *Educ* Winchester, Trinity Coll Dublin; *Heir* yr bro, Timothy Adam Goulding (b 1945, educated Winchester, m 1971 Patricia Mohan, of Dublin); *Career* formerly with Conzinc Rio Tinto of Aust; former mangr Rionore; racing driver; headmaster Headfort Sch 1977- (asst master 1974-76); *Style*— Sir Lingard Goulding, Bt; Dargle Cottage, Enniskerry, Co Wicklow, Eire

GOULDING, Marrack Irvine; CMG (1983); s of Sir (Ernest) Irvine Goulding, *qv*, and Gladys Ethel, *née* Sennett (d 1981); *b* 2 Sept 1936; *Educ* St Paul's, Magdalen Coll Oxford (BA); *m* 1961, Susan Rhoda, da of Air Marshal Sir John D'Albiac, KCVO, KBE, CB, DSO (d 1963); 2 s, 1 da; *Career* HM Dip Serv 1959-85; served Lebanon, Kuwait, London, Libya, Egypt, London (private sec to Min State FCO, seconded Cabinet Office CPRS), Portugal, UN (New York); ambass to Angola and (concurrently but non-resident) to Sao Tome and Principe 1983-85, UN Secretariat 1986-, under sec gen for special political affairs UN, New York 1986-; *Recreations* travel, bird-watching; *Clubs* Royal Over-Seas League; *Style*— Marrack Goulding, Esq, CMG; 82 Claverton St, London SW1V 3AX (☎ 071 834 3046); 40 East 61st St, NY, NY 10021, USA (☎ 212 935 6157)

GOULDING, Timothy Adam; s of Sir (William) Basil Goulding, 3 Bt (d 1982), and Hon Lady Goulding, *qv*; hp of bro, Sir (William) Lingard Goulding, 4 Bt; *b* 1945; *m* 1971, Patricia Mohan, of Dublin; *Style*— Timothy Goulding, Esq; Dargle Cottage, Enniskerry, Co Wicklow

GOULDING, Hon Lady (Valerie Hamilton); *née* Monckton; da of 1 Viscount Monckton of Brenchley, GCVO, KCMG, MC, PC, QC (d 1965); *b* 1918; *Educ* National Univ of Ireland; *m* 28 Aug 1939, Wing Cdr Sir (William) Basil Goulding, 3 Bt (d 1982); 3 s (Sir Lingard G, 4 Bt, *qv*; Timothy b 1945; Hamilton Paddy b 1947); *Career* ATAS 1941-45, late Subaltern WRAC (Reserve); stood as Fianna Fail candidate for Dun Laoghaire for Dail Gen Election 1982 (former senator of Republic of Ireland); chm Central Remedial Clinic Ireland; fndr memb: Nat Rehabilitation Bd, Union of Voluntary Orgns for the Handicapped; memb: Bd of Govrs St Patrick's Hosp, Mgmnt Ctee Mater Hosp, Advsy Ctee American/Ireland Fund; dir Ansbacher Merchant Bank Ireland; Hon LLD NUI, Hon Dr of Humanities Stonehill Coll Boston USA 1989; Dame of Honour and Devotion SMOM; *Style*— The Hon Lady Goulding; Dargle Lodge, Enniskerry, Co Wicklow; Central Remedial Clinic, Penny Ansley Memorial Building, Vernon Avenue, Clontarf, Dublin 3 (☎ 332206)

GOUMAL, Jose Luis; s of Gregorio Goumal, of London and Barcelona, and Ana, *née* Jimenez; *b* 5 Jan 1946; *Educ* St Michaels and Acland (UK), Don Manuel (Spain); *m* 1, 17 Sept 1966, Madeleine, da of Edward Raymond Yescombe, MBE, of Bedfordshire; 1 da (Amanda b 1967); m 2, 1 March 1978, Sandie Bennett, da of Joseph Edward Bennett (d 1981), of Buckinghamshire; 2 s (Jamie b 1978, Dominic b 1980); *Career* CA; princ Anderson Goumal & Co, ptnr Anderson Shaw & Co; dir: Sanchez Fin Servs Ltd, Counthurst Ltd, Albrissi Ltd, Russell Holdings Investments; FCA, FCCA, FBIM; *Recreations* music, the arts, golf, country walks, work; *Style*— Jose L Goumal, Esq; Clive Court, Maida Vale, London W9; 169-173 Regent Street, London W1 (☎ 071 439 1371, fax 071 439 4108)

GOURIET, Maj John Prendergast; s of Sqdn Ldr Alfred William Edward (Wings) Gouriet, RFC, RAF (d 1973), of Luxborough, Som, and Mary Douglas, *née* Prendergast (d 1977); *b* 1 June 1935; *Educ* Charterhouse, RMA Sandhurst, RMC Shrivenham and Staff Coll Camberley; *m* 4 April 1963, Sarah Julia Wheate, da of Maj Frank Henry Wheate Barnett (ka Dunkirk), of Glympton Park, Oxon; 3 s (James Edward Frank b 1966, Michael David b 1967, Rupert John b 1969); *Career* 15/19 Hussars, Sqdn Ldr and Ops Offr NATO 1956-70, Co 2 i/c Somaliland Scouts 1959-60, Adj Trucial Oman Scouts 1961-63, Staff GSO 3 Intelligence, dir of Ops Borneo 1965-66, DAA & QMG MOD (Ops and Plans) 1971-72; PA to Sir Walter Salomon Rea Brothers bankers 1973-75, dir Nat Assoc for Freedom 1975-78; co dir and conslt incl: Park Air Travel Ltd, Stevens-Lifield Ltd (chm), Wild Life Conservation Project (USA); chm: Freedom in Action, Voters' Res Assoc; PR dir CHREST (Charity Film Making on Christian origins), govr Int Policy Forum (US); hon memb: Inst of Econ Affrs, Nat Right to Work Ctee (US), Colditz Soc; FRGS; awarded Polish Gold Cross 1976; *Books* incl Checkmate Mr President; *Recreations* all forms of sport, hunting, polo, racing, fishing, mountaineering, big game hunting, stalking; *Style*— Maj John Gouriet; Upper Enham House, nr Andover, Hants (☎ 0264 351495); office: (☎ 071 225 3909, fax 071 225 3921)

GOURLAY, Gen Sir (Basil) Ian Spencer; KCB (1973), CVO (1990), OBE (1956, MBE 1948), MC (1944); s of Brig K I Gourlay, DSO, OBE, MC (d 1970); *b* 13 Nov 1920; *Educ* Eastbourne Coll; *m* 1948, Natasha, da of late Col Dimitri Zinovieff, and late Princess Elisaveta Galitzine; 1 s, 1 da; *Career* cmmnd RM 1940, Capt 1949, Maj 1956, Lt-Col 1963, CO 42 Commando 1963, Col 1965, actg Brig 1966, cdr 3 Commando Bde RM 1966, Maj-Gen 1968, cdr Trg Gp RM 1968-71, Lt-Gen 1971, Gen 1973, Cmdt-Gen RM 1971-75, ret; vice pres Utd World Colleges 1990- (DG 1975-90); *Clubs* Royal Over-Seas, MCC, Army and Navy; *Style*— Gen Sir Ian Gourlay, KCB, CVO, OBE, MC; c/o Lloyds Bank Ltd, 15 Blackheath Village, London SE3

GOURLAY, Dr (Robert) John; OBE (1983); s of Robert James Gourlay (d 1965), of Kilmacolm, Renfrewshire, Scotland, and Annie, *née* Patterson (d 1958); *b* 28 Aug 1912; *Educ* Morrison's Acad Crieff Perthsire, Univ of Glasgow (MB ChB, MD), Univ of Leeds (DPH), Univ of Oxford (BSc); *m* 1, 1940 (m dis), Elizabeth Thackeray; 1 s (Robin b 1941), 1 da (Elizabeth b 1943); m 2, 1962, Joan Glenys (d 1985); m 3, 3 Aug 1986, Jacqueline Dorothy Juanita, da of Maj John Edward Power, (d 1938), of Camden to Bletchingly; *Career* supt Wharfedale Isolation Hosp 1939-46, dep MOH Oxford City 1948-51, asst SMO NW Metro Regnl Hosp Bd London 1951-57, sr lectr and head Dept Social and Preventive Med Univ of WI 1957-66, chief MO (formerly SMO) Bermuda 1966-82; memb (Bermuda): 1966-72 Kiwanis Club, Age Concern, Probus; memb: CGA, Oxford Soc, Local Cons Assoc; Freeman City of Glasgow (qua weaver) 1945; FFCM 1985, FRSH 1960; *Recreations* golf, woodwork, music; *Clubs* Bermuda Mid-Ocean Golf 1970-85, The Naval; *Style*— Dr John Gourlay, OBE; Lyneham, High Ham, Langport, Somerset TA10 9DF (☎ 0458 250 091)

GOURLAY, Hon Mrs (Patricia Drake); *née* Normand; da of Baron Normand (Life Peer) (d 1962); *b* 1917; *m* 1948, Douglas William Gourlay; *Style*— The Hon Mrs Gourlay; c/o Craigmuie, Moniaive, Thornhill, Dumfriesshire

GOURLEY, Alan Stenhouse; s of Archibald Gourley, and Elizabeth Paterson, *née* Ednie; *b* 13 April 1909; *Educ* Glasgow Acad, DA Edinburgh; *Career* artist: head of design Johannesburg Tech Coll, designed and executed stained glass windows at Johannesburg and Pretoria Cathedrals, elected memb Royal Inst of Oil Painters 1965 (pres 1978-82), has works in Port Elizabeth, Luxemburg and RA galleries; John Laing painting prize 1985; *Style*— Alan Stenhouse Gourley

GOVETT, (Clement) John; LVO (1990); s of Clement Charles Govett (d 1963), and Daphne Mary, *née* Norman (d 1964); *b* 26 Dec 1943; *Educ* St Paul's, Pembroke Coll Oxford (MA); *m* 14 June 1975, Rosalind Mary, da of Geoffrey Fawn (d 1988); 3 da (Helen b 1977, Sarah b 1978, Joanna b 1981); *Career* Price Waterhouse 1966-69, dir J Henry Schroder Wagg & Co Ltd 1980-90 (joined 1969); dir: City & Commercial Investmt Tst plc 1981-, Schroder Ventures Ltd 1985-, SIM Unit Tst Mgmnt Ltd 1987-; chm Schroder Properties Ltd 1987-, dep chief exec Schroder Investmt Mgmnt Ltd 1987-; *Recreations* bridge, tennis, gardening; *Style*— John Govett, Esq, LVO; 29 Marchmont Road, Richmond, Surrey TW10 6HQ (☎ 01 940 2876); 36 Old Jewry, London EC2 R8BS (☎ 071 382 6000)

GOVETT, Peter John; s of late Francis Govett; *b* 3 Sept 1935; *Educ* Harrow; *m* 1, 1964, Janet Adorian; 1 s, 1 da; m 2, 1978, Carolyn Odhams; *Career* commodity broker; dir Lehman Brothers Ltd; *Recreations* theatre; *Style*— Peter Govett, Esq; 114 Pavilion Rd, London SW1 (☎ 071 235 7381); The Old Chapel, Ashampstead Green, Newbury, Berks (☎ 063522 512)

GOVETT, William John Romaine; s of John Romaine Govett, and Angela Mostyn, *née* Pritchard; *b* 11 Aug 1937; *Educ* Sandroyd, Gordonstoun; *m* 1 (m dis 1970), Mary Hays; 2 s (Charles b 20 March 1965, Alexander b 3 May 1967), 1 da (Laura b 12 Dec 1968); m 2, 1970, Penelope Ann Irwin, *née* Connolly; 1 da (Romaine b 4 Jan 1973); *Career* Nat Serv cmmnd Royal Scots Greys; chm John Govett and Co Ltd 1974-86 (dep chm 1986-); directorships incl: Legal & General Group plc 1972-, Govett Oriental Investment Trust 1972, Basinghall Securities Ltd 1975-, General Overseas Investments Ltd 1975-, Govett Equity Trust Ltd 1975-, Govett Strategic Investments

Trust plc 1975-, Scottish Eastern Investment Trust plc 1977-, Corney & Barrow Ltd 1979-, Govett Atlantic Investment Trust plc 1979-, Energy & Resources International Ltd 1981-, Union Jack Oil Co Ltd 1981-, LEP Group plc 1983-, Investors in Industry Group plc 1984-, CIN Management Ltd 1985-, Berkeley Atlantic Income Ltd 1986-, Berkeley Govett & Co Ltd 1986-, Govett American Endeavour Fund Ltd 1988-, Ranger Oil (UK) Ltd 1988-; tstee Nat Arts Collection Fund 1985, tstee Tate Gallery 1988; *Recreations* modern art, fishing; *Style—* William Govett, Esq; 62 Glebe Place, London SW3 5JB; Fosbury House, Marlborough, Wilts SN8 3NJ; John Govett & Co Ltd, Shackleton House, 4 Battle Bridge Lane, London SE1 2HR (☎ 071 378 7979, fax 071 638 6468, telex 884266)

GOW, John Stobie; s of David Gow (d 1988), of Sauchie, Alloa, Scotland, and Ann Frazer, *née* Scott (d 1984); *b* 12 April 1933; *Educ* Alloa Acad, Univ of St Andrews (BSc, PhD); *m* 29 Dec 1955, Elizabeth, da of James Henderson (d 1963), of Alloa; 3 s (Iain b 1958, Alan b 1961, Andrew b 1964); *Career* prodn mangr Chem Co of Malyasia 1966-68; ICI: res mangr Agric Div 1968-72, gen mangr Catalysts Agric Div 1972-74, res dir Organics Div 1974-79, dep chm Organics Div 1979-84, md speciality chemicals 1984-86; non-exec dir W & J Foster Ltd 1984; sec gen Royal Soc of Chem 1986-, memb Cncl Fedn Euro Chem Socs, assessor SERC; elder Utd Reformed Church; FRSE 1978, FRSC 1986, FRSA; *Style—* John Gow, Esq, FRSE; 19 Longcroft Ave, Harpenden, Herts AL5 2RD (☎ 05827 64889); Royal Society of Chemistry, Burlington House, Piccadilly, London (☎ 071 437 8656, fax 071 437 8883, telex 268001)

GOW, Gen Sir (James) Michael; GCB (1983, KCB 1979); s of J C Gow (d 1927); *b* 3 June 1924; *Educ* Winchester; *m* 1946, Jane Emily, da of Capt Mason H Scott, RN (ret); 1 s, 4 da; *Career* served WWII 2 Lt Scots Gds, Lt-Col cmdg 2 Bn Scots Gds 1964-67, Brig cmdg 4 Gds Bde 1967-70, Brig-Gen Staff (Intelligence & Security) HQ BAOR 1971-73, Col Cmdt Intelligence Corps 1972-86, GOC 4 Div 1973-75, dir Army Trg MOD 1975-78, GOC Scotland and Govr Edinburgh Castle 1979-80, C-in-C BAOR and Cdr NATO N Army Gp 1980-83, ADC Gen to HM The Queen 1981-84, Cmdt RCDS 1984-86, Brig Queen's Body Gd for Scotland (Royal Co of Archers); cmmr Br Scouts Western Europe 1980-83, vice pres Royal Patriotic Fund Corp 1984-88; pres: Royal Br Legion Scot, Earl Haig Fund Scot 1986-; *Recreations* sailing, travel, music, reading; *Clubs* Pratt's, New (Edinburgh); *Style—* Gen Sir Michael Gow, GCB; 18 Ann St, Edinburgh EH4 1PJ

GOW, Sheriff Neil; QC (Scot 1970); s of Donald Gow, of Glasgow; *b* 24 April 1932; *Educ* Merchiston Castle Sch, Univ of Edinburgh, Univ of Glasgow (MA, LLB); *m* 1959, Joanna, da of Cdr S D Sutherland, of Edinburgh; 1 s; *Career* Capt Intelligence Corps (BAOR); Carnegie scholar in History of Scots Law 1956, advocate 1957-76, Standing Cncl to Miny of Soc Security (Scot) 1964-70, Contested (C) Kircaldy Burghs Gen Elections 1964 and 1966, Edinburgh East 1970, memb Regnl Cncl Scottish Con Assoc, Sheriff of Lanarkshire 1971; Sheriff of South Strathclyde at Ayr; pres Auchinteck Boswell Soc; FSA (Scot); *Books* A History of Scottish Statutes (1959), An Outline of Estate Duty in Scotland (jt ed 1970), and numerous articles and broadcasts on legal topics and Scottish affairs; *Recreations* golf, books, antiquities; *Clubs* Prestwick GC, Western (Glasgow); *Style—* Sheriff Gow, QC; Old Auchenfail Hall, By Mauchline, Ayrshire (☎ 0290 50822)

GOWANS, Sir James Learmonth; CBE (1971); s of John Gowans and Selma Josefina Ljung; *b* 7 May 1924; *Educ* Trinity Sch Croydon, King's Coll Hosp Med Sch, Lincoln Coll Oxford, Pasteur Inst Paris, Exeter Coll Oxford; *m* 1956, Moyra Leatham; 1 s, 2 da; *Career* aon dir MRC Cellular Immunology Unit 1963-77, sec MRC 1977-87, sec gen Human Frontier Sci Program Strasbourg 1989-; memb Advsy Bd for Res Cncls 1977-; Royal Soc Royal medal, foreign associate US Nat Acad of Sciences; hon fell: St Catherine's Coll Oxford, Exeter Coll Oxford 1983, Lincoln Coll Oxford 1984; Hon MD: Edinburgh, Southampton; Hon ScD Yale; Hon DSc: Chicago, Birmingham, Rochester NY; FRCP, FRS (prof 1962-77, vice pres and memb Cncl 1973-75); kt 1981; *Style—* Sir James Gowans, CBE, FRS; 75 Cumnor Hill, Oxford OX2 9HX

GOWDY, (David) Clive; s of Samuel David Gowdy (d 1977), and Eileen, *née* Porter; *b* 27 Nov 1946; *Educ* Royal Belfast Academical Inst, Queen's Univ Belfast (BA, MSc); *m* 27 Oct 1973, Linda Doreen, da of Eric Anton Traub, of Belfast; 2 da (Claire b 1978, Alison b 1980); *Career* asst princ Miny of Fin 1970-73, dep princ Civil Serv Cmmn 1973-76, sec Rowland Cmmn 1978-79, princ NI Office 1979-81 (dep princ 1976-78), exec dir Industl Devpt Bd for NI 1985-87, under sec Dept of Economic Devpt 1987-90 (asst sec 1981-85), Dept of Health and Social Servs 1990-; *Recreations* running, tennis, archery, music, reading; *Style—* Clive Gowdy, Esq; Dept of Health and Social Services, Castle Buildings Stormont, Belfast 4 (☎ 0232 763939)

GOWENLOCK, Prof Brian Glover; CBE (1986); s of Harry Hadfield Gowenlock (d 1976), of Oldham, Lancs, and Hilda, *née* Glover (d 1977); *b* 9 Feb 1926; *Educ* Hulme GS Oldham, Univ of Manchester (BSc, MSc, PhD), Univ of Birmingham (DSc); *m* 24 July 1953, Margaret Lottie, da of Luther John Davies (d 1981), of Swansea; 1 s (Stephen David b 1958), 2 da (Cathren Elizabeth b 1959, Judith Margaret b 1964); *Career* lectr in chemistry Univ Coll of Swansea Univ of Wales 1951-55 (asst lectr 1948-51), sr lectr in chemistry Univ of Birmingham 1964-66 (lectr 1955-64); Heriot-Watt Univ Edinburgh: prof of chemistry 1966-90, dean Faculty of Sci 1987-90 (and 1969-72), Leverhulme emeritus fell 1990-; Erskine visiting fell Univ of Canterbury NZ 1976; memb Univ Grants Ctee 1976-85 (vice chm 1983-85); local preacher Methodist Church 1948-; FRSC 1966, FRSE 1969; *Books* Experimental Methods in Gas Reactions (with Sir Harry Melville, 1964), First Year at The University (with James C Blackie, 1964); *Recreations* genealogy; *Style—* Prof Brian Gowenlock, CBE; 49 Lygon Rd, Edinburgh EH16 5QA (☎ 031 667 8506); Dept of Chemistry, Heriot-Watt University, Edinburgh EH14 4AS (☎ 031 449 5111)

GOWER, David Ivon; s of Richard Hallam Gower (d 1973), and Sylvia Mary, *née* Ford (d 1986); *b* 1 April 1957; *Educ* King's Sch Canterbury, Univ Coll London; *Career* cricketer; Leicestershire Hampshire and England, Capt England 1984-86 and 1989; 8,000 plus test runs including 18 test centuries; dir David Gower Promotions Ltd; *Recreations* tennis, golf, skiing, Cresta run; *Clubs* St Moritz Tobagganing, East India; *Style—* David Gower, Esq; Hampshire CCC, Northlands Rd, Southampton S09 2TY (☎ 0703 333788)

GOWER, David William; s of John Maudslay Gower (d 1969), of Moseley, Birmingham, and Betty, *née* Church; *b* 3 Nov 1945; *Educ* Oundle, Fitzwilliam Coll Cambridge (MA); *m* 12 Feb 1972, Madelyn, da of John Hiram Kirkham; 3 s (John David b 8 Aug 1972, Richard Max b 2 Aug 1973, Roger Charles b 10 May 1978); *Career* asst slr Clifford Turner 1970-73, ptnr Pinsent & Co 1975- (articled clerk 1968-70); former memb Revenue Law Ctee Law Soc 1978-88); *Recreations* golf, sport, reading, travel, Spain; *Clubs* MCC, Aberdovey Golf, Edgbaston Golf, Edgbaston Priory, Warwickshire CCC; *Style—* David Gower, Esq; Pinsent & Co, Wesleyan House, Colmore Circus, Birmingham 4

GOWER, His Hon Judge John Hugh; QC (1967); s of Henry John Gower, JP (d 1951), of Penbury, Kent, and Edith, *née* Brooks (d 1926); *b* 6 Nov 1925; *Educ* The Skinners' Co Sch Tunbridge Wells, Inns of Court Sch of Law; *m* 20 Feb 1960, Shirley Maureen, da of William Henry Darbourne (d 1977), of Carshalton Beeches, Surrey; 1 s (Peter b 1960), 1 da (Anne b 1962); *Career* RA Serv Corps 1945-48, Staff Sgt; called to the Bar Inner Temple 1948, circuit judge 1971-, resident judge and liaison judge East Sussex Crown Courts 1986-; pres: Kent Assoc of Parish Cncllrs 1962-71, Tunbridge Wells DC of Voluntary Serv 1974-88; vice pres Kent Cncl of Voluntary Serv 1971-86, chm Southdown and Eridge Hunt 1985-91; *Recreations* fishing, fox-hunting, gardening; *Style—* His Hon Judge Gower, QC; The Coppice, Lye Green, Crowborough, E Sussex TN6 1UY (☎ 08926 4395); The Crown Court, Lewes, Sussex

GOWER-SMITH, (Nicholas) Mark; s of Charles Samuel Smith (d 1983), of Tunbridge Wells, and Margaret Brenda, *née* Isaac; *b* 20 March 1955; *Educ* The Skinners' Sch Tunbridge Wells; *m* 25 July 1987, Christine Lorraine, da of Leslie Frank George Allan, (d 1981); 1 s (Charles b 1989); *Career* CA; sr ptnr Norman Cox & Ashby 1984-, proprietor Gower-Smith & Co 1984-; ACA 1981; *Recreations* music, photography, philately; *Clubs* Royal Cwlth Soc; *Style—* Mark Gower-Smith, Esq; Grosvenor Lodge, 72 Grosvenor Rd, Tunbridge Wells, Kent TN1 2AZ (☎ 0892 22551)

GOWERS, Andrew Richard David; s of Michael David Warren Gowers, of Limpsfield, Surrey, and Florence Anne Dean, *née* Sykes; *b* 19 Oct 1957; *Educ* Trinity Sch Croydon, Gonville and Caius Coll Cambridge (MA); *m* 1982, Finola Mary, *née* Clarke; *Career* Reuters: graduate trainee 1980, Brussels Bureau 1981-82, Zurich corr 1982-83; Financial Times: foreign staff 1983-84, agric corr 1984-85, commodities ed 1985-87, ME ed 1987-90, features ed 1990-; jt winner Guardian/NUS Student Journalist of the Year award 1979; Behind the Myth: Yasser Arafat and the Palestinian Revolution (1990); *Recreations* cinema, reading, opera, music of all kinds; *Style—* Andrew Gowers, Esq; Financial Times, 1 Southwark Bridge, London SE1 (☎ 071 873 3000)

GOWERS, Gillian Carol; da of John Edward Gowers, and Irene, *née* Strong (d 1985); *b* 9 April 1964; *Educ* Hove GS, Chelsea Coll Eastbourne (BSc); *Career* badminton player; Cwlth Games: team Gold medal (twice), ladies doubles Gold and Silver medals; Euro Championships: ladies doubles Gold medal, mixed doubles Silver medal; mixed doubles Bronze medal World Championships; GB Nat Championships: 5 times ladies doubles winner, 2 times mixed doubles winner; winner of several Grand Prix World titles; Silver medal World Team Championships (Uber Cup), finalist All England Ladies Doubles and Mixed Doubles; *Style—* Ms Gillian Gowers

GOWING, Nik; s of Donald James Graham Gowing (d 1969), and Prof Margaret Mary, *née* Elliott; *b* 13 Jan 1951; *Educ* Latymer Upper Sch, Simon Langton GS Canterbury Kent, Univ of Bristol (BSc); *m* 10 July 1982, Judith Wastall, da of Dr Peter Venables, of 29 The Avenue, Andover, Hants; 1 s (Simon Donald Peter b 9 Feb 1987), 1 da (Sarah Margaret b 23 Dec 1983); *Career* reporter Newcastle Chronicle 1973-74, presenter-reporter Granada TV 1974-78; ITN 1978-: Eastern Europe corr 1980-83, foreign affrs corr 1983-87, dip corr 1987-89, dip ed 1989-; *Books* The Wire (1988); *Recreations* cycling, skiing, authorship; *Style—* Nik Gowing, Esq; 200 Gray's Inn Rd, London WC1 (☎ 071 430 4215, fax 071 430 4607 telex 266448)

GOWLAND, Robert George; s of George Fredrick Gowland (d 1978), of Enfield, Middlesex, and Meta, *née* Emck; *b* 27 Jan 1943; *Educ* Haileybury and ISC, Royal Agricultural Coll (CLAS); *m* Anne Sandra, da of Douglas Markes; 1 s (Benjamin Thomas George b 1976), 1 da (Nicola Louise b 1973); *Career* chartered surveyor; Strutt & Parker (Ipswich) 1961-62 and 1964-65, Weller Eggar & Co (Guildford) 1965-67, King & Co (London) 1968, WS Johnson & Co (Leighton Buzzard and Buckingham) 1969-70; ptnr: Wyatt & Son (Havant and Chichester) 1970-73, E J Brooks & Son (Oxford) 1973-79; Phillips International Auctioneers 1979-, pres Phillips New York 1980, md Phillips Chester and North West 1981-; main author Furniture and Works of Art Syllabus for RICS (chm Ctee 1984-87); auctioneer of historical golfing memorabilia 1982-; hon sec Soc of Fine Art Auctioneers 1976-80 and 1981-87 (chm 1987-), memb Br Hallmarking Cncl 1985-; Liveryman Worshipful Co of Clockmakers; FRICS 1974 (Arics 1966); *Recreations* restoring historic golf clubs and furniture, golf, game fishing and shooting; *Clubs* Chester City, Artists' (Liverpool); *Style—* Robert Gowland, Esq; Phillips, New House, 150 Christleton Rd, Chester CH3 5TD (☎ 0244 313936/7, fax 0244 340028)

GOWLLAND, Robin Anthony Blantyre; s of Reginald Blantyre-Gowlland (d 1974), of London and Hawkley, Hants, and Pauline, *née* Broomfield (d 1981); *b* 6 Sept 1932; *Educ* RNC Dartmouth and Greenwich, IMEDE Lausanne (Dip), Harvard Business Sch (MBA); *Career* RN 1946-62, served UK, Med, Far East and Suez Campaign 1956 (ret as Lt); mgmnt conslt and dir Egon Zehnder International 1969- (md UK 1969-81, chm 1981-); dir Videotron Corporation Ltd 1990- (chm 1989-90); chm: ERI 1973-90, ABGH 1979-, G & B Media 1988-; sr res fell Cranfield Inst of Technol 1964-66; sr conslt and ptnr Harbridge House Inc 1966-69, vice chm London Fedn of Boys Clubs 1976- (dir Int Fedn), dep chm Christian Assoc of Business Execs (chm 1976-80), dir Inst of Business Ethics, chm Downside Settlement 1983- (hon sec 1966-73, vice chm 1973-83), memb Cncl Playing Fields Soc; KHS 1985; Hon Lt Col Alabama State Militia (USA), Hon Citizen City of Mobile (USA); FRSA 1989, KSG 1983, KHS 1985; *Recreations* cricket, squash, real tennis, sailing, travel, theatre, art; *Clubs* Brooks's, Royal Yacht Sqdn, MCC, Naval and Military, Royal Thames, Anglo-Belgian, Jesters; *Style—* Robin A B Gowlland, Esq; Tann House, Crondall, Hants GU10 5QU (☎ 0252 850700); 4 Sloane Gate Mansions, London SW1X 9AG (☎ 071 730 2121); Egon Zehnder International, Devonshire House, Mayfair Place, London W1X 5FH (☎ 071 493 3882)

GOWRIE, 2 Earl of (UK 1945); Alexander Patrick Greysteil Hore Ruthven; PC (1984); also Baron Ruthven of Gowrie (UK 1919), Baron Gowrie (UK 1935), and Viscount Ruthven of Canberra (UK 1945); in remainder to Lordship of Ruthven of Freeland (officialy recognised in the name of Ruthven by Warrant of Lord Lyon 1957); s of Maj Hon Patrick Hore Ruthven (s of 1 Earl of Gowrie, VC, GCMG, CB, DSO, PC, who was govr gen and C-in-C of Australia 1936-44 and 2 s of 9 Lord Ruthven of Freeland); suc gf 1955; *b* 26 Nov 1939; *Educ* Eton, Balliol Coll Oxford, Harvard; *m* 1, 1962 (m dis 1974), Xandra, yr da of Col Robert Bingley, CVO, DSO, OBE; 1 s; *m* 2, 1974, Countess Adelheid, yst da of Count Fritz-Dietlof von der Schulenburg; *Heir* s, Viscount Ruthven of Canberra; *Career* former lectr and tutor: State Univ of New York, UCL, Harvard; Cons whip 1971-72, lord in waiting 1972-74, oppn spokesman Economic Affrs 1974-79; min of state: Dept of Employment 1979-81, NI Office 1981-83, Privy Cncl Office (and min for The Arts) 1983-84; chllr of the Duchy of Lancaster (and min for The Arts) 1984-85; chm: Sotheby's Int 1985-86, Sotheby's UK 1987-; *Books* A Postcard from Don Giovanni (1971); jtly: The Genius of British Painting (1975), Derek Hill, An Appreciation (1985), The Conservative Opportunity (1976); *Style—* The Rt Hon the Earl of Gowrie, PC; House of Lords SW1

GOYDER, Daniel George; s of George Armin Goyder, CBE, of Long Melford, Suffolk, and Rosemary Bernard Goyder; *b* 26 Aug 1938; *Educ* Rugby, Univ of Cambridge (MA, LLB), Harvard Law Sch (LLM); *m* 28 July 1962, Jean Mary, da of Kenneth Godfrey Arthur Dohoo (d 1944) of Malaysia; 2 s (Andrew b 1968, Richard b 1970), 2 da (Joanna b 1963, Elizabeth b 1965); *Career* admitted slr 1962, conslt Birkett Westhorp Long (formerly Birketts) Ipswich 1983- (ptnr 1968-83), pt/t lectr Dept of Law Univ of Essex 1981-; memb MMC 1980-, chm St Edmundsbury and Ipswich Diocesan Bd of Fin 1977-85; memb Law Soc; *Books* The Antitrust Laws of the USA (with Sir Alan Neale, 3 edn 1980), EEC Competition Law (1988); *Recreations* sport, choral singing; *Clubs* Ipswich and Suffolk (Ipswich); *Style—* Daniel Goyder, Esq;

Manor House, Old London Rd, Capel St Mary, Ipswich, Suffolk (☎ 0473 310 583); Birkett Westhorp & Long Solictors, 20-32 Museum St, Ipswich (☎ 0473 232 300, fax 0473 230 524, telex 98597)

GOYMER, Andrew Alfred; s of Richard Kirby Goymer (d 1986), of Keston, Kent, and Betty Eileen, *née* Thompson; *b* 28 July 1947; *Educ* Dulwich, Pembroke Coll Oxford (BA, MA); *m* 30 Sept 1972, Diana Mary, da of Robert Harry Shipway, MBE, of Heathfield, E Sussex; 1 s (Patrick b 1977), 1 da (Eleanor b 1980); *Career* called to the Bar Gray's Inn 1970; SE Circuit 1972-, asst rec 1987-, admitted to the Bar NSW Aust 1988; Gerald Moody entrance scholar 1968, Holker sr exhibitioner 1970, Arden Atkin and Mould prizeman 1971; *Style—* Andrew Goymer, Esq; 6 Pump Court, Temple, London EC4Y 7AR (☎ 071 353 7242, fax 071 583 1667)

GRAAFF, David de Villiers; s and h of Sir de Villiers Graaff, 2 Bt, MBE; *b* 3 May 1940; *Educ* Diocesan Coll S Africa, Stellenbosch Univ, Grenoble Univ, Magdalen Coll Oxford; *m* 1969, Sally, da of Robin Williams; 3 s, 1 da; *Career* farmer Hex River; dir: Graaff's trust, Milnerton Estates, Deciduous Fruit Bd, MP Wynberg; *Recreations* tennis; *Clubs* West Province Sports, West Province Cricket, City and Civil Service; *Style—* David Graaff, Esq; PO Box 1, Hex River, Cape, South Africa 6855 (☎ 02322 8708)

GRAAFF, Sir de Villiers; 2 Bt (UK 1911), of Cape Town, Cape of Good Hope Province of Union of South Africa; MBE (1947); s of Sir David Pieter de Villiers Graaff, 1 Bt, sometime high cmmr for Union of S Africa in London, Cabinet minister and mayor of Cape Town (d 1931); *b* 8 Dec 1913; *Educ* Diocesan Coll Cape Town, Univ of Cape Town (BA), Magdalen Coll Oxford (BCL, MA), Leyden Univ Holland; *m* 1939, Ena, da of Frederick Voigt; 2 s, 1 da; *Heir* s, David de Villiers Graaff; *Career* war service in SA Forces 1941 (POW); advocate S African Supreme Ct 1938-, leader of the Oppn in SA 1957-77 (MP 1948-77); farmer of pedigree Friesian cattle; dir: Graaff's Trust, Milnerton Estates; Hon LLD Rhodes Univ, Hon DLit Univ of SA; Decoration for Meritorious Serv 1978; *Recreations* fishing, riding, cricket; *Clubs* Civil Service, Kelvin Grove, Western Province Cricket; *Style—* Sir de Villiers Graaff, Bt, MBE; De Grendel, Private Bag, GPO, Cape Town 8000, S Africa (☎ 0102721 582068, 01027 21 4616613)

GRABHAM, Sir Anthony Herbert; *b* 19 July 1930; *Educ* St Cuthberts GS Newcastle upon Tyne, Univ of Durham (MB BS); *m* 1960, Eileen Pamela; *Career* conslt Surgn Kettering Gen Hosp 1965-; chm: Jt Conslt Ctee 1984-, BMA Cncl 1979-84; FRCS; Kt 1987; *Clubs* Army and Navy; *Style—* Sir Anthony Grabham; Rothesay House, Headlands, Kettering, Northants NN15 6DG; BMA House, Tavistock Sq, London WC1 (☎ 071 387 4499)

GRABINER, Anthony Stephen; QC (1981); s of Ralph Grabiner (d 1985), and Freda, *née* Cohen (d 1989); *b* 21 March 1945; *Educ* Central Fndn Boys' GS London, LSE, London Univ (LLB, LLM); *m* 18 Dec 1983, Jane Aviva, da of Dr Benjamin Portnoy, of Hale, Cheshire; 2 s (Joshua b 1986, Daniel b 1989); *Career* called to the Bar Lincoln's Inn 1968; standing jr counsel to the DTI Export Credits Guarantee Dept 1976-81; jr counsel to the Crown 1978-81; bencher Lincoln's Inn 1989, rec S Eastern circuit 1990; memb Ct of Govrs LSE 1990-; *Books* Sutton & Shannon on Contracts (7 edn 1970), Banking Documents in Encyclopedia of Forms and Precedents (1986); *Recreations* theatre, swimming; *Clubs* Garrick, RAC, MCC; *Style—* Anthony Grabiner, QC; 1 Essex Court, Temple, London EC4Y 9AR (☎ 071 583 2000)

GRABOWSKI, Stanislaw; s of Col Zygmunt Grabowski (Polish Army), MC, TD (d 1968), of Barons Court, London, and Anna, *née* Edemska (d 1959); *b* 6 Sept 1919; *Educ* Mil Academy (Poland), Univ of Cambridge (MA), Polytechnic Sch of Architecture (Dip Arch); *m* 19 Sept 1947, Maria, da of Col Benedykt Chlusewicz (d 1951), Col Polish Army; 1 s (Marek Bohdan b 1948); *Career* Capt Polish Army CO Squadron of Tanks 1 Polish Armd Div 1944-45, France, Belgium, Holland and Germany; Platoon Cdr in France 1940; architect in private practice, conslt since 1986; FRIBA; Knight Order of Leopold 1946, Croix de Guerre 1946, War Cross 1944, Cross of Merit 1946 (TD); *Clubs* White Eagle; *Style—* Stanislaw Grabowski, Esq; 99 The Ridgeway, Gunnersbury Park, London W3 8LP (☎ 081 992 8196); 12 Sutton Row, London W1V 6AB (fax 071 734 1793)

GRACEY, Howard; s of Charles Douglas Gracey (d 1968), and Margaret Gertrude Gracey; *b* 21 Feb 1935; *Educ* Birkenhead Sch; *m* 8 June 1960, Pamela Jean, da of William Thomas Bradshow (d 1988); 1 s (Mark), 2 da (Kathryn, Rachel); *Career* Nat Serv 2 Lt RA 1959-61; Royal Insurance Co 1953-69, consulting actuary and ptnr R Watson & Sons 1970-; pres Pensions Mgmnt Inst 1983-85; memb: General Synod C of E 1970-, C of E Pensions Bd 1970- (chm 1980-); Church Cmmr 1978-, treas S American Missionary Soc 1975-; FIA 1959, FIAA 1982, FPMI 1977, ASA 1978; *Recreations* fellwalking, photography; *Clubs* Army and Navy; *Style—* Howard Gracey, Esq; Timbers, Broadwater Rise, Guildford, Surrey GU1 2LA (☎ 0483 659 63); R Watson & Sons, Watson Ho, London Rd, Reigate, Surrey RH2 9PA (☎ 073 72 41144)

GRACEY, John Halliday; CB (1984); s of Halliday Gracey, and Florence Jane, *née* Cudlipp; *b* 20 May 1925; *Educ* City of London Sch, Brasenose Coll Oxford (MA); *m* 1950, Margaret Procter; 3 s; *Career* served Army 1943-47; joined Inland Revenue 1950, HM Treasy 1970-73; dir: Bd of Inland Revenue 1973-85, Gen (Mgmnt) 1981-85; hon treas Nat Assoc for Care and Resettlement of Offenders 1987; *Recreations* walking, beekeeping; *Clubs* Reform; *Style—* John Gracey, Esq, CB; 3 Woodberry Down, Epping, Essex (☎ 0378 72167)

GRACEY, Lionel Rodney Hubert; s of Dr Ivan Hubert Gracey, of 8 Clarendon Place, Leamington Spa, and Kathleen Gracey, *née* McCarthy (d 1984); *b* 31 July 1928; *Educ* Beaumont Coll, Jesus Coll Cambridge, St Bart's Hosp (MA, MB MChir); *m* 13 Feb 1971, Angela Mary, da of Edmund Henry Fleming (d 1972); 3 s (John b 1971, Charles b 1973, Thomas b 1982); 3 da (Emma b 1974, Laura b 1975, Sarah b 1977); *Career* conslt surgn: Royal Free Hosp, King Edward VII Hosp for Offrs, Hosp of St John and St Elizabeth; hon consulting surgn Italian Hosp; FRCS, FRCSEd; *Recreations* golf, tennis, skiing; *Clubs* Royal and Ancient, Sunningdale, Hawks, Ski (GB); *Style—* Lionel Gracey, Esq; 149 Harley St, London W1N 2DE (☎ 071 935 4444)

GRACEY, Peter Bosworth Kirkwood; s of Lt-Col H M K Gracey (d 1972), of Tonbridge, Kent, and E M Gracey (d 1946); *b* 12 Dec 1921; *Educ* Wellington, Brasenose Coll Oxford (MA); *m* 1, June 1953 (m dis 1982), Ruth Mary, da of Charles Young (d 1960), of Berrow Manor, Burnham-on-Sea, Somerset; 1 s (Guy b 1958), 2 da (Sylvia b 1960, Pippa b 1962); m 2, May 1982, Jane (d 1987), da of Vernon Owen (d 1980), of Mockbeggar, Playden, Rye, E Sussex; m 3, 4 Feb 1989, Andra Julia Mary, da of Capt A C Duckworth, DSO, DSC, RN (d 1987), of Myskyns, Ticehurst, E Sussex; *Career* WWII cmmnd RE 1941, 2 Lt 280 Parachute Sqdn RE, 81 Inf Div HQ, West African Engrs RWAFF, Capt RE OC Gold Coast Field Co 1946; Tate & Lyle Ltd 1948-62 (London mangr tport 1955), gen mangr and dir Sturgeons Transport 1963, gen mangr Marley Tile Transport 1968, distribution dir Lyons Bakery Ltd 1973; dir: Bosworth & Co Ltd (music publishers) 1973, Hill Samuel Investment Servs Ltd, Royal Life Financial; memb Ctee Nat Freight Tport Assoc 1976; pres Oxford and Cambridge Golfing Soc 1987-91 (hon sec 1959-64, capt 1970-71); Freeman City of London 1970, memb Worshipful Co of Wax Chandlers 1970; *Recreations* golf, sport; *Clubs* MCC, Naval and Military, Royal and Ancient Golf, Rye Golf; *Style—* Peter Gracey, Esq; The Oast House, Houghton Green Lane, Playden, Rye, E Sussex TN31 7PJ (☎ 079 78 269)

GRADE, Baron (Life Peer UK 1976), of Elstree, Co Herts; Sir Lew Grade; s of Isaac and Olga Winogradsky; bro of Lord Delfont, *qv*; *b* 25 Dec 1906; *Educ* Rochelle St Sch London; *m* 1942, Kathleen Sheila, da of John Moody; 1 s (adopted); *Career* jt md Lew and Leslie Grade to 1955; pres ATV 1977-82, chm and chief exec: ACC 1973-82, Embassy Communications International 1982-; chm and md ITC Entertainment 1958-82; chm: Bentray Investments 1979-82, Stoll Moss Theatres 1969-82, ACC Enterprises Inc 1973-82, chm and chief exec The Grade Company 1985-; Kt Cdr of St Silvester; OStJ; kt 1969; *Style—* The Rt Hon the Lord Grade; 8 Queen St, London W1X 7PH

GRADE, Michael Ian; s of late Leslie Grade and n of Lords Grade and Delfont; *b* 8 March 1943; *Educ* St Dunstan's Coll; *m* 1, 1967 (m dis 1981), Penelope Jane, *née* Levinson; 1 s, 1 da; m 2, 1982, Hon Sarah Jane Grade, *qv*, *née* Lawson, yst da of Lt-Col 5 Baron Burnham, JP, *qv*, of Hall Barn, Beaconsfield, Bucks; *Career* sports columnist Daily Mirror 1964-66 (trainee journalist 1960), theatrical agent Grade Organisation 1966, jt md London Management and Representation 1969-73, dir of progs and bd memb LWT 1977-81 (dep controller of progs 1973), pres Embassy TV Los Angeles 1982-83, chm and chief operating offr The Grade Co (ind tv and motion picture prodn co) 1983-84, controller BBC 1 1984-86, dir of progs BBC TV 1986-87, chief exec Channel 4 1988-; memb Cncl LAMDA 1981-; *Recreations* entertainment; *Style—* Michael Grade, Esq; Channel Four Television, 60 Charlotte St, London W1P 2AX (☎ 071 631 4444)

GRADE, Paul Nicholas; only child (adopted) of Baron Grade; *b* 1952; *m* Lisa, *née* Pearce; 1 s (Daniel b 1978), 1 da (Georgina b 1980); *Career* dir The Ivy Restaurant; book and record publisher; *Style—* Paul Grade, Esq; c/o ATV House, Great Cumberland Place, W1

GRADE, Hon Mrs (Sarah Jane); *née* Lawson; da of Lt-Col 5 Baron Burnham, JP, DL, *qv*; *b* 7 Oct 1955; *Educ* Heathfield; *m* 1982, as his 2 w, Michael Ian Grade, *qv*; *Career* slr Macfarlanes 1976-80, agent Curtis Brown 1980-82, vice-pres Devpt TV D L Taffner Ltd 1982-84, pres Taft Entertainment/Lawson Group 1985-; *Recreations* theatre; *Style—* The Hon Mrs Grade

GRADIDGE, (John) Roderick Warlow; s of Brig John Henry Gradidge, OBE, and Lorraine Beatrice Warlow, *née* Warlow-Harry; *b* 3 Jan 1929; *Educ* Stowe, Arch Assoc Sch of Arch; *Career* architect specialising in repair, alteration and additions to major country houses particularly work of Edwin Lutyens and contemporaries; recent work incl: interior Bodelwyddan Castle Clwyd (Museum of the Year 1989), extension St Edmund's Coll Cambridge, new entrance Nat Portrait Gallery; currently recreating Victorian interiors Northampton Guildhall; property corr: The Field 1984-87, Country Life 1988-; memb: Ctee Victorian Soc, The Thirties Soc, Lutyens Tst; master Art Workers Guild 1987 (hon sec 1978-84); *Books* Dream Houses - The Edwardian Ideal (1980), Edwin Lutyens - Architect Laureate (1981), Surrey, A House and Cottage Handbook (1990); *Recreations* enjoyment of early twentieth century architecture and appreciation of its potential; *Clubs* Art Workers Guild; *Style—* Roderick Gradidge, Esq; 21 Elliott Rd, London W4 1PF (☎ 081 995 6490, fax 081 995 6490)

GRAEF, Roger Arthur; s of Irving Philip Graef (d 1978), and Gretchen Waterman Graef (d 1984); *b* 18 April 1936; *Educ* Horace Mann Sch NY, Putney Sch Vermont, Harvard Univ (BA Hons); *m* 1, 26 Nov 1971 (m dis 1983), Karen Bergermann (d 1986); 1 s (Maximilian James b 26 July 1979), 1 da (Chloe Fay b 26 Nov 1972); m 2, 20 July 1986, Susan Mary, da of Sir Brooks Richards, KCMG, DSc, of Farnham, Surrey; *Career* writer, prodr and dir; dir 26 plays and operas USA and two dramas for CBS TV; dir Period of Adjustment (Royal Court); writer prodr and/or dir films for TV incl: Police series (BBC) 1980-82 (BAFTA award 1982), Police: Operation Carter 1981-82, The Secret Policeman's Ball (Amnesty Int) 1977-78, Closing Ranks (Zenith/ Central) 1987, Decision: Steel, Oil, Rates (ITV/Granada), Decision: British Communism (Royal TV Soc award 1978), The Space Between Words (BBC/KCET), A Law in the Making: Four Months Inside The Ministry (Granada), Inside The Brussels HQ (Granada), Is This the Way to Save a City (BBC) 1975, Nagging Doubt (Channel 4) 1984, Maybe Baby (BBC) 1985, The Secret Life of the Soviet Union (Channel 4) 1990; series ed: Who Is? (BBC), Inside Europe (ITV), Signals (Channel 4); co-designer London Transport Bus Map, pt/t lectr Diploma Sch Assoc Sch of Architecture; memb Bd Govrs BFI 1975-79; memb Bd: London Transport Exec 1976-79, Channel Four TV 1980-85; memb Cncl: ICA 1971-83, BAFTA 1976-77, AIP 1987-90 (chm 1988-89); memb: Devpt Control Review (the Dobry Ctee) DOE 1975-77, Ctee for Control of Demolition DOE 1976; chm Study Gp for Public Involvement in Planning 1975-77, fndr ICA Architectural Forum, memb Br Soc of Criminology, pres Signals Int Tst; *Books* Talking Blues: The Police in Their Own Words (1989); numerous articles in: The Times, The Independant, The Observer, The Telegraph, The Sunday Telegraph, Independent on Sunday, The Guardian, Police Review; *Recreations* tennis, music, photography; *Clubs* Beefsteak, Groucho; *Style—* Roger Graef, Esq; 72 Westbourne Park Villas, London W2 5EB (☎ 071 727 7868)

GRAESSER, Col Sir Alastair Stewart Durward; DSO (1945), OBE (1963), MC (1944), TD (1950); s of Norman Hugo Graesser, JP (d 1970), and Annette (d 1970), da of James Durward; *b* 17 Nov 1915; *Educ* Oundle, Gonville and Caius Coll Cambridge; *m* 1939, Diana Aline Elms Neale; 1 s (Simon), 3 da (Dawn, Camilla, Emma); *Career* served WWII (France and Germany): cmmnd 4 Bn (TA) Royal Welsh Fus 1939, cmd 158 Bde Anti Tank Co (later became 53 Welsh Div Reconnaissance Regt) 1940-46, Cheshire Yeo 1949-64, Hon Col 3 RWF 1972-80; md R Graesser Ltd 1947-1972, dir Lancashire Tar Distillers Ltd 1949-1972, chm Welsh Industl Estates Corp 1971-75, former pres Industl Assoc Wales and Monmouth; former chm: Wales Regnl Cncl CBI, Central Trg Cncl for Wales; former memb: Merseyside N Wales Electricity Bd, Devpt Corp Wales and Monmouth, Wales and the Marches Postal Bd, Welsh Cncl; former managing tstee Municipal Mutual Insurance Ltd, former dir Chester Grosvenor Hotel Co Ltd, tstee Wales and Border Counties TSB; hon vice-pres Nat Union Cons and Unionist Assoc (chm 1974-75, pres 1984-85); High Sheriff Flintshire 1963, Vice Lord-Lt Clwyd 1980-83; JP 1956-78; CStJ 1980; kt 1973; *Recreations* boxing (half Blue), rugby football, rowing, shooting, gardening; *Clubs* Hawks (Cambridge), Leander, Naval and Military; *Style—* Col Sir Alastair Graesser, DSO, OBE, MC, TD; Sweet Briar, Berghill Lane, Babbinswood, Oswestry, Salop SY11 4PF (☎ 0691 662395)

GRAESSER, (Norman) Rhidian; s of Norman Hugo Graesser (d 1970), and Annette Stewart, *née* Durward (d 1970); *b* 21 Oct 1924; *Educ* Oundle, RNC Dartmouth; *m* 2 July 1952, Stella Ainley, da of Philip Nicholson Hoyle (d 1982); 2 s (Jonathan b 1953, Max b 1957), 1 da (Fern b 1970); *Career* RN 1942-48, invalided out with rank Lt; served Mediterranean, N Atlantic, E and W Indies; dir James Lithgow Ltd 1953-86; *Recreations* countryside, golf, bridge; *Clubs* Lansdowne; *Style—* Rhidian Graesser, Esq; Fron Fanadl, Llandyrnog, Denbigh, Clwyd LL16 4HR (☎ 08244 349)

GRAFFTEY-SMITH, John Jeremy (Jinx); s of Sir Laurence Barton Grafftey-Smith, KCMG, KBE (d 1989), and Mrs Vivien Isobel Tennant-Eyles, *née* Alderson; *b* 13 Oct 1934; *Educ* Winchester, Magdalen Coll Oxford (MA); *m* 23 Jan 1964, Lucy, da of Maj John Fletcher, MBE, of Sussex; 2 s (Alexander b 1967, Toby b 1970), 1 da (Camilla b 1968); *Career* 2 Lt Oxfordshire & Bucks LI 1953-55; banker; Samuel Montagu 1958-

66, Wallace Bros 1966-76, res dir Allied Med Gp Saudi-Arabia 1977-81, Euro rep and mangr corr banking Nat Commercial Bank of Saudi-Arabia 1982-, dir Saudi NCB Securities Ltd (IMRO memb); memb Saudi Br Soc Ctee, govr Brendoncare Fndn; *Recreations* golf, shooting, tennis, music, wine, bridge; *Clubs* Cavalry and Guards', City of London, Hong Kong, Green Jackets, Ashridge Golf, Rye Golf, The Benedict's Soc; *Style*— Jinx Grafftey-Smith, Esq; Burcott Hill House, Wing, Leighton Buzzard, Bedfordshire LU7 0JU; National Commercial Bank, Bevis Marks House, Bevis Marks, London EC3A 7SB

GRAFFTEY-SMITH, Roger Tilney; s of Sir Laurence Barton Grafftey-Smith, KCMG, KBE (d 1989), and Mrs Vivien Isobel Tennant-Eyles, *née* Alderson; *b* 14 April 1931; *Educ* Winchester, Trinity Coll Oxford; *m* 28 March 1962, Jane Oriana Mary, da of Sir John Pollen-Bart; 2 s (Simon b 1968, Max b 1974), 1 da (Selina b 1971); *Career* 2 Lt Queens Bays 1949-51; md Galban Lobo (England) Ltd 1962-72, vice chm N Wilts Dist Cncl 1980-82; managing ptnr Grafftey-Smith & Associates Financial Conslts 1982, chm Unilab Corporation 1985; dir: Utilitech 1988, Biolytic Systems Ltd 1990-; *Recreations* shooting, fishing; *Style*— Roger T Grafftey-Smith, Esq; Monks Farm House, Sherborne, Cheltenham, Glos; Grafftey Smith Associates, 133 Thomas More House, Barbican, London EC2Y 8BU (☎ 071 638 1937, fax 071 920 9262)

GRAFTON, Duchess of; (Ann) Fortune FitzRoy; GCVO (1980, DCVO 1970, CVO 1965), JP; o da of late Capt (Evan Cadogan) Eric Smith, MC, LLD; *m* 12 Oct 1946, 11 Duke of Grafton, *qv*; 2 s, 3 da; *Career* SRCN Great Ormond St 1945, pres W Suffolk Mission to the Deaf, vice pres Suffolk Br Royal British Legion Women's Section; govr: Felixstowe Coll, Riddlesworth Hall; JP: Co of London 1949, Co of Suffolk 1972; memb Bd of Govrs Hosp for Sick Children Great Ormond St 1952-66, pres Great Ormond St Nurses League, vice pres Trinity Hospice (Clapham Common); lady of the bedchamber to HM The Queen 1953-66, mistress of the robes to HM The Queen 1967-; pres W Suffolk Decorative and Fine Art Soc; *Style*— Her Grace the Duchess of Grafton, GCVO, JP; Euston Hall, Thetford, Norfolk IP24 2QP (☎ 0842 3282)

GRAFTON, 11 Duke of (E 1675); Hugh Denis Charles FitzRoy; KG (1976), DL (Suffolk 1973); also Earl of Euston, Viscount Ipswich and Baron Sudbury (E 1672); patron of four livings; Hereditary Ranger of Whittlebury Forest; s of 10 Duke of Grafton (d 1970), and Lady Doreen Buxton, 2 da of 1 Earl Buxton; *b* 3 April 1919; *Educ* Eton, Magdalene Coll Cambridge; *m* 12 Oct 1946, Fortune (*see* Grafton, Duchess of, GCVO); 2 s, 3 da; *Heir* s, Earl of Euston; *Career* Grenadier Gds ADC to Viceroy of India 1943-46; memb: Historic Bldgs Advsy Ctee to English Heritage, Historic Churches Ctee Nat Tst Properties Ctee, Royal Fine Art Cmmn; pres: Soc for the Protection of Ancient Buildings, Architectural Heritage Tst; nat pres Cncl of Br Soc of Master Glass Painters; chm: Cathedrals Advsy Cmmn for England, Tstees Historic Churches Preservation Tst, Tstees Sir John Soane's Museum; vice-chm tstees Nat Portrait Gallery; patron Hereford Herd Book Soc; Hon Air Cdre No 2633 RAuxAF Regt Sqdn 1982-; Hon LLD Univ of East Anglia 1990; *Clubs* Boodle's; *Style*— His Grace the Duke of Grafton, KG, DL; Euston Hall, Thetford, Norfolk IP24 2QP (☎ 0842 753282)

GRAFTON, Col Martin John; CBE (1976, OBE 1964, MBE 1944), TD (1958); s of Vincent Charles Grafton (d 1949), of Worcester and Tewkesbury, and Maud Isabel, *née* Brazier (d 1968); *b* 28 June 1919; *Educ* Bromsgrove Sch; *m* 7 Aug 1948, Jean Margaret (Jennifer), da of James Drummond-Smith, OBE (d 1945), of Daventry; 2 da (Fiona, Caroline); *Career* WWII RE 1940-46; cmmnd 1941, Capt 1943, served Normandy and NW Europe 1944-46; RE TA 1947-66: served 101 (London) FD Engr Regt, Maj 1954, Lt-Col 1960, cmd 101 FD Engr Regt 1960-64, Col 1964, Dep Chief Engr E Anglian Dist 1964-66; John Lewis Partnership: joined 1948, gen mangr Peter Jones 1951-53, dir bldg 1954-60, md 1960-63; dir gen Nat Fedn Bldg Trades Employers (now Bldg Employers Confedn) 1964-79, dir Alfred Booth & Co Ltd 1979-80; memb: EDC for Bldg 1964-75, Cncl CBI 1964-79, Nat Consultative Cncl for Bldg and Civil Engrg 1964-79; DL Gtr London 1967-83; Freeman City of London 1978, memb Worshipful Co of Builders 1977-80; FFB 1968-80, hon FCIOB 1978; *Recreations* travel, reading, music; *Style*— Col Martin Grafton, CBE, TD; Urchfont Hse, Urchfont, nr Devizes, Wilts SN10 4RP (☎ 038 084 404)

GRAFTON, Peter Witheridge; CBE (1972); s of James Hawkins Grafton and Ethel Marion, *née* Brannan; *b* 19 May 1916; *Educ* Westminster City Sch, Sutton Valence Sch, Coll of Estate Mgmnt; *m* 1, 1939, Joan (d 1969), da of late Rear Adm Hubert Bleackley, CBE, MVO; 3 da and 1 s (1 s and 1 da decd); m 2, 1971, Margaret Ruth, da of John Frederick Ward; 2 s; *Career* Nat Serv WWII Queen's Westminster Rifles, Dorsetshire Regt and RE, UK and Far E (Capt); chartered quantity surveyor, ptnr G D Walford & Partners 1949 (sr ptnr 1978-82); pres Royal Inst Chartered Surveyors 1978-79 (vice pres 1974-78, first chm Policy Review Ctee), memb and past chm Quantity Surveyors Cncl (first chm Building Cost Info Serv), memb Cncl Construction Industs Res and Info Assoc 1963-69, memb Res Advsy Cncl to Min of Housing and Construction 1967-71, memb Nat Cncl for Building and Civil Engrg Industs 1968-76, memb Nat Jt Consultative Ctee for Building Indust 1970-77, (chm 1974), memb Br Bd of Agrément 1973-88; tstee United Westminster Schs, chm of govrs Sutton Valence Sch 1976-91, former chm Old Suttonians Assoc; contested (Lib) Bromley 1959; fndr and chm Public Schs Old Boys Golf Assoc, co-donor Grafton Morrish Trophy, past capt Chartered Surveyors Golfing Soc; Master Worshipful Co of Chartered Surveyors 1983-84; FRICS, FCIArB; *Publications* author of numerous articles on tech and other professional subjects; *Recreations* golf, writing; *Clubs* Reform, Rye Golf, Tandridge golf; *Style*— Peter Grafton, Esq, CBE; Longacre, Hookwood Park, Limpsfield, Oxted, Surrey RH8 0SQ (☎ 0883 716685)

GRAHAM, Alan Philip; s of Aaron Goldstein (d 1981), of Edgware, Middx, and Helen, *née* Brown; *b* 4 Dec 1947; *Educ* Orange Hill Boys GS; *m* Jennifer, da of Charles Phillips; 2 da (Caroline Louise b 14 Jan 1977, Lucie Vanessa b 11 April 1979); *Career* merchant banker; N M Rothschild & Sons Group: Credits Div 1967-68, money market dealer 1968-69, assigned to Manchester Branch 1969-71, Foreign Exchange and Bullion Dealing Room 1971-77, mangr 1974, md and chief exec NMR Metals Inc NY (memb Precious Metals Ctee NY Commodity Exchange) 1977-79, asst dir 1980, Int Banking Div London 1980-83, exec dir and head Banking Div NM Rothschild & Sons (CI) Limited Guernsey and dir Old Court Currency Fund Ltd 1984-88, exec dir N M Rothschild & Sons Limited 1988- (dir Treasy Div, head Treasy Admin, non-exec dir N M Rothschild & Sons (CI) Ltd, memb Northern Advsy Bd, chm Treasy Ctee, memb Credits Ctee); Freeman City of London 1977; memb Chartered Inst of Bankers 1967; *Recreations* soccer, music, theatre, tennis; *Clubs* Overseas Bankers; *Style*— Alan Graham, Esq; N M Rothschild & Sons Ltd, New Court, St Swithin's Lane, London EC4P 4DU (☎ 071 280 5000, fax 071 929 1643)

GRAHAM, (John) Alistair; s of Robert Graham (d 1968), and Dorothy, *née* Horner; *b* 6 Aug 1942; *Educ* Royal GS Newcastle upon Tyne; *m* 1967, Dorothy Jean, da of James Clark Wallace, of Morpeth, Northumberland; 1 s (Richard b 1974), 1 da (Polly b 1972); *Career* gen sec The Civil and Public Servs Assoc 1982-86, Industl Soc 1986; *Recreations* music, theatre; *Clubs* RAC; *Style*— Alistair Graham, Esq; The Industrial Society, Peter Runge House, 3 Carlton House Terrace, London SW1Y 5DG (☎ 071 839 4300)

GRAHAM, Major Andrew John Noble; s and h of Sir John Alexander Noble Graham, 4 Bt, GCMG, *qv*; *b* 21 Oct 1956; *Educ* Eton, Trinity Coll Cambridge; *m* 7 July 1984, Susan Mary Bridget, da of Rear Adm John Patrick Bruce O'Riordan, of The Manor House, Islip, Northants; 2 da (Katharine b 1986, Louisa b 1988), 1 s (James b 1990); *Career* Maj Argyll and Sutherland Highlanders; *Recreations* outdoor sports, piping; *Clubs* Army and Navy, MCC, RGS; *Style*— Maj Andrew Graham; c/o RHQ The Argyll and Sutherland Highlanders, The Castle, Stirling

GRAHAM, Andrew Winston Mawdsley; s of Winston Graham, OBE, of Abbotswood, Buxted, Sussex, and Jan Mary, *née* Williamson; *b* 20 June 1942; *Educ* St Edmund Hall Oxford (MA); *m* 1970, Peggotty, da of E L Fawssett; *Career* econ asst: Nat Econ Devpt Office 1964, Dept of Econ Affrs 1964-66, asst to the Econ Advsr To The Cabinet 1966-68, econ advsr to the PM 1968-69, fell and tutor in economics Balliol Coll Oxford 1969- (univ lectr 1970-), policy advsr to the PM 1974-76, estates bursar Balliol Coll Oxford 1978 (investmts bursar 1979-83, vice master 1988); memb: The Wilson Ctee on the Functioning of Fin Insts 1977-80, Econs Ctee SSRC 1978-80; non-exec dir of the Br Tport Docks Bd 1979-82, memb ILO/JASPA Employment Advsy Mission to Ethiopia 1982, head of Queen Elizabeth House Food Studies Gp advising the Govt of the Republic of Zambia 1984, conslt to BBC 1990-; *Publications* Government and Economics in the Postwar World (ed, 1990); *Recreations* windsurfing; *Style*— Andrew Graham, Esq; Balliol Coll, Oxford OX1 3BJ

GRAHAM, Antony Richard Malise; s of Col Patrick Ludovic Graham, MC, (d 1958), and Barbara Mary Jury (d 1964); *b* 15 Oct 1928; *Educ* Nautical Coll Pangbourne; *m* 1958, Gillian Margaret, da of L Bradford Cook (d 1941); 2 s (Ludovic b 1961, Thomas b 1962); 1 da (Lucy b 1965); *Career* Merchant Navy 1945-55 (Master Mariners Cert 1955); Stewarts and Lloyds Ltd 1955-60, PE Consulting Group 1960-72 (regnl dir 1970-72), under sec DTI 1972-76; dir: Barrow Hepburn Gp plc, Maroquinerie Le Tanneur du Bugey SA 1976-81; chm Paton & Sons (Tillicoultry) Ltd 1981-82, DTI 1983-85, dir Clive & Stokes Inetrnational 1985-; Parly candidate (C) Leeds East 1966; FIMC; *Style*— Antony Graham, Esq; 1 The Gardens, Nun Appleton Hall, York YO5 7BG (☎ 0904 84533)

GRAHAM, Beatrice, Lady; Beatrice Mary; *née* Spencer-Smith; OBE (1982); o da of Lt-Col Michael Seymour Spencer-Smith, DSO, MC (d 1928, yr bro of Sir Drummond Hamilton-Spencer-Smith, 5 Bt), and (Evelyn) Penelope (d 1974, having m 2, 1934, Elliot Francis Montagu Butler), yr da of Rev Arthur Delmé-Radcliffe and Beatrice, da of Hon Frederick Dudley Ryder, 3 s of 1 Earl of Harrowby; *b* 27 March 1909; *m* 16 Sept 1939, Sir Richard Bellingham Graham, 10 Bt, OBE, JP, DL, (d 1982); 3 s; *Style*— Beatrice, Lady Graham; Norton Conyers, Ripon, N Yorks (☎ 076 584 333)

GRAHAM, Lord Calum Ian; s of 7 Duke of Montrose; *b* 22 July 1958; *Educ* St Andrew's Coll Grahamstown, Univ of Cape Town, Institut Européen d'Administration des Affaires (INSEAD); *Career* finance; *Clubs* Caledonian; *Style*— The Lord Calum Graham; Montrose Estate Office, Drymen G63 OBQ

GRAHAM, Charles Kenneth Colles; s of Malcolm Vaughan Graham, of 17 Ailesbury Drive, Dublin, and Daphne Mary Nurmahal, *née* Dooley; *b* 24 April 1956; *Educ* Shrewsbury, Tinity Coll Cambridge; *Career* admitted slr 1980, ptnr Cole and Cole 1986-, slr to Oxfordshire Health Authy 1986-; memb Law Soc; *Recreations* golf, church wardenship; *Style*— Charles Graham, Esq; 29 Southdale Rd, Oxford OX2 7SE (☎ 0865 52039), Cole & Cole, St George's Mansions, George St, Oxford OX1 2AR (☎ 0865 791122)

GRAHAM, Maj Sir Charles Spencer Richard; 6 Bt (GB 1783), of Netherby, Cumberland; s of Lt-Col Sir (Frederick) Fergus Graham, 5 Bt, KBE, TD (d 1978), and Mary Spencer Revell, CBE (d 1985), da of Maj-Gen Raymond Northland Revell Reade, CB, CMG; *b* 16 July 1919; *Educ* Eton; *m* 1944, Susan, da of Maj Robert Lambton Surtees, OBE; 2 s, 1 da; *Heir* s, James Fergus Surtees Graham; *Career* Maj Scots Gds, served 1940-50, NW Europe (despatches), Malaya; High Sheriff of Cumberland 1955-56, Lord-Lt Cumbria 1983- (DL Cumberland 1970); pres Country Landowners Assoc 1971-73, memb Nat Water Cncl 1973-83; Master Worshipful Co of Farmers 1982-83; KStJ; *Clubs* Brooks's, Pratt's; *Style*— Maj Sir Charles Graham, Bt; Crofthead, Longtown, Cumbria CA6 5PA (☎ 0228 791231)

GRAHAM, Clifford; s of James Mackenzie Graham (d 1983), and Monica, *née* Nelder (d 1973); *b* 3 April 1937; *Educ* Alsop HS Liverpool, Univ of London (LLB); *m* 2 s (Nicholas b 1961, Robin b 1965), 1 da (Carolyn b 1968); *Career* Nat Serv RAF Aden 1955-57; clerical offr Admty 1954-59, exec offr Customs and Excise 1959-65, called to the Bar Grays Inn 1969, asst sec Miny of Health 1975-82 (higher exec offr 1965-68, princ 1969-74), under sec DHSS 1983-85, sr res fell on sabbatical LSE 1985-87, under sec Priority Care Div Dept of Health (formerly DHSS) 1987-90, dir (on secondment) Inst of Health Kings Coll London; memb Gen Cncl Bar 1969; *Books* incl: Public Administration and Health Services in England (1983), Oxford Textbook of Public Health (contrib, 1984), In praise of the Civil Service (1986), Listen to the Individual Person (1987), numerous articles in jls and DHSS reports; *Recreations* cycling, rambling, reading, music, opera; *Clubs* Gray's Inn; *Style*— Clifford Graham, Esq; Highcroft, Milton Clevedon, Stepton Mallet, Somerset BA4 6NS (☎ 0749 830308); Department of Health, Richmond House, 79 Whitehall, London SW1A 2NS (☎ 071 210 5446); King's College London, Kensington Campus, Hill Rd, London W8 (☎ 071 333 4646, fax 071 937 5690)

GRAHAM, Colin; s of Fredrick Eaton Graham-Bonnalie (d 1975), of Edinburgh, and Alexandra Diana Vyvyan Findlay (d 1988); *b* 22 Sept 1931; *Educ* Stowe, RADA; *Career* artistic dir: English Opera Group 1966-75, Aldeburgh Festival 1968-90, English Music Theatre 1976-, Banff Opera Canada 1984-; ass dir of prodn Sadler's Wells Opera 1968-76, dir of prodn ENO 1979-84, vice pres Aldeburgh Festival 1990-, Orpheus award for Prodn 1972, Winston Churchill fellowship 1979, Opera America award 1988; ordained min Christian Church 1987, memb: Br Actors' Equity 1933, AGMA 1973 Hon D of Arts Webster Univ St Louis; *Books* A Penny for a Song (Libretto 1966), The Golden Vanity (Libretto 1980), The Postman Always Rings Twice (Libretto 1985), Joruri (Libretto 1987); *Recreations* the Bible, movies, motor-cycles, weight-training; *Style*— Colin Graham, Esq; PO Box 13148, Saint Louis, Missouri 63119, USA (☎ 010 314 961 0171, fax 010 314 961 7463)

GRAHAM, Hon Mrs (Daphne); *née* Bootle-Wilbraham; da of 6 Baron Skelmersdale (d 1973), and Ann, da of Percy Quilter (d 1974, s of 1 Bt); *b* 14 Oct 1946; *m* 1980, Jocelyn Peter Gore Graham, s of Brig Peter Alastair John Gore Graham, of Chalkpit Cottage, Blewbury, Oxon; 1 da (Tamsin b 1985); *Style*— The Hon Mrs Graham; 11 Rosenau Rd, London, SW11 4QN

GRAHAM, David James Ogle; s of Dr Frank Ogle Graham, of Stokesly, Cleveland, and Annie Campbell, *née* McLeod; *b* 7 May 1932; *Educ* Taunton Sch Somerset; *m* 6 Sept 1960, Marion Emma, da of David William Ralph Knighton (d 1983); 1 s (Robert b 7 April 1985), 1 da (Sarah Jane b 8 May 1983); *Career* slr; former: ptnr Bentleys Stokes & Lowless, chm Admiralty Solicitors Group, memb Admty Ct Ctee; govr St Albans HS for Girls; memb Law Soc; *Recreations* golf, fly fishing; *Style*— David Graham, Esq; Fairway, 38 The Ave, Potters Bar (☎ 0707 55909)

GRAHAM, (Stewart) David; QC (1977); s of Lewis Graham (d 1985), of Harrogate, and Gertrude, *née* Markman (d 1989); *b* 27 Feb 1934; *Educ* Leeds GS, St Edmund Hall Oxford (MA, BCL); *m* 20 Dec 1959, Corinne, da of Emile Carmona (d 1984), of London; 2 da (Jeanne (Mrs Zane), Angela); *Career* called to the Bar Middle Temple

1957; Harmsworth Law scholar 1958, ret from Bar 1985, dir Coopers and Lybrand and Cork Gully 1985-; chm: law Parly and Gen Purpose Ctee of Bd of Deputies of Br Jews 1983-88, Editorial Bd of Insolvency Intelligence 1988-; memb: Cncl of Justice 1976-, Insolvency Rules Advsy Ctee 1984-86; editor of various works on Insolvency Law; *Recreations* biography, travel, music, history of insolvency law; *Style—* David Graham, Esq, QC; 133 London Rd, Stanmore, Middx HA7 4PQ (☎ 081 954 3783); Shelley House, 3 Noble St, London EC2V 7DQ (☎ 071 606 7700, fax 071 606 9887, telex 884730 CORK GXG)

GRAHAM, Lord Donald Alasdair; s of 7 Duke of Montrose; *b* 28 Oct 1956; *Educ* St Andrew's Coll Grahamstown, Univ of St Andrew's Scotland (BSc), INSEAD (MBA); *m* 1981, Donalda Elspeth, da of Maj Allan John Cameron, of Allangrange, Munlochy, Ross-shire; 1 s (Alasdair b 1986, d 1988), 1 da (Caitriana b 1984); *Career* MBCS; *Recreations* windsurfing, tennis, piping; *Clubs* New (Edinburgh); *Style—* Lord Donald Graham; Nether Tillyrie, Milnathort, Kinross-shire, Scotland; Adam & Company plc, 22 Charlotte Square, Edinburgh EH2 4DF

GRAHAM, Donald Henry (Don); s of Alan Wilson Graham (d 1985), of Woodvale, Storrs Park, Windermere, and Mary Margaret, *née* Addison; *b* 13 July 1945; *Educ* Heversham GS; *m* 12 May 1973, (Norah) Christine, da of John O'Connor (d 1979), of Wigan; 1 s (Michael b 11 Oct 1976), 1 da (Anna b 6 May 1983); *Career* CA; ptnr Jackson and Graham 1968-; sidesman St Mary's Church Windermere, govr St Mary's Sch Windermere 1982-88; hon auditor for various local charities: Save the Children, St Mary's Church, St Martin's Church, Windermere Jr Sch; FICA 1973 (assoc memb 1968); *Style—* Don Graham, Esq; Maudlands, Maude Street, Kendal, Cumbria (☎ 0539 720526)

GRAHAM, Dr Douglas; s of David Sims Graham (d 1974), of Cheshire, and Freda Wilson, *née* Pearce; *b* 18 Jan 1946; *Educ* Rutherford Coll of Technol (BSc), Univ of Newcastle (PhD); *m* 16 April 1966, Rosemary Anne Graham; 1 s (Anthony Edmund b 5 Aug 1967), 1 da (Rosalynde Michelle b 11 Nov 1969); *Career* res engr CA Parsons 1966-71, fin controller ICFC 1972-76, chief exec Indespension Ltd 1977-; chm Bolton Business Ventures; MIMechE (1972); *Style—* Dr Douglas Graham; Moorlands, Chapeltown Rd, Bromley Cross, Bolton (☎ 0204 53 850); Indespension Ltd, Belmont Rd, Bolton, Lancs (☎ 0204 309797, fax 0204 309148)

GRAHAM, (Malcolm Gray) Douglas; s of Malcolm Graham, of Farmcote Hall, Claverley, nr Wolverhampton, and Annie Jeanette Sankey, *née* Robinson (d 1976); *b* 18 Feb 1930; *Educ* Shrewsbury; *m* 18 April 1980, Sara Ann, da of William Patrick Whitelaw Anderson (d 1976), of Feckenham, Worcs; 2 step s (Colin William Edward Elwell b 12 Jan 1971, James Peter Elwell b 24 April 1973); *Career* chm: The Midland News Assoc Ltd 1984-, Express & Star Ltd, Shropshire Newspapers Ltd 1980-; pres: Young Newspapermen's Assoc 1969, W Midlands Newspaper Soc 1973-74; chm Evening Newspaper Advtg Bureau 1978-79; *Recreations* shooting; *Style—* Douglas Graham, Esq; Roughton Manor, Worfield, nr Bridgnorth, Shropshire (☎ 074 64 209); Express and Star, Queen St, Wolverhampton, W Midlands (☎ 0902 313131)

GRAHAM, Duncan Gilmour; CBE (1987); s of Robert Gilmour Graham, of Glasgow, and Lilias Turnbull, *née* Watson; *b* 20 Aug 1936; *Educ* Hutchesons' Sch Glasgow, Univ of Glasgow (MA), Jordanhill Coll of Educn (Cert Ed); *m* 26 Dec 1962, Margaret Gray, da of Maj James Brown Cairns R E (d 1984), of Eaglesham; 2 s (Roderick b 1966, Duncan b 1969), 1 da (Kirsty b 1967); *Career* teacher of history Whitehill and Hutchesons' Sch's Glasgow 1959-65, lectr Craigie Coll of Educn Ayr 1965-68, asst then sr dep dir of educn Renfrewshire 1968-74, sr dep dir of educn Strathclyde Regnl Cncl 1974-79, co educn offr Suffolk CC 1979-87, chief exec Humberside CC 1987-88, chm and chief exec Nat Curriculum Cncl 1988-; advsr to Convention of Scottish Local Authys and Scottish Teachers' Salaries Ctee 1974-79, advsr Assoc of CC 1983-88, memb Burnham Ctee 1983-87, chm Assoc of Educn Offrs 1984, sec Soc of Co Educn Offrs 1985-87, Arts Cncl nominee on Lincoln and Humberside Arts; memb: BBC North NE Advsy Panel, Cncl Industl Soc; FBIM 1972, FRSA 1981; *Books* Those Having Torches (1985), In the Light of Torches (1986), Mathematics For Ages 5-16 (1988); *Recreations* golf, sailing, fishing, the Arts; *Clubs* Caledonian, Western Gailes, Royal Overseas League; *Style—* Duncan Graham, Esq, CBE; 1 Dunroyal Close, Helperby, York; National Curriculum Council, Albion Wharf, 25 Skeldergate, York YO1 2XL (☎ 0904 622533, fax 0904 622921)

GRAHAM, Euan Douglas; CB (1985); yr s of Brig Lord (Douglas) Malise Graham, CB, DSO, MC (d 1979; 2 s of 5 Duke of Montrose), and Hon Rachael Mary Holland (d 1977), da of 2 Viscount Knutsford; *b* 29 July 1924; *Educ* Eton, Ch Ch Oxford (MA); *m* 1, 3 June 1954 (m dis 1970), Pauline Laetitia, eldest da of Hon David Francis Tennant, and former w of Capt Julian Lane-Fox Pitt Rivers; m 2, 1972, Caroline Esther, da of Sheriff Kenneth Middleton, of Ledwell, Oxon; 2 da (Sarah b 1973, Alexandra b 1976); *Style—* Euan Graham, Esq, CB

GRAHAM, (Norman) Garrick; s of Cecil Davies Graham (d 1969), and Martha Berneice Isabel, *née* Glass, of Auckland, New Zealand; *b* 15 Dec 1932; *Educ* King's Coll Auckland NZ, Otago Univ Med Sch Dunedin NZ (MB ChB, univ cricket XI); *m* 15 Dec 1956, Joy Frances, *née* Bayly; 1 s (Michael Ian b 24 Oct 1958), 2 da (Kathryn Denise b 22 Nov 1960, Jacky Joy b 20 Dec 1965); *Career* house surgn Auckland Hosps NZ 1957-58, surgical registrar Auckland Pub Hosp NZ 1959, anatomy demonstrator Otago Univ Med Sch 1960, rotating surgical registrar Auckland Hosps 1961-62, surgical registrar St Mary's Hosp Portsmouth Eng 1963-64, lectr and sr registrar Professiorial Surgical Unit The Gen Infirmary Leeds 1964-67, conslt gen surgn Huddersfield Hosps 1967-, pt/t unit gen mangr Huddersfield Royal Infirmary 1986-; memb: BMA, Assoc of Surgns of GB and Ireland, Br Soc of Gastro-Enterology; FRACS 1962, FRCS 1963; author numerous papers in med jls relating to gastro-intestinal and biliary tract surgery; *Recreations* golf, cricket, travel, reading; *Style—* Garrick Graham, Esq; Unit General Manager and Consultant Surgeon, Huddersfield Royal Infirmary, Lindley, Huddersfield, W Yorkshire (☎ 0484 421191)

GRAHAM, Geraldine, Lady; Geraldine; *née* Velour; da of Austin Velour, of Brooklyn, NY; *m* 1949, as his 2 w, Sir Ralph Wolfe Graham, 13 Bt (d 1988); 2 s (Sir Ralph Stuart, 14 Bt, *qv*, Robert Bruce b 1953); *Style—* Geraldine, Lady Graham; 134 Leisureville Boulevard, Boynton Beach, Florida 33435, USA

GRAHAM, Gordon; CBE (1980); s of late Stanley Bouch Graham and Isabel Hetherington; *b* 4 June 1920; *Educ* Creighton Sch, Nottingham Sch of Architecture (Dip Arch 1949); *m* 1946, Enid Pennington; 3 da; *Career* sr ptnr Gordon Graham and Ptnrs, pres RIBA 1977-79; *Style—* Gordon Graham, Esq, CBE; Lockington Hall, Lockington, Derby DE7 2RH

GRAHAM, (William) Gordon; MC (1944); s of Thomas Graham (d 1944), and Marion Walker Hutcheson (d 1979); *b* 17 July 1920; *Educ* Hutchesons' GS Glasgow, Univ of Glasgow (MA); *m* 1948, Friedel, da of Emil Gramm (d 1966); 2 da (Fiona, Sylvia); *Career* Nat Serv Queen's Own Cameron Highlanders 1941-46, Capt 1944, Maj 1945, GSO II India Office 1946 serving in India and Burma; newspaper corr and publishers' rep in India 1946-56; vice pres McGraw-Hill Book Co NY 1961-74 (int sales mangr 1956-63); md McGraw-Hill: UK, Europe, ME, Africa 1963-74; chief exec Butterworth Publishers 1975-88 (gp chm 1975-90), ed Logos 1990-; chm: International Electronic Publishing Research Centre Ltd 1981-84, Publishers Databases Ltd 1982-84, R R Bowker NY 1985-90; dir: W & R Chambers Edinburgh 1974-83, International Publishing Corporation 1975-82, Reed Publishing Group 1982-90; pres Publishers' Assoc of GB 1985-87 (memb Cncl 1972-88), memb Bd Br Library 1980-86; FRSA; *Recreations* reading, writing, skiing, gardening; *Style—* Gordon Graham, Esq, MC; 5 Beechwood Drive, Marlow, Bucks SL7 2DH (☎ 0628 483371)

GRAHAM, Prof Hilary Mavis; da of Joseph Anderson Swenarton (d 1964), and Mavis Gertrude, *née* Simmons; *b* 13 Dec 1950; *Educ* Sherborne Sch for Girls, Univ of York (BA, MA, PGCE, PhD); *m* 24 Oct 1970, Alan Thomas Graham, s of Thomas Graham, of Helen's Bay, Co Down, NI; 1 s (Luke b 1972), 2 da (Ruth b 1974, Carrie b 1982); *Career* res fell Univ of York 1975-79, lectr in social policy Univ of Bradford 1979-85, head of dept Coventry Poly 1986-87, prof of applied social studies Univ of Warwick 1988-; memb: Coventry Diocesan Bd of Social Responsibility, Social Policy Assoc, Br Sociological Assoc, Social Res Assoc, Bd of Govrs Tile Hill Coll Coventry; *Books* Women, Health and the Family (1984), Health and Welfare (1985); *Recreations* gardening, rock music, squash; *Style—* Prof Hilary Graham; Department of Applied Social Studies, University of Warwick, Coventry CV4 7AL (☎ 0203 523523 ext 3173, fax 0203 461606)

GRAHAM, Ian David; s of David Patton Graham (d 1984), of Alnwick, Northumberland, and Elsie, *née* Pate (d 1990); *b* 9 May 1955; *Educ* The Duke's Sch Alnwick, Ch Ch Oxford (Harmsworth exhibitioner, Asbury scholar, MA); *Career* called to the Bar Middle Temple 1978; *Recreations* opera, chess, traditional catholic theology music and ceremony; *Style—* Ian Graham, Esq; 36 Burdon Terrace, Jesmond, Newcastle upon Tyne (☎ 091 2811670), New Ct Chambers, Broad Chare, Newcastle Upon Tyne (☎ 091 2321980)

GRAHAM, Col Ian Derek; TD, DL (Humberside 1974-); s of Maj Ernest Frederic Graham, MBE, MC (d 1985), of Rowan, The Park, Swanland, N Humberside, and Muriel, *née* Fell (d 1970); *b* 27 Feb 1928; *Educ* Sedbergh, Univ of Hull, Univ Coll London (LLB); *m* 1, 24 July 1955 (m dis 1984), Margaret Edwards; 3 da (Fiona Clare b 1956, Janet Elaine b 1958, Sally Anne b 1962); m 2, 1985, Betty, da of Thomas Vessey Whittaker (d 1954); *Career* cmmnd RA 1947, TA 1949-71, Lt-Col 440 LAD Regt RA 1967, Col Cmdt Humberside ACF 1971-79; admitted slr 1954; sr ptnr Graham & Rosen; memb Nat Cncl ACF Assoc (currently chm Shooting Ctee), vice chm Yorks and Humberside TAVRA 1987-90; local chm Nat Insur and Social Security Appeal Tbnl 1970-; memb Law Soc; *Recreations* game shooting; *Style—* Col Ian Graham, TD, DL; Kelsey Cottage, Hariff Lane, Burstwick, North Humberside (☎ 0964 622429); Graham & Rosen, 8 Parliament St, Hull (☎ 0482 23123)

GRAHAM, Marquess of; James; s and h of 7 Duke of Montrose; *b* 6 April 1935; *Educ* Loretto; *m* 1970, Catherine Elizabeth MacDonnell, da of Capt Norman Alexander Thompson Young (d 1942), Queen's Own Cameron Highlanders of Canada; 2 s (Lord Fintrie b 1973, Lord Ronald John Christopher b 1975), 1 da (Lady Hermione Elizabeth b 1971); *Heir* s, Lord Fintrie; *Career* Brig Royal Co of Archers (Queen's Body Guard for Scotland) 1986-; memb Cncl Scottish Nat Farmers' Union 1981-86 and 1987-90; OStJ 1978; *Clubs* Hon Memb RNVR (Scotland), Royal Scottish Pipers Soc, Royal Highland and Agricultural Soc of Scotland; *Style—* Marquess of Graham; Auchmar, Drymen, Glasgow (☎ 0360 60307)

GRAHAM, Sir James Bellingham; 11 Bt (E 1662), of Norton Conyers, Yorkshire; er s of Sir Richard Graham, 10 Bt, OBE, JP, DL (d 1982); *b* 8 Oct 1940; *Educ* Eton, Christ Church Oxford; *m* 1986, Halina, yr da of late Major Wiktor Grubert; *Heir* yr bro, William Reginald Graham, *qv*; *Career* Res Asst Cecil Higgins Museum and Art Gallery Bedford; *Books* Guide to Norton Conyers (1976), Cecil Higgins, Collector Extraordinary (jtly with wife 1983), A Guide to the Cecil Higgins Museum and Art Gallery (1987); *Recreations* history, sightseeing; *Style—* Sir James Graham, Bt; 1 Oberon Court, Shakespear Rd, Bedford MK40 2EB

GRAHAM, James Fergus Surtees; s and h of Maj Sir Charles Graham, 6 Bt; *b* 29 July 1946; *Educ* Milton Abbey; *m* 1975, Serena Jane, da of Ronald Frank Kershaw; 1 s (Robert b 1985), 2 da (Catherine b 1978, Iona b 1980); *Style—* James Graham, Esq; The Tower, Kirkandrews-on-Eden, Longtown, Cumbria (☎ 0228 791262); 35 Drayton Court, Drayton Gardens, London SW10 (☎ 071 370 7245)

GRAHAM, James Lionel Malin; s of Christopher Colin Graham (d 1980), of Offchurch, Leamington Spa, and Evelyn Gladys, *née* Pridmore (d 1987); *b* 2 Sept 1927; *Educ* All Saints Sch Bloxham, Lincoln Coll Oxford; *m* 28 Oct 1961, Valerie Maddalena, da of Dr William Herbert Cotton Croft (d 1990), of Kineton, Warwick; 2 s (Christopher b 1962, Stephen b 1963), 1 da (Sarah b 1969); *Career* Army 1945-48, cmmnd RASC, demobbed Lt; Thomson McLintock & Co 1948-52, qualified as CA 1953, md J & J Cash Ltd 1959-73, dir Coventry Provident Building Soc 1970-81, fin dir John Trelawny Ltd 1975-77, md Br Transfer Printing Co Ltd 1978-88, ret 1988; magistrate Coventry Bench 1969-75, gen cmmr of income tax 1979; High Sheriff Warwicks 1985-86; pt/t conslt Display Prodrs and Screenprinters Assoc London 1989- (treas 1984-88), tstee Coventry TSB 1966-80; memb Coventry C of C 1970-82, memb Regnl Bd TSB of Eng and Wales Birmingham 1984-89; former pres: Coventry Textile Soc, Warwicks Soc of CAS; mangr Newfield Sch 1966-72, tstee Bonds Hosp Estates Charity 1958, Edwards Charity 1962, Samuel Smith's Charity 1965, Newfield Charitable Tst 1972, Sir Thomas White's Charity 1971, Coventry Church Charities 1978; Liveryman Worshipful Company of Weavers 1966 (Upper Bailiff 1986-87); Fellowship: Drapers Coventry 1959 (past master), Broadweavers and Clothiers 1957 (past master); FCA 1953; *Recreations* skiing, gardening, philately, golf, collecting and hoarding generally, overseas travel; *Style—* James Graham, Esq; Gable House, Offchurch, Leamington Spa, Warwicks CV33 9AP; La Coquille, Braye Rd, Alderney, CI

GRAHAM, Sir John Alexander Noble; 4 Bt (UK 1906), of Larbert; GCMG (1985, KCMG 1979, CMG 1972); s of Sir Reginald Graham, 3 Bt, VC, OBE (d 1980), and Rachel, *née* Sprot (d 1984); *b* 15 July 1926; *Educ* Eton, Trinity Coll Cambridge; *m* 1956, Marygold Ellinor Gabrielle, da of Lt-Col Clive Austin, JP, DL (d 1974), and Lady Lilian Lumley, sis of 11 Earl of Scarbrough, KG, GCSI, GCVO, TD, PC; 2 s, 1 da; *Heir* s, Maj Andrew Graham; *Career* joined FO 1950, served Amman, Kuwait, Bahrain, Belgrade, Benghazi, and as cnsllr and head of Chancery Washington; ambass Iraq 1974-77, FCO dep under sec 1977-79 and 1980-82, ambass Iran 1979-80, ambass and UK perm rep NATO Brussels 1982-86; dir Ditchley Fndn 1987-; *Recreations* outdoor activities; *Clubs* Army and Navy; *Style—* Sir John Graham, Bt, GCMG; Ditchley Park, Enstone, Oxford OX7 4ER; The Withies, Long Parish, Andover, Hants SP11 6PD

GRAHAM, Maj-Gen John David Carew; CB (1978), CBE (1973, OBE 1967); s of Col John Alexander Graham (d 1957), of The White House, Nettlestone, IOW, and Constance Mary, *née* Carew-Hunt (d 1987); *b* 18 Jan 1923; *Educ* Fernden Sch Haslemere, Cheltenham; *m* 17 Nov 1956, Rosemary Elaine, da of James Basil Adamson (d 1946), of Georgetown, British Guyana; 1 s (John Christopher Malcolm b 1959), 1 da (Jacqueline Patricia Anne b 1957); *Career* cmmnd Argyll and Sutherland Highlanders 1942 (despatches), served 5 Bn The Parachute Regt 1946-49, Br Embassy Prague 1949-50, HQ Scottish Cmd 1956-58, mil asst to CINCENT Fontainebleau 1960-62, cmd 1 Bn The Parachute Regt 1964-66, instr Staff Coll Camberley 1967, Regtl Col The Parachute Regt 1968-69, Cdr Sultan's Armed Forces Oman 1970-72, Indian Nat Def Coll 1973, asst Chief of Staff HQ AFCENT 1974-76; GOC Wales 1976-78, Hon Col Kent ACF 1981-88 (chm Kent ACF Ctee 1979-86), Hon

Col 203 Welsh Gen Hosp, RAMC, TA 1983-89; OStJ (chm St John Cncl for Kent 1978-86), CStJ; Order of Oman; *Recreations* gardening, walking, travel; *Style—* Major-General John Graham, CB, CBE; c/o National Westminster Bank, Riverhead, Sevenoaks, Kent TN13 2DA

GRAHAM, John Malcolm; s of Malcolm Pullen Graham (d 1989), of Oxford, and Edna Stanhope, *née* Davis; *b* 9 Feb 1940; *Educ* Uppingham, Pembroke Coll Oxford (MA, BM BCh), Middx Hosp; *m* 15 Jan 1966, Sandy Judy, da of Wing Cdr Eduardo Walpole Whitaker, DFC (d 1985); 1 s (Alastair b 25 April 1966), 2 da (Harriet b 9 June 1976, Emily b 17 Jan 1978); *Career* conslt ENT surgn UCH, Middlesex and Royal London Homeopathic Hosp 1979-; author of various sci papers, contrib chapters on subjects incl: tinnitus in adults and children, cochlear implants, electric response audiomentry; Freeman City of London 1988, Liveryman Worshipful Soc Apothecaries; memb: BMA, RSM; FRCS, FRCSE; miembro correspondiente Societad del ORL de Uruguay; *Recreations* music, construction; *Style—* John Graham, Esq; 16 Upper Wimpole Street, London W1 (☎ 071 486 9583)

GRAHAM, Sir John Moodie; 2 Bt (UK 1964), of Dromore, Co Down; s of Sir Clarence Johnston Graham, 1 Bt (d 1966); *b* 3 April 1938; *Educ* Trinity Coll Glenalmond, Queen's Univ Belfast; *m* 1970 (m dis 1982), Valerie Rosemary, da of late Frank Gill, of Belfast; 3 da; *Career* pres N Ireland Leukaemia Res Fund, dir John Graham (Dromore) Ltd, Electrical Supplies Ltd, Concrete (NI) Ltd, Ulster Quarries Ltd, G H Fieldhouse Plant (NI) Ltd; memb Lloyds 1978-; ret 1983; *Style—* Sir John Graham, Bt; Lista de Correos, 07819 Jesus, Ibiza, Baleares, Spain (☎ 010 34 71 31 38 34); Les Bordes d'Arinsal, Principat d'Andorra (☎ 010 33 863)

GRAHAM, Judy; da of Norman Flowers Graham, of Milwaukee, Wisconsin, USA, and Virginia Tallmadge, *née* Smith (d 1977); *b* 13 July 1942; *Educ* Shorewood HS Milwaukee Wisconsin USA, Carroll Coll Waukesha Wisconsin (BA), Columbia Univ NY (MA); *m* 28 Dec 1978, Jonathan Roy Blair, s of Dr Maurice Blair, of Brighton, Sussex; 1 s (Benjamin b 25 Nov 1979), 1 da (Tanya b 27 March 1973); *Career* dir of social servs and community organiser NENA Health Centre NY 1969-72, Women's Med Centre NY 1972-74, dir of social servs alcohol treatment St Luke's Hosp NY 1974-79, dir Alcohol Recovery Project London 1979-85, grants dir Charity Projects 1986-; vice chm Fedn of Alcohol Rehabilitation Establishments; memb Greenpeace, Anti Apartheid, Islington Woodcraft Folk; memb Professional Acad of Social Workers USA; *Recreations* tennis; *Style—* Mrs Judy Graham; 9 Highbury Crescent, London N5 1RN (☎ 071 700 4168); Charity Projects, 48 Leicester Square, London WC2H 7QD (☎ 071 930 0606, fax 071 839 3704)

GRAHAM, Marigold Evelyn; JP (Clwyd 1983); da of Sir J Crosland Graham (d 1946), and Violet Kathleen, *née* Brinkley (d 1985); *b* 17 Feb 1931; *Educ* St Leonard's Sch, Univ of St Andrew's; *Career* farmer; High Sheriff Clwyd 1981, N Wales regnl rep Riding for Disabled Assoc 1970-77, vice pres BRCS Denbighshire, tstee Clwyd Special Riding Tst, chm of tstees 1987-90 Clwyd Fine Arts Tst; *Recreations* hunting, travel, sport, fine arts; *Style—* Miss Marigold Graham, JP; Plas-yn-Rhos, Ruthin, Clwyd (☎ 08242 2048)

GRAHAM, Sir (Alexander) Michael; GBE (1990), JP; s of Dr Walter Graham (d 1985), of 66 Acacia Rd, London, and Suzanne, *née* Simon (d 1976); *b* 27 Sept 1938; *Educ* St Paul's; *m* 6 June 1964, Carolyn, da of Lt-Col Alan Wolryche Stansfeld, MBE, of Dellview Cottage, St Ippollytts, Hitchin, Herts; 3 da (Lucy b 1967, Catriona b 1969, Georgina b 1970); *Career* Nat Serv Lt The Gordon Highlanders 1957-59, 4/7 Bn The Gordon Highlanders, 3 Bn and HQ 152 Highland Bde (TA) 1959-67; underwriting memb Lloyd's; Frizzell Group Ltd (insurance brokers): joined 1957, md 1973-90, dep chm 1990; Common Councilman City of London 1978-79, Alderman for Ward of Queenhithe 1979-, Sheriff City of London 1986-87, Lord Mayor London 1990-91; govr: St Paul's Sch, St Paul's Girls' Sch, The Hall Sch, Christ's Hosp, King Edward's Whitley; memb: Cncl Gresham Coll, Tstees Morden Coll; pres Queenhithe Ward Club; Churchwarden All Saints, St Paul's Walden 1981-84; Freeman of City of London, Liveryman Worshipful Co of Mercers 1971 (Master 1983-84), HM Lt City of London 1989; FCII 1964, FBIBA 1970, MBIM 1971, FRSA 1980; CStJ 1987; Ordre de Wissam Alouite (Morocco) 1987; *Recreations* golf, swimming, shooting, tennis, wine, silver, bridge; *Clubs* Carlton, City Livery, Highland Brigade, Royal Worlington Golf; *Style—* Sir Alexander Graham, GBE, JP; Walden Abbotts, Whitwell, Hitchin, Herts (☎ 0438 87223); The Frizzell Group Ltd, Frizzell House, 14-22 Elder St, London E1 6DF (☎ 071 247 6595, fax 071 377 9114, car 0860 339 399)

GRAHAM, Prof Neil Bonnette; s of George Henry Graham (d 1979), of Liverpool, and Constance, *née* Bonnette (d 1986); *b* 23 May 1933; *Educ* Alsop HS Liverpool, Univ of Liverpool (BSc, Phd); *m* 16 July 1955, Marjorie, da of William Edwin Royden (d 1937), of Liverpool; 1 s (Paul b 19 Sept 1957), 3 da (Kim b 7 Oct 1959, Michele b 14 May 1965, Lesley b 6 Aug 1967); *Career* res scientist Canadian Industries Ltd McMasterville PQ Canada 1956-67, gp head ICI Petrochemical and Polymer Laboratory Runcorn Cheshire 1967-73 (former assoc gp head), res prof of chemical technol Univ of Strathclyde 1983- (Young Prof 1973-83), fndr and tech dir Polysystems Ltd Clydebank 1980-90; memb DHSS Medicines Div Regulatory Advsy Ctee on Dental and Surgical Materials; tstee: McKinnon McNeil Tst, James Clerk Maxwell Tst; govr Keil Sch; holder of more than 50 patents; ALCM, CChem, FRSC, FPRI, FRSE; *Recreations* walking, sailing, music; *Style—* Prof Neil Graham; 6 Kilmardinny Grove, Bearsden, Glasgow G61 3NY (☎ 041 942 0484); 5 Clyde St, Millport, Cumbrae Island, Scotland; University of Strathclyde, Dept of Pure & Applied Chemistry, Thomas Graham Building, 295 Cathedral St, Glasgow G1 1XL (☎ 041 552 4400, fax 041 552 5664, telex 77472 UNSLIB G)

GRAHAM, Norman Sidney; s of Sidney Graham (d 1975), of Cheshire, and Esther, *née* Shipley (d 1983); *b* 19 Sept 1928; *Educ* Birkenhead Sch, St Catharine's Coll Cambridge (MSc); *m* 1954, Gwendolen Mary, da of William Hughes (d 1965), of Cheshire; 1 s (Philip b 1958); *Career* chm Intermediaries Ctee Assoc of Br Insurers; ex pres Manchester Actuarial Soc; Actuary to three Charitable Disaster Funds; govr Cncl Coll of Insurance; gen mangr chief Actuary, General Accident Life Assurance Ltd York 1980 (dir 1983); FIA, FCII; *Recreations* golf, bridge, music, hill-walking; *Clubs* Yorkshire, Gallio Dining; *Style—* Norman Graham, Esq; 41 Hillcrest Ave, Nether Poppleton, York YO2 6LD (☎ 0904 795 111); General Accident Life Assurance Ltd, Rougier St, York YO1 1HR (☎ 0904 28 982)

GRAHAM, Sir Norman William; CB (1961); s of late William McLeod Graham; *b* 11 Oct 1913; *Educ* Glasgow HS, Univ of Glasgow; *m* 1949, Catherine Mary, *née* Strathie; 2 s, 1 da; *Career* PPS to Min of Aircraft Prodn 1944-45, asst sec Dept of Health for Scotland 1945, under sec Scottish Home and Health Dept 1956-63, sec Scottish Educn Dept 1964-73; kt 1971; *Clubs* New (Edinburgh); *Style—* Sir Norman Graham, CB; Chesterhall Steading, Longniddry, East Lothian (☎ 0875 52130)

GRAHAM, Hon Mrs (Pamela Winifred); *née* Whitelaw; yst da of 1 Viscount Whitelaw, *qv*; *b* 1951; *m* 1974, Malise Charles Richard Graham; 4 da (Arabella Mary Susan b 1975, Georgina Carol Cecilia b 1977, Laura Meliora Winifred b 1981, Victoria Malise Samantha b 1985); *Style—* The Hon Mrs Graham; The Cottage, Sproxton, Melton Mowbray, Leicestershire (☎ 0476 860266)

GRAHAM, Sir (John) Patrick; s of Alexander Graham (d 1942), of Shrewsbury; *b* 26 Nov 1906; *Educ* Shrewsbury, Gonville and Caius Coll Cambridge; *m* 1931, Annie Elizabeth Newport, da of Newport Granger Willson, of Fordham, Ely; 4 s (Anthony John, Robert Alexander, William Patrick Newport, Dan Washington); *Career* served WWII Gp Capt RAFVR, chief planning branch PR Div SHAEF; called to the Bar Middle Temple 1930, QC 1953, bencher 1961, treas 1979, dep-chm Salop Quarter Sessions 1961-69, judge of the High Court of Justice (Chancery Div) 1969-81; memb Standing Ctee on Structural Safety 1975-; kt 1969; *Books* Awards to Inventors; *Recreations* golf, fishing; *Style—* Sir Patrick Graham; Tall Elms, Radlett, Herts WD7 8JB (☎ 0923 856307)

GRAHAM, Peter; CB (1982), QC (1990); s of Alderman Douglas Graham, CBE (d 1981), of Huddersfield, Yorkshire, and Ena May, *née* Jackson (d 1982); f was Mayor of Huddersfield 1966-67, and Freeman of Borough 1973; *b* 7 Jan 1934; *Educ* St Bees Sch Cumberland (scholar), St John's Coll Cambridge (scholar, MA, LLM); *m* 1, Judith Mary Dunbar; 2 s (Ian b 1960, Alistair b 1962); m 2, Anne Silvia, o da of Benjamin Arthur Garcia; *Career* called to the Bar Grays Inn 1958, Parly counsel 1972-86, second Parly counsel 1987-; *Recreations* village organist, gardening, bridge; *Clubs* The Sette of Odd Volumes; *Style—* Peter Graham, Esq, CB, QC; Parliamentary Counsel Office, 36 Whitehall, London SW1A 2A7

GRAHAM, Sir Peter Alfred; OBE (1969); s of Alfred Graham and Margaret, *née* Winder; *b* 25 May 1922; *Educ* St Joseph's Coll Beulah Hill; *m* 1953, Luned Mary, *née* Kenealy-Jones; 2 s, 2 da; *Career* chm: Standard Chartered Merchant Bank 1977-83, Standard Chartered Bank Ltd 1987-, Crown Agents 1983-; FIB, CBIM; kt 1987; *Style—* Sir Peter Graham, OBE; 3 Somers Crescent, London W2 2PN

GRAHAM, Peter Louis; s of David Barnett Graham, and Hannah, *née* Hyams; *b* 15 June 1946; *Educ* St Paul's, Magdalene Coll Cambridge (exhibitioner, scholar, BA, LLB, MA); *m* 25 June 1981, Susan Jane, da of Dr Benjamin Gottlieb; 1 s (Edward James b 21 June 1982); *Career* Norton Rose Botterell & Roche (now Norton Rose): articled clerk 1969-71, asst slr 1971-76, ptnr 1977-; on secondment to Cleary Gottlieb Steen & Hamilton Paris 1973-74; assoc memb Inst of Taxation 1971, memb Co Law Ctee Law Soc 1980-; Freeman City of London Slrs Co 1977; memb: Law Soc 1971, Int Bar Assoc 1985; *Recreations* theatre, chess, classical music; *Style—* Peter Graham, Esq; Norton Rose, Kempson House, Camomile St, London EC3A 7AN (☎ 071 283 2434, fax 071 588 1181)

GRAHAM, Maj-Gen Peter Walter; CBE (1981, OBE 1978, MBE 1972); s of Dr Walter Graham (d 1985), of London, and Suzanne, *née* Simon (d 1976); *b* 14 March 1937; *Educ* Fyvie Sch Aberdeenshire, Hall Sch Hampstead, St Pauls Sch London, RMA Sandhurst; *m* 23 March 1963, Alison Mary, da of David Begg Morren, TD, of Huntly, Aberdeenshire; 3 s (James b 1964, Roderick b 1967, Douglas b 1970); *Career* cmmnd The Gordon Highlanders 1956; regtl appts 1957-62: Dover, BAOR, Scot, Kenya; Staff Capt HQ Highland Bde Perth 1962, Adj 1 Gordons 1963-66 Kenya, Scotland, Borneo (despatches), Staff Capt HQ 1 Br Corps BAOR 1966-68, Staff Coll Aust 1968, Co Cdr 1 Gordons BAOR 1969, BM 39 Inf Bde Ulster 1970-72; 2 i/c 1 Gordons 1972-74, Scot, Ulster, Singapore; MA to Adj Gen MOD 1974-76; CO 1 Gordons 1976-78, Scot, Ulster, Chester; COS HQ 3 Armd Div BAOR 1978-82, Cdr UDR (despatches) 1982-84, Nat Def Coll Canada 1984, dep mil sec B MOD 1985-87, Col The Gordon Highlanders 1986, GOC Eastern Dist 1987-89, Cmdt RMA Sandhurst 1989-; memb: The Queen's Bodyguard for Scot Royal Co of Archers 1985, RUSI; *Books* Gordon Highlanders Pipe Music Collection (with Pipe Major B McRae, vol 1 1983, vol 2 1985); *Recreations* shooting, fishing, hill walking, gardening under wife's supervision, pipe music; *Clubs* Caledonian; *Style—* Maj-Gen Peter Graham, CBE; c/o National Westminster Bank, Cropthorne Court, Maida Vale, London W9 1TA

GRAHAM, Sir Ralph Stuart; 14 Bt (E 1629); er s of Sir Ralph Wolfe Graham, 13 Bt (d 1988), and his 2 w, Geraldine, *née* Velour; *b* 5 Nov 1950; *Educ* Hofstra Univ; *m* 1, 1972, Roxanne (d 1978), da of Mrs Lovette Gurzan, of Elmont, Long Island, New York; m 2, 1979, Deena Louise, da of William Robert Vandergrift, of 2903 Nemesis, Waukegan, Illinois; 1 child; *Career* self-employed (maintenance company); singer/songwriter (recorded three gospel albums, including Star of the Show, One by One); *Recreations* bible fellowships, performing music; *Style—* Sir Ralph Graham, Bt; 904 Earps Court, Nashville, Tennessee 37221, USA

GRAHAM, Col Richard Harold; MBE (1979); s of Harold Ernest Graham (d 1970), and Vera Irene Greta, *née* Wenman; *b* 20 Jan 1941; *Educ* Gillingham Sch, Jesus Coll Cambridge (MA, MPhil), Staff Coll Camberley, Nat Defence Coll Latimer; *m* 28 Dec 1963, Ruby Primula Cécile, da of Walter Edwin Down, of Guernsey; 1 s (Justin Èmile b 15 Oct 1969), 1 da (Sarah Louise b 10 Aug 1965); *Career* cmmnd Middlesex Regt 1964, served in Gibraltar, Lybia, Br Guiana, NI, BAOR 1964-83, DAA and QMG 8 Inf Bde 1974-78; (despatches) 1977; CO 3 Bn The Queen's Regt 1981-83, Cdr battle gp trainer 1984-86, COS 1 Armed Div 1986-88, Cmdt Jr Div The Staff Coll 1989-, Dep Col The Queen's Regt 1989-; Croix D'Honneur avec Rosette De L'ordre De La Maison D'Orange - Netherlands 1983; *Recreations* cricket, golf, music; *Clubs* Royal Guernsey Golf; *Style—* Col Richard Graham, MBE; Junior Division, The Staff College, School of Infantry, Warminster, Wiltshire BA12 0DJ (☎ 0985 214000 ext 2479)

GRAHAM, Robert Martin; s of Francis P Graham (d 1979), of Dublin, and Margaret, *née* Broderick; *b* 20 Sept 1930; *Educ* CBS Synge St Dublin; *m* 8 Sept 1959, Eileen, da of Francis Hoey (d 1981); 2 s (Peter b 2 July 1960, James b 11 July 1962), 2 da (Susan b 14 May 1965, Catherine b 28 Jan 1972); *Career* chief exec BUPA 1984- (dep chief exec 1982-84); pres Int Fedn of Voluntary Health Serv Funds 1988-90, vice pres Int Assoc of Mutualities (AIM); *Clubs* RAC, London Irish Rugby Football; *Style—* Robert Graham, Esq; Provident House, Essex St, London WC2R 3AX (☎ 071 353 5212)

GRAHAM, Ronald Cairns; s of Thomas Graham (d 1967), of Airdrie, Lanarkshire, and Helen Waugh, *née* Cairns (d 1989); *b* 8 Oct 1931; *Educ* Airdrie Acad, Univ of Glasgow (MB, ChB), Univ of Edinburgh (Dip Social Med); *m* 9 Oct 1959, Christine Fraser, da of James Cunningham Osborne (d 1982), of Airdrie; 2 s (Colin Thomas b 1961, Alistair James b 1971), 1 da (Rhona Osborne Walker b 1963); *Career* Nat Serv Capt RAMC 1957-59; dep med supt Royal Infirmary of Edinburgh 1962-65, asst sr med offr S Eastern Regnl Hosp Bd 1965-69, dep MO rising to sr MO Eastern Regnl Hosp Bd 1969-73, gen mangr Tayside Health Bd 1985- (chief med offr 1973-85); FFPHM 1973, FRCP (Edinburgh) 1983; *Recreations* golf, fishing; *Style—* Dr Ronald Graham; 34 Dalgleish Rd, Dundee DD4 7JT (☎ 0382 455426); Tayside Health Board, PO Box 75, Vernonholme, Riverside Drive, Dundee DD1 9NL (☎ 0382 645151, fax 0382 69734)

GRAHAM, (George) Ronald Gibson; CBE (1986); s of Dr James Gibson Graham, (d 1987) and Elizabeth, *née* Waddell (d 1987); *b* 15 Oct 1939; *Educ* Glasgow Acad, Loretto, Oriel Coll Oxford (MA), Univ of Glasgow (LLB); *m* 23 July 1965, Mirren Elizabeth, da of (James) Forrest Carnegie, of 35 Lauder Road, Edinburgh; 3 s (Peter Carnegie Gibson b 4 Jan 1967, Alan Ronald b 18 Nov 1969, Douglas James Gibson b 28 May 1974); *Career* ptnr Maclay Murray & Spens Solicitors Glasgow Edinburgh and London 1968-, coordinator of Dip in Legal Practice Univ of Glasgow 1979-83, dir Scottish Widows' Fund and Life Assurance Society 1984; clerk to Gen Cncl Univ of Glasgow 1990-; Law Soc of Scotland: memb 1965-, memb Cncl 1977-89, pres 1984-85; *Books* Stair Memorial Encyclopaedia of the Laws of Scotland (contrib); *Recreations* fishing, golfing, swimming; *Clubs* Wester Baths (Glasgow); *Style—* Ronald G Graham, Esq, CBE; 44 Kingsborough Gardens, Glasgow G12 9NL (☎ 041 334 2730); 151 St Vincent St, Glasgow G2 5NJ (☎ 041 248 5011, fax 041 248 5819)

GRAHAM, Sandra Denise (Mrs John Bridger); da of James Graham, of Pinxton, Notts, and Joyce N Elizabeth, *née* Botham; *b* 28 Sept 1957; *Educ* Fylde Lodge HS Stockport Cheshire, Manchester Poly (BA); *m* 13 Sept 1986, John Christopher Bridger, s of Lt Henry Chris Bridger, of Bournemouth, Dorset; 1 da (Sarah b 4 Nov 1990); *Career* admitted slr 1984; ptnr Penningtons Bournemouth, specialist in liquor licensing law; nat rep Bournemouth and Dist Young Slrs Gp; memb: Law Soc Nat Ctee, Gen Ctee Bournemouth and dist Law Soc; memb Law Soc; *Recreations* squash, cake decorating (memb Br Sugarcraft Guild), sailing, travel; *Clubs* South Dorset Squash; *Style*— Ms Sandra Graham; 70 Richmond Hill, Bournemouth, Dorset BH2 6JA (☎ 0202 551991, fax 0202 27742, telex 41223 EURLAW G, car 0831 168951); Clement House, 99 Aldwych, London WC2B 4JL (☎ 01 242 4422, fax 01 430 2210, telex 22509)

GRAHAM, Stuart Twentyman; CBE (1981), DFC (1943); s of Twentyman Graham (d 1923); *b* 26 Aug 1921; *Educ* Kilburn GS; *m* 1948, Betty June, *née* Cox; 1 s (Neil); *Career* Sqdn Ldr RAF 1940-46; Midland Bank Ltd 1938-1982: joined 1938, jt gen mangr 1966-70, asst chief gen mangr 1970-74, chief gen mangr 1974-81, dir 1974-85, gp chief exec 1981-82; dir: Allied-Lyons plc 1981-, Sheffield Forgemasters Holdings plc 1983-85, Aitken Hume International plc 1985-, Efamol Holdings plc 1985-; chm: Northern Bank Ltd (head office Belfast) 1982-85, Int Commodities Clearing House Ltd 1982-86; *Recreations* music, reading, photography; *Clubs* RAF; *Style*— Stuart Graham, Esq, CBE, DFC

GRAHAM, (Arthur) William; JP (1979); s of William Douglas Graham (d 1970), and Eleanor Mary Scott, *née* Searle; *b* 18 Nov 1949; *Educ* Monkton Coll, Coll Estate Mgmnt London; *m* 20 June 1981, Elizabeth Hannah, da of Joshua Griffiths, of Gwent; 1 s (William James b 1982), 2 da (Sarah Jane Mary b 1984, Hannah Victoria b 1987); *Career* cncllr Gwent 1985, elected to Newport BC 1988; FRICS 1980; *Recreations* breeder of pedigree suffolk sheep; *Clubs* IOD; *Style*— William Graham, Esq, JP; The Volland, Lower Machen, Newport, Gwent NP1 8UY (☎ 440419, 254825); 114 Commercial St, Newport, Gwent NP9 1LW

GRAHAM, William Reginald; 2 s of Sir Richard Bellingham Graham, 10 Bt, OBE (d 1982); bro and h of Sir James Graham, 11 Bt, *qv*; *b* 7 July 1942; *Educ* privately; *Style*— William Graham, Esq; Rock House, Botton Danby, Whitby, North Yorkshire

GRAHAM, Winston Mawdsley; OBE (1983); s of Albert Henry Graham, and Anne, *née* Mawdsley; *b* 30 June 1912; *m* 1939, Jean Mary, da of Cdr Samuel Arthur Williamson, RN; 1 s (Andrew), 1 da (Rosamund); *Career* published novelist since age of 23, books translated into 17 languages, six novels made into feature films incl Marnie (directed by Alfred Hitchcock); TV films: The Sleeping Partner 1967, The Forgotten Story (six instalments) 1983, The Poldark novels (twenty-nine instalments) 1975-77; other works incl: Angell, Pearl and Little God, The Walking Stick, The Grove of Eagles, The Spanish Armadas, Poldark's Cornwall, The Green Flash, The Tumbled House, The Twisted Sword; FRSL; *Clubs* Savile, Beefsteak; *Style*— Winston Graham, Esq, OBE; Abbotswood House, Buxted, Sussex TN22 4PB

GRAHAM-BOWMAN, Judyth Jacqueline; JP; da of Ernest Vivian Mason (d 1954), of Stockton-on-Tees, and Grace Helen, *née* White, JP; *b* 14 Sept 1939; *Educ* Harrogate Coll; *m* 4 April 1964, Anthony Robert (d 1988), s of Lt Col Gerald Wilberforce Graham-Bowman, OBE, MC, DL (d 1968), of Carlisle; 1 da (Vanessa Elizabeth b 29 May 1965); *Career* fndr memb North Tees Community Health Cncl 1974-81, memb Cleveland FPC 1982-85, nat chm Nat Assoc for Welfare of Children in Hosp 1987-89 (memb exec ctee 1985-89), vice chm North Tees DHA 1989 (memb 1981), memb Bd of Mgmnt Children's Fndn (Newcastle upon Tyne) 1990); *Recreations* opera-going, collecting antique maps, needlepoint, reading; *Style*— Mrs A R Graham-Bowman, JP; 2 Malvern Road, Oxbridge Lane, Stockton-on-Tees, Cleveland TS18 4AU (☎ 0642 674776)

GRAHAM-BROWN, Dr Robin Alan Charles; s of Maj Lewis Hilary Graham-Brown, of Oast Cottage, Bells Farm Lane, Kent, and Elizabeth Constance, *née* Blaxland; *b* 14 Aug 1949; *Educ* Sevenoaks Sch, Royal Free Hosp Sch of Med (BSc, MB BS); *m* 13 Sept 1975, Dr Margaret Marie Rose Anne Graham-Brown, da of Dr Robert Graham, of 19 Grassholme Dr, Loughborough; 3 s (James Robert Philip b 1980, Matthew Paul Mark b 1982, John Joseph Dominic b 1987); *Career* conslt dermatologist 1982-; Leicester Royal Infirmary, Leicester Gen Hosp, Market Harborough Hosp, BUPA Hosp Leicester; clinical teacher Univ of Leicester Sch of Med 1982-; editorial rep section of dermatology RSM, local sec Br Assoc Dermatologists 1987-88; MRCP 1974, FRCP 1990; *Books* Skin Disorders in the Elderly (1988); *Recreations* horseriding, cricket, opera; *Clubs* MCC, Dowling; *Style*— Dr Robin Graham-Brown; Killiecrankie, 3 Brickwood Place, Burton on the Wolds, Nr Loughborough, Leicestershire LE12 5AW (☎ 0509 880558); Dept of Dermatology Leicester Royal Infirmary Leicester LE1 5WW (☎ 0533 541414)

GRAHAM BRYCE, Dame Isabel; *née* Lorrain-Smith; DBE (1968); da of late Prof J Lorrain-Smith, FRS; *b* 30 April 1902; *Educ* St Leonards Sch, St Andrew's Univ of Edinburgh (MA); *m* 1934, Alexander Graham Bryce (d 1968); 2 s; *Career* investigator Industl Fatigue Res Bd 1926-27, HM inspector of factories 1928-34, organizer WRVS Manchester 1938-39, dir of orgn Ontario div Canadian WRVS 1941-42, tech advsr American WRVS 1942-43, res fell Fatigue Lab Harvard Univ 1943-44; Nat Cncl of Women: chm Manchester Branch 1947-50, vice chm Educn Ctee 1950-51; vice pres Princess Christian Coll Manchester, JP and memb Juvenile Ct Panel Manchester City 1949-55, vice chm Assoc of HMC's 1953-55; memb: Nurses and Midwives Whitley Cncl 1954-60, Gen Nursing Cncl 1956-61, public health inspr Educn Bd 1958-64, ITA 1960-65, ATV Network Ltd 1968-72; chm: Oxford Regnl Hosp Bd 1963-72, Nat Staff Ctee and Nat Nursing Staff Ctee of NHS 1967-75; memb Bd: Br Tport Hotels 1962-78, Oxford Poly 1969-70; pres Goring & Dist Day Centre for the Elderly, life memb Br Fedn Univ Women, hon memb Oxford Br Zouta Int; memb: Edinburgh Univ Graduates Assoc, Oxford Br Nat Cncl of Women; pres League of Friends Radcliffe Infirmary Oxford, patron Oxford Branch Motor Neurone Disease Assoc; *Style*— Dame Isabel Graham Bryce, DBE; 1 Quinton House, 98 Woodstock Rd, Oxford OX2 7HE (☎ 0865 513168)

GRAHAM-BRYCE, Dr Ian James; s of late Alexander Graham-Bryce, and Dame Isabel Graham-Bryce; *b* 20 March 1937; *Educ* William Hulmes' GS, Univ of Oxford (BA, MA, BSc, DPhil); *m* 1959, Anne Elisabeth; 1 s , 3 da; *Career* res asst Univ of Oxford 1958-61, lectr Dept of Biochemistry and Soil Science Univ Coll of N Wales 1961-64, sr scientific offr Rothamsted Experimental Station 1964-70, sr res offr ICI Plant Protection Div Jealott's Hill Res Station Bracknell 1970-72, special lectr Pesticide Chemistry Imperial Coll of Sci and Technol Univ of London 1970-72, dep dir Rothamsted Experimental Station 1975-79 (head Dept Insecticides and Fungicides 1972-79), visiting prof Imperial Coll of Sci and Tecnol Univ of London 1976-79, hon lectr Univ of Strathclyde 1977-80, dir East Mailing Res station 1979-85, conslt dir Cwlth Bureau of Horticulture and Plantation Crops, hon conslt Zoecon Corp Calif; pres Soc of Chemical Indust 1982-84, memb Br Nat Ctee for Chemistry 1982-84; govr: Long Ashton Res Station 1979-85, Imperial Coll of Sci Technol Univ of London 1985; chm Agrochemical Planning Gp Int Orgn for Chem Scis in Devpt 1985-87, tstee Devpt and Endowment Fund Br Soc for Horticultural Res 1987-, pres Assoc of Applied Biologists 1988-89, chm Working Gp on Enviromental Auditing, Enviromental Cmmn Int CofC 1988-, memb Global Warming Gp Int Petroleum Indust Enviromental Conservation Assoc 1988-, vice chm Environmental Res Working Gp Industl Res and Devpt Advsy Ctee to the Euro Communities 1988-; memb: Scientific Ctee Euro Chem Indust Ecology and Toxicology Centre 1988-, Cncl UK Natural Enviroment Res Cncl 1989-, Tech Assoc Coal Indust Advsy Bd Global Warming Ctee 1989-; Freeman City of London 1981, Liveryman Worshipful Co of Fruiterers 1981; *Books* Physical Principles of Pesticide Behaviour; *Recreations* music (especially opera), squash racquets, fly-fishing, windsurfing; *Clubs* Athenaeum; *Style*— Ian Graham-Bryce, Esq; Environmental Affairs Division, Shell International Petroleum Mastschappij B V, Postbus 162, 2501 AN Den Haag, Netherlands

GRAHAM-CAMPBELL, Hon Mrs (Sarah Grenville); *née* Peyton; o da of Baron Peyton of Yeovil, PC (Life Peer); *b* 4 Sept 1948; *m* 1971, Dugald Graham-Campbell; issue; *Style*— The Hon Mrs Graham-Campbell; 14 Ewald Rd, London SW6

GRAHAM-CLARKE, Philip Audley; s of Gerald Graham-Clarke (d 1961); *b* 6 Oct 1924; *Educ* Eton, Univ of Edinburgh; *m* 1960 (m dis 1974), Nora Margaret, *née* Keep; 1 da (Emma Marjorie b 1962); *Career* Maj RA (India, BAOR, W Africa, USA); CA 1966; DL Monmouthshire 1963-73; co cmmr for Scouts Monmouthshire 1962-69; *Style*— Philip Graham-Clarke, Esq; Hortons, The Street, Broughton Gifford, Melksham, Wiltshire (☎ 0225 782586); Norman & Pike, 11 Edward St, Westbury, Wilts (☎ 0373 822290)

GRAHAM-DIXON, Anthony Philip; QC (1973); Leslie Charles Graham-Dixon, QC (d 1986), and Dorothy, *née* Rivett (d 1979); *b* 5 Nov 1929; *Educ* Westminster, ChCh Oxford (MA); *m* 15 Dec 1956, Margaret Suzanne, da of Edgar Hurmon Villar (d 1953); 1 s (Andrew b 1960), 1 da (Elizabeth b 1965); *Career* Mid Special Branch RN 1953-55, Lt Special Branch RNVR 1956; called to the Bar Inner Temple 1956; bencher 1982, memb Advsy Bd Competition Law in Western Europe and the USA 1976-87; chm London Concertino Ltd 1982-90; memb Cncl Charing Cross Hosp Med Sch 1976-83, dep chm Public Health Laboratory Serv 1988- (bd memb 1987-), tstee Soc for Promotion of New Music 1988-, govr Bedales Sch 1988-; Liveryman Worshipful Co of Goldsmiths; *Recreations* music, gardening, tennis, walking, trees; *Style*— Anthony Graham-Dixon, Esq, QC; 31 Hereford Sq, London SW7 4NB (☎ 071 370 1902), Masketts Manor, Nutley, East Sussex (☎ 082 571 2719)

GRAHAM-DIXON, Francis; s of Michael Stuart Graham-Dixon, of Asthall, Oxfordshire, and Anita, *née* Falkenstein; *b* 21 March 1955; *Educ* Stowe; *m* 19 Dec 1980, Emma Charlotte Louise, *née* Kentish; 2 s (Freddie Francis b 9 March 1981, Charlie Isaac b 26 Oct 1984), 1 da (Celia Rosie b 6 May 1989); *Career* Sotheby's London 1973-78, Record Merchandisers 1978-79, Warner Brothers 1979-80, Heiman Music 1980-81, BBC 1982-87, opened own gallery 1987; govr Winchester Sch of Art 1989-; *Recreations* our children, looking at art, music, sport; *Clubs* MCC, Chelsea Football; *Style*— Francis Graham-Dixon, Esq; Francis Graham-Dixon Gallery, 17-18 Great Sutton St, London EC1V ODN (☎ 071 250 1962, fax 071 490 1069)

GRAHAM-HARRISON, Robert Montagu; s of Francis Laurence Theodore Graham-Harrison, CB, of London, and Carol Mary St John, *née* Stewart; *b* 16 Feb 1943; *Educ* Eton, Magdalen Coll Oxford (BA); *m* 30 April 1977, Kathleen Patricia, *née* Maher; 2 da (Emma b 24 July 1978, Laura b 15 Aug 1980); *Career* VSO India 1965, ODA (formerly Miny of Overseas Dept) 1967, World Bank Washington 1971-73, private sec Min of Overseas Devpt 1978, asst sec ODA 1979; head: Br Devpt Div Eastern Africa 1982, Eastern Asia Dept ODA 1986, UK alternate exec dir World Bank 1989; *Style*— Robert Graham-Harrison, Esq; Overseas Devpt Admin, Eland House, Stag Place, London SW1 (☎ 071 273 3000)

GRAHAM-JONES, Oliver; s of late Andrew Vaughan Jones, and Ethel Mabel, *née* Smith; *b* 17 Feb 1919; *Educ* King Edward's GS, RVC London Univ (FRCVS); *m* 23 March 1958, Gillian Margaret (d 1990), da of Basil Dent (d 1948); 2 s (Piers Dominic b 1965, Peregrine Jasper b 1967); *Career* WWII cmmnd RAVC served Italy 1943-44; vet surgn in private practice 1941-50, sr vet offr Zoological Soc of London 1960-66 (vet offr 1951-60), sr lectr RVC 1966-79 (asst lectr 1950-51); conslt vet offr: Nat Hosp for Nervous Diseases 1967-, London Hosp Med Sch 1967-, Royal Nat Orthopaedic Hosp; prof vet med and surgn to Sultan of Oman 1972-79; past pres: Br Small Animal Vet Assoc, Central Vet Soc; vet steward Nat Greyhound Racing Club; expert witness in many cases involving wild and domestic animals, licensed zoo inspector; awards: Livesey Medal RCVS, Victory Medal, Sir Arthur Keith Medal; Hon Col Legion of Frontiersmen Mounted Sqdn; FRCS; *Books* First Catch Your Tiger; author of numerous contributions to learned journals and magazines; *Recreations* horse driving, polo; *Clubs* RSM; *Style*— Oliver Graham-Jones, Esq; 45 Clayton Rd, Selsey, Chichester PO20 9DF (☎ 0243 602838, fax 0243 605596)

GRAHAM-MOON, Sir Peter Wilfred Giles; 5 Bt (UK 1855), of Portman Square, Middx; s of Sir Wilfred Graham Moon, 4 Bt (d 1954), by his 2 w, Doris, *née* Jobson (d 1953); *b* 24 Oct 1942; *Educ* Lancing; *m* 1967, Mrs Sarah Chater, da of Lt-Col Michael Smith, MC, of The Grange, Headley, Hants (gs of Sir Thomas Smith, 1 Bt, KCVO, Hon Serjeant-Surgeon to King Edward VII); 2 s; *Heir* s, Rupert Graham-Moon; *Career* chm Trans Continental Corpn Ltd, md Langbury Property Investments (Pty) Ltd SA; *Recreations* golf, shooting, horse racing; *Clubs* Royal Cork Yacht; *Style*— Sir Peter Graham-Moon, Bt; Battens Farm House, Lambourn Woodlands, Newbury, Berks RG16 7TN

GRAHAM-MOON, Rupert Francis Wilfred; s and h of Sir Peter Graham-Moon, 5 Bt; *b* 29 April 1968; *Educ* Marlborough; *Style*— Rupert Graham-Moon, Esq

GRAHAM OF EDMONTON, Baron (Life Peer UK 1983), of Edmonton in Greater London; (Thomas) Edward Graham; s of Thomas Edward Graham, of Newcastle-upon-Tyne; *b* 26 March 1925; *Educ* WEA Co-Op Coll, Open Univ (BA); *m* 1950, Margaret Golding, da of Frederick and Alice Golding, of Dagenham; 2 s (Hon Martin Nicholas b 1957, Hon Ian Stuart b 1959); *Career* various posts Co-operative Movement 1939-; memb and leader Enfield Cncl 1961-68, national sec Co-Op Party 1967-74, MP (Lab and Co-Op) Enfield Edmonton Feb 1974-83, PPS to Min of State Prices and Consumer Protection 1974-76, lord cmmr Treasury 1976-79; oppn front bench spokesman on: Environment 1981-, Sport, Defence, N Ireland; oppn whips office, oppn chief whipp 1990, sec All Pty Gp on Retail Trade; Hon MA 1989; pres Inst of Meat, FBIM. FRSA; *Style*— The Rt Hon the Lord Graham of Edmonton; 17a Queen Anne's Grove, Bush Hill Park, Enfield, Middx EN1 1BP (☎ 081 360 0985); House of Lords, London SW1 (☎ 071 219 3234)

GRAHAM-SMITH, Prof Sir Francis; s of Claud Henry Smith, of April Cottage, Fairlight, Sussex (d 1963), and Cicely Winifred Kingston (d 1946); *b* 25 April 1923; *Educ* Epsom Coll, Rossall Sch, Downing Coll Cambridge (MA, PhD); *m* Dorothy Elizabeth, da of Reginald Palmer, of Ecclestone House, Mildenhall, Suffolk (d 1949); 3 s, 1 da; *Career* dir Royal Greenwich Observatory 1976-81, pres Royal Astronomical Soc 1975-77, prof of radio astronomy Univ of Manchester 1964-74 and 1981-90, dir Nuffield Radio Astronomy Laboratories 1981-88, Astronomer Royal 1983-90; physical sec Royal Soc 1988-, pro vice chllr Univ of Manchester 1988-90; FRS; kt 1986; Hon fell Downing Coll Cambridge 1970; Royal Soc Royal medal 1987; *Recreations* sailing, badminton, gardening; *Style*— Sir Francis Graham-Smith, FRS; Old School House, Henbury, Macclesfield, Cheshire SK11 9PH (☎ 0625 612657); Nuffield Radio Astronomy Laboratories, Jodrell Bank, Macclesfield, Cheshire (☎ 0477 71321)

GRAHAM-VIVIAN, Henry Richard; TD (1955), JP (Cornwall 1970), DL (1982); s of (Richard) Preston Graham-Vivian, MVO, MC, sometime Norroy and Ulster King of Arms (d 1979, himself 2 s of Sir Richard Graham, 4 Bt, JP, DL, and Lady Mabel Duncombe, who in her turn was da of 1 Earl of Feversham), by his w Audrey, da of Henry Wyndham Vivian (which surname Preston assumed by Royal Licence 1929), himself n of 1 Baron Swansea and gn of 1 Baron Vivian; *b* 13 April 1923; *Educ* Eton, Ch Ch Oxford; *m* 1955, Rosemary, da of Lt-Col Giffard Loftus Tyringham (d 1976); 1 s, 1 da; *Career* Capt Coldstream Guards Normandy, territorial serv with Duke of Cornwall Light Infantry 1946-60, High Sheriff Cornwall 1965; *Recreations* shooting, fishing; *Clubs* Army and Navy; *Style*— Henry Richard Graham-Vivian, Esq, TD, JP, DL; Bosahan, Manaccan, nr Helston, Cornwall TR12 6JL (☎ 032 623 330)

GRAHAM-WOOD, David; TD (1952); s of Sir Edward Graham Wood, JP (d 1930), and Dorothy, MBE, *née* Harwood (d 1956); *b* 14 March 1919; *Educ* Oundle, Univ of London; *m* 15 April 1950, Joan Helen, da of Lt-Col John Stratton Storrar, MC (d 1946); 2 s (Malcolm b 1957, Maxwell b 1959), 2 da (Fiona b 1951, Gillian b 1954); *Career* TA 42 (E Lancs) Div, WWII serv UK, BEF (despatches), N Africa, Italy; chm and fndr Graham Wood Steel Gp plc 1952-78, dir and later chm Lilleshall Co plc 1979-87; serv on Surrey CC and later Finance Office for the Euro Constituency of Surrey; Freeman City of London, Liveryman Worshipful Co of Glaziers and Painters of Glass (Master 1977/78); OStJ 1986; *Recreations* sailing, stained glass; *Clubs* Royal Thames Yacht, City Livery, MCC; *Style*— David Graham-Wood, Esq, TD; Little Chartham, Shalford, Guildford, Surrey GU4 8AF (☎ 0483 62429)

GRAHAME-SMITH, Prof David Grahame; s of George Edward Smith (d 1968), Leicester, and Constance Alexandra Smith (d 1974); *b* 10 May 1933; *Educ* Wyggeston GS for Boys Leicester, St Mary's Hosp Med Sch Univ of London (MB BS, MRCS, LRCP, MRCP, PhD), Univ of Oxford (MA); *m* 25 May 1957, Kathryn Frances, da of Dr Francis Robin Beetham (d 1985), of Leeds, 2 s (Harvey Neil b 1958, Henry Peter b 1964); *Career* Capt RAMC 1957-60; house physician Paddington Gen Hosp 1956, house surgn Battle Hosp Reading 1956-57, H A M Thompson scholar Royal Coll of Physicians 1961-62 (FRCP), hon med registrar Professorial Medical Unit St Mary's Hosp Paddington 1961-66 (registrar and sr registrar in medicine 1960-61), Saltwell res scholar Royal Coll of Physicians 1962-65, Wellcome Tst res fell 1965-66, MRC travelling fell Dept of Endocrinology Vanderbilt Univ Nashville Tennessee 1966-67, sr lectr and reader in clinical pharmacology and therapeutics St Mary's Hosp Med Sch Univ of London 1967-71, hon consIt physician St Mary's Hosp Paddington 1967-71, Rhodes prof of clinical pharmacology Univ of Oxford 1971-, hon dir MRC Unit of Clinical Pharmacology Radcliffe Infirmary Oxford 1971, hon consIt physician in gen internal medicine and clinical pharmacology Oxford AHA 1971-, fell Corpus Christi Coll Oxford 1971-, hon dir Oxford Univ-Smith Kline Beecham Centre of Applied Neuropsychobiology 1989-; consIt clinical pharmacologist RAF 1985-, visiting prof in clinical pharmacology Peking Union Med Coll Beijing China 1985-, consIt in pharmacology to the Army 1986-, William Potter lectr Thomas Jefferson Univ of Philadelphia 1988; examiner in medicine UK and abroad 1974- (incl principle examiner final BM BS Examinations Univ of Oxford 1990-); memb Editorial Bd: Archives Internationale de Pharmacodynamic et de Therapie (Belgium), Pharmacopsychiatria (Berlin), Br Journal of Clinical Pharmacology (chm 1987-), Pharmacology and Therapeutics, Psychological Medicine; memb: Br Nat Pharmacological Ctee 1974-79, Clinical Trials and Toxicity Sub Ctee of Ctee on Safety of Medicines 1974-86 (memb Main Ctee 1975-86), Clinical Medicine Faculty Bd 1976-80; vice chm Clinical Medicine Faculty Bd Univ of Oxford 1978-80; memb: Res Ctee Mental Health Res Fund 1978-80, Ctee Clinical Pharmacology Section Br Pharmacological Soc 1978-81, Scientific Ctee Migraine Tst 1980-86; tstee Sheik Rashid Diabetes Tst Oxford 1986; cncllr: Collegium Internationale Neuro-Psychopharmacologium 1988-, Clinical Section International Union of Pharmacology 1988-; pres Oxford Div BMA 1989-90; chm UK Advsy Ctee on Misuse of Drugs 1988-; memb: Br Pharmacological Soc, Biochemical Soc (memb Neurochemical Gp Sub Ctee 1971-74), Med Res Soc, Assoc of Physicians of GB and Ireland, Int Soc of Neurochemistry, Brain Res Assoc, Br Assoc of Psychopharmacology; assoc memb Royal Coll of Psychiatrists; *Books* Carcinoid Syndrome (1972), Oxford Textbook of Clinical Pharmacology and Drug Therapy (with JK Aronson, 1984); *Recreations* piano, horse riding; *Style*— Prof David Grahame-Smith; MRC Unit of Clinical Pharmacology, Radcliffe Infirmary, Woodstock Rd, Oxford OX2 6HE (☎ 0865 241091, fax 0865 791712)

GRAINGER, (Leonard) Cherry; s of George Grainger (d 1936), and Lucy, *née* Cherry (d 1974); *b* 12 March 1919; *Educ* Westminster Catering Coll (Dip), Ecole Des Hoteliers Zurich; *m* 17 June 1944, (Yvonne) Claudia Marshall, da of Victor Stanley Chambers, OBE (d 1954); 1 s (Cdr RN Robert Marshall b 1955), 2 da (Lynne b 1945, Jacki b 1947); *Career* RN: Fleet Air Arm 1940-42, Paymaster 1942-46; fndr and chm Graison (Caterers) Ltd 1946-; Chevalier Du Tastevin 1964; chm: London Ctee Catering Trades Benevolent Assoc, tstees Reunion Des Gastronomes (former pres); memb: Ctee Br Hotels & Restaurants Assoc, Mgmnt Ctee City & Guilds; govr Westminster Coll 1981-; Freeman City of London 1964, Liveryman Worshipful Co of Distillers 1964-, Master Worshipful Co of Cooks 1988-89; FCA, FHCIMA, FRSH; *Recreations* swimming, travel; *Clubs* City Livery, RAC; *Style*— Cherry Grainger, Esq; 102 Hayes Way, Beckenham, Kent BR3 2RS (☎ 081 650 4727, 081 650 4727); Casa 22, Puebla Blanca, Torreblanca, Malaga, Spain

GRAINGER, Frederick George Edward (Stewart); s of Frederick Thomas Grainger (d 1978), of Ashcott, Somerset, and Alice Mary, *née* Syrett; *b* 23 June 1936; *Educ* Dr Mogan's Sch Bridgwater, RMA Sandhurst, Medway Coll of Technol (Dip Civil Engrg), Open Univ (BA), RMCS Shrivenham, RAF Staff Coll, NDC; *m* 31 Oct 1959, Shirley Dorothy, da of Harold Pole (d 1965), of Bridgwater, Somerset; 2 s (Ian Anthony b 10 April 1968, Peter Edward b 8 Feb 1971), 1 da (Karen Shirley b 1 Aug 1965); *Career* Paratrooper 1959-62, army pilot 1965-68, jr exec estab Directorate of Army Air Corps 1970-72, offr i/c 60 Field Sqdn 1972-73, CO 72 Engr Regt (Vol) 1976-78, mil advsr to Chief Scientist of the Army 1979-80, sr mil advsr to Dir RAE Farnborough 1983, CRE 1 Armd Div 1983-86, Col Doctrine and Weapons RE 1986-89; barrier systems mangr Royal Ordnance plc; chm Army Canoe Union 1975-83 (sec 1970-72); FBIM 1980, AMRAeS 1983; *Recreations* canoeing, skiing; *Clubs* Civil Service, Royal Aeronautical Soc; *Style*— Stewart Grainger, Esq; 24 Studley Crescent, New Barn, Longfield, Kent DA3 7JL; Royal Ordnance plc, Blackburn, Lancashire BB1 2LE (☎ 0254 55131 ext 4996)

GRAINGER, Margaret Ethel; OBE (1979); da of Walter James Grainger (d 1980), and Mabel Ethel, *née* Peacock (d 1986); *b* 28 Oct 1922; *Educ* Ealing Co Sch for Girls; *Career* meteorologist WAAF 1942-46, section offr 1944-46, flying offr WRAF VR 1949-54; HM Civil Serv: sr princ Dept of Social Security 1978-80, asst sec, sec and controller of the exec office to the Occupational Pensions Bd 1980-82; emeritus fell pensions Mgmnt Inst, fndr chm The Occupational Pensions Advsy Serv 1982-, public speaker, TV and radio appearances, writer on occupational pensions; vice chm Civil Serv Sports Cncl, life vice pres of Dept of Social Security Recreational Assoc; memb: Nat Tst, RSPB, Eng Heritage; *Recreations* golf, conservation; *Clubs* RAF; *Style*— Miss Margaret Grainger, OBE; 7 Chester Gardens, Argyle Road, Ealing, London W13 8EP (☎ 081 997 6971); Occupational Pensions Advisory Service, 11, Belgrave Rd, London SW1V 1RB (☎ 071 233 8080)

GRAMMENOS, Prof Costas Theophilos; s of Theophilos C Grammenos, and Iro, *née* Spanakos; *b* 23 Feb 1944; *Educ* State School in Athens, Pantion Univ (BA), Univ of Wales (Msc); *m* 20 Nov 1972, Anna, da of Constantinos A Papadimitriou; 1 s (Theophilos Grammenos b 6 April 1975); *Career* Nat Serv Greek Navy 1968-70; Nat Bank of Greece 1962-75 (shipping fin expert, head office 1973-74); City Univ Business Sch London: visiting prof 1982-86, dir Int Centre for Shipping, Trade and Finance 1984-, prof of shipping, trade and finance 1986-; author of various studies in int banking and shipping investmt and finance; *Books* Bank Finance for Ship Purchase (1979); *Recreations* music, theatre, walking; *Clubs* Travellers; *Style*— Prof Costas T Grammenos; 139 Defoe House, Barbican, London EC2; City University Business School, Frobisher Crescent, Barbican Centre, London EC2Y 8HB (☎ 071 920 0111, telex 263896, fax 071 588 2756)

GRANARD, 9 Earl of (I 1684); Sir Arthur Patrick Hastings Forbes; 10 Bt (S 1628), AFC (1941); also Viscount Granard, Baron Clanehugh (both I 1675) and Baron Granard (UK 1806, title in House of Lords); s of 8 Earl of Granard (d 1948, eighth in descent from 1 Earl, who was himself ggs of Hon Patrick Forbes, 3 s of 2 Lord Forbes); *b* 10 April 1915; *Educ* Eton, Trinity Coll Cambridge (BA 1937); *m* 1949, Marie Madeleine Eugène, yst da of late Jean Maurel, of Millau, Aveyron, and formerly w of late Prince Humbert de Faucigny Lucinge; 2 da (Lady Moira Beatrice b 1951, Lady Georgina Anne b 1952); *Heir* nephew, Peter A H Forbes, *qv*; *Career* Air Cdre RAFVR, served WW II (despatches, Cdr Legion of Honour, offr of American Legion of Merit, 4 Class Order of George I of Greece with crossed swords, French Croix de Guerre, Polish Cross of Valour); *Clubs* White's, Pratt's, Kildare Street, RYS, Jockey (France), Royal St George Yacht; *Style*— The Rt Hon the Earl of Granard, AFC; Castle Forbes, Newtown Forbes, Co Longford, Republic of Ireland ; 11 Rue Louis de Savoie, Morges, Switzerland

GRANBY, Marquess of; David Charles Robert Manners; s & h of 10 Duke of Rutland, CBE, JP, DL, by his 2 w, Frances; *b* 8 May 1959; *Educ* Wellesley House Broadstairs Kent, Stanbridge Earls; *Career* dir: Belvoir Management Ltd, Belvoir Arms and Armour; agent Elderkins (gunsmiths) Spalding Lincs; Freeman City of London, Liveryman Worshipful Co of Gunsmiths; *Recreations* shooting, fishing; *Clubs* Turf, Annabel's; *Style*— Marquess of Granby; The Old Saddlery, Belvoir, Grantham, Lincs

GRANBY, Nicholas Charles; s of Paul Granby (d 1982), of London, and Lydia Barbara, *née* Goulding; *b* 19 Nov 1945; *Educ* Westminster Sch, London Sch of Film Technique (Dip); *m* Pauline Sylvia, da of Arthur Hapgood Rice (d 1975); 1 da (Sarah b 1967); *Career* Film & TV dir, writer and prodr; films incl: Closed Circuit (1987, prize winner Barcelona Film Festival); documentaries incl: The Queen in Arabia 1979, To Win at all Costs - The Story of the America's Cup 1983-84 (prize-winner Houston Int Film Festival and UK Video Awards), The Queen in Jordan 1984; stage musical Mesmer (1988); dir: Nicholas Granby Prodns Ltd, Orbit TV and Film Ltd, Para-Shoot Enterprises Ltd; *Clubs* BAFTA; *Style*— Nicholas C Granby, Esq; c/o Valerie Hoskins, Eagle House, 109 Jermyn St, London SW1Y 6HB (☎ 071 839 2121)

GRANDY, Marshal of the RAF Sir John; GCB (1967, KCB 1964, CB 1956), GCVO (1988), KBE (1961), DSO (1945); s of Francis Grandy (d 1932), and Nellie, *née* Lines (d 1948); *b* 8 Feb 1913; *Educ* Univ Coll Sch; *m* 1937, Cecile Rankin, yr da of Sir Robert Rankin, first and last Bt (d 1960); 2 s; *Career* RAF 1931, Adj and Flying Instr London Univ Air Sqdn 1937-39, cmd 249 Sqdn Battle of Britain, Wing Cdr Flying RAF Coltishall 1941, cmd RAF Duxford 1942, cmd HQ 210 Gp No 73 Operational Training Unit and Fighter Conversion Unit Abu Sueir 1943, cmd 341 Wing SE Asia 1944-45, Air Cdre 1956, AVM 1958, Cdr 2 TAF and C-in-C RAF Germany 1961-63, Air Marshal 1962, AOC-in-C Bomber Cmd 1963-65, C-in-C Br Forces Far East and UK Mil Advsr SEATO 1965-67, Air Chief Marshal 1965, Chief of Air Staff 1967-71, Marshal of RAF 1971, govr and C-in-C Gibraltar 1973-78, constable and govr Windsor Castle 1978-88; chm tstee Imperial War Museum 1978-89, dep chm Cncl RAF Benevolent Fund, RAF tstee Burma Star Assoc, tstee Shuttleworth Remembrance Trust and chm Aerodrome Ctee 1978-88, past sr pres Offrs Assoc, vice pres Offrs Pension Soc, pres Disablement in City; tstee: St Clement Danes RAF Church, Prince Philip Trust Fund Royal Borough of Windsor and Maidenhead; vice pres: Nat Assoc of Boys Clubs, RNLI; dir Brixton Estate 1971-73 and 1978-83; memb Ctee Royal Humane Soc, patron Polish Air Force Assoc in GB; pres Air League 1984-87; Freeman City of London, Hon Liveryman Haberdashers Co; KStJ; *Clubs* White's, Pratt's, Royal Yacht Sqdn, RAF; *Style*— Marshal of the RAF Sir John Grandy, GCB, GCVO, KBE, DSO; c/o White's, St James's St, London SW1

GRANGE, Hugh; s of James Grange (d 1968), of Inver Green House, Inver, Larne, Co Antrim, and Ruth, *née* Gourley; *b* 26 Nov 1943; *Educ* Trinity Coll Dublin (MA, LLB); *m* 18 Sept 1971, Janet, da of Maj K C B Golding, TD, JP (d 1977), of Court Farm, Hedgerley, Bucks; *Career* called to the Bar NI 1970, practised NI 1970-73, called to the Bar Gray's Inn 1974, worked for HM Procurator Gen and Treasy Slr 1974-87, seconded Attorney Gen Chambers Law Offrs Dept 1987- (responsible for NI matters), protocol offr Law Offrs Dept 1988; memb: RSL, Compilation Team Burkes Irish Family Records (1975); *Recreations* history, literature, genealogy, walking, pictures, travel; *Style*— Hugh Grange, Esq; Lyndhurst, Jordans Lane, Jordans, Beaconsfield, Bucks HP9 2SW (☎ 02407 71055); The Attorney General's Chambers, Legal Secretariat to the Law Officers, 9 Buckingham Gate, London SW1

GRANGE, Kenneth Henry; CBE (1984); s of Harry Alfred Grange, and Hilda Gladys, *née* Long; *b* 17 July 1929; *Educ* Willesden Coll of Art; *m* 21 Sept 1984, Apryl Jacqueline, da of Deric Swift; *Career* tech illustrator RE 1947-48; architectural asst Bronek Katz & Vaughan 1949-50; designer: Gordon Bowyer 1950-52, Jack Howe & Ptnrs 1952-58; fndr Kenneth Grange Design London 1958, fndr ptnr Pentagram Design 1972-; winner of 10 Design Cncl awards and Duke of Edinburgh Prize for Elegant Design 1963; work represented in collections of: V & A, Design Museum London, State Museum Munich; one man shows: Kenneth Grange at the Boilerhouse V & A 1983, The Product Designs of Kenneth Grange of Pentagram XSITE Tokyo Japan 1989; master Faculty of Royal Design for Indust 1985-87 (memb 1969); Design Cncl: Cncl memb, industl design advsr 1971, memb Advsy Bd on Product Design; chm Br Design Export Gp, consIt design dir Wilkinson Sword Ltd, cncl memb and ct memb RSA; Hon Dr RCA 1985, Hon DUniv Herriot-Watt Univ 1986; FCSD 1965 (pres 1987-99); RDI 1969; *Books* Living by Design (jtly 1977); *Recreations* tennis, model making and building; *Clubs* RAC; *Style*— Kenneth Grange, Esq, CBE; Pentagram, 11 Needham Rd, London W11 2RP (☎ 071 229 3477, fax 071 727 9932, telex 9852000 PENTA G)

GRANGER, Dr John Douglas; s of Dr Edmund Douglas Granger (d 1961), of Dorset, and Kathryn Edith Emily Granger (d 1982); *b* 16 Aug 1926; *Educ* Stowe, Magdalen Coll Oxford, St Thomas's Hosp (BM, BCL, MRCCP, QRCOG); *m* 25 March 1961, Mary Sylvia, da of George William Back, of Kent; 2 s (William b 1965, Oliver b 1966), 2 da (Cressida b 1963, Annabel b 1969); *Career* gen med practitioner; MO, Flt Lt, RAF Malaya 1952-54; house surgn St Thomas's Hosp 1951; *Recreations* golf; *Clubs* Parkstone Golf; *Style*— Dr John D Granger; St Just, Sandbourne Rd, Bournemouth (☎ 0202 752550); Westbourne Medical Centre, Milburn Rd, Bournemouth (☎ 0202

752550)

GRANGER, Penelope Ruth; da of Eric Frank Hardy, of Stowmarket, Suffolk, and Ruth Susannah, *née* Turner; *b* 14 July 1947; *Educ* Norwich HS for Girls, Univ of Sheffield (BA), Homerton Coll Cambridge; *m* 11 July 1970, Richard John; 1 s (Timothy b 1976), 1 da (Caroline b 1973); *Career* memb Gen Synod of the C of E 1980, church cmmr 1983, GS Standing Ctee 1985-90, chm Ely Diocesan Synod House of Laity 1988; broadcaster, musician; *Recreations* walking; *Clubs* Royal Cwlth Soc; *Style*— Mrs Penny Granger; 88 Queen Edith's Way, Cambridge, CB1 4PW (☎ 0223 246392)

GRANT; *see*: Macpherson-Grant

GRANT, Prof Alan Archie; s of Archie William Grant (d 1968), and Elizabeth, *née* Hooper; *b* 17 March 1930; *Educ* Univ of Melbourne (BDSc, MDSc, DDSc), Univ of Manchester (MSc); *m* 28 Dec 1961, Annemarie, da of Paul Fisch (d 1963); 2 s (Matthew b 1963, Nicholas b 1965), 1 da (Helen b 1968); *Career* sr lectr in dental prosthetics Univ of Melbourne 1964-69 (lectr 1960-64), visiting assoc prof N Western Univ Chicago 1965-66; Univ of Manchester: prof of restorative dentistry 1970, pro vice chllr 1983-86, dean of Dental Sch 1988- (1977-81); Health Authy memberships: Rochdale 1973-77, Central Manchester 1982-88; memb: Standing Dental Advsy Ctee 1980-88, Gen Dental Cncl 1982-88, Inter Univ Cncl 1982, IADR 1953, BSSPD 1970, BSDR 1970; FRACDS; *Books* Training Manual for Dental Nurses (1965), Dental Assistants Manual (1969), The Selection and Properties of Materials for Dental practice (1973), An Introduction to Removable Denture Prosthetics (1984); *Recreations* Bonsai; *Style*— Prof Alan Grant; 297 Ashley Rd, Hale, Altrincham, Cheshire WA14 3NH (☎ 061 928 2738); University of Manchester, Oxford Rd, Manchester M13 9PL (☎ 061 275 6670, fax 061 275 6776)

GRANT, Alexander Marshall; CBE (1965); s of Alexander Gibb Grant, and Eleather May, *née* Marshall; *b* 22 Feb 1925; *Educ* Wellington Coll New Zealand; *Career* princ dancer Royal Ballet (now English National Ballet) 1946-76, dir Ballet for All 1971-76, artistic dir Nat Ballet of Canada 1976-83, princ dancer London Festival Ballet 1985-; judge at int ballet competitions: Moscow, Mississippi, Paris, Helsinki; created many ballet roles particularly for Sir Frederick Ashton, guest artist with Royal Ballet and Joffrey Ballet; *Recreations* gardening, cooking; *Style*— Alexander Grant, Esq, CBE; English National Ballet, Markova House, 39 Jay Mews, London SW7 2ES (☎ 071 581 1245)

GRANT, (Duncan) Alistair Antoine; s of Duncan George Grant (d 1968), of London, and Germaine Victoria, *née* Ramet Cousin (d 1970); *b* 3 June 1925; *Educ* Froebel E Sheen, Whitehall Glasgow, Birmingham Sch of Art, RCA; *m* Phyllis (d 1988), da of late William Fricker, of Guildford; 1 da (Emma b 12 Sept 1954); *Career* Aircrew RAF 1943-47; artist, painter and printmaker; art teacher 1951-53: St Martin's Sch of Art, Hammersmith Sch of Art, Sidcup Sch of Art, Colchester Sch of Art; RCA: tutor Printmaking Dept 1955-70, head Printing Dept 1970-84, head of Printmaking 1984-90; numerous exhibitions 1951- including: Redfern Gallery London 1952-87, Nat Arts Cncl of Southern Rhodesia 1957, Tel Aviv Museum Israel 1959, Zwemmer Gallery London 1961 and 1962, AAA Gallery NY 1967, Portland Museum Oregon 1971, Carcow Print Biennale (prize) 1972, Calgary Graphics Canada 1973, Limited Editions London 1979, Mullhouse Print Biennale 1982 and 1986, Le Cadre Gallery Hong Kong 1985; works in the collection of: V & A Museum, The Arts Cncl, The Tate Gallery, Dallas Museum USA, Museum of Modern Art NY USA, Vancouver Art Gallery Canada, Tel Aviv Museum Israel, Cairo Art Gallery Egypt, Nat Gallery of S Aust, Mobil Oil, BP Int, Unilever, Br Museum, Hunterian Museum Glasgow; memb RBA; *Clubs* Chelsea Arts; *Style*— Alistair Grant, Esq

GRANT, Allan Wallace; OBE (1974), MC (1941), TD (1947); s of Henry Grant (d 1929), and Rose Margaret, *née* Sheppard (d 1947); *b* 2 Feb 1911; *Educ* Dulwich, Univ of London (LLB); *m* 1, 31 Aug 1939, Kathleen Rachel, *née* Bamford; 1 da (Hilary b 1944); m 2, Mary, *née* Wyles; *Career* Sharpshooters: Trooper 23 London Armd Car Co 1929 (2 Lt 1938), Capt 3 Co London Yeo 1940 (Maj 1941, 2 i/c 1942); md Ecclesiastical Insurance Office Ltd 1952-75 (chm 1975-81, pres 1981-87); pres Sharpshooters Regtl Assoc 1969-, chm Clergy Orphan Corp 1967-80 (vice pres 1980-), govr St Mary's Sch Wantage 1967-81; memb: Worshipful Co of Goopers (Master 1984-85), Worshipful Co of Insurers (asst from fndn); Hon Dr Canon Law Lexington USA 1970; FCII 1970-71 (pres); *Recreations* golf; *Clubs* City Livery's, Richmond Golf (Capt 1974); *Style*— Allan Grant, Esq, OBE, MC, TD; 5 Queen's Court, Queen's Rd, Richmond, Surrey TW10 6LA (☎ 081 940 2626)

GRANT, Anne Caroline; da of Maj Gen Ferris Nelson Grant, of Ropley, Hants, and Patricia Anne Grant (d 1988); *b* 18 Feb 1951; *Educ* Hall Sch Wincanton, Exeter Tech Coll, Royal Naval Sch of Physiotherapy; *Career* NHS Univ Coll Hosp 1974-75, Hosp de Zone Payerne Switzerland 1975-76, Hosp Orthopaedic Lausanne Switzerland 1976-78, La Cassage Home Ecole FMC Lausanne 1978-80, Catholic Relief Servs Thailand 1980-82, personal physiotherapist to HRH Sheik Rashid Dubai 1983, private practice London 1984-; memb Chartered Soc Physiotheraphy, MCSP, SRP; *Recreations* tennis, skiing, travel, photography; *Style*— Miss Anne Grant; 10 Gowrie Rd, London SW11 5NR (☎ 071 228 4748); Cannons, Cousin Lane, London EC4R 3TE (☎ 071 283 0108)

GRANT, Anthony Ernest; s of Ernest Grant (d 1986), of Sheffield, and Doris, *née* Hughes; *b* 23 April 1940; *Educ* King Edward VII GS Sheffield, Keble Coll Oxford (MA); *m* 14 April 1962, Darel Avis, da of Frederick John Atkinson (d 1980), of Sheffield; 3 da (Henrietta b 1965, Sarah b 1966, Philippa b 1969); *Career* Coopers & Lybrand CA 1961-: Sheffield 1961-68 (qualified 1964, mangr 1966, later ptnr), E Malaysia and Brunei 1968-72, London 1972-73, Madrid 1973-75, Leeds 1976- (office ptnr 1984-); dep chm Leeds Poly, treas Leeds C-of-C, memb Ctee Friends of Br Limbless Ex-Servicemen's Assoc Leeds; FCA 1965; *Recreations* riding, bridge; *Clubs* Leeds; *Style*— Anthony Grant, Esq; Albion Ct, 5 Albion Pl, Leeds (☎ 0532 431343, fax 0532 424009, telex 556230)

GRANT, Sir (John) Anthony; MP (C) SW Cambridge 1983-; s of Arthur Ernest Grant; *b* 1925,May; *Educ* St Paul's, BNC Oxford; *m* 1953, Sonia Isobel, da of late George Henry Landen; 1 s, 1 da; *Career* served WWII Capt 3 Dragoon Gds; admitted slr 1952; MP (C) Harrow Central 1964-1983, oppn whip 1966-70, Parly sec BOT 1970; Parly under-sec: trade 1970-72, industl devpt 1972-74, DTI; chm Cons Back Bench Trade Ctee 1979-83, memb Foreign Affrs Select Ctee 1980-83, chm Econ Ctee Cncl of Europe 1980-84; memb Trade and Indust Select Ctee 1987-, pres Guild of Experienced Motorists 1987-; Freeman City of London (Master 1978-79), Liveryman Worshipful Co of Slrs; kt 1982; *Style*— Sir Anthony Grant, MP; House of Commons, London SW1

GRANT, Bernard Alexander Montgomery (Bernie); MP (L) Tottenham 1987-; s of Eric and Lily Grant; *b* 17 Feb 1944; *Educ* Stanislaus Coll Guyana, Tottenham Tech Coll; *m* separated; 3 s; *Career* analyst Demerara Bauxite Co Guyana 1961-63, clerk BR 1963-65, telephonist Int Telephones 1969-78, area offr NUPE 1978-83, devpt worker Black Trade Unionists Solidarity Movement 1983-84, sr housing offr London Borough Newham 1985-87; fndr memb and chair Parly Black Caucus 1987, memb Nat Exec Anti-Apartheid Movement 1988, launched and ed of The Black Parliamentarian magazine 1989, elected chair Socialist Campaign Gp of Lab MP's 1990; ldr Harringay Cncl London; *Style*— Bernard Grant, Esq, MP; House of Commons, London SW1A 0AA

GRANT, His Hon (Hubert) Brian; *b* 5 Aug 1917; *Educ* Trinity Coll Cambridge (MA); *m* 1946, Jeanette Mary; 1 s (Paul), 3 da (Susan, Elizabeth, Jane); *Career* served WWII, No 10 Commando 1942-44; called to the Bar Gray's Inn 1945, circuit judge Sussex and Kent (formerly judge County Courts) 1965-82, memb Lord Chllr's Law Reform Ctee 1970-74; vice chm Nat Marriage Guidance Cncl 1970-72; fndr pres Parenthood 1979; hon librarian Br Deaf Assoc 1985-88; *Publications* Marriage, Separation and Divorce (1946), Family Law (1970), Conciliation and Divorce (1981), The Quiet Ear (1987), The Deaf Advance (1990); *Clubs* Penrith Golf; *Style*— His Hon Brian Grant; Eden Hill, Armathwaite, Carlisle CA4 9PQ

GRANT, Hon Mrs (Caroline Elizabeth); *née* Goschen; da of 3 Viscount Goschen, KBE (d 1977); *b* 24 July 1963; *m* 19 Jan 1991, William E J Grant, er s of M Alistair Grant, of Campden Hill Square, London W8; *Style*— The Hon Mrs Grant

GRANT, Christopher; s of Christopher Grant, of Bolton-on-Swale, North Yorkshire, and Margaret Rose, *née* Fulcher; *b* 14 Oct 1956; *Educ* Ridsdale Sch; *m* 4 June 1984, Dawn Heather, da of Roy Green; *Career* national hunt jockey; Dennys Smith stable 1972-88; Arthur Stephenson stable 1988-; *Recreations* our dogs at home, eating, holidays in the sun; *Style*— Christopher Grant, Esq; Crake Scar Cottage, Hamsterley, Bishop Auckland, Co Durham DL13 3QP (☎ 0388 710425)

GRANT, David James; CBE (1980), JP (1988); s of Frederick Grant, MC, QC (d 1954), of London, and Grace Winifred, *née* McLaren (d 1966); *b* 18 Jan 1922; *Educ* Fettes, Oriel Coll Oxford (MA); *m* 10 Sept 1949, Jean Margaret, da of Gp Capt TEH Birley, OBE (d 1985), of Durham; 2 s (James b 1951, Frederick b 1954), 1 da (Rosalind b 1958); *Career* Nat Serv RAF (vol) 1940, cmmnd navigator 1941; served: Bomber Cmd 218 Sqdn 1941-42, 215 Sqdn India and Burma 1942-43, glider towing and supply drops Tport Cmd 271 Sqdn 1944, Navigation Offr 267 Sqdn Burma 1945; demobbed Flt Lt 1945; md Darchem Ltd 1959-87, dep chm William Baird PLC 1981- (dir 1961-); memb Northern Econ Planning Cncl 1968-79, chm Northern Regnl Cncl CBI 1973-75; memb: NE Industl Devpt Bd 1975-85, Exec Ctee NE Devpt Cncl 1982-85; chm: Northern Regnl Bd BIM 1982-88, Cncl Univ of Durham 1988-; govr Teesside Poly 1989; ex officio: co pres Cncl of St John, memb Scout Assoc; High Sheriff Co Durham 1985-86, Lord-Lt Co Durham 1988- (Vice Lord Lt 1987, DL 1980); Hon DCL: Univ of Durham 1988, Newcastle upon Tyne 1989; CBIM, FBIM 1978; *Clubs* Naval and Military; *Style*— David Grant, Esq, CBE, JP; Aden Cottage, Whitesmocks, Durham DH1 4HJ (☎ 091 386 7161)

GRANT, Delma; da of William Grant (d 1983), of Rugby, Warwicks, and Rosalys Louise, *née* Skinner; *b* 10 Sept 1939; *Educ* Rugby GS, City of Bath Coll (Teaching Dip); *Career* teacher, artist photographer, writer; annual Delma Design Exhibitions: Design Centre London 1974-88, Design and Industry Bd of Trade Exhibition (London and touring) 1984; writer children's books; *Books* incl 12 poetry and Bear prose books 1986-89; Goodnight (1986), Goodmorning (1986), New Nonsense and other Rhymes (1986); *Recreations* gardening, photography, museum collation, snouting in junk shops, interiors, mountains, entertaining nieces, art galleries and museums, horse and cart driving, viewing beautiful houses, churches, nattering, thinking, good food, fine architecture, woodlands; *Clubs* Parrot; *Style*— Miss Delma Grant; PO Box 99, 17 West St, Alresford, Hants (☎ 0425 272876, fax 0962 63516)

GRANT, Dr Douglas; TD; s of Robert Grant (d 1957) and Ierne Grant (d 1963); *b* 6 Jan 1918; *Educ* George Watson's Coll, Univ of St Andrews; *m* 1948, Enid Whitsey, da of Raymond Whitsey Williams (d 1985); 3 s (William Neil b 1953, Richard Martin b 1955, Peter Michael b 1958); *Career* WWII Lt-Col RA (served W Africa and staff) 1939-46; Scot Widows Fund 1936-39; dir: Oliver and Boyd Ltd 1947-67, Edinburgh C of C 1952-56, New Education Ltd 1962-66, Bracken House Publications Ltd 1963-67, Sprint Productions Ltd 1963-80, E & S Livingston Ltd 1963-67, Darien Press Ltd 1963-68, R & R Clark Ltd 1963-80, Port Seton Offset Printers Ltd 1965-75, T & A Constable Ltd 1965-75, Br Jl of Educnl Psychology 1970-, Pindar (Scot) Ltd 1986-89, Macdonald Lindsay (Printers) Ltd 1988-89; chm: Scot Journal of Theology Ltd 1948-, Robert Cunningham & Sons Ltd 1952-76, Hunter and Foulis Ltd 1963-75, Port Seton Offset Printers Ltd 1965-75, Multi Media (AU) Services Ltd 1967-75, Ch of Scot Publications Ctee 1971-76; Scotland Academic Press Ltd 1969-, Scotland International Review Ltd 1970-75, The Handsel Press Ltd 1975-, Scotland Academic Press (Jls) Ltd 1976-, Clark Constable Printers Ltd 1978-89; tstee: The Lodge Tst (Natural History) 1949-85, Darling (Ogilby) Investment Tst 1955-78, Kilwarlin Tst 1964-, Esdaile Tst 1975-, The Soc for the Benefit of Sons and Daughters of the Clergy of the Church of Scotland 1990-; memb Ctee: The Scot Cncl of Law Reporting 1950-, Police Dependents Tst (Lothian and Borders Police) 1956-, NEDO 1968-75, New Coll Univ of Edinburgh (Fin) 1970-, Univ of Edinburgh Ct 1972-84, The Scot Arts Cncl 1975-79; Pres: Edinburgh Master Printers Assoc 1962-64, Edinburgh Bookseller Soc 1977-80, Edinburgh Amateur Angling Club 1978-80; Hon DLitt Univ of St Andrew's; FRSE (1949); *Clubs* New (Edinburgh), Hon Co of Edinburgh Golfers; *Style*— Dr Douglas Grant, TD, FRSE; 2 Pentland Road, Edinburgh EH13 0JA (☎ 031 441 3352)

GRANT, Francis Tollemache; s of late Capt Sir Francis Grant, 12 Bt; hp of bro, Sir Archibald Grant, 13 Bt; *b* 18 Dec 1955; *Recreations* salmon fly-fishing; *Style*— Francis Grant, Esq; The Malt House, Kingston House Estate, Kingston Bagpuize, Abingdon, Oxon OX13 5AX

GRANT, Dr James Shaw; CBE (1968, OBE 1956); s of William Grant (d 1932), of Stornoway, Isle of Lewis, and Johanna, *née* Morison (d 1952); *b* 22 May 1910; *Educ* Nicolson Inst Stornoway, Univ of Glasgow (MA); *m* 25 July 1951, Catherine Mary (1988), da of Norman Stewart (d 1945), of Back, Isle of Lewis; *Career* journalist and author; ed Stornoway Gazette 1932-63, chm Crofters Common 1963-78, dir Grampian TV 1969-80; plays incl: Tarravore (1944), The Magic Rowan (1947), Legend is Born (1948), Comrade the King (1951); books incl: Highland Villages (1977), Their Children will See (1979), The Hub of My Universe (1982), Surprise Island (1983), The Gaelic Vikings (1984), Stornoway and the Lewis (1985), Discovering Lewis and Harris (1987), Enchanted Island (1989); memb: Highlands and Islands Advsy Panel 1954-65, Highlands and Islands Devpt Bd 1970-82, Scottish Advsy Ctee Br Cncl 1972-; Hon LLD Univ of Aberdeen 1979; FRSE 1982, FRAGS 1973; *Recreations* walking, photography; *Clubs* Royal Overseas League, Highland; *Style*— Dr James Shaw Grant, CBE, FRSE; Ardgrianach, Inshes, Inverness (☎ 0463 231 476)

GRANT, John Donald; s of Ian Campbell Grant (d 1960), and Eleanor Sage, *née* Maley (d 1984); *b* 31 Oct 1926; *Educ* Univ of Cambridge (MA); *m* 14 July 1951, Helen Bain Fairgrieve, da of James Wilson (d 1984); 2 s (Alasdair b 1953, Robin b 1956); *Career* Lt REME 1947-49, Lt London Rifle Bde 1949-56; N Thames Gas Bd 1949-60, ICI plc 1960-83, chief exec FIMBRA (formerly NASDIM) 1983-88, ptnr Grant and Fairgrieve 1988-; chm: The Strategic Planning Soc 1989-, Fedn of Software Systems 1989-; *Clubs* United Oxford and Cambridge; *Style*— John Grant, Esq

GRANT, John Douglas; *b* 16 Oct 1932; *Educ* Stationers' Company's Sch Hornsey; *m* 1955, Patricia Julia Ann; 2 s, 1 da; *Career* journalist, author, conslt; reporter Daily Express 1955-70 (chief industl corr 1967-70); Parly candidate (L) Beckenham 1966, MP (L) Islington East 1970-74 (Islington Central 1974-83, (L) to Nov 1981, SDP to 1983); chm Lab and Industl Correspondents' Gp 1967, oppn front bench spokesman Bdcasting and Press Policy 1974, Parly sec CSD 1974; Parly under-sec state: Overseas Devpt Miny 1974-76, Department of Employment 1976-79; oppn (L) front bench spokesman employment 1979-81, SDP employment and industry spokesman 1982-83, Parly advsr to First Div Assoc (a sr civil servants' trade union) 1982-83; head of communication Electrical Electronic Telecommunication and Plumbing Union 1984-89; memb Radio Authy 1990-; tstee Fedn for Industl Understanding, dir Social Market Fndn; *Style—* John Grant, Esq; Branscombe, Upper St, Kingsdown, Nr Deal, Kent CT14 8BJ (☎ 0304 363991)

GRANT, Dr John William; s of John MacDonald Grant, and Isabella Grigor Clark, *née* Morrison; *b* 27 May 1953; *Educ* Dingwall Acad Ross & Cromarty, Univ of Aberdeen (MB ChB, MD); *m* 14 Nov 1980, Daniela, da of Hans Felix, of Bex, Switzerland; 2 da (Joanna b 1983, Marsali b 1986); *Career* registrar pathology Ninewells Hosp Dundee 1979-81, sr registrar in neuropathology and histopathology Southampton Gen Hosp 1981-86, Oberarzt Inst of Pathology Univ of Zurich Switzerland 1986-88; conslt histopathologist Addenbrooke's Hosp Cambridge 1988-, assoc lectr Univ of Cambridge 1989-, fell Emmanuel Coll Cambridge; memb: BMA, Pathological Soc, Br Neuropathology Soc, Swiss Neuropathology Soc; MRCPath 1984; *Recreations* skiing, photography, squash; *Style—* Dr John W Grant; 4 The Stakings, Mill Lane, Sawston, Cambridge CB2 4DF (☎ 0223 835383); Histopathology Dept, Addenbrooke's Hosp, Hills Rd, Cambridge CB2 2QQ (☎ 0223 216744, fax 0223 216980)

GRANT, Keith Wallace; s of Randolph Grant (d 1977), and Sylvia, *née* Hawks (d 1983); *b* 30 June 1934; *Educ* Trinity Coll Glenalmond, Clare Coll Cambridge (MA); *m* 1968, Deanne, da of Dr Arnold Bergsma (d 1972), of S Africa; 1 s (Sam b 1975), 1 da (Katherine b 1977); *Career* account exec W S Crawford Ltd 1958-62; gen mangr Royal Opera Co Covent Garden and English Opera Gp 1962-73; sec RSA 1973-77, dir Design Cncl 1977-82, dean Faculty of Design Kingston Poly 1988-; *Recreations* music, reading, gardening; *Clubs* Garrick, Arts; *Style—* Keith Grant, Esq; c/o Garrick Club, Garrick St, London WC2

GRANT, Very Rev Malcolm Etheridge; s of Donald Etheridge Grant, and Nellie Florence May, *née* Tuffey; *b* 6 Aug 1944; *Educ* Dunfermline HS, Univ of Edinburgh (BSc, BD); *m* 1984, Katrina Russell, da of David Burn Skinner Dunnett; 1 s (Iain b 1989), 1 da (Alison b 1987); *Career* asst curate St Mary's Cathedral Glasgow 1969-72, team vicar of Earlesfield Grantham 1972-78, priest-in-charge St Ninian's Invergordon 1978-81, examining chaplain to Bishop of Moray Ross and Caithness 1979-81, provost and rector St Mary's (Scot Episcopal) Cathedral Glasgow 1981-; memb Highland Cncl Educn Ctee 1979-81; *Style—* The Very Rev Malcolm Grant; 45 Rowallan Gardens, Glasgow G11 7LH (☎ 041 339 4956); St Mary's Cathedral, 300 Great Western Road, Glasgow G4 9JB (☎ 041 339 6691)

GRANT, Prof Malcolm John; s of Francis William Grant (d 1987), and Vera Jessica, *née* Cooke; *b* 29 Nov 1947; *Educ* Waitaki HS Oamaru NZ, Univ of Otago (LLB, LLM, LLD); *m* 13 July 1974, Christine Joan, da of Thomas John Endersbee, ISO (d 1986); 2 s (Nikolas b 1976, Thomas b 1980), 1 da (Joanna b 1978); *Career* sr lectr in law (former lectr) Univ of Southampton 1972-86, prof of law UCL 1988- (sr lectr 1986-88); ed Encyclopaedia of Planning Law and Practice 1982-; *Books* Planning Law Handbook (1981), Urban Planning Law (1982), Rate Capping and the Law (2nd edn, 1986), Permitted Development (1989); *Recreations* Italy; *Style—* Prof Malcolm Grant; The Cricketers, Top Green, Lockerley, Romsey, Hants SO5 0JP (☎ 0794 41104); Faculty of Laws, University College London, Bentham House, 4-8 Endsleigh Gdns, London WC1H 0EG (☎ 071 387 7050 ext 2134, fax 071 387 9597)

GRANT, Lady; Margaret Katharine; da of J W Milne; *m* 1936, Rt Hon Lord (William) Grant, TD (d 1972; sometime Lord Justice-Clerk of Scotland); *Style—* Lady Grant; 30 Moray Place, Edinburgh (☎ 031 225 4406)

GRANT, Prof Michael; CBE (1958, OBE 1946); s of late Col Maurice Harold Grant, and late Muriel, *née* Jörgensen; *b* 21 Nov 1914; *Educ* Harrow, Trinity Coll Cambridge (MA, LittD); *m* 1944, Anne Sophie Beskow, of Norrköping, Sweden; 2 s; *Career* Army first Br Cncl Rep Turkey 1940-45 (acting Capt War Office 1939-40); fell Trinity Coll Cambridge 1938-49, prof of humanity Univ of Edinburgh 1948-59, first vice-chllr Univ of Khartoum 1956-58, pres and vice-chllr Queen's Univ Belfast 1959-66; medallist Royal Numismatic Soc 1962 (pres 1953-56), J H Gray lectr Cambridge 1955; chm: Cwlth Conf on Teaching of English as Second Language Makerere Uganda 1961, Nat Cncl for Supply of Teachers Overseas 1963-66; pres: Virgil Soc 1963-66, Classical Assoc 1977-78; Hon LittD Dublin 1961, Hon LLD QUB 1967; hon fell Royal Numismatic Soc 1984; memb American Numismatic Soc (Huntingdon medallist) 1965, FSA; Gold medal for Educn (Sudan) 1977; *Books* From Imperium to Auctoritas (1946), Aspects of the Principate of Tiberius (1950), Birth of Western Civilization (ed, 1964), Who's Who in Classical Mythology (with J Hazel, 1973), A Guide to the Ancient World: dictionary of ancient place names (1986), The Visible Past (1990); *Clubs* Athenaeum; *Style—* Prof Michael Grant, CBE; Le Pitturacce, Gattaiola, Lucca, Italy

GRANT, Newton Keene; OBE, JP (formerly of Surrey, now City of London 1974-); s of Cyril Ernest Newton Oscar Grant (d 1947), of London, and Ethel, *née* Keene (d 1958); *b* 25 June 1931; *Educ* Eggars GS Alton Hants; *m* 30 Aug 1958, Mary Elizabeth, da of Joseph Henri Jules Romagny (d 1971), of Soissons, France; 3 da (Nicole Mary (Mrs Corbin) b 1962, Carolyn Gillian b 1966, Marie-Anne Hélène b 1969); *Career* Nat Serv RAPC; sr ptnr: Pridie Brewster CAs (ptnr 1960); pres Chartered Assoc of Certified Accountants 1983-84, chm Hearing Aid Cncl; memb Worshipful Co of Horners 1971 (memb Ct of Assts and Master); FCCA 1955, FCA 1960, FCIArb 1970; *Recreations* music, cookery, antique silver; *Clubs* Savage, City Livery; *Style—* Newton Grant, Esq, OBE, JP; Treworas House, Ruanhighlanes, Truro, Cornwall TR2 5LN (☎ 0872 501759); 96 Thomas More House, Barbican EC2Y 8BU Carolyn House, 29-31 Greville St, London EC1N 8RB (☎ 071 831 8821, fax 071 404 3069, telex 296326)

GRANT, (Ian) Nicholas; s of Hugo Moore Grant (d 1987), of Herts and Cara Phyllis, *née* McMullen-Pearson; *b* 24 March 1948; *Educ* Durham Sch, Univ of London (LLB), Univ of Warwick (MA); *m* 5 Nov 1977, Rosalind Louise, da of Winston Maynard Pipe; 1 s (Robert b 1979), 1 da (Rosemary b 1981); *Career* chm Pearson Grant Assocs, pub affs advsr to Robert Maxwell 1985-89; dir of info Lab Pty 1983-1985, head of res and PR Confedn of Health Serv Employees 1972-82; memb: Lambeth Borough Cncl (Lab) 1978-84, West Lambeth Dist Health Authy 1982-84; Parly candidate (L) contested Reigate 1979; *Books* Economics of Prosperity (1980), Political Communication for British General Election (1983); *Recreations* walking, music, photography; *Clubs* Reform; *Style—* Nicholas Grant, Esq; 23 Orlando Rd, Clapham, London SW4 0LD (☎ 071 720 1091)

GRANT, Prof Nigel Duncan Cameron; s of Alasdair Cameron Grant (d 1957), of Inverness, and Anne Blythe Munro, *née* Blythe (d 1989); *b* 8 June 1932; *Educ* Inverness Royal Acad, Univ of Glasgow (MA, MED, PhD); *m* 15 July 1957, Valerie Keeling, da of Dr W S Evans (d 1952), of Glasgow; 1 s (David b 2 Feb 1966), 1 da (Alison b 25 Oct 1963); *Career* Nat Serv gunner RA 1955-57; teacher of English in Glasgow secdy schs 1957-60, lectr in educn Jordanhill Coll 1960-65, lectr then reader Univ of Ediburgh prof of educn Univ of Glasgow 1978-; memb: Lab Pty, Br Comparative and Int Educn Soc (past chm and pres), Scottish Educnl Res Assoc (past chm), Advsy Cncl for the Arts in Scotland; chm Scottish Univs Cncl for Studies in Educn; memb: AUT, SERA, BCIES, CESE, Glasgow Educnl Colloquium (hon pres 1989); *Books* Soviet Education (1964, 1968, 1972 and 1979), Society, Schools and Progress in Eastern Europe (1969), Education and Nation-building in the Third World (jtly, 1971), A Mythology of British Education (jtly, 1973), Scottish Universities: The Case for Devolution (jtly, 1975), Patterns of Education in the British Isles (jtly, 1977), The Crisis of Scottish Education (1982); *Recreations* lanuages, poetry, music, theatre, ornithology, travel, history; *Clubs* Glasgow University College; *Style—* Prof Nigel Grant; 4A Sydenham Rd, Glasgow, Scotland G12 9NS (☎ 041 357 1549); Department of Education, The University, Glasgow G12 8QQ (☎ 041 339 8855 ext 6030 5528)

GRANT, (Alastair) Norman; s of Alexander Grant (d 1985), of Carrbridge, Scotland, and May Grant, *née* Robertson; *b* 18 Nov 1943; *Educ* Royal Acad Inverness, Grays Sch of Art Aberdeen, (Dips Silversmithing and Graphic Design); *m* 3 July 1965, Jess Sloss Innes, da of Dr William Paterson (d 1968), of Glenrothes, Fife; 1 s (Rob b 1973), 1 da (Romany b 1966); *Career* fndr and md Dust Jewellery Ltd 1966-88, co fndr and md Grant Walker Ltd (the first jewellery design conslt working internationally for UN, EEC, UK and other govts and private co's), art coll business studies advsr; Freeman: City of London 1981, Worshipful Co of Goldsmiths 1981; *Recreations* travel, Scottish cottage; *Style—* Norman Grant, Esq; 55 Ridge Rd, London N8 9LJ (☎ 081 341 6104); Grant Walker Ltd, 4-5 Broadbent Close, Highgate Village, London N6 5JP (☎ 081 341 9119, fax 081 348 0078)

GRANT, Capt Pauline Ann; da of Sqdn Ldr John James Woods, RAF, DFC, of Kipscombe, 15A Church Street, Steeple Ashton, Trowbridge, Wilts, and Nancy Farran, *née* Caldecott; *b* 17 Jan 1956; *Educ* Stover Sch Newton Abbot Devon, Trowbridge High Sch Wilts, Loughborough Univ of Technol (BA); *Career* WRAC, UK and N Ireland (despatches), Capt 1978-84; project ldr Racal Vodafone 1984-86, info systems mangr and supervisory conslt Learmouth and Burchett Mgmnt Services plc 1987-89; project ldr Norwich Union 1990-; *Recreations* eating out and gardening; *Clubs* Br Computer; *Style—* Capt Pauline Grant, WRAC; 17 Crawford Rd, Camberwell, London SE5 9NF (☎ 0603 810990); Norwich Union Insur Gp, Norvic House, Chapelfields Rd, Norwich, Norfolk (☎ 0603 680429)

GRANT, Robin William; s of Rt Hon Lord (William) Grant (d 1972), Lord Justice-Clerk of Scotland, and Lady Margaret, *née* Milne, *qv*; *b* 14 May 1938; *Educ* Rugby, Univ of Oxford (MA); *m* 4 May 1968, Hilary Beryl, da of Air Cdre Peter H Hamley (d 1978); 1 s (Jonathan b 1972), 1 da (Veronica b 1970); *Career* Royal Scots 1956-58, 2 Lt 1957; CA; Baring Bros & Co 1966-71, dir Williams Glyn & Co 1971-75, Charterhouse Bank Ltd 1984- (joined 1977); FCA; *Recreations* golf, music, skiing; *Clubs* Denham Golf; *Style—* Robin Grant, Esq; 14 Cumberland Rd, Barnes, London SW13 9LY (☎ 081 748 7760); Charterhouse Bank Ltd, 1 Paternoster Row, St Paul's, London EC4M 7DH (☎ 071 248 4000, fax 071 248 1998)

GRANT, Russell John d'Ammerall; s of Frank William Grant and Joan Alice Peverall; *b* 5 Feb 1952; *Educ* Abbotsfield; *Career* TV presenter; presenter Star Choice (ITV), The Zodiac Game (ITV); radio presenter Believe It or Not (BBC Radio 4), original presenter BBC Breakfast Time; pres Emeritus Br Astrological Psychic Soc, hon life memb Astrologer's Guild of GB; *Books* Your Sun Signs, Your Love Signs; *Recreations* collector of Br maps and gazetteers, county of Middlesex memorabilia; *Style—* Russell Grant, Esq; BBC TV (☎ 081 743 8000); TV Times Magazine (☎ 081 323 3222)

GRANT, Susan Lavinia; da of Donald Blane Grant, of Dundee, Scotland, and Lavinia Ruth, *née* Ritchie; *b* 29 Jan 1948; *Educ* St Leonards Sch St Andrews Scotland, Goldsmiths Coll London; *m* 1, 1969 (m dis 1973), Charles Sharpe; m 2, 1975 (m dis 1983), Ian Woolgar; 1 s (Edward Rupert b 1980), 1 da (Lavinia Unity b 1977); *Career* res exec J Walter Thompson 1968-74, researcher BBC Publications then publicity exec BBC TV 1974-78, publicity mangr Hamlyns 1978-82, account mangr then account dir Good Relations 1982-86, fndr dir and memb Bd The Communication Group 1986-; MIPR; *Recreations* tennis, golf, waterskiing, Scotland, painting; *Clubs* Riverside Racquets, Panmure Golf; *Style—* Ms Susan Grant; The Communication Group, 19 Buckingham Gate, London SW1 (☎ 071 630 1411)

GRANT, William; s of A S Grant (d 1967), and Dr F M Grant (d 1962); *b* 27 March 1938; *Educ* Wellington, Univ of Cambridge (MA); *m* 1 Sept 1961, Jane Margaret Grant; 3 da (Louise b 6 Jan 1966, Polly b 5 July 1969, Belinda b 5 Jan 1972); *Career* Nat Serv RAF 1956-58; admitted slr 1965, ptnr Linklaters and Paine 1970; Freeman City of London, memb Worshipful Co of Pewterers; Law Soc; *Recreations* skiing, walking, art; *Clubs* Roehampton; *Style—* William Grant, Esq; Barrington House, 59/67 Gresham St, London EC2V 7JA (☎ 071 606 7080, telex 884349, fax 071 606 5113, car 0860 327628)

GRANT-DALTON, Maj Nathaniel Duncan Spry; s of Lt-Col Duncan Grant-Dalton, CMG, DSO (d 1969), of Place House, St Anthony-in-Roseland, Portslatho, Truro, Cornwall, and Gwavas May, *née* Spry (d 1955); *b* 24 July 1922; *Educ* Clifton Coll; *m* 19 Sept 1950, Valentia, da of Hon Francis Alexander Innys Eveleigh-de-Moleyns (d 1964), of Balnagown Castle, Kildary, Ross-shire, Scotland; 1 s (Kevin Duncan Spry b 23 Dec 1952), 2 da (Miranda b 14 Jan 1955, Nicola b 15 Feb 1957); *Career* joined army 1941, cmmnd RA 1942, war serv Western Desert and Italy, Flying Instr AOP 1946-53, Long Gunnery Staff Course Larkhill 1954, Gunnery SO Hohne Germany 1955-57, RHA 1957-59, ret 1959; working memb Lloyds 1959-72; High Sheriff of Cornwall 1986-87, local cncllr; *Recreations* shooting, sailing; *Style—* Maj Nathaniel Spry Grant-Dalton; Place House, St Anthony-in-Roseland, Portscatho, Truro, Cornwall (☎ 087 258 447)

GRANT-FERRIS, The Rev the Hon Dom Piers Henry Michael; s of Baron Harvington, PC, AE (Life Peer), *qv*; *b* 9 April 1933; *Educ* Ampleforth, Strawberry Hill Teaching Coll; *Career* Lt Irish Gds, served Germany 1953 and Egypt 1954; monk of St Benedict 1959, priest 1964-, teacher Ampleforth Prep Sch 1965-75, asst priest Workington 1977-89, Leyland 1989-; chaplain of Magistral Obedience SMO Malta 1980; OSB 1959; *Recreations* mountaineering, swimming, skiing, riding, photography; *Clubs* British Ski, Kandahar Ski, Alpine Ski, Achille Ratti Climbing; *Style—* The Rev the Hon Dom Piers Grant-Ferris, OSB; St Mary's Priory, Broadfield Walk, Leyland, Preston PR5 1PD (☎ 0772 421183)

GRANT OF DALVEY, Sir Patrick Alexander Benedict; 14 Bt (NS 1688); Chieftain of Clan Donnachaidh Grants; s of Sir Duncan Alexander Grant of Dalvey, 13 Bt (d 1961), of Polmaily, Glen Urquhart, Inverness-shire, and Joan Penelope, *née* Cope (d 1991); *b* 5 Feb 1953; *Educ* Fort Augustus Abbey Sch, Glasgow Univ (LLB); *m* 1981, Carolyn Elizabeth, da of Dr John Highet, of Pollokshields, Glasgow; 2 s (Duncan b 1982, Neil b 21 Oct 1983); *Heir* s, Duncan Archibald Ludovic Grant of Dalvey b 19 April 1982; *Career* deerstalker/gamekeeper 1969-71, inshore fisherman/skipper Scottish Highlands W Coast 1971-76; chm and md Grants of Dalvey Ltd 1987-; *Recreations* deerstalking, Scottish piping; *Clubs* New (Edinburgh); *Style—* Sir Patrick Grant of Dalvey, Bt; Tomintoul House, Flichity, Farr, Inverness-shire IV1 RXD; Grants of Dalvey Ltd, Alness, Ross-shire IV17 0XT

GRANT OF GARTENBEG, Rear Adm John; CB (1960), DSO (1942); s of Maj-Gen Sir Philip Grant, KCB, CMG (d 1943), and Lady Annette Mary Grant, *née* Coventry (d 1963), descendant Earls of Coventry, Lords St John of Bletsoe and Lords Seton of Barnes; *b* 13 Oct 1908; *Educ* Eastbourne, RNC Dartmouth, RNC Greenwich, JSSC, RCDS; *m* 1935, Ruth, da of Richard Slade (d 1915); 2 s (Duncan, Andrew), 2 da (Tessa, Grizel); *Career* RN; CO HM Ships: Beverley, Philante (Atlantic, Med, Russia) 1940-43, HMS Opportune, Fame, Crispin, Cleopatra, Vernon 1943-56; Flag Offr Cmdg Reserve Fleet Vanguard 1959-61; ret 1961; Rank Organisation 1961-65, dir Conf of

Electronics Industry 1965-71; CBIREE, FRSA until 1970; *Clubs* Hurlingham; *Style*— Rear Adm John Grant, CB, DSO; 9 Rivermead Ct, Ranelagh Gardens, London SW6 3RT

GRANT OF GLENMORISTON, (14 Laird of) Ian Faulconer Heathcoat; JP (1982); s of John Augustus Grant, DL (d 1978), and Gwendolen Evelyn Mary Knight; *b* 3 June 1939; *Educ* Sedbergh, Liverpool Coll of Commerce; *m* 1964, Sarah Bonita, da of Kenneth Lincoln Hall, CBE (d 1981); 1 s (John b 1976), 3 da (Amabel b 1966, Miranda b 1968, Iona b 1970); *Career* md Glenmoriston Estates Ltd, chm Pacific Assets Trust plc, dir: The Royal Bank of Scotland Group plc, Worldwide Value Fund Inc; *Recreations* gardening; *Clubs* New (Edinburgh); *Style*— Ian Grant of Glenmoriston, JP, DL; Bhlaraidh House, Glenmoriston, Inverness; Duncow House, Kirkmahoe Dumfries DG1 1TA, Glenmoriston Estates Ltd, Glenmoriston, nr Inverness (☎ 0320 51202)

GRANT OF GRANT, Hon Amanda Caroline; da of 5 Baron Strathspey and 32 Chief of the Clan Grant, by his 2 w, Olive; *b* 16 Feb 1955; *Educ* St Margaret's Sch Bushey, Central Sch of Art & Design; *Career* graphic designer; *Style*— The Hon Amanda Grant of Grant; Flat D, 25 Nevern Sq, London SW5

GRANT OF GRANT, Hon (Geraldine) Janet; da of 5 Baron Strathspey; *b* 10 June 1940; *m* 1963 (m dis 1972), Neil Hamish Cantlie, s of Adm Sir Colin Cantlie, KBE, CB, DSC (d 1967); resumed maiden name of Grant of Grant; *Style*— The Hon Janet Grant of Grant; c/o Royal Bank of Scotland, 14 George St, Edinburgh EH2 2YF

GRANT OF GRANT, Hon Michael Patrick Francis; s of 5 Baron Strathspey; *b* 22 April 1953; *Educ* Harrow, Oriel Coll Oxford (MA); *Career* real estate conslt and fast food restaurateur, franchise conslt, dir Blythe Management Ltd 1984-; ARICS; *Recreations* sailing (yacht 'Blue Daiquiri'); *Style*— The Hon Michael Grant of Grant; 3 Ifield Road, London SW10 9AZ (☎ 01 351 1868)

GRANT OF MONYMUSK, Sir Archibald; 13 Bt (NS 1705), of Cullen, Co Buchan; s of Capt Sir Francis Cullen Grant, 12 Bt (d 1966, himself tenth in descent from Archibald Grant, whose f d 1553 and whose er bro John was ancestor of the Barons Strathspey), by his w Jean, only da of Capt Humphrey Tollemache, RN (s of Hon Douglas Tollemache, 8 s of 1 Baron Tollemache); *b* 2 Sept 1954; *Educ* Trinity Coll Glenalmond, RAC Cirencester (Dip Farm Mgmnt); *m* 31 Dec 1982, Barbara Elizabeth, eldest da of A G D Forbes, of Druminnor Castle, Rhynie, Aberdeenshire, and Mrs Alison Forbes; 2 da (Christian Mariot b 31 March 1986, Catriona Elizabeth b 14 April 1988); *Heir* bro, Francis Tollemache Grant; *Career* farmer; *Recreations* hill-walking, shooting, water-divining; *Clubs* Royal Northern; *Style*— Sir Archibald Grant of Monymusk, Bt; House of Monymusk, Monymusk, Inverurie AB51 7HL (☎ 046 77220, office 046 77250)

GRANT OF ROTHIEMURCHUS, John Peter; DL; s of Lt-Col John Grant of Rothiemurchus, MBE (d 1987), and Lady Katherine Grant of Rothiemurchus, *qv*; *b* 22 Oct 1946; *Educ* Gordonstoun; *m* 1973, Philippa, da of John Chance, of Widmer Lodge, nr Princes Risborough; 1 s, 2 da; *Style*— John Grant of Rothiemurchus, DL

GRANT OF ROTHIEMURCHUS, Lady Katherine; *née* Greaves; 2 da of Countess of Dysart (d 1975, the 10 holder of the title) and Maj Owain Greaves, DL, RHG (d 1941); hp to sis, Countess of Dysart (11 holder of the title); *b* 1 June 1918; *m* 1941, Lt-Col John Peter Grant of Rothiemurchus, MBE (d 1987), *qv*, Lovat Scouts, s of late Col John P Grant of Rothiemurchus, CB, TD, JP, DL; 1 s (John Peter m Philippa Chance), 1 da (Jane m A R F Buxton); *Style*— The Lady Katherine Grant of Rothiemurchus; Rothiemurchus, Aviemore, Inverness-shire

GRANT-SUTTIE, James Edward; s and h of Sir (George) Philip Grant-Suttie, 8 Bt; *b* 29 May 1965; *m* 10 Nov 1989, Emma Jane, yr da of Peter Craig, of Innerwick, E Lothian; *Style*— James Grant-Suttie, Esq; Sheriff Hall Farm, North Berwick, E Lothian

GRANT-SUTTIE, Sir (George) Philip; 8 Bt (NS 1702); s of late Maj George Grant-Suttie, gs of 2 Bt; suc kinsman, Sir George Grant-Suttie, 7 Bt, 1947; *b* 20 Dec 1938; *Educ* Sussex Composite HS New Brunswick, McGill Univ; *m* 1962 (m dis 1969), Elspeth Mary, da of Maj-Gen Robert Elliott Urquhart, CB, DSO; 1 s; *Heir* s, James Grant-Suttie; *Career* farmer, writer, pilot; *Recreations* fishing, forestry, flying (owner: Cessna 206); *Style*— Sir Philip Grant-Suttie, Bt; The Granary, Sheriff Hall, North Berwick, E Lothian EH39 5BP (☎ 0620 2569; office 3750)

GRANTCHESTER, 2 Baron (UK 1953); Kenneth Bent Suenson-Taylor; CBE (1985), QC (1971); s of 1 Baron Grantchester, OBE (d 1976), and Mamie (d 1976), da of Albert Suenson, of Copenhagen; *b* 18 Aug 1921; *Educ* Westminster, Christ's Coll Cambridge; *m* 12 April 1947, Betty, da of Sir John Moores, CBE, *qv*; 3 s, 3 da; *Heir* s, Hon Christopher Suenson-Taylor; *Career* former Lt RA; called to the Bar Middle Temple 1946, ad eundem Lincoln's Inn; pres VAT Tribunals 1972-87 (chm 1988-90), rec of the Crown Cts 1975-89, chm Licensed Dealers' Tribunal 1976-88, pres Aircraft and Shipping Industs Arbitration Tribunal 1980-83; chm: Dairy Produce Quota Tribunal 1984-, Financial Services Tribunal 1987-; dep chm in House of Lords 1988-; *Clubs* Buck's; *Style*— The Rt Hon the Lord Grantchester, CBE, QC; The Gate House, Coombe Wood Rd, Kingston Hill, Surrey KT2 7JY

GRANTHAM, Adm Sir Guy; GCB (1956, KCB 1952, CB 1942), CBE (1946), DSO (1941); s of Charles Fred Grantham, JP (d 1922); *b* 9 Jan 1900; *Educ* Rugby; *m* 1934, Beryl Marjory Mackintosh-Walker, CStJ; 2 da; *Career* joined RN 1918, Capt 1937, served WWII (despatches 2), Rear Adm 1947, Flag Offr Submarines 1948-50, Flag Offr (Air) 2 in Cmd Mediterranean Fleet 1950-51, Vice Chief of Naval Staff 1951-54, Vice Adm 1950, Adm 1953, C-in-C Mediterranean Station and Allied Forces Mediterranean 1954-57, C-in-C Portsmouth and Allied C-in-C Channel and S North Sea NATO 1957-59, govr and C-in-C Malta 1959-62, first and princ naval ADC to HM The Queen 1958-59, ret; vice-chm Cwlth War Graves Cmmn 1963-70; govr Corps of Commissionaires 1964-; *Style*— Adm Sir Guy Grantham, GCB, CBE, DSO; Tandem House, Nayland, Colchester, Essex EO6 4JF

GRANTHAM, (Robert) James; s of Walter Leslie Grantham, and Marcia Anne Howard, *née* Macdonald; *b* 20 Sept 1947; *Educ* Stowe, Wolverhampton Poly (BA); *m* 6 April 1985, Cecilia Anna Eloise, da of Kapten Karol Wickström; 1 da (Isabella b 1986), 1 step s (Marcus b 1971), 2 step da (Matilda b 1970, Emily b 1979); *Career* Spillers 1969-71, investmt analyst Sternberg Thomas Clarke & Co 1972-77, mangr Fixed Interest and Money Market Servs Dept Phillips & Drew 1977-86, dir County NatWest (formerly County Gp) 1986-, i/c convertibles and warrants research County NatWest Woodmac (formerly County Securities and County NatWest Securities) 1986-; memb Int Stock Exchange 1986; *Style*— James Grantham, Esq; County Natwest WoodMac, 135 Bishopsgate, London EC2M 3XT (☎ 071 375 6818, fax 071 375 6481)

GRANTLEY, Baroness; Lady Deirdre Freda Mary; *née* Hare; da of 5 Earl of Listowel, GCMG, PC; *b* 1935; *Educ* Lady Margaret Hall Oxford; *m* 1955, 7 Baron Grantley, *qv*; *Style*— The Rt Hon the Lady Grantley; Markenfield Hall, Ripon; 53 Lower Belgrave St, London SW1

GRANTLEY, 7 Baron (GB 1782); John Richard Brinsley Norton; MC (1944); s of 6 Baron Grantley (d 1954, ggs of George Norton by his w Caroline, herself gda of the playwright Sheridan), and Jean, da of Brig-Gen Sir David Kinloch, 11 Bt, CB, MVO; *b* 30 July 1923; *Educ* Eton, New Coll Oxford; *m* 18 Jan 1955, Lady Deirdre Elisabeth Freda Hare, eldest da of 5 Earl of Listowel; 2 s; *Heir* s, Hon Richard Norton, *qv*; *Career* served WWII Capt Grenadier Gds; memb Lloyd's; *Clubs* White's, Pratt's; *Style*— The Rt Hon the Lord Grantley, MC; Markenfield Hall, Ripon, N Yorks; 53 Lower Belgrave St, London SW1 (☎ 071 730 1746)

GRANVILLE, 5 Earl (UK 1833); Granville James Leveson-Gower; MC (1945); also Viscount Granville, of Stone Park (UK 1815), and Baron Leveson, of Stone (UK 1833, eldest s and h usually styled simply Lord Leveson); s of 4 Earl Granville (d 1953, gs of 1 Earl, who was himself yr bro of 1 Duke of Sutherland), and Lady Rose Bowes-Lyon, da of 14 Earl of Strathmore and sis of HM Queen Elizabeth The Queen Mother; through his mother Lord Granville is therefore first cous of HM The Queen; *b* 6 Dec 1918; *Educ* Eton; *m* 1958, Doon, da of Flt Lt Hon Brinsley Sheridan Plunket (2 s of 5 Baron Plunket, gs of 1 Marquess of Dufferin and Ava, and gggs of the playwright Sheridan); 2 s, 1 da; *Heir* s, Lord Leveson; *Career* Maj Coldstream Gds, Supply Reserve; pres Navy League 1953-66; served WWII N Africa & Italy; dir Lilleshall plc 1948-; DL Inverness 1974, Vice Lord Lieut Western Isles (Islands Area) 1976-83, Lord Lieut 1983-; *Style*— The Rt Hon the Earl Granville, MC; Callernish, Sollas, N Uist, Outer Hebrides, Inverness-shire; 49 Lyall Mews, London SW1 (☎ 071 235 1026)

GRANVILLE, Hon Linda Elizabeth Mary; only child of Baron Granville of Eye (Life Peer *qv*); *b* 10 Feb 1949; *Educ* Univ of London (BA); *Recreations* eventing and dressage, opera; *Clubs* Lansdowne; *Style*— The Hon Linda Granville; c/o Rt Hon Lord Granville of Eye, 112 Charlton Lane, Cheltenham

GRANVILLE, Richard de la Bere; JP; s of Richard St Leger Granville (d 1972), of Frays, Weston, Herts, and Barbara Lempriere, *née* Wells (d 1983); *b* 20 June 1938; *Educ* Eton; *m* 1966, Christina Veronica, da of Philip Debell Tuckett (d 1967); 1 da (b 1968); *Career* Lt Coldstream Gds 1957-59; assoc memb Hoare Govett Ltd (stockbrokers) 1986 (joined Hoare & Co 1959); memb: Stock Exchange 1964, Cncl of Stock Exchange 1981-84; dir J S Gadd Holdings Ltd and various other cos; *Recreations* country pursuits; *Clubs* Boodle's, Pratt's; *Style*— Richard Granville, Esq, JP; 116 Woodsford Sq, London W14 8DT; J S Gadd Holdings Ltd, 45 Bloomsbury Square, London WC1A 2RA (☎ 071 242 5544, telex 23260 ARCADY G)

GRANVILLE OF EYE, Baron (Life Peer UK 1967), of Eye, Co Suffolk; Edgar Louis Granville; s of Reginald Granville, of Brighton; *b* 12 Feb 1899; *Educ* High Wycombe, Melbourne Australia; *m* 1943, Elizabeth, da of late Rev William Cecil Hunter; 1 da (Hon Linda Elizabeth Mary b 1949); *Career* sits in Lords as an Independent Peer; served WWI and II; former md E L Granville & Co; MP (Lib) Suffolk Eye 1929-51; PPS to: Sir Herbert Samuel 1931, Sir John Simon (National Govt) 1931-36; *Recreations* skiing, writing autobiographies, poetry and novels, watching 3 day events; *Style*— The Rt Hon the Lord Granville of Eye; Charlton Lane, Cheltenham, Glos

GRANVILLE WEST, Hon Gerald Hugh; s of Baron Granville West (Life Peer, d 1984); *b* 1942; *m* 1969, Barbara, da of Arthur Strath, of Ellwood Deane, Kilndown, Cranbrook, Kent; children; *Style*— The Hon Gerald Granville West

GRATTAN, Dr Donald Henry; CBE (1989); s of Arthur Henry Grattan (d 1980), and Edith Caroline, *née* Saltmarsh (d 1980); family of Henry Grattan, Irish PM; *b* 7 Aug 1926; *Educ* Harrow County GS, Kings Coll Univ of London (BSc), Open Univ (DUniv); *m* 1950, Valmai, da of Richard Edward Morgan (d 1978); 1 s (David), 1 da (Jennifer); *Career* jr res offr TRE Gt Malvern 1945-46; sch master Chiswick GS 1946-50, sr master Downer GS 1950-56; television prodr BBC 1956-61, ed further educn BBC 1961-63, head of continuing educn BBC TV 1963-71, controller educnl broadcasting BBC TV 1971-84; memb: Cncl Open Univ 1972-84, Cncl Educnl Technol 1972-84, Advsy Cncl for Adult and Continuing Educn 1979-83; chm: UDACE (Unit for Devpt of Adult Continuing Educn) 1984-, Nat Cncl for Educnl Technol 1985-; memb: Mathematical Assoc, Royal TV Soc, Assoc for Sci Educn, Marlow Soc, Open University Visiting Ctee 1987-, Open Coll Cncl 1987-89; FRSA 1988; *Publications* Science and the Builder, Mathematics Miscellany; *Recreations* dinghy sailing, foreign travel; *Style*— Dr Donald Grattan, CBE; Delabole, Gossmore Close, Marlow, Bucks SL7 1QG (☎ 0628 473571)

GRATWICK, John; OBE (1978); s of Percival John Gratwick (d 1957), of Brands Hatch Place, Fawkham, Kent, and Kathleen Mary, *née* Lunnon (d 1970); *b* 23 April 1918; *Educ* Cranbrook, Imperial Coll London (BSc); *m* 14 Feb 1944, Ellen Violet, da of W H Wright (d 1942), of Coventry, Warwicks; 2 s (John Michael b 1948, Christopher Andrew b 1950), 2 da (Susan Anne b 1953, Jennifer Jane b 1955); *Career* asst prodn mangr Armstrong Siddeley Motors Ltd 1941-45; Urwick Orr & Ptnrs Ltd: joined 1945, dir 1959, md 1968, vice-chm 1971-72; vice-chm: Lake & Elliot Ltd 1971-85, George Bassett Holdings plc 1977-80; dir: R Kelvin Watson Ltd 1976-86, The Export Fin Co Ltd 1984-89; chm: Empire Stores Group plc 1973-90, Guild Sound & Vision Ltd 1976-85, Lovat Enterprise Fund Ltd 1980-88; chm Clothing Indust Econ Devpt Ctee 1985-90 (memb 1967-90); ret 1990; memb: Senate of Univ of London 1967- (memb Ct 1987-), MMC 1969-76, Bd of CAA 1972-75; FCGI, CEng, MIMechE, CBIM, FIMC, FRSA; *Recreations* golf, sailing, photography, philately; *Clubs* RAC, City Livery, Wentworth; *Style*— John Gratwick, Esq, OBE

GRAUBARD, Lady Mary Jane; *née* Cavendish-Bentinck; da of 9 and last Duke of Portland, CMG (d 1990); *b* 1929; *m* 1, 1963 (m dis 1978), Alexander Georgiades; 2 s; m 2, 1978, Prof Stephen Graubard; *Style*— The Lady Mary Graubard; 8 Maple Avenue, Cambridge, Mass 02139, USA

GRAVE, (George) Frank; s of George Grave (d 1965), and Mary, *née* Litt-Wilson (d 1983); *b* 14 Dec 1928; *Educ* Palmers Sch, The London Hosp Med Coll (MB BS); *m* 2 Oct 1954, Rosemary Marjorie, da of Walter L Gurd, of 10 Smiths Field, Cirencester; 3 da (Jane b 1956, Joanna b 1958, Catherine b 1966); *Career* sr surgn, head Surgery Dept Bulawayo and MPILO Central Hosps Bulawayo Rhodesia 1966-79, conslt surgn The Alexandra Hosp Redditch Worcs 1979-; FRCS (Edin); *Recreations* sailing, golf, gardening; *Style*— G Frank Grave, Esq; Lychgate Cottage, Salwarpe, nr Droitwich (☎ 0905 773696); The Alexandra Hospital, Redditch (☎ 0527 503030)

GRAVELL, David William; s of Canon William James Gravell (d 1968); *b* 9 June 1925; *Educ* Marlborough, Trinity Coll Cambridge; *m* 1955, Cecil Katharine, *née* Eastwood; 3 s, 1 da; *Career* shipbroker; chm: Exec Ctee Br Philippine Soc 1966-67, Killick Martin & Co 1975-89 (dir 1954-89), St Olave's Hart St Patronage Tst 1980-89, London C of C SE Asia Ctee 1982-85; pres Malaysia, Singapore and Brunei Assoc 1987-89; memb Br Waterways Bd 1980-83; *Recreations* watching cricket, listening to music, seeing the world; *Clubs* MCC, IOD; *Style*— David Gravell, Esq; Great Barnetts, Leigh, Kent

GRAVES, Francis Charles; OBE (1983), DL (West Midlands 1982); s of Capt Jack Graves (d 1942), of Whitby, Yorkshire, and Lily, *née* Porter (d 1980); *b* 9 June 1929; *Educ* Whitby GS, Birmingham Coll of Technol (now Aston Univ), Coll of Estate Mgmnt London; *m* 24 Nov 1951, Phyllis May, da of Abraham Arthur Woolhouse (d 1940), of Birmingham; 1 s (Richard John Charles b 22 March 1956), 1 da (Helen Margaret b 28 June 1953); *Career* Capt RE 1953-56; chartered quantity surveyor; articled pupil Maxwell Harrison & Ptnrs 1948-52, asst surveyor Wilfred Hiles & Son 1952-53, chm and ptnr Francis C Graves & Ptnrs 1956-; West Midlands RICS 1960-: chm junior organisation branch ctee 1960-61, chm quantity surveyors branch ctee 1969-71, chm branch ctee 1973-74, nat pres quantity surveyors div 1980-81; memb Cncl: Royal Soc of Health 1969-75, Birmingham Engrg and Bldg Centre 1969-83, Univ of Birmingham 1989-; project controller construction NEC Birmingham 1972-76 (project controller extensions 1978-), memb W Midlands Economic Planning Cncl 1975-79; chm: Building Ind Gp W Midlands 1976-80, NEDO report Construction for Industrial Recovery 1977-78; dir Birmingham Hippodrome Theatre Tst 1979-; memb: Midlands Electricity Bd 1980-, Redditch Development Corp 1981-85, PSA Advsy Bd 1981-85; pres Birmingham Chamber of Indust and Commerce 1985-86 (memb 1977-, vice pres 1983-85), memb Home Office Prison Bldg Bd 1987-; High Sheriff Co of West Midlands 1988-89; Freeman: City of London, Worshipful Co of Paviors 1977; FRICS 1961, FRSH 1965, FCIOB 1980; *Recreations* sport generally, cricket (memb ctee Warwicks CCC), golf, football (vice pres Aston Villa FC), gardening, travelling; *Style*— Francis Graves, Esq, OBE, DL; Aldersyde, Broad Lane, Tanworth in Arden, Solihull, W Midlands B94 5DY (☎ 05644 2324); 9 Frederick Rd, Edgbaston, Birmingham B15 1TW (☎ 021 455 9521, fax 021 454 9643, telex 338024)

GRAVES, John Derek; s of Capt Eric Christie Graves (d 1981), of Harrogate, Yorks, and Joyce, *née* Reffitt (d 1981); *b* 30 April 1938; *Educ* Rossall; *m* 1, 28 April 1962, Lorna Sugden (d 1978), da of Robin Sugden Moore (d 1976); 2 s (Nicholas Jonathan b 1965, Stephen Robert b 1968), 1 da (Caroline Frances b 1966); m 2, 30 Dec 1978, Pauline, da of Cyril Henry Stoyle (d 1943), of Totnes, Devon; 1 step s (Hedley Triggs b 1970); *Career* chartered surveyor: Hollis & Webb Leeds 1955-63, Frank Richardson & Co Leeds 1963-68; chief valuation surveyor Leeds Permanent Building Soc 1985- (chartered surveyor 1968-83, sr valuation surveyor 1983-85); FRICS 1961; *Recreations* golf, gardening, reading; *Clubs* Pannal Golf; *Style*— John Graves, Esq; 31 Harlow Manor Park, Harrogate, N Yorks (☎ 0423 568278); Leeds Permanent Building Soc, Permanent House, 72 The Headrow, Leeds LS1 1NS (☎ 0532 352930)

GRAVES, John William; s of Richard Arthur Graves of Bridge House, Swineshead Bridge, nr Boston, Lincs, and Janet Irene, *née* Lyon; *b* 25 March 1960; *Educ* Oakham Sch; *Career* Rugby Union player Rosslyn Park FC; clubs: Bedford RUFC 1979-80 (44 appearances, scored 179 points), Boston RUFC, Rosslyn Park FC 1980- (250 appearances, scored 2000 points); rep: Leics Schs, Lincs Colts 1978-79 (capt), Notts & Lincs Derbys U23 1981-82 (capt), Surrey, London Div (reserve), Midlands Div (reserve); farmer, business mangr Samsonite UK Ltd; *Recreations* photography, travel, wildlife (safaris, nature), theatre, opera; *Style*— John Graves, Esq; 8 Jeremy Court, The Chase, Clapham, London SW4 0NQ (☎ 071 627 2035); Rosslyn Park FC, Priory Lane, Upper Richard Rd, Roehampton, London SW15 5JH (☎ 081 876 1879)

GRAVES, Prof Norman John; s of George Alfred Graves (d 1977), of Worthing, Sussex, and Andrée Adèle Céline, *née* Carrel (d 1986); *b* 28 Jan 1925; *Educ* Highbury County Sch, LSE, Univ of London (BSc, MA, PhD); *m* 28 July 1950, Mireille Camille, da of Camille Joseph Dourguin, Croix de Guerre, of Saint Rémy de Provence; 1 s (Francis Alan b 26 Feb 1954), 1 da (Hélène Monica (Mrs Osborne) (twin)); *Career* school teacher 1950-60, lectr in educn Univ of Liverpool 1961-63, prof (formerly sr lectr, reader) Inst of Educn Univ of London 1963-, prof and dir Inst of Educn 1984-90; pres Geographical Assoc 1979, chm World Educn Fellowship 1985-; FRGS; *Books* Geography in Secondary Education (1970), Geography in Education (1975-84), Curriculum Planning in Geography (1979), The Educational Crisis (1988), New UNESCO Source Book for Geography Teaching (ed, 1982), Initial Teacher Education: Politics and Progress (ed, 1990); *Recreations* walking, gardening, decorating; *Style*— Prof Norman Graves; Institute of Education, Univ of London, 20 Bedford Way, London WC1H OAL (☎ 071 636 1500, fax 071 436 2186)

GRAVES, 8 Baron (I 1794); Peter George Wellesley Graves; s of 7 Baron (d 1963); *b* 21 Oct 1911; *Educ* Harrow; *m* 1960, Winifred (the actress Vanessa Lee), da of Alfred Moule, and wid of Warde Morgan; *Heir* 2 cous once removed, Maj Evelyn Graves; *Career* actor; *Recreations* lawn tennis (played Wimbledon championships 1932-33); *Clubs* All England Lawn Tennis; *Style*— The Rt Hon the Lord Graves; Nelson House, Dolphin Square, London SW1

GRAVES, Richard Perceval; s of John Tiarks Ranke Graves (d 1980), of Amesbury, and Mary, *née* Wickens; *Educ* Charterhouse, St John's Coll Oxford (MA); *m* 1970 (m dis 1988), Anne Katharine, da of Richard Lewis Fortescue; 2 s (David John Perceval b 21 Aug 1972, Philip MacCartney b 26 March 1974), 1 da (Lucia Mary b 17 Jan 1977); *Career* temp teaching posts: Arnold Lodge Prep Sch 1968, Harrow 1969; teacher: Holme Grange Prep Sch 1969-71, Ellesmere Coll 1971-73; writer; books: Lawrence of Arabia and his World (1976), A E Housman: The Scholar - Poet (1980), The Brothers Powys (1983), Robert Graves: The Assault Heroic 1895-1926 (1986), Robert Graves: The Years with Laura 1926-1940 (1990); memb: Whittington Parish Cncl, Oswestry Borough Cncl 1976-83, Shropshire Community Health Cncl 1987-; memb Soc of Authors; *Recreations* reading, walking, watching films, talking to strangers in pubs; *Clubs* Salop; *Style*— Richard Graves, Esq; 21 Bishop St, Cherry Orchard, Shrewbury SY2 5HB (☎ 0743 365 413); Rachel Calder, Curtis Brown, 162-168 Regent St, London W1R 5TB (☎ 071 872 0331, fax 071 872 0332)

GRAVES, Rodney Michael; s of Brian William Graves (d 1971), of Surrey, and Helen, *née* O'Brien (d 1986); *b* 13 Jan 1941; *Educ* Downside, Pembroke Coll Cambridge (MA, Boxing blue); 1 s (Julian Philip David b Sept 1966); *Career* articled clerk Cooper Brothers 1963-69; ptnr Singleton Fabian Derbyshire & Co 1969-74; BDO Binder Hamlyn (following merger): ptnr 1974-, nat dir of corporate fin 1985, regnl managing ptnr for SW and Wales, memb London Partnership Ctee, dir mgmnt consultancy; dir and memb Cncl The Downside Settlement 1991-; FCA; *Recreations* squash, bridge, tennis; *Clubs* The Hawks, Lansdowne; *Style*— Rodney Graves, Esq; BDO Binder Hamlyn, 20 Old Bailey, London EC4M 7BH (☎ 071 489 6014, fax 071 489 6280)

GRAVES-JOHNSTON, Hon Mrs (Carolyn Meliora); da of Rt Hon Viscount Whitelaw (Viscount 1983); *b* 1946; *m* 1, 1973 (m dis 1979), Robert Donald Macleod Thomas; 2 da (Miranda b 1974, Rhoda b 1977); m 2, 1983, Michael Francis Graves-Johnston; 2 da (Cleopatra Frances b 1985, Helen Mercedes b 1987); *Style*— The Hon Mrs Graves-Johnston; 54 Stockwell Park Rd, London SW9

GRAVESTOCK, Peter Stanley; s of Herbert Stanley Gravestock, of W Bromwich, W Midlands, and Phyllis Gwendoline, *née* Bye; *b* 6 June 1946; *Educ* W Bromwich GS; *m* 9 Dec 1973, Cynthia Anne, da of Maj Philip John Radford, of Walsall, W Midlands; 1 da (Elisabeth b 1977); *Career* sr lectr W Bromwich Coll of Commerce and Technol 1971-79 (lectr 1967-71), fndr ptnr Gravestock and Owen 1974-; lectr in taxation Inst of Taxation; former pres Wolverhampton Branch Inst of CAs, memb Ctee Staffs Salop and Wolverhampton Dist Soc Inst of CAs; memb Cncl: Inst of Taxation, Assoc of Taxation Technicians; memb ICEAW, FCA 1967, FTII 1978, ATT 1990; *Books* Tolleys Taxwise Workbooks (jtly, published annually), Sweet & Maxwell's Personal Tax Manual (consulting ed); *Recreations* travelling, walking, reading; *Clubs* Nat Tst; *Style*— Peter Gravestock, Esq; 2 Grasmere Ave, Little Aston, nr Lichfield, Staffs (☎ 021 353 5482); Gravestock and Owen, 1 Walsall St, Willenhall, W Midlands (☎ 0902 601 166, fax 0902 606 925, car 0831 552 377)

GRAY; *see*: Campbell-Gray

GRAY, Adam Thomas; s of David Frederick Gray, of 12 Princess Road, London NW1, and Ilse Erica, *née* Krott; *b* 6 July 1963; *Educ* Haverstock Comp Chalk Farm London, St Martins Sch of Art (BA); *Career* artist; worked in studio Camden Town 1985-87; co-fndr: Angel Studios 1987, Southgate Road Studios Islington 1990; solo exhibitions Anderson O'Day Gallery London 1987 and 1989; group exhibitions incl: Whitechapel Open 1986, 1987, 1988, Oxford Gallery 1988, Flowers East 1989 and 1990, Curwen Gallery 1990, Thumb Gallery 1990, Mario Flecha 1989; taught at various art colls; under 25 prize Athena Art awards 1987; *Recreations* playing piano, tennis, cinema, travel, procrastinating in the early hours of the morning, painting; *Style*— Adam Gray, Esq; 95a Albion Rd, Stoke Newington, London N16 9PL (☎ 071 249 6630, 071 254 6485); Anderson O'Day Gallery, 255 Portobello Rd, London W11 1LR (☎ 071 221 7592)

GRAY, Alistair William; s of John Lambert Gray (d 1980), of St Andrews, and Agnes Roberts, *née* Pow; *b* 6 Sept 1948; *Educ* The Madras Coll St Andrew Fife, Univ of Edinburgh (MA); *m* 7 April 1972, Sheila Elizabeth, da of Walter Harold Rose, of Preston, Lancs; 2 da (Kathryn Julia b 1976, Nicola Elizabeth b 1978); *Career* asst mill mangr Wiggins Teape Ltd 1970-72, divnl mangr Unilever Ltd 1972-78, exec dir John Wood Group plc 1978-81, dir strategic mgmnt consltg Arthur Young 1982-87, mangr of strategy PA Consulting Group 1987-; visiting lectr Univ of Stirling, chm Scottish Hockey Union; memb: Scottish Sports Cncl, IOD; Burgess of Aberdeen 1980; FInstM, ACMA, MInstD, MBIM, MRSH; *Books* The Managers Handbook (1986); *Recreations* hockey, golf, squash; *Clubs* Western Hockey, New Golf (St Andrews), Royal Northern and Univ; *Style*— Alistair Gray, Esq; Westfield, 26 Glenburn Rd, Bearsden, Glasgow (☎ 041 943 0252); PA Consulting Group, 2 Blythswood Sq, Glasgow (☎ 041 221 3954)

GRAY, Andrew Aitken; MC (1945); s of John Gray (d 1956), and Margaret Eckford, *née* Crozier (d 1960); *b* 11 Jan 1912; *Educ* Wyggeston Sch Leicester, Ch Ch Oxford (MA, BSc); *m* 1, 5 Nov 1939, Eileen Mary (d 1980), da of George Augustus Haines (d 1959), of Leicester; 3 s (John Aitken b 1942, Andrew George Aitken b 1944, Duncan Aitken b 1950); m 2, Jess, *née* Carr; *Career* WWII RE 1939-45 (despatches), Maj 1942; Unilever 1935-52, Wellcome Foundation Ltd 1952-77 (chm 1970); chm Hertfordshire AHA 1973-77; Commendatore Order of Merit Italy 1976, Ord Merito Agricola Spain 1969; *Recreations* theatre, fishing, gardening; *Clubs* East India; *Style*— Andrew Gray, Esq, MC; Rainhill Spring, Bovingdon, Herts HP3 0DP (☎ 0442 833 277)

GRAY, Master of; Hon Andrew Godfrey Diarmid Stuart Campbell-Gray; Master of Gray; s and h of 22 Lord Gray; *b* 3 Sept 1964; *Educ* Craigflower Prep Sch, Trinity Coll Glenalmond, Edward Greene's Tutorial Estab Oxford, Exeter Univ (BA); *Style*— The Master of Gray; Airds Bay House, Taynuilt, Argyll PA35 1JR (☎ 086 62 232)

GRAY, 22 Lord (S 1445); Angus Diarmid Ian Campbell-Gray; s of Maj the Hon Lindsay Stuart Campbell-Gray, Master of Gray, MC (d 1945), and Doreen, *née* Tubbs (d 1948); suc grandmother, Lady Gray, 21 holder of the title 1946; *b* 3 July 1931; *Educ* Eton; *m* 1959, Patricia Margaret (d 1987), da of Capt Philip Alexander (d 1953, gs of 3 Earl of Caledon), of Lismore, Co Waterford, Ireland; 1 s, 3 da; *Heir* s, The Master of Gray; *Clubs* Carlton, MCC; *Style*— The Rt Hon the Lord Gray; Airds Bay House, Taynuilt, Argyll PA35 1JR

GRAY, Charles Antony St John; QC (1984); s of Charles Gray (d 1982), and Catherine, *née* Hughes (d 1986); *b* 6 July 1942; *Educ* Winchester, Trinity Coll Oxford (MA); *m* 7 Sept 1967, Rosalind Macleod, da of Capt R F Whinney, DSO, RN, of Lymington, Hants; 1 s (Alexander Charles Macleod b 1974), 1 da (Anya Catherine Macleod b 2 Nov 1972); *Career* called to the Bar Gray's Inn 1966, in practice Midlands and Oxford Circuit, rec 1990; *Recreations* tennis, skiing, walking; *Clubs* Brooks's; *Style*— Charles Gray, Esq, QC; 45 Ladbroke Grove, London W11 3AL (☎ 071 727 2655); Matravers House, Uploders, Dorset (☎ 0308 85222); 10 South Square, Gray's Inn, London WC1R 5EV (☎ 071 242 2902, fax 071 831 2686)

GRAY, Charles Donald Marshall; s of Capt Donald Gray, RE (d 1975), of Bournemouth, and Maude Elizabeth Gray; *b* 29 Aug 1928; *Career* actor; stage debut Regents Park Open Air Theatre, has acted with the RSC and at the Old Vic, roles incl: Achilles in Troilus and Cressida, Bolingbroke in Richard II; West End plays incl: Expresso Bongo, Everything in the Garden, Poor Bitos, The Philanthropist; Broadway: Right Honourable Gentlemen, Kean, Poor Bitos; numerous films incl: You Only Live Twice, The Man Outside, The Night of the Generals, Secret War of Harry Frigg, The Devil Rides Out, The Executioner, Cromwell, Diamonds are Forever, The Beast Must Die, The Rocky Horror Picture Show, The Seven Per Cent Solution, Seven Nights in Japan, The Silver Bears, The Legacy, The Mirror Crack'd, Shock Treatment, The Jigsaw Man; TV: Hay Fever, The Moon and Sixpence, Ross, Richard II, Julius Caesar, An Englishman Abroad, Comedy of Errors, Sherlock Holmes, Bergerac, Small World, Blind Justice; *Style*— Charles Gray, Esq; c/o London Mgmnt, 235-241 Regent St, London W1A 2JT (☎ 071 493 1610)

GRAY, Charles Ireland; JP; s of Timothy Gray (d 1971), and Janet McIntosh, *née* Brown (d 1968); *b* 25 Jan 1929; *Educ* Coatbridge HS; *m* 14 June 1952, Catherine Creighton, da of James Gray; 3 s (Donald b 22 March 1953, James b 30 Sept 1955, Charles b 17 Sept 1958), 2 da (Rosemary b 12 July 1960, Jacqueline b 2 Oct 1964); *Career* 40 yrs serv BR, now ret; rep Chryston Lanark CC until 1974, first Lab chm Lanark's Ninth Dist Cncl, regnl memb Chryston/Kelvin Valley 1974, first vice-convener Strathclyde, currently ldr Strathclyde Regnl Cncl (former first chm Planning and Devpt Ctee, chm Policy and Resources Ctee); former memb: Bd Clyde Port Authy, Sec of State's Advsy Ctee for Travelling People; vice-chm East Kilbride Devpt Corp 1974-86 (vice-chm planning exchange 1976-86); memb Bd: Scot Devpt Agency 1975-85, SECC 1986; regnl rep Glasgow Action 1986, memb Mgmt Advsy Bd Glasgow Garden Festival 1986, memb Scottish Local Govt Info Unit Jt Ctee 1986, ldr COSLA Lab Gp 1988; memb: Single Market Ctee Scottish Econ Cncl 1989, Euro Consultative Cncl Local and Regnl Authys 1989; *Recreations* politics, music and reading; *Style*— Charles Gray, Esq, JP; 9 Moray Place, Chryston, Glasgow G69 (☎ 041 779 2962); Strathclyde Regnl Cncl, Strathclyde House, 20 India St, Glasgow G2 4PF (☎ 041 227 3400, fax 041 227 2870)

GRAY, Lt-Col Charles Reginald; MBE (1945), TD (1950); s of Charles Wilson Gray (d 1969); *b* 3 July 1920; *m* 1941, Anne, da of Ewart Bradshaw (d 1959), of Greyfriars Hall, nr Preston; 2 s; *Career* Lt-Col WWII; md then chm The Dutton-Forshaw Group Ltd 1969-81; former chm: Sterling Wygate Ltd, Wygate Holdings, Sterling Foods Ltd, William Clarke (Bradford) Ltd, Cabana Soft Drinks Ltd, Tammy Pet Foods Ltd, Cabana (Holdings) Ltd; former dep chm Jack Barclay Ltd; currently chm: Williams & Gray Ltd, Greyfriars Estates Ltd, Icee (UK) Ltd, PER 4M Ltd; *Recreations* shooting; *Clubs* Cavalry and Guards'; *Style*— Lt-Col Charles Gray, MBE, TD; Wennington Old Farm, Wennington, nr Lancaster (☎ 05242 21330)

GRAY, David; MBE (1987); s of George William Gray (d 1979), and Florence Harriet, *née* Jones; *b* 11 July 1932; *Educ* Stamford Sch, Univ of Nottingham (BMus); *Career* teacher, composer, violinist; compositions incl orchestral works and an opera for children A Christmas Carol 1960, princ conductor Ernest Read Jr orchestral course 1960-, dir Brighton Youth Orchestra 1961-; hon assoc Mount Royal Coll Calgary Canada; ISM; Citation Distinguished Serv to Youth Music Pa USA 1970; *Recreations* gardening; *Style*— David Gray, Esq, MBE; 3 Railway Cottages, Ripe Lane, Firle, E Sussex BN8 6NJ (☎ 032 183 488); Rue de l'Independance, Montolieu 11170, Aude, France (☎ 68 24 8842); Brighton Polytechnic, Falmer, E Sussex BN1 9PH (☎ 0273 606622)

GRAY, David Francis; s of John Morris Gray (d 1975), and Alice Kathleen, *née*

Winsor (d 1982); *b* 18 May 1936; *Educ* Rugby, Trinity Coll Oxford (MA); *m* 11 Sept 1970, Rosemary Alison Elizabeth, da of Horace William Parker (d 1987); 2 s (James b 1975, Oliver b 1981), 1 da (Fiona b 1977); *Career* admitted slr 1960; articled clerk Coward Chance 1957-60; slr: Coward Chance 1960-62, Bischoff & Co 1962-63; ptnr: Lovell White & King 1966-88 (slr 1963-65), Lovell White Durrant 1988-; vice pres, jt sec and chm ctee City of London Law Soc 1985-88, asst treas Int Bar Assoc 1988- (memb 1972-), hon auditor Law Soc 1988-90 (memb 1960-), tstee Trinity Coll Oxford Soc (hon sec 1979-88); City of London Slrs Co: asst to the Ct 1974-, Master 1984-85, Almoner 1988-; Liveryman: Worshipful Co of Slrs, Worshipful Co of Glaziers; *Recreations* skiing, golf, tennis, swimming; *Clubs* Ski of GB, Liphook Golf; *Style—* David Gray, Esq; 65 Holborn Viaduct, London EC1A 2DY (☎ 071 236 0066, fax 071 248 4212)

GRAY, Hon (James Northey) David; s of Baron Gray of Contin (Life Peer), and Judith Waite, *née* Brydon; *b* 30 April 1955; *Educ* Fettes Coll, Bristol Univ; *m* Lynda Jane, *née* Harlow; 2 da (twins b 1984); *Career* head of English Leeds GS; *Style—* The Hon David Gray; 11 Vancouver Rd, Forest Hill, London

GRAY, Dr Denis Everett; CBE (1983, MBE 1972), JP (Solihull 1982-); s of late Charles Norman Gray, and Kathleen Alexandra, *née* Roberts; *b* 25 June 1926; *Educ* Bablake Sch Coventry, Univ of Birmingham (BA), Univ of London, Univ of Manchester (PhD); *m* 1949, Barbara Joyce, da of Edgar Ewart Kesterton (d 1970); *Career* sr lectr Univ of Birmingham 1957-84, chm of Bench 1971-75; chm: Jt Negotiating Ctees for Justices' Clerks and Magistrates Courts Staff 1978-86, Central Cncl of Magistrates' Courts Ctees 1980-86; memb Magistrates' Courts Rule Ctee 1982-86; *Books* Spencer Perceval the Evangelical Prime Minister (1963); *Recreations* travel, church architecture, reading; *Style—* Dr Denis Gray, CBE, JP; 11 Brueton Ave, Solihull, West Midlands (☎ 021 705 2935)

GRAY, The Rev Canon Dr Donald Clifford; TD (1970); s of Henry Hackett Gray (d 1959), of Manchester, and Constance Muriel, *née* Bullock; *b* 21 July 1930; *Educ* Newton Heath Tech HS Manchester, King's Coll London (AKC), Univ of Liverpool (MPhil), Univ of Manchester (PhD); *m* 1955, Joyce, da of Walter Mills Jackson (d 1979), of Oldham; 1 s (Timothy), 2 da (Clare, Alison); *Career* curate Leigh Parish Church 1956-60, chaplain TA & TAVR 1958-77, vicar St Peter Westleigh 1960-67, vicar of All Saints' Elton 1967-74, rector of Liverpool 1974-87, hon chaplain to HM The Queen 1974-77, proctor in convocation 1964-74 and 1980-87, rural dean of Liverpool 1975-81, canon diocesan of Liverpool 1982-87, hon chaplain to HM The Queen 1982-, canon of Westminster, rector of St Margaret's Westminster, chaplain to the Speaker of the House of Commons 1987-; memb Liturgical Cmmn 1968-86, chm Soc for Liturgical Study 1978-84, memb Jt Liturgical Gp 1969- (sec 1980-89, chm 1989-), pres Societas Liturgica 1987-89; FRHistS; OStJ 1982 (chaplain 1990); *Books* Earth and Altar (1986), contributions to Worship and the Child (1975), Getting the Liturgy Right (1982), Liturgy Reshaped (1982), Nurturing Children in Communion (1985), ed Holy Week Services (1983), ed The Word in Season (1988), Chaplain to Mr Speaker (1991); *Recreations* watching cricket, reading modern poetry; *Clubs* Athenaeum (Liverpool), Liverpool Artists'; *Style—* The Rev Canon Dr Donald Gray, TD; 1 Little Cloister, Westminster Abbey, London SW1P 3PL (☎ 071 222 4027)

GRAY, Prof Douglas; s of Emmerson Walton Gray, and Daisy Gray; *b* 17 Feb 1930; *Educ* Wellington Coll NZ, Victoria Univ of Wellington (MA), Univ of Oxford (MA); *m* 3 Sept 1959, Judith Claire, da of Percy Campbell; 1 s (Nicholas b 1961); *Career* asst lectr Victoria Univ of Wellington 1953-54, lectr in English Pembroke and Lincoln Colls Oxford 1956-61, fell in English Pembroke Coll 1961-80 (emeritus fell 1980-), univ lectr English language 1976-80, JRR Tolkien prof English literature and language 1980-, professorial fell Lady Margaret Hall 1980-; FBA 1989; *Books* Themes & Images in the Medieval English Religious Lyric (1972), A Selection of Religious Lyrics (1975), Robert Henryson (1979), The Oxford Book of Late Medieval Verse and Prose (1985); *Style—* Prof Douglas Gray; Lady Margaret Hall, Oxford OX2 6QA (☎ 0865 274300)

GRAY, Dulcie Winifred Catherine (Mrs Michael Denison); CBE (1983); da of Arnold Savage Bailey, CBE (d 1935), of Kuala Lumpur, and Kate Edith, *née* Clulow-Gray (d 1942); *b* 20 Nov 1920; *Educ* St Anthony's Wallingford Berks, Luckley Wokingham Berks, Leeson House Langton Matravers Dorset, St Mary's Kuala Lumpur; *m* 29 April 1939, (John) Michael Terence Wellesley Denison, CBE, *qv*, s of Gilbert Dixon Denison (d 1959); *Career* actress 1939-; first part Sorel in Hay Fever at His Majesty's Aberdeen; ENSA 1944; more than 40 plays in West End incl: Brighton Rock, Candida, Where Angels Fear to Tread, Bedroom Farce, School for Scandal; tv plays incl: The Governess, The Letter, Beautiful for Ever, Three Up Two Down; most recently playing Kate Harvey in BBC TV's Howards' Way; memb exec Cncl and Fin Ctee Actor's Charitable Tst, numerous appearances for charities; FLS, FRSA; *Books* 24 published books incl: Baby Face, Murder in Mind, The Murder of Love, Butterflies on My Mind (winner Times Educnl Supplement Sr Info Award 1978), The Glanville Women, Looking Forward - Looking Back (autobiography); *Recreations* swimming, butterflies; *Clubs* The Lansdowne; *Style—* Miss Dulcie Gray, CBE; Shardeloes, Amersham, Bucks; c/o International Creative Managment, 388-396 Oxford St, London W1N 9HE (☎ 071 629 8080)

GRAY, (Edna) Eileen Mary; OBE (1978); da of William Thomas Greenway (d 1957), of Reigate, Surrey, and Alice Evelyn Mary, *née* Jenkins (d 1983); *b* 25 April 1920; *Educ* St Saviours and St Olaves GS for Girls London; *m* 25 Aug 1946, Walter Herbert Gray, s of Walter James Gray (d 1947), of London; 1 s (John Andrew b 25 Nov 1947); *Career* inspectorate fighting vehicles 1940-45; invited to ride aboard Br womens cycling team 1946, int delegate Paris 1957, organiser first int competition for women in UK 1957, campaigner for int recognition of women in cycling and team mangr inaugural womens world championship 1958, elected Exec Ctee Br Cycling Fedn 1958-87 (chm Fin Ctee, pres), elected to Fedn International Amateur de Cyclism 1977, elected vice chm BOA 1988; int official Cwlth Games Edmonton and Brisbane, special Gold award Min of Educn Taiwan; Mayor Royal Borough of Kingston upon Thomas 1990-91; memb: Womans Int Cmmn for Cycling, Br Int Sports Ctee (BISC); chm housing leisure Royal Borough Kingston upon Thames; Freeman City of London 1987, dep grandmaster Hon Fraternity Ancient Freemasons (women); *Style—* Mrs Eileen Gray, OBE; 129 Grand Ave, Surbiton, Surrey KT5 9HY (☎ 081 399 0068)

GRAY, Geoffrey George; s of Geoffrey Frederick Gray, of Northants and Rita, *née* Peacock; *b* 24 Nov 1950; *Educ* Wellingborough GS; *m* 22 Sept 1987, Rosalind Margaret, da of Robert Evitts, of Leamington Spa; 2 s (George b 1987, William b 1990); *Career* Cannon Assurance Ltd 1970-78, sales dir TSB Tst Co Ltd 1978; *Clubs* Abbotts Ann Cricket (Capt); *Style—* Geoffrey Gray, Esq; Ash Meadows, Clanville, Nr Andover, Hampshire SP11 9HZ; TSB Trust Company, Charlton Place, Andover, Hampshire SP10 1RE (☎ 0264 56789, fax 0264 50091 ext 93, telex 477018 TSB TCLK)

GRAY, George Bovill Rennie; OBE (1991), DL (E Lothian 1984); s of John Rennie Gray (d 1937), of Smeaton-Hepburn, E Lothian, and Margaret, *née* Bovill (d 1958); *b* 5 March 1920; *Educ* Clayesmore Iwerne Minster, E of Scotland Coll of Agric; *m* 30 Jan 1946, Anne Constance, da of John Robert Dale, of Auldhame, N Berwick; 4 s (John b Dec 1946, Kenneth b May 1948, Duncan b Sept 1949, Quentin b Feb 1954), 2 da (Ruth b June 1952, Joanna b Sept 1956); *Career* chm G B R Gray Ltd Farmers 1952-; convenor Cereals Ctee NFUScot 1955-58, dir Scot Soc for Res in Plant Breeding 1957-; memb: Pig Indust Devpt Authy 1958-68, Agric and Vet Sub-ctee of UGC 1972-82, Scotland Advsy Bd Br Inst of Mgmnt 1978-90; vice pres Animal Diseases Res Assoc Moredum 1974-, vice chm Hanover Housing Assoc Ltd Scotland 1989-; elder Church of Scotland; memb: Boy Scout Assoc E Lothian, Garleton Div Lothian Regnl Cncl 1974-82; FBIM 1978; *Recreations* gardening, arboriculture; *Clubs* Caledonian; *Style—* George Gray, Esq, OBE, DL; Smeaton-Hepburn, East Linton, East Lothian EH40 3DT (☎ 0620 860275)

GRAY, George Gowans; *b* 21 Jan 1938; *Educ* Linlithgow Acad, Univ of Edinburgh (BSc), Univ of Cambridge (PhD); *Career* engr: Pratt & Whitney Canada 1960-63, RCA Limited Canada 1963-69; researcher Univ of Cambridge 1969-71, md Serv Div RCA Limited Sunbury-on-Thames 1974-87 (mangr 1971-74), chm Serco Group plc 1987-; FIMechE; *Publications* contrib with K L Johnson: Journal of Sound and Vibration (1972), The Institution of Mechanical Engineers Proceedings (1975); *Clubs* Oxford and Cambridge; *Style—* George Gray, Esq; Serco Group plc, Lincoln Way, Windmill Rd, Sunbury-on-Thames, Middx TW16 7HW (☎ 0932 785511, fax 0932 782714, telex 24246)

GRAY, His Eminence Cardinal Gordon Joseph; s of Francis Gray, and Angela Gray; *b* 10 Aug 1910; *Educ* Holy Cross Acad Edinburgh, St Joseph's Coll Mark Cross, St John's Seminary Wonersh, St Andrew's Univ (MA); *Career* asst priest St Andrew's 1935-41, parish priest Hawick 1941-47, rector Blairs Coll Aberdeen 1947-51, cardinal 1969, archbishop of St Andrew's and Edinburgh 1951-85; Hon FEIS 1970; Hon DUniv Heriot-Watt 1981, Hon DD St Andrew's Univ 1967; *Recreations* joinery, gardening, local historical research; *Style—* His Eminence Cardinal Gordon Joseph Gray; The Hermitage, St Margaret's Convent, Whitehouse Loan, Edinburgh EH9 1BB (☎ 031 447 6210)

GRAY, Harold James; CMG (1956); s of John William Gray (d 1930), and Amelia Francis, *née* Miller (d 1961); *b* 17 Oct 1907; *Educ* Dover County Sch, Univ of London (BSc, MSc, LLB), Gray's Inn, Harvard (MPA); *m* 1928, Katherine, da of Sydney George Starling (d 1956); 1 da (Ann); *Career* civil servant 1927-61, examiner Patent Office 1935-39, asst sec Miny of Supply 1939, Cwlth Fund Fellowship 1949-50, under sec BOT 1954, UK sr trade cmmr; econ advsr to: UK High Cmmr Aust 1954-58, S Africa 1958-60; dir: Nat Union of Mfrs 1961-65, CBI 1965-72; chm Numas Management Service Ltd 1970-74 (dir 1961-70); author of various booklets on small firms in UK 1965-72; CPhys, MInstP, FRSA; *Books* Electricity in Service of Man (1949), Economic Survey of Australia (1955), Dictionary of Physics (1956), New Dictionary of Physics (1975); *Recreations* horse riding, swimming, golf; *Style—* Harold Gray, Esq, CMG; Copper Beeches, 58 Tudor Avenue, Maidstone, Kent ME14 5HJ (☎ 0672 685978)

GRAY, Henry Withers; s of Henry Withers Gray (d 1958), and Jean Allen, *née* Cross; *b* 25 March 1943; *Educ* Rutherglen Acad, Univ of Glasgow (MD); *m* 5 July 1967, Mary Elizabeth, da of Angus Henry Shaw, of Arbeadie Rd, Banchory, Aberdeenshire; 1 s (Stuart Henry b 1968), 2 da ((Elizabeth) Anne b 1970, Karen Louise b 1981); *Career* conslt physician in med and nuclear med 1977; FRCP 1978, FRCPG 1984; *Style—* Henry Gray, Esq; 4 Winton Park, E Kilbride, Glasgow G75 8QW (☎ 03552 29525); The Department of Nuclear Medicine, The Royal Infirmary, Alexandra Parade, Glasgow (☎ 041 552 3535, fax 041 552 5943)

GRAY, Dr James Allan; s of Maj (James) Douglas Allan Gray, TD, of 32 W Grange Gardens, Grange Loan, Edinburgh, and Agnes Dorothy, *née* Sloan (d 1985); *b* 24 March 1935; *Educ* St Pauls, Faculty of Med Univ of Edinburgh (MB ChB); *m* 17 Sept 1960, Jennifer Margaret Newton, da of Maj Eric Newton Hunter, MC, TD (d 1983), of Sheildaig Cottage, Badachro, Westerross; 1 s (Hugh Douglas Allan b 5 March 1962), 2 da (Emma Elizabeth b 15 Sept 1966, Alison Lucy McLullich b 11 Nov 1967); *Career* cmmnd Flying Offr RAF, unit MO RAF Finningley Yorks 1960-62, Flt Lt OC Med Div RAF Hosp Khormaksar Beach Aden 1962-63; house surgn and physician posts Edinburgh and Middlesborough 1959-60, house physician sr house offr and res fell posts Edinburgh 1964-67, registrar Bristol Royal Infirmary 1967-68, sr registrar Dept of Infectious Diseases Royal Free Hosp London 1968-69, conslt in communicable diseases Regnl Infectious Diseases Unit City Hosp Edinburgh 1969-, pt/t sr lectr Dept of Med Univ of Edinburgh 1969-, asst dir of med studies Edinburgh Postgrad Bd for Med 1976-84, PMO Scottish Widows Fund Edinburgh 1990- (asst PMO 1979-1990); fndr and ed Research Medica 1957-58, asst ed Journal of Infection 1979-86, numerous pubns on infection, immunisation and antimicrobial chemotherapy; FRCPE 1974, fell Royal Med Soc, sr pres Royal Med Soc 1958-59, pres Br Soc for the Study of Infection 1989-91 (vice pres 1987-89); Freeman City of London, Liveryman Worshipful Soc of Apothecaries London (Yeoman 1958); *Books* Antibacterial Drugs (jtly, 1983), Colour Aids: Infectious Diseases (jtly, 1984); *Recreations* hill walking, pottery collecting; *Style—* Dr James Gray; St Andrews Cottage, 15 Lauder Rd, Edinburgh EH9 2EN (☎ 031 667 4124); Regional Infectious Diseases Unit, City Hospital, Greenbank Drive, Edinburgh EH10 5SB (☎ 031 447 1001, fax 031 452 8363)

GRAY, James Laird; s of John Marshall Gray (d 1957), of Glasgow, and Jessie Cameron Smith (d 1968); *b* 11 Jan 1926; *Educ* Hyndland Secdy Sch Glasgow, Univ of Glasgow (BSc); *m* 1954, Mary, da of Thomas Magee; 2 s (Thomas Alexander b 1955, John James b 1963), 1 da (Susan b 1956); *Career* apprentice Yarrow and Co Glasgow, asst engr Steam Turbine Design Dept English Electric Co Ltd (now GEC) 1946-48, Br Electricity Authy (now CEGB) 1948-75 (latterly head Turbine - Generator Design Branch), chief engr Generation Design and Construction South of Scotland Electricity Bd 1989-90 (mangr of Generation Design and Tech Servs 1975-89), ret 1990; Thomas Hawksley Gold Medal, James Clayton Award of IMechE; FIMechE 1960, FEng 1985; *Recreations* sailing, gardening; *Clubs* Royal Northern and Clyde Yacht; *Style—* James L Gray, Esq; Woodburn, Garelochhead, Helensburgh G84 0EG (☎ 0436 810403)

GRAY, John; s of William Bernard Gray, of Epsom, Surrey, and Frances, *née* Powell; *b* 25 Feb 1947; *Educ* Glyn Sch Epsom, Univ of London (MB BS); *m* 22 Sept 1973, Janette Mary, da of Walter Manning Cotsworth, of Sheringham, Norfolk; 1 s (Matthew b 1981), 1 da (Katy b 1985); *Career* conslt medical microbiologist N Staffs Health Authy 1978-, dir Stoke-on-Trent Public Health Laboratory; FRCPath 1988; *Recreations* gardening, local history; *Style—* John Gray, Esq; The Chancery, 32 Heathfield Rd, Audlem, Crewe CW3 0HH (☎ 0270 811405); Public Health Laboratory, Central Pathology Laboratory, Hartshill, Stoke-on-Trent ST4 7PX (☎ 0782 46956, fax 0782 744568)

GRAY, Sir John Archibald Browne; s of Sir Archibald Montague Henry Gray, KCVO, CBE (d 1967); *b* 30 March 1918; *Educ* Cheltenham, Clare Coll Cambridge (MA, MB, ScD); *m* 1946, Vera Kathleen, da of Charles Anthony Mares, of Highgate; 1 s, 1 da; *Career* Surgn Lt RN Pacific Fleet; physiologist; prof of physiology UCL London 1959-66, sec MRC 1968-77, memb external scientific staff MRC Marine Biological Assoc Laboratories Plymouth 1977-83; hon fell Clare Coll 1976; Hon DSc Exeter 1985; FIBiol, FRCP, FRS; kt 1973; *Recreations* sailing (35 ft sloop 'White Seal II'); *Clubs* Royal Cruising, Royal Plymouth Corinthian Yacht, Royal Western Yacht; *Style—* Sir John Gray, FRS; Seaways, North Rock, Kingsand, Torpoint, Cornwall (☎ 0752 822745)

GRAY, Vice Adm Sir John Michael Dudgeon; KBE (1967, OBE 1950), CB (1964);

s of Col Arthur Claypon Horner Gray, OBE (d 1963), of Nayland, Suffolk, and Dorothy, *née* Denham; *b* 13 June 1913; *Educ* RNC Dartmouth; *m* 1939, Margaret Helen, da of Arthur Purvis, of Cairo; 1 s, 1 da; *Career* joined RN 1926, served WWII: in HMS Hermes and Spartan, with US in Anzio, with 8 Army in Italy, with French Army in France (despatches); Cdr 1947, Capt 1952, cmd HMS Lynx 1955, cmd HMS Victorious 1960, Rear Adm 1962, dir gen Trg MOD (RN) 1962-65, Vice Adm 1965, C-in-C S Atlantic and S America 1965-57, ret; sec The Oriental Ceramic Soc; *Clubs* Naval and Military; *Style*— Vice Adm Sir John Gray, KBE, CB; 55 Elm Park Gardens, London SW10 (☎ 071 352 1757, office 071 636 7985)

GRAY, John Montgomery; s of Dr John Montgomery Gray (d 1984), and Margaret Elizabeth, *née* Welsh (d 1986); *b* 17 Oct 1938; *Educ* Tonbridge, Brasenose Coll Oxford (BA); *m* 2 Sept 1972, Susan Caroline, da of Maj Humphrey Pares, TD; 1 s (Jonathon b 13 March 1974), 2 da (Theresa b 20 May 1976, Anna b 11 May 1978); *Career* called to the Bar Inner Temple 1962, Inner Temple Major scholar 1962-65, recorder 1986; *Recreations* gardening, cabinet making; *Style*— John Gray, Esq; 1 Crown Office Row, Temple, London EC4Y 7HH (☎ 071 583 9292, fax 071 353 9292)

GRAY, Maj-Gen (Reginald) John; CB (1973); s of Dr Cyril Gray (d 1951), and Frances Anne, *née* Higgins (d 1953), of Higginsbrook, Trim, Co Meath; *b* 26 Nov 1916; *Educ* Ascham House Gosforth, Rossall Sch, Durham Univ; *m* 1943, Esme, da of late Maj G R G Ship; 1 s, 1 da; *Career* served 1939-45 in India, Burma, later in NW Europe, Egypt, Malta, BAOR; Gold Staff Offr 1953, dep dir-gen AMS 1967-69, QHS 1970-73, med dir UKLF 1972-73, CMO BRCS 1974-83, dir Int Generics Ltd 1974-83, Col Cmdt RAMC 1977-81; chm: RAMC Assoc 1980-88, BMA Armed Forces Ctee 1981-85; memb BMA and Casualty Surgns Assoc; memb (hon caus) St AAA and Inst of Civil Defence; FRSM, FFCM (fndr fell), FFPHM; CStJ 1971 (OStJ 1957); *Recreations* growing some things, repairing others; *Style*— Maj-Gen John Gray, CB; 11 Hampton Close, Wimbledon, London SW20 0RY (☎ 081 946 7429)

GRAY, John Walton David; CMG (1986); s of Myrddin Gray (d 1943), of Llanelly, Carmarthenshire, and Elsie Irene, *née* Jones (d 1983); *b* 1 Oct 1936; *Educ* Queen Elizabeth GS Devon, Blundell's Sch Tiverton Devon, Christ's Coll Cambridge (BA, MA), ME Centre Oxford, American Univ Cairo; *m* 22 Sept 1957, Anthoula, da of Nicholas Yerasimou, of Nicosia, Cyprus; 1 s (Nicholas Myrddin Christopher b 1971), 2 da (Helen Irene (Mrs Carless) b 1961, Clare Marian (Mrs Rees) b 1963); *Career* 2 Lt RASC 1954-56; Foreign Serv: joined 1962, serv MECAS 1962-63, political offr Bahrain 1964-67, FO 1967-70, Geneva 1970, UK delgn to Conf on Security and Co-operation in Euro 1973-74, head of chancery Sofia 1974-77, cnsllr Jedda 1978-81, head of dept FCO 1982-85, ambass Beirut 1985-88, UK permanent rep OECD Paris 1988-; *Recreations* watching sport, reading history, Wales; *Clubs* Athenaeum, Royal Cwlth Soc; *Style*— John W D Gray, Esq, CMG; c/o Foreign and Commonwealth Office, King Charles St, London SW1A 2AH; UK Delegation to OECD, 19 rue de Franqueville, 75116 Paris, France (☎ 010 33 145249820)

GRAY, Margaret Caroline; da of A Herbert Gray (d 1956), and Mary Christian, *née* Dods (d 1957); *b* 25 June 1913; *Educ* St Mary's Hall Brighton, Newnham Coll Cambridge (MA), Smith Coll Northampton Massachusetts USA; *Career* asst mistress History Dept Westcliff HS 1937-38, head of History Dept Mary Datchelor Sch Camberwell London 1939-52; headmistress: Skinners' Co Sch for Girls London 1952-63, Godolphin and Latymer Sch London 1963-73; chm: Ctee Assoc Headmistresses 1970-72, Nat Advsy Centre on Careers for Women 1970-; vice chm Cncl Francis Holland Schs; memb: Secdy Heads Assoc, AA, Nat Tst, RSPB, Rose Soc; *Recreations* gardening, travelling, books, theatre; *Style*— Miss Margaret Gray

GRAY, (Stephen) Marius; s of Basil Gray, CB, CBE, of Long Wittenham, Oxford, and Nicolete Mary, *née* Binyon; *b* 3 Aug 1934; *Educ* Westminster, New Coll Oxford (MA); *m* 2 Sept 1961, Clare Anthony, da of Sir Anthony Horace Milward, CBE (d 1981); 1 s (Theodore b 1964), 3 da (Emma b 1962, Bridget b 1967, Jacquetta b 1971); *Career* Nat Serv 2 Lt RCS 1953-55; CA 1962; non-exec dir: Davies Turner Ltd 1970-, Abingworth plc 1973-, Folkestone Ltd 1977-, Br Bio-Technology Group PLC 1982-, Assoc Newspapers Hldgs plc 1983-, Daily Mail and Gen Tst plc 1985-; sr ptnr Dixon Wilson 1981 (ptnr 1967); chm: British Real Estate Group PLC 1989-, special tstees The London Hosp 1974-, mgmnt ctee The King's Fund 1985-; govr The London Hosp Med Coll 1984-89; FCA; *Clubs* Savile; *Style*— Marius Gray, Esq; 47 Maze Hill, London SE10 8XO; Dixon Wilson, Rotherwick House, PO Box 900, 3 Thomas More St, London E1 9YX (☎ 071 628 432, fax 071 702 9769, telex 883967)

GRAY, Martin David; s of Barry Gray, of 22 Hornby Avenue, Sedgefield, Co Durham, and Sylvia, *née* Schollick; *b* 17 Aug 1971; *Educ* Sedgefield Community Coll; *Career* professional footballer Sunderland FC, 9 appearances on loan Aldershot; Durham county cap 1988-89 (capt youth team 1987-89); former player Ferryhill Athletic (winners Vauxhall Centenary Trophy 1988); *Recreations* snooker, keep-fit, tennis, horse racing, football; *Style*— Martin Gray, Esq; 22 Hornby Avenue, Sedgefield, Co Durham (☎ 0740 21272); Sunderland FC, Roker Park, Sunderland (☎ 091 514 0332)

GRAY, Dr Michael Ian Hart (Mike); s of Harry Lesley Gray, of London, and Edith Louise, *née* Hart; *b* 12 July 1940; *Educ* Dartford GS, Univ of St Andrews (MB ChB), RAF Inst of Aviation Med (DAvMed); *m* 22 July 1964, Patricia Margaret (Trish), da of Capt William Thompson Stewart, of Dundee, Scot; 1 s (Jeremy Rupert Andrew Hart b 1968); *Career* cmmnd RAMC 1963, Regtl MO 4/7 Royal Dragoon Gds 1966-68, pathologist Queen Alexandra Mil Hosp London 1972-74 (trainee since 1969), trainee in aviation med Army Air Corps Centre 1974-76, awarded Helicopter Wings 1975, specialist in aviation med Army Air Corps Centre 1976-77, advsr in aviation med (Lt-Col) to dir Army Air Corps 1977-79, conslt in aviation med (Flt Surgn) King Abdul Aziz Mil Hosp Tabuk Saudi Arabia 1979-83; chief med offr Gulf Air Bahrain 1986-88 (sr med offr 1983-86), aviation med specialist Military Aircraft Div Br Aerospace 1989-; memb: Br Acad of Forensic Scis 1971, Soc of Occupational Med 1978; MFOM 1981, MRAeS 1984; *Recreations* reading, gardening, sailing, shooting; *Clubs* Cavalry and Guards; *Style*— Dr Mike Gray; Nut Tree Cottage, Lower Chicksgrove, Tisbury, Salisbury, Wiltshire SP3 6NB (☎ 072 270 382)

GRAY, Lt-Gen Sir Michael Stuart; KCB (1986), OBE (1971); s of Lt Cdr Frank Gray, RNVR (ka 1940); *b* 3 May 1932; *Educ* Christ's Hosp Horsham, RMA Sandhurst; *m* 1958, Juliette Antonia; 3 children; *Career* Reg Offr Br Army; Staff College: student 1963, instr 1971-73; memb RCDS 1976; Cdr: 16 Parachute Bde 1977, 6 Field Force and COMUKMF 1977-79; Cdr Br Army Staff and mil attaché (with additional responsibilities of head Br Def Staff and Def Attaché) Washington 1974-81, GOC SW Dist 1981-83, COS HQ BAOR 1984-85, GOC SE Dist (cmd Joint Force HQ) 1985-88, ret 1988; Col Cmdt The Parachute Regt 1990-; conslt Brittany Ferries 1988-, def industs advsr Wardle Storeys plc 1989-; area organiser (NE England) King Georges Fund for Sailors 1988-; chm: Airborne Assault Normandy Tst 1978-, Mil and Aerospace (Aldershot) Tst 1989-, Airborne Forces Museum Airborne Forces Charities Devpt Tst; pres Forces Retirement Assoc, tstee Airborne Forces Security Fund, dir Airborne Initiative Ltd, chm The Praetorian Project (Redmont Promotions Ltd); Parachute Regimental Assoc: pres, pres Portsmouth Branch; vice pres: Army Parachute Assoc, Normandy Veterans Assoc Goole Branch; patron Combined Ex Services Assoc Bridlington, memb Amicable Soc of Blues, hon tstee Br Support Ctee Meml Museum Caen Normandy; Freeman City London; FBIM, FInstD; *Recreations* military history, gardening and house maintenance; *Style*— Lt-Gen Sir Michael Gray, KCB, OBE; c/o National Westminster Bank plc, 60 Market Place, Beverley, North Humberside

GRAY, Milner Connorton; CBE (1963); s of Archibald Campbell Gray (d 1952), of Eynsford, Kent, and Katherine May, *née* Hart; *b* 8 Oct 1899; *Educ* Privately, Colfe Sch Lewisham, Goldsmiths' Coll London; *m* 12 July 1934, Gnade Grace, da of William Osbourne-Pratt, of Northampton; *Career* 19 London Regt 1917, transferred RE Experimental Section Sch of Camouflage 1917-19, gunner HAC (TA) 1923-31, admitted Veteran Co 1931; fndr and sr ptnr Basset Gray (multi-discipline design practice) 1922-35, sr ptnr Industl Design Ptnrship (reorganisation of former practice) 1935-40, princ Sir John Cass Sch of Art 1937-40, head and princ design advsr Exhibitions Branch Miny of Info 1940-44, fndr ptnr Design Res Unit 1945-80, conslt 1980-; work incl: rendering of Royal Coat of Arms Crown and Royal Cipher for Coronation Souvenirs 1952-53, design conslt Royal Mint for coin inscriptions 1961-, design of armorial bearings and common seal PO 1970, design of official emblem for Queen's Silver Jubilee for use on street decorations and souvenirs; fndr memb FCSD 1930 (pres 1943-49 and 1966-67); memb Cncl: Design and Industs Assoc 1935-38, RSA 1959-65; memb: Miny Educn Advsy Ctee for Art Examinations 1947-52, Alliance Graphique Internationale 1950 (Br pres 1963-71), Royal Mint Advsy Ctee 1952-86, fndr Ctee Int Cncl Soc Industl Design 1956, Miny Educn Advsy Cncl on Art Educn 1973-76; Design Centre award 1957, Queen's Silver Jubilee medal 1977; Freeman City of London 1981; Hon DA Manchester 1965, hon fell Soc Typographic Designers 1979, hon Dr RCA 1979; RDI 1938, FInstPack 1947, AGI 1950; *Books* numerous publications, lectures and broadcasts on design; *Clubs* Arts; *Style*— Milner Gray, Esq, CBE; Felix Hall, Kelvedon, Essex CO5 9DG; 8 Holly Mount, Hampstead, London NW3 6SG (☎ 071 435 4238)

GRAY, Dr (James) Nicol; s of Capt George Nicol Gray (d 1961), and Elsie May, *née* Scott (d 1966); *b* 29 March 1922; *Educ* George Watsons Coll Edinburgh, Univ of Edinburgh, Royal Sch of Med; *m* 28 Nov 1953, Pamela Ann, da of James MacDonald Walker, DFC (d 1942); 1 s (Ian b 1958), 2 da (Lesley b 1954, Moira b 1962); *Career* Canadian mangr Benger Laboratories Ltd 1957-61, res grantee Arthritis and Rheumatism Cncl 1964-66, GP 1965-78, police surgn 1967-87; med advsr 1978-85: Lothian Regnl Cncl, Lothian and Border Police, Lothian and Border Fire Brigade; LRCPE, LRCSE, LRFPS, DMJ, AFOM, FRSM; memb: BMA, BSMDH, Assoc Police Surgns, Faculty Occupational Medicine RCP 1981; *Recreations* golf, photography; *Clubs* Luffness New; *Style*— Dr Nicol Gray

GRAY, Nicolete Mary; *née* Binyon; da of Laurence Binyon, CH (d 1943), and Cicely, *née* Powell (d 1962); *b* 20 July 1911; *Educ* St Paul's Girls Sch, Univ of Oxford (MA), Br Sch at Rome; *m* 20 July 1933, Basil Gray, s of Charles Gray (d 1915), of London; 2 s (Marius b 1934, Edmund b 1939), 3 da (Camilla b 1936 d 1971, Cecilia b 1940, Sophia b 1943); *Career* asst princ Miny of Food 1940-43, pt/t teacher Convent of Sacred Heart Hammersmith 1948-51, lectr in lettering Central Sch of Art & Design London 1964-81; *Lettering works incl* alphabet of relief Egyptians 1959, whole wall relief inscription Shakespeare Centre Stratford 1964, tombstone of Cardinal Heenan 1976, entrance Mosaic Westminster Cathedral 1981, various tombstones; *Exhibitions organised* Abstract abd Concrete (first exhibition of int abstract art in Br) 1936, Lettering for Arts Cncl of GB 1963, Lettering for Assoc Typographique Int 1981, introductions to Helen Sutherland Collection 1970 and to David Jones 1989; *Books* XIX Century Ornamented Types and Title Pages (1938 and 1976), The Paleography of Latin Inscriptions in Italy 700-1000 AD (1948), Rossetti, Dante and Ourselves (1947), Jacob's Ladder (a bible picture book for children from Anglo-Saxon Mss) (1949), Lettering on Buildings (1960), Lettering as Drawing (1971), The Painted Inscriptions of David Jones (1981), A History of Lettering (1986), The Paintings of David Jones (1989); *Clubs* Double Crown; *Style*— Mrs Nicolete M Gray; Dawbers House, Long Wittenham, Abingdon, Oxon OX14 4QQ

GRAY, Paul Richard Charles; s of Rev Sidney Albert Gray (d 1981), of Thaxted, Essex, and Ina, *née* Maxey; *b* 2 Aug 1948; *Educ* Wyggeston Boys Sch, LSE (BSc); *m* 15 April 1972, Lynda Elsie, da of James Benjamin Braby, of Loughton, Essex; 2 s (Simon b 1978, Adam b 1980); *Career* HM Treasy 1969-77, corp planning exec Booker McConnell Ltd 1977-79; HM Treasy: princ Agric Div 1979-83, asst sec Gen Expenditure Div 1984-86, asst sec Indust and Employment Div 1987-, under sec Monetary Gp 1990; econ affrs private sec to PM 1988-90; *Recreations* family, walking, gardening; *Style*— Paul Gray, Esq; c/o H M Treasury, London SW1

GRAY, Peter Francis; s of Rev George Francis Selby Gray; *b* 7 Jan 1937; *Educ* Marlborough, Trinity Coll Cambridge; *m* 1978, Fiona Elspeth Maude Lillias, da of late Arnold Charles Verity Bristol; 2 s; *Career* Nat Serv Lt Royal Fus attached to 4 Kings African Rifles Uganda 1956-58; Coopers & Lybrand 1967-69, Samuel Montagu & Co 1970-77, head of Investmt Div Crown Agents for Overseas Govts and Admins 1977-83, md and chief exec Touche Remnant & Co and Touche Remnant Holdings 1983-87, dir TR Industrial & General Trust plc 1984-88; dep chm The Assoc of Investmt Tst Cos 1985-87, chm Exmoor Dual Investment Trust 1988, dir NZ Investment Trust 1988-, dir Gartmore Value Investments; FCA; *Clubs* Brooks's, Buck's; *Style*— Peter Gray, Esq; 1 Bradbourne St, London SW6 (☎ 071 731 4950)

GRAY, Philip Malcolm James; s of James Carter Gray (d 1932), and Lucy Venetia Emily, *née* Robson (d 1972); *b* 17 Jan 1927; *Educ* Eastbourne Coll, Royal Sch of Mines, Univ of London (BSc); *m* 18 Aug 1949, Joan, da of Alfred Thomas Houldsworth; *Career* scientific offr AERE Harwell 1947-51, res offr Cwlth Scientific and Res Orgn Melbourne Aust 1951-55, metallurgist and devpt mangr Imperial Smelting Corporation Avonmouth UK 1955-64 (tech mangr 1964-71), chief metallurgist Non-Ferrous Div Davy Corporation London 1971-78, metallurgical conslt and ptnr Philip M J Gray and J Gray London 1978-; pres Inst of Mining and Metallurgy 1984-85 (Capper Pass award 1952 and 1955), Waverly Gold medal 1955; Freeman City of London 1984, Liveryman Worshipful Co of Engineers; ARSM, FIMM 1973 (MIMM 1953), fell Aust Inst Mining and Metallurgy 1970 (memb 1952), FEng 1984; *Books* The Profitable Development of Sulphide Ore Resources (with P Loffler and G Bielstein, 1985), numerous contribs to learned pubns (1951-); *Recreations* bell ringing, opera, musical appreciation, looking at paintings, golf, cricket, travel; *Clubs* Lansdowne; *Style*— Philip Gray, Esq; 24 Quickswood, Primrose Hill, London NW3 3RS (☎ 071 722 8513); Philip M J Gray and J Gray, 24 Quickswood, Primrose Hill, London NW3 3RS (☎ 071 722 8513, fax 071 483 2966)

GRAY, Dr (John) Richard; s of Capt A W Gray, RN, of Bournemouth, and Christobel Margaret, *née* Raikes; *b* 7 July 1929; *Educ* Charterhouse, Downing Coll Cambridge (MA), SOAS London (PhD); *m* 30 March 1957, Gabriella, da of Dr Camillo Cattaneo (d 1956); 1 s (Camillo b 1959), 1 da (Fiammetta b 1965); *Career* lectr Univ of Khartoum 1959-61; SOAS: res fell 1961-63, reader 1963-72, prof of African history 1972-89; chm: African Centre Covent Garden 1967-72, Br Zimbabwe Soc 1981-84; Equitem Ordinis Sancti Silvestri Papae 1966; *Books* The Two Nations (1960), A History of the Southern Sudan (1961), Cambridge History of Africa (ed vol 4, 1975), Black Christians and White Missionaries (1990); *Style*— Dr Richard Gray; 39 Rotherwick Rd, London NW11 7DD

GRAY, Roger Ibbotson; QC (1967); s of Arthur Gray (d 1959), and Mary, *née*

Ibbotson (d 1982); *b* 16 June 1921; *Educ* Wycliffe Coll, Queen's Coll Oxford (BA); *m* 1, 1952, Anne Valerie, da of Capt G G P Hewett, CBE, RN (d 1966), of Folkestone; 1 s (Randal b 1952); m 2, 1987, Lynne Jacqueline, da of Eric Towell, of Spain; *Career* cmmnd RA 1942, with Ayrshire Yeo 1942-45, Normandy and NW Europe, GSO 3 8 Corps 1945, GSO 3 (Mil Ops) GHQ India 1946; called to the Bar Gray's Inn 1947; rec of Crown Ct 1972-; Parly candidate (C) Dagenham 1955; *Recreations* cricket, reading; *Clubs* Carlton, Pratt's, MCC; *Style*— Roger Gray, Esq, QC; The Old Cottage, 20 Friday St, Minchinhampton, Glos Gl6 9JL; Queen Elizabeth Building, Temple, London EC4 (☎ 071 583 7837)

GRAY, Ronald George; s of Henry Gray (d 1958), and Elizabeth Campbell, *née* Cowan (d 1942); *b* 12 July 1929; *Educ* Royal HS Edinburgh, Univ of Edinburgh (MA); *m* 26 June 1954, Diana Ravenscroft, da of Francis Henry Houlston (d 1983); 3 da (Karen b 14 Oct 1955, Francesca b 14 Sept 1958, Fiona b 10 March 1960); *Career* trainee Unilever 1953; dir: Elida Gibbs Ltd 1967-72, Unilever Co-ordination 1973-80; chm: Elida Gibbs (Germany) 1981-84, Lever Bros Ltd 1984-; chm: CTFA (Cosmetic Toiletry and Fragrance Assoc) 1970-72, SDIA (Soap and Detergent Industry Assoc) 1985-89; pres ISBA 1988-90, memb IBA Advertising Advsy Ctee; govr: Dulwich Coll, Alleyns Sch; *Style*— Ronald Gray, Esq; Lever Brothers Ltd, Lever House, 3 St James's Rd, Kingston-on-Thames, Surrey KT1 2BA (☎ 081 541 8200)

GRAY, Rosemarie Hume; *née* Elliott-Smith; da of Air Cdre C H Elliott-Smith, AFC, of Eggleston Hall, Barnard Castle, Co Durham, and Margot Agnes, *née* Piffard (d 1977); *Educ* privately; *m* 22 April 1954, William Talbot Gray (d 1971), s of Sir William Cresswell Gray, 2 Bt (d 1978); 1 s (Sir William Hume Gray, 3 Bt, *qv*), 2 da (Victoria (Mrs Straker) b 15 July 1958, Emma Mary b 7 Oct 1962); *Career* dir: Eggleston Estate Co, Talbot Gray Ltd; govr Polam Hall Sch; non-exec memb SW Durham Health Authy; High Sheriff of Co Palatine of Durham 1986; *Recreations* gardening, travel; *Style*— Mrs William Talbot Gray; Eggleston Hall, Barnard Castle, Co Durham (☎ 0833 50403); 483 Fulham Palace Rd, London SW6

GRAY, Prof Sidney John; s of Sidney George Gray (d 1978), and Mary Angeline, *née* Birch (d 1974); *b* 3 Oct 1942; *Educ* Bedford Mod Sch, Univ of Sydney (BEc), Univ of Lancaster (PhD); *m* 23 July 1977, Hilary Fenella, da of William Leonard Jones, of Drymen; 1 s (Peter b 1985), 1 da (Helen b 1981); *Career* exec: Peirce Leslie & Co Ltd UK and India 1961-67 (factory mangr 1966-67), Burns Philp & Co Ltd Aust 1967-68; tutor in accounting Univ of Sydney 1972, lectr Univ of Lancaster 1974-78 (res scholar 1973-74), prof of accounting and fin Univ of Glasgow 1978- (head of dept 1980-87); sec gen Euro Accounting Assoc 1982-83, memb UK Accounting Standards Ctee 1984-87, vice-pres Europe Int Assoc for Accounting Educn and Res 1986-, chm Br Accounting Assoc 1987; ACIS 1971, FCCA 1980, MBIM 1973; *Books* International Accounting and Transnational Decisions (1983), Information Disclosure and the Multinational Corporation (1984), International Financial Reporting (1984), Mega-Merger Mayhem (1989); *Recreations* tennis, golf; *Clubs* East India; *Style*— Prof Sidney Gray; Dept of Accounting and Finance, University of Glasgow, 65-71 Southpark Ave, Glasgow G12 8LE (☎ 041 330 5426, fax 041 330 4442)

GRAY, Simon James Holliday; s of Dr James Davidson Gray, and Barbara Cecelia Mary, *née* Holliday; *b* 21 Oct 1936; *Educ* Westminster, Dalhousie Univ, Trinity Coll Cambridge (MA); *m* 1965, Beryl Mary, *née* Kevern; 1 s (Ben), 1 da (Lucy); *Career* res student and Harper-Wood travelling student 1960, sr instr in English Univ of Br Columbia 1963-64, lectr QMC London 1965-85; author and playwright; *Plays*: Wise Child (1968), Sleeping Dog (1968), Dutch Uncle (1969), The Idiot (1971), Spoiled (1971), Butley (1971), Otherwise Engaged (1975, voted Best Play 1976-77 by NY Drama Critics Circle), Plaintiffs and Defendants (1975), Two Sundays (1975), Dog Days (1976), Molly (1977), The Rear Column (1978), Close of Play (1979), Stage Struck (1979), Quartermaine's Terms (1981), The Common Pursuit (1984), Plays One (1986), Melon (1987), After Pilkington (1987, televised 1987), Old Flames (televised 1990), Hidden Laughter (1990), The Holy Terror and Tartuffe (1990), They Never Slept (1991); *Books* Colmain (1963), Simple People (1965), Little Portia (1967, as Hamish Reade), A Comeback for Stark (1968), An Unnatural Pursuit and Other Pieces (1985), How's That For Telling 'em Fat Lady? (1988); *Recreations* watching cricket and soccer; *Clubs* Dramatist, Groucho; *Style*— Simon Gray, Esq; c/o Judy Daish Assoc, 83 East Bourne Mews, London W2 6LQ

GRAY, Simon Talbot; s of Dr John Talbot Carmichael Gray (d 1961), of Ealing, and Doris Irene, *née* Baker; *b* 1 June 1938; *Educ* Westminster; *m* 1963, Susan, da of Felix William Grain, of Ealing; 2 s (Nicholas b 1965, Julian b 1968); *Career* CA; sr tax ptnr Smith & Williamson; dir: S & W Securities, S & W Trust Corporation, S & W Nominees, S & W Insurance Consultants, Yattendon Investment Trust Ltd, Syndicate Administration Ltd, Hartridge Investment Ltd, Chichester Estate Company, Yattendon Holdings plc; special tstee of St Bartholomew's and St Marks Hospitals 1982-; memb City & Hackney Health Authy 1983-90; memb Ct Worshipful Co of Glass Sellers (Master 1978); *Recreations* yachting (yacht 'Fast Anchor'); *Clubs* City of London, City Livery, Royal Lymington Yacht, Royal Thames Yacht; *Style*— Simon Gray, Esq; Brackens, Captains Row, Lymington, Hants SO41 9RP (☎ 0590 677101); 44 Minster Court, Hillcrest Rd, Ealing W5 1HH (☎ 081 997 6447); 1 Ridinghouse St, London W1 (☎ 071 637 5377, telex 25187, fax 071 631 0741)

GRAY, Sir William (Stevenson); JP (Glasgow 1965), DL (City of Glasgow 1976); s of William Gray; *b* 3 May 1928; *Educ* Univ of Glasgow (BL); *m* 1958, Mary Rodger; 1 s, 1 da; *Career* slr and Notary Public; City of Glasgow: hon treas 1971-72, magistrate 1961-64, memb Corp 1958-75, chm Property Mgmnt Ctee 1964-67; former chm Irvine New Town Devpt Corp; chm: Gap (formerly World of Property Housing Scottish) Housing Assoc 1974-, Third Eye Centre 1975-85, Scottish Devpt Agency 1975-79, The Oil Club 1975-, Glasgow Ind Hosp 1982-89, The Barrel Selection 1986-, WPHT Scotland Ltd 1987-, Norcity plc 1988-, Clan Homes plc 1988-, Healthcare Gp plc 1989-, Norhomes plc 1989-, Manchester Village Homes plc 1989-, Gap Housing Association (Ownership) Ltd 1989-, Dermalose Ltd 1989-, First Tax Homes plc 1989-, Second Tax Homes plc 1989-, Norcity II plc 1989-; vice pres Glasgow Citizens' Theatre 1975-; memb: Scottish Opera Bd 1971-72, Nat Tst Scotland 1971-72, Ct of Glasgow Univ 1972-75, Clyde Port Authy 1972-75, Advsy Cncl Energy Conservation 1974-85, Glasgow Advsy Ctee on JPs 1975- (patron), Scottish Youth Theatre 1976-86, Scottish Pakistani Soc 1983-; vice pres: Charles Rennie Mackintosh Soc 1974-, Scottish Assoc for Care and Resettlement of Offenders 1975-82; Lord Provost City of Glasgow, Lord Lt Co of the City of Glasgow 1972-75 (DL 1971-72); kt 1974; *Style*— Sir William Gray, JP, DL; 13 Royal Terrace, Glasgow G3 7NY (☎ 041 332 8877, fax 041 332 2809)

GRAY, Sir William Hume; 3 Bt (UK 1917), of Tunstall Manor, Hart, Co Durham; s of late William Talbot Gray, s of 2 Bt; suc gf, Sir William Gray, 2 Bt, 1978; Sir William Cresswell Gray, 1 Bt, was chm William Gray & Co Ltd, a memb of Lloyds Register Ctee and first chm of the S Durham Steel and Iron Co Ltd in 1889; *b* 26 July 1955; *Educ* Eton, Polytechnic of Central London (Dip Arch); *m* 1984, Catherine, yst da of late John Naylor, of The Mill House, Bramley, Hants; 1 s, 2 da; *Heir* s, William John Cresswell Gray b 1986; *Career* architect; *Style*— Sir William Gray, Bt; Eggleston Hall, Eggleston, Barnard Castle, Co Durham

GRAY-CHEAPE, Hamish Leslie; JP (Warwickshire 1985), DL (Warwickshire 1990); s of Lt-Col Leslie George Gray-Cheape, of Carse Gray, Forfar, Angus, Scotland, and Dorothy Evelyn, *née* Thomas (d 1986); *b* 18 March 1942; *Educ* Eton; *m* 6 Oct 1965, Fiona Mariella, da of Brig Sir Harry Ripley Mackeson (d 1964, 1 Bn late Royal Scots Greys); 2 s (James b 1968, George b 1971); *Career* Capt Grenadier Gds 1961-71; High Sheriff of Warwickshire 1984; farmer 1972-; memb Queens Body Guard for Scotland (The Royal Co of Archers) 1972; *Style*— Hamish Gray-Cheape, Esq, JP, DL; Great Alne (☎ 0789 488420); Hill House, Walcote, Alcester, Warwickshire B49 6LZ

GRAY OF CONTIN, Baron (Life Peer UK 1983), of Contin in the District of Ross and Cromarty; Hamish James Hector Northey Gray; PC (1982), DL (1989); s of James Northey Gray, JP (d 1979), of Inverness; *b* 28 June 1927; *Educ* Inverness Royal Acad; *m* 1953, Judith Waite, da of Noel M Brydon, MBE, of Ayr; 2 s (Hon (James Northey) David b 1955, Hon Peter b 1959), 1 da (Hon Sally (Hon Mrs Brown) b 1957); *Career* served Queen's Own Cameron Highlanders (Lt) 1945-48; memb Inverness Cncl 1965-70; former dir: Drumry Testing Co Hillington, James Gray (Inverness) Ltd, and others; MP (C) Ross and Cromarty 1970-83; asst govt whip 1971-73, lord cmmr Treasury 1973-74, oppn whip 1974-75, oppn spokesman on energy 1975-79; min of state: Energy 1979-83, Scottish Office 1983-86, public affrs business and Parly conslt 1986-; *Recreations* golf, cricket, walking; *Clubs* Highland (Inverness); *Style*— The Rt Hon Lord Gray of Contin, PC, DL; Achneim House, Flichity, Inverness-shire IV1 2XE (☎ 08083 211); House of Lords, London SW1

GRAYBURN, Jeremy Ward; s of Sqdn Ldr Robert William Grayburn (d 1982), of Silverdale, Lancs, and Moira Wendy, *née* Fry; *b* 24 Aug 1952; *Educ* Lancaster Royal GS; *m* 7 Feb 1976, Pamela Anne, da of Flt Lt Graham Ross; 2 da (Nichola, Caroline); *Career* Allied Dunbar Assurance plc: joined 1971, divnl dir 1984-85, exec dir 1985-, sr exec dir 1990; *Style*— Jeremy Grayburn, Esq; York Cottage, Long Lane, Shaw, Newbury, Berks RG16 9LJ (☎ 0635 34437); Allied Dunbar Assurance plc, Allied Dunbar Centre, Swindon, Wiltshire (☎ 0793 514514, fax 0793 512301)

GRAYDON, Air Vice Marshal Sir Michael James; KCB (1989), CBE (1984); s of James Julian Graydon (d 1985), and Rita Mary, *née* Alkan; *b* 24 Oct 1938; *Educ* Wycliffe Coll; *m* 25 May 1963, (Margaret) Elizabeth, da of Arthur Ronald Clark (d 1972); *Career* RAF Coll Cranwell 1957-59, QFI No 1 Fts 1960-62, No 56 Sqdn Wattisham 1963-64, 226 OCU 1965-67, Flt-Cdr No 56 Akrotiri 1967-69, RAF Staff Coll Bracknell 1970, PSO to D/CINCENT HQAFCENT 1971-73, ops staff MOD 1973-75, NDC Latimer 1975-76, OC No 11 Sqdn Binbrook 1977-79, MA to CDS MOD 1979-81, OC RAF Leuchars 1981-83, OC RAF Stanley FI 1983, RCDS London 1984, SASO HQ 11 Gp Bentley Priory 1985-86, ACOS policy SHAPE Belgium 1986-89, Air Marshal and AOC-in-C RAF Support Cmd 1989-; govr Wycliffe Coll; *Recreations* golf, photography; *Style*— Air Vice Marshal Sir Michael Graydon, KCB, CBE; AOC-in- C, RAF Support Command, Brampton, Huntingdon, Cambs PE18 8QL (☎ 0480 52151)

GRAYSON, Edward; *b* 1 March 1925; *Educ* Taunton's Sch Southampton, Exeter Coll Oxford; *m* 27 May 1959, (Myra) Wendy Shockett; 1 s (Harry b 26 March 1966); *Career* RAF 1943-45; called to the Bar Middle Temple 1948; uninterrupted practice: Lincoln's Inn 1949-53, Temple and SE circuit 1953-; author and communicator; contrib: legal, sporting and nat jls, newspapers, BBC, ITV, various radio stations; contrib and conslt to Centl Cncl of Physical Recreation and Sports Cncl, hon legal advsr Freedom in Sport Int; memb Br Assoc of Sports Med; *Books* Corinthians and Cricketers (1955, re-issued as Corinthian-Casuals and Cricketers 1983), The Royal Baccarat Scandal (jtly, second edn 1988), The Way Forward: The Gleneagles Agreement (1982), Sponsorship of Sport, Arts and Leisure (jtly, 1984), Sport and The Law (second edn 1988); *Recreations* working and creative thinking; *Clubs* MCC, Harlequins, Corinthian-Casuals, Sussex, Surrey CC, Littlehampton Town FC; *Style*— Edward Grayson, Esq; 1 Brick Court, Temple, London EC4Y 9BY (☎ 071 583 6287); Temple Gate, Shaftesbury Rd, Rustington, West Sussex (☎ 0903 783823); 4 Paper Buildings, Temple, London EC4Y 7EX (☎ 071 583 7765, fax 071 353 4674: Groups 2 & 3)

GRAYSON, Sir Rupert Stanley Harrington; 4 Bt (UK 1922); s of late Sir Henry Grayson, 1 Bt, KBE (d 1951); suc n Sir Ronald Henry Rudyard Grayson, 3 Bt (d 1987); unc of Lord Rawlinson, of Ewell, QC and the Earl of Munster; *b* 22 July 1897; *Educ* Harrow; *m* 1, 1919, Ruby Victoria, da of Walter Henry Banks; m 2, 1950, Vari Colette, da of Maj Henry O' Shea, Royal Dublin Fus, of Cork; *Heir* n, Jeremy Brian Vincent Grayson b 1933; *Career* Ensign in Irish Gds (twice wounded) 1914-18, King's Foreign Serv Messenger 1939-45; novelist, constant traveller; Kt of Order of Holy Sepulchre; *Books autobiographies* Voyage Not Completed, Stand Fast The Holy Ghost; *fiction* 26 Gun Cotton, Secret Service Adventures; *Style*— Sir Rupert Grayson, Bt; c/o Midland Bank, Hythe, Kent

GRAZEBROOK, Lt-Col Adrian Michael; TD (1974); s of Brig (Tom) Neville Grazebrook, CBE, DSO (d 1967), of Sheepscombe House, Gloucestershire, and (Marion) Betty, *née* Asplin; *b* 25 March 1943; *Educ* Sherborne; *m* 22 Sept 1984, Susan Mary, da of (Frank) Geoffrey Outwin, of Barnwood, Gloucester; *Career* cmmnd TA 1962, Lt-Col 1984-; admitted slr 1966; ptnr Wilmot & Co 1968-; memb Cncl Racehorse Owners' Assoc; memb Law Soc 1966; *Recreations* racing, choral singing; *Clubs* Army and Navy; *Style*— Adrian Grazebrook, Esq, TD; The Shepherd's Cottage, Hilcot End, Ampney Crucis, Cirencester, Gloucestershire GL7 5SG (☎ 0285 851507); 38 Castle St, Cirencester, Gloucestershire GL7 1QH (☎ 0285 650551, fax 0285 654007, car 0836 502757)

GRAZEBROOK, Donald McDonald Denis Durley; s of Kenrick Denis Durley Grazebrook (d 1957), and Evelyn, *née* Griffiths; *b* 17 Jan 1927; *Educ* privately, UCL (LLB); *m* 17 April 1953, Mabel, da of Charles Gawler (d 1970), of Stalbridge, Dorset and Anglesey; *Career* called to the Bar Lincoln's Inn 1952, entered Govt Legal Serv 1952; serv: Miny of Nat Insur 1952-61, Miny of Lab (later Dept of Employment) 1961-78; ind legal advsr 1979; UKAEA 1982-: legal advsr 1982-88, conslt 1988-; pres Conseil D' Administration Assoc Int du Droit Nucléaire 1990 (memb 1983, 2 vice pres 1987); *Recreations* fox and stag hunting; *Clubs* East India; *Style*— Donald Grazebrook, Esq; Pine Ridge, Peaslake, Surrey; Atomic Energy Authy, 11 Charles II St, London SW1

GREATOREX, Raymond Edward (Ray); s of Percy Edward Greatorex (d 1985), and Lilian Alice, *née* George (d 1986); *b* 28 May 1940; *Educ* Westcliff HS, Lewes County GS; *m* 1, 3 Sept 1966 (m dis 1982), Brenda Margery, da of Edward James Rands (d 1990); m 2, 27 May 1982, Barbara Anne, da of Mark Booth; 1 step da (Joanna Dawn Carty b 16 Sept 1974); *Career* CA 1965; ptnr: Sydenham & Co 1970 (merged to form Hodgson Harris 1980), Hodgson Impey (after merger) 1985; int ptnr Kidsons Impey (after merger) 1990; memb ctees SE Soc of CA's; Freeman City of London; FCA; *Recreations* travelling, horse breeding and racing, gardening; *Style*— Ray Greatorex, Esq; Beeches Brook, Wisborough Green, W Sussex RH14 OHP (☎ 0403 700 796); Peel House, Barttelot Rd, Horsham, Sussex RH12 1DQ (☎ 0403 51666, fax 0403 51466)

GREATREX, Geoffrey Harold; s of Harold Victor Greatrex, of Essex, and Henrietta; *b* 3 March 1933; *Educ* Gosfield Sch, Durham Univ Newcastle upon Tyne (MB BS), Toronto Univ, Harvard Univ; *m* 1968 (m dis 1976), Tatiana, da of Mikhail Swetchin (d 1967), of Toronto; 1 da (Alexandra b 1973); *Career* Capt RAMC attached parachute regt Cyprus 1958-61; conslt surgn Central Notts Health Authy 1977-, dir Nottingham private med conslts 1983-; memb ct of examiners RCS (Eng) 1986-; *Recreations* arts, fell walking, tree felling; *Clubs* Flyfishers, Royal Society of Medicine; *Style—* Geoffrey Greatrex, Esq; Greenfields, Quaker Lane, Farnsfield, Notts NG22 8EE; Kings Mill Hospital, Sutton-in-Ashfield, Notts

GREAVES, Brian John; s of John Greaves (d 1976), and Beatrice Mabel, *née* Siddon (d 1961); *b* 25 April 1935; *Educ* Clark's Coll Putney, Poly of Central London; *m* 1, (m dis); 2 s (Richard John b 1962, Andrew Peter b 1963), 1 da (Dawn Elizabeth b 1960); m 2, 1986, Hazel, da of Alan John Osborne Robinson; 1 s (John Michael b 25 June 1984); *Career* Nat Serv RAF 1953-55; Wallace Heaton: trainee photographer 1951-53, fine art photographer 1955-62, mangr photographic studio (New Bond St London) 1962-64; Agfa Ltd: trained as tech rep Leverkusen W Germany 1964-70, colour specialist Industl Dept (Agfa-Gevaert Ltd) 1970-76, colour mktg specialist Professional Sales Dept 1976-83, prod mangr Paper and Chemicals Photofinishing Professional Dept 1983, currently prod mangr Colour Paper and Film Business Group; pt/t lectr in photography: Regent St Poly 1962-64, Paddington Coll 1970-88; club instr Br Sub Aqua Club 1975; FBIPP 1982, fell Master Photographers Assoc 1988; *Recreations* boating, sub-aqua; *Clubs* Middle Thames Yacht (rear cdre); *Style—* Brian Greaves, Esq; Agfa Gevaert Ltd, Great West Rd, Brentford, Middlesex TW8 9AW (☎ 081 542 9692, fax 081 569 7817)

GREAVES, James Peter (Jimmy); s of James Greaves (d 1989), and Mary Greaves; *b* 20 Feb 1940; *Educ* Kingswood Secdy Sch Hainault; *m* Irene, *née* Barden; 3 s (Jimmy b 1960 d 1960, Daniel b 1962, Andrew b 1966), 2 da (Lynn b 1959, Mitzi b 1964); *Career* professional footballer 1957-71: debut Chelsea Aug 1957, AC Milan Italy, Tottenham Hotspur, West Ham Utd; non-league clubs: Chelmsford, Brentwood, Barnet, Woodford Town; 57 full England caps (44 goals) 1959-67; scored total of 491 goals in first class games (357 in Div 1) 1957-71; honours with Tottenham Hotspur: FA Cup winners' medal 1962 and 1967, Euro Cup Winners' medal 1963; TV presenter and football analyst 1980-, tv previewer TV-AM 1983-, jt presenter Saint & Greavsie Show ITV 1985-; three times winner TV Times Readers' Popularity awards; *Books* 14 with Norman Giller incl: This One's On Me (autobiography, 1981), It's A Funny Old Life (autobiography, 1990); *Recreations* watching football, cricket and rugby, playing golf, gardening, trying to keep pace with seven grandchildren; *Clubs* Alcoholics Anonymous; *Style—* Jimmy Greaves, Esq; TV-AM, Hawley Crescent, London NW1 (☎ 071 267 4300); Greaves Insurance Co, Elm Rd, Leigh-on-Sea, Essex (☎ 0707 77773); c/o Barry Brown Management, 47 West Square, London SE11 4SP (☎ 071 582 6622)

GREAVES, (Ronald) John; s of Ronald Greaves, and Rose Mary, *née* Nugent; *b* 7 Aug 1948; *Educ* Donai Martyrs Ickenham Middx, Central London Poly (LLB); *m* 1, 3 July 1970 (m dis 1980), Angela, da of Stanley Menze; m 2, Margaret Dorothy, da of Denis John O'Sullivan, of Thornhill, Lincoln Drive, Winterton, S Humberside; 1 s (Patrick John b 30 Sept 1987), 1 da (Caroline Frances b 28 July 1984); *Career* called to the Bar Middle Temple 1973; currently in practice SE Circuit; Parly candidate (Lab) St Albans 1974; memb: Justice Ctee of Compensation for Wrongful Imprisonment, Soc of Labour Lawyers; *Style—* John Greaves, Esq; 51 Kingsend, Ruislip, Middlesex HA4 7DD (☎ 0895 632676); 4 Paper Buildings, Temple, London EC4Y 7X (☎ 071 583 7765, fax 071 353 4674)

GREAVES, Jonathan Frederick Anthony (Jon); s of Geoffrey Greaves (d 1991), of Rock, Cornwall, and Edith Helen, *née* Wolfe; *b* 20 June 1939; *Educ* Haileybury, Grenoble Univ, High Wycombe Coll of Further Educn; *m* Susan Mary, da of late A G Drayson, of Sutton Valence, Kent; 1 s (Jeremy b 14 July 1968), 1 da (Victoria b 9 April 1971); *Career* mktg mangr Greaves & Thomas 1964-68, md Quantic Ltd 1968-; MInstM 1974, MIPA 1975; *Recreations* sailing, skiing, shooting, tennis, photography; *Style—* Jon Greaves, Esq; Fitzjohns, Great Canfield, Dunnow, Essex CM6 1JZ (☎ 0371 820 448); Bay Cottage, Rock, N Cornwall PL27 6LB; Quantic Ltd, The Old Bakery, High Wych, Harlow, Essex CM21 0HZ (☎ 0279 726990, fax 0279 726851, car 0860 746422)

GRECIAN, Nicholas James (Nick); s of John Livingstone Grecian, of Sonning-on-Thames, Berkshire, and Margaret Joyce, *née* McElderry; *b* 1 Sept 1963; *Educ* Loretto, Nene Coll Northampton; *Career* Rugby Union wing threequarter London Scottish RFC; clubs: Chingford RFC 1982-83, Northampton RFC 1983-88 (76 appearances), London Scottish RFC 1988-; rep: Essex, Eastern Counties, E Midlands, Public Sch Wanderers, Anglo-Scots, Scotland U21, Scotland B (debut v Ireland 1990); area account mangr Barbour Index; *Recreations* Scottish history, real ale, shooting; *Style—* Nick Grecian, Esq; London Scottish FC, Richmond Athletic Ground, Kew Foot Rd, Richmond, Surrey

GREELEY, Paul William; s of Thomas Greeley, of Huddersfield, and Mary Greeley, of Huddersfield; *b* 5 Oct 1939; *Educ* St Josephs Acad Blackheath; *m* 10 April 1976, Moya Patricia, da of A Basil Pippet; 2 s (Justin b 1978, Andrew b 1984), 2 da (Susanna b 1980, Sophia b 1982); *Career* CA; public practice; FCA, ATII; *Recreations* cricket, chess, literature; *Clubs* Challoner; *Style—* Paul Greeley, Esq; Four Stacks, 6 Peaks Hill, Purley, Surrey CR8 3JE (☎ 081 668 5789); 1433B London Rd, Norbury, London SW16 4AW (☎ 081 679 5722, fax 081 773 2267)

GREEN, Alan Laurence; s of Samuel Ben Green (d 1967), of Manchester, and Miriam, *née* Berkovitch; *b* 2 Feb 1946; *Educ* Carmel Coll, Altrincham GS, Univ of Sussex (BA); *m* 12 Dec 1977, Charlotte Ann Maud, da of Maj Basil Wade Coxeter (d 1988), of Blakeney, Norfolk; 2 s (Tom b 1978, George b 1980); *Career* called to the Bar Grays Inn 1973; practising barr 1973-80, head of chambers 1985-90; *Recreations* walking, sailing, skiing; *Style—* Alan Green, Esq; 2 Harcourt Buildings, Temple, London EC4Y 9DB (☎ 071 353 1394, fax 071 353 4134)

GREEN, Alan Michael; s of Frank Joseph Green (d 1966), and Hilda, *née* Bowden; *b* 22 Dec 1932; *Educ* Colfes GS Lewisham, Beckenham Sch of Art (NDD), RCA (major travelling scholar, ARCA); *m* 30 Aug 1958, June, da of Oswald Barnes; 2 da (Paula b 5 July 1960, Julia b 26 July 1961); *Career* artist, pt/t and full time teacher in art colls until 1972; regular solo exhibitions in Europe America and Japan 1963-; paintings in perm museum collections worldwide incl: The Tate Gallery London, Solomon R Guggenheim Museum New York, Tokyo Metropolitan Art Museum; Grand Prix 4th Norwegian Int Print Biennale, Nat Museum of Art Osaka prize 11th Print Biennale Tokyo; *Style—* Alan Green, Esq; Annely Juda Fine Art, 23 Dering St, London W1R 9AA (☎ 071 629 7578, fax 071 491 2139)

GREEN, Alison Anne; da of Sam Green, CBE, of Holly Lodge, 39 Westmoreland Rd, Bromley, Kent, and Lilly, *née* Pollak; *b* 18 March 1951; *Educ* Bromley HS, UCL (LLB, LLM), Univ of Louvain; *Career* called to the Bar Middle Temple 1974; lectr in law Univ of Surrey 1976-78; tutor in law: QMC London 1978-79, UCL 1979-81; memb ctee Br Insur Law Assoc, memb IBA; *Books* Insurance Contract Law (ed advsr 1988), Current Law (ed Euro Communities section); *Recreations* music, tennis, ballet; *Clubs* Hurlingham; *Style—* Miss Alison Green; Queen Elizabeth Building, Temple, London EC4Y 9BS (☎ 071 353 9153, fax 071 583 0126)

GREEN, Sir Allan David; KCB (1991), QC (1987); s of Lionel Green, and Irene Evelyn, *née* Abrahams (later Mrs Axelrad, d 1975); *b* 1 March 1935; *Educ* Charterhouse, St Catharine's Coll Cambridge (MA); *m* 21 Feb 1967, Eva Brita Margareta, da of Prof Artur Attman (d 1988), of Gothenburg, Sweden; 1 s (Robin b 1969), 1 da (Susanna b 1970); *Career* serv RN 1953-55; called to the Bar Inner Temple 1959; sr prosecuting counsel to Crown Central Criminal Ct 1979-85 (jr prosecuting counsel 1977-79), rec Crown Ct 1979-87, bencher 1985, first sr prosecuting counsel Crown Central Criminal Ct 1985-87, dir Public Prosecutions and head Crown Prosecution Serv 1987; non-exec dir Windsmoor plc 1986-87; *Recreations* music, studying calligraphy; *Style—* Sir Allan Green, KCB, QC; 4-12 Queen Anne's Gate, London SW1H 9AZ

GREEN, Andrew Fleming; s of Gp Capt Joseph Henry Green, CBE (d 1970), and Beatrice Mary, *née* Bowditch; *b* 6 Aug 1941; *Educ* Haileybury, Magdalene Coll Univ of Cambridge (BA, MA); *m* 21 Sept 1968, Catherine Jane, da of Lt Cdr Peter Norton Churchill, RN (d 1940); 1 s (Stephen b 1973), 1 da (Diana b 1970); *Career* short serv cmmn Royal Greenjackets 1962-65; Dip Serv: MECAS Lebanon 1966-68, second sec Aden 1968-70, asst political agent Abu Dhabi 1970-73; first sec: FCO 1973-77, UK Del OECD Paris 1977-80, FCO 1980-82; political cnsllr Washington 1982-85, consul gen and head of chancery Riyadh 1985-88, cnsllr FCO 1988; *Recreations* tennis, sailing, bridge; *Style—* Andrew Green, Esq; c/o Foreign and Commonwealth Office, King Charles St, London SW1A 2AH

GREEN, Anthony Eric Sandall; s of Frederick Sandall Green (d 1961), of 17 Lissenden Mansions, London, and Marie-Madeleine (Mrs Joscelyne), *née* Dupont (d 1969); *b* 30 Sept 1939; *Educ* Highgate Sch, Slade Sch of Fine Art UCL (Dip Fine Art); *m* 29 July 1961, Mary Louise, da of Gordon Roberts Cozens-Walker (d 1981); 2 da (Katharine Charlotte b 1965, Lucy Rebecca b 1970); *Career* artist; Harkness Fellowship USA 1967-69, over 40 one man shows worldwide; UK public collections: Tate, V & A, Arts Cncl of GB, Br Cncl, and others; foreign public collections at: The Met Museum of Art NYC, various museums in Japan and Brazil, and others; RA 1977; *Books* A Green Part of the World (with Martin Bailey, 1984); *Recreations* family, travel; *Clubs* Arts; *Style—* Anthony Green, Esq; 17 Lissenden Mansions, London NW5 1PP (☎ 071 485 1226)

GREEN, Antony John Stephen; s of Edwin Stephen Green, of Lyndhurst, and Eileen, *née* Rigby; *b* 6 Jan 1935; *Educ* Merchant Taylors' Sch Crosby, Univ of Bristol; *m* 30 March 1962, Valerie Anne, da of late Herbert Stanley Exworth; 2 c (Sarah Caroline b 14 Sept 1964, Christopher Stephen Antony b 19 Jan 1966); *Career* Nat Serv RN 1958-59; mgmnt apprentice Trust Houses Ltd 1959-62, various admin and mgmnt posts Trust House Forte Ltd 1962-84, dir Evergreen Hotels Ltd (fndr 1984, proprieter Crown Hotel Lyndhurst); Master Innholder 1987, Freeman City of London 1987; MBIM 1968, FHCIMA 1972; *Recreations* sailing, cooking; *Clubs* Island Cruising (Salcombe); *Style—* Antony Green, Esq; Evergreen Hotels Ltd, Crown Hotel, High St, Lyndurst, Hants SO43 7NF (☎ 0703 282922, fax 0703 282751)

GREEN, Arthur; s of Arthur Henry Green (d 1953), and Elizabeth Burns, *née* Stewart (d 1978); *b* 15 June 1928; *Educ* Liverpool Collegiate; *m* 26 July 1952, Sylvia, da of Harold Myatt (d 1982); 1 s (Andrew Paul b 13 July 1960), 1 da (Sally Linda b 29 Jan 1962); *Career* qualified CA 1950; ptnr Bryce Hanmer & Co (now Grant Thornton) 1954; Grant Thornton: nat managing ptnr 1974-83, chm and md Grant Thornton International 1984-87, sr ptnr 1984-88; pres: Liverpool Soc of CAs 1971-72, ICAEW 1987-88; Freeman City of London 1987, memb CAs Livery Co 1987; FCA; *Recreations* tennis, swimming, walking, watching soccer; *Style—* Arthur Green, Esq; Up Yonder, Herbert Rd, Salcombe, Devon TQ8 8HP (☎ 054 884 2075)

GREEN, Rev Father (Humphrey Christian) Benedict; CR; s of Rev Canon Frederick Wastie Green (d 1953), and Marjorie Susan Beltt, *née* Gosling (d 1978); *b* 9 Jan 1924; *Educ* Eton, Merton Coll Oxford (MA); *Career* RNVR 1943-46, cmmnd Sub-Lt 1944, served Intelligence Staff E Indies Station 1944-45, SEAC (Kandy and Singapore) 1945-46; ordained Diocese of London: deacon 1951, priest 1952; asst curate St Marys Northolt 1951-56, lectr Theol Faculty Kings Coll London 1956-60 (sub-warden Theol Hostel 1957-); entered Community of Resurrection Mirfield 1960, professed 1962, princ Coll of the Resurrection Mirfield 1975-84 (vice princ 1965-75), assoc lectr Dept of Theol and Religious Studies Univ of Leeds 1967-87 (memb Univ Ct 1981-); *Books* The Gospel of Matthew (1975); *Recreations* walking, music, travel (according to opportunity); *Style—* The Rev Father Benedict Green, CR; House of the Resurrection, Mirfield, W Yorks WF14 0BN (☎ 0924 494318)

GREEN, Rev Bernard; s of George Samuel Green (d 1988), of Rushden, Northants, and Laura Annie Agnes, *née* Holliday (d 1974); *b* 11 Nov 1925; *Educ* Wellingborough Sch, Bristol Baptist Coll and Univ of Bristol (BA), St Catherine's and Regent's Park Colls Oxford (MA), Univ of London (BD); *m* 19 July 1952, Joan, da of Harry Viccars (d 1954), of Rushden, Northants; 2 s (Roger Malcolm b 1954, Martin James b 1961), 1 da (Pamela Mary Overend b 1958); *Career* Baptist minister: Yardley Baptist Church Birmingham 1952-61, Mansfield Rd Baptist Church Nottingham 1961-76, Horfield Baptist Church Bristol 1976-82; gen sec Baptist Union of GB 1982-, moderator Free Church Federal Cncl 1988-89; dir: Baptist Union Corp Ltd 1982-, London Baptist Property Bd Ltd 1982-, Baptist Holiday Fellowship Ltd 1982-, Baptist House Ltd 1989-, Baptist Times Ltd 1982-, Baptist Insurance Co plc 1982-; broadcaster and memb Religious Advsy Panel; BBC Radio Nottingham 1970-76, BBC Radio Bristol 1977-82; *Recreations* gardening, walking, listening to music, reading, spectator sport; *Style—* The Rev Bernard Green; Baptist Union of Great Britain, Baptist House, PO Box 44, 129 Broadway, Didcot, Oxon OX11 8RT (☎ 0235 512077)

GREEN, Prof Brynmor Hugh (Bryn); s of Albert Walter Green (d 1971), and Margaret Afona, *née* Griffiths (d 1971); *b* 14 Jan 1941; *Educ* Dartford GS, Univ of Nottingham (BSc, PhD); *m* 14 Aug 1965, Jean, da of (Thomas) Norman Armstrong (d 1981); 2 s (David Ellis, Simon Gareth); *Career* lectr Dept of Botany Univ of Manchester 1965-67; Nature Conservancy Cncl: dep and SE regnl offr 1967-74, chief sci team 1974; lectr and sr lectr Wye Coll 1974-87, Sir Cyril Kleinwort prof of countryside mgmnt Wye Coll 1987-; memb Eng Ctee Nature Conservancy Cncl 1983-90, vice chm Kent Farming and Wildlife Advsy Group; Countryside Cmmr 1984-; FRSA 1989; *Books* Countryside Conservation (2 edn, 1985), contrib sci papers to numerous books; *Recreations* golf, watercolour sketching, ornithology; *Style—* Prof Bryn Green; 19 Chequers Park, Wye, Ashford, Kent TN25 5BB (☎ 0233 812575); Dept of Agriculture, Horticulture and Environment, Wye Coll, Univ of London, Wye, Ashford, Kent TN25 5AH (☎ 0233 812401, fax 0233 813320, telex 96118 ANZEEC G)

GREEN, Charles; s of Jacob Green, of Leicester, and Anna, *née* Ostersetzer; *b* 26 March 1950; *Educ* London Sch of Film Technique; *m* 20 May 1972, Toni, da of Leibish Engelberg, of Antwerp, Belgium; 1 s (Kenny b 23 Jan 1975), 2 da (Michelle b 4 June 1977, Davina b 6 June 1986); *Career* photographer, opened portrait studio Edgware 1978; Master Photographer of the Year award 1985, Court of Honour award of excellence Professional Photographers Soc of NY USA 1986, 9 Kodak Gold awards for tech excellence and creativity 1988-89, Gold Certificate for Achievement World Cncl of Professional Photographers 1989; exhibition The Forgotten People 1990, portrait chosen by Professional Photographers of America for exhibition Epcot Centre Florida 1990; FBIPP 1985 (assoc BIPP 1983), fell The Master Photographers' Assoc, FRPS, FRSA; *Books* Shooting For Gold (1987); *Style—* Charles Green, Esq; 309 Hale Lane, Station Rd, Edgware, Middlesex HA8 7AX (☎ 081 958 3183, fax 081 958 1947)

GREEN, Charles Frederick; s of George Frederick Green (d 1987), and Ellen Maud Mary, *née* Brett (d 1987); *b* 20 Oct 1930; *Educ* Harrow Co Sch; *m* 1956, Elizabeth

Pauline Anne, da of Egbert Joseph William Jackson, CB, MC (d 1975); 2 s (Nicholas b 1957, Martin b 1959), 1 da (Mary b 1963); *Career* joined National Provincial Bank 1946 (sec 1967-70); National Westminster Bank: head of planning 1970, dir and gen mangr Fin Control Div 1982, dep gp chief exec 1986-89; md Centre File 1974-76; memb Industl and Econ Affrs Ctee C of E 1986, Multinational Affrs Panel CBI/ICC 1982-87, Overseas Ctee CBI 1987-89; dir Business in the Community 1983-90 (vice chm 1983-89); memb General Synod 1980-90, vice chm C of E Bd for Social Responsibility 1983 (memb 1980); tstee Church Urban Fund 1987-89, treas Policy Studies Inst 1984; *Recreations* opera, concert music, drama; *Clubs* National, Langbourn Ward, Athenaeum; *Style—* Charles Green, Esq; The Old House, Parks Farm, Old Sedbury, Bristol BS17 6PX (☎ 0454 311936)

GREEN, Christopher Edward Wastie (Chris); s of James Wastie Green, and Margarita, *née* Mensing; *b* 7 Sept 1943; *Educ* St Paul's, Oriel Coll Oxford (MA); *m* 1966, Mitzie, da of Dr Joachim Petzold, of Lugano, Switzerland; 1 s (James b 1971), 1 da (Carol b 1969); *Career* BR mgmnt trainee 1965, area mangr Hull 1973, passenger ops mangr BRB 1978, regnl ops mangr Scotland 1980, dep gen mangr Scot Rail 1983, gen mangr Scot Rail 1984, md Network South East 1990- (dir 1986); FCIT; *Recreations* architecture, music, hill walking; *Style—* Chris Green, Esq; British Rail, Euston, London NW1 (☎ 071 928 5151)

GREEN, Dr Christopher John Charles; s of Eric Frederick Green, and Muriel Mary, *née* Rice; *b* 3 Nov 1942; *Educ* Northgate GS for Boys Ipswich, Univ of Leeds (BA, PhD); *m* 3 Aug 1968, Sylvia Alice, da of Robert Buckenham; 2 s (Jonathan James b 13 Dec 1971, Richard Charles b 27 April 1975); *Career* lectr Enfield Coll of Technol 1971-73 (Hockerill Coll 1968-71), sr lectr Middx Poly 1973-76, head of dept Essex Coll of Higher Educn 1981-89 (Chelmer Coll of Higher Educn 1976-81), project dir Essex Centre Anglia Coll of Higher Educn 1989-;sr music critic E Anglian Daily Times; dir Essex Radio plc; artistic dir Trianon Music Gp 1959-, chm Nat Assoc of Youth Orchestras 1975-78, artistic dir Ipswich Festival 1980-83, chm Chelmsford and Dist Mental Health Centre 1983-, chm Essex Radio Helping Hands Tst 1989, chm Ipswich Arts Assoc 1989-; assoc fell Br Psychological Soc 1989; *Recreations* reading, music, theatre; *Style—* Dr Christopher Green

GREEN, Hon Mrs (Claerwen); *née* Gibson-Watt; er da of Baron Gibson-Watt, MC, PC; *b* 20 Oct 1952; *Educ* Queensgate London, Châtelard Switzerland; *m* 1, 1970 (m dis 1979), Enrique Rene Ulvert, s of Marcel Ulvert-Portocarrero, sometime Nicaraguan ambass in London; 2 s (Marcel David Joaquin b 1971, Charles Nicholas b 1972); m 2, 4 Sept 1980, John (James) Randal Green, s of John Richard Daniel Green, and Hon Jane Smith, da of 2 Baron Bicester; 3 s (Toby James Ralf b 1982, Richard John Daniel b 1984, David Peter Julian (twin) b 1984); *Style—* The Hon Mrs Green; Foxboro' Hall, Melton, nr Woodbridge, Suffolk IP12 1ND

GREEN, David John Mark; s of John Geoffrey Green, of Woodford Green, Essex, and Margaret Green; *b* 8 March 1954; *Educ* Christs Hosp Horsham, St Catharine's Coll Cambridge (MA); *m* 7 June 1980, Katherine, da of James Sharkey, of Woodford Green; 1 s (Dominic James Millican), 1 da (Clemency Alice); *Career* Def Intelligence Staff MOD 1975-78; called to the Bar Inner Temple 1979; *Style—* David Green, Esq; 5 King's Bench Walk, Temple, London EC4 (☎ 071 353 4713, fax 071 353 5459)

GREEN, David Michael; s of John Barrington Green, of Brisbane, Australia, and Nance, *née* O'Brian; *b* 28 Feb 1960; *Educ* St Pauls Brisbane Australia; *m* 4 Dec 1981, Lucinda Jane, da of Maj-Gen G E Prior Palmer; 1 s (Freddie David b 9 April 1985), 1 da (Lissa Bella b 3 Feb 1989); *Career* horserider; competitions incl: Badminton Horse Trials: 6 place (Mairangi Bay) 1982, 11 place (Walkabout) 1984; winner int three-day event Punchestown Ireland (Botany Bay) 1982, 5 place American three-day event championships Chesterland (Walkabout) 1983; Euro Championships: Burghley (Walkabout) 1985, (Count de Bolebec) 1987; winner Hasselt Belgium (The Bushby Solider) 1987, winner Samur France (Ayres Rock) 1988; memb Aust team: World Championships Luhmulen Germany (Mairangi Bay) 1982, Seoul Olympics (Ayres Rock) 1988, World Equestrian Games 1990; placed in top fifteen world ranking system 1987-88; *Recreations* scuba diving, skiing; *Style—* David Green, Esq; The Tree House, Appleshaw, Andover, Hants SP11 9BS (☎ office 0264 773905)

GREEN, David William; *b* 5 March 1950; *Career* conslt anaesthetist; dir Care Gp Anaesthetics and Intensive Care Depts; memb: BMA, POWAR King's Coll Hosp; *Books* A New Short Textbook of Anaesthetics (jtly, 1986); *Style—* David Green, Esq; 65 Court Lane, Dulwich, London SE21 7EF; Dept of Anaesthetics, King's College Hospital, Denmark Hill, London SE5 9RS (☎ 071 326 3154/3358)

GREEN, Ernest; s of Luke Green (d 1944), and Daisy Sarah Lydia, *née* Smeeton; *b* 22 Dec 1929; *Educ* Westminster Tech Coll; *m* 1 Sept 1951, May, da of John Menzies Kennedy (d 1959), of Scot; 3 s (Graham Ernest b 1955, Russell Ian b 1959, Elliot Luke b 1973), 1 da (Susan Debra (Mrs Wright) b 1957); *Career* Nat Serv Sgt RE 1949, MONS OTC, cmmnd 1952; served: 3 TRRE, 9 TRRE, 114 Army Engr Regt, 101 Field Engr Regt, ret RE TA 1957; gained experience in various civil and structural consulting offices, fndr own pratice Ernest Green Hldgs (first consulting engr on London Stock Exchange) 1985; memb Assoc of Consulting Engrs; Freeman City of London 1960, Liveryman Worshipful Co of Basketmakers 1960, Freeman Guild of Air Pilots and Navigators 1974; FIStructE 1955, FICE 1957; *Recreations* motor yachting, flying; *Clubs* City Livery, Belfry; *Style—* Ernest Green, Esq; The White Hse, L'Eree, St Peters in the Wood, Guernsey, CI (☎ 0481 643 85, fax 0481 650 85)

GREEN, Dr Frank Alan; s of Frank Green (d 1943), and Winifred Hilda, *née* Payne; *b* 29 Oct 1931; *Educ* Mercers Sch, Univ of London (BSc, PhD); *m* 30 March 1957, Pauline Eleanor, da of George Edward Tayler (d 1980); 1 s (Paul b 19 July 1963), 2 da (Gail b 17 April 1958, Sally b 18 Sept 1960); *Career* md AE Group subsid 1962-66, tech advsr Consormex SA Mexico City 1966-68, mfrg dir Stewart Warner Corp 1968-72, dir market devpt Calor Group 1972-74, md British Twin Disc Ltd (dir Twin Disc International SA) 1974-80, industl advsr (under sec) DTI 1981-84; currently: md Charing Green Ltd, sr conslt Centre for Consultancy Ltd, dir General Technology Systems (Scandinavia), dir Gen Technol Systems (Portugal); advsr to Mexican Govt on mfrg 1966-68, dep chm Newcastle Technol Centre 1983; memb: Kent CBI Ctee and CBI SE Regnl Ctee 1974-80, Professional Bd Inst of Metals 1986- (chm Gen Educn Ctee 1986-88, chm Initial Formation Ctee 1988-, memb Cncl 1990-); currently involved in Understanding Indust Initiative; Freeman City of London 1953; CEng, FIM, FBIM; *Recreations* wine, photography, hill walking, military and local history; *Clubs* Old Mercers; *Style—* Dr Frank Green; Courtwood House, Burleigh Rd, Charing, Kent TN27 OJB (☎ 023 371 3152); Centre for Consultancy Ltd, Boxley Rd, Maidstone, Kent ME14 3DN (☎ 0622 692919, fax 0622 692920)

GREEN, Geoffrey David; s of Ronald Green (d 1977), of Enfield, and Ivy May, *née* Steggles (d 1988); *b* 17 March 1946; *Educ* George Spicer Central Sch Enfield; *m* 3 April 1969, Rosmarie, da of Dominik Raber, of Affoltern Am Albis, Switzerland; 2 da (Natasha b 1970, Vanessa b 1972); *Career* dir: Bisgood 1985, Co Securities 1986, Co Nat West 1986, Co Nat West Wood MacKenzie 1988; memb Stock Exchange 1970; *Recreations* cycling, gardening, travel, reading; *Style—* Geoffrey Green, Esq; Hadleigh, 35 Carnaby Rd, Broxbourne, Hertfordshire

GREEN, Geoffrey Edward; s of Edward Bowyer Green (d 1990), of Beaconsfield, and Clara Jane, *née* Allen (d 1972); *b* 27 March 1929; *Educ* High Wycombe Royal GS, Law Society's Coll of Law, Univ of London (LLB); *m* 2 Jan 1954, Joy Anne, da of William Robert Willcocks (d 1963), of Beaconsfield; 1 da (Nichola Joy (Mrs Blunt) b 1955); *Career* admitted slr 1951; asst to late Sir Cullum Welch, Bt, PA to late Sir Frank Medlicott, CBE, MP 1952-54, sole practice and ptnr central London 1954-61, practice in Beaconsfield 1962-; appointed NP 1969, underwriting memb Lloyds 1972-; Parly candidate (C) Manchester Openshaw Gen Election 1974, memb Soc of Cons Lawyers (memb Exec Ctee 1974-77), fndr memb (former memb Cncl) Central and S Middx Law Soc; Freeman City of London 1951, Liveryman Worshipful Co of Slrs 1974; memb: Law Soc, Soc of Notaries, Berks Bucks and Oxon Law Soc; *Recreations* reading, travel, gardening; *Clubs* Arts, Wig & Pen; *Style—* Geoffrey Green, Esq; Tumblers Chase, 8 Stratton Rd, Beaconsfield, Bucks HP9 1HS (☎ 0494 674406)

GREEN, Dr Geoffrey Frederic; s of George Hanson Green (d 1987), of Guiseley, West Yorks, and Elizabeth, *née* Kershaw; *b* 22 Aug 1947; *Educ* Bootham Sch York, Univ of Edinburgh (MA, PhD); *m* 25 Nov 1974, Ellen Clare, da of Edmund Favre Hughes (d 1987), of New Orleans; 1 s (Christopher George b 24 April 1985), 1 da (Emily Anais b 31 Oct 1983); *Career* md T&T Clark academic publishers 1987- (publishing dir 1977-87); *Clubs* Edinburgh Croquet, Carlton Cricket, Edinburgh Univ Staff, Penn; *Style—* Dr Geoffrey Green; 35 Dick Place, Edinburgh, Scotland (☎ 031 667 2028); T&T Clark, 59 George St, Edinburgh (☎ 031 225 4703, fax 031 220 4260, telex 728134)

GREEN, Geoffrey Stephen; s of John Geoffrey Green, of Essex, and Margaret Rowena, *née* Millican; *b* 3 Sept 1949; *Educ* Forest Sch, St Catharine's Coll Cambridge (MA); *m* 1 (m dis 1980), Fiona Mary Inglis; m 2, 30 Dec 1982, Sarah Charlton Green, da of Wing Cdr Arthur Chesshire; 3 s (Alexander Thomas Charlton b 29 Dec 1983, Frederick Robert b 3 June 1986, Henry George Rollo b 30 July 1990); *Career* admitted 1975; ptnr Ashurst Morris Crisp 1979-; *Recreations* tennis, cricket, golf; *Clubs* Hurlingham; *Style—* Geoffrey Green, Esq; Broadwalk House, 5 Appold Street, London EC2A 2HA (☎ 071 638 1111)

GREEN, Maj George Hugh; MBE (1958), MC (1946), TD (1947), DL (Caithness 1965); s of George Green (d 1952), and Charlotte, *née* Steven (d 1952); *b* 21 Oct 1911; *Educ* Wick HS, Univ of Edinburgh (MA); *m* 1936, Isobel Elizabeth (d 1987), da of Peter Myron (d 1953); 2 s (George, Patrick); *Career* served WWII: N Africa, Sicily, NW Europe, TA 1935-63 incl active serv; headmaster until 1977; Vice-Lt Caithness 1973-86; *Recreations* gardening, beekeeping; *Clubs* Highland Bde; *Style—* Maj George Green, MBE, MC, TD, DL; Tjaldur, Gerston, Halkirk, Caithness (Tel: 084 783 639)

GREEN, Gerald John; s of Alfred Stanley Green (d 1988), of Margerstan House, Northleach, Glos, and Mary Ellen, *née* Flynn (d 1981); *b* 14 Sept 1928; *Educ* Westwoods GS; *Career* ROC 1944-45, Palestine Police Force 1946-48, GOC Haifa Volunteer Force 1948; building control offr Local Govt Serv 1950-90; memb: Nat Cncl of Faculty of Architects and Surveyors 1967-88, Building and Civil Engrg Cncl BSI 1972-; tstee Northleach Town 1972- (hon surveyor to tstees 1974-), chm Glos Branch Faculty of Architects and Surveyors 1972-73, High Bailiff of Northleach Town 1979-80, memb Nat Cncl of Architects and Surveyors Inst 1989 (chm Glos Branch 1989); Andrew Byrne Cup from Faculty of Architects and Surveyors 1985; Freeman City of London 1978, fndr memb and Liveryman Worshipful Co of Arbitrators 1981; FASI 1960, FSVA 1963, FIAS 1983, FCIArb 1972, MIBC 1973; *Books* FAS Short Form of Building Contract (LA version with J W Stephenson, 1964); *Recreations* travel, flying, collecting autographed first edition books; *Clubs* Special Forces; *Style—* Gerald Green, Esq; Margerstan House, Northleach, Glos GL54 3PG (☎ 0451 60272)

GREEN, Helen Janet; da of William Ernest Green, and Edna Winifred, *née* Thompson; *b* 24 Feb 1942; *Educ* Haberdashers' Aske's, Architectural Assoc, Univ of London (Dip Arch, Dip Restoration and Conservation of Historic Bldgs); *Career* Hist Bldgs Div GLC 1968-70, project architect Kent CC 1970-73, princ architect Company of Designers PPI 1973-76, Property Servs Agency Dept of the Environment 1977-; memb: Mid Kent Branch RIBA (Planning Ctee 1973-74), Tunbridge Wells Branch RIBA; memb: Architectural Assoc 1960-, RIBA 1968-, ARCUK (registered architect) 1968-, SPAB 1969-, ASCHB 1970-; fell ASI 1979-, RIBA SE Regnl Rep Woman of Kent 1980 and 1986; *Recreations* country pursuits, photography, reading, driving, Kentish buildings research; *Style—* H J Green

GREEN, Helen Therese; da of Francis Joseph Morgan (d 1962), of Liverpool, and Helen Josephine, *née* Hanley; *b* 15 Oct 1925; *Educ* Notre Dame Convent Liverpool, Univ of Liverpool (MB ChB, MD); *m* 26 April 1952, Prof Leslie Leonard Green, CBE, s of Leonard Green (d 1972), of Leicester; 1 s (Paul b 1959), 1 da (Sarah b 1956); *Career* sr lectr in med microbiology Univ of Liverpool 1975-77, hon conslt med microbiologist Royal Southern Hosp and David Lewis Northern Hosp 1975-77, conslt med microbiologist S Sefton Health Authy 1977-90; memb: BSAG, AMM, BSSI, BMA, ACP; MD, FRCPath 1984; *Recreations* music, hill walking; *Style—* Ms Helen Green; Seafield Cottage, De Grouchy Street, West Kirby, Merseyside L48 5DX (☎ 051 625 5167)

GREEN, James C R; s of James Gatherer Green (d 1967), and Jeannie Black, *née* Thompson (d 1984); *b* 19 Sept 1949; *Educ* John Neilson Inst Paisley Scotland, Univ Coimbra Portugal, Univ S Nebraska, Univ of Birmingham; *m* 11 Oct 1969, da of William John Johnston, of 11 Novi Lane, Leek, Staffs; *Career* directorships in companies in USA and UK incl: publishers, bookselling, printing indust; company offr of COHSE fin servs, freelance prodr and presenter BBC Radio; translator of many Spanish and Portuguese poets, numerous pubns on subjects incl gliding, vegetarian ethics, diet therapy, drug addiction; memb and chm: Birmingham Poetry Centre, Iolaire Arts Assoc; memb and vice chm Birmingham and Midland Inst; memb: Writers Guild of GB, Cncl of Authors Leading and Copyright Soc; ATII 1971, MBIM 1986; *Books* Lisbon Revisited: selected poems of Fernando Pessao; *Recreations* rugby union, drama, gliding; *Clubs* Wig & Pen, London Scottish; *Style—* James Green, Esq; PO Box 18, 109 Spring Gardens, Buxton, Derbyshire SK17 6YP (☎ 0298 72471); 298a High Rd, Wood Green, London N22 4JR (☎ 081 888 5743); Prospice Publishing Ltd, PO Box 418, Leek, Staffordshire ST13 8UX (☎ 0358 399608, telex 94017237 AQLA G, fax 0298 72402)

GREEN, Hon Mrs (Jane Beatrix Randal); *née* Smith; yr and o surviving da of 2 Baron Bicester (d 1968); *b* 12 Feb 1928; *m* 21 April 1949, John Richard Daniel Green, *qv*; 1 s, 2 da; *Style—* The Hon Mrs Green; Appleshaw Manor, Nr Andover, Hampshire SP11 9BH (☎ 026477 2255)

GREEN, John Dennis Fowler; s of Capt Henry Green (d 1947), of The Manor, Chedworth, Cheltenham, and Amy Gertrude, *née* Rock (d 1950); *b* 9 May 1909; *Educ* Cheltenham, Peterhouse Cambridge (MA); *m* 6 May 1946, (Diana) Judith, da of Col HC Elwes, MVO, DSO; *Career* called to the Bar Inner Temple; special agric mission to Aust and NZ MAFF 1945-47, controller Talks Div BBC 1956-61, chm Agric Advsy Cncl 1964-70, memb Nat Exec CPRE 1967-80 (pres Glos branch); pres Nat Pigbreeders Assoc 1954-55, chm Cirencester and Tewkesbury Cons Assoc 1964-78, tstee and dep pres RASE 1984; *Books* Mr Baldwin: A Study in Post War Conservatism (1933); *Recreations* forestry, field sport; *Clubs* Bucks, Oriental, Naval & Military, Farmers; *Style—* John Green, Esq; The Manor, Chedworth, Cheltenham (☎ 028 57 233)

GREEN, Dr John Edward; s of John Green (d 1957), and Ellen, *née* O'Dowd (d 1974);

b 26 Aug 1937; *Educ* Birkenhead Inst GS, St John's Coll Cambridge (BA, MA, PhD); *m* 12 June 1959, Gillian Mary, da of Harold Barker Jackson (d 1988); 1 s (John b 1966), 1 da (Imogen b 1964); *Career* student apprentice Bristol Aircraft Ltd 1956, tech asst De Havilland Engine Co 1959-61, dir of project time and cost analysis MOD (PE) HQ 1981-, dep head of defence staff and min cllr of defence eqipment Br Embassy Washington 1984-85, dep dir of aircraft Royal Aircraft Estab 1985-87 (aerodynamics 1964-81, head of various res divs 1971-78, head of Aerodyanamics Dept 1978-81), chief exec Aircraft Res Assoc Ltd 1988-; memb Cncl: Royal Aeronautical Soc, Assoc of Ind Res & Technol Orgns; UK rep on Int Cncl of Aeronautical Sciences, memb of Court Cranfield Inst of Technol; FRAeS 1978; *Recreations* mountain walking, music; *Style—* Dr John Green; Aircraft Research Association Ltd, Manton Lane, Bedford MK41 7PF (☎ 0234 350681, fax 0234 328584, telex 825056)

GREEN, John Michael; CB (1976); s of George Morgan Green (d 1949), and Faith Mary, *née* Sage (d 1988); *b* 5 Dec 1924; *Educ* Merchant Taylors', Jesus Coll Oxford (MA); *m* 1951, Sylvia, da of Rowland Yorke Crabb (d 1972); 1 s (David), 1 da (Barbara); *Career* Royal Armoured Corps, Capt 1943-46; entered Civil Serv (Inland Revenue) 1948, HM Treasy 1956-57; memb: Bd of Inland Revenue 1971 (dep chm of Bd 1973-85), N West Surrey Health Authy 1989-; *Recreations* gardening; *Clubs* Reform; *Style—* John Green, Esq, CB; 5 Bylands, Woking GU22 7LA

GREEN, John Richard Daniel; yr s of John Everard Green (d 1966); *b* 8 Oct 1926; *Educ* Harrow, Christ Church Oxford; *m* 4 April 1949, Hon Jane Beatrix Randal Smith, *qv*; 1 s, 2 da; *Career* Sub-Lt RNVR, Home Fleet; chm Blackwall Green Gp Ltd and subsids 1970-, insur broker at Lloyd's; chm Cowes Combined Clubs 1982-; *Recreations* yacht racing, fishing, shooting; *Clubs* Royal Yacht Squadron, Pratt's, City of London, Seawanhaka Corinthian; *Style—* John Green, Esq; Appleshaw Manor, Appleshaw, Andover, Hants SP11 9BH; Blackwall Green Group Ltd, 4 Botolph Alley, London EC3R 8DR (☎ 071 626 5161)

GREEN, Sir Kenneth; s of James William Green, and Elsie May Green; *b* 7 March 1934; *Educ* Helsby GS, Univ of Wales Bangor (BA), Univ of London (MA); *m* 1961, Glenda, *née* Williams; 1 da (Lindsey); *Career* Nat Serv 2 Lt S Wales Borderers 1955-57; trainee mangr Dunlop Rubber Co Birmingham 1957-58, asst teacher Speke Secdy Modern Sch Liverpool 1958-60, lectr I Widnes Tech Coll 1961-62, lectr II Stockport Coll of Technol 1964-68, head of educn City of Birmingham Coll of Educn 1968-72, visiting lectr Univ of Warwick 1972-73, dean Faculty of Community Studies and Educn Manchester 1973-81, dir Manchester Poly 1981-; memb: Cncl for Nat Academic Awards 1985-, Ct Univ of Salford 1985-, Univs Funding Cncl 1989-, Bd of Govrs Sheffield City Polytechnic 1989-, Mgmnt Bd Polytechnics and Colleges Employers' Forum 1989-, Bd Manchester Trg and Enterprise Cncl 1989-, Manchester Literary and Philosophical Soc; Hon Memb RNCM 1987, FRSA 1987; kt 1988; *Recreations* rugby football; *Style—* Sir Kenneth Green; 40 Royden Ave, Runcorn, Cheshire WA7 4SP (☎ 09285 75201); Manchester Polytechnic, All Saints, Manchester M15 6BH (☎ 061 247 1560, fax 061 236 7383)

GREEN, Kenneth Charles; s of Louis Charles Green (d 1950), of Wimbledon, and Rose Elizabeth, *née* Hyatt (d 1965); *b* 18 Feb 1940; *Educ* Hinchley Wood Commercial Sch Esher Surrey; *m* 18 Sept 1971, Margaret Jean; *Career* devpt mangr Zurich Insur Gp 1969-72, md Midland Bank Insur Servs Ltd 1972-88, gen mangr Clydesdale Bank plc 1988-90, md Prosperity Financial Services Group (subsid of Municipal Mutual Insurance) 1990-; former chm City Forum; Freeman City of London, memb Worshipful Co of Insurers; FCII 1969; *Recreations* cricket, golf, walking, travel; *Clubs* MCC, Reform, Surbiton Golf (former tstee); *Style—* Kenneth Green, Esq; c/o Prosperity Financial Services Group, 22 Old Queen Street, London SW1H 9HW (☎ 071 222 7933, fax 071 233 0145)

GREEN, Kenneth David; s of William Haskell Green, of California, USA, and Zelma Grace, *née* Galyean; *b* 11 April 1944; *Educ* El Camino HS, UCLA (BA, MBA); *m* 12 April 1969, Anne Elizabeth, da of late William Fred Fremdling; 1 s (Michael b 1972), 1 da (Melissa b 1975); *Career* sr vice pres Bank of America 1968-86, md Bank of America International Ltd 1980-86; dir: Barclays de Zoete Wedd Holdings Ltd 1986-, Barclays de Zoete Wedd Ltd 1986-; md Barclays de Zoete Wedd Capital Markets Ltd 1986-, dir Barclays de Zoete Wedd Government Securities Inc 1987-; *Recreations* tennis, travel, family; *Clubs* St George's Hill Lawn Tennis, Annabel's; *Style—* Kenneth Green, Esq; The Lake House, 29 Broadwater Close, Walton-on-Thames, Surrey (☎ 0932 247398); 2 Swan Lane, London EC4R 3TS (☎ 071 623 2323, fax 071 895 1525)

GREEN, Prof Leslie Leonard; CBE (1989); s of Leoard Green (d 1975), and Victoria, *née* Hughes (d 1978); *Educ* Alderman Newtons Sch Leicester, King's Coll Cambridge (MA, PhD); *m* 26 April 1952, Helen Therese, da of late Francis Morgan; 1 s (Paul Nicholas b 25 April 1959), 1 da (Elizabeth Sarah b 1956); *Career* Univ of Liverpool: lectr 1948, reader 1962, prof (now emeritus) 1964, dean Faculty of Sci 1976-79, pro vice chllr 1977-80; dir SERC Daresbury Laboratory 1981-88; FInstP, CPhys; *Style—* Prof Leslie Green, CBE; Seafield Cottage, De Grouchy St, West Kirby, Merseyside L48 5DX (☎ 051 625 5167)

GREEN, Lewis Homer; s of Ernest Sydney Green (d 1980); *b* 14 Nov 1935; *Educ* Sherrardswood Sch, London Coll of Printing; *m* 1961, Mary Valentine; 3 children; *Career* printer; md Unwin Brothers Ltd 1974-79, dir Staples Printers Ltd 1975-81, dir and chief exec Martins Publishing Gp 1979-81; dir: Taylowe Ltd 1981-89, BPCC Packaging Ltd 1989; Freeman Worshipful Co of Stationers; *Books* Confessions of a Woodpecker (ed), The Wood Engravings of George Mackley; *Recreations* the wood engravings of George Mackley and Gertrude Hermes, sport, homemaking, private press work; *Style—* Lewis Green, Esq; The Knoll, Shiplake, Henley-on-Thames, Oxon RG9 3JT; BPCC Packaging Ltd, Furze Platt, Malvern Rd, Maidenhead, Berks (☎ 0628 23311)

GREEN, Lucinda Jane; MBE (1977); da of Maj-Gen George Erroll Prior-Palmer, CB, DSO (d 1977), by his 2 w, Lady Doreen, *qv*; *b* 7 Nov 1953; *Educ* St Mary's Wantage, Idbury Manor Oxon; *m* 1981, David Michael Green, yr s of Barry Green, of Brisbane, Australia; 1 s (Frederick b 1985), 1 da (Lissa b 1989); *Career* formerly known as Lucinda Prior-Palmer; winner Badminton Horse Trials Championships 1973, 1976, 1977, 1979, 1983, and 1984; Individual Euro Championships 1975, and 1977; memb Olympic Team Montreal 1976, winning Euro Championship Team Burghley 1977, World Championship Team Kentucky 1978; memb World Championship-winning Br 3-Day Event Team Luhmühlen (W Germany) 1982, also winner of individual championship; Silver medallist Euro Championship Frauenfeld 1983, memb Silver medal-winning Olympic Team 1984, winning Euro Championship Team Burghley 1985; TV co-presenter of 6 part documentary Horses 1987; *Books* Up, Up and Away (1978), Four Square (1980), Regal Realm (1983), Cross Country Riding (1986); *Clubs* Mount Kenya Safari; *Style—* Mrs David Green, MBE; The Tree House Appleshaw Andover, Hants (☎ 026 477 3322)

GREEN, Dr Malcolm; s of James Bisdee Malcolm Green, of 90 Lexden Rd, Colchester, Essex, and Frances Marjorie Lois, *née* Ruffel; *b* 25 Jan 1942; *Educ* Charterhouse, Trinity Coll Oxford (BA, BSc, BM BCh, MA, DM), St Thomas' Hosp Med Sch; *m* 21 April 1971, Julieta Caroline, da of William Preston (d 1984); 2 s (Andrew b 28 Feb 1974, Marcus b 1979), 3 da (Nicola b 8 March 1972, Alexandra b 26 Dec 1975 d 1978, Camilla b 1980); *Career* lectr in med St Thomas' Hosp 1970-74 (house physician 1968-69), Radcliffe travelling fell Oxford Univ to Harvard Univ Med Sch 1971-73, conslt physician and conslt i/c Chest Dept St Bart's Hosp 1975-87, conslt physician in chest med and sr lectr Royal Brompton Hosp 1975-, dean Nat Heart & Lung Inst Univ of London 1988-90, dir Br Postgrad Med Fedn 1991-; hon treas United Hosps SC 1977-87, chm Cncl and exec Br Lung Fndn 1985-; author of chapters, reviews and articles on gen med, respiratory med and physiology; Freeman City of London 1968, Liveryman Worshipful Co of Apothecaries 1965; MRCP 1970, FRCP 1980; *Recreations* sailing, skiing; *Clubs* WMYC, Imperial Poona Yacht; *Style—* Dr Malcolm Green; 38 Lansdowne Gdns, London SW8 2EF (☎ 071 622 8286); Royal Brompton Hosp, London SW3 6HP (☎ 071 351 8058)

GREEN, Malcolm Leslie Hodder; s of Leslie Ernest Green (d 1946), and Ethel Sheila, *née* Hodder; *b* 16 April 1936; *Educ* Denstone Coll, Acton Tech Coll (BSc), Imperial Coll London (PhD, DIC); *m* 2 Jan 1965, Jennifer Clare, da of Philip Leo Bilham (d 1956); 3 c (Russel Philip Malcolm b 1969, Sophie Anne Jennifer b 1970, Matthew Charles Hereward b 1973); *Career* res assocs fell Imperial Coll 1959-60, asst lectr in inorganic chemistry Univ of Cambridge 1960-63 (fell Corpus Christi Coll 1961); Univ of Oxford: septcentenary fell of inorganic chemistry Balliol Coll 1963-88, departmental demonstrator 1963, univ lectr 1965-88, vice master Balliol Coll 1987, prof of inorganic chemistry and head of dept 1989-, fell St Catherine's Coll; visiting prof: Univ of W Ontario 1971, Ecole de Chimie and Institute des Substances Naturelles 1972; A P Sloan visiting prof Harvard Univ 1973, Pacific W Coast lectr in inorganic chemistry, Br Gas Royal Soc sr res fell 1979-86, Sherman Fairchild visiting scholar Caltech 1981, Karl Ziegler Gastprofessor Max Planck Inst Mulheim 1983, Hutchinson lectr Univ of Rochester 1983, Univ lectr in chem Univ of W Ontario 1984, Wuhan Univ PRC 1985, Debye lectr Cornell Univ 1985, Julius Stieglitz lectr Univ of Chicago 1986, Frontiers of Science lectr Texas A & M Univ 1987; memb: Governing Body Inst of Plant Sci Res, Inorganic Chemistry Ctee SERC; conslt to: Medisense, BP, ICI; Corday-Morgan medal and prize 1974, RSC medal in Organometallic Chemistry 1986, JC Bailar medal Univ of Illinois 1983, American Chemical Soc annual award for Inorganic Chemistry 1984, Tilden prize 1982; Chem, FRSC, FRS 1985; *Recreations* family; *Style—* Prof Malcolm Green, FRS; St Catherine's College, Oxford

GREEN, Dr Malcolm Robert; s of Frank Green (d 1970), and Margery Isabel Green; *b* 4 Jan 1943; *Educ* Wyggeston GS Leicester, Magdalen Coll Oxford (MA, DPhil); *m* 18 Dec 1971, Mary Margaret, da of Leonard Charles Pratley (d 1987); 1 s (Alasdair Calum b 1981), 2 da (Eleanor b 1975, Sally b 1978); *Career* lectr in Roman history Univ of Glasgow 1967-; memb: Corpn of Glasgow 1973-75, Strathclyde Regnl Cncl 1975-; chm: Scottish Teachers and Lectrs Negotiating Ctee 1977-90, Nat Ctee for In-Serv Trg of Teachers 1977-86, Scottish Ctee for Staff Devpt in Educn 1987-, Educn Ctee of Convention of Scottish Local Authys 1978-90; Scottish cmmr MSC 1983-85, fin chm Scottish Examination Bd 1984-90; active in community based housing assoc movement 1975-; FScotvec; *Style—* Dr Malcolm Green; 46 Victoria Crescent Rd, Glasgow G12 9DE (☎ 041 339 2007); Strathclyde House, India St, Glasgow G2 4PF (☎ 041 227 3447)

GREEN, Martin; s of Samuel Green (d 1967); *b* 7 Oct 1933; *Educ* Whittinghame Coll Brighton, Univ of Manchester; *m* 1960 (m dis 1980), Gillian Susan; 3 s, 1 da; *Career* md: Adsega Ltd 1960-65, Wrensons Stores Ltd, David Greig Ltd, Lampa Ltd 1971-74; dir: Scottish Heritable Trust Ltd 1976-82, Associated Tooling Industries Ltd 1978-, The Jessel Trust Ltd 1981-; *Style—* Martin Green, Esq; 101 Dovehouse St, London SW3 (☎ 071 352 2783)

GREEN, Dame Mary Georgina; DBE (1968); da of Edwin Green, of Wellingborough; *b* 27 July 1913; *Educ* Wellingborough HS, Westfield Coll London; *Career* govr BBC 1968-73, chm Gen Optical Cncl 1979-85, former headmistress Kidbrooke Sch London; *Recreations* gardening; *Style—* Dame Mary Green, DBE; 45 Winn Rd, London SE12 9EX

GREEN, Rev Prof (Edward) Michael Bankes; s of Rev Edward Bankes Green (d 1985), and Beatrice Emily, *née* Smith (d 1980); *b* 20 Aug 1930; *Educ* Clifton, Exeter Coll Oxford (scholar, BA), Queens' Coll and Ridley Hall Cambridge (BA, BD, Fencing blue, Carus New Testament and Selwyn New Testament prizes); *m* 12 Sept 1957, Rosemary Wake, da of Lt-Col Charles Felix Stoehr, OBE (d 1932); 2 s (Timothy b 1960, Jonathan b 1966), 2 da (Sarah b 1962, Jenny b 1964); *Career* Nat Serv Lt RA 1953-55; ordained deacon 1957, ordained priest 1958, curate Holy Trinity Eastbourne 1957-60; tutor in New Testament: London Coll of Divinity 1960-69, Univ of London 1960-69, Univ of Nottingham 1969-75; princ St John's Coll Nottingham 1969-75, rector St Aldgate's Church Oxford 1975-86, prof of evangelism Regent Coll Vancouver Canada 1987-; pres Christian Union Oxford 1955-57, memb Studiorum Novi Testamenti Societas 1960-69, conslt at Lambeth Conf 1968, rep of Anglican Communion 1969-75; *Books* Called to Serve (1964), Evangelism in the Early Church (1970), I Believe in the Holy Spirit (1975), You Must Be Joking (1976), The Truth of God Incarnate (ed 1977), I Believe in Satan's Downfall (1981), To Corinth With Love (1982), Evangelism through the Local Church (1990); *Recreations* fishing, walking, squash; *Style—* Rev Prof Michael Green; Regent College, 5800 University Boulevard, Vancouver, BC V6T 2E4, Canada (☎ 604 224 3245, fax 604 224 3097)

GREEN, Prof Michael Boris; s of Absalom Green, of London, and Genia, *née* Osherovitz; *b* 22 May 1946; *Educ* William Ellis Sch, Churchill Coll Cambridge (BA, PhD); *Career* res fell: Inst for Advanced Study Princeton NJ USA 1970-72, Cavendish Laboratory Cambridge 1972-77, Dept of Theoretical Physics Oxford 1977-79; Nuffield Science fell 1984-86, prof Physics Dept Queen Mary Coll 1985- (lectr 1979-85), sr fell SERC 1986-91 (advanced fell 1977-79), Distinguished Fairchild fell California Inst of Technol 1990; Maxwell medal and prize Inst of Physics 1987, Hopkins prize Cambridge Philosophical Soc 1987, DIRAC medal Int Centre of Theoretical Physics 1989, FInstP, FRS 1989; *Books* Superstring Theory Vols 1 and 2 (with J H Schwarz and E Witten) Cambridge University Press, 1987; *Style—* Prof Michael Green, FRS; Physics Dept, Queen Mary and Westfield College, Mile End Rd, London E1 4NS (☎ 071 975 5078, fax 081 981 9465)

GREEN, Michael James Bay; s of Patrick Green, OBE, and Eileen Brenda Green; *b* 4 June 1943; *Educ* Harrow; *m* 26 Aug 1971, Ann Eila, da of James Kennedy Elliott, OBE; 1 s (Edward James Patrick b 27 Nov 1973), 1 da (Caroline Eila b 6 Oct 1975); *Career* articled clerk Peat Marwick Mitchell & Co 1960-65, mangr G W Green & Sons 1965-71; Kleinwort Benson Ltd: joined 1971, dir 1978, chm and md Kleinwort Benson Australia Ltd 1981-84; md Hill Samuel Bank Ltd 1991- (dir and head corporate planning 1988-91); FCA; *Recreations* opera, tennis, shooting, flying (gained private pilot's licence); *Style—* Michael Green Esq; Hill Samuel Bank Ltd, 100 Wood St, London EC2P 2AJ (☎ 071 628 8011, fax 071 588 5292)

GREEN, Michael Philip; s of Cyril Green, and Irene, *née* Goodman; *b* 2 Dec 1947; *Educ* Haberdashers' Aske's; *m* 1, 12 Oct 1972 (m dis 1989), The Hon Janet Francis, da of Lord Wolfson of Marylebone; 2 da (Rebecca b 1974, Catherine b 1976); m 2, 15 June 1990, Theresa, *née* Buckmaster; *Career* chm and chief exec Carlton Communication plc; chm: Open Coll, Tangent Charitable Tst; *Recreations* bridge, television; *Clubs* Portland, Carlton; *Style—* Michael P Green, Esq; 15 St George Street, Hanover Sq, London W1R 9DE (☎ 071 499 8050)

GREEN, Prof Mino; s of Alexander Green (d 1969), and Elizabeth Rachel Gorodetsky;

b 10 March 1927; *Educ* Dulwich, Univ Coll Durham (BSc, PhD, DSc, rugby XV); *m* 1951, Diana Mary, da of Rev Arthur William Allen; 1 s (David Mino Allen b 12 Aug 1952), 1 da (Penelope Susan b 31 Dec 1955); *Career* gp ldr Lincoln Laboratory MIT 1951-55, post-doctoral fell Chemistry Dept Imperial Coll London 1955-56, div chief (res) Zenith Radio Corp Chicago USA 1956-60, assoc dir Electrochemistry Laboratory Univ of Pennsylvania 1960-62, dir Zenith Radio Res Corp (UK) Ltd 1962-72; Electrical Engrg Dept Imperial Coll London: res fell 1972-73, lectr 1973-76, reader in electrical materials 1976-83, prof of electrical device sci 1983-; visiting prof in physical chemistry Univ of Bradford 1967-72; FIEE 1986; *publications*: Solid State Surface Science (ed, 3 volumes, 1969, 1970, 1972), over 100 papers in scientific jls; *Recreations* walking, tennis, art appreciation; *Clubs* Hurlingham; *Style*— Prof Mino Green; 55 Gerard Rd, London SW13 9QH (☎ 081 748 8689); Imperial College of Science, Technology and Medicine, Department of Electrical Engineering, Exhibition Rd, London SW7 2BT (☎ 071 589 5111, fax 071 823 8125, telex 929484)

GREEN, Sir Owen Whitley; *b* 14 May 1925; *m* Doreen Margaret Spark; 1 s, 2 da; *Career* chm BTR 1984- (formerly md); former Businessman of the Year; FCA; kt 1984; *Style*— Sir Owen Green; BTR Ltd, Silvertown House, Vincent Square, London SW1P 2PL (☎ 071 834 3848)

GREEN, Brig Percy William Powlett; CBE (1960, OBE 1956), DSO (1946); s of Brig Gen Wilfrith Gerald Key Green, CB, CMG, DSO (d 1937), and Minnie Lilian, *née* Powlett (d 1962); *b* 10 Sept 1912; *Educ* Wellington, RMC; *m* 27 Nov 1943, Phyllis Margery Fitzgerald, da of late Lt-Col Arthur Henry May, OBE; 1 s (Guy b 24 July 1947), 1 da (Susan b 20 Nov 1944); *Career* cmmnd Northamptonshire Regt, served ops NW Frontier India 1936-37, BEF France 1939-40; Cdr: 2 Bn W Yorks Regt Burma and Java 1945-46 (despatches), 1 Bn Malay Regt 1946-47, 4 Bn KAR (ops in Kenya) 1954-56 (despatches); Col Gen Staff WO 1956-57, Brig COS E Africa Cmd 1957-60, dep dir Mil Intelligence WO 1961-63, COS NI Cmd 1963-65, ADC to HM The Queen and Dep Cdr Aldershot Dist 1965-67, Dep Col Royal Anglian Regt 1966-76, ret 1967; *Recreations* field sports; *Clubs* Army and Navy; *Style*— Brig Percy Green, CBE, DSO; Grudds, South Warnborough, Basingstoke, Hants RG25 1RW (☎ 0256 862 472)

GREEN, Peter Frederick; s of Frederick Arthur Green (d 1964); *b* 5 Sept 1922; *Educ* Berkhamsted; *m* 1949, Ruth Joy Griggs; 1 s, 1 da; *Career* dir LCP Hldgs Ltd 1975-85, chm Evans Halshaw Hldgs Ltd 1975-87, non-exec dir Evans Halshaw Hldgs plc; *Recreations* golf, rugby; *Style*— Peter Green, Esq; Windrush, Wawensmere Rd, Wootton Wawen, Warwickshire (☎ 056 42 2395)

GREEN, Prof Peter Morris; s of Arthur Green, CBE (d 1976), and Olive Emily, *née* Slaughter (d 1985); *b* 22 Dec 1924; *Educ* Charterhouse, Trinity Coll Cambridge (open major scholar, sr fndn scholar, res scholar, BA, MA, PhD); *m* 1, 28 July 1951 (m dis 1975), Lalage Isobel, da of late Prof R J V Pulvertaft; 2 s (Timothy Michael b 1955, Nicholas Paul b 1958), 1 da (Sarah Francesca b 1960); m 2, 18 July 1975, Carin Margreta, da of late G N Christensen, of Saratoge, USA; *Career* WWII RAFVR 1943-47; dir of studies in classics Selwyn Coll Cambridge 1952-53, fiction critic London Daily Telegraph 1953-63, literary advsr The Bodley Head 1957-58, sr conslt ed Hodder & Stoughton 1960-63, TV critic The Listener 1961-63, film critic John o'London's 1961-63, emigrated to Greece as full-time writer 1963-71, lectr in Greek history and lit Coll Year in Athens Greece 1966-71 (memb Bd of Advsrs 1984); Univ of Texas: visiting prof of classics 1971-72, prof of classics 1972-, James R Dougherty jr centennial prof of classics 1982- (memb numerous univ ctees and Classics Dept ctees 1974-); visiting prof UCLA 1976, Mellon prof of humanities Tulane Univ 1986; numerous public lectures; memb Book Soc Selection Ctee 1959-62; former memb selection ctees for literary prizes: Heinemann award, John Llewelyn Rhys, WH Smith £1000 award for Literature; memb: APA, AIA, Classical Assoc UK, Soc for Promotion of Hellenic Studies UK, FRSL 1956 (memb Cncl 1958); *Books* The Expanding Eye (1953), Achilles His Armour (1955), Cat in Gloves (pseudonym Denis Delaney, 1956), The Sword of Pleasure (W Heinemann award for Lit 1957), Kenneth Grahame 1859-1932: A Study of his Life, Work and Times (1959), Essays in Antiquity (1960), Habeas Corpus and other stories (1962), Look at the Romans (1963), The Laughter of Aphrodite (1965), Juvenal: The Sixteen Satires (trans, 1967), Armada from Athens: The Failure of the Sicilian Expedition 415-413 BC (1970), Alexander the Great: a biography (1970), The Year of Salamis 480-479 BC (1971), The Shadow of the Parthenon (1972), Alexander of Macedon 356-323 BC: a historical biography (1974), Ovid: The Erotic Poems (trans, 1982), Beyond the Wild Wood: the World of Kenneth Grahame (1982), Medium and Message Reconsidered: the changing functions of classical translation (1986), Classical Bearings: interpreting ancient history and culture (1989), Alexander to Actium: The Historical Evolution of the Hellenistic Age (1990); *Recreations* squash, tennis, travel, avoiding urban life; *Clubs* Savile; *Style*— Prof Peter Green; 1619 Sunny Vale, Austin, Texas 78741, USA (☎ 512 443 7550); Department of Classics, The University of Texas, Austin Texas 78712, USA (☎ 512 471 8502/5742)

GREEN, Peter Smart; MBE (1972), MC (1944), JP (Gwent 1960), DL (Gwent 1978); s of (Abel Arthur) Aylmer Green (d 1949), and (Sarah) Maria, *née* Edwards (d 1955); *b* 8 Dec 1918; *Educ* Colston's Sch Bristol; *m* 26 April 1952, Phyllis Joyce, da of Albert Edmund Edwards (d 1985), of Weston-Super-Mare; 2 s (Martyn b 1953, Richard b 1956), 1 da (Helen b 1962); *Career* WWII RA: 2 Lt 1940, Lt 1941, Capt 1942-46; md Davies Bros (Debee) Ltd (Builders Merchants) 1947-82 (dir 1944-47), chm and md Davies Bros (Newport) Holdings Ltd 1961-, chm Monmouthshire Building Society 1977- (dir 1962-77), dir Aberthaw Cement Co plc 1972-82; magistrate Gwent 1960; memb: Tax Cmmn Gwent, Fin and Gen Purposes Ctee Gwent Branch BRCS; chm SSAFA Gwent 1978-90; Freeman City of London 1977, Liveryman Worshipful Co of Builders Merchants 1977; FIBM; *Recreations* golf, bridge; *Clubs* Newport Golf; *Style*— Peter Green, Esq, MBE, MC, JP, DL; 38 Chepstow Rd, Newport, Gwent NP9 1PT (☎ 0633 63963)

GREEN, Dr Philip Charles; s of Thomas James Green (d 1979), and Alice, *née* Theakston (d 1953); *b* 13 Nov 1929; *Educ* Bridlington Sch, Univ of Cambridge (MA, MB BChir), St George's Med Sch London; *m* 3 Sept 1955, Judy Frances, da of Francis Harris Laraman, of Trentham Lodge, Wellington Rd, Enfield; 3 s (Jeremy b 1957, Barnaby b 1958, Leander b 1964), 2 da (Stella b 1962, Candida b 1967); *Career* house offr: St Peter's Chertsey 1956, St George's 1956; res clinical pathologist St George's 1957-58, princ GP Beaconsfield 1960-89 (ret 1989), trainer in gen practice 1974-88, visiting MO Katherine Knapp Home for the Blind, Bucks Co MO Red Cross 1974-82 (local MO 1962-74); govr Oakdene Sch for Girls 1982- (chm Bd 1986-88); Freeman City of London 1975, Liveryman Worshipful Co of Barbers; LMSSA 1955, MRCGP 1979; *Recreations* shooting, sailing, bridge; *Style*— Dr Philip Green; Barritshayes Farm, Colyton, East Devon EX13 6DU (☎ 0297 52485)

GREEN, Richard Chevallier; s of Lionel Green, MBE, JP, DL (d 1969), of The Whittern, Lyonshall, Kington, Herefords, and Phyllis Chalmers, *née* Jameson, (d 1977); *b* 22 May 1924; *Educ* Wellington, RAC Cirencester; *m* 1959, Julia, da of Roger de Wesselow (d 1960); 1 s (Jonathan b 1966), 3 da (Nicola, Joanna, Sara); *Career* Lt RNVR 1942-46, Escort Vessels N Atlantic and MTBs English Channel; farmer; dir The Whittern Farms Ltd; High Sheriff Herefords & Worcs 1981-82; *Recreations* fishing, travel, boating (yacht 'Rondone'); *Clubs* Royal Yacht Squadron, Farmers'; *Style*— Richard Green, Esq; The Whittern, Lyonshall, Kington, Herefordshire (☎ 05448 241/205); 65 Burton Court, London SW3 (☎ 071 730 0420); Cancello Rosso, Giuncarico (GR), Italy (☎ 010 39 566 88228)

GREEN, Richard David; s of Bernard Green, and Flora Amelia, *née* Wartski; *b* 25 May 1944; *Educ* Highgate Sch, Queens' Coll Oxford (BA); *Career* PA to chm/md John Wyeth & Co Ltd 1966-67; Keyser Ullman Investmt Mgmnt Ltd: investmt analyst 1967-68, gp economist and fund mangr 1970-72; Hill Samuel Investmt Mgmnt Ltd: economist Res and Unit Tst Mgmnt 1973, inst funds mangr 1974-76, sr investmt mangr 1976-77 (dir 1979); former dir Hill Samuel Asset Mgmnt 1981 (global investmt), exec dir and chief investmt offr Daiwa Int Capital Mgmnt (UK) Ltd 1988; memb: Soc of Business Economists, London Oil Analysts Gp, Soc of Investmt Analysts; *Recreations* skiing, travel, water sports, theatre; *Style*— Richard Green, Esq; The Cottage, Whitestone Lane, London NW3 1EA (☎ 071 435 3497); 14 St Paul's Churchyard, London EC4M 8BD (☎ 071 248 1515)

GREEN, Richard Desmond; s of Walter Herbert Green, FCA, of Winchester, and Nina Margaret, *née* Hellyar; *b* 3 June 1947; *Educ* Allhallows, Rousdon Devon; *m* 16 Aug 1986, Margaret Ann, da of Frederick Richard Lisle (d 1985); *Career* CA 1970; dir: Int Thomson Publishing Servs Ltd 1988-, Routledge, Chapman & Hall Ltd 1988-; *Recreations* golf, amateur operatics and dramatics; *Style*— Richard Green, Esq; ITPS Ltd, Cheriton House, North Way, Andover, Hants SP10 5BE (☎ 0264 332424)

GREEN, Richard Paul; s of Hugh Claude Green (d 1990), of Effingham, Surrey, and Betty Rosina, *née* Blake (d 1983); *b* 17 April 1950; *Educ* King's Coll Sch Wimbledon, City of Westminster Coll London; *m* 29 Sept 1973, (Sheila) Marilyn, da of Lionel Francis Guillem, of Fetcham, Surrey; 3 da (Nicola b 1976, Elizabeth b 1976, Susannah b 1981); *Career* CA; ptnr Arthur Young 1979-87, dir Svenska International plc 1987-89, gp fin dir Abaco Investments PLC 1989-; chm Guildford Round Table 1988-89, vice pres French C of C in GB 1984-89; govr Royal Russell Sch Croydon 1987-, Freeman City of London 1981, memb Worshipful Co of Glovers 1981; FCA 1971; *Recreations* gardening, family, motor sport; *Clubs* RAC; *Style*— Richard Green, Esq; Tanglewood, Aldersey Rd, Guildford, Surrey GU1 2ES (☎ 0483 32 216); Abaco Investments plc, King's House, 36/73 King Street, London EC2U 8BE (☎ 071 600 0840)

GREEN, (Aylmer) Roger; s of Aylmer Green (d 1983), and Irene Cameron, *née* Hunt; *b* 15 April 1949; *Educ* Wycliffe Coll; *m* 27 July 1974, (Aud) Reidunn Teodora, da of Einar Alfred Pedersen (d 1968), of Sarpsborg, Norway; 2 s (Eric b 1978, Christian b 1988), 1 da (Elizabeth b 1976); *Career* conslt plastic surgn Mersey Regnl Plastic Surgery and Burns Centre Liverpool 1987-, clinical lectr plastic surgery Univ of Liverpool 1987-; memb: Br Assoc Plastic Surgns, Br Assoc Aesthetic Plastic Surgns; LRCPI, LRCSI 1974, FRCS 1981, FRSM 1983; *Recreations* walking, skiing, fishing; *Style*— Roger Green, Esq; Rowan House, 8 Roehampton Drive, Blundellsands, Liverpool L23 7XD (☎ 051 924 5823); Mersey Regional Plastic Surgery and Burn Centre, Whiston Hospital, Prescot, Liverpool L35 5DR (☎ 051 426 1600 ext 262); 31 Rodney St, Liverpool L1 9EH (☎ 051 709 8522)

GREEN, Sam; CBE (1960); s of Fred Green (d 1951), and Alice Ann, *née* Wrigley (d 1950); *b* 6 Feb 1907; *Educ* Oldham Tech Coll (HNC), Manchester Coll of Technol; *m* 18 July 1942, Dr Lilly, da of Lugwig Pollak (d 1942); 1 da (Alison Anne b 18 March 1951); *Career* apprentice Platt Bros electrical and mechanical engrs, Br Northrop Automatic Loom Co 1934-39 (invented Box Motion Automatic Loom), chief engr Betts & Co London 1939-42, works mangr Morphy-Richards 1942-44, gen works mangr Horoplast Ltd 1944-47, indust advsr Industl & Commerical Fin Corpn 1948-52, md Remploy Ltd 1952-65, chm and md Ralli Bros Industs Ltd 1965-70, chm (govt appt) Dula UK Ltd 1969-, chm and chief exec Spears Bros Ltd 1970-; non-exec dir: Grampion Lighting Co Ltd 1966-69, J E Lesser Co Ltd 1969-74, New Day Hldgs Ltd 1966-69; lectr Workingmens Coll Crowndale Rd Kings Cross 1949-51, chm and vice pres Inst of Patentees & Inventors 1952-, vice pres Int Fedn of Inventors Assocs 1968-, memb Industl Advsrs to the Blind 1965-72; Royal Br Legion 1965-: memb Benevolent Ctee, dir and vice chm Poppy Factory, dir of industs Maidstone Kent; CEng, FIEE, FIProdE, Fell IOD; 1984 Gold medal for Services to Invention by WIPO UN; *Recreations* reading, gardening, walking, cycling; *Clubs* Reform, Pickwick Bicycle; *Style*— Sam Green, Esq, CBE; Holly Lodge, 39 Westmoreland Rd, Bromley, Kent BR2 0TF (☎ 081 460 3306); Spear Bros Ltd, 1 Southlands Rd, Bromley, Kent BR2 2QR (☎ 081 460 0039)

GREEN, Lt-Col Simon Lycett; TD, JP (Wakefield), DL (W Riding Yorks); s of Sir Edward Green, 3 Bt (d 1941); hp of bro, Sir (Edward) Stephen Green, 4 Bt, CBE; *b* 11 July 1912; *Educ* Eton, Magdalene Coll Cambridge (BA); *m* 1, 3 Jan 1935 (m dis 1971), Gladys, eldest da of late Arthur Ranicar, JP; 1 da; m 2, 1971, Mary, da of late George Ramsden, of Wakefield; *Career* Lt-Col cmdg Yorks Dragoons Yeo 1947-51; chm Green's Economiser Group Ltd 1956-83, ret; *Recreations* shooting, racing; *Clubs* White's; *Style*— Lt-Col Simon Green, TD, JP, DL; Cliff Bank, N Rigton, Leeds LS17 0BZ (☎ 0423 734582)

GREEN, Solomon Jacques; s of Alexander Benjamin Green, (d 1957), of Cairo, and May Maisie Green; *Educ* English Sch Cairo, St Paul's, Christ's Coll Cambridge (MA); *m* 1959, Gillian Anne, da of Cyril Heafield; 1 s (Alexander William b 1962), 2 da (Rachel May b 1960, Lisa Shoshana b 1969); *Career* 3 class clerk Prudential 1953-59, actuarial asst Duncan C Fraser & Co 1960-61, pension fund sec GEC 1961-64, pension fund mangr ICT 1965-68; investmt mangr BOAC 1969-71, md Fraser Green 1971-; fndr memb Worshipful Co of Actuaries 1980-; FIA 1961, ASIA 1968, MBAE 1989; *Recreations* beach combing, cooking, walking and writing; *Style*— Solomon Green, Esq; Fraser Green, 2 Friars Lane, Richmond, Surrey TW9 1NL (☎ 081 948 0164)

GREEN, Stephen Edgar Alexander; s of Rev Ernest Edgar Montague Green (d 1972), of Ryde, IOW, and Frances Ethel Isabella, *née* Coryton (d 1972); *b* 24 May 1943; *Educ* Monkton Combe Sch, Brasenose Coll Oxford (BA, MA), Univ of Liverpool (Dip Archive Admin); *Career* asst archivist Northants Record Office 1966-68, curator, librarian and archivist MCC 1968-; hon archivist St Martin in the Fields, hon sec The Brasenose Soc, pres IOW Assoc of Cricket Umpires; memb: Soc of Archivists, Museums Assoc; *Books* St James' Church, Ryde, Isle of Wight-A Short History (1975), Backward Glances (1976), Cricketing Bygones (1982), Oxford and Cambridge Cricket (contrib, 1989), My Lord's (contrib, 1990); *Recreations* travel, exploring churches and local history; *Style*— Stephen Green, Esq; Flat 15, Richmond House, 4 The Strand, Ryde, Isle of Wight PO33 1JD (☎ 0753 889897), Lord's Ground, London NW8 8QN (☎ 071 2891611, fax 071 2899100, telex 297 329 MCCG G)

GREEN, Sir (Edward) Stephen Lycett; 4 Bt (UK 1886), CBE (1964), JP (Norfolk 1946, supp list 1980); s of Sir Edward Arthur Lycett Green, 3 Bt (d 1941), and Elizabeth Williams (d 1964); *b* 18 April 1910; *Educ* Eton, Magdalene Coll Cambridge; *m* 1935, Constance Mary, da of late Ven Harry Sydney Radcliffe, Archdeacon of Lynn; 1 da; *Heir* bro, Simon Lycett Green; *Career* served WWII in Army 1939-45; called to the Bar 1933; farmer and landowner; cncllr 1946-49, dep chm Norfolk Quarter Sessions 1948-71, chm E Anglian Regnl Hosp Bd 1959-74, DL 1961-90, High Sheriff Norfolk 1973-74; *Style*— Sir Stephen Green, Bt, CBE, JP; Ken Hill, Snettisham, King's Lynn, Norfolk (☎ 0485 70001)

GREEN, Stephen Peter; s of James Dean Green, and Ruth, *née* Marley; *b* 2 Jan 1937; *Educ* Kingswood Sch Bath, Univ of Manchester (LLB); *m* 1 (m dis 1979); 3 da (Clarissa Jane b 10 July 1965, Philippa Lucy b 17 Jan 1967, Victoria Alice b 16 Sept 1971); m 2, 2 Aug 1979, Margaret Owen, da of Cdr John Irwin, RD, RNR (ret), of Swanland, N Humberside; *Career* admitted slr 1963; chief exec Pannone March Pearson (a memb of Pannone de Backer EEIG) Manchester; pres Manchester Consular Assoc 1988 (sec 1990); Netherland Consul for: Greater Manchester, E Lancs, E Cheshire, NW rep, Netherlands; memb Ctee Manchester and Dist Housing Assoc (chm No 2 Assoc); memb: Law Soc, Licensing Exec Soc; *Recreations* opera, music, gardening; *Clubs* St James' (Manchester), Royal Over-Seas League; *Style—* Stephen Green, Esq; Cottage of Content, Off London Rd, Buxton, Derbyshire SK17 9NL; March Pearson and Skelton, 41 Spring Gardens, Manchester M2 2BB (☎ 061 832 7290, fax 061 832 2655)

GREEN, Rev Vivian Hubert Howard; the man on whom John Le Carré partly modelled the character of George Smiley in Tinker, Tailor, Soldier, Spy, The Honourable Schoolboy and Smiley's People; s of Hubert James Green (d 1963); *b* 18 Nov 1915; *Educ* Bradfield Coll Berks, Trinity Hall Cambridge (MA, DD); *Career* deacon 1939, priest 1940; former chaplain and asst master Sherborne Sch; rector Lincoln Coll Oxford 1983-87 (chaplain 1951-69, fellow and history tutor 1951-83, sr tutor 1953-62 and 1974-77, sub-rector 1970-83, hon fellow 1987-); FRHistS; *Publications* Bishop Reginald Pecock (1945), The Hanoverians (1948), From St Augustine to William Temple (1948), Renaissance and Reformation (1952), The Later Plantagenets (1955), Oxford Common Room (1957), The Young Mr Wesley (1961), The Swiss Alps (1961), Martin Luther and the Reformation (1964), John Wesley (1964), Religion at Oxford and Cambridge (1964), The Universities (1969), Medieval Civilization in Western Europe (1971), A History of Oxford University (1974), The Commonwealth of Lincoln College 1427-1977 (1979), Love in a Cool Climate, Letters of Mark Pattison and Meta Bradley 1879-1884 (1985); Memoirs of an Oxford Don, Mark Pattison (edited with an introduction, 1988); A Question of Guilt: the murder of Nancy Eaton (with William Scoular 1989); contrib to Dictionary of English Church History, The Oxford Dictionary of the Christian Church, The Oxford History of the University, Encyclopaedia of Oxford (ed C Hibbert), The Quest for Le Carré (ed Alan Bold, 1988); *Style—* The Rev Vivian Green; Lincoln College, Oxford OX1 3DR (☎ 0865 279830); Calendars, Sheep St, Burford, Oxon (☎ 099 382 3214)

GREEN-ARMYTAGE, John McDonald; *m* 1977, Susan Rosemary, da of Lt-Col Hugh Shelley Le Messurier and Rosemary Alice Champney, *née* (maternal gda of 21 Baron Forbes and paternal ggda of Sir James Walker, 1 Bt, of Sand Hutton); 1 s (Matthew b 1978), 3 da (Anna b 1981, Camilla b 1983, Elizabeth b 1985); *Career* md Guthrie Corpn 1982-; *Style—* John Green-Armytage, Esq; c/o The Guthrie Corporation plc, 6 Devonshire Square, London EC2M 4LA

GREEN-PRICE, Lady; Jean Chalmers Scott; da of David Low Stark, of Arbroath, and widow of Thomas Scott; *m* 17 Oct 1956, as his 2 w, Capt Sir John Green-Price, 4 Bt (d 1964); *Style—* Lady Green-Price; Gwernaffel, Knighton, Powys

GREEN-PRICE, (Powell) Norman Dansey; 2 s of John Powell Green-Price (d 1927, 5 s of Sir Richard Green-Price, 2 Bt), and Julia Helen Ouchterlony Norman, da of Harold Manners-Norman; adopted by his uncle Sir Robert Green-Price, 3 Bt, 1944; hp to his nephew Sir Robert Green-Price, 5 Bt; *b* 22 July 1926,in India; *Educ* Shrewsbury; *m* 1963, Ann Stella, da of late Brig Harold George Howson, CBE, MC, TD, of North House, Carlton-in-Lindrick, Worksop, Notts; 1 s (Simon Richard b 1964), 1 da (Stella Rachel b 1965); *Career* Lt Welsh Guards; High Sheriff of Radnorshire; chm of magistrates; MFH; *Style—* Norman Green-Price, Esq; Hivron, Bleddfa, Knighton, Powys LD7 1NY

GREEN-PRICE, Sir Robert John; 5 Bt (UK 1874), of Norton Manor, Radnorshire; s of Capt Sir John Green-Price, 4 Bt (d 1964); *b* 22 Oct 1940; *Educ* Shrewsbury; *Heir* uncle, Powell Norman Dansey Green-Price JP, *qv*; *Career* Capt (ret) RCT; ADC to Govr of Bermuda 1969-72; *Style—* Sir Robert Green-Price, Bt; Gwernaffel, Knighton, Powys (☎ 0547 528580)

GREENACRE, Andrew John; s of late John Edwin Greenacre; *b* 5 May 1931; *Educ* East Ham GS, Trinity Coll Oxford; *Career* 2 Lt Royal Artillery Germany; fin dir: Glaxo Laboratories Ltd 1975-78, Glaxo Operations UK Ltd 1978-82, Glaxo Pharmaceuticals Ltd 1982-85; *Clubs* Oxford and Cambridge Univ; *Style—* Andrew Greenacre, Esq; 10 Hayes Court, Sunnyside, Wimbledon, London SW19 (☎ 081 946 9413)

GREENACRE, Maj David Laurence; JP (1979); s of Brig Walter Douglas Campbell Greenacre, CB, DSO, MVO (d 1978), and Gwendolen Edith, *née* Fisher-Rowe (d 1978); *b* 19 June 1929; *Educ* Eton; *m* 1, 26 May 1960 (m dis 1970), Lady Elizabeth Marjory Lindesay-Bethune, da of The Earl of Lindsay (d 1986); 2 s (Philip b 1961, Andrew b 1969), 1 da (Louise b 1967); m 2, 1 June 1971, Pauline Daphne, da of Alexander Wilberforce Bird; *Career* Welsh Gds 1953-69, Maj; banker: Page & Gwyther 1969-72, Charterhouse Japhet 1973-84; *Clubs* Pratt's, SCGB, Colchester Garrison Officers; *Style—* Maj David L Greenacre, JP; Alresford Lodge, Alresford, Colchester, Essex CO7 8BE (☎ 020682 2926)

GREENACRE, Lady Elizabeth Marjory Beatrice; *née* Lindesay-Bethune; er da of 14 Earl of Lindsay, DL (d 1985); *b* 31 May 1932; *m* 26 May 1960 (m dis 1970), Maj David Laurence Greenacre, late Welsh Gds, eld s of Brig Walter Douglas Campbell Greenacre, CB, DSO, MVO; 2 s, 1 da; *Style—* The Lady Elizabeth Greenacre; Selby House, Ham Common, Richmond, Surrey (☎ 081 940 8012)

GREENALL, Dr Hon Gilbert; 2 s of 3 Baron Daresbury, *qv*; *b* 16 Aug 1954; *m* 1983, Sarah Elizabeth, er da of Ian C Mouat, of Stetchworth, Suffolk, and former w of Robert Greville Kaye Williamson; 3 s (Gilbert Edward b 1984, Frederick John b 1986, Alexander b 1988), 1 da (Amelia Frances b 1990); *Career* MB ChB, MBA; *Style—* Dr The Hon Gilbert Greenall; 2 Windsor Terrace, Clifton, Bristol

GREENALL, John Desmond Thomas; s of Thomas Henry Greenall (d 1941), and Joan Clare Walker, *née* Ridgway; *b* 11 April 1939; *Educ* Winchester; *m* 30 Jan 1965, Margaret Anne, da of Sir Iain Maxwell Stewart; 1 s (Damian b 1968), 2 da (Melissa b 1967, Cleonie b 1974); *Career* stockbroker; dir: The Securities Assoc Ltd, Greig Middleton and Co Ltd, Chart Serv plc, Local Stores Ltd, Small Shops Assoc, REES Geophysical Ltd; chm Gavel Securities; *Recreations* shooting, cricket; *Clubs* Prestwick Golf, The Hon Co of Edinburgh Golfers, Royal and Ancient Golf, MCC; *Style—* John Greenall, Esq; Greig, Middleton & Co Ltd, 139 St Vincent St, Glasgow G2 5JP (☎ 041 221 8103)

GREENALL, Hon John Edward; 3 and yst s of 3 Baron Daresbury, *qv*; *b* 22 July 1960; *Educ* Fettes; *m* 1985, Gabrielle, da of Stephen James, of Lymington, Hants; 1 s (James b 1988), 1 da (Katie b 1986); *Style—* The Hon John Greenall; Lullington House, Lullington, Burton on Trent, Staffs

GREENALL, Peter Gilbert; s of Hon Edward Gilbert Greenall, of Crossbow House, Trinity, Jersey, CI, and Margaret Ada, *née* Crawford; *b* 18 July 1953; *Educ* Eton, Univ of Cambridge (BA), London Business Sch (Sloan fellowship); *m* 11 Sept 1982, Clare Alison, da of Christopher N Weatherby, MC, of Whaddon House, Whaddon, Bucks; 3 s (Thomas b 1984, Oliver b 1986, Toby b 1988); *Career* md Greenalls Brewery, dir Greenall-Whitley plc, chm Aintree Racecourse Co Ltd; *Recreations* hunting, skiing, tennis, golf; *Clubs* Jockey, White's, Turf, MCC; *Style—* Peter Greenall, Esq; Hall Lane Farm, Daresbury, Warrington, Cheshire WA4 4AF (☎ 0925 74212); Greenall-Whitley plc, PO Box 2, Wilderspool Brewery, Warrington, Cheshire WA4 6RH (☎ 0925 51234, car 0860 336810 and 0836 701526)

GREENALL, Philip Dalton; s of William Sydney Greenall (d 1959), of Mill Hill, London, and Frances May, *née* Dalton (d 1958); *b* 25 April 1915; *Educ* Christ's Coll Finchley, UCL (MSc); *m* 4 April 1963, Stella Margaret, da of Colin Dring Draycott (d 1959), of Rivelin Sheffield; *Career* WWII, RAF 1940-47 (Sqdn Ldr 1944); tutor to HIH Grand Duke Vladimir of Russia 1937; memb Scientific Civil Serv 1947-74 (sr princ sci offr 1957-): head Grants Div Dept of Sci and Industl Res 1957-62, memb cncls numerous industl res assocs 1962-64, secretariat UGC 1964-67, memb RN Sci Serv 1970-74; formerly: memb Nat Exec Ctee Fabian Soc, chm Govrs Camden Adult Educn Inst 1976-82, memb Cncl Westfield Coll Univ of London 1983-89; tstee Hampstead Wells and Campden Tst 1988-; memb Hampstead Heath Consultative Ctee Corpn of London 1989-, awarded Labour Pty Nat Exec Ctee Cert of Merit 1989; FSS 1948, FBPsS 1961, FIMA 1964, FRNS 1966; *Recreations* photography, numismatics, chess (capt & first bd UCL 1936/37), walking, local community affairs; *Clubs* London Numismatic (pres 1981-83), Civil Serv; *Style—* Philip Greenall, Esq; 20 Gardnor Mansions, Church Row, Hampstead NW3 6UR (☎ 071 435 5667)

GREENAWAY, Prof David; s of David Greenaway (d 1986), and Agnes MacKechnie, *née* Parker; *b* 20 March 1952; *Educ* Eastbank Acad Glasgow, Henry Mellish GS Nottingham; *m* Elizabeth, da of William Hallam, of 16 Flamsteed Rd, Strelley, Nottingham; 2 s (Stuart David b 1978, Daniel Christopher b 1980); *Career* lectr in econs Leicester Poly 1975-78; prof of econs: Univ of Buckingham 1986-87 (lectr sr lectr and reader 1979-86), Univ of Nottingham 1987-; visiting prof: Lehigh Univ Pennsylvania 1982 and 1987, Claremont Graduate Sch California 1989; conslt: UNIDO 1983 and 1985, World Bank 1986 and 1988; memb: Royal Econ Soc 1978-, Euro Econ Assoc, Cncl Royal Econ Soc 1990-; *Books* An Introduction to International Economics (1979), International Trade Policy (1983), Current Issues in International Trade (1985), The Economics of Intra Industry Trade (1986), Macroeconomics: Theory and Policy in the UK (2 edn with G K Shaw, 1988), Pioneers of Modern Economics in Britain (1989), Current Issues in Macroeconomics (1989); *Recreations* squash, football, wine, travel; *Clubs* Victoria; *Style—* Prof David Greenaway; 238 Ruddington Lane, Wilford, Nottingham (☎ 0602 810773), Dept of Economics, University of Nottingham, University Park, Nottingham NG7 2RD (☎ 0602 484848)

GREENAWAY, Sir Derek Burdick; 2 Bt (UK 1933), of Coombe, Co Surrey; CBE (1974), TD, JP (Kent 1962), DL (1973); s of Sir Percy Walter Greenaway, 1 Bt (d 1956); *b* 27 May 1910; *Educ* Marlborough; *m* 28 April 1937, Sheila Beatrice, o da of Richard Cyril Lockett (d 1950); 1 s, 1 da; *Heir* s, John Michael Burdick Greenaway, Lois Weedon House, Weedon Lois, Towcester, Northants; *Career* Hon Col 44 (HC) Signal Regt (Cinque Ports) (TA) 1966-67, Hon Col 36 (Eastern) Signal Regt (V) 1967-74; High Sheriff Kent 1971-72; life pres Daniel Greenaway & Son Ltd printers; jt Master Old Surrey and Burstow Fox Hounds 1958-66, pres Sevenoaks Div Cons Assoc 1963-66 (formerly chm), chm SE Area Nat Union of Cons Assocs 1975-79 (hon treas 1969-75); Liveryman Worshipful Co of Stationers and Newspaper Makers (Master 1974-75, Silver Medal 1984); *Recreations* hunting, shooting, fishing; *Clubs* Carlton, City of London, MCC; *Style—* Sir Derek Greenaway, Bt, CBE, TD, JP, DL; Dunmore, Four Elms, Edenbridge, Kent TN8 6NE (☎ 073 270 275)

GREENAWAY, John Michael Burdick; s and h of Sir Derek Greenaway, 2 Bt, CBE, TD, JP, DL, of Dunmore, Four Elms, Edenbridge, Kent; *b* 9 Aug 1944; *Educ* Harrow; *m* 1982, Susan, da of Henry Birch, of Lion House, Tattenhall, Cheshire; 1 s (Thomas), 1 da (Camilla); *Career* Lt Life Gds (ret); dir Daniel Greenaway & Sons Ltd 1970-79; farmer 1980-; *Recreations* skiing, tennis, riding; *Style—* John Greenaway, Esq; Blackford, Cornwood, nr Ivybridge, Devon (☎ 075 537 297)

GREENAWAY, Michael Philip; s of Alan Pearce Greenaway, of E Sussex, and Patricia Frances, *née* Wells (d 1982); gs of Sir Percy Greenaway, Lord Mayor of London 1932-33 and Sir Frederick Wells, Lord Mayor of London 1947-48; *b* 14 Dec 1949; *Educ* Harrow; *m* 28 Jan 1978, Alison Robyn, da of Geoffrey Douglas Cohen, of W Sussex; 1 s (Daniel Pearce b 1981), 2 da (Hannah Kate b 1980, Rebecca Lucy b 1984); *Career* fin dir Cormon Ltd 1984-, dir Charles Clarke Printers Ltd 1984; Dip Mgmnt Studies 1983; Liveryman of Stationers and Newspaper Makers Co; FCA; *Recreations* tennis, skiing, family; *Clubs* Royal Automobile, City Livery; *Style—* Michael P Greenaway, Esq; Criplands, Gravelye Lane, Lindfield, W Sussex RH16 2SL (☎ 0444 483196); Cormon House, South Street, Lancing, W Sussex BN15 8AJ (☎ 0903 766861, telex 877885, fax 0903 763192)

GREENBAUM, Prof Sidney; s of Lewis Greenbaum (d 1949), and Nellie Greenbaum (d 1963); *b* 31 Dec 1929; *Educ* Hackney Downs (Grocers) GS, Univ of London (BA, MA, PhD); *Career* visiting asst prof Univ of Oregon 1968-69, assoc prof Univ of Wisconsin Milwaukee 1969-72, visiting prof of Hebrew Univ of Jerusalem 1972-73, prof Univ of Wisconsin Milwaukee 1972-83, Quain prof of English language and literature UCL 1983-90, (dir of Survey of English Usage 1983-); memb Senate Univ of London 1985-90, dean Faculty of Arts Univ of London 1986-88 and UCL 1988-90; *Books* Studies in English Adverbial Usage (1969), Verb-Intensifier Collocations in English (1970), Elicitation Experiments in English (jtly, 1970), A Grammar of Contemporary English (jtly, 1972), A University Grammar of English (jtly, 1973), Acceptability in Language (ed, 1977), Studies in English Linguistics (jt ed, 1980), A Comprehensive Grammar of the English Language (jtly, 1985), The English Language Today (ed, 1985), Studying Writing (jt ed, 1986), Gowers Complete Plain Words (jt revisor 1986), Good English and the Grammarian (1988), Guide to English Usage (jtly 1988), A College Grammar of English (1989), A Student's Grammar of the English Language (jtly, 1990); *Recreations* reading novels; *Clubs* Reform; *Style—* Prof Sidney Greenbaum; Dept of English, Univ Coll London, Gower St, London WC1E 6BT (☎ 071 387 7050)

GREENBOROUGH, Sir John Hedley; KBE (1979, CBE 1975); s of William Greenborough (d 1953), and Elizabeth Marie, *née* Wilson; *b* 7 July 1922; *Educ* Wandsworth Sch London; *m* 1951, Gerta Ebel; 1 step s; *Career* served WWII pilot RAF later Fleet Air Arm; exec vice pres Shell Argentina 1960-66, area co-ordinator (Far East) Shell International Petroleum Co 1967-68, md (mktg) Shell-Mex & BP Ltd 1969-71, chief exec and md Shell-Mex & BP Ltd 1971-75, md Shell UK 1976-78, dep chm Shell UK 1976-80; chm Newarthill 1980-; dep chm: Bowater Industries 1984-87; dir: Lloyds Bank 1980- (dep chm 1985), Hogg Group 1980-, Laporte Industries (Hldgs) 1983-86; pres: CBI 1978-80, Nat Cncl for Voluntary Orgns 1980-86, Strategic Planning Soc 1986; govr Ashridge Mgmnt Coll 1972- (chm 1977-); chm: Governing Cncl United Med and Dental Schs of Guy's and St Thomas' Hosps 1982-90, Nursing and Professions Allied to Medicine Pay Review Body 1983-86, Civic Tst 1983-86; Liveryman Co of Distillers 1975-, Freeman City of London; Hon LLD Birmingham 1983; *Style—* Sir John Greenborough, KBE; 30 Burghley House, Oakfield, Somerset Rd, Wimbledon Common, London SW19 5JB; Newarthill plc, 40 Bernard St, London WC1N 1LG (☎ 071 837 3377, fax 071 833 4102)

GREENBURY, Edward Charles; s of Albert Lewis Greenbury (d 1955), of London, and Marjorie Sara, *née* Lang (d 1961); *b* 15 Jan 1928; *Educ* Univ Coll Sch Hampstead; *m* 1955 (m dis) Linda Robina Schneiderman; 1 s (James Brett b 15 April 1961), 2 da

(Susan Hilary Michaels b 6 March 1957, Melissa Anne Donald b 29 July 1964); m 2, 1973, Valerie June Ross; *Career* RAF 1946-49; articled clerk Mordant Jarvis Garvin & Co 1944-50, George A Touche & Co 1950-52, Summers Greenbury & Co 1952-70, managing ptnr Hacker Young 1986-90 (joined 1970); non-exec dir: Marling Industries plc 1991-, Timbmet Ltd 1991-, Pearl Paints Ltd 1991-; dep cmdt Jewish Lads & Girls Brigade 1987- (chm Cncl 1982-); FCA; *Clubs* Serpentine Swimming (vice pres); *Style*— Edward Greenbury, Esq; Hacker Young, St Alphage House, Fore St, London EC2Y 5DH (☎ 071 588 3611)

GREENBURY, Richard; s of Richard Oswald Greenbury (d 1974), and Dorothy, *née* Lewis (d 1980); *b* 31 July 1936; *Educ* Ealing County GS; *m* 1, 1959 (m dis), Sian, da of Dr T Eames Hughes, CBE; 2 s (Jonathan Harri b 1963, Adam Richard b 1966), 2 da (Alyson Jane b 1960, Rosalind b 1970); m 2, Gabrielle Mary, *née* McManus; *Career* Marks & Spencer plc: alternate dir 1970, full dir 1972, jt md 1978, chief operating offr 1986, chief exec offr 1988, chm and chief exec 1991-; non-exec dir: British Gas plc 1976-87, Metal Box 1985-89; memb Br American C of C; *Recreations* tennis; *Clubs* All England Lawn Tennis, Int Lawn Tennis of GB; *Style*— Richard Greenbury, Esq; c/o 27 Baker St, London W1A 1DN; Marks & Spencer plc, Michael House, 47-57 Baker St, London W1A 1DN (☎ 071 935 4422)

GREENBURY, Toby Jonathan; s of Coleman Leonard Greenbury (d 1989), of Henley-on-Thames, Oxon, and Hannah Judith Pamela Greenbury; *b* 18 Sept 1951; *Educ* Clifton, UCL; *Career* asst slr Stephenson Harwood 1976-79 (articled clerk 1974-76), seconded assoc Lord Day & Lord 1976-77, ptnr D J Freeman & Co 1980- (asst slr 1979-80); Freeman: City of London 1987, Worshipful Co London Slrs 1985; memb: Law Soc, NY Bar; *Recreations* gardening, sport and music; *Clubs* RAC; *Style*— Toby Greenbury, Esq; D J Freeman & Co, 43 Fetter Lane, London EC4A 1NA (☎ 071 583 4055, fax 071 353 7377, telex 894579)

GREENE, Dr Alice Mary; da of Col Dr Charles Westland Greene (d 1984), and Capt Dr Elizabeth M Greene, *née* Rees; *b* 19 Sept 1952; *Educ* Wesley Coll Dublin, Trinity Coll Dublin (MB BCh, BAO, BA, Univ colours Hockey); *Career* jr house offr Sir Patrick Dun's Hosp Dublin 1977-78, St James' Hosp 1978-79, paediatric med and surgery Crumlin Children's Hosp Dublin 1980, registrar med Royal London Homoeopathic Hosp 1982-83, GP S Kensington 1983, clinical asst Royal London Homoeopathic Hosp 1983-85 GP clinical asst NHS practice 1983-87, opened private practice Hampstead 1983-89, Letchworth Centre for Homoeopathic and Complementary Medicine 1985-, private practice Harley St 1989-; pt/t lectr Faculty of Homoeopathy Royal London Homoeopathic Hosp 1985-, lectr Br Assoc for Autogenic Trg and Therapy; post grad qualifications: DCH NUI, DORCPI 1980, Family Planning Certificate 1980, certificate of prescribed/equivalent experience JCPTGP 1983; MRCGP 1981, MFHOM 1982; memb: Br Assoc for Autogenic Trg and Therapy 1988 (hon sec 1988-), Br Holistic Med Fndn, Scientific and Med Network, chairwoman London Med Post Grad Homoeopathic monthly meetings; *Style*— Dr Alice Greene; The Fourth Floor Flat, 86 Harley St, London W1N 1AE (☎ 071 580 4188)

GREENE, Hon Mrs (Amanda Louise Massy); *née* Edwardes; o da of 8 Baron Kensington; *b* 22 May 1962; *Educ* St Annes Sch for Girls SA; *m* 1984, Anthony Michael Greene; 1 s (James Stuart b 1985), 2 da (Stephanie Louise Massy b 1987, Rachel Delia b 1988); *Style*— The Hon Mrs Greene; Mansfield Farm, PO Box 130, Nottingham Road, Natal, S Africa

GREENE, Graham; OM (1986), CH (1966); 3 s of Charles Henry Greene (himself yr bro of Sir Graham Greene, KCB, JP (decd), and 1 cous of Sir Edward Greene, 1 Bt); er bro of Sir Hugh Carleton Greene, KCMG, OBE, *qv*; bro of Elisabeth Dennys (*see* Dennys, Rodney); *b* 2 Oct 1904; *Educ* Berkhamsted, Balliol Coll Oxford (hon fell 1963); *m* 1927, Vivien Muriel, da of Sidney Roderick Browning, of Clifton; 1 s (Francis b 1936), 1 da (Caroline b 1933); *Career* author, dramatist, story writer, essayist; The Times 1926-30, literary ed The Spectator 1940-41, FO 1941-44, former dir Bodley Head and Eyre & Spottiswoode; memb Panamanian Delgn to Washington for signing of Canal Treaty 1977; *Awards* Shakespeare prize Hamburg 1986, John Dos Passos prize 1980, Jerusalem prize 1980; Hon LittD Cantab 1962; Hon Dlitt: Edinburgh 1967, Oxon 1979; Hon Doctorate Moscow Univ 1988; Chevalier de la Lègion d'Honneur 1967, medal City of Madrid 1980, hon citizen Anacapria 1978, Grand Cross Order of Vasco Nurez de Balboa (Panama) 1983, Commander des Arts des Lettres (France) 1934, Order of Ruben Dario (Nicaragua) 1987; *Publications* Babbling April (1925), The Man Within (1929), The Name of Action (1930), Stamboul Train (1932), It's a Battlefield (1934), The Old School (ed, 1934), The Bear Fell Free (1935), England Made Me (1935), The Basement Room (short stories, 1935), Journey without Maps (1936), A Gun for Sale (1936), Brighton Rock (1938), The Lawless Roads (1939), The Confidential Agent (1939), The Power and the Glory (1940, Hawthornden prize 1940), British Dramatists (1942), The Ministry of Fear (1943), The Heart of the Matter (1948), The Third Man (1950), The End of the Affair (1951), The Lost Childhood and other essays (1951), Essais Catholiques (1953), Twenty One Stories (1954), Loser Takes All (1955), The Quiet American (1955), Our Man in Havana (1958), A Burnt-Out Case (1961), In Search of a Character, Two African Journals (1961), A Sense of Reality (1963), The Comedians (1966), May we Borrow your Husband? and other comedies of the Sexual Life (short stories, 1967), Collected Essays (1969), Travels with my Aunt (1969), A Sort of Life (autobiography, 1971), The Pleasure-Dome; The Collected Film Criticism 1935-40 (ed John Russell Taylor, 1972), Collected Stories (1972), The Honorary Consul (1973), Lord Rochester's Monkey (1974), An Impossible Woman: the Memories of Dottoressa Moor of Capri (ed, 1975), The Human Factor (1978), Dr Fischer of Geneva (1980), Ways of Escape (autobiog, 1980), J'Accuse: the Dark Side of Nice (1982), Monsignor Quixote (1982), Getting to Know the General (1984), The Tenth Man (1985) The Captain & The Enemy (1988), Reflections (collection of journalism, 1990) *Plays* The Living Room (1953), The Potting Shed (1957), The Complaisant Lover (1959), Carving A Statue (1964), The Return of A J Raffles (1975), Yes and No (1980), For Whom the Bell Chimes (1980), The Great Jowett (1981); *Children's Books* The Little Train (1947), The Little Fire Engine (1950), The Little Horse Bus (1952), The Little Steamroller (1953); *Screenplays* Brighton Rock (1948), The Fallen Idol (1948), The Third Man (1948), Our Man in Havana (1960), The Comedians (1967); *Style*— Graham Greene, Esq, OM, CH; c/o Reinhardt Books, 27 Wrights Lane, London W8 5TZ

GREENE, Graham Carleton; CBE (1986); er s of late Sir Hugh Carleton Greene; *b* 10 June 1936; *Educ* Eton, Univ Coll Oxford (MA); *m* 1, 1957 (m dis), Hon Judith Margaret, da of late Baron Gordon-Walker, CH, PC (Life Peer); m 2 , 1976, Sally Georgina Horton, da of Sidney Wilfred Eaton; 1 s; *Career* merchant banking Dublin, New York and London 1957-78; publishing: Secker & Warburg Ltd 1958-62, Jonathan Cape 1962-90 (dir 1962-90, md 1966-88); dir: Chatto Virago, Bodley Head and Jonathan Cape 1969-88 (chm 1970-88), Random House UK Ltd 1988-90, Jackdaw Publications (chm 1964-88), Cape Goliard Press 1967-88, Guinness Mahon Holdings 1968-79, Australasian Publishing Co Pty 1969-88 (chm 1978-88), Sprint Productions 1971-80, Book Reps (NZ) 1971-88 (chm 1984-88), CVBC Services Ltd (chm 1972-88), Guinness Peat Group 1973-87, Grantham Book Storage (chm 1974-88), Triad Paperbacks 1975-88, Chatto Virago, Bodley Head and Jonathan Cape Australia (chm 1977-88), Greene King & Sons 1979-, Statesman & Nation Publishing Co 1980-85 (chm 1981-85), Statesman Publishing Co 1980-85 (chm 1981-85), New Society (chm 1984-86), Random House Inc 1987-88, pres Publishers Assoc 1977-79 (memb Cncl 1969-88); memb: Book Devpt Cncl 1970-79 (dep chm 1972-73), Int Ctee Int Publishers Assoc 1977-88 (Exec Ctee 1981-88), Groupe des Editeurs de Livres de la CEE (EEC) 1977-86 (pres 1984-86), Arts Cncl Working Party Sub Ctee on Public Lending Right 1970, Paymaster Gen's Working Party on Public Lending Right 1970-72, Bd British Cncl 1977-88; chm Nat Book League 1974-76 (dep chm 1971-74), Gen Ctee Royal Literary Fund 1975; Br Museum: tstee 1978-, chm Devpt Tst 1986-, pres Br Museum Fndn Inc 1989-90, chm Br Museum Pubns 1988-; chm GB - China Centre 1986-; Merlin Int Green Investment Trust plc 1989-; Chev L'Ordre des Arts et des Lettres, 1985 (France); *Style*— Graham C Greene, Esq, CBE; 11 Lord North St,London SW1P 3LA (☎ 071 799 6808)

GREENE, Jenny; da of James Wilson Greene, (d 1945), of Cork, and Mary Emily, *née* Dickson (d 1971); *b* 9 Feb 1937; *Educ* Rochelle Sch Cork, Trinity Coll Dublin (BA), Univ of Montpellier France (Dip d' Etudes Francais); *m* 1 April 1971 (m dis 1987), John Gilbert, s of Capt James Gilbert (d 1987), of Johannesburg; *Career* researcher 1963-64, account exec Central News 1964-65, Pembertons Advertisers 1965-66, publicity exec Revlon 1966-71, beauty ed Woman's Own 1971-75, features writer and drama critic Manchester Evening News 1975-77, asst ed Woman's Own 1977-78, ed Homes and Gardens 1978-86, fndr ed A la Carte 1984-85, ed Country Life 1986-; contrib to numerous papers and magazines incl: The Times, The Independent, Daily Mail, BBC Today, Observer; memb Guild of Writers; *Recreations* gardening, cookery; *Style*— Miss J Greene; Michaelmas House, Churchyard, Kimbolton, Cambs PE18 0HH; Country Life, IPC Magazines, Kings Reach Tower, Stamford St, London SE1 (☎ 071 261 7070)

GREENE, Hon Judith; *see*: Dawson-Gowar

GREENE, Lesley; *b* 25 March 1950; *Career* exhibitions organiser Scottish Arts Council 1973-79, visual arts offr Greater London Arts 1979-83, dir Public Art Development Trust 1983-; chairwoman Public Art Forum, tstee Forest of Dean Sculpture; memb: Govt Art Collection Ctee, Art Advsy Ctee Br Library, Percent for Art Steering Ctee Arts Cncl, Art for Architecture Res Team DOE, Art for Architecture Awards Scheme Ctee DOE/RSA; *Recreations* gardening, walking, reading, embroidery; *Style*— Ms Lesley Greene; Public Art Development Trust, 1A Cobham Mews, Agar Grove, London NW1 9SB

GREENE, Roger David; s of Francis Leonard Greene, and Jean Paterson, *née* Hale; *b* 3 Aug 1953; *Educ* St Edwards Coll Liverpool, Univ of Leeds (Gulbenkian scholar, BA, PhD, 1st XV Rugby), Consejo Superior de Investiqaciones Cientificas (post grad scholar); *m* 7 April 1979, Anne Noreen Victoria, da of Charles Anthony Wratislaw; 3 da (Alexandra Marie b 21 Dec 1982, Samantha Noreen b 14 Nov 1985, Rachael Anne b 24 Jan 1989); *Career* NHS: graduate admin trainee 1980-83, asst unit admin Peterborough Dist Hosp 1983-86, asst gen mangr Derby City Hosps Unit 1986-89, unit gen mangr Clareadon Wing Unit Leeds Gen Infirmary 1989-; assoc memb Inst of Health Services Mgmnt; *Style*— Roger Greene, Esq; Leeds Western Health Authority, General Infirmary at Leeds, Gt George St, Leeds LS1 3EX (☎ 0532 437107)

GREENE OF HARROW WEALD, Baron (Life Peer UK 1974), of Harrow, Greater London Sidney Francis Greene; CBE (1966); s of Frank James Greene, of London; *b* 12 Feb 1910; *m* 1936, Masel Elizabeth Carter; 3 da; *Career* gen sec NUR 1957-74, chm TUC 1969-70; dir: Bank of England 1970-78, Trades Union Unit Tst 1970-, RTZ 1975-80; independent nat dir Times Newspaper Hldgs 1980-82; JP London 1941-65; FCIT; kt 1970; *Style*— Rt Hon Lord Greene of Harrow Weald, CBE; 26 Kynaston Wood, Boxtree Rd, Harrow Weald, Middx

GREENER, Anthony Armitage; s of William Martin Greener, and Diana Marianne, *née* Muir; *b* 26 May 1940; *m* Audrey, da of Patrick Ogilvie (d 1944); 1 s (Charles b 5 May 1981), 1 da (Claire b 20 Oct 1977); *Career* dir and gp mangr Dunhill Holdings plc 1974-87; dir: Guinness plc 1986-, Reeves Communications (USA) 1986-, Reed International 1990-; md Utd Distillers 1987-; *Recreations* ocean racing, skiing; *Clubs* Royal Ocean Racing; *Style*— Anthony Greener, Esq; Holly House, Church St, Chiswick, London W4; Utd Distillers plc, Landmark House, Hammersmith Bridge Rd, Hammersmith, London W6 9DP (☎ 081 846 8040 office)

GREENER, Maj (William) John Martin; s of William James Greener, JP (d 1977), of Huntspill Court, Bridgwater, Somerset, and Joyce Durbin, *née* Glass Hooper; *b* 19 Sept 1929; *Educ* Abberley Hall Worcs, Harrow; *m* 14 Jan 1964, (Gillian Diana) Juniper, da of Lt-Col (Arthur) Patrick Sykes, MBE, of Lydham Manor, Bishops Castle, Shropshire; 1 s (James b 1967), 1 da (Juliet b 1970); *Career* cmmnd 2 Lt Coldstream Gds 1948, Capt 1952, Adj Mons OCS 1956-58, Maj 1959, MA to MOD (Army) and to Dep Sec of State 1964-67, ret 1968; Wright Deen & Co Ltd 1968-74 (dir 1972-74); Richards Longstaff Ltd: dir 1974-86, md 1977-86, chm 1986-88 (resigned 1988); dir: Lautro Ltd 1986-, Winterbourne Hosp plc 1982-88; chm P and D Associates Ltd 1989-, conslt to Laurence Keen (stockbrokers) 1989-; St John Ambulance Bde: area cmmr Somerset 1968-71, cmmr Co of Bristol 1971-73, cmmr Co of Avon 1973-77, cdr Co of Avon 1977-87; chm: Dorset Health Tst, Dorset Respite and Hospice Tst, St Christopher's Sch Burnham-on-Sea; memb: BIBA 1974, IBRC 1976; KStJ 1984; Chevalier Legion d'Honneur; *Recreations* gardening, country pursuits; *Clubs* Cavalry and Guards; *Style*— Maj John Greener

GREENER, Michael John; s of late Gabriel William Greener, and late Morfydd, *née* Morgan; *b* 28 Nov 1931; *Educ* Douai Sch Wolverhampton, Univ of Wales Cardiff (BA); *m* 17 May 1964 (m dis 1973), Heather, da of James Balshaw; 1 s (Matthew Dominic b 16 Feb 1965); *Career* sr clerk Doloitte Plender Griffiths Cardiff 1956-58 (articled clerk 1949-56), asst to Sec Western Mail and Echo 1958-59, asst lectr then lectr Coll of Commerce Wednesbury Staffs 1959-62, dir then md Greener & Sons Ltd 1963-; author of over 60 articles in professional jls 1958-; FCA 1967 (ACA 1957); *Books* Problems for Discussion in Mercantile Law (1968), Between the Lines of the Balance Sheet (1968, revised 1980), Penguin Dictionary of Commerce (1970, revised 1980), Penguin Business Dictionary (1987); *Recreations* Open University, freelance journalism, reading, bridge, walking; *Style*— Michael Greener, Esq; 33 Glan Hafren, The Knap, Barry, South Glamorgan CF6 8TA (☎ 0446 732867); 10 Broad St, Barry, S Glamorgan CF6 8AA (☎ 0446 735747)

GREENFIELD, Christopher John; s of Leonard George Greenfield, of Oldland Common, Nr Bristol, and Betty Joan, *née* Griffiths; *b* 28 Dec 1948; *Educ* Kingswood GS, Univ of Leeds (BA), Michigan State Univ (MA); *m* 23 June 1984, Gillian, da of George Orme (d 1984), of Newcastle upon Tyne; 1 s (George b 1987), 1 da (Laura b 1989); *Career* researcher Rowntree Tst 1971-73, asst to Richard Wainwright MP 1974-77, teacher in Huddersfield and Bahrain 1978-82, Quaker ME sec 1982-86, headmaster Sidcot Sch 1986-; memb Leeds CC 1973-76, Lib Parly candidate Leeds NE 1974 and Leeds W 1979; memb: W Yorks CC 1976-80, Winscombe Parish Cncl 1988-; tstee Rowntree Reform Tst 1983-; memb Soc of Headmasters of Ind Schs 1986; *Recreations* local history, walking; *Clubs* National Liberal, Penn; *Style*— Christopher Greenfield, Esq; Hawkstone, Sidcot, Avon BS25 1LU (☎ 093 4842809); Sidcot School, Winscombe, Avon BS25 1PD (☎ 093 4842340)

GREENFIELD, Jonathan (Jon); s of John Frederick Greenfield, of Hatfield, and Mary Decimer, *née* Metivier; *b* 17 April 1959; *Educ* Hatfield GS, Univ of Manchester Sch of

Architecture (BA, BArch); *Career* architect; office jr Sir Basil Spence Partnership 1978, trg with Trevor Dannatt & Partners 1980-81; project architect Chapman Taylor Partners (shopping devpts in Stockport and Coventry), Pentagram Design Ltd (reconstruction of Shakespeare's Globe in Southwark, campaign designs for the Rose Theatre Tst); UNESCO travelling scholar Verona 1980, winner Mid Herts Rotary debating competition 1976; memb RIBA; *Recreations* drawing and painting; *Clubs* Friends of Shakepeare's Globe, Charter 88; *Style—* Jon Greenfield, Esq; 4 Brunswick House, 94 Balcombe St, London NW1 6NG (☎ 071 402 0132); Pentagram Design Ltd, 11 Needham Rd, London W11 2RP (☎ 071 229 3477, fax 071 727 9932)

GREENFIELD, Hon Julius MacDonald (Julian); CMG (1954), QC (1949); s of Rev C E Greenfield (d 1940), and Jeannie, *née* Henderson (d 1948); f served as chaplain Royal Scots Greys S African War 1899-1902; *b* 13 July 1907; *Educ* Milton HS Bulawayo, Univ of Capetown (BA, LLB), Univ of Oxford (BA, BCL); *m* 1935, Florence Margaret, da of John Cardno Ogston Couper (d 1913), of Craigiebuckler, Aberdeen; 2 s (Ewen, Thomas), 1 da (Caroline (decd)); *Career* called to the Bar Gray's Inn 1933, advocate S Rhodesia, princ legal advsr to Lord Malvern and later to Sir Royal Welensky at numerous conferences with UK Govt 1951-63; memb: Parliament SR 1948-53, Fedn of Rhodesia and Nyasaland 1954-63; min of: Justice SR 1950-54, Law Fedn of Rhodesia and Nyasaland 1954-63; puisne judge High Ct Rhodesia 1948-74; ret; *Books* Testimony of a Rhodesian Federal 1978; *Clubs* Bulawayo, Harare, Cape Town (City and Civil Serv); *Style—* Hon J M Greenfield, CMG, QC; Flat 40, Berkeley Sq, 173 Main Rd, Rondebosch 7700, Cape, S Africa

GREENFIELD, Dr Peter Rex; QHP (1987); s of Rex Youhill Greenfield (d 1962), and Elsie Mary *née* Douthwaite (d 1987); *b* 1 Dec 1931; *Educ* Cheltenham, Pembroke Coll Cambridge (BA, MB BChir), St Georges Hospital Med Sch (DObst RCOG, MA); *m* 24 Sept 1954, Faith Stella Greenfield, da of George William Gigg, of Old Beetley, Dereham, Norfolk; 8 s (James b 1956, Simon b 1958, Richard b 1960, Michael b 1961, Andrew b 1963, Nicholas b 1965, Edward b 1966, Timothy b 1974), 2 da (Christine b 1954, Lucy b 1967); *Career* GP Robertsbridge 1959-69; DHSS: MO 1969-73, sr MO 1973-78, princ MO 1978-82, sr princ MO 1983-; chief med advsr DSS 1983-86, Hon Physician to The Queen 1987-90; memb Jt Formulary Ctee Br Nat Formulary 1978-82, chm Informal Working Gp on Prescribing 1980-81, divnl surgn St John Ambulance Bde 1964-, tstee Chaseley Home for Disabled ex-servicemen Eastbourne; memb: BMA, Br Geriatrics Soc; assoc RCGP; *Recreations* golf, walking; *Style—* Dr Peter Greenfield, QHP; Lorne House, Bellhurst Rd, Robertsbridge, E Sussex TN32 5DW (☎ 0580 880209); Department of Health, Alexander Fleming House, Elephant & Castle, London SE1 6BY (☎ 071 972 4420, fax 071 972 4422)

GREENGROSS, Prof Sir Alan; DL (1986); s of Morris Philip Greengross, OBE (d 1970), and Miriam Greengross (d 1969); *b* 15 April 1929; *Educ* Univ Coll Sch, Trinity Coll Cambridge (sr scholar, MA); *m* 26 May 1959, Sally; 1 s (Peter b 1962), 3 da (Gail b 1960, Joanna b 1961, Claire b 1964); *Career* chm Memfagimal Group; dir: Indusmond Ltd, Blazy and Clement Ltd, BC Blazy and Clement Ltd; dir Port of London Authy 1979-84; memb Holborn Borough Cncl 1957-64; memb Cncl London Borough of Camden 1965-84: chm planning and communications 1967-71, dep oppn ldr 1971-74, oppn ldr 1974-79; memb GLC 1977-86: chm Covent Garden Ctee, chm N London Area Planning Ctee, ldr Planning and Communications Policy Ctee 1979-81, dep ldr of oppn 1982-83, ldr of oppn 1983-86;visiting prof City of London Poly, chm Bloomsbury and Islington Health Authy; govr Univ Coll Sch, memb London Regnl Passenger Ctee, fndr memb Inst for Metropolitan Studies; kt 1986; *Clubs* Hurlingham; *Style—* Prof Sir Alan Greengross, DL; 9 Dawson Place, London W2; Batworthy on the Moor, Devon

GREENGROSS, Lady; Sally; *b* 29 June 1935; *Educ* Brighton & Hove HS, LSE (BA); *m* 26 May 1959, Prof Sir Alan Greengross; 1 s (Mark Peter b 6 Nov 1962), 3 da (Stephanie Gail b 24 April 1960, Joanna Louise b 31 Oct 1961, Claire Juliet b 10 Feb 1964); *Career* former linguist, exec in indust, lectr and researcher; dir Age Concern Eng 1987- (asst dir 1977-82, dep dir 1982-87), sec gen Eurolinkage 1981-, presently Euro vice pres Int Fedn on Ageing (sec gen 1982-87), coordinator Prog for Elderly People Within Second EEC Prog to Combat Poverty 1985-89, memb Standing Advsy Ctee on Transport for Disabled and Elderly People 1986-88, jt chm Bd Age Concern Inst of Gerontology King's Coll London 1987-; ind memb: UN Network on Ageing 1983-, WHO Network on Ageing 1983-; former memb: Inner London Juvenile Ct Panel, Mgmnt Bd Hanover Housing Gp; UK Woman of Europe 1990; FRSH; *Books* Ageing, an Adventure in Living (ed, 1985), The Law and Vulnerable Elderly People (ed, 1986), Loving and Ageing (1989), and others; *Recreations* countryside, music; *Clubs* Reform, Hurlingham; *Style—* Lady Greengross; Age Concern England, 60 Pitcairn Rd, Mitcham, Surrey CR4 3LL (☎ 081 640 5431, fax 081 648 7221)

GREENHALF, (William) Douglas George; s of late John William Greenhalf, and Mabel Gertrude Greenhalf (d 1985); *b* 8 May 1918; *m* 1966, Phyllis Doreen; 1 s (Stephen b 1952); *Career* dir Shipton Communications Ltd; *Recreations* work, swimming, reading; *Style—* Douglas Greenhalf, Esq; En-Joie, Henton, Oxford (☎ 0844 52922)

GREENHALGH, Arthur Frederick; s of James Arthur Didsbury Greenhalgh (d 1971), of Liverpool, and Blanche, *née* Durschnabel (d 1988); *b* 30 Dec 1932; *Educ* Merchant Taylors; *m* 18 March 1961, Nancy Winifred, da of John Owen Parry; 1 s (Mark Duncan Arthur b 30 March 1966); *Career* Flying Offr RAF 1957-59; CA 1957; articled clerk Glass & Edwards Chartered Accountants 1951-56, accountant A W Webb & Co Ltd 1959-64; md: Wright of Wisbech Ltd 1965-68, Craners of Burton Ltd 1968-71; currently sr ptnr Greenhalgh & Co (fndr 1972, merged with Kidsons 1978-86); chm Burton Abbey Round Table 1972-73, sec Burton upon Trent chamber of Trade 1976-, memb Cncl Burton upon Trent and S Derbyshire C of C and Indust 1982-91; pres: Rotary Club of Burton upon Trent 1983-84, Derby Soc of CAs 1990-91; FCA 1967; *Recreations* skiing, badminton, bridge, golf; *Clubs* The Burton, Ski Club of Great Britain, Rotary, Burton Golf; *Style—* Arthur Greenhalgh, Esq; The Pebble, Somersal Herbert, Derby DE6 5PD (☎ 0283 78253); Greenhalgh & Co, Chartered Accountants, 240 Branston Rd, Burton Upon Trent, Staffs DE14 3BT (☎ 0283 31711, fax 0283 510825)

GREENHALGH, David Anthony; s of Rowland William Greenhalgh (d 1972), and Barbara Emily, *née* Edwards (d 1989); *b* 4 Dec 1943; *Educ* Sedbergh; *m* 24 May 1980, Jill Marian, da of John Donaldson, of Walton-on-Thames, Surrey; *Career* articled clerk March Pearson & Skelton Manchester 1963-68; admitted slr 1968; corporate tax ptnr Linklaters & Paines (joined 1969, ptnr 1974); memb: Law Soc 1968, Revenue Law Sub Ctee City of London Law Soc; *Recreations* golf, gardening; *Clubs* West Sussex Golf, St George's Hill Golf; *Style—* David Greenhalgh, Esq; Linklaters & Paines, Barrington House, 59-67 Gresham St, London EC2V 7JA (☎ 071 6067080, fax 071 6065113, telex 884349)

GREENHALGH, Peter Andrew Livsey; s of Herbert Livsey Greenhalgh, (d 1973), of Heywood, Lancashire, and Elsie, *née* Wright; *b* 18 Oct 1945; *Educ* Bury GS, King's Coll Cambridge (Douton scholar, sr scholar, BA, Carrington-Koe student, MA, PhD); *m* 1968, Anna Mary Beatrice, da of Prof Kendal Dixon; 1 da (Clare Elizabeth Jane b 1978); *Career* res student and coll supervisor in classics and ancient history King's Coll Cambridge 1967-70, mgmnt trainee Reckitt & Colman PLC 1970-71, asst mangr corporate fin Hill Samuel & Co Ltd London 1972-76, sr lectr then assoc prof of classics Univ of Cape Town 1977-82, conslt in corp fin systems QB On-Line Systems England 1979-, asst gen mangr (corp fin) Hill Samuel Merchant Bank S Africa 1982-84, dir Hill Samuel Securities London 1985, dir and head corp fin Arbuthnot Lathan Bank London 1985-88, fin conslt London 1988-89, chief exec AAF Investmt Corp PLC and md AAF Consultants Ltd 1989-90, pres Mobibau Inc (USA) 1990, md (corp fin) Chartered WestLB Ltd London 1990-; non-exec dir: Teamcor Ltd (S Africa) 1983-90, Dyfast Ltd (UK) 1986-90, Auspharm International Ltd (Aust) 1986-88, AAF Investment Corp PLC (UK) 1988-89, Swaziland Scaffolding Ltd (Swaziland 1989-90, Guyrex (Botswana) Pty Ltd 1989-90, Guyrex Equipment Ltd (UK) 1989-90; chm Premier Construction Co Ltd (UK) 1989-90; non-exec dir: Mobilbau Inc (USA) 1990, Preferred Medical Enterprises Inc (USA) 1990; chm Diamond Engineered Space Inc (USA) 1990; *publications* books: Early Greek Warfare (1973), The Year of the Four Emperors (1975), Pompey: The Roman Alexander (1980), Pompey: The Republican Prince (1981), Deep into Mani: A Journey to the Southern Tip of Greece (1985, German edn 1987); radio plays: The Tragedy of King Oedipus (1983), The Wrath of Achilles (1983), Pompey the Great (1984), The Return of Odysseus (1985); *Recreations* reading, writing, walking, travel, theatre; *Clubs* Athenaeum; *Style—* Peter Greenhalgh, Esq; 138 Humber Rd, Blackheath, London SE3 7LY (☎ 081 858 6807, 071 220 8431); Chartered West LB Limited, Merchant Bankers, 33-36 Gracechurch St, London EC3V 0AX

GREENHALGH, Robert; s of Robert Greenhalgh, of 42 Barley Cop Lane, Lancaster, Lancs, and Bertha Platt (d 1980); *b* 15 March 1942; *Educ* Lancaster Royal GS, Open University (BA); *m* 17 July 1965, Elizabeth, da of John Richard Higdon, of The Old Barn, West End, Kemsing, Kent; *Career* princ RNIB Nat Rehabilitation Centre 1975-83, UK and Int conslt for Low Vision Int 1982-, princ of trg South Regnl Assoc for the Blind 1983-; hon chm: Mobility of the Blind Assoc 1973-76, Partially Sighted Soc 1980-88; memb Nat and Int Light for Low Vision Ctee 1977- (ed Handbook), memb Nat Light and Health Panel 1981-, Br Assoc Social Workers 1970; Freeman City of Lancaster; *Recreations* music, good food, writing; *Style—* Robert Greenhalgh, Esq; 15 Belsize Park Mews, London NW3 5BL (☎ 071 794 4861); South Regional Association for the Blind, 55 Eton Ave, London NW3 3ET (☎ 071 722 9703)

GREENHALGH, Prof Roger Malcolm; s of Maj John Greenhalgh (d 1977), of IOM, and Phyllis, *née* Poynton; *b* 6 Feb 1941; *Educ* Ilkeston Sch, Clare Coll Cambridge (MA, MD MChir), St Thomas' Hosp; *m* 30 July 1964, Karin Maria, da of Dr Karl Gross, and Lucia Hammer; 1 s (Stephen John b 4 Sept 1967), 1 da (Christina Elizabeth b 26 June 1970); *Career* house surgn St Thomas' Hosp London 1967, lectr in surgery Bart's 1972, sr lectr in surgery Charing Cross Hosp London 1976 (hon conslt surgn 1976-), head Dept of Surgery Charing Cross Hosp Med Sch 1981 (prof of surgery London Univ 1982), head Dept of Surgery Univ of London at Charing Cross and Westminster Hosp Med Schs 1989 (prof 1984-), cncl memb Assoc of Surgns of GB and Ireland 1987, Hunterian prof RCS of Eng 1980, vice pres Section of Surgery RSM 1986; chm Editorial Bd European Journal of Vascular Surgery 1987, offr and memb Cncl Euro Soc for Vascular Surgery 1987, sec gen and chm Exec Ctee Assoc of Int Vascular Surgn 1987; FRCS 1971; *Books* Progress in Stroke Research (1978), Smoking and Arterial Disease (1979), Hormones and Vascular Disease (1980), Femoro Distal Bypass (1981), Extra Anatomical Bypass and Secondary Arterial Reconstruction (1982), Progress in Stroke Research 2 (1983), Vascular Surgical Tecniques (1984), Diagnostic Techniques and Investigative Procedures (1985), Vascular Surgery: Issues in Current Practice (1986), Indications in Vascular Surgery (1987), Limb Salvage and Amputation in Vascular Surgery (1988), Vascular Surgical Techniques: An Atlas (2 edn, 1989), The Cause and Management of Anemysms (1990), The Maintainance of Arterial Reconstruction (1991); *Recreations* tennis; *Clubs* Roehampton; *Style—* Prof Roger Greenhalgh; 271 Sheen Lane, London SW14 8RN (☎ 081 878 1110); Department of Surgery, Charing Cross Hospital, London W6 8RF (☎ 081 846 7316)

GREENHILL, Dr Basil Jack; CB (1981), CMG (1967); s of Basil Greenhill (d 1979), of Nailsea, Somerset, and Edith, *née* Holmes (d 1964); *b* 26 Feb 1920; *Educ* Bristol GS, Univ of Bristol (BA, PhD); *m* 1, 1950, Gillian (d 1959); 1 s (Richard); m 2, 1961, (Elizabeth) Ann, da of Walter Ernest Giffard, JP (d 1970), of Lockeridge, Wiltshire; 1 s (James); *Career* Lt RN (Air Branch) 1941-45; HM Dip Serv cnsllr 1946-67; dir Nat Maritime Museum 1967-83; chm: Dulwich Picture Gallery 1980-88, SS Great Britain Project 1982-, The Royal Armouries 1983-88, Univ of Exeter Maritime History Project 1985-, Govt Advsy Ctee on Histories Wreck Sites 1986-, The Royal Air Force Museum 1987-; princ advsr BBC TV series: The Commanding Sea 1980-81, Trade Winds 1985-86; BBC Radio series The British Seafarer 1980-81; frequent radio and television appearances; fell Univ of Exeter; Order of White Rose Finland 1980; *Books* Boats and Boatmen of Pakistan (1971), Westcountrymen In Prince Edward's Isle (3 edn 1990, filmed and televised, American Assoc award), Archaeology of the Boat (1976), The Merchant Schooners (4 edn 1988), The Life and Death of the Sailing Ship (1980), Seafaring Under Sail (1982), The Grain Races (1986), The British Assault on Finland 1854-55 (with Ann Giffard, 1988), The Evolution of the Wooden Ship (1988), The Fletcher (ed of N Mary and preface, 1990), The Herzog in Cecilie (1991); *Recreations* gardening, walking, sailing (Nugget), travel; *Clubs* Arts, Royal Western Yacht, Nautical (Mariehamn Finland); *Style—* Dr Basil Greenhill, CB, CMG; West Boetheric Farm, St Dominic, Saltash, Cornwall PL12 6SZ

GREENHILL, 3 Baron (UK 1950), of Townhead in the City of Glasgow; Malcolm Greenhill; yr s of 1 Baron Greenhill, OBE, LLD (d 1967), and Ida, *née* Goodman (d 1985); suc bro, 2 Baron 1989; *b* 5 May 1924; *Educ* Kelvinside Acad Glasgow, Glasgow Univ (BSc); *Heir* none; *Career* chartered patent agent; memb UK Scientific Mission to Washington USA 1950-51, UKAEA 1954-73, MOD 1973-89; *Recreations* gardening; *Style—* The Rt Hon the Lord Greenhill; 28 Gorselands, Newbury, Berks RG14 6PX (☎ 0635 45651)

GREENHILL, Baroness; Margaret Jean; da of Thomas Newlands, of Hamilton, Ontario, Canada; *m* 1946, 2 Baron Greenhill, MD, DPH (d 1989); 2 da (Hon Mrs Youngren, Hon Mrs Davidson, *qqv*); *Style—* The Rt Hon the Lady Greenhill; Greenhill, 10223 137th Street, Edmonton, Alberta, Canada T5N 2G8

GREENHILL OF HARROW, Baron (Life Peer UK 1974), of Royal Borough of Kensington and Chelsea; Sir Denis Arthur Greenhill; GCMG (1972, KCMG 1967, CMG 1960), OBE (mil 1941); s of James Greenhill, of Ashfields, Loughton, Essex; *b* 7 Nov 1913; *Educ* Bishop's Stortford Coll, Christ Church Oxford (MA); *m* 1941, Angela Doris, da of late William Leitch McCulloch, of Helensburgh; 2 s (Hon Nigel Denis St George b 1942, Hon Robin James b 1945, d 1986); *Career* Col RE; served WWII: ME, N Africa, Italy, Asia; FO 1946-73, PUS FCO and head Dip Serv 1969-73; govr BBC 1973-78; dir: BP 1973-78, BAT Industries 1974-82, British Leyland 1974-77, Leyland International 1977-82, Clerical Medical & General Life Assurance 1973-, Hawker Siddeley Group 1974-84, S G Warburg & Co Ltd 1974-, The Wellcome Foundation Ltd 1974-85; dep chm BUPA 1978-84; chm Governing Body: SOAS 1978-85, King's Coll Hosp Med Sch Cncl 1977-83; memb select ctees House of Lords 1974-; pres: Royal Soc for Asian Affrs 1976-84, Anglo-Finnish Soc 1981-84; tstee Rayne Fndn 1974-; govr Wellington Coll 1974-83; hon student ChCh Oxford 1973, FKC 1984; *Clubs* Travellers'; *Style—* The Rt Hon the Lord Greenhill of Harrow, GCMG, OBE; 25 Hamilton House, Vicarage Gate, London W8 (☎ 071 937

8362)

GREENING, Christopher Seymour; s of John Seymour Greening (d 1971), and Natalie, *née* Robertson; *b* 26 Nov 1938; *Educ* Highgate Sch, RCM, Clare Coll Cambridge (MA); *m* Jane, da of Eric and Sylvia Alexander; 2 c (Julia Natalie b 1974, Robert Charles Alexander b 1979); *Career* Nat Serv Irish Gds 1957-60; advertising exec; graduate trainee J Walter Thompson 1963, copywriter McLaren Dunkley Friedlander 1964-70, vice chm Charles Barker City 1980- (creative dir 1970-80), md Christopher Greening Ltd 1980-83; creative dir: Valin Pollen 1983-91, Gavin Anderson & Co 1991-; *Recreations* music, family life; *Clubs* 23; *Style—* Christopher Greening, Esq; The Want House, Barkway, nr Royston, Herts SG8 8EG (☎ 076 384 208); Gavin Anderson & Co, 18 Grosvenor Gdns, London SW1W ODH (☎ 071 730 3456, fax 071 730 7445)

GREENING, (Pamela) Margaret Evelyn; da of Philip Vincent Pelly, of Wilts, and Pamela Mary, *née* de Veoux (d 1971); *b* 22 July 1933; *Educ* The Study Wimbledon; *m* 6 Jan 1957, Maurice John Greening; 3 s (Harold John b 1958, James Timothy b 1960, Dominic Maurice Vincent b 1964), 1 da (Mary Jacqueline b 1962); *Career* md family firm M J Greening; memb several diocesan ctees Glos Dio, chm Smooth Coat Chihuahua Club, sec West Country Chihuahua Club, ctee memb W of E Ladies Kennel Soc, treas Rural Theology Assoc, church warden St Mary's Acton Turville, moderator for Gloucester Movement of Ordination of Women, diocesan sec SPCK, memb Parish Cncl; *Recreations* running, photography, gardening, breeding dogs, church work; *Clubs* Royal Over-Seas League, IOD; *Style—* Mrs Margaret Greening; Ladyfield, Acton Turville, Badminton (☎ 0454 21 314/628)

GREENING, Rear Adm Sir Paul Woollven; KCVO; s of Capt Charles Greening, DSO, DSC, RN; *b* 1928; *Educ* Mowden Sch Brighton, Nautical Coll Pangbourne; *m* 1951, Monica; 1 s, 1 da; *Career* RN 1946; Capt Britannia Royal Naval Coll 1976-78, Naval Sec 1978-80, ADC to HM The Queen 1978, Flag Offr Royal Yachts 1981-85, Extra Equerry to HM 1983-; Master of HM Household 1986-; *Style—* Rear Adm Sir Paul Greening, KCVO; Kingsmead Cottage, Kingsmead, Wickham, Hants

GREENLAND, Prof Dennis James; s of James John Greenland (d 1976), and Lily Florence Greenland, *née* Gardener (d 1980); *b* 13 June 1930; *Educ* Portsmouth GS, ChCh Oxford (MA, DPhil); *m* 27 Aug 1956, (Edith) Mary, da of Albert Henry Johnston (d 1974); 1 s (Rohan James b 1961), 2 da (Judith Mary b 1956, Jennifer Helen b 1962); *Career* lectr Univ of Ghana 1956-60, reader Univ of Adelaide 1960-69, prof Univ of Reading 1970-79, dep DG Int RICE Res Inst 1979-87, dir sci servs CAB Int 1987-; hon DAgSci Univ of Ghent 1982; FIBiol 1974, FWA 1987; *Books* The Soil Under Shifting Cultivation (with P H Nye, 1960), Soil Conservation and Management in the Humid Tropics (ed with R Lal, 1977), Chemistry of Soil Constituents (ed with M H B Hayes, 1978), Soil Physical Properties and Crop Production in the Tropics (ed with R Lal, 1979), Characterization of Soils in Relation to their Classificaiton and Management for Crop Production: Some Examples from the Humid Tropics (ed, 1981), The Chemistry of Soil Processes (ed with M H B Hayes, 1981); *Recreations* golf, walking; *Style—* Prof Dennis Greenland; Low Wood, The Street, South Stoke, Oxfordshire (☎ 0491 873259), CAB International, Wallingford, Oxon OX10 8DE (☎ 0491 32111, fax 0491 33508, telex 847964)

GREENLAND, Michael Patrick; s of Patrick John Greenland, and Margaret Elsie, *née* Howlett; *b* 29 Nov 1941; *Educ* Gilbard Sch Colchester (ONC); *m* 28 May 1966, Susan, da of Henry Lavender Frost, OBE, of Tolleshunt Major, Essex; 2 s (Andrew b 1967, Howard b 1969), 1 da (Katherine b 1972); *Career* chm and md MPG Hydraulics Ltd 1971-; *Recreations* drinking fine wines, fishing, reading, charitable activities; *Style—* Michael P Greenland, Esq; MPG Hydraulics Ltd, Lynn Street, Swaffham, Norfolk PE37 7AT (☎ 0760 721707, fax 0760 23708)

GREENLY, Simon Stafford; s of Raymond Henry Greenly, of Corsham, and Brenda Margaret Agnes, *née* Stafford (d 1986); *b* 2 March 1945; *Educ* Uppingham, Univ of London (BSc); *Career* Beecham Group 1967-71 (from mgmnt trainee to int mktg exec); dir: Stafford Robert and Partners Management Consultants 1972-82, Greenly's Management Consultants 1983-; chm: Les Routiers 1983-90, ATA Selection plc 1986-88, Greenly's Holdings 1988-; assoc St George's House Windsor; *Recreations* fishing, racing, gardening; *Clubs* Carlton, RAC; *Style—* Simon Greenly, Esq; Wayside Cottage, Mincing Lane, Chobham, Surrey GU24 8RX; 39 Thames St, Windsor, Berks SL4 1PR (☎ 0836 292020)

GREENOCK, Lord; Charles Alan Andrew Cathcart; s and h of 6 Earl Cathcart, CB, DSO, MC, *qv*; *b* 30 Nov 1952; *Educ* Eton; *m* 1981, Vivien Clare, o da of Francis Desmond McInnes Skinner, of North Farm, Snetterton, Norfolk; 1 s (Hon Alan George b 16 March 1986), 1 da (Hon Laura Rosemary b 11 June 1984); *Heir* s, Hon Alan George Cathcart; *Career* late Scots Gds, cmmnd Scots Gds 1972-75; CA Ernst and Whinney 1976-83, Hogg Robinson plc 1983; ACA; *Clubs* Cavalry and Guards', City; *Style—* Lord Greenock; 18 Smith Terrace, London SW3; Gateley Hall, Dereham, Norfolk

GREENOGH, Hon Mrs (Mary Heritage); *née* Banbury; only da of Capt the Hon Charles William Banbury, Coldstream Gds (ka 1914); raised to rank of a Baron's da, 1938; *b* 28 March 1914; *m* 1, 1941, Siegfried Guido Buchmayr (d 1963); 3 s; m 2, 1964, Richard D Greenogh; *Style—* The Hon Mrs Greenogh; 120 East 79th St, New York, NY 10026, USA

GREENOUGH, Alan Edward; s of Edward Greenough (d 1987), and Nancy Dewar, *née* Houghton; *b* 14 July 1949; *Educ* Cowley GS St Helens, Univ of Bristol (LLB); *m* 16 Aug 1975, Sheila Mary, da of Francis Thomas Collins, of Rainhill, Merseyside; 2 da (Emma b 10 June 1978, Kate b 16 April 1980); *Career* slr; Alsop Wilkinson: ptnr 1979, sr ptnr 1989, sr corp fin ptnr NW 1989; non exec dir: Thames International plc 1989; exec dir Doctus plc 1990, commercial dir Microvitec plc 1990; memb Law Soc; *Recreations* rugby league, travel, cinema, most sports; *Style—* Alan Greenough, Esq; Southcroft, 30 Hough Lane, Wilmslow, Cheshire SK9 2LH (☎ 0625 533351); Doctus plc, Capital House, Waterfront Quay, Salford, Manchester M2 5TW (☎ 061 872 3809, fax 061 872 3375, mobile 0836 299318)

GREENOUGH, Michael Howarth; s of Arthur Greenough (d 1987) of Morecambe, Lancs, and Mary, *née* Morphet (d 1986); *b* 28 Dec 1936; *Educ* Morecambe GS, Fitzwilliam Coll Cambridge (MA); *m* 20 Dec 1958, Julie Margaret, da of Harry Gabbitas (d 1987), of 1 St Margaret's Court, Ilkley, West Yorkshire; 3 da (Amanda b 1960, Lucinda b 1965, Zoë b 1970); *Career* Nat Serv with RE, Farnborough, Chatham, Aldershot 1958-60; 2 Lt RE; assoc dir Burton Gp plc; md Montague Burton Property Investmt Ltd; dir: Burton Property Tst Ltd, Freebody Properties Ltd, FPI Devpt Co Ltd, MBPI Securities Ltd, Pengap Estates Ltd; FRICS; *Recreations* tennis, golf, skiing, riding, sailing; *Clubs* Royal Yachting Assoc, Great Middenden Lawn Tennis, Ilkley Golf; *Style—* Michael Greenough, Esq; 35/36 Grosvenor Street, London W1X 9FG (☎ 071 491 7823, fax 071 493 4075, telex 295253)

GREENSLADE, Roy; *b* 13 Dec 1946; *Educ* Dagenham County HS, Univ of Sussex (BA); *Career* journalist; Barking Advertiser 1962-66; sub ed: Lancashire Evening Telegraph 1966-67, Daily Mail Manchester 1967-69; dep chief sub ed The Sun 1969-71 and 1971-73, sub ed Daily Mirror 1971, pt/t sub ed Sunday Mirror 1975-79, news reader BBC Radio Brighton 1975-79, Daily Express and Daily Star 1979-81 (leaving as features ed), asst features ed The Sun 1981-86, managing ed (News) Sunday Times 1986-90, ed Daily Mirror 1990-; *Books* Goodbye to the Working Class (1975); *Style—* Roy Greenslade, Esq; Daily Mirror, Holborn Circus, London EC1P 1DQ (☎ 071 353 0246)

GREENSTOCK, Jeremy Quentin; s of Wilfrid Greenstock, of Sheepscombe, Glos, and Ruth Margaret, *née* Logan (d 1974); *b* 27 July 1943; *Educ* Harrow, Worcester Coll Oxford (exhibitioner, BA, rackets blue, tennis blue); *m* 12 April 1969, Anne Derryn Ashford Hodges, da of William Anthony Ashford Hodges, of Fritton, Norfolk; 1 s (Nicholas b 1973), 2 da (Katherine b 1970, Alexandra b 1975); *Career* asst master Eton 1966-69; HM Dip Serv: joined 1969, MECAS 1970-72, second then first sec Dubai 1970-74, private sec to HM Ambass Washington 1974-78, planning staff, personnel ops, Near E and N African Depts FCO 1978-83, commercial cnsllr Jeddah and Riyadh 1983-86, head Chancery Paris 1987-90, asst under sec of State Western and Southern Europe FCO 1990; *Recreations* travel, photography, court games; *Clubs* United Oxford and Cambridge Univ; *Style—* Jeremy Greenstock, Esq; Foreign and Commonwealth Office, Whitehall, London SW1A 2AH (☎ 071 270 3000)

GREENTREE, (William Wayne) Chris; s of James Murray Greentree (d 1987), and Grace Mary Florence, *née* Kastning; *b* 6 April 1935; *Educ* Moose Jaw Tech Saskatchewan, Univ of Alberta (BSc); *m* 1, 1956 (m dis 1990), Patricia Ann, *née* Hugo; 5 da (Cheryl Geoghegan b 1958, Valerie Ann b 1959 d 1989, Leanne Marie b 1960, Laurie Ellen b 1962, Leslie Patricia b 1964); m 2, 3 Nov 1990, Hilary Jane, da of Sidney James Wilson, of Potters Bar, Herts; *Career* tech and managerial appts onshore and offshore Shell Canada 1957-72, md Ranger Oil (UK) Ltd 1976-79 (managerial appts 1972-76), sr vice pres Exploration and Prodn Mapco Inc USA 1979-82, chief exec offr LASMO plc 1982-; memb Assoc of Professional Engrs of Alberta 1957, FInstPet 1984; Ordre National du Mérite Gabon 1987; *Recreations* golf, skiing, fishing; *Clubs* Highgate Golf, Petroleum (USA); *Style—* Chris Greentree, Esq; LASMO plc, 100 Liverpool St, London EC2M 2BB (☎ 071 945 4545, fax 071 606 2893, telex 8812970)

GREENTREE, Hedley Anthony; s of Bertram Albert Greentree (d 1963), of The Crossways, Portchester, and Dolly, *née* Snell (d 1956); *b* 17 April 1939; *Educ* St Johns Coll Southsea, Portsmouth Poly (Dip Arch); *m* 1 (m dis), Sandra Caroline, da of late Frank Paige; 1 s (Richard Anthony b 19 March 1971); m 2, 10 Jan 1976, Jennifer Mary, da of Douglas Stuart Edwin Gudgin, of Magnolia Cottage, Friarydene, Prinstead, nr Emsworth, W Sussex; 3 s (Benjamin Hedley b 4 Feb 1977, Thomas Anthony b 7 Aug 1979, Joseph Michael b 27 Oct 1981); *Career* Nat Serv Lance Corpl X-Technician Army Signals Regt 1959-61; fndr Hedley Greentree Ptnrship Hampshire 1968, chm HGP Greentree Allchurch Evans Ltd (incorporating HGP Conslts, Greentree Assoc Ltd and Marintech) 1987-; fndr and exec ctee memb Hampshire Devpt Assoc; former vice pres Portsmouth Junior C of C, former pres Hampshire branch RIBA, former dir Portsmouth Area Enterprise Bd, chm Bd of Govrs Portsmouth Coll of Art Design and Further Educn, memb Portsmouth Cathedral Businessman's Assoc; memb RIBA; *Recreations* windsurfing, tennis, swimming; *Style—* Hedley Greentree, Esq; Dormers, Crofton Ave, Lee-on-Solent, Hampshire(☎ 0329 661347); HGP Greentree Allchurch Evans Ltd, Furzehall Farm, Wickham Rd, Fareham, Hampshire PO16 7JG (☎ 0329 283225, fax 0329 237004, car 0836 598136)

GREENWAY, 4 Baron (UK 1927); Sir Ambrose Charles Drexel Greenway; 4 Bt (UK 1919); s of 3 Baron (d 1975); *b* 21 May 1941; *Educ* Winchester; *m* 1985, Mrs Rosalynne Peta Schenk, da of Lt Col Peter Geoffrey Fradgley, of Upcott Manor, Rackenford, N Devon; *Heir* bro, Hon Mervyn Greenway; *Career* marine photographer and writer, Yr Bro of Trinity House 1987; *Recreations* sailing, swimming; *Clubs* House of Lords Yacht; *Style—* The Rt Hon Lord Greenway; c/o House of Lords, London SW1

GREENWAY, Cordelia, Baroness; Cordelia Mary; da of Maj Humphrey Campbell Stephen, JP, of Dormansland, Surrey; *m* 1939, 3 Baron Greenway (d 1975); 3 s (incl 4 Baron); *Career* Freeman City of London 1978, memb Worshipful Co of Glovers 1979; *Style—* The Rt Hon Cordelia, Lady Greenway; 703 Collingwood House, Dolphin Square, London SW1

GREENWAY, Harry; MP (C) Ealing North 1979-; s of late John Kenneth Greenway, and Violet Adelaide, *née* Bell; *b* 4 Oct 1934; *Educ* Warwick Sch, Coll of St Mark and St John London, Caen Univ; *m* 1969, Carol Elizabeth Helena, da of Maj John Robert Thomas Hooper, Metropolitan Stipendiary Magistrate (d 1975); 1 s, 2 da; *Career* former schoolmaster, chm British Atlantic Educn Ctee 1970-84; dep headmaster: Sir William Collins Sch 1971-72, Sedgehill Sch 1972-79; chm All Party Adult Educn Ctee 1979-, memb Parly Select Ctee on Educn Science and Arts 1979-, vice chm Greater London Members 1981-, vice chm and hon sec Cons Parly Educn Ctee 1981-, vice chm Cons Pty Sports Ctee 1987; memb Cncl: Br Horse Soc 1973- (Award of Merit 1980), Open Univ 1982-; tstee Clare Coll Cambridge 1982-, pres Nat Equine Welfare Cncl 1989-; *Recreations* riding, hockey (fndr Lords & Commons Hockey Club, capt 1982), tennis, music, cricket, skiing; *Clubs* Ski Club of GB, St Stephen's Constitutional; *Style—* Harry Greenway, Esq, MP; House of Commons, London SW1 (☎ 071 219 4598)

GREENWAY, John Robert; MP (C) Ryedale 1987-; s of Thomas William, of 34 Melchett Cres, Rudheath, Northwich, Cheshire, and Kathleen Gregory; *b* 15 Feb 1946; *Educ* Sir John Deane's GS Northwich; *m* 24 Aug 1974, Sylvia Ann, da of James Francis Gant, of 4 Mulgrave Rd, Whitby, N Yorks; 2 s (Stephen, Anthony), 1 da (Louise); *Career* Midland Bank 1964-65, Met Police 1965-69, insur rep 1969-72, insur broker 1972; PPS to Baroness Trumpington, Min of State at Ministry of Agriculture, Fisheries and Food 1991-; memb House of Commons Select Ctee on Home Affrs, sec Cons Backbench Health Ctee; vice-chm: Cons Backbench Agric Ctee, Cons Backbench Home Affrs Ctee, All Pty Football Ctee; memb N Yorks CC 1985-87; pres York City FC; *Recreations* opera, football, wine, travel; *Style—* John Greenway, Esq, MP; 11 Oak Tree Close, Strensall, York YO3 5TE (☎ 0904 490535); 109 Town St, Old Malton, YO17 OHD (☎ 0653 692023); House of Commons, London SW1A 0AA (☎ 071 219 3000)

GREENWAY, Hon Mervyn Stephen Kelvygne; s of 3 Baron Greenway; bro and hp of 4 Baron Greenway; *b* 19 Aug 1942; *Educ* Winchester; unmarried; 1 da (Philippa Mary b 1980); *Career* stockbroker; Freeman City of London, Liveryman Worshipful Co of Vintners; FCA; *Recreations* racing, bridge, golf, cricket, tennis; *Clubs* Turf, MCC; *Style—* The Hon Mervyn Greenway; 605 Howard House, Dolphin Sq, London SW1 (☎ 071 821 1893)

GREENWAY, Hon Nigel Paul; yst s of 3 Baron Greenway (d 1975); *b* 12 Jan 1944; *Educ* Winchester; *m* 1979, Gabrielle, eldest da of late Walter Jean Duchardt, of Obenheim, Alsace; 2 s (Nicholas Walter Paul b 6 Dec 1988, Philippe Charles b 21 Jan 1991); *Style—* The Hon Nigel Greenway; 7 Rue du Colonel Oudot, 75012 Paris, France

GREENWELL, Sir Edward Bernard; 4 Bt (UK 1906), of Marden Park, Godstone, Co Surrey and Greenwell, Wolsingham, Co Durham; s of Sir Peter Greenwell, 3 Bt, TD (d 1978), and (Jean) Henrietta Rose (who m 2, Hugh Kenneth Haig, TD), da of Peter Haig Thomas and Lady Alexandra, *née* Agar, 2 da of 4 Earl of Normanton, DL; *b* 10 June 1948; *Educ* Eton, Nottingham Univ (BSc), Cranfield Inst of Technology (MBA); *m* 1974, Sarah, da of Lt-Col Philip Gore-Anley (d 1968), of Sculthorpe House, Fakenham; 1 s, 3 da; *Heir* s, Alexander; *Career* farmer; sometime chm Suffolk Coastal

District Cncl; *Clubs* Turf; *Style*— Sir Edward Greenwell, Bt; Gedgrave Hall, Woodbridge, Suffolk (☎ 0394 450440)

GREENWELL, Maj James Peter; JP (1986); 2 s of Sir Peter Greenwell, 3 Bt, TD, DL (d 1978); *b* 27 May 1950; *Educ* Eton; *m* 1979, Serena, da of Hon Colin Dalrymple, DL (4 s of 12 Earl of Stair, KT, DSO, JP, DL), by his 2 w Fiona (da of Adm Sir Ralph Edwards, KCB, KBE); 1 s, 1 da; *Career* Army 1968-81, Blues and Royals 1981; farmer 1981-; *Style*— Maj James Greenwell, JP

GREENWELL, (Arthur) Jeffrey; s of George Greenwell (d 1982), of Durham, and Kate Mary, *née* Fleming; *b* 1 Aug 1931; *Educ* Durham Sch, Univ Coll Oxford (MA); *m* 15 Aug 1958, Margaret Rosemary, da of Sidney David Barnard (d 1949); 1 s (David 1964), 2 da (Jane b 1960, Kate b 1962); *Career* Nat Serv RHA 1950-51; articled to Town Clerk Newcastle upon Tyne 1955-58, admitted slr 1958, law tutor Gibson and Weldon 1958-59, asst slr Birmingham Corporation 1959-61, dep clerk of the Cncl Hants CC 1967-74 (asst clerk 1964-67, asst slr 1961-64), dep clerk of the peace 1967-74, dep clerk Hants River Authy 1967-74, chief exec Northants CC 1974-, clerk of Lieutenancy Northants 1977-; pres Northants Assoc of Local Cncls, memb Peterborough Diocesan Synod, govr Nene Coll, tstee Central Festival Opera; hon sec: Assoc of Co Chief Execs 1980-84, Soc of Local Authy Chief Execs 1984-88; chm Home Office Gp on Juvenile Crime 1987, memb Bd Crime Concern, pres Soc of Local Authy Chief Execs 1991; FCIS 1982 (pres 1989); *Recreations* bridge, travel, local history; *Clubs* Northampton and County; *Style*— Jeffrey Greenwell, Esq; County Hall, Northampton NN1 1DN (☎ 0604 236050, fax 0604 236223)

GREENWOOD, Maj (Arthur) Alexander; s of Dr Augustus Charles Greenwood (d 1938), of Horncastle, Lincs; kinsman of: 2 Viscount Greenwood, cous of Gen Sir Roland Guy, Maj-Gen Richard Gerrard-Wright, *qqv* and Brian Beves; *b* 8 March 1920; *Educ* Oakham Sch, Sidney Sussex Coll Cambridge (PhD); *m* 1, 1946 (m dis 1970), Betty Doreen, da of Brig Sidney Albert Westrop, CBE, DSO, MC (d 1979), of Brattleby, Lincs; 1 s (Nicholas Alexander b 1948), 1 da (Jane Alexandra b 1947); m 2, 1976, Shirley Knowles, da of Wing Cdr Alec Knowles-Fitton, MBE, CC (d 1988), of Appletreewick, N Yorks; *Career* regular army, The Royal Lincs Regt 1939-59, serv WWII Norway 1940, Iceland 1940-41, India and Burma 1942-45 (despatches), ADC to FM Sir Claude Auchinleck, GCB 1943-44, GSO 2 (Int) GHQ Middle East Land Forces 1953-54, chief instr Sch of Mil Intelligence 1954-56; memb London Stock Exchange 1963-76; co dir 1977-; dir Lincolnshire Chickens Ltd 1965-87; Liveryman Worshipful Co of: Pattenmakers 1965, Chartered Secretaries 1978; memb: Authors Soc, Heraldry Soc, Soc of Genealogists; FCIS, FSCA, FRSA, FRGS, FREconS, FInstD; *Books* The Greenwood Tree in Three Continents (1988), Field-Marshal Auchinleck (1990); *Recreations* cricket, golf, shooting, genealogy; *Clubs* Carlton, Pilgrims, MCC; *Style*— Maj A A Greenwood; RR 1, Box 40, Madrona Drive, Nanoose Bay, BC, V0R 2R0 Canada (☎ 604 468 9770)

GREENWOOD, Allen Harold Claude; CBE (1974), JP (Surrey 1962, Hampshire 1987); s of Lt-Col Thomas Claude Greenwood (d 1958); *b* 4 June 1917; *Educ* Cheltenham, Coll of Aeronautical Engrg London; *Career* Lt Cdr (A) RNVR, pilot Fleet Air Arm 1942-52; chm: Sepecat SA 1964-73, Panavia GMBH 1969-72, Rookcliff Props 1973-87, Europlane Ltd 1974-83, British Aircraft Corp 1975-77, Remploy Ltd 1976-79, British Aerospace Inc (USA) 1977-81; dep chm British Aerospace 1977-83; pres: Euro Assoc Aero Cos 1974-76, Br Soc Aero Cos 1970-72; vice pres Engrg Employers' Fedn 1982-83, gen cmmr of Income Tax 1970-74; pres Cheltenham Cncl Coll, chm Cncl St John's Sch Leatherhead 1980-84; memb: Cncl Cranfield Inst of Technol 1970-79, Cncl CBI 1970-77, Ctee Governing Body of Public Schs 1981-84; Freeman City of London, Liveryman Coachmakers' Co, memb Guild of Air Pilots; *Recreations* sailing, motoring, travel; *Clubs* White's, RAC, Royal Lymington Yacht; *Style*— Allen Greenwood, Esq, CBE, JP; 2 Rookcliff, Milford-on-Sea, Lymington, Hampshire SO41 0SD (☎ 0590 42893)

GREENWOOD, (Geoffrey) Brian; JP (1969); s of Walter Greenwood (d 1971), of Rawdon, Leeds, and Anne, *née* Nellist (d 1973); *b* 20 Aug 1927; *Educ* Woodhouse Grove Sch; *m* 31 Aug 1949, Enid Dorothy, da of James Bennet (d 1955), of Stockton Heath, Cheshire; 1 s (David Brian b 1 June 1956), 1 da (Patricia Mary b 16 March 1951); *Career* chm: Greenwoods Menswear Group 1971-82 (dir 1949-82), Burley House Group 1982-; chm Woodhouse Grove Sch 1969-, govr St Martin's Coll Lancaster 1986-; *Recreations* shooting, fly-fishing, tennis; *Style*— Brian Greenwood, Esq, JP; Whittington Hall, Whittington, Carnforth, Lancashire LA6 2NR (☎ 05242 71249); Burley House, Burley-In-Wharfedale, Ilkley, West Yorks LS29 7DZ (☎ 0943 864333, fax 0943 864362)

GREENWOOD, Christopher John; s of Capt Murray Guy Greenwood, of Singapore, and Diana Maureen, *née* Barron; *b* 12 May 1955; *Educ* Wellingborough Sch, Magdalene Coll Cambridge (MA, LLB); *m* 5 Aug 1978, Susan Anthea, da of late Geoffrey James Longbotham; 2 da (Catherine b 1982, Sarah b 1985); *Career* called to the Bar Middle Temple 1978; Cambridge Univ: fell Magdalene Coll 1978-, dir studies in law 1982-, tutor 1989-, dean 1982-87, lectr Faculty of Law 1984- (asst lectr 1981-84); tutor 1989-, dir of studies in pub int law Hague Academy of Int Law 1989; visiting prof: West Virginia Univ 1986, Mississippi Univ 1989; jt ed Int Law Reports; *Recreations* politics, reading novels, walking; *Clubs* Oxford & Cambridge; *Style*— Christopher Greenwood, Esq; 2 Victoria Park, Cambridge CB4 3EL (☎ 0223 312105); Magdalene Coll, Cambridge CB3 0AG (☎ 0223 33 2100, fax 0223 63637)

GREENWOOD, 2 Viscount (UK 1937); Sir David Henry Hamar Greenwood; 2 Bt (UK 1915); also Baron Greenwood (UK 1929); s of 1 Viscount Greenwood, PC, KC (d 1948), and Dame Margery Spencer, DBE, da of Rev Walter Spencer (decd), of Fownhope Ct, Herefordshire; *b* 30 Oct 1914; *Educ* privately and Bowers Gifford; *Heir* bro, Hon Michael Greenwood; *Career* farmer; *Recreations* reading, walking, shooting; *Style*— The Rt Hon the Viscount Greenwood; 63 Portsea Hall, Portsea Place, London W2 2BY

GREENWOOD, Derek; s of Cyril Greenwood, of Tunbridge Wells, Kent, and Dorothy Alice Sarah, *née* Macdonald; *b* 5 Nov 1941; *Educ* Dulwich, Univ of London (BSc); *m* 17 April 1965, Kathleen Margaret, da of Harry Alderson; 1 s (Timothy William b 30 Aug 1969), 1 da (Fiona Clare b 20 June 1971); *Career* ptnr Seymour Pierce Stockbrokers 1967-87, jt md Seymour Pierce Butterfield Ltd 1987-; Freeman City of London; memb Stock Exchange 1967-; *Recreations* walking, tennis, classic cars; *Style*— Derek Greenwood, Esq; 10 Old Jewry, London EC2R 8EA (☎ 071 628 4981, fax 071 606 2405)

GREENWOOD, Prof Duncan Joseph; s of Herbert James Greenwood (d 1982), and Alison Fairgrieve Greenwood (d 1967); *b* 16 Oct 1932; *Educ* Hutton GS, Univ of Liverpool (BSc), Univ of Aberdeen (PhD, DSc); *Career* res fell Univ of Aberdeen 1957-59; Nat Vegetable Res Station: scientific offr Chemistry Section 1959-62, sr scientific offr 1962-66, head of soil sci 1966-87; head of soil science and plant nutrition AFRC Inst of Horticultural Res 1987-; Blackman lectr Univ of Oxford 1982, Distinguished Scholar Queens Univ of Belfast 1982, Hannaford lectr Univ of Adelaide 1985, Shell lectr Univ of Kent at Canterbury 1988, Amos lectr Wye Coll London 1989; visiting prof in plant scis Univ of Leeds, hon prof of agric chemistry Univ of Birmingham 1986; Res medal Royal Agric Soc of England 1979, Sir Gilbert Morgan medal Soc of Chemical Indust 1962; published over 130 scientific papers; pres Int Ctee of Plant Nutrition 1978-83; fell: Royal Chemical Soc 1977, Inst of Horticulture 1986; FRS 1985; *Style*— Prof Duncan J Greenwood, FRS; 23 Shelley Rd, Stratford-upon-Avon CV37 7JR (☎ 0789 204 735); Horticulture Research International, Wellesbourne, Warwick CV35 9EF (☎ 0789 470382, fax 0789 470552)

GREENWOOD, Prof Geoffrey Wilson; s of Richard Albert Greenwood (d 1987), of Bradford, W Yorkshire, and Alice Greenwood (d 1983); *b* 3 Feb 1929; *Educ* Grange GS Bradford, Univ of Sheffield (BSc, PhD, DMet, Brunton medal); *m* 1984, Nancy, *née* Cole; 2 s (John Stephen, Alan Richard), 1 da (Catherine Joyce); *Career* scientific then sr scientific offr AEA Harwell 1953-60, section head CEGB Berkeley Nuclear Laboratories 1960-65, res mangr of sciences Electricity Cncl Res Centre Capenhurst 1965-66, prof of metallurgy Univ of Sheffield 1966- (pro vice chllr 1979-83); LB Pfeil prize of Inst of Metals and Iron and Steel Inst 1972, Rosenhain medal 1975; FIM 1966, FInstP 1966, FEng 1990; pres Sheffield Metallurgical and Engrg Assoc 1981-82; *Recreations* music, oboe and piano playing, travel, various outdoor activities; *Clubs* Rotary; *Style*— Prof Geoffrey Greenwood; University of Sheffield, School of Materials, Mappin St, Sheffield S1 3JD (☎ 0742 768555 ext 5517, fax 0742 754325)

GREENWOOD, Prof James Russell; LVO (1975); s of James Greenwood (d 1974), of Stirking Hill Farm, Padiham, Lancs, and Lilian, *née* Moffat; *b* 30 April 1924; *Educ* Royal GS Clitheroe, Queen's Coll Oxford (BA, MA); *m* 17 June 1957, (Mary) Veronica, da of Dr David W Griffith (d 1975), of Sudbury, Suffolk; 1 s ((James) Martin Russell b 17 April 1960); *Career* private then cadet Queen's RR 1943-45, 2 Lt then Lt Intelligence Corps 1945-47; HM Dip Serv 1949-78 (served in Bangkok, Tokyo, Osaka, Rangoon, Rome), consul-gen Osaka 1973-77, cnsllr Br Embassy Tokyo 1968-73; PRO APV Co Ltd and APV International 1980-82, prof Asian Studies Univ of Matsusaka Japan 1983-; Order of the Sacred Treasure (3 class) Japan 1975; *Recreations* travel, golf, swimming; *Clubs* Utd Oxford and Cambridge Univ, MCC; *Style*— Prof James Greenwood, LVO; Apartment B, 48 Hirao Heights, Matsusaka, Mie Prefecture, Japan; Dept of Political Science, Matsusaka University, 1846 Kubo-cho, Matsusaka, Mie, Japan (☎ 010 81 0598 29 1122)

GREENWOOD, Jeffrey Michael; s of Arthur Greenwood (d 1981), of London, and Ada, *née* Gordon (d 1964); *b* 21 April 1935; *Educ* Raine's Foundation Sch, Downing Coll Cambridge (MA, LLM); *m* 1964, Naomi, da of Leo Grahame; 3 s (Matthew b 1967, Joel b 1970, Ethan b 1973), 1 da (Abigail b 1965); *Career* articled clerk Bartlett and Gluckstein 1959-60, admitted slr 1960; Nabarro Nathanson: ptnr 1963-; head of Property Dept 1972-87, sr ptnr 1987-; chm: Jewish Welfare Bd 1986-90, Jewish Care 1990-; memb Cncl: Business in the Community, Hampstead Garden Suburb Trust (Law Soc appointee 1984-87); dir: Bank Leumi (UK) plc, Jewish Chronicle Ltd; Freeman of the City of London, Liveryman of Glovers Company 1984; memb Law Soc 1960; *Recreations* running, swimming, skiing, literature, travel; *Clubs* RAC; *Style*— Jeffrey Greenwood, Esq; Nabarro Nathanson, 50 Stratton St, London W1X 5FL (☎ 071 493 9933, fax 071 629 7900)

GREENWOOD, Jeremy John; s of Basil Procter Greenwood (d 1963), of Langham, nr Holt, Norfolk, and Stephanie Kathleen, *née* Davidson Houston, MBE (d 1988); *b* 30 March 1936; *Educ* Haileybury, Peterhouse Cambridge (BA); *m* 26 Oct 1963, Annabel Elizabeth Marie-Gabrieile, da of Noel Carlile (d 1945); 1 s (Simon Harry b 1966), 2 da (Elinor Rose b 1971, Gemma Charlotte b 1972); *Career* publisher; various positions with: Cassell, Pergamon and Hutchinson Presses; dir Trade Div Cassell and Co 1977-81; property and managing dir Quiller Press 1981-; govr Runton Hill Sch for Girls; *Books* Sefton - Horse For Any Year (1983); *Recreations* horses, shooting, tennis, theatre; *Clubs* Cavalry and Guards; *Style*— Jeremy Greenwood, Esq; Sparrow Hall, Hindringham, nr Fakenham, Norfolk; Quiller Press Ltd, 46 Lillie Rd, London SW6 1TN (☎ 071 499 6529, fax 071 381 8941, telex 21120)

GREENWOOD, John Kenneth; s of Kenneth Greenwood, and Iris, *née* Humphries; *b* 24 Dec 1948; *Educ* Wellington, Manchester; *m* 21 June 1986, Jennifer Joy, da of R Hagan; 1 s (Maximilian Peter b 1983), 1 da (Tzigane Timanfaya Grace b 1985); *Career* dir Intercon Advertising 1971-78, shareholder Gen Advertising Co London Ltd 1978-87, proprietor Greenwood Hinds Advertising Ltd 1987-; MInstM, MInstDir, MBIM, MCAM; *Recreations* writing, golf; *Clubs* Foxhills, St Georges; *Style*— John Greenwood, Esq; Pendrick, Castle Rd, Weybridge, Surrey KT13 9QN (☎ 0932 858 652) Greenwood Hinds Advertising Ltd, 17 Church St, Epsom, Surrey KT17 4PF (☎ 0372 742 066, fax 03727 220 73)

GREENWOOD, Hon Michael George Hamar; yr son of 1 Viscount Greenwood (d 1948); hp of bro, 2 Viscount; *b* 5 May 1923; *Educ* Eton, ChCh Oxford, Webber-Douglas Sch of Singing and Dramatic Art; *Career* formerly with RCS; actor; West End theatre appearance in Joan of Arc at the Stake (with Ingrid Bergman); Feature films incl: The Big Money, House in the Woods, The Bank Raiders, Poor Cow, The Insomniac; TV appearances incl: Emergency Ward 10, Falstaff, Great Expectations, Charlie Drake Show, Dixon of Dock Green, Rob Roy, Lloyd George Documentary, Nixon at Nine, Adam Adamant Lives, Broaden Your Mind, Honey Lane, Gnomes of Dulwich, Eric Sykes Show, Nancy Astor; *Recreations* walking, dancing, reading, writing and rhythm; *Style*— The Hon Michael Greenwood; 63 Portsea Hall, Portsea Place, London W2 2BY (☎ 071 402 2975)

GREENWOOD, Prof Norman Neill; s of Prof John Neill Greenwood (d 1981), of Melbourne, Aust, and Gladys, *née* Uhland (d 1976); *b* 19 Jan 1925; *Educ* Univ HS Melbourne, Univ of Melbourne (BSc, MSc, DSc), Univ of Cambridge (PhD, ScD); *m* 21 Dec 1951, Kirsten Marie, da of Johannes Rydland (d 1978), of Bergen, Norway; 3 da (Karen b 1952, Anne b 1954, Linda b 1958); *Career* res tutor and lectr Trinity Coll Univ of Melbourne 1946-48, sr lectr (formerly lectr) in inorganic chemistry Univ of Nottingham 1953-61; prof and head of Dept Inorganic Chemistry Univ of Newcastle 1961-71, prof of inorganic and structural chemistry Univ of Leeds 1971-90; emeritus prof Univ of Leeds 1990- (dean Faculty of Sci 1986-88); visiting professorships: Aust, Canada, USA, Denmark, Japan; author of numerous books and res papers; chm Int Cmmn on Atomic Weights; pres: Inorganic Chemistry Div Int Union of Pure and Applied Chem 1977-81, Dalton Div Royal Soc of Chemistry 1979-81, Chemistry Section Br Assoc Advanced Science 1990-91; chm UK Ctee of Heads of Univ Chemistry Depts 1985-87; Freeman of Nancy (France) 1977; Hon Doctorate l'Univ de Nancy 1977; memb American Chem Soc 1958, FRSC 1960, FRS 1987, CChem; *Books incl*: Ionic Crystals, Lattice Defects and Nonstoichiometry (1968), Mössbauer Spectroscopy (with T C Gibb, 1971), Contemporary British Chemists (with W A Campbell, 1971), Boron (1973), Chemistry of the Elements (with A Earnshaw, 1984); *Recreations* skiing, music; *Style*— Prof Norman Greenwood, FRS; School of Chemistry, University of Leeds, Leeds LS2 9JT (☎ 0532 336406, fax 0532 336565, telex 556473 UNILDS G)

GREENWOOD, Paul Michael; s of Ernest Charles Greenwood, of Glasgow, and Marie Patricia, *née* Dunn; *b* 2 Aug 1943; *Educ* Alexandra GS Singapore, Wymondham Coll; *m* ;1 adopted da (Melissa); *Career* actor 1965-; tv appearances incl title role in Rosie BBC TV, Yelland in 'Spender' BBC TV; RSC 1980-; roles incl: Antipholus of Syracuse in A Comedy of Errors, Lysander in A Midsummer Night's Dream, Polixenes in The Winter's Tale, Cromwell in Henry VIII, Kent in King Lear, Scarecrow in the Wizard of Oz; *Style*— Paul Greenwood, Esq

GREENWOOD, Philip John; s of John Edward James Greenwood, and Betty, *née*

Roberts (d 1944); *b* 20 Nov 1943; *Educ* Dolgellau GS, Harrow Coll of Art (NDD), Hornsey Coll of Art (ATC); *m* 19 Oct 1974, Valery Jane (d 1985), da of Maj James Francis Ratcliff, of 242 Banstead Rd, Banstead, Surrey; 4 s (Huw b 27 Aug 1976, Jonathan b 26 Jan 1978, Owen (twin) b 26 Jan 1978, Ashley b 12 Oct 1981); *Career* artist; lectr in printmaking Herts Coll of Educn 1970-71; maj one-man exhibitions: Bohun Gallery UK 1974, Gallery Deux Têtes Canada 1976, Portland Gallery UK 1978, Galerie Tendenz Germany 1982, J One Fine Arts Japan 1983, CCA Japan 1985 and 1990; maj gp exhibitions: RA, RE, 1964-, RGI 1973, Br Cncl Gallery Greece 1976, Br Printmakers Aust 1976, V&A UK 1977, Tate Gallery UK 1981, Br Embassy Belgium 1983; public collections: Tate Gallery, Arts Cncl, Br Cncl, Nat Mus of Wales; memb Cncl Royal Soc of Painters Etchers 1983-; memb: ARE 1979, RE 1982; *Recreations* fishing, shooting; *Style—* Philip Greenwood, Esq; Oakleigh, 30 Leigh Hill Road, Cobham, Surrey KT11 2HX (☎ 0932 862383)

GREENWOOD, (John) Richard; DL (1988); s of John Eric Greenwood (d 1975), of The Priory of Lady St Mary, Wareham, Dorset; *b* 18 March 1926; *Educ* Eton; *m* 1953, Penelope Anne, da of Lt-Col Sir Walter Raymond Burrell, 8 Bt, CBE, TD, DL (d 1985), of Knepp Castle, Horsham; 2 s (John Simon, James Anthony), 2 da (Anne Lucinda, Fiona Mary); *Career* former Capt Grenadier Gds; JP 1966-74; CCncllr: E Sussex 1966-74, W Sussex 1974-85; High Sheriff Sussex 1971; *Recreations* shooting, more shooting, golf; *Clubs* White's; *Style—* Richard Greenwood, Esq, DL; Stone Hall, Balcombe, Haywards Heath, West Sussex RH17 6QN (☎ 0444 811371); Lairg Lodge, Sutherland (☎ 0549 2004)

GREENWOOD, Richard Kay (Dick); s of John Herbert Kay Greenwood (d 1975), of Stalybridge, Cheshire, and Hilda *née* Wild (d 1978); *b* 3 May 1928; *Educ* Manchester GS, Trinity Hall Cambridge (MA, MD, MChir); *m* 20 Feb 1961, Sandrina Margaruite, da of Lt-Col David Bishop Campbell, OBE (d 1969), of Sevenoaks, Kent; 1 s (Alastair b 11 Jan 1963), 1 da (Laura b 4 May 1968); *Career* jr surgical appts London Exeter and Glos 1953-65, demonstrator of anatomy Univ of Cambridge, dep dir of Surgical Unit St Thomas's Hosp London, surgical tutor St Thomas's Hosp Med Sch, clinical tutor and examiner Leics Univ Hosp Med Sch, conslt in gen and peripheral vascular surgery Leics DHA 1965-, sr surgn and chm Div of Surgery Leics; Wellcome res fell Mayo Clinic USA; contrib numerous articles in jls on: the gastroesophageal junction, gall bladder, fissure in ano, pilonidal sinus and peripheral vascular disease; ombudsman of the Jt Conslts Ctee, sub-chm of the Central Med Manpower Ctee; med examiner Health Ctee GMC and UKCC (Nursing), assessor of Health Serv Bd and Overseas Med Graduates, memb Ct of the Univ of Warwick; memb: BMA (memb Cncl), RSM, Assoc of Surgns of GB and Ireland, Vascular Surgical Soc of GB and Ireland; Freeman: City of London 1974, Worshipful Co of Makers of Playing Cards 1974; FRCS; *Recreations* mountaineering, rowing, bridge, croquet, politics; *Clubs* Leander Rowing; *Style—* Dick Greenwood, Esq; Herongate, 30 The Ridgeway, Rothley LE7 7LE (☎ 0533 303466); The Leicester Clinic, Scraptoft Lane, Leics LE5 1HY (☎ 0533 769502); The Leicester Royal Infirmary, Infirmary Square, Leics LE1 5WW (☎ 0533 541414); Glenfield General Hospital, Groby Rd, Leics LE3 9QP (☎ 0533 871471)

GREENWOOD OF ROSSENDALE, Baroness; Gillian; da of Leslie Crawshay Williams (himself s of Arthur John Williams, DL, MP, of Glamorgan) and Joyce, a portrait miniaturist and only child of Hon John Collier (2 s of 1 Baron Monkswell) and his 1 w Marian, da of Thomas Huxley, the scientist; *b* 11 April 1910; *m* 1940, Baron Greenwood of Rossendale, PC (d 1982), Min of Housing and Local Govt in Sir Harold Wilson's second govt; 2 da (Hon Mrs Gardiner, Hon Mrs Murray); *Style—* The Rt Hon the Lady Greenwood of Rossendale; 1 Oak Tree House, Redington Gardens, London NW3 7RY (☎ 071 435 7344)

GREER, Germaine; *b* 29 Jan 1939; *Educ* Star of the Sea Convent Gardenvale Victoria Aust, Univ of Melbourne (BA), Univ of Sydney (MA), Univ of Cambridge (PhD); *Career* sr tutor in English Univ of Sydney 1963-64, asst lectr then lectr Univ of Warwick 1967-72, broadcaster, journalist, columnist and reviewer 1972-79, lectr throughout N America with American Program Bureau 1973-78, prof of mod letters Univ of Tulsa 1983 (visiting prof Grad Faculty 1979), dir Stump Cross Books 1988, special lectr and unofficial fell Newnham Coll Cambridge 1989-; fndr ed of Tulsa Studies in Women's Literature 1981; fndr dir Tulsa Centre for the Study of Woman's Literature; *Books* The Female Eunuch (1969), The Obstacle Race: The Fortunes of Women Painters and their Work (1979), Sex and Destiny: The Politics of Human fertility (1984), Shakespeare (1986), Kissing the Rod: an Anthology of Seventeenth Century Women's Verse (ed with S Hastings, J Medoff, M Sansone, 1989), Daddy, We Hardly Knew You (1989), The Uncollected Verse of Aphra Behn (1989); *Style—* Miss Germaine Greer; c/o Aitken and Stone, 29 Fernshaw Rd, London SW10 0TG

GREEY, Edward Ronald; s of Derek Edward Horace Greey (d 1979), and Irene Osborne, *née* Taylor; *b* 26 April 1939; *Educ* Malvern Coll; *m* 1 Oct 1966, Gillian Frances Rippon, da of John Sargeant Hughes, of Woodlea, 371 Thorpe Rd, Longthorpe, Peterborough; 3 da (Sally b 1969, Wendy b 1972, Philippa b 1976); *Career* cmmnd 16/5 Queens Own Royal Lancers, TA Queens Own Staffs Yeo; stockbroker and co dir; memb Birmingham Stock Exchange 1965 (chm 1975-76); dir: Albert E Sharp & Co, Birmingham Stock Exchange Bldgs Co Ltd, Robinson Bros Ryders Green Ltd; guardian Birmingham Assay Office, chm Stock Exchange Midland and Western Unit 1979-80 (dep chm 1977-78), memb Governing Cncl Stock Exchange 1985-88, chm Regnl Ctee Int Stock Exchange; gen cmmr of Income Tax; govr Malvern Coll; *Recreations* golf, fishing, shooting; *Clubs* Blackwell Golf, Edgbaston Golf, Royal West Norfolk Golf; *Style—* Edward Greey, Esq; Peewit Cottage, Bittell Farm Rd, Barnt Green, Worcestershire B45 8BS (☎ 021 445 1672); Albert E Sharp & Co, Ltd, Edmund House, 12 Newham St, Birmingham B3 3ER (☎ 021 200 2244 fax 021 200 2245)

GREGG, Hubert Robert Harry; s of Robert Joseph (d 1955), of London, and Alice Maud, *née* Bessant (d 1956); *b* 19 July 1914; *Educ* St Dunstan's Coll, Webber-Douglas Acad; *m* 1980, Carmel Josephine, da of Laurence Maguire, of Dublin; 1 s (Robert b 1983), 1 da (Katherine b 1981); *Career* WWII Private Lincs Regt 1939, cmd 60 Rifles 1940, seconded to Intelligence, political warfare exec 1942 (duties included broadcasting in German); actor, composer, lyric writer, author, playwright and dir; first London appearance Julien in Martine 1933, Shakespearean roles in Open Air Theatre Regent's Park and Old Vic 1934-35, first NY appearance as Kit Neilan in French Without Tears 1937 (London 1938-39); London appearances incl: Pip in The Convict 1935, Frederick Hackett in Great Possessions 1937, Tom D'Arcy in Off the Record 1947, Peter Scott-Fowler in After The Dance 1939, Polly in Men In Shadow 1942, Michael Carraway in Acacia Avenue 1944, Earl of Harpenden in While the Sun Shines 1945-46, Gabriel Hathaway in Western Wind 1949, John Blessington-Briggs in Chrysanthemum (musical) 1958, Lionel Toop in Pools Paradise 1961; Chichester Festival Theatre: Alexander MacColgie Gibbs in The Cocktail Party, Antonio in The Tempest, Announcer in The Skin of Our Teeth 1968, Sir Lucius O'Trigger in The Rivals, Brittannus in Caesar and Cleopatra, Marcellin in Dear Antoine (also London) 1971; dir London: The Hollow (Agatha Christie's first stage success) 1951, The Mousetrap 1953-60, Speaking of Murder 1958, The Unexpected Guest 1958, From The French 1959, Go Back for Murder 1960, Rule of Three 1962; first solo performance Leicester 1970, subsequently performances in Britain and America (subjects include Shakespeare, Shaw, Jerome K Jerome, the London Theatre and the 20s, 30s, and 40s); films incl: In Which We Serve, Flying Fortress, Acacia Avenue, The Root of all Evil, Vote for Huggett, Once Upon a Dream, Robin Hood (Walt Disney), The Maggie, Svengali, Doctor at Sea (also wrote music and lyrics), Simon and Laura, Speaking of Murder, Final Appointment, Room in the House, Stars in Your Eyes (also co-dir and wrote music and lyrics); announcer BBC Empire Service 1934-35, weekly radio programmes with accent on nostalgia 1965-, chm BBC TV Brains Tst 1955, 40 week radio series on London theatres 1974-75, biography series I Call it Genius, I Call It Style 1980, ITV solo series 1982, 50 Years of Broadcasting (BBC celebration programme) 1984; directed, lectured and adjudicated at: Webber-Douglas Sch, Central Sch of Speech Training, RADA; patron Cinema Theatre Assoc 1973-; pres: Northern Boys' Club 1975-, Concert Artists Assoc 1979-80; Gold Badge of Merit; Freeman City of London 1981; Br Academy of Composers, Authors and Song Writers 1982; plays and screenplays: We Have Company (1953), Cheque Mate (dir and appeared in), Villa Sleep Four (1965), From the French (as Jean-Paul Marotte), Who's Been Sleeping...?, The Rumpus (1967), Dear Somebody (1984), After the Ball (screenplay adapted from own television biography of Vesta Tilley), Stars in your Eyes (screenplay), Geliebtes Traumbild (1984); author of over 200 songs incl: I'm Going to get Lit up, Maybe it's Because I'm a Londoner; *Books* April Gentleman (1951), A Day's Loving (1974), Agatha Christie and all that Mousetrap (1980), Thanks for the Memory (1983); *Clubs* Garrick; *Style—* Hubert Gregg, Esq; 260 King's Drive, Eastbourne, E Sussex BN21 2XD; c/o Broadcasting House, London W1A 1AA

GREGOR, Prof Ian Copeland Smith; s of John Gregor, and Teresa, *née* Copeland; *b* 20 Jan 1926; *Educ* Univ of Durham (BA, PhD), Wadham Coll Oxford; *Career* asst lectr Kings Coll London 1956-58, lectr Univ of Edinburgh 1958-65, prof Univ of Kent 1969- (sr lectr 1965-69); memb AUT; *Books* The Moral and Story (with Brian Nicholas, 1962), William Golding: a Critical Study (with Mark Kinkead-Weekes, 1967), Matthew Arnold's Culture and Anarchy: A Critical Edition (1971), The Great Web: The Form of Hardy's Major Fiction (1974), Reading the Victorian Novel: Detail into Form (ed, 1980); *Recreations* golf; *Style—* Prof Ian Gregor; 143 Old Dover Rd, Canterbury, Kent (☎ 0227 761098); Rutherford College, University of Kent, Canterbury, Kent (☎ 0227 764000)

GREGOR, Zdenek Jiri; s of Prof Ota Gregor, and Miroslava Gregor; *b* 27 March 1948; *Educ* Prague 7 HS, Westminster Med Sch of London; *m* 5 May 1972, Catherine Mary, da of Henry Lironi (d 1986); 1 s (Benjamin b 1973), 1 da (Camilla b 1977); *Career* house appts Westminster Hosp 1971-72, res surgical offr Moorfields Eye Hosp 1976-79, asst prof Univ of Southern California LA 1980-82, sr lectr ophthalmology Univ of London 1982-83, conslt ophthalmic surgn Moorfields Eye Hosp 1983-, numerous pubns and chapters on disorders and surgical treatment of the retina and the vitreous 1975-; memb: Oxford Ophthalmological Congress 1979, Euro Flouroscein Angiography Club 1977, Macular Soc of the US, Retina Soc of the US, Scientific Advsy Cncl, Opportunities for the Disabled; LRCP 1971, FRCS 1977, FRSM 1986 (and memb), fell Coll Ophthalmologists 1988; *Recreations* music, skiing; *Style—* Zdenek Gregor, Esq; 94 Harley Street, London W1N 1AF (☎ 071 935 0777, fax 071 935 0777); Moorfields Eye Hospital, City Rd, London EC1V 2PD (☎ 071 253 3411, fax 071 253 4696, telex 266129)

GREGORY, Conal Robert; MP (Cons) York 1983-; s of Patrick George Murray Gregory and Marjorie Rose, *née* Pointon; *b* 11 March 1947; *Educ* King's Coll Sch Wimbledon, Univ of Sheffield (BA), Master of Wine; *m* 1971, Helen Jennifer, da of Frederick Craggs; 1 s (Rupert), 1 da (Fiona); *Career* wine buyer Colman's of Norwich 1973-77, wine corr 1977-, ed Int Wine and Food Soc Jl 1980-83, dir Standard Fireworks 1987-; sec All Pty Parly Tourism Ctee 1983-; vice chm: Cons Parly Tourism Ctee 1985-; chm Cons Parly Food and Drinks Industs Ctee 1989- (vice chm 1985-88); vice chm: Cons Parly Tport Ctee 1987-89 and 1990- (sec 1983-87), All Party Parly Hospice Gp 1990-; sec UK Parly Isle of Man CPA Ctee, hon treas UK Parly Cyprus CPA Ctee; fell Indust and Parly Tst; Norfolk CC: memb 1977-81, vice chm Schs Ctee 1977-78; vice pres: Norwich Jr Chamber 1975-76, York Civic Tst, UN Assoc (York Branch); fndr and chm Bow Gp of E Anglia 1975-82; vice chm: Nat Bow Gp 1976-77, Eastern Area Cons Political Centre 1980-83; govr Univ of Sheffield 1978-, chm Norwich N Cons Assoc 1980-82; memb: E Anglia Tourist Bd 1979-81, Ct of govrs Univs of Hull and York 1983, York Archaeological Tst; pres York Young Cons 1982-; *Books* Caterer's Guide to Drinks, A Policy for Tourism? (co-author), Beers of Britain (co-author), Food for a Healthy Britain (co-author); *Clubs* Acomb Conservative; *Style—* Conal R Gregory, Esq, MP; House of Commons, London SW1A 0AA (☎ 071 219 4603)

GREGORY, David John; s of (Newton) John Gregory, of London, and Doris May, *née* Bennett; *b* 3 Dec 1942; *Educ* Loxford Sch, NE London Poly; *m* 20 Jan 1968, (Solveig) Anita, da of Artur John Niklasson, of Lerdala, Sweden; 2 da (Anna b 1971, Lisa b 1973); *Career* ptnr Keevil & Gregory Architects 1973-; chm: Awards Ctee ARCUK, Rothersthorpe Parish Cncl; memb Cncl Northamptonshire C of C and Indust; RIBA 1972; *Style—* David Gregory, Esq; 9 Berry Close, Rothersthorpe, Northampton NN7 3JQ; Keevil & Gregory Architects, 53 Derngate, Northampton NN1 1UE (☎ 0604 239300, fax 0604 232748)

GREGORY, David Noel; s of Charles Cope Gregory, and Caroline Ada Gregory; *b* 25 Dec 1944; *Educ* Hillcroft Sch London; *m* 19 Aug 1972, Angela Mary, da of Ernest John Day; 1 s (Daniel Mark b 24 Feb 1977), 1 da (Claire Louise b 9 Feb 1975); *Career* CA; articled clerk Evans Peirson & Co, gp fin controller James Walker Goldsmith & Silversmith plc; fin dir: Instore Enterprises Ltd (subsid Debenhams), Eurobrands Ltd (UK distribution co of Remy Martin & Co) 1987-; FCA (ACA 1969), ATII 1971, FCCA 1980, MBCS 1981; *Clubs* IOD, Twickenham on Thames Rotary; *Style—* David Gregory, Esq; Eurobrands Ltd, The Malthouse, 45 New St, Henley on Thames, Oxfordshire RG9 2BP (☎ 0491 410777)

GREGORY, Derek Edward; s of Edward Gregory (d 1970), of Ilkeston, and Hilda, *née* Stokeley (d 1989); *Educ* Ilkeston GS; *m* 1, 16 June 1962, Marjorie (d 1984), da of Lloyd Priest Newcastle (d 1976); 1 s (Philip Edward b 1965), 1 da (Tina Louise b 1968); m 2, 13 Dec 1986, Kate; *Career* fndr and sr ptnr Gregory Priestley & Stewart CA's Ilkeston Long Eaton Sutton in Ashfield 1970-; treas Stanton by Dale CC 1958-; FCA 1961; *Recreations* horse racing, cricket, gardening; *Style—* Derek Gregory, Esq; Rosemary Cottage, Bowling Close, Stanton By Dale, Ilkeston, Derby (☎ 0602 322 047); 16 Queen St, Ilkeston, Derbys (☎ 0602 326 726)

GREGORY, Geoffrey; s of Gilbert Gregory (d 1966), of Gatley, Cheshire, and Minnie Louisa, *née* Haag (d 1988); *b* 14 March 1929; *Educ* Manchester GS, St Johns Coll Cambridge (MA), Stanford Univ California (MS, PhD); *m* 26 Feb 1958, Brenda, da of John Harold Raymond Syers (d 1985), of Hale, Cheshire; 3 da (Janet b 1959, Sarah b 1961, Kate b 1963); *Career* Nat Serv RAF; statistician British Celanese Ltd 1952-57, staff tutor Univ of Birmingham 1958-59, sr lectr and reader Univ of Melbourne 1959-68, sr res fell Univ of Lancaster 1968-72, prof mgmnt studies Loughborough Univ of Technol 1973-; FSS; *Books* Mathematical Methods in Management (1983), Decision Analysis (1988); *Recreations* fell walking, bridge; *Style—* Prof Geoffrey Gregory; 3 Burton Street, Loughborough, Leicestershire LE11 2DT (☎ 0509 263262); Department of Management Studies, University of Technology, Loughborough,

Leicestershire LE11 3TU (☎ 0509 223100, telex 34319)

GREGORY, John Frederick; s of Arthur Frederick Gregory (d 1955), of London, and Marjorie Phyllis, *née* Williams; *b* 7 April 1935; *Educ* Ashburton HS; *m* 9 June 1956, Ethel Currie, da of Robert Burns, of Preston, Lancs; 1 s (David Russell b 14 Nov 1965), 2 da (Linda Ann b 21 May 1957, Alison Joy b 8 Dec 1960); *Career* RAF 1953-55; Capel-Cure Myers (now ANZ McCaughan): joined 1950-, ptnr 1979-85, dir 1985-89; dir Beeson Gregory plc 1989-, non-exec dir Cussins Property Gp plc 1983-; memb Stock Exchange 1972; *Recreations* music, painting, fell walking; *Clubs* Gresham; *Style—* John Gregory, Esq; 185 Ballards Way, Croydon, Surrey (☎ 081 657 6706); Sefton, Saltcote Lane, Rye, East Sussex; Beeson Gregory plc, The Registry, Royal Mint Court, London EC3

GREGORY, John James Conrad; s of Hubert Conrad Gregory (d 1955), of Newark House, 2 Gloucester Rd, Staple Hill, Bristol, and Mary McLachlan, *née* Drysdale (d 1976); *b* 3 April 1932; *Educ* Chipping Sodbury GS, Merchant Ventures Tech Coll Bristol (ONC), Gosta Green Coll of Technol (HNC); *m* 9 April 1955, Marion Elizabeth, da of Gilbert H Mart, of 49 Raynes Rd, Ashton Gate, Bristol; 1 s (Nigel James b 1959), 1 da (Sarah Louise b 1961); *Career* apprentice and draughtsman Gardiner Sons & Co 1948-55, sr draughtsman Boulton & Paul 1955-58, section ldr Metal Constructions Ltd 1958-61, sr design engr Norris Conslts 1961-64, chief draughtsman Johnson Structures 1964-65, princ Gregory & Assocs 1965-; cmmns include: catering estabs, food and chemical plants, multi-storey office blocks, schools and sports facilities; pres Chamber of Indust & Commerce Swindon 1986-87, memb Bd Great Western Enterprise, rep Br Standards Ctee; CEng, FIStructE (former memb Cncl London, twice branch chm Bedford), MConsE, FFB 1970 (vice chm West Anglia Branch), MInstD (chm S East Midlands Branch); *Recreations* propogation of plants, cooking & presentation of food; *Style—* John Gregory, Esq; Redcliffe House, 14 Thrapston Rd, Spaldwick, Huntingdon, Cambridgeshire PE18 0TA (☎ 0480 890 632); Gregory & Associates, Harpur House, 62 Harpur St, Bedford MK40 2RA (☎ 0234 360377/8, fax 0234 211 121); Gregory & Associates, Shaftesbury Centre, Percy St, Swindon, Wiltshire SN2 2AZ (☎ 0293 512 923, fax 0793 616837)

GREGORY, John Raymond; s of Raymond Gregory (d 1988), of Congleton, Cheshire, and Ivy Charlotte, *née* Bourne; *b* 18 April 1949; *Educ* St Ambrose Coll Hale Barns Cheshire, Univ of Hull; *m* 11 April 1981, Fiona Mary Kristin, da of Donald Walker, of Chorlton, Manchester; 2 s (Gordon b 1981, Lawrence b 1984), 2 da (Victoria b 1983, Elizabeth b and d 1987); *Career* called to the Bar Middle Temple 1972, in practice 1973-; chm Stretford Constituency Cons Assoc 1980-82; *Recreations* swimming, archaeology, writing, painting; *Style—* John Gregory, Esq; 1 Deans Ct, Crown Sq, Manchester (☎ 061 834 4097)

GREGORY, Kenneth John; s of Frederick Arthur Gregory (d 1971), of Belper, Derbyshire, and Marion, *née* Yates (d 1981); *b* 23 March 1938; *Educ* Herbert Strutt Sch Belper Derbyshire, UCL (BSc, PhD, DSc); *m* 25 Aug 1962, Margaret (Christine) da of Lawrence Wilmot (d 1974) of Belper, Derbyshire; 1 s (Jonathon b 1971), 2 da (Caroline b 1964, Sarah b 1966); *Career* reader in physical geography Univ of Exeter 1972-76 (lectr 1962-72), visiting lectr Univ of New England Armidale NSW Aust 1975, distinguished visiting prof Arizona State Univ 1978, visiting prof Univ Kebangsan Malaysia 1987, dep vice chllr Univ of Southampton 1988- (prof 1976-, dean of sci 1984-87); FRGS 1962; *Books* Southwest England (with A H Shorter and W L D Ravenhill, 1969), River Channel Changes (ed, 1977), Geomorphological Processes (with E Derbyshire and J R Hails, 1979 and 1980), Horizons in Physical Geography (ed with M J Clark and A M Gurnell, 1988), The Nature of Physical Geography (1985); *Recreations* gardening, travel; *Clubs* Geographical; *Style—* Prof Kenneth Gregory; 12 Beech Close, Chandlers Ford, Eastleigh, Hants SO5 1NE (☎ 0703 269196); Department of Geography, University of Southampton, Highfield, Southampton S09 5NH (☎ 0703 592215, fax 0703 593939, telex 47661)

GREGORY, Capt (Alexander) Michael; OBE (1987); s of Vice Adm Sir George David Archibald Gregory, KBE, CB, DSO (d 1975), of Greymount, Alyth, Perthshire, and Florence Eve Patricia, *née* Hill; *b* 15 Dec 1945; *Educ* Marlborough, BRNC Dartmouth; *m* 13 June 1970, Jean Charlotte, da of Lt Cdr Gerald Robin Muir, OBE, of Silverton Farm House Braco, By Dunblane, Perthshire; 4 da (Charlotte b 1971, Katherine b 1973, Helen b 1979, Sarah b 1982); *Career* HMS Albion and HMS Aisne 1965-66, HMS Narwhale 1966-67, HMS Otter 1967-68, HMS Warspite 1968-70, HMS Courageous 1970-73, HMS Odin (based in Australia) 1973-75, i/c HMS Finwhale 1976-78, HMS Repulse 1978-80, staff of US Third Fleet Hawaii 1980-82, i/c HMS Renown 1982-85, Cdr Tenth Submarine Sqdn and i/c HMS Resolution 1985-86, Jt Servs Def Coll 1987, MOD Directorate of Naval Warfare 1987-88, i/c HMS Cumberland 1988-; memb Royal Co of Archers (Queen's Bodyguard for Scotland); *Recreations* shooting, fishing, skiing, stalking, gardening; *Style—* Capt Michael Gregory, OBE, RN

GREGORY, Michael Anthony; OBE (1990); s of Lt-Col Wallace James Ignatius Gregory (d 1972), and Dorothy Isabel, *née* Malyon; *b* 8 June 1925; *Educ* Douai Sch, UCL (LLB); *m* 11 Aug 1951, Patricia Ann, da of Frank Thomas Hodges (d 1978); 3 s (Martin, Damien, Tristan), 5 da (Anne, Philippa, Lucy, Bernadette, Jane); *Career* Nat Serv WWII, joined RAF 1943, cmmnd 1945, Navigator 1945, demobbed as Flying Offr 1947; called to the Bar Middle Temple 1952, in practice 1952-60, Legal Dept Country Landowners' Assoc 1960-90 (chief legal advsr 1977-90); freelance journalist; chm: Mgmnt Ctee Catholic Social Serv for Prisoners 1960-71 and 1974-85 (memb 1952-), Fleet Branch Int Help for Children 1967-77; hon legal advsr Nat Anglers Cncl 1968-, fndr memb Agric Law Assoc 1975-, tstee Country Landowners Assoc Charitable Tst 1980-; memb: BSI Ctee on Installation of Pipelines 1965-83, Cncl Salmon and Trout Assoc 1980-90, Cncl Anglers' Cooperative Assoc 1980-, Ctee Fedn for Promotion of Hort for Disabled People 1981-(tstee 1987), Thames Water Authy Regnl Fisheries Advsy Ctee 1974-89, Inland Waterways Amenity Advsy Cncl 1982-(regnl rep SE 1990-); pres Douai Soc 1984-86, memb Advsy Ctee Nat River Authy (Thames Region) 1989-; Papal medal Pro Ecclesia Et Pontifice Papal 1988; *Books* Organisational Possibilities in Farming (1968), Joint Enterprises in Farming (with C Townsend, 2 edn 1973), Angling and the Law (2 edn 1974), All for Fishing (with R Seymour, 1970), Essential Law for Landowners and Farmers (with Margaret Parrish, 2 edn 1987, with Angela Sydenham, 3 edn 1990); *Recreations* ball games, angling, playing saxophones, watching wildlife; *Style—* Michael Gregory, Esq, OBE; 63 Gally Hill Rd, Church Crookham, Fleet, Hants GU13 0RU (☎ 0252 616 473)

GREGORY, Dr Paul Duncan; s of Thomas Gregory, of Troon, and Elsie, *née* Millward; *b* 1 Dec 1954; *Educ* Marr Coll Troon, Univ of Edinburgh (BCom, PhD); *m* 21 July 1978, Catherine Margaret, da of James Campbell, of Troon; 1 s (James Alexander b 1985), 1 da (Jennifer Alison b 1987); *Career* oil analyst Wood Mackenzie & Co Ltd 1981-85, asst dir Hill Samuel 1986-87, dir County Natwest Securities 1989- (assoc dir 1988-89); memb Inst of Petroleum, memb Edinburgh & Leith Petroleum Club; *Books* Factors Influencing the Export Performance of the Scottish Manufacturing Sector of the Offshore Supplies Industry (1982), World Offshore Markets: Can Britain Compete? (1986); *Recreations* golf, squash; *Clubs* Morton Hall Golf; *Style—* Dr Paul Gregory; 35 Gilmour Rd, Edinburgh EH16 5NS (☎ 031 667 5086); County Natwest Securities Ltd, Kintore House, 74-77 Queen St, Edinburgh EH2 4NS (☎ 031 225 8525, fax 031 243 4434, telex 72555)

GREGORY, Peter William; s of William Henry Gregory, of Thamesway, 9 Berkeley Gardens, Walton on Thames, Surrey, and Florence Mabel, *née* Peters; *b* 3 Oct 1934; *Educ* Surbiton GS, City & Guilds, Imperial Coll Univ of London, (BSc); *m* 16 Jan 1960, Angela Margaret; 1 s (Timothy b 10 March 1963), 2 da (Sarah b 14 March 1965, Susan b 22 April 1966); *Career* short service cmmn RAF 1958-61, Flt Lt 5003 Sqdn Alb in UK; civil engr; dep chm and jt mangr dir Laing Mgmnt Contracting Ltd 1986, md LMC 1985, md LMC (Scotland) Ltd, dir John Lain Construction Ltd 1984, dir Laingloy Ltd; MICE; *Recreations* game shooting, salmon fishing, gardening, golf; *Style—* Peter W Gregory, Esq; Target House, Hexham, Northumberland NE46 4LD (☎ 0434 604689); Laing Management Contracting Ltd, 37-39 Grey Street, Newcastle upon Tyne NE1 6EE (☎ 091 261 7574, fax 091 261 7288, car 0836 204750)

GREGORY, Philippa; da of Arthur Percy Gregory (d 1955), of Nairobi, and Elaine, *née* Wedd (d 1983); *b* 9 Jan 1954; *Educ* Duncan House Sch for Girls' Clifton, Colston's Girls' Sch Bristol, Univ of Sussex (BA), Univ of Edinburgh (PhD); *m* (m dis); 1 da (Victoria Elaine b 31 Jan 1982); *Career* work on: newspaper in Portsmouth 1972-75, BBC Radio Solent and BBC Radio Scotland 1978-82; freelance BBC Radio producer 1978-82; *Books* Wideacre (1987), The Favoured Child (1989), Princess Florizella (1989), Meridon (1990), Princess Florizella and the Wolves(1991); *Style—* Ms Philippa Gregory; Rogers Coleridge & White, 20 Powis Mews, London W11 1JN (☎ 071 221 3717)

GREGORY, Lt-Col Richard Boutcher; s of Capt Ernest Foster Gregory, CBE, RN (d 1940), and Evelyn Isabelle, *née* Browning (d 1990); *b* 6 May 1916; *Educ* Cranleigh Sch, RMA Woolwich, RMCS Shrivenham; *m* 30 Aug 1955, Alison, da of Vice-Adm Wion De Malpas Egerton, DSO, RN (ka 1943); 1 s (Andrew b 1957), 1 da (Jane b 1960); *Career* cmmnd RA 1936, served India until 1940, active serv W Desert and Eritrea 1940-42, D Day 1944 (wounded); princ regnl inspr (armaments) Scot and Northern Region 1958-60; memb staff of Sedbergh Sch 1960-72, Educn Books Div Encyclopaedia Britannica 1975-82; *Style—* Lt-Col Richard Gregory; Rosslyn, Charmouth Rd, Lyme Regis, Dorset DT7 3DW (☎ 02974 3260)

GREGORY, Richard John; s of John Gregory, and Joan, *née* Slingsby; *b* 18 Aug 1954; *Educ* Danum GS, Doncaster; *m* 14 Aug 1976, Elaine Margaret, da of (Herbert Charles) Ronald Matthews (d 1971); 2 da (Anna Marie b 11 Feb 1979, Antonia Faye b 11 Dec 1987); *Career* industl corr Morning Telegraph 1977-79, news ed Granada TV 1979-81; Yorkshire TV: news ed 1981-82, prodr 1982-84, ed Calendar 1984-; *Recreations* squash, swimming, riding, hill-walking; *Style—* Richard Gregory, Esq; Brooklands, Castleton Rd, Hope, Derbyshire; Yorkshire Television, Kirkstall Rd, Leeds LS3 1JS (☎ 0532 438283)

GREGORY, Prof Richard Langton; CBE (1989); s of CCL Gregory (d 1969), and Patricia, *née* Gibson (d 1988); *b* 24 July 1923; *Educ* King Alfred Sch Hampstead, Downing Coll Cambridge; *m* 1, 1953 (m dis 1966); 1 s (Mark Foss Langton), 1 da (Romilly Caroline Langton); m 2, 1976 (m dis); *Career* Univ of Cambridge: res MRC Applied Psychology Res Unit 1950-53, demonstrator then lectr Dept Psychology 1953-67, fell Corpus Christi Coll 1962-67; prof of bionics Dept Machine Intelligence and Perception Univ of Edinburgh 1967-70 (chm 1968-70), currently Brain and Perception Laboratory and emeritus prof Dept Psychology Univ of Bristol; visiting prof: UCLA 1963, MIT 1964, NY Univ 1966; Freeman Worshipful Co of Spectacle Makers; *Books* Recovery from Early Blindness (with Jean Wallace, 1963), Eye and Brain (1966, 4 edn 1990), The Intelligent Eye (1970), Illusion in Nature and Art (jt ed, 1973), Concepts and Mechanisms of Perception (1974), Mind in Science (1981), Oxford Companion to the Mind (1987); *Clubs* The Athenaeum, Saville; *Style—* Prof Richard Gregory, CBE; 23 Royal York Crescent, Clifton, Bristol BS8 4JX (☎ 0272 739701); University of Bristol, Dept of Psychology, Berkeley Square, Clifton, Bristol BS8 1HH (☎ 0272 303030, fax 0272 732657)

GREGORY, Roger Michael; s of Walter James Gregory (d 1967), and Catherine Emma, *née* Regan (d 1978); *b* 1 June 1939; *Educ* Gillingham GS; *m* 22 April 1961, Johanna Margaret, da of James Robb-Russell O'Rourke (d 1978); 5 s (Simon b 1964, Matthew b 1970, Steven b 1972, Mark b 1976, Andrew b 1979), 2 da (Claire b 1962, Rachel b 1966); *Career* joined Metropolitan Police Civil Staff 1957, dir Computing Services 1983-89, dep receiver for Met Police Dist 1989-; *Recreations* cricket, bridge, gentle gardening; *Style—* Roger Gregory, Esq; New Scotland Yard, 10 Broadway, London SW1H 0BG (☎ 071 230 2491)

GREGSON, Baron (Life Peer UK 1975), of Stockport in Greater Manchester; John Gregson; DL (Gtr Manchester 1979); s of John Gregson; *b* 29 Jan 1924; *Career* joined Stockport Base Subsidiary 1939, Fairey R&D team, appointed to Bd 1966; pt/t memb Br Steel plc 1976-; exec dir Fairey plc 1978; Manchester Industrial Centre Ltd 1982-; non exec dir: Lazard Defence Fund Mgmnt Ltd 1982-, Otto-Simon Carves Ltd, Electra Corporate Ventures Ltd; memb House of Lords Select Ctee on Sci and Technol 1980, pres Parly and Scientific Ctee 1986-, chm Finance and Indust Gp of Lab Party 1978-, vice-pres Assoc of Metropolitan Authorities 1984, pres Defence Manufacturers Assoc 1984- (chm 1980-84); memb Court Univ Manchester Inst of Sci and Technol 1976; pres Stockport Youth Orch, vice-pres Fedn of Br Police Motor Clubs; hon fell Manchester Poly 1983, Hon FIProdE 1982, Hon D Open Univ, Hon DSc Aston Univ; AMCT, CBIM; *Recreations* mountaineering, skiing; *Style—* The Rt Hon the Lord Gregson, DL; Fairey plc, Cranford Lane, Heston, Middx

GREGSON, Sir Peter Lewis; KCB (1988, CB 1983); s of Walter Henry Gregson (d 1961), and Lillian Margaret, *née* Lees; *b* 28 June 1936; *Educ* Nottingham HS, Balliol Coll Oxford (MA); *Career* Nat Serv 1959-61 (2 Lt RAEC, attached Sherwood Foresters); BOT 1961-66, private sec to PM 1968-72, sec Industl Devpt Advsy Bd 1972-74, sec NEB 1975-77, under sec Dept of Trade 1977-80, dep sec Dept of Trade 1980-81; dep sec Cabinet Office 1981-85; perm under sec of state Dept of Energy 1985-89; perm sec DTI 1989-; *Recreations* gardening, listening to music; *Style—* Sir Peter Gregson, KCB; Department of Trade & Industry, 1-19 Victoria St, London SW1H 0ET (☎ 071 215 4439)

GREGSON, William Derek Hadfield; CBE (1970), DL (1984); s of W Gregson (d 1929); *b* 27 Jan 1920; *Educ* King William's Coll IOM, Alpine Coll Villars Switzerland, Faraday House Engrg Coll (DFH); *m* 1944, Rosalind Helen, da of R M E Reeves; 3 s, 1 da; *Career* served RAF, Sqdn Ldr NW Europe 1941-45; dir: Ferranti New York 1969-83, Ferranti Holdings Ltd 1983-85 (asst gen mangr Ferranti (Scotland) Ltd 1959-83), Anderson Strathclyde plc, Brammer plc, BT (Scotland) 1977-85; conslt ICI; former memb: Electronic Engrg Assoc (pres 1963-64), Electronics EDC 1965-75, Scot Economic Planning Cncl 1965-71, Soc of Br Aerospace Cos (chm Equipment Gp Ctee 1967), Bd of Livingston New Town 1968-76, Scot Cncl CBI 1975-79, Machine Tool Expert Ctee 1969-70, BIM Cncl 1975-80, jt BIM and NEDO Professional Mgmnt Advsy Ctee on Industl Strategy; pres Br Electrical and Allied Mfrs Assoc; chm: BIM Advsy Bd Scotland 1970-75, Scot GPs Res Support Unit 1971-79, Mgmnt Assoc of SE Scotland 1980-81; dep chm: Br Airports Authy 1975-85, Scot Cncl Devpt and Indust, Scot Nat Orch; dir E of Scotland Industl Investmts, cmmr Northern Lighthouse Bd; memb Design Cncl; CEng, FIEE, CBIM, FIIM; *Recreations* reading, cabinet-making, automation in the home; *Clubs* RAF, New (Edinburgh); *Style—* William Gregson, Esq, CBE, DL; 15 Barnton Ave, Edinburgh EH4 6AJ (☎ 031 336 3896)

GREHAN, Maj Denis Stephen; s of Maj Stephen Arthur Grehan, OBE, MC (d 1972), of Clonmeen, Banteer, Co Cork, and Cecily Mary, *née* Gaisford St Lawrence (d 1973), of Howth Castle, Co Dublin; *b* 24 July 1927; *Educ* Ampleforth, RMA Sandhurst; *m* 9 Aug 1969, Jane, da of Maj Norman McCaskle, of Harefield House, Theale, Berks (d 1968); *Career* Regular Offr Irish Gds 1948-67; with Stewart Wrightson Insur Brokers 1971-; dir: Stewart Wrightson PFP Ltd, Valuers Auctioneers and Estate Agents Gp Insur Servs Ltd; *Recreations* sports, hunting, shooting, fishing, polo; *Clubs* Blue Seal; *Style—* Maj Denis Grehan; Olivers Cottage, Bramley Green, Basingstoke, Hants (☎ 0256 881340); Willis Wrightson House, Wood St, Kingston upon Thames, Surrey KT1 1QG (☎ 081 860 6000)

GREIG, (Henry Louis) Carron; CVO (1972), CBE (1986); s of Gp Capt Sir Louis Greig, KBE, CVO, DL, of Thatched House Lodge, Richmond Park; *b* 21 Feb 1925; *Educ* Eton; *m* 1955, Monica, da of Hon John Stourton, TD, *qv*; 2 s and twin s and da; *Career* Capt Scots Gds N W Europe 1945; gentleman usher to HM The Queen 1962-; chm H Clarkson & Co 1973-85 (md 1962-85, dir 1954-85); chm Horace Clarkson plc 1976-; dir: James Purdey & Sons 1972-, Williams & Glyn's 1983-85; Royal Bank of Scotland 1985-, chm Baltic Exchange 1983-85 (dir 1978-85); vice-chm Not Forgotten Assoc 1979-; *Clubs* White's; *Style—* Carron Greig, Esq, CVO, CBE; Binsness, Forres, Moray; Brook House, Fleet, Hants

GREIG, David Robert (Bob); s of Maj Samual Victor Greig (d 1942), and Winifred, *née* Robertson (d 1976); *b* 1 May 1932; *Educ* Stowe; *m* 4 Sept 1965, Wendy Margaret, da of Alan McDonald (d 1958), of Sydney, Australia; 1 s (Alan b 28 Aug 1969), 2 da (Julia b 18 July 1967, Robyn b 25 Jan 1972); *Career* Nat Serv cmmnd 2 Lt 1950-52; dir David Greig Ltd 1954-72 (joined 1949), fndr Robert Greig Ltd 1972; *Recreations* national hunt and point-to-point racing, rode over 70 winners; *Style—* Bob Greig, Esq; Pittance Farm, Smithwood Common, Cranleigh, Surrey GU6 8QY (☎ 0483 272737); Robert Greig Ltd, 22-30 Bridge St, Andover, Hants SP10 1BN (☎ 0264 332054, fax 0264 66213)

GREIG, Ian Alexander; s of Alexander Broom (Sandy) Greig, DSO, DFC (d 1990), of Sydney, Aust, and Josephine Emily (Joyce), *née* Taylor; *b* 8 Dec 1955; *Educ* Queens Coll Queenstown SA, Downing Coll Cambridge (Cricket and Rugby blues); *m* 8 Jan 1983, Cheryl Ruth, da of Kevin Francis Day; 1 s (Andrew Ian b 20 Jan 1987), 1 da (Michelle Elizabeth b 17 Dec 1984); *Career* Nat Serv SA Capt Defence Force XI 1975; professional cricketer; first class cricket debut Border SA 1974, Griqualand West SA 1975-76, capt Cambridge Univ 1979, capt Combined Univ tour Aust 1979-80; Sussex CCC: debut 1979, awarded county cap 1981, dismissed 1985; capt and coach Queensland Colts Aust 1986, capt Surrey CCC 1987- (awarded county cap 1987); 2 Test matches England v Pakistan 1982-; off-seasons: player and coach in Aust 1980-87, Queensland Univ 1980-82, Waverley District CC 1983-85 (player of the year 1983 and 1984), mktg and cricket exec Surrey CCC 1987-; scored 291 v Lancs 1990: highest score by Surrey capt, highest score by number seven batsman, record eight wicket partnership with Martin Bicknell for Surrey; *Recreations* fly fishing, watching rugby union; *Style—* Ian Greig, Esq; Surrey CCC, Kennington Oval, London SE11 5SS (☎ 071 582 6660, fax 071 735 7769)

GREIG, James Dennis; CMG (1967); s of Dennis George Greig, of Eccles (d 1971), and Florence Aileen, *née* Marjoribanks (d 1959); *b* 14 July 1926; *Educ* Winchester, Clare Coll Cambridge, LSE; *m* 1, 1952 (m dis 1960), Pamela Marguerite Stock; 1 s (Charles Andrew b 1955), 1 da (Nicola Hilary (Mrs Chater) b 1954); m 2, 1960 (m dis 1967), Mrs Elizabeth Ettenger Brown, da of Horace Melville Starke, of Charlotte, N Carolina, USA; 1 s (Justin Simon b 1962); m 3, 1968, Paula Mary, da of Percival Cook (d 1969), of Gillingham, Kent; 1 adopted s (Nigel Lewis b 1963); *Career* Lt The Black Watch RHR and Nigeria Regt 1944-47 served Burma; Colonial Serv: Nigeria 1949-59, fin sec Mauritius 1960-67, head of Africa and Middle East Bureau Int Planned Parenthood Fedn 1968-76, dir Population Bureau Miny of Overseas Devpt 1976-80; trader in commodity and fin futures; racehorse owner; *Recreations* national hunt racing, shooting, gardening, polo, bowls, cricket, squash, tennis, bridge, ballet; *Clubs* Hurlingham, Annabel's; *Style—* James Greig, Esq, CMG; The Braw Bothy, Eccles, Kelso, Roxburghshire (☎ 089 084544); 6 Beverley Close, Barnes, London SW13 0EH (☎ 081 876 5354)

GREIG, Lt Cdr Philip Guy Morland; s of Capt Philip Humphreys Greig, MC (d 1965), and Minnie Sylvia, *née* Baker (d 1966); *b* 19 Jan 1927; *Educ* The Old Malt House, RNC Dartmouth; *m* 18 Nov 1953, Susan, da of Harold Owen Stutchbury (d 1966), of W Byfleet; 2 da (Victoria b 1954, Charlotte (twin) b 1954), 2 s (William b 1956, Stephen b 1959); *Career* Lt Cdr RN; served WWII D Day 1944, Far East, Signal Offr HMS Belfast 1959-61, Fleet Electronic Warfare Offr Far East Fleet 1961-62, Naval Liaison Offr GCHQ 1967-73; fruit farmer 1977-; fndr and chm Upper Thames Protection Soc 1986; obtained certificate in arboriculture Royal Forestry Soc; *Recreations* watching cricket on TV, growing trees; *Style—* Lt Cdr Philip Greig; (☎ 0285 8102744)

GRENFELL, Francis Pascoe John; JP (1977); s of Maj Hon Arthur Grenfell (2 s of 1 Baron Grenfell) and Eleanor Dorothy Alice, da of Hon (Mr Justice) Sir Francis James, of Saltash; hp to first cous, 3 Baron Grenfell; *b* 28 Feb 1938; *Educ* Eton, ChCh Oxford; *m* 1977, Elizabeth, da of Hugh Kenyon and Mary (da of Sir Peile Thompson, 4 Bt); *Career* teacher Kitwood Boys' Sch Boston Lincs; memb Bd of Visitors HM Prison North Sea Camp 1969-; *Recreations* fishing, restoration of buildings and drains, gardening; *Style—* Francis Grenfell, Esq, JP; Lenton House, Lenton, Grantham, Lincs NG33 4HB

GRENFELL, Irene, Baroness; Irene Lilian; da of Harry Cartwright, of Buenos Aires; *m* 1946, as his 2 w, 2 Baron Grenfell (d 1976); 1 da (Hon Aline Grenfell, *qv*); *Style—* The Rt Hon Irene, Lady Grenfell; 13 Liphook Crescent, Honor Oak, Forest Hill, SE23 3BN (☎ 081 699 8528)

GRENFELL, 3 Baron (UK 1902); Julian Pascoe Francis St Leger Grenfell; s of 2 Baron Grenfell, CBE, TD (d 1976), and his 1 w, Elizabeth (gda of 1 Baron Shaughnessy); *b* 23 May 1935; *Educ* Eton, King's Coll Cambridge; *m* 1, 1961, Loretta, da of Alfredo Reali, of Florence; 1 da; m 2, 1970, Gabrielle, da of Dr Ernst Raab; 2 da (Hon Katharina Elizabeth Anne b 1973, Hon Vanessa Julia Claire b 1976); m 3, 27 June 1987, Mrs Elizabeth Porter, da of Buford Scott, of Richmond, Virginia; *Heir* first cous, Francis Grenfell; *Career* 2 Lt KRRC (60 Rifles), Capt Queen's Westminsters (TA) KRRC; chief of info and pub affrs World Bank Europe 1970, dep dir European office World Bank 1973, special rep for World Bank to UNO 1974-81, special advsr World Bank 1983-87, sr advsr 1987-90, head of external affairs European Office 1990-; *Books* Margot (1984); *Recreations* writing; *Clubs* Royal Green Jackets; *Style—* The Rt Hon the Lord Grenfell; The World Bank, European Office, 66 avenue d'Iena, 75116 Paris, France (☎ 1 40693012)

GRENFELL, Hon Natasha Jeannine Mary; da of 2 Baron St Just (d 1984), and his 2 w, Maria Britneva, the actress, da of Alexander Vladimirovitch Britnev (decd), of St Petersburg, Russia; *b* 1959; *Style—* The Hon Natasha Grenfell

GRENFELL, Simon Pascoe; s of Osborne Pascoe, of Saltburn, N Yorkshire (d 1971), and Margaret Grenfell, *née* Morris; *b* 10 July 1942; *Educ* Fettes, Emmanuel Coll Cambridge (MA); *m* 13 April 1974, Ruth de Jersey, da of John Peter de Jersey Harvard (d 1981), of Carlton-in-Cleveland, N Yorkshire; 1 s (Robin b 1981), 3 da (Rachel b 1975, Amelia b 1976, Philippa b 1978); *Career* barr; rec Crown Ct 1985; *Recreations* music, sailing, coarse gardening; *Style—* Simon P Grenfell, Esq; St John's House, Sharow Lane, Sharow, Ripon, N Yorks NG4 5BN (☎ 0765 5771); Park Court Chambers, 40 Park Cross Street, Leeds LS1 2QH (☎ 0532 4332677, telex 666135, fax 0532 421285)

GRENFELL-BAINES, Prof Sir George; OBE (1960), DL (Lancs 1982); s of Ernest Charles Baines and Sarah Elizabeth, *née* Grenfell; *b* 30 April 1908; *Educ* Roebuck St Council Sch, Harris Coll Preston, Manchester Univ (DipTP); *m* 1 (m dis 1952), Dorothy Hudson; 2 da; m 2, 1954, Milena Fleischman; 1 s, 1 da; *Career* architect planning conslt; fndr Grenfell Baines Gp 1940, fndr ptnr and chm Building Design Partnership 1959-74, prof and head of Dept of Architecture Univ of Sheffield 1972-75, emeritus 1976, fndr and dir The Design Teaching Practice Sheffield 1974-, former vice pres RIBA, hon fellow Manchester Polytechnic, hon vice-pres North Lancs Soc of Architects, Hon DLitt Sheffield 1981, hon fellow American Inst of Architects 1982; RIBA, FRIBA, FRTPI; kt 1978; *Style—* Prof Sir George Grenfell-Baines, OBE, DL; 60 West Cliff, Preston, Lancs (☎ 0772 55824); 56 West Cliff, Preston, Lancs PR1 8HU (☎ 0772 52131)

GRENIER, David Arthur; s of Rev George A Grenier (d 1973), and Dorothy Anita, *née* Burn (d 1990); *b* 12 Aug 1931; *Educ* St John's Sch Leatherhead, Jesus Coll Cambridge (MA), Sorbonne; *m* 22 Aug 1959, Janet Elizabeth, da of Ralph Thompson (d 1989); 3 s (Lewis b 1962, Julian b 1968, Michael b 1969); *Career* Capel-Cure Myers Ltd: dep chm 1975-77, chm 1977-79; ptnr Scott Goff Hancock & Co 1980-82, sr ptnr Scott Goff Layton & Co 1982-86, dir Smith New Court plc 1986-88, chief exec Ind Investmt Mgmnt Ltd 1989-; assoc memb Soc of Investmt Analysts 1968-, memb IOD; *Recreations* opera, gardening; *Clubs* Oxford & Cambridge, Coningsby; *Style—* David Grenier, Esq; Horncastle, Mount Pleasant, Guildford, Surrey GU2 5H2 (☎ 0483 570809); Independent Investment Management Limited, Warnford Court, 29 Throgmorton St, London EC2N 2AT (☎ 071 628 6021, fax 071 588 0386)

GRENIER, John Allan; s of Rev George Arthur Grenier; *b* 2 April 1933; *Educ* St John's Sch Leatherhead Surrey; *m* 1980, Valerie, da of James William Cocksey; 2 c; *Career* chm The HLT Group Ltd (Queen's Award for Export 1982); elected chm of British Mgmnt Trg Export Cncl 1985; FCA; *Recreations* off-shore cruising, water skiing; *Clubs* RAC, IOD; *Style—* John Grenier, Esq; The HLT Group Ltd, 200 Greyhound Road, London W14 9RY (☎ 071 385 3377, telex 266386 fax 071 381 3377); Plovers, Horsmonden, Kent

GRENIER, Rear Adm Peter Francis (Frank); CB; s of Dr Frank William Henry Grenier (d 1964), and Mabel, *née* Burgess (d 1985); *b* 27 Aug 1934; *Educ* Blundell's; *m* 15 Aug 1957, Jane Susan, da of Bert Bradshaw (d 1973), of Kent; 3 s (Timothy Francis b 1959 d 1960, Stephen Marcel b 1961, Matthew Peter b 1965), 1 da (Juliet b 1963); *Career* BRNC Dartmouth special entry scheme 1952, submarine serv HMS Dolphin 1956, first cmd submarine HMS Ambush Far East 1964, 2 i/c HMS Resolution (Polaris) 1968, Cmmnd HMS Valiant (Nuclear Attack) 1972-74, Capt 1976, cmd destroyer HMS Liverpool 1981, Capt Fleet 1983-85, Rear Adm 1985, COS to C in C Naval Home Cmd, Flag Offr submarines 1987-89; chm RNFG 1982-85, govr Blundells Sch 1985; Liveryman: Worshipful Co of Painters and Stainers, Worshipful Co of Glass Sellers; *Recreations* painting, sketching, glass engraving, golf; *Clubs* Army and Navy, West Wilts Golf; *Style—* Rear Adm Frank Grenier, CB; c/o Army and Navy Club, St James Square, London

GRENSIDE, Sir John Peter; CBE (1974); s of Harold Cutcliffe Grenside (d 1953), and Muriel Grenside (d 1970); *b* 23 Jan 1921; *Educ* Rugby; *m* 1946, Yvonne Thérèse, da of Ernest Albert Grau (d 1959); 1 s, 1 da; *Career* Capt RA, served UK, Europe, India; CA; sr ptnr Peat Marwick Mitchell & Co 1977-86, (ptnr 1960-86), chm Peat Marwick Int 1980-83; non-exec dir: Allied-Lyons 1986, Nomura International Bank 1987; pres ICEAW 1975-76; Master Chartered Accountants' Livery Co 1987-88; FCA; kt 1983; *Recreations* tennis, bridge; *Clubs* All England Lawn Tennis, MCC, Hurlingham, Pilgrims; *Style—* Sir John Grenside, CBE; 51 Cadogan Lane, London SW1X 9DT (☎ 071 235 3372)

GRENVILLE, Prof John A S; s of Adolf Abraham Guhrauer (d 1960), of London, and late Charlotte, *née* Sandberg; *b* 11 Jan 1928; *Educ* Cambridge Tech Sch, Birkbeck Coll London, LSE (BA, PhD, Hutchinson medal); *m* 1, 1960, Betty Anne, *née* Rosenberg (d 1974); 3 s (Murrey Charles b 1962, Edward Samson b 1964, George Daniel b 1966); m 2, 5 May 1975, Patricia, *née* Conway; 1 da (Annabelle Charlotte b 1979), 1 step da (Georgina Carrie b 1972); *Career* asst gardener Peterhouse Cambridge 1945-47, lectr and reader Univ of Nottingham 1953-66, Cwlth Fund fell 1959-60, postdoctoral fell Yale Univ 1961-64, prof of int history Leeds Univ 1966-69, prof of modern history and head of dept Univ of Birmingham 1969-; visiting prof: City Univ of NY and Hamburg Univ; conslt: American Biographical Serv Oxford and Santa Barbara Calif 1960-, on particular documentary history film productions for Second German Television Service and BBC 1984-; formerly: memb Cncl of the Royal Hist Soc, dir of films Hist Assoc; fndr Br Univs History Film Consortium 1968-; dir Leo Baeck Inst London 1987-; FRHistS 1960; *Books* Lord Salisbury and Foreign Policy (1964), Politics, Strategy and American Diplomacy (with G B Young, 1966), Major International Treaties 1914-1974 (1974), Europe Reshaped 1848-1878 (1976), World History of the Twentieth Century 1900-45 (1980), Major International Treaties Since 1945 (with B Wasserstein, 1987); *Film Documentaries* Munich Crisis 1968, End of Illusion (with Nicholas Provey) 1970, World of the Thirties (with Dieter Franck) 1986; *Recreations* meeting international colleagues, listening to music, ballet and opera; *Clubs* Athenaeum, Elizabethan (New Haven); *Style—* Prof John Grenville; School of History, University of Birmingham, PO Box 363, Birmingham, B15 2TT (☎ 021 414 5736, fax 021 414 3656)

GRESHAM, Prof (Geoffrey) Austin; TD; s of Thomas Michael Gresham (d 1939), of Wrexham, N Wales, and Harriet Ann, *née* Richards (d 1945); *b* 1 Nov 1924; *Educ* Grove Pk GS, Gonville and Caius Coll Cambridge (MA, DSc, MB BChir, MD), King's Coll Hosp London; *m* 1 July 1950, Gweneth Margery, da of Louis Charles Leigh (d 1983), of Cambridge; 3 s (Christopher b 1951, Andrew b 1955, Robert b 1957), 2 da (Diana b 1954, Susan b 1959); *Career* Lt and Capt RAMC 1950-52, Maj and Lt-Col RAMC (V) 1954-66; house physician King's Coll Hosp London 1949-50 (house surgn 1949); Univ of Cambridge: demonstrator in pathology 1953-58, fell and coll lectr (and sometime pres) Jesus Coll, sec Faculty Bd of Med 1956-61, lectr in pathology 1958-62 (sometime dep assessor to Regius prof of physic and supervisor of res Student Dept of Pathology); univ morbid anatomist and histologist Addenbrooke's Hosp Cambridge 1962- (jr asst pathologist 1953, conslt pathologist 1960), Home Office pathologist to Mid Anglia 1966- (prof of morbid anatomy and histology 1973); ed of Atherosclerosis, sci fell Zoological Soc London; FRCPath; *Books* A Colour Atlas of General Pathology (1971), A Colour Atlas of Forensic Pathology (1979), Post Mortem Procedures (1979), A Colour Atlas of Wounds and Wounding (1987); *Recreations* gardening, organ playing, wine, silver; *Style—* Prof Austin Gresham, TD; 18 Rutherford Rd, Cambridge (☎ 0223 841326); Addenbrooke's Hosp, Hills Rd, Cambridge (☎ 0223 217168, fax 0223 216980)

GRESLEY, Lady; Ada Mary; da of George Miller (decd); *m* 1924, Sir William Francis Gresley, 13 Bt (d 1976, when the title became extinct); *Style—* Lady Gresley; 59A

Grand Ave, Southbourne, Bournemouth, Dorset

GRETTON, Baroness; Jennifer; o da of Edmund Moore, of York; *m* 1970, 3 Baron Gretton (d 1989); 1 s (4 Baron), 1 da (Hon Sarah Margaret b 1971); *Style*— The Rt Hon Lady Gretton; Holygate Farm, Stapleford, Melton Mowbray, Leicestershire LE14 2XQ (☎ 057 284 540)

GRETTON, 4 Baron (UK 1944) John Lysander Gretton; o s of 3 Baron Gretton (d 1989); *b* 17 April 1975; *Style*— The Rt Hon Lord Gretton; Holygate Farm, Stapleford, Melton Mowbray, Leicestershire LE14 2XQ

GRETTON, Margaret, Baroness; (Anna Helena) Margaret; JP (Staffs 1943); er da of Capt Henrik Loeffler (decd), of Grosvenor Sq, London W1; *m* 1930, 2 Baron Gretton, OBE (d 1982); 2 s (decd), 2 da; *Style*— The Rt Hon Margaret, Lady Gretton, JP; The Old Rectory, Ufford, Stamford (☎ 0780 740198)

GREVILLE, 4 Baron (UK 1869); Ronald Charles Fulke Greville; s of 3 Baron, OBE, JP, DL (d 1952, ADC to govr of Bombay (Baron Northcote) 1900-03 and Mil Sec to same as Govr-Gen of Australia 1904-08) and Olive Grace (d 1959), da of J W Grace; *b* 11 April 1912; *Educ* Eton, Magdalen Coll Oxford; *Heir* none; *Recreations* golf, tennis, gardening, reading, swimming; *Clubs* Hurlingham; *Style*— The Rt Hon the Lord Greville; 75 Swan Court, Chelsea Manor St, London SW3 5RY (☎ 071 352 3444)

GREW, James; CBE (1989), JP (1974), DL (Co Armagh 1981); s of James Grew; *b* 25 Oct 1929; *Educ* Downside; *m* 1955, Pauline Peta, da of Prof John Cunningham; 2 s (Jonathan James b 1958, Christopher Nicholas b 1969), 2 da (Michaela Maria b 1962, Philippa Peta b 1967); *Career* md Abbicoil Spring Ltd 1957-; memb: NI Econ Cncl 1970-74, NI Community Relations Cmmn 1971-74, Craigavon Devpt Cmmn 1971-73, Crawford Ctee on Bdcasting Coverage 1973-74; dir Management Development Services Ltd 1975-; dir: IACOLE USA 1989-, Bannside Development Co Ltd 1990-, Portadown Integrated Primary School Ltd 1990-, NIR Leasing Ltd 1990-, Novatech Ltd 1990-; memb: BBC Advsy Ctee NI 1976-80, BBC Gen Advsy Cncl London 1976-80; chm Post Office Users Cncl NI 1976-81; memb: Post Office Users Nat Cncl London 1976-81, Standing Advsy Cmmn on Human Rights 1980-82, IBA Advsy Ctee N Ireland 1983-85; first chm Probation Bd for NI 1982-88, dir (Govt appointment) NI Transport Holding Co Ltd 1983-86, dir NI Railways 1986, dep chm TSB Fndn Bd N Ireland 1986; first chm Ind Cmmn for Police Complaints NI 1988, dir Abbey National NI Advsy Bd 1989; memb: TAVRA NI, Ulster Def Regt Advsy Cncl, Army Cadet Force Assoc; FInstD 1989; *Recreations* sailing; *Clubs* Chief Exec Club at Queens, Armagh, Royal Irish Yacht; *Style*— James Grew, Esq, CBE, JP, DL; Peacefield, Ballinacorr, Portadown, Co Armagh, N Ireland BT63 5RJ; Abbicoil Springs Ltd, Obin St, Portadown, Co Armagh, N Ireland (☎ 0762 333245)

GREY, Sir Anthony Dysart; 7 Bt (UK 1814); s of Capt Edward Elton Grey (d 1962), and Nancy, *née* Meagher; suc gf, Sir Robin Edward Dysart Grey, 6 Bt (d 1974); *b* 19 Oct 1949; *Educ* Guildford GS Western Australia; *Recreations* fishing, painting; *Style*— Sir Anthony Grey, Bt; 86 Ringsway Gardens, 38 Rings Park Rd, West Perth, Western Australia 6005, Australia

GREY, Dame Beryl Elizabeth; DBE (1988, CBE 1973); da of Arthur Ernest Groom (d 1983), and Annie Elizabeth, *née* Marshall (d 1952); *b* 11 June 1927; *Educ* Dame Alice Owen Professional Madeleine Sharp, Sadlers Wells Ballet Sch; *m* 15 July 1950, Dr Sven Gustav Svenson, s of Ernest Svenson (d 1967) of Heleneborg, Vadstena, Sweden; 1 s (Ingvar b 1954); *Career* ballerina; danced Swan Lake at 15, Giselle at 16, Sleeping Beauty at 19, prima ballerina Sadlers Wells, later Royal Ballet 1941-57; first foreign guest artist Bolshoi Ballet Moscow 1957, Peking Ballet 1964; dir gen Arts Educnl Sch 1966-68, artistic dir London Festival Ballet 1968-79, chm Imperial Soc of Teachers of Dancing 1984-; int guest dancer; prodr Giselle with W Aust Ballet 1980, Sleeping Beauty with Royal Swedish Ballet Stockholm 1985; pres Dance Cncl Wales, vice pres Royal Acad of Dancing 1980-, vice chm Dance Teachers Benevolent Fund London Coll of Dance; Hon DMus Univ of Leicester 1970, Hon DLitt City of London Univ 1974, Hon DEd CNAA 1989; FRSA, FISTD; *Books* Red Curtain Up, Through the Bamboo Curtain, Favourite Ballet Stories (ed); *Recreations* swimming, reading, playing piano, painting; *Clubs* Anglo-Belgian, Royal Thames Yacht; *Style*— Dame Beryl Grey, DBE; Fernhill, Forest Row, East Sussex RH18 5JE (☎ 0342 822539)

GREY, Lt-Col The Hon Jeremy Francis Alnwick; yr s of Baron Grey of Naunton, GCMG, GCVO, OBE (Life Peer), *qv*; *b* 1949; *Educ* Marlborough, RAC Cirencester; *m* 1973, Susan Elizabeth Louise, da of Duncan Richard Fraser, CBE, of Nairobi, Kenya; 2 s (Barnaby Nicholas Alnwick b 1976, Sebastian Jonathan Alnwick b 1979); *Career* Lt-Col, Maj (1982) 14/20 King's Hussars (Royal Armoured Corps); *Style*— Lt-Col The Hon Jeremy Grey; c/o Overbrook, Naunton, Glos

GREY, John Egerton; CB (1980); s of John Grey (d 1979), of 68 Abingdon Villas, London W8, and Nancy Augusta, *née* Nickalls (d 1984); *b* 8 Feb 1929; *Educ* Blundell's, BNC Oxford (MA, BCL); *m* 1961, Patricia, da of Col Walter Francis Hanna, MC (d 1963); 2 adopted s; *Career* called to the Bar Inner Temple 1954, practised at Chancery Bar 1954-59; various posts as clerk Parly Office 1959-74, clerk asst and clerk of public bills House of Lords 1974-88; advsr Colchester CAB 1989-; *Recreations* gardening, boating; *Clubs* Arts, West Mersea Yacht; *Style*— J E Grey, Esq, CB; 51 St Peter's Rd, West Mersea, Colchester, Essex CO5 8LL

GREY, Maj-Gen John St John; CB (1986); s of Maj Donald John Grey, RM (d 1942), and Doris Mary Grey, *née* Beavan; *b* 6 June 1934; *Educ* Christ's Hosp Sch, Royal Coll of Defence Studies, Army Staff Coll Camberley, US Marine Corps Cmd and Staff Coll, Nat Defence Coll; *m* 1958, Elisabeth Ann, da of late Frederick Charles Langley; 1 s (Angus Matthew St John b 1968), 1 da (Emelia St John b 1969); *Career* cmmnd 1952; Commando Serv: Malta, Egypt, Cyprus 1955-58; Support Co Cmd 43 Commando RM 1962-64, Cruiser HMS Lion 1964-65, Instr Army Sch of Infantry 1967-69, Rifle Co Cmd 41 Commando RM 1969-70, US Marine Corps 1970-71, Directorate Naval Plan MOD 1971-74, CO 45 Commando RM 1976-79, Mil Sec and Col Ops and Plans MOD 1979-84, Maj-Gen cmd Commando Forces 1984-87, Chief of Staff RM 1987-88, ret Oct 1988; Clerk Worshipful Co of Pewterers; *Recreations* sailing; *Clubs* Army and Navy, RYA, RNSA, Royal Marines Sailing; *Style*— Maj-Gen John Grey, CB; c/o Lloyds Bank Ltd, Teignmouth, Devon

GREY, Hon Jolyon Kenneth Alnwick; er s of Baron Grey of Naunton, GCMG, GCVO, OBE (Life Baron), *qv*; *b* 4 June 1946; *Educ* Marlborough, Pembroke Coll Camb (MA); *m* 1971, Sarah Jane, da of Lt-Col Samuel Brian Digby Hood, TD; 2 s (Tobias Alnwick b 1973, Matthew Samuel b 1976); *Career* Bar Inner Temple 1968; *Style*— The Hon Jolyon Grey; 36 Octavia St, London SW11

GREY, 6 Earl (UK 1806); Sir Richard Fleming George Charles Grey; 7 Bt (GB 1746); also Baron Grey of Howick (UK 1801) and Viscount Howick (UK 1806); s of Albert Grey (ggs of Adm Hon George Grey, himself 4 s of 2 Earl Grey, who was PM 1830-34); suc 2 cous twice removed 1963; *b* 5 March 1939; *Educ* Hounslow Coll, Hammersmith Coll of Bldg; *m* 1, 1966 (m dis 1974), Margaret, da of Henry Bradford, of Ashburton; m 2, 1974, Stephanie, da of Donald Gaskell-Brown, of Newton Ferrers, Plymouth, and formerly w of Surgn-Cdr Neil Denham, RN; *Heir* bro, Philip Grey; *Career* pres Cost and Exec Accountants Assoc 1978; memb Liberal Pty; *Style*— The Rt Hon the Earl Grey; c/o House of Lords, London SW1

GREY, Robin Douglas; QC (1979); s of Francis Temple Grey (d 1941), and Eglantine, *née* Ellice; *b* 23 May 1931; *Educ* Eastbourne Coll, King's Coll London (LLB); *m* 8 Aug 1969, Berenice Anna, da of Dennis Wheatley (d 1985); 1 s (Julian Alexander b 2 May 1970), 1 da (Louise Katherine b 20 Aug 1973); *Career* Nat Serv Army 1950-51; called to the Bar Gray's Inn 1957; crown counsel in Aden 1959-63: acting attorney gen then acting registrar gen then acting sr crown counsel; in practice SE circuit 1963-, dep circuit judge 1977-, rec 1979-; memb Soc Forensic Med 1976; *Recreations* tennis, golf, fishing; *Clubs* Hurlingham; *Style*— Robin Grey, Esq, QC; Dun Cottage, Hungerford, Berks RG17 0SN (☎ 0488 835 78); Queen Elizabeth Bldg, London EC4Y 9BS (☎ 071 583 5766)

GREY DE RUTHYN, Barony of (E 1324); see Lubienski Bodenham, Count Charles

GREY EGERTON, Sir (Philip) John Caledon; 15 Bt (E 1617), of Egerton and Oulton, Cheshire; s of Sir Philip Reginald Le Belward Grey Egerton, 14 Bt (d 1962); *b* 19 Oct 1920; *Educ* Eton; *m* 1, 1951, Margaret Voase (d 1971), da of late Rowland Rank, of Aldwick, Place, Aldwick, W Sussex, and wid of Sqdn-Ldr Robert Ullman, RAF; m 2, 1986, Frances Mary, da of late Col Robert Maximilian Rainey-Robinson, of Broadmayne, Dorchester, Dorset, and wid of Sqdn-Ldr William Dudley Williams, DFC; *Heir* bro, Brian Balguy Le Belward Egerton; *Career* late Capt Welsh Gds; *Style*— Sir John Grey Egerton, Bt; Rylstone, Martinstown, Dorchester, Dorset DT2 9JR (☎ 0305 889332)

GREY OF CODNOR, 5 Baron (E 1397); Charles Legh Shuldham Cornwall-Legh; CBE (1977, OBE 1971), AE (1946), DL (Cheshire 1949); s of Charles Henry George Cornwall-Legh (d 1934, sixth in descent from 16 and last Baron of Burford, so styled although the Barons were never summoned to Parliament; the 16 Baron was himself sixteenth in descent from Richard, King of the Romans, Earl of Cornwall and Provence, and Count of Poitou, 2 s of King John), and Geraldine Maud, *née* Shuldham (d 1957); suc as 5 Baron Grey of Codnor (abeyant since 1495) on termination of the abeyance in his favour 1989; *b* 10 Feb 1903; *Educ* King's Sch Bruton, Hertford Coll Oxford; *m* 8 Feb 1930, Dorothy Catherine Whitson, er da of late John Whitson Scott, of Seal, Sevenoaks, Kent; 1 s (Hon Richard Henry), 2 da (Hon Rosemary (Hon Mrs Laing) b 1932, Hon Julia Margaret (Hon Mrs Prola) b 1939); *Heir* s, Hon Richard Henry Cornwall-Legh, *qv*; *Career* Flight Lt AAF and RAF 1939-45, High Sheriff Cheshire 1939, JP 1938-74, co cllr 1949-77; chm: New Cheshire CC 1974-76, Cheshire Police Authy 1957-74; Freeman City of London, Liveryman Worshipful Co of Feltmakers; *Clubs* Carlton, MCC; *Style*— The Rt Hon the Lord Grey of Codnor, CBE, AE, DL; High Legh House, Knutsford, Cheshire WA16 0QR (☎ 092 575 3168)

GREY OF NAUNTON, Baron (Life Peer UK 1968), of Naunton, Co Gloucester; Sir Ralph Francis Alnwick Grey; GCMG (1964, KCMG 1959, CMG 1955), GCVO (1973, KCVO 1956), OBE (1951); s of Francis Arthur Grey (d 1917), an accountant in NZ, and Mary Wilkie, *née* Spence (d 1952); *b* 15 April 1910; *Educ* Wellington Coll NZ, Auckland Univ Coll (LLB), Pembroke Coll Cambridge; *m* 1 Nov 1944, Esmé Mae, DStJ, da of Albert Victor Kerry Burcher, of Remuera, NZ, and widow of Pilot Offr Kenneth Kirkcaldie, RAFVR; 2 s (Hon Jolyon Kenneth Alnwick b 1946, Hon Jeremy Francis Alnwick b 1949), 1 da (Hon Amanda Mary Alnwick (Hon Mrs das Neves) b 1951); *Career* barr and slr NZ; Colonial Serv Nigeria 1937, devpt sec 1952, sec to Govr-Gen and Cncl of Mins Nigeria 1954, chief sec Fedn of Nigeria 1955, dep govr-gen 1957-59; govr and C-in-C: British Guiana 1959-64, Bahamas 1964-68, Turks and Caicos Islands 1965-68, N Ireland 1968-73 (dep chm 1973-78); chm: Cwlth Devpt Corpn 1979-80, Central Cncl Royal Overseas League 1976-81 (pres 1981-); hon bencher Inn of Ct of Northern Ireland, Hon Freeman City of Belfast and Borough of Lisburn, Freeman City of London; pres: Chartered Inst of Secs NI 1970-, Britain-Nigeria Assoc 1983-89, Overseas Serv Pensioners' Assoc 1983-; chllr: New Univ of Ulster 1980-84, Univ of Ulster 1984-; Hon: LLD Queen's Univ Belfast, DLitt New Univ of Ulster, LLD Nat Univ of Ireland, DSc Univ of Ulster; GCStJ 1976; Lord Prior of the Order of St John 1988-91 (Kt Cdr of Commandery of Ards 1968-76, Bailiff of Egle 1975-87 (chllr 1987-88); Gd Cross of Merit Pro Merito Melitensi; *Recreations* golf; *Clubs* Travellers'; *Style*— The Rt Hon the Lord Grey of Naunton, GCMG, GCVO, OBE; Overbrook, Naunton, Glos (☎ 0451 850263)

GRIBBLE, Dorothy-Rose Jessie; da of Lt Charles Herbert Gribble (ka 1917), and Dorothy Phyllis, *née* Milton (d 1978); *b* 5 July 1917; *Educ* Wycombe Abbey, UCL; *Career* dir and fndr Plantagenet Productions, hon dir Westridge Open Centre for Healing Studies and the Arts; recitalist; *Books* And I am a Doggerel Bard, Gribble Annals (ed of family papers of 1816-), Milton Traditions (over 300 years); *Plays*: Blood Will Out, The On The Cards Series; *Recreations* reading, walking, driving, theatre, printing; *Style*— Miss Dorothy-Rose Gribble; Westridge Open Centre, Highclere, nr Newbury, Royal Berkshire

GRIBBON, Angus John St George; s of Maj-Gen Nigel St George Gribbon, OBE, of 99 Pump St, Orford, nr Woodbrige, Suffolk, and Rowan Mary, *née* McLeish; *b* 25 Dec 1951; *Educ* Rugby, New Coll Oxford (MA); *m* 15 May 1965, Mary-Anne, da of Hugh Wynwel Gamon, CBE, MC, of Black Charles Underriver, nr Sevenoaks, Kent; 1 s (Edward b 1981), 2 da (Mary-Clare b 1983, Caroline b 1985); *Career* Clifford-Turner Slrs 1974-79, slr Allied-Lyons plc 1979-89, legal advsr Securicor Group 1989-; *Recreations* sailing, skiing; *Style*— Angus Gribbon, Esq; Pedlam Brook, West Peckham, Maidstone, Kent ME18 5JS (☎ 0732 851732); Securicor Group plc, Sutton Park House, 15 Carshalton Rd, Sutton, Surrey SM1 4LE (☎ 081 770 7000, fax 081 643 1059, telex 8814827)

GRIBBON, Maj Gen Nigel St George; OBE (1960); s of late Brig W H Gribbon, CMG, CBE; *b* 6 Feb 1917; *Educ* Rugby, RMC Sandhurst; *m* 1943, Rowan Mary, *née* MacLiesh; 2 s, 1 da; *Career* Maj Gen cmmnd King's Own Royal Regt 1937, Iraq 1941 (wounded), Western Desert 1942, Staff Coll Quetta 1943, GSO 2 45 Inf Div 1944, AATDC 1945-46, Palestine 1946, BM 1 Para Bde 1946, Trieste 1947-48, GSO 2 GHQ FARELF, Malaysia 1948-50, RAF Staff Coll 1952, DAQMG WO 1935-55, Hong Kong 1956-57; cmd 5 King's Own 1958-60, AMS War Office 1960-62, cmd 161 Bde TA 1963-65, Canadian Nat Defence Coll 1965-66, staff of CDS MOD, BG5 (Intelligence) BAOR 1967-69, ACOS NORTHAG 1967-69, ACOS (Intelligence) SHAPE 1970-72; ret; vice-pres King's Own Royal Border Regt 1974-88; md Partnerplan Public Affrs Ltd 1973-75, chm Sallingbury Ltd 1975-77 (md 1977-84, chm 1985), dir Gatewood Engrs 1976-84, dep chm Sallingbury Casey Ltd (Saatchi & Saatchi Group) 1985-87, dir Chancellor Insurance Co Ltd 1986-; memb: Exec Ctee British Atlantic Ctee 1977-89 (Cncl 1977-), Euro-Atlantic Group 1977-86; pres Canada-UK C of C 1981; chm Falkland Islands Tst 1982-, co-chm Joint Ctee with Canadian C of C 1984-; Freeman City of London, Liveryman Worshipful Co of Shipwrights 1982; *Recreations* sailing, swimming, skiing; *Clubs* Army & Navy, Canada; *Style*— Maj Gen Nigel Gribbon, OBE; 99 Pump St, Orford, Woodbridge, Suffolk IP12 2IX (☎ 039 45 413)

GRICE, Prof Roger; s of Francis Grice (d 1965), and Phyllis Dale, *née* Fell; *b* 27 July 1941; *Educ* Ormskirk GS, Cambridge Univ (MA), Harvard Univ (PhD); *m* 15 Aug 1964, Patricia Margaret, da of James Edmund Lee, of Bathavon, Somerset; 3 da (Cordelia Kendal b 29 Sept 1967, Emma Dale b 19 April 1969, Guinevere Lee b 7 Nov 1974); *Career* lectr in theoretical chemistry Univ of Bristol 1968-69, sr asst and asst dir of res Univ of Cambridge 1969-76, prof of physical chem Univ of Manchester 1976-; author papers in: molecular physics, Faraday discussions, transactions of Royal Soc of Chemistry; Faraday cncl memb Royal Soc of Chemistry 1984-87; govr:

Manchester GS, Withington Girls Sch; *Recreations* fell walking, theatre, classical music; *Style—* Prof Roger Grice; Oaklea, 186 Grove Lane, Cheadle Hulme, Cheshire SK8 7NH; Chemistry Dept, Univ of Manchester, Manchester M13 9PL (☎ 061 275 4667, fax 061 275 4598)

GRIDLEY, 2 Baron (UK 1955); Arnold Hudson Gridley; s of 1 Baron, KBE (d 1965); *b* 26 May 1906; *Educ* Oundle; *m* 1948, Lesley Winifred, da of Leslie Wheen, of Shanghai; 1 s, 3 da; *Heir* s, Hon Richard Gridley; *Career* sits as Conservative in House of Lords; entered Colonial Civil Serv Malaya 1928, interned by Japanese in Changi Gaol 1941-45, WWII, actg dep comptroller Fedn Malaya 1956, ret 1957; memb Cncl Overseas Serv Pensions Assoc 1966-, memb Exec Ctee Overseas Serv Pensions Assoc 1966-, govt tstee Far East Fund 1973- (for POWs and Internees); life pres Centralised Audio Systems 1985, memb Parly delegation to BAOR 1979, visited Rhodesia during Lancaster House Conf, London 1980 and 1985; commendation WWII 1941-45, visit of HRH the Duke of Kent on special duty to Singapore & Malaya to honour Civilian War Dead of all Races, incl Br Overseas Civil Servants; *Clubs* Royal Overseas League; *Style—* The Rt Hon Lord Gridley; Coneygore, Stoke Trister, Wincanton, Somerset (☎ 0963 32209)

GRIDLEY, Hon Richard David Arnold; only s and h of 2 Baron Gridley; *b* 22 Aug 1956; *Educ* Monkton Combe Sch, Portsmouth Poly; *m* 1, 1979 (m dis), Amanda J, da of late Ian Mackenzie, of Felixstowe, formerly of Ceylon; m 2, 1983, Suzanne Elizabeth, *née* Ripper; 1 s (Carl Richard b 5 Feb 1981), 1 da (Danielle Lauren b 1983); *Career* project mangr Rush and Tompkins Gp plc, Ballast Nedam Construction UK; *Style—* The Hon Richard Gridley; 79 Purbrook Gardens, Purbrook, Hampshire

GRIER, (Hugh) Christopher; s of The Very Rev A R M Grier (d 1939), of Perth, Scotland, and Edith Mary, *née* Howes (d 1961); *b* 4 Dec 1922; *Educ* Glenalmand Sch, King's Coll Cambridge (MA, MusB); *m* 30 Nov 1950, Mary Elizabeth, da of Brig J C Martin, CBE, DSO, MC; 1 s (Nicholas John Macgregor b 8 Feb 1956); *Career* served WWII The Black Watch 1942-45; music offr Br Cncl Scandinavia 1947-49; music critic: The Scotsman 1949-63, The Evening Standard 1971-; London drama critic The Scotsman 1984-; freelance contrib London newspapers, magazines and music jls 1963-, involved with BBC progs and purveyor of prog notes to various orchs and festivals; memb Prog Ctee Edinburgh Festival 1951-63, lectr Royal Scot Acad of Music and Drama 1954-63, formerly prof at RCM and RAM, vice pres Int Ski Club of Journalists 1982-84; memb: Critics Circle 1958, Inst of Journalists, Royal Soc of Musicians of GB; hon memb: RCM, RAM; *Recreations* walking, reading; *Style—* Christopher Grier, Esq; 27 Eton Rise, Eton College Rd, London NW3 2DF (☎ 071 722 6755)

GRIER, Hon Mrs (Patricia Mary); *née* Spens; er da of 1 Baron Spens, KBE, PC; *b* 15 July 1919; *Educ* Heathfield; *m* 1946, Anthony MacGregor Grier, CMG (d 1989), s of Very Rev Roy MacGregor Grier, sometime Rector and Provost of St Ninian's Cathedral, Perth; 2 s (Richard, Francis), 1 da (Lynda); *Career* served WWII as Capt FANY SOE in Europe and Far East; past pres Hereford and Worcester Red Cross; *Recreations* golf, bridge; *Clubs* Special Forces; *Style—* The Hon Mrs Grier; Mulberry House, Abbots Morton, Worcester WR7 4NA (☎ 0386 792422)

GRIERSON, Lady Daphne Olive; *née* Lambart; da of 11 Earl of Cavan; *b* 22 Dec 1909; *Educ* Shrewsbury HS, LSE; *m* 1944, Kenneth (d 1976), s of Douglas Grierson, barrister, of Shirley, Warwicks; 1 s (William); *Career* painter; author; social worker; *Recreations* reading, needlework; *Style—* The Lady Daphne Grierson; 24f Four Limes, Wheathampstead, Herts AL4 8PW

GRIERSON, Sir Michael John Bewes; 12 Bt (NS 1685), of Lag, Dumfriesshire; s of late Lt-Col Alexander Grierson, RM, 2 s of 9 Bt; suc kinsman, Sir Richard Grierson, 11 Bt (d 1987); *b* 24 July 1921; *Educ* St Edmund's Sch Canterbury; *m* 1971, Valerie Anne, da of late Russell Wright, of Gidea Park, Essex; 1 da (Sarah Anne b 1973); *Style—* Sir Michael Grierson, Bt; 40c Palace Rd, Streatham Hill, London SW2 3NJ

GRIERSON, Robert McMorrine; s of Robert Grierson (d 1987), and Gertrude, *née* Warwick; *b* 4 May 1943; *Educ* Yewlands Sch; *m* 12 Oct 1968, Pamela Christine, da of Richard Prewett (d 1985); 1 s (John Robert McMorrine b 1980), 1 da (Heather Louise b 1976); *Career* CA Robert M Grierson & Co; dir: Upperdale Ltd, Sheffield Wednesday Football Club plc; formerly: chm Chapeltown Round Table, pres Chapeltown 41 Club; holder of Duke of Edinburgh's Gold award; FCA; *Recreations* squash, football; *Style—* Robert M Grierson, Esq; 2 Croft Close, Whirlow, Sheffield S11 9QP (☎ 0742 361774); Moor Oaks Lodge, 6 Moor Oaks Rd, Sheffield S10 1BX (☎ 0742 680357, fax 0742 666010)

GRIEVE, Alan Thomas; s of Lewis Miller Grieve (d 1963), of Stanmore, Middx, and Doris Lilian, *née* Amner (d 1975); *b* 22 Jan 1928; *Educ* Aldenham, Trinity Hall Cambridge (MA, LLM); *m* 1, 1957 (m dis 1971), Anne, da of Dr Lawrence Dulake, of The White House, Blandford Road, Reigate, Surrey; 2 s (Charles b 1960, Ivan b 1962), 1 da (Amanda (Baroness Harlech) b 1958); m 2, 1971, Karen Louise, da of Michael de Sivrac Dunn, of Awliscombe House, Awliscombe, Honiton, Devon; 1 s (Thomas de Sivrac b 1973), 1 da (Lara b 1974); *Career* Nat Serv 2 Lt 14/20 Kings Hussars, Capt City of London Yeo TA; admitted slr 1953; sr ptnr Taylor Garrett; dir: Baggeridge Brick plc, Reliance Resources Ltd, Stenham plc, Med Insur Agency Ltd, St George's Hosp Ltd and other cos; chm Racehorse Owners Award; govr Brendoncare for the Elderly; tstee: Br Racing Sch, The Jerwood Fndn, The Jerwood Award, Oakham Sch; friend RCP; memb Educnl Assets Bd; memb Law Soc; *Books* Purchase Tax (1958); *Recreations* skiing, racing, shooting; *Clubs* Boodle's, Aula, Asparagus; *Style—* Alan Grieve, Esq; Brimpton House, Brimpton, Reading, Berks (☎ 0734 71 2100); Taylor Joynson Garrett, 180 Fleet St, London EC4A 2NT (☎ 071 430 1122, fax 071 528 7145, telex 25516, car 0836 527369)

GRIEVE, William Percival (Percy); QC (1962); s of 2 Lt W Percy Grieve (ka Ypres 1915), of Kirkcudbrightshire and Argentina, and Dorothy Marie, *née* Hartley, who m 2, Dr William Cunningham, of Monkseaton, Northumberland; *b* 25 March 1915, (posthumously); *Educ* privately, Trinity Hall Cambridge; *m* 1949, Evelyn, da of Cmdt Hubert Mijouain, of Paris, and Liliane, da of Sir George Roberts, 1 and last Bt (d 1950); 1 s (and 1 s decd), 1 da (decd); *Career* late Maj Middx Regt; called to the Bar Middle Temple 1938, Hong Kong 1960; bencher Middle Temple 1969; rec: Northampton 1965-71, Crown Ct 1971; MP (Cons) Warwicks Solihull 1964-83, UK Delgn Cncl of Europe (chm Legal Affrs Ctee 1979-83) and WEU 1969-83, hon assoc Parly Assembly Cncl of Europe 1989 and WEU 1990; Officier de l'Ordre d'Adolphe de Nassau, Chevalier de l'Ordre de la Couronne de Chêne, Croix de Guerre avec Palmes Luxembourg 1945-46, Bronze Star USA 1945, Chevalier de la Légion d'Honneur France 1974, Cdr de l'Ordre de Mérite Luxembourg 1976, Offr de l'Ordre de la Couronne Belgium 1980, Cdr de L'Order de La Couronne de Chene 1990; *Recreations* swimming, travel, theatre; *Clubs* Carlton, Hurlingham, RAC, Special Forces; *Style—* Percy Grieve, Esq, QC; 1 King's Bench Walk, Temple, London EC4 (☎ 071 353 8436); 32 Gunterstone Rd, London W14 (☎ 071 603 0376)

GRIEVE, Hon Lord; William Robertson Grieve; VRD (1958); s of Robertson Grieve (ka 1917), of Glasgow; *b* 21 Oct 1917; *Educ* Glasgow Acad, Sedbergh, Univ of Glasgow; *m* 1947, Lorna (d 1989), da of Rear Adm Edward Benn, CB; 1 s, 1 da; *Career* late Lt Cdr RNVR; advocate 1947, QC 1957, Sheriff Princ Renfrew and Argyll 1964-72, judge of appeal Jersey & Guernsey 1971-72; senator Coll of Justice Scot (Lord of Session) 1972-88; chm: govrs Fettes Tst 1978-86, Fish Farm Advsy Ctee, Bd of Govrs St Columba's Hospice 1983-, procurator Church of Scotland 1968-72; *Recreations* golf, painting; *Clubs* New (Edinburgh), Hon Co of Edinburgh Golfers, W Sussex Golf; *Style—* The Hon Lord Grieve, VRD; 20 Belgrave Crescent, Edinburgh EH4 3AJ (☎ 031 332 7500)

GRIEVES, John Kerr; s of Thomas Grieves (d 1979), of Littlehampton, Sussex, and Annie, *née* Davis (d 1976); *b* 7 Nov 1935; *Educ* King's Sch Worcester, Oxford Univ (MA), Harvard Business Sch; *m* 21 Oct 1961, Ann Gorell, da of Vincent Charles Harris (d 1982), of London; 1 s (Thomas b 11 Jan 1969), 1 da (Kate b 25 May 1964); *Career* Pinsent and Co 1958-63, sr ptnr Freshfields (joined 1963, managing ptnr 1979-85); *Recreations* the arts, running; *Clubs* Athenaeum, Roehampton; *Style—* John Grieves, Esq; 7 Putney Park Ave, London SW15 5QN (☎ 081 876 1207); Whitefriars, 65 Fleet St, London EC4Y 1HS (☎ 071 936 4000, fax 071 248 3487, telex 889292)

GRIEW, Prof Edward James; s of Harry Griew (d 1949), and Sylvia, *née* Wetstein (d 1976); *b* 25 Aug 1930; *Educ* Haberdasher's Aske's, Emmanuel Coll Cambridge (MA, LLB); *m* 9 Sept 1959, Marian Esther, da of Hyman Green; 1 s (Simon b 1965), 1 da (Rachel b 1963); *Career* barr, in practice 1954-57 and 1959-66; dean Faculty of Law Univ of Leicester 1982-87 (sr lectr in law 1966-72, prof 1972-87, head of dept 1973-76), prof of common law Univ of Nottingham 1988-90; memb Working Pty on Judicial Trg (chm Lord Justice Bridge) 1975-78, chm exec Nat Marriage Guidance Cncl 1976-80, memb Law Cmmn Criminal Law Codification Team 1981-88; *Books* The Theft Acts 1968 and 1978 (6 edn 1990); *Recreations* music, scrabble; *Style—* Prof Edward Griew; 43 Hallfields, Edwalton, Nottingham NG12 4AA; Dept of Law, The University, Nottingham NG7 2RD (☎ 0602 484848)

GRIFFIN, Adm Sir Anthony Templer Frederick Griffith; GCB (1975, KCB 1971, CB 1967); s of late Col Forrester Metcalf Griffith Griffin, MC, and Beryl Alice Beatrix, *née* Down; *b* 24 Nov 1920; *Educ* RNC Dartmouth; *m* 1943, Rosemary Ann, da of late Vice Adm Harold Hickling, CB, CBE, DSO, of NZ; 2 s, 1 da; *Career* RN 1934-75; WWII E Indies, Mediterranean, N Atlantic; Capt 1956, Capt Ark Royal 1964-65, Rear Adm 1966, Vice Adm 1968, Adm 1971, Controller of Navy 1971-75 (Flag Offr Plymouth 1969-71, 2 i/c Cmd Far East Fleet 1968-69); chm Br Shipbuilders 1975-80; vice pres: Wellington Coll 1980-90, Br Maritime League 1987- (exec chm 1982-87); pres Royal Inst Naval Architects 1981-84, chm Br Maritime Charitable Fndn 1982-; hon fell RINA; Rear Adm of the UK 1986-88, Vice Adm 1988-90; *Recreations* sailing; *Clubs* Army and Navy, Pratt's; *Style—* Adm Sir Anthony Griffin, GCB; Moat Cottage, The Drive, Bosham, Chichester, W Sussex PO18 8JG (☎ 0243 573373)

GRIFFIN, Brian James; s of James Henry Griffin (d 1985), of Lye, Near Stourbirdge, W Midlands, and Edith Moore; *b* 13 April 1948; *Educ* Halesowen Tech Sch, Dudley Tech Coll, Manchester Poly Sch of Photography (ONC, Dip Photography, Dip Assoc of Manchester); *m* July 1980, Frances Mary, da of Morris Newman; 1 s (Danz James Sky b Aug 1983), 1 da (Layla Sky b Jan 1982); *Career* trainee draughtsman 1964-66, trainee estimator 1966-69, photography student 1969-72, photographer 1972; Premi Al Llibre Fotografic award for Work (Primavera Fotografica '90 Barcelona); Freeman City of Arles (France); *Books* Brian Griffin Copyright (1978), Power (1980), Open (1985), Portraits (1987), Work (1988); *Recreations* speedway racing; *Clubs* Groucho; *Style—* Brian Griffin, Esq; Brian Griffin Limited, 121/123 Rotherhithe St, London SE16 4NF (☎ 071 231 7251, fax 071 231 7564, car 0836 687 166)

GRIFFIN, Charles Frederick; ERD (1975); s of Frederick James Griffin, JP (d 1947), of Newton Court, Monmouth, and Rosamary, *née* Hardy (d 1923); *b* 25 April 1918; *Educ* Bromsgrove, Royal Agric Coll Cirencester; *m* 30 May 1959, Iris, da of Evan John Carne David, MC, TD, DL, JP; 1 s (Ralph (Capt Griffin) b 1963), 1 da (Wynona (Mrs Hollom) b 1960); *Career* WWII serv: sr offr Welch Regt 1938-46, Nigeria Regt 1942-45; JP Gwent 1959, High Sheriff of Gwent 1975-76; memb: Royal Anthropological Inst, Royal Forestry Soc, CLA, Timber Growers Assoc; *Recreations* (formerly) hunting, shooting, genealogy, heraldry; *Clubs* Army and Navy; *Style—* Charles Griffin, Esq, ERD; Newton Court, Monmouth (☎ 0600 2992)

GRIFFIN, Dr George Edward; s of Herbert Griffin (d 1973), of Hull, and Enid Mary, *née* Borrill; *b* 27 Feb 1947; *Educ* Malet Lambert Sch Hull, Kings Coll London (BSc), St Georges Hosp Med Sch (MB BS), Univ of Hull (PhD); *m* 15 April 1972, Daphne Joan, da of Lionel Haylor, of Romford; 2 s (James Edward b 1978, Andrew John b 1980), 1 da (Joanna Mary b 1983); *Career* Harkness fell Harvard Univ Med Sch 1975-76; St Georges Hosp Med: house physician 1974-79, lectr 1979-83, div head of communicable diseases; Wellcome Tst: sr lectr, reader in med, conslt physician 1983-; sec Med Res Soc 1988-, various pubns on pathogenesis of infection and metabolic response to infection; memb Br Soc of Gastroenterology; FRCP; *Recreations* mountain walking, gardening; *Style—* Dr George Griffin; Division of Communicable Diseases, St Georges' Hospital Medical School, Tooting, London SW17 0RE (☎ 081 672 9944, fax 081 672 4864, telex 945291 SAGEMS G)

GRIFFIN, Lady Jane; *née* Bingham; da of 6 Earl of Lucan, MC (d 1964); *b* 1932; *Educ* Badminton Sch Bristol, UCL (MB, BS); *m* 1960, James D Griffin; 3 s, 1 da; *Style—* The Lady Jane Griffin; 444 East Sixty-Sixth St, NY, NY 10021, USA

GRIFFIN, Jasper; s of Frederick William Griffin, and Constance Irene, *née* Cordwell; *b* 29 May 1937; *Educ* Christ's Hospital, Balliol Coll Oxford (BA, MA); *m* 10 Sept 1960, Miriam Tamara, da of Leo Dressler, of New York; 3 da (Julia b 1963, Miranda b 1966, Tamara b 1969); *Career* Jackson fell Univ of Harvard 1960-61, tutorial fell Balliol Coll Oxford 1963- (Dyson res fell 1961-63), T S Eliot lectr Univ of Kent 1984; FBA 1986; *Books* Homer on Life and Death (1980), Snobs (1982), Lakin Poets and Roman Life (1985), Virgil (1986), The Mirror of Myth (1986), Oxford History of the Classical World (ed, 1986), Homer: The Odyssey (1987); *Style—* Jasper Griffin, Esq; 17 Staverton Road, Oxford; Balliol College Oxford (☎ 0865 2777782, fax 0865 270708)

GRIFFIN, Sir John Bowes; QC (1938); only s of Sir Charles Griffin, QC (d 1962); *b* 19 April 1903; *Educ* Clongowes, Univ of Dublin, Univ of Cambridge (MA, LLD); *m* 1927, Eva Orrell (d 1977), da of John Mellifont Walsh, of Wexford; 2 da; m 2, 1984, Margaret Guthrie Lever, *née* Sinclair; *Career* called to the Bar Inner Temple 1926, admin offr Uganda 1927, registrar High Ct Uganda 1929, crown counsel Uganda 1933, attorney-gen Bahamas 1936, KC Bahamas 1938, slr-gen Palestine 1939, attorney-gen Hong Kong 1946, chief justice Uganda 1952, ret 1956; acting chief justice N Rhodesia 1957, speaker Uganda Legislative Cncl 1958-62 and Nat Assembly 1962-63, chm Public Serv Cmmn N Rhodesia 1963 and Zambia 1964-65, chm Constitutional Cncl N Rhodesia 1964, ret 1965; CStJ 1960, kt 1955; *Style—* Sir John Griffin, QC; 1 Marina Court, Tigne Sea Front, Sliema, Malta

GRIFFIN, Dr John Parry; s of David Joseph Griffin, of Ty-Coch, Station Rd, Llaniden, Cardiff, and Phyllis May Griffin (d 1989); *b* 21 May 1938; *Educ* Howardian HS Cardiff, London Hosp Med Coll (BSc, PhD, MB BS); *m* 31 March 1962, Margaret, da Frank Cooper (d 1975); 1 s (Timothy David b 1967), 2 da (Jane Rachel b 1963, Ruth Catherine b 1965); *Career* head of clinical res Riker Laboratories 1967-71, professional head of Medicines Div Dept of Health 1971-84, hon conslt Lister Hosp 1976-, dir Assoc Br Pharmaceutical Industry 1984-, author over 150 pubns; FRCP, FRCPath; *Books* Iatrogenic Diseases (4 edns), Manual of Adverse Drug Interactions (3 edns), Medicines Regulation Research & Risk; *Clubs* Atheneum; *Style—* Dr John Griffin; Association of The British Pharmaceutical Industry, 12 Whitehall, London SW1A 2DY (☎ 071 930 3477)

GRIFFIN, Patrick Charles Lake; s of John Griffin, of Top Farm, Highclere, Newbury, Berks, and Helen Evelyn, da of Sir Henry Bashford, Hon Physician to King George VI, knighted for servs to med 1937; *b* 15 Sept 1948; *Educ* Leighton Park Sch, Birmingham Sch of Architecture, Aston Univ (BSc); *m* 8 Sept 1973, Linda Dorothy, da of Reginald Mitchell (d 1955), of Yapton, W Sussex; 1 s (Thomas b 1978), 1 da (Joanna b 1980); *Career* chartered architect; chm Architectural Partnerships plc, md Sutton Griffin Morgan (architects, planners, landscape architects, surveyors) 1973-; received Civic Tst Award 1977, Berkshire Environmental Awards 1981, 1983, 1984, 1985, 1986, 1987, 1988; RIBA Housing Award 1987; vice chm Berks Soc of Architects 1988; ARIBA; *Recreations* cricket; *Style*— Patrick Griffin, Esq; Whitewood, The Mount, Highclere, Newbury, Berkshire (☎ 0635 253155); Sutton Griffin Morgan plc, Albion House, Oxford St, Newbury, Berks (☎ 0635 521100, fax 0635 44188)

GRIFFIN, Paul; MBE (1961); s of Maj John Edwin Herman Griffin, MC (d 1963), of Chingford, Essex, and Gertrude Lilian, *née* Farbridge (d 1968); *b* 2 March 1922; *Educ* Framlingham Coll, St Catharine's Coll Cambridge (BA, MA); *m* 24 March 1946, Felicity Grace, da of Canon Howard Dobson (d 1984), of Huntingfield, Suffolk; 1 s (Jonathan b 1949), 1 da (Angela b 1946); *Career* cmmnd 6 Gurkha Rifles 1941, Adj Capt 3/6 Gurkha Rifles North West Frontier 1942, GSO III Special Force (Chindits) 1943, served Burma 1944, Maj GSO II 34 Indian Corps 1944, served Malaya, transferred Suffolk Regt, demobbed 1945; asst master and head of English Dept Uppingham 1949-55, princ Eng Sch Cyprus 1956-60, headmaster Aldenham Sch 1962-74, princ Anglo World Language Centre Cambridge 1976-82; newsreader Cyprus Broadcasting Corpn 1957-60; memb: MENSA 1947 (treas 1948), Ct Corpn Sons of Clergy 1973 (sr treas 1982), Soc of Authors; *Books* collaborated in: the "How To" books (1985, 1987, 1989, 1990), The Dogsbody Papers (1988); *Recreations* literary competitions, sea angling, bridge; *Clubs* Army & Navy; *Style*— Paul Griffin, Esq, MBE; 1 Strickland Place, Southwold, Suffolk IP18 6HN (☎ 0502 723709)

GRIFFIN, Paul; s of Reginald Stuart Griffin, and Sylvia Mary, *née* Toyn; *b* 29 Dec 1955; *Educ* Magdalen Coll Oxford (MA, BCL); *m* 16 April 1983, Janet Mary, da of Cecil Sidney Turner; *Career* called to the Bar Grays Inn 1979; *Recreations* collecting furniture art books and wine, gardening, travel, skiing, music; *Style*— Paul Griffin, Esq; 77 Highbury Hill, London N5 1SX (☎ 071 359 8559); 2 Essex Ct, Temple London EC4Y 9AP (☎ 071 583 8381, fax 071 353 0998, telex 8812528 ADROIT G)

GRIFFITH, David Humphrey; s of Maj H W Griffith, MBE; *b* 17 Feb 1936; *Educ* Eton; *m* 1966, Philippa Claire, *née* Roberts; 1 s, 3 da; *Career* dir: Greenall Whitley & Co Ltd 1964-, Dennis Ruabon Ltd 1973-; *Recreations* gardening, fishing, shooting, racing; *Clubs* Boodle's; *Style*— David Griffith, Esq; Garthmeilio, Llangwm, Corwen, Clwyd, N Wales (☎ 049 082 269)

GRIFFITH, David Vaughan; s of Arthur Vaughan Griffith, of Cardiff, and Josephine Mary, *née* East; *b* 14 April 1947; *Educ* Cardiff HS, Balliol Coll Oxford (MA); *m* 21 May 1977, Tina, da of Edwin Frost (d 1968), of Epsom; 1 s (Owen b 1981), 5 da (Mary b 1980, Lucy b 1983, Sarah b 1985, Anna b 1987, Tessa b 1989); *Career* banker; with S G Warburg & Co Ltd 1970-73, Edward Bates & Sons Ltd 1973-75, Orion Bank Ltd 1975-76, Saudi Int Bank 1976-86, exec dir Banque Paribas; *Recreations* hill walking, theatre, railways; *Clubs* Reform; *Style*— David Griffith, Esq; 68 Lombard Street, London EC3 (☎ 071 9294545)

GRIFFITH, John McIver; TD; s of Edward Ernest Griffith (d 1974), and Mary Ann Fraser, *née* McIver; *b* 3 July 1932; *Educ* Shrewsbury; *m* 1976, Margaret Ann Allan, da of George A Rennie, of S Africa; 2 step s (Andrew b 1965, Nicholas b 1969), 1 da (Philippa b 1979), 1 step da (Caroline b 1962); *Career* Maj TA 5 Bn Kings Regt, 2 Lt East Lancs Regt served Middle East; dir: C T Bowring & Co (Insur) 1977, Bowring Servs Ltd 1985, Bowring Marine & Energy Ltd 1986, C T Bowring (Charities Fund) Ltd 1989, Bowring Marine Reinsurance Brokers (London) Ltd 1990-; *Style*— John Griffith, Esq, TD; The Old Post Office, Elmdon, nr Saffron Walden, Essex (☎ 0763 838221); The Bowring Bldg, Tower Place, London EC3 (☎ 071 283 3100)

GRIFFITH, Kenneth; brought up by grandparents Ernest and Emily Griffith; *b* 12 Oct 1921; *Educ* Tenby Cncl Sch, Tenby Green Hill GS; *m* three times (all dis); 3 s (David, Jono, Huw), 2 da (Eva, Polly); *Career* actor, writer and film maker; films incl: A Touch of Churchill, A Touch of Hitler (life of Cecil Rhodes), Hang Out Your Brightest Colours (life of Michael Collins - this film was suppressed), The Man on the Rock (last six years of Napoleon's life), The Sun's Bright Child (life of Edmund Kean), The Public's Right to Know (investigation into suppression of Collins films), Curious Journey (investigation into cause of Irish Republicanism - also suppressed), Black as Hell, Thick as Grass (the S Wales Borderers in the Zulu War of 1879), The Most Valuable Englishman Ever (the life of Thomas Paine), Clive of India, The Light (life of David Ben Gurion), Life of Paul Kruger, Life of Jawaharlal Nehru, Zola Budd, The Untouchable, Embassy to China; *Books* Thank God We Kept the Flag Flying (1974), Curious Journey (1982); *Recreations* travelling around the world; *Style*— Kenneth Griffith, Esq; 110 Englefield Rd, Islington, London N1 (☎ 071 226 9013)

GRIFFITH, (Edward) Michael Wynne; CBE (1987); s of Maj Humphrey Wynne Griffith, MBE (d 1986), and Phyllis Lilian Griffith, JP, *née* Theobalds; *b* 29 Aug 1933; *Educ* Eton, RAC; *m* 31 Oct 1959, Jill Grange, da of Maj D P G Moseley (d 1986), of Dorfold Cottage, Cheshire; 3 s (Edward James Wynne b 1964, Anthony David Wynne b 1966, Martyn b 1968 d 1969); *Career* memb: ARC 1973-82, Wales Ctee Nat Tst, Exec Ctee and Cncl Advsy Bd Nat West Bank 1974-; chm: Clwyd Health Authy 1980-90, Countryside Cncl for Wales 1991-; High Sheriff Denbighshire 1969, DL Clywd, Vice Lord-Lt Clwyd 1989-; *Clubs* Boodle's; *Style*— Michael Griffith, Esq, CBE; Greenfield, Trefnant, Denbigh, Clywd (☎ 074 574 633)

GRIFFITH, Owen Glyn; CBE (1980, OBE 1969), MVO (1954); s of William Glyn Griffith, MBE (d 1960), and Glwadys May Picton, *née* Davies (d 1981); *b* 19 Jan 1922; *Educ* Oundle, Trinity Hall Cambridge; *m* 1 Feb 1949, Rosemary Elizabeth Cecil, da of Dr John Cecil St George Earl (d 1973); 2 s (David b 1955, Michael b 1957); *Career* cmmnd Welsh Gds 1941-43, served Tunisia (wounded twice); Colonial Serv (later Overseas Colonial Serv) Uganda 1944-63: dist offr 1944-51, private sec to Govr 1952-54, dist cmmr 1954-61, perm sec Miny of Commerce and Indust 1961-63; HM Dip Serv 1963-82: princ CRO 1963, first sec and head of Chancery Khartoum Embassy 1965, first sec (commercial) Stockholm Embassy 1969, dep high cmmr Malawi 1973, inspectorate 1976, high cmmr Lesotho 1978; memb Exec Cncl Beaconsfield Cons Assoc; local rep Forces Help Soc and Lord Roberts Workshops; *Recreations* golf, fishing; *Clubs* Denham Golf; *Style*— Owen Griffith, Esq, CBE, MVO; The Sundial, Marsham Way, Gerrard's Cross, Buckinghamshire SL9 8AD; Blaengwilym, Rhydwilym, Clynderwen, Dyfed SA66 7QH (☎ 0753 882 438)

GRIFFITHS *see also*: Norton-Griffiths

GRIFFITHS, Alan Paul; s of Emrys Mathias Griffiths, and Jane, *née* Griffiths; *b* 21 Sept 1953; *Educ* St Davids Sch, Jesus Coll Oxford (Meyrick exhibitioner, BA, BCL, MA); *Career* fell and tutor in Law Exeter Coll Oxford 1977-88, called to the Bar Gray's Inn 1981, practising barrister 1987-; chm: Museum of Modern Art Oxford 1990-, Oxfordshire Community Rels Cncl 1978-80; memb Nat Ctee Child Poverty Action Gp 1987-; Oxford City Cncl 1980-88 (ldr and chm Fin Ctee); *Style*— Alan Griffiths, Esq; 1 Essex Court, Ground Floor, Temple, London EC4Y 9AR (☎ 071 583 2000, fax 071 583 0118, 071 353 8958)

GRIFFITHS, Allan; s of John Edward Griffiths (d 1972), and Loy, *née* Howson (now Mrs Loy Cottrell), of 2 Larch Way, Formby; *b* 1 May 1945; *Educ* Waterloo GS Crosby Liverpool; *m* 9 Sept 1967, Maureen Jean, da of late Leslie Howarth Dunn; 1 s (Philip Allan b 1 July 1975), 1 da (Ruth Helen b 12 March 1972); *Career* articled clerk Harmood Banner Liverpool 1961-66, qualified CA 1966, gp accountant Millers Engineering Group Wrexham 1967-70, fin dir Polythene Drums Ltd Skelmersdale 1972-75 (fin controller 1970-72); Grant Thornton: insolvency mangr 1975-78, ptnr Liverpool 1978-80, insolvency ptnr Manchester 1980-, managing ptnr, chm Insolvency Panel; memb: Insolvency Practitioners Assoc, Assoc Euro des Practiciens des Procédures Collective; MBIM, FCA (ACA 1966); *Recreations* golf and sport; *Clubs* St James (Manchester), Formby Golf; *Style*— Allan Griffiths, Esq; Tower Grange, 2 Grange Lane, Freshfield, Formby, Merseyside L37 7BR (☎ 07048 71136); Grant Thornton, Heron House, Albert Square, Manchester M2 5HD (☎ 061 834 5414, fax 061 832 6042, car 0836 609500)

GRIFFITHS, Air Vice-Marshal Arthur; CB (1972), AFC (1964); s of Edward Griffiths (d 1960), of Saltney, Chester, and Elizabeth Griffiths; *b* 22 Aug 1922; *Educ* Hawarden GS; *m* 1950, Nancy Maud, da of Herbert Sumpter, of Wansford; 1 da; *Career* RAF 1940-77 (served in UK, Germany, Canada, Far East, Australia); dir Trident Safeguards Ltd 1985-; *Clubs* RAF; *Style*— Air Vice-Marshal Arthur Griffiths, CB, AFC; Water Lane House, Marholm Rd, Castor, Peterborough, Cambs (☎ 0733 380 742)

GRIFFITHS, Bill (baptised Brian Bransom); s of William Eric Bransom Griffiths (d 1984), of Kingsbury, Middx, and Eileen Alexandra Hambleton; *b* 20 Aug 1948; *Educ* Kingsbury Co GS, UCL (BA), King's Coll London (MA, PhD); *Career* self employed writer and small press publisher runs Amra Imprint specialising in Old Eng Lit, memb Cncl and mangr Printshop Poetry Soc 1974, sec and chm Assoc of Little Presses 1989-; poetry pubns incl: War with Windsor (1974), For Rediffusion (1977), Tract Against the Giants (1984), A Text Book of Drama (1987); translator of Old Eng poems incl: Guthlac B, Dream of the Road, The Phoenix; other work in this field incl: An Old English Subject Reader (1990), The Battle of Maldon (1991); awards jt winner Nat Poetry Centre's Alice Hunt Barlett award 1974, winner Tha Engliscan Gesithas' Caedmon prize for Old English poetry 1988, artist in residence Westfield Coll London 1984; *Recreations* piano, keep-fit; *Style*— Bill Griffiths, Esq; 21 Alfred St, Seaham, Co Durham SR7 7LH (☎ 091 581 6738)

GRIFFITHS, Brian Arthur; s of James Griffiths (d 1986), and Constance Lizzie Griffiths (d 1977); *b* 28 Jan 1932; *Educ* Lawrence Sheriff GS, Rugby; *m* 6 Oct 1956, Stella, da of Robert Dunning (d 1970); 1 da (Christine Julia b 1963); *Career* slr; dir Spireglade Gp of Cos 1984-; *Recreations* travel, photography, wine; *Style*— Brian A Griffiths, Esq; 5 Greswolde Road, Solihull, West Midlands (☎ 021 704 1509); 5 Lower Temple Street, Birmingham B2 4JF (☎ 021 643 8075)

GRIFFITHS, His Hon Bruce Fletcher; QC (1970); s of Edward Griffiths (d 1944), of Llwydcoed, Aberdare, Glamorgan, and Nancy Olga, *née* Fuell; *b* 28 April 1924; *Educ* Whitchurch GS Cardiff, King's Coll London (LLB, Jelf medal); *m* 1952, Mary Kirkhouse, da of Judge George Kirkhouse Jenkins, QC (d 1967), of Bath, Avon; 2 s (David Edward b 1954, Richard Bruce b 1956), 1 da (Branwen Jane b 1962); *Career* RAF 1942-47; called to the Bar Gray's Inn 1952, chm Local Appeals Tbnl (Cardiff) Miny Social Security 1964-70, vice chm Mental Health Tbnl Wales 1968-72; asst rec: Birkenhead 1965, Cardiff Swansea & Merthyr Tydfil 1966-71; dep chm Glamorgan QS 1971, cmmr of Assize Royal Courts of Justice London 1971, memb Parole Bd 1983-85, circuit judge 1972-86; memb: Welsh Arts Cncl 1972-79 (chm Art Ctee 1975-79), pres Prov Court Church of Wales 1979 (memb Governing Body 1978); chm: Welsh Sculpture Tst, Contemporary Art Soc for Wales (purchaser 1975-76, vice chm 1977-87); Chllr Dio Monmouth 1977-, organising tstee Welsh Portrait Sculpture Fund; Silver medal for Services to Art (Czechoslovak Republic) 1986; *Clubs* Carlton, Naval and Military, Cardiff and County (Cardiff); *Style*— His Hon Bruce Griffiths, QC; 15 Heol Don, Whitchurch, Cardiff CF4 2AR (☎ 0222 625001); 15 Es Traves 07108 Port de Soller, Spain (☎ 010 3471 633800)

GRIFFITHS, His Hon Judge David John; s of John Griffiths (d 1936), and Anne Virgo, formerly Griffiths, *née* Jones (d 1967); *b* 18 Feb 1931; *Educ* St Dunstan's Coll; *m* 1, 1959, Joyce, da of Charles Gosling (d 1963); 3 s (John b 1961, Huw b 1963, Bryn b 1965), 1 da (Jane b 1960); *m* 2, 1972, Anita, da of William John Williams (d 1967); *Career* Royal Tank Regt, 5 Bn BAOR 1949-51, TA City of London Yeo 1951-56; slr Supreme Court 1957, own practise Bromley Kent 1961, acquires Harvey of Lewisham practise 1970, HM rec 1988, Circuit Judge 1984; hon slr Bromley Marriage Guidance Cncl 1969 vice chm Law Legal Aid Area Ctee 1983-84 (memb 1976), appt Panel of Chm of Nat Insur Local Tbnls, chm Bromley Cncl of Voluntary Servs 1980-87; Freeman City of London 1982; *Recreations* riding, music (male voice); *Style*— His Hon Judge Griffiths

GRIFFITHS, His Hon Judge David Laurence; s of Edward Laurence Griffiths (d 1959), and Mary Middleton, *née* Ewens, of Crewkerne, Somerset; *b* 3 Aug 1944; *Educ* Christ's Hosp Horsham, Jesus Coll Oxford (MA); *m* 13 Mar 1971, Sally, da of Canon Gerald Hollis, of Salisbury, Wilts; 4 da (Kate b 4 June 1973, Jane b 29 Jan 1975, Emily b 20 June 1977, Lucy b 5 June 1981); *Career* called to the Bar Lincoln's Inn 1967, asst rec 1981, rec 1985, judge Western Circuit; *Recreations* gardening, opera, running, sailing, amateur dramatics, swimming, walking, skiing; *Style*— His Hon Judge Griffiths; Lord Chancellor's Department, Trevelyan House, Great Peter St, London SW1P 3BY (☎ 071 210 8500, fax 071 210 8549)

GRIFFITHS, Ven David Nigel; RD; s of late William Cross Griffiths, LDS; *b* 29 Oct 1927; *Educ* Cranbrook Sch, Worcester Coll Oxford, Lincoln Theol Coll; *m* 1953, Joan, *née* Fillingham; 2 s (Martin Simon b 1955, Oliver Mark b 1959), 1 da (Rachel Helen (Mrs Peter Holmes) b 1957); *Career* ordained 1958, chaplain RNR; clerk in Holy Orders, vice chllr and librarian of Lincoln Cathedral 1967-73, rector of Windsor 1973-87, officiating chaplain to Household Cavalry 1973-87, chaplain to HM The Queen 1977-, rural dean of Maidenhead 1977-82 and 1985-87, hon canon of ChCh Oxford 1983-87, archdeacon of Berkshire 1987-; FSA; *Recreations* serendipity; *Style*— The Ven David Griffiths, RD, FSA; 21 Wilderness Road, Earley, Reading, Berks RG6 2RU (☎ 0734 663459); Choristers' Mews, 1A Nettleham Road, Lincoln LN2 1RF (☎ 0522 512014)

GRIFFITHS, Derek; *b* 15 July 1946; *Educ* Acland Burghley Comp, London Coll of Music; *Career* actor, lyricist and composer; teacher of drama: ILEA, Greenwich Theatre Co 1970-73; theatre work incl: Sing a Rude Song (Garrick Theatre) 1971, Two Gentlemen of Verona (Phoenix Theatre) 1972, Black Mikado (Cambridge Theatre), Alladin (Shaftesbury Theatre and Toronto Canada), Travelling Music Show (Her Majesty's Theatre) Fagin in Oliver Theatre Royal Plymouth; dir nat tour Twelfth Night; prodns at Royal Exchange Theatre Manchester: version Dick Whittington (writer & composer), The Three Musketeers (composer, co-writer and lyricist), Government Inspector, Bluebird of Unhappiness, The Nerd, Twelfth Night, The Odd Couple; TV work incl: BBC TV childrens progs, Two By Two (composer & lyricist), Animal Album, Heads and Tails (award winning nature series, composer); extensive work in film and radio, memb Performing Rights Soc; *Recreations* flying vintage aircraft (Tiger Moths, Stampes SV4B's); *Style*— Derek Griffiths, Esq

GRIFFITHS, Sir Eldon Wylie; MP (C) Bury St Edmunds May 1964-; s of Thomas Herbert Wylie Griffiths, of Dorset, and Edith May, *née* Jones; *b* 31 March 1989; *Educ* Ashton GS, Emmanuel Coll Cambridge, Yale Univ; *m* 1949, Sigrid Gante; 1 s (John), 1 da (Pamela); m 2, 1985, Elizabeth Marie Beatrix, da of Adriaan den Engelse (d 1985); *Career* former journalist; Parly sec Min of Housing and Local Govt 1970, Parly under-sec of state DOE and Min for Sport 1970-74, conslt Nat Police Fedn; Regents prof Univ of California Irvine, pres World Affrs Cncl Orange Co California, chm Lynton Delancey Ptnrs; chm: Br-Iranian and Br-Polish Gps, Indo Br Assoc, Special Olympics (UK); Hon Freeman City of London, Hon Citizen Orange County California; Gold Medal of Culture Republic of China Taiwan 1989; *Recreations* swimming, tennis, exploring wilderness America; *Clubs* Carlton, Overseas League; *Style—* Sir Eldon Griffiths, MP; The Wallow, Great Barton, Bury St Edmunds, Suffolk; House of Commons, London SW1

GRIFFITHS, Elizabeth Ann (Liz); da of Harry Stanley Griffiths (d 1981), of Harry Stanley Griffiths (d 1981), of Stoke-on-Trent, and Irene, *née* Pemberton; *b* 20 Nov 1952; *Educ* Endsor HS, Sixth Form Coll Stoke-on-Trent, Burslem Sch of Art, Leicester Poly, St Martin's Sch of Art (Leverhulme scholarship, BA), Royal Coll of Art (MA); *m* 18 July 1987, Alessandro Dalla-Grana, s of Antonio Dalla-Grana; 1 s (Francesco Winston b 6 Nov 1987); *Career* designer; freelance work designing and sketching for Gloria Sachs NY 1974-76, freelance colour and knitted ideas for Missoni and prints and shawl ideas 1976, dir of Art Studio and colourist (specialising mainly in knitted and woven fabrics and jaquard designs) Missoni 1977-; external accessor Central Sch of Art Textiles Sch 1980-84; *Recreations* swimming, reading, travelling, cinema, tennis; *Style—* Ms Liz Griffiths; Missoni Spa, Sumirago 21040, Varese, Italy (☎ 010 39 0331 909170, fax 909955)

GRIFFITHS, Gareth Lloyd; s of Curwen Lloyd Griffiths (d 1982), of Penarth, S Glam, and Doris Ceinwen, *née* Hughes; *b* 28 March 1954; *Educ* Penarth GS, Jesus Coll Oxford (BA, MA), City Univ, Cncl of Legal Educn; *Career* Thomson Regnl Newspapers 1975-78, Liverpool Post and Echo 1978-79, Financial Times 1979-84, dir Shandwick Conslts 1986-; called to the Bar Gray's Inn 1986; memb Paddington and N Kensington Community Health Cncl 1984-86; memb: Bodleian Library Appeal Ctee, Hon Soc of Cymroddorion; tstee Welsh Writers Tst; memb: Royal Inst of PA, Royal Inst of Int Affrs; *Books* A Study of Competition and the Opticians (1987); *Recreations* 19th century political and church history, walking; *Clubs* Reform, Glamorganshire Golf, London Welsh; *Style—* Gareth Griffiths, Esq; 2 St Donats House, Seaview Court, Kymin Rd, Penarth, S Glamorgan; Shandwick Consultants Ltd, Dauntsey House, Fredericks Place, Old Jewry, London EC2 (☎ 071 726 4291)

GRIFFITHS, Garry; s of Arthur Griffiths (d 1976), and Marion, *née* Taylor; *b* 12 June 1941; *Educ* Wellingborough GS, Leicester Poly (NDD); *m* 25 July 1964, Anna Margaret, da of Albert Hannington, of Priors Rd, Whittlesey, Peterborough, Cambs; 2 da (Catherine Ann b 1965, Lucy Ann b 1971); *Career* designer Design Res Unit 1963-66, lectr Middx Poly 1966-67; YRM 1967- (designer, assoc, patron 1986); md YRM Interiors 1986-; memb Nat Tst; FCSD; *Recreations* photography, travel; *Style—* Garry Griffiths, Esq; The Willows, 15 Willow Drive, High Barnet, Herts EN5 2LQ (☎ 081 449 6872); YRM Partnership Ltd, 24 Britton St, London EC1M 5NQ (☎ 071 253 4311, telex 21692, fax 071 250 1688)

GRIFFITHS, (William) Griffin Thomas; s of Maldwyn Thomas Griffiths, of The Gyrnos, Gwenddwr, Builth Wells, Powys, and Catherine Irene, *née* Powell; *b* 10 Nov 1940; *Educ* Univ Coll of Wales Aberystwyth (LLB); *Career* slr; sr ptnr Jeffreys & Powell; pres Herefords Breconshire and Radnorshire Law Soc 1989; *Recreations* farming; *Style—* Griffin Griffiths, Esq; Wye Lodge, Erwood, Builth Wells, Powys LD2 3PQ (☎ 09823 560307); 4 Lion St, Brecon, Powys LD3 7AU (☎ 0874 2106, fax 0874 3702)

GRIFFITHS, Harold Edward Dunstan; CBE (mil 1988), TD (1969); s of Maj Harold Griffiths, OBE, DL (d 1948), of Griffithstown, Monmouthshire, and Eileen Grace Oatridge, *née* Richards (d 1971); *b* 29 Nov 1927; *Educ* Christ Coll Brecon, St Mary's Hosp London (MB BS); *m* 15 Aug 1955, Rosa Mary, da of Francis John Hayward (d 1954), of Cranham, Glos; 2 s (Rupert b 1958, Andrew b 1961), 3 da (Jane b 1956, Susan b 1960, Vivien b 1964); *Career* Nat Serv RAMC Japan and Korea 1952-54, TA Col and CO of 219 (Wx) Field Hosp RAMC (V) 1954-88, Hon Col 219 (Wx) Field Hosp; formerly: house surgn St Mary's Hosp, Royal Nat Orthopaedic Hosp; orthopaedic registrar and sr registrar Western Infirmary Glasgow 1959-64, conslt orthopaedic surgn Southmead Frenchay and Winford Orthopaedic Hosps Bristol 1964-90; author of papers on orthopaedic topics in medical jls; FRCS, Fell Br Orthopaedic Assoc 1964; *Books* Operative Surgery and Management (contrib, 1981); *Recreations* gardening, choral and orchestral music; *Style—* Harold Griffiths, Esq, CBE, TD

GRIFFITHS, Howard; s of Bernard Griffiths (d 1984), and Olive, *née* Stokes (d 1982); *b* 20 Sept 1938; *Educ* Gowerton GS, LSE (MSc); *m* 27 July 1963, Dorothy, *née* Todd; 1 s (Andrew b 1968), 1 da (Emma b 1972); *Career* MOD: res offr 1963-69, princ Army Dept 1970-72, princ Central Staffs 1972-76, asst sec head Civilian Faculty Nat Def Coll 1976-78, asst sec Procurement Exec 1978-80, dep and cnsllr def UK Delgn Mutual and Balanced Force Reduction Talks Vienna 1980-84, asst sec Office Mgmnt and Budget 1984-86, head Def Arms Control Unit 1986-88, asst under sec (policy) 1988-; *Style—* Howard Griffiths, Esq; Ministry of Defence, Whitehall, London SW1A 2HB

GRIFFITHS, Baron (Life Peer UK 1985), of Govilon, Co Gwent; Sir (William) Hugh Griffiths; MC (1944), PC (1980), QC (1964); o s of Sir Hugh Ernest Griffiths, CBE (d 1961), and Doris Eirene, da of W H James; *b* 26 Sept 1923; *Educ* Charterhouse, St John's Coll Camb (MA); *m* 1949, Evelyn, da of Col A F Krefting; 1 s; 3 da; *Career* WW II Capt WG 1939-45; called to the Bar Inner Temple 1949; judge: High Ct of Justice (Queen's Bench Div) 1970-80, Nat Industl Relations Ct 1973-74; memb Advsy Cncl on Penal Reform 1967-70, chm Tbnl of Inquiry on Ronan Point 1968, vice chm Parole Bd 1976-77, memb Chancellor's Law Reform Ctee 1976-, pres Senate of Inns of Court and the Bar 1982-; a lord justice of appeal 1980-85, a lord of appeal in ordinary 1985-; chm Security Cmmn 1985-; hon memb Canadian Bar Assoc 1981; hon fell: American Inst of Judicial Admin 1985, American Coll of Trail Lawyers 1988; Hon LLD Wales 1987; hon fell Univ of Cambridge 1985 kt 1971; *Clubs* Garrick, MCC (pres 1990), Sunningdale Golf, R&A Golf; *Style—* The Rt Hon Lord Griffiths, MC, PC, QC; c/o House of Lords, London SW1

GRIFFITHS, Dr Hugh William; s of Peter Griffiths, of Downham, Essex, and Gwyneth Margaret, *née* Roberts; *b* 20 March 1957; *Educ* Brentwood Sch Essex, Univ of Newcastle upon Tyne (MB BS); *m* 28 June 1986 (m dis 1989), Gail, da of Angus Yoxall, of Newcastle upon Tyne; *Career* house offr Darlington Meml Hosp 1980-81, Newcastle Rotational Trg Scheme in psychiatry 1982-85, res registrar MRC 1985-86, sr registrar Northern Regnl Rotation 1986-88, conslt psychiatrist St George's Hosp 1988-; hon clinical lectr Univ of Newcastle upon Tyne; MRCPsych 1984; *Recreations* rugby union, skiing, motor sport, photography, music; *Clubs* Medical Institute (Newcastle); *Style—* Dr Hugh Griffiths; 16 Ousby Court, Kingston Park, Newcastle upon Tyne NE3 2TF; St George's Hospital, Morpeth, Northumberland NE61 2NU (☎ 0670 512121)

GRIFFITHS, (John) Hywel; s of Hopkin Griffiths (d 1989), and Gwendoline Margaret, *née* Howells; *b* 9 Oct 1933; *Educ* Caerphilly GS, UCNW, Trinity Hall Cambridge (BA); *m* 9 Sept 1960, Joan Ethel, da of Arthur Ernest Morton, of Croydon; 4 da (Meurig, Charlotte, Sarah, Louisa); *Career* provincial community devpt offr HMOCS Northern Rhodesia 1957-63, dir Br Cncl Centre Port Harcourt Nigeria 1963-65, lectr in community devpt Univ of Manchester 1965-70, dir NI Community Rels Cmmn 1970-72, prof of soc admin New Univ of Ulster 1972-79, conslt to Voluntary Serv Unit Home Office 1979-82, dir Wales Cncl for Voluntary Action 1982-89, m of CRM Consultants Ltd 1989-; tstee: Nat Aids Tst, HTV TV Tst, Welsh Voluntary Tst; *Books* Community Work & Social Change (jtly, 1969), Current Issues in Community work (jtly, 1973), The Development of Local Voluntary Action 1981); *Recreations* walking, gardening, bee-keeping; *Clubs* Royal Cwlth Soc; *Style—* Hywel Griffiths, Esq; Plymouth House, Caerphilly CF8 2RL (☎ 0222 885368)

GRIFFITHS, John Albert; s of Richard Griffiths, of Egham, Surrey, and Katie Joan, *née* Smithers; *b* 2 Dec 1943; *Educ* Tiffin Boys' Sch Kingston upon Thames; *m* Peggy-Ann Marie, *née* Waite, da of late Robert Mandel, of Calgary, Alberta, Canada; 2 s (James Richard b 28 Feb 1980, Charles Robert b 25 July 1984); *Career* reporter then sub-ed Survey Herald Group 1961-64, ed Blackheath Reporter 1965-66, PR offr Mannix Heavy Construction Group Calgary Alberta 1966-67, news ed The Albertan (Calgary morning newspaper) 1967-68, night ed and motoring corr Calgary Herald 1968-70; Financial Times: foreign staff 1974-76, night foreign news ed 1977, dep foreign news ed 1978-80; specialist writer on world motor industry and motor sport 1980-; memb World Land Speed Record Team (Richard Noble, Black Rock Desert Nevada 1983, 633-468 mph) and writer subsequent film (For Britain and the Hell of it), holder World Land Speed Record for a fire engine (Black Rock Nov 2 1982, 130-157 mph); *Recreations* motor racing (as driver); *Style—* John Griffiths, Esq; Financial Times, 1 Southwark Bridge, London SE1 9HL (☎ 071 873 3000, fax 071 873 3085)

GRIFFITHS, John Calvert; CMG (1983), QC (1972); s of Oswald Hardy Griffiths (d 1952), and Christina Flora Littlejohn; *b* 16 Jan 1931; *Educ* St Peter's Sch York, Emmanuel Coll Cambridge (BA, MA); *m* 17 May 1958, Elizabeth Jessamy Jean, eld da of Prof G P Crowden, OBE (d 1967); 3 da (Amanda b 1963, Anna b 1970, Alyson b 1973); *Career* Lt RE 1949-51; called to Bar Middle Temple 1959 (bencher 1983), Hong Kong Bar 1979, attorney gen of Hong Kong 1979-83, chm Hong Kong Law Reform Cmmn 1979-83, memb Court Hong Kong Univ 1980-84; memb Exec Ctee Prince Philip Cambridge Scholarships 1980-84, patron Matilda Hosp Charity for Handicapped Children 1981-83, treas Bar Cncl 1987; memb: Exec Ctee Gen Cncl of Bar 1967-71, senate Inns of Court & The Bar 1984-86 (Exec Ctee 1973-77), Cncl of Legal Educn 1983-, Nat Cncl of Social Service 1974-79, Gtr London CAB Exec Ctee 1978-79; *Recreations* fishing, first edns, gardening; *Clubs* Fly Fishers, Hurlingham, Hong Kong; *Style—* John Griffiths, CMG, QC; 1 Brick Court, Temple, London EC4 (☎ 071 583 0777, fax 071 583 9401)

GRIFFITHS, John Charles; JP (Cardiff 1959); s of Sir Percival Griffiths, KBE, and Kathleen, *née* Wilkes (d 1979); *b* 19 April 1934; *Educ* Uppingham, Peterhouse Cambridge (MA); *m* 1, 1956, Ann; 4 s (Timothy b 1957, Christopher b 1958, Gavin b 1961, Jonathan b 1964); m 2, 1983, Carole Jane; 1 da (Emily b 1984); *Career* pres: Thompson Newspapers 1958-61, BBC 1961-64; exec dir Nat Extension Coll 1964-67, PR advsr Br Gas 1969-73; chm and md: MSG PR Ltd 1973-78, Rodhales Ltd 1978-, Contact PR Ltd 1981-85, Minerra Arts Channel 1983-; dep gen mangr Press Assoc 1968-69; contested (Lib): Ludlow 1964, Wanstead & Woodford 1966, Bedford (Feb & Oct) 1974; pres Lib Pty 1982-83; *Books* The Survivors (1964), Afghanistan (1967), Modern Iceland (1969), The Science of Winning Squash, Three Tomorrows, Afghanistan, Key to a Continent (1980), The Queen of Spades (1983), Flashpoint Afghanistan (1987); *Recreations* reading, talking, squash, music; *Clubs* RAC; *Style—* John Griffiths, Esq, JP; Nevaddfach, Llangynidr, Crickhowell, Powys; Minerva Arts Channel, PO Box 9, Crickhowell, Powys NP8 1XJ (☎ 0874 730164, fax 0874 730164)

GRIFFITHS, John Egbert; s of Claude Griffiths (d 1975), of Bridgnorth, Shropshire, and Edith May, *née* Bradley; *b* 6 May 1939; *Educ* Tettenhall Coll Staffordshire, Kings Coll, Univ of Durham (BArch); *m* 12 Aug 1964 (m dis 1988), Joyce Margaret, da of Archibald Berrisford Collings; 2 da (Heidi Michelle b 1966, Sally Ann b 1969); *Career* architect and arbitrator; ptnr The Mason Richards Patnership 1972-; ARIBA 1965, ACIArb 1976; *Books* The Evolution of a Small Town (1962); *Recreations* countryside pursuits, painting & sketching, watching rugby union football, canoeing, running miniature steam trains on Welsh estate; *Clubs* Old Tettenhallians; *Style—* John Griffiths, Esq; The Fron, Glascwm Bwlch-y-Cibau, Llanfyllin, Moutgomeryshire, Powys, Wales SY22 5LU (☎ 093 884 204); St Marys Court, St Marys St, Bridgnorth, Shropshire WV16 4DZ; The Mason Richards Partnership, Architects Planners Consulting Engineers Landscape Architects, Highfield Court, 23/24 Highfield Rd, Edgbaston, Birmingham B15 3DP (☎ 021 456 1544, fax 021 456 1523, car 0836 515567)

GRIFFITHS, John Francis Philpin; s of James Maldwyn Griffiths, of Hayes, Bromley, Kent, and Joan, *née* Philpin; *b* 16 Sept 1948; *Educ* St Dunstan's Coll London, Clare Coll Cambridge (MA, DipArch); *m* 16 Sept 1972, Fiona Barbara, da of Lt Cdr Hugh Desmond Campbell Gibson, of Kilmelford, Argyll, Scotland; 1 s (Leo b 27 July 1980), 1 da (Anna b 16 Jan 1977); *Career* architect; Scarlett Burkett Assoc (Scarlett Burkett Griffiths 1986-): joined 1972, assoc 1975, ptnr 1978; chm: London Region Assoc of Conslt Architects 1988-90, AA Part III Examination Bd 1989-; Freeman City of London 1987, Liveryman Worshipful Co of Arbitrators 1987; memb RIBA 1974, FCIArb 1986, ACA 1985, memb AA 1987; *Recreations* reading, railway memorabilia, woodworking; *Style—* John Griffiths, Esq; Lyndhurst, 98 Hayes Rd, Bromley, Kent BR2 9AB (☎ 081 460 6246); Scarlett Burkett Griffiths, 14 Clerkenwell Close, London EC1R 0PQ (☎ 071 490 5002, fax 071 490 2160)

GRIFFITHS, John Greville; s of Orlando HG Griffiths (d 1961), and Florence, *née* Beck (d 1971); *b* 17 Sept 1935; *Educ* Dr Morgan's GS Bridgwater, Univ of Cambridge (MA); *m* 1 Sept 1962, Ruth, da of Edwin A Claypole, MM (d 1976); 1 da (Claire b 1966); *Career* Castrol: dir Europe 1975-90, dep md 1988-90; dir Burmah Castrol plc 1990-, md Foseco 1991-; *Recreations* archaeology, historical res, travel; *Style—* John Griffiths, Esq; Jenners, Poulton, Cirencester, Glos GL7 5JE (☎ 0285 851476); Castrol Ltd, Burmah House, Pipers Way, Swindon SN3 1RE (☎ 0793 512712, fax 0793 512 640)

GRIFFITHS, John Henry Morgan; s of Sir Eldon Griffiths, MP, and Sigrid, *née* Gante; *b* 3 Dec 1953; *Educ* Rugby, Emmanuel Coll Cambridge (BA); *Career* Lloyds Bank International 1975-79 (seconded to Bank of London & SA 1975-77, int mgmnt London 1977-79), Samuel Montagu & Co Ltd 1979-90 (syndications mangr 1981-83, dir and W Coast rep (USA) S M Inc 1983-87 (exec dir 1986-1990), des gen mangr Nomura Bank International plc 1990-; Hon MA Univ of Cambridge 1979; *Recreations* tennis, squash, shooting; *Clubs* San Francisco Bay, The Metropolitan; *Style—* John Griffiths, Esq; 6 West Mews, West Warwick Place, London SW1; Lynton Cottage, Ixworth Thorpe, Bury St Edmunds, Suffolk; Nomura Bank International plc, Nomura House, 1, St Martin's-Le-Grand, London EC1A 4NP (☎ 071 696 6891, fax 071 626 0851)

GRIFFITHS, John Pankhurst; s of William Bramwell Griffiths (d 1978), of Broadstairs, and Ethel Doris, *née* Pankhurst; *b* 27 Sept 1930; *Educ* Torquay GS, King

George V Sch Southport, Sch of Architecture Univ of Manchester (Dip Arch); *m* 1 Aug 1959, Helen Elizabeth, da of Leonard Ivor William Tasker (d 1976), of Bristol; 2 s (Jonathan b 1962, Matthew b 1963), 1 da (Janet b 1964); *Career* res architect Maxwell Fry N Nigeria 1956-58, staff architect Granada TV 1959, fndr and first dir Manchester Bldg Centre 1959-65, head of tech info MPBW (later DOE) 1965-77, fndr Bldg Conservation Assoc (now Bldg Conservation Tst at Hampton Court Palace) 1977; Freeman Worshipful Co of Tylers and Bricklayers 1981; RIBA 1956; *Recreations* designing odd things, examining buildings, cooking on solid fuel Aga; *Style—* John Griffiths, Esq; Building Conservation Tst, Apartment 39, Hampton Court Palace, E Molesey, Surrey KT8 9BS (☎ 081 943 2277)

GRIFFITHS, Prof Keith; s of Richard Griffiths (d 1975), and Lilian Griffiths, *née* Ebbs; *b* 1 April 1935; *Educ* Sir William Turner's Sch Coatham N Yorks, Univ of Edinburgh (BSc, PhD, DSc); *m* 6 Sept 1958, Veronica, da of Robert Henry Williams, of Llandaff Close, Penarth, S Wales; 2 s (David b 7 Nov 1960, Timothy b 3 June 1962); *Career* res assoc Dept of Histochemistry Univ of Minnesota Minneapolis USA 1960-61, lectr Dept of Steroid Biochemistry Univ of Glasgow 1961-66, dir of res Tenovus Inst for Cancer Res Univ of Wales Coll of Med 1966-, dir of res and prof of cancer res 1971-; memb Biochemical Soc 1958-; chm: Welsh Office Welsh Scientific Advsy Ctee 1975-84, Liaison Ctee Br Endocrine Socs 1987-90, Soc of Endocrinology 1987- (memb 1960-); *Recreations* gardening, cricket, motoring; *Style—* Prof Keith Griffiths; Tenovus Institute for Cancer Research, University of Wales College of Medicine, Heath Park, Cardiff CF4 4XX (☎ 0222 755944, fax 0222 747618)

GRIFFITHS, Kenneth Ernest Oliver; s of Ernest Griffiths (d 1948), of Neston, S Wirral, and Constance Annie, *née* Oliver (d 1970); *b* 1 May 1909; *Educ* Merchant Taylors'; *m* 26 June 1937, Joy Masters, da of Horace Rowland Hill (d 1968), of Petersfield, Hants; 2 s (Brian Oliver Hill b 1938, Robin Mark Hill b 1941), 1 da (Paula Louise Hill b 1944); *Career* insur practitioner; fndr ptnr Griffiths & Armour consulting insur brokers; *Recreations* travel, walking, bridge; *Clubs* Athenaeum (London and Liverpool), St Stephen's Constitutional, Artist's, Racquet (Liverpool); *Style—* Kenneth Griffiths, Esq; Brook Hey, Willaston, S Wirral (☎ 051 327 4220); Drury House, 19 Water Street, Liverpool L2 0RL (☎ 051 236 5656)

GRIFFITHS, Rev Dr Leslie John; s of Sydney John Griffiths (d 1987), and Olwen, *née* Thomas (d 1976); *b* 15 Feb 1942; *Educ* Univ of Wales (BA), Univ of Cambridge (MA), Univ of London (PhD); *m* 26 July 1969, Margaret, da of Alfred Rhodes (d 1989); 2 s (Timothy b 24 Sept 1972, Jonathan b 7 Jan 1974), 1 da (Ruth b 29 Oct 1975); *Career* lectr Univ of Wales 1964-67; methodist minister: Cambridge 1969-70, Haiti 1970-74 and 1977-80, Reading 1974-77, Loughton 1980-86, London 1986- (supt of West London Mission); regular contribs to radio bdcasting; chm Methodist Church Carribbean and Latin American Ctee 1981-89, govr Kingswood Sch Bath 1981-; KStJ 1989; *Recreations* rugby, snooker, reading, conversation; *Clubs* The Graduate Centre (Cambridge); *Style—* The Rev Dr Leslie Griffiths; 18 Beaumont St, London W1N 1FF (☎ 071 486 9924); The West London Mission, 19 Thayer St, London W1M 5LJ (☎ 071 935 6179)

GRIFFITHS, Mervyn Christopher; TD (1976); s of Rev Leonard Lewis Rees Griffiths, of Angle Cottage, Polecat Valley, Hindhead, Surrey, and Eileen Clarice, *née* Diffey; *b* 28 May 1936; *Educ* St George's Sch Windsor Castle, Uppingham, Corpus Christi Coll Cambridge (MA), Harvard Business Sch (PMD); *m* 27 April 1974, Barbara Marchant, da of Dr (Heneage) Marchant Kelsey, of Ramparts, Rudgwick, West Sussex; 1 step s (Mark Selway b 7 Feb 1964); *Career* 2 Lt 4/7 Royal Dragoon Gds 1954-56, Capt Queens Own Warwickshire & Worcestershire Yeo 1956-68; special constable Met Police 1973-76; asst mktg mangr W & T Avery Ltd 1959-65, PR exec McLeish Assoc 1965-66; Eurocard Int SA, Belgium: mktg mangr 1966-67, exec vice pres NY 1967-71, md London 1971-76; dir and dep chief gen mangr Alliance Building Society 1976-85, dir dep chief gen mangr and sec Alliance & Leicester Building Society 1985-89, dir Legal & General Mortgage Services 1990-; vice chm SE TAVRA; memb: Isfield PCC, NSPCC Nat Centenary Appeal Ctee 1984; govr: Handcross Park Sch Haywards Heath, St Bede's Sch Eastbourne; FCIM 1975; *Recreations* gardening, travel; *Clubs* Cavalry and Guards; *Style—* Mervyn Griffiths, Esq, TD; The Old House, Isfield, nr Uckfield, E Sussex TN22 5XU (☎ 082 575 446)

GRIFFITHS, Michael John; s of Sqdn Ldr J C Griffiths RAF; *b* 15 Dec 1934; *Educ* Peter Symond's Sch Winchester; *m* 10 Aug 1957, Jennifer Elizabeth (Jenny), da of the late Lt-Col E H Stafford, TD, of Witherley Lodge, nr Atherstone, Warwicks; 2 s (Jeremy Michael Christian b 10 July 1960, Andrew James Christian b 7 Oct 1961), 3 da (Sara Elizabeth (Mrs Hicklin) b 20 Nov 1958, Caroline Jane (Rosie) b 13 April 1964, Rebecca Lucy (Biba) b 5 June 1969); *Career* RAF Coll Cranwell 1952-55, GD Pilot 1955-62; md: Halls Oxford Brewery 1967, Benskins Brewery 1970, Taylor Walker 1979, Ind Coope 1985; dep chief exec Ansells Brewery Co 1974; dir: Friary Meux 1966, Allied Breweries 1979, Allied Lyons 1988-; chm: Victoria Wine Co 1988, Embassy Hotels 1989, J Lyons Catering Ltd 1989; memb Cncl Design Museum, chm London Brewers Cncl; Freeman City of London 1982; *Recreations* skiing, sailing, shooting, fishing; *Clubs* RAF; *Style—* Michael Griffiths, Esq; Mead Farm, Church Lane, Yarnton, Oxford (☎ 08675 3284); Allied Lyons plc, 24 Portland Place, London W1 (☎ 071 323 9000)

GRIFFITHS, Mike; *b* 18 March 1962; *Educ* Blaenclyoach Secdy Sch; *m* 27 Aug 1983, Anne, da of Haydn Arthur Griffiths; 2 s (Joel Michael b 25 Oct 1985, Luke Rhys b 29 Aug 1989); *Career* Rugby Union prop forward Cardiff RFC and Wales; Clubs: Ystrad Rhondda RFC, Bridgend RFC, Cardiff RFC; rep: Saltires, Crawshays, Barbarians, Wales B; Wales: debut v Western Samoa 1988, Five Nations debut v Scotland 1989; Br Lions tour Aust 1989; builder G D Griffiths & Sons (family business); *Recreations* mountain cycling, weight training, running; *Style—* Mike Griffiths, Esq; Cardiff RFC, Cardiff Arms Park, Westgate Street, Cardiff, South Glamorgan (☎ 0222 383546)

GRIFFITHS, Nigel; MP (Lab) Edinburgh South 1987-; s of Lionel Griffiths, of Edinburgh, and Elizabeth, *née* Murray; *b* 20 May 1955; *Educ* Hawick HS, Univ of Edinburgh (MA), Moray House Coll of Educn; *m* 1979, Sally, da of Hugh McLaughlin, of Kilmarnock; *Career* joined Lab Party 1970, pres Edinburgh Univ Lab Club 1976-77; rights advsr Mental Handicap Pressure Gp 1979-87, City of Edinburgh District cnclr; chm: Housing Ctee, Decentralisation Ctee; memb: Edinburgh Festival Ctee, Wester Hailes Sch Cncl 1980; *Books* Council Housing on the point of Collapse (1982), Welfare Rights Guide (1982, 83, 84, 85, 86), A Guide to DHSS Claims and Appeal (1983); *Recreations* travel, hill walking, rock climbing, architecture, politics; *Style—* Nigel Griffiths, Esq, MP; 39 Thirlestane Rd, Edinburgh EH9 1AP (☎ 031 447 1947); c/o Trevose House, Newburn St, London SE11; House of Commons, London SW1A 0AA (☎ 071 219 3442); Constituency Office, 93 Causewayside, Edinburgh (☎ 031 662 4520)

GRIFFITHS, Sir Percival Joseph; KBE (1963), CIE (1943); s of late J T Griffiths, of London; *b* 15 Jan 1899; *Educ* Central London Sch, Peterhouse Cambridge; *m* 1, 1924, Kathleen Mary (d 1979), da of late T R Wilkes, of Kettering; 3 s; m 2, 1985, Helen Marie Shirley Smith; *Career* served WW I, 2 Lt RFC 1917-18; entered ICS 1922, memb Indian Legislative Assembly 1937-47, leader European Gp 1946, central organiser Nat War Front India 1942-44, hon publicity advsr Govt of India 1942-47, hon advsr to India, Pakistan and Burma Assoc 1947-63, pres 1963, advsr to Indian Tea Assoc and Pakistan Tea Assoc 1947-63; co dir; kt 1947; *Style—* Sir Percival Griffiths, KBE, CIE; St Christopher, Abbots Drive, Wentworth, Virginia Water, Surrey

GRIFFITHS, Peter Harry Steve; MP (C) Portsmouth North 1979-; s of the late W L Griffiths, of West Bromwich; *b* 24 May 1928; *Educ* West Bromwich GS, City of Leeds Trg Coll, Univ of London, Univ of Birmingham; *m* 1968, Christine Jeannette, *née* Rubery; 1 s (John Paul) 1 da; *Career* former: headmaster, sr lectr, pres Young Cons; alderman Smethwick Borough Cncl 1964-66 (memb 1955-64), MP (C) Smethwick 1964-66, Parly candidate (C) Portsmouth North Feb 1974; Parly advsr MOD Staff Assoc; *Recreations* motoring, camping; *Clubs* Cons, Sloane; *Style—* Peter Griffiths, Esq, MP; House of Commons, London SW1A 0AA

GRIFFITHS, Peter John; s of Ronald Hugh Griffiths (d 1987), of Sutton, Surrey, and Emily Vera, *née* Cockshutt (d 1980); *b* 19 April 1944; *Educ* Battersea GS, Univ of Leicester (BA), McMaster Univ (MA); *m* 19 Aug 1968, Lesley Florence, da of Albert Palmer (d 1963), of Hull; 2 da (Helen b 1969, Clare 1972); *Career* Univ of London: asst to princ 1968-70, asst sec Ctee of Enquiry into the Governance of Univ of London 1970-72, special duties offr vice chllr's office 1972-78, dep head Legal and Gen Div Court Dept 1978-82, asst clerk of the court 1982-85, dep clerk 1985-87, clerk 1987-; memb Nat Conference of Registrars and Sec of UK Univs; *Recreations* choral singing Pro Musica Chorus of London; *Style—* Peter Griffiths, Esq; Upland House, Upland Rd, Sutton, Surrey SM2 5HW (☎ 081 643 3599); University of London, Senate House, Malet St, London WC1E 7HU (☎ 071 636 8000, fax 071 255 2171)

GRIFFITHS, Peter Kevin; s of Denis Griffiths, of Cardiff, and Elsie Joyce, *née* Linck; *b* 15 Oct 1956; *Educ* Llanishen HS Cardiff, Univ Coll Cardiff (BA); *Career* studio mangr BBC 1978; prodr Radio 4: Womans Hour 1981-82, Features Dept 1982-83, presentation 1983-85, Network Features Dept Manchester; sr prodr sport and outside bdcasts Radio 4 1985-, sr prodr Features, Arts and Education for Radio 4 and Radio 5 1990-; memb Radio Acad; *Recreations* music, friends; *Style—* Peter Griffiths, Esq; 3 Lancaster Cottages, Lancaster Park, Richmond, Surrey TW10 6AE; British Broadcasting Corporation, Broadcasting House, Portland Place, London W1A 1AA (☎ 071 927 4743, fax 071 580 5780)

GRIFFITHS, Peter Robert; s of Robert Amos Griffiths (d 1988), of Long Ridges, Shotover, Oxford, and Grace Margaret, *née* Wilson; *b* 1 Aug 1953; *Educ* Repton, St Catharines Coll Cambridge (MA); *m* 11 Dec 1981, (Julie) Marguerite, da of Hyltje Andrew Kamstra, of 74C Lairgate, Beverley, Humberside; 3 da (Victoria b 1983, Catharine b 1985, Sarah b 1988); *Career* Lt Inns of Court and City Yeomary 1981; called to the Bar Inner Temple 1977, joined chambers of TPE Curry, QC 1978; Freeman City of London 1985, Liveryman Worshipful Co of Merchant Taylors 1985; *Books* Atkins Court Forms (companies winding up, 1989); *Recreations* walking; *Clubs* Hurlingham; *Style—* Peter Griffiths, Esq; 4 Stone Buildings, Lincoln's Inn, London WC2A 3XT (☎ 071 242 5524, fax 071 831 7907, telex 892300 ADVICE G)

GRIFFITHS, Prof (Allen) Phillips; s of John Phillips Griffiths (d 1941), of Cardiff, and Elsie Maud, *née* Jones (d 1975); *b* 11 June 1927; *Educ* Univ Coll Cardiff (BA), Univ Coll Oxford (BPhil); *m* 1, 6 June 1948, Margaret (d 1974), da of John Henry Joseph Lock (d 1974); 1 s (John Benedict Phillips b 1960), 1 da (Sarah Katharine Phillips b 1961); m 2, 21 April 1984 (m dis 1990), Vera Clare, da of Patrick Dunphy; *Career* Sgt Intelligence Corps 1945-48 (despatches); lectr: Univ of Wales 1954-56, Birkbeck Coll London 1956-65; pro vice chllr Univ of Warwick 1970-76 (prof of philosophy 1965-); visiting prof: Swarthmore Coll Pa USA 1963, Univ of California 1967, Univ of Wisconsin 1965 and 1970, Carlton Coll Minnesota 1985; dir Royal Inst of Philosophy 1979-; hon fell Univ Coll Cardiff 1984; Queen's Jubilee medal 1977; memb Mind Assoc Aristotelian Soc 1955-; *Books* Knowledge and Belief (ed, 1967), Of Liberty (1983), Philosophy and Literature (1984), Philosophy and Practice (1985), Contemporary French Philosophy (1988), Philosophical Themes (1989), and numerous articles in philosophical journals; *Clubs* Conservative (Kenilworth); *Style—* Prof Phillips Griffiths; Dept of Philosophy, University of Warwick, Coventry CV4 7AL (☎ 0203 523320)

GRIFFITHS, Sir Reginald Ernest; CBE (1965); s of Arthur Griffiths; *b* 1910; *Educ* St Marylebone GS, Univ of London (externally); *m* 1935, Jessica Broad (d 1987); 2 s; *Career* dir of estabs LCC 1952-57; sec: Police Cncl, Nat Jt Industl Cncls (Local Authorities) 1957-72, Local Authorities Advsy Bd; memb Nat Industl Rels Ct 1972-74; industl arbitrator 1972-85; kt 1973; *Recreations* social work (voluntary), golf, gardening; *Style—* Sir Reginald Griffiths, CBE; 10 Woolbrook Park, Sidmouth, Devon (☎ 0395 514884)

GRIFFITHS, (William) Robert; s of William John Griffiths, of Haverfordwest, Dyfed, and Marjorie Megan, *née* Green; *b* 24 Sept 1948; *Educ* Haverfordwest GS, Open Scholar of St Edmund Hall Oxford (BA, BCL, MA); *m* 10 March 1984, Angela May, da of Robert Victor Crawford, of Manchester; 2 da (Anna-Victoria Sophia b 7 Oct 1986, Helena Elizabeth Rose b 13 Sept 1989); *Career* called to the Bar Middle Temple 1974, jr counsel to the Crown (common law) 1989; memb: Hon Soc of the Middle Temple, Hon Soc of Cymmrodorion; *Recreations* reading, collecting modern first editions, cricket; *Clubs* MCC; *Style—* Robert Griffiths, Esq; 4-5 Gray's Inn Square, Gray's Inn, London WC1R 5AY (☎ 071 404 5252, fax 071 242 7803)

GRIFFITHS, Robin John; s of David Gromwell Morgan Griffiths, and Elizabeth Hope, *née* Limbert; *b* 15 Dec 1942; *Educ* Bedford Sch, Univ of Nottingham (BA); *m* 6 Jan 1968, Esme Georgina (Gina), da of Willim Hunter (d 1967); 4 s (Mark David b 24 Sept 1971, Paul Robin b 6 Sept 1974, David James b 4 Aug 1977, Andrew William b 29 Nov 1979); *Career* Phillips & Drew 1964-68, ptnr Grieveson Grant 1968-84 (formerly Carr Sebag, previously W1 Carr), sr exec James Capel 1986-; chm Soc of Tech Analysts; memb: Nippon Tech Analysts Assoc, Int Fedn Tech Analysts; author and fndr The Amateur Chartist Newsletter; sailed the Atlantic with Robin Knox Johnston setting a Br record at the time; memb Stock Exchange 1971, FIMBRA 1987; *Recreations* sailing; *Style—* Robin Griffiths, Esq; James Capel & Co, Capel House, PO Box 551, 6 Bevis Marks, London EC3A 73Q

GRIFFITHS, Roger; s of William Thomas Griffiths (d 1979), of Barry, S Wales, and Annie Evelyn, *née* Hill; *b* 25 Dec 1931; *Educ* Lancing, King's Coll Cambridge (BA, MA), New Coll Oxford (BA, MA, DipEd); *m* 2 April 1966, Diana, da of Capt John Frederick Beaufoy Brown, OBE, DSC, RN (d 1979), of Burgess Hill, Sussex; 3 da (Elizabeth b 1966, Helen b 1968, Caroline b 1970); *Career* asst master Charterhouse 1956-64, headmaster Hurstpierpoint Coll 1964-86, sec HMC 1986-, dep sec SHA 1986-; JP Mid-Sussex Bench 1976-86, memb Mgmnt Ctee of Pallant House Chichester 1987-; govr: Mill Hill Sch 1987-, Tormead Sch Guildford 1987-, Prebendal Sch Chichester 1987-, Worth Sch 1990; Freeman City of London 1970, Master of the Wax Chandlers Co 1990-91; *Recreations* music, theatre, bowls, gardening; *Clubs* East India, Devonshire Sport, Public Schools, Sussex; *Style—* Roger Griffiths, Esq; Hanbury Cottage, Cocking, Midhurst, W Sussex GU29 0HF (☎ 073081 3503); The Headmasters' Conference, 1 Russell House, Bepton Rd, Midhurst, W Sussex GU29 9NB (☎ 073081 5635)

GRIFFITHS, Roy Garrad; s of William James Griffiths (d 1972), and Emma, *née* Garrad (d 1987); *b* 2 July 1934; *Educ* Ealing Coll; *m* 1, 26 Feb 1955 (m dis 1979), Sheila Elizabeth, da of Robert William Gerrish; 2 s (John Charles Roy b 30 Dec 1959, Paul James b 28 Nov 1965), 1 da (Anne Elizabeth b 21 Oct 1962); m 2, 8 May 1980, Christine Lillian Mackenzie Ronhof Gronbech, *née* Boote; *Career* md Clares Engrg Ltd

1967, dir: White Child and Beney plc 1972, Clares Refrigeration Ltd 1985; chm Clares Equipment Ltd 1978, chm and chief exec Clares Equipment Hldgs Ltd 1987; Freeman City of London, Liveryman Worshipful Co of Carmen; patron: Bath Rugby Club, Theatre Royal Bath; vice pres Somerset CCC; *Recreations* antiques, theatre, art, watching rugby and cricket; *Clubs* City Livery, MCC Lord Taverners; *Style*— Roy Griffiths, Esq; Clares Equipment Holdings Ltd, Parkwood Estate, Wells, Somerset BA5 1UT (☎ 0749 73688, fax 0749 73688, car phone 0860 327624, telex 449751 ROLPOL G)

GRIFFITHS, Trevor; s of Ernest Griffiths (d 1961), of Manchester, and Ann Veronica, *née* Connor (d 1976); *b* 4 April 1935; *Educ* St Bede's Coll Manchester, Univ of Manchester (BA); *m* 13 March 1960, Janice Stansfield (d 1977); 1 s (Joss b 1968), 2 da (Sian b 1965, Emma b 1967); *partner* Gillian Cliff; *Career* playwright; work incl: The Wages of Thin (first prodn Stables Theatre Manchester 1969), The Big House (1972, BBC Radio 4 1969), Occupations (1980, Stables Theatre Manchester 1970), Lay By (jtly 1971, Traverse Theatre Edinburgh), Apricots (1978, Basement Theatre London 1971), Thermidor (1978, Edinburgh Festival 1971), Sam, Sam (1972, Open Space 1972), The Party (1974, NT 1973), All Good Men and Absolute Beginners (1977, BBC TV 1974), Comedians (1976, Nottingham 1975), Through The Night and Such Impossibilities (1977, BBC TV 1975), Bill Brand (Thames TV 1976), The Cherry Orchard (new Eng version 1978, Nottingham Playhouse 1977), Deeds (jtly, Nottingham Playhouse 1978), Sons and Lovers (1982, BBC TV 1981), Country (1981, BBC TV 1981), Reds (jtly with Warren Beatty, 1981), Oi For England (1982, Central TV 1982), Judgement Over The Dead 1986, Central TV 1985), Real Dreams (1987, Williamstown Theatre Festival 1984), Fatherland (1987), Collected Plays for Television (1988), Piano (1990, NT 1990); memb: CND, The Reality Club (USA); fndr memb Charter '88; memb: The Writers' Guild of GB, The Writers' Guild of America (West), The Theatre Writers Union; *Recreations* chess, bridge, music, photography; *Style*— Trevor Griffiths, Esq; c/o Peters Fraser & Dunlop, 5th Floor, The Chambers, Chelsea Harbour, Lots Rd, London SW10 0XF (☎ 071 376 7676, fax 071 351 1756)

GRIFFITHS, Walter Lloyd; s of Joseph Ewance Griffiths (d 1974), and Josephine Mary, *née* Stokes (d 1972); *b* 24 June 1927; *m* 3 March 1962, Paula, da of Reginald Lord Hollebone (d 1953); 2 s (David b 13 Jan 1963, Mark b 23 Nov 1965 d 1969), 1 da (Julie b 24 March 1964); *Career* admitted slr 1960; sr ptnr Burnand and Burnand Hove and Worthing 1970- (ptnr 1961-70); NP 1966; Freeman City of London 1982 (Guild memb 1984), Liveryman Worshipful Co of Loriners 1982; memb: Law Soc 1960, Provincial Notaries Soc 1966; *Recreations* study of social and domestic life in Victorian England, gardening, travel; *Clubs* City Livery; *Style*— Walter Griffiths, Esq; Jefferies House, Jefferies Lane, Goring-by-Sea, Worthing, W Sussex (☎ 0903 43599); Burnand and Burnand, 39 Church Rd, Hove, E Sussex BN3 2BU (☎ 0273 734022, fax 0273 778760); 4 Aldsworth Parade, Goring-by-Sea, Worthing, W Sussex BN12 4UA (☎ 0903 502155, fax 0903 506731)

GRIFFITHS, William Arthur; s of Glyndwr Griffiths (d 1975), and Alice Rose Griffiths (d 1982); *b* 25 May 1940; *Educ* Owens' Sch Queens' Coll Cambridge, Univ of Manchester; *m* 23 May 1964 (m dis 1986), Margaret Joan Dodd; 2 s (Benjamin b 1 April 1965, Richard b 13 July 1966), 1 da (Elizabeth b 18 Oct 1964); *Career* probation serv 1965-72, Home Office 1972-77, chief probation offr NI 1977-87, dir NCVO 1985, mgmnt conslt Griffiths Seckerson 1986-; chm of fin Westminster City Cncl 1990, govr Pimlico Sch 1990; *Recreations* literature, theatre, travel; *Style*— William Griffiths, Esq; 86 Bryanston Court, George Street, London W1H 7HD (☎ 071 262 7589)

GRIFFITHS, Winston James (Win); MP (Lab) Bridgend 1987-; *b* 1943,Feb; *m* Elizabeth Ceri, *née* Gravell; 1 s, 1 da; *Career* teacher; MEP (Lab) S Wales 1979-89; *Style*— Win Griffiths, Esq, MP

GRIGG, Hon Anthony Ulick David Dundas; yr s of 1 Baron Altrincham, KCMG, KCVO, DSO, MC, PC (d 1955), and hp to Barony of bro, John Edward Poynder Grigg, *qv* (2 Baron, who disclaimed Peerage for life 1963); *b* 12 Jan 1934; *Educ* Eton, New Coll Oxford; *m* 1965, Eliane, da of the Marquis de Miramon; 2 s (Sebastian b 1965, Steven b 1969), 1 da (Casilda b 1967); *Career* late 2 Lt Grenadier Gds; *Style*— The Hon Anthony Grigg; 11 Horbury Mews, London W11 3NL (☎ 071 229 6005)

GRIGG, John Edward Poynder; s of 1 Baron Altrincham, KCMG, KCVO, DSO, MC, PC (d 1955), and Hon Joan Dickson-Poynder, da of 1 Baron Islington; disclaimed Barony for life 1963; *b* 15 April 1924; *Educ* Eton, New Coll Oxford; *m* 1958, Patricia, da of Harold Campbell CBE, of Belfast; *Heir* bro, Hon Anthony Grigg; *Career* served WWII Lt Grenadier Gds; Parly candidate (C) Oldham W 1951 and 1955; jounalist; ed Nat and English Review 1954-60, The Guardian 1960-70, The Times 1986-; chm London Library 1985-91; FRSL; *Books* Two Anglican Essays, The Young Lloyd George, Lloyd George: the People's Champion (Whitbread award, 1943), 1943: The Victory That Never Was, Nancy Astor: Portrait of a Pioneer, Lloyd George: From Peace to War (Wolfson award); *Style*— John Grigg; 32 Dartmouth Row, London SE10 (☎ 081 692 4973)

GRIGGS, (Frank) Douglas; s of Maj Frank Robertson Griggs, JP (d 1956), of Wirksworth, Derbyshire, and Katharine Emily Joan Griggs, *née* Legge (d 1951); *b* 11 Sept 1904; *Educ* Repton, Jesus Coll Cambridge (MA); *Career* timber importer Joseph Griggs & Co Ltd: dir 1939-69, chm 1970-83; *Clubs* Leander (Henley-on-Thames); *Style*— Douglas Griggs, Esq; c/o Lloyd's Bank plc, Montpellier, Cheltenham, Glos GL50 1SH

GRIGGS, Rt Rev Ian Macdonald; s of Donald Nicholson Griggs (d 1967), of Gt Easton, Essex, and Agnes Elizabeth, *née* Brown; *b* 17 May 1928; *Educ* Brentwood Sch, Trinity Hall Cambridge (BA, MA), Westcott House Cambridge; *m* 29 Aug 1953, Patricia Margaret, da of Ernest Charles Medland Vernon-Browne (d 1974), of Lindfield, Sussex; 3 s (Alistair b 1954, Mark b and d 1957, Julian b 1964), 3 da (Clare b 1956, Helen b 1959, Hilary b 1962); *Career* Essex Regt 1947-49; ordained: deacon 1954, priest 1955; asst curate St Cuthbert Portsmouth 1954-59, domestic chaplain bishop of Sheffield 1959-64, diocesan youth chaplain Sheffield 1959-64, vicar of St Cuthbert Firvale Sheffield 1964-71, vicar of Kidderminster 1971-83, hon canon Worcs 1977-84, archdeacon of Ludlow 1984-87, suffragan bishop of Ludlow 1987-; *Recreations* mountaineering, hill-walking; *Clubs* Lansdowne; *Style*— The Rt Rev Ian Griggs; Bishop's House, Halford, Craven Arms, Shropshire SY7 9BT (☎ 0588 673571)

GRIGGS, Jeremy David; s of Celadon Augustine Griggs, of Elm Tree Farm, East Brent, Highbridge, Somerset, and Ethel Mary, *née* Anderson; *b* 5 Feb 1945; *Educ* St Edward's Sch Oxford, Magdalene Coll Cambridge (MA); *m* 1, 1971 (m dis 1982), Wendy Anne Russell, *née* Culham; 2 s (Christopher b 1972, Tom b 1974), 1 da (Beth b 1976); m 2, 7 Sept 1985, Patricia Ann (the actress Patricia Maynard), da of Thomas Maynard, of Southfields, London; 2 step da (Hannah Waterman b 1975, Julia Waterman b 1979); *Career* called to the Bar Inner Temple 1968, memb Western Circuit, rec 1990, bar's rep CCBE 1990-; chm London Choral Soc 1986-90; *Recreations* choral singing, birdwatching, sailing; *Clubs* Groucho's, Hickling Broad Sailing; *Style*— Jeremy Griggs, Esq; The Old Vicarage, South Walsham, Nr Norwich, Norfolk NR13 6DQ (☎ 060 549 522); 24 Cholmeley Lodge, Cholmeley Park, Highgate, London N6 (☎ 081 340 2241); Lamb Building Temple, London EC4Y 7AS (☎ 071 353 6381, fax 071 583 1786)

GRIGGS, Patrick John Spear; s of John Garson Romeril Griggs (d 1987), of Jersey, CI, and Inez Frances, *née* Cole; *b* 9 Aug 1939; *Educ* Stowe, Tours Univ France, Law Soc Sch of Law London; *m* 4 April 1964, Marian Patricia, da of John Pryor Birch, of Mere, Wilts; 3 s (Simon Richard b 1967, Edward John b 1969, William Robert b 1972); *Career* slr 1963; joined Ince and Co 1958: ptnr 1966, sr ptnr 1989; Stanford Rivers Parish cncllr; Freeman City of London; *Books* Limitation of Liability for Maritime Claims (jtly, 1987); *Recreations* tennis, skiing, walking, cycling, hockey; *Clubs* Gresham; *Style*— Patrick Griggs, Esq; Ince & Co, Knollys Ho, 11 Byward St, London EC3 (☎ 071 623 2011, fax 071 623 3225, telex 8955043)

GRIGGS, Roy; s of Norman Edward Griggs, CBE, of 5 Gledhow Gardens, London SW5, and Livia Lavinia, *née* Levi; *b* 26 April 1950; *Educ* Westminster, Univ of Bristol (LLB); *m* 4 Jan 1975, Anita Gwendolyn, da of Humphrey Osmond Nunes (d 1972); 4 da (Flavia b 1979, Eleanor b 1982, Cordelia b 1986, Marina b 1989); *Career* slr: Norton Rose Botterell and Roche 1975-84 (seconded to Hong Kong office 1981-83), Cameron Markby 1984- (ptnr 1985); memb City of London Slr's Co; memb Law Soc; *Recreations* bridge, sailing, opera, skiing; *Clubs* Itchenor Sailing; *Style*— Roy Griggs, Esq; 2 Brechin Place, London SW7 4QA; Sceptre Court, 40 Tower Hill, London EC3 (☎ 071 702 2345, fax 071 702 2303)

GRIGSON, Dr Caroline (Mrs Colin Banks); da of Geoffrey Edward Harvey Grigson (d 1985), of Broad Town, Wiltshire, and Frances Franklin, *née* Galt (d 1937); *b* 7 March 1935; *Educ* Dartington Hall Sch, UCL (BSc), Inst of Archaeology London (PhD); *m* 18 Sept 1961, Colin Harold Banks, *qv*, of William James Banks (d 1985), of Faversham, Kent; 1 s (Joseph Caxton b 1967), 1 da (Frances Jenny Harriet b 1964, d 1978); *Career* archaeozoologist; asst curator Odontological Museum RCS 1973-87, Osman Hill curator 1987-; author of numerous scientific papers incl many on animal remains from archaeological sites in Br and the Near E; fndr memb Cncl of the Int Cncl for Archaeozoology (ICAZ); memb: Cncl Br Sch in Jerusalem, Cncl Br Inst in Amman, CBA Sci Ctee; co-organiser Fourth Int Conf in Archaeozoology Univ of London 1982, organizer Aims in Archaeozoology London Univ Inst of Archaeology 1985, former govr Kidbrooke Comprehensive Sch; memb: Prehistoric Soc, Quaternary Res Assoc, Assoc for Environmental Archaeology (AEA), Museums Assoc; FSA 1982; *Books* co-ed: Ageing and Sexing Animal Bones from Archaeological Sites (1982), Animals and Archaeology (4 vols, 1983 and 1984); Colyer's Variations and Diseases of the Teeth of Animals (jtly, 1990); *Recreations* excavation, travelling, gardening; *Style*— Dr Caroline Grigson, FSA; Odontological Museum, Royal College of Surgeons of England, 35-43 Lincoln's Inn Fields, London WC2A 3PN (☎ 071 405 3474 ext 3020, fax 071 831 9438)

GRILLER, Prof Sidney Aaron; CBE (1951); s of Salter Griller (d 1932), and Hannah, *née* Green (d 1963); *b* 10 Jan 1911; *Educ* London Co Sch, RAM; *m* 16 Dec 1932, Honor Elizabeth, da of James Linton, JP (d 1953); 1 s (Patrick Arnold), 1 da (Catherine Henry); *Career* Sgt RAF 1940-45; ldr Griller String Quartet 1924-63, lectr in music Univ of California Berkeley 1950-63, head of String Dept Royal Irish Acad of Music 1963-73, dir of chamber music RAM 1964-86; several world tours, tutor Menuhin Sch 1986-88; 20 string quartets dedicated to the Griller Quartet; Hon DUniv York; *Style*— Prof Sidney Griller, Esq, CBE; (☎ 071 937 7067)

GRILLS, His Hon Judge Michael Geoffrey; *b* 23 Feb 1937; *Educ* Royal GS Lancaster, Merton Coll Oxford (MA); *m* 1969, Ann Margaret Irene; 2 da (Alison, Victoria); *Career* ptnr Crombies, slr York 1965-73, dist registrar York and Harrogate 1973-90; rec of Crown Ct on N Eastern Circuit 1982-, dist judge 1990-; *Recreations* tennis, music; *Style*— His Hon Judge Grills; Aldwark House, Aldwark, off Goodramgate, York (☎ 0904 629935)

GRIMA, Andrew Peter; s of John Grima (d 1946), and Leopolda, *née* Farnese (descendant of Pope Paul III); *b* 31 May 1921; *Educ* St Joseph's Coll Beulah Hill London, Nottingham Univ; *m* 1977, Joanne Jill, da of Capt Nigel Maugham-Brown, MC (d 1970); 1 s, 3 da; *Career* served WW II Burma (despatches); chm Andrew Grima Ltd; jewellery designer to HM The Queen; Liveryman Worshipful Co Goldsmiths, Freeman City of London; Duke of Edinburgh Prize for Elegant Design 1966, Queen's Award for Export 1966, 11 Diamond Int Prizes New York; *Recreations* squash, tennis, cooking; *Clubs* RAC; *Style*— Andrew Grima, Esq; c/o Royal Automobile Club, 89-91 Pall Mall, London SW1

GRIMA, George Peter; s of John Grima (d 1945), and Leopolda, *née* Farnese (d 1984); *b* 31 July 1929; *Educ* St Joseph's Coll Beulah Hill, Northern Poly London (Dip Arch); *m* 14 Dec 1978, Christina Mary, da of Col Leslie Wright, TD, DL, of Bakewell, Derbyshire; *Career* Nat Serv RE 1955-57; architect; ptnr with bro Godfrey in Grima 1962-78; work incl: commercial centre Pomezia Rome 1970, ski resort Grimentz Val d'Anniviers Valais Switzerland 1972, jewellery shops for bro Andrew in London, Zurich, Sydney; worked with Raymond Erith on reconstruction of 10, 11 and 12 Downing St 1960; Royal Acad exhibitor 1970; ARIBA; *Recreations* gardening, antiquarian books, skiing, tennis; *Style*— George Grima, Esq; 33 Watery Lane, Sherbourne, Warwick CV35 8AL (☎ 0926 624 794)

GRIMALDI, Dr Barry; s of Angelo Grimaldi (d 1988), and Dorothy, *née* Coppola; *b* 10 Sept 1947; *Educ* Emanuel Sch, St Bartholemew's Hosp Med Sch and Univ of London (MB BS); *m* (m dis); *Career* RMO The London Clinic 1972-73, registrar in cardiology St Bartholemews's Hosp 1973, in private Gen Practice 1973-; med advsr Sports Cncl Working Party 1988, MRCS 1971, LRCP 1971, MRCP 1973, memb RSM 1986; *Publications* author of papers on med diagnosis and screening, and dance medicine; *Recreations* renaissance art, the oboe, riding, sky diving; *Clubs* Leander; *Style*— Dr Barry Grimaldi; 15 Harmont House, 20 Harley St, London W1N 1AL (☎ 071 631 7989, fax 071 323 5075)

GRIMBLE, Prof Michael John; s of Reginald William Parsons, of Truro, Cornwall, and Queenie Pearson; *b* 30 Oct 1943; *Educ* Rugby Coll of Engrg Technol (BSc), Imperial Coll London (PhD), Univ of Birmingham (MSc, DSc), Open Univ (BA); *m* 30 July 1966, Wendy, da of Noel Huntley (d 1975), of Grimsby; 1 s (Andrew Michael b 1977), 1 da (Claire Louise b 1975); *Career* sr engr GEC Electrical Projects 1971-75, reader in control engrg Sheffield City Poly 1975-81, prof of industl systems and dir Industrial Control Unit Univ of Strathclyde 1981-; tech dir: Industl Systems and Control Ltd 1987-, DTI Industl Club on Advanced Control Technol; over 150 papers on control systems engrg, estimation theory, etc; chm: Control Systems Soc Int Ctee IEEE (memb Bd of Govrs), Working Gp on Adaptive Systems IFAC (vice chm Control Theory Ctee); FIEE 1981, FIMA 1982, sr MIEEE 1983, FInstMC 1990; *Books* Control Systems Design II, Inst Measurement and Control (with MA Johnson and DH Owens, 1986), Optimal Control and Stochastic Estimation Vols I and II (with MA Johnson, 1988), Prentice Hall International Series on Systems and Control Engineering (ed), Prentice Hall International Series on Signal Processing (ed); *Recreations* reading; *Style*— Prof Michael Grimble; 9 Barrcraig Road, Carn Aosda, Bridge of Weir, Renfrewshire PA11 3HG; Industrial Control Unit, University of Strathclyde, Marland House, 50 George St, Glasgow G1 1QE (☎ 041 552 4400, fax 041 553 1232, telex 77472 UNSLIB G)

GRIME, Geoffrey John; s of Sqdn Ldr John Frederic Grime, DFC, of Blackpool, Lancs, and José Thompson, *née* Bennett; *b* 7 Feb 1947; *Educ* Sedbergh; *m* 19 June 1971, Margaret Joyce, da of Stanley Hamilton Russell, of St Helier, Jersey; 1 s (Charles b 1975), 1 da (Caroline b 1973); *Career* CA 1969; Coopers & Lybrand

Deloitte: joined 1969, ptnr 1972-, sr ptnr 1990; hon treas: Br Heart Fndn Jersey until 1987, Jersey Arts Cncl until 1985, Jersey Church Schs Soc 1987-; Freeman: City of London 1975, Worshipful Co of Musicians 1977; FCA 1969; *Recreations* veteran and vintage cars; *Clubs* Brooks's, Victoria (Jersey), United (Jersey), Muthaiga (Nairobi); *Style—* Geoffrey Grime, Esq; Pine Farm, Rue Du Douet, St Mary, Jersey, Channel Islands JE3 3EE (☎ 0534 36840); La Motte Chambers, St Helier Jersey, Channel Islands JE1 1BJ (☎ 0534 602000, fax 0534 602002, telex 4192231)

GRIME, Mark Stephen Eastburn; QC (1987); s of Roland Thompson, of Morfa Nefyn, and Mary Diana, *née* Eastburn; *b* 16 March 1948; *Educ* Wrekin Coll, Trinity Coll Oxford (Scholar, MA); *m* 29 July 1973, Christine, da of J H A Emck, of West Wittering, Sussex; 2 da (Eleanor b 1977, Isabel b 1981); *Career* called to the Bar Middle Temple 1970, Northern Circuit 1970-, rec 1990-; chm Disciplinary Appeal Tbnl UMIST 1980-, memb Cncl Northern Arbitration Assoc 1990-; *Recreations* antiquarian horology, sailing; *Style—* Stephen Grime, Esq, QC; Deans Court Chambers, Cumberland House, Crown Square, Manchester M3 3HA

GRIMLEY, Martyn Andrew; s of Ivor Trewartha Grimley, of Sale, Cheshire, and Shirley Elizabeth, *née* Vaughan; *b* 24 Jan 1963; *Educ* Sale GS, South Trafford Coll of Further Educn, Crewe & Alsager Coll of Higher Educn (BEd); *Career* teacher Banbury HS 1985, schoolmaster Dulwich Coll 1986-90; fin conslt Allied Dunbar 1990-; England Hockey player; Champions Trophy Tournament 1985-88, Silver medallist World Cup London 1986, Silver medallist Euro Cup Moscow 1987, Gold medallist Olympic Games Seoul 1988; *Recreations* reading, water sports, walking; *Style—* Martyn Grimley, Esq; Allied Dunbar Assurance plc, Richmond House, Runford Place, Liverpool L3 9QY (☎ 051 236 7536, fax 051 236 2591)

GRIMLEY EVANS, Prof John; s of Harry Walter Grimley Evans (d 1972), of Birmingham, and Violet Prenter, *née* Walker (d 1976); *b* 17 Sept 1936; *Educ* King Edward's Sch Birmingham, St John's Coll Cambridge (MA, MD), Balliol Coll Oxford (MA, DM); *m* 25 March 1966, Corinne Jane, da of Leslie Bernard Cavender (d 1947), of Edenbridge; 2 s (Edmund, Piers), 1 da (Freya); *Career* res fell med unit Wellington NZ 1966-69, lectr London Sch of Hygiene and Tropical Med 1969-71, conslt physician Newcastle Health Authy 1971-73, prof of med (geriatrics) Univ of Newcastle Upon Tyne 1973-84, prof of geriatric med Oxford Univ 1985- (fell Green Coll 1985-), ed Age and Ageing 1988-; FSS 1970, FRCP 1976, FFCM 1980; *Books* Care of the Elderly (jtly, 1977), Advanced Geriatric Medicine (jtly, 1981-88); *Recreations* fly fishing, photography; *Clubs* RSM; *Style—* Prof John Grimley Evans; Department of Geriatric Medicine, Radcliffe Infirmary, Oxford

GRIMOND, Hon Grizelda Jane; only da of Baron Grimond, PC, TD, by his w Laura, *née* Bonham Carter, *qqv*; *b* 1942; *Educ* St Paul's Girls' Sch, St Hugh's Coll Oxford; *Style—* The Hon Grizelda Grimond

GRIMOND, Baron (Life Peer UK 1983), of Firth, Co Orkney; Jo(seph); PC (1961), TD; s of Joseph Bowman Grimond, of St Andrew's, Fife, and Helen Lydia. *née* Richardson; *b* 29 July 1913; *Educ* Eton, Balliol Coll Oxford (hon fell 1984); *m* 1938, Hon Laura Miranda Bonham Carter (*see* Grimond, Baroness); 2 s (Hon John Jasper (*qv*), Hon (Thomas) Magnus b 13 June 1959) (and 1 s decd), 1 da (Hon Grizelda Jane b 1942); *Career* sits as Lib peer in House of Lords; served WWII: Maj, Fife and Forfar Yeo (despatches); called to the Bar Middle Temple 1937, contested (Lib) Shetland and Orkney 1945, personnel dir Euro Office UNRAA 1945-47, sec Nat Trust for Scotland 1947-49, MP (Lib) Orkney and Shetland 1950-83, chief Lib whip 1950, ldr of Parly Lib Pty 1956-67; rector: Univ of Edinburgh 1960-63, Univ of Aberdeen 1969-72; tstee Manchester Guardian and Evening News Ltd 1967-83; chllr Univ of Kent 1970-; ldr Parly Lib Pty May-July 1976; Chubb fellow Yale; Hon LLD: Edinburgh 1960, Aberdeen 1972, Birmingham, Buckingham 1983; Hon DCL Kent 1970; Hon DUniv Stirling 1984; *Publications include* The Liberal Future (1959), The Common Welfare (1978), Memoirs (1979), A Personal Manifesto (1983); *Style—* The Rt Hon the Lord Grimond, PC, TD; Old Manse of Firth, Orkney (☎ 085 676 393)

GRIMOND, Hon John Jasper; er s of Baron Grimond, TD, PC, by his w, Laura, *née* Bonham Carter *qv*; *b* 1946; *Educ* Eton, Balliol Coll Oxford, Harvard Univ (Nieman Fellow); *m* 1973, Kate, er da of Lt-Col Peter Fleming, OBE (d 1971), of Nettlebed, Henley-on-Thames; 3 da (Mary Jessie b 1976, Rose Clementine b 1979, Georgia Celia b 1983); *Career* The Economist: joined 1969, asst ed 1975-, Br ed 1976-79, American ed 1979-88, foreign ed 1989-; Harkness Fell 1974-75; *Books* The Economist Pocket Style Book (ed); *Style—* The Hon John Grimond; 49 Lansdowne Rd, London W11 2LG

GRIMOND, Baroness; Hon Laura Miranda; da of Sir Maurice Bonham Carter, KCB, KCVO, by his w, Baroness Asquith of Yarnbury, DBE (d 1969, who was Lady Violet Bonham Carter, da of 1 Earl of Oxford and Asquith, KG, PC, by his 1 w; the Earl was formerly Lib PM 1908-16); *b* 13 Oct 1918; *m* 1938, Baron Grimond, *qv*; 2 s, 1 da (and 1 s decd); *Style—* The Rt Hon the Lady Grimond; 24 Priory Avenue, London W4 1TY; The Old Manse of Firth, Kirkwall, Orkney

GRIMSBY, Bishop of 1979-; Rt Rev David Tustin; s of John Trevelyan Tustin (d 1983), and Janet Reynolds, *née* Orton; *b* 12 Jan 1935; *Educ* Solihull Sch, Magdalene Coll Cambridge (MA), Univ of Geneva; *m* 15 Aug 1964, Mary Elizabeth, da of Rev Prebendary John Moreton Glover (Prebendary of Hereford Cathedral, d 1979); 1 s (Nicholas b 1969), 1 da (Juliet b 1971); *Career* curate of Stafford 1960-63, asst gen sec C of E Cncl on Foreign Rels 1963-67; vicar: Wednesbury St Paul 1967-71, Tettenhall Regis 1971-79; rural dean of Trysull 1976-79; pres Anglican-Lutheran Soc, co-chm Anglican-Lutheran Int Cmmn; *Recreations* travel, music, European languages; *Style—* The Rt Rev the Bishop of Grimsby; Bishop's House, Church Lane, Irby upon Humber, Grimbsy DN37 7JR (☎ 0472 371715)

GRIMSHAW, Maj-Gen (Ewing) Henry Wrigley; CB (1965), CBE (1957, OBE 1954), DSO (1945); s of Lt-Col Ewing Wrigley Grimshaw (d 1916), and Geraldine Grimshaw; *b* 30 June 1911; *Educ* Brighton Coll, RMC Sandhurst; *m* 1943, Hilda Florence Agnes, da of Dr Allison (d 1942), of Coleraine, NI; 2 s (Ewing, Roland), 1 da (Hilary); *Career* joined Indian Army 1931, served war 1939-45, Western Desert, Burma, (despatches twice), transferred to The Royal Inniskilling Fus 1947, active service Malaya, Kenya, Cyprus, Suez (1956), GOC 44 Div (TA) and home counties dist 1962-65, Col The Royal Inniskilling Fus 1966-68, dep Col The Royal Irish Rangers 1968-73; *Style—* Maj-Gen Henry Grimshaw, CB, CBE, DSO; The Trellis House, Copford Green, Colchester CO6 1BZ

GRIMSHAW, Dr John Stuart; s of Neville Stuart Grimshaw (d 1978), and Sylvia May, *née* Taylor (d 1963); *b* 22 Sept 1934; *Educ* Repton, Jesus Coll Cambridge (MA), UCH Med Sch (MB BChir, DPM); *m* 12 July 1958, Anne, da of William James Vince (d 1986); 1 s (Robert b 13 March 1961), 1 da (Caroline b 14 Jan 1962); *Career* maj and sr specialist RAMC 1960-65; house physician and house surgn UCH 1959, house physician Whittington Hosp 1960, sr registrar Dept of Psychological Med St Thomas' Hosp and Knowle Hosp 1965-67, conslt psychiatrist Southampton Univ Hosps 1967-90, hon clinical tutor Univ of Southampton 1973-, chm Southampton Univ Hosps Med Exec Ctee 1977-80, chm Wessex Regnl Psychiatric Sub Ctee 1978-81, conslt rep Dist Mgmnt Team 1978-82; approval exercise convenor RCPsych 1973-77, examiner MRCPsych 1977-81 and 1983-87; memb: Panel of Observers MRCPsych exam 1987-, Central Policy Ctee Mental Health Act Cmmn 1983-89 (also second opinion doctor), memb Health Review Tbnl Wessex; FRCPE 1977, FRCPsych 1977; *Recreations* history, gardening, long distance walking and fell walking, numismatics; *Clubs* Royal Society of Medicine; *Style—* Dr John Grimshaw; The Orchard, Curdridge Lane, Curdridge, Southampton, Hampshire SO3 2BH (☎ 0489 782525); Marchwood Priory Hospital, Hythe Rd, Marchwood, Southampton S04 4WU

GRIMSHAW, Jonathan Michael; MBE (1990); s of George Brian Grimshaw (d 1989), of Whitley Bay, Tyne and Wear, and Pamela, *née* Chapman; *b* 2 April 1954; *Educ* Repton, The Kings Sch Tynemouth, Clare Coll Cambridge (BA, MA); *Career* TV prodn mangr 1981-84, co-fndr and sec of Body Positive, training offr of Nat AIDS Counselling Unit 1986-87, dir: The Landmark 1987-, Mainliners Ltd, Nat Aids Manual Ltd; memb: Inst of Med Ethics Working Party on AIDS, Prison Med Directorate AIDS Advsy Ctee; tstee: Nat AIDS Tst, Body Positive, CHART; patron of the London Lighthouse; *Recreations* travel, reading, trying to leave the office; *Style—* Jonathan Grimshaw, Esq, MBE; The Landmark, 47a Tulse Hill, London SW2 2TN (☎ 071 678 6686, fax 071 678 6825)

GRIMSHAW, Nicholas Thomas; s of Thomas Cecil Grimshaw (d 1942), and Hannah Joan, *née* Dearsley; *b* 9 Oct 1939; *Educ* Wellington, Edinburgh Coll of Art, Architectural Assoc Sch (Dip AA); *m* 20 Oct 1972, Lavinia, da of John Russell, CBE, of New York; 2 da (Chloe b 1973, Isabel b 1977); *Career* chm Nicholas Grimshaw & Ptnrs Ltd architects and industl designers; major projects incl: Channel Tunnel terminal for BR Waterloo, Br Pavillion for Expo '92 in Seville, Camden Superstore for J Sainsbury, HQ for BMW Bracknell, factory for Herman Miller Bath, Oxford Ice Rink, Gillingham Business Park for Grosvenor Devpts, res centre for Rank Xerox, printing plant for Financial Times; major awards and commendations incl: RIBA Awards 1975, 1978, 1980, 1983, 1986, 1989 and 1990, Financial Times Award for Industl Architecture 1977 and 1980, Structural Steel Design Awards 1969, 1977, 1980 and 1989, Civic Tst Award 1978, 1982, 1989 and 1990, Architectural Design Award 1974, Business and Indust Award Certificate of Merit 1977, Euro Award for Steel Structure 1981; memb: AA 1965, RIBA 1967; FCSD 1969; *Books* Nicholas Grimshaw & Partners Ltd Product and Process; *Recreations* sailing, tennis, skiing; *Style—* Nicholas Grimshaw, Esq; Nicholas Grimshaw & Partners Ltd, 1 Conway St, Fitzroy Sq, London W1P 5HA (☎ 071 631 0869, fax 071 636 4866)

GRIMSHAW, Hon Mrs (Shelagh Mary Margaret); *née* Milner; da of 1 Baron Milner, of Leeds, PC, MC, TD, (d 1967); *b* 1925; *m* 1948 (m dis 1965), Harry Barker Grimshaw; 1 s, 1 da; *Style—* The Hon Mrs Grimshaw; High Barn, Thorner, Yorks

GRIMSTON, Viscount; James Walter Grimston; s and h of 7 Earl of Verulam; *b* 6 Jan 1978; *Style—* Viscount Grimston

GRIMSTON, Hon (Cecil) Antony Sylvester; s of 1 Baron Grimston of Westbury (d 1979), and Sybil (d 1977), da of Sir Sigmund Neumann, 1 Bt; *b* 28 Feb 1927; *Educ* Eton, Magdalene Coll Cambridge (MA); *m* 1958, Dawn, da of Guy Janson, of Fair Hall, Southover, Lewes; 2 s; *Career* late Coldstream Gds; chartered surveyor, ptnr Strutt & Parker; FRSA, FRICS; *Recreations* shooting, sport; *Clubs* MCC, Naval & Military; *Style—* The Hon Antony Grimston; Wellingham Vane, nr Lewes, E Sussex (☎ 0273 812241)

GRIMSTON, Hon (Gerald) Charles Walter; 2 s of 2 Baron Grimston of Westbury and Hon June Ponsonby, da of 5 Baron de Mauley, JP; *b* 4 Sept 1953; *Educ* Eton, Univ of Exeter; *m* 10 May 1980, Katherine Evelyn, da of Maj Rupert Berkeley Kettle, DL, of Warwickshire; 2 s (Edward b 1985, Alexander b 1989); 1 da (Lucy b 1982); *Career* Maj Scots Gds 1973-83 (NI and Falklands); dir: Grimston Scott Ltd 1985-88, Woodcote Grove Estates Ltd 1988-, Heath Carroll and Partners Ltd 1988, Grimston Scott & Holman Ltd 1988-; *Recreations* cricket, skiing, real tennis; *Clubs* Royal Automobile; *Style—* Maj the Hon Charles Grimston; c/o Midland Bank, 69 Pall Mall, SW1

GRIMSTON, Hon Michael John Harbottle; yst s of 1 Baron Grimston of Westbury (d 1979); *b* 5 Jan 1932; *Educ* Eton; *m* 1957 (m dis 1978), Julia Mary, 3 da of Sir George Werner Albu, 2 Bt; 2 s, 2 da; *Clubs* Turf; *Style—* Hon Michael Grimston; Penny Hill, Bryanston, S Africa

GRIMSTON, Neil Alexander; TD (1982); s of Flt Lt Victor Gordon Manners Grimston (d 1966), and Adeline Jean Margaret Esson; *b* 8 Sept 1947; *m* 19 July 1975, Berylanne, da of David McNaught, of Thames Ditton, Surrey; 1 s (Alexander b 1979), 1 da (Henrietta b 1984); *Career* Private HAC 1970 (vet memb 1971-), cmmnd 2 Lt TA RCT 1971, Lt 1972, Capt 1976, cmd ind unit with BAOR 1977-82, Capt RARO 1983-; with Hill Samuel 1967-70, discount broker Smith St Aubyn 1970-73, discount broker Page and Gwyther Gp 1973-77, Chemical Bank 1977-, vice pres and mangr world insur gp (Asia) 1982-84, head city ints gp 1985-87, dir Chemical Bank tstee Co 1986-88, vice pres and head of Fin Insts (responsible for UK and Benelux Banks and Fin Insts) 1987-; memb Cncl London Borough of Richmond-upon-Thames 1971-74; vice chm Twickenham Cons Assoc 1969-71; memb: Lombard Assoc (City of London), approved list of Cons Party potential candidates for Westminster and Euro Parlys; chm Oxhott and Stoke Cons Assoc 1989-; Freeman City of London 1971, Liveryman Worshipful Co of Scriveners 1974; *Recreations* collecting prints, oriental rugs, wine drinking, photography; *Clubs* City Livery, Overseas Bankers, Singapore Cricket; *Style—* Neil A Grimston, Esq, TD; Willow, 29 D'Abernon Drive, Stoke D'Abernon, Cobham, Surrey KT11 3JE (☎ 0932 864973); Chemical Bank House, 180 Strand, London WC2R 1EX (☎ 071 380 5240, fax 071 380 5362, telex 264766)

GRIMSTON, Hon Robert (Robin) John Sylvester; er s and h of 2 Baron Robert Walter Sigismund (Lord Grimston of Westbury), The Old Rectory, Westwell, Burford, Oxfordshire, and June Mary, *née* Ponsonby; *b* 30 April 1951; *Educ* Eton, Reading Univ (BSc); *m* 1984, Emily Margaret, da of Maj John Evelyn Shirley, of Ormly Hall, Ramsey, IOM; *Career* Capt Royal Hussars (PWO) 1970-81; CA: Binder Hamlyn, Citicorp Scrimgeour Vickers Ltd; *Clubs* Cavalry and Guards; *Style—* The Hon Robin Grimston; 51 Alderbrook Rd, London SW12 8AD (☎ 081 673 4293)

GRIMSTON OF WESTBURY, 2 Baron (UK 1964); Sir Robert Walter Sigismund Grimston; 2 Bt (UK 1952); s of 1 Baron Grimston of Westbury (d 1979, er s of Canon Hon Robert Grimston, 3 s of 2 Earl of Verulam), and Sybil (d 1977), da of Sir Sigmund Neumann, 1 Bt (later anglicised to Newman); *b* 14 June 1925; *Educ* Eton; *m* 21 June 1949, Hon June Mary Ponsonby, er da of 5 Baron de Mauley; 2 s, 1 da; *Heir* s, Hon Robert Grimston; *Career* former Lt Scots Gds, WWII served NW Europe; formerly in oil and publishing, Hinton Hill & Coles Agencies Ltd (now Stewart Member's Agency Ltd) 1962-90; dir: Hinton Hill & Coles 1962-83, Stewart L Hughman Ltd 1983-86, River Clyde Holdings Ltd 1986-88; chm Gray's Inn (Underwriting Agency) Ltd 1970-87; Freeman City of London, Liveryman Worshipful Co of Gold and Silver Wyre Drawers; *Clubs* Boodle's, City of London; *Style—* The Rt Hon the Lord Grimston of Westbury; The Old Rectory, Westwell, Burford, Oxon OX8 4JT

GRIMSTONE, Gerald Edgar; s of Edgar Wilfred Grimstone (d 1986), and Dorothy Yvonne, *née* Martin; *b* 27 Aug 1949; *Educ* Whitgift Sch, Merton Coll Oxford (MA, MSc); *m* 23 June 1973, The Hon Janet Elizabeth Gudrun, da of 2 Baron Grantchester, CBE, QC; 1 s (Toby b 1975), 2 da (Jenny b 1979, Anna b 1982); *Career* Civil Serv 1972-86 (latterly asst sec HM Treasy), dir J Henry Schroder Wagg & Co Ltd 1986; dep chm Wimbledon House Residents Assoc 1986-88; *Recreations* shooting, skiing, children; *Clubs* Athenaeum; *Style—* Gerald Grimstone, Esq; 103 Home Park Rd,

London SW19 7HT; J Henry Schroder Wagg & Co Ltd, 120 Cheapside, London EC2V 6DS (☎ 071 382 6000)

GRIMSTONE, Hon Mrs (Janet Elizabeth Gudrun); *née* Suenson-Taylor; da of Kenneth Bent Suenson-Taylor, 2 Baron Grantchester, CBE, QC, of Kingston, Surrey; *b* 26 June 1949; *Educ* Cheltenham Ladies Coll, St Hilda's Coll Oxford (MA); *m* 1973, Gerald Edgar Grimstone, s of Edgar Wilfred Grimstone, of Sanderstead (d 1986); 1 s (Toby b 1975), 2 da (Jenny b 1979, Anna b 1982); *Career* conservator of paintings; *Recreations* fishing; *Style*— The Hon Mrs Grimstone; 103 Home Park Rd, London SW19 7HT

GRIMTHORPE, Dowager Baroness; Angela; da of Edward Courage; *b* 6 Oct 1901; *m* 1945, as his 2 w, 3 Baron Grimthorpe, TD (d 1963); 1 s (Hon William Beckett, *qv*); *Style*— The Rt Hon Dowager Lady Grimthorpe; Cross House, Ampleforth, N Yorks

GRIMTHORPE, 4 Baron (UK 1886); Sir Christopher John Beckett; 8 Bt (UK 1813), OBE (1958), DL (N Yorks, formerly E Riding, 1969), patron of 1 living; s of 3 Baron, TD (d 1963), by his 1 w Mary; through his gf's sis, Maud, Lord Grimthorpe is 2 cous of 22 Baron Hastings; *b* 16 Sept 1915; *Educ* Eton; *m* 1954, Lady Elizabeth, CVO, *née* Lumley, da of 11 Earl of Scarbrough (*see* Grimthorpe, Baroness); 2 s, 1 da; *Heir* s, Hon Edward Beckett; *Career* Brig (ret) 9 Queen's Royal Lancers, Lt-Col cmdg 1955-58, Col 9/12 Lancers 1973-77; Brig RAC HQ W Cmmd 1961-64, dep Cdr Malta & Libya 1964-67; ADC to HM The Queen 1964-68; dir: Standard Bdcasting Corp Canada (UK) Ltd 1972-83, Thirsk Racecourse Ltd 1972-, Yorkshire Post Newspapers 1973-85; *Clubs* Cavalry & Guards, Jockey; *Style*— The Rt Hon Lord Grimthorpe, OBE, DL; Westow Hall, York (☎ 065 381 225); 87 Dorset House, Gloucester Place, London NW1 (☎ 071 486 4374)

GRIMTHORPE, Baroness; Lady Elizabeth; *née* Lumley; CVO (1983); da of the late 11 Earl of Scarbrough, KG, GCSI, GCIE, GCVO, PC, TD, and Katharine, *née* McEwen, DCVO; *b* 22 July 1925; *m* 1954, 4 Baron Grimthorpe, *qv*; 2 s, 1 da; *Career* appointed lady of the bedchamber to HM Queen Elizabeth The Queen Mother 1973; *Style*— The Rt Hon the Lady Grimthorpe, CVO; Westow Hall, York (☎ 065 381 225)

GRIMWOOD, Nigel Manning; s of Maj Basil Joseph Grimwood, of Westhampnett, Sussex, and Kitty Nora, *née* Andrews (d 1986); *b* 10 March 1929; *Educ* King's Sch Ely, King's Coll London (LLB); *m* 3 Nov 1973, Diana Monica, da of Arthur Cecil Williams, of Surrey; 2 s (Toby b 1974, Hugo b 1985), 1 da (Lucy b 1976); *Career* admitted slr 1952, personal asst to Sir Archibald Forbes 1956-58, ptnr Clifford-Turner 1958-71, dir of public cos 1971-86; ret to devote more time to charitable work (particularly conservation); fndr: (with Dr Sir Norman Moore Bart) The Countryside Renewal Tst 1986, Ancient Tree Soc 1987; chm Edward Barnsley Workshop 1987; *Recreations* conservation; *Clubs* Travellers'; *Style*— Nigel Grimwood, Esq; Mayfield, Strettington, Chichester, W Sussex PO18 0LA (☎ 0243 773214)

GRINDROD, Most Rev John Basil Rowland; *see*: Brisbane, Archbishop of

GRINLING, Jasper Gibbons; CBE (1978); s of Lt-Col Anthony Gibbons Grinling, MBE, MC (d 1982), by his w Jean Dorothy Turing; *b* 29 Jan 1924; *Educ* Harrow, King's Coll Cambridge; *m* 1950, Gertrude Jane Moulsdale; 1 s, 2 da; *Career* served WWII 12 Lancers 1942-46, Capt; W & A Gilbey Ltd: joined 1947, dir 1952, md 1964; md IDV Ltd 1967; dir: N British Distillery Co 1968-86, corp affrs Grand Met Ltd 1981-85, trade relations Grand Met plc 1985-86; chm London Jazz Radio plc 1985-; vineyard proprietor; memb Cncl Scotch Whisky Assoc 1968-86; pres: EEC Confédération des Industs Agricoles et Alimentaires 1976-80, The Apple and Pear Devpt Cncl 1986-89; Chev l'Ordre National du Mérite (France) 1983; FRSA, CBIM; *Books* The Annual Report (1987); *Recreations* gardening, jazz drumming, painting; *Style*— Jasper Grinling, Esq, CBE; 94D Kensington Church St, London W8 (☎ 071 221 5377); The Old Vicarage, Helions Bumpstead, nr Haverhill, Suffolk CB9 7AS (☎ 044 084 316)

GRINSTEAD, Sir Stanley Gordon; s of Ephraim Grinstead; *b* 17 June 1924; *Educ* Strodes Sch Egham; *m* 1955, Joyce Preston; 2 da; *Career* served WW II in RN; chm and gp chief exec Grand Met plc 1982-86 (dep chm 1980-82, md 1980-86, with Grand Met 1957-62 and 1964-86), dir Reed Int plc 1981-90; tstee Fleet Air Arm Museum 1982-, Master Worshipful Co of Brewers' 1983-84; FCA, CBIM; kt 1986; *Recreations* gardening, cricket, racing, thoroughbred horse breeding; *Clubs* MCC, Surrey County Cricket; *Style*— Sir Stanley Grinstead

GRINYER, Prof John Raymond; *b* 3 March 1935; *Educ* Central Park Sch East Ham London, LSE (MSc); *m* 31 May 1958, Shirley Florence, da of Harry Alfred Marshall (d 1989), of Dagenham, Essex; 1 s (Christopher b 1967), 2 da (Julie b 1961, Sally b 1963); *Career* Nat Serv RAMC 1953-55; posts with LEB and Halifax Building Soc 1950-56, trg as CA Martin Redhead and Co, Hope Agar and Co 1956-61, sr audit asst Kemp Chatteris and Co 1962-63, lectr Harlow Tech Coll Essex 1963-66; sr lectr: City of London Poly 1967-71, Cranfield Sch of Mgmnt Bedfordshire 1971-76; Univ of Dundee 1976-: prof of accountancy and business finance, head of Dept 1976-90, dean Faculty of Law 1984-85 and 1991-; author of numerous articles in jls; chm: Assoc of Univ Teachers of Accounting 1980-81, Br Accounting Assoc 1990 (vice chm 1989), Polack Travelling Scholarship Fund Dundee; FCA 1961; *Recreations* golf, dinghy sailing; *Clubs* Royal Tay Yacht; *Style*— Prof John Grinyer; Department of Accountancy & Business Finance, The University, Dundee DD1 4HN (☎ 0382 23181, fax 0382 201604, telex 76293)

GRINYER, Prof Peter Hugh; s of Sydney George Grinyer, of Foxton, Cambs, and Grace Elizabeth, *née* Formals (d 1988); *b* 3 March 1935; *Educ* East Ham GS, Balliol Coll Oxford (BA, MA), LSE (PhD); *m* 6 Sept 1958, Sylvia Joyce, da of William James Boraston, of Chadwell Heath, Essex; 2 s (Paul Andrew b 27 July 1961, Nigel James b 12 May 1964); *Career* sr mgmnt trainee Unilever Ltd 1957-59, personal asst to md (later mangr of prodn planning and stock control) E R Holloway Ltd 1959- 61, asst lectr (later lectr and sr lectr) Hendon Coll of Technol 1961-64, lectr (later sr lectr and reader) Graduate Business Centre City Univ 1964-74, prof of business strategy City Univ Business Sch 1974-79; Univ of St Andrews: Esmee Fairbairn prof of economics 1979-85, vice princ 1985-87, actg princ 1986, actg chm Dept of Mgmnt 1987-90; memb Business and Mgmnt Studies Sub Ctee UGC 1979-85; non- exec dir: John Brown plc 1984-86, Don & Low Holdings (formerly Don Bros plc) 1985-, Ellis & Goldstein Hldgs plc 1987-88; fndr memb Glenrothes Enterprise Tst 1983-86; chm St Andrews Mgmnt Inst 1989-, chm St Andrews Strategic Management Ltd 1989-; memb: Royal Econ Soc, Scottish Econ Soc, Acad of Mgmnt, MInstD; *Books* Corporate Models Today (with J Wooller, second edn 1978), From Private to Public (with G D Vaughan and S Birley, 1977), Turnaround (with J C Spender, 1979), Sharpbenders (with D G Mayes and P McKiernan, 1988); *Recreations* golf, mountain walking; *Clubs* Royal and Ancient Golf; *Style*— Prof Peter Grinyer; Aberbrothock, 60 Buchanan Gdns, St Andrews, Fife KY16 9LX (☎ 0334 72966); University of St Andrews, Dept of Management, Kinnessburn, Kennedy Gdns, St Andrews, Fife KY16 9DJ (☎ 0334 76161)

GRISBROOKE, William Jardine; s of Joseph Henry Grisbrooke (d 1975), of Friern Barnet, Middx, and Lilian Maud, *née* Betts (d 1979); *b* 2 Feb 1932; *Educ* The Woodhouse Sch Finchley, Sidney Sussex Coll Cambridge (MA, BD); *m* 12 April 1955, Maureen, da of Albert Newton Tasker (d 1972), of Southport, Lancs; *Career* historian and theologian; lectr in theol Univ of Birmingham 1972-83 (res fell Inst for the Study of Worship and Religious Architecture 1967-72); lectr in liturgy: The Queen's Coll Birmingham 1972-80, St Mary's Coll Oscott Birmingham 1980-83; visiting lectr Pontifical Univ of Salamanca Spain 1974-80, visiting prof St George's Coll Jerusalem 1986-; author of numerous articles in jls and reviews; FRHistS; *Publications* Anglican Liturgies of the Seventeenth and Eighteenth Centuries (1958), Spiritual Counsels of Father John of Kronstadt (1967, 1981), The Liturgical Portions of the Apostolic Constitutions (1990), Dying, Death and Disposal, (contrib to symposia (1970), A Dictionary of Liturgy and Worship (1972), The Oxford Dictionary of the Christian Church (1974), The Study of Liturgy (1978), A Dictionary of Christian Spirituality (1983), The Study of Spirituality (1986), A New Dictionary of Liturgy and Worship (1986), Dizionario Patristico e di Antichità Cristiane (1985), The Unsealed Fountain: Essays in the Christian Spiritual Tradition (1987); *Recreations* music, reading, winemaking, cooking, walking, archery; *Style*— W Jardine Grisbrooke, Esq; Jokers, Bailey St, Castle Acre, King's Lynn, Norfolk PE32 2AG

GRISONI, Anthony Emilio (Tony); s of Mario Antonio Grisoni, and Peggy Winifred, *née* Domaille; *b* 28 Oct 1952; *Educ* St Peter's Sch Bournemouth, Poly of Central London (BA); *Career* mangr on commercials and pop promotion videos; writer 1984-; work cmmnd by: Zenith Film Prodns, BBC, Channel 4, German TV stations WDR and ZDF, Enterprise Pictures Ltd and various other ind cos; Queen of Hearts first full length script produced 1989; current projects incl: The Price of Love (a Thornzone Film), Gaia (a feature documentary for Brian Leith and ITEL), Fearless Heart (for The BBC), Angels-Body and Soul (for Granada TV), Scarlet Women (for Malcolm Craddock at Picture Palace); *Style*— Tony Grisoni, Esq; Linda Seifert Associates, 18 Ladbroke Terrace, London W11 3PG (☎ 071 229 5163, fax 071 229 0637)

GRIST, Graham John; s of John Alfred Grist, and Oenone Florence Muriel, *née* Butler; *b* 25 Dec 1946; *Educ* Southgate GS Herts, Ch Ch Oxford (MA), London Business Sch (Sloan Fellow 1976); *m* 3 June 1970 (m dis 1984), Deirdre Penelope, da of Joseph Robert Williams, of The Malt House, Upton on Severn, Worcestershire (d 1983); 1 s (Barnaby b 1972), 1 da (Natasha b 1975); *Career* IBM 1968-75, BICC 1977-80, fin dir Balfour Beatty 1981-86, dep chief exec British Satellite Broadcasting Ltd 1987-89; *Recreations* sailing, tennis, opera and music; *Clubs* United Oxford and Cambridge Univ; *Style*— Graham Grist, Esq; 49 Markham St, London SW3 3NR (☎ 071 351 1228)

GRIST, Ian; MP (C) Cardiff Central 1983-; s of the late Basil William Grist, MBE, and the late Leila Helen Grist; *b* 5 Dec 1938; *Educ* Repton, Jesus Coll Oxford; *m* 1966, Wendy Anne, *née* White, JP; 2 s; *Career* former plebiscite offr S Cameroons and stores mangr United Africa Co in Nigeria; info offr Wales Cons Central Office 1963-74, CRD 1970-74; MP (C) Cardiff N Feb 1974-83; chm Cons W Africa Ctee 1977-87, vice chm Cons Clubs Assoc 1978-82, PPS to Nicholas Edwards (sec of state Wales) 1979-81, parly under sec of state for Wales 1987-90; *Style*— Ian Grist, Esq, MP; 126 Penylan Rd, Cardiff; House of Commons, London SW1

GRIST, John Frank; s of late Capt Austin Grist, OBE, MC, and late Ada Mary Grist; *b* 10 May 1924; *Educ* Elizabeth Coll Guernsey, Ryde Sch IOW, St Edmund Hall Oxford, LSE, Univ of Chicago; *m* 8 Nov 1952, Christine Gilian (Jill), da of late Roger Cramage; 1 s (William Jonathan), 2 da (Caroline Anne, Nicola Helen); *Career* pilot RAF 1942-46 (ops coastal cmd 1944-45, latterly Flt Lt); BBC 1951-81: radio prodr North American Service 1951-53, Nigerian Broadcasting Serv 1953-56, prodr and ed of political progs 1957-81, head of Television Current Affrs 1967-71, controller English Regions 1972-78, American Rep New York 1978-81, md services Sound & Vision Corp 1981-88, broadcasting supervisor House of Commons 1989-; govr Royal Star & Garter Home Richmond; Press fell Wolfson Coll Cambridge; FRTS 1986; *Recreations* fell walking; *Clubs* Reform; *Style*— John Grist, Esq; House of Commons, London SW1 (☎ 071 219 5848/9)

GRIST, Prof Norman Roy; s of Walter Reginald Grist (d 1970), of Rothbury, Northumberland, and Florence Goodwin, *née* Nadin (d 1983); *b* 9 March 1918; *Educ* Shawlands Acad Glasgow, Univ of Glasgow (BSc, MB ChB); *m* 27 Feb 1943, Mary Stewart, da of Alexander McAlister (d 1926), of Cupertino, California; *Career* Univ of Glasgow: lectr in virus diseases 1952-62, reader in viral epidemiology 1962-65, prof of infectious diseases 1965-83; regnl advsr in virology to Scot Western Regnl Hosp Bd 1960-74, head regnl virus laboratory Ruchill Hosp Glasgow 1958-83; memb: Expert Advsy Panel on Virus Diseases WHO 1967-, BRAB of DSAC; pres: Br Soc for the Study of Infection 1982-83, Soc for the Study of Infectious Diseases 1971-72; chm Advsy Gp on Epidemiological and Other Aspects of Infection SHS Planning Cncl 1975-; memb: Jt Cmmn on Vaccination and Immunisation DHSS 1970-83, Dangerous Pathogens Advsy Gp 1978-80; memb Ctee Glasgow Branch Scot Ornithology Club 1984-, gen sec Glasgow Natural History Soc 1989- (memb Cncl 1988-); memb: Soc Gen Microbiology, Assoc Clinical Pathologists (hon memb 1989-), Br Soc for the Study of Infection, Pathological Soc of GB and Ireland; MRCPEd 1950, FRCPEd 1958, MRCPath 1959, FRCPath 1967, MRCP (Glasgow) 1980, FRCP (Glasgow) 1983; Orden Civ de Sanidad cat Encomienda Spain 1974, Bronze Medal Univ of Helsinki 1973; *Books* Diagnostic Methods in Clinical Virology (jtly, 3 edn 1979), Infections in Current Medical Practice (with Reid and Pinkerton, 1986), Diseases of Infection (jtly, 1988); *Recreations* music, natural history; *Clubs* Royal Scottish Automobile; *Style*— Prof Norman Grist; 5A Hyndland Ct, Glasgow G12 9NR (☎ 041 339 5242); Communicable Diseases Unit, Ruchill Hospital, Glasgow G20 9NB (☎ 041 946 7120, telex 776373, fax 041 946 4359)

GROB, Prof Paul Richard; s of Oscar Grob (d 1975), and Kathleen Ann, *née* Hogan; *b* 11 Feb 1936; *Educ* Guy's Hosp, Univ of London; *m* 1 July 1961, June, da of Herbert Fawcett (d 1957), of Zanzibar, Tanzania; 1 s (Stephen b 1963), 1 da (Catharine b 1962); *Career* visiting prof of gen practice and health care res Univ of Surrey 1980, chm Int Primary Care Network 1986, Lasdon Visiting Prof RSM Fndn 1987, pres Compton Heavy Horse Appreciation Soc; FRCGP, FRSM; *Recreations* sailing; *Style*— Prof Paul Grob; Abbots Garden, Eastbury Lane, Compton, Surrey GU3 1EE (☎ 0483 810410); Robens Institute, University of Surrey, Guildford (☎ 0483 38005, fax 0483 34154, telex 859331 UNIVSY G)

GROBBELAAR, Bruce David; s of Hendrik Gabriel Grobbelaar (d 1981), of Benlow, SA, and Beryl Eunice, *née* Banning; *b* 6 Oct 1957; *Educ* Mount Pleasant HS Hamilton Bulawayo; *m* 7 July 1983, Deborah Jane, da of Cecil Bernard Sweetland, of Ubley, Avon; 2 da (Tahli Mellisa b 6 Aug 1984, Olivia Gabrielle b 17 March 1988); *Career* Corpl 5 Ind Coy Rhodesian Army 1975-77; U13 and U14 cricket Rhodesian Fawns, U16 baseball Rhodesia and record holder for pitching strike outs, U16 soccer Rhodesia and N America Soccer League Champions 1979, goalkeeper Liverpool FC; English league champions 5 times, Milk and League Cup winners 3 times FA Cup winners twice, Euro Cup winners once, World Club Champions Cup finalist twice; memb Lords Taverners, involved with Variety Club of GB and with the blind on Merseyside; Freeman City of Vancouver 1979; memb Professional Footballers' Assoc; *Books* More Than Somewhat (with B Harris, 1986), Bring on the Clown (with B Harris, 1988); *Recreations* cricket, tennis, golf, squash, clay pigeon shooting; *Clubs* Heswall Golf, The Lord Taverners; *Style*— Bruce Grobbelaar, Esq; Novar, Tower Road North, Heswall, Wirral, Merseyside L60 6RT; Liverpool Football Club, Anfield Rd, Liverpool L4 OTH (☎ 051 260 3169)

GROBLER, Richard Victor; s of Harry Steyn Grobler (d 1970), and Edith Alice Grobler (d 1982); *b* 27 May 1936; *Educ* Diocesan Coll (Bishops) Cape Town, Univ of Cape Town (BA); *m* 1961, Julienne Nora Delacour, da of late Rev Canon Laurie Sheath; 1 s (Andrew b 1970), 3 da (Caroline b 1963, Rosemary b 1966, Elizabeth b 1975); *Career* barr Gray's Inn; dep clerk Central Criminal Ct 1970-72, dep courts admin 1972-74; courts admin: Inner London Crown Ct 1974-77, Centl Criminal Ct 1977-79; dep circuit admin SE Circuit 1979-84; dep sec of Cmmns Lord Chancellor's Dept 1984-; Liveryman Worshipful Co of Gold & Silver Wyre Drawers; *Recreations* gardening, swimming, golf; *Clubs* Temple Golf; *Style—* Richard Grobler, Esq; 26 Old Queen Street, London SW14 9HP (☎ 071 210 3479)

GROCHOLSKI, Count Alexander Luan; er s of Count Kazimierz Adam Grocholski, *qv*; *b* 30 Aug 1949; *Educ* French Lycée London, Study Centre for the History of the Fine and Decorative Arts London; *m* 1979, Bridget Caroline, da of Capt John Hamilton Fleming (d 1971); 1 da (Katherine Rose Mary b 1980); *Career* Phillips Son & Neale Ceramics Dept 1969-73, Sotheby's Valuation Dept 1973-78; Grocholski & Co Fine Art Valuers and Consultants 1978-; *Recreations* reading, walking, travel; *Clubs* Polish Hearth (London); *Style—* Count Alexander Grocholski; 27 Baalbec Road, London N5 1QN (☎ 071 226 8806)

GROCHOLSKI, Count Kazimierz Adam; yr s of Zdzislaw Henryk, Count Grocholski (d 1968), of Pietniczany and Poniatow, Poland, and Maria, *née* Countess Soltan; yr br and hp of Count Stanislas Bohdan Karol Grocholski, *qv*; *b* 21 Jan 1917; *Educ* Bielany Coll, Warsaw Univ, LSE; *m* 1, 1946 (m dis 1969, annulled 1981), Elzbieta Zofia (d 1987), da of Count Jerzy Bawrowski (d 1933); 2 s (Alexander, *qv*, Jacek), 2 da (Ida, Thea); *m* 2, 15 March 1989, Madame Anna (Nita) Mueller, *née* Svertschkov; *Career* Pilot Offr Polish Air Force; external rels offr Union of Polish Craftsmen and Workers in GB; editorial sec Polish Emigre Weekly; prog asst BBC Polish Section; freelance journalist and writer; *Recreations* reading, music, theatre, travel, swimming; *Clubs* Polish Air Force, Polish Hearth; *Style—* Count Kazimir Grocholski; 111 The Ave, London W13 8JT (☎ 081 997 3560); Flat 15, 169 Queen's Gate, London SW7 5HE; Villa Pampa, Ruetistrasse 16, CH-8702 Zollikon ZH, Switzerland

GROCHOLSKI, Count Stanislas Bohdan Karol; head of the family; s of Zdzislaw Henryk, Count Grocholski (d 1968), of Pietniczany and Poniatow, Poland, and Maria, *née* Countess Soltan (of an ancient Lithuanian-Ruthenian family of which Alexander Soltan, Treasurer and Court Marshal of the Gd Duchy of Lithuania, was a royal envoy to the courts of Europe in 15 cent); descendant of ancient Polish nobility of the Syrokomla clan known since 1347, who fought under their family banner at Grunwald against the Teutonic Knights in 1410, under the walls of Vienna against the Turks in 1683 and, after moving to Podolia in the 17 cent produced, among others, Martin, Palatine of Braclaw and Mikolaj, Govr of Podolia; gf Count Stanislaw Grocholski and his bro Count Tadeusz m Countesses Wanda and Zofia Zamoyska, while their sister Countess Maria m Prince Witold Czartoryski and as a widow entered the Carmelite Order; hereditary title of Count confirmed in Russia 1881; er br of Count Kazimierz Adam Grocholski, *qv*; *b* 4 Nov 1912; *Educ* Bielany Coll, Univ of Warsaw (MA), Warsaw Acad of Political and Social Studies; *m* 1980, Elisabeth Victoria Adelaide, da of Albert Edouard Janssen (d 1966), Belgian Min of State, and wid of Count Thaddée Plater-Zyberk; *Heir* br, Count Kazimierz Adam Grocholski, *qv*; *Career* Reserve Offr Polish Forces, vice consul Marseilles 1938-40, consul Dublin 1945-46, gen sec Fedn of Poles in Britain 1946-51, vice pres Anglo-Polish Soc 1955-, foreign affairs ed The Polish Daily 1959-74; chm Veritas Foundation 1965-89, vice chm and Polish rep The Euro Movement 1953-60, vice-chm Euro Liaison Gp 1970-; memb Catholic Union of Gt Britain 1972-; *Recreations* riding, tennis, swimming, travel; *Clubs* Special Forces, POSK (London); *Style—* The Count Grocholski; 111 The Avenue, London W13 8JT; Château de Valduc, 1320 Hamme-Mille, Belgium

GROCOTT, Bruce Joseph; MP (Lab) The Wrekin 1987-; s of Reginald Grocott; *b* 1 Nov 1940; *Educ* Univ of Leicester, Univ of Manchester; *m* 1965, Sally Barbara, *née* Ridgway; 2 s; *Career* lectr in politics 1965-74, television journalist and prodr Central Television 1979-87; MP (Lab) Lichfield and Tamworth 1974-79 pps to Min for Local Govt Planning 1975-76, Min of Agric 1976-78), currently dep shadow leader of the House and dep campaigns co-ordinator; *Clubs* Trench Labour; *Style—* Bruce Grocott, MP; House of Commons, London SW1A 0AA

GRODEN, Dr Bernard Melville; s of Louis Groden (d 1979), and Esther, *née* Goldberg (d 1978); *b* 1 Nov 1933; *Educ* Hutchesons Boys GS, Univ of Glasgow (MB ChB, MD); *m* 8 April 1964, Patricia Ruth, da of Cecil Freeman, of 1A Netherton Court, Newton Mearns, Glasgow; 3 da (Laura Rochelle b 1965, Carolyn Anne b 1967, Wendy Lorraine b 1969); *Career* conslt physician and cardiologist: Ballchmyle Hosp 1971-82, Crosshouse Hosp 1982-; hon clinical sub dean Univ of Glasgow 1988 (hon clinical lectr 1985); memb Br Cardiac Soc; chm: Mearns Community Cncl 1976-83, Eastwood Advanced Drivers Assoc 1983-87, Broom Cons Assoc 1986-89; memb BMA, FRCP Glasgow 1972, FRCPE 1974; *Recreations* sailing, golf, photography; *Style—* Dr Bernard Groden; 7 Broom Road East, Newton Mearns, Glasgow G77 5RQ (☎ 041 639 4432); Crosshouse Hospital, Kilmarnock (☎ 0563 21133)

GROGONO, James Lyon; s of Dr Eric Bernard Grogono, and Clare Anderton Gregono, JP, *née* Jolly; *b* 5 July 1937; *Educ* Oundle, London Hosp Med Coll London (MB BS); *m* 21 April 1972, Catherine Margaret, da of Dr Richard Bertram Morton, of 6 Hawk's Road, Hailsham, E Sussex; 1 s (Angus b 1974), 2 da (Emma b 1973, Dorothy b 1981); *Career* conslt surgn Wycombe Health Dist, surgical tutor RCS Eng; author; chm Windsurfing Ctee Royal Yachting Assoc, vice chm Multihull Ctee Iant Yacht Racing Union; FRCS, LRCP, DCH; *Books* Hydrofoil Sailing (1972), Icarus: The Boat the Flies (1987); *Recreations* sailing, wind surfing, sculling, skiing, skating, tennis, unicycling; *Clubs* Aldeburgh Yacht, Leander, Chiltern Med Soc; *Style—* James Grogono, Esq; The Garden House, Riverside, Marlow, Bucks (☎ 062848 4261)

GRONHAUG, Arnold Conrad; s of James Gronhaug, MBE (d 1951), and Beatrice May, *née* Guppy (d 1983); *b* 26 March 1921; *Educ* Barry GS, Cardiff Tech Coll (Dip Electrical Engrg); *m* 28 March 1945, Patricia Grace, da of Douglas Leslie Smith (d 1963), of Brighton; 2 da (Anne b 1946, Jennifer b 1952); *Career* electrical offr RNVR 1941-46; Air Miny Works Directorate 1946-63 (dep chief engrg (AMWD) RAF Germany 1960-63), Miny of Public Bldg and Works 1963-73 (JSSC 1964-65, superintending engr HQ 1967-71, dir Def Works Overseas 1971-73), Property Servs Agency DOE 1973-81 (dir Social and Res Servs 1973-75, dir and under sec Mechanical & Electrical Engrg Servs 1975-81); memb Nominations Ctee Engrg Cncl 1983-, chm Membership Ctee IEE 1979-82 (memb 1975-82), membership advsr IEE Surrey 1984-, memb Qualifications Bd CIBSE 1981-87; Freeman City of London 1979, Liveryman Worshipful Co of Engrs 1984; CEng, FIEE 1964, FCIBSE 1976, Hon FCIBSE 1980; *Recreations* photography, music; *Style—* Arnold Gronhaug, Esq; 6 Pine Hill, Epsom, Surrey KT18 7BG (☎ 0372 721888)

GRONOW, Dr Michael; s of Vivian Gronow (d 1970), and Mary Amelia, *née* Chappell; *b* 26 July 1937; *Educ* Cardiff HS, Univ Coll of S Wales (BSc), Trinity Coll Cambridge (PhD); *m* 20 Dec 1968, Janet Ruth, da of Guy Tomkins, of Ockley, Surrey; 1 s (Simon Richard b 19 March 1972), 1 da (Kathryn Louise b 26 Dec 1973); *Career* Univ of Cambridge: MRC res asst Dept of Radiotherapeutics 1963-65, demonstrator Dept of Chem 1962-65; res assoc Dept of Pharmacology Baylor Univ Houston Texas USA 1965-66, res assoc and demonstrator Dept of Biochem Univ of Oxford 1966-69, lectr Dept of Experimental Pathology and Cancer Res Univ of Leeds 1969-75, permanent sr res fell Cancer Res Unit Univ of York 1975-79; conslt PA Tech Centre Int 1979-80, head of biosciences PA Centre for Advanced Studies 1980-81, jt md and fndr Cambridge Life Science plc 1981-88, md CRL Ltd 1989, dir Aquamarine Sciences and Cambridge Phenomenom Promotions 1989; author of 50 pubns; memb: Biochemical Soc 1967, Br Assoc Cancer Res 1969; *Recreations* music, photography, hockey, chess, wine; *Style—* Dr Michael Gronow; Thornton House, 131 Waterbeach Rd, Landbeach, Cambridge CB4 4EA; Cambridge Research Laboratories, 181A Huntingdon Rd, Cambridge CB3 0DJ (☎ 0223 277744, fax 0223 276444)

GROOM, Brian William Alfred; s of Fred Groom (d 1978), of Manchester, and Muriel Edith, *née* Linfoot; *b* 26 April 1955; *Educ* Manchester GS, Balliol Coll Oxford (BA); *m* 1980, Carola May, da of Peter Withington; 1 s (Jack Edward b 4 Oct 1984), 1 da (Elinor Rose b 6 Aug 1987); *Career* trainee reporter and sports ed Goole Times 1976-78; Financial Times: Syndication Dept 1978-79, sub ed int edn 1979-81, labour reporter and mgmnt feature writer 1981-85, UK news ed 1985-88; dep ed Scotland on Sunday 1988-; Pfizer award NCTJ 1978; *Recreations* cricket, reading, hillwalking, cinema; *Style—* Brian Groom, Esq; 15 Gloucester Place, Edinburgh EH3 6EE (☎ 031 226 4295); Scotland on Sunday, 20 North Bridge, Edinburgh EH1 1YT (☎ 031 243 3485, fax 031 220 2443)

GROOM, Jeremy Richard; s of Peter Farrant Groom, of Walton on Thames, and Anne, *née* Dainty; *b* 2 May 1948; *Educ* King's Sch Canterbury, Lincoln Coll Oxford; *m* 9 April 1983, Jennifer, da of Sir Norman Richard Rowley Brooke, CBE, (d 1989), of Cardiff; 1 s (Pelham b 1989), 1 da (Camilla b 1984); *Career* joined Seymour Pierce and Co (memb Stock Exchange) 1972 (ptnr 1977-87), dir Seymour Pierce Butterfield Ltd 1987-; memb Stock Exchange 1975; *Recreations* music, theatre, cricket; *Clubs* MCC, Riverside Racquets; *Style—* Jeremy Groom, Esq; 32 Blandford Rd, Chiswick, London W4 1DX (☎ 081 994 8663); Seymour Pierce Butterfield Ltd, 10 Old Jewry, London EC2R 8EA (☎ 071 628 4981, fax 071 606 2405, telex 8811530)

GROOM, Maj-Gen John Patrick; CB (1984), CBE (1975, MBE 1963); s of Samuel Douglas Groom (d 1975), and Gertrude Groom, *née* Clinton; *b* 9 March 1929; *Educ* King Charles Sch Kidderminster, Rugby, RMA Sandhurst, Staff Coll Camberley, RCDS; *m* 1951, Jane Mary, da of Thomas Miskelly (d 1937); 3 da (Susan, Maryanne, Josephine); *Career* served Br Army N Africa, Egypt, UK, Aden, BAOR, Malaya, Singapore, Cyprus 1949-83 (despatches 1965); Col Cmdt Corps RE 1983, rep Col Cmdt 1986; dir gen Guide Dogs for the Blind Assoc 1983-89, vice pres Int Fedn Guide Dog Schs; Liveryman Worshipful Co of Plumbers; *Recreations* sailing (Anahita), ornothology, country pursuits; *Clubs* Royal Ocean Racing, Army & Navy, Royal Lymington Yacht; *Style—* Maj-Gen John Groom, CB, CBE; Bridge End Cottage, Walhampton, Lymington, Hants SO41 5RD (☎ 0590 675710)

GROOM, Michael John; s of Thomas Rowland Groom (d 1984), of Wolverhampton, and Elizabeth Groom (d 1971); *b* 18 July 1942; *Educ* St Chad's GS Wolverhampton, Cotton Coll N Staffs; *m* 4 June 1966, Sheila Mary, da of Harold Cartwright, of Wolverhampton; 2 da (Nichola b 1971, Sally b 1975); *Career* CA; Michael Groom & Co 1971-76 and 1981-, Tansley Witt 1976-80, Binder Hamlyn 1980-81, dir Professional Enterprise Group, lectr mgmnt and legistlation; ed 1975-81: Chartac Accounting Manual, Chartac Auditing Manual, Chartac Taxation Manual, Chartac Accounting and Auditing Model File; Financial Management in the Professional Office 1977, Cash Control in the Smaller Business 1978, Budgeting and Cash Management 1981; hon treas ICAEW (cncl memb 1975-); dep chm St Dominic's Ind Sch for Girls; Freeman Worshipful Co of CAs; FCA 1964; *Books* Chartac Adminstration Manual (1975); *Recreations* tennis, squash, photography, dog obedience training; *Clubs* Wolverhampton Lawn Tennis and Squash; *Style—* Michael Groom, Esq; 10 Clarendon St, Wolverhampton WV3 9PP (☎ 0902 773644)

GROOTENHUIS, Prof Peter; s of Johannes Christiaan Grootenhuis (d 1986), and Anna Christina van den Bergh; *b* 31 July 1924; *Educ* Netherlands Lyceum The Hague, Imperial Coll London (BSc Eng, DIC, PhD, DScENG); *m* 7 Aug 1954, Sara Joan, da of Maj Charles Campbell Winchester, MC, The Royal Scots (The Royal Regt) RR (ka 1940); 1 s (Hugh John b 30 April 1958), 1 da (Carol Felicity b 2 June 1955); *Career* apprenticeship rising to asst project engr Bristol Aero Engine Co Bristol 1944-46; Imperial Coll London: lectr in mech engrg 1946-59, reader in mech engrg 1959-72, prof 1972- (latterly emeritus prof), sr res fell 1989-, memb Bd of Studies of Civil and Mech Engrg 1959-89, memb Engrg Bd of Studies 1972-89, memb Governing Body Imperial Coll 1974-79; fndr Derriton Electronics Ltd 1960 (later tech dir Derriton Ltd), dir Derriton Environmental Systems Ltd 1981-84; ptnr Grootenhuis Allaway Associates (constg engrs) 1969-; conslt: Binnie and Partners 1962-64, Royal Armament R & D Estab 1963-64, Absorbit Ltd 1964-69, City of London Corp 1964-, Arup Assocs 1965-67, MOD 1965-84, Esso Chemicals Ltd 1968 and 1971, Union Electrica Madrid 1976-81; memb: Special Advsy Bd in Ergonomics Univ of London 1966-89 BSI Ctees 1967-, Ed Advsy Bd Journal of Environmental Engrg 1969-89 (chm 1974-89), jt MechE/Dutch Working Pty on Educn 1979-81; external examiner: The Coll of Technol Dublin 1971-79, Univ of Lagos Nigeria 1972-75, Univ of Bristol 1979-81; FIMechE 1979 (MIMechE 1952); Soc of Environmental Engrs: fndr memb 1959, fell 1964, pres 1964-67; MIM 1956-76, memb Br Acoustical Soc (now Inst of Acoustics) 1965 (memb Provisional Cncl 1964-66), AFRAeS 1950-75; Fell City and Guilds of London Inst 1976; F Eng 1982; chm: Imperial Coll Wine Ctee 1975-89, Knightsbridge Branch Cons Pty Assoc 1974-77; pres: Old Centralians 1988-89; *pubns* over 70 pubns in learned jls; *Recreations* gardening, sailing; *Clubs* Athenaeum; *Style—* Prof Peter Grootenhuis; Imperial College of Science, Technology & Medicine, Department of Mechanical Engineering, Exhibition Rd, London SW7 2BX (☎ 071 589 5111 ext 6144, fax 071 823 8845)

GROSBERG, Prof Percy; s of Rev Gershon Grosberg (d 1970), of Johannesburg and Tel Aviv, and Pearl, *née* Ornstein (d 1986); *b* 5 April 1925; *Educ* Parktown Boys' HS Johannesburg, Univ of the Witwatersrand (BSc, MSc, PhD), Univ of Leeds; *m* 5 Sept 1951, Queenie, da of Rabbi Dr Solomon Fisch (d 1985), of Leeds; 2 s (Jonathan b 25 Jan 1953, d 1980, David b 28 Jan 1957), 1 da (Gillian (Mrs Braunold) b 15 Aug 1955); *Career* sr res offr South African Wool Res Inst 1949-55; Univ of Leeds: lectr Dept of Textile Indust 1955-61, res prof of textile engrg 1961-90, head of Dept of Textile Indust 1973-83 and 1987-89; author of many papers in textile and other scientific jls; visiting prof Shenkar Coll of Textile Technol and Fashion Israel 1984; chm Leeds Friends of Bar-Ilan Univ Ramat-Gan Israel 1963-, rep of Chief Rabbi on Ct of Univ of Bradford, visiting expert for UNIDO to the Inst of Fibres and Forest Products Res Jerusalem 1969; Warner Meml Medal 1968, Textile Inst Medal 1972; MIMechE 1965, hon fell Textile Inst 1988 (fell 1966); Distinguished Serv Award Indian Inst of Technol Delhi 1986; *Books* An Introduction to Textile Mechanisms (1968), Structural Mechanics of Fibres, Yarns And Fabrics (1969); *Style—* Prof Percy Grosberg; 2 Sandringham Crescent, Leeds LS17 8DF (☎ 0532 687478); 3 Shilo St, Tel Aviv 64688, Israel; Dept of Textile Industries, Univ of Leeds, Leeds LS2 9JT

GROSE, Vice Admiral Sir Alan; KBE (1989); s of George William Stanley George (d 1986), and Anne May, *née* Stanford (d 1954); *b* 24 Sept 1937; *Educ* Strodes Sch, Britannia RNC Dartmouth; *m* 2 Sept 1961, Gillian Ann, da of Cdre Richard Paul

Dryden Dymond, of Simonstown, Cape Province, SA; 2 s (Jeremy b 1964, Matthew b 1968), 1 da (Sarah b 1969); *Career* Lt S Atlantic and Med 1957-67, qualified naval specialist 1964, Lt Cdr Home and Med Fleets 1967-71, Cdr 1972, Capt 1977; CO: HMS Eskimo 1974-75, HMS Bristol 1980-82, HMS Illustrious 1984-86; Rear Adm 1986, appointed to Def Staff MOD 1986-88, Flag Offr Flotilla Three 1988-1990, Vice Adm 1989, Flag Offr Plymouth 1990; pres RN and RM Rowing Assoc, Anchorite Assoc; RUSI 1964-, RCDS 1980; *Recreations* tennis, gardening, rowing (spectator); *Style*— Vice Adm Sir Alan Grose, KBE; c/o Barclays Bank, Princess Street, Plymouth, S Devon (☎ 0752 263333)

GROSE-HODGE, Peter Humfrey; s of Geoffrey Goldingham Grose-Hodge (d 1952), of Bedford, and Dorothy May, *née* Haydon; *b* 18 Dec 1929; *Educ* Bedford Sch, Rondebosch Coll Cape Town SA; *m* 25 June 1955, Jane, da of William Stanley Grossmith (d 1953), of Rustington, Sussex; 1 s (Simon Jeffrey b 29 Oct 1962), 1 da (Anne Susan b 15 Oct 1960); *Career* admitted slr 1952; ptnr: Speechly Bircham 1962-, Druces & Attlee 1990; memb: Holborn Law Soc, Law Soc Ctee on Family Law 1983-; pres Int Acad Matrimonial Lawyers 1989 memb Law Soc; *Recreations* motoring, gliding; *Clubs* Surrey and Hants Gliding, Ferrari Owners; *Style*— Peter Grose-Hodge; Brook End, Gosden Common, Bramley, Surrey GU5 0AE; Druces & Attlee, Salisbury House, London Wall, London EC2M 5PS (☎ 071 638 9271, fax 071 628 7525, telex 895 6278)

GROSS, Howard Anthony; s of Harold Victor Gross, of Southgate, and Pamela Alicia Tamara, *née* Rosen; *b* 24 May 1948; *Educ* Minchenden Sch, City of London Coll; *m* 4 Nov 1973, Beverley Myra, da of Bennett Teff, of Mill Hill; 2 da (Zoë b 1975, Amanda b 1978); *Career* CA; ptnr Gross Klein & Co 1968-; chm: fndr Hartley (now Paxus) Computer User Gp 1979-82, North London CAs 1984-85, Heathfield Sch Parent's Assoc (GPDST) 1985-89; London Soc ICA memb 1984, chm PR Ctee 1986-88, chm Advice and Servs Ctee 1988-89, chm memb Relations Ctee 1989-90, hon treas 1990-; Freeman City of London 1990; FCA 1971, ATII 1972, FCCA 1980; *Recreations* jogging (completed London marathon 1989); *Style*— Howard Gross, Esq; Gross Klein & Company, 6 Breams Buildings, London EC4A 1HP (☎ 071 242 2212, fax 071 404 4412)

GROSS, Dr Jeremy Martin; s of Donald Gross, and Sylvia, *née* Nussbaum; *b* 11 Nov 1939; *Educ* Spring Grove GS, Univ of Leicester (BSc, PhD); *m* 1, (m dis 1974), Diane Rose, *née* Jackson; 1 da (Deborah Sara b 20 Sept 1969); m 2, 1976, (m dis 1989), Pamela Margaret, *née* Davey; m 3, 1989, Diana Christine, da of Clement Trill; *Career* sr lectr (lectr) Sir John Cass Coll Univ of London 1965-69; mangr: GEC Computers 1969-71, ICL 1971-73; Triad Systems 1973-74; Data Logic 1974-90: chief conslt, tech dir, tech and mktg dir, divnl md; Independent Computer Consultant 1990-, Br Computer Soc, Computer Servs Assoc; Industl Advsry Gp: Brunel Univ, UMIST; various articles and chapters on computing; FRIC 1963, MBCS 1970, FInstD 1989; *Books* Principles of Physical Chemistry (1971); *Recreations* music, sport; *Clubs* Cricketers' London, IOD; *Style*— Dr Jeremy Gross; Lion Lodge North, Church Lane, Stoke Poges, Bucks SL2 4NZ (☎ 0753 21063)

GROSS, John Jacob; s of Abraham and Muriel Gross; *b* 12 March 1935; *Educ* City of London Sch, Wadham Coll Oxford; *m* 1965, Miriam May, *qv*, da of Kurt; 1 s, 1 da; *Career* former asst lectr London Univ, fellow King's Coll Cambridge 1962-65, literary ed New Statesman 1973, ed Times Literary Supplement 1974-81, tstee Nat Portrait Gallery 1977-84, dep chm George Weidenfeld & Nicolson Ltd 1982-83, staff writer NY Times 1983-89, theatre critic Sunday Telegraph 1990-; *Books* The Rise and Fall of the Man of Letters (1969, awarded Duff Cooper Meml Prize), Joyce (1971), The Oxford Book of Aphorisms (ed, 1983); *Style*— John Gross, Esq; 74 Princess Court, Queensway, London W2 4RE

GROSS, Dr Manfred Ferry; s of Leon Gross (d 1965), of London, and Else, *née* Schönfeld (d 1949); *b* 22 Dec 1907; *Educ* Das Graue Kloster Berlin Germany, Univs of: Berlin, Heidelberg, Würzburg and Edinburgh (MD, LRCP, LRCS, LRFPS (Edinburgh)); *m* 17 Aug 1963, Sylvia Edna, da of Lieut Patrick Webb (ka 1917); *Career* WWII despatches (Burma) 1945; res worker and conslt physician; worked as Br expatriate in Germany: Hufeland Hosp Berlin 1933-34, Virchow Hosp Berlin 1934-35, Hosp Persische Strasse Berlin 1935-36, Kerckoff Res Inst Bad Nauheim 1936-38; New End Hosp London 1942; War Serv RAMC 1943-46: 112 Br Gen Hosp India, 23 Indian Casualty Clearing Station Burma, cmd offr Mil Hosp Kodaicanal Mysore S India; hon conslt cardiologist New End Hosp London 1948-51, res work (with Prof Paul Niehans, Vevey, Switzerland) into Xenogenic cell implants (Cell Therapy) 1952-, res work into therapeutic application of ozone in cardio-vascular and other diseases 1965-; memb BMA 1942, FRSM 1952; memb: Med Assoc for Organo-Biotherapy (Germany) 1964, Med Assoc for Ozone Therapy (Germany) 1970; *Recreations* music and drawing cartoons; *Style*— Dr Manfred Ferry Gross; 3 Loom Place, Radlett, Hertfordshire WD7 8AF (☎ 0923 856339); 127 Harley St, London W1N 1DJ (☎ 071 224 5915)

GROSS, Dr Michael Lester Phillip; s of Harold Victor Gross, of Taemar, Abbotshall Ave, Southgate, and Pamela Alicia Tamar, *née* Rosen; *b* 31 March 1952; *Educ* Minchenden Sch Southgate, Sidney Sussex Coll Cambridge (BA, MA, MB BChir, MD), The London Hosp Med Coll; *m* 30 July 1974, Jennifer Ruth, da of Lawrence Hoffman, of 1 Lodge Close, Edgware, Middx; 2 da (Louise b 1977, Jemma b 1981); *Career* sr resident The Nat Hosp 1983-85, sr registrar St Marys Hosp and The Nat Hosp 1985-89, conslt neurologist Clementine Churchill Hosp; conslt neurologist Regnl Neurological Centre Royal Surrey Co Hosp Guildford and East Surrey Hosps; scientific papers and int presentations; treatment of Guillain-Barre syndrome, inflammatory polyneuropathy, experimental allergic neuritis, plasma exchange, rejection encephalopathy, gen neurology topics; memb Assoc of Br Neurologists; memb BMA, MRCP; *Books* The Therapeutic Modification of Inflammatory Polyneuropathy (1987); *Recreations* bridge, squash, photography, weight lifting, theatre; *Style*— Dr Michael Gross; Green Waters, Green Lane, Stanmore, Middlesex HA7 3AF (☎ 081 954 0987); Clementine Churchill Hospital, Sudbury Hill, Harrow, Middx (☎ 081 422 3464)

GROSS, Miriam Marianna; da of Kurt May, of Frankfurt, Germany, and Vera Hermine, *née* Freiberg; *b* 12 May 1939; *Educ* Dartington Hall Sch, St Anne's Coll Oxford (BA, MA, DipEd); *m* 1965, John Gross, *qv*, s of Abraham Gross; 1 s (Thomas b 1966), 1 da (Susanna b 1967); *Career* The Observer: joined as asst literary ed, dep literary ed 1964-81, woman's ed 1981-84, ed Book Choice Channel 4 1986-90, arts ed Daily and Sunday Telegraph 1986-; *Books* The World of George Orwell (1971), The World Raymond Chandler (1976); *Recreations* painting; *Style*— Mrs Miriam Gross; Daily Telegraph, South Quay Plaza, 181 Marsh Wall, London E14 (☎ 071 538 6400)

GROSS, Philip John; s of Juhan Karl Gross, and Mary Jessie Alison, *née* Holmes; *b* 27 Feb 1952; *Educ* Devonport HS Plymouth, Univ of Sussex (BA), Poly of North London (Dip Lib); *m* 1976, Helen, da of Leon Gamsa; 1 s (Jonathan Gamsa b 20 March 1982), 1 da (Rosemary Gamsa b 20 Aug 1978); *Career* worked in publishing and libraries; writer and poetry educator; poetry: Familiars (1983), The Ice Factory (1984), Cat's Whisker (1987), The Air Mines of Mistila (with Sylvia Kantaris, 1988), Manifold Manor (1989), The Son of the Duke of Nowhere (1991); novel The Song of Gail and Fludd (1991), play Internal Affairs (shared 1 prize BBC W of Eng playwriting comp); 1 prize National Poetry Competition 1982; *Clubs* Soc of Friends; *Style*— Philip Gross; 87 Berkeley Road, Bishopston, Bristol BS7 8HQ (☎ 0272 427190)

GROSS, Robert; *b* 16 Aug 1930; *Educ* Tulane Univ New Orleans Louisiana (BA); *m* 1952, Marilyn, da of Louis Heller (d 1956); 2 da; *Career* US Navy PRO, served Pacific (Korean War) 1952-56; chm and chief exec Geers Gross; author; *Books* Boy and Girl (1981); *Recreations* tennis, travel; *Clubs* Brooks's, Hurlingham, Queen's; *Style*— Robert Gross, Esq; Geers Gross plc, 110 St Martin's Lane, London WC2N 4DY (☎ 071 734 1655); 20 Ormonde Gate, London SW3; Beach Lane, Quogue, New York 11959, USA

GROSSART, Angus McFarlane McLeod; CBE (1990); s of William John White Grossart, JP (d 1980), and Mary Hay, *née* Gardiner; *b* 6 April 1937; *Educ* Glasgow Acad, Univ of Glasgow (LLD, MA, CA advocate); *m* 1978, Marion Gay Kerr Dodd; 1 da (Flure b 1982); *Career* chm and md Noble Grossart (merchant bank) 1969-; chm Scottish Investmt Tst plc 1973-; directorships incl: Alexander & Alexander Services Inc 1985-, American Trust plc 1973-, The Royal Bank of Scotland Group plc 1985-, Hewden Stuart plc; chm: Edinburgh Fund Managers plc 1983-, Scottish Television plc 1989; chm of tstees Nat Galleries of Scot; *Recreations* golf, castle restoration, decorative arts; *Clubs* New (Edinburgh), Royal and Ancient (St Andrews), Hon Co of Edinburgh Golfers; *Style*— Angus Grossart, Esq, CBE; 48 Queen St, Edinburgh EH2 3NR (☎ 031 226 7011, fax 031 226 6032)

GROSSMAN, Loyd Daniel Gilman; s of David K Grossman (d 1982), of Marblehead, Massachusetts, and Helen Katherine, *née* Gilman (d 1985); *b* 16 Sept 1950; *Educ* Boston Univ (BA), LSE (MSc); *m* 15 June 1985, Deborah Jane, da of David Puttman, CBE, *qv*, of London; 1 da (Florence b 1989); *Career* design ed Harpers & Queen 1981-84, contrib ed The Sunday Times 1984-86; presenter: Through The Keyhole ITV 1987-, Behind the Headlines BBC 1989-, Master Chef BBC 1990-; frequent bdcast appearances on ITV and BBC; writer for various pubns on: food, design, architecture; patron Nat Canine Def League; FSA Scot; *Books* The Social History of Rock Music (1975), Harpers & Queen Guide to London's 100 Best Restaurants (1987); *Recreations* fishing, looking at buildings; *Clubs* Flyfishers; *Style*— Loyd Grossman, Esq; c/o Peter Schnabl, Esq, 72 Vincent Square, London SW1P 2PA (☎ 071 630 6955)

GROSVENOR, Hon Hugh Richard; s of 4 Baron Ebury; *b* 1919; *Educ* Radley; *m* 1, 1939 (m dis 1952), Margaret, da of James Jacobs, of St Ives, Cornwall; 1 da (Margaret b 1947); m 2, 1955, Victoria, da of H Wright, of Newport, Salop; 1 s (William b 1959), 1 da (Rebecca b 1975); *Career* served WWII as Capt King's Shropshire LI; *Style*— The Hon Hugh Grosvenor; River Ridge, Courtlands Park, Carmarthen (☎ 0267 235610)

GROSVENOR, Hon Julian Francis Martin; s & h of 6th Baron Ebury by his 1 w; *b* 8 June 1959; *m* 15 April 1987, Danielle, 6 da of Theo Rossi, of Sydney, NSW, Australia; *Style*— The Hon Julian Grosvenor

GROSVENOR, Hon Laura Georgina Kiloran; *née* Grosvenor; reverted to maiden name by deed poll 1983; da (twin) of 5 Baron Ebury, DSO (d 1957), by 2 w, Hon Denise Yard-Buller (da of 3 Baron Churston); *b* 1946; *m* 1969, G R Mark Cross, only s of Geoffrey Cross, of Bray-on-Thames; *Style*— The Hon Laura Grosvenor; Bartons Lodge, Eversholt, Bletchley, Bucks (☎ 052 528 333) A333)

GROSVENOR, Peter George; s of George William Grosvenor, CBE (d 1979), of Combe Down, Bath, and Mabel Mary, *née* Mortimer (d 1976); *b* 4 May 1933; *Educ* Monkton Combe Sch Bath, Worcester Coll Oxford (MA), Indiana Univ USA; *m* 28 April 1962 (m dis 1982), Rita Mary, da of Charles Becker (d 1983), of Ealing, London; 3 s (Simon George b 5 Sept 1963, Paul William b 1 Jan 1965, Matthew Thomas b 25 March 1967); *Career* reporter: Daily Sketch 1954-55 and 1957-58, News Chronicle 1958-60; feature writer Reveille 1956-57, literary ed Daily Express 1962- (diarist William Hickey 1960-62); *Books* The British Genius (1973), We Are Amused — A History of Royal Cartoons (1978), Ian Woosnam's Golf Masterpieces with Peter Grosvenor (1988), Fred Trueman's Cricket Masterpieces with Peter Grosvenor (1990); *Recreations* watching cricket, playing golf; *Clubs* MCC, Royal Mid Surrey Golf, Garrick; *Style*— Peter Grosvenor, Esq; 46 King Henrys Rd, London NW3 3RP (☎ 01 586 8474); Daily Express, 245 Blackfriars Rd, London SE1 9UX (☎ 01 922 7049, fax 01 922 7970)

GROSVENOR, Hon Richard Alexander; s of 5 Baron Ebury, DSO, by his 2 w, Hon Denise Yarde-Buller (da of 3 Baron Churston); *b* 5 July 1946; *Educ* Milton Abbey, Perugia Univ, Montpelier Univ, Lyons Univ, Tours Univ, Munich Univ; *m* 1, 1970 (m dis 1986), Gabriella, da of Dr Xavier Speckert; 1 s (Bendorb 1977); m 2, 1989, Frances Ann, da of David Samuel Williams; 1 da (Letisah Emma b 1989); *Career* co dir; *Style*— The Hon Richard Grosvenor; c/o Messrs C Hoare & Co, 37 Fleet Street, London EC4P 4DQ

GROSVENOR, Hon (Robert) Victor; 2 s of 5 Baron Ebury, DSO TD (d 1957); by his 1 wife Anne (d 1982), da of Herbert Walter Acland-Troyte, MC; *b* 1936; *Educ* Eton, Gordonstoun; *m* 1959, Caroline, da of Ronald Higham by his w Hon Barbara, *qv*; 2 da (Rachel b 1963, Virginia b 1965); *Career* late 2 Lt Life Gds; *Clubs* Puffins (Edin); *Style*— The Hon Victor Grosvenor; Bennetts, Grafton, Oxford OX8 2RY

GROSVENOR, Hon William Wellesley; s of 5 Baron Ebury, DSO, and his 2 w, Hon Denise Yarde-Buller (da of 3 Baron Churston); *b* 12 Sept 1942; *Educ* Eton, Perugia Univ, Trinity Coll Oxford (MA); *m* 1966, Ellen, da of late Dr Günter Seeliger, sometime Fed German ambass to Mexico; 1 s, 1 da; *Career* conslt; *Recreations* shooting, fishing, bridge, golf; *Clubs* Portland, Buck's; *Style*— The Hon William Grosvenor

GROTRIAN, Sir (Philip) Christian Brent; 3 Bt (UK 1934); s of late Sqdn Ldr Robert Grotrian, s of 1 Bt, by 1 w, Elizabeth, da of late Maj Herbert Hardy-Wrigley; hp of unc, Sir John Grotrian, 2 Bt (d 1984); *b* 26 March 1935; *Educ* Eton, Trinity Coll Toronto; *m* 1960, Anne Isabel, da of Robert Sieger Whyte, of Toronto; 1 s; *Style*— Sir Philip Grotrian, 3 Bt; 295 Glen Rd, Toronto, Ontario, Canada

GROTRIAN, John Stephen Martin; s of Col Frederick Stephen Brent Grotrian, MC (d 1953), of Dumfries, Scot, and Eileen Gertrude, *née* Deane (d 1974); *b* 16 Sept 1925; *Educ* Ampleforth; *m* 25 April 1953, Clodagh, da of Maj Richard Shaw de Courcy Bennett (d 1959), of Collingwood Lodge, Camberley; 1 s (Jeremy Brent b 1959), 2 da (Amanda b 1955, Emma b 1963); *Career* Capt Grenadier Guards 1944-49; dir various advertising agencies, mktg conslt 1985-, garden design conslt 1987-; *Recreations* shooting, gardening, skiing; *Clubs* Cavalry and Guards; *Style*— John Grotrian, Esq; Lake House, Lake, Salisbury, Wilts (☎ 0980 262138)

GROTRIAN, Philip Timothy Adam Brent; s and h of Sir (Philip) Christian Brent Grotrian, Bt; *b* 9 April 1962; *Style*— Philip Grotrian Esq; c/o RR 3, Mansfield, Ontario L0N 1M0, Canada

GROUND, Alan Geoffrey; s of Reginald Ground (d 1975), of Pinner, Middx, and Ivy, *née* Irving; bro of R Patrick Ground, *qv*; *b* 5 April 1935; *Educ* Beckenham GS, Jesus Coll Cambridge (exhibitioner, LLB, MA); *m* Sarah Helen, *née* Russell; 3 s (Edward b 7 Oct 1970, Mark (twin) b 7 Oct 1970, Robert b 4 Nov 1972), 1 da Katherine b 18 Dec 1977); *Career* articled clerk Pollard Stallabrass 1959-62, ptnr Linklaters & Paines 1969- (joined 1962); memb: Int Ctee Law Soc, Human Rights Working Pty Liveryman City of London Slrs Co; *Books* Mergers & Acquisitions in Europe (EEC Merger Control); *Recreations* tennis, music, reading, theatre; *Clubs* RAC, Royal Overseas League; *Style*— Alan Ground, Esq; The Old Rectory, Dunsfold, Surrey GU8 4LT (☎ 048 649 438); Linklaters & Paines, Barrington House, 59-67 Gresham St, London EC2

(☎ 071 606 7080, fax 071 606 5113)

GROUND, (Reginald) Patrick; QC (1981), MP (C) Feltham and Heston 1983-; s of late Reginald Ground, and Ivy Elizabeth Grace, *née* Irving; bro of Alan G Ground, *qv*; *b* 9 Aug 1932; *Educ* Beckenham and Penge County GS, Lycée Guy Lussac Limoges, Selwyn Coll Cambridge (MA), Magdalen Coll Oxford (MLitt); *m* 1964, Caroline, da of Col J F C Dugdale, of 5 St Leonard's Terrace, London; 3 s (Andrew b 1967, Richard b 1970, Thomas b 1974), 1 da (Elizabeth b 1969); *Career* Sub Lt RNVR Med Fleet 1955-56; called to the Bar Inner Temple 1960; pres Univ of Oxford Cons Assoc 1958; memb Hammersmith Borough Cncl 1968-71; chm: Ctees responsible for Health and Social Servs 1969-71, Fulham Soc 1975-; PPS to the Slr Gen 1987-; *Recreations* lawn tennis, sailing, travel; *Clubs* Carlton, Brooks's; *Style*— Patrick Ground, Esq, QC, MP; 13 Ranelagh Ave, London SW6 3PJ; 8 New Square, Lincoln's Inn WC2A 3QP

GROUSE, Leonard David; s of Isaac Michael Grouse (d 1960); *b* 18 Sept 1930; *Educ* Bishopshalt Sch, LSE (BSc); *m* 1957, Jeannette Pauline, da of Leonard Thurgood (d 1944); 1 s, 1 da; *Career* HM Inspr of Taxes 1952-56; dir Noble Lowndes & Ptnrs Ltd 1964-65, md Gp Assurance Consultants 1965-71; dir: Stewart Wrightson Ltd 1971-77, Wigham Poland Hldgs 1977-81; md Leonard Grouse Associates Ltd; ATII, fell Pensions Mgmnt Inst; *Recreations* squash, chess, backgammon, reading, horse racing, crosswords; *Clubs* Savile, RAC; *Style*— Leonard Grouse, Esq; Highfield, Golf Side, Cheam, Surrey (☎ 01 642 1935)

GROUT, Noel Alfred Brian; s of Lt Noel Kenneth Grout (d 1964), and Violet Mary, *née* Jolleff; *b* 8 Aug 1927; *Educ* Culford Sch Bury St Edmunds; *m* 12 April 1958, Cynthia Audrey (Thea), da of Leonard Marks (d 1975); 1 s (Simon Kenneth b 1964); *Career* Nat Serv S Lancs Regt and RAOC, later HAC; press offr Western Union International, dir E K Monks Ltd 1963-72, chief exec Royal Masonic Benevolent Instn 1979- (asst sec 1972-78); Freeman: City of London 1979, Worshipful Co of Gold and Silver Wyre Drawers 1979; FBIM 1980; *Recreations* angling, bird watching, church architecture, walking; *Clubs* Royal Naval, Wig & Pen; *Style*— Noel A Grout, Esq; 61 Baston Rd, Hayes, Bromley, Kent BR2 7BS (☎ 081 462 3855); 20 Great Queen St, London WC2B 5BG (☎ 081 405 8341)

GROVE, Sir Charles Gerald; 5 Bt (UK 1874), of Ferne, Wilts; s of late Walter Peel Grove; suc bro, Sir Walter Grove, 4 Bt, 1974; *b* 10 Dec 1929; *Heir* bro, Harold Thomas Grove b 6 Dec 1930; *Style*— Sir Charles Grove, Bt; resident in USA

GROVE, Christopher John (Chris); s of Ronald Albert John Grove (d 1984), and Edna May, *née* Lazell; *b* 12 Dec 1947; *Educ* Manton House GS Goodmayes Essex, Thurrock Tech Coll Grays Essex; *m* 1 July 1972, Patricia Susan, da of Harold Charles Studholme, of South Ockendon, Essex; 2 s (Robert Allen b 2 Nov 1977, Jamie Oliver b 3 July 1979); *Career* gen mangr Rentmaster Ltd 1986-87, sales dir AI Int Ltd 1987-88, dir and ptnr Dickerson Tport Ltd; Nat Cricket Assoc: advanced coaching award, staff coach; *Recreations* coaching cricket, organising youth football; *Style*— Chris Grove, Esq; Dickerson Tport Ltd, Tomo Indust Estate, Stowmarket, Suffolk IP14 5AY (☎ 0449 615211, fax 0449 677733, car 0836 634900)

GROVE, (William) Dennis; s of William Grove (d 1968); *b* 23 July 1927; *Educ* Gowerton Sch, King's Coll London (BSc); *m* 1953, Audrey Irma, da of John Bernard Saxel (d 1961); 1 s, 1 da; *Career* Lt S Wales Borderers; overseas gen mangr Dunlop Group 1968-70, chm and chief exec Sonoco Europe and TPT Ltd 1970-85, chm NW Water 1985-; *Recreations* travel, golf; *Clubs* Bramall Park Golf; *Style*— Dennis Grove, Esq; Wilmslow, Cheshire

GROVE, Sir Edmund Frank; KCVO (1982, CVO 1974, MVO 4 Class 1963, MVO 5 Class 1953); s of Edmond Grove and Sarah Caroline, *née* Hunt; *b* 20 July 1920; *m* 1945, Grete Elisabet, da of Martinus Skou, of Denmark; 2 da; *Career* WWII RASC served ME; memb Royal Household 1946-82, chief accountant Privy Purse 1963-82, Sergeant-at-Arms to HM The Queen 1975-82, ret 1982; chev Order of Dannebrog (Denmark) 1974, offr Order of the Polar Star (Sweden) 1975, chev Légion d'Honneur (France) 1976; *Recreations* gardening; *Style*— Sir Edmund Grove, KCVO; Chapel Cottage, West Newton, Norfolk

GROVE, Rear Adm John Scott; CB (1984), OBE (1964); s of late William George Grove, and late Frances Margaret Scott Grove; *b* 7 July 1927; *Educ* Dundee HS, Univ of St Andrews (BSc); *m* 1950, Betty Anne Robinson; 1 s (Peter), 1 da (Diana, decd); *Career* RN 1948-85; qualified in submarines 1953, nuclear trg 1958-59, Cdr 1963, Capt 1970, Rear Adm 1980, first Sr Engr Offr HMS Dreadnought (first RN nuclear sub) 1960-64, RCDS 1974, CSO(E) to Flag Office Submarines 1975-77, Capt Fisgard 1977-79, Chief Strategic Systems Exec 1980-85, Chief Naval Engr Offr 1983-85, ret 1985; def conslt Babcock Energy Ltd 1986-, non-exec dir Devonport Mgmnt Ltd 1987-; Liveryman Worshipful Co of Engrs (Ct Asst); *Recreations* walking; *Clubs* Army and Navy, Royal Cwlth Soc; *Style*— Rear Adm John Grove, CB, OBE; Maryfield, South Close, Wade Court, Havant, Hants PO9 2TD (☎ 0705 475116)

GROVE, Josceline Philip; s of Brig Geoffrey Reginald Grove (d 1972), and Barbara Constance, *née* Woodburn; *b* 8 Nov 1938; *Educ* Hurstpierpoint Coll, RMA Sandhurst; *m* 8 April 1970, Jennifer Clifton, da of Maj E A Calvert, *qv*, of Rose Cottage Farmhouse, Faygate Sussex; 1 s (decd), 2 da (Miranda Clifton b 1974, Venetia Mary b 1976); *Career* RMA Sandhurst 1957-58, cmmnd 1 Bn Cheshire Regt 1958, Lt 1960, TA QRR 1963-66, 4 Vol Bn RGJ Capt 1966-71; mgmnt trainee J & P Coats Patons & Baldwins 1963, C T Bowring & Co 1964-65, The Economist 1966, The Sunday Times 1967-70, J Walter Thompson 1970-73, exec sec Wider Share Ownership Cncl 1976-78, dir Charles Barker 1978-83 (joined 1974), md Grandfield Rork Collins Financial 1983-; memb: City Branch Ctee BIM 1978-83, City Sponsor's Gp - Tower Hamlets Ltd, Business in the Community 1986-87; memb Ct of Assts, Worshipful Co of Bowyers; *Recreations* ocean racing, deer stalking, grand opera; *Clubs* Army & Navy, Brooks's, Northern Meeting (Invernesshire); *Style*— Josceline Grove, Esq; 27 Cloncurry St, London SW6 6DR (☎ 071 736 1533); Fasnakyle, Cannich, Invernesshire (☎ 045 65 202); Grandfield Rork Collins Financial, Prestige House, 14-18 Holborn, London EC1N 2LE (☎ 071 242 2002)

GROVE, Norman Harold; MBE (1986); s of Francis Harold Grove (d 1944), of Halesowen, and Lilian, *née* Hodgetts (d 1963); *b* 29 Dec 1914; *Educ* Wrekin Coll Wellington; *m* 1940, Lesley Joan, da of Frank Harvey (d 1973), of Kidderminster; 1 s (Peter b 1946), 1 da (Lesley b 1943); *Career* dir: James Grove & Sons Ltd 1940- (chm 1944-), Harbury & Cradley Building Society 1968-80; *Recreations* walking, travel, swimming, cricket; *Style*— Norman Grove, Esq, MBE; View Bank, Church Hill, Kinver, Stourbridge DY7 6HY (☎ 0384 877107); James Grove & Sons Ltd, PO Box 5, Stourbridge Road, Halesowen B63 3UW (telex 336921, fax 021 501 3905)

GROVE, Peter Ernest; s of Ernest Grove (d 1974), and Elsie May, *née* Silver; *b* 18 Nov 1949; *Educ* Heathcote Sch Chingford; *m* 27 Jan 1973, Catherine Anne, da of Joseph Frederick Jolly, of Wanstead, London E11; 1 s (Alexander b 28 April 1979), 2 da (Elizabeth b 10 Jan 1981, Caroline b 18 Jan 1982); *Career* dep underwriter: Willis Faber Underwriting Mgmnt Ltd 1977, Lloyd's Syndicates 197/726 561 & 566 1982; dir: Patrick Underwriting Agencies Ltd 1984, Bankside Syndicates Ltd 1987; active underwriter Lloyd's Syndicates 197 & 561 1988, dir Bankside Underwriting Agencies Ltd 1988; *Recreations* chess, reading; *Style*— Peter Grove, Esq; Patrick Underwriting Agencies Ltd, 5 Floor, Beaufort House, 15 St Botolph St, London EC3A 7PA (☎ 01 621 1862, fax 01 621 9917, telex 8814440)

GROVE, Peter Hulbert; TD (1975 and bar 1982); s of James Hulbert Grove (d 1985), and Elfrida, *née* Golby (d 1976); *b* 24 July 1936; *Educ* Whitgift Sch; *m* 1, 3 Oct 1964 (m dis 1984), Mary Frances, da of Harry Ingledew Hopper (d 1972); 1 s (William b 1967), 2 da (Catherine b 1969, Victoria b 1971); m 2, 19 Oct 1984, Mary, da of Dr Harry Graham Dowler (d 1989); *Career* joined HAC 1956, Nat Serv 15/19 Hussars 2 Lt 1958-60, resigned cmmn and rejoined HAC 1960, HAC re-cmmnd Lt 1964, Capt 1967; transfer: Queens Regt 1972, CVHQ RA 1977; Maj 1979, attached Staff of London Dist as SO2 (TA liason), ret 1986; Knox Cropper and Co: articled clerk 1952-58, rejoined after Nat Serv 1960, ptnr 1968, sr ptnr 1988; memb Fin and Gen Purposes Ctee of Royal Masonic Benevolent Inst 1987-, various mgmnt ctees of Royal Masonic Hosp 1976-86, Special Constable 1974-85, Divnl Offr in command of HAC Detachment of Met Special Constabulary 1984-85; Freeman City of London 1972, Liveryman Worshipful Co of Scriveners 1975; FCA 1965 (ACA); *Recreations* horology, Co of Pikemen and Musketeers HAC, canals, narrow boats; *Clubs* HAC, City Livery, XIX; *Style*— Peter Grove, Esq, TD; 121 Old Woking Rd, Woking GU22 8PF (☎ 0932 340620); Knox Cropper, 16 New Bridge St, London EC4V 6AX (☎ 071 583 8355, fax 071 583 2944)

GROVE, Valerie; da of Doug Smith (d 1973); *b* 11 May 1946; *Educ* Kingsbury Co GS, Girton Coll Cambridge (exhibitioner, MA); *m* 1, 1968, David Brynmor Jenkins; m 2, 1975, Trevor Charles Grove, s of Ronald Grove (d 1980); 1 s (Oliver b 1983), 3 da (Lucy b 1976, Emma b 1979, Victoria b 1981); *Career* reporter Shields Gazette 1965-66, feature writer Evening Standard 1968-87 (literary ed 1979-81 and 1984-87), columnist Sunday Times 1987-; *Books* Where I Was Young - Memories of London Childhood (1977), The Compleat Woman (1987); *Recreations* tennis, family; *Style*— Mrs Valerie Grove; The Sunday Times, News International, 1 Pennington St, London E1 (☎ 071 782 5000)

GROVE-WHITE, Robin Bernard; s of Charles William Grove-White, of Amlwch, Gwynedd, and Mary, *née* Dobbs; (*see* Burke's Irish Family Records); *b* 17 Feb 1941; *Educ* Uppingham, Worcester Coll Oxford (BA); *m* 1, 1970 (m dis 1974), Virginia Harriet, da of Christopher Ironside, OBE; 1 s (William b 1973); m 2, 1979, Helen Elisabeth, da of Sir Francis Graham Smith, of The Old School House, Henbury, Cheshire; 2 s (Simon b 1982, Francis b 1986), 1 da Ruth (b 1980); *Career* freelance writer for TV, radio, press in US, Canada and UK 1963-71, asst sec Cncl for the Protection of Rural England 1972-80, (dir 1981-87), vice-chm Cncl for National Parks; research fell Centre for Environmental Technology, Imperial Coll London 1987-89; sr res fell in Environmental Res Policy Lancaster Univ 1989-; contributor to various publications including The Times, Guardian, New Scientist, Nature; *Recreations* reading, walking, cricket; *Style*— Robin Grove-White, Esq; Conder Mill Cottage, Quernmore, Lancaster LA2 9EE (☎ 0542 382501); University of Lancaster, Bailrigg, Lancs (☎ 0542 65201)

GROVES, Brian Arthur; s of Alfred Edward Groves (d 1990) *qv*, and Winifred May, *née* Sheen, *qv*; *b* 3 July 1933; *Educ* Bishop Wordsworth Sch Salisbury; *m* 1 Aug 1955, Daphne Frances, da of Frederick Gale (d 1957); 2 da (Heather b 1956, Beverley, b 1957); *Career* journalist 1950-71, motoring ed Daily Mail 1968-71, advtg and PR dir Nissan UK Ltd 1983-88 (mktg dir 1975-83), chm David Ruskin Ltd 1988-; *Recreations* golf, swimming, boating, flying; *Style*— Brian A Groves, Esq; Sarum, Mare Hill, Pulborough, W Sussex (☎ 07982 3464, car 0836 256242)

GROVES, Sir Charles Barnard; CBE (1968, OBE 1958); *b* 10 March 1915; *Educ* St Paul's Cathedral Choir Sch, Sutton Valence Sch, Royal Coll of Music; *m* 1948, Hilary Hermione Barchard; 1 s, 2 da; *Career* conductor; BBC Northern Orchestra 1944-51, dir of Music Bournemouth Corp and conductor Bournemouth Municipal Orchestra 1951-54, conductor Bournemouth Symphony Orchestra 1954-61, resident musical dir WNO 1961-63, musical dir and resident conductor Royal Liverpool Philharmonic Orchestra 1963-77, assoc conductor Royal Philharmonic Orchestra 1967-, music dir ENO 1977-80, pres Nat Youth Orchestra of Great Britain 1977-; pres and artistic advsr English Sinfonia 1980-, princ conductor Guildford Philharmonic Orchestra 1987-; FRCM, Hon RAM, Hon FTCL, CRNCM, Hon GSM; Hon DMus Univ of Liverpool, Hon DUniv Open Univ, Hon DLitt Univ of Salford ; kt 1973; *Style*— Sir Charles Groves, CBE; 12 Camden Sq, London NW1 9UY

GROVES, Capt Peter Leslie John; s of Lt-Col Leslie Herbert Selby Groves, OBE (d 1961), of Dorset (gs of Sir John Groves, of Weymouth, dir John Groves & Sons, brewers), and Dorothy Olive Josephine Gundry (d 1969), of Bridport, Dorset; *b* 30 Dec 1925; *Educ* Eton; *m* 14 Dec 1956, Anthea Mary, da of Col Cuthbert Vaux, MC, TD (d 1960), of Richmond, N Yorks; 1 s (Michael b 1961), 2 da (Carol b 1958, Joanna b 1964); *Career* RMC Sandhurst 1945, cmmnd 1945, Adj 14/20 King's Hussars 1956-57, Adj Duke of Lancaster's Own Yeomanry TA 1952-55, instr Eaton Hall OCS 1957-58, temp Maj 1955 (ret 1960); exec Aspro-Nicholas 1961-70, sec Olympic Ski Appeal 1970-72, liaison offr SSAFA 1972-75, exec Help the Aged 1984-87, memb Ctee Wessex Area Cons Assoc 1970-72; underwriting memb Lloyds 1971; *Recreations* shooting; *Clubs* Army and Navy; *Style*— Capt Peter Groves; The Old Rectory, Great Langton, Northallerton, N Yorks DL7 0TA (☎ 0609 748 681)

GROVES, Philip Denys Baker; DL (Co of Hertford 1989); s of Joseph Rupert Groves (d 1958), of Watford, Herts, and Eva Lilian, *née* Baker (d 1986); *b* 9 Jan 1928; *Educ* Watford GS, Poly Sch of Architecture; *m* 21 June 1952, Yvonne Joyce, da of George Chapman (d 1971), of Rickmansworth; 2 s (Mark b 29 April 1957, Michael b 23 Sept 1965), 1 da (Sarah b 27 May 1961); *Career* RAF 1946-48; served: UK, Palestine, Egypt; chm Architects Co-Partnership 1980- (joined 1955, ptnr 1965); architect for educn and health care projects: UK, ME, Far East, Caribbean; vice pres RIBA Cncl 1972-75 and 1978-80 (memb 1962-81), chm Bd of Educn RIBA 1974-75 and 1979-80 (memb 1962-80), chm ARCUK 1971-74 (memb Cncl 1962-80); chm: Univ of York Centre for Continued Educn 1978-81, CPD in Construction GP 1986-; memb Comite De Liason Des Architects du Marche Commun 1972-80, external examiner at several schools of architecture in UK and overseas, British conslt Bureau (memb Cncl 1990-), dir Herts C of C (chm 1985-88, pres 1989), chm Herts Community Tst 1988-, dir Herts TEC 1989-; ARIBA 1955, FRIBA 1968, FRSA 1989; *Books* Design for Health Care (jtly, 1981), Hospitals and Health Care Facilities (jtly, 1990), Hospitals and Health Care Facilities (jtly, 1990); *Recreations* walking, reading, architecture; *Clubs* Reform; *Style*— Philip Groves, Esq, DL; The Dingle, Whisperwood, Loudwater, Rickmansworth, Hertfordshire WD3 4JU (☎ 0923 775921); Architects Co Partnership, Northaw House, Potters Bar, Hertfordshire EN6 4PS, (☎ 0707 51141)

GROVES, His Hon Judge Richard Bebb; TD (1966), RD (1979); s of George Thomas Groves (d 1965), and Margaret Anne Underhill, *née* Bebb; *b* 4 Oct 1933; *Educ* Bancroft's Sch Essex; *m* 1958, Eileen Patricia, da of Capt Graham Payne Farley (d 1942); 1 s (Christopher b 1963), 1 da (Caroline b 1961); *Career* Nat Serv 1952-54; TA 1954-70, Maj Intelligence Corps (TAVR) RNR 1970-83; Lt Cdr (SP) RNR PI Gp Nijmegen Medal Royal Netherlands League of Physical Culture 1965 and 1966; admitted slr 1960; ptnr: H J Smith & Co, Richard Groves & Co 1962-85; dep circuit judge 1978-80, rec Crown Ct 1980-85, circuit judge 1985; *Recreations* watching sport, playing tennis, walking, reading; *Clubs* RAC, Colchester Garrison Offrs, Chelmsford; *Style*— His Hon Judge Groves

GROVES, Richard Laurence; s of Wilfred Groves (d 1980), of Sheffield, and Ann

Groves; *b* 21 July 1944; *Educ* Rowlinson Secondary Sch Sheffield, Sheffield Poly (dip Municipal Admin), Manchester Poly (Dip Mgmnt Studies), Univ of Manchester (MA); *m* 1976, Christine, da of Gerard Grady; 1 s (Jonathan b 4 Jan 1979); *Career* clerical offr Sheffield City Cncl 1961-68, admin Tport and Town Clerks Depts Manchester City Cncl 1968-73, various managerial posts Manchester Regnl Hosp Bd N Western Regnl Health Authy 1973-75 (regnl servs planning offr 1975-86); N Manchester Health Authy: head of planning and admin 1986-88, unit gen mangr 1988-90, gen mangr and dep chief exec 1990-; *Recreations* football Sheffield Wednesday, tennis, walking; *Style*— Richard Groves, Esq; North Manchester General Hospital, North Manchester Health Authority, Central Drive, Crumpsall, Manchester M8 6RL (☎ 061 795 4567, fax 061 740 4450)

GROVES, Ronald Edward; CBE (1972); s of Joseph Rupert Groves (d 1958), of Watford, and Eva Lilian, *née* Baker (d 1986); *b* 2 March 1920; *Educ* Watford GS; *m* 16 Nov 1940, Beryl Doris Lydia, da of Frank William Collins (d 1940), of Watford; 2 s (Peter Warland b 1941, Richard Michael b 1958); 1 da (Mary Delia Margaret b 1945); *Career* Nat Serv RAF 1940-46, Flt Lt, seconded BOAC 1942, Capt 1943-46; pres Timber Trade Fedn 1969-71; chm: Meyer Int plc 1982-87, Int Timber plc 1976-87; pres Nat Cncl of Bldg Material Prodrs 1987-90; chm: Nat Sawmilling Assoc 1966-67, W Herts Main Drainage Authy 1970-74; dir Nat Bldg Agency 1978-82, Business in the Community 1984-87; memb: EDC for Bldg 1982-86, Cncl of London C of C 1982-, LCCI London Regnl Affrs Ctee 1980; London Regnl Cncl CBI 1983-87; cncllr Three Rivers Dist Cncl 1974- (chm 1977-78), Rickmansworth UDC 1950-74 (chm 1957-58, 1964-65, 1971-72); chm: Watford Boys GS 1980-, Watford Girls GS 1980-; *Style*— Ronald Groves, Esq, CBE; 8 Pembroke Rd, Moor Park, Northwood, Middx HA6 2HR (☎ 09274 23187)

GROVES, Terry Randolph Alexander; s of Dr T A Groves (d 1976), of Slegaby-Beg, Quarterbridge Rd, Douglas, IOM, and Daphne Carine, *née* Pruddah (d 1961); *b* 9 Aug 1946; *Educ* Shrewsbury; *m* 2 Sept 1972, Janet Pauline Elaine, da of H J Partington, JP, of 10 Lumley Rd, Chester; 2 s (Thomas Charles Alexander b 5 Nov 1974, Timothy Simon Robert b 7 Aug 1977); *Career* exec property devpt co 1969-75, property mangr South African Mutual Life (Natal region) 1975-77, ptnr Cowley Groves & Co (estate agents, surveyors and valuers) IOM 1977-86; dir: Cresta Hldgs Ltd, Cresta Properties Ltd 1986-89; bd memb Sun Alliance Ltd (IOM), dir Royal Skandia Lite Assurance Ltd, chm Ramsey Golf Links Ltd; former pres Ramsey Golf Club; memb: Mgmnt Ctee IOM Hospice Care Charity, Appeals Ctee IOM Cwlth Games Assoc; memb: (Cons) Chester City Cncl 1973-75, Rossall Sch Cncl; *Recreations* golf, tennis, gardening; *Clubs* Ramsey Golf (capt 1984-85), Castletown Golf, Executive (IOM); *Style*— Terry Groves, Esq; West Kella, Sulby, Lezayre, Isle of Man (☎ 0624 897904); Archbury Hse, Auckland Terrace, Ramsey, Isle of Man (☎ 0624 816090, fax 0624 816091)

GRUBB, Ralph Ernest Watkins; DL (E Sussex 1977); s of Rev Ernest Watkins Grubb (d 1914), and Mary Pauline, *née* Bevan (d 1946); *b* 12 April 1911; *Educ* Wellington, Trinity Coll Cambridge (BA); *m* 1944, Caroline Elizabeth Mabel (d 1989), da of William Reierson Arbuthnot (d 1938); 1 s, 2 da (and 1 decd); *Career* Inns of Court Regt TA 1936-46; Maj, GS Intelligence Palestine 1945-46; barr Inner Temple; High Sheriff Sussex 1972-73, vice chm E Sussex CC 1973-74 (memb 1954-74); chm: Plumpton Agricultural Coll 1966-69, Countryside Ctee 1969-74, Rye Harbour Nature Reserve 1969-80, Sussex County Playing Fields Assoc 1974-83; memb Nat Tst Regnl Ctee Kent and E Sussex 1974-84 (vice chm 1980); conservator Ashdown Forest 1958-74; FRICS; *Recreations* shooting, fishing, birdwatching; *Clubs* Farmers, Royal Cwlth Soc; *Style*— Ralph Grubb, Esq, DL; Mayes House, nr East Grinstead, Sussex (☎ 0342 810 597); Ottershatch, Beach St, Deal, Kent (☎ 0304 375533)

GRUBER, Christiana; da of Max Gruber, and Gloria Gruber; *b* 19 April 1953; *Career* former actress, TV presenter and character model for broadcast commercials; publicist: American Coll Leysan Switzerland, Montreux Jazz Festival, Formula One racing; coordinator VIP facility visits and tours UN Geneva, prodn asst to film dir Jean Négulesco Spain, researcher to Harry Gilmore Time Magazine, publicist Los Monteros Health and Sports Complex, Saatchi & Saatchi, Ellis & Barton (film prodrs), celebrity charity golf and tennis tournaments, promoted lifestyle magazine Metropolitan for Eppingfield, Redwood, contrib travel and arts pubns; ind gen PR conslt and practitioner: mktg and economic feasibility studies, lobbying, book launches, artistic ventures, design promotions, city firm of conslts, corp strategy recommendation for engrg co Egypt; sponsorship collaboration articles: on art, wine, gen interest; chm IPR Conslts Gp; memb: IPR, NUJ, Chartered Soc of Designers, Soc of Arts Publicists, Women in Art and Antiques, IPR, IPR Conslts Gp (Chm), Inst of Mktg Travel and Indust GP; *Recreations* cycling, music, reading, tennis; *Style*— Miss Christiana Gruber; 32 Anselm Road, London SW6 1LJ; 5 Dryden St, Covent Garden, London WC2E 9NW (☎ 071 829 8498/9, fax 071 240 5600, telex 299533)

GRUBMAN, Wallace Karl; s of Samuel Grubman (d 1988), of Philadelphia, Pa, USA, and Mildred, *née* Lippe (d 1985); *b* 12 Sept 1928; *Educ* Univ of Columbia NY (BS), Univ of New York (MS); *m* 29 July 1950, Ruth, da of Lewis Winer (d 1965); 3 s (James Wallace b 1954, d 1979, Steven Lee b 1956, Eric Peter b 1958); *Career* Nat Starch and Chemical Corp USA 1950-: corp vice pres 1971-75, gp vice pres 1976-77, dir 1978-, pres and chief operating offr 1978-83, chm and chief exec offr 1983-85; dir: United National Bank NJ USA 1978-86 (conslt to Bd 1986-), Unilever US 1981-86; dir and chemicals co-ordinator Unilever plc and Unilever NV 1986-; memb: Engrg Cncl Univ of Columbia NY, Chem Engrg Dept Studies Ctee Imperial Coll Sci and Technol, Royal Opera Covent Garden, Royal Acad, American Friends Gp; patron Met Opera Lincoln Centre NY; memb: American Inst Chem Engrs 1950, SCI 1978, FInstD 1986; *Recreations* sports, music; *Clubs* Wentworth Golf, Mid Ocean Bermuda, Roxiticus Golf (New Jersey), SKY and Princeton NY; *Style*— Wallace Grubman, Esq; Unilever House, Blackfriars, London EC4P 4BQ (☎ 071 822 6895); Nat Starch and Chemical Corp, Bridgewater, New Jersey 08807 (☎ 201 685 5161)

GRUEBEL-LEE, David Mark; s of Harry Gruebel-Lee (d 1959), of Johannesburg, SA; *b* 20 March 1933; *Educ* Parktown HS S Africa, Univ of Witwatersrand (MB BCh); *m* 14 April 1957, Lydia Deborah, da of Leonard Yale (d 1941), of Johannesburg; 1 s (Leonard b 1958), 2 da (Caroline b 1961, d 1984, Elizabeth b 1969); *Career* jr appts in orthopaedic surgery: St Mary's Hosp 1960-63, The London Hosp 1963-65; sr registrar St Thomas' Hosp 1965-1970, orthopaedic surgn to Albert Einstein Coll of Med Bronx NY 1967; conslt orthopaedic surgn: Frimley Park, Farnham and Fleet Hosps, King Edward VII Hosp (hon); fell BOA, FRCS, FRCSE; *Books* Disorders Of The Lumbar Spine (1978), Disorders Of The Foot (1980), Disorders Of The Hip (1983); *Recreations* sailing, photography, computers; *Style*— David Gruebel-Lee, Esq; Woodburn, 2 Middle Bourne Lane, Farnham, Surrey GU10 3ND; 70 East St, Farnham, Surrey GU9 7TP

GRUFFYDD, Prof (Robert) Geraint; s of Moses Griffith (d 1973), of Menai Bridge, Gwynedd, and Ceridwen, *née* Ellis (d 1982); *b* 9 June 1928; *Educ* Ardwyn GS Aberystwyth, Gordonstoun, UCNW Bangor (BA), Jesus Coll Oxford (DPhil); *m* 1 Oct 1953, (Elizabeth) Eluned, da of John Roberts (d 1965), of Holyhead; 2 s (Rhun b 4 March 1961, Pyrs b 26 Nov 1963), 1 da (Sian b 14 Oct 1957); *Career* asst ed Univ of Wales Dictionary of the Welsh Language 1953-55, lectr in Welsh UCNW Bangor 1955-70, prof of Welsh language and literature Univ Coll of Wales Aberystwyth 1970-79, librarian Nat Library of Wales 1980-85, dir Centre for Advanced Welsh and Celtic Studies Univ of Wales 1985-; chm: Welsh Books Cncl 1980-85, Welsh language section Yr Academi Gymreig (Welsh Acad) 1986-; memb Hon Soc of Cymmrodorion (ed of Transactions 1989-); *Books* ed: Cerddi '73 (1973), Meistri'r Canrifoedd (1973), Bardos (1982), Cerddi Saunders Lewis (1986), Dafydd ap Gwilym (1987), Yl Gair ar Waith (1988), Llenyddiaeth y Cymry (1989); *Recreations* meditating upon the uses of leisure; *Style*— Prof Geraint Gruffydd; Eirianfa, Caradog Rd, Aberystwyth, Dyfed (☎ 0970 623396); Centre for Advanced Welsh & Celtic Studies, The Old College, Aberystwyth, Dyfed (☎ 0970 622090)

GRUGEON, Sir John Drury; (DL Kent 1986); s of Drury Grugeon (d 1969), of Westfield Lodge, Broadstairs; *b* 20 Sept 1928; *Educ* Epsom GS, RMA Sandhurst; *m* 1, 1955 (m dis 1986), Mary Patricia, da of Walter James Rickards (d 1957), of Hoath Farm, Canterbury; 1 s, 1 da; m 2, 28 July 1989, Lois, widow of Dr Roland Phillips; *Career* served The Buffs 1948-60, Capt, Regimental Adj (later Adj 5 Bn); served: Europe, ME, Far East; chm Kent CC 1989 (elected 1967, ldr 1973-81, vice chm 1987-89) chm policy ctee Assoc CCs 1978-80, vice chm Assoc of CCs 1980-82; memb: Medway Ports Authy 1977-, Consultative Cncl Local Govt Fin; exec mangr Save & Prosper Gp Ltd (joined 1960); dir of Liverpool Int Garden Festival 1982-83, chm Tunbridge Wells Health Authy 1984-; kt 1980; *Recreations* shooting, cricket; *Clubs* Carlton, MCC, Kent CCC; *Style*— Sir John Grugeon, DL; 2 Shrublands Ct, Sandrock Rd, Tunbridge Wells, Kent TW2 3PS (☎ 0892 31936)

GRUMBALL, Clive Roger; s of Frederick William Grumball (d 1988), and Joan Doreen, *née* Ottewell (d 1976); *b* 17 Dec 1946; *Educ* Sir Roger Manwood's Sch Sandwich Kent, Welbeck Coll Worksop Notts, RMA Sandhurst; *m* 20 Feb 1971 (m dis 1986), Jennifer, da of David James Springhall, of Wallingford, Oxon; 1 s (Ian Nigel Clive b 1974), 2 da (Kirsty Elizabeth b 15 April 1973, Karen Louise d 1973); *Career* 2 Lt RCS 1967-68; asst to md Gillett Bros Discount Co Ltd 1969-77, asst treas Amex Bank Ltd 1977-80; dir: Nordic Bank plc 1980-85, County Gp Ltd 1985-87, treas Br and Cwlth Merchant Bank plc 1987-89, Yamaichi Bank (UK) plc 1989-; *Books* Managing Interest Rate Risks (1987); *Recreations* horse riding, hockey; *Style*— Clive Grumball, Esq; Guildhall House, 81-87 Gresham St, London EC2V 7NQ (☎ 01 600 1188, fax 01 600 1169, telex 919548 YBK LDN)

GRUNBERG, Michael; s of Solomon Aaron Grunberg, and Greta, *née* Fox; *b* 23 Sept 1956; *Educ* City of London Sch, LSE (BSc); *Career* CA, ptnr Stoy Hayward 1985, dir Stoy Hayward Consulting 1985; chm Steering Ctee Comic Relief; MIMC 1986, MIDPM 1987; *Recreations* fitness, squash, skiing, scuba diving; *Style*— Michael Grunberg, Esq; Stoy Hayward, 8 Baker Street, London W1M 1DA (☎ 071 486 5888, fax 071 487 3686, telex 267716 HORWAT G)

GRUNDY, David James; s of James Grundy, of Nantwich, Cheshire, and Edna, *née* Littler; *b* 27 Feb 1939; *Educ* St George's Hosp Med Sch London (MB BS); *m* 15 April 1972, Mary Ethel, da of Edmund Digby Buxton, of Alresford Hants; 2 da (Katharine b 1973, Joanna b 1976); *Career* sr MO and med supt Wusasa Hosp Nigeria 1973-79, conslt surgn Duke of Cornwall Spinal Treatment Centre Odstock Hosp Salisbury 1983-; FRCSEd 1969, FRCS 1970; *Books* ABC of Spinal Cord Injury (jtly, 1986); *Recreations* tennis, classical music; *Style*— David Grundy, Esq; The Old Post Office, Besomers Drove, Lover, Redlynch, Salisbury SP5 2PN (☎ 0725 22905); The Duke of Cornwall Spinal Treatment Centre, Odstock Hospital, Salisbury SP2 8BJ (☎ 0722 336262)

GRUNDY, Lady; Marie-Louise; da of Frederick Amaza Holder (d 1972), of Corsham, Wilts, and Ellen Mary, *née* Nation (d 1984), of Taunton, Somerset; *Educ* Univ of Exeter (BA); *m* 1975 (as his 2 w), Air Marshal Sir Edouard Grundy, KBE, CB (d 1987), s of Frederick Grundy (d 1924), of London; *Career* dir Pascall Group Melbourne Florida; chm American Legacy Foundation Inc, tstee Florida Inst of Technol, co chm Winston Churchill Meml Fund; former pres: Rotary Inner Wheel Singapore, Business and Professional Womens Club; *Recreations* sailing (yacht 'Fresh Aire'), genealogy, travel, chess, bridge; *Clubs* United Oxford and Cambridge, IOD, American, St James's, RAF, Eau Gallie Yacht, Goodwood Race Course; *Style*— Lady Grundy; 26 Basil Street London SW3 1AS (☎ 071 584 5117)

GRUNDY, Vincent Arthur; s of Cecil Frederick Grundy (d 1976), and Elizabeth Agnes, *née* Mason (d 1968); *b* 6 Dec 1931; *Educ* Worksop Coll; *m* 19 Oct 1957, Moira Patricia, da of George Barbour (d 1985); 1 da (Patricia b 1958); *Career* Nat Serv RE 1950-52; dir: Trafalgar House plc, John Brown plc; chm: Cementation Civil & Specialist Hldgs Ltd, Cementation Int Construction Hldgs Ltd, Cleveland Redpath Engrg Hldgs Ltd, Trafalgar House Offshore Ltd; md Trafalgar House Construction Hldgs Ltd; *Recreations* gardening, boating, shooting; *Clubs* Carlton; *Style*— Vincent Grundy, Esq; Camelford, Bradcutts Lane, Cookham Dean, Maidenhead, Berks SL6 9DN (☎ 06285 29069); Trafalgar House plc, 1 Berkeley St, London W1A 1BY (☎ 01 499 9020, fax 01 355 4418, telex 921341)

GRUNWELL, Peter Higson; s of Charles Arthur Grunwell (d 1959), of Worsley, Lancashire, and Elsie, *née* Higson; *b* 18 Dec 1936; *Educ* Canon Slade GS; *m* 20 Aug 1960, Vivian Mary, da of Roland Daintith (d 1974), of Mawdesley, Lancashire; 2 da (Ann Kathryn (Katy) b 26 Jan 1963, Joanne Mary b 11 Aug 1965); *Career* CA 1959; Pilkington plc: HQ ops incl transfer to plc 1961-70, dir Pilkington Flatglass Europe 1970-80, gp chief accountant 1980-85, dir Pilkington plc 1985-; dir: Pilkington International Holdings, Pilkington (NZ) Ltd, Pilkington (Aust) Ltd, Vidrieria Argentina SA, Santa Lucia Cristal SACIF, Santa Lucia Cristais Blindex Ltda, Pilkington Vidros Ltda, Glass South Africa, Pilkington South Africa Ltd, Ravenhead Renaisance; non-exec dir Rockwave Group plc; MCBI, BIM, FCA; *Recreations* golf, gardening, sports; *Style*— Peter Grunwell, Esq; Woodfield, Croasdale Drive, Parbold, Lancashire (☎ 025 76 2626); Pilkington plc, Prescot Rd, St Helens, Merseyside (☎ 0744 28882, fax 0744 30577, telex 627441)

GRYLLS, Brig (William) Edward Harvey; OBE (1945); er s of Maj (William) Edward John Grylls (d 1931), of Funtington Hall, nr Chichester, Sussex (*see* Burke's Landed Gentry, 18 Edn, vol II, 1969), and Helen Aline, *née* Combe (d 1941); *b* 11 July 1902; *Educ* Harrow, RMC Sandhurst; *m* 9 July 1929, Rachel Elizabeth (decd), o da of Brig-Gen Kempster Kenmure Knapp, CB, CMG (d 1948), of Brooke Lodge, Weedon, Northants; 1 s (William Michael John, *qv*), 1 da (Angela Mary Elizabeth b 18 June 1931, m Ronald Cathcart Roxburgh, *qv*); *Career* cmmnd 15/19 King's Royal Hussars 1923; instr Army Equitation Sch Weedon 1925-26; served: Tidworth, Egypt, India, NW Frontier, Mohmond War 1930-31, Shorncliffe, Tidworth, York 1934-38; instr RMC Sandhurst 1938-40, 2 i/c 15/19 King's Royal Hussars 1940, mission to USA to advise on tank design at Fort Knox 1941, dep dir armd fighting vehicles under Gen Montgomery 8 Army in Egypt 1942, served Sicily and Italy, returned to UK Dec 1943 with Gen Montgomery as dep dir armd fighting vehicles 21 Army Gp (serving from invasion of Normandy until surrender of Germany), Brig cmdg T Force (involved in reparations and intelligence), cmdt Sch of Tank Technol 1951; ret 1954; memb Dorset CC 1955-72, judge Br Show Jumping Assoc 1949-76, chm Hampshire and W of England United Retriever Club, memb ctee Golden Retriever Club; *Clubs* Army and Navy, Royal Cruising; *Style*— Brig W E H Grylls, OBE; Winterbourne Zelston House, Blandford, Dorset

GRYLLS, (William) Michael John; MP (C) NW Surrey 1974-; s of Brig (William) Edward Harvey Grylls, OBE, *qv*, and Rachel Elizabeth, *née* Knapp; *b* 21 Feb 1934; *Educ* RNC Dartmouth, Paris Univ, Madrid Univ; *m* 1965, Sarah, da of Neville Montague Ford, *qv*; 1 s, 1 da; *Career* served RM 1952-55; contested (C) Fulham 1964 and 1966, memb GLC 1967-70, chm Further and Higher Educn 1968-70, memb Nat Youth Employment Cncl 1968-70, dep ldr ILEA 1969-70; MP (C) Chertsey 1970-1974, memb Select Ctee Overseas Devpt 1970-78; chm: Small Business Bureau 1979-, Cons Industry Ctee 1981- (vice chm 1975-81); Hon Parly spokesman IOD 1979-; *Recreations* gardening, shooting, sailing, skiing; *Style*— Michael Grylls, Esq, MP; House of Commons, London SW1A 0AA (☎ 071 219 4193)

GUADACORTE, Marquis of; Don Rafael de Tramontana y Gayangos, Count of Casa Fuerte; s of Dr Rafael de Tramontana y Tramontana, Patrician of Messina (d 1964); gs of the Arabic author and scholar, Pasqual de Gayangos, who m an Englishwoman, Frances Revell, and who was k by a horsedrawn carriage and buried in Kensal Green cemetery; descendant of the noble family of Spain for whom the title of Marquis was created in 1690 and the title of Count in 1743; *b* 16 March 1947; *Educ* Areneros Madrid, Sherborne, License ès Sciences Econ Geneva; *Career* economist; chm Pasqual de Gayangos Arab-Hispanic Fndn, Carmona, Spain; memb Assoc of Hidalgos of Spain; Kt of Honour and Devotion SMO Malta, Kt of Justice Constantine Order of St George of Naples; *Recreations* horse-breeding, golf, polo, jogging, yachting; *Clubs* Royal Yacht Club of Gibraltar; *Style*— Marquis of Guadacorte, Count of Casa Fuerte; Felipe IV, 8 Madrid 14, Spain

GUASCHI, Francis Eugene; s of Gino Guaschi (d 1986), of Holborn EC1, and Catherine Bridget, *née* Smith (d 1982); *b* 5 April 1931; *Educ* St Marylebone GS; *m* 25 June 1960, Sylvia Rose, da of Douglas Jones Willesden (d 1959); 1 s (John b 27 Sept 1965), 1 da (Jane b 11 Aug 1967); *Career* Nat Serv 1955-57; asst gen mangr Mercantile and General Reinsurance Co Ltd 1980-85, ptnr Bacon and Woodrow Consulting Actuaries 1985-; FIA; *Recreations* playing the piano, mathematics, computers; *Clubs* Actuaries; *Style*— Francis Guaschi, Esq; 18 Clements Rd, Chorleywood, Rickmansworth, Herts WD3 5JT (☎ 0923 282425); Messrs Bacon & Woodrow Consulting Actuaries (telex 8953206 BWLONG)

GUDENIAN, John; s of Mihran Gudenian (d 1921), of London, and Nevric, *née* Mouradian (d 1941); *b* 27 April 1914; *Educ* Univ Coll Sch Hampstead, Hornsey Art Coll, St Martins Sch of Art; *m* 27 Aug 1955, Margaret, da of John Yateley (d 1984), of Newcastle; 2 da (Miranda Nevric b 1958, Christina Mary b 1961); *Career* WWII RAF UK N Africa, Italy; theatrical and film designer and costumier: BJ Simmons & Co Ltd 1931-39, J Arthur Rank Films 1946-50; dir LH Nathan Ltd 1950-72, dir and conslt Bermans & Nathans Ltd 1972-87; involved in tennis, cricket, ex-serv activities, Br Legion; Freeman City of London; *Style*— John Gudenian, Esq

GUDERLEY, Daisy Deborah; OBE (1974); da of Hyman Hyams, and Annie Hyams (d 1939); *b* 25 Nov 1912; *Educ* Coborn Secdy; *m* 1, 6 June 1936 Sidney Hart (d 1973); m 2, 2 May 1975, C Guderley; *Career* Tesco Stores: joined 1931, md Tesco Stores (Wholesale) Ltd 1970, dir Tesco Stores plc 1970-82; formerly involved with Food Trade (Regulation Labelling Ctee, Open Date Coding, Article Numbering), former memb: Retail Consortium Assoc, South Eastern Economic Ctee, Restrictive Practice Ct, Govt Metrication Bd 1970-79; *Style*— Mrs Daisy Guderley, OBE; 10 Noblefield Heights, Cherry Tree Hill, Great North Rd, Highgate, London N2 0NX (☎ 081 348 1591)

GUDKA, (Narendra) Naresh Zaverchand; s of Zaverchand Gosar, of Nairobi, Kenya, and Jiviben Zaverchand (d 1945); *b* 13 Jan 1942; *Educ* Duke of Gloucester Sch Nairobi Kenya, Balham and Tooting Coll of Commerce London; *m* 1 April 1967, Catherine Elizabeth, da of Michael Charles Tynan (d 1951), of Limerick; 2 da (Rita Claire b 13 Feb 1968, Michelle Christine b 11 Feb 1971); *Career* articled clerk Leslie Furneaux & Co 1961-66, qualified CA 1966, Peat Marwick McLintock 1967-68, J & A Scrimgeour & Co 1968-74, Banque Paribas Capital Markets Ltd 1974-82, Citicorp Scrimgeour Vickers & Co 1982-89, rejoined Banque Paribas Capital Markets Ltd 1989-; FCA 1967, ASIA 1975, TSA 1975; *Recreations* gardening, sports; *Clubs* MCC; *Style*— Naresh Gudka, Esq; 2 Aston Ave, Kenton, Middx HA3 ODB (☎ 081 907 3226); 33 Wigmore St, London W1H OBN (☎ 071 355 2000, fax 071 355 2020, telex 296723/23707)

GUERITZ, Rear-Adm Edward Findlay; CB (1971), OBE (1957), DSC (1942 and bar 1944); s of late Elton L Gueritz; *b* 8 Sept 1919; *Educ* Cheltenham; *m* 1947, Pamela Amanda Bernhardina, *née* Jeans; 1 s, 1 da; *Career* RN: 1939-45 War, Home, Med and Eastern Waters; Capt of Fleet Far East Fleet 1965-66, dir Def Plans (Navy) 1967, dir Jt Warfare Staff MOD 1968, Adm Pres RN Coll Greenwich 1968-70, Cmdt Jt Warfare Estab 1970-72, ret 1973; chief hon steward Westminster Abbey 1975-85, pres Soc for Nautical Res 1975-; dir Royal United Servs Inst for Def Studies 1979-81 (dep dir and ed 1976-79, dir and ed-in-chief 1979-81); vice chm: Cncl for Christian Approaches to Def and Disarmament 1974-80, Victoria League 1985-88, Marine Soc 1987-; *Publications* (jt ed) Ten Years of Terrorism, Will the Wells Run Dry, RUSI/Brassey's Defence Year Book (1978/79, 1980, 1981, 1982), Nuclear Attack/Civil Defence (1982); contributor: The Third World War (1978), The Second World War (1982), NATO's Maritime Strategy (1987); *Clubs* Army & Navy; *Style*— Rear Adm Edward Gueritz, CB, OBE, DSC; 56 The Close, Salisbury, Wilts (☎ 0722 3649)

GUERNSEY, Lord; Charles Heneage Finch-Knightley; s and h of 11 Earl of Aylesford; *b* 27 March 1947; *Educ* Oundle, Trinity Coll Cambridge; *m* 1971, Penelope Anstice, da of Kenneth A G Crawley (d 1988), of London; 1 s (Hon Heneage James Daniel b 29 April 1985); 4 da (Hon Rachel Louise b 1974, Hon Kate Pamela (twin) b 1974, Hon Alexandra Rosemary b 1977, Hon Laura Charlotte b 1982); *Heir* s, Hon Heneage James Daniel; *Recreations* shooting, archery, real tennis; *Style*— Lord Guernsey; Packington Hall, Meriden, nr Coventry, Warwicks CV7 7HF (☎ 0676 22274)

GUERRA, Maximiliano Guido; s of Guido Adolfo Guerra, of Buenos Aires, Argentina, and Maria del Carmen Maldonado; *b* 5 May 1967; *Educ* Superior Inst of the Arts, Colon Theatre Buenos Aires Argentina; *m* 28 May 1988, Sandra Beatrice, da of Gian Carlo Scanferlato; *Career* ballet dancer; princ dancer La Plata's Ballet del Teatro Argentino (work incl Alonso's Carmen), joined Colón Theatre's Ballet Buenos Aires 1985 (work incl: S American premiere of Dvořák Serenade, Balanchine's Four Temperaments, La Sylphide at III Int Dance Festival Rio de Janeiro with Prima Ballerina Eva Evdokimova, Bournonville's La Sylphide at the Colón Theatre); princ dancer Eng Nat Ballet (formerly London Festival Ballet) 1988-, roles incl: Siegfried in Makarova's Swan Lake, Nutcracker Prince and the Cavalier in Schaufuss' The Nutcracker, Franz in Hynd's Coppelia, Mercutio and Romeo in Ashton's Romeo and Juliet, Gennaro in Nappoli, Etudes and Le Corsaire Pas De Deux, Christopher Bruce's Land, the Golden Slave in Schéhérezade; toured USA with Eng Nat Ballet 1989 (performances incl: Bournonville's La Sylphide in Washington and the American premiere of Ashton's Romeo and Juliet at Metropolitan Opera House NY), performed Tchaikovsky-Carter's Swan Lake Colón Theatre Buenos Aires 1989, toured USSR 1989 and 1990 (prodns incl: Giselle, Swan Lake, Don Quixote, Vassilev's version of Prokofiev's Romeo and Juliet); most recent work incl: Vaganova's Diana and Acteon 1990, Piazolla-Lopez's Contrabajo para Hombre Solo and El Renidero 1990, Grigorovich's Spartacus with Novosibirsk Ballet Opera at St Petersburg's Renaissance 1991 (first non-Soviet dancer to perform this version of the ballet); performances at galas incl: Chicago Ballet Benefit Gala, XI Int Ballet Festival of Havana, V Ballet Royal Gala (Amsterdam), Montreal Canada, 40 Anniversary of Eng Nat Ballet London, XVIII Cervantino Int Festival; *awards* Grand Prix and Silver medal V Int Ballet Competition Ciudad de Trujillo Peru 1985, Silver medal NY Int Ballet Competition 1987, Gold medal at XIII Varna Int Ballet Competition 1988; *Recreations* sports; *Style*— Maximiliano Guerra, Esq; VEAB Producciones, Avenida Cordoba 807, 8voA, CP 1054, Buenos Aires, Argentina (fax 541 312 6245); Marco Borelli, Via Natale Battaglia 24, 20127 Milano, Italy (☎ 392 282 8077); London (fax 071 262 0254)

GUERRA-MALDONADO, Maximiliano Guido; *see*: Guerra, Maximiliano Guido

GUERRICO, Lady Moira Beatrice Forbes; da of 9 Earl of Granard; *b* 2 Feb 1951; *m* 1, 1971 (m dis 1975), HH Prince Charles Antoine Louis de Ligne de la Tremoille (who later m Princesse Aliette de Croy); m 2, 1978, José Guerrico; 1 s (Killian Arthur b 16 March 1987), 1 d (Shannon b 1983); *Style*— The Lady Moira Guerrico; 20 Avenue de l'Annonciade, Monte Carlo, Monaco

GUEST, Albert Sidney; s of Thomas Albert Guest (d 1978); *b* 17 Nov 1934; *Educ* Sladen Kidderminster, Univ of Birmingham; *m* 1962, Maureen, da of Frederick Corker (d 1961); 1 s, 1 da; *Career* 2 Lt RAPC; dir: Sheerloom Carpets 1977-81, (sales) Heckmondwike Carpets 1978-82; UK dir Besmer Carpets (UK) Ltd, Sub Besmer Sommer Germany 1982-; CMInstM; *Recreations* golf, walking; *Clubs* Woodsome Hall Golf (Huddersfield); *Style*— Albert Guest, Esq; 11 Fenay Crescent, Almondbury, Huddersfield, W Yorks (☎ 0484 532801)

GUEST, Dr Ann Hutchinson; da of Robert Hare Hutchinson (d 1975), of West Redding, Conn, USA, and Delia Farley, *née* Dana (d 1989); *b* 3 Nov 1918; *m* 20 Jan 1962, Ivor Forbes Guest, *qv*, s of Cecil Marmaduke Guest (d 1954), of Bickley, Kent; *Career* dancer in a series of successful musicals NY USA 1942-50; dance notator: Ballet Jooss 1938-39, NY City Ballet 1948-61; Dance Notation Bureau New York: fndr 1940, dir 1941-61, hon pres 1961-; fndr memb Int Cncl Kinetography Laban (pres 1985), fndr and dir Language of Dance Centre 1967-; dance reconstructor: Cachucha (Royal Ballet, Ballet for All 1967, Vienna Staatsoper 1969), Pas de Six, La Vivandière (Joffrey Ballet 1977, Sadler's Wells Royal Ballet 1982), L'Après-midi d'un faune (San Carlo Ballet Naples, Grands Ballets Canadiens, Juillard Dance Ensemble 1989); Hon LHD Marygrove Coll Detroit Univ 1977, Hon DHum Ohio State Univ 1987; *Books* Labanotration (1953), Your Move (1983), Dance Notation (1984), Choreo-Graphics (1989); *Recreations* photography; *Style*— Dr Ann Guest; 17 Holland Park, London W11 3TD (☎ 071 229 3780)

GUEST, Prof Anthony Gordon; CBE (1989), QC (1987); s of Gordon Walter Leslie Guest (d 1982), of Maidencombe, Devon, and Alice Marjorie, *née* Hooper; *b* 8 Feb 1930; *Educ* Colston's Sch Bristol, St John's Coll Oxford (MA); *Career* Lt RA (reg Army and TA) 1948-50; called to the Bar Gray's Inn 1956; memb Lord Chllr Law Reform Ctee 1963-84, UK del to UN Cmmn on Int Trade Law 1968-88, bencher Grays Inn 1978-; dean Univ Coll Oxford 1963-64 (fell and praelector 1955-65), prof of English Law Univ of London 1966-, reader Common Law Cncl of Legal Educn (Inns of Ct) 1967-80, fell Kings Coll London 1982-; memb bd govrs Rugby Sch 1968-88; FCIarb 1986; *Books* Anson's Law of Contract (21-26 edns 1959-84), The Law of Hire-Purchase (1966), Chitty on Contracts (gen ed, 23-26 edns 1968-89), Benjamin's Sale of Goods (gen ed, 1-3 edns 1974-86), Encyclopaedia of Consumer Credit (jt ed, 1975); *Clubs* Garrick; *Style*— Prof Anthony Guest, CBE, QC; 16 Trevor Place, London SW7 1LB (☎ 071 584 9260); 4 Raymond Buildings, Gray's Inn, London WC1 (☎ 071 405 7211)

GUEST, Hon Charles James; yst s of Maj 2 Viscount Wimborne, OBE (d 1967), and Lady Mabel Fox-Strangways, yr da of 6 Earl of Ilchester; *b* 10 July 1950; *Educ* Harrow, RMA Sandhurst; *m* 1976, Simone, da of Patrick Whinney, of Guernsey; 2 s, 1 da; *Career* served 9/12 Royal Lancers 1973, late Capt Royal Wessex Yeomanry; memb Int Stock Exchange 1986, with Cobbold Roach Ltd; *Recreations* shooting, fishing; *Clubs* Flyfishers', White's; *Style*— The Hon Charles Guest; Truckwell Manor Farm, Lydeard St Lawrence, Taunton, Somerset TA4 3PT (☎ 0984 56327)

GUEST, Hon David William Graham; er s (by 2 m) of late Baron Guest, PC (Life Peer); *b* 18 Sept 1943; *Educ* Charterhouse Cambridge, Clare Coll Cambridge (MA); *Career* CA; memb City of Edinburgh DC 1984-; *Style*— The Hon David Guest; 16 Deinhaugh Street, Edinburgh EH4 1LY

GUEST, Dr Douglas (Albert); CVO (1975); s of Harold Eastwood Guest (d 1948), of Henley-on-Thames, and Margaret Sarah, *née* Higgins; *b* 9 May 1916; *Educ* Reading Sch, RCM, King's Coll Cambridge (MusB, MA); *m* 4 Dec 1941, Peggie Florentia, da of Thomas Falconer (d 1934), of Amberley, Glos; 2 da (Susan Jennifer b 1943, Penelope Anne b 1946); *Career* WWII Maj RA, (despatches Normandy 1944), gazetted Hon Maj RA 1945; dir music Uppingham 1945-50; organist: Salisbury Cathedral 1950-57, Worcester Cathedral 1957-63; conductor 3 Choirs Festival 1957-63, organist and master of choristers Westminster Abbey 1963-81, prof RCM 1963-81, examiner Royal Schs Music 1948-86; Mus D (Cantab) 1981, MA Oxford by incorporation 1947; FRCM 1963, Hon RAM 1964, Hon FRCO 1966, FRSCM 1970; *Recreations* fly-fishing, golf; *Clubs* Flyfishers'; *Style*— Dr Douglas Guest, CVO; The Gables, Minchinhampton, Glos GL6 9JE (☎ 0453 883191)

GUEST, Dr George Howell; CBE (1987); s of Ernest Joseph Guest (d 1966), and Gwendolen, *née* Brown (d 1965); *b* 9 Feb 1924; *Educ* Chester Cathedral Choir Sch, Kings Sch Chester, Saint John's Coll Cambridge (MA, MusB); *m* 31 Oct 1959, Nancy Mary, da of William Peters Talbot; 1 s (David b 26 June 1963), 1 da (Elizabeth b 11 Oct 1965); *Career* WW II RAF (France and India) 1942-46; organist and dir of music St John's Coll Cambridge 1951-91, lectr in Music Univ of Cambridge 1956-82 (asst lectr 1953-56), examiner to Associated Bd of RSM 1959-, univ organist Cambridge 1973-91, dir Arts Theatre Cambridge; concerts with St John's Coll Choir incl: USA, Canada, Japan, Aust, Brazil, Western Europe, Philippines, S Africa; pres: Royal Coll of Organists 1978-80, Cathedral Organists Assoc 1980-82, Inc Assoc of Organists 1987-89; hon memb: RAM, Gorsedd y Beirdd Eisteddfod Genedlaethol Cymru; Mus D Lambeth 1977, Hon D Mus Univ of Wales 1989; FRCO 1942, FRSCM; *Recreations* Welsh language, Association football; *Clubs* United Oxford & Cambridge Univ, Clwb Ifor Bach (Cardiff); *Style*— Dr George Guest, CBE; 9 Gurney Way, Cambridge (☎ 0223 354932); Saint John's College, Cambridge (☎ 0223 338683)

GUEST, Ivor Forbes; s of Cecil Marmaduke Guest (d 1954); *b* 14 April 1920; *Educ* Lancing, Trinity Coll Cambridge; *m* 20 Jan 1962, Ann Hutchinson, *qv*, da of Robert Hare; *Career* slr, dance historian; sec Radcliffe Tst 1966-, chm Royal Acad of Dancing 1969-; *Books* incl: Napoleon III in England, The Ballet of the Second Empire, The Romantic Ballet in Paris, The Romantic Ballet in England, Fanny Elssler, Jules Perrot, Gautier on Dance, The Dancer's Heritage, Dr John Radcliffe and his Trust; FRAD; *Clubs* Garrick, MCC; *Style*— Ivor Guest Esq; 17 Holland Park, London W11 3TD (☎ 071 229 3780)

GUEST, Hon (Christopher) John Graham; only s (by 1 m) of Baron Guest, PC (Life Peer) (d 1984); *b* 30 July 1929; *Educ* Eton, Clare Coll Cambridge (BA); *m* 1960, Myrna Dukes, MD, Chicago; 1 s (Christopher b 1967), 1 da (Amanda b 1964); *Career* AA Dipl, RIBA; *Clubs* Chelsea Arts; *Style*— The Hon John Guest; 19 Cheyne Row,

London SW3 5HW

GUEST, Hon Julian John; 2 s of 2 Viscount Wimborne, OBE, JP, DL (d 1967); *b* 12 Oct 1945; *Educ* Stowe; *m* 1, 1970 (m dis 1978), Emma Jane Arlette, da of Cdr Archibald Gray, DSO, RN (ret), of Tilbridge, Gt Staughton, St Neots, Hunts; m 2, 1983, Jillian, da of late N S G Bannatine; *Style*— The Hon Julian Guest; 29 Bolton Gdns, London SW5

GUEST, Melville Richard John; s of Sqdn Ldr Ernest Melville Charles Guest, DSO, DFC, and Katherine Mary, *née* Hustler; *b* 18 Nov 1943; *Educ* Rugby, Magdalen Coll Oxford (MA); *m* 23 May 1970, (Beatriz Eugenia) Jenny, da of Horacio Alberto Lopez Colombres; 4 s (Edward, Benjamin, Alexander, William); *Career* entered FCO 1966, Tokyo 1967-72, PPS to Parly Under Sec FCO 1972-75, first sec commercial Paris 1975-79, FCO 1979-80, md Lucas France SA and dir Thomas-Lucas SA 1980-85, dir Channel Tunnel Group 1985-86, commercial cnsllr Br Embassy Tokyo 1986-89; *Recreations* tennis, golf, skiing; *Clubs* Oxford & Cambridge Univ, MCC, Hurlingham; *Style*— Melville Guest, Esq; FCO, King Charles St, London SW1A 2AH

GUEST, Hon Simon Edward Graham; WS; s of Baron Guest, PC (Life Peer, d 1984), by his 2 w, Catherine Hotham (gda of Adm of the Fleet Sir Charles Hotham, GCB, GCVO, and cous of Lord Hotham); *b* 22 April 1949; *Educ* Charterhouse, Univ of Dundee; *m* 1977, Fiona, da of Robert Wilson Taylor Lamont (1976); 1 s, 1 da; *Career* solicitor; *Recreations* golf; *Clubs* New (Edinburgh), Hon Co of Edinburgh Golfers (Muirfield); *Style*— The Hon Simon Guest, WS; 40 Hope Terrace, Edinburgh EH9 2AR (☎ 031 447 4075, office 031 226 6703)

GUEST ALBERT, Revel Sarah; da of Hon Oscar Guest (d 1958), of Hereford, and Susan Kathleen, *née* Paterson (d 1982); *b* 14 Sept 1931; *Educ* Bedgebury Pk Sch, LSE; *m* 26 Aug 1963, Robert Alan Albert, s of James Albert of Boston USA; 1 s (Justin Thomas b 19 Feb 1965), 1 da (Corisande Charlotte b 10 March 1967); *Career* private sec to Jo Grimond ldr Lib Pty 1949-51, contested gen election and LCC 1951 and 1952, asst ed Time & Tide magazine 1953-55, prodn asst and prodr Panorama BBC 1961-67, bureau chief Pub TV Laboratory of US 1967 and 1968, formed Transatlantic films 1968; prodr and dir 1968-, work incl: Greek Fire, The Horse in Sport, The Monastery of Mount Sinai, A Year in the Life of Placido Domingo, Four American Composers, In Search of Paradise, Paris Lost, Feliks Topolski, Self Encounter - Man in a Fog, Bold as Brass, If It Moves Shoot It, Makin' It, Norman Mailer V Fun City USA; Cons candidate LCC; memb Royal TV Soc; *Books* Lady Charlotte, A Biography of the Nineteenth Century (1989); *Recreations* horse riding; *Clubs* Turf; *Style*— Mrs Revel Guest Albert; Cabalva House, Whitney-on-Wye, Hereford (☎ 04973 232); 17 Girdlers Rd, London W14; 100 Blythe Rd, London W14 (☎ 071 727 0132, telex 21781, fax 071 603 0668, car 0860 333086)

GUEST de SWARTE, Lindsey (Lyn); da of Alfred John de Swarte, of Stanmore, Middx, and Anne, *née* Yashvin; *b* 12 June 1941; *Educ* Rosa Bassett Sch, St Martins Sch of Art; *m* 1, 1958 (m dis 1970), Frank Colin Sutton-McCrae; 2 s, 2 da; m 2, 1970 (m dis 1983), Raymond Guest; 1 s, 1 da; *partner* 1984, Catherine Gibb; *Career* publisher and managing ed Sportswoman 1984-86, dir Sportsworld International 1987, publisher and managing ed Sportscene 1988; freelance writer 1989-; elected Magazine Sportswriter of the Year 1988; life memb Nat Skating Assoc of GB (ice speed skating referee), helped found Women's Ice Hockey and League 1980, played for Streatham Strikers (league winners 1981) 1980-84; on Int Skating Union panel of Starters, referee Euro Youth Championships 1983; *Books* Women and Sport (1988); *Recreations* ice skating, reading, painting; *Clubs* Sports Writers Assoc of Gr Britain; *Style*— Ms Lyn Guest de Swarte; 21 Mount Earl Gdns, London SW16 (☎ 01 677 4985)

GUETERBOCK, Hon Mrs (Cynthia Ella); *née* Foley; da of Eva Mary FitzHardinge, Baroness Berkeley (16 in line, d 1964), and Col Frank Wigram Foley, CBE, DSO (d 1949); hp of sis, Baroness Berkeley (17 in line); *b* 31 Jan 1909; *m* 4 Aug 1937, Brig Ernest Adolphus Leopold Gueterbock, RE (d 1984), yst s of Alfred Gueterbock, of Bowdon, Cheshire; 1 s (Anthony FitzHardinge Gueterbock b 20 Sept 1939); *Recreations* golf, bridge; *Clubs* Naval and Military; *Style*— The Hon Mrs Gueterbock; The Plough, Terrick, Aylesbury, Bucks

GUILD, Ivor Reginald; CBE (1985), WS; s of late Col Arthur Marjoribanks Guild, DSO, TD, DL, and Phyllis Eliza, *née* Cox; *b* 2 April 1924; *Educ* Cargilfield, Rugby, New Coll Oxford, Univ of Edinburgh; *Career* ptnr Shepherd and Wedderburn WS, procurator fiscal of Lyon Court 1961-, clerk to Abbey Court of Holyroodhouse 1970-79, baillie of Abbey Ct 1979-, chm Nat Museum of Antiquities Scotland 1981-86; ed Scottish Genealogist 1959-, chllr of dioceses of Edinburgh and St Andrew's; *Recreations* golf, genealogy; *Clubs* New (Edinburgh); *Style*— Ivor Guild, Esq, CBE, WS; 16 Charlotte Square, Edinburgh EH2 4YS (☎ 031 225 8585; home 031 226 4882)

GUILD, Stuart Alexander; TD (1955), WS (1950); s of William John Guild (d 1958), of Belmont Gardens, Edinburgh, and Mary Margaret Morton Stuart (d 1968); *b* 25 Jan 1924; *Educ* Edinburgh Acad, George Watson's Coll, Queen's Univ Belfast, Univ of Edinburgh (BL); *m* 21 Nov 1950, Fiona Catherine, da of Andrew Francis MacCulloch (d 1952); 1 s (David b 1952), 2 da (Cathleen b 1955, Lesley b 1960); *Career* RA, served UK 1942-44, Burma 1944-45, French Indo-China 1945-46, Malaya 1946-47, TA RA 1947-65; ptnr (now conslt) Guild & Guild WS 1950-89; Notary Public; hon treas Army Cadet Force Assoc (Scot) 1976-91, cncl memb Army Cadet Force Assoc 1976-; memb RA Cncl of Scot 1985-, chm Scot Smallbore Rifle Assoc 1986-88, memb Scot Target Shooting Cncl 1986-88; govr Melville Coll Tst 1976-91, vice pres Lothians Smallbore Shooting Assoc 1985-91; chm Sandilands Memorial Tst 1985-; memb Worshipful Co of Merchants of the City of Edinburgh (asst Master's Ct) 1972-75; *Recreations* golf, target shooting, photography, collecting; *Clubs* Watsonian, Murrayfield Golf, Edinburgh Academical; *Style*— Stuart Guild, Esq, TD, WS; 5 Rutland Square, Edinburgh (☎ 031 229 5394)

GUILDFORD, 7 Bishop of 1983-; Rt Rev Michael Edgar Adie; s of Walter Granville Adie and Kate Emily, *née* Parish; *b* 22 Nov 1929; *Educ* Westminster, St John's Coll Oxford (MA); *m* 1957, Anne Devonald Roynon; 1 s, 3 da; *Career* former resident chaplain to Archbishop of Canterbury, vicar St Mark Sheffield 1960-69, rural dean of Hallam 1966-69, rector of Louth 1969-76, vicar of Morton with Hacconby 1976-83, archdeacon of Lincoln 1977-83; chm Gen Synod Bd of Educn and Nat Soc 1989-; *Style*— The Rt Rev the Lord Bishop of Guildford

GUILFORD, David John Scotchburn; s of Arthur Guilford, CBE (d 1975), of Banstead, and Nora Christine, *née* Snell (d 1987); *b* 4 Oct 1930; *Educ* Harrow, Christ's Coll Cambridge (MA); *Career* asst master Highfield Sch Liphook 1954-59, house master Eton Coll 1973-88 (asst master 1959-); winner of Eton Fives Amateur Championship Kinnaird Cup, govr Beaudesert Park Sch 1968-, vice pres Eton Fives Assoc 1975- (hon sec 1961-69); Liveryman Worshipful Co of Goldsmiths 1978; *Recreations* sport, contract bridge; *Clubs* Hawks (Cambridge), MCC, Jesters; *Style*— David Guilford, Esq; 1 Gulliver's, Eton College, Windsor, Berks SL4 6DB (☎ 0753 865045)

GUILFORD, 9 Earl of (GB 1752); Edward Francis North; DL (Kent 1976); also Baron Guilford (E 1683); patron of three livings; s of Major Lord North (k in accident 1940, himself er s of 8 Earl of Guilford), and Joan, da of Sir Merrik Burrell, 7 Bt, CBE; suc gf, 8 Earl; *b* 22 Sept 1933; *Educ* Eton; *m* 1956, Osyth Vere Napier, da of Cyril Leeston Smith; 1 s; *Heir* s, Lord North; *Style*— The Rt Hon the Earl of Guilford, DL; Waldershare Park, Dover, Kent (☎ 0304 820244)

GUILLAUME, John; s of Reginald Guillaume (d 1953), and Isabel, *née* Turton (d 1980); *b* 9 May 1925; *Educ* Cheltenham; *m* 1975, Angela Rae, da of Norman Moffett; 1 s, 2 da; *Career* Fleet Air Arm, Eastern Fleet; admitted slr 1950; conslt (formely sr ptnr) Guillaume & Sons Slrs; Master Worshipful Co of Solicitors of the City of London 1980-81; contrib Roving Commissions; *Recreations* cruising (yacht 'New Melody'), skiing, tennis, gardening, choral music; *Clubs* Carlton, Royal Cruising (hon slr 1985-), Royal Thames Yacht, Royal Lymington Yacht (vice-commodore 1987-90); *Style*— John Guillaume, Esq; c/o Guillaume & Sons Slrs, Dorchester House, Church St, Weybridge, Surrey (☎ 0932 840111, fax 0932 858092, telex 929843)

GUILOR, Ralph John; s of John Kenneth Guilor, and Ingeborg Elizabeth *née* Bambach; *b* 1 Jan 1955; *Educ* Dartford GS, Portsmouth Sch of Architecture; *m* 9 Sept 1979, Judith Elizabeth, da of Harold James Turner; 1 s (Edward Charles b 1985), 1 da (Rachel Elizabeth b 1983); *Career* architect; sr ptnr Guilor Petch Design Ptnrship, BArch, Dip Arch, RIBA; *Recreations* music, art, sport; *Style*— Ralph Guilor, Esq; c/o Barclays Bank, 1 Montpellier Exchange, Cheltenham, Glos; Suite 8, Bath Mews, 19 Bath Parade, Cheltenham, Glos (☎ 0242 521608)

GUINNESS, Sir Alec; CBE (1955); *b* 2 April 1914; *Educ* Pembroke Lodge Southbourne, Roborough Eastbourne; *m* 1938, Merula Silvia, da of M H Salaman; 1 s; *Career* RN Combined Ops WWII; actor; films incl: Oliver Twist, Kind Hearts and Coronets, The Lavender Hill Mob, The Bridge on the River Kwai (Best Actor of the Year Oscar 1957), Tunes of Glory, Lawrence of Arabia, Star Wars, A Handful of Dust; Special Oscar for Contribution to Film 1979, Laurence Olivier award for Services to the Theatre 1989; recent roles incl: *Plays* The Old Country, A Walk in the Woods; *TV* Tinker Tailor Soldier Spy, Smiley's People, Monsignor Quixote; Hon Doctor of Fine Arts Boston Coll, Hon DLitt Oxon; kt 1959; *Books* Blessings in Disguise (1985); *Clubs* Garrick, Athenaeum; *Style*— Sir Alec Guinness, CBE; c/o McReddie, 91 Regent Street, London W1

GUINNESS, Hon Catriona Rose; da of 2 Baron Moyne; *b* 13 Dec 1950; *Educ* Cranborne Chase and Winchester Co HS, LMH Oxford (MA); *Career* botanist and farm manager; *Style*— The Hon Catriona Guinness; Biddesdon Farm, Andover, Hants

GUINNESS, Hon Desmond Walter; s of 2 Baron Moyne; *b* 8 Sept 1931; *Educ* Gordonstoun, Ch Ch Oxford; *m* 1, 1954 (m dis 1981), HSH Princess Marie-Gabrielle Sophie Joti Elisabeth Albertine Almeria (d 1989), da of HSH Prince Albrecht Eberhard Karl Gero-Maria von Urach, Count of Wurttemberg; 1 s, 1 da; m 2, 1984, Penelope, da of Graham Cuthbertson; *Career* pres Irish Georgian Soc 1958-91; Hon LLD Trinity Coll Dublin; *Books* Georgian Dublin (1979), Irish Houses and Castles (jtly, 1971) The White House (1980), Palladio, a Western Progress (jtly, 1976), Newport Restored (jtly, 1981); *Style*— The Hon Desmond Guinness; Leixlip Castle, Co Kildare

GUINNESS, (Cecil) Edward; CVO (1986); er s of John Cecil Guinness (d 1970, gs of Richard Samuel Guinness, whose great uncle Arthur was the founder of the family brewing firm), of Clarehaven, Parbold, nr Wigan, Lancs; *b* 1924; *Educ* Stowe, Univ of Belfast, Sch of Brewing Birmingham; *m* 1951, Elizabeth Mary Fossett, da of George Alan Thompson (d 1971), of Albrighton Hall, nr Wolverhampton; 3 da; *Career* served WWII Offr Cadet RA (invalided out); vice chm Guinness Brewing Worldwide; dir: Guinness plc 1971-89, Wolverhampton and Dudley Breweries 1964-87; chm Harp Lager; vice pres Brewers' Soc (chm 1985-86); chm: governing body Dame Alice Owen's Sch Potters Bar, UK Tstees Duke of Edinburgh's Cwlth Study Cons 1971-86, Fulmer Parish Cncl, Licensed Trade Charities Tst; past pres and memb exec ctee Licensed Victuallers Nat Homes; memb: governing body Lister Inst, dept tst Queen Elizabeth's Fndn for the Disabled; Former Master Worshipful Co of Brewers; life memb Industl Soc; *Books* The Guinness Book of Guinness (1988); *Recreations* gardening, shooting, travel; *Style*— C Edward Guinness, Esq, CVO; Huyton Fold, Fulmer Village, Bucks (☎ 0753 663179)

GUINNESS, Hon Erskine Stuart Richard; s of 2 Baron Moyne; *b* 16 Jan 1953; *Educ* Winchester, Univ of Edinburgh; *m* 26 April 1984, Louise Mary Elizabeth, o da of late Patrick Dillon-Malone; 1 s (Hector b 1986), 1 da (Molly b 1985); *Career* MFH Tedworth Hunt 1981-84, memb Wilts CC 1979-81, farmer, tstee Guinness Tst Housing Assoc 1979-90, govr Chadacre Agric Inst 1982-88; *Recreations* bee-keeping, fishing, rare breeds; *Style*— The Hon Erskine Guinness

GUINNESS, Hon Mrs Diarmid; Felicity; da of Sir Andrew Hunter Carnwath, KCVO, *qv*; *b* 15 Nov 1942; *m* 1962, Hon Diarmid Edward Guinness (d 1977); 1 s, 3 da; *Style*— The Hon Mrs Diarmid Guinness; 2 Keats Grove, London NW3 2RT (☎ 071 435 5861)

GUINNESS, Hon Finn Benjamin; s of 2 Baron Moyne; *b* 26 Aug 1945; *Educ* Winchester, Ch Ch Oxford (MA), Inst of Animal Genetics Univ of Edinburgh (PhD); *Career* biologist; former pres Arabian Horse Soc; *Style*— The Hon Finn Guinness; Biddesden House, Andover, Hants

GUINNESS, Hon Fiona Evelyn; da of 2 Baron Moyne; *b* 26 June 1940; *Educ* Cranborne Chase, McGill Univ Canada; *Career* research zoologist; joint author of publication Red Deer, Behaviour and Ecology of Two Sexes; *Style*— The Hon Fiona Guinness; Isle of Rhum, Inner Hebrides, Scotland

GUINNESS, Lt Cdr Sir Howard Christian Sheldon; VRD (1953); s of Edward Douglas Guinness, CBE (d 1983), by his 1 w, Martha Letière, *née* Sheldon; er bro of John Guinness, CB, *qv*; *b* 3 June 1932; *Educ* Eton; *m* 1958, Evadne, da of Capt Evan Gibbs, Coldstream Gds (n of 1 Baron Wraxall); 2 s (Christopher b 1963, Dominic b 1966), 1 da (Annabel b 1959); *Career* served RNR, Lt Cdr; joined S G Warburg & Co 1955, exec dir 1970-85; dir Harris & Sheldon GP 1960-81; dir and dep chm Youghal Carpets (Hldgs) 1972-80; chm N Hants Cons Assoc 1971-74; Wessex Cons Assoc: vice chm 1974, chm 1975-78, treas 1978-81; dairy farmer, memb cncl English Guernsey Cattle Assoc 1963-72; kt 1981; *Clubs* White's; *Style*— Lt Cdr Sir Howard Guinness, VRD; The Manor House, Glanvilles Wootton, Sherborne, Dorset DT9 5QF

GUINNESS, James Edward Alexander Rundell; CBE (1986); s of Sir Arthur Guinness, KCMG (d 1951), of Hawley Place, Hants; *b* 23 Sept 1924; *Educ* Eton, Univ of Oxford; *m* 1953, Pauline, da of Vivien Mander; 1 s (Hugo), 4 da (Miranda (Mrs Keith Payne), Sabrina, Anita (Hon Mrs Amschal Rothschild), Julia (Hon Mrs Michael Samuel)); *Career* Sub Lt RNVR; chm Guinness Mahon Holdings, ret, dir Guinness Peat Gp, ret; chm Public Works Loan Bd, ret; *Recreations* fishing; *Clubs* Brooks's, Pratt's, Royal Yacht Sqdn; *Style*— James Guinness, Esq, CBE; Coldpiece Farm, Mattingley, Basingstoke, Hampshire (☎ 073 326 292)

GUINNESS, John Ralph Sidney; CB (1985); s of Edward Douglas Guinness, CBE (d 1983), by his 1 w, Martha Letière, *née* Sheldon; yr bro of Sir Howard Guinness, *qv*; *b* 23 Dec 1935; *Educ* Rugby, Trinity Hall Cambridge; *m* 1967, Valerie, da of Roger North, JP (7 in descent from Roger North, KC, MP Dunwich, memoirist and yr bro of 1 Baron Guilford, whose descendants became Earls of Guilford), whose m was Grace, da of Gen Hon Sir Percy Feilding, KCB, 2 s of 7 Earl of Denbigh, PC; 1 s, 1 da (and 1 s decd); *Career* Overseas Devpt Inst 1961-62; FO: joined 1962, Econ Rels Dept 1962-63, third sec UK Mission to UN NY 1963-64, seconded to UN Secretariat as special asst to Dep Under Sec (later Under Sec Econ and Social Affrs) 1964-66; FCO 1967-69, first sec (econ) High Cmmn Ottawa 1969-72, seconded to Central Policy Review Staff (Cabinet Off) 1972-75 and 1977-79, alternate UK rep to Law of the Sea

Conf 1975-77; transferred to Domestic Civil Serv 1980; under-sec Dept of Energy 1980-83 (dep sec 1983-); *Recreations* iconography; *Clubs* Brooks's, Beefsteak; *Style—* John Guinness, Esq, CB; Department of Energy, 1 Palace St, London SW1E 5HE (☎ 071 238 3129)

GUINNESS, Hon Jonathan Bryan; s and h of 2 Baron Moyne by his 1 w, Hon Diana, *née* Freeman Mitford (da of 2 Baron Redesdale and who subsequently m Sir Oswald Mosley, 6 Bt, *see* Mosley, Hon Lady); *b* 16 March 1930; *Educ* Eton (King's Scholar), Trinity Coll Oxford; *m* 1, 1951 (m dis 1963), Ingrid, da of Maj Guy Wyndham, MC (ggs of 1 Baron Leconfield), by his 2 w, Grethe; 2 s, 1 da; m 2, 1964, Mrs Suzanne Phillips, da of H W D Lisney, of Gerona, Spain; 1 s, 1 da; *Career* dir: A Guinness Son & Co, Leopold Joseph & Sons; former Reuters journalist, chm Monday Club 1972-77; *Clubs* Carlton, Beefsteak, Ibstock Working Men's; *Style—* The Hon Jonathan Guinness; 17 Kensington Square, London W8; Osbaston Hall, Market Bosworth, Nuneaton; Ermita de San Sebastian, Cadaques, Gerona, Spain

GUINNESS, Kenelm Edward Lee; s and h of Sir Kenelm Guinness, 4 Bt; *b* 30 Jan 1962; *Educ* Embry-Riddle Aeronautical U (BSc); *Career* commercial pilot; *Style—* Kenelm Guinness, Esq; Rich Neck, Claiborne, Maryland 21624, USA (☎ 301 745 5079)

GUINNESS, Sir Kenelm Ernest Lee; 4 Bt (UK 1867); s of Kenelm Edward Lee Guinness, MBE, RNVR (d 1937), and Josephine (d 1989), da of Sir Thomas Strangman, sometime Advocate Gen in Bombay; suc unc, Sir Algernon Guinness, 3 Bt, 1954; *b* 13 Dec 1928; *Educ* Eton, MIT (BSc); *m* 1961, Mrs Jane Nevin Dickson; 2 s; *Heir* s, Kenelm Edward Lee Guinness; *Career* late 2 Lt RHG; engr Int Bank for Reconstruction and Devpt (World Bank) 1954-75; ind consltg engr 1975-; *Clubs* Cavalry & Guards, Household Division Yacht; *Style—* Sir Kenelm Guinness, Bt; Rich Neck, Claiborne, Maryland, 21624, USA (☎ 301 745 5079)

GUINNESS, Hon Kieran Arthur; 5 s of 2 Baron Moyne, *qv*; *b* 11 Feb 1949; *Educ* Winchester, Ch Ch Oxford; *m* 4 Nov 1983, Mrs Vivienne Halban, da of André-Jacques van Amerongen, DFC, MB, of Grafton House, Blisworth, Northants; 2 s (Malachy b 1986, Lorcan b 1989), 1 da (Kate b 1985); *Career* botanist; *Style—* The Hon Kieran Guinness; Knockmaroon House, Castleknock, Co Dublin

GUINNESS, Hon Murtogh David; s of 1 Baron Moyne, DSO, TD, PC (assassinated in Cairo 1944); *b* 15 Nov 1913; *m* 1949, Nancy Vivian Laura, da of Cyril Edward Tarbolton (decd); *Style—* The Hon Murtogh Guinness; 117 E 80th St, New York, USA

GUINNESS, Hon Thomasin Margaret; da of 2 Baron Moyne; *b* 16 Jan 1947; *Educ* Cranborne Chase, Farnham Coll of Art; *Career* potter and painter; *Style—* The Hon Thomasin Guinness; Biddesden House, Andover, Hants

GUINNESS, Timothy Whitmore Newton (Tim); s of Capt Eustace Guinness, DSC, RN, and Angela Beryl, *née* Hoare (d 1990); *b* 20 June 1947; *Educ* Eton, Magdalene Cambridge (BSc), MIT (MSc); *m* 6 June 1974, Beverley Anne, da of George Mills, of Rotherfield, East Sussex; 2 s (Edward, Harry), 2 da (Mary, Katherine); *Career* Baring Bros & Co Ltd 1970-77, Guinness Mahon & Co 1977-87 (investmt dir 1982-87), md Guinness Flight Global Asset Mgmnt Ltd 1987-; *Recreations* sailing; *Clubs* City Univ, MCC, RYS; *Style—* Tim Guinness, Esq; 32 St Mary at Hill, London EC3P 3AJ (☎ 01 623 9333, fax 01 623 2760, telex 884035)

GUINNESS, William Loel Seymour; s of Gp Capt Loel Guinness, OBE (d 1988), and his 2 w, Lady Isabel Manners, yr da of 9 Duke of Rutland; bro of Marchioness of Dufferin and Ava, *qv*; *b* 28 Dec 1939; *Educ* Eton; *m* 1971, (Agnes Elizabeth) Lynn, da of Ian Day, of Brampton Ash, Northants; 2 s, 1 da; *Career* served Irish Gds 1959-61, Lieut; farmer; *Recreations* golf, skiing, shooting; *Clubs* White's, Pratt's; *Style—* William Guinness, Esq; 10 Bourne St, London SW1; Arthingworth Manor, Market Harborough, Leics

GUINNESS ASCHAN, Marit Victoria; da of Henry Samuel Howard Guinness (d 1975), of 6 Cheyne Walk, Chelsea, and Alfhild Holter (d 1983); *b* 28 Jan 1919; *Educ* PNEU, art schs in Munich, Florence and Paris; *m* 21 July 1937 (m dis 1963), Carl William Aschan, s of Judge Nils Aschan (d 1966), of Stockholm, Sweden; 1 s (David b 1943), 1 da (Juliet b 1945); *Career* Nat Serv MOI 1939-45; enamellist and painter; individual exhibitions incl: Beaux Arts Gallery London 1948, Van Diemen Lilienfield Galleries NY 1968 (also 1949, 1955, 1957, 1959, 1962, 1966), Inter Art Gallery Caracus 1973, Roy Miles Gallery London 1979, Saga Gallery London 1990, Gallery Galtung Oslo 1974, 1981, 1984 and 1990; cmmns and collections in England incl: Victoria and Albert Museum, Worshipful Co of Goldsmiths London; Focal Point on the Cross for the High Altar Exeter Cathedral, Hugo and Reine Pitman Collection, Paul Oppé Collection, Royal Norwegian Embassy Collection, The Lord and Lady Iliffe Collection, John Studzinski Collection; in Norway: HM King Olav of Norway, HM The Queen of Norway, Kunstindustrimuseet Oslo, Hans Rasmus Astrup Collection; in USA: Brooklyn Museum NY, Yale Univ Art Gallery, Nelson Gallery and Atkins Museum Kansas, New Orleans Museum of Art, North Carolina Museum of Art Raleigh, Ian Woodner Family Collection New York, Beal Fndn Collection Boston Mass; work in numerous other private collections worldwide; memb Chelsea Arts Club 1967, pres Artist Enamellers 1969-; *Books* incl: Modern Jewellers, The Art of Jewellery (1968), Enamels (ed, 1983); *Recreations* travelling; *Clubs* Chelsea Arts; *Style—* Mrs Marit Guinness Aschan; 25 Chelsea Park Gardens, London SW3 6AF (☎ 071 352 2562); Studios 3 and 4, Moravian Close, 381 Kings Rd, London SW10 0LP (☎ 071 352 3790)

GUIREY, Prince Azamat; yr s of Prince Kadir Guirey (d 1953), and his 2 w, Vaguidé, *née* Sheretlock (d 1975); family descends from Genghis Khan and were Khans of the Crimea until conquered by Catherine the Great of Russia in 1783 and later recognized as Princes by several Imperial Ukases; *b* 14 Aug 1924; *Educ* Hotchkiss Sch, Yale Univ (BA); *m* 1, 10 Aug 1957 (m dis 1963), Princess Sylvia, da of Prince Serge Platonovitch Obolensky-Neledinsky-Meletzky; 2 s (Kadir Devlet b 1961, Adil Sagat b 1964), 1 da (Selima b 1960); m 2, 25 Aug 1971, Fredericka Ann, da of Frederick Sigrist, co-fndr with Sir Thomas Sopwith of Hawker Siddeley Gp Ltd (d 1956); 1 s (Caspian b 1972); *Career* associated with Young & Rubicam, advertising agency; formerly dir Weidenfeld Publishers; *Recreations* hunting, shooting, fishing, golf; *Clubs* White's, Garrick, Pratt's, Beefsteak, Kildare St (Dublin), Brook (NY); *Style—* Prince Azamat Guirey; Bakchisarai, Lyford Cay, Nassau, Bahamas, PO Box N969 (☎ 809 32 64506)

GUISE, Christopher James (Jamie); s of Sir Anselm Guise, 6 Bt (d 1970), and Nina Margaret Sophie, *née* Grant; hp of bro, Sir John Guise, 7 Bt, *qv*; *b* 10 July 1930; *Educ* Stowe; *m* 7 Nov 1969, Carole Hoskins, eld da of Jack Hoskins Master (d 1979), and Ruth Master, of Longparish, Hants; 1 s (Anselm b 1971), 1 da (Ruth b 1972); *Career* dir: Shenley Trust Services Ltd, Winglaw Group Ltd, Purchasing Management Services Ltd, Just Ice (UK) Ltd, Pasta Galore Ltd; *Recreations* golf, shooting, fishing, gardening; *Clubs* Turf, White's, MCC; *Style—* Jamie Guise, Esq; Easton Town Farm, Sherston, Malmesbury, Wilts SN16 OPS (☎ 0666 840310); 106 Claxton Grove, London W6 (☎ 071 385 3803)

GUISE, James Theodore (Louis); TD (1946); s of John Dougal Guise (d 1952), of 25 Kensington Gate, London W8, and Laura Lilian, *née* Buckland (d 1950); *b* 26 Aug 1910; *Educ* Winchester, Trinity Coll Oxford (MA); *m* 22 June 1940, Barbara, da of Alfred Jefferson Brett (d 1958), of Mark Ash, Abinger Common, Surrey; 1 s (Richard b 10 Sept 1941); *Career* 2 Lt City of London Yeo RHA 1939, Adj 10 Lt AA Trg Regt 1940-41, Maj RA 14 Army Burma 1942-45, instr in Gunnery 1944-45; admitted slr 1935; sr ptnr Hunters Slrs Lincolns Inn 1968-69, dir Law Fire Insur 1955-65; gen cmmr of Income Tax 1957-67, first pres Holborn Law Soc 1967, chm Slrs Benevolent Assoc 1962, memb Lowtonian Soc; *Recreations* cricket, soccer, golf, skiing, tapestry work; *Clubs* MCC; *Style—* Louis Guise, Esq, TD; Greathed Manor, Lingfield, Surrey (☎ 0342 832884)

GUISE, Sir John; GCMG (1975), KBE (1975), MP (Ind) Papua New Guinea 1977-; *b* 1914; *Career* MHA Papua New Guinea 1964-67, speaker 1968-75, dep chief min and min for agric to 1975, govr-gen Papua New Guinea 1975-77; KStJ; *Style—* Sir John Guise, GCMG, KBE, MP; National Parliament, Port Moresby, Papua New Guinea

GUISE, Sir John Grant; 7 Bt (GB 1783), of Highnam Court, Glos; s of Sir Anselm Guise, 6 Bt, JP (d 1970), by his w Margaret, da of Sir James Grant, first and last Bt; *b* 15 Dec 1927; *Educ* Winchester, RMC Sandhurst; *Heir* bro, Christopher James Guise, *qv*; *Career* Capt 3 Hussars (ret 1959); Jockey Club official 1968-; patron of one living; *Clubs* Turf; *Style—* Sir John Guise, Bt; Elmore Court, Gloucester (☎ 0452 720293)

GULBENKIAN, Boghos Parsegh (Paul); s of Krikor Parsegh Gulbenkian (d 1968), of Beaulieu, Hants, and Vergine Gulbenkian (d 1965); *b* 23 March 1940; *Educ* Kings College Sch Wimbledon, LSE (LLB); *m* 1, Alice (d 1969); 1 da (Vergine b 24 Nov 1968); m 2, 23 May 1970 (m dis 1990), Vartouhi, da of Artin Costanian, of London; 1 da (Sylvia b 27 July 1972); m 3, 15 Dec 1990, Jacqueline, da of late Bedros Shambian; *Career* admitted slr 1965; sr ptnr 1989-; Isadore Goldman (ptnr 1970-89), Gulbenkian Harris Andonian; pt/t imigration adjudicator appointed by Lord Chllr 1989-; chm Camden CAB Serv Mgmnt Ctee 1978-83, pres Holborn Law Soc 1984-85, memb Legal Aid Appeal Panel 1984-89; tstee: St Sarkis Charity Tst various tst for benefit of Armenian Community; memb Law Soc 1968 (hon auditor 1988-89); *Recreations* music, tennis, squash, walking; *Style—* Paul Gulbenkian, Esq; 4 Regent's Court, St George's Avenue, Weybridge, Surrey KT13 0DQ; 181 Kensington High St, London W8 6SH (☎ 071 937 1542, fax 071 938 2059)

GULL, Sir Rupert William Cameron; 5 Bt (UK 1872); s of Sir Michael Swinnerton Cameron Gull, 4 Bt (d 1989), and his 1 w, Yvonne, *née* Heslop; *b* 14 July 1954; *Educ* Diocesan Coll Cape Town, Cape Town Univ; *m* 1980, Gillian Lee, da of Robert MacFarlaine; 2 da (Victoria Yvonne b 3 Nov 1984, Katie Alexandra b 9 Dec 1986); *Style—* Sir Rupert Gull, Bt; Moonrakers, 56 Linersh Wood Close, Bramley, Guildford, Surrey GU5 0EQ

GULLAN, Richard Wilson; s of Archibald Gordon Gullan, OBE, of Rickmansworth, Herts, and (Mary) Helena, *née* Todd; *b* 22 June 1953; *Educ* Merchant Taylors', Med Coll of St Bartholomew's Hosp (BSc, MB BS, MRCP); *m* 28 July 1979, Christine, da of Leslie Douglas Prime, of Wimbledon; 2 s (James Hector b 1985, Archie Charles b 1987), 2 da (Laura Jane b 1983, Helena Clare b 1988); *Career* surgical training rotator St Bartholomew's Hosp 1979-82 (house surgn Professorial Surgical Unit 1977-78); lectr in anatomy Univ of Manchester 1978-79, neurosurgical SHO Addenbrooke's Hosp Cambridge 1982-83, supervisor in anatomy Gonville and Caius Coll Cambridge 1982-83, neurosurgical registrar Edinburgh 1983-85; neurosurgical sr registrar: Guy's 1985-87, King's Coll Hosp 1985-87, Brook Regnl Unit 1987-88; conslt neurosurgeon SE Thames Regnl Neurosurgical Unit 1988-, hon conslt neurosurgeon Maudsley Hosp London 1988- (sr registrar 1985-87); memb Soc of Br Neurological Surgns, fndr memb Br Cervical Spine Soc; FRCS 1982, FRSM; *Recreations* music (violinist), golf; *Clubs* Moor Park Golf Herts; *Style—* Richard Gullan, Esq; South East Thames Regional Neurosurgical Unit, Brook Hospital, Shooters Hill, London SE18 4LW (☎ 081 856 5555)

GULLIVER, James Gerald; s of William Frederick Gulliver and Mary Gulliver; *b* 17 Aug 1930; *Educ* Campbeltown GS, Glasgow Univ, Harvard Univ; *m* 1, 1958, Margaret Joan, *née* Cormack; 3 s, 2 da; m 2, 1977, Joanne, *née* Sims; *Career* Nat Serv RN; mgmnt conslt Urwick Orr & Ptnrs Ltd 1961-65; md Fine Fare (Hldgs) Ltd 1965-72 (chm 1967-72); chm: Argyll Gp plc, James Gulliver Assocs Ltd 1977-, Alpine Hldgs Ltd 1977-, Gulliver Foods Ltd 1978-, Argyll Foods 1979-, Gulliver Hotels Ltd 1978-, Amalgamated Distilled Products; dir: Concrete (Scotland) Ltd 1960-61, Assoc Br Foods Ltd, Manchester Utd Football Club plc 1979-; memb cncl IOD, vice pres Mktg Soc, memb PM's Enquiry into Beef Prices 1973; Liveryman Worshipful Co of Gardeners; Guardian Young Businessman of the Year 1972; FBIM, FRSA; *Recreations* skiing, sailing, music, motoring; *Clubs* Carlton, Royal Thames Yacht; *Style—* James Gulliver, Esq; 27 Seymour Walk, London SW10 9NE; Argyll Group plc, Argyll House, Millington Rd, Hayes, Middx UB3 4AY (☎ 01 848 3801, telex 924888)

GULLIVER, Pamela Mary (Pam); da of Wilfred Arthur Glasby (d 1972), and Ada, *née* Featam (d 1970); *b* 10 Nov 1942; *Educ* Chorleywood Coll, Univ of Reading (BA), Open Univ; *m* 17 March 1962, William Albert (Bill) Gulliver, *qv*, s of Robert William Gulliver (d 1967); *Career* writer under pen names; dir: Int Tennis Servs 1981-, Anything Nostalgic 1983-, fndr own charity VARVES 1985 (Whitbread Community Care award 1989); served various charity ctees (often with husband); Books incl Bosminster Calendar (1980, as Victoria Thirsk, fiction), numerous magazine articles (as Mary Allerton-North, non fiction); *Recreations* voluntary work, good food, history; *Clubs* MENSA; *Style—* Mrs Pam Gulliver; The Neraldage, 35 Northcourt Ave, Reading RG2 7HE (☎ 0734 871479)

GULLIVER, Ronald; s of Ronald Charles Gulliver (d 1974), and Helen Christiana Duval; *b* 12 Aug 1940; *Educ* Kelvin Side Acad, King Alfred's Sch, Univ of London (LLB); *m* Daphne, da of Sir Henry Lushington, Bt; 1 s (Christopher Ronald b 5 April 1974), 1 da (Patricia Jean b 19 Jan 1976); *Career* articled clerk rising to ptnr Frye Sutton Morris & Co Chartered Accountants 1957-65, asst tech offr ICAEW 1965-67, ptnr P A Thomas & Co Chartered Accountants 1967-70, ptnr Nabarro Nathanson Solicitors 1974- (articled clerk 1970-74), chm Forminster plc 1988-; *awards* ICAEW: Plender prize, Sir Harold Howil prize, Morgan prize, certificate of merit; ACA 1963, memb Law Soc 1974; memb HAC 1963-; *Recreations* farming and wildlife; *Clubs* Naval and Military; *Style—* Ronald Gulliver, Esq; Nabarro Nathanson, The Old Chapel, New Mill, Eversley, Hants RG27 0RA (☎ home 0734 733194, office 0734 730300, fax 0734 730022)

GULLIVER, William Albert (Bill); s of Robert William Gulliver (d 1967), and Irene May, *née* Shaw; *b* 27 Aug 1935; *Educ* Sherborne, Univ of Reading, Univ of Bristol; *m* 17 March 1962, Pamela Mary, *qv*, da of Wilfred Arthur Glasby (d 1972), of Yorkshire; *Career* farmed on family farm near Bath; currently md: International Tennis Services, Anything Nostalgic, VARVES (a charity); prison visitor 1983-; author of mumerous articles on prison reform in nat and trade jls; memb: Reading C of C 1983-, Mgmnt Ctee The Keep; Whitbread Community Care Award 1989, HRH Duchess of Kent Community Serv Award (with w); *Books* Scottish Verse (compiler, 1989); *Recreations* international marathon running, tandem-riding, parties; *Clubs* IOD, Berkshire Hash House Harriers; *Style—* Bill Gulliver, Esq; The Neraldage, 35 Northcourt Avenue, Reading RG2 7HE

GULLY, Hon Edward James Hugh Grey; yr s of 3 Viscount Selby (d 1959), and Veronica Catherine, *née* Briscoe-George; *b* 17 March 1945; *Educ* King's Sch Canterbury; *m* 4 Dec 1971, Fiona Margaret, o da of Ian Strathaird Mackenzie (d 1984), of Iona; 2 s (James Ian Mackenzie b 3 Jan 1975, Andrew Donald Mackenzie b 28 March 1977); *Career* farmer; *Style—* The Hon Edward Gully; Dunmor, Easdale,

Isle of Seil, by Oban, Argyll (☎ 08523 434); Island of Shuna, Arduaine, by Oban, Argyll

GULLY, Hon Edward Thomas William; s and h of 4 Viscount Selby; *b* 21 Sept 1967; *Style—* The Hon Edward Gully

GUMBEL, (Henry) Edward; OBE (1989); s of Gustav Ludwig Gumbel (d 1942); *b* 31 Aug 1913; *Educ* Univs of Zürich (LLD), Geneva, Heidelberg and Berlin, LSE; *m* 1946, Ellen, *née* Frank; 3 s, 2 da; *Career* called to the Bar Middle Temple; dir: Willis Faber plc and assoc cos 1966-83, Storebrand (UK) 1972-85, Heddington Insurance Co (UK) 1983-, Allianz Legal Protection Co 1986-89; chm: Allianz International Insurance Co 1980-88, Tokio (UK) 1980-88, Tokio Reinsurance Co 1982-88; conslt Willis Group 1984-, hon pres Willis Faber Zurich 1988-; author numerous legal pubns; vice pres Chartered Insur Inst, chm Br Insur Law Assoc 1979 and 1980; ACIArb; Commander's Cross of Order of Merit (German Federal Republic) 1984; *Recreations* tennis, skiing, walking, music, reading; *Style—* H Edward Gumbel, Esq, OBE; Windybrae, The Highlands, E Horsley, Surrey; 15 Trinity Sq, London EC3P 3AX (☎ 071 481 7088)

GUMLEY, Frances Jane Miriah Katrina (Mrs A S Mason); da of Franc Stewart Gumley (d 1981), and Helen Teresa McNicholas (d 1987); *b* 28 Jan 1955; *Educ* St Augustine's and St Benedicts Ealing, Newnham Coll Cambridge (MA); *m* 2 July 1988, Andrew Samuel Mason 1988; 1 s; *Career* journalist, broadcaster, radio and television prodr; braille transcriber 1975, ed asst Catholic Herald 1975-76, staff reporter and literary ed 1976-79, ed Catholic Herald 1979-81, sr prodr religious broadcasting BBC 1981-88, series ed Channel 4 1988-89, acting exec prodr Religion BBC World Service 1989, guest prodr and scriptwriter BBC Radio 4 1989-91; Mistress of the Keys (Catholic Writers Guild) 1982-87; *Books* The Good Book (with Brian Redhead), The Christian Centuries (with Brian Redhead), The Pillars of Islam (with Brian Redhead); *Recreations* embroidery, deep sea diving; *Style—* Miss Frances Gumley; c/o Mr & Mrs M J Mason, 3 Hurst Close, London NW11

GUMLEY, Kenneth Louis; s of Lindsay Douglas Gumley, JP (d 1973); *b* 7 Oct 1932; *Educ* Fettes; *m* 1959, Anne Hogg, da of Lt-Col Robert Hogg Forbes, OBE (d 1978); 1 s (John Lindsay Robert b 1967), 1 da (Sally Catherine b 1961); *Career* chartered surveyor; md: The Joint Properties Ltd, Gogar Park Curling Club Ltd; *Recreations* curling, sailing (yachts: 'Bandit of Lorne',' Cromarty 36'); *Clubs* Royal Forth Yacht, Royal Highland Yacht Royal Caledonian Curling; *Style—* Kenneth L Gumley, Esq; Almondfield, 18 Whitehouse Rd, Edinburgh EH4 6NN (☎ 031 336 4839)

GUMMER, Rt Hon John Selwyn; PC (1985), MP (C) Suffolk Coastal 1983-; s of Canon Selwyn Gummer, and Sybille, *née* Mason; bro of Peter Gummer, *qv*; *b* 26 Nov 1939; *Educ* King's Sch Rochester, Selwyn Coll Cambridge; *m* 1977, Penelope Jane, yr da of John P Gardner; 2 s, 2 da; *Career* dir Shandwick Publishing Co 1966-81, md EP Gp of Cos 1975-80; chm: Selwyn Sancroft International 1976-81, Siemssen Hunter Ltd 1980 (dir 1973); MP (C): Lewisham W 1970-74, Eye Suffolk 1979-1983; vice chm Cons Pty 1972-74, PPS to Min of Agric 1972, govt whip 1981-83, under sec of state Employment June-Oct 1983, chm Cons Pty 1983-85; min of state: Employment 1983-84, Agric Fisheries and Food 1985-88; paymaster gen 1984-85, min for Local Govt 1988-July 1989, min Agric Fisheries and Food July 1989-; memb Gen Synod C of E 1978-, guardian of the Shrine of Our Lady of Walsingham 1983-; *Books* To Church with Enthusiasm (1969), The Permissive Society (1971), The Christian Calendar (1973), Faith in Politics (1987), Christianity and Conservatism (1990); *Recreations* reading, gardening, Victorian buildings; *Style—* The Rt Hon John Selwyn Gummer, MP; House of Commons, London SW1

GUMMER, Peter Selwyn; s of Rev Canon Selwyn Gummer, and Sybille, *née* Mason; bro of Rt Hon John Gummer, *qv*; *b* 24 Aug 1942; *Educ* Kings Sch Rochester, Selwyn Coll Cambridge (BA, MA); *m* 23 Oct 1982, Lucy Rachel, da of Antony Ponsonby Dudley-Hill (d 1969), of Sandle Manor, Fordingbridge, Hants; 1 s (James b 4 Aug 1990), 3 da (Naomi b 10 Jan 1984, Chloe b 17 Nov 1985, Eleanor b 5 Aug 1988); *Career* Portsmouth and Sunderland Newspaper Group 1964-65, Viyella International 1965-66, Hodgkinson & Partners 1966-67, Industrial & Commercial Finance Corporation (part of 3i Gp) 1967-74, chm Shandwick plc 1974-; non-exec dir CIA Group PLC 1990-; non-exec memb: London Bd Halifax Building Society 1990-, NHS Policy Bd 1991-; memb: Arts Cncl of GB, IOD, IPR, IOM; FRSA; *Recreations* opera, cricket, rugby; *Clubs* MCC, Hurlingham; *Style—* Peter S Gummer, Esq; Shandwick plc, 61 Grosvenor St, London W1X 9DA, (☎ 071 408 2232, fax 071 493 3048)

GUN-MUNRO, Sir Sydney Douglas; GCMG (1979), MBE (1957); s of Barclay Gun-Munro, and Marie Josephine Gun-Munro; *b* 29 Nov 1916; *Educ* Grenada Boys' Secdy Sch, King's Coll Hosp London; *m* 1943, Joan, *née* Benjamin; 2 s, 1 da; *Career* house surgn Horton EMS Hosp 1943, MO Lewisham Hosp 1943-46; dist MO Grenada 1946-49, surgn Gen Hosp St Vincent 1949-71, dist MO Bequia 1972-76, govr St Vincent 1977, govr gen St Vincent and Grenadines 1979-85; FRCS 1985; kt 1977; *Style—* Sir Sydney Gun-Munro, GCMG, MBE; Bequia, St Vincent and the Grenadines, West Indies (☎ 010 1 809 42 83261)

GUNDILL, (James) Norman; s of Maj (Henry) James Gundill (d 1979), of Pontefract, and Marjorie, *née* Sainter (d 1967); *b* 29 Oct 1942; *Educ* Sedbergh, The Coll of Law; *m* 5 Sept 1967, (Angela) Dianne, da of John Massarella (d 1988), of Almholme Grange, Doncaster; 1 s (John Edward b 4 Jan 1971); *Career* admitted slr 1966; sr ptnr Carter Bentley & Gundill 1987- (asst slr 1966-68, ptnr 1968-); pres Wakefield Incorporated Law Soc 1984-85 (sec 1976-79); Pontefract Park Race Co Ltd: dir 1972-, sec 1973-, md 1977-, clerk of the course 1983; chm Northern Area Racecourse Assoc 1988- (sec 1977-88), dir The Racecourse Assoc Ltd 1977-; memb Law Soc 1967-; *Recreations* racing, gardening, following cricket, keeping fit; *Style—* J Norman Gundill, Esq; The Coach House, Kirk Smeaton, Pontefract, West Yorks WF8 3JS (☎ 0977 620649); 33 Ropergate, Pontefract, West Yorks WF8 1LE (☎ 0977 703224)

GUNDRY, Hon Mrs (Caroline Anne Sabina); *née* Best; er da of 8 Baron Wynford, MBE; *b* 28 March 1942; *m* 1964, Edward Patrick Gundry; 1 s, 2 da; *Style—* The Hon Mrs Gundry; 15 Genoa Ave, London SW15

GUNDY, Dr Greville Henry; s of William Henry Gundy, MM (d 1986), and Gertrude Elizabeth, *née* York; *b* 19 March 1938; *Educ* Merrywood GS Bristol, Univ of Bristol (MB ChB); *Career* house physician Bristol Gen Hosp 1961-62, house surgn Bristol Royal Infirmary 1962; St George's Hosp London 1962-64, psychiatric unit St George's Hosp London 1964-65; sr registrar dept of psychological med St Thomas's Hosp 1965-68; conslt psychiatrist: Tooting Bec Hosp 1968-75, HM Prison Wandsworth (visiting) 1969-, Springfield Hosp 1975-; vice chm mgmnt ctee St Mungo's Bail Hostel (previously St Mungo Community Tst); MRC Psych (fndn memb 1971); *Recreations* reading, theatre, amateur dramatics; *Clubs* Royal Cwlth Soc; *Style—* Dr Greville Gundy; Springfield Hospital, 61 Glenburnie Rd, London SW17 7DJ (☎ 01 672 9911)

GUNN, Dr Alexander Derek Gower; OBE (1989); s of Col Alexander Joseph Gunn (d 1978), of West Bridgford, Nottingham, and Cassandra Valerie, *née* Hines (d 1978); *b* 27 Aug 1933; *Educ* William Hulme's GS Manchester, Univ of Sheffield; *m* 4 Jan 1956, Sheila Mary, da of Wilfred Gearey (d 1976), of Sale, Manchester; 1 s (Mark Alexander Gower b 25 Aug 1958), 1 da (Jessica Mary Cassandra b 21 April 1960); *Career* asst GP Darbishire House Health Centre Manchester 1961-64, asst MO Univ Health Serv Sheffield 1964-67, dir Univ Health Serv Reading 1971- (dep dir 1967-71); temp advsr WHO Geneva 1982; pres: Br Assoc Health Servs in Higher Educn (UK), Euro Union Sch and Univ Health Servs, Assoc of Welfare Offrs in Higher Educn (UK), Reading Diabetic Assoc; med advsr Berks Red Cross Soc; former govr: Nat Bureau for Handicapped Students, Norlands Trg Coll for Nursery Nurses Hungerford Berks; med author, ed and advsr to publishers; MRCS, LRCP, MRCGP, DPH, DObstRCOG; *Books* Privileged Adolescent (1970), International Handbook of Medical Science (1974), Uprooting - Psycho - Social Problems of Overseas Students (1983), Oral Contraception - 30 Year History (1986); *Recreations* wining, dining, gardening, boating; *Style—* Dr Alexander D G Gunn, OBE; The Old Barn, School Lane, Wargrave, Berks RG10 8AA (☎ 073 522 2845); University Health centre, 9 Northcourt Ave, Reading RG2 7HE (☎ 874551/2)

GUNN, Alexander Ewen (Ben); MBE; s of Lt Gunn (d 1987), of Elm Cottage, Castletown, Caithness, Scotland, and Christina Catto, *née* Ewen (d 1948); *b* 24 June 1923; *Educ* Whitehill Sch, RAF Coll Cranwell; *m* 23 Dec 1946, Geraldine (Gerry), da of James Phillips (d 1975), of Golders Green; 1 s (David b 19 May 1948); *Career* 501 Sqdn 11 Gp and 274 Sqdn 83 Gp 2 TAF 1943-45, test pilot A & AEE 1945-48; graduate Empire Test Pilot's Sch 1948, chief test pilot Boulton Paul Aircraft 1949-66, experimental test pilot Rover Gas Turbines 1966-67, regnl mktg dir Africa and ME Beagle Aircraft 1967-71, airport mangr Shoreham 1971-90, airport and aviation conslt 1990-; memb RAF Assoc; Upper Freeman Guild of Air Pilots and Navigators; Master Air pilot, AOPA Sword, Airport Operators Assoc Silver Medal (and hon memb); MRAeS; *Recreations* fishing; *Clubs* Royal Aero, RAF; *Style—* Ben Gunn, Esq, MBE; Four Winds, 69 Offington Lane, Worthing, W Sussex BN14 9RJ (☎ 0903 60840), Elm Cottage, Castletown, Caithness, Scotland

GUNN, Andrew; RD (1980); s of Andrew Gunn (d 1985), and Mary Anne Jane Murray Gunn (d 1979); *b* 6 March 1936; *Educ* Univ of Edinburgh (MB ChB); *m* 1 Dec 1962, Deirdre Elizabeth Mary, da of Edmond Richard Weld, of Kirkden House, By Letham, Angus; 1 s (Adrian Richard b 1965), 3 da (Hilary Mary b 1964, Clare Elizabeth b 1966, Phillippa Jane b 1967); *Career* RNR 1965-85; conslt surgn Tayside Health Bd, hon sr lectr Univ of Dundee, dir Iatros Ltd; pres Br Assoc of Endocrine Surgns 1988-90; FRCSEd 1962; *Books* Exploration of the Parathyroid Glands (1988); *Style—* Andrew Gunn, Esq, RD; Kirkden House, By Letham, Angus DD8 2QF (☎ 030 781 296); Ninewells Hospital & Medical School, Dundee DD1 9SY (☎ 0382 60111)

GUNN, Andrew Livingston; s of Alistair Livingston Gunn, VRD (d 1970), of Chislehurst, Kent, and Sybil Marion Gunn; *b* 11 Sept 1931; *Educ* Fettes, Clare Coll Cambridge, Guy's Hosp; *m* 15 Dec 1956, Elizabeth Baily, da of Charles Russell Baily Chiesman; 3 s (Robert Charles Livingston b 1959, James Andrew Livingston b 1962, Neil Alexander Livingston b 1966), 1 da (Felicity Jane Elizabeth Livingston b 1957); *Career* sr conslt orthopaedic surgn Ipswich Dist Hosp; fell Br Orthopaedic Assoc, memb SICOT; Liveryman Worshipful Soc of Apothecaries; FRSM 1968; *Clubs* MCC, London Scottish Football; *Style—* Andrew Gunn, Esq; Orthopaedic Department, Ipswich District Hospital, Heath Rd, Ipswich, Suffolk

GUNN, Bunty Moffat; OBE (1981), JP (City of Glasgow); da of William Morrison Johnston (d 1955), of Blairgowrie, and Dolina, *née* Moffat (d 1986); *b* 4 Sept 1923; *Educ* Grange Sch for Girls, Grangemouth HS; *m* 28 March 1946, Hugh McVane Houston Gunn, s of John Gunn (d 1962), of Rutherglen; 3 s ((Hugh) Cameron b 7 April 1952, (John) Niven b 24 Nov 1955, (William) Innes b 30 Dec 1960), 1 da ((Helen) Lindsey Morrison b 20 June 1960); *Career* memb: Lanarkshire Health Bd 1973-81, (chm 1981), Lanark CC 1970-73, Strathclyde Regnl Cncl 1973-82; chm Scot Cncl for Health Educn 1974-80, vice pres Royal Br Legion (CS & W Branch) 1978, memb CSA Mgmnt Ctee Scottish Health Serv 1985-; DSCHE 1978; *Recreations* music, reading, golf, grandchildren; *Clubs* Cathkin Braes Golf; *Style—* Mrs Bunty Gunn, OBE; 198 Dukes Road, Burnside, Rutherglen, Glasgow G73 5AA (☎ 041 647 8258); Lanarkshire Health Board, 14 Beckford St, Hamilton ML3 0TA (☎ 0698 281313)

GUNN, Catherine Rachel; da of John Sinclair Gunn, of Callow, Derbys, and Rosemary Elizabeth, *née* Williams; *b* 28 May 1954; *Educ* St Swithun's Sch Winchester, Univ of Durham (BA), Univ of Edinburgh (Dip Business Admin); *Career* investmt analyst Touche Remnant & Co 1976-78; fin writer: Investors' Chronicle 1978-80, The Times 1980-81, freelance 1981-83; fin writer and dep ed Financial Weekly, fin writer and dep city ed Today 1986 (city ed 1987-); memb NUJ 1978-; *Recreations* reading, travel, scribbling, entertaining; *Style—* Miss Catherine Gunn; Today, 1 Virginia St, London E1 9BS (☎ 071 782 4600)

GUNN, Prof John Charles; s of Albert Charles Gunn, of Charlwood, Surrey, and Lily Hilda Gunn; *b* 6 June 1937; *Educ* Brighton, Hove and Sussex GS, Reigate GS, Univ of Birmingham (MB ChB, MD), Univ of London (DPM); *m* 1, 9 Sept 1959 (m dis 1987), Celia Ann Frances (d 1989), da of Harry Richard Willis, of Charlwood, Surrey; 1 s (Richard Charles b 10 March 1962), 1 da (Frances Margaret b 28 Sept 1964); m 2, 11 Nov 1989, Pamela Jane, da of Rev P Geoffrey Taylor, of Liverpool; *Career* house offr Queen Elizabeth Hosp Birmingham 1961-63, registrar Maudsley Hosp London 1963-67; Inst of Psychiatry: res worker and lectr 1967-71, sr lectr 1971-75, prof of forensic psychiatry 1978-; dir Special Hosps Res Unit 1975-78; memb Home Sec's Advsy Bd on Restricted Patients, advsr House of Commons Social Servs Ctee 1985-86 (Ctee on Violence in Marriages 1975); MRCPsych 1971, FRCPsych 1980; *Books* Violence in Human Society (1973), Epileptics in Prison (1977), Psychiatric Aspects of Imprisonment (1978); *Recreations* walking, photography, theatre, opera, cinema; *Clubs* RSM; *Style—* Prof John Gunn; Inst of Psychiatry, De Crespigny Park, Camberwell, London SE5 8AF (☎ 071 703 5411, 071 701 7063)

GUNN, Prof Sir John Currie; CBE (1976); s of Richard Gunn, and Jane Blair Currie; *b* 13 Sept 1916; *Educ* Glasgow Acad, Glasgow Univ, St John's Coll Cambridge; *m* 1944, Betty Russum, OBE; 1 s; *Career* WWII researching for Admty; former applied mathematics lectr Manchester and London Univs; Cargill prof of natural philosophy Glasgow Univ 1949-82 (head of dept 1973-82, emeritus prof 1982-, dean of Faculties 1989-); former memb: Sci Res Cncl, UGC; Hon DSc: Heriot Watt Univ 1981, Univ Loughborough 1983; Hon DUniv Open Univ 1989; FRSE, FIMA, FInstP; *Style—* Prof Sir John Gunn, CBE, FRSE; 32 Beaconsfield Rd, Glasgow G12 0NY (☎ 041 357 2001)

GUNN, John Humphrey; s of Francis Gunn, of Northwich, Cheshire, and Doris, *née* Curbishley; *b* 15 Jan 1942; *Educ* Sir John Deane's GS, Univ of Nottingham (BA); *m* 2 Oct 1965, Renate Sigrid, da of Alfred Boehme (d 1968), 3 da (Ingrid b 1966, Alison b 1968, Natalie b 1968); *Career* Barclays Bank 1964-68, Astley & Pearce Ltd 1968-79, formed EXCO plc 1979, British & Commonwealth Holdings plc 1985-90; non-exec dir: Midland and Scottish Resources plc 1988, Smith New Court plc 1986, Silvermines plc 1985; chm Barnham Broom plc Norfolk, co fndr Inst of German, Austrian and Swiss Affairs Univ of Nottingham; *Recreations* golf, opera, skiing, walking, classical music; *Clubs* MCC; *Style—* John Gunn, Esq; c/o King's House, 36/37 King St, London EC2V 8BE (☎ 071 600 3000, fax 600 0734, telex 884095)

GUNN, His Excellency (Alan) Richard; CBE (1991); s of Alan Leslie Gunn (d 1960), of St Vincent and The Grenadines, and Violet Adeline, *née* Hazell; *b* 19 Jan 1936; *Educ* Boys GS St Vincent WI, Southern Coll of Art Portsmouth Hants, Regent St Poly London; *m* 28 April 1962, Flora Beryl, da of Charles Fitz-william Richardson (d 1962), of St Vincent and the Grenadines; 1 s (Anthony b 1962), 2 da (Cheryl b 1964, Beverley b 1970); *Career* dir Hazells 1964-74, chm and chief offr 1974-87, high cmmr for Eastern Caribbean States 1987-; pres St Vincent Chamber of Indust and

Commerce 1984-86, dir Caribbean Assoc of Indust and Commerce 1984-87; *Recreations* sailing; *Style—* His Excellency Richard Gunn, CBE; High Commission for Eastern Caribbean States, 10 Kensington Court, London W8 5DL (☎ 071 937 9522, fax 071 937 5514, telex 913047 ECACOM G)

GUNN, Robert Norman; s of Donald MacFie Gunn (d 1930), and Margaret, *née* Pallister (d 1965); *b* 16 Dec 1925; *Educ* Royal HS Edinburgh, Worcester Coll Oxford (MA); *m* 1956, Joan, da of Fredrick Parry (d 1972); 1 da (Jane Victoria b 1961); *Career* Lt RAC 1944-47; Boots Co plc: dir 1976-90, md industl div 1980-83, chief exec 1983-87, chm 1985-90; dir: Foseco plc 1984-, E Midlands Electricity plc 1989-; Nottingham Building Society 1990-, memb Bd: of Mgmnt Assoc Br Pharmaceutical Indust 1981-84 (vice pres 1983-84), Nottingham Devpt Enterprise 1988-; Cncl memb CBI 1985-90; CBIM 1983, FInstD 1985-90, PCFC 1988-; *Style—* Robert Gunn, Esq; Tor House, Pinfold Lane, Elston, Newark, Notts NG23 5PD

GUNN, Thom(son) William; s of Herbert Smith Gunn; *b* 29 Aug 1929; *Educ* Univ Coll Sch Hampstead, Trinity Coll Cambridge (BA); *Career* poet; teacher Univ of California at Berkeley, assoc prof of English 1958-66, freelance for 10 years, lectr in English 1976-; *Books of Poetry* Fighting Terms (1954), The Sense of Movement (1957), My Sad Captains (1961), Positives (with Ander Gunn, 1966), Touch (1967), Moly (1971), Jack Straw's Castle (1976), Selected Poems (1979), The Passages of Joy (1982), The Occasions of Poetry (1982); *Style—* Thom Gunn; 1216 Cole St, San Francisco, Calif 94117, USA

GUNNELL, (William) John; s of William Henry Gunnell (d 1961), of Kettering, Northants, and Norah, *née* Haughton (d 1965); *b* 1 Oct 1933; *Educ* King Edward Sch Birmingham, Univ of Leeds (BSc); *m* 8 Oct 1955, Jean Louise, da of Frank Lacey (d 1957); 3 s (Colin David John b 1957, Jeremy Mark William b 1961, Nicolas Daniel b 1965), 1 da (Sarah Imogen b 1966); *Career* teacher Leeds Modern Sch 1959-62, head Sci Dept UN Int Sch NY 1962-70, lectr Centre for Studies in Sci Educn Univ of Leeds 1970-88, dir Yorkshire Enterprise Ltd 1982- (chm 1982-90); chm: Yorks and Humberside Devpt Assoc 1981-, N of Eng Regnl Consortium 1984-; memb: W Yorks Metropolitan CC 1977-86 (leader 1981-86), spokesman for Metropolitan Cos in their campaign against abolition 1983-85, Leeds City Cncl 1986- (chair Social Servs Ctee 1990-, chair Crown Point Foods 1988-90); memb Audit Cmmn 1983-90, Leeds Devpt Corpn 1988-, Leeds Eastern Health Authy 1990-91; advsr Assembly of Regns of Europe 1986- (memb Bureau 1984-86); dir: Opera North 1982-, Leeds Theatre Tst (now West Yorkshire Playhouse) 1986-; *Publications* author of texts with E W Jenkins incl Selected Experiments in Advanced Level Chemistry (1975), contrib of Enterprise Boards: An Inside View to Local Economic Policy (ed M Campbell, 1990); *Recreations* opera, music, watching cricket and soccer; *Clubs* East Hunslet Labour, Warwickshire CCC, Yorkshire CCC; *Style—* John Gunnell, Esq; Yorkshire Enterprise, Elizabeth House, 9-17 Queen St, Leeds LS1 2TW (☎ 0532 420505, fax 0532 420266); Social Services Department, Leeds City Council, Sweet St, Leeds LS11 9DQ (☎ 0532 463424, fax 0532 440096); 6 Arthington View, Hunslet, Leeds LS10 2ND (☎ 0532 770592)

GUNNELL, Sally Jane Janet; da of Leslie Robert Gunnell, of Old Farm, Green Lane, Chigwell, Essex, and Doris Rosemary, *née* Mason; *b* 29 July 1966; *Career* athlete; Gold medal 100m hurdles Cwlth Games Edinburgh 1986; 400m hurdles: fifth place Seoul Olympics 1988 (first Briton to compete in the Olympic Games in 100m hurdles, 400m hurdles and 4x400m relay), second place Euro Cup 1989, Gold medal Euro Indoor Championship 1989, third place World Cup 1989, Gold medal Cwlth Games Auckland 1989; holder: UK record 400m hurdles, UK record 100m hurdles; *Style—* Miss Sally Gunnell

GUNNING, Ann, Lady; Ann (Helen Nancy); da of Vice Adm Sir Theodore John Hallett, KBE, CB (d 1957), and Helen Blanche, *née* Dakeyne; *m* 1934, Sir Robert Charles Gunning, 8 Bt (d 1989); 8 s, 2 da (and 1 da decd); *Style—* Ann, Lady Gunning; Box 6602, Peace River, Alberta T8S 1S4, Canada

GUNNING, Sir Charles Theodore; 9 Bt (GB 1778), CD (1964); s of Sir Robert Charles Gunning, 8 Bt (d 1989), and Ann (Helen Nancy), *née* Hallett; *b* 19 June 1935; *Educ* Royal Roads Mil Coll BC, RN Engrg Coll, Tech Univ of Nova Scotia; *m* 1, 1969 (m dis 1982), Sarah, da of Col Patrick Easton, of Tonbridge; 1 da (Caroline Ann b 1971); m 2, 1989, Linda; *Heir* bro, John Robert Gunning b 1944; *Career* Lt Cdr RCN/ Canadian Armed Forces 1952-80; engrg conslt; pres Ottawa Branch Royal Cwlth Soc 1975-78 and 1980-81, chm Nat Cncl RCS in Canada 1990- (vice chm 1980-90); Silver Jubilee medal 1977; PEng; *Recreations* squash, rugby (refereeing), skiing; *Clubs* RMC of Canada, Ottawa Athletic, Royal Cwlth Soc; *Style—* Sir Charles Gunning, Bt, CD; 2940 McCarthy Rd, Ottawa, Ontario K1V 8K6, Canada

GUNNING, Christopher; s of Alexis Lambertus Gunning (d 1962), of Cheltenham and London, and Janet Alice, *née* Bennett; *b* 5 Aug 1944; *Educ* Hendon Co GS, Guildhall Sch of Music and Drama (BMus); *m* 17 June 1974, Annie Christine, da of Flt Lt Clifford William Cornwall Farrow (d 1985), of Bristol; 4 da (Olivia b 1975, Pollyanna b 1977, Verity b 1981, Chloe b 1985); *Career* composer; TV and film scores incl: Day of the Triffids 1981, Rogue Male 1975, Charlie Muffin 1979, Wilfred and Eileen 1981, Flame to the Phoenix 1982, East Lynne 1982, Children's Opera Rainbow Planet 1983, Rebel Angel 1987, Porterhouse Blue 1987 (BAFTA Award for the Best Original TV Music), Hercule Poirot (BAFTA award for Best TV Music) 1989, When the Whales Came (Royal Premiere 1989, nominated British Film Institute Anthony Asquith award for Best Film Score 1990); composer dir PRS, fndr memb Assoc of Professional Composers; ARCM, AGSM; *Books* First Book of Flute Solos , Second Book of Flute Solos, Really Easy Flute Book, Really Easy Trumpet Book, Really Easy Horn Book (1987); *Recreations* sailing, walking, reading, horticulture, wine; *Style—* Christopher Gunning, Esq; The Old Rectory, Mill Lane, Monks Risborough, nr Aylesbury, Bucks HP17 9LG

GUNNINGHAM, John Robert; s of Howard James Gunningham (d 1974), and Zaida Zula (d 1946); *b* 26 March 1924; *Educ* Brentwood Sch, Oxford Univ (MA); *m* 22 July 1951, Philippa Anne, da of Brig Rev Charles Edwin Laurence Harris, of Church House, Sutton, Dover, Kent; 3 s (Robert b 1953, Paul b 1955, Charles b 1963); *Career* RCS 1942-47, 2 Lt 1944, T/Capt 1947; colonial serv and overseas civil serv Tanganyika E Africa 1951-61; dist cmmnr: Lushoto 1959, Manyoni 1960, Kahama 1960-61; admitted slr 1965-; ptnr: Chestermans 1966-67, Ford Gunningham & Co 1967-89; memb Law Soc; *Clubs* Leander (Henley); *Style—* John Gunningham, Esq; Thuja, Bath Rd, Marlborough, Wilts (☎ 0672 52777); Kingsbury House, Marlborough, Wilts (☎ 0672 52265, fax 0672 54891)

GUNNINGHAM, Hon Mrs (Mary Cynthia Burke); *née* Roche; da of 4 Baron Fermoy and Ruth, Lady Fermoy, DCVO, OBE, JP; aunt of HRH The Princess of Wales; *b* 19 Aug 1934; *m* 1, 1954 (m dis 1966), Hon Anthony Berry, MP (later Hon Sir Anthony Berry, d 1984), 6 s of 1st Viscount Kemsley; m 2, 1973 (m dis 1980), Dennis Roche Geoghegan; m 3, 1981, Michael Robert Fearon Gunningham; *Style—* The Hon Mrs Gunningham; 40 Chester Terrace, Regent's Park, NW1; Broadfield Hall Farm, Broadfield, Buntingford, Herts

GUNSTON, Sir Richard Wellesley; 2 Bt (UK 1938); s of Maj Sir Derrick Wellesley Gunston, 1 Bt, MC (d 1985), and Evelyn Bligh (Gardenia), OBE, da of Howard Bligh St George; *b* 15 March 1924; *Educ* Harrow, Clare Coll Cambridge; *m* 1, 1947 (m dis 1956), Elizabeth Mary, eldest da of Sir Arthur Colegate, MP; 1 da (Caroline Jane (Mrs Jonathan Peel) b 1950); m 2, 1959 (m dis), Joan Elizabeth Marie, o da of Reginald Forde, of Inanda, Johannesburg, S Africa, and Mrs Marie Louise Walker, of Somerset West, Cape Province, S Africa, and former w of H B Coldicott; 1 s (John Wellesley b 1962); m 3, 12 April 1976, Veronica Elizabeth, da of Maj Haynes, and wid of Capt Vivian Graham Loyd; *Heir* s, John Wellesley Gunston b 25 July 1962, m 1 Sept 1990, Rosalind G, yst da of Edward Gordon Eliott, of Bower's Mill House, nr Guildford, Surrey; *Career* Colonial Serv Nigeria, Nyasaland, Bechuanaland 1948-60; *Style—* Sir Richard Gunston, Bt

GUNSTONE, Prof Frank Denby; s of (Edwin) Leonard Gunstone (d 1981), and Adeline, *née* Benington (d 1969); *b* 27 Oct 1923; *Educ* Univ of Liverpool (BSc, PhD), St Andrews Univ (DSc); *m* 20 March 1948, Eleanor Eineen, da of Sidney John Hill (d 1949); 2 s (Douglas b 1950, John b 1952), 1 da (Penny b 1958); *Career* lectr Univ of Glasgow 1946-54, hon res prof of St Andrews 1989- (lectr 1954-59, sr lectr 1959-65, reader 1965-70, personal prof 1971-89); memb: American Oil Chemists Soc, RSE, Royal Soc of Chemistry 1945, Soc of Chemical Industry 1945; *Books* incl: A Text Book of Organic Chemistry (with J Reed, 1958), An Introduction to the Chemistry and Biochemistry of Fatty Acids and their Glycerides (1 edn 1958, 2 edn 1967), Programmes in Organic Chemistry Vol 1, Nomenclature of Aliphatic Compounds (1966), Programmes in Organic Chemistry Vol 6, Reactions of Amines, Alcohols and Alkyl Halides (1970), Guidebook to Stereochemistry (1975), Lipids in Foods; Chemistry, Biochemistry and Technology (with F A Norris, 1983), The Lipid Handbook (ed with F B Padley and J L Harwood, 1986) Critical Reports on Applied Chemistry Vol 15, Palm Oil (ed, 1987); *Recreations* gardening; *Clubs* University; *Style—* Prof Frank Gunstone; Rumgally House, Cupar, Fife KY15 5SY (☎ 0334 53613), Chemistry Dept, The University, St Andrews, Fife KY16 9ST (☎ 0334 76161, fax 78292)

GUNTER, John Forsyth; s of Dr Herbert Charles Gunter (d 1959), and Charlotte Rose Scott, *née* Reid; *b* 31 Oct 1938; *Educ* Bryanston, Central Sch of Art and Design; *m* 19 Dec 1969, Micheline, da of Col Maxwell S McKnight, of 520 N St SW, Washington DC; 2 da (Jessica b 4 June 1972, Nicolette b 16 Oct 1978); *Career* theatre designer; 28 prodns Royal Court Theatre 1965-66 incl: D H Lawrence Trilogy, Saved, The Contractor, The Philanthropist, West of Suez, Inadmissible Evidence; RSC: Juno and the Paycock, All's Well that Ends Well (produced on Broadway 1983), Mephisto 1986; National Theatre: Guys and Dolls (SWET award Best Designer), The Rivals, The Beggar's Opera, Wild Honey (SWET award Best Designer), The Government Inspector, Bay at Nice, Wrecked Eggs; West End: Comedians, Stevie, The Old Country, Rose, Made in Bangkok, High Society, Mrs Klein, Secret Rapture; opera designs incl: The Greek Passion WNO, Faust ENO, Peter Grimes Teatro Colon Buenos Aries, The Meistersinger Cologne, Un Ballo in Masquera Sydney Opera House, The Turn of the Screw Munich, Macbeth Leeds; for Sir Peter Hall Glyndebourne: Albert Herring, La Traviata 1987, Falstaff 1988; Porgy and Bess for Trevor Nunn Glyndebourne, Attila for Opera North Leeds 1990, Long Day's Journey Into Night National Theatre 1991, Marriage of Figaro Salzburg Festival Opera 1991, Madame Butterfly for Los Angeles Opera 1991; FRSA 1982; *Style—* John Gunter, Esq; agent: Peter Murphy, Curtis Brown, 162-168 Regent St, London W1R 5TB (☎ 071 872 0331)

GUPTA, Arvind Kumar; s of Purshottam Das Gupta, and Bala Devi Gupta; *b* 12 May 1943; *Educ* King George's Med Coll (MB BS, MD, MDPsych); *m* 5 May 1968, Indra, da of late Sri Ram Swaroop Gupta; 1 da (Sona b 18 June 1972); *Career* conslt clinical neurophysiologist W Birmingham Health Authy 1981-; author of several pubns on EEG and epilepsy; memb: ABCN, EEG Soc, ILEA, Br Epilepsy Assoc; *Style—* Arvind Gupta, Esq; EEG Department, Dudley Road Hospital, Dudley Road, Birmingham B18 7QH (☎ 021 554 3801, ext 4320)

GUPTA, Dr Nirmal Kumar; s of Kanti Bhushan Gupta (d 1964), of Agartala, India, and Kamala, *née* Sen Gupta (d 1948); *b* 13 June 1934; *Educ* Calcutta Univ (MB BS); *m* 28 Jan 1962, Namita, da of Nibaran Chandra Das Gupta (d 1982), of Assam, India; 2 da (Chandreyi b 1967, Sharmila b 1972); *Career* conslt in radiotherapy and oncology 1975-88 and dep dir in radiotherapy and oncology Christie Hosp and Holt Radium Inst Manchester; memb Sociedad Peruana de Radiologicá Lima 1982, pres The 1951 Club 1986-87; memb: Sub Ctee on Head and Neck Cancer UK Coordinating Ctee on Cancer Res 1988-, Int Collaborative Gp on Fractionation American Coll of Radiology Philadelphia 1988-; memb Cncl Faculty Bd of Radiotherapy and Oncology RCR 1988-89 (memb 1986-88); DMRT, FRCR, FFR; *Books* contrib: The Radiotherapy of Malignant Disease (1985), Clinical Radiology (1987), The British Journal of Radiology (1990); *Recreations* tasting good food, wine; *Style—* Dr Nirmal Gupta; The Christie Hospital & Holt Radium Institute, Withington, Manchester M20 9BX (☎ 061 4458123)

GURDON, Brig Adam Brampton Douglas; CBE (1980, OBE 1973); elder s of Maj-Gen Edward Temple Leigh Gurdon, CB, CBE, MC (d 1959), of Suffolk, and Elizabeth Madeleine, *née* Wilson (d 1967); *b* 4 May 1931; *Educ* Rugby; *m* 30 Aug 1958, Gillian Margaret, da of Col Charles Newbigging Thomson (d 1987), of Dundee; 4 da (Miranda b 1960, Madeleine Astrid (Mrs Andrew Lloyd Webber) b 1962, Melanie b 1966, Mary Louise b 1968); *Career* cmmnd Black Watch 1950, Korean War 1953-53, Mau Mau Kenya 1953-55, Adj Berlin 1956-57, Cyprus 1958, cmmnd Regtl Depot Perth 1960, KAR Tanganyka and Zanzibar 1961-62, Staff Coll 1963, DAA & QMG Gurkha Bde 1964-66, UN Cyprus 1967, MOD Mil Ops 1968-72, GSO1 Eastern Dist 1973-76, Mil Ops 1976-79 (while at MOD became involved in Lancaster House Settlement on Rhodesia, formulated Cwlth Monitoring Force, went to Rhodesia as COS to Maj-Gen Sir John Acland), RCDS 1981, Cabinet Office 1982-85, ADC to HM The Queen 1984-85, ret as Brig 1985; dir: St Edmundsbury Cathedral Appeal 1986-90, Chelmsford Cathedral Appeal 1990-; *Recreations* shooting, fishing, gardening; *Clubs* Army and Navy (vice chm 1986); *Style—* Brig Adam Gurdon, CBE; Burgh House, Woodbridge, Suffolk IP13 6PU (☎ 047 335 273); Cathedral Office, Guy Harlings, New St, Chelmsford, Essex (☎ 0245 496404)

GURDON, Prof John Bertrand; s of late W N Gurdon, DCM, of Suffolk, and late Elsie Marjorie, *née* Byass; *b* 2 Oct 1933; *Educ* Eton, ChCh Oxford (BA, DPhil, Beit meml fell); *m* 1964, Jean Elizabeth Margaret Curtis; 1 s, 1 da; *Career* Gosney res fell CA Inst of Technol 1962; Univ of Oxford: department demonstrator Dept of Zoology 1963-64, res student Christ Church 1962-72, lectr Dept of Zoology 1965-72; visiting res fell Carnegie Inst Baltimore 1965, head Cell Biology Div (MRC Laboratory of Molecular Biology Cambridge 1979-83), Fullerian prof of Physiology and Comparative Anatomy Royal Inst 1985-, numerous Univ lectures; fell: Churchill Coll Cambridge 1973-, Eton Coll 1978-; hon foreign memb American Acad of Arts and Sciences, Belgian Acad of Letters and Fine Arts 1984, foreign memb American Philosophical Soc 1983, hon student Christ Church; Hon DSc Chicago 1978, Paris 1982, Oxford 1985, Albert Brachet prize Belgian Royal Acad 1968, Scientific medal of Zoological Soc 1968, Feldberg Fndn award 1975, Paul Ehrlich award 1977, CIBA medal Biochemical Soc 1985, Comfort Crookshank award for Cancer Res 1983, William Bate Hardy prize Cambridge Philosophical Soc 1984, prix Charles Leopold Mayer Acad des Scis France 1984, Ross Harrison prize 1985, Royal medal Royal Soc 1985; FRS 1971; *Books* Control of Gene Expression in Animal Development (1974); author of articles in numerous scientific journals (especially on nuclear transplantation); *Recreations* tennis, skiing, horticulture, lepidoptera; *Clubs* Eagle Ski; *Style*— Prof John Gurdon, FRS; Whittlesford Grove, Whittlesford, Cambridge CB2 4NZ

GURNEY, Maj Carol James Hay; s of Brig Cecil Hay Gurney, CBE, and Elnyth Meryl, *née* Segar-Owen; *b* 24 Nov 1936; *Educ* Harrow; *m* 6 March 1964, Elizabeth Sara Ann, da of Brig Sir Frederick Coates, 2 Bt of Launchfield, Bryantspuddle, Dorchester, Dorset; 1 s (Christopher Hay b 22 April 1968), 1 da (Sara Catherine b 30 Aug 1965); *Career* served 60 Rifles and Royal Greenjackets 1955-69, seconded to Kenya Regt 1960-63, attended Indian Staff Coll 1967, memb HM Bodyguard of Hon Corps of Gentlemen of Arms 1989; Barclays Bank 1969- (local dir Norwich), farmer; *Recreations* field sports, gardening and forestry, travel; *Clubs* Army and Navy; *Style*— Maj Carol Gurney; Higham Lodge, Higham, Colchester, Essex (☎ 020637 217)

GURNEY, David Quintin; s of Richard Quintin Gurney (d 1980), and Elisabeth Margaret, *née* Boughey (d 1985); *b* 6 Feb 1941; *Educ* Harrow, Trinity Coll Cambridge, Grenoble Univ; *m* 1965, Jacqueline McLeod, *née* Rawle; 1 s, 2 da; *Career* banker, personal sector dir Barclays Bank Ltd Norwich 1988-; farmer, chm and dir Bawdeswell Farms Ltd, mangaging ptnr Breck Farms; dir: Tudor Hall Ltd, Camphill Communities E Anglia Ltd, Fakenham Race course Ltd; pres Norfolk branch Br Red Cross Soc 1989-; *Recreations* field sports; *Clubs* Farmers', MCC, Norfolk; *Style*— David Gurney, Esq; Bawdeswell Hall, East Dereham, Norfolk (☎ 036 288 307); Barclays Bank plc, Regional Office, Bank Plain, Norwich (☎ 0603 660255)

GURNEY, John; s of Sir Eustace Gurney, JP (d 1927); *b* 3 July 1905; *Educ* Eton, New Coll Oxford; *m* 1932, Ann, da of Capt Frederick Ogilvy, RN (3 s of Sir Reginald Ogilvy, 10 Bt, JP, DL, by his w Hon Olivia, da of 9 Lord Kinnaird, KT, PC); 4 da (Priscilla (Mrs Meath-Baker), Jean (Lady Mayhew), Elizabeth Olivia (Mrs Bristol), Christian (Mrs Forestier-Walker)), and 1 da decd (Elizabeth); *Career* served with Royal Norfolk Regt and W Africa Frontier Force 1939-43; chm and md Walsingham Estate Co 1928-, md Medici Soc 1935-; JP Norfolk 1930-75; *Recreations* photography; *Clubs* Norfolk (Norwich); *Style*— John Gurney, Esq; The Abbey, Walsingham, Norfolk

GURNEY, Dr Michael James Tyson; s of Norman James Stratton Gurney, of Highfield, Hillcourt Rd, Cheltenham, Glos, and Phyllis Anne May, *née* Tyson; *b* 8 Oct 1941; *Educ* Eastbourne Coll, The London Hosp Med Coll (MB BS); *m* 22 July 1967, Margaret, da of Arthur Thomas Woodward (d 1976), of Leigh on Sea, Essex; 1 s (Adrian Michael b 1 Dec 1977), 2 da (Nicola b 29 Nov 1970, Philippa b 4 Feb 1973); *Career* surgical registrar Cheltenham Gen Hosp 1969-71, orthopaedic registrar Bristol Royal Infirmary 1971-72, princ in GP ptnrship 1973-; FRCS 1971; *Recreations* squash, tennis, skiing; *Clubs* The Escorts Squash Rackets; *Style*— Dr Michael Gurney; Potters End, Buxted, E Sussex TN32 4PU (☎ 082 581 3249); Ireby Grange, Cumbria; The Meads, Grange Rd, Uckfield, E Sussex (☎ 0825 5777)

GURNEY, Hon Mrs ((Diana) Miranda); *née* (Hovell-Thurlow-) Cumming-Bruce; da of 8 Baron Thurlow, KCMG; *b* 6 July 1954; *m* 14 Feb 1981, Michael (Mike) J Gurney, s of J C Gurney; 1 s (Mungo b 1982), 1 da (Rowan); *Style*— The Hon Mrs Gurney

GURNEY, Prof Oliver Robert; s of Robert Gurney (d 1950), of Bayworth Corner, Boars Hill, Oxford, and Sarah Gamzu, *née* Garstang, MBE (d 1973); *b* 28 Jan 1911; *Educ* Eton, New Coll Oxford (MA, DPhil); *m* 23 Aug 1957, Diane Hope Grazebrook, da of Rene Esencourt; *Career* Capt RA 1939-45, Bimbashi Sudan Def Force 1940-44; Shillito reader in Assyriology Oxford 1946- (prof 1965-78), fell Magdalen Coll 1963, pres Br Inst of Archaeology at Ankara; Freeman City of Norwich; FBA 1959; *Books* The Hittites (latest edn 1981), Some Aspects of Hittite Religion (1977), The Middle Babylonian Legal and Economic Texts From Ur (1983); Literary and Miscellaneous Texts in the Ashmolean Museum (1989); *Recreations* golf; *Style*— Prof Oliver Gurney; Fir Tree House, Milton Lane, Steventon, Abingdon, Oxon OX13 6SA (☎ 0235 831 212)

GUROWSKA, Countess; Rosanna; only da of Maj 23 Knight of Kerry, 5 Bt, MC; *b* 5 Feb 1945; *m* 1964, 8 Count (Richard Melchior Beaumont) Gurowski (6 in descent from Raphael Gurowski, Chamberlain to Augustus III of Poland and who was cr Count by Letters Patent (1787) of Frederick William II of Prussia; the present Count Gurowski's mother was Angela, da of Peter Haig-Thomas by his w Lady Alexandra, *née* Agar, herself da of 4 Earl of Normanton); 2 da (Iona b 1967, Anya b 1970); *Style*— Countess Gurowska; North End House, Damerham, Fordingbridge, Hants (☎ 072 53 308)

GURR, Prof Michael Ian; s of Henry Ormonde Gurr (d 1988), of Braeview, Great Brickhill, Bletchley, Bucks, and Hilda Ruth Gurr (d 1978); *b* 10 April 1939; *Educ* Dunstable Sch, Univ of Birmingham (BSc, PhD); *m* 2 Aug 1963, (Elizabeth) Anne, da of Reginald Mayers, of 225 Aragon Rd, Morden, Surrey; 2 s (Nicholas b 5 Jan 1965, Stephen b 9 March 1968), 1 da (Eleanor b 18 April 1969); *Career* sr scientist Unilever Res 1967-78, head nutrition Nat Inst Res in Dairying Shinfield Reading 1979-85, head laboratory AFRC Inst Food Res Shinfield Reading 1985-86, nutrition conslt Milk Mktg Bd Thames Ditton Surrey 1986-90; visiting prof: Univ of Reading 1986-, Oxford Poly 1990-; memb: Ctee Med Aspects Food Policy 1985-90, Advsy Ctee Br Nutrition Fndn 1983-90; chm Ed Bd Br Jl Nutrition 1987-90; chm Sharnbrook Parish Cncl 1976; FIBiol 1980; memb: Biochemical Soc 1961, Nutrition Soc 1974, RSM 1987; *Books* Lipid Biochemistry: An Introduction (1971, 4 edn 1991), The Role of Fat in Food and Nutrition (1984); *Recreations* sailing, walking, piano playing, reading; *Style*— Prof Michael Gurr; Vale View Cottage, Maypole, St Mary's, Isles of Scilly TR21 0NU (☎ 0720 22224); Maypole Scientific Services, Vale View Cottage, Maypole, St Mary's, Isles of Scilly TR21 0NU

GURUSINGHE, Nihal Trevor; s of Hector Kingsley Gurusinghe, of Panadura, Sri Lanka, and Supriya, *née* Padmini; *b* 30 Oct 1946; *Educ* Univ of Ceylon (MB BS); *m* 6 Aug 1973, Indrani Lucille, da of Martin Kumaraperu (d 1974); 2 s (Dilnath b 1976, Lakmal b 1980); *Career* sr registrar in neurosurgery: Atkinson Morley's Hosp Wimbledon, Nat Hosp for Nervous Diseases London, Gt Ormond St Hosp London; currently conslt neurosurgn Royal Preston Hosp; chm Whittingham CC Preston, govr Queen Elizabeth GS Blackburn; FRCSEd 1980; memb: BMA, Soc of Br Neurological Surgns; *Recreations* cricket; *Style*— Nihal Gurusinghe, Esq; Holmwood, 4 Beech Drive, Fulwood, Preston, Lancs PR2 3NB (☎ 0772 862167); Neurosurgery Dept, Royal Preston Hospital, Sharoe Green Lane, Preston, Lancs PR2 4HT (☎ 0772 710574, car 0831 411227)

GUSCOTT, Jeremy Clayton; s of Henry Guscott, of Bath, and Susan Vivian, *née* Taylor; *b* 7 July 1965; *Educ* Ralph Allen Sr Sch Bath; *m* 14 July 1990, Jayne Irene Aland, da of Frederick Richard Simkiss; *Career* Rugby Union centre threequarters Bath RFC and England; clubs: Bath RFC 1972- (won Pilkington Cup 1989/90), Barbarians RFC; rep England B (2 caps) 1989; England: tour Romania 1989, debut v Romania 1989 (scored 3 tries), Five Nations debut v Ireland 1990; British Lions tour Aust 1989 (2 test appearances); pub relations offr; *Recreations* golf; *Style*— Jeremy Guscott, Esq; Bath RFC, Recreation Ground, Bath, Avon (☎ 0225 25192); British Gas Southwestern, Riverside, Temple St, Keynsham, Bristol BS18 1EQ (☎ and fax 0272 861717 ext 3151)

GUTHE, Alexander Digby; s of Digby Julius Ernest Guthe (d 1982), of Stay House, Kepwick, Thirsk, N Yorks, and Rosemary, *née* Reid; *b* 3 Jan 1966; *Educ* Haileybury, RAC Cirencester; *Career* Greenwell Montagu Securities (London) 1987-88, dir The West Hartlepool Steam Navigation Co Ltd (family co) 1989-; *Recreations* shooting, fishing, skiing; *Clubs* Schools; *Style*— Alexander Guthe, Esq; Stay House, Kepwick, Thirsk, N Yorks; 4 Church Square, Hartlepool, Cleveland

GUTHRIE, Lt-Gen Sir Charles Ronald Llewelyn; KCB (1990), LVO (1977), OBE (1980); s of Ronald Dalglish Guthrie (d 1982), of 35 Egerton Crescent, London SW3, and Nina, *née* Llewelyn (d 1987); *b* 17 Nov 1938; *Educ* Harrow, RMA Sandhurst; *m* 11 Sept 1971, Catherine, da of Lt-Col Claude Worrall, MVO, OBE (d 1973), of Bitham Hall, Avon Bassett, Warwicks; 2 s (David Charles b 21 Oct 1972, Andrew James b 3 Sept 1974); *Career* cmmnd Welsh Gds 1959, served BAOR and Aden, 22 SAS Regt 1965-69, psc 1972, mil asst to Chief of Gen Staff MOD 1973-74, Bde Maj Household Div 1976-77, CO 1 Bn Welsh Gds served Berlin and NI 1977-80, Col gen staff mil ops MOD 1980-82, cmd Br Forces New Hebrides 1980, 4 Armd Bde 1982-84, Chief of Staff 1 (Br) Corps 1984-86, GOC NE Dist cmd 2 Inf Div 1986-87, Asst Chief of the Gen Staff MOD, Cmd 1 Br Corps BFPO 39; Col Cmdt Intelligence Corps; Freeman City of London, Liveryman Worshipful Co of Painter-Stainers; *Recreations* tennis, skiing, travel; *Clubs* White's; *Style*— Lt-Gen Sir Charles Guthrie, KCB, LVO, OBE; Lloyds Bank, 79 Brompton Rd, London SW8 1LH

GUTHRIE, Sir Malcolm Connop; 3 Bt (UK 1936), of Brent Eleigh Hall, Co Suffolk; s of Sir Giles Guthrie, 2 Bt, OBE, DSC (d 1979), and Rhona, Lady Guthrie; *b* 16 Dec 1942; *Educ* Millfield; *m* 1967, Victoria, da of Douglas Willcock; 1 s, 1 da; *Heir* s, Giles Malcolm Welcome Guthrie b 16 Oct 1972; *Recreations* competitive shooting, deer stalking and hunting; *Style*— Sir Malcolm Guthrie, Bt; Brent Eleigh, Belbroughton, Stourbridge, Worcs DY9 0DW

GUTHRIE, Robert Isles Loftus (Robin); s of Dr W K C Guthrie (d 1981), and A M Guthrie; *b* 27 June 1937; *Educ* Clifton, Trinity Coll Cambridge (MA), Univ of Liverpool (CertEd), LSE (MSc); *m* 1963, Sarah Julia, da of J Weltman, OBE; 2 s (Andrew b 1965, Thomas b 1970), 1 da (Clare b 1969); *Career* 2 Lt Queens Own Cameron Highlanders 1956-58; head Cambridge House South London 1962-69, schoolteacher Kennington Sch Brixton 1964-66, social devpt offr Peterborough Devpt Corpn 1969-75, asst dir social work serv DHSS 1975-79, dir Joseph Rowntree Meml Tst 1979-88, chief charity cmmr England and Wales 1988-; memb Arts Cncl GB 1979-81 and 1987-88, chm Arts Assoc York 1984-88; chm Cncl: Regnl Arts Assoc 1985-88, Univ of York 1980-, Policy Studies Inst 1979-88; *Recreations* music (french horn), mountaineering, archaeology, travel; *Clubs* Utd Oxford and Cambridge Univs; *Style*— Robin Guthrie, Esq; Braeside, Acomb, York YO2 4EZ

GUY, Diana; da of Charles Stanley Eade (d 1964), of Broadstairs, Kent, and Vera Dorothy, *née* Manwaring; *b* 27 March 1943; *Educ* Queen Anne's Sch Caversham, Lady Margaret Hall Oxford (MA); *m* 25 May 1968, (John) Robert Clare Guy, s of Wilfred Guy (d 1965), of Sydenham, London; 2 s (Jonathan b 1972, Matthew b 1975); *Career* admitted slr 1968, ptnr Theodore Goddard 1973-; chm: Law Soc's Slrs Euro Gp 1985, Law Soc's 1992 Working Pty 1988; memb City of London Slrs Co 1985; memb Law Soc 1968; *Books* The EEC and Intellectual Property (with G I F Leigh, 1981); *Recreations* reading, opera; *Style*— Mrs Diana Guy; 29 Ennerdale Rd, Kew Gdns, Richmond, Surrey TW9 3PE (☎ 01 948 3594); Theodore Goddard, 16 St Martin's-Le-Grand, London EC1A 4EJ (☎ 01 606 8855, fax 01 606 4390, telex 884678)

GUY, Dr Keith William Arthur; s of Kenneth Leonard Guy (d 1977), of Portsmouth, and Margaret Olive Jesse, *née* Rose; *b* 14 Dec 1943; *Educ* Southern GS, Imperial Coll London (BSc, MSc, PhD, ACGI, DIC); *m* 5 April 1968 (m dis 1989), Penelope Ann, da of Peter Desmond Greenyer; 3 da (Tabitha Kate b 11 Sept 1971, Victoria Rose b 31 May 1973, Hannah Roberta b 9 Sept 1976); *Career* Air Products: joined 1970, mangr Staff Engrg 1974, mangr Engrg Design 1977, mangr Process and Proposals 1983, gp mangr Engrg 1985, tech dir 1987, mktg dir 1989; memb CEI 1979-83; chm: London and South East Branch Inst Chem Engrgs 1985-87, Engrg Practices Ctee Inst Chem Engrs 1989-, Mitcham and Morden C Assoc (now treas) 1983-88; SERC: Appointments to Interdiciplinary Res Centre at Imperial Coll 1989-, Process Engrg Ctee 1989-; FIChemE 1981, FEng 1988; *Books* numerous papers and co authorships on engrg; *Recreations* bridge, politics, golf, book collecting, church, music, travel, food; *Style*— Dr Keith Guy; Air Products plc, Hersham Place, Molesey Rd, Walton-on-Thames, Surrey KT12 4RZ (☎ 09322 49591, fax 09322 49565)

GUY, Neville Anselm; JP; s of Henry Anselm (d 1969), and Elsie Alice (d 1987); *b* 19 April 1936; *Educ* Ross-on-Wye Secdy Sch, Coventry Tech Coll, Lanchester Coll of Technol, S Birmingham Poly (Dip Mgmnt Studies); *m* 8 June 1957, Sheila Jean, da of Llewellyn Rees; 1 s (Richard Mark b 5 Dec 1962), 1 da (Sara Helen b 15 March 1965); *Career* Mil Serv RAF 1954-56; trainee British Acoustic Film Ltd 1952-54, quality control mangr H & G Thynne 1956-58, prodn mangr GEC 1958-60, works study offr Thomas Potterton Ltd 1962-64 (PA to MD 1964-66), gen mangr NHS 1966-; *Recreations* golf, walking; *Style*— Neville Guy, Esq, JP; Lottery Cottage, Hob Lane, Burton Green, nr Kenilworth CV8 1QA (☎ 0676 33747); North Birmingham Health Authority, Rectory Rd, Sutton Coldfield, West Midlands B75 7RR (☎ 021 37 2211, fax 021 311 1074)

GUY, Cdr Percy (Denis); s of Henry Percival Guy (d 1953), of New Barnet, Herts, and Elsie Dorothy, *née* Angell (d 1972); of the same family as Thomas Guy fndr of Guy's Hospital; *b* 22 Oct 1919; *Educ* Shoreham GS; *m* 1 July 1947, Norma, da of Norman Frank Kimber (d 1978); 1 s (Jonathan b 1959); *Career* Sub Lt RNVR 1941, Lt RN, engrg specialisation 1946, served Atlantic, ME, Far East, Med, E Africa; Cdr; sr ptnr consultancy practice; CEng, MIEE, FBIM, FIMC, FMS, FInstD; *Recreations* sailing, horse riding including dressage and show jumping; *Clubs* Naval and Military, Royal Naval, Royal Albert Yacht; *Style*— Cdr Denis Guy; Rowan Hill, Perrymead, Bath BA2 5AY (☎ 0225 834015, fax 0225 836176)

GUY, Richard Perran; s of Rev Wilfred Guy (d 1965) of Newlands Park, London, and Winifred Margaret Guy, *née* Hardesty (d 1988); *b* 10 May 1936; *Educ* Kingswood Sch Bath, Wadham Coll Oxford (MA); *m* 26 Sept 1981, Deborah Ann, da of Kenneth Owen, of Hillside Farm, Adlestrop, Glos; 1 s (Benjamin b 1983), 1 da (Georgina b 1986); *Career* Nat Serv 2 Lt CRMP 1955-57; called to the Bar Inner Temple 1970; memb: Hon Soc Inner Temple; *Recreations* tennis, theatre, skiing; *Clubs* RAC; *Style*— Richard Guy, Esq; 108 Barnsbury Rd, London N1 0ES (☎ 01 278 7220); Brynbanc Farm, Cwmbach, Whitland, Dyfed (☎ 09 946 317); Queen Elizabeth Buildings, Temple, London EC4 (☎ 01 353 7181, fax 01 353 3929)

GUY, Gen Sir Roland Kelvin; GCB (1987, KCB 1980), CBE (1978, MBE 1955), DSO (1972); s of Lt-Col Norman Greenwood Guy; *b* 25 June 1928; *Educ* Wellington, RMA Sandhurst; *m* 1957, Deirdre, da of Brig P Graves-Morris, DSO, MC; 2 da (Gillian, Nicola); *Career* cmmnd KRRC 1948; CO IRGJ 1969; Col GS HQ Near East Land Forces 1971, cmd 24 Airportable Bde 1972, RCDS 1975, princ staff offr to Chief of Def Staff 1976-78, chief of Staff HQ BAOR 1978-80, Col Cmdt Small Arms Sch Corps 1981-87, mil sec MOD 1980-83, Col Cmdt 1 Bn Royal Green Jackets 1981-86; rep Col Cmdt Royal Green Jackets 1985-86, Adj Gen MOD 1984-86, ADC Gen to HM the Queen 1984-87, govr Royal Hosp Chelsea 1987; chm Army Benevolent Fund 1987-, vice pres Wellington Coll 1990-, govr Milton Abbey Sch 1987-; *Recreations* music, skiing; *Clubs* Army & Navy; *Style*— Gen Sir Roland Guy, GCB, CBE, DSO

GUYMER, Patricia Lesley; *née* Bidstrup; er da of Clarence Leslie Bidstrup (d 1961), and Kathleen Helena (d 1968), *née* O'Brien; *b* 24 Oct 1916; *Educ* Kadina HS and Walford House Adelaide South Aust, Univ of Adelaide (MB BS, MD); *m* 18 April 1952,

Ronald Frank Guymer (d 1977), s of Frank Guymer (d 1958); 1 step s (Anthony b 1930), 1 step da (Jill b 1932); *Career* AAMC 1942-45; actg hon asst physician Royal Adelaide Hosp 1942-45, MO UN Relief & Rehabilitation Admin Glyn Hughes Hosp 1945-46, asst Dept Res in Industl Med MRC 1947-58, clinical asst St Thomas's Hosp 1958-76; memb: sci sub-ctee on Poisonous Substances used in Agric & Food Storage 1956-58, Industl Injuries Advsy Cncl 1970-83, med appeal tbnls 1970-88, Indust Health Fndn Ctee, Chromium Chemicals Environmental Health & Safety Ctee 1971-; examiner for Diploma in Indust Health Conjoint Bd and Dundee 1965-82, memb Cons Pty; Mayoress Royal Borough Kingston-upon-Thames 1959-60 and 1960-61; William P Yant Awardee American Industl Hygiene Assoc 1989; FRSM 1950, FRACP 1954, FRCP, FACOM 1958; *Books* Chromium (contrib, 1953), Cancer Progress (contrib, 1960), Toxicity of Mercury and its Compounds (1964), Prevention of Cancer (contrib, 1967), Clinical Aspects of Inhaled Particles (contrib, 1972); *Recreations* theatre, ballet, music; *Style*— Mrs Patricia Guymer; 11 Sloane Terrace Mansions, Sloane Terrace, London SW1X 9DG (☎ 071 730 8720)

GUZ, Prof Abraham; s of Akiwa Guz (d 1970), of London, and Esther Guz (d 1986); *b* 12 Aug 1929; *Educ* Grocers' Sch, Charing Cross Hosp Med Sch, Univ of London (MB BS, MD), MRCP; *m* 5 Nov 1989, Nita, *née* Florenz, da of Aaron Hollander (d 1973), of London; 3 da (Deborah b 1959, Gabrielle b 1961, Stephanie b 1964); *Career* Nat Serv 1954-56: Lt (later Capt) RAMC Br Army Hosp Hostert HQ BAOR; jr hosp appts 1952-53, asst lectr pharmacology Charing Cross Hosp Med Sch 1953-54, sr house offr Royal Posgrad Med Sch Hammersmith Hosp 1956-57; res fell: Harvard Med Sch 1957-59, Cardiovascular Res Inst Univ of California 1959-61; Charing Cross Hosp Med Sch 1961-82: lectr, sr lectr, reader, prof; prof med and head Dept of Med Charing Cross and Westminster Med Sch 1982-; hon sec MRS 1965-70, censor RCP 1979-81; FRCP 1969, memb RSM; *Recreations* family, violin in trio, Jewish culture study; *Style*— Prof Abraham Guz; 3 Littleton Rd, Harrow, Middlesex HA1 3SY (☎ 081 4222786); Dept of Medicine, Charing Cross and Westminster Medical School, Fulham Palace Rd, London W6 8RF (☎ 071 846 7181, fax 071 846 7170)

GWENLAN, Gareth; s of Charles Aneurin Gwenlan (d 1939), and Mary, *née* Francis (d 1980); *m* 1, 1962 (m dis); 1 s (Simon); m 2, 1986, Sarah Elizabeth, da of Peter Fanghanel; *Career* head of light entertainment BBC TV; prod and dir: Woodhouse Playhouse 1977, The Fall and Rise of Reginald Perrin 1978-80, Butterflies 1979-81, To The Manor Born 1978-81, Solo 1980, and approx 200 more programmes; *Recreations* dressage, eventing; *Clubs* Savage; *Style*— Gareth Gwenlan, Esq; Alderbourne Manor, Fulmer Lane, Gerrards Cross, Bucks; BBC TV Centre, Wood Lane, London W12 (☎ 01 743 8000)

GWILLIAM, Prof Kenneth Mason; s of John Gwilliam of Farnham, Surrey, and Marjorie, *née* Mason (d 1982); *b* 27 June 1937; *Educ* Latymer Upper Sch London, Magdalen Coll Oxford (BA); *m* 1, 1961 (m dis 1987), Jennifer Mary Bell; 2 s (David Richard b 30 Dec 1964, Michael James b 9 Jan 1967); m 2, 18 Dec 1987, Sandra, da of late John Robert; *Career* econ asst Fisons Ltd Felixtowe 1960-61, lectr in ind econs Univ of Nottingham 1961-65, lectr in econs Univ of E Anglia 1965-67, prof of tport econs Univ of Leeds 1967-89, prof of the econs of tport and logistics Erasums Univ Rotterdam 1989-; dir: Nat Bus co 1978-83, Yorkshire Ride 1985-87; specialist advsr to House of Commons tport ctee; FCIT; *Books* Transport and Public Policy (1964), Economics of Transport Policy (1975); *Recreations* badminton, golf, walking; *Style*— Prof Kenneth Gwilliam; Rotterdam Transport Centre, Erasmus University Rotterdam, PO Box 1738 (room H11-23), 300 DR Rotterdam, Netherlands (☎ 010 4081443, fax 010 4081495)

GWILLIAM, Russell; s of Ernest Charles Gwilliam, of London, and Jessie, *née* Mason; *b* 24 June 1931; *Educ* Mitcham Co GS For Boys, King's Coll London (BSc), Sch of Mil Survey Newbury, Victoria Univ, Univ of Manchester (DipTP); *m* 24 Oct 1953, Gillian Lesley, da of Leslie Hunkin (d 1980), of Richmond, Surrey; 2 s (Miles b 1962, Nigel b 1970), 2 da (Lesley b 1958, Stephanie b 1960); *Career* HM Colonial Serv Sarawak: asst dir of planning 1963-67, chief planning offr 1968-69; ptnr Peat Marwick & Ptnrs Canada 1973-74 (joined 1969), sr ptnr IBI Group Canada 1974-83, sometime independent conslt UK, awarded Heywood Silver medal for town & country planning; pres: Croydon Bowling Club (1749) Hldgs Ltd, Croydon Bowling Club Ltd; FRGS 1949, FRICS 1959, FRTPI 1963, MCIP 1975; *Recreations* reading, sport, travel; *Clubs* Royal Overseas League, Rugby Club of London; *Style*— Russell Gwilliam, Esq; Canon's End, 37 Canon's Hill, Old Coulsdon, Surrey CR5 1HB (☎ 0737 553 086)

GWILT, George David; s of Richard Lloyd Gwilt (d 1972); *b* 11 Nov 1927; *Educ* Sedbergh, St John's Coll Cambridge; *m* 1956, Ann Dalton, da of Arthur J Sylvester, of Connecticut, USA (d 1973); *Career* actuary; Standard Life Co 1949-: asst official 1956, asst actuary 1957, statistician 1962, mechanisation mangr 1964, systems mangr 1969, dep pensions mangr 1972, pensions actuary 1973, asst gen mangr and pensions mangr 1977, asst gen mangr (fin) 1978, gen mangr and actuary 1979; md and actuary 1985, ret 1988; dir: Hammerson Property Investment and Development Corp plc 1979-, Euro Assets Tst 1979-, Scottish Mortgage and Trust plc 1983-, Hodgson Martin Ltd 1989-; tstee TSB S Scotland 1966-83, pres Faculty of Actuaries 1981-83, memb Monopolies and Mergers Cmmn 1983-87, convener Scottish Poetry Library Assoc 1988-; *Recreations* flute playing; *Clubs* RAF, New (Edinburgh); *Style*— George Gwilt, Esq; 39 Oxgangs Rd, Edinburgh (☎ 031 445 1266)

GWYN, Capt Charles Anthony Hugh; s of Brig Rhys Anthony Gwyn, OBE (d 1987), of Menteith House, Port of Menteith, Perthshire, and Dorothy Elieen, *née* Macmillan; *b* 10 May 1943; *Educ* Abbotsholm Sch, Mons OCS; *m* 24 April 1971, Charnisay Ann, da of Col Sir Delaval Cotter, DSO, 6 Bt, of Green Lines, Child Oakford, nr Blanford, Dorset; 1 s (Simon Anthony Delaval b 19 March 1979), 3 da (Victoria Ann b 28 Nov 1972, Rebecca Louise b 13 Feb 1974, Jessica Harriett b 20 May 1976); *Career* cmmnd 2 Lt Scots Gds 1963; served: Malaysia, Germany, UK; ret Capt 1971; mangr Scottish and Newcastle Breweries Ltd 1971-74; dir: Christie & Co Ltd 1978-83 (mangr 1974-78), Christie Group plc 1983-88, chm and dir Town & Country Hotels Ltd 1988-; dir: Interchange Hotels Ltd 1988-, Picture of Health Ltd 1989-; dir and shareholder Bridghead 2000 Group; Freeman Worshipful Co of Merchants of Edinburgh 1983; memb: ISVA 1976-88, BHRCA 1988; *Recreations* shooting, tennis, wine and good food; *Style*— Capt Charles Gwyn; Humbie House, Humbie, East Lothian, Scotland (☎ 087 533606), 69/74 Bruntsfield Place, Edinburgh EH10 4HH (☎ 031 2291393, fax 031 2295634, telex 727897, car 0860 230751)

GWYN, Hon Mrs (Clare); *née* Devlin; er da of Baron Devlin, PC (Life Peer); *b* 2 March 1940; *m* 1961 (m annulled 1984), Julian Reginald Desgrand Jermy Gwyn, prof in history at Ottawa Univ, 3 s of Quintin P T J Gwyn, CD, of Thelwell House, Rosemere, Quebec (vice pres and dir Seagram Overseas Corp), and gs of late Maj Reginald P J Gwyn, of Stanfield Hall, Norfolk; 2 s (Christopher b 1965, Matthew b 1978), 3 da (Frances b 1962, Anya b 1963, Elin b 1964); *Style*— The Hon Mrs Gwyn

GWYN, Philip Hamond Rhys; s of Brig Rhys Anthony Gwyn, OBE (d 1987), and Dorothy Eileen, *née* Macmillan; is a collateral branch of Gwyn of Stanfield Hall, Norfolk (sold 1920), who can trace their ancestry back to Hwfa ap Cynddelw, Chief of the First Noble Tribe of Wales (19th in descent from Cunedda *fl* 400 AD); *b* 18 Aug 1944; *Educ* Eton, Trinity Coll Camb (MA); *m* 1970, Susan Alice Margaret, da of Brig Derek Shuldham Schreiber, CVO (d 1972); 1 s (Hwfa b 1980), 3 da (Katherine b 1972, Anna b 1974, Christina b 1977); *Career* called to the Bar Inner Temple 1968; chm Christie Gp plc, dir Alumasc Gp plc, SFV Communications Gp plc, etc; chm The Friends of Great Ormond St; *Recreations* sports, the arts; *Clubs* Brooks's; *Style*— Philip Gwyn, Esq; Dean House, Kilmeston, Alresford, Hants (☎ 096 279 287); 74 Ebury Street, London SW1 (☎ 01 730 7898); 2,4 & 6 York Street, London W1A 1BP (☎ 01 486 5974)

GWYNEDD, Viscount; David Richard Owen; s and h of 3 Earl Lloyd George of Dwyfor, *qv*; *b* 22 June 1951; *Educ* Eton; *m* 29 June 1985, Pamela Alexandra, o da of late Alexander Kleyff; 2 s (Hon William Alexander, Hon Frederick Owen b 15 Aug 1987); *Heir* s Hon William Alexander Lloyd George b 16 May 1986; *Career* Lloyd's broker; hon Adm Texas Navy; *Recreations* shooting; *Clubs* White's; *Style*— Viscount Gwynedd; Fulwood House, Longstock, nr Stockbridge, Hants SO20 6DW

GWYNN-JONES, Peter Llewellyn; s of Maj Jack Llewellyn Gwynn-Jones, of Kalk Bay, Cape Town, SA (d 1981); stepson and ward of Lt-Col Gavin David Young (d 1978), of Spring House, Long Burton, Dorset; *b* 12 March 1940; *Educ* Wellington, Trinity Coll Cambridge (MA); *Career* Bluemantle Pursuivant of Arms 1973-83, Lancaster Herald of Arms 1982-, House Comptroller College of Arms 1982; sec Harleian Soc 1982; *Recreations* local architecture, tropical forests, wildlife conservation, fishing; *Style*— Peter Gwynn-Jones, Esq; 79 Harcourt Terrace, London SW10 (☎ 071 373 5859); College of Arms, Queen Victoria St, London EC4 (☎ 071 248 0911)

GWYNNE, Derek Selby; OBE (1986); s of Samuel Frederick Gwynne (d 1975), and Margaret Martha, *née* Fayers (d 1973); *b* 17 June 1924; *Educ* Oxford Sch of Technol Art and Commerce; *m* 2 Sept 1950, Phyllis Gertrude, da of Joseph Edward Freeman (d 1955); 2 s (Derek b 1954, Robert b 1957), 1 da (Julie b 1951); *Career* md: Bentley Engineering Co Ltd 1975-88, Wildt Mellor Bromley Ltd 1983-88, Gwynne Associates Ltd 1986; chm: Br Textile Machinery Assoc, Leicester Engrg Trg Gp; Freeman City of London 1981, Liveryman Worshipful Co of Framework Knitters 1981; FIProdE 1965, FRS 1987; *Style*— Derek Gwynne, Esq, OBE, FRS; 3 Firle Drive, Seaford, E Sussex (☎ 0323 891 563, home 0323 891 563)

GWYNNE, Richard; s of Dr Edward Ieuan Gwynne, of Ystrad-Rhondda, Mid Glamorgan, and Mary Therese, *née* Downey; *b* 9 March 1955; *Educ* Porth County GS, Trinity Coll Cambridge (MA); *Career* admitted slr 1979, ptnr Stephenson Harwood 1986, chm mgmnt ctee of Fulham Legal Advice Centre 1987-; memb Worshipful Co of Slrs; memb IBA; *Recreations* opera, theatre, golf; *Style*— Richard Gwynne, Esq; Flat 3, 4 Oakhill Road, Putney, London SW15 2QU (☎ 01 8700494), Stephenson Harwood, One St Paul's Churchyard, London EC4M 8SH (☎ 071 3294422, fax 071 6060822, telex 886789)

GWYNNE-EVANS, Monica, Lady; Monica Dalrymple; *née* Clinch; da of Douglas Clinch, of Durban; *m* 1946, Sir Ian William Gwynne-Evans, 3 Bt (d 1986); *Style*— Lady Gwynne-Evans; 57 Eastood Road, Dunkeld, Johannesburg, S Africa

GYNGELL, Bruce; *b* 8 July 1929; *m* 1, 1957 (m dis), Ann Barr; 1 s, 2 da; m 2, 1986, Kathryn Rowan; 2 s; *Career* chief exec National Channel 9 Network Australia until 1969, md Seven Network 1969-72, dep chm and jt md ATV London 1972-75, fndr chm Aust Bdcasting Tbnl 1977-80, chm TV-am (UK) 1990- (md 1984-); *Style*— Bruce Gyngell, Esq; TV-am, Breakfast Television Centre, Hawley Crescent, London NW1 8EF (☎ 071 267 4300)

GYNN, Michael; s of A J Gynn, of Fields End Bridge Farm, Kings Dyke, Whittlesey, and Mary Gynn; *b* 19 Aug 1961; *Educ* Sir Harry Smith Community Coll, Peterborough Tech Coll, Henley Coll Coventry; *Career* professional footballer; Peterborough Utd: apprentice then professional, debut 1978, over 150 appearanaces, player of the year 1981, 1982, 1983; currently with Coventry City: over 200 appearances, FA Cup Winners Medal v Tottenham Hotspur 1987; *Recreations* record collecting, golf, good food; *Style*— Michael Gynn, Esq; Coventry City FC, Highfield Rd, King Richard St, Coventry

GYÖRKE, HE Dr Jósef; *b* 6 July 1942; *Educ* State Inst Foreign Relns (BA); *m* 1969, Eva; 1 s (Csaba b 1973), 1 da (Mariann b 1971); *Career* Miny For Affrs 1967, dip assignment Dar es Salaam 1969-71, Addis Abbaba 1971-73, dep head Dept of Central Ctee Hungarian Socialist Workers' Party (memb 1981-), Hungarian Ambass to London 1989-; *Recreations* tennis; *Style*— His Excellency Dr Jósef Györke; Embassy of the Hungarian People's Republic, 35 Eaton Place, London SW1X 8BY (☎ 071 235 4048, fax 071 823 1348)

GYSIN, John Max; MBE (1986); s of Max Gysin (d 1969), and Constance Marguerite, *née* Chesswas (d 1974); *b* 22 Jan 1935; *Educ* Cranleigh Sch Surrey; *m* 1, 1967 (m dis 1970), Ute Irmgard, *née* Festing; 1 s (Geoffrey 1967); m 2, 9 Sept 1978, Elisabeth Anna (Sissy), da of Kajetan Rainer, of Lienz, Austria; 1 s (Timothy b 1980), 1 da (Jennifer b 1984); *Career* RAF 1953-56; commercial offr: Embassy Bonn 1962-69, Embassy Berne 1969-70, vice consul (commercial) Zurich; MIL, RAFA, Br Legion; *Recreations* rugby referee (FSR), Victorian music hall, sailing, squash, tennis, skiing, aviation history; *Clubs* Old Cranleighon Soc, OC Rugby, Zurich Comedy, Zurich Rugby, IPMS; *Style*— John Gysin, Esq, MBE; British Consulate-General, Dufourstrasse 56, CH 8008 Zurich (☎ 01 2611520)

H

HAAN, Michael Robert Anthony; s of Joseph Patrick Haan (d 1989), and Mary Ailsa, *née* Richardson; *b* 24 Sept 1944; *Educ* Ledbury GS; *m* 26 May 1969, Margaret Mabel Haan, da of James Richard Dixon Delahay; 3 c (Rachel Elizabeth b 20 July 1971, Matthew Anthony b 12 June 1974, John Edward b 9 Aug 1978); *Career* chartered accountant Herbert Hill & Co 1969-71 (articled clerk 1964-69); Stoy Hayward: joined as supervisor following a merger 1971, ptnr 1974, chm of personnel, memb Fin Ctee, memb Lead Ptnrs; FCA (ACA 1969); *Recreations* golf, cricket and watching most sports, philately; *Style—* Michael Haan, Esq; Stoy Hayward, 8 Baker St, London W1M 1DA (☎ 071 486 5888, fax 071 487 3686)

HABAKKUK, Sir John Hrothgar; s of Evan Guest Habakkuk; *b* 13 May 1915; *Educ* Barry Co Sch, St John's Coll Cambridge; *m* 1948, Mary Richards; 1 s, 3 da; *Career* lectr Faculty of Economics Cambridge Univ 1946-50, dir of studies in history and librarian Pembroke Coll Cambridge 1946-50 (fell 1938-50, hon fell 1973), Chichele prof of econ history Oxford and fell All Souls 1950-67, princ Jesus Coll Oxford 1967-84, pres Univ Coll Swansea 1975-84, pro vice chllr Oxford Univ 1977-84 (vice chllr 1973-77); memb: Advsy Cncl Public Records 1958-70, SSRC 1967-71, Nat Libraries Ctee 1968-69, Admin Bd Int Assoc of Univs 1975-84, Royal Cmmn on Historical Manuscripts 1978-90; fell All Souls Coll Oxford 1988-; chm: Ctee of Vice Chllrs and Principals of Univs of UK 1976-77, Oxfordshire DHA 1981-84; former pres Royal Hist Soc; Hon DLitt: Wales 1971, Cambridge 1973, Pennsylvania 1975, Kent 1978, Ulster 1988; kt 1976; *Style—* Sir John Habakkuk; 28 Cunliffe Close, Oxford (☎ 0865 56583)

HABEL, Dr Alex; s of Jack Habel, of Bournemouth, and Gretel, *née* Berman (d 1978); *b* 31 May 1944; *Educ* Carmel Coll, Univ of Edinburgh (MB ChB); *m* 24 Feb 1972, Shay Trenchard, da of Arthur Torode; 2 s (Gideon, Rafael), 2 da (Ruth, Batsheva); *Career* lectr Dept of Child Life and Health Univ of Edinburgh 1973-78, conslt paediatrician W Middx Hosp 1978-; FRCP 1986 (MRCP 1970); *Books* Aids to Paediatrics (1982), Aids to Paediatrics for Undergraduates (1987), A Synopsis of Paediatrics (1991); *Recreations* taking children skiing; *Style—* Dr Alex Habel; 62 Burghley Rd, London SW19 5HN (☎ 01 946 9718, 01 944 1883); West Middlesex University Hospital, Isleworth TW7 6AF (☎ 071 867 5366)

HABERMAN, Prof Steven; s of Louis Haberman, of Essex, and Rita Lily, *née* Kaminsky; *b* 26 June 1951; *Educ* Ilford Co HS, Trinity Coll Cambridge (MA), City Univ (PhD); *m* 11 April 1976, Mandy Nicola, da of Arnold Brecker, of Herts; 1 s (Benjamin Adam b 18 Aug 1978), 2 da (Nadia Lia (twin) b 18 Aug 1978, Emily Michal b 15 Feb 1980); *Career* Prudential Assur Co 1972-74; dept Actuarial Sci City Univ: lectr 1974-79, sr lectr 1979-83, reader 1983-85, prof 1985-; memb Cncl Inst Actuaries; FIA 1975, ASA 1976, FSS 1979, AFIMA 1979, FRSA 1989; *Books* Pensions: The Problems of Today and Tomorrow (1987); *Recreations* badminton, reading, music; *Style—* Prof Steven Haberman; City University, Dept of Actuarial Science and Statistics, Northampton Square, London EC1V 0HB (☎ 01 253 4399, fax 01 250 0837)

HABGOOD, Anthony John; s of John Michael Habgood, MC, of Broad Farm, Salhouse, Norwich, and Margaret Diana Middleton, *née* Dalby; *b* 8 Nov 1946; *Educ* Gonville and Caius Coll Cambridge (MA), Carnegie Mellon Univ Pittsburgh USA (MS); *m* 29 June 1973, Nancy, da of Ray Nelson Atkinson, of 150 Sycamore, San Mateo, California, USA; 2 s (John Alan b 14 Nov 1979, George Michael (twin) b 14 Nov 1979), 1 da (Elizabeth Ann b 21 Sept 1975); *Career* memb Mgmnt Exec Ctee Boston Consulting Gp Inc 1979-86 (dir 1976-86); dir: Tootal Gp plc 1986-, Geest plc 1988-; *Recreations* country pursuits; *Clubs* Royal Norfolk and Suffolk Yacht, RAC; *Style—* Anthony Habgood, Esq; Tootal Group plc, 204 Great Portland St, London W1 (☎ 071 387 2817, fax 071 388 7115)

HABGOOD, Most Rev and Rt Hon John Stapylton; *see*: York, Archbishop of

HABIB, Mustafa Salmon; s of late Salmon Habib, and late Nadima, *née* Al-Wattar; *b* 23 Sept 1935; *Educ* Univ of London (B Pharm), Univ of Bradford (PhD); *m* May 1972, Rauntip, da of Dr Brig Koonaraksa, of Bangkok, Thailand; *Career* Iraq Petroleum Co 1965-68, researcher 1969-72, asst prof 1972-73, post doctoral fell 1973-74, co dir 1974-79; called to the Bar Lincoln's Inn 1980; various scientific and legal papers; MRPharmS, FRSH; *Books* various scientific legal papers; *Style—* Dr Mustafa Habib; 131 Gloucester Rd, London SW7 4TH (☎ 01 373 5344); 10 King's Bench Walk, Temple, London EC4 (☎ 01 353 7742, telex 916161 SELMAN G, fax 01 373 6145)

HACKER, Alan Ray; OBE; s of Kenneth Ray Hacker, and Sybil Blanche, *née* Cogger; *b* 30 Sept 1938; *Educ* Dulwich, RAM; *m* 1 (m dis 1976), Karen Wynne, *née* Evans; m 2, 1977, Anna Maria, *née* Skoks; 3 da (Alucin, Katy, Sophie); *Career* prof RAM, sr lectr Univ of York, conductor and teacher Royal Northern Coll; composer of maj modern clarinet works dedicated to HM Queen, revived Mozart bassett clarinet in the 1960's, pioneer of authentic classical performances in England, many first modern performances of classical works in the 1970's (Haydn to Mendlessohn), recent debut as operatic conductor; fndr: York early music festival (dir), York clarion band; memb of various arts Cncl Ctees, host Br Cncl; FRAM; *Books* Mozart's Clarinet concerto, Schumann's fantasy pieces (soirée stücke); *Recreations* cooking; *Style—* Alan Hacker, Esq, OBE; 7 Foxthorn Paddock, York YO1 5HJ (☎ 0904 410312); Haydn Rawstron Int Management, PO Box 654, London SE26 4DZ

HACKER, Richard Daniel; s of Samuel Hacker, of London, and Lilli Paula, *née* Eick; *b* 26 March 1954; *Educ* Haberdashers' Aske's, Downing Coll Cambridge (MA), Wiener Anspach scholar 1976, Université Libre De Bruxelles (Licencié Speciale En Droit Européen); *m* 25 March 1988, Sarah Anne, da of Richard Millar, of Bath; *Career* called to the Bar Lincoln's Inn 1977; Kennedy scholar 1977, Lincoln's Inn Student of the Year Prize 1977, Gray's Inn 1989; *Recreations* travel, gastronomy, opera; *Style—* Richard Hacker, Esq; 12 Belsize Rd, London NW6 4RD; 3-4 South Square, Gray's Inn, London WC1R 5HP (☎ 071 696 9900, fax 071 696 9911)

HACKET PAIN, Maj Wyndham Jermyn; JP (Surrey 1964), DL (Surrey 1986); eld s of Lt Col Michell Wyndham Hacket Pain (d 1971), of Surrey, and Audrey Ernestine Jermyn, *née* Ford; *b* 27 Dec 1921; *Educ* Harrow, RMA Sandhurst; *m* 6 Dec 1949, Wenllian Kennard, o da of Sir Godfrey Llewellyn, 1 Bt, CB, CBE, MC, JP, DL (d 1986); 2 s (Nicholas Wyndham Llewellyn Hacket Pain b 1953, Simon Michell Hacket Pain b 1956); *Career* serv Grenadier Guards: Western Desert, Italy (Salerno landing), Palestine (despatches), Malaya 1941-52; dir: Lloyd's brokers, Laurence Philipps and Co, Anderson Finch Villiers and Co 1953-67; memb Lloyds; chm Michell and Jermyn Co Ltd 1968-; chm Woking Cons Assoc 1965-68, serv SE Area Exec Ctee, area asst treas and serv on Central Bd of Finance 1973-74, elected SE Area rep Cncl of Nat Union 1969-74; chm: Woking Bench 1979-87, Surrey Magistrates' Courts Ctee 1984-87; appointed memb Ct Univ of Surrey 1986-; High Sheriff of Surrey 1988-89; *Recreations* shooting; *Clubs* Boodle's, Pratt's, City of London, MCC; *Style—* Major Wyndham Hacket Pain, JP, DL; Dixton Lodge, Hadnock, Monmouth (☎ 0600 6702); Michell and Jermyn Co Ltd, PO Box 24, Guildford, Surrey (☎ 0483 895020)

HACKETT, Cyril Charles; s of Charles Edward, (d 1967), and Letitia Elizabeth, *née* Husband (d 1982); *b* 27 April 1924; *Educ* SW Essex Tech Coll; *m* 29 Dec 1946, Peck, da of Joseph Frederick (d 1983); 2 s (Peter Andrew b 1948, Paul Charles b 1960), 2 da (Gillian Letitia b 1950, Francesca Jane b 1958); *Career* dir: Chingford Masonic Hall Ltd, French Kier (London) Ltd; Freeman City of London; *Recreations* community, church, DIY; *Clubs* Thulby; *Style—* Cyril C Hackett, Esq; Pippins, Chelmsford Road, Hatfield Heath, Bishops Stortford, Herts CM22 7BD (☎ 0276 (STD) 730470)

HACKETT, Dennis William Patrick; s of James Joseph Hackett (d 1961), of Sheffield, Yorks, and Sarah Ellen (d 1982); *b* 5 Feb 1929; *Educ* De La Salle Coll Sheffield; *m* 1, 1953 (m dis 1970); 2 s (Sean James b 15 Sept 1956, Michael Simon b 30 May 1961), 1 da (Anne-Marie b 10 Jan 1955); m 2, 10 Aug 1974, Jacqueline Margaret Totterdell; 1 da (Clare Siobhan b 11 Sept 1976); *Career* RN 1947-49; art ed The Observer 1960-62; ed: The Queen 1963-65 (dep ed 1962-63), Nova 1965-69; editorial dir George Newman (IPC) 1965-69, dir IPC Mirror Gp Newspapers 1969-71, assoc ed Daily Express 1973-74, dir HK Communications 1974-82, editorial conslt Assoc Newspapers 1982-86, TV critic The Times 1981-85; ed-in-chief: Today and Sunday Today 1986-87, The Observer Magazine 1987-88; ptnr Dennis Hackett Consultants 1982-86 and 1988-, dir Media Search & Selection 1988-; chm D & ADA 1968-69; *Books* The History of the Future: A History of the Bemrose Corporation 1826 (1976), The Big Idea: The Story of Ford in Europe (1978); *Recreations* reading, walking; *Clubs* RAC; *Style—* Dennis Hackett, Esq; 4 East Heath Rd, London NW3 1BN (☎ 071 784 1015, fax 071 431 4366)

HACKETT, Capt Edward Middleton; s of Maj Peter Middleton Hackett, of Broadstone, Dorset, and Hilda Margaret, *née* Thomas; *b* 28 Oct 1942; *Educ* Dauntsey's Sch, Britannia RNC; *m* 12 Dec 1981, Philippa Ann, da of Dr John Norcliffe Roberts, of London; 1 s (Jamie b 1987), 1 da (Flavia b 1984); *Career* RN: Dartmouth 1961, midshipman HMS Duchess, US Naval Coll Annapolis, navigating off HMS Puncheston 1965, served Borneo and Singapore Indonesian confrontation, Lt 1966, specialised aviation Flying Buccaneers 801 Sqdn HMS Hermes 1968, served Far East, Aust and SA, Flag Lt to Flag Offr Naval Air Cmd 1970, air warfare instr RNAS Lossiemouth, 809 Sqdn HMS Ark Royal served Western Atlantic and America, staff course RNC Greenwich, Lt Cdr 1974, instr Maritime Tactical Sch HMS Dryad (cdr 1977), cmd HMS Rhyl served W Indies, Directorate Naval Air Warfare MoD 1980-82, Cdr Air HMS Illustrious 1982, Staff Aviation Offr Staff of Flag Offr Third Flotilla 1984, Capt 1985, COS to Flag Offr Gibralta 1985-88, cmd HMS Coventry 1988, dep dir Naval Warfare (Air) MOD 1990; memb: Guild of Air Pilots and Air Navigators, Fleet Air Arm Offrs Assoc, RUSI; *Recreations* sailing, fishing, shooting; *Clubs* The Royal Navy of 1765 And 1785; *Style—* Capt Edward Hackett, RN; c/o Barclays Bank, Broadstone, Dorset BH18 8DS

HACKETT, John Charles Thomas; s of Thomas John Hackett, of 31 Ventnor Rd, Sutton, Surrey, and Doris, *née* Whitefoot (d 1978); *b* 4 Feb 1939; *Educ* Glyn GS Epsom, Univ of London (LLB); *m* 27 Dec 1958, Patricia Margaret, da of Eric Ronald Clifford Tubb, of 100 Kennel Lane, Fetcham, Surrey; *Career* prodn planning mangr Rowntree Gp 1960-64, prodn controller Johnson's Wax 1964, commercial sec Heating and Ventilating Contractors Assoc 1964-70, sec Ctee of Assocs of Specialist Engrg Contractors 1968-79, dir Br Constructional Steelwork Assoc 1980-84 (dep dir 1970-79); dir gen Br Insur and Investmt Brokers Assoc 1984-; memb Cncl CBI 1980-88; MInstD 1979, FBIM 1981; *Books* BCSA Members Contractual Handbook (1972, 1979); *Recreations* music, reading, walking, motoring; *Style—* John Hackett, Esq; 15 Downsway Close, Tadworth, Surrey KT20 5DR (☎ 0737 813024); The Br Insur and Investmt Brokers Assoc, Biiba House, 14 Bevis Marks, London EC3A 7NT (☎ 071 623 9043, fax 071 626 9676, telex 987321 Lloyds G)

HACKETT, Gen Sir John Winthrop; GCB (1967, KCB 1962, CB 1958), CBE (1953, MBE 1938), DSO (1942, Bar 1945), MC (1941), DL (Glos 1982); s of Hon Sir John Winthrop Hackett, KCMG, MLC, of Perth, WA (d 1916), and Deborah Vernon (d 1965, having m 2, 1918, Ald Sir Frank Beaumont Moulden, Lord Mayor of Adelaide (d 1932)), 2 da of Frederick Slade Drake-Brockman, of Guildford, WA; *b* 5 Nov 1910; *Educ* Geelong GS, New Coll Oxford (MA, BLitt); *m* 21 March 1942, Margaret, da of Joseph Frena (d 1953), of Graz, Austria, and widow of Friedrich Grossman; 1 da and 2 adopted step da; *Career* 2 Lt 8 Hussars 1931, served Palestine 1936 (despatches), seconded Transjordan Frontier Force 1937-39 (despatches), Syria (wounded), Western Desert (wounded), Italy 1943 (despatches), OC 4 Parachute Bde Arnhem 1944 (wounded), Temp Lt-Col 1942, Brig 1943, BGS (1) Austria 1946, OC Transjordan Frontier Force 1947, IDC 1951, Dep QMG BAOR 1952, OC 20 Armoured Bde 1954, Gen OC 7 Armd Div 1956, Maj-Gen 1957, Cmdt RMC of Sci 1958-61, Gen OC NI Cmd 1961-62, Dep Chief Imperial Gen Staff 1963-64, Dep Chief Gen Staff 1964-66, Gen 1966, C-in-C BAOR and Cdr Northern Army Gp in NATO 1966-68, ADC to HM The Queen 1967-68, Col QRIH 1969-75, Hon Col Univ of Oxford OTC 1967-78, 10 Para Bd TA 1967-78, Col Cmdt REME 1961-66, ret; princ King's Coll London 1968-75; pres: UK Classical Assoc 1971, UK English Assoc 1974; visiting prof of classics King's Coll; Hon LLD: Univ of WA, Queen's Univ Belfast, Univ of Exeter, Univ of Buckingham; Freeman City of London 1976; FRLS 1982; author; *Books* I Was A Stranger (1977), The Third World War (jtly, 1978), The Untold Story (1982), The Profession of Arms (1983), Warfare in the Ancient World (ed, 1989); *Recreations* music, wine, reading, travel, salmon and trout fishing; *Clubs* Cavalry and Guards, Carlton, United Oxford and Cambridge, White's; *Style—* Gen Sir John Hackett, GCB, CBE, DSO, MC, DL; Coberley Mill, nr Cheltenham, Glos GL53 9NH (☎ 024 287 207)

HACKETT, Keith Stuart; s of John Henry Hackett (d 1978), of Sheffield, and Sylvia, *née* Staniland (d 1972); *b* 22 June 1944; *m* 2 Dec 1968, Lynda Margaret, da of Rodgers William; 2 s (Paul b 15 May 1969, Michael b 30 Jan 1978); *Career* sales and mktg dir; football referee; games officiated incl: FA Cup final 1981, World Youth Cup 1982, Charity Shield 1983, Milk Cup Final 1986, Centenary FL 1988, Olympic Games 1989; MCIM, FISMM, FIFA referee 1981; *Books* Hacketts Law (1985); *Recreations* football refereeing; *Style*— Keith Hackett, Esq; 21 Arncliffe Drive, Chapeltown, Sheffield S30 4BS (☎ 0742 469289); Crosby Kitchens Ltd, Orgreave Drive, Sheffield S13 9NS (☎ 0742 697371, telex 547080, fax 0742 692586, car 0836 213104)

HACKING, Hon (Leslie) Bruce; s of 2 Baron Hacking (d 1971); *b* 16 June 1940; *Educ* Eton; *m* 23 Sept 1967, Hon Fiona Margaret Noel-Paton, da of Baron Ferrier (Life Peer); 1 s, 1 da; *Career* stockbroker, fund mangr currently compliance offr; apprenticed to Haberdashers' Co 1955, Liveryman 1962 (memb of Ct 1982); Freeman City of London 1962; *Clubs* Melbourne and Frankston Golf; *Style*— The Hon Bruce Hacking; Burchetts, Lower Mousehill Lane, Milford, Surrey GU8 5JX

HACKING, Daphne, Baroness; Daphne Violet; *née* Finnis; eld da of late Robert Finnis, of Kensington, W; *Educ* Priors Field, Godalming, and Paris; *m* 19 Feb 1936, 2 Baron Hacking (d 1971); 2 s (3 Baron, Hon Bruce Hacking), 2 da (Hon Mrs de Laszlo, Hon Mrs du Preez); *Style*— The Rt Hon Daphne, Lady Hacking

HACKING, 3 Baron (UK 1945); Sir Douglas David Hacking; 3 Bt (UK 1938); s of 2 Baron Hacking (d 1971); n of Hon Lady Waller *qv*; *b* 17 April 1938; *Educ* Aldro Sch, Charterhouse, Clare Coll Cambridge, (BA, MA); *m* 1, 31 July 1965 (m dis), (Rosemary) Anne (who m subsequently, 1982, Anthony Askew, of Highgate), da of the late Frank Penrose Forrest, FRCSE, of Lytchett Matravers, Dorset; 2 s (Hon Douglas Francis b 8 Aug 1968, Hon Daniel Robert b 27 May 1972), 1 da (Hon Belinda Anne b 1966); m 2, 1982, Dr Tessa Hunt, er da of Roland Hunt, CMG, of Whitchurch Hill, Berks; 3 s (Hon Alexander Roland Harry b 20 Jan 1984, Hon Maxwell David Leo b 8 July 1987, Hon Christian Eric George b 7 Dec 1989); *Heir* s, Hon Douglas Francis Hacking; *Career* Nat Serv RN 1956-58; Lt RNR (ret); sits as Independent peer in House of Lords (memb Select Ctee on Euro Community 1989-); barr 1963-76, Harmsworth Maj Entrance Exhibition and Astbury Scholar; attorney: New York State 1975, Simpson Thacher and Bartlett New York 1975-76; slr Supreme Court of Eng & Wales 1977; ptnr Richards Butler; Freeman: Worshipful Co of Merchant Taylors', City of London; *Clubs* MCC, Century (New York); *Style*— The Rt Hon the Lord Hacking; Richards Butler and Co, Beaufort House, 15 St Bitolph St, London EC3A 7EE (☎ 071 247 6555); 21 West Square, Kennington, London SE11 4SN (☎ 071 735 4400)

HACKING, Hon Edgar Bolton; MBE (1942), TD (1950); yr s of 1 Baron Hacking, PC, OBE (d 1950); *b* 31 May 1912; *Educ* Charterhouse, Clare Coll Cambridge, London Hosp (MA, MB BS, BCh); *m* 1, 3 April 1943, (m dis 1950), Winifred Mary, da of John Christie Kelly; 2 da; m 2, 5 July 1950, Evangeline Grace, da of late Percy Burstal Shearing; 2 s, 1 da; *Career* served with RAMC as anaesthetic specialist; Maj 1940-45; sr resident anaesthetist London Hosp 1939; MO to Queen's Westminsters (TA) 1938-40; sr asst anaesthetist Groote Schuur Hosp, anaesthetist instr Cape Town Univ 1946-51 and Stellenbosch Univ 1958; fellow Assoc of Anaestheists; MRCS, LRCP, FFARCS, DA; *Clubs* MCC and Western Province Sports; *Style*— The Hon Edgar Hacking, MBE, TD; Leeming, Alice Rd, Claremont, Cape Town, South Africa (☎ 01027 21 774 4544)

HACKING, Hon Mrs (Fiona Margaret); *née* Noel-Paton; da of Baron Ferrier (Life Peer); *b* 1943; *m* 1967, Hon (Leslie) Bruce Hacking, *qv*; *Style*— The Hon Mrs Hacking; Burchett's, Lower Moushill Lane, Milford, Surrey

HACKING, Dr Peter Michael; s of Lt-Col James Thompson Hacking (d 1975), of Exeter, and Ethel May, *née* Haddock; *b* 1 May 1929; *Educ* Exeter Sch, St John's Coll Cambridge (BA, MB BChir, MA, MD); *m* 27 June 1953, Helen Mary, da of Augustus William Wellings (d 1954), of Leamington Spa; 2 s (Nigel b 1956, Jeremy b 1960), 1 da (Julie b 1954); *Career* conslt diagnostic radiologist 1962-90, conslt in/c admin Radiology Dept Royal Victoria Infirmary Newcastle upon Tyne 1977-88, head Dept of Radiology Univ of Newcastle upon Tyne 1979-88; memb: Cncl RCR 1981-84, BMA 1953; BIR 1958, FRCR 1960; *Recreations* hill walking, gardening, opera going; *Clubs* Northern Counties; *Style*— Dr Peter Hacking; Holly House, 47 Main Rd, Long Hanborough, Oxford OX7 2BD (☎ 0993 882 336); Tenter Hill, Wooler, Northumberland NE71 6DB (☎ 0668 81628)

HACKNEY, Arthur; s of John Thomas (d 1971), of Stoke on Trent, and Annie, *née* Morris (d 1979); *b* 13 March 1925; *Educ* Burslem Sch of Art, RCA; *m* 14 Aug 1954, Mary Cecilia, da of Ernest Baker (d 1946), of Coventry; 2 da (Rosalind b 27 July 1956, Clare b 17 May 1961); *Career* WWII RN, serv Western Approaches 1943-46; RCA travelling scholarship 1949, lectr then princ lectr and head of dept W Surrey Coll of Art and Design 1949-85; work in pub collections incl: Bradford City Art Gallery, V & A, Ashmolean Gallery, Wellington Nat Gallery NZ, Nottingham Art Gallery, Keighley Art Gallery, Wakefield Art Gallery, Preston Art Gallery, Stoke on Trent Gallery; memb: Kent Educn Ctee, Staffs Educn Ctee, Fine Art Bd CNAA 1975-78; RWS, RE, ARCA; *Clubs* Chelsea Arts; *Style*— Arthur Hackney, Esq; Woodhatches, Spoil Lane, Tongham, Farnham, Surrey (☎ 0252 23919)

HACKNEY, Dr Roderick Peter (Rod); s of William Hackney, and Rose, *née* Morris; *b* 3 March 1942; *Educ* John Bright's GS Llandudno, Sch of Architecture Univ of Manchester (MA, BA, ARCH, PhD); *m* Christine (Tina); 1 s (Roan b 27 April 1982); *Career* architect Expo 1967 monorail stations Montreal Canada 1965-66, housing architect Libyan Govt Tripoli 1967-68, asst to Arne Jacobson Copenhagen 1968-71, established practice of Rod Hackney Architect in Macclesfield 1972, established a number of offices throughout the UK 1975-87, set up Castward Ltd building and devpt 1983; RIBA: elected nat memb to the cncl 1978, vice pres 1981-83, memb 3 man delgn to USSR under Anglo-Soviet Cultural Agreement 1984, chm The Times-RIBA Community Enterprise Scheme 1985-89, pres 1987-89; UIA: elected cncl for Gp 1 1981, memb ed bd Int Architect 1983 (Jl of Architect Theory and criticism 1988), vice pres 1985, pres 1987-90; visiting prof UP6 Paris 1984, pres Young Architect World Forum Sofia 1985, pres Building Communities Int Community Architecture Conf 1986, special prof in architecture Univ of Nottingham 1987-; first prize: DOE Awards for Good Design in Housing 1975, St Ann's Hospice Architectural Competition 1976; Prix Int d'Architecture de l'Institut National du Logement 1979, commended RICS and The Times Conservation Awards 1980, highly commended DOE Awards 1980, commended The Civic Tst Awards 1980, hon mention Sir Robert Matthews Award 1981, commended Civic Tst Awards 1981, President's award Manchester Soc for Architects 1982, commended Otis Award 1982; Gold medal: Bulgarian Inst of Architects 1983, Young Architect of the Biennale Sofia 1983; award of commendation Civic Tst Awards 1984, Grand medal of the Federation de Colegios de Arquitectas de la Republica Mexicana 1986, PA award for Innovation in Building Design and Construction 1988; hon fell: American Inst of Architects 1988, Federacion de Colegias de Arquitectos de la Republica Mexicana 1988, Utd Architects of the Philippines 1988, RAIC 1990, Indian Inst of Architects 1990; chm of Tstees Inner City Tst 1986-, presented the case for Int Year of Shelter for the Homeless to all Pty Confs 1986, pres Snowdonia Nat Park Soc 1987, patron Llandudno Museum and Art Gallery 1988, pres North Wales Centre of the Nat Tst; ARIBA 1969, FIArb 1977, MCIOB 1987, FFB 1987, PRIBA 1987; *Books* The Good, The Bad and The Ugly (1990); *Recreations* photography, butterflies, travelling, walking, outdoor pursuits, looking at buildings, speaking at conferences; *Clubs* Cwlth; *Style*— Dr Rod Hackney; St Peter's House, Windmill St, Macclesfield, Cheshire SK11 7HS (☎ 0625 431792, fax 0625 616929, car 0831 371034)

HACKNEY, Sqdn Ldr Roger Graham; s of Peter Neville Hackney, of Bache House, Bache, and Jean, *née* Ball; *b* 2 Sept 1957; *Educ* Univ of Birmingham (MB ChB); *m* 20 Jun 1981, Gillian Margaret, da of Charles Bernard Spurgin, of Leasingham, Sleaford, Lincs; 2 da (Alison Jean b 5 Nov 1986, Joanna Clare b 4 Jul 1988); *Career* unit MO RAF Cosford 1982-83, surgery trainee 1983-89, higher professional trg in orthopaedic surgery 1990-; athlete 3000 m steeplechase: debut for GB against USSR 1979, AAA champion 1980, semi-finalist Moscow 1980, UK champion 1981, AAA champion 1982, fifth place World Athletics Champsionships Helsinki 1983, finalist Los Angeles Olympics 1984, Silver medallist Cwlth Games Edinburgh 1986, finalist Euro Championships Stuttgart 1986, semi-finalist Seoul Olympics 1988; AAA 1500m indoor champion 1981, winner inaugural Euro Community Cross-Country 1988-89; asst sec Exec Cncl British Assoc of Sports and Medicine; *Books* AAA Guide to Athletics (contrib, 1988); *Recreations* sports medicine, ornithology, hifi, photography; *Clubs* Aldershot Farnham & Dist AC; *Style*— Sqdn Ldr Roger Hackney; Princess Mary's Hosptial, RAF Halton, Aylesbury, Bucks (☎ 0296 623535)

HADDAD, (Patricia) Faith; da of Lawrence Atkin (d 1987), and Letitia, *née* Green; *b* 7 Nov 1943; *Educ* Cleethorpes Girls' GS, Univ of Sheffield (MB ChB, MD, Dip Obstetrics); *m* 21 Feb 1972, Joseph Haddad; 1 da (Samantha Faith b 19 July 1976); *Career* pre-registration house offr Nottingham City Hosp 1967-68, pre-registration house surgn Sheffield City Gen Jan-July 1968; sr house offr: obstetrics and gynaecology Jessop Hosp Sheffield 1968-70, surgery Scunthorpe Gen Hosp 1970-71; registrar obstetrics and gynaecology Grimsby Gen Hosp 1971-72, sr med offr Hounslow and Surrey Public Health Dept 1972-75; registrar obstetrics and gynaecology Hillingdon Hosp 1975-76, W Middx Hosp 1976-79 (acting sr registrar); assoc specialist W London Hosp and Charing Cross Hosp 1982-85 (lectr in obstetrics and gynaecology 1979-82), conslt gynaecologist Garden Hosp London 1985-; memb: Working Pty for Change in Antenatal Care NCT 1981, Steering Ctee Forum on Maternity and Newborn, Advsy Ctee on Current Fertility Royal Coll of Gynaecologists 1984-86, Advsy Ctee for First Symposium on Preconception Care 1985, Advsy Ctee for Preconception Care Symposium City Univ 1987, recognized lectr to midwives; Lecture of the Year prize N of England Soc for Obstetrics and Gynaecology 1970; MRCOG 1972; memb: Inst of Psychosexual Med 1985, RSM, N of England Soc of Obstetrics and Gynaecology, Med Women's Fedn; fell Royal Coll of Gynaecologists; *publications:* author of numerous articles in various learned jls; *Recreations* music, sport; *Style*— Mrs Faith Haddad; Tara, Trout Rise, Loudwater, Rickmansworth, Herts WD3 4JY (☎ 0923 772971); 16 Upper Wimpole St, London W1M 7TB (☎ 081 906 4902)

HADDEN, Prof David Robert; s of Robert Evans Hadden (d 1978), of Portadown, and Marianne Baird, *née* Johnston; *b* 24 May 1936; *Educ* Campbell Coll, Queen's Univ Belfast (MB BCh, BAO, MD); *m* 7 April 1967, Diana Sheelah Mary, da of William Herbert Martin (d 1987), of Belfast; 1 s (Robert b 1968), 2 da (Katharine b 1970, Emily b 1971); *Career* house physician and res fell Royal Victoria Hosp Belfast 1959-62, Fulbright Travelling fellowship Johns Hopkins Hosp Baltimore USA 1962-64, MRC Infantile Malnutrition Res Unit Kampala Uganda 1965-66, Dept of Experimental Med Univ of Cambridge 1966-67, conslt physician Royal Victoria Hosp Belfast 1967-, prof of endocrinology Queen's Univ of Belfast 1990-; memb Assoc of Physicians of GB and I, Diabetes and Endocrinology Socs of GB and I, Europe, USA; FRCPE 1969, FRCP 1987, memb RSM; *Books* articles and chapters on diabetes and endocrinology in med lit; *Recreations* restoration and care of old houses and gardens; *Style*— Prof David Hadden; 10 Mount Pleasant, Belfast BT9 5DS (☎ 0232 667110); Sir George E Clark Metabolic Unit, Royal Victoria Hosptial, Belfast BT12 6BA (☎ 0232 240503, fax 0232 230788)

HADDINGTON, 13 Earl of (S 1619) John George Baillie-Hamilton; also Lord Binning (S 1613) and Lord Byres and Binning (S 1619); only s of 12 Earl (d 1986); *b* 21 Dec 1941; *Educ* Ampleforth, Trinity Coll Dublin, RAC Cirencester; *m* 1, 19 April 1975 (m dis 1981), Prudence Elizabeth, da of Andrew Rutherford Hayles, of Bowerchalke, Wilts; m 2, 8 Dec 1984, Susan Jane Antonia, da of John Heyworth, of Bradwell Grove, Burford, Oxon; 1 s (George Edmund Baldred, Lord Binning b 1985), 2 da (Lady Susan Moyra b 15 July 1988, Lady Isobel Joan b 16 June 1990); *Heir* s, George Edmund Baldred, Lord Binning b 27 Dec 1985; *Career* farmer, horse breeder; *Recreations* beekeeping, keeping finches, field sports, photography, racing, cereology; *Clubs* Turf, New, Puffin's, Chelsea Arts; *Style*— The Rt Hon the Earl of Haddington; Mellerstain, Gordon, Berwicks TD3 6LG

HADDINGTON, Dowager Countess of; Sarah; da of late George William Cook, of Westmount, Montreal, Canada; *m* 10 Oct 1923, George Baillie-Hamilton, 12 Earl of Haddington (d 1986); *Style*— The Rt Hon Dowager Countess of Haddington; Tyninghame Stables, Dunbar, E Lothian

HADDO, Earl of; Alexander George Gordon; s and h of 6 Marquess of Aberdeen, and Temair, *qv*; *b* 31 March 1955; *Educ* Harrow, Poly of Central London (Dip of Bldg Econs); *m* 30 May 1981, Joanna Clodagh, da of late Maj Ian George Henry Houldsworth, of Dallas Lodge, Forres, Moray; 3 s (George Ian Alastair, Hon Sam Dudley b 25 Oct 1985, Hon Charles David b 8 June 1990), 1 da (Lady Anna Katharine b 2 Sept 1988); *Heir* s, George Ian Alastair, Viscount Formartine b 4 May 1983; *Career* London & Edinburgh Trust plc 1986-; md Letinvest plc; dir: Washington Developments Ltd, Judlor Ltd, Sunderland Developments Ltd; landowner (10,000 acres); ARICS; *Recreations* sport, music, art; *Clubs* MCC, The Arts, London Scottish RFC; *Style*— Earl of Haddo; 22 Beauclerc Rd, London W6 0NS (☎ 081 748 4849); Estate Office, Haddo House, Aberdeen (☎ 065 15 664); London & Edinburgh Trust plc, 243 Knightsbridge, London SW7 1DH (☎ 071 581 1322)

HADDOCK, Peter; s of Thomas George Haddock (d 1978), and Agnes Haddock; *b* 9 Dec 1961; *Educ* Cramlington HS Northumberland; *m* 7 July 1984, Deborah, da of Frederick Carver; 2 s (Peter Ryan b 2 Dec 1985, Carl James b 18 Sept 1989); *Career* professional footballer; debut for Newcastle Utd 1981 (65 appearances), on loan to Burnley 1985 (7 appearances); Leeds Utd 1986-: over 120 appearances, Div 2 Championship 1990, player of the year 1987-88; *Recreations* golf, squash; *Style*— Peter Haddock, Esq; 3 Walnut Close, Saxton, North Yorkshire (☎ 093781 7199); Leeds United FC, Elland Rd, West Yorkshire

HADDON, Hon Mrs (Teresa Mary); da of 1 Viscount Head, GCMG, CBE, MC, PC (d 1983), and Dorothea, Viscountess Head (d 1987); *b* 20 June 1938; *m* 1972 (m dis), Richard Deacon Haddon; 2 s, 1 da (twin); *Style*— The Hon Mrs Haddon; The Granary, Fawler, Oxford OX7 3AH

HADDON-CAVE, Charles Anthony; s of Sir Philip Haddon-Cave, KBE, CMG, *qv*, of The Old Farmhouse, Tackley, Oxford, and Elizabeth, *née* Simpson; *b* 20 March 1956; *Educ* The King's Sch Canterbury, Pembroke Coll Cambridge (BA); *m* 2 Aug 1980, Amanda Charlotte, da of Timothy James Law, of Spire Hollen, Priorsfield Rd, Godalming, Surrey; 2 da (Alexandra Charlotte b 11 Feb 1987, Florence Caroline b 8 Jan 1991); *Career* called to the Bar: Gray's Inn 1978, Hong Kong 1980; *Recreations* tennis, squash; *Clubs* RAC; *Style*— Charles Haddon-Cave, Esq; 65 Bromfelde Rd,

Clapham Old Town, London SW4 6PP (☎ 071 622 2106); 2 Essex Court, Temple, London EC4Y 9AP (☎ 071 583 8381, fax 071 353 0998, telex 8812528)

HADDON-CAVE, Sir (Charles) Philip; KBE (1980), CMG (1973); s of Francis Macnamana Haddon-Cave; *b* 6 July 1925; *Educ* Tas Univ, King's Coll Cambridge; *m* 1948, Elizabeth Alice May, da of Frederick Alfred Simpson, 2 s, 1 da; *Career* joined Colonial Admin Service 1952; chief secretary Hong Kong 1981- (financial sec Hong Kong 1971-81); *Style—* Sir Philip Haddon-Cave, KBE, CMG; Government Secretariat, Hong Kong (☎ 95406); Victoria House, Hong Kong

HADEN, Harold John; s of Harold Stanley Haden (d 1979), and Eunice Escott, *née* Wood (d 1962); *b* 14 Feb 1941; *Educ* Wrekin Coll, Hackley Sch, NY (ESU Exchange Scholar), Univ of Birmingham (LLB); *m* 4 April 1964, (Elizabeth) Jane da of George Noel de St Croix, MBE; 1 s (Rupert b 1974), 2 da (Rachel b 1967, Philippa b 1970); *Career* pupillage practice 1964-65, barr 1966-69, loss adjuster 1970-72, M & G 1973, currently legal dir M & G Group plc (co sec until 1990); *Recreations* shooting, travel, theatre; *Style—* Harold Haden, Esq; M & G Limited, Three Quays, Tower Hill, London EC3R 6BQ (☎ 071 626 4588, fax 071 623 8615)

HADEN-GUEST, Hon Christopher; s and h of 4 Baron Haden-Guest; *b* 5 Feb 1948; *m* 1984, Jamie Lee Curtis, actress, eldest da of Tony Curtis, film actor; 1 da (Anne b 1986); *Career* actor; *Style—* The Hon Christopher Haden-Guest; 1242 South Camden Drive, Los Angeles, California 90035, USA; HC-64, Box 8018, Ketchum, Idaho 83340, USA

HADEN-GUEST, Dorothy, Baroness; Dorothy; da of Thomas Roseberry Good, late of Princeton, NJ; *m* 1968, as his 2 wife, 2 Baron Haden-Guest (d 1974); *Style—* The Rt Hon Dorothy, Lady Haden-Guest; 105 Bayard Lane, Princeton, New Jersey 08540, USA

HADEN-GUEST, Hon Hadley; da of 2 Baron Haden-Guest (d 1974); *b* 1949; *Style—* The Hon Hadley Haden-Guest; 37 Pleasant Lane, Southampton, NY 11968, USA

HADEN-GUEST, Hon Nicholas; 2 s of 4 Baron Haden-Guest; *b* 5 May 1951; *Educ* The New Sch for Social Research American Coll in Paris (BA), Stella Adler Inst, Herbert Berghof Studio; *m* 1, 11 May 1980 (m dis 1989), Jill Ellen, da of Harry Demby, USAF, of S Orange, New Jersey, USA; 1 da (Julia b 23 Sept 1988); m 2, 26 Nov 1989, Mrs Pamela Ann Seamon Rack, da of Lt Joseph G Seamon, USN, of Akron, Ohio, USA; 1 da (Elizabeth b 30 May 1990), 1 step s (William Rack b 24 Sept 1983); *Career* actor; feature films: The Long Riders (1979), Trading Places (1982), Appointment with Death (1987), The Assassin (1988), National Lampoon's Christmas Vacation (1989), The Grand Tour (1989); Aerosmith's Janie's Got a Gun (video) 1989; tv shows: Fathers and Sons (1986), The Return of Sherlock Holmes (1987), Zorro (1989), Hunter (1989); theatre: Vivien (Los Angeles) 1986; memb: Screen Actors' Guild, Actors' Equity Assoc, American Federated Television and Radio Artists, American Soc of Composers, Artists and Performers; wrote song Oralee Cookies for film Trading Places; *Style—* The Hon Nicholas Haden-Guest; P O Box 1069, Burbank, CA 91507, USA (☎ 0101 818 766 5432, fax 0101 818 760 2801)

HADEN-GUEST, 4 Baron (UK 1950); Peter Haden Haden-Guest; yr s (by 2 m) of 1 Baron, MC (d 1960); suc half-brother as 4 Baron 1987; *b* 29 Aug 1913; *Educ* City of London Sch, New Coll Oxford (MA); *m* 1945, Jean Pauline, da of late Dr Albert George Hindes, of Waverly Pl, New York City, USA; 2 s (Hon Christopher, *qv*, Hon Nicholas, *qv*), 1 da (Hon Mrs (Elissa) Smith, *qv*); *Heir* s, Hon Christopher Haden-Guest, *qv*; *Career* Lt RCNVR 1939-45; United Nations Official 1946-72 (Chief of Editorial Control, UN HQ; Chief Editor UN Office, Geneva, and Chief of Repertory Editing Gp, UN HQ, New York); *Style—* The Rt Hon the Lord Haden-Guest; 198 Old Stone Highway, East Hampton, New York 11937, USA

HADEN-TAYLOR, Anthony St John; s of Frank Pacey Haden-Taylor (d 1971), of Broughton House, Broughton Gifford, nr Melksham, Wilts, and Enid Christine, *née* Bushnell (now Mrs Bousfield); *b* 26 March 1948; *Educ* Kings Sch, Sherborne; *m* 15 April 1989, Hon Susan Rosemary, *née* Greenall, da of 3 Baron Daresbury, and former w of David St C O Bruton; 1 da (Pandora Eleanor Christine b 7 Nov 1989, d 1990); *Career* sr ptnr International Management Consultants SA 1970-82, chief exec Taylor Downs & Co 1987; Freeman City of London, Liveryman Worshipful Co of Basket Makers; *Recreations* polo, shooting; *Clubs* City Livery, Cirencester Polo; *Style—* Anthony Haden-Taylor, Esq; Bledisloe House, Coates, Cirencester, Glos, GL7 6NH (☎ 0285 770564, fax 0285 770710)

HADEN-TAYLOR, Hon Mrs (Susan Rosemary); *née* Greenall; o da of 3 Baron Daresbury, *qv*; *b* 18 Aug 1956; *m* 1, 1978 (m dis 1989), David St Clare Oswald Bruton; 1 s (Alastair Edward Oswald b 1985), 1 da (Natasha Charlotte b 1983); m 2, 15 April 1989, Anthony St John Haden-Taylor, *qv*, s of late Frank Pacey Haden-Taylor; 1 da (Pandora Eleanor Christine b 1989 d 1990); *Style—* The Hon Mrs Haden-Taylor; Bledisloe House, Coates, nr Cirencester, Glos GL7 6NH (☎ 0285 770564)

HADFIELD, Antony; s of Thomas Henry Hadfield, and Edna Hadfield; *b* 9 Sept 1936; *Educ* Sheffield, Brighton, Middx Poly (BA); *m* 1959, Dorothy Fay, da of Charles Edwin Osman (d 1976); 1 s (Warren b 1966); *Career* design engr Plessey 1958-62, design and project engr Metal Industries Group 1962-65, design engr CEGB 1965-67, sr engr and mangr Eastern Electricity 1967-77, area mangr Yorks Electricity 1977-79, dir of engrg Midlands Electricity 1979-85, dep chm and chief exec N Ireland Electricity 1985-, chm Livewire (NI) Ltd, memb Cncl CBI (and Irish), vice chm Power Div IEE, former chm NI centre IEE; visiting prof Queen's Univ Belfast, memb Advsy Ctee Duke of Edinburgh Award Scheme; *Recreations* mountaineering, sailing; *Clubs* Royal North of Ireland Yacht; *Style—* Antony Hadfield, Esq; Northern Ireland Electricity, PO Box 2, Danesfort, 120 Malone Rd, Belfast BT9 5HT (☎ 0860 616535)

HADFIELD, (Ellis) Charles Raymond; CMG (1954); s of Alexander Charles Hadfield (d 1926); *b* 5 Aug 1909; *Educ* Blundell's, St Edmund Hall Oxford (MA); *m* 1945, Alice Mary Miller, da of Lt-Col Henry Smyth, DSO (d 1943), of Brook Cottage, S Cerney, Glos; 1 s (and 1 s decd), 1 da; *Career* dir David & Charles 1960-64, memb Br Waterways Bd 1963-66; author; *Books* Afloat in America (with A M Hadfield, 1979), William Jessop, Engineer (with A W Skempton, 1979), The Canal Age (2 edn, 1981), British Canals: An Illustrated History (7 edn, 1984), World Canals: Inland Navigation Past and Present (1986), also a series by regions of the canals of Eng and Wales; *Recreations* writing, exploring canals; *Style—* Charles Hadfield, Esq, CMG; 13 Meadow Way, South Cerney, Cirencester, Glos GL7 6HY (☎ 0285 860422)

HADFIELD, James Irvine Havelock; s of Prof Geoffrey Hadfield (d 1970), of Ruperts Close, Henley-on-Thames, Oxon, and Sarah Victoria Eileen, *née* Irvine (d 1975); *b* 12 July 1930; *Educ* Radley, Brasenose Coll Oxford (BA), St Thomas' Hosp Med Sch (MA, BM BCh, MCh); *m* 5 Jan 1957, Ann Pickernell, da of Dr G C Milner (d 1974), of 3 Church Row, Rye, Sussex; 1 s (Geoffrey Irvine Havelock b 10 Jan 1964), 2 da (Esme Victoria b 12 Sept 1960, Helen Sarah (twin)); *Career* St Thomas' Hosp 1955-57: house surgn, casualty offr, lectr Dept of Anatomy; RAS St Thomas' Hosp Hysestile 1962, RSO Leicester Royal Infirmary 1962-64, surgical tutor Univ of Oxford 1964-66, first asst Nuffield Dept of Surgery 1964-66, conslt surgn and urologist Bedford Gen Hosp 1966, surgical and clinical tutor N Bedfordshire 1968-78; examiner: pathology MRCS and LRCP 1971-77, surgery Univ of Cambridge 1974-84; Univ of Cambridge: pt/t departmental demonstrator Dept of Anatomy, recognised teacher surgery 1974-; Arris and Gale lectr RCS 1975, conslt memb DMT 1979-84, chm Med Exec Ctee Bedford Gen Hosp 1979-84; memb: Ed Bd Health Trends 1972-77, Res and Devpt Ctee King Edwards Fund for London 1973-79; tstee Bedford Charity 1970-85, vice chm Estate Ctee Harpur Tst 1980-85 (govr 1970-85), pres Bedford Med Soc 1988; fell: Assoc Sports in Medicine, Assoc of Surgns Pakistan; FSZ (London), memb Anatomical Soc of GB, Ireland; boat club winner St Thomas' Hosp: sr fours, sr pairs, sr sculls, double sculls, United Hosps Regatta 1956 (15 races in 1 day); coach: Brasenose Coll 1951-80, St Thomas' Hosp Boat Club 1955-70, Oriel Coll Eight 1975-80; vice pres: Bedfords CC, Bedford RFC (qualified umpire ARA); memb Ctee Bedford Regatta; Freeman City of London, Liveryman Worshipful Co of Felmakers 1975-; FRCS, FRCSE 1960, FRSM, Fell Soc Clinical Anatomists, memb Assoc Urological Surgns; *Books* articles in med jls on: Venous Thrombosis, Intravenous Feeding and Topics in Urology; *Recreations* shooting, fishing, watching rowing, sport in general, hates gardening; *Clubs* London Rowing, Leander, Henley-on-Thames, Vincents (Oxford); *Style—* James Hadfield, Esq; Baker's Barn, Stagsden West End, Bedford MK43 8SZ (☎ 02302 4514); Porthiddy Cottage, St Davids, North Pembrokeshire SA62 6OW (☎ 03483 345)

HADFIELD, John Peter Brookes; JP (1969), DL (1986); s of John William Claude Hadfield (d 1965), of Devon, and Edith Annie, *née* Brookes; *b* 9 March 1926; *Educ* Brighton GS, Sandhurst; *m* 1949, Iris, da of Frederick Arthur Brailsford (d 1947), of Chesterfield; 2 da (Vivienne b 1954, Sarah b 1957); *Career* Mil Serv 1943-47 Sandhurst, 2 Recce Regt, 25 Dragoons RAC Capt served Far East 14 Army India, Malaya, Singapore, Sumatra; joined Bass Ratcliffe & Gretton Ltd 1947, md Bass Mitchells and Butlers (Northern) Ltd 1966; dir: Mitchells and Butlers Ltd, Bass Marketing Ltd, Bass UK Ltd 1968; md Bass (South West) Ltd 1975; chm and md Bass North West Ltd 1976-86, vice chm Bass North Ltd 1986 (ret March 1986); chm 1976-86: Bass Mitchells and Butlers (North West) Ltd, Bents Brewery Co Ltd, Catterall and Swarbricks Brewery Ltd, Fred Anderton Ltd, Gartsides (Brookside Brewery) Ltd, Masseys Burnley Brewery Ltd, Park Hall Leisure; dir: Telecable (Stockport) Ltd, Telecable (Macclesfield) Ltd; chm NW Regnl Bd Br Inst of Mgmnt and Nat Cncl; memb: CBI National Cncl, NW Regnl Cncl 1984; pres North Cheshire Branch BIM 1985; chm: Gtr Manchester Residuary Body, Trafford Park Devpt Corp, Mainkind Ltd, Gtr Manchester Property Tst, South Manchester Health Authy 1990-; dir: Gtr Manchester Economic Devpt Cncl, Central Station Properties Ltd, Lloyds Bank plc (NW Region), Burtonwood Brewery plc, Petros Devpts Ltd, Prestbury Golf Club, Savoy Hotel (Blackpool) plc, Manchester Chamber of Commerce; memb: Ctee Pattison Research Inst Manchester, Ct Univ of Manchester; Midland Hotel Crown Plaza Manchester; tstee The Hammond Sch Chester; patron Henshaws Soc for the Blind; memb Inst of Brewing; CBIM, FRSA; *Recreations* golf, shooting, gardening; *Clubs* St James's Manchester, Royal Lytham Golf, Prestbury Golf; *Style—* Peter Hadfield, Esq, JP, DL

HADFIELD, Hon Mrs (Maureen); elder da of Baron Segal (Life Peer; d 1985), and Molly, *née* Rolo (d 1989); *b* 15 Feb 1935; *Educ* St Anne's Coll Oxford (MA); *m* 6 Dec 1956, Jeremy Hadfield (d 1988), s of John Hadfield; 2 s; *Career* dir Economic Assocs 1969-76, economic advsr Price Cmmn 1976-78, dir Panther Hadfield Associates 1979-, mgmnt conslt Pannell Kerr Forster Associates 1985-88, advsr UNESCO 1989; chm Int Consulting Economics Assoc 1986-89; *Recreations* sailing; *Clubs* The Groucho; *Style—* The Hon Mrs Hadfield; 2 Park Town, Oxford OX2 6SH

HADFIELD, Maj (Robert) Michael; JP (Middx 1980); s of John William Claude Hadfield (d 1965), and Edith Anne, *née* Brookes; *b* 2 Sept 1928; *Educ* Brighton, RMA Sandhurst; *m* 29 Jan 1966, Helen Nancy, da of Rear Adm William Penrose Mark-Wardlaw, DSO, DSC, ADC (d 1952); 1 da (Rosemary Ann Elizabeth b 1972); *Career* cmmnd RA 1948 served: N Africa, Trieste, BAOR, Hong Kong; ret Major 1963; mangr gp public affrs Guinness plc (joined 1963, info offr Guinness Brewing 1971); memb Lloyd's; MIPR, MInstM, FRSA; *Recreations* arts, reading, gardening; *Clubs* Savile, Denham GC, Royal Western YC; *Style—* Major R M Hadfield, JP; Riverside House, East Chisenbury, Pewsey, Wilts SN9 6AQ (☎ 0980 70660); c/o Guinness plc, 39 Portman Square, London W1 (☎ 071 486 0288)

HADFIELD, Ronald; QPM (1989); s of George Hadfield (d 1975), of Oldham Lancs, and Phyliss Marjorie Hadfield (d 1983); *b* 15 July 1939; *Educ* Chadderton GS; *m* 1 April 1961, Anne Phylissia, da of Ernest Frederick Worrall, of Royton Lancs; 1 s (Neil Stuart b 25 April 1964), 1 da (Elaine Louise b 29 Dec 1962); *Career* Oldham Borough Police 1958-69 (Sgt 1965-67, Inspr 1967-69), Lancs Constabulary 1969-74 (Chief Inspr 1973), Greater Manchester Police 1974-81 (Supt 1975, Chief Supt 1980), Acting Dep Chief Constable Derbyshire 1984-86 (Asst Chief Constable 1981-84), Chief Constable Notts 1987-90 (Dep Chief Constable 1986-87), Chief Constable W Midlands Police 1990-; memb Nat Ctee Police Athletic Assoc, vice pres Co of Birmingham Scout Assoc; memb: Cncl St John, Steering Ctee Princes Trust, Exec Ctee Fedn of Boys' Clubs; *Recreations* golf; *Clubs* Warwickshire Co Cricket (vice pres); *Style—* Ronald Hadfield, Esq, QPM; Sherwood Lodge, Arnold Notts NG5 8PP (☎ 0602 670 999)

HADGRAFT, Prof Jonathan; s of John William Hadgraft (d 1984), and Doris, *née* Ayres; *b* 13 Dec 1950; *Educ* Queen Elizabeths Sch Barnet, University Coll Oxford (MA, DPhil); *m* 3 May 1975, Pauline Joyce, da of Thomas Henry Bilton, of Penarth, S Glamorgan; 1 da (Eleanor Tamsin); *Career* lectr in pharmaceutical chem Univ of Strathclyde 1977-79, lectr in pharmacy Univ of Nottingham 1979-85; CChem, FRSC 1983; *Recreations* squash; *Style—* Prof Jonathan Hadgraft; The Welsh School of Pharmacy, University of Wales, Cardiff CF1 3XF (☎ 0222 874000 ext 5800)

HADINGHAM, Reginald Edward Hawke (Buzzer); CBE (1988, OBE 1971), MC and bar (1944), TD; 2 s of Edward Wallace Hadingham (d 1973), and Ethel Irene Penelope (d 1936), 5 da of Sir William Gwynne-Evans, 1 Bt; *b* 6 Dec 1915; *Educ* St Paul's; *m* 1940, Lois, da of Edward Pope, of Montreal, Canada; 2 da (Susan, Stephanie); *Career* 67 ATK TA RA, served UK, Iraq, N Africa, Italy, actg Lt-Col; non exec chm Slazengers Ltd 1976-83 (joined 1933, Euro sales mangr 1936, export mangr 1949, sales dir 1952, joined bd 1952, md 1967, chm and md 1973); chm SPARKS (the Sportsman's Charity), dep chm Action Res for the Crippled Child, vice pres PHAB, sr memb and tres Sette of Odd Volumes (a dining club founded in 1878) 1957-; All Eng Lawn Tennis Club: elected Ctee 1976, chm 1984-89, vice pres 1990-, pres Int Lawn Tennis Club of GB 1990-; *Recreations* lawn tennis; *Clubs* All Eng Lawn Tennis, Queens LTC, Hurlingham, Lords Taverner; *Style—* Buzzer Hadingham, Esq, CBE, MC, TD; 118 Wimbledon Hill Rd, Wimbledon SW19 5QU (☎ 081 946 9611); All England Lawn Tennis Club (☎ 081 946 2244)

HADLEE, Roger Barrington; s of Barrington William Hadlee (d 1981), of Bishops Stortford, Herts, and Hilda Joan, *née* Newman; *b* 8 Jan 1935; *Educ* St Edwards Sch Oxford, Trinity Coll Oxford (MA); *m* 6 July 1960, (Alison) Jill, da of Harold Nettleton Broadley, of Folkestone, Kent; 3 da (Georgina b 1961, Caroline b 1964, Fiona b 1966); *Career* Subaltern 1 Royal Dragoons 1956-58; mktg exec: Pfizer Ltd 1958-63, Nabisco Foods 1963-65, Donald MacPherson Gp 1965-68, Br Printing Corpn 1968-74 (dir Publishing Gp); fndr Royal Exchange Art Gallery 1974; *Recreations* tennis, sailing, cricket; *Clubs* Cavalry & Guards, MCC, Free Foresters; *Style—* Roger Hadlee, Esq; The Old Rectory, Fairstead, Nr Chelmsford, Essex CM3 2BW (☎ 024533 246); Royal Exchange Art Gallery, 14 Royal Exchange, London EC3V 3LL (☎ 071 283 4400)

HADLEY, Anthony Francis (Tony); s of Henry Dennis Hadley (d 1957), of

Birmingham, and Lilian Winifred, *née* Bate; *b* 23 May 1953; *Educ* Blessed Humphrey Middlemore Sch, Madeley Coll of Higher Educn; *Career* athletics coach; represented GB 100m all levels sch to sr, Euro Catholic schs 100m and 200m champion 1970; coach 1976-, coached 24 sr internationals from sch to sr level in sprint and hurdle events incl: Phil Brown, Derek Redmond, Pat Beckford, Sonia Lanaman, Lincoln Asquith, Ainsley Bennett; coach Eng team Cwlth Games 1985; teacher of physical educn and drama; *Recreations* Beatles fanatic, theatre, producing musicals (various awards for school production of West Side Story 1990); *Style—* Tony Hadley, Esq; Birchfield Harriers, The Alexander Stadium, off The Walsall Rd, Great Barr, Birmingham

HADLEY, David Allen; CB (1991); s of Sydney Hadley (d 1980), and Gwendoline Alice, *née* Rodwell (d 1987); *b* 18 Feb 1936; *Educ* Wyggeston GS Leicester, Merton Coll Oxford (MA); *m* 1965, Veronica Ann, da of Stanley Hopkins, of Sussex; 1 s (Christopher b 1970); *Career* Miny of Agric 1959-75 and 1979-89, Treas 1976-78, Cabinet Office dep sec and head of European Secretariat 1989-; *Recreations* music, gardening; *Style—* David Hadley, Esq, CB; Cabinet Office, Whitehall, London SW1 (☎ 071 270 0044)

HADLEY, Graham Hunter; s of Albert Leonard Hadley (d 1973), and Lorna Elizabeth, *née* Hunter; *b* 12 April 1944; *Educ* Eltham Coll, Jesus Coll Cambridge (BA); *m* 1971, Lesley Mary Ann, da of Stanley Anthony Andrew Smith, of Kingston; 1 s (Andrew Hunter b 1978); *Career* Civil Service; asst princ: Miny of Aviation 1966, Miny of Technology 1968; princ: Miny of Aviation Supply 1971, Dept of Energy 1974; seconded to Civil Serv Cmmn 1976, asst sec Dept of Energy 1977, seconded to British Aerospace HQ Weybridge 1980, under sec Electricity Div Dept of Energy 1983 (asst sec 1981), seconded as sec of Bd CEGB 1983, permanent bd sec CEGB 1986-90; exec dir National Power plc 1990; *Recreations* cricket, history of architecture, theatre; *Clubs* RSA, Mandarins CC; *Style—* Graham Hadley, Esq; The Coach House, 14 Genoa Avenue, Putney, London SW15 (☎ 081 788 2698); National Power, Sudbury House, 15 Newgate Street, London EC1 (☎ 071 634 5111)

HADLEY, James; AE (1960); *b* 27 May 1923; *Educ* Berkhamsted Sch, QMC London, Université de Lyon; *m* 2 Feb 1966, Carlotta (Lottie) Edwina Gray, da of Lt-Col Gray Horton MC (d 1974); 1 da (Joanna Carlotta Gray b 5 Aug 1967); *Career* served WWII pilot RAF 1941-46, RAFVR 1946-60; called to the Bar Middle Temple; textile indust 1951-62, chief exec Export Cncl for Euro 1962-68, dir of cos construction and engrg industs 1968-76; dir: BTA 1970-72, Rank Prize Funds 1972-80, Franco-Br Cncl 1977-89; memb Euro Movement, chm Franco Br Soc 1984-90 (memb since 1953), tstee Euro Sch of Mgmnt(EAP) Oxford 1986-; memb Worshipful Ironmongers Co 1968; RIIA; Chevalier de la Légion d'Honneur France 1980, Officier de la Légion d'Honneur France 1984; *Books* History of France Society for International Understanding (1956); *Recreations* reading, walking, music; *Clubs* Garrick, Travellers; *Style—* James Hadley, Esq; Au Grand Broca, Béraut, 32100 Condom, France (☎ 62 28 33 24)

HADLEY, (Jennifer) Katharine; da of John Hadley, of Godmanchester, and Theresa Monica, *née* Ward (d 1986); *b* 20 March 1946; *Educ* Huntingdon GS, Univ of Reading; *m* 1, 1977 (m dis 1980), Dr Charles Hope, s of Sir Archibald Hope; 1 s (Thomas b 4 April 1978); m 2, Adrian Sington; 1 s (Hugh b 11 March 1981), 1 da (Angelica b 24 Feb 1986); *Career* womans ed The Sun 1973-81, asst ed Daily Express 1988 (womans ed 1981-88), womans ed Sunday Mirror 1988, exec ed Sunday Mirror Magazine 1989-; memb Network; *Recreations* needlepoint, collecting paintings, theatre, music; *Style—* Katharine Hadley; 39 Camberwell Grove, London SE5 8JA (☎ 071 701 7581); Sunday Mirror, High Holborn, London (☎ 071 822 2094)

HADLEY, Lady Paulina Mary Louise; *née* Pepys; yr da of 6 Earl of Cottenham (d 1943), and Sybil Venetia, *née* Taylor (now Countess of Devon); *b* 14 June 1930; *Educ* Lady Margaret Hall Oxford (MA 1956); *m* 1973, Denis Bernard Hadley; *Style—* The Lady Paulina Hadley; White Hill House, Upham, Hants

HADOW, Sir Gordon; CMG (1953), OBE (1945); s of Rev Frank Burness Hadow (d 1941), of Woolton, Liverpool, and Una, *née* Durrant; *b* 23 Sept 1908; *Educ* Marlborough, Trinity Coll Oxford; *m* 19 Oct 1946, Marie, da of Lionel Henry Moiser, of Coventry (d 1985); 2 s (Roger b 1947, Paul b 1950); *Career* entered Colonial Serv Gold Coast (now Ghana) 1932, dep fin sec Tanganyika 1946, under-sec Gold Coast 1948, sec for civil serv 1949, sec to govr and Exec Cncl Gold Coast 1950, dep govr Gold Coast 1954-57; kt 1956; *Clubs* Athenaeum; *Style—* Sir Gordon Hadow, CMG, OBE; Little Manor, Coat, Martock, Somerset

HADOW, Sir (Reginald) Michael; KCMG (1971, CMG 1962); s of Malcolm Macgregor Hadow (d 1921); *b* 17 Aug 1915; *Educ* Berkhamsted Sch, King's Coll Cambridge; *m* 1, 1943, Maria Anna Stefania Szemplinska; m 2, 1955, Dolores Frances, da of Alfred Fillibrow Main, of Mexico City; 1 step s, 1 step da; m 3, 1976, Daphne Madge Kerin (d 1988, formerly w of late Hon Michael Sieff, CBE), da of Cyril Aaron Michael, of London; 1 step s; *Career* entered ICS 1937, IPS 1941-47, transferred FO 1948, private sec to Min of State 1949-52, head of Chancery Mexico City 1952-54; cnsllr: FO 1958, Paris 1959-63; head of News Dept FO 1963-65; ambass to: Israel 1965-69, Argentine Republic 1969-72; ret; *Style—* Sir Michael Hadow, KCMG; Old Farm, Ashford Hill, Newbury, Berks RG15 8AX (☎ 0635 268335)

HADSLEY-CHAPLIN, (Edwin) Hadsley; s of Arthur Hadsley-Chaplin (d 1965), of Surrey, and Annie Violet Lewis (d 1983); *b* 27 Aug 1922; *Educ* Radnor House; *m* 1954, Margaret Mary, da of Robert Potter (d 1951); 2 s (Peter b 1957, Mark b 1961), 1 da (Anne b 1955); *Career* Capt RE 1941-46; chm: Rowe Evans Investment plc, Sungkai Holdings plc 1978, Bertam Holdings Ltd 1980, Beradin Holdings Ltd 1982-, Lendu Holdings plc 1983, Padang Senang Holdings plc, The Singapore Area Rubber Estates plc; chm Tropical Growers Assoc 1973-74 (memb); FCIS; *Recreations* watching cricket, travel, model railways, theatre; *Clubs* Oriental, Gresham; *Style—* Hadsley Hadsley-Chaplin, Esq; Norton House, Gatton Road, Reigate, Surrey (☎ 0737 246217)

HAENDEL, Ida; *b* 15 Dec 1928; *Educ* Warsaw Conservatoire (Gold Medal at age 7); *Career* violinist; began playing aged 3 1/2, studied with Carl Flesch and George Enescu in Paris, Br debut Brahm's Concerto Queen's Hall with Sir Henry Wood, gave concerts for Br and US troops and in factories WWII, has toured throughout Europe, N and S America, Scandinavia, Turkey, Israel, USSR and Far East; has accompanied for orchs incl: London Philharmonic, Scottish Nat, BBC Symphony, English Chamber (foreign tours incl Hong Kong, China, Aust and Mexico); has played with numerous foreign orchs incl: Bayerishe Rundfunk, Norddeutsche Rundfunk, Israel Philharmonic, Boston Symphony, New York Philharmonic, Montreal Symphony; numerous recordings with EMI; memb Jury: Carl Flesch Competition London, Sibelius Competition Helsinki Finland, International Violin Competition Cologne; winner Sibelius medal Sibelius Soc of Finland (on 25 Anniversary of Sibelius' Death); *Books* Woman with Violin (autobiog 1970); *Style—* Miss Ida Haendel; Harold Holt Limited, 31 Sinclair Road, London W14 ONS (☎ 071 603 4600)

HAERI, Anthony D; *b* 20 Jan 1940; *Educ* St Bartholomews Hosp Med Coll (MB BS); *m* 1963, Rosalind; 4 da (Philippa, Sarah, Amanda (Molly), Alexandra (Alex)); *Career* in trg: St Bartholomews Hosp, Queen Charlottes Hosp, St Thomas's Hosp; conslt gynaecologist: Ealing Gen Hosp, (and conslt obstetrician) Harley St; hon conslt gynaecologist Hammersmith Hosp; memb: BMA RSM, Hunterian Soc, Euro Soc of Hysteroscopy; FRCS, FRCOG; *Recreations* squash, tennis, skiing, sailing, walking; *Clubs* Royal Lymington Yacht; *Style—* Anthony Haeri, Esq; 73 Harley St, London W1N 1DE (☎ 071 935 5393)

HAGAN, David Lloyd; s of William Hamill Hagan (d 1984), of Liverpool, and Miriam Dilys, *née* Lloyd; *b* 21 May 1946; *Educ* Merchant Taylors Sch Crosby, Emmanuel Coll Cambridge; *m* 5 Dec 1981, Anita Janet Shepstone, da of Lennart Pettersson, of Karlstad, Sweden; 2 s (Charles b 1 Nov 1982, Felix b 14 Mar 1987), 1 da (Isabel b 4 Aug 1984); *Career* chm and chief exec Marlon House Hldgs Ltd 1974-83, dir Med and Professional Softwear Ltd 1984-, chm David Hagan Ltd 1986-, md Tullett & Tokyo Equities Ltd 1986-; memb Stock Exchange; FCA 1970, ATII 1970; offshore powerboat racing Class II World Champion; *Recreations* offshore powerboat racing, boatbuilding; *Clubs* Royal Thames Yacht, Royal Motor Yacht, The South West Shingles Yacht (Vice Cdr); *Style—* David Hagan, Esq; 46 Argyll Rd, London W8 7BS (☎ 071 937 7060); Tullett & Tokyo Equities Ltd, Cable House, 54-62 New Broad Street, London EC2M 1JJ (☎ 071 626 3741, fax 071 638 5751, car phone 0836 288 421, telex 941 3534)

HAGART-ALEXANDER, Claud; s and h of Sir Claud Hagart-Alexander, 3 Bt; *b* 5 Nov 1963; *Educ* Trinity Coll Glenalmond, Univ of Glasgow (BSc (Eng) Hons); *Career* electronics and electrical engr; *Style—* Claud Hagart-Alexander Esq; c/o Coutts & Co, Adelaide Branch, 440 Strand, London WC2R 0QS; Devron-Hercules Inc, 500 Brook Bank Ave, N Vancouver, British Columbia, Canada V7J 3S4 (☎ 604 980 3421)

HAGART-ALEXANDER, Sir Claud; 3 Bt (UK 1886), of Ballochmyle, Co Ayr; JP (1985); s of late Wilfred Archibald Alexander, 2 s of 2 Bt; suc gf 1945; additional surname Hagart recognised by decree of Lord Lyon 1948; Maj-Gen Sir Claud Alexander, 1 Bt, served in the Crimea and was MP for S Ayrshire (C) 1874-85; *b* 6 Jan 1927; *Educ* Sherborne, CCC Cambridge (BA); *m* 16 April 1959, Hilda Etain, yr da of late Miles Malcolm Acheson, of Ganges, BC, Canada; 2 s, 2 da; *Heir* s, Claud Hagart-Alexander, *qv*; *Career* Vice Lord-Lt Ayrshire and Arran (Strathclyde Region) 1983-; memb Inst of Measurement and Control (MInstMC); *Clubs* New (Edinburgh); *Style—* Sir Claud Hagart-Alexander, Bt, DL, JP; Kingencleugh House, Mauchline, Ayrshire KA5 5JL (☎ 0290 50217)

HAGDRUP, Alan; s of Sofus Vilhelm Hagdrup (d 1983), of Cheam; *b* 19 May 1932; *Educ* Epsom Coll, UCL; *m* 1958, Elizabeth, da of Lt-Col Harold Mason, OBE, TD (d 1960); 1 s, 2 da; *Career* dir: Hanson Transport Group 1969-, Hanson plc 1974-; ptnr Goulden's (slrs) 1962-69; *Recreations* golf, skiing, bridge, music; *Clubs* Walton Heath Golf; *Style—* Alan Hagdrup, Esq; The Mill House, Dorking Road, Tadworth, Surrey (☎ 073 7814522)

HAGER, David Paul; s of Donald Charles Hager, of Bournemouth, and Betty Kathleen, *née* Hewitt; *b* 7 Jan 1951; *Educ* Bournemouth Sch, Univ of Oxford (MA); *m* 10 Sept 1951, Jeanette Carolyn, da of Alan Peter Hares, of Chilbolton, Hants; 1 s (Tristram b 1984); *Career* investmt advsr N M Rothschild and Sons Ltd 1972-74; Bacon & Woodrow: joined 1975, ptnr in Investmt Dept 1976-85, ptnr 1987-; dir Co Investment Management 1985-87 (dir Co Group Ltd 1986-87); memb: FIA 1975, FPMI 1982; *Books* An Introduction to Institutional Investment (with AJ Frost, 1986), Debt Securities (with AJ Frost, 1990), Pension Fund Investment (with CD Lever, 1989); *Recreations* flying light aircraft; *Clubs* Oxford and Cambridge, Guild of Air Pilots and Navigators; *Style—* David Hager, Esq; Bacon and Woodrow, St Olaf House, London Bridge, London SE1 2PE (☎ 071 357 7171)

HAGERTY, William John Gell (Bill); s of William Hagerty, and Doris Julia, *née* Gell; *b* 23 April 1939; *Educ* Beal GS Ilford Essex; *m* 1965 (m dis 1990), Lynda Ann, *née* Beresford; 1 s (William Daniel b 22 Jan 1970), 1 da (Faith Georgia b 5 March 1975); *Career* Nat Serv RAF 1958-60; local newspapers 1955-58; local newspapers: Sunday Citizen, Daily Sketch, Daily Mirror 1960-67, various editorial positions The Mirror Group 1967-85, managing ed (features) Today 1986-87, ed Sunday Today 1987-88, conslt and advsr to the publisher Hola! Magazine (conslt Hello! Magazine) 1987-88; dep ed: Sunday Mirror 1988-90, Daily Mirror 1990-; *Books* Flash Bang Wallop! (with Kent Gavin 1978); *Recreations* cinema, theatre, swimming, lunch; *Style—* Bill Hagerty; Mirror Group Newspapers, Holborn Circus, London EC1P 1DQ (☎ 071 822 3544, fax 071 822 2098)

HAGGAR, Edward George (Eddie); s of Herbert Haggar, and Christina, *née* Burke; *b* 27 Jan 1936; *Educ* Christopher Wren Sch, Hammersmith Coll of Bldg (Dip Structural Engrg); *m* 29 Sept 1962, Carole Rosemary, da of Frank Henry Kelly; 1 s (Russell b 2 May 1969), 1 da (Claire b 15 Dec 1970); *Career* sr ptnr Jenkins & Potter Consulting Engineers 1986 (assoc ptnr 1964, ptnr 1967); chm Tport and Planning Ctee Camden Chamber of Commerce; memb Assoc Consltg Engrs; chm local Table Tennis Club; FIStructE, MInstR, MConsE; *Recreations* fell walking, table tennis; *Style—* Eddie Haggar, Esq; 24 Billy Lows Lane, Potters Bar, Herts EN6 1XN (☎ 0707 54335); 12-15 Gt Turnstile, London WC1V 7HN (☎ 071 242 8711, fax 071 404 0742, telex 21120)

HAGGARD, Prof Mark Peregrine; s of Capt Stephen H A Haggard (d 1943), and Morna Christian, *née* Gillespie (d 1977); *b* 26 Dec 1942; *Educ* Dollar Acad, Univ of Edinburgh (MA), Univ of Cambridge (PhD); *m* 22 Sept 1962, Elizabeth Gilmore, da of Thomas Jackson Houston (d 1943), of Hong Kong; 2 s (Stephen b 1963, Patrick b 1965); *Career* teaching offr and fell CCC Cambridge 1967-71, prof Queen's Univ of Belfast 1971-76, dir MRC Inst Hearing Res, chief advsr Hearing Res Tst, memb Neurosciences Bd MRC; FRSM 1977, FIOA 1978, fell Acoustical Soc America 1982; *Books* Hearing Science and Hearing Disorders (with M E Lutman, 1983), British Medical Bulletin: Hearing (with E F Evans, 1987), Screening Children's Hearing (with E A Hughes, 1991); *Recreations* skiing, choral singing, classical and mediaeval history; *Clubs* SCGB, Downhill Only (Wengen); *Style—* Prof Mark Haggard; 7 Elm Ave, Beeston, Nottingham NG9 1BU (☎ 0602 225761); 19A Lansdowne Crescent, London W11 2NS (☎ 071 221 6977); MRC Inst of Hearing Res, Univ of Nottingham, University Park NG7 2RD (☎ 0602 223431)

HAGGARD, Piers Inigo; s of Stephen Haggard (d 1943), of London, and Morna Christian, *née* Gillespie (d 1978); *b* 18 March 1939; *Educ* Dollar Acad Scotland, Univ of Edinburgh (MA); *m* 1, 1960, Christiane, *née* Stokes; 1 s (Philip Charles Napier b 1962), 3 da (Sarah Clemence b 1960, Claire Imogen 1961, Rachel Lindsay b 1961); m 2, Anna Maud, da of Grisha Sklovsky; 1 s (William Godfrey Abraham b 1975), 1 da ((Celia) Daisy Morna b 1978); *Career* theatre dir; started as asst dir Royal Court Theatre 1960; res dir: Dundee Repertory 1960-61, Glasgow Citizens 1961-62; asst The Nat Theatre 1963-65, trained with BBC TV 1965; tv incl: Pennies From Heaven (UK BAFTA award 1979) 1978, Mrs Reinhart 1981, Knockback (US ACE award 1985) 1984, Visitors 1987, Centrepoint 1990; films incl: Wedding Night 1969, The Blood on Satan's Claw 1970, The Quatermass Conclusion (Triest Festival award 1980) 1979, The Fiendish Plot of Dr Fu Manchu 1980, Venom 1982, A Summer Story 1988; also work in USA tv theatre and advtg; fndr The Directors Guild of GB and assoc organization The Directors' and Producers' Rights Soc; *Recreations* Swimming, landscape gardening, human nature; *Style—* Piers Haggard, Esq; Piers Haggard Productions Ltd, 26 Stockwell Park Crescent, London SW9 ODE (fax 071 737 4619)

HAGGART, Mary Elizabeth; OBE; s of John Neville Carpenter Scholes, and Margaret Elizabeth, *née* Hines; *b* 8 April 1924; *Educ* Wyggeston GS For Girls Leicester, Leicester Royal Infirmary and Children's Hosp (SRN), Guy's Hosp London

(CMB Part 1), Royal Coll of Nursing London (Admin Cert); *m* 3 April 1983, most Rev Alastair Iain MacDonald Haggart; *Career* matron Dundee Royal Infirmary (matron designate Ninewells Hosp Dundee) 1964-68, chief nursing offr Bd of Mgmnt Dundee Gen Hosps and Ninewells and Assoc Hosps 1968-73, chief area nursing offr Tayside Health Bd 1973-83; memb: Scottish Bd RCN 1965-70, Gen Nursing Cncl for Scotland 1966-70 and 1970-80, Standing Nursing and Midwifery Scottish 1971-74 (vice chm 1973-74), UK Central Cncl Nursing Midwifery and Health Visiting 1980-84, Bd of Mgmnt Carstairs State Hosp 1983-, Scottish Hosp Endowments Res Tst 1984-; pres Scottish Assoc of Nurse Admins 1973-77, chm Scottish Nat Bd for Nursing Midwifery and Health Visiting 1980-84; memb RCN; *Recreations* walking, music, travel; *Clubs* Royal Cwlth Soc; *Style—* Mrs Mary Haggart, OBE; 19 Eglinton Cres, Edinburgh EH12 5BY (☎ 031 337 8948)

HAGGER, Jonathan Osborne; s of Cyril Francis Osborne Hagger (d 1957), of Loughton, Essex, and Norah Harrison, *née* Broadley (d 1981); *b* 3 Feb 1949; *Educ* Chigwell Sch; *m* 27 April 1974, (Carol) Anne, da of Alan David Luton, of Loughton, Essex; 2 s (William b 1981, James b 1984); *Career* CA; Edward Moore & Sons (CAs) 1968-72, BUPA 1972-75, Willis Faber 1976-85; fin dir: Bain Clarkson 1985-89, FKB Group Plc 1990-, chief fin offr designate The Grosvenor Estate 1991-; Brook Street Bureau 1990-; church organist (deputises at King Charles the Martyr Tunbridge Wells); chm King Charles Music Soc; memb: The Nevill Tennis Club (Tunbridge Wells), Tunbridge Wells Civic Soc; ARCM 1968, FCA 1972; *Recreations* music, tennis; *Style—* Jonathan Hagger, Esq; 104 Warwick Park, Tunbridge Wells, Kent TN2 5EN (☎ 0892 29161)

HAGGETT, Prof Peter; s of Charles Frederick Haggett (d 1966), and Ethel Elizabeth Haines (d 1971); *b* 24 Jan 1933; *Educ* Dr Morgan's GS Somerset, St Catharine's Coll Cambridge (MA, PhD, ScD); *m* 28 July 1956, Brenda Mavis, da of Cyril Robert Woodley (d 1976); 2 s (Timothy b 1961, Andrew b 1965), 2 da (Sarah b 1960, Jacqueline b 1963); *Career* asst lectr UCL 1955-57, lectr Univ of Cambridge 1957-66, acting vice chllr Univ of Bristol 1984-85 (prof of urban and regnl geography 1966-); memb: SW Econ Planning Cncl, UGC 1985-89, Nat Radiological Protection Bd 1985-; Hon DSc York Canada 1983, Hon LLD Bristol 1985, Hon DSc Durham 1989; memb Euro Acad 1988; *Books* Geography: A Modern Synthesis (1983); *Clubs* United Oxford and Cambridge Univ; *Style—* Prof Peter Haggett; 5 Tunbridge Close, Chew Magna, Avon (☎ 0272 332780); Dept of Geography, University of Bristol, Bristol BS8 1SS (☎ 0272 303751)

HAGGETT, Stuart John; s of Wilfred Francis Haggett, West Kirby, Wirral, and Doreen Ada, *née* New; *b* 11 April 1947; *Educ* Dauntsey's Sch West Lavington, Downing Coll Cambridge (MA); *m* 2 Jan 1971, (Hilary) Joy, da of Maj Albert Hammond (d 1963), of Weymouth; 2 da (Laura Louise b 26 Feb 1978, Emily Frances b 23 Sept 1979); *Career* head of modern languages and housemaster Canford Sch Dorset 1973-83, second master King's Sch Rochester 1983-88, headmaster Birkenhead Sch 1988-; chm: Interact Club, Rotary Club of Birkenhead; memb: Medical Service Ctee, Wirral Family Health Services Authy, Secondary Heads Assoc 1983, Headmasters' Conference 1988; *Recreations* sport, reading and theatre, DIY, East India; *Style—* Stuart Haggett, Esq; 58 Beresford Rd, Oxton, Birkenhead, Merseyside L43 2JD (☎ 051 652 4014, fax 051 653 7412)

HAGGIE, David William; s of Richard Aubrey Garmondsway Haggie, of Aldborough Lodge, Aldborough, N Yorkshire, and Priscilla Mary, *née* Ramsden; *b* 23 Feb 1955; *Educ* Eton; *m* 7 Jan 1976, Fiona Ellalis Gray, da of Richard Gray Worcester; 1 s (Linford Richard David b 15 Aug 1978), 1 da (Calantha Alice b 15 June 1984); *Career* CA 1975, fin dir Molinare Holdings plc 1979-83, md Michael Peters Financial 1983-86, fndr The Haggie Group 1986 (comprising The Haggie Co, Fin Design Consultancy, Guideline Computer Management); *Recreations* collecting art and books, tennis, shooting, carpentry; *Style—* David Haggie, Esq; The Haggie Group, Saville House, 2 Lindsey St, London EC1A 9HP (☎ 071 796 3261, fax 071 796 3569)

HAGSTON, Prof Winston Edwin; s of Thomas Hagston, and Florence Maud, *née* Kirby; *b* 30 Nov 1941; *Educ* Beverley GS, Imperial Coll London (BSc), Univ of Hull (PhD), Univ of London (DSc); *m* 9 Nov 1963, (Sylvia) Heather, da of Harold Robinson (d 1982), of Melbourne, York; 2 s (Winston b 19 April 1964, Paul b 21 March 1967), 1 da (Michelle b 23 March 1966); *Career* postdoctoral res fell SRC 1966-68; Physics Dept Univ of Hull: lectr 1968-73, sr lectr 1973-80, reader in theoretical physics 1980, personal chair in theoretical physics 1986-; ARCS; *Recreations* fishing, shooting; *Style—* Prof Winston Hagston; The Wildfowlers, 7 Millbeck Close, Market Weighton, York YO4 3HT (☎ 0430 873158); Department of Applied Physics, The University, Cottingham Rd, Hull HU6 7BX (☎ 0482 46311 ext 5823)

HAGUE, Prof Sir Douglas Chalmers; CBE (1978); s of Laurence Hague; *b* 20 Oct 1926; *Educ* Moseley GS, King Edward VI HS Birmingham, Univ of Birmingham; *m* 1947 (m dis 1986), Brenda Elizabeth Fereday; 2 da; m 2, 1986, Janet Mary Leach; *Career* economist (mgmnt prof, conslt, co dir); chm Manchester Industl Relations Soc, dep chm Price Cmmn and pres NW Operational Res Gp, rapporteur to IEA 1953-78 (ed gen 1981-86), reader political economy Univ of London 1957, Newton Chambers prof of econs Univ of Sheffield 1957-63, visiting prof of economics Duke Univ N Carolina USA 1960-61, head business Studies Dept Univ of Sheffield 1962-63, prof of applied econs Univ of Manchester 1963-65, memb Cncl Manchester Business Sch 1964-81, prof of managerial economics 1965-81 (dep dir 1978-81); visiting prof Imp Coll London 1981-; fell Templeton Coll Oxford 1981-; personal econ advsr to Rt Hon Margaret Thatcher 1967-79 (incl Gen Election 1979), advsr PM's Policy Unit 1979-83; chm ESRC 1983-87; chm: Metapraxis Ltd 1984-90, Oxford Strategy Network 1984-; dir CRT plc 1990- kt 1981; *Recreations* Manchester Utd supporter, organist of classical music (granted permission to play at Blenheim Palace); *Clubs* Athenaeum; *Style—* Prof Sir Douglas Hague, CBE; Templeton College, Oxford OX1 5NY

HAGUE, Paul Nicholas; s of Bernard Hague, and Annie Nichols; *b* 3 Aug 1947; *Educ* Belle Vue Boys GS, Hatfield Coll, Durham Univ (BA); *m* 1969, Alice Christine, da of Alf Tyreman; 1 s (Nicholas James b 1974), 1 da (Chrissie Anne b 1976); *Career* chm Business & Market Research plc; *Books* The Industrial Market Research Handbook (1987), Do Your Own Market Research (1987), How To Do Market Research (1990), Handbook of Market Research Techniques (1990); *Recreations* athletics; *Style—* Paul Hague, Esq; 13 Marple Hall Drive, Marple, Stockport SK6 6JN (☎ 061 427 7552); Business & Market Research, High Lane, Stockport SK6 8DX (☎ 0663 765115)

HAGUE, William Jefferson; MP (Cons) Richmond Yorkshire 1989; s of Timothy Nigel Hague, of Wentworth, S Yorks, and Stella, *née* Jefferson; *b* 26 March 1961; *Educ* Wath upon Dearne Comp Sch, Magdelen Coll Oxford (BA, pres Oxford Union), INSEAD (MBA); *Career* temp special advsr to Chancellor of Exchequer 1983, mgmnt conslt McKinsey and Co 1983-88, PPS to Chancellor of Exchequer 1990-; *Style—* William Hague, Esq, MP; House of Commons, London SW1A 0AA (☎ 071 219 5867, fax 071 217 5970)

HAHN, Prof Frank Horace; s of Dr Arnold Hahn; *b* 26 April 1925; *Educ* Bournemouth GS, LSE; *m* 1946, Dorothy Salter; *Career* formerly: reader in mathematical econs Univ of Birmingham, lectr in econs Univ of Cambridge; prof of econs: LSE 1967-72, Univ of Cambridge 1967-72 (fell Churchill Coll); pres: Econometric Soc 1968, Royal Econ Soc 1986-89; hon memb American Econ Assoc 1986, foreign assoc US Nat Acad of Scis 1988; Hon DScoSci Birmingham 1983, D Honoris Causa Strasbourg 1984, Hon DLitt UEA 1984, Hon DSc (Econ) London 1985, hon fell LSE 1989; *Books* General Competitive Analysis (with K J Arrow), The Share of Wages in the National Income, Money and Inflation, Equilibrium and Macroeconomics (1984), Money Growth and Stability (1985); *Style—* Prof Frank Hahn; 16 Adams Rd, Cambridge; Churchill College, Cambridge

HAIG, 2 Earl (UK 1919); George Alexander Eugene Douglas Haig; OBE (1965), DL (Roxburghshire, Ettrick and Lauderdale 1976); also Viscount Dawick, Baron Haig (both UK 1919) and thirtieth Laird of Bemersyde Chief of the Haig family; s of Field Marshal 1 Earl Haig, KT, GCB, OM, GCVO, KCIE (d 1928), by his w, Hon Dorothy, GCStJ (d 1939), 2 da of 3 Baron Vivian; *b* 15 March 1918; *Educ* Stowe, Ch Ch Oxford (MA), Camberwell Sch of Arts and Crafts; *m* 1, 19 July 1956 (m dis 1981), Adrienne Thérèse, da of Derrick Morley; 1 s, 2 da; m 2, 1981, Donna Gerolama Lopez y Royo di Taurisano; *Heir* s, Viscount Dawick; *Career* Capt Royal Scots Greys M East Force 1939-42, POW 1942-45, Maj on disbandment of Home Gd; sits as Conservative Peer in House of Lords, train bearer at Coronation of King George VI; painter; holds exhibitions at regular intervals; memb: Royal Fine Art Cmmn for Scotland 1958-61, Scottish Arts Cncl (chm Art Ctee 1969-76); tstee: Nat Galleries of Scotland 1963-73, Scottish Nat War Meml 1961- (chm Bd of Tstees 1983-); pres: Border Area RBLS 1955-61, Scottish Crafts Centre 1953-1974; chm: Disablement Advisory Ctee SE Scotland 1960-73, Berwickshire Civic Society 1970-76; memb Bd of Dirs Richard DeMarco gallery 1986-87; chm Offr's Assoc (Scottish Branch) 1977-87; pres: OA Scottish Branch 1987-, Royal British Legion Scotland 1979-86 (nat chm 1963-66), The Earl Haig Fund Scotland 1979-86; vice-pres: Royal Blind Asylum, Scottish Nat Inst for War Blinded; DL Berwickshire 1953-76, Vice Lieut Berwicks 1967-70; memb Royal Co of Archers (Queen's Body Guard for Scotland); ARSA 1988, FRSA; KStJ; *Recreations* fishing, shooting; *Clubs* New (Edinburgh), Cavalry & Guards; *Style—* The Rt Hon the Earl Haig, OBE, DL; Bemersyde, Melrose, Roxburghshire (☎ 083 52 2762)

HAIG, Lady (Elizabeth) Vivienne Thérèse; da of 2 Earl Haig, OBE; *b* 1 March 1959; *Educ* St George's Edinburgh, Bedales Sch, St Martin's Sch of Art, Edinburgh Coll of Art; *Career* artist; *Style—* The Lady Vivienne Haig

HAIGH, Dr Clement Percy; *b* 11 Jan 1920; *Educ* Univ of Leeds (BSc), Kings Coll London (PhD); *m* 8 June 1945, (Ruby) Patricia, *née* Hobdey; 3 s ((Julian) Robin David b 5 July 1950, (Stephen) Patrick Hobdey b 19 Nov 1957, Jeremy Rupert Michael b 6 June 1961); *Career* with Radiochem Centre Thorium Ltd 1943-49, med physicist Barrow Hosp Bristol 1949-56; CEGB: joined 1956, dir Berkeley Nuclear Labs 1959-73, dep dir gen Design and Construction Div Gloucester 1973-78; dir of res BNOC 1978-81 (conslt 1981-), dir S Western Industl Res 1981-86; distinguished lectr American Nuclear Soc San Francisco 1965, assessor Nuclear Safety Advsy Ctee 1972-76; memb: BBC W Advsy Cncl 1972-76, Mech Engrg and Machine Tools Requirements Bd 1972-76, UK chm Jt UK/USSR Working Gp on Problems of Electricity Supply 1974-78, Offshore Engrg Technol Bd 1978-81, Nat Maritime Inst 1981-82; chm Programme Steering Ctee UK Offshore Steels Res Project 1981-87; CPhys, FInstP 1953, FRSA 1985; *Recreations* music; *Clubs* Savile, RAC; *Style—* Dr C P Haigh; Painswick, Old Sneed Pk, Bristol BS9 1RG (☎ 0272 68 2065); Duncombe, Wetherby Rd, Harrogate, N Yorks

HAIGH, Maurice Francis; s of late William Haigh and Ceridwen Haigh; *b* 6 Sept 1929; *Educ* Repton; *Career* barr Gray's Inn 1955, recorder Crown Ct 1981-, chm Medical Appeal Tribunals; *Clubs* English Speaking Union; *Style—* Maurice Haigh, Esq; 83 Bridge St, Manchester M3 23F (☎ 061 832 4036)

HAIGH, (John) Randal; s of Fred Willoughby Haigh (d 1956), of Holmfirth, Yorks; *b* 12 Dec 1919; *Educ* King James's Sch Almondbury, St Catharine's Coll Cambridge (MA); *m* 1952, Zara Mary, da of W Ronald Martin (d 1970), of Coulsdon; 1 s, 1 da; *Career* served Lt, Middle East and Italy; dir Imperial Gp Ltd 1972-81 (sec 1968-74, investment advsr 1974-81); dir of pension fund; FIA; *Recreations* golf, walking, music, watching cricket and rugby football; *Clubs* MCC, HAC, Denham Golf; *Style—* Randal Haigh, Esq; Gable End, Spurgrove, Frieth, Henley-on-Thames, Oxon, RG9 6PB (☎ 0494 882335)

HAILES, Julia Persephone; da of Lt-Col John Martin Hunter Hailes, of Chiselborough House, Stoke-sub-Hamdon, Somerset, and Marianne Carlyon, *née* Coates; *b* 23 Sept 1961; *Educ* St Mary's Sch Calne Wilts; *Career* Leo Burnett Advertising 1981-83; dir and co sec Sustain Ability Ltd; elected to UN Global 500 roll of honour for outstanding environmental achievements 1989; FRSA; *Books* Green Pages, The Business of Saving The World (1988), The Green Consumer Guide (1988), The Green Consumer's Supermarket Shopping Guide (1989), The Young Green Consumers Guide (1990); *Recreations* tennis, travel, bridge; *Style—* Miss Julia Hailes; 5 St Lawrence Terrace, London W10 5SU (☎ 01 968 9415); Sustain Ability Ltd, The People's Hall, 91-97 Freston Rd, London W10 4BD (☎ 071 243 1277, fax 071 243 0364)

HAILES, Leslie Sydney; s of Sydney Hailes (d 1979), and Hilda, *née* Turner (d 1974); *b* 14 June 1932; *m* 17 Dec 1955, Mary, da of Leonard Gomer (d 1976); 2 s (Stephen Christopher b 1956, Paul David b 1960), 1 da (Christine Lesley b 1962); *Career* md Robert Heyworth Gp Ltd 1977-, chm The Forum of Private Business 1979-; *Style—* Leslie S Hailes, Esq; Apt 6, West Lynn, Bowdon, Cheshire (☎ 061 926 9295); Heyworth House, Dakota Avenue, Salford M5 2PU, Needham Ave, Chorlton-cum-Hardy, Manchester M21 2AA (telex 665185, fax 061 872 8703)

HAILEY, Arthur; s of George Wellington Hailey, and Elsie Mary Wright; *b* 5 April 1920; *m* 1, 1944 (m dis 1950), Joan Fishwick; 3 s; m 2, 1951, Sheila Dunlop; 1 s, 2 da; *Career* Pilot RAF 1939-47, Flt Lt; emigrated to Canada 1947; various positions in indust and sales until becoming freelance writer 1956; author, books published in 35 languages; *Books* Flight into Danger (with John Castle, 1958), The Final Diagnosis (1959), Close-Up (collected plays, 1960), In High Places (1962), Hotel (1965, film 1966), Airport (1968, film 1970), Wheels (1971, film 1978), The Moneychangers (1975, film 1976), Overload (1979), Strong Medicine (1984, film 1986), The Evening News (1990); *Other Films* Zero Hour (1956), Time Lock (1957), The Young Doctors (1961); *Clubs* Lyford Cay (Bahamas); *Style—* Arthur Hailey, Esq; Lyford Cay, PO Box N7776, Nassau, Bahamas; office: Seaway Authors Ltd, 3400 First Canadian Place, PO Box 130, Toronto, Ontario M5X 1A4, Canada

HAILSHAM, Viscountcy of (UK 1929); *see*: Hailsham of St Marylebone, Baron

HAILSHAM OF ST MARYLEBONE, Baron (Life Peer UK 1970); Quintin McGarel Hogg; KG (1988), CH (1974), PC (1956); s of 1 Viscount Hailsham (d 1950) by his 1 w Elizabeth, da of Judge Trimble Brown, of Nashville, Tennessee, and widow of Hon Archibald Marjoribanks (4 s of 1 Baron Tweedmouth); disclaimed both Viscountcy and Barony for life 1963; 1 cous of Sir John Hogg, TD, *qv*; *b* 9 Oct 1907; *Educ* Eton, Ch Ch Oxford; *m* 1, 1931 (m dis 1943), Natalie Antoinette (d 1987), da of Alan Sullivan, of Sheerland House, Pluckley, Kent; m 2, 1944, Mary Evelyn (d 1978), o da of Richard Martin, of Kensington; 2 s, 3 da; m 3, 1986, Deirdre, er da of Mrs Margaret Briscoe and late Capt Peter Shannon; *Heir* (to Viscountcy and Barony of Hailsham, UK cr respectively 1928 & 1929, only) s, Hon Douglas Hogg, QC, MP; *Career* served WWII Rifle Bde; barrister 1932, QC 1953; MP (C) Oxford City 1938-58, St Marylebone 1963-70; first lord Admiralty 1956-57, min Educn 1957, lord pres of

Cncl 1957-59 and 1960-64, lord privy seal 1959-60, min Science and Technology 1959-64, ldr House of Lords 1960-63 (dep ldr 1957-60), lord chllr 1970-74 and 1979-88 (3 in precedence in Cabinet); chm Cons Pty Orgn 1957-59; rector Univ of Glasgow 1959; ed Halsbury's Laws of England (4th edn) 1972-; fellow All Souls Oxford 1951-38 and 1962-; Hon DCL Oxford, Hon LLD Cambridge; FRS 1973; *Style*— The Rt Hon the Lord Hailsham of St Marylebone,KG,CH,FRS,PC; Corner House, Heathview Gdns, London SW15 3SZ (☎ 081 789 3954/788 2256)

HAILSTONE, Dr (John) Donovan; s of Capt Frank Hailstone (d 1944), and Maud Eunice, *née* Greenhough; *b* 26 Feb 1930; *Educ* Univ of Nottingham (BSc), Univ of London (DipEd, DPM, MB BS); *m* 1, 2 Sept 1951 (m dis 1978), Pamela Margaret, da of Michael John Gray (d 1971), of Andover, Hants; 1 s (Julien John b 1965); m 2, 14 April 1979, (Beatrice) Jane; *Career* St George's Hosp London 1961-62, med resident NY and Boston 1962-63, sr registrar St Mary's Hosp London 1964-69, conslt physician in psychological med the Royal Free Hosp London 1970-, hon sr lectr Royal Free Hosp Med Sch 1970-; chm Hampstead Dist Med Ctee and Dist Mgmnt Team 1983-85, memb Hosp Advsy Serv 1989-, Lord Chllrs Med Visitor 1989-, memb Mental Health Tribunal 1990-; MRCS, LRCS 1960, MRCPsych 1973, FRCPsych 1983; *Books* Psychiatric Illness in the Medical Profession and the Clergy (1969); *Recreations* sailing, private flying; *Clubs* Royal Ocean Racing Club (RORC); *Style*— Dr Donovan Hailstone; 130 Harley St, London W1 (☎ 071 935 6558)

HAINES, Prof Andrew Paul; s of Charles George Thomas Haines, of 75 Tentelow Lane, Southall, Middx, and Lilian Emily, *née* Buck; *b* 26 Feb 1947; *Educ* Latymer Upper Sch, KCH Med Sch London (MB BS, MD); *m* 12 Feb 1982 (m dis 1989), June Marie Power; *Career* house physician and surgn KCH 1969, sr house offr Nat Hosp for Nervous Diseases 1972, MO Br-Nepal Med Tst 1973, memb scientific staff MRC, Epidemiology and Med Care Unit Northwick Park Hosp 1974-86, pt/t sr lectr in gen practice Middx Hosp Med Sch 1980-84, St Marys Hosp Med Sch 1984-87, prof of primary health care UC and Middx Sch of Med 1987-; author of papers on med subjects incl cardiovascular prevention, alcohol and care of the elderly; memb: Pub Health Laboratory Serv Bd 1983-86, Cncl Inst Physicians for the Prevention of Nuclear War 1982- (winners of Nobel Peace Prize 1985), Cncl Pugwash Orgn for Sci and World Affrs 1987-, Health Servs Res Ctee MRC 1989-, Working Pty on Prevention RCP 1989-; MRCP 1971, MRCGP 1976, MFPHM 1987; *Recreations* foreign travel, environmental and security issues; *Style*— Prof Andrew Haines; Flat 2, 62 Shepherds Hill, London N6 5RN (☎ 081 341 3388); Dept of Primary Health Care, University College and Middlesex School of Medicine, Whittington Hospital, Highgate Hill, London N19 5NF (☎ 071 272 3070 ext 4608)

HAINES, Dr Brian William; s of Brig William Haines (d 1939), of S Aust, and Vera, *née* Clutton-Williams (d 1949); *b* 24 Jan 1938; *Educ* Colfs GS, Univ of London (LLM), Univ of Ohio (PhD), Sch of Business Studies (MA); *Career* short story writer 1950-; called to the Bar Gray's Inn 1970; in practice 1970-86, published history on consensus agreements by contract 1973, claims conslt specialising in claims and negotiations on int agreements, founded Haines International (property consultancy); prospective Lib candidate 1964, prospective Euro MP Social Democrats 1980; memb Br Actors Equity 1960, fell Geologists Assoc 1960, memb American Soc of Int Law 1972, fell Inst of Arbitrators 1972, memb Law Inst Melbourne 1974; *Books* Guide to English Law (1960), Copyright in International Negotiations (1967), Presenting Your Case in Court (1969), Do Your Own Conveyancing (1970), How to Live Without a Solicitor (1979), The Householders Guide to Leaseholds (1983), Collected Short Stories (1987), Paula (1988), Irma (1988), Tales of Ginitelli (1989); *Recreations* fencing; *Clubs* Lansdowne, English Speaking Union; *Style*— Dr Brian Haines; Metherell, Beaworthy, Devon EX21 5TT

HAINES, Dr Charles Ian; s of Col George Harris Haines, MC, RAMC (d 1974), and (Laura) Ailsa, *née* MacPhail (d 1979); *b* 15 Sept 1934; *Educ* Marlborough, St Mary's Hosp Med Sch and Univ of London (MB BS); *m* 14 Sept 1963, Mollie Cynthia, da of James Reid Wheeler (d 1973); 1 s (Rupert b 1967), 3 da (Alexandra b 1965, Ruth b 1971, Lucy b 1974); *Career* Surgn Lt RN 1960-63; princ in gen practice 1963-66; conslt paediatrician: Bromsgrove and Kidderminster Gen Hosps, Alexandra Hosp Redditch 1974-; sr clinical lectr Dept of Paediatrics Univ of Birmingham 1988-; pres League of Friends Scott Atkinson Child Devpt Centre Redditch; FRCP 1984; *Recreations* gardening, golf, fishing, opera; *Clubs* Gentlemen of Worcs CC; *Style*— Dr Charles Haines; 34 Greenhill, Blackwell, Bromsgrove, Worcs B60 1BJ (☎ 021 445 1729); Alexandra Hospital, Woodrow Drive, Redditch, Worcs (☎ 0527 503030)

HAINES, Rev Dr Daniel Hugo; TD (1989); s of Dr Richard Wheeler Haines, of 54 Elm Grove, London SE15, and Ellen Stephanie, *née* Swift (d 1989); *b* 16 March 1943; *Educ* Abbotsholme Sch Derbyshire, Guys Hosp Dental Sch Univ of London (BDS, LDS), London Hosp Med Coll Univ of London, Staff Coll Camberley; *m* 20 July 1968, Dr Hilary Margaret Haines, da of Tudor Isaac, of 107 Alma Rd, Maesteg, Mid Glamorgan; 2 s (Tudor b 1972, Gwyn b 1977), 1 da (Catherine b 1974); *Career* Univ of London OTC 1962, Dental Offr 221 (Surrey) Field Ambulance RAMC (Capt) 1968, MO 217 (London) Gen Hosp RAMC (Maj) 1984; hon lectr in forensic dentistry London Hosp Med Coll 1968-75, med offr Govt of the Cayman Is 1975-77, chief med offr Usutu Forests Swaziland 1977-80, sr med offr Govt of the Falkland Is 1980-82, med and dental practitioner 1982-; ordained priest Southwark Cathedral 1984, hon curate St Catherine's Hatcham 1984-; Freeman City of London 1968, Liveryman Worshipful Soc of Apothecaries 1970; memb: BMA, BDA; FRSM, LRCP, MRCS, DRCOG; *Recreations* gardening, walking; *Style*— The Rev Dr Daniel Haines, TD; 56 Vesta Rd, London SE4 2NH (☎ 071 635 0305); The Surgery, 29 Crossway Ct, Endwell Rd, London SE4 2NQ (☎ 071 639 0654)

HAINES, Hon Mrs (Emma Charlotte); *née* Bancroft; o da of Baron Bancroft, GCB (Life Peer); *b* 1959; *Educ* Sheen Sixth Form Coll, Canterbury Coll of Art (BA); *m* 2 June 1984, Jeremy Guy Minton Haines, s of G D M Haines, of Uckfield, Sussex; 1 da (Phoebe b 1988); *Career* graphic designer; *Style*— The Hon Mrs Haines

HAINES, Joseph Thomas William (Joe); s of Joseph Haines, and Elizabeth Haines; *b* 29 Jan 1928; *m* 1955, Irene Lambert; *Career* political corr: The Bulletin (Glasgow) 1958-60 (Parly corr 1954-58), Scottish Daily Mail 1960-64, The Sun 1964-68; chief leader writer Daily Mirror 1978-90 (feature writer 1977-78), asst ed The Mirror 1985-90; dir: Scottish Daily Record and Sunday Mail Ltd, Mirror Group Newspapers 1986 (gp political ed 1984-90); columnist Daily Mirror, chief press sec to Harold Wilson as PM 1969-70 and 1974-76 and as Leader Oppn 1970-74 (dep press sec 1969); former chm Tonbridge & Malling Lab Pty (resigned), former memb Tonbridge UDC and Royal Cmmn on Legal Servs; *Books* The Politics of Power (1977), Malice in Wonderland (ed, 1986), Maxwell (1986); *Style*— Joe Haines, Esq; 1 South Frith, London Rd, Southborough, Tunbridge Wells, Kent (☎ 0732 365919)

HAINES, Prof Michael; *b* 13 Aug 1939; *Career* various appts then nat cooperation advsr Nat Agric Advsy Serv MAFF 1963-71, prof of agriculture and food mktg UCW Aberystwyth 1981- (lectr 1971-81); advsr Dyfed CC Econ Devpt Ctee 1983, memb Agric Advsy Panel to Sec of State for Wales, memb Bd Seafish Indust Authy 1987-; MInstM 1979-89, FCIM 1989, FSA 1989; *Books* An Introduction to Farming Systems (1982), Diversifying The Farm Business (1987); *Recreations* reading, gardening; *Clubs* Farmers; *Style*— Prof Michael Haines; University College of Wales, Aberystwyth, Dyfed SY23 3DD (☎ 0970 622242, fax 0970 617172 telex 35181 ABYUCW G)

HAINES, Michael Geoffrey Minton; s of Geoffrey Francis Minton Haines (d 1941), and Daphne Joan, *née* Thal, BEM (d 1979); *b* 30 Dec 1935; *Educ* Stowe; *m* 21 Dec 1973, Elizabeth, da of Lt-Col John Matthew Blakiston Houston, of Beltrim Castle, Gortin, Co Tyrone (d 1983); 2 s (Francis b 1975, Richard b 1977), 1 da (Rosie b 1979); *Career* Nat Serv cmmnd 2 Lt Rifle Bde 1959, 4 (Vol) Bn Royal Green Jackets TAVR 1961-70 (ret Maj 1970); accountant; ptnr KPMG Peat Marwick McLintock 1969- (joined 1954); dir: Shires Investment Trust 1971-80, Nationwide Anglia Building Soc 1984-88; dep dir Ind Devpt Unit 1975-76; treas: London & Quadrant Housing Tst 1970, E London Housing Assoc 1982-87, Sanctuary Housing Gp 1988-90; memb Overseas Projects Bd 1987-90; dir London Sinfonietta; Freeman City of London 1982, memb Worshipful Co of Playing Card Makers 1983; MICAS 1959; *Recreations* music, theatre, literature, military history, golf, squash; *Clubs* Brooks's, City of London; *Style*— Michael Haines, Esq; 82A Mortimer Rd, London N1 4LH (☎ 071 254 2339); KPMG Peat Marwick McLintock, 1 Puddle Dock, London EC4V 3PD (☎ 071 236 8000, fax 071 248 6552, telex 811541 PMMLON G)

HAINING, Thomas Nivison; CMG (1982); s of William Haining, of Ayrshire (d 1977), and Agnes Nivison, *née* Williamson; *b* 15 March 1927; *Educ* Univ of Edinburgh, Göttingen Univ; *m* 1955, Dorothy Patricia, da of late Leslie Robson, of Whitley Bay; 1 s (Nicholas); *Career* HM Dip Serv 1952-82, ambass consul gen to Mongolian People's Republic 1979-82, ret; conslt on int and personnel questions 1982-87; hon res assoc Dept of History Univ of Aberdeen 1988-, pres Chinese Study Gp; Freeman City of Rochester (NY State) 1972; FRGS; *Publication* Genghis Khan: His Life and Legacy (trans and ed, 1991); *Recreations* reading, historical travel studies, local historical studies, music golf; *Clubs* RAC, New Club (Brechin), Royal Northern and University (Aberdeen); *Style*— Thomas N Haining, Esq, CMG; Carseview, 7 The Banks, Brechin, Angus DD9 6JD (☎ 03562 2584)

HAINSWORTH, Prof Roger; s of Edward Trevor Hainsworth, of Wakefield, and Constance Mary, *née* White; *b* 23 Dec 1938; *Educ* Queen Elizabeth GS Wakefield, Univ of Leeds (MB ChB, PhD, DSc), Cardiovascular Res Inst San Francisco USA; *m* 24 July 1965, Janet Ann, da of Frederick Fisher (d 1985), of Cheadle, Cheshire; 2 s (Christopher Roger b 1967, Jonathan Peter b 1968), 2 da (Caroline Ann b 1971, Lucy Jane b 1982); *Career* house offr Leeds 1963-64; Univ of Leeds: lectr in physiology 1964-69, lectr Dept of Cardiovascular Studies 1970-76, sr lectr 1976-87, reader 1987-90, prof 1990-; Br-American res fell San Francisco 1969-70, hon conslt in clinical physiology Leeds Western DHA and Leeds Eastern DHA 1979-; memb: Physiological Soc, Systems Physiology Sub Ctee, Med Res Soc; *Books* Cardiac Receptors (with C Kidd and R J Linden, 1979), Acid Base Balance (1986), Cardiogenic Reflexes (with P N McWilliam and Mary Dasg, 1987); *Recreations* travel, photography, wine making; *Style*— Prof Roger Hainsworth; Dept of Cardiovascular Studies, University of Leeds, Leeds LS2 9JT (☎ 0532 334820, fax 0532 334803, tlx 556473)

HAIR, Prof Paul Edward Hedley; s of Thomas Edward Couchman Hair (d 1972), and Florence, *née* Hedley (d 1946); *b* 27 Jan 1926; *Educ* Berwick-upon-Tweed GS, St John's Coll Cambridge (MA), Nuffield and Balliol Colls Oxford (DPhil); *m* 5 Dec 1959, Margaret, da of Kenneth Alfred Edward Robinson (d 1961); 1 s (Christopher b 1963), 1 da (Ruth b 1966); *Career* res fell Univ of Ibadan Nigeria 1952-55, lectr Univ of Sierra Leone 1961-63, sr lectr African hist Univ of Khartoum 1963-65; Univ of Liverpool: lectr, sr lectr, reader Dept of History 1965-79, Ramsay Muir prof of mod history 1979-90, emeritus prof and sr fell 1990-; memb: Cncl Hakluyt Soc, Fontes Historiae Africanae Ctee Br Acad; chm: Local Population Studies Soc, Liverpool Med Hist Soc, Liverpool Soc for History of Sci and Technol; FRHistS; *Books* The Early Study of Nigerian Languages (1967), Before the Bawdy Court (1972), Liverpool, The African Slave Trade and Abolition (ed, 1976 and 1989), The Westward Enterprise (ed, 1978), East of Mina (1988), Coals on Rails (1988), To Defend Your Empire (1990); *Recreations* reading, television; *Style*— Prof Paul Hair; 17 Abbey Rd, West Kirby, Merseyside L48 7EN (☎ 051 625 5745); Department of History, University of Liverpool, PO Box 147, Liverpool L69 3BX (☎ 051 709 2366)

HAITINK, Bernard; Hon KBE (1977); *b* 1929; *Career* artistic dir Concertgebouw Orchestra Amsterdam 1964-88, artistic dir and princ conductor London Philharmonic Orchestra 1967-79, debut Royal Opera House 1977, musical dir Glyndebourne Opera 1978-88, appointed musical dir Royal Opera House Covent Garden 1986-; *Style*— Bernard Haitink, Esq, KBE; c/o Harold Holt Ltd, 31 Sinclair Rd, London W14

HAKEWILL SMITH, Lady; Edith Margaret; *née* Nelson; eldest da of late Brig-Gen Herbert Nelson, DSO (d 26 May 1949), of Shovel, N Petherton, Somerset, by his wife Edith Frances Wright, da of late Richard Cory, of Langdon Court, Devon; *m* 1928, Maj-Gen Sir Edmund Hakewill Smith, KCVO, CB, CBE (d 15 April 1986); 1 da; *Style*— Lady Hakewill Smith; 28 Tennis Court Lane, Hampton Court Palace, East Molesey, Surrey

HALAKA, Ahmed Nageeb; s of Ali Mohamed Halaka (d 1983), of Mansura, Egypt, and Nafisa Osman Abou-El-Khier (d 1983); *b* 8 Feb 1949; *Educ* Lycée la Liberté Mansura, Mansura Faculty Med Cairo Univ (MB BCh), Univ of Leeds (PhD); *m* 31 March 1979, Catherine Anne, da of Alan Hibbert, of 7 High Lane, Woodley, Stockport; 3 da (Sarah b 24 Aug 1980, Sophie b 7 June 1982, Suzanne b 29 March 1986); *Career* sr house offr orthopaedics Swansea 1973 (sr house offr neurosurgery 1972-73), sr house offr gen surgery N Allerton 1974-75, registrar neurosurgery Cardiff and Swansea 1975-77, conslt neurosurgn Leeds 1982- (sr registrar in neurosurgery 1977-82), author of papers on meningitis, pituitary absess and intracranial tumours; memb: SBNS, NENA, Egyptian Soc Neurosurgeons; FRCSEd; *Style*— Ahmed Halaka, Esq; 9 Fulwith Close, Harrogate, N Yorks HG2 8HP (☎ 0423 872542); BUPA Hospital, Roundhay Hall, Jackson Ave, Leeds LS8 1NT (☎ 0532 693939, fax 0532 681340)

HALAM, Ann; *see*: Jones, Gwyneth Ann

HALAS, John; OBE (1972); s of Victor Halas, and Bertha Halas; *b* 16 April 1912; *Educ* Acad of Arts Budapest, Institut De Beaux Arts Paris; *m* 1940, Joy Ethel, *née* Batchelor; 1 s (Paul b Feb 1949), 1 da (Vivien b July 1945); *Career* fndr: Halas & Batchelor Animation Studio 1940, Educnl Film Centre 1960, Great Masters Ltd 1981; dir and prodr of over 2000 animated films incl: Animal Farm (first Euro animated feature film), Dilemma (first computer generated film); winner of over 200 int awards, pres Br Fedn of Film Socs 1980-, hon pres Int Animated Film Assoc; Freeman San Francisco 1961; memb: BKSTS 1972, SFRCA 1988; *Recreations* arts, music, painting; *Style*— John Halas, Esq, OBE; 6 Holford Rd, Hampstead, London NW3 1AD (☎ 071 435 8674); 3-7 Kean St, London WC2B 4AT (☎ 071 836 5108, fax 071 836 5401, telex 269 496)

HALBERT, Trevor Anthony; s of Ronald Halbert, of Wirral, Cheshire, and Freda Mabel, *née* Impett; *b* 2 June 1952; *Educ* King's Sch Chester, Selwyn Coll Cambridge (MA); *m* 30 May 1983, Elaine Elizabeth Richardson, JP, da of William Alan Richardson, of Wirral, Merseyside; 2 s (Matthew b 1985, Simon b 1989); *Career* 2 Lt 3 Bn RWF 1975-77; called to the Bar Inner Temple 1975, standing counsel to DSS 1983- (Wales and Chester Circuit); *Recreations* mountaineering, music; *Style*— Trevor Halbert, Esq; Sedan House, Stanley Place, Chester CH1 2LU (☎ 0244 348282, fax 0244 42336)

HALDANE, Brodrick Vernon Chinnery; yr s of James Brodrick Chinnery-Haldane,

JP (d 1941), and Katherine Annie, *née* Napier (d 1957); bro of Alexander Chinnery Haldane of Gleneagles, *qv*; *b* 12 July 1912; *Educ* Lancing; *Career* served WWII with 83 Battery Light Artillery RA; actor (as Brodrick Haldane) 1932-35; appeared with Sir Philip Ben Greet's Shakespearian Theatre Co; films include: Two Hearts in Waltz Time, Happy, Murder in Monte Carlo; int society photographer 1930-; exhibitions held in Lausanne, Traquair House, Innerleithen 1982, Edinburgh Festival 1987; contributor to numerous books, magazines and newspapers; *Style*— Brodrick Chinnery Haldane, Esq; 56 India Street, Edinburgh EH3 6HD

HALDANE OF GLENEAGLES, Alexander Napier Chinnery; 25th of Gleneagles; er s of James Brodrick Chinnery Haldane, 24th of Gleneagles (d 1941), and Katherine Annie, *née* Napier (d 1957); sr male representative of the Haldanes of Gleneagles; *b* 17 June 1907; *Educ* Harrow, Wadham Coll Oxford; *Heir* kinsman, J Martin Haldane of Gleneagles, Younger, *qv*; *Career* Capt The Royal Scots Gds, served WWII; *Style*— Alexander Chinnery Haldane of Gleneagles; Gleneagles, Auchterarder, Perthshire PH3 1PJ (☎ 076482 249)

HALDANE OF GLENEAGLES, Younger, (James) Martin; er s of James Haldane (d 1990), of The Old Schoolhouse, Gleneagles, Auchterarder, and Joanna Margaret, *née* Thorburn; hp to Alexander Chinnery Haldane, 25th of Gleneagles, *qv*; *b* 18 Sept 1941; *Educ* Winchester, Magdalen Coll Oxford; *m* 5 Oct 1968, Petronella Victoria, da of Sir Peter Scarlett, KCMG, KCVO; 1 s, 2 da; *Career* chartered accountant; ptnr: Arthur Young 1970-89, Chiene & Tait 1989-; chm: Scottish Philharmonic Soc 1978-85, Scottish Chamber Orchestra 1981-85, Craighead Investments plc 1982-90; dir: Northern and Scottish Bd, Legal and General Assurance Soc 1984-87, Scottish Life Assurance Co 1990-; memb: Cncl Edinburgh Festival Soc 1985-89, D'Oyly Carte Opera Tst 1985-; memb Royal Co of Archers (Queen's Body Guard for Scotland); *Recreations* music, golf; *Clubs* Brooks's, New (Edinburgh); *Style*— J Martin Haldane of Gleneagles, Younger; Gleneagles, Auchterarder, Perthshire PH3 1PJ (☎ 076 482 388); 23 Northumberland Street, Edinburgh EH3 6LR (☎ 031 556 2924)

HALDANE-STEVENSON, Rev (James) Patric; TD (and Bar); s of Graham Morton Stevenson (d 1939), of Llandaff, Glam (descended from 3 Haldane Laird of Airthrey, later Campus of Univ of Stirling), and Jane Haldane, da of James Thomson, of Airdrie; *b* 17 March 1910; *Educ* King Edward's Sch Birmingham, St Catherine's Coll Oxford (BA, MA); *m* 1, 1938 (m dis 1967), Leila Mary, da of Arthur Flack; 2 s (Alan, Keith), 1 da (Janet); m 2, 1983, Mrs Joan Talbot Smith, o da of late Lt Cdr C W Wilson, of Par, Cornwall; *Career* served Br Reg Army 1946-55; Westminster Bank 1927-30; ordained Southwark 1935; rector: Hillington Norfolk (but on active serv 1939-46), Anglican Church in Wongan Hills Australia 1956-59; vicar N Balwyn Melbourne 1959-80, cmmr for Canon Law 1971-77; author; contrib to various books and jls, Aust corr Le Monde 1969-73; pres Cambrian Soc of ACT 1985-88, assoc memb Inst RE, memb Celtic Cncl of Australia; *Books* In Our Tongues (1944), Religion and Leadership (1948), Crisanzio and Other Poems (1948), Beyond the Bridge (1973), The Backward Look (1976); *Recreations* riding; *Clubs* Athenaeum, Quorn Hunt, Melbourne, Naval and Military (Melbourne), National Press (Canberra); *Style*— The Rev Patric Haldane-Stevenson, TD; 3 Argyle Square, Ainslie Avenue, Canberra 2601, Australia; c/o C Hoare & Co, 32 Lowndes St, London SW1X 9HX

HALE, Charles Martin; s of Charles Sydney Hale (d 1981), and Carmen, *née* de Mora; *b* 19 Jan 1936; *Educ* St Bernard's Sch NY, Culver Mil Acad, Stanford Univ (BSc), Harvard Business Sch (MBA); *m* 11 Feb 1967, Kaaren Alexis Hale; 2 da (Melissa b 18 May 1971, Amanda b 9 Nov 1976); *Career* USN: serv USS Union, Ensign i/c Boat Gp Div 1958, Lt 1960; gen ptnr Hirsch & Co London 1963-71, md and sr offr Europe AG Becker Inc 1971-83, gen ptnr Lehman Bros Kuhn Loeb Inc 1983-84, md and head of Int Div Donaldson Lufkin & Jenrette Securities Corp 1984-; chm UK Assoc of NY Stock Exchange Membs 1989-; memb: Harvard Business Sch Club of London, Stanford Univ Club of GB; *Recreations* tennis; *Clubs* Hurlingham, Vanderbilt, Annabel's, Harvard (New York); *Style*— Charles Hale, Esq; 33 Lyall Mews, London SW1 (☎ 071 245 9916); Donaldson, Lufkin & Jenrette Securities Corp, Jupiter House, Triton Court, 14 Finsbury Square, London EC2A 1BR (☎ 071 638 5822, fax 071 588 0120)

HALE, John Hampton; s of Dr John Hale, and Elsie Ledbrooke Coles; *b* 8 July 1924; *Educ* Eton, Magdalene Coll Cambridge (MA), Harvard Business Sch; *m* 1, 1950; 1 s (Jonathan), 2 da (Susan, Anne); m 2, 1980, Nancy Ryrie Birks; *Career* dir: Alcan Aluminium Ltd 1970-85 (joined 1949, exec vice pres Fin 1970-83), Pearson plc 1983- (md 1983-86), Economist Newspaper Ltd 1984-, Bank of Montreal 1985-, SSMC Inc 1986-89; lay memb Cncl Int Stock Exchange (London) 1987-, memb Ct of Assts Worshipful Co of Armourers and Brasiers 1985 (Master 1990); *Recreations* skiing, fishing, shooting; *Clubs* Royal Thames YC, Mount Royal, Toronto; *Style*— John Hale, Esq; Pearson plc, Millbank Tower, London SW1P 4QZ (☎ 071 828 9020, fax 071 828 3342, telex 8953869)

HALE, Prof Sir John Rigby; *b* 17 Sept 1923; *Educ* Eastbourne Coll and Jesus Coll Oxford (DLitt); *m* 1, 1952, Rosalind Williams; 1 s, 2 da; m 2, 1965, Sheila Haynes MacIvor, journalist; 1 s; *Career* prof of Italian history Univ Coll London 1970-89 (emeritus 1989-); chm of Tstees Nat Gallery 1974-80 (tstee 1973-80); tstee: V & A 1983-, British Museum 1985-, chm Govt Art Collection Advsy Cncl 1982-; author; FSA, FRHistS, FRSA, FBA; kt 1984; *Style*— Prof Sir John Hale, FSA; 26 Montpelier Row, Tickenham, Middx TW1 2NQ (☎ 081 892 9636)

HALE, (Mathew) Joseph Hovey; MC (1945), TD (1974); s of Mathew Robert Hale (d 1926), of Bognor Regis, and Grace Muriel, *née* Hovey (d 1962); *b* 14 Oct 1918; *Educ* St John's Coll Hurstpierpoint; *m* 28 Jan 1950, Gwenda, da of Sidney Herbert Roberts (d 1972), of Worthing, W Sussex; 2 da (Sheila b 1950, Sally b 1955); *Career* WWII 1939-46, cmmnd RA 1939, served N African and Italian Campaigns, Maj 1944; admitted slr 1947, in private practice; dir T R Beckett Ltd 1959-; chm: Beckett Newspapers Ltd 1967-, T R Beckett Ltd and subsid cos 1969-, Today Interiors Ltd 1976-; pt/t sec London Master Stevedares Assoc 1946-77, memb Exec Ctee Worthing Area Guild for Voluntary Serv 1974-, chm Govrs Our Lady of Sion Sch Worthing 1984-; memb Law Soc 1947; *Recreations* golf, walking, gardening; *Clubs* Army and Navy; *Style*— Joseph Hale, Esq, MC, TD; Stortford, Little Drove, Steyning, W Sussex (☎ 0903 814 852), 1 Commercial Rd, Eastbourne, E Sussex (☎ 0323 220 91)

HALE, Julian Anthony Stuart; s of James Peter Rashleigh Hale (d 1981), and Gillian Mariette Stuart, *née* Mason; *b* 27 Nov 1940; *Educ* Winchester, Christ Church Oxford (BA); *m* 1, 1963 (m dis 1970), Jennifer Monahan; m 2, 1971, Mary Kathleen Benét (d 1984); m 3, 18 April 1987, Helen Elizabeth Grace, da of Julian Likierman, of London; 1 s (Felix b 1990), 2 da (Laura b 1972, Tamara b 1988); *Career* books ed G G Harrap 1963-65, Italian prog organiser BBC External Servs 1972-73 (prodr and scriptwriter 1968-72), ed European Gazette 1973, writer 1973-; prodr BBC Radio 3 and 4 incl: In The Air, Wilke's Weekly, File On 4 1979- (also presenter European Journeys); *Books* incl: Ceausescu's Romania (1971), Radio Power (1975), Snap Judgement (1974), Vicious Circles (1978), Midwinter Madness (1979), Black Summer (1982); *Clubs* MCC; *Style*— Julian Hale, Esq; 11 Alexander St, London W2 5NT (☎ 071 229 0671); BBC Broadcasting House, London W1A 1AA (☎ 071 927 4664)

HALE, Michael; s of Bertram Hale (d 1986), of Dudley, W Midlands, and Nellie, *née* Cartwright (d 1977); *b* 20 June 1942; *Educ* Sir Gilbert Claughton GS; *m* 19 June 1965, Maureen Janet, da of John Thomas Shipley (d 1978), of Dudley; 1 s (Stephen Michael b 20 Nov 1971), 1 da (Helen Louise b 26 Oct 1975); *Career* dir: Central Manufacturing & Training Group 1975-80, Caparo Industries plc 1980-83, Glynwed Distribution Ltd 1983-86; md GEI International plc 1986-; FCMA 1969, ACIS 1971; *Recreations* tennis, walking; *Style*— Michael Hale, Esq; Lower House, 57A Norton Road, Stourbridge (☎ 0384 373789); GEI International plc, 42-44 West Street, Dunstable, Beds LU6 1TA (☎ 0582 601201, fax 0582 666930, telex 825261)

HALE, Norman Morgan; s of Thomas Norman Hale (d 1961), of Worcs, and Ada Emily, *née* Morgan (d 1969); *b* 28 June 1933; *Educ* Prince Henry's GS, St John's Coll Oxford (MA); *m* 1965, Sybil Jean, da of Stephen Leonard Maton (d 1974), of Glos; 1 s (Roger b 1966), 1 da (Alison b 1968); *Career* under sec (grade 3) Dept of Health (formerly DHSS) 1975-, Miny of Pensions and Nat Insur 1955, asst sec Assistance Bd 1966, Miny of Social Security 1966-70, Civil Serv Dept 1970-72; head Mental Health Div 1978-82, head Medicines Div 1982-87; currently head: Child Health, Maternity and Prevention Div (with AIDS Unit); *Recreations* gardening, historical geography; *Style*— Norman Hale, Esq; Dept of Health, Elephant and Castle, London SE1

HALE, Raymond; s of Tom Raymond Hale (d 1963), and Mary Jane, *née* Higgin; *b* 4 July 1936; *Educ* Baines GS Poulton-le-fylde; *m* 22 Aug 1956, Ann, da of George Elvidge of Thornton-Cleveleys; 1 s (Philip Raymond b 1963); *Career* RAF 1954-56; with Lancs CC 1952-61, Notts CC 1961-65, co treas Leics CC; treas: Leics Probation Serv, Magistrates Cts Serv, Leics & Rutland Police Authy, E Mids Area Museums Serv; vice chm Leics Guild of Physically Handicapped, treas Parkinson's Disease Soc (Leics Branch); IPFA 1959, FCCA 1981; *Recreations* DIY, gardening, rugby, cricket; *Style*— Raymond Hale, Esq; County Hall, Glenfield, Leicester, LE3 8RB, (☎ 0533 657830, fax 0533 657833, telex 341478)

HALE, Richard; *b* 19 July 1947; *Educ* Whitchurch GS Cardiff, UCL (LLB); *m* 14 Feb 1976, Jacqueline Mary; 1 s (Nicholas b 18 July 1979), 1 da (Elizabeth b 9 Nov 1980); *Career* admitted slr 1971; ptnr private practice Morgan Bruce & Harwickes (Cardiff, Swansea and Pontypridd) 1974-; memb Law Soc 1971; *Recreations* music, sailing, walking; *Clubs* Cardiff and County; *Style*— Richard Hale, Esq; Bradley Court, Park Place, Cardiff CF1 3DP (☎ 0222 233677, fax 0222 399288, car 0836 220135, telex 497902)

HALE, Robert; s of Roland Gilbert Hale, of Brierley Hill, and Ida Dorothy, *née* Atkins; *b* 29 Aug 1943; *Educ* Sir Gilbert Claughton GS Dudley; *m* 21 Sept 1968, Diane Elizabeth, da of William Henry Morris; 1 s (Simon Robert b 28 Nov 1972), 1 da (Rachel Elizabeth b 21 May 1970); *Career* Robson Rhodes: articled clerk 1962-67, qualified 1967, gen serv mangr 1970-73, ptnr (Gen Servs) 1974-88, ptnr Corp Fin Servs 1989-90; FCA (ACA 1967); *Recreations* golf, cricket, rugby, snooker; *Clubs* Forest of Arden Golf & Country; *Style*— Robert Hale, Esq; Battendown, Coton Rd, Nether Whitacre, Coleshill, Birmingham B46 2HH

HALES, Lady Celestria Magdalen Mary; da of 5 Earl of Gainsborough; *b* 27 Jan 1954; *Educ* St Mary's Convent Ascot, St Hilda's Coll Oxford; *m* 1 March 1990, Timothy Manville Hales, o s of late S W M Hales, MC; 1 da (Catherine Rose Mary b 11 June 1990); *Style*— The Lady Celestria Hales; 8 Peel St, London W8

HALES, Christopher Atherstone; s of Lt-Col Herbert Marwicke Atherstone Hales (d 1956), of Turweston, Bucks, and Mary, *née* Bell (d 1970); *b* 26 Aug 1931; *Educ* Wellingborough, HMS Worcester; *m* 17 May 1956, Barbara Mary, da of Edwin Arthur Ryan (d 1963), of London N18; 2 s (Julian b 1963, Adrian b 1966), 4 da (Katherine b 1958, Caroline b 1959, Antonia b 1961, Marie Louise b 1964); *Career* MN, midshipman to 2 Offr Blue Funnel Line 1949-58, Master Mariner 1957; barr Gray's Inn 1960, articled clerk Alsop Stevens and Co 1961-64, admitted slr 1964, asst slr Alsop Stevens and Co 1964, ptnr Holman Fenwick & Willan 1968- (asst slr 1965-67); dep dist judge; Freeman City of London, Liveryman Hon Co of Master Mariners; memb Law Soc; *Recreations* concert and theatregoing, history, following cricket; *Style*— Christopher Hales, Esq; Flat 4, 66 Gloucester St, London SW1V 4EF; Farthing Green, Elmdon, Saffron Walden, Essex; Holman, Fenwick & Willan, Marlow House, Lloyds Ave, London EC3N 3AL (☎ 071 488 2300, fax 071 481 0316)

HALES, Christopher James; s of James Camille Hales (d 1968), and Genefer Enid, *née* Ratcliff; *b* 12 Nov 1952; *Educ* Westminster, Univ Hall London (External BA); *Career* called to the Bar Gray's Inn 1979, slr Treasy 1990; *Recreations* composing songs, sport, art, karate, painting; *Style*— Christopher Hales, Esq; Treasury Solicitor Queen Anne's Chambers 28 Broadway London SW1 (☎ 210 3313)

HALES, (Charles) Nicholas; *b* 25 April 1935; *Educ* King Edward VI GS Stafford, Trinity Coll Cambridge (scholar, BA, MB BChir, MA, PhD, MRCPath, MRCP, MD); *Career* house physician UCH 1960 (house surgn 1959), Stothert res fell Royal Soc 1963-64, lectr in biochemistry Univ of Cambridge 1964-70, fell Downing Coll Cambridge 1964-70, hon conslt clinical biochemistry Addenbrooke's Hosp Cambridge 1968-70 (clinical asst 1961-68), prof in chm pathology Welsh Nat Sch of Med 1970-77, hon conslt in chem pathology Univ Hosp of Wales 1970-77, prof in clinical biochemistry Univ of Cambridge 1977-, hon conslt in clinical biochemistry Cambridge AHA 1977-; FRCP 1976, FRCPath 1980; *Recreations* music, fishing; *Style*— Prof Nicholas Hales; Dept of Clinical Biochemistry, Addenbrookes Hospital, Hills Road, Cambridge CB2 2QR (☎ 0223 336787)

HALEWOOD, David Frank; s of Thomas Halewood (d 1972), and Winifred, *née* Spencer (d 1974); *b* 28 April 1933; *Educ* Walton Tech Coll, Burton Tech Coll; *m* 29 Sept 1958, Eleanor Ann, da of John Smith (d 1970), of Burton on Trent; 2 da (Jacqueline b 1961, Jayne b 1965); *Career* jt md Chamberlain Phipps plc 1985; chm and md Chamter Ltd 1985; dir: Plasilem (Vic) Australia, Tanner Chemical USA 1984, CP Italia Spa 1983; CEng, MIMechE, MIProdE; *Recreations* golf, walking; *Clubs* Charnwood Forest; *Style*— David Halewood, Esq; 3 Paterson Drive, Woodhouse Eaves, Loughborough, Leics LE12 8RL (☎ 0509 890784); Wanlip Road, Syston, Leics (☎ 0533 601757, 34485)

HALEY, Prof (Keith) Brian; s of Arthur Leslie Haley (d 1972), and Gladys Mary, *née* Robson (d 1957); *b* 17 Nov 1933; *Educ* King Edward VI GS Birmingham, Univ of Birmingham (BSc, PhD); *m* 2 April 1960, Diana Elizabeth Haley, JP, da of Albert Bottrell Mason (d 1981); 1 s (Alan John b 1962); *Career* operational res scientist NCB 1957-59; Univ of Birmingham: lectr 1959, sr lectr 1963, prof operational res 1968, head of Dept of Engrg Prodn 1980; dir Centre for Applied Gerontology, govr and tstee Bromsgrove Sch 1969-, pres Operational Res Soc 1982-83, vice pres Int Fedn of Operational Res Socs 1983-86; FIMA 1968, FOR 1970, FIProdE 1982; *Books* Mathematical Programming for Business & Industry (1964), Operational Research 75 (1975), Operational Research 78 (1978), Operational Research in Search (1980), Operational Research in Fishing (1981); *Recreations* squash, bridge; *Style*— Prof Brian Haley; 22 Eymore Close, Selly Oak, Birmingham B29 4LB (☎ 021 475 3331); School of Manufacturing and Mechanical Engineering, The University of Birmingham, Edgbaston, Birmingham B15 2TT (☎ 021 414 4542)

HALEY, Geoffrey Norman (Geoff); s of Norman Haley (d 1966), of Pudsey, Yorkshire, and Grace Ward, *née* Cooke (d 1983); *b* 12 Oct 1944; *Educ* Accrington GS, Univ of London (BL), Brunel Univ and Henley Mgmnt Coll (MBA), Inst of Mktg (Dip Mktg); *m* 22 Oct 1966, Doreen Haley, da of Leslie Veitch; 1 s (Paul b 5 Sept 1974), 1 da (Julie b 24 June 1977); *Career* admitted slr 1971, dep gp legal advsr

Costain Gp 1974-78, dir Costain UK 1980-86 (legal advsr 1978-86), gen mangr Costain Ventures 1986-89, ptnr Theodore Goddard 1989-; legal advsr: Thames Barrier Consortium 1979-86, Channel Tunnel contractors Transmanche Link 1985; dir GKN Kwikform Ltd 1986-89, alternate dir Br Urban Devpt 1988-89; memb: Ascot Round Table, Law Soc, Strategic Planning Soc, Inst of Mktg, Greenlands Assoc, Soc of Construction Law, Inaugral Ctee Br Urban Regeneration Assoc; numerous articles in the field of construction law and private fin for transportation and infrastructure projects; MIStructE (memb Ctee on Design and Construction of Deep Basements), MInstPet; *Recreations* swimming, cycling, walking; *Style—* Geoffrey Haley, Esq; Tanglewood, 39A Llanvair Drive, S Ascot, Berks SL5 9LW (☎ 0344 27311); Theodore Goddard, Bastion House, 140 London Wall, London EC2Y 5AA (☎ 071 606 8855, fax 071 606 6100, telex 884678)

HALFORD, (James) Harold; s of James Henry Halford (d 1962), and Blanche Ida, *née* Cowling (d 1973); *b* 9 Jan 1923; *m* 4 Dec 1948, Norma; 1 s (Martin James b 28 Dec 1955), 1 da (Philippa Caroline (Mrs Gasson) b 19 Aug 1958); *Career* WWII 1942-45 cmmnd RE 1944; served: 210 Field Co (Holland, Belgium, Germany), HQ 30 Corps (Germany); Stirling Maynard and Ptnrs (formerly Maj E M Stirling): asst engr (later chief asst) 1946-55, ptnr 1955-75, sr ptnr 1975-86, conslt 1986-87, ret 1987; engrg advsr Nottingham Univ, former chm E Midlands ICE, pres Peterborough Rotary Club 1984; FICE 1954, MIHT 1954, MIWEM 1955, MConsE 1957, CEng; *Recreations* photography, wood turning, caravanning; *Clubs* Peterborough Rotary; *Style—* Harold Halford, Esq; Kirkby House, 94 Tinwell Road, Stamford, Lincs PE9 2SD (☎ 0780 54783)

HALFPENNY, The Ven Air Vice-Marshal Brian Norman; CB (1990); s of late Alfred Ernest Halfpenny, and Fanny Doris Halfpenny; *b* 7 June 1936; *Educ* George Dixon GS Birmingham, St John's Coll Oxford (BA, MA), Wells Theological Coll; *m* 15 July 1961, Hazel Beatrice, da of late Leslie Alfred Cross; 3 da (Sarah Jane b 1962, Deborah Anne b 1965, Naomi Ruth b 1967); *Career* ordained deacon 1962 and priest 1963 Salisbury Cathedral, asst curate Parish of Melksham Wiltshire 1962-65; RAF chaplain 1965-; served RAF stations: Cosford, Wildenrath, Leeming, Kai Tak, Brize Norton, Halton, Akrotiri; sr chaplain RAF Coll Cranwell 1982-83; asst chaplain-in-chief: RAF Support Command 1983-85, RAF Strike Command 1985-88; hon chaplain to HM The Queen 1985-91, chaplain-in-chief RAF 1988-91; prebendary St Botolph and canon of Lincoln Cathedral 1989-91; memb Gen Synod C of E 1988-91; *Recreations* music, theatre, running, fell walking; *Clubs* RAF, Oxford Union; *Style—* The Ven Air Vice-Marshal Brian Halfpenny, CB; Ministry of Defence, Adastral House, Theobalds Road, London WC1X 8RU (☎ 071 430 7268)

HALIFAX, Archdeacon of; *see*: Chesters, Ven Alan David

HALIFAX, 3 Earl of (UK 1944); Sir Charles Edward Peter Neil Wood; 7 Bt (GB 1784); DL (Humberside 1983); also Viscount Halifax (UK 1866), Baron Irwin (UK 1925); s of 2 Earl of Halifax (d 1980); *b* 14 March 1944; *Educ* Eton, ChCh Oxford; *m* 1976, Camilla, da of Charles Younger, of Gledswood, Melrose, Roxburghshire, and former w of Richard Eustace Parker Bowles; 1 s, 1 da (Lady Joanna b 1980); *Heir* s, Lord Irwin; *Career* dir Hambro's Bank; JP; High Steward of York Minster 1988; OStJ; *Style—* The Rt Hon the Earl of Halifax, DL; Garrowby, York YO4 1QD

HALL, Adrian Charles; s of Alexander Stephenson Hall, of Boarstall Tower, Boarstall, Aylesbury, Bucks, and Edith Mary Partington, *née* Smith (d 1975); *b* 8 June 1945; *Educ* Dragon Sch Oxford, Eton, Mansfield Coll Oxford (MA); *m* 17 Oct 1981, Magdalena Mary, da of Maj Edward Lewis Fiteni (ret RMA), of Morpeth Mansions, Morpeth Terrace, London SW1; 2 s (Richard b 27 June 1985, Edward (twin) b 27 June 1985), 1 da (Mary b 2 Dec 1982); *Career* asst slr Norton Rose (London) 1971-75, assoc barr/slr Borden & Elliot (Toronto) 1975-78, asst slr Allen & Overy 1978-82, sr legal mangr Standard Chartered Bank 1982-86, ptnr Turner Kenneth Brown slrs 1986-; memb: Law Soc of England and Wales 1971, International Bar Assoc, Canadian Bar Assoc; memb Worshipful Co of Slrs; *Recreations* historic motor racing, field game, cricket, classical music (oboe and cor anglais); *Clubs* MCC, Historic Sports Car, Classic Saloon Car, Eton Ramblers, Raffles, Alfa Romeo Owners; *Style—* Adrian C Hall, Esq; Turner Kenneth Brown, 100 Fetter Lane, London EC4A 1DD (☎ 071 242 6006, fax 071 242 3003, telex 297696)

HALL, Col Alan Edmund Matticot; TD (1975), DL (1985); s of Maj Edmund Hall (d 1983), of Helston, Cornwall, and Norah, *née* Carrick (d 1985); *b* 7 Oct 1935; *Educ* Emanuel Sch, Churchers Coll Petersfield, The Grammar Sch Enfield; *m* 8 Feb 1958, Diane Mary, da of Robert William Keyte (d 1969), of Cliftonville; 1 s (James b 1968), 2 da (Amanda b 1959, Nicola b 1962); *Career* Nat Serv 1955-57, Territorial Serv Royal Mil Police 1961-82; OC 44 Parachute Bde Provost Co 1965-67, OC 253 Provost Co 1969-76; appt Hon Col Royal Mil Police TA 1977-82; memb Ctee Greater London TAVRA: exec & fin, gen purpose & fin, HQ; Hon Col 36 Sig Regt 1990; md: Ind Coope East Anglia Ltd 1981-84, J & W Nicholson & Co 1984; dir of UK sales Löwenbräu Lager 1986-; pres The Licensed Victuallers National Homes 1990, former pres The Percheron Horse Soc, regnl chm The Wishing Well Appeal, pres NE London SSAFA & FHS, vice pres Essex Boy Scout Assoc; DL Co of London, rep DL London Borough of Redbridge; Freeman City of London 1984, Liveryman Worshipful Co of Broderers; FBIM 1979; *Recreations* shooting, wood working, curry cooking; *Clubs* Wig and Pen; *Style—* Col Alan Hall, TD, DL; Pippins, Tye Green, Good Easter, Essex (☎ 024 531 280); The Brewery, High St, Romford, Essex CMI 4SH (☎ 0708 762 839, 0708 722743, fax 0708 733407, car 0860 339 900, telex 265657 LOBRAU)

HALL, Alan Vivian; s of Walter Hall (d 1963), of Hull and Vera, *née* Thompson (d 1978); *b* 5 April 1930; *Educ* Hull GS, Nottingham Univ (BSc); *m* 26 June 1954, June Kathleen, da of William Redvers Beck (d 1977), of Hull; 2 s (Richard Guy b 1958, Jonathan Charles b 1961); *Career* RAF 1948-50; Shell-Mex and BP Ltd 1961-72, investmt mangr Shell Int Petroleum Co Ltd 1973-, memb Bd of Tstees Coll Retirement Equities Fund (USA) 1978-; Freeman City of London 1979, Liveryman Worshipful Co of Actuaries 1979; AIA 1958, FSS 1962, AMSIA 1961, FPMI 1978; *Recreations* travel, golf; *Clubs* MCC, Burhill GC; *Style—* Alan Hall, Esq; Shell Centre, London SE1 7NA (☎ 071 934 6261, telex 919651)

HALL, Alfred Charles; CBE (1977, OBE 1966); s of Alfred Hall (d 1951); *b* 2 Aug 1917; *Educ* Oratory Sch, Open Univ (BA); *m* 1946, Clara Georgievna, *née* Strunina, of Moscow; 5 s, 1 da; *Career* served WWII Intelligence Corps; HM Dip Serv; attached to embassies in: Cairo, Tehran, Moscow; first sec: India, Pakistan, Canada; cncllr: (info) Nigeria, Canberra; attached to Dept of Trade 1969-71, cncllr (econ and devpt) Nigeria 1972-75, dep high cmmr in S India 1975-77; grants offr Save the Children Fund 1979-82; *Recreations* gardening, journalism; *Clubs* Royal Cwlth; *Style—* Alfred Hall, Esq, CBE; White Cliff, St Margarets Bay, Kent (☎ 0304 852230)

HALL, Hon Mrs (Alison Elizabeth Vivienne); *née* Gridley; 2 da of 2 Baron Gridley; *b* 27 June 1953; *m* 1975, Michael John Hall; *Style—* The Hon Mrs Hall; c/o Rt Hon Lord Gridley, Coneygore, Stoke Trister, Wincanton, Somerset

HALL, Anthony John; s of late Maj Percy Edwin John Hall, and late Mabel, *née* Webster; *b* 27 Feb 1938; *Educ* Harrogate GS, UCL (MB BS); *m* 19 Aug 1967, Avis Mary, da of Dennis John Harbour (d 1973); 2 s (Simon John Webster b 3 March 1969, Charles b 9 Sept 1970), 1 da (Julia b 26 April 1974); *Career* conslt orthopaedic surgn Charing Cross Hosp, hon conslt Royal Marsden and Queen Charlotte's Hosps 1973-, regnl advsr in orthopaedics to NW Thames RHA 1987; memb: Ct of Examiners RCS 1985, Editorial Bd International Orthopaedics 1987, Cncl Br Orthopaedic Assoc, Int Soc of the Knee; nat delegate Société Internationale De Chirurgie Orthopaedique et de Traumatologie; past pres W London Medico Chirurgical Soc; FRCS; *Books* Manual of Fracture Bracing (ed, 1985), Orthopaedic Surgical Approaches (ed with C L Colton, 1991); *Recreations* sailing; *Style—* Mr Anthony Hall; 8 Campen House Close, Hornton St, London W8 7NU (☎ 071 937 6225); 126 Harley St, London W1N 1AH (☎ 071 486 1096, fax 071 224 2520, car 0860 362435)

HALL, Anthony Stewart (Tony); s of Albert Hall (d 1970), of Gillingham, Kent, and Dora Rose Ellen, *née* Rundle (d 1987); *b* 26 Oct 1945; *Educ* Gillingham GS, LSE (BSc); *m* 28 Dec 1968, Phoebe Katharine, da of John Leonard Souster; 1 s (Simon Anthony b 19 Dec 1973), 1 da (Katharine Phoebe b 17 May 1976); *Career* lectr mgmnt and orgn studies Nat Inst for Social Work Trg 1971-73, lectr in social admin Univ of Bristol 1971-78, dir Assoc of Br Adoption and Fostering Agencies 1978-80, dir and sec Br Agencies for Adoption and Fostering 1980-86, dir Central Cncl for Educn and Trg in Social Work 1986-; *Books* The Point of Entry: A Study of Client Reception in the Social Services (1974), Part-Time Social Work (with Phoebe Hall, 1980); *Recreations* photography, music, old films, genealogy, sport, stamps; *Style—* Tony Hall, Esq; 115 Babington Rd, Streatham, London SW16 6AN (☎ 081 769 1504); Central Council for Education and Training in Social Work, Derbyshire House, St Chad's St, London WC1H 8AD (☎ 071 278 2455)

HALL, Anthony William (Tony); s of Donald William Hall, and Mary Joyce, *née* Wallwork; *b* 3 March 1951; *Educ* King Edward's Sch Birmingham, Birkenhead Sch, Keble Coll Oxford (MA); *m* 6 Aug 1977, Cynthia Lesley, da of Arthur Robin Davis; 1 s (William Arthur Henry b 5 June 1989), 1 da (Eleanor Alice Mary b 30 Jan 1986); *Career* BBC TV: news trainee 1973, sr prodr World at One 1978, output ed Newsnight 1980, sr prodr Six O'Clock News 1984, ed Nine O'Clock News 1985, ed News and Elections '87 1987, dir News and Current Affrs TV 1990- (ed 1987-); contrib various pubns; Liveryman Worshipful Co of Painter Stainers 1985, Freeman City of London 1988; memb RTS; *Books* King Coal: A History of The Miners (1981), Nuclear Politics (1984); *Recreations* opera, church architecture, walking; *Clubs* Reform; *Style—* Tony Hall, Esq; BBC TV Centre, Wood Lane, London W12 (☎ 081 576 7312 fax 081 743 7882)

HALL, Sir Arnold Alexander; s of Robert Alexander Hall (d 1960), of Wirral, Cheshire, and Ellen Elizabeth, *née* Parkinson; *b* 23 April 1915; *Educ* Alsop HS, Clare Coll Cambridge (MA); *m* 29 Nov 1946, (Moira Constance) Dione, da of Rev J A Sykes, of Mugginton, Derby; 3 da (Caroline, Elizabeth, Veronica); *Career* Royal Aircraft Estab Farnborough: princ sci offr 1938-45, dir 1951-55; Hawker Siddeley Gp: dir 1955-86, vice chm 1963-67, md 1967-81, chm 1981-86, chm various subsidiary cos; md Bristol-Siddeley Engines 1959-63; dir: ICI, Lloyds Bank 1966-85, Phoenix Assur 1969-86, Lloyds Bank UK Mgmnt 1979-84, Rolls-Royce 1983-88; memb: Air Registration Bd 1963-73, Electricity Supply Res Cncl 1963-72, Advsy Cncl on Technol 1964-67, Def Industs Cncl 1969-77, Industl Devpt Advsy Bd 1973-75; dep chm Engrg Industs Cncl 1975-, chm Bd of Tstees Sci Museum 1984-86; pro chllr Univ of Warwick 1964-70, hon fell Clare Coll Cambridge 1966, foreign assoc US Nat Acad of Engrg 1976-, chllr Loughborough Univ of Technol 1980-89, hon memb American Soc of Mech Engrs 1981-, hon fell American Inst Aero Astronautics; Von Baumhauer Medallist of Royal Netherlands Aero Club 1959; Gold Medal: Royal Aeronautical Soc 1962, Br Inst of Mgmnt 1982; Hambro Award for Businessman of the Year 1975, Albert Medal Royal Soc of Art 1983; Freeman City of London 1988; FRS, FEng, Hon FAIAA, Hon FIMechE, Hon ACGI, Hon FIEE, Hon FRAeS; kt 1954; *Recreations* sailing; *Style—* Sir Arnold Hall, FRS; Wakehams, Dorney, nr Windsor, Berks SL4 6QD (☎ 0753 864916); c/o Hawker Siddeley Group plc, 18 St James's Sq, London SW1 (☎ 071 930 6177)

HALL, Col Austin Patrick; TD (1970); s of Austin Percy Stuart Hall (d 1984), of Harrogate, Yorks, and Lily, *née* Melloy (d 1981); *b* 13 March 1932; *Educ* King James GS Knaresborough, Bradford Coll of Advanced Technol (DipEng); *m* 1957, Dorothy, da of George Alfred Whitfield (d 1961), of Harrogate; 1 s (Richard), 2 da (Sarah, Fiona); *Career* Col Engr and Tport Staff Corps RE (TA), Hon Col Legion of Frontiersmen of the Cwlth; chartered civil engr and builder, chief exec Bovis Civil Engineering 1974-81, dir Bovis Ltd 1977-81, gp md Turriff Corporation plc 1981-84, exec dir ARC Properties Ltd; chm: The Bath & Portland Group plc, ARC Building Ltd, ARC Homes Ltd, ARC Services Ltd; exec dir: Westlea Developments Ltd, St Mellion Residential Ltd, ARC Property Investments Ltd, The Runnymede Centre Ltd, Kivel Properties Ltd, Marples Ridgeway Properties Ltd, Harlow Business Park Ltd; visiting industl fell Fac of Engrg Univ of Bristol; govr Dauntsey's Sch; Freeman City of London, Liveryman Worshipful Co of Arbitrators; EurIng, CEng, FICE, FCIOB, FCIArb, FIQA; *Recreations* golf, sailing, philately; *Clubs* IOD, Bath & County, Tracey Park Golf & Country, St Mellion Golf & Country, City Livery; *Style—* Col Austin Hall, TD; 12 Trossachs Drive, Bathampton, Bath, Avon BA2 6RP (☎ 0225 465957); ARC Properties Ltd, 20 Manvers St, Bath, Avon BA1 1LX (☎ 0225 444200)

HALL, Sir Basil Brodribb; KCB (1976), MC (1944), TD; s of Alfred Brodribb Hall; *b* 2 Jan 1918; *Educ* Merchant Taylors', London Univ (LLB); *m* 1955, Jean Stafford, da of Edgar Frederick Gowland; 2 s, 1 da; *Career* 12 Lancers France 1940, Maj 27 Lancers UK 1940-44, Italy 1944-45, Inns of Ct TA; admitted slr 1942, entered Treasy Slrs Dept 1946, HM procurator-gen and treasy slr 1975-80, chm Civil Serv Appeal Bd 1981-84 (former dep chm); legal advsr Broadcasting Complaints Cmmn 1981-, memb Euro Cmmn of Human Rights 1985-; memb Cncl Nat Army Museum 1981-, chm gen ctee Athenaeum 1983-86; *Recreations* military history; *Clubs* Athenaeum; *Style—* Sir Basil Hall, KCB, MC, TD; Woodlands, 16 Danes Way, Oxshott, Surrey KT22 OLX (☎ 0372 842 032)

HALL, Brian Allan; s of Harold Hall, of Manchester, and Barbara Violet, *née* Jeffkins; *b* 15 Aug 1947; *Educ* Ashton-under-Lyne GS, Kings Coll London (LLB); *m* 14 April 1973, Judith, da of Ronald Roberts, of Exeter; 1 s (Timothy b 29 Jan 1978), 1 da (Jenny b 11 May 1975); *Career* admitted slr 1972; ptnr Leeds Smith (now Leeds Day) 1976-; Dep Under Sheriff Beds 1979-, Notary Public 1981-; sec Biggleswade Chamber of Trade; memb: Law Soc, Provincial Notaries Soc, Shrievalty Assoc, Under Sheriffs Assoc; *Recreations* music, reading; *Clubs* John O'Gaunt Golf; *Style—* Brian Hall, Esq; Lodge Cottage, Church La, Hemingford Grey, Huntingdon, Cambs (☎ 0480 68631); Leeds Day Solicitors, 20 Hitchin St, Biggleswade, Beds (☎ 0767 315 040, fax 0767 316 573)

HALL, Dame Catherine Mary; DBE (1981, CBE 1967); da of Robert Hall, OBE (d 1955), and Florence Irene, *née* Turner (d 1975); *b* 19 Dec 1922; *Educ* Hunmanby Hall Sch for Girls Filey; *Career* nursing; Gen Infirmary Leeds 1941-53, asst matron Middx Hosp 1954-56, gen sec Royal Coll of Nursing 1957-82; memb GMC 1979-1989, chm UK Central Cncl for Nursing Midwifery and Health Visiting 1980-1985; pt/t memb: Cmmn on Industl Relations 1971-74, Br Regnl Bd (London and SE) 1975-77; Hon DLitt City Univ 1975; FRCN 1976; life vice pres Royal Coll of Nursing 1982; OStJ 1977; *Recreations* reading, gardening; *Style—* Dame Catherine Hall, DBE; Barnsfield, Barnsfield Lane, Buckfastleigh, Devon TQ11 0NP (☎ 0364 42504)

HALL, Christopher John; TD (1980); s of Maj Gordon Hamer Hall, of Watford,

Herts, and Esme, *née* Gaunt; *b* 13 Oct 1947; *Educ* Watford GS, Corpus Christi Coll Cambridge (MA); *m* 1, 31 Aug 1974, Susan Kathleen, da of Capt Sidney George Reynolds, of Watford, Herts; m 2, 14 April 1990, Sally Rose, da of Eric Charles Bateman Baker, of Waresly, Cambs; *Career* Univ of Cambridge OTC 1966-69 (cmmd 1968), 2 Lt (later Maj) 217 (London) FD Sqdn RE (V) and 73 Engr Regt (V) 1969-80, Maj 2 i/c III Engr Regt (V) 1981-83 and 1986-88 (Trg Maj 1984-86), Lt Col CO III Engr Regt (V) 1989-; CA; chief accountant SE Labs (EMI) Ltd 1976-80, fin dir and co sec Metal and Pipeline Endurance Ltd (Amec plc Gp), fin dir Biggs Wall & Co Ltd 1987; gp fin dir and co sec Penspen Ltd 1988-90; hon treas: Watford Operatic Soc 1976-86, St Neots and Dist Operatic Soc 1987-89; FCA 1972; *Recreations* cruising on inland waterways; *Style*— Christopher Hall, Esq, TD; 27 Sand Lane, Northill, nr Biggleswade, Beds SG18 9AD (☎ 0767 27723)

HALL, Capt Christopher John Pepler; RD (1976, Bar 1986); s of Cdr Harry John Hall, DSO, DSC, RD, of 5 De Vaux Place, Salisbury, Wiltshire, and Kathleen Gwladys, *née* Pepler; *b* 30 Dec 1940; *Educ* Marlborough, Univ of Edinburgh; *m* 8 July 1967, Patricia Valerie, da of Capt William Neil Kennedy Mellon Crawford, VRD (d 1978); 5 s (Richard b 1969, Ian b 1970, David b 1972, Alistair b 1976, Stephen (twin) b 1976); *Career* RNR 1960-; cmmnd 1961, Cdr 1978, Capt 1988, co HMS Claverhouse, Fourth Division RNR 1984-, currently Capt mobilisation and recruiting (Reserves); qualified CA 1966, Cooper Bros Mombasa 1967-68, ptnr Davidson Smith Wighton and Crawford Edinburgh 1970-82 (merged: Turquands Barton Mayhew 1978, Whinney Murray 1979-80, to form Ernst and Whinney), formed own accountancy mgmnt co Hall Management Servs Ltd 1982; diocesan sec and treas Diocese of Argyll and The Isles Scot Episcopal Church, memb finance Ctee Scot Episcopal Church; *Recreations* sailing, travel, reading, theatre; *Clubs* Caledonian (Edinburgh), RNSA; *Style*— Capt Christopher Hall, RD; 31 Stirling Rd, Edinburgh EH5 3JA (☎ 031 552 5991); 25 Dublin St, Edinburgh EH1 3PB (☎ 031 557 2400, fax 031 557 3285)

HALL, Christopher Myles; s of Gilbert Hall, of Gt Cutts Farmhouse, East Hyde, Beds, and Muriel, *née* Filsell; *b* 21 July 1932; *Educ* Berkhamsted, New Coll Oxford (BA); *m* 24 March 1957 (m dis 1980), Jennifer Bevan, da of late Harold Keech, of Woodbury, Devon; 1 s (Gilbert), 1 da (Jessica); *Career* Nat Serv RA 1951-52; reporter and feature-writer Daily Express, sub-ed and ldr-writer Daily Mirror, feature and ldr-writer Daily Herald and Sun; special asst (info) to: Min of Overseas Devpt, Miny of Tport 1965-69; chief info offr Miny of Tport 1969, ed The Countryman 1981-; Ramblers' Assoc: sec 1969-74, memb Exec Ctee 1982-, chm 1987-90, pres 1990-; dir Cncl for Protection of England 1974-80, ed South Eastern Rambler 1974-82; chm Save The Broad St Line Ctee 1963-65, hon sec Chiltern Soc 1965-68, memb Common Land Forum 1984-86; memb NUJ 1959-; *Recreations* country walking; *Style*— Christopher Hall, Esq; The Countryman, Sheep St, Burford OX8 4LH (☎ 099 382 2258)

HALL, Christopher Sandford; TD (1970), DL (East Sussex 1986); s of Brig Geoffrey Sandford Hall, TD, DL (d 1975), and Christine, *née* March; *b* 9 March 1936; *Educ* Rugby, Trinity Coll Cambridge (MA); *m* 8 July 1967, Susanna Marion, da of Richard Harry Bott, of Benington Lordship, Stevenage, Herts; 3 s (David b 1968, Colin b 1970, Philip b 1973); *Career* Nat Serv 5 Royal Inniskilling Dragoon Gds 1954-56 (TAVR 1956-70); admitted slr 1963, ptnr Cripps Harries Hall Tunbridge Wells 1964-; dir Mid Sussex and W Kent Water Cos; chm: A Burslem & Son Ltd, British Equestrian Promotions Ltd, S Eng Agric Soc 1984-90; chm Tstees Temple Grove Sch; memb: Cncl Br Horse Soc, Jockey Club 1990; steward Nat Hunt Ascot Folkestone and Plumpton; memb Law Soc; *Recreations* hunting, racing, farming; *Clubs* Cavalry and Guards'; *Style*— Christopher Hall, Esq, TD, DL; Great Danegate, Eridge Green, Tunbridge Wells, Kent (☎ 089 275 385); 84 Calverley Rd, Tunbridge Wells (☎ 0892 515 121)

HALL, Colin; s of Arthur Graham Henry Hall, of Enfield, Middlesex, and Winifred Martha, *née* Gray (d 1979); *b* 23 April 1945; *Educ* Stationer's Company's Sch, Univ of Bristol (LLB); *m* 29 Sept 1973, Philippa Margaret, da of Hac Collinson, of Sway, Hants; 4 s (Nicholas Justin b 1976, Oliver Rupert b 1978, Giles Edward b 1981, Rupert Charles (twin) b 1981); *Career* HM Dip Serv 1966-68, admitted slr 1971, ptnr Slaughter and May slrs 1978- (joined 1969); *Recreations* sailing, gardening, conservation; *Style*— Colin Hall, Esq; The Oast House, West End, Frensham, Surrey (☎ 025 125 3422); 35 Basinghall St, London EC2 (☎ 071 600 1200, fax 071 600 0289, telex 883486)

HALL, Colin David; s of Fredrick Ronald Hall, of 13 St Andrews Rd, Portsmouth, and Doreen Hall; *b* 3 July 1941; *Educ* Portsmouth Tech HS, Highbury Coll (Cert of Works Mgmnt), Open Univ (BA); *m* 30 Jan 1965, Muriel May (d 22 Sept 1989), da of Ernest William George Stares, of 41 Owens Rd, Winchester, Hants; 2 da (Jacqueline Grace b 3 Sept 1968, Katrina Marie b 12 June 1972); *Career* rubber technologist FPT Industries 1959-61, sr asst Yarsley Research Laboratories 1961-64, rubber and plastics technologist Plessey UK 1964-65; Ralli Bondite Ltd: chief chemist 1965-73, tech sales dir 1973-75, md 1975-; dir G & L Ralli Investment & Trustee Co Ltd 1978, chm Frowds Ltd 1989 (dir 1988); chm Br Adhesives and Sealants Assoc 1987-89; FInstD, FIIM, MBIM; *Style*— Colin Hall, Esq; 'Hillcroft', Day Lane, Lovedean, Portsmouth, Hampshire PO8 0SH (☎ 0705 593714); Ralli Bondite Ltd, Arnside Rd, Waterlooville, Hants PO7 7UJ (☎ 0705 251321, fax 0705 264307, car 08 6033 0408)

HALL, Darren James; s of James Henry Hall, and Ann Carol, *née* Stevens; *b* 25 Oct 1965; *Educ* Higham's Park Sr Sch; *Career* badminton player; has represented Eng approx 62 occasions; winner: every jr nat men's singles title from Under 13 to Under 21, Under 18 Six Nations' Men's Singles Championships, Men's Singles Eng Nat champion 1986, 1988, 1989, 1990 and 1991 (first man to win 4 times consecutively and equalling Ray Steven's record of 5 wins), German Open Men's Singles 1988, Euro Championships (first Englishman ever to win) Norway 1988, Silver medal Euro Championships 1990; Cwlth Games 1990: Gold medal in team event, Bronze medal in Men's Singles; reached World Grand Prix Semi-Finals Hong Kong 1988; *Recreations* golf, snooker and cars; *Style*— Darren J Hall, Esq; 28 Harford Rd, North Chingford, London E4 7NQ

HALL, David; CBE (1983), QPM (1977); s of Arthur Thomas Hall (d 1974), of London, and Dorothy May, *née* Bryant (d 1965); *b* 29 Dec 1930; *Educ* Richmond and East Sheen GS for Boys; *m* 14 June 1952, Molly Patricia, da of Roland Knight (d 1981), of London; 2 s (Philip David b 17 Oct 1956, Nicholas Peter b 29 Nov 1958); *Career* joined Met Police 1950, supt 1965; staff offr to Col Eric St Johnstone (chief inspr of Constabulary), asst chief constable Staffordshire 1970 (later dep chief constable), chief constable Humberside 1976-; memb St John Cncl; Freeman City of London 1987; CBIM 1987; *Recreations* music (playing the piano), gardening; *Clubs* Sloane; *Style*— David Hall, Esq, CBE, QPM; Humberside Police Headquarters, Queens Gardens, Kingston upon Hull HU1 3DJ (☎ 0482 26111, fax 0482 226 877)

HALL, David Bernard; s and h of Sir John Bernard Hall, 3 Bt, by his w Delia Mary (da of Lt-Col James Innes, DSO, by his 3 w, Evelyn (*see* Lady Joly de Lotbinière), gda of Hon William Dawnay, JP, DL, 6 s of 7 Viscount Downe); *b* 12 May 1961; *Educ* Eton, Univ of York; *Career* clerk Bank of America (Hamburg) 1980, Sales Dept United Biscuits 1985-, md All Blinds and Curtains 1988-; *Recreations* rugby, tennis; *Clubs* Lansdowne, Boodle's; *Style*— David Hall, Esq; Rose Cottage, Holly Lane, Haughton, Stafford

HALL, David Christopher; s of Sir Frederick Hall, 2 Bt (d 1949), and bro and h of Sir (Frederick) John (Frank) Hall, 3 Bt; *b* 30 Dec 1937; *m* 24 Nov 1962, Irene, da of William Duncan, of Kincorth, Aberdeen; 1 s, 1 da; *Career* joiner/cabinet maker 1962-79, woodwork teacher 1980-, antique restorer 1982-; *Style*— David Hall, Esq; Inverene, 368 Queens Rd, Aberdeen (☎ 0224 319766)

HALL, David John Lees; s of Herbert Vaughan Lees Hall (d 1974), of Tilneys, Hall Road, Rochford, Essex, and Nancy Dewar Hall (d 1989); *b* 19 Feb 1946; *Educ* Felsted, Univ of Nottingham (BSc); *m* 1 April 1972, Yvonne Pepita, da of Douglas Acock, of Westcliffe-on-Sea, Essex; 1 s (Christopher b 27 June 1974), 1 da (Katharine b 20 April 1982); *Career* chm Monometer Group Co Ltd 1974- (dir 1967-); AMIBF 1968; *Recreations* yachting, skiing, squash; *Clubs* Royal Ocean Racing, Royal Corinthian Yacht, Royal Burnham Yacht, Courtland Park Country, Ski Club of Great Britain; *Style*— David Hall, Esq; 1 Thorpe Bay Gardens, Thorpe Bay, Essex SS1 3NS (☎ 0702 582183); Monometer Group Co Ltd, Monometer House, Rectory Grove, Leigh-on-Sea, Essex (☎ 0702 72201, fax 0702 715112, telex 99381); car ☎ 0836 244979

HALL, Dr David Michael Baldock; s of Ronald Hall, and Gwen, *née* Baldock; *b* 4 Aug 1945; *Educ* Reigate GS, St George's Med Sch (MB BS); *m* 25 Aug 1966, Susan Marianne, da of Gordon Howard Luck; 2 da (Emma b 1969, Vanessa b 1971); *Career* paediatrician Baragwaath Hosp Johannesburg 1973-76, sr registrar Charing Cross Hosp 1976-78, conslt St George's Hosp 1978-; hon conslt: Spastic's Soc 1982-86, Tadworth Ct 1986-; med advsr Assoc for all Speech-Impaired Children, fndr memb Children's Head Injury Tst; memb Br Paediatric Assoc, MRCP 1972, FRCP 1986; *Books* The Child with a Handicap (1984), Health for all Children (1989); *Recreations* travel, reading, music, plumbing; *Style*— Dr David Hall; Park Farm House, 34 Heatherside Rd, W Ewell KT19 9QU (☎ 081 393 8001); Clare House, St George's Hospital, London SW17 0QT (☎ 081 672 9999, ext 215)

HALL, David Nicholas; s of William Noel Hall (d 1981), of London, and Louisa Augusta, *née* Palma; *b* 19 Nov 1933; *Educ* London Choir Sch, Carlisle & Gregson (Jimmy's), RMA Sandhurst; *m* 28 Dec 1963, Harriet Mary Arden, da of William Lloyd McElwee, MC, TD (d 1978); 3 da (Susannah b 25 Feb 1965, Phillie b 13 April 1967, Christina b 17 Oct 1969); *Career* active serv Korean War 1953, cmmnd RE served Cyprus, Congo (Zaire), Ghana, instr RMA Sandhurst, Staff Coll, staff appt with Engr-in-Chief, Sqdn Cdr Scotland and Gibraltar, Kirkcudbright, CO RE Depot 1974-77, technical staff appt 1977-79, Record Office RE 1979-81, ret Lt-Col 1981; author of various pubns on land navigation and expeditions; dir Fndn for Science and Technol 1981-, liaison offr Learned Socs 1981-; hon treas Palestine Exploration Fund 1983-90, chm Expeditions & Research Ctee RGS 1990- (hon foreign sec 1973-83, vice pres 1984-87, memb 1985-), first pres The Desert Dining Club 1980-, chm Young Explorers' Tst Screening 1983-; organiser and ldr Br Expedition to Air Mountains 1970, various camel journeys and scientific expeditions to arid regions; RMCS Heilbron Prize 1966, RGS Ness Award 1972; FICS, FRGS, FRSA; *Books* Expeditions (1977); *Recreations* exploration, fishing, wine, music; *Clubs* Athenaeum; *Style*— David Hall, Esq; 3 Spencer Rd, London SW18 2SP (☎ 081 228 8476); 12 Upper Belgrave St, London SW1X 8BB

HALL, Denis Whitfield; CMG (1962); s of Henry Rushton Hall (d 1945), of Haslemere, Surrey, and Marie Gabrielle Hall (d 1960); *b* 26 Aug 1913; *Educ* Dover Coll, Wadham Coll Oxford (BA); *m* 12 Sept 1940, Barbara, da of Boys Carman; 2 s (Richard Whitfield b 1941, Nigel Rushton b 1945); *Career* Colonial Admin Serv: dist offr cadet 1935, dist offr 1937, dist cmmr 1946, PA to Chief Native Cmmr 1948-51, sr dist cmmr 1955, prov cmmr 1959; dep chm Sussex Church Campaign 1965-73; *Recreations* walking, reading, sailing; *Clubs* Oxford Union, Oxford Univ Yacht; *Style*— Denis Hall, Esq, CMG; Martins Priory Close, Boxgrove, Chichester, Sussex PO18 OEA (☎ 0243 773 351)

HALL, Dr Derek Gordon; s of Gordon Ivor Hall (d 1986), of Dinas Powys, S Glam, and May Magaretta, *née* Horsey; *b* 17 April 1944; *Educ* Penarth Co Sch, UCL (BSc, PhD); *m* 1, 1967 (m dis 1971), Pauline Margaret Vivienne, *née* Coombe; 1 da (Samantha Kate b 1969); m 2, 6 Oct 1979, Susan Olga, da of Eric Eaton, of Cheltenham, Glos; 2 s (Guy Sebastian b 1968, Daniel Gordon b 1973); *Career* Mgmnt Consultancy Div Arthur Andersen & Co 1970-76; J P Morgan 1976-: vice pres 1978-87, sr vice pres 1987-; *Style*— Dr Derek Hall; J P Morgan Securities Ltd, PO Box 124, 30 Throgmorton St, London EC2N 2NT (☎ 071 600 7545, telex 895 4804/5)

HALL, Dinny; da of David Alexander Hall, of Shantock House, Bovingdon, Hertfordshire, and Susan Anne, *née* Martyr; *b* 28 April 1959; *Educ* Bourne Valley Comp Herts, Herts Sch of Art and Design St Albans, Central Sch of Art and Design (BA); *Career* jewellery designer; set up own business in Soho London 1983, clients incl: Harvey Nichols, Browns, Bergdorff Goodman (USA), Barneys (USA), Sabu (Japan) and fashion designers Rifat Ozbek and Bruce Oldfield in London and Isaac Mizrahi and Jennifer George NY; collections featured in magazines 1985- incl: Vogue, Harpers & Queen, Elle, Sunday Times, Sunday Telegraph; launched first range of jewellery using gold and precious stones 1990; Br Accessory Designer of the Year 1989; *Books* Creative Jewellery (1986); *Recreations* cooking, travelling, walking, reading, talking and writing; *Clubs* Groucho's; *Style*— Ms Dinny Hall; Dinny Hall Ltd, 43 Beak St, London W1R 3LE (☎ 071 437 8291, fax 071 287 9095)

HALL, Air Marshal Sir Donald Percy; KCB (1984, CB 1981), CBE (1975), AFC (1963); s of William Reckerby Hall, and Elsie Hall; *b* 11 Nov 1930; *Educ* Hull GS, RAF Coll; *m* 1953, Joyce, *née* Warburton; 2 da; *Career* AOC 38 Gp RAF 1980-83, dep CDS 1983-86, ret 1986; chm Marconi Def Systems 1987; FRAeS; *Style*— Air Marshal Sir Donald Hall, KCB, CBE, AFC; c/o Lloyds Bank, 6 Pall Mall, London SW1Y 6NH

HALL, Dorothy, Lady; Dorothy Maud; da of late William Laurence Jones; *m* 22 June 1957, Sir Neville Reynolds Hall, 13 Bt (d 1978); *Style*— Dorothy, Lady Hall; Ash Cottage, Ash, Dartmouth, S Devon

HALL, Sir Douglas Basil; 14 Bt (NS 1687), of Dunglass, Haddingtonshire; KCMG (1959, CMG 1958), JP (Devon 1964); s of Capt Lionel Erskine Hall (d 1948); suc bro Sir Neville Hall, 13 Bt 1978; *b* 1 Feb 1909; *Educ* Radley, Keble Coll Oxford; *m* 25 April 1933, Rachel Marion (d 1990), da of late Maj Ernest Gartside-Tippinge; 1 s, 2 da (and 1 s decd); *Heir* s, John Douglas Hoste Hall; *Career* entered HMOCS as a cadet N Rhodesia 1930, dist offr 1932-50, sr dist offr 1950-53, provincial cmmr 1953, admin sec 1955-56, sec for Native Affrs 1956, govr and C-in-C of Somaliland Protectorate 1959-60; memb Police Authy for Devon and Cornwall 1971-79; *Style*— Sir Douglas Hall, Bt, KCMG; Barnford, Ringmore, nr Kingsbridge, Devon (☎ 0548 810401)

HALL, Lady; Elinor Claire; da of Paul Hirschorn, of New York, and previously w of Eric H Marks; *m* 13 Sept 1946, as his 2 w, Sir Noel Frederick Hall (d 1983); former princ: Henley Mgmnt Coll 1946-60, Brasenose Coll Oxford 1960-73; 1 s (Jonathan b 1952), 1 da (Louise b 1950); *Clubs* Huntercombe Golf; *Style*— Lady Hall; 1 Northfield End, Henley-on-Thames, Oxon (☎ 0491 573 265)

HALL, Rear Adm Geoffrey Penrose Dickinson; CB (1973), DSC (1943), DL (1982); s of Maj Arthur Kenrick Dickinson Hall (d 1945), of Legbourne Abbey, Louth, Lincs, and Phyllis Mary, *née* Penrose (d 1969); maternal gf Brig-Gen Cooper Penrose, CB, CMG, cmd RE Southern Cmd; maternal ggf Thomas Greene DD was sec of the Gen Synod of the Church of Ireland for 40 years; ggf Thomas Dickinson Hall was High

Sheriff of Nottingham & Leicester, gf Frederick Dickinson Hall was rector of Manby and rural dean of Louthesk; *b* 19 July 1916; *Educ* Haileybury; *m* 1945, Mary Ogilvie, da of Henry George Carlisle (d 1954), of Ardlair, Heswall, Cheshire; 2 s (Nicholas, Adrian), 1 da (Virginia); *Career* Naval Offr 1934-75, cmd six of HM ships 1945-67, hydrographer of the Navy 1971-75, served in Atlantic, Iceland, W Africa, India, Burma & Far East 1939-45, hydrographic surveying in N and S Atlantic, Antarctic, Indian Ocean and NZ 1938-67, combined ops 1943-45, various appts within Admty and MOD 1954-75; landowner (6 acres); *Recreations* walking, writing, tennis, golf, croquet, dogs; *Clubs* Naval and Military, Royal Navy, Lincolnshire, Louth; *Style*— Rear Adm Geoffrey Hall, CB, DSC, DL; Manby Ho, Manby, Louth, Lincs LN11 8UF (☎ 0507 327777)

HALL, Prof Geoffrey Ronald; CBE (1985); s of Thomas Harold Hall, JP (d 1974), of Douglas, IOM; *b* 18 May 1928; *Educ* Douglas HS, Univ of Manchester (BSc); *m* 1950, Elizabeth, da of Thomas Day Sheldon (d 1951), of Manchester; 3 children; *Career* Colombo plan expert India 1956-58; prof (formerly reader) of nuclear technol Imperial Coll 1958-70, dir and prof Brighton Poly 1970-90; pres Br Nuclear Energy Soc 1970; memb: Cncl Engrg Cncl 1982-86, Sci and Engrg Res Cncl 1982-86, Nat Cncl for Vocational Qualification 1987-89; *Recreations* travel, golf, caravanning; *Style*— Prof Geoffrey Hall, CBE; 23 Firsdown R, High Salvington, Worthing BN13 3BG

HALL, Prof George Martin; s of George Vincent Hall (d 1971), of Bridlington, Yorks, and Dora Hortensia, *née* Beauchamp; *b* 14 May 1944; *Educ* Kind Edward VI Sch Lichfield, UCL (MB BS, PhD); *m* 9 Jan 1964, Marion Edith, da of Frank Gordon Burgin, MBE, of Gt Missenden, Bucks; 1 da (Katherine Elizabeth b 1965); *Career* prof of clinical anaesthesia Royal Postgrad Med Sch Univ of London 1989- (sr lectr 1976-85, reader 1985-89); hon sec to British Journal of Anaesthesia; *Books* contrib research papers on anaesthesia; *Recreations* running; *Style*— Prof George Hall; Dept of Anaesthetics, Hammersmith Hospital, Royal Postgraduate Medical School, London W12 0HS (☎ 081 740 3290)

HALL, Henry Robert (Bill); OBE (1982), TD (1952), DL; s of Samuel Ernest Hall, JP (d 1957), of Camberwell, London, and Kempsell Caroline, *née* Singer; *b* 25 May 1917; *Educ* Dulwich; *m* 22 Aug 1953, Margret (Greta) Lucy, da of Dan Dunglinson Stobart (d 1975), of Knebworth, Herts; 2 s (Robert b 14 Aug 1954, Nigel b 7 July 1957), 1 da (Caroline b 8 Sept 1959); *Career* Phillips and Drew: ptnr 1955-74, conslt 1974-88; JP 1961-78, chief scout cmmr 1976-82 (county scout GLS 1965-75), island cmmr Jersey 1978-80, cmmr income tax appeal Jersey 1989-; Freeman City of London 1956, memb Worshipful Co of Glaziers; memb of Stock Exchange 1947-75 and 1978-; *Recreations* scouting, walking, gardening, tennis; *Clubs* Victoria Jersey; *Style*— Bill Hall, Esq, OBE, TD, DL; La Landelle, Route Des Landes, St Ouen, Jersey CI (☎ 0534 82424, fax 83319)

HALL, Janice Elizabeth (Jan); da of John Brian Hall, and Jean, *née* Chadwick; *b* 1 June 1957; *Educ* Rutland Girls HS, St Anne's Coll Oxford (MA); *m* David Winston Constain; *Career* mktg exec ICI Paints Div 1979-83, chm and chief exec Coley Porter Bell 1983-, teaching assoc Ashridge Management Coll 1986-; non-exec dir: Allied Maples Group Ltd 1988-, Friends of the Earth Ltd 1990-; chm: Design Business Assoc 1988-90, Ashridge Coll Assoc; memb: DTI Small Firms Advsy Gp on the Single Market 1988-90, DTI BOTB Small Firms Ctee, BR (Southern) Board 1990-, Mktg Gp of GB 1991-, Forum UK 1990-; memb Cncl: CSD 1988-, IOD 1991-; winner Design Effectiveness awards 1990; FCSD 1989, FRSA 1990, FInstD; *Books* Management and Design (1991); *Recreations* travel, food, opera, riding, sailing; *Clubs* Aldeburgh Yatch; *Style*— Ms Jan Hall; Coley Porter Bell, 4 Flitcroft St, London WC2H 8JD (☎ 071 379 4355, fax 071 379 5164)

HALL, Joan Valerie; CBE (1990); da of Robert Hall (d 1979), and Winifred Emily, *née* Umbers; *b* 31 Aug 1935; *Educ* Queen Margaret's Sch Escrick nr York, Ashridge House of Citizenship; *Career* Cons candidate for Barnsley 1964 and 1966, MP (C) Keighley 1970-74; PPS to Min of State MAFF 1972-74; memb Cncl: Univ Coll Buckingham 1977-83, Central Tport Users' Consultative Ctee 1981-86; chm Sudan Studies Soc of the UK 1989-; *Style*— Miss Joan Hall, CBE; Mayfields, Darton Rd, Cawthorne, Barnsley, S Yorks S75 4HY (☎ 0226 790230)

HALL, John Anthony Sanderson; DFC (1944, Bar 1945), QC (1967); s of Rt Hon William Glenvil Hall, MP (d 1962), of Heath Mansions, Hampstead, and Rachel Ida, *née* Sanderson (d 1950); *b* 25 Dec 1921; *Educ* Leighton Park Sch, Trinity Hall Cambridge (MA); *m* 1, 27 Oct 1945 (m dis 1974), Nora Ella, da of Arthur Ulrich Crowe (d 1941); 1 s (Jonathan Mark Glenvil b 1950), 2 da (Sally Anne b 1946, Pamela Mary b 1952); m 2, 10 July 1976, Elizabeth Mary, da of Richard Wells; *Career* called to the Bar Inner Temple 1948, bencher Inner Temple 1975, dep chm Hants QS 1967-72, rec Swindon 1971, rec Crown Ct 1972-78; memb: Gen Cncl of the Bar 1964-68 and 1970-74, Senate Inns of Ct 1966-68 and 1970-74; chm UK Delgn Consultative Ctee of European Bars and Laws Socs 1978-79, govr St Catherine's Sch Guildford 1967; memb Worshipful Co of Arbitrators; FCIArb 1982; *Recreations* fly fishing, book collecting; *Clubs* RAF, Garrick; *Style*— John Hall, Esq, DFC, QC; Swallows, Blewbury, Oxon (☎ 0235 850511)

HALL, Sir John Bernard; 3 Bt (UK 1919), of Burton Park, Sussex; s of Lt-Col Sir Douglas Hall, 2 Bt, DSO (d 1962), and his 2 w, Nancie (who m 2, 1962, Col Peter J Bradford, DSO, MC, TD (d 1990)), o da of Col John Edward Mellor, CB, JP, DL; *b* 20 March 1932; *Educ* Eton, Trinity Coll Oxford (MA); *m* 19 Oct 1957, Delia Mary, da of Lt-Col James Innes, DSO (d 1949); 1 s, 2 da; *Heir* s, David Bernard Hall b 12 May 1961; *Career* Lt Royal Fus RARO; joined J Henry Schröder & Co (later J Henry Schröder Wagg & Co Ltd) 1955 (dir 1967-73), dir Bank of America Int 1974-82, vice pres Bank of America NT & SA 1982-90; md: European Brazilian Bank 1983-89, The Nikko Bank (UK) plc 1990-; former chm: Anglo-Colombian Soc, Assoc of British Consortium Banks; Liveryman and memb Ct of Assts Worshipful Co of Clothworkers (Warden 1987-89); FCIB 1976, FRGS 1988, FRSA 1989; *Recreations* travel, fishing; *Clubs* Boodle's, Lansdowne, Overseas Bankers; *Style*— Sir John Hall, Bt; Penrose House, Patmore Heath, Albury, Ware, Herts SG11 2LT (☎ 027 974 255); Inver House, Lochinver, Lairg, Sutherland IV27 4LJ

HALL, John Douglas Hoste; s and h of Sir Douglas Hall, 14 Bt, KCMG, of Barnford, Ringmore, Kingsbridge, Devon; *b* 7 Jan 1945; *Educ* Dover Coll, Gonville and Caius Coll Cambridge, Univ of Southampton; *m* 1972, Angela Margaret, da of George Keys, of 2 Barnsfield Lane, Buckfastleigh, S Devon; 2 s; *Career* poet; asst princ Dartington Coll of Art; *Books of Poetry* Between the Cities, Days, Malo-Lactic Ferment, Couch Grass, Repressed Intimations, Meaning Insomnia; *Style*— John Hall, Esq; Brook Mill, Buckfastleigh, S Devon TQ11 0HL (☎ 0364 42985)

HALL, Sir (Frederick) John Frank; 3 Bt (UK 1923), of Grafham, Surrey; s of Sir Frederick Henry Hall, 2 Bt (d 1949), and Olwen Irene, *née* Collis, who subsequently m Arthur Borland Porteous; *b* 14 Aug 1931; *Educ* Bryanston; *m* 1, 3 April 1956 (m dis 1960), Felicity Anne, da of late Edward Rivers-Fletcher, of Norwich; m 2, 3 June 1961 (m dis 1967), Patricia Ann, da of Douglas Atkinson (d 1973), of Carlisle; 2 da; re-m 9 Nov 1967, his 1 w, Felicity Anne; 2 da; *Heir* bro, David Christopher Hall; *Style*— Sir John Hall, Bt; Carradale, 29 Embercourt Rd, Thames Ditton, Surrey KT7 0LH (☎ 081 398 2801)

HALL, John Michael; s of Ernest Smith Hall (d 1964), of Solihull, West Midlands, and Joyce Kathleen, *née* Butler; *b* 30 Jan 1936; *Educ* Bloxham Sch; *m* 20 Oct 1962, Angela Phyllis, da of Ralph Dixon Coates, MBE, of Milford on Sea, Hampshire; 4 da (Katherine b and d 23 Jan 1964, Sophie b 6 Feb 1965, Lucy b 11 Nov 1967, Charlotte b 14 Nov 1969); *Career* Nat Serv 2 Lt RAPC 1959-61; CA; sr ptnr Halls CAs 1964-, non-exec dir Marley plc; chm Mgmnt Ctee Warren Pearl Marie Curie Centre, govr St Martin's Sch Solihull; FCA 1959; *Recreations* vintage and classic cars, messing with boats; *Style*— John Hall, Esq; New Oxford House, 16 Waterloo Street, Birmingham (☎ 021 643 3451, fax 021 643 3859, car 0836 507716)

HALL, John Piers; s of Dr Robert Noel Hall, of Park Farm House, Upper Harlestone, Northampton, and Doreen Cecilia, *née* Russell; *b* 26 June 1940; *Educ* Dragon Sch Oxford, Stowe; *m* 1965, Sarah Gillian, da of Gerard Thorpe Page; 4 s (James b 6 April 1966, Charles b 6 May 1968, Thomas b 1 April 1985, Freddie b 12 May 1987); *Career* trainee Read Hurst & Brown Stockbrokers 1958-65; Wontner Dolphin & Francis (merged to become Brewin Dolphin 1974, became Brewin Dolphin & Co Ltd 1987): joined 1965, ptnr 1967, memb Mgmnt Ctee 1974, md 1987; Freeman City of London 1970; memb Worshipful Co Livery of Merchant Taylors, memb Nat Autistic Care and Training Ctee Appeal; memb: Stock Exchange 1965, The Securities Assoc 1987, IMRO 1990; *Recreations* breeding British White cattle, sailing Dragons, golf; *Style*— John Hall, Esq; Chalkhouse, Green Farm, Kidmore End, nr Reading; Brewin Dolphin & Co Ltd, 5 Giltspur St, London EC1A 9DE (☎ 071 248 4400, fax 071 329 0949)

HALL, Brig Jonathan Michael Francis Cooper; OBE (1987); s of (Charles) Richard Hall (d 1982), of Horsham, and Rosemary Elizabeth, *née* Beckwith (d 1979); *b* 10 Aug 1944; *Educ* Taunton Sch, RMA Sandhurst; *m* 5 Oct 1968, Sarah Linda, da of Laurence Whitmarsh Hudson, of Cheltenham; 2 da (Candida Sarah b 1971, Rachel Katharine b 1973); *Career* cmmnd 3 Carabiniers 1965, Capt Adj 3 Carabiniers 1969-71, GSO 3 Ops Trg HQ Anzuk Bde Singapore 1971-73, Maj Royal Scots Dragoon Guards 1974-76, Staff Coll Camberley 1977, SO2 instr Jr Div Staff Coll 1978-79, Sqdn Ldr Royal Scots Dragoon Guards 1980-81, SO2 Personnel MOD 1982, Lt Col SO1 Censorship Study (Beach Ctee) MOD 1983, CO Royal Scots Dragoon Guards 1984-86, Col MS2 MOD 1986-88, student Higher Cmd and Staff Course 1988, Brig cmdg 12 Armoured Bde 1989-90; memb: Cavalry and Guards' Gen Ctee 1981-, Chalke Valley Deanery Synod 1978-79, Forces Archdeaconry Synod (Army) 1989-; *Recreations* country, walking, tennis, travel; *Clubs* Cavalry & Guards'; *Style*— Brig Jonathan Hall, OBE; c/o Home Headquarters, The Royal Scots Dragoon Guards, The Castle, Edinburgh

HALL, His Hon Judge Julian; s of Alexander Stephenson Hall, of Bucks, and Edith Mary Partington, *née* Smith (d 1975); *b* 13 Jan 1939; *Educ* Eton, Ch Ch Oxford (MA), Trinity Coll Dublin (LLB); *m* 1, 1968 (m dis 1988), Margaret Rosalind; 1 s (Benjamin b 1971), 1 da (Rebecca b 1969); m 2, 11 March 1989, Ingrid; *Career* industl res chemist 1961-63; called to the Bar Gray's Inn 1966; practicing Northern Circuit 1966-86, rec Crown Court 1982-86, prosecuting counsel Inland Revenue Northern Circuit 1985-86, circuit judge 1986-; ARCM; *Recreations* making music; *Clubs* Buxton Musical Soc, Music Camp; *Style*— His Hon Judge Julian Hall; Northampton Combined Court, 27 Guildhall Rd, Northampton NN1 1DP (☎ 0604 21083)

HALL, Dr Keith; s of Leslie Hall (d 1982), and Florence May, *née* Watson (d 1967); *b* 10 Jan 1944; *Educ* Chislehurst and Sidcup GS, Westminster Hosp Med Sch Univ of London (MB BS); *m* 12 Sept 1970, Valerie Jean, da of Harry Hancock (d 1972); 3 da (Gillian b 20 April 1973, Jennifer b 13 Dec 1977, Lucy b 6 Sept 1981); *Career* asst surgn P & O Lines 1968-69, conslt neuroradiologist 1979-; author of chapters and papers neuroradiology and management of pituitary disease; memb: RCR 1975, RSM 1980, BIR 1979, BSNR 1978; *Recreations* cycling, walking, golf, soccer, shopping; *Style*— Dr Keith Hall; Newcastle Gen Hosp, Dept of Neuroradiology, Regnl Neurological Centre, Westgate Rd, Newcastle upon Tyne, Tyne & Wear NE4 6BE (☎ 091 2738 811 telex 091 2722 641)

HALL, Keith Rawlings; TD; s of Alfred Brodribb Hall (d 1974), of Surrey, and Elsie Hilda, *née* Banks; *b* 10 June 1928; *Educ* Clayesmore, King's Coll Cambridge (MA); *m* 1958, Susan (Shoonan) Rosemary Lee, da of Sir Algernon Arthur Guinness, 3 Bt, and former w of Samuel Charles Gillchrest (d 1954); 2 s (Simon b 1959, Mark b 1967), 2 da (Susan b 1960, Jennifer b 1963); *Career* Maj 2 i/c Inns of Court and City Yeo 1962; chief exec and dir Legal & Gen PMC Ltd 1986, chm Dreamscape Ltd; vice chm: Donnington Tst, Exec Ctee St Loye's Coll; *Recreations* hunting, music; *Clubs* Cavalry and Guards'; *Style*— Keith Hall, Esq, TD; Higher Hewood, South Chard, Somerset (☎ 0460 20235)

HALL, Prof Laurance David; s of Daniel William Hall, of Stevenage, and Elsie, *née* Beard; *b* 18 March 1938; *Educ* Leyton Co HS, Univ of Bristol (BSc, PhD); *m* 1 Aug 1962, (Winifred) Margaret, da of Henry Arthur Golding; 2 s (Dominic Courtney St John b 15 Dec 1971, Brecken Guy D'Arcy (twin) b 15 Dec 1971), 2 da (Gwendolen Judith Virginia b 21 May 1963, Juliet Katharine Olivia b 1 July 1964); *Career* post doctoral fell Univ of Ottawa 1962-63, prof of chemistry Univ of Br Columbia Vancouver Canada 1963-84, first holder Herchel Smith prof of medicinal chem Univ of Cambridge Clinical Sch; FCIC 1974, FRS (Canada) 1982, CChem, FRSC 1985; *Recreations* wine-making, skiing, scientific research; *Clubs* Emmanuel Coll Cambridge; *Style*— Prof Laurance Hall, FRS; 22 Long Rd, Cambridge CB2 2QS (☎ 0223 336 805); Laboratory for Medicinal Chemistry, University Forvie Site, Cambridge CB2 2PZ (☎ 0223 336 805)

HALL, Leonard Graham; s of William Edwin Hall (d 1951), of Grimsby, and Nellie Alice, *née* Smith (d 1919); *b* 25 Feb 1917; *Educ* Humberstone Foundation Sch Cleethorpes, St John's Coll Cambridge (MA); *m* 1946, Betty, da of William James Minns (d 1939), of Grimsby; 2 s (William, John), 1 da (Rosalind); *Career* actuary; Clerical Medical and General Life Assurance Society: joined 1938, dep gen mangr 1961-75, gen mangr 1975-82, non exec dir 1982-90; dir: Lands Improvement Group, Sumit plc; chm: Soc of Investmt Analysts 1969-71, Life Offices Assoc 1979-81; vice pres Inst of Actuaries 1970-73; Master Worshipful Co of Actuaries 1984-85; *Recreations* music, travel, golf; *Clubs* United Oxford and Cambridge Univ, RAF, Northwood Golf; *Style*— Leonard Hall, Esq; Temple Bar, Green Lane, Northwood, Middlesex HA6 2UY; (☎ 09274 25942)

HALL, Viscountess; Marie-Colette; da of Col Henri Bach; *m* 1974, as his 3 w, 2 Viscount Hall (d 1984); *Style*— The Rt Hon Viscountess Hall; Solvain, 41210 St Viatre, Loir et Cher, France

HALL, Prof Michael Anthony; s of Frederick Lancelot Hall (d 1982), and Eva, *née* Bridgewood-Jeffes; *b* 7 July 1940; *Educ* Rutherford GS, Imperial Coll London (BSc, PhD, DSc); *m* 25 Aug 1964, Gillian, da of Frederick Barrone (d 1975); 1 da (Sara Jayne Barrone b 1 June 1969); *Career* Univ of California Riverside 1964-67, Scottish Hort Res Inst 1967-68, prof Univ Coll of Wales Aberystwyth 1968-; 150 pubns in professional jls; FIBiol, FRSA, ARCS; *Books* Plant Structure, Function and Adaptation (1976); *Recreations* skiing, music; *Style*— Prof Michael Hall; Glascoed, Piercefield Lane, Penparcau, Aberstwyth, Dyfed SY23 1RX (☎ 0970 612465); Department of Biological Sciences, University College of Wales, Aberystwyth, Dyfed SY23 3DA (☎ 0970 622313, telex 35181 ABYUCWG, fax 0970 617172)

HALL, (Haddon) Michael; s of William Haddon Hall (d 1972), and Mildred, *née* Brown, of London; *b* 28 June 1945; *Educ* Aristotle Sch; *m* 1, 24 Jan 1970 (m dis 1976), Kathleen Mary, da of William Suggitt; m 2, 25 April 1981 (m dis 1986), Suzanne Marie, da of Ronald M Bell; m 3, 11 May 1989, Victoria Ann, da of Bryan

John Vallas (d 1984); *Career* CA Barsham Nixon & Hamilton 1969-72 (joined as articled clerk 1961), qualified sr Stoy Hayward & Co 1972-74; Boty Cox Crawford & Ridley (merged Edward Moore & Sons 1975, which merged Rowland Nevill 1985 to become Moores Rowland): audit mangr 1974-79, ptnr 1979-, equity ptnr 1983-; FCA (1979, CA 1969); non-exec dir Croydon Business Venture Ltd 1990; *Recreations* applied philosophy, shooting, reading science fiction, collecting collectables; *Style—* Michael Hall, Esq; Moores Rowland, 9 Bedford Park, Croydon, Surrey CRO 2AP (☎ 081 686 9281, fax 081 760 0411, car 0860 834 122)

HALL, Michael Robert; s of Robert Hall (d 1980), of Cheshire, and Hannah Hall; *b* 9 May 1942; *Educ* William Hulmes Manchester; *m* 1969, Irene Mavis, da of Percy Cuthbert Archer, of Cheshire; 1 s (Robert Anthony b 1973), 1 da (Kathryn Elizabeth b 1971); *Career* gp md Thomas Robinson Gp plc, dir Selective Fin Servs Ltd 1987, Derby HS Ltd 1987, Heritage Brewery Museum 1987; chm: W Hawley & Son Ltd 1987, Selective Tech Innovations Ltd 1988, Construction Cosmetics Ltd 1988; FCT, FCA, FCMA; *Recreations* squash, walking, sailing; *Clubs* Duffield Derbyshire, Stakis Regency International; *Style—* Michael R Hall, Esq; Ecclesbourne House, Windley, Derbyshire

HALL, Michael Robert; s of Antony David Hall, of Bridgend, and Julia, *née* Hayes; *b* 13 Oct 1965; *Educ* Brynteg Comprehensive Sch, Univ Coll Cardiff, Wolfson Coll Cambridge (2 blues); *partner*, Rachel Ann Kidley; *Career* rugby player; teams played for: Maesteg RFC, Bridgend RFC, Barbarians, Welsh Students, Welsh Univs (capt), Br Students (capt); current club Cardiff RFC; 12 Welsh caps, memb Wales B team v France 1987, capt U21 Welsh team, memb Wales U20 team; toured: Wales to NZ 1988, Barbarians to Hong Kong Sevens 1989, Welsh Sevens to Aust 1988/89, Br Lions Tour of Aust 1989; memb World XV v South Africa (two tests) 1989; *Style—* Michael Hall, Esq; Cardiff County Football Club, Cardiff Arms Park, Westgate St, Cardiff

HALL, Nigel John; s of Herbert John Hall, of Chipping Sodbury, Avon, and Gwendoline Mary, *née* Olsen; *b* 30 Aug 1943; *Educ* Bristol GS, West of England Coll of Art (NDD), RCA (MArtRCA, Harkness Fellowship to USA); *m* 1986, Manijeh Yadegar; *Career* artist; tutor RCA 1971-74, princ lectr Chelsea Sch of Art 1974-81; solo exhibitions incl: Galerie Givaudan Paris 1967, Robert Elkon Gallery NY 1974, 1977, 1979, 1983, Annely Juda Gallery London 1978, 1981, 1985, 1987, Galerie Maeght Paris 1981 and 1983, Staatliche Kunsthaus Baden-Baden 1982, Nishimura Gallery Tokyo 1980, 1984, 1988, Hans Mayer Gallery Dusseldorf 1989, Garry Anderson Gallery Sydney 1987, 1990; gp exhibitions incl: Documenta VI (Kassel) 1977, British Sculpture in the Twentieth Century (Whitechapel Gallery London) 1981, Aspects of British Art Today (Tokyo Metropolitan Museum) 1982, Carnegie International (Carnegie Inst Pittsburgh) 1982, Britannica: Thirty Years of Sculpture (Le Havre Museum of Fine Art) 1988; work cmmnd by: Aust Nat Gallery Canberra, IBM London, Airbus Industrie Toulouse, Olympic Park Seoul, Museum of Modern Art Hiroshima, British Petroleum London; represented in numerous public collections incl: Tate Gallery London, Musée Nat d'Art Moderne Paris, Nat Galerie Berlin, Tel Aviv Museum, Power Inst Sydney; memb: Panel CNAA 1975-76, Faculty of Prix de Rome 1979-83; *Style—* Nigel Hall, Esq; 11 Kensington Park Gardens, London W11 3HD (☎ 071 727 3162); Annely Juda Fine Art, 23 Dering St, Lodnon W1R 9AA (☎ 071 629 7578, fax 071 491 2139)

HALL, Dr Peter; s of Arnost Hall (d 1971), of Bournemouth, and Margit, *née* Weiss (d 1979); *b* 30 Dec 1931; *Educ* Wyggeston Sch Leicester, Univ of Birmingham (MB ChB), Univ of Sheffield (PhD); *m* 12 Jan 1957, Gwynneth Anne, da of Harold Wallhouse (d 1989), of Warwick; 3 s (Nicholas b 1957, Jonathan b 1960, Timothy b 1963); *Career* Med Branch RAF 1956-59, RAFVR 1959-69, Wing Cdr 1969; fndn res fell Univ of Sheffield 1959-62, sr conslt psychiatrist Worcester 1963-, Upjohn lectr Canadian Med Assoc 1979, advsr Med Res Cncl 1981-84, memb Worcester Health Authy 1983-89; appointed doctor Mental Health Cmmn 1984-85, sr visiting conslt Woodbourne Clinic 1984-, advsr mental health WHO 1985-89, regnl tutor psychiatry W Midland Health Authy 1986-, advsr psychiatry Univ of Birmingham 1986-, memb Hosp Advsy Serv 1987, med examiner Gen Nursing Cncl 1988-, chm Individual Membs World Psychiatric Assoc 1989-90; DPM (RCP) 1961, FAmGerSoc 1972, FRCPsych 1973 (memb Bd Examiners), FICA 1977, FAASP 1980; *Books* Assessment in Cerebrovascular Insufficiency (1971), Chemotherapy of Schizophrenia (1983), Perspectives in Psychiatry (1988), The Closure of Mental hospitals (1990); *Recreations* inept gardening, package tourism, hopeless fishing; *Style—* Dr Peter Hall; Worcester Royal Infirmary, Worcester; Woodbourne Clinic, Edgbaston, Birmingham; Cotswold Hospital, Cheltenham; Wye Valley Hospital, Hereford; St Anne's Orchard Hospital, Malvern (☎ 0905 763333)

HALL, Peter Edward; CMG (1987); s of Bernard Hall, of Arden House, 31 The Highway, Hunton Bridge, Kings Langley, Herts, and Katherine Monica, *née* Blackbourn (d 1972); *b* 26 July 1938; *Educ* Portsmouth GS, Pembroke Coll Cambridge; *m* 6 May 1972, Marnie, da of Herbert Brumby Kay (d 1971); 1 s (Barnaby b 1975), 1 da (Amanda Hall b 1973); *Career* Nat Serv RAF 1956-58, offr cadet Jt Servs Sch for Linguists, cmmnd RAFVR 1958; FO 1961-63, third then second sec Warsaw 1963-66, second sec New Delhi 1966-69, first sec FCO 1969-72, first sec Brussels EEC 1972-76, first sec FCO 1976-77, cnsllr for econ and political affrs Caracas 1977-78; cnsllr and head of Br Info Servs: New York 1978-81, Washington 1981-83; dir of research FCO 1983-86, under sec Cabinet Office 1986-88, sabbatical Stanford Univ visiting scholar 1988-89, HM ambass Yugoslavia 1989-; memb: ESCR Govt and Law Ctee 1983-86, Exec Ctee Br Int Studies Assoc 1983-86; *Recreations* reading, music; *Clubs* Royal Air Force; *Style—* HE the British Ambassador; British Embassy, Generala Ždanova 46, 1100 Belgrade, Yugoslavia (☎ 010 38 11 645 055, telex 11468 probel yu, fax 010 38 11 659 651)

HALL, Prof Peter Geoffrey; s of Arthur Vickers Hall (d 1973), of Blackpool, and Bertha, *née* Keefe (d 1979); *b* 19 March 1932; *Educ* Blackpool GS, St Catharine's Coll Cambridge (MA, PhD); *m* 1, 7 Sept 1962 (m dis 1967), Carla Maria, da of Frank Wartenberg (d 1986); m 2, 13 Feb 1967, Magda, da of Antoni Mróz, of Warsaw; *Career* asst lectr then lectr Birkbeck Coll Univ of London 1957-65, reader in geography LSE 1966-67, prof of geography Univ of Reading 1968-89 (emeritus prof 1989-), visiting prof of city and regnl planning Univ of California 1980-; memb various govt bodies incl SE Regnl Econ & Planning Cncl 1960-79; FBA 1983, FRGS; *Books* London 2000 (1963), The Containment of Urban England (1973), Europe 2000 (1977), Great Planning Disasters (1980), High-Tech America (1986), Western Sunrise (1987), Cities of Tomorrow (1988), London 2001 (1989); *Recreations* walking; *Clubs* Athenaeum, RGS; *Style—* Prof Peter Hall; Institute of Urban and Regional Development, University of California at Berkeley, Berkeley CA 94720, USA (☎ 415 642 6579, fax 415 643 9576)

HALL, Sir Peter Reginald Frederick; KBE (1977, CBE 1963); s of Reginald Edward Arthur Hall, and Grace, *née* Pamment; *b* 22 Nov 1930; *Educ* Perse Sch Cambridge, St Catharine's Coll Cambridge (MA); *m* 1, 1956 (m dis 1965), Leslie Caron, the actress; 1 s, 1 da; m 2, 1965 (m dis 1981), Jacqueline Taylor; 1 s, 1 da; m 3, 1982 (m dis 1990), Maria Ewing, the mezzo-soprano; 1 da (Rebecca b 1982); *Career* dir: Oxford Playhouse 1954-55, Arts Theatre London 1955-57; fndr Int Playwrights' Theatre 1957, md RSC 1960-68 (created the RSC as a permanent ensemble, and opened the RSC's London home at the Aldwych Theatre), dir Nat Theatre of GB 1973-88, artistic dir Glyndebourne Festival Opera 1984-; assoc prof of drama Univ of Warwick; memb Arts Cncl of GB 1969-72; hon doctorates: York, Reading, Liverpool, Leicester, Cornell USA; winner Tony Award: 1967 for Pinter's Homecoming, 1981 for Shaffer's Amadeus; awarded Order des Arts et des Lettres, Sidney Edwards Award for Nat Theatre prodn of The Oresteia 1982; has directed over sixty major prodns in London, Stratford-upon-Avon and New York, including 19 Shakespeare plays, and the premieres of plays by Samuel Beckett, Harold Pinter, Tennessee Williams, Edward Albee, Jean Anouilh, Peter Shaffer, John Mortimer, John Whiting, Alan Ayckbourn; has directed opera at Covent Garden, Sadler's Wells, Glyndebourne, Geneva, Los Angeles, Houston, Chicago, the Metropolitan Opera New York and Bayreuth, and 8 films; productions incl: Waiting for Godot 1955, Gigi 1956, Love's Labours Lost 1956, Cat on a Hot Tin Roof 1958, Twelfth Night 1958, 1960 ad 1991, A Midsummer Night's Dream 1959 and 1963, Beckett 1961, The Collection 1962, The Wars of the Roses 1964, The Homecoming 1965 and 1973, The Magic Flute 1966, Macbeth 1967 and 1982, A Delicate Balance 1969, Perfect Friday 1969, La Calisto 1970, Bedroom Farce 1977, Don Giovanni 1977, Così Fan Tutte 1978 and 1988, The Cherry Orchard 1978, Betrayal 1978 and 1980, The Importance of Being Earnest 1982, Yonadab 1985, Carmen 1985 and 1986, Albert Herring 1985, Simon Boccanegra 1986, Salome 1986, La Traviata 1987, The Marriage of Figaro 1987, Entertaining Strangers 1987, Antony and Cleopatra 1988, The Winter's Tale 1988, Cymbeline 1988, The Tempest 1988, Orpheus Descending 1988, Falstaff 1988, The Merchant of Venice 1989, She's Been Away 1989, New Year 1989, The Wild Duck 1990; *Books* The Wars of the Roses (with John Barton), adaptation of Ibsen's John Gabriel Borkman (with Inga-Stina Ewbank), adaptation of George Orwell's Animal Farm, Peter Hall's Diaries; *Clubs* Garrick, Athenaeum, RAC; *Style—* Sir Peter Hall, KBE; The Peter Hall Co, 18 Exeter St, London WC2E 7DU (☎ 071 379 0438)

HALL, Prof Reginald; CBE (1989); s of Reginald Peacock Hall (d 1969), of Berwick upon Tweed, and Maggie Watson (d 1980); *b* 1 Oct 1931; *Educ* Univ of Durham (BSc, MB BS, MD); *m* 1, 1956, Joan, *née* Patterson (d 1959); 1 da (Susan b 1958); m 2, 11 June 1960, Molly, da of Clifford Vincent Hill (d 1977), of Frinton on Sea; 2 s (John b 1963, Andrew (twin) b 1963), 2 da (Amanda b 1962, Stephanie b 1966); *Career* Harkness fell Cwlth Fund and clinical res fell in med Harvard Univ and Mass Gen Hosp 1960-61, hon lectr in med Univ of Newcastle upon Tyne 1965-67 (Wellcome sr res fell in clinical sci 1964-67), hon conslt physician Royal Victoria Infirmary 1966-79; prof of med: Univ of Newcastle upon Tyne 1970-79, Univ of Wales Coll of Med 1980-; MRCP 1959, FRCP 1970; *Books* Fundamentals of Clinical Endocrinology (4 edn, 1989), Wolfe Atlas of Endocrinology (2 edn, 1990); *Style—* Prof Reginald Hall, CBE; 37 Palace Rd, Llandaff, Cardiff CF5 2AG; 22 Grantbridge St, Islington, London N1; 11 Brundholme Gardens, Keswick, Cumbria (☎ 0222 567 689)

HALL, Richard Iain; s of Harold Ross Hall, of Whitley Bay, Tyne and Wear, and Betty, *née* Little; *b* 4 Jan 1952; *Educ* Univ of Newcastle upon Tyne (MB BS, MD); *m* 13 Nov 1976, Fiona Lesley, da of Harry Smith Mackenzie (d 1987); 1 s (Christopher Richard b 1984), 2 da (Victoria Emma b 1978, Juliette Anna b 1980); *Career* first asst surgn Univ of Newcastle upon Tyne 1981-85, sr lectr and conslt surgn St James' Univ Hosp Leeds 1985-89, conslt surgn S Derbyshire Health Authy 1989; memb Br Soc of Gastroenterology 1985; FRCS; *Style—* Richard Hall, Esq; Derbyshire Royal Infirmary, London Rd, Derby (☎ 0332 47141)

HALL, Richard Martin; s of James Livingston Hall (d 1976), of Seaton, Devon, and Sybil, *née* Mycroft; *b* 8 July 1944; *Educ* Owen's Sch London, Balliol Coll Oxford (BA); *m* 2 Feb 1974, Caroline Jane, da of Gordon Ngaio Wright; *Career* Reckitt and Colman 1966-68, RHM Foods 1968-71, FGA Ltd 1971-76, Mettoy plc 1976-83, md FCO Ltd 1983-; *Recreations* golf, cricket; *Style—* Richard Hall, Esq; FCO Ltd, Eldon House, 1 Dorset St, London W1 (☎ 071 935 0334, fax 071 486 7092)

HALL, Robert; s of Lt-Col Henry Robert Hall, OBE, TD, DL, of La Landelle, Routex Des Landes, St Ouen, Jersey, CI, and Margaret Lucy, *née* Stobbart; *b* 14 Aug 1954; *Educ* Radley, Univ of Leeds (BA); *Career* reporter and presenter: Channel TV 1977-80, Yorkshire TV 1980-88; reporter ITN 1988-; *Recreations* walking, tennis, swimming; *Style—* Robert Hall, Esq; Independent Television News, 48 Wells St, London W1 (☎ 071 637 2424, fax 071 637 0349)

HALL, Robin Alexander; s of Leslie Alexander Hall (d 1984), and Sheila Mary, *née* Martin; *b* 19 May 1948; *Educ* Highbury Co GS; *m* 25 March 1977, Hazel Ann, da of Ronald William George Maidman; 2 s (James Alexander b 1978, Richard William b 1983), 1 da (Emma Rebecca b 1980); *Career* CA; audit mangr Arthur Young & Co 1969-75, investmt exec Nat Enterprise Bd 1976-79, fin dir Insac Products Ltd 1980-81, md CIN Venture Managers Ltd 1981-; non exec dir: RMT Group plc 1983-, Citylink Group plc 1983-, Gabicci plc 1984-, Sema Group plc 1985-; FCA 1972; *Style—* Robin Hall, Esq; CIN Venture Managers Ltd, Hobart House, Grosvenor Place, London SW1X 7AD (☎ 071 245 6911)

HALL, Ronald; s of John Hall (d 1960), and Amy Hall (d 1975); *b* 28 July 1934; *Educ* Dronfield GS, Pembroke Coll Cambridge (BA); *m* 1982, Christine; *Career* chief sub ed Topic Magazine 1962; Sunday Times: co-fndr Insight Team 1963, Insight ed 1964-66, asst ed 1966-68, managing ed of features 1969-77; ed Sunday Times Magazine 1978-81, jt dep ed Sunday Times 1981-82, ed Sunday Express Magazine 1982-86, associate ed London Daily News 1986-87, London ed Condé Nast Traveler New York 1987-, conslt ed Scotland on Sunday 1988-89; *Books* Scandal 63, A Study of The Profumo Affair (jtly), The Strange Voyage of Donald Crowhurst (with Nicholas Tomalin, 1970); *Recreations* chess, travel, building; *Style—* Ronald Hall, Esq; 13a Pond St, London NW3; (☎ 071 794 8849)

HALL, Simon Andrew Dalton; s of Peter Dalton Hall, CB, of Milton Keynes, Bucks, and Stella Iris, *née* Breen; *b* 6 Feb 1955; *Educ* Ampleforth, St Catharine's Coll Cambridge (MA), Coll of Law; *m* 26 Aug 1978, Teresa Ann, da of John Edmund Bartleet, of Great Tey, Colchester, Essex; 2 s (Teddy b 8 Dec 1980, Harry b 31 March 1983), 2 da (Rachael b 16 June 1979, Sophie b 18 March 1988); *Career* slr; articled clerk Freshfields 1977-79, seconded to Cravath Swaine & Moore 1983-84, Freshfields NY office 1984-85 (ptnr 1985); memb: Law Soc, Int Bar Assoc, City Slrs Co; *Books* Leasing Finance (jtly, 1985), Aircraft Financing (ed 1989); *Style—* Simon Hall, Esq; Freshfields, Whitefriars, 65 Fleet Street, London EC4Y 1HT (☎ 071 936 4000, fax 071 832 7001, telex 889292)

HALL, Simon Robert Dawson; s of Wilfrid Dawson Hall (d 1984), of Tunbridge Wells, and Elizabeth Helen, *née* Wheeler (d 1989); *b* 24 April 1938; *Educ* Tonbridge, Univ Coll Oxford (MA); *m* 30 Dec 1961, Jennifer, da of Cecil Henley Harverson; 2 s (Stephen b 1963, Andrew b 1964); *Career* 2 Lt 7 Royal Tank Regt 1956-58; asst master Gordonstoun 1961-65, jt head Dunrobin Sch 1965-68, housemaster and dep head Haileybury 1969-79, head Milton Abbey Sch 1979-87, warden Glenalmond Coll 1987-; FRSA 1983; *Recreations* reading, music, motoring, sailing, hill-walking; *Style—* Simon Hall, Esq; The Warden's House, Glenalmond College, Perth PH1 3RY (☎ 073 888 205)

HALL, Stephen Hargreaves; TD (1969); s of Walter Brian Hall (d 1987), and Marjorie Marian, *née* Hargreaves; *b* 30 April 1933; *Educ* Rugby, Christ's Coll

Cambridge (MA); *m* 9 July 1960, Nuala, da of Edward James Walker Stanley (d 1985); 2 s (Niall James b 1961, Patrick Thomas b 1963), 1 da (Victoria Jane b 1972); *Career* Nat Serv 2 Lt KOYLI Korea 1951-53, Maj TA 1953-70; ptnr Ernst & Young 1962-; non-exec dir: Yorkshire TV Holdings plc 1986-, Yorkshire TV Ltd 1973-; High Sheriff of Humberside 1981-82, memb Cncl Univ of Hull 1972-84; FCA; *Recreations* fishing; *Clubs* City of London, Army and Navy; *Style—* Stephen H Hall, Esq, TD; 10 Douro Place, London W8 5PH (☎ 071 937 1778); Becket House, 1 Lambeth Palace Rd, London SE1 7EU (☎ 071 928 2000, fax 071 928 1345)

HALL, Prof the Rev Stuart George; s of George Edward Hall (d 1980), of London, and May Catherine, *née* Whale; *b* 7 June 1928; *Educ* Univ Coll Sch, New Coll Oxford (BA, MA, BD); *m* 9 April 1953, Brenda Mary, da of Walter McLaren Henderson, OBE (d 1975), of Glasgow; 2 s (Lindsay b 1954, Walter b 1965), 2 da (Nicola (Mrs Nicholson) b 1956), Edith b 1959); *Career* Nat Serv RA/RAEC 1947-48; ordained: deacon 1954, priest 1955; asst curate Newark-upon-Trent 1954-58, tutor The Queen's Coll Birmingham 1958-62, lectr in theology Univ of Nottingham 1962-73 (sr lectr 1973, reader 1978), prof of ecclesiastical history King's Coll 1978-, ed Theologische Realenzyklopädie 1977-; memb: Studiorum Novi Testamenti Societas 1969, Academie Internationale de Science Religieuse 1983; *Books* Melito of Sardis and Fragments (1979); *Recreations* gardening, choral music, bad golf; *Clubs* Golf House (Elie); *Style—* Prof the Rev Stuart Hall; 15 High St, Elie, Leven, Fife KY9 1BY (☎ 0333 330 216); King's College, The Strand, London WC2R 2LS (☎ 071 836 5454, 071 673 5711)

HALL, Prof Stuart McPhail; s of Herman McPhail Hall (d 1980), of Kingston, Jamaica, and Jesse Merle, *née* Hopwood; *b* 3 Feb 1932; *Educ* Jamaica Coll, Merton Coll Oxford (Rhodes scholar, Jamaica scholar, BA, MA, DPhil); *m* 15 Dec 1964, Catharine Mary, da of Rev John Barrett; 1 s (Jesse b 1970), 1 da (Rebecca b 1968); *Career* lectr film and TV studies Chelsea Coll London 1961-64, dir Centre for Cultural Studies Univ of Birmingham 1968-79 (res fell 1964-68), prof of sociology The Open University 1979-; govr Poly of East London, tstee Photographer's Gallery, memb Advsy Ctee ICA; Hon DLitt Univ of Massachusetts 1988, hon fell Portsmouth Poly 1989, Centenary fell Thames Poly 1990; *Style—* Prof Stuart Hall; 5 Mowbray Road, London NW6 7QX (☎ 081 459 5372); Faculty of Social Science, The Open University, Walton Hall, Milton Keynes MK7 6AA (☎ 0908 653423)

HALL, Col Thomas Armitage; OBE (1966); o child of Athelstan Argyle Hall (d 1962), of Cricket St Thomas, Chard, Somerset; *Educ* Eton; *m* 24 Feb 1954, Mariette, da of Sir (Roger) Antony Hornby (d 1987); 2 s (Edward b 1960, John b 1964), 4 da (Jane b 1955, Annabel b 1956, Lucy (twin) b 1960, Catherine (twin) b 1964); *Career* Hon Col Royal Hussars 1974-83; Hon Corps of Gentlemen-at-Arms 1980-; High Sheriff Oxon 1981; dir Lloyds Bank 1982-, chm Int Language Centres 1971-88; *Recreations* skiing, shooting, travel; *Clubs* Cavalry and Guards'; *Style—* Col Thomas Hall, OBE; Marylands Farm, Chiselhampton, Oxford (☎ 0865 890350); 1 Riding House St, London W1 (☎ 071 637 5377)

HALL, Dr Trevor Henry; JP (Leeds 1959); s of H Roxby Hall, of Wakefield; *b* 28 May 1910; *Educ* Wakefield Sch, Trinity Coll Cambridge, Univ of Leeds (MA, PhD); *m* 1, 1937, Dorothy (d 1973), da of A Keningley, of Nostell; 1 s, 1 da; m 2, 1977, Marguerite, wid of Dr R McMorris; 1 step s, 1 step da; *Career* sr ptnr V Stanley Walker & Son Chartered Surveyors (Leeds, Wakefield, Rothwell, Morley and Bramhope) 1945-82; dir and former pres Huddersfield Bldg Soc (now Yorkshire Bldg Soc) 1958-82, dir and former chm (Northern and Scottish Bds) Legal & General Assur Soc 1962-82; chm Leeds Dist Ctee Nat Tst 1968-70, pres Leeds Library 1969-82; one of 300 invited fndr life members Cambridge Soc 1977; memb Oxford Univ Soc of Bibliophiles (lectr 1980 and 1982); Cecil Oldman Meml lectr in bibliography and textual criticism Univ of Leeds 1972; FSA, FRICS; *Books Incl:* The Testament of R W Hull (1945), The Strange Case of Edmund Gurney (1964), Strange Things (with Dr John Lorne Campbell, 1968), Sherlock Holmes, Ten Literary Studies (1969), Mathematical Recreations 1633: An Exercise in 17th Century Bibliography (1970), The Early Years of the Huddersfield Building Society (1974), Sherlock Holmes and his Creator (1978), Search for Harry Price (1978), The Strange Story of Ada Goodrich Freer (1979), Dorothy L Sayers: Nine Literary Studies (1980), The Leeds Library, A Check-List of Publications relating to its History from 1768 to 1977; *Style—* Dr Trevor Hall, JP; The Lodge, Selby, N Yorks YO8 0PW (☎ 0757 703372)

HALL, Dr Vernon Frederick; CVO (1960); s of Cecil Septimus Hall, and Maud Mary, *née* Fuller; *b* 25 Aug 1904; *Educ* Haberdashers' Aske's, King's Coll London, King's Coll Hosp Med Sch; *m* 19 Jan 1935, Constance Marcia, da of Rev H T Cavell, rector of Woodford Green, London; 1 s (Desmond Lawrence b 1937), 2 da (Judith Margaret b 1939, Janet Elizabeth b 1943); *Career* WWII RAMC advsr in anaesthetics to SE Asia Cmd, late dir of anaesthetics Indian and Burma Cmd, Brig; fell King's Coll London, fndr memb Faculty of Anaesthetists RCS, pres Assoc of Anaesthetics of GB & Ireland; anaesthetist to HM The Queen for births of her four children, also HRH The Princess Margaret and HRH Duchess of Kent, conslt anaesthetist King's Coll Hosp 1930 (dean Med Sch 1937-66); vice pres The Exmoor Soc; Univ of London: memb Senate, chm Bd of Advanced Med Studies, hon fell Faculty of Anaesthetists 1975, pres Assoc of Anaesthetists 1962-65 (hon fell); MRCS, LRCP, FFARCS; *Books* History of King's College Hospital Dental School, Scrapbook of Snowdonia; *Recreations* rugby, squash, tennis, riding; *Clubs* RAC; *Style—* Dr Vernon F Hall, CVO; 83A Foxgrove Rd, Beckenham, Kent BR3 2DA (☎ 081 650 2212)

HALL, Victor Edwin; s of Robert Arthur Victor James Hall (d 1978), of Selsey, Sussex, and Gladys, *née* Fukes (d 1986); *b* 2 March 1948; *Educ* Chichester HS for Boys, Univ of Hull (LLB); *m* 11 May 1974, Rosemarie Berdina, da of Walter Raymond Jenkinson, of Stoneygate, Eaton Hill, Baslow, Derby; 2 s (Timothy James b 24 July 1981, Matthew Peter b 16 Feb 1984); *Career* called to the Bar Inner Temple 1971; tenancy in chambers: Leicester 1972-89, London 1990-; rec Crown Ct 1988 (asst rec 1983-); memb Market Harborough Round Table 1981-88, vice chm E Farndon Parish Cncl 1987- (chm 1985-87), deacon Marlborough Evangelical Church 1989-; memb Inner Temple Soc; *Recreations* skiing, cooking, music, computers; *Style—* Victor Hall, Esq; 22 Old Buildings, Lincoln's Inn, London WC2A 3UJ

HALL, William; DFC (1944); s of Archibald Hall (d 1956), and Helen Macfadyen (d 1977); *b* 25 July 1919; *Educ* Paisley GS, Coll of Estate Mgmnt; *m* 1945, Margaret Semple, da of Robert Gibson (d 1965); 1 s (David b 1954), 3 da (Elinor b 1947, Elaine b 1951, Maureen b 1959); *Career* pilot RAF Bomber Cmd 1939-45, served Europe, M East and Burma (despatches); memb Lands Tbnl: Scotland 1971-, England & Wales 1979-; sr ptnr R & W Hall (chartered surveyors) 1949-79; chm RICS Scotland 1972; Hon Sheriff Paisley; *Recreations* golf; *Clubs* RAF; *Style—* William Hall, Esq, DFC; Windyridge, Brediland Road, Paisley PA2 9HF (☎ 050 581 3614)

HALL, Dr Zaida Mary; da of Maurice Megrah, QC (d 1985), and Jessie, *née* Halstead (d 1977); *b* 11 July 1925; *Educ* St Pauls Girls Sch, Univ of Oxford and St George's Hosp (MA, DM); *m* 1, 13 May 1950, Ruthven O Hall (d 1983); 4 s (Richard b 7 Dec 1953, David b 1 Sept 1955, Nigel b 19 Nov 1960, Peter b 16 Feb 1962); m 2, 6 July 1985, The Hon Sir Peter Ramsbotham, GCMG, GCVO, *qv*, s of The Right Hon Viscount Soulbury, GCMG, MC (d 1979); *Career* conslt psychiatrist 1971-; conslt psychotherapist Royal S Hants Hosp Southampton (currently hon res fell Dept of Psychiatry); special interests: gp therapy for identity problems of students, gp therapy for women victims of childhood sexual and emotional abuse; memb: Wessex Psychotherapy Soc, Waynflete Singers, Winchester Music Club; FRCPsych 1983, FRCP 1984, memb Gp Analytic Soc; *Books* Understanding Women in Distress (with Pamela Ashurst, 1989); *Recreations* choral singing, opera, gardening; *Clubs* The Lansdowne; *Style—* Dr Zaida Hall; Royal South Hants Hosp, Academic Department of Psychiatry, Southampton (☎ 0703 634288)

HALL-SMITH, Martin Clive William; s of Sydney Patrick Hall-Smith, of 30 The Drive, Hove, Sussex, and Angela Wilma, *née* Hall; *b* 21 July 1948; *Educ* Eton, Univ of Edinburgh (LLB), Selwyn Coll Cambridge (MA); *m* 17 Dec 1983, Victoria Mary, da of John Sherwood Stephenson, of West Mews, Wylam, Northumberland; 1 s (Edward b 28 July 1989), 2 da (Rose b 14 May 1985, Katharine b 21 April 1987); *Career* called to the Bar 1972; Freeman City of London 1978, Liveryman Worshipful Co of Loriners; *Recreations* music, skiing, walking, family life; *Clubs* City Livery; *Style—* M C W Hall-Smith, Esq; Chichester House, 64 High St, Hurstpierpoint, W Sussex; Goldsmith Building, Temple, London EC4 (☎ 071 353 7881, fax 071 353 5319)

HALL-THOMPSON, Maj (Robert) Lloyd; ERD (1953), TD (1956), JP (1959); s of Rt Hon Col Samuel Herbert Hall-Thompson JP, DL, MP (d 1954); *b* 9 April 1920; *Educ* Campbell Coll Royal Sch; *m* 1948, Alison (Freda), *née* Leitch; 1 s, 1 da; *Career* served RA, Maj 1939-56; joined Unionist Party 1938, vice pres Clifton Unionist Assoc (chm 1954-57), MP (U) Clifton 1969-73; memb (U) N Belfast NI Assembly 1973-75 (chief whip and ldr of Assembly 1974), memb (U) N Belfast NI Constitutional Convention 1975-76; dir of several companies; life govr and vice chm Samaritan Hosp Mgmnt Ctee 1958-73, memb NI Hosps Authy, pres and tstee N Belfast Working Men's Club 1954-90, pres Irish Draught Horse Soc, sec Half Bred Horse Breeders Soc; dep govr, chm of Exec and Mgmnt Ctee and steward of Down Royal Corp of Horse Breeders (incorp by Royal Charter 22nd Dec 1685 granted by King James II); chm Lagan Valley Cons Assoc, memb select vestry Holy Trinity Church Ballylesson Co Down, life memb Royal Ulster Agric Soc, memb Irish Thoroughbred Breeders Assoc, patron Friends of the Union; landowner; *Recreations* horse riding, hunting, racing, eventing, show jumping, horse breeding, golf, reading; *Clubs* Ulster; *Style—* Maj Lloyd Hall-Thompson, ERD, TD, JP; Maymount, Ballylesson, Co Down, N Ireland

HALLADAY, Eric; s of The Rev Albert Raymond Halladay (d 1969), of Loversal, Yorks, and Helena Nicholson, *née* Renton; *b* 9 July 1930; *Educ* Durham Sch, St John's Coll Cambridge (BA, MA), Ripon Hall Oxford; *m* 1 Aug 1956, Margaret Leslie, da of Leslie Baister (d 1946), of Newcastle; 1 s (Richard b 1963), 2 da (Claire b 1962, Katharine b 1966); *Career* Nat Serv 2 Lt 5 Regt RHA 1948-50; Exeter Sch 1954-60 (sr history master 1956-60), sr lectr RMA Sandhurst 1960-64; Grey Coll Univ of Durham 1964-: sr tutor 1964-80, vice master 1967-80, master 1980-89, rector 1989-, rector St Aidais Coll 1990-91, hon lectr in history; sec Durham Branch Soldiers Sailors and Airmen's Families Assoc 1976-89, memb N Eastern TA Volunteer Res Assoc 1978, pres and chm Durham Regatta 1982-88; *Books* The Buildings of Modern Africa (with D D Rooney, 1966), The Emergent Continent (1972), Rowing in England - A Social History (1990); *Recreations* rowing, gardening; *Clubs* Leander (Henley-on-Thames); *Style—* Eric Halladay, Esq; The Coign, Corbridge, Northumberland (☎ 0434 632838); Grey College, Durham (☎ 091 374 2961)

HALLAM, Edwin William Lewis; DFC (1945); s of Canon Henry James Brunsdon Hallam (d 1979), and Anita Muriel, *née* Lewis (d 1978); *b* 28 July 1923; *Educ* Denstone Coll Uttoxeter; *m* 14 Sept 1946, Barbara Mary, da of late Wilfred Anthony; 3 da (Elizabeth b 1950, Judith b 1953, Catherine b 1958); *Career* WWII 1942-46, RAF Aircrew 1942, cmmnd PO 1943, Flt Lt 1944, served 115 Sqdn Bomber Cmd (35 Ops); slr 1948, sr ptnr Thatcher and Hallam Slrs Midsomer Norton Bath 1949-89; pres Somerset Law Soc 1982-83, chm Cheshire Home Timsbury, memb Royal Br Legion; memb Law Soc; *Recreations* gardening, flying; *Clubs* RAF; *Style—* Edwin Hallam, Esq, DFC; Ragg House, Kilmersdon, nr Bath, Somerset (☎ 0761 32132); Island House, The Island, Midsomer Norton, nr Bath, Avon (☎ 0761 414646)

HALLAM, Bishop of (RC Diocese est 1980) 1980-; Rt Rev Gerald Moverley; s of William Joseph Moverley (d 1973), and Irene Mary, *née* Dewhirst (d 1964); *b* 9 April 1922; *Educ* St Bede's GS Bradford, Ushaw Coll Durham, Angelicum Univ Rome (JCD); *Career* ordained priest 1946, sec to Bishop of Leeds 1946-51, chllr Diocese of Leeds 1957, domestic prelate to HH Pope Paul VI 1965, titular bishop of Tinisa in Proconsulari (aux bishop of Leeds) 1968; *Style—* The Rt Rev the Bishop of Hallam; Quarters, Carsick Hill Way, Sheffield, S Yorks S10 3LT (☎ 0742 309101)

HALLAM, Valerie Jayne (Val); da of Joe Hallam (d 1987), of Derbyshire, and Margaret, *née* Goodwin; *b* 28 Dec 1960; *Educ* Buxton Girls' Sch (formerly Cavendish GS), Sheffield City Poly (BEd); *Career* hockey player; Buxton Mixed Club 1974-81, Staveley Women's Club 1981-86, Sheffield League Co team 1981-87, Rotherwick Women's Club 1986-; represented North 1983-87 (under 23 1982); England: under 23 1982, B 1982-83 and 1984-85, 27 full caps 1985-, played in World Cup Holland 1986 and Sydney 1990, played in Euro Cup London 1987 (Silver medal)); GB: 9 caps, played in Champions Trophy Germany 1989; player of the tournament Lada Tournament Luton 1989; represented Derbyshire Co netball 1975-81 (under 16, under 18, under 21), FA preliminary coach, memb Macclesfield Women's Football Club 1971-82; physical educn teacher Aston Comp Sch Rotherham 1986-; *Recreations* visiting places of antiquity, theatre, pop concerts, travelling, walking, playing and watching a wide range of sports; *Style—* Miss Val Hallam; 22 Sandy Acres Drive, Waterthorpe, Sheffield, South Yorkshire S19 6LS (☎ 0742 470983); All England Women's Hockey Assoc, 51 High St, Shrewsbury, Shropshire SY1 1ST (☎ 0743 233572, fax 0743 233583)

HALLATT, Ven David Marrison; s of John Vincent (d 1980), of Birkenhead, Cheshire, and Edith Elliott, *née* Leighton (d 1989); *b* 15 July 1937; *Educ* Birkenhead Sch, Univ of Southampton (BA), St Catherine's Coll Oxford (MA); *m* 19 Aug 1967, Margaret, da of Edmund Smitton, of Aughton, Ormskirk, Lancs; 2 s (Jonathan David b 1972, Timothy James b 1974); *Career* curate St Andrew's Maghull Liverpool 1963-67, vicar All Saints Totley Sheffield 1967-75, team rector St James and Emmanuel Didsbury 1975-89, archdeacon of Halifax 1989-; *Recreations* walking, birdwatching, crosswords, listening to music; *Style—* The Ven the Archdeacon of Halifax; 9 Healey Wood Gardens, Brighouse, W Yorks HD6 3SQ (☎ 0484 714553)

HALLCHURCH, David Thomas; TD; s of Walter William Hallchurch (d 1962), and Marjorie Pretoria Mary, *née* Cooper (d 1978); *b* 4 April 1929; *Educ* Bromsgrove, Trinity Coll Oxford (MA); *m* 1, 1954 (m dis 1972), Cherry, da of Basil Jagger (d 1980); 3 s (Nicholas b 1958, Nigel b 1960, Adrian b 1966); m 2, 1972, Susan Kathryn Mather Brennan, *née* Wilson; 2 step children (Myles b 1967, Kathryn b 1964); *Career* Maj Staffs Yeo (QORR) TA 1962; called to the Bar 1954, rec Crown Ct 1980; puisne judge of the High Ct of Botswana 1986-88; chm Mental Health Review Tbnl for W Mids 1979-86; *Recreations* tennis, golf; *Clubs* Vincent's (Oxford); *Style—* David Hallchurch, Esq, TD; Neachley House, Tong, nr Shifnal, Shropshire (☎ 090722 3542)

HALLER, (Bernard) John Frederick; s of Bernard Haller (d 1961), of Sheffield, and Ellen Louise Norah, *née* Holmes; *b* 1 Jan 1922; *Educ* Central Secdy Sch Sheffield, Univ of London (BSc); *m* 24 July 1948, Nora Mary (Lew), da of Charles David Lewis, MBE, of Hope, Derbys; 1 s (Nicholas b 1955), 2 da (Sally b 1957, Katherine b 1961); *Career* Beds & Herts Regt 1942-43, Glider Pilot Regt 1943-47 (despatches); GS master 1948-61; dir: Philip Harris Biological Ltd 1961-, Philip Harris Hldgs plc 1968- (md 1978-88, chm 1983-); involved in local charities incl St Giles' Hospice; FIBiol 1974; *Recreations* swimming, running, hill walking, amateur art; *Style—* John Haller, Esq; 54 Tudor Hill, Sutton Coldfield, W Mids B73 6BH (☎ 021 3546036); Philip Harris Hldgs plc, Lynn La, Shenstone, Staffs (☎ 0543 480 077, fax 0543 481 091)

HALLETT *see also*: Hughes Hallett

HALLETT, Heather Carol; QC (1989); da of Hugh Victor Dudley Hallett, QPM, of 20 Sportsfield, Sittingbourne Rd, Maidstone, Kent, and Doris Viola, *née* Churchill; *b* 16 Dec 1949; *Educ* Brockenhurst GS, St Hugh's Coll Oxford, (MA); *m* 20 April 1974, Nigel Vivian Marshall Wilkinson, s of John Marshall Wilkinson, of Saffronfield, Rowbarns Way, E Horsey, Surrey; 2 s (James b 1980, Nicholas b 1982); *Career* called to the Bar Inner Temple 1972; rec of Crown Court 1989; *Recreations* theatre, music; *Style—* Ms Heather Hallett, QC; 6 Pump Court, Temple, London EC4 (☎ 071 353 7242, fax 071 583 1667)

HALLETT, Jeffrey Paul; s of Raymond George Hallett (d 1985), of Weymouth, Dorset, and Norma Joan, *née* Humphries; *b* 14 Dec 1946; *Educ* Hardye's Sch Dorchester, St Peter's Coll Oxford (MA, BM BCh), Univ Coll Hosp Med Sch; *m* 21 March 1970, Margaret Elizabeth, da of Dr Henry Renwick Vickers; 1 s (David b 1974), 2 da (Mary b 1976, Susan b 1983); *Career* sr orthopaedic registrar on trg rotation of UCH and Westminster Hosp 1978-83, conslt orthopaedic surgn Ipswich Hosp 1983-; various pubns in jls; chm E Anglian Regnl (Med) Manpower Ctee; Br Orthopaedic Assoc: memb, chm Working Pty on Plaster Technicians, rep BSI Ctees HCC18 and HCC22; memb: BMA, RSM, Sesamoid Soc, UCH/Westminster Orthopaedic Club; cncllr and vice chm Pettistree Parish Cncl, hon treas Pettistree PCC; FRCS; *Books* Traction and Orthopaedic Appliances (jtly, 1983), Use of the Tourniquet in Hand Surgery (1984); *Recreations* sailing, bell ringing, sheep farming, Suffolk Punch horses, domestic poultry; *Clubs* Aldeburgh Yacht, Oxford & Cambridge Sailing Soc; *Style—* Jeffrey Hallett, Esq; The Laurels, The St, Woodbridge, Suffolk IP13 0HU (☎ 0728 746210); The Ipswich Hospital, Heath Rd, Ipswich, Suffolk IP4 5PD (☎ 0473 712233); 89 Berners St, Ipswich, Suffolk IP1 3LN (☎ 0473 251135)

HALLETT, Michael John; s of Arthur Ronald Hallett (d 1979), of Weymouth, Dorset, and Dorothy Muriel, *née* Stone; *b* 29 April 1940; *Educ* Weymouth GS, Bournemouth Municipal Coll of Art (IBP intermediate exam in Photography, City and Guilds final level exam in photography, Dorset County Athletics Colours), Manchester Poly UMIST (MPhil), Birmingham Poly (Dip in History of Art and Design); *m* 1970, Carol Ann, da of Norman Maurice Flint; 1 s (William James b 11 July 1977), 1 da (Emily Jane b 22 May 1975); *Career* photographer Studio 5 1959-60; lectr in photography: Leicester Coll of Art and Design 1960-65, Bournemouth and Poole Coll of Art 1965-66; lectr then sr lectr in photographic studies Manchester Coll of Art and Design and Manchester Poly 1966-69 and 1970-75, visiting prof Sch of Photographic Arts and Scis Rochester Inst of Technol NY 1969-70; Birmingham Poly: princ lectr Dept of Visual Communication 1975-82, head Sch of Photography 1975-78, dir BA (Hons) Graphic Design Course 1979, princ lectr Sch of History of Art Design and Contextual Studies Birmingham Inst of Art and Design 1982-; conf convenor for Rewriting Photographic History 1989, publishing ed Article Press 1990-; memb: Nat Cncl Inst of Incorporated Photographers 1966-69, Int Advsy Bd History of Photography jl 1988-, Associateship Panel and Fellowship Panel of History of Photography and Critical Writing Category RPS 1990-; dep chm Sector 7 Admissions and Qualifications Bd BIPP 1989-; Kodak Colour scholar Eastman Kodak Co 1964, life memb Stockport Harriers & Athletic Club 1975; FRSA 1964, FRPS 1967, FRIPP 1969, MBIM 1976, FCSD 1977; memb Euro Soc for the History of Photography 1981; *Books* Programmed Photography (with Jack Tait, 1967), Programmed Colour Photography (1970), Worcester Cathedral: A Grand View (1987), Arts Council Independent Photography Directory (with Barry Lane, 1989), Where to Study: Photography Film Video TV (1990), Rewriting Photographic History (1990), reg contrib British Journal of Photography, contrib Journal of Photography Annual 1970-88; *Style—* Michael Hallett, Esq; Holm Oak, 134 Henwick Rd, St Johns, Worcs, WR2 5PB (☎ 0905 425547); Birmingham Inst of Art and Design, Birmingham Polytechnic, Corporation St, Gosta Green, Birmingham B4 7DX (☎ 021 331 5881, fax 021 331 6543)

HALLGARTEN, Anthony Bernard Richard; QC; s of Fritz Hallgarten, and Friedel, *née* Liebmann (d 1986); *b* 16 June 1937; *Educ* Merchant Taylors', Downing Coll Cambridge (BA); *m* 16 Dec 1962, Katherine Anne, da of Kurt Borchard, and Ruth Borchard; 1 s (Joseph b 22 May 1970), 3 da (Ruth b 1 Feb 1965, Judy b 24 Oct 1966, Emily b 26 Oct 1972); *Career* called to the Bar, jr counsel 1962-78, leading counsel 1978-, bencher Middle Temple, advocate and arbitrator in commercial matters, head of chambers; chm: Inns of Ct/Bar Cncls Jt Regulations Ctee, chm Ctee on Waybills Br Maritime Law Assoc; chm Camden Victim Support, active in Soviet Jewry Movement; *Recreations* cricket, cycling, historical novels, visiting the Ariège; *Clubs* Garrick, MCC; *Style—* Anthony Hallgarten, Esq, QC; 3 Essex Court, Temple, EC4Y 9AL (☎ 071 583 9294, fax 071 583 1341, telex 893468)

HALLGARTEN, Dr Peter Alexander; s of Siegfried Salomon (Fritz) Hallgarten, and Friedel Liselotte, *née* Leibmann; *b* 29 Sept 1931; *Educ* Merchant Taylors, Univ of Zurich, Univ of London (PhD), Univ of Chicago; *m* 3 July 1960, Elaine, da of Sqdn Ldr Philip Braham, MBE; 2 s (Daniel Arthur b 1961, Simon Alfred b 1963), 1 da (Lisa Ann b 1966); *Career* chm Hallgarten Wines Ltd 1986- (joined 1958, md 1967); chm Wine and Spirit Assoc of GB and NI 1978-79; Liveryman Worshipful Co of Distillers 1968; FRSC, CChem; Chevalier De L'Ordre Du Merite Agricole France 1982; *Books* Liqueurs (special edn, 1973), Guide To The Wines Of The Rhone (1979), French and Danish Spirits and Liqueurs (special edn, 1983); *Recreations* golf, travel, music, theatre; *Style—* Dr Peter Hallgarten; 14 Antrim Grove, London NW3 4XR (☎ 071 722 1077); Dallow Rd, Luton, Beds LU1 1UR (☎ 0582 22538, fax 0582 23240)

HALLIBURTON, Ian Scott; s of George William Halliburton (d 1976), of Edinburgh, and Barbara Foster, *née* Grandage; *b* 30 Jan 1943; *Educ* Royal HS of Edinburgh; *m* 1, 14 June 1969 (m dis 1982), Patricia Mercer Harley (Pat); 1 s (Simon George b 1973), 1 da (Susan Gail (Susie) b 1975); m 2, 20 Aug 1982, Anne, da of George Morison Whitaker (d 1985), of Stornoway; *Career* gen banking trg 1961-63, RSAMD 1963-66, teacher trg Jordanhill Coll of Educn 1966-67, professional actor 1967-70, sales conslt Imperial Life Assurance Co of Canada 1970-71, asst dir Towry Law & Co (Scotland) Ltd 1971-78, dir James Finlay Services Ltd 1978-; vice chm Third Eye Centre (Glasgow) Ltd, chm Platform Music Socs Ltd, dir New Beginnings (Glasgow) Ltd; memb: Scottish Arts Cncl, Music Ctee Scottish Arts Cncl; *Recreations* hill walking, listening to music, supporting the arts; *Clubs* Western (Glasgow); *Style—* Ian Halliburton, Esq; James Finlay Financial Services Ltd, PO Box 58, 10-14 West Nile St, Glasgow G1 2PP (☎ 041 226 4451, fax 041 248 4751, telex 777844)

HALLIBURTON, Rev Canon (Robert) John; s of Robert Halliburton (d 1953), and Katherine Margery, *née* Robinson (d 1968); *b* 23 March 1935; *Educ* Tonbridge, Selwyn Coll Cambridge (BA, MA), Keble Coll Oxford (DPhil); *m* 15 April 1968, Jennifer Ormsby, da of John Walter Turner (d 1978); 2 s (Rupert Sinclair b 1969 d 1969, Julian Alexander John b 1972), 3 da (Rachel Helen b 1970, Naomi Katherine b 1975, Charlotte Sophia Louise b 1979); *Career* Nat Serv RCS 1956-58; asst curate St Dunstan's and All Saints Stepney 1961-67, vice princ St Stephen's House Oxford 1970-75 (tutor 1967-70), princ Chichester Theol Coll 1975-82, canon Chichester 1976-82, p-in-c All Souls St Margaret's-on-Thames 1982-90, canon residentiary St Paul's Cathedral London 1990-; conslt Anglican Roman Catholic Int Cmmn 1971-82, memb Doctrine Cmmn of C of E 1977-86; *Books* The Authority of a Bishop (1987), Educating Rachel (1988); contrib to: The Eucharist Today (1975), The Study of Liturgy (1979); *Recreations* music, gardening; *Clubs* Athenaeum; *Style—* The Rev Canon John Halliburton; 1 Amen Court, London EC4M 7BU (☎ 071 248 1817)

HALLIDAY, David Ralph; s of Walter Henry Halliday (d 1976), and Isabel Kathleen, *née* Blagdon; *b* 28 Sept 1952; *Educ* Devonport HS, Selwyn Coll Cambridge (MA); *Career* pension fund actuary; ptnr Bacon and Woodrow 1987- (joined 1974); FIA 1979; *Recreations* reading, bridge, opera, swimming, drinking; *Style—* David Halliday, Esq; 5 Sunnyside, Catford, London SE6 4UR; Bacon and Woodrow, St Olaf House, London Bridge City, London SE1 (☎ 071 357 7171, fax 071 378 8428, telex 8953206 BWLON G)

HALLIDAY, Mrs John; (Mary) Elizabeth; MBE (1980), JP (1958); da of Maj William Edmond Logan Stewart, DSO, JP, DL (d 1964), of Llanfair House, Llandovery, Dyfed, and Mary Adela Morland, *née* Rice (d 1969); *b* 20 Feb 1909; *Educ* St Mary and St Anne Abbots Bromley, Harcombe House, Mrs Hoster's Secretarial Training Coll; *m* 4 Dec 1935, (Ruthven) John Wyllie Halliday, s of Richard William Ruthven Halliday (d 1943), of Weston Mark, Upton Grey, Basingstoke, Hants; 1 s (David b 1939 d 1983); *Career* Army welfare offr and WVS canteen organiser WWII; gen cmmr of Income Tax 1959-84, borough cncllr 1957-62, pres Llandovery Royal Br Legion Women's Section 1958-, minister's rep Camarthenshire Exec Cncl and FPC (NHS) 1958-82; memb: Governing Body Church of Wales 1969-74, Cncl and Exec Trinity Coll Camarthen 1971-80; fndn memb Cncl of Coleg Elidyr Camphill Coll for Special Educn 1973-88; *Recreations* gardening, music; *Style—* Mrs John Halliday, MBE, JP; Llanfair House, Llandovery, Dyfed SA20 OYF (☎ 0550 20319)

HALLIDAY, Ian Francis; s of Michael Halliday; *b* 16 Nov 1927; *Educ* Lincoln Coll Oxford (MA); *m* 1952, Mary Busfield; 1 s, 2 da; *Career* chief exec Nat Enterprise Bd 1980, dir Lowndes Lambert Gp Ltd 1981-87, memb Bd Port of London Authy 1984-; FCA; *Style—* Ian F Halliday, Esq; 40 Finthorpe Lane, Huddersfield HD5 8TU (☎ 0484 530311)

HALLIDAY, James Gordon Tollemache; s of Col Cecil Alexander Tollemache Halliday, OBE, DL (d 1982), and Lilias Rollo Maitland, *née* Fischer; *b* 10 Feb 1947; *Educ* Beaumont Coll, Trinity Coll Dublin (MA); *m* 19 Sept 1970, (Mary Margaret) Anne, da of Patrick Joseph MacNamara; 1 s (Patrick b 1978), 2 da (Louise b 1974, Anna b 1981); *Career* slr; John Laing 1969-71, Foster Wheeler 1971-73, ptnr Foreman Laws Hitchin 1977-; memb Law Soc 1977; *Recreations* tennis, cricket, skiing, music; *Clubs* MCC; *Style—* James Halliday, Esq; Hillsbank House, Graveley, Herts (☎ 0438 355 477); Foreman Laws, 25 Bancroft, Hitchin Herts (☎ 0462 58 711, fax 0462 59 242)

HALLIDAY, Dr Norman Pryde; s of James Grieve Halliday (d 1962), of Tree House, Sandyford, Glasgow, and Jessie Thompson Hunter, *née* Pryde (d 1960); *b* 28 March 1932; *Educ* Woodside Glasgow, King's Coll London, KCH Med Sch London (MB BS, LRCP); *m* 25 Oct 1953, Eleanor, da of Alfred Walter Smith (d 1959), of Kingston-upon-Hull; 3 s (Allen Norman b 8 Sept 1955, Derek Clive b 17 March 1958, Jonathan Neil b 17 March 1963), 1 da (Susan Elaine b 25 Aug 1960); *Career* Nat Serv RAMC 1950-52; SRN 1955, qualified in med 1964; various appts: King's Coll Hosp, New End Hosp, Queen Mary's Hosp Kent, Royal Hosp Wolverhampton, Medway Hosp; Civil Serv 1970- (under sec 1977-); hon physician to HM The Queen; MRCS, DCH, FRSM; *Recreations* photography, sub-aqua diving, fashion, reading, DIY, cross-bow shooting; *Style—* Dr Norman Halliday; 12 Regalfield Close, Guildford, Surrey GU2 6YG (☎ 0483 236 267); Deptartment of Health, Alexander Fleming House, Elephant and Castle, London SE1 6BY (☎ 071 972 2829)

HALLIDAY, Vice Adm Sir Roy William; KBE (1980), DSC (1944); *b* 27 June 1923; *Educ* William Ellis Sch, Univ Coll Sch; *m* 1945, Dorothy Joan Meech; *Career* joined RN 1941, served WWII Fleet Air Arm (fighter pilot), test pilot Boscombe Down 1947-48, naval asst to Chief of Naval Info 1962-64, Cdr (Air) HMS Albion 1964-66, Capt 1966, Dep Dir Naval Air Warfare 1966-70, Capt D3 Far East Fleet and D6 Western Fleet 1971-73, Cdre (Intelligence) Def Intelligence Staff 1973-75, ADC to HM The Queen 1975, cmd Br Navy Staff Washington and naval attaché and UK nat liaison rep to SACLANT 1975-78, Dep CDS (Intelligence) 1978-81, dir gen Intelligence 1981-84; *Clubs* Royal Navy; *Style—* Vice Adm Sir Roy Halliday, KBE, DSC; Willow Cottage, Bank, nr Lyndhurst, Hants

HALLIDIE, Geoffrey Andrew; MBE (1942), TD (1945); s of Andrew Hallidie Smith Hallidie (d 1958), of Linton House, Linton, Cambridge, and Alice Maud Mary, *née* Deakin (d 1966); *b* 20 Nov 1904; *Educ* Radley, King's Coll Cambridge (MA); *m* 3 Aug 1929, (Marjorie) Zöe, da of Rev William Charles Eppstein (d 1928), of Lambourne Rectory, Abridge; 2 s (Mark b 5 May 1934, Nicholas b 8 Dec 1935); *Career* RE (TA) 1939, London Corps Troops Engrs 1939, Devon and Cornwall Engrs (TA) 1940, WO Demolition Greece 1941, Maj 27 Mil Mission 1942, OC 297 Corps FD Park Co Western Desert and later Italy, WO 1945, demobbed 1946, TARO until retiring age; Ransomes and Rapier Ltd 1926-28 (Egypt Nag Hamadi Barrage 1928-32), engr Guthries (sent to oil palm factory Malaya) 1934-38; farmer Suffolk 1945-65, Elvas Portugal 1965-88; sometime chm Serv Ctee Royal Br Legion (treas Bures Branch); MICE 1931; *Recreations* rowing, swimming; *Clubs* Royal Br Club (Lisbon); *Style—* Geoffrey Hallidie, Esq, MBE, TD; Quinta dos Passarinhos, Ribas de Cima, Bucelas 2760 Loures, Portugal (☎ 010 351 1985 5500)

HALLIFAX, Adm Sir David John; KCB (1983), KBE (1982); s of Vice Adm Ronald Hamilton Curzon Hallifax, CB, CBE, of Longcroft, Shedfield, Hants; *b* 3 Sept 1927; *Educ* Winchester; *m* 8 Dec 1962, Anne, da of Lt-Col John Matthew Blakiston-Houston (d 1984), of Beltrim Castle, Gortin, Co Tyrone; 2 s (Thomas b 1965, Matthew b 1967), 1 da (Louisa b 1964); *Career* joined RN 1945, Flag Offr 1 Flotilla 1978-80, COS to C-in-C Fleet 1980-82, Vice Adm and Dep Supreme Allied Cdr Atlantic 1982-84, Adm and Cmdt RCDS 1986-87; constable and govr Windsor Castle 1988-; *Recreations* sailing, woodwork, conchology, gardening; *Clubs* Royal Yacht Sqdn, Farmers', Pratt's, Pitt; *Style—* Adm Sir David Hallifax, KCB, KBE; c/o Lloyds Bank, Winchester, Hants

HALLINAN, Sir (Adrian) Lincoln; DL (Glam 1969); s of Sir Charles Hallinan, CBE (d 1981), of Cardiff, and his 1 w, Theresa Doris, JP (d 1961), da of Frederick William Holman, of Knole Park, Almondsbury, nr Bristol; *b* 13 Nov 1922; *Educ* Downside; *m* 1955, Mary Alethea (*see* Parry Evans, Mary), da of Dr Evan Parry-Evans, JP; 2 s, 2 da; *Career* called to the Bar 1950, recorder 1972, stipendiary magistrate S Glam 1976; Lord Mayor Cardiff 1969-70; Chevalier Palmes Academiques 1965, Chevalier Legion d' Honneur 1973; kt 1971; *Recreations* music, the arts; *Style—* Sir Lincoln Hallinan, DL

HALLINAN, Lady (Mary); *see*: Parry Evans, Mary

HALLISSEY, Michael; s of John Francis Hallissey, MBE (d 1986), and Mary, *née* Kendall; *b* 6 March 1943; *Educ* Royal GS Lancaster, Magdalen Coll Oxford (MA); *Career* CA; Price Waterhouse: staff accountant 1964-68, asst mangr Melbourne 1969-70, mangr Milan 1970-71, sr mangr London 1971-74, audit ptnr London 1974-79, practice devpt ptnr UK 1979-81, strategic planning ptnr UK 1981-82, corp fin ptnr London 1982-85, head corp fin servs UK 1985-87, head strategic planning world firm

1987-88, dir strategy Price Waterhouse Europe 1988-; FCA 1968, FRSA; *Books* numerous articles on corporate strategy, strategic planning, mergers and acquisitions; *Recreations* politics, sailing, music, opera, good food; *Style—* Michael Hallissey, Esq; 49 Whitelands House, Cheltenham Terrace, London SW3 4QX; Price Waterhouse, Southwark Towers, 32 London Bridge St, London SE1 9SY (☎ 071 407 8989, fax 071 378 0647, telex 884657)

HALLIWELL, Brian; s of Norman Halliwell (d 1980), of Preston, Lancs, and Emma, *née* Kay (d 1981); *b* 17 Dec 1930; *Educ* Preston GS, Central London Poly Sch of Mgmnt (DMS); *m* 2 March 1957, Agnes, *née* Lee; *Career* RAOC 1949-51; HM Customs and Excise: joined 1947, princ 1969, asst sec 1973, dep accountant gen 1976, accountant and comptroller gen 1980-85; head of VAT Servs KPMG Peat Marwick McLintock 1989- (VAT conslt 1985-); pres Customs Annuity and Benevolent Fund Inc 1985- (dir 1981-); FBIM 1985; *Recreations* chess, reading, sport; *Style—* Brian Halliwell, Esq; 3 Knollcroft, Ulster Ave, Shoeburyness, Southend-on-Sea SS3 9JY (☎ 0702 297 570); KPMG Peat Marwick McLintock, PO Box 486, 1 Puddle Dock, Blackfriars, London EC4V 3PD (☎ 071 236 8000 ext 6431, fax 071 248 6552 (gp 3))

HALLIWELL, Thomas Morton; s of Rev Dr Thomas Halliwell (d 1982), of Pembrokshire, and Kathleen, *née* Morton; *b* 17 June 1945; *Educ* Marlborough, Coll of Law; *m* 11 April 1970, Susan Winifred, da of Maj F Fitt, of Mallorca; 1 s (Giles b 1973), 1 da (Rebecca b 1971); *Career* admitted slr 1969, dist notary 1984, memb Regnl Duty Slrs Ctee 1985-90; memb Law Soc; *Recreations* fishing, photography, ceramics, music; *Style—* Thomas M Halliwell, Esq; Perrymead Dilwyn, Hereford (☎ 0544 318 514); Topaze, Anzere, Switzerland; The Old Merchants House, Leominster, Herefords (☎ 0568 6333, fax 0568 4013)

HALLSTROM, Dr Cosmo Oliver Sven; s of Björn Hallstrom (d 1969), and Lolo, *née* Bergenthal; *b* 21 Oct 1946; *Educ* Haberdashers' Aske's, Univ of Liverpool (MB ChB, MD); *m* 1 Sept 1984, Diana Wendy, da of Derek Buckland, of 49 Grove Way, Esher, Surrey; 1 s (Oliver b 1989), 1 da (Sophie b 1987); *Career* lectr Inst of Psychiatry 1977-79, res psychiatrist Rockland Res NY USA 1979-81, clinical asst prof of psychiatry Univ of NY 1980-82, conslt psychiatrist Charing Cross Hosp 1982-; pubns on tranquillizer addictions and the psychopharmacology of depression and anxiety; fndr memb Mgmnt Ctee of Broadway Housing, memb Tranx Steering Gp; MRCP, MRCPsych; *Recreations* countryside, family, friends, skiing, travel; *Style—* Dr Cosmo Hallstrom; Charing Cross Hosp, Dept of Psychiatry, Fulham Palace Rd, London W6 8RF (☎ 081 846 1502, fax 071 622 5402)

HALLSWORTH, Norris Edward; s of Norris Carl Hallsworth; *b* 9 March 1941; *Educ* Long Eaton GS; *m* 1964, Sylvia Christine, da of Leonard Smith; 2 s; *Career* chartered accountant; md Slack & Parr; holder of various other gp directorships; *Clubs* Longcliffe Golf; *Style—* Norris Hallsworth Esq; 28 Shepshed Rd, Hathern, Loughborough, Leics

HALLWORTH, David Malcolm; s of Frank Hallworth (d 1961), of Mapperley, 34 Arthog Rd, Hale, Altrincham, Cheshire, and Irene Mildred, *née* Perry (d 1973); *b* 17 April 1930; *Educ* Shrewsbury, Univ of Oxford (MA); *m* 16 May 1959, Joan Stewart, da of Leslie Arnold (d 1968), of Timperley, Altrincham, Cheshire; 3 da (Alison b 1961, Claire b 1963, Sarah b 1965); *Career* slr 1957; ptnr: Hall Brydon and Co Slrs Manchester 1959-79, Foysters Slrs Manchester 1979-89; conslt Davies Wallis Foyster Slrs 1989-; former memb Cncl Manchester Law Soc 1966-78 (hon treas 1976-78); Oxford half blue: for golf 1951 and 1952 (full blue 1953), for Eton fives 1953; memb: Law Soc 1957-, Manchester Law Soc 1960-; *Recreations* physical exercise, singing; *Clubs* Hale Golf, Royal St Davids Golf (Harlech), Bowdon Cricket Hockey and Squash; *Style—* David Hallworth, Esq; Redcroft, Belmont Rd, Hale, Altrincham, Cheshire (☎ 061 928 2346); 34 Ty Canol, Harlech, Gwynedd, N Wales; Davies Wallis Foyster, Harvester House, 37 Peter St, Manchester M2 5GB (☎ 061 228 3702, fax 061 835 2407)

HALPERN, Sir Ralph Mark; *b* 1938; *Educ* St Christopher Sch Letchworth; *m* Joan Halpern, JP, *née* Donkin; 1 da; *Career* trainee with Selfridges; The Burton Group 1961-90: joined Peter Robinson 1961, developed Top Shop chain 1968, chief exec Burton Retail, chm Peter Robinson and Top Shop 1977, chm The Burton Group plc 1981-90 (md 1978, chief exec 1978-90); Confederation of British Industry: chm Mktg and Consumer Affairs Ctee 1984-, memb City-Industry Task Force 1986-, memb President's Ctee; chm British Fashion Cncl 1990-; FInstD, CBIM; kt 1986; *Clubs* Reform; *Style—* Sir Ralph Halpern; c/o The Reform Club, 104 Pall Mall, London SW1Y 5EW

HALPIN, William Richard Crozier; yr s of William Henry Halpin (d 1937), of Ford Lodge, Cavan, Ireland, and Caroline Isabella Emma, da of Albert Hutton, JP, of Rockwood House, Swanlinbar, Co Cavan; *b* 28 June 1912; *Educ* Rugby, CCC Cambridge; *m* 25 Nov 1939, Hilary Alicia, da of Col Gilbert Henry Keighley-Bell, of Hurlingham Court, Putney; 1 s, 2 da; *Career* chm: Premier Consolidated Oilfields 1957-63, North Sea Oil Finders 1972-76, Albion 1974-80; dep chm: Fine Fare 1963-68, S & K Holdings 1970-72; fin controller Assoc Br Foods 1963-68, md Knight Wegenstein 1968-70; dir: Francis Industs 1972-83, Polly Peck 1983-; FCA; *Recreations* beagling; *Clubs* Carlton; *Style—* William Halpin, Esq; 11 Provost Rd, London NW3 4ST (☎ 071 722 4637)

HALSBURY, 3 Earl of (UK 1898); John Anthony Hardinge Giffard; also Baron Halsbury (UK 1885), and Viscount Tiverton (UK 1898); s of 2 Earl of Halsbury (d 1943; himself s of 1 Earl, lawyer, MP, solicitor-gen and lord chllr of three Conservative administrations), and Esmé Stewart Wallace (d 1973); *b* 4 June 1908; *Educ* Eton; *m* 1, 1 Oct 1930 (m dis 1936), Ismay Catherine, da of Lt-Col Lord Ninian Crichton-Stuart; 1 s; m 2, 12 Dec 1936, Elizabeth Adeline Faith (d 1983), da of Maj Harry Godley, DSO, and his w Elizabeth Mary (great niece of 3 Earl Annesley); 2 da; *Heir* s, Adam Edward Giffard (Viscount Tiverton, but does not use title); *Career* sits as Independent peer in House of Lords; md Nat Research Devpt Corp 1949-59; memb: DSIR Advisory Cncl 1950-55, SRC 1967-71; chm Science Museum Advsy Cncl 1951-65, first chllr Brunel Univ 1966, chm Meteorological Ctee 1970-82; memb: Standing Cmmn on Museums and Galleries 1960-76, MRC 1973-77, Ctee of Mangrs Royal Instn 1976-79; govr: LSE 1959-88, BBC 1960-62, UMIST 1966-; Hon DTech Brunel 1966, Hon DUniv Essex 1968; Hon FRSC, FEng, FRS; *Recreations* music, philosophy, mathematics; *Clubs* Athenaeum, RAC; *Style—* The Rt Hon the Earl of Halsbury, FRS; 4 Campden House, 29 Sheffield Terrace, London W8 7NE (☎ 071 727 3125)

HALSEY, Prof Albert Henry; s of William Thomas Halsey, and Ada, *née* Draper (d 1976); *b* 13 April 1923; *Educ* Kettering GS, LSE (BSc, PhD); *m* 12 April 1944, (Gertrude) Margaret, da of Herbert Arthur Littler (d 1979), of Winsford, Cheshire; 3 s (Robert William b 13 July 1958, David b 16 Feb 1966, Mark b 22 Dec 1967), 2 da ((Catherine) Ruth b 10 April 1955, Lisa Jane b 13 Oct 1964); *Career* RAF: Cadet Pilot 1942-45, Sgt 1945, Flt Sgt 1946-47; lectr in sociology Univ of Liverpool 1952-54, sr lectr in sociology Univ of Birmingham 1954-62, dir Dept of Social and Admin Studies Univ of Oxford 1962-, professorial fell Nuffield Coll Oxford 1962-, advsr to Sec of State for Educn 1964-66; Hon DSSC Univ of Birmingham 1987, Hon Doctorate Open Univ 1990, American Acad of Arts and Sciences 1988; *Books* Social Class and Educational Opportunity (with J E Floud and F M Martin, 1956), Technical Change and Industrial Relations (with W H Scott et al), The Sociology of Education - A Trend Reports and Bibliography (with J E Floud, 1958), Education, Economy and Society (with J E Floud and C A Anderson, 1961), Ability and Educational Opportunity (1962), Power in Co-operatives (with G N Ostergaard, 1965), Social Survey of the Civil Service (with Ivor Crewe, 1966-68), The British Academics (with Martin Trow, 1971), Trends in British Society Since 1900 (ed, 1972), Educational Priority (ed, 1972), Traditions of Social Policy (ed, 1976), Power and Ideology in Education (with J Karabel, 1977), Heredity and Environment (1977), Change in British Society (1978, 1981, 1986), Origins and Destinations (with A F Heath and J M Ridge, 1980), Faith in the City (1985), British Social Trends Since 1900 (1988), English Ethical Socialism: from Thomas More to R H Tawney (with N Dennis, 1988); author of over 250 articles in various learned jls; *Recreations* gardening and squash; *Style—* Prof A H Halsey; 28 Upland Park Rd, Oxford OX2 7RU (☎ 0865 58625); Nuffield College, Oxford, OX1 1NF (☎ 0865 278521)

HALSEY, Rev Sir John Walter Brooke; 4 Bt (UK 1920); s of Sir Thomas Edgar Halsey, 3 Bt, DSO (d 1970); *b* 26 Dec 1933; *Educ* Eton, Magdalene Coll Cambridge; *Heir* kinsman, Nicholas Guy Halsey, TD, b 1948; *Career* deacon 1961, priest 1962 Diocese of York, curate Stocksbridge 1961-65, brother in Community of the Transfiguration 1965-; *Style—* The Reverend Brother John Halsey; Community of the Transfiguration, 23 Manse Road, Roslin, Midlothian EH25 9LF

HALSEY, (James) Richard; s of James Henry Halsey (d 1989), of Tavistock, Devon, and May Doris, *née* Hunt; *b* 19 July 1946; *Educ* St Albans Sch; *m* 6 Jan 1973, Maureen Claire, da of Trevor Henry Alfred Taylor, of Tedburn St Mary, Devon; *Career* specialist antique dealer (early oak and walnut furniture and allied items), guest lectr on antiques and their devpt in the English home; former memb: Tedburn Village Hall Ctee, Tedburn Charity Ctee; former: parish cncllr for 10 years (chm 1984-86), sch govr; *Recreations* studying vernacular architecture, countryside; *Clubs* Veteran Car; *Style—* James R Halsey, Esq; Lower Cadham Farm, Jacobstowe, nr Okehampton, Devon (☎ 0837 85288)

HALSTEAD, Sir Ronald; CBE (1976); s of Richard Halstead, of Burton-in-Lonsdale, Lancs, and late Bessie, *née* Harrison; *b* 17 May 1927; *Educ* Lancaster Royal GS, Queens' Coll Cambridge; *m* 1968, Yvonne Cecile (d 1978), da of Emile de Monchaux (d 1970), of Australia; 2 s; *Career* chm Beecham Prods 1967-84; Beecham Group plc: md Consumer Prods 1973-84, chm and chief exec 1973-84; non-exec dir: Br Steel plc 1979- (dep chm 1986-), The Burmah Oil plc 1983-89, Davy Corporation plc 1986-, Gestetner Holdings plc 1983-89, American Cyanamid Co 1986-; chm: Knitting Sector Gp NEDC 1978-, Garment and Textile Sector Gp NEDC 1991-, Nat Coll of Food Technol 1978-83, Bd for Food Studies Univ of Reading 1978-83, Industl Devpt Advsy Bd DTI 1985- (memb 1983-); memb Cncl and Exec Ctee Food Mfrs Fedn Inc 1966-86 (pres 1974-76); memb Cncl: CBI 1970-86, Univ of Buckingham 1973-, Univ of Reading 1978, Trade Policy Res Centre 1985-89; vice chm The Advertising Assoc 1973-81, dir and hon treas Centre for Policy Studies 1984-, memb Priorities Bd for R & D in Agric and Food for MAFF 1984-87, tstee Inst of Econ Affrs 1980-, govr Ashridge Mgmnt Coll 1970- (vice chm 1977-); memb: Cncl Trade Policy Res Centre 1985-89, Newspaper Panel Monopolies and Mergers Cmmn 1980-; memb Cncl and Exec Ctee Imperial Soc of Knights Bachelor 1986-; Hon DSc: Reading 1982, Lancaster 1987; hon fell Queens' Coll Cambridge 1985; FBIM, FRSA, FRSC, FInstM (Hon 1982), FIGD, fell Mktg Soc, Hon FIFST; kt 1985; *Recreations* squash racquets, skiing; *Clubs* Brook's, Athenaeum, Carlton, Lansdowne, Royal Thames Yacht, Hurlingham; *Style—* Sir Ronald Halstead, CBE; 37 Edwardes Square, London W8 6HH (☎ 071 603 9010); British Steel plc, 9 Albert Embankment, London SE1 7SN (☎ 071 735 7654, telex 916061)

HALSTED, Nicolas; s of Erik Jacob Halsted (d 1976), and Winifred Lena Henrietta, *née* Lever; *b* 24 Oct 1942; *Educ* Westminster, Wadham Coll Oxford (MA); *m* 23 Sept 1972, Clare June, da of Sir Douglas Henley, KCB, of Banstead, Surrey; 2 s (Benjamin b 1977, Laurence b 1984), 1 da (Alexandra b 1981); *Career* admitted slr 1968; corporate legal advsr Reed Int plc 1983-; pres Amateur Fencing Assoc; memb Law Soc; *Recreations* fencing, tennis, theatre; *Style—* Nicolas Halsted, Esq

HALTON, Nicholas Allen; s of Eric Creighton Halton (ka 1941), of Carlisle, and Diana Mabel, *née* Carr (now Mrs Wilkinson); *b* 26 Aug 1940; *Educ* Marlborough, Emmanuel Coll Cambridge; *m* 1, 17 Sept 1966 (m dis 1981), Nicola Mary Wynne (d 1982), da of Gerald Mole (d 1971); 1 da (Candida b 27 Feb 1974); m 2, 21 Jan 1983 (m dis 1986), Diana Jane, *née* Hall; *Career* admitted slr 1966; Esso Group 1968-: legal advsr and co sec Esso Petroleum Co Ltd 1979-82, sr cncl Esso Europe Inc 1982-86, gen cncl Esso Europe-Africa Servs Inc 1986-; memb Putney Soc, hon treas Putney Cons Assoc 1985-90, memb Indust Tribunals 1977-87, exec tstee Petroleum and Mineral Law Educn Tst 1981-, chm Insolvency Practitioners Tribunal 1987-, vice chm and treas Section on Energy Law Int Bar Assoc; memb Law Soc 1966; *Recreations* sport, walking, reading; *Clubs* Roehampton; *Style—* Nicholas Halton, Esq; 36 Granard Ave, Putney, London SW15; Esso House, Victoria St, London SW1 (☎ 071 834 6677, fax 071 245 3146)

HALUCH, (Stefan) James; s of Stefan L Haluch, and Elizabeth, *née* Wallace; *b* 9 March 1944; *Educ* St Mary's Acad Bathgate; *m* 25 May 1968, Joyce Vevers, da of late George S McClelland; 2 s (James b 1969, Eoin b 1974), 2 da (Helena b 1965, Shelagh b 1971); *Career* sales mangr (advertising) Scotsman Publications Ltd 1965-70, sr ptnr Athol Business Consultants 1970-75, md Athol Restaurants Ltd (Hoteliers) 1975-88, chm Highland Coach Tour Hotels Ltd 1987-88, business and mktg conslt 1988-, UK sales trg mangr Sight and Sound Education Ltd 1988-; chm Isle of Arran Tourist Bd 1980-83, pres Isle of Arran Licensed Trade Assoc 1983-86; former councillor: Bathgate Town Cncl, W Lothian CC; MBIM; *Recreations* music, travel; *Style—* James Haluch, Esq; 150 Easter Bankton, Livingston, W Lothian, Scotland EH54 9BH

HAMADAH, Dr Kamel; s of His Honour Judge Ahmad Hamadah (d 1972), of Cairo, and Khadouga, *née* El Gindi (d 1950); *b* 20 April 1929; *Educ* Khaediveyah Sch Cairo, Cairo Univ Med Sch (MB BCh), Air Shams Univ Cairo (DPM & Neurology); *m* 27 March 1969, Brenda Olive, da of Capt Alfred Mullinger, DCM (d 1980), of London; *Career* conslt psychiatrist: SW Metropolitan Regnl Hosp Bd 1973-75, St Thomas' Health Dist 1975-; clinical tutor Tooting Bec Hosp 1973-74, hon assoc clinical tutor 1975-77, med administrator 1973-77; chm: Tooting Bec & St Thomas' Health Dist Rehabilitation Ctee 1975-85, Psychiatrists Ctee St Thomas' Health Dist 1979-82 (Psychiatry Mgmnt Team 1978-79), Southern Div RCPsych 1980-84 (hon sec 1977-80); examiner of RCPsych 1980-85 (sr organiser of membership examination 1978-), med advsr to Health Ctee GMC 1980- (med examiner 1980-), recognised teacher Univ of London 1982-, memb Visiting Team Health Advsy Serv 1984, dep regnl advsr in psychiatry South East Thames RHA 1984-90, nat advsr Nat Counselling and Welfare Serv for Sick Doctors 1985-, cmmr Mental Health Act Cmmn 1986- (appointed Dr 1983-); contrib: Lancet, British Medical Journal, Biochem Journal, Biochem Society Transcripts, British Journal of Psychiatry; LMSSA 1967, MRCPsych 1972, FRCPsych 1977; memb: Br Assoc of Psychopharmacology, Assoc of Univ Teachers, World Fedn In Mental Health; *Recreations* shooting, walking; *Style—* Dr Kamel Hamadah; St Thomas' Hospital, London SE1 7EH (☎ 071 928 9292)

HAMAL, Dr Prem Bikram; s of Maj Dala Bahadur Hamal (d 1968), of Kathmandu,

Nepal, and Sushila Devi Hamal (d 1982); *b* 22 Feb 1935; *Educ* Patan HS, Patna Univ of India, Univ of London (DPath, LRCP, MRCS); *m* 10 May 1961, Shanti, da of Mohan Singh Hamal, of Kathmandu, Nepal; 2 s (Abhinna Bikram b 1963, Bobby Kikram b 1970), 1 da (Anokha b 1965); *Career* served Nepalese Army MO 1960 at Nepal China Bordez; house offr King George's Med Coll India 1960; med offr: Sallyan Health Centre Sheoraj Hosp Nepal 1960-64, Pathology Laboratory Chest Clinic Kathmandu Nepal 1964-65; registrar Central Laboratory Portsmouth Hants 1965-66, house offr in medicine IOW Co Hosp 1966-67, registrar in pathology Birch Hill Hosp Rochdale 1967-69; Dudley Rd Hosp and Med Sch Birmingham: registrar in pathology 1969-71, sr registrar 1971-75; chm: Nepalese Drs Assoc UK 1985-87, Overseas Drs Assoc Wakefield 1986-90; MRCPath 1970, FRCpath 1982; *Recreations* gardening, badminton; *Style*— Dr Prem Hamal; 9 Attlee Crescent, Sandal, Wakefield, W Yorks WF2 6RF (☎ 0924 258347); Consultant Pathologist, Pinderfields General Hospital, Aberford Rd, Wakefield, W Yorks WF1 4DG (☎ 0924 375217)

HAMBLEDEN, Dowager Viscountess; Lady Patricia; *née* Herbert; GCVO (1990, DCVO 1953), JP (1961); da of 15 Earl of Pembroke and (12 Earl of) Montgomery, JP, DL (d 1960), by his w, Lady Beatrice Paget, CBE (yr da of Lord Alexander Paget, and sis of 6 Marquess of Anglesey, GCVO); *b* 12 Nov 1904; *m* 26 Sept 1928, 3 Viscount Hambleden (d 1948, s of 2 Viscount by Lady Esther Gore, 3 da of 5 Earl of Arran); 3 s (4 Viscount, Hon Richard and Hon Philip Smith, *qqv*), 2 da (Hon Mrs Brand, Hon Mrs Townend, *qqv*); *Career* lady-in-waiting to HM The Queen (now HM Queen Elizabeth The Queen Mother) 1937-; *Style*— The Rt Hon the Dowager Viscountess Hambleden, GCVO, JP; Hill House, Ewelme, Oxon (☎ 0491 39242)

HAMBLEDEN, 4 Viscount (UK 1891); William Herbert Smith; s of 3 Viscount (d 1948), and Lady Patricia Herbert (*see* Dowager Viscountess Hambleden); *b* 2 April 1930; *Educ* Eton; *m* 1955 (m dis 1988), Donna Maria Carmela Attolico di Adelfia, da of Conte Bernardo Attolico, of Rome; 5 s; m 2, 1988, Mrs Lesley Watson; *Heir* s, Hon William Henry Smith; *Style*— The Rt Hon the Viscount Hambleden; The Estate Office, Hambleden, Henley-on-Thames, Oxon RG9 6RJ

HAMBLEN, Prof David Lawrence; s of Reginald John Hamblen, of Woolwich, London, and Bessie, *née* Williams; *b* 31 Aug 1934; *Educ* Roan Sch Greenwich, The London Hosp Med Coll (MB BS); *m* 16 Nov 1968, Gillian Frances, da of Edgar Leonard Bradley, OBE, of Bearsden, Glasgow; 1 s (Neil Andrew b 1975), 2 da (Sarah Catherine b 1970, Clare Alison b 1974); *Career* Nat Serv RAMC 16 Para Bde, Maj TA 44 Para Bde, reg army res offr 1972-89; fell in orthopaedics Harvard Med Sch, clinical and res fell Mass Gen Hosp Boston USA 1966-67, lectr in orthopaedics Univ of Oxford 1967-68, sr lectr in orthopaedic surgery Univ of Edinburgh 1968-72, prof of orthopaedic surgery Univ of Glasgow; pres Br Orthopaedic Assoc; FRCS, FRCS Edinburgh, FRCS Glasgow; *Books* Outline of Orthopaedics (co-author 11 edn, 1990); *Recreations* golf; *Clubs* RSM; *Style*— Prof David Hamblen; 3 Russell Drive, Bearsden, Glasgow G61 3BB (☎ 041 942 1823); University Department of Orthopaedic Surgery, Western Infirmary, Glasgow G11 6NT (☎ 041 339 8822 ext 4678)

HAMBLEN, Nicholas Archibald; s of Derek Ivens Archibald Hamblen, CB, OBE, of Chelsea, London, and Pauline Alison, *née* Morgan; *b* 23 Sept 1957; *Educ* Westminster, St John's Coll Oxford (MA), Harvard Law Sch (LLM); *m* 13 July 1985, Catherine Gwenllian (Kate), da of Peter Hayden, of Chatcull House, Chatcull, Staffs; 1 da (Eleanor Rose b 16 Nov 1990); *Career* called to the Bar Lincoln's Inn 1981; barrister specialising in commercial law and arbitration; *Recreations* cricket, opera; *Clubs* MCC, Hurlingham; *Style*— Nicholas Hamblen, Esq; 3 Essex Court, Temple, London EC4Y 9AL (☎ 071 583 9294, telex 893468 SXCORT G, fax 071 583 1341)

HAMBLETON, Dr Garry; s of Gerald Hambleton, of Marple, Cheshire, and Margaret, *née* Hodson; *b* 26 Aug 1940; *Educ* Manchester GS, Wadham Coll Oxford, Guy's Hosp London (BM BCh, MA, LMSSA); *m* 28 Dec 1963, (Kathleen) Mary, da of James Alfred Salthouse (d 1976) of Accrington, Lancs; 2 da (Sophie b 1967, Anna b 1969); *Career* conslt paediatrician: Trafford Health Authy 1975-83, Salford Health Authy 1983-; FRCP 1980; *Books* Manual of Hospital Paediatrics (1988), scientific articles connected with paediatrics; *Recreations* singing, music, cricket, gardening, ornithology; *Style*— Dr Garry Hambleton; 8 Manor Close, Cheadle Hulme, Cheadle, Cheshire SK8 7DJ (☎ 061 485 8852); Royal Manchester Children's Hosp, Hospital Rd, Pendlebury, Manchester M27 1HA (☎ 061 794 4696)

HAMBLETON, Kenneth George; s of George William Hambleton (d 1972), of Chesterfield, Derbys, and Gertrude Ellen, *née* Brighouse (d 1981); *b* 15 Jan 1937; *Educ* Chesterfield GS, Queens' Coll Cambridge (MA); *m* 4 April 1959, Glenys Patricia, da of Horace Smith, of Hayling Island, Hants; 1 s (Neil b 1963), 1 da (Lindsey b 1965); *Career* res and devpt of semiconductor materials devices and applications Servs Electronics Res Lab Herts 1958-73, res and devpt on naval radars weapon systems and computers Admty Surface Weapons Estab 1973-81 (dep dir 1981-82), dir strategic electronics MOD 1982-85, asst chief sci advsr MOD (responsible for advising on sci content of all def projects and long term res progs) 1985-86; dir gen: Air Weapons and Electronic Systems 1986-90, Aircraft 3 1990-; CEng, FIEE 1982; *Recreations* bridge, chess, music, computing, golf; *Clubs* Woking Bridge, Woking 41; *Style*— Kenneth Hambleton, Esq; Prospect House, 100 New Oxford St, London WC1A 1HE (☎ 071 632 6543, fax 071 632 3979)

HAMBLETON, Roy David; s of Harry Hambleton, of Macclesfield, and Minnie, *née* Henshall; *b* 29 Aug 1944; *Educ* King's Macclesfield, Univ of Manchester (BSc); *m* 13 Aug 1966, Carol, da of Charles Arnold, of Macclesfield; 1 s (Mark James), 1 da (Lucy-Jane); *Career* prodn and projects mgmnt Staveley Chemicals 1967-68, md Graesser Laboratories 1986-88 (chief engr until 1981, ops dir 1981-86), currently dep md Nipa Laboratories Ltd; sec Trinity Fammau Scout Troop; graduate memb IChem 1966; *Recreations* walking, running, football spectating; *Style*— Roy Hambleton, Esq; Greenheys, Cefn Bychan Rd, Pantymwyn, Mold, Clwyd (☎ 0352 740 206); NIPA Laboratories Ltd, Graesser Works, Sandycroft, Deeside, Clwyd (☎ 0244 520 777, fax 0244 537 216, telex 61128 GRSL G)

HAMBLIN, Prof Terence John (Terry); s of John Gordon Hamblin (d 1978), of Farnham, Surrey, and Gladys Marjorie, *née* Allies; *b* 12 March 1943; *Educ* Farnborough GS, Univ of Bristol (MB ChB), Univ of Southampton (DM); *m* 22 July 1967, Diane Vivienne, da of George William Lay, of Farnham, Surrey; 2 s (Richard b 1971, David b 1980), 2 da (Karen b 1968, Angela b 1977); *Career* house physician Southmead Hosp Bristol 1967, house surgn Bristol Royal Infirmary 1968, MRC registrar med Univ of Bristol 1970-72, sr registrar haematology Poole Gen Hosp 1972-74, conslt haematologist Bournemouth 1974-, sr lectr immunology Univ of Southampton 1980-87, sr ed Transfusion Sci 1985-, memb Examining Panel RCPath 1986-, ed Leukaemia Res 1986-, prof immunohaematology Univ of Southampton 1987, memb Working Pty Adult Leukaemia MRC 1989-; chm Tenovus Bournemouth, deacon Lansdowne Baptist Church Bournemouth, pres Euro Soc Haemapheresis 1986; MRCP 1971, MRCPath 1973, FRCPath 1985, FRCP 1985; *Books* Plasmapheresis and Plasma Exchange (1979), Immunological Investigation of Lymphoid Neoplasms (1983), Haematological Problems in the Elderly (1987), Immunotherapy of Disease (1990); *Recreations* reading theology, refereeing children's football, writing funny articles, preaching, pond gardening, listening to Buddy Holly records, painting (houses); *Style*— Prof Terry Hamblin; 15 Queens Park, South Drive, Bournemouth BH8 9BQ (☎ 0202 391844); Department of Haematology, Royal Victoria Hospital, Shelley Rd, Bournemouth BH1 4JG (☎ 0202 395201); Tenovus Research Institute, Southampton General Hospital, Shirley, Southampton SO9 4XY (☎ 0703 777222)

HAMBLING, Gerald James; s of Ernest James Hambling (d 1965), and Elsie Maud, *née* Sedman (d 1971); *b* 14 June 1926; *Educ* Whitgift Middle Sch Croydon, Selhurst GS Thornton Heath Surrey; *m* 23 May 1954, Margaret, da of George Speakman (d 1945); 1 s (Robert b 31 July 1957), 1 da (Belinda b 18 Oct 1954); *Career* Coldstream Gds 1944-47; asst ed J Arthur Rank Two Cities Films 1947-50; sound ed: Herbert Wilcox Films 1950-54, Alexander The Great 1954, Freud - The Passion 1962, The Servant 1964, Pretty Polly 1966, Night of the Iguana 1966, Wuthering Heights 1970; film ed: Dry Rot 1955, The Whole Truth 1956, The Story of Esther Costello 1957, Sally's Irish Rogue 1958, Left Right and Centre 1959, The Bulldog Breed 1960, She'll Have to Go 1961, The Early Bird 1963, A Stitch in Time 1965, The Intelligence Men 1967, That Riviera Touch 1968, The Magnificent Two 1969, Roger Cherrill Ltd documentaries and commercials 1971-74, Bugsy Malone 1975, Moses - The Lawgiver 1976, Midnight Express 1977 (Br and American Acad nomination), Fame 1979 (Br Acad Award and American Acad nominations, Br Guild of Film Eds award, American Eds Guild nomination), Heartaches 1980, Shoot the Moon 1981, Pink Floyd - The Wall 1982, Another Country 1983 (Br Acad nomination), Birdy 1984 (Br Guild of Eds award), Absolute Beginners 1985, Angel Heart 1986 (Br Guild of Eds nomination), Leonard VI 1987, Mississippi Burning 1988; memb: Br Guild of Film Eds 1966-, American Acad of Arts and Scis 1980-, American Cinema Eds Guild 1980-; *Recreations* horology, fishing, antiques, photography; *Style*— Gerald Hambling, Esq; Ramblers, Skirmett, nr Henley-on-Thames, Oxon RG9 6TG (☎ 049 163 316)

HAMBLING, Sir (Herbert) Hugh; 3 Bt (UK 1924); s of Sir (Herbert) Guy Musgrave Hambling, 2 Bt (d 1966), and Olive Margaret Gordon, *née* Carter (d 1969); *b* 3 Aug 1919; *Educ* Eton; *m* 23 Sept 1950, Anne (d 1990), da of Judge Hugo Edmund Oswald Page (d 1932), of Seattle, USA; 1 s; *Heir* s, (Herbert) Peter Hugh, *qv*; *Career* RAF Training and Atlantic Ferry Cmd 1939-45; airline rep: BA 1956-74, Royal Brunei Airlines 1975-; mangr Sir Guy Hambling & Son 1956-; *Clubs* Seattle Tennis; *Style*— Sir Hugh Hambling, Bt; Rookery Park, Yoxford, Suffolk (☎ 072 877 310); 1219 Evergreen Point Rd, Bellevue, Washington 98004, USA

HAMBLING, Maggi; da of Harry Leonard Hambling, of Wistaria House, Hadleigh, Suffolk, and Marjorie Rose, *née* Harris (d 1988); *b* 23 Oct 1945; *Educ* Hadleigh Hall Sch, Amberfield Sch, Ipswich Sch of Art, Camberwell Sch of Art (DipAD Painting), Slade Sch of Fine Art (Higher Dip in Fine Art), Boise travel award NY 1969; *Career* first artist in residence Nat Gallery London 1980-81; works in public collections incl: Arts Cncl of GB, Birmingham City Art Gallery, Br Cncl, Br Museum, Christchurch Mansion Ipswich, Clare Coll Cambridge, Chelmsford and Essex Museum, Contemporary Art Soc, Eastern Arts Collection, Euro Parliament Collection, Fndn Du Musee De La Main Lausanne, GLC, Greene King Breweries, Gulbenkian Fndn, Haddo House Aberdeen, Harris Museum and Art Gallery Preston, HTV Bristol Imperial War Museum, Leics Educn Ctee, Minories Colchester, Morley Coll London, Nat Gallery, Nat Portrait Gallery, Petworth House, Rugby Museum, RAMC, Scottish Nat Gallery of Modern Art Edinburgh, Scottish Nat Portrait Gallery, Southampton Art Gallery, St Mary's Church Hadleigh Suffolk, St Mary's Coll Strawberry Hill London, St Mary's Hosp London, Tate Gallery, Unilever House London, Whitworth Art Gallery Manchester, William Morris Sch London; exhibited: Hadleigh Gallery Suffolk 1967, Morley Gallery London 1973, Warehouse Gallery London 1977, Nat Gallery London 1981, Nat Portrait Gallery London and Tour 1983, Serpentine Gallery London 1987, Richard Demarco Gallery Edinburgh 1988, Maclaurin Art Gallery Ayr 1988, Arnolfini Gallery Bristol and Tour 1988, Bernard Jacobson Gallery London 1990; *Clubs* Chelsea Arts; *Style*— Miss Maggi Hambling; c/o Bernard Jacobson Gallery, 14a Clifford Street, London W1X 1RF

HAMBLING, (Herbert) Peter Hugh; s and h of Sir (Herbert) Hugh Hambling, 3 Bt, *qv*; *b* 6 Sept 1953; *Educ* Univ of Washington (BSc), von Karman Inst for Fluid Dynamics (Dip), Yale Sch of Orgn and Mgmnt (Master Public & Private Mgmnt); *Career* high technol mgmnt; Strategic Planning Associates 1982-84, 3m Co 1984-87, Orbital Sciences Corp 1987-91, Digital Control Inc Seattle Washington 1991- (pres, chief operating offr and fndr); *Recreations* flying, sailing, skiing; *Clubs* Seattle Tennis, Corinthian Yacht (Seattle), Wings Aloft Flying, Felthorpe Flying; *Style*— Peter Hambling, Esq; Rookery Park, Yoxford, Suffolk

HAMBLY, Dr Edmund Cadbury; s of late Edmund Henry Hambly, and Elizabeth Mary, *née* Cadbury; *b* 28 Sept 1942; *Educ* Eton, Trinity Coll Cambridge (scholar, BA, MA, PhD); *m* 1964, Elizabeth Audrey, da of late Victor Alexander Gorham; 1 s (Edmund Tristram b 1971), 3 da (Elizabeth Loveday b 1967, Emma Karenza b 1969, Tamsin Alexandra (twin) b 1971); *Career* res fell Emmanuel Coll Cambridge 1967-69, asst engr Ove Arup & Ptnrs 1969-70, section engr Kier Ltd 1970-71, sr engr Gifford & Ptnrs 1971-74, consulting engr with own practice in civil, structural and offshore engrg 1974-; author of 25 tech papers published UK and USA (awarded prizes Inst of Structural Engrs 1976 and 1979), inventor True Triaxial Apparatus, visiting prof in principles of engrg design Univ of Oxford, tstee Bournville Village Tst 1979-88, chm Offshore Engrg Soc 1989-90; MASCE, FIStructE 1982, FEng 1984 (initiator of Engrg Guidelines for Warnings of Preventable Disasters 1990), FICE 1990, vice pres ICE 1991-; *Books* Plane Strain Behaviour of Soft Clay (1969), Bridge Deck Behaviour (1976, 2 edn 1991), Bridge Foundations and Substructures (1979); *Recreations* engineering, thinking, discourse, handiwork, bullnose, Robert Hooke; *Clubs* Scouts, Soc of Friends (Quakers); *Style*— Dr E C Hambly; Home Farm House, Little Gaddesden, Berkhamsted, Herts HP4 1PN (☎ 0442 843412, fax 0442 842741)

HAMBLY, Dr Michael Trevan; s of Dr Trevan Hambly, of Pondwell, Ryde, IOW, and Helena Geraldine, *née* Boughton; *b* 8 Nov 1942; *Educ* Blundell's, Bart's Med Sch; *m* 15 Oct 1966, Judith Anne (Judy), da of Felix John Patrick O'Connor (d 1971); 2 s (Patrick b 1969, Rupert b 1974); *Career* conslt psychiatrist to Cornwall and Isles of Scilly Health Authy 1977-; memb Exec Ctee SW Div RCPsych 1982-86, memb numerous med and psychiatric advsy ctees; MRCS, LRCP, DObst, MRCOG, DPM, MRCPsych; *Recreations* sailing, skiing; *Clubs* Royal Ocean Racing, Royal Cornwall Yacht; *Style*— Dr Michael Hambly; Chy Howlek, 28 Comfort Road, Mylor Bridge, Falmouth, Cornwall TR11 5SE (☎ 0326 72693); White House Cottage, Roscarrock Hill, Port Isaac, Cornwell PL29 3RG; Trengweath, Penryn Street, Redruth, Cornwall TR15 2SP (☎ 0209 219232)

HAMBRO, Charles Eric Alexander; s of late Sir Charles Hambro, KBE, MC, and Pamela, *née* Cobbold; *b* 24 July 1930; *Educ* Eton; *m* 1, 1954 (m dis 1976), Rose Evelyn, *née* Cotterell; 2 s, 1 da; m 2, 1976, Cherry Felicity, *née* Huggins; *Career* Coldstream Gds 1949-51; Hambros Bank Ltd: joined 1952, md 1957, chm 1972-83; non-exec dir: Taylor Woodrow plc 1962-, Hambros plc 1983-, Peninsular & Oriental Steam Navigation Co 1987-; non-exec chm Guardian Royal Exchange plc 1988-; dir: Instituto Bancario San Paolo Di Torino, General Oriental Investments Ltd; chm Royal Nat Pension Fund for Nurses 1968, tstee Br Museum 1984-; *Clubs* MCC, White's; *Style*— Charles Hambro, Esq; 69 Victoria Rd, London W8 5RH; Hambro plc, 41 Tower Hill, London EC3N 4HA (☎ 071 480 5000, fax 071 702 4424, telex 883851)

HAMBRO, James Daryl; s of Jocelyn Olaf Hambro, MC, *qv*; *b* 22 March 1949; *Educ*

Eton, Harvard Business Sch; *m* ; 3 c; *Career* exec dir Hambros Bank 1972-85, dir J O Hambro & Co 1986-, md J O Hambro Magan & Co 1988-; *Clubs* White's, Pratt's, Royal West Norfolk; *Style*— James Hambro, Esq; J O Hambro Magan & Co, 32 Queen Anne's Gate, London SW1H 9AL (☎ 071 233 1400, fax 071 222 4978)

HAMBRO, Jocelyn Olaf; MC (1944); eldest s of Ronald Olaf Hambro, JP, and Winifred, 5 da of Martin Ridley-Smith (ggs of Abel Smith, MP for Nottingham, consequently cousin to Lords Bicester and Carrington) by his 2 w (also his 1 w's sis), Cecilia, da of Henry Stuart, gs of 1 Marquess of Bute; *b* 7 March 1919; *Educ* Eton, Trinity Coll Cambridge; *m* 1, 28 March 1942, Ann Silvia (d 1972), da of Rowland Muir, of Binfield; 3 s (Rupert *qv*, Richard *qv*, James); m 2, 1976, Margaret Elisabeth (d 1983), da of late Frederick McConnel (she m 1, Lt-Col James Church, MC; m 2, 1954, 9 Duke of Roxburghe, who d 1974); m 3, 28 Jan 1988, Margaret Anne, formerly w of 7 Earl Fortescue, and da of Charles Michael Stratton; *Career* served WW II, Coldstream Gds; non-exec chm Charter Consolidated 1982- (dir 1965-); chm Hambros Ltd 1970-83 (pres 1983-); chm: Phoenix Assurance Co, The Hambros Tst, Hambros Investment Tst, HIT Securities, Hambros Diamond Investment Corpn, Hereditaments Ltd, Berkeley Hambro Property Co, Newmarket Estates & Property Co, Rosedimond Investment Tst, Waverton Property Co, Wiltons (St James's) Ltd; *Clubs* Jockey, White's, Pratt's; *Style*— Jocelyn Hambro, Esq, MC; Waverton House, Moreton-in-Marsh, Glos; 16 Victoria Rd, London W8 (☎ 071 937 4550/7573); Hambros, 41 Bishopsgate, London EC2P 2AA

HAMBRO, Peter Charles Percival; elder s of Lt-Col Everard Bingham Hambro, MBE (d 1971, ggs of Baron Hambro, cr a Danish Baron 1851, and fndr of the Hambros as British bankers, by his 1 w), of Durrington House, Old Harlow, Essex; *b* 18 Jan 1945; *Educ* Eton, Université d'Aix-Marseille; *m* 1968, Karen Guinevere Gould, da of Capt George Brodrick, of Dunley Manor, Whitchurch, Hants; 3 s; *Career* md: Smith St Aubyn & Co Hldgs to 1983, Richco Bullion Ltd 1982-83; dir Mocatta & Goldsmid Ltd 1985-90, md Peter Hambro Plc 1990-; dir City of Oxford Investment Tst; *Recreations* shooting, fishing, painting; *Clubs* Pratt's, White's; *Style*— Peter Hambro, Esq; 108 St George's Square, London SW1 (☎ 071 821 8400)

HAMBRO, (Alexander) Richard; s of Jocelyn Hambro, MC, *qv*; *b* 1 Oct 1946; *Educ* Eton; *m* 1, 1973 (m dis 1982), Hon Charlotte, da of Baron Soames, GCMG, GCVO, CH, CBE, PC, *qqv*; 1 da (Clementine b 1976, bridesmaid to Lady Diana Spencer at her marriage to HRH The Prince of Wales 1981); m 2, 12 July 1984, Juliet Grana Mary Elizabeth, da of Maj Thomas and Lady Mary Harvey; *Style*— Richard Hambro Esq; 49 Egerton Crescent, SW3

HAMBRO, Rupert Nicholas; eld s of Jocelyn Hambro, MC, *qv*, of Waverton House, Stow-on-the-Wold, Glos; *b* 27 June 1943; *Educ* Eton, Aix-en-Provence; *m* 1970, Mary, da of Francis Boyer; 1 s, 1 da; *Career* dir Racecourse Holdings Trust 1985-, chm Hambros Bank 1983-86 (dir 1969-89); dir: Anglo American Corp of SA 1981-, Daily Telegraph plc 1986-, Sedgwick Group plc 1987-; chm: Assoc of Int Bond Dealers 1979-82, Hamleys Ltd 1989-, J O Hambro Magan & Co 1988; non-exec dir Tiphook Plc 1990-; *Recreations* racing, shooting; *Clubs* White's, Portland, Jupiter Island; *Style*— Rupert Hambro, Esq; J O Hambro & Company, 30 Queen Anne's Gate, London SW1 9A (☎ 071 222 2020)

HAMBURGER, Michael Peter Leopold; s of late Prof Richard Hamburger, and Mrs L Hamburger, *née* Hamburg; *b* 22 March 1924; *Educ* Westminster, ChCh Oxford (MA); *m* 1951, Anne Ellen, *née* File; 1 s, 2 da; *Career* Army Serv 1943-47; freelance writer 1943-47, asst lectr in German UCL 1952-55, lectr rising to reader in German Univ of Reading 1955-64, Florence Purlington lectr Mount Holyoke Coll Mass 1966-67, visiting prof State Univ of NY 1969, visiting fell Centre for Humanities Wesleyan Univ Conn 1970; Regent's lectr Univ of Calif San Diego 1973; visiting prof: Univ of S Carolina 1973, Boston Univ 1975-77; pt/t prof Univ of Essex 1978, Bollingen Fndn fell 1959-61 and 1965-66; pubns incl: Flowering Cactus (1950), Poems 1950-51 (1952), The Dual Site (1958), Weather and Season 1963, Feeding the Chickadees (1968), Penguin Modern Poets (with A Brownjohn and C Tomilinson, 1969), Travelling (1969), The Truth of Poetry (1969), Travelling I-V (1973), Ownerless Earth (1973) Travelling VI (1975), Real Estate (1977), Moralities (1977), Variations (1981), Collected Poems (1984), Trees (1988), Selected Poems (1988); autobiography A Mug's Game (1973); translator of various poems letters and novels incl work by: Brertold Brecht, Goethe, Beethoven, Hölderlin, Enzenberger, N Sachs, P Bichsel; translation prizes: Deutsche Akademie für Sprache und Dichtung Darmstadt 1964, Arts Cncl 1969, Arts prize Inter Nationes Bonn 1976, medal Inst of Linguists 1977, Schlegel - Tieck prize London 1978 and 1981, Wilhelm-Heinse prize Mainz 1978, Goethe medal 1986, Austrian State prize for literary translation 1988, Euro Cmmn Translation prize 1990; Hon DLitt UEA; corresponding memb: Deutsche Akademie für Sprache und Dichtung Darmstadt 1973, Akademie der Künste Berlin, Akademie der Schönen Künste Munich; FRSL 1972-86; *Recreations* gardening, walking; *Style*— Michael Hamburger, Esq

HAMBURGER, Sir Sidney Cyril; CBE (1966), JP (Salford 1957), DL (Greater Manchester 1981); s of Isidore Hamburger (d 1953); *b* 14 July 1914; *Educ* Salford GS; *m* 1940, Gertrude, da of Morris Sterling (d 1951); 3 s; *Career* cncllr and Alderman Salford City Cncl 1946-71, Mayor Salford 1968-69; memb North Western Electricity Consultative Cncl 1953-70 (chm Manchester Area Ctee 1963-68, dep chm Cncl 1968-70); chm: NE Manchester Hosp Mgmnt Ctee 1970-74, NW Regnl Health Authy 1973-82, North West ASH 1977-; life pres: Manchester Jewish Homes for the Aged 1965, Zionist Central Cncl 1976 (pres 1967-70 and 1974-75); pres: Jewish Day Centre for the Elderly, Jewish Rep Cncl 1962-65, Trades Advsy Cncl (national), Jt Israel Appeal, Labour Friends of Israel; memb: Manchester Univ Ct 1972-83, Advsy Bd Salvation Army 1983; govr King David Schs, pres Manchester Ctee Bar-Ilan Univ Jerusalem, hon fell Bar-Ilan Univ 1979; Hon MA Salford 1979, Hon LLD Manchester 1983; Papal Award Cross Pro Ecclesia et Pontifice 1983; Supplementary Benefit Cmmn 1967-77, Bd of Gov Ben Gurion Univ 1979; chm: Age Concern Salford 1984, Manchester Cncl for Soviet Jewry 1984, Greater Manchester Citizens Advice Bureau 1985, Bnei Brith Annual award 1984; kt 1981; *Recreations* reading, public service, football; *Style*— Sir Sidney Hamburger, CBE, JP, DL; 26 New Hall Rd, Salford M7 0JU (☎ 061 834 5452)

HAMER, (Michael Howard) Kenneth; s of Mark Hamer (d 1970), and Feodora Leonora, *née* Abrahams (d 1958); *b* 27 July 1945; *Educ* Cheltenham, Sidney Sussex Coll Cambridge; *m* 20 Sept 1986, Victoria Hilda, da of Dr Thomas Walsh (d 1988); 1 da (Clara Ninette b 1989); *Career* admitted slr 1968, called to the Bar Inner Temple 1975; Westminster City cncllr 1974-78; *Recreations* cooking, opera, arts; *Clubs* Carlton; *Style*— Kenneth Hamer, Esq; 1 Harcourt Buildings, Temple, London EC4Y 9DA (☎ 071 353 0375, fax 071 583 5816); Iford Manor, Iford, nr Lewes, E Susex BN7 3EU (☎ 0273 472832)

HAMER, Dr Michelle Suzanne Fernande; da of Heraud Max Louis Leon, of Nimes France, and Simone Hortense, *née* Janvier; *b* 10 Aug 1952; *Educ* Lycee Montaury Nimes France (Baccalaureat), Montpellier Med Sch (MD, Diplome d'Etat); *m* 6 Aug 1977, Colin John Hamer, s of Eric John Hamer, of Ashford, Kent; 1 da (Jessica Maite Michelle b 1981); *Career* conslt anaethetist i/c intensive care Joyce Green Hosp Kent 1988-; memb: BMA, Assoc of Anaesthetists, Intensive Care Soc; FFARCS; *Recreations* travel, skiing, entertaining; *Style*— Dr Michelle Hamer; Intensive Therapy Unit, Joyce Green Hospital, Joyce Green Lane, Dartford, Kent DA1 5PL (☎ 0322 227242)

HAMER-HODGES, David William; s of Dr Robert James Hamer-Hodges (d 1961), of Portsmouth, and Priscilla, *née* Fowler; *b* 17 Oct 1943; *Educ* Portsmouth GS, UCH (MB BS, MS); *m* 10 Oct 1969, Gillian Landale, da of Richard Cameron Kelman (d 1978), of Aberdeen; 3 s (Christopher James b 1970, Gareth William b 1973, Anthony Paul b 1975), 1 da (Clair Gillian b 1980); *Career* res fell surgery Harvard 1973, sr registrar surgery Aberdeen 1974, res surgical offr St Mark's Hosp London 1971, conslt surgn and hon sr lectr surgery Edinburgh 1979-; memb socs involving gastroenterology, endocrinology and transplantation; memb RSM; FRCS, FRCSEd; *Recreations* gardening; *Style*— David Hamer-Hodges, Esq; 14 Moray Plc, Edinburgh EH3 6DT (☎ 031 225 4843)

HAMILL, Sir Patrick; QPM (1979); s of late Hugh Hamill; *b* 29 April 1930; *Educ* St Patrick's HS Dumbarton, Open Univ (BA); *m* 1954, Nell Gillespie; 4 s, 1 da; *Career* Dunbartonshire Police 1950, asst chief constable City of Glasgow Police 1972, chief constable Strathclyde Police 1977-85 (joined 1975), RCDS 1976; memb Bd of Govrs: Scot Police Coll 1977-85, St Aloysius Coll Glasgow 1983-90; Assoc of Chief Police Offrs (Scotland): rep to INTERPOL 1977-81, pres 1982-83, hon sec 1983-85; chm: Bd of Mgmnt St Margaret's Hospice Clydebank 1986-, Bd of Govrs St Andrew's Coll of Educn Bearsden 1987-88; OStJ 1977; kt 1984; *Recreations* walking, reading, history, golf; *Style*— Sir Patrick Hamill, QPM

HAMILTON *see also*: Douglas-Hamilton, Stirling-Hamilton

HAMILTON, Duke of; *see*: Hamilton and Brandon

HAMILTON, Adrian Walter; QC (1973); s of Walter George Morrell Hamilton (d 1957), and Sybil Emily, *née* Thomson (d 1972); *b* 11 March 1923; *Educ* Highgate, Balliol Coll Oxford (MA); *m* 1966, Jill Margaret Beverlie, da of Stanley Richard Brimblecombe, of Eastbourne; 2 da (Sarah b 1967, Philippa b 1970); *Career* Lt RNVR (Atlantic, Mediterranean, English Channel); called to the Bar Lincoln's Inn, Middle Temple and Inner Temple 1949, rec Crown Ct 1974; memb: Senate and Inns of Ct and the Bar 1976-82 (treas 1979-82), Cncl of Legal Educn 1977-87; inspr Peek Foods Ltd 1977-81, bencher Lincoln's Inn 1979; *Recreations* golf, sailing, family; *Clubs* Garrick, Roehampton, Piltdown Golf; *Style*— Adrian Hamilton, Esq, QC; 7 King's Bench Walk, Temple, London, EC4 (☎ 071 583 0404)

HAMILTON, Alex John; *b* 5 Nov 1936; *Educ* Brazil and Argentina, The Queen's Coll Oxford (Neale scholar, BA); *m* Stephanie Nettell; 2 s; *Career* novelist, journalist and broadcaster; work incl: ed Books and Bookmen, columnist The Times and The Glasgow Herald, various BBC World Service programmes, travel ed The Guardian 1981- (formerly features writer); winner James Fitzgerald Travel Writer of the Year award; *Books* The Siberian Track, Tall Dark and Gruesome, As If She Were Mine, Wild Track, Town Parole, If You Don't Watch Out (USA), Beam of Malice, Fly On The Wall, The Dead Needle, The Christmas Pudding That Shook the World; ed: Triangles, Splinters, Factions, The Gold Embrace, Best Horror Stories; *Recreations* photography; *Style*— Alex Hamilton, Esq; 24 Weymouth St, London W1N 3FA (☎ 071 580 3479); The Guardian, 119 Farringdon Road, London EC1R 3ER (☎ 071 278 2332, fax 071 837 2114)

HAMILTON, Andrew; s of Peter Hamilton, of Sussex, and Susie, *née* Blackwell; *b* 15 Jan 1950; *Educ* Univ Coll Sch, Coll of Estate Mgmnt Univ of Reading; *m* 23 July 1983, Fiona Ann, da of John Scott-Adie, of Perthshire; 1 s (Charles Scott-Adie b 1988); *Career* dir: John D Wood SA 1975-77, Haslemere Estates plc 1985-86, Ranelagh Development Ltd 1986-; md Culverin Holdings Ltd 1986-; FRICS 1986; *Recreations* opera, conservation, shooting; *Clubs* RAC; *Style*— Andrew Hamilton, Esq; 82 Park St, Mayfair W1Y 3HQ (☎ 071 408 1188, fax 071 493 8042)

HAMILTON, Andrew Caradoc; s and h of Sir (Robert Charles) Richard Caradoc Hamilton, 9 Bt, *qv*; *b* 23 Sept 1953; *Educ* Charterhouse, St Peter's Coll Oxford (MA); *m* 26 Oct 1984, Anthea Jane, da of Frank Huntingford, of Hindhead, Surrey; 2 da (Alice b 4 Dec 1986, Harriet b 18 March 1989); *Career* schoolmaster 1976-89; History Dept Woodrush HS nr Birmingham 1976-84, head of history Evesham HS Worcs 1984-89; restored Wellesbourne Watermill to full working order 1988-90, now promoting mill's stoneground products and mill as tourist attraction 1990-; memb Ctee: Warwickshire Fine Foods, Leamington Cricket Club, Moreton Morrell Real Tennis Club; *Recreations* cricket, real tennis, art, music, family; *Clubs* MCC, Leamington Cricket, Leamington and Moreton Morrell Real Tennis; *Style*— Andrew Hamilton, Esq; c/o Wellesbourne Watermill, Mill Farm, Kineton Road, Wellesbourne, Warwickshire CV35 9HG (☎ 0789 470237)

HAMILTON, Lord (Claud) Anthony; DL (Co Fermanagh 1979); s of 4 Duke of Abercorn (d 1979), and Lady Mary Kathleen, GCVO, *née* Crichton (d 1990), sis of 5 Earl of Erne; *b* 8 July 1939; *Educ* Eton; *m* 17 April 1982, Catherine Janet, eldest da of Dennis Faulkner, CBE, of Ringhaddy House, Killinchy, Co Down; 1 s (Alexander James b 1987), 1 da (Anna Kathleen b 1983); *Career* Lt Irish Gds; Capt RARO Ulster Def Regt 1979-; HS Co Fermanagh 1990; *Clubs* Kildare St and University; *Style*— Lord Anthony Hamilton, DL; Killyreagh, Tamlaght, Enniskillen, Co Fermanagh, N Ireland (☎ 0365 87 221)

HAMILTON, Hon Archibald Gavin; MP (C) Epsom and Ewell 1978-; yr s of 3 Baron Hamilton of Dalzell, GCVO, MC, JP (d 1990), and Rosemary Olive, *née* Coke; *b* 30 Dec 1941; *Educ* Eton; *m* 14 Dec 1968, Anne, da of late Cdr Trevelyan Napier, DSC, RN; 3 da; *Career* cncllr Kensington & Chelsea 1968-71; PPS to: Sec of State Energy 1979-81, Sec of State Transport 1981-82; asst govt whip 1982-84, lord cmmnr to the Treasy 1984-86, Parly under secretary of state (Defence Procurement) 1986-87, PPS to PM 1987-88, min of state (Armed Forces) 1988-; *Style*— The Hon Archibald Hamilton, MP; House of Commons, London SW1

HAMILTON, Arthur Campbell; QC (1982); s of James Whitehead Hamilton (d 1954), of Glasgow, and Isobel Walker, *née* McConnell; *b* 10 June 1942; *Educ* Glasgow HS, Univ of Glasgow, Worcester Coll Oxford (BA), Univ of Edinburgh (LLB); *m* 12 Sept 1970, Christine Ann, da of Thomas Carlyle Croll, of St Andrews, Fife; 1 da (Miranda b 1975); *Career* advocate, memb Faculty of Advocates 1968; standing jr counsel: Scot Devpt Dept 1975-78, Bd Inland Revenue (Scot) 1978-82; Advocate Depute 1982-85, judge of the Courts of Appeal of Jersey and Guernsey 1988-; *Recreations* hill walking, fishing; *Style*— Arthur Hamilton, Esq, QC; 8 Heriot Row, Edinburgh EH3 6HU (☎ 031 556 4663); Advocates Library, Parliament House, Edinburgh (☎ 031 226 5071, fax 031 225 3642)

HAMILTON, Dr Barbara; da of Herbert H Hunter, OBE (d 1980), of Belfast, and Margretta, *née* Hemphill; *b* 19 Feb 1944; *Educ* Methodist Coll Belfast, Queen's Univ Belfast (MB BCh, BAO), Univ of Aberdeen (Dip FP, Dip Psychotherapy); *m* 20 March 1971, David Stewart, s of David Hamilton (d 1981); 2 s (Michael b 1974, Colin b 1983), 3 da (Lisa b 1972, Barbara-Anne b 1973, Emma b 1977); *Career* hon lectr Univ of Aberdeen (former trainee psychiatrist and sr registrar), presently conslt psychiatrist; memb Exec RCPsych, gp supervision ldr Marriage Guidance Cncl Ayrshire; memb: BMA, AFT; MRCPsych; *Recreations* golf, music, dancing; *Clubs* Turnberry Golf; *Style*— Dr Barbara Hamilton; St Johns, Maybole, Ayrshire KA19 7LN (0655 82284); Isla Bank House, Keith, Banffshire AB5 3BS (☎ 05422 2322); Crosshouse Hospital, Kilmarnock (☎ 0563 21133)

HAMILTON, Brian Hamilton; s of Clarence Kent (d 1946), of 17 Mottram Rd, Hyde,

Cheshire, and Edyth (d 1963); *b* 29 Sept 1931; *Educ* Hyde GS, Univ of Salford (BSc); *m* 15 May 1954, Margery, da of Laurence Foulds (d 1974), of Vernon Rd, Bredbury, Cheshire; 1 s (Peter Hamilton b 15 April 1958), 2 da (Wendy Susan (Mrs Martin) b 13 July 1960, Linda Anne b 10 Oct 1961); *Career* Lt RN 1954-57; mangr Mather And Platt Contracting Ltd 1960, marketing dir Morganite Carbon Ltd 1965, md Alfa Laval UK Ltd 1970, exec chm Staveley Industries plc 1987- (chief exec and gp md 1980); former chm Industry and Parliamentary Tst, memb Cncl CBI; FIMechE (view pres), FIEE; *Recreations* boating, bridge, tennis; *Clubs* RAC, IOD; *Style—* Brian Hamilton, Esq; Collingwood, 16 Woodlands Rd, Surbiton, Surrey KT6 6PS (☎ 081 390 2232); Staveley House, 11 Dingwall Rd, Croydon, Surrey CR9 3DB (☎ 081 688 4404, telex 915 855, fax 081 760 0563, car 0860 364853)

HAMILTON, Baron Carl-Diedric Hugo Gustav; s of Baron Fredrik Adolf Hugo Johan Hamilton (d 1968), and Karin Odelstierna; *b* 7 Aug 1948; *Educ* Sigtuna Skolan, Stockholm Sch of Business; *m* 1976, Astrid Gudrun Ebba Charlotte, da of Erik Carleson (d 1959); 1 s (Carl-Johan b 1977), 2 da (Ebba b 1980, Louise b 1982); *Career* Capt Reserve Royal Swedish Lifeguards; dir Hambros Bank Ltd 1976-82; exec dir Enskilda Securities 1982-; *Style—* Baron Carl-Diedric Hamilton; 9 Queen Anne's Gdns, London W4 1TU (☎ 081 995 6768); Enskilda Securities, 26 Finsbury Square, London EC2A 1DS (☎ 071 638 3500, telex 8955951)

HAMILTON, David; s of C J Pilditch (d 1967), and Joyce Mary Hamilton (d 1970); *b* 10 Sept 1938; *m* 5 Nov 1962 (m dis 1977), Shelia Moore; 1 s (David b 1964), 1 da (Jane b 1963); *Career* Nat Serv RAF, broadcaster Br Forces Broadcasting Serv Germany 1959; writer weekly column in nat football magazine whilst at school, script-writer ATV 1956 (scripted Portrait of a Star 1957); continuity announcer: Tyne-Tees TV 1961, ABC TV (Manchester) 1962; former freelance announcer several ITV stations; work incl: pop and sports shows, beauty contests, quizzes; host All Clued Up ITV 1988-91; radio: first broadcast for BBC 1962, presented own daily show on Radio 1 and Radio 2 1973-86, currently presenter daily show for Capital Gold Radio London and weekly networked prog on ind radio stations UK; several appearances in films and maj pantomimes; hon pres Showbiz XI Football Team (memb for twenty years); *Books* The Music Game (autobiography, 1986); *Recreations* tennis; *Style—* David Hamilton, Esq

HAMILTON, Prof David Ian; s of Dr John Alexander King Hamilton, GM (d 1983), and Helen Eliza Bruce, *née* Kirk (d 1964); *b* 22 June 1931; *Educ* Leighton Park Sch, Middx Hosp Univ of London (MB BS); *m* 16 Nov 1957, Myra, da of Rev Malcolm James Alexander McAra (d 1981); 4 s (Ian b 1959, James b 1960, Alastair b 1963, Ross b 1965); *Career* RCS 1949-51 (Lt 1951); surgical registrar Dept of Surgical Studies Middx Hosp 1963 (house surgn 1957, surgical registrar in cardio-thoracic surgery 1961, surgical registrar 1962), surgical registrar Thoracic Unit Harefield Hosp 1964, sr surgical registrar Cardio-Thoracic Unit Broadgreen and The Royal Liverpool Children's Hosps 1965-68, Comyns Berkley travelling fell Presbyterian Med Centre San Francisco USA 1966-67; conslt cardiac surgn: Broadgreen Hosp Liverpool 1968, Royal Liverpool Children's Hosp 1969-86; fndn chair of cardiac surgery Univ of Edinburgh at The Royal Infirmary and Royal Hosp for Sick Children 1987; author of articles on congenital heart disease in children and infants 1969-; examiner in cardio-thoracic surgery RCS(Ed): Higher Specialist Fellowship examination 1981-89, Inter Collegiate examination 1989; memb: Surgical Sub-Ctee Nat Confidential Enquiry into Peri-operative Deaths 1988-89, Br Cardiac Soc 1969, Soc of Cardiothoracic Surgns of GB and I 1969 (pres elect 1989); hon memb Polish Assoc of Paediatric Surgns 1988; memb BMA 1957; FRCS 1961, FRCS(Ed) 1989; *Books* contrib: Textbook of Nursing (18 and 19 edns), Textbook of Operative Surgery, Reoperations in Cardiac Surgery (1989); *Recreations* golf; *Clubs* Royal Liverpool Golf, Luffness New Golf; *Style—* Prof David Hamilton; Colton, 44 Spylaw Bank Rd, Colinton, Edinburgh EH13 0JG (☎ 031 441 1934); Dept of Surgery, The Royal Infirmary, Lauriston Place, Edinburgh EH8 9AG (☎ 031 229 2477 ext 2268, fax 031 228 2661)

HAMILTON, Dr David Stewart; s of David Hamilton (d 1981), of Belfast, and Anne, *née* Stewart; *b* 3 June 1944; *Educ* Belfast Royal Acad, Queen's Univ Belfast (MB BCh, BAO, DRCOG); *m* 20 March 1971, Barbara, da of Herbert Hunter, OBE (d 1980), of Belfast; 2 s (Michael b 1974, Colin b 1983), 3 da (Lisa b 1972, Barbara b 1973, Emma b 1977); *Career* princ GP Belfast 1972-77, trainee psychiatrist Aberdeen 1977-84, conslt psychiatrist and sr lectr Univ of Aberdeen 1984-87, conslt psychiatrist Ayrshire 1987-; sec Mental Handicap Section RCPsych Scotland, vice chm Div of Psychiatry Ayrshire; memb: BMA, AFT; assoc RCGP 1978, MRCPsych; *Recreations* golf, music, restoration of mansion houses; *Clubs* Turnberry, Ayrshire Symphony Orch; *Style—* Dr David Hamilton; St John's, Maybole, Ayrshire KA19 7LN (☎ 0655 82284); Isla Bank House, Seafield Ave, Keith AB5 3BS (☎ 05422 2322); Crosshouse Hospital, Kilmarnock (☎ 0563 21133)

HAMILTON, Dr David Valentine; s of Prof William James Hamilton (d 1975), and Maimie Campbell, *née* Young (d 1989); *b* 14 Feb 1946; *Educ* Harrow, Queens' Coll Cambridge (MA), St Thomas' Hosp London (MB BChir, MRCP); *m* 17 May 1975, Cynthia Ann, da of Maj Sydney Allaway (d 1974); 1 s (Jonathan David b 21 July 1977), 1 da (Sarah Anne b 1 Jan 1979); *Career* conslt physician and nephrologist 1982-; memb: Renal Assoc, Euro Dialysis and Transplantation Assoc, Br Hypertension Soc; LRCS; *Recreations* squash, tennis; *Style—* Dr David Hamilton; 219 Newmarket Rd, Norwich NR4 7LA (☎ 0603 53859); Norfolk and Norwich Hospital, Brunswick Rd, Norwich (☎ 0603 628377)

HAMILTON, Douglas Owens; s of Oswald Hamilton (d 1949), and Edith Florence Hamilton (d 1987); *b* 20 April 1931; *Educ* John Fisher Sch Purley Surrey, London Univ (LLB); *m* 15 Sept 1962, Judith Mary, da of Harold Arthur Benjamin Wood (d 1979); 3 s (Giles Alexander Douglas, Angus James Douglas, Benjamin Charles Douglas); *Career* sr ptnr Norton Rose Slrs 1982-(ptnr 1959, fin ptnr 1970-76, exec ptnr 1978-82); memb Court of Benefactors of Oxford Univ, treas Br Polish legal Assoc; hon treas Br Maritime Charitable Fndn; Liveryman Worshipful Co of Shipwrights; memb: Law Soc 1955, Baltic Exchange 1970; *Recreations* tennis, golf, travelling; *Style—* Douglas Hamilton, Esq; Kempson House, Camomile St, London, EC3N 7AN (☎ 071 283 2434, fax 071 588 1181, telex 883652)

HAMILTON, Douglas Victor; s of Douglas William Hamilton (d 1959), and Evelyn Louise, *née* Hamilton (d 1968); *b* 1 Oct 1938; *Educ* Arbroath HS, Duncan of Jordanstone Coll of Art, Sch of Architecture (Dip Arch); *m* 20 Dec 1966 (m dis 1986), Pamela Isobel, *née* Bruce; 1 s (Paul Douglas b 1967), 1 da (Juliet Elizabeth b 1970); *Career* architect; Baxter Clark & Paul Dundee 1961-63, res architect Prefabricated Housing 1963-64, Baxter Clark & Paul Glasgow 1964-65, lectr Sch of Architecture Duncan Jordanstone Coll of Art 1965-72 (dir of live projects 1967-69), dir McLaren Murdoch & Hamilton Perth 1975- (architect 1972-); memb: RIBA, RIAS; *Recreations* squash, cricket, petanque; *Style—* Douglas Hamilton, Esq; No 3 St Martin's Mill, by Balbeggie, Perthshire PH2 6AQ (☎ 08214 571); Bowman-Route D'Uzes, Le Village, St Hippolyte de Montaigu, Gard, France; McLaren Murdoch & Hamilton, Chartered Architects, 2 Dundee Rd, Perth PH2 7DW (☎ 0738 27061, fax 0738 39938)

HAMILTON, (James) Dundas; CBE (1985); s of late Arthur Douglas Hamilton, and Jean Scott Hamilton; *b* 11 June 1919; *Educ* Rugby, Clare Coll Cambridge; *m* 1954, Linda Jean, da of late Sinclair Frank Ditcham; 2 da; *Career* Lt-Col RA, Europe and Far East 1939-46; memb Stock Exchange 1948- (cncl memb 1972-78, dep chm 1973-76), sr ptnr Fielding Newson-Smith & Co 1977-85, dep chm Br Invisible Exports Cncl 1976-86; chm: TSB Commercial Holdings Ltd 1984-90, Utd Dominions Trust Ltd 1984-90, Wates City of London Properties plc; dir: TSB plc 1985-90, LWT (Holdings) plc, WIB Publications Ltd; memb: Exec Ctee City Communications Centre 1977-87, Advsy Bd Royal Coll Def Studies 1980-87; govr Pasold Res Fund 1976-90; Parly candidate (C) East Ham North 1951; novelist and playwright; *Recreations* swimming, writing, golf, tennis; *Clubs* City of London, All England Lawn Tennis and Croquet, Royal and Ancient, Hurlingham, Worplesdon; *Style—* Dundas Hamilton, Esq, CBE; 45 Melbury Court, London W8 6NH (☎ 071 602 3157)

HAMILTON, Eben William; QC (1981); s of Rev John Edmund Hamilton, MC (d 1981), of Edinburgh, and Hon Lilias Maclay (d 1966); *b* 12 June 1937; *Educ* Winchester, Trinity Coll Cambridge (MA); *m* 1985, Themy Rusi, da of Brig Rusi Bilimoria (d 1963), of Bellagio, Warden Rd, Bombay, India; *Career* 4/7 Royal Dragoon Gds 1955-57, Fife and Forfar Yeo Scottish Horse TA 1957-68; called to the Bar Inner Temple 1962; bencher Inner Temple 1985;FRSA 1989; *Clubs* Garrick; *Style—* Eben Hamilton, Esq, QC; 28 Pembroke Square, London W8; Priests Island, Co Longford, Ireland; 1 New Square, Lincoln's Inn, London WC2

HAMILTON, Sir Edward Sydney; 7 Bt (GB 1776), of Marlborough House, Hampshire, and 5 Bt (UK 1819), of Trebinshun House, Brecknockshire; s of Sir (Thomas) Sydney (Percival) Hamilton, 6 and 4 Bt (d 1966); *b* 14 April 1925; *Educ* Canford; *Heir* none; *Career* RE 1943-47, 1 Royal Sussex Home Guard 1953-56; *Style—* Sir Edward Hamilton, Bt; The Cottage, East Lavant, nr Chichester, West Sussex PO18 OAL (☎ 0243 527414)

HAMILTON, Eric Brian Devon; s of James Hamilton (d 1966), of Birkenhead and Annalong, Co Down, NI, and Isobel, *née* Devon (d 1943); *b* 28 April 1927; *Educ* Rydal Sch, Christ's Coll Cambridge (MA), Middx Hosp Med Sch (MB BChir); *m* 6 Dec 1958, (Margaret) Claire, da of Myrddin Morris (d 1982), of Swansea; 4 s (Simon b 1959, Piers b 1961, Gavin b 1963, Timothy b 1967); *Career* Nat Serv RAF 1953-55; registrar MRC Rheumatism Unit Canadian Red Cross Hosp Taplow, conslt rheumatologist King's Coll Hosp 1963-; FRSM, FRCP; *Style—* Eric Hamilton, Esq; 11 Woodhall Drive, London SE21 7HJ (☎ 081 693 2880); King's College Hospital, Denmark Hill, London SE5 9RS (☎ 071 274 6222 ext 2353)

HAMILTON, Francis Rowan Oldfield de Courcy; s of James Percival de Courcy Hamilton, of Brightwell Baldwin, Oxon, and Elizabeth Millicent, *née* Oldfield; *b* 11 Feb 1940; *Educ* Winchester, Christ Church Oxford; *m* 22 July 1972, Catherine Rae, da of Lt Cdr William Alastair Robertson, CBE, DSC, RN, of Garvald, East Lothian; 1 s (Thomas b 1983), 2 da (Antonia b 1977, Olivia b 1979); *Career* The Economist Intelligence Unit 1965-72 (dir Mexico office from 1967), dir Samuel Montagu & Co Ltd 1978-86; chief of div and sr advsr Int Finance Corpn Washington DC 1986-; *Clubs* Travellers'; *Style—* Francis de C Hamilton, Esq; 4610 Chesapeake St, NW Washington, DC 20016 (☎ 010 202 362 9525); 44 Moreton St, London SW1 (☎ 071 828 5018)

HAMILTON, (Alexander) Gordon Kelso; s of Arthur Hamilton Kelso Hamilton, of Weybridge, Surrey, and Elizabeth Evelyn, *née* Williams; *b* 27 Aug 1945; *Educ* Charterhouse, Pembroke Coll Cambridge (MA); *m* 12 July 1980, France Elisabeth Mary Colette, da of Pierre Laurent Millet , of Paris, France; 1 s (Edward b 1984), 1 da (Georgina b 1986); *Career* CA; ptnr Mann Judd 1975-79, following merger ptnr Touche Ross & Co 1979-; tstee Pembroke Coll Cambridge (The Valence Mary (1997) Endowment Fund); memb Cncl of Management and Fin Ctee Royal Nat Inst for the Deaf, dir St George's Hill Golf Club Ltd; FCA; *Recreations* golf; *Clubs* R & A, St George's Hill Golf; *Style—* Gordon Hamilton, Esq; 19 Elm Park Road, London SW3 (☎ 071 352 2228)

HAMILTON, Iain Ellis; s of James Hamilton (d 1951), of London, and Catherine, *née* Ellis (d 1979); *b* 6 June 1922; *Educ* Mill Hill Sch, Royal Acad of Music (LRAM, ARAM), Univ of London (BMus); *Career* engr Handley Page Aircraft Co 1939-46; lectr: Morley Coll 1952-60, Univ of London 1952-60; Mary Duke Biddle prof of music Duke Univ N Carolina USA 1962-78; composer; works incl: Symphony No 1 (1948), Concerto for Clarinet and Orchestra (1949-50), Symphony No 2 (1951), The Bermudas (for chorus and orchestra, 1957), Sinfonia for Two Orchestra (1958), The Royal Hunt of the Sun (Opera in Two Acts, 1967-69), Alastor for Orchestra (1970), Anna Karenina (opera in two parts, 1979), St Mark Passion (1982), Piano Concerto No 2 (1988); Hon Doctorate of Music Univ of Glasgow 1970; FRAM; *Recreations* reading, walking; *Style—* Iain Hamilton, Esq; 1 King St, London WC2E 8HN (☎ 071 240 0040)

HAMILTON, Ian Gordon; s of Forrest Hamilton (d 1943), of Glasgow, and Jane Isobel Cameron (d 1964); *b* 2 Dec 1925; *Educ* Market Harborough GS, Royal Tech Coll Glasgow (BSc); *m* 2 July 1952, Jean, da of Duncan MacMillan; 1 s (Gordon Macmillan b 6 Feb 1954); *Career* metallurgist Stewarts & Lloyds Ltd 1946-51, asst to Chief Metallurgist Babcock & Wilcox Ltd 1951-56, chief metallurgist and welding engr Motherwell Bridge & Engineering Co Ltd 1956-57, dir Problematics Ltd (engrg conslts) 1957-59, dep chief metallurgist Babcock & Wilcox Ltd 1959-67, chief metallurgist Babcock & Wilcox (Operations) Ltd 1967-77, gp chief metallurgist Babcock Energy 1977-87, sr engr assoc CAPCIS-UMIST 1988-; pres Scottish Assoc for Metals 1978-79, awarded Brooker medal The Welding Inst; ARTC, FEng 1989, FIM, FWeldI; *Recreations* hill walking, literature, music; *Style—* Ian Hamilton, Esq; 88 Wester Rd, Glasgow G32 9JT (☎ 041 778 3057)

HAMILTON, (Robert) Ian; s of Robert Tough Hamilton (d 1951), and Daisy, *née* Mackay; *b* 24 March 1938; *Educ* Queen Elizabeth GS Darlington, Keble Coll Oxford (BA); *m* 1, 1963 (m dis 1979), Gisela Dietzel; 1 s (Matthew William b 1967); m 2, 1981, Ahdaf Soueif; 2 s (Robert b 1984, Richard b 1989); *Career* Nat Serv RAF 1956-58; poet and author; ed: The Review 1962-72, The New Review 1974-79; *Books* incl: The Visit (poems, 1970), A Poetry Chronicle (1973), The Little Magazines (1976), Robert Lowell: A Biography (1983), In Search of J D Salinger (1988), Fifty Poems (1988), Writers in Hollywood 1915-51 (1990); *Style—* Ian Hamilton, Esq; 54 Queens Rd, London SW19 (☎ 081 946 0291)

HAMILTON, Ian Robertson; QC (Scotland 1980); s of John Harris Hamilton (d 1968), of Paisley, Renfrewshire, and Martha, *née* Robertson (d 1976); *Educ* John Neilson Sch Paisley, Allan Glens Sch Glasgow, Univ of Glasgow (BL), Univ of Edinburgh; *m* 1 and 2; 1 s, 2 da; m 3, 4 April 1974, Jeanette Patricia Mairi, da of Sqdn Ldr James Mitchell Watson Stewart, MBE (d 1966), of Dimbula, Ceylon; 1 s (Ian Stewart b 26 Oct 1975); *Career* RAFVR 1944-48; called to the Scottish Bar 1954, advocate depute 1964, state advocate Zambia 1966, hon sheriff Lanarkshire 1968, called to the Canadian Bar 1982, sheriff of Strathclyde and Kelvin 1985 (resigned to return to private practice); fndr Castlewynd Printers Ltd 1954, fndr chm Whichway Tst for Young Offenders 1988; *Books* No Stone Unturned (1952), The Tinkers of the World (1958), A Touch of Treason (1990); *Recreations* oyster farming; *Style—* Ian Hamilton, Esq, QC; Parliament House, Edinburgh (☎ 031 226 2881, car 0860 820869)

HAMILTON, James; CBE (1979); s of late George Hamilton, of Baillieston, Lanarkshire; *b* 11 March 1918; *Educ* St Bridget's, St Mary's HS; *m* 1945, Agnes, da of Constantine McGhee; 1 s (and 1 s decd), 3 da; *Career* Reconnaissance Corps 1939-46, constructional engr, pres Constructional Engineering Union 1968-74, former co cncllr Lanarkshire; MP (Lab): Bothwell 1964-83, Motherwell North 1983-87; asst govt whip 1969-70, oppn whip 1970-74, lord commr of the Treasury 1974; vice chamberlain HM Household 1974-1978, comptroller 1978-79; former chm PLP Trade Union Gp, memb Select Ctee on Selection; *Style—* James Hamilton Esq, CBE; 12 Rosegreen Crescent, Bellshill, Lanarkshire (☎ 0698 2071)

HAMILTON, Sir James Arnot; KCB (1978, CB 1972), MBE (1952); *b* 2 May 1923; *Educ* Lasswade Sch, Univ of Edinburgh (BSc); *m* 5 Sept 1947 (m dis 1977), Christine Mary, da of Robert McKean, of Glasgow; 3 s (Robin b 1949, Gordon b 1954, Angus b 1956); *Career* Marine Aircraft Estab 1943-52 (head of Flt Res 1948), Royal Aircraft Estab 1952 (head of Projects Div 1964); dir Anglo-French Combat Aircraft Miny of Aviation 1965, dir gen Concorde Miny of Technol 1966-70, dep sec DTI 1971-73, dep sec Cabinet Office 1973-76, perm sec Dept of Educn and Sci 1976-83; dir: Hawker Siddeley Group 1983-, Smiths Industries 1984-, Devonport Royal Dockyard 1987-; memb Advsy Bd Brown & Root (UK) Ltd; tstee Br Museum (Natural History) 1984-88; vice chm Cncl UCL 1985-, vice pres Cncl Univ of Reading 1985-; Hon DUniv Heriot-Watt Univ 1983, Hon LLD CNAA 1983; FRSE 1981, FEng 1981, Hon FIMechE 1982, FRAeS 1960; *Clubs* Athenaeum; *Style—* Sir James Hamilton, KCB, MBE, FRSE; Pentlands, 9 Cedar Rd, Farnborough, Hants (☎ 0252 543254); Hawker Siddeley Group, 18 St James's Square, London SW1 (☎ 071 027 7500)

HAMILTON, Marquess of; James Harold Charles Hamilton; s and h of 5 Duke of Abercorn; *b* 19 Aug 1969; *Heir* bro, Lord Nicholas Hamilton; *Career* Page of Honour to HM The Queen 1982-84; *Style—* Marquess of Hamilton

HAMILTON, Jeremy Ian Macaulay (Jim); s of Zachary Macaulay Hamilton (d 1986), of Roe Downs House, Medstead, Alton, and Pamela Lucie, *née* Robson (d 1983); *b* 6 Jan 1944; *Educ* Canford Sch, Univ of Bristol (LLB); *m* 12 Mar 1977, Janet Lorna Joanna, da of David Morrice Man (d 1957), of Alresford, Hants; 2 s (James b 1977, Kit b 1979), 1 da (Nina b 1981); *Career* slr Beaumont & Son 1969-70, asst co sec Tioxide plc 1970-73, ptnr Grieveson Grant and Co 1980-85 (joined 1973); dir Kleinwort Benson Ltd 1986-; church warden; memb Law Soc 1970; *Recreations* salmon and trout fishing, wine; *Style—* Jim Hamilton, Esq; Kleinwort Benson Ltd, 20 Fenchurch Street, EC3P 3DS, (☎ 071 623 8000)

HAMILTON, His Hon Judge John; s of Cdr John Ian Hamilton, Kt SMOM, RN, of Bognor Regis, Sussex, and Margaret Elaine, *née* Rowe (d 1959); *b* 27 Jan 1941; *Educ* Harrow, Hertford Coll Oxford (MA); *m* 19 Feb 1965, Patricia Anne, da of Flt Lt Cedric Walter Clive Henman, of Pulham Market, Norfolk; 2 s (Mark b 1967, Rupert b 1969), 1 da (Stephanie 1972); *Career* called to the Bar Gray's Inn 1965, rec of the Crown Court 1983, circuit judge 1987-; English under eighteen golf international 1958, winner of Carris trophy 1958, runner of forty three marathons 1981-; Freeman City of London, Liveryman Worshipful Co of Merchant Taylors; Kt SMOM; *Recreations* jogging, golf, bridge, gardening; *Style—* His Hon Judge Hamilton; Red Stack, Anstey, nr Buntingford, Herts SG9 0BN (☎ 076 384 536)

HAMILTON, Adm Sir John Graham; GBE (1966, KBE 1963, CBE 1958), CB (1960); s of Col Ernest Graham Hamilton, CMG, DSO, MC (d 1950); *b* 12 July 1910; *Educ* RNC Dartmouth; *m* 1938, Dorothy Nina, da of Col John Eamer Turner, CMG, DSO (d 1955), of Sandhurst, Surrey; *Career* joined RN 1924; specialised in gunnery 1936; serv WWII, Capt 1949, dep dir Radio Equipment 1950-51, cmd 5 Destroyer Sqdn 1952-53, Dir of Naval Ordnance 1954-56, cmd HMS Newfoundland 1956-58, Rear Adm 1958, Naval Sec to First Lord of the Admiralty 1958-60, Flag Offr Flotillas (Home) 1960-62, Vice Adm 1961, Flag Offr Naval Air Command 1962-64, Adm 1964, C-in-C Med and C-in-C Allied Forces Med 1964-67, ret 1967; nat pres Inst of Marketing 1972-75; *Recreations* walking, climbing, photography; *Style—* Adm Sir John Hamilton, GBE, CB; Chapel Barn, Abbotsbury, Weymouth, Dorset DT3 4LF (☎ 0305 871507)

HAMILTON, Lawrence Austin; s of John A Hamilton (d 1978), of Liverpool, and Lilian, *née* Woodhouse; *b* 27 Oct 1929; *Educ* Liverpool Inst GS; *m* 3 April 1954, Judith Irene; 1 s (Ian Lawrence b 12 Jan 1955), 1 da (Valerie Christine b 14 Feb 1959); *Career* chartered insurer; Phoenix Assurance Co Ltd: joined Liverpool 1950, fire and accident superintendent City Branch 1964-68, (Newcastle upon Tyne 1960-64); fire and accident mangr United Standard Insurance Co Ltd (Provident Life Assurance Group) 1968-75, asst gen mangr London and Manchester Assurance Co Ltd 1978-82 (gen branch mangr 1975-78), md Wesleyan Assurance Society 1982-; dir: Wesleyan Home Loans Ltd, Wesleyan Development Ltd; tstee Wesleyan Employee Benefit Scheme; vice pres Insur Inst of London 1978-91, dep pres Exeter Insurance Inst 1981- 82; pres Birmingham Insurance Inst 1987-88; Freeman City of London, memb Worshipful Co of Insurers; FCII 1960; *Recreations* sport; *Style—* Lawrence Hamilton, Esq; 5 Netherstone Grove, Four Oaks, Sutton Coldfield, W Midlands B74 4DT (☎ 021 353 5310); Wesleyan Assurance Society, Colmore Circus, Birmingham B4 6AR (☎ 021 200 3003, fax 021 200 2971)

HAMILTON, Loudon Pearson; CB (1987); s of Vernon Hamilton (d 1980), of Glasgow, and Jean Mair (d 1987); *b* 12 Jan 1932; *Educ* Hutchesons' GS Glasgow, Univ of Glasgow (MA); *m* 15 Aug 1956, Anna Mackinnon, da of Hugh Young (d 1955), of Glasgow; 2 s (Hugh Vernon b 1958, Gavin Patrick b 1964); *Career* Nat Serv 2 Lt RA 1954-55; Dept of Agric (Scottish Off) 1960, private sec to Parly Under Sec of State for Scotland 1963-64, first sec Agric Br Embassy Copenhagen 1966-70, asst sec Dept of Agric and Fisheries for Scotland 1973-79, princ estabs offr Scottish Office 1979-84, sec Dept of Agric and Fisheries for Scotland 1984-; memb Agric and Food Res Cncl 1984-; *Recreations* hillwalking, bad bridge; *Clubs* Royal Cwlth Soc; *Style—* Loudon Hamilton, Esq, CB; DAFS Pentland House, Robbs Loan, Edinburgh EH14 1TW (☎ 031 556 8400)

HAMILTON, Dr Michael; OBE (1988); s of Dr Archibald Hamilton (d 1939), of Clifton End, Manningham Lane, Bradford, Yorks, and Silvia, *née* Wolf (d 1971); *b* 17 Feb 1923; *Educ* Bradford GS, Epsom Coll, St Mary's Hosp Med Sch, Univ of London (MB BS, MD); *m* 23 Nov 1946, Jane, da of Dr Edgar Bernard Argles (d 1955), of Amersham, Bucks; 2 s (David b 1948, Ian b 1951), 1 da (Susan b 1961); *Career* Flt Lt (later Sqdn Ldr) RAFVR serv, acting med specialist RAF Nocton Hall; house physician St Mary's Sector Hosps 1945-46, sr med registrar St Mary's Hosp 1949-52, sr med registrar RPMS Hammersmith Hosp 1952-56; Nuffield travelling res fell: Alfred Hosp Melbourne 1954, Univ of Otago Dunedin 1955; conslt physician Chelmsford Hosps 1956-81, hon conslt physician Mid Essex Health Authy 1981-; examiner in med: Univ of Glasgow, Royal Coll of Physicians; former memb: Chelmsford Hosp Mgmnt Ctee, NE Thames Regnl Hosp Bd, Essex AHA, Mid Essex DHA, Cncl RCP; memb: Int Soc of Hypertension 1966, BMA 1945, Assoc of Physicians 1966; MRCP 1946, FRCP 1966; *Books* Anti-Hypertensive Therapy (jtly, 1966), The Hypertensive Patients (jtly, 1980); *Recreations* gardening, golf; *Style—* Dr Michael Hamilton, OBE; 3 Barnfield Feering, nr Colchester, Essex CO5 9HP (☎ 0376 71914)

HAMILTON, Sir Michael Aubrey; s of Rt Rev Eric Hamilton, KCVO, sometime Bishop Suffragan of Shrewsbury, Registrar of the Most Noble Order of the Garter and Dean of Windsor, by his w Jessie, da of Sir Walter Cassels; *b* 5 July 1918; *Educ* Radley, Univ Coll Oxford; *m* 16 May 1947, Lavinia, da of Sir Charles Ponsonby, 1 Bt, TD; 1 s, 3 da; *Career* served WWII 1 Bn Coldstream Gds; MP (C): Wellingborough 1959-64, Salisbury 1965-83; asst govt whip 1961-62, Lord Cmmr Treasy 1962-64; UK rep UN Gen Assembly 1970, US Bicentennial Celebrations 1976; PPS to Francis Pym (Foreign Sec) 1982-83; kt 1983; *Style—* Sir Michael Hamilton; Lordington House, Chichester, W Sussex (☎ 024 34 371717)

HAMILTON, Michael John; s of William E Hamilton (d 1985), of Guelph, Canada, and Jean, *née* Clark; *b* 24 Oct 1939; *Educ* Univ of Western Ontario (BA), Univ of Oxford (MA); *m* 20 Sept 1967, Irena, da of Albert Rudusons (d 1962); 1 s (Andrew), 3 da (Katharine, Anna, Nina); *Career* jt md Mfrs Hanover Ltd 1969-73; exec dir: First Boston Corpn Europe Ltd 1973-78, Blyth Eastman Dillon Inc 1978-79; memb Euro Advsy Bd Nippon Telephone and Telegraph Inc 1986-, md Wallace Smith Tst Co Ltd 1980-; tstee St Margaret's Residential Estate; *Recreations* tennis, opera, cottage; *Clubs* City of London; *Style—* Michael Hamilton, Esq; Wallace, Smith Trust Co Ltd, 77 London Wall, London EC2 (☎ 071 638 6444, fax 071 588 6470)

HAMILTON, (Mostyn) Neil; MP (C) Tatton 1983-; s of Ronald Hamilton, of Southsea, Hants, and Norma, *née* Jones; *b* 9 March 1949; *Educ* Amman Valley GS, UCW Aberystwyth (BSc, MSc), Corpus Christi Coll Cambridge (LLB); *m* 4 June 1983, (Mary) Christine, da of Dr Edward Theodore Holman, of Manaccan, Cornwall; *Career* called to the Bar Middle Temple 1978; dir IOD 1982-83; contested (C): Abertillery 1974, Bradford N 1979; PPS to Min for Public Tport 1986-87, memb Treasy and Civil Serv Select Ctee 1987-90; sec Cons Pty Fin Ctee 1987-90; vice chm Cons Pty Trade and Industry Ctee 1987-90, govt whip 1990-, vice patron Small Business Bureau 1983-; *Books* The Facts of State Industry, US/UK Double Taxation Treaty (1980); *Recreations* bibliomania, gardening, architecture and conservation, silence; *Style—* Neil Hamilton, Esq, MP; House of Commons, London SW1A 0AA (☎ 071 219 4157)

HAMILTON, Nicholas Ian; s of Ian Archibald Hamilton, of Alnwick, Northumberland, and Billie (Kathleen), *née* Stocken; *b* 11 Nov 1949; *Educ* Epsom Coll, Univ of York (BA); *m* Nicola May, da of Kenneth Stephen Spooner; 2 da (Charlotte Emily May b 1976, Claudia Frances b 1980); *Career* Touche Ross & Co 1971-84, Schroders 1984-; FCA 1979, memb Stock Exchange 1986; *Recreations* tennis, riding; *Clubs* In and Out, MCC; *Style—* Nicholas Hamilton, Esq; Schroder Securities Ltd, 120 Cheapside, London EC2 (☎ 071 382 3000, fax 071 382 3057, car 0860 383825)

HAMILTON, Prof Nigel; s of Sir Denis Hamilton (d 1988), and Olive, Lady Hamilton, *née* Wanless; *b* 16 Feb 1944; *Educ* Westminster Sch, Univ of Munich, Trinity Coll Cambridge (BA, MA); *m* 1, 1966, Hannelore Pfeifer (d 1973); 2 s (Alexander b 1967, Sebastian b 1970); m 2, 1976, Outi Palovesi; 2 s (Nicholas b 1977, Christian b 1980); *Career* slave Andre Deutsch Publishing House 1965-66; fndr: The Greenwich Bookshop 1966, The Biography Bookshop 1987; freelance author, lectr and broadcaster 1969-; *publications* Royal Greenwich (with Olive Hamilton, 1969), The Brothers Mann, The Lives of Heinrich and Thomas Mann (1978), Monty: The Making of a General (1981), Monty: Master of the Battlefield (1983), Monty: The Field-Marshal (1986), Monty, The Man Behind the Legend (1987); writer and narrator, films incl: Monty, In Love and War (BBC TV 1987), Frontiers, Finland and the Soviet Union (BBC TV 1989); currently J F Kennedy scholar and visiting prof Univ of Moss Boston (working on a new complete life of President Kennedy 1917-63); *Awards* Whitbread prize for Best Biography 1981, Templer award for Best Contrib to Mil History 1987, Blue Ribbon award for Best Documentary (NY Film and Video Assoc) 1987; *Recreations* lake sailing; *Style—* Prof Nigel Hamilton; c/o David Higham Associates, 5-8 Lower John Street, London W1R 4HR

HAMILTON, Nigel James; *b* 27 March 1941; *Educ* Loretto; *m* 1966, Valerie Joan Moorwood; 1 s (James Andrew b 1968), 1 da (Fiona Allison b 1972); *Career* articled clerk Graham Proom & Smith Newcastle upon Tyne 1959-64; Ernest & Young ptnr 1975-, nat ptnr in charge of insolvency; vice pres Soc of Practitioners of Insolvency, chm Insolvency Practitioners Ctee ICAEW; ACA 1965; *Recreations* coaching rugby, football, golf, tennis, boats, opera, theatre; *Style—* Nigel J Hamilton, Esq; Lindenwood, Cokes Lane, Chalfont St Giles, Buckinghamshire HP8 4UD; Ernst & Young, Becket House, Lambeth Palace Rd, London SE1 7EU (☎ 071 928 2000)

HAMILTON, Nigel John Mawdesley; QC (1981); s of Archibald Dearman Hamilton, OBE, of 21 Briant's Piece, Hermitage, nr Newbury, Berks, and Joan Worsley, *née* Mawdesley; *b* 13 Jan 1938; *Educ* St Edward's Sch Oxford, Queen's Coll Cambridge (BA, MA); *m* 31 Aug 1963, Leone Morag Elizabeth, da of William Smith Gordon, CBE; 2 s (Andrew b 5 Oct 1966, William b 5 May 1970); *Career* Nat Serv 2 Lt RE; asst master: St Edward's Sch Oxford 1961-65, King's Sch Canterbury 1963-65; called to the Bar Inner Temple 1965, in practice Western Circuit, bencher Inner Temple 1989-; *Recreations* fishing; *Clubs* Flyfishers'; *Style—* Nigel Hamilton, Esq, QC; St John's Chambers, Small St, Bristol, BS1 1DW (☎ 0272 213456, fax 0272 294 821); 1 Essex Court, Temple, London EC4Y 9AR (☎ 071 936 3030, fax 071 353 8620)

HAMILTON, Sir Patrick George; 2 Bt (UK 1937), of Ilford, co Essex; s of Maj Sir (Collingwood) George Clements Hamilton, 1 Bt (d 1947), and Eleanor (d 1957), eld da of Henry Simon, of Manchester; *b* 17 Nov 1908; *Educ* Eton, Trinity Coll Oxford; *m* 17 Oct 1941, Winifred Mary Stone (Pix), CBE, and an assoc of Newnham, fndr chm Disabled Living Fndn and of Winged Fellowship Tst, memb Exec Cncl Royal Assoc for Disablement and Rehabilitation (Radar), da of late Hammond B Jenkins, of Maddings, Hadstock; *Heir* none; *Career* md and later chm Tyresoles Ltd 1934-53; dir: Simon Engineering Ltd 1937-78, Propellor Production Miny of Aircraft Prodn 1941-43, Renold Ltd 1952-78, Lloyds Bank Ltd 1953-79, Possum Controls Ltd; chm Expanded Metal Co Ltd 1955-78; tstee: Eleanor Hamilton Educational Trust, Disabled Living Fndn, Charitable Tst, Sidbury Tst; *Clubs* Carlton; *Style—* Sir Patrick Hamilton, Bt; 21 Madingley Rd, Cambridge CB3 0EG (☎ 0223 351577)

HAMILTON, Peter Boris; *b* 17 Oct 1928; *Educ* Bedford Sch, Univ of St Andrews (BSc), Harvard Univ (MBA); *m* 1951, Gwendolen Mary, *née* Clark; 1 s (Michael), 1 da (Susan); *Career* Pilot Offr RAF; chm and chief exec: Firth Cleveland Ltd 1977-79, GKN Engrg and Construction Servs Ltd 1978-79; gp chief exec APV Holdings plc 1980-84, chief exec Carrier Holdings Ltd 1985-; *Recreations* sailing (TSMY 'Moorea IV'), skiing, photography, politics; *Clubs* Royal Yacht Sqdn, Royal Thames Yacht, Royal Southampton Yacht; *Style—* Peter Hamilton, Esq; 31 Chantry View Rd, Guildford, Surrey GU1 3XW (☎ 0483 65318); Carrier Holdings Ltd, Carrier House, The Crescent, Leatherhead, Surrey KT22 8DY (☎ 0372 376000, fax 0372 377758)

HAMILTON, Peter Brian; s of Lt-Col Brian Hamilton, of Briar Lodge, Galmpton, S Devon, and Clara Maria, *née* Ertelthaler; *b* 7 Feb 1941; *Educ* Beaumont Coll Windsor, Plymouth Coll of Navigation (Diploma); *m* 1 (m dis); 1 s (James Drummond Alexander b 11 Sept 1977); m 2, 1979, Rosalind Mary, da of Bernard James Sanger (d 1990); 1 s (Edward Peter Willoughby b 14 Nov 1980), 1 step s (Charles Lindsay Jerrom b 11 May 1973), 1 step da (Amanda Suzanne Jerrom b 25 Aug 1970); *Career* PR exec; navigating cadet Shell Tankers Ltd 1957-60, reporter and feature writer Financial Times 1960-63, Planned Public Relations International (Young and Rubicam) 1963-75 (exec, account dir, md), dir public affairs Gulf Oil Corporation (Europe Africa and ME) 1975-80, dir Good Relations Group plc 1980-84; md: Hill & Knowlton Ltd London 1984-85, The Communication Group plc 1985-; winner of various awards for UK community affairs prog for Gulf Oil; author of various articles and essays on public relations; MIPR 1967, memb Int PR Assoc 1971; *Recreations* sailing, gardening, music, French railways; *Clubs* Salcombe Yacht; *Style—* Peter Hamilton, Esq; The Mill, West Farndon, Daventry, Northants NN11 6TU (☎ 0327 61727); The Communication

Group plc, 19 Buckingham Gate, London SW1E 6LB (☎ 071 630 1411, fax 071 931 8010)

HAMILTON, Maj Peter James Sidney; MBE (mil 1953); s of Maj Frank Carr Hamilton (d 1946), late RGA, of Bishop's Stortford, Herts, and Alice Joan, *née* Trumper (d 1973); *b* 19 Nov 1917; *Educ* Bishop's Stortford Coll; *m* 1962, Patricia Douglas, da of Robert Hirst (d 1940), of Croydon; 2 s (Andrew, Hamish), 2 da (Rosamund, Penelope); *Career* served WWII with Prince of Wales Own Regt of Yorkshire and on Gen Staff: N Africa, Palestine, Iraq, India, Burma, China, Malaya, Cyprus, attained rank of Maj; banker 1936-38; instr Mons Offr Cadet Sch 1951-54, Cyprus 1957-60, security advsr to PM of S Rhodesia 1961-62, dir Chubb Security Services Ltd 1972-78, md Zeus Security Consultants Ltd 1978-83, dep chm Zeus Security Ltd 1980-83, md Peter Hamilton (Security Consultants) Ltd 1983-89, jt md (with John Ingram) Hamilton Ingram Ltd 1989-90; twice chm Euro Chapter American Soc for Industl Security (dep chm 1990-); has lectured wideley in Europe, USA and Canada; hon fell Inst of Professional Investigators, memb Br Security Indust Assoc; assoc memb Nat Supervisory Cncl for Intruder Alarms; FRSA, FIPI, FInstD; *Books* editor Handbook of Security; *Publications* Espionage Terrorism and Subversion in an Industrial Society (1968 and 1980), Computer Security (1972), Business Security (1980), The Adminstration of Corporate Security (1987); several works translated into Japanese, Finnish and Italian; *Recreations* country life, fishing; *Clubs* Athenaeum, Army and Navy; *Style—* Maj Peter Hamilton, MBE; 37-39 Eastcheap, London EC3M 1DT (☎ 071 623 9913)

HAMILTON, Sir (Robert Charles) Richard Caradoc; 9 Bt (NS 1646), of Silvertonhill, Lanarkshire; s of Sir Robert Hamilton, 8 Bt (d 1959), and Irene (d 1969), 2 da of Sir Charles Mordaunt, 10 Bt; *b* 8 Sept 1911; *Educ* Charterhouse, St Peter's Coll Oxford; *m* 16 April 1952, Elizabeth Vidal, da of Sir William Pell Barton, KCIE, CSI, formerly of Lower Lodge, Ardingly, Sussex; 1 s (Andrew), 3 da (Susanna b 1956, Sophie b 1964, Penelope b 1966); *Heir* s, Andrew Caradoc Hamilton, *qv* b 23 Sept 1953; *Career* Intelligence Corps 1940-45; taught French and drama at Ardingly Coll 1945-61; church warden Walton d'Eivile 1970-, memb Warwickshire Co Cncl Educn Ctee 1965-73; govr Westham House Adult Educn Coll, memb Warwickshire CLA; plays acted at Margate, Dundee and Farnham Reps, five Shakespeare plays directed at the Minack Theatre; landowner (4000 acres); *Publications* de Luze's A History of the Royal Game of Tennis (trans, 1979), Barcellon's Rules and Principles of Tennis (trans, 1987); *Recreations* real tennis, playwright; *Style—* Sir Richard Hamilton, Bt; The Old Rectory, Walton, Warwick CV35 9HX (☎ 0789 840460)

HAMILTON, His Hon Judge Richard Graham; s of Henry Augustus Rupert Hamilton (d 1970), and Frances Mary Graham, *née* Abercrombie; *b* 26 Aug 1932; *Educ* Charterhouse, Univ Coll Oxford (MA); *m* 16 April 1960, Patricia Craghill, da of Willian Newton Ashburner (d 1954); 1 s (William Graham b 1963), 1 da (Susan Elizabeth b 1965); *Career* recorder of Crown Court 1974, chllr of Diocese of Liverpool 1976; *Books* Foul Bills and Dagger Money (1979), All Jangle and Riot (1986), A Good Wigging (1988); *radio plays* Van Gogh in England (1981), Voices from Babylon (1983), A Longing for Dynamite (1984), The Maybrick Trial (1988), The Veronica Meeting (1990); *Recreations* reading, walking, films; *Clubs* Athenaeum, Liverpool; *Style—* His Hon Judge Hamilton

HAMILTON, Robert Abraham; CBE (1971); s of Isaac Hamilton (d 1955), of Annalong, Co Down; *b* 5 Feb 1909; *Educ* Royal Belfast Academical Inst, Queen's Univ Belfast (BSc, BAgric), Fitzwilliam Hall Cambridge (DipAgric), Imperial Coll of Tropical Agric (AICTA); *m* 1935, Caroline Dorothea, da of Henry Adams (d 1934), of Belfast; 2 s; *Career* dir: Central Agric Control Board ICI Ltd 1944-58, Pharmaceutical Div ICI Ltd 1955-60, Billingham Div ICI Ltd 1958-64, Scottish Agric Industries Ltd 1959-64, W & HM Goulding Ltd 1964-71; dep chm Agric Div ICI Ltd 1964-71; chm: Plant Protection Ltd, Richardsons Fertilisers Ltd, Ulster Fertilisers Ltd 1964-71, Northern Ireland Agric Trust 1967-74, NI Tourist Board 1970-75, Pigs Marketing Board Investment Company 1971-77, Unipork Ltd 1976-78; pres Société Pour La Protection de L'Agriculture (Paris) 1967-71; sr pro chllr and senate chm Queen's Univ Belfast 1986- (sr pro chllr 1980-86); Hon DSc Queen's Univ 1973; *Recreations* gardening, travelling; *Clubs* Ulster, Farmers'; *Style—* Robert Hamilton, Esq, CBE; Riverside, 205 Mountsandel Rd, Coleraine, N Ireland BT52 1TB (☎ 0265 52022)

HAMILTON, Thomas Gottfried Louis; s of Louis Hamilton (d 1948), of 77 Ladbroke Grove, London W11, and Johanna Agnes Lucia, *née* Jahn (d 1956); *b* 29 March 1930; *Educ* The King's Sch Canterbury, UCL (BA); *m* 23 March 1957, Georgina Vera, da of Hugh Millen Craig (d 1956), of 3 Rose Park East, Belfast; 1 s (Richard b 1964), 1 da (Julia b 1962); *Career* asst architect: Bertram Carter 1956-58, Campbell-Jones & Ptnrs 1958-60; ptnr Hammett & Norton 1960-64, fndr ptnr McDonald Hamilton & Montefiore 1964-86, dir MHM Partnership Ltd 1986-; memb RIBA; *Recreations* painting, theatre, music, literature, winter sports; *Clubs* Arts; *Style—* Thomas Hamilton, Esq; 55 Addison Ave, London W11 4QU; Dorking Tye Cottage, Dorking Tye, Bures, Suffolk CO8 5JY; 102 Jermyn St, London SW1Y 6EE (☎ 071 930 3381, fax 071 839 1085)

HAMILTON, William McDonald (Bill); s of Cdr James Hamilton, VRD, RNR (ret), of St Andrews, Fife, Scotland, and Emily, *née* McDonald; *b* 22 Sept 1943; *Educ* Dundee HS, Monkwearmouth Coll Sunderland; *m* 5 Feb 1972, Gertrude Veronica, da of Michael Lee (d 1963), of Aughrim, Co Wicklow; 1 s (David b 1980), 1 da (Claire b 1973); *Career* reporter/news reader Tyne Tees TV 1966-70, sports prodr BBC radio 1970-71, reporter/presenter Border TV 1971-73, reporter/presenter BBC TV Scotland 1973-80, home affrs corr BBC TV news 1981-88, news and sports corr BBC TV News 1988-; memb Football Referees Assoc; hon special dep sheriff Essex Co, New Jersey, USA; *Books* I Belong to Glasgow (1975); *Recreations* association football referee (class 1); *Style—* Bill Hamilton, Esq; 39 Waverley Rd, St Albans, Hertfordshire, AL3 5PH (☎ 0727 869604); BBC Television Centre, Wood Lane, London W12 7RJ (☎ 081 576 7487, fax 081 576 1314)

HAMILTON, William Winter (Willie); s of J Hamilton, of Philadelphia, Co Durham; *b* 26 June 1917; *Educ* Washington GS Co Durham, Alderman Smith GS Co Durham, Univ of Sheffield (BA, DipEd); *m* 1, 1944, Joan Callow (d 1968); 1 s, 1 da; m 2, 1982, Mrs Margaret Cogle, of Newcastle Upon Tyne; *Career* serv WWII Middle East with RAF and Capt Pioneer Corps; joined Labour Pty 1936, contested (Lab) W Fife 1945; MP (Lab): W Fife 1950-74, Fife Central 1974-87; contested (Lab) S Hams 1987, ret; chm House of Commons Estimates Ctee 1964-70, vice chm PLP 1966-70, Members' chm of Euro Parl's Rules and Procedure Ctee, memb Euro Parl Ctees on Regnl Policy and Budgets, MEP 1975-79, contested and lost Lincs CC elections 1988; ret 1987; memb Public Accounts Ctee 1979-84; MEP 1975-79; noted for anti-monarchy views; sponsored MP for COHSE former schoolmaster; *Books* The Monarchy and its Future (contrib, 1969), The Queen (contrib, 1977), My Queen and I (1975); *Recreations* baiting establishment and other public menaces; *Style—* Willie Hamilton, Esq

HAMILTON AND BRANDON, 15 and 12 Duke of (S 1643, GB 1711); Angus Alan Douglas Douglas-Hamilton; also Earl of Arran (S 1503), Marquess of Douglas, Lord Abernethy and Jedburgh Forest (both S 1633), Marquess of Clydesdale, Earl of Arran and Cambridge, Lord Aven and Innerdale (all S 1643), Earl of Lanark, Lord Machansire and Polmont (both S 1661), Baron Dutton (GB 1711); Premier Duke in the Peerage of Scotland; Hereditary Keeper of Holyrood House; 18 Duke of Châtelherault (France 1549); s of 14 and 11 Duke of Hamilton and Brandon, KT, GCVO, AFC, PC (d 1973), and Dowager, Duchess of Hamilton and Brandon, *qv*; *b* 13 Sept 1938; *Educ* Eton, Balliol Coll Oxford (MA); *m* 1, 1972 (m dis 1987), Sarah, da of Sir Walter Scott, 4 Bt; 2 s (Alexander b 1978, John b 1979), 2 da (Eleanor b 1973, Anne b 1976); m 2, 1988, Jillian, da of Noel Robertson, formerly w of (1) Martin Page, and (2) Edward Hulton; *Heir* s, Alexander, Marquess of Douglas and Clydesdale b 1978; *Career* Flt Lt RAF until 1967, flying instructor 1965, instrument rating examiner 1966, sr commercial pilot's licence 1968, test pilot Scottish Aviation 1971-72; KStJ and Prior Order of St John in Scotland 1975-83, hon memb Royal Scottish Pipers Soc, memb Piobaireachd Soc, patron British Airways Pipe Band 1977, Hon Air Cdre No 2 (City of Edinburgh) Maritime HQ Unit RAuxAF 1982-; chm Hamilton & Kinneil Estates Ltd 1973; memb The Queen's Body Guard for Scotland (Royal Co of Archers); *Recreations* motorcycling, diving, piping; *Clubs* New (Edinburgh), RAF; *Style—* His Grace the Duke of Hamilton; Lennoxlove, Haddington, E Lothian EH41 4NZ (☎ 062 082 2156)

HAMILTON AND BRANDON, Dowager Duchess of; Lady Elizabeth Ivy; *née* Percy; OBE, DL; da of 8 Duke of Northumberland, KG, CBE, MVO (d 1930); *b* 25 May 1916; *m* 2 Dec 1937, 14 Duke of Hamilton and (11 of) Brandon, KT, GCVO, AFC, PC (d 1973); 5 s (including 15 Duke); *Style—* Her Grace the Dowager Duchess of Hamilton and Brandon, OBE, DL; North Port, Lennoxlove, Haddington, E Lothian (☎ 062 082 2478)

HAMILTON-BURKE, Ian Douglas; s of John Douglas Burke (ka 1944), and Jean Hamilton, *née* Drane; *b* 14 Oct 1943; *Educ* Liverpool Coll; *m* Joan, da of Harold Planche; 2 s (James Patrick Ian, Andrew Charles Raoul), 1 da (Victoria Roisin); *Career* articled clerk J Summerskill and Son 1960-66, accountant Cooper Brothers 1966-68, ptnr Poulsoms Chartered Accountants 1968-86; dir Minster Executive Ltd 1978-86; ptnr: Hodgson Impey 1986-90, Pannell Kerr Forster Chartered Accountants 1990-; dir Curtins Holdings plc 1990-; bd memb Liverpool Marie Curie Home, govr Liverpool Coll; memb Co of Pipe Makers and Tobacco Blenders, Freeman City of London 1982 (Liveryman); memb IOD, FCA; *Recreations* hockey, marathon running, fell walking; *Clubs* Lyceum (Liverpool), Rotary (Liverpool); *Style—* Ian Hamilton-Burke, Esq; Bellisle, Quarry St, Liverpool L25 6DY (☎ 051 428 3199); Pannell Kerr Forster, 52 Mount Pleasant, Liverpool L3 5UN (☎ 051 708 7773)

HAMILTON-DALRYMPLE, Lady Anne-Louise Mary; *née* Keppel; da of 9 Earl of Albemarle, MC, and his 2 w, Dame Diana Grove, DBE (*see* Countess of Albemarle); *b* 17 March 1932; *m* 25 Sept 1954, Maj Sir Hew Fleetwood Hamilton-Dalrymple, 10 Bt, KCVO, *qv*; 4 s; *Style—* The Lady Anne-Louise Hamilton-Dalrymple; Leuchie, North Berwick, East Lothian (☎ 0620 2903)

HAMILTON-DALRYMPLE, Sir Hew Fleetwood; 10 Bt (NS 1698), of North Berwick, Haddingtonshire; KCVO (1985, CVO 1974), JP (1987); s of Sir Hew Clifford Hamilton-Dalrymple, 9 Bt (d 1959), and Anne Dorothea Dyce Nicol, *née* Thorne (d 1979); *b* 9 April 1926; *Educ* Ampleforth; *m* 25 Sept 1954, Lady Anne-Louise Mary Keppel, *qv*; 4 s (Hew Richard b 1955, John James b 1957, Robert George b 1959, William Benedict b 1965); *Heir* s, Hew Richard Hamilton-Dalrymple; *Career* Maj Grenadier Gds, ret 1962; Capt Queen's Body Guard for Scotland (Royal Co of Archers) (Adjt 1964-85, pres Cncl 1988-); dir: Scottish & Newcastle Breweries 1967-86 (vice chm 1983-86), Scottish American Investment Co 1967- (chm 1985-); DL East Lothian 1964-87; Vice-Lieut East Lothian 1973-87; Lord Lieut East Lothian 1987-; *Clubs* Cavalry and Guards'; *Style—* Sir Hew Hamilton-Dalrymple, Bt, KCVO, JP; Leuchie, North Berwick, East Lothian (☎ 0620 2903)

HAMILTON-DALRYMPLE, Hew Richard; s and h of Sir Hew Hamilton-Dalrymple, 10 Bt; *b* 3 Sept 1955; *Educ* Ampleforth, Corpus Christi Coll Oxford (MA), Clare Hall Cambridge (MPhil), Birkbeck Coll London (MSc); *m* 1987, Jane Elizabeth, yr da of Lt-Col John Morris, of Leighterton, Glos; 1 s (Hew John Lucian Hamilton b 28 Aug 1990), 1 da (Hero Cecilia b 1989); *Career* Overseas Devpt Inst Fellowship Swaziland 1982-84, Peat Marwick Management Consultants 1984-; *Style—* Hew Dalrymple Esq; 1 Puddle Dock, London EC4 (☎ 071 236 8000)

HAMILTON-GRIERSON, Philip John; s of Philip Francis Hamilton Grierson (d 1963), of Edinburgh, and Margaret Bartholomew (d 1969); *b* 10 Oct 1932; *Educ* Rugby Sch, CCC Oxford (MA); *m* 1963, Pleasaunce Jill, da of Peter Gordon Cardew, of Somerset; 1 s (Philip b 1967), 2 da (Sophie b 1964, Katherine b 1966); *Career* PO RAF (Asst Adjutant 207 AFS); sec to Lib Party 1962-65; dir: Gallaher Ltd 1978-88, dep chm Highlands and Islands Devpt Bd 1988-; chm Highland Hospice Ltd 1988-, dir Cromarty Firth Port Authority 1989-; *Recreations* tennis, music, sailing; *Clubs* Highland; *Style—* Philip Hamilton-Grierson, Esq; Pitlundie, North Kessock, By Inverness 1V1 1XG (☎ 0463 73 392); Highland and Island Development Board, Bridge St, Inverness 1V1 1QR (☎ 0463 234 171)

HAMILTON-JONES, Maj-Gen John; CBE (1976); s of Capt George Hamilton-Jones, MBE (d 1985), of London, and Lilian, *née* Bolton (d 1981); *b* 6 May 1926; *Educ* Cranbrook Sch, Univ of Edinburgh; *m* 15 Nov 1952, Penelope Ann Marion, da of Robert Laurie Derry (d 1982), of Norfolk; 3 da (Janet b 1956, Diana b 1958, Kaye b 1962); *Career* commissioned 1945; served India, Burma and Malaya 1945-50, staff Coll 1959, DS 1966, cmd Artillery Regt 1967-70, MOD staff from Col through Brig to Maj-Gen 1971-81; vice pres of int mkting: Gen Def Corpn 1981-89, Allied Res Corpn 1989-; Lefroy Gold medallist 1972; MIERE 1960, FRAeS 1980, FBIM 1981, FInstD 1982; Cdr Assoc Franco Britannique 1980; *Recreations* rugby, rowing, flying, music; *Style—* Maj-Gen John Hamilton Jones, CBE; Lloyds Bank, Cox's and Kings Branch, 7 Pall Mall, PO Box 1190, London SW1Y 5NA

HAMILTON OF DALZELL, 4 Baron (UK 1886); James Leslie Hamilton; s of 3 Baron Hamilton of Dalzell, GCVO, MC (d 1990), and Rosemary Olive, *née* Coke; *b* 11 Feb 1938; *Educ* Eton; *m* 29 March 1967, (Ann Anastasia) Corinna Helena, da of Sir Pierson John Dixon, GCMG, CB (d 1965), and sis of Piers Dixon, *qv*; 4 s (Hon Gavin b 8 Oct 1968, Hon Robert b 29 July 1971, Hon John b (twin) 29 July 1971, Hon Benjamin b 5 Nov 1974); *Heir* s, Hon Gavin Hamilton b 8 Oct 1968; *Career* 2 Lt Coldstream Gds 1956-58; memb Stock Exchange 1967-80; dir Rowton Hotels plc 1978-82; govr Queen Elizabeth's Fndn for the Disabled 1978- (chm of appeals 1980-88, chm of executive 1989-); vice chm Surrey Branch CLA 1986-89, chm 1989; Freeman City of London, Liveryman Worshipful Co of Drapers 1977; *Recreations* shooting; *Clubs* Boodle's, Pratt's; *Style—* The Rt Hon the Lord Hamilton of Dalzell; Stockton House, Norton Shifnal, Shropshire (☎ 095 271 270); Betchworth House, Betchworth, Surrey RH3 7AE (☎ 073 784 3324)

HAMILTON OF DALZELL, Dowager Baroness; Rosemary Olive; er da of Hon Sir John Spencer Coke, KCVO (d 1957; 5 s of 2 Earl of Leicester, KG), and Hon Dorothy Olive Levy-Lawson (d 1937), o child of 1 and last Viscount Burnham, GCMG, CH; *b* 18 Nov 1910; *m* 4 March 1935, 3 Baron Hamilton of Dalzell, GCVO, MC (d 1990); 2 s (4 Baron, Hon Archie Hamilton, *qqv*), 1 da (Hon Janet (Hon Mrs Lane Fox), *qv*); *Style—* The Rt Hon the Dowager Lady Hamilton of Dalzell

HAMILTON-RUSSELL, Col Brian Gustavus; s of Brig The Hon R G Hamilton-Russell, DSO, LVO, DL, of S Hill House, Cornbury, Charlbury, Oxon, and Pamela Penelope, *née* Cayzer (d 1988); *b* 8 May 1940; *Educ* Eton, RMA Sandhurst; *m* 1, 8

Oct 1967 (m dis 1979), Lea Wild; 1 s (Henry b 28 Feb 1969), 1 da (Victoria b 9 March 1976); m 2, 19 July 1981, Sarah Julianne, *née* Colebrook-Robjent; *Career* cmmnd 1960, CO 17/21L 1980-83, Col MOD 1985, ret 1989; SAAB Training Systems 1989-; *Recreations* country sports; *Clubs* Cavalry and Guards'; *Style*— Col Brian Hamilton-Russell; Hardwickforge, Stottesdon, Kidderminster DY14 8TL (☎ 074 632 577)

HAMILTON-RUSSELL, Hon Gustavus (Tavie) Michael Stucley; s and h of 10 Viscount Boyne, JP, DL; *b* 27 May 1965; *Educ* Harrow, RAC Cirencester (Dip in Rural Estate Management); *Career* probationer RICS; *Recreations* cricket, skiing, travel; *Clubs* Turf, Annabel's; *Style*— The Hon Gustavus Hamilton-Russell; Burwarton House, Bridgnorth, Shropshire

HAMILTON-RUSSELL, Col James Gustavus; MBE (1976); s of Maj Hon John Hamilton-Russell (ka 1943), and Lady Diana, *née* Legge (d 1970); *b* 11 Sept 1938; *Educ* Eton; *m* 30 Oct 1965, Alison Mary, da of Dr Sydney Haydn Heard, MBE, of Channel Islands; 2 s (Mark b 1969, Edward b 1969), 1 da (Julia b 1967); *Career* Col; cmmnd Royal Dragoons 1958; served Middle East, Far East, Europe 1958-78; mil asst to Dep Supreme Allied Cdr Europe Shape 1978-80; CO The Blues and Royals 1980-82; Cdr: Household Cavalry and Silver Stick-in-Waiting 1983-86, Br Contingent UN Force in Cyprus 1986-88; asst mil attaché Br Embassy Washington 1988-; *Recreations* shooting, fishing, travel, golf, music; *Clubs* Cavalry and Guards'; *Style*— Col James G Hamilton-Russell, MBE; The Brewhouse, Dudmaston, Bridgnorth, Shropshire (☎ 0746 780094); British Defence Staff, British Embassy, Washington DC

HAMILTON-RUSSELL, Brig Hon Richard Gustavus; DSO (1943, and bar 1944), LVO (4 Class 1977), DL (N Yorks 1973); 2 s of 9 Viscount Boyne, JP, DL; *b* 4 Feb 1909; *Educ* Eton, RMC Sandhurst; *m* 17 July 1939, Hon Pamela Cayzer (d 1987), da of 1 Baron Rotherwick; 2 s (Brian, Richard), 1 da (Veronica); *Career* WWII N Africa & Italy (despatches 1945); Brig late 17/21 Lancers (Col 1957-65); memb HM's Body Guard of Hon Corps of Gentlemen at Arms 1956-79 (standard bearer 1977); High Sheriff Yorks 1968; *Clubs* Cavalry and Guards'; *Style*— Brig the Hon Richard Hamilton Russell, DSO LVO, DL; South Hill House, Cornbury Park, Charlbury, Oxfordshire OX7 3EU

HAMILTON-SMITH, Hon Timothy; s of late 2 Baron Colwyn; *b* 28 June 1944; *Educ* Cheltenham, Oxford Univ (MA); *m* 29 July 1967, Carolyn, da of Bernulf Llewelyn Hodge; 2 da; *Style*— The Hon Timothy Hamilton-Smith; 45 Third Ave, Claremont 7700, S Africa

HAMILTON STUBBER, Hon Mrs (Susanna Cynthia); *née* Brooke; The Hon; da of 2 Viscount Brookeborough, PC, DL; *b* 17 April 1962; *m* 29 April 1989, Richard J Hamilton Stubber, s of late Col John Hamilton Stubber; *Career* secretary; *Recreations* tennis, riding, swimming, travelling; *Style*— The Hon Mrs Hamilton Stubber

HAMILTON-TURNER, William Allen; s of Claude Frederic Hamilton-Turner (d 1988), of Castletown, IOM, and Mary Eileen, *née* Allen; *b* 16 July 1947; *Educ* Eton; *m* 4 Dec 1976, Dulcie Jill, da of Herbert Secretan Procter, of Ballasalla, IOM; 1 s (Henry b 1978), 1 da (Lucy b 1980); *Career* Brown Shipley & Co Ltd 1966-74, Singer & Friedlander (IOM) Ltd 1974-80, md Rea Bros (IOM) Ltd 1980-; Hon ADC to HE The Lieut Govr of the Isle of Man; Freeman City of London, Liveryman Worshipful Co of Skinners; ACIB 1972; *Recreations* golf; *Clubs* MCC; *Style*— William Hamilton-Turner, Esq; Ballaquayle, Princes Rd, Douglas, IOM (☎ 0624 624063); 29 Athol St, Douglas, IOM (☎ 0624 629696, fax 0624 622039, telex 627752)

HAMILTON-WEDGWOOD, Kenneth Roy; s of Thomas Hamilton-Wedgwood (d 1978), of Rustington, W Sussex, and Elsie Maude, *née* Kershaw (d 1978); *b* 11 Dec 1931; *Educ* Warwick and Whitgift Schs; *m* 19 May 1973 (m dis 1979), Rita, da of George William Gransden, of Hyde Home Farm, East Hyde, Luton, Bedfordshire; *Career* conslt/tech author (electronics) Environmental Instrumentation Satellite Data Collection (Argos) Oceanography; Nat Serv RAF; SAC airborne wireless communciations, early experimental decca navigator 1950-52; with Whessoe Ltd Darlington Co Durham, resident engr i/c instrumentation installation data measurement and transmission system for Esso West London Terminal (bulk fuel storage) 1960-67, with Ultra Electronics London 1968-69, Marine Electronics Ltd 1971-72; *Recreations* fully licensed radio amateur G3XKW, country walking, music, photography; *Style*— Kenneth Hamilton-Wedgwood, Esq; Rosedale, Redmoor, Bodmin, Cornwall PL30 5AR (☎ 0208 872608); Partech Electronics Ltd, Eleven Doors, Charlestown, St Austell, Cornwall PL25 3NN (☎ 0726 74856, telex 45362 G a/G PARTEK, fax 0726 68850)

HAMILTON-TEMPLE-BLACKWOOD, Lady Perdita Maureen; yr da of late 4 Marq of Dufferin and Ava (ka 1945); *b* 17 July 1934; *Career* racehorse breeder; *Style*— Lady Perdita Hamilton-Temple-Blackwood

HAMLIN, Patrick Lindop; s of Thomas Patrick Hamlin (d 1985), of Hong Kong, and Zehra Emena, *née* Mahmoud (d 1987); *b* 4 Aug 1947; *Educ* Birkenhead Sch, Inns of Ct Sch of Law; *m* 11 Sept 1976, Shelagh Joan, da of William Bernard Fitzpatrick (d 1985), of Wallasey; 1 s ((Edward) Ruari b 1985), 1 da (Georgina Louise b 1982); *Career* called to the Bar Gray's Inn (McCaskie scholar) 1970; private practice in common law and local authy, asst rec 1990; memb Lincoln's Inn Bar Rep Ctee, former memb Ctee London Common Law Bar Assoc; memb Lincoln's Inn and Gray's Inn; *Recreations* skiing, reading, Eng furniture; *Style*— Patrick Hamlin, Esq; 22 Old Buildings, Lincolns Inn, London WC2A 3UJ (☎ 071 831 0222, fax 071 831 2239)

HAMLYN, Michael John; s of Jack Trelawney Hamlyn (d 1990), and Agnes, *née* Ecob; *b* 26 March 1936; *Educ* Kimbolton Sch Cambs, St Peter's Coll Oxford (BA); *m* 1 July 1961, Claire Honor Annabel, da of Silvester Bolam; 2 s (Nicholas b 5 Dec 1961, Alexander b 12 Aug 1964), 1 da (Victoria b 28 Feb 1963); *Career* reporter The Journal Newcastle upon Tyne 1959-61; The Sunday Times: reporter 1961-65, news ed 1965-68, asst ed (news) 1968-70; The Times: asst ed (night) 1970-73, exec ed (night) 1973-81, chief of bureau NY Bureau News Ltd and Times Newspapers 1981-83, South Asia corr 1983-89, dep foreign ed 1989, chief night ed 1989-90, exec ed news 1990-; *Clubs* Savile; *Style*— Michael Hamlyn, Esq; 51 Lawrie Park Ave, London SE26 6HA (☎ 081 778 8449); The Times, 1 Pennington St, London E1 9XN (☎ 071 782 5128, fax 071 488 3242, car 0860 395147)

HAMLYN, Paul Bertrand; *b* 12 Feb 1926; *Educ* St Christopher's Sch Letchworth; *m* 1 s, 1 da; *Career* fndr Paul Hamlyn Ltd 1950 (developed Hamlyn Group which was sold 1965 and repurchased 1986), exec chm Octopus Publishing Group 1971-, formed Conran Octopus 1983 (merger with Heinemann Group 1985); directorships incl: Octopus Books Ltd 1979, Tigerprint Ltd 1980, The Hamlyn Publishing Group Ltd 1986, Dean & Sons Ltd 1986, Reed International plc 1987, Brandchart Ltd 1987, Chateau de Bagnols Ltd 1988, English Nat Ballet Ltd 1989; overseas dir Octopus Books Party Ltd and Bookworld Party Ltd 1989; involved with Paul Hamlyn fndn (promoting med in The Third World and fighting illiteracy in the UK); *Recreations* opera; *Style*— Paul Hamlyn, Esq; Octopus Publishing Group plc, Michelin House, 81 Fulham Rd, London SW3 6RB (☎ 071 581 9393, fax 071 589 8440)

HAMMENT, Hon Mrs (Tania Ann); *née* Campbell; eldest da of 6 Baron Stratheden and Campbell, *qv*; *b* 19 Sept 1960; *m* 1984, Paul Hamment; *Style*— The Hon Mrs Hamment; c/o The Rt Hon Lord Stratheden and Campbell, Ridgewood, MS 1064, Cooroy, Queensland 4563, Australia

HAMMER, James Dominic George; CB (1983); s of E A G Hammer, and E L G Hammer; *b* 21 April 1929; *Educ* Dulwich, Corpus Christi Coll Cambridge; *m* 1955, Margaret Eileen Halse; 2 s, 1 da; *Career* conslt in occupational health and safety; dep dir gen Health & Safety Exec 1985-89, vice chm Camberwell Health Authy, Southwark MENCAP; pres Int Assoc of Labour Inspection, tech dir UK Skills; chm: Nat Certificate Scheme for In Serv Inspection Bodies, UK Nat Organising Ctee for the Euro Year of Safety Hygiene and Health at Work 1992; *Style*— James Hammer, Esq, CB; 10 Allison Grove, Dulwich, London SE21 7ER

HAMMER, Rev Canon Dr Raymond Jack; s of Mendel Paul Hammer (d 1968), and Lily, *née* Simons (d 1972); *b* 4 July 1920; *Educ* Liverpool Inst, Oxford Univ (BA, Dip Theol, MA), London Univ (BD, MTheol, PhD); *m* 23 July 1949, Vera Winifred, da of Charles Thomas Reed (d 1947), of Hayes, Middx; 2 da (Alison b 1954, Elizabeth b 1956); *Career* ordained: deacon 1943, priest 1944; sr tutor St John's Coll Durham 1946-49, lectr in theology Univ of Durham 1946-49; prof: Central Theological Coll Tokyo 1950-64, St Paul's Univ Tokyo 1954-64; chaplain Br Embassy Tokyo 1954-64, lectr The Queen's Coll Birmingham 1965-77; lectr Dept of Theology Univ of Birmingham 1965-77; dir: W Midlands Ministry Course 1971-76, Bible Reading Fellowship 1977-85; tutor Open Univ 1978-85; external examiner for London, Warwick, Southampton and Exeter Univs; canon St Michael's Cathedral Kobe Japan 1964-; sec Archbishops' Interfaith Conslts 1981-, treas Studiorum Novi Testamenti Societas 1970-82; memb: SNTS, SOTS, SST; *Books* Japan's Religious Ferment, Commentary on Daniel, Oxford Dictionary of the Christian Church (contrib), Theological Word Book of the Bible; New Testament Times Bible Atlas (ed); contrib to: Shorter Books of the Apocrypha, Man and His Gods, Concise Dictionary of the Bible, Concise Dictionary of Christian Mission, World Religions; *Recreations* travel; *Clubs* Athenaeum, Sion Coll; *Style*— The Rev Canon Dr Raymond Hammer; 22 Midsummer Meadow, Inkberrow, Worcs WR7 4HD (☎ 0386 792 883)

HAMMERBECK, Brig Christopher John Anthony; s of Sqdn Ldr Olaf Rolf William Hammerbeck (d 1988), of Frinton on Sea, Essex, and Ivy Mary, *née* Musker; *b* 14 March 1943; *Educ* Mayfield Coll; *m* 23 March 1974, Alison Mary, da of Capt John Edward Felice, VRD, JP, RNR, of 7 Holcombe Ct, 9/11 Argyle Rd, Southport, Lancs; 1 s (Christian b 7 July 1976), 2 da (Lucy b 5 Oct 1977, Leonora b 26 Oct 1984); *Career* slr's articled clerk 1961-64; cmmnd 1965, Staff Coll 1975, DAA and QMG 12 Mech Bde 1976-78, DS Army Staff Coll 1982-84, CO 2 Royal Tank Regt 1984-87, ACOS G3 HQ 1 BR Corps 1987-88, RCDS 1989, cmd 4 Armd Bde 1990-; memb Exec Ctee Army Bobsleigh Assoc; MBIM 1981; *Recreations* sailing, cricket, skiing, bobsleigh; *Clubs* Army and Navy; *Style*— Brig Christopher Hammerbeck; HQ 4th Armoured Brigade, British Forces Post Office 17 (☎ 010 49 251 616350)

HAMMERSLEY, Rear Adm Peter Gerald; CB (1982), OBE (1965); s of the late Capt Robert Stevens Hammersley, of Endon, Stoke-on-Trent, and Norah, *née* Kirkham; *b* 18 May 1928; *Educ* Denstone Coll, RN Engrg Coll, RN Coll Greenwich, Imperial Coll London (DIC); *m* 1959, (Audrey) Cynthia Henderson, da of Pelham Bolton, of Wilmslow, Cheshire; 1 s (Robert), 1 da (Daphne); *Career* RN 1946-82, First Engr Offr First Br Nuclear Submarine HMS Dreadnought 1960-64, Capt RN Engrg Coll 1978-80, CSO (Engrg) to C-in-C Fleet 1980-82; chief exec Br Internal Combustion Engine Mfrs Assoc 1982-85, dir Br Marine Equipment Cncl 1985; Master Worshipful Co of Engrs 1988-89 (Freeman); *Recreations* walking, gardening; *Clubs* Army and Navy; *Style*— Rear Adm Peter Hammersley, CB, OBE; Wistaria Cottage, Linersh Wood, Bramley, nr Guildford, Surrey GU5 0EE (☎ 0483 898568); BMEC, 30 Great Guildford St, London SE1 0HS (☎ 071 928 9199)

HAMMERTON, Prof Max; *b* 16 Nov 1930; *Educ* Univ of London (BSc, BSc, PhD); *m* 15 Nov 1958 (m dis 1975), Elizabeth Mary, da of Rev Prof R V G Tasker; 1 s (Oliver David b 18 June 1962 d 1973); *Career* tech engr Br Aerospace 1953-59, res scientist MRC Cambridge 1960-73; visiting prof: UCLA 1969, St John's 1973; prof of psychology Univ of Newcastle upon Tyne 1973-89 (ret); visiting prof: VMI 1984, Murdock Univ 1986 and 1990, UNC(C) 1987; memb Soc of Friends of the Nat Army Museum; FUCLA 1969, FBIS 1954, MEPA 1962, RUSI 1970, FBPS 1973-88; *Books* Statistics for the Human Sciences (1974); *Recreations* history, cooking, shooting, SciFi; *Style*— Prof M Hammerton; Dept of Psychology, University of Newcastle, Newcastle upon Tyne, NE1 7RU (☎ 091 222 6000)

HAMMERTON, His Hon Judge Rolf Eric; s of Eric Maurice Hammerton (d 1967), and Dorothea Alice, *née* Zander (d 1970); *b* 18 June 1926; *Educ* Brighton and Hove GS, Peterhouse Cambridge (MA, LLB); *m* 1953, Thelma Celèstine, da of Vernon Peters Appleyard (d 1955); 1 s (Alastair Rolf b 1960), 3 da (Veronica Lesley b 1954, Andrea Frances b 1956, Lorraine Hilary b 1958); *Career* Capt R Sussex Regt seconded RWAFF 1946-48; called to the Bar Inner Temple 1952, circuit judge 1972, contrib to Butterworth Co Ct Precedents; Philip Teichman Prizeman 1953; *Recreations* cooking; *Style*— His Hon Judge Hammerton; The Old Rectory, Falmer, nr Brighton BN1 9PG

HAMMETT, Sir Clifford James; s of late Frederick John Hammett; *b* 8 June 1917; *Educ* Woodbridge Sch; *m* 1946, Olive Beryl, da of Frank A Applebee; 4 s, 1 da; *Career* serv WWII 1 Punjab Regt (despatches), POW Siam Railway 1942-45; called to the Bar Middle Temple 1948, chief justice: Tonga 1956-68, Fiji 1967-72; acting govr-gen Fiji 1971; kt 1969; *Style*— Sir Clifford Hammett; c/o Lloyds Bank, 6 Pall Mall, London SW1

HAMMICK, Paul St Vincent; s and h of Sir Stephen George Hammick, 5 Bt; *b* 1 Jan 1955; *Educ* Sherborne; *m* 11 July 1984, Judith Mary, da of Ralph Ernest Reynolds, of Wareham, Dorset; *Style*— Paul Hammick Esq

HAMMICK, Sir Stephen George; 5 Bt (UK 1834); DL (Dorset 1989); s of Sir George Frederick Hammick, 4 Bt (d 1964), and Mary Adeliza, *née* Welch-Thornton (d 1988); *b* 27 Dec 1926; *Educ* Stowe, RAC Cirencester; *m* 16 April 1953, Gillian Elizabeth, da of Maj Pierre Elliot Inchbald, MC (d 1959); 2 s (Paul b 1955, Jeremy b 1956), 1 da (Wendy b 1960); *Heir* s, Paul St Vincent Hammick; *Career* RN 1944-48, RAC Cirencester 1949-50, MFH Cattistock Hunt 1961 and 1962, CC Dorset 1958, farmer; High Sheriff Dorset 1981; vice chm Dorset CC (chm 1988); chm Cattistock Hunt; *Recreations* hunting, fishing, music; *Style*— Sir Stephen Hammick, Bt, DL; Badgers, Wraxall, Dorchester, Dorset DT2 0HN (☎ 093583 343)

HAMMON, Michael Antony; s of Arthur Stanley Hammon (d 1985), of Leam Bank Farm, Wappenbury, Leamington Spa, and Mary Augusta, *née* Salter; *b* 5 March 1937; *Educ* Oundle; *m* 8 Oct 1966, Letitia Sara, da of Henry Leslie Johnson, of Offchurch Bury, Leamington Spa; 2 s (Charles b 1969, George b 1973), 2 da (Sara b 1970, Elizabeth b 1972); *Career* slr and farmer; memb Warwick RDC 1965-70; Warwickshire CC 1967-81: chm Fin Educn and Policy and Resources Ctees, ldr of Cncl 1976-81; memb Coventry City Cncl 1987-; vice chm Warwick, Leamington and Kenilworth Cons Assoc 1970-73, lawyer memb W Midlands Rent Assessment Panel 1982-86; press and PR offr Warwickshire Law Soc 1984-89; dir: H H Goddard Ltd, Eathorpe Hall Farms Ltd, Marath Devpts Ltd; *Recreations* gardening, photography; *Clubs* Naval and Military; *Style*— Michael Hammon, Esq; Eathorpe Hall, Leamington Spa CV33 9DF (☎ 0926 632755); Lloyds' Bank Chambers, 53 Corporation St, Coventry CV11GL (☎ 0203 227537)

HAMMOND, Anthony Hilgrove; s of Col Charles William Hilgrove Hammond (d 1985), and Jesse Eugenia, *née* Francis (d 1940); *b* 27 July 1940; *Educ* Malvern, Emmanuel Coll Cambridge (open scholar, BA, LLB); *m* 29 Sept 1988, Avril, *née*

Collinson; *Career* admitted slr 1965, asst slr GLC (formerly London CC) 1965-68 (articled clerk 1962-65); Home Office: legal asst 1968-70, sr legal asst 1970-74, asst legal advsr 1974-80, princ asst legal advsr to Home Office and NI Office 1980-88, dep under sec of state and legal advsr 1988- (legal advsr NI Office 1988-); Freeman City of London 1991, memb Worshipful Co of Glass Sellers 1990; *Recreations* bridge, music, birdwatching; *Clubs* Athenaeum; *Style—* Anthony Hammond, Esq; Legal Adviser's Branch, Home Office, Queen Anne's Gate, London SW1H 9AT (☎ 071 273 2681)

HAMMOND, Col Catherine Elizabeth; CBE (1950); da of late Frank Ernest Rauleigh Eddolls; *b* 22 Dec 1909; *Educ* Lassington House Highworth, Chesterville Sch Cirencester; *m* 1, 1930, Albert Edward Haynes (decd); 1 s, 1 da; m 2, 1949, Aldwyn Hammond (d 1958), farmer and racehorse trainer; *Career* Col WRAC, dep dir HQ Eastern Cmd 1947-50, Hon Col 54 (E Anglian) Div/Dist WRAC (TA) 1964-68; chm WRAC Assoc Cncl 1966-70, life vice pres WRAC Assoc 1971-; chm Highworth Branch RNLI 1971-; pres: Highworth Royal Br Legion (Women's Section) 1977-86, Highworth Amateur Dramatic Soc 1982-86; town Mayor Highworth 1979-81 and 1984-85; SSStJ 1986; *Recreations* racing, hockey; *Style—* Col Mrs Catherine Hammond, CBE; Red Down, Highworth, Wilts (☎ 0793 762331)

HAMMOND, Donald William; s of Capt Eric Gardiner Hammond, of Bollington, and Mabel Joyce, *née* Buck; *b* 5 March 1948; *Educ* King's Sch Macclesfield, Univ of Lancaster (BA), Manchester Business Sch (DBA); *m* 19 March 1982, Carole Isobel Hammond; *Career* Turner & Newall Ltd 1969-73, account exec Citibank NA 1974-76, Banco Hispano Americano Ltd 1976-86; dir: Edington plc 1986-, Henry Cooke Gp plc 1988-, Naughton plc 1989-, William Hammond Ltd (currently); chm various schs in Ealing 1978-86, chm fin and dep ldr London Borough of Ealing 1983-86 (cncllr 1978-86); FInstD, Assoc MBA; *Recreations* riding, shooting, chess, reading science fiction; *Style—* Donald Hammond, Esq; The Butts, Smithy Lane, Gt Budworth, Ches; No 1 King St, Manchester (☎ 061 834 2535, fax 061 834 8650, car 0860 326948)

HAMMOND, Eric Albert Barratt; OBE (1977); s of Arthur Edgar Hammond (d 1963), and Gertrude May, *née* Barratt (d 1983); *b* 17 July 1929; *Educ* Corner Brook Sch Newfoundland; *m* 26 Sept 1953, Brenda Mary, da of George Edgeler; 2 s (Ivan b 1958, Shaun b 1961); *Career* Nat Serv REME 1950-52; EETPU: electrician 1952-64, exec cncllr 1964-84, gen sec 1984-; chm 5 N Fleet Scout Gp 1979-84; cncllr: Gravesend Borough DC 1957-60, Northfleet UDC 1960-63; *Recreations* gardening, photography, watching rugby, reading; *Clubs* Gravesend Rugby; *Style—* Eric Hammond, Esq, OBE; EETPU, Hayes Court, West Common Rd, Hayes Bromley, Kent (☎ 081 462 7755)

HAMMOND, Frederick Alexander; s of Frederick Hammond (d 1976), and Alice Hammond (d 1980); *b* 8 July 1936; *Educ* Ashton GS, Univ of Manchester (MSc); *m* 16 April 1960, Margaretta, da of Edward Thorpe (d 1974); 2 s (Nigel Derek b 1964, Nicholas Mark b 1965); *Career* sr ptnr The APC Int Gp; chm: Project Management Int plc, Rogers Chapman plc; *Recreations* golf, bridge, shooting; *Clubs* Brooks's, Burhill, City Livery; *Style—* Frederick Hammond, Esq; 3 Ince Rd, Burwood Park, Walton-on-Thames KT12 5BJ (☎ 0932 227686); The Lodge, Harmondsworth, West Drayton, Middx UB7 0LA (☎ 081 759 0966)

HAMMOND, (John) Martin; s of Rev Canon Thomas Chatterton Hammond (d 1981), Rector of Beckenham, and Joan, *née* Cruse; *b* 15 Nov 1944; *Educ* Winchester, Balliol Coll Oxford; *m* 25 June 1974, Meredith Jane, da of Kenneth Wesley Shier, of Ontario, Canada; 1 s (Thomas b 1976), 1 step da (Chantal b 1970); *Career* asst master St Paul's 1966-71, teacher Anargyrios Sch Spetsai Greece 1972-73, asst master Harrow 1973-74, master in coll Eton 1980-84 (head of Classics Dept Eton 1974-80); headmaster: City of London Sch 1984, Tonbridge Sch 1990; memb Gen Advsy Cncl of the BBC; *Books* Homer: The Iliad, A New Prose Translation (1987); *Style—* Martin Hammond, Esq; Tonbridge School, Tonbridge, Kent TN9 1JP (☎ 0732 365555)

HAMMOND, Michael David; s of Raymond Hammond, of Albury, Guildford, Surrey, and Linda Mary Underdown, *née* Tanner; *b* 25 Sept 1962; *Educ* Broadwater Secdy Sch Godalming; *Career* Nat Hunt Jockey; ridden 231 winners incl: Scottish Grand National 1986 (Hardy Lad), Glenlivet Liverpool 1988 (Royal Illusion), Lanzorotie Hurdle Kempton 1988 (Fredcoteric); Nat Hunt Jockey of the Year 1988, Pacemaker Int Jockey of the Year 1988, William Hill Golden Spur's award 1988; *Recreations* watching football (Leeds Utd and Glasgow Rangers); *Style—* Michael Hammond, Esq; Tupgil Park, Stables, Coverham, Middleham, North Yorkshire (☎ 0969 40228)

HAMMOND, Michael Harry Frank; CBE (1990), DL (Nottinghamshire 1990); s of Cecil Edward Hammond (d 1963), and Kate Hammond, *née* Lovell (d 1984); *b* 5 June 1933; *Educ* Leatherhead Co Secdy Sch; *m* 21 Aug 1965, Jenny, da of Dr George Macdonald Campbell (d 1981); 2 s (Ralph b 1968, Richard b 1971), 1 da (Sara b 1966); *Career* slr; dep town clerk: Newport Monmouthsire 1969-71, Nottingham 1971-73; chief exec and town clerk Nottingham City Cncl 1973-90 (prosecuting slr 1963-66); election supervisor Rhodesia Independence Elections 1980; chm: Assoc of Local Authy Chief Execs 1984-85, E Midlands Branch Soc of Local Authy Chief Execs 1988-90; pres Notts Law Soc 1989-90; Zimbabwe Independence medal 1980, Rhodesia medal 1980; *Recreations* walking, gardening, bowling; *Style—* Michael Hammond, Esq, CBE, DL; 41 Burlington Rd, Sherwood, Nottingham (☎ 0602 602 000)

HAMMOND, Valerie June; *née* Amas; da of Stanley F Amas (d 1972), and Eileen M Amas; *b* 22 Oct 1942; *Educ* Pendergast GS, Open Univ (BA); *m* 1982, A Knighton Berry; *Career* dir Ashridge Mgmnt Res Group 1980-, past pres European Women's Mgmnt Devpt Network; previously: project mangr Petroleum Indust Training Bd, Mobil Oil, Friden Ltd, Rank Screen Servs; *author*: Employment Potential: Issues in the Development of Women (with Ashridge team, 1980), The Computer in Personnel Work (with Edgar Wille, 1981), Tomorrow's Office Today (with David, Birchall 1981), No barriers here? (1982), Practical approaches to Women's Management Development (1984), Current Research in Management (1985), Men and Women in Organisations (with Tom Boydell, 1985), and jl articles from research and conferences; *Style—* Ms Valerie Hammond; Ashridge Mgmnt Coll, Berkhamsted, Herts HP4 INS (☎ 044 284 3491, telex 826434 Aschcol G)

HAMMOND-CHAMBERS, Robert Alexander (Alex); s of Maj Robert Rupert Hammond-Chambers (d 1952), and Leonie Elise Noble, *née* Andrews; *b* 20 Oct 1942; *Educ* Wellington, Magdalene Coll Cambridge (MA); *m* 24 Feb 1968, Sarah Louisa Madelaine, da of Col John Guy Dalrymple Fanshawe (d 1984); 2 s (Rupert, Jeremy), 1 da (Lucy); *Career* Ivory & Sime: joined 1964, ptnr 1969, dir 1975 (upon incorporation), dep chm 1982, chm 1985; first overseas govr Nat Assoc Securities Dealers Inc 1984-87; chm Edinburgh Green Belt Tst 1991, dir GBC North America Fund Inc, govr Fettes; memb Soc Investmt Analysts; *Recreations* golf, tennis, sailing, photography; *Clubs* New (Edinburgh); *Style—* Alex Hammond-Chambers, Esq; Grange Dell, Penicuik, Midlothian EH26 9LE; 49 Inlet Cove, Kiawah Is, S Carolina SC 29455; Ivory & Sime PLC, 1 Charlotte Square, Edinburgh EH2 4DZ (☎ 031 225 1357, fax 031 225 2375, telex 727242 IVORYS G)

HAMMOND INNES, Ralph; CBE (1978); s of William Hammond Innes and Dora Beatrice, *née* Crisford; *b* 15 July 1913; *Educ* Cranbrook Sch; *m* 1937, Dorothy Mary, da of William Cape Lang (d 1989); *Career* Maj RA WWII, served in ME; journalist Financial News 1934-40; author; landowner; Hon DLitt Univ of Bristol 1985; *Books* (all made into films): The Lonely Skier (1947), The White South (1949), Campbells Kingdom (1952), The Mary Deare (1956), Levkas Man (1971), Golden Soak (1973); other books incl: The Last Voyage: Captain Cook's Lost Diary (1978), Solomons Seal (1980), The Black Tide (1982), High Stand (1985), Medusa (1988); non-fiction incl: Harvest of Journeys (1960), Scandinavia (with the eds of Life, 1963), Sea and Islands (1967), The Conquistadors (1969), Hammond Innes Introduces Australia (1971), Hammond Innes' East Anglia (1986); plays incl: Campbells Kingdom (screenplay, 1957), The Story of Captain James Cook (TV play, 1975); *Clubs* Soc of Authors, PEN, Royal Yacht Sqdn, Royal Ocean Racing, Royal Cruising; *Style—* Ralph Hammond Innes, Esq, CBE; Ayres End, Kersey, Suffolk IP7 6EB

HAMMOND-MAUDE, Hon Mrs (Sonia Mary); *née* Peake; da of 1 Viscount Ingleby (d 1966); *b* 12 Dec 1924; *m* 1, 26 Oct 1946 (m dis 1958), David George Montagu Hay, GC, RN, later 12 Marquess of Tweeddale (d 1979); 3 s; m 2, 27 June 1966, Maj Michael William Vernon Hammond-Maude, JP, 5 Royal Inniskilling Dragoon Gds (ret); *Career* served WWII, WRNS; *Style—* The Hon Mrs Hammond-Maude; Mitton Cottage, Arncliffe, nr Skipton, N Yorks

HAMMOND-STROUD, Derek; OBE (1987); s of Herbert William Stroud (d 1951), of Stanmore, Middx, and Ethel Louise, *née* Elliott (d 1988); *b* 10 Jan 1926; *Educ* Salvatorian Coll Harrow, Trinity Coll of Music; *Career* RWAFF India, Burma 1944-47; concert and opera baritone, private study with Elena Gerhardt and Prof Gerhard Hüsch; Glyndebourne Festival Opera 1959-, ENO 1960-, Covent Garden Opera 1971-, Netherlands Opera 1976-87, Metropolitan Opera NY 1977-80, Teatro Colón Buenos Aires 1981, Munich State Opera 1983; Festivals: Edinburgh, Aldburgh, Vienna, Munich, Cheltenham, English Bach; concerts and recitals in Spain Iceland and Denmark; recordings: EMI, RCA, Philipps, Célèbre, Symposium Records; prof of singing RAM 1974-90; awarded Sir Charles Santley Memorial Gift by Worshipful Co of Musicians 1988; Freeman City of London 1952; ISM 1971; Hon: RAM 1976, FTCL 1982; *Recreations* chess, study of philosophy; *Style—* Derek Hammond-Stroud, Esq, OBE; 18 Sutton Rd, Muswell Hill, London N10 1HE (☎ 081 883 2120)

HAMOND; *see*: Harbord-Hamond

HAMPDEN, 6 Viscount (UK 1884); Anthony David Brand; DL (E Sussex 1986); s of 5 Viscount Hampden (d 1975), and Hon Imogen Rhys, da of 7 Baron Dynevor; *b* 7 May 1937; *Educ* Eton; *m* 27 Sept 1969 (m dis 1988), Cara Fiona, da of Capt Claud Proby, Irish Guards (d 1987), 2 s of Sir Richard Proby, 1 Bt, MC, JP, DL; 2 s (Hon Francis, Hon Jonathan Claud David Humphrey b 24 Aug 1975), 1 da (Hon Saracha Mary b 7 March 1973); *Heir* s, Hon Francis Anthony Brand b 17 Sept 1970; *Career* chm Emanuel Sch Governing Body 1985-; *Books* Henry and Eliza; *Clubs* White's; *Style—* The Rt Hon the Viscount Hampden, DL; Glynde Place, Glynde, Lewes, Sussex (☎ 079 159 337)

HAMPDEN, Imogen, Viscountess; Hon Imogen Alice; *née* Rhys; da of late 7 Baron Dynevor and Lady Margaret Child-Villiers, da of 7 Earl of Jersey; *b* 27 Aug 1903; *m* 14 July 1936, 5 Viscount Hampden (d 1975); 1 s (6 Viscount), 2 da (Hon Mrs Hodgson, Hon Mrs Chetwode); *Style—* The Rt Hon Imogen, Viscountess Hampden; Trevor House, Glynde, Lewes, Sussex

HAMPDEN, Leila, Viscountess; Leila Emily; only da of Lt-Col Frank Seely, JP, DL (d 1928, 3 s of Sir Charles Seely, 1 Bt), of Ramsdale Park, Notts; *b* 24 Aug 1900; *m* 26 July 1923, 4 Viscount Hampden, CMG (d 1965); 2 da (Lady Dacre, w of Hon William Douglas-Home; Hon Mrs Ogilvie Thompson) and 2 da decd; *Style—* The Rt Hon Leila, Viscountess Hampden; Mill Court, Alton, Hants (☎ 0420 23125)

HAMPEL, Ronald Claus; s of Karl Victor Hugo Hampel (d 1960), and Rutgard Emil Klothilde, *née* Hauck (d 1975); *b* 31 May 1932; *Educ* Canford Sch, CCC Cambridge (MA); *m* 11 May 1957, Jane Bristed, da of Cdr Wilfred Graham Hewson, RN, of Wellington, Som; 3 s (Andrew b 1960, Rupert b 1962, Peter b 1962), 1 da (Katharine b 1958); *Career* Nat Serv 2 Lt 3 RHA 1951-52; ICI: joined 1955, vice pres Americas 1973-77, gen mangr Commercial Gp 1977-80, chm Paints Div 1980-83, chm agrochemicals 1983-85, dir 1985-; non-exec dir: Powell Duffryn plc 1984-89, Commercial Union 1987-, Br Aerospace 1989-; memb: Br N American Ctee 1986- (Exec Ctee 1989), Bd American C of C 1988; CBIM 1985; *Recreations* skiing, tennis, golf; *Clubs* All England Lawn Tennis, MCC; *Style—* Ronald Hampel, Esq; ICI plc, ICI Group HQ, 9 Millbank, London SW1P 3JF (☎ 071 834 4444, fax 071 834 2042, telex 21324 ICI HQ G)

HAMPERL, John Frederick; s of Alois Hamperl (d 1987), of Watford, Herts, Copthorn, Sussex, and Fort George, Guernsey, and Pauline Wilhelmena, *née* Henne; *b* 6 April 1936; *Educ* Ardingly, Nat Coll of Food Technol London, Cassio Coll Watford; *m* 2 June 1963, Elaine Karen, da of Henry Holm (d 1979), of London; 1 s (Lawrence b 1965), 1 da (Karen b 1967); *Career* Nat Serv RASC 1955-57; serv Malaya and Singapore; dir: A Hamperl Ltd 1960-82, Porky Boy Products Ltd 1967-73, Alan Drew Ltd 1974- (chm 1987-); chm: Bushey and Oxhey Round Table 1970-71, Round Table Area 42 (The Chilterns) 1975-76, Fullerians Rugby Club 1982-85; memb: Herts RFU, Orders and Medals Res Soc; Freeman City of London, Liveryman Worshipful Co of Butchers 1959; *Recreations* vintage motor cars (especially Bentleys), rugby football, British Naval Medals; *Clubs* Durrant's, Bentley Drivers; *Style—* John Hamperl, Esq; Alan Drew Ltd, Caxton Way, Watford, Herts WD1 8UA (☎ 0923 817 933, fax 0923 37824, car 0860 414 520)

HAMPSHIRE, Sir Stuart Newton; s of G N Hampshire; *b* 1 Oct 1914; *Educ* Repton, Balliol Coll Oxford; *m* 1961, late Renée Ayer; m 2, 1984, Nancy, *née* Cartwright; *Career* served WWII; lectr in philosophy UCL 1947-50, fell New Coll Oxford 1950-55, domestic bursar and res fell All Souls' Coll Oxford 1955-60, Grote prof of philosophy of the mind and logic Univ of London 1960-63, prof of philosophy Princeton USA 1963-70, warden Wadham Coll Oxford 1970-83; FBA; kt 1979; *Books* Spinoza (1951), Thought and Action (1959), Freedom of the Individual (1965), The Socialist Idea (1975), Two Theories of Morality (1977), Morality and Conflict (1983), Innocence and Experience (1989); *Style—* Sir Stuart Hampshire; 7 Beaumont Road, The Quarry, Headlington, Oxford

HAMPSHIRE, Susan; da of George Kenneth Hampshire (d 1964), and June Hampshire (d 1967); *b* 12 May 1942; *Educ* Hampshire Sch Knightsbridge; *m* 1, 1967 (m dis 1974), Pierre Julian Granier-Deferre; 1 s, 1 da (decd); m 2, 1981, Eddie Kulukundis, *qv*; s of George Elias Kulukundis (d 1978); *Career* actress; plays: Express Bongo, Follow That Girl, Fairy Tales Of New York, The Ginger Man, Past Imperfect, The Sleeping Prince, She Stoops to Conquer, Peter Pan, A Dolls House, The Taming of The Shrew, Romeo and Jeanette, As You Like It, Miss Julie, The Circle, Arms and The Man, Man and Superman, Tribades, An Audience Called Edward, Crucifer of Blood, Night and Day, The Revolt, House Guest, The King and I, Blithe Spirit, Married Love, A Little Night Music; films: During One Night, The Three Lives of Thomasina, Night Must Fall, The Flighting Prince of Donegal, Paris in August, Monte Carlo or Bust, Violent Enemy, David Copperfield, A Time For Loving, Living Free, Baffled, Malpertius, Neither The Sea Nor The Sand, Roses and Green Peppers, Bang; TV incl: What Katy Did, The Andromeda Breakthrough, The Forsythe Saga 1970, Variety Fair 1971, The First Churchills 1973, The Pallisers 1975, Dick Turpin 1980, Barchester Chronicles 1982, Leaving, Going to Pot I, II and III (2 series); winner 3 Emmy Awards for Best Actress; Hon DLitt: Univ of London 1984, Univ of St Andrews 1986; *Books* Susan's Story, The Maternal Instinct, Lucy Jane at the Ballet,

Lucy Jane on Television, Lucy Jane and the Dancing Competition, Trouble Free Gardening, Every Letter Counts; *Recreations* gardening, writing, water skiing; *Style*— Miss Susan Hampshire; c/o Midland Bank Ltd, 92 Kensington High St, London W8

HAMPSON, Bernard William; s of James William Hampson, of Theakston Hall Stud, Theakston, Bedale, North Yorks, and Nellie Hampson; *b* 1 Feb 1942; *m* 16 Sept 1965, Pamela Jean, da of Arnold Pearson, DSO, DFC, of 9 Helmesly Way, Northallerton, North Yorks; 2 s (Simon b 1966, Jeremy b 1968), 1 da (Rebecca b 1970); *Career* chm and md Mavitta Holdings Ltd, md John Evans and Associates Ltd, dir PE International PLC; *Recreations* racehorse owner (horse, Madraco, won William Hill Stewards Cup), golf, cricket; *Style*— Bernard Hampson, Esq; 32 Mearse Lane, Barnt Green, Birmingham B45 8HL (☎ 021 445 3849); Systems House, 11 The Square Broad St, Birminghamn B15 1AS (☎ 021 236 5877)

HAMPSON, Christopher; s of Harold Ralph Hampson (d 1972), of Montreal, Canada, and Geraldine Mary, *née* Smith (d 1984); *b* 6 Sept 1931; *Educ* Ashbury Coll Ottawa Canada, McGill Univ Montreal Canada (BEng); *m* 18 Sept 1954, Joan Margaret Cassils, da of Lt-Col Arthur C Evans (d 1960), of Montreal; 2 s (Christopher Geoffrey b 1957, Harold Arthur b 1965), 3 da (Daphne Margaret (Mrs Kearns) b 1955, Sarah Anne (Mrs Claridge) b 1958, Aimée Joan Geraldine b 1966); *Career* CIL Inc Canada: vice pres and dir 1973-78, sr vice pres and dir 1982-; md and chief exec offr ICI Australia Ltd 1984-87, exec dir ICI plc 1987-; memb and chm Cncl BIM; FBIM 1988; *Recreations* tennis, skiing; *Clubs* York (Toronto), Mount Royal (Montreal), Hurlingham; *Style*— Christopher Hampson, Esq; Imperial Chemical Industries Plc, 9 Millbank, London SW1 (☎ 071 834 4444)

HAMPSON, Dr Keith; MP (C) Leeds North-West 1983-; s of Bert Hampson (d 1967), of Shildon, Co Durham; *b* 14 Aug 1943; *Educ* King James I GS Bishop Auckland, Univ of Bristol, Harvard (PhD); *m* 1975, Frances Pauline Einhorn (d 1975); m 2, 1979, Susan, da of John Cameron; *Career* former chm Bristol Univ Cons Assoc, PA to Rt Hon Edward Heath 1966 1968 and 1970; history (American) lectr Edinburgh Univ 1968-74, MP (C) Ripon 1974-1983 (contested same at by-election July 1973), vice chm Cons Educn Ctee 1975-79, vice pres WEA 1979-, vice chm Youthaid 1979-83; memb: Assoc of Business Execs 1979-, Educn Advsy Ctee of UK Cwlth for UNESCO 1980-84; PPS to Rt Hon Tom King as Min for Local Govt and Environmental Services 1979-83, PPS to Rt Hon Michael Heseltine Sec of State for Defence 1983-84; sec Cons Parly Def Ctee 1984-88, memb Trade and Indust Select Ctee 1988-; *Recreations* tennis, gardening, DIY; *Clubs* Carlton; *Style*— Dr Keith Hampson, MP; Pool House, Pool-in-Wharfedale, Leeds LS21 1LH

HAMPSON, Prof Norman; s of Frank Hampson (d 1967), and Elizabeth Jane, *née* Fazackerley (d 1946); *b* 8 April 1922; *Educ* Manchester GS, Univ Coll Oxford (MA), Univ of Paris (Docteur de l'Université), Univ of Edinburgh (DLitt); *m* 22 April 1948, Jacqueline Juliette Jeanne Marguerite, da of Charles Hector Gardin (d 1933); 2 da (Françoise b 1951, Michèle b 1955); *Career* RNVR 1941-45, Lt 1943; asst lectr then sr lectr Manchester Univ 1948-67; prof: Univ of Newcastle 1967-74, Univ of York 1989-; FRHS 1970, FBA 1980; *Books* La Marine de l'An II (1959), A Social History of the French Revolution (1963), The Enlightenment (1968), The First European Revolution (1969), The Life and Opinions of Maximilien Robespierre (1974), A Concise History of the French Revolution (1975), Danton (1978), Will and Circumstance 1983, Prelude to Terror (1987), Saint-Just (1990); *Recreations* gardening; *Style*— Prof Norman Hampson; 305 Hull Road, York, YO1 3LB (☎ 0904 412 661)

HAMPSTEAD, Archdeacon of; *see*: Coogan, Ven Robert Arthur William

HAMPTON, Barry Charles; s of Charles Frederick Ernest Hampton, of Chippenham; and Elsie Ray, *née* Watkins; *b* 22 Aug 1937; *Educ* Chippenham GS, Bath Tech Coll; *m* 11 June 1966, Lesley May, da of Lesley Matterson Massey (d 1967), of Corsham; 1 da (Susan Jane b 26 April 1968); *Career* ptnr Harvey McGill & Hayes 1979-; ctee memb W Counties Branch of CIArb (listed panel arbitrator), former chm SW branch Inst of Public Health Engrs, memb Rotary Int and Exeter C of C; memb: Royal Philatelic Soc London, Postal History Soc, Helvetia Philatelic Soc, Exmouth Stamp Club, Wessex Philatelic Fedn, Br Philatelic Fedn (lectr and judge); county timekeeper Amateur Swimming Assoc, fndr memb Chippenham Modern Pentathlon Club; Freeman: City of London 1987 Worshipful Co of Arbitrators 1987; CEng, FIStructE 1965, FIWEM 1972 FCIArb 1974, MConsE, FFS 1985; *Recreations* postal history, philately, sea fishing; *Style*— Barry Hampton, Esq; 188 Exeter Rd, Exmouth, Devon EX8 3DZ (☎ 0395 279 513); c/o Harvey McGill & Hayes, Northernhay House, Northernhay Place, Exeter, Devon EX4 3RY (☎ 0392 525 31, fax 0392 791 24)

HAMPTON, Bryan; s of William Douglas Hampton, of Ramsey, Isle of Man, and Elizabeth, *née* Cardwell; *b* 4 Dec 1938; *Educ* Harrow County GS for Boys; *m* 10 Oct 1964, Marilyn, da of Frank Joseph; 5 da (Alison Jane b 1967, d 1988, Kathryn Louise b 1968, Lucy Ann b 1972, Sarah Elizabeth b 1976, Emily Maria b 1976); *Career* exec offr BOT 1957, asst private sec to Parly Sec 1962, private sec to Min of State 1963, asst princ 1965, second sec Ukdel Efta Gatt Geneva 1966, princ DTI 1969, asst sec Dept of Energy 1974, cnsllr (energy) Br Embassy Washington 1981, dir of personnel Dept of Energy 1989; *Recreations* music, golf; *Clubs* Northwood Golf; *Style*— Bryan Hampton, Esq; Orchard House, Berks Hill, Chorley Wood, Herts WD3 5AG (☎ 0923 282311); Dept of Energy, 1 Palace St, London SW1E 5H3 (☎ 071 238 3800)

HAMPTON, Christopher James; s of Bernard Patrick Hampton, and Dorothy Patience, *née* Herrington; *b* 26 Jan 1946; *Educ* Lancing, New Coll Oxford (MA); *m* 1971, Laura Margaret de Holesch; 2 da; *Career* res dramatist Royal Court Theatre 1968-70, freelance writer 1970-; plays: When Did You Last See My Mother? 1966, Total Eclipse 1968, The Philanthropist 1970 (Evening Standard Best Comedy Award, Plays and Players London Theatre Critics Best Play), Savages 1973 (Plays and Players London Theatre Critics Best Play, Los Angeles Drama Critics Circle Award for Distinguished Playwriting 1974), Treats 1976, After Mercer 1980, The Portage to San Cristobal of A H (from George Steiner) 1982, Tales from Hollywood 1982 (Standard Best Comedy Award 1983), Les Liasons Dangereuses (from Laclos) 1985 (Plays and Players London Theatre Critics Best Play, Standard Best Play Award 1986, NY Drama Critics' Circle Best Foreign Play Award 1987, Laurence Olivier Award 1986); TV: Able's Will BBC 1977, The History Man (from Malcolm Bradbury) BBC 1981, The Price of Tea 1984, Hotel du Lac (From Anita Brookner) BBC 1986 (BAFTA Best TV Film Award 1987), The Ginger Tree (from Oswald Wynd) BBC 1989; Films: A Dolls House 1973, Tales From the Vienna Woods 1979 (Screen International Award 1980), The Honorany Consul 1983, The Good Father 1986 (Prix Italia 1988), Wolf at the Door 1986, Dangerous Liaisons 1988 (Writers Guild of America Award, BAFTA Award Academy Award); translations: Marya (by Isoac Babel) 1967, Uncle Vanya (by Chekhov) 1970, Hedda Gabler (by Ibsen) 1970, A Doll's House (by Ibsen) 1971, Don Juan (by Molière) 1972, Tales from the Vienna Woods (by Horváth) 1977, Don Juan Come Back from the War (by Horváth) 1978, Ghosts (by Ibsen) 1978, The Wild Duck (by Ibsen) 1979, The Prague Trial (by Chéreau and Mnouchkine) 1980, Tartuffe (by Molière) 1983, Faith, Hope and Charity (by Horváth 1989; *Recreations* travel, cinema; *Clubs* Dramatists'; *Style*— Christopher Hampton, Esq; 2 Kensington Park Gardens, London W11

HAMPTON, Prof John Reynolds; s of Eric Albert Hampton (d 1979), of Gorleston, Norfolk, and Norah Kathleen, *née* Johnson (d 1981); *b* 8 Nov 1937; *Educ* Gresham's, Magdalen Coll Oxford (BA, DM, DPhil, MA, BM BCh, MRCP), Radcliffe Infirmary Oxford; *m* 25 July 1964, Pamela Jean, da of Edmund Joseph Wilkins (d 1980), of Tunbridge Wells; 2 s (Christopher, Philip), 1 da (Joanna); *Career* house physician and surgn and sr house offr Radcliffe Infirmary 1963-64, jr lectr and lectr in med Univ of Oxford 1965-68, instr in med and jr assoc in med Harvard Univ and Peter Bent Brigham Hosp Boston Mass USA 1968-69; Univ of Nottingham 1969-: lectr, sr lectr in med and hon conslt physician to Nottingham Hosps 1970-74, reader in med and conslt physician Queen's Med Centre 1974-79, prof of cardiology 1980-; sec Atherosclerosis Discussion GP 1978-81; memb: Br Cardiac Soc, Assoc of Physicians; FRCP 1975; *Books* incl: Basic Electrocardiography - an audiovisual approach (1976), All about heart attacks: A guide for patients with heart disease and high blood pressure (1980), Integrated clinical science - cardiovascular disease (1983), The ECG made easy (3 edn, 1984), The ECG in practise (1986); *Recreations* sailing; *Style*— Prof John Hampton; Dept of Medicine, D Floor, S Block, Queen's Medical Centre, Nottingham NG7 2UH (☎ 0602 709346)

HAMPTON, 6 Baron (UK 1874); Sir Richard Humphrey Russell Pakington; 6 Bt (UK 1846); s of 5 Baron Hampton, OBE, FRIBA (d 1974), and Grace, da of Rt Hon Sir Albert Spicer, 1 Bt; *b* 25 May 1925; *Educ* Eton, Balliol Coll Oxford; *m* 25 Oct 1958, Jane, da of Thomas Arnott, OBE, TD; 1 s, 2 da; *Heir* s, Hon John Pakington; *Career* Sub Lt Fleet Air Arm, RNVR WW II; in advertising to 1958, CPRE Worcs 1958-71, with Tansley Witt and Co 1971-73; sits as a Liberal Democrat in House of Lords, Lib spokesman on NI 1977-87, pres South Worcestershire Lib Assoc 1978-88; *Books* The Pakingtons of Westwood (1975); *Style*— The Rt Hon Lord Hampton; Palace Farmhouse, Upton-upon-Severn, Worcs (☎ 068 46 2512)

HAMPTON, Robert Paul; s of Michael James Toop, of 35 Lyonsdown Ave, Barnet, Herts, and Jennifer Marie, *née* Slade; *b* 14 Feb 1962; *Educ* The Nicholas Legat Sch of Russian Ballet; *m* 16 July 1982, Fiona Jayne, da of Arthur James Legate-Dear; 1 s (Ross Michael b 17 June 1986); *Career* ballet dancer; first princ role James in Bournonville's La Sylphide 1983 (performed Spoleto Festival Charlston USA 1986); performed Peter Darrell's prodns: Othello 1984, Cinderella (Prince) 1984, Don José 1985, Cheri 1985, Nutcracker (Prince) 1985, Seigfried 1986, Albrecht 1987, Tales of Hoffman 1987; Cranko's Romeo 1988, only Euro dancer Japan Ballet Festival 1988; *Style*— Robert Hampton, Esq; The Scottish Ballet Co, 261 West Princes St, Glasgow G4 9EE (☎ 041 331 2931)

HAMPTON, Surgn Rear Adm Trevor Richard Walker; CB (1988); s of Percy Ewart Erasmus Hampton (d 1952), of King's Lynn, Norfolk, and Violet Agnes, *née* Neave (d 1987); *b* 6 June 1930; *Educ* King Edward VII GS King's Lynn, Univ of Edinburgh Sch of Med (MB ChB, MRCPE); *m* 1, 11 Aug 1952 (m dis 1976), (Celia) Rosemary, da of Stanley Day (d 1957), of Winchmore Hill; 3 da (Fiona, b 1956, Nicola b 1959, Judy b 1963); m 2, 12 Aug 1976, Jennifer Lily, da of Leonard R Bootle (d 1986), of Fillongley, Warwickshire; *Career* Surgn Lt RN 1955; serv: HMS Ganges, Harrier and Victorious; conslt physician RN Hosps: Plymouth, Haslar and Gibraltar; Surgn Cdr 1967, Surgn Capt 1977; med offr i/c RN Hosps: Gibraltar 1980-82, Plymouth 1982-84; Surgn Rear Adm 1984, Support Med Servs 1984-87, Operational Med Servs 1987-89; author of pubns on Waterhouse-Friderichsen Syndrome, inhalation injury, drowning and med screening; FRCPE 1975; *Recreations* professional and amateur theatre, music, writing; *Style*— Surgn Rear Adm Trevor Hampton, CB; Coombe House, Latchley, nr Gunnislake, Cornwall PL18 9AX (☎ 0822 832419)

HAMSON, John Everard; s of Vincent Everard Hamson (d 1978), of Croydon, and Florence, *née* Reynolds (d 1979); *b* 3 April 1925; *Educ* Bromley County GS, Bedford Evening Inst; *m* 1, 1949, Mary, da of Capt George Thomas (d 1965), of Beckenham; 2 da (Anna b 1958, Victoria b 1959); m 2, 1980, Cherry, da of Herbert Edwards, of Tenby; 1 s (Jack b 1983), 1 da (Rose b 1980); *Career* RAF (Warrant Offr) 1943-47; news reporter 1941-43; 1947-56; press and PR exec 1956- (Hamson and Hamson PR Conslts); *Recreations* bass trombone; *Clubs* Wig and Pen, Press (Birmingham); *Style*— John Hamson, Esq; 42 High Street, Bidford-on-Avon, Warwicks (☎ 0789 773347)

HAMYLTON JONES, Keith; CMG (1979); s of G Jones, of Fairholm, Sussex; *b* 12 Oct 1924; *Educ* St Paul's, Balliol Coll Oxford; *m* 1953, Eira, da of B Morgan; 1 da; *Career* serv WWII Capt HM Welsh Gds (Italy, Germany and S France); HM Foreign Serv 1949-: Warsaw, Lisbon, Manila, Montevideo, Rangoon; HM consul-gen to Katanga 1970-72; ambass: Costa Rica 1974-79, Honduras 1975-78, Nicaragua 1976-79; chm (for Devon and Cornwall) Operation Raleigh 1983-85 (led int expdn to Costa Rica 1985); nat chm: Anglo-Costa Rican Soc 1983-88; Anglo-Central American Soc 1988-91; *Recreations* reading, writing (pen-name Peter Myllent)· *Clubs* Chelsea Arts; *Style*— Keith Hamylton Jones, Esq, CMG; Morval House, Morval, nr East Looe, Cornwall (☎ 05036 2342)

HANAGAN, Patrick Sean; s of Maj John Thomas Frederick Hanagan, and Eva Helen, *née* Ross; *b* 9 Aug 1950; *Educ* Gordonstoun, St Johns Coll Coolhurst, Univ of Hull, London Univ (BA); *Career* involved in int banking, econ advice and research Royal Bank of Scotland 1974-81, exec fin info servs Reuters 1981-84, co founding dir Enigma Systems Ltd 1984, fndr Business Enterprise Award 1979, Art Exhibition 1985; Freeman City of London 1978, Liveryman Worshipful Co of Needlemakers 1983; *Recreations* oil painting, piano, music and opera, books, travel, walking, working, gardening; *Style*— Patrick Hanagan, Esq; 11 Welbeck St, London W1

HANBURY, Antony; s of 3 and yst s of Horace Hanbury, but yr s by Horace's 2 w Clara, da of Edward Matthew Howard, of Gosebrook House, Wolverhampton, Staffs; Horace was 3 s of Sir Thomas Hanbury, KCVO, who was seventh in descent from Philip Hanbury (b 1582), whose er bro John was ancestor of 1 Baron Sudeley. Philip and John's Hanbury ancestors were MPs for Worcester and Worcestershire in the fourteenth century; *b* 31 July 1922; *m* 1 Sept 1949, Elizabeth Anne (d 20 Sept 1982), sole da of Col Robert Edward Kennard Leatham, DSO; 1 s (Rupert b 1952: m 1979, Anne, da of Brig Alan and Hon Mrs Breitmeyer, *qv*), 2 da (Sarah b 1950, Jane b 1954); *Career* md Singer and Friedlander, to 1982 (remains as non-exec dir); *Style*— Antony Hanbury, Esq; c/o Singer and Friedlander plc, 21 New St, Bishopsgate, London EC2M 4HR (☎ 071 623 3000)

HANBURY, Benjamin John; s of Lt-Col Christopher Lionel Hanbury, MBE, TD, JP, DL, of Burnham, Bucks, and Lettice Mary Charrington (d 1980); *b* 19 Jan 1934; *Educ* Eton, ChCh Oxford; *m* 8 May 1962, Verena Elizabeth Anne Kimmins, da of Capt Anthony Martin Hannam Kimmins, RN, OBE (d 1964); 4 s (James b 1964, Timothy b 1967, Simon b 1969, Marcus b 1972), 1 da (Lucinda b 1963); *Career* dir: Charrington and Co Ltd, The Brewers' Soc, Procrescent Ltd, Temple Grove Sch Tst Ltd, Southover Manor Gen Educnl Tst Ltd, The Medical Cncl on Alcoholism; chm: Social Responsibility Ctee The Brewers' Soc 1978-90, Bd of Govrs Aldenham Sch 1985-90; Freeman City of London 1969, Master Worshipful Co of Brewers 1977-78; *Recreations* skiing, shooting, gardening; *Style*— Benjamin Hanbury, Esq; 8 Hans St, London SW1X 0NJ; Cogans Piltdown, nr Uckfield, Sussex TN22 3XR; 66 Chiltern St, London W1M 1PR

HANBURY, Maj Christopher Osgood Philip; s of Sqdn Ldr Osgood Villiers Hanbury, DSO, DFC (ka 1943), and Cecil Patricia Thompson, *née* Harman; *b* 16 Feb 1944; *Educ* Millfield, RAC Cirencester; *m* 2 Dec 1969, Bridget Anne, da of Charles Francis Birch (d 1974), of Southern Rhodesia; 2 s (Charles b 15 May 1986, George b

6 Nov 1987), 4 da (Zahra b 10 April 1971, Emma b 15 Jan 1973, Arabella b 13 Dec 1975, Jessica b 13 April 1979); *Career* Mons Offr Cadet Sch 1964, cmmnd Queens Royal Irish Hussars 1965; serv BAOR 1965, Hong Kong 1968-69, BAOR 1970-73, loan serv to Royal Brunei Malay Regt (equerry to HM Sultan of Brunei) 1974-81; dir Dorchester Hotel 1985; memb Cirencester Polo Club Ctee; Brunei SLJ 1975, SNB and PHBS 1976, DPMB 1978; *Recreations* racing, polo, shooting; *Clubs* Cavalry and Guards, Cirencester Polo; *Style—* Maj Christopher Hanbury; Lovelocks House, Shefford Woodlands, Hungerford, Berks RG17 OPU (☎ 048839 558)

HANBURY, Evan Robert (Joss); s of Lt-Col James Robert Hanbury (d 1971), of Burley on the Hill, Rutland, and Sarah Margaret, *née* Birkin (d 1976); *b* 17 March 1951; *Educ* Eton, RAC Cirencester; *m* 22 July 1974, Rosalind Jeannette, da of Derrick Alex Pease, of 2 Britten St, London SW3; 2 s (James Robert b 1979, William Edward b 1983), 1 da (Susanna Rosemary b 1977); *Career* farmer; master of foxhounds of Quorn and formerly Cottesmore; memb Rutland Dist Cncl 1972-73; *Recreations* riding, gardening; *Style—* Evan Hanbury, Esq; Chapel Farm, Oakham, Rutland (☎ 0572 812203)

HANBURY, Sir John Capel; CBE (1969); s of Frederick Capel Hanbury (d 1957), and Muriel Hope, *née* Franklin-Adams; *b* 26 May 1908; *Educ* Downside, Trinity Coll Cambridge, Univ of London; *m* 1, 29 May 1935, Joan Terry (d 1989), da of late Edward John Fussell, of Frinton-on-Sea, Essex; 2 s (and 1 s decd), 1 da; m 2, 26 April 1990, Rosemary Elizabeth, wid of Lt Cdr Paul Coquelle, RN, of Hunsdon, Herts; *Career* memb Pharmacopoeia Cmmn 1948-73, pres Assoc of Br Pharmaceutical Indust 1950-52, chm Assoc of Br Chemical Mfrs 1961-63; chm Central Health Servs Cncl 1970-76, memb Thames Water Authy 1974-79; FRSC, FRPS, Fell UCL 1977; kt 1974; *Clubs* Utd Oxford and Cambridge Univ; *Style—* Sir John Hanbury, CBE; Amwellbury House, Great Amwell, Ware, Herts (☎ 0920 462108)

HANBURY, Leslie Francis; s of Capt Robert Francis Hanbury (d 1960), of Kirkcudbright, and Margaret Lucy Hanbury, *née* Scott (d 1966); *b* 23 Sept 1926; *Educ* Eton, Magdalene Coll Cambridge (MA); *m* 23 April 1966, Daphne Gillian, da of Lt-Gen Charles James Briggs, KCB, KCMG (d 1941), of Suffolk; 2 da (Anna b 1973, Lucy b 1976); *Career* agriculturist, serv Capt RASC (MT) in Greece and Egypt 1945-48; arable farmer, hill sheep and cattle 1968; memb Inst of Agric Engrs, memb Ctee Br Soc for Res in Agric, friend of Rothamsted Agric Experimental Station, tax cmmr; *pubns incl*: Jl of Agric Sci (vol 68), various jls; *Recreations* rural conservation, gardening; *Style—* Leslie Hanbury, Esq; Manor House, Wickhambrook, nr Newmarket CB8 8XJ (☎ 0440 820 213)

HANBURY, Reginald FitzRoy (Reg); s of late Lt-Col Reginald Henry Osgood Hanbury, of Melgate, Slingsby, York, and Esmé Leila Gertrude, *née* Fitzroy; *b* 5 June 1938; *Educ* Eton, Sandhurst; *m* 23 Dec 1969, Elizabeth Gay Randal, da of Randal James Woollatt (d 1985); 1 s (Richard Timothy b 1972), 1 da (Samantha Fiona b 1970); *Career* offr of HM Armed Forces (served UK, NI, Kuwait, Malaysia, BAOR), Sqdn Ldr 15 and 19 King's Royal Hussars 1970-72, asst military study dir Project Foresight 1984-90; *Recreations* hunting, skiing, polo, tennis, shooting, fishing; *Clubs* Cavalry, South Dorset Foxhounds (jt master 1986-); *Style—* Reg Hanbury, Esq; Lorton Farm, 541 Dorchester Rd, Broadway, Weymouth, Dorset DT3 5BT (☎ 0305 815140)

HANBURY, Robert Edmund Scott; s of Capt Robert Francis Hanbury (d 1960), and Margaret Lucy, *née* Scott (d 1966); *b* 20 March 1925; *Educ* Eton, Scot Coll of Agric; *m* 28 Oct 1961, Celia, da of Lt-Col Gerald Ian Maitland-Heriot, MC, of SA; 1 s (Roland b 1964), 1 da (Melanie b 1967); *Career* serv W Seaforth Highlanders 1943-47; landowner; *Recreations* golf, shooting; *Style—* Robert Hanbury, Esq; Drumstinchall, Dalbeattie, Kirkcudbrightshire, Scotland DG5 4PD

HANBURY-TENISON, Richard; JP (Gwent 1979); s of Maj G E F Tenison (d 1954), sometime Jt MFH Essex and Suffolk, of Lough Bawn, Co Monaghan, Ireland, by his w Ruth (only da of John Capel Hanbury, JP, DL, who was n of 1 Baron Sudeley); *b* 3 Jan 1925; *Educ* Eton, Magdalen Coll Oxford; *m* 12 May 1955, Euphan Mary Hanbury-Tenison, JP, er da of Maj Arthur Wardlaw-Ramsay and Hon Mary, *née* Fraser, only da of 18 Lord Saltoun; 3 s (John b 1957, William b 1962, Capel b 1965), 2 da (Sarah b 1956, Laura b 1966); *Career* WWII Irish Gds NW Europe (wounded), Capt 1946; Foreign Serv 1949-75; first sec: Vienna, Phnom Penh, Bucharest; cnsllr: Bonn, Brussels; head Aviation and Telecommunication Dept FCO 1970-71, ret 1975; Timber Growers award for forestry and woodland management 1990; pres: Monmouthshire (later Gwent) Rural Community Cncl 1959-67, Gwent Community Servs Cncl 1975- (chm 1967-74); chm: Art Ctee Nat Museum of Wales 1986 (memb 1976-), S Wales Regnl Bd Lloyds Bank 1987-(dir 1980-); DL: Monmouthshire 1973, Gwent 1974; High Sheriff Gwent 1977, Lord Lt Gwent 1979-; Hon Col 3 Bn Royal Regt of Wales 1982-90, pres TA and VR Assoc for Wales 1985-90, South Wales Regn TAVRA 1990-, CStJ 1980, KStJ 1990; *Recreations* shooting, fishing, conservation; *Clubs* Boodles, Kildare St Univ (Dublin); *Style—* Richard Hanbury-Tenison, Esq, JP; Clytha Park, Abergavenny, Gwent (☎ 0873 840 300); Lough Bawn, Co Monaghan, Ireland

HANBURY-TENISON, (Airling) Robin; OBE (1981); s of Maj Gerald Evan Farquhar Tenison (d 1954), of Co Monaghan Ireland, and Ruth Julia Marguerite, *née* Hanbury; *b* 7 May 1936; *Educ* Eton, Magdalen Coll Oxford (MA); *m* 1, 14 Jan 1959, Marika (d 1982), da of Lt-Col John Montgomerie Hopkinson (d 1989), of Garwyns Farm, Sussex; 1 s (Rupert b 1970), 1 da (Lucy b 1960); m 2, 1983, Louella Gage, da of Lt-Col George Torquil Gage Williams, of Menkee, Cornwall; 1 s (Merlin b 1985); *Career* farmer, author, explorer, pres Survival Int 1984 (chm 1969-84); *Books* The Rough and The Smooth (1969), A Question of Survival (1973), A Pattern of Peoples (1975), Mulu: The Rain Forest (1980), The Yanomami (1982), Worlds Apart (1984), White Horses Over France (1985), A Ride along the Great Wall (1987), Fragile Eden (1989), Spanish Pilgrimage (1990); *Recreations* travelling, conservation; *Clubs* Kildare Street and Univ (Dublin), Groucho, Dorchester; *Style—* Robin Hanbury-Tenison, Esq, OBE; Maidenwell, Cardinham, Bodmin, Cornwall PL30 4DW (☎ 020 882 224)

HANBURY-TRACY, (Desmond) Andrew John; er s of Maj Claud Edward Frederick Hanbury-Tracy-Domvile, TD (d 1987), and his 1 w Veronica May (d 1985), da of Cyril Grant Cunard; hp of kinsman 7 Baron Sudeley, *qv*; *b* 30 Nov 1928; *Educ* Sherborne, RAC Cirencester; *m* 1, 22 June 1957 (m dis 1966), Jennifer Lynn, o da of Dr Richard Christie Hodges; 1 s (Nicholas Edward John b 13 Jan 1959); m 2, 4 April 1967 (m dis), Lilian, da of late Nathaniel Laurie; 1 s (Timothy Christopher Claud b 25 March 1968); m 3, 28 July 1988, Mrs Margaret Cecilia White, da of late Alfred Henry Marmaduke Purse, MBE; *Style—* Andrew Hanbury-Tracy, Esq; 7 Gainsborough Drive, Sherborne, Dorset DT9 6DS

HANBURY-TRACY, Hon Mrs (Blanche Mary); *née* Arundell; da of 15 Baron Arundell of Wardour (d 1944); *b* 5 Dec 1908; *m* 11 Jan 1935 (m dis 1954), Ninian John Frederick Hanbury-Tracy (d 1971), gs of 4 Baron Sudeley; 1 da; *Style—* The Hon Mrs Hanbury-Tracy; Maude, 10 Haldane Rd, London SW6; Casita Blanca, Nerja, Malaga, Spain

HANCOCK, Prof Barry William; s of George Llewellyn Hancock, of London, and Sarah Hancock (d 1973); *b* 25 Jan 1946; *Educ* E Barnet GS, Univ of Sheffield Med Sch (MB ChB, MD), Univ of London (DCH); *m* 5 July 1969, (Christine Diana) Helen, da of Alexander Moffatt Spray (d 1972); 1 s (David b 1974), 1 da (Caroline b 1971); *Career* medical registrar professorial therapeutics unit Royal Infirmary Sheffield 1973-74, lectr in med and sr registrar Professorial Medical Unit Royal Hosp Sheffield 1974-78, hon conslt physician and oncologist Royal Hallamshire and Weston Park Hosps Sheffield 1978-88; Univ of Sheffield: sr lectr in med 1978-86, reader in med 1986-88, prof of clinical oncology 1988-; hon dir Trent Region Palliative and Continuing Care Centre, trial co-ordinator Br Nat Lymphoma Investigation, divnl surgn N Derbs St John Ambulance Bde; MRCP 1973, FRCP 1985; *Books* Assessment of Tumour Response (ed, 1982), Immunological Aspects of Cancer (jt ed, 1985), Lymphoreticular Disease (jt ed, 1985), Lecture Notes in Clinical Oncology (jtly, 1986); *Recreations* railways, photography, philately, tennis; *Style—* Prof Barry Hancock; Treetops, 253 Dobcroft Rd, Ecclesall, Sheffield S11 9LG (☎ 0742 351433); YRCP, Dept of Clinical Oncology, Weston Park Hospital, Whitham Rd, Sheffield S10 2SJ (☎ 0742 670222, fax 0742 684193)

HANCOCK, (Doreen) Brenda; JP (Manchester City 1982); da of Edward William Hancock (d 1970), of Tunbridge Wells, and Gwennyth Gertrude, *née* King (d 1986); *b* 19 Jan 1932; *Educ* St Felix Sch, Bedford Coll London (scholar, BA), Univ of London Inst of Educn (PGCE), Univ of London (External DipEd); *Career* Kenya HS Nairobi 1956-60 (teacher of modern languages, housemistress), fndr princ Cobham Hall Kent 1961-71; Conservative Party Res Dept 1972-75, dir of social policy Equal Opportunities Commission 1989- (head Consumer Affairs Dept 1976-89); *Style—* Ms Brenda Hancock, JP; Equal Opportunities Commission, Overseas House, Quay St, Manchester M3 3HN (☎ 061 833 9244)

HANCOCK, Cyril James; s of Herbert James Hancock (d 1958), and Lilian, *née* Smith; *b* 9 Nov 1931; *Educ* Univ of Durham (BSc); *m* 9 July 1955, (Jean) Helen Spence, da of Samuel Steel (d 1967); 2 da (Karen b 1961, Ann b 1963); *Career* princ conslt and divnl dir PE Conslting Group 1961-78, dir Binder Hamlyn Fry 1979-81; non-exec dir: William Tathan Ltd 1981-, Wrights and Dobson Bros 1981-84, Shackleton Engrg 1984-86; princ Cyril Hancock Assocs 1981-; FIProdE, FIMC, MIMechE; *Recreations* walking, veteran bicycles and cycling, vintage cars; *Clubs* Vintage Sports Car; *Style—* Cyril Hancock, Esq; Fairacre, Bellingdon, Chesham, Bucks HP5 2XU (☎ 024 029 243)

HANCOCK, Sir David John Stowell; KCB (1985); s of Alfred George Hancock (d 1955), of Beckenham, Kent, and Florence, *née* Barrow (d 1988); *b* 27 March 1934; *Educ* Whitgift Sch, Balliol Coll Oxford (BA, MA); *m* 23 Dec 1966, Sheila Gillian (Gill), da of Dr Evan Finlay, of Walgrave, Northamptonshire; 1 s (John Farquharson b 1969), 1 da (Cordelia Jane b 1973); *Career* Nat Serv 2 Lt RTR 1953-54; BOT 1957-59; HM Treasy: joined 1959, under sec 1975-80, dep sec 1980-82; head Euro Secretariat Cabinet Office 1982-83, perm sec DES 1983-89, exec dir Hambros Bank Ltd 1989-, dir Hambros plc 1989-; Freeman City of London 1989; Hon DLL Poly of E London (CNAA) 1990; FRSA 1986, CBIM 1987; *Recreations* theatre, music, opera, reading, gardening, walking; *Clubs* Athenaeum; *Style—* Sir David Hancock, KCB; Hambros Bank Limited, 41 Tower Hill London EC3N 4HA (☎ 071 480 5000, fax 071 702 4424)

HANCOCK, David Martin; s of Henry Charles Hancock (d 1973), and Constance Catherine, *née* Martin (d 1990); *b* 1 May 1936; *Educ* Surrey County GS; *m* 30 March 1963, June Noreen, da of William Thomas (d 1990); 1 s (Thomas b 1971), 1 da (Emma b 1969); *Career* fin dir and gp commercial dir McCann Erickson Advertising Ltd 1965-82, gp vice chm and chief fin offr Grey Communications Group Ltd 1984-; FCCA 1961, FIOD 1977, FIPA 1990; *Recreations* music, reading, sport; *Clubs* Royal Automobile; *Style—* David Hancock, Esq; Grey Communications Group Ltd, 215/227 Great Portland St, London W1N 5HD (☎ 071 636 3399, fax 071 637 7473)

HANCOCK, John Norman David; s of John Norman Hancock, of Evington, Leicester, and Eunice Elizabeth, *née* Sturges; *b* 4 Oct 1939; *Educ* Wyggeston GS for Boys, Leics Poly (HNC); *m* 31 Aug 1963, Patience Anne, da of Philip James Taylor, of Cropston, Leics; 1 s (Mark James b 1965), 1 da (Jane Elizabeth b 1968); *Career* heating engr 1966-71, private narrow fabric mfr 1971-, chm and chief exec Hanro Gp of Cos 1975-; memb Ctee Br Narrow Fabrics Assoc; FInstD 1983; *Recreations* golf, sailing, aviation; *Clubs* Leics and Rothley Golf, Salcombe Yacht; *Style—* John N D Hancock, Esq; Hancock & Roberts Ltd, Stadon Rd, Anstey, Leics LE7 7AY (☎ 0533 357 520, fax 0533 353 912, car 0831 496 844, telex 341843)

HANCOCK, Marion; da of Thomas Douglas Archibald Hancock, and Doris, *née* Hornsby (d 1978); *b* 23 March 1954; *Educ* Gosforth GS Newcastle upon Tyne, Univ of Warwick (BA); partner, David Kirkpatrick; *Career* ed; PA to Dir Foyles Booksellers 1975-76; The British Council 1976-87: admin asst then project mangr design, prodn and publishing then dep ed press and info; ed Design Magazine The Design Council 1987-; *Recreations* making lists; *Style—* Ms Marion Hancock; Design Magazine, 28 Haymarket, London SW1Y 4SU (☎ 071 839 8000, fax 071 925 2130)

HANCOCK, Michael Anthony; s of Anthony Ilbert Hancock (d 1954), of Bickley, Kent, and Eileen Mary, *née* King; *b* 11 Sept 1943; *Educ* Tonbridge; *m* 11 July 1967 (m dis 1975), Diana Margaret, da of Albert Edward Peter; 1 s (Froude), 2 da (Claire, Emma); *Career* Bank of England 1961-63, ptnr WN Middleton & Co and Stock Exchange memb 1969-75, chm and chief exec Chart Estates Ltd 1985-; *Recreations* vintage cars, fine wines, antique furniture; *Clubs* Wig and Pen, Kent Woolgrowers; *Style—* Michael Hancock, Esq; Crabbe Farm, Lenham, Heath, Kent (☎ 0622 858 320); Bourg de Borreze, Dordogne, France

HANCOCK, Dr Robert Peter Dawbney; s of Sqdn Ldr Francis William Hancock, of Studland, Dorset, and Daphne Mary, *née* Baguley; *b* 21 April 1944; *Educ* Rugby, Guy's Med Sch; *m* 2 July 1966, Sonia Rosemary, da of Cdr Henry Petre, RN; 3 s (Benjamin b 1974, Toby b 1974, Bertie b 1979), 1 da (Scarlett b 1981); *Career* RAMC 1967-73, Capt surgical specialist mil hosps: Millbank, Woolwich Aldenshott, Rinteln BAOR, Regtl MO 3 Bn LI, princ in private practice GP; memb Private Practice Ctee BMA; hon clinical asst and gp ldr staff Support Gp ICRF Breast Unit Guy's 1985-88; vice chm Dulwich Dyslexia Soc; FRCS; *Recreations* tennis, skiing, sailing; *Style—* Dr Robert Hancock; Fordie House, 82 Sloane St, London SW1X 9PA (☎ 071 235 3002)

HANCOCK, Roger Markham; s of Howard Spencer Hancock, of Oxford, and Helen Marjorie, *née* Skelcher; *b* 4 Nov 1942; *Educ* Southfield Sch Oxford; *m* 14 Aug 1968, Marian Sheila, da of Arthur Herbert Holloway of S Tawton; 1 s (Mark Peter Skelcher b 25 Jan 1978), 1 da (Kirsty Sheila Bevis b 14 Aug 1975); *Career* articled clerk Wenn Townsend CAS Oxford 1959-65, mgmnt accountant British Motor Corporation 1965, mangr Morris & Harper CAS 1966, managing ptnr Whitley Stimpson & Partners 1987, (ptnr 1967-), ptnr Moores Rowland Banbury 1979-, memb Cncl Moores Rowland International 1985-; dir Nortec Training Agency Ltd 1986-; tstee Reed Coll of Accountancy 1988-; pres Banbury and District Chamber of Commerce 1989-90; FCA 1967 (ACA 1965); *Recreations* theatre, music, rugby football; *Style—* Roger Hancock, Esq; Whitley Stimpson & Partners, Neithrop House, Warwick Rd, Banbury, Oxon OX16 7AB (☎ 0295 270200, 0295 271784, fax 0295 272784)

HANCOCK, Ronald Philip; s of Philip Henry Hancock (d 1953), and Ann, *née* Lioni (d 1980); *b* 9 Aug 1921; *Educ* Epsom Coll; *m* 1958, Stella Florence (d 1988), da of Arthur Howard Mathias, CBE (d 1970); 2 s (William, Richard), 1 da (Anne-Marie); m 2, Pauline Mary, da of William Leighton Jones (d 1980); 1 step da (Susan); *Career* Lt RNVR, serv Atlantic and Pacific Oceans and with Coastal Forces in English Channel; memb Lloyd's, int insur conslt; farmer; forester; chm: Euro Risk Management Ltd

1972-77, A R M International Ltd 1972-84, Leumi Insurance Services (UK) Ltd 1983-87; dep chm Bland Welch and Co Ltd 1955-70 (dir 1946-70); dir: De Falbe Halsey and Co (Holdings) Ltd 1972-74, International Risk Management Ltd 1972-77, American Risk Management Inc (USA) 1972-77, Med Insurance Agency Ltd 1974-; memb Cncl: Royal Med Fndn of Epsom Coll 1969-, Br Horse Soc 1980-87; chm Horse Driving Trials Ctee 1983-87, memb Br Equestrian Fedn 1983-87; chm: Surrey PHAB (Physically Handicapped and Ablebodied) 1973-79, tstee PHAB 1979-; pt/t cmmr and memb Forestry Cmmn 1988-, memb Cncl Riding for the Disabled Assoc 1989-; Freeman City of London, memb Worshipful Co of Carmen; *Recreations* ocean racing and cruising, hunting, horse driving trials; *Clubs* Royal Thames Yacht, Lloyd's Yacht; *Style—* Ronald Hancock, Esq; Hillside Farm, Shere Rd, West Horsley, Surrey (☎ 04865 2098)

HANCOCK, Stephen Clarence; s of Norman Harry Hancock, of Brymore, West Parade, Llandudno, Wales, and Jean Elaine, *née* Barlow; *b* 1 Nov 1955; *Educ* King Edward VI Lichfield Staffs, City of Stoke-On-Trent Sixthform Coll, Sheffield Univ (LLB); *Career* admitted slr 1980; ptnr Herbert Smith Slrs 1986- (articled clerk 1978-80, asst slr 1980-86); memb Worshipful Co of Slrs; *Recreations* golf; *Clubs* Lakeside Golf and Country (Staffs); *Style—* Stephen Hancock, Esq; 1 Willow End, Surbiton, Surrey; Herbert Smith, Exchange House, Primrose St, London EC2A 2HS (☎ 071 374 8000)

HANCOCK, (John) Stuart; s of W J S Hancock; *b* 8 June 1941; *Educ* Dynevor Sch Swansea, Univ of Birmingham (BCom); *m* 1977, Marjorie Elizabeth; *Career* CA; ptnrship sec Edwards Geldard (slrs); FCA; *Recreations* travel, walking, gardening, golf; *Style—* Stuart Hancock, Esq; Somercombe House, 109 Higher Lane, Langland, Swansea SA3 4PS; Edwards Geldard, 16 St Andrews Crescent, Cardiff CF1 3RA (☎ 0222 238239, fax 237268)

HANCOX, Tony; s of Christopher Hancox (d 1957), of Nottingham, and Gwendoline, *née* Chapman (d 1975); *b* 1927; *Educ* Univ of Oxford (BA, MA); *m* 1949, Doreen, da of Thomas Bertie Anthony (d 1972), of London; 1 s (George b 1959), 1 da (Alcina b 1958); *Career* memb: Ct of Govrs London Inst 1986, Cncl of Coll for Distributive Trades 1981, Assoc Templeton Coll Oxford 1983-85, Careers Advsy Bd Univ of London 1970-80, Local Employment Ctee City of Westminster (dep chm 1969-72), Cncl Assoc of Retail Distributors 1970-72, employers sides Retail Wages Councils 1965-80, Steering Gp Retail Mktg Degree Manchester Poly 1987, Nat Cncl of Vocational Qualifications (supervisory and mgmnt awards) 1987; chm Hancox Management Services 1987, nat coordinator Nat Retail Trg Cncl 1987 (retail mangr, latterly in personnel mgmnt and trg 1952-87); memb faculty Euro Sch of Mgmnt Oxford 1987, moderator external exam Univ of Stirling 1986; capt Thames Rowing Club 1958, memb of Eng Eight Commonwealth Games (Bronze medallist) 1958; FIPM (1975), FInst Trg and Devpt 1987; *Recreations* music, reading, writing, rowing; *Clubs* Athenaeum, Leander; *Style—* Tony Hancox, Esq; National Retail Training Council, Trent House, 69-79 Fulham High St, London SW6 3JQ (☎ 071 371 5021)

HAND, Nicholas; s of Kenneth Robert Hand, of Bristol, and Josephine Mary, *née* Griffiths; *b* 4 Jan 1957; *Educ* Filton HS Bristol, King Edward XI GS Stafford, Stafford Coll of Further Educn, Bristol Poly (Post graduate Dip Graphic Design); *m* 10 April 1982, Katharine Elizabeth, da of Harry Graydon; 1 s (Laurence Daniel b 9 Nov 1990), 2 da (Eleanor Clare b 27 May 1984, Jessica Louise b 28 Nov 1986); *Career* designer; Creative Advertising 1978-80, ESL Bristol (design for audio visual presentations) 1980-82, sr designer Playne Design (graphic design for book packaging and gen print) 1982-85, freelance graphic design 1985-88, ptnrship with Len Upton forming Legend Design Consultants 1988-; lectured: Polytechnic South West, Bristol Poly, Gwent Coll of Higher Educn, Brunel Tech Coll; CSD: diploma memb 1977, charted memb 1982, chm SW Region 1987-90, hon sec 1990-; *Recreations* walking in the countryside, playing football and squash; *Style—* Nicholas Hand, Esq; Legend Design Consultants, 33 Eastfield Rd, Westbury-on-Trim, Bristol BS9 4AE (☎ 0272 621333, fax 0272 621117)

HANDA, Jawahar Lal; s of Dr SL Handa, of India, and Savitry, *née* Malhotra; *b* 30 Dec 1939; *Educ* Univ of Punjab (MB BS), Univ of Kanpur (MS); *m* 13 Sept 1967, Urmil, da of Dr K L Sethi, of India; 3 s (Sanjeev b and d 1972, Rahul Handa b 9 Nov 1973, Rohit b 24 April 1975); *Career* Army med corp 1963-67; res asst CISR 1967-69, sr house offr 1970-72, registrar 1972-79, sr registrar 1979-80, conslt 1980-; dir Hank Enterprises Ltd, ptnr A H & Co (property investment); memb: Asian Art Soc Glasgow, BMA; FRCS; *Recreations* lawn tennis, badminton, photography; *Style—* Jawahar Handa, Esq; 26 Locksley Crescent, Greenfaulds, Cumbernauld, Glasgow G67 4EL (☎ 0236 732300); Ent Department, Law Hospital, Carluke ML8 5ER (☎ 0555 351100)

HANDCOCK, John Eric; LVO (1991), DL (Royal Co of Berks 1986); s of Eric George Handcock (d 1979), and Gladys Ada Florence, *née* Prior, of Bolton Ave, Windsor; *b* 7 Oct 1930; *Educ* Aldenham, King's Coll London (LLB); *m* 1956, Joan Margaret, da of Wilfred Joseph Bigg, CMG (d 1983), of Swanage, Dorset; 2 s (David, Jonathan), 2 da (Sandra, Nicola); *Career* admitted slr 1954; sr ptnr Lovegrove and Durant of Windsor and Ascot 1966- (now Lovegrove & Eliot of Windsor, Ascot and Egham); pres Berks, Bucks and Oxon Incorporated Law Soc 1979-80, dir Solicitors' Benevolent Assoc 1981-88; Nat Assoc of Round Tables of GB and NI: chm Thames Valley Area 1964-65, memb nat Cncl 1966-68, nat exec convenor Rules and Special Purposes 1968-70; chm Berks Bucks and Oxon Prof Cncl 1981-82; govr St George's Choir Sch Windsor Castle 1975-, dep Capt lay stewards St George's Chapel Windsor Castle 1977-, tstee Prince Philip Tst for Windsor and Maidenhead 1978-; hon life memb River Thames Soc 1986; Citoyen d'Honneur de la Ville Royale de Dreux 1976; Freeman City of London 1984; *Recreations* history, travel, wine, books; *Clubs* Law Society; *Style—* John E Handcock, Esq, LVO, DL; Red Deer House, Kingswood Rise, Englefield Green, Surrey (☎ 0784 434289); Lovegrove and Eliot, 4 Park St, Windsor, Berks SL4 1JF (☎ 0753 851133, telex 849275 LOVDUR G)

HANDFORD, Peter Thomas; MBE (1945); s of Rev Hedley William Mountenay Handford (d 1928), Vicar of Four Elms, Edenbridge, Kent, and Helen Beatrice, *née* Crosse (d 1964); *b* 21 March 1919; *Educ* Christ's Hosp; *m* 12 May 1974, Helen Margaret; 2 da (Lyn Patricia (Mrs Hedges), Pamela Anne (Mrs Kucel)), both by previous m; *Career* WWII (Capt RA) serv incl 50 BFF and D Day landings 1939-46; sound recordist London Film Prodns 1936-39; after war worked with various film companies before becoming freelance; responsible for sound recording on more than 60 films incl: Room at the Top, Billy Liar, Out of Africa (won Academy (Oscar) and Bafta awards for sound track 1986), Murder on the Orient Express, Hope and Glory, Gorillas in the Mist, Dangerous Liaisons, White Hunter Black Heart, Havana; prodr Sounds of the Steam Age on records (awarded Grand Prix du Disque Paris 1964); memb Acad of Motion Picture Arts and Sciences 1986; *Books* The Sound of Railways (1980); *Recreations* gardening, sound recording, railway enthusiasm and travel, country pursuits; *Clubs* Academy of Motion Picture, Arts and Scis, Sloane; *Style—* Peter T Handford, Esq, MBE; Sandra Marsh Management, Post Box 37, Lee International Studios, Studios Road, Shepperton, Middx TW17 0QD (☎ 0932 568148, telex MOVIES G 929416)

HANDLER, Thomas Joseph; s of Nicholas Handler (d 1958), and Lily, *née* Singer (d 1986); *b* 25 May 1938; *Educ* Fort Street Boys' HS Sydney Australia, Univ of Sydney (Cwlth scholarship, BA, LLB); *m* 25 May 1970, Adrienne, da of Alajos Marxreiter; 2 da (Rebecca Louise b 21 Dec 1974, Sophie Melinda b 15 Aug 1976); *Career* slr; WC Taylor & Scott (Sydney) 1962-65 (articled clerk 1958-61), Simmons & Simmons (London) 1965-67, ptnr Baker & McKenzie 1973- (joined 1967); memb: Law Soc 1966, UK Environmental Law Assoc; *Recreations* reading, music, theatre, tennis, skiing, hiking, gardening; *Style—* Thomas Handler, Esq; Baker & McKenzie, Aldwych House, Aldwych, London WC2B 4JP (☎ 071 242 6531, fax 071 831 8611)

HANDLEY; *see*: Davenport-Handley

HANDLEY, Dr Anthony James; s of Wing Cdr Austyn James Handley, RAF (d 1985), of W Mersea, Essex, and Beryl Janet, *née* Ashling (d 1982); *b* 22 June 1942; *Educ* Kimbolton Sch, King's Coll London, Westminster Hosp Med Sch (MB BS, MD, MRCP); *m* 3 Dec 1966, Jennifer Ann, da of Noël Lindsay Ross Kane (d 1986), of Colchester, Essex; 1 s (Simon b 1973), 1 da (Juliette b 1971); *Career* Maj RAMC (TA) 1970-, chm Inter-Serv Cadet Rifle Matches Ctee; conslt physician NE Essex Health Authy 1974-, hon clinical tutor Charing Cross and Westminster Med Sch 1976-, clinical tutor Colchester Postgrad Med Centre 1980-85; vice pres and med advsr RLSS; county judge Essex Amateur Swimming Assoc; FRCP 1985, memb Br Cardiac Soc 1984, FRSM 1985, hon sec Resuscitation Cncl (UK) 1986; *Books* Thoracic Medicine (contrib, 1981), Resuscitation and First Aid (ed, 1986); *Recreations* swimming, squash, music (trombone player); *Style—* Dr Anthony J Handley; 40 Queens Rd, Colchester, Essex CO3 3PB (☎ 0206 562 642); 27 Oaks Drive, Colchester, Essex CO3 3PR (☎ 0206 573 253, fax 0206 571 032)

HANDLEY, Carol Margaret; da of Claude Hilary Taylor (d 1966), and Margaret Eleanor, *née* Peebles (d 1977); *b* 17 Oct 1929; *Educ* St Paul's Girls Sch, UCL (BA); *m* 30 July 1952, Prof Eric Walter Handley, s of Alfred Walter Handley (d 1976); *Career* N Foreland Lodge Sch 1952, Queensgate Sch 1952-56, headmistress Camden Sch for Girls 1971-85 (head of Classics Dept 1956-65, dep headmistress 1965-71); fell UCL 1977; memb Cncl: Royal Holloway Coll 1977-85, Middx Hosp Med Sch 1980-84, Bedford Coll 1981-85, Royal Holloway and Bedford New Coll 1985-; sr memb Wolfson Coll Cambridge 1989; *Style—* Mrs Carol Handley

HANDLEY, Prof Eric Walter; CBE (1983); s of Alfred Walter Handley (d 1974), and Ada Doris, *née* Cox (d 1944); *b* 12 Nov 1926; *Educ* King Edward's Sch Birmingham, Trinity Coll Cambridge, (BA, MA); *m* 31 July 1952, Carol Margaret, da of Claude Hilary Taylor (d 1966); *Career* UCL: lectr in greek and latin 1946-61, reader 1961-67, prof 1967-68, prof of greek and head of dept 1968-84; dir Inst of Classical Studies Univ of London 1967-84, regius prof greek Univ of Cambridge 1984, fell Trinity Coll 1984, hon fell UCL 1989, visiting lectr classics Harvard 1966, visiting memb Inst for Advanced Study Princeton 1971, visiting prof Stanford 1977 and Melbourne 1978, sr res fell Princeton 1981; foreign memb Societas Scientiarum Fennica 1984, memb Academia Europaea 1988, pres Classical Assoc 1984-85, chm Cncl Univ Classical Depts 1975-78 (sec 1969-70), FBA 1969 (for sec 1979-88), FRSA 1971; *Books* The Telephus of Euripides (with John Rea, 1957), The Dyskolos of Menander (1965), Relire Ménandre (with André Hurst, 1989); *Recreations* walking, travel; *Clubs* Utd Oxford Cambridge; *Style—* Prof Eric Handley, CBE; Trinity College, Cambridge CB2 1TQ (☎ 0223 3384130)

HANDLEY, James Arthur; s of Wilfred Arthur Handley, of Downside, Battledown Approach, Cheltenham, and Heather Elizabeth, *née* Magwick; *b* 18 Feb 1950; *Educ* Whitefriars Sch Cheltenham, Univ of Liverpool (BA, BArch); *m* 23 Dec 1978, Elizabeth, da of Capt Gerrald Kendrick Barnett, of 63 Grange Rd, Shrewsbury; 1 s (Rupert William b 26 June 1983), 2 da (Tamasin Lily b 23 July 1979, (Claire) Holly b 12 Aug 1981); *Career* Atelier Aubock Vienna 1972-73, Farman Farmaian Tehran 1975-78, Abbey Hanson Rowe 1978-; Rotarian; memb: RIBA, ARCUK; *Recreations* tennis, skiing, sailing; *Style—* James Handley, Esq; 54 The Hill, Grinshill, Shrewsbury SY4 3BU (☎ 093928 335); Abbey Hanson Rowe, 21 St Marys St, Shrewsbury SY1 1ED (☎ 0743 232905, fax 0743 232717, car 0860 524492)

HANDLEY JONES, Susan Kathleen (Sue); da of Patrick John Dickinson (d 1984), of Surrey, and Christine Margaret Wells, *née* Weston; *b* 13 July 1955; *Educ* Malvern Girls Coll, Univ of Warwick (BA); *m* 10 Sept 1983, Nicholas, s of Anthony Handley Jones, of Bucks; *Career* recruitment specialist Badenach and Clark, PR consultancy work for Honewell, Philips, Telephone Rentals 1981-83, recruitment and personnel work 1977-81; *Clubs* Oriental; *Style—* Mrs Susan Handley Jones; Westwood House, Westwood, Southfleet, Kent (☎ 047 483 2156); Badenoch and Clark, 16 New Bridge St, London EC4V 6AU (☎ 071 583 0073, fax 071 353 3908)

HANDS, Hargrave Patrick; *b* 2 Feb 1921; *m* 19 Aug 1947, Daphne Mary; 1 s (Jeremy b 1951), 1 da (Rowena b 1954); *Career* artist and illustrator; considerable work in all fields of publishing and advertising worldwide, regular contrib to newspaper magazines over past 30 years and pioneer of the realistic but decorative approach; specialist in anantomical, entomolgical, ornithological and horticultural illustration; awarded Grenfell Medal (RHS); *Recreations* music, golf; *Clubs* Flempton and SIA; *Style—* Hargrave Hands, Esq; Thatch End, Flempton, Suffolk IP28 6EG (☎ 0284 84467)

HANDS, Jeremy Gyles Hargrave; s of Hargrave Patrick Hands, of Thatch End, Flempton, Bury St Edmunds, Suffolk, and Daphne Mary, *née* Bolton; *b* 4 April 1951; *Educ* St Marylebone GS; *m* 4 June 1977, Julia Rae, da of Stanley Edward Bennett, of Knaresborough, N Yorks; 1 s (Tom b 20 Aug 1978), 1 da (Lucy b 4 Sept 1980); *Career* reporter: Hendon and Finchley Times 1970-74, Herald Express Torquay 1974; researcher Westward TV Plymouth 1974-77; reporter: Border TV Carlisle 1977-78, ITN 1978-89 (coverage of Falklands campaign, Gulf War, Lebanon, NI); presenter Anglia TV Norwich 1989-; *Books* with Robert McGowan: Don't Cry for Me, Sergeant Major (1983), Try Not to Laugh, Sergeant Major (1984); *Recreations* golf, writing, maritime history; *Clubs* Whipsnade Park Golf; *Style—* Jeremy Hands, Esq; Anglia TV, Norwich, Norfolk (☎ 0603 619261, telex 97424, fax 0603 615494)

HANDS, Newby Sophia; da of Anthony Richard Hands, of Oxford, and Yvonne, *née* Reeve; *b* 20 July 1963; *Educ* Headington Sch for Girls Oxford, Beechlawn Tutorial Coll Oxford; *Career* ed; trainee Harrods 1981-82, sec Woman's Own IPC 1983-84; fashion asst: Woman's Realm IPC 1984-87, Evening Standard 1987; style and beauty Daily Mail 1989- (dep fashion ed 1987-89); *Style—* Miss Newby Hands; Daily Mail, Northcliffe House, 2 Derry St, Kensington, London W8 5TT (☎ 071 938 6175, fax 071 937 3251)

HANDS, Lt-Col Sidney Edward; TD (1946); s of William Hands (d 1958), of High Wycombe, and Mary Annie, (d 1943); *b* 4 June 1903; *Educ* Royal GS High Wycombe; *m* 21 Dec 1938, (Edith) Irene, da of Arthur William Head (d 1953); 1 s (Christopher b 1949), 2 da (Rosemary Irene b 1943, Venetia Mary b 1948); *Career* WWII, gazetted 1938 RAPC, Lt/Staff Paymaster CII, TA 1939, Capt 1939, Maj and Staff Paymaster class II 1941, Lt-Col and Staff Paymaster class I 1944, discharged with hon rank Lt-Col 1945; W Hands and Son (est 1906): joined 1921, dir and sec 1935, md 1966, chm 1969-71, ret 1973; Old Wycombiesians RUFC: jt fndr 1929, Capt 1930-39, hon treas 1929-60, pres 1968-69; fndr H W Motor Cycle Club 1921; Royal Philatelic Soc London: hon treas 1949-67, vice pres 1965-69, pres 1969-71, hon life memb 1973; High Wycombe Rotary Club: joined 1953-, treas 1955-68, pres 1968-69; Freeman

Worshipful Co of Furniture Makers 1941 (life memb 1973); *Recreations* philately, gardening; *Style*— Lt-Col Sidney Hands, TD; 17 Brands Hill Ave, High Wycombe, Bucks HP13 5PZ (☎ 0494 25307)

HANDS, Terry; *b* 9 Jan 1941; *Educ* Univ of Birmingham (BA), RADA; *m* 1, 1964 (m dis 1967), Josephine Barstow; m 2, 1974, (m dis 1980), Ludmila Mikael; 1 da (Marina); m 3, 1988, Julia Lintott; 1s (Sebastian); *Career* fndr dir Liverpool Everyman Theatre 1964-66; RSC: joined 1966, artistic dir Theatreground (touring schs and community centres) 1966-68, assoc dir 1967, jt artistic dir 1978, chief exec 1986-91; dir many prodns for RSC at Stratford and Aldwych incl: The Merry Wives of Windsor 1968 (revived 1975/76), Pericles 1969, Henry V, Henry IV Parts I and 2 and The Merry Wives of Windsor (all subsequently transfd to Aldwych) for centenary season Stratford 1975, all 3 parts of Henry VI (1st time in entirety since Shakespeare's day, SWET award Dir of the Year) Stratford 1977, As You Like It, Richard II and Richard III (the latter two completing the entire Shakespeare history cycle, begun 1975, with Alan Howard in leading roles) Stratford 1982 , Much Ado About Nothing (Stratford) 1982, Poppy (Musical of the Year), Cyrano de Bergerac (SWET award for Best Dir) Barbican 1983, Red Noses 1985, Singer 1989, The Seagull 1990; dir: Richard III (Comedie Francaise) 1972, Twelfth Night 1976, Othello (Paris Opera, televised France 1978), Parsifal (Royal Opera House) 1979; conslt dir Comedie Française 1975-80; Hon DLitt; hon fell Shakespeare Inst; Chevalier des Arts et des Lettres; *Style*— Terry Hands, Esq; 54 Onslow Gardens, Muswell Hill, London N10 3JX (☎ 081 883 1545); Royal Shakespeare Company, Barbican Centre, Barbican, London EC2 (☎ 071 628 3351)

HANDSCOMBE, Richard Stanley; s of Stanley George Handscombe (d 1957), of Harrow, London, and Phoebe Blow; family traces ancestry back to hamlet of Hanscombe End, near Shillington, Bedfordshire— first published records 1222; *b* 31 March 1937; *Educ* Haberdashers' Aske's Hampstead, UCL (BSc); *m* 1, 10 Sept 1960, Jennifer Anne, da of Beresford Paul (d 1986), of Minchinhampton; 3 da (Fiona b 1966, Sophie b 1968, Naomi b 1971); m 2, 30 May 1978, Maria Theresia, da of Jan Bakker, of Amsterdam; *Career* mangr: ICI 1958-62, Mars 1962-65, Bernard Matthews 1965-68, Urwick Orr and Ptnrs 1968-76; md: Urwick Int N Europe 1973-76, Kepner Tregoe N Europe 1976-80; managing ptnr Richard S Handscombe and Ptnr 1980-; lectr and dir int mgmnt conf and courses; chm Br Business Assoc Netherlands 1976; FBIM, FInstD, FIMC, MIChemE; *Books* Bankers Management Handbook (ed in chief 1976), The Product Management Handbook (1989), Strategic Leadership - the Missing Links (1989); author of various contribs to handbooks and of c 100 articles; *Recreations* skiing, gardening, fishing, writing; *Style*— Richard S Handscombe, Esq; 10 Gloucester Place, Windsor, Berks (☎ 0753 863 947)

HANDY, Prof Charles Brian; s of Ven Brian Leslie Handy Archdeacon of Kildare, and Joan Kathleen Herbert, *née* Scott; *b* 25 July 1932; *Educ* Bromsgrove Sch, Oriel Coll Oxford (BA, MA), MIT (SM); *m* 5 Oct 1962, Elizabeth Ann, da of Lt-Col Rowland Fenwick Ellis Hill (d 1978); 1 s (Scott b 1968), 1 da (Kate b 1966); *Career* mktg exec Shell International Petroleum Co Ltd 1956-65, economist Charter Consolidated Co Ltd 1965-66, int faculty fell MIT 1966-67, London Business Sch 1967- (prof 1978-), warden St George's House Windsor Castle 1977-81, writer and broadcaster 1981-; chm RSA 1986-88, memb CNAA 1983-; Hon DLitt Bristol Poly 1988, Hon DUniv Open Univ 1989; *Books* Understanding Organizations (1983), Future of Work (1984), Gods of Management (1985), Understanding Schools (1986), Understanding Voluntary Organizations (1988), The Age of Unreason (1989), Inside Organisations (1990); *Recreations* theatre, cooking, travel; *Style*— Prof Charles Handy; 73 Putney Hill, London SW15 3NT (☎ 081 788 1610); Old Hall Cottages, Bressingham, Diss, Norfolk; Le Bagnaie, Castellina in Chianti, Siena, Italy; London Business Sch, Susssex Place, Regent's Park, London NW1 (☎ 071 262 5050)

HANDYSIDE, Robert Graham; s of George Robinson Handyside (d 1966), of Gwent, and Marion Handyside, *née* Graham; *b* 1 Aug 1938; *Educ* Bassaleg GS; *m* 25 Feb 1963, Rhona Nancy; 1 s (Richard b 1968), 1 da (Julie b 1966); *Career* CA; chm: Argosy Fin & Co Ltd 1970, Argosy Fin and Guarantees Ltd 1970, Glenwood Securities Ltd 1975, Office & Factory Engrg and Servs Ltd 1982; *Recreations* golf; *Clubs* RAC, Cardiff and County (Cardiff); *Style*— Robert Handyside, Esq; The Mews, 4 Cathedral Rd, Cardiff CF1 9RF (☎ 0222 372331, telex 497132, fax 0222 222624)

HANFORD, John; s of Joseph Henry Hanford (d 1965), and Caroline English, *née* Smith (d 1967); *b* 10 Dec 1932; *Educ* St James Choir Sch Grimsby, Loughborough Univ (BSc); *m* 13 Aug 1960, Rita Katrina, da of Herbert Arthur (d 1964); 2 s (Timothy John b 1964, James Philip b 1966); *Career* dir: Pencol Engineering Consultants, Manchester Jetline Ltd; Liveryman Worshipful Co of Engrs 1985, FICE, MIWEM; *Clubs* RAC; *Style*— John Hanford, Esq; Kingscliffe, Pinner Hill, Pinner, Middx HA5 3XU (☎ 081 866 6824)

HANHAM, Prof Harold John (Harry); s of John Newman Hanham (d 1960), and Ellie, *née* Malone (d 1977); *b* 16 June 1928; *Educ* Mount Albert GS, Auckland Univ Coll, Univ of NZ (BA, MA), Selwyn Coll Cambridge (PhD); *m* 27 Jan 1973, Ruth Soulé, da of Prof Daniel I Arnon, of Univ of California; *Career* asst lectr (latterly sr lectr) Univ of Manchester 1954-63, prof of politics Univ of Edinburgh 1963-68, prof of history Harvard Univ (also fell of Lowell House) 1968-73, prof of hist and political sci and dean sch of humanities social sci MIT 1973-85, hon prof of hist and vice-chllr Univ of Lancaster 1985-; memb Econ and Socl Res Cncl 1986-, memb Cncl for Mgmnt Educn and Devpt 1988-, Guggenheim Fell 1972-73; Hon AM Harvard Univ 1968; FRHistS, FAAAS; *Books* Elections and Party Management (1959), The Nineteenth Century Constitution (1969), Scottish Nationalism (1969), Bibliography of British History 1851-1914 (1976 awarded John H Jenkins prize); *Clubs* UTD Oxford and Cambridge Univ, St Botolph (Boston); *Style*— Prof HJ Hanham; The Croft, Bailrigg Lane, Lancaster, LA1 4XP (☎ 0524 63454); University House, University of Lancaster, Lancaster, LA1 4YW (☎ 0524 65201 ext 203, fax 0524 63808, telex 65111 LANCUL G)

HANHAM, Sir Michael William; 12 Bt (E 1667), of Wimborne, Dorsetshire, DFC (1944); s of Patrick Hanham (d 1965), by his 1 w, Dulcie, *née* Daffarn formerly Hartley (d 1979); 3 s of Col Phelips Hanham, bro of Sir John Hanham, 9 Bt; *b* 31 Oct 1922; *Educ* Winchester; *m* 27 Feb 1954, Margaret Jane, da of Wing-Cdr Harold Thomas; 1 s, 1 da; *Heir* s, William Hanham; *Career* Flying Offr RAF Pathfinder Force 1944-45, actg Flt Lt India 1946; BOAC 1947-61; own garden furniture workshop 1963-74; running family estate at Wimborne 1974-; KASG; *Clubs* Pathfinder; *Style*— Sir Michael Hanham, Bt, DFC; Deans Court, Wimborne, Dorset

HANHAM, William John Edward; s and h of Sir Michael Hanham, 12 Bt, DFC; *b* 4 Sept 1957; *Educ* Winchester, Courtauld Inst of Art (BA); *Career* press offr Christie's; *Recreations* painting, beekeeping, chess; *Style*— William Hanham, Esq; Christie's, King Street, London SW1 (☎ 071 839 9060)

HANKES-DRIELSMA, Claude Dunbar; *b* 8 March 1949; *Career* banker; Manufacturers Hanover 1968-72, Robert Fleming & Co Ltd 1972-77 (dir 1974-77); chm: Mgmnt Ctee Price Waterhouse and Partners 1983-89, British Export-Fin Advsy Cncl (BEFAC) 1981-, Export Finance Co Ltd 1982-89, Action Resource Centre 1986-; advsr to the Board of Corange (Boehringer Mannheim) 1988-; memb Cncl of Govrs Business in the Community 1986- (memb Pres Ctee 1988-); memb: Nat Cncl Young Enterprise 1987-, Cncl for Charitable Support 1989-, Deanery Synod 1984-, sr common room Corpus Christi Coll Oxford 1989-; assisted to Dr Fritz Leutwiler in his role as ind mediator between the South African Govt and foreign banks 1985, initiated attempt to secure Thyssen Collection for Britain 1988; *Publications* The Dangers of the Banking System: Funding Country Deficits (1975); *Recreations* gardening, walking, skiing, reading, ancient art; *Style*— Claude Hankes-Drielsma, Esq; Stanford Place, Faringdon, Oxon (☎ 0367 240547, fax 0367 242853)

HANKEY, Dr Hon Alexander Maurice Alers; s of 2 Baron Hankey, KCMG, KCVO; *b* 18 Aug 1947; *Educ* Rugby, Trinity Coll Cambridge, MIT (PhD), MERU (MSCI); *m* 1970, Deborah, da of Myron Benson, of Mass, USA; *Career* Greenlaw fell MIT 1969-71, Lindemann fellowship 1972-73 (held at Stanford Linear Accelerator Centre), teacher of transcendental meditation 1973-, asst prof of physics Maharishi Int Univ US 1973-74 (associate prof 1974-75, prof 1975-1978), prof of physics Maharishi Euro Res Univ of Switzerland and UK 1975-82, govr Age of Enlightenment 1977-, dean Faculty Maharishi Int Academy UK 1985-86, co dir Academy for the Science of Creative Intelligence Mass 1978, registrar Maharishi Univ of Natural Law North of England Campus 1986-, Leverhulme Foundation Res award 1986; *Recreations* skiing, tennis, hiking; *Clubs* Queen's, Royal Tennis; *Style*— Dr the Hon Alexander Hankey; 5 Rowan Lane, Woodley Park, Skelmersdale, Lancs WN8 6UL

HANKEY, Hon Christopher Alers; OBE (1958); s of 1 Baron Hankey, PC, GCB, GCMG, GCVO (d 1963); *b* 1911; *Educ* Rugby, Univ of Oxford (MA), Univ of London (BSc); *m* 1, 31 Oct 1945 (m dis 1957), Prudence May, da of Keith Brodribb; 1 da; m 2, 5 Sept 1958, Helen Christine, da of late Alexander John Cassavetti; 1 s; *Career* serv WWII, Maj RM; princ Miny of Overseas Devpt 1964-72, ret; exec Cncl for Tech Educn and Trg in Overseas Countries 1972-78; churchwarden St Mary's Church Westerham 1967-71, hon sec Parochial Church Cncl 1971-; *Recreations* amateur artist; *Style*— The Hon Christopher Hankey, OBE; New Cottage, French Street, nr Westerham, Kent

HANKEY, Hon Donald Robin Alers; s of 2 Baron Hankey, KCMG, KCVO, *qv*; *b* 12 June 1938; *Educ* Rugby, UCL; *m* 1, 1963 (m dis 1974), Margaretha Thorndahl; m 2, 1974, Eileen Désirée, da of Maj-Gen Stuart Hedley Molesworth Battye, CB; 2 da (Fiona, Beatrice (Bea)); RIBA; *Style*— The Hon Donald Hankey; 53 Woodfield Ave, London SW16 6LE

HANKEY, Hon Henry Arthur Alers; CMG (1959), CVO (1960); yst s of 1 Baron Hankey, GCB, GCMG, GCVO, PC (d 1963); *b* 1 Sept 1914; *Educ* Rugby, New Coll Oxford; *m* 1 Jan 1941, Vronwy, o da of late Rev Thomas Frederic Fisher, Rector of Stilton, Peterborough; 3 s (Christopher, Maurice, Peter), 1 da (Veronica); *Career* ambass to Panama 1966-69, under sec FCO 1969-74; dir: Lloyds Bank International 1975-80, Autofagasta (Chile) & Bolivia Railway Co 1975-82; sec Br N American Ctee 1981-85; *Clubs* SCGB, United University; *Style*— The Hon Henry Hankey, CMG, CVO; Hosey Croft, Westerham, Kent

HANKEY, 2 Baron (UK 1939); Robert Maurice Alers Hankey; KCMG (1955, CMG 1947), KCVO (1956); s of 1 Baron Hankey, GCB, GCMG, GCVO, PC, FRS, Sec of Cabinet 1915-38, Chllr Duchy of Lancaster 1940 and Paymaster-Gen 1941-42 (d 1963); *b* 4 July 1905; *Educ* Rugby, New Coll Oxford, Univ of Bonn, Sorbonne; *m* 1, 27 Sept 1930, Frances Beryl (d 1957), da of Walter Stuart-Menteth (4 s of Sir James Stuart-Menteth, 4 Bt); 2 s, 2 da; m 2, 2 Oct 1962, Joanna, da of Rev James Johnston Wright, late chaplain to Edinburgh Castle and asst St Giles Cathedral; *Heir* s, Hon Donald Hankey; *Career* sits as Ind Peer in House of Lords; FO 1927-65; served: Berlin, Paris, London, Warsaw, Bucharest, Cairo, Teheran, Madrid, Budapest; ambass Stockholm 1954-60, perm UK del OEEC and OECD and chm Econ Policy Ctee 1960-65; dir Alliance Building Society to 1983; vice pres Euro Inst of Business Admin Fontainebleau (INSEAD) 1966-80, pres Anglo Swedish Soc 1970-78; *Recreations* reading, skiing, tennis, golf; *Clubs* Royal Cwlth Soc; *Style*— The Rt Hon the Lord Hankey, KCMG, KCVO; Hethe House, Cowden, Edenbridge, Kent (☎ 0342 850538)

HANKINS, (Frederick) Geoffrey; s of Frederick Aubrey Hankins (d 1966), of Eltham, and Elizabeth, *née* Stockton (d 1957); *b* 9 Dec 1926; *Educ* St Dunstan's Coll; *m* 1951, Iris Esther, da of George Robert Perkins (d 1977), of Wotton-under-Edge; 2 da (Susan, Jane); *Career* served Army BAOR 1946-48; mgmnt trainee later mfrg mgmnt J Sainsbury 1949-55, gen mangr Allied Suppliers 1955-62, prodn dir Brains Food Prods 1962-69, Kraft Foods 1966-69; W L Miller and Sons Poole: gen mangr 1970-72, md 1972-82, chm 1975-85; Fitch Lovell plc: dir 1975-90, chief exec 1982-89, chm 1983-90; non-exec dir Booker plc 1990; dir: Blue cap Frozen Food Servs Ltd, Fitch & Son Ltd, Fitch Lovell Nominees Ltd, Hedges Frozen Foods Ltd, Jus-rol Ltd, L Noel & Sons Ltd, Lovell & Christmas (Canada) Inc, Newforge Foods Ltd, Parrish and Fenn Ltd, Robirch Ltd, Salaisons Le Vexin SA, Stocks Lovell Ltd, Trent Meat Co Ltd, W L Miller & Sons Ltd; FRSA; *Recreations* genealogy, antiques, practical pursuits; *Style*— Geoffrey Hankins, Esq; 51 Elms Ave, Parkstone, Poole, Dorset BH14 8EE

HANKINS, Prof Harold Charles Arthur; s of Harold Arthur Hankins (d 1982), of Crewe, Cheshire, and Hilda Hankins (d 1959); *b* 18 Oct 1930; *Educ* Crewe GS, Univ of Manchester (BSc, PhD); *m* 23 July 1955, Kathleen, da of Alec Higginbottom (d 1983), of Glossop, Derbyshire; 3 s (Anthony b 22 Dec 1957, Matthew b 9 July 1961, Nicholas b 21 Dec 1962); *Career* asst chief engr Metropolitan Vickers Electrical Co Ltd 1955-68; UMIST: lectr in electrical engrg 1968-71, sr lectr in electrical engrg 1971-74, prof of communication engrg and dir of Med Engrg Unit 1974-84, vice princ 1979-81, dep princ 1981-82, acting princ 1982-84, princ 1984-; non-exec dir Thorn EMI Lighting Ltd 1979-85; chm NW Centre Ctee Inst of Electrical Engrs 1977-78 (memb 1969-77); memb: Bd of Govrs Manchester Poly 1989-, Manchester Lit & Phil Soc 1983-; Mitchell Meml medal 1990; hon fell Manchester Poly 1984; CEng, FIEE 1975; *Recreations* hill walking, music, choral work; *Clubs* Athenaeum; *Style*— Prof Harold Hankins; Rosebank, Kidd Rd, Glossop, Derbyshire SK13 9PN (☎ 04574 3895); UMIST, P O Box 88, Manchester M60 1QD (☎ 061 236 3311, fax 061 228 7040, telex 666094)

HANKINS, Timothy Glyn; s of Maj Hankins, of Crittles Ct, Wadhurst, and Eileen Molly Hankins; *b* 19 March 1944; *Educ* Monmouth Sch, City Univ (BSc); *m* 30 May 1970, Susan Rosalie, da of Richard Stanley Oke (d 1982), of Cornwall; 2 da (Lucy Sarah b 1972, Emma Louise b 1975); *Career* divnl dir Honeywell Info Systems 1972-76, mktg dir Avery Label Systems 1976-81, md Alpha-Numeric Systems Ltd 1981-86, chm Alpha-Numeric Systems plc 1986-, pres Alpha-Numeric Systems SA (Spain) dir Aplha Numeric Developments Ltd; memb Ctee Automatic Identification Advsy Orgn; visiting lectr Univ of Keele; MInstD; *Recreations* wine collecting, skiing, water sports; *Clubs* Barnet RFC (vice pres); *Style*— Timothy Hankins, Esq; Charlton Cottage, 18 Copperkins Lane, Chesham Bois, Bucks (☎ 0494 725 385); Alpha-Numeric Systems plc, Alpha-Numeric Hse, Bourne End, Bucks (☎ 0628 810 180, fax 0628 810 157, car 0836 617 049)

HANKINSON, Alan; s of Robert Hankinson (d 1970), of Lancs, and Beatrice, *née* Nelson (d 1966); *b* 25 May 1926; *Educ* Bolton Sch, Univ of Oxford (MA); *m* 1952 (m dis 1984), Roberta Lorna, da of James Gibson (d 1977), of Bolton; 1 s (Robert James b 1958); *Career* news ed Nigerian Broadcasting Corp 1953-58, journalist ITN London 1958-75; author; *Books* The First Tigers (1972), The Mountain Men (1977), Man of Wars (1985), A Century on the Crags (1988); *Recreations* rock climbing, reading, tennis, squash, chess, fell walking; *Clubs* Keswick Chess, Keswick Squash; *Style*— Alan Hankinson, Esq; 30 Skiddaw St, Keswick, Cumbria CA12 4BY; (☎ 07687 73746)

HANKINSON, David Kyrle; s of Ernle George Hankinson (d 1959), of Upper Richmond Rd, London, and Hilda Muriel, *née* Sykes (d 1968); *b* 30 May 1928; *Educ* St Peter's Ct, RNC Dartmouth; *m* 1, 2 Aug 1958 (m dis 1965), Carolyn Anne, da of Capt Charles Keys, RN (d 1986), of Buckland Monachorum, Devon; 2 s (Mark b 1960, Piers b 1963); m 2, 2 Sept 1969, Lavinia Joan, da of Rt Hon Sir Alan Lascelles, GCB, GCVO, CMG, MC (d 1981), of Kensington Palace; *Career* sr in destroyers Home and Med Fleets 1945-59, specialised in gunnery 1955, Cdr 1962, cmd HMS Cambrian Near and Far East 1962-64, resigned 1966; portrait painter; *Recreations* landscape painting, walking and building stone walls; *Style*— David Hankinson, Esq; 12a Barkston Gdns, London SW5 0ER (☎ 071 370 4949)

HANKS, Capt (Alfred) Leonard; s of William Thomas (d 1941), and Emma Berry (d 1943); *b* 25 Oct 1918; *Educ* Chipping Campden GS; *m* 13 April 1941, Kathleen May (d 1988), da of Arthur John Catling (d 1976); 1 da (Judith Caroline b 1948); *Career* serv RA 1940-46, attached to Indian Army and serv in Far East (India and Burma); auctioneer and land agent, princ Tayler and Fletcher 1964-82, conslt 1982; *Recreations* all country sports; *Style*— Capt Leonard Hanks; High View, Lyneham, Oxford OX7 6QL (☎ 0993 830404); Tayler and Fletcher, Stow-on-the-Wold, Cheltenham, Glos GL54 1BL (☎ 0451 30383)

HANLEY, Brian Michael; s of Eric Thomas Hanley, and Constance Mary, *née* Garnett; *b* 3 April 1943; *Educ* John Fisher GS; *m* 19 Oct 1973, Rosalyn Alice, da of James Hancock (d 1971); 1 s (Christopher b 5 March 1981), 2 da (Michelle b 7 August 1974, Susan b 14 March 1978); *Career* various sr sales and mktg mgmnt appointments Honeywell Info Systems Ltd 1969-82; Perkin Elmer: nat sales mangr 1982-83, chm and md 1984-87, gen mangr Europe 1989 (concurrent with responsibility for ME, S America and Africa); md UK & International Motorola Computer Systems 1990-; *Recreations* water sports, tennis; *Style*— Brian Hanley, Esq; Motorola Computer Systems, 27 Market St, Maidenhead, Berks SL6 8AE

HANLEY, Ellery; MBE (1990); step s of Vincent Wendell Adams, of Leeds, s of Orene Muriel Hanley; *b* 27 March 1961; *Career* rugby league player; capt: GB 1987-, GB tour of Australasia 1988, Wigan, Yorkshire; Golden Boot winner (Player of the world) 1989, three times Man of Steel (Rugby League Personality of the Year); *Recreations* chess, squash, badminton, reading; *Style*— Ellery Hanley, Esq, MBE

HANLEY, Howard Granville; CBE (1975); s of Frederick Thomas (d 1951), of Bournemouth, and Edith, *née* Hill (d 1949); *b* 27 July 1909; *Educ* St Bees Sch Cumberland; *m* 7 Oct 1939, Margaret, da of James Jeffrey (d 1957), of Kensington; 2 s (David, Paul); *Career* Maj RAMC; civilian conslt urologist to Army 1950-65; urologist St Peter's Hosps 1945-65; conslt urologist: Italian Hosps 1948, St Luke's Hosp for Clergy 1948, Royal Hosp Chelsea 1950-65; urologist King Edward VII Hosp for Offrs 1950-68, dean Inst of Urology 1965-70 (chm and pres 1988); pres Br Assoc of Urological Surgns 1972-74 (memb Cncl), vice-pres RCS 1978-79 (dean basic scis 1971-76, Hunterian prof); visiting prof of urology: Univ of California, State Univ of Ohio Columbus, Univ of Texas, Univ of New Orleans; hon fell American Coll of Surgns 1967, corresponding fell American Assoc of Genitourinary Surgns 1962; Freeman City of London, Liveryman Worshipful Co Apothecaries 1958; FRCS, Hon FACS; *Books* Recent Advances in Urology (1957); *Recreations* gardening; *Clubs* Athenaeum; *Style*— Howard Hanley, Esq, CBE; Brandon House, North End Avenue, London NW3 7HP

HANLEY, Jeremy James; MP (C) Richmond and Barnes 1983-; s of Jimmy Hanley (d 1970), and Dinah Sheridan; *b* 17 Nov 1945; *Educ* Rugby; *m* 1973, Verna, Viscountess Villiers, da of Kenneth Stott of Jersey; 2 s, 1 da; *Career* CA; contested (C) Lambeth Central (by-election) 1978 and 1979; vice chm Cons Trade and Indust Ctee, memb House of Commons Select Ctee on Home Affrs; memb: House of Commons Select Sub Ctee on Race Relations and Immigration, Br-Irish Inter Parly Body; sec All Party Gp for Europe; PPS to: Min of State at Privy Cncl Office, Min for Civil Serv and the Arts (Rt Hon Richard Luce, MP) 1987-90, Sec of State for the Environment (Rt Hon Christopher Patten, MP) 1990-; under sec of state NI Office 1990-; Parly advsr Inst of CAs in England and Wales; dep chm Fin Trg Co; chm Nikko Fraser Green Ltd (memb of IMRO); Freeman City of London FCA, FCCA, FCIS; *Recreations* cookery, cricket, golf, chess, languages, the arts; *Style*— Jeremy Hanley, Esq, MP; House of Commons, London SW1A 0AA

HANLEY, Hon Lady (Lorna Margaret Dorothy); JP; da of Hon Claude Hope-Morley (d 1968), and sis of 3 Baron Hollenden; raised to rank of Baron's da 1977; *b* 1929; *m* 1957, Sir Michael Bowen Hanley, KCB, *qv*; 1 s (Peter b 1968), 1 da (Sarah b 1967); *Style*— The Hon Lady Hanley, JP

HANLEY, Sir Michael Bowen; KCB (1974); s of late Prof J A Hanley; *b* 24 Feb 1918; *Educ* Sedbergh, Queen's Coll Oxford; *m* 1957, Hon Lorna Margaret Dorothy, *qv*; *Career* served WWII; attached to MOD; *Style*— Sir Michael Hanley, KCB; Ministry of Defence, Whitehall, London SW1

HANLON, Lady Colleen; *née* Wellesley; da of late 4 Earl Cowley; *b* 1925; *m* 1945, Paul A Hanlon, MD, late Capt US Army; 5 s, 2 da; *Style*— Lady Colleen Hanlon; 543 Westmoreland Ave, Kingston, Pennsylvania 18704, USA

HANMER, Lady Frances Jane; *née* Cole; da of 5 Earl of Enniskillen, CMG (d 1963), and Irene Frances, *née* Miller Mundy; *b* 16 Dec 1914; *m* 1954, as his 2 w, Gp Capt Henry Ivan Hanmer, DFC, RAF, (d 1984) gggs of 2 Bt; 1 s (Thomas Edward decd); *Style*— Lady Frances Hanmer; 1 Church Way, Grendon, Northampton

HANMER, (Wyndham Richard) Guy; s and h of Sir John Wyndham Edward Hanmer, 8 Bt; *b* 27 Nov 1955; *Educ* Wellington; *m* 9 Aug 1986, Elizabeth, *née* Taylor, of Frampton on Severn; 1 s (Thomas Wyndham William b 10 May 1989); *Career* Blues and Royals, ret 1981-; now farming; *Style*— Guy Hanmer, Esq; The Stables, Bettisfield Park, Whitchurch, Shropshire

HANMER, Sir John Wyndham Edward; 8 Bt (GB 1774), of Hanmer, Flintshire, JP (Clwyd 1971), DL (1978); s of Lt-Col Sir Edward Hanmer, 7 Bt (d 1977), by his 1 w, Aileen; *b* 27 Sept 1928; *Educ* Eton; *m* 1954, Audrey, da of Maj Arthur Congreve, of the same family (which held land in Staffs from *temp* Edward II) as William Congreve, the Restoration playwright; 2 s; *Heir* s, Wyndham Hanmer; *Career* Capt late The Royal Dragoons; landowner and farmer; dir Chester Race Co 1978, Ludlow Race Club Ltd 1980; High Sheriff Clwyd 1977; *Recreations* shooting, racing; *Clubs* Army and Navy; *Style*— Sir John Hanmer, Bt, JP, DL; The Mere House, Hanmer, Whitchurch, Shropshire (☎ 094 874 383)

HANN, Derek William; s of Claude Tavener Hann (d 1974), of Williton, Somerset, and Ernestine Freda, *née* Bowerman; *b* 22 Aug 1935; *Educ* Dauntsey's Sch; *m* 1, 1958 (m dis), Jill Symonds; 1 s (Simon b 1961), 1 da (Carol b 1959); m 2, 1987, Sylvia Jean, da of Rev John Newton Holder, of Guildford; *Career* joined RAF 1954; served on 65, 201 and 203 Sqdns; OC No 42 Sqdn 1972-74, OC RAF St Mawgan 1977-79, dir Operational Requirements 2 (RAF) MOD 1981-84, COS HQ No 18 Gp 1984-87, dir-gen RAF Personal Servs MOD 1987-89, ret AVM 1989; art dealer; *Recreations* theatre, gardening, horology, music; *Style*— Derek Hann, Esq; The Hann Gallery, 2A York St, Bath BA1 1NG (☎ 0225 466904)

HANN, Judith; da of Ralph Hann of Derby, and Connie, *née* Buxton; *b* 8 Sept 1942; *Educ* Univ of Durham (BSc); *m* 17 Oct 1964, John Exelby; 2 s (Jake b 7 Jan 1970, Daniel b 6 Dec 1971); *Career* journalist trg Northern Echo and Westminster Press, won Glaxo award for science writers in 1960s and 70s, reporter BBC science and features (currently presenter Tomorrow's World); *Books* But What About the Children, The Perfect Baby, Family Scientist, Total Health Plan, The Food of Love; *Recreations* walking, herb gardening, cookery; *Style*— Ms Judith Hann; Tomorrows World, Kensington House, Richmond Way, London W14 0AX (☎ 081 895 6352)

HANNA, Herbert Frederick; s of Arthur F Hanna (d 1980), of Dublin; *b* 26 Oct 1934; *m* 12 Sept 1955, Vyvyenne, *née* Davis; 1 s (Arthur b 1958); *Career* gen mangr Basic System IBM Europe 1968-74; md: ITT Consumer Prods and dir ITT Europe 1974-82, Dataport-Parcon (Unitech Sudsid) 1982-86, FKI Metamec Dereham Norfolk 1986-89, Metramec clocks and Lighting 1989-; memb Norfolk C of C, vice chm Br Clock and Watchmakers Assoc; fell Worshipful Co of Clockmakers; MBHI; *Recreations* rugby, cricket, boating; *Clubs* Middx Co RU, Middx Cricket, Norfolk Broads Yacht; *Style*— Herbert Hanna, Esq; Fairbourne, 27 Norwich Rd, Dereham, Norfolk (☎ 0362 698219); Bristol Gardens, London W9; Cowper Rd, Rathmines, Dublin; FKI Metamec, South Green, E Dereham, Norfolk (☎ 0362 692121, fax 0362 693022)

HANNA, (James) Rainey; s of James Hanna (d 1964), of Coleraine Rd, Portrush, Co Antrim, and Margaret, *née* Henry; *b* 30 May 1924; *Educ* Enniskillen Model Sch, Portora Royal Sch, Queen's Univ Belfast (LLB); *m* 30 March 1950, Kathleen Isobel, da of Francis Wright Hoey (d 1968), of Dyan House, Caledon, Co Tyrone; 2 s (Jonathan b 1953, Paul b 1956); *Career* RAF 1943-46, Fl Sgt, Air Gunner; slr; chm Local Tbnls 1955-, HM coroner 1956-; memb: Inc Law Soc of NI 1948, Ctee of mgmnt Enniskillen Savings Bank 1960 (custodian tstee 1960); *Recreations* golf, music; *Clubs* Royal Cwlth Soc (life memb), Royal Overseas League, Fermanagh County, Enniskillen Golf; *Style*— Rainey Hanna, Esq; Larage Ho, Ballinamallard, Co Fermanagh (☎ 0365 230 90); 25 Darling St, Enniskillen, NI (☎ 0365 22 009); Main St, Fivemiletown, Co Tyrone, NI (☎ 03655 212 34); 92 Lisburn Rd, Belfast, NI (☎ 0232 683 126)

HANNA, William Alexander; s of William John Hanna (d 1952), of Gujarat, India, and Margaret, *née* Blair (d 1987); *b* 21 March 1927; *Educ* Campbell Coll Belfast, Univ of Edinburgh (MB ChB); *m* 9 Jan 1954, Patricia Ruth, da of Joseph Molyneaux Hunter, QHP (d 1973, hon physician to HM The Queen), of Helen's Bay, Co Down; 1 s (David b 1961), 2 da (Winifred b 1956, Patricia b 1957); *Career* MO Mission Hosps Gujarat India 1953-61, sr surgical registrar NI Hosps Authy 1961-65, conslt surgn Belfast City Hosp 1965-89; fell: Ulster Med Soc 1963, Assoc of Surgns of GB and I 1966; pres Belfast Geologists Soc 1988-90; FRCSEd 1958; *Books* Celtic Migrations (1985); *Recreations* ancient history, geology, music; *Style*— William Hanna, Esq; 8 Olde Forge Manor, Belfast, Northern Ireland, BT10 0HY, (☎ 0232 626331)

HANNAH, David Stuart; s of Daniel Hannah, of Appleton, Warrington, and Phyllis, *née* Mottershead; *b* 1 Jan 1953; *Educ* Royal GS Lancaster, Univ of Liverpool (LLB); *m* 26 March 1977, Joanne Alison, da of James Crichton, of Minchinhampton, Glos; 3 s (Daniel b 1981, Christopher b 1983, Michael b 1987), 1 da (Louise b 1979); *Career* admitted slr 1977; tutor in law of equity and trusts Univ of Liverpool 1974-78; memb Legal and Area Ctee Chester; *Recreations* swimming, photography, restoring classic cars; *Style*— David S Hannah, Esq; 1 Marlfield Rd, Grappenhall, Warrington WA4 2JT (☎ 0925 64974); 1 Victoria Rd, Stockton Heath, Warrington (☎ 0925 61354)

HANNAH, Gordon Marshall; s of Dr Daniel Marshall Hannah (d 1971, former Wing-Cdr), of Eccles, Manchester, and Kathleen Mary, *née* Schaap, JP; *b* 30 April 1940; *Educ* Ellesmere Coll Shropshire, Trinity Coll Cambridge (MA); *m* 14 March 1964, Carolyn Joyce, da of William Dancer, of Axminster, Devon; 2 da (Juliette b 29 June 1966, Vanessa b 8 Oct 1968); *Career* chief engr The Dredging & Construction Co Contractors 1972-76; ptnr: Brown Crozier & Wyatt Consultant Engineers 1976-79, Hannah Reed & Assocs 1979-; memb Cncl Inst of Civil Engrs 1982-85, past pres Rotary Club of Cambridge Rutherford; past chm: Cambridge Round Table, E Anglian Assoc of Inst of Civil Engrs; Eur Ing; FICE 1981, MConsE 1982, FIHT 1983, FRSA 1986; *Recreations* golf, gliding, gardening, modelmaking; *Clubs* Gog Magog Golf, Cambridge Univ Gliding; *Style*— Gordon Hannah, Esq; 1 Bunkers Hill, Girton, Cambridge (☎ 0223 276 399); Hannah Reed & Assocs, Telford Hse, Station Rd, Cambridge CB1 2JF (☎ 0223 68523, fax 0223 316 894, car 0831 511 665)

HANNAH, Prof Leslie; s of Arthur Hannah (d 1969), and Marie, *née* Lancashire; *b* 15 June 1947; *Educ* Manchester GS, St John's and Nuffield Colls Oxford (BA, MA, DPhil); *m* 29 Dec 1984, Nuala Barbara Zahedieh, da of Thomas Hockton, of Hove, Sussex; 1 s (Thomas b 1988), 2 step da (Sophie b 1977, Miranda b 1981); *Career* res fell St John's Coll Oxford 1969-73, lectr in econs Univ of Essex 1973-75, lectr Univ of Cambridge 1975-78 (fell Emmanuel Coll Cambridge, fin tutor 1977-78); LSE: dir Business Hist Unit 1978-88, prof 1982-; res fell Centre for Econ Policy Res London 1984-, visiting prof Harvard Business Sch 1984-85, assoc fellow Centre for Business Strategy London Business School 1988-89, invited lectr at univs in USA Europe and Japan; dir NRG Victory Holdings and other cos, fndr memb London Econs (specialist res conslt); referee/tstee for various res funding agencies, charities and jls; memb Social Sci Res Cncl (UK) 1982-84, chm Ed Advsy Bd Dictionary of Business Biography 1979-85, panel speaker Celebrity Speakers Int; MInstD; *Books* The Rise of the Corporate Economy (1976, 2 edn 1983, Japanese edn 1987), Management Strategy and Business Development (ed, 1976), Concentration in Modern Industry: Theory, Measurement and the UK Experience (jtly, 1977), Electricity Before Nationalisation (1977), Engineers, Managers and Politicians (1982), Entrepreneurs and the Social Sciences (1984), Inventing Retirement: The Development of Occupational Pensions in Britain (1986), Electricity Privatisation and the Area Boards: the Case for 12 (jtly, 1987), Pension Asset Management: An International Perspective (ed 1988); *Recreations* reading, walking, talking; *Style*— Prof Leslie Hannah; LSE, Houghton St, London WC2A 2AE (☎ 071 955 7110, fax 071 955 7730, telex 24655)

HANNAH, His Hon Judge William; s of William Bond Hannah (d 1952), and Elizabeth Alexandra, *née* Farrow (d 1982); *b* 31 March 1929; *Educ* Everton Sch Nottingham; *m* 1 July 1950, (Alma) June, da of James Marshall (d 1969); 1 s (William Robert b 1960), 1 da (Kay b 1953); *Career* RAF 1946-52; police serv (UK) 1952-77; Bar 1977, in practice Newcastle (chambers of David Robson, QC) 1977-88, rec 1987, circuit judge 1988-; *Recreations* golf, swimming, walking, theatre; *Clubs* South Shields Golf; *Style*— His Hon Judge Hannah; New Court Chambers, 3 Broad Chare, Quayside, Newcastle upon Tyne NE1 3DQ

HANNAM, Eric James Stanley; s of Capt Frank Stanley Hannam (d 1943), and Margaret Ada, *née* Collens (d 1956); *b* 13 Nov 1919; *Educ* Reading Sch Berks; *m* 1953, Betty Sinclair, da of Herbert George Cheel, MBE; 1 s (Mark James b 1955), 2 da (Sarah Margaret b 1957, Judith Emma b 1959); *Career* Inns of Ct Regt TA 1938, 2 Lt Shrops Yeo 1939, subsequently 76 (Shrops Yeo) Medium Regt RA, served with regt in ME and Italy 1942-46, demobbed Capt RA 1946, memb Regtl Ctee London 1946-; joined staff Nat Provincial Bank Ltd 1936 (subsequently Nat West Bank plc), ret as sr mangr London West End 1979; exec dir Leopold Joseph and Sons Ltd 1979-81; non-exec dir: London and Provincial Shop Centre (Holdings) plc 1980-87, Grillford Ltd Fine Art Printers Milton Keynes (chm 1982-); memb Harrow Cncl 1990-; Freeman City of London; Worshipful Co of Broderers: Freeman 1965, Liveryman 1965, Warden 1986, Master 1987; FCIB; *Recreations* theatre, reading, fine arts, watching sport;

Clubs Oriental; *Style*— Eric Hannam, Esq; 11 Oakhill Ave, Pinner, Middx HA5 3DL (☎ 081 866 3444); Grillford Ltd, 26 Peverel Drive, Granby, Bletchley, Milton Keynes MK1 1QZ (☎ 090 864 4123)

HANNAM, John Gordon; MP (C) Exeter 1970-; s of Thomas William Hannam (d 1955), and Selina, *née* Young (d 1986); *b* 2 Aug 1929; *Educ* Yeovil GS; *m* 1, 19 June 1956 (m dis 1981), Wendy, da of late Thomas Lamont Macartney, of Beckenham; 2 da (Amanda b 1961, Katie b 1976); m 2, 1983, Mrs Vanessa Wauchope, da of Wing Cdr Henry Albert Anson, RAF (d 1955; gs of 2 Earl of Lichfield); 1 step s, 3 step da; *Career* cmmnd 4 Royal Tank Regt 1947-48, 4 Bn Somerset LI (TA) 1949-51; md: Hotels & Restaurants Co 1952-61, Motels & Restaurants Co 1961-70; chm British Motels Fedn 1967-74, pres 1974-80; memb Cncl Br Travel Assoc 1968-69; PPS min Indust 1972-73, chief sec Treasy 1973-74; sec All-Pty Disablement Gp 1975-; chm: W Country Cons Backbench Ctee 1979-81, Cons Energy Ctee 1979-; capt: Lords and Commons Tennis Club 1975-, Lords and Commons Ski Club 1975-82; memb: Govt Advsy Ctee on Transport for Disabled, Cncl Action Res, Glyndebourne Festival Soc, Bd Nat Theatre; pres Br Motels Fedn 1974-79; vice pres Disabled Drivers' Assoc; dir Berkeley Exploration and Prodn plc; Hon MA Open Univ 1986; *Recreations* tennis (ex Somerset Singles Champion), skiing, sailing, music, singing, reading; *Clubs* All England Lawn Tennis, Royal Yacht Sqdn; *Style*— John Hannam, Esq, MP; 4 Thurleigh Rd, London SW12 8UG (☎ 081 673 5750); Pightel Cottage, Plymtree, Devon (☎ 088 47 332)

HANNAY, Anthony Hewitt Scott; s of Thomas Scott Hannay (d 1975), of Stable House, Chorlton-by-Backford, Chester, and Doreen, *née* Paul; *b* 2 May 1944; *Educ* Rugby, Univ of Liverpool (LLB); *m* 10 Oct 1970, Rosemary Susan, da of Maj Geoffrey Thomas St John Sanders, TD (d 1986), of Cirencester, Glos; 1 s (Andrew b 1975), 1 da (Diana b 1973); *Career* admitted slr 1968; ptnr: Laces & Co 1970-88, Lace Mawer 1988-; memb: Mersey RHA 1988-90, RNLI Mgmnt Ctee 1986 (chm Port of Liverpool and Dist Branch 1989); memb Law Soc; *Recreations* sailing, skiing, windsurfing; *Clubs* Liverpool Racquet; *Style*— Anthony Hannay, Esq; The Stray, School Lane, Hinderton, South Wirral L64 7TX (☎ 051 336 8455); Lace Mawer, Castle Chambers, 43 Castle St, Liverpool L2 9SU (☎ 051 236 2002, telex 627229, fax 051 236 2585, car 0860 800080)

HANNAY, Sir David Hugh Alexander; KCMG (1986, CMG 1981); s of J G Hannay (d 1972), of Aston Tirrold, nr Didcot, Oxon, and E M Hannay (d 1986), *née* Lazarus; *b* 28 Sept 1935; *Educ* Winchester, New Coll Oxford; *m* 1961, Gillian Rosemary, da of H Rex (d 1962), of Exmouth, Devon; 4 s (Richard, Philip, Jonathan, Alexander); *Career* 2 Lt 8 Kings Royal Irish Hussars 1954-56; joined FCO 1959, Tehran 1960-61, oriental sec Kabul 1961-63, Eastern Dept FO 1963-65, 2 and 1 sec UK Delgn to the EC 1965-70, 1 sec UK Negotiating Team with the Euro Community 1970-72, chef de cabinet to Sir Christopher Soames (vice pres of Cmmn of Euro Community) Brussels 1973-77, head Energy Sci and Space Dept FCO 1977-79, head ME Dept FCO 1979, asst under-sec of state (Euro Community) FCO 1979-84, min Washington 1984-85, ambass and UK perm rep to Euro Community 1985-90, UK perm rep to the UN New York 1990-; *Recreations* travel, gardening; *Clubs* Travellers'; *Style*— Sir David Hannay, KCMG; UK Missions to the United Nations, 10th Floor, 845 Third Avenue, New York, NY 10022

HANNAY OF KIRKDALE AND THAT ILK, Ramsay William Rainsford; s of Col Frederick Rainsford-Hannay, CMG, DSO, JP (d 1959), of Cardoness, Gatehouse-of-Fleet, Kirkcudbrightshire, and Dorothea Letitia May, *née* Maxwell (d 1981); *b* 15 June 1911; *Educ* Winchester, Trinity Coll Cambridge; *m* 19 Sept 1936, Margaret, 2 da of Sir William Wiseman, 10 Bt (d 1962), of Content, Montego Bay, Jamaica; 1 s (David Wiseman Ramsay b 3 Jan 1939), 1 da (Jessica Margaret b 2 Sept 1937); *Career* served WWII, cmmnd Highland Light Inf, serv with SOE in US and Europe, attached to Kings Liverpool Regt, demob as Maj; called to the Bar 1934, legal asst Bd of Trade 1937-59, asst slr Bd of Trade 1959-64 (ret to look after family estates in Galloway); appointed Hon Sheriff substitute Stewartry of Kirkcudbright; appointed Chief of Clan Hannay 1980 as Hannay of Kirkdale and of that Ilk and relinquished the surname of Rainsford; *Recreations* shooting, fishing, sailing; *Clubs* New (Edinburgh), Royal Ocean Racing; *Style*— Hannay of Kirkdale and of that Ilk; Cardoness House, Gatehouse-of-Fleet, Kirkcudbrightshire DG7 2EP (☎ 0557 24 207); Estate Office, Cardoness, Gatehouse-of-Fleet, Kirkcudbrightshire DG7 2EP (☎ 0557 24 288)

HANNEY, Douglas William John; s of Percy John Hanney, of Sidmouth, Devon, and Iris May, *née* Wright; *b* 9 May 1955; *Educ* Abingdon Sch; *m* 1 June 1982, Helen Anne, da of Donald Arthur Parkes, of Halesowen, W Midlands; 2 s (Jonathan b 16 June 1984, Mark b 18 April 1986); *Career* dir Baring Securities Ltd; *Recreations* horse racing, golf, flying; *Style*— Douglas Hanney, Esq; Hampton, Middx; Sidmouth, Devon; 1 Lloyds Chambers, 1 Portsoken St, London E1 (☎ 0860 818039)

HANNING, Hugh Peter James; s of John Rowland Hanning (d 1961, kinsman of John Hanning Speke who discovered source of the Nile), and Valentine Mary, *née* Bradshaw (d 1975); *b* 5 Feb 1925; *Educ* Winchester, Univ Coll Oxford; *m* 11 Dec 1954, Caragh, da of Arnold McClure Williams; 1 s ((Giles) James b 3 April 1956); *Career* Nat Serv cmmnd RNVR WWII; former def corr The Observer and def conslt The Guardian, ed Royal United Services Institute Jl 1967-70, sec C of E Int Ctee 1972-80, dir Br Atlantic Ctee (Govt financed) 3 times 1974-82, former advsr MOD and FO Disarmament Ctee (sent by FO to Biafra), vice pres Intermediate Technol Devpt Gp, UK dir Int Peace Acad NY, conslt (Africa) Int Inst for Strategic Studies; lectr and memb Ctee Chatham House (RIIA), current chm Fontmell Gp on Disaster Relief; *Books* The Peaceful Uses of Military Forces, A Global Strategy for Britain, Peace: The Plain Man's Guide (1988); *Recreations* piano, golf, painting; *Clubs* Army and Navy; *Style*— Hugh Hanning, Esq; 18 Montpelier Row, Blackheath, London SE3 0RL (☎ 081 852 4101)

HANNON, Lady Fiona Mary; *née* Graham; da of 7 Duke of Montrose, and his 1 w Isobel Veronica, *née* Sellar (d 1990); *b* 1 Jan 1932; *Educ* North Foreland Lodge; *m* 1 Oct 1966, Peter Alexander O'Brien Hannon, s of Ven Gordon Hannon (d 1978); 2 da (Catherine b 1968, Veronica b 1971); *Style*— The Lady Fiona Hannon; The Fort House, Dundooan, Coleraine, N Ireland BT52 2PX

HANRAHAN, Brian; s of Thomas Hanrahan, and Kathleen, *née* McInerney; *b* 22 March 1949; *Educ* St Ignatius Coll, Univ of Essex (BA); *m* 4 Jan 1986, Honor Catherine, *née* Wilson; *Career* BBC: Far East corr 1983-85, Moscow corr 1986-89, foreign affrs corr 1989-; *Style*— Brian Hanrahan, Esq; c/o BBC TV Centre, Wood Lane, London W12 (☎ 081 743 8000)

HANRATTY, Dr James Francis; OBE (1989); s of Dr James Joseph Hanratty (d 1968), of Huddersfield, and Elsie May, *née* Lycett (d 1987); *b* 27 July 1919; *Educ* Stonyhurst, Univ of Leeds (MB ChB); *m* 26 May 1945, (Mary) Irene Evangeline, da of Andrew Belton (d 1977); 4 s (James b 1946, John b 1949, Patrick b 1952, Peter b 1957), 1 da (Mary b 1947); *Career* Surgn Lt RNVR 1943-46 (despatches 1944); serv HMS Cam: Atlantic, Med, Normandy invasion; GP N Derbys 1946-78, med dir St Joseph's Hospice Hackney 1978-88, hon conslt physician Mildmay Hosp Shoreditch; lectr on terminal illness: RAMC, USA 1981, Sorbonne 1983, Hong Kong 1984, Brussels 1987, Hague 1987; former pres Derbys Branch BMA, memb Industl Injuries Med Bd Chesterfield 1949-78, master Guild of Catholic Doctors Nottingham 1975-78, govr Stonyhurst Coll 1975-81, fndr memb Cncl and tstee of Help the Hospices; MRCGP 1969, FRSM 1977; Knight of the Order of St Gregory the Great (Papal) 1988, Knight of the Order of the Holy Sepulchre of Jerusalem English Lieutenancy 1987; *Books* Control of Distressing Symptoms in the Dying Patient (1982); *Recreations* watching cricket, classical music; *Clubs* Naval, Hurlingham, Athenaeum; *Style*— Dr James Hanratty, OBE; 44 Westminster Gardens, Marsham St, London SW1P4JG (☎ 071 834 4660)

HANSARD, Gerald George Anthony; s of Capt Trevor Thomas Hansard (d 1961), of Merthyr Tydfil, and Helen Mary, *née* Brennan (d 1973); *b* 28 Oct 1935; *Educ* Downside; *m* 15 June 1963, Ursula St Clair, da of Dr Timothy Joseph Hurley (d 1980), of Cardiff; 1 s (Charles Christopher b 24 Aug 1964), 1 da (Philippa Clare b 12 Oct 1967); *Career* Nat Serv, 2 Lt S Wales Borderers 1954-56; dir Buckley's Brewery Plc 1978-87, self employed dir G H Trading 1988-; memb Brewers Soc 1983-87; *Recreations* gardening, photography; *Clubs* Cardiff and County; *Style*— Gerald Hansard, Esq; Beaufort Cottage, Reynoldston, Gower Swansea, West Glamorgan (☎ 0792 390075)

HANSCOMB, Hon Mrs (Elinor Ruth); *née* McNair; da of 1 Baron McNair, CBE, QC, LLD (d 1975); *b* 25 Feb 1924; *m* 24 March 1955, Raymond Hanscomb, MRCVS, s of William Hanscomb, of Chapel House, Overthorpe, Banbury, Oxon; 1 s (Benjamin Douglas b 30 Aug 1956), 1 adopted s (George Sebastian b 21 Dec 1965), 1 adopted da (Emma Frances Mary b April 1963); *Style*— The Hon Mrs Hanscomb; Powells End, Kempley, Dymock, Glos

HANSCOMBE, Philip Martin; s of Stanley William Hanscombe, MBE (d 1967), and Sylvia, *née* Gordon (d 1983); *b* 9 Jan 1930; *Educ* Giggleswick Sch, Univ of Liverpool (BA); *m* 17 Sept 1960, Margaret Winnifred, da of George Erskine (d 1981); 2 s (Jonathan b 1963, Nicholas b 1969, d 1973), 2 da (Philippa b 1964, Caroline b 1975); *Career* Nat Serv Corpl RE 1948-50; dir mktg Trend plc 1958-61; ICI Paints 1961-: mktg mangr 1965-72, dir 1972-89; self employed mktg conslt; *Recreations* golf, tennis, badminton, bridge, reading; *Clubs* Denham Golf; *Style*— Philip Hanscombe, Esq; (☎ 0494 67564)

HANSEN, Hon Mrs (Elizabeth Joan); *née* Bradbury; only da (by 1 m) of 2 Baron Bradbury; *b* 17 March 1940; *m* 1965, Warren G Hansen, s of Joseph H Hansen, of Dallas, Texas, USA; 1 s, 1 da; *Style*— The Hon Mrs Hansen; 2 Sargent Place, Waxahachie, Texas, 75167

HANSON, Sir Anthony (Leslie Oswald) Dominic Sean; 4 Bt (UK 1887), of Bryanston Sq, Co Middx; s of Sir Gerald Stanhope Hanson, 2 Bt (d 1946), and his 3 w Flora Libre, *née* Blennerhassett (d 1956); suc half-bro Sir Richard Leslie Reginald Hanson, 3 Bt, 1951; *b* 27 Nov 1934; *Educ* Hawtrey's, Gordonstoun, Exeter Univ (BEd); *m* 1964, Denise Jane, da of Richard S Rolph, BEM, of Stoke-sub-Hamdon, Somerset; 1 da (Charlotte b 1971); *Heir* none; *Career* served RN; farming to 1967; teacher to 1983; serious motorcyle accident 1980; *Recreations* riding, avoiding rows with wife, reading, working for Amnesty Int and Greenpeace, talking; *Style*— Sir Anthony Hanson, Bt; Woodland Cottage, Woodland, Ashburton, Devon (☎ 0364 52711)

HANSON, Brian John Taylor; s of Benjamin John Hanson (d 1978), of Norwood Green, Middx, and Gwendoline Ada, *née* Taylor; *b* 23 Jan 1939; *Educ* Hounslow Coll, Law Soc Coll of Law; *m* 10 June 1972, Deborah Mary Hazel, da of Lt-Col Richard Stewart Palliser Dawson, OBE, of Shrubbery Cottage, Stowting, Kent; 2 s (James b 1973, Crispin b 1982), 3 da (Sarah b 1975, Rebecca b 1979, Alice b 1986); *Career* slr ecclesiastical notary; slr 1963-65; slr church cmmnrs for Eng 1965-70, asst legal advsr: Gen Synod of C of E 1970-74; legal advsr Gen Synod 1974- (registrar 1980-), House of Bishops 1974-; registrar to the Convocation of Canterbury 1982-; memb Legal Advsy Cmmn of the Gen Synod 1980- (sec 1970-86); Guardian Shrine of Our Lady of Walsingham 1984-, memb cncl: St Luke's Hosp for the Clergy 1985-, The Ecclesiastical Law Soc 1987-; fell Woodard Corp 1987-, govr St Michaels Sch Burton Park 1987-, Bishop's Nominee on Chichester Diocesan Synod 1987-; memb: Law Soc 1963, Canon Law Soc of GB 1980; Ecclesiastical Law Assoc 1980-; Freeman: City of London, Worshipful Co of Glaziers and Painters of Glass; *Books* The Opinions of the Legal Advisory Commission (ed 6 edn, 1985), The Canons of the Church of England (ed 2 edn 1975, 4 edn 1986), Norwood Parish Church - A Short History (1970); *Recreations* the family, gardening, genealogy; *Clubs* RCS; *Style*— Brian Hanson, Esq; Daltons Farm, Bolney, W Sussex RH17 5PG (☎ 0444881 890); Church House, Deans Yard, London SW1 (☎ 071 222 9011)

HANSON, Christopher John; s of Laurence William Hanson (d 1966), of Oxford, and Carola Mary, *née* Hawes (d 1985); *b* 20 April 1940; *Educ* The King's Sch Canterbury, Univ of Oxford (MA); *m* 26 May 1975, Jayne Gwenllian, da of Evan Morgan Lewis, of Maidstone; 1 s (David William b 1976), 1 da (Elizabeth Jane b 1979); *Career* slr; ptnr Lovell White Durrant; memb Insolvency Jt Working Pty Bar and Law Soc 1977-, vice chm Insolvency Sub Ctee City of London Slrs Co; *Style*— Christopher Hanson, Esq; The Shaw, Brasted Chart, nr Westerham, Kent (☎ 0959 63 763); Lovell White Durrant, 21 Holborn Viaduct, London EC1A 2DY (☎ 071 236 0066, fax 071 248 4212, telex 887122 LWD G)

HANSON, Derek; *b* 17 June 1933; *Educ* Univ of Nottingham (BSc), Queen's Coll Cambridge (BA); *Career* various appts ICI plc 1957-71; John Brown plc: tech mangr 1971-78, md John Brown E & C Ltd 1979-90 (mktg dir 1978-79), dir 1989-, pres Chemetics International Co Ltd 1990-; FIChemE 1971, FEng 1986; *Recreations* sailing, cricket; *Clubs* MCC, Royal Naval; *Style*— Derek Hanson, Esq; John Brown plc, 1, Buckingham St, Portsmouth, Hants P01 1HN (☎ 0705 822300, fax 0705 812599)

HANSON, Derrick George; s of late John Henry Hanson; *b* 9 Feb 1927; *Educ* Waterloo GS, Univ of London, Univ of Liverpool; *m* 1 1951, Daphne Elizabeth (decd); 1 s, 2 da; m 2, 1974, Hazel Mary (decd); m 3, 1986, Patricia; *Career* dir and gen Mangr Martins Bank Trust Co 1968, Barclays Bank Trust Co 1969-76, chm Barclays Unicorn 1972-76, sr advsr (UK) Mfrs Hanover Trust Co 1977-79, chm City of London and Euro Property Co Ltd 1980-86, dir Phillips Fine Art Auctioneers 1977-82, memb Cncl Univ of Liverpool 1981-84; chm: Key Fund Managers Ltd 1984-87, Southport and Formby DHA 1986-89, Birmingham Midshires Building Society, Moneyguide Ltd; dir: Toye and Co Ltd, Albany Investment Trust Ltd, Br Leather Co Ltd, James Beattie plc; memb Nat Tst NW Regnl Cncl, pres Assoc of Banking Teachers 1979-88, chm Christian Arts Tst 1980-86; hon: fell City Univ Business Sch, Ch Inst of Bankers; *Books* Service Banking: The Arrival of the All-Purpose Bank (1982, sr prize of Chartered Inst of Bankers for outstanding contribution to banking literature), Moneyguide: the handbook of personal finance (1980), Dictionary of Banking and Finance (1985); *Recreations* golf, gardening, hill walking; *Clubs* RAC, Formby Golf; *Style*— Derrick Hanson, Esq; Bridgend, Deepdale Bridge, Patterdale, Cumbria; Grasshopper House, Freshfield Road, Formby, Merseyside

HANSON, (James) Donald (Don); s of Leslie Hanson (d 1977), of W Yorks, and Mary, *née* Haigh (d 1982); *b* 4 Jan 1935; *Educ* Heath GS Halifax W Yorks; *m* 1, 29 Aug 1959 (m dis 1977), (Patricia) Margaret, da of Frank Talent (d 1982), of Cheshire; 2 s (Steven b 1962, Scott b 1966); m 2, 8 July 1978, Anne Barbara Asquith; *Career* managing ptnr of strategical affrs and communications Athur Andersen & Co 1989- (joined 1958, estab NW practise 1966, manging ptnr 1968-82, sr ptnr of UK firm

1982-89); memb: Int Operating Ctee 1982-88, Int Bd of Ptnrs 1985-88; pres Manchester Soc of chartered Accountants 1979 (memb 1967-81); memb: Cncl of CBI 1982-, Cncl and Ct Univ of Manchester 1982-; memb Inst of Chartered Accountants, ACA 1956, FCA 1957; *Recreations* reading, tennis; *Clubs* Mark's, Groucho, Annabel's; *Style—* Don Hanson, Esq; Arthur Andersen & Co, 2 Arundel St, London WC2R 3LT (☎ 071 438 3693, telex 8812711, fax 071 438 3015, car 0860 265709)

HANSON, Geoffrey; s of John Hanson (d 1967), of Witney, Oxfordshire, and Grace Emily, *née* Elphick (d 1977); *b* 9 Dec 1939; *Educ* Eastbourne GS, Itchen GS Southampton, Trinity Coll of Music (GTCL, LTCL, ATCL); *m* 5 Aug 1961, (Alice) Janet, MBE, da of Frank Wyatt (d 1948), of Sussex; *Career* conductor and composer; conductor London Ripieno Soc 1962-, prof Trinity Coll of Music 1964-, conductor Square Singers of St James 1977-89; Telemann St Matthew Passion Camden Festival 1968; compositions incl: 3 Pieces for Organ 1970, A Trilogy of Psalms for chorus and orchestra 1973, Brecon Ser 1974, concerto for piano and orchestra 1977, concerto for oboe and strings 1978, Sinfonia Amoris for soloists chorus and orchestra 1981, War! Cry War! for soloists chorus and orchestra 1986, concerto for violin and orchestra 1986, concerto for clarinet and strings 1987, concerto for viola and orchestra 1990; hon fell Trinity Coll of Music London 1972; memb City of Westminster Arts Cncl; memb: Performing Rights Soc 1981, Composers Guild of GB 1983; *Recreations* swimming, walking; *Style—* Geoffrey Hanson, Esq; 89 Fordington Rd, Highgate, London N6 4TH (☎ 081 444 9214)

HANSON, Baron (Life Peer UK 1983), of Edgerton, Co of W Yorks; Sir James Edward Hanson; s of Robert Hanson, CBE (d 1973), and late Louisa Ann (Cis), *née* Rodgers; *b* 20 Jan 1922; *m* 1959, Geraldine, *née* Kaelin; 2 s, 1 da; *Career* chm: Hanson plc 1965-, Hanson Transport Group Ltd 1965-; tstee Hanson Fellowship of Surgery Oxford Univ; fell Cancer Research Campaign; Liveryman Worshipful Co of Saddlers, Freeman City of London; FRSA, CBIM; Hon LLD Leeds 1984; kt 1976; *Clubs* Brooks's, Huddersfield Borough, The Brook (New York), Toronto; *Style—* The Rt Hon the Lord Hanson; 1 Grosvenor Place, London SW1X 7JH (☎ 071 245 1245, telex 917202)

HANSON, Sir (Charles) John; 3 Bt (UK 1918), of Fowey, Cornwall; s of Sir Charles Edwin Bourne Hanson, 2 Bt (d 1958); *b* 28 Feb 1919; *Educ* Eton, Clare Coll Cambridge; *m* 1, 1944 (m dis 1968), Patricia Helen, da of late Adm Sir (Eric James) Patrick Brind, GBE, KCB; 1 s, 1 da; m 2, 1968, Violet Helen, da of late Charles Ormonde Trew, and formerly wife of late Capt Philip Cecil Langdon Yorke, OBE, RN; *Heir* s, Charles Rupert Patrick Hanson; *Career* late Capt, The Duke of Cornwall's Light Inf; serv WWII; *Clubs* Army and Navy, MCC; *Style—* Sir John Hanson, Bt; Gunn House, Shelfanger, nr Diss, Norfolk

HANSON, John Gilbert; CBE (1979); s of Gilbert Fretwell Hanson (d 1981), and Gladys Margaret, *née* Kay; *b* 16 Nov 1938; *Educ* Manchester GS, Wadham Coll Oxford (MA); *m* 1962, Margaret, da of Edward Thomas Clark, MBE, of Oxfordshire; 3 s (Mark b 1966, Paul b 1967, James b 1971); *Career* WO 1961-63; Br Cncl: Madras India 1963-66, MECAS Lebanon 1966-68, Bahrain 1968-72, London 1972-75, Tehran Iran 1975-79, London 1979-82, RCDS 1983; min (cultural affrs) Br High Cmmn New Delhi 1984-88; dep dir gen Br Cncl 1988-; memb Governing Cncl Br Inst Persian Studies, Royal Soc for Asian Affrs; *Recreations* books, music, sailing, sport, travel; *Clubs* Athenaeum, MCC, Gymkhana (Madras); *Style—* John Hanson, Esq, CBE; c/o The British Council, 10 Spring Gardens, London SW1A 2BN (☎ 071 930 8466)

HANSON, Prof Owen Jerrold; s of Lawrence Hanson-Smith (d 1972), of Cheltenham, and Edith Annette Audrey, *née* Waller; *b* 2 Jan 1934; *Educ* Wallington Co HS, Univ of Cambridge (BA, MA), Univ of London (MSc), City Univ (PhD); *m* 14 July 1965, Barbara Maria Teresa, da of Maj Albin Srodzinski; 2 da (Annette b 31 Aug 1967, Ilona b 9 March 1971); *Career* jr technician RAF 1952-54; works metallurgist Wilkinson Sword Co Ltd 1957-60, mangr works laboratory Gillete Industs UK Ltd 1962-64, systems analyst IBM UK Ltd 1964-70, head of Dept of Business Systems Analysis City Univ 1988 (sr lectr 1970, dir Centre for Business Systems Analysis 1983); FIDPM, MIM; *Books* Basic File Design (1978), Design of Computer Data Files (1982, 2 edn 1988), Essentials of Computer Data Files (1985); *Recreations* cross country running, tennis, squash; *Clubs* South London Harriers, Purley Cricket; *Style—* Prof Owen Hanson; City University, Northampton Square, London EC1V 0HB (☎ 071 253 4399 ext 3400, fax 071 608 1270, pager 528 9001, PAGER 814004)

HANSON, Prof Philip; s of Eric Hugh Cecil Hanson (d 1942), of London, and Doris May, *née* Ward (d 1980); *b* 16 Dec 1936; *Educ* Highgate Sch, Jesus Coll Cambridge (MA), Univ of Birmingham (PhD); *m* 22 Oct 1960, Evelyn, da of Sidney James Rogers (d 1968), of London; 2 s (Paul Edward b 1963, Nicholas James b 1972); *Career* Nat Serv Middx Regt and Intelligence Corps, Sgt mil interpreter (Russian); lectr in econs Univ of Exeter 1961-67, visiting prof of econs Univ of Michigan 1967-68; Univ of Birmingham 1968-: lectr, sr lectr, reader, currently prof of Soviet econs, dep dir Centre for Russian & East Euro Studies; first sec HM Embassy Moscow, sr res offr FCO 1971-72; visiting prof Univ of Michigan 1977, sr Mellon fell Harvard Univ 1986-87; conslt: Planecon Inc, Oxford Analytica, Radio Liberty; memb Ctee Birmingham Jazz 1978-83, memb E Europe Exec Birmingham C of C and Indust 1980-89, memb Cncl Univ of London Sch of Slavonic and East Euro Studies 1990-; MRIIA; *Books* Trade and Technology in Soviet-Western Relations (1981), The Comparative Economics of Research, Development & Innovation (with K Pavitt, 1987), Western Economic Statecraft in East-West Relations (1988); *Recreations* jazz, cricket; *Style—* Prof Philip Hanson; c/o Centre, University of Birmingham, Birmingham, B15 2TT, (☎ 021 414 6353 fax 021 414 3423)

HANSON, Richard William Durrant; TD (1969); s of William Gordon Hanson, OBE, and Dulce Durrant Hanson; *b* 11 Aug 1935; *Educ* Eton; *m* 23 June 1961, Elizabeth Deirdre Dewar, da of late Dr A D Frazer; 1 s (James b 1969), 2 da (Arabella b 1962, Georgina b 1963); *Career* 2 Lt 17/21 Lancers 1954-56, Maj Sherwood Rangers Yeo and Royal Yeo 1956-69; dir Hardys & Hansons plc; Kimberley Brewery Nottingham: joined 1962, md 1973, chm and md 1989; High Sheriff Nottinghamshire 1980-81; *Recreations* shooting, tennis; *Clubs* MCC; *Style—* Richard Hanson, Esq, TD; Budby Castle, Newark, Notts NG22 9EU (☎ 0623 822293); Hardys & Hansons plc, Kimberley Brewery, Nottingham NG16 2NS (☎ 0602 383611, fax 0602 459055)

HANSON, Hon Robert William; s of Baron Hanson (Life Peer); *b* 3 Oct 1960; *Educ* Eton, St Peter's Coll Oxford; *Career* NM Rothschild & Sons Ltd 1983-90, asst dir NM Rothschild's Sons Ltd 1990-, assoc dir Hanson plc 1990-; *Recreations* hunting, polo, helicopter flying, golf; *Clubs* White's, Brooks's, The Berkshire, Cirencester Polo, The Brook (NY); *Style—* The Hon Robert Hanson; 1 Grosvenor Place, London SW1X 7JH

HANSON, (Charles) Rupert Patrick; s and h of Sir (Charles) John Hanson, 3 Bt; *b* 25 June 1945; *Educ* Eton, Central London Poly; *m* 1977, Wanda, da of Don Arturo Larrain, of Santiago, Chile; 1 s (Alexis b 1978); *Career* tech, legal and commercial translator 1977-84; teacher of English as foreign language 1981-83; revenve offr Inland Revenue (HMIT Hove); *Recreations* classical music, writing poetry, tennis; *Style—* Rupert Hanson, Esq; 125 Ditchling Rd, Brighton, E Sussex BN1 4SE (☎ 0273 697882)

HANSON-SMITH, Christopher John; s of Herbert Cecil Smith, CBE (d 1981), of Monmouth, and Jane Bell, *née* Blair (d 1983); *b* 24 Dec 1927; *Educ* Winchester, New Coll Oxford; *m* 16 April 1955, Jennifer Margery, da of John Douglas Latta, MC (d 1973), of Ayr; 1 s (Julian b 1962), 3 da (Jane b 1956, Louise b 1957, Gabrielle b 1964); *Career* Lt Royal Norfolk Regt, India, BAOR 1946-48; dist offr HMOCS Nigeria 1950-59, vice consul Spanish Guinea 1957, export salesman British Celanese Ltd 1959-64, md Vine Fuels Ltd 1964-66, PR offr Nat Tst 1967-87 (conslt 1988-), project dir E Anglia Tourist Bd 1989-90; lectr for Nat Tst: NADFAS, ESU (USA); chm: Beatrix Potter Soc 1984-90, Food and Farming (Norfolk) 1989; MIPR; medals: Rhodesia (1980), Zimbabwe Independence (1980); *Recreations* photography, walking, fishing, travel; *Clubs* Lansdowne, Naval and Military; *Style—* Christopher Hanson-Smith, Esq; Roundabout Farm, Thurning, Dereham, Norfolk, NR20 5QS; National Trust, 36 Queen Anne's Gate SW1 (☎ 071 222 9251)

HANWORTH, 2 Viscount (UK 1936); Sir David Bertram Pollock; 2 Bt (UK 1922); also Baron Hanworth (UK 1926); s of Charles Pollock (s of 1 Viscount Hanworth, KBE, PC, JP, who d 1936 and was 5 s of George Pollock, himself the 3 s of Rt Hon Sir Frederick Pollock, 1 Bt, PC; his lordship m Laura, da of Sir Thomas Salt, 1 Bt, sometime MP for Stafford, JP, DL, whose w, Emma, was great-niece of Cardinal Manning); *b* 1 Aug 1916; *Educ* Wellington, Trinity Coll Cambridge; *m* 27 April 1940, (Isolda) Rosamond, JP, DL, FSA da of Geoffrey Parker (3 s of Hon Cecil Parker, JP, by his w Rosamond, da of Most Rev Charles Longley, DD, sometime Archbishop of Canterbury); *Heir* s, Hon (David) Stephen Geoffrey Pollock; *Career* formerly independent, then SDP, now sits as Social and Lib Democratic peer in House of Lords; barr 1958; late Lt-Col RE; CEng, MIMechE, FIEE, FIQA, FRPS; speaks particularly on all energy matters, author of books on colour photography; *Style—* The Rt Hon the Viscount Hanworth; Quoin Cottage, Shamley Green, Guildford, Surrey (☎ 0483 893 018)

HAPPOLD, Edmund; s of Prof Frank Charles Happold, of Three Roods, New Barnes Road, Arnside, Cumbria, and Margaret, *née* Smith (d 1988); *b* 8 Nov 1930; *Educ* Leeds GS, Bootham Sch York, Univ of Leeds (BSc); *m* 21 Dec 1967, Evelyn Clare, da of Charles Matthews of Hayle, Cornwall; 2 s (Matthew b 1969, Thomas b 1971); *Career* site engr Sir Robert MacAlpine and Sons 1952-54, asst engr OVE Arup and Ptnrs (worked on Coventry Cathedral, Sydney Opera House) 1956-58, engr Severud Elstad and Kruger NY (Lincoln Centre Yale Ice Hockey) 1958-60, exec ptnr (prev assoc, sr engr) OVE Arup and Ptnrs (projects incl: Conference Centres at Riyadh and Mecca, Knightsbridge Cavalry Barracks, Br Embassy Rome, Centre Pompidou Paris, Mannheim Lattice Shell), 1960-76; sr ptnr Buro Happold 1976- (projects incl: Dip Club Riyadh, Munich Aviary, 58 degrees N Alberta), prof bldg engr Univ of Bath 1976-; chm: advsy bd Const Indust Computer Assoc 1982-, Bldg Indust Cncl 1988-, Theatre Royal Bath 1988-; awards: Guthrie Brown Medal, 2 Oscar Faber Medals, Queen's Award for Indust 1987, Leslie Murray Medal; memb: Design Cncl 1988-, bd Property Servs Agency DOE 1981-86, BRAC 1988-; Freeman City of London, Liveryman Worshipful Co of Carmen; Hon DSc City Univ 1988; RDI, FEng, FICE, FIStructE (pres 1986-87), FCIOB, FHKIE, Hon FRIBA, Hon FCIBSE; *Books* author of numerous tech papers for learned jls; *Recreations* travel, family activities; *Clubs* Athenaeum; *Style—* Prof Edmund Happold; 4 Widcombe Terrace, Bath, Avon BA2 6AJ (☎ 0225 315 656); 32 Grosvenor St, London W1X 9FF; Buro Happold, Camden Mill, Lower Bristol Rd, Bath BA2 3DQ (☎ 0225 337510); Sch of Architecture and Building Engrg, Univ of Bath, Claverton Down, Bath (☎ 0225 826 622)

HAQQANI, Dr Mustafa Tahseen; s of Mohsinuddin Haqqani (d 1980), and Iqbal Fatima; *b* 6 Oct 1941; *Educ* Madrasa Aliya Hyderabad India, Osmania Univ Hyderabad India (MB BS), London (DPath); *m* 26 June 1966, Moina, da of Faizuddin (d 1954); 1 s (Ehsan Murtuza b 27 July 1978); *Career* demonstator in pathology 1965-68, registrar in pathology 1969-71, sr demonstrator in pathology 1971-73, sr registrar in pathology 1973-76, consIt pathologist 1976-; contrib to numerous learned sci jls; memb: assoc of clinical pathologists, int academy of pathology; FRCPath; *Recreations* chess, reading, gardening, travel; *Style—* Dr Mustafa Haqqani; Consultant Pathologist, Walton Hospital, Rice Lane, Liverpool L9 7AE (☎ 051 529 4585, 051 529 4416)

HARBERT, Walter Bertram; s of Bertie Francis Harbert (d 1979), of Mitcham, Surrey, and Maud Lily May, *née* Marchant (d 1967); *b* 12 Feb 1931; *Educ* Mitcham GS, Univ of Hull (dip social studies), Univ of Manchester (cert psychiatric social work); *m* 26 May 1962, Susan Pamela, da of Harold Hill (d 1976), of Birmingham; 2 s (Stephen b 1963, Richard b 1964), 3 da (Josephine b 1965, Gillian b 1968, Alison b 1970); *Career* Nat Serv radar operator RAF 1949-51; gen sec Liverpool Personal Serv Soc 1965-70; dir of social serv: London Borough of Hackney 1970-73, Avon CC 1973-90; exec dir UK Ops Help The Aged 1990-; Home Office: memb Advsy Ctee on Probation and After Care 1968-72, memb Working Pty on Community Serv Orders; DHSS: memb Finer Ctee on One Parent Families, Tutt Working Pty on Observation and Assessment of Children, Nodder Ctee on Mgmnt of Mental Illness Hosps; memb: Assoc of Psychiatric Social Workers 1960, Assoc of Dirs of Social Servs 1970 (pres 1978-79); *Books* Welfare Benefits Handbook (1968), Community-Based Care - The Avon Experience (1983), The Home Help Service (1983), The Welfare Industry (1988), Letters To My Staff (1989); *Recreations* writing, lecturing, walking, foreign travel; *Style—* Walter Harbert, Esq, OBE; 67 Bristol Rd, Keynsham, Bristol BS18 2BB (☎ 0272 865276); St James's Walk, London EC1R 0BT (☎ 071 253 0253, fax 071 895 1407)

HARBERTON, 10 Viscount (I 1791); Thomas de Vautort Pomeroy; also Baron Harberton (I 1783); s of 8 Viscount Harberton, OBE (d 1956); suc bro, 9 Viscount, 1980; *b* 19 Oct 1910; *Educ* Eton; *m* 1, 1939 (m dis 1946), Nancy, da of C Penoyer, of San Francisco; m 2, 1950, Pauline (d 1971), da of Wilfred Baker, of Plymouth; m 3, 1978, Vilma (Wilhelmine), widow of Sir Alfred Butt, 1 Bt; *Heir* bro, Hon Robert Pomeroy; *Career* Lt-Col Welsh Gds (1931-41) and RAOC from 1941; *Clubs* Cavalry and Guards; *Style—* The Rt Hon the Viscount Harberton; c/o Barclays Bank, High Street Branch, St Peters Port, Guernsey CI

HARBISON, Air Vice-Marshal William; CB (1977), CBE (1965), AFC (1956); s of William Harbison, of Garvagh, NI; *b* 11 April 1922; *Educ* Ballymena Acad; *m* 1950, Helen, da of William Blaine Geneva, of Bloomington, Illinois; 2 s; *Career* Cdr RAF Staff and air attaché Washington 1972-75, AOC HQ 11 Gp RAF 1975-77; vice pres Br Aerospace, Washington DC 1979-; *Recreations* motoring; *Clubs* RAF, Army and Navy (Washington); *Style—* Air Vice-Marshal William Harbison, CB CBE, AFC; c/o Cox's and King's Branch of Lloyds Bank, 6 Pall Mall, London SW1

HARBORD, Richard Lewis; s of Lewis Walter Harbord, of Norwich, and Dorothy Florence, *née* Mobbs; *b* 30 April 1946; *Educ* Minchenden GS, Anglian Regnl Mgmnt Centre (M Phil), Henley Coll of Mgmnt (Phd); *m* 2 May 1970, Jenny Ann, da of Herbert John Berry (d 1988), of London; 3 s (Mark b 26 Aug 1971, Adam b 5 Oct 1975, Guy b 21 June 1984); *Career* chief exec London Borough of Richmond Upon Thames 1988- (fin dir 1981-88); memb Cncl Ratings and Valuation Assoc 1987-, memb Ct Univ of Surrey; hon treas: Richmond Crossroads, Windlesham PCC; memb IPFA 1967, memb IDPM 1968, FCCA 1981, FRVA 1982; *Recreations* family; *Style—* Richard Harbord, Esq; Gooserye, Cooper Rd, Windlesham, Surrey GU20 6EA; York House, Twickenham (☎ 081 891 1411, fax 081 891 7703)

HARBORD-HAMOND, Hon Charles Anthony Assheton; s and h of 11 Baron Suffield, MC; *b* 3 Dec 1953; *Educ* Eton; *m* 10 Sept 1983 (m dis), Lucy Lennox

Scrope, yr da of Cdr A S Hutchinson, of Langford Grange, Lechlade, Glos; *Career* Capt Coldstream Gds 1972-79; temp equerry to HM The Queen 1977-79; Insur Broker, ACII; dir: Investmt Insur Int (mangrs) Ltd 1981-1985, Donner Underwriting Agencies Ltd, Lloyd's 1985, Philip N Christie & Co Ltd 1990-; OStJ; *Clubs* Pratt's, City of London; *Style—* The Hon Charles Harbord-Hamond; 12b Albert Bridge Road, London SW11 4PY

HARBORD-HAMOND, Hon John Edward Richard; 2 s of 11 Baron Suffield, MC, and Elizabeth Eve, *née* Edgedale; *b* 10 July 1956; *Educ* Eton, Coll of Law; *m* 1983, Katharine Margaret Lucy Seymour, only da of Maj and Hon Mrs Raymond Seymour, of Bucklebury, Berks; 1 s 1 da; *Career* memb Inner Temple; ptnr Cazenove & Co; *Style—* The Hon John Harbord-Hamond; 28 Swanage Road, London SW18 2DY

HARBORNE, Prof Jeffrey Barry; s of Frank Percy Harborne (d 1969), of Bristol, and Phyllis Maud, *née* Sherriff (d 1987); *b* 1 Sept 1928; *Educ* Wycliffe Coll Stonehouse Glos, Univ of Bristol (BSc, PhD, DSc); *m* 15 June 1953, Jean Charlotte, da of Dr John Buchanan (d 1935), of Bristol; 2 s (Alan Jeffrey b 1954, Derek Jeremy b 1958); *Career* biochemist John Innes Inst 1955-63, res fell Univ of Liverpool 1965-68, ed in chief jl Phytochemistry 1972-, prof in botany Univ of Reading 1976- (reader 1968-76); visiting prof Univ of Texas 1976, plenary lectr IUPAC Nat Prods Symposium 1976, visiting prof Univ of California 1977; Gold Medal in Botany Linnean Soc London 1985, Silver Medal Phytochemical Soc of Euro 1986; churchwarden Christ Church Reading 1972-85; memb: Royal Soc Chemistry 1956, Biochemical Soc 1957; FLS 1986; *Books* Biochemistry of Phenolic Compounds (1964), Comparative Biochemistry of the Flavonoids (1967), Phytochemical Phylogeny (1970), Phytochemical Ecology (1972), Phytochemical Aspects of Plant and Animal Coevolution (1978), Phytochemical Methods (2 edn, 1984), Plant Chemosystematics (1984), Introduction to Ecological Biochemistry (3 edn, 1988), The Flavonoids: Advances in Research Since 1980 (1988); *Recreations* rambling, classical music; *Style—* Prof Jeffrey Harborne; Univ of Reading, Plant Science Laboratories, Reading, Berks RG6 2AS (☎ 0734 318162, fax 0734 314404, telex 847813 RULIB G)

HARBORNE, Peter Gale; s of Leslie Herbert Harborne, of 24 Blounts Drive, Uttoxeter, Staffs, and Marie Mildred Edith, *née* Suckling; *b* 29 June 1945; *Educ* King Edwards Sch Birmingham, Univ of Birmingham (BCom); *m* 24 July 1976, Tessa Elizabeth Harborne, da of Dennis Frederick Joseph Henri, of 65 Water Orton Road, Castle Bromwich Birmingham; 2 s (James b 1980, Alexander b 1981); *Career* Home Civil Service 1966-72, HM Dip Serv 1972, Ottawa 1974-75, first sec commercial Mexico City 1975-78, Lloyds Bank Int 1979-81, FCO 1981-83, first sec and head of Chancery Helsinki 1983-87, counsellor and dep head of Mission Budapest 1988-; *Recreations* cricket, tennis; *Clubs* MCC; *Style—* Peter Harborne, Esq; c/o Foreign and Commonwealth Office, King Charles St, London SW1A 2AH; British Embassy, Budapest 1051, Harmincad 6, Hungary (☎ 010 36 1 118 2045, fax 010 36 1 118 0907, telex 224527)

HARBOTTLE, Rev Anthony Hall Harrison; LVO (1984, MVO 1979); s of Alfred Charles Harbottle (d 1938), of Topsham, Devon, and Ellen Muriel, *née* Harrison (d 1955); *b* 3 Sept 1925; *Educ* Sherborne, Christ's Coll Cambridge (MA), Wycliffe Hall Oxford; *m* 1955, Gillian Mary, da of Hugh Goodenough (d 1975); 3 s (Charles, Jonathan, David), 1 da (Jane); *Career* serv WWII RM (Corpl) Holland, NW Germany; deacon 1952, priest 1953; asst curacies: Boxley 1952-54, St Peter-in-Thanet 1954-60; rector of Sandhurst with Newenden 1960-68, chaplain Royal Chapel Windsor Great Park 1968-81, rector East Dean with Friston and Jevington 1981-; chaplain to: HM The Queen 1968-, Co of Sussex, Royal Br Legion 1982-; FRES; *Recreations* butterflies and moths, nature conservancy, entomology, ornithology, philately, coins, treasury and bank notes, painting, cooking, lobstering; *Style—* The Rev Anthony Harbottle, LVO; The Rectory, East Dean, Eastbourne, E Sussex BN20 0DL (☎ 032 15 3266)

HARBOTTLE, (George) Laurence; s of George Harbottle, MC, of Newcastle upon Tyne, and Winifred Ellen, *née* Benson (d 1982); *b* 11 April 1924; *Educ* The Leys Sch Cambridge, Emmanuel Coll Cambridge (MA); *Career* cmmnd RA 1942, Capt and Adj 9 Field Regt RA 1945-47; sr ptnr Harbottle and Lewis 1955-; first chm: Theatre Centre Ltd, Prospect Productions Ltd, Royal Exchange Theatre Co Ltd, Cambridge Theatre Co Ltd; formerly chm ICA, pres Theatrical Mgmnt Assoc and memb Arts Cncl, chm Central Sch of Speech and Drama; vice chm: Theatres Tst, Theatres Nat Ctee; dir Cambridge Arts Theatre Ltd, tstee Equity Tst Fund; memb Law Soc, The Bookmen Soc; *Recreations* works of art, gardening; *Clubs* The Savile; *Style—* G Laurence Harbottle, Esq; Hanover House, Hanover Square, London W1R 0BE (☎ 071 629 7633, fax 071 493 0451, telex 22233 HARLEX)

HARBOTTLE, Brig Michael Neale; OBE; s of Capt Thomas Cecil Benfield Harbottle, RN (d 1968), and Kathleen Millicent, *née* Kent (d 1937); *b* 7 Feb 1917; *Educ* Marlborough, RMA Sandhurst, Staff Coll Pretoria SA (psc); *m* 1, 1 Aug 1940 (m dis 1972), Alison Jean, *née* Humfress; 1 s (Simon Neale b 2 April 1942), 1 da (Carolyn Daphne b 6 Nov 1946); m 2, 5 Aug 1972, Eirwen Helen, da of Hugh Llewlyn Jones (d 1962); *Career* cmmnd The Oxfordshire and Buckinghamshire Light Inf 1937, WWII serv UK and Italy (despatches), GSO2 instr UK Army Staff Coll 1945, GSO2 staff duties WO 1950-52, GSO1 43 Inf Div TA/SW Dist 1957-59, CO 1 Green Jackets Regt 1959-62, Security Cdr and Cdr Aden Garrison 1962-64, Cdr 129 Inf Bde TA 1964-66, COS UN Peacekeeping Force Cyprus 1966-68, ret 1968; chief security offr Sierra Leone Selection Tst 1969-70, VP Int Peace Acad 1970-73, visiting sr lectr Sch of Peace Studies Univ of Bradford 1974-79; visiting prof: Univ of Cape Town SA 1976, Waterloo Univ 1979, Carleton Univ Canada 1979; head of dept Vietnamese Section Br Cncl for Aid to Refugees 1979-80, gen sec World Disarmament Campaign (UK) 1980-82, fndr and dir Centre for Int Peacebuilding 1983-, memb Generals for Peace and Disarmament, RIAA; *Books* The Impartial Soldier (1970), Blue Berets (1971), The Thin Blue Line (jtly, 1974), The Knaves of Diamonds (1976), The Peacekeepers' Handbook (1978), Reflections on Security in the Nuclear Age (jtly, 1988); *Recreations* cricket, tennis, hockey, golf; *Clubs* MCC; *Style—* Brig Michael Harbottle, OBE; 9 West St, Chipping Norton, Oxon (☎ 0608 642335); Centre for Int Peacebuilding, (fax 0608 642031, telex 932011 GEN FIN G)

HARBOTTLE, (Philip) Richard Milnes; s of Thomas Milnes Harbottle, CBE, MC (d 1961), of Ponteland, Northumberland, and Marion, *née* Learmount; *b* 19 March 1934; *Educ* The Leys Sch Cambridge, Trinity Hall Cambridge (MA); *m* 13 Aug 1960 (Jean Margaret) Elizabeth, da of John Talbot Hall (d 1958), of Sutton Coldfield; 3 da (Charlotte (Mrs Welch), Philippa (Mrs Sampson), Rebecca); *Career* ptnr Deloitte Haskins & Sells (and predecessor co) 1962-89, non-exec chm Northumberland Health Authy 1986-; non-exec dir: Northern Rock Building Society 1988-, C M Yuill Investments Ltd 1989-; chm Tyne & Wear Building Preservation Tst, treas Soc of Antiquaries of Newcastle upon Tyne; FCA (ACA 1960); *Recreations* gardening, history, walking; *Clubs* Northern Counties; *Style—* Richard Harbottle, Esq; Northumberland Health Authority, East Cottingwood, Morpeth, Northumberland NE61 2PD (☎ 0670 514331)

HARCOURT, Prof Geoffrey Colin; s of Kenneth Kopel Harcourt (d 1988), of 24 Faircroft Avenue, Gen Iris, Melbourne 3146, Aust, and Marjorie Rahel, *née* Gans (d 1981); *b* 27 June 1931; *Educ* Wesley Coll Melbourne, Queen's Coll Univ of Melbourne (BCom, MCom), King's Coll Cambridge (PhD, Litt D); *m* 30 July 1955, Joan Margaret, da of Edgar James Bartrop, OBE (d 1989), of 2 Haddon St, Ballarat, W Victoria, Aust; 2 s (Robert Geoffrey b 1961, Timothy William b 1965), 2 da (Wendy Jane b 1959, Rebecca Mary b 1968); *Career* Univ of Adelaide: lectr in economics 1958-62, sr lectr 1963-65, reader 1965-67, prof (personal chair) 1967-85 (prof emeritus 1988); Univ of Cambridge: lectr in economics and politics 1964-66, fell Trinity Hall 1964-66, fell Jesus Coll 1982-, lectr 1982-90, pres Jesus Coll 1988-89 and 1990-, reader in the history of economic theory (ad hominem) 1990-; memb Aust Labor Pty 1954; Howard League for Penal Reform S Aust branch: sec 1959-63, vice pres 1967-74, pres 1974-80; chm Campaign for Peace in Vietnam S Aust 1970-72 (1968), fell Acad of the Social Sciences in Aust 1971, memb Cncl Royal Economic Soc 1990; *Books* incl: Economic Activity (jtly, 1967), Capital and Growth, Selected Readings (ed with N F Laing, 1971), Some Cambridge Controversies in the Theory of Capital (1972), Theoretical Controversy and Social Significance: An Evaluation of the Cambridge Controversies (1975), The Microeconomic Foundations of Macroeconomics (ed, 1977), The Social Science Imperialists. Selected Essays (1982), Readings in the Concept and Measurement of Income (jt ed 1969, 2 edn 1986), Controversies in Political Economy Selected Essays (1986), International Monetary Problems and Supply-side Economics. Essays in Honour of Corie Tarshis (jt ed 1986); *Recreations* cricket, running; *Clubs* Melbourne Cricket, S Aust Cricket; *Style—* Prof Geoffrey Harcourt; 43 New Square, Cambridge CB1 1EZ (☎ 0223 60833); Austin Robinson Building, Faculty of Economics and Politics, University of Cambridge, Sidgwick Ave, Cambridge CB3 9DD (☎ 0223 335231); Jesus College, Cambridge CB5 8BL (☎ 0223 68611 ext 236)

HARCOURT, Palma; *see*: Trotman, Palma Noreen Sarah

HARCOURT-SMITH, Lt-Col Charles Simon; s of Simon Guisbert Harcourt-Smith (d 1982), of London, and Rosamund Hilda, *née* Miller (d 1987); *b* 11 Feb 1942; *Educ* Inst Auf Den Rosenberg Switzerland; *m* 10 July 1971, Sabrina Jane, da of Lt-Col Richard Harry Longland (d 1968), of IOW; 3 s (William b 1972, Alexander b 1974, Edward b 1977); *Career* Army Offr joined Life Gds 1962, attended Staff Coll 1976; serv: Germany, Libya, Far East, Middle East, Belgium, Holland, Army Helicoptor Pilot Far East 1966-68, Lt-Col 1984; *Recreations* shooting, fishing, sailing; *Clubs* Cavalry and Guards', Flyfishers, Bembridge Sailing; *Style—* Lt-Col Charles Harcourt-Smith; c/o Lloyds Bank, 6 Pall Mall SW1Y 5NH; MOD, Whitehall

HARCOURT-SMITH, Air Chief Marshal Sir David; GBE (1989), KCB (1984), DFC (1957); *b* 14 Oct 1931; *Educ* Felsted, RAF Coll; *m* 1957, Mary, *née* Entwistle; 2 s, 1 da; *Career* cmmnd RAF 1952, served with 11, 8 and 54 Squadrons, Staff Coll 1962, OC 54 Sqdn 1963-65, Cmdt RAF Coll Cranwell 1978-80, Asst CAS (Operational Requirements) 1980-, Air Marshal 1984, Air Office Commanding-in-Chief RAF Support Cmmd 1984, Controller Aircraft (MOD PE) and memb Air Force Bd 1986, Air Chief Marshal, 1987-89 (ret); aviation conslt; *Recreations* music, golf; *Style—* Sir David Harcourt-Smith, GBE, KCB, DFC; c/o Barclays Bank, 2/6 High Streeet, Salisbury SP1 2NP

HARDAWAY, (Adolph) James; s of Lawrence Hardaway (d 1960), of the USA, and Grace Maria, *née* Habig (d 1977); *b* 12 Sept 1929; *Educ* Brown Univ USA (BA); *m* 6 Sept 1961, Sheila Ann; *Career* stockbroker; memb The Stock Exchange; former chm: Whale Hardaway and Co Ltd (stock and share brokers), Toroak Investmt and Fin Servs, Met London Gp; exec dir Investmt and Fin Trg Ltd; former memb: Prov Stock Exchange, Pacific Coast Stock Exchange, NY Stock Exchange; FID; FESU; *Recreations* tennis, literature, theatre, music, travel, fine art; *Clubs* English Speaking Union London, Royal Torbay Yacht; *Style—* James Hardaway, Esq; c/o 7 Park Hill Rd, Torquay, Devon (☎ 0803 298743, fax 0803 292615)

HARDCASTLE, Prof Jack Donald; s of Albert Fenton Hardcastle, and Bertha, *née* Ellison; *b* 3 April 1933; *Educ* St Batholomew's GS Newbury, Emmanuel Coll Cambridge (BA, MB BChir, MA, MChir); *m* 18 Dec 1965, Rosemary, da of Col Cecil Hay-Shunker; 1 s (Philip b 3 May 1968), 1 da (Rachel b 19 June 1971); *Career* London Hosp: lectr and registrar 1963-65, sr registrar 1965-68; St Mark's Hosp: sr registrar 1968, sr lectr 1968-70; prof and head of Dept of Surgery Queen's Med Centre Univ of Nottingham 1970-; Sir Arthur Sims Travelling Prof 1985, Mayne Visiting Prof Univ of Queensland Aust 1987, Sir Alan Park Visiting Prof St Marks Hosp London 1991; chm Nottingham Ice Hockey Club; MRCP 1961, FRCS 1962, FRCP 1984; *Books* Isolated Organ Perfusion (jtly, 1973); *Clubs* RSM; *Style—* Prof Jack Hardcastle; Department of Surgery, University Hospital, Queen's Medical Centre, Nottingham NG7 2UH (☎ 0602 709245, fax 0602 709428)

HARDCASTLE, Leslie Jesse; OBE (1978); s of Francis Ernest Hardcastle, and Dorothy Alma, *née* Schofield; *b* 8 Dec 1926; *Educ* St Joseph's Coll Croydon; *m* 14 Sept 1968, (Vivienne Mansel) Wendy, da of Maj Trevor Richards (d 1968), of Red Tiles Farm, Fairwarp, Sussex; 2 s (Adam Alexander b 23 June 1972, Paul James b 3 Jan 1975); *Career* RN sick berth Br Pacific Fleet 1944-47; prodn Br Lion Film Studio 1943, admin Br Film Inst 1947, mangr Festival of Br Telekinema 1951, admin London Film Festival 1958-86, controller Nat Film Theatre 1968 (mangr 1952), creator Museum of Moving Image 1988, controller Br Film Inst South Bank (Nat Film Theatre and Museum of Moving Image) 1989; chm and pres Soho Soc, chm Housing Mgmnt Soho Housing Assoc; *Recreations* theatre, music, community work; *Style—* Leslie Hardcastle, Esq, OBE; 37 C Great Pulteney St, London W1 (☎ 071 437 5149); Woodlands Cottage, Nursery Lane, Fairwarp, Sussex (☎ 082 571 2887); NFT & Museum of Moving Image, South Bank Arts Complex, Waterloo SE1 (☎ 071 928 3535)

HARDCASTLE, Sarah; da of Geoff Hardcastle, and Anne, *née* Surgenor; *b* 9 April 1969; *Educ* Shoeburyness Comp, Thurrock Tech Coll; *Career* Southend Borough Swimming Club; first Jr Int 1981; 800m Freestyle: 5 place Cwlth Games Brisbane 1982, 3 place Euro Championships Rome, 3 place Olympic Games LA 1984, 2 place Euro Championships Bulgaria 1985, 1 place Cwlth Games Scot 1986; 400m Freestyle: 2 place Olympic Games LA 1984, 1 place Cwlth Games 1986, 3 place World Championships Spain 1986; Cwlth Games Scot 1986: 3 place 400m Individual medley, 2 place 4 x 200m, Br record 400m and 800m Freestyle, Euro record 800m Freestyle; gym instr Cottons Sports Club London 1987-89, temps controller Manpower Agency 1989-90, sec Personnel Dept Allders Dept Store Basildon 1990-; *Recreations* aerobics, reading, looking after my sister's children; *Style—* Ms Sarah Hardcastle; c/o Warrior Square Swimming Pool, Southend-On-Sea, Essex (☎ 0702 464445)

HARDEN, Maj James Richard Edwards; DSO (1945), OBE (1983), MC (1944), JP (Armagh 1956, Caernarvonshire 1971), DL (Armagh 1946, Caernarvonshire 1968); s of James Edwards Harden (d 1945), and Letita Grace Campbell Connal (decd); *b* 12 Dec 1916; *Educ* Bedford Sch, RMC Sandhurst; *m* 1948, Ursula Joyce, da of Gerald Murray Strutt (d 1956); 1 s (David), 2 da (Theresa, Carolyn); *Career* landowner and farmer; MP (UU) Armagh 1948-54; High Sheriff Caernarvonshire 1971-72, chm Regnl Land Drainage Ctee Welsh Water Authy 1973-83; landowner (5000 acres); *Recreations* shooting; *Style—* Maj James Harden, DSO, OBE, MC, JP, DL; Nanhoran, Pwllheli, Gwynedd LL53 8DL (☎ 0758 83610)

HARDEN, Prof Ronald McGlashan; s of Alexander Harden (d 1959), and Janet Roy, *née* McGlashan; *b* 24 Dec 1936; *Educ* Uddington GS, Univ of Glasgow (MB ChB, MD); *m* 4 Jan 1961, Sheila, da of James Harris (d 1956); 3 da (Susan b 28 Sept 1964,

Valerie b 31 July 1966, Jennifer b 3 July 1968); *Career* res and clinical posts Western Infirmary Glasgow 1960-70, sr lectr in med Univ of Glasgow 1970-72, postgrad dean of med Univ of Dundee 1985- (dir centre for med educn and hon conslt physician 1972), ed Medical Teacher and int authy on med educn with over 200 papers in scientific jls; chm Res Ctee Assoc Study of Med Educn; FRCP Glasgow 1975, FRCPS Canada 1988; *Recreations* gardening; *Clubs* Royal Society of Medicine; *Style*— Prof Ronald Harden; 10 Guthrie Terrace, Broughty Ferry, Dundee (☎ 0382 78130); Director, Centre for Medical Education, Level 8, Ninewells Hospital and Medical School, Dundee (☎ 0382 60111, ext 3050, fax 0382 645748)

HARDER, Ian Gray; s of Robert William Harder (d 1940), and Gladys Dorothy, *née* Mawby (d 1980); *b* 3 June 1931; *Educ* E Barnet GS, Univ of Southampton (BSc), Univ of London; *Career* Corpl RAF 1953-55; head Econ and Fin Dept EIU 1955-65, md New Ventures (Investments) Ltd 1965-68, chm and md Maxwell Stamp plc 1968-; *Recreations* music, theatre, walking; *Style*— Ian G Harder, Esq; 5 Blake Rd, New Southgate, London N11 2AD (☎ 081 368 6417); Maxwell Stamp plc, 2 Hat and Mitre Court, St John St, London EC1M 4EL (☎ 071 251 0147, fax 071 251 0140)

HARDESTY, Hon Mrs (Rachel Henrietta); *née* Cunliffe; o da of 3 Baron Cunliffe, *qv*; *b* 14 Feb 1960; *Educ* N London Collegiate Sch, Felsted, Cambridge Univ (BA), Manchester Univ, Univ of Minnesota; *m* 1987, Roger David Hardesty, s of late R D Hardesty, of Belle Mead, New Jersey, USA; *Style*— The Hon Mrs Hardesty

HARDIE, Andrew Rutherford; QC (1985); s of Andrew Rutherford Hardie, of 263 Ashley Terrace, Alloa, and Elizabeth Currie, *née* Lowe; *b* 8 Jan 1946; *Educ* St Modan's HS Stirling, Univ of Edinburgh (MA, LLB); *m* 16 July 1971, Catherine Storrar, da of David Currie Elgin, of Crescent Wood Rd, London; 2 s (Ewan b 1975, Niall b 1981), 1 da (Ruth b 1977); *Career* enrolled slr 1971, admitted memb Faculty of Advocates 1973; advocate depute 1979-83, standing jr counsel City of Edinburgh DC 1983-85 (sr counsel 1987-), treas Faculty of Advocates 1989-; *Clubs* Caledonian (Edinburgh), Murrayfield Golf; *Style*— Andrew Hardie, Esq, QC; 27 Hermitage Gdns, Edinburgh, EH10 6AZ (☎ 031 447 2917); Advocates Library, Parliament House, Edinburgh EH1 1RF (☎ 031 226 5071)

HARDIE, Sir Charles Edgar Mathewes; CBE (1963, OBE 1943); s of Dr Charles Frederick Hardie (d 1964), of Barnet, Herts, and Mrs R F Hardie, *née* Moore; *b* 10 March 1910; *Educ* Aldenham; *m* 1, 1937, Dorothy Jean Hobson (d 1965); 1 s (Jeremy, *qv*), 3 da; m 2, 1966 (m dis 1975) Angela, wid of Raymond Paul Richli, and da of George Street; m 3, 1975, Rosemary Margaret Harwood; *Career* WWII Col; sr ptnr Dixon Wilson and Co 1975-81 (joined 1934); chm: White Fish Authy 1967-73, BOAC 1969-70, British Printing Corporation 1969-76 (dir 1965-82), Fitch Lovell Ltd 1970-77; dir: Trusthouse Forte 1970- (dep chm 1983-), Royal Bank of Canada 1969-81, Hill Samuel Group 1970-77; FCA; Legion of Merit (USA); kt 1970; *Recreations* bridge; *Clubs* Phyllis Court; *Style*— Sir Charles Hardie, CBE; The Old School House, Sturminster Newton, Dorset (☎ 0258 72983); 25 New St, Henley on Thames, Oxon RG92 2BP (☎ 0491 577944)

HARDIE, David; WS (1982); s of John Hardie, of Gourock, Renfrewshire, Scot, and Amy Alfreda, *née* Masey; *b* 17 Sept 1954; *Educ* Glasgow Acad, Greenock HS, Univ of Dundee (LLB); *m* 27 Feb 1981, Fiona Mairi, da of Dr Alexander Donaldson Willox, MBE, of W Lothian, Scot; 3 s (Iain b 1981, Stewart b 1984, Alasdair b 1989); *Career* NP 1979, ptnr Dundas & Wilson CS 1983; memb: Law Soc of Scot, Int Bar Assoc; *Recreations* sailing, golf, swimming, cycling; *Clubs* Royal Forth Yacht; *Style*— David Hardie, Esq, WS; 25 Charlotte Square, Edinburgh EH2 4EZ (☎ 031 225 1234, fax 031 225 5594, telex 72404)

HARDIE, Maj (John) Donald Morrison; OBE (1987); s of Capt John David Hardie (d 1949), of Dallas, Morayshire, late Scottish Horse and Skinner's Horse, and Gertrude Louise, *née* Morrison; *b* 27 Sept 1928; *Educ* Beckenham GS, Univ of St Andrews (MA), Indiana Univ USA (MSc); *m* 9 Aug 1952, Sally Patricia, da of Thomas Whipple Connally (d 1928), of Atlanta, Georgia, USA; 2 s (David b 1954, Robin b 1957), 1 da (Katharine b 1960); *Career* Lt 1 Bn Queen's Own Cameron Highlanders 1952-56, Maj TA Bn 1956-67; dir Wood and Hardie Ltd 1961-82; currently dir: Bute Fabrics Ltd, McCann Erickson (Scotland) Ltd, McCann Ltd, Corporate Risk plc, Noble Situations plc; dir Scottish Div IOD 1980-; organised Yes campaign in Scotland for EEC referendum 1975; session clerk Humbie Kirk 1960-; memb Scottish XI (hockey) 1950-53; *Recreations* golf, shooting; *Clubs* Hon Co of Edinburgh Golfers, Royal and Ancient Golf (St Andrews), New (Edinburgh), Piedmont Driving, Peachtree Golf (Atlanta); *Style*— Maj Donald Hardie, OBE; Chesterhill House, Humbie, E Lothian EH36 5PL (☎ 087 533 648); Inst of Directors, 13 Great Stuart Street, Edinburgh EH3 7TP (☎ 031 225 8101)

HARDIE, Sir Douglas Fleming; CBE (1979), JP (1970); s of James Dunbar Hardie, JP, of 5 Invergowrie Drive, Dundee, and Frances Mary, *née* Fleming; *b* 26 May 1923; *Educ* Trinity Coll Glenalmond; *m* 5 Sept 1945, Dorothy Alice, da of Frederick William Warner (d 1971), of 8 North Rd, Ponteland, Newcastle upon Tyne; 2 s (Michael b 1948, Christopher b 1954), 1 da (Hilary b 1947); *Career* Trooper 58 Trg Regt RAC 1941, cmmnd RMA Sandhurst 1942, 1 Fife and Forfar Yeomanry Flamethrowing Tank Regt NW Europe 1942-46 (despatches), Maj; chm and md Edward Parker and Co Ltd 1960-, dep chm Scottish Development Agency 1978-; dir: H and A Scott (Holdings) Ltd 1964-84 (chm 1984-85), Dayco Rubber (UK) Ltd 1956-86, Clydesdale Bank plc 1981-, The Alliance Trust plc 1982-, The Second Alliance Trust plc 1982-, Alliance Trust (Finance) Ltd 1982-, SECDEE Leasing 1982-, Alliance Trust (Nominees) Ltd 1982-, A G Scott Textiles Ltd 1985-88; chm Grampian TV plc 1989- (dir 1984-); deacon convener Nine Incorporated Trades of Dundee 1951-54, pres Dundee Rotary Club 1967-68; memb: CBI Grand Cncl London 1976-85, Scot Econ Cncl 1977-, Cncl Winston Churchill Meml Tst 1985-; vice pres Fife and Forfar Yeo Regtl Assoc, elder Dundee Parish church (St Mary's), dir Prince's Scottish Youth Business Tst 1988; FRSA 1988, CBIM 1989; kt 1990; *Recreations* golf, fishing; *Clubs* Caledonian, Royal and Ancient Golf, Blairgowrie Golf, Panmure Golf; *Style*— Sir Douglas Hardie, CBE, JP; Grampian TV plc, Chairman's Office, 68 Albany Rd, Dundee DD5 1NW (☎ 0382 739363, fax 0382 74867)

HARDIE, (Charles) Jeremy Mawdesley; CBE (1983); s of Sir Charles Hardie, CBE *qv*; *b* 9 June 1938; *Educ* Winchester Coll, New Coll Oxford; *m* 1, 1962 (m dis 1976), Susan Chamberlain; 2 s, 2 da; m 2, 1978, Xandra, Countess of Gowrie, da of late Col Robert Albert Glanvill Bingley, CVO, DSO, OBE (d 1976); 1 da; *Career* Monopolies and Mergers Cmmn: memb 1976-, dep chm 1980-83; Nat Provident Inst: dir 1972-77, dep chm 1977-80, chm 1980-; dep chm Alexanders Discount Co (dir 1978-); dir: Unilever Pensions Investmt Mgmnt Ltd 1980-, Stockholders Investmt Tst 1979-, John Swire and Sons 1982-; ptnr Dixon Wilson and Co 1975-; chm Alexander Syndicate Mgmnt Ltd 1982-, memb local bd Bank of Scotland 1983-; Parly candidate (SDP) Norwich South 1983; memb Arts Cncl of GB 1984-; FCA; *Style*— Jeremy Hardie Esq, CBE; The Old Rectory, Netton, nr Cromer, Norfolk (☎ 026 376 765)

HARDIE, Michael Scott; s of Col Alan Scott Hardie, OBE, DL (d 1968), of Purves Hall, nr Greenlaw, Berwickshire, and Joan Lilian, *née* Powell (d 1968); *b* 31 Dec 1926; *Educ* Glenalmond; *m* 14 Feb 1953, Valerie Edith, da of Richard Everard Hambro (d 1968); 4 s (Nicholas A S b 19 Jan 1955, Christopher R S b 28 Feb 1957, Charles M S b 14 Nov 1961, Jonathan D S b 12 Feb 1965); *Career* RAF Hong Kong 1946-48, HAC 1953-58; qualified CA Scot 1951; Brown Fleming & Murray 1952-53, Mercantile Investment Tst 1955-57, Debenture Corpn Investment Tst 1957-59 (also 1953-55), dep Investment Mangr ICI Pension Fund 1959-71, investmt dir Friends Provident 1971-86; govr Glenalmond Coll Perthshire; memb Honarable Artiller Co 1953; FCA; *Clubs* Muirfield Golf, Royal Wimbledon Golf; *Style*— Michael Hardie, Esq; Wyndham Barns, Corton Denham, Sherborne, Dorset DT9 4LS (☎ 0963 22631, fax 0963 22738); Blue House, Trevose Estate, Constantine Bay, nr Padstow, Cornwall (☎ 0481 520331); c/o Shires Investment plc, 29 St Vincent Place, Glasgow G1 2DR (☎ 041 226 4585, fax 041 226 3632); c/o Larpent Newton & Co Ltd, 24-26 Baltic St, London EC1Y 0TB (☎ 071 251 9111, fax 071 251 2609)

HARDIE, Miles Clayton; OBE (1988); s of Frederick Russell Hardie (d 1930), of London, and Estelle Mary Harwood, *née* Clarke (d 1929); *b* 27 Feb 1924; *Educ* Charterhouse, Oriel Coll Oxford (MA); *m* 1, 22 July 1949 (m dis 1974), Pauline, da of Prof Sir Wilfrid Edward Le Gros Clark (d 1971), of Oxford; 2 s (Philip b 1952, Roger b 1953); m 2, 21 Nov 1974 (m dis 1985), (Katherine) Melissa Woelfel, da of the late James Edward Witcher, of USA; m 3, 20 April 1985, (Madeline) Elizabeth Spencer-Smith, da of the late Herbert Dudley Ash; *Career* WWII RAF Pilot 1943-46, demob Flt Lt; joined NHS 1949; sec: Victoria Hosp for Children Chelsea 1952-56, Bahrain Govt Med Dept 1956-58; joined King Edward's Hosp Fund for London 1958, dep dir King's Fund Centre 1963-66 (dir 1966-75), dir gen Int Hosp Fedn 1975-87; helped estab Br Hosps Export Cncl 1964 (hon sec and memb Cncl); served on various cncls and ctees incl: MIND, Mental Health Fndn, Centre for Policy on Ageing, Spinal Injuries Assoc, Volunteer Centre; advsr to WHO; memb Worshipful Co of Salters 1954, Hon Dr Admin Northland Open Univ Canada 1987; FHSM 1955; WHO Geneva Health for All Medal 1987; *Recreations* walking, gardening; *Style*— Miles Hardie, Esq, OBE; Tallow Cottage, Fishers Lane, Charlbury, Oxford OX7 3RX (☎ 0608 810088)

HARDING, Maj (George William) Cecil; s of Col George Harding, DSO, of Co Laois, Eire; *b* 12 July 1916; *Educ* Wellington, RMA; *m* 1947, Beatrice, da of Col Geoffrey Youl, MC, of Tasmania; 3 da; *Career* served RA (Europe, ME, Pacific) Maj, ret 1958; landowner (inherited from f) 1957-; chm: Capital Gearing Trust plc 1963-, Ewart New Northern plc 1977-86; *Recreations* travel; *Clubs* Naval and Military, Ulster (Belfast); *Style*— Maj Cecil Harding; Capital Gearing Trust plc, 34 Upper Queen Street, Belfast BT1 6HG (☎ 0232 244001)

HARDING, Charles Alvar; s of Charles Copeley Harding (d 1942), of 14 Holland Park, London W11, and Louise Victoria Alvar Woods, *née* Beckmann (d 1966); *Educ* Westminster, Gonville and Caius Coll Cambridge; *Career* Capt Royal Fus, ADC to Govr of Madras 1942-46; dir Trafford Gallery 1948-75; *Recreations* skiing, tennis, architecture, theatre; *Clubs* Travellers'; *Style*— Charles Harding, Esq; 47 Cadogan Square, London SW1X 0HX (☎ 071 235 7400)

HARDING, Cherry Jacinta; da of James Albert Harding, of Homer, Much Wenlock, Shropshire, and Pauline Mary, *née* Temlett; *b* 2 June 1956; *Educ* The Canon Slade GS Bolton Lancs, King's Coll London (LLB); *m* 8 July 1989, Michael Almond; *Career* called to the Bar Gray's Inn 1978; in practice 1980-, main area of work The Family Bar; *Recreations* theatre, cookery; *Style*— Miss Cherry Harding; 5th Floor, Gray's Inn Chambers, Gray's Inn, London WC1 (☎ 071 404 1111)

HARDING, Christopher George Francis; s of Frank Harding (d 1986), of Amersham, Bucks, and Phyllis Rachel Pledger Wise; *b* 17 Oct 1939; *Educ* Merchant Taylors', Corpus Christi Coll Oxford (MA); *m* 1, 1963 (m dis 1977), Susan Lilian; 1 s (Rupert b 1965), 1 da (Louise b 1966); m 2, 1978 (m dis 1988), Françoise Marie; *Career* head office ICI Ltd London 1961-65, agric div ICI Billingham 1966-69, Hanson Trust Ltd 1969-74, md Hanson Transport Group Ltd 1974-; non-exec dir: Hanson plc 1979-, British Nuclear Fuels plc 1984- (chm 1986-); memb Cncl: CBI 1986, Business in the Community 1989, Prince's Youth Business Tst 1988; memb: Br Nat Cmmn World Energy Conf 1986 (chm 1989), Ct UMIST 1987, Econ Res Cncl 1988, Br Assoc Sci & Indust Ctee 1989, govr World Energy Forum 1990-; hon fell: Huddersfield Poly 1990, City and Guilds of London Tst 1990; Freeman: City of London 1965, Worshipful Co of Merchant Taylors 1965 (Liveryman 1986); FRSA 1987, CBIM 1988; *Recreations* theatre, music, travel, tennis, pocillovy; *Clubs* Brooks's, Huddersfield Borough; *Style*— Christopher Harding, Esq; British Nuclear Fuels plc, 65 Buckingham Gate, London SW1E 6AP (☎ 071 222 9717, fax 071 222 1935, telex 8953101)

HARDING, Derek William; s of William Arthur Harding (d 1982); *b* 16 Dec 1930; *Educ* Glendale GS London, Univ of Bristol; *m* 1965, Daphne Sheila, *née* Cooke; 1 s, 1 da; *Career* engr Pye Ltd 1954-56, sr physics master Thornbury GS Bristol 1956-60; sr lectr: physical sci St Paul's Coll Cheltenham 1960-64, Nuffield Fndn 1964-69; registrar sec Inst Metallurgists 1969-76, sec gen Br Computer Soc 1976-86, exec sec Royal Statistical Soc 1986-; *Recreations* music, sailing; *Style*— Derek Harding Esq; 16 Exeter Rd, London N14 5JY

HARDING, Edward William; s of Ernest Edward Harding (d 1980), of Herne Place, Sunningdale, and Elizabeth Isabelle, *née* Owens; *b* 19 Feb 1949; *Educ* Alleyns Sch Dulwich; *m* 5 April 1947, Florence Elizabeth; 1 da (Emma Elizabeth b 30 Jan 1979); *Career* musician and writer; Spencer Davis Gp 1968-76; songs recorded by: Allman Bros, Sacha Distel, Donovan, Billy Ocean, Spencer Davis Gp, David Coverdale, Jimmy Helms, Chris Barber, Glen Hughes, Chris Thompson, Zak Starkey, Mike D'Abo, Joe Fagin, Twiggy, Cliff Richard, Jon Entwhistle, Steve Hackett, Tony Barton, Iris Williams, Vincent Price, Jon Lord, Tony Ashton, Ian Paice; memb Performing Rights Soc; *Clubs* Wig & Pen; *Style*— Edward Harding, Esq; Burleigh Court, Burleigh Rd, Ascot, Berks SL5 7LE (fax 0990 24919); Whitewalls, Bedford Lane, Sunningdale, Berks

HARDING, Frank Alexander; *b* 20 Sept 1937; *Educ* Malvern Coll, Ecole de Commerce de Neuchatel; *m* 30 Aug 1960, Belinda Ruth; 2 s (David b 1961, Thomas b 1968), 2 da (Kate b 1963, Amanda b 1967); *Career* CA 1961, ptnr KPMG Peat Marwick McLintock (formerly Thomson McLintock & Co) 1967- (joined 1955); memb Cncl: Inst of CAs of Scot 1980-85, Inst of CAs in Eng and Wales 1990-, Int Fedn of Accountants (UK rep) 1987-; memb Exec Ctee Union of Euro Accountants 1983-86; *Recreations* golf, tennis, opera, bridge; *Style*— Frank Harding, Esq; KPMG Peat Marwick McLintock, 1 Puddle Dock, London EC4V 3PD (☎ 071 236 8000, fax 071 248 6552, telex 8811541)

HARDING, Dr Geoffrey Wright; s of Jack Harding, of Gravesend, Kent, and Ethel Florence, *née* Wilkinson; *Educ* King's Coll London (LLB, AKC), Northwestern Univ Sch of Law Chicago (LLM), QMC London (PhD); *m* 7 Oct 1972, Margaret June, da of Eric Oscar Danger; 1 s (Peter James John b 1980), 1 da (Kate Joanna b 1978); *Career* Nat Serv RAF 1951-53; called to the Bar Gray's Inn 1957; asst sec FCEC 1958-60, legal advsr Br Insur (Atomic Energy) Ctee 1960-63, exchange lawyer under Harvard Law Sch Prog Isham Lincoln and Beale Attorneys Chicago 1963-64, asst slr Joynson Hicks 1965-67, ptnr Wilde Sapte (specialising in banking, consumer credit, competition and Euro Community law) 1967-; memb Bar and Law Soc Jt Working Pty on Banking Law; business advsr The Prince's Youth Business Tst; memb: Nat Autistic Soc, Kent Autistic Community Tst; Gen Electric Fndn fell Northwestern Univ Sch of Law Chicago; Freeman City of London 1986, memb Guild of Freemen of City of London; memb Law Soc; *Books* Banking Act 1987 - Current Law Annotated (1987), Encyclopaedia of Competition Law (jt consltg ed, 1987); *Recreations* piano playing, mountain biking, avoiding domestic DIY; *Style*— Dr Geoffrey Harding; Wilde Sapte, Queensbridge House, 60 Upper Thames St, London EC4V 3BD (☎ 071 236 3050, fax 071 236 9624, telex 887793)

HARDING, Prof Graham Frederick Anthony; s of Frederick William Harding, of Shenstone, and Elizabeth Louise Harding; *b* 19 March 1937; *Educ* Torquay GS, UCL (BSc), Univ of Birmingham (PhD), Univ of Aston (DSc); *m* 4 March 1961 (m dis 1989), Margaret, da of Reginald Francis Lloyd, of Sutton Coldfield; 2 da (Catherine Louise b 25 Oct 1965, Laura Jane b 14 Aug 1969); *Career* hon conslt electroencephalographer Wolverhampton Area Health Authy 1974-, hon conslt neuropsychologist Birmingham Area Health Authy 1974-, head of vision sciences Univ of Aston 1981-89 (res fell 1964-73, reader in neuropsychology 1973-78, head of neuropsychology unit 1969-78, prof of clinical neurophysiology 1978-); memb: Electroencephalographic Soc 1963- (memb Cncl 1971-75), Ctee on Clinical Neurophysiology W Midland RHA 1975-, Int Soc for Clinical Electrophysiology of Vision, Nat Conf of Univ Profs 1989; tstee Birmingham Eye Fndn 1989-, patron Birmingham Royal Inst for the Blind Appeal 1990-; FBPsS, CPsychol; *Books* Photosensitive Epilepsy (1975); *Recreations* railways, model railways, cottage renovation; *Style*— Prof Graham Harding; Vision Sciences Department University of Aston, Aston Triangle, Birmingham B4 7ET (☎ 021 359 3611, fax 021 359 6470, telex 336997)

HARDING, Lt-Col Henry Christian Ewart; MC (1945); s of Col George Harding, DSO (d 1957), of Tulach Nore, Leix, Eire, and Charlotte Hope, *née* Ewart (d 1934); *b* 8 Dec 1919; *Educ* Wellington, RMA Woolwich, Staff Coll Camberley; *m* 21 Nov 1958, Audrey Lennox, da of Maj Charles McNaughton Napier (d 1967), of Broadway, Worcs; 1 s (William b 1964), 2 da (Sarah b 1961, Susan b 1966); *Career* WWII cmmnd RA 1939, served Sicily and Italy 1943-45; instr of gunnery Sch of Artillery Larkhill 1945-47, Staff Coll Camberley 1948, regtl and staff UK and abroad 1949-65, GSO 1 head C-in-C Secretariat M East Cmd 1965-67, supt Proof and Experimental Estab Eskmeals 1968-69, ret 1969; dir: Capital Gearing Trust Ltd 1969-(co sec 1976-), Capital Gearing Management Ltd; tst mangr Paris Smith Randall Solicitors 1977-85; rep Kent Athletics 1939; dep chm New Forest Cons Assoc 1985-88 (pres 1990); ACIS 1974; *Recreations* sailing, photography, travel; *Style*— Lt-Col Christian Harding, MC; Furzey Lodge, Furzey Lane, Beaulieu, Hants (☎ 0590 612 283)

HARDING, John Glendower Rowe; s of His Hon Rowe Harding, of The Old Rectory, Ilston, Gower, Glamorgan, and Elizabeth Adeline, *née* Owen George; *b* 2 Aug 1934; *Educ* Stowe, Trinity Coll Cambridge (MA), SOAS Univ of London; *m* 24 Sept 1966, Georgina Elizabeth, da of Roger Brett Asplin, TD (d 1985), of Bridgetown, W Aust; 3 da (Emma Georgina b 1967, Victoria Alice Elizabeth b 1969, Joanna Natalie b 1970); *Career* Nat Serv 1952-54, cmmnd Welsh Gds 1953; Charles W Hobson Ltd advertising agents 1957-58, political offr Aden and S Arabia HMOCS 1959-65; articled clerk Markby Stewart & Wadesons 1965-69, Canberra Coll Advanced Educn 1970, admitted slr 1971, Tackley Fall and Read 1971-72, ptnr Norton Rose 1976- (joined 1973); pres Alpine Ski Club, tstee Alpine Club, hon legal advsr and memb Ctee Mount Everest Fndn, vice pres Eagle Ski Club; memb: Worshipful Co of Slrs; reg contrib to mountaineering pubns; memb Law Soc; FRGS; *Recreations* ski mountaineering, mountaineering, writing, music, photography; *Clubs* Alpine, Roehampton; *Style*— John Harding, Esq; Norton Rose, Kempson House, Camomile Street, London EC3A 7AN (☎ 071 283 2434, fax 071 588 1181, telex 883652)

HARDING, John Richard Vincent; s of William Henry Harding, (d 1981), and Winifred Elsie, *née* Brett; *b* 1 Sept 1939; *Educ* Enfield GS, Clare Coll Cambridge, (MA); *m* 30 March 1965 (m dis 1983), Janet Ann, da of Albert Norman Roué, of Kempston, Bedford; 2 da (Clare b 1966, Susan b 1968); *Career* graduate trainee rising to asst mangr Martins Bank Ltd 1962-70, vice-pres and asst gen mangr Republic Nat Bank of Dallas London 1970-76, mangr rising to dep gen mangr European Arab Bank Ltd 1977-85, gen mangr AK Int Bank 1985-; ACIB 1966; FCIB 1990; *Recreations* swimming, music, theatre, gardening, photography; *Style*— John Harding, Esq; 10 Finsbury Square, London EC2A 1HE (☎ 071 628 3844, fax 071 638 2037, telex 8955636)

HARDING, Dr (Leslie) Keith; s of Leslie Charles Harding (d 1964), of West Bromwich, and Priscilla Olive, *née* Mason (d 1984); *b* 3 Feb 1939; *Educ* Handsworth GS, Univ of Birmingham Med Sch (BSc, MB ChB, MRCP); *m* 18 Aug 1962, Carol Margaret, da of Dr Colin Starkie, of Kidderminster; 1 s (Nicholas b 1969), 1 da (Victoria b 1972); *Career* lectr in med Queen Elizabeth Hosp Birmingham, conslt in nuclear med Dudley Rd Hosp Birmingham 1982- (conslt physician in gen and nuclear med 1972-82), clinical sr lectr in med Univ of Birmingham 1982-; author of chapters on gastric emptying and bile reflux; papers on: gastro intestinal motility, the lung, radiation safety in nuclear med depts; memb Task Force on Nuclear Med and the Environment, Br del Euro Assoc of Nuclear Med; chm: Admin of Radioactive Substances Advsy Ctee, Regnl Scientific Ctee on Radiation Safety, W Birmingham Health Authy (former chm Med Exec Ctee and Dep Dist Gen Mangr), Radiology and Diagnostic Imaging Servs Ctee; vice chm Med Advsy Ctee, treas and past pres Br Nuclear Med Soc, sec Intercollegiate Standing Ctee on Nuclear Med; fndn govr King Edward VI Schs Birmingham, chm of govrs Five Ways Sch, memb Cncl Nat Assoc of Maintained Charitable Secdy Schs; FRCP 1980, FRCR 1990; *Recreations* maintaining a country cottage, gardening; *Clubs* Woolhope; *Style*— Dr Keith Harding; Huntroyd, 27 Manor Rd North, Edgbaston, Birmingham B16 9JS (☎ 021 454 2497); Birmingham Regional Radioisotope Centre, Physics and Nuclear Medicine Department, Dudley Road Hospital, Birmingham B18 7QH (☎ 021 554 3801 ext 4430/1, fax 021 523 0951)

HARDING, Michael John; s of Maurice John Harding (d 1949), of Colombo, Ceylon, and Dorchester, Dorset, and Wanetse Harding (d 1974); *b* 24 Aug 1933; *Educ* Canford, Gonville and Caius Coll Cambridge (BA, MA); *m* 6 June 1964, Inga Elisabeth, *née* Ericsson; 1 s (Michael James b 11 Aug 1969); *Career* Nat Serv 2 Lieut RA 1952-54; articled clerk Whinney Smith & Whinney 1958-62, seconded to Special Cmmn on Govt Ops Republic of Liberia 1962-63; Whinney Murray Ernst & Ernst: mangr Zurich 1964-67, ptnr Paris 1967-68, ptnr Frankfurt 1969-73, managing ptnr Germany 1974-85, pres Accountants Gp in Germany 1974-85; ptnr Ernst & Young London 1985-; FCA 1968 (ACA 1962), memb Institut der Wirtschaftspruerer 1968-85; *Recreations* golf, tennis, reading political and military biographies; *Clubs* RAC; *Style*— Michael Harding, Esq; Wellwaters, Dogmersfield, nr Basingstoke, Hants (☎ 0252 616717); Ernst & Young, Becket House, 1 Lambeth Palace Rd, London SE1 7EU (☎ 071 928 2000, fax 071 928 1345)

HARDING, Paul Anthony; s of Norman John Harding, and Yvonne Mary, *née* Rees; *b* 6 Oct 1955; *Educ* Hardye's GS Dorchester Dorset; *m* 18 Aug 1979, Deborah Anne, da of Roy William George Harvey, of Farnham, Surrey; 1 s (Benjamin James); 1 da (Alison Jane); *Career* slr: NCB 1979-82, Forsyte Kerman 1982-84, Titmuss Sainer Webb 1984-86 (ptnr 1986-); memb Law Soc; *Style*— Paul A Harding, Esq; Esher, Surrey; Titmuss, Sainer & Webb, 2 Serjeants' Inn, London EC4Y 1LT (☎ 071 583 5353, fax 071 353 0683)

HARDING, Peter Leslie; s of Leslie O'Brien Harding (d 1977), and Muriel Ellen, *née* Money (d 1966); *b* 22 Sept 1926; *Educ* Rugby, King's Coll Cambridge; *m* 6 Nov 1954, Nina Doris, da of Charles Downing Barnard (d 1967); 1 s (David b 30 July 1959), 1 da (Caroline b 23 March 1956); *Career* Union Castle Line 1947-53, dir Alexr Howden & Co Ltd 1960-67 (joined 1953); Baltic Exchange Ltd: dir 1969-73 and 1975-83, chm 1981-83; chm JE Hyde & Co Ltd 1986-(ptnr 1968-86); Freeman City of London 1982, Liveryman Worshipful Co of Shipwrights 1984; FICS; *Recreations* gardening, fly-fishing; *Style*— Peter Harding, Esq; Martlets, Greenways, Walton-on-The-Hill, Tadworth, Surrey (☎ 0737 813766); Baltic Exchange Chambers, 14-20 St Mary Axe, London EC3P 3EQ (☎ 071 283 4266, fax 071 283 2968, telex 885991)

HARDING, Air Chief Marshal Sir Peter Robin; GCB (1988, KCB 1982, CB 1980); s of Peter Harding, and Elizabeth, *née* Clear; *b* 2 Dec 1933; *Educ* Chingford HS; *m* 1955, Sheila Rosemary, da of Albert May; 3 s (Simon, Timothy, Stephen), 1 da (Katherine); *Career* joined RAF 1952, pilot 12 Sqdn 1954-57, QFI and Flt Cdr, RAF Coll Cranwell 1957-60, pilot 1 Sqdn RAAF 1960-62, Staff Coll 1963, Air Secretary's Dept MOD 1964-66, OC 18 Sqdn Gutersloh and Acklington 1966-69, Jt Serv Staff Coll Latimer 1969-70, Def Policy Staff MOD 1970-71, Dir Air Staff Briefing MOD 1971-74, station cdr RAF Bruggen 1974-76, Dir of Def Policy MOD 1976-78, Asst Chief of Staff (plans and policy) SHAPE 1978-80, AOC 11 Gp 1981-82, Vice Chief of Air Staff 1982-84, Vice Chief of Def Staff 1985, Air Offr C-in-C Strike Cmd and C-in-C UK Air Forces 1985-88, Chief of Air Staff 1988-; ADC to HM The Queen 1975-77, Air ADC to HM The Queen 1988; contrib articles to professional jls, magazines and books; memb Cncl Winston Churchill Meml Tst 1990, govr Charterhouse Hosp 1990; hon companion Royal Aeronautical Soc 1989; Liveryman Guild of Air Pilots and Navigators 1989; Hon DSc Cranfield 1990; FRAeS 1983, CBIM 1984, FRSA 1988; *Recreations* tennis, pianoforte, bridge, birdwatching and shooting (normally separately); *Clubs* RAF, Colonels (fndr memb); *Style*— Air Chief Marshal Sir Peter Harding, GCB; c/o Lloyds Bank plc, 6 Pall Mall, London SW1

HARDING, Philip; s of Douglas Harding, and Leonora, *née* Browne; *b* 28 April 1947; *Educ* Univ of York (BA); *m* 1979, Margo, da of Morris Blythman; 1 da (Laura b 1980); *Career* dep ed Nationwide 1980-81, dep ed Panorama 1981-83 (sr prodr 1978-80), ed London Plus 1984-86, asst head current affrs BBC TV 1986-87 (prodr 1972-78), ed Today BBC Radio Four 1987-; Emmy award for Best Documentary Who Killed Georgi Markov? 1980; Sony awards: Best Current Affrs Prog 1989, Best Response to a News Event 1989, Best Daily News Prog 1990, Best Response To A News Event 1990; NY Radio Festival: Silver medal (for Lockerbie coverage) 1989, Gold medal (for Romania coverage) 1990; *Recreations* swimming, walking, watching QPR; *Style*— Philip Harding, Esq; BBC Today Programme, Broadcasting House, London W1A 1AA (☎ 071 927 5532)

HARDING, Robert Alan; s of Alan Killoch Harding, of Farnham, Surrey, and Aileen Margaret, *née* McBride; *b* 6 Dec 1937; *Educ* Elmhurst Sch, Whitgift Sch, St Martins Sch of Art; *m* 1, 8 April 1961 (m dis 1972), (Elisabeth) Ann; 1 s (Rupert Gordon McBride b 16 April 1966), 1 da (Samantha Minou Kathleen (Mrs Haynes) b 13 June 1964); m 2, 6 Dec 1972, Dolores Brenda, da of Edward Warris Mantez (d 1969), of Ghana; 1 s (Robert Tony Nelson Mantez b 12 March 1974); *Career* dir: William Sommerville & Son plc 1966-, Conservation Papers Ltd 1989-; Br Paper and Bd Indust Fedn: chm Paper and Bd Trade Custom Ctee 1986-, chm 1992 working pty 1988-90, chm AMPW 1989-90 (and 1986-88); life memb London Soc RFU Referees, referee RFU and Surrey RFU 1967-72; *Recreations* rugby football, painting, calligraphy; *Style*— Robert Harding, Esq; 2 Barham Rd, Croydon, Surrey CR2 6LD (☎ 081 688 5409); Dalmore Mill, Milton Bridge, Penicuik, Midlothian EH26 0NE (☎ 0968 72 214, fax 01 681 1176/0968 73314, car 0860 327723, telex 72451 SOMPEN G)

HARDING, Robert John (Bob); s of John Henry Harding (d 1960), of Bideford, Devon, and Ethel, *née* Luxton; *b* 31 Oct 1923; *Educ* Bideford GS; *m* 24 Feb 1946, Dorothy Alice Harding, JP, da of Frederick George Holdsworth (d 1974); 1 s (David John b 16 Jan 1948), 1 da (Maureen Ann b 12 July 1953); *Career* RN and Combined Ops 1942-46; serv: Sicily, Italy, Normandy (D Day) Walcheren; Western Counties Building Soc: chief clerk 1946, asst sec 1954, sec 1970, dir 1980; W of Eng Bldg Soc: md 1985, ret 1986; memb Cncl Bldg Socs Assoc 1983-86 (rep Wales and W of Eng Assoc of Bldg Socs, past chm Regnl Assoc); fndr memb Bideford Round Table and 41 Clubs; past pres: Bideford C of C, Bideford Rotary Club; pres Torridgeside RNA, fndr govr Bideford Coll, memb Bd Bideford Housing Soc; ACIS 1954, FCBSI 1948; *Recreations* cricket and golf; *Clubs* Bideford Rotary, North Devon Cricket; *Style*— Bob Harding, Esq; 17 Rectory Park, Bideford, N Devon EX39 3AJ (☎ 0237 474199)

HARDING, Air Vice-Marshal Ross Philip; CBE (1968); s of late Philip James Harding, of Salisbury, and late Ellen Alice, *née* Mann; *b* 22 Jan 1921; *Educ* Bishop Wordsworth's Sch Salisbury, St Edmund Hall Oxford (MA); *m* 29 March 1948, (Laurie) Joy, da of late Edward James Gardner, of Salisbury; 3 s (Russell b 1950, Murray b 1957, Stuart b 1963); *Career* WWII serv No 41 Sqdn Fighter Cmd and 2 TAF 1943-45, RAF Staff Coll Andover 1951, ACAS (Ops) Air Miny 1952-54, CO No 96 Sqdn Germany 1955-58, dir staff RAF Staff Coll Andover 1958-60, CO Oxford Univ Air Sqdn 1960-62, dep chief Br Mil Mission Berlin 1963-65, CO RAF Valley 1965-68, sr dir staff (Air) Jt Servs Staff Coll 1968-69, def and air attaché Moscow 1970-72, dir Personal Servs I MOD (Air) 1973, sr RAF memb RCDS 1974-76, ret 1976; head Airwork Ltd Oman 1976-78, def advsr House of Commons Select Ctee on Def 1979-83; chm: Selection Bds Civil Serv and MoD 1979-, govrs Bishop Wordsworth's Sch; *Recreations* bridge, skiing; *Clubs* RAF; *Style*— Air Vice-Marshal Ross Harding, CBE; 8 Hadrian's Close, Lower Bemerton, Salisbury, Wilts (☎ 0722 336 075)

HARDING, Sir Roy Pollard; CBE (1978); s of William Foster Norman Harding, BEM (d 1966), of Cornwall, and Phebe Emma, *née* Pollard (d 1978); *b* 3 Jan 1924; *Educ* Liskeard GS, King's Coll London (BSc, DPA, AKC); *m* 1948, Audrey Beryl, da of Arthur Wimble Larkin (d 1973); 2 s (Alan, Paul), 1 da (Hilary); *Career* educationalist, ballistics res, sch and coll teacher until 1950; educn admin 1951-84: Wilts, Herts, Leics, Bucks (chief educn offr Bucks 1966-84); memb: Printing and Publishing Indust Trg Bd 1970-72, BBC Further Educn Advsy Ctee 1970-75, Burnham Ctee 1972-77, DES Local Authy Educnl Expenditure Gp 1976-84, Sec of State's visiting Ctee Cranfield Inst of Technol 1976-81, Cncls and Educnl Press Eds Advsy Panel 1977-87, Teaching of Mathematics in Schools (Cockcroft) Ctee 1978-81, Educnl Mgmnt Info Exchange 1981-89, Bd Nat Advsy Body for Higher Educn 1982-84, Open Univ Cncl 1985- (chm Bd for Professional Devpt of Teachers 1983-87), Higginson Ctee (A Level) 1987-88, CBI Educn Fndn Cncl 1990-, AEC Tst 1990; advsr: CC Assoc 1972-74, Assoc of City Cncls and Cncl of Local Educn Authys 1974-84; pres: Soc of Educn Offrs 1977-78 (exec 1974-79, chm Int Ctee 1978-83, gen sec 1984-89), Br Educnl Equipment Assoc 1980-83, Br Assoc Educn Section 1986-87, Nat Inst Adult & Continuing Educn 1988-, Inst of Mathematics and Applications 1990- (Cncl 1983-88, vice pres 1986-88, Fin Ctee 1986-); chm: Co Educn Offrs Soc 1978-79 (sec 1973-76), Educn Policy Interchange Ctee 1979-88, Further Educn Staff Coll 1986-, EMIS Ltd 1988-; vice chm Secdy Examinations Ctee 1983-86; Hon DUniv Open Univ 1985; FIMA, FZS; kt 1985; *Clubs* Royal Overseas; *Style*— Sir Roy Harding, CBE; 27 King Edward Ave, Aylesbury, Bucks HP21 7JE (☎ 0296 23006)

HARDING, Sir (George) William; KCMG (1983, CMG 1977), CVO (1972); s of Lt-Col George Richardson Harding, DSO, MBE (d 1976), and Grace Henley, *née* Darby; *b* 18 Jan 1927; *Educ* Aldenham, St John's Coll Cambridge; *m* 1955, Sheila Margaret Ormond, da of Maj John Ormond Riddel (d 1945), of Edinburgh; 4 s (Rupert, Simon,

Martin, James); *Career* Lt Royal Marines 1945-48; entered Dip Serv 1950, served Singapore, Burma, Paris, Santo Domingo, Mexico City, Paris; ambass Peru 1977-79, asst under sec of state FCO 1979-81, ambass Brazil 1981-84, dep under sec of state for Asia and the Americas FCO 1984-86; int advsr to bd and non-exec dir of Lloyds Bank plc 1988-, dir Lloyds Merchant Bank Holdings Ltd 1988-; visiting fell Harvard Univ Center for Int Affrs 1986; chm: First Spanish Investment Trust plc 1988-, Thai-Euro Fund Ltd 1988-, Govrs Centre for Int Briefing Farnham Castle 1987-; memb: Trilateral Cmmn 1987-, Cncl of Royal Inst of Int Affrs 1988-, Cncl of Royal Geographical Soc 1988-; *Clubs* Garrick, Beefsteak, Leander; *Style*— Sir William Harding, KCMG, CVO; Shelley Court, Tite St, Chelsea, London SW3 4JB; Lloyds Bank plc, 71 Lombard St, London EC3P 3BS

HARDING-JONES, David; s of Rev William Harding Jones (d 1981), of Seaford, Sussex, and Gertrude Alice, *née* Roberts; *b* 3 Aug 1936; *Educ* Bancrofts Sch, Charing Cross Hosp Med Sch (MB BS); *m* 2 April 1960, (Josephine) June Mary, da of Henry Thomas Hitchens, of Exeter; 3 s (Andrew David b 1964, Ian Richard b 1965, Neil Robert b 1967), 2 da (Alison Margaret b 1969, Fiona Marie b 1971); *Career* orthopaedic registrar Oswestry and Hereford 1968-69 (Westminster Hosp 1964-67), orthopaedic sr registrar Cardiff 1969-70, conslt orthopaedic surgn W Wales Gen Hosp Carmarthen 1971-; regnl advsr orthopaedics S Wales RCS England, chm Orthopaedic Advsy Ctee Wales; pres Rotary Club Saundersfoot 1980-81, past master Caerfyrddin Lodge 4928, previous convener S W Wales Orthopaedic Club 1972-88; memb: BMA, Hosp Conslts and Specialists Assoc; FRCS; *Recreations* travel; *Style*— David Harding-Jones, Esq; Dept of Orthopaedics, W Wales Gen Hosp, Glangwili, Carmarthen, Dyfed SA31 2AF (☎ 0267 235151 ext 2531)

HARDING OF PETHERTON, 2 Baron (UK 1958); John Charles Harding; o s of Field Marshal 1 Baron Harding of Petherton, GCB, CBE, DSO, MC (d 1989), and Mary, *née* Rooke (d 1983); *b* 12 Feb 1928; *Educ* Marlborough, Worcester Coll Oxford; *m* 20 June 1966, Harriet, da of Maj-Gen James Hare, CB, DSO (d 1970); 2 s (Hon William Allan John, Hon David Richard John b 1978), 1 da (Hon Diana Mary b 1967); *Heir* s, Hon William Allan John Harding b 5 July 1969; *Career* Maj 11 Hussars, ret 1968; farmer, ret 1991; *Style*— The Rt Hon the Lord Harding of Petherton; Barrymore Farm House, Huish Episcopi, Langport, Somerset TA10 9EZ

HARDINGE, Hon Andrew Hartland; 2 s of 5 Viscount Hardinge (d 1984), and Zoe Anne, *née* Molson; *b* 7 Jan 1960; *Educ* The Gow Sch New York USA, Trinity Coll Sch Ontario Canada; *m* 2 June 1990, Sophia Mary, o da of Capt (William) David Armstrong Bagnell, of East Worldham House, Alton, Hants; *Career* KCA Engineering Ltd: management trainee 1982-83, engrg asst 1983-85, asst gen mangr 1985-88, gen mangr 1988-; *Recreations* shooting, fishing; *Clubs* RAC; *Style*— The Hon Andrew Hardinge; The Garden Flat, 59 Redcliffe Gardens, London SW10 9JJ (☎ 071 370 6682); KCA Engineering Ltd, 3rd Floor, Columbia Centre, Market Street, Bracknell, Berks RG12 1PA (☎ 0344 860444, fax 0344 860094, telex 846258 KCA DRL G, car 0836 354719)

HARDINGE, 6 Viscount (UK 1846); Charles Henry Nicholas Hardinge; s of 5 Viscount Hardinge (d 1984), and 1 w (m dis 1982), Zoe Ann (Mrs C M H Murray), da of Hartland de Montarville Molson, OBE, of Montreal, Senator of Canada; *b* 25 Aug 1956; *Educ* Upper Canada Coll, Trin Coll Sch, McGill Univ; *m* 1985, Mrs Julie Therese Sillett, eldest da of Keith Sillett, of Sydney, Australia; 2 da (Hon Emilie Charlotte b 1986, Hon Olivia Margaux b 1989), and 1 step s (Matthew b 1982); *Heir* bro, Hon Andrew Hartland Hardinge, *qv*; *Career* Independant in House of Lords, mangr Private Banking, The Royal Bank of Canada; *Style*— The Rt Hon the Viscount Hardinge; 12 Streathbourne Rd, London SW17

HARDINGE, Florence, Viscountess; Florence Elisabeth; *née* Baroness von Oppenheim; da of late Baron Harold von Oppenheim, of Cologne; *Educ* Fondation Nationale des Sciences Politique (Paris), Université Paris II; *m* 1982, as his 2 w, 5 Viscount Hardinge; 1 da (Hon Georgia Victoria b 1984); *Recreations* shooting, skiing, music; *Style*— The Rt Hon Florence, Viscountess Hardinge; 5 Somerset Sq, London W14 8EE

HARDINGE, Margot, Viscountess; Margaret (Elizabeth Arnot); da of late Hugh Percy Fleming, of Wynyards, Rockcliffe, Ottawa; *m* 15 Sept 1928, 4 Viscount Hardinge, MBE (d 1979); 1 s (5 Viscount d 1984), 2 da (Hon Mrs Worsley, Hon Mrs Raymond); *Style*— Margaret, Viscountess Hardinge; 1523 Summerhill Ave, Montréal, Québec, Canada

HARDINGE, Sir Robert Arnold; 7 Bt (UK 1801), of Lurran, Fermanagh; s of Sir Robert Hardinge, 6 Bt (d 1973); *b* 19 Dec 1914; *Heir* kinsman, 5 Viscount Hardinge; *Style*— Sir Robert Hardinge, Bt

HARDINGE OF PENSHURST, 3 Baron (UK 1910); George Edward Charles Hardinge; s of 2 Baron, GCB, GCVO, MC, PC (d 1960), and Helen, Baroness Hardinge of Penshurst (d 1979); *b* 31 Oct 1921; *Educ* Eton, RNC Dartmouth; *m* 1, 22 July 1944 (m dis 1962), Janet (d 1970), da of Lt-Col Francis Balfour, CIE, CVO, CBE, MC (n of 1 and 2 Earls of Balfour); 3 s; m 2, 1966, Mrs Margaret Trezise, da of William Jerrum; 1 s, 1 adopted (step)s; *Heir* s, Hon Julian Hardinge; *Career* Lt Cdr RN ret; page of honour to HM 1933-38, train bearer at Coronation of George VI; 30 years as a professional publisher (Collins, Longmans, Macmillan); *Books* An Incompleat Angler (1976); *Clubs* Brooks's; *Style*— The Rt Hon Lord Hardinge of Penshurst; Bracken Hill, 10 Penland Road, Bexhill-on-Sea, E Sussex (☎ 0424 211866)

HARDINGHAM, Michael; s of Edmund Arthur Hardingham, and Winifred, *née* Leeding; *b* 16 Oct 1939; *Educ* West House and Solihull Sch, St Marys Hosp Univ of London (MB BS, LRCP); *m* 25 Sept 1982, Ellen, da of William McCafferty, of Pennsylvania, USA; 1 s (Henry b 1984), 1 da (Isabel b 1986); *Career* postgrad med trg London, Edinburgh and Sweden, trg in otorhinolaryngology St Mary's Royal Marsden Hosp, conslt ENT surgn Cheltenham Gen Hosp and Gloucestershire Royal Hosp 1974- (special interest head and neck oncology); memb Cncl Section of Laryngology RSM; memb: Assoc of Head and Neck Ocologists GB, Cheltenham Ctee for Nat Soc Cancer Relief, exec Ctee Nat Assoc of Laryngectomy Clubs UK; Gloucestershire Hosp rep to BMA annual rep body meeting, foreign corresponding memb American Soc of Head and Neck Surgns; memb and examiner for: DLO of RCS, Nursing Assoc of Midland Inst of Otology (formerly hon sec); BMA Gloucestershire Branch (formerly sec), MRCS 1964, FRCM, FRCS, FRSM; *Books* contrib: pubns to otolaryngolical clinics N America, asst ed ENT jl USA; *Recreations* theatre, opera, skiing; *Style*— Michael Hardingham, Esq; Gloucester Clinic, 5 Denmark Rd, Gloucester GL1 3HZ (☎ 0452 423601)

HARDMAN, Blaise Noel Anthony; s of Air Chief Marshal Sir Donald Hardman, GBE, KCB, DFC (d 1982), and Dorothy, *née* Ashcroft Thompson; *b* 24 Dec 1939; *Educ* Eton; *m* 1967, Caroline Marion, da of Sir Donald Cameron of Lochiel, KT, CVO, of Inverness-shire; 1 s (Thomas b 1977), 4 da (Jane b 1969, Annabel b 1971, Elizabeth b 1974, Rosanna b 1979); *Career* cmmnd 2 Lt HM Forces 1959, served 13/18 Royal Hussars 1959-61, Malaya 1961, BAOR; Morgan Grenfell and Co Ltd 1962-88, (dir 1971, chm 1987); dir: P and O Steam Navigation Co 1980-83, Matthew Clark and Sons (Holdings) 1982, Murray International plc 1988, Tokai International Ltd 1989, Whiteaway Laidlaw Bank Ltd 1989; vice chm Crediop Finance plc 1988; *Recreations* gardening; *Clubs* Boodles; *Style*— Blaise Hardman, Esq; Farley House, Farley Chamberlayne, nr Romsey, Hants; Morgan Grenfell and Co Ltd, 23 Great Winchester St, London EC2 (☎ 071 588 4545)

HARDMAN, Lady; Dorothy; da of William Ashcroft Thompson, JP, of Larkenshaw, Chobham; *m* 1930, Air Chief Marshal Sir (James) Donald Innes Hardman, GBE, KCB, DFC (d 1982); 2 s, 1 da (*see* North, Sir Jonathan, 2 Bt); *Style*— Lady Hardman; Dolphin Cottage, St Cross Hill, Winchester, Hants

HARDMAN, Sir Henry; KCB (1962, CB 1956); s of Harry Hardman (d 1957); *b* 15 Dec 1905; *Educ* Manchester Central HS, Univ of Manchester; *m* 1937, Helen Diana, da of late Robert Carr Bosanquet; 1 s, 2 da; *Career* economics tutor Univ of Leeds 1934-45; Miny of Food 1940-: dep head Br Food Mission to N America 1946-48, under-sec 1948-53; min UK delegn to NATO Paris 1953-54, dep sec MAFF 1955-60; dep sec Miny of Aviation 1960 (perm sec 1961-63), perm under-sec of state MOD 1963-66; memb MMC 1967-70 (dep chm 1967-68), chm Covent Garden Market Authy 1967-75, govr and tstee Reserve Bank of Rhodesia 1967-79, chm Home-Grown Cereals Authy 1968-77; *Style*— Sir Henry Hardman, KCB; 9 Sussex Square, Brighton, East Sussex BN2 1FJ (☎ 0273 688904)

HARDMAN, Victoria; da of Donald Hardman, of Lincolnshire, and Joan Frances, *née* Dolphin; *b* 5 Jan 1953; *Educ* Erdington GS Birmingham, Dorset Inst of HE (BA); *m* 1989, Michael Fairey; *Career* trg in NHS 1978-81, asst admin Guy's Hosp 1981-83, health serv planner NE Thames RHA 1983-86, gen mangr The Royal London Hosp 1986-; memb Inst of Health Servs Mgmnt 1979; *Recreations* opera, ballet, gardening; *Style*— Miss Victoria Hardman; The Royal London Hospital, Whitechapel, London E1 1BB (☎ 071 377 7491, fax 071 377 7291)

HARDSTAFF, Joseph (Joe); s of Joseph Hardstaff (d 1990), of Nottingham, and Cissy, *née* Rose (d 1981); *b* 28 Feb 1935; *Educ* Brunts Sch Mansfield; *m* 21 Dec 1963, Olive Mary, da of Thomas Nancekieville, of Torrington, Devon; 1 s (Joseph b 21 Dec 1967), 1 da (Lisa Jane b 20 Nov 1965); *Career* sec Middlesex CCC 1989-; gen duties offr pilot RAF 1953-88 (ret as Air Cdre); cricket player: RAF 1953-73 (capt 1964 and 1967-69), Combined Servs 1964; *Recreations* golf, walking, reading; *Style*— Joe Hardstaff, Esq; 5 Dial Close, Seend, Melksham, Wiltshire SN12 6NP (☎ 0380 828458); Middlesex CCC, Lord's Ground, London NW8 8QN (☎ 071 289 1300)

HARDWICK, Donald Hugh; s of Capt Donald Frederick Hardwick, MC (d 1967), of Purlands, Charing, Kent, and Adeline Marion, *née* Sulston (d 1966); *b* 28 Oct 1936; *Educ* St Edmund's Canterbury, Canterbury Coll of Art (Nat Dip Design); *m* 29 Feb 1964, Kathleen, da of Alfred George Englefield (d 1959); 2 s (Leigh Hardwick b 22 Nov 1967, Giles Hardwick b 27 Oct 1968); *Career* Nat Serv REME attached to 4 Gds Bde BAOR 1956-58; appts in advertising indust 1958-; dir: Appropriate Technology Ltd 1979-, Butler Borg Ltd 1986-89; md Jogdean Ltd 1979-; *Style*— Donald Hardwick, Esq; St Margarets, Rochester, Kent (☎ 0634 402632); 4 Gee's Court, Oxford St, London W1M 5HQ (☎ 071 408 2301, fax 071 408 0382, telex 267529)

HARDWICK, Mary Atkinson (Mollie); *née* Greenhalgh; da of Joseph Greenhalgh (d 1940), of Cheadle Hulme, Cheshire, and Anne Frances, *née* Atkinson (d 1959); *Educ* Manchester HS for Girls; *m* 1961, Michael Hardwick, s of George Drinkrow Hardwick, of Leeds, W Yorks; 1 s (Julian); *Career* announcer BBC North Region 1940-45, BBC (Radio) Drama Dept 1945-62; freelance author 1962-; FRSA; *Books* Stories from Dickens (1968), Emma, Lady Hamilton (1969), Mrs Dizzy (1972), Upstairs Downstairs: Sarah's Story (1973), The Years of Change (1974), The War to end Wars (1975), Mrs Bridges' Story (1975), The World of Upstairs Downstairs (1976), Alice in Wonderland (play, 1975), Beauty's Daughter (1976, Elizabeth Goudge Award for best historical romantic novel of year), The Duchess of Duke Street: The Way Up (1976), The Golden Years (1976), The World Keeps Turning (1977), Charlie is My Darling (1977), The Atkinson Heritage (1978), Thomas and Sarah (1978), Thomas and Sarah: Two for a Spin (1979), Lovers Meeting (1979), Sisters in Love (1979), Dove's Nest (1980), Willowwood (1980), Juliet Bravo 1 (1980), Juliet Bravo 2 (1980), Monday's Child (1981), Calling Juliet Bravo: New Arrivals (1981), I Remember Love (1982), The Shakespeare Girl (1983), By the Sword Divided (1983), The Merrymaid (1984), Girl with a Crystal Dove (1985), Malice Domestic (1986), Parson's Pleasure (1987), Uneaseful Death (1988), Blood Royal (1988), The Bandersnatch (1989), Perish in July (1989), The Dreaming Damozel (1990); with Michael Hardwick: The Jolly Toper (1961), The Sherlock Holmes Companion (1962), Sherlock Holmes Investigates (1963), The Man Who Was Sherlock Holmes (1964), Four Sherlock Holmes Plays (1964), The Charles Dickens Companion (1965), The World's Greatest Sea Mysteries (1967), Writers' Houses: a literary journey in England (1968), Alfred Deller: A Singularity of Voice (1968), Charles Dickens As They Saw Him (1969), The Game's Afoot (Sherlock Holmes Plays, 1969), Plays from Dickens (1970), Dickens's England (1970), The Private Life of Sherlock Holmes (1970), Four More Sherlock Holmes Plays (1973), The Charles Dickens Encyclopedia (1973), The Bernard Shaw Companion (1973), The Charles Dickens Quiz Book (1974), The Upstairs Downstairs Omnibus (1975), The Gaslight Boy (1976), The Hound of the Baskervilles and Other Sherlock Holmes Plays (1982); numerous plays and scripts for radio and television; contributions to women's magazines; *Recreations* reading detective novels; *Style*— Mollie Hardwick; 2 Church St, Wye, Kent TN25 5BJ (☎ 0233 813051)

HARDWICK, Michael John Drinkrow; s of George Drinkrow Hardwick (d 1964), and Katharine Augusta, *née* Townend (d 1964); *b* 10 Sept 1924; *Educ* Leeds GS; *m* 1961, Mollie, da of Joseph Greenhalgh (d 1940), of Cheadle Hulme, Cheshire; 1 s (Julian); *Career* Indian Army 1943-47, Capt, served in India and Japan; author and dramatist, reporter Morley Observer 1942-43; dir: NZ Nat Film Unit 1948-53, Freedom Newspaper NZ 1953-54, BBC Radio Drama Dept 1958-63; freelance author 1963-; FRSA; *Books* The Royal Visit to New Zealand (1954), Emigrant in Motley: letters of Charles Kean and Ellen Tree (1954), Seeing New Zealand (1955), Opportunity in New Zealand (ed with Baron Birkett, 1955), The Verdict of the Court (1960), Doctors on Trial (1961), The Plague and Fire of London (1966), The Worlds Greatest Air Mysteries (1970), The Discovery of Japan (1970), The Osprey Guide to Gilbert and Sullivan (1972), The Osprey Guide to Jane Austen (1973), A Literary Atlas and Gazetter of the British Isles (1973), The Osprey Guide to Oscar Wilde (1973); Upstairs Downstairs: Mr Hudson's Diaries (1973), Mr Bellamy's Story (1974), On with the Dance (1975), Endings and Beginnings (1975), The Osprey Guide to Anthony Trollope (1974), The Inheritors (1974), The Pallisers (abridger, 1974), The Four Musketeers (abridger, 1975), The Man Who Would be King (abridger, 1976), The Cedar Tree (1976), The Cedar Tree: Autumn of an Age (1977), A Bough Breaks (1978), Regency Royal (1978), Prisoner of the Devil (1979), Regency Rake (1979), Regency Revenge (1980), Bergerac (1981), The Chinese Detective (1981), Regency Revels (1982), The Barchester Chronicles (1982), The Private Life of Dr Watson (1983), Sherlock Holmes: my life and crimes (1984), Last Tenko (1984), Complete Guide to Sherlock Holmes (1986), The Revenge of the Hound (1987), Nightbone (1989); as John Drinkrow: The Vintage Operetta Book (1972), The Vintage Musical Comedy Book (1973); with Mollie Hardwick: The Jolly Toper (1961), The Sherlock Holmes Companion (1962), Sherlock Holmes Investigates (1963), The Man Who Was Sherlock Holmes (1964), Four Sherlock Holmes Plays (1964), The Charles Dickens Companion (1965), The World's Greatest Sea Mysteries (1967), Writers' Houses: a literary journey in England (1968), Alfred Deller: A Singularity of Voice (1968), Charles Dickens As They Saw Him (1969), Dicken's England (1970), The Private Life of Sherlock Holmes (1970), The Bernard Shaw Companion (1973), The Charles Dickens Encyclopaedia (1973), The Charles Dickens Quiz Book (1974), The Upstairs Downstairs Omnibus (1975), The Gaslight Boy (1976); plays: A Christmas Carol (1975), Four Sherlock Holmes Plays (jtly, 1964), The Game's Afoot (jtly, 1969), Four More Sherlock Holmes Plays (jtly, 1973), The Hound of the Baskervilles and other Sherlock Holmes Plays (1982); author of many plays and scripts for tv and radio; *Recreations* listening to music, watching old films on television; *Style—* Michael Hardwick, Esq; 2 Church St, Wye, Kent TN25 5BJ (☎ 0233 813 051)

HARDWICK, Dr Peter Bernard; s of Arthur William Hardwick (d 1976), of Rayleigh, Essex, and Nellie, *née* Love (d 1960); *b* 21 Sept 1933; *Educ* Southend-on-Sea HS for Boys, The Royal Free Hosp Sch of Med (MB BS); *m* 1961 (m dis 1988) Nancy, *née* Peters; 2 s (Nigel Peter Arthur b 1967, Matthew James Gerald b 1969), 2 da (Deborah Claire b 1962, Julia Dawn b 1964, d 1989); *Career* The Royal Free Hosp London: conslt anaesthetist, conslt i/c clinic for pain relief 1969-; memb Ct of Common Cncl Corp of City of London, Hon MO London and Schools ABA, dep dist surgn St John Ambulance Bde London Prince of Wales Dist; Liveryman: Worshipful Co of Barbers, Worshipful Soc of Apothecaries; OStJ; FFARCS; *Recreations* private flying, horse riding, cricket and rugby; *Clubs* MCC; *Style—* Dr Peter Hardwick; 126 Harley Street, London W1N 1AH (☎ 071 935 4895)

HARDWICKE, Countess of; Enid Munnick; *m* 1, Roy Boulting, the film producer and one half of the Boulting Bros; m 2, 1970, as his 2 w, 9 Earl of Hardwicke (d 1974); *Style—* The Rt Hon the Countess of Hardwicke

HARDWICKE, 10 Earl of (GB 1754); Joseph Philip Sebastian Yorke; also Baron Hardwicke (GB 1733) and Viscount Royston (GB 1754); s of Viscount Royston (d 1973, s and h of 9 Earl, who d 1974); *b* 3 Feb 1971; *Heir* kinsman, Richard Yorke; *Style—* The Rt Hon Earl of Hardwicke; 9 Fernshaw Rd, SW10

HARDY, Prof Barbara Gladys; da of Maurice Nathan (d 1962), and Gladys Emily Ann, *née* Abraham; *b* 27 June 1924; *Educ* Swansea HS for Girls, UCL (BA, MA); *m* 14 March 1946, Ernest Dawson Hardy (d 1977); 2 da (Julia b 1955, Kate b 1957); *Career* English Dept Birkbeck Coll London, prof of English Royal Holloway Coll Univ of London 1965-70; prof Enlish lit Birkbeck Coll London 1970-; pres Dickens Soc 1987-88; memb: Labour Pty, Welsh Acad; hon memb MLA; DUniv Open Univ 1981; *Books* The Novels of George Eliot (1959), The Appropriate Form (194), The Moral Art of Dickens (1970), The Exposure of Luxury radical themes in The Closeray (1972), Tellers and Listeners: the narative imagination (1975), A Reading of Jane Austen (1975), The Advantage of Lyric (1977), Particularities: readings in George Eliot (1982), Forms of Feeling in Victorian Fiction (1985), Narrators and Novalists: collected essays, (vol 1 1987); *Recreations* walking, acting; *Style—* Prof Barbara Hardy; Birkbeck College, Malet Street, London WC1E 7HX

HARDY, David Gordon; s of Gordon Patrick Hardy, of 33a High St Auchtermuchty, Fife, Scotland and Margaret Maud, *née* Cunningham; *b* 5 July 1940; *Educ* Daniel Stewart's Coll Edinburgh, Univ of Edinburgh (BSc, MB ChB), Univ of Cambridge (MA); *m* 8 Aug 1967, Maria Rosa (Rosemary), da of Johann Breu (d 1965), of Appenzell Switzerland; 1 s (James Patrick b 5 Oct 1971), 1 da (Ruth Maria b 10 Oct 1969); *Career* Fulbright Hayes scholar Univ of Florida 1977-78, sr lectr in neurosurgery London Hosp Med Coll 1979-80, conslt neurosurgn Addenbrooke's Hosp Cambridge 1980-, supervisor in anatomy Gonville and Caius Coll Cambridge (assoc lectr faculty of clinical med), visiting conslt Norfolk and Norwich Hosp; contrib various chapters and papers on various neurosurgical and anatomical subjects; memb Cncl Section of neurology RSM, FRCS Ed 1970, FRCS 1971, FRSM, Memb Soc of Br Neurosurgeons; *Recreations* gardening, walking; *Style—* David Hardy, Esq; Department of Neurosurgery, Addenbrooke's Hospital, Hills Rd, Cambridge CB2 2QQ (☎ 0223 216302)

HARDY, David William; s of Brig John Herbert Hardy, CBE, MC (d 1969), of Lancaster, and (Amy) Doris, *née* Bacon (d 1982); *b* 14 July 1930; *Educ* Wellington, Harvard Business Sch (AMP); *m* 11 Sept 1957, Rosemary Stratford, da of Sir Godfrey Ferdinando Stratford Collins, KCIE, CSI, OBE (d 1952); 1 s (Alexander David b 11 May 1968), 1 da (Sarah Elizabeth b 28 May 1964); *Career* 2 Lt 2 Royal Horse Artillery Germany 1953-54; dir: Funch Edye Co Inc 1960 (1954-64), Imperial Tobacco (vice pres fin and admin 1964-70), (fin) Tate and Lyle plc 1972-77, Ocean Transport and Trading plc 1977-83, Waterford Wedgwood Group plc 1984-90, Paragon Group Ltd 1984-88, Sturge Holdings plc 1985, Aberfoyle Holdings plc 1986, Tootal Group 1990-; chm: Ocean Inchcape Ltd 1980-83, Globe Investment Tst plc 1983-90 (dir 1976), London Park Hotels 1983-87, Docklands Light Railway 1984-87, Swan Hunter Ltd 1986-88, MGM Assur 1986- (dir 1985), Leisuretime International 1988-89, Buckingham International 1989, London Docklands Devpt Corp 1988-, DTI Engrg Markets Advsy Ctee 1988-90; dep chm: London Regnl Tport 1984-87, The Agricultural Mortgage Corp 1986 (dir 1973); secondment to HM Govt (co-ordinator of Industl Advsrs) 1970-72; memb: NEDC for Agriculture 1970-72, ECGD Advsy Cncl 1973-78, CBI Econs and Fiscal Ctee 1982-89; co-opted Cncl Inst CAs 1974-78, chm 100 Gp of Fin Dirs 1986-88; Freeman City of London; Liveryman: Worshipful Co of CA's, Worshipful Co of Shipwrights; FCA, FCIT, CBIM (chm Econs and Social Affrs Ctee 1974-78, memb Cncl 1974-79); *Recreations* flyfishing, shooting; *Clubs* Brooks's, MCC, HAC, The Philippics, Flyfishers; *Style—* David Hardy, Esq; 181 Marsh Wall, London E14 9TJ (☎ 071 512 3000, fax 071 512 0277, telex 894041)

HARDY, Hon Lady (Diana Joan); *née* Allsopp; da of 3 Baron Hindlip, OBE, JP, DL (d 1931), and Agatha (d 1962), da of John Thynne, DL (d 1918), who was 6 s of Rev Lord John Thynne, 3 s of 2 Marquess of Bath, KG (d 1837); *b* 1908; *m* 2 June 1930, Lt-Col Sir Rupert John Hardy, 4 Bt; 1 s, 1 da; *Style—* The Hon Lady Hardy; Gulliver's Lodge, Guilsborough, Northampton

HARDY, Graham John; s of William A Hardy (d 1976), and Lettie, *née* Lovell (d 1984); *b* 5 March 1938; *Educ* Llandaff Cathedral Sch, Cathays HS, Welsh Sch of Architecture Univ of Wales (BArch); *m* 7 Sept 1963, Sara Maureen, da of David Metcalfe Morgan, of Archer Road, Penarth; 1 s (Keiron b 1972), 2 da (Bridget b 1966, Elise b 1968); *Career* chartered architect and ecclesiastical surveyor; Prince of Wales Award 1984, St John Ev Church Grounds Cardiff; Prince of Wales Award 1984, Eglwysilian Church Mid Glam; Catnic UK Restoration Award 1981; first prize: Prince of Wales' Ctee (competition for Inner Areas) 1980; Civic Tst commendation Victoria Place Newport 1980; architect and surveyor to the Fabric: Margam Abbey, Old Priory Caldey Abbey, St Illtyds Church Llantwit Major St Germans Church Cardiff; architect to the Cathedral Parish of Llandaff; former pres Rotary Club of Cardiff East; ARIBA; *Clubs* Rotary; *Style—* Graham J Hardy, Esq; Timbers, 6 Cefn Coed Rd, Cyncoed, Cardiff CF2 6AQ (☎ 0222 752960); Graham J Hardy and Assoc, 6 Cefn Coed Rd, Cardiff CF2 6AQ

HARDY, Herbert Charles; s of Charles Hardy; *b* 13 Dec 1928; *Educ* Sandhurst; *m* 1960, Irene Burrows; 1 da; *Career* dir News Gp Newspapers Ltd 1969-78, md and chief exec News International Ltd 1976-78 (dir 1972-78), chief exec Evening Standard Co Ltd 1980-, md Associated Newspapers Ltd 1989-; *Style—* Herbert Hardy, Esq; 118 Fleet St, London EC4P 4DD (☎ 071 353 8000)

HARDY, Maj-Gen John Campbell; CB (1985), LVO (1978); s of Gen Sir Campbell Hardy, KCB, CBE, DSO (d 1984); *b* 13 Oct 1933; *Educ* Sherborne; *m* 1961, Jennifer Mary Kempton; 1 s, 1 da; *Career* joined RM 1952, 45 Commando 1954, HMS Superb 1956, instr NCOs' Sch at Plymouth 1957, 42 Commando 1959, 43 Commando 1962, Adj Jt Serv Amphibious Warfare Centre 1964, Co Cdr 45 Commando 1965, student RAF Staff Coll Bracknell 1966, instr RNC Greenwich 1967, extra equerry to HRH Prince Philip 1968-69, SO in Dept of Cmdt Gen RM 1969, Rifle Co Cdr 41 Commando 1971, student NDC Latimer 1972, staff of CDS 1973, SO HQ Commando Forces 1975, CO RM Poole 1977, Col 1978, COS and asst def attaché Br Def Staff Washington 1979, ADC to HM The Queen 1981-82, Maj-Gen 1982, COS to Cmdt Gen RM 1982-84, dep COS HQ AFNORTH 1984-87; dir Br Digestive Fndn 1987; *Recreations* current affairs, sailing; *Clubs* Army and Navy; *Style—* Maj-Gen John Hardy, CB, LVO; c/o National Westminster Bank, 51 The Strand, Walmer, Deal, Kent

HARDY, Laurence Carey; s of Herbert Ronald Hardy (d 1954); *b* 17 Nov 1929; *Educ* RNC Dartmouth; *m* 1953, Rebeka Ann; 1 s, 3 da; *Career* Lt RN served in Korea and Malaya; dir: Allied Leather Industs Ltd 1967-89, Freshfield Lane Brickworks Ltd 1980-; pres Southern Brick Federation Ltd 1988-91; High Sheriff E Sussex 1976; conservator Ashdown Forest 1977-, chm Franklands Village Housing Assoc Ltd 1987-; *Recreations* shooting, fishing, conservation, gardening; *Style—* Laurence Hardy, Esq; Latchetts Dane Hill, Haywards Heath, W Sussex RH17 7HQ (☎ 0825 790237); Freshfield Lane Brickworks Ltd, Dane Hill, Haywards Heath, W Sussex RH17 7HH (☎ 0825 790350)

HARDY, Peter; MP (Lab) Wentworth 1983-; s of Lawrence Hardy, of Wath-upon-Dearne; *b* 17 July 1931; *Educ* Wath-upon-Dearne GS, Westminster Coll, Univ of Sheffield; *m* 1954, Margaret Anne, *née* Brookes; 1 s; *Career* MP (Lab) Rother Valley 1970-83; PPS: to Sec of State for Environment 1974-76, for Sec 1976-79; vice chm Cncl of Europe Socialist Gp, chm C of E Environment Ctee sponsored by NACODS 1986-90, ldr of Lab delgn to Cncl of Europe 1983-, chm Energy Ctee; Parly Lab Pty; memb: Central Exec Cncl NSPCC, Cncl of World Wildlife Fund UK; Patron Yorkshire Wildlife Tst; *Books* A Lifetime of Badgers (1975); *Style—* Peter Hardy, MP; 53 Sandygate, Wath-upon-Dearne, Rotherham, S Yorkshire (☎ 0709 874590)

HARDY, Richard Charles Chandos; s and h of Lt-Col Sir Rupert Hardy, 4 Bt *qv*; *b* 6 Feb 1945; *Educ* Eton; *m* 1972, Venetia, da of Simon Wingfield Digby, TD, DL, MP; 4 da; *Career* insurance broker; *Recreations* hunting, point-to-pointing, racing; *Clubs* Turf; *Style—* Richard Hardy Esq; Springfield House, Gillingham, Dorset

HARDY, Richard Harry Norman; s of Norman Hardy (d 1938), of Amersham, Bucks, and Gladys Marjorie, *née* Berneys (d 1951); *b* 8 Oct 1923; *Educ* Marlborough, Doncaster Tech Coll (HNC); *m* 30 April 1949, (Anne) Gwenda, da of Leonard Aspinall (d 1961); 2 s (James b 1953, Peter Miles b 1958), 1 da (Anthea Jane b 1950); *Career* apprenticeship locomotive engrg and mgmnt Doncaster LNER 1941-45; mangr engine depots LNER and BR 1949-55: Woodford Halse, Ipswich, Battersea, dist motive power supt (formerly asst) Stratford 1955-62; divnl mangr: Kings Cross 1963-68, Liverpool 1968-73; advsr engrg and res personnel Br Railways Bd 1973-82; memb City Challenge Mgmnt Ctee 1973-87; dir Festiniog Railway 1977-87; chm Steam Locomotive Operators Assoc; CEng, FIMechE; *Books* Steam in the Blood (1971), Railways in the Blood (1985), Beeching, Champion of the Railways ? (1989); *Recreations* family and people, railways, writing, cricket, hunting, riding, dressage, gardening, photography; *Clubs* MCC; *Style—* Richard Hardy, Esq; Greenbank Hse, 20 South Rd, Amersham, Bucks HP6 5LU (☎ 0494 726281)

HARDY, Robert Hugh; JP (Berks 1984); s of Rev Charles Sidney Hardy (d 1965), of Curfew House, Sandwich, Kent, and Eva Meriel Violet, *née* Hodson; *b* 15 Aug 1932; *Educ* Winchester, Merton Coll Oxford (BA, MA); *m* 18 July 1970, Penelope Jean Maxwell, da of Robert Shersron (d 1982), of Ringwell House, Ditcheat, Somerset; 1 s (James b 1975), 1 da (Caroline b 1972); *Career* house master Eton Coll 1969-84 (asst master 1956-87), headmaster Milton Abbey Sch 1987-; govr N Foreland Lodge 1984; *Recreations* walking, fishing, cricket, antique glass; *Style—* Robert Hardy, Esq, JP; The Headmaster's House, Milton Abbey, Blandford Forum, Dorset DT11 ODA (☎ 0258 880500); Dorcas Cottage, Bicknoller, Taunton, Somerset TA4 4EG

HARDY, His Hon Judge; Robert James; s of James Frederick Hardy and Annie, *née* Higinbotham; *b* 12 July 1924; *Educ* Mostyn House, Wrekin, Univ Coll London (LLB); *m* 1951, Maureen Scott; 1 s, 1 da; *Career* barr 1950, circuit judge 1979-; *Style—* His Hon Judge Hardy; Smithy House, Sandlebridge, Little Warford, Cheshire SK9 7TY; Betlem, Mallorca

HARDY, (Timothy Sydney) Robert; CBE (1981); s of late Maj Henry Harrison Hardy, CBE, and Edith Jocelyn, *née* Dugdale; *b* 29 Oct 1925; *Educ* Rugby, Magdalen Coll Oxford (BA); *m* 1, 1952 (m dis), Elizabeth, da of late Sir Lionel Fox, and Lady Fox; 1 s; m 2, 1961 (m dis 1986), Sally, da of Sir Neville Pearson, 2 Bt, and Dame Gladys Cooper, DBE; 2 da; *Career* actor; early work incl: Shakespeare (Memorial Theatre) 1949-51, West End 1951-53, Old Vic Theatre 1953-54, USA 1954, 1956-58, 1963-64 (incl Hamlet and Henry V), Shakespeare (Memorial Theatre Centenary season) 1959; later work incl: Rosmersholm (Comedy Theatre) 1960, The Rehearsal (Globe Theatre) 1961, A Severed Heat (Criterion Theatre) 1963, The Constant Couple (New Theatre) 1967, I've Seen You Cut Lemons (Fortune Theatre) 1969, Habeas Corpus (Lyric Theatre) 1974, Dear Liar (Mermaid Theatre) 1982, Winnie Victoria (Palace Theatre) 1988; TV incl: David Copperfield 1960, Age of Kings 1960, Trouble-Shooters 1969-67, Elizabeth R 1970, Manhunt 1970, Edward VII 1973, All Creatures Great and Small 1978-90 Winston Churchill - The Wilderness Years 1981, Paying Guests 1986, Make and Break 1986, Churchill in The USA 1986, Hot Metal 1987-88, Northanger Abbey 1987; films incl: Torpedo Run 1956, The Spy Who Came in from the Cold, Ten Rillington Place, Young Winston, How I Won The War, Le Silencieux, La Gifle, The Far Pavilions 1983, The Shooting Party 1984, Jenny's War 1985, Paris by Night 1988, War and Remembrance 1988; author of TV documentaries: The Picardy Affair 1962, The Longbow 1972, Horses in our Blood 1977, Gordon of Khartoum 1982; conslt Mary Rose Tst 1979-, tstee WWF 1983-89, memb Bd Tstees Royal Armouries 1984-, chm Berks Bucks and Oxon Naturalists Tst Appeal 1985-90; Hon DLitt Reading 1990; Master Ct Worshipful Co Bowyers 1988-90; *Books* Longbow (1976); *Recreations* archery, horsemanship, bowyery; *Clubs* Buck's, Royal Toxophilite, Br Longbow; *Style—* Robert Hardy, Esq, CBE; Upper Bolney House, Upper Bolney, nr Henley-on-Thames, Oxon RG9 4AQ

HARDY, Lt-Col Sir Rupert John; 4 Bt (UK 1876), of Dunstall Hall, Co Stafford; s of Sir Bertram Hardy, 3 Bt (d 1953), and Violet, da of Hon Sir Edward Chandos Leigh, KCB, KC, JP (2 s of 1 Baron Leigh); *b* 24 Oct 1902; *Educ* Eton, Trinity Hall Cambridge; *m* 2 June 1930, Hon Diana *née* Allsopp, *qv*; 1 s (Richard *qv*), 1 da (Mrs Robert Black *see* Baronetage b 1931); *Career* Lt-Col Life Gds, served WW II 8 Army in W Desert, Palestine, Syria, France; ret from Army 1948; rejoined as RARO 1952, Lt-Col Cmdg Household Cavalry 1952-56; *Recreations* hunting, shooting; *Clubs* Turf; *Style—* Lt-Col Sir Rupert Hardy, Bt; Gulliver's Lodge, Guilsborough, Northampton (☎ 0604 375)

HARDY, Timothy; s of Robert Norman Hardy, of Seer Green, Beaconsfield, Buckinghamshire, and Patricia Margaret May, *née* Keen (d 1985); *b* 17 Feb 1956; *Educ* Royal GS High Wycombe, Balliol Coll Oxford (MA); *Career* admitted slr 1982; asst litigation slr Barlow Lyde & Gilbert 1982-87 (ptnr 1987-); memb: Br Insurance Law Assoc, Law Soc; *Recreations* theatre, film, modern history, cricket, hockey;

Clubs Dulwich Hockey, Nepotists Cricket; *Style*— Timothy Hardy, Esq; Barlow Lyde & Gilbert, Beaufort House, 15 St Botolph St, London EC3A 7NJ (☎ 071 247 2277, fax 071 782 8509, tlx 913281)

HARDY-ROBERTS, Brig Sir Geoffrey Paul; KCVO (1972), CB (1945), CBE (1944, OBE 1941), JP (W Sussex 1960), DL (W Sussex 1964); s of late Alfred Roberts; *b* 16 May 1907; *Educ* Eton, RMC Sandhurst; *m* 1945, Eldred, (d 1987) wid of Col John Ronald Macdonell, DSO (d 1944); *Career* regular cmmn 9 Lancers 1926-37, served WWII, ME, Sicily, Italy, NW Europe, Brig 1943; contested (C) Wimbledon 1945; sec-superintentent Middx Hosp 1946-67; master of HM's Household 1967-73, extra equerry to HM The Queen 1967-, memb W Sussex AHA 1974-81, dep chm King Edward VII Hosp Midhurst 1967-81; High Sheriff Sussex 1965; Offr Legion of Merit (USA) 1945; *Style*— Brig Sir Geoffrey Hardy-Roberts, KCVO, CB, CBE, JP, DL; The Lodge, Bury Gate House, Pulborough, W Sussex RH20 1HA (☎ 0798 831921)

HARDYMAN, Norman Trenchard; CB (1984); s of late Rev Arnold Victor Hardyman, and late Laura Hardyman; *b* 5 Jan 1930; *Educ* Clifton, Christ Church Oxford; *m* 1961, Carol Rebecca Turner; 1 s, 1 da; *Career* princ Miny of Educn 1960 (asst princ 1955), private sec to Sec of State 1966-68, under sec DES 1975-79 (asst sec 1968-75), under sec DHSS 1979-81, sec Univ Grants Ctee 1982-89, sec Univ Funding Cncl 1989-90, memb Univ Grants Ctee Univ of S Pacific 1990-; *Style*— Norman Hardyman, Esq, CB; 16 Rushington Ave, Maidenhead, Berks (☎ 0628 24179); 14 Park Crescent, London W1N 4DH (☎ 071 636 7799)

HARDYMAN, Paul; s of George Harry Hardyman, of Portsmouth, and Eileen Elsie, *née* Atkins; *b* 11 May 1964; *Educ* Great Salterns Secdy Sch Portsmouth, Highbury Tech Coll Portsmouth; *m* 22 June 1985, Hazel Ruth, da of William Parry; 2 s (Robert Paul b 14 May 1986, Mark William George b 6 Oct 1988); *Career* professional footballer; Portsmouth 1983-89: turned professional 1984, debut v Crystal Palace 1984, 135 appearances; transferred for £130,000 to Sunderland 1989- (over 70 appearances); 2 England under 21 caps (v Eire 1985 and v Denmark 1986): promoted to Div 1 with Portsmouth 1987 and Sunderland 1990, preliminary coaching certificate 1988; apprentice carpenter and joiner DOE 1980-83; *Recreations* golf, snooker; *Style*— Paul Hardyman, Esq; Sunderland FC, Roker Park, Grantham Rd, Roker, Sunderland SR6 9SW (☎ 091 5140332)

HARE, Hon Alan Victor; MC (1942); s of 4 Earl of Listowel, and Hon Freda, da of 2 Baron Derwent; *b* 14 March 1919; *Educ* Eton, New Coll Oxford (MA); *m* 1945, Jill, da of late Gordon North; 1 s (Alan b 1948), 1 da (Marcia b 1946); *Career* WWII Europe and Far East (MC); FCO 1947-61 (1 sec Br Embassy Athens 1957-60); dir Pearson Longman 1975-82, chm Industrial and Trade Fairs Holdings 1979-82 (dep chm 1977-79), chm Financial Times Ltd 1978-83 (chief exec 1975-83); pres Soc Civile du Vignoble du Chateau Latour 1983-90; dir: Economist Newspaper Ltd 1975-89 (dep chm 1985-89) dir English Nat Opera 1982-89; tstee Reuters 1985-; *Recreations* music, walking, opera; *Clubs* White's; *Style*— The Hon Alan Hare, MC; Flat 12, 53 Rutland Gate, London SW7 (☎ 071 581 2184)

HARE, Ann, Lady; Barbara Mary Theodora (Ann); da of Joseph Arthur Walton; *m* 1960, as his 3 w, Maj Sir Ralph Hare, 4 Bt (d 1976); 1 da (Mary-Ann b 1961); *Style*— Ann, Lady Hare; Stow Bardolph, King's Lynn, Norfolk PE34 3HU

HARE, Christopher Peter; s of Reginald Charles Hare (d 1980), and Mary Euphemia, *née* Lefroy (d 1988); *b* 6 Nov 1947; *Educ* Dover Coll; *m* (Dorothy) Jane, da of Richard Gough Dowell, of Middleton-on-Sea, Sussex; 2 s (Nicholas Anthony b 28 May 1977, Julian Charles b 17 Nov 1981), 1 da (Rebecca Anne b 14 Feb 1975); *Career* John Dickenson & Co 1966-68, Lyon Trail Attenborough (formerly Lyon Lohr & Sly) 1968-85; dir: Lyon Lohr Group Services 1979 (gp admin 1979-85), Lyon Lohr Int 1980, Fenchurch Underwriting Agencies 1986 (joined 1985); memb Lloyd's 1977-, chm City Forum 1983 (memb 1978, memb Ctee 1980-83); govr Dover Coll 1982- (memb Cncl and Fin Ctee 1982-), chm Ctee Old Dovorian Club 1984-90 (memb 1975-); Freeman City London, Liveryman Worshipful Co of Merchant Taylors 1978; *Recreations* cricket, tennis, squash; *Clubs* MCC, RAC; *Style*— Chistopher Hare, Esq; 40 Doneraile St, London SW6 6EP (☎ 071 736 4218); Fenchurch Underwriting Agencies Ltd, 136 Minories, London EC3N 1QN (☎ 071 488 2388, fax 071 481 9467, telex 884442)

HARE, Christopher William Trelawny; s of Wing Cdr Bertram William Trelawny Hare (d 1959), of S Devon, and Violet Evelyn Seaforth, *née* Fisher; *b* 17 April 1935; *Educ* Blundells, RAC; *m* 7 Aug 1965, Lavinia Frances, da of George Ronald Pigé Leschallas, of Kent; 3 s (Henry b 1966, Jonathan b 1968, James b 1971); *Career* farmer and landowner; *Recreations* fishing, shooting; *Style*— Christopher W T Hare, Esq; Henceford Farm, Black Dog, Crediton, Tiverton (☎ 860342)

HARE, David; s of Clifford Theodore Rippon, and Agnes Cockburn Hare; *b* 5 June 1947; *Educ* Lancing, Jesus Coll Cambridge; *m* 1970 (m dis 1980), Margaret Matheson; 2 s, 1 da; *Career* playwright; *Plays* Slag (1970), The Great Exhibition (1972), Brassneck (with Howard Brenton, 1973), Knuckle (1974), Teeth 'n' Smiles (1975), Fanshen (1975), Plenty (1978), A Map of the World (1983), Pravda (with Howard Brenton, 1985), The Bay at Nice and Wrecked Eggs (1986), The Knife (opera with Nick Bicat and Tim Rose Price, 1987), The Secret Rapture (1988), Racing Demon (1990); *Films* Wetherby (written and dir, 1985), Plenty (1985), Paris By Night (written and dir, 1988), Strapless (written and dir, 1988); *TV Plays* Licking Hitler (1978), Dreams of Leaving (1980), Saigon (1983), Heading Home (1991); *Style*— David Hare, Esq; c/o Margaret Ramsay Ltd, 14a Goodwin's Court, St Martins Lane, London WC2

HARE, Diane Margaret; da of Rowland Hare, of Ecclesall, Sheffield, and Edna, *née* Jepson; *b* 9 Dec 1948; *Educ* Abbeydale Girls' GS Sheffield, St Anne's Coll Oxford (BA, MA); *Career* barr Middle Temple 1973; lectr in law Lanchester Poly Coventry 1972-74, Univ of Manchester (dir studies in accounting and law 1984-) 1974-, writer and speaker corpn insolvency, commercial and co law; memb: res team Int Accounting Harmonization Network (and res cmmnd by Home Office), justice memb: Legal Action Gp, Child Poverty Action Gp, Stockport Garrick Theatre; local preacher Stockport Methodist Church; *Recreations* theatre, music, poetry, travelling; *Style*— Diane Hare; Faculty of Law, Univ of Manchester, Manchester M13 9PL (☎ 061 275 3560)

HARE, Hon Mrs Richard; Dora; da of late Mark Gordine, of St Petersburg, Russia; *m* 1936, Hon Richard Gilbert Hare, (d 1966 2 s 4 Earl of Listowel); *Career* FRBS; *Style*— The Hon Mrs Richard Hare; Dorich House, Kingston Vale, London SW15

HARE, John Neville; s of late Capt Lancelot Geldart Hare, MC (d 1957), and Esther Maria, *née* Whales (d 1969); *b* 11 Dec 1934; *Educ* St Edward's Oxford; *m* 17 Sept 1966, Pippa, da of Harding McGregor Dunnett, of Eliot Vale, Blackheath, London; 3 da (Charlotte b 1968, Henrietta b 1970, Emily b 1974); *Career* Lt Oxfordshire and Buckinghamshire LI Royal W Africa Frontier Force 1954-55; sr dist offr Colonial Serv Northern Nigeria 1957-64; dir Macmillan Education Publishers 1966-74, author and conslt Hodder and Stoughton Publishers 1980-89; UN Environment Prog 1989-; *Books* (under pseudonym of Dan Fulani): Hijack (1979), No Condition is Permanent (1979), Primary Hausa Course (1979), Sauna and the Bank Robbers (1980), Sauna, Secret Agent; Sauna to the Rescue (1981), Medicinal Pots of the Cham and Mwana Tribes (1985), No Telephone to Heaven (1985), God's Case No Appeal (1985), The Fight For Life (1986), The Power of Corruption (1986), Flight 800 (1986), The Price of Liberty (1987), Sauna and the Drug Pedlars (1988), Rhino's Horn (1988), Leopard's Coat (1989), Elephant's Tusk (1990); *Recreations* hunting, amateur dramatics, travel, writing; *Clubs* East India; *Style*— John Hare, Esq; School Farm, Benenden, Kent (☎ 0580 240 755)

HARE, Prof (Frederick) Kenneth; CC (1987, OC 1978); s of Frederick Hare; *b* 5 Feb 1919; *Educ* Windsor GS, King's Coll London (BSc), Univ of Montreal (PhD); *m* 1, 1941 (m dis 1952), Suzanne Bates; 1 s; m 2, 1953, Helen Neilson, da of Alvin Morrill (d 1954), of Montreal; 1 s, 1 da; *Career* served WWII Flt Lt RCAFVR; geographer; prof in geography Univ of Toronto 1969-, provost Trinity Coll Univ of Toronto 1979-86, chllr Trent Univ 1988-; IMO prize of the World Meteorological Orgn 1988; FRSC; Order of Ontario 1989; *Clubs* York (Toronto); *Style*— Prof F Kenneth Hare, CC; 301 Lakeshore Rd West, Oakville, Ontario, Canada L6K 1G2 (☎ 010 1 416 849 1374)

HARE, Philip Leigh; s of Edward Philip Leigh Hare (d 1954) and his 3 w, Lady Kathleen, *née* Stanhope (d 1971), da of 9 Earl of Harrington, and widow of Edward Morant, JP, of Brockenhurst Park, Hants; hp of cous, Sir Thomas Hare, 5 Bt, *qv*; *b* 13 Oct 1922; *m* 4 Nov 1950, Anne Lisle, 2 da of Maj Geoffrey Nicholson, CBE, MC; 1 s (Nicholas b 1955), 1 da (Louisa (twin) b 1955); *Style*— Philip Hare, Esq; The Nettings, Hook Norton, Oxon

HARE, (Thomas) Richard; *see*: Pontefract, Bishop of

HARE, Lady Rose Amanda; *née* Bligh; da (by 2 m) of 9 Earl of Darnley; *b* 1935; *m* 1961, Sir Thomas Hare, 5 Bt, *qv*; 2 da (Lucy b 1962, Elizabeth b 1964); *Style*— The Lady Rose Hare; Stow Bardolph, King's Lynn, Norfolk PE34 3HU

HARE, Sir Thomas; 5 Bt (UK 1818), of Stow Hall, Norfolk; s of Maj Sir Ralph Leigh Hare, 4 Bt (d 1976, an earlier Btcy in the family, dating from 1641, died out in 1764), and his 1 w, Doreen, da of Maj Sir Richard Bagge, DSO; *b* 27 July 1930; *Educ* Eton, Magdalene Coll Cambridge; *m* 1961, Lady Rose Amanda, *née* Bligh, *qv*; 2 da; *Heir* cous, Philip Leigh Hare, *qv*; *Career* Lt RARO Coldstream Gds; chartered surveyor, ARICS; landowner and farmer; *Clubs* RAC; *Style*— Sir Thomas Hare, Bt; Stow Bardolph, King's Lynn, Norfolk PE34 3HU

HARE DUKE, Michael Geoffrey; *see*: St Andrews, Dunkeld and Dunblane, Bishop of

HAREWOOD, 7 Earl of (UK 1812); George Henry Hubert Lascelles; KBE (1986); also Baron Harewood (GB 1796) and Viscount Lascelles (UK 1812); s of 6 Earl of Harewood, KG, GCVO, DSO, TD (d 1947), and HRH Princess Mary (The Princess Royal), CI, GCVO, GBE, RRC, TD, CD (d 1965), only da of HM King George V, *see* Debretts Peerage, Royal Family section; *b* 7 Feb 1923; *Educ* Eton, King's Coll Cambridge; *m* 1, 29 Sept 1949 (m dis 1967; she m 2, 1973, as his 2 w, Rt Hon Jeremy Thorpe), Maria Donata Nanetta Paulina Gustava Erwina Wilhelmina (Marion), o da of late Erwin Stein; 3 s (Viscount Lascelles b 1950, Hon James b 1953, Hon Jeremy b 1955); m 2, 31 July 1967, Patricia Elizabeth, o da of Charles Tuckwell, of Sydney, and former w of (Louis) Athol Shmith (d 1990); 1 s (Hon Mark b 1964); *Heir* s, Viscount Lascelles, *qv*; *Career* Capt late Grenadier Guards, serv WWII (wounded, POW); ADC to Earl of Athlone 1945-46; ed Opera magazine 1950-53, asst to David Webster at The Royal Opera Covent Garden 1953-60; artistic dir: Leeds Festival 1956-74, Edinburgh Festival 1961-65, Adelaide Festival 1988; md ENO 1972-85, govr BBC 1985-87, pres Br Bd of Film Classification 1985-; pres Leeds United Football Club 1962-, Football Assoc 1963-72; chllr Univ of York 1963-67; Hon LLD Leeds 1959, Aberdeen 1966, Hon DMus Hull 1962, Janáček Medal 1978, Hon RAM 1983, Hon DLitt Bradford 1983, Hon Doctorate York Univ 1983, hon fell King's Coll Cambridge 1984, hon memb Royal Northern Coll of Music 1984; Austrian Great Silver Medal of Honour 1959, Lebanese Order of the Cedar 1970; *Books* Kobbé's Complete Opera Book (ed), The Tongs and the Bones (memoirs 1981), The Illustrated Kobbé; *Recreations* looking at pictures, shooting, watching cricket, football, films; *Style*— The Rt Hon the Earl of Harewood, KBE; Harewood House, Leeds, LS17 9LG

HARFORD, Anstice, Lady; Anstice Marion; yst da of Sir Alfred Ernest Tritton, 2 Bt (d 1939), and Agnetta Elspeth, *née* Campbell (d 1960); *b* 17 July 1909; *m* 9 April 1931, Lt-Col Sir George Arthur Harford, 2 Bt, OBE (d 1967); 2 s (Sir Timothy *qv*, Piers b 1937), 1 da (Mrs Jeremy Glyn *see* Peerage B Wolverton); *Style*— Anstice, Lady Harford; Sutton Manor, Sutton Scotney, Winchester, Hants SO21 3JX (☎ 0962 760157)

HARFORD, Sir James Dundas; KBE (1956), CMG (1943); s of late Rev Dundas Harford; *b* 7 Jan 1899; *Educ* Repton, Balliol Coll Oxford; *m* 1, 1932, Countess Thelma, da of Count Albert Metaxa; 1 s; m 2, 1937, Lilias, da of Maj Archibald Campbell; 2 da; *Career* govr and C-in-C St Helena 1954-58; *Style*— Sir James Harford, KBE, CMG; Links Cottage, Rother Rd, Seaford, East Sussex (☎ 0323 892115)

HARFORD, Mark John; s and h of Sir Timothy Harford, 3 Bt; *b* 6 Aug 1964; *Style*— Mark Harford, Esq

HARFORD, Michael Gordon (Mick); s of John Harford, of 1a Stamford Ave, Humbledon, Sunderland, and Lydia, *née* Furness; *b* 12 Feb 1959; *Educ* St Josephs Secdy Modern; partner, S L White; 1 s (William Michael Joseph); *Career* professional footballer; 126 appearances Lincoln City 1977-80, 19 appearances Newcastle Utd 1980-81, 40 appearances Bristol City 1981-82, 109 appearances Birmingham City 1982-84, 186 appearances Luton Town 1984-90, transferred to Derby County 1990-; 2 England caps 1988-89 (1 B cap 1988); *Recreations* golf, cricket, reading; *Style*— Mick Harford, Esq; Derby County FC, Baseball Ground, Shaftesbury Crescent, Derby DE3 8NB (☎ 0332 40105)

HARFORD, Philip Hugh; er s of Mark William Harford (d 1969), of Horton Hall, Chipping Sodbury, and Little Sodbury Manor, Glos, and Elizabeth Ellen, da of late Brig-Gen Philip Leveson-Gower, CMG, DSO, DL, of Saltings, Yarmouth, IOW; gs of Hugh Wyndham Luttrell Harford (d 1920), who acquired Horton Hall; descended from William Harford, of Marshfield, Glos, living 1602 (*see* Burke's Landed Gentry, 18 edn, vol I, 1965); *b* 14 Aug 1946; *m* 11 June 1982, Willa, yr da of William Joseph Franklin, of North Lodge, Brill, Bucks; *Career* served LI; *Clubs* Royal Yacht Sqdn; *Style*— Philip Harford, Esq

HARFORD, Piers Scandrett; s of Sir George Arthur Harford, Bart (d 1967), and Anstice Marion, *née* Tritton; *b* 9 Sept 1937; *Educ* Eton, Worcester Coll Oxford (BA); *m* 1, Hyacinthe Cecilia, da of Nigel Walter Hoare; 1 s (Henry Scandrett b 17 July 1963), 1 da Anstice b 12 May 1965); m 2, Patricia Jane, da of Air Cdr Patrick Burnett; *Career* stockbroker; ptnr B S Stock Son & Co Bristol 1965 (joined 1961), Albert E Sharp 1990-; memb Stock Exchange 1965; *Recreations* various; *Style*— Piers Harford, Esq; The Old Rectory, Great Somerford, nr Chippenham, Wilts (☎ 0249 720135); Albert E Sharp & Co, Spectrum, Bond St, Bristol BS1 3DE (☎ 0272 260051, fax 0272 251869, car 0836 251 458)

HARFORD, Raymond Thomas (Ray); s of Thomas Harford, of Chelmsford, Essex, and Violet, *née* Breton; *b* 1 June 1945; *Educ* St Judes Southwark, Archbishop Temples Lambeth; *m* Maureen Rosemary, da of Charles McCall; 1 s (Paul Tomas b 21 Oct 1974); *Career* professional football manager; player: began career with Charlton Athletic 1964, 55 appearances Exeter City, 4 seasons with Lincoln City, Mansfield Town, Port Vale, Colchester Utd (player then coach); coach then mangr Fulham, coach then mangr Luton Town (mangr 1987-89); Wimbledon: coach March 1990, briefly caretaker mangr, mangr Dec 1990-; Littlewoods Cup winners Luton Town 1988 (runners-up 1989), Simod Cup winners 1988; *Recreations* reading; *Style*— Ray Harford, Esq; Wimbledon Football Club, Plough Lane, Wimbledon, London SW19 (☎ 081 946

6311)

HARFORD, Sir (John) Timothy; 3 Bt (UK 1934), of Falcondale, Co Cardigan; s of Lt-Col Sir George Arthur Harford, 2 Bt, OBE (d 1967), and Lady Harford *qv*, *née* Anstice Marion Tritton; *b* 6 July 1932; *Educ* Harrow, Worcester Coll Oxford, Harvard Business Sch; *m* 12 May 1962, Carolyn Jane, o da of Brig Guy John de Wette Mullens, OBE (d 1981), of North House, Weyhill, Andover; 2 s (Mark b 1964, Simon b 1966), 1 da (Clare b 1963); *Career* dir Singer & Friedlander Ltd 1970-88; dep chm: Wolseley Group plc 1983-, Wesleyan Assurance Society 1987-; dir: Provincial Group plc, ACT Group plc, Wagon Industries Holdings plc chm Kwiksave Group plc 1990-; *Clubs* Boodle's; *Style*— Sir Timothy Harford, Bt; South House, South Littleton, Evesham, Worcs (☎ 0386 830478)

HARGRAVE, David Grant; s of (Frank) Edward Hargrave, of 7 Henllys Rd, Cyncoed, Cardiff, and Margaret Constance Mabel, *née* Grant; *b* 11 April 1951; *Educ* Howardian HS Cardiff, Univ of Birmingham (BCom, MSc); *m* 13 Dec 1969, Celia, da of Harry Hawksworth (d 1963); 1 s (Neil David b 30 July 1974), 1 da (Emma Louise b 17 June 1970); *Career* actuary Duncan C Fraser & Co (later William M Mercer Fraser Ltd) 1973-79, ptnr Bacon & Woodrow (formerly TG Arthur Hargrave) 1979-, non-exec dir Homeowner's Friendly Soc 1982-; sec and treas Birmingham Actuarial Soc 1979-81; Nat Assoc Pension Funds Ltd (W Midlands): treas 1982-85, sec 1985-87, chm 1987-89; govr Yew Tree Sch 1988-; FIA 1977; *Recreations* long distance running, swimming, windsurfing, rugby; *Style*— David Hargrave, Esq; 41 Calthorpe Rd, Edgbaston, Birmingham B15 1TS (☎ 021 456 3040, fax 021 456 3041)

HARGREAVE, Colin Oliver; s of Oliver Hargreave (d 1948), of The Willows, Lytham, and Dorothy, *née* Whipp (d 1944); *b* 8 Jan 1915; *Educ* Le Rosey Switzerland, Hamburg Poly Germany; *m* 1951, Rachel Averina Grace (d 1987), da of Charles Sackville-Hamilton; 1 s (Jeremy David Hamilton b 26 Aug 1955); *Career* trainee pilot RAF 1938-43 (invalided out); stockbroker; Creighton Brothers & Townley Liverpool 1932-34, Bailey Kindersley 1934-36, sr ptnr MW Hargreave Hale and Co (founded by gf 1897) 1948- (joined 1943); chm Lytham St Annes Branch of NW kidney Res Assoc; memb Stock Exchange 1940-; *Recreations* golf, skiing, fishing; *Clubs* Royal Lytham St Anne's Golf; *Style*— Colin Hargreave, Esq; The Penthouse, The Willows, 10 Clifton Drive, Lytham, Lancs (☎ 0253 736455); MW Hargreave Hale & Co, 8-10 Springfield Rd, Blackpool, Lancashire (☎ 0532 21575, fax 0253 29511)

HARGREAVE, Dr Timothy Bruce; s of Lt Cdr John Michael Hargreave, VRD, and Margaret Isobel Hargreave; *b* 23 March 1944; *Educ* Harrow, Univ of London (MB BS, MS); *m* 27 March 1971, Molly; 2 da (Alison Lucinda b 1972, Sophie Louise b 1976); *Career* sr lectr Univ of Edinburgh, hon conslt urological and transplant surgn Lothian Health Bd; memb Steering Ctee WHO Infertility Task Force, chm Br Andrology Soc, memb Cncl Br Assoc of Urological Surgns, former sec Scot Urological Soc; FRCSE, FRCS; *Books* Male Infertility (1983), Practical Urological Endoscopy (1988), Management of Male Infertility (1990); *Recreations* skiing; *Style*— Dr Timothy Hargreave; Dept of Surgery, Western General Hospital, Edinburgh (☎ 031 332 2525)

HARGREAVES, Andrew Raikes; MP (C) Birmingham Hall Green 1987-; s of Col David William Hargreaves, and Judith Anne *née* Currie; *b* 15 May 1955; *Educ* Eton, St Edmund Hall Oxford (MA); *m* 1978, Fiona Susan, da of Guy William Dottridge; 2 s (William b 1985, Thomas b 1986); *Career* former auctioneer and valuer Christies 1977-81; exec Hill Samuel 1981-85; asst dir: Sawwa International 1983-85, Schroders 1985-87; *Recreations* fishing, gardening, walking; *Clubs* Boodle's; *Style*— Andrew Hargreaves, Esq, MP; 5 Glendevon Road, Birmingham, B14 5DD; House of Commons, Westminster, London SW1 (☎ 071 219 3000)

HARGREAVES, Maj (Edgar) Charles Stewart; s of Edgar Horace Hargreaves (d 1968), of Christchurch, NZ, and Ellen Margaret, *née* Stewart (d 1951); *b* 7 Sept 1917; *Educ* St Andrew's Coll Christchurch NZ; *m* 1, 19 Dec 1945 (m dis 1951), Betty, da of the late Duncan McFarlane, of NZ; 2 s (Guy b 22 March 1946, David b 21 Oct 1948); m 2, June 1952 (m dis 1955), Phyllis Kathleen Anderson; m 3, 14 Oct 1965, Valerie Dawn, da of Donald John Mackay (d 1968), of Berks; *Career* cmmnd Supplementary Reserve & Offrs Royal Armoured Corps 1937, NZ Divnl Cavalry Regt 1939-40, North Irish Horse 1940, 2 Cmd 1941, 11 Special Air Serv Bn, 1 Parachute Bn 1941, VIII King's Royal Irish Hussars, Parachute Instr, special serv with SOE Eastern Euro 1942-43 (POW 1943), Intelligence Unit in Halmahera Gp 1945; Intelligence Servs 1956, private sec Govr of Trinidad and Tobago 1957-58, comptroller to Duke of Bedford 1958-60, bursar Heathfields Sch 1962-63, Queen's Messenger 1963-76, opened Hatchlands Finishing Sch for Girls Surrey 1965, moved Finishing Sch to Scotland 1980, ret 1987; *Clubs* Cavalry & Guards', Special Forces, Highland; *Style*— Maj Charles Hargreaves; Cantray House, Croy, Inverness-shire IV1 2PW (☎ 06678 424)

HARGREAVES, David; s of Herbert Hargreaves (d 1959); *b* 3 June 1930; *Educ* Pocklington Sch; *m* 1978, Jill, da of Joseph Fuller (d 1977); 4 children; *Career* Lt E Yorks Regt, Malaya; chm: Hirst and Mallinson to 1980, Hestair plc and subsidiaries; FCA; *Recreations* sailing, golf, gardening, squash; *Clubs* Royal Ascot Squash, Foxhills Golf; *Style*— David Hargreaves Esq

HARGREAVES, Prof David Harold; s of Clifford Hargreaves (d 1977), and Marion, *née* Bradley (d 1961); *b* 31 Aug 1939; *Educ* Bolton Sch, Christ's Coll Cambridge (MA, PhD), Univ of Oxford (MA, DPhil); *Career* reader Dept of Educn Univ of Manchester 1964-79 (formerly lectr and sr lectr), reader in educn Univ of Oxford 1979-84 (fell Jesus Coll), chief inspr ILEA 1984-88, prof of educn Univ of Cambridge 1988- (fell Wolfson Coll); FRSA 1984; *Books* Social Relations in a Secondary School (1967), Interpersonal Relations and Education (1972), Deviance in Classrooms (1975), The Challenge for the Comprehensive School (1982); *Recreations* opera; *Clubs* Athenaeum; *Style*— Prof David Hargreaves; Dept of Educn, Univ of Cambridge, 17 Trumpington St, Cambridge CB2 1QA (☎ 0223 332 888)

HARGREAVES, Ian Richard; s of Ronald Hargreaves (d 1988), and Edna, *née* Cheetham; *b* 18 June 1951; *Educ* Burnley GS, Altrincham GS, Queens' Coll Cambridge; *m* 20 March 1972, Elizabeth Anne, da of Charles Crago, of Cornwall; 1 s (Ben b 20 Oct 1975), 1 da (Kelda b 23 June 1977); *Career* Bradford & District Newspapers 1973-76, Financial Times 1976-87, dir BBC News and Current Affrs 1987-90, dep ed Financial Times 1990-; *Recreations* tennis, football; *Style*— Ian Hargreaves, Esq; Financial Times, 1 Southwark Bridge, London SE1 9HZ (☎ 071 873 3000)

HARGREAVES, Prof John Desmond; s of Arthur Swire Hargreaves (d 1950), of Colne, Lancs, and Margaret Hilda, *née* Duckworth (d 1968); *b* 25 Jan 1924; *Educ* Ermysted's GS Skipton, Bootham, Univ of Manchester (BA, MA); *m* 30 Sept 1950, Sheila Elizabeth, da of George Samuel Wilks (d 1960), of Stockton, Warwickshire; 2 s (Alastair b 1952, Nicholas b and d 1957), 2 da (Sara b 1953, Catherine b 1959); *Career* 2 Lt The Loyal Regt 1944, served Germany 1945, Malaya 1945-46, T/Capt 1946; asst lectr and lectr in history Univ of Manchester 1948-52, sr lectr Fourah Bay Coll Sierra Leone 1952-54, Burnett-Fletcher prof of history Univ of Aberdeen 1962-85 (lectr 1954-62); visiting prof: Union Coll Schenectady NY 1960-61, Univ of Ibadan 1970-71; Hon DLitt Univ of Sierra Leone 1985; FRHistS 1963; *Books* Prelude to the Partition of West Africa (1963), West Africa Partitioned (two vols, 1974 and 1985), The End of Colonial Rule in West Africa (1979), Aberdeenshire to Africa (1981), Decolonisation in Africa (1988); *Recreations* hill walking, lawn tennis, theatre; *Style*— Prof John Hargreaves; Balcluain, 22 Raemoir Rd, Banchory, Kincardine AB3 3UJ (☎ 03302 2655)

HARGREAVES, Joseph Kenneth (Ken); MP (C) Hyndburn 1983-; s of James and Mary Hargreaves; *b* 1 March 1939; *Educ* St Mary's Coll Blackburn, Manchester Coll of Commerce; *Career* ACIS; *Recreations* music, theatre, travel; *Style*— Ken Hargreaves, Esq, MP; House of Commons, London SW1

HARGREAVES, Dr (George) Kenneth; s of Albert Hargreaves (d 1969), of St Annes on Sea, Lancs, and Ada, *née* Lord (d 1989); *b* 24 Oct 1928; *Educ* King Edward VII Sch Lytham, Univ of Edinburgh (MB ChB); *m* 24 March 1956, Hazel, da of James Nutter (d 1982), of Clithere, Lancs; 2 s (Timothy b 17 Feb 1957, John b 23 Sept 1961), 2 da (Gillian b 27 Feb 1959, Catherine b 10 Sept 1964); *Career* Nat Serv RAMC 1952-54, Capt 1953, OC MRS Hook of Holland 1954; conslt dermatologist: NW RHA 1962, Mersey RHA 1974, Trent RHA 1989; lectr Northern Coll of Chiropody 1962-86, hon lectr Univ of Manchester 1983; pres N of Eng Dermatological Soc 1981 (sec 1963-79); FRCPE 1971, FRSM; *Recreations* gardening, walking, music; *Style*— Dr Kenneth Hargreaves; 23 St John St, Manchester M3 4DT (☎ 061 834 5649)

HARGREAVES, (Thomas) Peter; s of Arthur Hargreaves, of Lancs, and Phylis Mary, *née* Seymour (d 1987); *b* 24 Oct 1934; *Educ* Shrewsbury, Queen Elizabeth's GS Blackburn; *m* 1958, Maureen Elizabeth, da of Francis Joseph Higginson (d 1985); 4 s (Arthur b 1959, Mark b 1960, Craig b 1966, Boyd b 1975); *Career* md: Enfield MFG Co Ltd, Hilden MFG Co Ltd, J B Smith and Co Ltd; *Style*— Peter Hargreaves, Esq; 10 Royds Avenue, Hollins Lane, Accrington, Lancs BB5 2LE (☎ 0254 233462); Hilden MFG Co Ltd, Clifton Mill, Pickup St, Oswald Twistle, Accrington, Lancs (☎ 0254 391131, fax 0254 386108)

HARGREAVES, Richard Strachan; MC (1944); s of Col James Hargreaves, of Parkhill, Lyndhurst, Hants (d 1980), and Mary, *née* Barton (d 1975); *b* 26 Sept 1919; *Educ* Dauntsey's Sch West Lavington Wiltshire; *m* 9 Oct 1945, Kathleen Jenny, da of Herbert Truman Nightingale (d 1951), of Harnham, Salisbury, Wilts; 1 s (Timothy b 28 June 1952), 3 da (Joanna b 23 Oct 1947, Judy b 12 Dec 1949, Sally (twin) b 12 Dec 1949); *Career* 2 Lt Royal Fusiliers TA 1939, Capt 12 Bn Royal Fusiliers 1942, Capt and Adj Parachute Regt 1942, Maj and Co Cdr 4 Bn Parachute Regt 1943; overseas serv: N Africa, Italy, France, Greece and Palestine; staff coll 1944, Bde Maj 4 Br Div Greece 1945-46, demobbed 1946; Peter Merchant Ltd 1946-56 (exec dir 1952-56), Gallaher Ltd 1956-68 (exec dir 1965-68), exec dir Savoy Hotel Ltd 1968-84, chm J A Devenish plc 1980-86 (non-exec dir 1986-90); Westminster City Cncllr 1973-77, dep Lord Mayor Westminster 1977; Freeman City of London 1960, Liveryman Worshipful Co Tobacco Pipe Makers and Tobacco Blenders (Master 1976); *Recreations* shooting, sailing, skiing, theatre; *Style*— Richard Hargreaves, Esq, MC; Church Walk, Little Bredy, Dorchester, Dorset (☎ 0308 482 356)

HARGROVES, Brig Sir (Robert) Louis; CBE (1965), DL (Staffs 1974); s of William Robert Hargroves (d 1946); *b* 10 Dec 1917; *Educ* St John's Coll Southsea; *m* 1940, Eileen Elizabeth, da of Lt-Col W M Anderson, CIE (d 1947); 4 da; *Career* served WWII Sicily and Italy, Brig 1964, Col The Staffordshire Regt (The Prince of Wales') 1971-77; kt 1987; *Recreations* field sports; *Style*— Brig Sir Louis Hargroves, CBE, DL; Hyde Cottage, Temple Guiting, Cheltenham, Glos GL54 5RT (☎ 0451 850 242)

HARINGTON, Gen Sir Charles Henry Pepys; GCB (1969, KCB 1964, CB 1961), CBE (1957, OBE 1953), DSO (1944), MC (1940); s of Col Hastings Harington (ka 1916), and Dorothy, da of Hon Walter Courtenay Pepys, (1914) 5 s of 1 Earl of Cottenham (Lord High Chllr of England 1836-41, and 1846-50); *b* 5 May 1910; *Educ* Malvern, Sandhurst; *m* 1942, Victoire Williams-Freeman; 1 s (Guy b 1946), 2 da (Louise (Hon Mrs Alan Gordon Walker) b 1949, Clare (Mrs Julian Calder) b 1956); *Career* cmmnd Cheshire Regt 1930, served WWII NW Europe Co and Bn Cdr, CO 1 Para 1949, Cdr 49 Bde Kenya 1955, Cmdt Sch of Infantry 1958, GOC 3 Div 1959, Cmdt Army Staff Coll 1961, C-in-C Middle East Cmd 1963, DCGS 1966, Chief of Personnel and Logistics to the 3 Services 1968-71, ADC (Gen) to HM The Queen 1969-71; vice pres Star and Garter Home; pres Hurlingham Club; *Style*— Gen Sir Charles Harington, GCB, CBE, DSO, MC; c/o The Huntingham Club, Ranelagh Gardens, London SW6

HARINGTON, David Richard; s of His Honour John Charles Dundas Harington, QC (decd), and Lavender Cecilia Harington (d 1982); hp of bro, Sir Nicholas Harington, 14 Bt *qv*; *b* 25 June 1944; *Educ* Westminster, ChCh Oxford; *m* 1983, Deborah Jane, da of Maurice William Catesby, MC, of Long Compton, Warks; 2 s (John b 1984, Christopher b 1986); *Style*— David Harington Esq; 7 Vale Grove, London W3 7QP (☎ 081 740 8382)

HARINGTON, Guy Charles; s of Gen Sir Charles Harington, GCB, CBE, DSO, MC, of London, and Victoire Marion, *née* Williams-Freeman; *b* 12 Dec 1946; *Educ* Malvern, Univ Coll Oxford (MA), Loughborough Univ of Technol (MSc); *m* 8 Sept 1984, Kay Elizabeth; 1 s (Charles Hasting b 1986), 1 da (Zara Elizabeth b 1988); *Career* BP 1969-71, dir J Henry Schroder Wagg & Co Ltd 1985- (joined 1971); *Recreations* swimming, skiing, music, reading; *Clubs* Hurlingham; *Style*— Guy Harington, Esq; 120 Cheapside, London EC2

HARINGTON, Dr Judith Mary; da of Herbert William Hutton, of Alhampton, Somerset, and Audrey Ellen, *née* Horton; *b* 17 April 1955; *Educ* Burton Sch for Girls Somerset, Univ of Southampton Med Sch (BM), Univ of Auckland (Dip Obstetrics and Gynaecology); *m* 27 Dec 1986, Henry William Berkeley Harington, s of Maj John Berkeley Harington, of Woking, Surrey; 1 s (James b 1988); *Career* registrar radiology Christchurch NZ 1980-83, sr registrar radiology Southampton 1983-86, conslt radiology Kingston upon Thames 1987-; fundraiser: hosp charities Br Ski Club for the Disabled; memb: BMA 1983, Br Med Ultrasound Soc 1986; FRACR 1982, FRCR 1986; *Recreations* windsurfing, sailing, skiing, photography; *Style*— Dr Judith Harington; X-Ray Department, Kingston Hospital, Wolverton Aveneu, Kingston upon Thames, Surrey (☎ 01 546 7711 Ext 352)

HARINGTON, Kenneth Douglas Evelyn Herbert; s of His Honour Edward Harington, JP (d 1937; 3 s of Sir Richard Harington, 11 Bt, JP, DL), and Louisa Muriel, *née* Vernon; bro Vernon Harington *qv*; *b* 30 Sept 1911; *Educ* Stowe; *m* 1, 1 March 1939, Lady Cecilia Bowes-Lyon (d 1947), er da of 15 Earl of Strathmore and Kinghorne, JP, DL, bro of HM Queen Elizabeth The Queen Mother; 2 s (Michael b 9 Aug 1951, Jonathan b 14 March 1953); m 2, 28 July 1950, Maureen Helen, da of Brig-Gen Sir Robert McCalmont, KCVO, CBE, DSO; *Career* served WWII, NW Europe, Maj Coldstream Gds; called to the Bar Inner Temple 1952; dep judge Crown Ct 1965, met stipendiary magistrate 1967-84; hon attaché Br Legation Stockholm 1930-32; *Recreations* shooting, fishing, gardening; *Style*— Kenneth Harington, Esq; Orchard End, Upper Oddington, Moreton-in-Marsh, Glos (☎ 0451 30989)

HARINGTON, Sir Nicholas John; 14 Bt (E 1611), of Ridlington, Rutland; s of His Hon late John Charles Dundas Harington, QC (s of Sir Richard Harington, 12 Bt); suc uncle, Sir Richard Harington, 13 Bt, 1981; *b* 14 May 1942; *Educ* Eton, ChCh Oxford; *Heir* bro, David Richard Harington, *qv*; *Career* barr; joined Civil Serv 1972; *Style*— Sir Nicholas Harington, Bt; The Ring o'Bells, Whitbourne, Worcester WR6 5RT

HARINGTON, (Edward Henry) Vernon; s of His Honour Edward Harington (d 1937; 3 s of Sir Richard Harington, 11 Bt, JP, DL), and Louisa Muriel, *née* Vernon (d 1963);

bro of Kenneth Harington, *qv*; *b* 13 Sept 1907; *Educ* Eton; *m* 1, 1937 (m dis 1949), Mary, da of Louis Egerton (ka 1917, s of Sir Alfred Egerton, KCVO, CB, and Hon Mary, *née* Ormsby-Gore, er da of 2 Baron Harlech) and Jane, er surviving da of Rev Lord Victor Seymour (s of 5 Marquess of Hertford, GCB, PC, DL); 1 da (Mrs Sidney Whitteridge b 1941) and 1 da decd; m 2, 1950, Mary Johanna Jean, JP, da of late Lt-Col R Cox, MC; 2 da (Marie Louisa (Mrs Robin Pagan Taylor) b 1951, Susan (Mrs David Scott) b 1953); *Career* served WWII, Maj Coldstream Gds and in War Office; called to the Bar 1930; ps to Lord Chllr and dep sergjeant-at-arms House of Lords 1934-40, served on Control Cmmn for Austria in the legal div 1945, asst sec to Lord Chllr for Commissions of the Peace 1945-46, a dep judge advocate 1946, AJAG 1955; dep chm Herefordshire QS 1969-71, recorder of Crown Ct 1972-74; cllr Malvern Hills Dist Cncl 1979-87; JP Herefordshire 1969-71; chm Hereford, Worcester, Warwicks and W Midlands Regnl Agric Wages Ctee; *Recreations* shooting, fishing; *Style*— Vernon Harington, Esq; Woodlands House, Whitbourne, Worcester (☎ 0886 21437)

HARKER FARRAND, Prof Margaret Florence; da of Dr Thomas Henry Harker (d 1947), of Southport, Lancashire and Ethel Dean, *née* Dyson (d 1975); *b* 17 Jan 1920; *Educ* Howell's Sch Denbigh (Draper's Co), Southport Sch of Art, The Polytechnic Regent St; *m* 20 Dec 1972, Richard George Farrand, s of Frederick George Farrand; *Career* photographer, historian, lecturer, author; architectural photographer 1941-59; The Polytechnic of Central London (formerly The Polytechnic Regent St) 1943-1980: lectr Sch of Photography 1943-59, head of Sch of Photography 1959-74, prof of photography 1972-, dean Sch of Communications 1974-75, pro rector (asst dir) 1975-80, emeritus prof of photography 1987-; RPS: memb Cncl 1951-76, pres 1958-60, chm Photographic Collection and hon curator of Photographs 1970-79 and 1982-86; memb Ctee for Art & Design 1977-83, chm Photography Bd 1978-83 (memb 1971-83); pres Euro Soc for The History of Photography 1985-, memb Advsy Ctee Nat Museum of Photography Film and Television Bradford 1983-, chm Tstees Photographers' Gallery 1987-, govr London Coll of Printing 1977-81 and 1982-5; Hon Dr of Arts CNAA 1987; hon fell Br Kinematograph Sound and TV Soc 1969; memb Deutsche Gesellschaft fur Photographie 1960; FRPS, FBIPP 1942 (pres 1964-65) FRSA 1962; *Books* Henry Peach Robinson, Master of Photographic Art 1830-1901 (1988), The Linked Ring, the Secession in Photography 1892-1910 (1979), Victorian and Edwardian Photographs (1975); *Recreations* gardening, swimming; *Style*— Prof Margaret Harker Farrand; Egdean House, Egdean, nr Pulborough, Sussex RH20 1JU (☎ 079 882 360); The Polytechnic of Central Lonodon, 309-311 Regent St, London W1R 8AL

HARKINS, His Hon Judge Gerard Francis Robert; s of Francis Murphy Harkins (d 1977), and Katherine, *née* Hunt; *b* 13 July 1936; *Educ* Mount St Mary's Coll Spinkhill, King's Coll Univ of Durham (LDS); *Career* dental surgn in gen practice Yorks 1961-70; called to the Bar Middle Temple 1969, in practice NE Circuit 1970-86, appointed circuit judge 1986-; *Style*— His Hon Judge Harkins; c/o The Law Courts, The Quayside, Newcastle upon Tyne (☎ 091 201 2000)

HARKNESS, Prof David William; s of William Frederick Samuel Harkness, and Rita Alice, *née* Barrett; *b* 30 Oct 1937; *Educ* Campbell Coll Belfast, Corpus Christi Coll Cambridge (BA, MA), Trinity Coll Dublin (PhD); *m* 29 Aug 1964, Hilary Katherine Margaret, da of William Walker Land (d 1987), of Wilmslow; 1 s (Patrick b 1972), 2 da (Emma b 1967, Lucy b 1969); *Career* RE 1956-58 (2 Lt 1957-58); sr lectr (former asst lectr and lectr) Univ of Kent 1965-75, prof Queen's Univ Belfast 1975-; memb: Irish Ctee of Historical Sciences 1976- (chm 1980-86), Bd Tstees Ulster Folk and Tport Museum 1978- (chm 1985-), BBC Gen Advsy Cncl 1979-84; FRHistS; *Books* The Restless Dominion (1969), The Post-War World (1974), Irish Historical Studies (ed, 1978-88), Northern Ireland since 1920 (1983); *Recreations* squash, running, travel; *Style*— Prof David Harkness; Dept of Modern History, Queen's University, Belfast BT7 1NN (☎ 0232 245133)

HARKNESS, Lt-Col Hon Douglas Scott; OC (1978), GM (1943), ED (1944), PC (Can 1957); s of William Harkness (d 1938); *b* 29 March 1903; *Educ* Alberta Univ (BA), Calgary Univ (LLD); *m* 1932, Frances Elisabeth, da of James Blair McMillan (d 1958); 1 s; *Career* Lt-Col RCA; teacher, farmer, formerly in oil business; Canadian politician: MP 1945-72, min of Agriculture 1957-60, min of Defence 1960-63; *Recreations* golf, reading, bridge; *Style*— Lt-Col Hon Douglas Harkness, OC, GM, ED, PC; 716 Imperial Way SW, Calgary, Alberta, Canada T2S 1N7 (☎ 403 243 0825)

HARKNESS, Rev James; OBE (1978), QHC (1982); s of James Harkness, of Dumfries, and Jane McMorn, *née* Thomson; *b* 20 Oct 1935; *Educ* Dumfries Acad, Univ of Edinburgh (MA); *m* 1960, Elizabeth Anne, da of George Tolmie (d 1959); 1 s (Paul b 1965), 1 da (Jane b 1962); *Career* joined RAChD 1961; DACG: NI 1974-75, 4 Div 1974-78; staff chaplain HQ BAOR 1978-80, asst chaplain gen Scotland 1980-81; sr chaplain: 1 (Br) Corps 1981-82, BAOR 1982-84; dep chaplain gen 1985-86, chaplain gen 1987-; OStJ 1988; *Clubs* New (hon memb, Edinburgh); *Style*— The Rev James Harkness, OBE, QHC, Chaplain General; (☎ 0276 71717); c/o The Royal Bank of Scotland, Holt's Whitehall Branch, Kirkland House, Whitehall, London SW1

HARKNESS, John Leigh (Jack); OBE; s of Verney Harkness, OBE (d 1980), and Olivia Austin (d 1941); *b* 29 June 1918; *Educ* Whitgift; *m* 1947, Betty, *née* Moore; 2 s, 1 da; *Career* rose breeder; md R Harkness and Co 1960-77; vice pres Royal Nat Rose Soc 1969-, sec Br Assoc of Rose Breeders 1973-85; *Books* Roses (1978), The World's Favourite Roses (1979), The Makers of Heavenly Roses (1985); *Style*— Jack Harkness, Esq, OBE; 1 Bank Alley, Southwold, Suffolk (☎ 0502 722030)

HARLAND, His Excellency (William) Bryce; s of Edward Dugard Harland (d 1939), and Annie Mcdonald Harland, *née* Gordon (d 1965); *b* 11 Dec 1931; *Educ* Victoria Univ of Wellington NZ (MA), Fletcher Sch of Law & Diplomacy Medford USA (AM); *m* 1, 15 June 1957 (m dis 1977), Rosemary Anne, *née* Gordon; 3 s (James b 1958, Andrew b 1960, d 1978, David b 1962); m 2, 29 June 1979, (Margaret) Anne, da of Andrew Blackburn, of Auckland NZ; 1 s (Thomas b 1981); *Career* joined NZ Foreign Serv 1953, third sec Singapore and Bangkok 1956-59, second sec NZ Mission to UN NY 1959-62, Dept External Affrs Wellington 1962-65, consellor NZ Embassy Washington 1965-69, Miny of Foreign Affrs Wellington NZ 1969-73, NZ ambass to China Peking 1973-75, asst sec Foreign Affrs NZ 1976-82, ambass and permananent rep to UN NY 1982-85, NZ high cmmr London 1985; chm Econ and Fin Ctee UN General Assembly 1984; memb Worshipful Co of Butchers 1986, Freeman City of London 1987-; KStJ 1985; *Recreations* history, music, walking; *Clubs* Brook's, East India, RAC; *Style*— Bryce Harland, Esq; New Zealand House, Haymarket, London, SW1 (☎ 01 930 8422)

HARLAND, Air Marshal Sir Reginald Edward Wynyard; KBE (1974), CB (1972), AE; s of Charles Cecil Harland (d 1945); *b* 30 May 1920; *Educ* Stowe, Trinity Coll Cambridge; *m* 1942, Doreen, da of William Hugh Cowie Romanis (d 1972); 2 s, 2 da (and 1 s decd); *Career* joined RAF 1939, served W Med 1942-45, Gp Capt 1960, STSO HQ 3 Gp Bomber Cmd 1962-64, STSO HQ FEAF 1964-1966, Air Cdre 1965, Harrier project dir Miny Technol 1967-69, idc 1969, AOC 24 Gp 1970, Air Vice-Marshal 1970, AO i/c E Air Support Cmd 1972, Air Marshal 1973, AOC-in-C RAF Support Cmd 1973-77; tech dir W S Atkins and Ptnrs Epsom 1977-82, engrg and mgmnt conslt 1982-; Parly candidate (Alliance) Bury St Edmunds 1983 and 1987; chm Suffolk Preservation Soc 1988-; CEng; *Recreations* politics, bridge, chess; *Clubs* RAF; *Style*— Air Marshal Sir Reginald E W Harland, KBE, CB, AE; 49 Crown St, Bury St Edmunds, Suffolk IP33 1QX (☎ 0284 763 078)

HARLE, John Crofton; s of Jack Harle, and Joyce, *née* Crofton; *b* 20 Sept 1956; *Educ* Newcastle Royal GS, Royal Coll of Music (Fndn scholar, ARCM); *m* 1985, Julia Jane Eisner; 2 s; *Career* saxophonist, composer, conductor, recording artist; ldr Myrha Saxophone Quartet 1977-82, formed duo with pianist John Lenehan 1979, saxophone soloist 1980-; concerto appearances incl: Carnegie Hall, South Bank Centre, The Proms, Germany, Switzerland, Far East; played with: LSO, English Chamber Orch, Basel Chamber Orch, London Sinfonietta, Northern Sinfonia, BBC Orchs; princ saxophone London Sinfonietta 1987-, prof of saxophone Guildhall Sch of Music and Drama 1988-; frequent soloist on TV and feature films (incl Prick Up Your Ears), regular broadcaster on BBC Radio, featured in One Man and his Sax BBC 2 TV 1988; EMI Classics Artist 1990-; saxophone ed Universal Edition Vienna; Cousins Meml Medal Kneller Hall 1976, Dannreuther Concerto Prize Royal Coll of Music 1980, GLAA Young Musician 1979 and 1980; FGSM 1990; *Books* John Harle's Saxophone Album (1986); *Recreations* family life, cooking, becoming a nicer person; *Style*— John Harle, Esq; c/o Horowitz Artists Management, Grosvenor Gardens House, 35-37 Grosvenor Gardens, London SW1W 0BS

HARLECH, 6 Baron (UK 1876); The Hon Francis David Ormsby Gore; s of 5 Baron Harlech, PC, KCMG (d 1985), and his 1 w Sylvia (d 1967), da of late Hugh Lloyd Thomas, CMG, CVO (*see* Peerage B Bellew); *b* 13 March 1954; *m* 1986, Amanda Jane, da of Alan T Grieve, of Brimpton House, Brimpton, Berks; 1 s (Jasset David Cody), 1 da (Tallulah Sylva Maria b 16 May 1988); *Heir* s, Hon Jasset David Cody Ormsby Gore b 1 July 1986; *Style*— The Rt Hon the Lord Harlech; The Mount, Race Course Rd, Oswestry, Shropshire

HARLECH, Pamela, Lady; Pamela; *née* Colin; o da of Ralph Frederick Colin (d 1985), of NY; *b* 18 Dec 1934; *Educ* Smith Coll, Finch Coll; *m* 1969, as his 2 wife, 5 Baron Harlech, KCMG, PC (d 1985); 1 da (Hon Pandora b 19 April 1972); *Career* journalist/producer; London ed for American Vogue 1965-69, contributing ed to British Vogue 1970-84; tstee V & A; memb: South Bank Bd, Arts Cncl, Cncl of Assoc for Business Sponsorship of the Arts, British-American Arts Assoc; chm: Women's Playhouse Tst, English Nat Ballet 1990-; *Books* Feast Without Fuss, Pamela Harlech's Complete Book of Cooking, Entertaining and Household Management, Vogue Book of Menus; *Style*— The Rt Hon Pamela, Lady Harlech

HARLEN, Dr Wynne; da of Arthur Mitchell, and Edith, *née* Radcliffe; *b* 12 Jan 1937; *Educ* Pate's GS for Girls Cheltenham, Univ of Oxford (MA), Univ of Bristol (MA, PhD); *m* 14 Aug 1958, Frank Harlen (d 1987); 1 s (Oliver b 1 Jan 1965), 1 da (Juliet b 9 July 1967); *Career* teacher Cheltenham 1958-60; lectr: St Mary's Coll Cheltenham 1960-64, Glos Coll of Art 1965-66; res fell: Univ of Bristol 1966-73, Univ of Reading 1973-77; sr res fell Univ of London 1977-84, Sidney Jones prof of sci educn Univ of Liverpool 1985-90, dir Scottish Cncl for Res in Educn 1990-; memb: Sec of State's Working Gp For Devpt of the Nat Sci Curriculum, Teaching Educn Ctee CNAA; memb: BERA, ASE, ASET, ASPE; *Books* incl: Science 5 to 13: A Formative Evaluation (1975), Guides to Assessment in Education: Science (1983), Teaching and Learning Primary Science (1985), Developing Primary Science (with S Jelly, 1989), Environmental Science in the Primary Curriculum (with Elstgeest, 1990); *Recreations* listening to music, walking; *Style*— Dr Wynne Harlen; Scottish Council for Res in Educn, 15 St John St, Edinburgh EH8 8JR (☎ 031 557 2944, fax 031 556 9454)

HARLEY, Maj-Gen Alexander George Hamilton; OBE (1981); s of Lt Col William Hamilton Coughtrie Harley (d 1973), of Warnham, Sussex and Eleanor Blanche *née* Jarvis; *b* 3 May 1941; *Educ* Caterham Sch, RMA Sandhurst; *m* 12 Aug 1967, Christina Valentine, da of Edmund Noel Butler-Cole, of Cross-in-Hand, Sussex, and Kathleen Mary, *née* Thompson; 2 s (Oliver b 1973, Angus b 1974); *Career* cmmnd RA 1962; 1963-72: served 7 Para Regt RHA, instr Jr Ldrs Regt RA, Staff Capt Miny of Def and Adj 36 Air Def Regt RA; Canadian Staff Coll 1972-73, Mil Asst Miny of Def 1974-75, Battery Cmdr 1975-78 (despatches 1978), memb Directing Staff Staff Coll 1978-79, CO 19 Field Regt RA 1979-82, Col Def Staff Miny of Def 1983-85, Cmdr 33 Armd Bde 1985-87, Asst Chief of Staff Ops N Army Gp 1988-90, Asst Chief of Def Staff (Overseas) Miny of Def 1990; Hon Regimental Col 19 Field Regt RA, pres Army Hockey; FBIM 1982; *Recreations* golf, hockey, fishing, clocks; *Clubs* Royal Cwlth Soc; *Style*— Maj-Gen A G H Harley, OBE; Ministry of Defence (ACDS (Overseas)), Main Building, Whitehall, London SW1A 2HB

HARLEY, Basil Hubert; s of Mervyn Ruthven Harley, JP (d 1973), of Stud Farm, Lamb Corner, Dedham, Essex, and Marion, *née* Parkinson (d 1973); *b* 17 July 1930; *Educ* Harrow, St John's Coll Oxford (MA); *m* 10 Oct 1959, Annette, da of Edgar Wolstan Bertram Handsley Milne-Redhead, ISO, TD, of Parkers, Bear St, Nayland, Suffolk; 3 da (Jane Elizabeth b 12 Oct 1960, Emma Katherine b 7 June 1962, Harriet Susanna b 15 May 1965); *Career* Nat Serv RA 1949-50, cmmnd 2 Lt 1949, 17 Trg Regt Oswestry 1949-50, Capt TA Queen's Own Oxfords Hussars & Royal Bucks Yeo 1950-60; md Curwen Press Ltd 1964-82; dir: Curwen Prints Ltd 1970, Wedge Entomological Res Fndn US at Nat Museum Natural History Washington DC 1974-; chm and md Harley Books Natural History Publishers (BH & A Harley Ltd) 1983-; memb Cncl Essex Naturalists' Tst 1975-78, chm Wynken de Worde Soc 1975, memb Exec Ctee Nat Book League 1974-78; Liveryman Worshipful Co of Stationers & Newspaper Makers 1973-; fell of Linnean Soc 1955, fell Royal Entomological Soc 1981; *Books* The Curwen Press A Short History (1970); *Recreations* natural history, reading; *Clubs* Utd Oxford and Cambridge Univ, Double Crown; *Style*— Basil Harley, Esq; Martins, Great Horkesley, Colchester, Essex CO6 4AH (☎ 0206 271 216)

HARLEY, Christopher Charles; JP (1960), DL (1987); s of Maj John Ralph Henry Harley, JP, DL (d 1960), of Brampton Bryan, and Rachel Mary, *née* Gwyer (d 1967); *b* 31 Dec 1926; *Educ* Eton, Magdalene Coll Cambridge; *m* 2 April 1959, Susan Elizabeth, da of Sir Roderick Barclay, GCVO, KCMG, of Latimer, Bucks; 4 s (Edward b 1960, John b 1961, Adrian b 1965, Philip b 1969); *Career* mech engr to 1956; landowner Brampton Bryan Herefords 1956-; High Sheriff of Hereford and Worcs 1987-88; memb Nat Tst Severn Regnl Ctee 1968-; CEng; *Recreations* shooting, forestry; *Style*— Christopher Harley, Esq, JP, DL; Brampton Bryan Hall, Bucknell, Salop SY7 0DJ (☎ 05474 241)

HARLEY, David Adams Henry; s of Robert Harley (d 1965), of 93 Wester Drylaw Ave, Edinburgh, and Ann Crighton, *née* Henry; *b* 15 April 1930; *Educ* Boroughmuir Sr Secdy Sch Edinburgh, James Gillespie Sch Edinburgh, Heriot-Watt Coll Edinburgh; *m* 26 Sept 1953, Irene Helen, da of John Walker Blanch, of 69 Murrayburn Park, Edinburgh; 2 s (Douglas Robert b 1955, Gordon David b 1965), 2 da (Dorothy Helen b 1958, Joyce Walker b 1961); *Career* Nat Serv RAF 1948-50; vice chm and trade rels dir United Distillers Ltd (formerly Arthur Bell and Sons Ltd); er Church Scotland 1964-, pres Perth Toastmasters Club 1970-71, capt King James VI GC 1975-77, pres Licensed Victuallers Nat Homes 1986-87, companion memb Br Inst Innkeeping; *Recreations* golf; *Clubs* Blair Gowrie Golf, King James VI Golf; *Style*— David Harley, Esq; Ellwyn, Craigie Knowes Rd, Perth PH2 0DG (☎ 0738 23 514); United Distillers UK, Cherrybank, Perth PH2 0NG (☎ 0738 21 111, fax 0738 38 739, telex 76 275)

HARLEY, Prof Ian Allan; s of Capt Gordon Nicol Harley (d 1986), of Maryborough, Queensland, and Bessie Winifred, *née* Shapcott (d 1975); *b* 4 April 1932; *Educ* Maryborough State HS, Univ of Queensland (BSc), Univ of London (PhD); *m* 11 Jan

1957, (Margaret) Wendy, da of Oswald Hoskin, (d 1941), of Brisbane, Queensland; 3 s (David b 1960, William b 1962, Robert b 1964), 1 da (Anne b 1966); *Career* surveyor Queensland surveyor-gen's dept 1953-59, surveyor Mount Isa Mines Ltd 1959, head of dept of surveying Univ of Queensland 1973-82 (staff memb 1963-82), res fell Alexander Von Humbolt fndn Univ of Stuttgart 1969, dean of faculty of engrg UCL 1985-88 (prof and head of dept of surveying and photogrammetry 1982-); FISAust 1968, FRICS 1983, FRSA 1984; *Recreations* music (all kinds), reading, walking, swimming; *Style*— Prof Ian Harley; 37 Ridgmount Gdns, London WC1E 7AT (☎ 01 580 3444); Dept of Photogrammetry and Surveying, University College London, Gower St, London WC1E 6BT (☎ 01 380 7225, fax 01 380 0453)

HARLEY, Paul Stuart; s of Brian Erskine Harley (d 1972), of Melbourne, Australia, and Elizabeth Ann Charlton, *née* Allan; *b* 20 June 1939; *Educ* St Lawrence Coll Kent, Univ Coll of N Staffs Keele (IEE PtIII); *m* 15 April 1963, Sally Ann, da of Eugene Prosser, of Wilts; 2 s (Nicholas b 1965, Adam b 1970), 1 da (Cherie-Ann b 1973); *Career* electrical engr, inventor of Welliwarma, md Wiltsavon Leisure Ltd 1984-86, proprietor Gloster Tech Chemicals, tech and mktg conslt to various cos; *Recreations* choral singing, riding; *Style*— Paul S Harley, Esq; The Old Farmhouse, Milbourne, Malmesbury, Wilts SN16 9JA (☎ 0666 824107)

HARMAN, Harriet; MP (Lab) Peckham 1982-; da of John Bishop Harman, and Anna Charlotte Malcolm Spicer; niece of Countess of Longford; *b* 20 July 1950; *Educ* St Paul's Girls' Sch, Univ of York; *m* Jack Dromey, Sec of SE Area TUC, nat sec TGWU; 2 s, 1 da; *Career* lawyer; memb Nat Cncl Civil Liberties; *Style*— Ms Harriet Harman, MP; House of Commons, London SW1

HARMAN, Hon Mr Justice; Hon Sir Jeremiah LeRoy Harman; s of late Rt Hon Sir Charles Harman; *b* 13 April 1930; *Educ* Eton; *m* 1960 (m dis 1986), Erica, da of Hon Sir Maurice Bridgeman, KBE (d 1980, 3 s of 1 Viscount Bridgeman); 2 s (Charles Richard LeRoy b 1963, Toby John b 1967), 1 da (Sarah b 1962); m 2, 1987, Katharine, da of late Rt Hon Sir Eric Sachs; *Career* served Coldstream Gds and Para Regt 1948-51; called to the Bar 1954, QC 1968, barr Hong Kong 1978, Singapore Bar 1980, High Ct judge (Chancery) 1982-; kt 1982; *Recreations* fishing, bird watching; *Style*— The Hon Mr Justice Harman; The Royal Courts of Justice, The Strand, London WC2A 2LL

HARMAN, Michael Godfrey; s of John Richard Harman (d 1986), and Elsie, *née* Stokes (d 1960); *b* 30 Jan 1937; *Educ* Mercers Sch, Magdalen Coll Oxford (BA); *m* 4 Sept 1971, Phyllis Eveline, da of John Henry North, of Thistlewood Farm, Sutton St James, Lincs; 1 s (Paul b 1972); *Career* chartered patent agent, European patent attorney; *Recreations* recreational mathematics; *Style*— Michael Harman, Esq; Holmwood, 37 Upper Park Rd, Camberley, Surrey GU15 2EG (☎ 0276 22985, telex 858902 BARON G, fax 0276 64091)

HARMAN, Robert Donald; QC (1974); s of late Herbert Donald Harman, MC; *b* 26 Sept 1928; *Educ* St Paul's, Magdalen Coll Oxford; *m* 1, 1960, Sarah (d 1965), *née* Cleverly; 2 s; m 2, 1968, Rosamond Geraldine Harman, JP, da of late Cdr G Scott, RN; 2 da; *Career* barr Gray's Inn 1954, bencher 1984; SE Circuit, treasy counsel Central Criminal Ct 1967-74, rec Crown Ct 1972-; judge Cts of Appeal Jersey and Guernsey 1986-; *Clubs* Garrick, Beefsteak, Pratt's; *Style*— Robert Harman, Esq, QC; 17 Pelham Cres, London SW7 (☎ 071 584 4304); 2 Harcourt Bldgs, Temple, London EC4 (☎ 071 353 2112)

HARMAR-NICHOLLS, Baron (Life Peer 1974), of Peterborough, Cambs; Sir Harmar Harmar-Nicholls; 1 Bt (1960), JP, MEP (EDG) Gtr Manchester S 1979-; s of Charles Nicholls; *b* 1 Nov 1912; *Educ* Queen Mary's GS Walsall; *m* 1940, Dorothy, da of James Edwards; 2 da (Hon Mrs Alan Aspden b 1941, Hon Susan, *qv*); *Career* takes Cons Whip in House of Lords; MP (C) Peterborough 1950-74; PPS to Asst Postmaster-Gen 1951-1955; Parly sec: MAFF 1955-57, Miny of Works 1957-60; chm Nicholls and Hennessy (Hotels) Ltd, Malvern Festival Theatre Trust Ltd; dir J and H Nicholls and Co, Radio Luxemburg (London) Ltd; Lloyd's underwriter; *Style*— The Rt Hon the Lord Harmar-Nicholls, JP, MEP; Abbeylands, Weston, Stafford (☎ 0889 252)

HARMAR-NICHOLLS, Hon Susan Frances Nicholls; da of Baron Harmar-Nicholls, JP, MEP (Life Peer and 1 Bt); *b* 23 Nov 1943; *Career* actress (Sue Nicholls); TV roles incl: Coronation Street (Audrey Roberts, *née* Potter), Crossroads, Rise and Fall of Reginald Perrin, Rent a Ghost, Up the Elephant, Village Hill; Royal Shakespeare Co, Broadway, In London Assurance; *Style*— The Hon Susan Harmar-Nicholls

HARMER, Dr Clive Lucas; s of Cecil Norman Harmer (d 1986), and Elizabeth Mary, *née* Lucas (d 1989); *b* 18 Aug 1940; *Educ* Westminster Hosp Med Sch (MB BS, MRCP); *m* 2 Jan 1965 (m dis 1977), Dr Margaret Flora Spittle; 2 da (Kasha b 1968, Victoria b 1971); *Career* instr Dept of Radiation Oncology Stanford Univ California 1970; conslt in radiotherapy and oncology: St Luke's Hosp Guildford 1970-73, St George's Hosp London 1973-; currently chm Dept of Radiotherapy and Oncology Royal Marsden Hosp London; examiner final fellowship RCR; chm Thyroid Unit Royal Marsden Hosp London and Sutton; memb: RSM, Br Inst Radiology; FRCR 1968; *Recreations* wildlife photography; *Clubs* Wig & Pen, Stocks; *Style*— Dr Clive Harmer; St George's Hospital, Blackshaw Rd, London SW17 0QT; Royal Marsden Hospital, Fulham Rd, London SW3 6JJ

HARMER, Sir (John) Dudley; OBE (1963), JP (Kent 1962); s of Ernest Harmer; *b* 27 July 1913; *Educ* Merchant Taylors', Wye Coll London; *m* 1947, Erika Minder-Lanz, of Switzerland; 2 s; *Career* farmer; dep chm Kent Agric Exec Ctee 1964-72, tstee Kent Incorp Soc for Promoting Experiments in Horticulture 1979-; chm SE Area Cons Prov Cncl 1966-71, pres E Kent Euro Cons Cncl 1982- (chm 1979-82); kt 1972; *Style*— Sir Dudley Harmer, OBE, JP; Stone Hill, Egerton, Ashford, Kent (☎ 023 376 241)

HARMER, Sir Frederic Evelyn; CMG (1945); s of late Sir Sidney Harmer, KBE; *b* 3 Nov 1905; *Educ* Eton, King's Coll Cambridge; *m* 1, 1931, Barbara (d 1972), da of late Maj J Hamilton, JP, of Fyne Court, Bridgwater; 1 s, 3 da (1 decd); m 2, 1973, Daphne Shelton Agar; *Career* with Treasy 1939-45, dep chm P and OSN Co 1957-70, govt dir BP 1953-70; kt 1968; *Style*— Sir Frederic Harmer, CMG; Tiggins Field, Kelsale, Saxmundham, Suffolk (☎ 0728 603156)

HARMER, Robert James Andrew; s of Sir Frederic Harmer, CMG, of Suffolk, and Barbara Susan, *née* Hamilton (d 1972); *b* 4 Oct 1936; *Educ* Eton, King's Coll Cambridge (MA); *m* 2 June 1962, Nichola Anne, da of Major Eric James Mather, MBE, of Argyll; 2 s (Andrew b 1964, Dominic b 1969), 1 da (Fiona b 1970); *Career* Lt RNR HM Subs; dir Overseas Containers Ltd 1975-85, chm F W Harmer (Holdings) Ltd and F W Harmer (Engineering) Ltd 1982- (dir 1971-82); dir: MAT Tport Mgmnt Ltd 1989-, SITPRO 1983-; *Recreations* sailing, fishing, opera; *Clubs* Lansdowne, Aldeburgh Yacht, Epée; *Style*— R James Harmer, Esq; Gruline House, Isle of Mull, Scotland (☎ 0680 300332); MAT Group Ltd, Arnold House, 36/41 Holywell Lane, London EC2P 2EQ

HARMSWORTH, Elen, Lady; Elen; da of Nicolaj Billenstein, of Randers, Denmark; *m* 1925, Sir Hildebrand Alfred Beresford Harmsworth, 2 Bt (d 1977); *Style*— Elen, Lady Harmsworth; Aucassin, Le Vallon, St Clair, Le Lavandon, France

HARMSWORTH, Hildebrand Esmond Miles; s and h of Sir Hildebrand Harold Harmsworth, 3 Bt; *b* 1 Sept 1964; *Educ* Dean Close Sch Cheltenham, Crewe and Alsager Coll; *m* 23 Dec 1988, Ruth Denise, da of Dennis Miles, of Cheltenham; 1 da (Alice Katherine Elspeth b 23 March 1990); *Recreations* hockey, golf; *Style*— Hildebrand Harmsworth, Esq

HARMSWORTH, Sir Hildebrand Harold; 3 Bt (UK 1922), of Freshwater Grove, Parish of Shipley, Co Sussex; s of Sir Hildebrand Alfred Beresford, 2 Bt (d 1977); *b* 5 June 1931; *Educ* Harrow, Trinity Coll Dublin; *m* 1960, Gillian Andrea, da of William John Lewis, of Tetbury, Gloucs; 1 s (Hildebrand, *qv*), 2 da (Claire b 1961, Kirsten b 1963); *Style*— Sir Hildebrand Harmsworth, Bt; Ewlyn Villa, 42 Leckhampton Rd, Cheltenham, Gloucs

HARMSWORTH, Lady Jessamine Cécile Marjorie; *née* Gordon; da of 3 Marquis of Aberdeen and Temair; *b* 14 Aug 1910; *Educ* privately; *m* 1937, Michael St John Harmsworth, TD, DL, Seaforth Highlanders (d 1981), nephew of Lords Northcliffe, Rothermere and Harmsworth; 2 s (Andrew b 1939, Peter b 1952), 4 da (Mrs Francis Pym b 1940, Mrs Petros Demitriades b 1946, Mrs Donald Sinclair b 1949, Mrs R MacLeod b 1951); *Career* chm County Multiple Sclerosis Soc; pres: Caithness County Music Ctee (former chm), County Children's League, County Save the Children Fund, Wick Choral Soc; vice pres Nat Deaf Children's Soc (Highland region); dir County Red Cross 1968-85, (currently hon vice pres and life memb receiving Badge of Honour for distinguished serv); BRCS Voluntary Med Service Medal 1983; nominated Citizen of the Year 1988 for services to the community by Wick Rotary Club; patron Thurso Live Music Assoc; *Recreations* music, singing, organist, grandmother to 22 grandchildren; *Style*— The Lady Jessamine Harmsworth; Thrumster House, Caithness (☎ 095 585 262)

HARMSWORTH, Hon (Harold) Jonathan Esmond Vere; s and h of 3 Viscount Rothermere; *b* 3 Dec 1967; *Style*— The Hon Jonathan Harmsworth

HARMSWORTH, Madeleine Thérèse Margaret; da of Eric Beauchamp Northcliffe, Harmsworth (d 1988), and Hélène Marie, *née* Dehove; *b* 10 July 1941; *Educ* Pole's Convent Ware Herts, Somerville Coll Oxford (MA); *Career* journalist; gen reporter 1962, film critic 1965-, theatre critic 1979-88, letters page ed 1985-, travel corr 1991-; freelance journalist (under pseudonym Hannah Carter) for nat newspapers and jls; memb BBC's Central Music Advsy Ctee 1973-80, govr Dr Johnson's Houst Tst 1982-; memb The Critic's Circle 1971-; *Recreations* cycling, trekking, swimming; *Style*— Ms Madeleine Harmsworth; 15 Sudeley St, London N1 8HP; Sunday Mirror, Holborn Circus, London EC1P 1DO (☎ 071 822 3605)

HARMSWORTH, 3 Baron (UK 1939); Thomas Harold Raymond Harmsworth; o s of Hon Eric Beauchamp Northcliffe Harmsworth (d 1988), and Hélène Marie, *née* Dehove (d 1962); suc uncle 2 Baron Harmsworth 1990; *b* 20 July 1939; *Educ* Eton, Christ Church Oxford; *m* 26 June 1971, Patricia Palmer, da of Michael Palmer Horsley, of Waltham House, Brough, N Humberside; 2 s (Hon Dominic Michael Eric b 18 Sept 1973, Hon Timothy Thomas John b 6 April 1979), 3 da (Hon Philomena Hélène Olivia b 10 Feb 1975, Hon Abigail Patricia Thérèse b 14 June 1977, Hon Pollyanna Mary Clare b 8 Sept 1981); *Heir* s, Hon Dominic Harmsworth b 18 Sept 1973; *Career* Nat Serv 2 Lt Royal Horse Gds 1957-59; in the City 1962-74, civil serv 1974-88, publisher 1988-; chm Dr Johnson's House Gough Square London; *Style*— The Rt Hon the Lord Harmsworth; The Old Rectory, Stoke Abbott, Beaminster, Dorset DT8 3JT

HARMSWORTH BLUNT, Margaret, Lady; Margaret Hunam; da of William Redhead, of Carville Hall, Brentford; *m* 1, 1920 (m dis 1938), 2 Viscount Rothermere (d 1978); 1 s (3 Viscount), 2 da (Hon Lady Cooper-Key, Countess of Cromer, *qv*); m 2, Capt Thomas Hussey, RN (ret); m 3, 1947, as his 2 w, Sir John Blunt, 10 Bt (d 1969); *Style*— Margaret, Lady Harmsworth Blunt; The Old Mill, Mayfield, Sussex

HARNDEN, Prof David Gilbert; s of William Alfred Harnden (d 1934), of London, and Anne McKenzie, *née* Wilson (d 1983); *b* 22 June 1932; *Educ* George Heriot's Sch Edinburgh, Univ of Edinburgh (BSc, PhD); *m* 9 Jul 1955, Thora Margaret, da of Alexander Ralph Seatter (d 1945), of Burray, Orkney; 3 s (Ralph b 1957, Mark b 1960, Richard b 1965); *Career* lectr Univ of Edinburgh 1956-57, sci memb MRC Harwell and Edinburgh 1957-69, res fell Univ of Wisconsin USA 1963-64, prof of cancer studies Univ of Birmingham 1969-83, dir Paterson Inst for Cancer Res Manchester 1983-, prof of experimental oncology Univ of Manchester 1983-; chm Br Assoc Cancer Res 1984-87, pres Assoc Clinical Cytogeneticists 1985-88, chm ed bd Br Journal of Cancer; many papers on cytogenetics and cancer published in learned jls and books; memb exec ctee Cancer Res Campaign; FIBiol 1970, FRCPath 1983, FRSE 1983, hon MRCP 1987; *Recreations* sketching, a little gardening; *Style*— Prof David Harnden; Tanglewood, Ladybrook Road, Bramhall, Stockport, Cheshire SK7 3NE (☎ 061 485 3214); Paterson Institute for Cancer Research, Christie Hospital and Holt Radium Institute, Wilmslow Road, Manchester M20 9BX (☎ 061 445 8123, fax 061 434 7728, telex 934999 TXLINKG)

HARNEY, Desmond Edward St Aubyn; OBE (1968); s of Edward Augustine St Aubyn Harney, KC, MP (d 1929), of London, and Kathleen, *née* Anderson (d 1973); *b* 14 Feb 1929; *Educ* Corby Sch Sunderland, Univ of Durham (BSc), Univ of Cambridge, SOAS London; *m* 10 July 1954, Judith Geraldine, da of Daniel McCarthy Downing (d 1940), of Dublin; 1 s (Richard Tindle b 16 Oct 1958), 2 da (Geraldine Anne b 3 July 1955, Bridget Clare b 14 Sept 1957); *Career* Nat Serv Sgt 1947-49, serv Canal Zone (Suez) and Pakistan; ICI 1954-56, cnsllr Dip Serv Iran and Kenya 1956-74, dir Morgan Grenfell & Co Ltd 1974-87; non-exec dir: London Brick plc 1981-85, Equatorial Bank plc 1986-, ME Consultants Ltd 1988-; chm Irano-British C of C 1976-79; memb Cncl: Royal Soc For Asian Affrs 1987-, Br Inst of Persian Studies 1987-; chm Chelsea Cons Assoc 1986-90, cncllr RBKC 1986-, govr Catholic Sixth Form Coll Kensington 1990-; *Recreations* photography, skiing, riding; *Clubs* Garrick; *Style*— Desmond Harney, Esq, OBE; 16 Stafford Terrace, London W8 7BH (☎ 071 938 3291); Broadwater House, 31 Sherborne, Cheltenham, Glos GL54 3DR; The Glassmill, Suite 13, 1 Battersea Bridge Rd, London SW11 3BG (☎ 071 924 2980, fax 071 924 2991)

HARNIMAN, John Phillip; OBE 1984; s of William Thomas Harniman (d 1941), and Maud Kate Florence, *née* Dyrenfurth (d 1980); *b* 7 May 1939; *Educ* Leyton CHS, Culham Coll (Dip Ed), Univ of London (BA), Université de Paris; *m* 26 August 1961, Avryl da of Harold Hartley (d 1953), 1 s (Denzil b 20 Nov 1971), 1 da (Claire-Elise b 24 Dec 1968); *Career* teacher William Morris Sch Walthamstow, lectr Ecole Normale Supérieure de St Cloud 1960-67; Br Cncl: Algeria 1967-70, asst dir personnel 1970-76, rep Singapore 1976-81, cultural attache Romania 1981-84, cultural cnsllr and rep for Belgium and Luxembourg 1984-87, dir of trg Br Cncl London 1988; *Recreations* music, reading, letter writing, cats; *Clubs* Anglo-Belgian; *Style*— John Harniman, Esq, OBE; The British Council, 10 Spring Gardens, London SW1A 2BN (☎ 01 930 8466, fax 071 839 6347, telex 8952201)

HARPER, Lt-Col Alexander Forrest (Alec); DSO (1946); s of Lt-Col Alexander Forrest Harper (d 1972), of Littoncheney, Dorset, and Clare Rosamund, *née* Rowlandson; *b* 12 July 1910; *Educ* Blundell's, RMC Sandhurst; *m* 18 Dec 1946, (Margaret Helen) Rosemary, da of Eric Hayward, of Dane St House, Chilham, Kent; 1 s (Alexander (Sandy) b 16 March 1948), 1 da (Caroline b 16 Sept 1950); *Career* Royal Deccan Horse IA 1931-44, Capt 1937, seconded cmdt Govr of Bengal's Bodyguard 1938-40, Maj 1942, 9 Gurkha Rifles (Chindits) 1944-47 (despatches 1944), Lt-Col 1944, Staff Coll Quetta 1947, ret 1948; jt md Bengal Distilleries Co Ltd 1948-55; hon sec Hurlingham Polo Assoc 1972-89; memb: Indian Cavalry Offrs Assoc, 9 Gurkhas Offrs Assoc, Ctee Cowdray Park Polo Club; *Recreations* polo (played for England 1951, 1953), field sports, fishing, hunting; *Clubs* Cavalry and Guards', Shikar; *Style*—

Lt-Col Alec Harper, DSO; Ambersham Farm, Midhurst, Sussex (☎ 079 85 254)

HARPER, Brig (Charles) Anthony des Noëttes; CBE (1969, OBE 1964); s of Dr Charles Harold Lefebvre Harper (d 1936), of Finchley; *b* 17 July 1916; *Educ* St Edward's Sch Oxford; *m* 1947, Francesca Marie, da of Col Frank John Beecham (d 1945), of Cape Town; 1 da; *Career* WWII served NW Europe, India, Malaya, Singapore, Germany; mil attaché Moscow 1966-68, Cdr Br Forces Antwerp 1969-71, security advsr HQ CENTO (Turkey) 1971-74, MOD HQ Intelligence Centre 1974-82; diplomat 1971-74, civil servant MOD 1974-82; ldr Ashford Borough Cncl 1985-90 (memb 1983-); *Clubs* Army and Navy; *Style—* Brig Anthony Harper, CBE; Venus House, The St, Appledore, Ashford, Kent TN26 2BU (☎ 023 383 375)

HARPER, Prof Anthony John; s of Maurice Colston Harper (d 1984), and Evelyn, *née* Thomas; *b* 26 May 1938; *Educ* Univ of Bristol (BA, MA), Univ of Edinburgh (PhD); *m* 4 April 1964, Sandra, da of Harold Green; 1 s (Stephen b 20 March 1971), 2 da (Veronica b 7 Oct 1965, Anne b 12 Nov 1967); *Career* lectr Univ of Edinburgh 1964-70 (asst lectr 1962-64), prof and head German studies Univ of Strathclyde 1979-; *Books* German Today (with E McInnes, 1967), David Schirmer - A Poet of the German Baroque (1977), Time and Change - Essays on German and European Literature (1982), Schriften zur Lyrik Leipzigs 1620-70 (1985), The Song Books of Gottfried Finckelthaus (1988); *Style—* Prof Anthony J Harper; 101 Stirling Drive, Bishopbriggs, Glasgow G64 3PG (☎ 041 772 2905); University of Strathclyde, Dept of Modern Languages, 26 Richmond St, Glasgow G64 3PG (☎ 041 552 4400)

HARPER, Douglas Ross; s of Louis R Harper (d 1973), of Aberdeen, and Margaret Hall, *née* Cartwright; *b* 16 Feb 1940; *Educ* Aberdeen GS; *m* 19 July 1968, Dorothy Constance, da of Norman F Wisely, of Methlick, Aberdeenshire; 1 s (Ross b 1973), 3 da (Caroline b 1969, Lorraine b 1971, Helen b 1977); *Career* jr surgical post Aberdeen Royal Infirmary 1967-73, sr surgical registrar Edinburgh Royal Infirmary 1973-76, conslt gen surgn Falkirk and Dist Royal Infirmary 1976-, clinical sr lectr Dept of Clinical Surgery Univ of Edinburgh 1976-; memb: Assoc of Surgns, Vascular Surgical Soc, Cncl of Mgmnt Strathcarrow Hospice; FRCSE 1971, FRCS 1972, FRCS Glasgow 1985; *Recreations* hillwalking; *Style—* Douglas Harper, Esq; Glenallan, 16 Upper Glen Rd, Bridge of Allan, Stirlingshire FK9 4PX (☎ 0786 832242); Falkirk & District Royal Infirmary, Major's Load, Falkirk, Stirlingshire (☎ 0324 24000)

HARPER, Elizabeth; da of Judge Norman Harper (d 1967), of Whinbrow, Cloughton, Nr Scarborough, N Yorks, and Irene, *née* Rawson (d 1989); *b* 29 Dec 1935; *Educ* Malvern Girls' Coll, St Anne's Coll Oxford (BA); *m* 15 July 1961, Frederick Rudolph Charles Such; 1 s (Rupert b 23 March 1964), 1 da (Sarah b 12 March 1967); *Career* called to the Bar Middle Temple 1960; chm Newcastle Social Security Appeal Tbnl 1985-; memb Tport Users Consultative Ctee N East Area 1975-81; *Recreations* reading, tennis; *Style—* Miss Elizabeth Harper; The Rift Barns, Wylam, Northumberland NE41 8BL (☎ 0661 852763); 71 Borough Rd, Middlesbrough, Cleveland (☎ 0642 226036)

HARPER, Gerald George Frederick; s of Ernest George Harper, and Mary Elizabeth, *née* Thomas; *Educ* Haileybury; *m* 1, 1958 (m dis), Jane Downe; 1 s (James), 1 da (Sarah b 1959); m 2, (m dis 1983), Carla, *née* Rabaiotti; *Career* Nat Serv 2 Lt Army 1947-49; actor; first appeared London stage Arts Theatre in How He Lied to Her Husband (He) 1951, Liverpool Repertory 1952, Cambridge Theatre London No News From Father 1955, Free as Air (Savoy) 1957, Broadway debut Old Vic 1960, NY Boing Boing 1965; other W End plays incl: House Guest, Baggage, Suddenly at Home, Royal Baccarat Scandal, Little Hut, The Crucifer of Blood; TV series Hadleigh and Adam Adamant (won most popular actor on TV awards); films incl: The Dambusters, The Young Ones, League of Gentlement, The Lady Vanishes; ten years broadcaster Capital Radio, current long running show BBC Radio 2; *Style—* Gerald Harper, Esq; London Management, 235 Regent St, London W1 (☎ 071 493 1610)

HARPER, Hon Mrs (Hazel Eleanor); da of Baron Woolley, CBE, DL (Life Peer); *b* 11 Dec 1938; *Educ* Malvern Girls' Coll; *m* 1961, William David Harper, only s of William Richard Harper, OBE; 2 s, 1 da; *Career* SRN; farmer; magistrate 1980-; *Recreations* golf, walking, family activities; *Clubs* Royal Liverpool Golf; *Style—* The Hon Mrs Harper; Clogwyn y Gwin, Rhyd Ddu, Beddgelert, Gwynedd (☎ 0766 86579)

HARPER, Heather (Mrs Eduardo Benarroch); CBE; da of Hugh Harper, of Belfast, and Mary Eliza, *née* Robb; *b* 8 May 1930; *Educ* Ashleigh House Sch Belfast, Trinity Coll of Music (LTCL); *m* 19 May 1973, Eduardo J Benarroch, s of Hector A Benarroch, of Buenos Aires; *Career* soprano; leading int opera and concert singer 1954-, has sung at all major opera houses and with all major symphony orchs in the world; recent seasons incl: Japan, Hong Kong, Australia, New York, Geneva, Rome, Milan, Madrid, Vienna, Paris, Amsterdam, Los Angeles; soprano soloist: first BBC Symphony Orch Far East tour 1982, first BBC Philharmonic Orch South American tour 1989; regular soloist: Covent Garden, New York Met, Teatro Colon Buenos Aires; notable performances incl: Elsa in Lohengrin (Bayreuth debut, conducted by Kempe), Countess in The Marriage of Figaro, Deutsche Opera Berlin (conducted by Barenboim), Arabella and Chrysothemis in Die Marschallin and Die Kaiserin by Richard Strauss; world premieres incl: Britten's War Requiem Coventry Cathedral 1962, Mrs Coyle in Britten's Owen Wingrave 1971, Tippett's Third Symphony 1972, Nadia in Tippett's The Icebreak Covent Garden 1975, Britten's Praise We Great Men 1985; recorded over 90 major works with all main recording cos in Britain and abroad; awards incl: Edison award for Britten's Les Illuminations, Grammy nomination for Berg's Seven Early Songs, Grammy award and Grand Prix du Disque for Peter Grimes, Grammy award Best Solo Recording for Ravel's Scheherazade 1984; prof of singing and conslt RCM 1985-, hon dir of singing studies Britten-Pears Sch Snape, visiting lectr RSAMD 1988- vice pres N Ireland Youth Symphony Orch; Hon DMUS Queen's Univ Belfast 1964; hon RAM 1972, FTCL, FRCM 1988, RSA 1989; *Recreations* reading, biographies, gardening; *Style—* Miss Heather Harper, CBE; 20 Milverton Rd, London NW6 7AS; Virrey Olaguer y Feliu 3444-8o, 1426@@ D Buenos Aires, Argentina

HARPER, James Norman; s of His Hon Judge Norman Harper (d 1967), and Iris Irene, *née* Rawson (d 1989); *b* 30 Dec 1932; *Educ* Marlborough, Magdalen Coll Oxford (BA); *m* 1956, Blanka Miroslava Eva, da of Miroslav Sigmund, of Henley on Thames; 1 s, 1 da; *Career* Lt RA (Nat Serv and TA for 3 years); called to the Bar Gray's Inn 1957, rec 1980; pres Northumberland Co Hockey Assoc 1982-; *Recreations* cricket, hockey; *Clubs* MCC; *Style—* James Harper, Esq; 59 Kenton Rd, Gosforth, Newcastle upon Tyne NE3 4NJ (☎ 091 285 7611)

HARPER, Prof John Lander; CBE (1989); s of John Hindley Harper, and Harriet Mary, *née* Archer; *b* 27 May 1925; *Educ* Lawrence Sheriff Sch Rugby, Magdalen Coll Oxford (MA, DPhil); *m* 8 Jan 1954, Borgny, da of Toralf Lero; 1 s (Jonathan b 24 Sept 1960), 2 da (Belinda b 19 Jan 1955, Claire b 20 Jan 1957); *Career* univ demonstrator Dept of Agric Univ of Oxford 1948-60, prof of botany Univ of N Wales 1967-82 (prof of agric botany 1960-67), emeritus prof Univ of Wales 1982-; memb: NERC 1971-78 and 1987-90, AFRC 1980-90, foreign assoc Nat Acad of Sci USA; Darwin medal 1990; Hon DSc Univ of Sussex 1984; FRS 1978 (memb Cncl 1987-89); *Books* Population Biology of Plants (1977), Ecology: Individuals, Populations and Communities (with M Begon and C Townsend, 1986); *Recreations* gardening; *Clubs* The Farmers; *Style—* Prof John Harper, CBE, FRS; Cae Groes, Glan-y-Coed Park, Dwygyfylchi, Penmaenmawr, Gwynedd LL34 6TL (☎ 0492 622362)

HARPER, John Mansfield; s of Thomas James Harper (d 1944), of Bucks, and May, *née* Charlton; *b* 17 July 1930; *Educ* Merchant Taylors', St John's Coll Oxford; *m* 1956, Berenice Honorine, da of Harold Haydon (d 1970), of Spain; 1 s (Neil Mansfield b 1960), 1 da (Ann Berenice b 1963); *Career* Civil Serv (PO) 1953-69, PO Telecommunications 1969-81, md Inland Div and memb Bd Br Telecom 1981-83 (ret 1983); special advsr to the bd NEC (UK) Ltd 1985-; CIEE, CBIM; *Recreations* reading, electronics, gardening, carpentry; *Style—* John Harper, Esq; 11 Lullington Close, Seaford, E Sussex BN25 4JH (☎ 0323 898316); NEC (UK) Ltd, 1 Victoria Rd, London W3 6UL (☎ 081 993 8111)

HARPER, Kenneth William; s of William Ernest Harper, of 52 Doagh Rd, Newton Abbey, and Elizabeth, *née* Thompson; *b* 1 Aug 1949; *Educ* Aunadale GS, Queen's Univ Belfast (BSc, MB, MD); *m* 8 July 1972, Rosemary, da of George Hewitt, of 222 Jordanstown Rd, Newton Abbey; 3 s (Gavin b 1974, Ian b 1976, Stuart b 1982), 1 da (Alison b 1983); *Career* jr hosp doctor in anaesthetics 1976-87, conslt anaesthetist 1987-; FCAnaes 1981; *Recreations* rugby football; *Style—* Kenneth Harper, Esq; 5 Castlehill Park, Belfast, N Ireland BT4 3GU (☎ 0232 63661); Royal Victoria Hospital, Belfast, N Ireland BT12 6BA (☎ 0232 240503)

HARPER, Martin John; s of Frank Harper, of Welford-on-Avon; *b* 26 March 1925; *Educ* King Edward's GS Birmingham, LSE; *m* 1949, Stella, da of Francis Beavis, of Birkdale, Southport; 1 s, 2 da; *Career* merchant banker and conslt; dir: Keyser Ullmann 1971, London Interstate Bank 1980, Charterhouse Japhet 1980 (md 1984-86); chm: Charterhouse Japhet Credit 1983, Johnson Matthey Bankers 1984, Royal Scottish Finance Group 1986-, Minories Finance 1986-; *Recreations* reading, music, walking; *Clubs* Carlton, Overseas Bankers; *Style—* Martin Harper, Esq; 123 Minories, London EC3 (☎ 071 488 2671); Martin Harper & Co, 46a Priestlands Park Rd, Sidcup, Kent DA15 7HJ (☎ 081 300 1264)

HARPER, Dr Peter George; s of Frederick Charles Harper (d 1965), of Bath, and Catherine Tryphosa, *née* McHattie; *b* 30 Aug 1945; *Educ* UCH and UCL (MB BS, LRCP, MRCP, MRCS); *m* 21 June 1971, Saga Margaret Elizabeth, da of Peter Guise Tyndale; 3 s (Benjamin b 1974, Sebastian b 1976, Maximillian b 1988), 1 da (Harriet b 1980); *Career* house offr then sr house offr UCH and Addenbrooke's Hosp Cambridge 1969-71, sr house offr and med registrar St Mary's Hosp 1972-76, sr med registrar UCH 1976-82, conslt physician and med oncologist Guy's Hosp 1982-; MRC: Lung Cancer Ctee, Gynaecological Malignancies Ctee, Genito-Urinary Malignancies Ctee; memb: UK Central Coordinating Cancer Ctee Br Prostate Gp, Hampstead Med Soc; FRCP 1987; *Books* numerous papers on aspects of cancer treatment; contrib chapters: The Treatment of Urological Tumours (1985), A Textbook of Unusual Tumours (1988); *Recreations* music (especially opera), walking, fly fishing, shooting; *Style—* Dr Peter Harper; 97 Harley St, London W1N 1DE (☎ 071 935 6698)

HARPER, Peter Philip Dudley; s of William John Harper (d 1984), and Ida Bertha, *née* Evans (d 1948); *b* 4 Nov 1930; *Educ* Richmond and East Sheen GS, UCL (LLB); *m* 15 Jan 1955, Joyce, da of Sidney Thomas White (d 1967); 1 s (Robert b 1966), 1 da (Vivien b 1960); *Career* Nat Serv 2 Lt RASC, Temp Capt Claims Cmmn 1955-57; admitted slr 1954, ptnr Warmingtons & Hasties (now Shoosmiths & Harrison since merger 1989) 1959-90; conslt Calvert Smith & Sutcliffe 1990-; Clerk to Worshipful Co of Woolmen 1970-75 (Liveryman 1975); memb Law Soc; *Style—* Peter P D Harper, Esq; 15 York Ave, East Sheen, London SW14 7LQ (☎ 081 876 4827); 151 Sheen Lane, London SW14 8LR (☎ 081 876 6268, fax 081 876 8943)

HARPER, Rev Roger; s of Albert William Harper (d 1979), of Peel, IOM, and Joyce, *née* Griffiths (d 1990); *b* 10 Jan 1943; *Educ* Merchant Taylors' Crosby, UMIST (BSc); *m* 26 July 1966, Joan, da of John Worthington, of Freckleton, Lancs; 2 da (Charlotte b 1967, Camilla b 1969); *Career* CA; ordained priest 1988 in diocese of Sodor and Man, chm Diocesan Bd of Fin 1984-; dir: Roach Bridge Holdings plc, Manx Industry Trust 1973-, Westmorland Smoked Foods 1988-; FCA; *Recreations* jt master IOM bloodhounds drag hunt; *Style—* Rev Roger Harper; Ballahowin House, St Marks, Ballasalla, Isle of Man (☎ 0624 851251); 5th Floor, Victory House, Prospect Hill, Douglas, Isle of Man (☎ 0624 64945, fax 64530, telex 629222)

HARPER, Prof (John) Ross; CBE (1986); s of Thomas Harper (d 1960), and Margaret Simpson, *née* Ross; *b* 20 March 1935; *Educ* Hutchesons' Boys' GS, Univ of Glasgow (MA, LLB); *m* 26 Sept 1963, Ursula Helga Renate, da of Hans Gathmann (d 1966), of Zimerstrasse, Darmstadt; 2 s (Robin b 1964, Michael b 1969), 1 da (Susan b 1966); *Career* slr Scot; sr ptnr Ross Harper & Murphy; pt/t prof of law Univ of Strathclyde; former pres: Law Soc of Scot, Scottish Cons and Unionist Assoc, Glasgow Bar Assoc; chm Gen Practice Section Int Bar Assoc, former chm Tory Reform Gp Scotland; *Books* Practitioners' Guide to Criminal Procedure, A Guide to the Courts, The Glasgow Rape Case, Fingertip Guide to Criminal Law; *Recreations* angling, bridge, shooting; *Clubs* RSAC, Glasgow and Western; *Style—* Prof Ross Harper, CBE; 97 Springkell Avenue, Pollokshields, Glasgow (☎ 041 427 3223); Ca 'd'oro, 45 Gordon St, Glasgow G1 3PE (☎ 041 221 8888)

HARPER GOW, (Maxwell) Eric; s of Sir (Leonard) Maxwell Harper Gow, MBE, of Eventyr, Longniddry, Lothian, and Lillian Margaret, *née* Kiaer; *b* 1 Aug 1945; *Educ* Rugby, Universite de Grenoble France; *m* 1 July 1972, Celia Marjorie, da of James William Macleod (d 1978); 1 s (Robert b 1978), 2 da (Marianne b 1973, Amalie b 1975); *Career* CA; Graham Smart & Annan Edinburgh 1964-69, Cooper Brothers & Co London 1970-73, fin controller sound and vision div Hayes Middx EMI Ltd 1973-78, fin dir Edinburgh and Reading Nuclear Enterprises Ltd 1978-81, co sec A H McIntosh & Co Ltd Kirkcaldy 1981-82, assoc dir corporate fin support servs Coopers & Lybrand Edinburgh 1982-; memb Inst CA Scotland 1969; *Recreations* sailing, skiing, silviculture; *Clubs* New Edinburgh; *Style—* Eric Harper Gow, Esq; Coopers & Lybrand, 126 George Street, Edinburgh (☎ 031 226 2595)

HARPER GOW, Sir (Leonard) Maxwell; MBE (1944); s of Capt Leonard Harper Gow (d 1965), and Eleanor Amelie Salvesen (d 1980); *b* 13 June 1918; *Educ* Rugby, CCC Cambridge; *m* 1944, Lillan Margaret, da of Aage Jul Kiaer (d 1931); 2 s (Maxwell, Leonard), 1 da (Karen); *Career* served war 1939-46, Maj RA 1 Commando Bde; shipowner; vice-chm Christian Salveson plc 1981- (dir 1952-, chm 1964-81); dir: The Royal Bank of Scotland plc 1965- (vice-chm 1981-85), The Royal Bank of Scotland Gp plc 1978-, Radio Forth Ltd 1973-, DFM Hldgs Ltd 1985, The Scottish Cncl Devpt and Indust 1972- (vice-pres 1985); memb cncl IOD, chm Scottish Widows' Fund and Life Assur Soc (past chm 1964-85), Edinburgh Investmt Tst plc 1965-85; memb: Queen's Body Guard for Scotland (The Royal Co of Archers), Lloyd's underwriter; Liveryman Worshipful Co of Shipwrights; chm Friends of the Queen's Hall Edinburgh 1980-85 (pres 1985); CBIM; kt 1985; *Recreations* hill farming, shooting, fishing; *Clubs* New (Edinburgh), Caledonian; *Style—* Sir Maxwell Harper Gow; Eventyr, Lyars Road, Longniddry, East Lothian EH32 0PT (☎ 0875 52142); 50 East Fettes Ave, Edinburgh EH4 1EQ (☎ 031 552 7101)

HARPHAM, Sir William; KBE (1966, OBE 1948), CMG (1953); s of William Harpham, of Grimsby (d 1932); *b* 3 Dec 1906; *Educ* Wintringham Secdy Sch Grimsby, Christ's Coll Cambridge; *m* 1943, Isabelle, da of Maurice Droz; 1 s, 1 da; *Career* HM Foreign Serv: dep to UK delgn to OEEC 1953-56, min Tokyo 1956-59, min (econ) Paris 1959-63, ambass to Bulgaria 1964-66, ret 1967; dir GB East Europe Centre

1967-80; *Clubs* RAC; *Style—* Sir William Harpham, KBE, CMG; 9 Kings Keep, Putney Hill, London SW15 6RA (☎ 081 788 1383)

HARPUR, Oonagh Mary; da of Dr William Ware Harpur, of Whincroft, Stubble Green, Drigg, Cumbria, and Patricia Elizabeth, *née* Coote; *b* 26 Sept 1953; *Educ* Univ of Keele (BA); *m* 18 Dec 1974, Peter Edward Clamp, s of Owen Gregory Edward Clamp, of 41 Richmond Rd, Caversham, Reading, Berks; 1 da (Jennifer Sarah b 23 Nov 1978); *Career* held various posts, especially advising bd membs and ctees NCB 1976-85, ldr Professional Practices Consulting Gp Spicer & Oppenheim 1985-87, assoc Strategic Planning Assoc Washington DC 1987-88, princ exec Berwin Leighton 1988-; former chm and current memb Network (orgn for top business women in the UK); *Recreations* clarinet playing especially chamber music, circle dancing, friends, going to opera and ballet; *Style—* Ms Oonagh Harpur; Berwin Leighton, Adelaide House, London Bridge, London EC4R 9HA (☎ 071 623 3144, fax 071 623 4416, telex 886420)

HARRAP, Robert Charles Henry; s of Robert Evan Harrap (d 1981), of Tunbridge Wells, and Gladys Mabel, *née* Webb (d 1972); *b* 2 Nov 1926; *Educ* Cranleigh Sch, Univ of London (LLB); *m* 30 March 1957, Anne Catherine, da of William Clark (d 1985), of Forest Row; 3 da (Claire b 1958, Judith b 1962, Elizabeth b 1966); *Career* admitted slr 1950; conslt Berrymans 1989- (ptnr 1954-, sr ptnr 1979-89); memb Coleman St Ward Club; Freeman City of London 1948, Liveryman City of London Slrs Co 1972; memb Law Soc 1950; *Recreations* walking, music; *Style—* Robert Harrap, Esq; Milton Cottage, Milton St, nr Alfriston, E Sussex BN26 5RN (☎ 0323 870882); Salisbury House, London Wall, London EC2M 5QN (☎ 071 638 2811, fax 071 920 0361, telex 892070)

HARRAP, Simon Richard; s of M W Harrap, of Marsh House, Bentley, and Cynthia Mary, *née* Darell; *b* 25 March 1941; *Educ* Harrow; *m* 24 May 1969, Diana, da of Ian Akers Douglas (d 1952); 1 s (Nicholas Guy 15 April 1975), 2 da (Louise Jane b 17 Oct 1971, Lara Sophie b 5 Jan 1979); *Career* Stewart Smith & Co 1960-71; dir: Stewart Wrightson N America Ltd 1971-88, Stewart Wrightson plc 1984-87, Willis Faber plc 1987-88, Gibbs Hartley Cooper Ltd 1988; *Style—* Simon Harrap, Esq; Gibbs Hartley Cooper Ltd, 27-33 Artillery Lane, London E1 7LP (☎ 071 247 5433)

HARRHY, Eiddwen Mair; *b* 14 April 1949; *Educ* St Winifred's Convent Swansea, Royal Manchester Coll of Music; *m* 23 Jan 1988, Gregory Strange; *Career* debut: Royal Opera House Covent Gdn 1974, English Nat Opera 1975; performances incl: Glyndebourne Festival, Scottish Opera, Welsh National Opera, Opera North, Teatro Colon Buenos Aires, La Scala Milan, Amsterdam Concertgebouw, Sydney Opera House, Hong Kong, NZ, LA, BBC Promenade concerts; recordings: EMI, Harmonia Mundi, Erato, Deutsche Grammophon, Virgin Classics; awards: Imperial League of Opera Prize Gold Medal, Miriam Licette Prize; *Recreations* chamber music concerts, watching rugby in Wales; *Clubs* Friends of the Musicians' Benevolent Fund; *Style—* Miss Eiddwen Harrhy; c/o Helen Sykes Artists' Management, 79 Bickenhall Mansions, Bickenhall Street, London W1H 3LD (☎ 071 224 3881)

HARRIES, Hon Mrs (Anne Marjorie); *née* Sidney; da (by 1 m) of 1 Visc De L'Isle, VC, KG, GCMG, GCVO, PC; descent King William IVs natural da Lady Sophia FitzClarence (d 1837) w 1 Baron De L'Isle and Dudley (d 1851); *b* 1947; *m* 1967, David Alexander Harries, s of Rear Adm David Hugh Harries, CB, CBE; 2 s (David b 1970, James b 1972), 1 da (Alexandra b 1968); *Style—* The Hon Mrs Harries; c/o Thomson Snell & Passmore, New Rents, Ashford, Kent

HARRIES, (John) Arthur Jones; CBE (1979), JP; s of Tom Llewelyn Harries, MBE, JP (d 1971), of Pilroath, Llangain, Carmarthen, Dyfed, and the late Muriel, *née* Thomas; *b* 24 Nov 1923; *Educ* Queen Elizabeth GS Carmarthen, Royal Veterinary Coll London; *m* 1, Nov 1950, Hazel (d 1982), da of Alec F Richards (d 1937), of Johnstown, Carmarthen; 2 s (Ieun, Gwyn), 2 da (Wendy, Julie); m 2, Margaret Mair; 2 s (Paul, Martin), 1 da (Annea); *Career* qualified vet 1946, self employed practice Carmarthen 1946-82; memb: Calvinistic and Deacon Moriah Chapel Llanstephan 1935-, cncl S Wales div Br Vet Assoc 1985-, cncl Br Vet Assoc 1966-86, cncl Trinity Coll Camarthen 1973-, Welsh Counties Ctee 1973- (ldr ind gp), cncl OU 1973, cncl Nat Eisteddfod 1975-84, Assoc of CCs 1976- (ind spokesman on educn and policy), nat steering gp Tech Vocational Educnl Initiative 1980-89, cncl Int Union of Local Authorities 1981-, cncl of Euro Municipalities 1981-, Welsh Adsvy Body 1984-89, ct and cncl Univ of Wales; chm Ctee for the Accreditation of Teacher Educn (SW Wales) 1990-, fndr (later sec, then pres) W Wales Vet Clinical Club 1950-, ldr Camarthenshire CC 1969-73 (memb 1966-73), vice chm Welsh Coll of Music and Drama Cardiff 1976-89; dir: WNO Co 1981-87, Business and Technician Educn Cncl 1986-; pres Camarthen Rotary Club 1982-83, admitted to the Druidical order of Gorsedd 1985, chm ctee Local Educn Authorities 1986-87; MRCVS 1946, memb BVA 1947; *Recreations* sailing, gardening; *Clubs* Rivertywi Yacht, Nat Liberal; *Style—* Arthur Harries, Esq, CBE, JP; 1 Whitehall Place, London

HARRIES, Rt Rev Richard Douglas; *see*: Oxford, Bishop of

HARRIES, Roy Edward; s of John Benjamin Harries (d 1983), and Elizabeth Anne, *née* Twigg; *b* 15 Sept 1943; *Educ* Rhondda County GS; *m* 21 Jan 1973, Caryl Ann Harries, da of Thomas James Jones (d 1965); 1 s (Neil Edward b 1976), 1 da (Joannie Louise b 1978); *Career* ptnr Barlow Mendham & Co 1974-75, sr ptnr Harries Watkins & Co (ptnr 1975); ACA 1972, FCA 1979; *Recreations* chess, reading, twentieth century history, music; *Style—* Roy Harries, Esq; Teg Fan, 67 Coychurch Rd, Pencoed, Mid-Glam (☎ 0656 865 683); 85 Taff St, Pontypridd, Mid Glam (☎ 01443 402 627); 16 Coychurch Rd, Pencoed, Mid-Glam (☎ 0656 863 000)

HARRIES-JENKINS, Dr Gwyn; s of Gwyn Charles Jenkins (d 1975), of Llanellen Gwent, and Olwen James; *b* 13 July 1931; *Educ* W Monmouth Sch, Univ Coll of Wales (LLB), Coll of Europe Bruges (Diplôme), Univ of E Anglia (MA, MPhil), Univ of Hull (PhD); *m* 24 March 1956, Williamina (Ina), da of George Mitchell Millar (d 1968), of Loddon, Norfolk; 3 da (Siona b 1957, Morag b 1960, Elaine b 1969); *Career* cmmnd RAF 1953: Flt Lt 1956, Sqdn Ldr 1963, ret 1970; dean of adult and continuing educn Univ of Hull 1987- (staff tutor in Social Studies 1969-77, sr lectr in adult educn 1977-83, dir of Dept of Adult Educn 1983-84); chm Fin and Gen Purposes Ctee Bishop Grosseteste Coll Lincoln, vice chm of Lincoln Diocesan Bd for Educn and Training; *Books* The Army in Victorian Society (1977), Armed Forces and the Welfare Societies (1982); *Recreations* reading and writing; *Style—* Dr Gwyn Harries-Jenkins; 6 The Ridings, Molescroft, Beverley, E Yorks HU17 7ER (☎ 0482 869902); School of Adult and Continuing Education, University of Hull HU6 7RX (☎ 0482 465937, fax 0482 465977, telex 592530 UNIHUL G)

HARRIMAN, Andrew Tuoyo; s of Chief H Harriman, of Windrush, Clare Hill, Esher, Surrey, and Irene, *née* Ogedegbe; *b* 13 July 1964; *Educ* Radley, Magdalene Coll Cambridge (exhibitioner, Rugby blue, Athletics blue); *Career* rugby player; Harlequins RFC: debut 1986, winner Middlesex 7s (three times), winner John Player Cup 1988; divnl rugby debut for London Oct 1988, int debut England v Australia Nov 1988 (injured thereafter), represented Barbarians RFC 1989; qualified chartered surveyor 1989-90, self-employed 1990-; GB U16 tennis doubles champion 1980; *Style—* Andrew Harriman, Esq; Harlequins RFC, Stoop Memorial Ground, Craneford Way, Twickenham, Middlesex

HARRIMAN, Hon Mrs (Pamela Beryl); da of late 11 Baron Digby, KG, DSO, MC, TD; *b* 1920; *m* 1, 1939 (m dis 1946), Maj the Hon Randolph Frederick Edward Spencer-Churchill, MBE (d 1968, eld s Rt Hon Sir Winston Churchill KG, PC, OM, CH, TD, DL (PM), and Baroness Spencer-Churchill (Life Peeress), *see* Peerage D of Marlborough); 1 s (Winston b 1940); m 2, 1960, Leland Hayward (d 1971); m 3, 1971, (William) Averell Harriman (d 1986); *Style—* The Hon Mrs Harriman; 3038 N Street NW, Washington DC, 20007, USA

HARRIMAN, Capt (Joseph) William Fletcher; TD (1989); s of Flt-Lt Joseph Fletcher Harriman MBE (d 1974), and Kathleen Harriman, *née* Robinson; *b* 27 April 1956; *Educ* Oakham Sch Rutland, Trent Poly Nottingham (BSc); *Career* S Notts Hussars Yeomanry RHA TA 1974-, troop commander 1986-88, seconded Royal Yeomanry as artillery advsr 1989; head of Catalogue Dept and princ valuer Weller and Dufty Auctioneers 1984-87 (conslt 1987-), ind conslt valuer and identifier of firearms 1987-, expert witness in ct cases for firearms and ballistics 1987; conslt to Br Assoc for Shooting and Conservation, conslt to BBC on arms and militaria, memb Panel of Experts Antiques Roadshow; assoc Inc Soc Valuers and Auctioneers; *Books* Experts on Antiques (contrib, 1987); *Recreations* shooting, riding, toxophily, wine, music; *Style—* William Harriman, Esq; 223 Chilwell Lane, Bramcote, Beeston, Nottingham NG9 3DU (☎ 0602 254417); Weller & Dufty Ltd, 141 Bromsgrove St, Birmingham B5 6RQ (☎ 021 692 1414, fax 021 622 5605, car 0860 247787)

HARRINGTON, Dr Christine (Mrs Maddocks); da of Edward Thomas Harrington, of Braintree, Essex, and Ida Oxborough, *née* Richardson (d 1981); *b* 21 Sept 1947; *Educ* Braintree County HS, Univ of Sheffield (MB ChB, MD); *m* 8 March 1982, John Leyshon Maddocks, s of Thomas Maddocks, of Mumbles, S Wales; 2 s (Geraint b 1983, Owen b 1986); *Career* conslt dermatologist 1980-; studies on bullous diseases, written works and nat and int lectures on diseases of the vulva; memb: Br Assoc of Dermatologists, N England Dermatological Soc, Euro Acad of Dermatology and Venereology; MRCP 1974, FRCP 1989; *Recreations* music, walking, gardening; *Style—* Dr Christine Harrington; Somersby, 3 Endcliffe Grove Ave, Endcliffe, Sheffield S10 3EJ (☎ 0742 667201); Dermatology Dept, Royal Hallamshire Hospital, Glossop Rd, Sheffield 10 (☎ 0742 766222)

HARRINGTON, Prof (John) Malcolm; s of John Roy Harrington, of Newport, Gwent, and Veda Naomi, *née* Harris; *b* 6 April 1942; *Educ* Newport HS, Kings Coll, Westminster Med Sch London (BSc, MB, BS, MSc, MD); *m* 20 May 1967, Madeline Mary, da of Brinley Hunter Davies (d 1971); 1 da (Kate b 27 Sept 1975); *Career* various hosp appts 1966-69, visiting scientist US Public Health Serv 1975-77, sr lectr in occupational med London Sch of Hygiene and Tropical Med 1977-80 (lectr 1969-75), fndn prof of occupational health Univ of Birmingham 1981-; chm Industrial Injuries Advsy Cncl, specialist advsr House of Lords select ctees, academic registrar Faculty of Occupational Med RCP, over 120 scientific papers published; memb: Soc Occupational Med, Soc Epidemiological Res, Int Epidemiology Assoc, Br Occupational Hygiene Soc; FRCP (MRCP, LRCP), MRCS, FFOM (MFOM), FACE USA; *Books* Recent Advances in Occupational Health (ed vol 2, 1984, ed vol 3, 1987), Occupational Health (with FS Gill, 1 edn 1983, 2 edn 1987, 3 edn 1991); *Recreations* music, theatre, gardening; *Style—* Prof Malcolm Harrington; Institute of Occupational Health, The University of Birmingham, Edgbaston, Birmingham B15 2TT (☎ 021 414 6022, fax 021 471 5208, telex 333762)

HARRINGTON, Dr Mary Gabrielle; *b* 28 Feb 1952; *Educ* St Hilda's Coll Oxford (MA), Middx Hosp Sch of Med (MB BS); *Career* res fell Hammersmith Hosp 1980-82, sr registrar Middx Hosp 1984-86, sr lectr King's Coll Sch of Med and Dentistry 1986-, conslt geriatrician King's Coll Hosp 1989-; MRCP 1980; *Style—* Dr Mary Harrington; 22 St George's Square, London SW1V 2HP (☎ 071 630 8128); King's College Hospital, Denmark Hill, London SE5 (☎ 081 693 3377)

HARRINGTON, Peter Roy; s of (Clifford) Roy Harrington, OBE, of Beeches, 33 Annings Lane, Burton Bradstock, Dorset, and Sylvia Abigail Bernadette, *née* Lilwall (d 1990); *b* 3 March 1951; *Educ* St John's Sch Leatherhead; *m* 8 Nov 1980, Sally Anne, da of John Leslie Boyer, OBE, of Friars Lawn, Norwood Green Road, Southall, Middx; 2 s (Oliver Brendan b 4 Sept 1981, Joshua Edward b 3 May 1984), 1 da (Pandora Jane b 11 Sept 1987); *Career* admitted slr 1977; ptnr 1978-: Kidd Rapinet, MacDonald Stacey; *Recreations* tennis, squash, golf, music; *Clubs* Royal Cwlth Soc; *Style—* Peter Harrington, Esq; 14/15 Craven St, London, WC2N 5AD (☎ 071 925 0303, fax 071 925 0334)

HARRINGTON, 11 Earl of (GB 1742); William Henry Leicester Stanhope; also Viscount Stanhope of Mahon, Baron Stanhope of Elvaston (both GB 1717), Baron Harrington (GB 1730), and Viscount Petersham (GB 1742); s of 10 Earl of Harrington, MC (d 1929, ggn of 4 Earl, inventor of the blend of snuff known as Petersham mixture, snuff being colour he used for his livery and equipage); suc kinsman, 7 and last Earl Stanhope, in the Viscountcy of Stanhope of Mahon and the Barony of Stanhope of Elvaston 1967; *b* 24 Aug 1922; *Educ* Eton; *m* 1, 1942 (m dis 1946), Eileen, da of Sir John Foley Grey, 8 Bt; 1 s (Viscount Petersham b 1945), 2 da (Lady Jane b 1942 d 1974, Lady Avena Maxwell b 1944); m 2, 1947 (m dis 1962), Anne, da of Maj Richard Chute, of Co Limerick; 1 s (Hon Steven b 1951), 2 da (Lady Trina b 1947, Lady Sarah Barry b 1951); m 3, 1964, Priscilla, da of Hon Archibald Cubitt (5 s of 2 Baron Ashcombe); 1 s (Hon John b 1965), 1 da; *Heir* s, Viscount Petersham, *qv*; *Career* Capt RAC serv WWII; landowner; adopted Irish citizenship 1965; *Clubs* Kildare Street (Dublin); *Style—* The Rt Hon the Earl of Harrington; Greenmount Stud, Patrickswell, Co Limerick, Ireland

HARRIS *see also*: Reader-Harris, Stuart-Harris, Sutherland Harris

HARRIS, Prof Adrian Llewellyn; s of Luke Harris, and Julia Wade; *b* 10 Aug 1950; *Educ* Liverpool Collegiate Sch, Univ of Liverpool (BSc, MB), Univ of Oxford (DPhil); *m* 7 July 1975, Margaret Susan, da of Rev Ronald Denman; *Career* clinical scientist Clinical Pharmacology Unit MRC Liverpool 1975-78, lectr med oncology Royal Marsden Hosp Oxford 1978-80, visiting fell ICRF 1981, prof of clinical oncology Univ of Newcastle 1981-88, ICRF prof of clinical oncology and dir of molecular laboratory Univ of Oxford 1988-; memb MRC; FRCP; *Recreations* swimming, walking, films and theatre; *Style—* Prof Adrian Harris

HARRIS, Prof Sir Alan James; CBE (1968); s of Walter Harris; *b* 8 July 1916; *Educ* Owen's Sch Islington, Northampton Poly, Univ of London (BSc); *m* 1948, Marie Thérèse, da of Prof Paul Delcourt (d 1976), of Paris; 2 s; *Career* WWII RE served NW Europe (despatches), Maj 1945; local govt engr 1933-40, sr ptnr (later conslt) Harris & Sutherland 1955-; memb Engrg Cncl 1982-85, emeritus prof of concrete structures Imperial Coll London 1981 (prof 1973-81), tstee Imperial War Museum 1983-89, pres Hydraulics Res Ltd 1989- (chm 1981-89); Hon DSc; FEng, FIStructE (pres 1978, gold medal 1984), FICE, MConsE; Croix de Guerre France 1945, Ordre du Mérite France 1978; kt 1980; *Recreations* sailing; *Clubs* Itchenor Sailing; *Style—* Prof Sir Alan Harris, CBE; 128 Ashley Gdns, Thirleby Rd, London SW1P 1HL (☎ 071 834 6924)

HARRIS, Alan John Fraser; s of Sqdn Ldr Nigel Mayne Wilfred Harris, of 16 Quaker Row, Coates, nr Cirencester, Glos, and Marion Lawrence, *née* Little; *b* 7 Jan 1942; *Educ* Charterhouse, Univ of Toronto (unfinished); *m* 18 June 1966, Veronica Fraser, da of Malcolm Carduff Calderwood (d 1985), of Eastbourne, E Sussex; 2 s (Malcolm b 3 July 1969, Rupert b 9 Feb 1971); *Career* investmt mangr; Black Geoghegan and Till

London 1960-66, Coopers and Lybrand Ltd Toronto 1966-68, Imperial Oil Ltd Toronto 1968-72, William Brandts Ltd London 1973-76, Lloyds Bank plc London 1976-85, Lloyds Merchant Bank Ltd London 1985-; asst treas East Chiltington PCC; Freeman City of London 1963, Liveryman Worshipful Co of Grocers 1977 (Freeman 1963); FCA 1975 (ACA 1965); *Recreations* football (soccer), cricket, golf; *Clubs* MCC, Old Carthusian Football; *Style—* Alan Harris, Esq; The Old Sch, Novington Lane, E Chiltington, Lewes, E Sussex BN7 3AX (☎ 0273 890 141); Lloyds Investmt Mangrs Ltd, 48 Chiswell St, London EC1Y 4GR (☎ 071 600 4500, fax 071 522 5412, telex 881 2696)

HARRIS, Ann Gertrude; MBE (1984); da of Reginald Thompson Harris (d 1956), of North Crawley, Newport Pagnell, Bucks, and Beatrice Amy, *née* Inglis (d 1961); *b* 27 July 1923; *Career* war work with Echo Radio Firm Aylesbury and Glasgow; camphill Rudolf Steiner Schs nr Aberdeen 1946-: trained under fndr Dr Karl Konig, involved with people with special needs and children with handicaps, fndr memb first communities in England The Sheiling Schs (Ringwood and Thornby nr Bristol), moved from Harley St office to Hertfordshire 1963 (responsible for arrangements for interviews, adults with mental handicaps and people who have undergone mental illness, addresses various gps of people to bring about a better awareness of people with handicaps); memb: Nationwide Counselling Serv, Nat Assoc for the Rehabilitation of Offenders, Nat Schizophrenic Fellowship, Assoc of Residential Communities, Assoc of Therapeutic Communities, Ctee Housing Assoc for Single People Islington; former memb Disablement Advsy Ctee for Watford area; called to address gps of: Soroptimists, Rotarians, Women's Insts; *Recreations* travel, including taking parties of handicapped people for 22 years abroad, keen interest in social problems and questions, but not biased politically; *Style—* Miss Ann Harris, MBE; The Camphill Village Trust, Delrow House, Aldenham, Watford, Herts (☎ 0923 856006)

HARRIS, Anthony David; LVO (1979); s of Reginald William Harris (d 1983), and Kathleen Mary, *née* Daw; *b* 13 Oct 1941; *Educ* Plymouth Coll, Exeter Coll Oxford; *m* 1, 1970 (m dis 1988), Patricia Ann, *née* Over; 1 s (Stuart Alexander Hugh b 1978); m 2, 6 March 1988, (Ann) Sophie, da of Prof Erik Kisling, of Brobyhus, OØrnholmvej 11, 3070 pr Snekkersten, Denmark; 2 s (Andreas William b 1988, Alexander Mattias b 1990); *Career* Dip Serv; joined 1964, Arabic Sch Lebanon 1965-67, third then second sec Jedda 1967-69, info offr Khartoum 1969-72, first sec and head of Chancery and HM Consul Abu Dhabi 1975-79, first sec UK perm mission to UN Geneva 1979-82, cnllr home inspectorate FCO 1982-83, regnl mktg dir Gulf States and Pakistan MOD 1983-86, cncllr and dep head of mission Cairo 1986-90, cncllr FCO 1990-; *Recreations* shooting (HM Queens prize Bisley 1964), skiing, climbing, diving, travel; *Clubs* North London Rifle (Bisley), British Cwlth Rifle (Bisley); *Style—* Anthony Harris, Esq, LVO; 13A Elm Bank Mansions, The Terrace, Barnes, London SW13 0NS (☎ 081 876 0081); HM Diplomatic Service, Foreign and Commonwealth Office, King Charles St, London SW1A 2AH (☎ 071 210 6159)

HARRIS, Sir Anthony Travers Kyrle; 2 Bt (UK 1953), of Chepping Wycombe, Bucks; s of Marshal of the RAF Sir Arthur Harris, 1 Bt, GCB, OBE, AFC, and 1 w, Barbara, da of Lt-Col E W K Money, 85th Regt (KSLI); *b* 18 March 1918; *Educ* Oundle; *Career* Nat Serv WWII, Queen Victoria's Rifles and Wilts Regt 1939-45, aux Units 1941, ADC to GOC-in-C Eastern Cmd 1944; reader for MGM 1951-52; subsequently work ed with antiques; *Recreations* music, horology; *Style—* Sir Anthony Harris, Bt; 33 Cheyne Ct, Flood St, London SW3

HARRIS, Cdr Antony John Temple; OBE (1963); s of George James Temple Harris (d 1929), and Eva Kenyon, *née* Green Wilkinson (d 1942); *b* 5 Aug 1915; *Educ* RNC Dartmouth, RNC Greenwich; *m* 25 April 1940, Doris (Deedee), da of Frank Dufford Drake (d 1981), of USA; 2 s (Michael b 1941, John b 1944); *Career* RN: Cadet 1933, Midshipman 1933-35, Home and Med Fleets 1937-38 (Sub Lt), Home Fleet China 1938-40 (Lt), Coastal Forces 1940-42, Long Anti-Submarine Course 1942, Escort Trg W Isles 1942-43, Lt and Lt Cdr E Indies and Pacific 1944-45, Naval Staff Course 1946, Torpedo Course 1946, Home Fleet 1947, TAS Course instr 1948, Cdr staff of C-in-C Home Fleet 1949-51, Jt Servs Staff Course 1951-52, Admty 1952-54, E Indies 1954-55, NATO (Gallant staff) USA 1958-60, NATO (staff of C-in-C North) Norway 1961-63, NATO (staff of C-in-C Channel) 1964-65, ret 1965; naval staff author MOD 1966-74; churchwarden St Nicholas Church Wickham 1965-72, field master Meon Valley Beagles 1969-74, memb Droxford RDC 1970-74; *Recreations* walking, beagling; *Style—* Cdr Antony Harris, OBE, RN; Hawthorns, Park Place, Wickham, Hants PO17 5EZ (☎ 0329 832 204)

HARRIS, Basil Vivian; s of Henry William Harris (d 1984), of Bexhill on Sea, and Sarah May, *née* Edwards (d 1983); *b* 11 July 1921; *Educ* Watford GS; *m* 15 May 1943, Myra Winifred Mildred, da of William Abbott Newport (d 1943), of Harrow; *Career* WWII RAF 1943-46; Engrg Res Dept GPO 1939-43 and 1946-63; FCO: Dip Wireless Serv 1963-71, dep chief engr Communications Div FCO 1971-79, chief engr 1979-81, ret 1981; contribs to numerous tech jls on communications; Civil Serv Cmmn 1981-87; CEng, MIEE 1956; *Recreations* golf, photography, travel; *Clubs* Royal Eastbourne Golf (formerly Capt); *Style—* Basil Harris, Esq; 13 Decoy Drive, Eastbourne, Sussex BN22 0AB (☎ 0323 505 819)

HARRIS, Brian Nicholas; s of Claude Harris (d 1976), and Dorothy, *née* Harris (d 1982); *b* 12 Dec 1931; *Educ* Coll of Estate Mgmnt Univ of London; *m* 18 March 1961, Rosalyn Marion, da of Geoffrey Alfred Caines (d 1982); 2 da (Suzanne b 1961, Jennifer b 1965); *Career* chartered surveyor; vice-chm: RICS Bldg Surveying Div 1976-77, RICS Continental Gp 1977-78; chm: Partnership of Richard Ellis 1984 (ptnr 1961), City Branch Royal CS 1984-85; memb Cncl: (and dep chm) London C of C 1985, Aust Br C of C (UK) 1988; govr (and dep chm) Woldingham Sch 1986; Liveryman and memb Ct of Assistants Worshipful Co of Glaziers and Painters of Glass 1975; *Recreations* flyfishing, gardening, golf; *Clubs* Carlton, Flyfishers', City of London; *Style—* Brian Harris, Esq; Grants Paddock, Grants Lane, Limpsfield, Surrey RH8 0RQ (☎ 0883 723215); Richard Ellis, 55 Old Broad St, London EC2M 1LP (☎ 071 256 6411, fax 071 256 8328)

HARRIS, Brian Thomas; OBE (1983), QC (1982); s of late Thomas John Harris, and late Eleanor May, *née* Roffey; *b* 14 Aug 1932; *Educ* Henry Thornton GS, King's Coll London; *m* 6 April 1957, Janet Rosina, da of Herbert W Hodgson; 1 s (Neil Andrew), 1 da (Jane Eleanor); *Career* called to the Bar Gray's Inn 1960, London Magistrates Ct 1963, clerk to the Justices Poole 1967-85, dir Professional Conduct Dept ICEAW 1985-; *Books* Criminal Jurisdiction of Magistrates (1986), The Rehabilitation of Offenders (1989) Halsburys Laws (contrib ed, Magistrates, 4 edn 1979); *Style—* Brian Harris, Esq, OBE, QC; Gloucester House, Silbury Boulevard, Central Milton Keynes, Bucks (☎ 0908 668833, fax 071 920 0547, telex 884443)

HARRIS, Bryan Kingston; s of Walter Henry Harris (d 1957), of Cambridge, and Ruth Olive, *née* Drake (d 1987); *b* 24 Dec 1932; *Educ* Cambridgeshire Tech Coll and Sch of Art, Univ of Nottingham (pres of Union 1958-59); *m* 4 Feb 1967, Elizabeth Ward, da of (Francis) Charles Wright (d 1986), of Burton-on-Trent; 1 s (Jonathan Kingston b 28 Nov 1967), 1 da (Charlotte Elizabeth b 21 Feb 1970); *Career* Nat Serv RASC 1951-53; studio mangr BBC External Servs 1959-64, current affrs prodr BBC Midland Region 1965-69, programme organiser BBC Radio Birmingham 1970-80; mangr: BBC Radio Cleveland 1980-82, BBC Radio Derby 1983-; chm Quarndon Parish Cncl 1987-, govr Mackworth Tertiary Coll Derby 1990-; memb: Derby Mozart Bi-Centenary Ctee, Derby Crime Prevention Panel, Derbyshire Ctee RNIB Looking Glass Appeal; vice pres Quarndon CC; *Recreations* pen and ink drawing, local history, travel; *Style—* Bryan Harris, Esq; Park Nook House, Inn Lane, The Common, Quarndon, Derby DE6 4LD (☎ 0332 553394); BBC Radio Derby, PO Box 269, Derby DE1 3HL (☎ 0332 361111, telex 37257, fax 0332 290794)

HARRIS, Carol Ruth; *née* Leibson; da of Dr Michael Leibson, and Sylvia, *née* Schwartz; *b* 2 Feb 1943; *Educ* Central Fndn Girls Sch, Highbury Hill HS, Univ of London (BSc); *m* 22 March 1964, Paul Harris, s of Sidney Harris, of Wanstead, London; *Career* conslt and trainer in personnel mgmnt and impression mgmnt 1986-; dir of personnel and admin Arts Cncl of GB 1979-86 (earlier posts in health serv, local govt, mgmnt consultancy and res), chm IPM Central London Gp, memb IPM Nat Ctees on Orgn and Manpower Planning and Public Serv, vice chm Alexandra Palace Action Gp; FIPM, MAIE; *Recreations* fencing, riding, collecting fans, Indian classical dance; *Style—* Mrs Carol Harris; 360 Alexandra Park Rd, London N22 4BD (☎ 081 889 6244)

HARRIS, Cecil Rhodes; s of Frederick William Harris (d 1954); *b* 4 May 1923; *Educ* Kingston GS; *m* 1946, Gwenyth, da of Hugh Llewelyn Evans (d 1956); 1 s, 2 da; *Career* Commercial Union Assur Co: asst gen mangr 1969-73, dep gen mangr and asst sec 1973-74, co sec 1974-78, dir 1975, exec dir 1976-, dep chief gen mangr 1980-82, chief exec 1982-85; dep chm Trade Indemnity plc 1986; FCIS, FSCA; *Recreations* bible study; *Style—* Cecil Harris, Esq; Ashley, 35a Plough Lane, Purley, Surrey CR8 3QJ (☎ 081 668 2820)

HARRIS, Charles James; s of Charles Allen Harris (d 1961), of 33 Ryebrook, Leatherhead, Surrey, and Ivy Irene, *née* Lipyear (d 1967); *b* 20 Dec 1958; *Educ* Harrow, Royal Acad of Arts (BA, MA); *Career* artist; protraits incl 1980-88: Rev Mother St Teresa's Convent, Col W.H.J. Sale, MBE, MC, Mr G Bulger (former pres Kerr McGee Oil), Eddie Durham (veteran jazz player); works incl: a picture requested by HRH Queen Elizabeth for the royal collection 1987, portrait of the Rt Hon David Steel MP 1987; awarded a sr academic cultural exchange to Russia 1987, lectures on traditional paintings 1987-88, Project 1988 (around the world painting tour on behalf of the World Wildlife Tst) 1988-89; Freeman City of London 1980, Liveryman Worshipful Co of Painters and Stainers 1983; *Books* The Primacy of Tone in Traditional Painting; *Recreations* sailing (Tasar Dingy World Championships); *Style—* Charles Harris, Esq; c/o Painters' Hall, 9 Little Trinity Lane, London EC4V 2AD

HARRIS, (Geoffrey) Charles Wesson; QC (1989); s of Geoffrey Hardy-Harris, of Tettenhall, nr Wolverhampton, Staffs, and Joan, *née* Wesson (d 1979); *b* 17 Jan 1945; *Educ* Repton, Univ of Birmingham (LLB); *m* 25 July 1970, Carol Ann, da of J D Alston, CBE, of South Lapham Hall, Norfolk; 2 s (Roger, Hugh), 1 da (Kate); *Career* called to the Bar Inner Temple 1967, in practice (Common law) London and Midlands 1968-, asst rec 1987-90, rec 1990-; Parly candidate (C) Penistone 1974; govr St Clement Danes C of E Primary Sch 1976-79; memb: Euro Bar Assoc, London Common Law and Commercial Bar Assoc; Liveryman Worshipful Co of Glaziers; *Books* contrib current edn Halsbury's Laws of England; *Recreations* history, stalking, skiing, architecture, shooting, fireworks; *Clubs* Carlton; *Style—* Charles Harris, Esq, QC; Westcot Barton Manor, Oxfordshire (☎ 0869 40624); 1 Harcourt Buildings, Temple, London EC4Y 9DA (☎ 071 353 0375, fax 071 583 5816)

HARRIS, Prof Christopher John; s of George Henry Harris, BEM, and Hilda Winifred, *née* Ward; *b* 23 Dec 1945; *Educ* Portsmouth GS, Univ of Leicester (BSc), Univ of Oxford (MA), Univ of Southampton (PhD); *m* 10 Sept 1965, (Ruth) Joy, da of Robert Garrod (d 1986); 1 s (Philip Jonathan b 1971), 2 da (Caroline Louise b 1968, Kathryn Ruth b 1978); *Career* lectr in electronics Univ of Hull 1969-72, lectr in control engrg and maths UMIST 1972-75, lectr and fell in engrg sci Univ of Oxford and St Edmund Hall 1976-80, prof and dep chief scientist MoD 1980-84, prof and chm of sch Cranfield Inst of Technol 1984-87, Lucas prof of aerospace Univ of Southampton 1987-; author of several scientific papers; CEng 1972, MIEE 1972, FIMA 1975; *Books* Mathematical Modelling of Turbulent Diffusion in the Environment (1979), Stability of Linear Systems (1980), Self Tuning and Adaptive Control (1981), The Stability of Input/Output Dynamic Systems (1983), Advances in Command, Control and Communication Systems (1987), Application of Artificial Intelligence to Command and Control Systems (1988); *Recreations* gardening, off-shore sailing, golf; *Style—* Prof Christopher Harris; Dept of Aeronautics & Astronautics, University of Southampton, Highfield, Southampton, Hants (☎ 0703 592353, fax 0703 593939, telex 47661 SOTONU G)

HARRIS, Christopher John Ashford; s and h of Sir Jack (Wolfred) Ashford Harris, 2 Bt; *b* 26 Aug 1934; *m* 1957, Anna, da of F de Malmanche, of Auckland, NZ; 1 s, 2 da; *Style—* Christopher Harris, Esq; 21 Anne St, Wadestown, Wellington, New Zealand

HARRIS, Rev Cyril Evans; JP (Beaconsfield 1976-); s of Arthur Frederick Harris (d 1982), of The Ridings, Angmering-on- Sea, Sussex, and Phillis, *née* Evans (d 1977); *b* 27 April 1930; *Educ* Cranleigh Sch, Eaton Hall Officer Cadet Sch, Lincoln Theol Coll, Central Sch for Arts and Crafts; *m* 29 May 1954, Heather Louie, da of George Frederick White; 3 s (Paul, Bruce, Martin), 2 da (Louise, Mary); *Career* Nat Serv 1948, cmmnd 2 Lt Essex Regt 1949, seconded Beds and Herts, served Greece 1949-50, Oxford and Bucks LI 1950; co mangr (theatrical supplies, TV, stage and screen) 1951-62, designer embroidery and costume; ordained: deacon 1963, priest 1964; curate and priest i/c Beaconsfield 1963-68, vicar St Giles Stoke Poges 1968-89; hon chaplain: Wexham Park Hosp 1987-, Educn Corps Wilton Park Beaconsfield, 4 Prince of Wales Offrs Assoc Gurkhas; chm: Stoke Poges First and Middle Schs, Stoke Common Tst; vice chm Stoke Poges Parish Cncl 1976-, tstee Lord Hastings Tst, govr Oakdene Sch Beaconsfield; fndr memb: Round Table, Beaconsfield Advsy Centre; memb: RSPB, Nat Tst; *Books* Guide to the Work and Life of Thomas Gray, Historical Guide of St Giles Stoke Poges; *Recreations* squash, tennis, hockey, art (oils), walking; *Clubs* Cranleigh Hockey; *Style—* The Rev Cyril Harris, JP; The Vicarage, Park Rd, Stoke Poges, Bucks (☎ 02814 4177)

HARRIS, David Anthony; MP (C) St Ives 1983-, MEP (EDG) Cornwall and Plymouth 1979-84; s of Edgar Courtenay Harris (d 1980), and Betty Doreen Harris (d 1977); *b* 1 Nov 1937; *Educ* Mount Radford Sch Exeter; *m* 1962, Diana Joan, *née* Hansford; 1 s (Justin b 1964), 1 da (Rebecca b 1967); *Career* journalist; W Country newspapers, political corr Daily Telegraph 1976-79 (joined 1961); *Clubs* Farmers; *Style—* David Harris Esq, MP; Trewedna Farm, Perranwell, nr Truro, Cornwall (☎ 0872 863200)

HARRIS, David Anthony; s of Dr Samuel Harris, and Joan, *née* Pegler; *b* 31 March 1954; *Educ* King Edward's Sch Birmingham, Univ of London (LLB); *m* 7 Nov 1987, Penelope Anne, da of Alfred Dalton, CB; 1 da (Sophie Olivia b 30 Sept 1988); *Career* admitted slr 1979; Field Fisher & Martineau 1977-82, ptnr Lovell White & King 1986 (joined 1982); Freeman Worshipful Co of Slrs; memb Law Soc; *Recreations* tennis, skiing, travel; *Style—* David Harris, Esq; Lovell White Durrant, 21 Holborn Viaduct, London EC1A 2DY (☎ 071 236 0066)

HARRIS, Prof David John; s of Sidney John William Harris, and Alice May, *née* Full (d 1955); *b* 3 July 1938; *Educ* Sutton HS Plymouth, Kings Col London (LLB), LSE (LLM, PhD); *m* 15 Aug 1964, Sandra, da of Denzil Nelson, of Arcadia, California; 2 s (Mark b 20 Sept 1967, Paul b 27 March 1972); *Career* asst lectr in law Queens Univ

Belfast 1962-63; Univ of Nottingham asst lectr in law 1963-65, lectr 1965-73, sr lectr 1973-81, prof of public int law 1981-, head of law dept; *Books* International Law: Cases and Materials (1973), Civil Liberties: Cases and Materials (1979), The European Social Charter (1984); *Recreations* walking, travel; *Style*— Prof David Harris; Department of Law, University of Nottingham, Nottingham (☎ 0602 484848)

HARRIS, David Keith; OBE (1987, MBE 1983), TD (1978); s of Edwin Harris (d 1974), of Epworth, Doncaster, and Mona Doreen, *née* Sleight; *b* 27 Jan 1945; *Educ* Worksop Coll, King's Coll London (LLB); *m* 25 Jan 1975, Veronica Mary, da of Arthur Vernon Harrison (d 1983), of Manor Farm, Finningley, Doncaster; *Career* Univ of London OTC 1963-67, cmmnd Royal Lincolnshire Regt TA 1967; served: 5 R Anglian 1967-78, 7 R Anglian 1978-80, SO2 G3 7 Field Force 1980-82, SO2 G3 49 Inf Bde 1982; cmd 7 R Anglian 1984-87, dep cdr 49 Inf Bde 1987-90, TA Col RMAS 1991-; admitted slr 1969, sr ptnr Richmonds 1987- (co dir); Parly candidate (Cons) for Bassetlaw Oct 1974 and May 1979; memb Law Soc 1967; ADC 1990; *Recreations* shooting, gardening, good food and wine; *Clubs* East India; *Style*— Col David Harris, OBE, TD; Green Hill House, Haxey, Doncaster, S Yorks DN9 2JU (☎ 0427 752794); Richmonds, 35 Potter St, Worksop, Nottingham S80 2AG (☎ 0909 474321, fax 0909 483852, car 0836 298307) and Gainsborough (☎ 0427 613831)

HARRIS, David Kingsley Neale; *b* 15 March 1947; *Educ* Sherborne, Oriel Coll Oxford (MA); *Career* asst slr Stephenson Harwood & Tatham 1973-74 (articled clerk 1970-73), ptnr Kenneth Brown Baker 1977-83 (asst slr Conveyancing Dept 1974-77), ptnr Turner Kenneth Brown (created by merger 1983) 1983-; *Style*— David Harris, Esq; 9 St Anne's Road, Barnes, London SW13 9LH

HARRIS, David Laurence; *b* 19 June 1944; *Educ* Liverpool GS, Coll of Law, Inst of Taxation (Law Soc prize); *m* 1973, Maureen Ann, *née* Cocklin; 2 s, 1 da; *Career* Govt serv exec various appts 1963-73, ptnr Tax Law Dept Nabarro Nathanson 1973-82; dir N M Rothschild & Sons Ltd 1982-, chief exec Rothschild Trust Corporation Ltd 1982, dir N M Rothschild & Sons (CI) Ltd 1985, non-exec dir N M Rothschild Asset Management Ltd 1984; memb Law Soc, fell Inst of Taxation; *Recreations* art, opera, sport, gardening; *Style*— David Harris, Esq; Director, N M Rothschild & Sons Limited, PO Box 185, New Court, St Swithin's Lane, London EC4P 4DU

HARRIS, David Leslie; s of Leslie Godfrey Harris (d 1959), and Frances Olive, *née* Jones (d 1974); *b* 24 April 1938; *Educ* Watford GS, Westminster Hosp Med Sch (MB BS, MS); *m* 22 Feb 1966, Patricia Ann (Trish), da of William Charles David Hooper (d 1978); 1 s (Stephen b 1967, d 1986), 3 da (Vanessa b 1967, Joanna b 1968, Sally b 1976); *Career* conslt plastic surgn and head of Dept Derriford Hosp Plymouth 1972-, civilian conslt in plastic surgery RN Hosp Stonehouse Plymouth 1978-86, chm Div of Surgery Plymouth Health Authy 1981-84, hon visiting conslt in plastic surgery to Gibraltar Health Authy St Bernard's Hosp Gibraltar 1985-, civilian conslt RN 1986-; numerous pubns on psychological aspects of plastic surgery and treatment of hypospadias; memb: Br Assoc of Plastic Surgns (pres 1989-), Int Soc of Aesthetic Plastic Surgns, Br Assoc of Aesthetic Plastic Surgns (pres 1989-90), Faculty Educnl Fndn MRCS 1961, FRCS 1966; *Recreations* garden, music, dining out, sailing; *Clubs* Plymouth Legal and Medical Dining, Royal Western Yacht; *Style*— David Harris, Esq; West Park House, Tamerton Foliot, Plymouth PL5 4NG (☎ 0752 773411); Nuffield Hospital, Derriford Rd, Plymouth PL6 8BG (☎ 0752 707345)

HARRIS, David Michael; QC (1989); s of Maurice Harris, of Liverpool, and Doris, *née* Ellis; *b* 7 Feb 1943; *Educ* Liverpool Inst HS for Boys, Univ of Oxford (BA, MA), Univ of Cambridge (PhD); *m* 16 Aug 1970, Emma Lucia, da of Dr Italo Calma, of Liverpool; 2 s (Julian b 3 July 1974, Jeremy b 9 May 1977), 1 da (Anna b 10 May 1980); *Career* asst lectr in law Univ of Manchester 1967-69, called to the Bar 1969, rec 1988- (asst rec 1984-88); *Books* Winfield & Jolowicz on Tort (co-ed, 1971), Supplement to Bingham's The Modern Cases on Negligence (co-ed, 1985); *Recreations* arts, travel, sport; *Style*— David M Harris, Esq, QC; 20 Aldbourne Ave, Liverpool L25 6JE (☎ 051 722 2848); Peel House, 3rd Floor, Harrington St, Liverpool L2 9XN (☎ 051 236 0718, fax 051 255 1085)

HARRIS, Prof David Russell; s of Dr Herbert Melville Harris (d 1976), of Oxford, and Norah Mary, *née* Evans (d 1985); *b* 14 Dec 1930; *Educ* St Christopher Sch Letchworth Herts, Univ of Oxford (MA, BLitt), Univ of California Berkeley (PhD); *m* 5 July 1957, Helen Margaret, da of Dr Gilbert Ingram Wilson (d 1980), of Stafford; 4 da (Sarah b 1959, Joanna b 1962, Lucy b 1964, Zoë b 1969); *Career* Nat Serv RAF 1949-50; teaching asst and instr Univ of California 1956-58, lectr Queen Mary Coll London 1958-64; UCL: lectr and reader 1964-79, prof of human environment Inst of Archaeology 1979- (dir 1989-); memb: Museum of London Archaelogy Ctee 1984-, English Heritage Sci and Conservation Panel 1985-; chm science-based archaeology Ctee SERC 1989-, pres Prehistoric Soc 1990-; FSA 1982; *Books* Plants, Animals and Man in the Outer Leeward Islands (1965), Africa in Transition (with B W Hodder, 1967), Human Ecology in Savanna Environments (1980), Foraging and Farming (with G C Hillman, 1989); *Recreations* hill walking, archaeo-ecological overseas travel; *Clubs* Athenaeum; *Style*— Prof David Harris; Institute of Archaeology, University College London, 31-34 Gordon Square, London WC1H 0PY (☎ 071 380 7483, fax 071 387 8057)

HARRIS, Prof (Norman) Duncan Campany; s of Willie Frederic Harris (d 1956), and Georgina Frances, *née* Campany; *b* 13 Dec 1933; *Educ* Heversham Sch Milnthorpe, Univ of Nottingham (BSc, MSc), Univ of Bath (PhD); *m* 8 April 1961, Patricia Mary, da of Wilfred Georgeson, of 20 Valley Rd, Macclesfield, Cheshire; 2 da (Jane b 1962, Susan b 1963); *Career* instr Lt served RN 1956-59 RN and RNR 1959-65, instr Lt-Cdr RNR 1965-69; Schoolmaster King Edward Sch Birmingham 1959-64, head of physics Ellesmere Port GS for Boys 1964-67, sr lectr Sch of Educn Univ of Bath 1980-85 (lectr 1967-80); Univ of Brunel: head Dept of Educn, prof of educn 1986-, dean of Faculty of Educn and Design 1989-; memb: Br Educnl Res Assoc, Assoc Educnl Trg and Tech, PCC St Michael's Church; FRSA 1987; *Books* incl: Aspects of Educational Technology VI (with K Austwick, ed 1972), Educational Technology in European Higher Education (1976), Preparing Educational Materials (1979), Guide to Evaluating Methods: Microtechnology Innovation (with R Strachan, 1983), Asssessing and Evaluating for Learning (with C D Bell, 1986 and 1990), Health Education (with C James and J Balding, 1988), also various pubns on educnl techniques; *Recreations* walking, gardening, classical music, theatre; *Style*— Prof Duncan Harris; Dept of Education, Runnymede Campus, Brunel University, Englefield Green, Egham, Surrey TW20 0JZ (☎ 0784 431341, fax 0784 72879, telex 261173 G)

HARRIS, Prof Frank; s of David Aaron Harris (d 1948), and Miriam, *née* Silber (d 1977); *b* 6 Oct 1934; *Educ* Univ of Capetown (MB ChB, MMed (paediatrics), MD); *m* 13 Mar 1963, Brenda Henriette, da of Samuel van Embden (d 1982); 2 s (David b 1964, Evan b 1965); *Career* Univ of Liverpool: prof of child health 1974-89, pro vice chllr 1981-84, dean Faculty of Med 1985-88; dean Sch of Med and prof of paediatrics Univ of Leicester 1990; memb: Liverpool Health Authy 1977-83, CRM 1981; Mersey RHA 1983-89, CSM 1990, Trent RHA 1990, GMC 1989, Leicestershire DHA 1990; FRCPE 1975, FRCP 1982; *Books* Paediatric Fluid Therapy (1973); *Recreations* golf; *Style*— Prof Frank Harris

HARRIS, (Walter) Frank; s of Walter Stanley Harris (d 1955), and Ellen, *née* Shackell (d 1985); *b* 19 May 1920; *Educ* King Edward VI Sch Birmingham, Univ of Nottingham (BCom), Univ of SA, Open Univ (BA); *m* 8 Aug 1941, Esther Blanche (Tessa), da of Harold Joe Hill; 2 s (Walter Douglas b 1945, Clive Richard b 1947), 2 da (Christine Mary Beatrice (Tina) b 1953, Sarah Elizabeth Frances b 1956); *Career* WWII RAFVR 1939-46, Coastal Cmd Pilot, demobbed as Flt Lt; Wood Bastow Nottingham 1948-49, Ford of Britain 1950-65, princ city offr and town clerk Newcastle upon Tyne 1965-69, dir Massey Ferguson 1969-71, fin dir Dunlop SA 1971-79, Dunlop Tyres 1980-81; parish and dist cncllr 1966-69; FCA, FCIS, FCMA; *Recreations* astrophysics, fell-walking, DIY; *Clubs* Reform, Beacon, Brunswick; *Style*— Frank Harris, Esq; Acomb High House, Northumbria NE46 4PH (☎ 0434 602844)

HARRIS, Geoffrey Ronald; s of Clarence Edgar Harris (d 1966); *b* 10 Sept 1926; *Educ* Whitgift; *m* 1953, Joan Lyn, da of George Jarvis; 2 s (Nigel David, Mark Stephen), 1 da (Sally Elizabeth); *Career* WWII Lt served Germany and India; insur broker; dir: Stewart Wrightson (Marine) 1965-88, Codresa (Spain) 1973-88, Stewart Wrightson Chile Ltd 1978-88, Stewart Wrightson Cusur (Argentina) 1978-88, Golding Stewart Wrightson 1985-88, insur conslt Alexander Howden Reinsurance Brokers Ltd 1989-; *Recreations* sport, travel; *Style*— Geoffrey Harris, Esq; Rookwood, Lower Park Rd, Chipstead, Surrey (☎ 0737 553768); Alexander Howden Reinsurance Brokers Ltd, 8 Devonshire Square, London EC2M 4PL (☎ 071 623 5500, telex 882171)

HARRIS, Geoffrey Thomas; CBE (1968); s of John Henry Harris (d 1937), of Lincoln; *b* 4 Aug 1917; *Educ* Lincoln Sch, Christ's Coll Cambridge (MA, PhD); *m* 1940, (Constance) Geraldine, da of Vernon Seymour White (d 1967), of Wallingford; 4 children; *Career* md Jessop-Saville Ltd Sheffield 1967-73 (res and tech dir 1951-61), directeur relations techniques Creusot-Loire SA (France) 1973-82, consltg engr 1982-; pres Iron and Steel Inst 1972-73; FEng; *Recreations* music (organ); *Clubs* Athenaeum; *Style*— Dr Geoffrey T Harris, CBE; 103 Oak Tree Rd, Tilehurst, Reading, Berks RG3 6LA (☎ 0734 417506)

HARRIS, 6 Baron Harris (UK 1815); George Robert John Harris; s of 5 Baron Harris, CBE, MC (d 1984), and Dorothy Mary (d 1981), da of Rev John Crookes; *b* 17 April 1920; *Educ* Eton, Christ Church Oxford; *Career* Capt RA; *Style*— The Rt Hon the Lord Harris; Huntingfield, Faversham, Kent (☎ 0795 282)

HARRIS, Glyn; s of Ivor Kenneth Harris, and Ivy Margaret, *née* Goddard; *b* 11 Sept 1950; *Educ* Whitchurch GS, Bristol Poly; *m* 29 June 1974, Jill Rosalind, da of Frank Colin Simon Sudbury; 1 s (Stephen Neil b 24 July 1975), 2 da (Sally Elizabeth b 3 April 1977, Amy Rebecca b 29 April 1981); *Career* fin dir and co sec Craig Shipping plc 1983 (joined 1967); memb Round Table; MCT; *Recreations* sailing, badminton; *Style*— Glyn Harris, Esq; 113-116 Bute Street, Cardiff, S Glamorgan CF1 6TE (☎ 0222 488636, fax 0222 494775, telex 498527)

HARRIS, Graham Derek; s of Philip Henry Harris, of 16 Hardwick Rd, Folkestone, Kent, and May Dorothy, *née* Perovich; *b* 28 Sept 1956; *Educ* King's Sch Canterbury Kent, Oriel Coll Oxford (MA); *m* 14 Feb 1987, Katarine Maria, da of Boris Stanislaus Brandl (d 1955), of Garstang, Lancs; 1 da (Philippa Josephine Brandl b 28 Sept 1989); *Career* slr; articled clerk Norton Rose Botterell & Roche 1979-83, admitted 1981, ptnr Richards Butler 1988- (joined 1983); SSC; *Style*— Graham Harris, Esq; Richards Butler, Beaufort House, 15 St Botolph St, London EC3A 7EE (☎ 071 247 6555, telex 949494 RBLAW G, fax 071 247 5091)

HARRIS, Prof Henry; s of late Sam Harris, and late Ann Harris; *b* 28 Jan 1925; *Educ* Sydney Boys' HS, Univ of Sydney (Garton scholar BA, MB BS, Freehill prize for Italian), Univ of Oxford (MA, DPhil, DM); *m* 1950, Alexandra Fanny Brodsky; 1 s, 2 da; *Career* resident med offr Royal Prince Albert Hospital Sydney Aust 1950, res offr Dept of Physiology Univ of Melbourne 1951, dir of res Br Empire Cancer Campaign at Sir William Dunn Sch of Pathology Oxford 1954-59, visiting scientist NIH USA 1959-60; head of Dept of Cell Biology John Innes Inst 1960-63, prof of pathology Univ of Oxford 1963-79, visiting prof Vanderbilt Univ 1968, Walker-Ames prof Univ of Washington 1968, foreign prof Collège de France 1974; memb: ARC 1968-78 (chm Animals Res Bd 1976-78), Cncl Euro Molecular Biology Orgn 1974-76, Cncl Royal Soc 1971-72, Scientific Advsy Ctee CRC 1961-85; govr Euro Cell Biology Orgn 1973-75; lectr numerous public lectures; corr memb: Aust Acad of Sci, American Assoc for Cancer Res, Waterford Striped Bass Derby Assoc (foreign correspondent); hon memb: American Assoc of Pathologists, German Soc for Cell Biology; foreign memb Max Planck Soc, foreign hon memb American Soc of Arts and Scientists, hon fell Cambridge Philosophical Soc; Hon DSc Univ of Edinburgh 1976; Hon MD: Univ of Geneva 1982, Univ of Sydney 1983; Hon FRCPath Aust, FRCP, FRCPath, FRS; *Publications* Nucleus and Cytoplasm (1968, 2 edn 1970, 3 edn 1974), Cell Fusion (1970), Le Fusion Cellulaire (1974), The Balance of Improbabilities (1987), papers on cellular physiology and biochemistry; *Style*— Prof Henry Harris, FRS; Sir William Dunn School of Pathology, South Parks Road, Oxford OX1 3RE (☎ 0865 275503)

HARRIS, Hugh Christopher Emlyn; s of T E Harris, CB, CBE, (d 1955), and M A Harris (d 1980); *b* 25 March 1936; *Educ* The Leys Sch, Trinity Coll Cambridge (MA); *m* 7 Sept 1968, Pamela Susan, da of R A Woollard (d 1980); 1 s (William b 1972), 1 da (Kate b 1970); *Career* Nat Serv Lt RA 1954-56; dir: BE Services Ltd 1979-, Houblon Nominees 1988-, The Securities Management Trust Ltd 1988-; Bank of England: joined 1959, chief of corp servs 1984-88, assoc dir 1988-; dir Solefield School Educational Trust Ltd, churchwarden St Margaret's Lothbury, hon treas Royal Br Legion Kemsing Branch, memb Cncl Business in the Community; ACIB, FIPM, FRSA; *Recreations* rugby, tennis; *Style*— Hugh Harris, Esq; Bank of England, London EC2R 8AH (☎ 071 601 3131)

HARRIS, Iain Grant Nicolson; *b* 17 March 1946; *Educ* George Heriot's Sch Edinburgh, Univ of Aberdeen (MA); *m* 8 Aug 1969, Jane Petrie, *née* Robertson; 1 s (Grant b 1975), 1 da (Rochelle b 1980); *Career* sales promotion mangr RMC Group 1968-73; dir: Parker PR Associates Ltd 1973-80, Shandwick Consultants Ltd 1980-82, Good Relations City Ltd 1982-85; chm: Lombard Communications Ltd 1985-90, Wolfe Lombard Ltd 1985-90, Lombard Group plc 1988-90, Lombard Consultants 1989-90, Lombard PR Ltd 1989-90, First Pacific Ltd 1990-; pres Lombard Communications Inc (USA) 1987-; pres: Windsor Soc for Mentally Handicapped Children and Adults, Windsor Talking Newspaper; tstee New Windsor Community Assoc, vice pres Royal Windsor Rose and Horticultural Soc, Mayor Royal Borough of Windsor and Maidenhead 1976-78 (borough cncllr 1970-79); Freeman City of London 1982; *Recreations* gardening supervision, travel; *Style*— Iain Harris, Esq; Chanonry, St Leonard's Hill, Windsor, Berks SL4 4AT (☎ 0753 863452)

HARRIS, Lt-Gen Sir Ian Cecil; KBE (1967, CBE 1958), CB (1962), DSO (1945); s of late J W A Harris; *b* 7 July 1910; *Educ* Portora Royal Sch Enniskillin, RMC Sandhurst; *m* 1945, Anne-Marie Desmotreux; 2 s; *Career* 2 Lt Ulster Rifles 1930, WWII served NW Europe and Burma (despatches), Lt-Col 1952, Brig 1958, Maj-Gen 1960, GOC Singapore Base Dist 1960-62, chief of staff Contingency Planning SHAPE 1963-66, Lt-Gen 1966, GOC NI 1966-69, ret; owner Victor Stud, memb of family partnership and mangr Ballykisteen Stud Tipperary, chm Irish Bloodstock Breeders Assoc 1977-; *Style*— Lt-Gen Sir Ian Harris, KBE, CB, DSO; Acraboy House, Monard, Co Tipperary, Ireland (☎ 052 51564)

HARRIS, Irene; da of Sydney Harris (d 1971), film prodr, and Kitty Harris (d 1963); *b* 11 May 1948; *Educ* Wessex Gdns and Whitefields Secdy Sch; *Career* special events dir UN, organiser Women of the Year Luncheon, convener Women of Tomorrow

Awards, fndr pres and memb Network, memb IOD; FRSA; *Recreations* films, communicating with others; *Style*— Ms Irene Harris; 8 Thornton Place, London W1H 1FGF (☎ 071 935 7059)

HARRIS, Sir Jack Wolfred Ashford; 2 Bt (UK 1932), of Bethnal Green, London; s of Rt Hon Sir Percy Harris, 1 Bt, PC, DL (d 1952); *b* 23 July 1906; *Educ* Shrewsbury, Trinity Hall Cambridge; *m* 1933, Patricia, da of Arthur Penman, of NSW; 2 s, 1 da; *Heir* s, Christopher John Ashford Harris; *Career* chm Bing Harris & Co NZ 1935-; past pres Wellington C of C; *Recreations* reading, gardening, swimming, writing; *Clubs* Wellington; *Style*— Sir Jack Harris, Bt; Flat 12, Quarterdeck, Carabella St, Kirribilli, NSW, Aust; Te Rama, Waikanae, New Zealand (☎ 5001)

HARRIS, Prof John Buchanan; s of John Benjamin Sargent Harris (d 1971), of Adelaide, Aust, and Mary Isobel, *née* Pratt; *b* 18 Jan 1940; *Educ* Tiffin Sch Kingston upon Thames, Univ of London (BPharm), Univ of Bradford (PhD); *m* 6 Sept 1965, Christine Margaret, da of Clifford Morton Holt (d 1983), of Bradford, W Yorks; 2 s (Joel b and d 1972, Jolyon Leo b 1974), 1 da (Danica Mathilde b 1981); *Career* res asst Univ of Bradford 1963-67; Univ of Newcastle: sr res asst 1967-72, princ res assoc 1972-74, sr lectr 1974-80, prof 1980-; res fell Univ of Lund Sweden 1970-71, UCLA America 1977-78, Monash Univ Melbourne Aust 1978; FIBiol; *Books* Muscular Dystrophy and other Inherited Diseases of Muscle in Animals (1979), Natural Toxins (1986), Muscle Metabolism (with D M Turnbull, 1990); *Recreations* reading, philately, walking; *Style*— Prof John Harris; 37 Bridge Park, Newcastle upon Tyne NE3 2DX (☎ 091 2854913); University of Newcastle School of Neurosciences, Muscular Dystrophy Group Laboratories, Regional Neurological Centre, Newcastle General Hospital, Newcastle upon Tyne NE4 6BE (☎ 091 2738811 ext 22632, fax 091 2722641)

HARRIS, John Charles; DL (S Yorks 1986); s of Sir Charles Joseph William Harris, KBE (d 1986), and Emily Kyle, *née* Thompson; *b* 25 April 1936; *Educ* Dulwich, Clare Coll Cambridge (BA, MA, LLB, LLM); *m* 1 April 1961, Alison Beryl, da of Dr Kenneth Reginald Sturley; 1 s (Edward John Charles b 16 June 1968), 1 da (Susan Alison b 15 Sept 1966); *Career* Nat Serv 2 Lt Intelligence Corps 1954-56; with UK AEA (seconded to OECD) 1959-63, Poole Borough Cncl 1963-67, admitted slr 1966, dep town clerk Bournemouth CB 1971-73 (offr 1967-73); S Yorks CC 1973-86: co sec 1973-83, chief exec and co clerk 1983-86, non-exec dir S Yorks Passenger Tport Exec, clerk to Lord-Lieut S Yorks 1983-86; conslt incl recruitment for PA Conslt Gp, admin Eng Camerata, freelance corr on public affrs, non exec dir Pontefract Health Authy 1990-; memb: Rampton Special Hosp Ctee, Arts Cncl Touring Advsy Bd, Bd Northern Counties Housing Assoc, Ctee Ackworth Gp Riding for the Disabled Assoc 1976-; fndr memb and sec Barnsley Rotary Club 1976-79, vice chm and sec Friends of Opera North 1978-87; Opera North plc: memb Cncl 1979-88, memb Devpt Ctee 1987-; nat chm Soc of Co Secs 1983, hon PR offr S Yorks and Humberside Region RDA 1983-; memb: Chief Exec Cncl Soc of Local Authys Chief Exec 1984-86, RDA Nat Pubns Ctee 1988-90; Freeman City of London 1957; FRSA 1984; *Recreations* foreign travel, opera, competitive trail riding; *Clubs* Leeds; *Style*— John Harris, Esq, DL; Long Lane Close, High Ackworth, Pontefract, Yorkshire, WF7 7EY (☎ 0977 795 450)

HARRIS, Prof John Edwin (Jack); MBE (1981); s of John Frederick Harris (d 1978), and Emily Margaret, *née* Prosser (d 1980); *b* 2 June 1932; *Educ* Larkfield GS Chepstow, Univ of Birmingham (BSc, PhD, DSc); *m* 9 June 1956, Ann, da of Peter James Foote (d 1976); 2 s (Peter b 28 March 1957, Ian b 17 May 1962), 2 da (Wendy b 3 Feb 1962, Perlita b 6 April 1966); *Career* res worker AEI John Thompson 1956-59; Berkeley Nuclear Laboratories CEGB: res offr 1959-64, section head 1964-88, univ liaison offr 1988; visiting prof of engrg Univ of Manchester 1989-; memb: Bd of Br Nuclear Energy Soc, Bd of Visitors Leyhill Open Prison 1967-; FIM 1974, FEng 1987, FRS 1988; *Books* Physical Metallurgy of Reactor Fuel Elements (ed), Vacancies (ed 1976); *Recreations* writing popular articles on sci; *Clubs* Cam Bowling (non playing memb); *Style*— Prof Jack Harris, MBE; Church Farm House, 28 Hopton Rd, Upper Cam, Dursley, Glos GL11 5PB (☎ 0453 543165)

HARRIS, John Eric; s of Jack Harris (d 1982), of Ilford, Essex, and Freda, *née* Jacobs (d 1979); *b* 29 April 1932; *Educ* Slough GS, Plaistow GS; *m* 1, 15 June 1958, Helene Hinda (d 1985), da of Aaron Coren (d 1960), of 19 Morton Way, Southgate, London N14; 1 s (Daniel Bruce b 1960), 1 da (Allyson b 1961); m 2, 10 Dec 1989, Jacqueline Maureen, da of Alfred Freeman (d 1989), of Kendene, Bishops Ave, London; wid of Philip Leigh; *Career* chm: Alba plc 1987, Harvard Int 1980-87, Bush Radio plc, Satellite Technol Systems Ltd; md Harris Overseas Ltd 1963-82; dir: Alba France SA, Hinari Deutschland GMbn; chm and tstee Helene Harris Meml Tst promoting res into ovarian cancer; *Recreations* reading, bridge, golf, theatre, opera; *Style*— John Harris, Esq; Arranmore, 19 Totteridge Village, London N20 8PN (☎ 081 446 3300); Harvard House, 14-16 Thames Rd, Barking, Essex OHX 1GII (☎ 081 594 5533, car 0034 214 309)

HARRIS, John Frederick; s of John Harris (d 1942), and Lily, *née* Heard (d 1985); *b* 9 Dec 1938; *Educ* Central GS Birmingham, Aston Tech Coll Birmingham, Univ of Aston; *m* 27 Aug 1960, Diana Joyce, da of Stanley John Brown, of Nottingham; 1 s (Alastair Charles b 1961), 2 da (Mary Julia b 1963, Susan Elizabeth b 1977); *Career* dep chm NORWEB 1979-82, dir Saudi Arabia BEI Ltd 1978-84, dir BEI Ltd 1982-87, chm EMEB 1982-90, chm East Midlands Electricity plc 1990-; pres Nottinghamshire VSO; memb: cncl IEE, Chartered Engr 1967; FIEE 1982, companion Br Inst of Mgmnt 1984; *Recreations* golf, opera, gardening; *Style*— John Harris, Esq; East Midlands Electricity plc, Coppice Rd, Arnold, Notts (☎ 0602 269711)

HARRIS, His Hon Judge John Percival Harris; DSC (1945), QC (1974); s of Thomas Percival Harris (d 1981), of Ebbor Hall, Somerset; *b* 16 Feb 1925; *Educ* Wells Cathedral Sch, Pembroke Coll Cambridge (BA); *m* 1959, Janet Valerie, da of Archibald William Douglas, of Jersey, CI; 1 s, 2 da; *Career* Sub Lt RNVR 1943-46, serv: Western Approaches, Far East, China, Japan; called to the Bar Middle Temple 1949 (master of the bench 1970), rec Crown Court 1972-80, circuit judge 1980-, dep sr judge of the Ct of the Sovereign Base Area Cyprus; *Recreations* golf, reading, Victorian paintings; *Clubs* Woking Golf, Rye, Golf, The Royal St George's Golf; *Style*— His Hon Judge Harris, DSC, QC; Tudor Court, Fairmile Park Rd, Cobham, Surrey KT11 2PP (☎ 0932 864756)

HARRIS, Prof John Raymond; s of John Seddon Harris (d 1974), of St Helens, Lancs, and Mary, *née* Eccleston (d 1954); *b* 14 May 1923; *Educ* Univ of Manchester (BA, MA, PhD); *m* 8 Aug 1953, Margaret Thelma, da of John Knockton (d 1980), of St Helens, Lancs; 2 s (Paul, Philip); *Career* Royal Signals, RAEC 1943-47; Dept of Economics Univ of Liverpool: tutor 1953, lectr 1957, sr lectr 1963, dir of social studies 1965, reader 1969; Univ of Birmingham: prof of econ history, head Dept of Econ and Social History 1970-90, dean Faculty of Commerce and Social Sciences 1978-81, dir Ironbridge Inst 1980-90, emeritus prof 1990-; chm Int Ctee for the Conservation of Industl Heritage 1981-84, tstee Ironbridge Gorge Museum, memb Cncl Econ History Soc 1963-; FRHistS; Chevalier de l'Ordre des Arts et des Lettres France 1990; *Books* Merseyside Town in Industrial Revolution (with T C Barker, 1954), Blue Funnel (with F E Hyde, 1956), The Copper King (1964), Liverpool and Merseyside (ed, 1969), British Iron Industry 1700-1850 (1989); *Style*— Prof John Harris; 5 Stretton Drive, Barnt Green, Birmingham B45 8XJ (☎ 021 445 3489); Economic and Social History Dept, School of Social Sciences, University of Birmingham, PO Box 363, Birmingham B15 2TT (☎ 021 414 6659, fax 021 414 6707)

HARRIS, John Robert; TEM (1945); s of Maj Alfred Harris, CBE, DSO, and Rosa Alfreda, *née* Alderson; *b* 5 June 1919; *Educ* Harrow, Architectural Assoc Sch of Architecture (AA Dip); *m* 10 June 1950, Gillian, da of Col C W D Rowe, CB, MBE, TD, JP, DL (d 1954), of Peterborough; 1 s (Mark b 27 Sept 1952), 1 da (Georgina b 7 Aug 1956); *Career* active serv and TA 1939-45, Lt RE Hong Kong 1940-41 (POW of Japanese 1941-45); memb: Br Army Aid Gp China 1943-45, Hong Kong Resistance 1942-45; architect; fndr and sr ptnr J R Harris Partnership 1949- (fndr and sr ptnr assoc firms in Brunei, Dubai, France, Hong Kong, Oman, Qatar, Spain); projects won in int competition: State Hosp Qatar 1953, New Dubai Hosp 1976, Corniche Devpt and traffic intersection Dubai 1978, HQ for Min of Social Affrs and Lab Oman 1979, Tuen Mun Hosp Hong Kong 1981; int assessment Rulers office devpt Dubai 1985, architect and planner Zhuhai New Town Econ Zone Peoples Republic of China 1984; major UK works incl: Stoke Mandeville Hosp 1983, Wellesley House and St Peters Ct Sch redevpt 1975; major overseas works incl: Int Trade Centre (40 storey) Dubai 1982, Br Embassy chancery offices and ambassador's residence Abu Dhabi 1982, Univ Teaching Hosp Maiduguri Nigeria 1982, dept stores 1973-83 (Antwerp, Brussels, Lille, Paris, Strasbourg); architect for the Dorchester Hotel 1985-90; pres Survey Club 1968 (pres 1960); FRIBA 1949, HKIA 1982, FRSA 1982; Membre de l'Ordre des Architects Francais 1978; *Books* John R Harris Architects (jtly, 1984); *Recreations* architecture, sketching, sailing (Dream Lady); *Clubs* Athenaeum, Royal Thames Yacht; *Style*— John Harris, Esq, TEM; 24 Devonshire Place, London W1N 2BX (☎ 071 935 9353, fax 071 935 5709)

HARRIS, John Simon; s of Donald Isadore Harris, Stanmore, Middx, and Dorothy Sarah, *née* Leewarden; *b* 20 March 1941; *Educ* Christs Coll GS Finchley, Hornsey Coll (NDD, commendation RSA Bursary award); *m* 17 March 1964, Caryl, da of late Louis Harris; 3 da (Selene b 1973, Sofie b 1977, Sarah b 1979); *Style*— John Harris, Esq; John Harris Design Consultants Ltd, 151a Gloucester Rd, London SW7 4TH (☎ 071 370 4191, fax 071 370 0956)

HARRIS, Joseph Hugh; JP (Penrith 1971), DL (1984); s of John Frederick Harris; *b* 3 June 1932; *Educ* Harrow, RAC Cirencester (DipAg); *m* 1957, Anne, da of Brig L H McRobert (d 1981); 3 s; *Career* Lt 11 Hussars PAO; chm Cumbrian Newspapers Ltd 1987- (formerly dir); farmer, landowner; memb Miny of Agric Northern Regnl Panel 1977-83, vice pres RASE 1980- (sr steward 1957-77, hon dir Royal Show 1978-82, dep pres 1986-87); High Sheriff Cumbria 1976-77; chm: govrs Aysgarth Sch 1975-85, Grasmere Sports 1977-, Penrith & Aston Magistrates Bench 1991-; *Recreations* shooting and field sports; *Style*— Joseph Harris Esq, JP, DL; Brackenburgh, Calthwaite, Penrith, Cumbria, CA11 9PW (☎ 076 885 253)

HARRIS, (Jonathan) Kim; s of Wilfrid John Harris, of Adelaide, South Australia, and Eileen Elsie, *née* Goodman; *b* 1 June 1944; *Educ* Wellingborough Sch, Brighton Sch Australia, Univ of Adelaide (BSc); *m* (m dis); 1 s (Jonathan Luke b 25 Sept 1977), 1 da (Beatrix Joanna b 28 July 1980); *Career* McCann Erikson 1962-70 (Aust, Chicago, London); dir: Brian Dowling Ltd 1970-76, Multicom Group 1976-83; chm PA 1983-86, dir City & Commercial Communications plc 1987-; FIPR (Aust) 1985- (memb 1964); *Recreations* yacht racing, sleeping; *Style*— Kim Harris, Esq; City & Commercial Communications plc, Bell Court House, 11 Blomfield St, London EC2M 7AY (☎ 071 588 6050, fax 071 920 9405)

HARRIS, Leslie George; MBE (1972); s of William George Harris (d 1935), of Birmingham, and Florence Ann, *née* Deakin (d 1943); *b* 20 June 1905; *Educ* Birmingham Central Secdy Sch; *m* 1942, Edith Mary, da of Frederick Wood (d 1975); 2 s (Andrew b 1944, Richard b 1945), 1 da (Geraldine b 1951); *Career* fndr chm L G Harris & Co Ltd Stoke Prior, chm L G Harris & Co (SA Party) Ltd; chm: L G Harris and Co (E Africa) Ltd 1964-84, Harris (Ceylon) Ltd 1968-, Harris Brushes (Far East) Ltd 1984-; chm Margery Fry Meml Tst 1963-72 (hostels for ex-prisoners, pres 1972-80), life govr Univ of Birmingham 1972-, chm Mgmnt Res Gps (Midlands) 1960-62, fndr chm Avoncroft Museum of Bldgs 1963-79 (vice pres 1979-), tstee Fircroft Coll Birmingham 1966-89; *Recreations* golf, forestry, music; *Clubs* Blackwell Golf; *Style*— Leslie G Harris, Esq, MBE; Ridge End, Hanbury, Worcs (☎ 052 784 359); L G Harris and Co Ltd, Stoke Prior, Worcs (☎ 0527 575441)

HARRIS, Lyndon Goodwin; s of late Sydney Ernest Harris, of Halesowen, and late Mary Elsie, *née* Tilley; *b* 25 July 1928; *Educ* Halesowen GS, Birmingham Coll of Art, Slade Sch of Fine Art (Dip Fine Art), Univ of London Inst of Educn (ATD), Courtauld Inst; *Career* artist; works exhibited at: Paris Salon (Gold medal in painting, hon mention in etching), RA, RSA, RI, RSW, RWA, RBA, RGI, NEAC; works in permanent collections incl: Govt Art Collection, UCL, Birmingham and Midland Inst; works reproduced in: Young Artists of Promise (Studio), The Artist (Masters of Water Colour and their Techniques), Royal Inst of Painters in Water Colours History and Membership List 1831-1981, Birmingham Post; scholarships: Leverhulme, Pilkington, Slade; Slade Anatomy Prizeman; memb: RI 1958, RSW 1952, RWA 1947; *Recreations* music (organ and pianoforte), cycling; *Style*— Lyndon Harris, Esq

HARRIS, Prof Malcolm; s of Ralph Harris, and Ada, *née* Greenbaum; *b* 8 Nov 1934; *Educ* Univ of Leeds Dental Sch (BchD), London Hosp Med Sch (MB BS), Univ of London (MD); *m* 10 Jan 1965, Naomi, da of Israel Cohen; 1 s (Daniel b 16 June 1971), 2 da (Gemma b 7 Aug 1967, Jessica b 11 July 1969); *Career* FDSRCS Eng, FFD RCS; *Books* Oral Surgery (with G R Seward and D M McGowan, 1988), Basic Manual of Orthognathic Surgery (with I Reynolds, 1990); *Recreations* work, painting, cooking and eating; *Clubs* Royal Society of Medicine; *Style*— Prof Malcolm Harris; 95 Wood Vale, London N10 3DL (☎ 071 883 1379); Eastman Dental Hospital, Grays Inn Rd, London WC1 8LD (☎ 071 837 3646, fax 071 833 3123)

HARRIS, Mark; s of Solomon Harris (d 1982), of London, and Eva, *née* Lazarus (d 1990); *b* 23 Feb 1943; *Educ* Central Fndn Boy's GS, LSE (LLB), The Law Soc Coll of Law; *m* 8 Oct 1972, Sharon Frances, da of Alex Colin (d 1981), of Essex; 1 da (Emma Tanya b 1975); *Career* admitted slr 1967; Dept of Employment: legal asst 1968, sr legal asst 1973-78, asst slr 1978-87, legal advsr 1987-88; asst treasy slr Dept of Educn and Sci 1988; *Recreations* travel, short-story writing (several published), painting, walking, London Jewish male choir (second tenor); *Style*— Mark Harris, Esq; Department of Education and Science, Elizabeth House, York Rd, London SE1 7PH (☎ 071 934 9762)

HARRIS, Prof Martin Best; s of William Best Harris (d 1987), of Plymouth, and Betty Evelyn, *née* Martin; *b* 28 June 1944; *Educ* Devonport HS for Boys Plymouth, Queens' Coll Cambridge (BA, MA), Univ of London (PhD); *m* 10 Sept 1966, Barbara Mary, da of Joseph Daniels (d 1971); 2 s (Robert b 1 July 1968, Paul b 13 June 1970); *Career* lectr in French linguistics Univ of Leicester 1967-72; Univ of Salford: sr lectr in French linguistics 1972-76, prof of romance linguistics 1976-87, dean social science and arts 1978-81, pro vice chllr 1981-87; vice chllr Univ of Essex 1987-, author of numerous books and articles on the romance languages; govr Colchester Sixth Form Coll; memb UGC 1984-87 (chm NI sub ctee 1985-89); chm: UFC NI Ctee 1989-, Nat Curriculum Working Party on Modern Languages 1989-90, govrs Centre for Information on Language Teaching 1990-, govr SOAS 1990-, memb Cncl Philological Soc; *Books* Evolution of French Syntax (1978), The Romance Verb (with N Vincent,

1983), The Romance Languages (with N Vincent, 1988); *Recreations* walking, gardening, wine; *Style—* Prof Martin Harris; University of Essex, Wivenhoe Park, Colchester, Essex, CO4 3SQ (☎ 0206 872000, fax 0206 869493)

HARRIS, (Maurice) Martin; s of Sidney Simon Harris, and Mignonette, *née* Jonas; *b* 29 Dec 1927; *m* 1, 21 June 1951, Betty (d 1981), da of Morris Rei (d 1967); 1 s (Philip Anthony b 15 Sept 1953), 1 da (Louise b 19 March 1955); m 2, 9 March 1983, June Marlene; *Career* Gaumont British News 1942-53, cmmnd photographer with Army Br W Africa 1947-49, started own film prodn co 1953, made over 40 films for Rank Film Distributors; exclusive film rights: Melbourne Olympics 1956, Investiture of Prince of Wales 1969; made feature film A Prince for Wales (incl first public interview with HRH The Prince of Wales); MRPS, MBKS; *Style—* Martin Harris, Esq; 14 Haywood Close, Pinner, Middx HA5 3LQ (☎ 081 866 9466)

HARRIS, Martin Richard; s of Col T B Harris, DSO (d 1965), of Bexhill-on-Sea, Sussex, and Phyllis Margaret, *née* Goode (d 1972); bro of Oliver Birkbeck Harris, *qv*; family members of Drapers' Co since 1760; *b* 30 Aug 1922; *Educ* Wellington Coll, Trinity Hall Cambridge; *m* 1952, Diana Moira, da of R W Gandar Dower (d 1967), of 15 Ennismore Gdns, London SW1; 4 s (Andrew, Colin, Thomas, Peter); *Career* WWII Capt RE serv Middle East and Italy 1941-46; CA; Price Waterhouse & Co 1946-74 (ptnr 1956-74), dir gen of the City Panel on Take-overs and Mergers 1974-77; dir: Reckitt and Colman 1977-82 (dep chm 1979-82), NatWest Bank 1977-, NatWest Investment Bank 1977-, Inmos International 1980-84, Equity and Law Life Assurance Society 1981-87 (dep chm 1983-87), The De La Rue Co 1981-, Westland 1981-85, TR Industrial and General Trust 1983-88; chm The Nineteen Twenty-Eight Investment Trust 1984-86; govr QMW London 1979- (chm 1989-), memb Cncl RCM 1985-; memb Ct: The Worshipful Co of Drapers 1978- (master 1987-88), Co of CAs 1972- (master 1983-84); FCA, FRCM, US Silver Star 1945; *Recreations* music, antique furniture and china, philately; *Clubs* Carlton, MCC, Pilgrims; *Style—* Martin Harris, Esq; 29 Belvedere Grove, Wimbledon, London SW19 7RQ (☎ 081 946 0951); Equitable House, 48 King William St, London EC4R 9DJ (☎ 071 623 0532)

HARRIS, Max; s of Harry Harris (d 1970), of London, and Tilly, *née* Stock (d 1975); *b* 15 Sept 1918; *m* 12 Aug 1953, Nanette Patricia May, da of Albert Rees (d 1946), of London, WC1; 1 s (Paul Avrom), 1 da (Sarah Ann); *Career* Sgt RA 1942, Capt RASC 1943; pianist, composer, arranger; TV themes incl: Sherlock Holmes, Gurney Slade, Poldark, Porridge, Open All Hours, Black Eyes, Singing Detective; radio musical dir: Round The Horn 1969, Frankie Howerd 1976, Arthur Askey 1985; radio themes: The Spy Who Came In From The Cold, Tinker Tailor Soldier Spy, Smiley's People; film themes: Carry On Sergeant, Baby Love, On The Buses, Christmas Wife; Novello award winner 1960-64, arranger on records by Stephan Grappelli and Yehudi Menuhin; memb Ctee Br Heart Fndn; MCPS 1954, PRS 1961; *Recreations* golf, pictorial art; *Clubs* Savage, Betchworth Park Golf; *Style—* Max Harris, Esq

HARRIS, Michael Abraham Philip; s of Louis Harris (d 1974), of 7 Clarendon Court, Clarendon Rd, Southsea, Hants, and Rebecca, *née* Peter; *b* 14 March 1937; *Educ* Portsmouth GS, Queen's Coll Oxford (MA); *m* 11 Aug 1963, Sylvia Freda, da of Joshua Berman (d 1969), of Grove Rd South, Southsea, Hants; 2 s (David, Jonathan), 1 da (Claire); *Career* admitted slr 1965; memb Hants Inc Law Soc 1965-, tstee and hon slr Portsmouth and Southsea Hebrew Soc; memb Law Soc 1965-; *Recreations* all sport (especially cricket and soccer), bridge, classical music; *Clubs* Old Portmuthian; *Style—* Michael A P Harris, Esq; 16 Burbidge Grove, Southsea, Hants, PO4 9RR (☎ 0705 825 129); 106 Victoria Road North, Portsmouth, Hants, PO5 1QG (☎ 0705 828 611, fax 0705 736 978)

HARRIS, Rear Adm Michael George Temple; s of Cdr Antony John Temple Harris, OBE, RN, of Wickham, Hants, and Doris, *née* Drake; *b* 5 July 1941; *Educ* Pangbourne, RNC Dartmouth; *m* 17 Oct 1970, (Caroline) Katrina, da of Gp Capt Patrick George Chichester, OBE, RAF (d 1983), of Hayne Manor, Stowford, Devon; 3 da (Tamsin b 1971, Rebecca b 1973, Emily b 1979); *Career* Sub Lt RN 1961, Lt 1963, Cdr 1975, Capt 1980, Rear Adm 1989; served: home, Med, submarines, Canada, long TAS course, submarine CO's Course, North Pole 1976, staff of flag offr submarines 1977-79, Capt HMS Cardiff 1980-82, Falklands Campaign, Capt 3 Submarine Sqdn 1982-85, central staff MOD 1985-87, Capt HMS Ark Royal 1987-89, asst chief of Def Staff (NATO UK) 1989-; yr bro of Trinity House 1989; Freeman and Shipwright City of London 1990; Liveryman Worshipful Co of Shipwrights 1991-; FRGS 1978, FNI 1988; *Recreations* fishing, reading, bellringing; *Clubs* Naval and Military; *Style—* Rear Adm Michael Harris; c/o Naval Secretary, Ministry of Defence, Spring Gardens, Whitehall, London SW1A 2BE

HARRIS, Capt Nicholas Richard; s of Sidney George Harris, of Sussex, and Jean Elliott (d 1986); *b* 24 Sept 1941; *Educ* South Africa and Nautical Coll General Botha; *m* 31 Dec 1966, Philippa Joan Harris, da of Col Donald Friswell Easten, MC, of Wormingford, Essex; 2 s (Rupert b 20 Oct 1967, Giles 16 July 1973), 2 da (Jessica 24 April 1971, Emily b 9 July 1983); *Career* BNRC Dartmouth 1963, qualified fixed wing pilot 1964-65; HMS Eagle 899 Sqdn 1965-66, 766 Sqdn RNAS Yeovilton 1967-68, 764 Sqdn RNAS Lossiemouth 1969-70, USN VF121 and Topgun NAS Mirimar California 1971-72, HMS Devonshire 1973, RN Staff Coll Greenwich 1974, directorate of Naval Air Warfare MOD 1975-76, CO 892 Sqdn 1977, Air Warfare Course RAF Cranwell 1978, RN presentation team 1979, directorate of Naval Manpower Planning MOD 1980-81, HMS Bristol 1982-83, Royal Coll of Defence Studies 1984-85, dept sec chief of staff ctee MOD 1986, naval attache Rome 1987-89, dir Mgmnt Strategy (Naval Personnel) MOD 1990; *Recreations* cricket, photography; *Clubs* Royal Over-Seas League; *Style—* Capt Nicholas Harris, RN; c/o Naval Secretary, Old Admiralty Building, Spring Gardens, London SW1A 2BE (☎ 071 218 9000)

HARRIS, Nigel Henry; *b* 11 July 1924; *Educ* Cambridge (MA, MB BChir); *Career* Nat Serv RAF 1949-52; house surgn: Orthopaedic Dept Middx Hosp 1947, N Middx Hosp 1952-53; in charge of Casualty and registrar to Orthopaedic Dept King Edward Meml Hosp Ealing 1953-55, surgical registrar Mile End Hosp 1955-56, surgical registrar Fulham Hosp 1958-59, orthopaedic registrar 1956-58, sr registrar Royal Nat Orthopaedic Hosp 1960 (registrar 1959-60), Euro travelling scholar 1962, conslt orthopaedic surgn to Thames Gp of Hosps 1963, conslt orthopaedic Surgn to Paddington Gp of Hosps and the London Foot Hosp 1964-67, asst hon orthopaedic surgn to the Hosp for Sick Children Gt Ormond St 1964-67, Geigy scholar 1967, hon conslt orthopaedic surgn St Mary's Hosp until ret from NHS 1990; orthopaedic surgn to: the Football Assoc, Arsenal Football Club; fell: Br Orthopaedic Assoc, RSM; memb: Br Orthopaedic Res Soc, Hosp Conslts and Specialists Assoc, Medico-Legal Soc, Br Acad of Experts, med Examiner for Football League Underwriters; tstee Metropolitan Police Convalescent and Rehabilitation Tst; FRCS; *Style—* Nigel Harris, Esq; 14 Ashworth Rd, London W9 (☎ 071 286 4725); 72 Harley St, London W1

HARRIS, Oliver Birkbeck; s of Col T B Harris, DSO, RE (d 1965), of Bexhill-on-Sea, Sussex, and Phyllis Margaret, *née* Goode (d 1972); bro of Martin Richard Harris, *qv*; *b* 28 Feb 1929; *Educ* Wellington Coll; *m* 20 Aug 1966, Caroline Mary, da of Lt-Col J Y B Sharpe, RA, of Godalming, Surrey; 2 s (John b 1967, Robert b 1972), 1 da (Felicity b 1968); *Career* Nat Serv cmmnd 2 Lt RE 1952-54; ptnr Rowley Pemberton Roberts 1959-69, sec Baring Brothers & Co Ltd and dir various subsid cos 1969-85; dir Nat Heritage Meml Fund 1988-89 (dep dir 1985-88), advsr American Friends of the Nat Gallery 1989-, assoc memb Lloyd's 1962 (memb 1968), memb Ctee of Mgmnt Abbotstone Agric Property Unit Tst 1975-; FCA, AMSIA, FRSA; *Recreations* gardening, heritage, history; *Clubs* City of London, Naval and Military, MCC; *Style—* Oliver Harris, Esq; Eden House, Winkworth Hill, Godalming, Surrey (☎ 048 632 236)

HARRIS, Patricia Ann; *b* 29 May 1939; *Educ* St Julian's HS Newport Monmouthshire, Trinity Coll Carmarthen; *m* 3 August 1963, The Rev James Nigel Kingsley Harris; 1 s (James Michael b 11 Oct 1967), 1 da (Sarah Ann b 25 June 1965); *Career* memb Diocesan: Houses Bd 1975, Synod 1980, Pastoral Ctee 1984-89, Educn Ctee 1986-89; Mothers' Union diocesan pres 1980-85, memb Gen Synod (House of Laity) 1985-, central pres Mothers' Union 1989-, memb Cncl of Churches for Britain and Ireland 1990-; *Recreations* watching Gloucester play rugby, swimming; *Style—* Mrs Patricia Harris; The Vicarage, Elm Rd, Stonehouse, Gloucester GL10 2NP (☎ 04538 22332); The Mary Sumner House, 24 Tufton St, London SW1P 3RB (☎ 071 222 5533, fax 071 222 6143)

HARRIS, Paul Haydn Beverley; s of late Michael James Harris, and Vivien Diana, *née* Hoyland; *b* 4 Sept 1945; *Educ* Emanuel Sch, Univ of Kent at Canterbury (BA); *m* 27 Oct 1979, Amanda Helen, da of late Arthur Robert Charles Stiby, TD, JP; 1 s (Kit b 1988); *Career* broadcaster and writer; radio and TV newsreader and presenter 1973-86, BBC staff 1970-80, freelance 1980-, currently specialising in prodn of commercial educnl and med videos and films; memb local RNLI Ctee, widely involved in charity fund raising in S of England; *Recreations* cricket, carriage driving, writing, fine art, ceramics; *Clubs* Hants CCC; *Style—* Paul Harris, Esq; Mile Tree House, Crawley, Winchester, Hampshire SO21 2QF (☎ 0962 885916)

HARRIS, Paul Ian; s of Alexander Munsie Harris (d 1988), and Sylvia, *née* Goodman (d 1989); *b* 13 Dec 1943; *Educ* Chatham House GS Ramsgate, Birmingham Univ (LLM); *m* 21 June 1967, Margaret Eve, da of Hayley Roer; 1 s (Keith Daniel b 1971), 1 da (Ruth Caroline b 1974); *Career* admitted slr 1969, ptnr Linklaters & Paines; tstee World Student Drama Tst; memb: Law Soc, Slrs Benevolent Assoc; *Books* Day & Harris Unit Trusts (1974), Linklaters & Paines Unit Trusts The Law and Practice (1989); *Recreations* bridge, sailing, watching football, theatre, cinema, sitting on committees; *Style—* Paul Harris, Esq; 59/67 Gresham St, London EC2V 7JA (☎ 071 606 7080, fax 071 606 5113, telex 884349)

HARRIS, Prof Peter Charles; s of David Jonathan Valentine Harris (d 1987), and Nellie Dean, *née* Blakemore (d 1986); *b* 26 May 1923; *Educ* St Olave's and St Saviour's GS, KCH London (MB BS, MD, PhD); *m* 1, 24 Jan 1952 (m dis 1982), Felicity Margaret, da of Prof Hamilton Hartridge (d 1977); 2 da (Sophie b 1956, Libbie b 1964); m 2, 13 Nov 1989, Frances Monkarsh; *Career* Simon Marks Prof of Cardiology Univ of London and physician Nat Heart Hosp 1966-88; Freeman: City of La Paz 1966, City of Winnipeg 1986; FRCP 1964; *Books* The Human Pulmonary Circulation (with D Heath, 1986); *Recreations* painting, music; *Style—* Prof Peter Harris; 42 Great Percy St, London WC1 (☎ 071 278 2911); Cannaregio 3698/A, Venezia, Italy

HARRIS, Gp Capt Peter Langridge; CBE (1988), AE (1961, and clasp 1971), DL (Gtr London 1986-); s of Arthur Langridge Harris (d 1975), of Eastbourne, and Doris Mabel, *née* Offen (d 1978); *b* 6 Sept 1929; *Educ* St Edward's Sch Oxford, Univ of Birmingham (BSc); *m* 29 Dec 1955, (Yvonne) Patricia, da of Arthur James Stone, DSM (d 1986), of Southsea; 2 da (Sally b 1960, Philippa b 1962); *Career* RAFVR 1947-60, RAuxAF 1960-88 (Gp Capt 1983, Inspr 1983-88), ADC to HM The Queen 1984-88, vice chm (air) TA & VR Assoc for Gtr London 1988-; chartered engr; Elliott Bros (London) Ltd 1952-55, Decca Navigator Co Ltd 1955-59, Elliott-Automation GEC plc 1959-89, ret 1989, memb Bd of Mgmnt Princess Marina House Rustington 1990-; FIEE 1976; *Recreations* travel, gardening; *Clubs* RAF; *Style—* Gp Capt Peter L Harris, CBE, AE, DL; 10 Dolphin Court, St Helen's Parade, Southsea, Hants (☎ 0705 817602); 29 Davenham Ave, Northwood, Middx

HARRIS, Sir Philip Charles; s of Charles William Harris, and Ruth Ellen, *née* Ward; *b* 15 Sept 1942; *Educ* Streatham GS; *m* 1960, Pauline Norma, da of Bertie William Chumley (d 1968); 3 s, 1 da; *Career* chm: Harris Queensway plc 1964-88 (chief exec 1987), Harris Ventures Ltd 1988, Carpetright of London 1988, CW Harris Properties 1988, Furniture City 1988; dir Harveys Holdings plc 1986; non-exec dir: Great Universal Stores 1986, Fisons plc 1986; memb: Br Showjumping Assoc, Cncl of Govrs United Med and Dental Schs of Guy's and St Thomas's Hosps 1984, Ct of Patrons RGOG 1984; govr Nat Hosp for Nervous Diseases 1985; Hambro Business Man of the Year 1983, hon fell Oriel Coll Oxford 1989; kt 1985; *Recreations* showjumping, cricket; *Style—* Sir Philip Harris; Harris Ventures Ltd, Central Court, Knoll Rise, Orpington, Kent BR6 0JA (☎ 0689 75135)

HARRIS, Philip James; s of Philip John Harris, of Avenue Decelles, Montreal, Canada, and Violet Edna May, *née* Fretwell; *b* 4 Oct 1936; *Educ* Northampton Sch of Art, Watford Coll of Technol; *m* 1, 20 April 1959 (m dis 1977), Audrey Mary, da of Richard Stanley Flawn (d 1968), of The Old Manor, Irthlingborough, Northants; 1 s (Philip Julian b 1964), 1 da (Susan Mary (Mrs Goodwin) b 1967); m 2, 21 March 1980, Esther Elizabeth, da of James Buchanan (d 1982), of Blunham, Beds; *Career* Parachute Regt 1955-58 active serv: Cyprus, Eoka Campaign, Suez; chief exec Reporter Newspapers Kent 1977-79, dir and gen mangr Middx Co Press 1979-83; md: B Lansdown & Sons Trowbridge 1983-87, Wessex Group of Newspapers Bath 1987-; former pres SW Fedn Newspaper Owners, vice pres Newsvendors Benevolent Inst; memb: Patrons Club, W Wilts Cons Assoc; MIIM 1979, memb Inst of Printing 1981, FBIM 1983, memb IOD 1985; *Recreations* horse racing, polo, rowing; *Clubs* Leander, Bath and County, Guards' Polo, Cirencester Park Polo; *Style—* Philip Harris, Esq; 18 Palairet Close, Bradford-on-Avon, Wiltshire (☎ 02 216 4223); Principal Office, Wessex Newspapers, Westgate St, Bath BA1 1EW (☎ 0225 444 044, fax 0225 446 495, car 0836 260 788)

HARRIS, Phillip; s of Simon Harris (d 1970), of Edinburgh, and Leah Sarah, *née* Horovits (d 1984); *b* 28 March 1922; *Educ* Royal HS Edinburgh, Univ of Edinburgh; *m* 7 Nov 1949, Sheelagh Shena, da of Harry Joshua Coutts (d 1977), of Glasgow; 1 s (Harvey b 14 May 1953), 1 da (Frances b 27 Oct 1950); *Career* Capt RAMC 1945-48; Univ of Edinburgh: sr conslt neurosurgeon dept of clinical neurosciences, sr lectr dept of surgical neurology, lectr dept of linguistics; visiting prof in Univs worldwide; pres Br Cervical Spine Assoc, sr del Br Neurosurgeons to the World Fedn of Neurological Surgery, pres Scottish Sports Assoc for the Disabled, dir and tstee Scottish Tst for the Physically Disabled, hon memb Scottish Paraplegic Assoc, cncl memb Thistle Fndn Scotland, memb Med Appeals Tbnl Scotland; ed Paraplegia (the int jl on the spine); LRCP Edinburgh, LRCS Edinburgh, LRFP Glasgow, LRCS Glasgow, FRCS Edinburgh, FRCP Edinburgh, FRCS Glasgow, FRSE 1967; hon memb: American Assoc of Neurological Surgeons, The Hong Kong Surgical Soc, Middle East Neurosurgical Soc; *Books* Head Injuries (ed 1971), Epilepsy (ed 1974), Spine (ed 1987); *Recreations* art, music, travel, golf; *Clubs* New (Edinburgh), Royal Scottish Automobile (Glasgow), Bruntsfield Links Golfing Soc (Edinburgh); *Style—* Phillip Harris, Esq; 4/5 Fettes Rise, Edinburgh EH4 1QH (☎ 031 552 8900); Paraplegia Journal, Royal College of Surgeons, Nicolson Street, Edinburgh EH8 9DW (☎ 031 668 2557); Murrayfield Hospital, 122 Corstorphine Road, Edinburgh (☎ 031 334 0363)

HARRIS, Raymond Govette; s of Walter Henry Harris (d 1957), of Cambridge, and

Ruth Olive, *née* Drake (d 1987); *b* 3 June 1928; *Educ* Perse Sch Cambridge, Architectural Assoc Sch of Architecture (AA Dip); *m* 16 Feb 1957, Rosemary, da of Rev Frederick Walter Palmer (d 1979), of Easebourne, W Sussex; 1 s (Thomas Edward Henry b 1964), 3 da (Katherine b 1958, Eleanor Rosemary b 1959, Hilary Juliet b 1962); *Career* architect; sr ptnr T P Bennett & Son 1982-85 (ptnr 1967-82), sr ptnr T P Bennett Partnership 1985-, architect to: The Middx Hosp, Rackhams Birmingham, Bentalls Kingston; works incl: Br Linen Bank Glasgow, Int Students House Park Crescent, Financial Times Bldg, Norwich Union HQ Norwich; chm Islington Soc; FRIBA 1968 (ARIBA 1951), FRSA 1973; *Recreations* watercolour drawing, cabinet making, music; *Clubs* Garrick; *Style—* Raymond Harris, Esq; Somerset Lodge, North St, Petworth, W Sussex (☎ 0798 43842); T P Bennett Partnership, 262 High Holborn, London WC1V 7DU (☎ 071 405 9277, fax 071 405 3568, telex 21671)

HARRIS, Ven Reginald (Brian); s of Reginald George Harris (d 1985), of Kent, and Ruby C Harris; *b* 14 Aug 1934; *Educ* Eltham Coll, Christ's Coll Cambridge (MA), Ridley Hall Cambridge; *m* 1959, Anne Patricia, da of George Frederick Hughes (d 1986); 1 s (Nigel b 1962), 1 da (Celia b 1963); *Career* curate: Wednesbury 1959-61, Uttoxeter 1961-64, vicar of St Peterbury 1964-70, vicar and rural dean of Walmsley 1970-80, archdeacon of Manchester 1980-, canon residentiary of Manchester Cathedral 1980-, sub dean 1986-; *Recreations* long distance walking, painting; *Style—* The Ven the Archdeacon of Manchester; 4 Victoria Ave, Eccles, Manchester M30 9HA (☎ 061 707 6444)

HARRIS, Richard Leslie; s of William Leslie Freer Harris (d 1956), of Romsley, Worcs, and Lucy Penelope Harris (d 1976); *b* 31 March 1927; *Educ* Shrewsbury; *m* 1955, Jane, da of Herbert Charles Oxenham, of Rhuallt, St Asaph; 2 s; *Career* stockbroker and CA; ptnr Harris Allday Lea and Brooks; chm: Royal Brierley Crystal Ltd, Newater Investmts Ltd; dir: Tewksbury Marina Ltd, Thomas Jones Estates Ltd; memb Stock Exchange 1961 and Stock Exchange Cncl; chm: Midlands and Western Stock Exchange 1969, Feoffees Old Swinford Hosp Sch; Freeman City of London; *Clubs* Birmingham; *Style—* Richard Harris, Esq; 23 Farlands Rd, Old Swinford, Stourbridge, W Midlands DY8 2DD (☎ 0384 395760); Harris Allday Lea and Brooks, Stock Exchange Buildings, 33 Great Charles St, Queensway, Birmingham B3 3JN (☎ 021 233 1222)

HARRIS, Richard Travis; 2 son of Douglas Harris (d 1964), and Emmeline, *née* Travis; *b* 15 April 1919; *Educ* Charterhouse, RMA Woolwich; *m* 1, 1941 (m dis 1953), June Constance, *née* Rundle; 2 da; m 2, 1953, Margaret Sophia Nye, *née* Aron; 1 s, 1 da; *Career* RCS 1939, France 1940, Western Desert 1941-43, Italy 1943, Staff Coll 1944, instr Sch of Inf 1944-45, BAOR 1945-46, Sudan Def Force 1947-50, ret Lt-Col 1950; md Rediffusion (Nigeria) Ltd 1951-54, dep gen mangr Assoc Rediffusion Ltd 1954-57, md Coates & Co (Plymouth) Ltd 1957-63, md Dollond & Aitchison Group Ltd 1964-70; dir: Dolland & Aitchison Group Ltd 1964-86 (chm and md 1970-78), Gallaher Ltd 1970-84 (dep chm 1978-84), Burton Group plc 1984-; chm IOD 1982-85 (vice pres 1985-89), Wider Share Ownership Cncl 1988-; govr Royal Shakespeare Theatre, memb Cncl Univ of Birmingham; *Recreations* flyfishing, theatre; *Clubs* Athenaeum; *Style—* Richard Harris, Esq; 21 Lucy's Mill, Mill Lane, Stratford-upon-Avon, Warwicks CV37 6DE (☎ 0789 299631)

HARRIS, Robert Dennis; s of Dennis Harris, and Audrey, *née* Hardy; *b* 7 March 1957; *Educ* King Edward VII Sch Melton Mowbray, Selwyn Coll Cambridge (BA, chm Cambridge Fabian Soc, pres Cambridge Union Soc); *m* 1988, Gillian, da of Sir Derek Hornby, *qv*; 1 da (Holly b 21 July 1990); *Career* res and film dir Current Affairs Dept BBC TV (progs incl Tonight, Nationwide and Panorama) 1978-81; reporter: Newsnight 1981-85, Panorama 1985-87; political ed Observer 1987-89, political reporter This Week (Thames TV) 1988-89, political columnist Sunday Times 1989-; author of: A Higher Form of Killing, The History of Gas and Germ Warfare (with Jeremy Paxman 1982), Gotcha! The Media, The Government and The Falklands Crisis (1983), The Making of Neil Kinnock (1984), Selling Hitler, The Story of the Hitler Diaries (1986, televised 1991), Good and Faithful Servant The Unauthorised Biography of Bernard Ingham (1990); *Style—* Robert Harris, Esq; 31 St Lawrence Terrace, London W10 5SR (☎ 081 960 1410)

HARRIS, Prof Robert James; s of Charles William Harris, of Sanderstead, Surrey, and Lucy Dorothea Emily, *née* Weller; *b* 10 March 1947; *Educ* The GS Enfield, Univ of Leeds (BA), McMaster Univ (MA), Univ of Manchester (DipAS), Univ of Birmingham (DSW); *m* 23 Feb 1974, Janet Nuttall, da of James Nuttall Horne (d 1987), of Ewell, Surrey; 1 s (George b 1982), 2 da (Ruth b 1978, Amelia b 1979); *Career* probation offr Middx 1973-75; lectr: social work and criminology Brunel Univ 1975-77, social work and criminal justice Univ of Leicester 1977-87; prof social work Univ of Hull 1987-; memb Humberside Probation Ctee; chm Humberside Child Protection Ctee; *Books* Educating Social Workers (1985), Practising Social Work (1987), Welfare, Power and Juvenile Justice (1987), The Law Report (1988); *Recreations* antiquarian book collecting, supporting Hull City AFC; *Style—* Prof Robert Harris; Yew Tree House, Station Walk, Cottingham, N Humberside HU16 4QU (☎ 0482 849961); The Univ of Hull, Dept of Social Policy, Hull HU6 7RX (☎ 0482 465784)

HARRIS, Prof Robin Kingsley; s of Alfred William Harris (d 1964), of Hornchurch, Essex, and Nellie, *née* Missen (d 1987); *b* 23 Dec 1936; *Educ* Royal Liberty GS Romford, Magdalene Coll Cambridge (BA, MA, PhD, ScD); *m* 6 Aug 1960, Maureen Elizabeth, da of James Samuel Reardon (d 1968), of Langley, Berks; 1 s (Nigel b 1962); *Career* fell in ind res Mellon Inst Pittsburgh 1962-64; prof of chemistry: Univ of East Anglia 1980-84 (lectr 1964-70, sr lectr 1970-73, reader 1973-80), Univ of Durham 1984-; fell Royal Soc of Chemistry, memb Ctee Sci and Engrg Res Cncl, sec gen Int Soc of Magnetic Resonance; *Books* High-Resolution Nuclear Magnetic Resonance Spectroscopy (with RM Lynden-Bell, 1969), Nuclear Magnetic Resonance Spectroscopy: A Physiochemical View (1983); *Recreations* gardening; *Style—* Prof Robin Harris; Dept of Chemistry, University of Durham, South Rd, Durham DH1 3LE (☎ 091 374 3121, fax 091 374 3745, telex 537351 DURLIB G)

HARRIS, Prof Rodney; s of Ben Harris (d 1966), and Toiby, *née* Davies (d 1958); *b* 27 May 1932; *Educ* Quarry Bank Sch, Univ of Liverpool (MD); *m* 1, Ruth, *née* Levy (d 1975); m 2, Hilary Jean, da of Eric Melsher, of Bowdon; 1 s (Richard Ben), 2 da (Alexandra Jane, Anne Tessa); *Career* prof of med genetics Manchester 1980-, advsr to Chief Med Offr at Dept of Health 1982-89; chm: Specialty Advsy Ctee RCP 1982-89, RCP Ctee on Clinical Genetics 1986-, NWRHA Clinical Genetics 1986-; memb Preston Health Authy 1986-; FRCP 1964; *Style—* Prof Rodney Harris; Medical Genetics, St Mary's Hospital, Manchester M13 0JH (☎ 061 276 6262, fax 061 274 3159)

HARRIS, Dr Roger James; s of Sidney George Harris (ka 1940), of Northampton, and Alfreda Mabel, *née* Sibley; *b* 29 Nov 1937; *Educ* Northampton GS, Univ of Bristol Med Sch (MB ChB, MD); *m* 20 April 1963, Mary Jennifer Evans; 1 s (Simon John b 1967), 3 da (Sarah Jane b 1964, Katherine (Kate) Martha b 1980, Emmeline (Mimi) Louisa May b 1982); *Career* currently conslt paediatrician Tower Hamlets DHA, sr lectr in child health London Hosp Med Coll 1975-; author of articles on paediatrics; examiner in paediatrics for RCP, rep for Tower Hamlets DHA on Regnl Advsy Paediatric Ctee, Chair of Children's Unit Appeal The Royal London Hosp, memb Area Child Protection Ctee; FRCP 1986; *Recreations* theatre, opera, playing cricket; *Style—* Dr Roger Harris; The Children's Dept, The Royal London Hospital, Whitechapel, London E1 1BB (☎ 071 377 7428)

HARRIS, Sir Ronald Montague Joseph; KCVO (1960, MVO 1943), CB (1956); only s of Rev Joseph Montague Harris and Edith Annesley, 4 da of George Forbes Malcolmson, whose w Catherine Annesley was paternal gda of Sir Henry Austen, JP, DL; Sir Henry's maternal grandmother was Hon Helen Thompson, da of 1 Baron Haversham (cr 1696) and Lady Frances Annesley, da of 1 Earl of Anglesey of the 1661 creation; *b* 6 May 1913; *Educ* Harrow, Trinity Coll Oxford; *m* 1, 1939, Margaret Julia (d 1955), eldest da of John Robert Wharton; 1 s (Jocelin), 3 da (Imogen, Celia, Olivia); m 2, 1957, Marjorie, widow of Julian Tryon and da of Sir Harry Verney, 4 Bt, DSO, and Lady Rachel, *née* Bruce, da of 9 Earl of Elgin and Kincardine; 1 step s (decd), 1 step da (Edith); *Career* Civil Serv 1936, Burma Office 1936-39, War Cabinet Secretariat 1939-44, India Office 1944-46, private sec to Sec of State for India and Burma 1946-47, Treasy 1949-52, Cabinet Office 1952-55, perm cmmr Crown Lands 1955, second Crown Estate cmmr 1956-60, third sec HM Treasy 1960-64, sec Church Cmmrs for Eng 1964-68, first Church Estates cmmr 1969-82, chm Central Bd of Fin 1978-82; dir General Accident Fire and Life Assurance Corporation 1970-84, govr Yehudi Menuhin Sch (chm 1989-90); *Books* Memory-soft the Air (recollections of life and service with Cabinet, Crown and Church) (1987); *Clubs* Boodle's; *Style—* Sir Ronald Harris, KCVO, CB; Slyfield Farm House, Stoke D'Abernon, Cobham, Surrey

HARRIS, Hon Mrs (Rosanne Monica Michelle); da of Baron Plurenden (Life Peer; d 1978), and Baroness Plurenden, *qv*; *b* 1960; *m* 21 June 1986, Robert William Kenneth Harris; *Career* farmer, co dir; *Recreations* horse breeding; *Style—* The Hon Mrs Harris; Court Lodge Oast, Bodiam, Robertsbridge, East Sussex TN32 5UJ

HARRIS, Rosemary Jeanne; da of Marshal of the RAF Sir Arthur Harris, 1 Bt, GCB, OBE, AFC (d 1984), and Barbara Daisy Kyrle (d 1986), da of Lt-Col E W K Money, KSLI; g and g-uncs were the famous ten Fighting Battyes chronicled by Younghusband's Story of the Guides and by Evelyn Battye in her book The Fighting Ten; *b* 20 Feb 1923; *Educ* privately, Thorneloe Sch Weymouth, Chelsea Sch of Art, Dept of Technol Courtauld Inst; *Career* author of fiction, thrillers and children's books; picture restorer 1949, reviewer of children's books for The Times 1970-73; *Publications* plays: Peronik (1976), The Unknown Enchantment (1981); books: The Summer-House (1956), Voyage to Cythera (1958), Venus with Sparrows (1961), All My Enemies (1967), The Nice Girl's Story (1968), A Wicked Pack of Cards (1969), The Double Snare (1975), Three Candles for the Dark (1976); for children: Moon in the Cloud (won Carnegie medal 1968), The Shadow on the Sun (1970), The Seal-Singing (1971), The Child in the Bamboo Grove (1971), The Bright and Morning Star (1972), The King's White Elephant (1973), The Lotus and the Grail (1974), The Flying Ship (1974), The Little Dog of Fo (1976), I Want to be a Fish (1977), A Quest for Orion (1978), Beauty and the Beast (1979), Greenfinger House (1979), Tower of the Stars (1980), The Enchanted Horse (1981), Janni's Stork (1982), Zed (1982), Heidi (adapted 1983), Summers of the Wild Rose (1987), Love and the Merry-go-Round (ed poetry anthology, 1988), Colm of the Islands (1989); *Recreations* music, reading, gardening; *Style—* Miss Rosemary Harris; c/o A P Watt Ltd, Literary Agents, 20 John St, London WC1N 2DL

HARRIS, Rosina Mary; da of Alfred Harris, DSO, CBE (d 1976), and Rosa Alfreda, *née* Alderson (d 1987); *b* 30 May 1921; *Educ* St Swithins Sch, St Hilda's Coll Oxford (MA, BCL); *Career* served with American Ambulance of GB 1941-45; called to the Bar Lincoln's Inn; solicitor; sr ptnr Joynston-Hicks 1977-86 (ptnr 1954-89), conslt Taylor Joynson Garrett 1989-; dep chm Blundell-Permoglaze Holdings plc 1981-86, non-exec dir London Brick plc 1983-84; Queen's Jubilee medal 1977; *Recreations* gardening, opera, theatre; *Style—* Miss Rosina Harris; 23 Devonshire Place, London W1N 1PD (☎ 071 935 6041); Taylor Joynson Garrett, 10 Maltravers St, London WC2R 2BR (☎ 071 836 8456)

HARRIS, Prof Roy; s of Harry Harris (d 1978), and Emmie Jessie, *née* Oaten (d 1978); *b* 24 Feb 1931; *Educ* Queen Elizabeth Hosp Bristol, St Edmund Hall Oxford (BA, MA, DPhil, PhD); *m* 14 July 1955, Rita Doreen, *née* Shulman; 1 da (Laura Doe b 1959); *Career* lectr: Univ of Leicester 1957-60, Univ of Oxford 1960-76, fell and tutor in romance philosophy Keble Coll Oxford 1967-76, prof of gen linguistics Univ of Oxford 1977-88 (prof of romance languages 1976-77), prof of English language Univ of Hong Kong 1988-; hon fell St Edmund Hall Oxford 1987; FRSA 1986; *Books* Synonymy and Linguistic Analysis (1973), The Language-Makers (1980), The Language Myth (1981), F De Saussure, Course in General Linguistics (trans 1983), The Origin of Writing (1986), Reading Saussure (1987), The Language Machine (1987), Language, Saussure and Wittgenstein (1988); *Recreations* cricket, modern art and design; *Style—* Prof Roy Harris; 2 Paddox Close, Oxford OX2 7LR (☎ 0865 54256)

HARRIS, Dr (Henry) Roy; s of Alfred Henry Harris (d 1957), and Grace, *née* Squire (d 1972); *b* 2 April 1932; *Educ* Univs of London, Nottingham, Oxford, Reading (BSc, MA, PhD); *m* 14 Dec 1963, (Alice) Joan, da of James Bainbridge Noble Hetherington (d 1988); *Career* called to the Bar Lincoln's Inn; princ Harrow Coll of Higher Educn 1975-; memb Cncl: Inst Chartered Secs and Admins, Soc of Company and Commercial Accountants; Liveryman: Worshipful Co of Chartered Secs, Worshipful Co of Scriveners, Worshipful Co of Arbitrators; FCIS, FSCA, FBIM, FCP; *Recreations* music; *Clubs* City Livery; *Style—* Dr Roy Harris; Harrow Coll of Higher Educn, Northwick Park, Harrow, Middx HA1 3TP (☎ 081 864 5422, fax 081 864 6664)

HARRIS, Susan Jane; da of Alfred Norman Harris, of Solihull, and Esme Joyce, *née* Skey; *b* 2 Jan 1959; *Educ* Tudor Grange Girls GS, Solihull Sixth Form Coll, St Catherine's Coll Oxford (BA, MA, Swimming half blue), Cranfield Sch of Management (MBA, PR Week scholar, Chartered Inst of Marketing (DipCIM); *Career* pre-doctoral res asst Univ of Leicester 1981-84 (res demonstrator 1984-85); Kempsters Communication Gp: tech conslt 1984-85, PR tech writer 1985, PR account exec 1985-87, PR dir 1987-89, gp business dir 1989-; memb Cranfield Mgmnt Assoc, MCIM, MIPR; *Style—* Ms Susan Harris; Kempsters Communications Group Ltd, Essex House, Essex Rd, Basingstoke, Hants RG21 1SU (☎ 0256 842274, fax 0256 469308)

HARRIS, Hon Mrs (Thelma Eirene); *née* Kitson; da of 2 Baron Airedale, JP; *b* 1902; *m* 1923, Noel Gordon Harris (d 1963), s of Sir Alexander Harris, KCMG, CB, CVO; 1 s (James b 1933, m Primrose Millicent Elaine, da of late Sir Philip du Cros, 2 Bt); 3 da (Joyce Estelle (Mrs Edward Griffith) b 1924, Leslie Beryl (Mrs Michael Johnson) b 1926, Jean Constance (Mrs James Arnot) b 1931); *Style—* The Hon Mrs Harris; 28 Lyttleton Court, Lyttleton Road, London N2 0EB

HARRIS, Thomas George; s of Kenneth James Harris, of Ferndown, Dorset, and Dorothy, *née* Barrett; *b* 6 Feb 1945; *Educ* Mercers' Sch, Haberdashers' Ashe's, Gonville and Cairns Coll Cambridge; *m* 21 Oct 1967, Mei-Ling, da of Kono Hwang (d 1976), of Kobe, Japan; 3 s (Ian Kenneth b 1969, Paul David b 1970, Simon Christopher b 1984); *Career* asst princ Bd of Trade 1966-68, third sec Br Embassy Tokyo 1969-71, asst private sec to Min for Aerospace 1971-72, princ Dept Trade and Ind 1972-76, Cabinet Office 1976-79, princ private sec to Sec of Stte for Trade and Indust 1978-79, asst sec civil aviation policy DTI 1979-83, commercial cnsllr Br Embassy Washington 1983-88, head chancery Br High Commn Lagos 1988-; *Recreations* reading; *Clubs* Metropolitan (Lagos); *Style—* Thomas Harris, Esq; c/o

FCO (Lagos), King Charles St, London SW1

HARRIS, Tim John; s of John Arthur Harris, of 14 Hillview, Pickenham, Swaffham, Norfolk, and Myrtle Ann, *née* Davies; *b* 21 Dec 1962; *Educ* Swaffham Hammonds HS Swaffham Norfolk; *Career* cyclist: Nat Professional Cycling Race Champion 1987, Nat Professional Cycling Road Racing Champion 1989; winner of five maj cycle races at: Sheffield, Fleetwood, Withernsea, Snarestone and Cork; memb: Br Cycling Fed; memb Professional Cycling Assoc; *Recreations* reading, cinema, driving; *Style—* Tim Harris, Esq; 4 Tenby Gardens, Balby, Doncaster DN4 8JH (☎ 0302 854 272)

HARRIS, Timothy Richard; s of Kenneth Morgan Harris, of Cardiff, and Margaret, *née* McLean; *b* 16 April 1945; *Educ* Cathays HS for Boys Cardiff; *m* 8 May 1971, (Marion) Julia, da of late Thomas Barlow; 2 da (Emma b 2 Dec 1975, Ellen Rachel b 19 June 1980); *Career* articled clerk Deloitte Plender Griffiths & Co Cardiff 1962; ptnr: Deloitte Haskins & Sells 1983-89, Coopers & Lybrand Deloitte 1990- (following merger), Cork Gully 1990-; vice pres London Welsh RFC; FCA 1969, FIPA 1980, MICM 1988, MSPI 1990; *Recreations* rugby union; *Style—* Timothy R Harris, Esq; Coopers & Lybrand Deloitte, PO Box 207, 128 Queen Victoria St, London EC4P 4XJ (☎ 071 236 6500)

HARRIS, William Barclay; QC (1961); s of William Cecil Harris (d 1942), and Rhoda Mary, *née* Barclay (d 1961); landed gentry family formerly of Westcotes; *b* 25 Nov 1911; *Educ* Harrow, Trinity Coll Cambridge (MA); *m* 1937, Elizabeth Hermione, da of Capt Sir Clive Milnes-Coates, 2 Bt, OBE, JP, and Lady Celia, *née* Crewe-Milnes, JP, da of 1 and last Marquess of Crewe, KG; 1 s (Jonathan), 2 da (Jessica, Hermione); *Career* WWII 1940-45 Coldstream Gds served: N Africa, Italy, Germany (despatches), demobbed Maj; called to the Bar Inner Temple 1937; chm Rowton Hotels 1965-83; Church cmmr 1966-82, chm Redundant Churches Ctee 1972-82, pres Georgian Gp 1990- (chm 1985-90); Liveryman Worshipful Co Merchant Taylors; *Recreations* shooting; *Clubs* Brooks's, Athenaeum, MCC; *Style—* William Harris Esq, QC; Moatlands, East Grinstead, West Sussex (☎ 0342 810228); 29 Barkston Gardens, London SW5 (☎ 071 373 8793)

HARRIS, Sir William Gordon; KBE (1969), CB (1963); s of Capt James Whyte Harris, RNR (d 1952); *b* 10 June 1912; *Educ* Liverpool Coll, Sidney Sussex Coll Cambridge (MA); *m* 1938, Margaret Emily, da of John Steel Harvie (d 1951); 3 s, 1 da; *Career* civil engr; joined Admty 1937, civil engr in chief Admty 1959, dir gen Navy Works Admty 1960-63; dir gen: Works MPBW 1963-65, Highways Miny of Tport (later Environment) 1965-73; ptnr Peter Fraenkel & Ptnrs 1973-78; chief Br del: Perm Int Assoc of Navigation Congresses 1969-85 (vice pres 1976-79), Perm Int Assoc of Road Congresses 1970-73; Hon Seabee (US Navy) 1961, Decoration for Distinguished Civilian Serv (US Army) 1985; pres: ICE 1974-75, Smeatonian Soc of Civil Engrs 1983-84; chm: Construction Indust Manpower Bd 1976-80, B & CE Holiday Mgmnt Co 1978-87, Dover Harbour Bd 1980-83; chm Br Sch of Osteopathy 1990-; Hon DSc City Univ 1977; FEng, FICE; *Recreations* gardening, walking, music, 10 grandchildren; *Style—* Sir William Harris, KBE, CB; 3 Rofant Rd, Northwood, Middx HA6 3BD (☎ 09274 25899)

HARRIS OF GREENWICH, Baron (Life Peer UK 1974); John Henry Harris; s of Alfred Harris; *b* 5 April 1930; *Educ* Pinner GS; *m* 1, 1952 (m dis 1982), Patricia, da of George Alstrom; 1 s (Hon Francis b 1961), 1 da (Hon Deborah b 1958); m 2, 1983, Angela, da of Joseph Arthur Smith; *Career* sits as Lib Democrat Peer in House of Lords; PA to ldr of oppn (Rt Hon Hugh Gaitskell) 1959, dir of publicity Lab Pty 1962-64; special asst to: Foreign Sec 1964-66, Home Sec 1966-67; Chllr Exchequer 1967-70, Min of State Home Office 1974-79; pres Nat Assoc of Sr Probation Offrs; chm Parole Bd England and Wales 1979-82; tstee Police Fndn (chm exec ctee); political corr The Economist 1970-74; *Style—* The Rt Hon the Lord Harris of Greenwich; House of Lords, London SW1

HARRIS OF HIGH CROSS, Baron (Life Peer UK 1979); Ralph Harris; s of William Henry Harris (d 1954); *b* 10 Dec 1924; *Educ* Tottenham GS, Queens' Coll Cambridge; *m* 1949, Jose Pauline, da of Roger Fredrick Jeffery (d 1975); 1 s (Hon Julian Paul), 1 da (and 1 s decd); *Career* sits as Independent Peer in Lords; contested (C): Kirkcaldy 1951, Edinburgh 1955; leading writer Glasgow Herald 1956, lectr in political economy Univ of St Andrews 1949-56, gen dir Inst of Econ Affrs 1957-87 (chm 1987-89, life pres 1990-), ind dir Times Newspapers 1988-, chm Bruges Group 1989-; memb Cncl Univ of Buckingham; tstee: Ross McWhirter Fndn, Wincott Fndn, Centre for Res into Communist Econs, Atlas Fndn (UK); chm: FARM (Africa) 1987-, Forest 1989-; *Books* Politics Without Prejudice, End of Government, Challenge of a Radical Reactionary, No Minister!; *Style—* The Rt Hon the Lord Harris of High Cross; 2 Lord North St, London SW1P 3LB (☎ 071 799 3745); 4 Walmar Close, Hadley Wood, Barnet, Herts EN4 OLA (☎ 081 449 6212)

HARRISON, Prof Alan; TD (1983) (Bar 1989); s of Lt-Col John Thomas West Harrison, TD, of West Kirby, Wirral, Merseyside, and Mona Evelyn, *née* Gee; *b* 24 July 1944; *Educ* Rydal Sch Colwyn Bay, Welsh Nat Sch of Med Dental Sch (BDS, PhD); *m* 1, (m dis 1980), Pauline Lilian, *née* Rendell; 1 s (Mark Richard b 26 Aug 1973), 1 da (Jane Lorrie b 11 March 1970); m 2, 1 Oct 1982, Margaret Ann, da of Alan William Frost (d 1973), of Leicester; 2 da (Kathryn Ruth b 24 Feb 1984, Sally Deborah b 24 April 1985); *Career* OC 390 Field Dental Team 1971-73, CO 308 Evacuation Hosp RAMC (V) (2 i/c 1988-89, training offr 1984-88); lectr Dept of Restorative Dentistry Dental Sch Cardiff 1970-78, visiting asst prof Univ of S Carolina USA 1974-75, sr lectr and hon conslt Sch of Dentistry Univ of Leeds, prof of dental care of the elderly and head Dept of Prosthetic Dentistry and Dental Care of the Elderly Univ of Bristol 1987-; FDSRCS; *Books* Overdentures in General Dental Practice (1988); *Recreations* tennis, walking, DIY schemes; *Style—* Prof Alan Harrison, TD; Department of Prosthetic Dentistry & Dental Care of the Elderly, Dental School, Lower Maudlin St, Bristol BS1 2LY (☎ 0272 226056, fax 0272 253724)

HARRISON, Alan James; s of Maj James Harrison (d 1972); *b* 8 Jan 1942; *m* Oct 1978, Dioné Anne, da of Rev William Austin; 1 s (Martin Richard b 1969), 2 da (Yvonne Jane b 1966, Victoria Dioné b 1981); *Career* London branch mangr Bank Sanaye Iran 1978-82; Multibanco Cotermex: gen mangr Singapore branch 1982-84, gen mangr London branch 1984-; memb Berks CC 1985-; Freeman City of London; assoc memb Chartered Inst of Bankers; *Clubs* Overseas Bankers, Guards Polo; *Style—* Alan Harrison, Esq; Hill Hampton Pines, Sunning Ave, Sunningdale, Ascot, Berks (☎ 0990 24252); 66 Gresham St, London EC2V 7BB (☎ 01 796 3244)

HARRISON, Anthony Augustus Bertie; s of Capt Augustus Bertie Harrison (d 1930), of 41 Cornwallis Rd, Holloway, London N7, and Dorothy Rosina, *née* Schafe-Harrissen (d 1980); *b* 4 June 1920; *Educ* Highgate Sch, Univ of Cambridge; *m* 1, 29 March 1959 (m dis 1970), Marie, *née* McKenna-Lewis; 1 da (Antonia Michelle b 11 Dec 1961); m 2, 26 March 1971, Veronica Lesley, da of Capt Norman Hack, of 67 Kent View Rd, Vange, Essex; *Career* enlisted RAC 1939, cmmnd 1940, appointed Capt in Field Western Desert Egypt 1942, demob 1946; chm: Harrison & Willis Ltd 1958-83, HW Task Force 1982-85, Peats Investments Ltd 1978-82; dir: Forrest Harrison Orgn 1950-53, Mervyn Hughes & Co 1953-58, Esquire Catering Co Ltd 1983-90; vice pres Variety Club of GB 1976-82, memb Ctee Save the Family Appeal 1982-, govr Royal Masonic Hosp; JP 1977-85; Freeman City of London 1980, memb Worshipful Co of Painter Stainers Co, Hon Citizen Arizona USA 1982; FBIM 1965, FIAA 1968, MIEC 1963, FRPS 1962, FInst D 1965; *Recreations* sailing, music; *Clubs* City Livery, Royal Temple Yacht, Coda (sec 1987-); *Style—* Anthony Harrison, Esq; 29 Thamespoint, Fairways, Teddington TW11 9PP (☎ 081 977 9473)

HARRISON, Prof Bernard Joseph; s of William Bernard Harrison (d 1964), of Bristol, and Camilla Victoria, *née* Davis; *b* 29 May 1933; *Educ* Dursley GS, Cheltenham GS, Univ of Birmingham (BA, MA), Univ of Michigan, Ann Arbor (PhD); *m* July 1956, Dorothy Muriel, da of George Harold White (d 1967), of Nottingham; 1 s (David Thomas b 24 Dec 1964), 2 da (Eva Tempe Jane b 1957, Katherine Lisa b 1960); *Career* lectr in philosophy Univ of Toronto 1960-62, asst lectr in philosophy Univ of Birmingham 1962-63, prof of philosophy Univ of Sussex 1985- (lectr 1963, reader 1972), E E Erickson porf of philosophy Univ of Utah 1991-; *Books* Meaning and Structure (1972), Form and Content (1973), Fielding's Tom Jones: The Novelist as Moral Philosopher (1975), An Introduction to the Philosophy of Language (1979), Inconvenient Fictions: Literature and the Limits of Theory (1991); *Style—* Prof Bernard Harrison; School of English and American Studies, The University of Sussex, Falmer, Brighton, E Sussex BN1 9QN (☎ 0273 606755); Department of Philosophy, University of Utah, Salt Lake City, Utah 84112, USA (Sept-Dec annually)

HARRISON, Dr Brian David Walter; s of Joseph Harrison (d 1955), and Constance Jennings, *née* Horsfall, of Lytham St Annes; *b* 24 April 1943; *Educ* Shrewsbury, St John's Coll Cambridge (MA, MB, BChir), Guy's Hosp (LRCP, MRCS); *m* 13 July 1968, Jennifer Anne, da of Dr John Fisher Stokes, of Stoke Row, Oxfordshire; 1 s (Ben b 1970), 1 da (Nicola b 1974); *Career* house physician Guy's Hosp 1967-68, house surgn Bolingbrooke Hosp London 1968-69, sr house offr New Cross Hosp London 1969, jr registrar cardiology and gen med Guy's Hosp 1969-70, hon clinical lectr inphysiology Brompton Hosp 1971-72 (house physician 1970-71), registrar to med professorial unit Westminster Hosp 1971-72, clinical lectr in physiology Brompton Hosp 1973, sr med registrar Ahmadu Bello Univ Hosp Zaria Nigeria 1973-74, lectr and sr registrar in thoracic and gen med Middlesex Hosp 1974-77; conslt physician: Norfolk and Norwich Hosp 1978-, West Norwich Hosp 1978-; memb Cncl ASH 1983 (fndr and first chm Norfolk ASH 1979); British Thoracic Soc: memb Res Ctee 1980-86, clinical coordinator Nat Pneumonia Study 1981-87, memb Educn Ctee 1986-89, chm Pneumonia Standing Sub Ctee 1987-89, chm Standards of Care Ctee 1989-, memb Cncl and Exec 1989-, coordinator conf to produce guidelines on the mgmnt of asthma in Britain 1990-; pres East Anglian Thoracic Soc 1982-84; MRCP 1970, FRCP 1987; FCCP 1990; author of numerous med pubns on pneumonia, smoking, asthma, pulmonary function respiratory failure, secondary polycythemia, chronic airflow obstruction, lung biopsy sarcoidosis; *Recreations* gardening, sailing, theatre, skiing, travel; *Clubs* Stranger's (Norwich); *Style—* Dr Brian Harrison; The White House, Church Avenue East, Norwich NR2 2AF (☎ 0603 56508); Norfolk and Norwich Hospital, Brunswick Road, Norwich NR1 3SR (☎ 0603 62837 ext 253/254); West Norwich Hospital, Bowthorpe Road, Norwich NR2 3TU

HARRISON, Brian Fraser; s of James Fraser Harrison (d 1971); *b* 6 Sept 1918; *Educ* St Christopher's Sch, Liverpool Coll for Boys; *m* 1939, Constance Kathleen Fraser, da of John Edward Bennion (d 1962); 1 s; *Career* WWII RASC (TA) served, Gold Coast Br West Africa; slr; ptnr Mace & Jones 1948-83, memb Lord Chllr's Circuit Advsy Ctee (Liverpool) 1972-81; professional mil artist 1983-; author; *Books* Advocacy at Petty Sessions, A Business of Your Own, A Business of Your Own Today, Work of a Magistrate, How to Select Your Professional Advisers - and Get the Best Out of Them, How to Make More Money as a Freelance Bookkeeper, How to Be a Successful Outside Caterer, How to Make Money as a Neighbourhood Handyman, How to Get What You Really Want Out of Life; *Recreations* art, writing, walking; *Style—* Brian Fraser Harrison, Esq; Peddars Cottage, The Street, Hessett, Bury St Edmunds IP30 9AX (☎ 0359 70409)

HARRISON, Brian William; s of Frank Harrison, of Auckland, NZ, and Priscilla Helen Harrison; *b* 30 Oct 1953; *Educ* Lynfield Coll Auckland NZ, Auckland Univ NZ (LLB); *m* 2 July 1988, Diana Durad, da of Pete Gibbons, of Auckland, NZ; 1 da (Jessica b 20 July 1989); *Career* admitted slr and barriste supreme Court of NZ 1976; Allen and Ovary: asst 1983-86, admitted slr 1985, ptnr 1987; Liveryman Worshipful Co of Slrs 1987; Law Soc 1985; *Recreations* yachting, skiing; *Clubs* Royal Ocean Racing, New York Yacht, Royal Hong Kong Yacht; *Style—* Brian Harrison, Esq; CI-Allen & Overy, 9 Cheapside, London EC2U 6AD (☎ 071 248 9898, telex 8812801, fax 071 236 2192)

HARRISON, Prof Bryan Desmond; CBE (1990); s of John William Harrison (d 1963), and Norah, *née* Webster; *b* 16 June 1931; *Educ* Whitgift Sch Croydon, Univ of Reading (Wantage scholar, BSc), Rothamsted Experimental Station Harpenden, Univ of London (PhD); *m* 13 Jan 1968, Elizabeth Ann, da of Vivian Francis Latham-Warde (d 1981); 2 s (Peter William b 1969, Robert Anthony b 1972), 1 da (Claire Janet b 1977); *Career* res scientist: Virology Section Scot Horticultural Res Inst Dundee 1954-57, Plant Pathology Dept Rothamsted Experimental Station Harpenden 1957-66; Scot Crop Res Inst Dundee (formerly Horticultural Res Inst): res scientist and head Virology Dept 1966-91, sr pso 1969, dep chief scientific offr 1981; hon prof Univ of St Andrews 1986-, hon visiting prof Univ of Dundee 1988-91, (prof Plant Virology June 1991-); Hon Doctorate in Agricultural Sci Univ of Helsinki 1990; hon memb: Assoc of Applied Biologists 1989, Soc for Gen Microbiology 1990; *Recreations* gardening; *Style—* Prof Bryan Harrison, CBE, FRS, FRSE; Scottish Crop Research Institute, Invergowrie, Dundee DD2 5DA (☎ 0382 562731, fax 0382 562426)

HARRISON, Christopher John; s of John Forth Harrison (d 1947), of Manchester, and Margaret Heywood, *née* Ham; *b* 20 Aug 1934; *Educ* St Edward's Sch Oxford; *m* 15 July 1961, Daphne Gwen, da of Trevor Spickett Roberts (d 1985), of Cardiff; 2 s (Robert, James); *Career* Price Waterhouse & Co 1958-61; ptnr: Richard Leyshon & Co 1961-64, Brown Harrison Weare & Co (formerly Longdon Griffiths Griffin & Co 1964-); pres Cardiff Caledonian Sec 1973-74 (sec 1964-73); FCA 1958; *Recreations* golf; *Clubs* Glamorganshire Golf, Rotary; *Style—* Christopher Harrison, Esq; Machrihanish, 16 Clinton Rd, Penarth CF6 2JB (☎ 0222 708 978); Brown Harrison Weare & Co, Midland Bank Chambers, 97-100 Bute St, Cardiff CF1 6PP (☎ 0222 480 167)

HARRISON, Claude William; s of Harold Harrison (d 1976), and Florence Mildred, *née* Ireton (d 1986); *b* 31 March 1922; *Educ* Hutton GS, Harris Art Sch Preston, Liverpool City Sch of Art, RCA (ARCA); *m* 1 March 1947, Audrey, da of Arthur John Johnson (d 1964); 1 s (Tobias b 1950); *Career* WWII RAF 1942-47; serv: India, Burma, China; painter of: conversation pieces, portraits, figure compositions; exhibitions: RA, London, Florida, NY, Chicago; RSPP 1961; *Books* The Portrait Painters Handbook (1968), Book of Tobit (1970); *Recreations* walking and reading; *Style—* Claude Harrison, Esq; Barrow Wife, Cartmel Fell, Grange over Sands, Cumbria LA11 6NZ (☎ 053 95 31323)

HARRISON, Sir (Robert) Colin; 4 Bt (UK 1922), of Eaglescliffe, Co Durham; s of late Sir John Fowler Harrison, 2 Bt, and Kathleen, Lady Harrison, *qv*; suc bro, Sir (John) Wyndham Harrison, 3 Bt 1955; *b* 25 May 1938; *Educ* Radley, St John's Coll Cambridge; *m* 1963, Maureen Marie, da of late E Leonard Chiverton ; 1 s, 2 da (Rachel b 1966, Claire b 1974); *Heir* s, John Wyndham Fowler Harrison b 14 Dec 1972; *Career* Nat Serv cmmnd 5 Royal Northumberland Fusiliers 1957-59; chm Young Master Printers Nat Ctee 1972-73; *Style—* Sir Colin Harrison, Bt; The Grange,

Rosedale Abbey, Pickering, N Yorks YO18 8RD (☎ 03475 226)

HARRISON, Dr David; CBE (1990); s of Harold David Harrison (d 1987), of Exeter, Devon, and Lavinia, *née* Wilson; *b* 3 May 1930; *Educ* Bede Sch Sunderland, Clacton Co HS, Selwyn Coll Cambridge (BA, PhD, MA, ScD); *m* 11 Aug 1962, Sheila Rachel, da of Denis Richardson Debes, of Little Budworth, Cheshire; 2 s (Michael b 1963, Tony b 1966, d 1986), 1 da (Sarah b 1965); *Career* Nat Serv 2 Lt REME 1949; Cambridge Univ: lectr 1956-79, fell Selwyn Coll 1957- (sr tutor 1967-79), chm bd of tstees Homerton Coll 1979-; visiting prof: Delaware Univ USA 1967, Sydney Univ Aust 1976; vice chllr: Keele Univ 1979-84, Exeter Univ 1984-; chm UCCA 1984-, pres Inst of Chem Engrs 1991; FEng 1987, FRSC, FRIC 1961, FIChemE 1968, FRSA 1985, CBIM 1990; *Books* Fluidised Particles (with J F Davidson, 1963), Fluidization (with J F Davidson and R Clift, 2 edn 1985); *Recreations* music, tennis, hill walking, good food; *Clubs* Athenaeum, Foundation House (Stoke-on-Trent); *Style—* Dr David Harrison, CBE; Redcot, Streatham Drive, Exeter; 7 Gough Way, Cambridge; University of Exeter, Northcote House, The Queen's Drive, Exeter (☎ 0392 263000, fax 0392 263008, telex 42894 EXUNIV G)

HARRISON, David Ernest; s of Ernest Harrison (d 1984), and Margaret Louise, *née* Robson (d 1976); *b* 14 July 1936; *Educ* Exeter Sch, St Catherine's Coll Oxford (MA), Stanford Univ Calif USA (MA); *m* 25 March 1961, Pamela Lilian, da of Stanley Brobyn; 1 s (Richard Stanley Ernest b 30 May 1964 d 1981), 2 da (Catherine Louise (Mrs Raba) b 21 Sept 1965, Rowan Jane b 11 April 1970); *Career* ATV 1959-68 (asst sales exec, sales exec, London sales mangr, dep sales controller), Tyne Tees Television 1968-71 (dep sales controller, sales dir); md: British Posters 1971-73, Media Div Lion International 1973; mktg dir: Credcrest Ltd 1973-74, E Gomme Ltd 1974-82; chm and chief exec Harrison Salinson & Co (part of TMDH 1989-) 1982-, memb Gp Bd TMDH 1990; govr RSC 1979-; *Recreations* amateur dramatics, cricket, soccer, rugby; *Style—* David Harrison, Esq; Harrison Salinson & Co Ltd, 55 North Wharf Rd, London W2 1RA (☎ 071 724 7244, fax 071 724 7620)

HARRISON, David Richard; s of Richard Frankland Harrison (d 1973), and Muriel Eileen, *née* Wilson (d 1963); *b* 3 June 1932; *Educ* Clayesmore; *m* 12 Sept 1959, Diana, da of Gerald Clay Megson (d 1982); 1 s (Richard b 31 Aug 1964), 1 da (Caroline b 8 Sept 1966); *Career* CA 1957; sec: Oldham C of C and Indust 1971, Oldham branch RNLI 1961; FCA 1962; *Recreations* golf, contract bridge; *Style—* David Harrison, Esq; 6 Beech Hill Rd, Grasscroft, Oldham, Lancs OL4 4DR (☎ 0457 873151); 8 Clydesdale St, Oldham, Lancs OL8 1BT (☎ 061 624 2482)

HARRISON, David Roger; s of John Charles Rowles Harrison, and Muriel Florence, *née* Hubbard; *b* 14 June 1942; *Educ* Wellingborough Sch; *m* 9 Sept 1965, Veronica Jean, da of Peter Kirkby, DFM; 1 s (Robert David b 6 Sept 1976), 3 da (Claire Veronica b 17 May 1968, Charlotte Jane b 13 March 1970, Bryony Jean b 1 Jan 1974); *Career* dir Duplex Plastics Ltd 1969-74; md: RC Harrison Ltd 1980-88 (dir 1973-88), Nylacast Systems Ltd 1982-; non-exec dir Kanoria Petro Prods Ltd Delhi India 1988-; chm Keyham Utd Charities 1972-80; Freeman City of Leicester 1964; MInstD; *Recreations* motor sport, skiing, swimming; *Clubs* Vintage Sports Car, Veteran Car Club of GB, Maserati Owners; *Style—* David Harrison, Esq; The Old Rectory, Hungarton, Leicester (☎ 053 750 639)

HARRISON, Sir Donald Frederic Norris; Kt (1990); s of Frederick William Rees Harrison, OBE, of Ludshott Court Hampshire, and Florence (d 1987); *b* 9 March 1925; *Educ* Newport HS Gwent, Guy's Hosp (MS, MD, PhD, Pembray prize, 12 Gold medals); *m* 29 Jan 1948, Audrey Dixon, da of Percival Clubb (d 1970); 2 da (Susan Patricia Denny b July 1949, Zoë Clare b March 1965); *Career* Nat Serv ENT specialist RAF 1950-52; 1963-90: Hunterian prof of Laryngology and Otology Univ of London, sr surgn Royal Nat ENT Hosp, ENT surgn Moorfields Eye Hosp London, dean Inst of Laryngology and Otology; pres Gatwick-Horley Div St John Ambulance, memb Cncl Roedean Girls Sch 1982-89; memb Worshipful Co of Apothecaries; FRCS 1955; memb: Royal Coll of Surgns Australia 1977 and Edinburgh 1981, S African Coll of Med 1988, American Coll of Surgns 1990, 40 nat and int learned socs; *Publications* 36 book chapters, Scientific Basis of Otolarynagology (1976), Dilemmas in Otorhinolaryngology (1988); *Recreations* heraldry, model making, comparative anatomy; *Style—* Sir Donald Harrison, Kt; Springfield, 6 Fishers Farm, Horley, Surrey RH6 9DU (☎ 0293 784307); Royal National ENT Hospital, 330 Grays Inn Rd, London (☎ 071 837 8855, fax 071 833 9480)

HARRISON, Air Cdre Donald James; CBE (1987); s of Charles Harrison, of 6 Houseman Park, School Drive, Bromsgrove, and Minnie Alice Eva, *née* David (d 1988); *b* 2 July 1937; *Educ* George Dixon GS Birmingham, Birmingham Coll of Tech; *m* 2 Jan 1960, Enda Teresa, da of Percy Lee-Cooper (d 1976); 1 s (Jeremy b 1966), 1 da (Valerie b 1967); *Career* cmmnd catering branch RAF 1956, appt catering staff HQ Bomber Cmd 1965-67, MOD staff 1967-70, RAF staff coll 1970, cmd catering staff HQASC and HQSTC 1970-75, OC trg wing RAF Hereford 1975-77, directorate of recruiting MOD 1977-79, command catering offr HQSTC 1980-82, dir of catering RAF 1982-86, appt Air Cdre, dep Air Offr admin HQRAF support command 1986-8, DPM Airmen RAF 1989; memb: RYA (dinghy instr and yacht master, offshore certified skipper), Nat Tst; Hon Freeman Worshipful Co of Cooks 1982, Freeman City of London 1983; FBIM 1989; *Recreations* sailing, gardening, choral music; *Clubs* RAF; *Style—* Air Cdre Donald Harrison, CBE; 29 Cordingley Close, Churchdown, Cloucester GL3 2EN (☎ 0452 856265); Director of Personnel Management (Airmen) (RAF), RAF Personnel Management Centre, RAF Innsworth, Gloucester (☎ 0452 712612 ext 7820)

HARRISON, Sir Ernest Thomas; OBE (1972); s of Ernest Horace Harrison by his w Gertrude Rebecca Gibbons; *b* 11 May 1926; *Educ* Trinity GS London; *m* 1960, Phyllis Brenda (Janie), *née* Knight; 3 s, 2 da; *Career* CA; Harker Holloway & Co, Nat Savings Movement 1964-76; Racal Electronics plc: joined 1951, dir 1958, dep md 1961, chief exec, chm 1966; chm Racal Telecom plc 1988; Capt of Industry (Livingston Industl and Commercial Assoc Edinburgh) 1980, Hambro Businessman of the Year 1981, Aims of Industry Nat Free Enterprise award 1982, Br Enterprise award for Racal 1982, received The 1990 Founding Society's Centenary award by Inst of Chartered Accountants; former memb Cncl Electronics Engrg Assoc and Nat Electronics Cncl; memb Worshipful Co of Scriveners'; Hon DSc Cranfield Inst of Technol, Hon DUniv Surrey, Hon DSc City Univ, Hon DUniv Edinburgh, Hon FCGI; memb RSA, FCA, ComplERE, ComplEE Companion Inst of Mgmnt; kt 1981; *Recreations* horse racing (owner and breeder), gardening, wild life, all sports (particularly soccer); *Clubs* Jockey; *Style—* Sir Ernest Harrison, OBE; Racal Electronics plc, Western Rd, Bracknell, Berks

HARRISON, Sir Francis Alexander Lyle (Frank); MBE (1943), QC (NI), DL (Co Down 1973); s of Rev Alexander Lyle Harrison; *b* 19 March 1910; *Educ* Campbell Coll Belfast, Trinity Coll Dublin; *m* 1940, Norah Patricia Rea; 2 da; *Career* called to the bar NI 1937, bencher Inn of Ct NI 1961, pres Lands Tbnl NI 1964-; fndr memb NI Assoc of Mental Health 1959, chm Glendhu Children's Hostel 1969-81; cmmr: Local Govt Boundaries NI 1971-72 and 1983-84, Dist Electoral Areas 1984; kt 1974; *Style—* Sir Frank Harrison, MBE, QC, DL; Ballydorn Hill, Killinchy, Newtownards, Co Down, NI (☎ 0238 541 250)

HARRISON, Gerald Stanley; s of Arthur Guiton Harrison, CBE (d 1976), of Jersey, and Noella Alice, *née* Laurens; *b* 5 May 1938; *Educ* Victoria Coll Jersey, Exeter Coll Oxford (MA, half blue Athletics); *m* 22 May 1961, Gillian Mary (d 1986), da of Michael Hubert Horris, of 15 Chilbury Gdns, Owermoigne, nr Dorchester, Dorset; 1 da (Catherine b 11 Sept 1964); *Career* dir Overseas Trading Corporation (1939) Ltd Jersey 1972-87 (mktg mangr 1962-72); capt Jersey Cwlth Games team 1958; memb ctee Jersey Cancer Relief; *Recreations* lawn bowls, swimming, gardening, travel; *Style—* Gerald Harrison, Esq; La Conchiere, La Rocque, Jersey (☎ 0534 534 19)

HARRISON, (James) Graham; s of Col Alfred Marshal Langton Harrison, CBE, MC (d 1986), of West Malvern, Worcs, and Violet, *née* Robinson (d 1988); *b* 3 July 1930; *Educ* The Elms Colwall Worcs, Bishop Cotton Sch Simla India, Geelong GS Victoria Aust, Uppingham; *m* 26 July 1958, June Eveline, da of Robert Eustace Taylor (d 1958), of Woodford Wells, Essex; 2 s (Robert b 1962, Nicholas b 1973), 1 da (Sarah (Mrs Moloney) b 1959); *Career* Nat Serv 2 Lt RHA 1954-56; TA: L/Bdr HAC 1956-59, Capt S Nottingham Hussars 1959-64; CA; articled Wright & Westhead 1948-54, qualified 1954, Price Waterhouse 1956-59, Chamberlain & Merchant 1959-64; sole practitioner: Sacker & Harrison Bournemouth 1964-70, Bicker & Co 1970-84, Thornton Baker 1985; fndr Harrison & Co 1986-; dir Portman Bldg Soc 1989-; chm: Wessex Branch Inst of Taxation 1978-80, Courses Ctee S Soc of CAs 1979-82; treas St Saviour's PCC 1984-90 (sec 1974-79, churchwarden 1979-84); FCA 1954, ATII 1963; *Books* Handbook on Taxation of Land (1982), Taxation of Income Arising From Furnished Lettings (1985); *Recreations* sport, music; *Clubs* Lanz Sportz Centre; *Style—* Graham Harrison, Esq; 45 Littledown Ave, Queens Park, Bournemouth, BH7 7AX (☎ 0202 393540); Rowland House, Hinton Rd, Bournemouth, BH1 2EG (☎ 0202 294 162, fax 0202 295 546)

HARRISON, Harry Cyril; CBE (1982); s of late Richard Harrison, and Elsie May; *b* 1 March 1920; *m* 1945, Joyce, da of Samuel Nicholls; 1 s (Geoffrey), 1 da (June); *Career* served Worcester Regt 1940-46 (despatches); chm: Simon Engrg plc 1982- (chief exec 1970-82), Warman Int Ltd, Simon Engrg plc, Dudley Business Venture, Dudley Zoo Dvpt Tst; dir: Simon US Corpn, Barclays Bank (Manchester local bd), John Folkes Hefo plc (non-exec); memb: CBI cncl London, 10D Manchester Branch Ctee, Engrg Industs Cncl, Ct of Univ of Manchester, Ct of Govrs Univ of Manchester Inst of Science and Technol; FRSA, MIBF, CBIM; *Recreations* golf, reading, travelling, swimming; *Style—* Harry Harrison, Esq, CBE; Tudor Lodge, Redlake Drive, Pedmore, Stourbridge, W Midlands DY9 0RX; Simon Engineering plc, Bird Hall Lane, Cheadle Heath, Stockport, Cheshire (☎ 061 428 3600)

HARRISON, Maj-Gen Ian Stewart; CB; s of Capt Leslie George Harrison (d 1930), and Evelyn Simpson, *née* Christie (d 1980); *b* 25 May 1919; *Educ* St Albans Sch; *m* 5 Dec 1942, Winfred (Wynne) Raikes, da of George Vose Stavert, of Endmoor, Kendal, Westmorland; 1 s (David Raikes Stewart b 11 June 1949), 1 da (Jenifer Anne b 15 April 1947); *Career* cmmnd RM 1937; serv at sea 1939-45: Norway, ME, Sicily, BAOR; student staff coll Camberley 1948, HQ 3 Commando Bde 1949-51, dir staff coll Camberley 1953-55, cmdt signal sch RM 1959-61, staff of cmdt gen RM 1962-63, chief instr Jt Warfare Estab 1963-65, CO RM barracks Eastney 1966-67, Br def staff Washington DC 1967-68, chief of staff RM 1968-70; ADC to HM The Queen 1966-67; dir gen: British Food Export Cncl 1970-78, British Consultants Bureau 1978-88; fndr tstee Brtish Sch of Brussels 1969-, chm Chichester Festivities 1979-89, Capt of Deal Castle 1980-; FBIM; *Recreations* golf, real tennis, sailing; *Clubs* Royal Yacht Squadron, Army and Navy, Royal St George's Golf; *Style—* Maj-Gen Ian Harrison, CB; Manor Cottage, Runcton, Chicester, W Sussex PO20 6PU (☎ 0243 785 480)

HARRISON, John; s of John Henry Jordan, of Grantham, Lincs, and Margaret, *née* Harrison; *b* 20 Feb 1944; *Educ* Silverdale Secdy Modern Sch, Sheffield Tech Coll; *m* 13 July 1968, Vivien Ann Eveline, da of Frederick Charles Hardisty (d 1988), of Brighton; 1 s (Mark b 31 July 1976); *Career* asst electrician to chief engr Harold Fielding 1961-63, lighting designer Theatre Projects Ltd 1964-68, prodn mangr and tech dir ENO 1968-74, theatre conslt John Wyckham Associates 1975-76; tech dir: WNO 1976-88, Vancouver Opera (Canada) 1984-88, Royal Opera House Covent Garden 1989-; md Cardiff Theatrical Services Ltd 1984-88; memb: Assoc of Br Theatre Technicians 1968, Soc of Br Theatre Designers 1964, Soc of Br Lighting Designers 1964; *Recreations* travel, gardening; *Style—* John Harrison, Esq; 6 Summerswood Close, Kenley Lane, Kenley, Surrey CR8 5EY; Royal Opera House, Covent Garden, London WC2E 9DD (☎ 071 240 1200, fax 071 836 1762, telex 27988 COVGAR G)

HARRISON, John; s of Kenneth Ridley Harrison (d 1960), of Stockton on Tees, and Margaret, *née* Calvert; *b* 12 Nov 1944; *Educ* Grangefield GS, Univ of Sheffield (BA); *m* 4 June 1969, Patricia Alice Bridget, da of Dr Harry Raymond Alban (d 1974), of London; 1 s (Joseph b 1979), 2 da (Rachel b 1971, Philippa b 1973); *Career* articled clerk Coopers & Lybrand 1966-70, Tillotson corp planner 1970-72, ptnr Touche Ross 1981- (mgmnt conslt 1972-); dir Granta Radio Ltd; FCA 1969, FIMC 1973, FRSA 1991; *Recreations* skiing, sailing, shooting; *Clubs* Royal Harwich Yacht; *Style—* John Harrison, Esq; Goodwin Manor, Swaffham Prior, Cambridge (☎ 0638 742 850); Touche Ross, Hill House, 1 Little New St, London EC4A 3TR (☎ 071 936 3000, fax 071 583 8517, telex 884739 TRLNDN G)

HARRISON, Surgn Vice Adm Sir John (Albert Bews); KBE (1981); s of Albert William Harrison (d 1959), of Dover, Kent, and Lilian Eda, *née* Bews (d 1973); *b* 20 May 1921; *Educ* St Bartholomew's Hosp; *m* 1943, Jane Harris; 2 s; *Career* RN Med Serv 1947-83, after serv with RM (and at sea), served in RN Hosps Plymouth, Hong Kong, Chatham, Malta and Haslar; advsr in radiology to Med DG Navy 1967-76, dep med DG and dir med Personnel and Logistics 1975-77, Dean Naval Med and Surgn Rear Adm in charge Inst of Naval Med 1977-80, QHP 1976-83, med DG Navy and Surgn Vice Adm 1980-83; memb MRC Decompression Sickness Panel, former memb Cncl for Med Postgrad Educn of Eng and Wales; pres: Radiology Section RSM 1984-85, Med Soc London 1985-86; FRCP, FRCR, DMRD; CStJ 1983 (OStJ 1975); *Recreations* fishing, cricket, photography; *Clubs* RSM, MCC; *Style—* Sir John Harrison, KBE; Alexandra Cottage, Swanmore, Hants SO3 2PB

HARRISON, John Clive; LVO (1971); s of Sir Geoffrey Wedgwood Harrison GCMG, KCVO, and Amy Katherine, *née* Clive; *b* 12 July 1937; *Educ* Winchester, Jesus Coll Oxford (BA); *m* 1967, Jennifer Heather, da of Cdr John Courtney Evered Burston, OBE, RN (d 1970); 1 s (James b 1968), 2 da (Carolyn b 1970, Sarah b 1972); *Career* dip serv offr, cnsllr head of Chancery Lagos 1981-84, head of Consular Dept FCO 1985-89, dep high cmmr Islamabad 1989-; *Recreations* gardening, golf, tennis; *Clubs* Mannings Heath Golf; *Style—* John C Harrison, Esq, LVO; Foreign and Commonwealth Office, King Charles St, London SW1

HARRISON, Col John George; OBE (1975), TD (1960), DL (1973); s of James Harrison (d 1960); *b* 15 March 1920; *Educ* Bridgend GS, St Luke's and Loughborough Colls; *m* 1946, Mona Patricia, da of Onslow Francis Froud (d 1950); 1 s, 2 da; *Career* served WWII with Inland Inf, cmd Devon 1 RV (TA) 1961-64, Dep Cdr 130 Inf Bde (TA) 1965-67, Territorial Col SW Dist 1967-68, Cmdt Devon ACF 1970-75; *Clubs* Exeter Golf and Country; *Style—* Col John Harrison, OBE, TD, DL; Ivy Cottage, 36 Buckerell Ave, Exeter, Devon EX2 4RD (☎ 0392 74959)

HARRISON, Julian Pitman Hyde; s of Lt-Col Jim Willoughby Hyde Harrison, MC (d 1958), and Sylvia Hayward, *née* Pitman (d 1956); *b* 21 Aug 1929; *Educ* Bryanston,

Magdalen Coll Oxford (MA); *m* 23 Jan 1965, June Selby, da of Herbert Saysell Colwill (d 1959); 1 s (James b 10 July 1967), 1 da (Sarah b 23 Aug 1965); *Career* memb Lloyd's 1957-, underwriter T R Mountain (and others) 1970-, chm A R Mountain & Son Ltd 1988-; councillor (Cons) Camden Borough 1968-71 and 1978-86; contested (C) Stoke-on-Trent (Central) 1959 and 1964; Liveryman Worshipful Co of Merchant Taylors' 1956; *Recreations* chess, reading, maintaining a country house; *Clubs* Carlton; *Style—* Julian Harrison, Esq; Danemore Park, Speldhurst, Kent TN3 0JP (☎ 0892 862 829); 37 Gayton Rd, London NW3 1UB; A R Mountain & Son Ltd, Lloyds, London EC3M 7HL (☎ 071 623 7100 ext 3153)

HARRISON, Kathleen, Lady; Kathleen; *née* Livingston; da of Robert Livingston, of The Gables, Eaglescliffe, Co Durham; *m* 29 April 1930, Sir (John) Fowler Harrison, 2 Bt (d 1947); 2 s (Sir (John) Wyndham, 3 Bt d 1953, Sir (Robert) Colin, *qv*), 1 da (Mrs Paul Standing); *Style—* Kathleen, Lady Harrison; Bonnie Banks, Sproxton, Helmsley, York YO6 5BJ (☎ 0439 70598)

HARRISON, Kenneth Arthur; TD (1965); s of Arthur Reginald Harrison (d 1969), and Agnes, *née* Hutcheson (d 1963); *b* 4 July 1930; *Educ* Denstone Coll Staffs, Univ of Manchester; *m* 12 Sept 1953, Christine Mary, da of Joseph Herrod; 2 s (Roger b 1955, Peter b 1960); *Career* chm: Harrison Industries plc 1971- (sr engr 1951-61, building design conslt 1961-65, md (engrg) 1965-70), Bostwick Doors (UK) Ltd (subsid; Queen's award for Export 1980); *Recreations* tennis, parachuting, business, golf, garden design; *Clubs* St James's (Manchester and London); *Style—* Kenneth Harrison, Esq, TD; White Cottage, Oldfield Rd, Altrincham, Cheshire; Shippon, Moelfre, Anglesey; Chesaux-Dessous, St Cergues, Switzerland; Bostwick Doors (UK) Ltd, Stockport, Cheshire (telex 667724)

HARRISON, Kenneth Cecil; OBE (1980, MBE (Mil) 1946); s of Thomas Harrison (d 1967), of Hyde, Cheshire, and Annie, *née* Wood (d 1976); *b* 29 April 1915; *Educ* Hyde GS Cheshire, Coll of Technol Manchester, RMA Sandhurst; *m* 26 Aug 1941, Doris, da of Frank Taylor (d 1927), of Hyde, Cheshire; 2 s (David John b 25 Aug 1944, Timothy Michael b 28 Aug 1948); *Career* WWII served: S Lancs Regt 1940-42, offr cadet RMC 1942, 2 Lt W Yorks Regt 1942, Lt E Yorks Regt 50 Div Western Desert 1942, platoon cdr Sicily Landing 1943, Capt 1943, Maj 1944, company cdr D-Day landing (wounded) 1944, Normandy and Arnhem 1944, Italy and Austria 1945; demob bd Maj 1946; borough librarian: Hyde and Glossop 1939, Hove 1947, Eastbourne 1950, Hendon 1958; city librarian Westminster 1961-80, chief exec Cwlth Library Assoc 1980-83, conslt librarian Ranfurly Library Serv 1983-90; vice pres City of Westminster Arts Cncl 1980-(hon sec 1965-80), govr Westminster Coll 1962-80, pres Paddington Soc 1982-90; memb Rotary Club: Hyde 1939-47, Hove 1947-50, Eastbourne 1950-58 (pres 1957-58), Hendon 1958-61; memb past Rotarians Club of Eastbourne and dist 1986-, memb Eastbourne Local History Soc 1987-; fell Library Assoc 1938-(pres 1973); memb Cwlth Library Assoc (pres 1972-75); Knight First Class Order of the Lion of Finland 1976; *Books* Public Libraries Today (1963), Facts at your Fingertips (2 edn, 1966), British Public Library Buildings (1966), Libraries in Britain (1968), Libraries in Scandinavia (2 edn, 1969), The Library and the Community (3 edn, 1977), Prospects for British Librarianship (ed, 1977), First Steps in Librarianship (5 edn, 1980); Public Library Policy (ed, 1981), Public Relations for Librarians (2 edn, 1982), Public Library Buildings 1975-83 (ed, 1987), International Librarianship (1989), Library Buildings 1984-89 (ed, 1990); *Recreations* reading, writing, travel, wine-bibbing, crosswords, cricket, zoo visiting; *Clubs* MCC, Cwlth Tst, Sussex CCC; *Style—* K C Harrison, Esq, OBE; 5 Tavistock, Devonshire Place, Eastbourne, East Sussex BN21 4AG (☎ 0323 26747)

HARRISON, Prof Martin; s of Wilfrid Harrison (d 1968), of Darlington Co Durham, and Isobel, *née* Armstrong; *b* 19 April 1930; *Educ* Queen Elizabeth GS Darlington, Univ of Manchester (BA), Univ of Oxford (PhD), Univ of Paris (DRESSP); *m* 23 April 1957, Wendy Handford, da of Robert Wood Hindle (d 1974), of Madeley Staffs; 2 s (Andrew b 1959, David b 1962), 1 da (Catherine b 1966); *Career* RAF 1952-54: PO 1953, flying offr 1954, Flt Lt 1954; res fell Nuffield Coll Oxford 1957-62, lectr then sr lectr Univ of Manchester 1963-66, pro vice chllr Univ of Keele 1985-88 (prof and head Dept of Politics 1966-, dep vice chllr 1979-82); chm Local Radio Advsy Ctee and BBC Radio Stoke-on-Trent 1982-85; memb: BBC Gen Advsy Ctee 1983-85, BBC Midlands Advsy Co 1983-86; chm: Beth Johnson Housing Gp 1983-, Editorial Bd Sociological Review; chm Bd of Social Scis Univ of Keele 1988- (1976-79), Co controller Staffs Radio Amateur Emergency Network; *Books* Trade Unions and the Labour Party (1960), De Gaulle's Republic (1960), Politics and Society in De Gaulle's Republic (1972), French Politics (1969), TV News: Whose Bias? (1985); *Recreations* amateur radio (G3USF), walking; *Style—* Prof Martin Harrison; 1 Church Fields, Keele, Newcastle-Under-Lyme, Staffs ST5 5AT (☎ 0782 627396); Dept of Politics, Keele University, Keele, Staffs ST5 5BG (☎ 0782 621111 ext 3999)

HARRISON, Martin Edward; *b* 4 April 1937; *Educ* Harrow, Oriel Coll Oxford (MA); *Career* with Samuel Montagu & Co Ltd 1961-75 (ending as asst dir), sr vice pres Morgan Guaranty Trust Co (joined 1975); chm: J P Morgan Investment Management Australia Ltd, J P Morgan Investment Management Pacific Ltd; memb Fin and Planning Ctee London Sch of Hygiene and Tropical Med; *Clubs* Brooks's, Utd Oxford and Cambridge; *Style—* Martin Harrison, Esq; Morgan Guaranty Trust Co, 83 Pall Mall, London SW1Y 5ES (☎ 071 839 9211, fax 071 839 3901, telex 896631 MGT G)

HARRISON, (George) Michael Antony; CBE (1980); s of George and Kathleen Harrison; *b* 7 April 1925; *Educ* Manchester GS, BNC Oxford (MA); *m* 1951, Pauline, *née* Roberts; 2 s, 1 da; *Career* chief educn offr City of Sheffield 1967-85, educn systems conslt 1985-; memb Engrg Cncl 1982-87; Hon LLD Sheffield; *Style—* Michael Harrison, Esq, CBE; (☎ 0742 553783)

HARRISON, Sir Michael James Harwood; 2 Bt (UK 1961); s of Col Sir Harwood Harrison, 1 Bt, TD (d 1980), MP (C) Eye 1951-79, of Little Manor, Woodbridge, Suffolk and Peggy Alberta Mary, *née* Stenhouse; *b* 28 March 1936; *Educ* Rugby; *m* 1967, Louise, da of Edward Buxton Clive (d 1975), of Swanmore Lodge, Swanmore, Hants; 2 s (Edwin b 1981, Tristan b 1986), 2 da (Davina b 1968, Priscilla b 1971); *Heir* s, Edwin Michael Harwood Harrison b 29 May 1981; *Career* Nat Serv 17/21 Lancers 1955-56; insur broker Lloyd's 1958-; chm: Leggett Porter and Howard Ltd 1981-, L P H Pitman Ltd 1987-; dir of private cos 1980-; memb Cncl Sail Training Assoc 1968-; Freeman City of London 1964-, Master Mercers' Co 1986 (Liveryman 1967), vice pres Assoc of Combined Youth Clubs 1983-; chm Management Ctee Assoc of Combined Youth Clubs 1987-; *Recreations* sailing (yacht 'Falcon'), skiing, riding (horse and bicycle), Daily Telegraph crossword; *Clubs* Boodle's, MCC, Royal Harwich Yacht; *Style—* Sir Michael Harrison, Bt; 35 Paulton's Square, London SW3 (☎ 071 352 1760); c/o L P H Pitman Ltd, St Michael's Alley, off Cornhill, London EC3 (☎ 071 283 7345)

HARRISON, Philippa Mary; da of Charles Kershaw Whitfield (d 1972), and Alexina Margaret, *née* Dykes; *b* 25 Nov 1942; *Educ* Walthamstow Hall, Univ of Bristol (BA), Courtauld Inst; *m* July 1967 (m dis), James Fraser Harrison; *Career* jt ed in chief Penguin Books 1979-80, ed dir Michael Joseph 1980-85, md and publisher MacMillan London 1986-88; md V and A Enterprises 1990-; memb: Literature Panel Arts Assoc 1988-, Bd of Book Marketing Cncl 1983-88; CBIM 1987; *Books* Publishing: The Future (contrib, 1988); *Recreations* walking, theatre, reading, the arts; *Clubs* Groucho; *Style—* Mrs Philippa Harrison; 105 Lofting Rd, London N1 (☎ 071 609 5516)

HARRISON, Reziya; da of Rasheed Ahmad (d 1960), of London, and Vera Margaret Evemy; *Educ* St Michael's Sch Surrey, Somerville Coll Oxford (BA); *m* 11 June 1965, Martin Edward Harrison, s of Edward Ernest Harrison; 1 s (Thomas b 15 Aug 1969), 1 da (Frances b 13 May 1966); *Career* called to the Bar Lincoln's Inn 1975; *Recreations* domestic life; *Style—* Mrs Reziya Harrison; 11 Old Square, Lincoln's Inn, London WC2A 3TS (☎ 071 430 0341, fax 071 831 2469)

HARRISON, Prof Sir Richard John; er s of late Geoffrey Arthur Harrison, MD, and Theodora Beatrice Mary, *née* West; *b* 8 Oct 1920; *Educ* Oundle, Gonville and Caius Coll Cambridge (MA, MD), Univ of Glasgow (DSc), St Bart's; *m* 1, 1943 (m dis), Joanna Gillies; 2 s, 1 da; m 2, 1967, Barbara (d 1988), da of late James Fuller, of Neston, Cheshire; m 3, 3 March 1990, Gianetta, widow of Cdr John Drake, RN (ret); *Career* prof of anatomy Cambridge Univ 1968-82 (later emeritus), fell Downing Coll Cambridge 1968-82 (hon fell 1982); chm Farm Animal Welfare Cncl 1979-88, memb Bd of Tstees Br Museum (natural history) 1984-; pres Int Fedn of Assocs of Anatomists 1985-87; FRS 1973; kt 1984; *Books* Handbook of Marine Mammals (vols I-IV, 1981), Research on Dolphins (1986), Whales, Dolphins and Porpoises (1988); *Recreations* gardening; *Clubs* Garrick; *Style—* Prof Sir Richard Harrison, FRS; 7 Aylesford Way, Stapleford, Cambridgeshire CB2 5DP (☎ 0223 843287)

HARRISON, (Desmond) Roger Wingate; s of Maj-Gen Desmond Harrison, CB, DSO, and Kathleen, *née* Hazley; *b* 9 April 1933; *Educ* Rugby, Worcester Coll Oxford (MA), Harvard Business Sch; *m* 1965, Victoria, MVO, da of Rear Adm John Lee-Barker; 1 s (decd), 4 da; *Career* 5 Royal Inniskilling Dragoon Guards 1955-57; freelance writer, principally for The Times 1951-57; writer The Times 1957-67; The Observer: joined 1967, dir 1970-, jt md 1977-84, chief exec 1984-87; dir: Capital Radio 1975-, LWT and LWT Hldgs 1976-, Duke of York's Theatre 1979-, Sableknight 1981-; exec dir The Oak Fndn (UK) Ltd 1987-; cncl memb Newspaper Publishers' Assoc 1967-87; govr Sadler's Wells Theatre 1984-; *Recreations* theatre, country pursuits, tennis; *Clubs* Cavalry and Guards', Flyfishers', Queens; *Style—* Roger Harrison, Esq; 35 Argyll Rd, London, W8 7DA (☎ 071 937 2770)

HARRISON, Terence; DL (Tyne and Wear 1989); s of Roland Harrison (d 1985), and Doris, *née* Wardle; *b* 7 April 1933; *Educ* Univ of Durham (BSc); *m* 9 July 1956, June, da of Mathew Forster; 2 s (Peter Forster b 18 May 1959, Mark Terence b 20 June 1962); *Career* Clarke Chapman Ltd: dir 1976, md 1977, merged with Reyrolle Parsons Ltd to become Northern Engineering Industries 1977; Northern Engineering Industries plc: dir 1977, md UK ops 1980, chief exec 1983, chm 1986-, merged with Rolls-Royce plc 1989 (dir Rolls-Royce plc 1989); non-exec dir: Local Bd Barclays Bank plc 1986-, Northumbrian Water Group plc 1989-, British Maritime Technology Ltd 1990-; author various tech and business papers on the mechanical engrg marine and mining industs; dir Centre for the Exploitation of Sci and Technol; pres: BEAMA 1989-90, NE Coast Inst of Engrs and Shipbuilders 1988-90; fndr chm Northern Engrg Centre; Freeman City of London, memb Worshipful Co of Engineers; FIMarE 1973, FIMechE 1984, FEng 1988; *Recreations* fell walking, gardening, golf; *Style—* Terence Harrison, Esq, DL, FEng; South Lodge, Hepscott, Morpeth, Northumberland NE61 6LH (☎ 0670 519228); Northern Engineering Industries plc, NEI House, Regent Centre, Newcastle upon Tyne NE3 3SB (☎ 091 284 3191, fax 091 284 4534, telex 537900)

HARRISON, Theophilus George; OBE (1971), JP; s of Alfred Harrison (d 1926), and Emma Edith Harrison (d 1966); *b* 30 Jan 1907; *m* 1935, Clarissa, da of Thomas Plevin; 1 da (Kathleen), 1 s (George); *Career* gen sec Nat Assoc of Powerloom Overlookers 1948-73; Swinton and Pendlebury Borough Cncl: memb 1941-56, alderman 1956-74, Mayor 1954-55, chm Housing Ctee and Youth Employment Ctee, chm Highways and Lighting Ctee, memb Div Planning Ctee; Lancs CC: chm Educn Ctee 1953-74 (memb 1946-74, vice chm 1951-53), chm Road Safety Ctee, vice chm Public Health and Housing Ctee; chm: Gtr Manchester Cncl 1973-75 (dep chm 1975-76), Gtr Manchester Tport Ctee; memb: Gen Cncl Lancs and Merseyside Ind Devpt Corp, N Counties Textile Trades Fedn Bd, Manchester Regnl Hosp BA 1961-74, Mental Health Review Tbnls 1961-70, Salford Community Health Cncl 1973-83, Assot Community Health Cncls 1973-83, vice pres Gtr Manchester Cncl for Voluntary Serv, dir RoSPA; Freeman of Swinton and Pendlebury 1973; *Recreations* reading, rugby league (spectator), political and public activities; *Style—* Theophilus Harrison, Esq, OBE, JP; 271 Rivington Crescent, Bolton Rd, Pendlebury, Manchester M27 2TQ (☎ 061 794 1112)

HARRISON, Timothy David Blair; s of Clair Wilfred Wortley Harrison, of The Coach House, Banwell, Avon, and Sheelagh Margurite Hildergarde, *née* Woolford (d 1972); *b* 13 Dec 1944; *Educ* Blundell's; *Career* UBM/MAC Group Bristol 1963-73, GKN Mills Building Services Ltd 1973-76, Norplant/Witpalm International Ltd 1976-79, Mallison-Denny Group 1979-86 (sales and mktg dir Formwood Ltd, md Bushboard Ltd), md GA Harvey Office Furniture Ltd 1986-88, Trafalgar House Building & Civil Engineering Holdings Ltd 1988-89 (dir, sector md), gp chief exec The Company of Designers plc 1989- (directorships and chm of 22 companies COD gp); Freeman City of London, memb Worshipful Co of Builders Merchants; *Recreations* rugby (watching now), running, rally driving; *Style—* Timothy Harrison, Esq; Mendip Croft, Celtic Way, Bleadon, nr Weston-Super-Mare, Avon BS24 0NA (☎ 0934 815331); The Company of Designers plc, The Malt House, Sydney Buildings, Bath BA2 6B2 (☎ 0225 465701, fax 0225 465714, car 0836 770424)

HARRISON, Tony; s of Harry Ashton Harrison (d 1980), and Florence Horner, *née* Wilkinson (d 1976); *b* 30 April 1937; *Educ* Leeds GS, Univ of Leeds (BA); *Career* poet and dramatist; pres Classical Assoc 1988, FRSL; *Books* Earthworks (1964), Aikin Mata (1965), Newcastle is Peru (1969), The Loiners (1970), The Misanthrope (1973), Phaedra Britannica (1975), The Passion (1977), Bow Down (1977), from The School of Eloquence (1978), Continuous (1981), A Kumquat for John Keats (1981), US Martial (1981), The Oresteia (1981), Selected Poems (1984), The Mysteries (1985), V (1985), Dramatic Verse 1973-85 (1985), The Fire-Gap (1985), Theatre Works 1973-85 (1986), Selected Poems (augmented edn 1987), The Trackers of Oxyrhynchus (performed ancient stadium of Delphi 1988, NT 1990); TV: The Oresteia (Channel 4 1982), The Big H (BBC 1984), The Mysteries (Channel 4 1985), Yan Tan Tethera (Channel 4 1986), Loving Memory (BBC 1986), V (Channel 4 1987 (Royal Television Soc Award)), The Blasphemers' Banquet; *Style—* Tony Harrison; c/o Peters Fraser & Dunlop, 5th Floor, The Chambers, Chelsea Harbour, Lots Rd, London SW10 0XF (☎ 071 376 7676, fax 071 352 7356)

HARRISON, Walter Paul; s of Walter Harrison, of Morecambe, and Margaret Hildred, *née* Buttery; *b* 19 March 1955; *Educ* Skerton Co Boys' Sch Lancaster, Preston Poly (OND, HNC), Leicester Poly (BA, Dip Arch); *Career* Cassidy & Ashton Partnership Preston 1973-75, W E Moore & Sons Leicester 1978-79 (ptnr and dir 1987), Robert Davies John West Assocs Staines 1981-88 (assoc 1986), ptnr local office Robert Davies John West & Assoc Crawley 1988-; RIBA, ARCUK; *Recreations* squash, badminton, cars, horse riding; *Clubs* Copthorne Country, Crawley; *Style—* Paul Harrison, Esq; Denholme, Crawley Rd, Horsham, West Sussex (☎ 0403 62224); Robert Davies John West & Associates, Buxton House, 2 East Park, Crawley RH10 6AS (☎ 0293 541581/2, fax 0293 548104)

HARRISON, William H; *Educ* Giggleswick Sch; *m* Angela; 4 c; *Career* ptnr Coopers

& Lybrand Deloitte (and predecessor firms) 1974-; memb Exec Cncl Bradford Common Purpose; ACA 1964; *Style*— William H Harrison, Esq; Coopers & Lybrand Deloitte, Albion Court, 5 Albion Place, Leeds LS1 6JP (☎ 0532 431 343, fax 0532 424009)

HARRISON, William Robert (Bill); s of William Eric Harrison, and Catherine Frances, *née* Dyson; *b* 5 Oct 1948; *Educ* George Dixon GS Birmingham, LSE (BSc, MSc); *m* 18 July 1970, Jacqueline Ann, da of Marwood Eric Brown, of Birmingham; 1 s (Nicholas David b 1977), 1 da (Charlotte Ann b 1976); *Career* md Shearson Lehman Hutton Inc, formerly dir J Henry Schroder Wagg & Co Ltd; *Recreations* soccer, cricket, music, gardening; *Style*— Bill Harrison; 1 Broadgate, London EC2 (☎ 071 601 0011)

HARRISS, Dr Gerald Leslie; s of Walter Leslie Harriss, and Mable Oblein, *née* Panchaud; *b* 22 May 1925; *Educ* Chigwell Sch, Magdalen Coll Oxford (MA, DPhil); *m* 8 Aug 1959, (Margaret) Anne Harriss; 2 s (Basil, Cyril), 3 da (Rachel, Ursula, Madeline); *Career* Nat Serv Sub Lt RNVR 1946; lectr Univ of Manchester 1955-56, lectr and reader Univ of Durham 1956-67, fell and tutor Magdalen Coll Oxford 1967- (reader in modern history 1990-); FRHistS 1960, FBA 1986; *Books* King, Parliament and Public Finance in England (1975), Henry V (1985), Cardinal Beaufort (1988); *Style*— Dr Gerald Harriss; Dean Court House, 89 Eynsham Road, Botley, Oxford OX2 9BY; Magdalen College, Oxford OX1 4AU (☎ 0865 276071)

HARROD, Maj-Gen Lionel Alexander Digby; OBE; s of Frank Henry Harrod, CBE (d 1958), of Coventry, and Charlotte Beatrice Emmeline Harrod (d 1981); *b* 7 Sept 1924; *Educ* Bromsgrove; *m* 2 Feb 1952, (Anne) Priscilla Stormont, da of Charles Cobden Stormont Gibbs (d 1969); 1 s (David b 1955), 2 da (Elinor b 1953, Catherine b 1959); *Career* Grenadier Gds 1943-63, Staff Coll 1955, Bde Maj 19 Bde 1956-58, GSO 2 SD2 WO 1961-63, 2 i/c 1 Bn The Welch Regt 1964-66, CO 1 Bn The Welch Regt 1966-69, Br Liaison Staff Washington 1969-70, def and mil attaché (Col) Baghdad 1971, Col Staff Duties HQ UKLF 1972, Chief (Brig) BRIX MIS 1974-76, ACOS Intelligence SHAPE 1976-79, Col The Royal Regt of Wales 1977-82, Inspr of Army Recruiting 1979-90; vice chm N Dorset Cons Assoc 1985-90, sec League of Remembrance 1990, chm Marnhull Br NDCA, pres Marnhull Br Legion, memb Ctee Mil Commentators Circle, active in Peace Through NATO and Br Atlantic Ctee; *Recreations* fishing, current affairs; *Clubs* Pratt's, Army and Navy, MCC, Pilgrim's, European Atlantic Gp; *Style*— Maj-Gen Lionel Harrod, OBE; The Grange, Marnhull, Dorset DT10 1PS (☎ 0258 820 256)

HARROD, Lady (Wilhelmine Margaret Eve); *née* Cresswell; da of Capt Francis Joseph (Joe) Cresswell (ka 1914), and Barbara, *née* ffolkes, wid of Gen Sir Peter Strickland, KCB; *b* 1 Dec 1911; *Educ* Langford Grove Maldon Essex; *m* 8 Jan 1938, Sir Roy Forbes Harrod (d 1978), s of Henry Harrod; 2 s (Henry b 1939, Dominick b 1940); *Career* involved in conservation countryside and bldgs; memb: Georgian Gp, Oxford Preservation Tst, Cncl Protection Rural Eng, Regnl Ctee Nat Tst, Historic Churches Preservation Tst, Norfolk Churches Tst (fndr and pres), various diocesan ctees; Hon DCL UEA 1989; fndr Norfolk Churches Tst; *Books* Shell Guide to Norfolk (jtly 1957), The Norfolk Guide (1988); *Recreations* gardening; *Clubs* The Norfolk (Norwich); *Style*— Lady Harrod; The Old Rectory, Holt, Norfolk NR25 6RY (☎ 0263 712 204)

HARROLD, Timothy John (Tim); s of Col W G Harrold (d 1969), and Christine Russell, *née* Kilburn Scott; *b* 12 May 1938; *Educ* Bryanston, Lausanne Univ Switzerland, Pembroke Coll Cambridge (MA); *m* 9 Sept 1967, Gillian Doris, da of Leslie Albert Cruttenden; 3 s (Simon Timothy b 14 March 1970, Michael Stephen b 24 March 1971, James Andrew b 15 Sept 1976), 1 da (Katherine b 2 Sept 1973); *Career* with ICI 1960-69, mktg dir Polydor Ltd London 1970-74, exec vice pres Phonodisc Inc NY 1974-75; pres: Polygram Inc Montreal 1975-81, Polydor Int Hamburg 1981-83; exec vice pres Polygram Int London 1983- (chm Polygram Classics, Decca Int); *Recreations* skiing; *Style*— Tim Harrold, Esq; Dunstanburgh, Downside Rd, Guildford, Surrey (☎ 0483 648 76); Polygram Int, 30 Berkeley Square, London (☎ 071 493 8800, car 0836 236 822)

HARROP, Sir Peter John; KCB (1984, CB 1980); s of Gilbert Harrop (d 1971), and Frances May, *née* Dewhirst; *b* 18 March 1926; *Educ* King Edward VII Sch Lytham, Peterhouse Cambridge (MA); *m* 1975, Margaret Joan, da of E U E Elliott-Binns; 2 s (Andrew b 1976, Nicholas b 1978); *Career* Sub Lt RNVR 1945-48; asst princ: Miny of Town and Country Planning 1949, Miny of Housing and Local Govt 1951, DOE 1970; regnl dir and chm Yorks and Humberside Econ Planning Bd 1971-73, HM Treasy 1973-76, Cabinet Office 1979-80, second perm sec DOE 1981-86; chm UK Ctee Euro Year of the Environment 1987, chm Nat Bus Co 1988; non-exec dir: Nat Home Loans plc, Thames Water plc; managing tstee Municipal Mutual Insurance Ltd, tstee Br Museum; *Recreations* sailing, golf; *Clubs* United Oxford and Cambridge, Roehampton; *Style*— Sir Peter Harrop, KCB; 19 Berwyn Road, Richmond, Surrey TW10

HARROP, Stuart Reginald; s of Reginald Harrop, of E Yorkshire, and Valerie Mary, *née* Hotham; *b* 11 Jan 1956; *Educ* Beverley GS, Univ of Leeds (LLB); *m* 30 April 1983, Tracy Ann, da of Dennis Roy Green; 2 s (Lee Stuart b 11 May 1986, Joel William b 3 Feb 1990); *Career* admitted slr 1980; slr Costain Gp plc 1982-84, co slr Albright & Wilson Ltd 1984-86, ICI plc 1986-88, dir legal servs Stock Exchange 1988-; memb Law Soc; *Recreations* freelance photography (natural history and business lifestyle); *Style*— Stuart Harrop, Esq; The Stock Exchange, Old Broad St, London EC2N 1HP (☎ 588 2355, fax 588 3886)

HARROWBY, 7 Earl of (UK 1809); Dudley Danvers Granville Coutts Ryder; TD (1953); also Baron Harrowby (GB 1776) and Viscount Sandon (UK 1809); er s of 6 Earl of Harrowby (d 1987), and Lady Helena Blanche, *née* Coventry (d 1974), sis of 10 Earl of Coventry; *b* 20 Dec 1922; *Educ* Eton; *m* 14 June 1949, Jeannette Rosalthé, yr da of Capt Peter Johnston-Saint (d 1974); 1 s, 1 da (Lady Frances Rundall, *qv*); *Heir* s, Viscount Sandon, *qv*; *Career* served WWII in NW Europe (wounded) with 59 Inf Div, 5 Para Bde; India and Java (political offr) 1941-45 56 Armoured Div; Lt-Col RA cmdg 254 (City of London) Field Regt RA (TA) 1962-64; dep chm National Westminster Bank plc 1971-87 (dir 1968); chm: International Westminster Bank plc 1977-87, National Westminster Investment Bank 1986-87; dep chm Coutts & Co 1970-89 (md 1949); chm: The Private Bank & Trust Co Ltd 1989-, Dowty Group plc 1986-; dir Saudi International Bank 1980-82 and 1985-87; chm Nat Biological Standards Bd 1973-88; memb: Trilateral Cmmn 1980-, Ctee of Mgmnt Inst of Psychiatry 1953-73 (chm 1965-73); Bd of Govrs: Bethlem Royal and Maudsley (Postgraduate Teaching) Hosps 1955-73 (chm 1965-73), Univ of Keele 1956-68, Lord Chancellor's Advsy Investmt Ctee for Ct of Protection 1965-77, Advsy Investmt Ctee for Public Tstee 1974-77, Psychiatry Research Tst (tstee) 1982-, Institut Internationale d'Etudes Bancaires 1977-87, Kensington Borough Cncl 1950-65 (chm GP Ctee 1957-59), Kensington and Chelsea Borough Cncl 1965-71 (chm Finance Ctee 1968-71); govr Atlantic Inst of Int Affairs 1983-88; hon treas: Staffs Soc 1947-51, Exec Ctee London Area Conservative Assoc 1949-50, Family Welfare Assoc 1951-65, S Kensington Conservative Assoc 1953-56, Central Cncl for Care of Cripples 1953-60; dir Dinorwic Slate Quarries Co Ltd 1951-69; mangr Fulham and Kensington Hosp Gp 1953-56, gen Commr for Income Tax 1954-71; dir: National Provincial Bank 1961-69, UKPI 1955-86 (dep chm 1956-64), Olympic Group 1968-73 (chm 1971-73), Powell Duffryn Gp 1976-86 (chm 1981-86), Sheepbridge Engineering Ltd 1977-79; chm: Orion Bank 1979-81, Bentley Engineering Co Ltd 1983-86; Freeman of City of London 1947, Liveryman Worshipful Co of Goldsmiths 1959; CBIM, MRIIA, hon fell Royal Coll of Psychiatrists 1983; *Style*— The Rt Hon the Earl of Harrowby, TD; 5 Tregunter Rd, London SW10 9LS (☎ 071 373 9276); Sandon Hall, Stafford ST18 OBY (☎ 08897 338); Burnt Norton, Chipping Campden, Glos (☎ 0386 840 358); 11 Old Town Close, Beaconsfield, Bucks (☎ 0494 671706, car 0836 327337)

HARSTON, Julian John Robert Clive; s of Col Clive Harston, of Surrey, and Kathleen Mary, *née* Grace; *b* 20 Oct 1942; *Educ* The King's Sch Canterbury, Univ of London (BSc); *m* 1966, Karen Howard Oake, da of Col T E Longfield (ka 1941); 1 s (Alexander b 1978); *Career* mangr Br Tourist Authy Copenhagen and Vancouver 1965-71, FO 1971, first sec/consul Hanoi 1973-74, first sec Blantyre 1975-79, first sec Lisbon 1982-84, cnsllr Harare 1984-88; *Recreations* travel, photography, Switzerland; *Clubs* East India, RAC, Gremio Literario (Lisbon), Harare; *Style*— Julian Harston, Esq; c/o Foreign and Commonwealth Office, King Charles St, London SW1

HART; *see*: Turton-Hart

HART, Alan; s of Reginald Thomas Hart (d 1980), of Haddenham, Bucks, and Lilian Clara, *née* Hanson; *b* 17 April 1935; *Educ* Univ Coll Sch Hampstead; *m* 16 Dec 1961, Celia Mary, *née* Vine, da of Raglan Keough; 2 s (David Alan b 31 Oct 1962, Andrew Dominic b 6 May 1965), 1 da (Gabrielle Louise b 13 Nov 1975); *Career* reporter: Willesden Chronicle and Kilburn Times 1952-58, Newcastle Evening Chronicle 1958, London Evening News 1958-59; editorial asst BBC Sportsview 1959-61, TV sports prodr BBC Manchester 1962-64, ed BBC Sportsview 1965-68 (asst ed 1964-65), ed Grandstand 1968-77, head of sport BBC TV 1977-81, controller BBC 1 1981-84, special asst to Dir Gen BBC 1985, controller Int Rels BBC 1986-91, chm Eurosport 1989-; FRTS; *Recreations* sport, walking, music; *Style*— Alan Hart, Esq; BBC, Henry Wood House, Langham Place, London W1A 1AA (☎ 071 927 5548, fax 071 637 0970)

HART, Anelay Colton Wright; s of Anelay Thomas Bayston Hart, of Orchard Close, Alne, York (d 1971), and Phyllis Marian, *née* Wright (d 1981); *b* 6 March 1934; *Educ* Stamford Sch, King's Coll London (LLB); *m* 22 March 1979, Margaret Gardner; *Career* admitted slr 1961, ptnr Appleby, Hope & Matthews 1963-; memb Cncl RSPCA 1969- (hon treas 1974-81, chm 1981-83, 1985-86 and 1988-90, vice chm 1983-84 and 1986-88); Queen Victoria Silver medal 1984; advsy dir World Soc for the Protection of Animals 1982-; pres Rotary Club of South Bank and Eston 1972-83; memb Law Soc; *Recreations* walking; *Clubs* Royal Over-Seas League; *Style*— Anelay Hart, Esq; Village Farm, Moulton, Richmond, North Yorkshire DL10 6QQ; 35 High St, Normanby, Middlesbrough, Cleveland TS6 OLE (☎ 0642 440444, fax 0642 440 342)

HART, (Thomas) Anthony Alfred; s of Rev Arthur Reginald Hart, and Florence Ivy Hart; *b* 4 March 1940; *Educ* City of Bath Sch, New Coll Oxford (BA, MA); *m* 1971, Daintre Margaret Withiel, *née* Thomas; 1 s, 1 da; *Career* served with VSO (Mzuzu Secdy Sch Nyasaland) 1959-60; asst princ rising to princ Miny of Tport 1964-69, seconded to Govt of Malawi as tport advsr 1969-70, princ DOE and Civil Serv Dept 1970-73, head Voluntary Servs Unit Home Office 1973-75, asst sec Civil Serv Dept and HM Treasy 1975-84; headmaster Cranleigh School 1984-; *Clubs* Travellers'; *Style*— Anthony Hart, Esq; The Headmaster's House, Cranleigh School, Cranleigh, Surrey GU6 8QQ

HART, Prof (Charles) Anthony; s of Edmund Hart, of Harrogate, N Yorks, and Alice Edna, *née* Griffin; *b* 25 Feb 1948; *Educ* St Michael's Coll Leeds, Royal Free Hosp Sch of Med Univ of London (MB BS, BSc, PhD); *m* 26 June 1971, Jennifer Ann, da of Keith Bonnett (d 1977); 3 da (Caroline Joanne b 23 March 1975, Rachel Louise b 6 Jan 1977, Laura Jane b 5 Feb 1980); *Career* res student and hon lectr Royal Free Hosp Sch of Med 1973-76, prof and hon conslt Dept Med Microbiology Univ of Liverpool 1986- (lectr 1978-82, sr lectr and hon conslt 1982-86), visiting prof Univ of Sante Tomas Manila Phillipines 1987-; MRCPath 1983; *Style*— Prof Anthony Hart; 104 Thurstaston Rd, Thurstaston, Wirral L61 0HG (☎ 051 648 1491); Dept of Medical Microbiology, University of Liverpool, PO Box 147, Liverpool L69 3BX (☎ 051 706 4381)

HART, Charles; s of George Hart, of Henley-on-Thames, and Juliet, *née* Byam Shaw; *b* 3 June 1961; *Educ* Desborough Comp Sch Maidenhead, Robinson Coll Cambridge (BA), Guildhall Sch of Music and Drama, Dartington Summer Sch of Music; *Career* composer and lyricist; composer Show Piece (overture for small orch BBC Radio 2) 1984; lyrics: The Phantom of the Opera (musical) 1986, Doretta's Dream (aria) 1987, Aspects of Love (musical, with Don Black) 1988-89; music and lyrics: Moll Flanders (musical) 1985, Watching (Granada TV) 1987, Love Songs (song cycle BBC Radio 2) 1988-89, Split Ends (Granada TV) 1989; winner: Best Musical for Phantom of the Opera, Olivier award 1987, Standard award 1987, Ivor Novello award 1987, Tony award 1988; memb Cncl and rep Composers' Jt Cncl BASCA; *Clubs* Groucho; *Style*— Charles Hart, Esq; c/o Marc Berlin, London Management, 235-241 Regent St, London W1R 7AG (☎ 071 493 1610, fax 071 355 3261)

HART, Dr (Francis) Dudley; s of Rev Canon Charles Dudley Hart (d 1952), of Southwell Cathedral, and Kate Evelyn, *née* Bowden (d 1961); *b* 4 Oct 1909; *Educ* Grosvenor Sch Nottingham, Univ of Edinburgh (MB ChB, MD); *m* 18 Dec 1944, Mary Josephine (Maureen), da of Luke Tully (d 1956), of Carrigaline, Co Cork, Ireland; 1 s (Paul b 1950), 2 da (Elizabeth b 1946, Clare b 1948); *Career* Maj (med specialist) and Lt-Col i/c Med Div RAMC 1942-46, civilian conslt physician Army 1972-74; house surgn: Royal Hosp for Sick Children Edinburgh 1933, Paddington Green Children's Hosp 1934; house physician Brompton Hosp 1937, med registrar Royal Northern Hosp 1935-37 (house physician 1935); currently consulting physician: Westminster Hosp (conslt physician and physician i/c rheumatism clinic 1946-74, med registrar 1939-42), Hosp St John and St Elizabeth St John's Wood London; former: memb and vice chm Ctee Review of Medicines, pres Heberden Soc (rheumatism res and educn); chm Ctee Tst Educn and Res Therapeutics, vice chm and memb Exec Ctee Arthritis and Rheumatism Cncl; Freeman City of London 1956, Liveryman Worshipful Soc of Apothecaries 1956; hon memb French Italian American Australian Rheum Socs, MRCP 1937, FRCP 1949, Hon FRSM; *Books* French's Index of Differential Diagnosis (ed 10-12 edns 1973-85), Drug Treatment of Rheumatic Diseases (3 edns, 1978-87), Overcoming Arthritis (1981), Practical Problems in Rheumatology (1983), Colour Atlas of Rheumatology (1987), Clinical Rheumatology Illustrated (1987); *Recreations* walking, snorkelling; *Style*— Dr Dudley Hart; 19 Ranulf Rd, London NW2 2BT (☎ 071 794 2525); 24 Harmont House, 20 Harley St, London W1N 1AN (☎ 071 935 4252)

HART, Garry Richard Rushby; s of Dennis George Hart (d 1984), and Evelyn Mary, *née* Rushby; *b* 29 June 1940; *Educ* Northgate GS Ipswich, UCL (LLB); *m* 1, 24 March 1966 (m dis 1986), Paula Lesley, da of Leslie Shepherd; 2 s (Alexander, Jonathan), 1 da (Kaley); m 2, 1986, Valerie Elen Mary, da of Cledwyn Wilson Davies; 2 da (Sarah, Stephanie (twins)); *Career* slr; ptnr Herbert Smith 1970- (head Property Dept 1988-); Freeman City of London, Liveryman Worshipful Co of Slrs; memb Law Soc 1966; *Books* Blundell and Dobrys Planning Appeals and Inquiries (jtly, 4 edn); *Recreations* farming, travel; *Clubs* Carlton; *Style*— Garry Hart, Esq; 36 Alwyne Road, London N1; Exchange House, Primrose St, London EC2 (☎ 071 374 8000, fax 071 496 0043, telex 886633)

HART, Dr George; s of George Hart, of Golborne, Lancs, and Mary, *née* Britton; *b* 7

June 1951; *Educ* Boteler GS, Churchill Coll Cambridge (BA, MA), Trinity Coll Oxford and Oxford Univ Clin Sch (BA, MA, BM, BCh), St Peter's Coll Oxford (DM); *m* 19 Jan 1980, Dr Judy Hart, da of Alfred Alan Reynolds (d 1988), of Bognor Regis, West Sussex; 2 s (Samuel b 1985, Joseph b 1986), 1 da (Alice b 1982); *Career* jr hosp posts 1975-77; registrar: cardiology Papworth Hosp 1977-78, med Addenbrooke's Hosp 1978-79; lectr in physiology Balliol Coll Oxford 1979-80, MRC res trg fell Physiology Laboratory Univ of Oxford 1979-82, Sidney Perry jr res fell St Peter's Coll Oxford 1979-82, sr registrar in cardiology Yorkshire Regnl Health Authy 1982-86, BHF clinical reader in cardiovascular med Univ of Oxford 1986-, hon conslt physician and cardiologist John Radcliffe Hosp Oxford 1986-, supernumerary fell Lady Margaret Hall Oxford 1986-; memb: Br Cardiac Soc, The Physiological Soc; chm Br Soc for Cardiovascular Res 1990-; MRCP 1977, FRCP 1990; *Recreations* preaching, cooking, music; *Style*— Dr George Hart; 82 Stanmore Rd, Oxford OX2 6RB; Cardiac Department, John Radcliffe Hospital, Headington, Oxford OX3 9DU

HART, Guy William Pulbrook; OBE (1985); s of Ernest Guy Hart (d 1966), of Guildford, and Muriel Lily, *née* Walkington (d 1965); *b* 24 Dec 1931; *Educ* Cranleigh Sch Surrey; *m* 14 Aug 1954, (Elizabeth) Marjorie, da of Charles Bennett (d 1963), of Caerleon; 1 s (Guy), 2 da (Victoria (Mrs Eley), Alexandra (Mrs Miller)); *Career* Nat Serv Army Offr Intelligence Corps 1951-61; Br Cellophane Ltd London 1961-62; civil service career; Cwlth Relations Office London 1962-63, consular offr Br High Cmmn Kuala Lumpur 1963-67, News Dept FCO 1971-73, second later first sec Br Mil Govt Berlin 1974-78, first sec commercial Br High Cmmn Port of Spain 1979-82, first sec commercial Br Embasssy Budapest 1982-85 (second sec information 1968-71), asst head Information Dept FCO London 1986, ambass Ulan Bator Mongolia 1987-89, Br High Cmmr Victoria Seychelles 1989-; *Recreations* Alpine sports, painting, gardening; *Clubs* Austrian Alpine; *Style*— Guy Hart, Esq, OBE; British High Commission, Victoria, Seychelles (☎ 010 248 25228, fax 010 248 25127, telex 2269 AB UKREP SZ)

HART, K Mortimer; s of Frank Mortimer (d 1969), and Minnie Anna, *née* Houlson (d 1968); *b* 24 March 1914; *Educ* Redland Hill House Sch Bristol; *m* 7 Dec 1946, Shirley, da of Percy Burkinshaw, of Wakefield and Sheffield; 1 da (Catherine Jane Mortimer b 23 June 1955); *Career* WWII RAFVR 1940-45, seconded Indian Air Force 1942-45; chartered surveyor and town planner; sr planning inspr: Miny of Housing, Local Govt, Welsh Office; surveyor and town planning conslt; chm Conwy Valley Civic Soc 1976-82; ARICS 1935, MRTPI 1945; *Books* Conwy Valley and the Lands of History (1988); *Recreations* formerly swimming, photography; *Clubs* Royal Cwlth Soc; *Style*— K Mortimer Hart, Esq; Pen Rhiw, Ro Wen, Conwy, Gwynedd LL32 8TR (☎ 0492 650 343)

HART, Prof Michael; s of Reuben Harold Victor Hart, of Melbourne, and Phyllis Mary, *née* White; *b* 4 Nov 1938; *Educ* Cotham GS Bristol, Univ of Bristol (BSc, PhD, DSc); *m* 16 April 1963, Susan Margaret, *née* Powell; 3 da (Linda b 29 Sept 1964, Janet b 20 June 1966, Rachel b 1 Jan 1969); *Career* res assoc Cornell Univ NY USA 1963-65; Univ of Bristol: res assoc 1965-67, lectr in physics 1967-72, reader 1972-76; sr res assoc Nat Res Cncl USA 1969-70, special advsr CPRS Cabinet Office 1975-77, Wheatstone prof and head of physics Kings Coll London 1976-84, prof of physics Univ of Manchester 1984, sci prog coordinator SERC Daresbury Laboratory 1985-87; winner CV Boys Prize of Inst of Physics and Warren Award of American Crystallographic Assoc; CPhys, FRS, FInstP; *Clubs* Athenaeum; *Style*— Prof Michael Hart, FRS; Department of Physics, Schuster Laboratory, The University, Manchester M13 9PL (☎ 061 275 4115, fax 061 273 5867)

HART, Michael Christopher Campbell; QC (1987); s of Raymond David Campbell Hart, and Penelope Mary, *née* Ellis; *b* 7 May 1948; *Educ* Winchester, Magdalen Coll Oxford (MA, BCL); *m* 12 Aug 1972, Melanie Jane, da of Richard Hugh Sandiford; 2 da (Jessie b 3 Oct 1973, Zoe b 13 Dec 1974); *Career* called to the Bar Gray's Inn 1970; fell All Soul's Coll Oxford 1970; *Style*— Michael Hart, Esq, QC; 2 New Square, Lincoln's Inn, London WC2A 3RU (☎ 071 242 6201, fax 071 831 8102)

HART, Michael John; s of Ernest Stanley Granville Hart (d 1982), of Theydon Bois, Essex, and Wilhelmine Patricia, *née* McClurg (d 1972); *b* 26 Dec 1932; *Educ* LSE (BSc); *m* 30 May 1964, (Ann) Sheila, da of William Severy Conrad Decker (d 1965), of Loughton, Essex; 1 s (Samuel b 19 Jan 1977), 1 da (Susan b 23 May 1975); *Career* Nat Serv RAF 1950-52; jt mangr Foreign and Colonial Investmt Tst 1969-, dep chm Foreign and Colonial Mgmnt 1986-; chm Assoc Investmt Tst Cos 1989-; ACIS 1956; *Recreations* tennis, cricket, gardening, reading biographies; *Style*— Michael Hart, Esq; Springs, Water End, Ashdon, Essex (☎ 079 984 259); Exchange House, Primrose St, London EC2A 2NY (☎ 071 628 8000)

HART, Prof Oliver Simon D'Arcy; s of Philip Montagu D'Arcy Hart, and Ruth Hart; *b* 9 Oct 1948; *Educ* Univ Coll Sch, King's Coll Cambridge (BA), Univ of Warwick (MA), Princeton (PhD); *m* 1974, Rita Goldberg; 2 s; *Career* lectr in economics Univ of Essex 1974-75, asst lectr then lectr in economics Univ of Cambridge 1975-81, fell Churchill Coll Cambridge 1975-81, prof of economics: LSE 1981-85, MIT 1985-; visiting Scholar Harvard Law Sch 1987-88, Marvin Bower fell Harvard Business Sch 1988-89; memb: Coordinating Ctee Social Sci Res Cncl Econ Theory Study Gp UK 1975-79, Prog Ctee Fourth World Congress of the Econometric Soc 1980, Editorial Advsy Bd Review of Econ Studies 1975-88, Editorial Advsy Bd Cambridge Surveys of Econ Lit Cup 1984-, Cncl Econometric Soc 1983-89 (memb Exec Ctee at large 1984-87), Nat Sci Fndn Economics Panel 1987-, Advsy Cncl Princeton Univ Economics Dept 1989-; assoc ed: Jl of Econ Theory 1976-79, Econometrica 1984-87, Games and Economic Behaviour 1988-, JL of Accounting Auditing and Finance 1989-; ed Review of Econ Studies 1979-83 (asst ed 1978-79), prog dir Centre for Econ Policy Res London 1983-84, res assoc Nat Bureau of Econ Res 1990-; fell: Econometric Soc 1979, American Acad of Arts and Scis 1988; *publications* author of numerous articles and chapters in various books; *Recreations* playing and watching tennis; *Style*— Prof Oliver Hart; Department of Economics, Mass Institute of Technology, Cambridge, Mass 02139, USA

HART, Peter Dorney; s of Sydney Charles Hart (d 1974), of Fulham and Croydon, and Florence Jane, *née* Dorney; *b* 24 June 1925; *Educ* Dulwich, Regent St Poly; *m* 18 March 1958, Paulette Olga, da of Julian Pearmain (d 1971), of Hayes, Kent; *Career* RE 1943-48, Capt attached to Indian Army 1945-48, RARO 1949-75; Walfords Chartered Quantity Surveyors: joined 1950, ptnr 1967, jt sr ptnr 1982, sr ptnr 1987-89, conslt 1989-91; sr ptnr PD Hact & Partners 1984-; dir Surveyors Pubns 1984-90; memb: Nat Jt Consultative Ctee for Bldg 1978-86, bd Coll of Estate Mgmnt Reading 1985- (hon treas 1989-); pres RICS: pres Quantity Surveyor's Divnl Cncl 1987-89 (vice-chm 1989-90), memb General Cncl 1988-91; tstee: Douglas Haig Meml Homes 1978-, Housing Assoc for Offrs Families 1988-; hon sec Surrey & N Sussex Beagles 1979-; pres The Surveyors' Club 1988; Freeman City of London 1977; Liveryman: Worshipful Co of Chartered Surveyors 1977, Worshipful Co of Carpenters 1984; FRICS 1965 (Assoc 1953); *Recreations* beagling, archaeology, local history; *Clubs* Athenaeum; *Style*— Peter Hart, Esq; The Coach House, 50 Lovelace Rd, Surbiton, Surrey KT6 6ND (☎ 081 399 8423); Walfords, 7/9 St James's St, London SW1A 1EN (☎ 071 930 4293, fax 071 839 2962)

HART, Philip; s of Jacob Hart, (d 1973), of Cape Town S Africa, and Rosa, *née* Suitkin (d 1979); *b* 5 Oct 1939; *Educ* South African Coll Sch, Coll of Law London; *m* 3 May 1960, Anita, da of Percy Bub (d 1982); 1 s (Gaon Leslie b 17 Oct 1965), 1 da (Shana b 31 Oct 1961); *Career* slr, fndr (sr ptnr) Hart Fortgang 1961; *Recreations* hiking, skiing; *Style*— Philip Hart, Esq; Princess House, 50 Eastcastle St, London W1A 4BY (☎ 071 436 3300, fax 071 255 3066, telex 8956086)

HART, Capt Raymond; CBE (1963), DSO (1945), DSC (1941, Bar 1943); s of Herbert Harry Hart (d 1955), of Bassett, Southampton, and Daisy Gladys, *née* Warn (d 1968); *b* 24 June 1913; *Educ* King Edward VI Sch Southampton, Naval Staff Coll, Jt Servs Staff Coll; *m* 16 June 1945, Margaret (Peggy) Evanson, da of Capt Samuel Barbour Duffin (d 1959), of Danesfort, Belfast; 2 s (Ian b 1950, Peter b 1956), 1 da (Nicola b 1952); *Career* RN 1937-63: WWII, HMS Hasty 2 destroyer flotilla 1939-42; i/c: HMS Vidette 1942-44, HMS Havelock 1944, HMS Conn (and sr offr 21st Escort Gp) 1944-45 (despatches 1944); 1 Lt HMS Vanguard Royal Cruise to S Africa 1947, promoted Cdr 1947, promoted Capt 1954, liaison offr CINC Allied Forces Southern Europe 1954-56, Capt i/c HMS Undine 6 Frigate Sqdn 1957-58, dep dir Plans Div Admty 1958-60, Cdre naval drafting 1960-62, ret RN 1963; Br Cwlth Shipping Co 1963-72, nautical dir (later fleet mangr) Cayzer Irvine & Co 1972-, ret 1976; memb Bd Br Cwlth 1966; vice pres: Seaman's Hosp Soc 1983, Marine Soc 1989; FRIN 1970, FNI 1966; Offr Order of Merit Republic of Italy 1958; *Recreations* golf, swimming, gardening; *Clubs* RN Club of 1765 and 1785, Liphook Golf; *Style*— Capt Raymond Hart, CBE, DSO, DSC; Three Firs Cottage, Bramshott Chase, Hindhead, Surrey

HART, Roger Dudley; s of Alfred John Hart (d 1975), and Emma Jane, *née* Turner (d 1984); *b* 29 Dec 1943; *Educ* St Olave's GS London Univ of Birmingham (BA); *m* 3 May 1968, Maria De Los Angeles De Santiago Jimenez (Angela), da of Lt-Col Arsenio De Santiago, of Madrid, Spain; 2 s (Stephen Andrew b 1969, Christopher Alexander b 1970); *Career* HM Dip Serv: third sec FO London 1965, third later second sec Br Mil Govt W Berlin 1967-70, second sec Political Residency Bahrain 1970-72, second later first sec FCO London 1972-75, first sec (AID) Br High Commission Nairobi 1975-78, first sec (commercial) Br Embassy Lisbon 1978-83, asst head Def Dept FCO London 1985-, int advsr Br Nat Space Centre London 1986, HM consul-gen Rio de Janeiro; citizen of Rio de Janeiro 1989-; awarded Pedro Ernesto Medal Brazil 1990; *Recreations* travel, reading, music, swimming; *Clubs* Paissandu, Rio De Janeiro; *Style*— Roger Hart, Esq; 7 Rosscourt Mansions, 4 Palace St, London SW1E 5HZ (☎ 071 834 6032); Rua Paulo Cesar De Andrade, 232/1101, Laranjeiras, Rio De Janeiro, Brasil (☎ 010 5521 205 6698); British Consultate General, Praia Do Flamengo, 284-2 Andar, Flamengo, Rio De Janeiro, CEP 22210 Brasil (☎ 010 5521 552 1422, fax 021 552 5796, telex 021 21577 A/B EIG BR)

HART, Timothy Frederick (Tim); s of Louis Albert Hart, (d 1977) of Dynes Hall, Halstead, Essex, and Theresa Elsie Hart; *b* 7 Dec 1947; *Educ* Westminster, Jesus Coll Cambridge (MA); *m* Stefa Belitis, da of Vladimir Daskaloff; 3 s (Samuel b Sept 1974, Edward b Aug 1976, James b March 1982); *Career* Henry Ansbacher and Co 1969-73, Lehman Brothers Inc 1974-79; purchased Hambleton Hall 1979 (opened as Country House Hotel 1980); fndr chm and chief exec Hart Hambleton plc 1986, purchased and redeveloped Ram Jam Inn 1986, chm Br Section of Relais ex Chateaux 1987-90; govr Oakham Sch 1990-; *Recreations* hunting, shooting, fishing, gastronomy, oenology, literature, gardening, watercolour painting, deer stalking; *Style*— Tim Hart, Esq; Hart Hambleton plc, Hambleton Hall, Hambleton, Oakham, Rutland LE15 8TH (☎ 0572 2756991, fax 0572 724721)

HART, Timothy Guy Collins; s of Dr Robert John Collins Hart (Lt-Col RAMC), of Budleigh Salterton, Devon, and Mary Winifred, *née* Sawday; *b* 31 Aug 1953; *Educ* The Kings Sch Canterbury, Oxford Poly; *m* 2 Aug 1980, Judith Charlotte, da of Brig Bernard Cyril Elgood, MBE, of Pauntley, Glos; 2 s (Thomas b 1982, Nicholas b 1985), 1 da (Jennifer b 1988); *Career* Arthur Young 1974-83, Prudential Assurance 1983-85, Phildrew Ventures Advisers 1985-; ACA 1980; *Recreations* tennis, golf, skiing; *Style*— Timothy Hart, Esq; Herberts Hole Cottage, Ballinger, Gt Missenden, Bucks HP16 0RR; Phildrew Ventures, Triton Ct, 14 Finsbury Sq, London EC2A 1PD (☎ 071 628 6366, fax 071 638 2817)

HART, William Stephen; s of John Edward Cecil Hart (d 1980), and Evelyn Lucy, *née* Bateman; *b* 10 Dec 1955; *Educ* The Cathedral Sch Bristol, Univ of Exeter (LLB); *m* 14 July 1976, Jill, da of John Edwin Vaughan (d 1978); *Career* called to the Bar Middle Temple 1979; practising in Bristol; *Recreations* riding, sport, photography, ornithology; *Style*— William Hart, Esq; Albion Chambers, Broad Street, Bristol BS1 1DR (☎ 0272 272144)

HART-DAVIS, (Peter) Duff; s of Sir Rupert Hart-Davis, of Marske-in-Swaledale, Yorks, and Comfort Borden, *née* Turner (d 1970); *b* 3 June 1936; *Educ* Eton, Univ of Oxford (BA); *m* 1961, Phyllida, da of Col John Barstow; 1 s (Guy b 1965), 1 da (Alice b 1963); *Career* journalist and author, graduate trainee Western Mail Cardiff 1960; Sunday Telegraph: asst to Literary Ed 1961-63, ed Close-Up (news background) team 1968-70, literary ed 1976-77, asst ed 1977-78, editorial advsr 1980-85; contrib Country Matters column The Independent 1986-; *Books* novels: The Megacull (1968), The Gold of St Matthew (1970), Spider in the Morning (1972), The Heights of Rimring (1980), Level Five (1982), Fire Falcon (1983), The Man-Eater of Jassapur (1985), Horses of War 1991; non-fiction: Peter Fleming (1974), Ascension (1976), Monarchs of the Glen (1978), Hitler's Games (1986), The Letters and Journals of Sir Alan Lascelles (2 vol, 1986 and 1988), Armada (1988), Country Matters (1989), The House the Berrys Built (1990); *Recreations* opera, gardening, deer stalking, splitting wood; *Clubs* Garrick; *Style*— Duff Hart-Davis, Esq

HART-DAVIS, Sir Rupert Charles; s of Richard Vaughan Hart-Davis and Sybil Cooper (sister of Rt Hon Sir Alfred Duff Cooper, GCMG, DSO, 1 Viscount Norwich, da of Sir Alfred Cooper, FRCS, and Lady Agnes, *née* Duff, 4 of da 5 Earl of Fife and sister of 1 Duke of Fife); *b* 28 Aug 1907; *Educ* Eton, Balliol Coll Oxford; *m* 1, 1929 (m dis), Dame Peggy Ashcroft, *qv*; m 2, 1933 (m dis), Catherine Comfort Borden-Turner; 2 s (Duff b 1936, Adam b 1943), 1 da (Lady Silsoe, *qv*); m 3, 1964, Winifred Ruth (d 1967), da of C H Ware and wid of Oliver Simon; m 4, 1968, June, née Clifford, wid of David Williams; *Career* ed, author, publisher; dir Rupert Hart-Davis Ltd (and fndr) 1946-68 (former dir Jonathan Cape Ltd), vice pres Ctee of London Library 1971- (former chm); ed letters of: Oscar Wilde, Max Beerbohm, the Lyttleton Hart-Davis Letters, and Siegfried Sassoon Diaries 1920-22; kt 1967; *Books* Hugh Walpole: a Biography (1952), The Arms of Time: a Memoir (1979); *Style*— Sir Rupert Hart-Davis; The Old Rectory, Marske-in-Swaledale, Richmond, N Yorks

HART DYKE, Sir David William; 10 Bt (E 1677), of Horeham, Sussex; s of Sir Derek Hart Dyke, 9 Bt (d 1987); 2 Bt m Anne, da and heir of Percival Hart of Lullingstone Castle, 5 Bt unsuccessfully claimed the Barony of Brayes of which he was a co heir through the Harts 1836; *b* 5 Jan 1955; *Heir* Uncle (Oliver) Guy Hart Dyke b 1928; *Style*— Sir David Hart Dyke, Bt; 28 King St West, Apt B14, Stoney Creek, Ontario, Canada

HART DYKE, Trevor; DSO (1944), DL (Derbys 1981); er s of Col Percyvall Hart Dyke, DSO (whose gf Thomas was 2 s of Sir Percival Hart Dyke, 5 Bt); *b* 19 Feb 1905; *Educ* Marlborough; *m* 1, 1933 (m dis 1965), Eileen Joyce, er da of John Niblock-Stuart, of Nairobi; 1 s (Terence b 1934), 1 da (Jennifer (Mrs Vaudrey) b 1939); m 2, 1965, Mary Eliot, da of J A Roberts and wid of Maj D E Lockwood;

Career Brig Queen's Royal Regt, serv WWII, Gibraltar, NW Europe, SE Asia; *Style*— Brig Trevor Hart Dyke, DSO, DL; Clough House, Bamford, Derbys

HART-LEVERTON, Colin Allen; QC (1979); s of Morris Hart-Leverton, of London; *b* 10 May 1936; *Educ* Stowe; *m* 1990, Kathi, *née* Davidson; *Career* called to the Bar Middle Temple 1957, dep circuit judge 1975, attorney-at-law Turks and Caicos Islands 1976, Crown Ct rec 1979; occasional radio and TV broadcasts in UK and USA; memb Taxation Inst 1957; *Recreations* table tennis, jazz; *Style*— Colin Hart-Leverton, Esq, QC; 10 King's Bench Walk, London EC4Y 7EB (☎ 071 353 2501)

HART OF SOUTH LANARK, Baroness (Life Peer 1988), of Lanark, Co Lanark; Judith Constance Mary Hart; DBE (1979), PC (1967); da of Harry and Lily Ridehalgh; *b* 18 Sept 1924; *Educ* Clitheroe Royal GS, LSE (BA); *m* 1946, Anthony Bernard Hart; 2 s; *Career* Parly candidate (Lab): Bournemouth West 1951, Aberdeen South 1955; MP (Lab): Lanark 1959-1983, Clydesdale 1983-87; jt Parly under sec Scotland 1964-66, min of state Cwlth Office 1966-67, min for Social Security 1967-68, paymaster gen with Seat in Cabinet 1968-69, min for Overseas Devpt 1969-70 (1974-75 and 1977-79), front bench oppn spokesman Overseas Aid 1979-80; memb: Lab Party NEC 1969-83 (chm 1981-82, vice chm 1980-81), Lab Party-TUC Liaison Ctee to 1982-83 (chm Industl Policy Sub-Ctee until 1983); hon fell Inst of Devpt Studies Univ of Sussex 1984; vice chm UN Assoc 1989-; vice pres World Univ Service 1986-; *Books* Aids and Liberation; *Recreations* gardening; *Style*— The Rt Hon Baroness Hart of South Lanark, DBE, PC; 3 Ennerdale Rd, Kew Gdns, Richmond, Surrey (☎ 081 948 1989)

HARTE, Geoffrey Charles; s of Charles Fredrick Harte (d 1982); *b* 16 Sept 1923; *Educ* Plympton GS; *m* 1950, Moira, da of James Kennedy (d 1958); 1 s; *Career* engr; pres J and S Marine Ltd; former non-exec dir Cray Electronics Holdings, ret, non-exec chm Cray Marine Ltd; *Recreations* music, photography, books; *Clubs* IOD; *Style*— Geoffrey Harte, Esq; Combers Week, Harracott, Barnstaple, N Devon (☎ 0271 85448)

HARTE, John Denis; MBE (1981); s of Frank Harry Roach Harte (d 1980), and Beatrice Mary, *née* de Looze (d 1971); *b* 14 March 1926; *Educ* Clapham Secdy Sch; *m* 23 Feb 1952 (m dis 1983), (Kathleen) Joan, da of Percy Joseph Cater (d 1971), of Farnborough Park, Kent; 2 s (Jeremy Mark b 30 Nov 1960, Joby John b 30 Jan 1982), 1 da (Judith Anne b 15 July 1955); m 2, 25 April 1983, Jane Nicholson, da of John Kennedy; 1 step da (Joanna Louise b 26 July 1973); *Career* admitted slr 1952, ptnr Goodwin Harte & Co Harrow; NP; legal advsr St Marylebone CAB 1958-87; chm Mgmnt Ctee: Westminster CAB 1980-85, Elstree CAB 1981-86; memb Law Soc; *Style*— John Harte, Esq, MBE; The Grotto, Yanwath, Penrith, Cumbria (☎ 0768 63288, fax 0768 63432)

HARTE, Dr Michael John; s of Harold Edward Harte, of Sussex, and Marjorie Irene, *née* Scaife; *b* 15 Aug 1936; *Educ* Charterhouse, Trinity Coll Cambridge (BA), UCL (Dip Biochem Engrg, PhD); *m* 1, 1962 (m dis); m 2, 1975, Mrs Mary Claire Preston, da of D J Hogan (d 1972); 4 step-da (Caroline b 1962, Emma b 1964, Abigail b 1966, Lucy (twin) b 1966); *Career* chm NATO Budget Ctees 1981-83; asst under sec: Dockyard Planning Team MOD 1985, Air Personnel MOD 1987, Resources MOD 1990-; *Recreations* wine, walking, weeding; *Style*— Dr Michael Harte; Greenman Farm, Wadhurst, Sussex TN5 6LE (☎ 0892 88 3292)

HARTGILL, John Claverling; s of Maj-Gen William C Hartgill, CB, MC, OBE, KHS (d 1969), and Katherine Robertson, *née* Lowe, MM (d 1970); *b* 26 July 1925; *Educ* Wanganui Collegiate NZ, Univ of Otago NZ, The London Hosp; *m* 1 July 1961, Unni, da of Otto Aass (d 1971), of Drammen, Norway; 2 s (Paul b 9 April 1963, Tom b 26 Sept 1966), 1 da (Katrina b 24 March 1968); *Career* sr registrar Dept of Obstetrics The London Hosp 1958-61, asst Lege Ulleval Hosp Oslo Norway 1962-66, conslt obstetric and gynaecological surgn The London Hosp 1966-; sr lectr London Hosp Med Coll 1966-; examiner 1966-: Univ of Cambridge, RCOG, Univ of London; jt ed Int Journal of Lymphology 1967-72; memb: Gynaecological Visiting Soc of GB & I, Sydenham Med Club, The Blizard Club (London Hosp Med Sch); Liveryman Worshipful Soc of Apothecaries 1973, Freeman City of London; FRCSEd, FRCOG, MRCS, LRCP, FRSM 1958; awarded Norske Medicinske Seiskap Medal 1964; *Books* Ten Teachers Obstetrics (jtly 12, 13, 14 edns 1976-85), Diseases of Women (jtly 12 edn 1976), Ten Teachers Gynaecology (jtly 13 and 14 edns 1980-85); *Clubs* Wig and Pen; *Style*— John Hartgill, Esq; Bridge House Farm, Felsted, Great Dunmow, Essex CM6 3JF (☎ 0371 820349), 121 Harley St, London W1N 1DM (☎ 071 935 7111, car 0836 260530)

HARTIG, Hon Mrs (Linda); *née* Nivison; er da of 3 Baron Glendyne; *b* 23 Oct 1954; *m* 1976, Dr Count Nikolaus Hartig; 1 s, 1 da; *Style*— The Hon Mrs Hartig; Heuberggasse 9, A-1170 Vienna, Austria

HARTILL, (Edward) Theodore; s of Clement Augustus Hartill, of Shropshire, and Florence Margarita, *née* Ford (d 1989); *b* 23 Jan 1943; *Educ* Priory Sch for Boys Shrewsbury, Coll of Estate Mgmnt, Univ of London (BSc); *m* 1, 2 s (Jeremy b 1969, Richard b 1972); m 2, 1975, Gillian Ruth, da of Harold Todd (d 1963); 2 s (Andrew b 1977, Giles b 1981); *Career* joined Messrs Burd and Evans Land Agents Shrewsbury 1963; Estates Dept Legal and Gen Assurance Society 1964-73, Property Investmt Dept Guardian Royal Exchange Assurance Group 1973-85, The City Surveyor Corp of London 1985-; visiting lectr in law of town planning and compulsory purchase Hammersmith and West London Coll of Advanced Business Studies 1968-78, jr vice chm Gen Practice Div RICS 1990-91; memb of Br Schs Exploring Soc; Liveryman Worshipful Company of Chartered Surveyors 1985-; FRICS; *Recreations* travel, hill walking, cinema, family; *Style*— E T Hartill Esq; 215 Sheen Lane, East Sheen, London SW14 8LE (☎ 081 878 4494); The City Surveyor, City Surveyor's Dept, Corporation of London, PO Box 270, Guildhall, London EC2P 2EJ (☎ 071 260 1500, fax 071 260 1119, telex 265608 LONDON G)

HARTINGTON, Marquess of; Peregrine Andrew Morny Cavendish; s and h of 11 Duke of Devonshire, MC, PC, and Hon Deborah (Debo) Freeman-Mitford (sis of Nancy, Jessica and Unity Mitford, *see* Treuhaft, Hon Mrs, and Hon Lady Mosley), da of 2 Baron Redesdale; *b* 27 April 1944; *Educ* Eton, Exeter Coll Oxford; *m* 28 June 1967, Amanda Carmen, da of late Cdr Edward Gavin Heywood-Lonsdale, RN; 1 s, 2 da (Lady Celina Imogen b 1971, Lady Jasmine Nancy b 1973); *Heir* Earl of Burlington b 1969; *Style*— Marquess of Hartington; Beamsley Hall, Skipton, N Yorks BD23 6HD (☎ 075 671 419/424)

HARTLAND, Neil Arthur; s of Robert Arthur Hartland, of Westwinds, Hazelwood Lane, Chipstead, Surrey, and Jean Beryl Helen, *née* Flindell; *b* 14 Aug 1953; *Educ* Sutton Valence, Kingston Poly (BA); *m* 17 Aug 1979, Christel Ulrike, da of Friedrich Hachenburg, of 26A Spesenrotherweg, 5448 Kastellaun, W Germany; 2 s (Sebastian Neil b 12 July 1982, Joshua Stefan b 4 July 1985), 1 da (Jennifer Felicitas (twin) b 4 July 1985); *Career* div dir McColl 1987 (assoc 1982), md interior design Aukett Assocs 1987, main bd dir operations McColl 1988; memb CSD 1982; *Recreations* squash, sailing, walking, reading, photography, drawing; *Style*— Neil Hartland, Esq; McColl, 64 Wigmore St, London W1H 9DJ (☎ 071 935 4788, telex 27392 SMCOLL, fax 071 935 0865)

HARTLAND, Robert Arthur; s of William Thomas Hartland (d 1956), of Croydon, and Alice Jane, *née* Woodman (d 1958); *b* 13 May 1926; *Educ* Whitgift Middle Sch; *m* 17 July 1948, Jean Beryl Helen, da of Arthur Robert Flindell (d 1984), of London; 1 s (Neil b 1953); *Career* RE 1944-48; Sir Frederick Snow & Partners (formerly Frederick Snow & Partners): articled pupil 1948, assoc 1960, ptnr 1965, sr ptnr 1984; chm Snow Group plc 1989; Constantine Gold medal Manchester Soc of Engrs 1978; Freeman: City of London 1977, Worshipful Co of Constructors 1977, Worshipful Co of Engrs 1985; CEng 1952, FICE 1965, MConsE 1967, memb Inst of Demolition Engrs (pres 1983 and 1984), The Concrete Soc (sr vice pres 1988, pres 1990-91); *Books* Design of Precast Concrete (1975); *Recreations* hill walking, gardening; *Clubs* IOD; *Style*— Robert Hartland, Esq; West Winds, Hazelwood Lane, Chipstead, Surrey CR3 3QZ (☎ 07375 53939); Ross House, 144 Southwark St, London SE1 0SZ (☎ 071 928 5688, fax 01 928 1774, telex 917478 SNOMEN G)

HARTLAND-SWANN, Julian Dana Nimmo; s of Prof John Hartland-Swann (d 1961), and Kenlis, *née* Taylour (d 1957); *b* 18 Feb 1936; *Educ* Stowe, Lincoln Coll Oxford (BA); *m* 22 Oct 1960, Ann Deirdre, da of Lt Cdr Robert Green, DSO, of St Helier, Shotley Gate, nr Ipswich; 1 s (Piers b 1961), 1 da (Justina b 1963); *Career* Nat Serv RA 1955-57; Dip Serv 1960-; 3 sec late 2 sec Bangkok Embassy 1961-65, 1 sec FO 1965-68, head of External Dept Br Mil Govt Berlin 1968-71, 1 sec and head of chancery Vienna 1971-74, FCO 1975-77, cnsllr 1977, ambass to Mongolian People's Republic 1977-79, cnsllr and head of chancery Brussels 1979-83, head of SE Asian Dept FCO 1983-85, consul gen Frankfurt 1986-90, ambass to Union of Myaumar Burma 1990-; *Recreations* French food, sailing, restoring ruins; *Style*— Julian Hartland-Swann, Esq; c/o Foreign and Commonwealth Office, London SW1A 2AH

HARTLEY, Air Marshal Sir Christopher Harold; KCB (1963, CB 1961), CBE (1957, OBE 1949), DFC (1945), AFC (1944); s of Brig-Gen Harold Hartley, GCVO, CH, CBE, MC, FRS (d 1972); *b* 31 Jan 1913; *Educ* Eton, Balliol Coll Oxford, King's Coll Cambridge; *m* 1, 1937 (m dis 1943), Anne Sitwell; m 2, 1944, Margaret Watson (d 1989); 2 s; *Career* zoologist Univ of Oxford Expeditions: Sarawak 1932, Spitsbergen 1933, Greenland 1936; asst master Eton 1937-39; joined RAFVR 1938, served WWII, Gp Capt 1952, Air Cdre 1958, AOC 12 Gp Fighter Cmd 1959, Air Vice-Marshal 1960, asst chief Air Staff (Operational Requirements) Air Miny 1961-63, Air Marshal 1963, dep chief Air Staff 1963-66, controller of Aircraft Miny of Aviation 1966, ret 1970; dir Westland Aircraft Ltd 1971-83, dep chm British Hovercraft Corp 1979-83 (chm 1974-79); *Recreations* fishing; *Clubs* Travellers'; *Style*— Air Marshal Sir Christopher Hartley, KCB, CBE, DFC, AFC; c/o Barclays Bank, Bank Plain, Norwich, Norfolk

HARTLEY, Christopher Ian James; s of C J Hartley (d 1987), and Rosemary Pamela Metcalf, *née* Horne; *b* 10 Aug 1961; *Educ* St Edward's Sch Oxford, Univ of Bristol (BSc); *Career* business mangr; ICI Fire Chemicals (ICI C & P Ltd) 1985-86, ICI Australia 1988-90, int sales mangr carpets ICI Fibres 1990-; Bristol Univ Red (rowing); *Style*— Christopher I J Hartley, Esq; Greenhayes, Grove Hill, Dedham, Colchester, Essex; c/o ICI Fibres, Harrogate, N Yorks

HARTLEY, David Fielding; s of Robert Maude Hartley (d 1980), of Hebden Bridge, Yorks, and Sheila Ellen, *née* Crabtree (d 1977); *b* 14 Sept 1937; *Educ* Rydal Sch, Clare Coll Cambridge (MA, PhD); *m* 23 April 1960, Joanna Mary, da of John Stanley Bolton (d 1988), of Halifax; 1 s (Timothy b 1965), 2 da (Caroline (Mrs Eatough) b 1963, Rosalind b 1968); *Career* Univ of Cambridge: sr asst in res 1964-65, asst dir of res 1966-67, lectr Mathematical Laboratory 1967-70; jr res fell Churchill Coll 1964-67, dir computing serv 1970-, fell Darwin Coll 1969-86, fell Clare Coll 1987-; dir: Lynxvale Ltd, Cad Centre Ltd, chm and dir NAG Ltd; memb: Computer Bd for Univs and Res Cncls 1979-83, PM's Info Technol Advsy Panel 1981-86, BBC Sci Consultative Gp 1984-87, vice pres Br Computer Soc; Freeman: City of London 1988, Co of Info Technologists 1988; FBCS 1967; Medal of Merits Nicholas Copernicus Univ Poland 1984; *Style*— Dr David Hartley; 26 Girton Rd, Cambridge (☎ 0223 276 975); Univ of Cambridge, Computer Laboratory, New Museums Site, Pembroke St, Cambridge (☎ 0223 334 703)

HARTLEY, Sir Frank; CBE (1970); s of Robinson King Hartley (d 1916), and Mary, *née* Holt (d 1959); *b* 5 Jan 1911; *Educ* Nelson Municipal Secondary Sch, Sch of Pharmacy Univ of London, UCL, Birkbeck Coll London (PhD); *m* 1937, Lydia May England; 2 s; *Career* dean Sch of Pharmacy Univ of London 1962-76, vice chllr Univ of London 1976-78; chm Br Pharmacopoeia Cmmn 1970-80, vice chm Medicines Cmmn 1974-83; chm: Cmmrs Lambeth Southwark and Lewisham Health Area 1979-80, Consortium of Charing Cross and Westminster Med Schs 1981-84, Br Cncl for Prevention of Blindness 1988-; hon fell Imperial Coll London 1990-, Hon FRCP (London) 1979, Hon FRCS (London) 1980; Hon DSc Warwick 1978, Hon LLD Strathclyde 1980, Hon LLD London 1987; Charter Gold medal Royal Pharmaceutical Soc of GB 1974; FRPharmS, FRSC; kt 1977; *Recreations* reading; *Clubs* Athenaeum; *Style*— Sir Frank Hartley, CBE; 24 Old School Close, St Mary's Mead, Merton Park, London SW19 3HY

HARTLEY, Prof Frank Robinson; s of Sir Frank Hartley, CBE, of Old School Close, Merton Park, London SW19 3HY, *qv*, and Lydia May, *née* England; *b* 29 Jan 1942; *Educ* King's Coll Sch Wimbledon, Magdalen Coll Oxford (MA, DPhil, DSc); *m* 12 Dec 1964, Valerie, da of George Peel (d 1984), of Silksworth, Co Durham, and Watchfield, Oxon; 3 da (Susan b 1967, Judith b 1971, Elizabeth b 1974); *Career* res fell Div of Protein Chem CSIRO (Aust) 1966-69, ICI res fell and tutor in chem UCL 1969-70, lectr chem Univ of Southampton 1970-75, princ and dean RMCS 1982-89 (prof chem 1975-82), vice chllr Cranfield Inst of Technol 1989-; non-exec dir: T & N plc 1989-, Eastern Regnl Bd National Westminster Bank plc 1990-; special advsr to PM on Defence Systems 1988-; memb: Parly Scientific Ctee 1987-, Oxon Soc of Rugby Football Referees; FRSC 1977, FRSA 1988; *Books* Chemistry of Platinum and Palladium (1973), Elements of Organometallic Chemistry (1974), Solution Equilibria (1980), Supported Metal Complexes (1985), Chemistry of the Metal-Carbon Bond (vol 1 1983, vol 2 1984, vol 3 1985, vol 4 1987, vol 5 1989); Chemistry of Organphosphones Compounds (vol 1 1990); *Recreations* rugby refereeing, swimming, cliff walking, reading, gardening, squash; *Clubs* Shrivenham, IOD; *Style*— Prof Frank Hartley; Cranfield Institute of Technology, Cranfield, Bedford MK43 0AL (☎ 0908 674 444, fax 0908 674 422)

HARTLEY, Rev Godfrey; s of Isaac Hartley, and Hannah, *née* Lowther; *b* 26 Aug 1937; *Educ* Clare Hall Sch, Manchester Univ, Cuddesdon Coll Oxford; *m* 17 Aug 1963, Maureen Ruth, da of Norman Harding Goldsworth, of Nottingham; 2 s (António b 1965, Richard b 1974); *Career* Nat Serv RAF 1956-58; chaplain RNR 1973-, chaplain of the Fleets Representative Ships Bldg Clyde 1974-89; ordained: deacon 1964, priest 1965; curate St Giles Balderton Diocese of Southwell 1964-67, port chaplain Missions to Seamen, rector St George Beira Mozambique 1968-73, sr chaplain and sec for Scotland Missions to Seamen 1974-89, priest i/c St Gabriel's Govan 1974-89, chaplain the Missions to Seamen in Cornwall 1989; memb: SSC, Int Christian Maritime Assoc; Freeman City of Glasgow 1979, memb Incorporation of Coopers of Glasgow 1979; *Recreations* skiing, photography, painting, reading; *Clubs* Army and Navy, Naval, Ski of GB, Glasgow Press, Bearsden Ski, Skal of Scotland; *Style*— The Rev Godfrey Hartley; Sandoes Gate, Feock, Truro, Cornwall TR3 6QN (☎ 0872 865863)

HARTLEY, Prof Keith; s of W Hartley, of Leeds, and Ivy, *née* Stead; *b* 14 July 1940; *Educ* Univ of Hull (BA, PhD); *m* 12 April 1966, Winifred; 1 s (Adam b 27 Feb 1969), 2 da (Lucy b 18 Oct 1970, Cecilia b 20 July 1975); *Career* visiting prof: Univ of Illinois,

Univ of Malaysia; Inst for Res in Social Sciences Univ of York; *Books* Nato Arms Co-operation (1983); *Recreations* angling, football, reading; *Style*— Prof Keith Hartley; Institute for Research in Social Sciences, University of York, York YO1 5DD (☎ 0904 433680, telex 0904 433433)

HARTLEY, Richard Cedric; s of Gp Capt Cedric Mozart Powers Hartley (d 1971), and Georgette, *née* Herckerbout (d 1988); *b* 13 Sept 1928; *Educ* Sedbergh, Univ of Birmingham (MB ChB, CHM); *m* 22 Aug 1959, Dorothy Mary, da of Joseph Howarth (d 1989); 1 s (Richard Robert b 1962), 1 da (Jane b 1960); *Career* Lt RAMC 1953-54, Capt 1954-55; conslt surgn N Manchester Gen Hosp 1967; memb: Ct of Examiners RCS 1984, Assoc of Surgns of GB and Ireland, Br Soc of Gastroenterology; FRCS 1959; *Recreations* skiing, sailing; *Clubs* Naval and Military; *Style*— Richard Hartley, Esq; Lilac Cottage, Horrocks Fold, Bolton, Lancashire BL1 7BX (☎ 0204 51641); 21 St John St, Manchester M3 4DT (☎ 061 832 5212)

HARTLEY, Roger Anderson; s of John Herbert Hartley (d 1975), of Clevedon House, Ranmoor, Sheffield, and Hilda Mary, *née* Sowerby (d 1987); *b* 28 May 1942; *Educ* Shrewsbury, St Catharine's Coll Cambridge (MA); *m* 1, 4 Oct 1969 (m dis 1981), Roslynne Mary, *née* Vincent-Jones; 1 s (Peter Anderson b 16 July 1974), 1 da (Sarah Catharine b 26 April 1977); m 2, 9 July 1984, Tina Elizabeth, da of Jack Alderson, of Woodthorpe, York; 1 da (Rebecca Elizabeth b 25 Jan 1989); *Career* slr 1970; slr to Malton Town Cncl, memb Ryedale DC 1979-83, clerk to Fearnsides and Stephensons Charities 1970-84; memb: Law Soc, Yorks Law Soc; *Recreations* boating, walking, music; *Style*— Roger Hartley, Esq; Melrose, Sandsend, Whitby, N Yorks YO21 3SZ (☎ 0947 83250); 13 Yorkersgate, Malton, N Yorks YO17 0AA (☎ 0653 693101/2)

HARTLEY, Timothy Guy; s of Brig Harry Leslie Hartley, of 14 Macaulay Buildings, Widcombe Hill, Bath, and Gwen, *née* Woolfitt; *b* 30 Oct 1947; *Educ* King's Sch Canterbury, Univ of Bristol (LLB); *m* 2 Sept 1972, Jacqueline Therese Lucie, da of Charles Herrmann, of Les Deux H, Meounes Les Montrieux, France; 1 s (Anthony b 1979), 2 da (Heloise b 1976, Emma-Fleur b 1982); *Career* called to the Bar Grays Inn 1970, lectr Inns of Ct Sch of Law 1970-72, in practice NE circuit 1972-; counsel to inquiries into: food poisoning at Stanley Royd, Bradford Football Stadium fire, Cleveland Child abuse; Parly candidate (C) Barnsley West and Penistone 1983; *Recreations* photography, wine, riding, idling; *Style*— Timothy Hartley, Esq; Tholthorpe Hall Farm, Tholthorpe, York YO6 2JN (☎ 03473 586); Park Court Chambers, Leeds (☎ 0532 433277, fax 0532 421285); 4 Paper Buildings, Temple, London

HARTMAN, (Gladys) Marea; CBE 1978 (MBE 1967); *Career* head of Delgn Eng Int Athletics Teams and Cwlth Games Athletics Teams 1978-, runner for Spartan Athletic Club and Surrey County, team mangr Br Athletics Team at Olympic and Euro Games and Eng Athletics Team at Cwlth Games 1956-78, memb Women's Cmmn of Int Amateur Athletic Fedn 1958- (chm 1968-81), chm Br Amateur Athletics Bd 1989- (hon treas 1972-84, life vice pres 1980), hon sec Women's Amateur Athletic Assoc 1960- (hon treas 1950-60, life vice pres 1970, vice chm 1981-), hon treas CCPR 1984- (dep chm 1981-83), hon life memb IAAF (Women's Ctee) 1987, FIPM; *Recreations* music, reading, theatre; *Style*— Marea Hartman, CBE; Women's Amateur Athletic Association, Francis House, Francis Street SW1P 1DE (☎ 071 828 4731, fax 071 630 8820, telex 8956058)

HARTMANN, Dr Reinhard Rudolf Karl; s of Walther Eduard Hartmann, of Vienna, Austria, and Gerta Emilia Stanislawa, *née* Müllner; *b* 8 April 1938; *Educ* Vienna GS, Vienna Sch of Economics (BSc and Doctorate), Univ of Vienna (Dip Translation), Southern Illinois Univ (MA); *m* 22 June 1965, Lynn, da of Kingston Vernon Warren, of Droylsden, Manchester; 1 s (Stefan b 1967), 1 da (Nasim b 1965); *Career* lectr modern languages UMIST 1964-68, lectr applied linguistics Univ of Nottingham 1968-74, dir Dictionary Res Centre Univ of Exeter 1984- (sr lectr applied linquistics and dir Language Centre 1974-); memb Ctee Dirs UK Univ Language Centres, pres Euro Assoc Lexicography (former sec and fndr); memb: BAAL 1967, LAGB 1970, SLE 1972, ALLC 1975, EURALEX 1983, DSNA 1984; *Books* Dictionary of Language and Linguistics (jtly, 1972), Contrastive Textology (1980); ed: Lexicography Principles and Practice (1983), Lexeter '83 Proceedings (1984), The History of Lexicography (1986), Lexicography in Africa (1990); *Recreations* listening to music, table tennis; *Style*— Dr Reinhard Hartmann; The Language Centre, University of Exeter, Queen's Building, Exeter, Devon EX4 4QH (☎ 0392 264302, fax 0392 263108, telex 42894 EXUNIVG)

HARTNELL, Dr George Gordon; s of Francis George Hartnell, of Holywell Lake, Somerset, and Margaret, *née* Gordon; *b* 19 July 1952; *Educ* Abingdon Sch, Univ of Bristol (BSc, MB ChB); *Career* registrar in cardiology Harefield Hosp 1979-81, registrar and sr registrar Royal Postgrad Med Sch Hammersmith Hosp London 1983-87, currently conslt and sr lectr Dept of Radiodiagnosis Univ of Bristol; memb: Br Cardiovascular Intervention Soc, Br Soc of Interventional Radiology; MRCP 1982, FRCR 1985; *Recreations* sailing, skiing; *Style*— Dr George Hartnell; Department of Radiodiagnosis, Bristol Royal Infirmary, Bristol BS2 8HW (☎ 0272 282731)

HARTNETT, Frank Ernest Lawrence; OBE (1988); s of John Richard Hartnett (d 1966), of Odiham, Hampshire, and Eva Marjorie, *née* Maybanks (d 1970); *b* 3 Sept 1940; *Educ* Lord Wandsworth Coll, Univ of London (BSc), Univ of Southampton (Cert Ed), Univ of Sussex (Dip Ed Tech); *m* 27 Dec 1961, Catherine Mary, da of Thomas Adams; 1 s (Richard Lawrence b 25 Feb 1964), 1 da (Katherine Louise b 9 Nov 1966); *Career* head of economics Cheshunt GS 1962, cmmnd RAF 1965, post grad dip Sussex 1971, lead role in achieving organisational change in RAF trg 1972-75, involvement with fast jet ops RAF Germany 1975-78, introduction of Tornado into RAF serv 1979-81, chm Offr and Aircrew Selection Panel 1982; cmdg Offr: Training Wing RAF Hereford 1982-85, Admin Wing RAF Cosford 1985-87; gen mangr: Maternity and Child Health Services Grampian 1987-89 (winner Sunday Times Hosp of the Year and UK's Best Teaching Hosp 1989), Mental Health Services Grampian 1990-; *Recreations* hillwalking, badminton, golf, shooting; *Clubs* RAF; *Style*— Frank Hartnett, Esq, OBE; Grampian Health Board, Mental Health Services, Royal Cornhill Hospital, Cornhill Rd, Aberdeen (☎ 0224 681818 ext 57314)

HARTOP, Barry; s of Philip William Hartop (d 1954), of Lowestoft, and Constance Winifred Hartop; *b* 15 Aug 1942; *Educ* Lowestoft GS, Univ of Durham (BSc); *m* 30 July 1965, Sandra, da of Alan Walter Swan (d 1976), of Lowestoft; 1 s (James), 1 da (Anna); *Career* mgmnt trainee Unilever, prodn mangr Lever Bros, Unilever Coordination, Unilever Res Div (Euro Operational Res Rotterdam), head Euro Market Devpt and Application Centre Utrecht, chm and md Lever Industries UK, md Gestetner Group (office prods), dir Gestetner Holdings PLC; *Style*— Barry Hartop, Esq; Field Cottage, The Ridgeway, Guildford, Surrey (☎ 0483 577617); 66 Chiltern St, London W1M 2AP (☎ 071 465 1000)

HARTSHORNE, Dennis; *b* 1946; *Educ* Heanor GS Derbyshire, Univ of Lancaster (BA), Univ of Southampton (PGCE), Univ of Leicester (MA); *m* Janet; 2 s (Edward, James); *Career* dir: Birmingham Technol Ltd, Aston Sci Park, W Midlands Enterprise Bd, Birmingham Innovation and Devpt Centre; ed Br Atlantic Publications; Parly candidate (C) Stoke-on-Trent South 1987; memb Birmingham City Cncl: Fin and Mgmnt Ctee, Business and Investmt Ctee, Educn Ctee, Tourism and Promotions Ctee, Jt Consultative Ctee, Employment Ctee (chm 1982-84), Personnel Ctee, Gen Purposes and Licensing Ctee, Aid-To-Indust Ctee; memb Cncl Br Atlantic Ctee; chm: SW Birmingham CPC 1973-83, Bournville Cons Assoc 1981-82 (pres 1983-88); memb Exec Ctee Birmingham Cons Gp (responsible for local policy and election planning), chm Govrs Cadbury Coll; voluntary PR work for NATO (NATO fell 1980); MBIM; *Recreations* historical research; *Style*— Dennis Hartshorne, Esq; Chenda, 59 Bittell Rd, Barnt Green, Worcs (☎ 021 445 1645)

HARTSHORNE, (Bertram) Kerrich; s of Bertram Charles Hartshorne (d 1949), of Alexandria, Egypt, and Beatrice Mabel, *née* Spencer (d 1974); *b* 24 Nov 1923; *Educ* Charterhouse, Clare Coll Cambridge (MA), Birmingham Univ (MSc); *m* 27 Sept 1952, Jean Irving, da of Oswald Irving Bell (d 1946), of Dumfries; 3 s (David b 1954, Christopher b 1955, James b 1965), 1 da (Pamela b 1958); *Career* WWII RE 1942-47; cmmnd 1943, active serv with Royal Bombay Sappers and Miners in India, Burma and Indo-China (despatches 1946); commanded: field sqdn 1945, depot bn 1946-47; Sir William Halcrow & Ptnrs civil engrs: joined 1949, assoc 1969-73, ptnr 1973-84, conslt 1984-; dir Halcrow Fox & Assocs 1977-83; chm: Halcrow Surveys 1982-84, Sir William Halcrow & Ptnrs Scotland 1983-84; sr ptnr The Hartshorne Ptnrship 1985-; involved with many major projects incl: Volta River Project Ghana 1950-60, Pangani River Basin and Nym Dam Tanzania 1961-68, Orange Fish Tunnel 1963-64, military and civil devpt projects Sultanate of Oman 1973-79; FICE 1968, FInstHE 1970, memb ACE 1973; *Books* Transport Survey of the Territories of Papua and New Guinea (1971); *Recreations* sailing, landscape gardening, travelling; *Style*— Kerrich Hartshorne, Esq; Mill House, Irongray, Dumfries DG2 9SQ (☎ 038773 417); The Hartshorne Partnership, Oakwood Farm, Irongray, Dumfries DG2 9SQ (☎ 038773 493)

HARTWELL, Sir Brodrick William Charles Elwin; 5 Bt (UK 1805), of Dale Hall, Essex; s of Sir Brodrick Hartwell, 4 Bt (d 1948), and his 2 w, Joan; *b* 7 Aug 1909; *Educ* Bedford Sch; *m* 1, 1937 (m dis 1950), Marie, da of Simon Mullins; 1 s; m 2, 1951, Mary, MBE, da of J Church; (1 s, 1 da both decd); *Heir* s, Francis Antony Charles Peter Hartwell, *qv*; *Career* served RAF 1928-29, Army 1931-48 (Capt Leics Regt); *Style*— Sir Brodrick Hartwell, Bt; 50 High St, Lavendon, nr Olney, Bucks (☎ 0234 712619)

HARTWELL, Eric; CBE (1983); s of Alfred Hartwell (d 1932), of Holmleigh, West Parade, Worthing, Sussex, and Edyth Maud, *née* Brunning (d 1980); *b* 10 Aug 1915; *Educ* Mall Sch Twickenham, Worthing HS; *m* 1, 1937 (m dis 1951), Gladys Rose, *née* Bennett; 1 s (Anthony Charles b Jan 1939), 1 da (Susan b Jan 1946); m 2, 14 June 1952, Dorothy Maud, da of late Harold Mowbray, MM, of Edgware, Middx; 1 s (Keith Alan b Sept 1958), 1 da (Janine Erica b June 1956); *Career* served WWII with RE 1940-46 (QMSI); chief exec Trusthouse Forte plc 1978-83 (vice chm 1972-), chm Br Hotels Restaurants and Caterers Assoc 1981-84; memb Cncl CBI 1972-87 (memb Fin and Gen Purposes Ctee and chm Fin Sub Ctee 1980-87), fndr memb LV Catering Educnl Tst, vice chm Thames Heritage Tst 1983-87, memb Inner Magic Circle; Freeman City of London, Liveryman Worshipful Co of Upholders; CBIM, FHCIMA, FRSA, MIMC; *Recreations* yachting (yacht 'Kandora'), painting, photography, golf, magic; *Clubs* Thames Motor Yacht, South Herts Golf, Terenure Country, Inner Magic Circle; *Style*— Eric Hartwell, Esq, CBE; Tall Trees, 129 Totteridge Lane, London N20 8NS (☎ 081 445 2321); Trusthouse Forte plc, 166 High Holborn, London WC1V 6TT

HARTWELL, Francis Anthony Charles Peter; s and h of Sir Brodrick William Charles Elwin Hartwell, 5 Bt, *qv*; *b* 1 June 1940; *Educ* Thames Nautical Trg Coll, HMS Worcester, Cadet RNR, Univ of Southampton (Sch of Navigation-Master Mariner); *m* 26 Oct 1968, Barbara Phyllis Rae, da of Henry Rae Green (d 1985), of Sydney, Aust; 1 s (Timothy b 1970); *Career* P and OSNCO/Inchcape Gp 1958-69 and 1972-75: Chief Offr/Cadet trg Offr, Mate/master, OCL (London) 1969-71, Cargo Supt 1975-, Overseas Managerial Services for marine and port ops contracts, pt/t ind marine and cargo surveyor; nominated surveyor for Lloyd's Agency (Port Moresby) and The Salvage Assoc 1981-86; Port Advsy ctee 1981-82, memb Arbitration Tbnl 1982-83 and 1985 for Papua New Guinea Govt; gen mangr Marine Services-Port and Agency-WA Liner Agencies; memb Fed of Aust Underwater Instructors (FAUI), MCIT, MRIN; *Recreations* scuba diving, water skiing, photography, reading, philately; *Clubs* Master Mariners (Southampton), Old Worcester's Assoc; *Style*— Francis Hartwell, Esq; c/o Barclays Bank, 11 High St, Olney, Bucks

HARTWELL, Baron (Life Peer UK 1968), of Peterborough Court in the City of London; Hon (William) Michael Berry; MBE (1945), TD; 2 s of 1 Viscount Camrose; hp to bro, 2 Viscount; *b* 18 May 1911; *Educ* Eton, Ch Ch Oxford; *m* 1936, Lady Pamela, *née* Smith (d 1982), yr da of 1 Earl of Birkenhead; 2 s (Hon Adrian b 1937, Hon Nicholas b 1942), 2 da (Hon Harriet b 1944, Hon Eleanor b 1950); *Career* served WWII, Lt-Col 1944; dir Daily Telegraph plc, tstee Reuters 1963-89, ed Sunday Mail (Glasgow) 1934-35, managing ed Financial Times 1937-39, chm Amalgamated Press Ltd 1954-59; chm and ed-in-chief: Daily Telegraph 1954-87, Sunday Telegraph 1961-87; *Clubs* White's, Royal Yacht Sqdn, Beefsteak; *Style*— The Rt Hon Lord Hartwell, MBE, TD; Oving House, Oving, Aylesbury, Bucks (☎ 0296 641307); 18 Cowley St, London SW1 (☎ 071 222 4673)

HARTWELL, Roger John; s of John Stanton Hartwell (d 1978), and Eva, *née* Chapman; *b* 21 Feb 1943; *Educ* Magdalen Coll Sch Brackley, Univ of Bristol (LLB); *m* 3 June 1967, Rosemary Malvyn, da of Sydney Jackson (d 1969), of 15 Vale Walk, Worthing; 1 s (Nicolas Mark b 11 Feb 1969), 1 da (Suzanne Michelle b 21 Nov 1970); *Career* admitted slr 1966; ptnr Donne Mileham Haddock 1973-; pres: Worthing Lions Club 1973, Worthing Rotary Club 1984, Worthing and Dist Law Soc 1989-; vice-chm Worthing CAB; memb: Worthing Health Authy, Worthing Law Soc; *Recreations* triathlons, railways; *Style*— Roger Hartwell, Esq; Hythe Lodge, Hythe Rd, Worthing, Sussex BN11 5DA (☎ 0903 49625); 15a Chapel Rd, Worthing, W Sussex (☎ 0903 35026, fax 0903 30041)

HARTY, Bernard Peter; s of William Harty (d 1975), and Eileen Nora, *née* Canavan; *b* 1 May 1943; *Educ* St Richard's Coll Droitwich, Ullathorne GS Coventry; *m* 12 Aug 1965, Glenys Elaine, da of Ernest Simpson (d 1969); 1 da (Sarah Jane b 1970); *Career* accountant Coventry City Cncl 1961-69; forward budget planning offr Derbys CC 1969-72, chief accountant Bradford City Cncl 1972-73, chief fin offr Bradford Met Dist Cncl 1972-73, co treas Oxon County Cncl 1976-83; Chamberlain of Corp of London 1983-, chm Fndn for Information Technol in Local Govt; Liveryman Worshipful Co of Tallow Chandlers, Freeman Worshipful Co of Info Technol; IPFA, MBCS; *Recreations* Nat Tst, music cricket; *Style*— Bernard Harty, Esq; Chamberlain of London, Guildhall, London EC2P 2EJ (☎ 071 260 1300)

HARTY, Martin John; *b* 22 April 1952; *Educ* Ullathorne GS, Brasenose Coll Oxford (Ma); *m* 2 April 1982, Eily Goodall; 3 c; *Career* called to the Bar Middle Temple 1976; in practice at the Bar 1976-86, Phillips and Drew 1986-87, currently gp legal and compliance dir Credit Lyonnais Capital Markets plc; *Style*— Martin Harty, Esq; Credit Lyonnais Capital Markets PLC, Broadwalk House, 5 Appold Street, London EC2 (☎ 071 214 5250, fax 071 588 0299)

HARVEY, Alan Frederick Ronald; OBE (1970); s of Edward Frederick Harvey (d 1966), and Alice Sophia, *née* Cocks (d 1963); *b* 15 Dec 1919; *Educ* Tottenham GS; *m* 28 July 1946, Joan Barbara, da of Albert Henry Tuckey (d 1976), of Barnes; 1 s (Ian b 16 March 1952); *Career* RAF 1940-45: RAF station Amman 1940, Br Embassy Ankara

1942, Br Embassy Paris 1945; Air Miny 1946-49; Dip Serv: FO 1949-52, vice consul Turin 1953-55; second sec: Rome 1956, Tokyo 1957-59; consul (info) Chicago 1959-62, FO 1963-65; first sec (commercial): Belgrade 1965-67, Tokyo 1967-72; commercial cnsllr: Milan 1973-74, Rome 1975-76; consul gen Perth 1976-78; *Recreations* golf, gardening; *Clubs* Royal Cwlth Soc, Civil Serv, Windwhistle Golf, Squash and Country; *Style—* Alan Harvey, Esq, OBE; The Mews, Leigh Court, Forton, Chard, Somerset TA20 4HW

HARVEY, Anthony Peter; s of Frederick William Henry Harvey, of Kettering, Northants, and Fanny Evelyn, *née* Dixon (d 1978); *b* 21 March 1940; *Educ* Hertford GS; *m* 16 Jan 1963, Margaret, da of Walter Henry Hayward, of Hastings, Sussex; 3 s (Terence b 7 Jan 1966, Iain b 7 June 1967, Kevin b 18 March 1972), 1 da (Joanne b 24 Sept 1970); *Career* British Museum (Natural History) now The Natural History Museum: head Dept of Library Servs 1981-88, coordinator of planning and devpt 1985-88, head Dept of Marketing and Devpt 1988-; dir The Natural History Museum Devpt Tst 1990- (sec 1988-); author of numerous papers in professional journals; Freeman of the City of London 1985, Liveryman of Worshipful Co of Marketors 1990-; MInstInfSci, FRGS, FRHS, memb Soc for History of Natural History; *Books* Directory of Scientific Directories (1969, 2 edn 1972, 4 edn 1986), Guide to World Science (1974), Geoscience Information: an international state-of-the-art review (ed 1979), Walford's Guide to Reference Material (ed 1980), Natural History Manuscript Resources in the British Isles (jt ed 1980), European Sources of Scientific and Technical Information (jt ed 1981, 1983, 1984), The Petrology of Archaeological Artifacts (jt ed 1984); *Recreations* books, music, countryside, gardens and gardening; *Clubs* City Livery; *Style—* Anthony Harvey, Esq; Ragstones, Broad Oak, Heathfield, E Sussex TN21 8UD (tel/fax 04352 2012); Natural History Museum, London SW7 5BD (☎ 071 938 8962, fax 071 938 9066)

HARVEY, Barbara Fitzgerald; da of Richard Henry Harvey (d 1960), of Teignmouth, and Anne Fitzgerald, *née* Julian (d 1974); *b* 21 Jan 1928; *Educ* Teignmouth GS, Bishop Blackall Sch Exeter, Somerville Coll Oxford (BLitt, MA); *Career* asst lectr Dept of Scottish History Univ of Edinburgh 1951-52, lectr Dept of History Queen Mary Coll London 1952-55, vice princ Somerville Coll Oxford 1981-83 (tutor in medieval history 1955-, fell 1956-, vice princ 1976-79), reader (ad hominem) Oxford Univ 1990-; fell: Royal Historical Soc 1960- (vice pres 1986-90), Br Acad 1982-; memb Royal Cmmn on Historical Manuscripts 1991-; *Books* Westminster Abbey and its Estates in the Middle Ages (1977), The Westminster Chronicle 1381-1394 (ed with L C Hector, 1982); *Clubs* University Women's; *Style—* Miss Barbara Harvey; 66 Cranham St, Oxford OX2 6DD (☎ 0865 54766); Somerville College, Oxford OX2 6HD (☎ 0865 270600)

HARVEY, Prof Brian Wilberforce; s of Gerald Harvey, and Noelle, *née* Dean; *b* 17 March 1936; *Educ* Clifton, St John's Coll Cambridge (choral scholar, MA, LLM); *Career* slr 1961, lectr Univ of Birmingham 1962-63, sr lectr Nigerian Law Sch 1965-67; Queen's Univ of Belfast 1967-73: lectr, sr lectr, prof of Law; pro vice chllr Univ of Birmingham 1986- (prof of property law 1973-), chm: Medical Appeals Tbnls and Social Security Appeals Tbnls Birmingham 1982-, Consumer Credit Appeals 1990-; memb Br Hallmarking Cncl 1989, tstee Ouseley Tst 1988-; *Books* Settlements of Land (1973), Law of Consumer Protection and Fair Trading (1978, 3rd edn 1987), Law of Auction (jtly, 1985), Law of Producing and Marketing Goods and Services (jtly, 1990); *Recreations* theological speculation, studying violins, music; *Style—* Brian Harvey, Esq; c/o Faculty of Law, The University, Birmingham B15 2TT (☎ 021 414 5936)

HARVEY, (Sir) Charles Richard Musgrave; 3 Bt (UK 1933), of Threadneedle St, City of London; does not use title; s of Sir Richard Musgrave Harvey, 2 Bt (d 1978), and Frances, *née* Lawford (d 1986); *b* 7 April 1937; *Educ* Marlborough, Pembroke Coll Cambridge; *m* 1967, Celia Vivien, da of George Henry Hodson; 1 s, 1 da (Tamara b 1977); *Heir* s, Paul Richard Harvey b 2 June 1971; *Career* fell Inst of Devpt Studies Univ of Sussex; *Style—* Charles Harvey, Esq; 33 Preston Park Avenue, Brighton, Sussex BN1 6HG; IDS, University of Sussex, Brighton BN1 9RE (☎ 0273 606261, telex 877159 RR HOVE IDS)

HARVEY, Cynthia Theresa; da of Gordon G Harvey, of Greenville, S Carolina, and Clara de Ojeda Harvey; *b* 17 May 1957; *Educ* San Marin HS NY USA; *Career* ballerina; American Ballet Theatre: joined 1974, soloist 1978-, princ dancer 1982, danced maj roles in all classical ballets incl Swan Lake, Giselle, Romeo and Juliet; Royal Ballet (Covent Gdn): joined as first American ballerina 1986, roles inc Sleeping Beauty, Odine, Manon, Meyerling; symphonic variations created roles in Wayne Eagling's Beauty and the Beast, David Bintley's Still Life of the Penguin Cafe, danced premier of Anthony Dowell's Swan Lake; co starred in video film Don Quixote with Mikhail Baryshnikov, appeared in Channel 4 prodn Tehaikow; Skys Women 1988; memb Bd of Dirs Sightsavers Int; received John Anthony Bittson Award (for achievement in dance) 1974; *Recreations* football supporter, body conditioning, theatre goer, snorkeling; *Style—* Miss Cynthia Harvey; c/o Royal Ballet, Royal Opera House, Covent Garden WC2E 9DD (☎ 071 240 1200)

HARVEY, Prof David R; s of Capt John Harvey (d 1983), of New Milton, Hants, and Ann, *née* Dodgson; *b* 24 Oct 1947; *Educ* Berkhamsted Sch, Univ of Newcastle (BSc), Univ of Manchester (MA, PhD); *m* 1, (m dis 1984), Catherine, *née* Whitehead; 2 s (Daniel John b 1975, James b 1977); m 2, 9 April 1985, Joan, da of John Hayward, of Ripon, Yorks; 1 s (John b 1985); *Career* asst lectr Univ of Manchester 1972-73, sr economist of agric Ottawa Canada 1977-79 (economist of agric 1973-76); prof: Univ of Reading 1984-86, Univ of Newcastle 1986- (lectr 1979-83); memb Nat Ctee SDP 1983-87; *Books* Costs of The Common Agricultural Policy (1982); *Style—* Prof David Harvey; Dept of Agricultural Economics and Food Marketing, The University, Newcastle upon Tyne NE1 7RU (☎ 091 222 6000 ext 6872, fax 091 261 1182, telex 53654)

HARVEY, Dr David Robert; s of Cyril Francis Harvey (d 1971), of Orpington, Kent, and Margarita, *née* Cardew-Smith (d 1986); *b* 7 Dec 1936; *Educ* Dulwich, Guy's Hosp Med Sch (MB BS); *Career* held jr appointments in paediatrics: Guy's Hosp, Gt Ormond St, Hammersmith Hosp; conslt paediatrician: Queen Charlotte's Maternity Hosp 1970-, St Charles Hosp 1971-, St Mary's Hosp 1987-; hon sec: Neonatal Soc 1974-79, British Paediatric Assoc 1979-84, British Assoc for Perinatal Paediatrics 1983-86; dir: Terence Higgins Tst 1983-88, Radio Lollipop; Freeman of City of London, memb Worshipful Soc of Apothecaries; MRCP 1963, FRCP 1976; *Books* articles on general and neonatal paediatrics and child health, A New Life (1979), New Parents (1988); *Recreations* opera, learning Chinese, using word processor; *Style—* Dr David Harvey; 2 Lord Napier Place, Upper Mall, London W6 9UB (☎ 081 748 7900); Queen Charlotte's and Chelsea Hospital, Goldhawk Road, London W6 OXG (☎ 081 740 3918)

HARVEY, David Stanley; s of Stanley Joseph Harvey (d 1964), and Edna Nancy May, *née* Harvey; *b* 2 Aug 1952; *Educ* Gresham's; *m* 3 April 1981, Kerry Louise, da of David Owen; 2 s (James b 1978, Travis b 1982), 1 da (Lucy b 1986); *Career* slr; memb Law Soc; *Recreations* sailing, swimming; *Style—* David S Harvey, Esq; 11 Street on Gurrow, St Ives, Cornwall (☎ 0736 793786)

HARVEY, David William; s of Frederick Hercules Harvey, MBE (d 1963), and Doris Maude, *née* Morton (d 1977); *b* 31 Oct 1935; *Educ* Gillingham GS, St John's Coll Cambridge (BA, MA, PhD); *Career* lectr Univ of Bristol 1961-69, prof of geography The John Hopkins Univ Baltimore 1969-89, Halford Mackinder prof of geography Oxford Univ 1987-; fell Inst Br Geographers, memb Assoc of American Geographers; Anders Retzius Gold medal Swedish Anthropology and Geography Soc 1989, Gill Meml Royal Geographical Soc 1972; *Books* Explanation in Geography (1969), Social Justice and the City (1973), The Limits to Capital (1982), The Urbanisation of Capital (1985), Consciousness & The Urban Experience (1985), The Urban Experience (1989), The Condition of Postmodernity (1989); *Style—* Prof David Harvey; 27 Hart St, Jericho, Oxford OX2 6BN (☎ 0865 511412); School of Geography, University of Oxford, Mansfield Rd, Oxford OX1 3TB (☎ 0865 271930, fax 0865 270708)

HARVEY, Ian Alexander; s of Dr Alexander Harvey (d 1987), and Mona, *née* Anderson; *b* 2 Feb 1945; *Educ* Cardiff HS, Univ of Cambridge (MA), Harvard Business Sch (MBA); *m* 21 Nov 1976, Dr DeAnne Julius, da of Prof Marvin Julius, of Ames, Iowa, USA; 1 s (Ross b 1980), 1 da (Megan b 1979); *Career* apprentice mech engr Vickers Ltd 1963-69, project engr Laporte Industs 1969-73, sr loan offr World Bank 1975-82, ptnr Logan Assocs Inc 1984-85, chief exec Br Technol Gp 1985-; memb: Cabinet Office Advsy Cncl on Sci and Technol, Res and Mfrg Ctee CBI, Sci and Industl Ctee Br Assoc for Advancement of Sci; CBIM 1987; *Recreations* piano, skiing, sailing, windsurfing; *Style—* Ian Harvey, Esq; British Technology Group, 101 Newington Causeway, London SE1 6BU (☎ 071 403 6666, fax 071 403 7586, telex 894397)

HARVEY, Jane Margaret; da of Dr William James Harvey, of The Hirsel, Coldstream, Berkwicks, and Ann Margaret, *née* Shaw; *b* 10 June 1958; *Educ* St Mary's Convent Longridge Towers Berwick upon Tweed, Univ of Edinburgh (Bsc, Dip MBA); *m* 28 June 1986, Timothy Ernest Myer, s of Henry Ernest Myer, of 86 Deacons Hill Rd, Elstree, Herts; *Career* res analyst: McKinsey and Co Inc 1982-84, The Mac Gp 1984-85; mktg mangr One to One 1985-86, account dir Shandwick Communications 1986-88, ptnr Harrington Communications; *Style—* Mrs Jane Harvey; 44 Burtonhole Lane, London NW7 1AL (☎ 081 959 3475); Harrington Communications, 16-17 Junction Mews, Clapham, London W2 1PN (☎ 071 723 3633)

HARVEY, Jean; da of Lt WJ Harvey, DSM (d 1983), of Harrow, Middx, and Amy, *née* Benfield (d 1979); *b* 19 Sept 1936; *Educ* Univ of London (BA); *Career* Sunday Times 1963-69, fndr Jean Harvey Group 1969 (publishing, PR, fundraising, entertainment), publicity dir Methodist Homes for the Aged; MIPR 1988, MICFM 1990; *Books* Jean Harvey's Bedside Book (1986); *Videos* Charity Fundraising (1989 and 1990); *Recreations* photography, antiquarian book collecting; *Clubs* Groucho, University Women of America; *Style—* Ms Jean Harvey; Wheelwright's Cottage, Litton Cheney, Dorchester, Dorset DT2 9AR

HARVEY, John Charles Tolmie; s of John St Clair Harvey (d 1959), and Carol May, *née* Tolmie (d 1960); *b* 10 Sept 1937; *Educ* Harrow, Clare Coll Cambridge (MA); *m* 6 June 1961 (m dis), (Irene Margaret) Rosamund, *née* Gillespie; 2 da (Julia Carol b 22 June 1962, Mary Elizabeth b 20 July 1964); m 2, 13 Feb 1971, Elizabeth Laura, *née* Bradish-Ellames; 1 s (John James Russell b 10 March 1975), 1 da (Kate Sally b 19 June 1972); *Career* Nat Serv 2 Lt 1 Queen's Royal Lancers 1956-58, Lt Royal Gloucestershire Hussars TA; int trade dir Harveys of Bristol; pres Bristol Children's Help Soc, warden Soc of Merchant Venturers, former pres Grateful Soc, chm Harrow Assoc; Freeman: City of Bristol, City of London; memb Worshipful Co of Vintners; *Recreations* racing, fishing; *Clubs* Army and Navy, Clifton; *Style—* John Harvey, Esq; 1 Miles Rd, Clifton, Bristol BS8 2JN (☎ 0272 253253); John Harvey & Sons Ltd, 12 Denmark St, Bristol BS1 4DD (☎ 0272 836161, fax 0272 833878, telex 44100)

HARVEY, Prof Jonathan Dean; s of Gerald Harvey, and Noelle Heron, *née* Dean (d 1969); *b* 3 May 1939; *Educ* St Michael's Coll Tenbury, Repton, St John's Coll Cambridge (MA, DMus), Univ of Glasgow (PhD); *m* 24 Sept 1960, Rosaleen Marie, da of Daniel Barry (d 1949); 1 s (Dominic b 3 May 1967), 1 da (Anna Maria b 13 Jan 1964); *Career* composer; lectr Univ of Southampton 1964-77, Harkness fell Princeton Univ 1969-70, prof of music Univ of Sussex 1980- (reader 1977-80); works performed at many festivals and int centres; compositions: Persephone Dream (for orchestra, 1972), Inner Light (trilogy for performers and tape, 1973-77), Smiling Immortal (for chamber orchestra, 1977), String Quartet (1977), Veils and Melodies (for tapes, 1978), Magnificat and Nunc Dimitis (for choir and organ, 1978), Album (for wind quintet, 1978), Hymn (for choir and orchestra, 1979), Be(com)ing (for clarinet and piano, 1979), Concelebration (instrumental, 1979 and 1981), Mortuos Plango Vivos Voco (for tape, 1980), Passion and Resurrection (church opera, 1981), Resurrection (for double chorus and organ, 1981), Whom ye Adore (for orchestra, 1981), Bhakti (for 15 instruments and tape, 1982), Easter Orisons (for chamber orchestra, 1983), The Path of Devotion (for choir and orchestra, 1983), Nachtlied (for soprano piano and tape, 1984), Gong-Ring (for ensemble with electronics 1984), Song Offerings (for soprano and players, 1985), Madonna of Winter and Spring (for orchestra synthesizers and electronics, 1986), Lightness and Weight (for tuba and orchestra, 1986), Forms of Emptiness (for choir, 1986), Tendril (for ensemble, 1987), Timepieces (for orchestra, 1987), From Silence (for soprano 6 instruments and tape, 1988), Valley of Aosta (for 13 players 1988), String Quartet No 2 (1989), Ritual Melodies (for tape, 1990), Cello Concerto (for cello and orchestra, 1990); memb Academia Europaea 1989, Hon D Mus Univ of Southampton 1990; *Books* The Music of Stockhausen (1975); *Recreations* tennis, meditation; *Style—* Prof Jonathan Harvey; 35 Houndean Rise, Lewes, Sussex BN7 1EQ (☎ 0273 471 241)

HARVEY, Lawrence M; s of Charles Harry Harvey, and Queenie, *née* Schryber; *b* 19 Sept 1951; *Educ* UCS, UCL (LLB); *m* 14 Oct 1982, Marian, da of Philip Rosenblatt (d 1974), of London; 1 s (Daniel Philip b 13 July 1985), 1 da (Rebecca Louise b 10 June 1987); *Career* dir Anglo-Continental Gp and Wessex Homes Gp 1974-78; md: Harvey Gp 1978-87, Metfield Estates 1987-; chm Supporting Ctee for Nat Assoc Mentally Handicapped Children 1972-78, prison visitor 1974-82; Freeman City of London 1982, Liveryman Worshipful Co of Glovers 1982; MInstD; *Recreations* bridge, golf, theatre; *Clubs* City Livery, RAC; *Style—* Lawrence Harvey, Esq; 305 Ballards Lane, London N12

HARVEY, (Graham) Lionel; s of C Harvey, of 36 Westway, Stoneleigh, Epsom, Surrey, and BMH Harvey (d 1980); *b* 29 Aug 1936; *Educ* Reading Sch, Queen's Coll Oxford (MA); *m* 1 (m dis 1980), J Harvey; 4 s (Philip b 1962, Robert b 1966, James b 1967, Jonathan 1971), 5 da (Carolyn b 1963, Jane b 1964, Samantha b 1965, Katherine b 1970, Victoria b 1972); m 2, 25 Sept 1981, Rosemary Joyce, da of RJ Harvey, of Keynsham; *Career* planning mangr GE (USA) 1966-69, corp planning dir Lex Serv plc 1978 - (corp planning mangr 1969-78); chm of several local PTA'S, memb CBI Econ Ctee; *Recreations* cycling, walking, food and wine; *Style—* Lionel Harvey, Esq; Lex Service plc, 17 Connaught Place, London W2 2EL (☎ 071 723 1212)

HARVEY, Lady Mary Katherine; *née* Coke; da of 4 Earl of Leicester (d 1949), and Marion, da of Col Hon Walter Trefusis, CB (3 s of 19 Baron Clinton by his w, Lady Elizabeth Kerr, da of 6 Marquess of Lothian); *b* 7 March 1920; *m* 1940, Maj Thomas Harvey, CVO, DSO, *qv*; 1 s (David b 1941), 2 da (Mrs Nicholas Raison b 1943, Mrs Richard Hambro b 1947); *Career* woman of the bedchamber to HM Queen Elizabeth The Queen Mother 1961-63; *Style—* The Lady Mary Harvey; Warham House, Warham, Wells-next-the-Sea, Norfolk (☎ 0328 710457)

HARVEY, Michael; s of Owen Harvey (d 1961), of Bishop's Waltham, Hants, and Amy

Marie Elise, *née* Wood; *b* 12 April 1934; *Educ* Winchester, Oriel Coll Oxford (MA); *m* 1 Oct 1970, Susan (d 1988), da of Hans Schaffner-Buerli, of Baden, Switzerland; 1 da (Deborah Ann b 1973); *Career* Nat Serv Rifleman KRRC, 2 Lt Royal Hampshire Regt 1952-54; Shell Cos (Indonesia, Argentina, Switzerland, France, Nigeria, The Netherlands) 1957-86, gp treas Royal Dutch Shell Gp of Cos London 1986-; ACIS; *Style—* Michael Harvey, Esq; 12 Melton Court, Old Brompton Rd, London SW7 3JQ; Shell International Petroleum Co Ltd, Shell Centre, London SE1 7NA (☎ 071 934 4064, fax 071 934 8060, telex 919651)

HARVEY, Michael Anthony; s of Edgar Charles Harvey (d 1975), of Dorking, Surrey, and Evelyn May, *née* Klein (d 1976); *b* 22 Aug 1921; *Educ* Bryanston, Selly Oak Coll Woodbrooke Birmingham, Wimbledon Sch of Art (Intermediate Exam in Art and Crafts, Nat Dip in Design); *m* 30 Oct 1965 (m dis 1973), (Anne) Jennifer; 1 s (Anthony b 1966); *Career* Friends' Ambulance Unit 1940-42, Fishing Fleet 1942-43, MN 1943-55, awarded Africa Star 1945; artist; teacher: Royal Alexandra and Albert Schs Reigate 1957-59, Ewell Castle Sch Surrey 1959-64, Tollington Park Sch 1965-69, Ct Lodge Sch Horley 1970-76; exhibited paintings: Qantas Gallery W1 1964, Royal Acad 1965, Fine Arts Gallery W1 1967, John Whibley Gallery W1 1969-70, Rutland Gallery W1 1970-71, Royal Inst of Oil Painters, Royal Soc of Br Artists, Royal Inst of Oil Painters Aust 1977, Silver Longboat Exhibition Portsmouth and Oslo 1988 and 1990; awarded Linton prize for Painting 1972, art critic Surrey Mirror Group of Newspapers 1973-80, art corr Croydon Advertiser Group 1975-78; memb: Chichester Art Soc, Ctee Reigate Soc of Artists; tutor and memb Bognor Regis Art Soc, life memb Int Assoc of Art 1970, memb Cncl Soc of Graphic Fine Art 1980-; FRSA; *Recreations* sailing; *Clubs* Royal Soc of Arts; *Style—* Michael Harvey, Esq; 15 Waterloo Sq, Bognor Regis, W Sussex (☎ 0243 863 732)

HARVEY, Michael Francis Charles; s of William Charles Harvey (d 1980), and Winifred Esther, *née* Harwood Butler (d 1986); *b* 23 July 1935; *Educ* Colchester Royal GS, Univ of Oxford (BA); *m* 24 Oct 1964, Julie Erwina, da of Dr Joseph Gaston (d 1952); 1 s (Mark Gaston Charles b 19 Dec 1967), 1 da (Ruth Philippa b 7 May 1966); *Career* Nat Serv RAF 1953-55; asst slr Reading CBC 1962-65, sr asst slr East Suffolk CC 1965-68; county prosecuting slr: Suffolk Police Authy 1968-74, Suffolk CC 1974-86; chief crown prosecutor Norfolk Suffolk area 1986-; vice pres Felixstowe Rotary Club; *Recreations* gardening, foreign travel; *Style—* Michael Harvey, Esq; 33 Cordy's Lane, Trimley St Mary, Ipswich, Suffolk 1P10 0UD (☎ 0394 282822); Saxon House, Cromwell Sq, Ipswich, Suffolk 1P1 1TS (☎ 0473 230332, fax 0473 231377)

HARVEY, Michael Llewellyn Tucker; QC (1982); s of Rev Victor Llewellyn Tucker Harvey, of Suffolk, and Pauline, *née* Wybrow; *b* 22 May 1943; *Educ* St John's Sch Leatherhead, Christ's Coll Cambridge (BA, LLB, MA); *m* 2 Sept 1972, Denise Madeleine, da of Leonard Walter Neary, of London; 1 s (Julian b 19 June 1976), 1 da (Alexandra b 30 June 1973); *Career* called to the Bar Gray's Inn 1966, recorder 1986; *Books* Damages in Halsbury's Laws of England (jt contrib, 4 edn 1975); *Recreations* shooting, golf; *Clubs* Athenaeum, Hawks (Cambridge); *Style—* Michael Harvey, Esq, QC; 2 Crown Office Row, Temple, London EC4Y 7HJ (☎ 071 353 9337, fax 071 583 0589, telex 8954005 TWOCOR G)

HARVEY, Prof Paul Dean Adshead; s of John Dean Monroe Harvey (d 1978), and Gwendolen Mabel Darlington, *née* Adshead; *b* 7 May 1930; *Educ* Bishop Feild Coll St John's Newfoundland, Warwick Sch, St John's Coll Oxford (BA, MA, DPhil); *m* 6 July 1968, Yvonne, da of Howard Leonard Crossman (d 1965); *Career* asst archivist Warwick Co Record Off 1954-56, asst keeper Dept of Manuscripts Br Museum 1957-66, sr lectr Dept of History Univ of Southampton 1970-78 (lectr 1966-70), prof of medieval history Univ of Durham 1978-85 (emeritus prof 1985-); gen ed: Southampton Records Series 1966-78, Portsmouth Record Series 1969-; vice pres Surtees Soc 1978, memb Advsy Cncl on Public Records 1984-89, hon fell Portsmouth Poly 1987; FRHistS 1961, FSA 1963; *Books* The Printed Maps of Warwickshire 1576-1900 (with H Thorpe 1959), A Medieval Oxfordshire Village: Cuxham 1240-1400 (1965), Manorial Records of Cuxham Oxfordshire 1200-1359 (ed, 1976), The History of Topographical Maps (1980), The Peasant Land Market in England (ed, 1984), Manorial Records (1984), Local Maps and Plans from Medieval England (ed with R A Skelton, 1986); contrib to: Victoria History of Oxfordshire Vol 10 (1972), History of Cartography Vol 1 (1987), Agricultural History Review, Economic History Review, Past and Present; *Recreations* Br topography; *Style—* Prof P D A Harvey; Lyndhurst, Farnley Hey Road, Durham DH1 4EA (☎ 091 386 9396)

HARVEY, Peter; CB (1980); s of George Leonard Hunton Harvey (d 1948), and Helen Mary, *née* Williams (d 1973); *b* 23 April 1922; *Educ* King Edward VI HS Birmingham, St John's Coll Oxford (MA, BCL); *m* 1950, Mary Vivienne, da of John Osborne Goss (d 1971); 1 s (Roderick), 1 da (Vivienne); *Career* RAF 1942-45; called to the Bar Lincoln's Inn 1948, legal asst Home Office 1948, princ asst legal advsr Home Office 1971-77, legal advsr Dept of Educn and Sci 1977-83, conslt Legal Advsr's Branch Home Office 1983-86, asst to Speaker's Counsel House of Commons 1986-; *Publications* contrib to 3 and 4 edns of Halsbury's Laws of England; *Recreations* walking, history; *Style—* Peter Harvey, Esq, CB; Mannamead, Old Ave, Weybridge, Surrey KT13 0PS (☎ 0932 845133)

HARVEY, Peter Martin Seaver; s of George Edward Harvey (d 1960); *b* 16 July 1927; *Educ* St John's Coll, Hurstpierpoint Coll of Estate Mgmnt; *m* 1962, Maureen Richardson, da of Dr Arthur Gray (d 1979); 1 s, 1 da; *Career* Capt India and Malaya; md Herring Son and Daw (chartered surveyors) 1976-79 (ptnr-dir 1964-75); FRICS; *Recreations* shooting, fly-fishing, squash; *Clubs* Army and Navy; *Style—* Peter Harvey, Esq; Flat 5, 26/28 Sackville St, London W1 (☎ 071 734 8155); Kempson House, Whitchurch, Bucks (☎ 0296 641 205)

HARVEY, Hon Philip William Vere; s of Baron Harvey of Prestbury (Life Peer), and Jacqueline Anne, *née* Dunnet; *b* 4 March 1942; *Educ* Eton, Geneva Univ; *Career* insur broker; md Harvey and Boyd Ltd; *Recreations* skiing; *Style—* The Hon Philip Harvey

HARVEY, Richard Charles; s of Cyril Joseph Harvey (d 1988), and Elsa, *née* Syer (d 1977); *b* 5 Sept 1935; *Educ* Caterham Sch, Merton Coll Oxford (MA); *m* 22 Sept 1962, Susan Rae, da of Bernard Sidney Keeling, of Southwold, Suffolk; 1 s (Ben b 29 Aug 1967), 1 da (Sarah b 4 June 1965); *Career* Nat Serv 2 Lt RASC; ptnr Slaughter and May 1969-; Liveryman Worshipful Co of Slrs; memb Law Soc (cncl memb 1980, chm Trg Ctee 1986-89); *Recreations* golf, skiing, fly fishing, tennis; *Clubs* Hurlingham, Royal Wimbledon Golf, Leander; *Style—* Richard Harvey, Esq

HARVEY, Robert Lambart; *b* 21 Aug 1953; *Educ* Eton, Christ Church Oxford; *Career* contested (C): Caernarvon Oct 1974, Merioneth 1979; MP (C) Clwyd South West 1983-87; memb: NUJ, Bow Gp; BBC broadcaster, asst ed The Economist, columnist The Daily Telegraph; *Style—* Robert Harvey, Esq

HARVEY, Maj Thomas Cockayne; CVO (1951), DSO (1944), ERD; s of Col John Harvey, DSO, whose mother, Rosa, was 6 da of Adm Hon Keith Stewart, CB (2 s of 8 Earl of Galloway), by Mary Fitzroy (paternally ggda of 3 Duke of Grafton and maternally gda of 4 Duke of Richmond); *b* 22 Aug 1918; *Educ* Radley, Balliol Coll Oxford; *m* 1940, Lady Mary Katherine, *qv*; 1 s, 2 da; *Career* joined Scots Gds 1938, serv Norway 1940, Italy 1944; private sec to HM The Queen 1946-51, extra gentleman usher to HM King George VI 1951-52 (to HM The Queen 1952-); regnl dir Lloyds Bank 1980-85; Capt The Royal and Ancient Golf Club of St Andrews 1976-77; *Recreations* golf, shooting; *Clubs* White's, Beefsteak; *Style—* Maj Thomas Harvey, CVO, DSO, ERD; Warham House, Warham, Wells-next-the-Sea, Norfolk (☎ 0328 710 457)

HARVEY-JONES, Sir John Henry; MBE (1952); s of Mervyn Harvey-Jones, OBE, and Eileen Harvey-Jones; *b* 16 April 1924; *Educ* Tormore Sch Deal, RNC Dartmouth; *m* 1947, Mary Evelyn Atcheson, er da of E F Bignell and Mrs E Atcheson; 1 da; *Career* served in RN 1937-56, submarines and naval intelligence, qualifying as German and Russian interpreter; ICI: joined as work study offr 1956, dir 1973-, dep chm 1978-81, chm 1982-87 (dep chm Heavy Organic Chemicals Div, chm ICI Petrochemicals Div); former chm Phillips-Imperial Petroleum, memb NE Devpt Bd 1971-73; dir: Carrington Viyella Ltd 1974-79 and 1981-82, Reed Int plc 1975-84; dep chm: Grand Metropolitan Plc 1987 (joined 1983), GPA Ltd 1989- (joined 1987); chm: The Economist 1989 (joined 1987), Parallax Enterprises 1987-, Burns Anderson 1987-90 (non-exec dir 1987); non-exec chm Business International Ctee 1988-, memb Advsy Bd New European 1987; TV presenter Troubleshooter (BBC) 1990; vice pres Indust Participation Assoc 1983; memb: Cncl British-Malaysian Soc 1983-, Advsy Cncl Prince's Tst 1986-, Bd Welsh Devpt Int 1989; vice chm: Policy Studies Inst 1980-85, BIM 1980-; hon vice pres Inst of Mktg 1982-89; pres: Conseil Européen des Fédérations de l'Industrie Chimique (CEFIC) 1984- (vice pres 1982-84), Book Tst Appeal Fund 1987, Wider Share Ownership Cncl 1988-; tstee: Science Museum 1983-, Police Fndn (chm of tstees) 1984-; hon fell: Royal Soc or Chemistry 1985, Inst of Chemical Engrs 1985; Hon LLD: Univ of Manchester 1985, Univ of London 1988, Univ of Nottingham 1988, Univ of Keele 1989; DUniv Surrey 1985; Hon DSc: Univ of Bradford 1986, Univ of Leicester 1986; Hon DBA Int Mgmnt Centres 1990; sr ind fell Leicester Poly 1990; memb: Soc of Chemical Indust 1978-, RSA 1979 (vice pres 1988); patron: Cambridge Univ Young Entrepreneurs Soc 1987-, Manpower Servs Cmmn Nat Trg awards 1987-, Steer Orgn, Nat Canine Defence League 1990-; vice patron Br Polio Fellowship 1988-; vice pres: Hearing and Speech Tst 1985-, Heaton Woods Tst 1986; chllr Univ of Bradford 1986-; BIM Gold medal 1985, Soc of Chemical Indust Centenary medal 1986, Jo Hambro Businessman of the Year 1987, Assoc of Business Communications award of excellence in communication 1987, Radar Man of the Year 1987; Cdr's Cross Order of Merit of Fed Republic of Germany 1985; kt 1985; *Books* Making it Happen (1988), Troubleshooter (1990), Getting it Together (1991); *Recreations* ocean sailing, swimming, the countryside, cooking, contemporary literature; *Clubs* Athenaeum, The Groucho; *Style—* Sir John Harvey-Jones, MBE; Parallax Enterprises, PO Box 18, Ross-on-Wye, Herefordshire HR9 7TL (☎ 098 985 430, fax 098 985 427)

HARVEY-KELLY, (Hugh) Denis; s of Lt-Col Charles Hamilton Grant Harvey-Kelly, DSO (d 1982), of Clonhugh, Mullingar, and Sybil Mary, *née* Nuttall (d 1980); paternal (Kelly) lineage listed in Burke's Irish Family Records; *b* 5 March 1932; *Educ* Wellington, RMA Sandhurst; *m* 20 June 1964, Jennifer Rosemary, da of John Elton-Phillips (d 1943); 1 da (Sarah b 1971); *Career* Capt 8KRI Hussars Germany and Aden 1949-57; Vickers da Costa Stockbrokers London 1958-84, Dudgeon & Sons Stockbrokers Dublin; dir: Investment Bank of Ireland 1968-85, Marlborough Prodns plc 1985-87; chm: Ovidstown Bloodstock 1984-, Dolormore plc 1985-87; master of Foxhounds Westmeath Hunt 1979-83; *Recreations* hunting, shooting, fishing; *Clubs* Kildare St University; *Style—* Denis Harvey-Kelly, Esq; 16 Philbeach Gardens, London SW5 9KK (☎ 071 370 1098, fax 071 370 6630); Pinel-Hante Rive 47380, Mouclar, France (☎ 53010445)

HARVEY OF PRESTBURY, Baron (Life Peer UK 1971); Arthur Vere Harvey; CBE (1942); s of Arthur Harvey; *b* 31 Jan 1906; *Educ* Framlingham Coll; *m* 1, 1940 (m dis 1954), Jacqueline, da of W Dunnett; 2 s (Hon Philip *qv*, Hon Guy *qv*); m 2, 1955 (m dis 1975), Hilary (d 1975), da of David Charles and formerly w of Lt-Col Brian Robertson Williams; m 3, 1978, Carol, da of late Austin Cassar-Torregiani; 3 adopted da (Charmaine, Romona, Petra); *Career* Air Cdre RAuxAF; served RAF 1925-30, Flying Instructor; dir Far East Aviation Co and Far East Flying Training Sch 1930-35; advsr to S Chinese AF and Sqdn Ldr AAF, served WWII France (despatches twice); MP (C) Macclesfield 1945-71, chm 1922 Ctee 1966-70; chm CIBA-GEIGY (UK) Ltd 1957-72, dir Tradewinds Airways; Hon DSc Salford; FRAeS; Order of Orange Nassau; kt 1957; *Clubs* Royal Yacht Sqdn, Buck's, RAF; *Style—* The Rt Hon the Lord Harvey of Prestbury, CBE; Rocklands, Les Vardes, St Peter Port, Guernsey, CI

HARVEY OF TASBURGH, 2 Baron (UK 1954); Sir Peter Charles Oliver Harvey; 5 Bt (UK 1868); s of 1 Baron, GCMG, GCVO, CB, Ambass France 1948-54 (d 1968), and Maud, da of Arthur Williams-Wynn (gn of Sir Watkin Williams-Wynn, 4 Bt); *b* 28 Jan 1921; *Educ* Eton, Trinity Coll Cambridge; *m* 1957, Penelope, yr da of Lt-Col Sir William Makins, 3 Bt; 2 da (Hon Juliet b 1958, Hon Miranda b 1960); *Heir* bro, Hon John Harvey *qv*; *Career* served WWII RA N Africa and Italy; CA investmt conslt Brown Shipley and Co 1978-81; formerly with Bank of England, Lloyd's Bank Int Ltd, English Transcontinental Ltd; *Clubs* Brooks's; *Style—* The Rt Hon the Lord Harvey of Tasburgh; Crownick Woods, Restronguet, Mylor, Falmouth, Cornwall TR11 5ST

HARVEY-SMITH, Dr Edmund Andrew; s of Harold William Victor Harvey Smith (d 1975), and Violet May, *née* Self (d 1985); *b* 22 May 1929; *Educ* Latymer Upper Sch, St John's Coll Cambridge (BA, MA), Westminster Med Sch (MB BChir); *m* 26 Jan 1957 (m dis 1987), Anne, da of Dr Philip Chandler (d 1980); 2 s (Andrew Justin b 24 Aug 1961, Mark Jeffrey b 20 Sept 1963), 1 da (Caroline Jane (Mrs Bolter) b 12 July 1957); *Career* Nat Serv Royal Corps of Signals 2 Lt (actg Capt) 1948-50; house physician Westminster Hosp 1956, various posts in cardiology, chest diseases, neurology, rheumatology, endocrinology and kidney disease at The Brompton, Hammersmith, St Stephens and Westminster Hosps 1956-62, sr registrar in psychotherapy Maudsley Hosp 1966 (registrar 1962-66); currently conslt psychiatrist 1967-: Warlingham Park, Mayday and Purley Day Hosps; conslt Shirley Oaks and Hayes Grove Priory Hosps; BMA: UK chm Hosp Jr Staff Ctee 1960-66, memb Cncl 1966-67, memb Jr Staff Ctee 1960-66, fell 1966; chm Dist Hosp Med Ctee 1985-89, memb Exec Team (Dist Mgmnt Team) Croydon Health Authy 1985-89, MRCP 1962, FRCPsych 1980; *Recreations* good company, walking, ball games, reading; *Style—* Dr Edmund Harvey-Smith; 33 Wolverton Ave, Kingston-upon-Thames, Surrey KT2 7QF (☎ 071 546 5052); Mayday Hospital, Mayday Rd, Croydon CR4 7YE (☎ 088362 2101); Warlingham Park Hospital, Warlingham, Surrey

HARVIE, Alida Gwendolen Rosemary; *née* Brittain; da of Sir Harry Brittain, KBE, CMG (d 1974), and Dame Alida Luisa Brittain, *née* Harvey (d 1943); *b* 23 June 1910; *Educ* St George's Sch Harpenden, Hanover Germany; *m* 3 Oct 1950, Maj John Keith Harvie (d 1971), s of John Walter Harvie (d 1939); *Career* Staff Offr Army Educnl Corps (home cmd), Sr Cdr (Maj) ATS 1943-46; memb Kensington Borough Cncl and London CC 1949-54, WHO 1947-48, LCC lectr 1949-57; fund raising for Tree Replacement 1977-87; *Books* Those Glittering Years (1980 biography of Sir Harry Brittain), The Rationed Years (1982), The Sundial Years (1984 biography of J K Harvie), The Doom-Laden Years (1985); *Recreations* reading, history study, history research, classical music; *Clubs* Royal Over-Seas League London; *Style—* Mrs A G R Harvie; 15 Brackens Way, Martello Rd South, Poole, Dorset (☎ 0202 700734)

HARVIE-WATT, Sir James; 2 Bt (UK 1945), of Bathgate, Co Linlithgow; er s of Sir George Steven Harvie-Watt, 1 Bt, TD, QC (d 1989), and Jane, *née* Taylor; *b* 25 Aug 1940; *Educ* Eton, ChCh Oxford (MA); *m* 28 May 1966, Roseline, da of Baron Louis de Chollet (d 1972), of Fribourg, Switzerland; 1 s (Mark b 19 Aug 1969), 1 da (Isabelle b 19 March 1967); *Heir* s, Mark Louis Harvie-Watt b 19 Aug 1969; *Career* Lt London Scottish (TA) 1959-67; with Coopers and Lybrand 1962-70, exec Br Electric Traction Co Ltd and dir of subsid cos 1970-78, md Wembley Stadium Ltd 1973-78; memb: Exec Ctee London Tourist Bd 1977-80, Sports Cncl 1980-88 (vice chm 1985-88); chm Crystal Palace Nat Sports Centre 1984-88, dir Lake & Elliot Industries Ltd 1988-, chm Cannons Sports & Leisure Ltd 1990-; memb of Mgmnt Ctee: The Nat Coaching Fndn 1984-88, The Nat Water Sports Centre Holme Pierrepont 1985-88; memb: Sports Cncl Enquiries into Financing of Athletics in UK 1983, Karate 1986, Cncl NPFA 1985-; OStJ 1964 (memb London Cncl of the Order 1975-84); FCA 1975 (ACA 1965), FRSA 1978; *Recreations* tennis, golf, shooting, photography, philately; *Clubs* White's, Pratt's, Sunningdale, Queen's (chm 1990 -, vice chm 1987-90); *Style*— Sir James Harvie-Watt, Bt; 15 Somerset Sq, London W14 8EE (☎ 071 602 6944)

HARVIE-WATT, Bettie, Lady; Jane Elizabeth (Bettie); o da of late Paymaster-Capt Archibald Taylor, OBE, RN; *m* 4 June 1942, Sir George Steven Harvie-Watt, 1 Bt, TD, QC (d 1989); 2 s (Sir James, 2 Bt (*qv*), Euan b 24 Dec 1942), 1 da (Rachel (Mrs Iain Gordon Fraser) b 31 May 1944); *Style*— Bettie, Lady Harvie-Watt; Sea Tangle, Earlsferry, Fife KY9 1AD (☎ 0333 330506)

HARVINGTON, Baron (Life Peer UK 1974); Robert Grant Grant-Ferris; AE (1942), PC (1971); s of Dr Robert Grant-Ferris; *b* 30 Dec 1907; *Educ* Douai, Woolhampton Berks; *m* 1930, Florence, da of Maj William De Vine, MC; 1 s, 1 da; *Career* Wing Cdr Auxiliary (now Royal) AF, WWII: Europe, Malta, Egypt, India; called to the Bar Inner Temple 1937; MP (C): N St Pancras 1937-45, Nantwich 1955-74; dep speaker House of Commons and chm Ways and Means Ctee 1970-74; KStJ; kt 1969; *Recreations* (formerly) golf, motor yachting, cricket; *Clubs* Carlton, Royal Thames Yacht, RAF, Royal and Ancient Golf, MCC, Royal Yacht Sqdn; *Style*— The Rt Hon Lord Harvington, AE, PC; La Vieille Maison, The Bulwarks, St Aubin, Jersey, CI

HARWOOD, Hon Mrs (Elizabeth Margaret); *née* Leonard; da of Baron Leonard, OBE (Life Peer, d 1983); *b* 1946; *Educ* Univ of Wales (LLB); *m* 1963, Michael Harwood, of The Hague, Netherlands; *Style*— The Hon Mrs Harwood

HARWOOD, Lady Felicity Ann; *née* Attlee; 2 da of Rt Hon Clement Attlee, 1 Earl Attlee, KG, OM, CH, PC (d 1967; PM 1945-51); *b* 22 Aug 1925; *Educ* St Felix Sch Southwold, Rachel McMillan Trg Coll Deptford; *m* 1955, (John) Keith Harwood, OBE (d 1989); 1 s (Richard b 1963), 3 da (Penelope b 1956, Joanna b 1958, Sally b 1960); *Career* teacher; headmistress New Gregorys Sch Beaconsfield 1972-74; memb: Beaconsfield Ctee, Save The Children Fund; *Recreations* bridge, gardening, reading, travel; *Style*— Lady Felicity Harwood; Whinbury, 6 Hogback Wood Rd, Beaconsfield, Bucks HP9 1JR (☎ 04946 73284)

HARWOOD, Giles Francis; JP (North Avon); s of Basil Antony Harwood, QC, *qv*, and Enid Arundel, *née* Grove (d 1990); *b* 31 Jan 1934; *Educ* Douai Sch, ChCh Oxford (MA); *m* 1, 5 Jan 1963 (m dis 1979), Ursula Mary, da of Norman Humphrey, OBE (d 1965), of Exeter; 3 s (Francis, Dominic, Nicholas), 2 da (Monica, Bridget); m 2, 31 March 1983, Diana Mary, da of Maj Gerald Cuthbert Galahad Roe (d 1957), of Birkdale; *Career* Nat Serv 2 Lt RA 1956-58, Asst Adj/BHQ Troop Cdr Sch of Anti-Aircraft Artillery and Guided Weapons Manorbier (TA) HAC G Battery 1959-66, Veteran Co 1966-88; called to the Bar Inner Temple 1956; London and Western Circuit 1959-70, sr state counsel Kenya 1970-72, first Parly counsel Kenya 1972-75, legal advsr St Vincent and The Grenadines 1976-78, chief Parly draftsman Malawi 1978-83, chief justice Tonga 1983-85, pt/t chm Social Security Appeal Tbnls 1986, chm Registered Homes Tbnl 1987, law revision cmmr Grenada 1988; ACIArb 1985; *Books* Odgers' Principles of Pleading and Practice (17-20 edns, 1960-71); *Recreations* music, travel; *Clubs* Nairobi; *Style*— Giles Harwood, Esq, JP; Fernhill House, Almondsbury, Bristol BS12 4LX (☎ 0454 616 755)

HARWOOD, Gillian Margaret; da of Herbert Norton Harwood, of Kyrenia, Cyprus, and Margaret, *née* Gadsby; *b* 29 Nov 1942; *Educ* Farrington Girls' Sch, Institut Brittanique Paris; 2 da, (Hester Allen b 4 April 1974, Flossie Allen b 28 Nov 1975); *Career* worked with: Mather & Crowther Ltd 1962-64, WGBH TV Boston USA 1964-66, CBC News London 1966-68; involved in antique selling, BBC drama and gardening business 1968-78, worked converting redundant indust buildings into managed workspace for small and growing firms; md: Omnibus Workspace Ltd, Forum Workspace Chichester, The Old Needlemakers Lewes, Tideway Yard Mortlake, United House Islington; opened The Depot Winebar Mortlake 1986; dir City and Inner London North TEC; winner: Options/TSB Tst Co Women Mean Business Award 1988, The Times/RICS Conservation Award, Business in the Community Environment Award 1990; *Recreations* gardening, breeding Staffordshire Bull Terriers; *Style*— Miss Gillian M Harwood; 35 Gorst Road, London, SW11; Podmore's Farm, Tillington, Petworth, Sussex; 12 Flitcroft St, London, WC2 (☎ 071 836 7580, fax 379 4671)

HARWOOD, Prof John Leander; s of Capt Leslie James Harwood, of Tunbridge Wells, and Lt Beatrice, *née* Hutchinson; *b* 5 Feb 1946; *Educ* King Edwards GS Aston, Univ of Birmingham (BSc, PhD, DSc); *m* 27 Aug 1967, Gail, da of Harry Burgess (d 1968); 1 s (Nicholas James b 27 Feb 1969); *Career* Post doctoral res Univ of California Davis 1969-71 and Univ of Leeds 1971-73, personal chair Univ Coll Cardiff 1984 (lectr 1973, reader 1980), over 150 scientific pubns; guide book writer for S Wales Mountaineering Club and The Climbers Club; memb: Biochemical Soc, Phytochemical Soc, Soc of Experimental Biology; *Books* SE Wales A Rock Climbers Guide (ed, 1977), Lipids of Plants and Microbes (1984), The Lipid handbook (jt ed, 1986), Plant Membranes (jt ed, 1988); *Style*— Prof John Harwood; Department of Biochemistry, University of Wales College of Cardiff, PO Box 903, Cardiff CF1 1ST (☎ 0222 874108)

HARWOOD, John Warwick; s of Denis George Harwood, of West Camel, Somerset, and Winifred, *née* Hoatson; *b* 10 Dec 1946; *Educ* Catford Sch, Univ of Kent (BA), Univ of London (MA); *m* 4 Oct 1967, Diana Margaret, da of Harford Thomas, of Kingston, near Lewes, Sussex; 1 s (Jonathan b 1971), 1 da (Rebecca b 1974); *Career* admin offr GLC 1968-73, private sec to Sir Ashley Bramall ldr ILEA 1973-77, asst chief exec London Borough Hammersmith and Fulham 1979-82 (head chief exec's office 1977-79); chief exec Lewisham Borough Cncl 1982-88, Oxfordshire CC 1989-; dir: N Oxfordshire Business Venture Ltd, Heart of Eng Trg and Enterprise Cncl, Thames Business Advice Centre, Thames Valley Technol Centre; memb Exec Ctee Town and Country Planning Assoc 1981-89, clerk S London Consortium 1983-89, memb SOLACE; *Recreations* walking, cooking, squash; *Style*— John Harwood, Esq; County Hall, Oxford OX1 1ND (☎ 0865 815330, fax 0865 726155); West End House, Wootton, nr Woodstock, Oxfordshire OX7 1DL

HARWOOD, Lee; s of Wilfrid Travers Lee-Harwood (d 1969), of Chertsey Surrey, and Grace, *née* Ladkin; *b* 6 June 1939; *Educ* St George's Coll Weybridge Surrey, QMC London (BA); *m* 1, (m dis), Jenny Goodgame; 1 s (Blake b 1962); m 2, (m dis), Judith Walker; 1 s (Rafe b 1977), 1 da (Rowan b 1979); *Career* poet; collections published: title illegible (1965), The Man with Blue Eyes (1966), The White Room (1968), Landscapes (1969), The Sinking Colony (1971), HMS Little Fox (1976), Boston-Brighton (1977) All the Wrong Notes (1981), Monster Masks (1985), Dream Quilt (1985) Rope Bay to the Rescue (1988), Crossing the Frozen River: selected poems (1988); translations: Tristan Tzara selected Poems (1975) Tristan Tzara - Chanson Dada: Selected Poems (1987); chm: Nat Poetry Secretariat 1974-76, Poetry Soc London 1976-77; *Awards* Poetry Fndn (NY) annual award 1966, Alice Hunt Bartlett prize Poetry Soc London 1976; *Recreations* mountaineering and hill walking, the countryside; *Style*— Lee Harwood, Esq

HARWOOD, Richard Cecil; s of Cecil Albert Harwood, of 7 Cherry Orchard, Ashtead, Surrey, and Gladys Merrells, *née* Davis (d 1979); *b* 21 Sept 1943; *Educ* Sutton HS for Boys, Tiffin Boys Sch Kingston-on-Thames, The City Univ London (BSc Hons, Sir Walter Puckey prize), The City Univ Business Sch (SSRC scholar, MSc); *m* 26 Aug 1967, da of Egund Alexander Møller; 1 s (Alexander Richard b 27 June 1977), 2 da (Cordelia Anne b 16 April 1970, Amanda Kirsten b 28 Sept 1972); *Career* Smiths Industries: student apprentice 1962-67, asst works mangr 1967-68, Divnl Corp Planning 1968-69; res ptnr Scott Goff Hancock (investmt analyst 1969-73), dir Smith Newcourt Agency 1986, res dir Morgan Grenfell Securities 1986-89, dir UK Research Schroder Securities 1989-; no 1 Office equipment sector analyst Extel and Institutional Investor surveys 1973-88; memb Cncl Soc of Investmt Analysts 1981-89 (chm Educn Ctee 1984-87); memb: Stock Exchange 1971, Lloyds 1987; MIProdE, CEng, FSIA; *Books* Institutional Investment Research; *Recreations* classic cars, family, travel; *Style*— Richard Harwood, Esq; Homestead Farm, Burtons Lane, Chalfont St Giles, Bucks HP8 4BL (☎ 0494 763043); Schroder Securities Ltd, 120 Cheapside, London EC2V 6DS (☎ 071 382 3263, fax 071 382 3079)

HARWOOD, Ronald; s of Isaac Horwitz (d 1950), and Isobel, *née* Pepper (d 1985); *b* 9 Nov 1934; *Educ* Sea Point Boys' HS Capetown, RADA; *m* 1959, Natasha, da of William Charles Riehle, MBE (d 1979); 1 s (Antony), 2 da (Deborah, Alexandra); *Career* actor 1953-60; writer 1960-; artistic dir Cheltenham Festival of Lit 1975; presenter: Kaleidoscope BBC 1973, Read All About It BBC TV 1978-79; wrote and presented All The World's A Stage for BBC TV; chm Writers Guild of GB 1969; memb Lit Panel Arts Cncl of GB 1973-78; visitor in theatre Balliol Coll Oxford 1986; pres PEN (Eng) 1989; FRSL; *TV Plays* incl The Barber of Stamford Hill (1960), Private Potter (1961), The Guests (1972), adapted several Roald Dahl's Tales of the Unexpected for TV 1979-80, Breakthrough at Reykjavik (1987), Countdown to War (1989); *Screenplays* incl A High Wind in Jamaica (1965), One Day in the Life of Ivan Denisovich (1971), Evita Peron (1981), The Dresser (1983), The Doctor and the Devils (1985), Mandela (1987); *Books* All the Same Shadows (1961), The Guilt Merchants (1963), The Girl in Melanie Klein (1969), Articles of Faith (1973), The Genoa Ferry (1976), César and Augusta (1978); short stories: One Interior Day (adventures in the film trade 1978), New Stories 3 (ed, 1978); biography: Sir Donald Wolfit, CBE - his life and work in the unfashionable theatre (1971); essays: A Night at the Theatre (ed, 1983), The Ages of Gielgud (1984), Dear Alec (1989); others: All The World's A Stage (1984); *Plays* Country Matters (1969), The Ordeal of Gilbert Pinfold (from Evelyn Waugh, 1977), A Family (1978), The Dresser (New Standard Drama Award, Drama Critics Award, 1986), After the Lions (1982), Tramway Road (1984), The Deliberate Death of a Polish Priest (1985), Interpreters (1985), J J Farr (1987), Ivanov (from Chekov 1989), Another Time (1989); *Musical Libretto* The Good Companions (1974); *Recreations* tennis, cricket; *Clubs* Garrick, MCC; *Style*— Ronald Harwood, Esq; c/o Judy Daish Associates, 83 Eastbourne Mews, London W2 6LQ

HARWOOD-LITTLE, Maj Mark Guy; s of Lt-Col Cuthbert Joseph Harwood-Little, OBE (d 1963), of Chichester, and Barbara Fox, *née* Dodgson (d 1962); *b* 30 Oct 1924; *Educ* Wellington, Peterhouse Cambridge (MA); *m* 10 Dec 1949, Josephine Mary, da of Maj Aidan Staples (d 1942); 1 s (David b 1955), 1 da (Philippa b 1952); *Career* Maj RE 1942-60, served India, BAOR; psc; Lucas Industries 1960-78; dir Ironbridge Gorge Museum Devpt Tst 1978-89; Upper Severn Navigation Tst 1980-, dir St Johns Ambulance Devpt Fund Shropshire 1990; FRSA; *Recreations* sailing, industrial archaeology; *Clubs* Pilgrims; *Style*— Maj Mark G Harwood-Little; The Old Rectory, Stapleton, Dorrington, Shrewsbury SY5 7EF (☎ 074 373 220)

HARWOOD-SMART, Philip Mervyn Harwood; s of Harold Leslie Harwood Smart (d 1976), of High Point, Cuckfield, Sussex, and Moira Veronica, *née* Scanlon (d 1986); *b* 1 Oct 1944; *Educ* Eastbourne Coll, Univ of Lancaster (BA); *m* Juliet Marion Frances, da of Keith Mackay Campbell (d 1990), of West Bagborough, Somerset; 2 da (Venetia Louise b 14 June 1977, Davina Brietzcke b 17 Feb 1980); *Career* 4/5 Bn KORR Lancaster (TA) 1964-67, cmmnd 1965, memb HAC 1986-; admitted slr 1971, assoc ptnr Herbert Smith & Co 1973-75, asst slr Farrer & Co 1977-80, ptnr Ashurst Morris Crisp 1984-; chm Owslebury and Morestead Cons Assoc, hon sec Old Eastbournian Assoc 1970; memb: Sussex Archaeological Soc, Cncl of Friends of Winchester Cathedral, Sussex Record Soc, Royal Archaeological Inst, Alresford Agricultural Soc; Freeman: City of London 1973, Worshipful Co of Slrs 1973; *Books* The History of Jevington (1962, second edn, 1972); *Recreations* heraldry, genealogy; *Clubs* Carlton, Bishops Gate Ward, Coleman Street Ward, Inns of Ct, City Yeo Luncheon, Henley Royal Regatta; *Style*— Philip Harwood-Smart, Esq; Thimble Hall, Owslebury, Winchester, Hants; Broadwalk House, 5 Appold St, London EC2 (☎ 071 638 1111, fax 071 972 7990, telex 887067)

HASELER, Prof Stephen Michael Alan; s of Maj Cyril Percival Haseler (d 1973); *b* 9 Jan 1942; *Educ* Westcliff HS for Boys, LSE (BSc, PhD); *m* 24 Feb 1968, Roberta Berenice Haseler; *Career* prof of govt: City of London Poly 1968-, Univ of Maryland 1982-; visiting prof: Georgetown Univ Washington DC 1978, John Hopkins Univ 1984; chm Gen Purposes Ctee GLC 1973-75 (memb 1973-77), fndr memb SDP 1981, chm Radical Soc 1987- (fndr memb); Parly candidate (Lab): Saffron Walden 1966, Maldon 1970; hon prof Univ of Maryland 1986-; *Books* The Gaitskellites (1969), The Tragedy of Labour (1976), Eurocomunism (1978), Thatcher & The New Liberals (1989); *Clubs* IOD; *Style*— Prof Stephen Haseler; 2 Thackeray House, Ansdell Street, Kensington, London W8 (☎ 071 937 3976)

HASELHURST, Alan Gordon Barraclough; MP (C) Saffron Walden 1977-; s of late John Haselhurst, and late Alyse, *née* Barraclough; *b* 23 June 1937; *Educ* Cheltenham, Oriel Coll Oxford; *m* 1977, Angela, da of John Bailey; 2 s, 1 da; *Career* MP (C) Middleton and Prestwich 1970-74, PPS to Sec of State Educn 1979-81; chm of Trustees Community Projects Fndn 1986-; *Recreations* music, gardening, watching cricket; *Style*— Alan Haselhurst, Esq, MP; House of Commons, London SW1

HASELTINE, Barry Albert; s of Albert Edward Haseltine (d 1974), of 53 Clarence Rd, Horsham, Sussex, and Lillian Sarah Louise, *née* Payne; *b* 17 June 1933; *Educ* Collyers Sch Horsham, Imperial Coll London (BSc, DIC); *m* 7 July 1956, Sylvia Ethel, da of Arthur George Jones (d 1975), of Gloucester; 1 s (Richard Barry b 16 Feb 1963), 1 da (Susan Jane b 8 March 1966); *Career* Flying Offr RAF 1955-57; ptnr Jenkins and Potter Consulting Engrs 1967-; chm: Euro Cmmns Code of Practice Ctee for Masonry, several Br Standards Inst Ctees, Int Standards Orgn Ctee; FEng, FICE, FIStructE, MConsE, FICERAM, FCGI; *Books* Bricks and Brickwork (1974), Handbook to BS5628: Part 1 (1980); *Recreations* gardening, golf, skiing; *Clubs* RAF, Copthorne Golf (Sussex); *Style*— Barry Haseltine, Esq; Jenkins and Potter, 12-15 Great Turnstile, London WC1V 7HN (☎ 071 242 8711, fax 071 404 0742, telex 21120 ref 2060)

HASHEMI, Kambiz; s of Hussain Hashemi, of Tehran, Iran and Aghdas, *née* Tehrani; *b* 13 Aug 1948; *Educ* Greenmore Coll Birmingham, Univ of Birmingham (MB ChB, MD); *m* 11 Sept 1974, Elahe, da of Dr Abbas Hashemi-Nejad, of Tehran, Iran; 1 s (Nima b 14 Nov 1978), 1 da (Neda b 14 May 1989); *Career* surgical registrar United Birmingham Hosp 1974-82, sr registrar in accident and emergency med Dudley Rd and East Birmingham Hosp 1982-85, dir of accident and emergency serv Croydon Health Authy 1985-, conslt in trauma and hand surgery Mayday Univ Hosp Croydon 1985-; author numerous scientific pubns in med jls; memb: Manpower Advsy Ctee, Dist Child Accident Prevention Gp, Dist Ethics Ctee, Academic Ctee BAEM, Med Cmmn for Accident Prevention, BMA, BAEM, The Emergency Med Res Soc, The Iran Soc; FRCS, FRSM; *Books* Hazards of Forklift Truck (1989); *Recreations* squash, tennis, photography, theatre and opera; *Style—* Kambiz Hashemi, Esq; 14 Hartley Old Rd, Purley, Surrey CR8 4HG (☎ 081 668 1176); Accident and Emergency Unit, Mayday University Hospital, Mayday Rd, Thornton Heath, Surrey CR7 7YE (☎ 081 684 6999, fax 081 683 0279)

HASHMI, Dr Farrukh Siyar; OBE (1974); s of Dr Ziaullah Qureshi (d 1983), and Majida, *née* Mufti (d 1987); *b* 12 Sept 1927; *Educ* Punjab Univ (MB BS), King Edward Med Coll Lahore Pakistan (DipPsychological Med); *m* 11 Feb 1972, Shahnaz Hashmi, JP, da of Khalifa M Nasimullah, of Karachi, Pakistan; 1 s (Zia b 2 Sept 1977), 2 da (Mahnaz b 1 Jan 1973, Noreen b 16 Sept 1974); *Career* asst med offr for health Bewickshire 1957, scholar Volkart Fndn Switzerland 1958-60, registrar Uffculme Clinic and All Saints Hosp 1960-63, res fell Dept of Psychiatry Univ of Birmingham 1969- (sr registrar 1966-69), psychotherapist HM Prison Stafford 1973-; memb: Health and Welfare Advsy Panel Nat Ctee Cwlth Immigrants 1966-81, Home Secs Advsy Ctee On Race 1976-81; cmmr Cmmn for Racial Equality 1980-86, memb Working Pty on Community and Race Rels Trg Home Office Police Trg Cncl 1982-83, GMC memb Tbnl on Misuse of Drugs 1983-, advsy conslt C of E Bd for Social responsibility 1984-86; memb: Race Rels Bd W Midlands Conciliation Ctee 1968-81, Regnl Advsy Ctee BBC 1970-77; fndr and chm Iqbal Acad Coventry Cathedral 1972-86; memb: Warley Area Social Servs Sub Ctee 1973-81, Mental Health Servs Ctee RHA 1976-; chm Psychiatric Div W Birmingham Health Dist 1977-83 and 1989, memb Central DHA Birmingham 1982-90; individual memb World Psychiatric Assoc, fndr pres and patron Overseas Drs Assoc UK, memb World Fedn for Mental Health; FRCPsych 1971; *Books* Pakistani Family in Britain (1965), Psychology of Racial Prejudice (1966), Mores Migration and Mental Illness (1966), Community Psychiatric Problems Among Birmingham Immigrants (1968), In a Strange Land (1970), Measuring Psychological Disturbance in Asian Immigrants to Britain (1977); *Recreations* writing, reading music; *Clubs* The Oriental, Rotary Int, Edgbaston Priory (Birmingham); *Style—* Dr Farrukh Hashmi, OBE; Shahnaz, 5 Woodbourne Rd, Edgbaston, Birmingham B15 3QJ (☎ 021 523 5151)

HASKARD, Sir Cosmo Dugal Patrick Thomas; KCMG (1965, CMG 1960), MBE (1945); s of Brig-Gen John McDougall Haskard, CMG, DSO (d 1967), and Alicia Isabel, *née* Hutchins (d 1960); *b* 25 Nov 1916; *Educ* Cheltenham, RMC Sandhurst, Pembroke Coll Cambridge (MA); *m* 3 Aug 1957, Phillada, da of Sir Robert Christopher Stafford Stanley, KBE, CMG (d 1981); 1 s (Julian Dominic Stanley b 1962); *Career* 2 Lt TA 1938; emergency cmmn RIF attached KAR, served 2 Bn E Africa Ceylon Burma, Maj WWII 1944; Colonial Serv Tanganyika 1940 (suspended for War Serv), subsequently Nyasaland 1946 (dist cmmr 1948), memb Nyasaland Mozambique Boundary Cmmn 1951-52, provincial cmmr Nyasaland 1955, acting sec for African Affairs 1957-58; sec: Labour and Social Devpt 1961, sec for Local Govt 1962, sec for Natural Resources 1961-64, govr and C-in-C Falklands Is and high cmmr for British Antarctic Territory 1964-70; tstee Beit Tst 1976-; *Style—* Sir Cosmo Haskard, KCMG, MBE; Tragariff, Bantry, Co Cork, Ireland

HASKELL, Prof Francis; *b* 1923; *Educ* Eton, King's Coll Cambridge; *m* 1965, Larissa Salmina; *Career* fell King's Coll Cambridge 1954-57, librarian Fine Arts Faculty Univ of Cambridge 1962-67, prof history of art Univ of Oxford 1967-; tstee Wallace Collection 1976-; Serena Medal for Italian Studies British Acad 1985, Officer de L'Ordre des Arts et des Lettres 1990; hon fell King's Coll Cambridge 1986, foreign hon memb American Acad of Arts and Sciences 1979-; corresponding memb: Academia Pontaniana Naples 1982-, Ateneo Veneto 1986-; hon memb Academia Clementina of Bologna 1990-; FBA 1971; *Books* Patrons and Painters (1963), Rediscoveries in Art (1976), L' Arte e ilLiguaggio Della Politica (1978), Taste and the Antique (with Nicholas Penny, 1981), Past and Present in Art and Taste (1987), The Painful Birth of the Art Book (1987); *Style—* Prof Francis Haskell; Department of History of Art, University of Oxford, 35 Beaumont St, Oxford OX1 2PG (☎ 0865 278290)

HASKELL, (Donald) Keith; CVO (1979); s of Lt Donald Eric Haskell, RN, of Southsea, Hants, and Beatrice Mary, *née* Blair (d 1985); *b* 9 May 1939; *Educ* Portsmouth GS, St Catharine's Coll Cambridge (BA, MA); *m* 7 Feb 1966, Maria Luisa Soeiro, da of Dr Augusto Tito de Morais (d 1981); 3 s (Donald Mark b and d 1972, Jonathan b 1974, Paul b 1976), 3 da (Lysa b 1970, Anne-Marie b 1979, one other unnamed b and d 1969); *Career* HM Dip Serv 1961-: language student MECAS Shemlan Lebanon 1961-62 and 1968-69, third sec Br Embassy Bahgdad Iraq 1962-66, second sec FO London 1966-68, first sec and consul Br Embassy Benghazi Libya 1969-70, first sec Br Embassy Tripoli Libya 1970-72, first sec FCO London 1972-75, chargé d'affaires and consul gen Br Embassy Santiago Chile 1975-78, cnsllr and consul gen Br Embassy Dubai UAE 1978-81, head Nuclear Energy Dept FCO London 1981-83, head ME Dept FCO London 1983-84, cnsllr Br Embassy Bonn W Germany 1985-88, seconded to indust 1988-89, ambass to Peru 1990-; target rifle shooting half blue 1960-61, shot for Hampshire Eng and GB on various occasions; *Recreations* target shooting, squash, tennis, skiing, wine and food; *Clubs* Hawks (Cambridge); *Style—* Keith Haskell, Esq, CVO; c/o Foreign and Commonwealth Office, King Charles Street, London SW1A 2AH

HASKELL, Richard; s of Jack Herbert Haskell (d 1982), and Marjorie Rose, *née* Damerum; *b* 19 June 1936; *Educ* King Edward VI Royal GS Guildford, KCH (MB BS, BDS); *m* 16 April 1959, Marion, da of John Lucas Gregory (d 1973); 1 da (Greer Myra b 2 June 1964); *Career* conslt oral surgn Guys Hosp and Greenwich Health Dist 1974-, hon civilian conslt to Queen Elizabeth Military Hosp Woolwich 1981-; memb: Dental Advsy Bd, Bd of Faculty of Dental Surgery RCS 1990-, Med Protection Soc; Cncl Br Assoc of Oral and Maxillofacial Surgns; FDS RCS (chm of examiners 1988-89), MRCP; *Books* Atlas Of Orofacial Diseases (jtly 1971), Clinical Oral Medicine (2 edn jtly, 1977); *Style—* Richard Haskell, Esq; 19 Pembridge Square, London W2 4EJ (☎ 071 229 3552); Guys Hospital, St Thomas Street, London SE1 9RT (☎ 071 955 4449)

HASKINS, Samuel Joseph (Sam); s of Benjamin George Haskins (d 1970), and Anna Elizabeth Haskins (d 1983); *b* 11 Nov 1926; *Educ* Helpmekaar HS SA, Witwatersrand Tech Coll SA, London Coll of Printing; *m* 1952, Alida Elzabe, da of Stephanus Johanne van Heerden; 2 s (Ludwig b 1955, Konrad b 1963); *Career* photographer; estab: freelance advertising studio Johannesburg SA 1952, Haskins Studio and Haskins Press London 1968; solo exhibitions incl: Haskins Photographs (Johannesburg) 1953, Sam Haskins (Pentax Gallery Tokyo) 1970, Haskins Posters (The Photographers Gallery) 1972, FNAC Gallery Paris 1973, The Camera Gallery Amsterdam 1974, Scandiniavian Landscape (Isetan Gallery Tokyo) 1973, Sam Haskins a Bologna (Bologna) 1984, The Best of Sam Haskins (Pentax Forum Gallery Tokyo) 1986, The Image Factor (Pentax Forum Gallery Tokyo) 1990; books incl: Five Girls (1962), Cowboy Kate and Other Stories (1964, Prix Nadar), November Girl (1966), African Image (1967, Silver medal Int Art book competition 1969), Haskins Posters (1972, Gold medal NY Art Directors Club 1974), Photographics (1980, Kodak Book of the Year award 1980), Sam Haskins a Bologna (1984); *Recreations* vintage car rallying, sculpting, joinery, painting, craft and antique collecting, horticulture; *Style—* Sam Haskins, Esq

HASLAM, Rear Adm Sir David William; KBE (1984, OBE 1964), CB (1979); s of Gerald Haigh Haslam and Gladys, *née* Finley; *b* 26 June 1923; *Educ* Bromsgrove; *Career* hydrographer of the Navy 1975-85; pres Directing Ctee, Int Hydrographic Bureau Monaco 1985-; *Style—* Rear Adm Sir David Haslam, KBE, CB; Palais Saint James, 5 Avenue Princesse Alice, Monte Carlo MC 98000, Principaute de Monaco

HASLAM, John; LVO; s of William Haslam; *b* 17 June 1931; *Educ* King George V GS Southport, Univ of Liverpool; *m* 1953, Jean Anne, *née* Capstick; 2 s; *Career* joined BBC 1955, mangr BBC Radio Outside Broadcasts 1974-81, dep press sec to HM The Queen 1988- (asst press sec 1981-88); *Recreations* fell-walking, reading, music, Times crossword; *Style—* John Haslam, Esq, LVO; 4 The Old Barracks, Kensington Palace, London W8 4PU

HASLAM, Dr Michael Trevor; s of Gerald Haslam (d 1946), of Leeds, England, and Edna Beatrice, *née* Oldfield; *b* 7 Feb 1934; *Educ* Sedbergh, St John's Coll Cambridge (MA, MD), Bart's (MB BChir, DPM, DMJ); *m* 2 May 1959, Shirley Dunstan, da of Alfred Walter Jeffries (d 1985); 1 s (Michael b 1965), 2 da (Fiona b 1962, Melanie b 1966); *Career* RAMC 1960-62, Lt, Capt, Actg Maj; registrar in psychiatry York 1962-64, sr registrar Newcastle upon Tyne 1964-67; conslt in psychological med: Doncaster 1967-70, York 1970-89; assoc clinical prof St George's Univ Grenada 1987-90, med dir The Harrogate Clinic 1989; hon sec Soc of Clinical Psychiatrists; former: chm Clinical Tutors Ctee Royal Coll of Psychiatrists, hon sec and chm Leeds Regnl Psychiatrists Assoc; Liveryman Worshipful Soc of Apothecaries 1971, Freeman City of London 1971; FRCPS (Glasgow) 1979, FRCPsych 1980; *Books* Psychiatric Illness in Adolescence (1975), Sexual Disorders (1978), Psychosexual Disorders (1979), Psychiatry Made Simple (1987); *Recreations* fives, squash, croquet, music; *Clubs* Authors; *Style—* Dr Michael Haslam; Chapel Garth, Crayke, York YO6 4TE; Medical Director, The Harrogate Clinic, 23 Ripon Rd, Harrogate HG1 2JL (☎ 0423 500599, car 0836 328204)

HASLAM, Baron (Life Peer UK 1990), of Bolton in the County of Greater Manchester; Sir Robert Haslam; s of Percy Haslam (d 1971); *b* 4 Feb 1923; *Educ* Bolton Sch, Univ of Birmingham (BSc); *m* 1947, Joyce, da of Frederick Quinn (d 1937); 2 children; *Career* dep chm ICI plc 1980-83; chm: Tate and Lyle plc 1983-86, Br Steel Corporation 1983-86; dir Bank of England 1985-, chm Br Coal 1986-90, advsy dir Unilever plc 1986-; Hon: DTech Brunel Univ 1987, DEng Birmingham Univ 1987; FIMinE; kt 1985; *Recreations* golf, travel; *Clubs* Brooks's, Wentworth; *Style—* The Rt Hon Lord Haslam; c/o House of Lords, London SW1A 0PW

HASLAM, Simon Mark; s of Peter Haigh Haslam, of 21 The Green, Allestree, Derby, and Elizabeth Anne, *née* Gallimore; *b* 29 May 1957; *Educ* Ecclesbourne Sch Duffield Derbys, Magdalen Coll Oxford (BA, MA); *m* 15 May 1982, Catherine (Kate) Nina (who retains her maiden name), da of Capt Robert Kenneth Alcock, CBE, RN, of The Court House, Brantham Court, Manningtree, Essex; 1 s (Thomas b 9 July 1987), 1 da (Eleanor (twin) b 9 July 1987); *Career* CA; Touche Ross & Co (formerly Spicer & Pegler): articled clerk 1978-81, mangr 1984-86, ptnr 1986-; dist councillor Welwyn Hatfield 1990-; memb: Ward Ctee Welwyn and Hatfield Cons Assoc; ACA 1981; *Recreations* choral societies, walking, reading; *Style—* Simon Haslam, Esq; 11A Guessens Rd, Welwyn Garden City, Herts AL8 6QW (☎ 0707 325 117); Touche Ross, Friary Ct, 65 Crutched Friars, London EC3N 2NP (☎ 071 480 7766, fax 071 480 6958, telex 884257 ESANO G)

HASLEHURST, Peter Joseph Kinder; s of Col Arthur Kinder Haslehurst, TD (d 1987), and Beatrice Elizabeth, *née* Birkinshaw; *b* 4 March 1941; *Educ* Repton, Univ of Loughborough (DLC); *m* 29 Oct 1977, Susan Marilyn, da of Geoffrey W Y Heath; 1 s (Thomas William Kinder b 22 May 1983); *Career* md Wellman Mechanical Engrg Ltd 1969-81, chm Flexibox Int Ltd 1986- (chief exec 1981-86), currently chief exec EIS Gp plc; current chairmanships incl: Francis Shaw plc, PLCV Ltd, Hick Hargreaves & Co Ltd, C F Taylor (Hurn) Ltd, Beagle Aircraft Co Ltd, Zwicky Engineering Ltd, C F Taylor (Skyhi) Ltd, Floataire Ltd, The Mollart Engineering Co Ltd, Airpel Filtration Ltd, Golden Super BV Netherlands; currently pres: Flexibox SA France, Flexibox Spa Italy, Hibon International SA; memb Anglo Soviet Econ Conf, ldr Indust Missions to E Europe and Latin America, chm Br Metalworking Plant Makers Assoc 1974 and 1980, memb Jt Trade Cmmn with Czechoslovakia 1978-80, industl advsr to Min of State on official visit to Czechoslovakia 1978, ldr Metals Soc Team N E China 1979; memb: Materials Chemicals and Vehicles Requirement Bd Dept of Indust 1981-84, Br Hydromechanics Res Assoc 1984-89; Eisenhower Fell 1980; CEng, FIMechE, FIProdE, FIM, CBIM; *Recreations* sailing and the countryside; *Clubs* Naval and Military, Royal Thames yacht; *Style—* Peter Haslehurst, Esq; EIS Group plc, 6 Sloane Sq, London SW1W 8EE (☎ 071 730 9187)

HASSALL, Nicholas Steward; s of Harry Thomas Hassall, of Sussex, and Joyce Dinah, *née* King; *b* 25 May 1934; *Educ* City of London Sch, Wadham Coll Oxford (BA); *m* Oct 1966, Alison Jane, da of Cecil Marks; 2 da (Natasha b July 1968, Catriona b Feb 1971); *Career* articled clerk Guscotte Fowler & Cox 1959-62, ptnr Messrs Boodle Hatfield 1970- (asst slr 1962-70); *Style—* Nicholas Hassall, Esq; Beeches, 16 Eton Rd, Datchet, Berkshire (☎ 0753 43324); Messrs Boodle Hatfield, 43 Brook St, London W1

HASSALL, Tom Grafton; s of William Owen Hassall, of The Manor House, Wheatley, Oxford, and Averil Grafton, *née* Beaves; *b* 3 Dec 1943; *Educ* Dragon Sch, Lord Williams's GS Thame, Corpus Christi Coll Oxford (BA); *m* 2 Sept 1967, Angela Rosaleen, da of Capt Oliver Goldsmith (d 1944), of Thirsk; 3 s (Oliver b 28 Nov 1968, Nicholas b 30 April 1970, Edward b 10 July 1972); *Career* asst local ed Victoria County History of Oxford 1966-67, dir Oxford Archaeological Excavation Ctee 1967-73, dir Oxford (formerly Oxfordshire) Archaeological Unit 1973-85, fell St Cross Coll Oxford (emeritus fell 1988-), assoc staff tutor Dept for External Studies Univ of Oxford 1978-85, sec Royal Cmmn on the Historical Monuments of England 1986-; tstee Oxford Preservation Tst 1973-, chm Standing Conf of Archaeological Unit Mangrs 1980-83, pres Cncl for Br Archaeology 1983-86, chm Br Archaeological Awards 1983-87, pres Oxfordshire Architectural and Historical Soc 1984-; Freeman City of Chester 1973; FSA 1971, MIFA 1985; *Books* Oxford, The Buried City (1987); *Recreations* gardening; *Style—* Tom Hassall, Esq, FSA; The Manor House, Wheatley, Oxford OX9 1XX (☎ 08677 4428); The Little Cottage, Cley-next-the-Sea, Holt, Norfolk; The Royal Commission on the Historical Monuments of England, Fortress House, 23 Savile Row, London W1X 2JQ (☎ 071 973 3350)

HASSAN, The Hon Sir Joshua Abraham; GBE (1987, CBE 1957), KCMG (1985), LVO (1954), QC (Gibraltar 1961), JP (Gibraltar 1949); s of late Abraham M Hassan; *b* 21 Aug 1915; *Educ* Line Wall Coll Gibraltar; *m* 1, 1945 (m dis 1969), Daniela, *née* Salazar; 2 da; m 2, 1969, Marcelle, *née* Bensimon; 2 da; *Career* called to the Bar Middle Temple 1939; dep coroner for Gibraltar 1941-64, mayor of Gibraltar 1945-50 and 1953-69, MEC and MLC Gibraltar 1950-64 (chief memb 1958-64), chief minister of Gibraltar 1964-69 and 1972-87, ldr of oppn House of Assembly 1969-72, hon bencher Middle Temple 1983-; Hon LLD Univ of Hull; kt 1963; *Clubs* United Oxford and Cambridge Univ, Royal Gibraltar Yacht; *Style*— The Hon Sir Joshua Hassan, GBE, KCMG, LVO, QC, JP; 11-18 Europa Rd, Gibraltar (☎ 010 350 77295); 57 Line Wall Rd, Gibraltar (☎ 010 350 79000)

HASSELL, Christopher Derek; s of Leonard Arthur Hassell (d 1954), and Evelyn Mary, *née* Pease; *b* 27 Nov 1942; *Educ* Ewell Boys Sch, Ewell Co Secdy Sch; *m* 19 June 1965, (Eleanor) Claire, da of Douglas Reid; 1 s (Richard Douglas b 12 April 1975), 2 da (Amanda Claire b 28 Sept 1968, Sandra Carole b 10 Dec 1969); *Career* articled clerk (chartered accountants) 1960; Crystal Palace FC: admin asst 1961, asst sec June 1963, sec Dec 1963; sec: Everton FC 1973-75, Preston North End FC 1975-77; asst sec Arsenal FC 1977-78; sec Lancashire CCC 1978-; FA referee (class one) 1960, FA preliminary coach 1961; Surrey combination Football League (press fixtures and bulletin sec, vice chm, currently vice pres), memb Surrey Football Assoc Cncl 1968-73, chm Town Green Boys FC 1973-80, hon treas Football League Secretaries and Mangrs Assoc 1968-78 (asst sec 1965-68); memb: Addiscombe & Shirley Round Table 1971-73, Maghull & District Round Table 1973-84; Area 8 Lancs and Manx Round Table Cncl: sports offr 1980-81, vice chm 1981-82, chm 1982-83; memb Ctee Lords Taverners (NW); vice pres: Croydon Schs FA, Lancashire Schs Cricket Assoc; *Clubs* Rainford 41, MCC, The Forty; *Style*— Christopher Hassell, Esq; Lancashire County Cricket Club, Old Trafford, Manchester M16 OPX (☎ 061 848 7021, fax 061 848 9021)

HASSELL, Prof Michael Patrick; s of Maj Albert Marmaduke Hassell, MC, of Mayfield House, Clench, nr Marlborough, Wilts, and Gertrude, *née* Loeser (d 1973); *b* 2 Aug 1942; *Educ* Whitgift Sch, Clare Coll Camb (MA), Oriel Coll Oxford (DPhil); *m* 1, 7 Oct 1966 (m dis), Glynis Mary Ethel, da of John Everett; 2 s (Adrian Michael b 6 Feb 1971, David Charles b 2 April 1973); m 2, Victoria Anne, da of Reginald Taylor (d 1984); 1 s (James Mark b 10 June 1986), 1 da (Kate Helen b 18 April 1988); *Career* Imperial Coll London: lectr Dept of Zoology and Applied Entomology 1970-75, reader in insect ecology Dept of Zoology and Applied Entomology 1975-79, prof of insect ecology Dept of Pure and Applied Biology 1979-, dep head Dept of Pure and Applied Biology 1984, dir Silwood Park 1988-; FRS 1986; *Books* The Dynamics of Competition and Predation (1976), The Dynamics of Arthropod and Predator-Prey Systems (1978); *Recreations* walking, natural history, croquet; *Style*— Prof Michael Hassell, FRS; Silwood Lodge, Silwood Park, Ascot, Berks SL5 7PZ; Imperial Coll at Silwood Park, Dept of Pure & Applied Biology, Ascot, Berks SL5 7PY (☎ 0344 23911, fax 0344 20094)

HASTIE-SMITH, Richard Maybury; CB (1984); s of Engr Cdr D Hastie-Smith, and H I Hastie-Smith; *b* 13 Oct 1931; *Educ* Cranleigh Sch, Magdalene Coll Cambridge (MA); *m* 1956, Bridget Noel Cox; 1 s, 2 da; *Career* entered Civil Service (War Office) 1955-: private sec to Perm Under Sec 1957, asst private sec to Sec of State 1958, princ 1960, asst sec to Sec of State for Defence 1965, private sec to Min of Defence (Equipment) 1968 (asst sec 1969), RCDS 1974, under sec MOD 1975, Cabinet Office 1979-81, dep under sec of state MOD 1981-; *Style*— Richard Hastie-Smith, Esq, CB; 18 York Ave, East Sheen, London SW14 (☎ 081 876 4597)

HASTINGS; *see*: Abney-Hastings

HASTINGS, Rev Prof Adrian Christopher; s of William George Warren Hastings (d 1952), and Mary Hazel, *née* Daunais; *b* 23 June 1929; *Educ* Douai Abbey Sch Woolhampton, Worcester Coll Oxford (BA, MA), Univ of Cambridge (DipEd), Urban Univ of Rome (DTheol); *m* 31 March 1979, (Elizabeth) Ann, da of Mervyn Spence, of Bristol; *Career* priest Diocese of Masaka Uganda 1958-66, visiting prof of theol Univ of Lovanium Kinshasa Zaire 1963-64, editor Post Vacation II Tanzania 1966-68, ecumenical lectr Mindolo Ecumenical Fndn Kitwe Zambia 1968-70, res offr Sch of Oriental & African Studies London 1973-76, fell St Edmund's House Cambridge 1974-76, lectr in religious studies Univ of Aberdeen 1976-80 (reader 1980-82), prof of religious studies Univ of Zimbabwe Harare 1982-85, prof of theology Univ of Leeds 1985-, Prideaux lectr Univ of Exeter 1990-; ed Journal of Religion in Africa; tstee Yorkshire Historic Churches Tst; *Books* books include: Prophet and Witness in Jerusalem (1958), Church and Mission in Modern Africa (1967), A Concise Guide to the Documents of the Second Vatican Council (2 Vol 1968-69), Christian Marriage in Africa (1973), The Faces of God (1975), A History of African Christianity 1950-75 (1979), A History of English Christianity 1920-85 (1986), African Catholicism (1989), The Theology of a Protestant Catholic (1990); *Recreations* walking, cutting hedges, doing jigsaw puzzles; *Style*— The Rev Prof Adrian Hastings; 3 Hollin Hill House, 219 Oakwood Lane, Leeds LS8 2PE (☎ 0532 400154); The Hillside Cottage, Chase End, Bromsberrow, Ledbury, Herefordshire; The Dept of Theology and Religious Studies, The University of Leeds, Leeds LS2 9JT (☎ 0532 333641, fax 0532 336017, telex 556473 UNILDS G)

HASTINGS, Christine Anne; da of Peter Edwards Hastings, and Anne Fauvel, *née* Picot; *b* 15 Feb 1956; *Educ* Whyteleafe GS; *m* 5 May 1985 (m dis 1988), Lawrie Lewis; *Career* dir: Pact Ltd (PR Consultancy) 1980-86, Biss Lancaster plc 1986-88; managing ptnr Quadrangle Mktg Servs Ltd 1988-, founding dir Quadrangle Communications Ltd 1989-; *Style*— Miss Christine Hastings; Quadrangle Communications Ltd, 81 Dean St, London W1V 5AB (☎ 071 287 2262, fax 071 439 1537, telex 894767)

HASTINGS, 22 Baron (E 1290); Sir Edward Delaval Henry Astley; 12 Bt (E 1660); s of 21 Baron (d 1956), and Lady Marguerite Nevill, da of 3 Marquess of Abergavenny; *b* 14 April 1912; *Educ* Eton, abroad; *m* 1954, Catherine, yr da of Capt Harold Virgo Hinton, and formerly w of Vernon Coats; 2 s, 1 da; *Heir* s, Hon Delaval Astley; *Career* Maj Coldstream Gds, ret; patron of eight livings; lord-in-waiting to HM The Queen 1961-62, jt Parly sec Min Housing and Local Govt 1962-64; former farmer S Rhodesia (now Zimbabwe); pres: British-Italian Soc 1972-, Br Epilepsy Assoc 1965-; govr: Br Inst Florence, Royal Ballet; grand offr Order of Merit (Italy); *Clubs* Brooks's, Army and Navy, Northern Counties (Newcastle), Norfolk (Norwich); *Style*— The Lord Hastings; Seaton Delaval Hall, Northumberland (☎ 091 237 0786)

HASTINGS, Hon Mrs (Eileen Ellen); *née* Wise; da of Baron Wise (d 1968), and Kate Elizabeth, *née* Sturgeon; *b* 28 Sept 1916; *m* 1940, Sqdn Ldr Gerald Edmund Hastings; s of Alfred Philip Hastings (d 1984); 3 da (Tanera, Eileen, Bridget); *Style*— The Hon Mrs Hastings; Bridge Cottage, Rousdon Lymeregis, Dorset (☎ 029 743433)

HASTINGS, Hon Lady (Elizabeth Anne Marie Gabrielle); *née* FitzAlan-Howard; yr da of 2 and last Viscount FitzAlan of Derwent, OBE (d 1962), and Joyce Elizabeth, now Countess Fitzwilliam, *qv*; *b* 26 Jan 1934; *m* 1, 17 Jan 1952 (m dis 1960), Sir Vivyan Naylor-Leyland, 3 Bt; 1 s; m 2, 1975, Sir Stephen Lewis Edmonstone Hastings, MC, *qv*; *Career* MPhil, Egyptologist; hon res asst Dept of Egyptology Univ Coll London; jt master Fitzwilliam Hounds; chm Badminton Conservation Tst; *Style*— The Hon Lady Hastings; Milton, Peterborough, Cambridgeshire (☎ 0733 380780)

HASTINGS, (Andrew) Gavin; s of Clifford N Hastings, of Edinburgh, and Isobel, *née* Macallum; *b* 3 Jan 1962; *Educ* George Watsons Coll Edinburgh, Paisley Coll of Technol, Magdalene Coll Univ of Cambridge (Rugby blue); *Career* Rugby Union full back Watsonians FC and Scotland (30 caps); clubs: Univ of Cambridge 1984-85, London Scottish FC (capt and winners 3 Div Championship 1989-90), Watsonians RFC, Barbarians FC (v NZ 1989); rep Scotland B (debut 1984, 5 caps); Scotland: tour North America 1985, debut v France 1986, shared Five Nations Championship (with France) 1986, 4 appearances World Cup 1987, memb Grand Slam winning team 1990, tour NZ 1990; Scotland records: most points scored (52) in a Five Nations Championship 1985-86, most points in an international (27) v Romania 1987, most conversions in internationals (37) 1986-90, most conversions in an international (8) v Zimbabwe 1987 and v Romania 1987, most penalty goals in a Five Nations Championship (14) 1985-86; Br Lions: tour Aust 1989 (3 tests) with S Hastings, *qv* first Scottish brothers to play together in a Lions Test; agency surveyor Richard Ellis Chartered Surveyors Glasgow; *Recreations* golf (7 handicap), squash, travelling; *Style*— Gavin Hastings, Esq; c/o Scottish Rugby Union, MurrayField, Edinburgh EH12 5PJ (☎ 031 337 9551, fax 031 313 2810)

HASTINGS, George Frederick; s of J Maurice Hastings (d 1965), of Rainthorpe Hall, and Rosemary Crane Hastings (d 1983); *b* 17 June 1932; *Educ* Eton, Christ Church Oxford (MA); *m* 1, 17 April 1965 (m dis 1974), Alys, da of Viggo Kihl (d 1969), of Canada; 1 s (Magnus b 1968), 1 da (Sophie b 1966); m 2, 7 Oct 1983, Melissa, da of Peter Cuyler Walker, of Washington DC; 1 s (Samuel b 1984); *Career* Nat Serv Pilot Offr RAF, 245 Day Fighter Sqdn 1950-52; called to the Bar Inner Temple 1972; memb Parish Cncl 1979-86; *Recreations* writing, shooting, sylviculture; *Clubs* Brooks's, Norfolk; *Style*— George Hastings, Esq; Rainthorpe Hall, Tasburgh, Norfolk NR15 1RQ (☎ 0508 470 618)

HASTINGS, Max Macdonald; s of Douglas Macdonald Hastings (d 1982), and Anne Scott-James (Lady Lancaster); *b* 28 Dec 1945; *Educ* Charterhouse, Univ Coll Oxford; *m* 1972, Patricia Mary, da of Tom Edmondson, of Leics; 2 s (Charles b 1973, Harry b 1983), 1 da (Charlotte b 1977); *Career* author, journalist and broadcaster; reporter: London Evening Standard 1965-70, BBC TV 1970-73; ed Evening Standard Londoner's Diary 1976-77; columnist and contrib: Evening Standard, Daily Express, Sunday Times 1973-86; The Daily Telegraph: ed 1986, ed in chief 1990, The Daily Telegraph plc 1989; fell World Press Inst St Paul USA 1967-68; *Books* The Fire This Time (1968), The Struggle for Civil Rights in Northern Ireland (1970), The King's Champion (1976), Hero of Entebbe (1979), Bomber Command (1979, Somerset Maugham Prize), The Battle of Britain (with Len Deighton, 1980), Das Reich (1981), The Battle for the Falklands (with Simon Jenkins 1983, Yorkshire Post Book of the Year Prize), Overlord: D-Day and The Battle for Normandy (1984, Yorkshire Post Book of the Year Prize), Victory in Europe (1985), The Oxford Book of Military Anecdotes (ed, 1985), The Korean War (1987), Outside Days (1989); *Recreations* shooting, fishing; *Clubs* Brooks's, Beefsteak, Saintsbury; *Style*— Max Hastings, Esq; Guilsborough Lodge, Northamptonshire, 32 Chepstow Court, London W11; The Daily Telegraph, South Quay Plaza, London E14 9SR (☎ 071 538 5000)

HASTINGS, Scott; *b* 4 Dec 1964; *Educ* George Watsons Coll, Newcastle upon Tyne Poly; *m* Sept 1990, Jenny; *Career* Rugby Union Centre Watsonians and Scotland (29 caps); clubs: Newcastle Poly RFC, Northern FC 1982-85, Watsonians RFC 1986- (capt 1987-88 and 1988-89), Barbarians RFC, Scottish Sch 1983 (3 caps), Northumberland 1984, Anglo Scots 1984, Edinburgh 1985- (incl grand slam appearances 1986, 1987 and 1988), Scotland U21 (3 caps) 1984, Scotland B 1985; Scotland: debut v France 1986, memb World Cup squad (4 appearances) 1987, memb Grand Slam sinning team 1990, tour NZ 1990 (2 test appearances); Br Lions tour Aust (2 test appearances) 1989; with Gavin Hastings, *qv*, became first Scottish brothers to play together in a Lions test; account exec Barkers; *Recreations* golf, all sporting and leisure activities, underwater snooker, mixed mud wrestling; *Style*— Scott Hastings, Esq; Scottish Rugby Union, Murrayfield, Edinburgh, Lothian (☎ 031 337 2346)

HASTINGS, Lady Selina Shirley; da of 15 Earl of Huntingdon (d 1990), and his 2 w, Margaret Lane; *b* 5 March 1945; *Educ* St Paul's Girls' Sch, St Hugh's Coll Oxford (MA); *Career* writer; literary ed Harper's and Queen; *Books* Sir Gawain and the Green Knight, Sir Gawain and the Loathly Lady, Nancy Mitford a Biography; *Style*— The Lady Selina Hastings; c/o Rogers, Coleridge & White, 20 Powis Mews, London W11

HASTINGS, Sir Stephen Lewis Edmonstone; MC (1944); s of Lewis Aloysius Macdonald Hastings, MC (d 1966), and Meriel, *née* Edmonstone (d 1971); *b* 4 May 1921; *Educ* Eton, RMC Sandhurst; *m* 1, 1948 (m dis 1971), Harriet Mary Elizabeth, da of late Col Julian Latham Tomlin, CBE, DSO; 1 s (Neil), 1 da (Carola); m 2, 1975, Hon Elizabeth Anne Marie Gabrielle Naylor Leyland, *née* Fitzalan Howard, *qv*; *Career* served Scots Gds 1939-48: 2 Bn Western Desert 1941-43 (despatches), SAS Regt 1943; later served with: Special Forces in Italy, Br Troops in Austria; FO 1948, Br Legation Helsinki and Embassy Paris 1952-58, first sec Political Office ME Forces 1959-60; MP (C) Mid-Bedfordshire 1960-83; dir of various cos; chm: BMSS Ltd, BFSS 1982-88; thoroughbred breeder Milton Park Stud; kt 1983; *Publications* The Murder of TSR2 (1966); *Recreations* field sports, painting; *Clubs* White's, Buck's, Pratt's; *Style*— Sir Stephen Hastings, MC; Milton Hall, Peterborough (☎ 0733 380 780); 12a Ennismore Gardens, London SW7 (☎ 071 589 6494)

HASTINGS, Steven Alan; s of Thomas Alan Hastings, OBE, of Larchmont, Crab Hill, Beckenham, Kent, and Margaret Elizabeth, *née* Webber; *b* 18 Sept 1957; *Educ* Dulwich, Univ of Bristol (BSocSci); *m* 19 July 1987, Teresa Lynne Eugenie, da of John Wimbourne, of Esher, Surrey; 1 s (Thomas Magna b 1 April 1989); *Career* jr planner Leagas Delaney 1980-83, planner D'Arcy McManus & Masius 1983-84, sr planner Lowe Howard-Spink 1984-88, planning dir BBDO UK Ltd 1988-; memb: MRS, Account Planning Gp, Euro Soc for Opinion and Market Res; *Recreations* running classic cars; *Clubs* Naval and Military; *Style*— Steven Hastings, Esq; 49 Westbourne Gardens, London W2 5NR (☎ 071 229 3898); BBDO, 10 Cambridge Terrace, London NW1

HASTWELL, Vincent Edward; s of Dennis Edward Hastwell (d 1972), and Monica Dorothy Grace, *née* Lawson-White (d 1971); *b* 9 May 1943; *Educ* Chichester HS for Boys, Architectural Assoc Sch of Architecture (AA Dipl); *m* 7 Oct 1968, Lynne, da of Douglas Richardson (d 1986), of Bersted, Sussex; 1 s (Leon Alastair b 1971), 1 da (Anya Victoria b 1978); *Career* ptnr Hastwell Associates Chartered Architects 1977-; joint first prize Millbank competition 1977 for Crown Estates; RIBA 1972 (chm Kingston Branch 1990-), memb ARCUK Bd of Architectural Educn 1990-; *Recreations* walking, music, collecting vintage guitars; *Clubs* Architectural Assoc; *Style*— Vincent Hastwell, Esq; Old Nags Head Cottage, Horsham Rd, Homwood, nr Dorking, Surrey RH5 4ED; 11-13 Sheen Rd, Richmond, Surrey TW9 1AD (☎ 081 940 8096)

HASWELL, Maj Chetwynd John Drake (Jock); s of Brig Chetwynd Henry Haswell, CIE (d 1956), and Dorothy Edith, *née* Berry (d 1973); *b* 18 July 1919; *Educ* Winchester, RMC Sandhurst; *m* 25 Oct 1947, (Charlotte) Annette, da of Richard Cecil Petter (d 1971); 2 s (Richard b 1948, Charles b 1956), 1 da (Frances b 1950); *Career* cmmnd The Queen's Royal (W Surrey) Regt 1939-60, ret offr grade II (author) Intelligence Centre 1966-84; tech writer and PR offr Messrs Spembly Ltd 1960-64, md Southern Sales Promotion Ltd 1964-66; memb: Nat Tst, English Heritage, CPRE; chm Regimental Museum Managing Tstees,l historian for The Queen's Regt; *Books* under pen name George Foster: Indian File (1960), Soldier on Loan (1961); under own name Jock Haswell: The Queen's Royal Regiment (1967), The First Respectable Spy (1969), James II Soldier and Sailor (1972), British Military Intelligence (1973), Citizen Armies

(1973), The British Army (1975), The Battle for Empire (1976), The Ardent Queen-Margaret of Anjou (1976), Spies and Spymasters (1977), The Intelligence and Deception of the D Day Landings (1979), The Tangled Web-Tactical and Strategic Deception (1985), The Queen's Regiment (1985), Spies and Spying (1986); *Recreations* gardening, carpentry, building; *Style—* Maj Jock Haswell; The Grey House, Lyminge, Folkestone, Kent CT18 8ED (☎ 0303 862232)

HASWELL, (Anthony) James Darley; OBE (1985); s of Brig Chetwynd Henry Haswell, CIE (d 1956), and Dorothy Edith, *née* Berry (d 1976); *b* 4 Aug 1922; *Educ* Winchester, St John's Coll Cambridge (MA); *m* 6 July 1957, Angela Mary, da of Guy Blondel Murphy (d 1949), of Harrow, Middx; 3 s (Timothy b 1958, Jonathan b 1960, Jeremy (twin) b 1960), 1 da (Kate b 1965); *Career* cmmnd DCLI (TA) 1951, Capt Army Legal Servs Staff List (now Army Legal Corps) 1952, Capt Legal Staff MELF 1953-55, Temp Maj 1956, Maj 1960, DADALS HQLF 1965-67, Lt-Col 1967, ADALS NELF Cyprus 1968-71, CO HQ Army Legal Aid 1971-73, Legal Offr Army Legal Aid BAOR 1974-80, Army Legal Aid Aldershot 1980-81, ret 1981; admitted slr of Supreme Ct 1949; Legal Dept RAC 1949, asst slr Reginald Rogers & Co Helston 1950-51, first Insur Ombudsman 1981-89; chm and playing memb Insur Orchestral Soc; Freeman City of London, Liveryman Worshipful Co Insurers 1987; *Books* Insurance Ombudsman Annual Reports (1981-88); *Recreations* music, theatre, painting, woodwork; *Style—* James Haswell, Esq, OBE; 31 Chipstead St, London SW6 3SR (☎ 071 736 1163)

HASZARD, Maj (Jacinth) Rodney; s of Col Gerald Fenwick Haszard, CBE, DSC, JP, DL (d 1967), of Milford Hall, Stafford, and Dyonese Rosamund, *née* Levett; *b* 24 Oct 1933; *Educ* RNC Dartmouth; *m* 28 Oct 1980, Anna Serena, da of Paul Henry Hawkins (d 1984), of Chetwynd Knoll, Newport, Shropshire; 1 step s (Charles Roarie Scarisbrick), 1 step da (Arabella Domenica Scarisbrick); *Career* served Kings Shropshire LI; Platoon Cdr: 1 Bn BAOR 1952-55, Mau Mau rebellion Kenya 1955-56, Arabian Peninsula Dhala battle of Jebel Jihaf 1957; ADC to HE Govr and C-in-C Tanganyika 1959-60; Adj Herford LI 1960-65, Co Cdr 3 Bn LI Plymouth, Malaya 1965-67, Trg Maj 5 Bn LI (TA) 1968-71; regnl sec CLA 1971-78, agent to tstees of the Earl of Lichfield 1978-; underwriting memb Lloyds 1976; JP Stafford 1974-89; gen cmmr of Income Tax 1985-88; High Sheriff of Staffordshire 1978; *Recreations* shooting, fishing, arboriculture; *Style—* Maj Rodney Haszard; Barwhinnock, Twynholm, Kirkcudbright; (☎ 0557 6212); Yeld Bank Farm, Knightley, Stafford (☎ 0785 284682); Lichfield Estate Office, Ranton Abbey, Lawnhead, Stafford (☎ 0785 282659)

HATCH, David Edwin; s of Rev Raymond Harold Hatch (d 1967), and Winifred Edith May, *née* Brookes (d 1987); *b* 7 May 1939; *Educ* St John's Leatherhead, Queens' Coll Cambridge (MA, DipEd); *m* 1964, Ann Elizabeth, da of Christopher Martin (d 1945); 2 s (Christopher b 1967, Richard b 1970), 1 da (Penelope b 1965); *Career* co starred with John Cleese, Graham Chapman, Bill Oddie and Tim Brooke Taylor in Cambridge Footlights Revue Cambridge Circus 1963; BBC: actor and writer I'm Sorry I'll Read That Again (Radio Light Entertainment) 1965, exec prodr Prog Devpt 1971, ed Radio Network Manchester 1978, head of Radio Light Entertainment 1978, controller Radio 2 1980, controller Radio 4 1983, dir of Progs 1986-87, md Network Radio 1987-, vice chm BBC Enterprises Ltd; vice chm The Servs Sound and Vision Corp, vice pres Euro Bdcasting Union's Radio Prog Ctee; FRSA; *Recreations* Bruegel Jigsaws, family, laughing; *Style—* David Hatch, Esq; The Windmill, Ray's Hill, Chesham, Bucks HP5 2UJ; Broadcasting House, Langham Place, London W1A 1AA (☎ 071 927 5460)

HATCH, Prof David John; s of James Frederick Hatch, of 20 Mount Pleasant Ave, Hutton, Essex, and Marguerite Fanny, *née* Forge; *b* 11 April 1937; *Educ* Caterham Sch, UCL (MB BS, LRCP); *m* 4 June 1960, Rita, da of William Henry Wilkins Goulter (d 1956); 2 s (Michael b 1963, Andrew b 1969), 2 da (Susan b 1964, Jane b 1967); *Career* fell in anaesthesiology Mayo Clinic Rochester Minnesota 1968-69, conslt in anaesthesia and respiratory measurement Hosp for Sick Children Gt Ormond St 1969-91 (chm Div of Anaesthesia 1984-87), sub dean Inst of Child Health Univ of London 1974-85, prof of paediatric anaesthesia Univ of London 1991-; hon sec Assoc of Paediatric Anaesthetists 1979-86; memb Cncl: Assoc of Anaesthetists of GB and Ireland 1982-86, Coll of Anaesthetists 1986-; MRCS, FFARCS 1965, FCAnaes 1988; *Books* with Sumner: Neonatal and Perioperative Care (1981), Clinics in Anaesthesiology: Paediatric Anaesthesia (1985), Textbook of Paediatric Anaesthetic Practice (1989); *Recreations* squash, sailing; *Clubs* RSM; *Style—* Prof David Hatch; 6 Darnley Rd, Woodford Green, Essex IG8 9HU (☎ 081 504 4134); The Institute of Child Health, 30 Guildford Street, London WC1N 1EH (☎ 071 242 9789)

HATCH, John Vaughan; s of Brian Hatch, of Rippingale, Lincs, and Eileen Mabel, *née* Woodmansey; *b* 25 May 1949; *Educ* Worksop Coll, Mansfield Coll Oxford (MA), St Anthony's Coll Oxford (MPhil); *m* 30 June 1973, Sally Margaret, da of Geoffrey William Randle Brownscombe (d 1950), of Hove, Sussex; 2 da (Rebecca b 1978, Amber b 1982); *Career* mgmnt conslt Deloitte Haskins & Sells 1973-82, dep dir of Investmt Water Authorities Superannuation Fund 1982-84, md Venture Link (Hldgs) Ltd 1984-87, chm and md Venture Link Investors Ltd 1987-; memb: Nat Consumer Cncl 1980-86, Gen Optical Cncl 1984-88; cncllr Oxfordshire 1973-77; non-exec dir: Century Publishing Co Ltd 1982-85, Century Hutchinson Ltd 1985-89; chm Electricity Consumers' Cncl 1984-90, Nat Grid Co plc 1990-; ccncllr Oxfordshire 1973-77; memb Nat Consumer Cncl 1980-86, Gen Optical Cncl 1984-88; pres Blewbury and Upton Cricket Club; Freeman: City of London 1985, Worshipful Co of Info Technologists 1989; ACMA 1980; *Books* Controlling Nationalised Industries (with John Redwood, 1982), Value For Money Audits (with John Redwood, 1981); *Recreations* cricket, bridge; *Clubs* City of London, Lansdowne; *Style—* John Hatch, Esq; Rose Cottage, High St, Upton, Nr Didcot, Oxfordshire (☎ 0235 850 671); Tectonic Place, Holyport Rd, Maidenhead, Berks (☎ 0628 771 050, fax 0628 770 392)

HATCH OF LUSBY, Baron (Life Peer UK 1978); John Charles Hatch; s of John James Hatch; *b* 1 Nov 1917; *Educ* Keighley Boys' GS, Sidney Sussex Coll Cambridge; *Career* sits as Labour Peer in House of Lords; journalist (on New Statesman), broadcaster, author, lecturer; national organiser ILP 1944-48, head Cwlth Dept Lab Pty HQ 1954-61, first dir Inst of Human Relations Zambia Univ until 1982, dir emeritus Inter-Univ African Studies Programme Houston Texas, hon sr lectr Sch of Devpt Studies UEA; Hon DLitt St Thomas Univ Houston 1981; *Books* A History of Post-War Africa, Africa Emergent, Two African Statesmen; *Recreations* cricket, music; *Clubs* MCC and Royal Cwlth Soc; *Style—* The Rt Hon the Lord Hatch of Lusby; House of Lords, London, SW1A 0PW (☎ 071 219 5353)

HATCHARD, Frederick Harry; s of Francis Joseph (d 1960), and May Evelyn, *née* Tyler (d 1982); *b* 22 April 1923; *Educ* Yardley GS, Univ of Birmingham; *m* 22 Oct 1955, Patricia Evelyn, da of Frederick Edward Egerton (d 1955), of Sutton Coldfield; 2 s (Simon b 1959, Michael b 1962); *Career* pilot RAF 1942-46, RAFVR 1950-55; admitted slr 1958; justices clerk: Sutton Coldfield 1963-67, Walsall 1967-81; stipendary magistrate Birmingham 1981-; *Recreations* sport, gardening; *Style—* Frederick Hatchard, Esq; 3b Manor Rd, Streetly, Sutton Coldfield, W Midlands

HATCHER, Mark; s of Peter Thomas Hatcher, of Great Bookham, Surrey, and Joan Beatrice, *née* Crisp; *b* 16 Oct 1954; *Educ* Sutton Valence Sch Kent, Exeter Coll Oxford (BA, MA); *m* 9 July 1988, Clare Helen, eld da of Prof Hugh Lawrence, of London; 1 da (Sophie b 13 Nov 1990); *Career* called to the Bar Middle Temple 1978 (ad eundem Lincoln's Inn), private practice 1978-80, legal asst Law Cmmn 1980-83, dep legal and sr legal asst Legislation Gp Lord Chancellor's 1980-88, Cts and Legal Servs Gp 1988-89; mgmnt conslt Coopers & Lybrand Deloitte 1989-; memb Greenwich Soc (conservation); memb Gen Cncl of Bar; asst sec Law Reform Ctee 1984-88; *Books* Financial Control (contrib); *Recreations* windsurfing, second-hand books, cooking; *Style—* Mark Hatcher, Esq; 37 Ashburnham Grove, Greenwich, London SE10 8UL (☎ 081 691 7191); Coopers & Lybrand Deloitte, Management Consultants, PO Box 198, Hillgate House, 26 Old Bailey, London EC4M 7PL (☎ 071 583 5000, fax 071 236 2367, telex 8955899)

HATCHETT, Alan George; CBE (1987); s of Ralph Hatchett (d 1929); *b* 3 Oct 1924; *Educ* William Ellis Sch Hampstead; *m* 1960, Margaret Kathlyn, da of Albert Victor Brockhurst; 1 child; *Career* dir: The Australia Japan Container Line, Federal Steam Navigation Co, P & O Lines, The Peninsular and Oriental Steam Navigation Co; dep chm Overseas Containers Ltd 1983-, jt md (fleet mgmnt) 1983-; *Recreations* gardening, fishing; *Clubs* Oriental; *Style—* Alan Hatchett, Esq, CBE; St Ronans, Wonersh Park, Wonersh, Surrey; Overseas Containers Ltd, Beagle House, Braham St, London E1 8EP (☎ 071 488 1313)

HATELY, Dr William; s of William Williamson Hately (d 1956), and Janet Favard, *née* Roxburgh (d 1983); *b* 19 Dec 1935; *Educ* George Heriot's Sch Edinburgh, Univ of Edinburgh (MB ChB, DMRD); *m* 19 Sept 1959, Gillian, da of Charles William Massot, of Flat 12, Crowholt, The Chine, Echo Barn Lane, Farnham, Surrey; 2 da (Ruth b 12 Nov 1964, Diane b 16 April 1969); *Career* Nat Serv med branch RAF 1959-62; conslt radiologist The London Hosp 1968-, dir X-Ray Dept The London Clinic; vice pres Br Inst of Radiology; FRCR, FRCPE; *Recreations* swimming, travel; *Style—* Dr William Hately; 4 Hitherwood Drive, London SE19 1XB (☎ 081 670 7644); Casa Jinty 459, Mijas La Nueva, Mijas, Malaga, Spain; Alexandra Wing X-Ray Dept, The Royal London Hospital, Whitechapel, London E1 1BB (☎ 071 377 7657); X-Ray Dept, The London Clinic, 20 Devonshire Place, London W1 (☎ 071 935 4444)

HATFIELD, Dr Adrian Richard William; *b* 15 May 1946; *Educ* Univ of London (MB BS, LRCP, MRCP, MD); *Career* conslt gastroenterologist: Middx Hosp London, King Edward VII Hosp for Offrs London; memb: Br Soc of Gastroenterology, Royal Soc of Med; FRCP; *Style—* Dr Adrian Hatfield; 18 Upper Wimpole St, London W1M 7TB (☎ 071 224 4598)

HATHAWAY, Derek Charles Derek; *Career* chm: Dartmouth Investments, Ashby Leisure Products, Combat Engineering, Energy Machine Tools, Lawton Pressings; *Style—* Derek Hathaway, Esq; Dartmouth Investments Ltd, Bilston Trading Estate, Oxford St, Bilston, Staffs

HATHERLEY, John; s of Harold Norman Hatherley (d Margate S Africa 1986), and Hester Van Heerden (d 1972); *b* 18 Oct 1926; *Educ* Christian Bros Coll Boksburg S Africa, Univ of Witwatersand (BA), Univ of Cape Town (MA); *m* 5 Jan 1955, Gertruida Johanna, da of Jacobus Mattys-Botha; 1 s (Peter b 1957), 1 da (Anita b 1956); *Career* accountant Gearings Water Boring and Equipment Co Ltd 1950-51; teacher: Charterhouse, King's Coll Sch Wimbledon; head of Econ and Politics Dept Purley HS and Wimbledon Coll; assoc memb Chartered Inst of Secs 1953; memb: Exec Ctee Econ Res Cncl, Econ and Social Sci Res Assoc; sec Centre for Incentive Taxation; pres Sutton Educn Assoc; prospective Parly candidate (Lib) Carshalton (Sutton) 1975-83, London Lib Party Exec and Policy Panel 1974-83; *Recreations* esoteric philosophy, new economics, economic reform (especially as regards taxation, inner city decay), education reform, freelance writing (mostly economics and poetry); *Clubs* Gladstone; *Style—* John Hatherley, Esq; 16 Brighton Rd, Coulsdon, Surrey CR5 2BA (☎ 081 668 4038)

HATHERTON, 8 Baron (UK 1835) Edward Charles Littleton; only s of Mervyn Cecil Littleton (d 1970), gs of 3 Baron, by his w, Margaret Ann, da of Frank Sheehy; *b* 24 May 1950; *m* 1974, Hilda Maria Robert, of San Jose, Costa Rica; 1 s (Hon Thomas), 2 da (Hon Melissa Ann b 1975, Hon Valerie Anne b 1981); *Heir* s, Hon Thomas Edward, b 1977; *Style—* The Rt Hon Lord Hatherton; PO Box 3358, San José, Costa Rica

HATHORN, Eric Anthony; s of James Hathorn, of Edinburgh; *b* 18 June 1929; *Educ* Wellington, Merton Coll Oxford; *m* 1966, Hon Jean Rosemary *qv*, da of Lord Evans, GCVO (d 1963); 2 s, 1 da; *Career* 2 Lt Grenadier Gds; with ICI 1952-68, joined L Messel and Co (Stockbrokers) 1968; ptnr: Beardsley Bishop Escombe 1973-83, Henderson Crosthwaite 1983-; *Recreations* travel, theatre, opera, gardening; *Clubs* City University; *Style—* Eric Hathorn, Esq; 51 Netherhall Gdns, London NW3 (☎ 071 794 6892); Henderson Crosthwaite Ltd, 32 St Mary-at-Hill, London EC3 (☎ 071 283 8577)

HATHORN, Hon Mrs (Jean Rosemary); *née* Evans; da of 1 and last Baron Evans, GCVO (d 1963); *b* 14 April 1934; *m* 1966, Eric Anthony Hathorn, *qv*; 2 s, 1 da; *Style—* The Hon Mrs Hathorn; 51 Netherhall Gdns, London NW3 (☎ 071 794 6892)

HATT-COOK, Mark Edward; RD (and Bar); s of Lt-Col John Edward Hatt-Cook, MC, of The Courtyard, Stoke Farthing, Broadchalke, Salisbury, Wilts, and Lavender Helen, *née* Covernton; *b* 18 Dec 1942; *Educ* Bradfield; *m* 18 Oct 1969, Susan Georgina, da of Lt-Col Ronald John Henry Kaulback, OBE, of Altbough, Hoarwithy, Hereford; 2 da (Catherine Emma b 13 Aug 1974, Georgina Alice b 13 June 1977); *Career* cmmnd RMR 1963, 45 Commando S Arabia 1963 (active serv), 42 Commando Malaysia 1969, 41 Commando N Ireland 1970, qualified Arctic survival instr 1980, TAVR staff course Camberley 1981, USMC staff course Quantico 1984, Lt-Col CO RMR City of London 1990; articled with Hunters and with Bichoffs, admitted slr 1970, asst slr Deacons Hong Kong, ptnr Wilsons Salisbury; memb regnl Br Olympic Ctee 1988, pres Salisbury Slrs Assoc 1989; Freeman City of London 1981; memb Law Soc; *Recreations* shooting, skiing, numismatics; *Style—* Mark Hatt-Cook, Esq, RD; Mascalls, Broadchalke, Salisbury, Wilts (☎ 0722 780 480); Steynings House, Salisbury, Wilts (☎ 0722 412412, fax 0722 411 500)

HATTERSLEY, Lt Cdr Charles William; s of Maj J S Hattersley, of 17 Conference Way, Colkirk, Fakenham, Norfolk; *b* 22 March 1949; *Educ* Marlborough, Univ of Durham (BA), Guildford Coll of Law; *m* 30 July 1988, Rebecca Jane, da of Capt David Vernon Smith, of Guildford, Surrey; *Career* Britannia RN Coll Dartmouth 1971-72, Seaman Offr HMS Ark Royal 1972-73, Navigating Offr HMS Olympus 1973-74, 4 i/c HMS Courageous 1974-76; 3 i/c: HMS Walrus 1976-77, HMS Conqueror 1977-79; 2 i/c HMS Opportune 1979-81; memb: Jt Servs Team to Phabrang 21000 Peak India, Jt Servs Team to Manaslu North 24000 Nepal, Jt Servs Team to North face of Everest reached 27,200 feet; Capt 5 Bn Royal Anglian's TA Peterborough, (2 i/c of Company 1988-); articled clerk Holman Fenwick London 1985-87; admitted slr 1988; maritime lawyer Norton Rose London 1988-; lectr RGS and Alpine Club, played for Naval and Military Club in Bath Cup London; Liveryman Worshipful Co of Skinners 1981; FRGS, MNI; *Recreations* mountaineering, skiing, squash, golf; *Clubs* Naval and Military, Alpine; *Style—* Lt Cdr Charles Hattersley; 45 Layton Cresent, Brampton, Huntingdon PE18 8TS (☎ 0480 453 889); Norton Rose, Kempson House, PO Box 570, London EC3A 7AN (☎ 071 282 2434, fax 071 588 1181, telex 883652)

HATTERSLEY, Prof (William) Martin; s of Col Sidney Martin Hattersley, MC, late RAMC (ka 1943), and Vera, *née* Blackbourn (d 1962); *b* 31 March 1928; *Educ* Marlborough, Univ of London (BSc); *m* 1, 1 Sept 1950 (m dis 1982), Shena Mary, da of Sydney Drummond Anderson (d 1961); 3 da (Susan Mary (Mrs Boyce) b 13 Jan

1955, Clare Helen (Mrs Papavergos) b 6 June 1956, Diana Rosine (Mrs Warner) b 5 Nov 1957); m 2, 1 Oct 1982, May Ling, da of Wee Bin Chye (d 1949), of Singapore; *Career* probationary 2 Lt RM 1946, Lt RM 1948, resigned cmmn 1950, elected memb HAC 1988; Gerald Eve & Co (chartered surveyors): improver 1950-54, tech asst 1954-58, ptnr 1958, responsible for all overseas assignments 1962-86, responsible for Brussels Office 1975-83; chief resident valuation offr Kuala Lumpur Municipal Cncl 1959-61, prof and head of Dept of Property Valuation and Mgmnt City Univ; memb: RNLI, Lavant Valley Decorative and Fine Arts Soc, Emsworth Maritime and Historical Tst, Solent Protection Soc, Chichester Canal Soc; friend of: Chichester Festival Theatre, National Maritime Museum, Redgrave Theatre, Yvonne Arnard Theatre, National Library of Wales; pres: BSc Estate Mgmnt Club 1970, Rating Surveyors' Assoc 1978; Freeman City of London 1950; Liveryman: Worshipful Co of Skinners 1963, Worshipful Co of Chartered Surveyors 1977; FRICS 1963, FISM 1968, FSVA 1971; memb: RNSA 1946, RYA FIABCI 1973, IRRV 1986, ACIArb 1990; FIABCI Medaille d'Honor for Leadership of Professional Standards Ctee (France 1986); *Books* Valuation: Priniciples into Practice (contrib 1988); *Recreations* sailing; *Clubs* Carlton, Naval and Military, City Livery; *Style*— Prof Martin Hattersley; 4 Roundhouse Meadow, Emsworth, Hants PO10 8BD (☎ 0243 375664, fax 0243 378464); Dept of Property Valuation and Management, City University, Northampton Square, London EC1V OHB (☎ 071 253 4399, ext 3950)

HATTERSLEY, Rt Hon Roy Sydney George; PC (1975), MP (Lab) Birmingham Sparkbrook 1964-; s of late Frederick Hattersley (Lord Mayor Sheffield 1981-), and Enid Hattersley; *b* 28 Dec 1932; *Educ* Sheffield City GS, Hull Univ; *m* 1956, Molly (Edith Mary, headmistress Creighton Sch London, formerly ctee chm Headmistresses' Assoc and pres Secondary Heads Assoc, asst educn offr in charge of teaching staff ILEA 1982-), da of Michael Loughran; *Career* journalist; exec Health Serv and memb Sheffield City Cncl; PPS to Min of Pensions and Nat Insurance 1964-67, jt Parly sec Employment 1967-69, min of defence for admin 1969-70; Lab spokesman: defence 1972, Educn and Science 1972-74; min of state FCO 1974-76, prices and consumer protection sec 1976-79; chief oppn spokesman on: Environment 1979-80, Home Affairs 1981-83, Treasy and Econ Affairs 1983-87, Home Affairs 1987-; stood in Lab leadership and dep leadership elections, elected dep ldr Oct 1983-; named columnist of the year 1982 What the Papers Say (Granada TV); re-elected to shadow cabinet and appointed chief oppn spokesman Treasury and Econ Affrs 1983-; *Style*— The Rt Hon Roy Hattersley, MP; 14 Gayfere St, London SW1P 3HP (☎ 071 222 1309)

HATTON, Christopher John Bower; s of Alan Herbert Hatton (d 1960); *b* 5 March 1933; *Educ* Charterhouse; *m* 1962, Alison Myfanwy, da of Robert Faulkner Armitage (d 1982); 3 c; *Career* slr 1956; chm: Greenall Whitley plc (brewers), de Vere Hotels Ltd; dir Northern Advsy Bd National Westminster Bank, North Western Bd Sun Alliance Assurance Co; *Style*— Christopher Hatton, Esq; Robert Davies & Co Solicitors, PO Box 1, 21 Bold St, Warrington, Cheshire (☎ 0925 50161)

HATTRELL, Michael Walter; s of (Walter) Stanley Hattrell (d 1977), of The Limes, Brancaster, Norfolk, and Pauline Gertrude, *née* Herbert; *b* 1 May 1934; *Educ* Ampleforth , Trinity Coll Cambridge (MA); *m* 2 Sept 1967, Charmian Adele, da of Louis Larth, of Brimpsfield, Glos; 2 da (Samantha b 1968, Victoria b 1971); *Career* Nat Serv cmmnd Green Howards, served Canal Zone and Cyprus 1952-54; architect ptnr WS Hattrell & Ptnrs 1961-75, currently in practice as Michael Hattrell & Assoc 1975-; works incl: St Andrews Shared Church Slough 1970, works for house of Stanley Kubrick in St Alban's 1977, works at Brocket Hall Herts 1985-89; hon sec: Chilterns Cricket League, Soc of Int Christian Artists; Freeman City of London, Liveryman Worshipful Co Coach Makers and Coach Harness Makers; FRIBA; *Recreations* cricket, golf; *Style*— Michael Hattrell, Esq; Priory Cottage, Stomp Rd, Burnham, Bucks (☎ 06286 5030); 29 Trott St, London SW11 3DS (☎ 071 228 1672)

HATTY, Sir Cyril James; s of James Hatty; *b* 22 Dec 1908; *Educ* Westminster City Sch; *m* 1937, Doris Evelyn Stewart; 2 s; *Career* dep dir O and M Div UK Treasy to 1947; MP for Bulawayo S Rhodesia 1950-62 (min of Treasy 1954-62, min of Mines 1956-62); min of Fin Bophuthatswana 1979-82; tstee Zimbabwe Nat Conservation Tst; FCIS, FCMA; kt 1963; *Style*— Sir Cyril Hatty; Merton Park, Norton, Zimbabwe

HAUGHEY, Edward; OBE (1987), JP (1986); s of Edward Haughey (d 1943), of Kilcurry House, Dundalk, Co Louth, and Rose, *née* Traynor; *b* 5 Jan 1944; *Educ* Christian Brothers Secdy Sch Dundalk; *m* 5 Jan 1972, Mary Gordon, da of William Alfred Young (d 1977); 2 s (Edward, James), 1 da (Caroline); *Career* chm: Norbrook Laboratories Ltd 1969-, Norbrook Hldgs 1988; dir Short Brothers 1989; memb: Cncl CBI (NI) 1983-89, Bd of S ITEC 1985-89; chm IOD (NI branch) 1986-87 (1985-86), memb NI Fire Authy 1986-89, dir Advsy Bd Bank of Ireland 1987; memb Bd: Warrenpoint Harbour Authy 1989 (also 1986), Industl Tbnls 1990-; FID; *Recreations* study of architectural history; *Clubs* Savage (London); *Style*— Edward Haughey, Esq, JP, OBE; Carpenham, Rostrevor, Co Down, N Ireland; Norbrooks Laboratories Ltd, Station Works, Camlough Rd, Newry, Co Down, N Ireland ☎ 0693 64435, telex 747048, fax 0693 61721

HAVARD, Dr John David Jayne; CBE (1989); s of Dr Arthur William Havard (d 1964), of Lowestoft, and Ursula Jayne Vernon, *née* Humphrey (d 1990); *b* 5 May 1924; *Educ* Malvern, Jesus Coll Cambridge (MA, MD, LLM), Middx Hosp Med Sch (MRCP); *m* 1, Sept 1950 (m dis 1982), Margaret Lucy, da of Albert Lumsden Collis, OBE (d 1963), of Wimbledon; 2 s (Jeremy Michael Jayne b 18 April 1952, Richard William b 27 Jan 1954), 1 da (Amanda b 12 May 1956); m 2, July 1982, Anne Audrey, da of Rear Adm Lawrence Boutwood, CB, OBE (d 1982), of Tideford, Cornwall; *Career* Nat Serv Actg Sqdn Ldr RAF Med Serv 1950-52; called to the Bar Middle Temple 1954, house physician Professorial Med Unit Middx Hosp 1950, GP Lowestoft 1952-58, sec E Suffolk LMC 1956-58; staff BMA 1958-89, sec BMA 1979-89; former dep chm Staff Side Whitley Cncl (Health Servs), chm Sci Ctee Int Driver Behaviour Res Assoc, pres Br Acad of Forensic Sciences 1985, sec and treas Cwlth Med Assoc 1986-; memb Gen Medical Cncl 1989-; Stevens Medallist (RSM) 1984, Green Coll lectr Oxford 1989; Widmark award (Int Ctee on Alcohol, Drugs and Traffic Safety) Chicago Oct 1989, Gold medal for Distinguished Merit of BMA 1990; MRCP (UK) 1987; *Books* Detection of Secret Homicide (Cambridge Studies in Criminology Vol XI 1960), Medical Negligence: The Mounting Dilemma (1989), author of chapters in text books on legal med, alcohol, drugs, etc; *Recreations* Bach Choir, country walks; *Clubs* United Oxford and Cambridge University, Achilles; *Style*— Dr John Havard, CBE; 1 Wilton Sq, London N1 3DL (☎ 071 359 2802); Golden Cap, Tideford, Saltash, Cornwall; Commonwealth Medical Association, BMA House, Tavistock Square, London WC1H 9JP (☎ 071 383 6266, fax 071 383 6233, telex 265929)

HAVARD, (Michael) Robin; s of Capt Cyril Havard, of The Pound, St Nicholas, nr Cardiff, and Elizabeth Mary Morgan Havard, JP, *née* Williams; *b* 7 May 1957; *Educ* Epsom Coll, Univ Coll Cardiff (BSc); *m* 4 Dec 1982, Ann, da of Kenneth John Evans (d 1976); 1 da (Abigail Tanya b 31 May 1987); *Career* slr; ptnr: Loosemore 1981-83, Watkin Jones & Co 1984-85, Morgan Bruce 1985-; memb Law Soc 1981; *Recreations* rugby, sailing, golf; *Clubs* Bridgend, London Welsh, Swansea, Newport, Glamorgan County, WRU Presidents XV; *Style*— Robin Havard, Esq; 216 Heol Hir, Thornhill, Cardiff (☎ 0222 754284), Morgan Bruce, Bradley Court, Park Place, Cardiff CF1 3DP (☎ 0222 233677, fax 0222 399288, telex 497902)

HAVELOCK, Sir Wilfrid Bowen; s of Rev E W Havelock (d 1916), and F H Bowen; *b* 14 April 1912; *Educ* ISC Windsor; *m* 1, 1938 (m dis 1967), Mrs Muriel Elizabeth Pershouse, *née* Vincent; 1 s; m 2, 1972, Mrs Patricia Mumford; *Career* served in 3/4 African Rifles 1940-42; MLC Kenya 1948-63 (min Local Govt, Health and Lands 1954-62, min Agric and Animal Husbandry 1962-63), dep chm Kenya Agriculture Finance Corporation 1964-84, memb Nat Irrigation Bd Kenya 1974-79, dir Bamburi Portland Cement Co 1974-86; dir: Baobab Farm Ltd Bamburi 1974-, African Fund for Endangered Wildlife Ltd (Kenya); chm Kenya Assoc of Hotelkeepers and Caterers 1973-76, memb Hotels and Restaurant Authy 1975-82; kt 1963; *Clubs* Muthaiga Country (Nairobi), Mount Kenya Safari (Nanyuki) fell Royal Commonwealth Soc (London, Nairobi, Mombasa); *Style*— Sir Wilfrid Havelock; No 63 Lakeview Estate, PO Box 30181, Nairobi, Kenya (☎ 010 254 2 732142)

HAVELOCK-ALLAN, Sir Anthony James Allan; 4 Bt (UK 1858), of Lucknow; s of Allan Havelock-Allan (2 s of Sir Henry Havelock-Allan, 1 Bt, VC, GCB, MP, DL and his w Lady Alice Moreton, da of 2 Earl of Ducie), and Annie Julia, da of Sir William Chaytor, 3 Bt; suc bro, Sir Henry Ralph Moreton Havelock-Allan, 3 Bt, 1975; *b* 28 Feb 1905; *Educ* Charterhouse, Switzerland; *m* 1, 12 April 1939 (m dis 1952), (Babette) Valerie Louise (the film actress Valerie Hobson; she m 2, 1954, John Dennis Profumo, CBE), da of late Cdr Robert Gordon Hobson, RN; 2 s (Simon Anthony Henry b 1944 d 1991, (Anthony) Mark David b 1951); m 2, 1979, Maria Theresa Consuela (Sara), da of late Don Carlos Ruiz de Villafranca (formerly Spanish ambass to Chile and Brazil); *Heir* s, (Anthony) Mark David Havelock-Allan b 1951; *Career* film producer; formerly produced quota films for Paramount, produced for Pinebrook Ltd and Two Cities Films 1938-40, assoc producer to Noel Coward 1941, with David Lean and Ronald Neame formed Cineguild 1942, producer, assoc producer and in charge of production for Cineguild 1942-47, formed Constellation Films 1949, formed with Lord Brabourne and Maj David Angel Br Home Entertainment (first co to attempt to introduce pay TV by cable) 1962; chm British Film Academy 1952, govr Br Film Inst (memb Inst's Production Ctee) 1958-65, chm Council of Soc of Film and Television Arts (now BAFTA) 1962 and 1963; *Style*— Sir Anthony Havelock-Allan, Bt; c/o Messrs Gorrie Whitson and Sons, 9 Cavendish Sq, London W1

HAVERS, Christopher Antony Gore; s of Antony Cecil Oldfield Havers, of Berks, and Barbara Harrison Havers; *b* 30 April 1950; *Educ* Repton, Trinity Coll Dublin (BA); *m* 6 May 1978, Christine Mary, da of Kevin Patrick Moore, of Coventry; 2 s (Timothy b 1981, Patrick b 1984), 1 da (Rosie b 1988); *Career* called to the Bar Inner Temple 1975; dir: Through Transport Mutual Services Ltd 1985, West of England Ship Owners Insurance Services 1987; *Recreations* shooting, sailing, farming; *Style*— Christopher A G Havers, Esq; West of England Services, International House, 1 St Katharine's Way, London E1 9UE

HAVERS, Baron (Life Peer 1987), of St Edmundsbury, Co Suffolk; (Robert) Michael Oldfield; PC (1977), QC (1964); s of Sir Cecil Havers, sometime High Ct judge, by his w Enid, da of William Oldfield Snelling, JP, of Norwich; *b* 10 March 1923; *Educ* Westminster, Corpus Christi Coll Cambridge; *m* 1949, Carol Elizabeth, da of Stuart Lay, of London; 2 s; *Career* called to the bar Inner Temple 1948, dep chm W Suffolk QS 1961-65 (chm 1965-71); rec: Dover 1962-68, Norwich 1968-71, Crown Ct 1972; slr gen 1972-74, shadow attorney gen and legal advsy to shadow cabinet 1974-79, attorney gen 1979-87, Lord Chllr July-Oct 1987; chllr: Diocese of St Edmundsbury and Ipswich 1965-73, Diocese of Ely 1969-73; MP (C) Wimbledon 1970-87; hon fell Corpus Christi Coll Cambridge 1988; kt 1972; *Clubs* Garrick, Pratts; *Style*— The Rt Hon Lord Havers, PC, QC; 5 King's Bench Walk, Temple, London EC4 (☎ 071 353 4713); White Shutters, Ousden, Newmarket, Suffolk (☎ 063 879 267)

HAVERS, Hon Nigel; yr s of Baron Havers, *qv*; *b* 6 Nov 1951; *m* 1, 1974 (m dis 1989), Carolyn Gillian, da of Vincent Cox; 1 da (Katharine b 1977); m 2, 12 Dec 1989, Mrs Polly Bloomfield; *Career* actor; The Glittering Prizes, Nicholas Nickleby, Horseman; TV: A Horseman Riding By, Upstairs Downstairs, Nancy Astor, Strangers and Brothers, Don't Wait Up, The Charmer, A Perfect Hero, Sleepers; films: Chariots of Fire, A Passage to India, Burke and Wills, The Whistle Blower, Empire of the Sun, Farewell to the King; *Recreations* keeping fit, reading, gardening; *Clubs* Garrick; *Style*— The Hon Nigel Havers; 125 Gloucester Rd, London SW7

HAVERS, Hon Philip; er s of Baron Havers (Life Peer); *b* 16 June 1950; *Style*— The Hon Philip Havers; 74 Cadogan Terrace, London SW1

HAVERY, Richard Orbell; QC (1980); s of Joseph Horton Havery, of London, and Constance Eleanor, *née* Orbell (d 1987); *b* 7 Feb 1934; *Educ* St Paul's, Magdalen Coll Oxford (BA, MA); *Career* barr, rec of Crown Ct 1986 (asst rec 1982), bencher Middle Temple 1989; *Books* Kemp and Kemp The Quantum of Damages (jt ed 3 edn, 1967); *Recreations* music, croquet, steam locomotives; *Clubs* Garrick, Hurlingham; *Style*— Richard Havery, Esq, QC; 11 Alderney St, SW1V 4ES; 4 Raymond Buildings, Gray's Inn London WC1R 5BP (☎ 071 405 7211, fax 071 405 2084)

HAVILAND, Christopher Philip; s of late Col Philip Haviland Haviland, OBE, and Molly Gwendoline Parker, *née* Butt; *b* 9 Feb 1940; *Educ* Trinity Coll Dublin (MA, LLB); *m* 1970, Catherine Margaret Joan, da of George Ernest Swanson, of Colinton, Lothian; 2 s (Philip Julian Swanson b 27 Jan 1972, Adrian Christopher Clemow (twin) b 27 Jan 1972), 1 da (Fiona Mary Katharine b 30 June 1975); *Career* merchant banker; dir: N M Rothschild & Sons (CI) Ltd 1975-81, N M Rothschild & Sons Ltd 1976-81, Barclays Merchant Bank Ltd 1981-86, Barclays de Zoete Wedd Ltd 1986-, Barclays Bank (regnl dir) 1987-, Korea Merchant Banking Corp 1987-, Barclays Trust & Banking (Japan) Ltd 1987-, Seibu Barclays Finance Ltd 1987-; *Recreations* swimming, tennis, walking; *Style*— Christopher Haviland, Esq; 4 Royal Mint Court, London EC3N 4HJ (☎ 071 626 1567)

HAVILAND, Julian Arthur Charles; er s of Maj Leonard Proby Haviland (d 1971, Indian Cavalry), by his w, Helen Dorothea (d 1972), only da of Sir Charles Fergusson, 7 Bt, GCB, GCMG, DSO, MVO; *b* 8 June 1930; *Educ* Eton, Magdalene Coll Cambridge; *m* Sept 1959, Caroline Victoria, yst da of late George Freeland Barbour, by his w Hon Helen Victoria, da of 8 Lord Polwarth; 3 s (Peter b 1961, Charles b 1964, Richard b 1967); *Career* political ed The Times 1981-85 (suc Fred Emery, who became home ed), political ed ITN to 1981; has worked for: Surrey Advertiser, Evening Standard, Daily Telegraph; *Style*— Julian Haviland, Esq; 39 Cator Rd, London SE26 5DT (☎ 081 778 4428)

HAVILL, Brian Bond; s of Arthur Ernest Havill (d 1971), and Violet May, *née* Williams; *b* 31 Aug 1939; *Educ* Hafod-y-Ddol GS, Univ of Sheffield (BSc), Harvard Business Sch (PMD); *m* 29 Nov 1969, Ann Jennifer, da of late Charles Rooke; 2 s (Gervase Bond b 2 April 1972, Giles Dominic b 3 Feb 1976); *Career* joined ALCAN Group as graduate trainee 1961, mktg dir Haden Carrier 1974, vice pres of ops Thomas Tilling 1974, dir and vice pres Citicorp Inc 1983, md Painewebber International 1986-; memb: Harvard Business Sch Assoc, Br American C of C; *Recreations* golf, literature, music; *Clubs* Royal Wimbledon Golf; *Style*— Brian Havill, Esq; 19 Lingfield Rd, Wimbledon, London SW19 4QD (☎ 081 946 5422); Paine Webber International (UK) Ltd, 1 Finsbury Ave, London EC2M 2PA (☎ 071 377 0055, fax 071 247 0871, car 0836 261 705)

HAVILLE, Robert William; s of James Haville (d 1983), and Eileen Haville; *b* 27 July 1955; *Educ* Marlborough GS, Univ of Lancaster (BA), Univ of Bradford (MBA); *m* 18

Oct 1980, Hazel Dawn, da of George Burke, of London; 1 s (James b 1988), 2 da (Rosalind b 1986, Sarah b 1990); *Career* fin analyst Kimberley Clark 1976-77; investmt analyst: McAnally Montgomery 1978-81, James Capel 1982-87, Morgan Stanley 1988-; memb Business Graduates Assoc; *Clubs* RAC; *Style—* Robert Haville, Esq; Morgan Stanley International, Kingsley House, 1A Wimpole St, London W1 (☎ 071 709 3000)

HAW, David William Martin; s of Rev Albert Haw, MC (d 1931), and Kathleen Ellen, *née* Turk (d 1970); *b* 17 March 1926; *Educ* Kingswood Sch, Leeds Univ Med Sch (BSc, MB ChB); *m* 27 March 1948, Dr Marjorie Elise Haw, da of Arthur Hetherington (d 1933); 2 s (Roger b 1952, Marcus b 1967), 3 da (Judith b 1949, Catherine b 1951, Sally b 1955); *Career* short service cmmn Flt lt 1952-55; house physician Harrogate Gen Hosp 1951-52, gen duties MO RAF 1952-55, demonstrator in anatomy 1955-56, house surgn Leeds Gen Infirmary 1956-57 (house physician 1951), sr house surgn Manchester Royal Infirmary 1957-58, registrar surgn Ashton-u-Lyme Gen Infirmary 1958-59, sr house offr Royal Nat Orthopaedic Hosp Stanmore 1959-60; orthopeadic registrar: Lord Mayor Treloar Hosp 1960-61, Guy's Hosp 1961-63; sr registrar Leeds Regnl Bd 1963-65: Hull Royal, Bradford Royal, Leeds Gen Infirmary; conslt orthopaedic surgn York Dist 1965-; represented England at annual triangula 3 miles 1947; pres Northern Veterans Athletic Assoc 1975-77, former chm Thirsk and Malton Cons Dining Club, pres Holdsworth Travelling Orthopaedic Club 1989 (sec 1978-85) FRCS, FBOA; *Recreations* oil painting, gardening, athletics; *Clubs* The Lord Mayor Treloar and Gauvain Dining, The Ryedale Cons Assoc Dining; *Style—* David Haw, Esq; East Court, Shipton by Beningbrough, York YO6 1AR (☎ 0904 470324); The Purey Cust Nuffield Hospital, Precentors Ct, York (☎ 0904 641571); The District Hospital, Wiggington Rd, York (☎ 0904 631313)

HAW, Jonathan Stopford; s of Denis Stopford Haw (d 1979), of Sidcup, Kent, and Elisabeth Mary Dorothy, *née* Mack; *b* 16 March 1945; *Educ* Radley, Keble Coll Oxford (MA); *m* 20 Dec 1969, Hélène Lucie, da of Louis Lacuve, Chevalier de L'Ordre National du Mérite, of Perpignan, France; 1 s (Alexander b 1973), 1 da (Katherine b 1976); *Career* slr; Slaughter and May: ptnr 1977-, first ptnr New York 1984-87; memb Ctee Bassishaw Ward Club London; memb Bd of Dirs The Juvenile Diabetes Fndn (UK); Freeman City of London 1970, Liveryman Worshipful Co of Armourers and Brasiers, memb City of London Slrs Co; memb: Law Soc, Int Bar Assoc; *Recreations* tennis, reading, wine; *Clubs* Leander; *Style—* Jonathan S Haw, Esq; Goldhill House, East Garston, Newbury, Berks (☎ 0488 39 265); 27 St Paul's Place, Islington, London N1 2QG; 35 Basinghall St, London EC2V 5DB (☎ 071 600 1200, fax 071 600 0289, 071 726 0038, telex 883486/888926)

HAWARDEN, 8 Viscount (I 1793); Sir Robert Leslie Eustace Maude; 10 Bt (I 1705); also Baron de Montalt (I 1785); s of 7 Viscount (d 1958), by his w Marion (da of Albert Wright, whose w Margaretta was sis of 20 Baron FitzWalter); *b* 26 March 1926; *Educ* Winchester, ChCh Oxford; *m* 1957, Susannah, da of Maj Charles Gardner (gggs of 1 Baron Gardner); 2 s, 1 da; *Heir* s, Hon Connan Maude; *Career* served Coldstream Gds 1944-45; landowner and farmer; *Style—* The Rt Hon the Viscount Hawarden; Wingham Court, Canterbury, Kent CT3 1BB (☎ 0227 720222)

HAWES, Roger Stapeldon; s of Esmond Montague Hawes, and Daisy Marion, *née* Grout; *b* 30 Oct 1949; *Educ* King's Sch Worcs, Univ of Sheffield (LLB); *m* 18 March 1972, Hilary Stella; 1 s (Rupert David b 1976), 3 da (Lucy Frances b 1979, Bryony Isobel b 1988, Rowan Bethany Ruth b 19 Feb 1990); *Career* admitted slr 1974; ptnr Cobbett Leak Almond; memb 41 Club, Jr Chamber Int Senator; memb Law Soc; *Recreations* keep fit; *Style—* Roger Hawes, Esq; Cobbett Leak Almond, Ship Canal House, King St, Manchester (☎ 061 833 3333, fax 061 833 3030)

HAWES RICHARDS, Derek; s of Arthur Hawes Richards (d 1971), and Eva Evelyn, *née* Small (d 1987); *b* 2 Feb 1933; *Educ* South Devon Technical Coll Torquay; *m* 29 Aug 1959, Hazel Anne, da of Victor Maddison, of Kent; 2 da (Lisa b 1966, Sophie b 1973); *Career* memb Liberal Party 1964-, cnclr Pembury Parish 1974-82, cnclr Kent County Cncl 1985-, pres Tunbridge Wells C of C 1988-89; FRIBA; *Recreations* cricket, snooker, music, reading; *Style—* Derek Hawes Richards, Esq; Hop Press Oast, Mascalls Court Road, Paddock Wood, Kent TN12 6NB (☎ 0892 834692); 4 St Johns Road, Tunbridge Wells, Kent TN4 9ND (☎ 0892 38777, fax 0892 49849)

HAWKE, Hon Edward George; s and h of 10 Baron Hawke, *qv*; *b* 25 Jan 1950; *Educ* Eton; *Style—* The Hon Edward Hawke; c/o The Rt Hon Lord Hawke, Old Mill House, Cuddington, Northwich, Cheshire

HAWKE, Ina, Lady; Ina Mary Faure Hawke; *née* Faure Walker; er da of Henry Faure Walker (d 1940), of Highly Manor, Balcombe, Sussex and Edith Ina, *née* Bartholomew (d 1940); *b* 20 Oct 1912; *m* 1 Nov 1934, 9 Baron Hawke (d 1985); 7 da (who include the w of Nicholas Scott, MP, *qv*); *Style—* The Rt Hon Ina, Lady Hawke; Faygate Place, Faygate, Sussex

HAWKE, Cdr Michael George Richard; s of Peter Kenneth Nöel Hawke (d 1979), and Mary Olivia, *née* Wilson; *b* 29 Oct 1940; *Educ* RNC; *m* 20 July 1971, Juliet Beaumont Fullerton, da of Cdr Leslie George Wilson, OBE, of Dunbartonshire; 1 s (Simon Andrew b 1977), 2 da (Harriet b 1973, Catherine b 1974); *Career* joined BRNC Dartmouth 1959, appointed to HMS Loch Alvie 9 Frigate Sqdn, joined HMS Dolphin 1962 (subs), HMS Ocelot 1963-64, CO HMS Oberon 1972-73, memb C-in-C Fleet Staff (CTF 345) 1973-75, OC NUSCOT 1978, CO HMS Repulse 1981-84, Cdr HMS Dryad 1987-89; staff Comnasouth Izmir 1989-; chm Nautical Inst Scot Branch 1979, fell Nautical Inst 1988-; *Recreations* sailing, walking, music, shooting, fishing, model making; *Style—* Cdr Michael G R Hawke; Yew Tree House, Nicholashayne, Wellington, Somerset TA21 9QY (☎ 0884 40302); Comnasouth Staff Izmir

HAWKE, 10 Baron (GB 1776); (Julian Stanhope) Theodore; s of 8 Baron Hawke (d 1939), and Frances Alice, *née* Wilmer (d 1959); suc bro, 9 Baron Hawke (d 1985); *b* 19 Oct 1904; *Educ* Eton, King's Coll Cambridge (MA); *m* 1, 17 Feb 1933 (m dis 1946), (Angela Margaret) Griselda (d 1984), o da of Capt Edmund William Bury (d 1918); 2 da; m 2, 22 May 1947, Georgette Margaret, o da of George Davidson, of 73 Eaton Square, London; 1 s, 3 da; *Heir* s, Hon Edward George, *qv*; *Career* Wing Cdr AAF 1945, W Africa; with Manchester textile firm 1926-69; dir Glazebrook Steel Ltd 1932-69; *Recreations* golf, gardening, shooting; *Style—* The Rt Hon the Lord Hawke; The Old Mill House, Cuddington, Northwich, Cheshire (☎ 0606 882248)

HAWKEN, Lewis Dudley; CB (1983); s of Richard Hawken, and Doris May Evelyn Hawken; *b* 23 Aug 1931; *Educ* Harrow Co Sch for Boys, Lincoln Coll Oxford (MA); *m* 1954, Bridget Mary Gamble (d 1989); 2 s, 1 da; *Career* dep chm Bd of Customs and Excise 1980-87; *Style—* Lewis Hawken, Esq, CB; 19 Eastcote Rd, Ruislip, Middx

HAWKER, Christopher Henry Acton; MBE (1972); s of Lt-Col (Albert) Henry Hawker, CMG, OBE, of Bowling Green Farm, Cottered, nr Buntingford, Herts, and Margaret Janet Olivia Hawker (d 1980); *b* 6 Dec 1945; *Educ* Kenton Coll Nairobi Kenya, Haileybury, RMA Sandhurst, Exeter Coll Oxford; *m* 29 July 1977 (m dis 1988), (Sarah) Jane, da of Prof G I C Ingram, of Staple Lees, Hastingleigh, Ashford, Kent; 1 s (Nicholas b 24 Aug 1982), 1 da (Kate b 23 Jan 1985); *Career* cmmnd Royal Green Jackets 1966, 1 Bn Berlin 1966-67, 1 and 3 Bn 1970-75, Adj 3 Bn 1973-75, ret 1975; co-founding dir Ridgeway Int Ltd (int freight forwarders) 1975-; MInstD; *Recreations* sailing, skiing, squash, tennis, walking; *Clubs* Army and Navy, Vincents (Oxford); *Style—* Christopher Hawker, Esq, MBE; c/o Ridgeway International Ltd, 69 High Street, Wallingford, Oxon OX10 0BX, (☎ 0491 39780, fax 0491 39765, telex 847994)

HAWKER, Rt Rev Dennis Gascoyne; s of Robert Stephen Hawker, of Ashtead Surrey (d 1983), and Amelia Caroline, *née* Gascoyne (d 1984); *b* 8 Feb 1921; *Educ* Addey and Stanhope GS London, Queens' Coll Cambridge (MA), Cuddesdon Theological Coll Oxford; *m* Margaret Hamilton, da of Robert Henderson, of Brockley SE14 (d 1980); 1 s (Martin Robert b 1946), 1 da (Alison Margaret b 1954); *Career* Major Royal Marines 1940-46; curate SS Mary and Eanswythe Folkestone 1950-55, vicar St Mark S Norwood 1955-60, St Hughs missioner Diocese of Lincoln 1960-65, vicar St Mary and James Gt Grimsby 1965-72, bishop of Grantham 1972-87; *Recreations* walking, gardening, naval and military history; *Clubs* Army and Navy; *Style—* The Rt Rev D G Hawker; Pickwick Cottage, Hall Close, Heacham, nr Kings Lynn, Norfolk PE31 7JT (☎ 0485 70450)

HAWKER, Geoffrey Fort; TD; *b* 20 Dec 1929; *Educ* Univ of London (BSc); *m* ;2 da; *Career* chartered civil engr 1956; called to the Bar Grays Inn 1970; in practice as conslt and arbitrator; pres Soc of Construction Arbitrators 1986-89; Liveryman: Worshipful Co of Arbitrators, Worshipful Co of Engrs; CEng, FEng, FICE, FIEI, FIStructE, Eur Ing, MSocIS (France), MConsE, FCIArb; *Books* A Guide to Commercial Arbitration under the 1979 Act (with R Gibson-Jarvis, 1980), The ICE Arbitration Practice (with Uff and Timms, 1986); *Style—* Geoffrey Hawker, Esq, TD; 199 The Strand, London WC2R 1DR (☎ 071 497 9757, fax 071 497 9710, DX 1014)

HAWKES, Dr Christopher Hickman; s of Austin John Hawkes (d 1979), of Dawlish, Devon, and Irene, *née* Hickman (d 1986); *b* 2 June 1939; *Educ* Liverpool HS, Univ of Liverpool (BSc), Univ of Edinburgh (MB ChB, BSc, MD); *m* 1, 1965 (m dis 1981), Bernadette June, *née* Hamilton; 2 s (Martin Hamilton b 14 Oct 1968, Malcolm Alexander b 10 July 1970), 1 da (Anne-Marie b 27 Nov 1966); m 2, 1982, Mahboub Belghes, da of General Mahmood Ghezel-Ayagh; 2 da (Elizabeth Dolatshahy b 8 Aug 1985, Catherine Dolatshahy b 20 July 1987); *Career* conslt neurologist Ipswich Hosp 1976-, hon lectr Inst Neurology London 1976-, clinical teacher Univ of Cambridge Med Sch 1983-; many articles on neurology and med 1970-; vice pres: Ipswich Parkinson's Disease Soc 1983-, Ipswich Multiple Sclerosis Soc 1987-; memb: Assoc Br Neurologists 1974, BMA 1975; MRCP 1968, FRCP 1985; *Recreations* sailing, squash, computing; *Clubs* Waldringfield Sailing, Ipswich Sports; *Style—* Dr Christopher Hawkes; 22 Henley Rd, Ipswich IP1 3SL (☎ 0473 254543); Dept of Neurology, Ipswich Hosp, Heath Rd, Ipswich IP4 5PD (☎ 0473 704044)

HAWKES, Prof Donald Durston; s of Clifford George Durston Hawkes (d 1983), of Cardiff, and Mabel Sophia Stephens (d 1979); *b* 18 July 1934; *Educ* Canton GS, Univ of London (BSc), Univ of Birmingham (MSc, Phd); *m* 22 July 1958, Janet Beatrice, da of Enoch Francis Davies (d 1988), of Cardiff; 1 s (David b 1965), 1 da (Jane b 1960); *Career* geologist: Br Antarctic Survey 1956-59, Overseas Geological Survey 1959-62; lectr then sr lectr Fourah Bay Coll 1963-70; prof and head of geology: Univ of Sierra Leone 1970-72, Univ of Aston 1972-88; prof and head of earth sciences Univ of Birmingham 1988-; author of numerous scientific pubns; FGS 1957, MIGeol 1978, FRSA 1981; *Recreations* sea fishing, gardening; *Style—* Prof Donald Hawkes; School of Earth Sciences, The University of Birmingham, Edgbaston, Birmingham B15 2TT (☎ 021 4143344

HAWKES, Jacquetta; *see*: Priestley, (Jessie) Jacquetta

HAWKES, Prof John Gregory; s of Charles William Hawkes (d 1964), and Gertrude Maude, *née* Chappell (d 1970); *b* 27 June 1915; *Educ* Cheltenham GS, Christ's Coll Cambridge (BA, MA, PhD, ScD); *m* 20 Dec 1941, (Ellen) Barbara, da of Charles Henry Leather (d 1954); 2 s (Anthony Christopher b 1950, Peter Geoffrey b 1950), 2 da (Phillada Daphne (Mrs Collins) b 1944, Stephanie Katherine (Mrs Hazeldine) b 1946); *Career* Cwlth Bureau of Plant Breeding and Genetics 1939-48, dir Colombian Miny of Agric Res Station 1948-52; Univ of Birmingham: lectr and sr lectr in botany 1952-61, prof of plant taxonomy 1961-67, prof and head Plant Biology Dept 1967-82, emeritus prof plant biology 1982-; hon life memb: Euro Assoc for Research in Plant Breeding 1989, Potato Assoc of America 1989; fell Linnean Soc 1945 (pres 1991-); FInstBiol 1976; *Books* incl: Reproductive Biology and Taxonomy of Vascular Plants (ed, 1966), Chemotaxonomy and Serotaxonomy (ed, 1968), The Potatoes of Argentina, Brazil, Paraguay and Uruguay (jtly, 1969), A Computer-Mapped Flora (jtly, 1971), Crop Genetic Resources for Today and Tomorrow (jt ed, 1975), Conservation and Agriculture (ed, 1978), The Diversity of Crop Plants (1983), Revised Edition of Salaman's History and Social Influence of the Potato (ed, 1985), The Potatoes of Bolivia (jtly, 1989), The Potato-Evolution, Biodiversity and Genetic Resources (1990); *Recreations* gardening, travel; *Clubs* Athenaeum; *Style—* Prof John Hawkes; University of Birmingham, PO Box 363, Birmingham B15 2TT (☎ 021 414 6170)

HAWKES, Michael John; s of Wilfred Arthur Hawkes (d 1968), and Anne Maria Hawkes (d 1966); *b* 7 May 1929; *Educ* Bedford Sch, New Coll Oxford (MA); *m* 1, 7 Dec 1957 (m dis 1973), Gillian Mary, *née* Watts; 2 s (James b 1964, Jason Michael b 1967), 2 da (Louise b 1963, Laura b 1966); m 2, 10 July 1973, Elizabeth Anne, *née* Gurton; *Career* banker; former chm: Kleinwort Benson Ltd, Sharps Pixley Ltd; former dep chm Kleinwort Benson Gp; *Recreations* walking, gardening; *Style—* Michael Hawkes, Esq; Brookfield House, Burghfield Common, Berks (☎ 0734 83 2912)

HAWKES, (Anthony) Paul; s of Reginald Ernest Hawkes, and Maria Campbell, *née* Straton-Ferrier; *b* 19 April 1951; *Educ* City of London Sch, Brighton Poly (BA), Harvard Business Sch; *m* 6 Oct 1984, Marjorie, da of Frederick Smith; 2 s (Lee b 13 May 1980, Benjamin b 26 July 1985); *Career* mgmnt trainee: Shlackman & Son 1969, Alders of Croydon 1971-72; area mangr EF Student Services 1974-75, mktg mangr American Express 1977-78 (mktg exec 1975-77); Time-Life Books (Europe) Inc: mail order mangr 1978-80, Eng area mangr 1980-82, Euro mktg vice pres 1982-86; dir: Abram Hawkes Associates Ltd 1987-, BDMA 1988-, IMC Ltd 1989-, The Campbell Stratton Group 1989-; MBIM 1987, MInstD 1987, CIM 1984; *Style—* Paul Hawkes, Esq; 10 Stanton Rd, West Wimbledon, London SW20 8RL (☎ 081 946 9353); Abram, Hawkes Associates, Oakfield House, 35 Perrymount Rd, Haywards Heath, West Sussex RH16 3BW (☎ 0444 441176, fax 0444 441268)

HAWKES, (Henry) William; s of late William Neville Hawkes, of Honington, Warwicks, and Marjorie Elsie, *née* Jackson; *b* 4 Dec 1939; *Educ* Uppingham, Cambridge Univ (MA, Dip Arch); *m* 22 Oct 1966, Hester Elizabeth, da of David Foster Gretton (d 1967); 3 da (Harriet b 1967, Polly b 1969, Olivia b 1972); *Career* architect, dir Stoneleigh Abbey Preservation Tst 1980-; chm Coventry Diocesan Advsy Ctee 1986-, tstee Coventry and Warwickshire Historic Churches Tst 1986-; memb Georgian Gp Exec Ctee 1985-; publications on 18th Century Gothic Revival; *Recreations* hand printing, cycling, architectural history; *Style—* William Hawkes, Esq; 20 Broad Street, Stratford upon Avon, Warwickshire (☎ 0789 66415); Hawkes and Cave, 1 Old Town, Stratford upon Avon, Warwickshire (☎ 0789 298877)

HAWKESBURY, Viscount; Luke Marmaduke Peter Savile Foljambe; s and h of 5 Earl of Liverpool; *b* 25 March 1972; *Style—* Viscount Hawkesbury; Barham Court, Exton, Oakham, Rutland, Leics LE15 8AP

HAWKESFORD, John Ernest; s of Ernest Hawkesford (d 1965), of Rushwick Grange, Rushwick, Worcestershire, and Sarah Elizabeth, *née* Jones; *b* 29 Nov 1946; *Educ* Warwick Sch Warwick, Univ Coll Med Sch London; *m* 29 June 1974, Barbara, da of Alexander Howe, of 54 Dovedale Gardens, Low Fell, Gateshead, Tyne and Wear; 3 da (Abigail Lisa b 1976, Julia Marie b 1979, Rachel Chloe b 1989); *Career* registrar in oral maxillo-facial surgery Stoke Mandville Hosp Bucks 1973-76, sr registrar in oral maxillo-facial surgery W of Scotland Plastic Surgery Unit Canniesburn Hosp Beardsden Glasgow, hon clinical lectr in oral surgery and oral med Univ of Glasgow 1976-79; conslt in oral maxillo-facial surgery 1979: Newcastle Health Authy (teaching), Northern RHA; hon clinical teacher in oral and maxillo-facial surgery Univ of Newcastle upon Tyne 1979-, clinical dir of oral and maxillo-facial surgery Newcastle Gen Hosp; memb: RSM, BDA, Br Assoc of Oral Maxillo-Facial Surgery; *Recreations* squash, swimming; *Style*— Mr John Hawkesford; The Quarry, 31 Batt House Rd, Stocksfield, Northumberland NE43 7RA (☎ 0661 842338); Oral and Maxillo Facial Surgery Department, Newcastle General Hospital, Westgate Rd, Newcastle upon Tyne NE4 6BE (☎ 091 2738811 ext 22204)

HAWKESWORTH, John Stanley; s of Lt-Gen Sir John Ledlie Inglis Hawkesworth, KBE, CB, DSO (d 1945), and Helen Jane, *née* McNaughton (d 1966); *b* 7 Dec 1920; *Educ* Rugby, Queen's Coll Oxford (BA); *m* 10 April 1943, Hyacinthe Nairne Marteine, da of Maj-Gen Philip Saxon George Gregson-Ellis, CB (d 1956); 1 s (Philip b 1949); *Career* WWII Capt Grenadier Gds served France, Belgium, Holland, Germany 1941-46; entered film indust 1946 as asst to Vincent Korda (London Films); art dir: The Third Man (1949), Sound Barrier (1952), The Heart of the Matter (1953); writer/producer: Rowlandson's England (1956), Tiger Bay (1959); for TV (creator/producer/writer): The Goldrobbers (LWT 1967), Upstairs Downstairs (LWT 1970-75), The Duchess of Duke St (BBC 1976-77), Danger UXB (Euston Films 1979), The Flame Trees of Thika (Euston Films 1981), QED (CBS 1982), The Tale of Beatrix Potter (BBC 1983), Oscar (BBC 1985), By The Sword Divided (1983-85); for TV (writer/developer) The Adventures and the Return of Sherlock Holmes (Granada 1984-88); developer Campion (BBC 1989), co-creator Chelworth (BBC 1989); painter; exhibitions: one man Show Watercolour Paintings (73 Glebe Place 1989), Film Designs from the Fifties (Austin/Desmond Gallery 1991); chm Rutland Branch Mental Health Fndn, pres Rutland and Leics Branch Grenadier Guards Assoc; awards incl: BAFTA, Writers Guild GB, Emmy (US), Critics Circle (US), Peabody Award Univ of Georgia; *Books* Upstairs, Downstairs (1972), In My Lady's Chamber (1973); *Recreations* hunting, tennis; *Style*— John Hawkesworth, Esq; Fishponds House, Knossington, Oakham, Rutland LE15 8LX (☎ 066 477 339); Flat 2, 24 Cottesmore Gardens, London W8 (071 937 4869)

HAWKESWORTH, Rex; s of Christopher Gilbert Hawkesworth (d 1963), and Queenie Victoria Hawkesworth; *b* 8 Sept 1939; *Educ* Portsmouth Northern GS; *m* 25 Oct 1961, Pauline Mary; 2 da (Ruth b 1962, Lee b 1965); *Career* architect; freelance 1972-, specialist in private houses and estates in S Hampshire; author of articles on building, architecture and environment in nat and local magazines and newspapers; *Recreations* athletics coaching; *Clubs* Portsmouth Fareham and Dist Ladies Athletics; *Style*— Rex Hawkesworth, Esq; 4 Rampart Gdns, Hilsea, Portsmouth, Hants (☎ 0705 662330)

HAWKESWORTH, (Thomas) Simon Ashwell; QC (1982); s of Charles Peter Elmhirst Hawkesworth, and Felicity, *née* Ashwell; *b* 15 Nov 1943; *Educ* Rugby, Queen's Coll Oxford (MA); *m* 1970 (m dis 1989), Jennifer, da of Dr Thomas Lewis (d 1944); 2 s (Thomas b 1973, Edward b 1978); m 2, 1990, Dr May Bamber; *Career* called to the Bar Gray's Inn 1967; appointed rec of the Crown Ct 1982, elected bencher Gray's Inn 1990; *Style*— Simon Hawkesworth, Esq, QC; Tanner Beck House, Staveley, Knaresborough, N Yorks HG5 9LD (☎ 0423 340 604); 2 Harcourt Buildings, Temple, London EC47 9DB

HAWKINGS, Christopher Robert; s of Reginald Hawkings (d 1983), and Molly Hawkings (d 1988); *b* 24 Aug 1937; *Educ* Berkhampsted Sch; *m* 25 April 1965, Sandra, da of James Kerr (d 1984); 2 s (Simon b 18 Dec 1965, Timothy b 25 Nov 1971), 1 da (Caroline (twin) b 18 Dec 1965); *Career* Phillips Auctioneers: joined 1957, md 1972, dep chm 1989; FIAScot; *Style*— Christopher Hawkings, Esq; Phillips Auctioneers, 7 Blenheim St, London W1Y 0AS (☎ 071 629 6602, fax 071 629 8876)

HAWKINGS, Patrick Stanley; s of late Stanley Albert Hawkings, and late Edith Laura Hawkings; *b* 5 May 1914; *Educ* Laxton Sch Oundle; *m* 4 June 1945, Sylvia Hilda, *née* Chamberlain; *Career* WWII serv Maj Middle E and BAOR 1939-46; ptnr: Wood Albery and Co 1948-74, Baker Rooke 1974-80; dir London and Associated Investment Trust plc 1974-; former dir Cordova Land Co and Klerksdoorp Gold Mines, London Australian Gen Exploration Co; Freeman City of London; FCA; *Style*— Patrick Hawkings, Esq; 3 Red Lodge Gardens, Graemesdyke Rd, Berkhamsted, Hertfordshire HP4 3LW (☎ 04428 75744)

HAWKINS, Andrew John; s of Austen Ralph Hawkins, of Bournemouth, and May, *née* O'Donnell; *b* 24 Sept 1958; *Educ* Bedford Modern Sch, Univ of Lancaster (BA), Kellogg Grad Sch of Mgmnt Northwestern Univ Evanston Illinois (MBA); *m* 16 Nov 1990, Karen, da of Gerald Edward Pursey; *Career* graduate trainee Ogilvy and Mather 1982, account dir Publicis (formerly McCormick Publicis) 1985 (account mangr 1983); GGK London: joined Bd 1988, dep md Jan 1990, md Nov 1990; *Recreations* waterskiing, skiing, movies, the occasional marathon; *Style*— Andrew Hawkins, Esq; 80A Camden Mews, London NW1 9BX (☎ 071 485 3491); GGK London, 76 Dean St, London W1V 5HA (☎ 071 734 0511, fax 071 437 3961, car 0831 393675)

HAWKINS, Prof Anthony Donald; s of Kenneth St David Hawkins, and Marjorie, *née* Jackson; *b* 25 March 1942; *Educ* Poole GS, Univ of Bristol (BSc, PhD); *m* 31 July 1966, Susan Mary; 1 s (David Andrew b 23 Feb 1973); *Career* dir of Fisheries Res Scotland 1987-, chief scientific offr SO 1987-, hon prof Univ of Aberdeen 1987; FRSE 1988; *Recreations* whippet racing; *Style*— Prof Anthony Hawkins, FRSE; Kincraig, Blairs, nr Aberdeen (☎ 0224 868984); Marine Laboratory, PO Box 101, Victoria Rd, Torry, Aberdeen (☎ 0224 876544, fax 0224 879156, telex 73587)

HAWKINS, Sir Arthur Ernest; s of Rev Harry Robert Hawkins (d 1942); *b* 10 June 1913; *Educ* The Blue Sch Wells, Gt Yarmouth GS, London Univ (BSc); *m* 1939, Laura Judith Tallent, da of Albert Draper (d 1956); 1 s, 2 da; *Career* memb CEGB 1970- (chm 1972-77), memb Nuclear Power Advsy Bd 1973-; kt 1976; *Recreations* fell walking, swimming; *Clubs* The Hurlingham; *Style*— Sir Arthur Hawkins; 61 Rowan Rd, Brook Green, London W6 7DT (☎ 071 603 2849)

HAWKINS, Blanche, Lady; (Marjorie) Blanche; da of A E Hampden-Smithers, of Springs, Transvaal; *m* 1920, Sir Villiers Geoffrey Caesar Hawkins, 6 Bt (d 1955); *Style*— Blanche, Lady Hawkins; 187 Lynnwood Rd, Brooklyn, Pretoria, Transvaal, S Africa

HAWKINS, Catherine Eileen Mary; da of Stanley Richard Hawkins, of Thornhill Cottage, Meadow Rd, Cockington, Torquay, and Mary-Kate Hawkins (d 1984); *b* 16 Jan 1939; *Educ* La Retraite HS for Girls Clifton Bristol; *Career* Capt TA QARANC 219 Wessex Gen Hosp 1962-69; project mangr Bahrain 1964-66, teacher Field Work Bristol 1966-68; admin: Health Centre Bristol 1968-70 and 1971-72, Res Div Health Educn Cncl 1970-71; area nursing offr Gloucestershire Cncl 1972-74, area nurse Avon Area Health Authy 1974-79; chief nursing offr: Bristol and Weston DHA 1979-82, Southmead DHA 1982-84; regnl gen mangr and regnl nursing offr South West Regional Health Authority 1984-; *Recreations* travel, DIY, walking, opera, ballet; *Style*— Ms Catherine Hawkins; South Western Regional Health Authority, Kings Square House, 26/27 King's Square, Bristol, Avon (☎ 0272 427820)

HAWKINS, Christopher James; MP (C) High Peak 1983-; *b* 26 Nov 1937; *Educ* Bristol GS, Bristol Univ; *Career* Courtaulds Ltd 1959-66; sr lecturer economics Southampton Univ 1966-83; *Style*— Christopher Hawkins, Esq, MP; House of Commons, London SW1

HAWKINS, Dave; s of George Vincent, of London, and Irene Lavina, *née* Mallett; *b* 22 Dec 1948; *Educ* St Bonaventure's GS, Univ of York (BA); *m* 4 June 1978, Chris, da of Leslie George Rodgers, of London; 2 s (Elliott Alexander b 1981, Bradley Wade b 1987), 1 da (Cassie Louise b 1982); *Career* Benton & Bowles Advertising Agency 1970-73, Ogilvy & Mather 1973-83 (dir 1982-83), exec dir McCann Erickson 1983-85; fndr Beard Hawkins Direct 1985-90, Hawkins Direct 1990-; memb: MRS 1974, Mktg Soc 1984, IOD 1984; *Clubs* The Rugby; *Style*— Dave Hawkins, Esq; Hawkins Direct, Southbank House, Black Prince Rd, London SE1 7SJ (☎ 071 587 0175, fax 071 587 1589, telex 295555 LSPG)

HAWKINS, Prof Denis Frank; s of Frank Reginald Hawkins (d 1970), and Elsie Anne May, *née* Sallis (d 1986); *b* 4 April 1929; *Educ* Alleyn's Sch Dulwich, UCL, UCH (BSc, MB BS, PhD, DSc); *m* 10 July 1957, Joan Dorothy Vera, da Walter James Taynton (d 1949); 2 s (Robert James b and d 1960, Richard Frank b 1961), 2 da (Valerie Joan b 1958, Susan Pauline b 1966); *Career* prof and chm of obstetrics and gynaecology Univ of Boston 1965-68, conslt obstetrician and gynaecologist Hammersmith Hosp 1968-, emeritus prof of obstetric therapeutics Univ of London 1989- (lectr 1961-65, sr lectr 1968-74, reader 1974-79, prof 1979-89), ed Jl of Obstetrics and Gynaecology 1980-; memb: Br Fertility Soc, BMA, Br Pharmacological Soc, Italian Soc for Perinatal Med, RSM; Freeman City of London 1985, Liveryman Worshipful Soc of Apothecaries 1987; MRCOG 1962, DObst RCOG 1957, FRCOG 1970; *Books* Obstetric Therapeutics (1974), The Intrauterine Device (1977), Human Fertility Control (1979), Gynaecological Therapeutics (1981), Drugs and Pregnancy (1 edn 1983, 2 edn 1987), Perinatal Medicine (1986), Advances in Perinatal Medicine (1988), Diabetes and Pregnancy (1989); *Recreations* Arabian primitive rock carvings, Greek archeology; *Clubs* Savage; *Style*— Prof Denis Hawkins; Dept of Obstetrics and Gynaecology, Hammersmith Hospital, Ducane Rd, London W12 0HS, (☎ 081 740 3268, fax 081 740 3920, telex 926 128)

HAWKINS, Prof Eric William; CBE (1973); s of James Edward Hawkins (d 1958), of West Kirby, Wirral, and Agnes, *née* Clarie Hawkins (d 1973); *b* 8 Jan 1915; *Educ* Liverpool Inst, Trinity Hall Cambridge; *m* 12 Aug 1938, Ellen Marie Baunsgaard, da of Prof Peder Thygesen (d 1955), of Copenhagen; 1 s (John b 1947), 1 da (Anne b 1939); *Career* WWII 1940-46 Offr 1 Bn Loyal Regt served: N Africa (wounded), Anzio beachhead (despatches), Adj 1944-45; headmaster: Oldershaw GS Wallasey 1949-53, Calday Grange GS West Kirby Cheshire 1953-65; Univ of York: reader in educn 1965-67, prof of language educn and dir Long Teaching Centre 1967-79, emeritus prof 1979-; hon prof UCW Aberystwyth 1985; memb: Plowden Ctee Nat Advsy Educn Cncl 1963-67, Nat Ctee for Cwlth Immigrants 1965-68, Ctee of Inquiry Educn of Children of Ethnic Minorities 1979-81; FIL 1973; Commandeur dans l'Ordre des Palmes Académiques France 1985; *Books* Modern Languages in the Curriculum (2 edn 1987), Awareness of Language - An Introduction (2 edn 1987); *Recreations* cello, walking; *Clubs* Royal Cwlth; *Style*— Prof Eric Hawkins, CBE

HAWKINS, Howard Caesar; s and h of Sir Humphry Villiers Caesar Hawkins, 7 Bt; *b* 17 Nov 1956; *Educ* Hilton Coll; *Career* S African Air Force 1975; *Style*— Howard Hawkins, Esq; 1279 Homestead Avenue, Wallnut Creek, California 94598, USA (☎ 0101 415 932 6743)

HAWKINS, Sir Humphry Villiers Caesar; 7 Bt (GB 1778); s of Sir Villiers Geoffrey Caesar Hawkins, 6 Bt (d 1955); *b* 10 Aug 1923; *Educ* Hilton Coll, Witwatersrand Univ (MB ChB); *m* 1952, Anita, da of Charles H Funkey; 2 s, 3 da; *Heir* s, Howard Hawkins; *Career* European War 1942-45 with 6 S African Armoured Div; medical practitioner; *Clubs* Johannesburg County; *Style*— Sir Humphry Hawkins, Bt; 41 Hume Rd, Dunkeld, Johannesburg, S Africa

HAWKINS, Josephine; da of Joseph Hawkins (d 1951), of London, and Emily, *née* Tarr (d 1974); *b* 28 Feb 1938; *Educ* City of London Coll; *Career* dir PR Co 1959-62, fndr PR consultancy 1963; MIPR 1962, MJI 1962, MAIE 1964, FSAE 1982, FPA 1984; *Recreations* writing, gardening, cooking; *Clubs* British Pottery Mfrs, Wig & Pen, London Press, Foreign Press; *Style*— Miss Josephine Hawkins; M16 Victoria House, Vernon Place, London WC1B 4DA (☎ 071 404 0520, fax 071 242 4996, telex 83147 INTERUNI)

HAWKINS, Keith John; *b* 19 Nov 1947; *m* 23 April 1977, Linda Claire; 1 s (Richard b 1979), 1 da (Philippa b 1982); *Career* admitted slr 1974; ptnr Dutton Gregory & Williams; memb Law Soc 1974; *Style*— Keith Hawkins, Esq; 29 Hocombe Wood Rd, Chandlersford, Hants (☎ 0703 261026); Dutton Gregory and Williams, 96 Winchester Rd, Hants (☎ 0703 267222, telex 477921 DGWLAW G, fax 0703 251436)

HAWKINS, Kenneth Ernest; s of Ernest Leslie Hawkins (lost at sea 1941), of Roby, Merseyside, and Edith, *née* Saunders; *b* 18 July 1933; *Educ* Prescot GS Merseyside, Liverpool Coll of Commerce; *m* 1, 9 April 1955 (m dis 1970), Doris, da of George Henry Pye; 2 s (Keith Stephen b 26 Oct 1955, Roy Andrew b 25 June 1957), 1 da (Amanda Jayne b 25 Nov 1960); m 2, 16 July 1986, Joan Ellis; *Career* Nat Serv RAF 1951-53, Royal Liver Friendly Soc 1949- (sec 1985-); ACII 1974; *Clubs* W Kirby Light Opera Soc (memb Chorus and former sec 1979-89); *Style*— Kenneth Hawkins, Esq; Royal Liver Friendly Society, Royal Liver Building, Pier Head, Liverpool L3 1HT (☎ 051 236 1451 ext 3311, fax 071 236 2122)

HAWKINS, Louis; s of Edgar Ernest Hawkins, of Harrow, Middlesex, and Winifred Elizabeth, *née* Stevens; *b* 19 Aug 1945; *Educ* Chandos Secdy Mod Stanmore, Willesden Tech Coll, Poly of Central London (Dip Arch); *m* 20 Aug 1966, Patricia Anne, da of Douglas Herbert Jarvis (d 1976), of Godstone, Surrey; 1 s (Joseph b 1983), 1 da (Harriet b 1980); *Career* architect; chm: Devon Branch of the Assoc of Conslts, ACA Quality Assur Working Pty 1988; vice chm govrs Upottery C P Sch 1986-88; ARIBA; *Recreations* photography, fell walking, music; *Style*— Louis Hawkins, Esq; Stoneburrow Cottage, Rawridge, Upottery, Honiton, Devon EX14 9PY (☎ 0404 86 533); The Louis Hawkins Practice, Chartered Architects, School House, Old School House Court, High St, Honiton, Devon EX14 8NZ (☎ 0404 45528/9)

HAWKINS, Michael Richard; OBE (1987); s of William Hawkins, MM (d 1987), of Minehead, Somerset, and Winifred May, *née* Strawbridge (d 1985); *b* 27 Nov 1927; *Educ* Minehead GS; *m* 1, 20 May 1950 (m dis 1977), Doreen, *née* Went; 2 s (Malcolm b 1951, Lyndsay b 1953); m 2, 4 Feb 1978, Judith Carole, da of Leslie Fauxton Yelland, of Newquay; *Career* borough engr Torquay 1965-68, dir of tech servs Torbay 1968-74, co engr and planning offr Devon 1974-90; pres: Inst of Municipal Engrs 1982-83, Co Surveyors Soc 1987-88; chm: Nat Ctee Reporting On Cause And Remedies Of Alkali Silica Reaction In Concrete, Br Nat Ctee of PIARC; vice pres Concrete Soc, vice chm South Devon Healthcare Trust; hon memb Dartmoor Rescue Serv; Freeman City of London, Liveryman Worshipful Co of Paviors; FICE 1981, FIStructE 1962, MRTPI 1963, FIHT 1969, FRS 1986; *Books* Devon Roads (1988); *Recreations* walking, collecting antique maps; *Clubs* RAC; *Style*— Michael Hawkins, Esq, OBE; 19 Mead Road, Livermead, Torquay TQ2 6TG (☎ 0803 607819)

HAWKINS, Sir Paul Lancelot; TD (1945); s of Lance G Hawkins (d 1947) and Mrs Hawkins (*née* Peile); *b* 7 Aug 1912; *Educ* Cheltenham; *m* 1, 1937, Joan Snow (d 1984); 2 s, 1 da; m 2, 1985, Christine M Daniels; *Career* served Royal Norfolk Regt

(TA) 1933-45 (POW Germany 1940-45); chartered surveyor 1933, having joined family firm 1930; co cncllr Norfolk 1949-70, alderman 1968-70, MP (C) SW Norfolk 1964-87, asst govt whip 1970-71, lord cmmr of Treasury (govt whip) 1971-73, vice-chamberlain of HM Household 1973-74; memb: Select Ctee House of Commons Servs 1976-87, Delgn to WEU and Cncl Europe 1976-87; chm Agric Ctee Cncl of Europe 1985-87; kt 1982; *Recreations* gardening, travel; *Style—* Sir Paul Hawkins, TD; Stables, Downham Market, Norfolk

HAWKINS, Peter John; s of Derek Gilbert, of Ariége, France, and Harriet Joanne, *née* Mercier; *b* 20 June 1944; *Educ* private tutors, Hawtreys, Eton, Univ of Oxford (MA); *Career* dir Christies 1973-, md Christies Monaco (Monte Carlo) sale room 1987-89; Freeman City of London, Liveryman Worshipful Co of Gunmakers; *Recreations* shooting, foxhunting, fishing, driving collectors' cars, skiing, skindiving, collecting antiques, travel, art; *Clubs* Turf, Carlton House Terrace; *Style—* Peter Hawkins, Esq; 20 Ennismore Gdns, London SW7; Caroline Cottages, Hull Farm, Chipping Norton, Oxon; 8 King St, St James's, London SW1 (☎ 071 839 9060)

HAWKINS, His Hon Judge Richard Graeme; QC (1984); s of late Denis William Hawkins, of Frinton-on-Sea, Essex, and Norah Mary Hawkins, *née* Beckingsale; *b* 23 Feb 1941; *Educ* Hendon County Sch, UCL (LLB); *m* 1969, Anne Elizabeth, da of Dr Glyn Charles Edwards, of Bournemouth, Dorset; 1 s (Benjamin b 1975), 1 da (Victoria b 1972); *Career* called to the Bar Gray's Inn 1963, in practice South Eastern Circuit, rec of Crown Ct 1985, circuit judge 1989-; *Recreations* sailing; *Clubs* Royal Thames Yacht; *Style—* His Hon Judge Richard Hawkins, QC; The Crown Ct, Inner London Sessions House, Newington Causeway, London SE1 6AZ (☎ 071 407 7111)

HAWKINS, Capt Richard Henry; s of Maj H Hawkins, OBE (d 1930), of Everdon Hall, Daventry, Northants, and Dorothy Kathleen, *née* Hanmer (d 1957); *b* 1 Sept 1922; *Educ* Stowe, RMC Sandhurst; *m* 12 April 1944 (m dis 1964), Elizabeth Heather, da of Maj Robert Stafford, MC (d 1959), of Elvaston Place; 1 s (Anthony Richard b 1 Oct 1946), 1 da (Anne Elizabeth b 29 July 1949); *Career* 4 Bn Coldstreams Gds 1942-46; handicapper under Jockey Club rules of racing and Nat Hunt rules 1947-59, currently steward Warwick and Towcester; memb: Cross Arrows CC, I'Zingari, R H Hawkins XI; jt master Grafton Hounds 1953-54 and 1961-85; former memb Bucks and Guards Club; *Recreations* hunting, cricket; *Clubs* Farmers, Forty, MCC; *Style—* Capt Richard Hawkins; Everdon Hall, Daventry, Northants NN11 6BG (☎ 032 7367 207)

HAWKINS, Richard Ingpen Shayle; s of Vice Adm Sir Raymond Hawkins, KCB (d 1987), and Rosalind Constance Lucy, *née* Ingpen (d 1990); *b* 20 June 1944; *Educ* Bedford Sch; *m* 26 July 1969, Amanda Louise, da of Rear Adm E F Gueritz, CB, OBE, DSC, *qv*, of Salisbury, Wilts; 2 s (William b 1973, George b 1976); *Career* cmmnd 2 Lt RM 1962, Lt 42 Commando Far East 1964-65, 43 Commando UK 1965-66, 45 Commando Aden and UK 1967-69, Capt 40 Commando Far East 1970-71, GSO3 HQ Commando Forces 1971-73, Adj RMR Tyne 1973-75, Army Staff Coll Camberley 1976, Co Cdr 45 Commando UK, Maj Instr Sch of Inf 1978-80, GSO2 Dept of Cmdt Gen RM MOD 1980-82, ret 1982; dir: Burgoyne Alford Ltd 1983-85, Richards Longstaff (Insur) Ltd 1985-87, Baillie Longstaff Ltd 1989-; pres Bedwyn and Dist Royal Br Legion; *Recreations* sailing, field sports; *Clubs* Royal Yacht Sqdn; *Style—* Richard Hawkins, Esq; The Old Forge, Upton, Andover, Hants SP11 OJS (☎ 026 476 269)

HAWKINS, Dr Thomas James; TD; s of Douglas William Richard Hawkins, of Yeovil, Somerset, and Caroline Emily Maria, *née* Drury (d 1982); *b* 16 May 1937; *Educ* Colfe's GS, Royal Free Hosp Sch of Med Univ of London (MB BS, DA); *m* 19 Nov 1960, Sylvia Colleen, da of Alan Adrian Parsons (d 1971), of Dorchester, Dorset; 1 s (Simeon b 1966), 1 da (Sarah b 1964); *Career* Lt-Col RAMC (TA): CO 144 Parachute Field Ambulance RAMC (Vol) 1983-86, offr i/c Resuscitation and Anaesthesia 257 Gen Hosp RAMC (Vol) 1987-88, lectr BATLS specialist trg team 1988-, offr in cmd 363 Field Surgical Team RAMC (Vol) 1989-; house surgn Dreadnought Seamen's Hosp 1961, jr casualty offr and anaesthetist Royal Free Hosp 1962, house physician St Alfege's Hosp 1962-63, sr res anaethetist and sr house offr Royal Free Hosp 1963-64; registrar in anaesthesia: Peace Meml Hosp 1964-66, London Chest Hosp 1966-68, Charing Cross Hosp 1968-69; sr registrar in anaesthesia and chief asst St Bartholomew Hosp 1969-73; memb: Assoc of Anaesthetists of GB and I, Assoc of Cardio-thoracic Anaesthetists, Sheffield and E Midlands Soc of Anaesthetists, World Anaesthesia, Airborne Med Soc, BMA, Nottingham Medico-Chirurgical Soc, TA Med Offr Assoc; assoc memb Tri-Serv Anaesthetic Soc; FFARCS; *Recreations* model railways, kit car building, gardening; *Style—* Dr Thomas Hawkins, TD; Weatherbury, 119 Main St, Willoughby on the Wolds, Loughborough, Leicestershire LE12 6SY (☎ 0509 880912); Dept of Anaesthesia, University Hospital, Queen's Medical Centre, Nottingham NG7 2UH (☎ 0602 421421)

HAWKINS, Lady; Virginia Anne Noel; da of Gp Capt Noel Heath, OBE; *b* 31 Dec 1925; *Educ* Ascham Sch Sydney, Frensham Mittagong Australia; *m* 1947, Maj Sir Michael Hawkins, KCVO, MBE (d 1977; private sec to HRH The Duke of Gloucester), s of Lancelot Hawkins, of Bilney Hall, Norfolk; 1 da; *Recreations* gardening, reading, travelling; *Style—* Lady Hawkins; 37 Rumbold Rd, London SW6 2HX (☎ 071 736 3701)

HAWKSEY, Brian Foran; s of Joseph Osmund Hawksey (d 1979), of Manchester, and Mary Susan, *née* Foran (d 1981); *b* 22 Aug 1932; *Educ* St Bede's Coll Manchester, Douai Sch Woolhampton; *m* 19 June 1965, (Patricia) Anne, da of Patrick Maginnis, of Bognor Regis, W Sussex; *Career* materials mangr Smiths Industry Ltd 1973-77, dep dir of trg Purchasing Economics Ltd 1977-79, ptnr Brian Hawksey & Assoc 1979-80, purchasing devpt & trg mangr Thorn-EMI plc 1981-86; dir Purchasing and Materials Mgmnt Servs 1986-; FInstPS, MBIM; *Recreations* music, photography; *Style—* Brian Hawksey, Esq; Tall Trees, Egypt Lane, Farnham Common, Bucks SL2 3LD (☎ 0753 642698); Purchasing & Materials Management Services, PO Box 4, Lytham, Lytham St Annes, Lancs FY8 2EL (☎ 0753 642698)

HAWKSLEY, John Richard; s of Richard Walter Benson Hawksley (d 1976), and Jean Lilley of Norwich; *b* 11 March 1942; *Educ* Haileybury; *m* 9 March 1968, Jane, da of Col Hugh Pettigrew; 2 s (Benjamin b 26 Nov 1968, David b 23 April 1971), 1 da (Victoria b 11 Dec 1973); *Career* qualified chartered accountant 1965; Deloitte Haskins & Sells: ptnr 1975, ptnr i/c Reading 1981-85, ptnr i/c Birmingham 1986-1990, regnl ptnr i/c Midland Region 1987, ptnr i/c Birmingham Coopers & Lybrand Deloitte (following merger) 1990-; chm Public Arts Cmmn Agency 1988-, memb Cncl Birmingham C of Indust & Co 1990-, govr City Technol Coll 1988-, dir DTI Business Action Team 1989-; FCA (ACA 1965), FRSA, MInstD; *Recreations* cricket, golf, horse racing (owner), watching all sport, opera, theatre, music; *Clubs* MCC, Stratford Oaks Golf; *Style—* John Hawksley, Esq; Coopers & Lybrand Deloitte, 35 Newhall St, Birmingham B3 3DX (☎ 021 200 4000, fax 021 200 2829)

HAWLEY, Sir Donald Frederick; KCMG (1978, CMG 1970), MBE (1955); s of Frederick George Hawley (d 1973), of Little Gaddesden, Herts; *b* 22 May 1921; *Educ* Radley, New Coll Oxford (MA); *m* 1964, Ruth Morwenna Graham, da of Rev Peter Graham Howes (d 1964), of Charmouth, Dorset; 1 s, 3 da; *Career* served WWII Capt RA; called to the Bar Inner Temple 1951; Sudan Govt and Sudan Judiciary 1944-55; Dip Serv 1956-81: ambass Muscat 1971-75, asst under sec of state 1975-77, Br high cmmr Malaysia 1977-81; chm The Centre for Br Teachers 1987-; dir Ewbank & Ptnrs 1981-, chm Ewbank Preece Ltd 1982-86 (special advsr 1986-); memb London Advsy Ctee Hong Kong and Shanghai Banking Corp 1981-; pres of Cncl Univ of Reading, vice pres Anglo-Omani Soc 1981-, chm Br Malaysian Soc 1983-, chm Confedn of Br SE Asian Socs 1988-, govr ESU 1989; *Books* Handbook for Registrars of Marriage and Ministers of Religion (Sudan Govt, 1963), Courtesies in the Trucial States (1965), The Trucial States (1971), Oman and its Renaissance (1977), Courtesies in the Gulf Area (1978), Debrett's Manners and Correct Form in the Middle East (1984); *Recreations* tennis, golf, travel; *Clubs* Travellers', Beefsteak; *Style—* Sir Donald Hawley, KCMG, MBE; Little Cheverell House, nr Devizes, Wilts (☎ 0380 813 322)

HAWLEY, James Appleton; TD (1968), JP (Staffs 1969-), DL (Staffs 1978-); s of John James Hawley (d 1968), of Longdon Green, Staffs, and Ethel Mary Hawley, JP; *b* 28 March 1937; *Educ* Uppingham, St Edmund Hall Oxford (MA); *m* 8 April 1961, Susan Anne Marie, da of Alan Edward Stott, JP, DL, of Armitage, Staffordshire; 1 s (Charles John b 1965), 2 da (Catherine Marie b 1963, Jane Rachel b 1968); *Career* 2 Lt S Staffs Regt 1955-57, Nat Serv Cyprus, TA 2 Lt to Maj Staffs Yeo 1957-69; called to the Bar Middle Temple 1961; chm and md: John James Hawley Ltd 1961-, J W Wilkinson & Co Ltd 1970-; dir Stafford Railway Bldg Soc 1985-, High Sheriff Staffs 1976-77; chm Walsall Soc for Blind 1979-; Freeman City of London 1987, Liveryman Worshipful Co of Saddlers 1988; *Recreations* fishing, shooting; *Clubs* United Oxford & Cambridge; *Style—* James Hawley, Esq, TD, JP, DL; John James Hawley (SW) Ltd, Lichfield Rd, Walsall, West Midlands WS4 2HX (☎ 0922 25641, fax 0922 720163, telex 335056 JJHWAL G)

HAWLEY, Peter Edward; s of Albert Edward Hawley (d 1962), of Leicester, and Winifred, *née* Skinner; *b* 20 July 1938; *Educ* Wyggeston Sch, Magdalene Coll Cambridge (MA, LLB); *m* 19 Sept 1964, (Mary) Tanya, da of John Ounsted, of Appletree Cottage, Woodgreen Common, Fordingbridge, Hants; 1 da (Sasha Louise b 26 Aug 1967); *Career* Nat Serv, Sgt (RAEC) attached 99 Gurkha Inf Bde Johore Malaya 1957-59; admitted slr 1967; Walker Martineau (now Walker Martineau Stringer Saul): articled clerk 1964-67, asst slr 1967-69, ptnr 1970-, managing ptnr 1983-; hon treas Magdalene Coll Assoc 1975-87 (hon sec 1970-75), hon treas Whitchurch-on-Thames Twinning Assoc 1980-89; Freeman City of London 1989, Freeman Worshipful Co of Slrs 1988; MIOD 1984; *Recreations* hogging shade in hot climates; *Clubs* Gresham; *Style—* Peter Hawley, Esq; Whitchurch House, Whitchurch on Thames, Reading; 55-57 Gloucester Road, London SW7; Walker Martineau Stringer Saul, 64 Queen Street, London EC4 (☎ 071 236 4232, fax 071 236 2525)

HAWLEY, Peter Robert; s of Robert Thomas Hawley, of Tunbridge Wells, and Edna May, *née* Tadman; *b* 16 Aug 1933; *Educ* Kings Coll Sch Wimbledon, UCL, UCH (MB MS); *m* 16 Sept 1960, Valerie Geraldine, da of Stanley Bernard Warder (d 1971), of Reigate, Surrey; 2 s (Graham Robert Warder b 1964, David Richard Thomas b 1966), 1 da (Alison Margaret b 1962); *Career* conslt surgn: St Marks Hosp London, King Edward VII's Hosp for Offrs London and Midhurst; articles and chapters on gastrointestinal surgery incl large bowel cancer and inflammatory bowel disease; fell UCL; fell Assoc of Surgns of GB and Ireland, memb Br Soc of Gastroenterology: FRSM, FRCS 1960; *Recreations* sailing, golf; *Style—* Peter Hawley, Esq; 149 Harley St, London W1N 2DE

HAWLEY, Dr Richard Martin; s of Donald Pearson Hawley, of Duffield, Derbys, and Margaret, *née* Robinson; *b* 17 April 1955; *Educ* King Edwards Sch Birmingham, Ecclesbourne Sch Derbys, Univ of Birmingham (MB ChB); *Career* clinical lectr psychiatry Univ of Birmingham 1983-84, conslt psychiatrist S Western RHA 1985-, clinical lectr mental health Univ of Bristol 1985-; MRCPsych 1983; *Recreations* travel; *Style—* Dr Richard Hawley; 41 St John's Rd, Clifton, Bristol BS8 2HD; Southmead Hospital, Westbury-on-Trym, Bristol BS10 5NB

HAWLEY, Dr Robert; s of William Hawley (d 1960), and Eva, *née* Dawson; *b* 23 July 1936; *Educ* Wallasey GS, Wallasey Tech Coll, Birkenhead Tech Coll, Kings Coll Durham (BSc, PhD), Univ of Newcastle upon Tyne (DSc); *m* 17 Jan 1962, Valerie, da of Colin Clarke; 1 s (Nicholas Richard b 30 July 1968), 1 da (Fiona Jane b 10 Dec 1966); *Career* CA Parsons: head of res Di-electrics 1961-64, electrical designer Generators 1964-66, dep chief generator engr 1966-70, dir and chief electrical engr 1973-74 (chief electrical engr 1970-73), dir Prodn and Engrg 1974-76; NEI plc: md NEI Parsons Ltd 1976-84, md Power Engineering Gp 1984-88, dir 1984-88, md Ops 1989-; dir Rolls Royce plc 1989; IEE Achievement Medal 1989, CAA Parsons Meml lectr 1977, Hunter Meml lectr 1990; Freeman City of London; FIEE 1970, FInstP 1970, FEng 1979, FIMechE 1987; *publications:* author of numerous scientific papers; *Recreations* gardening, philately; *Clubs* Athenaeum; *Style—* Dr Robert Hawley; Northern Engrg Industries plc, NEI House, Regent Centre, Gosforth, Newcastle upon Tyne NE3 3SB (☎ 091 284 3191, fax 091 284 4534)

HAWORTH, Christopher; s and h of Sir Philip Haworth, Bt, *qv*, Cheshire, and Joan Helen, *née* Clark; ggf Sir Arthur Addlington Haworth (Liberal MP); *b* 6 Nov 1951; *Educ* Rugby, Univ of Reading (BSc); *Career* dir: Sheraton (UK) Ltd 1989-91, Dunlin Devpt Ltd 1987-; chm Chelsea Harmonic Soc 1987-90; ARICS; *Recreations* shooting, fishing, skiing, squash, ornithology, singing; *Clubs* Ski of GB, RAC, Lansdowne; *Style—* Christopher Haworth, Esq; 11 Mossbury Rd, London SW11 2PA (☎ 071 350 2941); Sheraton Securities International plc, Leconfield House, Curzon St, London W1Y 7FB (☎ 071 629 4049)

HAWORTH, Hon Mrs (Hester Josephine Anne); *née* Freeman-Grenville; yr da of Lady Kinloss; *b* 9 May 1960; *m* 9 June 1984, Peter Haworth, s of Arnold F C Haworth, of Flat 1, Huttons Ambo Hall, nr Malton, York; 3 s (Joseph Anthony b 1985, David Arnold b 1987, Christopher John b 1989); *Career* cordon bleu cook; *Style—* Hon Mrs Haworth; The Laurels, Tholthorpe, Yorks YO6 2JN

HAWORTH, Lionel; OBE (1958); s of John Bertram Haworth (d 1953), of Trooilaps Pan, Via Upington, Cape, Province, SA, and Anna Sophia, *née* Ackerman (d 1916); *b* 4 Aug 1912; *Educ* Rondebosch Boys HS Cape Town SA, Univ of Cape Town (BSc); *m* 1 Dec 1956, Joan Irene, da of Wilfred Bertram Bradbury, of Whitchurch, Shrops; 1 s (John Andrew), 1 da (Erica Jane); *Career* graduate apprentice Assoc Equipment Co 1934; Rolls Royce Ltd: designer 1936, asst chief designer 1944, dep chief designer 1951, chief designer (civil engines) 1954, chief engr (turboprops) 1962; Bristol Siddeley Engines Ltd: chief design conslt 1963, chief designer 1964, dir of design Aero Div Rolls Royce Ltd 1968-77; Br Gold Medal for Aeronautics 1971; RDI 1976; fndr and sr ptnr Lionel Haworth & Assocs 1977; FRS 1971, FEng 1976, GIMechE 1936, FIMechE 1954, FRAeS 1959; *Recreations* sailing, walking; *Clubs* Bristol Scientific, Trent Valley Sailing, Is Cruising (Salcombe); *Style—* Lionel Haworth, Esq, OBE; 10 Hazelwood Road, Sneyd Park, Bristol, BS9 1PX (☎ 0272 683032)

HAWORTH, Sir Philip; 3 Bt (UK 1911), of Dunham Massey, Co Cheshire; s of Sir Geoffrey Haworth, 2 Bt (d 1987); *b* 17 Jan 1927; *Educ* Reading Univ (BSc); *m* 1951, Joan Helen, da of Stanley Percival Clark (decd), of Ipswich; 4 s, 1 da; *Heir* s Christopher b 1951, *qv*; *Career* agriculture; *Recreations* music; *Clubs* Farmers; *Style—* Sir Philip Haworth, Bt; Free Green Farm, Over Peover, Knutsford, Cheshire

HAWORTH, Richard Anthony; s of George Ralph Haworth, and Joan Kershaw, *née* Taylor; *b* 3 Sept 1955; *Educ* Oundle, Univ of Leeds (LLB); *Career* called to the Bar Inner Temple 1978; *Recreations* shooting, fishing; *Clubs* East India; *Style—* Richard Haworth, Esq; 14 Winckley Square, Preston, Lancashire (☎ 0772 52828, fax 0772

58520)

HAWORTH, (John) Vernon Stewart; s of Lt Richard Haworth (d 1957), and Irene, *née* Holt (d 1961); *b* 24 Feb 1928; *Educ* Ackworth Sch, Univ of Leeds (BCom); *m* 11 April 1953, Heather Margaret, da of Lt-Col James Barker (d 1971); 2 s (John b 1954, Richard b 1961), 1 da (Sarah b 1957); *Career* served RN 1946-48; master printer; chm of dirs Japa Paper Products Ltd (joined bd 1955); *Recreations* golf, sailing; *Style*— Vernon Haworth, Esq; 23 Park Lane, Leeds LS8 2EX (☎ 0532 663980); Laneside Mills, Churwell, Morley, Leeds LS27 7NP (☎ 0532 532661)

HAWS, Edward Thomas; s of Edward Haws (d 1983), of Southend-on-Sea, and Phyllis Annie, *née* Thomas; *b* 19 Jan 1927; *Educ* Southend-on-Sea HS, St John's Coll Cambridge (MA); *m* 26 Aug 1950, Moira Jane, da of John Forbes (d 1958), of Moulin, Perthshire; 2 s (Gordon b 1951, Tony b 1958), 1 da (Linda b 1954); *Career* Sir Alexander Gibb & Ptnrs 1947-63: res engr Meig Dam, res engr Atiamuri Power Project, engr i/c Tongariro River Power Devpt; John Mowlem & Co Ltd 1963-78: dir Soil Mechanics Ltd, md Engrg & Resources Consllts; Rendel Palmer & Tritton 1978-: chm, md, dir of 4 assoc cos; chm: Br Nat Ctee on Large Dams 1986-89, Br Hydromechanics Res Assoc 1978-81, Ctee on the Environment of Int Cmmn on Large Dams 1981-; project engr Mersey Tidal Power Barrage; MICE 1952, FIPENZ 1959, FICE 1962, FEng 1989; *Books* contrib Chapter 5 (Diaphragm Walls) in Civil Engineering for Underground Rail Transport (1990), author of 33 technical papers; *Recreations* golf, hill walking, photography, music; *Style*— Edward Haws, Esq; Rendel Palmer & Tritton, 61 Southwark St, London SE1 1SA (☎ 071 928 8999, fax 071 928 5566, telex 919553 RENDEL G)

HAWSER, Anthony Greatrex; s of His Hon Judge Lewis Hawser, QC (d 1990), and Phyllis, *née* Greatrex, JP; *b* 23 May 1946; *Educ* Westminster, Christ Church Coll Oxford (MA), The Coll of Law; *m* 1, 5 March 1970 (m dis 1981), Anna Maria, da of Dugan Chapman; m 2, 1 March 1984, Carol Ann, da of Philip Corell (d 1980), of New York; 1 da (Eloise Elizabeth b 1985), 1 step s (Matthew Alexander b 1976); *Career* called to the Bar Inner Temple 1970; md The Reject Shop plc 1973-; *Recreations* tennis, skiing, ballet; *Clubs* Turf, Queens, Sunningdale; *Style*— Anthony Hawser, Esq; 15 Townmead Road, London SW6 (☎ 071 736 7474, fax 071 731 5409, telex 914177)

HAWTHORNE, James Burns; CBE (1982); s of Thomas Hawthorne (d 1980), of Belfast, and Florence Mary Kathleen, *née* Burns (d 1977); *b* 27 March 1930; *Educ* Methodist Coll Belfast, Queen's Univ, Stranmillis Coll Belfast (BA); *m* 1958, Sarah Patricia, da of Thomas Allan King (d 1975); 1 s (Patrick), 2 da (Fiona, Deirdre); *Career* joined BBC 1960, Schools prodr i/c NI, chief asst BBC NI 1969-70, controller Television Hong Kong 1970-72, dir Broadcasting Hong Kong 1972-77, controller BBC NI 1978-87; media consllt James Hawthorne Assocs 1988-; gave 1988 Listener lecture; NI Cncl for Educnl Devpt 1980-85; memb: Fair Employment Agency NI 1987-89, Accreditation Panel Hong Kong Acad for Performing Arts 1988-; chm: Health Promotion Agency 1988-, Cultural Traditions Gp 1988-, NI Community Relations Cncl 1989-; Winston Churchill Fellowship 1968, Hon LLD Queens Univ Belfast 1988; memb RTS (Cyril Bennett Award 1986), FRTS 1988; *Books* Two Centuries of Irish History (ed, 1967), Reporting Violence from Northern Ireland (1981); *Recreations* music, angling; *Clubs* BBC; *Style*— Dr James Hawthorne, CBE; 5 Tarawood, Cultra, Holywood, Co Down, N Ireland BT18 0HS (☎ 02317 5570, fax 02317 7749)

HAWTHORNE, Prof John Nigel (Tim); s of Ralph William Hawthorne (d 1970), of Dudley, and Alice Maud, *née* Baker (d 1965); *b* 7 March 1926; *Educ* Dudley GS, Univ of Birmingham (BSc, PhD, DSc); *m* 1, 21 Aug 1954 (m dis 1984), Jennifer, da of Dr Samuel Noel Browne (d 1971), of Church Stretton, Salop; 1 s (Barnabas b 1958), 2 da (Deborah b 1956, Prudence b 1962); m 2, 1984, Valerie Wallace; *Career* reader Univ of Birmingham 1966-69 (lectr in med biochemistry 1956-62, sr lectr 1963-65); prof of biochemistry: Univ of Calgary Alberta Canada 1970-72, Univ of Nottingham 1986- (prof and head of biochemistry 1972-85, pro-vice chancellor 1982-86); chm Int Soc for Neurochemistry Ltd 1987-89 (co sec 1987-); FIBiol 1973; *Books* Questions of Science and Faith (1960), Phospholipids (jtly, 1982), Windows On Science and Faith (1986); *Recreations* music, gardening; *Style*— Prof Tim Hawthorne; 5 Lucknow Ave, Mapperley Park, Nottingham NG3 5AZ (☎ 0602 621477); Dept of Biochemistry, Medical School, Queen's Medical Centre, Nottingham NG7 2UH (☎ 0602 709361, fax 0602 422225)

HAWTHORNE, Nigel Barnard; CBE (1987); s of Dr Charles Barnard Hawthorne (d 1969), of Coventry, and Agnes Rosemary Rice (d 1982); *b* 5 April 1929; *Educ* Christian Brothers' Coll Cape Town, Univ of Cape Town; *Career* actor and writer; Privates on Parade (1976/77), Uncle Vanya (Hampstead), The Magistrate (National Theatre 1986), Hapgood (1988), Shadowlands (London 1989-90, NY 1990-91); TV: Yes Minister, Yes Prime Minister, Barchester Chronicles, Mapp and Lucia; Hon MA Univ of Sheffield 1987; *Recreations* writing, gardening; *Style*— Nigel Hawthorne, Esq, CBE; c/o Ken McReddie, 91 Regent St, London W1R 7TV

HAWTHORNE, Dr William McMullan; s of Thomas Hawthorne (d 1980), of Belfast, and Florence Mary Kathleen, *née* Burns (d 1977); twin bro of Dr James Burns Hawthorne, *qv*; *b* 27 March 1930; *Educ* Methodist Coll Belfast, Stranmillis Coll Belfast, Univ of London, Queen's Univ Belfast (BSc, PhD); *m* 18 Dec 1957, Isobel Irene, da of Hamilton Donaldson (d 1976); 2 s (Michael Laurence Forsythe b 7 Jan 1959, Julian Thomas Hedley b 5 Dec 1969); *Career* sr lectr in mathematics Stranmillis Coll Belfast 1963-75, consllt to African and Caribbean educn systems, sr res fell in mathematics educn Univ of Ibadan 1975-79, inventor HMX Ciphersystem; currently md Gelosia Ltd Norwich; *Books* author of numerous books on mathematics incl: Mathematics for West Cameroon Schools (1966), Mathematics for Nigerian Schools (1980), Continuing Mathematics (1982); *Recreations* angling, boating; *Style*— Dr William Hawthorne; Kenmare, Bramerton Rd, Surlingham, Norwich NR14 7DE (☎ 05088 249); Gelosia Ltd, Upper St Giles St, Norwich (☎ 0603 617506)

HAWTHORNE, Prof Sir William Rede; CBE (1959); s of William Hawthorne, and Elizabeth Hawthorne; *b* 22 May 1913; *Educ* Westminster, Trinity Coll Cambridge (MA, ScD), MIT (ScD); *m* 1939, Barbara Runkle, of Cambridge, Mass; 1 s, 2 da; *Career* devpt engr Babcock and Wilcox 1937-39, sci offr RAE 1940-44, seconded to Sir Frank Whittle Power Jets Ltd (developed combustion chambers for first jet engine) 1940-41, Br Air Cmmn Washington USA 1944-45, dep dir Engine Res Miny of Supply London 1945-46, George Westinghouse prof of mech engrg MIT 1948-51 (assoc prof 1946-48, Jerome C Hunsaker prof of aeronautical engrg 1955-56, visiting inst prof 1962-63), Hopkinson and ICI prof of applied thermodynamics Univ of Cambridge 1951-80 (head Engrg Dept 1968-73, master Churchill Coll 1968-83); dir: Dracone Developments 1958-87, Cummins Engine Co Inc 1974-86; chm: Home Office Sci Advsy Cncl 1967-76, Def Sci Advsy Cncl 1969-71, Advsy Cncl on Energy Conservation 1974-79; former memb: Electricity Supply Res Cncl, Energy Cmmn, Cmmn on Energy and Environment; tstee Winston Churchill Fndn of USA 1968-, govr Westminster Sch 1956-76; has published numerous papers on fluid mechanics, aero-engines, flames and energy in scientific and tech jls; FRS (vice-pres 1969-70 and 1979-81), FEng, FIMechE, Hon FRAeS, Hon FAIAA; Hon DEng Univ of Sheffield 1976; Hon DSc: Univ of Salford 1980, Univ of Strathclyde 1981, Univ of Bath 1981, Univ of Oxford 1982, Univ of Sussex 1984; Hon DEng Univ of Liverpool 1982, Hon FRSE 1983, fell Imperial Coll of Sci and Technol 1983; kt 1970; *Clubs* Athenaeum, Pentacle (Cambridge); *Style*— Prof Sir William Hawthorne, CBE, FRS, FRSE; Churchill College, Cambridge CB3 0DS (☎ 0223 61 200); 19 Chauncy St, Cambridge, Massachusetts 02138, USA

HAWTHORNE LEWIS, Lady; Geraldine Susan Maud; da of Prof James Edward Geoffrey de Montmorency (d 1934), and Maud (d 1973), 3 da of Maj-Gen J de Havilland; *Educ* Blackheath HS, Cheltenham Ladies Coll, UCL; *m* 1957, as his 2 w, Sir William Hawthorne Lewis, KCSI, KCIE (d 1970), govr of Orissa 1941-46, s of William Crompton Lewis (d 1928) sometime dir of Public Instruction, UP India; *Career* librarian of Univ of London Inst of Education 1925-57; awarded UNESCO travelling fellowship 1952; FLA; *Recreations* travel, reading, gardening; *Clubs* English Speaking Union; *Style*— Lady Hawthorne Lewis; The Bridge House, Wilton, nr Salisbury, Wilts SP2 0BG (☎ 0722 742233)

HAWTIN, Michael Victor; s of Guy Hawtin, and Constance Hawtin; *b* 7 Sept 1942; *Educ* Bournemouth Sch, St John's Coll Cambridge (MA), Univ of Calif Berkeley (MA); *m* 1966, Judith Mary, *née* Eeley; 1 s, 1 da; *Career* princ HM Treasy 1969-77 (asst princ 1964-69), seconded to Barclays Bank 1969-71, asst sec HM Treasy 1977-83, under sec (princ fin offr) PSA 1983-86, under sec HM Treasy 1986-88, dir Resource Mgmnt Gp and princ estab and fin offr Export Credits Guarantee Department 1988-; *Recreations* music, travel; *Clubs* Overseas Bankers'; *Style*— Michael Hawtin, Esq; Export Credits Guarantee Department, Export House, 50 Ludgate Hill, London EC4M 7AY (☎ 071 382 7008)

HAXBY, David Arthur; s of Arthur Nugent Haxby, of Filey, North Yorkshire, and Alice Jane Milner; *b* 16 June 1941; *Educ* Bridlington GS, Univ Coll London (LLB); *m* 29 April 1968, Eileen Margaret, da of James Gallagher; 1 s (Daniel James b 31 Aug 1971), 3 da (Jane Louise b 14 Dec 1969, Sarah Kate b 5 Nov 1972, Linda Claire b 5 April 1978); *Career* Whitehill Marsh Jackson London 1963-68; Arthur Andersen & Co: Manchester 1968-75, Leeds 1975-, managing ptnr of regnl practice 1986-; FCA; *Recreations* sport (playing and spectating); *Style*— David Haxby, Esq; Arthur Andersen & Co, St Paul's House, Park Square, Leeds LS1 2PJ (☎ 0532 438222, fax 0532 459240)

HAY; *see*: Dalrymple-Hay

HAY, Alexander Douglas; s of Lt-Col George Harold Hay, DSO (d 1967), of Duns Castle, Duns, Berwickshire, and Patricia Mary, *née* Hugonin; *b* 2 Aug 1948; *Educ* Rugby, Univ of Edinburgh (BSc); *m* 20 Jan 1973, Aline Mary, da of Robert Rankine Macdougall; 1 s (Robert Alexander b 29 July 1976), 1 da (Caroline Laura b 9 July 1978); *Career* ptnr Greaves West & Ayre CAs Berwick upon Tweed 1978- (joined 1975); chm: Scottish Episcopal Church Widows & Orphans Fund Corp Ltd 1980-89, Borders Area Scout Cncl, Roxburgh & Berwickshire Cons & Unionist Assoc; memb Queens Body Guard for Scotland (The Royal Co of Archers); MICAS 1975; *Recreations* golf; *Clubs* Hon Co Edinburgh Golfers; *Style*— Alexander Hay, Esq; Duns Castle, Duns, Berwickwshire (☎ 0361 83211); 1-3 Sandgate, Berwick upon Tweed, TD15 1EW (☎ 0289 306688)

HAY, Hon Mrs (Amanda Jane); eldest da of Baron Mackenzie-Stuart (Life Peer); *b* 29 April 1954; *m* 1977, Michael George Hay, s of George Ronald Hay; 2 da (Daisy Elizabeth b 1981, Marianna Clare b 1985); *Style*— The Hon Mrs Hay; 3 Blenheim Drive, Oxford

HAY, Lord Andrew Arthur George; s of 12 Marquis of Tweeddale, GC (d 1979); *b* 1959,(twin); *Educ* Fettes, RAC Cirencester; *m* 6 Sept 1986, Rosanna Meryl, *née* Booth; *Career* chartered surveyor Knight Frank and Rutley; *Recreations* avoiding wheel clamps and over zealous traffic wardens; *Style*— Lord Andrew Hay; 21 Martindale Rd, London SW12 9PW

HAY, Andrew Mackenzie; CBE (1968); s of Ewen James Mackenzie Hay (d 1961), and Bertine Louise Vavasseur, *née* Buxton; *b* 9 April 1928; *Educ* Blundell's, St John's Coll Cambridge (BA, MA); *m* 30 July 1977, Catherine, da of Cdr Horace Newman, US Navy (d 1975); *Career* Intelligence Corps and RAEC 1946-48, demob 1948; commodity exec London and Colombo Ceylon 1950-54, pres and chief exec offr Calvert Vavasseur Co Inc NYC 1962-78 (vice pres 1954-61), merchant banking exec NY 1979-81, int trade consllt Portland Oregon 1982- (also HM hon consul at Portland); pres: Br American C of C 1966-68, American Assoc of Exporters and Importers NYC 1977-79; memb Bd and tstee Winston Churchill Fndn of US 1970-75, exec dir Pacific NW Int Trade Assoc 1986-; memb Advsy Ctee of Tech Innovation US Nat Acad of Sci; *Books* A Century of Coconuts (1972); *Recreations* photography, food and wine, books; *Clubs* Arlington, University; *Style*— Andrew Hay, Esq, CBE; 3515, SW Council Crest Drive, Portland, Oregon 97201; 5595 Norwester, Oceanside, Oregon 97134 (☎ 503 224 5163, 503 227 5669)

HAY, Anthony Michael; s of Norman Leslie Stephen Hay (d 1979), and Joan Agnes Eileen, *née* Watson; *b* 17 Sept 1936; *Educ* St Paul's Sch West Kensington; *m* 25 Nov 1967, Gayle Dales-Howarth; 1 s (Julian b 1970), 2 da (Francesca b 1969, Victoria b 1973); *Career* chm Norman Hay plc 1983-(dir Norman Hay Ltd 1963-83); *Recreations* cricket, tennis; *Style*— Anthony Hay, Esq; Mossat Farm, Gracious Pond, Chobham, Surrey; Norman Hay plc, Bath Rd, Harmondsworth, West Drayton, Middx UB7 0BU (☎ 081 759 1911, fax 081 897 3060, telex 933036)

HAY, Sir Arthur Thomas Erroll; 10 Bt (NS 1663), of Park, Wigtownshire; s of Sir Lewis John Erroll Hay, 9 Bt (d 1923); *b* 13 April 1909; *Educ* Fettes, Liverpool Univ (Dip Arch); *m* 1, 1935 (m dis 1942), Hertha Hedwig Paula Louise, da of late Ludwig Stölzle, of Nagelberg, Austria, and widow of Walter Biheller; 1 s; m 2, 1943, Mrs Rosemary Anne Weymouth, da of late Vice-Adm Aubrey Lambert; *Heir* s, John Hay; *Career* WWII served RE 1939-45, 2 Lt 1943, Lt 1944; retired civil servant; ARIBA, Companion ISO 1974; *Style*— Sir Arthur Hay, Bt; c/o Lloyds Bank, Castle St, Farnham, Surrey

HAY, David John MacKenzie; s of Ian Gordon McHattie Hay, of Inverness, and Ishbel Jean Hay, *née* MacKenzie; *b* 30 June 1952; *Educ* Inverness Royal Acad, Univ of Edinburgh (MA), Magdalene Coll Cambridge (MA, LLM); *Career* called to the Bar Inner Temple 1977, managing ed Atkin's Encyclopaedia of Court Forms 1984-85, ed R & D 1985-86, managing ed Electronic Forms Publishing 1986-88, ed Halsbury's Laws of England (reissue) 1989-; memb The Barley Players; *Recreations* music, enjoying the countryside, reading, travel; *Style*— David Hay, Esq; The Cottage, School Lane, Barley, nr Royston, Herts SG8 8JZ (☎ 076 384 8110); Butterworth Law Publishers Ltd, 88 Kingsway London WC2B 6AB (☎ 071 405 6900, fax 071 405 1332, telex 95678)

HAY, Dennis; s of James Glegg Hay, of 34d Cattofield Place, Aberdeen, and Elsie Whyte, *née* Beattie; *b* 5 Oct 1940; *Educ* Aberdeen GS, Jordanhill Coll of Educn; *m* 20 Dec 1968, Elizabeth Anne, *née* Davidson; 3 s (Brian b 12 Oct 1970, Alan b 14 July 1972, Neil b 13 Nov 1975); *Career* hockey coach; club player: Glasgow Western 1963-66, Inverleith 1966-74, Perthshire 1974; Scotland: schoolboy caps 1957-58, 62 outdoor caps 1964-74, 11 indoor caps 1973-74; GB: 17 outdoor caps 1966 and 1970-72, tour Aust 1966 and India 1971, played in Olympic Games Munich 1972; coach: Scot Schs 1976-82, Scot men indoor 1973-75, Scot women indoor 1976-77, Scot women outdoor 1982-86 (World Cup 1983 and 1986), GB women outdoor 1985- (fourth place Olympic Games Seoul 1988); teacher: various schs Renfrew 1963-66, Melville Coll 1966-74, David Stewart's Sch 1972-74), Perth GS 1974-80, Drummond

Community HS 1980-87, Balerno Community HS 1987- (currently asst princ teacher guidance); *Recreations* hill walking; *Style*— Dennis Hay, Esq; c/o Scottish Hockey Union, Caledonian House, South Gyle, Edinburgh EH12 9DQ

HAY, Elizabeth Joyce (Jocelyn); *née* Board; da of William George Board (d 1951), and Olive Price Jones (d 1962); *b* 30 July 1927; *Educ* Open Univ (BA); *m* 26 Aug 1950, William Andrew Hunter Hay, TD, s of Sheriff J C E Hay, CBE, MC, TD, DL (d 1975); 2 da (Penelope Jill b 1960, Rosemary b 1961); *Career* freelance writer and broadcaster 1954-83; work incl: Forces Broadcasting Serv, Womans' Hour BBC Radio 2 and 4; head of press and PR Dept Girl Guides Assoc, Cwlth HQ 1973-78, fndr London Media Workshops 1978-, fndr and chm Voice of the Listener 1983-; FIPR; *Recreations* gardening, bee-keeping; *Style*— Mrs Jocelyn Hay; 101 Kings Dr, Gravesend, Kent, (☎ 0474 564676)

HAY, Lord Hamish David Montagu; s of 12 Marquess of Tweeddale, GC (d 1979); *b* 1959,(twin); *Educ* Fettes, Wadham Coll Oxford (BA Botany), Kings Coll Hosp Medical Sch (MB BS); *Career* Doctor; *Style*— Lord Hamish Hay; c/o Lord Andrew Hay, 21 Martindale Road, Balham London SW12

HAY, Ian Wood; s of John William Hay (d 1977), of Harwich, Essex, and Winifred May, *née* Fox (d 1975); *b* 25 Jan 1940; *Educ* Colchester Sch of Art (NDD), RCA; *m* 26 March 1968, Teresa Mary, da of Stanislav Antoni Sliski, of Harwich, Essex; 2 s (James b 1978, Rupert b 1982); *Career* visiting lectr: St Martins Sch of Art 1963-77, Norwich Sch of Art 1971-75; sr lectr in drawing Sch of Art Colchester Inst 1988-, RCA prize for landscape painting 1963; known for pastel paintings of London and The Thames; many one man and group shows in Essex and London in The Minories and Phoenix Art Gallery; works in private and public collections incl: Guildhall Art Gallery, Sheffield Art Gallery, Doncaster City Art Gallery, Univ of Essex; memb Colchester Art Soc; ARCA (1963); *Recreations* travel; *Style*— Ian Hay, Esq; 32 Tall Trees, Mile End, Colchester, Essex CO4 5DU (☎ 0206 852 510)

HAY, John Erroll Audley; s and h of Sir Arthur Hay, 10 Bt; *b* 3 Dec 1935; *Educ* Gordonstoun, St Andrew's Univ (MA); *Style*— John Hay, Esq

HAY, Lady Marioth Christina; resumed use of maiden name Hay 1971; da of Lt-Col Lord Edward Hay, DL (3 s of 10 Marquess of Tweeddale, KT, DL) by his 1 w, Violet, da of Maj Cameron Barclay; sis of 12 Marquess of Tweeddale; raised to rank of a Marquess's da 1970; *b* 1 Sept 1918; *m* 1, 1940 (m dis 1954), Lt-Col George Trotter (2 s of Col Algernon Trotter, DSO, MVO, JP, DL, by Lady Edith Montgomerie, yr da of 15 Earl of Eglinton and Winton); 2 s (Richard b 1941, m Marian Campbell; Edward b 1943, m Jemima Mills), 1 da (Bridget Mary b 1944, m John Ellwood); m 2, 1954, as his 2 w, Sqdn Ldr Sir Gifford Fox, 2 and last Bt (d 1959); m 3, 1963 (m dis 1971), Sir John James, KCVO, CB; *Style*— The Lady Marioth Hay; Forbes Lodge, Gifford, East Lothian (☎ 062 081 212)

HAY, Lady Melissa Ann; el da of 15th Earl of Kinnoull; *b* 25 Sept 1964; *Educ* Heathfield, Manchester Coll Oxford; *Recreations* scuba diving, tennis, squash; *Style*— Lady Melissa Hay; 15 Carlyle Sq, London SW3

HAY, Lady Olga; *see*: Maitland, Lady Olga

HAY, Peter Laurence; s of Norman Leslie Stephen Hay (d 1979); *b* 7 March 1950; *Educ* St Paul's, Brunel Univ; *m* 19 July 1985, Perdita Sarah Amanda Lucie Rogers; *Career* dir: Norman Hay plc, Borough Plating Ltd, Montgomery Plating Co Ltd, Armourcote Surface Treatments Ltd, Techniplate Ltd, Plasticraft Ltd; *Recreations* flying helicopters; *Clubs* Lamborghini UK (chm); *Style*— Peter Hay, Esq; Windlesham Grange, Kennel Lane, Windlesham, Surrey GU20 6AA (☎ 0276 72 980); Norman Hay plc, Bath Rd, Harmondsworth, West Drayton, Middx UB7 0BU (☎ 081 759 1911, telex 933036 HAYNOR G, fax 081 897 3060)

HAY, Peter Rossant; s of Vincent Hay, and Marie Winifred, *née* Chase; *b* 11 Oct 1948; *Educ* Clifton; *m* 14 April 1973, Christine Maria; 2 s (Alexander William Rossant b 11 Feb 1978, James Vincent Rossant b 10 Aug 1985), 1 da (Nicola Marie b 8 March 1975); *Career* admitted slr 1973; currently fin ptnr Penningtons (ptnr 1973); chm Richmond Athletic Assoc Ltd 1986-, hon slr The Royal Scot Corp 1985-; non-exec dir Meat Trade Suppliers plc 1988-89; *Recreations* golf, skiing, swimming, ex-rugby and rowing; *Clubs* Caledonian, London Scottish FC, Sunningdale; *Style*— Peter Hay, Esq; Penningtons, 37 Sun St, London EC2M 2PY (☎ 071 377 2855, fax 071 256 5319, telex 25910 Penton G)

HAY, Richard; s of Prof Denys Hay, of Edinburgh, and Sarah Gwyneth, *née* Morley; *b* 4 May 1942; *Educ* George Watson's Coll Edinburgh, Balliol Coll Oxford; *m* 1969, Miriam Marguerite Alvin, da of Charles Arthur England (d 1975); 2 s (Jonathan b 1971, Timothy b 1973); *Career* dir gen Personnel and Admin Euro Cmmn Brussels 1986-; *Style*— Richard Hay, Esq; 200 Rue de la Loi, 1049 Brussells, Belgium (☎ 235 1111)

HAY, Rita, Lady; Rita; da of John Munyard; *m* 1940, Sir Ronald Nelson Hay, 11 Bt (d 1988); 1 s (Sir Ronald Frederick Hamilton, 12 Bt), 1 da (Pamela Rosemary (Mrs Finnegan) b 1945); *Style*— Rita, Lady Hay; 17 Murrumbeena Crescent, Murrumbeena, Victoria 3163, Australia

HAY, Sheriff Robert Colquhoun; CBE (1988); s of J B Hay (d 1971), of Stirling, and J Y Hay (d 1971); *b* 22 Sept 1933; *Educ* Univ of Edinburgh (MA, LLB); *m* 14 June 1958, Olive, da of J C Black; 2 s (Robin b 2 March 1959, Michael b 17 Oct 1967), 2 da (Penelope b 1 Jan 1961, Elizabeth b 28 Dec 1975); *Career* private legal practice 1959-63 and 1968-76, dep procurator fiscal Edinburgh 1963-68, pres Industl Tribunals (Scot) 1981-89 (chm 1976-81), temp Sheriff 1984-89, Sheriff Princ of N Strathclyde 1989-; cmmnr Northern Lights 1989-, memb Sheriff Ct Rules Cncl 1990-; *Books* The Laws of Scotland: Stair Memorial Encyclopaedia (contrib); *Recreations* sailing, hillwalking, gardening; *Clubs* Western (Glasgow), Royal Northern and Clyde Yacht; *Style*— Sheriff Robert Hay, CBE, WS; Sheriff Principal's Chambers, Sheriff Court House, St James St, Paisley PA23 2HW (☎ 041 887 5291)

HAY, Robin William Patrick Hamilton; s of William Reginald Hay (d 1975), of Nottingham, and (Mary Constance) Dora, *née* Bray; *b* 1 Nov 1939; *Educ* Eltham, Selwyn Coll Cambridge (MA, LLB); *m* 18 April 1969, Lady Olga Maitland, *qv*, er da of 17 Earl of Lauderdale; 2 s (Alastair b 18 Aug 1972, Fergus b 22 April 1981), 1 da (Camilla b 25 June 1975); *Career* called to the Bar Inner Temple 1964, rec of Crown Ct 1985; ILEA candidate (Cons) Islington S and Finsbury 1986, chm Young Musicians Symphony Orch; *Recreations* gastronomy, church tasting, choral singing; *Style*— Robin Hay, Esq; 21 Cloudesley St, London N1 0HX (☎ 071 837 9212); Mill Farm, Wighton, Norfolk; Goldsmith Bldg, Temple, London EC4Y 7BL (☎ 071 353 7881, fax 071 353 5319)

HAY, Sir Ronald Frederick Hamilton; 12 Bt (NS 1703), of Alderston; o s of Sir Ronald Nelson Hay, 11 Bt (d 1988), and Rita, *née* Munyard; *b* 1941; *m* 1978, Kathleen, da of John Thake; 2 s (Alexander James b 1979, Anthony Ronald b 1984), 1 da (Sarah Jane b 1981); *Heir* s, Alexander James Hay b 1979; *Style*— Sir Ronald Hay, Bt; Aspendale, Victoria 3195, Australia

HAY-DRUMMOND, Lady Betty Mary Seton; *née* Montgomerie; da of late 16 Earl of Eglinton and Winton by 1 w, Lady Beatrice Dalrymple, da of 11 Earl of Stair; *b* 1912; *m* 1933, Capt George Vane Hay-Drummond, ggs of Lt-Col the Hon Charles Hay-Drummond (s of 11 Earl of Kinnoull); 1 s, 1 da; *Style*— Lady Betty Hay-Drummond; Vane House, 1 The Glebe, Dunning, Perthshire

HAYCRAFT, Anna Margaret; da of John Richard Alfred Lindholm (d 1960), and Gladys Irene Alexandra, *née* Griffith; *b* 9 Sept 1932; *Educ* Bangor County GS for Girls, Liverpool Art Coll; *m* 1956, Colin Berry Haycroft, *qv*, s of Maj William Church Stacpoole Haycraft, MC (d 1929); 5 s (William, Joshua d 1978, Thomas, Oliver, Arthur), 2 da (Rosalind d 1970, Sarah); *Career* writer; dir G Duckworth and Co Ltd 1975; *Books* The Sin Eater (Welsh Arts Cncl award, 1977), The Birds of the Air (1980), The 27th Kingdom (Booker prize nomination 1982), The Other Side of the Fire (1983), Unexplained Laughter (1985), The Clothes in The Wardrobe (1987), The Skeleton in the Cupboard (1988), Natural Baby Food (1977), Darling, You Shouldn't Have gone To So Much Trouble (1979), Home Life (1986), Secrets of Strangers (1986), More Home Life (1987), Home Life III (1988), The Loss of the Good Authority (1989), Wales: an Anthology (1989), The Fly in the Ointment (1989), Home Life IV (1989), The Inn at the Edge of the World (1990), A Welsh Childhood (1990); weekly column: Home Life in Spectator 1985-89, The Universe 1989-; *Style*— Anna Haycraft; 22 Gloucester Crescent, London NW1 7DS (☎ 071 485 7408)

HAYCRAFT, Colin Berry; s of Maj William Church Stacpoole Haycraft, MC (and bar) (ka 1929), and Olive Lillian Esmée Haycraft, *née* King (d 1976); *b* 12 Jan 1929; *Educ* Wellington (open scholar and foundationer), The Queen's Coll Oxford (open classical scholar, MA, Squash blue, Lawn Tennis blue, Rackets blue); *m* 1956, Anna Margaret, *qv*, (pseudonym Alice Thomas Ellis, novelist), da of John Alfred Lindholm (d 1961); 5 s (William, Joshua d 1959, Thomas, Oliver, Arthur), 2 da (Rosalind d 1970, Sarah); *Career* on staff Daily Mirror Newspapers Ltd 1955-, editorial staff Observer 1959-; dir: Weidenfeld and Nicolson Ltd, Weidenfeld (Publishers) Ltd 1962-; chm and md Gerald Duckworth and Co Ltd 1971- (jt md 1968-); *Recreations* real tennis; *Clubs* Vincents, Jesters, Queen's, Beefsteak; *Style*— Colin Haycraft, Esq; 22 Gloucester Crescent, London NW1 7DS (☎ 071 485 7408); Gerald Duckworth and Co Ltd, The Old Piano Factory, 43 Gloucester Crescent, London (☎ 071 485 3484)

HAYCRAFT, John Bernard; s of Bernard Gottfried Haycraft, of Bucks, and Diana Margery, *née* Brockwell; *b* 1 Sept 1942; *Educ* Eversley Sch Southwold, Marlborough Coll; *m* 1, 1 Oct 1966, Marie Luize, da of Bryan Hervey Talbot, of Runcorn, Cheshire; 3 s (Alexander Richard b 1969, Oliver Talbot b 1972, Simon Hervey b 1973); m 2, 7 May 1982, Paula Celeste, da of Franco C Vegnuti, of Rowington, Warks; 1 s (Thomas Julian b 1984), 1 da (Jessica Celeste b 1987); *Career* fine art auctioneer and valuer; regnl dir Phillips 1981-; *Recreations* squash, badminton, hockey; *Clubs* Warwick Hockey; *Style*— John Haycraft, Esq; 4 Little Kineton Cottages, Little Kineton, Warks (☎ 0926 641409); Phillips, The Old House, Station Rd, Knowle, Solihull, W Midlands B93 0HT

HAYCRAFT, John Stacpoole; CBE (1981); s of Maj William Stacpoole Haycraft, MC (d 1929), and Olive Lillian, *née* King (d 1978); *b* 11 Dec 1926; *Educ* Wellington, Jesus Coll Oxford (MA), Yale; *m* 17 Oct 1953, Brita Elisabeth, da of Gösta Langenfelt (d 1965), of Stockholm; 2 s (Richard b 1959, James b 1964), 1 da (Katinka b 1957); *Career* Guardsman Coldstream Gds 1945, 2 Lt Queen's Regt 1945, Lt 8 Punjabis 1946, Lt E Surrey Regt 1947; fndr: Academia Britannica 1953, Int Language Centre 1959, Int Teacher Trg Inst 1962, Int House 1964, Eng Teaching Theatre 1969, Eng Language Services International Ltd 1974; founded schs: Cordoba 1953, London 1959, Algiers 1963, Tripoli 1965, Rome 1967, Osaka 1968, Paris 1969; ARELS 1962; *Books* Babel in Spain (1958), Getting on in English (1964), Babel in London (1965), Choosing your English (1972), Introduction to English Language Teaching (1978), Italian Labyrinth (1985), In Search of the French Revolution (1989); *Recreations* tennis, swimming, chess, reading; *Clubs* Canning; *Style*— John Haycraft, Esq, CBE; 79 Lee Rd, London SE3 9EN (☎ 081 852 5495); International House, 106 Piccadilly, London W1 (☎ 071 499 0177, fax 071 495 0284, telex 918162 INTHSE G)

HAYDAY, Sir Frederick; CBE (1963); s of late Arthur Hayday, sometime MP for W Notts; *b* 26 June 1912; *Career* national industrial offr National Union of General and Municipal Workers 1946-71; General Cncl TUC: memb 1950-72, chm 1962-63, vice-chm 1964-69; memb Police Complaints Bd 1977-; kt 1969; *Style*— Sir Frederick Hayday, CBE; 42 West Drive, Cheam, Surrey (☎ 081 642 8928)

HAYDAY, Terence John (Terry); s of John Alfred Hayday (d 1978), and Annie Dorothy, *née* Tebby; *b* 23 June 1947; *Educ* Hampton GS, Univ of Sussex (BA); *m* 9 June 1973, Susan Pamela, da of Gordon Grenville Dean; 2 s (Nicholas b 1977, Christopher b 1979), 1 da (Annabel b 1987); *Career* Lloyd's broker Leslie & Godwin Ltd 1965-67, Lloyd's underwriting asst R W Sturge & Co 1967-69, reinsur underwriter Slater Walker Insurance Co Ltd 1972-76, dir Holmes Kingsley Carritt Ltd (now Holmes Hayday Underwriting Agencies Ltd) 1976-79 (dep Lloyd's underwriter), underwriter Lloyd's Syndicate 694 1980-; chm Holmes Hayday (Underwriting Agencies) Ltd 1988- (md 1980-88), non-exec dir Newman & Stuchbery Ltd 1988-; memb Ctee Insur Inst of London, chm and memb various Sub Ctees at Lloyd's; FCII 1976; *Recreations* sailing, rugby, theatre, literature; *Clubs* Lloyd's Yacht, Twickenham Yacht, Haywards Heath Rugby Football; *Style*— Terry Hayday, Esq; Holmes Hayday (Underwriting Agencies) Ltd, 9 Devonshire Square, London EC2M 4YL (☎ 071 623 8317 ext 4040, fax 071 623 8254)

HAYDEN, William Joseph (Bill); CBE (1976); s of George Hayden (d 1977), of Henley in Arden, Warwickshire, and Mary Ann Overhead; *b* 19 Jan 1929; *Educ* Romford Tech Coll; *m* 1954, Mavis, da of Redvers Ballard (d 1957), of Elm Park Essex; 2 s (Christopher, Andrew), 2 da (Elisabeth, Tracey); *Career* dir: Ford Netherlands 1970-81, Ford Britain 1972-; vice pres mfrg Ford of Europe 1974-, corporate vice pres Ford US 1974-, chm and chief exec Jaguar Cars Ltd 1990-; *Recreations* golf, gardening, soccer; *Clubs* Thorndon Park Golf; *Style*— Bill Hayden Esq, CBE; Coventry, West Midlands (☎ 0203 402121, telex 31622)

HAYDON, Hon Mrs (Kathleen Mary); *née* Seely; da of 1 Baron Mottistone, CB, CMG, DSO, TD (d 1947); *b* 1907; *m* 1946, (Clement) Maxwell Winton Haydon; *Style*— The Hon Mrs Haydon; Paddock Hill, Lymington, Hants

HAYDON, Sir Walter Robert (Robin); KCMG (1980, CMG 1970); s of Walter Haydon (d 1946), and Evelyn Louise, *née* Thom; *b* 29 May 1920; *Educ* Dover GS; *m* 1941, Joan Elizabeth (d 1988), da of Col Reginald Tewson (d 1948); 1 s (decd), 1 da (decd); *Career* WWII served: France, India, Burma; head News Dept FO 1967-71, high cmmr Malawi 1971-73, chief press sec 10 Downing Street 1973-74, high cmmr Malta 1974-76, ambass to Republic of Ireland 1976-80, ret; dir: Imperial Group 1980-84, Imperial Tobacco 1984-88; govr: ESU 1980-86 and 1987, Dover GS; memb: Reviewing Ctee on Export of Works of Art 1984-87, Tobacco Advsy Cncl 1984-88; *Recreations* tennis, walking, swimming; *Clubs* Travellers', Special Forces; *Style*— Sir Robin Haydon, KCMG; c/o Lloyds Bank, Cox's and King's Branch, 6 Pall Mall, London SW1

HAYES, Dr Alan; s of Ernest Hayes, and Annie, *née* Draycott; *b* 12 June 1930; *Educ* Newton Heath Tech Sch Manchester, Royal Tech Coll Salford (BSc), Univ of Cambridge (PhD); *m* 26 Dec 1955, Audrey, da of Henry Leach; 1 s (Stephen b 12 May 1966), 2 da (Alison b 30 Oct 1959, Wendy b 4 July 1961); *Career* Nat Serv RAF 1954-56; ICI plc Pharmaceuticals 1950-78: res scientist, dir, dep chm; chm ICI Agrochemicals 1979-, princ exec offr ICI Seeds 1985-; chm Euro Trade Ctee DTI, memb Bd BOTB; FRSC 1984; *Recreations* music (opera), gardening; *Style*— Dr Alan Hayes, Esq; ICI Agrochemicals, Fernhurst, Haslemere, Surrey GU27 3JE (☎ 0428 655106, fax 0428 655123, telex 858270 ICIPPFG)

HAYES, Chief Constable Brian; QPM (1985); s of James Hayes (d 1984), and Jessie, *née* Spratt; *b* 25 Jan 1940; *Educ* Plaistow Co GS, Univ of Sheffield (BA); *m* 8 Oct 1960, Priscilla Rose, da of Thomas Bishop; 1 s (Stephen Mark b 1962), 3 da (Priscilla Dawn b (twin) 1962, Jacqueline Denise b 1963, Emma Lucy b 1975); *Career* Met Police 1959-77: seconded Northern Ireland 1971-72, police advsr Mexico 1975-76 and Colombia 1977, Br Police rep EEC 1976-77; asst Chief Constable Surrey 1977-81, dep Chief Constable Wilts 1981-82, Chief Constable Surrey 1982-; 1 vice-pres Assoc of Chief Police Offrs, chm Police Athletic Assoc 1989- (nat sec 1984-88), pres Union Sportive des Polices d'Europe 1990-; Police Long Serv and Good Conduct medal 1982; OStJ 1987; *Recreations* martial arts, running, sailing, golf; *Style—* Chief Constable Brian Hayes, QPM; Surrey Constabulary, Mount Browne, Sandy Lane, Guildford, Surrey GU3 1HG (☎ 0483 571212, ext 2000, fax 0483 300279, telex 859273)

HAYES, Sir Brian David; GCB (1988, KCB 1980, CB 1976); s of Charles Wilfred Hayes (d 1958); *b* 5 May 1929; *Educ* Norwich Sch, CCC Cambridge (MA, PhD); *m* 1958, Audrey, da of Edward Mortimer Jenkins (d 1973); 1 s (Edward b 1963), 1 da (Catherine b 1962); *Career* 2 Lt RASC Home Cmd 1948-49; civil servant; perm sec: MAFF 1979-83, Dept of Indust 1983, DTI 1985-89 (jt perm sec 1983-85); dir: Guardian Royal Exchange plc, Tate and Lyle plc 1989-; advsy dir Unilever plc 1990-; *Recreations* reading, watching cricket; *Style—* Sir Brian Hayes, GCB; c/o Tate and Lyle plc, Lower Thames Street, London EC3

HAYES, (Francis) Brian; s of Col Pierse Francis Hayes, OBE, RE, of The Apple House, 2 Davis Close, Marlow, and Sheila Mary, *née* O'Brien; *b* 22 April 1942; *Educ* Downside, Worcester Coll Oxford (BA); *m* 18 May 1968, Lesley Anne, da of Oliver Roy Holcroft (d 1984), of Endon Hall, Pershore, Worcs; 8 s (William b 1969, Alexander b 1970, Oliver b 1974, Toby b 1977, Benedict b 1979, Damian b 1981, Matthew b 1985, Theodore b 1987), 2 da (Rebecca b 1972, Decima b 1990); *Career* CA; memb Governing Bd Coopers & Lybrand 1988-90 (joined 1964, ptnr 1971); memb Partnership Bd Coopers & Lybrand Deloitte 1990-; tstee Clyclotron Tst 1984-; memb Historic Houses Assoc; memb ICAEW 1967; *Books* UK Taxation Implications International Trade (1985); *Recreations* shooting, riding; *Style—* Brian Hayes, Esq; Holt Castle, Holt Heath, Worcester WR6 6NJ (☎ 0905 621065); Coopers & Lybrand, Plumtree Court, London EC4 (☎ 071 583 5000, fax 071 822 8278)

HAYES, Sir Claude James; KCMG (1974, CMG 1969); s of James Benjamin Fidge Hayes (d 1951); *b* 23 March 1912; *Educ* Ardingly, St Edmund Hall Oxford (MA, MLitt), Sorbonne Univ Paris, New Coll Oxford; *m* 1940, Joan, da of Edward McCarthy Fitt (d 1984); 2 s (Peter, Robert), 1 da (Rosemary); *Career* Lt-Col BEF 1939, N Africa, Sicily, Italy, Combined Ops NW Europe; Civil Serv Cmmr 1949, HM Treasy 1957-64, princ fin offr Miny of Overseas Devpt 1965-68, chm Crown Agents for Oversea Govts and Admins 1968-74; vice chm E D Sassoon Banking Co Ltd 1968-72; interim cmmr for W Indies 1968-85; *Recreations* garden maintenance and betterment, old oak furniture, Georgian domestic chattels, Wealden timber houses; *Style—* Sir Claude Hayes, KCMG; Prinkham, Chiddingstone Hoath, Kent (☎ 0342 850 335)

HAYES, David Nelson; s of Peter Nelson Hayes, of 249 Norwich Rd, Fakenham, Norfolk, and Gwyneth Harper, *née* Jones; *b* 11 Feb 1943; *Educ* The Leys Sch Cambridge, Sidney Sussex Coll Cambridge; *m* 1, 7 Feb 1970 (m dis 1981), Wendy Vanessa, da of William Herbert Nowell, of 24 The Warren, Old Catton, Norwich, Norfolk; 2 da (Melissa b 1973, Sarah b 1977); m 2, 11 Sept 1981, Susan Lee, da of Henry Robins Cook (d 1980); 3 step s (Timothy b 1971, Nicholas b 1973, Benjamin b 1977); *Career* slr 1967, legal memb Mental Health Review Tbnl 1986; pres: W Norfolk and King's Law Soc 1987-88, Fakenham Day Centre for Physically Handicapped 1981-; chm Fakenham and Dist Care Attendant Scheme 1983-; *Recreations* gardening and walking; *Style—* David Hayes, Esq; Green Farm House, Little Snoring, Fakenham, Norfolk NR21 OHU (☎ 0328 878772); Hayes and Storr, 18 Market Place, Fakenham, Norfolk NR21 9BH (☎ 0328 863231, fax 0328 55455)

HAYES, Derek William; s of George Hayes (d 1985), and Marjorie, *née* Frodsham; *b* 8 June 1952; *Educ* Upholland GS, Manchester Poly Sch of Art, Sheffield Poly Sch of Art (DipAD), Nat Film and TV Sch; *Career* film and video producer; dir Albion (film BBC Bristol) 1978, animation and effects Great Rock and Roll Swindle 1979-80; co-fndr (with Phil Austin) Animation City 1979; commercials incl: Lego Spaceland, Halls Mentholyptus, Delight Margarine, Golden Vale, Our Price; pop videos incl: Dire Straits (Brothers In Arms), Madonna (Dear Jessie), Elton John (Club at the End of the Street), London Boys (Harlem Desire, London Nights, My Love), Tom Jones (Couldn't Say Goodbye); TV title sequences: Blott on the Landscape, Porterhouse Blue, Forever Green, Jeeves and Wooster, Challenge Anneka; TV station promotional graphics: Autumn on Four, New Year on Four, Spring on Anglia, MTV; various documentary, corp and instructional videos and graphics; films for Channel 4: Skywhales, The Victor, Binky & Boo, Arcadia; Mari Kuttna award 1985; chm Jury Br Animation Awards 1988; judge: Channel 4 MOMI Awards 1990, Br Assoc Film Animators Awards 1989; external assessor Film Dept RCA 1991, memb Int Animation Festival Advsy Ctee 1981-; memb: ACTT 1979, IPPA 1984, Guild of Br Animators 1985; *Recreations* drawing, cycling, walking, reading everything, staring into space; *Style—* Derek Hayes, Esq; Animation City A C Live, 69 Wells St, London W1P 3RB (☎ 071 494 3084, fax 071 436 8934)

HAYES, Prof (John) Desmond; s of William John Hayes (d 1947), and Annie Matilda, *née* Butler (d 1975); *b* 27 July 1931; *Educ* Narberth GS, Univ Coll of Wales (BSc) Univ of Wisconsin (MS), Univ of Wales (PhD); *m* 21 Aug 1959, Nansi, da of David John Lewis (d 1965); 3 s (John Daniel b 1966, Michael Edward b 1970, Timothy Lewis b 1973), 1 da (Sharon Ann b 1964); *Career* King George VI Meml Fell 1954-55, head of Arable Crops Breeding Dept Welsh Plant Breeding Station 1955-77, sci advsr to Agric Res Cncl 1977-79, prof of agric 1979-; memb Governing Bodies: NSDO, SCRI, NVRS, AGRS; memb of UK Seeds Exec; memb IOB, AAB, NIAB, BGS, AEA, Eucarpia; FInstBiol, fell Indian Soc of Genetics and Plant Breeding; *Recreations* family, rugby, gardening, rambling, travel, exploring villages; *Clubs* Farmers; *Style—* Prof Desmond Hayes; Dunstall, Borth, Dyfed SY24 5NN (☎ 0970 871255); Department of Agricultural Sciences, University College of Wales, Penglais, Aberystwyth (☎ 0970 622260, fax 0970 617172)

HAYES, (George) Forbes; s of Raymond Stanley Hayes JP (d 1956), of Bryngarw Bridgend, and Gladys Vera, *née* Keating (d 1981); *b* 22 April 1977; *Educ* Wycliffe Coll Stonehouse Glos, Trinity Coll Cambridge (MA); *m* 5 Sept 1942, Jean, da of Charles Cory; 1 s (John Forbes Raymond, *qv*, b 21 Oct 1948), 1 da (Ann Caroline Milne b 14 Nov 1945); *Career* 2 Lieut 81 Field Regt RA (TA) 1938-39, Maj REME WWII 1943-46; apprentice engr TH & J Daniels Stroud 1934-38, dir and chm Sheppard & Sons (later Hayes Industries) 1946-66, dir Hill Samuel & Co Ltd 1966-76, chm Henley Forklift 1973-75; High Sheriff Glamorgan Co 1972-73; pres: Engrg & Employers Fedn S Wales 1960-61, Indust Assoc of Wales & Mons 1964; fndr chm CBI Cncl Wales 1965; UWIST: memb Cncl 1973, chm Cncl 1974-82, vice pres 1982-88; vice pres Univ of Wales Coll of Cardiff 1988- (memb Cncl 1988); Freeman City of London 1951, memb of Court of Assts Worshipful Co of Tin Plate Workers 1961- (memb 1951, Master 1975-76), govr: RAS, Bath and West Soc; CEng, FIMechE, FRHS, FRAS, CStJ; *Recreations* music, garden, golf, travel; *Clubs* Farmers, City Livery, Cardiff & County, Royal (Porthcawl); *Style—* Forbes Hayes, Esq; Brocastle, Bridgend, Mid Glamorgan CF35 5AU (☎ 0656 660600)

HAYES, Francis Edward Sutherland; s of Raymond Stanley Hayes, JP (d 1956), of Bryngarw, Brynmenyn, Bridgend, and Gladys Vera, *née* Keating (d 1981); *b* 14 May 1930; *Educ* Wycliffe Coll Stonehouse Gloucester, Jesus Coll Cambridge; *m* 26 April 1958, (Nesta) Suzanne, da of Maj Sir William Reardon-Smith Bt, RA, of Rhode Farm, Romansleigh, South Molton, N Devon; 1 s (Patrick b 5 Nov 1961), 3 da (Thira b 5 April 1960, Elizabeth b 27 July 1964, Philippa b 21 Sept 1966); *Career* Nat Serv Sub Lt RNR 1950-52; gen cmmr Inland Revenue 1976-, chm Gresswell Valves Ltd 1977-, dir AB Electronic Products Gp plc 1982-, dep chm Wales Regnl Bd TSB Eng & Wales 1987-89 (dir 1984), dir Bruno Electrical Ltd 1983-; High Sheriff S Glamorgan 1977-78; fell The Woodard Corp 1973-; chm The Br Valve Mfrs Assoc 1984, chm of govrs The Cathedral Sch Llandaff Cardiff 1985-, chm CLA Game Fair 1990; Freeman: City of London 1966, Worshipful Co of Farriers 1966; *Recreations* music, sailing, shooting; *Clubs* Cardiff & County, Naval; *Style—* Francis Hayes, Esq; Llansannor House, Cowbridge, South Glamorgan CF6 7RW (☎ 044 63 5453); New Worcester Works, Elkington St, Birmingham B6 4SL (☎ 021 359 2052, fax 021 359 5938, telex 337114)

HAYES, Jeremy Joseph James (Jerry); MP (Cons) Harlow 1983-; s of Joseph B Hayes, of Theydon Mount, Essex, and Daye Julia Hayes; *b* 20 April 1953; *Educ* Oratory Sch, Univ of London (LLB); *m* 22 Sept 1979, Alison Gail, da of Frederick John Mansfield (d 1985), of Epping, Essex; 1 s (Lawrence Frederick b 1986), 1 da (Francesca Julia b 1984); *Career* barr at law, practising on SE circuit; memb Select Ctee on Social Servs, jt sec Backbench Cons Health Ctee, hon dir State Leadership Fndn; Freeman: City of London, Worshipful Co of Fletchers, Worshipful Co of Watermen and Lightermen; *Clubs* Carlton; *Style—* Jerry Hayes, Esq, MP; House of Commons, London SW1A 0AA (☎ 071 219 6349)

HAYES, John Forbes Raymond; s of George Forbes Raymond Hayes, of Brocastle, Bridgend, Mid Glamoragan, and Jean Hayes, OBE, *née* Cory; *b* 21 Oct 1948; *Educ* Harrow, Trinity Hall Cambridge (MA); *m* 1 May 1976, Nicola Anne, da of Brian Thomas Reilly (d 1988); 4 s (Charles, Hugh, Matthew, Benjamin Thomas); *Career* accountant; Coopers & Lybrand Deloitte: articles 1971, conslt 1980, dir Nigerian firm 1982-84, dir UK firm 1986-, chm UK Investment Gp 1990; Freeman City of London 1970, memb Worshipful Co of Tin Plate Workers 1970 (Gen Purposes Ctee 1989), under-warden 1990; FCA 1980 (ACA 1975); *Recreations* music, shooting, sailing; *Clubs* Leander; *Style—* John Hayes, Esq; Crompton Hall, South Park, Gerrards Cross, Bucks SL9 8HE (☎ 0753 887094); Plumtree Court, London EC4A 4HT (☎ 071 583 5000, 071 822 4715, fax 071 822 4652, telex 887470)

HAYES, Vice Adm Sir John Osler Chattock; KCB (1967, CB 1964), OBE (1945); s of Maj Lionel Chattock Hayes, RAMC (d 1962); *b* 9 May 1913; *Educ* RNC Dartmouth; *m* 1939, Hon Rosalind Mary, *qv*, da of 2 and last Viscount Finlay; 2 s (Colin b 1943, Malcolm b 1951), 1 da (Griselda b 1954); *Career* entered RN 1927; served WWII, Atlantic, Far East (HMS Repulse), Arctic Convoys, Malta; naval sec to First Lord of Admiralty 1962-64, Flag Offr 2 i/c Western Fleet 1964-66, flag offr Scotland and N Ireland 1966-68; pres King George's Fund for Sailors (Scotland) 1968-79; memb Queen's Body Guard for Scotland 1969-; dep chm Gordonstoun Sch 1970-86; chm Cromarty Firth Port Authy 1974-77; HM Lord-Lt of Ross and Cromarty, Skye and Lochalsh 1977-88; *Recreations* walking, music, writing; *Style—* Vice Adm Sir John Hayes, KCB, OBE; Wemyss House, Nigg, by Tain, Ross and Cromarty (☎ 086 285 212)

HAYES, John Philip; CB (1984); s of late Harry Hayes, and late G E Hayes, *née* Hallsworth; *b* 1924; *Educ* Cranleigh, CCC Oxford; *m* 1956, Susan Elizabeth, da of Sir Percivale Liesching, GCMG, KCB, KCVO; 1 s, 1 da; *Career* WWII RAFVR 1943-46; political and econ planning 1950-53, OEEC 1953-58, Int Bank For Reconstruction and Devpt 1958-64, head Econ Devpt Div OECD 1964-67, dir World Economy Div (Econ Planning Staff) Miny of Overseas Devpt 1967-69, dep dir gen Econ Planning Miny of Overseas Devpt and Overseas Devpt Admin 1969-71; dir: Econ Program Dept (later Econ Analysis and Projections Dept) Int Bank for Reconstruction and Devpt 1971-73, Trade and Fin Div Cwlth Secretariat 1973-75; asst under sec of state (economics) FCO 1975-84; sr fell Trade Policy Res Centre 1984-89; *Books* Economic Effects of Sanctions on Southern Africa (1987); *Recreations* music, travel; *Style—* J P Hayes, Esq, CB; 51 Enfield Rd, Brentford, Middx TW8 9PA (☎ 081 568 7590)

HAYES, Dr John Trevor; CBE (1986); s of Leslie Thomas Hayes (d 1976), of London, and Gwendoline, *née* Griffiths (d 1976); *b* 21 Jan 1929; *Educ* Ardingly Coll Sussex, Keble Coll Oxford (MA), Courtauld Inst of Art Univ of London (PhD), Inst of Fine Arts NY; *Career* dir: London Museum 1970-74 (asst keeper 1954-70), Nat Portrait Gallery 1974-; visiting prof in history of art Yale Univ 1969; hon fell Keble Coll Oxford; FSA 1975; *Books* The Drawings of Thomas Gainsborough (1970), Gainsborough as Printmaker (1971), Rowlandson Watercolours and Drawings (1972), Gainsborough Paintings and Drawings (1975), The Art of Graham Sutherland (1980), The Landscape Paintings of Thomas Gainsborough (1982); *Recreations* music, walking, gardening, travel; *Clubs* Beefsteak, Garrick, Arts; *Style—* Dr John Hayes, CBE, FSA; National Portrait Gallery, 2 St Martin's Place, London WC2H OHE (☎ 071 306 0055, fax 071 306 0056)

HAYES, Michael Anthony; s of Brian George Gerard Hayes (d 1983), of Wimbledon and Dorking, Surrey, and June Louise, *née* Wenner (d 1967); *b* 10 Jan 1943; *Educ* Wimbledon Coll, Univ Coll Oxford (MA); *m* 5 June 1971, Jacqueline Mary, da of Peter Kenneth Judd; 2 s (Dominic b 11 Aug 1972, William b 13 Feb 1978), 1 da (Victoria b 25 April 1974); *Career* admitted slr 1968; ptnr Macfarlanes 1974- (articled clerk 1966-68, asst slr 1968-71, assoc 1971-74); memb Ctee: City of London Law Soc 1978- (Distinguished Service award 1987), Law Soc Standing Ctee on Entry and Trg 1987-89, Law Soc Wills and Equity Ctee 1989-; vice chm Advsy Ctee of City of London CAB 1988- (chm 1985-88), tstee Tower Hamlets Tst; Freeman Worshipful Co of Slrs 1978-; memb Law Soc; *Recreations* jazz, wine, windsurfing; *Clubs* Wig and Pen, Roehampton; *Style—* Michael Hayes, Esq; 10 Norwich St, London EC4A 1BD (☎ 071 831 9222, fax 071 831 9607)

HAYES, Roger Peter; s of Peter Hall, and Patricia Mary, *née* Lacey; *b* 15 Feb 1945; *Educ* Isleworth GS, Univ of London, Univ of Southern California (BSc, MA); *m* 15 Feb 1974, Margaret Jean Hayes; 1 s (Nicolas Alexander b 25 Nov 1983); *Career* corr Reuters Paris 1967-72, dir and vice pres Burson Marsteller 1972-79, PA mgmnt conslt 1979-83, dir of corporate communications Thorn EMI plc 1985-88, dir IT World 1985-, chm Hayes Macleod International and Investor Corporate Communications 1988-, dir the Watts Group plc 1989; numerous articles in jls; vice chm Fulham Conservatives; chm: City and Fin Gp Inst of Public Relations, Tstees Int Foundation of Public Affrs; memb: Nat Ctee Tory Reform GP, CBI Multinationals Panel; hon sec general Int Public Relations Assoc and memb of Bd 1988-; FRSA 1987, FIPR 1988; *Books* Corporate Revolution (jtly, 1986), Experts in Action (jtly, 1988); *Recreations* tennis, travel, books, music, international relations; *Clubs* RAC, Hurlingham, Savile; *Style—* Roger Hayes, Esq; 11 Doneraile St, London SW6 6EL (☎ 071 731 1255); Hayes Macleod, 52 St John Street, Smithfield, London EC1M 4DT (☎ 071 490 4747, fax 071 490 4628)

HAYES, Hon Lady (Rosalind Mary); da of 2 and last Viscount Finlay (d 1945), and Beatrice Marion Hall (d 1942); *b* 27 Dec 1914; *m* 1939, Vice-Adm Sir John Osler

Chattock Hayes, KCB, OBE, *qv*; 2 s (Colin b 1943, Malcolm b 1951), 1 da (Griselda b 1954); *Recreations* horses, walking, gardening, music; *Style*— The Hon Lady Hayes; Wemyss House, Nigg, by Tain, Ross and Cromarty (☎ 086 285 212)

HAYES, Hon Mrs (Sarah); da of 2 Baron Maclay, KBE (d 1969); *b* 1937; *m* 1968, David Richard Hayes, s of Eric Gerald Hayes (d 1958); *Style*— The Hon Mrs Hayes; Muir of Knock, Pityoulish, Aviemore, Inverness-shire

HAYES, Dr William; s of Robert Hayes (d 1986), and Eileen, *née* Tobin (d 1985); *b* 12 Nov 1930; *Educ* Univ Coll Dublin (BSc, PhD), Univ of Oxford (MA, DPhil); *m* 28 Aug 1962, Joan Mary, da of John Ferriss (d 1986); 2 s (Robert b 1973, Stephen b 1974), 1 da (Julia b 1970); *Career* offical fell and tutor in physics St John's Coll Oxford 1960-67, 1851 overseas scholar 1955-57, sr fell American Nat Sci Fndn Purdue Univ USA 1963-64, visiting prof Univ of Illinois USA 1971, princ bursar St John's Coll Oxford 1977-87, dir and head Clarendon Laboratory Oxford 1985-87, pres St John's Coll Oxford 1987-; Hon DSc Nat Univ of Ireland 1988; *Books* Scattering of Light by Crystals (with R Loudon, 1978), Defects and Defect Processes in Non-Metallic Solids (with A M Stoneham, 1985); *Recreations* walking, reading, listening to music; *Clubs* Utd Oxford and Cambridge; *Style*— Dr William Hayes; President's Lodgings, St John's Coll, Oxford (☎ 0865 277 424); St John's Coll, Oxford (☎ 0865 277 419)

HAYGARTH, (Edward James) Anthony; s of Edward Haygarth (d 1961), and Sarah Agnes, *née* McGill (d 1949); *b* 28 March 1931; *Educ* Birkenhead Sch, Univ of Liverpool (BCom); *m* 29 Oct 1957, Catherine Patricia, da of Henry William Carpenter (d 1953); 1 s (Edward b 1972); *Career* Nat Serv PO RAF 1956-58; dir Combined English Stores Gp plc 1972-87; FCA; *Recreations* tennis; *Clubs* Cumberland LTC, Hampstead CC; *Style*— Anthony Haygarth, Esq

HAYGARTH-JACKSON, Angela Ray; OBE (1984); da of Harold Haygarth-Jackson, MC (d 1972), and Frieda, *née* Barraclough (d 1979); *b* 25 July 1929; *Educ* Cheltenham Ladies' Coll, Univ of Manchester (BSc, MSc); *Career* mangr Info Servs Section ICI Pharmaceuticals 1956-86, info sci conslt 1986-; pres Inst of Info Scientists 1983-84; chm: Editorial Bd of Journal of Documentation 1984-, Royal Soc of Chemistry Pubns Info Bd 1988-; memb: Royal Soc Sci Info Ctee 1978-86, Br Library Advsy Cncl 1981-86; external examiner Dept of Info Studies Univ of Sheffield 1983-87; memb UK delgn to advise the People's Republic of China on library and info matters 1984; author of many papers on info sci and lectures in UK and overseas; FIInfSc; *Recreations* travel, bridge, gardening, DIY, photography, original tapestry; *Style*— Miss Angela Haygarth-Jackson, OBE; Highwayside, Bowdon, Altrincham, Cheshire WA14 3JD

HAYHOE, Rt Hon Sir Barney (Bernard) John; PC (1985), MP (C) Brentford and Isleworth 1983-; s of Frank Hayhoe and Catherine Hayhoe; *b* 8 Aug 1925; *Educ* Borough Poly; *m* 1962, Anne Gascoigne *née* Thorton; 2 s, 1 da; *Career* MP (C): Heston and Isleworth 1970-74, Hounslow Brentford and Isleworth 1974-1983; CRD 1965-70, PPS to Lord Pres and Ldr of the Commons 1972-74, additional oppn spokesman Employment 1974-79, Parly under sec Def (Army) 1979-81; min of state: CSD 1981, Treasy 1981-85, min for Health 1985-86; kt 1987; *Style*— The Rt Hon Sir Barney Hayhoe, MP; 20 Wool Rd, London SW20 0HW (☎ 081 947 0037)

HAYHURST, Andrew Neil; s of William Hayhurst, of Manchester, and Margaret, *née* Wilson; *b* 23 Nov 1962; *Educ* Worsley Wardley HS Swinton, Eccles Sixth Form Coll, Carnegie Coll of Physical Educn (BA), Leeds Poly; *m* 17 Feb 1991, April, da of David Cauldwell; *Career* professional cricketer; Lancashire CCC 1985-89, Somerset CCC 1990-; represented England under 19 1981, played in Tasmania winters 1987 and 1988; scored century on debut Somerset 1990; advanced cricket coach, numerous coaching awards in other sports; winter teaching: Worsley Sixth Form Coll Manchester 1985, Blackburn Sixth Form Coll 1986, Broadoak Secdy Sch Weston-Super-Mare 1990; represented Greater Manchester under 19 soccer 1981; *Recreations* watching and participating in all sports, animals, music, decorating; *Style*— Andrew Hayhurst, Esq; c/o Somerset County Cricket Club, The County Ground, St James Street, Taunton TA1 1JT (☎ 0823 272946)

HAYHURST-FRANCE, Christopher; s of Capt George Frederick Hayhurst-France, DSO, MC (d 1940), and Joyce Lilian, *née* Le Fleming (d 1961); *b* 6 Feb 1927; *Educ* Durham Sch, Coll of Estate Mgmnt; *m* 6 Sept 1956, Suzanne, da of Howard Spackman Ferris (d 1973), of Swindon; 2 s (David b 1957, Jonathan b 1960), 2 da (Sarah b 1959, Rachel b 1965); *Career* RM 1945 (invalided out), Lt 3 Glos Bn HG 1952-56; chartered surveyor, auctioneer, valuer; ptnr Moore Allen & Innocent Lechlade 1954-87 (currently conslt); pres Central Assoc Agric Valuers 1975-76, dir Stroud Building Society 1970-, chm Stroud & Swindon Building Society 1986-, sec Berners Estate Co Faringdon 1988-; vice pres Oxfordshire Fedn Young Farmers Clubs; FRICS 1951, FAAV 1956; *Recreations* gardening; *Clubs* Faringdon Rotary; *Style*— Christopher Hayhurst-France, Esq; 9 Orchard Hill, Faringdon, Oxon SN7 7EH (☎ 0367 20433); Moore Allen & Innocent, Lechlade, Glos GL7 3AJ (☎ 0367 52541)

HAYKLAN, Stephen Paul; s of Michael Bernard Hayklan, and Marjorie Elizabeth, *née* Cochrane; *b* 19 April 1934; *Educ* Christ's Hospital; *m* 1959, Barbara Anne, da of Richard Kingston Bayes (d 1975); 1 s (Guyon), 1 da (Sofia); *Career* chm and chief exec Wiggins Gp plc 1981-, chm Abingdon Gp of Cos 1970; fell Incorp Soc of Valuer and Auctioneers; *Recreations* sailing, shooting; *Clubs* Naval and Military; *Style*— Stephen Hayklan, Esq; 18 Rutland Gate, London SW7 1BB (☎ 071 589 3082)

HAYLER, Clive Reginald; s of Reginald Hayler (d 1985), and Dorothy Edith Hayler; *b* 11 Aug 1955; *Educ* Steyning GS, Univ of Liverpool (BSc), Univ of Exeter; *m* ; 2 s (Richard Mark b 1984, Christopher James b 1985); *Career* mktg mangr Beckman RIIC Ltd 1979-83, UK Sales Person of the Year 1981; md Hawksley & Sons Ltd 1985- (gen mangr 1983-85); ctee memb BSI; FInstD, CBiol, ABHI, FSI, FInstSMM; *Recreations* running, swimming, karate, reading, theatre, skiing; *Clubs* IOD; *Style*— Clive Hayler, Esq; Hawksley & Sons Ltd, Marlborough Rd, Lancing, W Sussex (☎ 0903 752815, fax 0903 766050, tlx 87134 HAWSON)

HAYLEY, Dr Thomas Theodore Steiger; s of Otto Johannes Steiger (d 1945), and Constance Mary, *née* Hayley (d 1971); *b* 4 Oct 1913; *Educ* Clifton, Univ of Cambridge (MA), Univ of Oxford (MA), Univ of London (PhD); *m* 7 Sept 1946, Audrey, da of Sir Keith Cantlie, CIE (d 1977); 3 s (Keith b 1952, Clive b 1957, Robin b 1962), 2 da (Ann b 1954, Emma b 1973); *Career* field work in social anthropology among Lango Tribe Uganda 1936 and in Brahmaputa Valley of Assam 1947-50; Indian Civil Serv: dep cmmr, sec to the Govt of Assam in the depts under the PM 1938-50; asst dir Br Branch Int C of C 1950; psychoanalyst; memb Br Psychoanalytical Soc 1956- (chm and vice pres 1969-72); editor: Int Journal of Psycho-Analysis 1978-, Int Review of Psychoanalysis 1978-; *Publications*: The Anatomy of Lango Religion and Groups (monograph), Ritual Pollution and Social Structure in Hindu Assam (PhD Thesis); *Style*— Dr Thomas T S Hayley; Old East Haxted, Edenbridge, Kent TN8 6PT (☎ 0732 862276); 5 Upper Wimpole St, London W1M 7TD (☎ 071 935 9305); 63 New Cavendish St, London W1M (☎ 071 580 5625)

HAYMAN, Sir Peter Telford; KCMG (1971, CMG 1963), CVO (1965), MBE (1945); s of Charles Henry Telford Hayman (d 1950), of The Manor House, Brackley, Northants; *b* 14 June 1914; *Educ* Stowe, Worcester Coll Oxford; *m* 1942, Rosemary Eardley, da of Lt-Col Wilmot Blomefield, OBE, RE (d 1926, yst s of Sir Thomas Wilmot Peregrine Blomefield, 4 Bt); 1 s (Christopher b 1947), 1 da (Virginia b 1944); *Career* WWII Maj Rifle Bde 1942-45; entered Home Office 1937, Miny of Home Security 1939-41, asst sec MOD 1950, cnsllr UK Delgn to NATO, transfd FO 1954, cnsllr Belgrade 1955-58, info advsr to Govr of Malta 1958-59, cnsllr Baghdad 1959-61, dir gen Br Info Servs NY 1961-64, min and dep cmdt Br Mil Govt Berlin 1964-66, asst under-sec of state FO 1966-69, dep under-sec of state 1969-70, high cmmr Canada 1970-74, ret; *Recreations* fishing, travel; *Clubs* MCC; *Style*— Sir Peter Hayman, KCMG, CVO, MBE; Uxmore House, Checkendon, Oxon (☎ 0491 680 658)

HAYMAN, Ronald; s of John Hayman (d 1954), of Bournemouth, and Sadie, *née* Morris (d 1989); *b* 4 May 1932; *Educ* St Paul's, Trinity Hall Cambridge; *m* 11 Nov 1969, Monica, da of Hew Lorimer; 2 da (Imogen Hayman b 9 Jan 1971, Sorrel Trechard b 16 Dec 1981); *Career* author and theatre dir; actor in repertory and TV, first play to be staged The End of an Uncle 1959, memb Royal Court Writers Gp 1959, dir Arts Theatre and Stratford East, trainee dir Northampton Repertory Co (under Associated Rediffusion trainee dirs scheme); prodns as freelance dir incl: An Evening with GBS, a Peter Handke play at the Open Space, a Fassbinder play at the Traverse Edinburgh; author and broadcaster 1967-; *Books* Samuel Beckett (1968), Harold Pinter (1968), John Osborne (1968), John Arden (1968), Techniques of Acting (1969), John Whiting (1969), Robert Bolt (1969), Tolstoy (1970), Arthur Miller (1970), Arnold Wesker (1970), John Gielgud: A Biography (1971), Edward Albee (1971), Eugène Ionesco (1972), Playback (1973), The Set-Up an Anatomy of English Theatre Today (1974), The First Thrust (1975), The German Theatre (ed, 1975), How to Read a Play (1976), Leavis (1976), The Novel Today 1967-75 (1976), Artaud and After (1979), Tom Stoppard (1977), My Cambridge (ed, 1977), De Sade: A Critical Biography (1978), British Theatre since 1955 (1975), Theatre and Anti-Theatre (1979), Nietzsche: A Critical Life (1980), K: A Biography of Kafka (1981), Brecht: A Biography (1983), Brecht: The Plays (1984), Fassbinder: Film-Maker (1984), Secrets: Boyhood in a Jewish Hotel (1985), Writing Against: A Biography of Sartre (1986), Proust: A Biography (1990); *Recreations* tennis; *Style*— Ronald Hayman, Esq; Aitken & Stone, 29 Fernshaw Rd, London SW10 OTG (☎ 071 351 7561, fax 351 9268)

HAYMAN, Prof Walter Kurt; s of Prof Franz Samuel Haymann (d 1947), of Oxford, and Ruth Matilde Therese, *née* Hensel (d 1979); *b* 6 Jan 1926; *Educ* Gordonstoun, St John's Coll Cambridge (BA, MA, ScD); *m* 20 Sept 1947, Margaret Riley, da of Thomas William Crann (d 1978), of 48 Hawthorn Terr, New Earswick, York; 3 da (Daphne Ruth b 1949, Anne Carolyn b 1951, Gillian Sheila b 1956); *Career* lectr Univ of Newcastle 1947, fell St John's Coll Cambridge 1947-50, reader in mathematics Univ of Exeter 1953-56 (lectr 1947-53), dean Royal Coll of Sci Imperial Coll London 1978-81 (first prof of pure mathematics 1956-85), pt/t prof Univ of York 1985-; fndr with Mrs Hayman Br Mathematic Olympiad; memb: Cncl of RS 1962-63, Finnish Acad of Arts and Scis 1978, Bavarian Acad 1982, Accademia Dei Lincei (Rome) 1985, London Mathematic Soc, Cambridge Philosophical Soc, Soc Protection of Sci and Learning (memb Cncl); Hon DSc: Univ of Exeter 1981, Univ of Birmingham 1985; FRS 1956, FIC 1989; *Books* Multivalent Functions (1958), Meromorphic Functions (1964), Research Problems in Function Theory (1967), Subharmonic Functions (vol 1 with PB Kennedy, 1976, vol 2 1989); *Recreations* music, travel, television; *Style*— Prof W K Hayman, FRS; 24 Fulford Park, Fulford, York YO1 4QE (☎ 0904 637713); 3 Lancaster Cottages, Goathland, Whitby, N Yorks YO22 5NQ (☎ 0947 86319); Department of Maths, University of York, Heslington, York YO1 5DD (☎ 0904 433 076)

HAYMAN-JOYCE, James Leslie; s of Maj Thomas F Hayman-Joyce, RA (d 1946), and B C Hayman-Joyce; *b* 12 May 1945; *Educ* Radley, RAC; *m* 3 March 1973, Charlotte Alexandra Mary, da of J P Crump, DFC, of Cold Aston, Gloucs; 2 s (Thomas b 1981, Simon b 1983); *Career* qualified chartered surveyor, ptnr Blinkhorn & Co 1983, dir Sandoes Nationwide Anglia Estate Agents 1988-; FRICS 1970; *Style*— James Hayman-Joyce, Esq; Bakers Farmhouse, Barton-on-the-Heath, Moreton-in-Marsh, Gloucs GL56 0PN (☎ 0608 74 291); 22 High St, Moreton-in-Marsh, Gloucs (☎ 0608 50564)

HAYMAN-JOYCE, Maj-Gen Robert John; CBE (1989, OBE 1979); s of Maj Thomas Fancourt Hayman-Joyce (d 1946), and Betty Christine, *née* Bruford; *b* 16 Oct 1940; *Educ* Radley, Magdalene Coll Cambridge (MA); *m* 19 Oct 1968, Diana, da of Maj Neil Livingstone-Bussell, of East House, Sydling St Nicholas, Dorchester, Dorset; 2 s (Richard Livingstone b 21 Oct 1973, Alexander Robert b 11 Dec 1976); *Career* cmmnd 11 Hussars (PAO) 1963, cmd Royal Hussars (PWO) 1980-82, Cdr RAC BAOR 1983-85, dep cmdt RMCS 1987, dir UK tank prog 1988, dir gen fighting vehicles MOD(PE) 1989, dir gen land fighting systems MOD (PE) 1990; *Recreations* skiing, horses, sailing, reading, music; *Clubs* Cavalry and Guards, Leander (Henley-on-Thames); *Style*— Maj-Gen Robert Hayman-Joyce, CBE; c/o Barclays Bank, 5 High St, Andover, Hants; MOD (PE), St Christopher House, Southwark St, London SE1 0TD (☎ 071 921 1975)

HAYNES, David Francis (Frank); MP (L) Ashfield 1979-; *b* 4 March 1926; *Career* NUM former branch official; memb: Nottinghamshire CC 1965-, Select Ctee on Parly Cmmn for Admin 1979-; *Style*— Frank Haynes Esq, MP; House of Commons, London SW1

HAYNES, Edwin William George; CB (1971); s of Frederick William George Haynes (d 1934), and Lilian May, *née* Armstrong (d 1950); *b* 10 Dec 1911; *Educ* Univ of London (BA, LLM); *m* 1942, Dorothy Kathleen; 1 s (Andrew), 1 da (Kathleen); *Career* barr Lincoln's Inn; civil servant, under sec DTI; ret; *Recreations* books, gardens; *Clubs* Civil Service; *Style*— Edwin Haynes, Esq, CB; 92 Malmains Way, Beckenham, Kent (☎ 081 650 0224)

HAYNES, John Harold; *b* 25 March 1938; *Educ* Sutton Valence Sch Kent; *m* Annette Constance; 3 s (John b 1967, Marc b 1968, Christopher b 1972); *Career* wrote and published first book 1956, ret from RAF as Fl-Lt 1967 to take up full-time publishing, having founded J H Haynes and Co 1960; chm and chief exec Haynes Publishing Group plc; dir: J H Haynes and Co Ltd 1960-, Haynes Publications Inc (USA) 1984, GT Foulis and Co Ltd 1977-, Haynes Developments Ltd 1979-, J H Haynes (Overseas) Ltd 1979-, John H Haynes Developments Inc (USA) 1979-, Oxford Illustrated Press Ltd 1981-, Gentry Books Ltd, Camway Autographics Ltd 1984-, Oxford Publishing Co 1988-, Patrick Stephens Ltd 1990-; *Recreations* cycling, walking, veteran and vintage cars, reading; *Clubs* Southern Milestone Motor (pres), Guild of Motoring Writers; *Style*— John H Haynes, Esq; Sparkford, Somerset BA22 7JJ (☎ 0963 40635, telex 46212); 861 Lawrence Drive, Newbury Park, Ca 91320 USA (☎ 818 889 5400, telex 0236662406)

HAYNES, Michael John; s of Ronald John Haynes, of Bucks, and Barbara Marion, *née* Paine; *b* 15 Jan 1956; *Educ* Highgate Public Sch, Univ of Leicester (LLB), Cncl of Legal Educn; *m* 17 May 1980, Caroline Alma, da of William Edmonds, of North Kensington; *Career* called to the Bar Gray's Inn 1979, practice from D Medhurst Chambers London; *Recreations* wine, karate, photography; *Clubs* Int Food and Wine Soc; *Style*— Michael Haynes, Esq; Top Floor, 4 Brick Ct, Temple, London EC4 (☎ 071 353 1492, fax 071 583 8645)

HAYNES, Hon Mrs (Penelope Margaret); *née* Gilbey; da of 10 Baron Vaux of Harrowden; *b* 1942; *m* 1965, John Charles Haynes; 2 s, 2 da; *Style*— The Hon Mrs Haynes; Evelith Mill, Shifnal, Shropshire

HAYNES, The Very Rev Peter; s of Francis Harold Stanley Haynes (d 1978), of

Bristol, and Winifred Annie, *née* Ravenhill (d 1970); *b* 24 April 1925; *Educ* St Brendan's Coll Clifton, Selwyn Coll Cambridge (MA), Cuddesdon Coll Oxford; *m* 1952, Ruth, da of Dr Charles Edward Stainthorpe (d 1971), of Newcastle upon Tyne; 2 s (Richard b 1953, Michael b 1956); *Career* RAF coastal cmd 1943-47; Barclays Bank 1941-43; ordained deacon York Minister 1952; asst curate: Stokesley 1952-54, Hessle 1954-58; vicar St John's Drypool Hull 1958-63, bishop's chaplain for youth, asst dir of religious educn Dioc Bath and Wells 1963-70; vicar of Glastonbury 1970-74, archdeacon of Wells 1974-82, dean of Hereford 1982-; *Recreations* sailing, model engineering; *Style—* The Very Rev the Dean of Hereford; The Deanery, The Cloisters, Hereford HR1 2NG (☎ 0432 59880)

HAYNES, Philip Edmund; s of Herbert Thomas Haynes, of Hove, Sussex, and Hilda, *née* Buckle (d 1981); *b* 8 July 1938; *Educ* Reigate GS; *m* 12 June 1965, Susan Edna, da of Cecil Lewis Blackburne; 2 s (Stephen b 4 March 1968, Michael b 2 April 1970); *Career* Nat Serv RAF 1956-58; articled clerk Hughes & Allen 1958-63, qualified CA 1964, ptnr Halletts (later Kidsons then Kidsons Impey) 1969-; memb Tech (Accounts & Audit) Sub Ctee LSCA 1975-76, chm Auditing Discussion Gp LSCA 1974-78; FCA 1969 (ACA 1964); *Recreations* photography, reading, gardening, theatre, classical music; *Style—* Philip Haynes, Esq; Kidsons Impey, Spectrum House, 20-26 Cursitor St, London EC4A 1HY (☎ 071 405 2088, fax 071 831 2206)

HAYNES, (Frank) Richard; s of Frank Sydney Haynes (d 1964), and Ethel Lulu, *née* Winfield (d 1963), gf William Haynes, master clockmaker, installed clock in St Paul's Cathedral and in many other churches and public bldgs; *b* 8 Dec 1936; *Educ* Cheltenham; *m* 7 Feb 1959, Patricia Saunders, da of Dr James Bryn Saunders Morgan (d 1987); 2 s (Michael b 1960, David b 1963), 1 da (Kathryn b 1967); *Career* jeweller; chm and md John D Eaton Ltd 1967- (dir 1960, md 1964); memb Royal Hort Soc Orchid Ctee 1985-, Br Orchid Cncl Judge 1986; *Recreations* orchid growing and breeding, golf, badminton; *Style—* Richard Haynes, Esq; Esseburne, 272 Broadway, Derby DE3 1BN (☎ 0332 557491); 4 Main Centre, Derby DE1 2PE (☎ 0332 44884)

HAYNES, Richard Stainthorpe; s of The Very Rev Peter Haynes, of The Deanery, Hereford, and Ruth, *née* Stainthorpe; *b* 17 June 1953; *Educ* Wells Cathedral Sch, Ealing Business Sch (BA, Dip MRS); *m* 2 June 1979, Penelope Jane, da of Robert Oliver Prentice, MC, of Ipswich; 1 s (Robert Alexander b 1987), 1 da (Sophie Elizabeth b 1984); *Career* Shell UK Oil: mgmnt trainee 1971-73, sponsored business studies student 1973-77, advertising exec 1977-78; mktg devpt mangr/int mktg Fisons Ltd 1978-83, mktg conslt Gwyn-Thomas Assocs Ltd 1983-85, unit tst mktg mangr TSB Tst Co Ltd 1985-87, mktg communications mangr TSB Gp plc 1987-88, investmt mktg dir Abbey Life Gp plc 1988-; MCIM; *Recreations* classical guitar, hill walking, choral music, organic gardening; *Style—* Richard Haynes, Esq; Abbey Life Group plc, 80 Holdenhurst Rd, Bournemouth BH8 8AL (☎ 0202 401 602)

HAYNES, Roger John; s of Thomas William (d 1974), of Haslemere, Surrey, and Phyllis, *née* Turner; *b* 26 April 1937; *Educ* Trinity Sch Croydon; *m* 20 March 1964, Caroline, da of late Maurice Nitsch, of Guildford; 2 s (Jon Charles, Will Benedict); *Career* formerly sr ptnr Brewers CA's, ptnr Smith & Williamson (chartered accountants); dir: Smith and Williamson Securities, County Sound plc; hon treas Surrey Cncl, Order of St John; *Recreations* music, golf, reading, gardening, people; *Clubs* County (Guildford); *Style—* Roger Haynes, Esq; Onslow Bridge Chambers, Bridge St, Guildford, Surrey GU1 4RA (☎ 0483 302 200, fax 0483 301 232)

HAYNES-DIXON; *see*: Godden, Rumer

HAYR, Air Marshal Sir Kenneth William; KCB (1988, CB 1982), CBE (1976), AFC (1963 and bar 1972); s of Kenneth James Maxwell Hayr (d 1990) of Auckland NZ, and Jeannie Templeton Hayr, *née* Crozier; *b* 13 April 1935; *Educ* Auckland GS, RAF Coll Cranwell; *m* 1961, Joyce (d 1987), da of T Gardner (d 1954); 3 s (Simon, James, Richard); *Career* RAF Offr, Fighter Pilot 1957-71, OC RAF Binbrook 1974-76, Inspr of Flight Safety 1976-79, Asst Chief of Air Staff (Ops) 1981-82, Air Offr cmdg No 11 Gp 1982-85, Cdr Br Forces Cyprus and Admin of the Sovereign Base Areas 1985-88, Dep CinC Strike Cmd/COS UKAIR 1988-90, Dep Chief Def Staff (Commitments) 1989-; *Recreations* tennis, hang gliding, windsurfing, skiing, parachuting; *Clubs* RAF; *Style—* Air Marshal Sir Kenneth Hayr, KCB, CBE, AFC; MOD (Room 6290), Main Building, Whitehall, London SW1A 2HB (☎ 071 218 6762)

HAYTER, Alison, Baroness; (Margaret) Alison; da of J G Pickard, of Leicester; *m* 1949, as his 2 w, 2 Baron Hayter (d 1967); *Career* sculptress, exhibitor Royal Academy; *Style—* The Rt Hon Alison, Lady Hayter; 31 Iverna Gdns, Kensington, W8 (☎ 071 937 6860)

HAYTER, (John) David Henzell; s of Lt-Col Herbert Roche Hayter, DSO (d 1952), and Elsie Helen Evelyn Winterton, *née* Pidcock-Henzell (d 1978); *b* 2 Oct 1921; *Educ* Marlborough, Clare Coll Cambridge (MA); *m* 17 April 1948, Mary Vivien, da of late Richard Vyvyan Mansell, OBE; 3 da (Vivien Helen (Mrs Cassel), Rosemary Margaret (Mrs Walker), Susan Carolyn (Lady Muir-Mackenzie)); *Career* Univ of Cambridge Air Sqdn, joined RAF, pilot Canada 1942-43, cmmnd Pilot Offr, instr Fleet Air Arm RAF Station Kingston Ontario Canada, returned UK 1945, instr RAF Little Rissington and RAF Turnhill, demobbed; Rootes Group Motor Manufacturing 1946; purchased farm at Methven Castle Perthshire 1953, sold castle and farm 1981, purchased Hollington Estate Highclere Newbury Berks 1982, sold 1989; involved with political and church affrs, agric orgns; *Recreations* shooting, yachting; *Clubs* Royal Perth Golfing Soc, Royal Solent Yacht; *Style—* David Hayter, Esq; Adbury Court, Newtown, Newbury, Berks RG15 9BP (☎ 0635 40372)

HAYTER, Hon Mrs (Deborah Gervaise); *née* Maude; da of Baron Maude of Stratford-upon-Avon (Life Peer); *b* 1948; *Educ* Univ of Bristol (BA); *m* 1973, Paul David Grenville Hayter (reading clerk House of Lords); 2 s (William b 1978, Giles b 1981), 1 da (Arabella b 1984); *Style—* The Hon Mrs Hayter; Williamscot, nr Banbury, Oxon

HAYTER, Dianne; da of Flt Lt Alec Bristow Hayter (d 1972), and Nancy, *née* Evans (d 1959); *b* 7 Sept 1949; *Educ* Penrhos Coll, Aylesbury HS, Trevelyan Coll Univ of Durham (BA); *Career* res asst GMWU 1970-72; res offr: Euro Trade Union Confedn Brussels 1973, Trade Union Advsy Ctee to OECD Paris 1973-74; gen sec Fabian Soc 1976-82 (asst gen sec 1974-76), journalist Channel 4's A Week in Politics 1982-83, dir Alcohol Concern 1983-90, chief exec Euro Party Lab Pty 1990-; memb: Exec Ctee NCVO 1987-90, Exec Ctee Fabian Soc 1986-, Royal Cmmn on Criminal Procedure 1978-81 London Lab Pty Exec 1976-82, Executive Fabian Soc 1986-, Lab Pty Nat Constitutional Ctee 1987-; JP Inner London 1976-90; *Style—* Ms Dianne Hayter; EPLP, 2 Queen Anne's Gate, London SW1H 9AA (☎ 071 222 1719)

HAYTER, 3 Baron (UK 1927); Sir George Charles Hayter Chubb; 3 Bt (UK 1909), KCVO (1977), CBE (1976); s of 2 Baron (d 1967), by his 1 w Mary; *b* 25 April 1911; *Educ* Leys Sch, Trinity Coll Cambridge; *m* 1940, Elizabeth Anne Hayter, MBE, da of Thomas Rumbold (ggs of Sir Thomas Rumbold, 1 Bt); 3 s, 1 da; *Heir* s, Hon George Chubb; *Career* chm Chubb and Son's Lock and Safe Co 1957-81 (md 1941-57), dir Charles Early and Marriott (Witney) Ltd 1952-83; pres Royal Warrant Holders Assoc 1967; dep chm House of Lords 1982-; govr King Edward's Hosp Fund for London 1983-86 (chm Mgmnt Ctee 1965-82); *Style—* The Rt Hon the Lord Hayter, KCVO, CBE; Ashtead House, Ashtead, Surrey (☎ 03722 73476)

HAYTER, John William; DL; s of C W J H Hayter (d 1985), of Farnfield Farm, Privett, Alton, Hampshire, and Edith Munro, *née* Fraser; *b* 31 Aug 1937; *Educ* Marlborough; *m* 1, 13 Sept 1961 (m dis 1966), Belinda, da of Lt-Col J H Walford, DSO (d 1976), of The Old House, Wolverton, Basingstoke, Hants; 1 da (Sarah b 13 Sept 1964); m 2, 6 Dec 1971 (m dis 1977), Constance Rowse, *née* Macandrew; m 3, 30 Aug 1983, The Hon Emma Jane Arlette Guest, da of Cdr A Gray, DSO, DL, of Tilbridge, Great Straughton, Huntingdon; 1 s (Charles b 29 July 1984); *Career* Capt 60 Rifles and Queen Victoria's Rifles; chm Hayter Brockbank Gp plc; former dir: Wm Brandts Underwriting Agencies Ltd, R W Sturge & Co Ltd, Pickford Dawson & Holland Ltd, Jardine Matheson Underwriting Agencies Ltd; *Recreations* racing, shooting; *Clubs* Royal Green Jackets (chm), Bucks, City of London, The Brook (NY); *Style—* John Hayter, Esq, DL; 18 Rood Lane, London EC3

HAYTER, Paul David Grenville; s of Rev Canon Michael George Hayter, and Katherine Patricia, *née* Schofield; *b* 4 Nov 1942; *Educ* Eton (King's scholar), ChCh Oxford (MA); *m* 1973, Hon Deborah Gervaise, da of Baron Maude of Stratford-upon-Avon ; 2 s, 1 da; *Career* House of Lords: clerk Parliament Office 1964, seconded as private sec to Ldr of the House and Chief Whip 1974-77, clerk of ctees 1977, princ clerk of ctees 1985-90, reading clerk and princ fin offr 1991-; sec Assoc of Lord-Lieuts 1977-; *Recreations* music, gardening, botanising, archery, painting; *Style—* Paul Hayter, Esq; Williamscot, Banbury, Oxon

HAYTER, Peter Reginald; s of Reginald James Hayter, of Bushey, Herts and Lucy Gertrude Gray; *b* 13 March 1959; *Educ* Aldenham Sch Elstree Herts, Goldsmith's Coll London (BA); *m* 28 Nov 1987, Mary Ann, da of late Geoffrey William Hamlyn; 1 s (Maximilian Geoffrey Reginald Hamlyn b 28 Dec 1990); *Career* journalist; Hayter's Sports Reporting Agency 1982-86 (office boy, jr reporter, reporter, managing ed, regular by-line in Mail on Sunday), football corr Sportsweek Magazine 1986-87; freelance writer 1987-88 (football diarist, writer and cricket writer Independent, football writer Observer, features ed Allsport Photographic), editorial prodr Running Late (C4 sports discussion prog) 1988, cricket corr The Mail on Sunday; *Books* Visions of Sport (1988), The Ashes: Highlights since 1948 (with BBC Test Match Special Team, 1989), Cricket Heroes (1990), Great Tests Recalled (1991), England v West Indies: Highlights since 1948 (with BBC Test Match Special Team, 1991); *Recreations* cricket, theatre, cinema, mind expanding drugs, hard liquor; *Clubs* MCC, The Cricketers Club of London, Stanmore Cricket, Icogniti Cricket, Fleet St Strollers Cricket; *Style—* Peter Hayter, Esq; The Mail On Sunday, Northcliffe House, Derry Street, London W8 5TT

HAYTER, Reginald James; s of late Reginald Hayter, and late Elizabeth, *née* Mills; *b* 4 Dec 1913; *Educ* St Marylebone GS; *m* 23 April 1939, Lucy Gertrude, da of late William Robert Gray; 2 s (Philip b 21 Jan 1947, Peter b 13 March 1959), 3 da (Sally b 21 Sept 1940, Mary b 2 June 1946, Elizabeth b 21 Feb 1950); *Career* RAPC 1941-45; reporter of cricket and football for Cricket Reporting Agency 1934, special reporter for Reuters and Press Assoc of MCC tours of: SA 1948-49, Aust 1950-51, W Indies 1953-54; fndr Hayters (Britain's leading freelance sports agency) 1955, ed Cricketer Magazine 1978-82; co fndr Br Empire Cricket XI during WW II; memb NUJ; *Books* Arsenal Football Book 4 edn (1972), Best of the Cricketer 1921-1981 (1981), Observer Book of Cricket 5 edn (1982); *Recreations* active cricketer; *Clubs* MCC, Lord's Taverners, Surrey CCC (hon life member), Forty, Stanmore CC (pres and former Capt), St George's Day; *Style—* Reginald Hayter, Esq

HAYTER, Sir William Goodenough; KCMG (1953, CMG 1948); s of Sir William Goodenough Hayter, KBE (d 1924); *b* 1 Aug 1906; *Educ* Winchester, New Coll Oxford; *m* 1938, Iris Marie, da of Lt-Col C H Grey (formerly Hoare), DSO (d 1955); 1 da; *Career* entered FO 1930, asst under sec of State 1948-49, min Paris 1949-53, ambass to USSR 1953-57, dep under sec of State FO 1957-58; warden New Coll Oxford 1958-76, tstee Br Museum 1960-69; fell Winchester Coll 1958-76, hon fell New Coll Oxford 1976; *Books* The Diplomacy of the Great Powers (1961), The Kremlin and the Embassy (1966), Russia and the World (1970), William of Wykeham (1970), A Double Life (autobiography, 1974), Spooner (1977); *Style—* Sir William Hayter, KCMG; Bassetts House, Stanton St John, Oxford (☎ 086 735 598)

HAYTON, Prof David John; s of Flt Lt Arthur Hayton, of 18 Colston Way, Beaumont Park, Whitley Bay, Tyne and Wear, and Beatrice, *née* Thompson; *b* 13 July 1944; *Educ* Royal GS Newcastle, Univ of Newcastle (LLB, LLD), Jesus Coll Cambridge (MA); *m* 17 March 1979, Linda Patricia, da of James David Rae (d 1974); 1 s (John James b 28 July 1990); *Career* called to the Bar Inner Temple 1968; lectr Univ of Sheffield 1968-69 (asst lectr 1966-68), in practice Lincoln's Inn 1970-85, fell Jesus Coll Cambridge 1973-87, dean Faculty of Law King's Coll London 1988-90 (prof of law 1987-), in practice Temple 1988-; head of UK delgn to Hague Conf On Private Int Law 1988 (1984); coach Cambridge RFC I XV 1980-83; *Books* Registered Land (3 edn, 1981), Cases and Commentary On Law Of Trusts (8 edn, 1986), Law Of Trusts and Trustees (14 edn, 1987), Law of Trusts (1989); *Recreations* playing cricket and squash, watching rugby; *Clubs* Royal Cwlth; *Style—* Prof David Hayton; Queen Elizabeth Building, Temple, London EC4Y 9BS (☎ 071 936 3131); School of Law, King's College, London University, London WC2R 2LS (☎ 071 836 5454, fax 071 873 2452)

HAYTON, Philip John; s of Rev Austin Hayton, of Mansfield, Notts, and Jennie Margaret Violet, *née* Errington; *b* 2 Nov 1947; *Educ* Fyling Hall Sch Robin Hood's Bay Yorks; *m* 22 Dec 1972, Thelma Susan, da of James Gant; 1 s (James b 1980), 1 da (Julia Elizabeth b 1988); *Career* various posts incl: teacher in Jordan, foundry worker, lavatory assembler, valet, doughnut salesman; pirate radio disc jockey and advertising salesman 1967-, reporter and prodr BBC Radio Leeds 1968-71; BBC TV 1971: reporter and presenter Look North Leeds 1971-74, nat news reporter (covering: Belfast, Beirut, Iranian Revolution, Ugandan War, Cod War, Rhodesian War) 1974-80, S Africa corr (also covering Argentina during Falklands War) 1980-83, reporter and newscaster (One, Six and Nine O'Clock News); *Recreations* sailing, theatre, walking, restaurants; *Style—* Philip Hayton, Esq; BBC TV, Television Centre, Wood Lane, London W12 7RJ (☎ 081 743 8000)

HAYWARD, Sir Anthony William Byrd; s of Eric Hayward (d 1964), of Dane St House, Chilham, nr Canterbury, and Barbara Olive, *née* Bird (d 1976); *b* 29 June 1927; *Educ* Stowe, ChCh Oxford; *m* 1955, Jenifer Susan, da of Dr Francis Howard McCay (d 1985); 2 s, (Simon, Charles), 2 da (Charlotte, Emma); *Career* temp Sub-Lt RNVR 1945-48, served in Scotland, SE Asia, Persian Gulf; family business in India 1948-57, dir Shaw Wallace and Co India 1957-78 (chm and md 1970-78), pres Associated Chambers of Commerce and Indust of India 1977-78, md Guthrie Berhad Singapore 1978-81, pres and chief exec offr Private Investmt Co for Asia (PICA) SA 1982-84, dir of various cos; FRSA; kt 1978; *Recreations* shooting, fishing, golf, photography; *Clubs* Boodles, Oriental, Rye Golf; *Style—* Sir Anthony Hayward; Dane St House, Chilham, nr Canterbury, Kent (☎ 0227 730221)

HAYWARD, Barry Charles; s of Peter Alfred Edward Hayward, of 3 Glossop Close, E Cowes, Isle of Wight, and Muriel Hilda, *née* Gillard; *b* 30 July 1953; *Educ* Carisbrooke GS, Univ of London (LLB); *m* 21 April 1979, Christine, da of Albert George Glenister, of Ashford, Middx; 1 s (Colin Charles b 1982), 1 da (Verity Jane b 1985); *Career* Messrs Owen White & Catlin Slrs Feltham: articles 1976-78, asst slr 1978-82, ptnr 1982-85; ptnr Hayward Parker Slrs 1985-; memb Law Soc 1976;

Recreations swimming, gardening; *Style*— Barry Hayward, Esq; 28 Inglewood Avenue, Heatherside, Camberley, Surrey (☎ 0276 62 921); 265 Yorktown Rd, College Town, Camberley, Surrey (☎ 0276 32 543, fax 0276 33 194)

HAYWARD, Sir Jack Arnold; OBE (1968); s of late Sir Charles Hayward, CBE, and Hilda, *née* Arnold; *b* 14 June 1923; *Educ* Stowe; *m* 1948, Jean Mary, *née* Forder; 2 s, 1 da; *Career* RAF 1941-46 (flying trg in Florida, active service pilot in SE Asia, demobilized as Flt Lt); served S Africa Branch Rotary Hoes Ltd until 1950 (joined 1947), fndr USA ops Firth Cleveland gp of cos 1951, joined Grand Bahama Port Authority Ltd 1956, chm Grand Bahama Development Co Ltd and Freeport Commercial and Industrial Ltd 1976-; pres: Lundy Field Soc, Wolverhampton Wanderers FC; vice pres SS Great Britain Project, hon life vice pres Maritime Tst 1971, Paul Harris fell (Rotary) 1983; Hon LLD Exeter 1971; William Booth award Salvation Army 1987; Kt 1986; *Recreations* promoting British endeavours (mainly in sport), watching cricket, amateur dramatics, preserving the British landscape, keeping all things bright, beautiful and British; *Clubs* MCC, Pratt's, RAF, RAC; *Style*— Sir Jack Hayward, OBE; Seashell Lane, (PO Box F-99), Freeport, Grand Bahama Island, Bahamas (☎ 010 809 352 5165)

HAYWARD, Prof Jack Ernest Shalom; s of Menachem Hayward (d 1961), of Vancouver, Canada, and Stella, *née* Isaac (d 1959); *Educ* Horsley Hall, LSE (BSc, PhD); *m* 10 Dec 1965, Margaret Joy, da of Harold Clow Glenn (d 1985), of Adelaide, Australia; 1 s (Alan b 1973), 1 da (Clare b 1971); *Career* Nat Serv flying offr RAF 1956-58; asst lectr and lectr Univ of Sheffield 1959-63, lectr and sr lectr Univ of Keele 1963-73, sr res fell Nuffield Coll Oxford 1968-69; visiting prof: Univ of Paris III 1979-80, Inst d'Etudes Politiques Paris 1990-91; prof of politics Univ of Hull 1973-; vice pres Political Studies Assoc of the UK 1981- (chm 1975-77, pres 1979-81); chev de l'Ordre Nat de Mérite France 1980, fell Br Acad; *Books* Private Interests and Public Policy, The Experience of the French Economic and Social Council (1966), The One and Indivisible French Republic (1973), Planning Politics and Public Policy: The British French and Italian Experience (with M Watson, 1975), Planning in Europe (with O Narkiewicz, 1978), State and Society in Contemporary Europe (with R Berki, 1979), The Political Science of British Politics (with P Norton, 1986), The State and the Market Economy: Industrial Patriotism and Economic Intervention in France (1986), Developments in French Politics (with P Hall and H Machin); *Recreations* music, books, walking; *Clubs* Royal Commonwealth Soc; *Style*— Prof Jack Hayward; Hurstwood, Church Lane, Kirk Ella, North Humberside HU10 7TA (☎ 0482 655027); Dept of Politics, The University, Hull HU6 7RX (☎ 0482 465961, fax 0482 466366)

HAYWARD, Joan Alice; *b* 14 June 1919; *m* 6 Sept 1942, husband decd; 1 s (John b 1948), 2 da (Celia (Mrs Stanley) b 1944, Julia (Mrs Cooke) b 1955); *Career* chm Shropshire CC 1964-; *Style*— Joan Hayward; Golden Plackett, 31 High St, Hadley, Telford, Shrops (☎ 0952 40445); Shire Hall, Shrewsbury

HAYWARD, Leslie Roy; s of George Rolph Hayward (d 1971), of Bengeo, Herts, and Maud Rose, *née* Thompson (d 1973); *b* 29 Jan 1928; *Educ* Tottenham Tech Coll; *m* 1, 4 Aug 1951 (m dis 1970), (Meriel) Ann, da of Maj George Cramp Bond (d 1970), of Hawthorns, Bath Rd, Taplow, Bucks; m 2, 11 June 1977, Rosemary Anne, da of George Lawrence Hart (d 1963), of 57 Mandrake Rd, London; *Career* fndr Ariel Plastics Group 1962 which grew into a notable orgn with depots in: Glasgow, Wakefield, Birmingham, Hertford, Alton; chm of parent Bd until ret 1984; *Recreations* motor racing, off-shore sailing, vintage car restoration, architecture, skiing; *Style*— Leslie Hayward, Esq; Lawrence House, Monkwood, nr Alresford, Hants SO24 0HB (☎ 0962 772468, car 0836 273 779)

HAYWARD, Mark Reece; s of Brian Walter Hayward, of Redbourn, Herts, and Rosalie Gordon, *née* Richards; *b* 27 Nov 1959; *Educ* Ellesmere Coll Shropshire; *Career* Central Selling Organisation De Beers 1978-79, H M Dip Serv 1979, apptd to Lord Carrington's private office 1981-82; theatre mangr: Comedy Theatre London 1982-84, Queens Theatre London 1984-87, Phantom of the Opera 1988; *Recreations* swimming, squash; *Style*— Mark Hayward, Esq; 43 Grosvenor Rd, Twickenham, Middx TW1 4AD; Her Majesty's Theatre, Haymarket, London, SW1Y 4QL (☎ 071 930 5337)

HAYWARD, Lady Patricia Mary; *née* Stopford; eldest da of 7 Earl of Courtown (d 1957), and Cicely Mary, *née* Birch; *b* 1 Feb 1906; *m* 26 May 1934, Maurice John Hayward, Malayan Civil Service (ret), s of Sir Maurice Henry Weston Hayward, KCSI; 1 s, 3 da; *Style*— The Lady Patricia Hayward; White Hart House, Haddenham, Aylesbury, Bucks (☎ 0844 291474)

HAYWARD, Peter Allan; s of Peter Hayward (d 1953), and Anne, *née* Jackson (d 1975); *b* 27 March 1932; *Educ* Haileybury, Trinity Coll Cambridge, (BA, MA); *m* 13 March 1954, Elizabeth Layton, da of John Layton Smith (d 1976); 1 da (Pandora b 1962); *Career* at RA 1952; called to the Bar Lincoln's Inn 1958 (Cassell scholar), practised at Patent Bar 1958-68, lectr UCL 1959-60, fell and tutor in jurisprudence St Peter's Coll Oxford 1968-, dir Intellectual Property Law Centre 1990-; memb Gen Bd of Faculties Univ of Oxford 1980-85; memb Holborn Borough Cncl 1962-66; *Books* Halsbury Laws of England (3 edn), Trade Marks and Designs (contrib, 1962), Annual survey of Commonwealth Law (contrib, 1970-73), Reports on Patent Cases (ed, 1970-74), Hayward's Patent Cases 1600-1883 (11 vols, 1988); *Style*— Peter Hayward, Esq; St Peter's College, Oxford, OX1 2DL (☎ 0865 278885); Priorton, Vernon Ave, Harcourt Hill, Oxford OX2 9AU (☎ 0865 248102)

HAYWARD, Peter Wilfred; JP (1965); s of Douglas Wilfred Hayward (d 1978), of Bournemouth, and Isobel Rosser, *née* Tovey (d 1988); *b* 3 May 1931; *Educ* Queen's Coll Taunton; *m* 6 Sept 1958, Jill Eileen, da of Alfred Victor Shelton (d 1989), of Poole; 1 s (Christopher Michael b 13 Aug 1959), 1 da (Wendy Mary b 11 July 1962); *Career* Nat Serv RAF 1953-55; currently chm and gp md W Hayward & Sons Ltd (joined 1951); memb Rotary Club, former memb Round Table; magistrate 1965 (chm of Bench 1986-88); FCIOB; *Recreations* chm AFC Bournemouth; *Clubs* Rotary; *Style*— Peter Hayward, Esq, JP; Pontresina, 105 Lilliput Rd, Canford Cliffs, Poole, Dorset BH14 8JY (☎ 0202 700937); W Hayward & Sons (Holdings) Ltd, 398/400 Holdenhurst Road, Bournemouth, Dorset BH8 8BW (☎ 0202 309575, fax 0202 303869)

HAYWARD, Redmond (John); *b* 12 July 1954; *Educ* More House Sch Surrey; *m* 4 May 1985, Phillipa Jane, *née* Williams; 1 da (Caitlin Rose b 25 Aug 1989); *Career* hotel proprietor; Ealing Hotel Sch 1973-75; Michelin Red M 1986-91, AA Rosette 1987-91, Egon Ronay Star 1989-91, commended in the top twelve The Times 1989 Awards for Good Taste, Good Food Guide Country Restaurant of the Year 1990, Good Food Guide 4/5 1991; *Clubs* 190 Queen's Gate; *Style*— Redmond Hayward, Esq; Redmond's, Cleeve Hill, Cheltenham, Glos GL52 3PR (☎ 0242 672017)

HAYWARD, Sir Richard Arthur; CBE (1966); s of late Richard Bolton Hayward, and Jessie Emmeline Elisabeth Hayward; *b* 14 March 1910; *Educ* Catford Central Sch; *m* 1936, Ethel Wheatcroft; 1 s, 1 da; *Career* dep gen sec Union of PO Workers 1951 (asst sec 1947), sec gen Civil Serv Nat Whitley Cncl 1956-66; chm: Supplementary Benefits Cmmn 1966-69, NHS Staff Cmmn 1972-75, New Towns Staff Cmmn 1976-77; memb: Civil Serv Security Appeals Panel 1967-82, PO Bd 1969-71, Home Office Advsy Panel on Security (Immigration Act 1972) 1972-81, Parole Bd for England and Wales 1975-79, Slrs Disciplinary Tbnl 1975-82; life vice pres: Civil Serv Sports Cncl 1973- (chm 1968-73), Assoc of Kent Cricket Clubs 1984- (pres 1970-84); govr Guy's Hosp 1949-72, tstee Kent County Playing Fields Assoc 1975-89, chm Southborough Soc 1983-87; pres Civil Serv: Cricket Assoc, Assoc Football; hon life memb Nat Assoc of Young Cricketers; Freeman City of London 1980; kt 1969; *Recreations* sport, history of Southwark; *Style*— Sir Richard Hayward, CBE; Lower Cowley, Parracombe, Barnstaple, N Devon EX31 4PQ (☎ 059 83 373)

HAYWARD, Richard Wellesley; s of Harold Joseph Hayward, MC, and Olive Mary, *née* Stanley (d 1988); *b* 4 Aug 1928; *Educ* Colston's Sch Bristol, Brixton Sch of Bldg (now S Bank Poly); *m* 14 June 1952, Jill Patricia, da of Wing Cdr Arthur Leslie Grice (ka), of Hatch End, Middlesex; 1 da (Jenny (Mrs Spivey) b 29 July 1958); *Career* sr ptnr Burrell Hayward and Budd 1974-80; memb Gen Cncl RICS 1971-79, chm RICS (Central London Branch) 1979-80, dir and sec School Mistresses and Governesses Benevolent Inst 1980-; memb The Clapham Soc; Freeman: City of London 1977, Worshipful Co of Tallow Chandlers 1978, Worshipful Co of Chartered Surveyors 1977-87; ARICS 1954, FRICS 1965; *Recreations* reading, walking the dog, Georgian and Victorian glass; *Style*— Richard Hayward, Esq; Flat 3, 23 West Side, Clapham Common, London SW4 9AN (☎ 071 228 5232); SGBI Office, Queen Mary House, Manor Park Rd, Chislehurst, Kent BR7 5PY (☎ 081 468 7997)

HAYWARD, Robert Antony; MP (C) Kingswood 1987; s of Ralph Hayward, of Swinford Farm, Eynsham, Oxon, and Mary Patricia, *née* Franklin; *b* 11 March 1949; *Educ* Maidenhead GS, Univ of Rhodesia (BSc); *m* 1981, Gillian Mary, da of Raymond Icke (d 1985); *Career* vice chm Nat Young Cons 1976-77, City cllr Coventry 1976-78; memb Select Ctee on Energy 1983-85; MP (C) Kingswood 1983-87, PPS Parly to Under Sec of State Trade and Indust 1985-87, miny for Indust 1986-87, and to Sec of State for Transport 1987-; *Recreations* rugby refereeø, psychology; *Style*— Robert Hayward, Esq, MP; House of Commons, London SW1 0AA; 2 Bracey Drive, Downend, Bristol B516 2UG

HAYWARD, (Christopher) Timothy Esmond; s of Tom Christopher Hayward, CBE, DL (d 1975), and Sybil Lisette, *née* Grainger-Brunt; *b* 13 Sept 1940; *Educ* Eton, CCC Cambridge (MA); *m* 9 June 1964 (m dis 1976), Charmian Rosalind, da of Derek Leaf (d 1943); 1 s (Derek Christopher b 1967), 1 da (Chloe Amanda b 1969); *Career* qualified CA 1965, ptnr Peat Marwick Mitchell and Co 1977 (joined 1962), sr ptnr corp recovery KPMG Peat Marwick McLintock 1987; ICAEW 1966, FCA; *Recreations* shooting, tennis; *Clubs* Bucks, MCC; *Style*— Timothy Hayward, Esq; 8 Claridge Ct, 41-43 Munster Rd, London SW6 4EX (☎ 071 736 5226); 1 Puddle Dock, Blackfriars, London EC4V 3PD (☎ 071 236 8000, fax 071 248 1790, telex 8811541 PMM LON G)

HAYWARD, Ven (John) Derek Risdon; s of Eric Hayward (d 1964), of Dane Street House, Chilham, nr Canterbury, and Barbara Olive, *née* Bird (d 1976); *b* 13 Dec 1923; *Educ* Stowe, Trinity Coll Cambridge (exhibition, BA, MA, Capt polo); *m* 15 Oct 1965, Teresa Jane (Tessa), da of Nicholas Astell Kaye, MBE, of Quinta doVale, Manjoeira, Loures nr Lisbon, Portugal; 1 s (Leo Nicholas Eric b 1966), 1 da (Natasha Jane Dacomb); *Career* WWII Lt 27 Lancers, served Italy 1944-45 (twice wounded); asst curate St Mary Bramall Lane Sheffield 1957-59; vicar: St Silas Sheffield 1959-63, All Saints Isleworth 1964-; archdeacon of Middx 1974-75, gen sec Diocese of London 1975-; Bronze Star (US) 1945; *Recreations* skiing; *Style*— The Ven Derek Hayward; 61 Church Street, Isleworth, Middlesex TW7 6BE (☎ 081 560 6662, fax 081 847 0660); London Diocesan House, 30 Causton St, London SW1P 4AU (☎ 071 821 9357, fax 071 821 9859)

HAYWARD, Maj-Gen (George) Victor; s of George Harold Hayward (d 1971), of Stratford-on-Avon, and Daisy, *née* Ball (d 1975); *b* 21 June 1918; *Educ* Blundell's, Univ of Birmingham (BSc); *m* 18 July 1953, Gay Benson, da of Hamilton Barrett Goulding (d 1947), of Dublin; 1 s (Stephen George Hamilton b 1954), 1 da (Victoria Clare b 1956); *Career* served WWII 1939-45, cmmnd 1940, transf to REME 1942, GSO1 REME Training Centre 1958, Cdr REME 2nd Div 1960, asst mil sec WO 1962, Col RARDE, Fort Halstead 1963, CO 38 Central Workshop 1965, Dep Cmdt Technical Gp REME 1966, Cmdt REME Trg Centre 1969, Cmdt Technical Gp REME 1971-73, Col Cmdt REME 1973-78, planning inspr DOE 1973-88; CEng, FICE, FIMechE, FBIM; *Recreations* sailing, skiing, shooting; *Clubs* Army and Navy; *Style*— Maj-Gen Victor Hayward; Chart Cottage, Chartwell, Westerham, Kent TN16 1PT (☎ 0732 866253)

HAYWARD SMITH, Rodger; QC (1988); s of Frederick Ernest Smith, of Ingatetone, Essex, and Heather Hayward, *née* Rodgers; *b* 25 Feb 1943; *Educ* Brentwood Sch Essex, St Edmund Hall Oxford (MA); *m* 4 Jan 1975, (Gillian) Sheila, *née* Johnson; 1 s (Richard b 1976), 1 da (Jane b 1978); *Career* called to the Bar Gray's Inn 1967, recorder 1986- (asst recorder 1981-86); memb Legal Aid Ctee of Law Soc 1983-; *Style*— Rodger Hayward Smith, Esq, QC; 1 King's Bench Walk, Temple, London, EC4Y 7DB (☎ 071 583 6266)

HAYWOOD, Brenda Gail; da of George N Harvey, of South Africa, and Rita Valerie, *née* Niemand; *b* 27 Sept 1954; *Educ* Queenstown Girls HS South Africa, Modern Methods Business Coll South Africa; *m* (m dis); 1 da (Simone Clementine b 22 Nov 1977); *Career* events organizer Inst of Personnel Mgmnt S A 1972, co admin Inst of Pub Rels SA 1974; prodn ed: Management Magazine SA 1975, City Magazines 1979, Cosmopolitan Magazine 1980, Working Woman Magazine 1984; prodn exec Associated Newspapers 1985, managing ed Telegraph Weekend Magazine 1987, assoc publisher of magazines Daily Telegraph 1989, ed mangr Daily and Sunday Telegraph Newspapers 1990-; memb Br Soc of Magazine Eds; *Recreations* being a parent, sport, (tennis, swimming, gym), German lessons; *Clubs* The Groucho; *Style*— Ms Brenda Haywood; The Daily Telegraph, Peterborough Court at South Quay, 181 Marsh Wall, London E14 9SR (☎ 071 538 7503, fax 071 538 3810, car 0836 256657)

HAYWOOD, Bryan; s of Arthur Haywood; *b* 1 May 1939; *Educ* King Edward VII Sch Leics; *m* (m dis); 1 s (Timothy); *Career* certified accountant; dir: Balfour Kilpatrick Ltd 1975-88, Balfour Kilpatrick International Ltd UK, Kilpatrick Group of Cos; chm Xianity Galore Investments 1988-; *Recreations* country life; *Style*— Bryan Haywood, Esq; 35 Kent Road, East Molesey, Surrey (☎ 081 979 9714)

HAYWOOD, Christopher Warren; s of Oliver Pilling Haywood, JP (d 1973), of Bolton, and Audrey Lillian Openshaw, *née* Warren; *b* 17 Nov 1945; *Educ* St Bees Cumbria; *m* 27 March 1981, Julie Anne, da of Peter Orrell Kirkpatrick, of 139 Turton Road, Tottington, Bury; 4 s (Charles Alexander b 1973, Edward Christopher b 1982, Michael Henry b 1983, Oliver Peter b 1985), 1 da (Katie Victoria b 1971); *Career* pres Bolton Soc of Chartered Accountants 1974; dir: Victor New Homes Ltd 1979-, Forshaw Watson Holdings Ltd 1986-; ptnr Touche Ross & Co CAs; chm Bolton Club 1985-87, treas Bolton Lads Club 1973-, pres Bolton Chamber of Commerce and Industry 1989-91 (memb Cncl 1984-); FCA, FBIM, ATII; *Recreations* golf, skiing, family pursuits; *Clubs* Bolton Golf, The Bolton, Markland Hill LTC, Windermere Motorboat Racing; *Style*— Christopher Haywood, Esq; Elsinore, 32 Albert Rd, Heaton, Bolton BL1 5HF (☎ 0204 42958); Acresfield House, Exchange St, Bolton (☎ 0204 22611, fax 0204 35210)

HAYWOOD, Sir Harold; KCVO (1988), OBE (1974), DL (1983); s of Harold Haywood (d 1988), of Burton on Trent, and Lillian, *née* Barratt (d 1929); *b* 30 Sept 1923; *Educ* Guild Sch Burton on Trent Staffs, Westhill Coll Birmingham, Ecumenical Inst Geneva; *m* Jan 1944, Amy, da of Charles William Richardson (d 1955), of Burton on Trent; 3 s; *Career* RN 1943 med discharge; organiser St Johns Clubland Sheffield 1948-51, lectr Westhill Coll of Educn 1951-53, regnl organiser Methodist Youth Dept Birmingham

1954-55 and vice pres Methodist Assoc of Youth Clubs, nat tutor King George VI leadership course 1955-57, educn offr Nat Assoc of Mixed Clubs and Girls Clubs 1957-77, dir of trg Nat Assoc of Youth Clubs 1966-74, gen sec Educn Interchange Cncl 1974-78, dir Royal Jubilee and Princes Tsts 1978-88, nat chm YMCA 1989 (former chm of Nat Coll Cncl, memb Bd of London Central YMCA and memb of Nat Exec and Nat Bd); chm Gen and Liberal Studies Dept Dacorum Coll of Further Educn Herts and vice chm of govrs 1965-69, memb Univ of Leeds Inst of Educn res project on Carnegie Community Sch 1966-74, external examiner Roehampton Inst and Rolle and St Lukes Colls Univ of Exeter 1969-74, visiting fell Inst of Technol Melbourne Aust 1987, currently govr Bell Educational Tst Cambridge; int organisations: advsr to Malaysia Dept of Social Welfare 1962, gen sec Educational Interchange Cncl and memb Advsy Ctee on Exchange Br Cncl 1974-78, memb Bd Anglo Austrian Soc 1974-81, UK rep Cncl of Europe and overseas advsr and delegate to S E Asia USA Scandinavia Hong Kong and N Africa; vice chm Br Nat Ctee World Assembly of Youth 1964-66, memb Young Vol Force Fndn Mgmnt Ctee 1970-74, chm Nat and Voluntary Youth Servs PR Gp 1974-78, memb Sec of State for Educn's Nat Advsy Cncl for the Youth Serv 1985-88, memb Bd Nat Youth Theatre 1987-, patron Nat Assoc for Young People in Care from inception to 1988; memb: Home Sec's Advsy Cncl on the Misuse of Drugs 1970-75, Peterborough Devpt Corporation, Cresset Neighbourhood Mgmnt Bd 1971-74, Exec Ctee Fndns forum 1986-88; chm BBC IBA Central Appeals Advsy Ctee 1988-, memb BBC Gen Advsy Cncl 1988-; tstee: Charities All Fndn 1989, Children in Need Tst 1989; church: lay preacher 1946-, former Methodist Church tstee, sec Local Church Neighbourhood Ctee; FRSA 1985; *Books* A Role for Voluntary Work (1970), Partnership With the Young (1979); *Recreations* the garden, books; *Clubs* Royal Over-Seas, Civil Service, Penn; *Style—* Sir Harold Haywood, KCVO, OBE, DL

HAYWOOD, Ian Robert; s of Walter Robert Haywood (d 1974), of Finchley, and Eileen Mary, *née* Warren (d 1987); *b* 13 Oct 1941; *Educ* Bedford Sch, St Thomas' Hosp Med Sch Univ of London; *m* 28 March 1970, Margaret Comrie, da of John Hannah, MBE (d 1984), of Annan, Dumfries and Galloway; 2 da (Jennifer b 1971, Susan b 1973); *Career* cmmnd Beds Regt TA 1959, reg cmmn RAMC 1965-; house appts: St Thomas' Hosp, Addenbrookes Hosp Cambridge; regtl med offr RWF, jr staff appts in surgery RAMC 1968-78, lectr in surgery Westminster Hosp Med Sch 1975, lectr Bart's Hosp Med Sch 1977-78, conslt surgn RAMC 1978, jt prof of mil surgery RCS and Royal Army Med Coll 1985, Ben Eiseman visiting prof Uniformed Univ Health Scis Bethesda Maryland 1987, examiner RCSE; author of numerous papers in learned jls; memb Exec Cncl Br Assoc for Immediate Care (chm Inter-Serv Liason and Disaster Planning Ctee); FRSM, FRCS 1970, FRCSE 1989; OStJ; *Books* Medicine for Disasters (contrib, 1988), Problems in General Surgery (contrib, 1989); *Recreations* history and photography; *Style—* Ian Haywood, Esq

HAYWOOD, Janette; da of Ronald Haywood, of Borehamwood, Herts, and Evelyn, *née* Jefferson; *b* 22 May 1952; *Educ* Copthall Mill Hill, Univ Coll Cardiff (LLB), UCL (LLM); *m* 2 July 1988, Jonathan Michael Anderson, s of John Anderson, JP, of Morecombelake, nr Chideock, Dorset, and Rosamund, *née* Baines; *Career* called to the Bar Middle Temple 1977; memb Family Law Bar Assoc; *Recreations* travel, interior design, theatre; *Style—* Miss Janette Haywood; 53 Ennismore Gardens, Knightsbridge, London SW7; 9 Holland Park Mansions, Holland Park Gardens, London W14 (☎ 071 371 6827); 1 Essex Ct, Temple, London EC4 (☎ 071 583 7759, fax 071 353 8620)

HAYWOOD, John (Barry); s of Bernard Haywood (d 1986), of Macclesfield, Cheshire, and Joyce Haywood, *née* Walker; *b* 18 Sept 1945; *Educ* King's GS Macclesfield, Leeds Poly; *m* 11 May 1968, Ann, da of George Gosling (d 1986), of Macclesfield, Cheshire; 2 da (Melanie b 1968, Kirstyn b 1971); *Career* mgmnt conslt and co dir; fndr, chm and dir IMO Group 1976; chief conslt Algerian Miny of Water Resources 1977-78, Algerian Miny of Oil 1978-79; MBIM 1977, AIL 1977, MIEx 1977, FInstD 1977, FIMC 1981; *Recreations* international travel, French and German language; *Clubs* IOD; *Style—* J Barry Haywood, Esq; Willow End, 5 Daisybank Drive, Congleton CW12 1LS

HAYWOOD, Roger; s of Maj George Haywood, of Norwich, and Ethel Florence, *née* Reynolds; *b* 24 July 1939; *Educ* Westcliff Sch Westcliff-on-Sea; *m* 30 June 1962, Sandra Leonora, da of George Yenson (d 1972); 2 s (Ian b 1965, Mark b 1966), 2 da (Sarah b 1963, Laura b 1971); *Career* mktg positions with Dunlop, Dexion and in various advertising agencies, Euro PR mangr Air Products 1971-75; md: Haywood Hood & Associates Ltd 1975-78, Tibbenham Group 1981; chm: Roger Haywood Associates Ltd 1982-, Worldcom Inc 1989-; pres Inst PR 1990; vice chm: Chartered Inst Mktg, PR Consults Assoc; Freeman City of London, memb Worshipful Co of Marketors; FCIM, ABC, FCAM, FIPR; *Books* All about Public Relations (1985, 2 edn 1990); *Recreations* music, classic cars; *Style—* Roger Haywood, Esq; 103 St Georges Square Mews, London SW1V 3QP (☎ 071 821 6739); Keswick Mill, Norwich, Norfolk; Roger Haywood Assocs Ltd, 7 Eccleston St, London SW1 (☎ 071 823 4125, car 0860 343015, fax 071 730 5300)

HAYZELDEN, John Eastcott; s of Allan Frederick George Hayzelden (d 1955), of Kinnersley, Woodhall Ave, Pinner, Middx, and Grace Winifred, *née* Hutton (d 1987); *b* 20 June 1936; *Educ* Merchant Taylors', St John's Coll Oxford (MA); *m* 8 June 1963, Susan Clare, da of Dr Robert Strang (d 1977), of The White House, Penn, Bucks; 2 da (Clare b 11 Nov 1964, Gillian b 17 Sept 1966); *Career* 2 Lt RA 1956-57; called to the Bar Middle Temple 1968; Home Office: princ 1966-73, asst sec 1973-88, head Passport Dept 1988-91, chief executive United Kingdom Passport Agency 1991-; *Recreations* tennis, golf, reading; *Clubs* Tring LTC (former chm); *Style—* John Hayzelden, Esq; Uplands, 39 Mortimer Hill, Tring, Herts (☎ 044 282 3563); Home Office, Queen Annes Gate, London SW1

HAZELL, Ven Frederick Roy; s of John Murdoch Hazell (d 1978), and Ruth, *née* Topping (d 1960); *b* 12 Aug 1930; *Educ* Hutton GS, Fitzwilliam Coll Cambridge (MA), Cuddesdon Coll Oxford; *m* 1956, Gwendoline Edna, da of Percival Vare (d 1975); 1 step s (James William Douglas Armstrong b 1945); *Career* vicar Marlpool Derbyshire 1959-63, chaplain Univ of West Indies 1963-66, vicar Holy Saviour Croydon 1968-84, rural dean Croydon 1972-78, archdeacon Croydon 1978-; *Recreations* listening to music, swimming, history; *Style—* The Ven the Archdeacon of Croydon; 246 Pampisford Rd, South Croydon CR2 6DD (☎ 081 688 2943); St Matthew's House, 100 George St, Croydon CR0 1PE (☎ 081 681 5496)

HAZELL, Quinton; CBE (1978, MBE 1961), DL (Warwicks 1982); s of Thomas Arthur Hazell (d 1962), of Colwyn Bay, N Wales; *b* 14 Dec 1920; *Educ* Manchester GS; *m* 1942, Morwenna Parry-Jones; 1 s; *Career* served WWII RA; chm and md Quinton Hazell Holdings 1946-73, chm Supra Group 1973-82, non-exec chm F and C Enterprise Tst plc 1981-86; dir: Edward Jones (Contractors) Ltd 1962-74, Phoenix Assurance 1968-86, Foreign and Colonial Investment Trust 1978-, Winterbottom Trust 1978-82, Hawker-Siddeley 1979-; non-exec dir: Banro Industs plc 1985-88, F and C Mgmnt Ltd 1985-86; chm: W Midlands Econ Planning Cncl 1971-77, Aerospace Engrg plc 1986-90; FIMI; *Style—* Quinton Hazell, Esq, CBE, DL; Wootton Paddox, Leek Wootton, Warwick CV35 7QX (☎ 0926 50704)

HAZELL, Robert John Davidge; s of Peter Hazell, of 86 Naunton Lane, Cheltenham, and Elizabeth Complin, *née* Fowler; *b* 30 April 1948; *Educ* Eton, Wadham Coll Oxford (BA); *m* 27 June 1981, Alison Sophia Mordaunt, da of Arthur Hubert Mordaunt Richards (d 1982); 2 s (Alexander Robert Mordaunt b 5 May 1982, Jonathan William Joshua b 4 Jan 1985); *Career* barr 1973-75; numerous depts of Home Office 1975-89, Nuffield and Leverhulme travelling fellowship to study freedom of info in Aust, Canada and NZ 1986-87, dir Nuffield Fndn 1989-; magistrate 1978-; vice chm Assoc of Charitable Fndns 1990-91; *Books* Conspiracy and Civil Liberties (1974), The Bar on Trial (1978); *Recreations* opera, badgers, bird watching, canoeing; *Style—* Robert Hazell, Esq; 94 Constantine Rd, London NW3 2LS (☎ 071 267 4881); Nuffield Foundation, 28 Bedford Square, London WC1B 3EG (☎ 071 631 0556, fax 071 323 4877)

HAZELWOOD, Maurice Harry; s of George William Hazelwood (d 1967), of Heckington, and Nellie Hazelwood; *b* 24 May 1933; *Educ* Carrington Sch; *m* Monicar Ruth Marshall (d 1959); 3 s (Mike b 1958, Tim b 1961, George b 1968), 1 da (Gillian b 1956); *Career* Nat Serv Army 1952-54; water skiing administrator; began water skiing 1964; memb Lincs Speed Boat Club 1966, chm Castle Water Ski Club 1970-83; Br Water Ski Assoc: joined 1967, team capt and mangr 1972-90, chm 1982-89, vice chm and hon memb 1989-; football referee 1951-65; lorry driver 1948-52 and 1954, potato merchant 1955; proprietor: Hazelwood Haulage Ltd 1960, Hazelwood Distribution Ltd 1982-, Hazelwood Ski World 1984-; *Recreations* Hazelwood Ski World; *Style—* Maurice Hazelwood, Esq; Hazelwood Ski World, Moor Lane, Thorpe-on-the-Hill, Lincoln LN6 9DA (☎ 0522 688245)

HAZLEHURST, Capt (Charles) Patrick; DL (1987); s of Capt Charles Arthur Cheshyre Hazlehurst (d 1953), and Evangeline Vere Eben, *née* Edwards (d 1980); *b* 2 April 1924; *Educ* Wellington; *m* 30 Sept 1965, Annsybella Sarah Penelope, da of Brig Archer Francis Lawrence Clive, DSO, MC, DL, of Perrystone, Ross-on-Wye, Herefords; 1 s (Charles Dominic b 1966), 1 da (Annsybella Emma Lucinda b 1969); *Career* joined 60 Rifles 1942, cmmnd 1943; serv: Italy 1944-45, Tripoli N Africa 1946; ADC to Lt-Gen Sir Evelyn Barker 1946-48 (when GOC-in-C: Palestine 1946-47, Eastern Cmd Hounslow 1947-48), Capt 1948, ret 1949; fndr Woodcemair Ltd (bldg prods) 1952 (md 1952-64, chm 1965-71), chm Torvale Gp Ltd (incl Woodcemair Ltd) 1972-; High Sheriff Hereford and Worcester 1985-86; *Recreations* shooting, fishing, field trials; *Clubs* Boodles', Flyfishers, Royal Greenjackets; *Style—* Capt Patrick Hazlehurst, DL; Broomy Ct, Llandinabo, Hereford HR2 8JB (☎ 0981 540215); Torvale Gp Ltd, Pembridge, Leominster, Herefordshire (☎ 05447 262, fax 05447 426, telex 35265)

HAZLEMAN, Dr Brian Leslie; s of Eric Edward Hazleman (d 1981), of Reading, Berks, and Gladys Marjorie, *née* Wells; *b* 4 March 1942; *Educ* Leighton Park Sch Reading, London Hosp Univ of London (MB BS), Univ of Cambridge (MA); *m* 29 Jan 1972, Ruth Margaret, da of Douglas Eynon, of Bristol; 3 da (Anna b 1973, Christina b 1976, Sarah b 1983); *Career* London Hosp 1966-71: house physician and surgn 1966-67, registrar rheumatology 1968-69, registrar med 1969-71; sr registrar med and rheumatology: Radcliffe Infirmary Oxford 1971-73, Nuffield Orthopaedic Hosp 1971-73; conslt physician: Addenbrookes Hosp Cambridge 1973, Newmarket Hosp 1973-; hon conslt Strangeways Res Laboratory Cambridge 1973-, dir Rheumatology Res Unit Cambridge 1975-, assoc lectr Univ of Cambridge 1975- (fell CCC 1982); memb Ed Bd: Br Jl of Rheumatology, Jl of Orthopaedic Rheumatology and Sports Med and Soft Tissue Trauma; winner: Begley prize RCS 1965, Margaret Holyrode prize Heberden Soc 1975-; FRCP; *Books* The Sclera and Systemic Disorders (1976), Rheumatoid Arthritis Pathology and Pharmacology (1976), The Shoulder Joint (1989); *Recreations* sailing, photography, travel; *Clubs* Royal Harwich (Suffolk); *Style—* Dr Brian L Hazleman; Church End House, Weston Colville, Cambs CB1 5PE (☎ 0223 290 543); Dept of Rheumatology, Addenbrokes Hospital, Hills Road, Cambridge (☎ 0223 217457)

HAZLERIGG, 2 Baron (UK 1945); Sir Arthur Grey; 14 Bt (E 1622), MC (1945), JP (Leics 1946), DL (1946); s of 1 Baron (d 1949); *b* 24 Feb 1910; *Educ* Eton, Trinity Coll Cambridge; *m* 1945, Patricia (d 1972), da of John Pullar, of Natal, S Africa; 1 s, 2 da; *Heir* s, Hon Arthur Hazlerigg; *Career* served WW II Maj RA (TA) and Leics Yeo; FRICS; *Recreations* golf; *Clubs* Army and Navy, MCC; *Style—* The Rt Hon the Lord Hazlerigg, MC, JP, DL; Noseley Hall, Billesdon, Leicester LE7 9EH (☎ 053 775 322)

HAZLERIGG, Hon Arthur Grey; s and h of 2 Baron Hazlerigg, MC; *b* 5 May 1951; *m* 1986, Laura, eld d of Sir William Dugdale, 2 Bt; 1 s (Arthur William Grey b 13 May 1987), 2 da (Eliza Patricia b 1989, Amelia Frances b (twin) 1989); *Clubs* Leicester Tiger Old Players, MCC; *Style—* The Hon Arthur Hazlerigg; The Chapel House, Noseley, Billesdon, Leics LE7 9HE (☎ 053 755 606)

HAZLERIGG, Hon Robert Maynard; yst s of 1 Baron Hazlerigg (d 1949); *b* 21 July 1916; *Educ* Eton, Trinity Coll Cambridge (BA); *m* 9 Jan 1942, Rose, da of Charles Cox; 2 da; *Career* Major RA (TA); ARICS; farmer; *Clubs* Oriental; *Style—* The Hon Robert Hazlerigg; Cottonsfield Farm, Three Gates, Billesdon, Leicester (☎ 053 755 382)

HAZLERIGG, Hon Thomas Heron; 2 s of 1 Baron Hazlerigg (d 1949), and Dorothy Rachel, *née* Buxton (d 1972); *b* 17 Jan 1914; *Educ* Eton, Trinity Coll Cambridge (BA); *m* 1, 28 March 1942 (m dis 1956), Audrey Cecil, da of late Maj Cecil Robert Bates, DSO, MC; 2 s; m 2, 31 Jan 1957 (m dis 1974), Doussa da of Fahmy Bey Wissa, of Ramleh, Egypt, formerly w of Maj Harold Stanley Cayzer; m 3, 1978, Anne Frances Roden, da of Capt Roden Henry Victor Buxton, RN, of Rodwell House, Loddon, Norfolk; *Career* Maj Leics Yeo, formerly Flying-Offr RAF Reserve; banker; *Recreations* skiing, Cresta Run, golf, shooting; *Clubs* White's, Pratt's, MCC; *Style—* The Hon Thomas Hazlerigg; Caflida, Klosters, Switzerland

HAZLEWOOD, Gerald Alan (Gerry); OBE (1986); s of Reginald Hazlewood, of Okanagan Centre, BC, Canada, and Lilian May, *née* Lofts; *b* 25 July 1939; *Educ* Royal GS, High Wycombe; *m* 6 Sept 1961, Toni Gay, da of Sqdn Ldr Edward John Lisle, of Mundaring, Western Australia; 1 s (Daniel b 1979), 2 da (Christine b 1967, Helen b 1965); *Career* chm Westwood Engineering Ltd 1986- (dir 1967-86); *Recreations* golf; *Style—* Gerry Hazlewood, Esq, OBE; Midland Bank plc, City Centre, Old Town St, Plymouth PL1 1DD; Westwood Engineering Ltd, Bell Close, Newnham Industrial Estate, Plympton, Plymouth PL7 4JH (car ☎ 0836 502067)

HAZLEWOOD, Maurice Charles; s of Alfred Ernest Hazlewood (d 1981), of Liverpool, and Laura, *née* Hughes (d 1972); *b* 16 Oct 1927; *Educ* Liverpool Coll, Liverpool Univ (BSc), St Peter's Hall Oxford; *m* 6 Aug 1955, Morfydd Elizabeth, da of John Rowlands (d 1972), of Rhyl; 1 s (Richard b 1960), 1 da (Mary b 1959); *Career* called to the Bar Gray's Inn 1952, practised Northern Circuit; joined Royal Dutch Shell Gp 1958, head of chemical licensing and Legal Div Shell Int Chemical Co Ltd 1961-68 (gen mangr Chemicals New York 1969-74), pres N American Plant Breeders Inc 1972-74; vice-pres: Masterflex Rubber Corpn, Sureflex Rubber Co 1972-74, Akzona Inc New York 1974-76 (conslt 1976-79); practised in Temple 1979-85; memb Police Complaints Authy 1985-88; *Recreations* gardening, viticulture (memb English Vineyards Assoc), cricket; *Clubs* MCC; *Style—* Maurice Hazlewood, Esq; Whitethorne, Chapel Rd, Limpsfield Common, Oxted, Surrey RH8 0SX (☎ 088 372 2345)

HAZLITT, Simon Charles; s of Denis Roy Hazlitt, of Woking, Surrey, and Jennifer Anne Margaret, *née* Dick; *b* 16 Oct 1966; *Educ* Clifton Coll Bristol, Univ of Nottingham (BA); *Career* entered Sandhurst 1988, cmmnd 2 Lt 2 Bn The Light Infantry 1989-; Hounslow Hockey Club: 13 England Caps 1987-, 12 GB Caps 1987-;

also played Co Combined Servs; Gold medal Sultan Azlan Shah Tournament Ipon Malaysia 1989 (Bronze 1987); *Recreations* golf, cricket, English and Russian lit, USSR; *Clubs* Hounslow Hockey, Oatlands Park Cricket; *Style—* Simon Hazlitt, Esq

HAZZARD, (Lawrence) Gordon; s of Frederick Hazzard, and Minnie; *b* 1925; *Educ* Waverley GS Birmingham; *m* 1, 1956 (m dis), Margery Elizabeth Charles; 1 da (Clare); m 2 1985, Miyuki Sedohara; *Career* served WWII, RAF 1943-47; gp md MK Elec Hldgs until 1980; dep chm (later chm) Grosvenor Gp plc 1981-86; chm: Wigfalls plc 1981-88, Waingate Insurance Ltd 1985-88, HB Electronic Components plc 1983-85, Toby Lane Ltd 1984-, Gordon Hazzard Ltd Anglo Japanese Business Advsrs 1988-, Green Park Health Care plc 1989-; former: memb Cncl CBI (former memb Industl Policy Cmmn), memb Bd ASTA, vice chm EIEMA, dep pres Br Electric and Allied Mfrs Assoc; memb: Econ Res Cncl, Japan Soc, Japan Assoc, Japan-Br Soc of Hiroshima; FIOD, CMIM; *Recreations* music; *Clubs* Oriental, RAC; *Style—* Gordon Hazzard, Esq; 5 Balfour Place, London W1Y 5RG (☎ 071 408 0626, fax 071 629 8105)

HEAD, His Honour Judge Adrian Herbert; s of His Honour Judge George Herbert Head (d 1927), of The Lodge, Acomb, York, and Geraldine Maria, *née* Pipon (d 1959); *b* 4 Dec 1923; *Educ* RNC Dartmouth (invalided polio), privately, Magdalen Coll Oxford (BA, MA); *m* 22 July 1947, Ann Pamela, da of John Stanning (d 1928), of Engoshura Farm, Nakuru, Kenya; 3 s (Henry b 1948, Christopher b 1954, David b 1955); *Career* called to the Bar Gray's Inn 1947 (Holker exhibition 1945, Arden scholar and Holker Sr exhibitioner 1947), subs ad eundem Inner Temple; chm Norfolk Lavender Ltd and Chilvers & Son (1874) Ltd 1958-71 (dir 1953-58), chm Agricultural Land Tbnls (SE Regn) 1971, dep chm Middx QS Sessions 1971, circuit judge 1972-; memb Law Advsy Bd UEA 1979-, co-fndr and sr tstee Norfolk Family Conciliation Serv 1983-, pres West Norfolk and Fenland Marriage Guidance Cncl (now Relate) 1984-; reader C of E 1961-; Hon D Civil Law UEA 1987; *Books* The Seven Words and the Civilian (1946, awarded the Tredegar Meml Lectureship RSL 1948), Essays by Divers Hands (contrib, 1953), Safety Afloat (trans from Dutch, 1965), Consumer Credit Act Supplement to McCleary's County Ct Forms (1979), Poems in Praise (1982), Butterworths County Ct Precedents and Pleadings (devised and gen ed 1985, contrib 1985-, consulting ed 1987-), Poems in Praise (2 edn, 1987); *Recreations* writing, painting, sailing, trees; *Clubs* Norfolk, RNSA, Cruising Assoc, St Katharine Haven Yacht; *Style—* His Honour Judge Adrian Head; Overy Staithe, King's Lynn, Norfolk PE31 8TG (☎ 0328 738312); 5 Raymond Bldgs, Gray's Inn, London WC1 5BP (☎ 071 405 7146)

HEAD, Audrey M; da of Eric Burton Head (d 1969), of Guildford, Surrey, and Kathleen Irene Head (d 1978); *b* 21 Jan 1924; *Educ* St Catherine's Sch Bramley, Surrey; *Career* md Hill Samuel Unit Trust Managers 1976-86 (dir 1973-86); dir: Hill Samuel Investment Management 1974-86, Hill Samuel Life Assurance 1983-86; chm Unit Trust Association 1983-85, dir Trades Union Unit Trust Manager 1986-89, memb Monopolies and Mergers Cmmn 1986-89; chm governing body St Catherine's Sch Bramley 1988- (govr 1979-), non-exec memb Royal Surrey and St Luke's NHS Trent 1990-, govr Cranleigh Sch 1988-; nominated Business Woman of the Year 1976, Silver Jubilee medal 1977; *Recreations* golf, gardening; *Clubs* Sloane; *Style—* Ms Audrey Head; West Chantry, 4 Clifford Manor Rd, Guildford, Surrey GU4 8AG

HEAD, Dennis Alec; CBE (1979); s of Alec Head (d 1953), of London, and Florence Lilian, *née* Childs (d 1991); *b* 8 Nov 1925; *Educ* Whitgift Sch, Peterhouse Cambridge (MA); *m* 23 April 1966, Julia May, da of Samuel Irving Rosser-Owen (d 1972), of Shrewsbury; 1 s (Richard Alexander b 20 June 1968); *Career* RN: Air Arm 1943, Midshipman 1944, sub Lt RNVR 1945-47; Rolls Royce Ltd: graduate trainee 1949, mangr design servs 1962, dir of personnel 1967, md Derby 1973, md Aero Div 1976, md ops 1980; dir ops Shorts Bros 1982, quality dir STC Manufacturing 1987, gen mangr STC Cardiff 1990; memb E Midlands Cncl for Further Educn 1968-73, memb Policy Ctee Engrg Employers Fedn 1978-82, memb NI Devpt Bd Res Devpt Educn Ctee 1983-86; FRAeS 1977; *Recreations* photography, history, music; *Style—* Dennis Head, Esq, CBE; Bodman's 48 D, High Street, Marshfield, Wilts (☎ 0225 891868); Well House, 27 Cultra Avenue, Holywood, Co Down BT18 OA7 (☎ 02317 5583)

HEAD, Eric Howard; TD (1968); s of Thomas Howard Head (d 1953), of Sussex, and Jane, *née* Baxter (d 1963); *b* 6 Dec 1919; *Educ* Brighton Coll; *m* 18 June 1949, Carol Elizabeth, da of Walter Bridgwood Batkin (d 1977), of Hertfordshire; 3 da (Victoria, Erica, Joanna); *Career* private KOYLI 1940, 2 Lt Royal Sussex Regt 1940, Maj 6/19 Hyderabad Regt Indian Army 1940-46, Lt-Col APIS (TA) 1952-67; CA: ptnr 1950, sr ptnr 1980-85, ret 1985; dir: Astral Computer Services Ltd 1980, R L Glover Underwriting Agency 1985; master Tower Ward Club 1984-85, pres Bishopsgate Ward Club 1986-87; memb: IOD, Guild of Freemen, Royal Soc of St George; assoc memb Lloyd's 1954-; Freeman: Worshipful Co of Horners, Worshipful Co of Chartered Accountants; FCA; *Recreations* golf, foreign travel; *Clubs* City of London, City Livery, Haywards Heath Golf, St Enodoc Golf, United Wards; *Style—* Eric Head, Esq, TD; Russell's Farmhouse, St Georges Lane, Hurstpierpoint, W Sussex BN6 9QX (☎ 0273 833174); Fairwinds, Trebetherick, Cornwall (☎ 020 886 3371)

HEAD, Major Sir Francis David Somerville; 5 Bt (UK 1838); s of Sir Robert Pollock Somerville Head, 4 Bt (d 1924), and Grace Margaret, *née* Robertson (d 1967); *b* 17 Oct 1916; *Educ* Eton, Peterhouse Cambridge; *m* 1, 11 Feb 1950 (m dis 1965), Susan Patricia, da of late Arthur Douglas Ramsay, OBE; 1 s, 1 da; m 2, 25 Jan 1967, Penelope Marion Acheson, yr da of late Wilfrid Archibald Alexander; *Heir* s, Richard Douglas Somerville Head, *qv*; *Career* Maj (ret) Queen's Own Cameron Highlanders; served WW II (wounded, POW); *Clubs* Naval and Military; *Style—* Major Sir Francis Head, Bt; 63 Chantry View Rd, Guildford, Surrey GU1 3XU

HEAD, Michael Edward; s of Alexander Edward Head (d 1971), of Kingston on Thames, Surrey, and Wilhelmina Head (d 1963); *b* 17 March 1936; *Educ* Leeds, Kingston and Woking GS's, UCL (BA), Univ of Michigan USA (MA); *m* 21 Sept 1963, Wendy Elizabeth, da of Richard and Florence Davies, of Hayes, Middlesex; 2 s (Andrew Justin Nicholas b 1965, Timothy Richard Alexander b 1972), 2 da (Gillian Lucy b 1967, Philippa Jane b 1970); *Career* Nat Serv 1958-60 2nd Lt RA 29th Field Regt; Home Office: asst princ 1960 (Immigration and Gen Depts 1960-64), private sec to Parly Under Sec of State 1964-66 (Fire Dept and Gen Dept 1966-74), asst sec Probation and Aftercare Dept 1974-78, asst sec Equal Opportunities Dept 1978-81, asst sec Criminal Dept 1981-84, asst under sec of state and head of Gen Dept 1984-86, head of Criminal Justice and Constitutional Dept 1986-, registrar of Baronetage 1984; *Recreations* theatre, reading, golf; *Clubs* Reform, Rotary (Woking); *Style—* Michael Head, Esq; Byways, The Ridge, Woking, Surrey GU22 7EE (☎ 0483 772929); Home Office, Queen Anne's Gate, London SW1 9AT (☎ 071 273 3918)

HEAD, 2 Viscount (UK 1960); Richard Antony Head; s of 1 Viscount Head, GCMG, CBE, MC, PC (d 1983), MP (C) for Carshalton 1945-60, Sec of State for War 1951-56, Minister of Def 1956-57, first high cmmr to Fedn of Nigeria 1960-63, high cmmr to Fedn of Malaysia 1963-66, and Lady Dorothea Louise (d 1987), da of 9 Earl of Shaftesbury; *b* 27 Feb 1937; *Educ* Eton, RMA Sandhurst; *m* 1974, Alicia Brigid, da of Julian John William Salmond, of The Old Manor Farmhouse, Didmarton, Badminton, Avon; 2 s (Hon Henry Julian b 30 March 1980, Hon George Richard b 20 July 1982), 1 da (Hon Sarah Georgiana b 26 Nov 1984); *Heir* s, Hon Henry Head; *Career* served Life Guards 1957-66, Capt ret; trainer of racehorses 1968-83; *Recreations* sailing, golf; *Clubs* White's, Cavalry and Guards'; *Style—* The Rt Hon the Viscount Head; Throope Manor, Bishopstone, Salisbury, Wilts (☎ 072 277 318)

HEAD, Richard Douglas Somerville; s and h of Sir Francis David Somerville Head, 5 Bt; *b* 16 Jan 1951; *Educ* Eton, Magdalene Coll Cambridge, Bristol (Art Coll) Poly; *Career* gardener The Royal Hort Soc Wisley Garden; *Recreations* music, painting, drawing, skiing; *Style—* Richard Head, Esq; 69 High Rd, Byfleet, Weybridge, Surrey KT14 7QN

HEAD, Sarah Daphne (Sally); da of Richard George Head, of Lavalow, Sithney Green, Helston, Cornwall, and Daphne Grace, *née* Henderson; *b* 20 Feb 1951; *Educ* Ancaster House Sussex, St Maurs Convent Weybridge; *m* 25 Sept 1975 (m dis 1987), Francis Vincent Keating, s of Bryan Keating; *Career* Sally Head Poetry Corner Radio London 1969, story of Warner Bros (Europe) 1972-75, script ed BBC and Thames TV 1976-84; prodr BBC Drama 1984-88: First Born, Marksman, Life and Loves of a She Devil, Breaking Up, The Detective, Inside Out; *Recreations* gardening sailing, theatre, pubs; *Clubs* Helford River Sailing, Stand-on-the-Green Sailing; *Style—* Miss Sally Head; 1 Hearne Road, Stand-on-the-Green, London

HEAD, Hon Simon Andrew; s of 1 Viscount Head, GCMG, CBE, MC, PC (d 1983), and Dorothea, Viscountess Head, *qv*; *b* 1944; *Educ* Eton, ChCh Oxford, Berkeley Univ Calif; *Career* asst ed Far Eastern Economic Review in Hong Kong 1966-67, corr in S E Asia for Financial Times 1970-72, New York corr New Statesman 1974-76; contrib on foreign affairs New York Review of Books 1973-; contested S Dorset (SDP-Lib) 1983; *Style—* The Hon Simon Head; 155 Cranmer Court, Sloane Ave, London SW3

HEADFORT, 6 Marquess of (I 1800); Sir Thomas Geoffrey Charles Michael Taylour; 9 Bt (I 1704); also Baron Headfort (I 1760), Viscount Headfort (I 1762), Earl of Bective (I 1766), and Baron Kenlis (UK 1831, which sits as); s of 5 Marquess, TD (d 1960), by his w Elsie, widow of Sir Rupert Clarke, 2 Bt, and da of James Tucker; *b* 20 Jan 1932; *Educ* Stowe, Christ's Coll Cambridge Univ (MA); *m* 1, 1958 (m dis 1969), Hon Elizabeth Nall-Cain, da of 2 Baron Brocket; 1 s, 2 da; m 2, 1972, Virginia, da of Mr Justice Nable, of Manila; *Heir* s, Earl of Bective; *Career* 2 Lt Life Gds 1950, actg PO RAFVR 1952; holds Commercial Pilot's Licence; Freeman Guild of Air Pilots and Air Navigators; dir Bective Electrical Co 1953, sales mangr and chief pilot Lancashire Aircraft Co 1959; Lloyd's Underwriter; Inspector Royal Hong Kong Aux Police 1977; FRICS, FCIArb, MIAUI; *Style—* The Most Hon The Marquess of Headfort; 1425 Figueroa St, Paco, Manila, Philippines (☎ 5220218, 593829, telex 64792 HORT PN); Affix Ltd, Room 601 Kam Chung Bldg, 54 Jaffe Road, Wanchai, Hong Kong (☎ 5 286011/2); Ellerslie Manor, Crosby, IOM (☎ Marown 851521)

HEADING, Prof John; s of Arthur Heading (d 1973), of Norwich, and Ada Lily, *née* Morley (d 1974); *b* 3 Dec 1924; *Educ* City of Norwich Sch, St Catharine's Coll Cambridge (BA, MA, PhD, ScD); *m* 31 Aug 1951, Margaret Helen, *née* Harris; 2 s (Jeremy b 1956, Peter b 1959); *Career* RCS lineman mechanic 1943-46; lectr in mathematics SW Essex Tech Coll 1953-56, sr lectr in mathematics West Ham Coll of Technol 1956-59, Univ of Southampton 1960-67 (lectr, sr lectr, reader), prof of applied mathematics Univ Coll of Wales Aberystwyth 1968-89; ed: Precious Seed magazine 1962-85, Developments in Electromagnetic Theory and Applications 1983-; author numerous scientific and biblical pubns in jls; fell Cambridge Philosophical Soc 1951-87; *Books* Matrix Theory for Physicists (1958), An Introduction to Phase-Integral Methods (1962), Mathematical Methods in Science and Engineering (1963), Acts, a Study in New Testament Christianity (1974), From Now to Eternity, the Book of Revelation (1978), What the Bible Teaches, Vol 2: Matthew (1984), Ten Thousand Lines Across Europe (1986), What the Bible Teaches, Vol 6: John (1988), The Servant-Son: Mark (1990); *Recreations* bible teaching, writing books; *Style—* Prof John Heading; Gorwel Deg, Piercefield Lane, Aberystwyth, Dyfed SY23 1RX (☎ 0970 612770)

HEADLEY, 7 Baron (I 1797); Sir Charles Rowland Allanson-Winn; 7 and 13 Bt (GB 1776, of Warley; E 1660, of Nostell); s of 5 Baron by his 1 w Teresa, *née* Johnson; suc bro, 6 Baron, 1969; *b* 19 May 1902; *Educ* Bedford Sch; *m* 1927, Hilda (d 1989), da of Thomas Thorpe; 1 s (decd), 3 da; *Heir* bro, Hon Owain Gwynedd Allanson-Winn; *Style—* The Rt Hon Lord Headley; Dreys, 7 Silverwood, West Chiltington, West Sussex RH20 2NG (☎ 0798 813083)

HEADLEY, (William) Robert; s of William James Headley (d 1982), of Desford, Leicestershire, and Alice Mary, *née* Horspool (d 1977); *b* 8 April 1922; *Educ* Hammersmith Sch, Architectural Assoc Sch of Architecture (AA Dip); *m* 1, 18 Aug 1946, Margaret Elizabeth Vining, *née* Harris (d 1973); 2 da (Jennifer b 1948, Carolyn b 1950), 1 s (Nigel b 1955); m 2, 27 May 1978, Anne Julia (d 1990), da of Maj Richard Clive Strachey, MC (d 1980); 1 step da (Francesca b 1954), 1 step s (Dominic b 1959); *Career* architect: dep chief architect Western Region BR 1947-55 (responsible for modernisation programme incl Plymouth and Banbury), chief architect Midland Region BR 1955-63 (responsible for all architectural bldgs incl electrification programme from London to Manchester and Liverpool); major new stations: Coventry, Piccadilly Manchester, Stafford; GMW Ptnrship Chartered Architects: ptnr 1963-68, sr ptnr 1968-89, conslt 1989- (major projects incl New Covent Garden Market, New College and HQ RMA Sandhurst, Coll of Science Shrivenham, responsible for overall mgmnt of practices in UK, Hong Kong, Singapore, Saudi Arabia); Freeman City of London, Worshipful Co of Chartered Architects; FRIBA, HKIA; *Recreations* music, cricket; *Clubs* MCC, Arts, Oriental, Roehampton; *Style—* Robert Headley, Esq; Funtington Lodge, Funtington, W Sussex PO18 9LG (☎ 0243 575 205); GMW Partnership, PO Box 1613, 239 Kensington High St, London W8 6SL (☎ 071 937 8020, telex 28566, fax 071 937 5815)

HEADY, Donald Edward; s of Albert Edward Heady (d 1957), of London, and Edith, *née* Hunt (d 1984); *b* 28 Sept 1933; *Educ* Southend on Sea HS for Boys; *m* 22 Sept 1956, Doreen Joan, da of Arthur Sharpe (d 1969), of Essex; *Career* CA; conslt; pres South Essex Soc of CA's 1980-81; memb: Cncl The Inst of CA's in England and Wales 1981-, Accounting Standards Ctee of the Consultative Ctee of Accountancy Bodies 1982-85; Freeman City of London, Liveryman Worshipful Co of CA's 1978-; FCA 1958, ATII 1962; *Recreations* swimming, still learning to play the piano and organ; *Style—* Donald Heady, Esq; 2 Great Lawn, Ongar, Essex CM5 0AA (☎ and fax 0277 362905)

HEAL, Susan (Sue); da of Raymond Heal, of Bridgwater, Somerset, and Florence May Heal (d 1971); *b* 1 March 1951; *Educ* Westover Secdy Modern Sch Bridgwater, Bridgwater Girls' GS, Univ of Nottingham (BA); *Partner* Stephen Fleming; *Career* res The Financial Times 1974-78, campaign organiser Abortion Law Reform Assoc 1978-80, freelance feature writer 1980-82, features writer then asst features ed Woman's Own 1982-84, The Six O'Clock Show LWT 1984-85, freelance feature writer for nat papers and magazines 1986-88, film critic Today 1988- (contrib to The Observer, Homes & Gardens, also various magazines UK and abroad); first Br journalist to expose The Moonies; memb Nat Critics Circle 1989; *Recreations* Italy, opera, taking driving tests; *Clubs* Groucho; *Style—* Ms Sue Heal; Today, News International, 1 Pennington St, London E1 (☎ 071 782 6000, fax 071 630 6839)

HEAL, Sylvia Lloyd; JP (Surrey) 1973, MP (Lab) Mid Staffordshire March 1990; da of John Lloyd Fox (d 1974), of Ewloe, N Wales, and Ruby, *née* Hughes; *b* 20 July 1942; *Educ* Elfed Secdy Mod, Coleg Harlech Harlech N Wales, Univ of Swansea (BSc); *m*

1965, Keith Heal, s of Cecil Heal; 1 s (Gareth Aneurin b 12 Aug 1973), 1 da (Joanne Siân Lloyd b 14 Sept 1970); *Career* med records clerk Chester Royal Infirmary 1957-63, social worker Health Service 1968-70 and 1983-90; memb GMBU; *Recreations* walking, male voice choirs, theatre's; *Style*— Ms Sylvia Heal, JP, MP; House of Commons, London SW1A 0AA (☎ 071 219 5895, 0889 579797)

HEALD, Lady; Daphne Constance; *née* Price; CBE (1976); da of Montague Price; *b* 1904; *Educ* privately; *m* 1929, as his 2 w, Rt Hon Sir Lionel Heald, PC, QC, JP, sometime MP Chertsey and attorney-gen (d 1981); 2 s, 1 da; *Career* connected with many voluntary organizations; Dame OStJ; *Recreations* gardening; *Style*— Lady Heald, CBE; Chilworth Manor, Guildford, Surrey (☎ 0483 61414)

HEALD, Kenneth; OBE (1991); s of Jesse Heald (d 1970), and Olive, *née* Whitham (d 1973); *b* 1 March 1933; *Educ* Pudsey GS; *m* 13 Nov 1954, Mary, da of Hugh Coulson (d 1970); 1 s (Christopher b 1964); *Career* Nat Serv Intelligence Corps 1951-53; FO: joined 1954, Madrid 1957-59, Mogadishu 1959-61, Brussels 1961-63, third sec Havana 1963-65, Vice-Consul Caracas 1966-70, second sec Santiago 1970-73; FCO: HQ 1973-76, second sec Ottawa 1976-78, consul Toronto 1978-80, first sec Geneva 1981-85, sr asst Inspr 1985-89, HM consul gen Madrid 1989-; *Recreations* walking, swimming, gardening; *Clubs* Civil Service; *Style*— Kenneth Heald, Esq, OBE; British Consulate General, Centro Colon, Marques De La Ensenada, 28004 Madrid, Spain (☎ 308 5201, fax 308 08 82, tlx 46664 A/B BRMADE)

HEALD, Mervyn; QC (1970); s of Rt Hon Sir Lionel Frederick Heald, PC, QC, MP (d 1982), and Daphne Constance Heald, CBE; *b* 12 April 1930; *Educ* Eton, Magdalene Coll Cambridge; *m* 1954, Clarissa, da of Harold Bowen; 1 s, 3 da; *Career* called to the Bar Middle Temple 1954; bencher 1978, cmmr Social Security 1988-; *Recreations* country pursuits; *Style*— Mervyn Heald Esq, QC; Headfoldswood, Loxwood, Sussex

HEALD, Nicholas Francis Barry; s of Maj Barry Harvey Heald, of Leamington Spa, Warwicks, and Jean Patricia, *née* Watts; *b* 12 Nov 1947; *Educ* Harrow Co Sch for Boys; *m* 4 Sept 1971, Mary Elizabeth, da of George Edward Goodhall; 2 da (Elizabeth b 1972, Katharine b 1974); *Career* admitted slr 1972; ptnr Simmons & Simmons 1977-; Freeman City of London 1977, Liveryman Worshipful Co of London Slrs 1977; memb Law Soc; *Recreations* travel especially to Spain, gardening, photography, DIY; *Style*— Nicholas Heald, Esq; Heatherdale, 49A Copperkins Lane, Amersham, Bucks HP6 5QP (☎ 0494 721720); 14 Dominion Street, London EC2M 2RJ (☎ 071 628 2020, fax 071 588 4129, telex 888562)

HEALD, Oliver; s of John Anthony Heald, of Folkestone, and Joyce, *née* Pemberton; *b* 15 Dec 1954; *Educ* Reading Sch, Pembroke Coll Cambridge (MA), Coll of Law; *m* 18 Aug 1979, Christine Janice, da of Eric Arthur Whittle (d 1980), of Eastbourne; 1 s (William b 1987), 2 da (Sarah b 1985, Victoria b 1989); *Career* called to the Bar Middle Temple 1977, SE Ciruit; parly candidate (C) Southwark and Bermondsey 1987; memb Hon Soc of Middle Temple; *Recreations* travel, gardening, sports; *Clubs* St Stephens Constitutional, Cambridgeshire County Farmers; *Style*— Oliver Heald, Esq; The Acacias, The Green, Royston, Herts SG8 7AD (☎ 0763 247640); Fenners Chambers, Madingley Rd, Cambridge (☎ 0223 68761)

HEALD, Owen Hubert; s of Henry Claypole Heald (d 1974), and Lilian May, *née* Cranness (d 1974); *b* 17 Jan 1925; *Educ* Westcliff HS; *m* 8 Nov 1947, Georgina Ruth, da of George Warman (d 1969); 1 da (Carole b 1949); *Career* oil indust exec Shell Petroleum Co Ltd and subsidiary cos 1949-85, vice-pres Shell Int Trading Co 1975-76, dir Shell UK Ltd 1979-84; bd memb The Oil and Pipeline Agency 1985- (chm 1988); *Recreations* sailing, golf; *Clubs* Thames Estuary Yacht; *Style*— Owen Heald, Esq; 6 Wyatts Drive, Thorpe Bay, Essex SS1 3DH (☎ 0702 468226); The Oil and Pipeline Agency, 35/38 Portman Square, London W1H 0EU (☎ 071 935 2585)

HEALD, Richard John; s of late John Eric Heald, and late Muriel Heald; *b* 11 May 1936; *Educ* Berkhamsted Sch, Gonville and Caius Coll Cambridge, Guys (MA, MB MChir); *m* 3 da (Sara b 1970, Lucy b 1972, Anna b 1977); *Career* ships surgn Union Castle Line; conslt surgn Basingstoke Dist Hosp, author books and papers on surgery of rectal cancer; cncl memb RCS, former pres Section of Surgery RSM; FRCS, FRCSEd; *Recreations* sailing; *Style*— Richard Heald, Esq; The Hampshire Clinic, Basing Rd, Basingstoke, Hampshire RG24 0AL (☎ 0256 54747, fax 0256 27670)

HEALD, Robert Douglas Spencer; s of Douglas Ernest Heald, of Longsdon Staffordshire, and Margaret Joyce, *née* Owen; *b* 9 Feb 1956; *Educ* Repton; *m* 18 March 1978, Jacqueline Ann, da of Frank Savin; 1 s (Oliver Robert Douglas b 6 March 1985), 3 da (Rebekeh Ann b 9 Oct 1977, Natalie Jane b 5 Dec 1979, Nicola Joyce b 25 Nov 1981); *Career* Wallaker & Co Ltd: apprenticed as probationer surveyor 1976-, assoc 1983, full equity ptnr 1987, md 1988; dir and divisional exec Britannia Estate Agencies Ltd 1989; FRICS 1989 (ARICS 1982); *Recreations* golf, shooting (clay and game); *Style*— Robert Heald, Esq; 1 St Matthew's Avenue, Surbiton, Surrey KT6 6JJ (☎ 081 390 6715); Britannia Estate Agencies Ltd, (formerly Wallaker & Co Ltd), 69 Victoria Rd, Surbiton, Surrey KT6 4NX (☎ 081 399 5381, fax 081 390 8775)

HEALD, His Hon Judge; Thomas Routledge; *b* 19 Aug 1923; *m* 1950, Jean Campbell; 2 s, 2 da; *Career* barr Middle Temple 1948; prosecuting cncl to Inland Revenue Midland Circuit 1965-70; dep chm: Lindsey QS 1965-71, Notts QS 1969-71; circuit judge 1970-; memb Matrimonial Causes Rule Ctee to 1983; pres Cncl of HM's Circuit Judges 1988 (sec 1984-85); memb Cncl Nottingham Univ 1975-; *Style*— His Hon Judge Heald; Rebbur House, Nicker Hill, Keyworth, Nottingham NG12 5ED

HEALD, Timothy Villiers; s of Col Villiers Archer John Heald, CVO, DSO, MBE, MC (d 1972), of Wilts, and Catherine Eleanor Jean, *née* Vaughan; *b* 28 Jan 1944; *Educ* Sherborne, Balliol Coll Oxford (MA); *m* 1968, Alison Martina, da of Norman Alexander Leslie, of Bucks; 2 s (Alexander b 1971, Tristram b 1977), 2 da (Emma b 1970, Lucy b 1973); *Career* contrib to various newspapers and magazines, writer Sunday Times Atticus Column 1965-67; features ed: Town Magazine 1967, Daily Express 1967-72; assoc ed Weekend Magazine Toronto 1977-78, thriller reviewer The Times 1983-89, Pendennis (The Observer) 1990; *Books* Simon Bognor Mystery novels (televised by Thames, 1973-), Networks (1983), Class Distinctions (1984), Red Herrings (1985), The Character of Cricket (1986), Brought to Book (1988), The Newest London Spy (ed, 1988), The Rigby File (ed, 1989), Business Unusual (1989), 150 Years of The Royal Warrant and Its Holders (by appt, 1989), My Lord's (ed, 1990), A Classic English Crime (ed, 1990); *Recreations* real tennis, spectator sports, lunch; *Clubs* MCC, Crime Writers Assoc (chm 1987-88), PEN (int co-ordinator Writers-in-Prison Ctee 1986-89), Society of Authors; *Style*— Timothy Heald, Esq; 305 Sheen Rd, Richmond-upon-Thames, Surrey TW10 5AW (☎ 081 878 2478)

HEALEY, Rt Hon Denis Winston; CH (1979), MBE (1945), PC (1964), MP (Lab) Leeds E 1955-; s of William Healey, of Keighley, Yorks; *b* 30 Aug 1917; *Educ* Bradford GS, Balliol Coll Oxford; *m* 1945, Edna May, da of Edward Edmunds, of Coleford, Glos; 1 s, 2 da; *Career* Lab Pty: int sec 1946-52, memb parly Ctee 1959, MP Leeds SE 1952-55, sec state for def 1964-70, oppn spokesman foreign and Cwlth affrs 1971, shadow chllr 1972-74, chllr of exchequer 1974-79; dep ldr 1981-83, shadow sec foreign and Cwlth affrs 1981-87; hon fell Baliol Coll Oxford 1980, former exec memb Fabian Soc; Freeman City of Leeds 1991; Hon DLitt Bradford 1983, Hon Dr Law Sussex 1989; Grand Cross Order of Merit Germany 1979; *Books* The Curtain Falls (1951), New Fabian Essays (1952), Neutralism (1955), Fabian International Essays (1956), A Neutral Belt in Europe (1958), NATO and American Security (1959), The Race Against the H Bomb (1960), Labour Britain and the World (1963), Healey's Eye (photographs, 1980), Labour and a World Society (1985), Beyond Nuclear Deterrence (1986), The Time of My Life (autobiography, 1989), When Shrimps Learn to Whistle (1990); *Style*— The Rt Hon Denis Healey, CH, MBE, MP; House of Commons, London SW1

HEALEY, Deryck John; s of Leonard Melvon Healey, of Natal, SA, and Irene Isabella, *née* Ferguson; *b* 30 Jan 1937; *Educ* Northlands HS Natal SA (Dip AD), Manchester Poly (DipAD); *m* 30 Sept 1962, Mary Elizabeth Pitt (decd), da of Col Philip Booth (d 1978), of Hay-on-Wye; 2 s (Paul Melyvon b 29 Aug 1963, Timothy Mathew b 29 Jan 1966); *Career* designer, artist sculptor, poet, design mangr Good Hope Textiles SA 1959-66; chm: Deryck Healey Associates 1966-85, Deryck Healey International 1969-85; design mangr WPM Wallpaper Manufacturers 1966-68, mangr ICI Design Studio 1968-80; dir: MMI 1987-89, Comcorp 1988-90, Retail Detail 1988-90; conslt: Texfi Industries USA 1970-80, Mrubeni Japan 1974-85, SA Nylon Spinners 1975-83; one man painting and sculpture exhibition 1990: Have I got your Number (London), Big Names (Venice), Silent Poems (London); int art fair exhibitions: Cologne, Frankfurt, Chicago; chm Textile and Fashion Bd CNAA 1971-81; memb: Art and Design Ctee CNAA 1971-81, Design Working Pty Clothing and Allied Products Trg Bd, Textile and Design Selection Ctee Design Cncl 1978-87; Crafts Cncl Bd: memb Textile Panel 1980-87, memb Fin and Gen Purposes Ctee 1983-85, chm Textile Devpt Gp 1982-84, memb Projects and Orgns Ctee 1983-85; patron New Art Tate Gallery 1983-, memb RSA Bursary Bd 1982-88, govr London Coll Fashion 1978, external examiner numerous CNAA BA and MA courses; COID Design award 1964, Queen's award to Indust for Export 1974, RSA Bicentenary Medal 1981, Textile Inst Design medal 1982; FRSA 1978, FCSD (FSIAD 1964); *Books* contrib Colour (1980), Living with Colour (1982), The New Art of Flower Design (1986); *Recreations* travel, painting, sculpture; *Style*— Deryck Healey, Esq

HEALEY, Dr Norman John; s of Dr Ronald Jack Healey, of Launceston, Cornwall, and Monica Mary Patricia, *née* Gibbins; *b* 2 Sept 1940; *Educ* Mount House Sch Tavistock, Epsom Coll, Guy's Univ of London (Kitchener scholarship 1959, MRCS, LRCP, DA, DObstRCOG, 1st XV Rugby); *m* 24 June 1978, Maureen Anne, da of Clarence Meadows Brock; 3 da (Rebecca Jane b 10 Feb 1980, Alicia June b 13 Sept 1981, Nicola Joy (twin) b 13 Sept 1981); *Career* Surgn Lt RN 1965-71, RN Hosp Haslar Dept of Anaesthetics 1966-68, HMS Albion serv in Far East 1968-69, RM Depot Deal 1970-71; sr house offr Obstetrics and Gynaecology Royal Bucks Hosp Aylesbury 1972, London Coll of Osteopathic Med 1973-74; clinical asst Dept of Rheumatology and Rehabilitation St Mary's Hosp London 1975-82; full time private practice as osteopathic physician and specialist in musculo-skeletal med 1975-; hon conslt St Luke's Hosp London 1987-; hon sec Br Osteopathic Assoc 1976-82, memb Cncl Br Assoc of Manipulative Med 1980-83; MRO 1975, fell London Coll of Osteopathic Med 1979, memb Br Soc of Rheumatology 1984, FRSM 1985; *Recreations* country walks, swimming; *Clubs* Royal Western Yacht, Incogniti Cricket; *Style*— Dr Norman Healey; Osteopathic Physician, 37 Devonshire Place, London W1N 1PE (☎ 071 487 3162)

HEALEY, Prof Patsy; da of Prof C T Ingold, CMG, of Benson, Oxon, and L M Ingold, *née* Kemp; *b* 1 Jan 1940; *Educ* Walthamstow Hall Sevenoaks Kent, UCL (BA), LSE (PhD), Regents St Poly (DipTP), Univ of Wales (Dip Ed); *m* 25 June 1961, Dr Ian Nevill Healey (d 1972), s of Douglas Healey (d 1978); m 2, 9 July 1977, David Reiach Hunter (d 1979), s of David Reiach (d 1919); *Career* sch teacher 1962-65, planning offr London Borough of Lewisham GLC 1965-69, sr res fell LSE 1970-72, lectr in planning Kingston Poly 1969-70 and 1972-74, lectr then head of dept and dean Oxford Poly 1974-87, prof and head of Dept of Town and Country Planning Univ of Newcastle upon Tyne 1988-; memb: ctees CNAA, Cncl and ctees RTPI, ctees ESRC; *Books* Professional Ideals and Planning Practice (with J Underwood, 1979), Planning Theory: Prospects for the 1980s (ed with G McDougall and M Thomas, 1982), Local Plans in British Land Use Planning (1983), Land Policy: Problems and Alternatives (ed with S M Barrett, 1985), A Political Economy of Land (with A Gilbert, 1985), Land Use Planning and the Mediation of Urban Change (with P F McNamara, M J Elson and A J Doak, 1988), Land and Property Development in a Changing Context (ed with R Nabarro, 1990); *Recreations* reading, walking, swimming, travelling; *Style*— Prof Patsy Healey; Department of Town and Country Planning, University of Newcastle upon Tyne, NE1 7RU (☎ 091 222 6000, fax 091 261 1182, telex UNINEW 953654)

HEALEY, Dr Tim; s of Thomas Henry Healey, of N Skelton, Cleveland, and Evelyn, *née* Hamilton; *b* 23 April 1935; *Educ* Boys HS Middlesbrough, Univ of Sheffield (MB ChB); *m* 18 Aug 1958, Ruth, da of Albert Edward Stagg (d 1977), of Northwich, Cheshire; 1 s (Trevor b 13 Sept 1960), 2 da (Janet b 9 March 1963, Sandra b 27 April 1969); *Career* house surgn Sheffield Royal Infirmary 1960 (house physician 1959), sr house offr orthopaedics Royal Hosp Sheffield 1960- (sr house offr in radiology 1960-61), sr registrar Leicester Royal Infirmary 1964-65 (registrar 1961-64), sr registrar United Sheffield Hosps 1965-66, conslt radiologist Barnsley 1966-; author of numerous articles on subjects incl: med, sci, history, philology; Br Inst Radiology: memb Cncl, memb N Branch 1987-, sec 1982-87, pres 1987-; hon doctorate in med history World Univ 1989; FFRRCS, FRCR, FRAI, FRSA, MINucE, FIDiagE; *Recreations* writing, collecting; *Style*— Dr Tim Healey; Northfield, Salisbury St, Barnsley, S Yorks S75 2TL (☎ 0226 205348); Barnsley District General Hospital, Barnsley, South Yorks S75 2EP (☎ 0226 730000)

HEALING, Hon Mrs (Elisabeth Mary Lionel Margaret); da of 16 Baron Petre (d 1915); *b* 1915,(posthumous); *m* 1935, Robert Peter Healing (1991); 1 s, 2 da; *Style*— The Hon Mrs Healing; The Priory, Kemerton, Glos

HEALY, David Elliott; s of Fergus Healy, of Singapore, and Gladys, *née* Elliott; *b* 11 Jan 1947; *Educ* St Marys Nairobi Kenya, Barts, Royal Dental Hosp (BDS); *Career* house surgn Royal Dental Hosp 1972-73 (pt/t teacher 1973); dentist: in private practice Harley Street 1973-80, refugee camps Singapore and Indonesia 1980-83, in private practice Upper Wimpole Street 1984-; winner American Soc of Endodentists award 1971; memb BDA 1972; *Style*— David Healy, Esq; 20 Upper Wimpole St, London W1M 7TA (☎ 071 935 8655)

HEALY, Prof John Francis; s of John Healy (d 1968), of Bishopsteignton, Devon, and Iris Maud, *née* Cutland; *b* 27 Aug 1926; *Educ* Trinity Coll Cambridge (BA, MA, PhD); *m* 1, 5 Jan 1957 (m dis 1985), Carol A McEvoy; 1 s (John Matthew Charles b 18 Oct 1964); m 2, 21 Sept 1985, Barbara Edith, da of John Douglas Henshall (d 1988), of Macclesfield; *Career* War Serv Essex Regt and Intelligence Corps 1944, Capt Intelligence Corps JAG Dept Singapore 1946-48 (Lt 1945-46); lectr in classics and classical archaeology Univ of Manchester 1953-61 (hon curator of coins 1958-80); Univ of London: reader in Greek Bedford Coll 1961-66, dean Faculty of Arts and Music Royal Holloway Coll 1978-81, chm Bd of Classical Studies 1979-81, emeritus prof of classics Royal Holloway and Bedford New Colls 1988-90, (chm Classics Dept 1985-88), head of dept Royal Holloway Coll 1966-85; chm Fin Sub Ctee Inst of Classical Studies 1966-88; pres Windsor Art Soc; FRNS 1950, FRSA 1971, memb Royal Inst of GB 1979; *Books* Cyrenaican Expeditions of the Manchester University Museum (1955-57) (with A Rowe, 1959), Mining and Metallurgy in the Greek and Roman World (1978), Sylloge Nummorum Graecorum VII, Manchester University Museum: The Raby and

Güterbock Collections (1986); *Recreations* music, travel, creative gardening (alpines); *Clubs* Cambridge Union; *Style—* Prof John Healy; c/o Royal Holloway and Bedford New College (University of London), Egham, Surrey TW20 0EX (☎ 0784 434455, fax 0784 37520, telex 935504)

HEALY, Maurice Eugene; s of Thomas Shine Healy (d 1961), and Emily Mary, *née* O'Mahoney (d 1980); *b* 27 Nov 1933; *Educ* Downside, Peterhouse Cambridge (BA); *m* 20 Dec 1958, Jose Barbara Speller, da of John Edward Dewdney (d 1971); 3 da (Kate b 1961 d 1977, Lulu b 1963, Jessica b 1964); *Career* Nat Serv 2 Lt RA 1954-56; asst princ Bd of Trade 1956-60, Consumers Assoc 1960-76; Which?: ed-in-chief and head of Ed Div 1973-76, project offr, dep ed, ed (Motoring Which, Handyman Which); dir Nat Consumer Cncl 1987-(joined 1977); memb Highgate Primary Sch Soc, chm Highgate Wood Sch 1982-86 (govr 1976-86, Soc memb); FRSA; *Recreations* jazz, Irish music, gardening, walking; *Style—* Maurice Healy, Esq; 15 Onslow Gardens, Muswell Hill, London N10 3JT (☎ 081 883 8955); National Consumer Council, 20 Grosvenor Gardens, London SW1W 0DH (☎ 071 730 3469)

HEALY, Prof Thomas Edward John; *b* 11 Dec 1935; *Educ* Guy's Hosp Univ of London; *m* 3 Nov 1966, Lesley Edwina; 1 s (Thomas b 19 April 1979), 3 da (Maria b 23 March 1968, Michaela b 8 Dec 1970, Laura b 28 Jan 1975); *Career* elected to Parish Cncl Stanton-on-the-Wolds, memb Dist Health Authy S Manchester 1981-87; author of over 100 published papers, ed Monographs in Anaesthesiology; memb Cncl: Assoc of Anaesthetists 1973-76, Anaesthetic Res Soc Cncl 1978-80, RSM 1985- (hon sec Ed Ctee), Coll of Anaesthetists 1989-, Postgrad Medical Fellowship 1990-; Freeman Worshipful Soc of Apothecaries, Freeman City of London; FCA, Academician Euro Acad of Anaesthesiology; *Books* Aids to Anaesthesia Book 1: Basic Science, Aids to Anaesthesia Book 2: Clinical Practice; *Recreations* reading; *Clubs* Royal Commonwealth Soc; *Style—* Prof Thomas Healy; Department of Anaesthesia, The University of Manchester, Withington Hospital, Manchester M20 8LR (☎ 061 447 3863, fax 061 445 1186)

HEANEY, Henry Joseph; s of Michael Heaney (d 1951), of Newry, Co Down, and late Sarah, *née* Fox; *b* 2 Jan 1935; *Educ* Abbey GS Newry Ireland, Queen's Univ Belfast (BA, MA); *m* 19 March 1976, Mary Elizabeth, da of Desmond Moloney, of Dublin; *Career* asst librarian Queen's Univ Belfast 1959-63, librarian Magee Univ Coll Londonderry 1963-69, dep librarian New Univ of Ulster Coleraine 1967-69, asst sec Standing Conf of Nat and Univ Libraries 1969-72, librarian Queen's Univ Belfast 1972-74, librarian and dir Sch of Librarianship Univ Coll Dublin 1975-78, librarian and keeper of the Hunterian Books and Manuscripts Univ of Glasgow 1978-; memb Br Library Bd; tstee: Nat Library of Scotland, Nat Manuscripts Conservation Tst; sec Advsy Ctee on Res Collections Standing Conf of Nat and Univ libraries, memb: Ctee Univ and Libraries Section Int Fedn of Library Assoc, Br Ctee Eighteenth Century Short Title Catalogue; ALA 1962, FLA 1967; *Books* World Guide to Abbreviations of International Organisations (9 edn, 1991); *Clubs* XIII (Glasgow); *Style—* Henry Heaney, Esq; 50A Sherbrooke Ave, Glasgow G41 4SB (☎ 041 427 1518); Glasgow Univ Library, Hillhead Street, Glasgow G12 8QE (☎ 041 330 4283)

HEANEY, John Bryan; s of Brig George Frederick Heaney (d 1983), and Doreen Marguerite, *née* Hammersley-Smith; *b* 26 Feb 1931; *Educ* Marlborough, Christ's Coll Cambridge (MA); *m* 19 Nov 1955, Catherine Ann, da of Lt Cdr Eliot Phillip Rayleigh Haller, RNVR (ka 1940); 1 s (Quintin John b 1957), 1 da (Alison Mary b 1959); *Career* cmmnd RE 1950, surveyor on first land based expedition to S Georgia Falkland Islands 1951-52, led expdn to Gough Island S Atlantic 1955-56; Shell International Petroleum Cos 1956-79, fndr and chief exec Saxon Oil plc 1980-85, chm Waveney Apple Growers Ltd 1987-; *Clubs* IOD; *Style—* John Heaney, Esq; Oldhouse Farm, Wakes Colne, Colchester, Essex CO6 2DR (☎ 0787 222287, fax 0787 224313)

HEAP, Sir Desmond; s of William and Minnie Heap, of Burnley, Lancs; *b* 17 Sept 1907; *Educ* Burnley GS, Univ of Manchester (LLB, LLM); *m* 6 Oct 1945, Adelene Mai, da of Frederick Lacey, of Harrogate; 1 s (John Nicholas Desmond b 5 July 1951), 2 da (Sally Elizabeth Adelene b 10 Aug 1946, Joanna Mary Alison b 29 April 1948); *Career* admitted slr 1933; chief asst slr City of Leeds 1938-40 (prosecuting slr 1935-38), dep town clerk Leeds 1940-47, comptroller and city slr to Corporation of London 1947-73; lectr Leeds Sch of Architecture 1935-47; RTPI: legal memb 1935-, memb Cncl 1947-77, pres 1955-56; assoc memb RICS 1953- (memb Cncl 1957-84); memb: Colonial Office Housing and Town Planning Advsy Panel 1953-65, Editorial Bd of Planning and Environment Law 1948-, Cncl on Tbnls 1971-77; vice pres Statute Law Soc 1982-, dep pres City of London Branch BRCS 1956-76, chm govrs Hurstpierpoint Coll 1975-82; hon assoc Worshipful Co of Solicitors of City of London 1987, Liveryman Worshipful Co of Carpenters, hon memb Ct Worshipful Co of Chartered Surveyors; Law Soc: memb Cncl 1954-78, chm Law Reform Ctee 1955-60, chm Town Planning Ctee 1964-70, pres 1972-73; Hon LLD Univ of Manchester 1973; FRSA (memb Cncl 1974-78); kt 1970; *Books* Planning Law for Town and Country (1938), Planning and the Law of Interim Development (1944), An Outline of Planning Law (1949, 10 edn 1991), Encyclopaedia of Planning Law and Practice (1960), Encyclopaedia of Betterment Levy (1967), How to Control Land Development (1974, 2 edn 1981); *Recreations* swimming, pedal biking, stage and theatre; *Clubs* Athenaeum, City Livery, Guildhall; *Style—* Sir Desmond Heap; Sugden and Spencer, Arndale House, Charles St, Bradford BD1 1ER (☎ 0274 732271)

HEAP, Peter William; CMG (1987); s of Roger Heap (d 1966), and Dora Heap, *née* Hosier; *b* 13 April 1935; *Educ* Bristol Cathedral Sch, Merton Coll Oxford (BA); *m* 1, 1960; 2 s (Alan, Derek d 1989), 2 da (Angela, Jane); m 2, 1986, Ann, *née* Johnson; 1 step s (Christopher), 1 step da (Sabrina); *Career* former posts HM Dip Serv in Dublin, Ottawa, Colombo, NY, Caracas, FCO London; high cmmr Nassau Bahamas 1983-86, min Lagos 1986-89, Br sr trade cmmr Hong Kong 1989-; *Clubs* Royal Cwlth Soc, Hong Kong; *Style—* Peter Heap, Esq, CMG; 6 Carlisle Mansions, Carlisle Place, London SW1; c/o Foreign and Commonwealth Office, King Charles St, London SW1

HEAPS, Christopher Seymour; s of Capt Christopher Robert Milner Heaps, TD (d 1962), and Peggy Margaret Catherine, *née* Mill (d 1984); *b* 15 Nov 1942; *Educ* Dorking GS, Univ of Exeter (LLB); *m* 14 March 1970, Ann Mary, da of Capt Peter Frederick Dudley Mays, of Dorking; 2 da (Grace b 1973, Elizabeth b 1975); *Career* slr 1967-; ptnr Jaques & Lewis (formerly Jaques & Co) 1971-; pres Holborn Law Soc 1983-84, memb Cncl Law Soc 1985-; memb: TUCC for London 1981-84, London Regnl Passengers Ctee 1984-(dep chm 1985-), Advsy Panel Railway Heritage Tst 1985-; chm Dorking Round Table 1978-79, pres Dorking Deepdene Rotary Club 1986-87, tstee Harrowlands Appeal (Dorking Hosp), govr Parson's Mead Sch Ashtead; Liveryman: Worshipful Co of Curriers 1976, Worshipful Co of Coachmakers and Coach Harness Makers 1985; MCIT 1988; *Books* London Transport Railways Album (1978), Western Region in the 1960's (1981), This is Southern Region Central Division (1982), B R Diary 1968-1977 (1988); *Recreations* transport and transport history; *Style—* Christopher Heaps, Esq; Pinecroft, Ridgeway Rd, Dorking, Surrey RH4 3AP (☎ 0306 881752); 33 Wendron St, Helston, Cornwall; 2 South Square, Gray's Inn, London WC1R 5HR (☎ 071 242 9755, fax 071 405 4464, telex 27938)

HEARD, Peter Graham; CB (1987); s of Sidney Horwood Heard (d 1959), of Devon, and Doris Winifred Heard, *née* Gale, MBE (d 1982); *b* 22 Dec 1929; *Educ* Exmouth GS, Coll of Estate Mgmnt; *m* 1953, Ethne Jean, da of Denys Stanley Thomas (d 1956), of Devon; 2 da (Tessa Jane b 1956, Julie Ann b 1957); *Career* chartered surveyor, Inland Revenue Valuation Office 1950-89; served in: Exeter, Kidderminster, Dudley, Leeds; district valuer Croydon 1971, superintending valuer Head Office 1973-, asst sec Somerset House 1975, superintending valuer Midlands 1978, asst chief valuer Head Office 1978, dep chief valuer Head Office 1983-89, ret 1989; FRICS; *Recreations* cricket, golf, theatre, countryside, walking the dog; *Clubs* MCC, Civil Serv; *Style—* Peter Heard, Esq, CB; Romany Cottage, High St, Lindfield, Sussex (☎ 0444 482095)

HEARD, Steven Philip; s of Brian Sidney Heard (d 1990), and Janet Louise, *née* Thomsett, of Saltwood, nr Hythe, Kent; *b* 29 April 1962; *Educ* Harvey GS Folkestone, Univ of Aston (BSc); *m* 9 May 1987, Sandra Jane, da of Sidney John Hammon; *Career* int athlete 1981-, memb 4 x 400m Relay Team Cwlth Games 1986, winner Euro Indoor 800m The Hague 1989; civil engr Knight Piesold & Partners Consultants 1984-; *Recreations* athletics; *Clubs* Wolverhampton & Bilston Athletic, International Athletes; *Style—* Steven Heard, Esq; Knight Piesold & Partners Consultants, 35/41 Station Rd, Ashford, Kent TN23 1PP (☎ 0233 628951)

HEARLEY, Timothy Michael; s of Maurice James Goodwin Hearley, CBE (d 1975); *b* 10 March 1942; *Educ* Malvern, Lincoln Coll Oxford (MA); *m* 1966, Pauline Muriel, *née* Dunn; 3 s (Philip Michael b 1967, James Paul b 1970, Richard Matthew b 1973); *Career* chm: The Beaver Group Ltd, CH Industrials plc, Rolfe and Nolan Computer Servs plc, Tickford Ltd; dir: Westbury plc, Interbrand Group plc, Commercial Holdings Ltd, Protea Commercial Properties Ltd; memb Soc of Investmt Analysts; memb Stock Exchange; *Recreations* tennis, piano, ballet, theatre; *Clubs* Reform; *Style—* Timothy Hearley, Esq; Rush Leys, 4 Birds Hill Rise, Oxshott, Surrey (☎ 037284 2506); CH Industrials plc, 33 Cavendish Sq, London W1M 9HF (☎ 071 491 7860, telex 266498)

HEARN, Clive Lennard; s of Lennard Clarence Hearn (d 1981), of London, and Doris Susannah, *née* Goodwin (d 1977); *b* 8 July 1926; *Educ* Collegiate Sch London; *m* 1 Sept 1951, Audrey Elizabeth, da of Capt Edward John Smith (d 1972), of London; 2 s (Andrew b 1956, Jonathan b 1967), 1 da (Karen b 1953); *Career* CA; dir: George Carter Ltd 1962-, Alfred Booth and Co Ltd 1965-81, Hazel Heath Homes Ltd 1984-, Maulden Homes Ltd 1988-; treas Cuffley Free Church 1960-81; govr: Stormont Sch Potters Bar 1962-, Lochinver House Sch Potters Bar 1966-; *Recreations* cricket, football; *Clubs* City Pickwick, Reform, Hove, MCC, Sussex CCC; *Style—* Clive Hearn, Esq; 15 The Ridgeway, Cuffley, Potters Bar, Herts EN6 4AY (☎ 0707 873084); 30 Market Place, Hitchin, Herts SG5 1DT (☎ 0462 437117/8)

HEARN, Donald Peter; s of Peter James Hearn, and Anita Margaret Hearn; *b* 2 Nov 1947; *Educ* Clifton, Selwyn Coll Cambridge; *m* 21 July 1973, Rachel Mary Arnold; 2 da (Emma b 1975, Sarah b 1977); *Career* Ernst & Young 1969-79, gp fin controller Saga Holidays 1979-83, chief fin offr Lee Valley Water Co 1983-86, sec Royal Horticultural Soc 1989- (fin dir 1986); Gen Cmmr of Taxes, govr Woldingham Sch; *Style—* Donald Hearn, Esq; The Royal Horticultural Society, 80 Vincent Square, London SW1P 2PE

HEARN, Hon Mrs (Kathleen Gertrude); *née* O'Grady; only child of 6 Viscount Guillamore (d 1927); *b* 21 April 1914; *m* 1945, Capt Geoffrey Hearn, Somersetshire LI; 1 s; *Career* late Junior Com ATS; *Style—* The Hon Mrs Hearn; Badgers Mount, Bottle Square Lane, Radnage, Bucks

HEARN, Stephen Robert; s of (Robert) Andrew Hearn, of Hill Farm, Gainfield, Buckland, Faringdon, Oxon, and Caroline Mary, *née* Warner; *b* 30 Jan 1970; *Educ* Burford Sch and Community Coll, Wye Coll London; *Career* target archer; memb: Royal Military Coll of Science Archery Club 1980-84, Buscot Park Archery Club 1984-; winner various nat jr titles 1983-87, nat champion 1989 (jr champion 1987); maj appearances: Grand Prix de Roma 1990, Grand Prix Dusseldorf 1990, Euro & Med Target Championships Barcelona 1990 (Jr Championships Luxembourg 1987); *Style—* Stephen Hearn, Esq; Hill Farm, Gainfield, Buckland, Faringdon, Oxon SN7 8QJ (☎ 036787 660)

HEARNE, Graham James; CBE; s of Frank Hearne, and Emily, *née* Shakespeare; *b* 23 Nov 1937; *Educ* George Dixon GS Birmingham; *m* 1961, Carol Jean, *née* Brown; 1 s, 3 da; *Career* admitted slr 1959, practised law in UK and USA 1959-67; exec Industl Reorgn Corpn 1967-70, exec dir N M Rothschild and Sons Ltd 1970-77, fin dir Courtaulds 1977-81, chief exec Tricentrol 1981-83, gp md Carless Capel and Leonard plc 1983-84, chief exec Enterprise Oil plc 1984-; *Clubs* Reform, MCC; *Style—* Graham Hearne Esq, CBE; 8 Church Row, London NW3 6UT (☎ 071 794 4987); One Hook Lane, Bosham, Chichester, W Sussex PO18 8EY (☎ 0243 572351); Enterprise Oil plc, 5 Strand, London WC2N 5HR (☎ 071 930 1212, fax 071 930 0321, telex 8950611)

HEARNE, John Michael; s of Reginald Hearne (d 1974), of Ipplepen, Devon and Mary Rachel, *née* Rees; *b* 19 Sept 1937; *Educ* Torquay GS, St Luke's Coll Exeter, Univ Coll of Wales Aberystwyth (BMus, MMus); *m* 6 July 1974, Margaret Gillespie, da of Archibald Jarvie, of Glasgow; *Career* teacher Tónlistarskóli Borgarfjardar (Rural Music Sch) Iceland 1968-69, lectr Aberdeen Coll of Educn 1970-87; composer, singer (bass-baritone) and conductor; compositions incl: Piano Sonata 1968, Piano Trio 1981, Songs and Choral Music, String Quartet 1971, Triduum (Festival Oratorio) 1982, Channel Firing 1979, The Four Horsemen (brass, percussion) 1985; Trumpet Concerto (BBC Scot Cmmn) 1990, self publishing Longship Music; performances incl: reader in Sincerely Edvard Grieg (compilation of Grieg's letters, songs, piano music), regular concert appearances in Scot, conductor Stonehaven and Dist Choral Soc; chm: Scot Soc of Composers, Aberdeen branch ISM, Aberdeen Scandinavian Soc, Scot Music Advsy Ctee BBC; memb Lions Club Garioch; *Recreations* classic motoring - 1954 Daimler Conquest Roadster; *Style—* John Hearne, Esq; Smidskot, Fawells, Keith-Hall, Inverurie, Aberdeenshire AB5 0LN (☎ 0651 82274); Longship Music, Smidskot, Fawells, Keithhall, Inverurie AB51 0LN (☎ 0651 82274)

HEARNE, Peter Ambrose; s of Dr Arthur Ambrose Hearne (d 1976), of Anecourt, Stony Hill, Jamaica, and Helen Mackay, *née* Noble (d 1981); *b* 14 Nov 1927; *Educ* Tonstall Sch Sunderland, Sherborne, Loughborough Coll (DLC), Coll of Aeronautics Cranfield (MSc); *m* 19 April 1952, Georgine Gordon; da of Alexander Gordon Guthrie (d 1986), of Farningham, Kent; 3 s (Patrick Gordon b 7 June 1956, Mark Alexander b 3 Feb 1958, Charles Peter Garrett b 24 May 1962); *Career* aerodynamicist Saunders Roe IOW 1946-47, Ops Devpt Unit BOAC 1949-54, helicopter project engr BEA 1954-58, mangr Guided Weapons Div Elliott Bros 1959, asst gen mangr Guided Flight Group Elliott 1960-65, dir and gen mangr Elliot Flight Automation (subsequently GEC Avionics) 1965-66, md GEC Avionics 1966-67, pres (Us Ops) GEC Marconi 1990- (asst md 1967-90); pres: Royal Aeronautical Soc 1980, Cranfield Soc 1979-87; FEng 1984, hon fell Aeronautical Soc 1990; *Recreations* gliding, flying, model railways; *Clubs* Surrey & Hants Gliding, Aero Club Alpin, Southwold Sailing; *Style—* Peter Hearne, Esq; 108 Quay St, Alexandria, Virginia, 22314 USA (☎ 703 549 3871); 1111 Jefferson Davis Highway, Suite 800, Arlington, VA 22202 USA (☎ 703 553 5582, 703 553 0274)

HEARSE, Prof David James; s of James Read Hearse (d 1974), of Holt, Wilts, and Irene Annetta, *née* Nokes (d 1982); *b* 3 July 1943; *Educ* John Willmott GS, Univ of Wales (BSc, PhD, DSc); *Career* instr in pharmacology New York Univ Med Centre 1968-70, res fell Br Heart Fndn Imperial Coll London 1970-76, hon sr lectr St Thomas's Hosp Med Sch 1976-86, prof of cardio vascular biochemistry United Med and Dental Schs Guys Hosp and St Thomas's Hosp, dir cardiovascular res The Rayne Inst St Thomas Hosp; author of 8 books and over 500 scientific papers in areas of res into heart disease; fell American Coll of Cardiology 1980; memb: RSM, Br Cardiac Soc; *Recreations* furniture, house restoration, photography, carpentry; *Clubs* RSM; *Style*— Prof David Hearse; Cardiovascular Res, Rayne Inst, St Thomas' Hosp, London SE1 (☎ 071 928 9292 ext 2990)

HEARSEY, David Glen; s of Leonard Walter Hearsey (d 1985), of London, and Gwenda Kathleen, *née* Taylor; *b* 7 Feb 1948; *Educ* Willesden Coll of Tech; *m* 23 Dec 1972 (m dis 1987); 1 s (Lee James b 26 Sept 1979), 1 da (Sophie Jane b 28 Sept 1976); *Career* David Glen Assocs (consulting engrs): fndr 1969, ptnr 1970, sr ptnr 1980-; sr ptnr Glen Leasing 1981-86; conslt engr in respect of over 300 major construction projects worldwide; memb Cons Assoc; Freeman City of London 1973, Liveryman Worshipful Co of Plumbers; MRSH 1970, MIP 1972, TEng CEI 1972, AMI Mun BM 1979, MSAME 1980; *Recreations* offshore sailing, skiing, shooting, golf, squash, tennis, chess, fishing; *Clubs* City Livery; *Style*— David Hearsey, Esq; David Glen Assocs Consulting Engineers, 2 Princess Lane, Ruislip, Middx HA4 8LE (☎ 0895 638007, fax 0895 679121)

HEARST, Stephen; CBE (1979); s of Dr Emanuel Hirschtritt (d 1962), of Harley St, London, and Claire Hearst (d 1980); *b* 6 Oct 1919; *Educ* Rainer Gymnasium Vienna, Vienna Univ Med Faculty, Univ of Reading, Brasenose Coll Oxford (MA); *m* 17 July 1948, Lisbeth Edith, da of Dr Ludwig Neumann (d 1979), of Haifa, Israel; 1 s (David Andrew b 1954), 1 da (Daniela Carol (Mrs Pountney) b 1951); *Career* joined Pioneer Corps 1940, Corpl Home Serv 1940-42, cmmnd 1943, served N Africa 1943, Beach Landing Bde 5 Army Salerno Landing 1943, posted Allied Mil Govt 1944 (served Florence, Bologna and Piacenza), Capt 1945, camp cmdt POW Camps Palestine 1945, demobbed 1946; BBC TV: newsreel writer 1952, trainee prodr 1952-53, writer for Richard Dimbleby documentaries 1953-55, documentary writer and prodr 1955-64, exec prodr arts programmes 1965-67, head of arts features 1967-71; controller BBC Radio 3 1972-78, controller Future Policy Gp BBC 1978-82, dir Orsino Prodns 1980-, special advsr to Dir-Gen BBC 1982-86; visiting fell Inst for the Advanced Study of the Humanities Univ of Edinburgh 1988; memb BAFTA; FRSA 1980; *Books* 2000 Million Poor (1965), The Third Age of Broadcasting (jtly, 1984); *Recreations* reading, gardening, swimming, golf; *Style*— Stephen Hearst, Esq, CBE; The British Academy of Film and Television Arts, 195 Piccadilly, London SW1

HEARTH, John Dennis Miles; CBE (1983); s of Cyril Howard Hearth, MC (d 1973), of Leicester, and Pauline Kathleen, *née* O'Flanagan (d 1989); *b* 8 April 1929; *Educ* The King's Sch Canterbury, Brasenose Coll Oxford (MA); *m* 1959, Pamela Anne, da of Arthur Gilbert Bryant, MC (d 1966), of Speldhurst, Kent; 2 s (Jonathan, Dominic), and 1 s decd; *Career* Nat Serv Intelligence Corps 1947-49; admin offr Overseas Civil Serv Br Solomon Islands Protectorate 1953-60, ed Fairplay Shipping Journal Fairplay Pubns Ltd 1961-66; The Cunard Steamship Co Ltd: special asst 1966-67, gp planning advsr 1967-68, jt ventures dir 1971; chief exec Royal Agric Soc of Eng 1972-89, tstee Rural Housing Tst (village homes for village people) 1988-; chm: Rural Enterprise Unit 1988-, BBC Rural and Agric Affrs Advsy Ctee 1990-; pres Nat Pig Breeders Assoc 1990-91; treas Univ of Warwick 1989- (memb of Ct 1985-); *Recreations* golf, theatre, travel, history; *Clubs* Farmers', Anglo-Belgian; *Style*— John D M Hearth, Esq, CBE; Bayard's, Fenny Compton, nr Leamington Spa, Warwicks CV33 0XY; Arthur Rank Centre, NAC, Stoneleigh, Kenilworth, Warwicks CV8 2LZ (☎ 0203 696969, fax 0203 696900)

HEASLIP, Rear Adm Richard George; CB (1987); s of Eric Arthur Heaslip, and Vera Margaret Heaslip, *née* Bailey (d 1986); *b* 30 April 1932; *Educ* Chichester HS, RN Coll Dartmouth; *m* 1959, Lorna Jean, da of Alfred D Grayston (d 1976), of Canada; 3 s (Edmund b 1960, Christopher b 1964, Paul b 1966), 1 da (Lorna b 1960); *Career* Capt second submarine sqdn 1975-76, CO HMS Conqueror 1971-72, exec offr of first RN nuclear submarine HMS Dreadnought 1965-67, CO HMS Sea Devil 1961-62; NATO Defence Coll Rome 1979-80; dir of Defence Policy MOD 1982-84; asst Chief of Staff Operations SHAPE 1984; ADC 1984; Flag Offr Submarines and NATO COMSUBEASTLANT 1984-87; dir gen English Speaking Union 1987-; chm RN Football Assoc 1977-84; pres London Submarine Old Comrades Assoc 1987; *Recreations* walking, music; *Style*— Rear Adm Richard Heaslip, CB; South Winds, Wallis Rd, Waterlooville, Hants (☎ 0705 241679); Dartmouth House, Charles St, London W1 (☎ 071 493 3328)

HEASMAN, Dr Michael Anthony; s of Alfred Heasman (d 1967), of Colchester, Essex, and Grace Ethel, *née* Woods (d 1970); *b* 9 Sept 1926; *Educ* Felsted, Univ of London St Mary's Hosp (DPH, MRCS, LRCP); *m* 17 Aug 1948, Barbara Nelly, da of Douglas Pickering Stevens (d 1963), of Taunton, Somerset; 1 s (Robert b 1949), 1 da (Patricia b 1955); *Career* RAF Med Branch Sqdn Ldr 1948-53; med statistician Gen Register Office 1956-61, sr med offr Miny of Health 1961-65, princ med offr Scottish Home & Health Dept 1965-74, dir Scottish Health Serv Info Servs Div 1974-86, hon sr lectr Univ of Edinburgh 1974-86; pubns incl articles on epidemiology and health statistics, expert in health statistics WHO 1967-87; FFCM 1974, FRCPE 1977, FFPHM 1989; *Recreations* hill walking, philosophy of science, literature; *Clubs* RAF; *Style*— Dr Michael Heasman; The Old Granary, 1 Monkrigg Steading, Haddington, East Lothian EH41 4LB

HEATH, Adrian Lewis Ross; s of Percy Charles Petgrave Heath (d 1952), of Monkton House, Monkton Combe, Bath, and Adria, *née* Porter (d 1972); *b* 23 June 1920; *Educ* Bryanston, Slade Sch UCL; *m* 1953, Corinne Elizabeth, da of Charles Jesse Lloyd; 1 s (Damon Lewis b 1955), 1 da (Clio b 1957); *Career* artist; served Bomber Cmd RAF 1940-45 (POW 1942-45); solo exhibitions incl: Musée de' Carcassonne France 1948, Lords Gallery London 1957, Hanover Gallery London 1959, 1960 and 1962, Redfern Galley London 1966, 1973, 1975, 1978, 1981, 1983, 1988, and 1990, Retrospective Exhibition (City Art Gallery Bristol 1971, Graves Art Gallery Sheffield 1972), Compass Gallery Glasgow 1981, Barbizon Gallery Glasgow (with Terry Frost) 1989; numerous gp exhibitions 1951-85 (most recent being Recalling the Fifties at Serpentine Gallery and St Ives, Twenty Five Years of Painting, Sculpture and Pottery at the Tate); pub collections incl: Arts Cncl of NI, Arts Cncl of GB, Br Cncl, Br Museum, Tate Gallery, V & A Museum, Nat Gallery of Victoria Aust, Boston Museum of Fine Arts; visiting lectr: Bath Acad of Art 1956-76, Univ of Reading 1980-85; memb: Art Panel of Arts Cncl 1964-71, Panel of Assessors Nat Cncl for Diplomas in Art and Design, Ctee of Art and Design Cncl Nat Acad Awards 1975-82; judge John Moores Exhibition Liverpool 1967, artist in residence Univ of Sussex 1969; chm London Gp Artists Int Assoc 1954-64 and 1967 and 1976; *Clubs* Beefsteak; *Style*— Adrian Heath, Esq; 28 Charlotte St, London W1P 1HJ (☎ 071 636 1957); Redfern Gallery, 20 Cork St, London W1X 2HL (☎ 071 734 1732/0578, fax 071 494 2908)

HEATH, Bernard Oliver; OBE (1980); s of Bernard Ernest Heath (d 1951), and Ethel May, *née* Sweeting (1981); *b* 8 March 1925; *Educ* Bemrose Sch, Derby Sch, Univ Coll Nottingham (BSc), Imperial Coll of Sci and Technol (DIC); *m* 1948, Ethel, da of Sidney Riley (d 1954); 1 s (Robert b 1951); *Career* Panavia: dir Systems Engineering (Warton) 1969-81, dir Tech Div 1978-81; divnl dir Advanced Engrg Br Aerospace Warton Div 1981-84; chm SBAC Tech Bd 1980-82 (memb 1975-84); prof Br Aerospace Integrated Chair in aeronautical engrg Univ of Salford 1983-89; CEng, FRAeS; *Recreations* military history, history of transport; *Style*— Bernard Heath, Esq, OBE

HEATH, Catherine Judith; da of Samuel Michael Hirsch (d 1976), and Anna, *née* de Boer (d 1980); *b* 17 Nov 1924; *Educ* Hendon Co Sch, St Hilda's Coll Oxford (MA); *m* 19 July 1947 (m dis 1977), Dennis Heath, s of Frederick Heath (d 1958); 1 s (David b 1955), 1 da (Anne b 1953); *Career* novelist, theatre critic; *Books* Stone Walls (1973), The Vulture (1974), Joseph and the Goths (1975), Lady on the Burning Deck (1978), Behaving Badly (1984, TV adaptation 1989); *Recreations* theatre, conversation, walking; *Clubs* PEN, Soc of Authors, Oxford and Cambridge; *Style*— Mrs Catherine Heath; 17 Penarth Ct, Devonshire Ave, Sutton, Surrey SM2 5LA (☎ 081 661 0213)

HEATH, Christopher John; s of Lt-Gen Sir Lewis Macclesfield Heath (d 1954), of Bath, and Katherine Margaret, *née* Lonergan (d 1984); *b* 26 Sept 1946; *Educ* Ampleforth; *m* 14 June 1979, Margaret Joan, da of Col Richard Arthur Wiggin, TD, JP, DL (d 1977), of Ombersley, Worcs; 1 s (William Henry Christopher b 29 April 1983); *Career* commercial asst ICI 1964-69; sales exec George Henderson & Co 1969-75; ptnr Henderson Crosthwaite & Co 1975-84; md Baring Securities Ltd 1984-; memb: Nat Appeals Ctee Cancer Res Campaign, Joy to the World (Save the Children Fund); memb Stock Exchange and TSA; *Recreations* fishing; *Clubs* Turf, Flyfishers'; *Style*— Christopher Heath, Esq; Baring Securities Ltd, Lloyds Chambers, 1 Portsoken St, London E1 8DF (☎ 071 621 1500)

HEATH, David Arthur; s of Richard Arthur Heath, of Chesterfield, and Gladys Heath; *b* 6 Sept 1946; *Educ* Chesterfield Boys GS, Glos Coll of Art and Design (Dip Arch), RIBA; *m* 27 June 1973, Angela Mary, da of late James Joseph Niall Hardy, of Chesterfield; 2 s (Richard b 1978, John b 1980); *Career* architect; ptnr Heath Avery Ptnrship 1980-, dir Heath (Properties) Ltd 1986; Cheltenham Civic award 1987 and 1989 (commendations 1986, and 1987); *Recreations* motor racing, music, reading; *Style*— David Heath, Esq; 11A The Verneys, Old Bath Rd, Cheltenham, Glos (☎ 0242 42066); 17 Imperial Square, Cheltenham, Glos (☎ 0242 529169, fax C 224069)

HEATH, David Michael William; s of Stanley Heath (d 1976), and Lucy May Heath (d 1982); *b* 14 Dec 1931; *Educ* Moseley GS Birmingham; *m* Patricia Ann, da of Eric Money Hazel; 1 s (Martin David b 26 Nov 1958), 3 da (Karen Hazel b 24 July 1961, Susan Patricia b 14 Aug 1965, Jacqeline Ann b 5 July 1969); *Career* cricket administrator; sales and mktg Imperial 1955-86 (latterly gen mangr Lea & Perrins Ltd), gen sec Warwickshire CCC 1986-; pres Moseley CC; chm: Birmingham and Dist Cricket League (pres 1988), Warwicks Old County Cricketers' Assoc, Cricket Ctee NCA; former cricket player: 10 first class appearances Warwickshire CCC (debut v Surrey 1949), RAF and Combined Servs 1951-52, Capt Moseley CC 1956-59, capt Birmingham & Dist Cricket League Rep XI; *Style*— David Heath, Esq; Secretary, c/o Warwickshire County Cricket Club, County Ground, Edgbaston, Birmingham B5 7QU (☎ 021 446 4422, fax 021 446 4544)

HEATH, David William St John; CBE (1989); s of Eric William Heath of Street, Somerset, and Pamela Joan *née* Bennett; *b* 16 March 1954; *Educ* Millfield Sch, St John's Coll Oxford (MA), The City Univ; *m* 15 May 1987, Caroline Marie Therese da of Harry Page Netherton, of Alicante, Spain; 1 da (Bethany b 31 March 1988); *Career* optician; memb: Somerset CC 1985 (ldr 1985-89), Nat Exec Lib Pty 1986-87, Fed Exec Lib Democrats 1989-; parly conslt to Worldwide Fund for Nature 1990; *Recreations* rugby football, cricket, pig-breeding; *Clubs* Nat Lib; *Style*— David Heath, CBE, Esq; 34, The Yard, Witham Friary, Nr Frome, Somerset (☎ 074 985 458); County Hall, Taunton, Somerset (☎ 0823 255065, fax 0823 255 258, telex 46682)

HEATH, Rt Hon Edward Richard George; MBE (1946), PC (1955), MP (C) Bexley Sidcup 1974-; s of late William George Heath and his 1 w Edith Annie, *née* Pantony; the family has been traced back in a continuous male line to one William Heath, of Cliston in Blackawton, Devon (d 1546); Mr Heath's f was a builder, his gf a railwayman, his ggf a merchant seaman, his gggf a coastguard, his ggggf a mariner; *b* 9 July 1916; *Educ* Chatham House Sch Ramsgate, Balliol Coll Oxford; *Career* served WWII RA (Maj 1945, despatches); Lt-Col cmdg 2 Regt HAC (TA) 1947-51; Master Gunner within the Tower of London, 1951-54; admin civil service 1946-47, worked in journalism and merchant banking 1947-50; MP (C) Bexley 1950-74, oppn leader 1965-70 and 1974-75, PM 1970-74; asst oppn whip 1951, lord cmmr Treasury 1951, jt dep chief whip 1952, dep chief whip 1953-55, parly sec Treasy and govt chief whip 1955-59, min Labour 1959-60, lord privy seal with FO responsibilities (negotiating UK entry EEC) 1960-63, sec state Indust, Trade, Regnl Devpt and pres BOT 1963-64; memb of Ind Cmmn on Int Devpt Issues (the Brandt Cmmn 1977-80 Advisory Ctee), chm IRIS 1981-83; chm LSO Tst 1963-70 (memb 1974-), vice pres Bach Choir 1970-, pres EEC Youth Orch 1977-, hon memb LSO 1974-; lectures: Godkin at Harvard 1968, Cyril Foster Meml Oxford 1965, Montagu Burton Leeds 1976, Edge Princeton 1976, Romanes Oxford 1976, Ishizaka Japan 1979, Felix Neubergh Gothenburg 1979, 10 STC Communication London 1980, Noel Buxton Univ of Essex 1980, Alastair Buchan Meml London 1980; Hoover Univ of Strathclyde 1980; Stanton Griffs Disting, Cornell Univ 1981; Edwin Stevens, RSM, 1981; William Temple, York 1981; City of London, Chartered Insce Inst 1982; John Findley Green, Westminster Coll, Missouri 1982; Mizuno, Tokyo, 1982; ITT European, Brussels, 1982; Bruce Meml, Univ of Keele 1982; Gaitskell, Univ of Nottingham 1983; Trinity Univ, San Antonio 1983; lectr to mark opening Michael Fowler Centre, Wellington, NZ 1983; Bridge Meml, Guildhall 1984; David R Calhoun Jr Meml Washington Univ, St Louis 1984; Corbishley Meml RSA 1984; John Rogers Meml Llandudno 1985; George Woodcock, Univ of Leicester 1985; Royal Inst of Int Affairs, Chatham House 1985; Int Peace Lecture, Univ of Manchester 1985; London Business Sch Lecture, Regent's Park 150 Anniversary of the Tamworth Manifesto 1985; 4 Annual John F Kennedy Meml Lectr, Oxford 1986; Employment Inst, Josiah Mason Lectr, Birmingham 1986; The Netherlands Inst for Int Relations 1986; address to both Houses of the Swiss Parliament, Zurich 1986; Lothian Fndn lectr 1987, Maitland, Edward Boyle Meml lectr, Sir John Keswick Meml lectr Southern Methodist Univ Texas 1988, Edward Boyle Meml Lectr Univ of Leeds 1988; visiting Chubb fell Yale 1975, Montgomery fell Dartmouth Coll 1980; Hon: DCL Oxford, DTech Bradford, DCL Kent; Hon Doctorate Sorbonne; hon fell: Balliol Coll Oxford, Queen Mary and Westfield Coll; Nuffield Coll Oxford, Inst of Devpt Studies at Univ of Sussex; hon: FRCM, FRCO, fell Royal Canadian Coll of Organists, Hon DL Westminster Coll Fulton Missouri; Liveryman Worshipful Co of Goldsmiths, Hon Freeman Musicians' Co; *Books* One Nation: A Tory Approach to Social Problems (co-author 1950), Old World, New Horizons (1970), Sailing - A Course of My Life (1975), Music - A Joy for Life (1976), Travels - People and Places in My Life (1977), Carols - The Joy of Christmas (1977); music chm London Symphony Orch Tst 1963-70, 1971 conducted Orch in Elgar's 'Cockaigne' Overture at its gala concert in the Royal Festival Hall London; has since conducted orchestras: in London, Cologne, Bonn; also conducted: Royal Philharmonia Orchestra, Philharmonia, London Sinfonia, Liverpool Philharmonic Orch, Bournemouth Symphony Orch, Bournemouth Sinfonia, the English Chamber Orch, the Thames Chamber Orch and the Sarum Chamber Orch, Berlin Philharmonic Orch, Chicago Symphony Orch, Philadelphia Symphony Orch, Cleveland Symphony Orch, the Minneapolis Symphony Orch, the Grand Teton Festival, the Jerusalem Symphony Orch, The Shanghai Philharmonic Orch, the Beijing Central Symphony Orch, the Swiss-Italian Radio Television Symphony Orch and the Zurich Chamber Orch, Singapore Symphony Orchestra, Leningrad Conservatoire Orch; was instrumental in founding the European Community Youth Orch of which he is pres, and conducted it on its 1978 Easter tour and 1978, 1979 and 1980 Summer tours of Europe. He has also conducted at the World festival of Youth Orchs in Aberdeen in 1977 and 1978 (Freiherr Von Stein Fndn prize; Charlemagne prize 1963, Estes J Kefauver prize 1971; Stresseman Gold medal 1971; Gold medal of City of Paris, 1978; World Humanity award 1980; Gold medal European Parl); sailing (bought ocean racer 'Morning Cloud' 1969, won Sydney to Hobart race 1969, Capt British team Admiral's Cup 1971 and 1979, Capt British team Sardinia Cup 1980), (winner Sydney to Hobart Ocean Race 1969); *Recreations* music, sailing; *Clubs* Royal Yacht Sqdn, Buck's, Carlton, St Stephen's; *Style—* The Rt Hon Edward Heath, MBE, MP; House of Commons, London SW1A 0AA

HEATH, Lady Emma Cathleen; da of 12 Marquess of Queensberry by his 1 w; *b* 13 Sept 1956; *Educ* Middlesex Poly (BA), RCA (MA); *Career* painter; *Style—* The Lady Emma Heath

HEATH, Dr Gordon William; s of Frederick William Heath (d 1971), and Edith Mary, *née* Nelder; *b* 7 Dec 1926; *Educ* Thornbury GS, Univ of Durham (BSc), Univ of London (PhD, CBiol); *m* 2 Aug 1952, Margaret Patricia, da of Aloysius Benjamin Cole (d 1951); 1 s (William b 1964), 3 da (Clare b 1955, Sarah b 1960, Helen b 1963); *Career* res scientist (biologist) Rothamstead Experimental Station 1952-54, 1959-65, Colonial Services (Nyasaland) 1956-59, PSO NERC 1965-78, biol conslt Heath and Ptnrs 1978; contrib numerous sci papers in entomology, soil sci and marine biology; memb Lib Pty Cncl 1982-87 (Nat Exec 1984) with Euro Affrs main political interest, vice chm Lib Pty Agric Panel, chm Devon and Cornwall Lib Pty 1984-87, conslt to Euro Fedn of Lib Democratic and Reform Parties 1987-89; memb Exec Bd Environmental Concern Centre for Europe 1989-; govr and vice chm Plymouth Poly; *Books* incl: Principles of Agricultural Entomology (with C A Edwards, 1964), Future of Man (with J Ebling, 1972), Marine Environment Research (ed, 1980-86); *Style—* Dr Gordon W Heath; 52 Kings Rd, Paignton, Devon TQ32 AW; ELDR European Parliament, 97 Rue Belliard, 1040 Brussels, Belgium

HEATH, (Dennis) Ivan Ewart; s of Joseph Henry Heath (d 1952), of Southend-on-Sea, and Elsie Anne, *née* Moore (d 1943); *b* 20 Nov 1915; *Educ* Sir George Monoux GS, Chelsea Coll of Tech Sci; *m* 16 Oct 1939, da of Albert Henry Wakeling (d 1945), of Leigh-on-Sea; *Career* WWII RAF 1941-46: AC2, LAC, PO 1942, Flying Offr 1943, Flt Lt 1944, Sqdn Ldr 1944; md Perivan Press Ltd 1938, memb Lloyds 1973, jt gp md Williams Lea Gp Ltd 1964-74 (dep gp md 1974-78), ret 1978; hon treas Printers Charitable Corp; Freeman City of London, Liveryman Worshipful Co of Stationers and Newspaper Makers; MInstD 1944; *Recreations* golf; *Clubs* RAF Piccadilly; *Style—* Ivan Heath, Esq; Acres Gate, 18 Woodside, Leigh-on-Sea, Essex SS9 4QU (☎ 0702 525 645)

HEATH, Sir Mark Evelyn; KCVO (1980), CMG (1980); s of Capt John Moore Heath, RN and Hilary Grace Stuart, *née* Salter; *b* 22 May 1927; *Educ* Marlborough, Queens' Coll Cambridge; *m* 1954, Margaret Alice, da of Sir Lawrence Bragg, CH, OBE, MC (d 1971); 2 s (Nicholas, William), 1 da (Clare); *Career* RNV(S)R 1945-48; HM Dip Serv 1950-85, Br ambass to Holy See 1982-85 (upgraded from representation as min which rank held from 1980), inspr FCO 1978-80, head W African Dept FCO and ambass Chad 1975-78, on secondment to Cabinet Office 1974-75, dep head UK Delgn to OECD 1971-74, formerly served Jakarta, Copenhagen, Sofia, Ottawa; dir protocol Hong Kong Govt 1985-88; chm Friends of the Anglican Centre Rome 1984-90; *Clubs* Athenaeum, Nikaean; *Style—* Sir Mark Heath, KCVO, CMG; St Lawrence, Lansdown Road, Bath, Avon BA1 5TD (☎ 0225 428272)

HEATH, Air Marshal Sir Maurice Lionel; KBE (1962, OBE 1946), CB (1957), CVO (1978); s of late H Lionel Heath (princ Mayo Sch of Arts, Lahore, India) and Maggie, *née* Forsyth; *b* 12 Aug 1909; *Educ* Sutton Valence Sch, RAF Coll Cranwell; *m* 1, 1938, Kathleen Mary (d 1988), da of Boaler Gibson, of Bourne Lincs; 1 s (James), 1 da (Julia); m 2, 7 Dec 1989, Lisa, wid of Col J M B Cooke, MC; *Career* joined RAF 1927, served in Nos 16 and 28 Sqdns 1929-32, specialist armament duties 1933-43, OC Bomber Station 5 Gp Bomber Cmd 1944-45 (despatches), dep to Dir Gen Armament Air Miny 1946-48, CO Central Gunnery Sch 1948-49, sr Air Liaison Offr Wellington NZ 1950-52, CO Bomber Cmd Bombing Sch 1952-53, Air Cdre 1953, idc 1954; Dir Gen Plans Air Miny 1955, Dep Air Sec 1955-57; Air Vice-Marshal 1956, Cdr Br Forces Arabian Peninsula 1957-59, Cmdt RAF Staff Coll Bracknell 1959-62, Air Marshal 1962, COS Allied Air Forces Central Europe 1962-65, ret 1965; chief hon steward Westminster Abbey 1964-74, Gentleman Usher to HM The Queen 1966-79 (Extra Gentleman Usher 1979-), dir Boyd and Boyd Estate Agents 1971-76; memb Cncl Offrs Pension Soc 1974-83, KCH appeal dir 1977-79, appeal conslt Voluntary Res Tst KCH 1979-84, private agent Henderson Fin Mgmnt 1980-88, DL W Sussex 1977-84; *Recreations* reading, gardening, travel; *Clubs* RAF; *Style—* Air Marshal Sir Maurice Heath, KBE, CB, CVO; Heronscroft, Rambledown Lane, W Chiltington, Pulborough, W Sussex RH20 2NW (☎ 079 83 2131)

HEATH, (Bryan) Michael; s of (George) Bryan Stevens Heath, of Buckingham, and Euphemia, *née* Wilson; *b* 16 June 1944; *Educ* Keswick Sch, Univ of Manchester (BSc); *m* 4 Dec 1976, Patricia Jane Margaret, da of late Francis Johnston; 1 da (Jane Mary Felicity b 1979); *Career* analyst Esso Petroleum 1965-67, ptnr Arthur Andersen and Co 1977 (joined 1967); *Style—* Michael Heath, Esq; Putney, London SW15; Olney, Bucks; Arthur Andersen & Co, 2 Arundel St, London WC2R 3LT (☎ 071 438 3316, fax 071 831 1133, telex 8812711)

HEATH, Michael Robert; s of George Ernest Heath (d 1988), and Kathleen Mary, *née* Van Der Pant (d 1980); *b* 9 Nov 1937; *Educ* Fernden Sch, Hurstpierpoint Coll; *m* 1, 1967 (m dis 1986), Judith Susan Heath; 3 s (Benjamin Elliot b 28 Nov 1968, Oliver Gideon b 29 April 1970, Samuel Barnaby b 1 Aug 1971); m 2, 1 Sept 1987, Lucinda Rosslyn, da of Frank Arnold Instone of Tunbridge Wells; 1 s (Joshua Joel b 27 Sept 1989); *Career* md Smith New Court plc; memb Stock Exchange; *Recreations* skiing, windsurfing, sub-aqua; *Style—* Michael Heath, Esq; Chetwynd House, 24 St Swithins Lane, London EC4N 8AE (☎ 071 626 1544)

HEATH, Prof Raymond Bartlett; s of Frederick William Heath (d 1930), and Elizabeth Augusta Heath (d 1958); *b* 14 March 1928; *Educ* Royal Masonic Sch, Univ of Sheffield (MB ChB, MD); *m* 1952, Edith, da of Edwin Swift (d 1966); 1 s (David b 1953 d 1978), 1 da (Katherin b 1955); *Career* RAF 1946-48; prof of virology St Bartholomews Hosp 1975-90 (sr lectr 1960-74); memb Soc Gen Microbiology; memb RSM, MRCPath; *Books* Modern Trends in Virology (co-ed, vol 1 1967, vol 2 1970), Virus Diseases (ed, 1979), Virus Diseases and the Skin (1983); *Recreations* golf, gardening, birdwatching; *Clubs* Athenaeum; *Style—* Prof Raymond Heath; The Cottage, Leybourne Rd, Broadstairs, Kent (☎ 0843 61618); Dept of Virology, St Bartholomew's Hospital, London EC1A 7BE (☎ 071 601 7351)

HEATH, Samuel Bonython; s of Denis William Heath (d 1983), of S Australia, and Ada Bray, *née* Bonython (d 1988); *b* 11 Feb 1938; *Educ* Rugby; *m* 1, 11 Feb 1961 (m dis 1978), Jill, da of Philip Brandon Angas Parsons; 2 s (Guy Samuel b 12 Dec 1961, Christopher Angas b 24 June 1963), 1 da (Stephanie Ann b 17 Jan 1965); m 2, 1981, Bobbi, da of Thomas Cruickshanks; 2 step da (Bobbi b 29 Nov 1972, Shona b 24 May 1974); *Career* Nat Service cmmn RAF 1956-58; chm and md Samuel Heath & Sons plc 1970- (dir 1961, jt md 1963-70); *Recreations* travel, languages, jazz; *Style—* Samuel Heath, Esq; c/o Samuel Heath & Sons plc, Leopold St, Birmingham B12 0UJ (☎ 021 772 2303, fax 021 772 3334, telex 336908)

HEATH-STUBBS, John Francis Alexander; OBE (1989); s of Francis Heath-Stubbs (d 1938), and Edith Louise Sara, *née* Marr (d 1972); *b* 9 July 1918; *Educ* Bembridge Sch, Worcester Coll for the Blind, Queen's Coll Oxford (BA, MA); *Career* English master The Hall Sch Hampstead 1944, ed asst Hutchinsons 1944-45, Gregory fell in poetry Univ of Leeds 1952-55, visiting prof of English Univ of Ann Arbor Michigan 1960-61, lectr in English Coll of St Mark & St John Chelsea 1962-72, non-stipendary lectr Merton Coll Oxford 1972-; Queen's medal for Poetry 1973; memb: English Assoc, Folklore Soc, Poetry Soc, Omar Khayyam Soc (pres 1989-90); FRSL; *Style—* John Heath-Stubbs, Esq, OBE; 22 Artesian Road, London W2

HEATHCOAT AMORY, Sir Ian; 6 Bt (UK 1874), of Knightshayes Court, Tiverton, Devon; JP, DL (Devon 1981); s of Sir William Heathcoat Amory, 5 Bt, DSO (d 1982), by his w Margaret, da of Col Sir Arthur Doyle, 4 Bt, JP (d 1948); *b* 3 Feb 1942; *Educ* Eton; *m* 1972, Frances Louise, da of Jocelyn Francis Brian Pomeroy (ggs of 4 Viscount Harberton); 4 s; *Heir* s, William Francis Heathcoat Amory b 19 July 1975; *Style—* Sir Ian Heathcoat-Amory, Bt, JP, DL; Calverleigh Court, Tiverton, Devon

HEATHCOAT-AMORY, Hon Mrs (Angela Jane); *née* Borwick; eldest da of 4 Baron Borwick, MC, *qv*; *b* 12 July 1955; *Educ* St David's Convent; *m* 1988, Charles William Heathcoat-Amory, 2 s of Sir William Heathcoat-Amory, 5 Bt, DSO (d 1982); *Career* trainer of competition horses; *Style—* The Hon Mrs Heathcoat-Amory; Pound House, Krowstone, South Molton, Devon

HEATHCOAT-AMORY, David Philip; MP (C) Wells 1983-; s of Brig Roderick Heathcoat Amory, and Sonia Heathcoat Amory; *b* 21 March 1949; *Educ* Eton, ChCh Oxford (MA); *m* 1978, Linda Adams; 2 s, 1 da; *Career* CA, asst fin dir Br Technol Gp 1980-83; contested (C) Brent S 1979, PPS to Home Sec 1987-88, asst whip 1988-89; Parly Under Sec of State: DOE 1989-90, Dept of Energy 1990-; FCA; *Recreations* walking, talking; *Style—* David Heathcoat-Amory, Esq, MP; House of Commons, London SW1

HEATHCOAT-AMORY, Hon Mrs (Margaret Irene Gaenor); JP (1968); da of 8 Baron Howard de Walden (d 1945); *b* 2 June 1919; *Educ* Benenden; *m* 1938, Richard Frank Heathcoat-Amory, s of Lt Col Harry William Ludovic Heathcoat-Amory (d 1945); 1 s, 2 da; *Career* Parly candidate (L) contested Taunton 1964 and 1966; *Style—* The Hon Mrs Heathcoat-Amory, JP; Hele Manor, Exebridge, Dulverton, Somerset TA22 9RN (☎ 0398 23307)

HEATHCOAT-AMORY, Margaret, Lady; Margaret Isabella Dorothy Evelyn; yr da of Sir Arthur Doyle, 4 Bt, JP, sometime ADC to Prince Edward of Saxe Weimar, by his w Joyce, da of Hon Greville Howard (himself 2 s of 17 Earl of Suffolk and (10 of) Berkshire); *b* 1907; *Educ* privately; *m* 1933, Lt-Col Sir William Heathcoat-Amory, 5 Bt, DSO (d 1982), sometime memb Queen's Bodyguard of Hon Corps of Gentlemen-at-Arms; 2 s (6 Bt, Ian), 2 da (Mrs Peter Sichel, Mrs David Cavender); *Style—* Margaret, Lady Heathcoat-Amory; 14 Pomeroy Rd, Tiverton, Devon (☎ 0884 254033)

HEATHCOAT-AMORY, Michael FitzGerald; only s of Maj Edgar Heathcoat-Amory (gs of Sir John Heathcoat-Amory, 1 Bt, JP, DL), by his w Sonia, da of Capt Edward Conyngham Denison, MVO, RN (whose f Henry was s of 1 Baron Londesborough by his 2 w, and half-bro of 1 Earl of Londesborough); *b* 2 Oct 1941; *Educ* Eton, Christ Church Oxford; *m* 1, 1965 (m dis 1970), Harriet Mary Sheila, da of Lt-Gen Sir Archibald Nye, GCSI, GCMG, GCIE, KCB, KBE, MC (d 1967); 1 s (Edward); m 2, 1975, Arabella, da of late Raimund von Hofmannstahl, and formerly w of Piers de Westenholz; 2 da (Lucy, Jessica); *Career* md Jupiter Tarbutt Merlin Ltd, farmer; chm London and Devonshire Tst; High Sheriff of Devon 1985-86; *Clubs* Whites, Pratts; *Style—* Michael Heathcoat-Amory, Esq; Chevithorne Barton, Tiverton, Devon; 2 Montrose Court, London SW7

HEATHCOTE, Brig Sir Gilbert Simon; 9 Bt (GB 1733), CBE (Mil 1964, MBE 1945); s of Lt-Col Robert E M Heathcote, DSO (d 1969), of Manton Hall, Rutland (he was gggs of Sir Gilbert Heathcote, 3 Bt, MP, who was gs of Sir Gilbert Heathcote, 1 Bt, one of the originators of the Bank of England and Lord Mayor of London 1711, also bro of Samuel, ancestor of Heathcote, Bt of Hursley), and Edith Millicent Heathcote (d 1977); suc kinsman, 3 Earl of Ancaster, 8 Bt, KCVO, TD, JP, DL, who d 1983; *b* 21 Sept 1913; *Educ* Eton; *m* 1, 1939 (m dis 1984), Patricia Margaret, da of Brig James Leslie, MC, of Sway, Hants; 1 s, 1 da; m 2, 1984, Ann Mellor, widow of Brig J F C Mellor, DSO, OBE; *Heir* s, Mark Simon Robert Heathcote, *qv*; *Career* 2 Lt RA 1933, served WWII NW Europe, Lt-Col 1953, Brig 1960, COS Mid E Cmd 1962-64, Brig RA Scottish Cmd 1964-66, ret 1966; *Recreations* sailing, skiing, equitation; *Clubs* Garrick, Army and Navy, Royal Yacht Squadron; *Style—* Brig Sir Gilbert S Heathcote, Bt, CBE; The Coach House, Tillington, nr Petworth, Sussex

HEATHCOTE, Mark Simon Robert; OBE (1988); s and h of Brig Sir Gilbert Simon Heathcote, 9 Bt, CBE, *qv*, and Patricia Margaret, Lady Heathcote, *née* Leslie, *qv*; *b* 1 March 1941; *Educ* Eton, Magdalene Coll Cambridge (BA); *m* 1976, Susan, da of Lt Col George Ashley, of Torquay (d 1963); 2 s (Alastair b 1977, Nicholas b 1979); *Career* Peninsular and Orient Steamship Co 1963-70; Dip Serv; first sec: Athens, Buenos Aires, Islamabad; *Recreations* water sports; *Style—* M S R Heathcote, Esq, OBE; c/o Upton Dean, Upton, nr Andover, Hants; Foreign and Commonwealth Office, London SW1

HEATHCOTE, Sir Michael Perryman; 11 Bt (GB 1733); s of Sir Leonard Vyvyan Heathcote, 10 Bt (d 1963); in remainder to the Earldom of Macclesfield; *b* 7 Aug 1927; *Educ* Winchester, Clare Coll Cambridge; *m* 2 June 1956, Victoria, da of Cdr James Edward Rickards Wilford, RD, RNR, of Ackland Cottage, Shirley Holms, Lymington, Hants; 2 s, 1 da; *Heir* s, Timothy Heathcote; *Career* 2 Lt 9 Lancers; farmer; *Style—* Sir Michael Heathcote, Bt; Warborne Farm, Boldre, Lymington, Hants (☎ 0590 673478)

HEATHCOTE, Michael Ryley; s of Col Lewis Heathcote, DL (d 1975), of York; *b* 23 Sept 1934; *Educ* Felsted; *m* 1961, Sally, da of Gilbert Burton (d 1975), of Brough, E Yorks; 4 children; *Career* corporate financier; former dir: Allied Plant Gp plc, Allied Residential plc, London and Foreign Investmt Tst plc; chm Humberside Industl Tst Ltd and Wightwood Industs Ltd; *Recreations* cricket; *Clubs* MCC, Farmers', Lloyds; *Style—* Michael Heathcote, Esq; Westgate House, North Cave, E Yorks HU15 2NJ (☎ 043 02 2481)

HEATHCOTE, Dr (Frederick) Roger; s of Frederic William Trevor Heathcote, of 6 Adrian Croft, Moseley, Birmingham, and Kathleen Annie, *née* Muckley; *b* 19 March 1944; *Educ* Bromsgrove Sch, Univ of Birmingham (BSc, PhD); *m* 1, 26 Sept 1970 (m dis 1986), Geraldine Nixon; m 2, 20 Dec 1986, Mary Campbell Syme Dickson; 1 s (David Frederic b 9 Jan 1988), 1 step da (Sarah Louise Campbell Cragg b 21 Feb 1984); *Career* res assoc Univ of Birmingham 1969-70; civil servant; Miny of Technol and DTI: joined 1970 as asst princ Oil Div 4, admin trainee 1971, transfd to Tariff Div 2 (a) 1971, higher exec offr (a) 1972, private sec to Sec (Industl Devpt) 1973; Dept of Energy: private sec to Perm Under Sec of State 1974, princ 1974, transfd to Offshore Technol Branch 1975 (sec Offshore Energy Technol Bd), asst sec Offshore Technol Unit 1978, transfd to Branch 1 Petroleum Engrg Div 1981, transfd to Branch 2 Gas Div 1982, transfd to Branch 1 Electricity Div 1984, transfd to Branch 3 Establishment and Fin Div 1987, promoted to Grade 4 and appointed dir of resource mgmnt

Establishment and Fin Div 1988, promoted to Grade 3 and appointed head of Coal Div 1989; *Recreations* reading, gardening, painting; *Style—* Dr Roger Heathcote; Department of Energy, 1 Palace St, London SW1E 5HE (☎ 071 238 3209, fax 071 238 3481)

HEATHCOTE, Timothy Gilbert; s and h of Sir Michael Perryman Heathcote, 11 Bt; *b* 25 May 1957; *Style—* Timothy Heathcote, Esq

HEATHER, Kenneth Thomas; s of Capt Thomas William Heather, MC (d 1968), and Marjorie, *née* Williams (d 1977); *b* 29 May 1921; *Educ* Uppingham, Jesus Coll Cambridge (BA, MA); *m* 12 June 1954, (Constance) Olive, da of James Findlay (d 1968); 1 s (Peter b 1958), 1 da (Kaeren b 1960); *Career* WWII service: Lt (Special Branch) RNVR 1945, trg HMS Victory, temp Sub Lt (Special Branch) RNVR 1942-43, HMS Belfast Russian Convoys NW Approaches, HMS Faulkner (8 Destroyer Flotilla) 1943, Salerno and Anzio landings Invasion of Sicily, HMS Grenville (25 Destroyer Flotilla) 1944, D Day Landings, Br Pacific Fleet land posting Sydney and Hong Kong 1945-46, demobbed 1947; GEC Res Laboratories Wembley 1947-49 (responsible for first radio-TV link, London to Birmingham), asst mangr Special Projects GEC Head Office 1950-60, sales mangr Elliott Automation & Tally Ltd 1960-71; Pragma Ltd: dir 1971-79, chm and md 1979-88, ret and sold co 1988; Freeman City of London, Liveryman Worshipful Co of Playing Card Makers; CEng 1960, MBIM 1965, MIEE; *Recreations* DIY, rambling; *Clubs* Naval; *Style—* Kenneth Heather, Esq; 33 Westbury Road, Northwood, Middx (☎ 09274 23474)

HEATHER, Stanley Frank; CBE (1980); s of Charles Heather (d 1954), of Ilford, Essex, and Jessie, *née* Powney (d 1953); *b* 8 Jan 1917; *Educ* privately, Downhills Sch, Univ of London; *m* 11 March 1946, Janet Roxburgh (Bunty) (d 1989), da of William Adams (d 1951), of 2 Croft Park, Craigie, Perth, Scotland; 1 s (Gerald Roxburgh b Jan 1949), 1 da (Gillean Alison Elsie b Aug 1951); *Career* WWII 1939-45, cmmnd RAC 1941, served Burma and India; admitted slr 1959; in private practice Horsham 1959-63, legal advsr City of London Police Force 1974-80, comptroller and city slr Corp of London 1974-80 (dep comptroller 1968-74, asst slr 1963-68); as comptroller was hon slr to: Museum of London, City Arts Tst, City Educnl Tsts Fund, City Archaeological Tst Fund, Sir WM Coxon Tst Fund, William Lambe Charity (also tstee), Sir John Langham Tst Fund, The Wilson Tst, Leonidas Alcibiades Oldfield Charity, The City Almshouse Charities; attorney and gen counsel to City of London (Arizona) Corp; Freeman City of London 1965, Liveryman Worshipful Co of Slrs 1965; Hon Liveryman Worshipful Co of: Clothworkers, Engrs 1983; FRSA 1981; *Recreations* golf, fishing; *Clubs* City Livery, Guildhall; *Style—* S F Heather, Esq, CBE; 71 Rosehill, Billingshurst, West Sussex RH14 9QQ (☎ 0403 783981)

HEATLEY, Dr (Richard) Val; s of Walter Russell Heatley, of Greenclose, Pitmans Lane, Morcombe Lake, Bridport, Dorset and Constance Marjorie, *née* Davis; *b* 11 Oct 1947; *Educ* Latymer Upper Sch, Welsh Nat Sch of Med (MB BCh, MD); *m* 5 May 1979, Ruth Mary, da of William Elderkin, of 5 Romway Close, Shepshed, Leics; 2 s (Richard Piers b 1986, Matthew Connel b 1987), 2 da (Kirsteen Ruth b 1980, Francine Mary b 1982); *Career* clinical fell Sr Res Dept of Med Univ of McMaster Hamilton Ontario 1978-80, sr lectr in med Welsh Nat Sch of Med and conslt physician Univ Hosp of Wales 1981-82, sr lectr in med Univ of Leeds 1982-, conslt physician St James's Univ Hosp Leeds 1982-; memb: Br Soc of Gastroenterology and Immunology, Bd Gut and Aliment Pharmacology and Therapeutics, Int Union of Nutritional Sci's Ctee for Nutrition and Immunology; FRCP; *Books* Constipation, Piles and Other Bowel Diseases (1984), Nutrition in Gastroenterology (1986), Campylobacter pylori and Gastroduodenal Disease (1989); *Recreations* children, music, travel, walking; *Style—* Dr Val Heatley; Dept Medicine, St James's Univ Hospital, Leeds LS9 7TF (☎ 0532 433144)

HEATLY, Sir Peter; CBE (1971), DL (1984); s of Robert Heatly (d 1968), of Edinburgh, and Margaret Ann, *née* Sproull (d 1955); *b* 9 June 1924; *Educ* Leith Acad, Edinburgh Univ (BSc); *m* 1, 3 April 1948, (Jean) Robertha Johnston (d 1979), da of William Brown Hermiston, of Ashley Grange, Balerno, Edinburgh; 2 s (Peter Hermiston b 20 Aug 1955, Robert Johnston b 31 Aug 1958), 2 da (Ann May b 27 May 1949, Jane Margaret b 9 May 1951); m 2, 7 Dec 1984, Mae Calder Cochrane, OBE; *Career* lectr in civil engrg Univ of Edinburgh 1947-50; md Peter Heatly & Co Ltd 1950-; chm: Scottish Sports Cncl 1975-87, Cwlth Games Fedn 1982- (Cwlth Diving Champion: 1950, 1954, 1958); govr Scottish Sports Aid Fndn; Master Mercant Co of Edinburgh 1988-90; convener of trades of Edinburgh 1971-75; FICE; kt 1990; *Recreations* swimming, gardening, travel; *Clubs* New (Edinburgh); *Style—* Peter Heatly, Esq, CBE, DL; Lanrig, Balerno, Edinburgh EH14 7AJ (☎ 031 449 3998); 1 Fidra Court, North Berwick, East Lothian; 17 Elbe St, Leith, Edinburgh (☎ 031 554 3226)

HEATON; *see*: Henniker-Heaton

HEATON, Maj Basil Hugh Philips; MBE; s of Cdr Hugh Edward Heaton, JP, DL (d 1964), and Gwenllian Margaret, *née* Philips, CBE, TD (d 1979); *b* 23 Dec 1923; *Educ* Shrewsbury, Queen's Univ Belfast; *m* 1, 30 June 1955, Bronwyn Margaret Knox (d 1978), da of Capt Bryan Cudworth Halsted Poole (d 1971), of Sydney, NSW; 3 da (Sara Margaret b 28 April 1956, Julia Mary b 2 Aug 1959, Victoria Bronwyn b 5 July 1971 d 1979); m 2, 22 Nov 1979, Jennifer, da of Sir Francis Williams, 8 Bt, of Bodelwyddan; *Career* WWII cmmnd RA 1943, served BLA (landed on D Day); serv: Japan, Hong Kong, Malaya, Korea 1951-53; Staff Coll 1956, ret 1965; landowner and dairy farmer; chm and pres: Flintshire NFU, Flintshire CLA; High Sheriff Flintshire 1971; *Books* A Short History of Rhûal (1987); *Recreations* shooting, fishing; *Style—* Maj Basil Heaton, MBE; Rhual, Mold, Clywd CH7 5DB (☎ 0352 700457)

HEATON, Very Rev Eric William; s of late Robert William Heaton, and late Ella Mabel, *née* Brear; *b* 15 Oct 1920; *Educ* Ermysted's Skipton, Christ's Coll Cambridge (MA); *m* 1951, Rachel Mary, da of late Rev Charles Harold Dodd, CH; 2 s (Jeremy Paul William b 1952, Nicholas Giles b 1968), 2 da (Anne Caroline b 1954, Josephine Charlotte b 1960); *Career* dean of Christ Church Oxford 1979-, pro vice chllr Univ of Oxford 1984-; hon fell: Champlain Coll Univ of Trent Ontario Canada 1973-, St John's Coll Oxford 1979, Christ's Coll Cambridge 1983; *Books* His Servants the Prophets (1949), The Old Testament Prophets (1958, 2 edn 1977), The Book of Daniel (1956), Everday Life in Old Testament Times (1956), Commentary of the Sunday Lessons (1959), The Hebrew Kingdoms (1968), Solomon's New Men (1974); *Style—* The Very Rev Eric Heaton; The Deanery, Christ Church, Oxford OX1 1DP (☎ 0865 276162, office: 0865 276161)

HEATON, Frances Anne; da of John Ferris Whidborne (d 1985), and Marjorie Annie, *née* Maltby (d 1989); *b* 11 Aug 1944; *Educ* Queen Anne's Sch Caversham, Trinity Coll Dublin (BA, LLB); *m* 26 April 1969, Martin Christopher Crispin Heaton, s of Ralph Neville Heaton, CB; 2 s (Mark Christopher Francis b 14 April 1972, Andrew John Ralph b 9 Nov 1974); *Career* called to the Bar Inner Temple 1967; Dept Econ Affrs 1967-70, HM Treasy 1970-80 (seconded S G Warburg & Co Ltd 1977-79), dir Lazard Brothers & Co Ltd 1986- (joined 1980); *Recreations* riding, gardening, bridge; *Style—* Mrs Frances Heaton; Lazard Brothers & Co Ltd, 21 Moorfields, London EC2 (☎ 071 588 2721, fax 071 628 4439)

HEATON, Lady Jane; *née* Butler; da of 6 Marquess of Ormonde, CVO, MC (d 1971); *b* 1925; *m* 1945 (m dis 1952), Lt Peter Heaton, RNVR; 1 s; *Style—* Lady Jane Heaton; La Chapelle St Jean, La Garde Freinet, Var, France

HEATON, Dr Kenneth Willoughby; s of Philip John Heaton (d 1971), of Salisbury, and Anna Stenberg (d 1963); *b* 3 Aug 1936; *Educ* Marlborough, Univ of Cambridge, Middx Hosp Med Sch; *m* 15 July 1961, Susan Tandy, da of Dr Brian Victor O'Connor (d 1968), of Jersey; 2 s (Philip b 1964, John b 1975), 1 da (Jenny b 1962); *Career* res fell Duke Univ Med Center N Carolina 1966-67, reader in med Univ of Bristol 1979- (lectr 1968-72, conslt sr lectr 1972-79), author of numerous pubns on gastrointestinal physiology, disease and nutrition; hon sec RCP Working Party on Dietary Fibre, chm RSM Forum on Food and Health, former chm Div of Med Bristol and Weston Health Dist; cncl memb: Br Soc of Gastroenterology, RSM; memb: Ed Bd of Gut, COMA Panel on Dietary Sugars and Human Disease, Nutrition Soc; memb Assoc of Physicians of GB and I; FRCP 1973; *Books* Bile Salts in Health and Disease (1972), Dietary Fibre: Current Developments of Importance to Health (1978), Dietary Fibre, Fibre-depleted Foods and Disease (contrib, 1985); *Recreations* music, walking; *Style—* Dr Kenneth Heaton; University Department of Medicine, Bristol Royal Infirmary, Bristol BS2 8HW (☎ 0272 282313)

HEATON, Mark Frederick; s of Peter Heaton (d 1965), and Rachael, *née* Frampton; *b* 20 Dec 1951; *m* 1, 24 July 1976 (m dis 1986), Lorna, da of Col Ralph Stewart-Wilson, MC; 2 s (Henry Peter Frederick b 14 April 1980, Oliver James Stewart b 12 Jan 1983); m 2, 18 March 1988, Naomi Claire Helen, *qv*, da of Dr Antony Jarrett; *Career* farmer in Gloucs; ptnr C and M Farms Eastleach Glos; dep chm Leo Burnett Advertising Ltd (joined 1972); chm: Frederick Co Ltd, Lowerfield Rentals Ltd; memb: CLA, Br Field Sports Soc, Racehorse Owners Assoc, Lloyds, BSAC; *Recreations* racing, skiing, shooting; *Clubs* Whites, MCC; *Style—* Mark Heaton, Esq; Manor Farm, Ampney St Mary, Cirencester, Gloucesterhsire GL7 5SP (☎ 028585 1321); 32 Bryanston Square, London W1H 7LS (☎ 071 262 0665); Leo Burnett Ltd, 48 St Martins Lane, London WC2N 4EJ (☎ 071 836 2424, fax 071 829 7026, telex 24243)

HEATON, Naomi Claire Helen; *née* Jarrett; da of Dr Boaz Antony Jarrett, of 43 Strand on the Green, Chiswick, London, and Patricia Evelyn *née* White; *b* 11 Sept 1955; *Educ* Walthamstow Hall Sch for Girls, St Hilda's Coll Oxford (BA); *m* 18 March 1988, Mark Frederick Heaton *qv*; *Career* graduate trainee Leo Burnett Advertising 1977-82, appt Main Bd Saatchi & Saatchi Advertising 1984 (joined 1982), main bd dir Young & Rubicam 1985-86; estab: Manor Properties 1986-, The Frederick Co Ltd 1988-, Lowerfield Rentals Ltd (property rental) 1989-, London Central Portfolio Ltd (investmt property search) 1989-; *Recreations* skiing, horse racing; *Clubs* Boodles; *Style—* Mrs Mark Heaton; 32 Bryanston Square, London W1; Manor Farm, Ampney St Mary, Cirencester, Gloucs (☎ 071 224 5366)

HEATON, Noel Thomas; *Educ* Manchester Coll of Technol; *m* 1, 1946, Sheila Mary, *née* McAndry; 1 da; m 2, 1983, Maria, *née* Kukulska; *Career* dir mktg Wickman Machine Tools UK Ltd 1970-79 (USA 1976-82, France 1976-82, John Brown Machine Tool Div 1980-82), conslt Telford Development Corporation 1982-89, mgmnt and business conslt 1989-; *Recreations* special constabulary (div cmdt Warwicks, ret); *Style—* Noel Heaton Esq; 21 Convent Close, Kenilworth, Warwicks CV8 2FQ (☎ 0926 53598)

HEATON, Roger Lambert; s of Col Benjamin William Heaton, MC, JP, DL (d 1964), of The White Hall, Little Budworth, Cheshire, and Mary Frances, *née* Wood (d 1979); *b* 31 Aug 1929; *Educ* Harrow, Trinity Coll Cambridge (BA); *m* 18 Feb 1965, Nancy Joyce, da of Robert Lyle Dobell (d 1969), of The Mount, Waverton, Chester; 1 s (Peter Robert Lambert b 1965), 1 da (Alice Mary b 1967); *Career* chm and co sec Wm Lawrence & Sons Ltd 1974-; JP Cheshire 1962; *Recreations* racing (owner); *Style—* R L Heaton, Esq; Wm Lawrence & Sons Ltd, Lyons Lane Mills, Chorley, Lancs (☎ 025 72 62294, fax 025 72 60023)

HEATON, Stuart Michael; s of Arthur Heaton (d 1965); *b* 29 May 1924; *Educ* Ledbury GS Hereford; *Career* WWII, Flt Lt Bomber Cmd 1944-45; dir Alfred Herbert (India) Ltd 1947-58, chm and md Ciro plc (joined 1964, ret 1989); *Recreations* having nothing to do; *Clubs* Oriental; *Style—* Stuart Heaton, Esq; 6 Daleham Gdns, Hampstead, London NW3 5DA (☎ 071 794 0893)

HEATON-ARMSTRONG, Anthony Eustace John; s of William Henry Dunamace Heaton-Armstrong, of 1 Blandys Lane, Upper Basildon, Nr Pangbourne, Berks, and Idonea, *née* Chance; *b* 27 Sept 1950; *Educ* Ampleforth, Univ of Bristol (LLB); *m* 1, 10 Feb 1973 (m dis 1977), Susan *née* Allnutt; m 2, 20 May 1982, Anne Frances, da of late Ethel Robigo; 1 s (John William b 15 Feb 1983), 2 da (Eleanor b 8 May 1985, Celestine b 3 Sept 1988); *Career* called to the Bar Gray's Inn 1973, in practice 1973-; expert on police evidence; numerous legal articles in jls; Int Cmmn of Jurists' observer at trials overseas involving alleged human rights adbuses, tstee Aldo Tst; *Recreations* gardening, wildlife and the countryside; *Clubs* Garrick; *Style—* Anthony Heaton-Armstrong, Esq; 11 South Square, Grays Inn, London WC1 (☎ 071 831 6974)

HEATON-ARMSTRONG, Bridget Almina Suzanne; MBE (1988); da of Sir John Heaton-Armstrong, MVO (d 1967), of 46 Carlisle Mansions, Carlisle Place, London SW1, and Suzanne Laura (d 1972), *née* Bechet de Balan; *b* 9 Aug 1920; *Career* L/72 voluntary aid detachment Br Red Cross Soc; hosp nurse: Red Cross 1939-42, St Bart's Hosp 1942-44; organiser hosp car serv 1944-46, Cmdt L/72 1944-48, awarded Def Medal 1939-43; sec Victoria League for Cwlth Friendship 1948-53, PA Earl Marshal's Office 1953, awarded Queen Elizabeth II Coronation Medal 1953, asst home sec Royal UK Benevolent Assoc 1957-62, int sec Nat Assoc of Youth Clubs 1964-70, advsr Citizen Advice Bureau 1972-80, chm Kensington and Chelsea Arthritis Care, res asst Radio Therapy Dept Royal Marsden Hosp, hon life govr and memb Royal UK Benevolent Assoc, key memb Wimbledon Branch Cancerlink; *Style—* Miss Bridget Heaton-Armstrong, MBE

HEATON-WARD, Dr (William) Alan; s of 2 Lt Ralph Heaton-Ward (d 1921), of Durham City, and Mabel, *née* Orton (d 1964); *b* 19 Dec 1919; *Educ* Queen Elizabeth's Hosp Clifton Bristol, Univ of Bristol (MB ChB, DPM); *m* 28 March 1945, Christine Edith, da of Maj David Fraser, DSO, MC, RHA (d 1943), of Nairn, Scotland; 2 da (Nicola (Mrs Kennedy), Lindsay (Mrs Maldini)); *Career* Local Def Vols and HG 1940-41, Surgn Lt-Cdr and neuropsychiatrist Nore Cmd RNVR 1946-48; dep med supt Hortham/Brentry Hosp Gp Bristol 1950-54, clinical teacher in mental health Univ of Bristol 1954-78; Stoke Park Hosp Gp Bristol: med supt 1954-61, hon conslt 1978-; Lord Chllr's med visitor Ct of Protection 1978-89, Blake Marsh lectr RCPsych 1976, Burden Res Gold medal and prize 1978; Br Cncl visiting lectr Portugal 1971, vice pres RCPsych 1976-78, pres Br Soc for Study of Mental Health Subnormality 1978-79, vice pres Fortune Centre Riding for the Disabled 1980-; memb: Advsy Cncl Radio Bristol 1985-88, Police Liaison Ctee 1988-90; Bristol Medico-Legal Soc, Bristol Medico-Chirurgical Soc; memb BMA, FRCPsych 1971; hon memb American Assoc of Physician Analysts 1978; *Books* Notes on Mental Deficiency (3 edn, 1955), Mental Subnormality (4 edn, 1975), Left Behind (1978), Mental Handicap (jtly, 1984); *Recreations* following all forms of sport, asking "Why", gardening; *Clubs* Bristol Savages, Bristol Football; *Style—* Dr Alan Heaton-Ward; Flat 2, 38 Apsley Rd, Clifton, Bristol BS8 2SS (☎ 0272 738971)

HEATON-WARD, Patrick Francis; s of Kenneth Pearce Heaton-Ward (d 1985), and Joan Moria Stuart, *née* Wilson-Steele; *b* 3 Oct 1939; *Educ* Bristol GS, Brasenose Coll Oxford (sr scholar, MA); *m* 18 June 1966, Danielle Paulette Michele, da of Hurbert

Mussot; 2 da (Anne Christine b 13 April 1971, Alice Mary b 24 June 1977); *Career* Bowater Paper Corporation 1962-64; Ogilvy Mather 1964-: account dir 1970, on secondment to Ogilvy & Mather Milan as client serv dir 1976-77, on secondment to Livraghi Ogilvy & Mather Milan as dir 1982-88, dir Ogilvy Adams & Rinehart 1988-; MIPA 1990; *Recreations* skiing, opera, ballet; *Style*— Patrick Heaton-Ward, Esq; Ogilvy Adams & Rinehart Ltd, Chancery House, Chancery Lane, London WC2A 1QU (☎ 071 405 8733, fax 071 831 0339)

HEATON WATSON, Richard Barrie; s of Kenneth Walter Heaton Watson (d 1981), of Albufeira, Portugal, and Jean Alexandra, *née* Harvey (d 1958); *b* 29 April 1945; *Educ* Harrow, Queen's Univ Belfast (BA), Univ of Cambridge (PGCE); *m* 29 July 1978, Caroline Ann, da of Leonard Cyril Mckane, MBE, *qv*, of Ampney St Peter, Glos; 1 s (Dominic b 1982), 2 da (Lucy b 1979, Fenella b 1987); *Career* head of dept Charterhouse 1975-84, housemaster Weekites 1985-; memb GA 1971; FRGS 1989; *Recreations* antiques, theatre, skiing; *Clubs* 1900, Golf Soc of GB; *Style*— Richard Heaton Watson, Esq; 20 Bywater St, London SW3 4XD; Brooke Hall, Charterhouse, Godalming, Surrey GU7 2DX (☎ 0483 426808)

HEBBLETHWAITE, (Richard) Jeremy; TD; s of Lt-Col Roger Vavasour Hebblethwaite, MC (d 1976), and Susan, *née* Hawkins; *b* 5 Dec 1933; *Educ* Wellington, Univ of Nottingham; *m* 1, 1966 (m dis 1988), Sara Elisabeth, da of James Stucker Offutt (d 1985); 2 s (Richard Alexander Vavasour b 1968, James Andrew Lewis b 1971); m 2, 1988, Josceline Mary, da of Sir Harry Phillimore, OBE; *Career* Nat Serv 2 Lt 2 RHA, Capt TA; dir Save & Prosper Gp 1969-87 (fin and mktg advsr 1987-); chm: Lancaster Hilton plc, Perceptive Research Ltd, X-Ling Press Ltd; memb: Organising Ctee Mktg Investmt Bd 1985-86, Norman Fowler's Pension Advsy Gp 1986-87, Occupational Pensions Bd 1987-; FCA 1969 (ACA 1959); *Recreations* sailing, opera, horticulture, golf; *Clubs* City, New (Edinburgh); *Style*— Jeremy Hebblethwaite, Esq, TD; 89 Cornwall Gardens, London SW7 4AX

HEBBLETHWAITE, Peter; s of Charles Hebblethwaite (d 1971), and Elsie Ann, *née* McDonald (d 1989); *b* 30 Sept 1930; *Educ* Xaverian Coll Manchester, Campion Hall Oxford (Heath Harrison scholarship, MA), Les Fontaines France, Heythrop Coll (LTh); *m* 31 July 1974, Margaret Isabella Mary, da of George Victor Speaight; 2 s (Dominic Paul b 7 Sept 1976, Benedict Charles b 15 March 1982), 1 da (Anna Cordelia b 17 July 1978); *Career* ed The Month 1967-73 (literary ed 1965-67), asst ed Frontier 1974-76, lectr in French Wadham Coll Oxford 1976-79, freelance writer and writer on Vatican affrs The National Catholic Reporter 1979- (Rome 1979-81, Oxford 1981-); writer of many articles in: The Observer, The Sunday Times, The Guardian, The TLS, The Tablet, and other jls; memb NUJ; *Books* George Bernanos: Studies In Modern European Literature and Thought (1965), Atheism and the Council Fathers (1967), Theology of the Church (1967), The Runaway church (1975), Christian-Marxist Dialogue and Beyond (1977), The Year of Three Popes (1979), Introducing John Paul II (1982), John XXIII Pope of the Council (1984), Synod Extraordinary (1986), In The Vatican (1987); *Recreations* walking and talking; *Style*— Peter Hebblethwaite, Esq; 45 Marston St, Oxford OX4 1JU (☎ 0865 723771)

HEBDITCH, Maxwell Graham (Max); s of Harold Oliver Hebditch (d 1975), of Yeovil, Somerset, and Lily, *née* Bartle; *b* 22 Aug 1937; *Educ* Yeovil Sch, Magdalene Coll Cambridge (MA); *m* 1 June 1963, Felicity Margaret, da of William Brinley Davies (d 1982); 2 s, 1 da; *Career* Nat Serv pilot offr (Secretarial Branch) RAF 1956-58; field archaeologist Leicester Museum 1961-64, asst curator Archaeology City Museum Bristol 1965-71 (latterly curator Social History); dir: Guildhall Museum London 1971-75, Museum of London 1977- (dep dir 1975-77); pres Museum Assoc 1990-, chm UK Ctee Int Cncl of Museums 1981-87; FSA, FMA; *Publications* contribs to specialist and academic jls; *Style*— Max Hebditch, Esq, FSA; Museum of London, London Wall, London EC2Y 5HN (☎ 071 600 3699, fax 071 600 1058)

HEBER PERCY, Lady Dorothy; *née* Lygon; 4 and yst da of 7 Earl Beauchamp (d 1938); *b* 22 Feb 1912; *m* 1985, as his 2 w, Robert Vernon Heber Percy (d 1987), 4 and yst s of late Maj Algernon Heber Percy, JP, DL, of Hodnet Hall, Salop; *Career* late section offr WAAF; *Style*— The Lady Dorothy Heber Percy; Lime Tree Cottage, 7 Coach Lane, Faringdon, Oxford SN7 8AB

HEBER-PERCY, Algernon Eustace Hugh; DL (Shropshire 1986); s of Brig Algernon George William Heber-Percy, DSO (d 1961), of Hodnet Hall, and Daphne Wilma Kenyon, *née* Parker Bowles; *b* 2 Jan 1944; *Educ* Harrow; *m* 6 July 1966, Hon Margaret Jane, *qv*, *née* Lever, yst da of 3 Viscount Leverhulme, KG, TD; 1 s ((Algernon) Thomas Lever b 29 Jan 1984), 3 da (Emily Jane b 19 Feb 1969, Lucy Ann b 29 Dec 1970, Sophie Daphne b 22 Jan 1979); *Career* Lt Grenadier Gds 1962-66; farmer; chm Ctee: Mercian Region Nat Tst 1979-90, Walker Trust; chm Pines and Lyneal Tst; memb Historic Houses and Gardens Ctee; fell Woodard Schs; High Sheriff of Shropshire 1987; *Recreations* gardening, country sports; *Clubs* Cavalry and Guards'; *Style*— Algernon Heber-Percy, Esq, DL; Hodnet Hall, Hodnet, Market Drayton, Shropshire TF9 3NN (☎ 063 084 202)

HEBER-PERCY, Hon Mrs (Margaret Jane); *née* Lever; da of 3 Viscount Leverhulme, KG, TD; *b* 1947; *m* 1966, Algernon Eustace Hugh Heber-Percy; 1 s, 3 da; *Recreations* gardening, fishing; *Style*— The Hon Mrs Heber-Percy; Hodnet Hall, Market Drayton, Shropshire

HECKENDORN, Hon Mrs (Roselle Sarah); *née* Bruce-Gardyne; o da of Baron Bruce-Gardyne (Life Peer) (d 1990); *b* 7 Dec 1959; *Educ* St Paul's Girls' Sch, Durham Univ; *m* 26 Sept 1978, David Heckendorn, o s of C H Heckendorn, of Beaux Arts Village, Washington, USA; *Style*— The Hon Mrs Heckendorn; 13 Kelso Place, London W8

HECKS, Malcolm; s of Ronald Frederick Hecks, of Chippenham, Wilts, and Ivy, *née* Rose (d 1962); *b* 5 Dec 1942; *Educ* Chippenham GS, Univ of Bath (BSc, BArch); *m* 12 Aug 1967, Donna Leslie, da of Robert Leslie Pratt, of Cape Town, SA; 1 s (Oliver Lewis Ledoux b 1978), 1 da (Alexandra Sophie Ivy b 1975); *Career* conslt architect; sr ptnr Malcolm Hecks Assocs Hants 1970-; designed World Wildlife HQ Bldg Godalming 1982; FRIBA 1971, MBIM 1978, FFAS 1985; *Recreations* music, theatre, travel, films, history of art and architecture, ecology; *Style*— Malcolm Hecks, Esq; Kinley House, Durford Wood, Petersfield, Hampshire GU31 5AS

HECTOR, Gordon Matthews; CMG (1966), CBE (1961, OBE 1955); s of George Pittendrigh Hector (d 1962), of 51 Forest Rd, Aberdeen, and Helen Elizabeth, *née* Matthews (d 1963); *b* 9 June 1918; *Educ* St Mary's Sch Melrose, Edinburgh Acad, Lincoln Coll Oxford (MA); *m* 28 Aug 1954, Mary Forrest, da of Robert Gray (d 1933); 1 s (Alistair b 5 Oct 1955), 2 da (Jean b 30 April 1957, Katy b 12 Oct 1961); *Career* cmmnd RASC 1939, served with E Africa Forces 1940-45; dist offr Kenya 1946, asst sec 1950, sec to Road Authy 1951, sec to Govt of Seychelles 1952, actg govr 1953, dep res cmmr and govt sec Basutoland 1956, dep Br Govt rep Lesotho 1965; dep sec Univ of Aberdeen 1976 (clerk to Univ Ct 1967-76), sec Assembly Cncl of Gen Assembly Church of Scot 1980-85; chm: Victoria League for Cwlth Friendship Scot 1983-89, W End Community Cncl Edinburgh Dist 1986-89, Gt North of Scotland Railway Assoc; vice pres The St Andrew Soc Edinburgh; Burgess of Guild City of Aberdeen 1979; fell Cwlth Fund 1939; *Recreations* town and country walking, railways, grandchildren; *Clubs* Royal Over-Seas League, Vincents (Oxford); *Style*— Gordon Hector, Esq, CMG, CBE; 4 Montgomery Court, 110 Hepburns Gardens, St Andrews KY16 9LT

HECTOR, Gp Capt Peter John; s of Harry Hector (d 1963), of Brigstock, Northants, and Edith Mary, *née* Farrer; *b* 5 Sept 1934; *Educ* Kettering GS, Rugby Coll of Technol; *m* 24 March 1956, Ann Helen Elizabeth, da of Herbert Hetterley, of Weldon, Northants; 1 s (Paul b 1958), 2 da (Sarah b 1963, Jane b 1965); *Career* RAF engr branch, PO 1956, Gp Capt 1978, ret 1988; freelance conslt in mgmnt and trg 1988-, int affairs conslt to Engrg Cncl 1988-, assoc Neale and Ptnrs 1989-; Hon Freeman Weston-super-Mare 1977-80; FRAeS 1978, FBIM 1985, MITD 1989, Eur Ing 1990; *Recreations* painting, reading, music, walking; *Clubs* RAF; *Style*— Gp Capt Peter Hector; Wentworth, 21 Cotterstock Rd, Oundle, Peterborough PE8 5HA (☎ 0832 272067)

HEDDEN, Robert; s of Frederick Hedden (d 1982), of Okehampton, Devon, and Winifred Elizabeth, *née* Trenaman; *b* 22 Feb 1948; *Educ* Okehampton GS, King's Coll, London (LLB, AKC); *m* 10 Sept 1977, Jean Mary, da of Walter John Worboyes (d 1982), of London; 1 s (Oliver Michael Ward), 1 da (Rachel Louise Worboyes); *Career* admitted slr 1972, ptnr Herbert Smith 1980-; memb Ctee Anglo-Polish Legal Assoc, assoc memb The Dirs Guild of GB; Freeman Worshipful Co of Slrs; memb Law Soc; *Recreations* theatre (making and watching), music (making and listening), tennis, skiing, swimming, travel; *Clubs* Broadgate, Croydon Stagers; *Style*— Robert Hedden, Esq; 25 Lewin Rd, London SW16 6JZ; Herbert Smith Exchange House, Primrose St, London EC2A 2HS (☎ 071 374 8000, telex 886633, fax 071 496 0043)

HEDGECOE, Prof John; s of William Alec Hedgecoe (d 1983), of Priory Farm, Lt Dunmow, Essex, and Kathleen Alice, *née* Don (d 1981); *b* 24 March 1937; *Educ* Gulval Village Sch, Guildford Sch of Art, Epsom Sch of Art, Ruskin Coll Oxford, RCA (Dr RCA); *m* 3 Oct 1959, Julia, da of Sidney Mardon (d 1971), of Bishops Stortford, Herts; 2 s (Sebastian John b 1961, Auberon Henry b 1968), 1 da (Imogen Dolly Alice b 1964); *Career* Nat Serv RAF SAC 1955-56; staff photographer Queen Magazine 1957-72; freelance: Sunday Times and Observer 1960-70, most int magazines 1958-; RCA: fndr photography sch 1965, head dept and reader and head in Photography Dept 1965-74, fell 1973, Chair of Photography 1975, fndr Audio/Visual Dept 1980, fndr Holography Unit 1982, managing tstee 1983; portrait of HM The Queen for Br and Aust postage stamps 1966, photographer The Arts Multi-Projection Br Exhibition Expo Japan Show 1970, visiting prof Norwegian Nat TV Sch Oslo 1985; dir: John Hedgecoe Ltd 1965-, Perennial Pictures Ltd 1980-90; md Lion & Unicorn Press Ltd 1986; illustrator of numerous books 1958-, contributor to numerous radio broadcasts; TV: Tonight (Aust) 1967, Folio (Anglia) 1980, eight programmes on photography (Channel Four) 1983 (repeated 1984), Winners (Channel Four) 1984, Light and Form (US Cable TV) 1985; exhibitions: London, Sydney, Toronto, Edinburgh, Venice and Prague; collections: V & A, Museum Art Gallery of Ontario, Nat Portrait Gallery, Citibank London, Henry Moore Fndn, Museum of Modern Art NY, Leeds City Art Gallery; govr W Surrey Coll of Art 1975-80 (memb Acad Advsy Bd 1975-80), memb Photographic Bd CNAA 1976-78, acad govr Richmond Coll London; Laureate and medal for achievement in photography Czechoslovakia Govt (1989); FRSA; *Books* Henry Moore (1968, prize best art book world-wide 1969), Kevin Crossley-Holland book of Norfolk Poems (jtly 1970), Photography, Material and Methods (jtly 1971-74 edns), Henry Moore Energy in Space (1973), The Book of Photography (1976), Handbook of Photographic Techniques (1977, 2 edn 1982), The Art of Colour Photography (1978), Possession (1978), The Pocket Book of Photography (1979), Introductory Photography Course (1979), Master Classes in Photography: Children and Child Portraiture (1980), Poems of Thomas Hardy (illustrated 1981), Poems of Robert Burns (illustrated), The Book of Advanced Photography (1982), What a Picture! (1983), The Photographer's Work Book (1983), Aesthetics of Nude Photography (1984), The Workbook of Photo Techniques (1984), The Workbook of Darkroom Techniques (1984), Pocket Book of Travel and Holiday Photography (1986), Henry Moore: his ideas, inspirations and life as an artist (1986), The Three Dimensional Pop-up Photography Book (with A L Rowse, 1986), Shakespeare's Land (1986), Photographers Manual of Creative Ideas (1986), Portrait Photography (with A L Rowse, 1987), Rowse's Cornwall (1987), Practical Book of Landscape Photography (1988), Hedgecoe on Photography (1988), Hedgecoe on Video (1989), Complete Guide to Photography (1990); *Recreations* sculpture, building, gardening; *Clubs* Arts; *Style*— Prof John Hedgecoe; Royal College of Art, Kensington Gore, London SW7

HEDGES, Anthony John; s of Sidney George Hedges (d 1974), and Mary, *née* Dixon; *b* 5 March 1931; *Educ* Bicester GS, Keble Coll Oxford (BA, BMus, DipEd, MA); *m* 28 Aug 1957, (Delia) Joy, da of Maj Albert Marsden (d 1971); 2 s (Nicholas b 28 Oct 1964, Simon b 10 May 1966), 2 da (Fiona b 25 Feb 1959, Deborah b 4 March 1961); *Career* Nat Serv Royal Signals Band 1955-57; teacher and lectr Royal Scottish Acad of Music 1957-63; Univ of Hull: lectr 1963, sr lectr 1968, reader in composition 1978-; princ compositions incl; orchestral: Comedy Overture 1962 (revised 1967), Overture Oct '62 1962 (revised 1968), Variations on a Theme of Rameau 1969, Festival Dances 1976, Four Breton Sketches 1980, Sinfonia Concertante 1980, Scenes from the Humber 1981, Symphony 1972-73, A Cleveland Overture 1984, Concertino for Horn and String Orchestra 1987; choral: Epithalamium 1969, Psalm 104 1973, The Temple of Solomon 1979, I Sing the Birth (Canticles for Christmas) 1985, I'll make me a world 1990; chamber music: String Quartets 1970 and 1990, Piano Trio 1977, Flute Trios 1985 and 1989, Clarinet Quintet 1988; Sonatas for Piano 1974, Flute 1989, Cello 1982, Viola 1982, Wind Quintet 1984; opera: Shadows in the Sun 1976; musical: Minotaur 1978; miscellaneous: anthems, partsongs music for TV, film and stage, complete archive in Hull Central Library; memb Cncl The Composers Guild of GB (memb Exec Ctee 1969-73 and 1977-81, chm 1972-73); memb: Cncl Central Music Library Westminster 1970-, SPNM Cncl 1974-81; memb Music Panels: Yorkshire Arts 1974-75, Lincs and Humberside Arts 1975-78, memb Music Bd CNNA 1974-77; LRAM; *Books* Basic Tonal Harmony (1988), An Introduction to Counterpoint (1988); *Recreations* reading, playing chamber music; *Style*— Anthony Hedges, Esq; Malt Shovel Cottage, 76 Walkergate, Beverley, E Yorks HU17 9ER (☎ 0482 860580); Department of Music, University of Hull, Cottingham Rd, Kingston upon Hull HU6 7RX (☎ 0482 465998)

HEDGES, George Arthur; s of George Arthur Hedges (d 1942), of Enfield, Middx, and Leah Anna, *née* Ferguson (d 1986); *b* 5 April 1936; *Educ* Mill Hill, Northern Poly Holloway Road; *m* 30 Jan 1980, Sheena, da of Robert McLelland Craig (d 1986), of Gwynedd, N Wales; *Career* CA in private practice; ARIBA; *Recreations* water sports; *Clubs* Cheyne (life memb), Mombasa, Victoria Craig-y-Don (Llandudno); *Style*— George A Hedges, Esq; c/o Lloyd Chambers, Reform Street, Llandudno, Gwynedd, N Wales (☎ 0492 879444)

HEDGES, Neil Francis; s of Kenneth Francis Chevalier, of Walmer, Kent, and Peggy, *née* Best; *b* 12 Dec 1956; *Educ* Watford Boys' GS, Univ of Sheffield (BA); *m* 19 Sept 1981, Katherine Anne, da of Trevor Noel Louis, of Bushey Heath, Herts; 2 da (Frances b 13 Feb 1986, Alexandra b 18 March 1989); *Career* md Valin Pollen Ltd 1988- (asst md 1985, account exec 1980); *Recreations* music, cinema, walking, family; *Style*— Neil Hedges, Esq; 7 Nicholas Rd, Elstree, Herts (☎ 01 207 5559); Valin Pollen Ltd, 18 Grosvenor Gardens, London SW1H 0DH (☎ 01 730 3456, fax 01 730 7445, telex 296846)

HEDLEY, Prof Anthony Johnson; s of Thomas Johnson Hedley (d 1977), of Yealmpton, Plymouth, Devon, and Winifred, *née* Duncan; *b* 8 April 1941; *Educ* Rydal Sch Colwyn Bay, Univ of Aberdeen (MB ChB, MD), Univ of Edinburgh (Dip Soc Med); *m* 2 Aug 1967, Elizabeth-Anne, da of William Henry Walsh; *Career* Aberdeen Univ OTC 1960-63; res fell dept of therapeutics and pharmacology Univ of Aberdeen 1968-69 (Philipps and Garden fell 1986-68), hon asst dept of pharmacology and therapeutics Univ of Dundee 1969-73, fell community med Scottish Health Serv 1973-74, lectr community med Univ of Aberdeen 1974-76, sr lectr community health Univ of Nottingham 1976-83, Henry Mechan prof and head Dept of Community Med Univ of Glasgow 1984-88 (titular prof and Henry Mechan prof-designate 1983-84), prof of community med Univ of Hong Kong 1988-, memb: Thyroid Club, Soc for Social Med, Nottingham Medico Chirurgical Soc, Hong Kong Med Assoc, Burton Joyce Preservation Soc, Cathay Camera Club; Hon MD Khon Kaen Univ Thailand 1983, FFCM 1981, FRCP (Edin) 1981, FRCP (Glas) 1985 FRCP (Lond) 1987; *Clubs* Freelancers (Nottingham), Rydal Veterans (Colwyn Bay), Aberdeen Boat Hong Kong; *Style—* Prof Anthony Hedley; 39 Foxhill Rd, Burton Joyce, Notts NG14 5DB (☎ 0602 31 2558); Flat 8 Block 2, Tam Towers, 25 Shawan Dr, Pokfulam, Hong Kong (☎ 5 819 4708); Department of Community Medicine (☎ 5 8199 280, fax 852 5 479 907)

HEDLEY, Mark; s of Peter Hedley, of Windsor and Eve, *née* Morley; *b* 23 Aug 1946; *Educ* Framlingham Coll, Univ of Liverpool (LLB); *m* 14 April 1973, Erica Rosemary, da of late John Capel Britton, of Ashbourne; 3 s (Michael b 1975, Steven b 1981, Peter b 1982), 1 da (Anna b 1978); *Career* called to the Bar Gray's Inn 1969; rec of Crown Ct 1988; reader C of E, chm Liverpool Diocesan Assoc of Readers; *Recreations* cricket, railways; *Style—* Mark Hedley, Esq; 55 Everton Rd, Liverpool 6 (☎ 051 227 1081, fax 051 236 1120)

HEDLEY, Dr Ronald Henderson; CB (1986); s of Henry Armstrong Hedley (d 1970), of Scarborough, Yorks, and Margaret, *née* Hopper (d 1950); *b* 2 Nov 1928; *Educ* Durham Johnston Sch, Univ of Durham (BSc, PhD), Univ of Newcastle Upon Tyne (DSc); *m* 28 Feb 1957, Valmai Mary, da of Roy Griffith (d 1971), of Taihape, NZ; 1 s (Iain b 18 June 1960); *Career* cmmnd RA 1953-55; Br Museum Natural History: sr and princ scientific offr, dep keeper of zoology 1955-71, dep dir 1971-76, dir 1976-88; nat res fell NZ 1960-61; author of tech papers on biology and cytology of protozoa; memb Cncl Fresh Water Biol Assoc 1972-76, tstee Percy Sladen Meml Fund 1972-77, pres Br Soc of Protozoa 1975-78, memb Cncl and govr Marine Biology Assoc 1976-, vice pres Zoological Soc of London 1980-85 (hon sec 1977-80); memb Cncl: Royal Albert Hall 1982-88, Nat Tst 1986-88; FZS 1960, FIBiol 1970, FRSA 1988; *Books* Foraminifera Vols 1-3 (1974-78), Atlas of Testate Amoebae (1980); *Recreations* horology, horticulture, humour; *Style—* Dr Ronald Hedley, CB; Pineways, Halley Rd, Broad Oak, Heathfield, E Sussex TN21 8TG

HEDLEY-DENT, Maj Ronald Peter; er s of Lt-Col William Edward Hedley-Dent (d 1980), of Shortflatt Tower, Belsay, Northumberland, and Renée Maude (d 1978), er da of Sir Arthur Philip du Cros, 1 Bt; descended from William Hedley, Mayor of Newcastle 1778, whose s William m Anne, sis and eventual heiress of John Dent, of Shortflatt Tower, which was inherited by their gs William Dent Hedley (later William Dent Dent) 1831; the additional surname and arms of Hedley were re-assumed in 1926 (*see* Burke's Landed Gentry, 18 edn, Vol III, 1972); *b* 29 June 1921; *Educ* Eton; *m* 24 June 1964, Nancy, da of Bryant H Dixon, of Rockaway Valley, Boonton, New Jersey, USA; 1 adopted da (Octavia b 23 Sept 1967); *Career* served in Welsh Gds 1941-62, ret as Maj; Northern Inspr of Courses for the Jockey Club 1964-86; chm: Belsay Parish Cncl, Northern Branch Mental Health Fndn; High Sheriff of Northumberland 1974-75; *Recreations* travelling, racing, farming, gardening; *Style—* Major Ronald Hedley-Dent; Shortflatt Tower, Belsay, Newcastle-upon-Tyne NE20 OHD (☎ 0661 881609)

HEDLEY LEWIS, Vincent Richard; s of John Hedley Lewis (d 1976), of Birkholme Manor, Corby Glen, and Sheelagh Alice Hedley, *née* De Paravicini; *b* 24 May 1941; *Educ* Wellesley House, Harrow; *m* 17 June 1978, Penelope Ann, da of A C Hobson, MC; 3 da (Selina Priscilla b 27 Sept 1980, Melissa Sheelagh b 12 Sept 1982, Amanda Jane b 28 Jan 1985); *Career* articled to M R Crouch, Crough Chapman & Co 1960-56, CA 1966, ptnr Spicer and Pegler (now Touche Ross) 1975, ptnr i/c Touche Ross Agribusiness Div 1975-; memb: Lincolnshire Jt Devpt Ctee 1981-, Econ Advsy Panel Rural Deupt Cmmn 1989-, Country Landowners Taxation Ctee 1989-; dir Peterborough Devpt Agency 1987-, farmer of 700 acres Carby Glen Lincs; memb SKGB (Gold medallist), ran London Marathon 1989; *Books* Contract Farming (1990); *Recreations* cricket, skiing, tennis, golf, shooting; *Clubs* Farmers, Marylebone Cricket, Free Foresters Cricket, Luffenham Heath Golf, Lincolnshire; *Style—* Vincent Hedley Lewis, Esq; Birkholme Manor, Corby Glen, Grantham, Lincolnshire NG33 4LF (☎ 047684 255); Touch Ross & Co, Leda House, Station Rd, Cambridge CB1 2RN (☎ 0223 460222, 0223 350839, car 0860 683542)

HEDLEY-MILLER, Dame Mary Elizabeth; DCVO (1989), CB (1983); da of late J W Ashe; *b* 5 Sept 1923; *Educ* Queen's Sch Chester, St Hugh's Coll Oxford (MA); *m* 1950, Roger Latham Hedley-Miller; 1 s, 2 da (of whom Rosalind, *qv*); *Career* under sec HM Treasy 1973-83, ceremonial offr Cabinet Office 1983-88; *Style—* Dame Mary Hedley-Miller, DCVO, CB; 108 Higher Drive, Purley, Surrey

HEDLEY-MILLER, Rosalind; da of Roger Latham Hedley-Miller, and Dame Mary Elizabeth, *née* Ashe, DCVO, CB, *qv*; *b* 25 Nov 1954; *Educ* St Paul's Girls' Sch, St Hugh's Coll Oxford (MA), Harvard Univ; *Career* Investmt Dept J Henry Schroder Wagg & Co Ltd 1977-79; Kleinwort Benson Ltd: corp fin dept 1979-, dir 1987-; non-exec dir Bejam Group plc 1987-88, non-exec TV-am plc 1990-; *Recreations* chamber music, orchestra, singing, bridge, tennis; *Style—* Miss Rosalind Hedley-Miller; 11 Manchuria Rd, London SW11 6AF; 20 Fenchurch St, London EC3P 3DB (☎ 071 623 8000, fax 071 623 5535)

HEEKS, Alan David; s of Leonard Frank Heeks, and Peggy Eileen, *née* Lawless; *b* 20 Aug 1948; *Educ* Reading Sch, Balliol Coll Oxford, Harvard Business Sch (MBA); *m* 7 Aug 1971, Ruth Frances, da of Arthur Stone; 2 da (Elinor b 1977, Frances b 1979); *Career* brand mangr Procter & Gamble 1969-73, mangr mktg and new prods Hygena Kitchens 1976-78; dir mktg and sales: Chloride Standby Systems 1978-81, Redland Roof Tiles 1981-83; md: Redland Prismo 1983-86, Caradon Twyfords Ltd 1986-89 (exec dir Caradon plc); dir: Nat Home Improvement Cncl 1986-90, Winchester Consulting Group 1989-; FInstM; *Recreations* design, the arts, walking; *Style—* Alan Heeks, Esq; 9 Hockley Cottages, Twyford, Winchester, Hants, SO21 1PJ, Winchester Consltg Gp, St Thomas House, St Thomas St, Winchester SO23 9HE (☎ 0962 856495)

HEELIS, Robert McRae; s of Robert Loraine Heelis (d 1971), of Mickledore, West Bridgford, Notts, and Susannah Heelis; *b* 20 June 1930; *Educ* Repton, Nottingham Univ (LLB); *m* 1, 23 July 1955 (m dis 1965), Elizabeth Isobelle, *née* Radford; m 2, 20 Dec 1968, Patricia Margaret, *née* Fletcher; 2 s (Robert Alexander Piers b 2 Dec 1970, Toby Edward Loraine b 12 May 1973), 1 da (Sarah Caroline Nesbitt); *Career* Nat Serv 2 Lt 1953-55, Capt Leics and Derbys Yeo 1955-68; memb E Midland T & AVRA cncl; slr 1953; ptnr Taylor Simpson & Mosley, Derby and Nottingham; sec Derby & Derbyshire Disabled Soldiers Settlement, cncllr Derby Borough Cncl 1967-70; Under Sheriff Derbyshire 1980-; *Recreations* shooting, vintage car racing; *Clubs* County Derby, VSCC, BOC; *Style—* Robert Heelis, Esq; Shaw House, Melbourne, Derby (☎ 0332 863827); 35 St Mary's Gate, Derby (☎ 0332 372311)

HEEPS, William (Bill); CBE; s of William Headrick Heeps (d 1980), and Margaret, *née* Munro (d 1978); *b* 4 Dec 1929; *Educ* Graeme HS Falkirk; *m* 1, 1956, Anne Robertson Paton (d 1974); 2 da (Elaine b 1958, Donna b 1961); m 2, 1983, Jennifer Rosemary, da of Jack Evans, of Hay-on-Wye ; 1 step da (Sarah-Jane, name changed to Heeps by deed poll); *Career* reporter Falkirk Mail 1943-52, reporter/sports sub-ed Daily Record (Kemsley Newspapers) 1952-54, joined ed staff of Evening Dispatch (later Evening News and Dispatch) of Scotsman Publications Ltd 1954 (asst ed 1962), asst to md Belfast Telegraph 1965-66, ed Middlesbrough Evening Gazette 1966-68; md: Celtic Newspapers 1968-72, Teesside 1972-75, Evening Post (Luton) and Evening Echo (Watford) 1975-77, Thomson Magazines 1977-80, Thomson Data 1980-82; chm and chief exec Thomson Regional Newspapers 1984- (ed dir 1982-83, md and ed-in-chief 1983-84); memb Bd The Thomson Corp (previously International Thomson Organisation) 1984-; elder of Church of Scot; dir: Thomson Regional Newspapers Ltd, Chester Chronicle and Associated Newspapers Ltd, North Eastern Evening Gazette Ltd, Belfast Telegraph Newspapers Ltd, Aberdeen Journals Ltd, The Scotsman Publications Ltd, Thomson International Press Consultancy Ltd; chm Royal Caledonian Schs, former pres Newspaper Soc, tstee The Thomson Fndn, vice pres The Boys Brigade; CBIM; *Recreations* golf, badminton; *Clubs* Caledonian; *Style—* Bill Heeps, Esq, CBE; The Vicarage, Pipers Hill, Great Gaddesden, Herts HP1 3BY (☎ 0442 253524); Hannay House, 39 Clarendon Rd, Watford, Herts WD1 1JA (☎ 0923 55588, telex 915054)

HEESOM, Tom Michael Anthony; s of Dr A H B Heesom (d 1955), of Redhill, Surrey, and Gwendoline Mary Heesom; *b* 26 Feb 1937; *Educ* Marlborough, Guys Hosp; *m* 23 March 1966, Willo Elizabeth, da of Dr W H Murby, of Toronto, Canada; *Career* gen dental surgn in private practice, visiting conslt in preventive dentistry State of Qatar 1979-82; chm Pankey Assoc (UK) 1985; fell: Int Coll Dentists 1988, Int Acad of Ornathology 1990; LDS, BDS, MGDS; *Recreations* vintage cars, walking, travel, music, gardening; *Style—* Tom Heesom, Esq; The Old Bothy, Norwood Hill, Horley, Surrey RH6 OHP (☎ 0293 862622); The Wall House, Yorke Rd, Reigate, Surrey RH2 9HG (☎ 0737 247424)

HEFFER, Eric Samuel; MP (Lab) Liverpool Walton 1964-; s of William Heffer, and Annie, *née* Nicholls; *b* 12 Jan 1922; *Educ* Longmore Sr Sch Hertford; *m* 1945, Doris Murray; *Career* served WWII RAF; Lab front bench spokesman industl rels 1970-72, min state DOI 1974-75, memb Lab NEC 1975- (chm Orgn Sub-Ctee to 1982), chm Lab Pty 1983-84, memb Shadow Cabinet and oppn front bench spokesman: Euro and Community Affrs (incl responsibility for planning UK withdrawal from EEC in event of Lab electoral victory) 1981-1983, housing and construction Nov 1983-; vice pres League Against Cruel Sports; pamphlets incl Democratic Socialism, Why You Should Vote Labour, Forward to Socialism; former columnist: The Times, New Statesman, Tribune, Liverpool Daily Post & Echo; contrib to numerous foreign and Br newspapers and jls; *Books* Class Struggle in Parliament, Labour's Future - Socialist or SDP Mark II, Faith in Politics (jtly); *Style—* Eric Heffer Esq, MP; House of Commons, London SW1

HEFFER, John N M; s of late Sidney Heffer; *b* 8 Jan 1919; *Educ* Leys Sch Cambridge; *m* 1944, Margaret, *née* Moore; 3 s; *Career* Flt Lt RAF WWII; bookseller and stationer, dep chm W Heffer and Sons Ltd; *Recreations* sailing, gardening, shooting; *Style—* John Heffer, Esq; Solway, Dry Drayton, Cambridge (☎ 0954 780628)

HEFFER, Simon James; s of James Heffer (d 1971), of Woodham Ferrers, Essex, and Joyce Mary, *née* Clements; *b* 18 July 1960; *Educ* King Edward VI Sch Chelmsford, Corpus Christi Coll Cambridge (BA, MA); *m* 31 July 1987, Diana Caroline, da of Sqdn Ldr P A Clee, of Marlow, Buckinghamshire; *Career* med journalist 1983-85, freelance journalist 1985-86; Daily Telegraph: leader writer 1986-, dep political corr 1987-88, political sketch writer 1988-91, political columnist 1990-; *Books* A Century of County Cricket (ed, 1990), A Tory Seer (jt ed with C Moore, 1989); *Recreations* cricket, music, ecclesiology, bibliophily, my wife; *Clubs* Essex County Cricket; *Style—* Simon Heffer, Esq; The Daily Telegraph, 181 Marsh Wall, London E14 9SR (☎ 071 538 5000, direct 071 538 6304)

HEFFERNAN, John Francis; *b* 1 Sept 1927; *Educ* Gunnersbury GS, Univ of London (BCom); *m* 19 July 1952, Veronica, da of Dr John Laing, of 7 Corfton Rd, Ealing; 2 da (Maureen, Catherine); *Career* called to the Bar Inner Temple 1954; Daily Express (later Evening Standard) 1941-45, chm and princ proprietor City Press Newspaper 1965-75; city ed: Yorkshire Post 1986-, United Provincial Newspapers Ltd 1965-; vice pres Free Trade League; hon sec: Assoc Regnl City Eds, Yorks and Humberside Devpt Assoc London Ctee; memb Ct Worshipful Co of Basketmakers; *Clubs* City Livery (memb Cncl); *Style—* John Heffernan, Esq; 1 Fern Dene, Ealing, London W13 8AN; United Newspapers, 23-27 Tudor St, London EC4Y OHR (☎ 071 353 3424, fax 071 353 7796)

HEFFERNAN, Patrick Benedict; s of Dr Daniel Anthony Heffernan, of Sutton, Surrey, and Margaret, *née* Donovan; *b* 17 March 1948; *Educ* Wimbledon Coll, Jesus Coll Cambridge (MA); *m* 5 May 1973, Elizabeth, da of Robert Essery (d 1966), of Huddersfield and Melbourne; 1 s (Thomas b 1984), 1 da (Miranda b 1987); *Career* slr 1974, ptnr Clyde & Co 1988-; *Recreations* times crossword, sport, reading; *Style—* Patrick Heffernan, Esq; 9 Victoria Rd, London N22 4XA (☎ 081 888 0349); Clyde & Co, 51 Eastcheap, London EC3M 1JP (☎ 071 623 1244, fax 071 623 5427, telex 884886)

HEFFLER, Lady Tara Francesca; *née* Fitz-Clarence; er da of 7 Earl of Munster, and his 1 w, Louise Marguerite Diane Delvigne; descended from William, Duke of Clarence (later King William IV) and Dorothy Jordan; *b* 6 Aug 1952; *m* 1979, Ross Jean Heffler, s of Dr Leon Heffler (d 1983); 1 s (Leo Edward Michael b 1985); 1 da (Alexandra Louise b 1982); *Career* mangr Sotheby Fine Art Auctioneers; *Recreations* family, travelling, the arts; *Style—* The Lady Tara Heffler; 146 Ramsden Rd, London SW12 8RE (☎ 01 673 4017)

HEGARTY, Paul Anthony; s of James Hegarty, of 3 Woodhall Avenue, Juniper Green, Edinburgh and Elizabeth, *née* Currie; *b* 25 July 1954; *Educ* St Anthony's Sch; *m* 12 June 1976, Linda Anne, da of James Higgins; 4 s (Paul Stephen b 23 Jan 1979, Mark David b 8 May 1981, Christopher James b 24 July 1984, Stephen Anthony b 14 Jan 1990); *Career* professional football player and manager; player: Hamilton Academicals 1972-74 (110 appearances), Dundee Utd 1974-90 (782 appearances, capt 1978-86), St Johnstone 1990 (15 appearances); player and mangr Forfar Athletic 1990-; Scotland: 4 under 21 caps, 1 league int cap, 8 full caps (capt v NI 1983); Scottish footballer of the year 1979; *Books* Heading for Glory (autobiography); *Recreations* golf; *Style—* Paul Hegarty, Esq; Forfar Athletic Football Club, Station Park, Forfar, Angus

HEGG, Warren Kevin; s of Kevin Hegg, of Bury, and Glenda, *née* Wright; *Educ* Castlebrook HS Unsworth, Stand Coll Whitefield; *Career* cricketer, wicketkeeper; first team debut: Stand CC 1983, Tonge CC 1984; professional 1985; Lancashire CCC 1989: capped 1989, toured WI 1986-87, toured Zimbabwe 1988-89, highest score 130 v Northants 1987, jt world record holder for 11 catches v Derbyshire 1989; represented: England North v Bermuda 1985, Young England v Sri Lanka 1987, Young England v Australia (Bicenterary) 1988, MCC v Worcester 1990, England A v Pakistan

1991; *Recreations* golf, fishing; *Style—* Warren Hegg, Esq

HEGGARTY, Hugh J; s of John Heggarty (d 1957), and Cecilia, *née* McGuire; *b* 28 Feb 1938; *Educ* St Aloysius Coll Glasgow, Univ of Glasgow (MB ChB, MRCP (Glas)); *m* 4 Jan 1964, Ann, da of late JS Hudson; 3 s (Kevin John b 6 Dec 1964, Paul Andrew b 15 July 1967, James Michael b 19 Sept 1970), 2 da (Marie Clare b 29 Feb 1972, Catherine Anne 15 April 1977); *Career* med registrar Univ of Zimbabwe 1964, res fell Iowa and Baltimore 1974, visiting prof Univ of Grenada W Indies 1987, currently conslt paediatrician York Dist Hosp; lectr: Canada, USA, Zimbabwe, Saudi Arabia, Iran, Libya, India; author of numerous med pubns on paediatric topics; memb: Br Paediatric Assoc, Life, SPUC; MRCP, MRCP (Glas), FRCPG, FRCPS; *Recreations* soccer, golf; *Clubs* York Golf; *Style—* Hugh Heggarty, Esq; 8 Hobgate, Acomb Rd, York YO2 4HF, (☎ 0904 791240); York District Hospital, Wigginton Rd, York YO3 7HE, (☎ 0904 31313)

HEGGS, Geoffrey Ellis; s of George Heggs, MBE (d 1972), of Guernsey, and Winifred Grace Ellis (d 1974); *b* 23 Oct 1928; *Educ* Elizabeth Coll Guernsey; *m* 28 March 1953, (Renée Fanny) Madeleine, da of Emilio Calderan (d 1940), of London; 2 s (Christopher b 1957, Oliver b 1964), 1 da (Caroline b 1960); *Career* admitted slr 1952; asst sec to The Law Soc 1956-58, practised as a slr in London 1958-77, chm of Industl Tbnls 1977-, rec Crown Ct SE circuit 1983-, regnl chm of London North region Industl Tbnls 1990-; Freeman City of London; memb: City of London Slrs Co, Law Soc; *Recreations* military history, music, painting; *Style—* Geoffrey Heggs, Esq; 19-29 Woburn Place, London WC1H 0LU (☎ 071 239 9265)

HEGINBOTHAM, Stafford; s of Stafford Heginbotham, of Oldham; *b* 12 Sept 1933; *Educ* Greenhill GS Oldham; *m* 1963, Lorna, da of Alfred Silverwood, of Leeds; 2 s (Simon b 1965, James b 1967); *Career* served RAF; chm and md Tebro Toys Ltd 1966-, chm Bradford AFC 1965-73; dir: Carlton Diecasters 1976-80, Douglas Plastics 1976-80; *Recreations* racing (racehorses: Cutler Heights, Tebro Teddy), golf, int travel; *Style—* Stafford Heginbotham Esq; The Pastures, Tong Village, Bradford, W Yorks (☎ 0532 853661)

HEGINBOTHAM, Prof Wilfred Brooks; OBE (1978); s of Fred Heginbotham (d 1958), of Bordsley, Ashton-under-Lyme, Lancs, and Alice, *née* Brooks (d 1986); *b* 9 April 1924; *Educ* pt/t student (ONC-HNC), UMIST (BSc, MSc, PhD, DSc); *m* 1957, Marjorie, *née* Pixton; 3 da (Janet Anne b 9 Oct 1958, Judith Rose b 11 Dec 1960, Robina Alice b 29 Jan 1963); *Career* jr clerk 1938-40, apprentice wood pattern maker 1940-46, textile machine designer 1944-46, prodn engr Textile Machinery 1950-51, lectr in prodn engrg subjects UMIST 1951-58; Univ of Nottingham: sr lectr in prodn engrg Dept of Mechanical Engrg 1958-61, fndr BSc course in prodn engrg (first in UK) 1961, head Dept of Prodn Engrg and Prodn Mgmnt 1961-64, Cripps prof of prodn engrg 1964-79, dean Faculty of Applied Science 1968-1971; DG Prodn Engrg Res Assoc 1979-84, assoc prof Univ of Warwick 1979-89, emeritus prof of prodn engrg Univ of Nottingham 1990 (special prof 1982-85); visiting prof: Univ of Warwick 1979-89, Dept of Electrical and Electronic Engrg Queen's Univ Belfast 1986-89, Univ of Rhode Island Sept-Dec 1987; visiting res fell Univ of Birmingham 1989-, freelance author lectr and conslt 1984-89; fndr Wolfson Industl Automation Gp Univ of Nottingham 1965; developed with Dept of Electronic and Electrical Engrg Univ of Nottingham: first programmable assembly machine in Europe 1967, first potentially practical assembly robot with artificial vision 1971; Robot Inst of America Joseph Engelburger award 1983; Hon DSc Aston Univ, Hon DTech Univ of Eindhoven (Holland); British Robot Assoc: fndr chm 1977-81, pres 1981-84, hon memb 1984-; memb ACARD 1980-83, emeritus memb Int Coll for Prodn Engrg Res 1990- (memb 1965-89), CEng, FEng 1985, FIProdE, MIMechE; *Books* Programmable Assembly (ed, 1984), Robot Grippers (ed with Dr D T Pham, 1986); *Recreations* gliding, remotely controlled model aircraft, micro computing; *Clubs* Derbyshire & Lancs Gliding, Notts Radio Control Soc, Rolls Royce Model Aircraft, Ten Ton (1000 mph); *Style—* Prof Wilfred Heginbotham, OBE; Bardsley Brow, 14 Middleton Crescent, Beeston, Notts NG9 2TH (☎ 0602 257796)

HEHIR, Peter Noel; s of Valentine Hehir, MBE (d 1977), and Hazel Florence Hehir (d 1989); *b* 22 Dec 1944; *Educ* Paisley GS; *m* (m dis); 3 s (Alexander John 23 May 1972, Stuart Michael b 2 Feb 1974, Christopher Valentine b 12 Dec 1981); *Career* journalist Paisley and Renfrewshire Gazette 1963-65, PR asst later PR exec later chief press offr Milk Marketing Bd 1965-68, news ed The Grocer 1969-73, md and chm Countrywide Communications 1973-; pres N Oxfordshire Sports Advsy Cncl; *awards* Oxfordshire Service to Sport award 1987, Consultancy of the Year 1989 and 1990; FIPR 1965, memb Inst of Grocery Distribution 1973, InstD 1975; *Recreations* reading, sport; *Clubs* Reform, West Bromwich Albion; *Style—* Peter Hehir, Esq; Countrywide Communications Group Ltd, Bowater House East, 68 Knightsbridge, London SW1X 7LH (☎ 071 584 0122, fax 071 584 6655)

HEILBRON, Hilary Nora Burstein; QC (1987); da of Dr Nathaniel Burstein, and Hon Dame Rose Heilbron, DBE, *qv*; *b* 2 Jan 1949; *Educ* Huyton Coll, LMH Oxford (MA); *Career* called to the Bar Gray's Inn 1971; *Style—* Miss Hilary Heilbron, QC; Brick Court Chambers, 15/19 Devereux Court, London WC2R 3JJ (☎ 071 583 0777)

HEILBRON, Dame Rose; DBE (1974); da of late Max Heilbron, and Nellie Heilbron; *b* 19 Aug 1914; *Educ* Belvedere Sch, Univ of Liverpool (LLM); *m* 1945, Dr Nathaniel Burstein; 1 da; *Career* Lord Justice Holker scholar Gray's Inn 1936, called to the Bar Gray's Inn 1939, QC 1949, bencher 1968, recorder and hon rec of Burnley 1972-74, memb Bar Cncl 1973-74, joined Northern Circuit (ldr 1973-74), judge of the High Court of Justice Family Div 1974-88, chm Home Sec's Advsy Gp on Law of Rape 1975-, presiding judge 1979-82; treas Gray's Inn 1985; hon fell: Lady Margaret Hall Oxford 1976, UMIST 1986; Hon LLD: Univ of Liverpool 1975, Univ of Warwick 1978, Univ of Manchester 1980, CNAA 1988; Hon Col WRAC(TA); *Style—* Dame Rose Heilbron, DBE; Strand, London WC2A 2LL

HEILIJGERS GOUGH, Anita Norma (Annie); da of Horace Kilian (d 1987), of Baddow Park, Gt Baddow, Essex, and Ruby Kilian; *b* 28 May 1930; *Educ* Benenden Sch Kent; *m* 22 July 1950 (m dis 1970), Hugh Patrick Gough, s of Hubert Vincent Gough (d 1986), of 33 Shooters Hill, Pangbourne, Berks; 2 da (Deirdre Caroline b 26 Sept 1952, Henrietta Joanna Louise b 22 July 1954); m 2, May 1990, Eri Heilijgers; *Career* memb Ballet Rambert Co 1948-50, fndr Fashion Design Co 1968-85; numerous private cmmns incl: HRH Princess Michael of Kent, Deborah Kerr, Hannah Gordon, Lisa Goddard; chm gp of packaging companies 1981-; *Recreations* vintage cars, interior design, country pursuits; *Style—* Mrs Annie Heilejgers Gough; The Stables, Little Horwood Manor, Little Horwood, Bucks NK17 0PH (☎ 029671 3703); H Kilian Ltd, Baddow Park, Gt Baddow, Essex CM2 7SY (☎ 0245 72361, telex 885225)

HEIM, Paul Emil; CMG (1988); s of George Heim, of London, and Hedy, *née* Herz; *b* 23 May 1932; *Educ* Prince of Wales Sch Nairobi, Univ of Durham (LLB); *m* 31 Aug 1962, Elizabeth, da of Lt-Col Geoffrey Morris Allen, MBE (d 1962), of Karen, Kenya; 1 s (Mathew Jacques b 1968), 2 da ((Elizabeth) Andrea b 1964, (Susan) Dominique b 1965); *Career* called to the Bar Lincoln's Inn 1955, magistrate, dep registrar and actg registrar HM Supreme Ct, Kenya (HMOCS) 1955-65, admin and princ admin Cncl of Europe 1965-73, head div and dir Euro Parl 1973-82, registrar Euro Ct of Justice 1982-88; chm: Fin Servs Tribunal, VAT Tribunal; pres FIMBRA Appeal Tribunals; visiting prof Univ of Leicester; Hon res fell Univ of Exeter; Bencher Lincoln's Inn; *Style—* Paul Heim, Esq, CMG; Wearne Wych, Picts Hill, Langport, Somerset TA10 9AA

HEIMANN, Hon Mrs (Diana Hester); *née* Macleod; da of Rt Hon Iain Norman Macleod, MP (d 1970), and Baroness Macleod of Borve (Life Peer); *b* 1944; *m* 1968, David Heimann; 3 s; *Style—* The Hon Mrs Heimann; Hertfordshire House, Coleshill, Bucks

HEIN, (Joseph Paul) Raymond; QC (Mauritius 1976); s of Sir Raymond Hein, QC (d 1983), and Lady Hein, *née* Marcelle Piat (d 1981); *b* 23 Jan 1929; *Educ* Royal Coll Mauritius, Wadham Coll Oxford (MA); *m* 1962, (Amélie Sybille) Marie Josée, da of E Jacques Harel (d 1962); 2 s (b 1965 and 1969); *Career* barr Middle Temple 1955, Mauritius 1955; municipal cncllr Port Louis 1956-69, mayor Port Louis 1963, chm Mauritius Bar Cncl 1973 (memb 1972-73); dir: Mauritius Commercial Bank Ltd, New Mauritius Dock Co Ltd, Union SE Co Ltd, Constance and La Gaieté SE Co Ltd, Harel Frères Ltd, Beau Plan SE Co Ltd, Bel Air St Félix Co Ltd, Promotion and Devpt Co Ltd; *Recreations* reading, hunting; *Clubs* Mauritius Turf, Mauritius Gymkhana; *Style—* J Raymond Hein, Esq, QC; Floreal, Mauritius (☎ 230 6861782); chambers: Cathedral Sq, Port Louis, Mauritius (☎ 230 2120327/230 2081044)

HEINDORFF, Michael; *b* 1949; *Educ* Art Coll and Univ of Braunschweig, Royal Coll of Art London; *Career* artist; teacher Royal Coll of Art London 1980-; solo exhibitions: Gallerie Axiom Cologne 1977, Bernard Jacobson Gallery London 1978, 1981-83, Bernard Jacobson Gallery NY 1983, Middendorf-Lane Washington 1983, Stadia Graphics Sydney 1983, Bernard Jacobson Gallery LA 1981, 1982 and 1984, Jacobson/Hochman Gallery NY 1981 and 1982, Mathildenhoehe Darmstadt Germany 1983, Villa Massimo Rome 1984, Bernard Jacobson Gallery NY and London 1985-87, Northern Centre for Contemporary Art Sunderland 1987, group exhibitions incl: John Moore's Liverpool Exhibitions 1976, Air Gallery 1977, Royal Coll of Art London (Annual Exhibitions) 1977, Whitechapel Art Gallery London 1979, Serpentine Gallery London (Summer show 1) 1980, Anne Berthand Gallery London 1981, Herzog Anton Ulrich-Museum Braunschweig 1981, Bradford Print Biennale 1982, Paton Gallery London (Alternative Tate) 1982, Ashmolean Museum Oxford (Innovations in Contemporary Printmaking) 1982, Third Biennale of European Graphic Art Baden-Baden 1983, Bruecke Museum Berlin 1984, Museum of Modern Art NY 1984, Univ of Maryland USA 1985, Bank of America San Francisco 1985, V&A Museum London 1986, Sunderland Arts Centre & Laing Art Gallery Newcastle 1987, Royal Acad of Art London 1988, Royal Coll of Art 150th Anniversary Show 1988, Imperial War Museum London (On Commission) 1989, Nat Gallery Washington USA 1989, Bernard Jacobson Gallery London 1990; work in the collections of: Royal Coll of Art, Univ of Liverpool, V&A, Vicaria di Santiago de Chile, Herzog Anton Ulrich-Museum Braunschweig, State of Niedersachsen Germany, Arts Cncl of GB, The Br Cncl, Bank of America LA, Security Pacific Bank LA, The Museum of Modern Art NY, The Bank of Montreal London, Bradford Municipal Museum, Green Coll Oxford, Imperial War Museum, Nat Gallery Washington USA; Awards: German Nat Scholarship Fndn scholar 1972-76, DAAD scholarship for London 1976-77, John Moore's Liverpool award 10 1976, State of Niedersachsen scholarship 1980, Schmidt-Rotluff prize 1981, Rome prize Villa Massimo 1981; fell Royal Coll of Art; *Clubs* Chelsea Arts (life memb); *Style—* Michael Heindorff, Esq

HEINEY, Paul; *see*: Ms Libby Purves

HEININGER, Patrick; s of John Jacob Heininger, of Pittsburgh, Pa, USA, and Catherine Ann, *née* Gaffney (d 1944); *b* 22 June 1942; *Educ* American Univ Washington DC (BA), Georgetown Univ Washington DC (LLM, JD); *m* 10 Oct 1987, Caroline, da of Eric Atack, of Essex; *Career* barr: Dist of Columbia 1967, NY 1971; lawyer Debevoise & Pimpton NY 1969-71, lectr and advsr Univ of Nairobi and Govt of Kenya 1971-73, legal advsr fin World Bank Washington DC 1973-82, dir Baring Bros Ltd 1982-90; *Books* Liability of US Banks for Deposits Placed in Their Foreign Branches, Law & Policy in International Business (1979); *Recreations* tennis, squash, chamber music; *Style—* Patrick Heininger, Esq; 18 Clarendon St, London, SW1V 4RD (☎ 071 828 5034); Sweetslade Farm, nr Bourton-on-the-Water, Glos GL54 3BL

HEISBOURG, Francois Louis Joseph; s of Georges Heisbourg, Ambass of Luxembourg (ret), of Luxembourg, and Hélène, *née* Pinet; *b* 24 June 1949; *Educ* Landon Sch Bethesda Maryland, Collége Stanislas Paris, Sciences-Po Paris, École Nationale d'Administration Paris; *m* 24 June 1989, Elyette, da of Georges Levy, of 118 Rue Monge, 75005 Paris; *Career* French Foreign Miny: memb Policy Planning Staff 1977-81, mission first sec to UN NY; int security advsr French MOD 1981-84, vice pres Co-operative Ventures Thomson - CSF Paris 1984-87, dir Int Inst Strategic Studies London 1987-; memb: Int Res Cncl CSIS Washington, Bd Aspen Inst Berlin; Gt Cross W German Order of Merit, Spanish Military Medal (first class), Offr of Togolese Nat Order, Knight French Nat Order of Merit; *Books* La Puce les Hommes et la Bombe (with M Boniface, 1986), The Conventional Defence of Europe (jtly, 1986), The Changing Strategic Landscape (ed, 1989); *Recreations* walking, chess; *Clubs* Travellers (Paris); *Style—* Francois Heisbourg, Esq; International Institute for Strategic Studies, 23 Tavistock St, London WC2E 7NQ (☎ 071 379 7676, fax 071 836 3108, telex 93212102499 G)

HEISER, Sir Terence Michael; KCB 1987 (CB 1984); s of David and Daisy Heiser; *b* 24 May 1932; *Educ* Windsor Co Boys' Sch Berks, Birkbeck Coll London (BA); *m* 1957, Kathleen Mary Waddle; 1 s, 2 da; *Career* served RAF 1950-52; joined Civil Serv 1949, served with Colonial Office, Miny of Works, Miny of Housing and Local Govt; perm sec DOE 1985-; fell Birkbeck Coll London (govr 1990); Freeman City of London 1990; Hon DLitt Univ of Bradford 1988; *Style—* Sir Terence Heiser, KCB

HELAL, Basil; s of Ibrahim Helal, CBE (d 1972), of Cairo, and Helena, *née* Sommerville (d 1942); *b* 28 Oct 1927; *Educ* English Sch Cairo, Univ of London (MB BS), Univ of Liverpool (MCh); *m* 1, 10 Oct 1954, Stella, *née* Feldman (d 1987); 1 s (Adam b 1965), 2 da (Dina b 1956, Manda b 1958); m 2, 30 Jan 1988, Susan Carolyn, *née* Livett; 2 s (Matthew b 1974, Simon b 1978); *Career* sr registrar St George's Hosp 1962-65; orthopaedic conslt: London Hosp 1965-88, Royal Nat Orthopaedic Hosp and Enfield Gp of Hosps 1965-88; emeritus hon conslt; orthopaedic advsr Br Olympic Assoc 1972-, vice pres Coll Internationale Du Chirurgie Medelin Du Pied 1980-, memb Cncl Br Orthopaedic Assoc 1980-82, co fndr Rheumatoid Arthritis Surgical Soc 1983 (former pres), pres Br Orthopaedic Foot Surgery Soc 1983 (fndr 1975), first pres Egyptian Med Soc UK 1984; pres: Br Soc Surgery of the Hand 1985, Br Assoc of Sport and Med 1987-; former vice pres and chm BASM; pres elect Orthopaedic Div RSM 1991-92, memb: BMA 1951, BOA 1957, BSSH, Hunterian Soc; FRCS, FRCSEd; *Books* Surgical Repair and Reconstruction in Rheumatoid Disease (1980), Sports Injuries (1986), The Foot (1988); *Recreations* squash, scuba diving, golf, swimming; *Clubs* Savage, Blizzard; *Style—* Basil Helal, Esq; The Corner House, 23 St Catharines Rd, Broxbourne, Herts EN10 7LD (☎ 0992 466688); 152 Harley St, London W1N 1HH (☎ 01 363 6384, car 0860 385515)

HELE, (James) Warwick; CBE (1986); s of John Warwick Hele (Capt Border Regt, d 1954), of Cumbria, and Elizabeth, *née* Gibb (d 1966); *b* 24 July 1926; *Educ* Sedbergh, Hertford Coll Oxford, Trinity Hall Cambridge (MA); *m* 3 April 1948, Audrey, da of Thomas Davenport Whalley (d 1969), of Bournemouth; 4 da (Elizabeth Ann b 1949, Jane Mary (twin) b 1949, Sarah Catherine b 1956, Rachel Shirley b 1964); *Career*

Royal Armoured Corps 1944-48, Lt 5 Royal Inniskilling Dragon Guards 1946-48; schoolmaster Kings Coll Sch Wimbledon 1951-55; Rugby Sch: schoolmaster 1955-73, housemaster Kilbracken 1965-73, second master 1970-73; high master St Paul's Sch 1973-86; chm: Headmaster Conf 1982 (memb 1973-86), Advsy Ctee Ind Schs Jt Cncl 1983-89, Sherborne Sch 1989-, History Ctees Secondary Examinations Cncl 1986-88, Combined Trusts Scholarship Trust; govr: Port Regis Sch Shaftesbury 1986-, Rossall Sch 1986-89, Uppingham Sch 1986-, Sherborne Sch 1986-; memb Exec Ctee GBA 1988-; tstee Brathay Hall 1977, Clouds House East Knoyle Wilts 1989-; conslt Depart of Education and Science (City Technol Colls) 1986-, non-exec dir Dorset Family Health Serv Authy 1990; *Recreations* gardening, hill-walking; *Clubs* East India and Public Schools; *Style*— Warwick Hele, Esq, CBE; Hillside, Hawkesdene Lane, Shaftesbury, Dorset SP7 8EX (☎ 0747 54205)

HELEY, Richard William; s of Wilfred Charles Heley, of Shaw, Newbury, Berks, and Joyce, *née* Chalker; *b* 9 Oct 1948; *Educ* Forest Sch, Univ of Wales (BA), Univ of Sussex; *m* 7 Sept 1974, Barbara Alessandra, da of Alexander Kirk Kidd, Banbury Rd, Oxford; 1 s (Adam Frederick Peter b 1983), 1 da (Lara Alessandra Cornelia Constantina b 1985); *Career* Int Fin Dept Phillips & Drew 1969-74, dir Corporate Fin Dept Hill Samuel & Co Ltd 1974-86, head of corporate fin Barclays de Zoete Wedd Ltd 1986-89, md UK corp fin Citibank NA 1989-90, exec dir corp fin Hill Samuel Bank Ltd 1990-; ASIA; *Books* Profit Forecasting (1981); *Recreations* riding; *Style*— Richard Heley, Esq; Hope Villa, 1 Wallace Rd, London N1 2PG (☎ 071 226 8698); Citibank NA, Coltons Centre, Hays Lane, London SE1 2QT (☎ 071 234 5678, fax 071 234 5550)

HELLER, Michael Aron; s of Simon Heller, of Harrogate, Yorks, and Nettie, *née* Gordon; *b* 15 July 1936; *Educ* Harrogate GS, St Catharine's Coll Cambridge (MA); *m* 1965, Morven, da of Dr Julius Livingstone; 2 s (John b 1966, Andrew b 1968), 1 da (Nicola b 1981); *Career* chm: London and Assoc Investment Tst plc, Bisichi Mining plc, Electronic Data Processing plc; non exec dir Utd Biscuits (Hldgs) plc; FCA; *Recreations* collecting modern British paintings; *Clubs* RAC; *Style*— Michael Heller, Esq; 30-34 New Bridge St, London EC4V 6LT

HELLER, Robert Gordon Barry; s of late Norman Joseph Heller, and Helen, *née* Flatto; *b* 10 June 1932; *Educ* Christ's Hosp, Jesus Coll Cambridge (BA); *m* 8 Jan 1955, Lois Ruth, da of Michael Malnick; 1 s (Matthew Jonathan b 1960), 2 da (Jane Charlotte b 1962, Kate Elizabeth b 1965); by Angela Mary Flowers, 1 da (Rachel Pearl b 1972); *Career* 2 Lt RASC 1950-52; industl corr (later diary ed and US corr) Financial Times 1955-63, business ed Observer 1963-65, ed (later ed-in-chief and editorial dir) Management Today 1965-87, editorial dir Haymarket Publishing 1978-85; chm: Graduate Gp, Heller Arts, Kate Heller Gallery; dir: Angela Flowers Gallery plc 1970-, Sterling Publishing plc 1985-, The Watts Gp plc, Media Search and Selection, Magazines Int, Business Newsletters; *Books* Superman, Can you Trust your Bank? (with Norris Willatt), The European Revenge (with Norris Willatt), The Naked Investor, The Common Millionaire, The Once and Future Manager, The Business of Winning, The Business of Success, The Naked Market, The Pocket Manager, The New Naked Manager, The State of Industry, The Supermanagers, The Supermarketers, The Age of the Common Millionaire, Unique Success Proposition, The Decision Makers, The Best of Robert Heller, Culture Shock; *Recreations* modern art, food and wine, books, music, exercise; *Style*— Robert Heller, Esq; Sterling Publishing Gp plc, 86/88 Edgware Rd, London W2 2YW (☎ 071 258 0066)

HELLICAR, Michael William; s of Jonathan Ernest Hellicar, of London, and Eileen May, *née* Williams (d 1983); *b* 3 April 1941; *m* 1962, June Betty, da of Charles Edward Pitcher; 3 da (Nicola Jane b 24 May 1965, Justine Louise b 28 July 1966, Charlotte Laura b 18 April 1979); *Career* journalist; apprentice reporter South London Observer 1956-60, asst news ed and feature writer New Musical Express 1960-63, news ed Rave Magazine 1963-64, feature writer Daily Sketch 1964-67; Daily Mirror: feature and leader writer 1967-72, ed Inside Page 1972-73, features ed 1973-76, sr writer 1976-81; asst ed Daily Star 1989- (chief feature writer 1982-89); *Recreations* causing trouble, whingeing; *Style*— Michael Hellicar, Esq; 13 Charlecote Grove, London SE26 4BW (☎ 081 699 8289); Daily Star, Express Newspapers plc, Ludgate House, 245 Blackfriars Rd, London SE1 9UX (☎ 071 928 8000, fax 071 922 7962)

HELLIKER, Adam Andrew Alexander; s of Maurice William Helliker, DFC, AFC (d 1984), and Jane Olivia, *née* Blunt; *b* 13 Sept 1958; *Educ* King's Sch Bruton, Somerset Coll of Arts and Technol; *Career* reporter: Western Times Co Ltd 1978-81, Daily Mail 1981-86; dep diary ed: Daily Mail 1986-, Mail on Sunday 1988; contrib to several nat magazines; Freeman: City of London 1989, Worshipful Co of Wheelwrights 1989; FRGS, FRSA, memb Royal Soc of Lit; *Books* The Debrett Season (ed, 1981), The English Season (contrib, 1988); *Recreations* shooting, book collecting, idle gossip; *Clubs* Naval, St James's, Wig & Pen, Mortons, RAC; *Style*— Adam Helliker, Esq; 1 Sandilands Rd, London SW6 2BD (☎ 071 736 9388); Coombe Hill House, Keinton Mandeville, Somerset (☎ 0458 223228); Daily Mail, 2 Derry St, London W8 5TT (☎ 071 938 6154; car 0860 446284)

HELLINGS, Brian Aliol; s of Robert Aliol Hellings (d 1984), of Falmouth, Cornwall, and Phyllis Selena, *née* Ferris (d 1987); *b* 12 Jan 1936; *Educ* Truro Cathedral Sch; *m* 23 May 1959, Ann, da of Edward Robert Rule (d 1961); 3 s (Mark Robert Aliol b 6 Oct 1962, James Edward Aliol b 16 May 1970, Charles Mathew Aliol b 9 Sept 1978), 3 da (Caroline Gail b 21 June 1961, Joanne Elizabeth b 24 April 1964, Sarah Victoria b 9 Sept 1978); *Career* articled Lodge & Winter 1953-59, audit clerk Deloitte Plender Griffiths & Co 1959-61, dir PB Cow & Co Ltd 1967-68 (fin comptroller and co sec 1961-68); sr dir responsible for fin Hanson plc 1988- (fin comptroller 1968, fin dir 1973); FCA (1959); *Recreations* fishing, gardening, reading; *Style*— Brian Hellings, Esq; Riverlands, W River Rd, Rumson, NJ 07760, USA (☎ 201 842 7005); 2 Third Street, Rumson, NJ, USA (☎ 201 549 7058, fax 201 549 7058, telex 132222, car 201 715 9742)

HELLINIKAKIS, Capt George John; JP (1980); s of John Michael Hellinikakis (d 1979), of Sitia, Crete, Greece, and Claire, *née* Mavroleon (d 1966); *b* 2 Feb 1930; *Educ* Greek Gymnasium, Navy Sch; *m* 29 Aug 1953, Yvonne Alice, da of Charles Richard Barraclough ICS (d 1964); 2 s (John George b 1954, Nicolas George b 1962); *Career* Capt served Navy till 1960; marine conslt Unitor Group of Cos 1960-; *Recreations* sailing, walking; *Clubs* American, Nat Lib, Marine, Master Mariners, Marine Engrs, Propeller (USA); *Style*— Capt George Hellinikakis, JP; 48 Brackley Square, Woodford Green, Essex IG8 7LL (☎ 081 504 0874); Unitor Ships Service Ltd, 3 High Street, Rickmansworth, Herts WD3 1SW (☎ 0923 777 484)

HELLYER, Robert Charles Orlando; s of Graham Hellyer, of North Humberside, and Lois Anness, *née* Anderton; *b* 8 Sept 1952; *Educ* Shrewsbury, Trinity Coll Dublin (BBS); *m* 14 June 1980, Elizabeth Ann, da of William Alan Rutherford; 3 da (Georgina b 9 April 1983, Chloë b 25 March 1987, Alexandra b 10 March 1989); *Career* CA 1980; KPMG Peat Marwick McLintock (formerly Peat Marwick Mitchell) 1976-82, co sec Charterhall plc 1982-86, fin dir J Hambro & Co Ltd 1986-; *Recreations* shooting, fishing; *Style*— Robert Hellyer, Esq; J Hambro & Co Ltd, 30 Queen Anne's Gate, London SW1H 9AL (☎ 071 222 2020, fax 071 222 1993)

HELM, Michael Thomas; s of Rev Thomas Helm (d 1978), of Tunbridge Wells, and Kathleen, *née* Hall (d 1976); *b* 17 May 1939; *Educ* Tonbridge; *m* 17 Oct 1973, Christine Jennifer, da of Stanley Alfred Henry Slattery, of Chislehurst, Kent; 1 s (Sebastian b 1974), 1 da (Alexandra b 1976); *Career* co sec Nitrate Corp of Chile Ltd 1969-78; fin dir: Croom-Helm Ltd 1978-86, WH Allen and Co Plc 1986-90, fin controller Granta Publications Ltd 1990, fin sec Glass & Glazing Federation 1991; FCA 1963; *Recreations* Napoleonic studies, opera, art; *Style*— Michael Helm, Esq

HELME, Hon Mrs (Mirabel Jane); *née* Guinness; da of 2 Baron Moyne; *b* 1956; *Educ* Cranborne Chase and E Anglia Univ (BA); *m* 10 August 1984, Patrick Ian Helme, interior designer; 2 da (Alice Mirabel b 1987, Tyga Elisabeth b 1990); *Career* equestrienne; MFH Tedworth Hunt 1986-; *Books* Biddesden Cookery (1987); *Style*— The Hon Mrs Helme; Mount Orleans, Collingbourne Ducis, Marlborough, Wilts

HELMORE, Charles Patrick; s of Patrick Helmore, of Crumlin Lodge, Inverin, Co Galway, Ireland, and Mary, *née* Hull; *b* 26 May 1951; *Educ* Eton, Magdalene Coll Cambridge (MA), INSEAD Fontainebleau (MBA); *m* 16 May 1981, Rachel, da of Bertram Aykroyd (d 1983), of Treyford Manor, Sussex; 2 s (Max b 1984, Caspar b 1987); *Career* called to the Bar Middle Temple, in practice 1973-75; Jardine Matheson Co Ltd 1975-78, Paine Webber Mitchell Hutchins 1979-82, dir Foreign & Colonial Mgmnt 1982-90, Enskilda Asset Managment Ltd 1990-; *Recreations* fishing, shooting, reading; *Style*— Charles Helmore, Esq; Wyndham Cottage, Rogate, nr Petersfield, Hants; Enskilda Asset Managment Ltd, 30 Finsbury Square, London EC2 (☎ 071 374 6133, fax 071 867 9084)

HELMORE, Roy Lionel; CBE (1980); s of Lionel John Helmore (d 1972), and Ellen, *née* Gibbins (d 1983); *b* 8 June 1926; *Educ* Montrose Acad, Univ of Edinburgh (BSc), Univ of Cambridge (MA); *m* 5 April 1969, Margaret Lilian, da of Ernest Martin (d 1971); *Career* various lectr posts in electrical engrg 1949-57, head of dept Electrical Engrg and Sci Exeter Tech Coll 1957-61; princ: St Albans Coll 1961-77, Cambridgeshire Coll of Arts & Technol 1977-86; fell Hughes Hall Univ of Cambridge 1982-; JP St Albans 1964-78, pres Assoc of Princs of Tech Insts 1972-73 (hon sec 1968-71), vice chm Technician Educn Cncl 1973-79, memb MSC 1974-82, chm of cncl Assoc of Colls for Further and Higher Educn 1987-88, hon memb City and Guilds of London Inst 1987; FIEE, FBIM; *Books* CCAT A Brief History (1989); *Recreations* gardening, watercolours, opera; *Style*— Roy Helmore, Esq, CBE; 5 Beck Rd, Saffron Walden, Essex CB11 4EH (☎ 0799 23981)

HELPS, Dr (Edmund) Peter Wycliffe; s of Edmund Arthur Plucknett Helps (d 1975), of Roscarberry, Eire, and Lucy Laura Frida, *née* Wycliffe-Taylor (d 1971); *b* 28 Sept 1921; *Educ* Radley, Bart's Hosp, Univ of London (LRCP, MRCP, MB BS, MD); *m* May 1950, Heather Bell, da of Andrew Hood (d 1965), of Brook, Hants; 1 s (Dominic b 1956), 1 da (Sarah b 1952); *Career* Capt RAMC 1945-48, staff surgn Bannu NWFP India 1945; house surgn Bart's 1944, house physician Hammersmith Hosp and Postgraduate Med Sch 1948, med registrar UCH 1950-57, med fell John Hopkins Hosp and Univ Baltimore USA 1956-57; conslt physician: Lambeth Gp London 1958-62, Dept of Med for Elderly Charing Cross Hosp 1963-88; inscribed in BMA Book of Valour 1978, Peter Helps Ward at Charing Cross Hosp Inaugurated 1989, author of articles on circulation and ageing topics; memb: BMA, Br Geriatrics Soc; FRCP 1973, FRSM; *Books* Today's Treatment (contrib 1978); *Recreations* boating, deerhounds, tennis; *Style*— Dr Peter Helps; Porch House, Coleshill, nr Amersham, Bucks HP7 0LG (☎ 0494 727584)

HELSBY, George; s of George Isaac Helsby (d 1948); *b* 9 Dec 1941; *Educ* Ellergreen HS; *m* 1964, Joyce, da of Thomas Walls (d 1984); 2 da; *Career* formerly chm and chief exec Burnett and Hallamshire Hldgs plc, chm and chief exec TPM Systems Ltd; *Recreations* music, philosophy; *Clubs* Clubs Int; *Style*— George Helsby Esq

HELSBY, Hon Nigel Charles; s of Baron Helsby (Life Peer d 1978), by his w Wilmett Mary (who m 2, Rex Hines), da of William Granville Maddison (d 1953), of Durham; *b* 26 July 1941; *Educ* Wellington, Keble Coll Oxford (MA); *m* 1969, Sylvia Rosena, da of Ronald Brown, of Burnham-on-Crouch; 2 da (Rebecca, Genevieve); *Career* electronics engr; mangr Electronics Centre Univ of Essex 1977-87, dir Radiocode Clocks Ltd 1983-; *Style*— The Hon Nigel Helsby; Abbots Wood, The Street, Salcott-cum-Virley, Maldon, Essex CM9 8HW (☎ 0621 860416); Radiocode Clocks Ltd, Radiocode House, Kernick Rd, Penryn Cornwall TR10 9LY (☎ 0326 76007)

HELSBY, Richard John Stephens (Rick); s of John Michael Helsby (d 1972), and Margaret Stella, *née* Andrews; *b* 10 Jan 1949; *Educ* Magdalen Coll Sch Oxford, Warwick Univ (BA), Oxford Univ (Dip Ed); *m* 27 July 1968, Kathryn Diana, da of Robert Alan Langford, of Abingdon, Oxford; 3 s (James b 1968, Nathan b 1972, William b 1986); *Career* HM inspr of Taxes Oxford 1972-78, sr inspr of Taxes Inland Revenue Enquiry Branch 1978-84, sr tax mangr Deloitte Haskins & Sells 1984-87, ptnr Tax Investigators Coopers & Lybrand Deloitte 1987-; *Books* Trouble with the Taxman (1985), Offshore Survival (with Jim McMahon, Bernard McCarthy 1988); *Recreations* squash, football, theatre, cinema, snooker; *Style*— Rick Helsby, Esq; 44 Tredegar Sq, Bow, London E3 5AE (☎ 081 981 1422); Coopers & Lybrand Deloitte, Hillgate House, 26 Old Bailey, London EC4M 7PL (☎ 071 583 5000, fax 071 454 8600)

HELVIN, Marie; da of Hugh Lee Helvin, of Honolulu, Hawaii, USA, and Linda S Helvin; *b* 13 Aug 1952; *m* 1975 (m dis 1985), David Bailey, *qv*; *Career* model; Vogue 12 covers; modelled for: (designers) St Laurent, Armani, Valentino, Chanel, Calvin Klein, (photographers) Lartique, Helmut Newton, David Bailey; presenter Frocks on the Box (ITV series); appeared in the film The Children (dir Tony Palmer 1990); author of articles for: The Independent, The Sunday Telegraph, Time Out; memb Cncl Aids Crisis Tst; patron: Foster Parents Plan, Frontliners, Zoo Check, Lynx; *Books* Catwalk - The Art of Model Style (1985); *Style*— Miss Marie Helvin; 23 Eyot Gardens, London W6 9TN (☎ 081 846 8070, fax 081 746 5334)

HELY HUTCHINSON, Hon Mark; yr s of late 7 Earl of Donoughmore; *b* 19 May 1934; *Educ* Eton, Magdalen Coll Oxford (BSc, MA), MIT USA (SM); *m* 1962, (Rosita) Margaret, yr da of late Dr Robert Rowan Woods, of Dublin; 2 s, 1 da; *Career* 2 Lt Irish Gds; joined Arthur Guinness Group 1958, md Guinness Ireland 1975-82; chief exec Bank of Ireland 1983-90 (dir 1975); *Style*— Mark Hely Hutchinson, Esq; Larch Hill, Coolock Lane, Dublin 17, Ireland (☎ 428718)

HELY HUTCHINSON, Hon Nicholas David; 3 s of 8 Earl of Donoughmore, *qv*; *b* 30 April 1955; *Educ* Harrow; *m* 1982, Fiona Margaret MacIntyre, da of late Maj W R Watson; 1 s (Seamus David b 1987), 1 da (Flora Clare b 1984); *Clubs* Beefsteak, Chelsea Arts; *Style*— The Hon Nicholas Hely Hutchinson; c/o The Rt Hon the Earl of Donoughmore, The Manor House, Bampton, Oxon OX8 2LQ

HELY HUTCHINSON, Hon Ralph Charles; 4 and yst s of 8 Earl of Donoughmore; *b* 16 Dec 1961; *Educ* Eton; *Career* stockbroker Phillips & Drew 1985-88, asst dir Hoare Govett 1988-; *Recreations* food and wine, racing, travel; *Style*— The Hon Ralph Hely Hutchinson; 8 Kensington Palace Gardens, London W8 (☎ 071 229 7127)

HELY HUTCHINSON, Hon Timothy Mark; 2 s of 8 Earl of Donoughmore; *b* 26 Oct 1953; *Educ* Eton, Oxford; *Career* md: Macdonald & Co (Publishers) Ltd 1982-86, Headline Book Publishing plc 1986-; FRSA; *Clubs* Groucho; *Style*— The Hon Timothy Hely Hutchinson; 2 Redan St, London W14 0AD

HEMANS, Simon Nicholas Peter; CVO (1983); s of Brig P R Hemans, CBE, of Hants, and M E Hemans, *née* Melsome; *b* 19 Sept 1940; *Educ* Sherborne, LSE

(BSc); *m* 1970, Ursula Martha, da of Herr Werner Naef (d 1972); 3 s (Alexander b 1967, Oliver b 1974, Anthony (twin) b 1974), 1 da (Jennifer b 1972); *Career* FO 1964, Br Embassy Moscow 1966-68, dep cmmr Anguilla 1969, FCO 1969-71, UK Mission to UN NY 1971-75, Br Embassy Budapest 1975-79, asst head Southern African Dept FCO 1979-81, dep high cmmr Nairobi 1981-84, cnsllr and head of chancery Moscow 1985-87, appt head of Soviet Dept FCO 1987-90; asst under-sec of state (Africa) FCO 1990-; *Recreations* travel, ballet, opera; *Style—* Simon Hemans, Esq, CVO; FCO, King Charles St, London SW1A 2AH (☎ 071 270 2202)

HEMERY, David Peter; MBE (1969); s of Peter Ronald Bentley Hemery, of Boston, Mass, USA, and Eileen Beatrice, *née* Price (d 1985); *b* 18 July 1944; *Educ* Endsleigh Sch Colchester, Thayer Acad USA, Boston Univ USA (BSc, DEd) St Catherine's Coll Oxford (CertEd), Harvard (MEd); *m* 31 July 1981, Vivian Mary, da of Alan Patrick William Bruford; 2 s (Adrain David b 6 Aug 1982, Peter Robert b 28 Oct 1984); *Career* former international athlete; achievements incl: AAA jr 120 yards high hurdles champion 1963, Gold medal 120 yards high hurdles Cwlth Games 1966, AAA 400m hurdles champion 1968, Gold medal 400m hurdles Olympic Games 1968, American Nat Collegiate 400m hurdles champion 1968, Silver medal 110m high hurdles Euro Championships 1969, Gold medal 110m high hurdles World Student Games 1970, Gold medal 110m high hurdles Cwlth Games 1970, Silver medal 4 x 400m relay Olympic Games 1972 (Bronze 400m hurdles); records: UK indoor 60 yards high hurdles 1966, Euro indoor 600 yards 1966, UK 120 yards high hurdles 1966 and 1969, UK 400m hurdles 1968, Olympic and world 400m hurdles 1968, world 300m hurdles 1972; winner Br Superstars 1973 and 1976, winner Br Past Masters Superstars 1983; gen clerk National Westminster Bank London 1962-63, computer and settlement clerk National Shawmut Bank Boston 1963-64, res Rank Audio-Visual London 1968-69, teacher and housemaster Millfield Sch 1972-73, dir Sobell Sports Centre 1974-75, head track coach and lectr Boston Univ 1976-83, fndr and presenter human devpt courses Nat Coaching Fndn 1984-; chm Int Athletics Club 1973-75; memb: Grants Ctee Sports Aid Fndn 1986-90, Educn Ctee BOA 1986-; Churchill Fell 1972; Euro athlete of the year 1968, Br Athletic Writers' Assoc athlete of the year 1968 and 1972, Track Field News world runner of the year 1968, New England coach of the year 5 times 1978-83; *Books* Another Hurdle (autobiography, 1976), Sporting Excellence (1986), Athletic in Action (1988), Winning Without Drugs (1990); *Recreations* physical, psychological and spiritual development and intergration - personal and human kind; *Style—* David Hemery, Esq, MBE; White Acre, Fyfield, Marlborough, Wiltshire SN8 1PX (☎ 0672 86645)

HEMINGFORD, 3 Baron (UK 1943), of Watford, Co Hertford; (Dennis) Nicholas Herbert; s of 2 Baron Hemingford (d 1982), and Elizabeth McClare, *née* Clark (d 1979); *b* 25 July 1934; *Educ* Oundle, Clare Coll Cambridge (MA); *m* 8 Nov 1958, Jennifer Mary Toresen, o da of Frederick William Bailey (d 1986), of Harrogate; 1 s (Hon Christopher Dennis Charles b 1973), 3 da (Hon Elizabeth Frances Toresen b 1963, Hon Caroline Mary Louise b 1964, Hon Alice Christine Emma b 1968); *Heir* s, Hon Christopher Dennis Charles Herbert b 1973; *Career* remains known professionally as Nicholas Herbert; journalist Reuters Ltd London and Washington DC 1956-61; joined The Times 1961: asst Washington correspondent 1961-65, Middle East correspondent 1965-69, dep features ed 1969-70; ed Cambridge Evening News 1970-74, editorial dir Westminster Press 1974-, pres Guild of Br Newspaper Editors 1980-81 (vice pres 1979-80); hon sec Assoc of British Editors 1985-; chm East Anglia Regnl Ctee Nat Tst; pres Huntingdonshire Family History Soc, resigned 1990; Liveryman Worshipful Co of Grocers; FRSA; *Recreations* genealogy, Victorian military history, destructive gardening; *Clubs* Commonwealth Trust, City Livery; *Style—* The Rt Hon the Lord Hemingford; The Old Rectory, Hemingford Abbots, Huntingdon, Cambs PE18 9AN (☎ 0480 66234); Westminster Press Ltd, 2 Common Lane, Hemingford Abbots, Huntingdon, Cambs PE18 9AH (☎ 0480 492133, fax 0480 492805)

HEMINGWAY, Prof Anne Patricia; da of Stanley Redgrave Hemingway, of Emsworth, Hants, and Grace Elizabeth, *née* Higgs (d 1983); *b* 1 March 1951; *Educ* Southend HS for Girls, Guy's Hosp Med Sch (BSc, MB BS, DMRD); *m* Dr David C M Evans; 1 da (Elizabeth Jane b 1989); *Career* house surgn Guy's Hosp 1975, house physician Greenwich Dist Hosp 1976, jr registrar in cardiology and med Guy's Hosp 1976-77, sr house offr Brook Hosp London 1977-78, registrar KCH 1978-79, sr lectr and conslt radiologist Royal Postgrad Med Sch London 1983-87 (registrar 1979-83), Kodak Prof of radiodiagnosis Univ of Sheffield 1987-; contrib to numerous learned jls; memb: Handicapped Childrens Pilgrimage Tst, Hosanna House Tst; memb: BMA, GMC, Radiological Soc of N America; FRCP, FRCR; *Recreations* cooking, reading, gardening, knitting, philately; *Style—* Prof Anne Hemingway; Academic Dept of Radiology, Royal Hallamshire Hospital, Glossop Rd, Sheffield S10 2JF (☎ 0742 724760, fax 0742 724760)

HEMINGWAY, Peter; *b* 19 Jan 1926; *m* 1952, June; *Career* ptnr John Gordon Walton and Co 1959-62, dir and chief gen mangr Leeds Permanent Building Society 1982-87 (joined as sec 1962), local dir (Leeds) Royal Insurance (UK) Ltd 1983-; chm Yorks and N Western Assoc of Bldg Socs 1984-86 (hon sec 1970-82); memb Cncl: Bldg Socs Assoc 1981-87, Chartered Bldg Socs Inst 1982-87; vice pres Northern Assoc of Bldg Socs 1988-; *Recreations* travel, motor racing, music, gardening; *Style—* Peter Hemingway, Esq; Old Barn Cottage, Kearby, nr Wetherby, Yorks (☎ 0532 886380)

HEMINGWAY, Wayne Andrew; s of Chief Billy Two Rivers (chief of Khanawake Tribe (Mohawk) Quebec Canada), and Maureen, *née* Hemingway; *b* 19 Jan 1961; *Educ* Queen Elizabeth's GS Blackburn, UCL (BSC); *m* Gerardine Mary, da of Ken Astin; 1 s (Jack b 22 June 1986), 2 da (Tilly b 23 July 1987, Corey b Aug 1990); *Career* fndr Red or Dead fashion design co 1982, expanded business from Camden Market Stall to (currently) 6 UK shops as mail order business and a whole sale network, designer Red or Dead own label shoe collection; regular speaker to fashion colls and footwear assocs on shoe, clothing and interior design; work shown in numerous exhibitions of Br design incl: Boymans Museum Rotterdam, Orange County California, V & A London; second place Young Business Person of the Year 1990; *Recreations* cricket; *Clubs* Stage Cricket; *Style—* Wayne Hemingway, Esq; Red or Dead, Pop-In Commercial Centre, South Way, Wembley, Middx HA9 0HD (☎ 081 903 2062/6777/9889/1490, fax 081 903 5111)

HEMMING, Alice Louisa; OBE (1974); da of William Arthur Weaver (d 1958), of Penticton, BC, and Alice Louisa, *née* Chorley (d 1964); *b* 18 Sept 1907; *Educ* Vancouver HS, Univ of Br Columbia (BA); *m* 5 March 1931, (Henry) Harold Hemming, OBE, MC, s of Henry Keane Simmons Hemming, of Charlottestown, Prince Edward Island, Canada; 2 c (Louisa b 13 Dec 1931, John b 5 Jan 1935); *Career* journalist Vancouver Sun 1928-30, Marquis of Donegall Cork Sunday Despatch 1939-41, columnist Vancouver Province 1940-44, broadcaster 1940-43, info offr Nat Film Bd of Canada 1943-44, ed advsr Municipal Journal 1948-68, dir Municipal Gp; pres Cwlth Countries League 1948-, vice pres Women's Cncl; memb: Br American Assocs, Cncl Canadian Univs Soc, Ctee Woodstock, Hampstead Old People's Housing Tst, Canadian Ctee of London House (for overseas graduates), Jt Cwlth Socs Cncl; govr CCLA Ed Ctee; *Recreations* dancing, entertaining for charities; *Style—* Ms Alice Hemming, OBE; 35 Elsworthy Rd, London NW3 3BT (☎ 071 722 6619)

HEMMING, Dr John Henry; s of Lt-Col Henry Harold Hemming, OBE, MC (d 1977), of London, and Alice Louisa, OBE, *née* Weaver; *b* 5 Jan 1935; *Educ* Eton, McGill Univ, Univ of Oxford (MA, DLitt); *m* 19 Jan 1979, Sukie Mary, da of Brig Michael J Babington-Smith, CBE (d 1984); 1 s (Henry Sebastian b 1979), 1 da (Beatrice Margaret Louisa b 1981); *Career* charity dir Royal Geographical Soc 1975-; publisher; jt chm: Hemming Publishing Ltd (formerly Municipal Jl Ltd) 1976- (dir 1962, dep chm 1967-76), Municipal Group Ltd 1976-; chm: Brintex Ltd 1979- (md 1962-71), Newman Books Ltd 1979-, Museum of Empire & Cwlth Tst; ldr Maracà Rainforest Project Brazil 1987-89; fndr tstee and sponsor Survival Int; memb Cncl/Ctee: Lepra, Anglo-Brazilian Soc, Geographical Club, L S B Leakey Tst, Gilchrist Educnl Tst, Inst of Latin American Studies, Museum of Empire & Cwlth Tst, Margaret Mee Tst, Cncl of Br Geography; Hon DLitt Univ of Warwick 1989; Founders medal RGS 1990, Mungo Park medal Royal Scottish Geographical Soc 1988; Orden de Mérito (Peru) 1987, hon corr memb Academia Nacional de Historia Venezuela; Freeman Worshipful Co of Stationers and Newspapermakers; *Books* The Conquest of the Incas (1970), Tribes of the Amazon Basin in Brazil (1973), Red Gold (1978), The Search for El Dorado (1978), Machu Picchu (1981), Monuments of the Incas (1982), Change in the Amazon Basin (1985), Amazon Frontier (1987), Maracá (1988), Roraima, Brazil's northernmost frontier (1990); *Recreations* writing, travel; *Clubs* Beefsteak, Bootle's, Geographical; *Style—* Dr John Hemming; 10 Edwardes Sq, London W8 6HE (☎ 01 602 6697); 32 Vauxhall Bridge Rd, London SW1V 2SS (☎ 071 973 6404, fax 071 233 5049, telex 262568 MUNBEX G)

HEMMING, Lindy; da of Alan Hemming (d 1983), of Crug-y-Bar, Llanwrda, Dyfed, and Jean, *née* Alexander; *b* 21 Aug 1948; *Educ* RADA; Bob Starrett; 1 s (Daniel Grace b 16 Nov 1974), 1 da (Alexandra Grace b 30 Jan 1969); *Career* costume designer in theatre, tv and film 1972-; Hampstead Theatre Club 1974-79: Abigail's Party, Ecstasy, The Elephant Man, Uncle Vanya, Clouds; RSC 1978-84: Juno and the Paycock, Mother Courage, All's Well That Ends Well; National Theatre Co: Death of a Salesman, Schweyk in the Second World war, Pravda, A View from the Bridge, A Small Family Business, Waiting for Godot; West End theatre: Donkeys Years, Brighton Beach Memoirs, Steel Magnolias, Clouds, Chorus of Disapproval, King (musical 1990); film and tv: Wetherby, 84 Charing Cross Rd, Abigail's Party, My Beautiful Laundrette, High Hopes, Meantime, Porterhouse Blue, Queen of Hearts, The Kray's; memb Soc Br Theatre Designers; *Recreations* cycling, walking, eating, drinking coffee, watching people; *Style—* Ms Lindy Hemming; 8 Bewdley St, London N1 1HB (☎ 01 607 6107)

HEMMINGS, Edward Ernest; s of Edward Hemmings and Dorothy Phyllis Hemmings; *b* 20 Feb 1949; *Educ* Campion HS; *m* 1971, Christine Mary; 2 s (Thomas, James); *Career* professional cricketer, starter 1965; *Style—* Edward Hemmings, Esq; Nottinghamshire CCC; Trent Bridge, Nottingham (☎ 821525)

HEMPHILL, Dr Barry Francis; s of Robert John Hemphill (d 1963), and Dorothy Mary, *née* Witherdin (d 1982); *b* 30 March 1934; *Educ* De la Salle Coll Armidale, Univ of Sydney (Cwlth scholarship and Univ exhibition, BDS, MDS), RCS (FDS), St Bartholomew's Hosp (LRCP, MRCS, MB BS); *m* 17 Oct 1964, Shelagh Veronica, da of Oscar Ronald Gilbey; 1 s (Guy Francis b 22 March 1966), 2 da (Beth Frances b 15 Jan 1969, Sophia Frances b 15 Sept 1970); *Career* sr teaching fell Faculty of Dentistry Univ of Sydney, studying and practising 1956-59, in specialised dental practice 1970-; Capt Royal Australian Army Dental Corps, former pres Br Endodontic Soc, former memb Cncl Odontological Soc of RSM; Freeman City of London 1981, Liveryman Worshipful Co of Barbers 1982; FRACDS 1964, FRSM 1972, fell Int Coll Dental Surgeons 1976; memb: BDA 1959, BMA 1970, Br Endodontic Soc 1974; *Books* Preservation of Pulpal Vitality (Master's thesis, 1959); *Recreations* art, music, theatre, swimming, rugby football; *Clubs* Athenaeum, Savage, Lansdowne; *Style—* Dr Barry Hemphill; 40 Harley St, London W1N 1AB (☎ 071 580 3299)

HEMPHILL, 5 Baron (UK 1906); Peter Patrick Fitzroy Martyn Martyn-Hemphill; assumed the additional surname of Martyn by deed poll of 1959; s of 4 Baron (d 1957); *b* 5 Sept 1928; *Educ* Downside, Brasenose Coll Oxford (MA); *m* 1952, Olivia, da of Major Robert Ruttledge, MC, of Co Mayo, and sis of Lady Edward FitzRoy (herself da-in-law of 10 Duke of Grafton); 1 s, 2 da; *Heir* s, Hon Charles Martyn-Hemphill; *Career* memb Turf Club and former sr steward; memb Irish Nat Hunt Steeplechase Ctee and former sr steward; Cross of Order of Merit, Order of Malta; *Clubs* White's, RIYC, Irish Cruising, RIAC, County (Galway); *Style—* The Rt Hon the Lord Hemphill; Raford House, Kiltulla, Co Galway, Ireland (☎ 010 353 091 48002)

HEMSLEY, Hon Mrs (Gwenllian Ellen); *née* James; eldest da of 4 Baron Northbourne; *b* 9 Sept 1929; *m* 1, 14 June 1952 (m annulled 1960), Michael Hugh Rose, 3 s of late Rt Rev Alfred Carey Wollaston Rose, Bishop of Dover; m 2, 9 Nov 1960, Thomas Jeffrey Hemsley, s of Sydney William Hemsley, of Hugglescote, Leics; 3 s; *Style—* The Hon Mrs Hemsley; 10 Denewood Rd, Highgate, London N6

HEMSLEY, Henry Neville (Harry); DL (Leics); s of Neville Hemsley (d 1948), of Jersey, CI, and Mary Florence Eliza, *née* Farran (d 1968); *b* 27 Nov 1922; *Educ* Sherborne, Univ of Cambridge (MA); *m* 26 Feb 1949, Margaret Ruth, da of Hon William Borthwick (d 1956); 2 s (John Neville b 1956, Oliver Charles b 1960), 2 da (Patricia Mary b 1964, Clare Margaret b 1953); *Career* Lt (E) Temp RN 1942-46; farmer 1961-; dep chm Rutland Magistrates Ct 1990- (chm 1987-90); memb Bd of Vistors Ashwell Prison 1969-, chm LRC Ashwell Prison 1990-, former chm local NAVSS, memb Nat Mgmnt Ctee NAVSS 1982-87, former cdre Rutland Sailing Club; *Recreations* shooting, bridge; *Style—* Henry Hemsley, Esq, DL; Langham Lodge, Oakham, Rutland LE15 7HZ (☎ 0572 722912)

HEMSLEY, Michael John; s of Reginald James Hemsley (d 1968), and Therese Elizabeth Hemsley (d 1987); *b* 9 March 1940; *Career* slr; fndr and princ Hemsleys Slrs Chester; *Style—* Michael J Hemsley, Esq; Spring Villa, Liverpool Road, Chester (☎ 0244 371125); Upper Northgate, Chester (☎ 0244 382400, fax 0244 372335)

HEMSLEY, Michael Stuart; s of Alan Fraser Hemsley, of Totton, Southampton, Hants, and Janet Enid Taylor; *b* 13 July 1957; *Educ* Beverley Boys Sch New Malden Surrey, Salisbury Coll of Art; *m* 30 May 1981, Catherine Bernadette Hemsley da of Thomas Oswald O'Keeffe; 2 s (Thomas Joseph b 26 Sept 1986, Robert Michael b 19 Oct 1988); *Career* professional photographer; Colt International Ltd Havant: trainee Photographic Dept 1974, photographed industl sites for advtg and promotional use until 1981; industl and commercial photographer Walter Gardiner Photography Worthing 1981-; photographic assignments in UK and abroad incl: submarines, toothpaste, sewage works and dead bodies in coffins; winner Bausch and Lomb Young Photographer of the Year 1982, Ilford Photographer of the Year 1985, 1989, winner Peter Grudgeon award for best fellowship application 1986; FBIPP (1986); *Style—* Michael Hemsley, Esq; Walter Gardiner Photography, Southdown View Rd, Worthing, W Sussex BN14 8NL (☎ 0903 200528, fax 0903 820830)

HEMSLEY, Thomas Jeffrey; s of Sydney William Hemsley (d 1986), of Little Eversden, Cambs, and Kathleen Annie, *née* Deacon (d 1976); *b* 12 April 1927; *Educ* Ashby-de-la-Zouch Boys GS, Brasenose Coll Oxford (MA); *m* 9 Nov 1960, Hon Gwenllian Ellen James, *qv*, s of Walter Ernest Christopher James, 4 Baron Northbourne (d 1982), of Northbourne Ct, Deal, Kent; 3 s (William b 1962, Matthew b

1963, Michael b 1965); *Career* PO RAF 1948-50; vicar choral St Paul's Cathedral 1950-51, opera debut Mermaid Theatre 1951, Glyndebourne Festival Opera debut 1953 (first of many appearances until 1983), princ baritone: Stadttheater Aachen 1953-56, Deutsche Oper am Rhein 1957-63, Opernhaus Zurich 1963-67; freelance singer 1967-: Covent Garden, ENO, Scottish Opera, WNO, Kent Opera, Glyndebourne Festival, Edinburgh Festival, Bayreuth Festival (1968-70); soloist for many orchs throughout Europe; teaching incl: RNCM, Guildhall Sch of Music of Drama, Royal Danish Acad of Music, Britten-Pears Sch; TV masterclasses: Denmark 1971, BBC TV 1976; opera prodr: RNCM, Dallas Public Opera, Kent Opera; jury memb at many singing competitions, Cramm lectr Univ of Glasgow 1976; Hon RAM (1974), Hon FTCL 1988; memb: ISM 1953, Equity 1953; *Recreations* gardening, mountain walking; *Clubs* Garrick; *Style—* Thomas Hemsley, Esq; 10 Denewood Rd, London N6 4AJ (☎ 081 348 3397)

HENCKE, David Robert; s of Charles Ewald Hencke London, and Enid, *née* Rose; *b* 26 April 1947; *Educ* Tulse Hill Comp Sch, Univ of Warwick (BA); *m* 5 July 1969, Margaret Mary, da of Laurie Langrick; 1 da (Anne Margaret b 14 Aug 1979); *Career* jr reporter Northamptonshire Evening Telegraph 1968-71, reporter: Western Mail 1971-73, Times Higher Educational Supplement 1973-76; The Guardian: reporter 1976-79, planning corr 1979-81, social servs corr 1981-86, Westminster corr 1986-; Reporter of the Year: E Midlands Allied Press 1971, Br Press awards 1989 (specialist writer of the year 1981); *Books* Colleges in Crisis (1976); *Recreations* theatre, walking, gardening, cooking; *Style—* David Hencke, Esq; The Guardian, 119 Farringdon Rd, London EC1R 3ER (☎ 071 278 2332, 071 219 6769, fax 071 222 1321)

HENDER, John Derrik; CBE (1986), DL (W Midlands 1973); s of Jesse Peter Hender (d 1944), and Jennie, *née* Williams (d 1965); *b* 15 Nov 1926; *Educ* Great Yarmouth GS; *m* 29 Oct 1949, Kathleen Nora, da of Frederick William Brown (d 1945); 1 da (Annetteb 6 May 1955); *Career* RN 1944-47; chief exec Coventry City 1969-73 (city treas 1964-69), chief exec W Midlands CC 1973-86, public sector conslt 1986-; hon fell Inst of Local Govt Studies Univ of Birmingham; FCA, IPFA; *Style—* J D Hender Esq, CBE, DL; 5 Cringleford Chase, Cringleford, Norwich NR4 7RS (☎ 0603 503747)

HENDERSON, Alan Brodie; *b* 30 July 1933; *Educ* Eton; *m* 9 June 1969; 4 s, 1 da; *Career* Capt Welsh Gds 1952-59; with James Capel (Stockbrokers) 1959-63, md Henderson Administration Ltd 1965-77 (joined 1963), chm Henderson Unit Trust Co Ltd 1974-77; dir: Mackay Shields Financial Corporation NY 1974-77, Schlesinger Investment Management Services Ltd 1977-81; md Schlesinger Trust Managers Ltd 1979-81, non-exec chm Newmarket Venture Capital plc 1972-; non-exec dir: Aberdeen Trust Holdings Ltd, Greenfriar Investment Co plc Frobisher Fund, Aetna International (UK) Ltd, Ranger Oil Ltd, Ranger Oil (UK) Ltd; *Clubs* Whites, City of London; *Style—* Alan Henderson, Esq; Ranger Oil (UK) Ltd, Ranger House, 71 Great Peter St, London SW1P 2BN (☎ 071 222 4363, fax 071 233 2997)

HENDERSON, Dr Alexander George; s of Alexander George Henderson (d 1961), and Ethel Kate, *née* Kilpatrick (d 1967); *b* 18 June 1924; *Educ* Whitgift Sch Croydon Surrey, Kings Coll London, Kings Coll Hosp Med Sch (MB BS); *m* 6 June 1953, Adrienne Mae, da of the late Ernest John Crump; 2 s (James b 1958, Alexander b 1972), 4 da (Rosemary b 1954, Margaret b 1956, Kathryn b 1961, Elizabeth b 1963); *Career* sr registrar Dept of Anaesthetics United Cardiff Hosps 1954-56 (registrar 1951-54), conslt anaesthetist Luton and Dunstable Hosp 1956-89; memb: The Pain Soc, Assoc of Anaesthetists; FFARCS 1954, FRSM 1956; *Recreations* church activities, walking, photography, reading; *Style—* Dr Alexander G Henderson; 62 Holywell Rd, Studham, Dunstable, Beds LU6 2PD (☎ 0582 873303)

HENDERSON, (James Stewart) Barry; s of James Henderson, CBE; *b* 29 April 1936; *Educ* Lathallan Sch, Stowe; *m* 1961, Janet; 2 s; *Career* Nat Serv Scots Gds 1954-56; info offr Scot Cons Cent Off 1966-70; posts in: info technol 1971-75, mgmnt consltancy 1975-86, paper indust 1987-90, dir Br Paper and Board Indust Fedn 1990-; Parly candidate (Cons): Edinburgh E 1966, E Dunbartonshire 1970; MP (Cons): E Dunbartonshire Feb-Oct 1974, Fife E 1979-83, NE Fife 1983-87; chm Scot Cons Backbench Ctee 1983; memb: Select Ctee for Scottish Affrs 1979-87, vice chm Parly Info Technol Ctee 1986-87, Commons Chm's Panel 1981-83; treasy PPS 1984-87; MBCS; *Style—* Barry Henderson, Esq; 10 White Hart Court, Fairford, Glos GL7 4AG (☎ 0285 713385)

HENDERSON, Bernard Vere; CBE (1988); s of Col P C Henderson, OBE (d 1961), and Ruth, *née* Morphew; *b* 8 June 1928; *Educ* Ampleforth; *m* Valerie Jane, da of Capt Charles Cairns (d 1931); 2 s (Mark, Paul), 1 da (Annabel); *Career* md PC Henderson Group 1956-79; dir: Davis & Henderson Assoc 1978-, Water Training International 1983-, Greyrule Ltd 1988-, Water Aid 1989-, Water Research plc 1989-; chm: Anglian Water plc 1981-, Water Services Association 1990-; memb Essex County Cncl 1970-74, magistrate 1974-80; *Recreations* countryside, narrow boat cruising and music; *Style—* Bernard Henderson, Esq, CBE; Anglian Water plc, Ambury Rd, Huntingdon, Cambs PE18 8PY (☎ 0480 443184, fax 0480 414866, telex 32175, car 0860 578873)

HENDERSON, Charles Edward; s of David Henderson (d 1972), and Georgiana Leggatt, *née* Mackie; *b* 19 Sept 1939; *Educ* Charterhouse, Univ of Cambridge; *m* 1966, Rachel, da of Dr A S Hall, of Bucks; 1 da (Catherine b 1970), 1 s (Luke b 1971); *Career* asst investmt sec Equity and Law Life Assurance Soc Ltd 1966-70, princ Export Credits Guarantee Dept DTI, asst sec Dept Energy 1976-82 (princ 1971-75), head Atomic Energy Div 1982-84, head Oil Div 1984-85, princ estab and fin offr 1985-88, head Office of Arts and Libraries 1989-; FIA; *Recreations* music (listening and playing), golf, reading, mountain walking; *Style—* Charles Henderson, Esq; 33 Fairfax Rd, London W4 1EN (☎ 081 994 1345); Office of Arts & Libraries, Horse Guards Rd, London SW1P 3AL (☎ 071 270 5811)

HENDERSON, Rt Rev Charles Joseph; s of Charles Stuart Henderson (d 1977), and Hanora, *née* Walsh (d 1970); *b* 14 April 1924; *Educ* Mount Sion Schs, Waterford, St John's Seminary Waterford; *Career* curate: St Stephen's Welling Kent 1948-55, English Martyrs Streatham 1955-58; chllr RC Dio of Southwark 1958-70; vicar gen: RC Dio of Arundel and Brighton 1965-66, RC Archdio of Southwark 1969-; episcopal vicar for religion 1968-73, parish priest St Mary's Blackheath 1969-82, canon Cathedral Chapter 1972- (provost 1973-), auxiliary bishop of Southwark and titular bishop of Tricala 1972-, area bishop SE Southwark 1980-; memb: Ecumenical Cmmn for England and Wales 1976-83, Nat Ctee for Racial Justice 1978-81, English Anglican/RC Ctee 1982- (co-chm 1983-), Methodist/RC Nat Ecumenical Ctee 1983- (co-chm 1984-), Pontifical Cncl for Inter Religious Dialogue 1990-; chm RC Ctee for Dialogue with other Faiths 1984-, RC consultor-observer BCC 1982-86, Papal Chamberlain 1960, prelate Papal Household 1965; Freeman City of Waterford 1973; Canon Law Soc of GB and Ireland 1959; Knight Cdr with Star of the Equestrian Order of the Holy Sepulchre of Jerusalem 1973-; *Recreations* special interest in sports and in art; *Style—* The Rt Rev Charles Henderson; Park House, 6A Cresswell Park, Blackheath, London SE3 9RD (☎ 081 318 1094, fax 081 318 9470)

HENDERSON, (George) Clifford McLaren; s of Robert McLaren Henderson (d 1962), and Stella, *née* Walter; *b* 7 Feb 1938; *Educ* Bembridge Sch IOW; *Career* dir: Frank Partridge 1973-77, Stair and Co New York 1977-79; antiques conslt 1979-88, exec dir Partridge Fine Arts Ltd 1988; *Recreations* music, swimming, theatre, bridge; *Style—* Clifford Henderson, Esq; 18 Lochmore House, Ebury St, London SW1W 9JX (☎ 071 730 2725)

HENDERSON, David Alexander; s of George Alexander Henderson (d 1973), of Edinburgh, and Jessie, *née* Wilson; *b* 16 Sept 1944; *Educ* Broughton HS; *m* 5 April 1970, (Constance) Mary, da of Adam Renton (d 1986), of Edinburgh; 1 s (Bryan b 1973), 1 da (Dayle b 1977); *Career* audit mangr Scott Mancrieff Thomson-Sheills 1969-71; gen mangr Scottish Equitable Life 1987- (asst gen mangr 1984-87, chief acountant 1979-84, accountant 1974-79, asst accountant 1971-74); FCCA 1968; *Recreations* golf, rugby; *Clubs* Watsonian, Morton Hall Golf; *Style—* David Henderson, Esq; 28 St Andrew Square, Edinburgh (☎ 031 556 9101)

HENDERSON, Sir Denys Hartley; *b* 11 Oct 1932; *Educ* Univ of Aberdeen (MA, LLB); *m* ; 2 da; *Career* slr; non exec dir: Dalgety plc 1981-87, Barclays Bank plc 1983-, Barclays Bank plc 1985-, Barclays International Ltd 1985-87; chm Imperial Chemical Industries plc 1987 (dir 1980-), non exec dir The RTZ Corp plc 1990-; chm: Stock Exchange Listed Cos Advsy Ctee, Ct of Govrs Henley Mgmnt Coll; memb: President's Ctee CBI, Br Malaysian Soc, Advsy Cncl of The Prince's Youth Business Tst, Opportunity Japan Campaign Ctee, Appeal Cncl Winston Churchill Memb Tst, President's Ctee Advertising Assoc, Save the Children Fund Indust and Commerce Gp; patron AIESEC, pres Soc of Business Economists, tstee Natural History Museum; DUniv Brunel 1987, Hon LLD Aberdeen 1987, Hon DSc Cranfield Inst of Technol 1989, Hon LLD Univ of Nottingham 1990; memb Law Soc of Scot; Hon FGCI, FCIM (hon vice pres), FRSA, CBIM; *Recreations* family life, swimming, reading, travel, minimal gardening, unskilled but enjoyable golf; *Clubs* Royal Automobile; *Style—* Sir Denys Henderson; Imperial Chemical Industries plc, ICI Group Headquarters, 9 Millbank, London SW1P 3JF (☎ 071 834 4444)

HENDERSON, Douglas John (Doug); MP (Lab) Newcastle upon Tyne North 1978-; s of John Henderson, and Joan, *née* Bryson; *b* 9 May 1949; *Educ* Waid Acad, Central Coll Glasgow, Univ of Strathclyde (BA); *m* 1974, Janet Margaret, da of Robert Graham (d 1984), of Scotland; 1 s (Keir John b 1986); *Career* apprentice Rolls Royce Glasgow 1966-68; Trade Union organisor (GMWU later GMB) 1973-87; memb Exec Scottish Cncl Lab Pty 1979-87 (chm 1984-85), memb NEDO Sector Working Pty 1981-84, industry spokesperson for Lab Pty; *Recreations* athletics, mountaineering; *Clubs* Lemington Labour, Newburn Memorial, Dinnington, Cambuslang Harriers, Elswick Harriers, Desperados Climbing; *Style—* Doug Henderson, Esq, MP; Ossian, 4 Parkside, Throckley, Newcastle upon Tyne NE15 9AX (☎ 091 267 2427); House of Commons (☎ 071 219 5017)

HENDERSON, Douglas Lindsay; s of Capt Arthur Henderson, of Sydney, Australia, and Sheila Lindsay, *née* Russel; *b* 17 Dec 1947; *Educ* Univ of New England (BA), Univ of NSW Australia (MBA, PhD); *m* 20 Jan 1970, Marilyn Gail, da of Ronald Clifford (d 1982), of Sydney, Australia; 3 s (Angus Arthur Lindsay b 1975, Duncan Ronald Alan b 1978, Stuart b 1987); *Career* lectr Univ of NSW Aust 1972-74; vice pres Bank of America Northern Territory and S Aust 1973-83, first vice pres and dir Swiss Bank Corporation 1983-89; memb: Graduate Business Assoc, AIB; *Clubs* Royal Over-Seas League; *Style—* Douglas Henderson, Esq

HENDERSON, Hon Mrs (Elizabeth Frances); *née* May; o da of 1 Baron May, KBE (d 1946), and Lily Julia, *née* Strauss (d 1955); *b* 29 June 1907; *m* 10 June 1955, George Leonard Brunton Henderson, MRCVS, s of late Edward Joseph Henderson; 2 s; *Career* served WW II as Flt Capt ATA (award for valuable service in the air 1945); *Style—* The Hon Mrs Henderson; Oak Lodge, Oak Hill Grove, Surbiton, Surrey KT6 6DS

HENDERSON, Hon Mrs (Flora Elizabeth); *née* Hewitt; da of 8 Viscount Lifford; *b* 1947; *m* 1965 (m dis 1975), Edward Bell Henderson; 2 da (Samantha b 1967, Amanda b 1971); *Style—* The Hon Mrs Henderson

HENDERSON, George Poland; s of George James Henderson (d 1963), and Emma Rouse Wilson (d 1949); *b* 24 April 1920; *Educ* Westminster City, Univ of London; *m* 27 April 1953, (Shirley) Prudence Ann Cotton, da of Kenneth W Cotton, librarian of Bank of England (d 1942); 2 s (Crispin Alastair Poland b 1955, Antony James Willis b 1957); *Career* Capt RA 1940-46; commercial reference librarian Guildhall Library London 1946-63, dir Kellys Directories Ltd 1963-66; pres: Assoc of Br Directory Publishers 1974-75, Euro Assoc of Directory Publishers 1976-78; Freeman City of London 1961; FInstD 1970; *Books* Current British Directories (6 edns, 1953-71), European Companies, A Guide to Sources of Information (3 edns, 1961-72), Directory of British Associations (10 edns, jtly, 1965-90); *Recreations* travel, gardening, postal history; *Style—* George Henderson, Esq; CBD Research Ltd, 15 Wickham Rd, Beckenham, Kent BR3 2JS (☎ 081 650 7745, fax 081 650 0768)

HENDERSON, Giles Ian; s of Charles David Henderson (d 1980), of Henfield, Sussex, and Joan, *née* Firmin; *b* 20 April 1942; *Educ* Michaelhouse Natal SA, Witwatersrand Univ SA (BA), Magdalen Coll Oxford (MA, BCL); *m* 21 Aug 1971, Lynne, da of Charles William Fyfield, OBE, of Alnmouth, Northumberland; 2 s (Mark b 1974, Simon b 1975), 1 da (Clare b 1978); *Career* admitted slr 1970, ptnr Slaughter and May 1975-; *Recreations* sport, music; *Style—* Giles Henderson, Esq; Slaughter and May, 35 Basinghall St, London EC2V 5DB (☎ 071 600 1200, fax 071 726 0038, 071 600 0289, telex 883486)

HENDERSON, Henry Merton (Harry); s of John Ronald Henderson, and Sarah Katherine, *née* Beckwith-Smith (d 1972); *b* 25 April 1952; *Educ* Eton; *m* 4 Feb 1977, Sarah Charlotte Margaret, *née* Lowther; 1 s (Harry Oliver b 24 March 1979), 1 da (Katie Sarah Henderson b 7 April 1981); *Career* ptnr Cazenove & Co 1982-; dir: Updown Investment Co plc 1984-, Witan Investment Co plc 1988-, Hotspur Investments plc 1990-; md Cazenove Unit Trust Managements Ltd; memb Stock Exchange; *Recreations* skiing, shooting, squash, golf; *Clubs* White's; *Style—* Harry Henderson, Esq; Bennetts Farm, West Woodhay, Newbury, Berkshire RG15 0BL (☎ 048 84 233); Cazenove & Co, 12 Tokenhouse Yard, London EC2R 7AN (☎ 071 588 2828, fax 071 606 9205)

HENDERSON, Hugh Peter; s of Dr Peter Wallace Henderson (d 1984), and Dr Stella Dolores Henderson of Langport, Somerset; *b* 23 Oct 1945; *Educ* Radley, St Catharine's Coll Cambridge, St Thomas's Hosp (MB BChir); *m* 11 Dec 1971, Elizabeth Anne Lynette, da of The Hon Mr Justice Arthur Douglas Davidson (d 1977), of Johannesburg, SA; 1 da (Fiona Elizabeth b 1984); *Career* trg as plastic surgn 1975-82, conslt plastic surgn 1982-; author of articles in plastic surgery on subjects incl: thermography, hypospadias, palate fistulae; Br Assoc of Plastic Surgns: memb Career Structure Sub Ctee, memb Res and Educn Sub Ctee; memb Br Assoc of Aesthetic Plastic Surgns; FRCS 1975; *Books* Questions and Answers in General Surgery, Questions and Answers in Surgery for Students; *Style—* Hugh Henderson, Esq; Nether Hall, Snows Lane, Keyham, Leics LE7 9JS (☎ 0537 50214); Leicester Royal Infirmary, Leicester LE1 5WW (☎ 0533 541414, fax 0533 720666, car 0533 718 994); The Bupa Hospital, Gartree Rd, Oadby, Leicester

HENDERSON, Ian James Sinclair; s of James Muirhead Henderson (d 1979), and Constance Jessie, *née* Sinclair; *b* 7 Jan 1933; *Educ* Chigwell Sch, Wadham Coll Oxford; *m* 1960, Jean, da of Ernest Thomas Fryer; 2 s (Mark Jeremy b 1959, d 1981, Philip James b 1962), 1 da (Judith Claire b 1969); *Career* Instr Lt RN 1954-60; Norwich Union Life Insurance Society 1960-63, asst actuary Scottish Union & National Insurance Company 1963-68; Scottish Equitable Life Assurance Society: asst actuary

1968, investment mangr 1972, dep gen mangr 1977-80; dir London and Manchester Group plc 1981-86 (gen mangr (investmt) 1980-81), dir Gartmore American Securities plc 1983-; chm 1986-: Ian Henderson Associates Ltd, Sinclair Henderson Ltd, Exeter Fund Managers Ltd; FIA 1962; *Style—* Ian Henderson, Esq; Ian Henderson Associates Ltd, 23 Cathedral Yard, Exeter EX1 1HB (☎ 0392 53225, fax 0392 412133)

HENDERSON, Ian Ramsay; s of David Hope Henderson (d 1977), of Achie Farm, New Galloway, Kirkcudbrightshire, and Eleanora Anderson, *née* Spence; *b* 21 June 1917; *Educ* Eton, Univ of Edinburgh (MA, LLB); *m* 28 Oct 1978, Virginia Theresa, da of Lt-Col John E B Freeman (d 1986), of Buxhall Vale, Buxhall, Stowmarket, Suffolk; 3 s (Alexander b 1982, Charles b 1984, George b 1987); *Career* Peat Marwick Mitchell & Co 1972-76, Morgan Grenfell & Co 1977-82; md Wardley Marine Int Investmt Mgmnt Ltd 1985 (dir 1982), dir Wardley Investment Servs Int Ltd 1987-; ACA 1975, FCA 1980; *Recreations* golf, tennis, windsurfing; *Clubs* Brook's, St James's; *Style—* Ian Henderson, Esq; 20 Westbourne Park Rd, London W2 5PH; 3 Harbour Exchange Square, London E14 9GJ

HENDERSON, Dr James Ewart; CVO; s of Rev James Ewart Henderson (d 1968), of Trinity Manse, Beith, Ayrshire, and Agnes Mary, *née* Crawford (d 1957); *b* 29 May 1923; *Educ* Univ of Glasgow, Univ of Edinburgh (MA, DSc); *m* 1, 20 Aug 1949, Alice Joan, da of Horace James Hewlitt (d 1958), of Herts; 1 da (Joanna b 1956); m 2, 17 Jan 1966, Nancy Maude da of Henry Tothill Dominy (d 1958), of Cornwall; 2 s (Jamie b 1966, Crawford b 1969); *Career* scientist, operational res (air rockets and guns) MAP 1943-44, hon cmmn RAFVR 1944-46, operational res air attacks in Belgium, Holland and Germany, 2 TAF 1944-45; experimental res: fighter armament RAF APC Germany 1945-46, fighter and bomber capability also use of radar and radio aids Fighter Cmd 1946-49 (subsequently Centl Fighter Estab 1949-52), weapons effects and capability Air Miny 1952-54; AWRE 1955, Air Miny 1955-58, asst scientific advsr (ops) Air Miny 1958-63, dep chief scientist (RAF) MOD 1963-69, chief scientist (RAF) and memb Air Force Bd 1969-73; aviation conslt Hawker Siddeley Aviation Ltd 1973-77, fin conslt Charles Stapleton and Co Ltd 1973-78, freelance operational res and mgmnt conslt 1974-78, dir Lewis Security Systems Ltd 1976-77, sci advsr Br Aerospace 1978-82, chm TIB Netherlands 1982-86, chm and md Mastiff Electronic Systems Ltd 1985-90 (dir 1977-82, md 1982-84), pres and chief exec Mastiff Systems (US) Inc 1982-88; pres Air League 1987- (memb Cncl 1979-80, chm 1981-87); author of tech papers on operational capability of aircraft and weapons 1949-73, UK Manual on Blast Effects of Nuclear Weapons (1955); *Recreations* sailing, golf, opera; *Clubs* Naval and Military, Royal Scottish Automobile, Royal Western Yacht, Moor Park Golf, New Zealand Golf; *Style—* Dr James E Henderson, Esq, CVO; Mastiff Electronic Systems Ltd, Little Mead, Cranleigh, Surrey (☎ 0483 272097, telex 859307 MASTIF G, fax 0483 276728)

HENDERSON, Hon James Harold; s and h of 3 Baron Faringdon; *b* 14 July 1961; *m* 1986, Lucinda, yr da of Desmond Hanson, of Knipton, nr Grantham, Lincs; *Style—* The Hon James Henderson

HENDERSON, Sir James Thyne; KBE (1959), CMG (1952); s of Sir Thomas Henderson (d 1951); *b* 18 Jan 1901; *Educ* Sedbergh, Queen's Coll Oxford; *m* 1929, Karen Margrethe, da of R P Hansen, of Denmark; 1 s, 4 da; *Career* entered FO 1925, consul-gen Houston 1949-53, min Iceland 1953-56, ambass Bolivia 1956-60, ret; chm Cwlth Inst Scotland 1963-73; *Style—* Sir James Henderson, KBE, CMG; 43 Gillespie Crescent, Flat 14, Edinburgh EH10 4HY (☎ 031 229 8191)

HENDERSON, John Crombie; s of Maj Morrice Pitcairn Henderson, TD; *b* 8 April 1939; *Educ* Uppingham; *m* 1968, Marylou Susan, da of Maj-Gen Sir Francis de Guingand, KBE, CB, DSO (d 1979); 2 da; *Career* Lt Black Watch 1959-63; memb Stock Exchange 1969, chief exec Capel-Cure Myers Capital Mgmnt Ltd 1988- (joined 1964); *Recreations* shooting, fishing, golf; *Clubs* Turf, Berkshire Golf; *Style—* John Henderson, Esq; 125 Abbotsbury Rd, London W14 8EP

HENDERSON, John Ronald; CVO (1986), OBE (1985, MBE 1944); s of late Maj R H W Henderson, and Marjorie, *née* Garrard; *b* 6 May 1920; *Educ* Eton, Univ of Cambridge; *m* 1, 1949, Katherine Sarah (d 1972), yr da of Maj-Gen Merton Beckwith-Smith, DSO, MC (d 1942); 2 s (Nicholas b 1950, Henry b 1952), 1 da (Joanna b 1955); m 2, 1976, Catherine, da of Geoffrey William Barford, JP, and wid of Lt-Col John Monsell Christian, MC; 1 step s, 2 step da; *Career* chm Updown Investmt Tst; dir: Howard De Walden Estates, Whitbread Investmt Tst; Lord Lt Berks 1989 (Vice Lord Lt 1979, formerly DL); *Recreations* racing, shooting, hunting; *Clubs* White's; *Style—* John Henderson Esq, CVO, OBE; West Woodhay House, Newbury, Berks (☎ 048 84 271); 3/4 Balfour Place, London W1 (☎ 071 629 4861)

HENDERSON, John Wilson; OBE (1978); s of Frederick James Henderson (d 1977), and Bertha May, *née* Wilson; *b* 8 July 1935; *Educ* Perse Sch Cambridge, Luton Coll of Technol; *m* 1963, Vivienne, da of Ronald Cedric Parker (d 1969); 1 s (David John Charles b 1967), 1 da (Sarah Jayne b 1970); *Career* dir: George Kent (Malaysia) BHD 1963-78, George Kent (Singapore) Pte Ltd 1965-78, Kent Precision Engineering Pte Ltd 1964-78, George Kent International Ltd 1979-86, Brown Boveri Kent (E Asia) Pte Ltd 1980-87, Kent Belgium SA 1983-87, Compteurs Kent SA 1983-87, Kent Meters Ltd 1985-; *Clubs* Penang (Malaysia); *Style—* John Henderson, Esq, OBE; April Cottage, West Wickham, Cambridge CB1 6SB (☎ 0223 290243); Kent Meters Ltd, Pondwicks Rd, Luton, Beds (☎ 0582 402020, fax 0582 36657, telex 825367)

HENDERSON, Hon Launcelot Dinadan James; er s of Baron Henderson of Brompton (Life Peer), and Susan Mary, *née* Dartford; *b* 20 Nov 1951; *Educ* Westminster, Balliol Coll Oxford; *m* 1989, Elaine Elizabeth, er da of Kenneth Frank Webb, of Dringhouses, York; 1 s (Peter George Galahad b 12 Aug 1990); *Career* called to the Bar Lincoln's Inn 1977; appointed standing jr counsel Chancery to the Inland Revenue 1987; fell All Souls Coll Oxford 1974-81 and 1982-89; *Style—* The Hon Launcelot Henderson; 17 Carlisle Road, London NW6 6TL

HENDERSON, Mark Ian; s of Ian Sidney Campbell Henderson (d 1954), and Patricia Joyce, *née* Muers; *b* 10 April 1947; *Educ* Stowe, CLP (BA); *m* 1970, Ann, da of Albert Edwin Reed (d 1982); 1 s (James b 1978), 1 da (Johanna b 1976); *Career* md RCB International Ltd 1987-89; dir: Hill Samuel Pensions Investment Management 1981-87 (md 1986-87), Mpalanganga Estates (Malawi) 1983-, Hill Samuel Asset Management 1984-87, Hill Samuel Investment Management 1985-87, American Distributors plc (formerly Sapphire Petroleum plc) 1985-88, Touche Remnant 1989-; memb Worshipful Co of Curriers; memb Lloyd's, assoc London Oil Analysts Gp; ASIA; *Publications* numerous articles on investmt mgmnt; *Recreations* running, music, scuba diving; *Clubs* Carlton; *Style—* Mark Henderson, Esq; 39 Winsham Grove, London SW11 6NB (☎ 071 228 9880); Touche, Remnant & Co, 2 Puddle Dock, London EC4V 3AT (☎ 071 236 6565)

HENDERSON, Michael John Glidden; s of William Glidden Henderson (d 1946), and Aileen Judith, *née* Malloy; *b* 19 Aug 1938; *Educ* St Benedict's Sch Ealing; *m* 29 Sept 1965, Stephanie Maria, da of John Dyer, of Hampton Court, Surrey; 4 s (Nicholas b 1966, Simon b 1968, Angus b 1972, Giles b 1976); *Career* chm and chief exec Cookson Gp plc; dir: Cookson Overseas Ltd, Cookson Investmts Ltd, Cookson America Inc, Cookson (Europe) SA, Cookson Hong Kong Ltd, Cookson India, Cookson Australia Pty Ltd, LIG Canada Inc, Spinnaker Insur Co Ltd Gibraltar, Mainsail Insur Co Ltd Bermuda, Guiness Mahon Hldgs Plc; FCA 1961; *Recreations* tennis, cricket; *Style—* Michael Henderson, Esq; Langdale, Woodland Drive, East Horsley, Surrey (☎ 048 65 3844); Cookson Group plc, 130 Wood St, London EC2V 6EQ (☎ 071 606 4400, fax 071 606 2851, telex 884141)

HENDERSON, Nicholas John; s of J R Henderson, of West Woodhay House, Newbury, Berks, and Sarah Becwith-Smith (d 1973); *b* 10 Dec 1950; *Educ* Eton; *m* 10 June 1978, Diana Amanda, da of John Thorne; 3 da (Sarah Lucy b 5 Dec 1981, Tessa Jane b 8 Dec 1983, Camilla Penny b 3 Nov 1987); *Career* horse trainer; asst trainer to Fred Winter 1973-78, amateur rider 1970-78 (rode 75 winners incl The Imperial Cup Sandown and Liverpool Foxhunters); trainer 1978-; trained over 500 winners incl See You Then (3 Champion Hurdles 1985, 1986, 1987), Brown Windsor (Whitbread gold Cup), The Tsarevich (16 races and 2 place in Grand National), Zongalero (won Mandarin Chase and 2 place in Grand National), First Bout (Daily Express Triumph Hurdle); leading nat hunt trainer 1986-87 and 1987-88, Piper Heidsick trainer of the Year 1986, 1987, and 1988; dir Berkeley Hotel; *Recreations* golf, shooting; *Style—* Nicholas Henderson, Esq; Windsor House, Lambourn, Newbury, Berks RG16 7NR (☎ 0488 72259, fax 0488 71596)

HENDERSON, Sir (John) Nicholas; GCMG (1977, KCMG 1972, CMG 1965), KCVO (1991); s of Prof Sir Hubert Henderson; *b* 1 April 1919; *Educ* Stowe, Hertford Coll Oxford; *m* 1951, Mary Barber, *née* Cawadias; 1 da (Alexandra m 1978 Viscount (Henry Dermot Ponsonby) Moore, *qv*); *Career* private sec to Foreign Sec 1963-65, min Madrid 1965-69; ambass: Poland 1969-72, W Germany 1972-75, France 1975-79, USA (Washington) 1979-82; dir: M and G Reinsurance 1982-89, Foreign and Colonial Investmt Tst plc 1982-89, Hambros plc 1983-89, Tarmac plc 1983-, F and C Eurotrust plc 1984-, Sotheby's 1989-; chm: Channel Tunnel Gp 1985-86, Fuel Tech NV; Lord Warden of the Stannaries, Keeper of the Privy Seal of the Duchy of Cornwall, vice chm of the Prince of Wales Cncl 1985-; tstee Nat Gallery 1985-89; Hon Fell Hertford Coll Oxford 1975, Hon DCL Oxford; *Books* Prince Eugen of Savoy (biography), The Birth of NATO (1982), The Private Office (1984), Channels and Tunnels (1987); *Recreations* gardening; *Clubs* Brooks's, Garrick, Beefsteak, Pratt's; *Style—* Sir Nicholas Henderson, GCMG, KCVO; 6 Fairholt St, London SW7 1EG (☎ 071 589 4291); School House, Combe, Newbury, Berks (☎ 04884 330)

HENDERSON, Adm Sir Nigel Stuart; GBE (1968, OBE 1944), KCB (1962, CB 1959), DL (Kirkcudbrightshire 1973); s of Lt-Col Selby Herriott Henderson (d 1935); *b* 1 Aug 1909; *Educ* Cheltenham; *m* 1939, Catherine Mary, *née* Maitland; 1 s, 2 da; *Career* RN 1927, served WWII, Cdr 1942, Capt 1948, Rear Adm 1957, Vice Adm 1960, Adm 1963, chm Mil Ctee NATO 1968-71, ret 1971; Rear Adm of UK 1973-76, Vice Adm of UK and Lt of the Admty 1976-79; pres Royal Br Legion Scotland 1974-80; *Style—* Adm Sir Nigel Henderson, GBE, KCB, DL; Hensol, Mossdale, Castle Douglas, Kirkcudbrightshire, Scotland (☎ 064 45 207)

HENDERSON, Oscar William James; OBE (1984), DL (Belfast 1977); s of Cdr Oscar Henderson, CVO, CBE, DSO (d 1969); bro of Robert B Henderson, *qv*; *b* 17 Aug 1924; *Educ* Brackenber House Belfast, Bradfield; *m* 1949, Rachel Primrose, da of Col John Vincent Forrest, CMG, of Belfast; 3 da; *Career* served WWII NW Europe, Capt Irish Gds 1942-47; chm Universities Press (Belfast) Ltd, Ewart plc; dir Ulster TV plc, FBIM; *Recreations* gardening, fishing; *Clubs* Ulster Reform (Belfast); *Style—* Oscar W J Henderson, Esq, OBE, DL; Glenalmond, Quarry Rd, Belfast, NI BT4 2NQ (☎ 0232 63145)

HENDERSON, Paul; s of Gen Frederick Paul Henderson, of New Jersey, USA, and Eva Holland Henderson (d 1990); *b* 2 Dec 1938; *Educ* Purdue Univ USA (BA), Wharton Sch Univ of Pennsylvania USA (MBA); *m* 1963, Kay Carathers; *Career* served US Marine Corps 1962-66; McKinsey & Co 1968-74, World Wildlife Fund 1974-77; proprietor Gidleigh Park Devon; *awards* Egon Ronay Guide: Wine Cellar of the Year 1982, Hotel of the Year 1990; Country House Hotel of the Year (Good Food Guide) 1983; Good Hotel Guide Ceasar Awards: Hauteur of Cuisine 1984, Most Sumptuous Country House Hotel 1989; Grand award (The Wine Spectator, USA) 1984, 1987 and 1990, Hotel Restaurant of the Year (The Times) 1989, English Country Hotel of the Year (The Hideaway Report, USA) 1990, 3 Red Stars and Rosette for restaurant (AA Guide) 1991, Blue Ribbon award (RAC Guide) 1991, Four Leaf Clover symbol Ackerman Guide; *Recreations* walking, travel; *Clubs* Stockey Furzen Cricket & Croquet; *Style—* Paul Henderson, Esq; Gidleigh Park Hotel, Chagford, Devon TQ13 8HH (☎ 0647 432367, fax 0647 432574)

HENDERSON, Philip David; s of David Hope Henderson, and Eleanora Anderson, *née* Spence; *b* 17 Feb 1947; *Educ* Eton, RAC Cirencester; *Career* assoc Henderson Thellusson; underwriting memb Lloyds; dep chm Courtfield Ward Cons Assoc 1977; FRICS; *Recreations* shooting, sailing, art; *Clubs* Brooks's, Hurlingham, Annabels; *Style—* Philip Henderson, Esq

HENDERSON, Philip William Alexander; s of Edgar Stuart Henderson (d 1974), of Bournemouth, Hants, and Dora Amelia, *née* Sizer (d 1956); *b* 3 April 1939; *Educ* Aldenham; *m* 29 June 1963, Patricia Elizabeth, da of Albert Edgar Civati (d 1976), of Wallington, Surrey; 1 da (Claire Annette b 1 April 1965, d 10 Jan 1972); *Career* articled clerk Viney Price and Goodyear 1956-61; stockbroking analyst: Vickers da Costa 1961-67, Laurence Keens Gardner 1967; ptnr James Capel and Co 1967-73, fndr Canadean Ltd 1973-76, ptnr Henderson Crosthwaite 1976-80, gp exec Strategy Dalgety plc 1980-82, mangr Ensign Tst 1985-91; exec chm Carmichael Participations 1976-; dir: Banque Bruxelles Lambert 1987-91, Seguin Moreau 1989-90, Meghraj Gp 1981-91, Clydesdale Investmt Tst 1987-89, Ensign Tst 1986-19, India Fund 1986-91, Aberdeen Tst Hldgs 1988-91, Worth Investmt Tst 1989-91; Argosy Asset Mgmnt 1985-91; chm: Filmtrax plc 1987-90, Figurehead Fin plc; organiser: Vamps Ball June 1985, Golddiggers Ball June 1987, Sweethearts Ball 1989, Ensign Prize RCA 1988-89; *Recreations* charity work, popular music 1900-69; *Clubs* City of London; *Style—* Philip Henderson, Esq; 15 Rothwell St, London N41 8YH (☎ 071 483 1873)

HENDERSON, Hon Richard Crosbie Aitken; yr s of Baron Henderson of Brompton, KCB (Life Peer), and Susan Mary, *née* Dartford; *b* 27 March 1957; *Educ* Westminster, Magdalen Coll Oxford (MA, DPhil), Univ of Nottingham (Dip Th); *m* 1985, Anita Julia, da of Antony Gerald Stroud Whiting; *Style—* The Hon Richard Henderson; 16 Pelham St, London SW7 2NG

HENDERSON, Robert Alistair; s of Robert Evelyn Henderson (himself er bro of Rt Hon Sir Nevile Henderson, GCMG, PC (d 1942), ambass to Germany 1937-39 and eld s of Robert Henderson, of Sedgwick Park, nr Horsham) and Beatrice (d 1980), o da of Sir William Clerke, 11 Bt (d 1930); R A Henderson is bro of 7 Earl Fortescue's first wife and 2 cous of 2 Baron St Just; *b* 4 Nov 1917; *Educ* Eton, Magdalene Coll Cambridge; *m* 1947, Bridget Elizabeth, only da of Col John Lowther, CBE, DSO, MC, TD, DL (yr bro of Sir Charles Lowther, 4 Bt) and Hon Lilah White (er da of 3 Baron Annaly); 2 s (Robert b 1948, James b 1955), 1 da (Emma b 1950); *Career* served WW II, Capt 60 Rifles (KRRC); chm: Kleinwort Benson Group plc 1978-88, Kleinwort Benson 1975-83, Kleinwort Benson Inc 1971-83, Kleinwort Benson (Tstees) Ltd 1975-83, Cross Investmt Tst (now Kleinwort Development Fund plc) 1969-; pres Klescan Investmts 1971-83; dir: Inchcape plc 1967-88, Hamilton Oil (GB) plc 1973-88; dep chm: Cadbury Schweppes plc 1977-, Hamilton Bros Oil and Gas Ltd 1981-88, BA plc 1985-89; memb BA 1981-85; former pres Equitable Life Assur Soc; *Clubs* Brooks's, RAC, White's; *Style—* Robert Henderson, Esq; 7 Royal Ave, London SW3

4QE (☎ 071 730 1104); North Ecchinswell Farm, Ecchinswell, nr Newbury, Berks RG15 8UJ (☎ 0635 268 244); Kleinwort Benson Group plc, 20 Fenchurch St, London EC3P 3DB (☎ 071 623 8000), N Ecclinaswell Farm, Newbury, Berks

HENDERSON, Robert Brumwell; CBE (1979); s of Cdr Oscar Henderson, CVO, CBE, DSO, RN (d 1969); bro of Oscar W J Henderson, *qv*; *b* 28 July 1929; *Educ* Brackenber House Sch Belfast, Bradfield, Trinity Coll Dublin (MA); *m* 1970, Patricia Ann, da of Mathew Davison, of Belfast; 2 da; *Career* journalist 1951-59; dir: ITN 1964-68, Ind TV Pubns 1968-87; chm: Ulster TV 1983-90 (md 1959-, dep chm 1977-83), Laganside Ltd 1987-; dep chm Powerscreen International plc, vice pres Co-Operation North; chm: Cinema and TV Benevolent Fund NI, Cncl of the Royal TV Soc 1982-84; pres: Assocs of Ulster Drama Festivals 1983-, Northern Ireland C of C and Indust 1979-80; memb Cncl IOD 1972-; DLitt Ulster 1982; *Books* Midnight Oil (1961), A Television First (1977), Amusing (1984); *Recreations* reading, theatre, cinema, golf; *Clubs* Naval and Military, Royal County Down Golf, Malone Golf; *Style*— Robert Brumwell Henderson, Esq, CBE; (☎ 0232 328122); 8 Crabtree Rd, Ballynahinch, Co Down, N Ireland BT24 8RH

HENDERSON, Hon Roderic Harold Dalzell; granted title rank and precedence of a Baron's son 1935; s of Lt-Col Hon Harold Greenwood Henderson, CVO, MP (d 1922), and Lady Violet Dalzell, da of 14 Earl of Carnwath (d 1956); bro of 2 Baron Faringdon; *b* 3 March 1909; *Educ* Eton, Pembroke Coll Cambridge; *Career* hon attaché Br Legation Stockholm 1932-33, HM Embassy Uruguay; civil attaché and private sec: HM Embassy Buenos Aires 1943-46, Stockholm 1946, Rome 1946, ret; *Recreations* swimming; *Style*— The Hon Roderic Henderson; 565 Tuckerman Ave, Middletown, Rhode Island 02840, USA (☎ 0101 401846 9358); 100 Alhambra Pl, W Palm Beach, Florida, USA 33405 (☎ 0101 407586 2829)

HENDERSON, Roger Anthony; QC (1980); s of Dr Peter Wallace Henderson (d 1984), and Dr Stella Dolores, *née* Morton; *b* 21 April 1943; *Educ* Radley, St Catharines Coll Cambridge; *m* 1968, Catherine Margaret; 3 da (Camilla, Antonia, Venetia); *Career* called to the Bar 1964, rec 1983; pres Br Acad of Forensic Sci 1986, memb Cncl Legal Educn 1986-90; chm: Public Affrs Ctee of the Bar 1989 and 1990, Special Ctee of St Peter's Hosps Gp 1989-; govr London Hosp Med Coll 1989-; *Recreations* fly-fishing, shooting; *Style*— R A Henderson, Esq, QC; 9 Brunswick Gardens, London W8 (☎ 071 727 3980); 2 Harcourt Buildings, Temple, London EC4 (☎ 071 583 9020, fax 071 583 2686); Holbury Mill, Lockerley, Hants; Upper Round Rd, St John's Parish, Nevis, West Indies

HENDERSON, Thomas Wilson; s of Walter Broadfoot Henderson (d 1989), of Selkirk, and Elizabeth Scott, *née* Wilson (d 1985); *b* 28 Sept 1941; *Educ* Selkirk Sch, Selkirk HS, Scottish Coll of Textiles Galashiels, Paisley Coll of Technol; *m* 1, 1961 (m dis 1972) Jean Scott Landels; 2 s (Alisdair b 15 Dec 1968, Kenneth b 21 Nov 1969); m 2, 9 April 1976, Catherine Helen, da of George Herbert (d 1973), of Selkirk; *Career* 4 Bn KOSB TA Mil Band 1958-62; dyer George Roberts & Co Ltd Selkirk 1957-61, asst dyehouse mangr William C Gray & Sons Ltd 1965-70 (dyer 1961-65), trg offr Kemp Blair & Co Ltd Galashiels, dyer RTN Yarns Ltd Selkirk 1971-74; John Turnbull & Sons Ltd Hawick: dyer 1975-78, asst mangr 1978-83, dir 1983-; memb: Selkirk Town Cncl 1973-75, Ettrick and Lauderdale DC 1974-; Provost of Selkirk 1978-; corp memb Soc of Dyers and Colourists 1973; *Recreations* horse riding, hillwalking, jazz, reading, cricket, football, rugby; *Style*— Thomas Henderson, Esq; Triglav, 29 Shaw Park Crescent, Selkirk TD7 4EX (☎ 0750 20821); John Turnbull & Sons Ltd, Slitrig Dyeworks, Slitrig Crescent, Hawick (☎ 0450 72305)

HENDERSON, Sir William MacGregor; s of William Simpson Henderson (d 1948); *b* 17 July 1913; *Educ* George Watson's Coll Edinburgh, Univ of Edinburgh (BSc, DSc); *m* 1941, Alys Beryl, da of Owen Cyril Goodridge (d 1932); 4 s; *Career* asst Dept of Med Royal Veterinary Coll Edinburgh 1936-38, dep dir sci Animal Virus Res Inst Pirbright 1955-56 (memb: Sci Staff 1939-55); dir: Pan-American Foot and Mouth Disease Centre Rio de Janiero 1957-65, ARC Inst for Res on Animal Diseases Compton 1967-72 (dep dir 1966-67); sec Agric Res Cncl 1972-78, chm Genetic Manipulation Advsy Gp 1979-81; memb Sci Cncl Celltech Ltd 1980-82 (Bd of Dirs 1982-84), Bd Wellcome Biotechnology Ltd 1983-89; pres: Zoological Soc of London 1984-89, Royal Assoc of Br Dairy Farmers 1985-87; FRS, FRSE; kt 1976; *Clubs* Athenaeum, New (Edinburgh); *Style*— Sir William Henderson; Yarnton Cottage, Streatley, Berks (☎ 0491 872162)

HENDERSON-STEWART, Sir David James; 2 Bt (UK 1957), of Callumshill, Co Perth; s of Sir James Henderson-Stewart, 1 Bt, MP (d 1961); *b* 3 July 1941; *Educ* Eton, Trinity Coll Oxford; *m* 1972, Anne, da of Count Serge de Pahlen; 3 s, 1 da; *Heir* s, David Henderson-Stewart b 2 Feb 1973; *Clubs* Travellers'; *Style*— Sir David Henderson-Stewart, Bt; 90 Oxford Gardens, London W10 (☎ 081 960 1278)

HENDRIE, Dr Gerald Mills; s of James Harold Hendrie (d 1981), and Florence Mary, *née* MacPherson (d 1968); *b* 28 Oct 1935; *Educ* Framlingham Coll Suffolk, RCM, Selwyn Coll Cambridge (MA, MusB, PhD); *m* 1, 11 July 1962, Dr Dinah Florence Barsham (d 1985); 2 s (Piers Edward b 13 May 1968, Dorian Mills b 15 Sept 1969); m 2, 15 Feb 1986, Dr Lynette (Lynne) Anne Maddern; *Career* dir of music Homerton Coll Cambridge 1962-63, lectr in history of music Univ of Manchester 1963-67, prof and chm Dept of Music Univ of Victoria Canada 1967-69, reader in music then prof Open Univ 1969-90, dir of studies in music St John's Coll Cambridge 1981-84, visiting fell in music Univ of Western Australia 1985; active as organist and composer; memb Cncl Handel Inst; FRSA 1981, FRCO, ARCM; *Recreations* windsurfing, reading; *Style*— Prof Gerald Hendrie; The Garth, 17 The Ave, Dallington, Northampton NN5 7AJ

HENDRIE, Robert Andrew Michie; s of John Hendrie (d 1978), of Edinburgh, and Effie Campbell, *née* Mackay; *b* 4 May 1938; *Educ* Bradford GS, Trinity Hall Cambridge (BA, MA); *m* 4 May 1964, Consuelo Liaño Solórzano, da of Ismael Liaño Fernández (d 1956), of Torrelavela, Spain; 2 da (Jessica Elena b 11 July 1967, Olivia Caroline b 24 Nov 1973); *Career* entered Foreign Serv MECAS 1961, political residency Bahrain 1962-65, HM Embassy Tehran Iran 1965-68, HM Embassy Tripoli Libya 1968-69, latin-american dept FCO 1969-73, HM Embassy Lima Peru 1973-75, HM Embassy Buenos Aires Argentina; FCO 1980-86: head Central African Dept, head Middle East Dept, Information Dept, HM consult Lille France 1986; MBIM 1985, MIL 1988; *Recreations* reading, walking, (watching) rugby, languages; *Style*— Robert Hendrie, Esq; British Consultate-General, 11 Square Dutilleul, 59800 Lille, France (☎ 010 33 20 57 87 90, fax 010 33 20 54 88 16, telex 120169); c/o Foreign & Commonwealth Office, King Charles St, London SW1A 2AH

HENDRY, Prof Arnold William; s of George Hendry (d 1953), of Buckie, and Mary, *née* Grassick (d 1921); *b* 10 Sept 1921; *Educ* Buckie HS, Univ of Aberdeen (BSc, PhD, DSc); *m* 1, 27 June 1946, Sheila Mary Cameron (d 1966), da of William Nicol Roberts (d 1962); 2 s (George b 1953, Eric b 1958, d 1978), 1 da (Margaret b 1948); m 2, 28 Dec 1968, Elizabeth Lois Alice, da of Harry R G Inglis (d 1939); *Career* civil engr Sir William Arrol & Co 1941-43, lectr Univ of Aberdeen 1943-49, reader King's Coll London 1949-51, prof of civil engrg Univ of Khartoum 1951-57, prof of bldg sci Univ of Liverpool 1957-63, prof of civil engrg Univ of Edinburgh 1964-88 (prof emeritus); memb Cncl The Cockburn Assoc Edinburgh 1978-87, pres Scottish Assoc for Public Tport; FICE, FIStructE, FRSA, FRSE; *Recreations* reading, walking, travel, DIY; *Style*— Professor Arnold Hendry, FRSE; 146/6 Whitehouse Loan, Edinburgh EH9 2AN (☎ 031 447 0368); Dept of Civil Engineering, The King's Buildings, Edinburgh EH9 3JL (☎ 031 667 1081)

HENDRY, (Edward) Colin James; s of Edward Alexander James Hendry, of Keith, Grampian, Scotland, and Anne, *née* Mackie; *b* 7 Dec 1965; *Educ* Keith GS; *m* Denise, da of David Duff; 1 da (Rheagan b 21 Aug 1989); *Career* professional footballer; 44 appearances Dundee 1984-87, 99 appearances Blackburn Rovers 1987-89 (joined for a fee of £25,000), transferred for a fee of £700,000 to Manchester City 1989-; Scotland B cap v E Germany 1990; Full Members Cup Blackburn Rovers 1987 (scored winning goal); young player of the year Dundee 1985; player of the year: Blackburn Rovers 1988, Manchester City 1990; *Recreations* family, music; *Style*— Colin Hendry, Esq; c/o Paul Stretford Esq, 5 Briarwood, Wilmslow Rd, Wilmslow, Cheshire SK9 2DN (☎ 061 745 9583)

HENDRY, Prof David Forbes; s of Robert Ernest Hendry, of 1 Bruce Gardens, East Watergate, Fortrose, and Catherine Elizabeth, *née* Mackenzie; *b* 6 March 1944; *Educ* Glasgow HS, Univ of Aberdeen (MA), LSE (MSc, PhD); *m* 7 Oct 1966, Evelyn Rosemary, da of Rev John Vass (d 1974), of Aberdeen; 1 da (Vivien Louise b 1977); *Career* prof of econs: LSE 1977-81 (lectr 1969-73, reader 1973-77), Univ of Oxford 1982-; visiting prof: Yale Univ 1975, Univ of California Berkeley 1976, Catholic Univ of Louvain-la-Neuve 1980, Univ of California San Diego 1981 and 1989-90; special advsr House of Commons Select Ctee on the Treasy and Civil Serv 1979-80, memb Academic Panel of HM Treasy 1976-89, Guy medal in Bronze of the Royal Statistical Soc 1986; Hon LLD Univ of Aberdeen 1987; fell Econometric Soc 1976, FBA 1987; *Books* Econometrics and Quantitative Economics (with K F Wallis, 1984), PC-Give: An Interactive Econometric Modelling Systems (1989); *Recreations* squash, cricket; *Style*— Prof David F Hendry; 26 Northmoor Rd, Oxford OX2 6UR (☎ 0865 515588); Nuffield College, Oxford OX1 1NF (☎ 0865 278587, fax 0865 278 621)

HENDRY, Hon Mrs (Elspeth Mariot); da of 1 Baron Ironside, GCB, CMG, DSO (d 1959, former Field Marshal); *b* 8 Jan 1917; *m* 1941, Capt Andrew Gilbert Hendry, Black Watch (Royal Highland Regt), s of Andrew Hendry, slr, of Dundee; 3 s; *Career* regnl cllr Tayside Region 1973-; *Recreations* tennis, gardening, travelling; *Clubs* New Cavendish; *Style*— The Hon Mrs Hendry; Kerbet House, Kinnettles, nr Forfar, Angus (☎ 030 782 286)

HENDRY, James David (Jim); s of Alexander Hendry (d 1986), of Perth, and Ethel, *née* Stephen (d 1990); *b* 10 Oct 1939; *Educ* Perth Sr Acad; *m* 1 Sept 1969, Georgina, da of Edwin John Adkins (d 1989), of Wibarston, Leics; *Career* housing offr: Perth Town Cncl 1955-61, Glenrothes Devpt Corpn 1961-65; dist housing offr Corby Devpt Corpn 1965-76, sr housing offr Corby Town Cncl 1976-79; Br Cycling Fedn: offr and coach nat team mangr 1969-79, dir racing 1979-85, dir coaching devpt 1985-89, chief exec 1987-; club div and nat offr Scottish Cyclists Union 1956-62; memb: Soc of Assoc Execs 1988-, Bri Assoc Nat Coaches 1979; *Books* BCF Training Manual (1987), Take Up Cycle Racing (1989); *Recreations* cycling, sea fishing; *Style*— Jim Hendry, Esq; British Cycling Federation, 36 Rockingham Rd, Kettering, Northants NN16 8HG (☎ 0536 412211, fax 0536 412142)

HENDRY, Stephen Gordon; s of Gordon John Hendry, of Edinburgh, and Irene Agnes, *née* Anthony; *b* 13 Jan 1969; *Educ* Inverkeithing HS; *Career* professional snooker player 1985-; winner Rothmans Grand Prix 1987, world doubles champion 1987, Australian Masters champion 1987, Br Open champion 1988, NZ Masters champion 1988, Scottish champion 1988 (1986 and 1987), Benson & Hedges champion 1989, Asian champion 1989, Regal Masters champion 1989, Dubai Classic champion 1989; Embassy World champion 1990; memb Lords Taverners Scotland; *Recreations* golf, music; *Style*— Stephen Hendry, Esq; Stephen Hendry Snooker Ltd, Kerse Rd, Stirling FK7 7SG Scotland (☎ 0786 62634, fax 0786 50068, car 0836 547147)

HENDRY, William Forbes (Bill); s of Duncan William Hendry, and Edna Beatrice, *née* Woodley; *b* 15 June 1938; *Educ* Uppingham, Univ of Glasgow (MB ChM); *m* 1961, Christina Marie (Chirsty), da of Donald MacDonald (d 1990), of 4 Brue Barvas, Isle-of-Lewis; 2 s (Duncan Forbes b 1962, Alexander Donald (Sandy) b 1968), 1 da ((Catherine) Louise b 1965); *Career* Univ of Glasgow Air Sqdn 1957-60; conslt urologist St Bartholomews Hosp and Royal Marsden Hosp London, civilian conslt in urology to the RN, Hunterian prof and Sir Arthur Sims Cwlth travelling prof RCS; FRCS; *Books* Recent Advances in Urology/Andrology edn (5 edn 1991); *Recreations* gardening, fishing, cycling, skiing; *Clubs* RSM; *Style*— Bill Hendry, Esq; Dene Cottage, 6 Fulford Rd, Ewell, Epsom Surrey KT19 9QX (☎ 081 393 2527); 149 Harley St, London W1N 2DE (☎ 081 636 7426)

HENDY, Anne-Marie; da of Hans A Sterchi, of 24 Ave Ruchonnet, Lausanne, Switzerland, and Marie, *née* Schori; *b* 9 Oct 1945; *Educ* College du Belvedere Lausanne, Deutsches Gymnasium Bayreuth, Univ of Geneva (BA, BA); *m* 26 July 1969, Robin Hendy, s of Capt Charles MacLaren Hendy (d 1983); 2 s (Marcus b 1977, d 1981, Nicholas b 1981), 1 da (Alexandra b 1983); *Career* freelance translator and interpreter Int Orgn and Municipality of Lausanne Switzerland 1967-69, translator Charter Consolidated Ltd 1969-71, res conslt on scripophily Stanley Gibbons Ltd 1978-81, dir Westcombe Investments Ltd 1987-; author articles 1978-85: Antique Collector, Stamp Magazine, Coin Monthly, Friends of Financial History (New York), Bond and Bank Note News, BSS Jl, Jl of the Bond and Share Soc; ctee memb Bond and Share Soc 1978-, memb Nat Tst, involved with local church help gps; *Books* American Railroad Stocks (1980); *Recreations* tennis, skiing, windsurfing, sailing, music (piano); *Clubs* RAC, Oxshott Village Tennis; *Style*— Mrs Anne-Marie Hendy

HENDY, John; QC (1987); s of Jack Hendy, of Penzance, and Mary, *née* Best; *b* 11 April 1948; *Educ* London Univ (LLB), Queens Univ Belfast (LLM); *Career* called to the Bar 1972; chm Inst Employment Rights 1989-; memb Hon Soc of Gray's Inn 1966; ACIArb 1989; *Style*— John Hendy, Esq, QC; 15 Old Sq, Lincoln's Inn, London WC2A 3UH (☎ 071 831 0801, fax 071 405 1387)

HENDY, Hon Mrs (Mary Jemima); *née* Best; da of 6 Baron Wynford, DSO (d 1940), and Hon Eva Napier, da of 2 Baron Napier of Magdala; *b* 1912; *m* 1944, John Hendy; 2 s; *Style*— The Hon Mrs Hendy; 1 Portherras Cross, Pendeen, Penzance, Cornwall

HENGHES, Hon Mrs (Penelope Kathryn Teresa); *née* Balogh; da of Baron Balogh (d 1985), and his 1 wife, Penelope Noel Mary Ingram, *née* Tower (d 1975); *b* 17 Oct 1957; *m* 1988, Ian Henghes, o s of Heinz Henghes (d 1975), and Daphne, *née* Gow; *Style*— The Hon Mrs Henghes; 10 St George's Terrace, Regents Park, London, NW1

HENHAM, His Hon Judge; John Alfred Henham; s of Alfred and Daisy Henham; *b* 8 Sept 1924; *m* 1946, Suzanne Jeanne Octavie Ghislaine, *née* Pinchart (d 1972); 2 s; *Career* stipendiary magistrate 1975-83, rec 1979, circuit judge 1983-; *Style*— His Hon Judge Henham; Crown Court, Castle St, Sheffield 3 8LW (☎ 0742 737511)

HENIG, Prof Stanley; s of Sir Mark Henig (d 1978), of Leicester, and Grace, *née* Cohen; *b* 7 July 1939; *Educ* Wyggeston Sch Leicester, CCC Oxford (BA), Nuffield Coll Oxford (MA); *m* 27 March 1966, Ruth Beatrice, da of Kurt Munzer, of Leicester; 2 s (Simon Antony b 10 June 1969, Harold David b 27 May 1972); *Career* MP Lancaster 1966-70; lectr: Civil Serv Coll 1972-75, Lancashire Poly 1976- (dean faculty of health and social studies 1985-90); head Centre of European Studies 1990-, govr Br Inst Recorded Sound 1975-80, chm Ct Royal Northern Coll of Music 1986-89 (hon memb 1989), ldr Lab Group Lancaster Cncl 1989-, memb Univ Assoc Contempory Euro

Studies 1970-; sec: Historic Masters Ltd 1984-, Historic Singers Tst 1985-; *Books* European Political Parties (1969), External Relations of European Community (1971), Political Parties in the European Community (1979), Power and Decision In Europe (1980); *Recreations* listening to opera, collecting records; *Style*— Prof Stanley Henig; 10 Yealand Drive, Lancaster LA1 4EW (☎ 0524 69624); Lancashire Polytechnic, Corporation St, Preston (☎ 0772 201201)

HENKEL, Dr David John; *b* 13 Jan 1921; *Educ* Univ of Natal (BSc), Univ of London (PhD), Imp Coll London (DIC); *Career* served WWII SACS 1941-45; head Soil Mechanics section Nat Bldg Res Inst Pretoria 1945-49, lectr then sr lectr in civil engrg Imp Coll of Sci and Technol and conslt on foundations dams landslides and harbours 1949-63, prof of soil mechanics Indian Inst of Technol and conslt to Indian Govt 1963-65, prof of civil engrg and head Dept Geotechnical Engrg Cornell Univ NY 1965-70, conslt Ove Arup & Ptnrs 1986-87, (geotechnical conslt and advsr 1970-77, dir 1977-85, concerned with; foundation stability of offshore oil platforms and major bldgs worldwide, problems of ground subsidence in Nigeria, Das Island and S Africa, design and construction of Dubai dry docks and underground stations for the Hong Kong Mass Transit Railway , slope stability problems in Hong Kong), chm Geotechnique Advsy Panel 1976-79; geotechnical advsr: Dept of Energy, Singapore Mass Rapid Transit Railway; advsr: DOE, CEGB; ret 1987; FICE, FEng, FGS; *Publications* The Measurement of Soil Properties in the Triaxial Test (with A W Bishop, 1957), The Shear Strength of Saturated Remoulded Clays (1960), Local Geology and the Stability of Natural Slopes (1967), Geology and Foundation Problems in Urban Areas (1969), The Role of Waves in Causing Submarine Landslides (1970) The 22nd Rankine Lecture, Geology Geomorphology and Geotechnical Engineering (1982); *Style*— Dr D J Henkel

HENLEY, Sir Douglas Owen; KCB (1973, CB 1970); *b* 5 April 1919; *Educ* Beckenham Co Sch, LSE (BSc); *m* 1942, June Muriel, da of Thomas Ibbetson; 4 da; *Career* served WWII Queen's Own Royal W Kent Regt N Africa Italy Greece (despatches twice); joined Treasy 1946; asst then dep under sec Dept of Econ Affrs 1964-69, second perm sec Treasy 1972-76, comptroller and auditor gen 1976-81, advsr Deloitte Haskins and Sells (accountants) 1982-90; memb Cncl GPDST 1981-, govr Alleyn's Coll of God's Gift Dulwich 1981-90; Hon LLD Bath 1981; *Style*— Sir Douglas Henley, KCB; Walwood House, Park Rd, Banstead, Surrey (☎ 0737 352626)

HENLEY, Nancy, Baroness; Nancy Mary; da of Stanley Walton, of The Hill, Gilsland, Carlisle; *m* 1949 (m dis 1975), as his 2 w, 7 Baron Henley (d 1977); *Style*— Nancy, Lady Henley; 10 Abbey St, Cerne Abbas, Dorchester, Dorset DT2 7JQ

HENLEY, 8 Baron (I 1799); Oliver Michael Robert Eden; also (and sits as) Baron Northington (UK 1885); s of 7 Baron (d 1977) by his 2 w Nancy, da of S Walton, of Gilsland, Cumbria; *b* 22 Nov 1953; *Educ* Dragon Sch Oxford, Clifton, Durham; *m* 11 Oct 1984, Caroline Patricia, da of A G Sharp, of Mackney, Oxon; 1 s (Hon John Michael Oliver b 1988), 1 da (Hon Elizabeth Caroline b 26 Feb 1991); *Heir* s, Hon John Michael Oliver Eden b 30 June 1988; *Career* sits as Cons in House of Lords; called to the Bar Middle Temple 1977; memb Cumbria CC 1986-89, chm Penrith and The Border Cons Assoc 1987-89; Lord in Waiting Feb-July 1989; Parly under-sec Dept of Social Security July 1989-; *Clubs* Brooks's, Pratt's; *Style*— The Rt Hon the Lord Henley; Scaleby Castle, Carlisle, Cumbria

HENLEY, Cdr Robert Stephen; OBE (1969), DSC (1942); s of Capt Charles Beauclerk Henley, RIM (d 1945), and Nellie Barbara, *née* Stranack (d 1962); *b* 4 July 1917; *Educ* Nautical Coll Pangbourne; *m* 31 July 1940, (Cecile) Noreen Sheila, da of Eric Hudson (d 1968); 4 s (Nigel b 1942, Timothy b 1945, Basil b 1953, Jonathan b 1956); *Career* RN; Cadet 1935, Lt 1940 qualified as Pilot, Lt Cdr 1944, Cdr 1955, Naval Attaché Madrid 1966-69; mangr Container Tport Int 1970-72; Amphibious Container Leasing Ltd: fndr 1972, md 1972-88, chm 1988-; MBIM 1970; *Recreations* riding; *Clubs* Naval and Military; *Style*— Cdr Robert Henley, OBE, DSC; Eden Lodge, West Liss, Hampshire (☎ 0730 892 325); Amphibious Container Leasing Ltd, Farnham Rd, West Liss, Hants (☎ 0730 892 611, fax 0730 894 352, telex 86576)

HENN, Alan Wesley; s of Thomas Wesley Henn; *b* 24 Sept 1930; *Educ* Uppingham; *m* 1956, Anne Whishaw, *née* Webb; 1 s, 2 da; *Career* Lt RA; chm: TA Henn and Son Ltd and assoc cos, Beacon Broadcasting of Communications Ltd (W Midland ILR Station), chm Jewellers of GB and Ireland Ltd; dir Severn-Trent plc; pres Nat Assoc of Goldsmiths (former chm), former pres Br Horological Inst; Master Worshipful Co of Clockmakers; FRSA; *Recreations* shooting, fishing; *Style*— Alan Henn, Esq; Abbeywell House, Much Wenlock, Shropshire (☎ 0952 727723)

HENNELL, Prof Michael Anthony; s of John Francis Hennell (d 1980), and Jean Marion, *née* Speirs (d 1959); *b* 9 Sept 1940; *Educ* Univ of London (BSc, MSc, PhD); *m* 6 March 1965, Margaret Linda May, da of Leslie Ernest Cannon Smith (d 1989); 1 s (Ian Jon b 6 Nov 1970), 2 da (Sheena Linda b 10 Feb 1967, Katherine Jean b 21 May 1968); *Career* currently prof Dept of Statistics and Computational Maths, Univ of Liverpool; *Style*— Prof Michael Hennell; Statistics and Computational Maths Dept, University of Liverpool, Liverpool L69 3BX, (☎ 051 794 4736, fax 051 709 2027)

HENNESSY; *see*: Pope-Hennessy

HENNESSY, Helen Julia; da of Frank Arthur Conway, and Joan Dorothy, *née* Shearman; *b* 7 Oct 1955; *Educ* Southend HS for Girls; *m* 2, 31 May 1987, James Edward Davis; 1 s; *Career* chief housing offr Borough of Broxbourne 1980-86, mgmnt conslt specialising in interpersonal and mgmnt training 1986-, private practice as a qualified psychosynthesis cnsllr; FIH; *Recreations* husband, home, friends, TM (Transcendental Meditation); *Style*— Mrs Helen Hennessy; 46 Peel Rd, London E18 2LG (☎ 081 505 7850)

HENNESSY, Sir James Patrick Ivan; KBE (1982, OBE 1968, MBE 1959), CMG (1975); s of Richard Hennessy, DSO, MC; *b* 26 Sept 1923; *Educ* Bedford Sch, Sidney Sussex Coll Cambridge, LSE; *m* 1947, Patricia, da of Wing Cdr F Unwin, OBE; 1 s (decd), 5 da; *Career* served RA 1942, seconded to IA (Adj) 1944, Battery Cdr 6 Indian FD Regt 1945; entered Colonial Admin Serv 1948; appts incl: dist offr Basutoland 1948, judicial cmmr 1953, jt sec Constitutional Cmmn 1957-59, sec to Exec Cncl 1960, seconded to Br High Cmmr's Office Pretoria 1961-63, electoral cmmr 1963; perm sec: Miny of Local Govt 1964, Home Affrs and Internal Security 1965, External Affrs and PM's Office 1966, ret; entered Dip Serv 1968; appts incl: chargé d'affaires Montevideo 1971-72, high cmmr to Uganda and non resident ambass to Rwanda 1973-76, consul-gen Cape Town 1977-79, govr and C-in-C Belize 1980-81, ret 1982; HM Chief Inspr of Prisons for Eng and Wales 1982-87; memb Parole Bd 1988-; tstee Butler Tst 1988-; *Clubs* Naval and Military, Royal Cwlth Soc; *Style*— Sir James Hennessy, KBE, CMG; Dolphin Square, London SW1

HENNESSY, Prof Peter John; s of William Gerald Hennessy, and Edith, *née* Wood-Johnson (d 1986); *b* 28 March 1947; *Educ* Marling Sch Stroud, St John's Cambridge (BA, PhD), LSE, Harvard Univ USA; *m* 14 June 1989, Enid Mary *née* Candler; 2 da (Cecily b 1976, Polly b 1979); *Career* lobby corr Financial Times 1976, reporter Br Section The Economist 1982; The Times: reporter Higher Educ Supplement 1972-74, reporter 1974-76, Whitehall corr 1976-82 ldr writer 1982-84; columnist: New Statesman 1986-87, Whitehall Watch The Independent 1987-; presenter Analysis BBC Radio Four 1986-, columnist Director Magazine 1989-, visiting prof of govt Univ of Strathclyde 1989-, co fndr and dir Inst Contemporary Br History 1986-89; visiting fell: Policy Studies Inst 1986-; Dept of Politics Univ of Reading 1988-, Politics Dept Univ of Nottingham 1989-, RIPA 1989-; hon res fell Brikbeck Coll London 1990-; tstee Atlee Fndn 1986-; *Books* States of Emergency (jtly, 1983), Sources Close to the Prime Minister (jtly, 1984), What the Papers Never Said (1985), Cabinet (1986), Ruling Performance (jt ed, 1987), Whitehall (1989); *Recreations* running, listening to music; *Clubs* Attlee Mem Runners; *Style*— Prof Peter Hennessy; Inst Contemporary Br History, 34 Tavistock Sq, London WC1H 9EZ (☎ 071 387 2331)

HENNIKER, Adrian Chandos; s and h of Brig Sir Mark Chandos Auberon Henniker, 8 Bt, CBE, DSO, MC; *b* 18 Oct 1946; *Educ* Marlborough; *m* 1971, Ann, da of Stuart Britton, of Malvern House, Fairwater Rd, Llandaff, Cardiff; 2 da (twins); *Style*— Adrian Henniker, Esq; Llwyndu, Abergavenny, Gwent

HENNIKER, 8 Baron (I 1800); Sir John Patrick Edward Chandos Henniker; 9 Bt (GB 1765), KCMG (1965, CMG 1956), CVO (1960), MC (1945); also Baron Hartismere (UK 1866); s of 7 Baron Henniker (d 1980), and Molly (d 1953), da of Sir Robert Burnet, KCVO, MD; *b* 19 Feb 1916; *Educ* Stowe, Trinity Coll Cambridge (MA); *m* 1, 18 Dec 1946, (Margaret) Osla (d 1974), da of James Benning, of Montreal; 2 s, 1 da; m 2, 1976, Mrs Julia Poland, da of George Mason, of Kew; *Heir* s, Hon Mark Henniker-Major; *Career* serv WWII Rifle Bde, Maj, mil mission to Yugoslav Partisans; For Serv 1938-68: ambass Jordan 1960-62, ambass Denmark 1962-66, asst under sec FO 1967-68; dir-gen Br Cncl 1968-72, dir Wates Fndn 1972-78; tstee City Parochial Fndn 1973-90, govr Cripplegate Fndn 1979-90; memb: Parole Bd 1979-83, Mental Health Review Tbnl (Broadmoor), Cncl UEA 1974-86; dep chm Toynbee Hall 1980-87 (memb Cncl 1978-87); vice pres Nat Assoc Victims Support Schemes 1986-90; pres Rainer Fndn (chm Intermediate Treatment Fund 1985-90); chm: Suffolk Rural Housing Assoc 1985-, Suffolk Community Alcohol Servs 1983-90; pres Community Cncl for Suffolk 1988, vice pres Suffolk Tst for Nature Conservation, pres Suffolk and N Essex Br Inst of Mgmnt 1985-88, govr Stowe Sch 1982-90; lay canon St Edmundsbury Cathedral 1986-; DL (Suffolk 1988), pres Suffolk Agric Assoc 1989; Hon DCL UEA 1989; *Clubs* Special Forces; *Style*— The Rt Hon the Lord Henniker, KCMG, CVO, MC; The Red House, Thornham Magna, Eye, Suffolk (☎ 037 983 336)

HENNIKER, Brig Sir Mark Chandos Auberon; 8 Bt (UK 1813), CBE (1953, OBE 1944), DSO (1944), MC (1933), DL (Gwent 1963); s of late Frederick Chandos Henniker (d 1953, ggs of 1 Bt); suc cous, Lt-Col Sir Robert John Aldeborough, MC (d 1958); *b* 23 Jan 1906; *Educ* Marlborough, RMA Woolwich, King's Coll Cambridge; *m* 1945, Kathleen Denys, da of John Anderson (d 1930), and Mrs John Anderson, of Pilgrim's Way, Farnham, Surrey; 1 s, 1 da; *Heir* s, Adrian Chandos Henniker; *Career* served RE 1925-58: Mohmand Ops 1933, WWII 1939-45 France, N Africa, Sicily (wounded), Italy and NW Europe, Malaya 1952-54 (despatches), Suez 1956 (despatches), ret Brig 1958; worked in industry 1959-62, self-employed in oil business 1963-77; *Books* Memoir of a Junior Officer (1951), Red Shadow over Malaya (1955), An Image of War (1987); *Recreations* appropriate to age and rank; *Clubs* Athenaeum; *Style*— Brig Sir Mark Henniker, Bt, CBE, DSO, MC, DL; 27 Western Rd, Abergavenny, Gwent, NP7 7AB

HENNIKER HEATON, Lady; Margaret Patricia; da of late Lt Percy Wright, Canadian Mounted Rifles; *m* 1948, as his 2 w, Wing-Cdr Sir (John Victor) Peregrine Henniker Heaton, 3 Bt (d 1971); *Style*— Lady Henniker Heaton; c/o Mrs I J S Mann, 10 The Street, Hoole Bank, Hoole Village, Chester

HENNIKER HEATON, Sir Yvo Robert; 4 Bt (UK 1912); s of Wing-Cdr Sir (John Victor) Peregrine Henniker Heaton, 3 Bt (d 1971); *b* 24 April 1954; *m* 1978, Freda, da of B Jones; *Heir* 1 cous, John Lindsey Henniker Heaton; *Style*— Sir Yvo Henniker-Heaton, Bt; 6 Lord Nelson St, Sneinton, Nottingham

HENNIKER-HEATON, (John) Lindsey; eld s of Clement Algernon Henniker-Heaton, CBE (d 1983; 3 s of late Sir John Henniker-Heaton, 2 Bt), and (Marjorie) Peggy, da of W E Speight, of Bournemouth; hp of 1 cous, Sir Yvo Henniker-Heaton, 4 Bt; *b* 19 June 1946; *Educ* Wellington, Emmanuel Coll Cambridge (MA); *m* 1970, Elisabeth Gladwell; 2 s (James b 1974, Robert b 1978); *Career* Br Aircraft Corpn 1964-74, RTZ Gp 1974-; CEng, FIMechE, MBIM; *Style*— Lindsey Henniker-Heaton, Esq; Northwoods House, Northwoods, Winterbourne, Bristol BS17 1RS (☎ 0454 775002)

HENNIKER-MAJOR, Hon Charles John Giles; 2 s of 8 Baron Henniker, KCMG, CVO, MC; *b* 1949; *Educ* Stowe; *m* 1980, Mrs Sally D M Kemp, da of Donald Newby, of Halesworth, Suffolk; 1 s (Thomas Charles John b 1982), 2 da (Osla Mary b 1981, Ruth Felicity b 1985); *Style*— The Hon Charles Henniker-Major; Great Chilton Farm, Ferryhill, Co Durham DL17 0JY

HENNIKER-MAJOR, Hon Mark Ian Philip Chandos; s and h of 8 Baron Henniker, KCMG, CVO, MC, by his w, Margaret Osla Benning (d 1974); *b* 29 Sept 1947; *Educ* Eton, Trinity Coll Cambridge (MA), UCL (LLM); *m* 1973, Mrs Lesley Antoinette Masterton-Smith, da of Wing Cdr G W Foskett, of Spitchwick Farm, Poundsgate, Newton Abbot, Devon; 2 s (Frederick John Chandos b 1983, Edward George Major b 1985), 3 da (Jessica b 1977, Josephine b 1979, Harriet b 1981); *Career* slr; co-fndr (1982) and ptnr Henniker-Major and Co of Ipswich, Felixstowe, Needham Market and Dovercourt/Harwich; dir: Foxwest Ltd, Anglia Business Conslts Ltd, Medvei John and Co; memb: Harwich Harbour Bd, CLA Suffolk; memb: Royal Aeronautical Soc, Br Insur Law Assoc, Law Soc; FCIArb; *Recreations* squash, chess, bridge; *Clubs* Ipswich and Suffolk, MCC; *Style*— The Hon Mark Henniker-Major; c/o Henniker-Major and Co, 1 and 3 Upper Brook St, Ipswich, Suffolk IP4 1EG (☎ 0473 212681, telex 98221, fax 0473 215118)

HENNIKER-MAJOR, Hon Richard Arthur Otway; s of 7 Baron Henniker (d 1980); *b* 1917; *Educ* Stowe, Magdalene Coll Cambridge (BA); *m* 1946, Nancy Pauline, da of late Sir John Armitage Stainton, KCB, KBE, QC; 2 s, 1 da; *Career* served WW II, Lt RA (POW); slr 1948; *Style*— The Hon Richard Henniker-Major; 13 Market Cross Place, Aldeburgh, Suffolk

HENNING, Kathleen Ann (Kathy); da of Robert Albert Henning, and Glenys Doreen, *née* Jones; *b* 26 April 1956; *Educ* Falmouth HS, Cornwall Tech Coll, Thames Polytechnic Business Sch; *Career* creative mangr Mary Quant Cosmetics 1978-83, gp product devpt mangr then product devpt dir Rimmel Int 1983-89; product devpt conslt Creative Force (own business) 1990-; *Style*— Ms Kathy Henning; 135 Gloucester Terrace, London W2 2DY (☎ 071 402 4857)

HENNING, Matthew Clive Cunningham; s of Matthew Henning (d 1982), of Co Londonderry, and Olivia Mary, *née* Cunningham (d 1990); *b* 4 Jan 1934; *Educ* St Andrew's Coll Dublin, Coll of Architecture Oxford (Dip Arch); *m* 27 Sept 1972, Vivien Margaret, da of David Ernest Walker (d 1971), of Armagh; 1 s (Daniel Clive Walker b 1978), 1 da (Kate Louise b 1982); *Career* conslt architect in private practice; formerly princ architect for the Southern Educn and Library Bd 1966-78; ARIBA; *Recreations* Golf; *Clubs* Portadown Golf, Tandragee Golf, Bushfoot Golf, County (Armagh), City (Amargh); *Style*— Matthew C.C. Henning, Esq; The Roost, Ridgeway Park South, Portadown, Craigavon, Co Armagh, NI BT62 3DQ (☎ 0762 331489); Bawnmore, Castlerock, Coleraine, Co Londonderry; Clive Henning Architects, 12 Market St, Portadown, Co Armagh (☎ 0762 338811)

HENRI, Adrian Maurice; s of Arthur Maurice Henri (d 1970), and Emma, *née* Johnson (d 1970); *b* 10 April 1932; *Educ* St Asaph GS N Wales, Dept Fine Art King's Coll Newcastle, Univ of Durham (BA); *m* 28 Oct 1959 (m dis 1974), Joyce (d 1987), da of Inspr Joseph Wilson; *Career* poet and painter; lectr: Manchester Coll of Art 1961-64, Liverpool Coll of Art 1964-67; led poetry-rock gp Liverpool Scene 1967-70, freelance poet, painter, singer songwriter and playwright 1970-; writer in res: The Tatterhall Centre Cheshire 1981-82, Dept of Educn Univ of Liverpool 1989; princ one-man shows: ICA London 1968, Art Net London 1975, Williamson Art Gallery Birkinhead 1976, Retrospective 1960-76, Wolverhampton City Art Gallery 1976, Demarco Gallery Edinburgh 1978, The Art of Adrian Henri 1933-85, South Hill Park Bracknell and touring 1986-87, John Moores Liverpool Exhibitions 1962, 1963, 1967, second prizewinner 1972, 1974, 1978, 1980, 1989; TV plays: Yesterday's Girl 1973, The Husband, The Wife and The Stranger 1986; pres: Merseyside Arts Assoc 1978-80, Liverpool Acad of Arts 1972-81; Hons D Litt Liverpool 1990; Books: Collected Poems (1986), Wish You were Here (poems 1990); for children: The Phantom Lollipop Lady (poems 1986), Rhinestone Rhino (poems 1989), Eric the Punk Cat (1980), Eric and Frankie in Las Vegas (1987), The Postman's Palace (1990); for teenagers: Box and Other Poems (1990), The Mersey Sound (with Roger McGough and Brian Patten, 1967, 3 edn, 1983), New Volume (1983); plays: I Wonder (with Michael Kustow, 1968), I Want (with Nell Dunn, 1983), The Wakefield Mysteries (1988), Fears and Miseries of the Third Term (1989); *Recreations* watching Liverpool FC, food and wine, travel, crime and Gothic novels and films; *Clubs* Chelsea Arts; *Style*— Adrian Henri, Esq

HENRICK, Ernest John; DFM (1945); s of Ernest Alfred, DCM, MM (d 1977), of London, and Mary, *née* Taylor (d 1978); *b* 10 May 1924; *Educ* Borough Poly; *m* 10 Nov 1945, Elizabeth Rose, da of Albert Edward McKenzie (d 1967), of London; 1 s (John Christopher b 13 March 1947), 1 da (Christine Mary Rose b 11 April 1950); *Career* WWII RAF 1942-46, Sgt Pilot 1943, 601 Sqdn (Spitfires) Italy 1944, Fl Sgt 1944, cmmnd Pilot Offr 1945, 253 Sqdn 1945, Flying Offr 1945, 91 Sqdn Duxford 1946, demob 1946; Sulzer Bros (UK) Ltd: mangr Manchester branch 1956, UK branch 1964, dir 1969-84, ret 1984; Freeman City of London, memb Worshipful Co of Fan Makers; CEng, MIEE 1956, FCIBS 1956, MIMechE 1960; *Recreations* golf, gardening; *Clubs* Wig and Pen, Hindhead Golf; *Style*— Ernest Henrick, Esq, DFM; Pine Hurst, Headley Hill Rd, Headley Bordon, Hants GU35 8DX (☎ 0428 713630)

HENRIKSEN, Bent; OBE (Hon 1983); *b* 20 March 1938; *Educ* Handelsskole Horsens Denmark, Forsvarets Gymnasium Copenhagen, Copenhagen Business Sch, Holbeck Denmark, Manchester Business Sch, Imede Lausanne Switzerland; *m* 12 Oct 1963, Hanne; 2 s (Troels b 1964, Rasmus b 1975), 1 da (Mette b 1966); *Career* Nat Serv Danish Army 1958-60, UN Army Force ME 1961-62; vice pres Elmwood Sensors Inc Providenc USA 1971-83, md Elmwood Sensors Ltd 1974-83, chief exec TSL Group plc Wallsend-on-Tyne 1983-87, chm Pharma Nord (UK) Ltd, dir IPM Victor Ltd Scotland; vice chm Newcastle Poly Prods Ltd; govr Newcastle upon Tyne Poly, chm Export Ctee Tyne & Wear C of C; FInstD 1975, FRSA 1982; *Recreations* riding, badminton; *Style*— Bent Henriksen, Esq, OBE; Spital Hall, Mitford, Morpeth, Northumberland NE61 3PN (☎ 0670 518667)

HENRIQUES, Lady; Marjory Brunhilda; *née* Burrows; *m* 1938, Sir Cyril Henriques, QC (d 1982), sometime pres Ct of Appeal Jamaica; 2 da; *Style*— Lady Henriques; Caribocho Rios Aptmts Ltd, Apt 111 Ocho Rios, St Ann, Jamaica (☎ 0974 5003)

HENRIQUES, Richard Henry Quixano; QC (1986); s of Cecil Quixano Henriques, of Thornton, Cleveleys, and Doreen Mary Henriques (d 1965); *b* 27 Oct 1943; *Educ* Bradfield, Worcester Coll Oxford (BA); *m* 14 July 1979, Joan Hilary (Toni), da of Maj Percy Sheard Senior (d 1947); 1 s (Daniel b 1981), 1 step s (David b 1970); *Career* called to the Bar Inner Temple 1967; rec of the Crown Ct 1983; memb Cncl Rossall Sch; *Style*— Richard Henriques, Esq, QC; Ilex House, Woodhouse Rd, Little Thornton, Lancashire FY5 5LQ (☎ 0253 826199); Deans Court Chambers, Crown Sq, Manchester (☎ 061 834 4097)

HENRY, Alan Lewis; s of John Clifford Lewis Henry, and Margaret Grae, *née* Cocks; *b* 9 June 1947; *Educ* Westcliff HS for Boys; *m* Ann; 1 s (Nicholas b 1980), 2 da (Emma b 1984, Charlotte b 1986); *Career* freelance motor sports journalist 1968-70, ed weekly specialist magazine 1987-89 (appointed to editorial staff 1970, Grand Prix corr 1973-87), motor racing corr The Guardian 1987-, ed Autocourse Annual; contrib to many pubns in Europe and Japan incl Autocar and Motor; *Books* Ferrari - The Grand Prix Cars (1984), Jackie Stewart's Principles of Performance Driving (1986), Derek Bell - My Racing Life (1988), The Turbo Years (1990); *Recreations* occasional golf; *Style*— Alan Henry, Esq; Alan Henry Associates, Old Reddings East, Tillingham, Essex CM0 7NX (☎ 0621 779 558/779608, fax 0621 778169)

HENRY, Hon Mrs ((Christian) Alison); da of The Rt Hon Lord Hughes, CBE, PC, and The Rt Hon Lady Hughes, *née* Gordon; *b* 2 March 1952; *Educ* Dundee HS, Univ of Strathclyde (BSc); *m* 1973, Allan Cameron Cassells, s of Allan Douglas Henry, of Hamilton; 1 s (Graham b 1984), 2 da (Gillian b 1977, Elaine b 1980); *Career* md Comrie (Dispensary) Ltd; *Style*— The Hon Mrs Henry; Tigh-an-Lios, The Ross, Comrie, Perthshire (☎ 0764 70864); Comrie (Dispensary) Ltd, Drummond St, Comrie (☎ 0764 70210)

HENRY, Anthony Patrick Joseph; s of Patrick Joseph Henry (d 1944), of Nottingham, and Helen Alethea, *née* Green; *b* 19 April 1939; *Educ* Epsom Coll Surrey, St Thomas Hosp Med Sch London (MB BS); *m* 1973, Patricia Mary, da of Kenneth Spiby, of Packington, Nr Ashby De La Zouch, Leics; 2 s (Joseph Patrick b 1974, George Michael b 1981), 1 da (Sarah Louise b 1977); *Career* TA Artists Rifles 21 SAS 1959-61; lectr in anatomy Univ of Alberta Canada 1966-67, res in surgery Durban S Africa 1968-70, sr registrar in orthopaedics Nottingham 1972-76, conslt orthopaedic surgn Derby 1976-, lectr in anatomy Derby Sch of Occupational Therapy 1974-; examiner in surgery Br Assoc of Occupational Therapists 1976-88, govr St Wynstans Sch Repton 1980-86; memb BMA 1963, FRCS 1971, fell Br Orthopaedic Assoc 1976; *Recreations* sailing, tennis, cricket; *Style*— Anthony Henry, Esq; Four Winds, Wagon Lane, Bretby, Derbys DE15 0QF (☎ 0283 217358); Orthopaedic Dept, Derbyshire Royal Infirmary, Derby DE1 2QY (☎ 0332 47141)

HENRY, Brian Glynn; s of Glynn Henry (d 1979), of Cookham, Berks, and Edith, *née* Jones (d 1982); *b* 5 Feb 1926; *Educ* Stowe, Trinity Coll Cambridge (MA); *m* 1, 10 June 1950, Elizabeth Jean, da of Ernest Craig (d 1977); 1 s (Julian b 1959), 3 da (Susan b 1951, Louise b 1953, Deborah b 1959); m 2, 30 June 1982, Jan Barney; *Career* Lt RNVR Home Fleet and Far East 1943-47; former co dir: Southern TV 1961-81, Remploy 1982-85, Wadlow Grosvenor 1982-84, Riviera TV 1982-84; dir Western Orchestral Soc Bournemouth Symphony Orchestra 1977-82, chm Oxford Playhouse 1988, vice pres Bournemouth and Poole Coll of Art and Design 1990, govr hist of Advertising Tst Atlantic Coll; FICM 1989; *Books* TV Advertising in Britain; The First 30 Years (1986); *Recreations* walking, photography, cycling; *Clubs* Buck's, Special Forces; *Style*— Brian Henry, Esq; Bere House, Pangbourne, Berks RG8 8HT (☎ 0734 843676)

HENRY, Clare; da of Walter Price Jenkinson (d 1989), and Marjorie Amy, *née* Bratley; *b* 21 Feb 1947; *Educ* Queen Elizabeth GS, Univ of Reading (BA); *m* 1 s (Damian b 25 Dec 1969), 1 da (Zara b 29 Nov 1976); *Career* researcher Paul Mellon Fndn of Br Art 1968-70, art critic Glasgow Herald 1980-, Scot ed Artline Scottish TV 1984- (Scot ed Arts Review 1984-87), currently arts contrib to BBC radio and tv, contrib to various magazines and exhibition catalogues; exhibition curator: New Scottish Prints (NY) 1983, London's Serpentine Summer Show 1985, Artists at Work (Edinburgh Festival) 1986, The Vigorous Imagination (Nat Gallery of Scot, Edinburgh Festival) 1987, Scotland at the Venice Biennale 1990; memb: Glasgow Print Studio 1973-80, NUJ, AICA, Visiting Arts Br Cncl; fndr memb SALVO; *Style*— Clare Henry

HENRY, Sir James Holmes; 2 Bt (UK 1923), CMG (1960), MC (1944), TD (1950), QC (Tanganyika 1953, Cyprus 1957); s of Rt Hon Sir Denis Stanislaus Henry, 1 Bt (d 1925), 1 Lord Chief Justice of NI, and Violet (d 1966), da of Rt Hon Hugh Holmes (former Lord Justice, Court of Appeal Ireland); *b* 22 Sept 1911; *Educ* Mount St Mary's Coll Chesterfield, Downside, UCL; *m* 1, 1941 (m dis 1948); m 2, 1949, Christina Hilary, da of Sir Hugh Oliver Holmes, KBE, CMG, MC, QC, and wid of Lt-Cdr Christopher Hayward Wells, RN; 3 da; *Heir* nephew, Patrick Denis Henry; *Career* served WW II (wounded), Capt London Irish Rifles (Royal Ulster Rifles); barr Inner Temple 1934, crown counsel Tanganyika 1946, legal draftsman 1949, slr-gen 1952, attorney-gen Cyprus 1956; memb Foreign Compensation Cmmn 1960-83 (chm 1977-83), ret; *Clubs* Travellers', Royal Cwlth Soc; *Style*— Sir James Henry, Bt, CMG, MC, TD, QC; Kandy Lodge, 18 Ormond Ave, Hampton-on-Thames, Middx

HENRY, Dr John Anthony; s of John Aloysius Henry, and Emma Susanna, *née* Elphick; *b* 11 March 1939; *Educ* St Josephs Acad Blackheath, Kings Coll London and KCH (MB BS); *Career* conslt physician Guys Hosp 1982-, conslt physician Nat Poisons Information Serv 1982-; FRCP 1986; *Books* ABC of Poisoning (jtly, 1984), BMA Guide to Medicines and Drugs (1988); *Recreations* walking; *Style*— Dr John Henry; 6 Orme Court, London W2 4RL; Guys Hospital, St Thomas St, London SE1 9RT (☎ 071 639 4831, fax 071 639 2101)

HENRY, Keith Nicholas; s of Kenneth George Henry, of 108 Montrose Ave, Luton, Beds, and Barbara, *née* Benns (d 1989); *b* 3 March 1945; *Educ* Bedford Sch, Univ of London (BSc), Univ of Birmingham (MSc); *m* 1974, Susan Mary, da of Roy Horsburgh; 2 da (Lucy Elizabeth b 1976, Claire Suzanne b 1978); *Career* engr mangr Brown & Root de France SA 1975-77, md Far East area Brown & Root (Singapore) Ltd 1977-80; Brown & Root (UK) Ltd: sr mangr 1980-83, chief engr 1983-85, commercial dir 1985-87 ; md: Brown & Root Vickers Ltd 1987-89, Brown & Root Marine 1989-90; chief exec Brown & Root (UK) Ltd 1990-; FEng, FICE, MInstD; *Recreations* shooting, sailing, golf; *Clubs* RAC; *Style*— Keith Henry, Esq; Brown & Root (UK) Ltd, 150 The Broadway, Wimbledon, London SW19 1RX (☎ 081 879 6601, fax 081 543 4895)

HENRY, Michael Meldrum; s of Cdre J M Henry, of Fieldside, Prinsted Lane, Prinsted, Hants, and Helen Muriel, *née* Davies (d 1971); *b* 19 Aug 1946; *Educ* Steyning GS, Univ of London (MB, BS); *m* 3 Aug 1981, Christine Mary, da of Alfred Douglas Parkyn (d 1985); *Career* lector to Trinity Coll Cambridge and lectr in surgery Cambridge Univ 1976-78, Hunterian prof RCS 1980, conslt surgn Dept of Gastroenterology Central Middlx Hosp London, sr lectr Academic Surgical Unit St Marys Hosp London; hon conslt surgn: St Marks Hosp for Diseases of Colon and Rectum London, St Lukes Hosp for the Clergy London; Freeman Worshipful Soc of Apothecaries; memb: BMA, RSM; FRCS; *Books* Coloproctology & The Pelvic Floor (1985), Surgery of Prolapse & Incontinence (1988); *Recreations* modern history, opera; *Clubs* Athenaeum; *Style*— Michael Henry, Esq; 26 Langham Mansions, Earls Court Square, London SW5 9UJ (☎ 071 370 7551); 106 Harley St, London W1N 1AF (☎ 071 935 3889)

HENRY, Richard Charles; TD (1976); s of John Richard Henry, OBE, JP, of Hilltop Cottage, Hopgoods Green, Bucklebury, Berks, and Blanche Catherine, *née* Barrett; *b* 26 Feb 1941; *Educ* Sherborne; *m* 15 April 1976, Judy Ann, da of Roger Massey (d 1974), of Stock, Essex; 1 s (Charles b 1977), 3 da (Belinda b 1979, Jane b 1979, Margaret b 1983); *Career* Capt HAC (TA) 1961-76, Ct of Assts HAC 1975-, treas 1990; articled Deloittes 1960, Coopers & Lybrand Assoc 1978-84; dir: Universal News Servs 1986, Tellex Monitors 1988, PNA Servs 1989, CRG 1990; fin dir Press Assoc 1989 (joined 1984); Freeman City of London 1986, Liveryman Worshipful Co of Barbers 1989; FCA 1966, memb IOD; *Recreations* TA, bridge, fishing; *Clubs* Army and Navy, Muthaiga; *Style*— Richard Henry, Esq, TD; Bailiffs Farmhouse, Ibworth, Basingstoke, Hants RG26 5TJ (☎ 0256 850 270); The Press Assoc, 85 Fleet St, London EC4P 4BE

HENRY, Stephen James Bartholomew; s of John Keith Maxwell Henry (d 1979), and Jose Isobel Prendergast, *née* Bartholomew (d 1975); *b* 21 Sept 1955; *Educ* Cranleigh Sch, St Catherine's Coll Oxford (BA, Shelley-Mills prize); *m* 18 Oct 1986, Angela Marie, da of Michael Coates; 1 da (Sophia Dominique Marie b 19 Nov 1989); *Career* copywriter: Crawfords 1979-81, Gold Greenlees Trott 1981-85; copywriter and creative gp head Wight Collins Rutherford Scott 1985-87, fndr and creative ptnr Howell Henry Chaldecott Lury 1987-; agency of year Campaign magazine 1989, winner of awards for various advertising campaigns; MIPA; *Recreations* swimming, reading, writing, being with my daughter; *Style*— Stephen Henry, Esq; Howell Henry Chaldecott Lury, Kent House, 14-17 Markets Place, Great Titchfield Street, London W1N 7AJ (☎ 071 436 3333, fax 071 436 2677)

HENSHALL, John Mark; s of John Henshall, of Stockport, and Margaret Winifred, *née* Passmore (d 1989); *b* 6 Jan 1942; *Educ* Queen Elizabeth GS Wakefield, Stockport GS; *m* 21 Sept 1979, Paulien, da of Dr Pieter Roorda, of Haarlem, Netherlands; 1 s (John Pieter b 12 May 1987), 2 da (Annelies b 11 Jan 1981, Martien b 13 July 1984); *Career* lighting dir BBC TV Serv 1975-76 (asst cameraman 1961-64, camera operator 1964-74), dir of photography and dir John Henshall Associates Ltd 1978-; recent prodns as dir of photography incl: Spitting Image, Sticky Moments, Network Seven, Seven Sport, MTV Europe, Dance Energy, The Winjin' Pom; recent prodns as dir: A Good Day's Fishing, Images, Amstrad commercials, Bic Razor commercial; co dir Telefex Ltd; lectr on various subjects incl: still photography, tv and video, lighting; Guild of TV Cameramen's award 1975-76, ITVA Gold awards of excellence: 1979, 1980, 1982; Advertising Assoc Gold and Silver award for best videotape commercials 1981, George Sewell trophy RPS 1986 and 87; memb Ctee Soc of TV Lighting Dirs 1986- (assoc memb 1975, full memb 1977); Guild of TV Cameramen: hon life memb 1978, vice chm 1974-78, hon fell 1984; memb Cncl RPS 1988- (memb Ctee Film and Video Gp 1986-89), pres BIPP 1991-92 (memb Cncl 1986-); FRGS 1967, FRPS 1985, FBIPP 1985; *Books* Dealers in Coins (1969), Sir H George Fordham, Cartobibliographer (1969); author of numerous articles; *Recreations* tennis, philately, philogyny, philomathy; *Style*— John Henshall; John Henshall Associates Ltd, 58 Kew Rd, Richmond, Surrey TW9 2PQ (☎ 081 940 1155, fax 081 940 8855, cellphone 0836 263000)

HENSHALL, Ruthie; da of David Henshall, of 1 Pond Cottages, Manningtree Rd, Stulton, Suffolk, and Gloria Diana, *née* Wilson; *b* 7 March 1967; *Educ* Bullswood GS Chislehurst Kent, Laine Theatre Arts Coll Epsom Surrey; *Career* theatre work: Mitzi in the Pied Piper of Hamlyn (Churchill Theatre Bromley) 1985, Ethel Dobbs in Fainettes (Bromley) 1985, lead role in Cellulord City Dandini in Cinderella (Aldershot) 1986, Maggie in A Chorus Line (nat tour) 1987, Jemima/Demeter/Grizabella/Griddlebone in Cats (New London Theatre) 1987-89, Ellen in Miss Saigon (Theatre Royal London) 1989-90, Aphra in Children of Eden (The Prince Edward Theatre) 1990-91; singer and dancer: Mack and Mabel (charity performance for Theatre Royal), summer season (Francis Golightly Clacton); billed solo singer (Clacton); TV work:

Wogan (BBC), Friday Live (Censtral), Children in Need (BBC), Secrets Out (BBC), Save The Children (Thames); contribs to numerous recording sessions; *Recreations* water skiing, diving, snow skiing, keeping fit, swimming; *Style*— Ms Ruthie Henshall; Hilary Gagan, Daly Gagan Associates, 68 Old Brompton Rd, London SW7 3LQ (☎ 071 581 0121, fax 071 589 2922)

HENSHAW, Brig Clinton Lionel Grant; CBE (1985), ADC (1988); s of Col C F G Henshaw, OBE, TD (d 1972), and Joan Aymer, *née* Ainslie; *b* 27 June 1936; *Educ* Wellington, RMA Sandhurst; *m* 15 Feb 1964, Suzanne Elliot, da of Cdr J A Philips (d 1986); 2 da (Caroline Emma Grant b 24 Sept 1965, Nichola Elizabeth b 25 July 1967); *Career* cmmnd Kings Royal Rifle Corps 1956; served: BAOR, Berlin, Guiana, Zimbabwe, France, Canada, NI; CDS staff MOD 1975-77, CO Rifle Depot 1977-79, DA Zimbabwe 1980-82, head DI ROW MOD 1982-85, cabinet office 1985-87, MA Paris 1988-; FBIM; *Recreations* fishing, shooting, golf, gardening; *Clubs* Army and Navy, Cercle Inter Alliée Paris; *Style*— Brig Clinton Henshaw, CBE, ADC; Plantation Cottage, Sutton Scotney, Winchester, Hants SO21 3NZ (☎ 0962 760844); Military Attache, British Embassy, 35 Rue De Faubourg St Honore, 75383 Paris Cedex 08, France (☎ 010 331 42669142))

HENSHAW, Hugh Nigel; s of Harold Henshaw (d 1955), of Rottingdean, Sussex, and Evelyn Louise, *née* Henshaw; *b* 28 Sept 1935; *Educ* Sherborne; *m* 29 March 1980, Anne Victoria Helen, da of Henry Thomas Hamilton Foley, MBE, JP (d 1959), of Stoke Edith Park, Hereford; 1 s (Thomas b 1983), 1 da (Katharine b 1981); *Career* Nat Serv 2 RHA 1954-55; admitted slr 1961; Clifford Turner, Freshfields, ptnr Lovell White & King 1968 (former memb), ptnr Lovell White Durrant 1988; memb Law Soc 1961; *Recreations* travel, opera, gardening; *Clubs* Bucks, HAC; *Style*— Hugh Henshaw, Esq; Lovell White Durrant, 65 Holborn Viaduct, London EC1A 2DY (☎ 071 236 0066, fax 071 248 4212, telex 887122 LWD G)

HENSHAW, John Trueman; OBE (1976); s of John Henshaw (d 1937), of Salford, Lancs, and Faith, *née* Trueman (d 1960); *b* 26 Nov 1913; *Educ* Royal Tech Coll Salford, Univ of Salford (MSc, PhD); *m* 14 May 1941, Elsie, da of Miles Goddard, of Mellor, Cheshire (d 1956); 1 s (David John b 1953), 1 da (Jennifer b 1950); *Career* head of design and weapons res AV Roe and Co Ltd 1954-55 (engrg designer aircraft 1937-46, exec designer 1946-54), sr lectr aircraft design Univ of Salford 1955-89, md Castlemere Engineering Ltd 1985-; fndr chm Whaley Bridge Amenity Soc (Civic Tst), fndr chm Whaley Bridge Branch Action Res for the Crippled Child Charity, co fndr and tech dir NW Orthotic Unit; FRAeS 1965, CEng 1968; *Books* Airframe Construction & Repair (1943), Aircraft Mechanics Pocket Book (1944), Supersonic Engineering (ed, 1962); *Recreations* walking and thinking; *Style*— John Henshaw, Esq, OBE; Taxal View, Fernilee, Whaley Bridge SK12 7HD; Castlemere Engineering Ltd, Sella Buildings, Market St, Whaley Bridge SK12 7AA

HENSMAN, Hon Mrs ((Mary) Sheila); *née* Wakefield; da of 1 Baron Wakefield, of Kendal (d 1983), and Rowena Doris, *née* Lewis (d 1981); *b* 29 April 1922; *Educ* Francis Holland Sch, Downe House Newbury; *m* 6 July 1945, Brig Richard Frank Bradshaw Hensman, CBE (d 1988), s of Capt Melvill Hensman, DSO, RN (d 1967), of South Hay House, Bordon, Hants; 1 s (Peter Richard Wavell b 30 Aug 1948), 1 da (Suzannah Mary b 9 Feb 1953); *Career* dir: Battlefields (Holdings) Ltd, Shapland & Petter Holdings Ltd, Lake District Estates Co Ltd, Ullswater Navigation & Transit Co Ltd, Ravenglass & Eskdale Railway Co Ltd; pres DHO Ski Club 1975-80, Ladies Ski Club 1987-90; vice-pres and chm Cumbria Tourist Bd 1990; *Recreations* skiing, walking, gardening; *Clubs* Lansdowne, Ski Club of Great Britain; *Style*— The Hon Mrs Hensman; Lindum Holme, Stricklandgate, Kendal, Cumbria LA9 4QG (☎ 0539 25093)

HENSON, Brian David; s of James Maury Henson, of New York and London, and Jane Anne Nebel Henson; *b* 3 Nov 1963; *Educ* Phillips Acad Andover USA, Univ of Colorado USA; *Career* film dir, puppeteer, animatronics performance co-ordinator and conslt: special effects technician and performer The Great Muppet Caper 1981 and The Muppets Take Manhattan 1983, performer of Jack Pumpkinhead in Return to Oz 1984, princ performer and performer co-ordinator Labyrinth 1984-85, princ performer Little Shop of Horrors 1986, princ performance co-ordinator Storyteller (TV series) 1987, dir Mother Goose Stories (TV) 1988, princ performer Jim Henson Presents: Living with Dinosaurs and Monster Maker (TV) 1988; memb: SAG, AFTRA, Equity (UK), ACTT, DGA; *Recreations* skiing, squash, cars, dogs, travelling, fashion; *Style*— Brian Henson, Esq; 1b Downshire Hill, London NW3 (☎ 071 431 2818)

HENSON, Nicholas Victor Leslie; s of Leslie Lincoln Henson, and Billie Dell, *née* Collins; *b* 12 May 1945; *Educ* St Bedes Eastbourne, Charterhouse, RADA; *m* 1, 1968 (m dis 1975), Una Stubbs; 2 s (Christian b 25 Dec 1971, Joe b 18 Sept 1973); m 2, 1 Aug 1986, Marquerite Ann Porter; 1 s (Keaton b 24 March 1988); *Career* former popular song writer incl 3 year writing contract with The Shadows and Cliff Richard, fndr memb Young Vic Co 1970; plays: All Square (Vaudeville) 1963, Camelot (Drury Lane) 1964, Passion Flower Hotel (Prince of Wales) 1965, London Laughs (Palladium) 1966, Canterbury Tales (Phoenix) 1968, The Ride Across Lake Constance (Hampstead and Mayfair) 1973, Hamlet (Greenwich) 1973, Mind Your Head (Shaw) 1973, A Midsummer Nights Dream (Open Air) 1973, Taming of the Shrew (Shaw) 1973, Cinderella (Casino) 1973, Mardi Gras (Prince of Wales) 1976, Rookery Nook (Her Majesty's) 1979, Noises Off (Lyric and Savoy) 1982, The Relapse (Lyric) 1983, Sufficient Carbohydrate (Hampstead and Albery) 1983, Journeys End (Whitehall) 1988, Ivanov (Strand) 1989, Much Ado About Nothing (Strand) 1989, Three Sisters (Royal Court) 1990; Young Vic: Waiting for Godot, Scapino, The Soldier's Tale, She Stoops to Conquer, Measure for Measure, Oedipus, Wakefield Nativity Plays, Romeo and Juliet, The Maids, Deathwatch, Look Back in Anger, Rosencrantz and Guildenstern are Dead, Charleys Aunt; NT 1978-: The Cherry Orchard, MAcbeth, The Women, The Double Dealer, A Fair Quarrel, The Browning Version, Harlequinade, The Provok'd Wofe, The Elephant Man, Mandragola, Long Time Gone; RSC: Man and Superman 1977, As You Like It 1985-86, Merry Wives of Windsor 1985-86; TV: A Midsummer Night's Dream, Absurd Person Singular, Seasons Greetings, Love After Lunch, Thin Air, Startrap 1988, Inspector Morse 1988, Boon 1989, After Henry 1990, The Upper Hand 1990; The Green Man 1990; films: appearances in over 25 incl: Theres A Girl in My Soup, Witch Finder General, Tom Jones, Number One of The Street Service; *Recreations* snooker; *Style*— Nicky Henson, Esq; c/o Richard Stone Partnership, 25 Whitehall, London SW1 2BS (☎ 071 839 6421)

HENTON, Roger Gordon; s of (William) Gordon Henton, of Lincoln, and Pamela, *née* Evans (d 1983); *b* 2 Aug 1940; *Educ* Bedford Sch; *m* 25 June 1966, Susan Eleanor, da of John Richmond Edwards; 1 s (Thomas b 1972), 1 da (Isabel b 1970); *Career* Streets & Co CAs Lincoln 1959-64, Coopers & Lybrand Geneva 1965-67, pa to md AAH plc Lincoln 1968-72, dir Camamile Assocs Lincoln 1973-77, fndr and sr ptnr Henton & Peycke CAs Leeds 1978-; ACA 1964, FCA; *Recreations* squash, golf; *Clubs* RAC, Scarcroft Golf; *Style*— Roger Henton, Esq; 12 York Place, Leeds, West Yorks (☎ 0532 457553, fax 0532 420474, car 0836 742200)

HENTY, Jonathan Maurice; s of Richard Iltid Henty (d 1954), of Fairy Hill, Chichester, Sussex, and Lettice Ellen, *née* Moore-Gwyn (d 1987); *b* 22 Dec 1933; *Educ* Eton, New Coll Oxford (MA); *m* 1, July (Margaret) Louise (d 1972), da of David Sadler (d 1954), of Biggar; 2 s (Richard Edward Jonathan b 9 March 1959, Charles James Christian b 4 July 1963), 1 da (Julia Rose b 7 April 1961); m 2, 26 March 1977, Veronica Mary Francis, da of Lt-Col Miller, of Bracken House, Crawley Drive, Camberley, Surrey; 2 da (Josephine Frances Veronica b 4 Aug 1978, Clemency Margaret Anne b 1 April 1983); *Career* called to the Bar Lincoln's Inn 1957, bencher Lincoln's Inn 1989, chllr Dioces of Hereford 1977; *Recreations* shooting, fishing, architecture; *Clubs* Athenaeum; *Style*— Jonathan Henty, Esq; Fisher Hill House, Northchapel, Petworth, Sussex GU28 9EJ (☎ 042 878 659); 24 Old Buildings, Lincoln's Inn, WC2 (☎ 071 404 0946, fax 071 405 1360)

HENWOOD, Roderick Waldemar Lisle; s of Noel Gordon Lisle Henwood (d 1972), and Daphne Muirhead, *née* Schroeder; *b* 29 Nov 1963; *Educ* Dollar Acad, Univ of Geneva, New Coll Oxford (BA); *Career* controller of prog business affrs Central Independent TV plc 1988-; *Recreations* snooker, golf; *Style*— Roderick Henwood, Esq; Central Independent Television PLC, Central House, Broad St, Birmingham B1 2JP ☎ 021 643 9898 Ext 4357, telex 338966, fax 021 643 4897

HEPBURN, Gavin Andrew Harley; s of John Harley Hepburn, JP (d 1966), of Kirkcaldy, and Lena Champbell, *née* Ritchie; *b* 6 Dec 1937; *Educ* Loretto, Dundee Tech Coll; *m* 28 Sept 1966, Anne Margaret, da of James Mitchell, Girvan, Ayrshire; 2 s (Alastair b 11 March 1968, David b 3 Feb 1976), 1 da (Katherine b 8 July 1967); *Career* md: Fife Forge Co Ltd 1973 (co sec 1966), Fife Indmar plc 1981 (chm 1981, dir 1988); dir: Robert Taylor Hldgs 1981-88, Bruntons plc Musselburgh 1983-86, Smith Anderson Ltd Leslie 1986-, Scotfresh Ltd Eyemouth 1987-89; pres Kirkaldy Jr C of C 1963, dir Kirkaldy C of C 1976-80; memb: Scot Cncl CBI 1976-82, Scot Cncl Devpt & Indust 1982-86; chm Forth Ports Authy 1980-86, dir Glenrothes Devpt Corp 1984-89, tstee Scot Hosps Tst 1985-, dir Edinburgh Acad Sch 1986-; memb Williams Ctee of Enquiry into Scot Agric Colls 1989; memb Incorporation of Hammermen (Edinburgh); ACMA, ACIS; *Recreations* fishing, golf, bridge, curling; *Clubs* New (Edinburgh), Elie Golf House; *Style*— Gavin Hepburn, Esq; 22 Mansion Ho Rd, Edinburgh EH9 2JD (☎ 031 667 7767); Fife Indmar plc, Smeaton Rd, Kirkcaldy, Fife (☎ 0592 533 88, fax 0592 549 88, car 0836 702 526, telex 72378)

HEPBURN, (James) Michael Harley; s of John Harley Hepburn, JP (d 1966), of Kirkcaldy, Fife; *b* 7 July 1934; *Educ* Loretto; *m* 1953, Ethne Margaret Forbes, da of Dr Percival Binnington (d 1944), of Hull; 3 da; *Career* served Lt 1 Royal Scots Korea 1952-53; dir: Fife Indmar plc 1969-, The Girls Sch Co 1970-82, Scottish Music Info Centre 1985-, Paton Holdings Ltd 1985-; md William Paton Ltd 1980; Punch Holdings (UK) Ltd 1989 MInstMSM, FinstD; *Recreations* skiing, marathon running, hill walking, choral singing; *Style*— Michael Hepburn, Esq; Upper Gavilmoss, Lochwinnoch, Renfrewshire (☎ 0505 843071); William Paton Ltd, Johnstone Mill, High St, Johnstone, Renfrewshire (☎ 0505 216333, telex 777841)

HEPBURN, Prof Ronald William; s of William George Hepburn (d 1961), of Aberdeen and Grace Ann, *née* Fraser (d 1974); *b* 16 March 1927; *Educ* Aberdeen GS, Univ of Aberdeen (MA, PhD); *m* 16 July 1953, Agnes Forbes, da of Rev William Anderson, of Edinburgh (d 1969); 2 s (David W b 1954, Antony R b 1957), 1 da (Catriona M b 1972); *Career* Nat Serv Army 1944-48; asst then lectr Dept of Moral Philosophy Univ of Aberdeen 1952-60, visiting assoc prof Univ of NY 1959-60, prof of philosophy Univ of Nottingham 1960-64, prof of moral philosophy Univ of Edinburgh 1975- (prof of philosophy 1964-75); various contribs to books, articles and broadcasts; *Books* Christianity & Paradox (1958 2 edn 1966 3 edn 1968), 'Wonder' Other Essays (1984); *Recreations* music, hill-walking, photography; *Style*— Prof Ronald Hepburn; Department of Philosophy, University of Edinburgh, David Hume Tower, George Square, Edinburgh EH8 9JX (☎ 031 6671011)

HEPBURNE SCOTT, Hon Francis Michael; MC; raised to rank of Baron's son 1945; 2 s of Capt Hon Walter Thomas Hepburne Scott (eldest s of 9 Baron Polwarth, decd); bro of 10 Baron Polwarth, TD; *b* 1920; *Educ* Eton, King's Coll Cambridge; *m* 1946, Marjorie Hamilton, da of Horatio John Ross; 2 s, 1 da; *Career* sometime Maj Lothians and Border Horse; farmer; FRICS (ret); *Style*— The Hon Francis Hepburne Scott; Newhouse, Lilliesleaf, Melrose, Roxburghs (☎ 083 57 307)

HEPHER, Michael Leslie; s of Leslie and Edna Hepher; *b* 17 Jan 1944; *Educ* Kingston GS; *m* 1971, Janice Morton; 1 s (Daniel b 1980); 2 da (Kelly b 1973, Erin b 1975); *Career* chm and md Lloyds Abbey Life plc 1980-; FIA, FCIA, ASA, FLIA; *Recreations* tennis, reading; *Style*— Michael Hepher, Esq; Lloyds Abbey Life plc, 205 Brooklands Rd, Weybridge, Surrey KT13 0PE (☎ 0932 850 888)

HEPPEL, Peter John Merrick; s of John Edward Thomas Heppel (d 1964), of Romford, Essex, and Ida Florence, *née* Ford (d 1983); *b* 31 March 1948; *Educ* Royal Liberty Sch Romford Essex, Univ of Hull (LLB), UCL (LLM); *m* 20 Sept 1980, Janice, da of John Coulton, of Southport, Merseyside; 2 s (Edward b 1981, William b 1986), 2 da (Charlotte b 1979, Indea b 1982); *Career* called to the Bar Middle Temple 1970, in practice NE Circuit 1972-, rec 1988-; *Recreations* family, music, reading; *Clubs* Sloane; *Style*— Peter Heppel, Esq; Warriston, Parkfield Ave, N Ferriby, Humberside HU14 3AL (☎ 0482 631657); 2 Harcourt Buildings, Temple, London EC4 (☎ 071 353 1394); Wilberforce Chambers, 171 High St, Hull HU1 1NE (☎ 0482 23264)

HEPPELL, Thomas Strachan; CB (1986); s of Leslie Thomas Davidson Heppell, and Doris Abbey, *née* Potts; *b* 15 Aug 1935; *Educ* Acklam Hall GS Middlesborough, The Queen's Coll Oxford (BA); *m* 1963, Felicity Ann, da of Lt-Col Richard Bernard Rice (ka 1943); 2 s (Jeremy Strachan b 1965, Martin Richard b 1967); *Career* princ Nat Assistance Bd 1963 (asst princ 1958); DHSS: asst sec 1973, under sec 1979, dep sec 1983; *Recreations* gardening, travelling; *Style*— Strachan Heppell, CB; Lloyds Bank, 6 Holborn Circus London EC1N 2HP; Department of Health, Richmond House, Whitehall, SW1

HEPPER, Anthony Evelyn; s of Lt-Col John E Hepper (d 1967), and Rosalind, *née* Bowker; *b* 16 Jan 1923; *Educ* Wellington, Loughborough Coll; *m* 1970, Jonquil Francesca; *Career* served RE (N Africa, Sicily, Italy, France, Belgium, Holland, Norway, Palestine, Egypt), Maj; dir Cape plc 1968-, chm Hyde Sails Ltd 1984-; CEng, FIMechE; *Recreations* golf; *Clubs* Boodle's; *Style*— A E Hepper, Esq; 70 Eaton Place, London SW1X 8AT (☎ 071 235 7518)

HEPPLE, Prof Bob Alexander; s of Alexander Hepple (d 1983), of Canterbury, and Josephine, *née* Zwarenstein; *b* 11 Aug 1934; *Educ* Univ of Witwatersrand (BA, LLB), Univ of Cambridge (LLB, MA); *m* 7 July 1960, Shirley Rona, da of Morris Goldsmith (d 1972), of London; 1 s (Paul Alexander b 11 Dec 1962), 1 da (Brenda (Mrs Henson) b 7 July 1961); *Career* practising attorney Johannesburg 1958, lectr law Univ of Witwatersrand 1959-62, practising advocate Johannesburg 1962-63, called to the Bar Grays Inn 1966, lectr law Univ of Nottingham 1966-68, fell Clare Coll and lectr law Cambridge 1968-76, prof comparative social and labour law Univ of Kent 1976-77, chm Industl Tbnls England and Wales 1977-82 (pt/t chm 1974-77 and 1982-); UCL: prof Eng law 1982-, dean faculty of laws and head Dept of Laws 1989-; memb: Cmmn on Racial Equality 1986-90, Tbnls Ctee Judicial Studies Bd 1988-; *publications:* numerous books and articles on labour law and industl rels, race rels and discrimination, law obligations in general; *Recreations* theatre, music, reading, walking, gardening; *Style*— Prof Bob Hepple; Faculty of Laws, University College, Bentham House, Endsleigh Gardens, London WC1H 0EG (☎ 071 387 7050, fax 071 387 9597)

HEPPLE, Keith Michael; s of Peter David Hepple (d 1982), and Patricia Mary, *née* Heppel (now Mrs Fitzsimmons); *b* 31 July 1965; *Educ* Knavesmire Secdy Modern Sch York, York Coll of Arts and Technol (Dip Fashion), Trent Poly of Art and Design

(BA); *Career* styled Benettons winter 1985/86 collection 1985, fashion asst to Debbi Mason at the launch of Br Elle Magazine 1985, finalist Smirnoff UK Fashion awards 1986, Paris corr to Thom O'Dwyer Fashion Weekly 1986-87, illustration cmmn for Warehouse 1987, conslt to John Partridge menswear 1987, lectr Trent Poly 1987, dep fashion ed Fashion Weekly 1987 (DR magazine 1988), author of articles for various fashion magazines; *Recreations* swimming, reading, books; *Clubs* The Daisy Chain (Brixton); *Style—* Keith Hepple, Esq; International Thomson Business Publishing, 100 Avenue Rd, London NW3 (☎ 081 965 6611 ext 2238, fax 071 722 4920, telex 299973 ITPLN G)

HEPPLE, (Robert) Norman; s of Robert Watkin Hepple, and Ethel Louise, *née* Wardale; *b* 18 May 1908; *Educ* Colfe GS, Goldsmith's Coll Art Sch, Royal Acad Schs; *m* 1948, Jillian Pratt; 1 s, 1 da; *Career* portrait artist; portraits incl: HM The Queen, HM The Queen Mother, HRH Prince Philip, HRH Prince Charles, HRH Princess Alice, HRH Princess Marina, HRH Princess Alexandra; The Dukes of Westminster Portland Rutland Roxburgh, many distinguished membs of the Church, industry and the professions; figure subject and landscape painter; RA 1961 (ARA 1954), PRP 1979 (RP 1948), NEAC 1950; *Style—* Norman Hepple, Esq; 10 Sheen Common Drive, Richmond, Surrey TW10 5BN (☎ 081 878 4452)

HEPTONSTALL, Cyril Philip; s of Lt-Col Robert Allatt Heptonstall (d 1969), and Mary Aline, *née* Dixon (d 1969); *b* 7 July 1924; *Educ* Tonbridge, St John's Coll Cambridge (MA, LLM); *m* 24 April 1954, Cora Arline Mary, da of Ernest Henry Smith (d 1971); 1 s (Hugh b 1956), 2 da (Julia b 1955, Anna b 1959); *Career* RAFVR 1943-46, Flying Offr (pilot); admitted slr 1951; practised at bar 1956-59; practising slr 1959-; *Recreations* fishing, shooting, photography; *Style—* Cyril Heptonstall, Esq; Martins, Howden, nr Goole, N Humberside DN14 7ER (☎ 0430 430519); 11/13 Gladstone Terrace, Goole, N Humberside DN14 5AH (☎ 0405 765661, fax 0405 764201, telex 57579)

HEPWORTH, David; s of Ernest Hepworth (d 1981), of Ossett, Yorkshire, and Sarah Marjorie, *née* Rollinson; *b* 27 July 1950; *Educ* Queen Elizabeth GS Wakefield, Trent Park Coll of Educn Barnet Herts (BEd); *m* 5 Sept 1979, Alyson, da of Ronald Elliott, of Hove, Sussex; 1 s (Henry b 1987), 1 da (Clare b 1982); *Career* freelance journalist 1975-79; ed: Smash Hits 1980-82, Just Seventeen 1983-85; editorial dir Emap Metro 1984-; presenter: BBC TV Whistle Test 1980-86; BBC Radio GLR; Periodical Publishers' Assoc: Ed of the Year 1985, Writer of the Year 1988; *Recreations* books, tennis, music; *Style—* David Hepworth, Esq; 48 The Mall, London N14 6LN (☎ 081 882 5963); 42 Great Portland St, London W1 (☎ 071 436 5430, fax 071 631 0781)

HEPWORTH, Brig Nicholas George Rispin; OBE (1985); s of Lt-Col Alfred Geoffrey Edwards Hepworth, of N Yorks, and Mary Rispin, *née* Humble; *b* 16 Aug 1941; *Educ* Daniel Stewart's Coll Edinburgh, RMA Sandhurst; *m* 6 April 1974, Teresa Jane, da of John Guy Henderson Huntley (d 1953); 1 s (Charles David Huntley b 15 May 1976), 1 da (Virginia Mary Louise b 26 May 1978); *Career* cmmnd 2 Lt King's Regt 1961; served 1961-74: Eng, Berlin, Br Guiana, seconded Sultan's Armed Forces Oman Dhofar War 1968-70, BOAR, Ulster, MOD 1975-79: Maj, Army Staff Coll, rifle company cdr 1 Bn King's Regt (Ulster, UN Forces Cyprus, England), Bde Maj BAOR; 1980-85: Lt-Col, DS Army Staff Coll Camberley, CO 1 Bn King's Regt BAOR and Ulster, MOD; Col PSO Sultan's Land Forces Oman 1985-86; Brig, cdr Br Forces Belize, Indian NDC New Delhi 1987-89; *Recreations* walking, travelling, reading; *Clubs* Army and Navy, Lansdowne; *Style—* Brig Nicholas Hepworth, OBE; c/o ANZ Grindlays Bank, 13 St James's Square, London SW1Y 4LF

HERBECQ, Sir John Edward; KCB (1977); s of Joseph Edward, and Rosina Elizabeth Herbecq; *b* 29 May 1922; *Educ* Chichester HS for Boys; *m* 1947, Pamela Filby; 1 da; *Career* joined Colonial Office 1939; private sec to chm UKAEA 1960-62, asst sec Treasy 1964; Civil Serv Dept: asst sec 1968, under sec 1970, dep sec 1973, 2 perm sec 1975-81; church cmmr 1982-; *Style—* Sir John Herbecq, KCB; Maryland, Ledgers Meadow, Cuckfield, Haywards Heath, W Sussex RH17 5EW (☎ 0444 413387)

HERBERT, Anthony James; s of Maj Kenneth Faulkner Herbert, MBE, of Park Rd Nursing Home, Winchester, and Kathleen Ellis, *née* Robertson; *b* 28 March 1940; *Educ* Eton, King's Coll Cambridge (MA); *m* 4 May 1968, Lowell, da of George M Pelton, of Nova Scotia, Canada; 2 s (Dominic b 9 April 1971, Daniel b 21 Feb 1973), 1 da (Julia b 21 March 1978); *Career* admitted slr 1965, ptnr Allen & Overy 1970- (asst slr 1965-69); memb: Law Soc 1965, Int Bar Assoc, City of London Law Soc; *Recreations* painting, tennis, skiing; *Clubs* Roehampton; *Style—* Anthony Herbert, Esq; 16 Woodborough Rd, London SW15 6PZ (☎ 081 788 7042); c/o Allen & Overy 9 Cheapside, London EC2V 6AD (☎ 071 248 9898, fax 071 236 2192, telex 8812801)

HERBERT, Arthur James (Jim); CBE (1982); s of Arthur Stephens Herbert (d 1959), of Middx, and Ethel Mary Ferguson (d 1954), of Tasmania; *b* 24 Oct 1918; *Educ* Sydney C of E GS, Merchant Taylors', Pembroke Coll Cambridge (MA); *m* 1948, Pamela Mary, da of Capt John Gyde Heaven (d 1923), of Bristol; 1 s (Richard b 1949), 3 da (Caroline b 1951, Nicola b 1955, Linda b 1958); *Career* serv WWII Maj RE (granted rank of Hon Maj on demob, despatches); chm Herbert & Sons Ltd; dir: Swift Scale Co Ltd, Lion Electronics Ltd, Meatex Ltd; pres Nat Fed Scale & Weighing Machine Mfrs 1966-68 and 1982-84; memb Engr Employers Fed Policy Ctee 1982-89 and Mgmnt Bd 1981-90, pres E Anglian Engr Employers Assoc 1980-82 and 1986-88; chm Bury St Edmunds Constituency Cons Assoc 1972-80 (pres 1980-86), chm Suffolk & SE Cambs Euro Constituency Cons Assoc 1987-89 (pres 1989-), pres S Suffolk Constituency Cons Assoc 1987-90; Freeman City of London; *Recreations* gardening; *Clubs* Hawks, (Cambridge), East India and Sports, MCC; *Style—* Jim Herbert, Esq, CBE; 18 Rookwood Way, Haverhill, Suffolk CB9 8PD (☎ 0440 703551, telex 817931 HERBRT G, fax 0440 62048)

HERBERT, Austin Godfrey Vivian; s of John George Herbert (d 1947), of 202 Ross Rd, Hereford, and Alice Susannah, *née* Blackford (d 1927); *b* 30 April 1907; *Educ* Hereford HS, Leicester Coll of Technol, Birmingham Commercial Coll; *m* 14 Nov 1953, Joan, da of Archibald Howard Osborne, MBE (d 1964); 1 da (Alison Sybil b 29 March 1957); *Career* Herefordshire Regt TA 1924-29, RAFVR 1939-45, Fighter Cmd 1939-41, SE Asia Cmd 1941-45, Sqdn Ldr; serv: Malaysia, Java, Aust, Sri Lanka, India; chief fin offr Tamworth DC 1928-31, clerk of the cncl Ross-on-Wye DC 1932-35, chief exec C B Buxton Ltd London 1935-39, co sec Bakelite Ltd 1945-65, dir of admin BXL (now part of BP) 1965-69, dir of courses and sr lectr S W London Coll 1969-77, business conslt 1977-; past pres and cncl memb Inst of Chartered Secs and Administrators, memb Cncl (former chm) Corp of Secs 1955-70, sr vice pres ICSA Registrars Gp 1961-, memb Exec Ctee Chemical Industs Assoc 1967-69, cnsllr Second Careers for RN Offrs 1971-81, memb Industl Tbnl Panel 1973-80; involved with Penn Parish Church; Freeman: City of London 1961, Worshipful Co of Scriveners 1961; FCIS 1938, FBIM 1959, FAIA 1964; *Clubs* The Naval, Mansfield Law; *Style—* Austin Herbert, Esq; 19 Hogback Wood Rd, Beaconsfield, Bucks HP9 1JR (☎ 0494 674650)

HERBERT, Barry; s of Harold John Herbert (d 1985), of N Humberside, and Gladys Irene Everitt, *née* Wade; *b* 13 April 1938; *Educ* Beverley GS; *m* 3 Sept 1966 (m dis 1990), Margaret Avril, da of Norman Nicholson, MBE (d 1962), of Humberside; 1 s (Christopher John b 1974), 1 da (Julia Anne b 1972); *Career* jt md Atlas Caravan Co Ltd 1978-; FCCA; DMS; MInstM; *Recreations* traction engine, organ restoration; *Clubs* Nat Traction Engine Tst, Leeds and Dist Traction Engine, East Riding Engine, Stanley Museum of America; *Style—* Barry Herbert, Esq; Owl Hill, 29 Old Village Rd, Little Weighton, East Yorks HU20 3US (☎ 0482 849380); Atlas Caravan Co Ltd, Wykeland Ind Estate, Wiltshire Rd, Hull, North Humberside HU4 6PH (☎ 0482 562101)

HERBERT, Hon Caroline Mary Louise; 2 da of 3 Baron Hemingford; *b* 4 Oct 1964; *Educ* Perse Sch for Girls Cambridge, Liverpool Poly, Univ of Lancaster (BEd); *Career* sch teacher (primary); *Recreations* reading, sewing, outdoor activities; *Style—* The Hon Caroline Herbert; The Old Rectory, Hemingford Abbots, Huntingdon, Cambs

HERBERT, Hon Christopher Dennis Charles; only s and h of 3 Baron Hemingford; *b* 4 July 1973; *Educ* King's Coll Choir Sch Cambridge, Oundle; *Recreations* cricket, fives; *Style—* The Hon Christopher Herbert

HERBERT, David Mark; s of Rt Rev Percy Mark Herbert, Bishop of Norwich, KCVO (d 1968), and Hon Elaine Laetitia Algitha, *née* Orde Powlett; *b* 2 Jan 1927; *Educ* Rugby, Trinity Coll Cambridge (BA, MA); *m* 1 Jan 1955, (Monica) Brenda, da of Lawrence Edmund Swann (d 1980); 1 s (Charles b 1959), 1 da (Emma b 1961); *Career* asst master: Eton Coll 1953, Christ's Hosp 1954-61; publishing dir and chief exec Studio Vista Publishing Co 1966-74 (ed dir 1963-66); md Rainbird Publishing Group Ltd 1974-77, md and chm Herbert Press Ltd 1976-, md Paul Elek Publishing 1977, publishing conslt to Benn Bros plc 1980-84; Hon Freeman of Shrewsbury 1972; *Books* Penguin Book of Narrative Verse (ed, 1960), Comic Verse (ed, 1962), Keats (ed, 1963), George Herbert (ed, 1963), Romeo and Juliet (ed, 1965), The Operas of Benjamin Britten (1979), Everyman Book of Evergreen Verse (1981), The Gallery of World Photography: The Human Figure (1982), Everyman Book of Narrative Verse (1990); *Recreations* writing, acting, tennis, travel, photography; *Clubs* The Garrick; *Style—* David Herbert, Esq; 46 Northchurch Rd, London N1 4EJ (☎ 071 254 4379); Stormy Castle, Church Path, Faringdon, Oxon

HERBERT, David Passmore; s of late A H Herbert; *b* 11 Jan 1935; *Educ* The Leys Sch, Queens' Coll Cambridge; *m* 1966, Rosemary Elaine, *née* Bawtree; 2 s; *Career* slr; ptnr Triggs Turner and Co 1962-71, gp sec and slr Davies and Newman Group of Cos 1971-78; dir: Davies and Newman Holdings plc 1978-, Smedvig Ltd 1979-90, Dan-Smedvig Supply Ships Ltd 1983-90, Dan-Air Services Ltd 1978-; dep chm Davies and Newman Holdings plc 1985-90, chm Vernon Educnl Trust Ltd 1989; *Recreations* sailing, gardening, reading; *Style—* David P Herbert, Esq; Meadowfold, South Rd, Liphook, Hants GU30 7HS (☎ 0428 722029); Davies & Newman Holdings plc, Newman House, Victoria Rd, Horley, Surrey RH6 7QG (☎ 0293 820700, fax 0293 774717, telex 877677)

HERBERT, Prof David Thomas; s of Trevor John Herbert, of Rhondda, and (Winifred) Megan, *née* Pearce (d 1990); *b* 24 Dec 1935; *Educ* Rhondda Co GS, Univ of Wales (BA, Dip ED), Univ of Birmingham (PhD); *m* 30 Dec 1968, Tonwen, da of Thomas John Maddock (d 1957); 1 s (David Aled b 1971), 1 da (Nia Wyn b 1973); *Career* Nat Serv RAF 1954-56; lectr Univ of Keele 1963-65; Univ of Wales Swansea: lectr 1965, sr lectr 1973, reader 1977, prof 1980, dean 1981-84, vice princ 1986-89; visiting prof: Univ of Toronto 1965, Univ of Manitoba 1967, Univ of York Ontario 1969, Univ of Leuven 1973, Univ of Colorado 1979, Univ of Oklahoma 1980, Univ of Sudan 1982, Univ of Warsaw 1987 (1985), Univ of Calgary 1989; memb: Inst of Br Geographers (formerly on Cncl) Geographical Assoc, Gen Dental Cncl, Sports Cncl for Wales, Pembrokeshire Coast Nat Park, Welsh Jt Educn Ctee; former memb Social Sci Res Cncl, chm Swansea Crime Prevention Panel; *Books* incl: Urban Geography: A Social Perspective (1972), Geography of Urban Crime (1982), Cities in Space: City as Place (with C J Thomas, 1990), Heritage Sites: Strategies for Marketing and Development (jtly, 1989), Geography and the Urban Environment (ed with RJ Johnston), Social Problems and the City (ed with DM Smith); *Recreations* tennis, fishing, skiing, reading, music; *Style—* Prof David Herbert; 36 Rhyd Y Defaid Drive, Sketty, Swansea SA2 8AJ (☎ 0792 204143); Department of Geography, University College, Swansea SA2 8PD (☎ 0792 295229, telex 48358 ULSWAN G, fax 0792 205556)

HERBERT, Hon Edward David; *b* 1 July 1958; *Educ* Bryanston, Univ of Lancaster (BSc), Spurgeon's Coll (BA); *m* 1985, Diana Christine, eld da of Cedric Shore; 1 s (David Andrew b 1988), 1 da (Joy Sarah b 1986); *Career* ACMA; *Style—* The Hon Edward Herbert; c/o The Rt Hon the Earl of Powis, Marrington Hall, Chirbury, Powys

HERBERT, Elizabeth Anne Morse; da of late Lt-Col H G Herbert, and late Elizabeth Vera, *née* Morse; *b* 9 Feb 1948; *Educ* St Swithun's Sch Winchester; *Career* res mangr Kuoni Travel E Africa 1969-81, various posts in PR and mktg 1981-, dir ABS Communications, dir Professional Connections; MIPR 1984; *Style—* Miss Elizabeth Herbert; 47 Westmoreland Terrace, London SWN 4AQ (☎ 071 630 9349); Willow Cottage, Broads Green, Gt Waltham, Essex CMS LDX (☎ 0245 360 746);14 Kinnerton Place South, Kinnerton St, London SW1X 8EH (☎ 071 245 6262, fax 071 235 3916)

HERBERT, Hon Harry - Henry Malcolm (Harry); yr s of 7 Earl of Carnarvon; *b* 1959; *Educ* Eton; *Career* md HMH Mgmnt, Bloodstock Mgmnt Co, dir Hogg Rosinson Agric; *Recreations* golf, tennis; *Style—* The Hon Harry Herbert

HERBERT, (Edward) Ivor (Montgomery); s of Sir Edward Herbert, OBE (d 1963), and Lady Sybil, *née* Davis (d 1989); *b* 20 Aug 1925; *Educ* Eton, Trinity Coll Cambridge (MA); *m* 1, 1950 (m dis), Jennifer, da of D R McBean, MC; 1 s (Nicholas b 1954); m 2 (m dis), Gilly, da of Dr Peter Steele-Perkins; 2 da (Kate b 20 Sept 1970, Jane b 11 March 1972); *Career* served Capt Coldstream Gds 1944-47 (seconded to Intelligence Germany 1945-47); PA to Chm then asst md Charterhouse Finance Corporation 1949-54, columnist Evening News Associated Newspapers 1954-70, racing corr and features columnist Sunday Express 1970-80, racing ed and main travel writer Mail on Sunday 1980-; ptnr: Bradenham Wines 1970-, Equus Productions 1974-; trained Nat Hunt racehorses 1947-62 (winner Cheltenham Gold Cup with Linwell 1957); scriptwriter and playwright: The Great St Trinian's Train Robbery, Night of Blue Demands; TV documentaries incl: Odds Against, Stewards' Enquiry, Classic Touch and The Queen's Horses; chm Bradenham Parish Cncl 1966-; memb: Soc of Authors, Writers Guild; *Books* 23 incl: Arkle, Red Rum, The Winter Kings, Winter's Tale, The Diamond Diggers; novels incl: The Filly, Revolting Behaviour; *Recreations* tennis, travel, riding, restaurants; *Clubs* Turf; *Style—* Ivor Herbert, Esq; The Old Rectory, Bradenham, nr High Wycombe, Bucks HP14 4HD (☎ 024 024 3310, fax 024 024 4504)

HERBERT, James; s of H Herbert, of London, and Catherine, *née* Riley; *b* 8 April 1943; *Educ* Our Lady of the Assumption Sch Bethnal Green, St Aloysius Coll Highgate, Hornsey Coll of Art Highgate; *m* August 1967, Eileen; 3 da (Kerry Jo b 22 July 1968, Emma Jane b 21 April 1972, Casey Lee b 31 Oct 1983); *Career* author; typographer John Collings Advertising 1962, Charles Barker Advertising 1965-77 (art dir, gp head, assoc dir); *books* The Rats (1974), The Fog (1975), The Survivor (1976), Fluke (1977), The Spear (1978), Lair (1979), The Dark (1980), The Jonah (1981), Shrine (1983), Domain (1984), Moon (1985), The Magic Cottage (1986), Sepulchre (1987), Haunted (1988), Creed (1990); *films* The Rats, The Survivor; awarded Avoriaz Grand Prix pour Literature Fantastique (for The Survivor) 1977; *Recreations* guitar, piano, painting, book design, swimming; *Style—* James Herbert, Esq; David Higham Associates, 5-8 Lower John St, Golden Square, London W1R 4HA (☎ 071 437 7888, fax 071 437 1072)

HERBERT, Jocelyn; da of A P Herbert, and Gwendolen Quilter; *b* 22 Feb 1917; *Educ* St Paul's Girls Sch Paris and Vienna; *m* 1937, Anthony Lousada (m dis 1960); 1 s, 3 da; *Career* theatre designer, film prodn designer; memb Eng Stage Co Royal Court Theatre 1956, freelance designer 1958-; designed at Royal Court: The Chairs (Ionesco) 1957, Purgatory (W B Yeats) 1957, Sport of my Mad Mother (Jellico) 1958, Krapps' Last Tape (Beckett) 1958, Roots (Wesker) 1959, Serjeant Musgrave's Dance (Arden) 1959, Chicken Soup with Barley 1960, I'm Talking about Jerusalem (Wesker) 1960, Trials by Logue, Antigone, The Trial of Cob and Leach (Logue) 1960, The Changling 1961, The Kitchen (Wesker) 1961, Luther (Osborne) 1961, A Midsummer Night's Dream 1962, Chips With Everything (Wesker) 1962, Happy Days (Beckett) 1962, Skyvers (Reckford) 1963, Exit the King (Ionesco) 1963, Inadmissible Evidence (Osborne) 1964, A Patriot for Me (Osborne) 1965, The Lion and the Jewel (Solrenka) 1966, Life Price (O'Neil & Seabrook) 1969, Three Months Gone (Donald Howarth) 1970, The Changing Room (Storey) 1971, Krapps Last Tape and Not 1 (Beckett) 1973, Savages (Hampton) 1973, Life Class (Storey) 1974, What the Butler Saw (Orton) 1975, End Game and Not 1 (Beckett) 1973; other theatre prodns incl: Richard III (RSC), Baal (Phoenix) 1963, The Merchant (NY) 1977, Ghosts (Aldwych) 1967, Hamlet (Roundhouse) 1967, Pygmalion (His Majesty's) 1967, Portage to San Christabel of Adolf Hitler (Mermaid) 1982, The Devil and the Good Lord (Lyric Hammersmith) 1984, Gigi (Lyric) 1985, J J Fahr (Phoenix) 1987, Timon of Athens (Haymarket Leicester) 1988, Julius Caeser (Haymarket Leicester) 1988, Creon (Haymarket Leicester) 1988, The Threepenny Opera (NY) 1989, Krapps Last Tape (Haymarket Leicester), Riverside (Paris); prodns for NT incl: Othello 1964, A Women Killed by Kindness 1966, Mother Courage 1965, Tyger 1967, Early Day's 1980, Galhiteo 1980, The Oreseia 1981, March on Russia 1988, Trackers 1989 and 1991; opera prodns incl: Orpheus and Euridice (Sadler's Wells) 1967, The Force of Destiny (Paris Opera) 1975, Lulu (Metropolitan NY) 1977, The Entfuhrung aus dem Sevail (Metropolitan NY) 1979, The Mask of Orpheus (Coliseium) 1986; colour and costume conslt film Tom Jones 1961; prodn designer on films incl: Isadora 1968, JF 1969, New Kelly 1970, Hamlet 1969, O Lucky Man 1972, Hotel New Hampshire 1983, The Whales of August 1986; Hon FRCA, Hon FRA, RDI; *Style*— Ms Jocelyn Herbert; 45 Pottery Lane, London W11

HERBERT, John Anthony; s of Rev Canon Frank Selwood Herbert (d 1978), of Nuneaton, Warks, and Joan Mary Walcot Herbert, *née* Burton (d 1976); *b* 10 Sept 1939; *Educ* Dean Close Sch, Cheltenham, Exeter Univ; *m* 2 Aug 1962, Michelle, da of Nigel Forbes Dennis, of Malta; 2 da (Rebecca b 1964, Tamsin b 1968); *Career* over 250 films and documentaries to credit, on archaeological, mil trg and historical subjects (clients inc Saudi Arabian TV, MOD, oil indust), ed: Quaryat Al fau (1981), Al Rabadhah (1984), books of archaeological excavations; contrib Illustrated London News on Arabian archaeology; photo exhibitions London and Paris 1986; Gold award for Excellence Int Video and Cinema Awards Festival for Film for Fighting the Good Fight 1990; FRGS; *Recreations* France, English wine growing, sailing; *Clubs* The Anglo-Arab Assoc, The Georgian Gp, The Historic Houses Assoc, English Vineyards Assoc; *Style*— John A Herbert, Esq; Much Hadham Hall, Much Hadham, Herts SG10 6BZ (☎ 0279 842663)

HERBERT, Martin Geoffrey Greenham; s of Geoffrey Basil Herbert (d 1974), and Alice Margery, *née* Greenham; *b* 9 Dec 1946; *Educ* Rugby, Balliol Coll Oxford (BA); *m* 10 June 1981, Alicia Malka, da of Dr Benjamin Abraham Jolles (d 1985); 1 s (Edward b 1987), 2 da (Susannah b 1982, Katharine b 1985); *Career* slr 1971, ptnr Clifford Chance (formerly Coward Chance) 1977-; *Recreations* sailing, tree planting; *Clubs* Royal Fowey Yacht, Royal Harwich Yacht; *Style*— Martin Herbert, Esq; 23 Alwyne Road, London, N1; The Gables, East Bergholt, Suffolk; Clifford Chance, Royex House, Aldermanbury Sq, London, EC2V 7LD (☎ 071 600 0808, fax 071 726 8561, telex 8959991)

HERBERT, Hon Mrs Mervyn; Mary Elizabeth; da of J E Willard (former US Ambassador to Madrid); *m* 1921, Hon Mervyn Robert Howard Molyneux Herbert (3 s of 4 Earl of Carnarvon and who died 1929); 1 s, 2 da; *Style*— The Hon Mrs Mervyn Herbert; 25 Eaton Sq, London SW1

HERBERT, Michael; CBE (1991); s of W R Herbert (d 1982), of Kent, and Eileen, *née* McKee; *b* 16 Aug 1933; *Educ* King's Sch Canterbury, St Edmund Hall Oxford (MA); *m* 1967, Anna Vibeke, da of Christian Madsen (d 1971), of Denmark; *Career* Nat Serv in RHA Germany 1956-58, 2 Lt; CA; chief exec: Tussaud Gp, Madame Tussauds Ltd, Chessington World of Adventures Ltd, Warwick Castle Ltd; FCA; *Recreations* walking, cricket, speaking Danish; *Clubs* Travellers', Hurlingham, MCC, Kent CC; *Style*— Michael Herbert, Esq, CBE; 14 Eaton Place, London SW1X 8AE (☎ 071 935 6861, fax 071 935 8906); Knudseje, 9352 Dybvad, Denmark

HERBERT, Hon Michael Clive; 2 s of 7 Earl of Powis, *qv*; *b* 22 Aug 1954; *Educ* Wellington, Christ's Coll Cambridge (MA), London Business Sch (MSc); *m* 1978, Susan Mary, da of Guy Baker (d 1982), of Welshpool, Powys; 2 s (Thomas Guy Clive b 1981, Mark Philip Clive b 1983), 1 da (Joanna Frances Clare b 1987); *Style*— The Hon Michael Herbert; Wicken Hall, Wicken, Ely, Cambs CB7 5XT

HERBERT, Hon Oliver Hayley Dennis; yst s of 1 Baron Hemingford, KBE, PC (d 1947); *b* 14 Aug 1919; *Educ* Oundle, Wadham Coll Oxford; *m* 1976 (m annulled), Rosemary Muriel, da of Rev Canon Roland Bate; *Career* formerly Maj Queen's Royal Regt, attached Indian Army; former treas and exec ctee memb Anglican Soc; *Style*— The Hon Oliver Herbert

HERBERT, Adm Sir Peter Geoffrey Marshall; KCB (1982), OBE (1969); s of A G S Herbert, and P K M Herbert; *b* 28 Feb 1929; *Educ* Dunchurch Hall, RN Coll Dartmouth; *m* 1953, Ann Maureen, *née* McKeown; 1 s, 1 da; *Career* served in submarines 1949-63, Cdr Nuclear Submarine HMS Valiant 1963-68, Capt appts 1966-76, cmd HMS Blake 1974-75, dep chief Polaris Exec 1976-78, Flag Offr Carriers and Amphibious Ships 1978-79, DG Naval Manpower and Trg 1980-81, Flag Offr Submarines and Cdr Sub Area E Atlantic 1981-83, Adm 1983, Vice Chief of Def Staff (Personnel and Logistics) 1983-85; def conslt; non-exec dir Radamec Group 1985-, chm SSAFA Cncl, memb Exec Ctee White Ensign Assoc; CBIM, MINucE; *Recreations* golf, swimming, woodwork, gardening; *Clubs* Army and Navy; *Style*— Adm Sir Peter Herbert, KCB, OBE; Dolphin Sq, London SW1

HERBERT, Peter George; s of George Frederick Herbert (d 1974), of London, and Ellen Alice, *née* Reed (d 1980); *b* 11 June 1926; *Educ* Dulwich and Rossall, Royal College of Music (scholarship); *m* 1, 1951, (m dis 1977), Pip, *née* Harkell; 2 s (Leigh Seaton b 1953, Robin Harkell Seaton b 1960), 1 da (Jennifer Reed b 1958); m 2, 1978, Susan Alison, da of Dr Gilbert Edward Hicks; 2 da (Joanna Kate b 1980, Nicola Jane b 1982); *Career* served Royal Fusiliers & Royal Sussex Reg 1944-48; trg in family hotel business then Austria & France 1948-50; md: Gore Hotel & Elizabethan Rooms London 1950-67, The Yard Arm Club Westminster 1963-67; chm Gravetye Manor Hotel East Grinstead W Sussex 1957-; Chevalier du Tastevin 1958, fell HCIMA 1960; *Recreations* sailing, game fishing, opera (Glyndebourne), gardening; *Style*— Peter Herbert, Esq; Gravetye Manor, nr East Grinstead, W Sussex RH19 4LJ (☎ 0342 810567); Gravetye Manor Hotel and Country Club Ltd, nr East Grinstead, W Sussex RH19 4LJ (☎ 0342 810567, fax 0342 810080)

HERBERT, Hon Peter James; 3 s of 7 Earl of Powis, *qv*; *b* 26 Dec 1955; *Educ* Wellington; *m* 1978, Terri, yr da of Sean McBride, of Callan, Co Kilkenny; 1 s (Oliver George Laurie b 1983), 2 da (Sophie Louise Mary b 1980, Lucy Alison Julia b 1988); *Style*— The Hon Peter Herbert; Wade Tower, Wade Ct, Havant, Hants

HERBERT, Wally; s of Capt Walter William Herbert, RAPC (d 1972), and Helen, *née* Manton (d 1982); *b* 24 Oct 1934; *m* 24 Dec 1969, Marie Rita, da of Prof Charles McGaughey (d 1982); 2 da (Kari b 17 Sept 1970, Pascale b 30 March 1978); *Career* RE 1950-54; trained as surveyor Sch of Mil Survey, serv in Egypt 1953-54; surveyor Falklands Islands Dependencies Survey based at Hope Bay Antarctica 1955-58, hitch hiked 15,000 miles Montivideo Uruguay to UK 1958-59, expeditions to Lapland and Spitzbergen 1960, surveyor with NZ Antarctic Expdn based at Scott Base McMurdo Sound 1960-62; ldr: Expdn NW Greenland (retracing route of Dr Frederick Cook) 1967-68, Br Trans-Arctic Expdn (first surface crossing of Arctic Ocean from Alaska via N Pole to Spitzbergen, a 3,800 mile journey with dog teams which took 16 months to complete) 1968-69, Expdn to NW Greenland (travelling over 4,000 miles with Eskimos) 1971-73, winter Expdn to Lapland 1974, Br N Polar Expdn (attempting to circumnavigate Greenland with dog teams and Eskimo skin boat) 1977-80, Expdn to NW Greenland 1980; conducted feasibility study for an Explorers Museum at Sir Francis Drake's house (Buckland Abbey) 1981-84; writing and filming biog of Adm Robert E Perry 1985-88, filming in NW Greenland 1987 with second visit to N Pole 1987; total time spent in polar regions 13 yrs, total distance travelled by dog sledges and in open boats in polar regions over 25,000 miles; Polar medal (1962, Clasp 1969) awarded for Antarctic and Arctic exploration, Livingstone Gold Medal RGS (Scot) 1969, Founders Gold Medal RGS 1970, City of Paris Medal 1983, French Geog Soc Medal 1983, Explorers Medal 1985, Finn Ronne Award 1985; hon memb Br Schs Exploring Soc, hon pres World Expeditionary Assoc; FRGS; *Books* A World of Men (1968), Across the Top of the World (1969), The Last Great Journey on Earth (1971), Polar Deserts (1971), Eskimos (1976), North Pole (1978), Hunters of the Polar North (1982), The Noose of Laurels (1989); *Recreations* painting; *Clubs* Lansdowne, Explorers; *Style*— Wally Herbert, Esq; c/o Royal Geographical Society, 1 Kensington Gore, London SW7 2AR

HERBERT, Lord; William Alexander Sidney Herbert; s and h of 17 Earl of Pembroke and Montgomery; *b* 18 May 1978; *Style*— Lord Herbert

HERBERT-JONES, Hugo Jarrett; CMG (1973), OBE (1963); s of Capt H Herbert-Jones (d 1923), of Llanrwst, Denbighshire, and Dora Jarrett, *née* Rowlands, MBE (d 1974); *b* 11 March 1922; *Educ* Bryanston, Worcester Coll Oxford (BA); *m* 1954, Margaret, da of Rev J P Veall (d 1971), of Eastbourne; 1 s (Nicholas), 2 da (Sarah, Siân); *Career* served Welsh Gds 1941-46, (wounded NW Europe 1944), Maj; HM Foreign later Dip Serv 1947-79; dir int affrs CBI 1979-87, chm The Aldeburgh Soc 1988-; *Recreations* sailing, golf, shooting, music, spectator sports; *Clubs* Garrick, MCC, London Welsh Rugby Football, Aldeburgh Yacht, Aldeburgh Golf; *Style*— Hugo Herbert-Jones, Esq, CMG, OBE; Priors Hill, Aldeburgh, Suffolk IP15 5ET (☎ 0728 453335); 408 Nelson House, Dolphin Sq, SW1V 3NZ (☎ 071 821 1183)

HERBERTSON, (Robert) Ian; s of Robert Hopkirk Herbertson (d 1969), and Winifred Rose, *née* Rawlinson; *b* 30 Dec 1953; *Educ* Selhurst GS, Birkbeck Coll London (BA); *m* 22 March 1985, Joanna Hazel, da of Reginald Bernard North, of Gwent 2 da (Rebecca Elizabeth b 1987, Emma Louise b 1990); *Career* Bank of England 1985- (audit mangr 1990-), dir Claridge Press 1987-88; memb: Inst of Fiscal Studies, Aristotelian Soc, Convocation Univ of London 1984, Ctee Ct of Electors Birkbeck Coll London 1987-90; C Dip AF 1985, FIAP 1986; *Recreations* philosophy, literature; *Clubs* Challoner; *Style*— Ian Herbertson, Esq; 21 Euston St, Huntingdon, Cambs (☎ 0480 455601); 15 Dovercourt Ave, Thornton Heath, Surrey (☎ 081 684 9218); Bank of England, Threadneedle St, London (☎ 071 601 4210)

HERBISON, Rt Hon Margaret McCrorie; PC (1964); *b* 11 March 1907; *Educ* Bellshill Acad, Univ of Glasgow; *Career* MP (Lab) N Lanark 1945-70, jt Parly under sec Scottish Office 1950-51, chm Lab Pty 1957, min Pensions and Nat Insur 1964-66, min Social Security 1966-67, former memb NEC; Lord High Cmmr to Gen Assembly of Church of Scot 1970-71, memb Royal Cmmn on Standards of Conduct in Pub Life 1974-; Scots Woman of Year 1970; Hon LLD Glasgow; *Style*— The Rt Hon Margaret Herbison; 8 Mornay Way, Shotts, Lanarks ML7 4EG (☎ 0501 21944)

HERD, (James) Peter; MBE (1946), WS (1949); s of Maj Walter Herd, MC (d 1951), of Kirkcaldy, Fife, and Sigrid, *née* Russell Johnston (d 1972); *b* 18 May 1920; *Educ* Edinburgh Acad, St Andrews Univ, Edinburgh Univ; *m* 5 Aug 1943, Marjory Phimister, da of James Mitchell (d 1961), of Aberdeen; 3 s (Michael b 1945, David b 1949, Malcolm b 1955), 2 da (Katherine b 1947, Penelope b 1959); *Career* Maj The Black Watch (RHR) 1939-46, serv in UK and SE Asia; ptnr Beveridge Herd & Sandilands 1951-, local dir Royal Insurance Group 1952-, tstee Kirkcaldy & Dist Tstee Savings Bank 1952-83, Notary Public 1952; dir Kirkcaldy Abbeyfield Soc; Hon Sheriff Kirkcaldy; *Recreations* curling, gardening; *Clubs* New (Kirkcaldy); *Style*— Peter Herd, Esq, MBE, WS; Nether Strathore, Thornton, Fife KY1 4DY (☎ 0592 773 863); 1 East Fergus Place, Kirkcaldy, Fife KY1 4DY (☎ 0592 261 616)

HERD, Hon Mrs (Sheelagh Margaret); *née* Monckton; eld da of 12 Viscount Galway; *b* 1945; *m* 1967, William Arthur Herd; *Style*— The Hon Mrs Herd; 726 Galloway Crescent, London, Ontario N6J 2Y7, Canada

HERDMAN, Dr John Macmillan; s of William Morrison Herdman (d 1975), of Edinburgh, and Catherine, *née* Macmillan; *b* 20 July 1941; *Educ* Merchiston Castle Sch, Magdalene Coll Cambridge (MA, PhD); *m* 30 July 1983, Dolina, da of Angus Maclennan (d 1950), of Marvig, Isle of Lewis; *Career* writer; awarded Scottish Arts Cncl bursaries 1976 and 1982, creative writing fell Univ of Edinburgh 1977-79, winner book award 1978, Hawthornden Writer's fellowship 1989, William Soutar Writer's fellowship 1990-; *Books* Descent (1968), A Truth Lover (1973), Clapperton (1974), Pagan's Pilgrimage (1978), Stories Short and Tall (1979), Voice without Restraint: Bob Dylan's Lyrics and their Background (1982), Three Novellas (1987), The Double in Nineteenth Century Fiction (1990); *Recreations* reading, walking, listening to music, medieval church history; *Style*— Dr John Herdman; 28 Pipeland Rd, St Andrews, Fife KY16 8AH

HERDMAN, (John) Mark Ambrose; LVO (1979); s of Cdr Claudius Alexander Herdman, DL, RN, of Braewood, Sion Mills, Strabane, Co Tyrone, NI, and Joan Dalrymple, *née* Tennant (d 1937); *b* 26 April 1932; *Educ* St Edward's Sch Oxford, Univ of Dublin (BA, MA), Queen's Coll Oxford; *m* 29 June 1963, Elizabeth Anne, da of Rupert McLintock Dillon (d 1972), of Dublin; 1 s (Patrick b 1969), 2 da (Deirdre b 1966, Bridget b 1970); *Career* HMOCS Kenya 1954-64; FCO (formerly CRO): London 1964-65, MECAS Lebanon 1965-66, Amman 1966-68, FCO 1969-71, Lusaka 1971-74, Jedda 1974-76, FCO 1976-78, Lilongwe 1978-81, FCO 1981-83, dep govr Bermuda 1983-86, govr Br Virgin Is 1986-; *Recreations* golf, fishing, philately; *Clubs* Royal Cwlth Soc, Ebury Court; *Style*— Mark Herdman, Esq, CBE, LVO; Government House, Tortola, British Virgin Islands (☎ 49 43400); c/o FCO (Tortola), King Charles St, London SW1A 2AH

HEREFORD, Dean of; *see*: Haynes, The Very Rev Peter

HEREFORD, Archdeacon of; *see*: Woodhouse, Ven Andrew Henry

HEREFORD, 103 Bishop of (cr 676) 1990-; Rt Rev John Oliver; s of Walter

Keith Oliver (d 1977), of Danehill, Sussex, and Ivy, *née* Nightingale (d 1981); *b* 14 April 1935; *Educ* Westminster, Gonville and Caius Coll Cambridge (BA, MA, MLitt); *m* 16 Sept 1961, Meriel, da of Sir Alan Moore, Bt (d 1959), of Battle, Sussex; 2 s (Thomas b 1964, Henry b 1968), 1 da (Mary b 1971); *Career* curate Hilborough Gp of Parishes Norfolk 1964-68, chaplain and asst master Eton Coll 1968-72; team rector: S Molton Gp 1973-82 (rural dean 1974-80), Central Exeter 1982-85; archdeacon of Sherborne, canon of Salisbury and P-in-C W Stafford 1985-90; *Recreations* railways, music, architecture, walking; *Style*— The Rt Rev the Bishop of Hereford; The Bishop's House, The Palace, Hereford (☎ 0432 271355)

HEREFORD, 18 Viscount (E 1550); Sir Robert Milo Leicester Devereux; 15 Bt (E 1611); Premier Viscount in the Peerage of England; s of Hon Robert Godfrey de Bohun Devereux (d 1934, s of 17 Viscount) and Audrey, who m, as her 2 husb, 7 Earl of Lisburne; suc gf 1952; *b* 4 Nov 1932; *Educ* Eton; *m* 1969, Susan Mary, only child of Maj Maurice Godley, of Sevenoaks; 2 s (Hon Charles, Hon Edward Mark de Breteuil b 1977); *Heir* s, Hon Charles Robin de Bohun Devereux b 11 Aug 1975; *Style*— The Rt Hon the Viscount Hereford; Lyford Cay Club, PO Box N-7776, Nassau, Providence, Bahamas

HEREN, Louis Philip; s of William F Heren (d 1924), and Beatrice, *née* Keller (d 1988); *b* 6 Feb 1919; *m* 1948, Patricia, *née* Cecilioàregan (d 1974); 1 s (Patrick b 1952), 3 da (Katherine b 1956, Sarah b 1958, Elizabeth b 1964); *Career* army 1939-46; The Times: reporter 1946-47, foreign corr (India 1947-48, Israel and ME 1948-50, SE Asia 1951-53, India 1953-55, Germany 1955-60), US chief corr and America ed 1960-700, war corr (Kashmir 1947, Israel-Arab War 1948, Korea 1950, Indo-China 1951), foreign ed and dep ed 1970-78, dep ed 1978-82; Int Reporter of the Year Br Press Award 1967, John F Kennedy Memorial Award 1968; FRSL 1974; *Books* New American Commonwealth (1965), No Hail, No Farewell (1970), Growing Up Poor In London (1973), The Story Of America (1976), Growing Up On The Times (1978), Alas, Alas For England (1981), The Power Of The Press? (1985), Memories Of Times Past (1988); *Recreations* enjoying life; *Clubs* Garrick; *Style*— Louis Heren, Esq; Fleet House, Vale of Health, London NW3 1AZ (☎ 071 435 0904)

HERFORD, Henry (Richard); s of Philip Henry Herford (d 1982), of Glasgow, and Elisabeth Jean, *née* Hawkins; *b* 24 Feb 1947; *Educ* Trinity Coll Glenalmond, Kings Coll Cambridge, Univ of York, Royal Manchester Coll of Music; *m* 14 Feb 1982, Jane Lindsay, da of Peter John; 2 s (Thomas Hal b 31 Oct 1982, John Peter b 19 Jan 1985), 1 da (Alice Jane b 5 March 1988); *Career* opera and concert singer; performances incl: Forester in Janacek's Cunning Little Vixen (Glyndebourne Touring Opera) 1977, Debussy and Caplet (Nash Ensemble, Wigmore Hall) 1979, Count in Mozart's Marriage of Figaro (Opera '80 Tour) 1980-81, Demetrius in Britten's Midsummer Night's Dream (Glyndebourne Touring Opera) 1981, recital (Carnegie Hall NY) 1982, song cycles (American Symphony Orch, Carnegie Hall NY) 1984, Vaughan Williams' Serenade To Music (Last Night of the Proms) 1984, Walton's Gloria (Last Night of the Proms) 1985, Maxwell Davies's The Lighthouse (Glasgow and Orkney), Osborne's Electrification of Soviet Union (Glyndebourne, BBC) 1987 (Berlin) 1988, Poulenc with Koenig Ensemble (Rome) 1989, Roderick in Debussy's Fall of the House of Usher (Queen Elizabeth Hall London, Lisbon) 1989, Handel Bach, Schubert, Brahms (Jerusalem) 1990, Smirnov in Walton's The Bear (Newcastle) 1990, Demetrius in Midsummer Night's Dream (Sadler's Wells) 1990; recordings incl: Rameau's Castor et Pollux with Farncombe and EBF (Erato) 1982, Bridge's The Christmas Rose with Howard Williams and Chelsea Opera Gp (Pearl) 1983, Handel's Messiah (excerpts) with George Malcolm and Scot Chamber Orch (Contour) 1983, Peter Dickinson's Dylan Thomas Song Cycle with Robin Bowman (Conifer) 1986, Britten's A Midsummer Night's Dream with Richard Hickox and City of London Sinfonia (Virgin) 1990, Charles Ives Song Recital I and II with Robin Bowman (Unicorn-Kanchana) 1990 and 1991; Curtis Gold medal for singing RNCM 1976, Benson and Hedges Gold award 1980, first prize Int American Music Competition 1982; *Recreations* family, house restoration, chamber music (cello), reading, walking; *Style*— Henry Herford; Pencots, Northmoor, Oxon OX8 1AX (☎ 0865 300884); c/o Ron Gonsalves, 10 Dagnan Rd, London SW12 9LQ (☎ 081 673 6507, fax 081 675 7276)

HERINCX, (Raymond Frederick) Raimund; s of Florent Herincx (d 1974), and Marie Therese Lucia, *née* Cheal; *b* 23 Aug 1927; *Educ* St Mary Abbot's Kensington, Thames Valley GS Twickenham, Univ of London; *m* 27 March 1954, Margaret Jean, aka Astra Blair, da of Lt-Col Douglas Waugh; 1 s (Gareth James) 2 da (Nicole Elaine, Gemma Marelen); *Career* Educn Offr Household Cavalry 1946-48; memb Royal Opera House Chorus 1949-53, joined Welsh Nat Opera 1956, joined Sadler's Wells Opera (now English Nat Opera) 1957 and Royal Opera House Covent Garden 1968, joined Met Opera House (NY) 1976; prof of voice RAM 1970-77, sr voice teacher NE of Scotland Music Sch 1979-, lectr Univ Coll Cardiff 1984-87; voice therapist 1979-, music critic 1987-; many commercial recordings incl creators' recordings and first recordings; fndr: Quinville Tst (for Handicapped Children), Sadler's Wells Soc; fndr memb Assoc of Artists Against Aids; world record for no of operatic roles and concert works sung (468); int music awards opera medal 1968, Hon RAM 1971; *Recreations* wine and its history, vine and plant breeding; *Style*— Raimund Herincx, Esq; Monks' Vineyard, Larkbarrow, East Compton, Pilton, Shepton Mallet, Somerset (☎ 0749 344462)

HERITAGE, John Langdon; CB (1990); s of Francis John Heritage, OBE, ISO (d 1967), and Elizabeth, *née* Langdon (d 1960); *b* 31 Dec 1931; *Educ* Berkhamsted Sch, Exeter Coll Oxford; *m* 3 April 1956, Elizabeth Faulkner, da of Charles Jamieson Robertson (d 1957); 2 s (Charles Francis b 1957, Edward John b 1965), 1 da (Rebecca Jane b 1960); *Career* Nat Serv Royal Hants Regt and RWAFF; called to the Bar Middle Temple 1956; sr legal asst Treasy Slr's Office 1964 (legal asst 1957), asst slr Lord Chllr's Dept 1973, under sec Royal Cmmn on Legal Servs 1983 (sec 1976-79); circuit admin S Eastern Circuit 1983-88, head of judicial appts 1989-; dir Chesham Building Society 1989-; author of articles in legal jls and reference books; *Recreations* painting, making things; *Clubs* Utd Oxford and Cambridge Univ; *Style*— John Heritage, Esq, CB; Lord Chancellor's Department, House of Lords, London SW1A 0PW (☎ 071 219 5554)

HERITAGE, Robert Charles; CBE (1980); s of Charles John Heritage, and Daisy May, *née* Clay; *b* 2 Nov 1927; *Educ* King Edwardes GS Birmingham, Birmingham Coll of Art and Industl Design, RCA Furniture Sch (MDes); *m* 4 April 1953, Dorothy, da of William Shaw; 2 s (Paul Robert b 1956, Michael Justin Lawrence b 1965), 1 da (Rachael Francesca b 1958); *Career* design conslt in private practice 1953-; *awards* Br Aluminium Design award 1966; Cncl of Industl Design awards for: Hamilton Sideboard 1958, Wall Units 1963, Oregon Dining Chair 1963, Memory Master Clock 1964, Quartet Major 1965, Silverspan fluroescent Fitting 1968, Restaurant Chair 1969, Superjet 1969, Powerflood 1971, Pan Parabolic 1971, Effect Lighting Lumiere Projector 1972, Lytespan 7 Track 1973, Eurospot 1973; Bundespreise 1972 for: Powerflood, Litespan 7, Eurospot, Pan Parabolic; prof of furniture design RCA 1974-85, appointed Royal Designer for Industry 1963; Liveryman Worshipful Co of Furniture Makers 1962-, hon fell RCA, FRSA, FCSD; *Recreations* salmon fishing, tennis; *Style*— Robert Heritage, Esq, CBE

HERMAN, Dr Stephen Sydney; s of Maurice Herman (d 1975), and Deborah, *née* Dutkevitch (d 1980); *b* 7 July 1942; *Educ* Central Foundation Boys GS, King's Coll London, St George's Hosp Med Sch (MB BS); *m* 21 June 1966, Yvette Hannah, da of Isaac Solomons (d 1964); 1 s (Simon b 13 March 1969), 2 da (Rachel b 31 July 1970, Ruth b 5 May 1973); *Career* conslt paediatrician Central Middlesex and Royal Nat Orthopaedic Hosps 1974; hon clinical sr lectr: St Mary's Hosp Med Sch Univ of London, Inst of Orthopaedics Univ of London; memb: Br Paediatric Assoc 1974, Neonatal Soc 1972; FRCP 1981; *Recreations* short wave and vintage radio; *Style*— Dr Stephen Herman; Barbary House, California Lane, Bushey Heath, Herts WD2 1EX (☎ 081 950 1006); 25 Wimpole St, London W1M 7AD (☎ 071 323 4959)

HERMAN-SMITH, Robert; s of Herman Geldert Smith (d 1985), of Carver House, Norton Rd, Stourbridge, W Midlands, and Alice, *née* Power (d 1989); *b* 12 Jan 1940; *Educ* Seabright Sch, Univ of Birmingham (BSc, Postgrad Dip); *m* 17 Sept 1964, (Florence) Jennifer Elizabeth, da of Gerald Munday, of Church Farm, Swindon, W Midlands; 2 da (Mary Louise b 23 July 1965, Suzanne b 12 June 1967); *Career* jt md and dep chm Herman Smith plc 1961-85, dir Darchem Engineering Ltd 1985-, mktg and business conslt 1985-; memb Charitable Tst Pedmore Sporting Club; *Recreations* fishing, shooting; *Style*— Robert Herman-Smith, Esq; Halfpenny Manor, Bobbington, Stourbridge, W Midlands DY7 5EG (☎ 0384 88261, fax 0384 56632)

HERMON-TAYLOR, Prof John; s of Hermon Taylor, of Bosham, W Sussex, and Marie Amelie, *née* Pearson (d 1981); *b* 16 Oct 1936; *Educ* Harrow, St John's Coll Cambridge (BA, MB BChir, MChir), The London Hosp Med Coll; *m* 18 Sept 1971, Eleanor Ann, da of Dr Willard S Pheteplace (d 1985), of Davenport, Iowa, USA; 1 s (Peter Maxwell b 1979), 1 da (Amy Caroline b 1975); *Career* various NHS and Univ trg posts in surgery 1963-68, MRC travelling fell in gastrointestinal physiology Mayo Clinic USA 1968-69, reader in surgery The London Hosp Med Coll 1971-76 (sr lectr 1970-71), prof and chm of surgery St George's Hosp Med Sch 1976-, conslt in gen surgery RN 1989, author of numerous scientific and med res articles; memb: Cncl Assoc of Surgeons of GB and Ireland 1980-83, Clinical Panel The Wellcome Tst 1985-88, Cncl Action Res for the Crippled Child 1988; winner: The Times Newspaper/ Barclays Bank Innovator of the Year award 1988, Hallet prize; FRCS 1963, memb Biochem Soc; *Recreations* sailing, shooting; *Clubs* Royal Thames Yacht; *Style*— Prof John Hermon-Taylor; 11 Parkside Avenue, Wimbledon, London SW19 5ES (☎ 081 946 0557); Dept of Surgery, St George's Hosp Medical Sch, London SW17 ORE (☎ 081 767 7631, fax 081 767 4696)

HERMSEN, (Adriaan) John; s of Adriaan Marinus Christiaan Hermsen (d 1982), of Broadway, Worcestershire, and Margaret, *née* Stanley (d 1989); *b* 20 Aug 1933; *Educ* Salvatorian Sch, Royal West of England Acad Sch of Architecture; *m* 23 March 1963, Jean Russell, da of Charles Herbert Simmonds (d 1971), of Durban, S Africa; 2 s ((Adriaan) Keir b 1968, Mark Christian Piers b 1971); *Career* Howard Lobb & Partners 1956-57, Richard Sheppard Robson & Partners 1957-59, R D Russell & Partners 1961-62, Douglas Stephen & Partners 1962-64, Nat Building Agency 1964-71, ptnr and dir Ahrends Burton & Koralek 1976- (joined 1971), rep Miny Housing & Local Govt on Br Standard Ctee 3921 1969-71; ARIBA 1962, FRIBA 1969, ACIArb 1984; *Recreations* construction law, walking and sailing; *Style*— John Hermsen, Esq; 18 Frogmore Close, Hughenden Valley, High Wycombe, Buckinghamshire HP14 4LN (☎ 024 024 2260); Ahrends Burton & Koralek, Unit 1, 7 Chalcot Rd, London NW1 8LH (☎ 071 586 3311, fax 071 722 5445)

HERON, (John) Brian; s of John Henry Heron (d 1944), of Leeds, and Dorothy, *née* Hinton; *b* 22 Jan 1933; *Educ* Manchester GS, St Catharine's Coll Cambridge (MA); *m* 7 Sept 1968, Margaret, da of Harvey Jessop (d 1965), of Heywood; 1 s (John Michael b 16 Nov 1972), 1 da (Joanne Elizabeth b 29 July 1970); *Career* dir: TBA Indust Products Ltd 1969, Deeglass Fibres 1969; chief exec and dep chm TBA 1968-89; chm: TBA (Pty) Aust 1986-89, Moor Plastics Ltd 1988-89, Telford Rubber Processors Ltd 1986-89, Fratherm GmbH 1987-89; vice pres Bentley-Harris Inc 1988-89; chm Textilver SA 1988-89; dir Manchester Sci Park, govr UMIST (chm Ct), memb Rochdale Dist Health Authority; chm: Indust Scis Gp UMIST, Rochdale Trg & Enterprise Cncl 1989-; *Recreations* sailing, motoring; *Clubs* Cambridge Univ Cruising, Oxford and Cambridge Sailing Soc, Royal Yachting Assoc, Hollingworth Lake Sailing; *Style*— Brian Heron, Esq; Cleggswood Heys Farm, Hollingworth Lake, Littleborough, Lancs (☎ 0706 73292)

HERON, Sir Conrad Frederick; KCB (1974, CB 1969), OBE (1953); s of Richard Foster Heron, of South Shields, and Ida Fredrika Heron; *b* 21 Feb 1916; *Educ* South Shields HS, Trinity Hall Cambridge; *m* 1948, Envye Linnéa, da of Hermann Gustafsson, of Sweden; 2 da; *Career* entered Miny of Labour 1938, dep chm Cmmn on Industl Relations 1971-72, perm sec Dept of Employment 1973-76, ret; *Style*— Sir Conrad Heron, KCB, OBE; Old Orchards, West Lydford, Somerton, Somerset (☎ 096 324 387)

HERON, Dr James Riddick; s of James Riddick Heron (d 1959), of Birmingham, and Sophia, *née* Leatham (d 1956); *b* 21 Jan 1932; *Educ* King Edward's Sch Birmingham, Univ of Birmingham (MB ChB); *m* 27 May 1961, Ann Fionnuala, da of Dr Richard Raphael Gamble (d 1955); 2 s (Richard b 31 May 1962, Robert b 24 Oct 1973), 3 da (Fiona b 27 April 1963, Elizabeth b 8 July 1964, Caroline b 15 Dec 1969); *Career* registrar: in neurology Royal Free Hosp London 1963-65, Nat Hosp For Nervous Diseases 1965-66; sr registrar Queen Elizabeth Hosp and United Birmingham Hosps 1966-67, clinical tutor in neurology Univ of Birmingham 1966-67, conslt neurologist N Staffs Royal Infirmary and N Staffs Hosp Centre 1967-; visiting neurologist: Burton-on-Trent Hosps 1967-, Robert Jones and Agnes Hunt Orthopaedic Hosp 1967-; sr lectr in neurology Univ of Keele 1980 (hon res fell Dept of Communication and Neuroscience 1969, sr res fell Dept of Postgraduate Med 1978), Wellcome res travelling fell Univ of Oslo 1967, Med Gilliand travelling fell to Centres in the United States of America 1982, assoc examiner opthalmology RCS 1987-90; ed N Staffs Med Inst Journal 1971-85; author of numerous articles and papers on neurological sci; memb Cncl Assoc of Br Neurologists 1984-87, former sec and pres Midland Neurological Soc, former chm W Midlands Regnl Advsy Ctee in Neurosurgery and Neurology, chm Stoke-on-Trent and N Staffs Theatre Tst, pres Bedford Singers, govr Newcastle-under-Lyme Sch; FRCP, FRCPE, FRSA; *Books* Metamorphoses (1985), Trees (1988), Improvisations (1990); *Recreations* poetry and literature, music, history of medicine, natural phenomena; *Clubs* Osler; *Style*— Dr James Heron; Willowbrake, 6 Granville Ave, Newcastle, Staffordshire ST5 1JH (☎ 0782 617766); Department of Neurology, North Staffordshire Royal Infirmary, Princes Rd, Hartshill, Stoke-on-Trent ST4 7LN (☎ 0782 49144)

HERON, Michael Gilbert (Mike); s of Gilbert Thwaites Heron (d 1962), and Olive Lilian, *née* Steele; *b* 22 Oct 1934; *Educ* St Joseph's Acad Blackheath, New Coll Oxford (MA); *m* 16 Aug 1958, Celia Veronica Mary, da of Capt Clarence Hunter (d 1960); 2 s (Jonathan, Damian), 2 da (Louise, Annette); *Career* Lt RA 1953-55; dir BOCM Silcock 1971-76, chm Batchelors Foods Ltd 1976-82, dep co-ordinator Food and Drinks Co-ordination Unilever 1982-86, dir Main Bd Unilever plc and NV 1986-; Food and Drink Fedn: memb Exec Ctee, memb Cncl, chm Food Policy Res Ctee; memb Armed Forces Pay Review Bd 1981 and 1982; *Recreations* very keen sportsman in the past, now a viewer; *Style*— Mike Heron, Esq; Paradise Cottage, Paradise Lane, Bucklebury, Berks RG7 6NU (☎ 0734 712 228); Garden flat, 19 Kensington Court,

London W8 5DW (☎ 071 937 2615); Unilever plc, Unilever House, Blackfriars, London EC4P 4BQ (☎ 071 822 6317, fax 071 822 5630, telex 28395 Unil G)

HERON, Robert; CVO (1988); s of James Riddick Heron (d 1959), and Sophie Lockhart, *née* Leathem (d 1956); *b* 12 Oct 1927; *Educ* King Edward's Sch Birmingham, St Catharine's Coll Cambridge (MA); *m* 8 Aug 1953, Patricia Mary, da of Frank Robert Pennell (d 1945); 2 s (Andrew, Neil), 1 da (Susan); *Career* housemaster: Strathallan Sch Perthshire 1953-59, Christ Coll Brecon 1959-62; headmaster King James I Sch IOW 1962-66, head educnl bdcasting ATV London (responsible for TV series incl sciences and social documentaries), del Euro Broadcsting Union (Paris, Rome, Stockholm, Basle), prog dir EVR Partnership (CBS USA, ICI UK, Ciba-Geigy UK) 1970, md EVR Enterprises Nippon EVR 1976-78, dir Duke of Edinburgh's Award 1978-87; Freeman City of London 1981; FRGS 1988; *Recreations* former memb 6/7 Bn The Black Watch RHR TA, athletics, rugby football, America's Cup Challenge; *Clubs* Army and Navy, ISC (Cowes), Port Pendennis, Hawks (Cambridge), Achilles (Oxford and Cambridge); *Style—* Robert Heron, Esq, CVO; The Oast House, Ingleden Park, Tenterden, Kent

HERON-MAXWELL, Geraldine, Lady; Dorothy Geraldine Emma; yr da of late Claud Paget Mellor, of Victoria, BC; *m* 1942, Sir Patrick Heron-Maxwell, 9 Bt (d 1982); 3 s (Nigel M, 10 Bt *qv*, Colin, Paul); *Style—* Geraldine, Lady Heron-Maxwell; 9 Cowslip Hill, Letchworth, Herts

HERON-MAXWELL, Sir Nigel Mellor; 10 Bt (NS 1683), of Springkell, Dumfriesshire; s of Sir Patrick Ivor Heron-Maxwell, 9 Bt (d 1982), sr male rep of the Maxwells of Pollock and the Clydesdale Maxwells; *b* 30 Jan 1944; *Educ* Milton Abbey; *m* 1972, Mary Elizabeth Angela, da of W Ewing, of Co Donegal; 1 s, 1 da (Claire Louise b 1977); *Heir* s, David Mellor Heron-Maxwell b 22 May 1975; *Career* navigation apprentice London and Overseas Freighters Ltd 1961-65, navigation offr Royal Fleet Aux Service 1966-76, flying instr 1976-80; commercial pilot 1980-83; asst data controller SmithKline & French Research Ltd 1983-85; analyst/programmer: SmithKline & French Laboratories Ltd 1985-89, SmithKline Beecham Pharmaceuticals 1989-; *Style—* Sir Nigel Heron-Maxwell, Bt; 105 Codicote Rd, Welwyn, Herts AL6 9TY (☎ 0438 820387); SmithKline Beecham Pharmaceuticals, Mundells, Welwyn Garden City, Herts AL7 1EY (☎ 0707 325111)

HERRIES, Sir Michael Alexander Robert Young; OBE (1968), MC (1945), JP; s of Lt-Col William Dobree Young-Herries, and Ruth Mary, *née* Thrupp; *b* 28 Feb 1923; *Educ* Eton, Trinity Coll Cambridge (MA); *m* 1949, Elizabeth Hilary Russell, *née* Smith; 2 s, (William, Robert), 1 da (Julia); *Career* served KOSB 1942-47; chm and md Jardine Matheson and Co 1963-70 (joined 1948), dir Scottish Widows Fund and Life Assur Soc 1974-, chm Royal Bank of Scotland 1976- (dir 1972-, vice chm 1974-75, dep chm 1975-76), dep chm Williams and Glyn's Bank 1978-85, dir Banco de Santander SA 1989-; memb Queen's Body Guard for Scotland (The Royal Co of Archers) 1973-, Lord Lt Dumfries and Galloway 1989 (DL 1983), Stewartry of Kirkudbright; kt 1975; *Style—* Sir Michael Herries, OBE, MC, JP; c/o Royal Bank of Scotland plc, 42 St Andrew Sq, Edinburgh EH2 2YE (☎ 031 556 8555); Spottes, Castle Douglas, Stewartry of Kirkcudbright, Scotland (☎ 055 666 202); 30 Heriot Row, Edinburgh (☎ 031 226 2711); Flat 14, Lochmore House, Cundy St, London SW1W 9JX (☎ 071 730 1119)

HERRIES OF TERREGLES, Lady (14 holder of S Lordship 1490); Lady Anne Elizabeth; *née* Fitzalan-Howard; eldest da of 16 Duke of Norfolk, KG, GCVO, GBE, TD, PC (d 1975, when the Dukedom and all other honours save the Lordship passed to his kinsman, 17 Duke, *qv*; the late Duke's mother was Lady Herries of Terregles *suo jure* following the death of her f, the 11 Lord), and Lavinia, Duchess of Norfolk, LG, CBE (*qv*); *b* 12 June 1938; *m* 1985, as his 2 w, (Michael) Colin Cowdrey, CBE, *qv*; *Heir* sis, Lady Mary Mumford, *qv*; *Career* racehorse trainer; *Style—* The Rt Hon the Lady Herries of Terregles; Angmering Park, Littlehampton, West Sussex (☎ 090 674 421)

HERRIN, John Edward; CBE (1985); s of Harold John Herrin (d 1974), of Humecourt, Hythe, Kent, and Gertrude Mary, *née* MacDermot (d 1989); *b* 15 Sept 1930; *Educ* Bancrofts Sch, Rugby Coll of Technol; *m* 4 April 1959, Heather Yeoman, da of Leslie Kirkpatrick Reid, JP (d 1980), of Mill House, Hale, Cheshire; 1 s (Jeremy b 1970), 2 da (Johanna b 1961, Caroline b 1962); *Career* Lt Cdr RNR 1953-55; chm Welwyn Electronics Ltd 1972; md: Royal Worcester plc 1975-83, Crystalate Holdings plc 1983-88; dir: Oxley Developments Co Ltd 1989-, Queensgate Instruments Ltd 1989-, Croster Electronics Ltd 1990-; chm Yeoman Technology 1989-; pres Euro Electronics Component Mfrs Assoc 1986-88; memb: Cncl of Electronic Component Indust Fedn (chm 1981-82), Nedo Electronics SG; chm N Regnl Cncl for Sport and Recreation 1982-84; Freeman City of London, Liveryman Worshipful Co of Scientific Instrument Makers (Master 1991-91); CEng, FIEE; *Recreations* sailing, shooting, fishing; *Style—* John Herrin, Esq, CBE; Petteridge Oast, Matfield, Kent TN12 7LX

HERRING, Dr Antony Babington; s of Charles Kemp Herring (d 1950), and Beatrice May, *née* Doudney; *b* 23 Sept 1931; *Educ* Chichester HS for Boys, BNC Oxford (MA, BSc), St Thomas' Hosp London (BM BCh); *Career* Nat Serv RAMC Capt and jr med specialist 1960-62, RMO Royal Devon and Exeter Hosp 1959-60, neurology registrar St Thomas' Hosp 1962-64 (casualty offr and house physician 1957-59), resident house physician The Nat Hosp for Nervous Diseases 1964-65, sr neurology registrar The London Hosp 1965-67, conslt neurologist Cornwall Health Authy 1967-; FRCP 1976 (MRCP 1959); *Style—* Dr Antony Herring; Brentwood, 19 Penweathers Lane, Truro, Cornwall TR1 3PW (☎ 0872 73678); Royal Cornwall Hospital (Treliske), Truro, Cornwall (☎ 0872 74242)

HERRING, Timothy Stephen; s of Cdr Philip Maurice Herring, RNVR (d 1982), and Flora Pepita Herring (d 1985); *b* 25 May 1936; *Educ* Bishops Stortford Coll; *m* 22 April 1960, Cathleen Elizabeth, da of Thomas Stephen Nevin (d 1972); 2 s (Stephen Ashley b 26 Nov 1960, Andrew Philip b 15 March 1963); *Career* Lamson Engrg 1956-66; proprietor: Julie's Restaurant 1969-, Portobello Hotel 1970-, Ark Restaurant USA 1983-; yachtsman, winner: Britannia Cup, Queen's Cup, Queen Victoria Cup; Freeman City of London 1961, memb Worshipful Co of Blacksmiths 1961; *Recreations* yachting; *Clubs* Royal Burnham Yacht, Royal Thames Yacht; *Style—* Timothy Herring, Esq; 127 Elgin Crescent, London W11 (☎ 071 727 2776); Quaycote, Burnham-on-Crouch, Essex

HERRINGTON, Timothy John; s of John Herrington, of 16 Scotney Rd, Basingstoke, Hants, and Barbara Jean Margaret, *née* Toon; *b* 22 April 1954; *Educ* Queen Mary's GS Basingstoke Hants, Univ of Bristol (LLB); *m* 20 Feb 1982, Kathleen Mary, da of Peter Loy Chetwynd Pigott, of Botswana; 1 s (James b 1987); *Career* admitted slr 1978; ptnr: Coward Chance 1985 (joined 1976), Clifford Chance 1987-; memb Law Soc Standing Ctee on Co Law 1988- (chm Fin Servs Gp); Freeman: City of London 1977, The Worshipful Co of solicitors 1985; memb Law Soc; *Books* Life After Big Bang (contrib, 1987); *Recreations* cricket, travel, walking, gardening; *Clubs* Hampshire CCC; *Style—* Timothy Herrington, Esq; Clifford Chance, Royex House, Aldermanbury Square, London EC2V 7LD (☎ 071 600 0808, fax 071 726 8561)

HERRON, Very Rev Andrew; s of John Todd Herron, and Mary Skinner, *née* Hunter; *b* 29 Sept 1909; *Educ* Glasgow Albert Road Acad, Univ of Glasgow (MA, BD, LLB); *m* 26 Dec 1935, Joanna Fraser (Queenie), da of David Neill (d 1914), of Forfar; 4 da (Ann b 1938, Lorna b 1940, Eleanor Isobel b 1942, Muriel b 1944); *Career* ordained min Church of Scotland 1934; min: Linwood 1936-40, Houston and Killellan 1940-59; clerk to Presbytery of Glasgow 1959-81, moderator Gen Assembly of Church of Scotland 1971-72 (covener: Dept of Publications 1959-69, Business Ctee 1972-76), special lectr in practical theol Univ of Glasgow 1968-85 (Baird lectr 1985, Barclay lectr 1989); Hon DD Univ of St Andrews 1975, Hon LLD Univ of Strathclyde 1983, Hon DD Univ of Glasgow; *Books* Record Apart (1974), Guide to the General Assembly (1976), Guide to Congregational Affairs (1979), Guide to Presbytery (1982), Kirk by Divine Right (1985), Guide to the Ministry (1987), Guide to Ministerial Income (1987), Record Apart (1990); *Style—* The Very Rev Andrew Herron; 36 Darnley Rd, Glasgow G41 4NE (☎ 041 423 6422)

HERRON, Anthony Gavin; TD (1972); s of Gavin Bessell Herron, of The Wilderness, Maresfield Park, Sussex, and Irene Dorothy, *née* Peel (d 1986); *b* 10 April 1934; *Educ* Canford Sch, LSE (BSc); *m* 5 July 1958, Gray, da of Henry Francis Gray (d 1987); 1 s (Angus b 1966), 1 da (Tracy b 1964); *Career* ptnr Touche Ross and Co 1966- (currently i/c Corporate Fin Gp, seconded to Postal Servs as dir of postal fin and corp planning 1973-75), dir Expamet International 1974-; past treas and vice pres HAC; FCA; *Recreations* golf, swimming, walking, antiques; *Clubs* RAC; *Style—* Anthony Herron, Esq, TD; Hill House, 1 Little New St, London EC4A 3TR; (☎ 071 353 8011, telex 884739 TRLNDNG)

HERSCHEL-SHORLAND, John; s of Christopher William Shorland (d 1982), and Eileen Dorothea, *née* Herschel (d 1980); descendant of Sir William and Sir John Herschel pioneers of science and astronomy; *b* 23 May 1935; *Educ* Wellington, UCL (BSc); *m* 19 Sept 1959, (Christian) Esther Flowerdew, da of John Noel Mason Ashplant Nicholls, OBE, KPM (d 1987); 1 s (William b 1966), 2 da (Amanda b 1961, Catherine b 1962); *Career* with Rolls Royce 1960-86 (latterly exec mangr Ind Gas Turbine Div); *Recreations* photography, sailing, music, real tennis; *Style—* John Herschel-Shorland, Esq

HERSCHELL, David John; s of (Leslie) William Herschell, (d 1990), of Bridport, Dorset, and (Florence) Georgette, *née* Page (d 1966); *b* 26 Oct 1944; *Educ* Kingston Tech Sch; *m* 7 Sept 1974, Hazel Joyce, da of Frederick Arthur Giddins (d 1989); 1 s (James Bruce b 1977), 1 da (Helen Georgette b 1976); *Career* banking 1961-83; self-employed printer 1983-90; tstee and exec memb The Scottish Tartans Soc Comrie Perthshire 1981-90; curator Scottish Tartans Museum Comrie Perthshire 1990-; ed of Tartans (jl of the Scottish Tartans Soc), convenor of jr section of The Scottish Tartans Soc 1985-; FSA Scot (1984); *Recreations* Scottish history and culture, reading, walking; *Style—* David Herschell, Esq; Braidon, Ancaster Lane, Comrie, Crieff, Perthshire, Scotland PH6 2DT (☎ 0764 70666)

HERSCHELL, Baroness; Lady Heather Margaret Mary; *née* Legge; da of late 8 Earl of Dartmouth; *b* 1925; *m* 1948, 3 Baron Herschell, *qv*; *Style—* The Rt Hon the Lady Herschell; Westfield House, Ardington, Wantage, Berks

HERSCHELL, 3 Baron (UK 1886); Rognvald Richard Farrer; s of 2 Baron, GCVO (d 1929), and Vera (d 1961), da of Sir Arthur Nicolson, 10 Bt; *b* 13 Sept 1923; *Educ* Eton; *m* 1 May 1948, Lady Heather Mary Margaret Legge, o da of 8th Earl of Dartmouth; 1 da; *Heir* none; *Career* page of hon to King George VI, King Edward VIII and King George V; Capt Coldstream Gds (ret); *Style—* The Rt Hon the Lord Herschell; Westfield House, Ardington, Wantage, Oxfordshire OX12 8PN (☎ 0235 833224)

HERSEY, David Kenneth; s of Charles Kenneth Hersey, and Ella, *née* Morgan; *b* 30 Nov 1939; *Educ* Oberlin Coll; *m* 1, 1962 (m dis 1967), Ellen Diamond; m 2, 1967 (m dis 1972), Juliet Case; 1 da (Miranda Louise b 1969); m 3, 25 Sept 1976, Demetra, da of Demetrius Maraslis; 1 s (Demetri Alexander b 1978), 1 da (Ellen Katherine b 1980); *Career* lighting designer; West End and Broadway prodns: Miss Saigon, Baker's Wife, Les Miserables (Tony Award 1987, Los Angeles Drama Critics Circle Award 1988, Dora Mavor Moore Award 1989), Cats (Tony Award 1983, Drama Desk Award 1983, Dora Mavor Moore Award 1984), Starlight Express, Chess, Metropolis, Song and Dance, The Little Shop of Horrors, Evita (Los Angeles Drama Critics Circle 1979, Tony Award 1980), Nicholas Nickleby, Merrily We Roll Along; NT prodns: Bartholomew Fair, Ghetto and many others; prodns for RSC; numerous operas and ballets: Royal Opera House, ENO, Ballet Rambert, London Contemporary Dance, Scot Ballet, Glyndebourne; fndr DHA Lighting, lighting conslt NT 1974-84, chm Assoc of Lighting Designers 1984-86; *Recreations* sailing; *Style—* David Hersey, Esq; DHA Lighting Ltd, 3 Jonathan St, London SE11 5NH (☎ 071 582 3200, fax 071 582 4779, car 0860 689345)

HERSEY, Hon Mrs (Katherine Viola); *née* James; da of 4 Baron Northbourne; *b* 1940; *m* 1963, John Wharton Hersey; 3 s; *Style—* The Hon Mrs Hersey; Thorneyburn Old Rectory, Tarset, Northumberland

HERTFORD, 8 Marquess of (GB 1793); Hugh Edward Conway Seymour; DL (Warwicks 1959); also Lord Conway, Baron Conway of Ragley (E 1703), Baron Conway of Killultagh (I 1712), Viscount Beauchamp, Earl of Hertford (both GB 1750), and Earl of Yarmouth (GB 1793); patron of 3 livings; s of Brig-Gen Lord Henry Seymour, DSO (2 s of 6 Marquess), and Lady Helen Grosvenor, da of 1 Duke of Westminster; *b* 29 March 1930; *Educ* Eton; *m* 1956, Comtesse Pamela Thérèse Louise de Caraman-Chimay, da of Lt-Col Prince Alphonse de Chimay, TD (d 1973), by his w, Brenda (d 1985), da of Lord Ernest Hamilton (7 s of 1 Duke of Abercorn); 1 s, 3 da; *Heir* s, Earl of Yarmouth; *Career* late Lt Grenadier Gds; Hertford PRs Ltd; estate mangr and prop of Ragley Hall; *Clubs* White's, Pratt's, Turf; *Style—* The Most Hon the Marquess of Hertford; Ragley Hall, Alcester, Warwicks (☎ 0789 762455)

HERTFORD, Bishop of; Rt Rev Robin Jonathan Norman Smith; *b* 1936; *Educ* Worcester Coll Oxford (BA, MA), Ridley Hall Cambridge; *m* 1961, Hon Lois Jean Pearson, da of Baron Pearson, CBE, PC (Life Peer, d 1980); *Career* ordained: deacon 1962, priest 1963; curate St Margaret's Barking 1962-67, chaplain Lee Abbey Lynton 1967-72, vicar St Mary's Chesham Bucks 1972-80, rural dean Amersham 1979-82, rector Great Chesham 1980-90, consecrated Bishop Suffragan of Hertford 1990; *Recreations* walking, travel, washing up; *Style—* The Rt Rev the Bishop of Hertford; Hertford House, Abbey Mill Lane, St Albans, Herts AL3 4HE (☎ 0727 866420)

HERTZOG, Dr Christopher Barry; s of Dr Willem Hertzog, of Ramsey, Cambs, and Elfreda Hertzog; *b* 21 Aug 1939; *Educ* Uppingham Sch, Cambridge (MA, PhD); *m* 21 Aug 1963, Dr Jeanne Lovell, da of William Brough (d 1939); 3 da (Sophia b 1964, Zoë b 1967, Justine b 1969); *Career* sr lectr in law Surrey Cricket 1974-89; conslt Deanplace plc; PBIM; *Recreations* flying, skiing, tennis, photography, travel, archaeology; *Clubs* IOD, RAC, Aircraft Owners' and Pilots' Assoc, Jaguar Drivers'; *Style—* Dr Christopher Hertzog; 5 Mountside, Guildford, GU2 5JD (☎ 0483 68679)

HERVEY, Rear Adm John Bethell; CB (1982), OBE (1970); s of Capt Maurice William Bethell Hervey, RN (d 1965), of Lee Common Bucks, and Joan Hanbury (d 1975); f served in both World Wars and was in HMS Ocean at the Dardanelles and in HMS Colossus at Jutland; *b* 14 May 1928; *Educ* Marlborough; *m* 1950, Audrey Elizabeth, da of Leonard Mallett Mote (d 1947), of Colombo; 2 s (Nicholas, Jonathan), 1 da (Katrina); *Career* RN 1946, specialized in submarines 1950, nuclear submarines 1968; cmd appts: HMS Miner VI 1956, HMS Aeneas 1956-57, HMS Ambush 1959-62, HMS Oracle 1962-64, Sixth Submarine Div 1964-66, HMS Cavalier 1966-67, HMS

Warspite 1968-69, Second Submarine Sqdn 1973-75, HMS Kent 1975-76; Staff appts: Course offr RN Petty Offrs Leadership Sch 1957-59, Submarine Staff Offr to Canadian Maritime Cdr Halifax Nova Scotia 1964-66, Flotilla Ops Offr to Flag Offr Submarines 1970-71, Def Operational Requirements Staff 1971-73, Dep Chief Allied Staff to: C-in-C Channel, C-in-C E Atlantic 1976-80, Hon ADC to HM The Queen 1979, Cdr Br Navy Staff and Br Naval Attaché Washington; UK Nat Liaison Rep to Saclant 1980-82, Rear Adm 1980, ret; mktg vice pres Western Hemisphere MEL 1982-86, ind naval conslt 1986-; *Recreations* walking, talking, reading; *Clubs* Army and Navy, Royal Navy of 1765 and 1785, Anchorites (pres 1988); *Style*— Rear Adm John Hervey, CB, OBE; c/o Nat Westminster Bank, 26 Haymarket, London SW1Y 4ER

HERVEY, Lord (Frederick William Charles) Nicholas Wentworth; s of 6 Marquess of Bristol (d 1985), and his 2 w, Lady Anne Juliet Dorothea Maud Fitzwilliam da of 8 Earl Fitzwilliam; hp of half-bro, 7 Marquess of Bristol; *b* 26 Nov 1961; *Educ* Eton, Yale; *Career* pres and fndr: Rockingham Club, Woodhouse Ltd; vice chllr and memb Grand Cncl of Monarchist League (fndr and pres of its Youth Assoc); tstee Yale Club of GB; vice pres: ESU Appeals Ctee, ESU Eastern Regn; *Recreations* skiing, swimming, golf; *Clubs* Turf, Brooks's, CLA, The Pundits Soc of Yale Univ; *Style*— The Lord Nicholas Hervey; 128 Pavilion Road, London SW1X 0AX (☎ 071 245 0906)

HERVEY-BATHURST, Sir Frederick Peter Methuen; 6 Bt (UK 1818), of Lainston, Hants; s of Maj Sir Frederick Edward William Hervey-Bathurst, 5 Bt, DSO (d 1956); *b* 26 Jan 1903; *Educ* Eton; *m* 1, 1933 (m dis 1956), Maureen Gladys Diana, da of Charles Gordon (d 1957), of Boveridge Park, Salisbury; 1 s, 1 da; m 2, 1958, Cornelia, da of late Frederic White Shepard, of New York, USA, and widow of Dr John Lawrence Riker, of Rumson, NJ, USA; *Heir* s, Frederick Hervey-Bathurst; *Career* former: Capt Grenadier Gds, estate agent; ret; *Recreations* sailing, flying, climbing; *Clubs* Cavalry and Guards, Royal Ocean Racing; *Style*— Sir Frederick Hervey-Bathurst, Bt; Bellevue Avenue, Rumson, New Jersey 07760, USA (☎ 842 0791)

HERVEY-BATHURST, (Frederick) John Charles Gordon; s and h of Sir Frederick Peter Methuen Hervey-Bathurst, 6 Bt; *b* 23 April 1934; *Educ* Eton, Trinity Coll Cambridge; *m* 1957, Caroline Myrtle, da of Sir William Randle Starkey, 2 Bt; 1 s, 2 da (*see* Portal, Sir Jonathan, Bt, and Colthurst, Sir Richard, Bt); *Career* Lt Grenadier Gds (Reserve); dir Lazard Bros and Co Ltd; *Style*— John Hervey-Bathurst Esq; Somborne Park, King's Somborne, Hants (☎ 079 47 322); Lazard Bros and Co Ltd, 21 Moorfields, London EC2P 2HT (☎ 071 588 2721)

HERVEY-BATHURST, Hon Mrs (Sarah Rachel); *née* Peake; 2 da of 2 Viscount Ingleby, of Northallerton, Yorks, *qv*; *b* 27 Nov 1958; *Educ* Queensgate Sch, UCL; *m* 25 Sept 1982, James Felton Somers Hervey-Bathurst , er s of Maj Benjamin Hervey-Bathurst, OBE, DL (half-bro of Sir Frederick Hervey-Bathurst, 6 Bt); 2 da (Imogen b 1986, Isabella b 1990); *Style*— The Hon Mrs Hervey-Bathurst; Eastnor Castle, Ledbury, Herefordshire (☎ 0531 2849)

HERWALD, Basil Mark Jonathan; s of Samuel Herwald, and Enid, *née* Brodie; *b* 27 July 1953; *Educ* Salford GS, Queens' Coll Cambridge (MA); *Career* admitted slr 1978; ptnr Herwald Seddon; city cncllr 1980-86; chm: Salford Victims Support Scheme, Festival 200 (Manchester Jewry Bicentennial Cmmn), Pendleton Coll Govrs, Mandley Park Sch; memb LS Lowry Centenary Festival Ctee; *Recreations* painting, etching, rambling; *Style*— Basil Herwald, Esq; Herwald Seddon, Solicitors, 306 Gt Cheetham St E, Salford, Lancs (☎ 061 792 2770)

HERXHEIMER, Dr Andrew; s of Herbert G J Herxheimer (d 1985), of London, and Ilse M, *née* König (d 1980); *b* 4 Nov 1925; *Educ* Highgate Sch, St Thomas's Hosp Med Sch (MB, BS); *m* 1, 4 March 1960 (m dis 1974), Susan Jane, da of Harry Collier (d 1983), of London; 2 da (Charlotte b 1961, Sophie b 1963); m 2, 24 March 1983, Dr Christine Herxheimer, da of Willrecht Bernecker (d 1942), of Stuttgart, Germany; *Career* lectr and sr lectr pharmacology London Hosp Med Coll 1959-76, sr lectr clinical pharmacology Charing Cross Med Sch (now Charing Cross and Westminster Med Sch) 1976-, extraordinary prof clinical pharmacology Univ of Groningen Netherlands 1968-77, ed Drug and Therapeutics Bulletin 1963-, med advsr Consumers' Assoc, vice-pres Coll of Health, chm Int Soc of Drug Bulletins; FRCP 1977, memb Br Pharmacological Soc 1960; *Books* Drugs and Sensory Functions (ed, 1968), Pharmaceuticals and Health Policy (jt ed, 1981); *Recreations* reading, travel; *Style*— Dr Andrew Herxheimer; Dept of Clinical Pharmacology & Therapeutics, Charing Cross Hospital, London W6 8RF (☎ 081 846 7329, fax 081 846 7253)

HERZBERG, Charles Francis; s of Franz Herzberg (d 1971), of Hundith Hill, Cockermouth, Cumbria, and Marie Louise, *née* Oppenheimer (d 1986); *b* 26 Jan 1924; *Educ* SHL Sigtuna Sweden, Fettes, Univ of Cambridge (MA); *m* 10 March 1956, Ann Linette, da of Lt Cdr (Keith) Robin Hoare, DSO, DSC; 1 s ((Francis) Robin b 18 Dec 1956), 2 da ((Elizabeth) Jane b 21 Jan 1961, Victoria Ann b 15 July 1964); *Career* industl conslt; dir: Commercial Plastics 1955-66, Robin Willey (United Gas) 1966-70; md Churchill Gears (TI GP) 1970-72, regnl industl dir DTI Northern Region 1972-75; dir: industl planning Northern Engineering Industries plc 1975-88, Northern Investors Co Ltd 1983-88, Newcastle-upon-Tyne Polytechnic Products Ltd; former pres Tyne & Wear C of C; memb: Northern Cncl CBI, Northern Ctee IOD; govr Newcastle-upon-Tyne Poly; CEng, FIMechE, MIGasE; *Recreations* shooting; *Clubs* East India, Public Schools; *Style*— Charles Herzberg, Esq

HERZBERG, Henry Joseph; s of Georges Herzberg (d 1989), and Nancibel, *née* Joseph; *b* 7 Oct 1943; *Educ* Ashburton Secdy Sch, Selhurst GS, Architectural Assoc London, RIBA (AADipl); *m* 6 Aug 1976, Kate, da of Thomas Bampton, 1 s (Joseph Daniel b 4 July 1977), 3 da (Chloe Zylpha b 18 Feb 1972, Anna Zimena b 12 Sept 1973, Rachel Henrietta b 4 April 1982); *Career* architect; in professional practice Ahrends, Burton and Koralek 1966-67; site architect: Sir Robert McAlpine Ltd 1969-71, Wates Ltd 1971-72; Lethaby and Bannister Fletcher scholar Soc for the Protection of Ancient Buildings 1972; project architect Wimpey Ltd 1973-75, Ahrends Burton Koralek 1975; bldg ed Architects Journal 1975-77; architect (work includes): Colin St John Wilson & Ptnrs (The Br Library Euston) 1977-79, YRM (Central Med Stores and Laundry Bahrain) 1979-80; Chapman Taylor Partners: architect (Ridings Shopping Centre Wakefield) 1980-, assoc (The Poplars Supermarket and District Centre Stevenage, Orchard Square Shopping Centre Fargate Sheffield) 1983-, ptnr (refurbishment of Octagon Shopping Centre High Wycombe, Lakeside Regnl Shopping Centre Priory Park Merton, Vicarage Field Shopping Centre Barking) 1986-; Euro award Int Cncl of Shopping Centres (for The Ridings Wakefield) 1983, Br Cncl of Shopping Centres award (for Orchard Square Sheffield) 1987, Br Cncl of Shopping Centres award of merit (refurbishment of The Octagon Centre High Wycombe) 1990; ARIBA 1970; memb: AA 1970, Soc for the Protection of Ancient Buildings 1971, Victorian Soc, Georgian Soc, Wind and Windmill Soc; *Style*— Henry Herzberg, Esq; 18 Patshull Rd, London NW5 2JY (☎ 071 485 9031); Chapman Taylor Partners, 96 Kensington High St, London W8 4SG (☎ 071 938 3333, fax 071 937 1391, car 0836 239336)

HERZBERG, Dr Joseph Larry; s of Adolf Heinrich Herzberg, of London, and Pearl, *née* Mesh; *b* 10 May 1953; *Educ* Carmel Coll Berks, Hasmonean Sch London, The London Hosp Med Coll (BSc, MB BS, MPhil); *m* 13 Feb 1977, Helene Ruth, da of Harry Gordon, of London; 1 s (Laurence b 1982); *Career* sr house offr and registrar in psychiatry London Hosp 1980-84 (house physician 1979-80); sr registrar in psychiatry: St Mary's Hosp London 1984-85, The Bethlem Royal and Maudsley Hosps London 1986-87; conslt psychogeriatrician Guy's 1987-, sr lectr UMDS Guy's Campus 1987-; various scientific papers on: social psychiatry, neuropsychiatry, psychogerintries, psychiatric educn; clinical tutor in psychiatry Guy's, scheme organiser UMDS and SE Thames Regnl Registrar Rotation in Psychiatry, clinical advsr UMDS; FRSM, MRCPsych 1983; *Recreations* music, particularly opera, theatre; *Style*— Dr Joseph Herzberg; 82b Ashley Gardens, Thirleby Rd, Westminster, London SW1P 1HG; Guy's Hospital, St Thomas St, London SE1 9RT (☎ 071 955 5000)

HESELTINE, John Wasney; s of William Wasney Heseltine, of Sway, Hants, and Freda Constance Edwards (d 1968); *b* 22 Aug 1951; *Educ* King's Sch Ely, Princeton HS USA, UCL (BA, MA); *m* 1985, Flavia Rosamund, da of James Howard, of Blackheath, London; 2 da (Nathalie b 22 Aug 1987, Tara b 18 Feb 1990); *Career* sub ed Marshall Cavendish Ltd 1979-83, freelance photographer specialising in landscape, travel, food and interiors 1983-; clients incl many maj magazines, book publishers and advertising agencies worldwide; AFAEP; *Publications* photographer for eleven travel books (for Ward Lock and George Philip) and 20 volumes on food and drink; *Recreations* gardening, music; *Style*— John Heseltine, Esq; 7 Cedar Way, Camley St, London NW1 0PD (☎ 0836 681233)

HESELTINE, Rt Hon Michael Ray Dibdin; PC (1979), MP (C) Henley 1974-; s of Col R D Heseltine; *b* 21 March 1933; *Educ* Shrewsbury, Pembroke Coll Oxford; *m* 1962, Anne Harding Williams; 1 s, 2 da; *Career* Nat Serv Welsh Gds; contested (C): Gower 1959, Coventry N 1964; MP (C) Tavistock 1966-74; oppn spokesman Tport 1969, parly sec Miny Tport June-Oct 1970, parly under sec Environment 1970-72, min Aerospace and Shipping (DTI) 1972-74, oppn spokesman Indust 1974-76, Environment 1976-79, sec of state for Environment 1979-83; sec of state for Def 1983-86; sec of state for the Environment 1990-; dir Bow Pubns 1961-65, chm Haymarket Press 1966-70; pres: Assoc Cons Clubs 1978, Nat YCs 1982-83 (vice pres 1978); *Books* Where There's A Will (1987), The Challenge of Europe, Can Britain Win? (1989); *Style*— The Rt Hon Michael Heseltine, MP; House of Commons, London SW1

HESELTINE, Richard Mark Horsley; s of late Edwin Oswald Heseltine, and Penelope Horsley, *née* Robinson; *b* 3 Oct 1945; *Educ* Winchester, New Coll Oxford (MA), Wharton Sch, Univ of Pa USA; *m* 1976, Joanna Elisabeth, da of Ronald C Symonds, CB, of London; 2 da (Catherine b 1978, Emma b 1981); *Career* Corp Fin Dept Morgan Grenfell 1969-71, dir Croda Int plc 1981- (exec 1971-80), non-exec dir Ramus Hldgs plc; cncllr London Borough of Islington (SDP) 1986-90; *Recreations* yacht racing; *Clubs* Reform, Oxford and Cambridge Sailing Soc; *Style*— Richard Heseltine, Esq; 29 Gibson Square, London N1 (☎ 071 359 0702); Passage House, The Quay, Dittisham, nr Dartmouth, S Devon; Croda International plc, 168 High Holborn, London WC1 (☎ 071 836 7777)

HESELTINE, Rt Hon Sir William Frederick Payne; KCB (1986, CB 1978), GCVO, (1988, KCVO 1981, CVO 1969, MVO 1961), PC (1986), AC (1988); s of Henry William Heseltine (d 1984), of Fremantle, W Aust, and Louise Mary Gwythyr, *née* Payne (d 1966); *b* 17 July 1930; *Educ* Christ Church GS Claremont, Univ of Western Aust (BA); *m* 1, Ann (d 1957), da of late L Turner, of Melbourne; m 2, 1959, Audrey Margaret, da of late Stanley Nolan, of Sydney; 1 s (John b 1964), 1 da (Sophy b 1961); *Career* Aust Civil Serv; PM's Dept Canberra 1951-62, private sec to PM of Aust (Sir Robert Menzies) 1955-59; asst fed dir Lib Pty of Aust 1962-64; press sec to HM The Queen 1967-72 (asst press sec 1960-61 and 1965-71), private sec to HM The Queen 1986- (asst private sec 1972-77, dep private sec 1977-86); *Clubs* Boodle's, Press, BAFTA; *Style*— The Rt Hon Sir William Heseltine, GCVO, KCB, AC; The Old Stables, Kensington Palace, London W8 4PU

HESFORD, Stephen; s of Bernard Hesford, of The Garth, Grammar School Rd, Lymm, Cheshire, and Nellie, *née* Haworth; *b* 27 May 1957; *Educ* Univ of Bradford (BSc), Poly of Central London (Postgrad Dip Law); *m* 21 July 1984, Elizabeth Anne, da of Dudley Henshall, of 3 Harlyn Ave, Bramhall, Cheshire; 2 s (John b 1986, David b 1988); *Career* called to the Bar Gray's Inn 1981; memb: Fabian Soc, Lab Pty; *Recreations* cricket, politics, antiquarian books, biographies; *Clubs* Lancashire County Cricket (life memb); *Style*— Stephen Hesford, Esq; 56 The Downs, Altrincham, Cheshire WA14 2QJ (☎ 061 928 1046); 6th Floor, Sunlight House, Quay St, Manchester M3 3LE (☎ 061 833 0489, fax 061 835 3938)

HESKETH, (Claude Robert) Blair; s of Maj Claude Walter Hesketh (d 1964), and Antoinette Roberta, *née* Bull; *b* 15 Jan 1939; *Educ* Stowe; *m* 10 April 1974, Margaret Isabel, da of Col Hubert Bromley Watkins, DSO (d 1984); 1 s (Rollo b 1975), 1 da (Arabella b 1977); *Career* dir Hill Samuel Aust Ltd 1969-78, md Hill Samuel Pacific Ltd 1978-84, dir Hill Samuel Bank Ltd 1984-; govr Cheam Sch; FCA 1962; *Recreations* music, shooting, racing, golf; *Clubs* Turf; *Style*— Blair Hesketh, Esq; The Close, Odiham, Hants (☎ 0256 703746); 100 Wood St, London EC2 (☎ 071 628 8011, fax 071 726 2789)

HESKETH, Dowager Baroness; Christian Mary; OBE (1984); da of Sir John McEwen, 1 Bt, JP, DL, and Bridget, da of Rt Hon Sir Francis Lindley, GCMG, CB, CBE, and Hon Etheldreda Fraser, 3 da of 13 Lord Lovat; *b* 17 July 1929; *Educ* John Watson's Sch, St Mary's Convent Ascot; *m* 22 Nov 1949, 2 Baron Hesketh, DL (d 1955); 3 s (incl 3 Baron); *Career* county organiser WRVS 1952-83; chm Daventry Cons Assoc 1964-74; memb Arts Cncl 1960-63; High Sheriff Northants 1981; Hon LLD Leicester 1982; *Books* Tartans (1961), The Country Home Cookery Book (with Elisabeth Luard and Laura Blond, 1985), For King and Conscience: John Graham of Claverhouse, Viscount Dundee (with Magnus Linklater, 1989); *Style*— The Rt Hon the Dowager Lady Hesketh; 20a Tregunter Rd, London SW10 (☎ 071 373 9821); Pomfret Lodge, Towcester, Northants (☎ 0327 50526)

HESKETH, Baroness; Hon Claire Georgina; *née* Watson; eldest da of 3 Baron Manton; *b* 7 Feb 1952; *m* 1977, 3 Baron Hesketh *qv*; 1 s, 2 da; *Style*— The Rt Hon the Lady Hesketh; Easton Neston, Towcester, Northants (☎ 0327 50969)

HESKETH, Lady Mary Constance; *née* Lumley; OBE (1974), DStJ; eld da of 11 Earl of Scarbrough, KG, GCSI, GCIE, GCVO, TD, PC (d 1969), and Katharine Isobel, DCVO, da of Robert McEwen, of Marchmont and Bardrochat; *b* 20 April 1923; *m* 23 Aug 1952, Col Roger Fleetwood Hesketh, OBE, TD; 1 s, 2 da (1 da decd); *Style*— The Lady Mary Hesketh, OBE; North Meols Lodge, Moss Lane, Southport, Lancs (☎ 0704 28689)

HESKETH, 3 Baron (UK 1935); Thomas Alexander Fermor-Hesketh; 10 Bt (GB 1761); s of 2 Baron Hesketh (d 1955), and Dowager Lady Hesketh, *qv*; *b* 28 Oct 1950; *Educ* Ampleforth; *m* 1977, Hon Claire *qv*, da of 3 Baron Manton; 1 s, 2 da; *Heir* s, Hon Frederick Hatton Fermor-Hesketh b 13 Oct 1988; *Career* govt whip House of Lords 1986-, Parly under sec of state DOE 1989-, Min of State DTI 1990-; *Clubs* Turf, White's; *Style*— The Rt Hon the Lord Hesketh; Easton Neston, Towcester, Northants (☎ 0327 50445; office 50969, fax 0327 51751)

HESLOP, Colin Bernard; s of Air Vice-Marshal Herbert William Heslop, CB, OBE (d 1976), of Sonning-on-Thames, Berks, and Phyllis Bletsoe, *née* Brown; *b* 16 Sept 1943; *Educ* Millfield; *m* 6 May 1967, Penelope, da of Arthur Huw Stow (d 1973), of Shoreham by Sea, Sussex; 2 s (Durran Bernard b 25 Aug 1968, Gordon Piers b 29 Feb 1972); *Career* trainee Thornton Baker 1960-64; accountant: Landau Morley &

Scott 1965-66, James Cowper 1967, Michael Beckett Ltd 1968; co sec: St Swithins Hldgs 1969-77, Cascom Ltd 1978; sr ptnr CB Heslop Co 1979-; chm: Thatcham C of C, W Berks Trg Consortium; former pres and chm Thatcham Rotary and Round Table Clubs; FCA; *Recreations* motor boating, classic car restoration; *Clubs* RYA, STA; *Style—* Colin Heslop, Esq; C B Heslop & Co, 1 High St, Thatcham, Newbury, Berks, RG13 4JG (☎ 0635 68202, fax 0635 68880, telex 849125)

HESLOP, Nigel John; *b* 4 Dec 1963; *Career* Rugby Union wing threequarter Orrell RUFC and England (7 caps); clubs: Waterloo FC, Liverpool St Helens FC, Orrell RUFC; rep: Eng Colts 1980, England B 1990 (2 caps), England XV Rovigo 1990; England: debut v Argentina 1990, tour Aregntina 1990; police offr; *Style—* Nigel Heslop, Esq; Orrell RUFC, Edgehall Road, Orrell, Wigan WN5 8TL (☎ 0695 623 193)

HESLOP, Richard William; s of Richard Basil Heslop (d 1962), of Nottingham, and Edith Margaret, *née* Butler; *b* 12 May 1931; *Educ* Nottingham HS, Univ of Birmingham (BSc, MB ChB); *m* 12 Sept 1959, Jean Elizabeth, da of A J N Gammond (d 1977), of Rudhall, Ross on Wye, Herefordshire; 1 s (Richard b 1962), 2 da (Janet b 1960, Elizabeth b 1964); *Career* Capt RAMC Hong Kong 1956-58; registrar and sr registrar Utd Birmingham Hosps 1960-66, conslt urologist Hull and E Riding of Yorks 1967-; surgn to Corpn of Hull Trinity House, memb Hull Health Authy; memb: BMA, Br Assoc of Urological Surgns; FRCS; *Recreations* freemasonry, motor sport, photography; *Style—* Richard Heslop, Esq; Eata House, Etton, North Humberside HU17 7PJ (☎ 0430 810488); The Nuffield Hospital, 81 Westbourne Ave, Hull (☎ 0482 42327); Princess Royal Hospital, Saltshouse Road, Hull (☎ 0482 701151)

HESS, Nigel John; s of John Hess, of Weston-Super-Mare, Somerset, and Sheila, *née* Merrick; *b* 22 July 1953; *Educ* Weston-Super-Mare GS for Boys, St Catharine's Coll Cambridge (MA); *m* Lynda, *née* Smith; 1 da (Alice Elizabeth b 31 Aug 1990); *Career* composer and conductor in TV theatre and film; music scores for TV incl: A Woman of Substance, Deceptions, Anna of the Five Towns, All Passion Spent, Vanity Fair, Campion, Summer's Lease, The London Embassy, The One Game, Testament, Chimera, Titmuss Regained; co music dir and house composer RSC 1981-85; contrib music scores to 14 prodns incl: Troilus and Cressida, Much Ado About Nothing, Julius Caesar, Cyrano de Bergerac, Comedy of Errors, Hamlet, Othello, The Winter's Tale, The Swan Down Gloves; West End prodns incl: The Secret of Sherlock Holmes, A Room of One's Own; UK films incl: Exploits at West Poley, The Spice of Wickedness; composer many chamber vocal and orchestral pieces; commercial recordings incl: The Swan Down Gloves (London Cast Album), Much Ado About Nothing (RSC original score), Chameleon (New Age Concept Album), Screens and Stages (TV and Theatre Themes compilation); winner: NY Drama Desk award Outstanding Music in a Play (RSC Much Ado About Nothing & Cyrano de Bergerac on Broadway) 1985, Novello award for Best TV Theme (Testament) 1988, Television & Radio Industs Club award for Best Theme (Summer's Lease) 1989; *Recreations* travel and photography; *Clubs* Assoc of Professional Composers; *Style—* Nigel Hess, Esq; Nigel Britten, Lemon Unna & Durbridge, 24 Pottery Lane, Holland Park, London W11 4LZ (☎ 071 727 1346, fax 071 727 9037)

HESSAYON, Dr David Gerald; s of Jack Hessayon (d 1958), and Lena Hessayon (d 1933); *b* 13 Feb 1928; *Educ* Univ of Leeds, Univ of Manchester; *m* 1951, Joan Parker, da of Weeden T Gray, of USA; 2 da; *Career* chm: Pan Britannica Industs 1972-, Turbair 1970-, Expert Publications 1988-, Br Agrochemicals Assoc 1980-81; Freeman City of London, memb Worshipful Co of Gardeners; *Books* The House Plant Expert, The Rose Expert, The Tree and Shrub Expert, The Armchair Book of the Garden, The Flower Expert, The Lawn Expert, The Vegetable Expert, The Indoor Plant Spotter, The Garden Expert, The Home Expert, The Gold Plated House Plant Expert, Rose Jotter, House Plant Jotter, Vegetable Jotter, Be Your Own Greenhouse Expert, The Bio Friendly Gardening Guide, The Fruit Expert, The Bedding Plant Expert; *Recreations* Times crossword, American folk music; *Clubs* London Press; *Style—* Dr David Hessayon; Hilgay, Mill Lane, Broxbourne, Herts EN10 7AX (☎ 0992 463490); PBI Ltd, Britannica House, Waltham Cross, Herts EN8 7DY (☎ 0992 23691, telex 23957 fax 0992 26452)

HESSE AND THE RHINE, HRH The Princess of; Hon Margaret Campbell; *née* Geddes; o da of 1 Baron Geddes, PC, GCMG, KCB, TD (d 1954), and Isabella Gamble, *née* Ross (d 1962); *b* 18 March 1913, Dublin; *m* 17 Nov 1937, HRH Prince Louis (Ludwig) Hermann Alexander Chlodwig of Hesse and the Rhine (b 1908, d 1968), whose mother, elder brother, sister-in-law and two nephews were killed in an aircrash 1937. Prince Louis' aunt, on his f's side, Alexandra, m Emperor Nicholas II and was murdered at Ekaterinburg 1918. Another aunt, Victoria, m 1 Marquess of Milford Haven and was mother of late 1 Earl Mountbatten of Burma, and also gm of HRH Prince Philip, Duke of Edinburgh. His paternal gm was Princess Alice, 2 da of Queen Victoria; 1 adopted s (Moritz, Prince and Landgrave of Hesse b 1926); *Style—* HRH The Princess of Hesse and the Rhine; Schloss Wolfsgarten, 6070 Langen, Hessen, W Germany

HESSIAN, Toby Paul; s of Paul Francis Hessian, of 2 Longacre, Bingham, Notts, and Dorothy, *née* Middleton; *b* 17 June 1969; *Educ* Becket RC Sch West Bridgford, West London Inst of Higher Educn; *Career* oarsman; memb Nottinghamshire County Rowing Assoc; achievements incl: jr world champion coxless four Cologne 1987, represented GB Lucerne 1989 and 1990, Gold medal lightweight coxless four Under 23 World Championships Austria 1990, Bronze medal lightweight eight World Championships Tasmania 1990; Henley Royal Regatta: winner Wyfold Challenge Cup 1988, winner Ladies Plate 1989, winner Thames Cup 1990, established record by competing alongside three brothers 1987; records: Br lightweight eights, Br heavyweight eights, world lightwieght eights Lucerne 1990; *Recreations* reading, sports psychology, history, african continent, golf, skiing, football, rugby, cricket, squash, tennis, swimming, cycling; *Style—* Toby Hessian, Esq; 2 Longaire, Bingham, Notts NG13 8BG (☎ 0949 838709); Amateur Rowing Association, 6 Lower Mall, Hammersmith, London

HESTER, Rev Canon John Frear; s of William Hester (d 1978), and Frances Mary, *née* Frear (d 1964); *b* 21 Jan 1927; *Educ* West Hartlepool GS, St Edmund Hall Oxford (MA), Cuddesdon Coll Oxford; *m* 1959, Elizabeth Margaret, da of late Sir Eric Riches, of Rutland Gate, London; 3 s (Robert b 1963, James b 1965, Alexander b 1971); *Career* clerk in holy orders, rector of Soho 1963-75, vicar of Brighton 1975-85, chaplain to HM The Queen 1984-, canon residentiary and precentor of Chichester Cathedral 1985-; chm Chichester Diocesan Overseas Cncl 1985-; *Books* Soho Is My Parish (1970); *Recreations* travel (real and imaginary), theatre, soccer; *Style—* The Rev Canon John Hester; The Residentiary, Canon Lane, Chichester PO19 1PX (☎ 0243 782961)

HESTER, Prof Ronald Ernest; s of Ernest Hester, of Heworth Place, York, and Rhoda Pennington, *née* Lennox (d 1985); *b* 8 March 1936; *Educ* Royal GS High Wycombe, Univ of London (BSc, DSc), Cornell Univ (PhD); *m* 30 Aug 1958, Bridget Ann, da of Sqdn Ldr Ernest Francis Maddin (d 1988); 2 s (Stephen b 1960, David b 1965), 2 da (Alison b 1962, Catherine b 1968); *Career* res fell Univ of Cambridge 1962-63, asst prof Cornell Univ USA 1963-65, prof Univ of York 1965- (former lectr, sr lectr, reader); approx 200 pubns in sci jls; chm: SERC Chemistry Ctee 1988-90, Euro Res Cncls Chemistry Ctee 1990-; memb: UGC Equipment Ctee 1987-89, SERC Sci Bd 1988-90, SERC Cncl 1990-, Royal Soc of Chemistry, RSA; FRSC 1970, CChem 1970; *Books* Physical-Inorganic Chemistry (1965), Understanding our Environment (1985), Advances in Spectroscopy vols 1-19 (1975-90); *Recreations* squash, tennis, skiing, travel; *Style—* Prof Ronald E Hester; The Old Rectory, Crayke, York YO6 4TA; Dept of Chemistry, University of York, York YO1 5DD (☎ 0904 432557, fax 0904 432516, telex 57933 YORKUL)

HETHERINGTON, Prof (Hector) Alastair; s of Sir Hector J W Hetherington, KCB (d 1965), and Alison, *née* Reid (d 1966); *b* 31 Oct 1919; *Educ* Gresham's, Corpus Christi Coll Oxford (BA, MA); *m* 1, 27 June 1957 (m dis 1977), (Helen) Miranda, da of Prof Richard Oliver, of Manchester; 2 s (Thomas b 1959, Alexander b 1961), 2 da (Lucy b 1963, Mary b 1965); m 2, 26 Oct 1979, Sheila Janet Cameron, wid of Hamish Cameron; *Career* WWII serv Maj RAC 1940-46; reporter Glasgow Herald 1946-50; Manchester Guardian (Later The Guardian): joined 1950, foreign ed 1953-56, ed 1956-75; BBC in Scotland 1976-79, res prof in media studies Univ of Stirling 1982-87 (emeritus prof 1987-), hon fell Corpus Christi Coll Oxford; Freeman City of Lille 1989; *Books* Guardian Years (1981), News Newspapers and Television (1985), Perthshire in Trust (1988), News in the Regions (1989), Highlands and Islands - A Generation of Progress (1990), Cameras in the Commons (1990); *Recreations* hill walking, golf; *Clubs* Athenaeum, Caledonian; *Style—* Prof Alastair Hetherington; 38 Chalton Rd, Bridge of Allan, Stirling FK9 4EF (☎ 0786 832168); High Corrie, Isle of Arran KA27 8JB (☎ 0770 81 652)

HETHERINGTON, Anthony Richard; s of Richard Ernest Hetherington, of Hants, and Charlotte Alice Annie, *née* Miller; *b* 6 Nov 1940; *Educ* Preston Manor Sch, Law Soc Sch of Law; *m* 1, 19 June 1965, Jacqueline, da of Auguste Théophile Duteil, of Paris; 2 s (David Anthony St Clare b 1967, Julian Anthony St John b 1968), 2 da (Sarah Jane and Joanna Mary b 1967); m 2, 14 Feb 1977, Hazel Mary, da of late George Gorman, of Hamps; *Career* slr; Cmmr for Oaths; dep registrar of the High Ct of Co Ct 1975-; Freeman City of London, Liveryman Worshipful Co of Arbitrators 1981; sec The Pulmerston Forts Soc 1986-; FCIArb; *Recreations* mucis, fly fishing, shooting, military history, travel, book, dogs; *Clubs* Fly Fishers'; *Style—* Anthony R Hetherington, Esq; Folly House, The Crescent, Alverstoke, Hants; 10 Stokesway, Stoke Rd, Gosport, Hants

HETHERINGTON, Sir Arthur Ford; DSC (1944); s of Sir Roger Gaskell Hetherington, CB, OBE (d 1952), and Honoria, *née* Ford; *b* 12 July 1911; *Educ* Highgate Sch, Trinity Coll Cambridge (BA); *m* 1937, Margaret Lacey; 1 s, 1 da; *Career* serv WWII RNVR; chm: Southern Gas Bd 1961-64 (dep chm 1956-61), E Midlands Gas Bd 1964-66, Br Gas Corp (formerly Gas Cncl) 1972-76 (memb 1961, dep chm 1967-72); kt 1974; *Clubs* Athenaeum, Royal Southampton Yacht; *Style—* Sir Arthur Hetherington, DSC; 32 Connaught Sq, London W2 (☎ 071 723 3128)

HETHERINGTON, Lt-Col John David; s of Howard Walklett Hetherington (d 1977), of Berks, and Doris Amy, *née* Dowling; *b* 28 Feb 1934; *Educ* Hailybury and ISC, Eaton Hall, Def Serv Staff Coll India; *Career* 2 Lt The Sherwood Foresters 1953 served: BAOR, Far E, India, Cyprus; Lt-Col OIC The Worcestershire and Sherwood Foresters Regt 1972-74, ret 1979; memb Co Ctee TA & VRA Derbyshire 1984-, memb Ctee ABF Derbyshire 1984-; vice chm and tech del The Midlands Driving Trials Gp 1984-; dep pres The Sherwood Foresters Assoc 1985-; memb Ctee Royal Windsor House Show 1986-; memb Burton Dist Ctee Staffs Agric Soc 1988-; chm BBC Radio Derby Advsy Cncl 1990-; OStJ Derbyshire: cdr 1986-88, cmmr 1987-88; land owner; *Recreations* competition carriage driving, ornithology; *Style—* Lt-Col John D Hetherington; The Stud Farm, Byrkley, Rangemore, Burton upon Trent, Staffordshire (☎ 0283 712368)

HETHERINGTON, Sir Thomas Chalmers; KCB (1979), CBE (1970), TD, QC (1978); s of W Hetherington; *b* 1926; *Educ* Rugby, Ch Ch Oxford; *m* 1953, June Catliff; 4 da; *Career* barr 1952, bencher 1978; former dep Treasy slr; dir of Public Prosecutions 1977-87, War Crimes Inquiry 1988-89; *Books* Prosecution and the Public Interest (1989); *Style—* Sir Thomas Hetherington, KCB, CBE, TD, QC; Rosemount, Mount Pleasant Road, Lingfield, Surrey RH7 6BM

HEUVEL, Christopher John; s of Desmond John Heuvel, of Lower Earley, and Joan Margaret, *née* Hooper; *b* 22 Oct 1953; *Educ* Douai Sch Woolhampton, Univ of Newcastle-upon-Tyne (BA, BArch), Poly of Central London (DipTP); *m* 7 March 1986, Diana Crystal, da of James William Joseph Collis (d 1981), of Ipswich, Suffolk; 1 s (Benjamin b 1985), 1 da (Beatrice b 1986); *Career* architect, princ one-man private practice; planning conslt; sr lectr City Coll Norwich; *Recreations* the arts, landscape; *Clubs* RIBA; *Style—* Christopher J Heuvel, Esq; 9 Earlham Rd, Norwich NR2 3AA (☎ 0603 629746); Le Belvedere, 46150 Saint Denis Catus, France (☎ 65227440)

HEWARD, Air Chief Marshal Sir Anthony Wilkinson; KCB (1972, CB 1968), OBE (1952), DFC (and Bar), AFC; s of late Col E J Heward; *b* 1 July 1918; *m* 1944, Clare Myfanwy, da of Maj-Gen Charles Brian Wainright, CB (d 1968); 1 s, 1 da; *Career* Gp Capt RAF 1956, Air Cdre 1963, Air Vice-Marshal 1966, Dep Cmdr RAF Germany 1966-69, AOA Air Support Cmmd 1969-70, Air Marshal 1970, COS RAF Strike Cmd 1970-72, AOC 18 (Maritime) Gp 1972-73, Air memb for supply and orgn MOD 1973-76, Air Chief Marshal 1974, ret 1976; CC Wilts 1981-89; *Clubs* RAF, Flyfishers'; *Style—* Air Chief Marshal Sir Anthony Heward, KCB, OBE, DFC, AFC; Home Close, Donhead St Mary, nr Shaftesbury, Dorset (☎ 0747 828 339)

HEWARD, Edmund Rawlings; CB (1984); s of late Rev Thomas Brown Heward, and Kathleen Amy Rachel Rawlings; *b* 19 Aug 1912; *Educ* Repton, Trinity Coll Cambridge; *m* 1945, Constance Mary Sandiford, da of late George Bertram Crossley, OBE; *Career* served WWII 1940-46 RA, Maj; admitted slr 1937, ptnr Rose, Johnson and Hicks 1946; chief master of the Supreme Ct (Chancery Div) 1980-85 (master 1959-79); *Books* incl: Guide to Chancery Practice (1962), Matthew Hale (1972), Lord Mansfield (1979), Chancery Practice (1983), Chancery Orders (1986); *Style—* Edmund Heward, Esq, CB; 36a Dartmouth Row, Greenwich SE10 8AW (☎ 081 692 3525)

HEWER, Prof Richard Langton; s of Dr Christopher Langton Hewer (d 1986), of London, and Doris Phoebe, *née* Champney (d 1978); *b* 29 March 1930; *Educ* St Lawrence Coll Ransgate, Bart's Univ of London (MB BS); *m* 21 June 1958, Jane Ann, da of Robert Wotherspoon, of St Helens, Lancs; 1 s (Simon Christopher b 9 Nov 1962), 2 da (Marian Jane b 19 April 1961, Sarah Ann b 21 Jan 1965); *Career* Nat Serv, RAF; chief asst Professorial Neurology Unit Oxford 1965-68, conslt neurologist Bristol 1968-, prof of neurology Univ of Bristol 1990-; fndr chm: Friedreich's Ataxia Gp 1963-75, Bristol Stroke Fndn 1983-; fndr and dir experimental Stroke Res Unit 1975, sec and chm RCP Disability Ctee 1978-, memb Cncl Assoc Br Neurologists 1987- (1981-84), chm Assoc Br Neurologists' Serv (Policy) Ctee 1983-, sec Working Gp on physical disability RCP 1986, chm Med Disability Soc 1986-88; memb: World Fedn of Neurology, Med Disability Soc, Soc for Res in Rehabilitation, Chest Heart and Stroke Assoc; FRSM, FRCP; *Books* Stroke - A Critical Approach to Diagnosis Treatment and Management (jtly, 1985), Stroke - A Guide to Recovery (with D T Wade, 1986), Modern Medicine (ed, 1975, 1979, 1983), The Oxford Companion to the Mind (1987), Rehabilitation of the Physically Disabled Adults (1988), More Dilemmas in the Management of the Neurological Patient (1987), The Management of Motor Neurone Disease (1987); *Recreations* sailing, walking; *Style—* Prof Richard Langton Hewer; Dept of Neurology, Frenchay Hospital, Bristol BS16 1LE (☎ 0272 701212)

HEWES, Robin Anthony Charles (Bob); s of Leslie Augustus Hewes, of Colchester, Essex, and Lily Violet, *née* Norfolk (d 1979); *b* 15 April 1945; *Educ* Colchester Royal GS, Univ of Bristol (LLB); *m* 23 Sept 1967, Christine Diane, da of Geoffrey William Gosnell Stonebridge (d 1983); 1 s (Stephen b 24 Dec 1969) 2 da (Kirstie b 11 March 1972, Rachel b 26 Jan 1977); *Career* HM Inspr of Taxes Inland Revenue 1966-7, princ Dept of Indust 1974-80 (asst sec 1980-85), non-exec dir Comfort-Vickers 1983-88, Machinery of Govt Div Cabinet Office (MPO) 1985-87, dir Enterprise and Deregulation Unit DTI 1987-88, head of regulatory services Lloyds of London 1988-; vice pres and past chm Brentwood Swimming Club; hereditary Freeman Borough of Colchester 1966-; *Recreations* swimming; *Style*— Bob Hewes, Esq; 38 Plovers Mead, Wyatts Green, Brentwood, Essex CM15 0PS (☎ 0277 822891); Lloyd's of London, One Lime St, London EC3M 7HA (☎ 071 327 6711, fax 071 626 2389, telex 987321 Lloyds G)

HEWETSON, Sir Christopher Raynor; TD (1967), DL (1986); s of Harry Raynor Hewetson, MRCVS (d 1976), of Southport, and Emma, *née* Seed (d 1989); *b* 26 Dec 1929; *Educ* Sedbergh, Peterhouse Cambridge (MA); *m* 5 May 1962, Alison May, da of Prof Allan Watt Downie, FRS (d 1988); 2 s (Charles b 1964, Richard b 1970), 1 da (Jane b 1966); *Career* Nat Serv 2 Lt 4 RHA 1951-53, 359 Medium Regt RA (TA) 1953-68 (Lt-Col cmdg 1965-68); admitted slr 1956; ptnr Lace Mawer Slrs 1961; memb Cncl Law Soc 1966-87, pres Liverpool Law Soc 1976, pres Law Soc 1983 (vice pres 1982); kt 1984; *Recreations* golf, walking; *Clubs* Army and Navy, Athenaeum (Liverpool), Royal Birkdale Golf; *Style*— Sir Christopher Hewetson, TD, DL; 24c Westcliffe Rd, Birkdale, Southport, Merseyside PR8 2BU (☎ 0704 67179); Lace Mawer, 43 Castle St, Liverpool L2 9SU (☎ 051 236 2002)

HEWETT, Kenneth Arthur John; s of Arthur Charles Frederick Hewett (d 1961); *b* 17 April 1921; *Educ* Westminster City Sch; *m* 1945, Jean Rosaline, *née* Nye; 1 s, 1 da; *Career* co dir shipping, jt md and vice chm Davies Turner and Co Ltd, dir Davies Turner Motors Ltd, Manchester International Terminal Ltd; memb Cncl Inst of Freight Forwarders Ltd; *Recreations* golf, music, swimming; *Clubs* E India, Devonshire (Eastbourne); *Style*— Kenneth Hewett, Esq; 41 St James Rd, Mitcham, Surrey (☎ 081 640 7268)

HEWETT, Sir Peter John Smithson; 6 Bt (UK 1813), of Nether Seale, Leics; MM; s of Sir John George Hewett, 5 Bt, MC (d 1990), and Yuilleen Maude, *née* Smithson (d 1980); *b* 27 June 1931; *Educ* Bradfield, Jesus Coll Cambridge (BA); *m* 1958, Jennifer Ann Cooper, da of E T Jones, OBE, of Nairobi, Kenya; 2 s (Richard Mark John b 1958, David Patrick John b 1968), 1 da (Joanna Yuilleen b 1960); *Heir* s, Richard Mark John Hewett b 1958; *Career* barr Gray's Inn 1954; practising advocate Kenya; *Recreations* windsurfing, birdwatching; *Clubs* Muthaiga Country, Karen Country, Naivasha Yacht; *Style*— Sir Peter Hewett, Bt, MM; P O Box 15669, Nairobi, Kenya

HEWETT, Richard William; s of Brig W G Hewett, OBE, MC (d 1976); *b* 22 Oct 1923; *Educ* Wellington; *m* 1954, Rosemary, da of B E Cridland, MC, TD (d 1979); 2 da (Vanessa, Virginia); *Career* Nat Serv WWII Army, Europe, Far East, Maj; regular offr to 1962; dir Reader's Digest Assoc Ltd UK (joined 1962), vice pres and dir Int Ops Readers Digest Assoc Inc NY USA; *Recreations* fishing, tennis; *Clubs* Buck's; *Style*— Richard Hewett, Esq; Chestnut House, Kirdford, W Sussex RH14 0LT (☎ 040377 553)

HEWINS, John Francis; s of late John Hewins, and Gladys Maud, *née* Van Mierlo; *b* 19 March 1936; *Educ* Mount St Marys Coll; *m* 20 Oct 1964, Valerie, da of late John Fife Mortimer; 1 s (Dominic John b 12 July 1969), 2 da (Natalie Brigid b 2 May 1966, Frances Camille b 2 Jan 1968); *Career* Nat Serv; student apprentice Davy Utd 1953, md Davy McKee Sheffield 1988 (sales dir 1977, gen mangr 1983, md 1983-90); dir: Hallamshire Investmts, S Yorks Supertram; Freeman Cutlers Co in Hallamshire, FRSA; *Recreations* garden, mediocre tennis, mountain bike, running, walking; *Style*— John Hewins, Esq; The Homestead, Nether Shatton, Bamford, Hope Valley, Derbyshire (☎ 0433 51201)

HEWISH, Prof Antony; s of Ernest William Hewish (d 1975), and Francis Grace Lanyon, *née* Pinch (d 1970); *b* 11 May 1924; *Educ* King's Coll Taunton, Gonville and Caius Coll Cambridge (MA, PhD); *m* 19 Aug 1950, Marjorie Elizabeth Catherine, da of Edgar Richards (d 1954); 1 s (Nicholas b 1956), 1 da (Jennifer b 1954); *Career* RAE Farnborough 1943-46; Univ of Cambridge: res fell Gonville and Caius Coll 1952-54, asst dir of res 1954-62, fell Churchill Coll 1962-, lectr in physics 1962-69, reader 1969-71, prof of radioastronomy 1971-; dir Mullard Radio Astronomy Observatory 1982-87; discovered pulsars (with S J Bell-Burnell) 1967; Nobel Prize for Physics (with M Ryle) 1974, Hughes Medal Royal Soc 1974-; prof of astronomy Royal Inst 1977-81; govr Knight's Templar Sch Baldock, churchwarden Kingston Parish Church Cambridge; Hon DSc: Leicester 1976, Exeter 1977, Manchester 1989; FRS 1968, foreign hon memb American Acad of Arts and Scis, foreign fell Indian Nat Sci Academy 1982; *Recreations* sailing, gardening; *Style*— Prof Antony Hewish, FRS; Pryor's Cottage, Field Rd, Kingston, Cambridge CB3 7NQ (☎ 0223 262 657); Cavendish Laboratory, Madingley Road, Cambridge CB3 0HE (☎ 0223 337 296)

HEWITT, Anthony Ronald; s of Ronald Berwick Hewitt, of Hemel Hempstead, Herts, and Phyllis Lavina, *née* Tammadge; *b* 9 May 1949; *Educ* St Albans GS, Open University (BA); *m* 11 Nov 1978, Felicity Heather, da of Roy Chalice Orford, CBE, of Budleigh Salterton, Devon; 2 s (Richard b 1980, Edward b 1987), 2 da (Penelope b 1981, Deborah b 1984); *Career* cmmnd serv RN 1968-88: submarine cmdg offr's course 1979, submarine tactics and weapons gp 1981-83, exec offr HMS Churchill 1980, starboard crew HMS Revenge 1983-86, SO strategic systems (submarines) Directorate of Naval Warfare MOD 1986-88; sec Cable Authy 1989-90, dep sec Ind TV Cmmn 1991-; MBIM 1988, FCIS 1990, MRTS 1990; *Recreations* choral music, house renovation, kite flying; *Style*— Anthony Hewitt, Esq; 1 Highlands Close, Leatherhead, Surrey KT22 8NG (☎ 0372 362917); Independent Television Commission, 70 Brompton Rd, London SW3 1EY (☎ 071 584 7011, fax 071 589 5533)

HEWITT, David Stuart; s of Geoffrey Walter Hewitt, of 10 Rosecroft Court, The Kings Gap, Holylake, Merseyside, and Margery Jessie, *née* Stuart (d 1984); *b* 30 Oct 1932; *Educ* Calday Grange GS, Wrekin Coll; *m* 24 June 1961, Susan, da of Sidney Milton Heathcote Caddick (d 1984); 2 s (Richard David b 19 April 1968, Nicholas Michael (twin) b 19 April 1968), 2 da (Jennifer Mary (Mrs Kevin Owens) b 22 July 1962, Helen Judith b 20 Feb 1965); *Career* Nat Serv cmmnd RA 1951-53; articled clerk Dawson Graves & Co Liverpool 1953-58, qualified chartered accountant 1958, joined Whinney Smith & Whinney 1959; became: Whinney Murray & Co 1965, Ernst & Whinney 1979, Ernst & Young 1989; FCA (ACA 1958); *Recreations* golf, family, bridge; *Clubs* St James's (Manchester), Heswall Golf; *Style*— David Hewitt, Esq; Ridgewood, 41 Quarry Road East, Heswall, Merseyside L60 6RB (☎ 051 342 3440); Ernst & Young, Commercial Union House, Albert Square, Manchester M2 6LP (☎ 061 953 9000, fax 061 832 4124)

HEWITT, Hon Mrs (Diana Marie Faith); raised to the rank of a Baron's da 1948; da of late Hon Edward Crofton (s of late 5 Baron Crofton); *b* 1927; *m* 1, 1949, Cdr Hugh May, RN; 1 s, 1 da; m 2, 1963, Cdr Edward Michael George Hewitt, RN; 1 s, 1 da; *Style*— The Hon Mrs Hewitt; Flat H, 63 Drayton Gdns, SW10

HEWITT, Edwin John; s of Sydney Hewitt (d 1968); *b* 14 April 1934; *Educ* Berkhamsted; *m* 1957, Jennefer Judy, née Oakley; 3 c; *Career* dir and joint gen mangr Co-operative Bank plc; dir: FC Finance Ltd, Centenary Finance (Glasgow) Ltd, Crowngap Ltd; FCA; *Recreations* riding, music, chess; *Style*— Edwin Hewitt, Esq; Co-operative Bank plc, PO Box 101, 1 Balloon Street, Manchester M60 4ET; Tudor Lodge, Lyme Green, nr Macclesfield, Cheshire (☎ 026 05 2209)

HEWITT, Ewan Christian; s of Dr Rupert Conrad Hewitt (d 1981), of Glenbeigh, Frinton-on-Sea, Essex, and Gladys Muriel, *née* Christian (d 1967); *b* 13 April 1928; *Educ* Wellington, Gonville and Caius Coll Cambridge (BA, MA), Manchester Business Sch; *m* 1, 25 July 1959 (m dis 1973), Gaylor Margaret Joyce, da of Henry Fraeke, of Westerham, Kent; m 2, 14 Dec 1973, Susan Mary, da of Donald James Maclachlan, of Hull, Yorkshire; 2 da (Annabel Elizabeth Christina b 16 Sept 1974, Lucinda Katherine Mary b 11 March 1977); *Career* Nat Serv Royal Engrs 1946-48; apprentice Davy Paxman & Co Ltd Colchester 1949; Davy & United Engineering Co Ltd Sheffield: apprentice 1952-54, sales engr 1954-56, contract mangr Durgapur Steelworks Project 1956-57, sr sales engr 1957-59, liaison engr Pittsburgh Pennsylvania 1959-60, asst chief engr Proposals 1961-64, tech sales mangr 1964-67, tech asst to MD 1967-68; tech dir: Davy Construction Co Sheffield 1971-72 (mangr tech services 1968-71), Davy Ashmore Ltd Stockton-on-Tees 1972-73, Davy-Loewy Ltd 1973-88, Davy McKee Ltd 1973-88 (dir tech mktg 1988-); Metals Soc Ablett prize; Metals Soc/Inst of Metals memb: Engrg Ctee 1974-85, Iron and Steel Ctee 1975-, Cncl 1981-87; memb Rolling Gp Inst of Metals 1989-, memb Bd Manufacturing Industs Div IMechE 1981-87; memb: Assoc of Iron and Steel Engrs USA 1959, Iron and Steel Soc of AIME USA 1982, Iron and Steel Inst (Metals Soc) Inst of Metals 1973, Sheffield Metallurgical and Engrg Assoc 1976; MIMechE 1954, FIMechE 1976, FEng 1989; *Recreations* photography, fly-fishing, bridge, gardening, walking, riding, jazz record collection; *Style*— Ewan Hewitt, Esq; Ash Cottage, Clarendon Rd, Fulwood, Sheffield S10 3TQ (☎ 0742 303197); Dir of Technical Marketing, Davy McKee (Sheffield) Ltd, Prince of Wales Rd, Sheffield S9 4EX (☎ 0742 449971, fax 0742 449641)

HEWITT, Gavin Wallace; s of Rev George Burrill Hewitt, TD (d 1976), and Elisabeth Murray, *née* Wallace (d 1976); *b* 19 Oct 1944; *Educ* George Watson's Coll Edinburgh, Univ of Edinburgh (MA); *m* 6 Oct 1973, Heather Mary, da of Trevor Shaw Clayton, of Whaley Bridge, Derbyshire; 2 s (Alexander Francis Reid b 3 Nov 1977, Peter James Clayton b 26 Jan 1982), 2 da (Claire Rebecca b 20 March 1975, Mary Elisabeth Courtney b 29 Sept 1979); *Career* asst princ Miny of Tport 1967-70, second sec UK delegation to the Euro Communities Brussels 1970-72, first sec Br High Cmmn Canberra 1973-78, first sec and head of chancery Br Embassy Belgrade 1981-84, dep permanent rep UK mission UN Geneva 1987-; vice chm Bd of Govrs Geneva English Sch 1989-; *Style*— Gavin Hewitt, Esq; Foreign and Commonwealth Office, King Charles St, London SW1A 2AH (☎ 071 270 3000)

HEWITT, Gillian Beresford; da of Hilary Max Torry (d 1987), of Cheshire, and Margaret Beresford, *née* Theaker; *b* 20 June 1946; *Educ* Birkenhead HS, Brighton Coll of Art; *m* 7 April 1970, Richard Frank Hewitt, s of Frank Lambert Hewitt; 1 da (Emma b 1978); *Career* dir Austin Reed Ltd 1983-; *Recreations* travel, literature, art; *Clubs* Arts; *Style*— Mrs Gillian Hewitt; 10 St Paul's Place, London N1 2QE (☎ 071 226 3125); Austin Reed, 103-113 Regent St, London W1 (☎ 071 734 6789)

HEWITT, Prof, Dr Godfrey Matthew; s of Horace John Hewitt, of Worcester and Hereford, and Violet May, *née* Hann (d 1989); *b* 10 Jan 1940; *Educ* Worcester Cathedral King's Sch, Univ of Birmingham (BSc, PhD, DSc); *m* 23 June 1963 (m dis 1982), Elizabeth June, da of Ivor Cecil Shattock, of 30 Freemantle Rd, Taunton, Somerset; 3 s (Daniel John b 14 July 1965, Matthew Alexander b 27 March 1967, James Justin b 20 May 1968); *Career* Fulbright fell Univ of California 1965-66, visiting fell: Gulbenkian Fndn Lisbon 1970, Aust Nat Univ Canberra 1973-74, Univ of Hawaii 1979; prof UEA 1988- (lectr 1966-75, reader 1975-88); numerous pubns in learned sci jls; memb: SERC Ctee, NERC Ctee, Genetical Soc, Soc Study of Evolution, Euro Soc of Evolution; FIBiol 1975, FLS 1987, FRES; *Books* Animal Cytogenetics-Grasshoppers and Crickets (1979); *Recreations* alpine hiking, jazz, running, cooking; *Style*— Dr Godfrey Hewitt; 25 Camberley Rd, Norwich NR4 6SJ (☎ 0603 58142); School of Biological Sciences, University of East Anglia, Norwich NR4 7TJ (☎ 0603 56161, fax 0603 259492, telex 975334)

HEWITT, His Hon Judge Harold; s of George Trueman Hewitt (d 1958), and Bertha Lillian Hewitt, *née* Teasdale (d 1984); *b* 14 March 1917; *Educ* King James I GS Bishop Auckland; *m* 1946, Doris Mary; 2 s (Christopher, Timothy); *Career* circuit judge 1980-90; *Clubs* Carlton; *Style*— His Hon Harold Hewitt; Longmeadows, Etherley, Bishop Auckland, Co Durham

HEWITT, Jeremy Robert (Jerry); s of Ernest Thomas Hewitt, of Moseley, Birmingham, and Gwendolen Mary, *née* Harris; *b* 7 Sept 1948; *Educ* King Edward VI GS Chelmsford, Hammersmith Sch of Architecture, Univ of Aston Sch of Architecture Birmingham, Architectural Assoc Sch of Architecture (AA Dipl); *m* 1, 7 Aug 1971 (m dis 1987), Angela Denise, da of Raymond Woods; m 2, 1 Nov 1990, Jillian Camelia Deborah Burgess, da of Trevor Ball (d 1990); *Career* architect; Murray Ward & Partners 1972-73, private practice 1973-76, ptnr Patterson & Hewitt 1976-83, dir BBA Patterson Hewitt Ltd 1983-85, dir Patterson Hewitt & Partners Ltd 1985-90, head of Environment Newell & Sorrell Ltd 1990-; finalist Redditch Community Housing Competition 1972, exhibitor Art Into Landscape Exhibition (Serpentine Gallery) 1972; exhibitor RA Summer Exhibition 1981 and 1983; memb Architectural Assoc; *Recreations* flying, books, cinema, theatre, music, art, travel; *Clubs* Chelsea Arts; *Style*— Jerry Hewitt, Esq; 54 Methley St, London SE11 (☎ 071 820 1644)

HEWITT, Col John Michael (Jim); OBE (1981); s of Harry Hewitt (d 1987), and Beatrice Eileen, *née* Goodman (d 1987); *b* 17 June 1936; *Educ* Plymouth Coll, RMA Sandhurst, Army Staff Coll, United States Army Command and General Staff Coll; *m* 14 Aug 1969, Janice Mary, da of Frank Sutcliffe, of 7 New Park Rd, Plympton, Plymouth, Devon; 2 s (James Paul b 14 Oct 1973, Charles Alexander b 13 June 1975); *Career* CO 11 Bn UDR 1979, Lt Col HQ Allied Command Euro Mobile Force 1981, sec to Chief of Staff HQ Allied Forces North Oslo 1984, Divnl Col Prince of Wales Div 1987; dir Br Gear Assoc 1989; FBIM 1989; *Recreations* golf, squash, skiing; *Clubs* Commonwealth Society; *Style*— Col Jim Hewitt, OBE; St James's House, Frederick Rd, Edgbaston, Birmingham B15 1JJ (☎ 021 456 3445, fax 021 456 3161)

HEWITT, Marguerite, Lady; Marguerite; da of Charles Burgess, of Deepdene, Filey; *m* 1940, Maj Sir Joseph Hewitt, 2 Bt (d 1973); *Style*— Marguerite, Lady Hewitt; Lebberston Hall, nr Scarborough

HEWITT, Michael Earling; s of Herbert Erland Hewitt (d 1938), and Dorothy Amelia, *née* Morris; *b* 28 March 1936; *Educ* Christ's Hosp, Merton Coll Oxford (MA), Univ of London (BSc); *m* 10 Aug 1961, Elizabeth Mary Hughes, da of Maj Arnold James Batchelor (d 1956); 1 s (Thomas b 1970), 1 da (Joanna b 1974); *Career* Gunner RA 1955-57; Bank of England: joined 1961, seconded econ advsr Govt Bermuda 1970-74, asst advsr oil 1974-76, fin forecaster 1976-78, advsr fin insts 1981-83 (asst advsr 1979-81), head fin supervision gen div 1984-87, head fin and indust area 1987-88, sr advsr fin and indust 1988-90, dir Central Banking Studies 1990-; memb: EEC Central Bank Gp Experts Money Supply 1976-78, Br Invisible Exports Cncl 1987-90, Dearing Ctee on Making of Accounting Standards 1988, City Advsy Panel City Univ Business Sch 1988-; chm: City EEC Ctee 1987-90, OECD Gp Experts Securities Mkts 1988-90; assoc memb Soc Investment Analysts 1979-; *Recreations* chess, travel, wine; *Style*— Michael Hewitt, Esq; Bank of England, Threadneedle St, London EC2R 8AH (☎ 071 601 4657, fax 071 601 4830, telex 885001)

HEWITT, Sir Nicholas Charles Joseph; 3 Bt (UK 1921); s of Maj Sir Joseph Hewitt, 2 Bt (d 1973); *b* 12 Nov 1947; *m* 1969, Pamela Margaret, da of Geoffrey J M Hunt, TD, of Scalby, Scarborough; 2 s, 1 da; *Heir* s, Charles Edward James Hewitt b 15 Nov 1970; *Style*— Sir Nicholas Hewitt, Bt; Colswayn House, Huttons Ambo, York

HEWITT, Patricia Hope; da of Sir (Cyrus) Lenox Simson Hewitt, OBE, of Sydney, Aust, and (Alison) Hope Hewitt; *b* 2 Dec 1948; *Educ* Girl's GS Canberra, Aust Nat Univ Canberra, Newnham Coll Cambridge (MA), Univ of Sydney (AMusA); *m* 1, 8 Aug 1970 (m dis 1978), (David) Julian Gibson Watt, s of Baron Gibson-Watt, *qv*; m 2, 17 Dec 1981, William Jack Birtles, s of William George Birtles (d 1976), of Shepperton, Middx; 1 s (Nicholas b 1988), 1 da (Alexandra b 1986); *Career* gen sec NCCL 1974-83, policy coordinator to Ldr of the Opposition 1988-89 (press and broadcasting sec 1983-88), dep dir and sr res fell Inst for Public Policy Res 1989; assoc Newnham Coll Cambridge; memb: bd Int League for Human Rights, exec ctee Fabian Soc, Sec of State's Advsy Ctee on the Employment of Women 1977-83; Parly candidate Leicester East 1983; *Books* The Abuse of Power: Civil Liberties in the United Kingdom (1983); Your Second Baby (with Wendy Rose-Neil, 1990); *Recreations* gardening, music, theatre, cooking; *Style*— Ms Patricia Hewitt; 21 Rochester Sq, London NW1 9SA (☎ 071 267 2567); Institute for Public Policy Research, 30-32 Southampton Street, London WC2E 7RA (☎ 071 379 9400)

HEWITT, Dr Penelope Boulton; da of Leslie Frank Hewitt (d 1967), of Cheam, Surrey, and Beryl Boulton (d 1978); *b* 23 July 1938; *Educ* Sutton HS GPDST, Guy's Hosp, Univ of London (MB BS, LRCP); *Career* res anaesthetist Guy's Hosp 1962-63; registrar in anaesthetics 1963-67: Nat Hosp for Nervous Diseases Queen Square London, St Mary's Hosp, Guy's Hosp; conslt anaesthetist Guy's Hosp 1972- (sr registrar 1967-72), recognised teacher in anaesthetics Univ of London 1974-; approved lectr: Central Midwives Bd 1979-83, English Nat Bd 1983-, combined Guy's and St Thomas' Hosp Schs of Midwifery; anaesthetics tutor Faculty of Anaesthetists RCS Guy's Hosp 1980-87, regnl assessor in anaesthetics for confidential enquiries into maternal deaths SE Thames Region Dept of Health 1981-, hon sec and treas SE Thames Soc of Anaesthetics 1984-87, anaesthetic assessor confidential enquiry into perioperative deaths Nuffield Prov Hosp Tst 1985-87, examiner for fellowship examination of the Coll of Anaesthetists 1986-, memb Cncl anaesthetics section RSM (hon sec 1987-89), hon asst sec and ed of proceedings Assoc Dental Anaesthetists 1989-; MRCS 1961, FFARCS 1966; *Books* Emergency Anaesthesia (1986); *Recreations* golf, gardening; *Clubs* Addington Golf; *Style*— Dr Penelope B Hewitt; Department of Anaesthetics, Guy's Hospital, St Thomas's St, London SE1 9RT (☎ 071 955 4051/ 5000)

HEWITT, Peter McGregor; OBE (1967); s of Douglas McGregor Hewitt (d 1984), and Audrey Vera, *née* Walker; *b* 6 Oct 1929; *Educ* De Aston Sch Market Rasen Lincs, Keble Coll Oxford (MA); *m* 23 June 1962, Joyce Marie, da of Robert J Gavin (d 1982); 3 da (Clare b 1963, Katherine (twin) b 1963, Sarah b 1965); *Career* Army 1947-49; HM Overseas Civil Serv 1952-64: Malaya, N Borneo; Dip Serv 1964-71: FO, Shanghai, Canberra; Home Serv 1971-89, regnl dir E Midlands DOE and Dept of Tport 1984-89; *Recreations* cricket, gardening, music; *Clubs* Royal Cwlth Soc; *Style*— Peter Hewitt, Esq, OBE; Dept of the Environment & Transport, Cranbrook House, Cranbrook St, Nottingham NG1 1EY (☎ 0602 476121)

HEWITT, Thomas; s of Thomas Hewitt (d 1981), and Helen, *née* Graham; *b* 10 June 1950; *Educ* Central Sch Jarrow, S Shields Marine and Tech Coll, Gateshead Tech; *Career* engr, energy conservation, civil servant, DoE/Property Servs Agency; treas Friends of Jarrow Hall, tstee St Paul's Jarrow devpt tst; *Recreations* gardening, crosswords, genealogy, DIY, reading; *Style*— Thomas Hewitt, Esq; 65 Underwood Grove, Northburn Grange, Cramlington NE23 9UT (☎ 0610 731848); Dept of Environment, Government Buildings, Broadway West, Gosforth (☎ 091 2857171)

HEWLETT, Hon (John) Richard; s of Baron Hewlett (Life Peer d 1979); *b* 1955; *Educ* Oundle, Bath Acad of Art; *Style*— The Hon Richard Hewlett

HEWLETT, Hon Thomas Anthony; s of Baron Hewlett, CBE (Life Peer, d 1979), and Millicent, *née* Simpson; *b* 31 March 1952; *Educ* Oundle, Magdalene Coll Cambridge (BA, MA); *m* 2 Oct 1980, Jane Elizabeth, da of Brian A Dawson, of Aldeburgh, Suffolk; 2 s (Harry b 30 Dec 1986, Charles b (twin) 30 Dec 1986), 2 da (Emily b 14 Feb 1984, Georgina b 24 July 1985); *Career* dir: Anchor Chemical Gp plc 1976-83, V Berg & Sons Ltd 1986-; vice- pres Morgan Guaranty Tst 1974-84; owner Portland Gallery 1985-; Freeman City of London, Liveryman Worshipful Co of Tin Plate Workers; *Books* Cadell - A Scottish Colourist (1988); *Recreations* golf, tennis, shooting; *Clubs* Aldeburgh Golf, Denham Golf, Vanderbilt; *Style*— The Hon Thomas Hewlett; Kyson House, Woodbridge, Suffolk IP12 4DN (☎ 03943 3441); Portland Gallery, 2 Holland Park Terrace, Portland Rd, London W11 4ND (☎ 071 221 0294)

HEWS, Richard Greenslade; s of Gordon Rodney Donald Hews (d 1988), of Canterbury, Kent, and Renee Maureen, *née* Smith; *b* 4 Jan 1948; *Educ* King's Sch Canterbury, RMA Sandhurst; *m* 4 Oct 1980, Diana Elizabeth, da of Maj Gen Mervyn Jones, CB, CBE; *Career* cmmnd 14/20 Kings Hussars 1970, Royal Armoured Corp Parachute Sqdn 1975-76, GSO 3 HQ NI 1978-80, advertisement mangr Surrey Advertiser Group 1980-84; account mangr: Eurocenter Communications 1984-86, Streets Financial Strategy 1986-88; dir Streets Communications Ltd 1989- (assoc dir 1988-89); *Recreations* tennis, gardening, antiques; *Style*— Richard Hews, Esq; Streets Communications Ltd, 18 Red Lion Court, Fleet Street, London EC4A 3HT (☎ 071 353 1090)

HEWSON, Michael John; s of George Alfred Hewson (d 1959), of Portsmouth, and Marjorie Phyllis, *née* Hall; *b* 17 March 1944; *Educ* Southern GS Portsmouth, MBA; *m* 21 July 1970, Sharland Elisabeth, da of Frank Templeman, of Grimsby; 1 s (Martin Philip b 1970); *Career* Nationwide Anglia Building Society branch mangr Oxford 1982-85 (Northampton 1976-81, Boston Lincs 1973-75), regnl mangr S E London 1988-90 (Surrey 1987, S E 1986), area mangr South 1990-91, quality conslt 1991-; FCBSI 1973, MBIM 1973; *Recreations* mountaineering, rock climbing; *Style*— Michael Hewson, Esq

HEWSON, Paul; *see*: Bono

HEWSON, Roy Gregory; s of Alfred Bertram Hewson, ISM (d 1981), of London, and Rosa Elder, *née* Eggleton (d 1964); *b* 27 Aug 1930; *Educ* East Barnet GS, City of London Coll; *m* 16 April 1955, Pamela Noreen, da of Lawson Hartley Birch (d 1960), of Leek, Staffordshire; 1 s (Paul b 1961), 2 da (Claire b 1958, Nicola b 1970); *Career* Nat Serv RAF 1952-54; mgmnt trainee GEC Ltd 1946-52, sec Britannia Bldg Soc 1985- (joined 1954, exec appt 1965-); pres local branch CBSI; FCBSI 1963, FCIS 1973; *Recreations* walking, swimming, gardening; *Clubs* Rotary; *Style*— Roy Hewson, Esq; Newton House, PO Box 20, Leek, Staffs ST13 5RG (☎ 0538 399 399, fax 0538 399 149)

HEXHAM AND NEWCASTLE, Bishop of 1974-; Rt Rev Hugh Lindsay; s of William Stanley Lindsay (d 1966), and Mary Ann, *née* Warren (d 1958); *b* 20 June 1927; *Educ* St Cuthbert's Coll Ushaw Durham; *Career* RAF 1945-48; priest 1953, asst diocesan sec Hexham and Newcastle 1953-59; asst priest: St Lawrence Newcastle 1953-54, St Matthew Ponteland 1954-59; diocesan sec 1959-69, auxiliary bishop of Hexham & Newcastle 1969-74; *Recreations* walking; *Style*— The Rt Rev the Bishop of Hexham and Newcastle; Bishop's House, East Denton Hall, 800 West Road, Newcastle upon Tyne NE5 2BJ (☎ 091 228 0003)

HEY, Prof John Denis; s of George Brian Hey, of Adlington, Cheshire, and Elizabeth Hamilton, *née* Burns; *b* 26 Sept 1944; *Educ* Manchester GS, Univ of Cambridge (BA), Univ of Edinburgh (MSc); *m* 18 Oct 1968, Marlene Robertson, da of Thomas Bissett (d 1958), of Perth; 1 s (Thomas b 1981), 2 da (Clare b 1979, Rebecca b 1984); *Career* econometrician Hoare & Co Stockbrokers 1968-69; lectr in econs: Univ of Durham 1969-73, Univ of St Andrews 1974-75; prof of econs and statistics Univ of York 1984- (lectr in social and econ statistics 1975-81, sr lectr 1981-84), ed Economic Journal 1986-, co-dir Centre for Experimental Econs 1986-, author of articles for numerous jls; memb: RES, AEA; *Books* Statistics in Economics (1974), Uncertainty in Microeconomics (1979), Britain in Context (1979), Economics in Disequilibrium (1981), Data in Doubt (1984); *Recreations* squash, walking, eating; *Style*— Prof John Hey; 49 Monkgate, York, N Yorks (☎ 0904 621 333); Dept of Economics and Related Studies, University of York, Heslington, York, N Yorks YO1 5DD (☎ 0904 433 786, fax 0904 275 433, telex 57933)

HEYCOCK, Hon Clayton Rees; o s of Baron Heycock, CBE (Life Peer, d 1990), and (Elizabeth) Olive, *née* Rees; *b* 1941; *Educ* Univ of Wales Swansea (MSc 1970), Univ of Leicester (MA 1971); *m* 1964, Lynda, *née* Williams; 2 da (Alyson Sian b 1970, Rebecca Louise b 1973); *Career* sec Welsh Jt Educn Ctee; *Style*— The Hon Clayton Heycock; 6 Tanygroes Place, Taibach, Port Talbot, W Glam

HEYDERMAN, Dr Eadie; da of Reuben Kirstein (d 1969), of London, and Sarah, *née* Haskell (d 1967); *b* 8 Oct 1931; *Educ* Central Foundation Sch for Girls London, UCH Dental Sch (BDS LDS RCS), UCH Med Sch (MB BS), St Thomas Hosp Med Sch London (MD); *m* 29 April 1956, Dennis Manfred Heyderman, s of Leopold Heyderman (d 1966), of London; 2 s (Robert Simon b 16 July 1960, John Bernard b 23 Sept 1962), 2 da (Emma Louise b 21 March 1966, Laura Jane b 8 Sept 1967); *Career* pt/t dental practice 1953; UCH: dental house surgn 1953, hon clinical asst (Dental Sch) 1958-59, house surgn 1959; house physician N Middx Hosp 1959-60; fndr (with husband) John Dobbie Educational Toy Stores 1963-73 (memb Ctee and lectr in design Design Centre); John Marshall fell (later Grahame scholar in morbid anatomy) UCH 1974-75, clinical scientist and hon pathologist Ludwig Inst for Cancer Res Royal Marsden Hosp Sutton 1975-79, locum res asst (clinical) and hon sr registrar in pathology St Mary's Hosp 1979, sr lectr and hon sr registrar Dept of Histopathology St Thomas's Hosp Med Sch 1979-80 (sr lectr and hon conslt 1980-86), reader in histopathology and hon conslt UMDS St Thomas's Hosp 1986-; memb Editorial Bd: Jl of Clinical Pathology 1979-84, Jl of Immunological Methods 1989-88; Bristol Myers Travelling Fellowship 1986; former examiner at various univs incl: Cambridge, London, Bristol and Surrey; papers presented in many countries incl: USA, Sweden, W Germany, Brazil, Holland and Switzerland; author of numerous papers and chapters in books and lectr on main res field of Immunology to Chemistry in Cancer; memb: Cncl Assoc of Clinical Pathologists 1984-89 (pres SE branch 1989-), Pathological Soc of GB and Ireland, Int Acad of Pathology, Assoc of Clinical Pathologists, Br Assoc for Cancer Res, Br Soc of Endocrine Pathologists, Pulmonary Pathology Club, RSM; *Recreations* theatre, reading, visual arts; *Style*— Dr Eadie Heyderman

HEYES, John Graham; s of Thomas Henry Heyes, of Edinburgh, and Margaret Sullivan Heyes; *b* 11 March 1945; *Educ* George Watson's Boys' Coll Edinburgh, Univ of Edinburgh (BDS); *m* 5 Aug 1972, Zena Noreen; 1 s (Graham b 1974), 2 da (Helen b 1976, Siân 1985); *Career* sr registrar Liverpool Dental Hosp 1977-80, conslt and head Orthodontic Dept South Clwyd 1980-; memb: English Heritage, Woodland Tst; govr Welshampton Sch; FDSRCS 1974, DOrth RCS 1975, DDOrth RCPS Glasgow 1975; *Recreations* swimming, beekeeping, family man; *Style*— John Heyes, Esq; Wrexham Maelor Hospital, Croesnewydd Rd, Wrexham, Clwyd LL13 7TD

HEYGATE, Sir George Lloyd; 5 Bt (UK 1831); s of Sir John Edward Nourse Heygate, 4 Bt (d 1976); *b* 28 Oct 1936; *Educ* Repton, Trinity Cambridge; *m* 1960, Hildegard Mathilde, da of August Anton Kleinjohann, of Wildstrasse 69, Duisburg, Germany; twin da (Joanna b 1977, Catherine b 1977); *Heir* bro, Richard Heygate; *Career* slr 1965; *Style*— Sir George Heygate, Bt; Willow Grange, Wissett, Halesworth, Suffolk

HEYGATE, Richard Gage; s of Sir John Edward Nourse Heygate, 4 Bt (d 1976), and hp of bro, Sir George Lloyd Heygate, 5 Bt; *b* 30 Jan 1940; *Educ* Repton, Balliol Oxford; *m* 1968 (m dis 1972), Carol Rosemary, da of late Cdr Richard Michell, RN, of Leith House, Amberley, Sussex; *Style*— Richard Heygate, Esq

HEYGATE, (Arthur) Robert; JP, DL (Northants 1983); s of Arthur Robert Heygate (d 1963), and Frances Amelia Heygate (d 1958), of Stone House, Bugbrooke; descendant of Thomas Heygate, of Highgate, Essex and Hayes, Middx, who in 1562 was given land in Northants; *b* 15 March 1914; *Educ* Oakham Sch; *m* 1940, Phyllis Mary, da of Rev John Foster Williams; 1 s (Robert), 1 da (Rosemary); *Career* landowner, farmer, flour miller; *Recreations* shooting; *Style*— A Robert Heygate, Esq, JP, DL; Lichborough Hall, Towcester, Northants NN12 8JF (0327 830240); Bugbrooke Mills, Northampton NN7 3QH (☎ 0604 830381)

HEYHOE FLINT, Rachael; *née* Heyhoe; MBE (1971); da of Geoffrey Heyhoe (d 1972), of Penn, Wolverhampton, and Roma Kathleen, *née* Crocker (d 1978); Heyhoe is an Anglo-Saxon farming name derived from Hey Mow; *b* 11 June 1939; *Educ* Wolverhampton Girls' HS, Dartford Coll of Physical Educn (Dip Phys Ed); *m* 1 Nov 1971, Derrick Flint, s of Benjamin Flint, of Underwood, Notts; 1 s (Benjamin b 8 June 1974); *Career* Women's Cricket Int England 1960-83, Capt 1966-77, scored 179 v Aust (Oval) 1976 (world record score for England, fourth highest score by woman in test); Women's Hockey Int England 1964; journalist; Guild of Professional Toastmasters Best After Dinner Speaker 1972; *Books* Fair Play, History of Women's Cricket (1976), Heyhoe (autobiography 1978); *Recreations* golf, squash; *Clubs* South Staffs Golf, Wig and Pen, Sportwriters' Assoc, La Manga (Spain), Patshull Park Golf and Country (Wolverhampton); *Style*— Mrs Rachael Heyhoe Flint, MBE; Danescroft, Wergs Rd, Tettenhall, Wolverhampton, Staffs (☎ 0902 752103)

HEYLIN, Angela Christine Mary (Mrs Maurice Minzly); da of Bernard Heylin (d 1985), and Ruth Victoria Heylin; *b* 17 Sept 1943; *Educ* Apsley GS, Watford Coll; *m* 13 March 1971, Maurice Minzly, s of Salem Minzly (d 1974); 1 s (James b 1982); *Career* dir FJ Lyons; Charles Barker Lyons: dir 1976, jt md 1980, chief exec 1984; dir Charles Barker Gp 1984 (chm and chief exec 1988); tstee Int Fndn for PR Studies 1987, chm PRCA 1990; FInstM 1987, FIPR 1987; *Recreations* theatre, piano, entertaining; *Style*— Miss Angela Heylin; 46 St Augustine's Rd, London NW1 9RN (☎ 071 485 4815); Charles Barker, 30 Farringdon St, London EC4A 4EA (☎ 071 634 1011, fax 071 236 0170, car 0860 318 205, telex 883588/887928)

HEYMAN, Sir Horace William; *b* 13 March 1912; *Educ* Ackworth Sch, Technische Hochschule Darmstadt, Univ of Birmingham (BSc); *m* 1, 1939; 1 s (Timothy), 1 da (Helen Thompson); m 2, 1966, Dorothy Forster Atkinson; *Career* chm English Industrial Estates Corporation 1970-77, pres Northumbria Tourist Bd 1983-86, govr Newcastle-on-Tyne Poly 1974-86 (vice-chm 1983-86, hon fell 1985), dir various UK and European engrg and travel cos; FIEE, FRSA, CEng; kt 1976; *Style*— Sir Horace Heyman; 20 Whitburn Hall, Whitburn, Sunderland SR6 7JQ

HEYMANN, Bernard; s of Joseph Heymann (d 1954) and Luise Irene Heymann (d 1977); *b* 19 Jan 1937; *Educ* Quintin Sch London, Univ of Durham (BA); *m* 10 Sept 1966, Anne Catherine Valentine, da of Melville Elphinstone Thomson; 1 s (dec'd), 1 da (Anne Belinda b 29 July 1968); *Career* dir: Leopold Joseph & Sons Ltd 1985-88 (conslt 1976-85), Highland Forest Products plc 1986-88, Location of Indust Bureau Ltd 1986-90, Milner Delvaux Ltd 1987-; FCA, FBIM; *Recreations* gardening; *Clubs* Old Quintinian; *Style—* Bernard Heymann, Esq; 5 Ranulf Rd, London NW2 2BT; 2 Scott House, Sekforde St, London EC1R OHH (☎ 071 490 3464, fax 071 490 4202)

HEYMANN, Prof Franz Ferdinand; s of Paul Gerhard Heymann (d 1981), and Magdalena Petronella, *née* Botha (d 1937); *b* 17 Aug 1924; *Educ* Ficksburg HS SA, Univ of Cape Town (BSc), Univ of London (PhD); *m* 15 Dec 1950, Marie, da of Alfred William Ewart Powell (d 1966), of Swinton, Lancs; *Career* lectr Cape Town 1945-47, res engr Metropolitan Vickers 1947-50; UCL: asst lectr 1950-53, lectr 1953-60, reader 1960-66, prof 1966-75, Quain Prof of physics and head of dept 1975-87, emeritus prof 1987-; author of numerous scientific papers in professional jls; memb numerous nat scientific ctees; CPhys, FInstP; *Recreations* music, gemmology, gardening; *Style—* Prof Franz Heymann; Dept of Physics & Astronomy, University College London, Gower St, London WC1E 6BT

HEYNES, David Gordon; s of Gordon Albert Arthur Heynes; *b* 17 April 1945; *Educ* Charterhouse; *m* 1968, Jennifer Jane, *née* Dreyer; 2 s, 1 da; *Career* CA, Hill Samuel and Co Ltd 1969-71, chief exec Park Place Investmts Ltd 1981 (dir 1972-); *Recreations* shooting and motor racing; *Style—* David Heynes, Esq; Newton Lodge, Buckland, Faringdon, Oxfordshire 036787 225

HEYWOOD, Francis Melville; s of Rt Rev Bernard Oliver Francis Heywood (d 1960), Bishop of Southwell, Hull and Ely, and Maude Marion, *née* Lempriere (d 1957); *b* 1 Oct 1908; *Educ* Haileybury, Gonville and Caius Coll Cambridge (BA, MA); *m* 28 Dec 1937, Dorothea Kathleen (d 1983), da of Sir Basil Edgar Mayhew, KBE (d 1966), of Felthorpe Hall, Norwich; 1 s (Simon b 1945, d 1985), 2 da (Susan, Janion), 1 adopted s (Michael b 1940); *Career* asst master Haileybury 1931-35, fell asst tutor and praelector Trinity Hall Cambridge 1935-39, master of Marlborough 1939-52, warden of Lord Mayor Treloar Coll 1952-69; *Books* A Load of New Rubbish (1985); *Recreations* formerly: cricket, rugby, squash, gardening; now walking; *Style—* F M Heywood, Esq; 30 The Bayle, Folkestone, Kent (☎ 0303 52366)

HEYWOOD, John Edwin; s of George Edwin Heywood (d 1971), of Tring, Hertfordshire, and Vera, *née* Heron (d 1967); *b* 8 April 1938; *Educ* Lower Sch of John Lyon Harrow; *m* 2 June 1962, Ann Patricia, da of William Hiram Wootton (d 1987), of West Bridgford, Nottingham; 4 da (Susan b 1964, Wendy b 1966, Helen b 1967, Katherine b 1971); *Career* Nat Serv REME attached to Army Air Corps 1960-62; D Napier and Son Ltd Acton 1955-60, Mission Aviation Fellowship in UK Kenya and Ethiopia 1963-68, chief engr Rogers Aviation Ltd Cranfield 1968-69, dep chief engr Safari Air Services Nairobi Kenya 1969-73, airworthiness surveyor CAA in Eng and Scot 1973-84, md J E Heywood Ltd Glenrothes 1984-89, dir of engrg Air Service Training Ltd 1989-90, conslt aeronautical engr 1990-; chm Nairobi branch Soc of Licensed Aircraft Engrs and Technologists 1971-73; CEng 1974, FRAeS 1987; *Books* Light Aircraft Inspection (1977), Light Aircraft Maintenance (1983); *Recreations* photography, hillwalking; *Style—* John Heywood, Esq; 2 Birch Place, Perth PH1 1DX (☎ 0738 20180)

HEYWOOD, John Kenneth; *b* 29 Jan 1947; *Educ* Shebbear Coll, UCL (LLB), INSEAD Fontainebleau; *m* 1976, Susan Ann Heywood; 2 s (James b 1980, William b 1983), 1 da (Sophie b 1990); *Career* joined Price Waterhouse 1968 (ptnr 1980-); FCA; *Recreations* golf, tennis; *Style—* John Heywood, Esq; Price Waterhouse, Southwark Towers, 32 London Bridge St, London SE1 9SY (☎ 071 939 3000)

HEYWOOD, Keith Alban; s of John Alban Heywood (d 1955), and Kittie Elizabeth, *née* Rennie; *b* 7 Oct 1948; *Educ* The Royal Masonic Sch; *m* 26 Aug 1968, Vivien, da of Alan Irwin (d 1979); 1 s (Jason b 1972), 1 da (Kirsten b 1970); *Career* CA; Crane Christmas & Co 1965-, ptnr Jeffreys Ubysz and Co 1975, slr practitioner Heywood & Co 1982, ptnr Brett Jenkins & Ptnrs 1987, fin conslt 1988, sole practitioner Keith A Heywood FCA 1990; former sec Old Masonians Assoc; FCA; *Recreations* painting, reading, walking, classic car restoration; *Clubs* The Royal Soc of St George, Silverstone Racing; *Style—* Keith Heywood, Esq; 10 Green End St, Aston Clinton, Aylesbury, Bucks HP22 5JE (☎ 0296 630114)

HEYWOOD, Peter; s and h of Sir Oliver Kerr Heywood, 5 Bt; *b* 10 Dec 1947; *Educ* Bryanston, Univ of Oxford; *m* 1970, Jacqueline Anne, da of Sir Robert Frederick Hunt, CBE, *qv*; 2 da; *Career* account director; *Style—* Peter Heywood, Esq; 64 Newbridge Rd, Weston, Bath, Avon BA1 3LA

HEYWOOD, Hon Mrs (Rosalind Louise Balfour); *née* Bruce; er da of 3 Baron Aberdare, GBE (d 1957); *b* 11 Nov 1923; *m* 25 Sept 1956, Benjamin Coote Heywood, s of late Col Henry Frank Heywood, MC; 2 da; *Career* served 1943-46 WRNS; *Style—* The Hon Mrs Heywood; 1 Elm Park Rd, SW3 6BD (☎ 071 352 0429)

HEYWOOD, Lady Sophia Hester; *née* Meade; 6 and yst da of 6 Earl of Clanwilliam (d 1989); *b* 14 Oct 1963; *m* 22 Dec 1990, Jonathan G Heywood, s of Brig Anthony Heywood, of Monkton House, Monkton Deverill, Wilts; *Style—* The Lady Sophia Heywood

HEYWOOD-LONSDALE, Hon Mrs (Jean Helen); *née* Rollo; da of 12 Lord Rollo; *b* 2 Dec 1926; *m* 1952, Lt-Col Robert Heywood-Lonsdale, MBE, MC, DL, Gren Gds, s of John Heywood-Lonsdale, DSO, OBE, TD, JP, sometime MFH The Bicester, and Hon Helen Annesley, 3 da of 11 Viscount Valentia; 1 s, 3 da; *Style—* The Hon Mrs Heywood-Lonsdale; Mount Farm, Churchill, Oxon

HEYWORTH, James David; s of James Heyworth, of Read, nr Burnley, and Margaret, *née* Myerscough; *b* 18 July 1950; *Educ* St Mary's Coll Blackburn, Univ of London (LLB); *m* 1, 26 July 1975 (m dis), Margaret Helen; 1 s (James Edward Watson b 1977); m 2, 23 Dec 1982, Hayden Boethman; 1 s (Christopher David b 1983); *Career* slr; ptnr Donald Race and Newton; *Recreations* shooting, farming, working gun dogs; *Style—* James Heyworth, Esq; Harwes Farm, Black Lane Ends, Colne, Lancaster (☎ 0282 864383); 59 Albert Rd, Colne (☎ 0282 864500, fax 0282 869579)

HEYWORTH, John; s of Lt-Col Reginald Francis Heyworth (ka 1941), and Hon Moyra, *née* Marjoribanks, da of 3 Baron Tweedmouth; *b* 21 Aug 1925; *Educ* Eton; *m* 10 June 1950, Susan Elizabeth, da of Sir John Henry Burder, ED, of Burford, Oxford; 1 s (Reginald b 1961), 3 da (Caroline b 1952, Jane b 1953, Joanna b 1957); *Career* Royal Dragoons NW Europe 1943-47; farmer and owner of Wild Life Park; High Sheriff Oxon 1962; *Style—* John Heyworth, Esq; Bradwell Grove, Burford, Oxford (☎ 099 382 3154)

HEYWORTH, Baroness; Lois; da of Stevenson Dunlop, of Woodstock, Ontario, Canada; *m* 1924, 1 and last Baron Heyworth (d 1974); *Style—* The Rt Hon the Lady Heyworth; 20 Sussex Sq, London W2

HEZLET, Vice Adm Sir Arthur Richard; KBE (1964), CB (1961), DSO (and Bar 1944, 1945), DSC (1941); s of Maj-Gen Robert Knox Hezlet, CB, CBE, DSO (d 1963); *b* 7 April 1914; *Educ* RNC Dartmouth, RNC Greenwich; *m* 1948, Anne Joan Patricia, *née* Clark; 2 adopted da; *Career* served WWII submarines, dir RN Staff Coll Greenwich 1956-57, Rear Adm 1959, Flag Offr Submarines 1959-61, Flag Offr Scotland and NI 1961-64, Vice Adm 1962, ret 1964; area pres Royal Br Legion NI, a vice pres RNLI; *Books* The Submarine and Sea Power (1967), Aircraft and Sea Power (1970), Electron and Sea Power (1975), The B Specials (1972); *Clubs* Army and Navy, Royal Ocean Racing; *Style—* Vice Adm Sir Arthur Hezlet, KBE, CB, DSO, DSC; Bovagh House, Aghadowey, Co Londonderry, N Ireland BT51 4AU (☎ 0265 868 206)

HIBBARD, Prof Bryan Montague; s of Montague Reginald Hibbard (d 1972), of Norfolk, and Muriel Irene, *née* Wilson (d 1989); *b* 24 April 1926; *Educ* Queen Elizabeth's Sch Barnet, St Bartholomew's Hosp Med Coll and Univ of London (MB BS, MD), Univ of Liverpool (PhD); *m* 30 July 1955, Elizabeth Donald, da of Dr James Campbell Grassie (d 1976), of Aberdeen; *Career* sr lectr Univ of Liverpool 1963-73, prof and head of Dept of Obstetrics and Gynaecology Univ of Wales Coll of Med 1973-; memb Advsy Sub Ctee in Obstetrics and Gynaecology Welsh Office 1974-, central assessor and memb Editorial Bd Confidential Enquiries into Maternal Deaths DHSS 1988-; memb: Ctee on Safety of Meds 1980-84, Maternity Servs Advsy Ctee DHSS 1980-85, Ctee Gynaecological Cytology DHSS 1983-89, S Glamorgan Health Authy 1983-88, Cncl RCOG 1982-88 and 1989- (curator of instruments 1986-, chm Library Ctee 1987-); pres: Welsh Obstetric and Gynaecological Soc 1985-86, Meds Cmmn 1986-89; chm Jt Standing Advsy Ctee on Obstetric Anaesthesia 1988-, RCOG and Royal Coll of Midwives 1988-; FRCOG 1965 (memb 1956); *Books* Principles of Obstetrics (1988), The Obstetric Forceps (1988); *Recreations* 18th century glass, fell walking, coarse gardening; *Clubs* RSM; *Style—* Prof Bryan Hibbard; The Clock Hse, Cathedral Close, Llandaff, Cardiff CF5 2ED; Dept of Obstetrics & Gynaecology, Univ of Wales Coll of Medicine, Health Park, Cardiff CF4 4XN (☎ 0222 747747)

HIBBERD, Dr Joan Louise; da of Peter Nalty (d 1943), of Queensland, Aust, and Jean, *née* Byrne (d 1987); *b* 28 Nov 1930; *Educ* Sacre Coeur Sch Melbourne, Univ of Melbourne, Univ of Toronto (LDS), Dept of Oral Med and Periodontology Royal London Hosp Med Coll Univ of London (PhD); *m* 1, 1953, Prof John Hunt Hibberd (d 1972); 6 s (Peter Hunt b 1954, Michael John b 1955, Graeme Robert b 1957, John Anthony b 1965, Christopher Richard b 1966, Robert James b 1970), 2 da (Jennifer Ann b 1959, Catherine Mary b 1969); m 2, 1984, Geoffrey Edwards (d 1990); *Career* conslt Queen Elizabeth Centre for Handicapped 1964-67, in gen practice 1964-67 then practice with Medical Arts Bd Toronto, assoc in dentistry Univ of Toronto Ontario 1975-77; Royal London Hosp Med Coll: lectr and clinical teacher in periodontology 1978-81, dep dir Sch of Dental Hygiene 1981-82, hon lectr 1981-83; in practice in periodontics Harley St 1983-; Specialist in Periodontics award RCDS Canada 1981; fell Int Coll of Dentistry 1985; memb: Canadian Dental Assoc 1975, FDI 1975, Int Assoc for Dental Res 1980, BDA 1981, Br Soc of Periodontology 1981, Canadian Acad of Periodontology 1981; FRSM; *Recreations* family, fishing, swimming, reading; *Clubs* Royal Canadian Yacht; *Style—* Dr Joan Hibberd; 70 Harley Street, London W1 (☎ 071 580 4082)

HIBBERT, Christopher; MC (1945); s of Canon H V Hibbert (d 1980); *b* 5 March 1924; *Educ* Radley, Oriel Coll Oxford (MA); *m* 1948, Susan, da of Rayner Piggford (d 1978); 2 s (James, Tom), 1 da (Kate); *Career* Capt London Irish Rifles Italy 1944-45; ptnr firm of land agents and auctioneers 1948-59; author 1959-; Heinemann award for Lit 1962, McColvin medal 1989; FRSL, FRGS; *Books Incl:* The Destruction of Lord Raglan (1961), Corunna (1961), Benito Mussolini (1962), The Battle of Arnhem (1962), The Court at Windsor (1964), The Roots of Evil (1964), Agincourt (1965), Garibaldi and his Enemies (1966), The Making of Charles Dickens (1967), London: Biography of a City (1969), The Dragon Wakes: China and the West (1970), The Personal History of Samuel Johnson (1971), George IV (2 vols 1972, 1973), The Rise and Fall of the House of Medici (1974), Edward VII (1976), The Great Mutiny: India 1857 (1978), The French Revolution (1980), Rome: Biography of a City (1985), The English: A Social History (1986), The Grand Tour (1987), Venice: The Biography of a City (1988), The Encyclopaedia of Oxford (ed, 1988), The Virgin Queen: The Personal History of Elizabeth I (1990), Redcoats and Rebels: The War for America, 1770-1781 (1990); *Recreations* cooking, gardening, travel; *Clubs* Army and Navy, Garrick; *Style—* Christopher Hibbert, Esq, MC; 6 Albion Place, West Street, Henley-on-Thames, Oxfordshire

HIBBERT, (Caroline) Maria; da of Sir John Lucas-Tooth, 2 Bt, *qv*; *b* 12 May 1956; *Educ* St Paul's Girls' Sch, Oxford Poly (BA); *m* 19 April 1980, William John Hibbert, s of Sir Reginald Hibbert, KCMG, of Machynlleth, Powis; 2 da (Cosima Mary b 1984, Clover Frances b 1988); *Career* ed Compliance Case Law, previously dir Capel-Cure Myers Capital Mgmnt; *Style—* Mrs Maria Hibbert; 39 Lancaster Rd, London W11 (☎ 071 727 2807)

HIBBERT, Sir Reginald Alfred; GCMG (1981, KCMG 1979, CMG 1966); s of Alfred Hibbert, of Sawbridgeworth; *b* 21 Feb 1922; *Educ* Queen Elizabeth's Sch Barnet, Worcester Coll Oxford; *m* 1949, Ann Alun, da of His Honour Sir Alun Pugh (d 1971), of Dunsfold, Surrey; 2 s, 1 da; *Career* served WWII, SOE and 4 Hussars (Albania and Italy); FO 1946-, served: Bucharest, Vienna, Guatemala, Ankara, Brussels; chargé d'affaires Ulaan Bator (Mongolian People's Republic) 1964-66, res fell Univ of Leeds 1966-67, Political Advsr's Office Singapore 1967-69, political advsr to C-in-C Far East 1970-71, min Bonn 1972-75, asst under-sec state FCO 1975-76, dep under-sec 1976-79, ambass France 1979-82, ret 1982; dir Ditchley Fndn 1982-87, chm Franco-Br Soc 1990-; visiting fell Nuffield Coll Oxford 1984-88; hon res fell Univ Coll Swansea; *Publications* The Albanian National Liberation Struggle: The Bitter Victory (1991); *Clubs* Reform; *Style—* Sir Reginald Hibbert, GCMG; Frondeg, Pennal, Machynlleth, Powys SY20 9JX (☎ 0654 791220)

HIBBERT, William John; s of Sir Reginald Hibbert, GCMG, of Machynlleth, Powys, and Ann Alun, *née* Pugh; *b* 23 Feb 1957; *Educ* Charterhouse, Worcester Coll Oxford (BA); *m* 19 April 1980, (Caroline) Maria, da of Sir John Lucas-Tooth, 2 Bt, of East Hagbourne, Oxon; 2 da (Cosima b 1984, Clover b 1988); *Career* called to the Bar Inner Temple 1979; *Style—* William Hibbert, Esq; 39 Lancaster Rd, London W11 1QJ (☎ 071 727 2807); 9 Devereux Court, London WC2R 3JJ (☎ 071 353 0924, fax 071 353 2221)

HIBBITT, Brian Leslie; s of Edgar Bennett Hibbitt (d 1977), and Kathleen Marion, *née* Groom (d 1965); *b* 15 July 1938; *Educ* SW Essex County Tech Sch, London Coll of Printing; *m* 1963, Jill Mavis, da of Albert Henry Oakley (d 1983); 2 s (Timothy John b 1964, Andrew James b 1968); *Career* md: Greenaway Harrison Ltd 1984-89, Turnergraphic Ltd 1989-; chm Br Printing Industs Fedn Industl Rels Ctee SE Region 1986-; *Recreations* local affairs, gardening, theatre; *Style—* Brian L Hibbitt, Esq; Tharance House, Priors Wood, Crowthorne, Berkshire RG11 6BZ (☎ 0344 772215); Winchester Rd, Basingstoke, Hants RG22 4AA (☎ 0256 59252, fax 0256 51501)

HIBBITT, Dr Kenneth George; s of Reginald Ennever Hibbitt (d 1967), of Bristol, Avon, and Helen Grace, *née* Millard (d 1974); *b* 12 Sept 1928; *Educ* St Brendan's Coll Bristol, Univ of Bristol Sch of Veterinary Sci (BVSc), Univ of Bristol Dept of Physiology (PhD); *m* 1 Sept 1962, Helen Teresa, da of Alfred Henry James Bown, OBE (d 1957), of Sunderland; 1 s (Richard b 12 Feb 1969), 1 da (Wendy b 20 May 1967); *Career* gen vet practice 1954-57, res and lectr dept of physiology Univ of Bristol 1957-62; Inst for Res on Animal Diseases Compton Newbury Berks: dep head of biochem 1962-72, head of Dept of Immunology and Parisitology 1972-85, head of Div of Immunopathology 1985-88, ret 1988; memb: Govrg Body Schs of St Helen and St Katharine Abingdon Oxon, St Helens Tst, Biochem Soc 1962; sometime chm

Steventon branch Wantage Constituency Cons Assoc; MRCVS 1954, memb BVA 1954, MRCVS 1954, AVTRW 1964; *Books* Production Disease in Farm Animals (co-ed with Payne and Sansom, 1973); *Recreations* walking, gardening, music, theatre; *Clubs* Farmers', Veterinary Res London; *Style*— Dr Kenneth Hibbitt; Whitecleave House, Burrington, Umberleigh, North Devon EX37 9JN (☎ 07693 468)

HICHENS, Antony Peverell; RD; s of Lt Cdr Robert Peverell Hichens, DSO and bar, DSC and two bars, RNVR, and Catherine Gilbert Enys; *b* 10 Sept 1936; *Educ* Stowe, Magdalen Coll Oxford, Univ of Pennsylvania; *m* 1963, Sczerina Neomi, da of Dr F T J Hobday; 1 da; *Career* Nat Serv Midshipman RNR 1954-56, ret as Lt Cdr 1969; called to the Bar Inner Temple, dep md Redland Ltd 1979 (fin dir 1972), md fin Consolidated Gold Fields plc 1981-89; chm: Caradon plc 1987-89, Y J Lovell (Holdings) plc 1990, MB Caradon plc 1990; dir: Greenfriar Investment plc 1985, Candover Investment plc 1989, SW Electricity plc 1990, Courtaulds Textiles plc 1990; *Recreations* travel, shooting, wine; *Clubs* City of London, Naval and Mil; *Style*— Antony Hichens, Esq; Slape Manor, Netherbury, Nr Bridport, Dorset (☎ 0308 88232); 55 Onslow Gardens, London SW10 (☎ 071 373 7355)

HICK, Graeme Ashley; s of John Douglas Baskerville Hick, of Trelawney Estate, PO Box 20, Trelawney, Zimbabwe, and Eva Francis Lister, *née* Noble; *b* 23 May 1966; *Educ* Prince Edward Boys' HS Harare Zimbabwe; *Career* cricketer; achievements incl: thousand runs before end of May 1989, highest individual innings 405 not out, youngest player to play in World Cup; *Style*— Graeme Hick, Esq

HICKEY, (James) Kevin; MBE (1987); s of James Francis Hickey (d 1972), of Blackpool, and Mary Veronica, *née* Queenan; *b* 25 July 1941; *Educ* St Joseph's Coll Blackpool, De La Salle Coll Middleton, St Mary's Coll Twickenham; *m* Kyra Marjorie, da of George C Collen; 2 s (Sean Francis b 11 May 1965, Adrian Kevin b 12 April 1966), 1 da (Katherine Kyra b 24 Nov 1969); *Career* sports coach and administrator; teacher 1962-69, sr nat coach ABA 1969-73, nat coach and dir of coaching 1973-89, tech dir BOA 1989-; vice chm Euro Coaches Fedn 1982-89, chm Br Assoc of Nat Coaches 1986-89, dir Mgmnt Bd Nat Coaching Fndn (former chm Tech Ctee); memb: Grants Ctee Sports Aid Fndn, Cncl Br Inst of Sports Coaches, World Safety Cmmn 1986-89; contrib to various coaching gps incl Coaching Review Panel 1989-90, lectured worldwide; conceived and implemented: Schs ABA Standards Scheme, Golden Gloves Award; sporting achievements: rugby and athletics co youth player, represented London Colls rugby and athletics, amateur boxing champion 1955-57; coaching achievements: coached GB boxing team Olympic Games 1972, 1976, 1980, 1984, 1988 (total 7 medals), coached England boxing team Cwlth Games 1970, 1974, 1978, 1982, 1986 (total 33 medals), every English boxer won medals Cwlth Games 1984 and 1988; fell Br Inst of Sports Coaches 1989, Sports Writers' J L Manning award 1987, UK coach of the year Br Assoc of Nat Coaches 1989; *Books* ABA Coaching Manual; *Recreations* keep fit activities including running and weight training, outdoor pursuits, fell walking, squash, golf; *Style*— Kevin Hickey, Esq, MBE; 180 West Park Drive, Blackpool, Lancs FY3 9LW (☎ 0253 64900); BOA, 1 Wandsworth Plain, London SW18 1EH (☎ 081 871 2677, fax 081 871 9104)

HICKLING, Rev Canon Colin John Anderson; s of Charles Frederick Hickling, CMG (d 1977), of Totteridge, and Margery Ellerington, *née* Blamey (d 1978); *b* 10 July 1931; *Educ* Haverfordwest GS, Taunton Sch, Epsom Coll, King's Coll Cambridge (BA, MA); *Career* Nat Serv E Surreys, Royal W Sussex 1949-50; ordained: deacon 1957, priest 1958; asst curate St Luke's Pallion Sunderland 1957-61, asst tutor in Old Testament Chichester Theol Coll 1961-65, asst priest vicar Chichester Cathedral 1963-65, asst lectr in New Testament studies King's Coll London 1968-84 (lectr 1968-84), hon asst curate St Mary Magdalene's Munster Square 1965-68, dep minor canon St Paul's Cathedral 1969-78, hon asst curate St John's E Dulwich 1970-84, priest in ordinary to HM The Queen 1974-84 (dept priest in ordinary 1971-74), canon theologian Leicester Cathedral 1982-, tutor Queen's Coll Birmingham 1984-85, EW Benson fell Lincoln Theol Coll 1985-86, vicar Arksey 1986-; memb: Soc for Old Testament Study 1963-, Studiorum Novi Testamenti Societas 1974-, Soc for the Study of Theology 1964-; Queen's Jubilee medal 1977; *Books* contribs include: Church Without Walls (1968), Bible Bibliography 1967-73 (1974), What about the New Testament? (jt ed, 1975), L'Evangile de Jean (1977), The Ministry of the word (1979), This is the word of the Lord (1980), Logia - Sayings of Jesus (1982), The Bible in Three Dimensions (1990), A Dictionary of Biblical Interpretation (1990); *Recreations* music; *Clubs* Nikaean, Arksey Victoria Social; *Style*— The Rev Canon Colin Hickling; All Saints' Vicarage, Station Road, Arksey by Doncaster, S Yorks DN5 0SP (☎ 0302 874445)

HICKMAN, Alan John; s of William Ralph Hickman, of Kent, and Mabel Ethel, *née* Johnson; *b* 10 March 1946; *Educ* Hayes Sch Kent (various engrg qualifications); *m* 25 July 1970 (m dis 1988), Leone, da of Donald Andrewartha, of Devon; 1 s (Scott John b 1976), 1 da (Carly Caroline b 1973); *Career* workstudy engr Osram GEC Ltd; work study offr: London Borough of Bromley, Sevenoaks Dist Cncl; work study team ldr Buckinghamshire CC, mgmnt servs offr Thames Valley Police (HQ Oxon), Force Organisation and method offr Devon and Cornwall Constabulary (HQ Exeter); MIMS; *Recreations* raquet sport, literature, art, theatre, architecture; *Style*— Alan J Hickman, Esq; 6 Hillside Avenue, Pennsylvania, Exeter, Devon EX4 4NN (☎ 0392 427527)

HICKMAN, Anthony Stanley Franklin; JP (1984); s of Franklin Hickman (d 1981), of Wargrave, Berks, and Kathleen Irene, *née* Hancock (d 1955); *b* 12 April 1931; *Educ* Edward VII Royal GS Guildford, Kingston Sch of Art (Dip Arch); *m* 6 Jan 1962, Brenda Valerie, da of Gp Capt Eric Passmore, CBE (d 1982), of Seychelles; 1 s (Christopher John b 3 June 1965), 1 da (Charlotte Sarah b 20 May 1963); *Career* Nat Serv RAF, cmmn PO 1956, qualified navigator, ret 1958, appointed flying offr in res; John R Harris 1955-56 and 1958-64, gp architect BPB Industs plc 1964-71, assoc ptnr Adams Holden and Pearson 1971-74, ptnr Stevens Scanlan and ptnrs 1974-; commendation: Financial Times Ind Architecture Award 1971, Civic Tst; various articles in Architects Journal, sec gen Franco-Br Union of Architects London and Paris 1963-; Freeman City of London 1983; FRIBA; Chevalier dans l'Ordre des Palmes Académiques (France) 1990; *Recreations* architecture, gardening, making things, music; *Style*— Anthony Hickman, Esq, JP; Stevens Scanlan & Partners, 56 Buckingham Gate, London SW1E 6AH (☎ 071 834 4806, fax 071 630 8246)

HICKMAN, Frederick; QPM (1985); s of John Harry Hickman (d 1955), and Lucy Maria, *née* Bloomer (d 1982); *b* 2 Nov 1926; *Educ* Rowley Regis Central GS; *m* 1, 2 June 1951, Doreen Mary (d 1955), da of Wilfred Millington, of Halesowen, W Mids; m 2, 28 June 1958, Joy Maureen, da of John Aubrey Jones (d 1965); 1 s (Steven b 4 June 1961), 1 da (Sharon b 10 March 1960); *Career* Nat Serv RCS 1945-48, UK and Germany; Worcestershire Constabulary 1948-67; Mercia Constabulary 1967-85; positions incl: detective supt Ops and dep 4 Dist (Midland) Regnl Crime Squad 1970-76 (detective chief supt co-ordinator 1976-82), i/c W Mercia Constabulary Force Inspectorate and Systems Devpt Depts 1982-85; civil servant 1985-; *Recreations* shooting, historic bldg restoration, travel; *Style*— Frederick Hickman, Esq, QPM; Thatch Cottage, Danes Green, Claines, Worcester

HICKMAN, Sir (Richard) Glenn; 4 Bt (UK 1903), of Wightwick, Tettenhall, Staffordshire; s of Sir Alfred Howard Whitby Hickman, 3 Bt (d 1979), and Margaret Doris, *née* Kempson; *b* 12 April 1949; *Educ* Eton; *m* 1981, Heather Mary Elizabeth, er da of Dr James Moffett (d 1982), of Westlecot Manor, Swindon, and Dr Gwendoline Moffett (d 1975); 2 s (Charles Patrick Alfred b 1983, Edward William George b 1990), 1 da (Elizabeth Margaret Ruth b 1985); *Heir* s, Charles; *Clubs* Turf; *Style*— Sir Glenn Hickman, Bt; 13 Gorst Rd, Wandsworth Common, London SW11 6JB

HICKMAN, John Kyrle; CMG (1977); s of John Barlow Hickman (d 1932), and Joan Hickman, of Cirencester, Glos; *b* 3 July 1927; *Educ* Tonbridge, Univ of Cambridge (BA); *m* 1956, Jennifer, da of Reginald Kendall Love (d 1976); 2 s (Matthew, Andrew), 1 da (Catherine); *Career* HM Forces 1948-50 2 Lt RA, asst princ WO 1950; princ CRO 1958, first sec Wellington 1959, CRO 1962, FO 1964, first sec Madrid 1966, cnsllr 1967, consul gen Bilbao 1967, dep high cmmr Singapore 1969, head SW Pacific Dept FCO 1971, cnsllr Dublin 1974 (chargé d'affaires 1976), HM ambass Quito 1977-80, attached to Inchape Gp plc 1981-82, HM ambass Santiago 1982-1987; dir Anaconda (S America) Inc 1988; business conslt; tstee New Theatre Royal Portsmouth, Chartered Express Distribution Services plc 1990, FRGS; *Books* The Enchanted Islands: The Galapagos Discovered (1985); *Recreations* golf, tennis, skiing, history; *Clubs* Garrick, Los Leones Golf (Santiago), Prince of Wales (Santiago); *Style*— J K Hickman, Esq, CMG; Ivy Bank, Oare, nr Marlborough, Wiltshire SN8 4JA (☎ 0672 63462)

HICKMAN, Margaret, Lady; Margaret Doris; o da of Leonard Kempson, of Potters Bar, Middx; *m* 1, 1942 (m dis 1946), as his 1 w, Denis Thatcher (later Sir Denis Thatcher, 1 Bt); m 2, 1948, Sir (Alfred) Howard Whitby Hickman, 3 Bt (d 1979); 1 s (Sir Glenn Hickman, 4 Bt, *qv*); *Style*— Margaret, Lady Hickman; Leaper Cottage, Letchmore Heath, Herts WD2 8ES

HICKMAN, His Hon Judge Michael Ranulf; s of John Owen Hickman (d 1949), and Nancy Viola, *née* Barlow (d 1963); *b* 2 Oct 1922; *Educ* Wellington, Trinity Hall Cambridge (MA); *m* 1943, Diana, da of Col Derek Charles Houghton Richardson (d 1975); 1 s (Peter), 1 da (Susan); *Career* Flt Lt RAFVR 1940-46, serv in Atlantic and SE Asia Coastal Cmd; called to the Bar Middle Temple 1949; dep chm Hertfordshire Quarter Sessions 1965-72, rec 1972-74, circuit judge 1974-; *Recreations* shooting, fishing, gundog training; *Style*— His Hon Judge Michael Hickman; The Acorn, Bovingdon, Herts (☎ 0442 832226); St Albans Crown Court (☎ 0727 834481)

HICKMAN, Beryl, Lady; Nancy Beryl; da of Capt Trevor George Morse-Evans (d 1972); *m* 1940, as his 2 w, Sir Alfred Edward Hickman, 2 Bt (d 1947); *Style*— Beryl, Lady Hickman; Holmbuch House, Faygate, Horsham, Sussex GL54 5JH

HICKMAN, Peter Leslie Victor; OBE (1983); *Career* ret Br Aerospace 1988; currently euro conslt SPAR Aerospace Ltd (Canada); *Clubs* Naval and Military; *Style*— Peter Hickman Esq, OBE; Nottingham Farm, Cottered, Buntingford, Herts SG9 9PU (☎ 076 381 308; fax 076 381 431)

HICKMAN, Roger Christopher; s of Joseph Green Hickman (d 1986), of Blakedown, nr Kidderminster, and Mary Elizabeth, *née* Richardson; *b* 21 Oct 1938; *Educ* Bilton Grange Sch, Rugby, Malvern Coll; *m* 1969 (m dis), Margaret Isabel, da of Leslie Hackett, of Worcs; 1 s (David Christopher b 1970); *Career* chm of the South Staffs Gp Ltd 1985-; *Recreations* motor racing; *Style*— Roger Hickman, Esq; Birch Hollow, Ct Farm Way, Churchill, Worcs DY10 3LZ; South Staffs Group Ltd, New Rd, Dudley, Worcs (☎ 0384 455121)

HICKMOTT, Sqdn-Ldr Maurice Ernest John; DFC (1955); s of Arthur John Hickmott (d 1989), and Winifred Violet, *née* Wood (d 1986); *b* 11 July 1924; *Educ* Windsor GS and in USA; *m* 10 Sept 1952, Joan Mackrell; 2 s (Paul J M b 1953, Simon J B b 1959), 1 da (Jane E M b 1956); *Career* Sqdn Ldr RAF UK and Far East Air Force 1946-71; conslt aircraft flt and maintenance crew trg equipment and systems; Freeman City of London 1964, Liveryman Guild of Air Pilots and Navigators 1964; FRAeS; *Recreations* tennis, swimming, cricket, golf; *Clubs* RAF, City of London Liverymen; *Style*— Sqdn-Ldr Maurice Hickmott, DFC; 39 Hawkhurst Way, Bexhill, Sussex TN39 3SG (☎ 0424 345 88)

HICKOX, Richard Sidney; s of Sidney Edwin Hickox (d 1988), and Jean MacGregor, *née* Hillar; *b* 5 March 1948; *Educ* Royal GS High Wycombe, Royal Acad of Music (LRAM), Queens' Coll Cambridge (MA, ChM); *m* 1, 1970 (m dis), Julia Margaret, *née* Smith; m 2, 1976, Frances Ina, *née* Sheldon-Williams; 1 s (Thomas Richard Campbell b 1981); *Career* organist and master of music St Margaret's Westminster 1972-82, Promenade debut 1973, artistic dir: Wooburn Festival 1967-, St Endellian Festival 1974-, ChCh Spitalfields Festival 1978-, Truro Festival 1981-, Northern Sinfonia 1982, Chester Summer Music Festival 1989-; London Symphony Chorus 1976-, asst conductor LSO, conductor and musical dir City of London Sinfonia, Richard Hickox Singers, conductor; regular conductor: LSO, RPO, Bournemouth Symphony Orchestra and Sinfonietta, Royal Liverpool Philharmonic Orchestra, BBC Symphony and Welsh orchestras; performances incl: ENO 1979, Opera North 1982 and 1986, Scottish Opera 1985 and 1987, Royal Opera 1985, Los Angeles Opera 1986; conductor for many overseas orchestras; over 100 recordings for Virgin, EMI, Decca, Chandos, ASV; FRCO (cncl memb); ARAM; *Recreations* watching football and tennis, surfing, politics; *Style*— Richard Hickox, Esq; Intermusica, 16 Duncan Terrace, London N1 8BZ (☎ 071 278 5455)

HICKS; *see*: Steele, Tommy

HICKS, Air Cdre Alan George; CBE (1990); s of William John Hicks, TD, of Verwood, Dorset, and Ellen Rose, *née* Packer; *b* 18 Feb 1936; *Educ* Fosters Sch Sherborne, St Catharine's Coll Cambridge (MA); *m* 30 Oct 1961, Jessie Elizabeth, da of James Hutchison, of Perth Scotland; 1 s (Jeremy b 8 Aug 1962), 3 da (Cressida b 22 Aug 1963, Gemma b 10 June 1965, Clare b 27 March 1967); *Career* cmmnd RAF 1957, 42 Sqdn 1962-65, 204 Sqdn 1965-67, Avionics Spec RAF Coll Manby 1969-71, Flt Cdr 203 Sqdn Malta 1973-76, OC 42 Sqdn 1976-78, directing staff RAF Staff Coll 1978-80, Central Tactics and Trials Orgn 1981, Station Cdr RAF Turnhouse 1982-84, MOD Concepts staff 1985-87, MOD dir of Def Commitments (non NATO) 1987-90; chm United Servs Catholic Assoc 1984-90; CEng, MRAeS 1971; *Recreations* music, books, local history; *Clubs* RAF; *Style*— Air Cdre Alan Hicks, CBE; c/o National Westminster Bank, 50 Cheap Street, Sherborne, Dorset

HICKS, Dr Brendan Hamilton; s of Bryan Hamilton Hicks (d 1968), of London, and Winefrede, *née* O'Leary; *b* 22 Feb 1942; *Educ* St Brendan's Coll Bristol, Univ of London (BSc, MB BS, MD); *m* 8 Oct 1966, Jacqueline Ann Hamilton, da of William R Box, of Reading; 1 s (Benjamin John Hamilton b 18 June 1974), 1 da (Amelia Clare Hamilton b 10 Oct 1970); *Career* lectr in med Guys Hosp Med Sch 1969-72, NIH int fell of the US Public Health Serv 1972-73, postgrad dean to United Med and Dental Schs of Guys and St Thomas' Hosps Univ of London 1985- (sr lectr in med and conslt physician and endocrinologist 1974-84); chm Educn Section and memb Cncl Br Diabetic Soc; Freeman City of London, Freeman Worshipful Soc of Apothecaries 1985 (memb ct of examiners); FRCP 1982; *Books* contrib A New short Textbook of Medicine (1988); *Recreations* good books, theatre & films, cocker spaniels, sailing and walking; *Style*— Dr Brendan Hicks; Pembury House, 3 Brewery Rd, Bromley Common, Kent BR2 8LG (☎ 081 462 3244); Guy's Hospital, Department of Endocrinology, London SE1 9RT (☎ 081 955 5000)

HICKS, Charles Antony; s of Peter Rivers Hicks, OBE, of Kent, and Felicity Hicks, *née* Hughes; *b* 31 July 1946; *Educ* Marlborough, Clare Coll Cambridge (MA); *m* 1, 1969, Jennifer Joy (*née* Boydell); 1 s (James b 1972), 1 da (Emma b 1974); m 2, 1980,

Virginia Helen Juliana, da of Col John Robert Guy Stanton, of Derbyshire; 1 s (Oliver b 1981), 2 da (Camilla b 1983, Sophia b 1985); *Career* ptnr Wedlake Bell (slr) 1972, non-exec dir Platignum plc 1982, ward clerk of Walbrook 1975; *Clubs* Boodles; *Style—* Charles Hicks, Esq; 26 Lonsdale Square, London N1 1EW (☎ 071 607 4602); 16 Bedford St, Covent Garden, London WC2E 9HF (☎ 071 379 7266, telex 25256, fax 071 836 6117)

HICKS, Dr Colin Peter; s of George Stephen Frederick Hicks (d 1976), and Irene Maud, *née* Hargrave; *b* 1 May 1946; *Educ* Rutlish Sch Merton, Univ of Bristol (BSc, PhD); *m* Elizabeth Joan, da of Rev Sidney Eric Escourt Payne of Birmingham, England; 2 da (Rachel Heather b 1970, Joanna Katharine b 1972); *Career* lectr in chemistry Univ of the West Indies 1970-73, ICI research fell Univ of Exeter 1973-75, researcher Nat Physical Laboratory 1975-80, various research positions DTI 1980-83, tech advsr Barclays Bank 1983-84, dep dir Laboratory of the Govt Chemist 1984-87, sec Industl Devpt Advsy Bd 1988-90, undersec i/c res and technol policy DTI 1990-; sec Teddington Baptist Church 1979-1990, memb London Baptist Assoc Cncl 1986-, FRSC 1985; *Recreations* computing; *Style—* Dr Colin Hicks; Research and Technology Policy Division, Department of Trade and Industry, 151 Buckingham Palace Road, London SE1 (☎ 071 215 1659)

HICKS, David Nightingale; s of Herbert Hicks (d 1940), of The Hamlet, Coggeshall, Essex, and Iris Elsie, *née* Platten; *b* 25 March 1929; *Educ* Charterhouse, Central Sch of Art and Design; *m* 1960, Lady Pamela Carmen Louise, *qv*, yr da of 1 Earl Mountbatten of Burma, KG, OM, DSO, FRS (d 1979); 1 s (Ashley Louis David b 1963), 2 da (Edwina Victoria Louise (Mrs Jeremy Brudenell) b 1961, India Amanda Caroline, b 1967, bridesmaid to Lady Diana Spencer at her marriage to HRH The Prince of Wales 1981); *Career* interior, product and garden designer; author; *Books* David Hicks on Decoration (1966), David Hicks on Living ... With Taste (1968), David Hicks on Bathrooms (1970), David Hicks on Decoration With Fabrics (1971), David Hicks on Decoration - 5 (1975), David Hicks on Flower Arranging (1976), David Hicks Living With Design (1979), David Hicks Garden Design (1982), David Hicks Style & Design (1987); *Recreations* gardening, shooting; *Style—* David Hicks, Esq; The Grove, Brightwell Baldwin, Oxon OX9 5PF; Albany, Piccadilly, London W1; David Hicks International, 4a Barley Mow Passage, London W4 4PH (☎ 081 994 9222, fax 081 742 2560)

HICKS, His Hon Judge John Charles; QC (1980); s of Charles Hicks (d 1963), and Marjorie Jane, *née* Bazeley (d 1980); *b* 4 March 1928; *Educ* King Edward VI GS Chelmsford, King Edward VI GS Totnes, Univ of London (LLB, LLM); *m* 1957, (Elizabeth) Mary, da of Rev John Barnabas Jennings (d 1979); 1 s (David, decd), 1 da (Elizabeth); *Career* Nat Serv RA (Gunner) 1946-48; slr 1952-66, ptnr Messrs Burchells 1954-65; Methodist Missionary Soc (Caribbean) 1965-66; barr 1966-88, rec Western Circuit 1978-88, circuit judge 1988; *Recreations* music, theatre, opera, squash racquets, the Methodist constitution; *Style—* His Hon Judge John Hicks, QC; Flat 3, 17 Montagu Square, London W1H 1RD (☎ 071 935 6008)

HICKS, John Geoffrey; s of John Albert Hicks (d 1971), of Redhill, Surrey, and Blanche Christian, *née* Arnot (d 1979); *b* 7 April 1936; *Educ* The Perse Sch for Boys Cambridge, Downing Coll Cambridge (MA); *m* 1, 1967 (m dis 1976), Janice Marilyn Denson; 1 s (David Markham John b 1971); m 2, 1983, Janet Florence Morrison; 1 s (Peter John Cameron b 1983); *Career* Vickers Armstrongs (Aircraft) Ltd/British Aircraft Corp 1954-64 (apprentice, stressman, section ldr), The Welding Institute 1964-75 (investigator, head of Design Advsy Serv, mangr UK Offshore Steels Res Project), conslt Sir William Halcrowd Partners 1976 (former sr project engr), advsr Standards and Quality HM Treas 1987-90, sec gen Int Inst of Welding 1990-; memb Worshipful Co of Engineers 1990, Freeman City of London; MRAes 1963; fell: Welding Inst 1973, American Welding Soc 1977, Welding Technol Inst of Aust 1980, Inst of Quality Assurance 1985, Assoc of Quality Mgmnt Conslts, ACIArb 1987, FEng 1990; *Books* Welded Joint Design (1979, 2 edn 1987), A Guide to Designing Welds (1989); *Recreations* church organ playing, creative gardening; *Style—* John Hicks, Esq; International Institute of Welding, Abington Hall, Abington, Cambridgeshire CB1 6AL (☎ 0223 891162)

HICKS, Martin Leslie Arther; s of Sgt William James Hicks (d 1968), of St Albans, Herts, and Elizabeth, *née* White; *b* 23 Dec 1953; *Educ* Bedford Sch, (BA, LLB); *m* 7 July 1984, Peta Alexandra, da of Capt Michael Stuart Hughes, MN (d 1982), of Wheathampstead, Herts; *Career* called to the Bar Inner Temple 1977, memb David Dethridee's Chambers 1980-, Aldun Property Co Ltd 1984-, Sec Oakbrave Ltd 1988-; memb: Civic Soc 1985; Hon Soc of Inner Temple 1977; *Recreations* squash, skiing, seafood; *Style—* Martin Hicks, Esq; 3 Temple Gardens, London EC4Y 9AU (☎ 071 583 0010, fax 071 353 3361)

HICKS, Maureen Patricia; MP (C) Wolverhampton North East 1987-; da of Ronald Cutler, of Bucks, and Norah, *née* O'Neill; *b* 23 Feb 1948; *Educ* Ashley Secondary Sch, Brockenhurst GS, Furzedown Coll of Educn London; *m* 1973, Keith Henwood Hicks, s of Thomas Henwood Hicks, of Australia; 1 s (Marcus b 1979), 1 da (Lydia b 1982); *Career* teacher; asst area educn offr 1974-75, Marks and Spencer mgmnt 1970-74; dir Stratford Motor Museum 1975-83 (consltdir 1983-); sec House of Commons Backbench Tourism Ctee 1987-; Stratford dist cncllr 1979-84; *Recreations* amateur dramatics, golf, travel; *Clubs* Royal Overseas; *Style—* Mrs Maureen Hicks, MP; c/o House of Commons, London SW1

HICKS, Michael Charles; s of Charles Peter Hicks, of Isleworth, Middlesex, and Sheila Mary, *née* Curtis; *b* 11 June 1953; *Educ* Brighton Coll, Trinity Coll Cambridge (entrance scholarship); *m* 22 Dec 1979, Sarah, da of Peter John Wallace, of Home Farm, Stretton Under Fosse, Warwicks; 1 s (Charles William Peter), 1 da (Georgina Mary Sarah); *Career* called to the Bar 1976; sailor: Nat Scorpion Class Champion 1976, Int Star Class UK Fleet champion 1985-87; *Recreations* sailing; *Clubs* Oxford and Cambridge Sailing Soc; *Style—* Michael Hicks, Esq; 3 Pump Ct, The Temple, London EC4 (☎ 071 583 5110, fax 071 583 1130, car 0836 295805)

HICKS, Maj-Gen (William) Michael Ellis; CB (1983), OBE (1969); s of Gp Capt William Charles Hicks, AFC (d 1939), and Nellie Kilbourne Kay (d 1970); *b* 2 June 1928; *Educ* Eton, RMA Sandhurst; *m* 1950, Jean Hilary, da of Brig William Edmonstone Duncan, CVO, DSO, MC (d 1970); 3 s (William, Peter, Alistair); *Career* Army Offr, cmmnd 1948, attended Staff Coll 1958; GSO1 MOI 1967-70, CO 1 Bn Coldstream Guards 1970-72, attended RCDS 1973, cmd 4 Guards Armd Bde 1974-75, BGS Trg HQ UKLF 1976-78, GOC NW Dist 1980-83, ret 1983; sec RCDS 1983-; *Recreations* golf, gardening; *Style—* Maj-Gen Michael Hicks, CB, OBE; c/o Cox and Kings, PO Box 1190, 7 Pall Mall, London SW1Y 5NA

HICKS, Michael Frank; s of Frank Henry Hicks (d 1985), and Annie Elizabeth Lydia, *née* Beeson (d 1988); *b* 11 March 1935; *Educ* Fairlop Secdy HS Hainault, Dane Secdy Modern Ilford; *m* 19 Sept 1959, Veronica Constance, da of Frederick Edwin Martin; 2 da (Corinne Veronica b 14 May 1962, Anne Christine b 15 April 1964); *Career* Nat Serv RAF 1953-55, serv Aden; stockbroker: HE Goodison 1948-56, Blount 1956-59; ptnr Simon and Coates 1959-80, equity ptnr Statham Duff Stoop 1980-86, dir Prudential Bache Capital Funding 1986-89, dir Soc Generale Strauss Turnbull Securities Ltd 1989-; chm Stock Exchange 20 Over Cricket League; *Recreations* walking; *Style—* Michael F Hicks, Esq; Spring Hill, Stoke by Nayland, Suffolk (☎ 020 637 321); Exchange House, Primrose St, Broadgate, London EC2A 2DD (☎ 071 638 5699)

HICKS, Nicola Katherine; da of Philip Lionel Shalto Hicks, of Radcot House Bampton Oxfordshire, and Jill Tweed; *b* 3 May 1960; *Educ* Frensham Heights Sch, Chelsea Sch of Art (BA), RCA (MA); *m* (m dis); ptnr Dan Flowers; *Career* artist; solo exhibitions incl: Angela Flowers Gallery London 1985 and 1986, Angela Flowers (Ireland) Inc, Co Cork, Ireland 1986, Beaux Arts Gallery Bath 1987, Flowers East London 1988, Tegnerforbundet Oslo Norway 1991; gp exhibitions incl: Christie's Inaugural Graduate Exhibition London 1982, Current Issues (RCA London) 1982, Portland Clifftops Sculpture Park 1983, Sculptural Drawings (Ruskin Coll Oxford) 1983, Int Garden Festival Liverpool: Sculpture Garden 1984, Hayward Annual (Hayward Gallery London) 1985, Basel Art Fair Switzerland 1985 and 1986, '85 Show (Serpentine Gallery London) 1985, Opening Exhibition (Damon Brandt Gallery NY) 1985, Sixteen (Angela Flowers Gallery London) 1986, The Living Art Pavillion (The Ideal Home Exhibition London) 1986, Beaux Arts Summer Exhibition Bath 1986, Chicago Art Fair 1987 and 1988, The Scottish Gallery Edinburgh 1987, Art In The City (Lloyds Building London) 1987, Rocket 6-1 (installed at the Economist Building Piccadilly London) 1988, Hakone Open Air Museum 1988, Veksolund Udstilling For Sculptor Copenhagen 1988, Out of Clay (Manchester) 1988, Daley Hicks Jeffries Jones Kirby Lewis (Flowers East London) 1989, Los Angeles Art Fair 1990, Sculptors Drawings (Cleveland Bridge Gallery Bath) 1990; work in various pub collections incl: Contemporary Arts Soc, Chase Manhattan Bank, Arthur Andersen; cmmn for monument in Battersea Park; artist in residence Brentwood HS; *Recreations* poker, backgammon, dice, dog and horse racing, travelling, searching for horned rhino on elephantback and white water surfing; *Clubs* Chelsea Arts; *Style—* Ms Nicola Hicks; c/o Flowers East, 199/205 Richmond Rd, Hackney, London E8 3NJ (☎ 081 985 3333)

HICKS, Lady Pamela Carmen Louise; *née* Mountbatten; yr da of 1 Earl Mountbatten of Burma, KG, GCB, OM, GCSI, GCIE, GCVO, DSO, PC, FRS (assas 1979); sister of Countess Mountbatten of Burma, *qv*; *b* 19 April 1929; *m* 13 Jan 1960, David Nightingale Hicks, *qv*; 1 s, 2 da; *Career* bridesmaid to HRH The Princess Elizabeth at her marriage 1947; lady-in-waiting to HM The Queen on her tour of Aust and NZ 1953-54; patron The Leukaemia Care Soc; vice-pres SSAFA; pres King Edward VII British-German Fndn; govr United World Coll of the Atlantic; memb Inst King Edward VII Hosp Midhurst; patron The Girls' Nautical Trg Corps 1955-79; pres: Royal London Soc for the Blind 1960-82, The Embroiderers' Guild 1970-80; *Style—* The Lady Pamela Hicks; Albany, Piccadilly, London W1 (☎ 071 734 3183); The Grove, Brightwell Baldwin, Oxon (☎ 0491 35353)

HICKS, Philip; s of Brig Philip Hugh Whitby Hicks, CBE, DSO, MC (d 1967), and Patty, *née* Fanshawe (d 1985); *b* 11 Oct 1928; *Educ* Winchester, RMA Sandhurst, Royal Acad Schs (Dip RAS); *m* 22 July 1952, Jill, da of Maj Jack Tweed (d 1979); 1 s (David b 1971), 1 da (Nicola b 1960); *Career* Irish Gds 1946-47, 2 Lt Royal Warwicks Regt 1948-49; pt/t teacher various art schs 1960-85, concentrated full time on painting 1986-; solo exhibitions incl: Camden Arts Centre 1971, Richard Demarco Gall Edinburgh 1971, Robert Self Gall London 1971, Imperial War Museum 1975, Galerie VFCU Antwerp 1977-79, Battersea Arts Centre 1977, Gallery 22 Dublin 1980, New Art Centre (London) 1980-82, Galleri Engstrom Stockholm 1985, Gallery 10 London 1986-91, Bohun Gall Henley 1986-90, mixed exhibitions incl: Tate Gallery London 1976, Mall Galleries London 1980, Israel Israel Mus Jerusalem 1980-81, Serpentine Gallery London 1982, Angela Flowers Gallery 1985, Art '89 London 1989; works in pub collections incl: Tate Gall, Comtemporary Art Soc, V & A, Imp War Mus; Br Cncl award 1977; also performs professionally as a jazz pianist; hon treas and memb cncl Artists Gen Benevolent Inst; *Recreations* music; *Clubs* Cheslea Arts, Arts; *Style—* Philip Hicks, Esq; Radcot House, Buckland Rd, Bampton, Oxford OX8 2AA (☎ 0993 850347)

HICKS, Robert Adrian; MP (C) Cornwall 1983-; s of W H Hicks of Horrabridge, Devon; *b* 18 Jan 1938; *Educ* Queen Elizabeth GS, Univ Coll London, Exeter Univ; *m* 1962 (m dis 1987), Maria, da of Robert Gwyther of Plympton, Devon; 2 da; *Career* nat vice chm Young Cons 1964-66, tech coll lectr 1964-1970, contested (C) Aberavon 1966, MP (C) Bodmin (formerly held by Libs) 1970-74 and 1974-1983; chm Horticultural Ctee 1971-73, asst govt whip 1973-74, memb Select Ctee on European Secdy Legislation 1973-; vice chm: Cons Pty Agric Ctee 1971-73 and 1974-81, Cons Pty European Affrs Ctee 1979-81; chm: Westcountry Cons Membs Ctee 1977-78 (sec 1970-73), UK branch Parly Assoc for Euro-Arab Co-operation 1983-, Cons Pty Agric Ctee 1988-90; treas Cons Pty Middle East Cncl 1979-; Parly advsr: Br Hotels Restaurants and Caterers Assoc 1974-, Milk Mktg Bd 1985-; *Clubs* MCC; *Style—* Robert Hicks, Esq, MP; Little Court, St Ive, Liskeard, Cornwall; 7 Carew Wharf Torpoint Cornwall

HICKS, Robin Edgcumbe; s of Ronald Eric Edgcumbe Hicks, of Alendale Cottage, Clifton, Bristol, and Freddie Hicks; *b* 6 Dec 1942; *Educ* Bancrofts' Sch, Seale Hayne Coll (NDA, Dip Farm Mgmnt), Univ of Reading (DipAgEngrg); *m* 19 Sept 1970, Sue, da of Peter Dalton, of Downton, Salisbury, Wiltshire; 1 s (Robert b 1977), 1 da (Sarah b 1976); *Career* agric advsr Ministry of Agriculture Fisheries & Food 1966-68, prodr BBC 1968-77 (London, Norwich, Birimingham, Edinburgh), head of mktg and devpt RASE Stoneleigh 1977-79, head Network Radio South & West BBC Bristol 1979-88, chief exec RASE 1989 (chief exec designate 1988-89); former memb: Bristol & Weston Health Authy, SW Concerts Bd, Cncl The Radio Academy; former tstee St Georges Music Tst; tstee: Rural Housing Tst, Head Injury Res Tst; Freeman City of London 1979, Liveryman Worshipful Co of Drapers 1981; *Recreations* narrow boats, gardening, photography, family farmers, anglo Belgium; *Clubs* Farmers, Anglo Belgium; *Style—* Robin Hicks, Esq; 9 Clarendon Crescent, Royal Leamington Spa, Warwickshire CV32 5NR (☎ 0926 422001); Royal Agricultural Society of England, National Agricultural Centre, Stoneleigh Park, Warwickshire CV8 2LZ (☎ 0203 696969, fax 0203 696900, telex 31697, car 0836 371 672)

HICKS BEACH, Hon David Seymour; s of 2 Earl St Aldwyn, PC, GBE, TD, JP, DL; *b* 1955; *Educ* Eton, Royal Agricultural Coll Cirencester; *Career* a page of honour to HM The Queen 1969-71, agriculture; *Recreations* natural history, fishing, shooting, travel; *Clubs* Royal Agricultural Soc of England, Royal Geographical Soc; *Style—* The Hon David Hicks Beach; Williamstrip Park, Cirencester, Glos GL7 5AT

HICKSON, Joan Bogle (Mrs Eric Butler); OBE (1987); da of Harold Alfred Squire Hickson, and Edith Mary, *née* Bogle; *b* 5 Aug 1906; *Educ* Castle Hall Sch Northampton, Castle Bar Sch London, Oldfeld Sch Swanage; *m* 29 Oct 1932, Eric Norman Butler, s of Thomas Harrison Butler (d 1944), of Hampton-in-Arden, Warwickshire; 1 s (Nicholas Andrew Mark b 24 May 1936), 1 da (Caroline Margaret Julia b 3 May 1939); *Career* actress, trained RADA; debut His Wife's Children 1927, first London appearance The Tragic Muse 1928; appeared in numerous plays incl: Appointment with Death, See How They Run, The Guinea Pig, A Day in the Life of Joe Egg, Forget-me-not-Lane, Bedroom Farce (won Miss Hickson a Tony award in NY); made many films incl: The Guinea Pig, The Magic Box, Seven Days to Noon; numerous tv appearances incl 9 adaptations of Agatha Christie novels in which she played Miss Marple 1984-87; Hon MA Univ of Leicester 1988 F; *Recreations* reading; *Clubs* New Cavendish; *Style—* Miss Joan Hickson, OBE; Terence Plunkett Greene, 4

Ovington Gardens, London SW3 1LS (☎ 071 584 0688)

HICKSON, Peter Hanam; s of Capt Keneth Roy Hickson, CBE, AFC, RN, of 4A Hollow Lane, Hayling Island, Hants, and Mary, *née* Hilary; *b* 31 Oct 1949; *Educ* Churchers Coll, Univ of Southampton (BSc); *m* 2 Oct 1976, Janet Fay, da of Thomas Robinson, of 37 Goodman Crescent, London SW2; 1 s ((Philip) Guy Hanam b 1981), 1 da (Ella Jocelyn b 1985); *Career* drilling engr: Burmah Oil Co 1971-74, Chevron Petroleum 1974-75; Houlder Offshore Ltd: asst ops mangr 1976-77, devpt mangr 1978-80, gen mangr 1980-82, md 1982-89, md and owner PHI Associates 1990-; memb Exec Ctee Hayling Island Sailing Club 1978-79 (gen ctee 1974-77); *Recreations* sailing, food, wine, squash, jogging; *Clubs* Hayling Island Sailing, St Katherines Yacht; *Style*— Peter Hickson, Esq; 59 Lafone St, London EC3 (☎ 071 357 7317, fax 071 403 8201, telex 884801)

HIDALGO, Alexander; s of Alexander Hidalgo, of Moca, Puerto Rico, USA, and Estebania Hidalgo; *b* 31 Dec 1938; *Educ* Brooklyn Tech HS New York, Brooklyn Coll Univ of the City of New York (BA, academic honour roll), Queen's Univ Belfast; *m* 27 Nov 1973, June Anne, da of Edward Arnold Davies (d 1964); 1 da (Theodora Juana Alexandra b 23 Dec 1972); *Career* conservator Royal Albert Memorial Museums Exeter 1969-72, curator Kirkaldy Museums & Art Gallery Fife 1972-75, dep dir Aberdeen Art Gallery & Museums 1975-89, head of ops Arts & Museums 1989-; memb Museums Assoc 1969, FSAS 1973, memb ICOM 1978, MBIM 1989; memb British Cactus and Succulent Soc; *Style*— Alexander Hidalgo, Esq; The Emmarick, Parkhill, By Dyce, Aberdeen AB2 0AT (☎ 0224 770244); Head of Operations, Arts & Museums, City Arts Dept, Aberdeen District Council, Schoolhill, Aberdeen AB9 1FQ (☎ 0224 646333, fax 0224 632133)

HIDE, Prof Raymond; CBE (1989); s of Stephen Hide (d 1940), and Rose Edna, *née* Cartlidge (now Mrs Thomas Leonard); *b* 17 May 1929; *Educ* Percy Jackson GS, Univ of Manchester (BSc, Samuel Bright prize, H G J Moseley prize), Univ of Cambridge (PhD, ScD); *m* 1958, (Phyllis) Ann, da of Gerald James William Licence (d 1946); 1 s (Stephen), 2 da (Julia, Kathryn); *Career* res assoc in astrophysics Univ of Chicago 1953-54, sr res fell Gen Physics Div AERE Harwell 1954-57, lectr in physics Univ of Durham 1957-61, prof of geophysics and physics MIT 1961-67, head Geophysical Fluid Dynamics Laboratory UK Meteorological Office 1967-90, head Robert Hooke Inst Oxford 1990-; visiting prof Dept of Meteorology Univ of Reading 1970-, Dept of Mathematics UCL 1970-82, Depts of Earth Scis and Maths Univ of Leeds; Adrian fell Univ of Leicester 1980-83 (Hon DSc 1985), fell Jesus Coll Oxford 1983-, Gresham prof of astronomy Gresham Coll City of London 1985-90; author of numerous scientific papers in learned jls; pres: RMS 1975-76 (hon fell 1989), Euro Geophysical Soc 1982-84 (hon fell 1988), RAS 1983-85; fell American Acad of Arts and Scis 1964; FRS 1971, Academia Europaea 1988; *Awards* Charles Chree medal and prize Inst of Physics 1974, Holweck medal and prize Société Française de Physique and Inst of Physics 1982, Gold medal Royal Astronomical Soc 1989; *Style*— Prof Raymond Hide, CBE, FRS; Robert Hooke Inst, Old Observatory, Clarendon Lab, Parks Rd, Oxford OX1 3PU (☎ 0865 272084)

HIDER, Dr Calvin Fraser; *b* 29 May 1930; *Educ* George Watsons Coll, Univ of Edinburgh (MB, CLB); *m* 1, 16 Jan 1959, Jean Margaret Douglas (d 1988), da of Prof N Dott, CBE; 3 da (Jacqueline b 1960, Katherine b 1962, Susan b 1965); m 2, 8 Sept 1990, Frances Ann Smithers; *Career* RNR 1955-64, Surgn Lt Cdr; sr conslt anaesthetist Cardiothoracic Unit Edinburgh 1964; FFARCS; *Recreations* fishing, riding, shooting, breeding Jacob sheep, sailing, Ocean Yacht Masters cert BOT; *Clubs* Sloane; *Style*— Dr Calvin Hider; Marchwell Cottage, Penicuik, Mid Lothian (☎ 0968 72680); Royal Infirmary, Edinburgh (☎ 031 229 2477)

HIDER, (Kenneth) Mark; s of Kenneth George Hider of Sevenoaks, Kent, and Marion, *née* Richards; *b* 18 Sept 1953; *Educ* Sir William Borlase's Sch Marlow, Trinity Coll Oxford (MA); *m* 20 June 1981, Nicola Louise, da of John Haigh; 2 s (Tom, Ben); *Career* started at Scottish Television and became media res controller, analysist rising to a sr planner Masius, planning dir Ogilvy & Mather 1988- (started as a sr planner, estab the Strategic Analysis Unit); memb: Mktg Soc, Market Res Soc, The Account Planning Group; MIPA; *Recreations* cricket, soccer, theatre, walking the dog, watching Brentford, travel; *Style*— Mark Hider, Esq; Ogilvy & Mather Ltd, Brettenham House, Lancaster Place, London WC2E 7EZ (☎ 071 836 2466, fax 071 497 2733, car 083 1102273)

HIGGIN, Capt William Bendyshe; s of Maj Walter Wynnefield Higgin, DL (d 1971), of Cheshire, and Olive, *née* Earle (d 1978); *b* 14 Feb 1922; *Educ* Gresham's Sch Holt, Royal Agric Coll; *m* 26 March 1947, Mary Patricia, da of Capt George Lee-Morris, RNVR (d 1983), of Cheshire; 2 s (Mark b 1954, Jonathan b 1956), 1 da (Gail b 1947); *Career* WWII co cdr 5/10 Baluch Regt IA 1941, ADC to GOC N India 1943-44, invalided out 1946; landowner in Clwyd and Anglesey; *Recreations* game shooting, gardening, restoring old houses; *Clubs* Sind, Shropshire; *Style*— Capt William Higgin; Mellus Manaw, Bodedern, Anglesey; Rhyd-Y-Gwtta, Waen, St Asaph, Clwyd, Wales

HIGGINS, Dr Andrew James; s of Edward James Higgins (d 1966), and Gabrielle Joy, *née* Kelland; *b* 7 Dec 1948; *Educ* St Michael's Coll, RVC, Univ of London (BVetMed, PhD), Centre for Tropical Veterinary Med Univ of Edinburgh (MSc); *m* 19 Dec 1981, Nicola Lynn, da of Peter Rex Eliot (d 1980); 1 s (Benjamin b 1982), 2 da (Amelia b 1984, Joanna b 1986); *Career* cmmnd RAVC 1973, Capt, served Dhofar War 1974; veterinary offr HM The Sultan of Oman 1975-76, vet advsr The Wellcome Fndn 1977-82, conslt Food and Agric Orgn of the UN 1981-, dir Animal Health Tst 1988-; memb Cncl Soc for the Protection of Animals in N Africa (vice chm 1987-89); memb: Conservation and Welfare Ctee Zoological Soc of London 1987-, Cncl Br Equine Vet Assoc 1984- (hon sec 1984-88), Editorial Advsy Bds Equine Veterinary Journal; dep ed British Veterinary Journal 1990-; hon vet advsr to Jockey Club 1988-; winner Equine Veterinary Journal Open Award 1986, Ciba-Geigy prize for res in animal health 1985, awarded Univ of London Laurel 1971; MRCVS; *Books* An Anatomy of Veterinary Europe (contrib, 1972), The Camel in Health and Disease (ed & contrib, 1986), many papers in scientific and general pubns and communications to learned societies; *Recreations* skiing, riding, opera, camels; *Clubs* Buck's; *Style*— Dr Andrew Higgins; Animal Health Trust, PO Box 5, Newmarket, Suffolk CB8 7DW (☎ 0638 661111, fax 0638 665789, telex 818418 ANHLTH G)

HIGGINS, Prof (John) Christopher; s of Sidney James Higgins (d 1958), of Surbiton, Surrey, and Margaret Eileen, *née* Dealtrey (d 1973); *b* 9 July 1932; *Educ* King George V Sch Southport, Gonville and Caius Coll Cambridge (BA, MA), Bedford Coll London (MSc), Birkbeck Coll London (BSc), Univ of Bradford (PhD); *m* 24 Sept 1960, Margaret Edna, da of William John Howells, of 17 Rookwood Close, Llandaff, Cardiff; 3 s (Peter John b 1962, David Richard b 1964, Mark Robert b 1969); *Career* short serv cmmn RAF 1953-56; conslt Metra Gp 1964-67, dir econ planning and res IPC Newspapers Ltd 1967-70, prof mgmnt sci 1970-89, dir Mgmnt Centre Univ of Bradford 1972-89, non exec dir Amos Hinton & Sons plc 1980-84; tstee Wool Fndn; memb: DTI Regnl Industl Devpt Bd, CS Scientific Advsrs Branch Air Miny 1962-64, various govt ctees 1976-; FIEE 1981, CBIM 1982; *Books* Last Two Strategic and Operational Planning Systems, Computer Based Planning Systems; *Recreations* music, fellwalking, bridge; *Clubs* Royal Over-Seas League; *Style*— Prof Christopher Higgins; 36 Station Rd, Baildon, Shipley, W Yorks (☎ 0274 592836); Univ of Bradford, Richmond Rd, Bradford BD7 1DP (☎ 0274 733466)

HIGGINS, Sir Christopher Thomas; s of Thomas Higgins (d 1964), and Florence Maud, *née* Wilkinson (d 1966); *b* 14 Jan 1914; *Educ* West Kensington Central Sch, Univ of London; *m* 1936, Constance Joan, da of Walter Herbert Beck (d 1951); 1 s (Geoffrey b 1944), 1 da (Jacqueline b 1939); *Career* serv WWII Lt RA; Acton Borough Cncl 1945-64, Mayor 1957; memb: Middx Co Cncl 1952-55 and 1958-64, GLC 1964-67, Hemel Hempstead Devpt Corp 1947-52, Bracknell Devpt Corp 1965-68; chm: Peterborough Devpt Corp 1968-81, North Thames Gas Consumers' Cncl 1969-79; kt 1977; *Style*— Sir Christopher Higgins; Coronation Cottage, Wood End, Little Horwood, Milton Keynes, Bucks MK17 0PE (☎ 029 671 2636)

HIGGINS, John Andrew; s of George Henry Higgins, of 80 Elphinstone Rd, Hastings, Sussex, and Mildred Maud, *née* Ullmer (d 1985); *b* 19 Feb 1940; *m* 18 Sept 1965, Susan Jennifer, da of George Alfred Mathis (d 1964); 1 s (Simon David b 1966); *Career* Exchequer and Audit Dept: asst auditor 1958, auditor 1968, sr auditor 1971, chief auditor 1977, dep dir 1981; Office of the Auditor Gen of Canada 1983-84; asst auditor gen NAO 1988- (dir 1984); govr (CIPFA Educn and Trg Centre Croydon, memb Crawley and Horsham Organists' Assoc; ARCO 1988; *Recreations* golf, bridge, classical organ playing; *Clubs* Ifield Golf and Country; *Style*— John Higgins, Esq; Zaria, 65 Milton Mount Ave, Pound Hill, Crawley, Sussex RH10 3DP (☎ 0293 883869); National Audit Office, Buckingham Palace Rd, London SW1W 9SP (☎ 071 798 7380, fax 071 828 3774)

HIGGINS, John Dalby; s of Frank Edward John Higgins, of Clifftop, Burlington Rd, Swanage, Dorset, and Edith Florence, *née* Dalby (d 1986); *b* 7 Jan 1934; *Educ* KCS Wimbledon, Worcester Coll Oxford (BA); *m* 3 Sept 1977, Linda Irene, da of Edward Sidney Christmas (d 1983); *Career* Nat Serv PO RAF; Fin Times: features ed 1962-64, arts ed 1963-69, literary ed 1966-69; The Times: arts ed 1970-88, chief opera critic 1988-, obituaries ed 1988-; memb: Ctee Royal Literary Fund 1969-, Advertising Ctee Musicians' Benevolent Fund 1985-; Chevalier de l'Ordre des Arts et des Lettres France 1973, Ehrenkreuz für Kunst und Wissenschaft (first Class) Austria 1977, Goldene Verdienstzeichen des Landes Salzburg Austria 1985, Officer de L'Orde des Arts et des Lettres France 1989; *Books* Travels in the Balkans (1970), The Making of An Opera (1977), Glyndebourne: A Celebration (ed, 1984), British Theatre Design 1978-88 (contrib, 1989); *Recreations* claret, watching Chelsea FC; *Clubs* Garrick; *Style*— John Higgins, Esq; The Times, Virginia St, London E1 9BD (☎ 071 782 5868, telex 262141)

HIGGINS, Prof Peter Matthew; OBE (1986); s of Peter Joseph Higgins (d 1952), of Stamford Hill, London, and Margaret, *née* De Lacey (d 1981); *b* 18 June 1923; *Educ* St Ignatius Coll, London, UCL, UCH (MB BS); *m* 27 Sept 1952, Jean Margaret Lindsay, da of Capt Dr John Currie, DSO (d 1932), of Darlington; 3 s (Nicholas b 1954, Anthony b 1956, David b 1958), 1 da (Jane b 1959); *Career* Capt RAMC 1948-49; asst med registrar UCH (house physician med unit 1947 and 1950, res med offr 1951-52); princ in gen practice: Rugeley Staffs 1954-65, Castle Vale Birmingham 1966-67, Thamesmead London 1968-88; prof in gen practice Guys Hosp Med Sch 1974-88 (sr lectr 1968-73); vice chm SE Thames RHA 1976- (memb 1974-); chm: Thamesmead Family Serv Unit (memb Nat Cncl of Family Serv Units) 1983-, Kent Family Health Servs Authy 1990-; memb: Attendance Allowance Bd 1971-74, Standing Med Advsy Ctee DHSS 1970-74; tstee: Thamesmead Community Assoc, Tst Thamesmead; formerly vice chm of govrs Linacre Centre for Study of Med Ethics; FRSM 1950, FRCP, FRCGP; *Recreations* reading, music, squash; *Style*— Prof Peter Higgins, OBE; Wallings, Heathfield Lane, Chislehurst, Kent BR7 6AH (☎ 081 467 2756)

HIGGINS, Rodney Michael; s of Ronald George Platten Higgins (d 1952), and Mina Emily, *née* Botterill; *b* 24 Oct 1927; *Educ* Hurstpierpoint Coll, Univ of Durham (BSc); *m* (Lilian) Joyce, da of late Thomas Bookless (d 1956); 1 s (Michael), 3 da (Lesley, Frances, Nicola); *Career* RE 1946-50; engr; designer and estimator British Reinforced Concrete 1952-54, designer Clarke Nichols & Marcel Bristol 1954-55, Kellogg International Corporation 1955-56, in private practice London 1958-64; princ: Cooper Higgins & Ptnrs Newcastle 1964-76, RM Higgins Assocs Newcastle 1976-; FRSA 1960, FIStructE 1966, MConsE 1966; *Recreations* industrial archaeology, folklore traditions of wild flowers, genealogy, local history; *Style*— Rodney Higgins, Esq; Somerville Hse, Allendale Rd, Hexham, Nmberland NE46 2NB (☎ 0434 602941); RM Higgins Assocs, 135 Sandyford Rd, Newcastle upon Tyne NE2 1QR (☎ 091 281 1307, fax 091 281 8430)

HIGGINS, Ronald Trevor; s of Robert Mold Higgins, Winchester, and Jean, *née* Richmond; *b* 10 July 1929; *Educ* Kingsbury, LSE (BSc), Magdalen Coll Oxford; *m* 16 Sept 1978, Dr Elizabeth Mary Bryan, da of Sir Paul Bryan, MC, DSO, of Westminster and North Yorks; *Career* Nat Serv 1947-48; HM Dip Serv 1954-68: third sec Tel Aviv 1956-58, second sec Copenhagen 1958-59, asst private sec to Lord Privy Seal Edward Heath 1960-62, sr resident clerk 1963-66, first sec Jakarta 1966-67, resigned 1968; special advsr to ed Observer 1968-76; patron of Safer World Fndn, dir Dunamis Forum St James's Church Piccadilly 1980-; hon res fell Richardson Inst Univ of Lancaster; memb Cncl ISIS (memb 1980-), chm Champernowne Tst; *Books* The Seventh Enemy (1974), Plotting Peace (1990); *Recreations* gardening, poultry breeding, music; *Style*— Ronald Higgins, Esq; Little Reeve, Vowchurch, Hereford HR2 0RL (☎ 0981 550307); Dunamis, St. James's, 197 Piccadilly, London W1V 9LF (☎ 071 437 6851)

HIGGINS, Rosalyn; da of Lewis Cohen, and Fay, *née* Inberg; *b* 2 June 1937; *Educ* Burlington GS London, Girton Coll Cambridge (Minor and Major scholar, Campell Scholar, Bryce-Tebbs scholar, BA, MA, LLB, Montefiore Award), Yale (JSD); *m* ; 1 s, 1 da; *Career* UK interne Office of Legal Affairs UN 1958, Cwlth Fund fell 1959, visiting fell Brooking's Inst Washington DC 1960, jr fell in int studies LSE 1961-63, staff specialist in int law RIIA 1963-74, visiting lectr in law Yale Law Sch 1966 and 1975, visiting fell LSE 1974-78; visiting prof of law: Stanford Law Sch 1975, Yale Law Sch 1977; prof of int law: Univ of Kent Canterbury 1978-81, Univ of London 1981-; bencher Inner Temple 1989; memb: UN Ctee on Human Rights 1984-, Advsy Cncl British Inst of Int and Comparative Law; external examiner (Univ of Cambridge, Centre for Petroleum and Mineral Law Studies Dundee), guest lectr at numerous univs in Europe and America, memb Bd of Eds American Jl of Int Law 1975-85; lectr for HM Govt on variety of int law matters; former vice pres American Soc Int Law 1972-74 (former memb Exec Cncl); memb: Int Bar Soc, Energy Law Ctee Int Law Assoc; Ordre des Palines Académiques; *Books* The Development of International Law Through the Political Organs of the United Nations (1963), Conflict of Interests: International Law in a Divided World (1965), The Administration of the United Kingdom Foreign Policy Through the United Nations (1966), UN Peacekeeping: Documents and Commentary (Vol I ME 1969, Vol II Asia 1970, Vol III Africa 1980, Vol IV Europe 1981), Law in Movement-Essays in Memory of John McMahon (jt ed with James Fawcett, 1974), The Taking of Property by the State (1983); author of numerous articles for law jls and jls of int relations; *Recreations* golf, cooking, eating; *Style*— Prof Rosalyn Higgins, QC; London School of Economics, Houghton St, London WC2A 2AE (☎ 071 955 7250, fax 071 242 0392, telex 24655 LSELONG G)

HIGGINS, Rt Hon Terence Langley; PC (1979),DL (W Sussex 1988), MP (Cons) Worthing 1964-; s of Reginald Higgins; *b* 18 Jan 1928; *Educ* Alleyn's Sch Dulwich, Gonville and Caius Coll Cambridge (MA); *m* 1961, Prof Rosalyn, *née* Cohen; 1 s, 1 da;

Career fin sec to Treasy 1971-74 (Min of State 1970-72), oppn spokesman Treasy and Econ Affrs 1974 (and 1966-70), Trade 1974-76; chm: Cons Parly Sports Ctee 1979-81, Tport 1979-90, House of Commons Liaison Ctee 1983-, Treasy and Civil Serv Select Ctee 1983- (memb 1980-); memb: Pub Accounts Cmmn 1983-, Cncl Inst of Advanced Motorists; govr Dulwich Coll 1978-; memb Cncl: Inst of Econ Affrs 1989-, Policy Studies Inst 1988-; tstee Indust and Parly Tst 1987-; NZ Shipping Co 1948-55, Unilever 1959-64; dir: Warne Wright Gp 1976-84, Lex Serv Gp 1980-; former memb Br Olympic Athletics Team (1948, 1952), lectr on econ principles Yale, pres Cambridge Union Soc 1958; *Style—* The Rt Hon Terence Higgins, DL, MP; House of Commons London SW1

HIGGINS, Rear Adm William Alleyne; CB (1985), CBE (1980); s of Cdr Henry Gray Higgins, DSO, RN (d 1977), of Winterbourne, Dauntsey, Salisbury, and Lilian Anne, *née* Leete (d 1980); *b* 18 May 1928; *Educ* Wellington; *m* 1963, Wiltraud, da of Josef Hiebaum (d 1968), of Innsbruck, Austria; 2 s (Charles, David), 1 da (Selina); *Career* joined RN 1945, Rear Adm 1982, Last Flag Offr Medway and Port Adm Chatham 1982-83, dir gen Naval Personal Servs 1983-86, sec Defence Press and Bdcasting Ctee 1986-; *Recreations* rock climbing, mountaineering; *Style—* Rear Adm William Higgins, CBE, CB

HIGGS, Air Vice-Marshal Barry; CBE (1981); s of Percy Harold Higgs (d 1973), of Hitcham, Ipswich, Suffolk, and Ethel Eliza, *née* Elliot; *b* 22 Aug 1934; *Educ* Finchley Co GS; *m* 30 March 1957, Sylvia May, da of Harry Wilks; 2 s (David Stanford b 1958, Andrew Barry b 1959); *Career* 1955-70 served with Sqdn nos: 207, 115, 138, 49, 51; RAF Staff Coll 1968, Directorate of Forward Policy RAF 1971-73, Nat Def Coll 1974, cmd 39 (PR) Sqdn 1975-77, Asst Dir of Def Policy 1978-79, cmd RAF Finningley 1979-81, Royal Coll of Def Studies 1982, Dep Dir of Intelligence 1983-85, Asst Chief of Def Staff (overseas) 1985-87; dir gen Fertiliser Mfrs Assoc 1987-; *Recreations* sailing (cruising), bridge, gardening, theatre; *Clubs* RAF, Farmers; *Style—* Air Vice-Marshal Barry Higgs, CBE; 33 Parsonage St, Cambridge CB5 8DN (☎ 0223 69062); FMA, Ltd Greenhill House, Thorpe Wood, Peterborough PE3 6GF (☎ 0733 331303, fax 0733 333617)

HIGGS, Brian James; QC (1974); s of James Percival Higgs (d 1984), of Brentwood, and Kathleen Anne, *née* Sullivan; *b* 24 Feb 1930; *Educ* Wrekin Coll, London Univ; *m* 1, 1953 (m dis), Jean Cameron Dumerton; 2 s (Jeremy b 1963, Jonathan b 1963), 3 da (Antonia b 1955, Nicola b 1962, Juliet b 1969); m 2, Vivienne Mary, da of Vivian Oliver Johnson, of Essex; 1 s (Julian b 1982); *Career* cmmnd RA, serv 1948-50; called to the Bar Grays Inn 1955, bencher 1986, rec Crown Ct 1974; *Recreations* gardening, golf, wine, chess, bridge; *Clubs* Thorndon Park Golf; *Style—* Brian Higgs, Esq, QC; Butt Hatch House, Dunmow Road, Fyfield, Essex (☎ 0277 899509); 9 Kings Bench Walk, Temple, London EC4 (☎ 071 353 5638)

HIGGS, Derek Alan; s of Alan Edward Higgs (d 1979), and Freda Gwendoline, *née* Hope (d 1984); *b* 3 April 1944; *Educ* Solihull Sch, Univ of Bristol (BA); *m* 1970, Julia Mary, da of Robert T Arguile, of Leics; 2 s (Oliver b 1975, Rowley b 1980), 1 da (Josephine b 1976); *Career* md S G Warburg Gp plc, head of corporate fin S G Warburg & Co Ltd; FCA; *Style—* Derek Higgs, Esq; 41 Upper Addison Gardens, London W14; 2 Finsbury Ave, London EC2 (☎ 071 860 1090)

HIGGS, Roger Junior; JP (1971); s of Roger Higgs (d 1948), of Caversham, Reading, and Joyce Kearle Rich, *née* Maggs; *b* 8 March 1932; *Educ* St Edward's Sch Oxford, Harper Adams Agric Coll; *m* 7 Feb 1953, Daphne Jean, da of Robert Victor Gray (d 1968), of Knebworth, Herts; 1 s (Timothy b 1955), 2 da (Janferie b 1954, Sarah b 1957); *Career* farmer; gen cmmr of Income Tax 1974, currently chm bd of govrs Nat Soc For Epilepsy (govr 1985), dir NSE Enterprises Ltd (later chm) 1986; *Recreations* sailing, travel; *Clubs* Rotary, Royal Southampton Yacht; *Style—* Roger Higgs, Esq; 9 Calshot Court, Ocean Village, Southampton SO1 1GR

HIGHAM, Hon Mrs (Barbara Constance); da of 3 Viscount Hampden, GCVO, KCB, CMG (d 1958); *b* 1907; *m* 1934, Ronald Harry Higham (d 1966); 1 s (Robin David b 1939), 1 da (*see* Grosvenor, Hon Mrs Victor); *Style—* The Hon Mrs Higham; Flat 6, 212 Old Brompton Rd, London SW5

HIGHAM, Geoffrey Arthur; s of late Arthur Higham, and late Elsie Higham; *b* 17 April 1927; *Educ* King Williams Coll Isle of Man, St Catharine's Coll Cambridge (MA); *m* 1951, Audrey, da of Charles W Hill; 1 s (Nicholas b 1 June 1954), 1 da (Susan b 20 Sept 1957); *Career* served RE 1945-48, Metal Box Co 1950-64, Montague Burton 1964-65; Cape Industries: joined 1965, md 1971-80, chm 1980-85; industl dir Charter Consolidated plc 1980-87, non-exec chm The Rugby Group plc 1986- (dir 1979-); non-exec dir: Pirelli General plc 1987-, Travers Morgan Ltd 1988-, Try Group plc 1989-; vice chm Cncl BIM 1984-88 (chm BIM fndn 1981-83); memb United Kingdom South Africa Trade Assoc; CBIM 1975, FRSA 1989; *Recreations* music, cricket, gardening; *Clubs* Army & Navy, Middlesex Cricket; *Style—* Geoffrey Higham, Esq; 32 East St Helen St, Abingdon, Oxfordshire OX14 5EB (☎ 0235 529815); The Rugby Group plc, Crown House, Rugby, Warwickshire (☎ 0788 542666, fax 0788 546726, telex 31523, car 0831 116226)

HIGHAM, Martin Pownall; s of Denis Higham, of Shepperton, Surrey, and Winifred Mary, *née* Bussey; *b* 3 May 1949; *Educ* Reigate GS; *m* 1974, Ann, da of Edward McMullen (d 1967); 1 s (Daniel Edward b 1978), 1 da (Emma Lucy b 1980); *Career* cashier and supervisor Barclays Bank Ltd 1969-71; Dexion International Ltd 1971-74 (asst press offr, press offr); account exec: James Mills & Associates 1974-75, Bastable Public Relations 1975-77; dir Kestrel Communications Ltd 1977-; ptnr: Kestrel Services 1981-, Broadway Partnership 1987-; memb of winning team Queen Mother's Birthday award 1990 (environment servs); MIPR; *Recreations* squash, travel, theatre; *Style—* Martin Higham, Esq; Kestrel Communications Ltd, Broadway House, The Broadway, Wimbledon SW19 1RL (☎ 081 543 2299, car 0836 240 734, fax 081 543 2296)

HIGHE, Jackie; da of John Barraclough (d 1988), and Lily, *née* Senior (d 1989); *b* 17 Sept 1947; *Educ* Univ of Leeds; *m* 5 April 1968, Brian Highe, s of Philip Highe, of Yorkshire; 1 s (Philip b 1971), 1 da (Jane b 1969); *Career* assoc ed Living Magazine 1984-86, ed Parents Magazine 1986-88; ed in chief: Bella Magazine 1988-90, First For Women 1990-; memb: UK Women's Forum, Br Soc of Magazine Eds; *Recreations* music, walking, reading; *Style—* Mrs Jackie Highe; First For Women, 270 Sylvan Ave, Englewood Cliffs, NJ 07632, USA

HIGHETT, Hon Mrs (Jean Mary); *née* Montagu; o da of 3 Baron Swaythling, OBE (d 1990), and his 1 w, Mary Violet, *née* Levy; *b* 8 Aug 1927; *m* 28 Nov 1951, Lintorn Trevor Highett, MC, s of Maj Trevor Cecil Highett, of Wainsford House, Lymington, Hants; 1 s (Paul Lintorn b 11 May 1958), 2 da (Clare Joanna b 9 Aug 1956, Stephanie Jane b 20 Nov 1963); *Style—* The Hon Mrs Highett; 2A Gore St, London SW7

HIGHFIELD, (William) Barry; s of Alfred Highfield (d 1978), of Sevenoaks, Kent, and Eileen Margaret, *née* Leavey; *b* 22 May 1934; *Educ* Tonbridge, Brooksby Hall Leics; *m* 2, 8 Feb 1980, Rosemary Helen, da of Lt Cdr Ian Nagle Douglas Cox, DSC, RN (d 1990); 1 s (David b 1965), 1 da (Jane b 1963), 2 step s; *Career* Nat Serv RAF 1952-54; farmer intensive livestock Kent and Sussex 1959-76; mangr Albany Life Assur 1980-, dir Hurstdens Ltd (gen insur brokers); assoc memb Life Assur Assoc; *Recreations* golf; *Clubs* Sloane, Tavistock Golf; *Style—* Barry Highfield, Esq; 30 West St, Tavistock, Devon PL19 8JY

HIGHFIELD, Dr Roger; s of Ronald Albert Highfield, of Enfield, Middx, and Dorothea Helena, *née* Depta; *b* 11 July 1958; *Educ* Christ's Hosp Horsham Sussex, Pembroke Coll Oxford (Domus scholar, MA, DPhil), Queen Elizabeth House Oxford (Leverhulme fell); *partner*, Julia Brookes; *Career* news/clinical reporter Pulse 1983-84 (dep features ed), news ed Nuclear Engineering International 1984-86; The Daily Telegraph: technol corr 1986, technol ed 1987, science ed 1988-; *awards* Med Journalist of the Year 1987, Science Writer of Year 1988, Specialist Corr of the Year (Br Press Awards) 1989; cited by Save British Science as Campaigning Journalist of the Year; memb RSC; *Books* The Arrow of Time (1990); *Recreations* swimming, drinking; *Style—* Dr Roger Highfield; Daily Telegraph, 181 Marsh Wall, London E14 9SR (☎ 071 538 5000, fax 071 538 7842)

HIGHLEY, Ian Godfrey; s of Capt Godfrey Wentworth Highley, OBE (d 1944 Abadan, Iran), and Gladys Mary, *née* Forrest (d 1988); *b* 11 April 1928; *Educ* Presteigne Co Sch Powys, Highgate Sch London; *m* 22 Dec 1956, Loraine Lee; 1 s (Richard Ian b 3 Jan 1963), 2 da (Denise Mary (Mrs Hollands) b 4 Oct 1957, Gwenyth Daphne (Mrs Archer) b 27 Feb 1959); *Career* Nat Serv RN 1947-49; articled clerk Jacob Cavenagh & Skeet Chartered Accountants 1944-47 and 1949, qualified 1949; Peat Marwick Mitchell: joined 1950, Hong Kong 1951, co sec and fin controller Eastern Shipping Group Hong Kong; ptnr West and Drake London and Reading 1958-71; fndr and ptnr: Highley & Co Insolvency Accountants, Highley & Partners Chartered Accountants 1971-; Insolvency Practitioners Assoc: memb Cncl 1984-90, chm Fin Ctee, chm Educn and Trg Ctee, ret 1990; memb Insolvency Licensing Ctee ICAEW 1986-; Berks CC (Pangbourne Ward) 1966-67; hon sec Thames Valley Branch IOD 1978-84, sec Padworth Coll Tst 1963-, tstee Reading Dispensary Tst 1982-, memb Lloyd's 1978-; FCA (ACA 1949), FIPA 1973, FCCA 1984, FInstD 1978; memb: Aberdeen Angus Cattle Soc 1982-, Association Européene des Practiciens des Procédures Collective 1982-; *Recreations* breeding pedigree Aberdeen Angus cattle, golf, gardening, reading; *Clubs* Phyllis Court, Henley-on-Thames, Oxon; *Style—* Ian Highley, Esq; 74 South St, Reading, Berkshire

HIGHMORE, Neil Sinclair; s of John Sinclair Highmore (Maj ret), of Rookdykes, Corse, by Huntly, Aberdeenshire, and Margaret Boyes Highmore, *née* Sinclair (d 1974); *b* 27 May 1948; *Educ* Broughton Secdy Sch, Edinburgh Art Coll, Heriot Watt Univ (BArch); *Career* ptnr in architectural practice Patience and Highmore, former chm of Borders Architectural Gp; RIBA, ARIAS; *Recreations* squash, gardening, angling; *Style—* Neil Highmore, Esq; Tighcarr, St Ronan's Terrace, Innerleithen, Peeblesshire (☎ 0896 830128); Quadrant, 17 Bernard St, Edinburgh EH6 6PW (☎ 031 555 0644)

HIGLETT, Simon Ian; s of John Higlett, of Allesley, Coventry, and Patricia Anne, *née* Such; *b* 30 May 1959; *Educ* Wimbledon Sch of Art (BA), Slade Sch of Fine Art (Higher Dip in Fine Art, Leslie Hurry prize for Theatre Design); *m* 21 Aug 1988, Isobel, da of Alan Arnett, of Tuffley, Gloucester; *Career* asst to Tim Goodchild 1982-84; costume designer for: Der Rosenkavalier (Marseilles Opera) 1984, A Midsummer Nights Dream and Ring Round the Moon (New Shakespeare Co) 1985, Night and Day and See How They Run (Theatre Clwyd) 1985, Medea (Young Vic) 1985, Taming of the Shrew and Antony and Cleopatra (Haymarket) 1986, Daughter in Law and School for Scandal (Birmingham Repertory) 1987, Hobson's Choice, Plotters of Cabbage Patch Corner, Mrs Warren's Profession, Gingerbread Man (all at Leeds Playhouse, 1988), Midsummer Nights Dream, The Contractor, The Railway Children (all at Birmingham Repertory, 1988, A Midsummer Night's Dream and Babes in Arms (New Shakespeare Co) 1988, Winnie (Victoria Palace) 1988, Last Waltz (Greenwich) 1989, A Month in the Country (Leeds Playhouse) 1989, A Midsummer Night's Dream, Twelfth Night, Swaggerer (all at New Shakespeare Co, 1989), An Inspector Calls (Plymouth Theatre Royal) 1989, Boys from Syracuse (Crucible Theatre Sheffield) 1989, Singer (RSC Barbican) 1990, Kean (Old Vic London and Canada) 1990, Scenes from a Marriage (Chichester) 1990, Some Like it Hot (West Yorkshire Playhouse) 1990, Don Giovanni and The Marriage of Figaro (Jugendstil Theater Vienna) 1991; *Recreations* reading, drawing, theatre; *Style—* Simon Higlett, Esq; 9 Park Crescent, Worthing, West Sussex BN11 4AH (☎ 0903 204480)

HIGNETT, John Mulock; s of Reginald Arthur Hignett (d 1975), and Marjorie Sarah Louise Hignett; *b* 9 March 1934; *Educ* Harrow, Magdalene Coll Cambridge; *m* 5 Aug 1961, Marijke Inge, da of Rudolf-Jeorje de Boer (d 1988), of Amsterdam; 1 s (Martin b 26 Nov 1962), 1 da (Karin b 4 March 1965); *Career* Lazard Bros: joined 1963, mangr Issues Dept 1971, dir 1972, head corp fin 1980-81, on secondment 1981-84, md 1984-88; former non-exec dir Carless Capel and Leonard, fin dir Glaxo Hldgs plc 1988-; non-exec dir: TI Group, Whitbread Investment Gp; dir gen Panel on Takeovers and Mergers 1981-84, CSI 1983-84 (first time these two posts have been held by one person); Boxing blue 1955 (capt 1956); FCA 1961; *Recreations* growing orchids; *Clubs* MCC, Hawks (Cambridge), Royal Southern Yacht; *Style—* John M Hignett, Esq; Glaxo Holdings plc, Lansdowne House, Berkeley Square, London W1X 6BP (☎ 071 493 4060)

HIGNETT, (John) Michael; TD (1967), JP (1980); s of Lt-Col John Derrick Hignett, DL, JP, of East Langton Grange, Market Harborough, Leics, and Alice Gwendoline, *née* Manners (d 1965); *b* 29 Sept 1928; *Educ* Stowe, Trinity Coll Cambridge (BA, MA); *m* 23 April 1960, Mary Beatrice Margaret Mella, da of Osborne Risk Burchnall (d 1970), of The Manor House, Aston Flamville, Leics; 2 s (Rupert b 1967, Edward b 1971), 1 da (Charlotte b 1969); *Career* Queen's Own Warwicks and Worcs Yeo 1952-64; Bass plc 1952-84: dir Bass UK 1970-81, vice chm Charrington & Co Ltd 1981-84 (md 1975-81); chm London Brewer's Soc 1970-84; High Sheriff of Leicester 1970; memb Ctee Leics and Rutland Army Benevolent Fund, tstee Fernie Hunt (chm Supporters Assoc), Woodm£n of Arden; memb Ct Worshipful Co of Brewers 1977-84; memb Inst of Brewing; *Recreations* foxhunting, fishing, shooting; *Clubs* Boodles, St James'; *Style—* Michael Hignett, Esq, TD, JP; Clipston Court, Market Harborough, Leics LE16 7RU (☎ 085 886 230)

HIGTON, Dennis John; s of John William Higton (d 1966), of Surrey, and Lillian Harriet, *née* Mann (d 1932); *b* 15 July 1921; *Educ* Guildford Tech Sch, RAE Farnborough Tech Sch (CEng); *m* 1945, Joy Merrifield, da of William Merrifield Pickett (d 1964), of Wilts; 1 s (Peter William b 1962), 1 da (Priscilla Margaret b 1949); *Career* engrg student apprentice RAE 1938-42, aerodynamic flight res RAE 1942-52, fighter and naval aircraft flight testing A and AEE 1953-66, def staff Washington DC USA 1966-70, asst dir Aircraft Prodn 1972-74 (dir 1974-76), dir gen (under sec) MOD (PE) 1976-81; conslt to aviation indust and dir 1981-88; bd chm Civil Serv Cmmn 1981-; chm S Wilts and Salisbury NSPCC 1982-; FIMechE, FRAeS; *Recreations* sailing, skiing, painting, bee keeping; *Style—* Dennis Higton, Esq; Jasmine Cottage, Rollestone Rd, Shrewton, Salisbury, Wilts SP3 4HG (☎ 0980 620276)

HILARY, David Henry Jephson; s of Robert Jephson Hilary (d 1937), and Nita Margaret Macmahon, *née* Mahon (d 1972); *b* 3 May 1932; *Educ* King's Coll Cambridge (MA); *m* 22 June 1957, Phoebe, da of John James Buchanan (d 1983); 2 s (John b 1964, Henry b 1968), 2 da (Miriam b 1967, Rachel b 1970); *Career* RA 1953-54; HO 1956-87, Cabinet Office 1967-69 and 1981-83; asst under sec of state 1975-87, receiver for Met Police Dist 1987-; *Recreations* cricket, bridge, family pursuits; *Clubs* RAC, MCC; *Style—* David Hilary, Esq; c/o New Scotland Yard, Broadway, London

SW1

HILDER, Rowland; OBE (1985); *b* 28 June 1905; *Educ* Askes Hatcham, Goldsmith's Coll Sch of Art; *m* 17 Dec 1929, Edith Hilder; 1 s (Anthony b 1936), 1 da (Mary b 1945); *Career* artist; exhibited Hayward Gallery London 1983; illustrated edns of: Moby Dick 1926, Treasure Island 1929, Precious Bane 1930, The Bible for Today 1940, The Guide to Flowers of the Countryside (with Edith Hilder) 1955; RI 1936, RSMA 1938, RE 1986; *Books* Starting with Watercolours (1966), Painting Landscapes in Watercolours (1982), Rowland Hilder's England (1986), Rowland Hilder Country 1987, Rowland Hilder Sketching Country (1991); *Recreations* sailing; *Style—* Rowland Hilder, Esq, OBE; 7 Kidbrooke Grove, Blackheath, London SE3 0PG (☎ 081 858 3072)

HILDESLEY, Michael Edmund; s of Paul Francis Glynn Hildesley, and Mary, *née* Morgan; *b* 16 Oct 1948; *Educ* Sherborne, Trinity Coll Oxford (MA); *m* 1972, Judith Carol, da of George Michael Pistor, of USA; 3 s (Robert b 1980, David b 1982, Charles b 1982); *Career* merchant banker; dir Morgan Grenfell & Co Ltd 1984-; *Style—* Michael Hildesley, Esq; 23 Gt Winchester Street, London EC2P 2AX (☎ 071 588 4545)

HILDRETH, Henry Hamilton Crossley (Jan); s of Maj-Gen Sir John Hildreth, KBE, and Joan Elsie Hallett, *née* Hamilton (d 1975); gf Alfred H J Hamilton, of Dibden Manor, descended from Hugh Hildreth, s of Sir James Hildreth who went to Ireland 1616, and hence of Hamiltons who arrived England mid 10 century, see Hildreth and Abercorn in Burkes P and B and Irish FR; *b* 1 Dec 1932; *Educ* Wellington, The Queen's Coll Oxford (MA); *m* 1958, Wendy Moira Marjorie, da of Arthur Harold Clough, CMG (d 1967), of Penn, Bucks; 2 s (Gerald, Gavin), 1 da (Frances); *Career* Nat Serv 1952-53, 2 Lt RA, TA 44 Para Bde; memb Baltic Exchange 1956; Royal Dutch Shell Gp Philippines and London 1957, Kleinwort Benson Ltd 1963, dir and asst chief exec John Laing and Son Ltd 1972, exec dir Minster Tst Ltd, non-exec dir Monument Oil and Gas plc 1984-88; chm: Sea Catch plc 1987-, Carroll Securities Ltd 1986-, Scallop Kings plc; dir numerous cos, ind conslt; memb NEDO 1965- (memb of 3 EDC's), memb Bd London Tport 1968, memb Cncl The Spastics Soc 1980-, dir Contact A Family 1980-; govr: Wellington Coll 1974, Eagle House Sch 1986-; chm Wimbledon Cons Assoc 1986-89; memb: Cncl Br Exec Serv Overseas, IOD (dir gen 1975-78), Ctee GBA 1978-86, Cncl ISIS 1979-82 (life), Industl Soc (memb Ctee 1973-83), Accounting Standard Advsy ctee 1976-79; *Recreations* running, watermills, gardening, photography; *Clubs* Athenaeum, Vincent's (Oxford), Thames Hare and Hounds, The Political Economy, Achilles; *Style—* Jan Hildreth, Esq; 50 Ridgway Place, Wimbledon SW19 4SW (☎ 081 946 0243); The Mill, Ponsworthy, Newton Abbot, Devon; Minster House, Arthur St, London EC4 R9HB (☎ 071 623 1050)

HILDRETH, Maj-Gen Sir (Harold) John Crossley; KBE (1964, CBE 1952, OBE 1945); s of Lt-Col Harold Crossley Hildreth, DSO, OBE (d 1936); *b* 12 June 1908; *Educ* Wellington, RMA Woolwich; *m* 1950, Mary Hildreth, da of George Wroe; 2 s, 3 da; *Career* 2 Lt RA 1928, Capt RAOC 1935, served WW II, Col 1943, Brig 1958, DOS BAOR 1957-59, Inspr RAOC 1959-61, Maj-Gen 1961, DOS WO 1961-64, ret; Col Cmdt RAOC 1963-70; md: Army Kinema Corpn 1965-69, The Services Kinema Corpn 1969-75; chm Gtr London Branch SS and AFA 1977-; *Style—* Maj-Gen Sir John Hildreth, KBE; 59 Latymer Court, London W6 (☎ 081 748 3107); 56 The Cottages, North St, Emsworth, Hants (☎ 024 34 3466)

HILDYARD, Hon Mrs (Aislinn Mary Katharine); *née* Morris; JP; eldest da of 2 Baron Morris (d 1975), and Jean Beatrice, *née* Maitland-Makgill-Crichton (d 1989, having m 2, Baron Salmon (Life Peer), *qv*); *b* 22 April 1934; *m* 1954, Capt Angus Jeremy Christopher Hildyard, DL, *qv*; 1 s (Nicholas Alexander Cyril b 1954), 1 da (Charlotte (Lady Tyrwhitt) b 1958); *Style—* The Hon Mrs Hildyard, JP; Goxhill Hall, Goxhill, Barrow-upon-Humber, South Humberside DN19 7LZ (☎ 0469 30121)

HILDYARD, Capt Angus Jeremy Christopher; DL (1977); s of Maj Donald Maxwell Dunlop (d 1963), and Noel Florence Dora, *née* Hildyard (who m 2, Col Alexander Bainbridge Craddock, CIE, OBE, and d 1963); changed surname by Deed Poll from Dunlop to mother's maiden name Hildyard 1945; sr co-heir of the Barony of Le Scrope of Masham through his grandmother, as sr descendant of Catherina d'Arcy, w of Sir Robert Hildyard, 3 Bt; *b* 15 Feb 1928; *Educ* Charterhouse, RMA Sandhurst; *m* 1954, Hon Aislinn Mary Katharine, *née* Morris, *see* Hon Mrs Hildyard; 1 s (Nicholas Alexander Cyril b 1954), 1 da (Charlotte (Lady Tyrwhitt) b 1958); *Career* Adj 17 Trg Regt Staff Capt RA 2 Inf Div, ret 1960; High Sheriff of Humberside 1978-79; chm Georgian Soc for E Yorks; gen cmmr Income Tax; vice chm Yorks Ctee Historic Houses Assoc; hon memb Yorks Tourist Bd; past pres Humberside Victims Support Scheme; *Recreations* gardening, classical architecture; *Style—* Capt Angus Hildyard, DL; Goxhill Hall, Goxhill, Barrow-upon-Humber, South Humberside DN19 7LZ (☎ 0469 30121)

HILDYARD, Sir David Henry Thoroton; KCMG (1975, CMG 1966), DFC (1943); s of His Hon Gerard Moresby Thoroton Hildyard, QC, DL (d 1956), of Flintham Hall, Newark, and Sybil Hamilton Hoare (d 1978); *b* 4 May 1916; *Educ* Eton, ChCh Oxford; *m* 1947, Millicent, da of Sir Edward Baron (d 1962), and widow of Wing Cdr R M Longmore; 1 s (Robert b 1952), 1 da (Marianna b 1955); *Career* served WWII RAF; joined Foreign Serv 1948, cnsllr Mexico 1960-65, head of Econ Rels Dept FO 1965, min and alternate UK delegate to UN 1968, ambass Chile 1970-73, ambass and perm rep to UN (Geneva) 1973-76, head UK Delgn to CSCE 1974-75; dir Lombard Odier Int Portfolio Mgmnt 1980; *Clubs* Garrick, Reform, Hurlingham; *Style—* Sir David Hildyard, KCMG, DFC; 97 Onslow Square, London SW7 (☎ 071 584 2110)

HILDYARD, Myles Thoroton; MBE, MC, TD, JP, DL; s of His Hon G M T Hildyard, KC (d 1956), of Flintham Hall, Newark, and Sybil, *née* Hamilton Hoare (d 1978); *b* 31 Dec 1914; *Educ* Eton, Magdalene Coll Cambridge; *Career* WWII Notts Sherwood Rangers Yeo; landowner, farmer, local historian; md Newfield Farm Ltd; pres Thoroton Soc of Notts and CPRE, vice chm Nat Tst Eastern Midlands Region; Lord of Manors of Flintham and Screveton Notts, patron of living of Flintham; FSA; *Clubs* Brook's; *Style—* Myles T Hildyard, MBE, MC, TD, JP, DL, FSA; Flintham Hall, Newark (☎ 0636 525214)

HILDYARD, Robert Henry Thoroton; s of Sir David Hildyard, KCMG, DFC, of 97 Onslow Square, London, and Millicent, *née* Baron; *b* 10 Oct 1952; *Educ* Eton, ChCh Oxford (BA); *m* 9 Aug 1980, Isabella Jane, da of James Rennie (d 1964); 3 da (Catherine b 31 Oct 1983, Camilla b 15 May 1985, d 1987, Alexandra b 15 Sept 1988); *Career* called to the Bar Inner Temple 1977; *Books* contrib to: Forms and Precedents: Company Law, Tolleys Company Law; *Recreations* tennis, shooting; *Clubs* Queen's, Hurlingham; *Style—* Robert Hildyard, Esq; 4 Stone Buildings, Lincoln's Inn, London WC2A 3VT (☎ 071 242 5524, fax 071 831 7907)

HILES, Andrew Nash; s of (Walter) Stanley Vernon Nash Hiles (d 1953), of Derby, and Ivy Mary Hiles; *b* 11 March 1941; *Educ* Bemrose Sch Derby, Univ of Manchester; *m* 1, 20 March 1962 (m dis 1976), Audrey; 3 s (Sean b 1963, Martin b 1965, Stuart b 1970); m 2, 25 Feb 1976, Lola Tillie, da of James Brass, of London; 1 s (Dominic b 1977); *Career* cmmnd pilot offr RAF 1965, Flt Lt ret 1975; mgmnt servs projects mangr and orgn and methods mangr London Tport 1975-84, business systems conslt PO 1984-86, computer servs mangr Harwell Laboratory 1986 (using CRAY, IBM and DEC systems); author of numerous articles on disaster recovery and information technol; fndr numerous user gps incl Public Servs Payrolls Forum 1989, fndr chm disaster recovery gp Survive; MBCS, MIDPM; *Recreations* work, dogs; *Style—* Andrew Hiles, Esq; 10 Exmoor Rd, Thatcham, Berkshire RG13 4UY (☎ 0635 67073); Harwell Laboratory, Harwell, Oxon OX11 0RA (☎ 0235 432958, telex 831135, fax 0235 432375)

HILEY, Carole Shirley; da of George Quastel (d 1976), of London, and Golda Gertrude Quastel (d 1982); *b* 25 Aug 1931; *Educ* Colwyn Bay Secdy Sch North Wales; *m* 1, 17 Aug 1952 (m dis 1972), Stanley S Cowan, s of William Cowan (d 1958); 1 s (Simon Anthony b 1955), 1 da (Suzanne b 1956); m 2, 6 June 1975, Ronald H Hiley, s of Charles Henry Hiley (d 1941); *Career* professional childcarer; fndr and md: Beck Kindergartens Ltd 1959-80, Kindergartens for Commerce Ltd 1966-80, Our Childrens World Ltd, Childrens World Ltd 1980, World of Children Ltd 1980-, Babycare Centres Ltd, Daycare Centres Ltd, Playcare Centres Ltd; *Recreations* children, gardening; *Clubs* Network, Phylis Court Henley, Women In Business, Variety Club of GB; *Style—* Mrs Carole S Hiley; Pankridge Manor, Bledlow Ridge, Buckinghamshire HP14 4AE (☎ 024 027 521 and 305); 10 Lincoln Park Business Centre, Cressex, High Wycombe, Bucks HP12 3RD (☎ 0494 25051)

HILEY, Peter Haviland; s of Sir (Ernest) Haviland Hiley, KBE (d 1943), of Cambridge, and Brenda Lee, *née* Lord (d 1961); *b* 19 Feb 1921; *Educ* Eton, Grenoble Univ; *m* 21 May 1955, (Isabel) Susan, da of Herbert George Hope, MBE (d 1956), of Blackmoor, Hants; 1 s (William b 1960); *Career* WWII Intelligence Corps 1941-45; Br Cncl 1945-49, joined Laurence Olivier Productions Ltd 1949; current dir: Wheelshare Ltd (formerly Laurence Olivier Productions Ltd), The Oliver Fndn, Old Vic Tst Ltd, Royal Victoria Hall Gdn; govr Petersfield Comprehensive Sch 1965-, gen cmmr Income Tax 1966-; *Recreations* theatre, sightseeing; *Style—* Peter Hiley, Esq; Byways, Steep, Petersfield, Hants GU32 1AD; 102 Valiant House, Vicarage Crescent, London SW11 3LX

HILL, Alan John Wills; CBE (1972); s of William Wills Hill (d 1974), of London, and May Francis Victoria, *née* Dixon (d 1962); *b* 12 Aug 1912; *Educ* Wyggeston GS Leicester, Jesus Coll Cambridge (MA); *m* 1939, Enid Adela, da of Frederick Malin (d 1915), of Leicester; 2 s (Stephen, David), 1 da (Carolyn); *Career* RAF 1940-45, Sqdn Ldr Europe; publisher; dir William Heinemann Ltd 1956-79, chm and md Heinemann Education Books Ltd 1961-79, md Heinemann Gp 1972-79; contrib many articles in jls; govr Nuffield Chelsea Curriculum Tst 1979-, hon public rels offr Prehistoric Soc 1988-; hon fell King's Coll London; *Books* In Pursuit of Publishing (1988); *Recreations* swimming, mountain walking; *Clubs* Athenaeum, Garrick, RAF, PEN; *Style—* Alan Hill, Esq, CBE; 56 Northway, London NW11 6PA (☎ 081 455 8388); New House, Rosthwaite, Borrowdale, Cumbria (☎ 059 684 687); Heinemann, Halley Ct, Jordan Hill, Oxford OX2 8EJ (☎ 0865 311 366, telex 837292)

HILL, Alastair Malcolm; QC (1982); s of Sir Ian George Wilson Hill, CBE, TD (d 1982); *b* 12 May 1936; *Educ* Trinity Coll Glenalmond, Keble Coll Oxford (BA); *m* 1969 (m dis 1977), Elizabeth Maria Innes; 2 children; *Career* barr Gray's Inn 1961; recorder Crown Ct SE Circuit 1982-; *Recreations* flyfishing, collecting watercolours and prints, opera; *Style—* Alastair Hill Esq, QC; New Court, Temple, London EC4Y 9BE (☎ 071 583 6166)

HILL, Alfred Edward; s of Mervyn Ewart Phillips Hill, of Gozo, and Betty Deborah Jane Matilda, *née* Bennett; *b* 29 Aug 1945; *Educ* Clifton Coll Imede (MBA); *m* 14 July 1973, Rosemary Sarth, da of John William Chandos Lloyd-Kirk; 2 c (Charlotte Rosina b 13 Aug 1975, Rupert Alfred b 23 Dec 1977); *Career* articled clerk: Monahans Swindon 1964-66, Grace Ryland (formerly CJ Ryland & Co) 1966-69; qualified CA 1969, seconded to Spafax SA 1972; ptnr: Thomson McLintock 1974-, KPMG Peat Marwick McLintock (following merger) 1987-; underwriting memb Lloyd's 1979, govr Clifton Coll 1989-; FCA 1979 (ACA 1969); *Clubs* Clifton, Bristol Savages; *Style—* Alfred Hill, Esq; Campfield, Church Rd, Abbots Leigh, nr Bristol, Avon BS8 3QU (☎ 0275 372104); KPMG Peat Marwick McLintock, 15 Pembroke Rd, Clifton, Bristol BS8 3BG (☎ 0272 732291, fax 0272 732196)

HILL, (George) Andrew; s of Cdr George Walter Hill (d 1974), of Orlestone Grange, Ashford, Kent, and Kathleen Mary Kynaston, *née* Jacques (d 1986); *b* 15 April 1939; *Educ* Winchester, Christ Church Oxford (MA); *m* 17 June 1972, Margaret Mary Katherine, da of Harold Arthur Armstrong While, MBE, TD (d 1983); 1 s (Timothy Trigger b 5 May 1976), 1 da (Lucy Kynaston b 14 Dec 1974); *Career* slr 1966, ptnr Monier Williams; memb Ctee Holborn Law Soc 1985-; Freeman City of London 1986, Liveryman Worshipful Co of Tin Plate Workers 1986 (clerk 1980-88); *Recreations* golf, gardening, wine and watercolours; *Clubs* City Livery, Royal Wimbledon Golf, Trevose Golf; *Style—* Andrew Hill, Esq; 235 Sheen Lane, London SW14 8LE (☎ 081 876 2055); 71 Lincoln's Inn Fields, London WC2A 3JF (☎ 071 405 6195)

HILL, Lady Anne Catherine Dorothy; *née* Gathorne-Hardy; da of 3 Earl of Cranbrook (d 1915), and Lady Dorothy Montagu Boyle, da of 7 Earl of Glasgow; *b* 12 Oct 1911; *m* 1938, George Heywood Hill (d 1986); 2 da (Harriet, Lucy); *Style—* The Lady Anne Hill; Snape Priory, Saxmundham, Suffolk IP17 1SA

HILL, 8 Viscount (UK 1842); Sir Antony Rowland Clegg-Hill; 10 Bt (GB 1727); also Baron Hill of Almarez and of Hardwick (UK 1816); strictly speaking the full title of the Viscountcy is: Viscount Hill of Hawkstone and of Hardwick; s of 7 Viscount Hill (d 1974, fourth in descent from John, er bro of 1 Viscount, who commanded Adam's Brigade in the Battle of Waterloo, was second in command of the Army of Occupation (of France) 1815-18 and was C-in-C 1828-42) by his 1 w Elisabeth, *née* Smyth-Osbourne (d 1967); *b* 19 March 1931; *Educ* Kelly Coll, RMA Sandhurst; *m* 1, 1963 (m dis 1976), Juanita, da of John Pertwee, of Surrey; m 2, 11 May 1989, Elizabeth Harriett, da of Ronald Offer, of Salisbury, Wilts; *Heir* cous, Peter Clegg-Hill; *Career* late Capt RA; has freedom of Shrewsbury; *Style—* The Rt Hon Viscount Hill; c/o House of Lords, SW1

HILL, Brian; CBE (1990), DL (Lancs 1977); *b* 16 Oct 1930; *Educ* Wigan GS, Univ of Manchester (LLB); *m* 3 July 1954, Barbara, *née* Hickson; 1 da; *Career* admitted slr 1953, asst slr Manchester Corpn 1953-56; Lancs CC: sr slr and second dep clerk 1956-74, dep clerk 1974-76, chief exec and clerk 1977-90; clerk of Lancs Lieutenancy 1977-90, co electoral returning offr 1977-90; sec: Lancs Advsy Ctee 1977-90, Lord Chllr's Advsy Ctee on Gen Cmmrs of Income Tax 1977-90, Lancs Probation and After Care Ctee 1977-; chm: Local Govt Legal Soc 1970-71, Soc of County Secretaries 1976-77, NW Branch SOLACE 1985; chm Assoc of County Chief Execs 1989-90 (advsr to Policy Ctee 1987-); co sec: Lancs Enterprises Ltd 1982-89, Lancs Co Enterprises Ltd 1989-; memb MSC Area Manpower Bd 1983-86, sec Lancs Ctee Royal Jubilee and Prince's Tsts 1985-90; memb: ct Univ of Lancaster 1977-, Bd of Govrs Royal Northern Coll of Music 1990- (clerk to Ct 1977-89), Cncl Rossall Sch 1990-; dep chm Halle Concerts Soc 1990-, dir Lancashire Area West Trg and Enterprise Cncl 1990-; vice pres Lancs Youth Clubs Assoc 1977-, memb Preston Select Vestry 1977-; hon fell Lancs Poly 1990; hon degree Royal Northern Coll of Music 1979; FRSA 1983, CBIM 1987; *Recreations* music; *Clubs* Royal Over-Seas League; *Style—* Brian Hill, Esq, CBE, DL; The Cottage, Bruna Hill, Garstang, Preston PR3 1QB (tel/fax 0995 603315)

HILL, Sir Brian John; s of Gerald A Hill, OBE (d 1974); *b* 19 Dec 1932; *Educ* Stowe, Univ of Cambridge (MA); *m* 1959, Janet Joyce, da of Alfred S Newman, OBE; 3

children; *Career* Nat Serv Army; gp md Higgs and Hill Ltd 1972-83, chm and chief exec Higgs and Hill plc 1983-89 (exec chm 1989-); dir Building Centre 1981-85; memb: Advsy Bd Property Services Agency 1981-86, Lazard Property Unit Trust 1982-, Lancs and Yorks Property Management Ltd 1985-, Palmerston Property Development plc 1985-, Grainhurst Properties Ltd 1985-; dir: Southern Regnl Bd National Westminster Bank 1991-, Property Services Agency 1986-88; chm Vauxhall Coll of Bldg and Further Educn 1976-86, pres London Region of Bldg Trade Employers' Confedn NFBTE 1981-82; chm: Nat Contractors Group 1983-84, Chartered Inst of Bldg 1984- (pres 1987-88); govr Great Ormond Street Hosp for Sick Children; FRICS, past pres Chartered Inst of Bldg, Hon FIStructE; *Recreations* travelling, tennis, gardening; *Clubs* RAC; *Style—* Sir Brian Hill; Barrow House, The Warren, Kingswood, Surrey; Higgs and Hill plc, Crown House, Kingston Rd, New Malden, Surrey KT3 3ST (☎ 081 942 8921)

HILL, Brian Lionel; s of Lionel Hill (d 1965); *b* 21 Dec 1935; *Educ* Hornchurch GS; *m* 1960, Julia Mary, *née* Woolford; 1 s (Simon), 1 da (Penelope); *Career* engaged in fin and industl mgmnt; fin dir Meggitt plc; FCA; *Recreations* pretending to be a farmer; *Style—* Brian Hill, Esq; Meggitt plc, 4 West St, Wimborne, Dorset BH21 1JN (☎ 0202 842915, fax 0202 881251); Northwood House, North Gorley, Hants SP6 2PL (☎ 0425 657455)

HILL, Rev Canon Christopher; s of Leonard Hill, of Kinver, Staffs, and Frances Vera, *née* Bullock; *b* 10 Oct 1945; *Educ* Sebright Sch Worcs, King's Coll London (BD, MTh, AKC); *m* 21 Dec 1976, Hilary Ann, da of Geoffrey James Whitehouse, of Brewood, Staffs; 3 s (Vivian b 1978, Adrian b 1982, Edmund b 1983), 1 da (Felicity b 1980); *Career* ordained Lichfield Cathedral (deacon 1969, priest 1970); asst curate: St Michael's Tividale Diocese of Lichfield 1969-73, St Nicholas Codsall 1973-74; asst chaplain to Archbishop of Canterbury for foreign rels 1974-81, co sec Anglican-RC Int Cmmn 1974-81 and 1983-, sec Anglican-Lutheran Euro Cmmn 1981-82, canon of Canterbury Cathedral 1982-89, sec for ecumenical affrs to Archbishop of Canterbury 1982-89, chaplain to HM the Queen 1987-, select preacher Univ of Oxford 1990, canon residentiary of St Paul's Cathedral 1989-; *Recreations* reading, walking, eating and drinking, classical music; *Clubs* Athenaeum, Nikaean (Guestmaster 1982-89), The Sette of Odd Volumes; *Style—* The Rev Canon Christopher Hill; 3 Amen Court, London EC4M 7BU (☎ 071 236 4532); The Chapter House, St Paul's Churchyard London EC4M 8AD (☎ 071 236 4128, fax 071 248 3104)

HILL, (John Edward) Christopher; s of Edward Harold Hill (d 1965), and Janet Augusta, *née* Dickenson (d 1964); *b* 6 Feb 1912; *Educ* St Peter's Sch York, Balliol Coll Oxford (BA, MA, DLitt); *m* 1, 1944 (m dis), Inez Bartlett; 1 da (Fanny Catherine d 1989); m 2, 1956, Bridget Irene, da of the Rev Harry Sutton; 1 s (Andrew Oliver b 16 June 1958), 1 da (Dinah Jane b 8 June 1960); *Career* Army and FO 1940-45; fell All Souls Coll Oxford 1934-38, asst lectr in modern history UC Cardiff 1936-38, master Balliol Coll Oxford 1965-78 (fell and tutor in modern history 1938-40 and 1945-65); Ford lectr Oxford 1962, visiting prof Open Univ 1978-80; Milton Soc of America award 1978, WH Smith literary award 1989; FRHistS 1948, FBA 1965; foreign hon memb: American Acad of Sciences 1973, Hungarian Acad of Sciences 1982; *Books* The English Revolution 1640 (1940), Lenin and the Russian Revolution (1947), Economic Problems of the Church (1956), Puritanism and Revolution (1958), The Century of Revolution (1961), Society and Puritanism (1984), Intellectual Origins of the English Revolution (1965), Reformation to Industrial Revolution (1967), God's Englishman: Oliver Cromwell (1970), Antichrist in 17th Century England (1971), The World Turned Upside Down (1972), Change and Continuity in 17th Century England (1974), Milton and the English Revolution (1977), Some Intellectual Consequences of the English Revolution (1980), The Experience of Defeat: Milton and Some Contemporaries (1984), Writing and Revolution in 17th Century England (1985), Religion and Politics in 17th Century England (1986), People and Ideas in 17th Century England (1986), A Turbulent, Seditious and Factious People: John Bunyan and His Church (1988), A Nation of Change and Novelty: Radical Politics, Religion and Literature in 17th Century England (1990); *Style—* Christopher Hill, Esq; Woodway House, Sibford Ferris, Banbury, Oxon OX15 5RA

HILL, Christopher Richard; s of Horace Rowland Hill (d 1966), of Trotton Place, near Petersfield, Hants, and Gwendolen Edith, *née* Smith (d 1987); *b* 4 March 1935; *Educ* Radley, Trinity Coll Cambridge (MA); *Career* HM Foreign Office 1958-62, asst dir Inst of Race Rels London 1962-65, lectr in govt Univ Coll of Rhodesia 1965-66, lectr in politics Univ of York 1966- (sr lectr 1982-), dir Centre for S African Studies 1972-82, visiting fell Cranleigh Sch 1988-90; Liveryman Worshipful Co of Leathersellers 1956; *Books* Bantustans – The Fragmentation of South Africa (1964), Rights and Wrongs – Some Essays on Human Rights (contrib ed, 1969), European Business and South Africa: An Appraisal of the EC Code of Conduct (contrib ed, 1981), Change in South Africa: Blind Alleys or New Directions (1983), Horse Power: The Politics of the Turf (1988); *Recreations* gardening, travel, journalism; *Clubs* Athenaeum, Travellers', Yorkshire; *Style—* Christopher Hill, Esq; Rother Cottage, Dodsley Grove, Midhurst, West Sussex GU29 9AB; Dept of Politics, University of York, Heslington, York YO1 5DD

HILL, David Beatty; s of Frederick Charles Hill (d 1964), and Jane Elizabeth, *née* Garlick (d 1934); *b* 5 Nov 1918; *m* 29 March 1952, Patricia, da of Thomas Walsh (d 1982), of Cornell House, Manor Park, Chislehurst, Kent; 2 da (Stevanne, Nikki); *Career* WWII RN 1939-40, special ops 1940-44, Fleet Air Arm 1944-45; asst ed Kentish Times 1946; ed: Ford Times 1946, European Esquire 1951; asst ed Daily Sketch 1953, ed-in-chief and md: Harmsworth Publications 1958, Weekend Publications 1958 (ed 1956), Harmsworth Press 1977; dir Associated Newspapers 1979; hon citizen New Orleans USA 1969; Freeman City of London 1967, Liveryman Worshipful Co Stationers and Newspaper Makers; *Books* The Cat Race (1952); *Recreations* golf, indolence as a fine art; *Clubs* Special Forces; *Style—* D Beatty Hill, Esq; Hill Court, Manor Park, Chislehurst, Kent

HILL, David Blyth; s of Ernest William Blyth Hill, of NSW, Aust, and Mary Frazer, *née* Snaddon; *b* 21 May 1946; *Educ* Normanhurst Boys HS; *m* ; 1 s (Julian Mark Geoffrey b 5 Sept 1980), 1 da (Jane Elizabeth Blyth b 15 July 1977); *Career* journalist Sydney Daily Telegraph 1964, COS ABC-TV 1968, vice pres Network Sports Nine Network Australia 1977-88, Sky Television London 1988-; *Recreations* fly fishing, surfing, reading, hiking; *Style—* David Hill, Esq; British Sky Broadcasting, Champion Television Ltd, 23 Iyot Gardens, London W6 5TR (☎ 081 746 5432, fax 081 746 5431)

HILL, David Layland; s of James Duncan Hill (d 1979), of Huddersfield, and Margaret, *née* Sykes; *b* 8 May 1935; *Educ* Bradford GS; *m* 1958, Pauline, da of Jack Steel (d 1976), of Huddersfield; 1 s (Michael b 1961); *Career* RAPC 1959-62, Lt in Singapore 1960-62; CA, sr ptnr Wheawill and Sudworth, former pres of Huddersfield Soc of CAs 1985; FCA 1959; *Recreations* golf; *Clubs* Woodsome Hall; *Style—* David Hill; 24 Dean Brook Road, Armitage Bridge, Huddersfield, West Yorkshire HD4 7PB (☎ 0484 666770); 35 Westgate, Huddersfield, West Yorkshire HD1 1PA (☎ 0484 423691, fax 0484 518803)

HILL, David Roderick; s of Desmond D'Artrey Hill, of Beaconsfield, Bucks, and Margaret Angela Ellis, *née* Hughes; *b* 28 Feb 1952; *Educ* Merchant Taylors'; *m* 6 April 1988, Jane Frances, da of Jack Collins, of Canterbury, Kent; 1 s (Henry Orlando b 7 April 1989); *Career* violin maker; Freeman City of London, Liveryman Worshipful Co of Musicians 1973; *Recreations* fishing, shooting, art, music; *Clubs* MCC; *Style—* David Hill, Esq; Haredell, Martinsend Lane, Great Missenden, Buckinghamshire

HILL, Duncan James Stanier; s of Maj Harold James Hill, of Cosford Grange, Shifnal, Shropshire, and Sheila, *née* Hughes; *b* 16 March 1956; *Educ* Shrewsbury, Magdalene Coll Cambridge (MA); *m* 16 Dec 1989, Tanya, *née* Marshall; *Career* md George Hill Industries Ltd 1987-; *Recreations* hunting, three day eventing; *Style—* Duncan Hill, Esq; Catherton Farm, Cleobury Mortimer, Kidderminster, Worcs (☎ 0299 270726); George Hill Industries Ltd, Halesfield 21, Telford, Shropshire (☎ 0952 586460, fax 0952 581522, telex 35881 GRANGE)

HILL, Edward Ewart; s of John Edward Hill (d 1982), of Crosshills, Yorkshire, and Janet Mary, *née* Ramsden (d 1989); *b* 13 June 1926; *Educ* Keighley Boys GS, Univ of Liverpool (BArch, MCD); *m* 22 July 1985, Kathleen Gertrude (Kate), da of Jonathan Wright (d 1965), of Keighley, Yorkshire; 3 s (Nicholas b 1951, Simon b 1953, Adam b 1959), 2 da (Jane b 1957, Emily b 1965); *Career* Nat Serv RN 1944-47; architect; articled pupil J B Bailey and Son 1941-44, Lord Esher's Office 1953-57, Building Design Partnership 1957- (ptnr 1964-); designs incl: Gen Infirmary and Med Sch Leeds, Queen's Med Centre Nottingham; memb and chm Penrith and Border Lib Democrats (Euro Parly candiate Cumbria and Lancashire N 1989); ARIBA 1953; *Recreations* fell running; *Clubs* Farmer's; *Style—* Edward Hill, Esq; Thorn House, Hartsop, Penrith, Cumbria CA11 0NZ (☎ 07684 82359)

HILL, Dame Elizabeth Mary; DBE (1976); *b* 24 Oct 1900; *Educ* Univ and King's Colls London (BA, PhD, MA); *m* 1984, Stojan J Veljković; *Career* slavonic specialist Miny of Info; univ lectr in Slavonic 1936-48, dir Intensive Jt Servs Courses Univ of Cambridge 1939-65, visiting prof Cornell Univ, prof of Slavonic studies Univ of Cambridge 1948-68, Andrew Mellon prof of Slavic languages and literatures Pittsburgh Univ 1968-70; fell: UCL, Girton Coll Cambridge; hon fell Univ of London SSEES 1990; Hon LittD UEA 1978; *Style—* Dame Elizabeth Hill, DBE; 10 Croft Gardens, Cambridge

HILL, Hon (Emma Louise Angela); da of 3 Baron McGowan; *b* 1963; *m* 7 Nov 1987, Guy H C Hill, eldest s of R J C Hill, of Croxton Kerrial, Leics, and Mrs J P Pollock, of Upper Froyle, Hants; *Style—* The Hon Mrs Hill; 14 Thirsk Rd, London SW11

HILL, Air Cmdt Dame Felicity Barbara; DBE (1966, OBE 1954); da of late Edwin Frederick Hill, and Frances Ada, *née* Cocke; *b* 12 Dec 1915; *Educ* St Margaret's Sch Folkestone; *Career* joined WAAF 1939, cmmnd 1940, inspr of WRAF 1956-59, OC RAF Hawkinge 1959-60, OC RAF Spitalgate 1960-65, dir of the WRAF 1966-69; Hon ADC to HM The Queen 1966-69; *Clubs* RAF; *Style—* Air Cmdt Dame Felicity Hill, DBE; Worcester Cottage, Mews Lane, Winchester, Hants

HILL, George Raymond; s of George Mark Hill, and Jill Hill; *b* 25 Sept 1925; *Educ* St Dunstan's Coll London; *m* 1948, Sophie, *née* Gibert; 2 da; *Career* Lt RM 1943-46; Distillers Co Ltd (Industl Gp) 1952-66, BP Chems Ltd 1967-69, chief exec Br Transport Hotels Ltd 1970-76 (chm 1974-76), dir Bass plc 1976-84 (memb Exec Ctee); chm: Bass UK Ltd 1978-80, Howard Machinery plc 1984-85, Channel Tunnel Nat Tourism Working Pty 1986-89, Crest Hotels Investment Ltd 1982-89, Sims Catering plc 1984-87, Liquor Licensing Ctee (Br Tourist Authy), Regal Hotel Group plc 1989-; dir Chester International Hotel plc 1987-, Ashford International Hotel plc 1988-; memb Br Tourist Authy Bd 1982-89; FCA, FCIT, FHCIMA, FRSA 1980; *Recreations* music, theatre, works of art, country life; *Clubs* RAC; *Style—* George Hill, Esq; 23 Sheffield Terrace, W8 (☎ 071 727 3986); The Paddocks, Chedworth, Gloucestershire

HILL, Gillian (Mrs Gillian Miller); da of Roger John Wright (d 1979), of Biggleswade, Beds, and Vera Florence, *née* Camp; *b* 18 Feb 1947; *Educ* Sacred Heart Convent Hitchin; *m* 1, 15 Aug 1968, George Hill; 1 da (Samantha Julia b 1973); m 2, 20 July 1978, Royston Miller, s of William Miller (d 1958); *Career* Lloyds Bank 1964-69, md Windscreens (Biggleswade) Ltd 1968-73, exec offr Br Water Ski Fedn 1974-; memb and sec Biggleswade Water Ski Club 1970-73, chair: Int Water Ski Fedn Barefoot Cncl 1980-, Br Assoc of Nat Sports Administrators 1980; *Recreations* water skiing, tennis, squash, reading; *Style—* Ms Gillian Hill; 390 City Rd, London EC1V 2QA (☎ 071 833 2855, fax 071 837 5879)

HILL, Graham Starforth; s of Capt Harold Victor John Hill (d 1955), of Alresford, Hants; *b* 22 June 1927; *Educ* Dragon Sch Oxford, Winchester, St John's Coll Oxford; *m* 1952 (m dis), Margaret Elise, da of Charles Ambler (d 1952), of Itchen Abbas, Hants; 1 s, 1 da; *Career* Flying Offr RAF Fighter Cmd UK 1948-50; called to the Bar Gray's Inn 1951; crown counsel Colonial Legal Serv Singapore 1953-56; slr 1961, ptnr (later sr ptnr) Rodyk and Davidson Advocates and Slrs Singapore 1957-76, chm Guinness Mahon & Co Ltd 1979-83 (dir 1977-79); conslt to: Frere Cholmeley 1984, Rodyk & Davidson (Singapore) 1985-; chm London City Ballet Tst 1981-82; tstee: Southwark Cathedral Devpt Tst Fund 1980-84, Royal Opera House Tst 1982-85; pres Law Soc of Singapore 1970-74; Cavaliere della Solidarieta 1975, Commendatore al Merito 1977-; *Recreations* music, Italy; *Clubs* Garrick, Costa Smeralda Yacht (Italy); *Style—* Graham Hill, Esq; 10 St Thomas St, Winchester, Hants SO23 9HE (☎ 0962 854146); Casa Claudia, 07020 Porto Cervo, Italy (☎ 0789 92157)

HILL, Gregory John Summers; s of Frederick John Hill (d 1987), and Margaret May, *née* Greenwood; *b* 5 May 1949; *Educ* Weston-super-Mare GS for Boys, Exeter Coll Oxford (MA, BCL); *m* 10 Sept 1977, Anne Gillian, da of William Spencer Barretta, of Clifton, Bristol; 1 s (Richard b 1982), 1 da (Alison b 1985); *Career* called to the Bar Lincoln's Inn 1972; in practice 1973-; *Books* Securities for Advances: Encyclopaedia of Banking Law (jtly, 1982-); *Style—* Gregory Hill, Esq; 17 Old Buildings, Lincoln's Inn, London WC2A 3UP (☎ 071 405 9653, fax 071 404 8089)

HILL, Harold James; s of Arthur Frederick Hill (d 1952); *b* 18 May 1920; *Educ* Wolverhampton GS; *m* 1949, Sheila Gwendolen, da of Hughes Alfred Thomas (d 1966); 2 c; *Career* chm: George Hill Industries Ltd, Grange Fencing Ltd, Grange Fencing Erectors Ltd; *Style—* H James Hill, Esq; Cosford Grange, Shifnal, Shrops (☎ 090 722 2501); George Hill Industries Ltd, Halesfield 21, Telford, Shropshire TF7 4PA (☎ 0952 588088, fax 0952 581522, telex 35881)

HILL, Harry Douglas; s of Jack Hill, of S Yorks, and Katheline Francis, *née* Curran; *b* 4 April 1948; *Educ* Holgate GS Barnsley; *m* 1 (m dis 1979), Glenis Margaret, *née* Brown; 2 s (Jonathan b 1973, Matthew b 1975); m 2, 23 Nov 1985, da of Frederick Aldred, of Downham Market, Norfolk; 2 s (William b 1986, Joshau b 1987); *Career* surveyor; articles A E Wilby & Son Barnsley 1964-67, various surveying appts 1967-74; ptnr: David Bedford Norfolk 1974-82, Hill Nash Pointen 1982-84, James Abbott Ptnrship 1984-86; dir Mann & Co 1986-87, md Hambro Countrywide plc 1988- (dir 1987-88); *Style—* Harry Hill, Esq; Hambro Countrywide Plc, 1-5 Ingrave Road, Brentwood, Essex CM15 8TB (☎ 0277 264466, fax 0277 217916, car 0836 290027)

HILL, (Michael) Hedley; s of late Kenneth Wilson Hill, and Dorothy, *née* Etchells (d 1984); *b* 3 Feb 1945; *Educ* Rydal Sch Colwyn Bay, St John's Coll Cambridge; *Career* admitted slr 1969; NP; ptnr Weightman Rutherfords Liverpool 1971-; treas Liverpool Law Soc, former chm Liverpool Young Slrs Gp; former pres Old Rydalian Club; memb: Law Soc, Liverpool Law Soc; *Recreations* canal boating, oenology; *Clubs* Liverpool Racquet, Union Soc Cambridge; *Style—* Hedley Hill, Esq; Fulwood Park

Lodge, Liverpool L17 5AA (☎ 051 727 3411); Weightman Rutherfords, Richmond House, 1 Rumford Place, Liverpool L3 9QW (☎ 051 227 2601, fax 051 227 3223, telex 627538)

HILL, Ian Canning; s of Hamilton Erskine Hill (d 1985), of Barnton, Edinburgh, and Janet MacColl, *née* Canning; *b* 20 Feb 1943; *Educ* Blackburn Tech and GS, George Heriot's Edinburgh, Univ of Strathclyde (Stenhouse scholar, MBA); *Career* inspr Royal Exchange Assurance 1960-66, mgmnt asst Northern Assurance Co Ltd 1966-67; Royal Insurance Holdings plc 1968-: head of mktg 1968-70, Mgmnt Res Unit 1970-72, asst agency mangr 1972-75, asst mktg mangr 1975-78, gp staff pensions mangr 1978-; FCII; *Recreations* golf; *Style—* Ian Hill, Esq; Schiehallion, 7 Links Close, Raby Mere, Wirral, Merseyside (☎ 051 334 5519); Group Staff Pensions Manager, Royal Insurance Plc, PO Box 144, New Hall Place, Liverpool L69 3EN (☎ 051 224 3443, fax 051 224 4490)

HILL, Ian Frederick Donald; JP (1978); s of Frederick Donald Banks Hill (d 1952); *b* 14 May 1928; *Educ* Shrewsbury; *m* 1955, Marlene Elizabeth, da of Norman Vincent Rushton (d 1971); 2 c; *Career* ptnr Arthur Young 1958-88, chm Kwik Save Group plc 1973-, dir Park Food Gp plc 1983-; chm Royal Liverpool Children's Hosp NHS Tst 1990-; FCA; *Recreations* golf; *Clubs* Royal Birkdale Golf; *Style—* Ian Hill, Esq, JP; 22 Hastings Rd, Southport, Merseyside PR8 2LW (☎ 0704 68398)

HILL, (Stanley) James Allen; MP (C) Southampton Test 1979; s of James Hill, and Florence Cynthia Hill, of Southampton; *b* 21 Dec 1926; *Educ* Regent's Park Sch, N Wales Naval Coll, Univ of Southampton; *m* 1958, Ruby Evelyn, da of Ross Albert Ralph, of Clanfield Farm, Basingstoke; 2 s, 3 da; *Career* Royal Fleet Aux 1941-46, served 11 yrs on BOAC flying staff; sr ptnr firm of Estate Agents; memb: UN Assoc, Southampton City Cncl 1966-; MP (C) Southampton Test 1970-74 and 1979-, sec Cons Backbench Ctee on Housing and Construction 1971-73, memb Select Ctee on Expenditure 1972-73, UK memb Euro Parl Strasbourg 1972-75 (chm Regnl Policy and Tport Ctee 1973-75, govt whip to Cncl of Europe and WEU 1979-90); memb Select Ctees: Euro Legislation 1979-83, Indust and Trade 1979-83; memb Mr Speaker's Panel of Chairmen, vice chm Cons Constitutional Affrs Ctee, chm Housing Improvement Ctee; *Clubs* St Stephen's Constitutional, Carlton; *Style—* James Hill, Esq, MP; c/o House of Commons, London SW1, Gunfield Lodge, Melchet Pk, Plaitford, Hants

HILL, Sir James Frederick; 4 Bt (UK 1916), of Bradford; s of Sir James Hill, 3 Bt (d 1976); *b* 5 Dec 1943; *Educ* Wrekin Coll, Univ of Bradford; *m* 1966, Sandra Elizabeth, da of late J C Ingram, of Ilkley; 1 s, 3 da; *Heir* s, James Laurence Ingram Hill b 22 Sept 1973; *Career* exec chm Sir James Hill and Sons Ltd; dir: Yorks Bldg Soc, Airedale DHA, Br Rail Eastern Region; *Recreations* tennis, sailing, golf; *Clubs* RAC, Bradford, Ilkley; *Style—* Sir James F Hill, Bt; Roseville, Moor Lane, Menston, Ilkley, W Yorks LS29 6AP (☎ 0943 74624)

HILL, Jeremy Adrian; s of Lt-Col Cecil Vivian Hill (d 1978); *b* 16 Jan 1940; *Educ* Eton, Ch Ch Oxford; *m* 1965, Virginia Ann, da of Maj Gordon Darwin Wilmot; 3 s; *Career* dir: J Henry Schroder Wagg and Co, Korea Europe Fund plc; *Recreations* tennis, shooting; *Style—* Jeremy Hill, Esq; Peyton Hall, Bures, Suffolk; J Henry Schroder Wagg and Co Ltd, 120 Cheapside, London EC2V 6DS (☎ 071 382 6000, telex 885029)

HILL, Hon John; s of Baron Hill of Luton, PC (Life Peer; d Aug 1989), and Marion Spencer, *née* Wallace (d Nov 1989); *b* 29 June 1945; *Educ* Epsom Coll, Cambridge Univ (MA), Univ of NSW; *m* 1974, Dawn Kay, da of Ian Hamilton Lance, of West Pennant Hills, NSW Aust; 2 s (Simon b 1975, Charles b 1977), 1 da (Melanie b 1979); *Career* system studies offr Aust Safeguards Office 1981-; *Recreations* amateur theatre; *Clubs* Sydney Journalists; *Style—* The Hon John Hill; 1 Oatley Park Ave, Oatley, NSW 2223 (☎ 02 570 6052); Australian Safeguards Office, PO Box KX 261, Kings Cross, NSW 2011 (☎ 02 358 6255)

HILL, John Andrew Patrick; CBE (1978); s of Henry Wilfred Hill and Beatrice Rose, *née* Smith; *b* 8 Feb 1936; *Educ* Ealing Tech Coll, MECAS; *m* 1960, Barbara Anne, da of Maj Frederick Joseph Knifton (d 1965); 2 s (Andrew, Timothy), 1 da (Philippa); *Career* served RAF 1954-56; banker; British Bank of the ME 1956-78, Hongkong and Shanghai Banking Corporation Hong Kong 1979-89; dir 1990- British Bank of the ME, Saudi British Bank, Hongkong Egyptian Bank, Cyprus Popular Bank, Wardley Cyprus Ltd, Arabian Gulf Investments (Far East) Ltd, Harper Hill Ltd, Hartley Wood & Co Ltd; memb Lloyd's; *Recreations* organ playing, travel, photography, fishing; *Clubs* Oriental, Hongkong, Royal College of Organists; *Style—* J A P Hill, Esq, CBE; Hawkwood Manor, Sible Hedingham, Essex

HILL, John Cameron; TD (1959); s of Maj Raymond Cameron Hill (d 1975), and Margaret, *née* Chadwick; *b* 8 April 1927; *Educ* Bishop Vesey's GS Sutton Coldfield, Trinity Coll Oxford, Coll of Estate Mgmnt Univ of London (BSc); *m* 12 Sept 1957, Jane Edna, da of Ernest Leslie Austin (d 1984); 1 s (Charles Austin b 1961), 1 da (Sally-Ann b 1957); *Career* RA 1945-49 (cmmnd 1947), Major RA TA and RHA 1949-73, Met Special Constabulary 1973-86 (Cmdt 1981); ptnr Hillier Parker May and Rowden 1963-88 (joined 1953); memb Lands Tribunal 1987-; Freeman City of London 1982; FRICS 1955; *Books* The Handbook of Rent Review (conslt ed), Valuations Principles Into Practice (part author); *Recreations* shooting; *Clubs* Army and Navy, Honourable Artillery Company; *Style—* John Hill, Esq, TD; Hastoe House, Hastoe, Tring, Herts HP23 6LU (☎ 044282 2084); Lands Tribunal, 48-49 Chancery Lane, London WC2A 1JR (☎ 071 936 7200)

HILL, John Edward Bernard; s of Capt Robert William Hill (ka 1917), and Marjorie Jane Lloyd-Jones, *née* Scott-Miller (d 1981); *b* 13 Nov 1912; *Educ* Charterhouse, Merton Coll Oxford (MA); *m* 7 July 1944, Edith, wid of Cdr R A E Luard, RNVR, and da of John Maxwell (d 1940), of Cove, Dumbartonshire; 1 adopted da (Linda (Mrs Jackson) b 7 March 1943); *Career* cmmnd RA (TA) 1938, air observation post pilot RA WO 1942 (wounded Tunisia 1943), specially employed WO 1944, invalided out 1945; called to the Bar Inner Temple 1938; farmer in Suffolk 1946-; memb CLA Exec 1957-59 and 1977-82; MP (C) South Norfolk 1955-74, govt whip and lord cmmr of Treasy 1959-64, memb Cncl of Europe and WEU 1970-72, MEP 1973-74; memb: E Suffolk and Suffolk Rivers Bd 1952-62, Governing Body Charterhouse Sch 1957-90, Exec Ctee GBA 1966-83, Bd of Govrs Suttons Hosp in Charterhouse 1966-, Cncl UEA 1975-82; *Clubs* Garrick, Farmer's; *Style—* JEB Hill, Esq; Watermill Farm, Wenhaston, Halesworth, Suffolk IP19 9BY (☎ 050 270 207)

HILL, Sir John Maxwell; CBE (1969), DFC (1945), QPM; s of late L S M Hill, of Plymouth; *b* 25 March 1914; *Educ* Plymouth Coll; *m* 1939, Marjorie Louisa Reynolds; 1 s, 1 da; *Career* served WW II Flying Offr Bomber Cmd RAFVR; HM inspr of Constabulary 1965-66; asst cmmr: Admin and Ops 1966-68, Personnel and Trg Met Police 1968-71; dep cmmr 1971-72, chief inspr of Constabulary Home Office 1972-75; kt 1974; *Recreations* golf, walking; *Clubs* RAC, RAF; *Style—* Sir John Hill, CBE, DFC, QPM; 4 The Kingsway, Epsom, Surrey KT17 1LT

HILL, Sir John McGregor; s of John Campbell Hill (d 1982); *b* 21 Feb 1921; *Educ* King's Coll London, St John's Coll Cambridge; *m* 1947, Nora Eileen, *née* Hellett; 2 s, 1 da; *Career* Flt Lt RAF 1941; UKAEA: joined 1950, memb of prodn 1964-67, chm 1967-81; chm: Br Nuclear Fuels Ltd 1971-83 (hon pres 1983-86), Amersham International plc 1975-88, Aurora Holdings 1984-88, Rea Bros Ltd 1987-; memb: Advsy Cncl on Technol 1968-70, Nuclear Power Advsy Bd 1973-81, Energy Cmmn 1977-79; FRS, FInstP, FIChemE, FInstE, FEng; Chevalier de la Légion d'Honneur; kt 1969; *Recreations* golf, gardening; *Clubs* East India; *Style—* Sir John Hill, FRS; Dominic House, Sudbrook Lane, Richmond, Surrey TW10 7AT (☎ 081 940 7221)

HILL, John Michael; s of Stanley Hill, of Oxshott, Surrey, and Ellen May, *née* Rose; *b* 28 Aug 1944; *Educ* St Dunstan's Coll Catford, Jesus Coll Cambridge (MA); *m* 25 Jan 1973, (Jean) Shirley, da of Jan Jakub Spyra (d 1979), of Cheadle; 1 s (Jeffrey), 1 da (Nicola); *Career* R Watson & Sons Consulting Actuaries 1970- (ptnr 1974); FIA 1971, FPMI 1981; *Recreations* music, keeping fit; *Style—* John Hill, Esq; 4 Underhill Park Rd, Reigate, Surrey RH2 9LX (☎ 0737 249 473); R Watson & Sons, Watson House, Reigate, Surrey RH2 9PQ (☎ 0737 241 144, fax 0737 241 496, telex 946070)

HILL, Dr Jonathan Charles; s of Frederick Charles Hill, of Witney, Oxon, and Joan Emily, *née* Sedgwick; *b* 29 Nov 1956; *Educ* Univ of Liverpool; *m* 21 July 1981, Gillian, da of Donald Knowles, of St Helens, Merseyside; 1 s (Jamie b 19 Feb 1987), 1 da (Miranda b 25 May 1985); *Career* conslt radiologist N Western Health Authy 1988; MB ChB 1981, DMRD 1984; memb BNMS 1989, FRCR 1985; *Recreations* fell walking, swimming, shooting; *Clubs* Bobbin Mill; *Style—* Dr Jonathan Hill; Royal Preston Hospital, Sharoe Green Lane, Fulwood, Preston, Lancs (☎ 0772 716565)

HILL, Judith Lynne; da of Dr Michael James Raymond, of Ley House, Worth, Sussex, and Joan, *née* Chivers; *b* 8 Oct 1949; *Educ* Brighton and Hove HS, Univ of Cambridge (MA); *m* 1, 9 Oct 1976 (m dis 1986), Brent Arthur Hill; 1 da (Olivia b 1981); m 2, 6 March 1987, Edward Richard Regenye, s of Edward Joseph Regenye (d 1987), of Rochelle Park, New Jersey, USA; *Career* admitted slr 1975, ptnr Farrer and Co 1986; dir: Melloward Ltd, WRVS Office Premises Ltd; memb Bd of Royal Hosp and Home Putney; memb Law Soc; *Recreations* travel, water-skiing, tennis; *Clubs* Reform; *Style—* Mrs Judith Hill; Messrs Farrer & Co, 66 Lincoln's Inn Fields, London WC2A 3LH (☎ 071 242 2022, telex 24318, fax 071 831 9748)

HILL, Julian; s of Harold Brian Cunningham Hill (d 1980), and Elise Magdalen, *née* Jeppe (d 1971); *b* 9 Aug 1932; *Educ* Rottingdean Sch, Eastbourne Coll; *m* 20 March 1956, (Ruth) Monica, da of late Paul Sekvens Toll, of 10 Villagatan, Stockholm; 2 s (Rowland b 1956, Michael b 1960), 1 da (Anne-Louise b 1963); *Career* Nat Serv 2 Lt 22 Cheshire Regt 1952-54; dir various cos operating UK and overseas for Unilever plc 1954-77; chm and md: Scanhill Ltd 1977-, Julian Hill Ltd 1977-; commercial advsr UN 1977-; Freeman City of London 1982, Liveryman Worshipful Co of Marketors 1984; FBIM, MCIM; *Recreations* sailing, skiing, cricket, opera; *Clubs* MCC, Naval & Military; *Style—* Julian Hill, Esq; Huntsland Cottage, Huntsland Lane, Crawley Down, Sussex RH10 4HB (☎ 0342 712 286); Julian Hill Ltd, 26 Wilfred St, Westminster, London SW1E 6PL (☎ 071 828 7494, fax 071 630 9256, telex 8950933 TEAPOT)

HILL, Kenneth George; s of George Bertram Hill (d 1982), and Ethel Dora, *née* Gibbs; *b* 11 June 1932; *m* 20 April 1968, Diana Sylvia Mary, da of Richard Harold Piper, TD (d 1977), of Weir Courtney, Lingfield, Surrey; 1 da (Sophie Diana Alexandra b 11 Feb 1969); *Career* King's Troop RHA 1950-52; Mullens and Co Stockbrokers 1952-86, Bank of England 1986-87; hon treas: E Sussex Branch of Distressed Gentlefolks Aid Assoc, The Old Surrey and Burstow Foxhounds; govr Moira House Sch Eastbourne; Freeman Worshipful Co of Loriners; *Recreations* country sports; *Style—* Kenneth Hill, Esq; Duckyls Holt, West Hoathly, Sussex

HILL, Lewis; s of Maurice Hill (d 1942), and Nettie, *née* Friedberg; *b* 19 July 1915; *Educ* St Paul's; *m* 28 Aug 1955, Caryll Edwina, da of Leonard Samuel Davis-Marks (d 1980); 2 da (Lesley Jane, Stephanie Lynn); *Career* cmmnd RASC 1940, served 8 Army Western Desert, Capt 1942, Maj 1944, served 21 Army Gp in invasion of Europe, OC Amphibious Unit Force 135; chm and md: L Hill (Properties) Ltd, L Hill (Investments) Ltd, Dykes & Co Ltd; Furniture Trade Benevolent Assoc (FTBA): pres London area 1967, nat pres 1979, chm Exec Ctee 1983-86, hon vice pres and tstee 1986; Freeman: City of London 1953, Worshipful Co of Furniture Makers 1953 (Liveryman 1979); *Recreations* travel, bridge, sport; *Style—* Lewis Hill, Esq; Links Cottage, Holders Hill Crescent, London NW4 1NE (☎ 081 203 3379)

HILL, Lady; Lorna; da of J F Wheelan, and B E Wheelan; *b* 1 March 1925; *Educ* Univ of Aberdeen (MB ChB, MD, DPM); *m* 1962, as his 2 w, Prof Sir (John) Denis Nelson Hill (d 1982), s of Col Hill, of Orleton Manor, Salop; 1 s (Richard b 1963), 1 da (Annabel b 1968); *Career* conslt psychiatrist KCH 1958-90; hon conslt Maudsley Hosp; FRCPsych; *Recreations* reading, painting, walking; *Style—* Lady Hill; 71 Cottenham Park Rd, Wimbledon, London SW20 0DR (☎ 081 946 6663)

HILL, Marjory, Lady; Marjory; JP; da of late Frank Croft, of Brocka, Lindale, Grange-over-Sands; *m* 1930, Sir James Hill, 3 Bt (d 1976); *Style—* Marjory, Lady Hill; Brea House, Trebetherick, Wadebridge, Cornwall

HILL, (Charles) Mark Roper; s of Charles Guy Roper Hill, MC (d 1977), of Lathom, Lancs, and Ethel Wilma, *née* Fair; *b* 28 Oct 1943; *Educ* Marlborough; *m* 6 Aug 1982, Judith Mary, da of John Clancy, of Ormskirk; 1 s (James b 1983), 1 da (Emily b 1986); *Career* admitted slr 1967, clerk to cmmrs of Income Tax 1971, ret; NP 1977; tstee Ormskirk Postgrad Med Tst; memb Law Soc 1967; *Recreations* golf, fell walking, gardening; *Clubs* Ormskirk Golf, Liverpool Ramblers AFC; *Style—* Mark Hill, Esq; Dickinson Parker Hill & Son, 22 Derby St, Ormskirk, Lancs L39 2BZ (☎ 0695 574201)

HILL, (Eliot) Michael; QC (1979); s of late Cecil Charles Hill, and late Rebecca Betty Hill; *b* 22 May 1935; *Educ* Bancroft's Sch Woodford Green Essex, BNC Oxford (MA); *m* 27 April 1965, Kathleen Irene (Kitty), da of late Rev Tom Venables Hordern; 1 s (Jonathan Edward Venables b 3 Oct 1970), 2 da (Penelope Gillian b 8 Dec 1968, Carolyn Patricia b 24 Nov 1972); *Career* called to the Bar Gray's Inn 1958, bencher 1986, memb Wine Ctee SE Circuit 1972-89; treasy counsel: Inner London Sessions Inner London Crown Court 1969-74, Central Criminal Court 1974-79; Senate of the Inns of Ct and the Bar and Gen Cncl of the Bar 1976-79 and 1982-90; Criminal Bar Assoc: fndr memb 1969, memb Ctee 1970-86, sec 1972-75, vice chm 1979-82, chm 1982-86; memb: Criminal Law Revision Ctee 1983-, Exec Ctee Soc for the Reform of Criminal Law 1987-; *Style—* Michael Hill, Esq, QC; 36 Essex St, London WC2 3AS (☎ 071 413 0353, fax 071 413 0374)

HILL, Michael William; s of Geoffrey William Hill (d 1961), of Cadewell Park, Torquay, and Dorothy, *née* Ursell (d 1973); *b* 27 July 1928; *Educ* King Henry VIII Sch Coventry, Nottingham HS, Lincoln Coll Oxford (MA, BSc); *m* 1, 1957, Elma Jack, *née* Forrest (d 1967); 1 s (Alastair Geoffrey Frank b 1961), 1 da (Sally Ann b 1959); m 2, 1969, Barbara Joy, *née* Youngman; *Career* Sgt and instr RAEC 1947-49; res scientist Laporte Chemicals Ltd 1953-56, res and prodn mangr Morgan Crucible Group 1956-64, asst keeper Br Museum 1964-68; dir: Nat Reference Library of Sci and Invention 1968-73, Sci Reference Library Br Library 1973-86; assoc dir sci technol and industry Br Library 1986-88, jt series ed Butterworths Guides to Information Sources; UK del to CEC Working Parties on Patents and on Info for Indust 1973-78; memb: UK Chemical Info Serv Bd 1974-77, Advsy Ctee for Scot Sci Reference Library 1983-88; vice pres Int Assoc of Technol Univ Libraries 1976-81; chm: Circle of State Librarians 1977-79, Cncl ASLIB 1979-81; pres Int Fedn for Info and Documentation 1984-90; FRSA, MRSC, FIInfSci; *Books* Patent Documentation (with Wittmann and Schiffels, 1979), Michael Hill on Science Invention and Information (1988), National Surveys of Library & Information Services: Yugoslavia (1990); *Clubs* United Oxford & Cambridge

Univ; *Style—* Michael Hill, Esq; Jesters, 137 Burdon Lane, Cheam, Surrey SM2 7DB (☎ 081 642 2418)

HILL, Peter; s of Percy Hill (d 1964), and Mary Anne, *née* Coffey (d 1982); *b* 22 Oct 1934; *Educ* Univ of Cambridge; *m* 2 Aug 1969, Sandra; 1 s (Ben b 1977); *Career* surgical registrar Royal Melbourne Hosp 1964-67, orthopaedic registrar and sr registrar Bristol Royal Infirmary 1969-73, conslt orthopaedic surgn N Staffs Hosp Centre 1973-; FRCS, FBOA; *Recreations* golf, gardening; *Style—* Peter Hill, Esq; 8 Queen St, Newcastle, Stoke-on-Trent, Staffs (☎ 0782 620201)

HILL, Dr Peter David; s of Derryck Albert Hill (d 1988), and Phyllis Mary, *née* Carn; *b* 16 March 1945; *Educ* Leighton Park Sch, Univ of Cambridge (MA, MB BChir); *m* 10 June 1972, Christine Margaret, da of Stanley William Seed, of Seaton, Devon; 2 s (Gulliver b 1974, Luke b 1976), 1 da (Jessica b 1981); *Career* registrar then sr registrar Maudsley Hosp 1972-79, sr lectr and head of section and conslt in child and adolescent psychiatry St George's Hosp and Medical Sch 1979-, hon conslt St Thomas' Hosp 1981-, conslt Tadworth Court Children's Hosp 1987-; tstee Children's Head Injury Tst, visiting conslt Nat Autistic Soc, trg and examining posts RCPsych; MRCP 1972, FRCPsych 1980 (MRCPsych 1975); *Books* Essentials of Postgraduate Psychiatry (with R Murray and A Thorley, 1979 and 1986), A Manual of Practical Psychiatry (with P Bebbington, 1986), Adolescent Psychiatry (1989), The Child Surveillance Handbook (with D Hall and D Elliman, 1990); *Recreations* jazz trumpet, house restoration; *Style—* Dr Peter Hill; Strand End, 78 Grove Park Rd, London W4 3QA (☎ 081 994 4349); Department of Mental Health Sciences, St George's Hospital Medical School, Cranmer Terrace, London SW17 0RE (☎ 081 672 9944)

HILL, Raymond Stanley; s of Stanley George Hill (d 1985), of Birchington, Kent, and Esther Frances, *née* Busby (d 1975); *b* 28 Nov 1934; *Educ* Haberdashers' Aske's; *m* 1958 (sep); 2 s (Martyn George b 13 June 1962, Jonathan Edmond b 2 June 1965), 1 da (Kathryn Alison b 3 Nov 1968); *Career* Nat Serv mil police; joined Royal Insurance Group 1951; Prudential Insurance Company: joined as underwriter 1958, asst city mangr 1973, asst gen mangr Gen Branch Ops 1981; gp chief exec Iron Trades Group and md subsid Iron Trades Insurance Co Ltd 1990- (chief exec and gen mangr 1987); lectr on tech and managerial topics 1970-; Freeman City of London 1984, Liveryman Worshipful Co of Insurers 1984; FCII 1960 (vice pres 1989-, chm Soc of Fellows 1989-), FBIM 1980; *Recreations* golf, freshwater angling, assoc football; *Clubs* Wig and Pen, City Livery, Harry's Bar; *Style—* Raymond Hill, Esq; Iron Trades Insurance Group, 21-24 Grosvenor Place, London SW1X 7JA (☎ 071 235 6033, fax 071 245 6308, car 0860 250225)

HILL, Reginald Charles; s of Reginald Hill (d 1961), and Isabel, *née* Dickson; *b* 3 April 1936; *Educ* Carlisle GS, St Catherine's Coll Oxford (BA); *m* 1960, Patricia, da of Leslie Ruell; *Career* worked for Br Cncl Edinburgh 1960-61; Eng teacher: Royal Liberty Romford Essex 1962-64, Fryerns Sch Basildon Essex 1964-67; Eng lectr Doncaster Coll of Educn 1967-81; author; novels incl: A Killing Kindness (1980), Who Guards A Prince (1982), Traitor's Blood (1983), Deadheads (1983), Exit Lines (1984), No Man's Land (1985), Child's Play (1987), The Collaborators (1987), Under World (1988), Bones and Silence (1990); novels under the pseudonym of Patrick Ruell incl: The Long Kill (1986), Death of a Dormouse (1987), Dream of Darkness (1989); novels under the pseudonym of Dick Morland: Heart Clock (1973), Albion! Albion! (1974); novels under the pseudonym of Charles Underhill: Captain Fantom (1978); short story collections: Pascoe's Ghost (1979), There are No Ghosts in the Soviet Union (1987); plays: An Affair of Honour (BBC, 1972), Ordinary Levels (Radio 4, 1982); Crimewriters' Assoc Gold Dagger award (for the best crime novel) 1990; memb: Crime Writers' Assoc 1971, The Detection Club 1978, Soc of Authors 1984; *Recreations* fell walking, listening to classical music, watching rugby, Siamese cats; *Style—* Reginald Hill, Esq; Caradoc King, A P Watt Ltd, Literary Agents, 20 John St, London WC1N 2DR (☎ 071 405 6774, fax 071 831 2154)

HILL, Reginald John Tower; er s of Lt-Col Francis Tower Hill (d 1974), of Holfield Grange, Essex, and Judith Mary, *née* Newall (d 1986); gs of Reginald Duke Hill, JP, DL (d 1922), who acquired Holfield Grange through his marriage to Flora, *née* Tower, widow of Osgood Beauchamp Hanbury (d 1889), whose family had owned it since the 18 century (*see* Burke's Landed Gentry, 18 edn, Vol I, 1965); *b* 25 Jan 1925; *Educ* Harrow; *m* 1, 30 April 1953, Anne Horsman (d 1980), da of Maj Vivian Horsman Bailey, MC, of Collyweston Manor, Stamford, Lincs; 1 s (Christopher Francis Edward b 12 May 1955), 1 da (Caroline Anne (Mrs Everard) b 19 March 1957); m 2, 25 Sept 1985, Jennifer Ann, da of Cdr E J Tamlyn, RN, and widow of William R C Quilter; *Career* Lt The Rifle Bde 1943-48; landowner and farmer; *Recreations* shooting, fishing, racing; *Clubs* Cavalry and Guards'; *Style—* Reginald Hill, Esq; Holfield Grange, Coggeshall, Essex (☎ 0376 61409)

HILL, Richard; JP (Avon 1974); s of Charles Loraine Hill, JP (d 1976), of Grove House, Alveston, nr Bristol, and Mary Anabel, *née* Harford (d 1966); *b* 25 July 1921; *Educ* Eton; *m* 17 April 1948, (Jean) Mary Vernon, da of Sir George Vernon Proctor Wills, Bt (d 1931), of Coombe Lodge, Blagdon, nr Bristol; 1 s (Charles Peter Loraine b 1954), 3 da (Angela Mary Loraine (Mrs Stone) b 1949, Caryll Loraine (Mrs Ingerslev) b 1951, Sarah Loraine b 1957); *Career* RE 1944-46, demobbed as Capt; Charles Hill of Bristol Ltd 1939-81 (chm 1968-81), chm Bristol City Line of Steamships 1968-81; memb: Exec Cncl Shipbuilding Conf 1955-68, SW Regnl Bd for Indust 1961-65; chm Dry Dock Owners and Repairers Central Cncl 1962-63; memb: SW Region Econ Planning Cncl 1965-66, Shipbuilding and Shiprepairing Cncl 1966-68; chm Statistics Working Pty 1967-68, memb Grand Cncl of the Confedn of Br Indust 1967-82; chm: Maritime Tport Res Steering Panel 1967-77, SW Regnl Cncl CBI 1968-70, Dart Containerline Bermuda Ltd 1969-72; memb Gen Ctee Lloyd's Register of Shipping 1973-77; directorships incl: Heeman Gp Ltd, Prince of Wales Dry Dock Co Ltd, Lovells Shipping and Tport Ltd, Dart Containerline Inc; nat and local involvement incl: memb Lloyd's Underwriters 1951-, pro chllr Univ of Bristol 1986- (memb Cncl 1959-, chm of Cncl 1972-86), tstee Bristol Municipal Charities 1962-, memb Nat Assoc of Youth Clubs (now Youth Clubs UK) 1964- (chm Exec Ctee 1964-70, later vice pres), chm W of England Branch IOD 1967-69 and 1972-75, memb SW Electricity Bd 1972-77, memb Appeal Ctee Wells Cathedral Appeal 1976-84, memb Ctee AA 1979-89, memb St George's House Assoc 1982- chm Bristol Local Ctee Br Assoc for Advancement of Sci 1984-87; Freeman: City of London 1954, City of Bristol 1957, Soc of Merchant Venturers (Master 1975-76), Worshipful Co of Shipwrights (Prime Warden 1976-77); JP Somerset 1962-74; High Sheriff of Somerset 1964; Hon LLD Univ of Bristol 1976; CEng, FRINA 1967 (assoc memb 1955); *Recreations* fishing, shooting, skiing, painting; *Style—* Richard Hill, Esq

HILL, Sir Richard George Rowley; 10 Bt (I 1779) of Brook Hall, Londonderry; MBE (1974); s of Sir George Alfred Rowley Hill, 9 Bt (d 1985); *b* 18 Dec 1925; *Educ* Clayesmore Sch, Glasgow Univ; *m* 1, 1954, Angela Mary (d 1974), da of Lt-Col Stanley Herbert Gallon (d 1986), of Berwick-on-Tweed; m 2, 1975 (m dis 1985), Zoreen Joy MacPherson, da of late Norman Warburton Tippett, of Kirkland, Berwick-on-Tweed, and widow of Andrew David Wilson Marshall, KOSB; 2 da; m 3, 1986, Elizabeth Margaret, *née* Tarbitt, widow of Laurence Sage, RNVR/FAA; *Career* Maj KOSB (ret); *Style—* Sir Richard Hill Esq, Bt, MBE; 21 Station Approach, Great Missenden, Bucks HP16 9AZ (☎ 02406 5536)

HILL, Richard John; s of John Lewin Hill, of Compton Dando, nr Bristol, and Audrey, *née* Chatterton; *b* 4 May 1961; *Educ* Bishop Wordsworth's GS Salisbury, Sch of Educn Univ of Exeter; *m* 3 Aug 1985, Karen Jane, da of Terry Shrapnell; 1 s (Joshua b 17 March 1987), 1 da (Natalie b 20 April 1988); *Career* Rugby Union scrum-half Bath RFC and England (18 caps); Salisbury RFC 1979-84, Exeter Univ RFC 1980-83 (capt 1982-83), replacement England Colts (under 19) v Wales and France 1980, English Univs and England Students 1982; Bath RFC: debut v Maesteg 1983, 185 appearances (incl 6 cup final victories) 1983-91; England: debut v South Africa Port Elizabeth 1984, NZ 1985, capt for 3 matches 1987, World Cup 1987, first try v Wales Twickenham 1990, toured Argentina 1990; physical educn teacher, fin conslt Noble Lowndes Bristol; *Recreations* family, travel; *Style—* Richard Hill, Esq; 10 Melrose Terrace, Ragland Lane, Fairfield Park, Bath, Avon (☎ 0225 312057); Bath Rugby Football Club, Recreation Ground, Bath (☎ 0225 425192)

HILL, Rear Adm (John) Richard; s of Stanley Hill (d 1963), of Standlake, Oxon, and May, *née* Henshaw (d 1969); *b* 25 March 1929; *Educ* RNC Dartmouth, King's Coll London; *m* 21 July 1956, Patricia Anne, da of (Leslie) Edward Sales, of Upwey, Dorset; 1 s (Nigel b 1959), 2 da (Anna b 1960, Penelope b 1960); *Career* Naval Offr (Navigation Specialist) HM ships to 1962, MOD, Flag Offr Admty Interview Bd 1981-83, ret 1983; under treas The Hon Soc of The Middle Temple 1983-, sec Cncl of the Inns of Ct 1987-; ed The Naval Review 1983-; *Books* The Royal Navy Today and Tomorrow (1981), Anti-Submarine Warfare (1984), British Seapower in the 1980s (1985), Maritime Strategy for Medium Powers (1986), Air Defence at Sea (1988), Arms Control at Sea 1988; articles incl: Survival, Navy Int, Naval Forces, NATO's 16 Nations, Brassey's Annual, Defence and Diplomacy, World Survey, The Naval Review; *Recreations* amateur theatre, crumbly cricket; *Clubs* Royal Cwlth Soc; *Style—* Rear Adm Richard Hill; Cornhill House, Bishop's Waltham, Southampton, Hants; Carpmael Building, Temple, London EC4Y 7AT; Treasury Office, Middle Temple, London EC4Y 9AT (☎ 071 353 4355, fax 071 583 3220)

HILL, Richard Kenneth; TD (1972); s of Lt-Col Peter Kenneth Hill, TD (d 1988), of 248 Thorpe Rd, Longthorpe, Peterborough, and Sylvia Mary Jephson, *née* Widdowson; *b* 20 April 1941; *Educ* Oakham Sch; *m* 29 April 1967, Pip Mary, da of Bernard Shipman, of Belton, nr Grantham, Lincolnshire; 1 s (Timothy Kenneth b 6 Sept 1969), 1 da (Zoë Louise b 31 Dec 1971); *Career* TA served: 8 Bn Sherwood Foresters, 5/8 Bn Sherwood Foresters, 4/5 Bn Northamptonshire Regt, 5 (volunteer) Bn Royal Anglian Regt, Maj 1970 (served as OC HQ at Peterborough); admitted slr 1964, sr ptnr Wyman & Abbott Peterborough; fndr vice pres of Rotary Club of the Ortons, chm Cambridgeshire TAVR Assoc, pres Peterborough Branch of Northants Regtl Comrades Assoc; memb Law Soc; *Recreations* gardening, field sports; *Clubs* Royal Over-Seas League; *Style—* Richard Hill, Esq, TD; Cherry Orton Farm, Orton Waterville, Peterborough (☎ 0733 231495); 35 Priestgate, Peterborough PE1 1JR (☎ 0733 64131)

HILL, Hon Robert; s of Baron Hill of Luton, PC (Life Peer; d Aug 1989), and Marion Spencer, *née* Wallace (d Nov 1989); *b* 1938; *Educ* Epsom Coll, Harper Adams' Agric Coll; *m* 1960, Ann, da of E Williamson, of Southampton; issue; *Career* agric; gp sec NFU; *Style—* The Hon Robert Hill; 33 Meadow View, Dunvant, Swansea, W Glam SA2 7UZ

HILL, Robin Murray; s of Albert Edward Hill, of Bramshot Dr, Fleet, Hampshire, and Phyllis, *née* Edgeler; *b* 13 Nov 1942; *Educ* Lancing; *m* Susan Margaret, da of Dr Gordon Carter, of Sheephatch Farm, Tilford, Farnham, Surrey; 2 da (Victoria b 1968, Vanessa b 1972); *Career* chartered surveyor Jones Lang Wootton 1972-79, ptnr Clifford Tee and Gale (architects and surveyors) 1979-; FRICS 1967; *Recreations* equestrian sports, skiing, gardening; *Clubs* Athenaeum; *Style—* Robin Hill, Esq; Southdown House, Lower Froyle, Alton, Hampshire GU34 4NA (☎ 0420 22187); Clifford Tee & Gale, 5 Eccleston St, London SW1W 9LY (☎ 071 730 9633)

HILL, Dr Ronald David; s of David Josiah Hill (d 1974), and Theresa, *née* Handy; *b* 20 June 1932; *Educ* Coventry Tech Coll, Guy's Hospital (MB BS); *m* 27 June 1957, Juliet Dorothea, da of Charles William Webb; 1 s (Simon Peter b 1966), 1 da (Sarah Louise b 1968); *Career* Nat Serv, NCO RAMC 1952-54; sr registrar Guy's Hosp 1967-70 (res fell 1967), conslt physician Wessex RHA 1970-; memb Br Diabetic Assoc, fndr chm Wessex Diabetes and Endocrine Assoc; FRCP 1978, MRCS, fell Assurance Med Soc 1989; *Books* contrib: Essentials Clinical Medicine (1984), Compendium of Anaesthetic and Resuscitative Data (1984), Microalbuminuria (1988); Diabetes Health Care (1987); *Recreations* sailing, walking, gardening; *Clubs* Royal Motor Yacht; *Style—* Dr Ronald Hill; Marlow Grange, 20 Martello Rd, Poole, Dorset BH13 7DH (☎ 0202 708917); Dept of Diabetes, Poole General Hospital, Poole, Dorset (☎ 0202 675100)

HILL, Rosalind Margaret; da of Brian Percival Hill, and Joan Barbera Warren, *née* Rollinson; *b* 18 April 1955; *Educ* St Margaret's Convent Sussex, Univ of Exeter (BA); *Career* CA; Ernst & Whinney 1977, J Henry Schroder Wagg & Co Ltd 1986, dir corporate fin P & P plc 1988-; memb Home Farm Tst; ACA 1981; *Recreations* travel, entertaining, the arts; *Style—* Miss Rosalind Hill; Hamilton House, 1 Temple Ave, London EC4Y OHA (☎ : 071 353 4212, fax 071 353 2105, telex 926604)

HILL, Hon Mrs (Rosamund Shirley); da of Baron Crowther-Hunt (Life Peer); *b* 1950; *m* 1978, John Christopher Hill; issue; *Style—* Hon Mrs Hill; 104 Ridgeway, Weston Favell, Northampton

HILL, Roy Gray; s of Martin Spencer Hill (d 1968), and Erwina, *née* Lancaster (d 1971); *b* 5 Jan 1922; *Educ* Chigwell Sch Essex; *m* Norah Olive, *née* Parker; 1 s (Martin Gray b 12 May 1953), 1 da (Elizabeth Ann b 21 Sept 1949); *Career* served WWII; slr; Hill Dickinson & Co: joined specialising in marine and commercial law 1947, ptnr 1951-84, sr ptnr 1984-87, chm 1987-89; chm Hill Dickinson Davis Campbell 1989-; former examiner Slrs Qualifying Examination Commercial Paper, mangr The Liverpool and London War Risks Insurance Assoc Ltd 1965-, served various ctees on Br Shipping incl Law of the Sea and Collision Regulations 1955-65, legal advsr to various Pension Funds (including within the Shipping Indust), chm Tstees Union of Marine Aviation and Shipping Transport Offrs 1985-; memb: Law Soc 1947, Liverpool Law Soc; *Recreations* gardening, walking, swimming, writing, music and opera; *Clubs* RAC, Royal Horticultural Soc, Alvis Owners', The Sloane; *Style—* Roy Hill, Esq; Lombardy, Telegraph Rd, Caldy, Wirral, Merseyside L48 2NY (☎ 051 625 8768); Hill Dickinson Davis Campbell, Pearl Assurance House, Derby Square, Liverpool L2 9XL (☎ 051 236 5400, fax 051 236 2175)

HILL, Roy Thomas; s of John Thomas Hill DSM, (d 1977), of Bury St Edmunds, Suffolk, and Lucy Clara Hill; *b* 4 Jan 1935; *Educ* Culford Sch Suffolk; *m* 12 March 1963, Ann Elizabeth, da of Arthur Chambers, 1 s (Stephen b 1964), 2 da (Sharon b 1967, Paula b 1970); *Career* United Dominions Tst plc (credit investigators) 1959-66, R T Hill and Co CAs 1966-67, sr ptnr Clayton and Brewill CAs 1967-; chm Bridgeway Fin Ltd, W Bridgford 41 Club; fin dir S Notts Trg Agency Ltd, treas 3 W Bridgford Friary Scout Gp; FCA 1958, FCMA 1961; *Recreations* golf, half marathon running; *Clubs* 41, Ruddington Grange Golf; *Style—* Roy Hill, Esq; Bridgeway House, 308 Loughborough Rd, W Bridgford, Nottingham (☎ 0602 503044); Cawley House, 149-153 Canal St, Nottingham (☎ 0602 503044)

HILL, Shaun Donovan; s of George Herbert Hill (d 1969), and Molly, *née* Cunningham, of London; *b* 11 April 1947; *Educ* The London Oratory, St Marylebone

GS; *m* 11 June 1966, Anja Irmeli, da of Martti Toivonen, of Lahti, Finland; 1 s ((Kim) Dominic b 18 Jan 1967), 2 da (Maija b 9 April 1972, Minna b 10 June 1975); *Career* cook: Carrier's Restaurant (London) 1968-71, The Gay Hussar (London) 1972-74, Intercontinental Hotel (London) 1975-76; head chef: Capital Hotel (Knightsbridge) 1976-77, Blakes (Chelsea) 1978-80, Lygon Arms (Broadway Worcs) 1981-82; chef and patron Hill's (Stratford upon Avon) 1983-85, chef and md Gidleigh Park (Chagford Devon) 1985-; memb Academie Culinaire de France 1982, elected master chef by Master Chefs Inst 1983; *Recreations* eating and drinking (not necessarily in that order); *Style—* Shaun Hill, Esq; 14 Oaktree Park, Sticklepath, Devon EX20 2NB (☎ 0837 840062); Gidleigh Park, Chagford, Devon TQ13 8HH (☎ 0647 433578, fax 0647 432574)

HILL, Stanley Arthur; s of John Henry Hill (d 1976), and Edith Muriel, *née* Mathews (d 1985); *b* 22 May 1935; *Educ* Townsend C of E Sch St Albans; *m* 9 July 1960, Elizabeth Scott (Betty), da of James McKay, of Forsyte Shades, Canford Cliffs, Poole, Dorset; 2 da (Elizabeth Scott b 19 Feb 1962, Catherine McKay b 11 Nov 1963); *Career* Nat Serv RMP 1953-55, served ME; md: Coopers Holdings Ltd, Coopers Metal Holdings Ltd, Coopers (Metals) Ltd, United Ferrous Supplies, Marple & Gillott Ltd, Coopers Wednesbury, Swindon Car and Commercials, Glos Steel Stock; dir: Coopers Non Ferrous Ltd, Cooper Barnes Metal Ltd, Norton Barrow Holdings Ltd, Norton Barrow Metals Ltd, Coopers Robinson Metals Ltd, Cooper Friswell Ltd; memb Bd Nat Cncl Br Scrap Fedn, memb Ctee Mid-West Scrap Assoc, chm Br Scrap Fedn Exporters Ctee, vice pres Ctee BIR; memb Ctee: 1986 Indust Year, Lechlade Soc; capt Burford Golf Club 1973-74; MIOD 1967-; *Recreations* cricket, golf; *Clubs* Burford Golf, Parkstone Golf, Swindon Golf; *Style—* Stanley Hill, Esq; The Butts, Bryworth Lane, Lechlade, Gloucestershire (☎ 0367 52598); Bridge House, Gipsy Lane, Swindon, Wilts SN2 6DZ (☎ 0793 532111, fax 0793 614 214, car 0836 597 483, telex 44251)

HILL, His Hon Judge (Ian) Starforth; QC (1969); s of Capt Harold Victor John Hill (d 1967), and Helen Dora, *née* Starforth; *b* 30 Sept 1921; *Educ* Dragon Sch Shrewsbury, BNC Oxford (MA); *m* 1, 1950 (m dis), Bridget Mary Footner; 1 s (David b 1951), 2 da (Jane b 1953, Juliet b 1956); m 2, 1982 (m dis), Greta Grimshaw; m 3, Wendy Elizabeth Stavert; *Career* Capt Indian Army 1940-45, India, Africa, Italy (despatches); called to the Bar 1949; dep chm IOW Quarter Sessions 1968-71, rec Crown Ct 1972-74, circuit judge 1974, memb Parole Bd 1983-84, resident judge Winchester Combined Court Centre 1990-; *Recreations* gardening, games, amateur theatre; *Clubs* Hampshire; *Style—* His Hon Judge Starforth Hill, QC; Tulls Hill, Preston Candover, Hants RG25 2EW

HILL, Stephen; s of Vincent Wolstenholme Hill (d 1959), of Edenfield, Lancs, and Ruth Emily Hill; *b* 27 Oct 1937; *Educ* Bury GS; *m* 21 Sept 1963, Elaine Margaret, da of Horace Sheldon (d 1979), of Tottington; 1 s (Richard b 1972), 2 da (Alison b 1965, Elizabeth b 1968); *Career* ptnr Grundy Middleton & Co CAs 1963-69, ptnr Hill Eckersley & Co 1969-; govr Bury GS, former memb Radcliffe Round Table; FCA 1960; *Recreations* golf, walking, skiing, gardening; *Clubs* Bury GSOB, Rossendale Golf; *Style—* Stephen Hill, Esq; Wyvern, 935 Walmersley Rd, Bury, Lancs BL9 5LL (☎ 061 764 5931); Hill Eckersley & Co, Chartered Accountants, 62 Chorley New Rd, Bolton BL1 4BY (☎ 0204 22113)

HILL, Susan; da of R H Hill, and Doris, *née* Bailey; *b* 5 Feb 1942; *Educ* Scarborough Convent, Barr's Hill Sch Coventry, King's Coll London (BA); *m* Prof Stanley Wells; 3 da (Jessica b 1977, Imogen b 1984 d 1984, Clemency b 1985); *Career* novelist, playwright, book reviewer; novels: The Enclosure (1961), Do Me A Favour (1963), Gentleman and Ladies (1968), A Change for the Better (1969), I'm the King of the Castle 1970, The Albatross (1971), Strange Meeting (1971), The Bird of Night (1972), A Bit of Singing and Dancing (collected short stories, 1973), In the Springtime of the Year (1974), Air and Angels (1991); ghost story The Woman in Black 1983; autobiography: The Magic Apple Tree (1982), Family (1989); children's books: One Night at a Time, Mother's Magic, Can it be true?, Suzy's Shoes, Pirate Poll, Septimus Honeydew, I won't go There Again, Stories of Codling Village, The Glass Angel, I've Forgotten Edward; ed: The Distracted Preacher and other stories (Thomas Hardy), The Walker Book of Ghost Stories, The Penguin Book of Modern Women's Short Stories; plays: The Cold Country, and other plays for radio; *Style—* Miss Susan Hill; Midsummer Cottage, Church Lane, Beckley, Oxford OX3 9UT (☎ 086 735 252, fax 086 735 8929)

HILL, Vince; s of late William Hill, and late Lillian Hill; *b* 16 April 1937; *Educ* educated in Coventry; *m* 4 June 1959, Annie; 1 s (Athol Vincent William b 19 Oct 1971); *Career* Nat Serv Band of Royal Corps of Signals; former baker and miner Keresley Colliery Coventry; singer; operatic baritone touring and appearing at prestigious venues, fndr of vocal gps: Four Others, The Raindrops; solo performer 1962-; singles incl: The Rivers Run Dry, Edelweiss 1967, Roses of Picardy, Look Around; Cabaret Performer of the Year; composer of musicals: Tolpuddle (played the lead role in BCC Radio 4 broadcast), Zodiac (with Alan Plater and Johnny Worth); radio series incl: Vince Hill's Solid Gold Music Show, Simply Vince (1991); TV series: The Musical Time Machine, They Sold a Million; stage acting debut as Ivor Novello in My Dearest Ivor (1990); successes in int song festivals as singer and composer, winner of many awards and recognised as one of Britain's top male vocalists, appeared as guest on numerous TV and radio shows in Britain and Europe, toured overseas, featured as subject of This is Your Life; *Style—* Vince Hill, Esq; George Bartram Associates, Creative House, 5 Commercial St, Birmingham B1 1RS (☎ 021 643 2323, fax 021 633 3469)

HILL, Hon Mrs (Wendy Helen); *née* Fitzherbert; yst da of 14 Baron Stafford (d 1986), and Morag Nada, *née* Campbell; *b* 28 April 1961; *Educ* Convent of the Sacred Heart Woldingham; *m* 1983, Jeremy John Maurice Hill, eld s of Lt-Col Colin Hill (d 1985), of Coley Court, Coley, East Harptree, Bristol, 2 s (Thomas b 1985, Nicholas b 1987); *Recreations* skiing; *Style—* The Hon Mrs Hill; 66 Scarsdale Villas, London W8 6PP

HILL, Prof William George; s of William Hill (d 1984), of Hemel Hempstead, Herts, and Margaret Paterson, *née* Hamilton (d 1987); *b* 7 Aug 1940; *Educ* St Albans Sch, Wye Coll Univ of London (BSc), Univ of California Davis (MS), Iowa State Univ, Univ of Edinburgh (PhD, DSc); *m* 1 July 1971, (Christine) Rosemary, da of John Walter Austin, of Kingskerswell, Devon; 1 s (Alastair b 1977), 2 da (Louise b 1973, Rachel b 1974); *Career* Univ of Edinburgh: prof of animal genetics 1983- (lectr 1965-74, reader 1974-83), head Inst of Cell, Animal and Population Biology 1990-; visiting prof and visiting res assoc: Univ of Minnesota 1966, Iowa State Univ 1967-78, N Carolina State Univ 1979 and 1985; memb: Sci Study Gp Meat and Livestock Cmmn 1969-72, AFRC Animals Res Grant Bd 1986-, Dirs Advsy Gp AFRC Animal Breeding Res Orgn 1983-87, AFRC Inst of Animal Physiology and Genetics Res 1987-; FRSE 1979, FRS 1985; *Books* Benchmark Papers on Quantitative Genetics (1984), Evolution and Animal Breeding (1989); *Recreations* farming, bridge; *Clubs* Farmers'; *Style—* Prof William Hill, FRS, FRSE; 4 Gordon Terr, Edinburgh EH16 5QH (☎ 031 667 3680); Institute of Cell, Animal and Population Biology, University of Edinburgh, West Mains Rd, Edinburgh EH9 3JT (☎ 031 650 5456, fax 031 667 3210, telex 727 442)

HILL, William Sephton; s of William Thomas Hill (d 1969), and Anne May, *née* Sephton (d 1972); *b* 24 July 1926; *Educ* Cowley Sch St Helens Merseyside, Emmanuel Coll Cambridge (BA, LLB); *m* 30 Jan 1954, Jean, da of Philip Wedgwood (d 1976); 1 da (Tracy); *Career* RAF 1944-47, served in Far East: India, Burma Malaysia, Hong Kong, Japan; Japanese interpreter; called to the Bar Gray's Inn 1951, Legal Dept HM Customs and Excise 1954-85 (departmental slr 1981-85), advsr euro affrs to Br American Tobacco Co 1985-89, Duty Free Confedn Brussels 1989-; *Recreations* golf, music, bridge; *Clubs* Moor Park Golf Herts; *Style—* William Hill, Esq; 31 Hill Rise, Richmansworth, Herts WD3 2NY (☎ 0923 774756, 0923 897004)

HILL, Hon Mrs (Yvonne Aletta); da of late 2 Baron de Villiers; *b* 1913; *Educ* LMH Oxford; *m* 1939, James Kenneth Hill; 3 s, 1 da; *Style—* The Hon Mrs Hill; Edgehill, 22 Wyndlorn Ave, Buderim, Queensland, Australia

HILL-NORTON, Vice Adm the Hon Nicholas John; s of Baron Hill-Norton, GCB (Life Peer); *b* 1939; *Educ* Marlborough Coll, RNC Dartmouth; *m* 1966, Ann Jennifer, da of Vice-Adm Dennis Mason, CB, CVO; 2 s (Simon b 1967, Tom b 1975), 1 da (Claudia b 1969); *Career* RN: Capt HMS Invincible 1983-84, Flag Offr Gibraltar 1987-90, Flag Offr Flotilla Three and Cdr Anti-Submarine Warfare Striking Force 1990; *Style—* Rear Admiral The Hon Nicholas Hill-Norton; Fort Southwick, Hants

HILL-NORTON, Adm of the Fleet Baron (Life Peer UK 1978); Peter John; GCB (1970, KCB 1967, CB 1964); s of Capt Martin John Norton (d 1928); *b* 8 Feb 1915; *Educ* RNCs Dartmouth and Greenwich; *m* 1936, Eileen, da of Carl Adolph Linstow (d 1947); 1 s, 1 da; *Career* Independent peer in House of Lords; RN 1932, served WWII Arctic Convoys and NW Approaches, Capt 1953, Rear Adm 1962, ACNS 1962-64, Flag Offr 2 in cmd Far East Fleet 1964-66, Vice Adm 1965, dep CDS (Personnel and Logistics) 1966-67, Second Sea Lord 1967, vice CNS 1967-68, Adm 1968, C-in-C UK Forces Far East 1969-70, CNS and First Sea Lord 1970-71, Adm of the Fleet 1971, CDS 1971-74, chm NATO Mil Ctee 1974-77; memb Steering Ctee for Volunteer Home Def Force 1983, fndr pres Br Maritime League; Freeman City of London 1974, Liveryman Wroshipful Co of Shipwrights 1974; *Books* No Soft Options (1978), Sea Power (1982); *Recreations* gardening, shooting; *Clubs* Army and Navy, Royal Navy of 1765; *Style—* Adm of the Fleet the Rt Hon the Lord Hill-Norton, GCB; Cass Cottage, Hyde, Fordingbridge, Hants (☎ 0425 652392)

HILL SMITH, Marilyn; da of George Francis Smith, and Irene Charlotte, *née* Clarke; *b* 9 Feb 1952; *Educ* Nonsuch HS For Girls Ewell Surrey, Guildhall Sch of Music & Drama; *m* 7 Dec 1974, Thomas Peter Kemp, s of Thomas William Kemp; *Career* opera singer; soprano soloist: Viennese Gala Performances Southbank and touring 1975-80, Gilbert & Sullivan For All touring England Australasia (1974) USA/Canada (1975-76) 1969-75; debut: BBC Radio 1975, princ soprano ENO 1978 (memb co 1978-84), Royal Opera House 1981, New Sadlers Wells Opera 1981, Canadian Opera 1984, Welsh Nat Opera 1987, Scottish Opera 1988, New D'Oyly Carte Opera 1990; festivals incl: Aldeburgh, Henley, Versailles, Nurenburg, Cologne, Athens, Granada, Bologna, Siena, Rome, Hong Kong; TV incl: Top C's and Tiaras (C4) 1983, Queen Mother's 90 Birthday Celebration 1990; recordings incl: Dixit Dominus (CBS Masterworks) 1977, The Songwriters (BBC) 1978, Christopher Columbus (Opera Rara) 1978, La Princesse de Navarre (Erato) 1980, Dinorah (Opera Rara) 1980, Robinson Crusoe (Opera Rara) 1981, Count of Luxembourg and Countess Maritza (New Sadlers Wells Opera) 1983, Vienna Premiere Vol I (Chandos, Music Retailers Assoc award 1984) 1983, Friday Night is Music Night (BBC Records) 1985, Treasures of Operetta Vol I (Chandos Retailers Assoc award 1985) 1985, Vienna Premiere Vol II (Chandos) 1987, Ruddigore (New Sadlers Wells) 1987, Candide (Bernstein, Scottish Opera) 1988, Treasures of Operetta Vol III (Chandos) 1989, Pirates of Penzance (New D'Oyly Carte) 1990, Student Prince (TER) 1990; *Recreations* cooking, reading, sleeping; *Style—* Ms Marilyn Hill Smith; c/o Music International, 13 Ardilaun Rd, Highbury, London N5 2QR (☎ 071 359 5183, fax 071 226 9792)

HILL-SMITH, His Hon Judge Derek Edward; VRD; s of Charles George Hill-Smith (d 1942), and Ivy Downs (d 1985); gf G E Hill-Smith entrepreneur and importer of silks and fine cloth from Far East last century; *b* 21 Oct 1922; *Educ* Sherborne, Trinity Coll Oxford; *m* 1950, Marjorie Joanna, da of His Hon Judge Montague L Berryman, QC (d 1974), of Essex; 1 s (Alexander b 1955), 1 da (Nicola b 1958); *Career* RNVR 1942-46, served in Atlantic 1942, cmmnd 1943, fighter direction offr 1943, attack on Tirpitz 1944, Normandy landings May 1944, FDO Flagship SE Asia, cmmnd 1945 Relief of Singapore, Lt-Cdr RNR; in business 1947-50, taught classics 1950-54, called to the Bar Inner Temple 1954; chm Kent Quarter Sessions 1970, rec 1971, circuit judge 1972-87; *Recreations* theatre, tennis, sailing, painting, restoring Old Masters; *Clubs* Bar Yacht, Garrick; *Style—* His Hon Judge Derek Hill-Smith, VRD; c/o National Westminster Bank, 7 North St, Bishops Stortford, Herts; Crown and County Courts in London and Home Counties

HILL-TREVOR, Hon Nevill Edward; JP (Berwyn Div 1971), DL (Denbighshire, now Clwyd 1965); s of 3 Baron Trevor (d 1950); *b* 1931; *m* 1963, Deborah, da of late W T B Jowitt, of Killinghall, Harrogate; 2 da; *Career* Flying Offr RAF Regt (ret), ADC to C-in-C Fighter Cmd 1958-59, ADC to Chief of Air Staff 1959-61; High Sheriff Denbighshire 1965-66; joint master: Border Counties (NW) Otter Hounds 1950-59, Sir W W Wynn's Foxhounds 1970-78; *Style—* The Hon Nevill Hill-Trevor, JP, DL; Plas Lledrod, Llansilin, Clwyd

HILL-WOOD, Sir David Basil; 3 Bt (UK 1921); s of Sir Basil Samuel Hill Hill-Wood, 2 Bt (d 1954), by his w, *see* Hon Lady Hill-Wood; *b* 12 Nov 1926; *Educ* Eton, *m* 1970, Jennifer Anne McKenzie Stratmann (assumed surname, Stratmann, by deed poll 1960), da of Peter McKenzie Strang (Japanese POW, presumed d 1943); 2 s, 1 da; *Heir* s, Samuel Thomas Hill-Wood b 24 Aug 1971; *Career* Lt Grenadier Gds (Palestine) 1945-48; Morgan Grenfell 1948-55; sr ptnr Myers and Co stockbrokers 1971-74 (ptnr 1955); dir: Capel Cure Myers 1974-77, Guinness Mahon and Co 1977-; High Sheriff Berks 1982-83; former pres Victoria FA (Aust), Aust rep on FA 1977; *Recreations* tennis, farming; *Clubs* White's, Melbourne (Australia); *Style—* Sir David Hill-Wood, Bt; Dacre Farm, Farley Hill, Reading, Berks (☎ 0734 733185); 58 Cathcart Rd, London SW10 (☎ 071 352 0389); Guinness Mahon and Co Ltd, 32 St Mary at Hill, London EC3P 3AJ (☎ 071 623 9333)

HILL-WOOD, Hon Lady - Hon Joan Louisa; *née* Brand; da of 3 Viscount Hampden, GCVO, KCB, CMG (d 1958); *b* 1904; *m* 1925, Capt Sir Basil Samuel Hill Hill-Wood, 2 Bt (d 1954); 1 s (David, 3 Bt *qv*), 1 da; *Style—* The Hon Lady Hill-Wood; Knipton Lodge, Grantham, Lincs (☎ 047 682 226)

HILLABY, John; s of Albert Ewart Hillaby (d 1967), and Mabel, *née* Colyer (d 1977); *b* 24 July 1917; *Educ* Woodhouse Grove Sch Leeds Yorks; *m* 1, 1940 (m dis 1966), Eleanor, *née* Riley; 2 da (Susan b 1947, Felicity b 1949); m 2, 1966, Thelma, *née* Gordon (d 1972); m 3, 1981, Kathleen (formerly Mrs Burton); *Career* WWII RA Field Gunner 1939-44, served briefly in France; author, journalist, TV and radio presenter, long distance walker; local journalism until 1939, magazine contrib and bdcaster 1944, zoological corr Manchester Guardian 1949, euro sci writer New York Times 1951-, biological conslt New Scientist 1953; former dir Univs Fedn for Animal Welfare, fndr pres Backpackers Club; travelled on foot through parts of: Boreal Canada, Eastern USA, Central and N Eastern Africa (incl Zaire, Ituri Forest and Mountains of the Moon Ruwenzoni), Sudan, Tanzania; three months foot safari with camels to Lake Rudolf; walked from: Lands End to John O'Groats, The Hague to Nice via the Alps, Provence to Tuscany, Athens to Mt Olympus via the Pindus Mountains; Woodward lectr Yale

1973; radio and TV series incl: Men of the North, Expedition South, Alpine Venture, Hillaby Walks, Globetrotter; fell Scientific Zoological Soc of London; *Books* Within The Streams (1949), Nature and Man (1960), Journey to the Jade Sea (1964), Journey Through Britain (1968), Journey Through Europe (1972), Journey Through Love (1976), Journey Home (1983), John Hillaby's Yorkshire (1986), John Hillaby's London (1987), Walking in Britain (1988), Journey to The Gods (1991); *Recreations* rectification of mis-spent youth by reading, slight academic instruction and observant travel; *Clubs* Savage; *Style—* John Hillaby, Esq; London & Yorks; c/o Constable Publisher, 10 Orange St, London WC2

HILLAND, Robert James McNally; s of Richard McNally Hilland (d 1978), of Scotland, and Grace McClymont, *née* Blackwell; *b* 31 July 1939; *Educ* Stranraer HS, Univ of Strathclyde (BA), Jordanhill Coll of Educn (DCE); *m* 15 Sept 1989, Rosalie Elizabeth, *née* Middleton; *Career* merchant banker; dir: Scottish Allied Investors Ltd 1982-88, Kirkby Central Gp Ltd 1984-89, Charterhouse Devpt Capital Ltd 1985, Charterhouse Devpt Ltd 1985, Nat Commercial and Glyns Ltd 1986, Royal Bank Devpt Ltd 1986, NW Independent Hosps Ltd 1987, Dean Smith Garages Ltd 1987, Realwood Ltd 1989, McMasters Stores Scot Ltd 1989, Bothwell Park Brick Co Ltd 1989, Echo Hotel plc 1989, Beatlight Ltd 1989; memb Scottish Venture Capital Forum; *Recreations* shooting, fishing, golf, theatre; *Clubs* St James, Mere Golf Country; *Style—* Robert Hilland, Esq; 24 Heriot Row, Edinburgh EH3 6EN (☎ 031 225 6699); Auchencloy Cottage, Stoneykirk, Stranraer, Wigtownshire (☎ 077682367); Charterhouse Devpt Capital Ltd, 26 St Andrew Square, Edinburgh EH2 1AF (☎ 031 556 2555, fax 031 557 2900, car 0836 605637)

HILLARY, Sir Edmund P; KBE (1953); s of Percival Augustus Hillary, of Remuera, Auckland, New Zealand; *b* 20 July 1919; *Educ* Auckland GS, Auckland Univ Coll; *m* 1, 1953, Louise Mary Rose (d 1975); 1 s, 2 da (and 1 da decd); m 2, 21 Dec 1989, June Mulgrew; *Career* served WWII with RNZAF; explorer, author, lectr; memb: Br Mount Everest Expdn (reached summit with Sherpa Tensing) 1953, Cwlth Antarctic Expdn 1957-58; leader Himalayan Sch House Expdn 1963; pres NZ Voluntary Service Abroad; dir Field Educn Enterprises of Australasia Pty Ltd conslt to Sears Roebuck and Co (USA); *Style—* Sir Edmund Hillary, KBE; 278a Remuera Rd, Auckland, New Zealand

HILLEARD, Darrell Alfred Frederick; s of Alfred George Hilleard (d 1956), and Catherine Emily, *née* Wager (d 1970); *b* 21 May 1930; *Educ* Kings Sch, King Edward VII Naval Coll, Vienna Univ, Coll of Technol Kingston Poly (Dip); *m* 23 Dec 1961, Pamela, da of Harold Richard Snook, of East Molesey, Surrey; 2 da (Charmain b 14 Feb 1973, Sharon (twin) b 14 Feb 1973); *Career* indentured apprentice and 3 offr MN 1947-54, served on Christian Salveson Antarctic South Georgia Station 1948-49; mgmnt conslt Peat Marwick Mitchell 1965-74, euro admin Eaton Corp 1974-77, business conslt Prodn Engrg Res Assoc 1977-78, md Cardale Gp 1978-81, sr inspection coordinator Fluor-Norsk Stat Pipe 1981-82, res engr Br Ports Assoc 1982-84, sr tech offr Inst Prodn Engrs 1984-87, business mangr Royal Borough Kensington and Chelsea 1987-90, industl estates devpt offr Bedfordshire Co Cncl; fndr memb Comcentre (the UK communications centre) 1987; professional inst rep: BSI, SERC, NEDO, Euro Community economic and social ctees; CEng 1964, MIMechE 1964, MIMarE 1964, MIMC 1971, MMS 1984; *Recreations* reinstatement and restoration of buildings of architectural interest, swimming, walking, attending professional instns' meetings, participating in specialist discussions on art and antiques; *Style—* Darrell Hilleard, Esq; 52 Priory Rd, Kew Green, Richmond, Surrey TW9 3DH (☎ 081 940 6509); Gorse Farm, Cotton End, Bedfordshire MK45 3AB; Economic Development Unit, Bedfordshire County Council, County Hall, Cauldwell St, Bedford MK42 9AP

HILLEARY, Hon Mrs (Fiona Mary); yst da of 3 Baron Burton, *qv*, and his 1 w, Elizabeth Ursula Forster, *née* Wise; *b* 31 Oct 1957; *Educ* West Heath Sevenoaks; *m* 1982, Alasdair Malcolm Douglas Macleod Hilleary, eldest s of Maj Ruaraidh Hilleary, of Logie Farm, Glen Ferness, Nairn, and Edinbaine, Isle of Skye; 2 da (Flora Elizabeth Macleod b 1985, Rosannagh Catriona b 1988); *Recreations* riding, stalking; *Style—* The Hon Mrs Hilleary; Greenhill House, Redcastle, Muir of Ord, Ross-shire

HILLEARY, Hon Mrs (Grace Janet Mary); *née* Best; eldest da of 6 Baron Wynford, DSO (d 1940), and Hon Eva Napier, da of 2 Baron Napier of Magdala; *b* 27 Aug 1907; *m* 12 Nov 1930, Edward Kenneth Macleod Hilleary, MVO, 2 s of Maj Edward Langdale Hilleary, OBE, TD, DL; 3 da; *Style—* The Hon Mrs Hilleary; Nettlebed House, Droxford, Hants

HILLEN, John Malcolm; s of Clarence Albert Hillen, of Great Barr, Birmingham, and Winifred Mary Hillen, *née* Bristow; *b* 13 May 1952; *Educ* King Edward VI GS Aston, Lincoln Coll Oxford (BA, MA); *m* 5 Oct 1985, Monica Lillian Marie, da of Harry Frewin Curtice, of Aldwick, West Sussex; 1 s (Guy Albert Curtice b 23 March 1989), 1 da (Florence Elizabeth b 11 Dec 1987); *Career* called to the Bar Middle Temple 1976; memb: South Eastern Circuit, Central Criminal Ct Bar Mess, Kent Bar Mess, Criminal Bar Assoc; *Recreations* theatre, cinema; *Style—* John Hillen, Esq; 9 King's Bench Walk, Temple, London EC4Y 7DX (☎ 071 353 5638/9, fax 071 353 6166)

HILLER, Robin John Cecil; s of Cecil Bernard Hiller (d 1966) and Esmé Leonora Patience Hiller, *née* Hughes; *b* 31 Oct 1933; *Educ* Epsom Coll; *m* 17 June 1961, Ann Margaret, da of Edwin Walter Booth, of Limpsfield, Surrey; 1 s (Mark Andrew Robin b 1962), 1 da (Alison Claire b 1963); *Career* Lt RNR Nat Serv; CA Annan Dexter to BDO Binder Hamlyn 1951-87, (fin dir and conslt); memb: Royal Surgical Aid Soc 1979-89, King Edward VII Fund Grant Ctee 1982-85; Liveryman Worshipful Co of Glovers; Lloyds underwriter 1972-; *Recreations* charitable work, skiing, golf; *Clubs* Reform, City Livery, City of London, Naval; *Style—* Robin J C Hiller, Esq; Bydown, 73 Blue House Lane, Limpsfield, Surrey RH8 0AP

HILLER, Susan; *b* 1942; *Educ* Smith Coll US (AB), Tulane Univ (MA); *Career* artist; solo exhibitions incl: Gallery House 1973, Hester van Royen 1976 and 1978, Serpentine Gallery 1976, Museum of Modern Art Oxford 1978, Gimpel Fils London (various 1980-84), A Space Toronto 1981, Akumulatory Warsaw 1982, Roslyn Oxley Gallery Sydney 1982, Interim Art 1984, ICA 1986, Pat Hearn NY 1988-90, Kettle's Yard Cambridge 1989, Mappin Gallery Sheffield 1990, Matt's Gallery London 1991; group exhibitions incl: From Britain '75 (Taidehall Helsinki) 1975, Hayward Annual 1978, Sydney Biennale 1982, The British Art Show (Arts Cncl of GB) 1984, Kunst mit Eigen-Sinn (Museum Moderner Kunst, Vienna) 1985, Staging the Self (Nat Portrait Gallery) 1986, Towards a Bigger Picture (V & A) 1987, 100 Years of Art in Britain (Leeds City Museum) 1988, Lifelines (Br Cncl, BASF, Tate, Ludwigshafen and Liverpool) 1989-90, Great British Art (Maclellon Galleries Glasgow) 1990, Ten Artists (Ceibu Caison Tokyo) 1990; public collections incl: Arts Cncl of GB, Tate Gallery, V & A Museum, Contemporary Arts Soc; works incl: Belshazzar's Feast (video installation), Monument (photography and audio), Midnight, Baker Street (self-portrait), Home Truths (series of paintings); lectr Maidstone Coll of Art and tutor St Martin's Sch of Art 1975-80, post grad tutor Slade Sch of Art UCL 1980-, distinguished visiting prof Dept of Art Calif State Univ Long Beach 1988, visiting lectr in New Genres Univ of Calif LA 1991, external examiner CNAA (various BA and MA Fine Art courses); memb Visual Arts Panel Greater London Arts Assoc 1976-81; Arts Cncl of GB: memb Subctee Support Schemes for Artists 1978-82, judge Student Film and Video Awards 1986 (memb Purchasing Panel 1990-); artist in residence Univ of Sussex 1975, Visual Artist's Award GB (Gulbentian Fndn) 1976 and 1977, Nat Endowment for the Arts Fell (USA) 1982, Visual Arts Bd Travelling Fell (Aust) 1982; *Books* Dreams - Visions of the Night (co-author), The Myth of Primitivism (ed), various artists books and monographs; *Style—* Ms Susan Hiller; 83 Loudoun Rd, London NW8 0DL (☎ 071 372 0438)

HILLER, Dame Wendy; DBE (1975, OBE 1971); da of Frank Watkin, and Marie Hiller; *b* 1912; *Educ* Winceby House Bexhill; *m* 1937, Ronald Gow; 1 s, 1 da; *Career* actress; plays incl: Love on the Dole (Garrick London and Shubert NY), Twelfth Night (war factory tour), Tess of the d'Urbervilles (Picadilly), The Heiress (Biltmore NY) 1948, Old Vic Season 1955-56, Aspern Papers (NY) 1962, The Wings of the Dove (Lyric) 1963, The Sacred Flame 1967, Crown Matrimonial (Haymarket), John Gabriel Baskman (National) 1975, The Importance of Being Earnest (Royalty) 1987, Driving Miss Daisy (Apollo) 1988; *films incl:* Pygmalion, Major Barbara, Sons and Lovers, A Man for all Seasons, David Copperfield, Separate Tables (won an Oscar), Murder on the Orient Express, The Elephant Man, The Lonely Passion of Judith Hearne; *Style—* Dame Wendy Hiller, DBE; c/o ICM, 388 Oxford St, London

HILLHOUSE, (Robert) Russell; s of Robert Hillhouse, of Newton Mearns, Glasgow, and Jean Russell; *b* 23 April 1938; *Educ* Hutchesons' GS Glasgow, Univ of Glasgow (MA); *m* 4 June 1966, Alison Janet, da of Barclay Stewart Fraser, of Edinburgh; 2 da (Catriona b 1967, Susanna b 1969); *Career* entered Home Civil Serv; SO: asst princ Educn Dept 1962, princ 1966, treasy 1971, asst sec 1974, Home and Health Dept 1977, princ fin offr 1980, sec Educn Dept 1987 (under sec 1985), perm under sec of state 1988; *Recreations* making music; *Style—* Russell Hillhouse, Esq; c/o St Andrews House, Regent Rd, Edinburgh

HILLIARD, Spenser Rodney; s of Alfred Hilliard (d 1982), of 62 Water Lane, London, and Kathleen Claribelle Hilliard; *b* 14 March 1952; *Educ* City of London Sch, QMC, Univ of London (LLB); *Career* called to the Bar Middle Temple 1975, practising barr; memb Hon Soc of Middle Temple; non-exec dir N Middx Hosp 1990-; *Recreations* wine; *Clubs* Bar Yacht, Academy; *Style—* Spenser Hilliard, Esq; Lamb Building, Temple, London EC4Y 7AS (☎ 071 353 0774, fax 017 353 0535, telex 265871 MONREF G INK 3025)

HILLIER, Jack Ronald; s of Charles Edward (d 1938), of Fulham, London, and Minnie Mimosa, *née* Davies (d 1970); *b* 29 Aug 1912; *Educ* Fulham Central Sch; *m* 28 May 1938, Mary Louise, da of Henry James Palmer (d 1957); 1 s (Bevis b 1940), 1 da (Mary Alison b 1943); *Career* RAF 1940-45 (Middle East 1943-45); conslt on Oriental Art to Sotheby's London 1953-77; Uchiyama prize Japan 1982 and 1988; memb: Soc for Japanese Arts & Crafts Netherlands, Ukiyoe Soc of Japan Tokyo; *Books* Old Surrey Water Mills (1951), Hokusai, Paintings, Drawings and Woodcuts (1955), Japanese Drawings from 17th to end of 19th Century (1965), Catalogue of The Gale Collection of Japanese Paintings and Drawings (1970), The Uninhibited Brush: Japanese Art in the Shijo Style (1974), Japanese Prints and Drawings from the Vever Collection (1976), The Art of The Japanese Book (1987); *Recreations* wood engraving, water colour painting, classical music; *Style—* Jack Hillier, Esq; 30 Clarence Rd, Meadvale, Redhill, Surrey RH1 6NG (☎ 0737 241123)

HILLIER, Dr (Edward) Richard; s of Cdr Edward Alan Hillier (d 1980), of Teignmouth, Devon, and Muriel Stella, *née* Hudson (d 1987); *b* 11 March 1940; *Educ* Christ's Hosp Horsham Sussex, St Bartholomew's Hosp London (MB BS, MD); *m* 16 April 1966, Anne, da of John Curtis Houldershaw (d 1986); 5 s (Charles b 1967, Henry b 1970, George b 1973, Ben b 1978, William b 1986), 5 da (Margaret b 1969, Katie b 1972, Elizabeth b 1975, Helen b 1976, Mary b 1980); *Career* res fell MRC Laboraties Hampstead 1965-70, princ in gen practice Exeter and Portsmouth 1972-77, sr lectr in palliative med Southampton Univ Hosps 1981- (conslt physician and med dir 1977), base cdr and MO Br Antartic Survey Base 'H' Signy Islands Antarctic Peninsula 1986-88, former advsr Swedish Health Bd on palliative care servs Guernsey CI; pubns in jls and books on palliative med incl: pain, symptom control, psychological issues, operational res; convenor and first sec Assoc for Palliative Med, first pres Scientific Ctee and cox convenor Euro Assoc for Palliative Med; memb: BMA, Int Assoc for Study of Pain; past memb Cncl Nat Soc for Cancer Relief; MRCOG, MRCGP; *Recreations* the family, walking, debating; *Style—* Dr Richard Hillier; The Cams, 11 Grove Rd South, Southsea, Hants PO5 3QR (☎ 0705 817222); Countess Mountbatten House, Moorgreen Hospital, West End, Southampton, Hants SO3 3JB (☎ 0703 477414)

HILLIER, William Edward; s of William Edward Hillier (d 1976), and Ivy, *née* Elliott; *b* 11 April 1936; *Educ* Acton Co GS, Luton Tech Coll (HNC, DMS), Open Univ (BA); *m* 12 April 1958, Barbara Mary, da of William Victor Thorpe (d 1980); 1 s (William Edward b 1963), 1 da (Joy Marie b 1961); *Career* Nat Serv 1955-57; work with missile electronic systems De Havilland Propellors Ltd 1957, in semiconductor mfrg Texas Instruments Ltd 1960, dir Racal-Redac Ltd 1974 (involved with computer aided engrg systems 1970), in computer integrated mfrg Racal Group Services 1984, dir of Application of Computing to Manufacturing-Engineering Dept Science and Engineering Research Council 1989; IEE: hon ed Computer Aided Engineering Journal, memb Computing and Control Bd, memb Management and Pension Bd; CEng, FIEE, FBIM; *Recreations* railway preservation; *Style—* William Hillier, Esq; Science & Engineering Research Council, Polaris House, North Star Ave, Swindon SN2 1ET (☎ 0793 411474, fax 0793 411105)

HILLINGDON, Baroness; Phoebe Maxwell; da of late Capt Mervyn James Hamilton, of Cornacassa, Monaghan, by his w, Hildred (da of Hon Bernard Ward, CB, 4 s of 3 Viscount Bangor); *b* 25 June 1918; *m* 1, Lt-Cdr John Sholto Fitzpatrick Cooke, CBE, RNVR; m 2, John Cooper; m 3, as his 2 wife, 4 Baron Hillingdon (d 1978); *Style—* The Rt Hon the Lady Hillingdon; Shalom Hall, Layer Breton, Colchester, Essex

HILLMAN, David; s of Leslie Hillman (d 1969), and Margery Joan, *née* Nash (d 1988); *b* 12 Feb 1943; *Educ* Aristotle Central Sch, London Sch of Printing (Graphic Art NDD); *m* 1, 27 Oct 1963 (m dis 1983), Eileen Margaret, *née* Griffin; 1 s (Stephen b 1968), 1 da (Jane b 1965); m 2, 2 July 1983, Jennie Diana, da of Max David Keith Burns, of Bye Cottage, Shappen Bottom, Burley, Hants BH24 4AG; *Career* asst Sunday Times Magazine 1962-65; art ed: London Life 1965-66, Sunday Times 1966-68; ed Design for Living Section Sunday Times Magazine 1968-75, art dir and dep ed Nova Magazine 1968-75; Designers and Art Dirs Assoc: Gold Award for Design 1973, Silver Award 1972-73 1975, 1983, 1984 and 1989; freelance practice London 1975-76; art dir: Wolff Olins Ltd 1976-77, Le Matin De Paris 1977-78; ptnr Pentagram Design 1978; memb AGI, FCSD; *Books* Ideas on Design (co ed 1986), Puzzlegrams (1989), Pentagames (1990); *Style—* David Hillman, Esq; 19 Westbourne Park Rd, London W2 5PX (☎ 071 229 1887); Pentagram Design Ltd, 11 Needham Rd, London W11 2RP (☎ 071 229 3477, fax 071 727 9932)

HILLMAN, Ellis Simon; s of David Hillman (d 1974), of 91 Priory Rd, West Hampstead, London NW6, and Annie, *née* Roland (d 1967); *b* 17 Nov 1928; *Educ* York House Sch, Univ Coll Sch, Chelsea Coll of Science and Technol (BSc); *m* 10 Dec 1967, Louise, da of Jack Shalom (d 1971), of 9 Barlow Moor Court, Manchester; 1 s (Eli Yaakov b May 1974); *Career* ground wireless mechanic RAF 1947-49, instr Empire Radio Sch RAF Debden 1948-49; scientific tech offr: Soil Mechanics Ltd 1955,

NCB Field of Investigation Gp 1956-59; secondary sch teacher 1960-64, admin offr Architectural Assoc 1964-69, lectr Kilburn Poly 1969-70; NE London Poly: sr lectr 1970-73, princ lectr in environmental studies 1973-, (head of Int Off 1981-85); princ lectr Sch of Architecture Sch of Ind Studies 1985-; elected to: LCC Norwood 1958, GLC, ILEA Hackney 1964-81; chm: London Subterranean Survey Assoc 1968-, GLC Arts and Recreation Ctee 1977-81, Further and Higher Educn Ctee ILEA 1977-81; vice chm ILEA 1980-81, cncllr Colindale Barnet 1986-, govr Imperial Coll of Science and Technol 1969-90; memb: Lee Valley Regnl Park Authy 1973-81, Sports Cncl 1975-81, Water Space Amenity Cmmn 1977-80, Inland Waterways Amenity Advsy Cncl 1977-80; govr: Museum of London 1973-82, Archaeology Ctee Museum of London 1980-; pres Lewis Carroll Soc; FRSA; *Books* Essays in Local Government Enterprise (3 vols 1964-67), Towards a Wider Use (1976), London Under London (with John Murray, 1985); *Recreations* walking, classical music, reading, writing poetry; *Style—* Ellis S Hillman, Esq; Poly of East London (☎ 081 590 7722 ext 3239/ 3229)

HILLMAN, Prof John Richard; s of Robert Hillman, of 20 Beechwood Ave, Farnborough, Orpington, Kent, and Emily Irene Hillman; *b* 21 July 1944; *Educ* Chislehurst and Sidcup GS, Univ Coll of Wales (BSc, PhD); *m* 23 Sept 1967, Sandra Kathleen, da of George Palmer, of 16 Alton Rd, Luton, Beds; 2 s (Robert George b 1968, Edmund John b 1969); *Career* lectr in physiology and environmental studies Univ of Nottingham 1969-71 (asst lectr 1968-69); Univ of Glasgow: lectr in botany 1971-77, sr lectr 1977-80, reader 1982-86, prof 1982-86; visiting prof: Univ of Dundee 1986-, Univ of Strathclyde 1986-, Univ of Edinburgh 1988-; author of papers in scientific jls and books on plant physiology and plant biochemistry; dir Scottish Crop Res Inst 1986-; FIBiol, CBiol 1985, FLS 1982, FBIM 1987, FRSE 1985; *Books* ed: Isolation of Plant Growth Substances (1978), Biosynthesis and Metabolism of Plant Hormones (with A Crozier, 1984), Biochemistry of Plant Cell Walls (with C T Brett, 1985); *Recreations* landscaping, building, renovations, horology, reading; *Clubs* Farmers; *Style—* Prof John Hillman, FRSE; Scottish Crop Res Inst, Invergowrie, Dundee DD2 5DA (☎ 0382 562 731, fax 0382 562 426, telex 265871 MONREF G Quote Ref NQQOO3)

HILLS, Barrington William; s of William George (d 1967), of Upton on Severn Worcs, and Phyllis, *née* Biddle; *b* 2 April 1937; *Educ* Ribston Hall Gloucester, St Mary's Convent Newmarket, Mr Whittaker's Worcester; *m* 1, 21 Nov 1959 (m dis 1977), Maureen, da of late Patrick Newson; 3 s (John b 1960, Michael b 1963, Richard b 1963); m2, 1 Sept 1977, Penelope Elizabeth May, da of John Richard Woodhouse, of Roehoe Lodge, Widmerpool, Notts; 2 s (Charles b 1978, George b 1983); *Career* Nat Serv King's Troop RHA, racehorse trainer 1969-; won: Prix de L'Arc de Triomphe, Budweiser Irish Derby, 2000 Guineas Newmarket, 1000 Guineas Newmarket; second place Epsom Derby three times; held open day at Manton Stables for charity 1987; *Recreations* hunting, shooting, golf; *Clubs* Turf; *Style—* Barrington W Hills, Esq; Manton House, Marlborough, Wilts SN8 1PN (☎ 0672 54871); BW Hills Southbank Ltd, Manton House Estate, Marlborough, Wilts SN8 1PN (☎ 0672 54901, fax 0672 54907, car 0836 203 641, telex 44322)

HILLS, Hon Mrs (Brenda); *née* Stallard; da of Baron Stallard (Life Peer); *b* 1949; *m* 1972 (m dis 1987) Colin Hills, of Kentish Town, London; 2 da (Claire, Kerry); *Style—* The Hon Mrs Hills

HILLS, David Henry; s of Henry Stanford Hills (d 1945), and Marjorie Vera Lily, *née* Constable; *b* 9 July 1933; *Educ* Varndean Sch Brighton; Univ of Nottingham (BA); *m* 1957, Jean Helen, *née* Nichols; 1 s (Simon b 1962); 2 da (Susan b 1959, Jacqueline b 1960); *Career* MOD: 1956-67, dir of mktg Defence Sales Orgn 1979-82, dir econ and logistic intelligence 1982-88, dir gen of intelligence 1988-; NBPI 1967-70; Nat Indust Rels Ct 1971-73; *Recreations* gardening; *Clubs* Royal Cwlth Soc; *Style—* David Hills, Esq; Ministry of Defence, Main Building, Whitehall, Londn SW1A 2HB

HILLS, David William; s of Frank Woodhatch Hills (d 1960), and Hilda, *née* Jessop (d 1975); *b* 9 March 1925; *Educ* Ilford Co HS Essex, Brasenose Coll Oxford (MA); *m* 1 Jan 1948, Joan Mary (d 1971), da of Arthur Cruise (d 1969); 1 s (Timothy David b 11 March 1950), 1 da (Susan Mary b 28 Sept 1959); m 2, 6 Jan 1973, Phyllis; *Career* chm TBA Industl Prods Ltd 1968-75; dir: Turner & Newall plc 1976-87 (divnl chm 1969-87), Whitecroft plc 1985-87; chm Nimtech 1990-, dir Inward 1990-; memb Cotton and Allied Industs Trg Bd 1976-78, chm of cncl and pro-chllr Univ of Salford; Freeman: City of London, Worshipful Co of Horners 1978; Hon DSC Salford 1988; FBIM 1965; *Recreations* swimming, clock making; *Clubs* Lansdowne; *Style—* David Hills, Esq; 12 Oakley Park, Bolton BL1 5XL (☎ 0204 45063); Via Mucciana 10, 50026 San Casciano, Val di Pesa, Florence, Italy

HILLS, Prof Peter John; s of Maj Neville Morris Hills, TD, of Ashtead, Surrey, and Geraldine Yvonne, *née* Cazalet; *b* 17 Aug 1938; *Educ* Sutton Valence Sch Maidstone Kent, Imperial Coll London (BSc), Univ of Birmingham (MSc); *m* 26 July 1968, Lesley Edna, da of Albert Edward Slater (d 1957); 2 da (Karin Elizabeth b 1970, Fiona Suzanne b 1972); *Career* asst engr Miny of Transport 1962-63 (Buchanan Report working gp), lectr and conslt Imperial Coll London 1964-72, asst res dir Inst for Transport Studies Univ of Leeds 1972-77, prof of transport engrg Univ of Newcastle Upon Tyne 1977- (dir Transport Ops Res Group 1977-); vice pres Instn of Highways and Transportation 1989, memb Transportation Bd Instn of Civil Engrs 1989; ACGI 1961, CEng, MICE 1967, (MIHT 1963), FIHT 1976, MCIT 1971, FCIT 1978; *Books* Traffic In Towns (jtly, 1963), Motorways in London (jtly, 1969), Urban Transportation Planning Techniques (jtly, 1976), Roads and Traffic in Urban Areas (jtly, 1987); *Recreations* jazz, 20 Century History; *Clubs* National Liberal; *Style—* Prof Peter Hills; 5 Rectory Terrace, Gosforth, Newcastle Upon Tyne, Tyne and Wear NE3 1XY (☎ 091 285 5157); Division of Transport Engineering, The University, Claremont Tower, Newcastle Upon Tyne, Tyne and Wear NE1 7RU (☎ 091 222 6547, fax 091 222 8352)

HILLS, Richard James; s of Barrington Willian Hills, of Lambourn, and Maureen, *née* Newson; *b* 22 Jan 1963; *m* 16 Nov 1988, Jaci Mary Taylor; 1 s (Patrick James b 29 April 1989); *Career* flat race jockey; wins incl: Prince of Wales Stakes Ascot on Mtoto 1987, Norfolk Stakes Ascot (twice) on Sizzling Melody 1986 and Petillante 1989, Gold Cup Ascot on Ashal 1990, John Porter Stakes Newbury on Alwasmui 1989, Blue Ribband Stakes Epsom on Shuja 1988; *Recreations* golf, shooting, hunting and breeding ornamental water fowl; *Style—* Richard Hills, Esq; 12 The Green, Tuddenham, St Marys, Bury St Edmunds; The Gables, Bury Rd, Kentford, Suffolk (☎ 0638 750379/ 751421)

HILLS, Lady Rosemary Ethel; *née* Baring; da of 2 Earl of Cromer, GCB, GCIE, GCVO, PC (d 1953) and Lady Ruby Elliot, da of 4 Earl of Minto; *b* 1908; *m* 1932, Lt-Col John David Hills, MC (d 1976), former headmaster of Bradfield Coll; 1 s (John), 2 da (Jean, Margaret); *Career* FRGS; *Recreations* mountaineering; *Style—* The Lady Rosemary Hills; House by the Dyke, Chirk, Wrexham, Clwyd

HILLS, Timothy James; s of Brig James Hills, DSO (d 1982), of The Old Vicarage, Easton Royal, Pewsey, Wilts, and Erica Dorothea Mabel, *née* Jeudwine; *b* 18 Sept 1943; *Educ* Rugby; *m* 31 May 1980, Susannah, da of Brig Harry Hopkinson, MBE (d 1983), of Coopers, Woolstone, nr Uffington, Oxon; 2 s (James b 1982, Harry b 1986); *Career* called to the Bar Lincoln's Inn 1968, ad eundem Western Circuit 1969-; memb Family Law Bar, tstee of Redland Parish Church Tst; *Recreations* vintage motoring, painting, keep-fit, village cricket; *Clubs* HAC, VSCC, Thames Hare and hounds; *Style—* Timothy Hills, Esq; Albion Chambers South, Broad St, Bristol BS1 1DR (☎ 0272 272144)

HILLSBOROUGH, Earl of; Arthur Francis Nicholas Wills Hill; s and h of 8 Marquess of Downshire; *b* 4 Feb 1959; *m* 28 April 1990, Diana Jane (Janey), o da of Gerald Leeson Bunting, *qv*, of Otterington House, Northallerton, N Yorkshire; *Style—* Earl of Hillsborough

HILLYER, John Selby; OBE (1975); s of Stanley Gordon Hillyer, OBE (d 1965), and Margaret, *née* Selby (d 1990); *b* 14 Feb 1925; *Educ* Stowe, Trinity Coll Oxford (MA); *m* 2 June 1951, Elizabeth Ann, da of Sinclair Jeavons Thyne, CBE, of Tasmania; 1 s (James b 1952), 2 da (Sarah b 1955, Caroline b 1958); *Career* Lt Coldstream Gds; called to the Bar Inner Temple 1949; ptnr Hill Vellacott CA 1954-88, sr ptnr Chantrey Vellacott 1988-89; dir: T H White Ltd 1954-, Capel-Cure Myers Unit Trust Management Ltd; chm Cncl Barnardo's 1970 (memb 1962-); Master Worshipful Co of Fanmakers 1969; *Recreations* gardening, keeping ornamental ducks; *Clubs* Royal Automobile, City Livery; *Style—* John S Hillyer, Esq, OBE; Copden House, Biddenden, Kent

HILMI, Hon Mrs (Mary Trevor); *née* Bruce; yr da of Baron Bruce of Donington (Life Peer); *b* 1945; *m* 1968, Shuhada Hilmi; *Style—* The Hon Mrs Hilmi

HILSUM, Prof Cyril; CBE (1990); s of Benjamin Hilsum, and Ada Hilsum; *b* 17 May 1925; *Educ* Raines GS, UCL (BSc, PhD); *m* 16 Aug 1947, Betty (d 1987), da of Herbert Cooper; 2 da (Karen b 1954, Lindsey b 1958); *Career* Admty HQ 1945-47, Admty Res Laboratory 1947-50, Servs Electronics Res Laboratory 1950-64, RSRE 1964-83, dir of res GEC plc 1983-, visiting prof of physics UCL; foreign assoc US Nat Acad, FRS, FEng, FInstP, FIEE; *Books* Semiconducting III - V Compounds (1961), Handbook of Semiconductors (1984); *Recreations* tennis, chess; *Style—* Prof Cyril Hilsum, CBE; Hirst Research Centre, GEC, East Lane, Wembley, Middx HA9 7PP (☎ 081 908 9006)

HILTON, Anthony Victor; s of Maj Raymond W Hilton (d 1975), of Huntly, Aberdeenshire, and Miriam Eileen Norah, *née* Kydd; *b* 26 Aug 1946; *Educ* Woodhouse Grove Sch Bradford Yorks, Aberdeen Univ (MA); *m* 1, 30 March 1969 (m dis 1973); 1 s (Steven b 1970); m 2, Cyndy Miles; 2 s (Michael b 1985, Peter b 1987); *Career* city ed The Times 1982-83, md (Evening Standard 1989- (city ed 1984-89), dir Associated Newspapers plc 1989-; *Books* Employee Reports (1978), City within a State (1987); *Recreations* after dinner speaking; *Clubs* Lansdowne; *Style—* Anthony Hilton, Esq; Evening Standard, Northcliffe House, Derry St, London W8 (☎ 071 938 6000)

HILTON, Colin John; s of Herbert Jackson Mason Hilton, of Daggers Drawn, North End, Swineshead, Boston, Lincs, and Marjorie, *née* Wray (d 1975); *b* 17 Aug 1945; *Educ* Boston GS, Univ of Newcastle Med Sch (MB BS); *m* 15 Feb 1969, Helen, da of Flt Lt Joseph William Atkinson, DFC, of 11 Studley Villas, Forest Hall, Newcastle upon Tyne; 1 da (Nicola b 27 Sept 1972); *Career* locum registrar in thoracic and gen surgery Queen Elizabeth Hosp Birmingham and Wolverhampton Royal Infirmary 1973, locum sr registrar in cardiothoracic surgery Harefield Hosp 1975-76 (registrar 1973-75), registrar in cardiac surgery Nat Heart Hosp 1976, sr registrar in cardiothoracic surgery Papworth Hosp Cambridge 1976-77, res fell Brown Univ Providence Rhode Is 1978, sr registrar St Bartholomew's Hosp 1979, conslt cardiothoracic surgn Freeman Hosp Newcastle 1979-; postgrad dean Soc of Cardiothoracic Surgns 1991-; memb Ctee Soc of Cardiothoracic Surgns of GB and NI; FRCS 1973; *Recreations* golf, skiing; *Clubs* Northumberland Golf; *Style—* Colin Hilton, Esq; Rodborough, 8 Westfield Grove, Gosforth, Newcastle upon Tyne NE3 4YA (☎ 091 2847394); Regional Cardiothoracic Centre, Freeman Hospital, Freeman Rd, High Heaton, Newcastle upon Tyne NE7 7DN (☎ 091 2843111 ext 26587, fax 091 2131968)

HILTON, (Wilfrid) Graham; s of Harry Hilton, and Doris *née* Dawson; *b* 18 May 1937; *Educ* Manchester GS, St John's Coll Oxford (BA); *m* 17 Sept 1966, Hilary, da of Rev Charles Frederick Jones; 1 s (Jonathan b 1974), 1 da (Sunita Claire b 1971); *Career* slr and in private practice 1965-; dep coroner High Peak Dist 1979-, dir Sports and Leisure Foods Ltd 1974-; chm Stockport Harriers and AC 1984-; *Recreations* sport, athletics, marathon running, squash, bird watching; *Clubs* Stockport Harriers and AC, RSPB; *Style—* W G Hilton, Esq; Beacom Villa, Compstall, Stockport SK6 5JZ (☎ 061 427 2519); Pricketts Ingham Wainwright, 32 Union Rd, New Mills, Stockport SK12 3EU (☎ 0663 743367)

HILTON, Isabel N; da of Dr Raymond W Hilton (d 1975), and Miriam Evelyn, *née* Kydd; *b* 25 Nov 1947; *Educ* Bradford Girls GS, Walnut Hills HS Ohio USA, Univ of Edinburgh (MA), Peking Languages Inst Univ of Fudan Shanghai (scholar); *m* 1, 1970 (m dis 1975), John Armstrong Black; m 2, Charles Neal Ascherson; 1 s (Alexander Stephen Thomas b 5 March 1985), 1 da (Iona Susan b 23 May 1988); *Career* journalist; teaching asst Chinese Dept Univ of Edinburgh 1972-73, Scottish TV 1976-77, Sunday Times 1977-86 (special corr China, feature writer, news reporter, Latin America ed, asst foreign ed); The Independant: Latin America ed 1986, Euro Affrs ed 1989, chief feature writer 1991-; memb: Chatham House (RIIA) 1977, Br Assoc of China Studies 1978, IISS 1989; *Books* The Falklands War (jtly, 1982), The Fourth Reich (jtly, 1984), Betrayed (contrib, 1988), The General (1990); *Recreations* family, gardening; *Clubs* Groucho; *Style—* Ms Isabel Hilton; The Independant, 40 City Rd, London EC1Y 2DB (☎ 071 956 1504, fax 071 960 0017)

HILTON, (Alan) John Howard; QC (1990); s of Alan Howard Hilton, (d 1986), of Bowdon, and Barbara Mary Campbell, *née* Chambers, (d 1958); *b* 21 Aug 1942; *Educ* Haileybury, Univ of Manchester (LLB); *m* 21 Dec 1978, Nicola Mary, da of Percy Harold Bayley (d 1977), of Brighton; 1 s (Felix b 24 Dec 1983); *Career* called to the Bar 1964, in practice 1964-, recorder 1985; *Books* Fish Cookery (1981), Opera Today (1985); *Recreations* opera, conjuring, 19 century females in oils, cooking; *Style—* John Hilton, Esq, QC; Queen Elizabeth Building, Temple EC4 (☎ 071 583 5766)

HILTON, Prof Julian; s of R K Hilton; *b* 11 Sept 1952; *Educ* Canford, BNC Oxford, Univ of Grenoble, Munich and Salamanca (MA, D Phil); *m* 10 July 1976, Hanne, da of H J Boenisch; 1 da (Ruth b 18 Feb 1978); *Career* res fell Alexander van Humboldt Stiftung 1976, fell Stiftung Maximilianeum Munich 1977, prof of drama and communications UEA 1988- (lectr 1977, sr lectr 1987, dir audio-visual centre 1987-); fndr and ptnr Technol Arts Info 1985-, project mangr AIM prog EC 1989-91; bd memb Theatre Royal Norwich, vice chm Norfolk Arts Forum, chm Artificial Intelligence and Interactive Systems Gp; fell Swedish Center for Working Life, jt project mangr COMETT proj EC 1991-, visiting prof Tech Univ Vienna; *Books* Georg Buchner (1982), Performance (1987); Plays incl: The Enchanted Bird's Nest (1985), Broken Ground (1986), The Marriage of Panurge (1986), Courage (1989); *Recreations* opera, walking, shopping; *Style—* Prof Julian Hilton; Audio-Visual Centre, University of East Anglia, Norwich (☎ 0603 592833, fax 0603 507721)

HILTON, Prof Kenneth; s of Arthur William Hilton (d 1985), and Rosaline Maud, *née* King (d 1960); *b* 2 Sept 1937; *Educ* Liverpool Inst HS, Univ of Liverpool (BA), Univ of Manchester, Univ of Southampton (PhD); *m* 20 July 1963, Dorothy, da of Alfred Mercer, of Sheffield; 1 s (Timothy b and d 1967), 3 da (Fiona Jane b 1965, Penelope Anne b 1968, Sally Victoria b 1971); *Career* asst lectr Univ of Reading 1961-62, dep vice chllr Univ of Southampton 1984-86 (lectr and sr res fell 1962-70, prof of fin control 1970-, dean of social scis 1975-78); hon fell Portsmouth Poly; FCIS; *Books* The

Economic Study of the United Kingdom (jt ed 1970), Control Systems for Social and Economic Management (1974); *Recreations* wine, bridge, sailboarding, swimming; *Style—* Prof Kenneth Hilton; Univ of Southampton, Dept of Accounting and Management Science, Southampton SO9 5NH (☎ 0703 592563)

HILTON, Mark William; s of Peter Entwistle Hilton, of Ripley, N Yorks, and Monica, *née* Smith; *b* 15 July 1958; *Educ* Wrekin Coll Wellington Shropshire, Univ of Leeds (LLB); *m* 25 April 1987, Catharine, da of George Canavan, of Ripon; *Career* slr; articled clerk Last Suddards Bradford 1980-82, Barlow Lyde & Gilbert London 1982-85, ptnr Last Suddards Leeds 1986-88 (joined 1982), ptnr Hammond Suddards Leeds 1988-; memb Law Soc 1980-, ACIArb; *Recreations* skiing, scuba diving, tennis; *Clubs* RAC, Pall Mal; *Style—* Mark Hilton, Esq; Hammond Suddards, Britannia Chambers, 4/5 Oxford Place, Leeds LS1 3AX (☎ 0532 444921, telex 557 202, fax 0532 44794, car 0836 735407) 0836 735407)

HILTON, Nicholas David; s of John David Hilton, of Wyndsway, Woodside Hill, Chalfont Heights, Gerrards Cross, Bucks, and Dorothy Gwendoline, *née* Eastham; *b* 27 June 1952; *Educ* Marlborough; *m* 14 July 1984, Vanessa Jane, da of Brig W John Reed of Frensham, Surrey; 1 da (Lucy Vanessa b 1989); *Career* CA 1974; ptnr Moore Stephens 1979-90, nat exec ptnr Moore Stephens (UK) 1990-; memb ICAEW, FCA 1979; *Recreations* golf, skiing, mah-jong, entertaining; *Clubs* Richmond Golf, Cygnets Hockey; *Style—* Nicholas Hilton, Esq; St Paul's House, Warwick Lane, London EC4P 4BN (☎ 071 248 4499, fax 071 248 3408, telex 884610)

HILTON, Prof Rodney Howard; *b* 17 Nov 1916; *Educ* Manchester GS, Balliol Coll Oxford, Merton Coll Oxford (BA, DPhil); *Career* served WWII 46 Bn RTR 1940-45 (served Middle East and Italy), served Indian Army 1945-46; lectr, reader and prof of medieval social history Sch of History Univ of Birmingham 1946-84, dir Inst for Advanced Res in the Humanities Univ of Birmingham 1984-87; memb Editorial Bd jl Past and Present 1952-87; memb Past and Present Soc 1952-; FBA 1977, fell Inst for Advanced Res in the Humanities 1987; *Books* The Economic Development of Some Leicestershire Estates in the 14th and 15th Centuries (1947), The English Rising of 1381 (with H Fagan, 1950), A Medieval Society: the West Midlands at the End of the 13th Century (1966), Bond Men Made Free: Medieval Peasant Movements and the English Rising of 1381 (1973), The English Peasantry in the Later Middle Ages (Ford lectures, 1975), Class Conflict and the Crisis of Feudalism: Essays in Medieval Social History (1985); *Style—* Prof Rodney Hilton

HIME, Martin; CBE (1987); s of Percy Joseph Hime (d 1966), and Esther Greta, *née* Howe (d 1974); *b* 18 Feb 1928; *Educ* King's Coll Sch Wimbledon, Trinity Hall Cambridge (MA, lawn tennis blue); *m* 1, 1960 (m dis 1971), Henrietta Mary Elisabeth, *née* Fehling; 1 s (Martin b 1962), 3 da (Marigold b 1964, Juliet b 1966, Jessica b 1967); m 2, 1971, Janina Christine, *née* 1 da (Cordelia b 1973); *Career* RA 1946-48; called to the Bar Inner Temple 1951; Marks & Spencer 1952-58; Dip Serv 1960-, HM consul gen Houston Texas 1985-88, assessor Foreign and Cwlth Office 1988-; Freeman: Louisville Kentucky 1982, State of Texas 1985; *Recreations* golf, lawn tennis, table games, reading; *Clubs* All England Lawn Tennis, Royal Wimbledon Golf, Hawke's, Cambridge; *Style—* Martin Hime, Esq, CBE; Foreign and Commonwealth Office, Whitehall, London SW1

HIMSWORTH, Sir Harold Percival; KCB (1952); s of Arnold Himsworth (d 1960); *b* 19 May 1905; *Educ* Almondbury GS, UCL, Univ Coll Hosp London (MD); *m* 1932, Charlotte Gray; 2 s; *Career* prof of med Univ of London 1939-49; dep chm MRC 1967-68 (memb 1948-49, sec 1949-68); *Clubs* Athenaeum; *Style—* Sir Harold Himsworth, KCB; 13 Hamilton Terrace, London NW8 (☎ 071 286 6996)

HINCHCLIFFE, Peter Robert Mossom; CMG (1987), CVO (1979); s of Herbert Peter Hinchliffe (d 1978), and Jeannie, *née* Wilson (d 1973); *b* 9 April 1937; *Educ* Radley, Trinity Coll Dublin (MA); *m* 1965, Archbold Harriet Hinchcliffe, MBE, da of Hugh Edward Siddall, of Dublin; 3 da (Fiona b 1967, Sally b 1969, Clare b 1972); *Career* Military Serv W Yorks Regt 1955-57, 2 Lt (Suez Campaign 1956), HMOCS Aden, political offr 1961-67, acting dep high cmmr 1967; joined FCO 1969, first sec UK mission to UN 1971-74, first sec and head of chancery Kuwait 1974-76, asst head of Sci and Tech Dept and Central and Southern African Dept 1976-78, counsellor and dep high cmmr Dar es Salaam 1978-81, consul gen Dubai, UAE 1981-85, head Info Dept FCO 1985-87, HM ambass Kuwait 1987 Br high cmmr Lusaka 1990; *Recreations* golf, tennis; *Clubs* East India, Royal Co Down Golf; *Style—* Peter Hinchcliffe, Esq, CMG, CVO; c/o Foreign and Commonwealth Office, King Charles St, London SW1A 2AH; British High Commission, PO Box 50050, Lusaka, Zambia

HINCHCLIFFE, Prof Ronald; s of Charles Hinchcliffe, and Fenella, *née* Pearce; *b* 20 Feb 1926; *Educ* Bolton Sch, Univ of Manchester, Harvard, Univ of London; *m* 4 July 1953 (m dis 1980), Doreen, *née* Lord; *Career* Sqdn Ldr and RAF med servs offr i/c RAF Acoustics Laboratory 1951-55; hon conslt neuro-otologist Royal Nat ENT Hosp London 1967-, prof of audiological med Univ of London 1977-; vice pres Int Soc of Audiology; memb Collegium Otorhinolaryngologicum Amicitiae Sacrum 1969; *Books* Scientific Foundations of Otolaryngology (jt ed, 1976), Hearing and Balance in the Elderly (ed, 1983); *Recreations* skiing, sailing; *Clubs* Athenaeum; *Style—* Prof Ronald Hinchcliffe; Institute of Laryngology and Otology, 330 Gray's Inn Rd, London WC1X 8EE (☎ 071 837 8855, fax 071 278 8643)

HINCHLIFF, Rev Canon Peter Bingham; s of Rev Samuel Hinchliff (d 1975), of Cape Town, SA, and Brenda, *née* Bagshaw; *b* 25 Feb 1929; *Educ* St Andrew's Coll Grahamstown SA, Rhodes Univ SA (BA, PhD), Univ of Oxford (MA, DD); *m* 16 April 1955, Constance Penford (Bunty), da of Edwin Lisle Whitehead (d 1980), of Uitenhage, SA; 3 s (Nicholas b 1956, Richard b 1959, Jeremy b 1963), 1 da (Susan b 1957); *Career* ordained: deacon 1952, priest 1953; prof of ecclesiastical hist Rhodes Univ Grahamstown SA 1960-69, canon Grahamstown 1964-69, sec Bd of Mission and Unity of the Gen Synod of C of E 1969-72, chaplain and fell Balliol Coll Oxford 1972-, canon theologian Coventry Cathedral 1972-; *Books* The South African Liturgy (1959), The Anglican Church in South Africa (1963), John William Colenso, Bishop of Natal (1964), The One-Sided Reciprocity: A Study of the Modification of the Establishment in England (1966), Calendar of Cape Missionary Correspondence (1967), The Church in South Africa (1968), The Journal of John Ayliff (1971), Cyprian of Carthage and the Unity of the Christian Church (1974), The Human Potential (with David Young, 1981), Holiness and Politics (The Bampton Lectures for 1982), Benjamin Jowett and the Christian Religion (1987); *Clubs* Oxford and Cambridge United Univs; *Style—* The Rev Canon Peter Hinchliff; Balliol College, Oxford OX1 3BJ (☎ 0865 277731)

HINCHLIFF, Stephen; CBE (1976); s of Gordon Henry Hinchliff (d 1976), and Winifred, *née* Ellis (d 1955); *b* 11 July 1926; *Educ* Almondbury GS Huddersfield, Boulevard Nautical Coll Hull, Huddersfield Coll of Tech (Dip Mech Engrg), Cranfield Inst of Tech (MSc); *m* 1, 1951 (m dis 1987), Margaret Arrundale Crossland; 1 s, 1 da; m 2, 1987, Ann Fiona Maudsley; 1 da; *Career* cadet and deck offr MN 1943-48; prodn engr Dowty Auto Units Ltd Cheltenham 1953; Dowty Seals Ltd: chief prodn engr 1953, works mangr 1954, prodn mangr 1956, dir 1958, dep md 1967; dep chm Dowty Group Ltd 1972 (dir 1968), md Dowty Group Industl Div 1973-76, chm and md Dexion Group 1976-; dir: Dacorum Enterprise Agency, Business in the Community; memb Ct Cranfield Inst of Technology; CEng, FIMechE, FIProdE, CBIM, FRSA; *Recreations* squash, badminton, tennis, fishing; *Style—* Stephen Hinchliff, Esq, CBE; Bowmore Farm, Hawridge Common, nr Chesham, Bucks HP5 2UH (☎ 024029 237)

HINCHLIFFE, David Martin; MP (Lab) Wakefield 1987-; s of Robert Victor Hinchliffe (d 1982), of Wakefield, and Muriel, *née* Preston (d 1987); *b* 14 Oct 1948; *Educ* Cathedral Secdy Mod Sch Wakefield, Wakefield Tech and Art Coll, Leeds Poly, Univ of Banford (MA), Hudderfield Poly (CertEd); *m* 17 July 1982, Julia, da of Harry North, of Mold, Clwyd; 1 s (Robert b 10 Oct 1985), 1 da (Rebecca b 24 May 1988); *Career* princ social worker Leeds Social Servs Dept 1974-79, social work tutor Kirklees Cncl 1980-87; cncllr: Wakefield City Cncl 1971-74, Wakefield DC 1978-88; former vice pres: Wakefield and Dist Trades Cncl, Wakefield Constituency Lab Pty; vice pres Wakefield Trinity RLFC; *Recreations* rugby league, Wakefield Trinity RLFC; *Style—* David Hinchliffe, Esq, MP; 21 King Street, Wakefield, W Yorks (☎ 0924 290134)

HINCHLIFFE, Ralph Eric; s of Lawrence Hinchliffe (d 1974); *b* 30 Jan 1931; *Educ* Royds Hall Grammar; *m* 1957, Jean Lesley, da of Vernon Rawlings (d 1978), of Huddersfield; 3 c; *Career* Nat Serv Corpl Royal Pay Corps; ptnr Smith and Garton CAS Huddersfield 1957-69; chm Heywood William Gp plc 1981-(joined 1969); FCA, FCMA; *Recreations* all sports; *Clubs* Woodsome Hall Golf, Yorkshire CCC, Liverpool FC; *Style—* Ralph Hinchliffe Esq; Bank House, New Mill, Huddersfield, W Yorks HD7 7HU (☎ 0484 682104); Heywood Williams Group plc, Waverley, Edgerton Rd, Huddersfield, W Yorks HD3 3AR (☎ 0484 435477)

HINCHLIFFE, Stephen Leonard; s of William Leonard (d 1974), and Ilse, *née* Sparer; *b* 2 Jan 1950; *m* 14 July 1973, Marjorie, da of Eric Wood (d 1971); 1 s (James b 1975), 1 da (Julia b 1978); *Career* accountant Sheffield Twist Drill, Trent Regnl Hosp Bd; chm and chief exec: Wade Group of Co's Ltd, James Wilkes plc, Lynx Holdings plc; FBIM, FSMM; *Recreations* helicopter flying, golf, motoring, shooting; *Clubs* Dore and Totley Golf; *Style—* Stephen L Hinchliffe, Esq; Beauchief Hall, Beauchief, Sheffield (☎ 0742 670076/620062, fax 0742 352144, car 0836 521521)

HINCKLEY, Gilbert Clive; OBE (1988); s of Capt Gilbert Percy (d 1972), of Hinckley, and Dorothy Kate, *née* Bown; *b* 6 July 1937; *Educ* The Leys Sch, Clare Coll Cambridge (MA); *m* 1 (m dis 1977), Jane Susan, *née* Bourne; 1 da (Hannah Jane b 1979); m 2, 21 Aug 1981, Karen Ann, da of Gerald Wilson; *Career* 2 Lt pack tport RASC 1957-58, TA 1959-64 Lt Queens Own Yorks Yeo; Hinckley Gp of Assoc Cos: gp dir 1962-, jt chief exec 1976-82, chm Flogates Div, dep chm KSR Int Div, gp md 1982-; chm of Derbyshire Cncl Order of St John, memb of Ct Cutlers Co Hallamshire; FIOD, Fell Inst Br Foundrymen, memb Inst of Metals; *Recreations* game shooting, fishing, riding; *Clubs* Cavalry & Guards; *Style—* Gilbert Hinckley, Esq, OBE; Amber House, Kelstedge, Amber Valley, Derbyshire S45 0EA; The Hinckley Group of Assoc Companies, Abbey Lane Beauchief, Sheffield S72 2RA (☎ 0742 369 011, fax 0742 364 775, telex 54496)

HIND, Andrew Charles; s of John William Hind (d 1986), of Grayshott, and Evelyn May, *née* Sidford (d 1986); *b* 10 July 1943; *Educ* Sutton County GS; *m* 27 Dec 1969, Janet Margaret, da of Norman William George Scullard (d 1983), of Hove; 1 s (Duncan William b 1976), 3 da (Joanna Scullard b 1973, Annalee Scullard b 1975, Suzanne Catherine b 1985); *Career* Lovell and Rupert Curtis Ltd (advertising): joined 1966, dir 1974, md 1984, chm and md 1987; chm The Garrick Gp 1988, dir Butler Borg Miller & Fraser LRC Ltd 1990; MIPA, FInstD; *Clubs* Naval and Military; *Style—* Andrew Hind, Esq; Cranley Cottage, Guildford, Surrey (☎ 0483 32120); 4 Gees Court, Oxford St, London W1M 5HQ (☎ 071 408 2301, fax 071 408 0382)

HIND, Dr Charles Robert Keith; s of Col (Robert) Keith Hind, of Kegworth House, Derby, and Dorothy, *née* Kinsey; *b* 7 June 1953; *Educ* Kings Coll Taunton, Univ of London Med Sch (BSc, MB, BS, MD, MRCP); *m* 21 July 1985, Fiona, da of Maj Alexander Hugh Fraser, of Calduthel, Cradley, Worcs; 1 s (James b 1986), 1 da (Eleanor b 1989); *Career* conslt physician gen and respiratory med Royal Liverpool Hosp and The Cardiothoracic Centre Liverpool 1987; *Books* X-Ray Interpretation for the MRCP (1983), Short Cases for the MRCP (1984), Amyloidosis and Amyloid P Component (1986); *Style—* Dr Charles Hind; 45 Rodney St, Liverpool L1 9EW (☎ 051 708 0842, fax 051 709 5679); Royal Liverpool Hospital, University of Liverpool, Liverpool L7 8XP (☎ 051 706 3571, fax 051 709 5806); The Cardiothoracic Centre, Liverpool L14 3LB (☎ 051 228 4878 ext 3553, fax 051 220 8573)

HIND, John; s of Warrant Offr George Hind, of 2 Woodlands Ave, Wheatley Hill, Co Durham, and Marjorie, *née* Terry; *b* 6 Aug 1954; *Educ* AJ Dawson GS, Newcastle upon Tyne Poly (BA), RCA (MA); *Career* Vogue Magazine: art ed 1980-85, art dir 1985-89, creative dir 1990-; memb D & ADA 1982-; *Style—* John Hind, Esq; 28 Park Rd, Chiswick, London W4 3HN (☎ 071 994 2583); Condenast Publications, 1 Hanover Sq, London W1 (☎ 071 499 9080)

HIND, Rt Rev John William; *see*: Horsham, Bishop of

HIND, Kenneth Harvard; MP (C) West Lancashire 1983-; *b* 15 Sept 1949; *Educ* Woodhouse Grove Sch, Bradford Yorks, Univ of Leeds; *m* Patricia Anne *née* Millar; 1 s, 1 da; *Career* called to the Bar Gray's Inn 1973, practising barr Leeds until 1983; PPS: Lord Trefgarne MOD 1986-87, John Cope Min DOE 1987-90, Rt Hon Peter Brooke Sec of State for NI 1990-; chm De Keyser Europe Ltd, dir Doctus PLC; vice pres: Central & W Lancs C of C, Merseyside C of C; chm W Lancs Employers Assoc; MInstD; *Recreations* sailing, skiing; *Clubs* Headingley Rugby Union Football (vice pres); *Style—* Kenneth Hind, Esq, MP; House of Commons, London SW1

HINDE, David Richard; s of Walter Stanley Hinde (d 1952), and Marjorie Jewell Grieg, *née* Butcher (d 1970); *b* 16 Aug 1938; *Educ* Marlborough, Univ of Cambridge (LLB); *m* 1963, Rosemary Jill, da of Malcolm Hartree Young (d 1965); 3 da (Sasha Karen b 1966, Rachel Olivia b 1968, Anna-Louise b 1972); *Career* asst slr Slaughter and May 1961-69; exec dir: Wallace Bros Gp 1969-77, Wardley Ltd 1977-81, Samuel Montagu and Co Ltd 1981-; *Recreations* skiing, gardening, travel; *Clubs* MCC, City of London; *Style—* David Hinde, Esq; Flat 2, 17 Clarendon Rd, London W11; The Glebe House, Great Gaddesden, Hemel Hempstead, Hertfordshire HP1 3BY; Samuel Montagu and Co Ltd, 10 Lower Thames Street, London EC3R 4AE (☎ 071 260 9699, fax 071 623 5512, telex 887213)

HINDE, Keith Stevens Gleave; TD (1969); s of Wing Cdr Sydney Arthur Hinde, OBE, DL (d 1977), of W Mersea, Essex, and Guinevere Waneeta Ashore, *née* Gleave (d 1974); *b* 4 Oct 1934; *Educ* Colchester Royal GS, CCC Cambridge (MA); *m* 8 May 1965, Gillian Myfanwy, da of William Godfrey Morgan (d 1955), of Coventry; 1 s (Edward Morgan Stevens b 1976); *Career* 2 Lt RA 1953-55, Battery Capt Suffolk & Norfolk Yeo 1955-67, Maj Suffolk/Cambs Regt (S and NY) 1967-69; admitted slr 1961; ptnr Pothecary & Barratt; tstee: Stretham Engine Tst, Suffolk & Norfolk Yeo Tst; cncl memb and hon slr King George's Fund for Sailors; Master Worshipful Co of Slrs 1988-89 (Liveryman 1966, Clerk 1969-76), Clerk Worshipful Co Cutlers 1975-; *Books* Steam in the Fens (1974); *Recreations* history (local and general), country pursuits; *Clubs* Utd Oxford & Cambridge; *Style—* Keith Hinde, Esq; Denny House, Waterbeach, Cambs (☎ 0223 860895); Pothecary & Barratt, Talbot House, Talbot Court, Gracechurch St, London EC3 (☎ 071 623 7520)

HINDE, Prof Robert Aubrey; CBE (1988); *b* 26 Oct 1923; *Educ* Oundle, St John's Coll Cambridge (BA), Univ of London (BSc), Univ of Oxford (DPhil), Univ of Cambridge (ScD); *Career* res asst Edward Grey Inst Dept of Zoology Univ of Oxford 1948-50, curator Ornithological Field Station Dept of Zoology Univ of Cambridge 1950-63; St John's Coll Cambridge: res fell 1951-54, steward 1956-58, tutor 1958-63, fell 1958-, master 1989-; res prof Royal Soc 1963-89, Hitchcock prof Univ of Calif 1979, Green visiting scholar Univ of Texas 1983, Croonian lectr Royal Soc 1990; vice pres Ex-Servicemen's Campaign for Nuclear Disarmament; FRS 1974 (memb Cncl 1985-87); hon fell: American Ornithologists Union 1976, British Psychological Soc 1981, Balliol Coll Oxford 1986, Royal Coll of Psychiatry 1988, Trinity Coll Dublin 1990; hon dir Medical Res Cncl Unit on the Devpt and Integration of Behaviour 1970-89; Docteur honoris causa: dans la faculte des Sciènces Pychologiques et Pedagogiques Université Libre Bruxelles 1974, Universite de Paris Nantere 1978, foreign hon memb American Acad of Arts and Scis 1974; hon memb: Assoc for Study of Animal Behaviour 1987, Deutsche Ornithologische Gesellschaft 1988; memb Academia Europaee 1990; Zoological Soc's Scientific medal 1961, Osman Hill medal Primate Soc of GB 1980, Leonard Cammer award NY Psychiatric Inst Columbia Univ 1980, Albert Einstein Award for Psychiatry Albert Einstein Coll of Medicine NY 1987, Huxley medal Royal Anthropological Inst 1990; *Books* Animal Behaviour: A Synthesis of Ethology and Comparative Psychology (1966, 2 edn 1970), Biological Bases of Human Social Behaviour (1974), Towards Understanding Relationships (1979), Ethology: Its Nature and Relations with Other Sciences (1982), Individuals, Relationships and Culture: Links between Ethology and the Social Sciences (1987); *Style*— Prof Robert Hinde, CBE, FRS; The Master's Lodge, St John's College, Cambridge (☎ 0223 338635)

HINDLE, Timothy Simon; s of Edwin Frederick Branwell Hindle (d 1969), and Joan Marjorie, *née* Pearson; *b* 7 June 1946; *Educ* Shrewsbury, Worcester Coll Oxford (MA), Heriot Watt Univ Edinburgh (Postgrad Dip Fin Studies); *m* 11 June 1975, Ellian Lea, da of Eli Aciman, of Istanbul; 1 s (Alexis b 1982), 1 da (Alara b 1979); *Career* dep ed The Banker 1978; The Economist: banking corr 1980, fin ed 1983, world business ed 1985; ed EuroBusiness 1988; VSO Dacca Bangladesh 1968-69; *Books* Pocket Banker (1984); *Recreations* reading novels, cinema, water skiing; *Style*— Timothy Hindle, Esq; 22 Royal Crescent, Holland Park, London W11 (☎ 071 602 2601); EuroBusiness, 28 Great Queen St, London WC2 (☎ 071 430 1240, fax: 071 430 0020)

HINDLIP, 5 Baron (UK 1886); Sir Henry Richard Allsopp; 5 Bt (UK 1880), JP (Wilts 1957), DL (1956); s of 3 Baron Hindlip, OBE, JP, DL, by his w Agatha (herself da of John Thynne, who was in his turn 6 s of Rev Lord John Thynne, 3 s of 2 Marquess of Bath); suc er bro (4 Baron) 1966; *b* 1 July 1912; *Educ* Eton, Sandhurst; *m* 1939, Cecily, da of Lt-Col Malcolm Borwick, DSO, JP, DL, (nephew of 1 Baron Borwick); 2 s, 1 da; *Heir* s, Hon Charles Allsopp; *Career* 2 Lt Coldstream Gds 1932, Maj 1941, ret 1948, served WWII NW Europe; *Clubs* White's, Pratt's, Turf; *Style*— The Rt Hon the Lord Hindlip, JP, DL; Tytherton House, East Tytherton, Chippenham, Wilts

HINDMARSH, Irene; JP (Birkenhead 1966, Durham 1974); da of Albert Hindmarsh, and Elizabeth, *née* White; *b* 22 Oct 1923; *Educ* Heaton HS, Lady Margaret Hall Oxford (MA), Univ of Durham (PGCE); *Career* teacher: St Paul's Girls' Sch London 1947-49, Rutherford HS Newcastle-upon-Tyne 1949-59 (interchange teacher Lycée de Jeunes Filles Dax Landes France 1954-55), headmistress Birkenhead HS GPDST 1964-70, second pro vice-chllr Univ of Durham 1982-85 (lectr in educn and french King's Coll 1959-64, princ St Aidan's Coll 1970-88); visiting prof 1962: NY State Univ, Syracuse, Cornell, Harvard; del Int Fedn of Univ Women UNO NY to Cmmns on Human Rights and Status of Women 1962, del and translator int conf FIPESO 1963-70; visiting prof: Fu-Dan Univ Shanghai 1979 (1980 and 1986), SW China Teachers' Univ Beibei Sichuan 1986; chm: int ctee Headmistresses' Assoc 1966-70, Int Panel of Jt Four 1967-70; Fell Royal Soc For The Encouragement Of Arts Manufactures and Commerce; *Books* History of Durham from the Air (contrib, St Aidan's Coll), numerous articles and seminar papers; *Recreations* travel, music, fine art, architecture, theatre and films; *Style*— Miss Irene Hindmarsh, JP; 8 Dickens Wynd, Merryoaks, Elvet Moor, Durham DH1 3QR (☎ 091 386 1881)

HINDMARSH, John Reed; s of Maj Frederick Denis Hindmarsh, TD, (d 1984), of Newcastle on Tyne, and Frances Myrtle Reed; *b* 28 Aug 1944; *Educ* Sedbergh Sch, Univ of Newcastle (MB BS, MD); *m* 29 June 1974, Katharine Rosemary, da of Maj Charles Henry Anthony Howe (d 1978), of Saltburn on Sea, North Yorks; 1 s (Richard b 1978), 1 da (Rachel b 1977); *Career* clinical tutor Univ of Edinburgh 1978-81, sr lectr Univ of London 1981-84; conslt urologist: St Peters Hosp London 1981-84, South Tees Health Authy 1984-; FRCS, FRCSEd 1975, memb Br Assoc of Urological Surgns 1977; *Recreations* fishing, shooting, music, wine, philately; *Clubs* RSM; *Style*— John Hindmarsh, Esq; Croft House, Hurworth Place, Croft on Tees, Nr Darlington (☎ 0325 720684)

HINDS, Joan Patricia Dobson; da of Ernest Ivor Dobson, and Muriel Augusta, *née* Rees; *b* 4 March 1950; *Educ* Bible Coll of Wales, Girls GS Neath, Univ of London (BA), Univ of Wales, London Business Sch (Sloan Fell); *m* 28 Sept 1974, Dr Charles Johnston, s of Dr Sydney Johnston Hinds; *Career* dep hosp sec The London Hosp 1975-76, dep house govr Moorfields Eye Hosp 1976-81, sec NHS National Staff Ctee, Admin and Clerical Staff (DHSS princ) 1981-84; mgmnt conslt Hay MSL 1985-86, fundraiser Advance in Medicine 1987-; *Recreations* opera, ballet, theatre, skiing, gardening, husband-minding; *Clubs* Network, The Blizard; *Style*— Mrs Joan Hinds; 38 Langton Way, Blackheath, London SE3 (☎ 081 853 0955); The Royal London Hospital Medical Coll, Turner St, London E1 2AD (☎ 071 377 7471, telex 893750, fax 071 377 7677)

HINDS, Ralph William Gore; s of Lt-Col Walter Augustus Gore Hinds, MC (d 1975), of Bournemouth, and Honoria Mary, *née* Quinn (d 1965); *b* 27 April 1925; *Educ* Cheltenham, Sandhurst; *m* 1, 23 Feb 1952, Barbara Diana, da of late John Sidey, of Bournemouth; 1 s (Nigel b 1955), 1 da (Hilary b 1958); *m* 2, 29 April 1982, Judith Margaret, da of William Henry Williams (d 1962), of Devon; *Career* served WWII 1943-46, Lt 1 Royal Dragoons; admitted slr 1950; in practice until 1990; *Recreations* jazz music, philately; *Style*— Ralph W G Hinds, Esq; 5 Cliff Lodge, 5 Boscombe Overcliff Drive, Bournemouth BH5 1JB (☎ 0202 303397)

HINDS, William James; MBE (1969), JP; s of Ben Hinds; *b* 9 Sept 1910; *Educ* Queen Elizabeth's GS Carmarthen, Pibwrlwyd Farm Inst, UCW; *m* 1938, Gwendolen, da of Thomas Harries; *Career* farmer; memb: (S Wales) Milk Marketing Bd 1952-1962 and 1965-83, Cncl Royal Welsh Agric Soc 1983-91 (pres 1987), Ct of Govrs UCW Aberystwyth; former memb S W Wales River Authy, hon life memb Camarthanshire NFU 1984; High Sheriff Dyfed 1981-82; FRAGS 1988; *Recreations* fishing, rugby; *Style*— William Hinds Esq, MBE, JP; Danyrallt, Abergorlech Rd, Carmarthen, Dyfed SA32 7AY (☎ 0267 290233)

HINDSON, William Stanley; CMG (1962); s of William Abner Lucas Hindson, of Darlington, Co Durham, and Mary Jane, *née* Richmond; *b* 11 Jan 1920; *Educ* Darlington GS, Coatham Sch Redcar, Constantine Tech Coll Middlesbrough, London Univ (BSc); *m* 1, 1944 Mary Sturdy (d 1961); 1 s (William Richard Forster b 1948), 1 da (Rosemary Ann Allen b 1946); m 2, 11 Jan 1965, Catherine Berthe Leikine of Paris, France; 1 s (William Alexander Joseph b 1966); *Career* devpt engr Dorman Long (Steel) Ltd 1946 (steel plant mangr 1945-46); chief engr and md: Metallurgical Equipment Export Co Ltd 1956-57, Indian Steelworkers Construction Co Ltd 1962-69; dir: Anglo German Bosphorus Bridge Consortium, British Bridge Builders Consortium 1969-71; md Humphreys & Glasgow Ltd 1972-74 (dir of engrg 1971-72), engrg and metallurgical conslt 1975-88; FIMechE, MIM; *Recreations* chess, philately, history; *Style*— William Hindson, Esq, CMG; 36 Eresby House, 19 Rutland Gate, London SW7 1BG (☎ 071 589 3194)

HINE, Andrew Charles; s of John Stanley Hine, and Gillian Mary Hine; *b* 30 Sept 1964; *Educ* Stowe, Univ of Reading (BSc); *Career* gold and silver trader bullion dept N M Rothschilds & Sons 1986-88, prof polo player 1988-; highlights of career incl: winner Br Open Cowdray Park Gold Cup 1983, Best Young Players 1983 and 89, Player of the Year Guards Polo Club 1989, winner Queens Cup, winner Coronation Cup Eng v Aust Cartier Day 1989; *Recreations* skiing, hunting; *Clubs* Annabels; *Style*— Andrew Hine, Esq; 51a St Georges Sq, Pimlico, London SW1 (☎ 071 821 9834)

HINE, Air Chief Marshal Sir Patrick Bardon (Paddy); GCB (1989, KCB 1983); s of Eric Graham Hine (d 1971) and Cecile Grace, *née* Philippe (d 1971); *b* 14 July 1932; *Educ* Peter Symonds Sch Winchester; *m* 1956, Jill Adèle, da of James Charles Gardner (d 1984); 3 s (Nicholas b 1962, Andrew b 1966, Jeremy b 1969); *Career* joined RAF 1950, memb Black Arrows aerobatic team 1957-59, cmd RAF Wildenrath 1974-75, dir P/R RAF 1975-77, SASO HQ RAF Germany 1979, ACAS rank of Air vice Marshal (Policy) MOD 1979-83, Air Marshal 1983, C-in-C RAF Germany and Cdr Second Allied Tactical Air Force 1983-85, Vice CDS 1985-87, Air Memb for Supply and Organisation 1987-88, AOC-in-C Strike Cmd and C in C UK Air Forces 1988; Air ADC to The Queen; FRAeS, CBIM; *Recreations* golf, skiing, fell walking, photography, military history; *Clubs* RAF, Brokenhurst Manor Golf; *Style*— Air Chief Marshal Sir Patrick Hine, GCB; Lloyds Bank plc, Cox's & King's Branch, 6 Pall Mall, London SW1Y 5NH

HINE, Royston Graeme; s of Graeme Douglas Hine, of Purley Way, Pangbourne, Berkshire, and Verena Morella, *née* Belt; *b* 10 May 1943; *Educ* Pangbourne Sch, Reading Tech Coll, Distributive Trades Coll; *m* 14 Dec 1961, Heather Eileen, da of Bernard Frank Brown; 1 s (Stephen John), 4 da (Linda Anne, Caroline Anne, Sarah Anne, Barbara Anne); *Career* Colebrook & Hedges, controller Keymarkets Ltd 1969-72, assoc dir Asda Stores Ltd 1972-78, dir Borthwick plc 1978-86; currently dir: Hine Meats Ltd, Scobie of Junor Ltd; fndr memb Meat Forum, vice pres Butchers and Drovers Charitable Inst; Freeman City of London 1979, Liveryman Worshipful Co of Butchers 1980; fell Inst of Meat 1986 (former chm); *Recreations* shooting, snooker, tennis; *Clubs* City Livery; *Style*— Royston G Hine, Esq; Summertrees, 48A Allcroft Rd, Reading RG1 5HN (☎ 0734 874 498); 10 Whitchurch Rd, Pangbourne, Berks RG8 7BP (☎ 0734 842063, fax 0734 845396, car 0831 491556)

HINES, Anthony James; s of James Alfred Hines, of Colchester, and Gladys Margaret, *née* Chalk; *b* 26 May 1939; *Educ* Felsted; *m* 31 July 1965, Carol Eleanor, da of R C P Wheeler (d 1988); 1 s (Philip b 23 Aug 1974), 1 da (Nicki b 3 Nov 1972); *Career* articled clerk Bland Fielden and Co 1956-61, Farrow Bersey Gain Vincent 1961-63, Whinney Smith and Whinney 1963-65; fin dir: E N Mason and Sons Ltd 1965-69, Van Heughten Bros Ltd 1969-73; gp fin dir UCC, md UCC International Ltd 1981-; FCA 1962; *Recreations* hockey, golf, bridge; *Clubs* Stowmarket and Thetford; *Style*— Anthony Hines, Esq; International House, Mill Lane, Thetford, Norfolk IP24 3BZ (☎ 0842 752443, fax 0842 762490)

HINES, (Melvin) Barry; s of Richard Lawrence Hines (d 1963), and Annie Westerman; *b* 30 June 1939; *Educ* Ecclesfield GS, Loughborough Coll of Educn (Teaching Cert); *m* (m dis), Margaret; 1 s (Thomas b 1969), 1 da (Sally b 1967); *Career* writer; teacher in various schs: London 1960-62, S Yorkshire 1963-72; books: The Blinder 1966, A Kestrel for a Knave 1968, First Signs 1972, The Gamekeeper 1975, The Price of Coal 1979, Looks and Smiles 1981, Unfinished Business 1983; films: Kes 1970, Looks and Smiles 1981; TV: Billy's Last Stand 1970, Speech Day 1973, Two Men From Derby 1976, The Price of Coal (two films, 1977), The Gamekeeper 1979, A Question of Leadership 1981, Threads 1984, Shooting Stars 1990; hon fell Sheffield City Poly 1985; FRSL 1977; *Style*— Barry Hines, Esq; c/o Lemon, Unna & Durbridge Ltd, 24 Pottery Lane, Holland Park, London W11 4LZ (☎ 071 229 9216)

HINGLEY, Gerald Bryan Grosvenor; s of Martin Ward Hingley, of White House Farm, S Broughton, Middlesborough, Cleveland, and Mary Hingley; *b* 2 July 1943; *Educ* Shrewsbury, Univ of Nottingham (BA); *m* 28 July 1978, Veronica Mary, da of John Hird (d 1972), of York; 2 s (John b 1981, David b 1986), 1 da (Helen b 1979); *Career* admitted slr 1970; ptnr Wragge & Co 1974-; memb advsy bd of W Midlands Salvation Army; tstee: Sense-in-the-Midlands Fndn, Kilcuppes Charity; memb Law Soc; *Recreations* swimming; *Clubs* Edgbaston Priory, English Speaking Union; *Style*— Gerald Hingley, Esq; Wragge & Co, Bank House, 8 Cherry St, Birmingham B2 5JY (☎ 021 632 4131, fax 021 643 2417, telex 338728 WRAGGE G)

HINGSTON; *see*: Hibbert-Hingston

HINKS, Frank Peter; s of Henry John Hinks, of Stamford, Lincs, and Patricia May, *née* Adams; *b* 8 July 1950; *Educ* Bromley GS, St Catherine's Coll Oxford (BA, BCL, MA); *m* 31 July 1982, Susan Mary, da of Col John Arthur Haire, of Bickley, Kent; 3 s (Julius b 1984, Alexander b 1985, Benjamin b 1987); *Career* called to the Bar Lincoln's Inn 1973, Chancery Bar 1974-; memb Shoreham PCC; Freeman Worshipful Co of Innholders 1988; *Recreations* poetry, gardening, collecting jugs; *Style*— Frank Hinks, Esq; The Old Vicarage, Shoreham, Sevenoaks, Kent (☎ 095 92 4480); 13 Old Square, Lincoln's Inn, London WC2 (☎ 071 242 6105, fax 071 405 4004)

HINNELLS, Prof John Russell; s of William Hinnells (d 1978), and Lilian, *née* Jackson; *b* 27 Aug 1941; *Educ* Derby Coll of Art, Kings Coll London (BD, AKC), Sch of Oriental and African Studies London; *m* 24 June 1965, Marianne Grace, da of William Bushell (d 1973); 2 s (Mark b 11 June 1966, Duncan b 9 Oct 1968); *Career* lectr Univ of Newcastle 1967-70, prof Univ of Manchester 1970- (dean Faculty of Theology 1987-88); visiting appts: sr lectr Open Univ 1975-77, govt res fellowship lectr Bombay 1975, Shann lectr Univ of Hong Kong 1986, Ratanbai Katrak lectr Univ of Oxford 1986; author of numerous articles on religious and theological topics published in books and jls; sec gen Soc for Mithraic Studies, fndr and first sec Shap Working Pty on world Religions in Educn 1968-75, memb Governing Cncl Br Inst of Persian Studies, convenor Int Congress of Mithraic Studies (second) Tehran 1975 (first, Manchester 1971), chm UNESCO Int Symposium on the Conception of Human Rights in World Religions Inter-Univ Centre Dubrovnik 1985, chief speaker American Acad of Religious Conference LA USA 1985, office bearer of Assoc of Univ Depts of Theology and Religious Studies 1986-87; FSA, FRAS; *Books incl*: Hinduism (ed, 1972), Persian Mythology (1974), Mithraic Studies (2 vols, ed 1975), Spanning East and West (1978), Zorastrianism and Parsis (1981), Penguin Dictionary of Religions (ed, 1984), Handbook of Living Religions (ed, 1985); *Recreations* drawing, painting, photography; *Style*— Prof John Hinnells; 10 St Brannocks Rd, Chorlton cum Hardy, Manchester M21 1UP (☎ 061 860 5972); Department of Comparative Religion, The University, Oxford Rd, Manchester M13 9PL (☎ 061 275 3615)

HINSLEY, Prof Sir (Francis) Harry; OBE (1946); s of Thomas Henry Hinsley (d 1956), and Emma, *née* Adey (d 1980); *b* 26 Nov 1918; *Educ* Queen Mary's GS Walsall, St John's Coll Cambridge (MA); *m* 1946, Hilary Brett, da of Herbert Francis Brett Smith (d 1952); 2 s (Charles b 1947, Hugo b 1950), 1 da (Clarissa b 1954); *Career* HM FO (war serv) 1939-46; Univ of Cambridge: res fell St John's Coll 1944-50, tutor St John's Coll 1956-63, lectr of history 1949-65, reader in history of int relations

1965-67, prof of history of int relations 1969-83, chm Faculty Bd of History 1970-72, master 1979-89, vice chancellor 1981-83; FBA 1981; kt 1985; *Clubs* Oxford and Cambridge United Univ; *Style*— Prof Sir Harry Hinsley, OBE; St John Coll, Cambridge CB2 1TP (☎ 0223 355075)

HINSON, Kenneth Jack (Ken); s of Thomas Walter Hinson (d 1980), of Leicester, and Doris Elizabeth, *née* Stuart (d 1967); *b* 19 Sept 1943; *Educ* Wandsworth GS; *m* 1, 11 Jan 1962 (m dis 1989), Janet Elizabeth, da of William Taylor (d 1985), of Banstead, Surrey; 1 s (Gary Thomas b 1962), 1 da (Lorna Elizabeth Bland b 1963); m2, 12 April 1989, Christina Page Holt, da of George Christopher Anderson (d 1988), of Nottingham; *Career* Harvey Preen & Co London: articled 1961, audit mangr 1968, qualified CA 1970, ptnr 1972-77; currently md Böttcher UK Ltd; chm BRMA Roller Coverers Section, memb CBI Welsh Cncl; FCS 1970, FIAA 1975, FBIM 1977; *Recreations* game shooting and fishing, vintage cars; *Clubs* IOD; *Style*— Ken Hinson, Esq; Onen House, The Onen, Monmouth, Gwent NP5 4EN (☎ 0600 85570); Böttcher UK Limited, CWM Draw, Newtown, Ebbw Vale, Gwent NP3 6AE (☎ 0495 350300, fax 0495 350064, telex 498347, car 0836 316982)

HINTON, Graham Peter Henry; s of Anthony Henry Hinton (d 1989), and Gwendoline Mary, *née* Coleman; *b* 27 Jan 1946; *Educ* Epsom Coll, LSE, Kingston Poly, Univ of London (BSc); *m* 9 May 1970, Deborah Poland, da of Dr John Anthony Poland Bowen; 3 s (Tom Henry b 15 Oct 1978, Dudley John b 17 Oct 1980, Joshua James b 18 Oct 1985), 2 da (Kirsty Miranda b 21 Oct 1976, Abigail Liesel b 5 March 1984); *Career* graduate trainee then account supervisor SSCB Lintas 1969-74, exec dir then head of account mgmnt McCann-Erickson 1974-81, currently jt chm chief exec and regnl md Europe DMB & B (joined 1981); *Recreations* children, squash, tennis, theatre, classical guitar; *Clubs* RAC, St James, Champneys; *Style*— Graham Hinton, Esq; D'Arcy Masius Benton & Bowles, 2 St James Square, London SW1 (☎ 071 839 3422)

HINTON, Jennifer (Jennie); da of William Francis Young (d 1949), of Surrey, and Mary Louisa, *née* Siddall (d 1978); *b* 26 Nov 1934; *Educ* Crouch End HS for Girls London; *m* 15 July 1959, Dr (John) Michael Hinton, s of Robert Joseph Hinton (d 1985), of Bristol; 2 s (Mark b 1961, Timothy b 1962), 1 da (Kate b 1965); *Career* chm: Bd of Govrs Fordwater Sch Chichester, Opera 70 Tstees; exec: Sussex Rural Community Cncl, Chichester Festivities; memb: Mgmnt Ctee Sussex Heritage Tst, Ct Univ of Sussex; chm Chichester Civic Soc 1980-84; FRSA 1976; *Recreations* listening to music, admiring gardens; *Clubs* Royal Overseas; *Style*— Mrs Michael Hinton; Stoke Dorothy, West Burton, Pulborough RH20 1HD (☎ 0798 831237)

HINTON, Michael Herbert; JP; s of Walter Leonard Hinton (d 1979), of Thorpe Bay, Essex, and Freda Millicent Lillian, *née* Crowe; *b* 10 Nov 1934; *Educ* Ardingly; *m* 1, 4 April 1955 (m dis 1982), Sarah, da of Oliver Gordon Sunderland, DL (d 1967); 1 s (Timothy b 1964), 2 da (Catherine b 1956, Jennifer b 1960); m 2, 5 Nov 1984, Jane Margaret, da of Arthur Crichton Howell; *Career* CA; ptnr Griffin & ptnrs; Alderman City of London 1970-81 (Sheriff 1977-78, memb Ct of Common Cncl 1968-70); Freeman: City of London, Worshipful Co of Watermen & Lightermen of the River Thames; Liveryman and Master Worshipful Co of Farmers 1981-82; Liveryman: Worshipful Co of Wheelwrights, Worshipful Co of Arbitrators; FCA, FRSA, FICM, FFA, ACInsARB; *Recreations* cricket, assoc football, travel, theatre, collecting; *Clubs* Farmers, MCC, City Livery (pres 1976); *Style*— Michael Hinton, Esq, JP; 9E Brechin Place, London SW7 4GB; Quags, Lower Oddington, Glouc; Practice 38 Grosvenor Gdns, London SW1W OEB (☎ 071 730 6171, fax 071 730 7165)

HINTON, Nicholas John; CBE (1985); s of the Rev Canon John Percy Hinton (d 1990), of Wiltshire, and Josephine Eleanor Hinton (d 1971); *b* 15 March 1942; *Educ* Marlborough, Selwyn Coll Cambridge (MA); *m* 1971, Deborah Mary, da of The Hon Douglas Vivian (d 1974); 1 da (Josephine Mary b 1984); *Career* dir: Nat Assoc for the Care and Resettlement of Offenders 1973-77, Nat Cncl for Voluntary Orgns 1977-84; dir gen The Save The Children Fund 1984-; *Recreations* music; *Style*— Nicholas J Hinton, Esq, CBE; 22 Westmoreland Place, London SW1V 4AE (☎ 071 828 3965); Mary Datchelor House, Grove Lane, London SE5 8RD (☎ 071 703 5400, fax 071 703 2278)

HINTON, Russell Fletcher; TD (1968); s of Arthur Russell Hinton (d 1974), of Middlesbrough, and Muriel Isabel, *née* Fletcher; *b* 22 July 1931; *Educ* Uppingham, Keble Coll Oxford (MA); *m* 13 May 1961, Patricia Anne, da of Terence Edward Maguire (d 1990), of Nottingham; 3 da (Claire b 1962, Elizabeth b 1963, Ruth b 1966); *Career* Maj REME, DAA and QMG 151 Inf Bde (TA), Maj Green Howards; mangr consumer res Agric Div ICI plc 1955-72, dir Amos Hinton and Sons plc 1972-84, chm Scarborough Health Authy 1986-; MIPM 1988; *Recreations* beagling, beekeeping, riding; *Style*— Russell Hinton, Esq, TD; Croft House, Sowerby, Thirsk, N Yorks (☎ 0845 522514); Toutvent Bas, 24580 Rouffignac, France; Scarborough Hospital, Scalby Rd, Scarborough (☎ 0723 386 111)

HINTON COOK, Gavin; s of Ronald Edward William Cook, and Gwendolin Bessie Hinton; *b* 9 April 1947; *Educ* Kingsbury GS, Architectural Assoc Sch of Architecture (AA Dipl); *m* 11 Sept 1971, Janine Dewar, da of Wing Cdr William Charles Ramsay (d 1979); *Career* chartered architect: WF Johnson and Assoc, Melvin and Lansley, London Borough of Lambeth, Philip Mercer RIBA; project architect Milton Keynes Devpt Corp 1976-79 (chief architect 1979-85, completed 2400 houses and co-ordinated Energy World at MK); md Orchard Design 1985- (39 current design projects, complete site development, engrg and total integration managed); lectr architectural studies Birmingham Univ; awards: Arch Design Magazines, Best of Br Architecture Design Award Commendation, RIBA S Regn Energy Award; ARIBA; *Recreations* sailing, squash, cycling, marathon running; *Style*— Gavin Hinton Cook, Esq; The Orchard, Mentmore, Leighton Buzzard, Beds LU7 0QE; Orchard Design Studio, Mentmore, Leighton Buzzard, Beds LU7 0QF

HINWOOD-ZEIDLER, Kathleen Mary (Kay); da of Lt Robert Wylie, MC (d 1941), of 43 Rodway Rd, Bromley, Kent, and Maimie Emilie, *née* Malling (d 1981); *b* 26 Nov 1920; *Educ* Stratford House Sch Bickley Kent; *m* 1, 26 July 1941, George Yorke Hinwood (d 1960), s of late Frederick Hinwood, of Malmesbury, Wilts; 1 s (Peter Wylie b 17 May 1946), 1 da (Georgina Mary (Mrs Fowkes) b 18 April 1942); m 2, 17 Feb 1966, Lt Cdr Douglas Louis Zeidler (d 1967); *Career* ambulance driver CD 1939-41; studied art: studio of Edouard MacAvoy Paris 1937, privately in London, with Sonia Mervyn, final studies with Kratochwil Kathleen Brown Studios Chelsea; exhibitions: RP, RBA, ROI, NEAC, SWA, Pastel Soc, UA; paintings in private collections in: Eng, France, Spain, Canada, USA, Aust; winner of Award for Pastel 1986 from Mall Galleries (UA exhibition 1984); memb: Pastel Soc, United Soc of Artists, Fedn Br Artists; signs work K Hinwood; *Recreations* reading, writing, photogaphy; *Clubs* Chelsea Arts; *Style*— Mrs Kay Hinwood-Zeidler

HIORNS, Brennan Martin; s of Hubert Hiorns (d 1986), of Pengam, Gwent, and Catherine Mary, *née* Brennan; *b* 21 Sept 1943; *Educ* The Lewis Sch Pengam, Univ of Birmingham (BSc, PhD), Univ of London (Dip in Arch); *m* 1969, Mary Diana, da of Ernest Long; 1 s (Christopher Brennan b 1972), 1 da (Catherine Victoria b 1970); *Career* res engr Plastics Div ICI 1970-74; Kleinwort Benson Securities (Grieveson Grant until taken over): investment analyst Chemicals, Paper and Textiles 1974-77, fund mangr 1977-79, equity salesman 1979-87, ptnr (Grieveson Grant) 1983-84, head of res 1987-90, dep md 1990-; AMSIA 1976, memb Prehistoric Soc 1978, memb Stock Exchange 1983; *Recreations* archaeology, military and naval history, English literature; *Style*— Brennan Hiorns, Esq; 16 Prospect Lane, Harpenden, Hertfordshire AL5 2PL (☎ 0582 761386)

HIPKIN, Hubert (Raymond); s of Hubert John Hipkin (d 1969), of The Limes, Stickford, Boston, Lincolnshire, and Mary Hannah Hipkin, *née* Truman (d 1967); *b* 17 Oct 1928; *Educ* King Edward VI GS Spilsby, Univ of Sheffield (ARIBA); *m* 26 March 1958, Janet Ann, da of Sydney Bacon (d 1973); 3 s (Gregory b 1959 (decd), Robert b 1961, Michael b 1963); *Career* sr ptnr and fndr Architectural Practice 1969-; fell of Melton Mowbray Town Estate 1980-; (town warden 1977-80); govr: Melton Mowbray Coll of FE, Ferneley High Sch, Melton Mowbray; ARIBA; *Recreations* golf, game shooting, foreign travel; *Style*— Raymond Hipkin, Esq; Waverley House, The Park, Melton Mowbray, Leicestershire (☎ 63208); 44 Asfordby Road, Melton Mowbray, Leicestershire (☎ 63288)

HIPKIN, Dr, Col Leslie John; TD (1987); *b* 10 July 1935; *Educ* Birkenhead Sch, Univ of Liverpool (MB ChB, MD, PhD, LRCP); *m* 5 July 1958, Marjorie June; 1 s (John b 1966), 1 da (Sally 1972); *Career* cmmnd RAMC Vols 1974 (CO 208(m) Gen Hosp); lectr in endocrine pathology Univ of Liverpool 1963-71, Carlsberg-Wellcome fell Copenhagen 1969-70, sr lectr in endocrine pathology 1971-, hon conslt in endocrinology Liverpool DHA and Mersey RHA 1972-; MRCS, FRCPath 1982; *Books* Clinical Endocrine Pathology (with J C Davis); *Style*— Dr Leslie Hipkin, TD; 3 Poplar Rd, Oxton, Birkenhead, Merseyside L43 5TB (☎ 051 652 2021); University Department of Chemical Pathology (Endocrine Section), Alder Hay Hospital, Eaton Rd, Liverpool L12 2AP (☎ 051 220 5577)

HIPWOOD, Lady Camilla Diana; da of 15 Earl of Westmorland; *b* 26 Dec 1957; *m* 25 Sept 1985, Howard J Hipwood; 1 s (Sebastian John b 1988), 1 da (Rosanna Charlotte b 1986); *Style*— The Lady Camilla Hipwood; New Priory Farm, Kington St Michael, Chippenham, Wilts SN14 6JP

HIPWOOD, Julian Brian; s of Brian John Hipwood, of Thame, Oxon and Marion Barbara Sharpe, *née* Brice; *b* 23 July 1946; *Educ* Kohat Sch Pakistan, St George's Sch Amberley, Tech Stroud; *m* 1, 11 Oct 1969 (m dis 1980), Zofia Krystina, da of Col Przemyflaw Kazimerz Kaminski, Polish Army (d 1985); 1 s (Tristan Julian b 28 Feb 1976), 1 da (Accalia Colette b 14 March 1971); m 2, 1 April 1980, Patricia Anne Secunda, da of Maj Neal Lane McRoberts, US Army (d 1966), of The Old Hall, Ashwell, Leics; *Career* professional polo player 1964, England capt 1971-76 and 1978-90; captained England to win the Coronation Cup: against Mexico 1979, USA 1988 and 1989, and 1990 against France; first player to have won World Cup in five consecutive years 1980-84, twice Br Open Winner, twice French Open winner, once US Open Winner; memb Ctee Cowdray Park Polo Club; *Recreations* racing and breeding of thoroughbreds; *Style*— Julian Hipwood, Esq; Lychgate Cottage, Easebourne, Midhurst, West Sussex (☎ 073 081 3293); 12665 Shady Pines Ct, West Palm Beach, Florida 33414 USA (☎ 407 793 1327)

HIRD, Thora (Mrs Scott); OBE; da of James Henry Hird (d 1946), and Mary Jane, *née* Mayor (d 1942); *b* 28 May 1911; *m* 3 May 1937, James Scott, s of James Scott (d 1942); 1 da (Janette (Mrs Radenmaekers) b 14 Dec 1938); *Career* actress of stage and screen; theatre starred in: The Queen Came By (Duke of Yorks) 1949, Tobacco Road (Playhouse) 1951, The Happy Family (Duchess) 1951, The Same Sky (Duke of Yorks) 1952, The Troublemakers (The Strand) 1952, The Love Match (Palace) 1953, TV Comedy series: Meet the Wife, In Loving Memory, Hallelusah, Last of the Summer Wine; TV drama series: First Lady, Flesh and Blood, Romeo and Juliet, Cream Cracker Under The Setee; presenter Praise Be BBC TV; has appeared in numerous Br Films; fndr The Thora Hird Charitable Tst; Hon DLitt; *Books* Scene and Hird (autobiography, 1976), Thora Hird's Praise Be Notebook (1990), Thora Hird's Praise Be Christmas Book (1991); *Style*— Miss Thora Hird; c/o Felix de Wolfe, Manfield House, 376/378 The Strand, London WC2R OLR (☎ 071 379 5769)

HIRSCH, Prof Sir Peter Bernhard; s of Ismar Hirsch; *b* 16 Jan 1925; *Educ* Sloane Sch Chelsea, St Catharine's Coll Cambridge (MA, PhD); *m* 1959, Mabel Anne, *née* Stephens, wid of James Kellar; 1 step s, 1 step da; *Career* reader in physics Cambridge 1964-66, fell St Edmund Hall Oxford 1966-, Isaac Wolfson prof of metallurgy Oxford 1966-; pt/t chm Atomic Energy Authy 1982-84; hon fell: RMS, Christ's Coll Cambridge 1978 (fell 1960-66), St Catharine's Coll Cambridge 1983, Imperial Coll 1988-; Hon DSc: Newcastle, City Univ, Northwestern, E Anglia; FRS; kt 1975; *Style*— Prof Sir Peter Hirsch, FRS; 104A Lonsdale Rd, Oxford; Dept of Materials, University of Oxford, Parks Rd, Oxford OX1 3PH (☎ 0865 273737)

HIRSCH, Prof Steven Richard; *b* 12 March 1937; *Educ* Amherst Coll Mass USA (BA), Johns Hopkins Univ USA (MD); *m* Teresa; 1 s (Phineas), 3 da (Georgina, Collette, Eleanor); *Career* attached res worker MRC social psychiatry Maudsley Hosp 1971-73 (sr registrar and lectr 1967-71), sr lectr and hon conslt Westminster and Queen Mary's Hosp 1973-75, prof of psychiatry and Head Dept of Psychiatry Charing Cross and Westminster Med Sch and hon conslt Charing Cross Hosp 1975-; former pres of Psychiatry Section RSM, former chm Assoc of Univ Teachers of Psychiatry, dep chm Mental Health Cmmn BMA; FRCPsych 1979, FRCP 1983; *Books* Themes and Variations in European Psychiatry: An anthology (ed with M Shepherd, 1974), Abnormalities in Parents of Schizophrenics: Review of the Literature and an Investigation of Communication Defects and Deviances (with J Leff, 1975), The Suicide Syndrome (ed with R Farmer, 1980), Social Behaviour Assessment Schedule. Training Manual and Rating Guide (with S Platt and A Weyman, 1983), The Psychopharmacology and Treatment of Schizophrenia (ed with PB Bradley, 1986), Consent and the Incompetent Patient: Ethics, Law and Medicines (ed with J Harris, 1988), Learning Psychiatry through MCQ: a comprehensive text (with TE Sensky, C Thompson et al, 1988); Piccola Biblioteca Di Neurologia E Psichiatra (with J Leff, 1976), author of Report of a Working Party of the Section for Social and Community Psychiatry of the Royal College of Psychiatrists; *Recreations* sport; *Style*— Prof Steven Hirsch; 20 Mansel Rd, London SW19 4AA; Department of Psychiatry, Charing Cross & Westminster Medical School, St Dunstan's Rd, London W6 8RP (☎ 081 846 7390, fax 081 846 7372)

HIRSHFIELD, Baron (Life Peer UK 1967); Desmond Barel Hirshfield; s of Leopold Hirshfield; *b* 17 May 1913; *Educ* City of London Sch, Birkbeck Coll London; *m* 1951, Bronia, da of Joseph Eisen, of Tel Aviv; *Career* jt sr ptnr Stoy Horwath and Co (CA) 1975-82, int pres Horwath and Horwath Int 1984-85 (pres 1978-84); chm Horwath and Horwath (UK) 1967-85; fndr chm Trades Union Unit Tst Mangrs Ltd 1961-83 and chm TUUT Charitable Tst 1961-83; chm: Norwood Charitable Tst 1971-83, Norwood Fndn 1971-83; dep chm MLH Conslts 1973-83, memb Top Salaries Review Body 1976-84; dir: Woodmond Securities, Ralmond Securities, Ralwood Securities, Fieldwood Securities, London Soloists 1983; govr LSE; pres Br Assoc Hotel Accountants 1971-83; treas UK Ctee UNICEF 1975-83 and 1986-87; FCA; *Recreations* painting, drawing, travelling; *Style*— The Rt Hon the Lord Hirshfield; House of Lords, Westminster, London SW1A OPW

HIRST, Christopher Halliwell; s of John Kenneth Hirst, of Oulston Close, Hutton Buscel, nr Scarborough, Yorks, and Marian Harrison, *née* Smith; *b* 27 May 1947; *Educ* Merchant Taylor's, Trinity Hall Cambridge (MA); *m* 1, 12 Aug 1972 (m dis 1985),

(Moira) Cecilia, da of Arthur Tienken, of Minneapolis, USA; 1 s (William b 1974), 1 da (Elizabeth b 1976); m 2, 28 March 1987, Sara Louise, da of Arthur James Petherick, of Bodmin, Cornwall; 2 da (Victoria b 1988, Catherine b 1989); *Career* trainee exec Bank of London & S America Chile 1969-71; housemaster Radley Coll 1978-85 (asst master 1978-85), headmaster Kelly Coll Tavistock 1985-; *Recreations* antiquarian, literary, sporting; *Clubs* East India, Free Foresters, Jesters, MCC; *Style*— Christopher Hirst, Esq; Headmaster's House, Kelly Coll, Tavistock, Devon PL19 0HZ (☎ 0822 616 677); Kelly Coll, Tavistock (☎ 0822 613 005)

HIRST, David Brian Addis; s of Harold Rupert Hirst, CBE (d 1990), and Maureen, *née* Doherty; *b* 31 Aug 1938; *Educ* St George's Coll Weybridge; *m* 20 Dec 1969, Honoria (Nora) Bernadette, da of Dr P W Kent, OBE, of Orlingbury, Northants; 2 s (Richard b 15 June 1973, Michael b 28 Nov 1977), 2 da (Patricia b 30 Sept 1971, Anthea b 4 May 1976); *Career* Coopers & Lybrand Deloitte: articled 1956-61, ptnr 1970, ptnr i/c Cardiff Office 1970-83, ptnr i/c East Regn 1983-, memb Cncl of Partners 1988-; KSG 1984, KHS 1985; FCA 1972 (ACA 1962); *Recreations* sailing, golf; *Clubs* Royal Cwlth Soc, Northampton and County, Wellingborough Golf; *Style*— David Hirst, Esq; Home Farm House, Rectory Lane, Orlingbury, Kettering NN14 1JH (☎ 0933 678 250); Coopers & Lybrand, Oriel House, 55 Sheep St, Northampton NN1 2NF (☎ 0604 230770, fax 0604 238001)

HIRST, Hon Mr Justice; Hon Sir David Cozens-Hardy Hirst; er s of Thomas William Hirst (d 1965), of West Lodge, Aylsham, Norfolk, and Margaret Joy, *née* Cozens-Hardy (niece of 1 Baron Cozens-Hardy) (d 1984); *b* 31 July 1925; *Educ* Eton, Trinity Coll Cambridge; *m* 1951, Pamela Elizabeth Molesworth, da of Col Temple Percy Molesworth Bevan, MC, of London (s of Hon Charlotte Molesworth, 2 da of 8 Viscount Molesworth); 3 s, 2 da; *Career* served WWII, RA and Intelligence Corps, Capt 1946; called to the Bar Inner Temple 1951, QC 1965, High Ct judge (Queen's Bench) 1982; memb: Lord Chllr's Law Reform Ctee 1966-80, Cncl on Tbnls 1966-80, Ctee to Review Defamation Act, Supreme Ct Rule Ctee 1984-; chm of the Bar 1978-79 (vice chm 1977-78); kt 1982; *Recreations* shooting, theatre and opera, growing vegetables; *Clubs* Boodle's, MCC; *Style*— The Hon Mr Justice Hirst; Royal Courts of Justice, Strand, London WC2

HIRST, Hubert John; s of John Hirst (d 1983), of Oldham, and Elsie, *née* Makin; 1857 ggf (John Hirst) purchased Oldham Chronicle; *b* 24 Jan 1940; *Educ* Hulme GS Oldham, Manchester Coll of Sci and Technol (AMCST); *m* 1965, Kay Bradbury, da of James Gwylfa Roberts (d 1966); 2 s (Nigel b 1969, Roger b 1971); *Career* chm Hirst Kidd and Rennie Ltd 1985 (dir 1965, md 1983); *Recreations* photography, walking, Rotary, good food; *Style*— Hubert J Hirst, Esq; 21 Tandle Hill Rd, Royton, Oldham OL2 5UU; Hirst, Kidd-Rennie Ltd, PO Box 47, 172 Union St, Oldham OL1 1EQ (☎ 061 633 2121)

HIRST, Jonathan William; QC (1990); s of Sir David Cozens-Hardy Hirst, *qv*, and Pamela Elizabeth Molesworth, *née* Bevan; *b* 2 July 1953; *Educ* Eton, Trinity Coll Cambridge (MA); *m* 20 July 1974, Fiona Christine Mary, da of Dr Peter Anthony Tyser; *Career* called to the Bar Inner Temple 1975; SE Circuit; memb Gen Cncl of Bar 1986; *Recreations* shooting, gardening, music; *Clubs* Boodle's; *Style*— Jonathan Hirst, Esq, QC; Brickcourt Chambers, 15-19 Devereux Court, Temple, London WC2R 3JJ (☎ 071 583 0777)

HIRST, Michael William; s of John Melville Hirst (d 1969), and Christina Binning, *née* Torrance; *b* 2 Jan 1946; *Educ* Glasgow Acad, Univ of Glasgow (LLB), Univ of Iceland; *m* 1, 21 Sept 1972, Naomi Ferguson, da of Robert Morgan Wilson (d 1977); 1 s (John b 1976), 2 da (Sarah b 1974, Kate b 1979); *Career* qualified CA 1970; ptnr Peat Marwick Mitchell & Co 1977-83, conslt Peat Marwick McLintock 1983-, ptnr Michael Hirst Assocs 1987-; MP (C) Strathkelvin and Bearsden 1983-87, PPS Dept of Energy 1985-87, vice chm Scottish Cons Pty 1987-89, pres SCUA 1989-; er Kelvinside Hillhead Parish Church 1975-; memb: exec ctee Princess Louise Scottish Hosp 1979-, Nat Exec Cncl Br Diabetics Assoc; govr The Queen's Coll Glasgow (chm Fin and Gen Purposer Ctee), chm The Park Sch Educn Tst, dir Weavers Soc of Anderston 1981-; *Recreations* golf, hill walking, theatre, skiing; *Clubs* Carlton, Western (Glasgow); *Style*— Michael Hirst, Esq; Enderley, Milngavie, Glasgow G62 8DU

HIRST, Prof Paul Heywood; s of Herbert Hirst (d 1971), of Huddersfield, and Winifred, *née* Michelbacher; *b* 10 Nov 1927; *Educ* Huddersfield Coll, Trinity Coll Cambridge (BA, MA), Univ of London (Dip), ChCh Oxford (MA); *Career* lectr and tutor Dept of Educn Univ of Oxford 1955-59, lectr in philosophy of educn Univ of London Inst of Educn 1959-65; prof of educn: Kings Coll London 1965-71, Univ of Cambridge 1971-88 (fell Wolfson Coll 1971-); visiting prof Univ of: BC, Malawi, Otago, Melbourne, Puerto Rico, Sydney, Alberton, London; CNAA: vice chm Ctee for Educn 1975-81, chm Res Ctee 1988-; memb: Cncl Royal Inst of Philosophy 1972-89, educn Sub Ctee UGC 1974-80, Ctee for Enquiry into the Educn of Children from Ethnic Minorities (Lord Swann Ctee) 1981-85; *Books* Knowledge and the Curriculum (1974), Moral Education in a Secular Society (1974), Education and its Foundation Disciplines (jtly, 1983), Initial Teacher Training and the Role of the School (jtly, 1988); *Recreations* music (especially opera); *Clubs* Athenaeum; *Style*— Prof Paul H Hirst; Flat 3, 6 Royal Crescent, Brighton BN2 1AL (☎ 0273 684118)

HIRST, Prof Paul Quentin; s of Henry Hirst, of Plymouth, and Joyce Evelyn, *née* Schaeffer; *b* 20 May 1946; *Educ* Public Secdy Sch for Boys Plymouth, Univ of Leicester (BA), Univ of Sussex (MA); *m* 16 Feb 1981, Penelope Ann Franklin, da of Alexander J Woolley, of Elsted W Sussex; 1 s (James Alexander Henry b 26 Feb 1981); *Career* Birkbeck Coll Univ of London: lectr 1969-74, reader in social theory 1978-85, prof 1985-; memb: Lab Pty, Charter 88, Fabian Soc, Editorial Bd of The Political Quarterly; *Books* incl: Durkheim Bernard and Epistemology (1975), Mode of Production and Social Formation (with B Hindess, 1977), On Law and Ideology (1979), Social Relations and Human Attributes (with P Woolley, 1982), Marxism and Historical Writing (1985), After Thatcher (1989), Representative Democracy and its Limits (1990); *Style*— Prof Paul Hirst; Dept of Politics, Birkbeck College, Malet St, London WC1E 7HX (☎ 071 631 6402, fax 071 631 6270)

HIRST, Rachel; da of Sir David Hirst, and Pamela, *née* Bevan; *b* 14 Nov 1960; *Educ* Cranborne Chase Sch; *Career* Good Relations 1982-85, dir Valin Pollen 1990- (joined 1985); memb UK Ctee of Br-American C of C 1990-; *Style*— Ms Rachel Hirst; Valin Pollen, 18 Grosvenor Gardens, London SW1W ODH (☎ 071 730 3456, fax 071 730 7445)

HISCOCK, David Miles; s of Jeffrey Hiscock, of Coombe Bissett, nr Salisbury, Wilts and Rosalind Mary, *née* Marshall; *b* 20 Sept 1956; *Educ* Bishop Wordsworths GS, Salisbury Art Sch, St Martin's Sch of Art (BA), RCA (MA); *Partner* Isobel Teresa, da of Michael Deeley; *Career* freelance photographic asst London 1979-82, freelance photographer: magazine work 1982-, advertising cmmns 1985-; currently pt/t lectr in photography RCA; solo exhibitions: RPS Bath 1987, Pomeroy Purdey Gallery London 1988 and 1990, Parco Gallery Tokyo 1990, Norwich Arts Centre Norwich 1990, The Chateau D'Eau Gallery Toulouse France 1991; selected gp exhibitions 1990: Identities (Philadephia Art Alliance USA), Rencontres Photographiques (Carcassonne France), Face On (Zelda Cheatle Gallery London), David Hiscock and Calum Colvin (Seagate Gallery), Dundee and Theatre Clwyd (Mold); work in exhibitions: Madame Tussauds's London, Nat Portrait Gallery, Haggerty Museum USA, Chateau D'Eau, Toulouse; Pentax bursaries 1983-85, Vogue award for photography 1985, Madame Tussaud's award for figarative work 1985; *Style*— David Hiscock Esq; c/o Pomeroy Purdy Gallery, Jacob St Studios, Mill Street, London SE1 2BA (☎ 071 237 6062, 071 252 0511)

HISCOCK, Robert Heath; s of Frederick Heath Hiscock (d 1963), of Highfields, 257 Singlewell Rd, Gravesend, Kent, and Edith Rose, *née* Turnbull (d 1984); *b* 18 Aug 1920; *Educ* Kings Sch Rochester, Univ of London (LLB); *m* 2 July 1947, Mrs (Kathleen) Patricia Tong, da of Herbert Septimus Humphreys, of Powers Ct, 25 The Avenue, Gravesend, Kent (d 1952); 1 s (Robert Grigor b 1948), 1 da (Catherine Patricia (Mrs Leadbetter) b 1952), 1 step s (Michael Ronald Tong b 1943); *Career* Sgt HG; admitted slr 1944, ptnr Tolhurst & Hiscock 1948, successor The Martin Tolhurst Partnership 1970-90 (conslt 1990-); Notary Public; memb: Gravesend Historical Soc, Kent Archaeological Soc, Gravesend Cons Assoc; contrib Archaeologia Cantiana; memb Law Soc, FSA; *Recreations* gardening, walking; *Style*— Robert Hiscock, Esq, FSA; 10 Old Road East, Gravesend, Kent (☎ 0474 567 378); 7 Wrotham Rd, Gravesend, Kent DA11 OPD (☎ 0474 325 531, fax 0474 560 771)

HISCOX, Lady Julia Elizabeth; *née* Meade; 3 da of 6 Earl of Clanwilliam (d 1989); *b* 31 Dec 1953; *m* 12 Oct 1985, Robert R S Hiscox, o son of Ralph Hiscox, CBE (d 1970); 2 s (Milo b 1987, Henry b 1989); *Style*— The Lady Julia Hiscox; Rainscombe Park, Oare, Marlborough, Wilts SN8 4HZ (☎ 0672 63491)

HISCOX, Robert Ralph Scrymgeour; s of Ralph Hiscox, CBE (d 1970), of Scotts Farm Chobham, Surrey, and Louisa Jeanie, *née* Boal; *b* 4 Jan 1943; *Educ* Rugby, Corpus Christi Coll Cambridge (MA); *m* 1, 1966 (m dis 1978), Lucy, da of Charles Henry Mills; 2 s (Renshaw b 5 June 1968, Frederick b 5 June 1972); m 2, 1985, Lady Julia Elizabeth, da of 6 Earl of Clanwilliam; 2 s (Milo Edmund b 4 Jan 1987, Henry Charles b 23 Sept 1989); *Career* chm Roberts & Hiscox Ltd 1974-; chm: Hiscox Holdings Ltd, Beazley Furlonge & Hiscox Ltd, Payne Hiscox Ltd, Harrison Holdings and other cos in Hiscox Group; treas Cncl of Friends of the Tate Gallery 1990 (memb of Cncl 1986-); chm Lloyd's Underwriting Agents Assoc 1991; memb of Lloyd's 1967-; *Recreations* art, the country; *Clubs* City of London; *Style*— Robert Hiscox, Esq; Rainscombe Park, Oare, Marlborough, Wilts SN8 4HZ (☎ 0672 63491); Hiscox Holdings Ltd, St Helens, 1 Undershaft, London EC3A 8LD (☎ 071 929 5531, fax 071 929 1251)

HISKEY, Rex Arthur; s of Harry Charles Hiskey, and Gwynneth, *née* Bush; *b* 9 March 1947; *Educ* Univ of Birmingham (LLB); *m* 2 Oct 1971, Christine Elizabeth, da of Maurice Henry Cobbold; 1 s (Thomas b 1981), 2 da (Florence b 1986, Clara b 1990); *Career* slr; in private practice holding various local appts, ptnr Hayes & Storr; *Recreations* reading, sailing; *Style*— Rex Hiskey, Esq; Chancery Lane, Wells-next-the-Sea, Norfolk (☎ 0328 710210, fax 0328 711261)

HISLOP, Ian; s of late David Atholl Hislop, and Helen Hislop; *b* 13 July 1960; *Educ* Ardingly Coll Sussex, Magdalen Coll Oxford (BA); *m* 16 April 1988, Victoria, *née* Hamson; 1 da (Emily Helen b 3 Oct 1990); *Career* scriptwriter Spitting Image 1984-89, columnist The Listener 1985-89, ed Private Eye 1986-; regular book reviewer and contrib to various newspapers and magazines, writer and broadcaster for radio and TV; *publications incl:* various Private Eye compilations; *Style*— Ian Hislop, Esq; Private Eye, 6 Carlisle St, London W1V 5RG

HISTON, John Robert; s of Robert Histon (d 1986), of Cheshire, and Elizabeth, *née* Eshelby; *b* 16 Aug 1938; *Educ* Wellington Boys Sch, Altrinchan GS, Univ of Manchester; *m* 1966, Susan Alicia, da of William Ronald Missett, of Cheshire; 2 da (Samantha Charlotte b 1967, Sophie Fleur b 1970); *Career* chartered architect; sr ptnr Covell Mattews Histon Partnership; dir: Corell Matthews Partnership, Marthal Investments; ARIBA 1972, FCIArb 1984; *Recreations* sailing, offshire racing, carriage driving; *Clubs* Royal Thames Yacht, Pwllheli Sailing, Irish Sea Offshore Racing Assoc, Cheshire Carriage Driving; *Style*— John Histon, Esq; The Hermitage, Holmes-Chapel, Cheshire CW4 8DP (☎ 0477 33130); 20 Kennedy Street, Manchester M2 4BS (☎ 061 236 9000, fax 061 228 1515)

HITCH, Brian; CMG (1985), CVO (1980); s of Richard Souter Hitch (d 1986), of Wisbech, Cambridge, and Gladys Evelyn, *née* Harley (d 1989); *b* 2 June 1932; *Educ* Wisbech GS, Magdalene Coll Cambridge (BA, MA); *m* 4 Sept 1954, Margaret (Margot) Kathleen, 2 da (Susan Jennifer Magdalene b 1956, Caroline Margaret b 1959); *Career* diplomat FO 1955-; language student, second (formerly third) sec Tokyo 1955-61, Far Eastern Dept FO 1961-62, first (formerly second) sec Havana 1962-64, language student first sec Athens 1965-68, head of Chancery Tokyo 1968-72, asst head Southern European Dept FCO 1972-73, head (formerly dep head) Marine and Transport Dept FCO 1973-75, cncllr (Bonn Gp) Bonn 1975-77, cncllr and consul gen Algiers 1977- 80, consul gen Munich 1980-84, min Tokyo 1984-87, high cmmr Malta 1988-; LRAM 1949. FRCO 1950; *Recreations* music; *Clubs* Utd Oxford & Cambridge Univ; *Style*— Brian Hitch, Esq; British High Commission, 7 St Annes's St, Floriana, Malta GC (☎ 233134-8, telex MW 1249)

HITCHCOCK, Dr Anthony; s of Dr Ronald Hitchcock (d 1976), of Bishops Waltham, Hants, and Hilda *née* Gould; *b* 26 June 1929; *Educ* Bedales Petersfield Hants, Manchester GS, Trinity Coll Cambridge (BA, PhD), Univ of Chicago; *m* 6 June 1953, Audrey Ellen (d 1990), da of William Ashworth, of Hartshill, Stoke-on-Trent; 1 s (Piers J b 1957), 2 da (Rowena b 1959, Elfrida b 1963); *Career* UKAEA (Risley, Harwell, Windscale, Winfrith) 1953-67, head of safety and transportation Tport and Road Res Laboratory 1967-76 and 1979-89, DOE 1976-79, conslt Prog for Advanced Technol for the Highway Univ of Calif Berkeley 1990-; CPhys 1959, MCIT 1976; *Books* Nuclear Reactor Control (1960); *Recreations* Bridge; *Style*— Dr Anthony Hitchcock; 41 Schooner Court, Richmond, Calif, 4804 USA (☎ 0101 415 236 5560)

HITCHCOCK, Prof Edward Robert; s of Edwin Robert Hitchcock, and Martha Mary, *née* Roberts; *b* 10 Feb 1929; *Educ* Lichfield GS, Univ of Birmingham (MB ChB); *m* 29 Sept 1953, Jillian, da of Harry Thompson Trenowath; 3 s (Jeremy b 28 March 1955, Julian b 22 July 1957, Timothy b 10 June 1961), 1 da (Charlotte b 12 Dec 1964); *Career* Capt RAMC MO 2 Ba Scots Guards 1954-56; Univ of Birmingham: ldr Spitzbergen Expdn 1951, lectr anatomy 1953; registrar traumatic surgery: Birmingham Gen Hosp 1956, UCH 1957-59; sr registrar neurosurgery Radcliffe Infirmary and Manchester Royal Infirmary 1960-65, clinical res fell MRC 1960; res fell Univ of Oxford 1962, sr lectr and reader Dept Surgical Neurology Univ of Edinburgh, examiner RCSE; memb and chm BSI Neurological Implants Ctee, pres Walsall Branch Parkinsons Disease Soc; memb: Advsy Cncl Soc Neurological Surgns, DHA, American Assoc of Neurological Surgns, Scandinavian Neurological Soc, American Neurological Soc, American Physiological Soc; hon specialist Brazilian Neurosurgical Soc 1980; ESFSN (pres), WSSFN (bd dir); *Recreations* history, fishing, capology, flying; *Clubs* Army & Navy, Arctic, 1942; *Style*— Prof Edward Hitchcock; Cubbold House, Ombersley, nr Droitwich, Worcs WR9 0HS; Dept of Neurosurgery, Univ of Birmingham, Midland Centre for Neurosurgery and Neurology, Birmingham, West Midlands (☎ 021 538 3232)

HITCHCOCK, Robert Edward; s of Edward Hitchcock (d 1976), of Clavering, Essex, and Isobel Mary, *née* Balch; *b* 1 May 1936; *Educ* Gresham's, Emmanuel Coll Cambridge (BSc); *m* 27 Feb 1965, Vera Eileen, da of Gilbert Thomas Boyce (d 1977); 2 da (Vanessa b 20 May 1967, Christina b 18 March 1969); *Career* md various subsids

RTZ 1960-69; dir Bd: McKechnie plc 1970-88, Lilleshall plc 1988-; non-exec dir Philip Harris Holdings plc 1986-; Freeman Worshipful Co of Farmers 1960; MInstM 1962, C Eng 1970; *Style—* Robert Hitchcock, Esq; Abbotswood, Orchard Coombe, Whitchurch Hill, Reading, Berks (☎ 0734 843656); Lilleshall plc, Old Drummers House, 18 Northcroft Lane, Newbury, Berks (☎ 0635 528200, fax 0635 528112, car 0836 603995)

HITCHCOCK, (Manfred) Witgar Sweetlove; s of Manfred Cooper Hitchcock (d 1957), of The Mill House, Bures, Suffolk, and Margaret, *née* Sweetlove, MBE (d 1987); *b* 7 June 1923; *Educ* Gresham's Sch Norfolk, St Catharine's Coll Cambridge (MA); *Career* scientific staff ARC 1944-47; C Hitchcock Ltd (animal feed mfrs): joined 1947, dir 1952, chm and jt md 1957-68, chm and md 1968-; treas Bures Victory Hall 1955-62, former treas and chm Bures and Dist Agric Club, ctee memb Bures and Dist Local History and Natural Soc; assoc memb Inst of Commercial and Agric Merchants 1948; *Recreations* tennis, walking, travel, reading, researching family history; *Style—* Witgar Hitchcock, Esq

HITCHING, His Hon Judge Alan Norman; s of Norman Henry Samuel Hitching (d 1987), and Grace Ellen, *née* Bellchamber; *b* 5 Jan 1941; *Educ* Forest Sch Snaresbrook, ChCh Oxford (MA, BCL); *m* 1967, Hilda Muriel, da of Arthur William King (d 1984); 2 s (Malcolm b 1972, Robert b 1977), 1 da (Isabel b 1969); *Career* called to the Bar Temple 1964, rec 1985-87, circuit judge 1987-; *Style—* His Hon Judge Alan Hitching; 9 Monkhams Drive, Woodford Green, Essex

HITCHINGS, Russell Walter; s of Walter Hitchings (d 1956), and Gladys Magdelin, *née* Bell; *b* 22 March 1922; *Educ* Rutlish Sch, RMC Sandhurst; *m* 1, 1941 (m dis 1956), Joan Kathleen Hughes (d 1980); 1 s (Derek Russell b 1947, d 1979); 2 da (Janet Kathleen b 1943, Ann Kathleen b 1948); m 2, 1956 (m dis 1961), Olga Dubska (d 1975); m 3, 24 Jan 1963, Betty Jean, JP, da of Keith Robinson (d 1978); 1 da (Julia Betty b 1964); *Career* TA Middx Yeo 1939, Cadet RMC Sandhurst 1942-43, Royal Tank Regt 1943-46; organiser Liberal Pty Orgn 1946-50, gen mangr Pilot Travel Ltd 1950-51, exec Eldridge and Co Ltd 1951-53; H J Symons (agencies) Ltd: dir 1953-55, md 1955, managing ptnr; H J Symons Gp of Cos: chm and chief exec 1960, exec and pres 1987, ret 1988; forestry owner, underwriting memb Lloyd's, memb Liberal Pty; Freeman City of London 1969, Freeman Worshipful Co of Blacksmiths; FCIB 1955; *Recreations* sailing, gardening; *Clubs* Royal Thames Yacht, Royal Ocean Racing, Lloyd's YC, City Livery; *Style—* Russell Hitchings, Esq; The Mount, South Godstone, Surrey RH9 8JD (☎ 0342 892176, 893488)

HITCHINSON, David Anthony; s of The Rev Prebendary William Henry Hitchinson, of 66 Waller Dr, Northwood, Middx, and Joan Lucretia, *née* Blakeley; *b* 8 July 1948; *Educ* Merchant Taylors, Rose Bruford Coll of Speech and Drama (RBC Dip), Univ of Kent (BA); *m* Jean, *née* Braithwaite; 1 step da (Sarah Bell); *Career* BBC: radio drama 1972-80, Radio 4 newsreader 1980-85, sr prodr drama World Serv 1985-; *Recreations* music, swimming, theatre; *Style—* David Hitchinson, Esq; BBC World Service Drama, Bush House, London WC2B 4PH (☎ 071 240 3456, telex 265781)

HITCHMAN, Frank Hendrick; s of Sir (Edwin) Alan Hitchman, KCB (d 1980), of London, and Katharine Mumford, *née* Hendrick; *b* 21 July 1941; *Educ* Westminster, Univ of St Andrews (BSc); *Career* Coopers & Lybrand 1964-69, Samuel Montagu & Co Ltd 1970-73, Sedgwick Gp plc 1973-89 (sec 1980-85), dir E W Payne Co Ltd 1985-89; dep gp fin dir and gp sec Greig Fester Gp Ltd 1989-; FCA 1978; *Recreations* opera, travel, collecting; *Style—* Frank Hitchman, Esq; 9 West Warwick Place, London SW1V 2DL (☎ 071 821 1695); Upper End, Chaddleworth, Newbury, Berks RG16 0EA; Regis House, 43-46 King William St, London EC4R 9AD (☎ 071 623 3177, fax 071 623 8735, telex 883206)

HITCHMAN, Prof Michael L; s of Leslie S Hitchman, of Bearsden, and Grace H Hitchman, *née* Callaghan; *b* 17 Aug 1941; *Educ* Stratton GS Biggleswade, QMC London (BSc), King's Coll London (PGCE), Univ Coll Oxford (DPhil); *m* 8 Aug 1964, Pauline J, da of George V Thompson, of Benfleet; 1 s (Timothy b 8 Feb 1973), 2 da (Natasha b 8 July 1971, Fiona E b 17 May 1977); *Career* asst lectr in chemistry Leicester Regnl Coll of Technol 1963-65, jr res fell Wolfson Coll Oxford 1968-70, ICI Postdoctoral Res fell Physical Chemistry Laboratory Oxford 1968-70, chief scientist Orbisphere Corpn Geneva 1970-73, staff scientist Laboratories RCA Ltd Zurich 1973-79, lectr then sr lectr Univ of Salford 1979-84, vice dean Faculty of Sci Univ of Strathclyde 1989- (Young Prof of Chemical Technol 1984-, chm of Dept of Pure and Applied Chemistry 1986-89); treas Electrochemistry Gp RSC 1984-90, chm Electroanalytical Gp RSC 1985-88; memb SERC Ctees on: chemistry 1987-90, semi-conductors 1989-90, non-metallic materials 1986-88; co-chm of W Scotland Sci Park Advsy Ctee; memb: Electrochemical Soc, Int Soc of Electrochemistry, Br Assoc of Crystal Growth; CChem, FRSC; *Books* Ring Disk Electrodes (jtly, 1971), Measurement of Dissolved Oxygen (1978); *Recreations* family, keep fit, walking, sailing, skiing, DIY, theatre, opera; *Style—* Prof Michael Hitchman; Dept of Pure and Applied Chemistry, University of Strathclyde, 295 Cathedral St, Glasgow G1 1XL (☎ 041 552 4400, telex 77472 UNSLIB G, fax 041 552 5664)

HITCHON, George Michael; s of Alfred Clifford Hitchon (d 1987), and Beatrice Helen, *née* Daniels (d 1982); *b* 26 Nov 1944; *Educ* King Edward's Five Ways Sch, Newent Sch, Univ of Nottingham (MSc); *Career* horticulturist at West of Scot Agric Coll 1969-; dir Ayrshire Arts Festival 1983-, pres Kyle and Carrick Civic Soc 1981-; *Recreations* music, conservation, architectural history, curling; *Clubs* Auchincruive Curling; *Style—* George M Hitchon, Esq; The Scottish Agric Coll, Auchincruive, Ayr KA6 5HN (☎ 0292 520331)

HITMAN, Dr Graham Alec; s of Maxwell Hitman (d 1987), and Annette Hitman (d 1976); *b* 19 Jan 1953; *Educ* Bromley GS, Univ Coll Hosp Med Sch (MB BS); *m* Avril Fiona, da of Ivor Sevitt, of 63 Court Rd, Eltham; 1 s (Oliver b 1980), 1 da (Nadia b 1978); *Career* sr house offr and registrar Kings Coll Hosp London, RD Lawrence res fell St Bartholomew's Hosp; London Hosp: lectr Med Unit, asst dir, sr lectr, hon conslt; memb: Br Diabetic Assoc, Med Res Soc; FRCP; *Publications* incl: Polymorphisms in the 5'flaking region of the insulin gene and non-insulin dependent diabetes (jtly, 1984), Type 1 diabetes and a highly variable locus close to the insulin gene on chromosome 11 (jtly, 1985), New HLA DNA polymorphism associated with auto-immune diseases (jtly, 1986), Genes and diabetes mellitus (with MJ Niven, 1986), The genetic predisposition to fibrocalculous pancreatic diabetes (jtly, 1989), 2'-5' oligoadenylate synthetare and its relationship to HLA and genetic markers of insulin dependent diabetes mellitus (jtly, 1989); *Recreations* windsurfing, tennis; *Style—* Dr Graham Hitman; 7 Toynbec Close, Chislehurst, Kent BR6 7TH (☎ 081 467 3331); Medical Unit, The London Hospital, Whitechapel, London E1 1BB (☎ 071 377 7111, fax 071 377 7677)

HITNER, Stella Annette; da of Alfred Wright, of Thame, Oxfordshire, and Esmé Ada Lillian, *née* Lovell; *b* 5 Nov 1946; *Educ* Holton Park Girls' GS Oxford, Oxford Poly; *m* 1, 27 March 1967 (m dis); m 2, 20 April 1985, Robert Ian Hitner, s of Laurence Hitner; 1 s (Philip Robert b 20 Nov 1984), 1 da (Claudia Elizabeth b 25 April 1974); *Career* Warren Cook & Partners (PR consultancy) London: sec and PA 1965-68, asst PR offr 1968-69, jr ptnr 1969-74; freelance PR conslt 1974-79, account dir Datanews Ltd (PR consultancy) Luton 1979-83; md: Media Communications and Marketing 1983-85, Datanews Ltd (strategic mktg communications & PR consultancy) 1985-; dist cncllr Aylesbury Vale Dist Cncl 19780-74, dir and organiser Bedfordshire Country Festival 1979-83; MIPR 1983, MInstD 1989, corporate memb PR Conslts Assoc 1989; *Recreations* golf, family, working; *Clubs* Wig & Pen; *Style—* Mrs Stella Hitner; Hillcroft, Stewkley Rd, Soulbury, Leighton Buzzard, Beds LU7 0DH (☎ 0525 270687); Datanews Ltd, Datanews House, 482 Dunstable Rd, Luton, Beds LU4 8DL (☎ 0582 490430, fax 0582 490414, car 0860 395018)

HIVES, Hon David Benjamin; s of 1 Baron Hives, CH, MBE (d 1965); *b* 1931; *Educ* Repton; *m* 1954, Shirley, da of late Harold Walker, of Duffield, Derbys; 1 s, 2 da; *Career* Gp Capt RAF (ret); Air Attaché The Hague 1976-78, Cdr RAF Hong Kong 1981-83; *Recreations* fishing, shooting, skiing; *Style—* The Hon David Hives; Cumberhill House, Duffield, Derbys DE6 4HA

HIVES, Hon Mrs Peter; Dinah; *née* Wilson-North; da of F Wilson-North, of Walcott, Norfolk; *b* 13 Dec 1928; *m* 1956, Hon Peter Anthony Hives (d 1974); 1 s, 3 da; *Style—* The Hon Mrs Peter Hives; Harmer Garry, Harmer Green Lane, Welwyn, Herts

HIVES, Hon Michael Bruce; s of 1 Baron Hives, CH, MBE (d 1965); *b* 1926; *Educ* Repton; *m* 1951, Janet Rosemary, da of late W E Gee, of Lynngarth, Duffield, Derby; 2 s, 1 da; *Style—* The Hon Michael Hives; Fairfield, The Pastures, Duffield, Derbys

HO-YEN, Dr Darrel Orlando; s of Basil Orlando Ho-Yen, and Cicely Ho-Yen; *b* 1 May 1948; *Educ* Univ of Dundee (BMSc, MB, ChB, MD); *m* 18 July 1975, Jennifer, da of Arthur Maxwell Nicholls; 2 s (Gregory Orlando b 9 Aug 1977, Colan Maxwell b 2 Oct 1979); *Career* dir: S Toxoplasma Reference Laboratory 1987-, S Hydatid Reference Laboratory 1987-; conslt microbiologist Raigmore Hosp Inverness 1987-, hon clinical sr lectr Univ of Aberdeen 1987-; memb: Br Soc for Study of Infection, Assoc of Clinical Pathologists, Pathology Soc of GB & Ireland Soc of Authors; MRCPath 1986; *Books* Better Recovery From Viral Illness (2 edn 1987), Diseases of Infection (jt 1987); *Style—* Dr Darrel Ho-Yen; Microbiology Department, Raigmore Hospital, Inverness (☎ 0463 234151)

HOARE, Capt (Edward Melvill) Brodie; DSC (1944); s of Joseph Brodie Hoare (d 1962), of Meole Brace Hall, Shrewsbury, and Gwendolen Margaret, *née* Melvill; *b* 18 Dec 1918; *Educ* RNC Dartmouth; *m* 20 Dec 1951, Nancy Beatrix, da of Maj John Edward Mountague Bradish-Ellames (d 1984), of Manor House, Little Marlow, Bucks, and 9 West Eaton Place, London, SW1; 2 s (Antony b 1953, Mark b 1957), 1 da (Caroline b 1955); *Career* RN 1932-69; WWII, served Home Waters and Pacific 1939-45, Cdr 1952, Jt Planning Staff MOD 1954-57, asst sec COS Ctee MOD 1959-61, Capt 1960, Queen's Harbourmaster Gilbraltar 1961-63, COS to C-in-C Portsmouth 1965-67, Cdre Def Intelligence Staff MOD 1967-69; ADC to HM The Queen 1968-69; dir Br Shippers' Cncl 1970-79, pres Soc of Shipping Execs 1980-87; underwriting memb of Lloyd's 1973-; *Recreations* country living, music; *Clubs* Army and Navy; *Style—* Capt Brodie Hoare, DSC, RN; Velhurst Farm, Alfold, Cranleigh, Surrey (☎ 0403 752 224)

HOARE, Prof Charles Antony Richard; s of late Henry Samuel Malortie Hoare, of 54 Copers Cope Rd, Beckenham, Kent, and Marjorie Francis, *née* Villiers; *b* 11 Jan 1934; *Educ* King's Sch Canterbury, Merton Coll Oxford (MA), Moscow State Univ; *m* 13 Jan 1962, Jill, da of John Pym, of Foxwold, Brasted Chart, Westerham, Kent; 2 s (Thomas b 1964, Matthew b 1967, d 1981), 1 da (Joanna b 1965); *Career* Nat Serv RN 1956-58, Lt RNR 1958; Elliot Bros Ltd 1960-69: programmer, chief engr, tech mangr, chief scientist; prof of computer sci Queen's Univ Belfast 1969-77, prof of computation Univ of Oxford 1977-; Turing award 1980, Faraday medal 1985; Hon DSc: Univ of Southern Calif (1979), Univ of Warwick (1985), Univ Pennsylvania (1986), Queen's Univ Belfast (1987), Univ of York (1989); Soc Stran Accad dei Lincei 1988; FBCS 1978, FRS 1982; *Books* Structured Programming (1972), Communicating Sequential Processes (1985), Essays in Computing Science (1988); *Recreations* reading, walking, swimming, music; *Style—* Prof C A R Hoare, FRS; 22 Chalfont Rd, Oxford OX2 6TH (☎ 0865 58933); Computing Laboratory, 8-11 Keble Rd, Oxford OX1 3QD (☎ 0865 273 841, fax 0865 273 839)

HOARE, Lady Christina Alice; *née* McDonnell; only da of 8 Earl of Antrim, KBE, JP, DL (d 1977), and Angela Christina, *née* Sykes (d 1984); *b* 18 Sept 1938; *Educ* Les Oiseaux Convent, Slade Sch of Art (Dip of Fine Arts); *m* 23 Jan 1963, Joseph Andrew Christopher Hoare, *qv*, s of Sir Reginald Hoare, KCMG (d 1954); 1 s (Charles William Reginald b 1966), 2 da (Jane Alice Patience (Mrs Patrick Warrington) b 1963, Lucy Mary Christina b 1968); *Career* artist; sponsored exhibition Padre Dio and the Gargano Landscape (Westminster Cathedral 1986, tour 1987), inaugurated Christian Arts Centre London 1988, retrospective exhibition Bell Gallery Belfast 1989, painted images of Divine Mercy (St Bridgets Church Belfast) 1990, exhibition Charlotte Lampard Gallery 1990; chm Br Italian Soc Ball 1990; memb: Lloyd's 1979-, Latin Mars Soc, Soc of Catholic Artists, Christian Arts, Catholic Union, Confraternity of St James, Movement for Christian Democracy; *Recreations* country walks, travel, sketching, reading, seeing friends; *Clubs* Arts; *Style—* The Lady Christina Hoare; Hartridge Manor Farm, Cranbrook, Kent TN17 2NA

HOARE, David John; s of Sir Peter William Hoare, 7 Bt (d 1973), and hp of bro, Sir Peter Richard David Hoare, 8 Bt; *b* 8 Oct 1935; *Educ* Eton; *m* 1, 1965, Mary Vanessa, yr da of Peter Cardew, of Westhanger, Cleeve, Bristol, 1 s (Simon b 1967); m 2, 1984, Virginia Victoria Labes, da of Michael Menzies, of Long Island, NY; *Career* banker and farmer; dep chm of family co C Hoare & Co; govr Hawtrey's Sch; *Recreations* fishing, shooting, golf, skiing; *Clubs* White's, Royal St George's Golf, Swinley; *Style—* David Hoare, Esq; 21 Kelso Place, London W8 (☎ 071 937 9925); Luscombe Castle, Dawlish, Devon; C Hoare and Co, 37 Fleet St, London EC4P 4DQ (☎ 071 353 4522)

HOARE, Hon Mrs (Frances Evelyn); *née* Hogg; da of Baron Hailsham of St Marylebone (Life Peer); *b* 1949; *Educ* St Paul's Girls' Sch, Homerton Teacher Training Coll Cambridge; *m* 1970, Richard Quintin Hoare; 2 s, 1 da; *Style—* The Hon Mrs Hoare; 1 Logan Place, London W8

HOARE, (Ernest) George; *b* 9 June 1927; *Educ* Saltash GS; *m* 1950, Nancy Beatrice; 3 s; *Career* chm J & F Pool (Holdings) Ltd 1983-87 (md 1970-83), dir Western Motor Holdings 1980-84, Conservatives CI Group plc 1987-88, assoc memb Devon and Cornwall Development Co Ltd 1988-; memb Industl Tbnls Panel 1976-, dir Western Enterprise Fund 1982-84; chm: Cornwall Gp CBI 1984-85, Cornwall and Devon Area Manpower Bd 1986-88, Cornwall Hosp Ind Tst 1989- (dir 1979-), Cornwall Coll 1989- (govr 1984-); memb SW Industl Devpt Bd 1986-89, Devon and Cornwall Bd Prince's Youth Tst 1988-; cnsllr DTI Enterprise 1988-91; FCA, MInstD; *Recreations* gardening, ctee work; *Style—* George Hoare, Esq; 51 Pendarves Rd, Camborne, Cornwall (☎ 0209 714332)

HOARE, Henry Cadogan; s of Henry Peregrine Rennie Hoare (d 1981), and Lady Beatrix Lilian Ethel Cadogan (*see* Lady Beatrix Fanshawe); *b* 23 Nov 1931; *Educ* Eton, Trinity Coll Cambridge (BA); *m* 1, 30 May 1959 (m dis 1970), Pamela Saxon, da of late Col G F Bunbury, OBE; 2 s (Timothy b 1960, Nicholas b 1964), 1 da (Arabella b 1968); m 2, 16 June 1977, Caromy Maxwell Macdonald, da of Robert Jenkins, CBE, JP; *Career* chm C Hoare & Co 1988 (managing ptnr 1959); *Style—* Henry Hoare, Esq

HOARE, John Michael; s of Leslie Frank Hoare (d 1976), of Leatherhead, and Gladys, *née* Mepham; *b* 23 Oct 1932; *Educ* Raynes Park GS, Christ's Coll Cambridge (BA); *m* 3 Aug 1963, Brita Gertrud, da of Gustav Hjalte (d 1978), of Falkenberg,

Sweden; 1 s (Nicholas b 1968), 1 da (Katherine b 1966); *Career* Nat Serv 2 Lt RA 1951-52; asst sec Utd Bristol Hosps 1960-62, house govr St Stephen's Hosps 1963-65, asst clerk of govrs St Thomas's Hosp 1965-67, admin Northwick Park Hosp Gp 1967-73, regnl gen mangr Wessex RHA 1984-89 (regnl admin 1973-84); memb Inst Health Serv Mgmnt 1960-; *Recreations* reading, music, walking, squash; *Style*— John Hoare, Esq; 24 Clausentum Rd, Winchester SO23 9QE

HOARE, Jonathan Michael Douro; s of Capt Michael Douro Hoare, of Downsland Court, Ditchling, Sussex, and Valerie Ann, *née* James; *b* 21 Oct 1953; *Educ* Eton, Oriel Coll Oxford (BA, MA); *m* 7 Aug 1982, Clare Elizabeth, da of Peter Parsons, of The Grove, Stocklinch, Somerset; 2 s (Timothy Jonathan b 4 Oct 1986, Sebastian Michael b 18 Dec 1989), 1 da (Natasha Ruth b 1984); *Career* advertising mangr The Economist 1977-83, business devpt mangr Valin Pollen 1983-85, chief exec BMP Business 1985-; memb: Publicity Club, IAA, IPA, Inst of Mktg; *Books* Racial Tension in the Twelfth Century in the Holylands (1975), The Third Crusade (1974); *Recreations* tennis, cricket, real tennis, golf, shooting; *Clubs* RAC, Queens, Piltdown Golf; *Style*— Jonathan Hoare, Esq; BMP Business, 54 Baker St, London W1 (☎ 071 486 5566, fax 071 262 0564, car 0836 248732)

HOARE, Joseph Andrew Christopher; o s of Sir Reginald Hervey Hoare, KCMG (d 1954), and Lucy Joan (d 1971), da of William George Frederick Cavendish-Bentinck, JP, and sis of 8 and 9 Dukes of Portland; *b* 23 March 1925; *Educ* Le Rosey, Eton, Univ of Southampton, Balliol Coll Oxford (MA); *m* 23 Jan 1963, Lady Christina Alice McDonnell, *qv*, o da of 13 Earl of Antrim, KBE, DL (d 1977); 1 s, 2 da; *Career* Flying Offr: RAF Regt BAOR 1946-47, 604 Sqdn (Co of Essex Fighter Sqdn) 1951-57; dir of Canadian Overseas Packaging Industries 1962-; farmer 1972-88; property developer 1986-; memb Stock Exchange 1957-77, chm Assoc of Chartered and Tech Analysts 1970-73; underwriting memb Lloyd's 1985-; *Recreations* devising and maintaining models for forecasting 11 leading world economies, keeping cats and bantams, avoiding urban contamination; *Clubs* Brooks's; *Style*— J A C Hoare, Esq; Hartridge Manor Farm, Cranbrook, Kent TN17 2NA

HOARE, Kenneth Ninian; MBE (1977); s of Capt Frank Edgar Hoare, RAOC (d 1958), and Mabel Elizabeth, *née* Powell (d 1987); *b* 4 March 1916; *Educ* Cardiff HS, Jesus Coll Oxford (MA); *m* 1, 18 June 1940 (m dis 1970), Marion Gertrude, da of Rev Dr Frederick Augustus Morland Spencer, of Oxford; 2 da (Gillian Sheila (Mrs Button) b 1947, Celia Jennifer (Mrs Reading) b 1952); m 2, 17 June 1971, Daphne Josephine, da of Donald Elstob Lubbock (d 1979), of Leatherhead, Surrey; *Career* cmmnd RA 1938, SO (Intelligence) 1939-40, invalided 1940; dir admin Res Assoc for the Paper & Bd and Printing & Packaging Indust UK 1945-79, hon sec gen Int Assoc of Res Insts for Graphic Arts Indust Switzerland 1965-; Liveryman Worshipful Co of Stationers 1977; FInstD; *Books* Graphic Arts Research (1972, 1973, 1984); *Recreations* reading, travel, gardening; *Clubs* IOD, Oxford Union; *Style*— Kennneth Hoare, Esq, MBE; Fetcham Park, Leatherhead, Surrey; Old Bell Cottage, Ferring, W Sussex

HOARE, Laura, Lady; Laura Ray; o da of Sir John Esplen, 1 Bt, KBE (d 1930); *m* 10 July 1929, Sir Peter William Hoare, 7 Bt (d 1973); 2 s; *Style*— Laura, Lady Hoare; Luscombe Castle, Dawlish, Devon

HOARE, Michael Rollo; s of Rollo Hoare (d 1983), of Dogmersfield, and Elizabeth, *née* Charrington; *b* 8 March 1944; *Educ* Eton, New Coll Oxford; *m* 1, 1965 (m dis 1978), Penelope, da of Sir Charles Mander, 3 Bt, *qv* ; 2 da (Venetia b 1965, Fiona b 1969); m 2, 1981, Caroline Jane, da of Derek Abele; 1 s (Rollo b 1987), 1 da (Isabella b 1985); *Career* memb Stock Exchange 1977-81, managing ptnr C Hoare & Co 1982-; govr RAM 1984-; *Recreations* hunting, skiing, singing, gardening; *Clubs* Brooks's; *Style*— Michael Hoare, Esq; C Hoare & Co, 37 Fleet St, London EC4P 4DQ

HOARE, Sir Peter Richard David; 8 Bt (GB 1786); s of Sir Peter William Hoare, 7 Bt (d 1973), of Luscombe Castle, Dawlish, Devon; *b* 22 March 1932; *Educ* Eton; *m* 1961 (m dis 1967), Jane, da of late Daniel Orme, m 2, 1978 (m dis 1982), Katrin Alexa, da of late Erwin Bernstiel, m 3, 1983, Angela Francesca de la Sierra, da of late Fidel Fernando Ayarza, of Santiago, Chile; *Heir* bro, David John Hoare; *Career* co dir; *Clubs* Royal Automobile; *Style*— Sir Peter Hoare, Bt; c/o Crèdit Andorrà, Av de Princep Benlloch 19, Andorra La Vella, Principality of Andorra

HOARE, Quintin Vincent; OBE (1944); s of Maj Vincent Robertson Hoare (ka 1915), and Elspeth Florence, *née* Hogg (d 1965); *b* 21 June 1907; *Educ* Eton, Oriel Coll Oxford; *m* 1, 2 May 1936 (m dis 1948), Lucy Florence, da of Very Rev Gordon Selwyn, Dean of Winchester; 3 s ((Benjamin) Quintin b 1938, Gavin Quintin b 1940 d 1986, Richard Quintin (Tigger) b 1943); m 2, Rosemary, da of Lt-Col Charles Hezlet, DSO (d 1965); 2 s (David Quintin b 1954 d 1981, Nicholas Quintin b 1956), 1 da (Belinda Rosemary Cash b 1958); *Career* 2 Rangers TA 1933-36, 8 KRRC 1939-45, AA and QMG (formerly SO) 6 Armed Div 1940-45; sr ptnr C Hoare & Co (joined 1928, managing ptnr 1935); *Recreations* golf, bridge; *Clubs* White's, Portland, Royal St George's Golf, Royal Cinque Ports Golf, Rye Golf; *Style*— Quintin Hoare, Esq, OBE; Stuart House, Delf St, Sandwich, Kent (☎ 0304 612 133); 37 Fleet St, London EC4 (☎ 071 353 4522)

HOARE, Richard John; s of Wing Cdr Charles Frederick Hoare, of Farnham, Surrey, and Joyce Mary, *née* Stamp; *b* 5 Oct 1952; *Educ* Mill Hill Sch; *Career* slr Barlow Lyde and Gilbert 1973- (ptnr 1983); govr W Surrey Coll of Art and Design; Freeman: City of London 1984, City of London Slrs Co; memb Law Soc 1978; *Recreations* gardening, sport, fine arts; *Style*— Richard Hoare, Esq; Barlow Lyde & Gilbert, Beaufort House, 15 St. Botolph Street, London EC3A 7NJ (☎ 071 247 2277, telex 913281, fax 071 782 8500)

HOARE, Richard Quintin; s of Quintin Vincent Hoare, OBE, and Lucy Florence, *née* Selwyn; *b* 30 Jan 1943; *Educ* Eton; *m* 19 Oct 1970, Hon Frances Evelyn Hogg, da of Lord Hailsham of St Marylebone, KG; 2 s (Alexander b 1973, Charles b 1976), 1 da (Elizabeth b 1978); *Career* HAC 1 RHA 1963-68, Home Serv Force HAC Detachment 1985-88; managing ptnr Hoare and Co Bankers 1969, chm Bulldog Securities Ltd 1986 (dir 1964); dir William Weston Gallery Ltd 1986; govr Westminster Med Sch 1972-76; memb: African Med Res Fndn 1977-84, BBA; *Recreations* travel, walking, stalking; *Clubs* White's; *Style*— Richard Hoare, Esq; Tangier House, Wootton St Lawrence, Basingstoke, Hants RG23 8PH (☎ 0256 780 240); 37 Fleet St, London EC4 P4DG (☎ 071 353 4522, fax 071 353 4521, telex 24622)

HOARE, Rev Dr Rupert William Noel; s of Julian Hoare, and Edith, *née* Temple; *b* 3 March 1940; *Educ* Dragon Sch, Rugby, Trinity Coll Oxford (MA), Kirchliche Hochschule Berlin, Fitwilliam House and Westcott House (MA), Univ of Birmingham (PhD); *m* Jan 1965, Gesine Pflüger; 3 s (Christopher, Martin, Nicholas), 1 da (Rebecca); *Career* curate St Mary's Oldham 1964-67, ordained priest 1965, lectr Queen's Coll Birmingham 1968-72, canon theologian Coventry Cathedral 1970-75, rector parish of the Resurrection Beswick E Manchester 1972-78, canon residentiary Birmingham Cathedral 1978, princ Westcott House Cambridge 1981-; *Recreations* walking, gardening (sometimes); *Style*— Rev Dr Rupert Hoare; Westcott House, Jesus Lane, Cambridge CB5 8BP (☎ 0223 350074)

HOARE, Sarah, Lady; Sarah Lindsay; *née* Herald; o child of Robert Irwin Herald (d 1956), of Glengyle, Belfast, and Alma May, *née* Sinanian (d 1969); *Educ* Ashleigh House Belfast; *m* 1, James Henry Bamber (d 1978); m 2, 24 March 1984 (m dis 1986), as his 3 w, Sir Frederick Alfred Hoare, 1 and last Bt (d 1986); *Recreations* music, sailing; *Style*— Sarah, Lady Hoare; c/o Midland Bank, 202 Sloane St, London SW1

HOARE, SaraJane; da of Jeff Hoare, of 53 Strand on the Green, London, and Elizabeth Jane Hoare; *b* 27 June 1955; *Educ* Univ of Warwick (BA); *Career* fashion ed Observer newspaper 1985-87, sr fashion ed Vogue 1987-; fashion dir British Vogue 1989- (fashion ed 1987-89); *Style*— Miss SaraJane Hoare; Vogue House, 1 Hanover Square, London W1 (☎ 071 499 9080, fax 493 1345, telex 27338 VOLON G)

HOARE, Sir Timothy Edward Charles; 8 Bt (I 1784); s of Sir Edward O'Bryen Hoare, 7 Bt (d 1969); *b* 11 Nov 1934; *Educ* Radley, Worcester Coll Oxford (MA), London Univ (MA); *m* 1969, Felicity Anne, da of Peter Boddington; 1 s, 2 da (twins Louisa Hope and Kate Annabella b 1972); *Heir* s Charles James Hoare b 15 March 1971; *Career* dir: Career Plan Ltd, New Metals and Chems Ltd; memb: Gen Synod of C of E 1970-, Chadwick Cmmn on Church and State, Crown Appointments 1987-; dir World Vision of Br, govr Canford Sch; Fell Linnean Soc, FZS; *Recreations* music, literature, natural history, Arsenal FC; *Clubs* MCC; *Style*— Sir Timothy Hoare, Bt; 10 Belitha Villas, London N1 1PD (☎ 071 607 7359)

HOBAN, (Brian) Michael Stanislaus; s of Capt Richard Aloysius Hoban (d 1930), and Ivy Kathleen, *née* Davis (d 1974); *b* 7 Oct 1921; *Educ* Charterhouse, Univ Coll Oxford (scholar, MA); *m* Jasmine Jane, da of Jasper Cyril Holmes (d 1978); 1 s (Patrick Nicholas b 1957), 2 da (Bryony Jane b 1953 d 1959, Deirdre Elizabeth b 1954); *Career* RAC 1940-45, cmmnd Westminster Dragoons 1941, Capt 1945 (despatches 1945), Capt Northamptonshire Yeo TA 1950-59; asst master: Uppingham 1949-52, Shrewsbury 1952-59; headmaster: St Edmunds Sch Canterbury 1960-64, Bradfield 1964-71, Harrow 1971-81; JP Berks 1967-71; hon assoc memb HMC 1981- (hon treas 1975-81); pt/t chm various Civil Serv Cmmn Selection Bds 1984-, sometime memb Central Advsy Bd for RAF Coll Cranwell, govr Wellington 1981-; *Books* Jesu Parvule (with Donald Swann, 1965); *Recreations* music, gardening, reading, walking; *Clubs* East India, Vincent's Oxford; *Style*— Michael Hoban, Esq; Upcot, Wantage Rd, Streatley, Berks RG8 9LD (☎ 0491 873419)

HOBAN, Russell Conwell; s of Abram Hoban, and Jenny, *née* Dimmerman; *b* 4 Feb 1925; *Educ* Lansdale HS Pennyslvania, Philadelphia Museum Sch of Industl Art; *m* 1, 1944 (m dis 1975), Lillian Aberman; 1 s, 3 da; m 2, 1975, Gundula Ahl; 3 s; *Career* Army, served 339 Infantry 85 Div 5 Army Italian Campaign (Bronze Star Medal); various jobs 1946-56 incl TV art dir Batten Barton Durstine & Osborn; freelance illustrator 1956-65; assignments incl: Sports Illustrated, Fortune, Time; copywriter Doyle Dane Bernbach NY 1965-67; full-time author 1967-; novels: The Mouse and His Child (1967, made into film 1977, The Lion of Boaz-Jachin and Jachin-Boaz (1973), Kleinzeit (1974), Turtle Diary (1975, made into film 1984), Riddley Walker (1980, John W Campbell Meml award 1982, Aust Sci Fiction Achievement award 1983), Pilgermann (1983) The Medusa Frequency (1987); author of 55 children's picture books incl: Charlie the Tramp (1966, Boys' Club Junior Book Award 1968), Emmet Otter's Jug-Band Christmas (1971, Lewis Carroll Looking-Glass Shelf award and Christopher award 1972) How Tom Beat Captain Najork and His Hired Sportsmen (1974, Whitbread award 1974); also author of numerous essays and fragments, short stories verse for children, and theatre pieces; *Style*— Russell Hoban, Esq; c/o David Higham Associates, 5-8 Lower John Street, Golden Square, London W1R 4HA (☎ 071 437 7888)

HOBART, Caroline, Lady; Caroline Fleur; yr da of Col Henry Monckton Vatcher, MC, of Valeran, St Brelade's, Jersey (d 1954), and Beryl Methwold, *née* Walrond; *m* 1, 22 Feb 1955, as his 3 w, 11 Duke of Leeds (d 1963); m 2, 30 March 1968 (m dis 1975), Peter Hendrik Peregrine Hoos; m 3, 1975, as his 2 w, Lt Cdr Sir Robert Hampden Hobart, 3 Bt (d 1988); *Career* artist (paints under name of Caroline Leeds); *Style*— Caroline, Lady Hobart; 42 Egerton Gardens, London SW3 2BZ

HOBART, Sir John Vere; 4 Bt (UK 1914); s of Sir Robert Hampden Hobart, 3 Bt (d 1988), and his 1 w Sylvia, *née* Argo (d 1965); gggs of 3 Earl of Buckinghamshire and h p to kinsman 10 Earl; *b* 9 April 1945; *m* 1980, Kate, o da of late George Henry Iddles, of Cowes, Isle of Wight; 2 s (George Hampden, James Henry Miles b 1986); *Heir* s, George Hampden Hobart b 10 June 1982; *Style*— Sir John Hobart, Bt; Shore End, Queen's Road, Cowes, Isle of Wight

HOBART, Leonard Frederick; s of Leonard Francis Hobart, of Clacton, Essex, and Margaret Kate, *née* Wilkinson; *b* 2 March 1926; *Educ* William Ellis Sch London, Regent St Poly (Dip Arch); *m* 19 Oct 1947, Ida Evelyn, da of Carlo Rasmussen, of Kolding, Denmark (d 1977); 2 s (Martin Leonard b 1949, Colin Frederick b 1952); *Career* Army 1944-47; architect; sr ptnr Culpin Partnership; Freeman City of London 1987, Liveryman Worshipful Co of Glaziers and Painters of Glass 1989; FRIBA, FCIArb; *Recreations* travel; *Clubs* Danish; *Style*— Leonard Hobart, Esq; 68 Galley Lane, Barnet, Herts ENS 4AL (☎ 081 449 0344)

HOBBS, Edward Cullen; s of Charles Hobbs (d 1958), of 7 Railway Terrace, Ilkley, Yorks, and Gertrude Louisa, *née* Cullen (d 1960); *b* 25 Oct 1905; *Educ* Ilkley GS; *m* 29 Sept 1932, Ida Mary, da of Ralph Gozney (d 1915), of Shireoaks, Worksop, Notts; 2 s (John Peter, Richard Gozney), 2 da (Gillian Mary (Mrs Fraser), Margaret (Mrs Evans)); *Career* WWII Air Raid Warden; articled to N Williamson & Co CA's 1923; FCA 1928, ACIS 1927; *Recreations* gardening, reading; *Style*— Edward Hobbs, Esq; Flat 6, Belgrave Mansions, South Marine Parade, Bridlington, N Humberside (☎ 0262 675747); Exchange St, Retford, Notts (☎ 0777 703623)

HOBBS, Grete; da of Oscar V Fogh (d 1956), and Elly, *née* Petersen (d 1 1982); *b* 9 Dec 1927; *Educ* Ballerup Private Real Skole; *m* 15 Sept 1950, Joseph Hobbs (d 1984), s of late J W Hobbs; 1 s (Peter b 23 Nov 1955), 1 da (Annemarie b 28 March 1953); *Career* hotelier of 22 years; awards: Hotel of the Year 1971, Hotelier of the Year 1989, Scottish Free Enterprise award 1987, numerous hotel awards from different countries; *Recreations* golf, bridge; *Style*— Mrs Grete Hobbs; Inverlochy Castle, Fort William, Scotland PH33 6SN (☎ 0397 2177, fax 0397 2953, car 0860 332319)

HOBBS, John Michael (Jack); TD (2 bars); s of Alfred Robert Hobbs (d 1982), and Vera Mary, *née* Selwood; father founded family business in 1927 (Hobbs Hldgs Ltd); *b* 27 March 1936; *Educ* The Downs Sch Somerset, Allhallows Sch Devon; *m* 4 April 1964, Jea Irene, da of Charles Harris (d 1944); 2 s (Richard John b 1965, Graham Michael b 1967); *Career* Nat Serv 2 Lt Somerset LI Cyprus 1956-58; TAVR RE 1960, 111 Engr Regt (V) 1960-78 (specialist unit), quarry advsr to Army 1978-82, Home Def Force SW Dist 1983- (Maj); dir: Hobbs Quarries 1960-81, Llanwern Slag 1962-87, Wimpey Hobbs Ltd 1982-; dep chm Hobbs Hldgs Ltd 1981-, chm Hobbs (Cornelly) Ltd 1980-86; chm: West of England branch Inst of Quarrying 1983-84, cncl Inst of Quarrying (Int) 1987-88, SW section Fedn of Civil Engrg Contractors 1985-86, safety panel Br Aggregate Construction Materials Industs 1987-; FIQ, FIHT, MIAT, MITD; *Recreations* golf; *Style*— Jack Hobbs, Esq, TD; Wimpey Hobbs Ltd, 4 High St, Nailsea, Avon BS19 1BW (☎ 0272 858151)

HOBBS, Ven Keith; s of Percival Frank Hobbs (d 1962), and Gwennyth Mary Jenkins (d 1988); *b* 3 March 1925; *Educ* St Olave's GS, Exeter Coll Oxford (MA), Wells Theol Coll; *m* 1950, Mary, da of Louis Lingg Ruderman (d 1981); 2 s (Jonathan b 1955, d 1960, Robin b 1956); 1 da (Anne b 1953, d 1988); *Career* DSO Min of Supply 1945-46, Instr Branch RN (Lt Cdr) 1946-56; curate: Clewer St Stephen 1958-60, Soho St Anne 1960-62, St Stephen S Kensington 1962-78; lectr and counselling coordinator Borough

Rd Coll 1964-77, actg gen sec Church Union 1977-78, chaplain to Bishop of Chichester 1978-81, archdeacon of Chichester 1981-; *Style*— The Ven the Archdeacon of Chichester; 4 Canon Lane, Chichester, W Sussex PO19 1PX (☎ 0243 784260)

HOBBS, Prof Kenneth Edward Frederick; s of Thomas Edward Ernest Hobbs (d 1951), of Suffolk, and Gladys May, *née* Neave (d 1986); *b* 28 Dec 1936; *Educ* W Suffolk Co GS Bury St Edmunds, Guy's Hosp Med Sch Univ of London (MB BS), Univ of Bristol (ChM); *Career* surgical res fell Harvard Univ 1968-69, sr lectr in surgery Univ of Bristol 1970-73 (lectr 1966-70), prof of surgery Royal Free Hosp Sch of Med 1973-, vice dean Faculty of Med Univ of London 1986-90, (elected memb of Senate 1985-); memb MRC Ctee Systems Bd 1982-86, chm MRC Grants Ctee A 1984-86, memb UGC Med Sub Ctee (now Univ Funding Cncl) 1986-89; FRCS 1964; *Books* contrib: Liver and Biliary Disease (1985), Surgical Techniques Illustrated (1985), General Surgical Operations (1987), Operative Surgery and Management (1987), Surgery of the Liver and Biliary Tract (1988); *Recreations* gourmet dining, the countryside; *Clubs* Athenaeum; *Style*— Prof Kenneth Hobbs; The Rookery, New Buckenham, Norfolk NR16 2AE (☎ 0953 860558); University Department of Surgery, Royal Free Hospital, Pond St, London NW3 2QG (☎ 071 435 6121, fax 071 431 4528)

HOBBS, Maj-Gen Michael Frederick; CBE (1982, OBE 1979, MBE 1975); s of Brig Godfrey Pennington Hobbs (d 1985), and Elizabeth Constance Mary, *née* Gathorne Hardy (d 1952); *b* 28 Feb 1937; *Educ* Eton; *m* 1967, Tessa Mary, da of Gerald Innes Churchill, of Oxon; 1 s (William b 1978), 2 da (Elizabeth b 1969, Victoria b 1970); *Career* served Grenadier Gds 1956-80, DS Staff Coll 1974-77; MOD 1980-82; cdr 39 Inf Bde 1982-84; dir PR Army 1984-85; GOC 4 Armd Div 1985-87 (ret 1987); dir Duke of Edinburgh's Award Scheme 1988-; *Recreations* field sports, horticulture; *Clubs* Cavalry and Guards', MCC; *Style*— Maj Gen Michael Hobbs, CBE; The Red House, Kirby Cane, Bungay, Suffolk NR35 2HW; The Duke of Edinburgh's Award Scheme, 5 Prince of Wales Terrace, Kensington, London W8 5PG

HOBBS, Peter David; s of Anthony Lewis Hobbs, of Sandhill Farm, Bilbnook, Minehead, Somerset, and Barbara, *née* Thomas; *b* 9 Feb 1962; *Educ* Pyrland Hall Taunton, King's Coll Taunton, RAC; *m* 14 June 1989, Angela; *Career* jockey; turned professional 1984, ridden 300 winners incl 3 at the Cheltenham Nat Hunt Festival; first jockey to ride 4 winners in one afternoon at Cheltenham; *Recreations* golf, all sports; *Style*— Peter Hobbs, Esq; The Old Pump House, The Street, Washington, Pulborough, West Sussex (☎ 0903 743928, fax 0903 746074, car 0860 729794)

HOBBS, Peter Thomas Goddard; s of Reginald Stanley Hobbs, BEM (d 1970), of Gloucester, and Phyllis Gwendoline, *née* Goddard; *b* 19 March 1938; *Educ* Crypt Sch Gloucester, Exeter Coll Oxford (MA); *m* Victoria Christabel, da of Rev Alan Matheson (d 1988), of Clifton Campville, Staffs; 1 da (Katharine b 1971); *Career* Nat Serv 2 Lt RASC 1957-59, Capt RCT TA 1959-68; ICI Ltd 1962-79 (final position jt personnel mangr Mond Div), gp personnel dir Wellcome Fndn and Wellcome plc 1979-; Chemical Industs Assoc 1979-: chm Employment Affr Bd, chm Trg Ctee 1985-89, dep chm Pharmaceuticals and Fine Chems Jt Industl Cncl 1979-89 and 1990-91; dir Employment Conditions Abroad Ltd 1984-, vice pres Int Inst of Personnel Mgmnt 1987-89, dir Roffey Park Inst 1989, dir London Business Sch Centre for Enterprise 1989-, chm Employer's Forum for Disability 1990-, tstee Learning from Experience Tst; CIPM 1989, FInstD; *Recreations* history, topography, theatre, opera; *Clubs* United Oxford and Cambridge; *Style*— Peter Hobbs, Esq; Wellcome Foundation Ltd, 160 Euston Rd, London NW1 2BP (☎ 071 387 447, fax 071 388 5462, telex 8951486)

HOBBS, Philip John; s of Anthony Lewis Hobbs, and Barbara, *née* Thomas; *b* 26 July 1955; *Educ* Kings Coll Taunton, Univ of Reading (BSc); *m* 12 June 1982, Sarah Louise, da of Albert Edwin Hill; 3 da (Caroline Elizabeth, Katherine Louise, Diana Margaret); *Career* professional jockey for 10 years (160 winners); racehorse trainer 1985-: currently trg 50 horses, approx 140 winners incl Midlands Nat and Mackason Gold Cup; *Recreations* shooting, cricket, hunting; *Clubs* Sportsman; *Style*— Philip Hobbs, Esq; Sandhill, Bilbrook, Minehead, Somerset (☎ 0984 40366)

HOBBS, Ronald William; s of William Matthew Hobbs (d 1976), of Nailsea, Somerset, and Florence Harriet Martha, *née* Holder (d 1988); *b* 18 Oct 1923; *Educ* Cotham GS, Univ of Bristol (BSc); *m* 5 June 1948, (Beatrice) May, da of Albert Hilling (d 1966), of Broadstairs, Kent; 1 s (Malcolm b 20 Nov 1951), 1 da (Marilyn b 9 May 1954); *Career* Royal Aircraft Estab 1943-46; jr engr Oscar Faber & ptnrs 1946-48, Ove Arup & Partners 1948- (ptnr 1961), Arup Associates 1963- (fndr ptnr, chm 1981-84), Ove Arup Partnership 1969- (fndr dir, co chm 1984-); memb Awards Panel ARCUK 1970-, rep of ACE on Jt Contracts Tbnl 1979-, memb Cncl of Assoc of Consulting Engrs 1982-83 and 1985-87; past chm: S Bucks Lib party, Iver Parish Cncl; Hon DEng Heriot Watt 1990; FICE 1985, FIStructE 1981, FEng 1990, Hon FRIBA 1990; *Recreations* bridge, gardening, history, 18th century porcelain; *Style*— Ronald Hobbs, Esq; Ove Arup Partnership, 13 Fitzroy St, London W1P 6BQ (☎ 071 636 1531, fax 071 580 3924, telex 295341 OVARPART G)

HOBDAY, Thomas Lyrian; TD (1960), JP (Liverpool 1968), DL (Merseyside 1973); s of Thomas Owen Francis Hobday (d 1927), of Amlwch, Anglesey, and Elizabeth, *née* Denman (d 1937); *b* 22 Jan 1920; *Educ* Holt GS Liverpool, Univ of Liverpool (MB ChB, DPH, DPA); *Career* WWII 1939-46; army: cmmnd in Intelligence Corps, served in Norway, Africa, and Europe 1939-46; TA: Capt RAMC 1957, Lt-Col CO 126 Field Ambulance 1962, Col Co 208 General Hosp 1966; called to the Bar Inner Temple; princ med offr Health Dept Liverpool 1957-64, travelling fell WHO (India) 1960, sr lectr in epidemiology Univ of Liverpool 1964-85; conslt: Liverpool Health Authy, Merseyside Regnl Health Authy 1974-85; QHP 1967-70; contested (C) Huyton 1966, memb Liverpool City Cncl 1966-73; chief whip Cons Pty; chm: Fire Bde, Civic Undertakings, Health and Educn Ctees; memb Merseyside CC 1974-86; *Recreations* reading and swimming; *Clubs* Athenaeum (Liverpool); *Style*— T L Hobday, Esq, TD, JP, DL; 8 Princes Park Mansions, Toxteth, Liverpool, Merseyside L8 3SA (☎ 051 727 2297)

HOBHOUSE, Sir Charles John Spinney; 7 Bt (UK 1812), of Broughton-Gifford, Bradford-on-Avon, and of Monkton Farleigh, Wiltshire; o s of Sir Charles Chisholm Hobhouse, 6 Bt, TD (d 1991), and his 2 w Elspeth Jean, *née* Spinney; *b* 27 Oct 1962; *Heir* uncle, John Spencer Hobhouse, AFC b 1910; *Style*— Charles Hobhouse Esq; The Manor, Monkton Farleigh, Bradford-on-Avon, Wilts (☎ 0225 858558)

HOBHOUSE, (Mary) Hermione; MBE (1981); da of Sir Arthur Lawrence Hobhouse, JP (d 1965), of Somerset, and Konradin Huth Jackson (d 1965); *b* 2 Feb 1934; *Educ* Cheltenham Ladies' Coll, Lady Margaret Hall Oxford (MA); *m* 1958 (m dis 1988), Henry Trevenen Davidson Graham, s of W Murray Graham (d 1956), of Cairo; 1 s (Francis Henry b 1960), 1 da (Harriet Konradin b 1964); *Career* writer, conservationist, freelance journalist 1960-76, sec Victorian Soc 1976-82, gen ed Survey of London RCHM(E) 1983-; memb: Cncl Nat Tst 1983-, Royal Cmmn for 1851 Exhibition 1984-, Cncl Br Sch at Rome 1990-; FSA 1980; *Books* Thomas Cubitt: Master Builder (1971), Lost London (1971), Prince Albert: His Life and Work (1983); *Recreations* gardening, looking at buildings of all periods; *Clubs* Reform; *Style*— Miss Hermione Hobhouse, MBE, FSA; 61 St Dunstan's Road, Hammersmith, London W6 8RE; Survey of London, Royal Commission on Historical Monuments (England) Newlands House, Berners Street, London W1 (☎ 071 631 5065)

HOBHOUSE, Hon Mr Justice; Sir John Stewart; 2 s of Sir John Hobhouse, MC, JP (d 1961), and Catherine, yr da of Henry Stewart-Brown (3 cous of Sir William Brown, 2 Bt); Sir John was gn of 1 and last Baron Hobhouse; *b* 31 Jan 1932; *Educ* Eton, ChCh Oxford (BA, BCL); *m* 1959, Susannah Sybil Caroline, o da of Sir Ashton Wentworth Roskill, QC; 2 s (William b 1963, Sebastian s b 1964), 1 da (Charlotte b 1961); *Career* called to the Bar 1955, practised at Commercial Bar to 1982, QC 1973, High Ct judge (Queen's Bench Div and Commercial Ct) 1982-; chm Cncl of Legal Educn 1986-89; kt 1982; *Style*— The Hon Mr Justice Hobhouse; Royal Courts of Justice, Strand WC2 (☎ 071 936 6000)

HOBHOUSE, Penelope (Mrs Malins); da of Capt James Jackson Lenox-Conyngham Chichester-Clark, DSO, RN (d 1933), and Marion Caroline Dehra, *née* Chichester (d 1976); *b* 20 Nov 1929; *Educ* No Foreland Lodge Sch, Girton Coll Cambridge (BA); *m* 1, 17 May 1952 (m dis 1983), Paul Rodbard Hobhouse, s of Sir Arthur Hobhouse (d 1966), of Hadspen House, Castle Cary, Somerset; 2 s (Neil Alexander b 29 Aug 1954, David Paul b 9 Sept 1957), 1 da (Georgina Dehra Catherine b 9 March 1953); m 2, 1983, Prof John Melville Malins; *Career* writer and garden designer; books incl: The Country Gardener (1976), The Smaller Garden (1981), Gertrude Jekyll on Gardening (1983), Colour in Your Garden (1985), The National Trust: A Book of Gardening (1986), Private Gardens of England (1986), Garden (1988), Borders (1989), The Gardens of Europe (1990); *Style*— Ms Penelope Hobhouse; Tintinhull House, nr Yeovil, Somerset BA22 8PZ (☎ 0935 822509, fax 0935 826357)

HOBLEY, Brian; s of William Hobley (d 1959), and Harriet Hodgson (d 1976); *b* 25 June 1930; *Educ* Univ of Leicester (BA); *m* 1953, Florence Elisabeth, da of John Parkes (d 1976); 1 s (Paul), 1 da (Toni); *Career* chief urban archaeologist City of London 1973-89, dir Hobley Archaeological Consultancy Services Ltd 1989-; chm Standing Ctee Archaeological Unit Mangrs; jt sec: The Br Archaeologists and Developers Liaison Gp, City of London Archaeological Tst; dir: Citydig Ltd (Trading Co of City of London Archaeological Tst), Inst of Field Archaeologists (hon treas); FSA, AMA, MBIM, MIFA; *Books* Waterfront Archaeology in Britain and Northern Europe (jt ed, 1981), Roman Urban Defences in the West (jt ed, 1983), Roman Urban Topography in Britain and the Western Empire (jt ed, 1985), The Rebirth of Towns in the West AD 700-1050 (jt ed 1988), Roman and Saxon London: a Reappraisal (1986); reports in many learned jls; *Recreations* music, gardening, chess; *Style*— Brian Hobley, Esq, FSA; 21 St Martins Rd, Finham, Coventry (☎ 0203 411068, fax 0203 692180)

HOBLEY, Denis Harry; s of John Wilson Hobley, of Bolton, Cumbria, and Ethel Anne, *née* Dixon; *b* 6 Feb 1931; *Educ* King George V GS Southport; *m* 1 April 1957, June, da of Barnard Windle (d 1982); 3 s (Philip b 12 Jan 1961, David b 11 Oct 1962, Keith b 25 Oct 1964); *Career* Nat Serv RAPC 1953-55; qualified CA 1953, sr ptnr Lithgow Nelson and Co 1985- (joined 1948); pres Liverpool Soc of CAs 1986-87; memb: ctee many local charities, Methodist Church (memb dist, circuit and local ctees); FICA; *Style*— Denis Hobley, Esq; 11 Silverthorne Drive, Southport, Lancs (☎ 0704 25274); 399 Lord St, Southport, Lancs (☎ 0704 531888, fax 0704 548343)

HOBMAN, David Burton; CBE (1983); s of Joseph Burton Hobman (d 1953), and Daisy Lucy, *née* Adler (d 1961); *b* 8 June 1927; *Educ* Univ Coll Sch, Blundell's; *m* 1954, Erica, da of Hugh Irwin (d 1954); 1 s (Anthony), 1 da (Lucy Ann; *Career* community work Forest of Dean 1954-56, Br Cncl for Aid to Refugees 1957, Nat Cncl of Social Services 1958-67, visiting lectr in social admin Nat Inst for Social Work 1967, dir Social Work Advsy Service 1968-70, dir Age Concern England 1970-87 (vice pres 1988-); visiting prof Sch of Social Work McGill Univ Montreal 1977, memb: BBC/ITA Appeals Advsy Cncl 1965-69, Steering Ctee Enquiry into Homelessness Nat Assistance Bd 1967-68, Advsy Cncl Nat Corpn for Care of Old People 1970-74, Metrication Bd 1974-80, Lord Goodman's Ctee Reviewing Law and Charity 1975-76, Family Housing Assoc 1969-70; conslt UN Div of Social Affairs 1968-69; observer White House Congress on Ageing 1971-; pres Int Fedn on Ageing 1977-80 and 1983-87 (vice-pres 1974-77); memb: Personal Social Services Cncl 1978-80, Exec Ctee Nat Cncl of Vol Orgns 1981-83, Anchor Housing 1982-85, Ctee for Elderly Disabled People; special advsr Br Delgn to World Assembly on Ageing 1982, prodr Getting On (Central TV) 1987-88, exec sec Charities Effectiveness Review Tst 1986-, chm Office of Telecommunications 1987-; govr: Cardinal Newman Comprehensive Sch Hove 1971-76 (chm), Volunteer Centre 1975-79; dir Cinctel Ltd 1988-; conciliator The Shetland Housing Advice and Conciliation Service 1990-; KSG 1977; *Books* A Guide to Voluntary Service (1964, 2 edn 1967), Who Cares (1971), The Social Challenge of Ageing (1978), The Impact of Ageing (1981), The Coming of Age (ed 1987), Planning Your Retirement (1990), and numerous papers and broadcasts; *Recreations* travel, caravanning, reading, writing; *Clubs* Reform; *Style*— David Hobman Esq, CBE; Robinswood, George's Lane, Storrington, Pulborough, W Sussex RH20 3JH (☎ 0903 74 2987)

HOBSBAUM, Prof Philip Dennis; s of Joseph Hobsbaum (d 1970), and Rachel, *née* Sapera; *b* 29 June 1932; *Educ* Belle Vue GS Bradford, Downing Coll Cambridge (MA), Univ of Sheffield (PhD), Royal Academy of Music (LRAM), Guildhall Sch of Music (LGSM); *m* 1, 7 Aug 1957 (m dis 1968), Hannah Kelly, da of Khedourie Baruch Chaim (d 1945); m 2, 20 July 1975, Rosemary, *née* Phillips; *Career* asst master of English Tulse Hill Sch 1956-58, dir Philip Hobsbaum Studio London 1958-59, lectr in English Queen's Univ Belfast 1962; Univ of Glasgow: lectr, sr lectr in English Lit 1966, reader 1979, titular prof of English Lit 1985-; memb Soc of Teachers of Speech and Drama 1957-59, N Kelvin Community Cncl 1978-80, chm Schs-Univs Liaison Ctee for the Teaching of English 1979-88; *Books* incl: A Group Anthology (ed, with Edward Lucie-Smith, 1963), Coming Out Fighting: poems (1969), A Reader's Guide to Charles Dickens (1972), Tradition and Experiment in English Poetry (1979), Essentials of Literary Criticism (1983), A Reader's Guide to Robert Lowell (1988), William Wordsworth: Poetry and Prose (ed, 1989); *Recreations* dog-walking, piano-playing; *Style*— Prof Philip Hobsbaum; Department of English Literature, University of Glasgow, Glasgow G12 8QQ (☎ 041 339 8855, fax 041 330 4601, telex 777070 UNIGLA)

HOBSLEY, Prof Michael; TD (1969); s of Henry Hobsley (d 1950), and Sarah Lily, *née* Blanchfield (d 1959); *b* 18 Jan 1929; *Educ* La Martinière Coll Calcutta, St Xavier's Coll Univ of Calcutta, Sidney Sussex Coll Cambridge (BA, MA, MB MChir), Middx Hosp Med Sch (PhD); *m* 28 July 1953, Jane Fairlie, *née* Cambell, da of Neville Cambell (d 1963); 1 s (James Cambell b 1960), 3 da (Alison Fairlie b 1954, Clare Gillian b 1956, Katherine Sarah b 1963); *Career* Nat Serv Lt RAMC 1952-54 (Capt 1953), TA 1954-72 (Maj 1962); house offr, registrar and lectr The Middx Hosp, The Whittington Hosp and Chase Farm Hosp London 1951-64; The Middx Hosp and Med Sch: sr lectr Dept of Surgical Studies 1967-70 (lectr 1964-67), hon conslt surgn 1969-, reader in surgical sci 1970-75, prof of surgical sci 1975-83, prof of surgery and dir Dept of Surgical Studies 1983-88, prof of surgery and head Dept of Surgery 1988-; RCS: Hunterian prof 1962-63, examiner in applied physiology in Primary Examination for Fellowship of RCS 1968-74, Penrose-May tutor 1973-78, Sir Gordon-Taylor lectr 1980; Comyns Berkeley fell Gonville and Caius Coll Cambridge and The Middx Hosp 1965-66, Howard C Nafziger surgical res fell Univ of California San Francisco Med Center and Univ examiner in surgery 1966, visiting prof Harvard Med Sch Beth Israel Hosp Boston Mass USA 1966; examiner: in nursing studies Univ of London Dip of Nursing 1976-79, in MS Univ of London, in BS Univ of Nigeria 1977-79, in BS Univ of

West Indies 1978 and 1980, in MB ChB Univ of Bristol 1986-88, in MB BChir Univ of Cambridge 1986-, Dip of Sports Med The London Hosp 1987-, in surgery MB BS St Mary's Hosp Univ of London 1989; Windemere Fndn Travelling prof of surgery and visiting prof Monash Univ of Melbourne Aust 1984, guest American Surgical Assoc San Francisco 1988, visiting prof Dept of Surgery Univ of Louisville 1988; hon sec Br Soc of Gastroenterology 1976-80 (pres in waiting); hon fell: Assoc of Surgeons of India 1983, American Surgical Assoc 1989; pres Section of Measurement in Med RSM, pres elect Assoc of Professors of Surgery; memb: Soc of Authors (former chm Med Writers Gp), Soc of Apothecaries 1981-, Assoc of Surgeons, Br Assoc of Clinical Anatomists, Br Assoc of Surgical Oncology, North East Metropolitan Surgical Soc, Société Internationale de Chirurgiae, Collegium Internationale Chirurgiae Digestivae (Br del), Enfield Health Authy 1990-; Freeman City of London 1983; *Books* Pathways in Surgical Management (1979, 2 edn 1986), Physiological Principles in Medicine: Disorders of the Digestive System (1982), A Colour Atlas of Parotidectomy (1984), MCQ Tutor for Primary FRCS: Basic Science for the Surgeon (with P Abrahams and B Cardell, 1980), Current Surgical Practice Vols 1 - V (ed), Pathology in Surgical Practice (ed 1985, 2 edn 1988), numerous med pubns; *Recreations* cricket; *Clubs* Marylebone CC, Athenaeum; *Style*— Prof Michael Hobsley, TD; Fieldside, Barnet Lane, Totteridge, London N20 8AS (☎ 081 445 6507); Dept of Surgery, University Coll, London; The Rayne Institute, 5 University St, London WC1E 6JJ (☎ 071 387 1710, fax 071 387 1710)

HOBSON, Anthony Robert Alwyn; s of Geoffrey Dudley Hobson, MVO (d 1949), of 11 Chelsea Park Gardens, London SW3, and Gertrude Adelaide, *née* Vaughan; *b* 5 Sept 1921; *Educ* Eton, New Coll Oxford (MA); *m* 4 Dec 1959, (Elena Pauline) Tanya (d 1988), da of Igor Pavlovich Vinogradoff (d 1987), of 10 Gower St, London W1; 1 s (William b 1963), 2 da (Emma b 1960, Charlotte b 1970); *Career* WWII Scots Gds 1941-46, Capt Italy 1943-46 (despatches); assoc Sotheby & Co 1971-77 (dir 1949-71), Sandars reader in bibliography Univ of Cambridge 1974-75, Franklin Jasper Walls lectr Pierpont Morgan Library NY 1979 (hon fell 1983-), visiting fell All Souls Coll Oxford 1982-83, Rosenbach lectr Univ of Pennsylvania 1990, Lyell reader in bibliography Univ of Oxford 1990-91; pres: Assoc Internationale de Bibliophilie 1985-, Bibliographical Soc 1977-79, hon pres Edinburgh Bibliographical Soc 1971-; tstee: Eton Coll Collections Tst 1977-, Lambeth Palace Library 1984-; Socio Straniero Accademia Veneta 1987-; Freeman City of London, Liveryman Worshipful Co of Clothworkers; Cavaliere Al Merito della Repubblica Italiana; *Books* French and Italian Collectors and their Bindings (1953), Great Libraries (1970), Apollo and Pegasus (1975), Humanists and Bookbinders (1989); *Recreations* travel, opera, visiting libraries founded before 1800; *Clubs* Brooks's, Roxburghe; *Style*— Anthony Hobson, Esq; The Glebe House, Whitsbury, Fordingbridge, Hampshire SP6 3QB (☎ 072 53 221)

HOBSON, Sir Harold; CBE (1971); s of Jacob Hobson; *b* 4 Aug 1904; *Educ* Univ of Sheffield (LittD), Oriel Coll Oxford (MA); *m* 1, 1935, Gladys Bessie Johns (d 1979); 1 da; m 2, 1981, Nancy Penhale; *Career* special writer The Sunday Times 1976- (drama critic 1947-76); author; hon fell Oriel Coll Oxford 1974; Chevalier of The Legion of Honour; kt 1977; *Books* Devil in Woodford Wells, French Theatre, Indirect Journey, Theatre in Britain; *Recreations* cricket, reading seventeenth century French literature; *Clubs* Lasserre (Paris); *Style*— Sir Harold Hobson, CBE; Westhampnett Private Nursing Home, Westhampnett, Chichester, W Sussex

HOBSON, Valerie Babette Louise; da of late Robert Gordon Hobson, and late Violet, *née* Hamilton-Willoughby; *b* 14 April 1917; *Educ* St Augustine's Priory London, RADA; *m* 1, 1939 (m dis 1952), Anthony James Allan Havelock-Allan, now Sir Anthony Havelock-Allan, 4 Bt; 2 s (Simon (decd), Mark); m 2, 1954, John Profumo, CBE, *qv*; 1 s (David); *Career* stage, television and film actress; *Recreations* painting, reading, writing; *Style*— Miss Valerie Hobson

HOCKADAY, Sir Arthur Patrick; KCB (1978, CB 1975), CMG (1969); s of (William) Ronald Hockaday (d 1974), of Plymouth, and Marian Camilla Hockaday (d 1988); *b* 17 March 1926; *Educ* Merchant Taylors', St John's Coll Oxford; *m* 1955, Peggy, da of Hector Wilfred Prince, of Portsmouth; *Career* private sec to successive Mins and Secs of State MOD 1962-65, NATO Int Staff 1965-69, asst sec gen Def Planning and Policy 1967-69, asst under sec of state MOD 1969-72, under sec Cabinet Office 1972-73, dep under sec of state MOD 1973-76, second perm under sec of state MOD 1976-82; sec and DG Cwlth War Graves Cmmn 1982-89; *Books* contrib: Ethics and Nuclear Deterrence (1982), The Strategic Defence Initiative, New Hope or New Peril? (1985), Ethics and European Security (1986), Ethics and International Relations (1986), Just Deterrence (1990); *Recreations* fell-walking; *Clubs* Naval and Military, Civil Service; *Style*— Sir Arthur Hockaday, KCB, CMG; 11 Hitherwood Court, Hitherwood Drive, London SE19 1UX (☎ 081 670 7940)

HOCKLEY, Rev Canon Raymond Alan; s of Henry Hockley (d 1957), and Doris, *née* Stonehouse (d 1987); *b* 18 Sept 1929; *Educ* Firth Park Sch, Royal Acad of Music (BMus, RAM), Westcott House Cambridge (MA); *Career* curate St Augustine's Sheffield 1958-61, person i/c Holy Trinity Wicker Sheffield 1961-63, chaplain Westcott House Cambridge 1963-68, fell chaplain and dir of music Emmanuel Coll Cambridge 1968-76, canon residentiary precentor and chamberlain York Minster 1976-; Prize for Best Piece of Br Chamber Music (String Quartet) 1954, Oratorio, Suite for Orchestra; articles for learned journals; *Recreations* cooking; *Clubs* Yorkshire; *Style*— The Rev Canon Raymond Hockley; 2 Minster Court, York (☎ 0904 624965); Dean and Chapter of York (☎ 0904 642526)

HOCKMAN, Stephen Alexander; QC (1990); s of Dr Nathaniel Hockman, of Bromley, Kent, and Trude, *née* Schlossman; *b* 4 Jan 1947; *Educ* Eltham Coll London, Jesus Coll Cambridge; *m* 3 Sept 1972, Hilary Moira, da of Mark Mandleberg; 2 s (Benjamin b 12 Sept 1978, Samuel b 8 Sept 1982); *Career* called to the Bar Middle Temple 1970; rec Crown Court 1987; *Clubs* RAC; *Style*— Stephen Hockman, Esq, QC; 6 Pump Court, Temple, London EC4Y 7AR (☎ 071 353 7242, fax 071 583 1667)

HOCKNEY, David; s of Kenneth and Laura Hockney; *b* 9 July 1937; *Educ* Bradford GS, Bradford Sch of Art, RCA; *Career* artist, photographer, costume and set designer (opera); one-man shows incl: Kasmin Ltd London 1963, 1965, 1966, 1968, 1969, 1970, 1972, Alan Gallery New York 1964-67, Louvre Paris 1974, Knoeuller Gallery 1979, 1981, 1982, 1986, Tate 1986, Hayward Gallery 1983, 1985; Exhibn photographs Hayward Gall 1983; designer: The Rake's Progress Glyndebourne 1975, The Magic Flute 1978, costumes and sets for Met Opera N York 1980; ARA; *Books* The Glue Guitar (1977), China Diary (1982), Hockney Paints the Stage (1983); *Style*— David Hockney, Esq; 7506 Santa Monica Boulevard, Los Angeles, California 90048

HOCKNEY, Michael Brett; s of Stanley Waller Hockney, of St Annes-on-Sea, Lancs, and Jean, *née* Duston; *b* 29 July 1949; *Educ* King Edward VII Sch Lytham, Univ of Manchester, LSE; *m* 30 July 1983, Elizabeth Anne (Dr Elizabeth Hockney), da of Bruce Cryer, of Richmond, Surrey; *Career* dir and memb Exec Ctee of Boase Massimi Pollitt 1980-87, gp md BDDH Group plc 1987-; memb Cncl: Royal Sch of Church Music 1986, Inst of Practitioners in Advtg 1989-, Advtg Assoc 1989-; chm Nightingale Ball Charitable Tst 1990-, vice chm Berkley Square Ball Charity Ctee 1986-90; organiser and choir master All Saints Church London 1974; FCIM, FIPA, FBIM; *Recreations* church music, eighteenth century English porcelain; *Clubs* Athenaeum, IOD; *Style*— Michael B Hockney, Esq; 64 East Sheen Avenue, London SW14 (☎ 081 876 4391); Butterfield Day Devito Hockney Ltd, 47 Marylebone Lane, London W1 (☎ 081 224 3000)

HODDER, James Gordon; s of Arthur Sylvester Hodder (d 1974); *b* 14 Jan 1920; *Educ* Hardyes Sch Dorchester, London Univ; *m* 1950, Eileen Margaret, da of Thomas John Scott; 2 s; *Career* slr 1948; Gibson and Weldon 1948-50, Powers Samas Accounting Machines Ltd 1950-52, Marsh and Baxter Ltd 1952-57; vice-chm Metal Box Ltd 1979- (entered 1957, asst sec 1964, sec 1970, dir 1972); *Recreations* music, reading, cricket, swimming, walking, theatre; *Clubs* MCC, Wig and Pen; *Style*— James Hodder Esq; 7 South Drive, Wokingham, Berks (☎ 0734 780246)

HODDER-WILLIAMS, (John) Christopher Glazebrook; s of Capt Ralph Hodder-Williams, MC (d 1960), and Marjorie, *née* Glazebrook (d 1970); *b* 25 Aug 1926; *Educ* Eton; *m* Nov 1967, Deirdre, da of Wilfred Matthew (d 1988); 1 s (Simon), 1 da (Petra); *Career* RCS 1945-48, PA to Maj-Gen C M F White; novelist and songwriter; wrote over 70 songs for TV 1955-57; *Books* Chain Reaction, Final Approach, Turbulence, The Higher They Fly, The Main Experiment, The Egg Shaped Thing, Fistful of Digits, Ninety-Eight Point Four, Panic O'Clock, Cowards' Paradise, The Prayer Machine, The Silent Voice, The Thinktank That Leaked, The Chromosome Game; TV plays: The Ship That Couldn't Stop, The Higher They Fly (from the novel); *Recreations* flying, music; *Style*— Christopher Hodder-Williams, Esq; 19 Erpingham Rd, Putney, London SW15 1BE

HODDER-WILLIAMS, Mark; s of Paul Hodder-Williams, OBE, TD, of Somerset, and Felicity Blagden (d 1986); *b* 24 March 1939; *Educ* Rugby, Univ of Oxford (MA); *m* 1961, Janette Elspeth, da of Harry Archibald Cochran (d 1980), of Kent; 3 s (Andrew b 1963, James b 1964, Peter b 1968), 1 da (Susanna b 1969); *Career* book publisher; dir Hodder and Stoughton Holdings Ltd; FRSA 1990; *Recreations* golf, skiing, gardening, music; *Clubs* Vincents (Oxford), Wildernesse (Sevenoaks); *Style*— Mark Hodder-Williams, Esq; 38 Greenhill Road, Otford, Sevenoaks, Kent TN14 5RS; Hodder and Stoughton Ltd, Mill Road, Dunton Green, Sevenoaks, Kent TN13 2YA

HODDINOTT, Prof Alun; CBE (1983); s of Thomas Ivor Hoddinott, MM (d 1974), and Gertrude Jones (d 1964); *b* 11 Aug 1929; *Educ* Gowenton GS, Univ Coll Cardiff (Glamorgan music scholar, BMus, Walford Daues prize, Arnold Bax medal); *m* (Beti) Rhiannon Hoddinott, da of Rev Llewellyn C Huws (d 1982); *Career* lectr: Welsh Coll of Music and Drama 1951-59, Univ Coll Cardiff 1959-66; reader Univ of Wales 1966-67, prof and head Dept of Music Univ Coll Cardiff 1967-87, prof emeritus; list of works incl: String Trio (Cardiff) 1949, Concerto for Harp and Orchestra (Cheltenham Festival) 1957, concerto for piano, wind and percussion (London) 1960, Carol for SSA (Cardiff) 1961, Sinfonia for string orchestra (Bromsgrave Festival) 1964, Fiorture for orchestra (Aberdeen) 1968, Suite for orchestra (Southampton) 1970, the sun the great luminary music for orchestra (Swansea Festival) 1970, Sonata for horn and piano (St Donats) 1971, The Silver Swimmer (Manchip White) for mixed voices and piano duet (Austin Texas) 1973, Sinfonia fidei for soprano, tenor, chorus and orchestra (Llandaff Festival) 1977, Scena for String Quartet (Portsmouth) 1979, Six Welsh Folk Songs (Cardiff Festival) 1982, Ingravescentum Aetatem (Manhattan Kansas) 1983, Piano Sonata No 7 (London) 1984, Passacaglia and Fugue (St Davids) 1985, Concerto for Clarinet and Orchestra (Manchester) 1987, Piano Sonata No 9 (Cheltenham Festival) 1989, Emynau Pantycelyn (Rhymni) 1990; fndr and artistic dir Cardiff Festival of Music 1967-90, fndr and chm Oriana Records 1983-91, govr St Johns Coll Cardiff, patron Live Music Now; hon memb Royal Acad of Music, fell RNCM; *Style*— Prof Alun Hoddinott, CBE

HODGART, Alan William; s of William George Hodgart, of Australia, and Hilda Murial Herschel, *née* Hester; *b* 19 July 1940; *Educ* Univ of Melbourne (MA), Univ of Cambridge; *Career* mgmnt conslt Cortis Powell Ltd (UK) 1967-76, md DHS Conslts Ltd 1976-83, dep managing ptnr Deloitte Haskins & Sells (Australia) 1983-84 (dir int strategy NY 1984-88), md Spicers Conslts Gp Ltd (UK) 1988-90; Hodgart Temporal & Co 1990-; *Books* The Economics of European Imperialism (1978); *Recreations* literature, 19th century music, walking; *Clubs* Athenaeum, Princeton Univ; *Style*— Alan Hodgart Esq; 29 Micklethwaite Rd, London SW6 1QD (☎ 071 385 4548); Hodgart Temporal & Company, Bechtel House, 245 Hammersmith Rd, London (☎ 081 528 9875)

HODGE, James William; s of William Hodge, of Edinburgh, and Catherine, *née* Carden (d 1977); *b* 24 Dec 1943; *Educ* Holy Cross Acad Edinburgh, Univ of Edinburgh (MA); *m* 20 June 1970, Frances Margaret, da of Michael Coyne, of Liverpool; 3 da (Catherine b 1973, Fiona b 1975, Claire b 1979); *Career* Cwlth Office 1966, second sec Br Embassy Tokyo 1970-72 (third sec 1967-69), FCO 1972-75, first sec BHC Lagos 1975-78, FCO 1978-81, cnsllr (commercial) Tokyo 1982-86 (first sec 1981-82), cnsllr and head of Chancery Br Embassy Copenhagen 1986-90, cnsllr FCO 1990; MIL 1990; *Recreations* books, music, tennis, Scandinavian studies; *Clubs* Travellers', MCC; *Style*— J W Hodge, Esq; c/o Foreign and Commonwealth Office, King Charles St, London SW1A 2AH

HODGE, Jane Aiken; da of Conrad Potter Aiken, and Jessie McDonald; *b* 4 Dec 1917; *Educ* Hayes Court Hayes Kent, Somerville Coll Oxford (BA), Radcliffe Coll Cambridge Mass (AM); *m* 3 Jan 1948, Alan Hodge; 2 da; *Career* author; asst: Br Bd of Trade Washington DC 1942-44, Br Supply Cncl 1944-45; researcher: Time Inc NY 1945-47, Life Magazine London 1947-48; *Books* Maulever Mall, The Adventurers, Watch The Wall, My Darling, Here Comes a Candle, The Winding Stair, Marry in Haste, Greek Wedding, Savannah Purchase, Strangers in Company, Shadow of a Lady, One Way to Venice, Rebel Heiress, Runaway Bride, Judas Flowering, Red Sky at Night, Last Act, Wide is the Water, The Lost Garden, Secret Island, Polonaise, First Night, Leading Lady; non-fiction: The Double Life of Jane Austen, The Private World of Georgette Heyer; memb: Soc of Authors, Writers Guild of America, Authors' Lending & Copyright Soc, Lewes Monday Literary Club; *Style*— Mrs Jane Hodge; 23 Eastport Lane, Lewes, East Sussex BN7 1TL; David Higham, 5-8 Lower John St, Golden Square, London W1R 4HA

HODGE, Sir John Rowland; 2 Bt (UK 1921), MBE (1940); s of Sir Rowland Hodge, 1 Bt (d 1950); *b* 1 May 1913; *Educ* Wrekin Coll, and Switzerland; *m* 1, 1936 (m dis 1939), Peggy Ann, da of Sydney Raymond Kent; m 2, 1939 (m dis 1961), Joan, da of late Sydney Foster Wilson; 3 da; m 3, 1962 (m dis 1967), Jean Wood Anderson, da of late Cdr W E Buchanan, of Edinburgh; m 4, 1967, Vivien, da of Alfred Knightley, of Norwood; 1 s, 1 da; *Heir* s, Andrew Rowland Hodge b 4 Dec 1968; *Career* formerly Lt Cdr RNVR, formerly Lt Oxfordshire and Bucks LI, WWII 1939-46; *Clubs* British Racing Drivers, Naval, Royal Malta Yacht, Royal Yachting Assoc, Cruising Assoc; *Style*— Sir John Hodge, Bt, MBE; 16 Sutherland Drive, Gunton Park, Lowestoft, Suffolk NR32 4LP

HODGE, Sir Julian Stephen Alfred; s of Alfred Hodge, and Jane, *née* Simocks; *b* 15 Oct 1904; *Educ* Cardiff Tech Coll; *m* 31 Dec 1951, Moira, da of John Oswald Thomas (d 1983); 2 s (Robert b 24 April 1955, Jonathan b 3 April 1958), 1 da (Jane b 2 June 1953); *Career* former chm: Julian S Hodge & Co Ltd, Gwent Enterprises Ltd, Hodge Fin Ltd, Hodge Life Assur Ltd, Carlyle Tst Ltd; fndr Hodge & Co Accountants 1941; dir: Channel Islands Conslts Ltd 1968-89, Standard Chartered Bank 1973-75, Bank of Wales (IOM) Ltd 1974-85; chm: Avana Group Ltd 1973-81, Bank of Wales (Jersey) Ltd 1974-87, Carlyle Trust (Jersey) Ltd 1977-, St Aubins Investment Co Ltd 1986-;

fndr and chm Bank of Wales 1971-85, exec chm Hodge Group 1975-78 (chm and md 1963-75); fndr: Jane Hodge Fndn 1962, Sir Julian Hodge Charitable Tst 1964; UWIST: treas 1968-76, dep pres 1976-81, pres 1981-85, memb Cncl; treas Welsh Centre for Int Affrs 1973-84; memb: Industl Project Sub-Ctee Welsh Econ Cncl 1965-68, Welsh Cncl 1968-79, Duke of Edinburgh Conf 1974, Prince of Wales Ctee, Fndn Fund Ctee Univ of Surrey; former govr All Hallows (Cranmore Hall) Sch Tst Ltd, tstee Welsh Sports Tst, chm Aberfan Disaster Fund, pres S Glamorgan Dist St Johns Ambulance Bde; Hon LLD Univ of Wales 1971; FCCA 1930, FTII 1941, FRSA; KSG 1978, KStJ 1977 (CStJ 1972); kt 1970; *Books* Paradox of Financial Preservation (1959); *Recreations* golf, gardening, reading, walking; *Clubs* Victoria (St Helier), La Moye Golf (Jersey); *Style—* Sir Julian Hodge; Clos Des Suex, Mont De Coin, St Aubin, St Brelade, Jersey, Channel Islands

HODGE, Malcolm; s of Bertram William Hodge (d 1985), and Edith Olive, *née* Wilks (d 1968); *b* 5 Aug 1935; *Educ* Kings Coll Taunton; *m* 1968, Tyler, da of Henry Tyler; 1 s (James b 1971), 1 da (Emma Olivia b 1975); *Career* Lt 1 Bn Devonshire Regt Kenya; md Chevron Int Oil Co 1978-85, dir Chevron Oil Service Co 1985-87, chm Chevron Oil Service Co Ltd Pension Tstees 1985-87; *Recreations* gardening, sailing, golf; *Clubs* Chichester Yacht; *Style—* Malcolm Hodge, Esq; Great Thorndean House, Warninglid, Sussex

HODGE, Ronald Jacob; s of Jacob Hodge (d 1964); *b* 16 May 1926; *Educ* Wycliffe Coll Stonehouse, New Coll Oxford (MA); *m* 1956, Pauline Phyllis Beale; 3 da (Nicola, Alison, Virginia); *Career* Lt Middx Regt; chm Emhart International Ltd; dir of other cos in same gp in UK, USA, France, Germany, Japan, Sweden, Denmark, Finland, Australia, Spain 1971-86, chm BSA Guns Ltd 1986-, guardian Birmingham Assay Office 1989; FRSA 1985; *Recreations* golf, music, horticulture; *Clubs* Edgbaston Golf; *Style—* Ronald Hodge, Esq; Park Mount, 259 Bristol Rd, Birmingham B5 7SR (☎ 021 472 0683)

HODGES, Anthony; s of John Humphrey Hodges (d 1950), and Emma, *née* Fadil (d 1984); *b* 3 Oct 1947; *Educ* Harrow, Oriel Coll Oxford; *m* 4 Oct 1975, Deborah June, da of Maj Arthur Wright, REME, of Cheam, Surrey; *Career* dir Benton & Bowles Advertising Agency 1978-83 (joined 1970), fndr Tony Hodges & Ptnrs 1983; MIPA; *Recreations* tennis, fly-fishing, wine collecting; *Style—* Anthony Hodges, Esq; Honeysuckle Cottage, 31 Henning St, London SW11 (☎ 071 585 2116) Tony Hodges & Partners Ltd, Inner Court, 48 Old Church St, London SW3 5BY (☎ 071 351 4477, fax 071 351 2231, car 0860 713656)

HODGES, David Reginald Eyles; s of Edward Reginald George Hodges, of Dolphin Square, London, and Irene Muriel, *née* Turner; *b* 26 Aug 1942; *Educ* Mickleburgh; *m* 1, 19 Dec 1969, Yolande Wadih (d 1988), da of Joseph Yuja (d 1975), of San Pedro Sula, Honduras; 1 s (Crispin James David b 1973), 1 da (Patricia Irene b 1964); m 2, 22 July 1989, Patricia Emma, da of Cesar Augusto Pancorvo Noriega Del Valle (d 1983), of Lima, Peru; *Career* dir Cayzer Steel Bowater International Ltd 1975-86, dir and chm Ridgelawn Associates Ltd 1986-, conslt J H Davies (Underwriting Agency) Ltd 1986-; memb Lloyds; *Recreations* sailing, travel, skiing; *Clubs* Turf; *Style—* David Hodges, Esq; c/o Messrs C Hoare and Co, 37 Fleet St, London EC4 (☎ 071 481 4455 or 071 821 0179 or 0227 721224)

HODGES, Prof Douglas John; s of John Hodges of West Bromwich, and Gladys Maud, *née* Bayliss; *b* 11 April 1933; *Educ* West Bromwich GS, Univ of Nottingham (BSc, PhD); *m* 13 Aug 1955, Iris Pauline, da of Samuel Williams (d 1984); 2 da (Vickie b 1957, Josie b 1972); *Career* Univ of Nottingham: lectr 1960-70, reader 1970-78, prof 1978-; memb: Engrg Cncl, Coal Indust Welfare Orgn, Inst of Mining Engrs; CEng, FIMinE, FInstCES, FRICS; *Books* Optical Distance Measurement (1971); *Recreations* gardening, driving, travel; *Style—* Prof Douglas Hodges; University of Nottingham, University Park, Nottingham NG7 2RD (☎ 0602 484848 ext 2259)

HODGES, Air Chief Marshal Sir Lewis MacDonald; KCB (1968, CB 1963), CBE (1958), DSO (1944 and Bar 1945), DFC (1942 and Bar 1943); s of Arthur MacDonald Hodges (d 1940); *b* 1 March 1918; *Educ* St Paul's, RAF Coll Cranwell; *m* 1950, Elisabeth Mary, da of Geoffrey Blackett, MC (d 1977); 2 s; *Career* joined RAF 1937, serv WWII Bomber Cmd, SE Asia, Gp Capt 1957, Air Cdre 1961, Air Vice-Marshal 1963, ACAS (Ops) MOD 1965-68, AOC-in-C Air Support Cmd 1968-70, air memb Personnel Air Force Bd 1970-73, Air Chief Marshal 1971, dep C-in-C AFCENT 1973-76, Air ADC to HM The Queen 1973-76, ret; dir Pilkington Bros plc (Optical Div) 1979-83; govr British United Provident Assoc 1973-85, chm Govrs Duke of Kent Sch 1979-86, chm RAF Benevolent Fund Educn Ctee 1979-86; pres: RAF Escaping Soc 1979-, RAF Assoc 1981-84, Special Forces Club 1982-86, Old Pauline Club 1985-87, RAF Club 1985-; Croix de Guerre (Fr) 1944, Cdr Légion d'Honneur (Fr) 1948 (Grand Offr 1988); *Clubs* RAF, Special Forces; *Style—* Air Chief Marshal Sir Lewis Hodges, KCB, CBE, DSO, DFC; c/o Lloyds Bank, 6 Pall Mall, London SW1

HODGES, Mark Willie; s of William Henry Hodges (d 1924), of Newport, Monmouthshire, and Eva, *née* Smith (d 1964); *b* 20 Oct 1923; *Educ* Cowbridge GS, Jesus Coll Oxford (MA); *m* 11 May 1948, Glenna Marion, da of Alfred Leopold Peacock (d 1979), of Oxford; 1 s (Timothy b 1965), 1 da (Tessa b 1957); *Career* WWII Sub Lt RNVR 1942-45; lectr Univ of Sheffield 1950-54, Dept of Scientific and Industl Res 1954-56, asst scientific attaché Br Embassy Washington 1956-61, Office of the Min for Sci 1961-64, sec Royal Cmmn on Med Educn 1965-68; asst sec Dept of Educn and Sci 1968-79 (Arts and Libraries branch 1977-79), head Office of Arts and Libraries 1982-84 (joined 1979, under sec 1982, dep sec 1983); chm South Bank Theatre Bd 1984-(memb 1982-), memb: Cncl Royal Albert Hall 1983-, Cncl and Mgmnt Ctee Eastern Arts Assoc 1986-89; *Recreations* woodwork, computer programming, listening to music; *Clubs* Athenaeum, United Oxford and Cambridge; *Style—* Mark Hodges, Esq; The Corner Cottage, Church Way, Little Stukeley, Cambs PE17 5BQ (☎ 0480 459266)

HODGES, Hon Mrs (Naomi Katharine); *née* Lloyd; da of Baron Lloyd of Hampstead (Life Peer), and Ruth Emma Cecilia, da of late Carl Tulla; *b* 5 Nov 1946; *Educ* Arts Educational School, West London Institute of Higher Education; *m* 1967, Peter Campbell Hodges, s of Donovan Hodges; 1 s (Benjamin b 1974), 1 da (Katharine b 1971); *Career* primary sch teacher; *Style—* The Hon Mrs Hodges; 3 Cleveland Rd, Barnes, London SW13 OAA

HODGES, Dr Richard Andrew; s of Roy Clarence Hodges, of Box, Wiltshire, and Joan Mary, *née* Martnell; *b* 29 Sept 1952; *Educ* City of Bath Boys' Sch, Univ of Southampton (BA, PhD); *m* Deborah, da of FCP Peters; 1 s (William b 15 March 1984), 1 da (Charlotte b 25 Oct 1986); *Career* archaeologist; lectr Univ of Sheffield 1976-86 (sr lectr 1986-88); visiting prof: Suny-Binghamton 1983, Univ of Siena 1984-87, Univ of Copenhagen 1987-88; dir Br Sch at Rome 1988-; maj archaeological excavations: Roystone Grange Derbyshire 1978-88, San Vincenzo Al Volturno (1980-), Montarrenti Siena 1982-87; FSA 1984; *Books* The Hamwih Pottery (1981), Dark Age Economics (1982), Mohammed Charlemagne and Origins of Europe (1983), Primitive and Peasant Markets (1988), The Anglo-Saxon Achievement (1989), Wall-to-Wall History (1991); *Recreations* hill-walking, listening to classical music, tennis; *Style—* Dr Richard Hodges, FSA; British School at Rome, Via Gramsci 61, 00197 Roma, Italy FOREIGN (☎ 06 3214464, 06 321 3454, fax 06 3221201)

HODGES, Hon Mrs (Veronica Mary); *née* Addington; elder da of 7 Viscount Sidmouth; *b* 1944; *Educ* St Mary's Convent S Ascot Berkshire; *m* 1, 1982 (m dis 1987), Allan (Sam) Mainds, eldest s of George Mainds; 1 da (Phillipa); m 2, 1989, Michael Jeremy Hodges; *Career* teacher (BEd); *Style—* The Hon Mrs Hodges; 54a Cornwall Gardens, London SW7 4BG

HODGKIN, Sir Alan Lloyd; OM (1973), KBE (1972); s of George Lloyd Hodgkin (d 1918); *b* 5 Feb 1914; *Educ* Gresham's Sch Holt, Trinity Coll Cambridge (MA, ScD); *m* 1944, Marion de Kay, da of Francis Peyton Rous (d 1970); 1 s, 3 da; *Career* scientific offr working on radar for Air Miny and Miny of Aircraft Prodn 1939-45, lectr then asst dir of res Cambridge Univ 1945-52, Foulerton res prof Royal Soc 1952-69, J F Plummer prof of biophysics Cambridge Univ 1970-81, pres Royal Soc 1970-75, chllr Leicester Univ 1971-85, master Trinity Coll Cambridge 1978-84 (fell 1936-78 and 1984-); jt winner Nobel Prize for Medicine or Physiology 1963; FRS; *Recreations* travel, ornithology, fishing; *Style—* Sir Alan Hodgkin, OM, KBE, FRS; 18 Panton St, Cambridge CB2 1HP (☎ 0223 352707); Physiological Laboratory, Cambridge (☎ 0223 64131)

HODGKIN, Prof Dorothy Mary; OM (1965); da of John Winter Crowfoot, CBE (d 1959); *b* 1910; *Educ* Sir John Leman Sch Beccles, Somerville Coll Oxford; *m* 1937, Thomas Lionel Hodgkin (d 1982), s of Robert Howard Hodgkin (d 1951), sometime provost Queen's Coll Oxford; 2 s, 1 da; *Career* Univ of Oxford: official fell and tutor in natural sci at Somerville Coll, lectr and demonstrator 1946-56, reader 1956-60, Wolfson res prof of the Royal Soc 1960-77, emeritus prof 1977-; chllr Univ of Bristol 1970-88; Nobel Laureate in Chemistry 1964; FRS; *Recreations* archaeology, children; *Style—* Prof Dorothy Hodgkin, OM, FRS; Crab Mill, Ilmington, Shipston-on-Stour, Warwicks CV36 4LE (☎ 060 882 233); Laboratory of Chemical Crystallography, 9 Parks Rd, Oxford (☎ 0865 270833)

HODGKIN, (Gordon) Howard Eliot; CBE (1977); s of Eliot Hodgkin, and the Hon Katherine Mary Hodgkin, *née* Hewart; *b* 6 Aug 1932; *Educ* Camberwell Sch of Art London, Bath Acad of Art Corsham; *m* 16 April 1955, Julia Hazel Ann, da of Albert Ernest Lane; 2 s (Louis b 23 Oct 1957, Sam b 20 Feb 1960); *Career* artist; teacher: Charterhouse 1954-56, Bath Acad of Art Corsham 1956-66, Chelsea Sch of Art 1966-72; second prize John Moores' Liverpool exhibition 1976-80, visiting lectr Slade and Chelsea Schs of Art London 1976-77, tstee Nat Gallery London 1978-85, Br Pavilion Venice Biennale 1984, Turner prize Tate Gallery London 1985 (tstee 1970-86), hon fell Brasenose Coll Oxford 1988 (artist in res 1976-77); public collections incl: Arts Cncl of GB, Br Cncl London, Contemporary Art Soc London, Fogg Art Museum Cambridge Mass, Louisiana Museum Denmark, Oldham Art Gallery, Sao Paulo Museum Brazil, Tate Gallery London, Walker Art Center Minneapolis; one man exhibitions incl: Arthur Tooth and Sons London 1962, 1964 and 1967, Kasmin Gallery London 1969 and 1971, Arnolfini Gallery Bristol 1970, Galerie Muller Cologne 1971, Kornblee Gallery New York 1973, Museum of Modern Art Oxford, Serpentine Gallery London, Waddington/Kasmin Galleries London 1976, Andre Emmerich New York and Zurich 1977, Br Cncl touring India (graphics) 1978, Waddington Galleries London (graphics) 1980, M Knoedler & Co New York 1981, 1982, 1984, 1986, 1988, Bernard Jacobson London & Los Angeles (graphics), Macquarie Galleries Sydney 1981, Tate Gallery London 1982, Br Pavilion, Venice Biennale, Phillips Collection Washington DC 1984, Yale Center for Br Art Connecticut, Kestner-Gesellschaft Hanover, Whitechapel Art Gallery London, LA Louver Gallery Venice California, Tate Gallery London (graphics) 1985, Waddington Galleries London 1988; Hon DLitt Univ of London 1985; *Style—* Howard Hodgkin, Esq, CBE; 32 Coptic St, London WC1A 1NP (☎ 071 580 7970)

HODGKIN, Hon Mrs (Katharine Mary); da of 1 and last Viscount Hewart (d 1964); *b* 1907; *m* 1929, Eliot Hodgkin; 1 s, 1 da; *Style—* The Hon Mrs Hodgkin; Shelley's Hare Hatch, Twyford, Berks

HODGKINS, David John; s of Rev Harold Hodgkins, and late Elsie Hodgkins, of Rhos-on-Sea, Clwyd; *b* 13 March 1934; *Educ* Buxton Coll, Peterhouse Cambridge (MA); *m* 6 July 1963, Sheila; 2 s (James b 1964, Andrew b 1967); *Career* Miny of Labour 1956-64, Treasy 1965-68, Dept of Employment 1969-84, Health & Safety Exec 1984 (dir of Safety Policy 1984-); *Clubs* Royal Cwlth Soc; *Style—* David Hodgkins, Esq; Four Winds, Batchelors Way, Amersham, Bucks HP7 9AJ (☎ 0494 725207); Baynards House, Chepstow Place, London W2 (☎ 071 243 6370)

HODGKINSON, (James) Andrew; s of Peter George Hodgkinson (d 1986), of St Georges House, Lincoln, and Gwyneth Anne, *née* Evans (d 1984); *b* 22 Jan 1952; *Educ* City Sch Lincoln, Brighton Poly (BA); *m* 22 Jan 1952; *Career* dir John Michael Design Consultants 1975-80, fndr and md Simons Design 1980-, Main Bd dir and shareholder of The Simons Gp; patron of New Art Tate Gallery, memb IOD; CSD 1989; *Recreations* design art, polo and numerous sports, ethnography, natural history; *Style—* Andrew Hodgkinson, Esq; Simons Design Group, 245 Old Marylebone Rd, London NW1 5QT (☎ 071 229 9556, fax 071 221 3671, car 0860 311380)

HODGKINSON, (Anne) Catherine; da of Richard Hodgkinson, of Ledbury, Herefordshire, and (Joyce) Marten, *née* Green (d 1990); *b* 19 Dec 1946; *Educ* New Hall Chelmsford Essex, Institut D'Art et D'Archeologie Paris (LèsL); *m* 19 Dec 1975 (m dis 1985), John Louis Rishad Zinkin, s of Maurice Zinkin, OBE, of Kensington, London; 1 da (Kate b 1977); *Career* art dealer; md Lumley Cazalet Ltd 1973-; *Recreations* theatre, art, travel; *Clubs* The Arts; *Style—* Ms Catherine Hodgkinson; Lumley Cazalet Ltd, 24 Davies St, London W1Y 1LH (☎ 071 491 4767, fax 071 493 8644)

HODGKINSON, Air Chief Marshal Sir (William) Derek; KCB (1971, CB 1969), CBE (1960), DFC (1941), AFC (1942); s of late Ernest Nicholls Hodgkinson; *b* 27 Dec 1917; *Educ* Repton; *m* 1939, Nancy Heather Goodwin; 1 s, 1 da; *Career* joined RAF 1936, serv WWII (POW 1942-45), OC 210 and 240 (GR) Sqdns, DS Aust Jt Awti Sub Sch and jt serv Staff Coll 1946-58, Gp Capt 1958, ADC to HM The Queen 1959-63, Air Cdre 1963, IDC 1964, Commandant RAF Staff Coll Andover 1965, Air Vice-Marshal 1966, Asst Chief of Air Staff (ops reg) 1966-69, report on RAF offr Career Structure 1969, SASO RAF Trg Cmmd 1969, Air Marshal 1970, C-in-C NEAF 1970-73, commander Br Force NE and administrator Sovereign Base Areas Cyprus 1970-73, Air Sec 1973-76, Air Chief Marshal 1974, ret 1976; pres Regular Forces Employment Assoc 1982-86 (vice chm 1977-80, chm 1980-82); *Recreations* fishing, cricket; *Clubs* RAF, MCC; *Style—* Air Chief Marshal Sir Derek Hodgkinson, KCB, CBE, DFC, AFC

HODGKINSON, George Howard; s of Frank Howard Hodgkinson (d 1975), of Boxford, Colchester, Essex, and Dorothy Georgina, *née* Levis (d 1983); *b* 4 March 1945; *Educ* Rugby, St John's Coll Oxford (MA); *m* 12 July 1975, Sarah, da of Maj John Bruce Robertson, OBE (d 1973), of Fernden Hill, Haslemere; 2 s (Mark b 1980, Robert b 1984), 1 da (Katie b 1977); *Career* admitted slr 1970; asst slr: Coward Chance 1970-71 (articled clerk 1967), Legal and Claims Div B P Tanker Co Ltd 1971-73; ptnr: Sinclair Roche & Temperley 1975- (asst slr 1973), Sinclair Roche Hong Kong 1978-; taught English Simla Hills India with VSO 1962; Freeman Worshipful Co of Slrs; memb: Law Soc, Baltic Exchange 1988 (currently non-trading memb); *Recreations* dinghy racing (Wayfarers), tennis, golf; *Clubs* Aldeburgh Yacht (Wayfarer class capt 1989-90); *Style—* George Hodgkinson, Esq; Sinclair Roche & Temperley, Stone House, 128-140 Bishopsgate, London EC2M 4JP

HODGKINSON, Neville John; s of John Robert Hodgkinson, of Minehead, Somerset, and Joan Evelyn, *née* Tye; *b* 3 Feb 1944; *Educ* Whitgift Sch S Croydon, Univ of Durham; *m* 1965 (m dis 1990), Liz, *née* Garrett; 2 s (Tom b 10 April 1968, Will b 9 Dec 1969); *Career* Chronicle & Journal Newcastle upon Tyne (reporter, sub ed, leader writer) 1965-70, sub ed Daily Telegraph 1970-72, The Times (sub ed, reporter, social policy corr) 1972-77, medical corr Daily Mail 1977-80, freelance writer 1981-85, ed Best of Health Magazine 1985-86, medical corr Sunday Times 1986-89, medical ed Sunday Express 1989-; runner up Reporter of the Year IPC Press Awards 1976; student and lectr in meditation Brahma Kumaris World Spiritual Univ 1981-; *Books* Will to be Well, The Real Alternative Medicine (1984, Spectator Book of the Year); *Recreations* spiritual study, walking; *Style*— Neville Hodgkinson, Esq; Sunday Express, Ludgate House, 245 Blackfriars Road, London SE1 9UX (☎ 071 922 7349, fax 071 922 7964)

HODGKINSON, Paul Richard; s of Peter George Hodgkinson, DL (d 1986), of St Georges House, Lincoln, and Gwyneth Anne, *née* Evans (d 1984); *b* 9 March 1956; *Educ* Lincoln GS, Oxford Poly (BA, DipArch); *m* 13 Oct 1984, Catherine Ann, da of George Giangrande, of New Vernon, New Jersey, USA; 1 s (Christopher Peter); *Career* Shepherd Ipstein & Hunter 1975-76, Capital and Counties plc 1979-81, Simons Design Conslts 1981-86, chm and chief exec Simons Gp Ltd 1986-, gp chm Lincs CBI; tstee Harding House Arts Tst, RIBA 1980, IOD, RSA 1986, ARCUK; *Recreations* squash, cricket, reading, golf, walking, food, opera, skiing; *Style*— Paul Hodgkinson, Esq; Simons Gp Ltd, Beech House, Witham Park, Waterside South, Lincoln LN5 7JP (☎ 0522 514513, fax 0522 513520)

HODGKINSON, (Claude) Peter; s of Claude Harold Hodgkinson, of Stoke-on-Trent, and Gweneth Mary, *née* Cupit; *b* 26 June 1943; *Educ* Ratcliffe Coll Leicester, Manchester Univ (BA); *m* 27 Nov 1974, Julie Margaret Wesley Thompson, of Birmingham; 1 s (Oliver b 1976), 1 da (Sophie b 1982); *Career* dir: Hanley Econ Bldg Soc 1972-, Naybro Stone (Stoke-on-Trent) Ltd 1972-, A G (Plaster) Ltd 1978-, William Boulton Gp plc 1983-, Rose Vale Cement Tile Co Ltd 1984-, Cauldon Gp plc 1987-; FCA 1968; *Recreations* golf, squash; *Clubs* British Pottery Manufacturers Fedn, Trentham Golf; *Style*— Peter Hodgkinson, Esq; Holly Cottage, Maer, Newcastle, Staffs ST5 5EF (☎ 0782 680255); A G (Plaster) Ltd, Unit 19, Reddicap Trading Estate, Coleshill Rd, Sutton Coldfield, W Midlands (☎ 021 329 2874)

HODGKINSON, Simon David; s of Alan Hodgkinson, of Oakham, Leicestershire, and Joan Mary, *née* Hodgkinson; *b* 15 Dec 1962; *Educ* Stamford Sch Lincolnshire, Trent Poly; *Career* rugby player; Nottingham Rugby Club 1981-; ca 260 appearances; 10 caps for England; world record penalties in int match; nat record: points on debut, points in int match, conversions in int match; Midland U15 Cricket; sch master Trent Coll Nottingham, area sales mangr HFS Loans; *Style*— Simon Hodgkinson, Esq; Nottingham RFC, Ireland Ave, Beeston, Nottingham

HODGKISS, Christopher Ian; s of William Morris Hodgkiss, of York, and Sylvia, *née* Dorn; *b* 18 Sept 1961; *Educ* King's Sch Pontefract, York Coll of Art and Design, Liverpool Poly (BA); *Career* advertising exec; art dir Cogent (Cogent Elliott Group) London 1984-, principal accounts worked on incl: Cuprinol Ltd, Milton Keynes Development Corp, Thorntons plc, Vauxhall Motors (Network Q), ICI (Garden Div), Polycell, Pioneer Hi-Fi, Epson (UK) Ltd; *awards* Creative Circle Silver award 1986, D & ADA commendation (for Cuprinol TV commercial) 1988, Silver award and commendation Campaign Poster awards (for Milton Keynes poster) 1990, various DIY awards (for Cuprinol); *Recreations* films, books, theatre, shopping, drinking, collecting; *Style*— Christopher Hodgkiss, Esq; Cogent, 31 Palace Gate, London W8 5LZ (☎ 071 581 5566, fax 071 225 0823)

HODGSON, Alfreda Rose; da of Alfred Hodgson (d 1979), and Rose, *née* McAllister; *b* 7 June 1940; *Educ* Levenshulme HS, Northern Sch of Music Manchester, Graduate Northern Sch of Music; *m* 21 Dec 1963, Paul Frederick Blissett, s of Arthur John Blissett (d 1955); 2 da (Alison Ruth b 1968, Rosemary Anne b 1972); *Career* concert singer (contralto); concert debut with Royal Liverpool Philharmonic Orchestra 1964, Covent Garden debut 1983; has performed with major orchestras throughout the world with: Klemperer, Horenstein, Boult, Barbirolli, Abbado, Britten, Colin Davis, Haitink, Rattle, Mazel; Kathleen Ferrier Meml scholarship 1964, Sir Charles Santley Meml gift Worshipful Co of Musicians 1985; hon fell: Northern Sch of Music 1972, RNCM 1990; LRAM; *Style*— Ms Alfreda Hodgson; 16 St Marys Rd, Prestwich, Manchester M25 5AP (☎ 061 773 1541)

HODGSON, Allan Ferguson; s of Allan Ferguson Hodgson (d 1965), and Catherine, *née* Archibald; *b* 19 May 1945; *Educ* George Heriots Sch, Univ of Edinburgh (MA); *m* 2 July 1969, Irene Devine Finlay, da of John Rennie, of Falkirk; 2 da (Sara Margaret b June 1972, Amanda Catherine (twin)); *Career* economist: Edinburgh Investmt Tst 1967-70, Ivory & Sime 1970-76; jt investmt sec Scottish Widows' Fund 1976-80, md Hodgson Martin Ltd 1980-; govr Edinburgh Coll of Art; memb: Scottish Econ Cncl, Single Market Ctee of Scottish Econ Cncl; *Recreations* golf, jogging, opera, travel, antiquarian books; *Style*— Allan Hodgson, Esq; Hodgson Martin Ltd, 36 George Street, Edinburgh EH2 2LE (☎ 031 226 7644, fax 031 226 7647, telex 727039)

HODGSON, (Arthur) Brian; CMG (1962); s of Maj Arthur Hammond Francis Hodgson (d 1952), and Annie Isabel Wallace, *née* Kidston (d 1973); *b* 24 Aug 1916; *Educ* Eton, Oriel Coll Oxford (MA), Trinity Coll Cambridge; *m* 6 May 1945, Anne Patricia Halse, da of Lt-Col Edward Marlborough Ley, DSO, KRRC (d 1948); 2 s (William Francis Halse b 1 Sept 1947, Paul Edward Brian (twin) b 1 Sept 1947), 2 da (Isabel Ann Ley b 1 March 1951, Odeyne Alison Patricia b 21 Jan 1958); *Career* HM Colonial Serv Tanganyika Territory 1939-63: sr dist cmmr Tanganyika Admin 1956 (dist offr 1939, dist cmmr 1949), perm sec PM Office 1958-62, princ depot tech co-op London 1963; Br Red Cross Soc: sec 1964, asst dir gen 1967, dir gen 1970-75, conslt 1976-81; conslt League of Red Cross Socs Geneva 1981-89; memb: Br Refugee Cncl 1967-81, Appeals Ctee IBA and BBC 1971-75; Steward Henley Royal Regatta; *Recreations* walking, gardening, boating; *Clubs* Leander, Naval; *Style*— Brian Hodgson, Esq, CMG; Chandlers, Furners Green, Nr Uckfield, Sussex TN22 3RH (☎ 0825 790310)

HODGSON, Dr Courtney; s of Lt-Col Gordon Lothian Hodgson (d 1966), and Constance Emily, *née* Catcheside (d 1976); *b* 20 Jan 1929; *Educ* King Edward VI Sch Five Ways Birmingham, Univ of Birmingham (MB ChB, MD); *m* 21 Sept 1957, Thelma Royle, da of Dr John Newton Friend (d 1966); 1 s (Peter John Gordon b 3 May 1970), 1 da (Joy Margaret b 4 Nov 1967); *Career* Capt RAMC 1953-55, RMO 15/19 Kings Royal Hussars 1954-55; res assoc Univ of Pennsylvania USA 1960-61, pt/t memb Med Res Unit For The Experimental Pathology Of The Skin Birmingham 1966-76, conslt dermatologist Birmingham RHA 1966-; MRCS, LRCP 1951, MRCP 1959; memb: RSM 1960, Br Assoc of Dermatologists 1976, BMA, FRCP 1978; *Recreations* tennis, golf; *Clubs* Priory (Edgbaston); *Style*— Dr Courtney Hodgson; 134 Church Rd, Moseley, Birmingham B13 9AA (☎ 021 449 1908); 6 Northumberland St, Alnmouth, Northumbria; Priory Hospital, Priory Rd, Edgbaston, Birmingham B5 7UG (☎ 021 4402323, fax 021 4400804, telex 267335 AMILDN 6)

HODGSON, Gordon Hewett; s of John Lawrence Hodgson (d 1936), and Alice Joan, *née* Wickham (d 1966); *b* 21 Jan 1929; *Educ* Oundle, UCL (LLB); *m* 1958, Pauline Audrey, da of William George Gray (d 1979), of Pinner; 2 s (John, William); *Career* Nat Serv RAEC 1947-49; called to the Bar Middle Temple 1953, in private practice SE circuit 1954-83, asst boundary cmmr 1976-83, asst rec 1979-83; Master of the Supreme Court 1983-; chm Ctee Bentham Club 1990 (memb Ctee 1987); *Recreations* sailing, enjoying Tuscany; *Clubs* East India, Royal Corinthian, Bar Yacht; *Style*— Gordon Hodgson, Esq; Royal Courts of Justice, Strand, London WC1A 2LL (☎ 071 936 6031)

HODGSON, Guy Richard; s of Derek Hodgson, of 8 Lansdowne House, Wilmslow Rd, Manchester, and Doreen, *née* Fish; *b* 15 Dec 1955; *Educ* William Hulme's GS Manchester; *m* 1, 1981 (m dis 1987), Patricia Anne, *née* Sumner; 1 da (Josie Amber b 31 March 1982); m 2, Jennifer Louise, *née* Roberts; 1 da (Charlotte b 20 Jan 1989 d 1989); *Career* sports reporter and golf corr; Cadishead and Irlam Guardian 1974-76, Sale Guardian 1976-78, Birmingham Post 1978-80, BBC 1980-86, Independent 1986-89, Independent on Sunday 1989-; *Recreations* reading, playing golf, football, badminton, music; *Clubs* MCC; *Style*— Guy Hodgson, Esq; 9 St Margarets Place, Bradford-on-Avon, Wiltshire BA15 1DT (☎ 02216 5571); Independent on Sunday, 40 City Rd, London EC1Y 2DB (☎ 071 415 1322)

HODGSON, Howard Osmond Paul; s of Osmond Paul Charles Hodgson (d 1985), and Sheila Mary, *née* Kendrick (now Mrs Baker); *b* 22 Feb 1950; *Educ* Aiglon Coll Villars Switzerland, MBIFD, DipEd, AFFIL, RSH; *m* 12 Aug 1972, Marianne Denise Yvonne, da of Samuel Kaitibien, of Aix-en-Provence, France; 3 s (Howard James Paul b 20 Dec 1973, Charles Alexandre Howard b 11 Jan 1979 d 1982, Jamieson Charles Alexandre Howard b 30 May 1983), 1 da (Davinia Clementine Marianne b 27 June 1990); *Career* asst mangr Hodgson & Sons Ltd 1969-71, life assur exec 1971-75; acquired: Hodgson & Sons 1975 (floated USM 1986), Ingals from House of Fraser 1987; launched Dignity in Destiny Ltd 1989; merger with Pompes Funebres Generales of France, Kenyon Securities and Hodgson Hldgs plc to form PFG Hodgson Kenyon International plc 1989; launched: Bereavement Support Serv 1990, PHKI Nat Trg Sch 1990; Business Magazine top 40 under 40 1986, Sunday Times top dozen 1987, USM Entrepreneur of the Year 1987; hon vice pres Royal Soc of St George; *Recreations* cricket, yachting, skiing, history; *Clubs* RMYC; *Style*— Howard Hodgson, Esq; PFG Hodgson Kenyon International plc, 132-138 Freston Rd, London W10 6TR (☎ 071 727 1257, fax 071 221 3396)

HODGSON, Hon Mrs (Jean Margaret); *née* Brand; er da of 5 Viscount Hampden and sister of 6 Viscount; *b* 19 Aug 1938; *m* 1976, as his 2 w, Robert John Hodgson, only s of John Hodgson; 1 s (Thomas Edward b 1981); *Style*— The Hon Mrs Hodgson; 2 St Hilda's Rd, London SW13 9JQ (☎ 081 748 9689)

HODGSON, Jonathan James; s of John Hodgson, of Sutton Coldfield, and Barbara, *née* Middlemiss; *b* 6 May 1960; *Educ* Park Hall Comp, Solihull Coll of Technol, Liverpool Poly (BA), RCA (MA); *m* Sept 1990, Emma Mary, da of Brian Hubble; *Career* film and video dir; co fndr Unicorn Productions 1985; freelance dir: Barry Joll Associates 1985-88, Practical Pictures 1985-88, Felix Films 1988-90, Bermuda Shorts 1991-; commercials, title sequences and pop videos for clients incl: UN, Brooke Bond, McVities, MTV, Channel 4, BSB, Lambie-Nairn, English-Markell-Pockett Thames TV, Initial TV; films: An Unseen Flight 1980, Dogs (first prize Stuttgart Trickfilmtage) 1981, Experiments In Movement and Line 1981, Night Club (6 int awards) 1983, Menagerie 1984, Train of Thought 1985, The Doomsday Clock (cmmnd by UN) 1987; art work published in European Illustration 1981-; *Recreations* playing violin and guitar in rock group Crawling Kingsnakes; *Style*— Jonathan Hodgson, Esq; 36 Richmond Ave, Barnsbury, London N1 0ND (☎ 071 837 2331, 071 437 7335)

HODGSON, Kenneth; s of Joseph Hodgson (d 1982), and Margaret May, *née* Johnston; *b* 18 Nov 1950; *Educ* St Cuthbert's GS Newcastle, Newcastle Univ; *m* 30 July 1971, Judith Helen, da of Matthew Docherty Brown (d 1986); 2 s (Timothy b 1975, Nicholas b 1977); *Career* chm Caldaire Holdings Ltd 1986-, vice chm W Yorks Metro-Nat Ltd 1984-; dir: Yorks Woollen District Co Ltd 1984-, United Automobile Services Co Ltd 1987-, United Automobile Enterprises Ltd 1987-, Caldaire North East Ltd, Selby & District Co Ltd, Tees & District Ltd, Teesside Motor Services Ltd; *Recreations* theatre, swimming; *Style*— Kenneth Hodgson, Esq; Westgarth, 42 Creskeld Lane, Bramhope, W Yorks; 24 Barnsley Rd, Wakefield WF1 5JX

HODGSON, Sir Maurice Arthur Eric; s of late Walter Hodgson, and Amy, *née* Walker; *b* 21 Oct 1919; *Educ* Bradford GS, Merton Coll Oxford (MA, BSc); *m* 20 March 1945, Norma, da of late Tom Fawcett; 1 s (Howard b 1953), 1 da (Vivien (Mrs Webster) b 1949); *Career* chm: ICI 1978-82 (joined 1942, dep chm 1972-78), BHS 1982-87; non-exec dir Storehouse plc 1985-89; nominated memb Cncl of Lloyd's 1987-; chm: Civil Justice Review Advsy Ctee 1985-88, Dunlop Holdings plc 1984 (resigned 1984, non-exec dir 1982-83), Imperial Chemicals Insurance Ltd 1972-78; memb: Int Cncl Salk Inst 1978-, Cncl CBI 1978-82, Court Univ of Bradford 1979-, Int Advsy Ctee Chase Manhattan Bank 1980-83, President's Ctee The Advertising Assoc 1978-90, Euro Advsy Cncl Air Products and Chemicals Inc 1982-84, Int Advsy Bd AMAX Inc 1982-85; govr London Graduate Sch of Business Studies 1978-87; visiting fell Sch of Business and Organisational Studies Univ of Lancaster 1970-; hon fell Merton Coll Oxford 1979, hon fell UMIST; pres Merton Soc 1986-89; Hon DTech Univ of Bradford, Hon DUniv Heriot-Watt, Hon DSc Univ of Loughborough; Messel medal Soc of Chemical Indust 1980, George E Davis medal IChemE 1982; FEng 1979, FIChemE 1964, CChem 1978, FRSC 1978; kt 1979; *Recreations* racing, swimming; *Clubs* RAC; *Style*— Sir Maurice Hodgson; Suite 75/76, Kent House, 87 Regent Street, London W1R 7HF (☎ 071 734 7777)

HODGSON, Michael Patrick Sanford (Mick); s of Arthur Geoffrey Sanford Hodgson, MBE, of Geerings, Warnham, Horsham, W Sussex, and Sheila Beatrice, *née* Sheppard; *b* 19 April 1946; *Educ* Eton, Univ of London (BSc); *m* 21 Jan 1977, Gytha Margaret Kerr, JP, da of Gerald Lawrence Clarke, of Chesterley, Swanage; 2 s (Benjamin Gerald Sanford b 21 Jan 1978, Roger Geoffrey Sanford b 25 Nov 1983), 1 da (Erica Sarah b 21 Feb 1980); *Career* ptnr Edward Erdman Surveyors 1977-; chm Warnham Parish Cncl; Freeman City of London 1968, Liveryman Worshipful Co of Vintners 1973; ARICS 1969; *Recreations* skiing; *Style*— Mick Hodgson, Esq; Old Manor, Warnham, Horsham, West Sussex RH12 3SN (☎ 0403 65069); 6 Grosvenor St, London W1 (☎ 071 629 8191, fax 071 409 3124, telex 28169)

HODGSON, Patricia Anne; da of Harold Hodgson, of Brentwood, Essex, and Lilian Mary, *née* Smith; *b* 19 Jan 1947; *Educ* Brentwood Co High, Newnham Coll Cambridge (MA); *m* 23 July 1979, George Edward Donaldson, s of Edward George Donaldson, of Donington-le-Heath, Leics; 1 s; *Career* Cons Res Dept 1968-70; prodr for Open Univ BBC (specialising in history and philosophy) 1970, freelance journalist and broadcaster in UK and USA, with BBC secretariat 1982-83 (dep sec 1983-85, sec 1985-87), head of Policy and Planning Unit 1987-; TV series incl: English Urban History 1978, Conflict in Modern Europe 1980, Rome in the Age of Augustus 1981; chm Bow Group 1975-76, ed Crossbow 1976-80; memb London Electricity Consultative Cncl 1981-83; dir BARB 1987-; *Recreations* quietness; *Clubs* The Reform; *Style*— Miss Patricia Hodgson; BBC Broadcasting House, Portland Place, London W1 (☎ 071 927 4974, fax 071 436 0393, telex 265 781)

HODGSON, Peter Barrie; s of Clive Ward (d 1980), and Gladys Stewart, *née* Ross (d 1983); *b* 12 March 1942; *Educ* Clayesmore Sch, St Peter's Coll Oxford (BA); *m* 10 Feb 1973, Audrone Ona, da of Jonas Grudzinskas, of Sydney, Australia; 1 s (Lindsay

Matthew Oliver b 3 Aug 1977); *Career* dir: Opinion Res Centre 1973-75, Professional Studies Ltd 1975-77; md: Professional Studies Ireland 1977, Action Research Ltd 1977-78; chm and md Travel and Tourism Research Ltd 1978-, dir City Research Associates Ltd 1981-89; chm Assoc of Br Market Res Cos 1987-89; memb: Cncl Market Res Soc 1978-81, Tourism Soc 1981-84; fndr memb Social Res Assoc; fell: Tourism Soc 1980, Inst of Travel and Tourism; memb: Market Res Society, Euro Soc for Opinion & Marketing Res; published articles in: Marketing, Jl of the Market Res Soc, Jl of the Prof Mktg Res Soc of Canada, Tourism Management; *Recreations* opera, wine, travel; *Style*— Peter Hodgson, Esq; Travel and Tourism Research Ltd, 39c Highbury Place, London N5 1QP (☎ 071 354 3391, fax 071 359 4043, 262433 MONREF G 1148)

HODGSON, Peter Gerald Pearson; s of Thomas William Hodgson, of Elloughton, North Humberside, and Edna, *née* Pearson; *b* 13 July 1934; *Educ* Reade Sch Yorks, Hull Univ (BSc), Imperial Coll London (DIC); *m* 30 Sept 1956, Noreen, da of Albert James Warnes, of Byfleet, Surrey; 2 s (Michael Charles Peter b 1966, John Paul Richard b 1967); *Career* chm: Petrocon Gp plc 1963-89 (chief exec 1963-88), Richards Gp plc 1988-; MICheme 1965, FInstPet (1968); *Recreations* golf, horse racing (owner); *Clubs* MCC, RAC; *Style*— Peter Hodgson, Esq; Richards Group plc, 33 Lionel St, Birmingham B3 1AP (☎ 021 233 4566, fax 021 233 3095)

HODGSON, Peter John Dixon; OBE (1979); s of John Dixon Hodgson, of Manaton, Launceston, Cornwall, and Dorothy Blanche, *née* Saunders; *b* 21 March 1947; *Educ* Charterhouse; *m* 18 July 1970, Cecilia Anne, da of Brig Arnold de Lerisson Cazenove, CBE, DSO, MVO (d 1969); 2 s (James b 1973, Timothy b 1975), 1 da (Charlotte b 1977); *Career* CA; chm Fin Ctee Red Cross Cornwall, hon treas Western Provincial Area Nat Union of Cons and Unionist Assocs; FCA 1970; *Recreations* gardening, fishing; *Style*— Peter Hodgson, Esq, OBE; Manaton, Launceston, Cornwall PL15 9JE (☎ 0566 772880); John D Hodgson, 12 Southgate St, Launceston, Cornwall PL15 9DP (☎ 0566 772177)

HODGSON, (Adam) Robin; s of Thomas Edward Highton Hodgson, CB (d 1985), and Emily Catherine Hodgson; *b* 20 March 1937; *Educ* William Ellis Sch London, Worcester Coll Oxford (MA); *m* 1962, Elizabeth Maureen Linda, da of Vernon Gordon Fitzell Bovenizer, CMG, of Cambridge; 1 s (Harvey b 1971), 2 da (Kate b 1968, Amy b 1972); *Career* admitted slr 1964, asst slr LCC and GLC 1964-66, sr asst slr Oxfordshire CC 1966-71, asst clerk Northamptonshire CC 1972-74, dep co sec East Sussex CC 1974-77, dep chief exec and clerk Essex CC 1977-85, chief exec Hampshire CC 1985-; *Recreations* music, drama, geology; *Clubs* Law Soc; *Style*— Robin Hodgson, Esq; Tara, Dean Lane, Winchester S022 5RA (☎ 0962 62119); The Castle, Winchester SO23 8UJ (☎ 0962 841841)

HODGSON, Robin Granville; s of Henry Edward Hodgson, of Astley Abbotts, Bridgnorth, Shropshire, and Natalie Beatrice, *née* Davidson; *b* 25 April 1942; *Educ* Shrewsbury, Oxford Univ (BA), Wharton Sch Univ of Pennsylvania (MBA); *m* 8 May 1982, Fiona Ferelith, da of Keith Storr Allom; 3 s (Barnaby Peter Granville b 1986, James Maxwell Gower (twin) b & d 1986, Toby Henry Storr b 1988), 1 da (Poppy Ferelith Alice b 1990); *Career* Lt 4 Bn Kings Shrops LI TA 1960-64; md Granville & Co (investmt bankers) 1972-, chm Nasdim 1979-85, dir Securities & Investmt Bd 1985-89; non-exec chm: Spotcannel plc, Walter Alexander plc, Dominic Hunter plc; memb West Midland Industl Devpt Bd 1988-; treas Cons Party West Midlands Area 1985-, MP (C) Walsall North 1976-79, memb Exec Ctee Nat Union of Cons Assocs 1988-; tstee Friends of Shrewsbury Sch; Liveryman Worshipful Co of Goldsmiths; *Style*— Robin Hodgson, Esq; Astley Abbotts, Bridgnorth, Shropshire (☎ 074 623 122); 15 Scarsdale Villas, London W8 (☎ 071 937 2964); Granville & Co, Mint House, 77 Mansell Street, London E1 8AF (☎ 071 488 1212, fax 071 481 3911, telex 8814 884 GVILCO G)

HODGSON, Stuart Henry; s of Henry Stockdale Hodgson, and Edith, *née* Vickers; *b* 16 April 1935; *Educ* Lancaster Royal GS, Ermysteds Sch Skipton; *m* 7 Jan 1959 (m dis 1991), (Doreen) June, da of Lawrence Packham (d 1985), of Bolton le Sands, Lancs; 2 da (Linzi Jane (Mrs Bridson) b 19 April 1959, Amanda (Mrs Wrench) b 11 Sept 1961); *Career* Nat Serv RAF 1953-55; press photographer Westminster Press, advertisement mangr Utd Newspapers (Lancaster), pharmaceutical mktg Lederle Laboratories London, founded Porton Group of Cos 1970 (ret 1990), chm Bd St Martins in the Field Enterprises Ltd; city cncllr Scotforth Ward Lancaster City 1964-69; memb IPA; *Recreations* motor sport (historic racing), tennis, golf; *Style*— Stuart Hodgson, Esq; Cedars, Broadwater Close, Burwood Park, Walton-on-Thames, Surrey KT12 5DD (☎ 0932 232341)

HODGSON, Ven Thomas Richard Burnham; s of Richard Shillito Hodgson (d 1949), of Kendal, Westmorland, and Marion Thomasena Bertram, *née* Marshall (d 1974); *b* 17 Aug 1926; *Educ* Heversham GS, Univ of London, London Coll of Divinity (BD, ALCD); *m* 1952, Margaret Esther, da of Evan Makinson (d 1964), of Cumberland; 1 s (Richard Nicholas b 1954), 1 da (Rachel Margaret b 1957); *Career* ordained: deacon 1952, priest 1953; curate: Crosthwaite 1952-55, Stanwix 1955-59; vicar St Nicholas Whitehaven 1959-65, rector Aikton 1965-67, vicar Raughton Head 1967-73, domestic chaplain to Bishop of Carlisle 1967-73, dir of ordinands 1970-74, surrogate 1962-, hon canon of Carlisle 1972-, vicar of Grange-over-Sands 1972-79, rural dean of Windermere 1976-79, archdeacon West Cumberland 1979-, vicar of Mosser 1979-83; memb Carlisle Diocesan Bd of Fin; FRMetS; *Recreations* meteorology, geology, listening to music, vegetable gardening; *Style*— The Ven the Archdeacon of West Cumberland; Moorside, 50 Stainburn Road, Workington, Cumbria CA14 1SN (☎ 0900 66190)

HODIN, Prof (Josef) Paul; s of Edvard David Hodin (d 1942), of Prague, and Rosa Rachel, *née* Klug; *b* 17 Aug 1905; *Educ* Kleinseitner Realschule Prague, Neustädter Realgymnasium Prague, Charles Univ Prague (LLD), Dresden Art Acad, College de France Paris, Courtauld Inst London; *m* 1 (m dis), Birgit, *née* Akesson, of Stockholm; m 2, 22 May 1944, Doris Pamela, da of George W Simms, of Kuala Lumpur and Cornwall; 1 s (Michael b 1946), 1 da (Annabelle b 1948); *Career* author, art historian and critic; press attaché to Norwegian Govt London 1944-45; dir of studies and librarian ICA London 1949-54; hon memb Editorial Cncl Journal of Aesthetics and Art Criticism Cleveland 1955, memb Exec Ctee Editorial Consultative Ctee Br Soc of Aesthetics 1960-, pres Br section Int Assoc of Art Critics 1974-75, memb Int PEN; co ed: Prisme des Arts Paris 1956-59, Quadrum Brussels 1956-66; int dir: Rels Studio Int, Journal of Modern Art London 1965-75; winner first int prize for art criticism Biennale Venice 1954; Hon PhD Uppsala Univ 1969, Hon Prof Austria; DSM first class Czechoslovakia 1947, Cavaliere Ufficiale Italy 1956, St Olav Medal Norway 1958, Cdr OM Italy 1966, Grand Cross OM Austria 1968, OM first class Germany 1969, Silver Cross of Merit Vienna 1972, Grand Cross of the Order of Merit West Germany 1986; *Books* Monographs on Sven Erixson (1940), Ernst Josephson (1942), Edvard Munch (1948), Isaac Grünewald (1949), Art and Criticism (1944), J A Comenius and Our Time (1944), The Dilemma of Being Modern (1956), Henry Moore (1956), Ben Nicholson (1957), Barbara Hepworth (1961), Lynn Chadwick (1961), Alan Reynolds (1962), Bekenntnis zu Kokoschka (1963), Edvard Munch, Der Genius des Nordens (1963), Kokoschka The Artist and His Work (1966), Der Maler Walter Kern (1966), The Painter Ruszkowski (1967), Bernard Leach A Potter's Work (1967), Kokoschka Sein Leben, seine Zeit (1968), Kafka und Goethe (1968), Giacomo Manzu (1969), Emilio Greco His Life and Work (1970), Die Brühlsche Terrasse, Ein Künstler Roman (1970), The Painter Alfred Manessier (1971), Kokoschka, The Psychography of an Artist (1971), Edvard Munch (1972), Modern Art and the Modern Mind (1972), Bernard Stern, Paintings and Drawings (1972), Hilde Goldschmidt (1973), Ludwig Meidner (1973), Paul Berger-Bergner (1974), Die Leute von Elverdingen, Erzählung (1974), Kokoschka and Hellas (1976), Alfred Aberdam (1977), John Milne (1977), Else Meidner (1978), Elisabeth Frink (1981), Douglas Portway (1981), Franz Luby (1981), Mary Newcomb (1984), Dieses Mütterchen hat Krallen, Die Geschichte einer Prager Jugend (1986), FK Gotsch (1986), Verlorene Existenzen, Erzählungen (1987), Der Künstler Jan Brazda (1989), Manzu Pittore (1989); *Recreations* travel, reading; *Clubs* Athenaeum, Arts; *Style*— Prof Paul Hodin; 12 Eton Ave, London NW3 3EH (☎ 071 794 3609)

HODKINSON, James Clifford; s of John Eric Thomas Hodkinson (d 1985), of Ferndown, Dorset, and Edith Lilian, *née* Lord; *b* 21 April 1944; *Educ* Salesian Coll Farnborough Hants; *m* 8 Feb 1968, Janet Patricia, da of George William Lee (d 1941); 1 da (Justine b 30 April 1970); *Career* trainee mangr F W Woolworth 1962-71; B & Q plc: mangr Bournemouth Store 1971-74, sales mangr in South 1974-79, ops dir 1979-84, ops and personnel dir 1984-86, chief exec 1986-; memb Bd Nat Steering Ctee to Advsy Cncl Prince's Youth Business Tst; dir Nat Home Improvement Cncl; FInstD, CBIM; *Recreations* golf, shooting; *Style*— James Hodkinson, Esq; B & Q plc, Portswood House, Hampshire Corporate Park, Chandlers Ford, Eastleigh SO5 3YX (☎ 0703 256 256, fax 0703 256 030)

HODKINSON, Prof (Henry) Malcolm; s of Charles Hodkinson (d 1986), of Mossley, Lancs, and Olive, *née* Kennerley (d 1988); *b* 28 April 1931; *Educ* Manchester GS, Brasenose Coll Oxford (BA, BM BCh, MA, DM), Middx Hosp Med Sch (MRCP); *m* 1, 2 Jan 1956 (m dis 1980), Elaine Margaret, *née* Harris; 4 da (Sarah b 1958, Isabel b 1960, Ruth b 1965, Naomi b 1967); m 2, 22 Nov 1986, Judith Marie, *née* Bryant; *Career* conslt geriatrician N Middx and St Ann's Gen Hosps London 1962-70, conslt geriatrician and memb MRC scientific staff Northwick Park Hosp and Clinical Res Centre Harrow Middx 1970-78, sr lectr in geriatric med Royal Postgrad Med Sch Hammersmith Hosp 1978-79 (prof of geriatric med 1979-84), Barlow prof of geriatric med Univ Coll and Middx Sch of med UCL 1985-; govr Res into Ageing; Yeoman Worshipful Soc of Apothecaries; FRCP 1974; *Books* An Outline of Geriatrics (several edns, 1975-84), Common symptoms of disease in the elderly (several edns, 1976-83), Biochemical diagnosis in the elderly (1977), Clinical Biochemistry of the Elderly (1984); *Recreations* British glass and ceramics; *Style*— Prof Malcolm Hodkinson; 8 Chiswick Sq, Burlington Lane, Chiswick, London W4 2QG (☎ 081 747 0239); Dept of Geriatric Med, Univ Coll and Middx Sch of Med, UCL St Pancras Hosp, St Pancras Way, London NW1 0PE (☎ 081 387 4411)

HODKINSON, Paul James; s of Francis Raymond Hodkinson, of 4 Mintor Rd, Northwood, Kirkby, Merseyside, and Patricia Ann, *née* Fergus; *b* 14 Sept 1965; *Educ* St Kevin's Comp; *m* has issue, 2 s (Kevin James Walsh, Jason Walsh); *Career* professional boxer (featherweight); Br Champion 18 May 1988 (defended 14 Dec 1988), Euro Champion 12 April 1989 (defended 13 Dec 1989), won Lonsdale Belt outright 6 Sept 1989 (for defence of Br and Euro Championships), unsuccessful challenge World Boxing Cncl title 2 June 1990, further defence of Euro title 13 Oct 1990; record to date: fights 20, won 18, drawn 1, lost 1; Boxer of the Year award 1990, Dave Crawley Belt; *Style*— Paul Hodkinson, Esq; 4 Mintor Rd, Northwood, Kirkby, Merseyside (☎ 051 546 8280)

HODSON, Hon (Charles) Christopher Philip; s of Baron Hodson, MC, PC (Life Peer, d 1984); *b* 1922; *m* 1953, Rose (d 1986), da of Sir Charles Markham, 2 Bt; 1 s, 3 da; *Style*— The Hon Christopher Hodson; Stoney Hall, Hannington, Hants

HODSON, Daniel Houghton; s of Henry Vincent Hodson, of 105 Lexham Gdns, London, and Margaret Elizabeth, *née* Honey; *b* 11 March 1944; *Educ* Eton, Merton Coll Oxford (MA); *m* 22 Feb 1979, Diana Mary, da of Christopher Breen Ryde, of Middleton-on-Sea, W Sussex; 2 da (Susannah Fleur b 1980, Emma Katharine b 1982); *Career* Chase Manhattan Bank NA 1965-73, dir Edward Bates & Sons Ltd 1974-76 (joined 1973), gp fin dir Unigate plc 1981-87 (gp treas 1976-81), pres Unigate Inc 1986-87; dir: Girobank plc 1986-89, GT Symons (Holdings) Ltd 1990-; chm Davidson Pearce Group plc 1988 (chief exec 1987-88); dep chief exec and gp fin dir Nationwide Anglia Building Society 1989-, pt/t memb Bd Post Office Corporation 1984-, exec ed Corporate Finance and Treasury Management 1984-, vice pres Assoc of Corporate Treasurers 1990- (chm 1984-86), dep chief exec and gp fin dir Nationwide Anglia Building Soc 1989-; chm Fulham Carnival 1979-81, govr The Yehudi Menuhin Sch 1984-; memb Worshipful Co of Mercers 1965; FCT 1979; *Books* Businessman's Guide to the Foreign Exchange Market (jtly); *Recreations* music, travel, skiing, gardening; *Clubs* Brooks's; *Style*— Daniel Hodson, Esq; Treyford Manor, Midhurst, W Sussex GU29 OLD (☎ 073 0825 436); Nationwide Anglia Building Society, Chesterfield House, Bloomsbury Way, London WC1V 5PW

HODSON, His Hon Judge; His Hon (Thomas) David Tattersall; s of Thomas Norman Hodson (d 1987), and Elsie Nuttall Hodson (d 1987); *b* 24 Sept 1942; *Educ* Sedbergh, Univ of Manchester (LLB); *m* 9 Aug 1969, Patricia Ann, da of Robert Arthur Vint (d 1967); 2 s (Nicholas b 1970, Benjamin b 1979), 1 da (Philippa b 1972); *Career* leader writer The Yorkshire Post 1964-65, called to the Bar Inner Temple 1966, in practice Northern Circuit 1966-87 (jr 1968), rec Crown Court 1983-87, circuit judge 1987-; *Recreations* music, fell-walking, family history; *Clubs* Lancs CC; *Style*— His Hon Judge Hodson; c/o The Crown Court, Courts of Justice, Crown Square, Manchester (☎ 061 832 8393)

HODSON, Denys Fraser; CBE (1982); s of Rev Harold Victor Hodson, MC (d 1977), of Gloucestershire, and Marguerite Edmée, *née* Ritchie; *b* 23 May 1928; *Educ* Marlborough, Trinity Coll Oxford (MA); *m* 1954, Julie Compton, da of Harold Goodwin (d 1984), of Warwicks; 1 s (Nicolas b 1965), 1 da (Lucy b 1963); *Career* dir arts and recreation Thamesdown Borough Cncl 1970; chm: Southern Arts Assoc 1975-81 and 1985-87, Cncl Regnl Arts Assoc 1976-81, dir Oxford Playhouse Co 1974-86, govr Br Film Inst 1976-87, memb Arts Cncl GB 1987- (vice chm 1989-); *Recreations* arts, fishing, bird watching; *Style*— Denys Hodson, Esq, CBE; Manor Farm House, Fairford, Gloucestershire GL7 4AR (☎ 0285 712642); Arts and Recreation Gp, Civic Office, Euclid Street, Swindon, Wiltshire SN1 2JH (☎ 0793 493170)

HODSON, Geoffrey Allan; s of Capt Allan C Hodson, and Hylda, *née* Taylor; *b* 26 Nov 1947; *Educ* Emmanuel Coll Cambridge (MA), Harvard Business Sch (MBA); *m* 29 July 1972, Bridget Elizabeth, da of Cyril D Deans (d 1987); 1 s (James b 1978), 1 da (Sarah Louise b 1975); *Career* ICI 1970-72, conslt McKinsey & Co 1974-76, asst chief of staff Triad Holding Corporation 1976-78, vice-pres Bankers Trust International Ltd 1978-82, md mergers and acquisitions Merrill Lynch International & Co 1982-; *Recreations* photography, ornithology, railways, rowing; *Style*— Geoffrey Hodson, Esq; Kilmory, Guildford Road, Cranleigh, Surrey GU6 8LT (☎ 0483 276200); Merrill Lynch International & Co, Ropemaker Place, 25 Ropemaker Street, London EC2Y 9LY (☎ 071 867 4865)

HODSON, Sir Michael Robin Adderley; 6 Bt (I 1787), of Holybrooke House, Wicklow; s of Maj Sir Edmond Adair Hodson, 5 Bt, DSO (d 1972); *b* 5 March 1932;

Educ Eton; *m* 1, 16 Dec 1963 (m dis 1978), Katrin Alexa, da of late Erwin Bernstiel, of St Andrew's House, St Andrew's Major, Dinas Powis, Glam; 3 da; m 2, 1978, Catherine, da of John Henry Seymour; *Heir* bro, Patrick Hodson; *Career* Capt (ret) Scots Gds; *Style*— Sir Michael Hodson, Bt; The White House, Awbridge, Romsey, Hants

HODSON, Patrick Richard; s of Maj Sir Edmond Adair Hodson, 5 Bt, DSO (d 1972), and hp of bro, Sir Michael Robin Adderley Hodson, 6 Bt; *b* 27 Nov 1934; *Educ* Eton; *m* 1961, June, da of H M Shepherd-Cross, of The Old Rectory, Brandsby, Yorks; 3 s; *Career* Capt (ret) Rifle Bde; *Style*— Patrick Hodson, Esq; Shipton Slade Farm, Woodstock, Oxford

HODSON, Philip; s of Kenneth David Hodson, of Peterborough, and Freda Margaret, *née* Reedman; *b* 2 Oct 1944; *Educ* Oundle, St Edmund Hall Oxford (MA); *m* 3 Aug 1968, Diane Elizabeth, da of Sydney Farrar Stansfield, of Peterborough; *Career* admitted slr 1969; slr Manchester CC 1969-73, ptnr Cobbett Leak Almond 1974-; chm Manchester Young Slrs Assoc 1980, treas S Manchester Law Centre Mgmnt Ctee 1982-88 (chm 1988-89); pres Manchester Law Soc 1988-89; memb: Slr Disciplinary Tbnl 1989-, Salford Playhouse Mgmnt Ctee 1989-; *Recreations* squash, golf, theatre; *Clubs* St James's; *Style*— Philip Hodson, Esq; 12 Stafford Rd, Eccles, Manchester M30 9HW (☎ 061 789 6756); Cobbett Leak Almond, Ship Canal House, King St, Manchester M2 4WB (☎ 061 833 3333, fax 061 833 3030)

HODSON-PRESSINGER, Selwyn Philip; s of Thomas Hodson-Pressinger (d 1961), and Pamela, Lady Torphichen, *née* Howard Snow, who m 1973 as 3 w, 14 Lord Torphichen (d 1975); *b* 9 Dec 1954; *Educ* Ludgrove, Downside, Aix-en-Provence Univ; *Career* mgmnt conslt; MBIM; *Recreations* history, deer-stalking; *Clubs* Turf; *Style*— Selwyn P Hodson-Pressinger, Esq; 69 Cornwall Gardens, London SW7 (☎ 071 938 4009)

HOERNER, John Lee; s of Robert Lee Hoerner (d 1990), and Lulu Alice, *née* Stone, of St Louis, Missouri; *b* 23 Sept 1939; *Educ* Univ of Nebraska (BS, BA); *m* 1, 9 Aug 1959 (m dis 1971), Susan Kay, da of Fred W Morgan, of Lincoln, Nebraska; 1 s (John Scott b 30 May 1960), 1 da (Joanne Lynne b 21 Sept 1962); m 2, 16 Feb 1973, Anna Lea, da of Leonard O Thomas, of Kansas City, Missouri; *Career* Hovland-Swanson Lincoln Nebraska: trainee 1959-60, buyer 1960-62, merchandise mangr 1962-65, sr vice pres 1965-68; gen merchandise mangr: Woolf Brothers Kansas City Missouri 1968-72, Hahnes New Jersey 1972-73; pres and chief exec offr First 21st Century Corporation McLean Virginia; Hahnes NJ: gen merchandising mangr 1974-76, dir of stores/ops 1976-78, sr vice pres 1979-81; Associated Dry Goods Corporation/May Company: chm and chief exec H & S Pogue Co Cincinnati Ohio 1981-82, chm & chief exec LS Ayres & Co Indianapolis Indiana 1982-87; The Burton Group plc: chm Debenhams 1987-, chm Harvey Nichols 1988-, chief exec stores 1989, exec dir 1989-; former memb Bd of Dirs: Indianapolis C of C, Indianapolis Symphony; *Books* Ayres Adages (1983); *Recreations* riding, flying; *Clubs* Queen City (Cincinnati), Woodstock (Indianapolis), Indianapolis University; *Style*— John Hoerner, Esq; Debenhams, 1 Welbeck St, London W1A 1DF (☎ 071 927 3573, fax 071 493 0643)

HOFFBRAND, Prof (Allan) Victor; s of Philip Hoffbrand (d 1959), of Bradford, Yorks, and Minnie, *née* Freedman; *b* 14 Oct 1935; *Educ* Bradford GS, The Queen's Coll Oxford (MA, DM), London Hosp (BM BCh); *m* 3 Nov 1963, (Irene) Jill, da of Michael Mellows, of Wembley Park, Middx; 2 s (Philip b 11 May 1967, David b 12 July 1970), 1 da (Caroline b 21 March 1966); *Career* jr hosp doctor London Hosp 1960-62, lectr in haematology St Bart's Hosp 1966-67, MRC res scholar Tufts Univ Boston 1967-68, lectr and sr lectr in haematology Royal Postgrad Med Sch 1968-74 (registrar and res fell 1962-66), prof of haematology Royal Free Sch of Med 1974-; DSc 1987; hon FRCP (Ed) 1986, FRCP 1976, FRCPath 1980; *Books* Essential Haematology (jtly 1980, 2 edn 1984), Clinics in Haematology (ed 1976, 2 edn 1986), Clinical Haematology Illustrated (jtly, 1988), Recent Advances in Haematology (ed, 5 edn 1988), Sandoz Atlas: Clinical Haematology (jtly, 1988), Postgraduate Haematology (jt ed, 3 edn 1989); *Recreations* squash, chess, bridge, antiques, music; *Style*— Prof Victor Hoffbrand; 57 Camden Square, London NW1 9XE (☎ 071 485 6984); Department of Haematology, Royal Free Hosp, London NW3 2QG (☎ 071 794 0500 ext 3258)

HOFFMAN, Anthony Edward; s of Geoffrey Hoffman, and Jean Hoffman; *b* 21 Feb 1937; *Educ* City of London Sch; *m* 1, 1960 (m dis 1964); m 2, 1967 (m dis 1984); 3 da (Anna b 1968, Sofie b 1969, Kate b 1971); *Career* admitted slr 1960; sole practitioner Joelson & Co (now Joelson Wilson) 1962 (jr ptnr 1960), sr ptnr following amalgamation with Hamlin Brown Veale and Twyford 1968, acquired MA Jacobs & Co, merged with Southall & Knight 1981 and with Slowes 1984 to form Hamlin Slowe, merged with H Davis & Co 1987, merged with Jocabson Ridley 1990; memb Law Soc; *Recreations* walking, shooting, fishing; *Style*— Anthony Hoffman, Esq; PO Box 4SQ, Roxburghe House, 273-287 Regent St, London W1A 4SQ (☎ 071 629 1209)

HOFFMAN, George Henry; s of George Hoffman, of USA, and Anna Cecilia, *née* Hojnowski; *b* 30 Oct 1939; *Educ* Cornell Univ (BA), Columbia Univ (MA); *m* 1961, Pauline Margaret, da of Gilbert R Lewis, of London; 1 s (Philip b 1968), 2 da (Erika b 1962, Bridgit b 1965); *Career* chm and chief exec Hoffman Assocs Ltd, non-exec dir Wittmann Design Ltd; dir American C of C UK 1984-, chm Euro Affrs Ctee 1986-; *Recreations* tennis, skiing, photography; *Clubs* Les Ambassadeurs, Gravetye; *Style*— George Hoffman; Ranvers House, The Haven, Billingshurst, West Sussex RH14 9BS (☎ 0403 822860, fax 0403 823338)

HOFFMAN, Mark; s of Dr Mark Hoffman (d 1975), of USA; *b* 14 Dec 1938; *Educ* Harvard Coll (AB), Trinity Coll Cambridge (MA), Harvard Business Sch (MBA); *m* 1968, Mary Jo, da of John C Pyles, of Washington DC, USA; 3 s (Nicholas b 1969, John b 1972, James b 1978); *Career* East African Common Services Orgn/MIT (Africa/USA) 1964-66, World Banks Int Finance Corp (Washington) 1966-68, Olympic Investmt Gp (Paris) 1968-69; dir: Hambros Bank (UK) 1970-74, Millipore Corpn (USA) 1975-, George Weston Ltd (Canada) 1975- (fin dir 1975-80, pres Weston Resources 1980-82), Guinness Peat Gp plc (UK) 1982-84 (gp md 1982-83), LAC Minerals (Canada) 1984-86; princ: Hamilton Lunn Ltd (UK) 1988-, Advent Int Inc (Boston) 1989-, Guinness Flight Global Asset Mgmnt Ltd (UK) 1989-; chm: Int Financial Markets Trading Ltd (UK) 1984-, Cambridge Capital Limited 1990-; dir Harvard Alumui Assoc 1989-, chm Oxford and Cambridge Rowing Fndn 1990-; *Clubs* Boodle's, Leander, (Henley-on-Thames (chm)), Harvard Club of London (pres), Utd Oxford and Cambridge Univ, Hawks', Guards' Polo, Toronto, Royal Canadian Yacht; *Style*— Mark Hoffman, Esq; 21 Campden Hill Square, London W8; 1 Finsbury Avenue, London EC2M 2PA; Estabrook Woods, Concord, Mass, USA

HOFFMAN, Michael Richard; s of Sydney William Hoffman, of Letchworth, Herts, and Ethel Margaret Hoffman (d 1978); *b* 31 Oct 1939; *Educ* Hitchin GS, Univ of Bristol (BSc); *m* 1, 1963, Margaret Edith; 1 da (Rachel); m 2, 1982, Helen Judith; *Career* chm Perkins Engines Ltd, pres Farm and Industl Machinery Div Massey Ferguson Toronto; chief exec: Thames Water 1988-, Airship Industries Ltd 1987-88 (dep chm 1989-); md Babcock Int plc 1983-87, dep chm Cosworth Engrg Ltd 1988-; memb: Monopolies & Mergers Cmmn 1988-, Cncl Brunel Univ 1984; BOTB; *Recreations* shooting, sailing, real tennis; *Clubs* RAC, Reform, MCC; *Style*— Michael Hoffman, Esq; 43 De Vere Gardens, London W8 5AW (☎ 071 581 4612); 4 St Marks Mews, Leamington Spa, Warwicks CV32 6EJ (☎ 0926 429643)

HOFFMAN, His Hon Judge Paul Maxim Laurence; s of Gerard Hoffman (d 1985), and Laura Hoffman; *b* 29 July 1942; *Educ* Roundhay Boys Sch, Sheffield Univ (LLB); *m* 1 (m dis); 3 s (Oliver b 1970, Simon b 1971, Adam b 1974); m 2, 9 July 1989, Elaine Bailey King; *Career* called to the Bar Lincoln's Inn 1964, standing prosecuting counsel Inland Revenue NE Circuit 1985-91, rec 1985-91; circuit judge (North Eastern Circuit) 1991-; *Recreations* music, gardening, walking; *Style*— His Honour Judge Hoffman; 25 Park Square, Leeds

HOFFMAN, Thomas; s of Dirk Hoffman (d 1986), of Cambridge, and Marie-Luise, *née* Leyser; *b* 9 Aug 1945; *Educ* The Leys Sch Cambridge, Univ of Exeter (LLB); *m* June 1971, Verena; 1 s (Alexander b 1975); *Career* CA; Spicer & Oppenheim 1963-70, Arthur Andersen & Co 1970-71, Williams & Glyn's Bank 1971-76, Hill Samuel & Co Ltd 1976-78, dir capital mkts Lloyds Bank Int 1978-84, dep md Fuji Int Fin 1984-89, head of corporate banking in UK Algemene Bank Nederland NV 1989-; govr Corp of the Sons of the Clergy; hon treas Ward of Cordwainer Club London 1985-, memb Anglo Netherlands Soc 1990; Liveryman Worshipful Co of Tylers & Bricklayers; Fell Royal Cwlth Soc 1964, FCA 1971, memb Royal Society for Asian Affairs 1989, FRSA 1990; various articles in professional journals; *Recreations* gardening, opera, 17th century choral music; *Clubs* City Livery, Royal Cwlth; *Style*— Thomas Hoffman, Esq; Old Curteis, Biddenden, Ashford, Kent; 72 Gainsford St, Tower Bridge Sq, London SE1; 61 Threadneedle St, London EC2

HOFFMAN, Walter Max; s of Bernard Hoffman (d 1944), and Paula Kirschberger (d 1944); *b* 27 Sept 1929; *Educ* Manchester GS, Univ of Manchester (BA); *m* (Renate) Shoshanah, da of Max Plaut; *Career* trained as chartered accountant, qualified taking first place ICAEW final examination 1953, inspector under Companies Act to investigate Barlow Cloves affair; FCA (ACA 1953); *Recreations* theatre, music and travel; *Clubs* Athenaeum; *Style*— Walter Hoffman, Esq; Baker Tilly, Chartered Accountants, 2 Bloomsbury St, London WC1B 3ST (☎ 071 413 5100, fax 071 413 5101)

HOFMEYR, Stephen Murray; s of late Jan Murray Hofmeyr, of Cape Town, and Stella Mary, *née* Mills; *b* 10 Feb 1956; *Educ* Diocesan Coll Rondesbosch, Univ of Cape Town (BCom, LLB), Univ Coll Oxford (MA); *m* 28 June 1980, Audrey Frances, da of James Murray Cannan, of Cape Town; 2 s (Timothy b 6 July 1986, Paul (triplet) b 6 July 1986), 1 da (Rebecca (triplet) b 6 July 1986); *Career* called to the Bar Gray's Inn 1982; *Recreations* photography, bird watching; *Clubs* Vincents; *Style*— Stephen Hofmeyr, Esq; 34 Dudley Rd, Walton on Thames, Surrey KT12 2JU (☎ 0932 253614); 7 Kings Bench Walk, Temple, London EC4Y 7DS (☎ 071 583 0404, fax 071 583 0950, telex 887491-KBLAW)

HOGAN, Prof Brian; s of late Thomas Hogan, and Margaret Mary, *née* Murray (d 1958); *b* 4 May 1932; *Educ* St Mary's GS Darlington, Univ of Manchester (LLB); *m* 10 Aug 1957, Pauline, da of Walter Cox (d 1950); 1 s (Christopher Paul b 1964), 1 da (Catherine Margaret Mary Alice b 1966); *Career* called to the Bar Gray's Inn; lectr Univ of Nottingham 1956-67, prof of common law Univ of Leeds 1967- (pro-vice chllr 1981-83), ed Criminal Law Review 1966-73; visiting prof: Univ of Adelaide 1960, Villanova Univ 1962-63, Law Reform Cmmn of Canada 1975, Dalhousie Univ 1978-79, Vanderbilt Univ 1984; *Books* Smith and Hogan Criminal Law (ed, 6 ends), Smith and Hogan Cases and Materials on Criminal Law (ed, 3 edns); *Recreations* DIY, reading, music; *Style*— Prof Brian Hogan; 11 Lady Wood Rd, Leeds LS8 2QF (☎ 0532 658045); Faculty of Law, Univ of Leeds, Leeds LS2 9JT (☎ 0532 335014, telex 556473 UNILDS G, fax 0532 420090)

HOGAN, Eileen Mary; da of Thomas Matthew Hogan, of Woking, Surrey, and Marjorie Coyle (d 1982); *b* 1 March 1946; *Educ* Streatham Hill and Clapham HS, Camberwell Sch of Arts and Crafts, Royal Acad Schs, Br Sch of Archaeology Athens, RCA (BA, MA); *m* Kenneth Ersser; *Career* artist; visiting lectr Fine Art Dept Bristol Poly 1982-84; Camberwell Coll of Art and Crafts: visiting lectr 1975-76, sr lectr and course ldr 1976-85, princ lectr and course ldr in illustration and dir Camberwell Press 1985, dean Sch of Applied and Graphic Arts 1989; sole exhibitions: Br Cncl Athens 1971 and 1983, New Grafton Gallery 1972, RCA 1974 and 1977, Magdalene St Gallery Cambridge 1975, Orangerie Holland Park London 1977, Horniman Museum London 1977, Galerie Simons Laden Hamburg 1977, Cootes Gallery Lewes 1979, Festival Exhibition (Hiscock Gallery Portsmouth) 1979, The Fine Art Soc London 1980, 1982, 1984, 1985, 1986 and 1988, The Fine Art Soc Glasgow 1980, The Alden Library Ohio Univ 1982, The King Library Univ of Kentucky 1982, Bohun Gallery Henley upon Thames 1983, The Imp War Museum 1984, Morehead Univ Kentucky 1986, Jonleigh Gallery Wonersh 1988, Graduate Sch of Library Servs Univ of Alabama 1988; selected gp exhibitions: Hayward Gallery London 1969, Royal Acad Summer Show 1969, 1974, 1976-90, ICA London 1973, Serpentine Graphics '73 (Serpentine Gallery London) 1973, Asinus Gallery Hamburgh 1974, The English Landscape (Usher Gallery) 1975, Draw the Line (V & A Museum London) 1977, Open and Shut (V & A Museum London) 1979, British Fine Printing (London) 1984, The Barbican Centre 1985, London Ecology Centre 1987, West Virginia Inst of Technol Montgomery 1988, British Contemporary Paintings (St James Art Gp) 1989, The President's Choice (Royal Acad) 1989, 20th Century Br Art Fair London 1990, The Discerning Eye (Mall Galleries) 1990, Art 90 (London's Contemporary Art Fair) 1990; numerous cmmns incl: Women at Work in the Royal Navy (for Artistic Records Ctee of Imp War Museum) 1983-84, The Queen presenting Colours to the Portsmouth Fleet (for HMS Nelson) 1986, stamps for Royal Mail 1989, 1990; work in numerous public collections; *awards* Reeves purchase prize 1968, David Murray scholarship 1968, Br Inst fund 1968, Gtr London award for Young Artists 1969, Landseer scholarship 1970 and 1971, Royal Overseas League award 1970 and 1972, Walter Neurath prize 1970, Greek Govt scholarship 1971, Arts Cncl of GB award 1974, Gtr London Arts Assoc award 1975, Crafts Cncl Advsy Ctee grant 1978, Spirit of London award 1982; *Publications* Oedipus and Locaste (1972), Fragments from Sappho (1973), Variations (1974), Dream of Gerontius (1976), Ogham (1977), Morning Sea (1978), Haiku (1978), 500 Points of Good Husbandry by Thomas Tusser (1981), A Selection of Poems by C P Cavafy (1985), On Common Ground (1987), Anaskaphes (1989); *Clubs* Chelsea Arts; *Style*— Ms Eileen Hogan; Camberwell College of Arts, Peckham Road, London SW16 6RR (☎ 071 703 0987, fax 071 703 3689)

HOGAN, Fursa Francis; s of James Edmund (d 1961), and Frances Jane Pope (d 1986); *b* 1 Jan 1931; *Educ* Xaviers's Dublin, Trinity Coll Dublin; *m* 4 May 1954, Arlette Mary, da of James Grew, of Shrewsbury Rd, Dublin; 3 da (Mandy b 1954, Doon b 1957, Kate b 1964); *Career* chm and ptnr The Manchester Tobacco Co; *Recreations* golf, tennis, swimming; *Clubs* RAC; *Style*— Fursa Hogan, Esq; 42 St Lawrence Quay, Salford Quays, Port of Manchester M5 4XT; Manchester Tobacco Co, Ludgate Hill, Manchester M4 4DA (☎ car 0860 629243)

HOGAN, Thomas Patrick; s of Daniel Hogan (d 1920); *b* 4 Aug 1908; *Educ* Mount St Joseph Coll, Univ Coll Dublin; *m* 1949, Mary Joan, *née* Bourke; 5 children; *Career* chm: Mica and Micanite, Mallow Industries, Pye Ireland; hon consul-gen Iceland; Order of Falcon (Iceland); FIEE; *Recreations* golf, sailing; *Clubs* Royal Irish Yacht, Portmarnock Golf; *Style*— Thomas Hogan, Esq; Monkstown Castle, Co Dublin, Ireland (☎ 0001 808103)

HOGAN, William Patrick (Bill); s of William Daniel Hogan (d 1983), of Laindon, Essex, and Lilian, *née* Morley; *b* 7 Sept 1943; *Educ* Christ's Hospital; *m* 20 March 1971, Audrey Margaret, da of Arthur Willber; 2 c (Neil b 28 May 1975, Natalie b 15 Dec 1982); *Career* qualified chartered accountant 1966, ptnr Baker Tilly Chartered Accountants; int tax specialist; writer and lectr; FCA 1976 (ACA 1966); *Recreations* reading, golf, travel; *Clubs* Christ's Hospital; *Style—* Bill Hogan, Esq; Baker Tilly, 2 Bloomsbury St, London WC1B 3ST (☎ 071 413 5100, fax 071 413 5101)

HOGARTH, Prof Cyril Alfred; s of Alfred Hogarth (d 1975), of Chaston, Clacton-on-Sea, and Florence Mary, *née* Farrow (d 1981); *b* 22 Jan 1924; *Educ* Tottenham Co Sch, Queen Mary Coll London (BSc, PhD, DSc); *m* 4 Sept 1951, Audrey, da of Frederick Percy Jones (d 1975), of The Limes, Thorpe-le-Soken; 1 s (Adrian b 1960), 2 da (Celia (Mrs Stuart-Lee) b 1954, Yvonne (Mrs Goyder) b 1954); *Career* pt/t Lt Sp RNVR 1944-46; experimental offr Admty 1943-46, lectr Chelsea Coll 1948-49, sr sci offr Royal Radar Estab 1951-58, emeritus prof of physics Brunel Univ 1989- (head of dept 1958-82 and 1984-85, prof 1964-89); visiting prof: S Bank Poly 1987-, Univ of Keele 1989-; conslt to Westcode Semiconductors 1958-, examiner and conslt to many orgns, many sci pubns; memb: Parish Cncl Gerrards Cross 1975-, Nat Housing and Town Planning Cncl, S Bucks DC 1983; FInstP 1958, FRSA 1972, FIEE 1985; *Books* Techniques of Non-Destructive Testing (with J Blitz 1960), Materials used in Semi-Conductor Devices (1965); *Recreations* foreign travel; *Style—* Prof Cyril Hogarth; Shepherds Hey, Orchehill Ave, Gerrards Cross, Bucks SL9 8QG (☎ 0753 884217); Dept of Physics, Brunel University, Uxbridge, Middlesex UB8 3PH (☎ 0895 74000, fax 0895 72391)

HOGARTH, (Arthur) Paul; OBE (1989); s of Arthur Hogarth (d 1966), of Kendal, Cumbria, and Janet, *née* Bownass; *b* 4 Oct 1917; *Educ* St Agnes Sch, Manchester Coll of Art, St Martin's Sch of Art London, RCA (PhD); *m* 1, 1940, Doreen (d 1948), da of Albert Courtman, of Alderley Edge, Ches; m 2, 1949, Phyllis, *née* Pamplin (d 1962); 1 s (Toby Graham b 1 Aug 1960); m 3, 2 Feb 1963, Patricia Morgan Graham, *née* Douthwaite (d 1981); m 4, 1989, Diana Marjorie, *née* Cochran; *Career* painter in watercolours, illustrator, author and printmaker; sr tutor Faculty Graphic Art RCA 1964-71, cmmnd by Imperial War Museum to depict Berlin Wall 1981; drawings watercolours and prints in permanent collections: Fitzwilliam Museum, Whitworth Gallery, Univ of Manchester, City Art Gallery Manchester, V & A Museum, Library of Congress (Washington USA), Boston Public Library (USA), Yale Centre of Br Art (USA); Francis Williams Award for Best Literary Illustration (1982), Yorkshire Post award for Best Art Book (1986); memb Library Ctee Royal Acad of Arts (memb cncl 1979-80 and 1986-88), hon pres Assoc of Illustrators; ARA 1974, MRA 1984, RDI 1979, RE 1988, Fell CSD 1964; *Books* Looking at China (1955), Creative Pencil Drawing (1964, 2 edn 1981), Artists on Horseback (1972, USA only), Drawing Architecture (1973, 2 edn 1980), Arthur Boyd Houghton (1982), Artist as Reporter (1986); illustrated books in collaboration with authors notably: Brendan Behan's Island (with Brendan Behan, 1962), Majorca Observed (with Robert Graves, 1965), Graham Greene Country (with Graham Greene, 1986), The Mediterranean Shore (with Lawrence Durrell, 1988); *Clubs* Reform; *Style—* Paul Hogarth, Esq, OBE; c/o Tessa Sayle, 11 Jubilee Place, London SW3 (☎ 071 823 3883)

HOGARTH, Peter Laurence; s of Michael Hogarth, of Perranaworthal, and Joyce, *née* Ponder; *b* 10 July 1949; *Educ* Haileybury; *m* 15 July 1972, Margaret Rosemary, da of Alexander Sidney Alison; 1 s (Ian b 30 Jan 1982), 2 da (Rosemary b 6 June 1983, Juliet b 25 April 1988); *Career* CA 1972; Peat Marwick McLintock 1967-88, Société Generale Strauss Turnbull Securities 1988-90; International Stock Exchange 1991-; Liveryman Worshipful Co Joiners and Ceilers 1978; *Recreations* golf, bridge, chess, cooking; *Style—* Peter Hogarth, Esq; 6 Frank Dixon Way, Dulwich, London SE21 7BB (☎ 081 693 8881)

HOGBEN, Dr Neil; s of Eric O'Neill Hogben (d 1984), and Alma, *née* Ault (d 1986); *b* 23 March 1923; *Educ* St Paul's, Magdalene Coll Cambridge (scholarship in history), Univ of Durham (1851 exhibition postgrad res scholarship in naval architecture, BSc, PhD); *m* 1958, Edith Cornelia, da of Wilhelm Leister (d 1971); 1 s (Giles Dominic b 1971), 2 da (Anita Ruth b 1959, Kim Frances b 1960); *Career* serv WWII: gunner RA 1942-47, 72 Anti Tank Regt N Africa Italy Austria; mgmnt trainee JL Thompson Shipbuilders 1947-51, tech asst Rotol Propeller Co 1951-52; National Physical Laboratory (Ship Div merged to National Maritime Institute 1976 became NMI Ltd 1982): sr princ scientific offr (individual merit) 1967, dep chief scientific offr (individual merit) 1979, sr res advsr to NMI Ltd 1983-85; pt/t conslt BMT (British Maritime Technology) Fluid Mechanics Ltd 1985-; RINA: Silver medal (Experience in Computing Wave Loads on Large Bodies) 1974, Bronze medal (Wave Climate Synthesis Worldwide) 1984; ICE George Stephenson medal (Estimation of Fluid Loading on Offshore Structures) 1977, MOD award for Oceanography 1989 (from Soc for Underwater Technol); chm: Environmental Conditions Ctee of Int Ship Structures Congress 1964-70 and 1973-79, Working Gp on Surface Waves for Engrg Ctee on Oceanic Resources 1972-76; FRINA 1967, assoc memb NE Coast Instn of Engrs and Shipbuilders 1956, FEng 1988; *Books* Ocean Wave Statistics (co-author, 1967), Global Wave Statistics (co-author, 1986); contrib to: Advances in Hydroscience Vol 4 (1967), The Sea Vol 9 pt A (1990), Encyclopaedia of Fluid Mechanics Vol 10 (1990); *Recreations* music (piano playing of a sort); *Style—* Dr Neil Hogben; 60 Foley Rd, Claygate, Surrey KT10 0ND (☎ 0372 462966); BMT (British Maritime Technology) Fluid Mechanics Ltd, Orlando House, 1 Waldegrave Rd, Teddington, Middlesex TW11 8LZ

HOGBIN, Walter; CBE (1990); s of Walter Clifford John Hogbin (d 1969), and Mary, *née* Roberts; *b* 21 Dec 1937; *Educ* Kent Coll Canterbury, Queens' Coll Cambridge (MA); *m* 1968, Geraldine Anne-Marie, da of Gerald Castley; 2 s (Justin Walter b 1970, Mark Walter b 1972); *Career* jt md Taylor Woodrow plc, chm Taylor Woodrow International Ltd; dep chm Overseas Projects Bd, chm Export Gp Construction Indust 1988-90; CEng; *Recreations* golf, tennis, gardening; *Style—* Walter Hogbin, Esq, CBE; Taylor Woodrow International Ltd, Western Avenue, London W5 1EU (☎ 081 997 6641, telex 23502 TAYINT G, fax 081 991 3117)

HOGG, Sir Arthur Ramsay; MBE (1945); 7 Bt (UK 1846), of Upper Grosvenor St, Co Middlesex; s of Ernest Charles Hogg (d 1907), and Lucy (d 1924), da of late William Felton Peel, of Alexandria, Egypt; suc cous, Sir Kenneth Weir Hogg, OBE, 6 Bt (d 1985); *b* 24 Oct 1896; *Educ* Sherborne, Ch Ch Oxford (MA); *m* 1924, Mary Aileen Hester Lee (d 1980), da of late P H Lee Evans; 3 s (Michael, Mark, Simon), 1 da (Anthea); *Heir* s, Michael David, *qv*; *Career* WWI, Capt Royal W Kent Regt (twice wounded), WWII, Major (Gen List); *Style—* Sir Arthur Hogg, Bt, MBE; 27 Elgin Rd, Bournemouth, Dorset (☎ 0202 763287)

HOGG, Lady; Barbara Elisabeth; yr da of late Capt Arden Franklyn, of New Place, Shedfield, Hants, and 33 Bryanston Sq, London W1; *m* 1, 2 June 1936, Brig Viscount Garmoyle, DSO, late Rifle Bde (ka 1942); m 2, 28 Oct 1948, Sir John Nicholson Hogg, TD; 1 s, 1 da; *Style—* Lady Hogg; The Red House, Shedfield, Southampton, Hants

HOGG, (Andrew) Bruce Campbell; OBE (1989), QFSM (1982); s of David Ogilvie Brown Hogg (d 1958), and Catherine Downie, *née* Soppit Smith (d 1982); *b* 2 May 1934; *Educ* Acton Tech Coll; *m* 15 July 1961, Eileen Hilda; 4 da (Mary b 1964, Nancy b 1968, Lucy b 1970, Jean (twin) b 1970); *Career* Nat Serv RE bomb disposal 1952-59; fire serv 1959-89 (chief fire offr Norfolk 1979-89, princ fire advsr Central Electricity Generating Bd 1989-90, princ fire advsr Nuclear Electric 1990); Co Cmmr St John Norfolk 1984-89, offr brother Order of St John; fell: Inst Fire Engrg, Inst Risk Mgmnt; *Style—* Bruce Hogg, Esq, OBE, QFSM; Glebe Cottage, Church End, Twyning, Tewkesbury, Glos (☎ 0684 294499; Nuclear Electric, Barnett Way, Barnwood, Glos GL4 7RS (☎ 0452 652222, fax 0452 652776)

HOGG, Sir Christopher; *b* 2 Aug 1936; *Educ* Marlborough, Trinity Coll Oxford (MA), Harvard (MBA); *m* ; 2 da; *Career* Nat Serv 1956; IMEDE Business Sch Lausanne 1962, Philip Hill Higginson Erlangers Ltd (now Hill Samuel & Co Ltd) 1963-66, Industrial Reorganisation Corporation 1966-68; Courtaulds plc: joined 1968, dir 1973-, dep chm 1978, chief exec and chm designate 1979, chm 1980-; non-exec chm: Reuters Holdings plc 1985- (non-exec dir 1984-), Courtaulds Textiles plc 1990-; memb International Council of J P Morgan 1988-; memb: Bd of Tstees Ford Fndn 1987-, Dept of Industry's Industl Advsy Bd 1976-80; hon fell Trinity Coll Oxford 1982; Hon DSc Cranfield Inst of Technol 1986, Hon DSc Aston Univ 1988; Centenary medal Soc Chem Indust 1989, Alumni Achievement award Harvard Business Sch 1989, Gold medal BIM 1986; hon fell Chartered Soc of Designers 1987-; *Recreations* theatre, reading, skiing, walking; *Style—* Sir Christopher Hogg; Courtaulds plc, 18 Hanover Square, London W1A 2BB (☎ 071 629 9080, fax 071 629 2586, telex 28788)

HOGG, Douglas Martin; MP (C) Grantham 1979-; s of Baron Hailsham of St Marylebone, KG, PC (Life Peer 1970; suc as 2 Visc Hailsham 1950, disclaimed Viscountcy 1963); h to Viscountcy of Hailsham; does not use the courtesy prefix of Hon; *b* 5 Feb 1945; *Educ* Eton, Ch Ch Oxford; *m* 6 June 1968, Hon Sarah Elizabeth Mary, *qv*, da of Lord Boyd-Carpenter, PC (Life Peer); 1 s (Quintin b 12 Oct 1973), 1 da (Charlotte b 26 Aug 1970); *Career* pres Oxford Union 1965; called to the Bar Lincoln's Inn 1968; PPS to Leon Brittan (chief sec to Treasury) 1982-83, asst govt whip 1983-84, Parly under sec Home Office 1986-89, min of state for Indust and Enterprise 1989-90, min of state Foreign Office 1990-; *Style—* Douglas Hogg, Esq, MP

HOGG, Vice Adm Sir Ian Leslie Trower; KCB (1968, CB 1964), DSC (1941, and Bar 1944); s of Col John M T Hogg (d 1955); *b* 30 May 1911; *Educ* Cheltenham; *m* 1945, Mary Gwynneth Jean, da of Col Cecil W Marsden, MC (d 1973); 2 s; *Career* joined RN 1929, served WWII, Capt 1953, Cdre Cyprus 1960-62, Rear Adm 1963, Flag Offr Medway and Adm Supt HM Dockyard Chatham 1963-66, Vice Adm 1966, Def Servs Sec 1966-67, Vice Chief of Def Staff 1967-70, ret; Comptroller Royal Soc of St George 1971-74; dir Richard Unwin Int Ltd 1975-87; FRSA; *Recreations* china restoring; *Clubs* Naval; *Style—* Vice Adm Sir Ian Hogg, KCB, DSC; 21 Chapelside, Titchfield, Hampshire PO14 4AP (☎ 0329 47515)

HOGG, James Dalby; s of Sir James Cecil Hogg, KCVO (d 1973), of 2 Upper Harley St, London NW1, and Lady Hogg; *b* 9 July 1937; *Educ* Eton; *m* 19 Aug 1964, Joan, da of Richard Blackledge; 2 s (James b 1965, Samuel b 1966); *Career* reporter: Bolton Evening News 1960-64, Morning Telegraph Sheffield 1964-65, BBC Manchester 1965-66, BBC Leeds 1967-69, 24 Hours BBC London 1970-72, Nationwide 1972-83, Newsnight 1983-88; writer and presenter of numerous documentaries; *Recreations* keeping animals, reading, jazz, trying to play the piano; *Clubs* The Count Basie Soc; *Style—* James Hogg, Esq; Forge House, Therfield, Royston, Herts SG8 9QA (☎ 076 387 280); BBC TV, Television Centre, London W12 7RJ (☎ 081 743 8000)

HOGG, John Goldsborough; s of F G Hogg (d 1969); *b* 21 Jan 1925; *Educ* Harrow, Trinity Coll Cambridge; *m* 1955, Hon Sarah Edith, *qv*, yst da of 1 Baron Noel-Buxton, PC (d 1948); 2 da; *Career* insur broker Lloyd's 1947-85, dep chm Hogg Robinson Group 1979-85; *Recreations* golf, shooting, fishing, skiing, flying; *Clubs* Boodle's; *Style—* John Hogg, Esq; Old Broad Oak, Brenchley, Kent (☎ 089 272 2318); Hogg Group plc, Lloyds Chambers, 1 Portsoken St, London E1 8DF (☎ 071 480 4000, telex 884633)

HOGG, Sir John Nicholson; TD (1946); s of Sir Malcolm Hogg (d 1948, yr bro of 1 Viscount Hailsham and sometime dep chm Bombay Chamber of Commerce, banker and memb Viceroy's Legislative Cncl in India), and Lorna, da of Sir Frank Beaman, sometime High Court Judge Bombay; 1 cous of Lord Hailsham of St Marylebone, *qv*; *b* 4 Oct 1912; *Educ* Eton, Balliol Coll Oxford; *m* 1948, Barbara Elisabeth, *qv*, yr da of Capt Henry Arden Franklyn (d 1960), of Shedfield, Hants, and wid of Brig Viscount Garmoyle (who d 1942, of wounds received in action); 1 s (Malcolm b 1949), 1 da (Susan b 1954); *Career* served WWII KRRC (Greece, Crete, Western Desert, Tunisia, NW Europe); joined Glyn Mills and Co (later Williams and Glyn's Bank) 1934, md Glyn Mills and Co 1950-70 (dep chm 1963-68, chm 1968-70), dep chm Williams and Glyn's Bank plc 1970-83; fell Eton Coll 1951-70, memb Cwlth War Graves Cmmn 1958-64, Sheriff County of London 1960, chm ECGD's Advsy Cncl 1962-67, dep chm Gallaher Ltd 1964-78, tstee Imperial War Graves Endowment Fund 1965-87, chm Abu Dhabi Investmt Bd 1967-75, dir Royal Bank of Scotland Gp 1970-82, chm Banque Francaise de Crédit Int 1972-83, dir Prudential Corpn Ltd 1964-85; pres Eton Ramblers; Inst Child Health: hon treas 1974-87, hon fell 1987; kt 1963; *Style—* Sir John Hogg, TD; The Red House, Shedfield, Southampton SO3 2HN (☎ 0329 832121)

HOGG, Hon Katharine Amelia; da of Baron Hailsham of St Marylebone (Life Peer; disclaimed Viscountcy of Hailsham 1963), and Lady Hailsham, *née* Martin (d 1978); *b* 18 Oct 1962; *Educ* Roedean Sch, St Peter's Coll Oxford (BA); *Career* publishing (with Michael Joseph); *Style—* The Hon Katharine Hogg; 79 Church Rd, Richmond, Surrey (☎ 081 940 1456); Michael Joseph Ltd, 44 Bedford Square, London WC1 (☎ 081 323 3200

HOGG, Michael David; s and h of Sir Arthur Ramsay Hogg, 7 Bt, MBE, and Mary Aileen Hester Lee (d 1980), da of late Philip Herbert Lee Evans; *b* 19 Aug 1925; *Educ* Sherborne, Ch Ch Oxford; *m* 21 Jan 1956, Elizabeth Anne Thérèse, da of Sir Terence Edmond Patrick Falkiner, 8 Bt (d 1987); 3 s; *Career* WWII 1943-45, Capt Grenadier Guards; journalist; The Daily Telegraph 1951-87: ed Peterborough 1971-79, asst ed 1976, arts ed 1979-86, letters ed 1986-87; *Style—* Michael Hogg, Esq; 19 Woodlands Rd, Barnes, London SW13

HOGG, Norman; MP (Lab) Cumbernauld and Kilsyth 1983-; *b* 12 March 1938; *Educ* Ruthrieston Secdy Sch; *m* 1964, Elizabeth McCall Christie; *Career* dist offr Nat and Local Govt Offrs Assoc 1967-69, memb Tport Users' Consultative Ctee for Scotland 1977-79, sec Trade Unions' Ctee for the Electricity Supply Indust 1978-79; MP (Lab) E Dunbartonshire 1979-83; memb Select Ctee: Scottish Affrs 1979-82, Pub Accounts 1991-; Scottish Lab whip 1982-83, Lab dep chief whip 1983-87; oppn front bench spokesman for Scottish Affrs 1987-88; *Style—* Norman Hogg, Esq, MP; House of Commons, London SW1A 0AA (☎ 071 219 5095)

HOGG, Pam; da of Andrew Hogg, and Mary, *née* McLachlan; *Educ* Bearsden Acad, Glasgow Sch of Art, Royal Coll of Art (MA); *Career* fashion designer; collections: Psychedelic Jungle 1984, Hippies Forever 1985, D'Alice in Wonderland 1985, Best Dressed Chicken in the Town 1986, And God Created Woman 1986, Play Girl 1987, Splash 1987, Flower of Scotland 1988, Wild Wild Women of the West 1988, Warrior Queen 1989, Brave New World 1989, Lust for Life 1990, School for Scandal 1990; singer and songwriter with Garden of Eden 1988-89, designed and opened Pam Hogg Shop Soho 1989-; judge of numerous competitions; nominated finalist for Young Contemporary Designer 1989, winner Scottish Style award 1989; *Style—* Miss Pam

Hogg; 88-94 Caledonian Road, Kings Cross, London N1 9DN (☎ 071 278 8637)

HOGG, Rear Adm Peter Beauchamp; CB (1980); s of Beauchamp Hogg (d 1964), of Hungerford, Berks, and Sybil, *née* Medley (d 1967); *b* 9 Nov 1924; *Educ* Bradfield; *m* 1951, Gabriel Argentine, da of Argentine Francis Alington (d 1977), of Dorset; 2 s (Christopher b 1954, Gavin b 1960), 2 da (Catherine b 1956, Annabel b 1962); *Career* RN (engrg branch) 1943-80; final appt as Rear Adm 1977-80, def advsr Br High Cmmn Canberra and head of Br Def Liaison Staff; appeal sec and bursar i/c bldg modernisation Winchester Coll 1980-88; *Recreations* woodwork, furniture repairs, walking, gardening; *Style—* Rear Adm Peter Hogg, CB; Common Hill Farm, Fownhope, Hereford HR1 4PZ

HOGG, Rear Adm Robin Ivor Trower; CB (1987); s of Dudley William Bruce Trower Hogg, and Lillian Nancy Hogg; *b* 25 Sept 1932; *Educ* New Beacon Sevenoaks, Bedford Sch; *m* 1, 1958, Susan Bridget Beryl, da of Adm Sir Guy Grantham, GCB, CBE, DSO; 2 s, 2 da; m 2, 1970, Angela Sarah Patricia, da of Brig Rudolph Kirwan, CBE, DSO; *Career* RCDS 1977, RN Presentation Team 1978, Capt First Frigate Sqdn 1979-81, dir Naval Operational Requirements 1981-84, Rear Adm 1984, Flag Offr First Flotilla 1984-86, COS to C-in-C Fleet 1986-88, resigned RN; chief exec Colebrand Ltd 1988, md Raidfleet Ltd; *Recreations* private life; *Style—* Rear Adm Robin Hogg, CB; c/o Coutts & Co, Chandos, 440 Strand, London WC2R 0QS

HOGG, Hon Mrs (Sarah Edith Noel); *née* Noel-Buxton; yst da of 1 Baron Noel-Buxton, PC (d 1948); *b* 23 Jan 1928; *m* 2 June 1955, John Goldsborough Hogg, *qv*; 2 da; *Style—* The Hon Mrs Hogg; 11 Mallord Street, London SW3

HOGG, Hon Mrs (Sarah Elizabeth Mary); *née* Boyd-Carpenter; yr da of Baron Boyd-Carpenter, PC, DL (Life Peer), *qv*; *b* 14 May 1946; *Educ* St Mary's Convent Ascot, Lady Margaret Hall Oxford; *m* 6 June 1968, Douglas Hogg, MP, *qv*; 1 s, 1 da; *Career* Economist Newspaper 1968-82; economics ed: Sunday Times 1981-82, The Times 1983-86; presenter and economics ed Channel 4 News 1982-83; Wincott Fndn Financial Journalist of 1985; dir London Broadcasting Co 1985-90; govr Centre for Economic Policy Research 1985-; asst ed, business and fin ed The Independent 1986-89; economics ed The Daily Telegraph and The Sunday Telegraph 1989-90; head of Policy Unit No 10 Downing St with rank of second permanent sec 1990-; memb IDS, Hon MA Open Univ 1987; *Style—* The Hon Mrs Hogg; c/o 10 Downing St, London SW1

HOGGART, Dr (Herbert) Richard; s of Tom Longfellow Hoggart, and Adeline Hoggart; *b* 24 Sept 1918; *Educ* schs in Leeds, Univ of Leeds (MA, LittD); *m* 1942, Mary Holt France; 2 s, 1 da; *Career* served WWII RA; staff tutor and sr staff tutor Univ Coll Hull 1946-59, sr lectr in English Univ of Leicester 1959-62, prof of English Univ of Birmingham 1962-73 (dir Centre for Contemporary Cultural Studies 1964-73), visiting fell Inst of Dvpt Studies Univ of Sussex 1975, warden Goldsmith's Coll Univ of London 1976-84; visiting prof Rochester Univ (NY) 1956-57; hon prof Univ of E Anglia 1984-, Reith lectr 1971; memb: British Cncl Br Books Overseas Ctee 1959-64, BBC Gen Advsy Cncl 1959-60 and 1964-, Pilkington Ctee on Broadcasting 1960-62, Culture Advsr Ctee of UK Nat Cmmn for UNESCO (asst dir gen UNESCO 1970-75), Arts Cncl 1976-81 (chm Drama Panel 1977-80, vice-chm 1980-81), Editorial Bd New Univs Quarterly; chm: Advsy Cncl for Adult and Continuing Educn 1977-83, Euro Museum of the Year Award Ctee 1977-, Statesman and Nation Publishing Co 1978-81 (publishers New Statesman), Nat Broadcasting Res Unit 1981-; govr Royal Shakespeare Theatre until 1988; pres Br Assoc Former UN Civil Servants 1979-86; Hon DLitt OU 1973, Hon Dés Lettres Univ Bordeaux 1975, Hon DUniv Surrey 1981, Hon LLD Cncl for Nat Academic Awards 1982, Hon LLD York Univ Toronto, Hon DLitt Univ of Leicester, Hon DLitt Univ of Hull, hon fell Sheffield Poly 1983, Hon DUniv East Anglia 1986, Hon Dés Lettres Paris 1987; *Books* The Uses of Literacy (1957), various works on W H Auden, Speaking to Each Other (1970), Only Connect (1972), An Idea and Its Servants (1978), An English Temper (1982), An Idea of Europe (with Douglas Johnson, 1987), A Local Habitation (1988), A Sort of Clowning (1990); *Style—* Dr Richard Hoggart; Mortonsfield, Beavers Hill, Farnham, Surrey GU8 7DF (☎ 0252 715740)

HOGGART, Simon David; s of Dr (Herbert) Richard Hoggart, *qv*, of Farnham, Surrey, and Mary Holt, *née* France; *b* 26 May 1946; *Educ* Hymers Coll Hull, Wyggeston GS Leicester, King's Coll Cambridge (MA); *m* 9 July 1983, Alyson Clare, da of Cdr Donald Louis Corner, RN, of Rusper, Sussex; 1 s (Richard b 1988), 1 da (Amy b 1986); *Career* political corr: The Guardian 1973-81 (reporter 1968-71, NI corr 1971-73), Punch 1979-85; columnist The Observer 1989- (reporter 1981-85, US corr 1985-89); author; *Books* incl: The Pact (with Alistair Michie, 1978), Michael Foot: A Portrait (with David Leigh, 1981), On The House (1981), Back On The House (1982), House of Ill Fame (1985), House of Cards (ed, 1988), America-A User's Guide (1990); *Recreations* reading, writing, travel; *Style—* Simon Hoggart, Esq; The Observer, Chelsea Bridge House, Queenstown Road, London SW8 (☎ 071 627 0700)

HOGGE, Philip Arthur Fountain; s of Arthur Henry Hogge (d 1952), and Margaret Julia, *née* Large; *b* 2 Sept 1941; *Educ* Blundell's Sch Devon, CAT Hamble; *m* 3 Oct 1964, Joyce Ann, da of Herbert Vassall Southby, of Vancouver, Canada; 2 s (Gavin b 1965, Giles b 1972), 1 da (Alice b 1968); *Career* pilot: BOAC 1962, Capt 1975; flt trg mangr: 707 1978, 747 1981; mangr flt crew 747 1986, chief pilot 747 1988; Liveryman The Guild of Air Navigators; Freeman City of London; *Recreations* gardening, boats; *Style—* P A F Hogge, Esq; Magdalen House, Wharfe Lane, Henley-on-Thames, Oxon RG9 2LL; A311 TBA, British Airways, PO Box 10, Heathrow Airport, Hounslow, Middx TW6 2JA (☎ 081 562 5285)

HOGGER, Henry George; s of Rear Adm Henry Charles Hogger, CB, DSC (d 1982), and Ethel Mary, *née* Kreiner (d 1973); *b* 9 Nov 1948; *Educ* Winchester, Univ of Cambridge (MA); *m* 21 Oct 1972, Fiona Jane, da of Alexander Patrick McNabb (d 1971); 2 s (Charles b 1984, Harry b 1984), 2 da (Rosalind b 1979, Eleanor b 1982); *Career* joined FCO 1969; third sec Aden 1972, Caracas second sec 1972-75, first sec Kuwait 1975-78, first sec and head of chancery Abu Dhabi 1982-86, dep head of mission and consul gen Amman 1989- (cnsllr); memb Inst of Advanced Motorists; *Recreations* sailing, golf, guitar; *Style—* Henry Hogger, Esq; Shop Farm House, Briantspuddle, Dorchester, Dorset DT2 7HY (☎ 0929 471491); British Embassy, PO Box 87, Abdoun, Amman, Hashemite Kingdom of Jordan (☎ 823100, fax 813759, telex 22209 PRODRM JO)

HOGGETT, Prof Brenda Marjorie; QC (1989); da of Cecil Frederick Hale (d 1958), and Marjorie, *née* Godfrey (d 1981); *b* 31 Jan 1945; *Educ* Richmond (Yorks) HS for Girls, Girton Coll Cambridge (MA); *m* 1968, Anthony John Christopher Hoggett, QC, s of Christopher Hoggett, of Grimsby; 1 da (Julia b 1973); *Career* called to the Bar Gray's Inn 1969, asst rec 1984-89, rec 1989-; asst lectr Univ of Manchester 1966, lectr 1968, sr lectr 1976, reader 1981-, prof of law 1986-89; visiting prof of law King's Coll London; memb Cncl of Tribunals 1980-84, jt gen ed Journal of Social Welfare Law 1978-84, law cmmr 1984-; managing tstee Nuffield Fndn 1987-, chm Nat Family Conciliation Cncl 1989-, memb Human Fertilisation and Embryology Authy 1990-; Hon LLD Sheffield 1989; *Books* Mental Health Law (1976, 3 edn 1990), Parents and Children (1977, 3 edn 1987), The Family Law and Society - Cases and Materials (with D S Pearl 1983, 2 edn 1987), Women and the Law (with S Atkins 1984); many contribs to legal texts and periodicals; *Recreations* bridge; *Style—* Prof Brenda Hoggett, QC; Law Commission, Conquest House, 37/38 John St, London WC1N 2BQ

HOGGETT, Dr (Anthony) John Christopher; QC (1986); s of Christopher Hoggett (d 1989), and Annie Marie, *née* Barker; *b* 20 Aug 1940; *Educ* Leeds GS, Hymers Coll Hull, Clare Coll Cambridge (scholar, MA, LLB), Univ of Manchester (PhD); *m* 28 Dec 1969, Prof Brenda Marjorie Hoggett, da of Cecil Frederick Hale (d 1959); *Career* lectr in law Univ of Manchester 1963-69, res fell Univ of Michigan 1965-66; called to the Bar 1969; head of Chambers 1985, rec Crown Ct 1988, memb DOE's Final Selection Bd for Planning Insprs; *Recreations* swimming, walking; *Style—* Dr John Hoggett, QC; Flat 29, Chepstow House, Chepstow St, Manchester M1 5JF (☎ 061 236 7973); 40 King St, Manchester M2 6BA (☎ 061 832 9082, fax 061 835 2139)

HOGWOOD, Christopher Jarvis Haley; CBE (1989); s of Haley Evelyn Hogwood (d 1982), of Saffron Walden, Essex, and Marion Constance, *née* Higgott; *b* 10 Sept 1941; *Educ* Nottingham HS, Skinners Sch Tunbridge Wells, Univ of Cambridge (MA), Charles Univ Prague; *Career* conductor, writer on music, keyboard player, fndr memb Early Music Consort of London 1967-76, fndr and dir Acad of Ancient Music 1973-, Univ of Cambridge 1975- (hon fell Jesus Coll), dir Handel and Haydn Soc Boston USA 1986-, hon prof of music Univ of Keele 1986-89, dir of music St Paul Chamber Orch Minnesota USA 1987-; various pubns in jls; Freeman Worshipful Co of Musicians; FRSA; *Books* Music at Court (1978), The Trio Sonata (1978), Haydn's London Visits (1980), Music in Eighteenth Century England (jtly, 1983), Handel (1984), New Grove Dictionary of Music and Musicians (contrib); *Style—* Christopher Hogwood, Esq, CBE; 10 Brookside, Cambridge CB2 1JE (☎ 0223 63975)

HOGWOOD, Paul Arthur; s of Robert Thomas Hogwood, of Forest Hill, and Hilda Jesse, *née* Marshall; *b* 18 July 1949; *Educ* Haberdashers' Aske's, Univ of Hull (BSc); *m* 30 Oct 1971, Sylvia Ann, da of Gordon McCulloch (d 1971); 2 s (James b 1978, Christopher b 1980); *Career* CA; audit mangr Coopers & Lybrand 1970-78, project fin asst dir Morgan Grenfell & Co Ltd 1983-86 (chief internal auditor 1978-83); co sec: Morgan Grenfell Securities Hldgs Ltd 1986-88, Morgan Grenfell Asset Mgmnt Ltd 1989-, Anglo & Overseas Tst plc 1989-, The Overseas Investmt Tst plc 1989-; FCA 1974; *Recreations* travel; *Style—* Paul Hogwood, Esq; 10 Ravenshill, Chislehurst, Kent BR7 5PD (☎ 081 467 1918); Morgan Grenfell Asset Management Ltd, 20 Finsbury Circus, London EC2M 1NB (☎ 071 826 0036, telex 920286 MGAM G, fax 071 826 0331, car 0860 257895)

HOHMANN, Margaret Mary; MBE; da of James Joseph Kelly, of Liverpool, and Mary Elizabeth Kelly (d 1984); *b* 22 Sept 1956; *Educ* St James Sch for Girls, High Baird Coll of Further Educn; *m* 15 May 1982, David George Hohmann, s of William Franz Hohmann, of Nottingham; 1 s (Robert Alan b 16 June 1986); *Career* swimmer; memb Br Team 1988-90 (and 1973-80); competed Cwlth Games: 1974, 1978 (silver, two bronze), 1990; competed Olympics: 1976, 1980 (silver in relay), 1988; Br team capt 1976-80, World Championship bronze 1978, World Cup gold for breaststroke; *Style—* Mrs David Hohmann, MBE

HOHNEN, David Leslie; *b* 19 Jan 1935; *Educ* Merchant Taylors'; *Career* CA 1958; ptnr Somerset Cowper & Co 1963- (now Saffery Champness); Freeman City of London 1972, Master Worshipful Co of Fruiterers 1991 (Liveryman 1972-), Freeman Worshipful Co of CAs 1977; FCA 1968; *Clubs* RAC; *Style—* David Hohnen, Esq; Saffery Champness, Fairfax House, Fulwood Place, Gray's Inn, London WC1V 6UB (☎ 071 405 2828, fax 071 405 7887)

HOING, Roy Coote; s of Albert Edward Hoing (d 1978), and Vera Rubina, *née* Coote; *b* 1 June 1935; *Educ* Royal GS High Wycombe; *m* 25 June 1960, Gay Yvonne, da of Roland Kenneth Hatchett (d 1985); 1 s (Adrian Clive b 30 Jan 1967), 2 da (Frances Elizabeth b 25 April 1965, Laura Louise (twin) b 30 Jan 1967); *Career* Lt RAPC 1959, served Singapore; CA; ptnr Nash Broad Wesson (formerly Waller Broad) CAs 1965-; nat treas Assoc of Ex Tablers Clubs 1982-88; FCA 1958; *Recreations* badminton, British butterflies; *Clubs* MCC; *Style—* Roy Hoing, Esq; Coachmans, Whielden St, Old Amersham, Bucks (☎ 0494 726937); Nash Broad Wesson, 42 Upper Berkeley St, London W1 (☎ 071 723 7293)

HOLBEN, Terence Henry Seymour; s of Henry George Seymour Holben, and Ivy Blanche, *née* Blomfield; *b* 4 March 1937; *Educ* Mark House Sch, S W Essex Technical Coll, London Coll of Printing; *m* 7 Oct 1961, June Elizabeth, da of Alan John Elliot, of Uckfield, Sussex; 2 s (Matthew Seymour b 1966, Simon Lee b 1969); *Career* Royal Navy 1955-57; art dir advertising companies: McCann Erickson 1960-66, Graham and Gillies 1967-77; creative dir Ogilvy and Mather 1977- (dir 1983-); *Recreations* rowing, wife and two sons; *Style—* Terence H S Holben, Esq; Oakwood, 19 London Rd, Stanford Rivers, Essex

HOLBORN, Thomas; *b* 5 Sept 1936; *Educ* London Sch of Econ (BSc); *m* 1960, Maureen, 1 s (Neil b 1969); *Career* chm (md to 1982) Tobler Suchard (now Jacobs Suchard Ltd) 1982-; *Style—* Thomas Holborn, Esq; Old Pond House, Upper Dean, Huntingdon, Cambs PE18 0ND; c/o Tobler Suchard Ltd, Miller Rd, Bedford (☎ 0234 55141)

HOLBOROW, Christopher Adrian; OBE (1989), TD (1969); s of Rev Canon George Holborow (d 1966), of Northants, and Barbara Stella, *née* Watson (d 1971); bro of Geoffrey J Holborow, *qv*; *b* 24 Dec 1926; *Educ* Repton, Gonville and Caius Coll Cambridge (MA, MD), Middx Hosp; *m* 1, 1960, Wanda Margaret (d 1982), da of John Douglas Nickels (d 1963), of Bridgnorth; 1 s (John b 1967), 2 da (Caroline b 1961, Emma b 1963); m 2, 1984, Caroline Ann, da of Edward Percy Woollcombe, OBE (d 1975), of Somerset; *Career* Maj RAMC (RARO) City of London FD Regt RA TA 1955-80, served Germany 1953-55; conslt surgn Westminster Hosp and Westminster Childrens Hosp 1964-85; JP 1978-82; chm Cwlth Soc for the Deaf 1984- (med advsr 1964-84); asst to Ct Worshipful Co of Tallow Chandlers 1988; Cdr Order of The Republic of The Gambia 1984 (offr 1978); *Recreations* fishing, shooting, travel; *Clubs* Army and Navy; *Style—* Christopher Holborow, Esq, OBE, TD; Witham House, Witham Friary, Frome, Somerset (☎ 074 985 340); 2/129 Fentiman Rd, London SW8 1JZ (☎ 071 735 5609)

HOLBOROW, Geoffrey Jermyn; OBE (1979); yst s of Rev Canon George Holborow (d 1966), and Barbara Stella, *née* Watson (d 1971); bro of Christopher A Holborow, *qv*; *b* 17 Sept 1929; *Educ* Repton, RMA Sandhurst, Emmanuel Coll Cambridge (MA); *m* 1, 8 Aug 1959, Lady Mary Christina, JP, DStJ, *qv*, da of 8 Earl of Courtown, OBE (d 1976), of Marfield House, Gorey, Co Wexford; 1 s (Crispin b 1963), 1 da (Katharine b 1961); m 2, 1990, Robert Wild; *Career* jt sr ptnr Stratton and Holborow, Chartered Surveyors 1960-89; vice pres Chartered Land Agents Soc 1969, pres Land Agency Division RICS 1976, memb Gen Cncl RICS 1970-83; High Sheriff of Cornwall 1977; govr RAC Cirencester 1976-88, chm Assoc of Cornish Boys' Clubs 1965-83; *Recreations* gardening; *Style—* Geoffrey Holborow, Esq, OBE; Ladock House, Ladock, Truro, Cornwall (☎ 0726 882274)

HOLBOROW, Lady Mary Christina; *née* Stopford; JP (1970); da (by 1 m) of 8 Earl of Courtown, OBE , DL, TD (d 1976); *b* 19 Sept 1936; *m* 8 Aug 1959, Geoffrey Jermyn Holborow, OBE, *qv*; 1 s, 1 da; *Career* memb Regnl Bd Trustee Savings Bank 1981-89, dir South West Water plc; chm Cornwall Ctee; memb: Rural Devpt Cmmn, Devon and Cornwall Trg and Enterprise Cncl; cmmr St John's Ambulance Bd Cornwall 1982-87; DStJ 1987; *Style—* The Lady Mary Holborow, JP; Ladock House, Ladock, Truro, Cornwall (☎ 0726 882274)

HOLBROOK, David; s of Kenneth Redvers Holbrook (d 1968), of Norwich, and Elsie Eleanor Holbrook (d 1956); *b* 9 Jan 1923; *Educ* City of Norwich Sch, Downing Coll Cambridge (BA, MA); *m* 23 April 1949, (Frances Margaret) Margot, da of Charles Davies-Jones (d 1938), of Bedwas, Wales; 2 s (Jonathan b 1956, Thomas b 1966), 2 da (Susan (Suki) b 1950, Kate b 1953); *Career* Lt E Riding Yeomanry RAC 1942-45, serv Normandy Invasion and NW Europe; asst ed Bureau of Current Affrs 1947-52, tutor Bassingbourn Village Coll Cambridge 1954-61, fell Kings Coll Cambridge 1961-65, sr Leverhulme res fell 1965, writer in residence Dartington Hall 1971-73, fell and dir Eng studies Downing Coll 1981-88 (asst dir 1973-75), Hooker visiting prof MacMaster Univ Hamilton Ontario 1984, emeritus fell Downing Coll 1988-, sr Leverhulme res fell 1988-; Arts Cncl Writers Grant: 1968, 1976, 1980; memb Editorial Bd Universities Quarterly 1978-86, pres Forum for Educnl Therapy 1988-; *Books* Imaginings (1971), English for Maturity (1961), English for the Rejected (1964), The Quest for Love (1965), Flesh Wounds (1966), The Exploring Word (1967), Object Relations (1969), Human Hope and the Death Instinct (1971), The Pseudo-Revolution (1972), Gustav Mahler and the Courage to be (1974), A Play of Passion (1977), Selected Poems (1980), Nothing Larger than Life (1987), The Novel and Authenticity (1987), Worlds Apart (1988), Images of Woman in Literature (1990); *Recreations* oil painting, foreign travel, cooking, gardening; *Style—* David Holbrook, Esq; Denmore Lodge, Brunswick Gardens, Cambridge, CB5 8DQ (☎ 0223 315 081); Downing Coll, Cambridge (☎ 0223 334 800)

HOLCROFT, Charles Anthony Culcheth; s and h of Sir Peter George Culcheth Holcroft, 3 Bt, *qv*; *b* 22 Oct 1959; *m* 28 July 1986, Mrs Elizabeth Carter, yr da of John Raper, of Four Crosses, Powys; 1 s (Tobias David b 5 Feb 1990), 1 da (Samara b 29 Aug 1988), 1 step s (Jamie); *Style—* Charles Holcroft, Esq

HOLCROFT, Sir Peter George Culcheth; 3 Bt (UK 1921), JP (Shropshire 1976); s of Sir Reginald Culcheth Holcroft, 2 Bt, TD (d 1978), and his 1 w, Mary Frances, *née* Swire (d 1963); *b* 29 April 1931; *Educ* Eton; *m* 21 July 1956 (m dis 1987), Rosemary Rachel, yr da of late Capt George Nevill Deas, 8 Hussars; 3 s, 1 da; *Heir* s, Charles Anthony Culcheth Holcroft, *qv*; *Career* High Sheriff of Shropshire 1969; *Style—* Sir Peter Holcroft, Bt, JP; Berrington, Shrewsbury

HOLDEN, Anthony Ivan; s of John Holden (d 1985), of Southport, Lancs, and Margaret Lois, *née* Sharpe (d 1985); *b* 22 May 1947; *Educ* Oundle, Merton Coll Oxford (MA); *m* 1 May 1971 (m dis 1988), Amanda Juliet, da of Sir Brian Warren, KBE; 3 s (Sam b 1975, Joe b 1977, Ben b 1979); m 2, 21 July 1985, Cynthia Blake, da of Mrs Rosemary Blake, of Brookside, Mass, USA; *Career* trainee reporter Evening Echo Hemel Hempstead 1970-73; The Sunday Times: home and foreign corr 1973-77, Atticus column 1977-79; Washington and chief US corr The Observer 1979-81, Transatlantic Cables columnist Punch 1979-81, features ed and asst ed The Times 1981-82, exec ed Sunday Today 1985-86; Br press Awards: Young Journalist of the Year 1972, Reporter of the Year 1976, Columnist of the Year 1977; freelance journalist and author: Holden At Large column Sunday Express magazine 1982-85, presenter In the Air BBC Radio 4 1982-83; TV documentaries: The Men who Would be King 1982, Charles at Forty 1988; opera translations: Don Giovanni ENO 1985, La Boheme Opera North 1986, The Barber of Seville ENO 1987; memb Cncl The Matthew Tst, tstee Br-American Drama Acad; memb NUJ 1971; *Books* Aeschylus' Agammemnon (translated and ed, 1969), The Greek Anthology (contrib, 1973), Greek Pastoral Poetry (translated and ed, 1974), The St Albans Poisoner (1974), Charles, Prince of Wales (1979), Their Royal Highnesses (1981), Anthony Holden's Royal Quiz - The Penguin Masterquiz (1983), Of Presidents, Prime Ministers and Princes (1984), The Queen Mother (1985 revised edn 1989), Don Giovanni (1987), Olivier, A Biography (1988), Charles A Biography (1989), Big Deal: A Year as a Professional Poker Player (1990); *Recreations* music, poker, Arsenal FC, Lancashire CC; *Clubs* Barracuda, Victoria Casino; *Style—* Anthony Holden, Esq; c/o A P Watt Ltd, 20 John St, London WC1N 2DR (☎ 071 405 6774)

HOLDEN, Brian Peter John; s of Sir George Holden, 3 Bt (d 1976), and hp of n, Sir John Holden, 4 Bt; *b* 12 April 1944; *m* 1984, Bernadette Anne Lopez, da of George Gerard O'Malley; *Style—* Brian Holden, Esq

HOLDEN, Sir David Charles Beresford; KBE (1972), CB (1963), ERD (1954); s of Oswald Addenbrooke Holden (ka 1917), and Ella Mary Beresford (d 1960); *b* 26 July 1915; *Educ* Rossall, King's Coll Cambridge (MA); *m* 1948, Elizabeth Jean, da of Arthur Norman Odling, OBE (d 1975); 1 s, 1 da; *Career* served WWII RA, BEF 1939-40, India, Burma 1942-45; temp Maj; NI Civil Serv 1937-76: sec Miny of Fin 1970-76, head Civil Serv 1970-76, dir Ulster Office London 1976-77; *Style—* Sir David Holden, KBE, CB, ERD; Falcons, Wilsford Cum Lake, Amesbury, Salisbury, Wilts SP4 7BL (☎ 0980 622493)

HOLDEN, His Hon Judge Derek; s of Frederic Holden, of Sussex, and Audrey Lilian Holden (d 1985); *b* 7 July 1935; *Educ* Cromwell House, Staines GS; *m* 1961, Dorien Elizabeth, da of Henry Douglas Bell, of Sunningdale; 2 s (Derek Grant b 1968, Derek Clark b 1970); *Career* Lt East Surrey Regt 1953-56, ptnr Derek Holden and Co (slrs) 1966-82, rec Crown Ct 1980-84, circuit judge 1984-; pres 1990: Social Security Appeal Tbnls, Med Appeal Tbnls, Vaccine Damage Tbnls; chm Tbnls Ctee of Judicial Studies Bd 1990-; *Recreations* sailing, rowing, photography, music; *Clubs* Leander, Royal Solent Yacht, Remenham, Staines Boat, Burway Rowing, Eton Excelsior Rowing, Datchet Water Sailing, Western (Glasgow), Sonata Assoc; *Style—* His Hon Judge Derek Holden; c/o Court Administrator, Sessions House, Ewell Rd, Surbiton SY

HOLDEN, Sir Edward; 6 Bt (UK 1893), of Oakworth House, Keighley, Yorks; s of Sir Isaac Holden, 5 Bt (d 1962); *b* 8 Oct 1916; *Educ* Leys Sch, Christ's Coll Cambridge, St Thomas's Hosp (MRCS, LRCP); *m* 17 Oct 1942, Frances Joan, da of John Spark, JP, of Ludlow, Stockton-on-Tees; 2 adopted s; *Heir* bro, Paul Holden; *Career* conslt anaesthetist Darton and Northallerton Gp Hosp 1957-74; FFARCS; *Clubs* Farmers'; *Style—* Sir Edward Holden, Bt; Moorstones, Riverbury Lane, Osmotherley, Northallerton DL6 3BG

HOLDEN, Dr Harold Benjamin; s of Reginald Holden (d 1979), and Frances Hilda, *née* Haslett (d 1983); Haslett family built and manned the first lifeboats on the Sussex coast (circa 1880-1910); *b* 2 June 1930; *Educ* Highgate, Charing Cross Hosp Med Sch Univ of London (MB BS); *m* 1, Nov 1963, Ann, da of Archibald Sinclair, of Cardiff; 2 s (Andrew b 1964, Michael b 1970), 1 da (Sarah b 1966); m 2, March 1979, Lydia, da of Dr Ronals James, of Toronto, Canada; 2 s (Benjamin b 1978, Robin b 1979); *Career* surgn, dir ENT Unit Charing Cross and Westminster Hosp Med Sch Univ of London, previously postgraduate dean Charing Cross Hosp Med Sch; fell Harvard Univ; FRCS; *Recreations* yachting, flying, golf; *Clubs* Royal Southampton YC, British Med Pilots Assoc, St Georges Hill GC; *Style—* Dr Harold B Holden; Yew Tree Cottage, Hyde, Fordingbridge, Hants (☎ 0425 52564); 128 Harley St, London W1N 1AH (☎ 071 486 9400)

HOLDEN, Sir John David; 4 Bt (UK 1919), of The Firs, Leigh, Lancaster; s of late David George Holden (eldest s of Sir George Holden, 3 Bt); suc gf 1976; *b* 16 Dec 1968; *m* 29 Aug 1987, Suzanne, *née* Cummings; *Heir* unc, Brian Holden; *Style—* Sir John Holden, Bt

HOLDEN, Lady; Mabel; da of Harry Morgan, of Cwt Blethyn, Usk, and Ethel, *née* Jones; *m* 1941, Sir Michael Holden, CBE, ED (d 1982), sometime Chief Justice Rivers State, Nigeria; 2 s, 1 da; *Style—* Lady Holden; 3 Rushton Rd, Wilbarston, Market, Harborough (☎ 0536 771100)

HOLDEN, Dr Michael Preston; s of Capt Malcolm Holden (d 1971), and Mary Agnes, *née* Preston (d 1985); *b* 10 May 1939; *Educ* Friends Sch Lancaster, Univ of Leeds (MB ChB); *m* 1 April 1963, Susan Margaret, da of Raymond Ashton (d 1976), of Wilsden; 1 s (David Mark b 1970), 1 da (Helen Jane b 1967); *Career* lectr in anatomy Univ of Glasgow 1964, first asst cardiovascular surgery Auckland NZ 1973, sr registrar cardiothoracic surgery Leeds 1966, sr conslt cardiothoracic surgn Univ of Newcastle 1974; sr examiner RCS; FRCS 1967, DObst RCOG 1966, FACN 1982, FICS 1990, FACA 1976; *Books* Towards Safer Cardiac Surgery (1980), Cardiothoracic Surgery (1981); *Recreations* gardening, horse riding, wood turning, dogs; *Style—* Dr Michael Holden; Cardiothoracic Department, Freeman Hospital, Newcastle upon Tyne NE7 7DN (☎ 091 284 3111, car 4537)

HOLDEN, Patrick Brian; s of Reginald John Holden, of East Hampshire, and Winifred Isabel Holden; *b* 16 June 1937; *Educ* All Hallows Sch, St Catharine's Coll Cambridge (BA, MA); *m* 1972, Jennifer Ruth, da of Francis Meddings (d 1985); *Career* served Royal Hampshire Regt 1955-57, seconded 1 Ghana Regt RWAFF; sec Fine Fare Group 1960-69 (legal and property dir 1965-69), Pye of Cambridge 1969-74, dir Pye Telecom 1972-74, dir and sec Oriel Foods Group 1975-81, gp sec Fisons plc 1981-83, chm Steak Away Foods Ltd 1982-; sec New Town Assoc 1974-75; FCIS, FBIM; *Recreations* bridge, walking; *Clubs* Naval and Military; *Style—* Patrick Holden, Esq; The Old School House, Lower Green, Tewin, Welwyn, Herts AL6 0LD (☎ 043 871 7573)

HOLDEN, Paul; s of Sir Isaac Holden, 5 Bt (d 1962), and hp of bro, Sir Edward Holden, 6 Bt; *b* 1923; *m* 1950, Vivien Mary, da of late Hedley Broxholme Oldham, of Allesley, Coventry; 1 s, 2 da; *Career* software and quality mgmnt, ret; chm Understanding Disabilities Educnl Tst; *Recreations* cine and video photography; *Clubs* Lions, Surrey Border Film and Video Makers; *Style—* Paul Holden, Esq; Glenside, Rowhills, Heath End, Farnham, Surrey GU9 9AU (☎ 0252 24116)

HOLDEN, Robert David; s of Major Hubert Robert Holden, MC (d 1987), of Sibdon Castle Craven Arms, Shropshire, and Lady Elizabeth, *née* Herbert; *b* 14 Jan 1956; *Educ* Eton; *m* 18 June 1988, Susan Emily Frances, da of Sir Joshua Rowley, 7 Bt, *qv*; *Career* chm Robert Holden Ltd 1978-, dir Fine Arts Courses Ltd 1985-; patron of the living of Sibdon; *Clubs* Army & Navy; *Style—* Robert Holden, Esq; Sibdon Castle Craven Arms Salop; 34 Nevern Place, London SW5; 15 Savile Row, London W1 (☎ 071 437 6010)

HOLDEN, Robin John; s of John Holden (d 1985), of Southport and Margaret Lois, *née* Sharpe (d 1985); *b* 22 May 1942; *Educ* Oundle; *m* 19 Sept 1964, (Margaret) Susan, da of George Ingham Rushton (d 1984); 2 s (Richard Ingham b 10 Dec 1966, Jonathan Robin b 26 April 1969); *Career* Cooper & Lybrand Deloitte (formerly Cooper Brothers & Co): joined 1959, qualified CA 1964; treas and dir Manchester C of C and Indust 1982-, memb Cncl ICAEW 1989-; FCA 1974 (ACA 1964); *Recreations* travel, theatre, photography, collecting foreign bank notes and matchbooks, golf, snooker; *Clubs* Royal Over-Seas League, Manchester Literary & Philosophical Soc, Manchester Luncheon, Royal Birkdale Golf, Hale Golf; *Style—* Robin J Holden, Esq; Tall Trees, Barry Rise, Bowdon, Cheshire WA14 3JS (☎ 061 928 8700); Coopers & Lybrand Deloitte, Abacus Court, 6 Minshull St, Manchester M1 3ED (☎ 061 236 9191, fax 061 247 4000)

HOLDEN, William John; s of James Alfred Holden (d 1989), and Elsie Sophia, *née* Hinson (d 1979); *b* 7 Aug 1933; *Educ* Kings Sch Worcester, Aston Univ; *m* 17 July 1954, Cleone Winifred, da of Frank Henry Hodges, of Droitwich; 2 s (Jeremy b 1956, Simon b 1959), 1 da (Andrée b 1961); *Career* engr; fndr and chm Holden Hydroman plc 1969-87; chm Holden Heat plc 1987-88; FPRI; *Recreations* yachtsman, skiing; *Clubs* Sloanes; *Style—* William J Holden, Esq; The Old Rectory, Suckley, Worcester WR6 5DF (☎ 08864 337)

HOLDEN-BROWN, Sir Derrick; *b* 14 Feb 1923; *Educ* Westcliff; *m* 1950, Patricia Mary Ross Mackenzie; 1 s, 1 da; *Career* WWII Lt RNVR; CA 1948; vice chm Allied Breweries 1975-82 (dir 1967, fin dir 1972), dep chm Sun Alliance and London Insurance Co 1977-; chm: Allied-Lyons (beer, wine and spirits group) 1982-, White Ensign Assoc Ltd 1987-; chm: Brewers Soc 1978-80, Portsmouth Naval Tst 1989-; memb Alcohol Educn and Res Cncl 1982-85; kt 1979; *Recreations* sailing (yacht Aqualeo); *Clubs* Boodle's, Royal Yacht Squadron; *Style—* Sir Derrick Holden-Brown; Copse House, De La Warr Rd, Milford-on-Sea, Hants; Allied-Lyons plc, 24 Portland Place, London W1N 4BB (☎ 071 323 9000, fax 071 323 1741, telex 267605)

HOLDER, Derek Alfred; s of Jesse Alfred Holder, of 71 Crane Ave, Isleworth, Middx, and Vera Helen, *née* Haynes; *b* 7 Sept 1951; *Educ* Isleworth GS, Univ of Manchester (BSc); *Career* mgmnt trainee BOAC 1970-71, marketing graduate Ford Motor Company 1974-75, sales mangr then marketing mangr McGraw-Hill Book Company 1975-79, marketing mangr Readers Digest Assoc 1979-80, sr lectr then princ lectr Kingston Poly Business Sch 1980-87, md The Direct Marketing Centre 1987-; creator: BDMA Dip in Direct Marketing 1981, The Direct Marketing Centre (an Educational Trust); memb: Br Direct Marketing Assoc 1981, Direct Marketing Assoc (USA) 1983; FID 1985; *Recreations* squash, running, snooker, world travel; *Style—* Derek Holder, Esq; The Direct Marketing Centre, 1 Park Rd, Teddington, Middx TW11 0AR (☎ 081 977 5705, fax 081 943 2535)

HOLDER, Sir (John) Henry; 4 Bt (UK 1898), of Pitmaston, Moseley, Worcs; s of Sir John Eric Duncan Holder, 3 Bt; *b* 12 March 1928; *Educ* Eton, Univ of Birmingham (Dip Malting and Brewing); *m* 10 Sept 1960, Catharine Harrison, da of Leonard Baker (d 1973); 2 s (Nigel John Charles b 1962, Hugo Richard (twin) b 1962), 1 da (Bridget Georgina b 1964); *Heir* s, Nigel John Charles b 1962; *Career* prodn dir and head brewer Elgood and Son Ltd (Wisbech) 1975-; chm E Anglian Section Incorporated Brewers' Guild 1981-83; dip memb Inst of Brewing; *Recreations* sailing; *Clubs* Ouse Amateur SC; *Style—* Sir Henry Holder, Bt; 47 St Pauls Rd, Walton Highway, Wisbech, Cambs PE14 7DN

HOLDER, John Wakefield; s of Charles Holder (d 1969), of Superlatine, St George, Barbados, and Carnetta, *née* Blackman (d 1984); *b* 19 March 1945; *Educ* Combermere HS Barbados, Rochdale Coll; *m* Glenda Ann; 2 s (Christopher Paul b 1968, Nigel Anthony John b 1970); *Career* cricket umpire 1983-; playing career: Combermere HS 1959-63, Central CC Barbados 1964, Caribbean CC London 1965, BBC Motspur Park 1965-66, Hampshire CCC 1966-72; professional: Rawtenstall 1974, Norden 1975, Slaithwaite 1976, Royton 1977-78 and 1980-82, Austerlands 1979; test match umpire: debut England v Sri Lanka (Lords) 1988, England v Aust (Edgbaston) 1989, Pakistan v India series (Karachi, Faisalabad, Lahore, Sialkot) 1989, England v NZ (Edgbaston) 1990, England v India (Old Trafford) 1990; Texaco Trophy One Day Int umpire: England v Sri Lanka (Oval) 1988, England v Aust (Old Trafford) 1989, England v India (Headingley) 1990; umpire India Nehru Cup (Delhi, Bombay, Calcutta, Madras, Jullumder) 1989; reappointed to test panel 1991; first English umpire with John Hampshire to officiate in a test match series abroad Pakistan 1989; *Recreations* keep fit, supporting Manchester Utd FC; *Style—* John Holder, Esq; 1 Heald Close, Shawclough, Rochdale OL12 7HJ (☎ 0706 39554); Test & County Cricket Board, Lords Cricket Ground, London NW8 8QZ (☎ 071 286 4405/6)

HOLDER, Maj Nicholas Paul; TD (1982); s of Air Marshal Sir Paul Holder, KBE, CB, DSO, DFC, *qv*, of Innisfree, Bramshott Chase, Hindhead, Surrey, and Mary Elizabeth, *née* Kidd; *b* 10 Nov 1942; *Educ* Sherborne; *Career* Royal Scots Greys (2 Dragoons) 1963-71, Royal Scots Dragoon Gds Reserve of Offrs 1971-82; Inns of Ct and City Yeo; assoc dir Kleinwort Benson Ltd 1984-87, currently exec dir Fuji International Finance (merchant banking subsid of Fuji Bank Tokyo); memb: Br Jostedhals Glacier Expedition 1967, Br White Nile Hovercraft Expedition 1969; treas Br Ski Mountaineering Assoc; *Recreations* skiing, tennis; *Clubs* Bucks, Alpine; *Style*— Maj Nicholas Holder, TD; 92 Settrington Rd, London SW6 3BA (☎ 071 736 0072); Fuji International Finance Ltd, River Plate House, 7-11 Finsbury Circus, London EC2 (☎ 071 638 5743)

HOLDER, Nigel John Charles; s and h of Sir John Henry Holder, 4 Bt; *b* 6 May 1962; *Career* open water scuba instructor 1989, medic first aid instructor 1990, master scuba diver trainer 1990, IDC staff instructor 1990; memb PADI (Professional Assoc of Diving Instructors); *Recreations* scuba diving, motorcycling; *Style*— Nigel Holder, Esq; 47 St Paul's Rd North, West Walton Highway, nr Wisbech, Cambs PE14 7DN (☎ 0945 583493); Gildenburgh Water, Eastern Region Scuba Diving Centre, Eastrea Road, Whittlesey, Cambs PE7 2AR (☎ 0733 351288, fax 0733 351299)

HOLDER, Air Marshal Sir Paul Davie; KBE (1965), CB (1964), DSO (1942), DFC (1941); s of Hugh John Holder (d 1961); *b* 2 Sept 1911; *Educ* Bristol Univ (MSc, PhD), Univ of Illinois USA (Robert Blair Fell); *m* 1941, Mary Elizabeth Kidd; 2 s; *Career* cmmnd RAF 1936, CO No 218 Sqdn Bomber Cmd 1942, Admin Staff Coll Henley-on-Thames 1949, IDC 1956, AOC Singapore 1957, AOC Hong Kong 1958-59, ACAS (Trg) Air Miny 1960-63, AOC No 25 Gp Flying Trg Cmd, AOC-in-C Coastal Cmd, Cdr Maritime Air E Atlantic and Cdr Maritime Air Channel Cmd 1965-68, ret; memb Waverley Dist Cncl 1976-83; FRAeS; *Clubs* RAF; *Style*— Air Marshal Sir Paul Holder, KBE, CB, DSO, DFC; Innisfree, Bramshott Chase, Hindhead, Surrey GU26 6DG (☎ 042 873 4579)

HOLDER, Robert Woollard; s of Frank Douglas Holder, OBE, MC, JP, DL (d 1978), and Cynthia Olive Woollard, *née* Hart (d 1956); *b* 4 Dec 1924; *Educ* Charterhouse, Peterhouse Cambridge (MA); *m* 10 Sept 1949, Margaret Helen, da of Hubert Charles Baker (d 1948); 4 s (Robert George b 26 Sept 1950, Simon Edward b 18 July 1952, James Douglas b 22 June 1954, Benjamin William b 9 Jan 1969), 1 da (Charlotte Helen Cynthia (Mrs Crossley) b 16 July 1956); *Career* War Serv Lt Royal Devon Yeo RA 1943-46; admitted slr 1949; ptnr Dodson and Pulman Taunton 1951-60, md and chm Fairey Co Ltd Heston 1970-77 (Avimo Ltd Taunton 1960-71); chm: Bridport Gundry plc 1975-88, Longclose Ltd Leeds 1983-, Delta Communications plc 1984-89, Langdon Industries Ltd Taunton 1986-, Bridport-Gundry Ireland Ltd 1988-90; memb Ctee on the Intermediate Areas (the Hunt Ctee) 1968-70, chm SW Regnl Cncl CBI 1968-71, memb Cncl CBI 1968-78, memb Eng Industl Estates Corpn 1970-75, chm Industl Ctee SW Regnl Economic Cncl 1972-74; Univ of Bath: treas 1974-84, chm cncl 1984-86, pro chllr 1985-; chm Ctee for Investmt Lead Times 1977-78, dir Cncl for Small Businesses in Rural Areas 1981-85, memb Wessex Water Authy 1981-86; Hon LLD Univ of Bath 1986; FBIM; *Books* A Dictionary of American and British Euphemisms (1987), The Faber Dictionary of Euphemisms (1989); *Style*— Robert Holder, Esq; Langdon Industries Ltd, Walford Cross, Taunton, Somerset

HOLDERNESS, Martin William; s and h of Sir Richard William Holderness, 3 Bt; *b* 24 May 1957; *m* 1984, Elizabeth D, da of Dr R Thornton, of 5 Bristow Park, Belfast; 1 s (Matthew William Thornton b 23 May 1990); *Style*— Martin Holderness, Esq

HOLDERNESS, Baron (Life Peer UK 1979); Hon Richard Frederick Wood; PC (1959), DL (Yorks E Riding 1967); 3 s of 1 Earl of Halifax, KG, OM, GCSI, GCMG, GCIE, TD, PC, sometime Viceroy of India and Foreign Sec (d 1959), and Lady Dorothy Onslow, CI, DCVO, JP, DGStJ, yr da of 4 Earl of Onslow; unc of present (3) Earl of Halifax, 1 cous of 6 Earl of Onslow; *b* 5 Oct 1920; *Educ* Eton, New Coll Oxford; *m* 15 April 1947, Diana, o da of late Col Edward Orlando Kellett, DSO, MP (ka 1943; whose widow, Myrtle, m as her 2 husb Hon William McGowan, 2 s of 1 Baron McGowan); 1 s (Edward), 1 da (Emma, m Sir Nicholas Brooksbank, 3 Bt, *qv*); *Career* sits as Cons Peer in House of Lords; serv WWII, ME, Lt KRRC 1943, ret severely wounded, Hon Col 4 Bn Royal Green Jackets TAVR 1967-89; MP (C) Bridlington 1950-79; Parly sec to: Min of Pensions and Nat Insur 1955-58, Min of Labour 1958-59, Min of Power 1959-63, Min of Pensions and Nat Insur 1963-64, Min for Overseas Devpt 1970-74; chm Disablement Servs Authy 1987-; dir Hargreaves Group 1974-86; regnl dir Lloyds Bank 1980-89; Hon LLD: Sheffield 1962, Leeds 1978, Hull 1982; *Recreations* gardening, travel; *Style*— The Rt Hon Lord Holderness, PC, DL; House of Lords, London SW1; Flat Top House, Bishop Wilton, York YO4 1RY (☎ 075 96 266); 65 Collines de Guerrevieille, 83120 Ste Maxime, France

HOLDERNESS, Sir Richard William; 3 Bt (UK 1920), of Tadworth, Surrey; s of Sir Ernest William Elsmie Holderness, 2 Bt, CBE (d 1968); *b* 30 Nov 1927; *Educ* Corpus Christi Coll Oxford; *m* 1953, Pamela, da of Eric Chapman, CBE (d 1985); 2 s, 1 da; *Heir* s, Martin Holderness; 1 s (Matthew); *Career* ret as dist offr HM Overseas Civil Serv 1954; dir Whiteheads (estate agents and surveyors) 1967-86; FRICS 1976; *Recreations* golf, gardening; *Clubs* East India, West Sussex Golf; *Style*— Sir Richard Holderness, Bt; Bramfold Ct, Nutbourne, nr Pulborough, W Sussex

HOLDGATE, Dr Martin Wyatt; CB (1978); s of Francis Wyatt Holdgate, JP (d 1981), of Lancs, and Lois Marjorie, *née* Bebbington (d 1990); *b* 14 Jan 1931; *Educ* Arnold Sch Blackpool, Queens' Coll Cambridge (BA, MA, PhD); *m* 2 April 1963, Elizabeth Mary, *née* Dickason; 1 s (Nicholas Michael David b 1965); 1 step s (Martin Robert Arnold Weil b 1956); *Career* res fell Queens' Coll Cambridge 1953-56, sr scientist and jt ldr Gough Island Sci Survey 1955-56; lectr in zoology: Univ of Manchester 1956-57, Univ of Durham 1957-60; ldr Royal Soc expdn to Southern Chile 1958-59, asst dir of res Scott Polar Res Inst Cambridge 1960-63, sr biologist Br Antarctic Survey 1963-66, dep dir The Nature Conservancy 1966-70, dir Central Unit on Environmental Pollution DOE 1970-74, Inst of Terrestrial Ecology Natural Environment Res Cncl 1974-76, dir gen of res (and dep sec) DOE and Dept of Tport 1976-83, dep sec (environment protection) and chief enviroment scientist DOE 1983-88, chief sci advsr Dept of Tport 1983-88, dir gen Int Union for Conservation of Nature and Natural Resources (The World Conservation Union) 1988; UNEP 500 award 1988, UNEP Silver medal 1983, Bruce medal Royal Soc Edinburgh 1964; CBiol, FIBiol; *Books* Mountains in the Sea (1958), Antarctic Ecology (ed, 1970), A Perspective of Enviromental Pollution (1979), The World Environment 1972-82 (jt ed, 1982); numerous papers in biological and environmental journals and works on Antarctic; *Recreations* hill walking, local history, natural history; *Clubs* Athenaeum; *Style*— Dr Martin Holdgate, CB; International Union for Conservation of Nature and Natural Resources, Avenue du Mont-Blanc, CH-1196, Gland, Switzerland

HOLDING, Capt Alan Oswald; RN; s of James William Holding (d 1964), and Dorothy Florence, *née* Corney; *b* 15 Feb 1935; *Educ* Outram House Sch, Univ of Durham (BSc); *m* 13 Sept 1958, Pauline Frances (d 1989), da of Frederick James Eugene (d 1968); 1 s (Clive b 1962), 1 da (Paula b 1965); *Career* joined RN 1958; promoted: Cdr 1972, Capt 1981; dean RNEC Manadon 1982 (dep dean 1980), chief staff offr to C in C Naval Home Cmd 1984, dir naval educn and training support 1987, chief naval instr offr 1989-; C Eng, MRINA; *Recreations* golf, gardening; *Style*— Capt Alan Holding, RN; Calpe, 44 Hurstville Drive, Waterlooville, Hants (☎ 0705 252863); Ministry of Defence, Whitehall, London SW1

HOLDING, Malcolm Alexander; s of Adam Anderson Holding (d 1962), of Edinburgh, and Mary Lillian, *née* Golding; *b* 11 May 1932; *Educ* King Henry VIII Sch Coventry; *m* 28 Dec 1955, Pamela Eve, da of late Jack Hampshire; 2 da (Alison b 18 Aug 1959, Penelope b 14 Feb 1962); *Career* 2 Lt RCS 1951-53; Dip Serv: FO 1953-55, MECAS 1956-57, third sec commercial Br Embassy Tunis 1957-60, second sec commercial Br Embassy Khartoum 1960-64, second sec commercial (later first sec) Br Embassy Cairo 1964-66, Consul Bari 1968-69, FCO 1970-72, first sec Br Dep High Cmmn Madras 1972-74, FCO 1975-78, cnsllr 1978, Nat Def Coll Canada 1978-79, commercial cnsllr Br Embassy Rome 1979-81; Br consul gen: Edmonton 1981-85, Naples 1986; Commendatore dell'Ordine del Merito Italy 1980; *Recreations* sailing, skiing, travel, pottering; *Clubs* Rotary; *Style*— Malcolm Holding, Esq; Foreign and Commonwealth Office, London SW1A 2AH; British Consulate General, Via Crispi 122, I-80122 Naples Italy (☎ 39 81 663511)

HOLDSWORTH, Lt Cdr Arthur John Arundell; CVO (1980), OBE (1962), DL (Devon 1973), RN (ret); eld s of Frederick John Cropper Holdsworth, JP, DL, sometime Mayor of Totnes and Master of the Dart Vale Harriers (whose maternal grandmother was Hon Margaret, da of 1 Baron Denman); *b* 31 March 1915; *Educ* RNC Dartmouth; *m* 1940, Barbara Lucy Ussher, da of Lt-Col William Acton, DSO; 1 s (Nicholas b 1942), 1 da (Jane b 1945); *Career* served WWII at sea (despatches), Asst naval attaché Warsaw 1947-49; Br Jt Servs Mission Washington DC 1950-51, Naval Staff Germany 1954-56, Flag Lt to Admty Bd 1956-65; gentleman usher to HM The Queen 1967-85 (extra gentleman usher 1985-); steward Newton Abbot Racecourse 1967-85; dep pres Devon Branch BRCS 1971-85 (patron 1985-); High Sheriff Devon 1976-77, Vice Lord Lt Devon 1982-90; *Recreations* shooting, fishing; *Style*— Lt Cdr John Holdsworth, CVO, OBE, DL, RN; Holbeam Mill, Ogwell, nr Newton Abbot, Devon (☎ 0626 65547)

HOLDSWORTH, Brian John; s of Reginald Hugh Holdsworth, of Long Eaton, and Dorothy, *née* Ellis; *b* 27 Jan 1950; *Educ* Southwell Minster GS, Guy's Hosp Med Sch (BSc, MB BS); *m* 21 Sept 1974, Ursula Jean, da of Victor Robert Lees (d 1974), of Roehampton; 3 s (Matthew b 1978, Thomas b 1982, Christopher b 1989); *Career* house jobs Guy's Gp of Hosps 1973-76, registrar in surgery Royal Infirmary Sheffield 1976-78, sr orthopaedic registrar Nottingham Hosps 1981-86 (orthopaedic registrar 1978-81), conslt orthopaedic surgn Univ Hosp Nottingham and Harlow Wood Orthopaedic Hosp nr Mansfield 1986-; Frontiers of Fracture Management (contrib, 1989), FRCS 1978, fell Br Orthopaedic Assoc 1987; *Recreations* photography, picture framing, growing cacti; *Style*— Brian Holdsworth, Esq; 32 Victoria Cres, Sherwood, Nottingham NG5 4DA (☎ 0602 604142)

HOLDSWORTH, Nicholas John William Arthur; s of Lt Cdr (Arthur) John Arundell Holdsworth, CVO, OBE, of Newton Abbot, S Devon, *qv*, and Barbara Lucy Ussher, *née* Acton; *b* 10 May 1942; *Educ* Winchester; *m* 17 Sept 1966, Susan Antonia, da of Charles Anthony Fradgley, of Hill Hay, Combe Florey, Somerset; 2 s (Ben b 7 May 1968, Sam b 5 July 1970); *Career* Rifle Bde 1961-64, Lt; account exec Charles Hobson and Grey 1964-69, account mangr Lintas Ltd 1969-70, account dir Charles Barker Gp 1970-84 (dir Charles Barker City 1981-84), dir Dewe Rogerson 1984-; hon sec Weyfarers CC; *Recreations* cricket, national hunt racing; *Clubs* MCC, Hurlingham; *Style*— Nicholas Holdsworth, Esq; 32 Carmalt Gardens, Putney, London SW15 6NE (☎ 081 788 1240); Dewe Rogerson Ltd, 3 1/2 London Wall Buildings, London Wall, London EC2M 5SY (☎ 071 638 9571, fax 071 628 3444, telex 883610)

HOLDSWORTH, Sir (George) Trevor; s of William Holdsworth; *b* 29 May 1927; *Educ* Hanson GS Bradford, Keighley GS Yorkshire; *m* 1951, Patricia June Ridler; 3 s; *Career* Rawlinson Greaves and Mitchell 1944-51, Bowater Corpn Ltd 1952-63; joined Guest, Keen and Nettlefolds plc as dep chief accountant 1963, rising to dep chm 1974, md and dep chm 1977, gp chm 1980-88; dir: Thorn-EMI plc 1977-87, Midland Bank plc 1979-88; chm Allied Colloids Gp plc 1983-; chm British Satellite Broadcasting 1987-90, md National Power 1990-; vice pres: Engrg Employers' Fedn 1980-87, Ironbridge Gorge Museum Devpt Tst 1981-, BIM 1982- (vice chm 1978-80, chm 1980-82, vice pres 1982-); chm Brighton Festival Tst 1982 (tstee 1980-); dep chm Advsy Bd of Inst of Occupational Health 1980; tstee: Anglo-German Fndn for the Study of Industl Soc 1980-, Royal Opera House Tst 1981-86; memb Cncl: CBI 1974- (and Steering Gp on Unemployment 1982-83, Special Programmes Unit 1982-83, and chm Tax Reform Working Party 1984-85); dep pres CBI 1987; memb: Bd of Govrs Ashridge Mgmnt Coll 1978-, Engrg Industries Cncl 1980-87 (chm 1985-), Overseas Panel Duke of Edinburgh's Award 1980-, Ct Br Shippers' Cncl 1981-87, British-N America Ctee 1981-85, Cncl Royal Inst of Int Affrs 1983-85, Int Cncl of INSEAD 1985-; tstee UK & Int 1988; memb Worshipful Co of CAs 1977-; Hon DTech Loughborough 1981, Hon DSc Aston 1982, Hon DEng Bradford 1983, Hon DSc Sussex 1988; CAs Founding Socs' Centenary Award 1983; FCA; kt 1981; *Recreations* music, theatre; *Style*— Sir Trevor Holdsworth; National Power, 15 Newgate Street, London EC1A 7AU (☎ 071 634 5111)

HOLDSWORTH HUNT, Christopher; s of Peter Holdsworth Hunt, of Flat 4, 48 Queens Gate Gardens, London, and Monica, *née* Neville (d 1971); *b* 2 Aug 1942; *Educ* Eton, Univ of Tours; *m* 1, 24 Feb 1969 (m dis), Charlotte Folin; m 2, 24 June 1976, Joanne Lesley Starr Minoprio, *née* Reynolds; 2 s (Rupert Daniel b 10 Sept 1976, Piers Richard b 4 July 1980); *Career* cmmnd Coldstream Gds 1961-64; joined Murton & Adams Stockjobbers 1964 (firm acquired by Pinchin Denny 1969), memb Mgmnt Ctee Pinchin Denny 1985 (ptnr 1971, firm acquired by Morgan Grenfell 1986), dir Morgan Grenfell Securities 1987, fndr Peel Hunt & Company Ltd 1989-; Freeman City of London 1970; memb Ct of Grocers Co 1988 (memb Livery 1978); *Recreations* opera, ballet, theatre, golf, tennis, walking; *Clubs* White's, City of London, Vanderbilt, Berkshire Golf; *Style*— Christopher Holdsworth Hunt, Esq; 105 Elgin Crescent, London W11 2JF (☎ 071 221 5755); Peel, Hunt & Co Ltd, 37 Lombard St, London EC3V 9BQ (☎ 071 283 9666, fax 071 283 0219)

HOLE, Rev Canon Derek Norman; s of Frank Edwin Hole (d 1987), of Durban, 11 Widley Lane, Crownhill, Plymouth, Devon, and Ella Evelyn, *née* Thomas; *b* 5 Dec 1933; *Educ* Public Central Sch Plymouth, Lincoln Theol Coll; *Career* ordained Leicester Cath: deacon 1960, priest 1961; asst curate St Mary Magdalen Knighton Leicester 1960-62, domestic chaplain to Archbishop of Cape Town 1962-64, asst curate St Nicholas Kenilworth Warwicks 1964-67, rector St Mary the Virgin Burton Latimer Kettering Northants 1967-73, vicar St James the Greater Leicester 1973-, hon canon Leicester Cathedral 1983-, rural dean Christianity South 1983-, chaplain Leicester HS 1983-, chaplain to HM The Queen 1985-, The Chaplain to the High Sheriffs of Leicestershire 1980-85 and 1987; chm House of Clergy, vice pres Diocesan Synod, memb Bishop's Cncl 1986-, govr Alderman Newton's Sch Leicester 1976-82, tstee Leicester Church Charities 1983-, pres Leicester Rotary Club 1987-88; memb: Leicester Charity Orgn Soc 1983-, Victorian Soc 1986-; *Recreations* music, walking, reading biographies and Victorian history; *Clubs* The Leicestershire; *Style*— The Rev Canon Derek Hole; St James The Greater Vicarage, 216 London Rd, Leicester LE2 1NE (☎ 0533 542 111)

HOLEY, Brian; s of Clifford Holey (d 1966), of Harrogate, and Lillian Agnes, *née*

Chappell (d 1982); *b* 29 Sept 1928; *Educ* Ripon GS; *m* 10 Sept 1955, Joanne, da of George Henry Plews, of Norton, Cleveland; 1 s (Adrian b 1959); *Career* CA; ptnr Brough Holey & Peel 1953-55, sr ptnr Holey & Co 1955-, chm Ashworth Fin Ltd 1959-72 (dir 1955-59), chm Templey Homes Ltd 1964-82, ptnr Dickenson Keighley & Co Harrogate 1975-78, fin advsr Entergold Gp of Cos 1977-86; FCA 1951, FTII 1964; *Recreations* working, walking, music, theatre; *Style*— Brian Holey, Esq; Sheringham, Hornbeam Crescent, Harrogate, N Yorks; White Gates, Sedbusk, Hawes, N Yorks; Stuart House, 15/17 North Pk Rd, Harrogate, HG1 5PD (☎ 0423 566086)

HOLFORD, Francis Lindsay; s of Lindsay Tillestone Holford (d 1971), and Kathleen Swain (d 1942); *b* 1 April 1937; *Educ* Collyers Sch Sussex; *m* 1963, Jennifer Jane, da of Frederick Ferdinand Wolff, CBE; 2 s (Michael b 1964, John b 1973), 3 da (Clare b 1965, Catherine b 1967, Anna b 1969); *Career* chm and md Rudolf Wolff and Co Ltd (Metals and Commodities Futures and Options Traders); memb Bd Securities and Futures Authy; *Recreations* walking, reading, music; *Clubs* Gresham; *Style*— Francis Holford, Esq; Winton, 46 London Rd, Guildford, Surrey GU1 2AL (☎ 0483 69167); 2nd Floor, D Section, Plantation House, 31-35 Fenchurch St, London EC3M 3DX (☎ 071 626 8765, fax 071 626 3939, telex 885034)

HOLGATE, Peter Alan; s of Harold Holgate, of Leeds, and Ivy, *née* Instrell; *b* 8 Feb 1953; *Educ* West Leeds Boys HS, Univ of Bradford (MSc); *m* 1980, Dr Nelda Elizabeth Frater; 1 s (Andrew b 25 Nov 1985); *Career* articled clerk John Gordon Walton & Co CAs Leeds 1970-74, audit sr and asst mangr Coopers & Lybrand London and Nairobi 1975-78, fin controller Mitchell Cotts Kenya Ltd 1978-79, business planning mangr Hertz Europe Ltd London 1979-81; under sec then sec Accounting Standards Ctee 1981-86; sr tech mangr Deloitte Haskins & Sells 1986-90, tech ptnr Coopers & Lybrand Deloitte 1990-; author of numerous articles in professional jls, frequent speaker at accounting confs; memb: Fin Reporting Ctee and Res Bd ICAEW 1990-, Main Ctee and Tech Ctee LSCA 1990-; FCA; *Books* A Guide to Accounting Standards - Accounting For Goodwill (1985, updated 1990), A Guide To Accounting Standards - SSAP 23 Accounting For Acquisitions and Mergers (1986), A Guide to Accounting Standards - SSAP 12 revised Accounting for Depreciation (1987), Goodwill, Acquisitions & Mergers (1990); *Recreations* music, visiting second hand bookshops, reading; *Style*— Peter Holgate, Esq; Coopers & Lybrand Deloitte 128 Queen Victoria St, London EC4P 4JX (☎ 071 583 5000, fax 071 489 9597)

HOLKAR, Dr Vasant Eaknath; s of Eaknath Holkar (d 1947), of Holkar State, Indore, India, and Anandibai Holkar; *b* 1 July 1925; *Educ* Holkar Coll Indore India, Grant Med Coll Bombay, Univ of Bombay (MB BS); *m* 29 Mar 1963 (m dis 1984), Joan; 1 s (Mohan b 1967), 2 da (Veena b 1965, Sandya b 1970); *Career* Oldchurch Hosp: sr house offr in neurosurgery 1958, sr house offr in orthopaedics 1959, registrar accident and emergency 1960, registrar orthopaedics 1961-64; Law Hosp Lanarkshire 1964-66, registrar orthopaedics Queen Elizabeth II Hosp Welwyn Gd City 1966-68, conslt i/c Accident and Emergency Dept Old Church Hosp Romford 1970-; memb Casualty Surgns Assoc of GB, fell Br Orthopaedic Assoc; *Recreations* reading, travelling, photography; *Style*— Dr Vasant Holkar; Oldchurch Hospital, Romford, Essex RM7 0BE (☎ 0708 46090)

HOLL-ALLEN, Dr Robert Thomas James; s of Robert Thomas James Allen (d 1988), and Florence Janet Rachel (d 1972); *b* 3 Dec 1934; *Educ* Warwick Sch, Harvard Med Sch (BSc, MB BS, DLO); *m* 1, 2 June 1962 (m dis 1972), Barbara Mary, da of Leslie Thomas Holl (d 1971); 1 s (Jonathan Guy b 7 April 1966); m 2, 2 March 1974 (m dis 1989), Diane Elisabeth Tootill; 1 s (Robert (Robin) Gerald b 10 Jan 1975), 1 da (Amanda Jane b 23 Nov 1976); *Career* house physician UCH 1959, registrar Radcliffe Infirmary Oxford 1963-65, res fell Harvard Med Sch 1968-69, sr surgical registrar W Midland RHA 1966-72, conslt surgn E Birmingham Hosp 1972-, visiting overseas professorships; memb League of Friends of Solihull Hosp; fell RSM 1964, FRCS 1963, FACS 1974, fell Int Coll of Surgeons 1974; *Recreations* golf, travel, good food; *Clubs* Squire, Tennessee; *Style*— Dr Robert Holl-Allen; Dept of Surgery, East Birmingham Hosp, Bordesley Green East, Birmingham B9 5ST (☎ 021 766 6611)

HOLLAMBY, Edward Ernest; OBE (1970); s of Edward Thomas Hollamby (d 1979), of Kent, and Ethel May Kingdom; *b* 8 Jan 1921; *Educ* Sch of Arts and Crafts Hammersmith, Univ of London (Dip Town Planning and Civic Design); *m* 1941, Doris Isabel, da of William John Parker, of London; 1 s (Andrew b 1953), 2 da (Marsha b 1946, Jillian b 1948); *Career* Royal Marine Engrs Far East 1941-46; architect, designer, town planner; sr architect London CC 1949-62, dir of architecture and town planning London Borough of Lambeth 1969-81 (borough architect 1962-69), conslt London Docklands Development Corporation 1985-88 (chief architect and planner 1981-85); town planning projects incl: Erith Township Kent (Thamesmead prototype), Brixton Town Centre, relocation Covent Garden Market, Isle of Dogs, London Docklands, Wapping and Limehouse, Royal Docks, Becton; works incl conservation of historic bldgs: Brandon Est, Kennington, Offices and Rec Centre Brixton, Lambeth housing, Christopher Wren and Burlington Schs Hammersmith, special schs for handicapped children Brixton and Kennington, holiday home for disabled Netley, public library and civic hall W Norwood; numerous design awards including 2 DOE Bronze medals; RIBA: memb Cncl 1961-72, hon treas 1967-70, memb NW Kent Branch SE Region; memb: Historic Bldgs Cncl for Eng 1971-83, London Advsy Ctee Eng Heritage 1986-90, London Borough Bexley Cons Area Advsy Panel; fndr memb: William Morris Soc, Bexley Civic Soc; FRTPI, FRSA; Hon Assoc Landscape Institute; *Books* Docklands Heritage - A Study in Conservation and Regeneration in London Docklands (1987), Red House Bexleyheath 189 - The home of William Morris (1990); *Recreations* travel, music, theatre, opera, gardening; *Clubs* Arts; *Style*— Edward Hollamby, Esq, OBE; Red House, Red House Lane, Upton, Bexleyheath, Kent (☎ 081 303 8808)

HOLLAND, Anthony Delano Rokeby; s of late H D Holland; *b* 20 Feb 1929; *Educ* Harrow; *m* 1973, Anne Patricia Russell, da of Russell Lang, CBE; 1 da; *Career* former Lt Coldstream Gds, served Palestine; exec chm: The Lincroft Kilgour Group plc 1974-88, The Holland & Sherry Group Ltd, Kilgour French and Stanby Ltd; *Recreations* shooting, tennis, golf; *Clubs* MCC, Sunningdale Golf; *Style*— Anthony D R Holland, Esq; Windlesham Manor, Windlesham, Surrey (☎ 0276 72373); 9-10 Savile Row, London W1X 1AF (☎ 071 437 0404)

HOLLAND, Barbara Lambton; da of Frank Holland (d 1960), of Masham, and Dora, *née* Brown (d 1988); *b* 29 June 1926; *Educ* Ripon Girls HS, Dartford Coll of Physical Educn, Univ of London (Dip Physical Educn); *Career* teacher in physical educn Ripon Girl's HS 1951-62 (Allerton HS Leeds 1947-51), dep head Ripon GS 1968-87 (teacher in physician educn 1962-68); hockey player; hockey int 1954-56; memb touring teams to: SA 1954, Aust 1956, USA 1961; capt Yorks 1958-69; memb GB Women's Hockey Olympic Ctee; pres: Northern Co's Women's Hockey Assoc 1979-84, All Eng Women's Hockey Assoc 1986-; *Recreations* gardening, theatre, music; *Style*— Miss Barbara Holland; The Bungalow, Masham, nr Ripon, North Yorks HG4 4ER (☎ 0765 89345)

HOLLAND, Brian Arthur; s of George Leigh Holland, of Heysham, Lancs, and Hilda Holland, MBE, *née* Hogg; *b* 14 June 1935; *Educ* Manchester GS, Univ of Manchester (LLB); *m* 25 Sept 1964, Sally, da of Gordon W Edwards (d 1988), of E Sussex; 1 s (Andrew David b 1966), 1 da (Alison Mary b 1969); *Career* admitted slr 1961; joined PO Solicitors Dept 1961, head of civil litigation PO Slrs Office 1977-79 (dir of litigation and prosecutions 1979-81), slr to the PO 1981-; *Books* Halsbury's Laws of England (contrib 4 edn, vol 36); *Recreations* photography, studying railways, sketching, gardening; *Style*— Brian Holland, Esq; 23 Grasmere Rd, Purley, Surrey CR8 1DY (☎ 081 660 0479); Post Office Solicitors Office, Impact House, 2 Edridge Rd, Croydon, Surrey CR9 1PJ (☎ 081 681 9011, fax 081 681 9220)

HOLLAND, Christopher John; QC (1978); s of Frank Holland (d 1979), of Leeds, and Winifred Mary, *née* Pigott (d 1984); *b* 1 June 1937; *Educ* Leeds GS, Emmanuel Coll Cambridge (MA, LLB); *m* 11 Feb 1967, Jill Iona; 1 s (Charles Christopher b 20 May 1969), 1 da (Victoria Joanna b 1 June 1971); *Career* Nat Serv 3 Royal Tank Regt 1956-58; barr Inner Temple 1963; practised NE Circuit; bencher Inner Temple 1985; vice chm Ctee of Inquiry into the Outbreak of Legionnaires' Disease at Stafford 1986; chm Lower Washburn Parish Cncl 1976-; *Clubs* United Oxford and Cambridge Univ; *Style*— Christopher Holland, Esq, QC; Pearl Chambers, 22 East Parade, Leeds LS1 5BU (☎ 0532 452702, fax 0532 420683); 6 Pump Court, Temple, London EC4Y 7AR (☎ 071 583 6013, fax 071 353 0464)

HOLLAND, (Robert) Einion; s of Robert Ellis Holland, and Bene, *née* Williams; *b* 23 April 1927; *Educ* Univ Coll N Wales Bangor (BSc); *m* 1955, Eryl Haf (d 1988); 1 s (Gareth), 2 da (Sian, Eluned); *Career* Pearl Assurance plc: joined 1953, chief mangr 1977-83, dir and chm 1983-89; dir: Aviation and General Insurance Co Ltd 1973-89, Pearl Assurance (Unit Funds) Ltd 1975-89, Crawley Warren Group plc, New London Properties Ltd 1984-89, Queens Ice Skating Ltd 1984-89, Pearl Group plc 1986-90 (chm 1986-89), BR Property Board 1987-90; memb Cncl Univ of Wales 1990-; FIA; *Recreations* golf, Welsh lit; *Style*— Einion Holland, Esq; 55 Corkscrew Hill, West Wickham, Kent BR4 9BA (☎ 081 777 1861)

HOLLAND, Elisabeth, Lady; Elisabeth Hilda Margaret; only child of Thomas Francis Vaughan Prickard, CVO, JP, by his w Margaret, *née* Raikes, niece through her mother of 1st Baron Parmoor; *m* 1937, Sir Jim Sothern Holland, 2 Bt, TD (d 1981); 2 da; *Style*— Elisabeth, Lady Holland; Dderw, Rhayader, Powys LD6 5EY (☎ 0597 810226)

HOLLAND, Geoffrey; CB (1984); s of late Frank Holland, CBE, and Elsie Freda, *née* Smith; *b* 9 May 1938; *Educ* Merchant Taylors', St John's Coll Oxford (MA); *m* 1964, Carol Ann, da of Sidney Challen (d 1982); *Career* joined Miny of Labour 1961, asst private sec 1964-65, princ private sec to Sec of State for Employment 1971-72; Manpower Servs Cmmn: head of Planning 1973, dir of Special Programmes 1977, conslt Industl Ctee C of E Bd of Social Responsibility 1980-, second perm sec 1986, dir Manpower Servs Cmmn 1981-; *Recreations* journeying, opera, exercising the dog; *Clubs* East India; *Style*— Geoffrey Holland, Esq, CB; Manpower Services Commission, Moorfoot, Sheffield S1 4PQ

HOLLAND, Sir Guy Hope; 3 Bt (UK 1917), of Westwell Manor, Oxford; yr s of Sir (Alfred Reginald) Sothern Holland, 1 Bt, JP (d 1948), and Stretta Aimee, *née* Price (d 1949); suc er bro, Sir Jim Sothern Holland, 2 Bt, TD, 1981; descended from the Holland family of Pendleton, Lancashire, as recorded at the College of Arms; *b* 19 July 1918; *Educ* privately, ChCh Oxford; *m* 12 May 1945, Joan Marianne, da of late Capt Herbert Edmund Street, 20 Hussars; 2 da (Davina, Georgiana); *Heir* none; *Career* late Capt Royal Scots Greys; farmer; art dealer; *Recreations* hunting, shooting, gardening, travel; *Clubs* Boodle's, Pratt's; *Style*— Sir Guy Holland, Bt; Sheepbridge Barn, Eastleach, Cirencester, Glos GL7 3PS (☎ 036 785 296)

HOLLAND, James Sylvester; OBE (1951); s of James Holland (d 1940), and Mary, *née* Munden; *b* 19 Sept 1905; *Educ* Mathematical Sch Rochester, Rochester Sch of Art, Royal Coll of Art (ARCA), Central Sch of Art; *m* 1, 1936 (m dis 1950); 2 da (Susan (Mrs Gibson) b 1939, Vivien (Mrs Powell) b 1943; m 2, 1953, Jacqueline, *née* Arnall; 1 s (James Julian), 1 da (Jane Caroline); *Career* freelance graphic designer and illustrator 1929-; princ clients: Shell, Curwen Press, Imperial Airways, Empire Marketing Board, Stuarts Advertising, Bodley Head; display and exhibition design: Gas Light & Coke Co London, Empire Exhibition Glasgow 1938, Expo 1937 Paris Peace Pavilion, Exhibitions Div Miny of Info 1941-, Exhibitions Div Central Office of Info 1946-, Festival of Br Office 1949-51, Miner Comes to Town Central Office of Info 1947; co-ordinating designer and design gp memb Festival of Br; contrib to various design pubns, author Minerva at Fifty Jubilee History of SIAD (1980); FSIAD 1946 (pres 1960), FRSA 1951; *Style*— James Holland, Esq, OBE; Romford Cottage, Romford Rd, Pembury, Kent TN2 4BB (☎ 089 282 2382)

HOLLAND, John Anthony; s of Maj John Holland, of Cornerways, Southella Rd, Yelverton, Devon, and Dorothy Rita, *née* George; *b* 9 Nov 1938; *Educ* Ratcliffe Coll Leics, Univ of Nottingham (LLB); *m* 1 June 1963, Kathleen Margaret (Kay), da of John Smellie Anderson (d 1978); 3 s (Andrew John, Christopher Iain, Nicholas Alexander); *Career* admitted slr 1962, ptnr Foot & Bowden Plymouth; chm Social Security Appeals Tbnl; memb Marre Ctee; Law Soc: elected to Cncl 1976, vice pres 1989, pres 1990; govr Plymouth Coll 1979-, chm Regnl Advsy Cncl BBC SW 1984-87; pres: Plymouth Law Soc 1986, Cornwall Law Soc 1988; memb Law Soc 1962; *Books* Principles of Registered Land Conveyancing (1968), Landlord and Tenant (1970); *Recreations* opera, travel, sailing; *Clubs* Royal Western Yacht of England; *Style*— Anthony Holland, Esq; 46 Thornhill Way, Mannamead, Plymouth PL3 5NP (☎ 0752 220 529); 66 Andrewes House, Barbican, London EC2Y 8AY (☎ 071 638 5044); 70-76 North Hill, Plymouth, Devon P14 8HH (☎ 0752 663 416, fax 0752 671 802, telex 45223)

HOLLAND, John Lewis; s of George James Holland (d 1988), of Notts, and Esther, *née* Swindell; *b* 23 May 1937; *Educ* Nottingham Tech GS; *m* 1958, Maureen Ann, da of Leonard Adams (d 1973), of Notts; 1 s (Jeremy b 1965), 1 da (Lesley b 1959); *Career* reporter Nottingham Evening News 1954, sports ed Aldershot News Group 1956, sub ed Bristol Evening Post 1964, ed West Bridgford and Clifton Standard 1966, dep sports ed Birmingham Evening Mail 1972; ed: Sandwell Evening Mail 1979 (gen mangr 1981), The Birmingham Post 1984-90, Birmingham Post and Evening Mail 1986-90 (promotions dir); md Herts and Essex Newspapers Ltd; dir Birmingham convention and visitor bureau, pres Chartered Inst of Mktg (Birmingham); *Recreations* sport (playing squash), gardening, DIY, horses; *Style*— John Holland, Esq; Windgarth, Lynn Lane, Shenstone, Lichfield (☎ 0992 587826); 5 Maistrali II, Protaras, Cyprus; Herts and Essex Newspapers Ltd, 1 Fore Street, Hertford SG14 1DB

HOLLAND, Julian Miles (Jools); s of Derek Holland, of London, and June Rose, *née* Lane; *b* 24 Jan 1958; *Educ* Park Walk Sch, Invicta Sherington Sch, Shooters' Hill Sch; *partner 1* (until 1986), Mary Leahy; 2 c (George Soloman b 14 April 1984, Rosie Areatha Mae b 1 Oct 1985; *partner 2*, Christabel Durham; 1 da (Mabel Ray Brittania b 22 Nov 1990); *Career* pianist 1975-78; keyboard player Squeeze 1978- (hits incl: Take Me I'm Yours, Cool for Cats, Up The Junction, Hourglass, Annie Get Your Gun, Pulling Mussels from a Shell, Tempted, Slap and Tickle), regularly tours UK and US, concerts at Madison Square Garden and Royal Albert Hall; solo album A World of His Own (IRS) 1990; guested with numerous artists incl: Elvis Costello, Sting, Al Green, Dr John, The The, Fine Young Cannibals (The Raw and the Cooked); TV Presenter: The Tube (C4) 1981-86, Juke Box Jury (BBC 2) 1989-, Sunday Night (with David Sanborn, NBC) 1990, The Happening (BSB) 1990; actor The Groovy Fellers (C4 TV) 1988; *Recreations* sketching, giving advice; *Style*— Jools Holland, Esq; Helicon

Mountain Ltd, Helicon Mountain, London SE3 7LP (☎ 081 858 0984, fax 081 293 4555)

HOLLAND, Julie Dawn; da of Alexander Mason, of Barbados, and Ann Holland; *b* 20 Jan 1966; *Educ* Cardinal Newman HS, Xaverian Sixth Form Coll (Eng Schs Cross Country champion 1984), Univ of Leeds (BA); *Career* long-distance runner; ranked: 2 in GB over 5000m, 3 in GB over 10,000m, 9 in GB over 3000m, 17 in the world over 5000m, 40 in the world over 10,000m, 12 over 10,000m in Euro Track Championships 1990; promotions and mktg asst mangr for a sports co; *Clubs* Sale Harriers; *Style*— Ms Julie Holland

HOLLAND, Sir Kenneth Lawrence; CBE (1971), QFSM (1974); s of Percy Lawrence Holland (d 1966), of Colwyn Bay, Wales; *b* 20 Sept 1918; *Educ* Whitcliffe Mount GS Yorks; *m* 1941, Pauline Keith, da of George Mansfield (d 1925), of Oldham; 2 s, 1 da; *Career* entered fire serv Lancs 1937; chief fire offr: Bristol 1960-67, W Riding Yorks 1967-72; HM chief inspr of Fire Servs 1972-80; dir Gent Ltd Leicester 1981-; chm: Fire Services Central Examinations Bd 1978-84, Loss Prevention Certification Bd 1985-; tstee Fire Services Res and Trg Tst 1983-; hon treas Poole Arts Fedn (Friends of the Poole Arts Centre 1985-); OStJ 1964; pres Assoc Structure Fire Protection Contractors and Manufacturers; memb BS2 Bd, chm BSI Multitechnics cncl 1984-; kt 1981; *Recreations* motor sport, the arts (especially theatre); *Clubs* St John House, Royal Over-Seas League; *Style*— Sir Kenneth Holland, CBE, QFSM

HOLLAND, Hon Mrs (Margaret Catharine); *née* Edmondson; da of Rev 2 Baron Sandford, DSC, and Catherine Mary, da of late Rev Oswald Andrew Hunt; *b* 7 Nov 1947; *Educ* Downe House Newbury, Trinity Coll Dublin (Dip Social Studies), Bristol Univ (Cert in Applied Social Studies); *m* 1977, Charles Alan Simon Holland, s of Francis Holland; 2 da (Hannah b 1979, Venetia b 1981), 1 s (Hereward b 1984); *Career* social worker; ILEA Sch Health Serv 1969-72, psychiatric social worker Friern Barnet Hosp 1973-75, sr social worker Child Abuse Unit (Reading) 1977-79; gp ldr Reading Parents Anonymous 1980-83; garden designer 1983-; book-seller 1987-90; med social worker Watlington and Churchill Hosps Oxford 1990-; *Recreations* music, art, swimming, gardening; *Style*— The Hon Mrs Holland; Barncroft, Brightwell-cum-Sotwell, Wallingford, Oxon OX10 0RJ

HOLLAND, Gp Capt Peter; MBE (1967); s of Capt George William Holland (d 1956), and Margaret May, *née* Clark (d 1976); *b* 7 March 1935; *Educ* St Michael's Coll Leeds, Hastings GS; *m* 29 Jan 1962, Kerstin Viola Elisabet, da of Alfred Eugen Lindberg, of Stockholm; 2 s (Peter b 1962, David b 1964), 2 da (Kristina b 1966, Ann-Marie b 1979); *Career* RAF Regt 1952-61, cmmnd 1954, Supply and Mvmnts 1961-; sr air mvmnts offr: Akrotiri Cyprus 1962-64, RAF Colerne 1965-67, Anzuk Tengah Singapore 1971-74; instr Jt Warfare Estab 1974-77; CO RAF Mvmnts Sch 1977-78, command mvmnts offr HQ RAF Support Command 1978-81, CO Supply Wing RAF Henlow 1981-83, chief of material and mvmnts 2 ATAF Germany 1983-84, Gp Capt Supply and mvmnts and asst COS (logistics) HQ RAF Strike Cmd 1984-89, Future RAF Stockholding Policy Study 1989-90, ret RAF 1990; MBIM 1981, MILDM 1981; *Recreations* sailing, windsurfing, skiing, squash; *Clubs* RAF; *Style*— Gp Capt Peter Holland, MBE

HOLLAND, Peter Rodney James; s of Arthur Giles Stewart Holland (d 1981), and Elizabeth Hamilton, *née* Simpson; *b* 31 July 1944; *Educ* St Edmunds Canterbury, Univ Coll Oxford (MA); *m* 16 May 1975, Susan Elizabeth, da of Frederick Roger Okeby (d 1987); 1 s (William), 1 da (Philippa); *Career* slr 1968, ptnr Allen and Overy 1972-; chm Co Law Ctee Law Soc 1983-87; *Recreations* skiing, outdoor activities; *Style*— Peter Holland, Esq; Long Sutton, Basingstoke, Hants; Allen and Overy, 9 Cheapside, London EC2V 6AD (☎ 071 248 9898, fax 071 236 2192, telex 8812801)

HOLLAND, Sir Philip Welsby; s of late John Holland, of Middlewich, Cheshire; *b* 14 March 1917; *Educ* Sir John Deane's Sch Northwich; *m* 1943, Josephine Alma, da of Arthur Hudson, of Plymouth; 1 s; *Career* RAF 1936-46, cmmnd Electrical Engrg Branch 1943; memb Cncl Kensington 1955-59, fndr memb Cons Cwlth Cncl; MP (C): Acton 1959-64, Nottinghamshire (Carlton) 1966-83, Gedling 1983-87; PPS to: Min of Pensions and Nat Insur 1961-62, Chief Sec to Treasy 1962-64, Min for Aerospace 1970-72, Min for Trade and Indust 1972-74; chm Ctee of Selection 1979-84; personnel conslt Standard Telephones and Cables until 1981, memb Mr Speaker's Panel of Chm 1983-87; rector's warden St Margaret's Church Westminster Abbey 1990-; kt 1983; *Books* The Quango Explosion (1978), Quango Quango Quango (1979), The Governance of Quango (1981), Quelling the Quango (1982), Lobby Fodder (1988); *Style*— Sir Philip Holland; 53 Pymers Mead, West Dulwich, London SE21 8NH

HOLLAND, Robert Matthew Crowder; s of Maj Charles Matthew Holland (d 1959), and Roberta Violet Holland, JP, *née* Crowder; *b* 18 May 1948; *Educ* St Philip's GS Birmingham, Birmingham Art Coll, Oxford Poly Sch of Architecture; *m* 22 Sept 1973, Philippa Madeleine, da of Wilfred Tracy (d 1980); 2 s (Matthew, Thomas), 1 da (Elizabeth); *Career* bd dir CG Smedley & Assocs Ltd Advertising Agency 1978-89 (jr account exec 1969), proprietor The Holland Owen Partnership 1989-, bd dir The Birmingham Media Devpt Agency Ltd 1989-; memb Cncl Birmingham Publicity Assoc (chm 1987-88); hon sec Edgbaston Archery and Lawn Tennis Soc, hon trophies sec Warwicks Lawn Tennis Assoc; *Recreations* tennis, swimming, photography, reading; *Style*— Robert Holland, Esq; The Holland Owen Partnership, Blenheim House, 263 Alcester Rd South, King's Heath, Birmingham B14 6DT (☎ 021 441 2442, fax 021 441 2446)

HOLLAND, Maj Stanley; TD (1950), JP (1964); s of Albert John Holland (ka 1915), and Amy Alice Smith (d 1972); *b* 4 Aug 1912; *Educ* Lancashire Hill Sch, Stockport Coll; *m* 26 Feb 1946, Marjorie Edwina, da of John Edwin Haslam (d 1938), of Prestatyn, N Wales; *Career* TA RA Field Regt 1938, Staff Capt and instr Sch of Mil Engrg, Staff Maj G2 Supreme HQ Mil Mission to Denmark, ret Army Res 1962; incorporated commercial conslt; JP 1964-; memb Lloyd's 1970-; hon memb Anglo-Danish Soc, hon sr memb Univ of Kent at Canterbury 1989; memb: Devpt Bd Univ of Kent 1990, Court Univ of Kent 1990, Nat Tst; tstee Stockport Sunday Sch; vice pres Edenbridge and Oxted Agric Show; Freeman City of London 1970, Liveryman Worshipful Co of Wheelwrights 1970 (memb Court 1980); FBSC 1946 (sr vice pres); Knight (1 class) Order of Danneborg Denmark 1946, Decoration Honour (Denmark 1990); *Recreations* world travel, viewing wildlife; *Style*— Maj Stanley Holland, TD, JP

HOLLAND, Prof Walter Werner; s of Henry H Holland (d 1959), of London, and Hertha, *née* Zentner; *b* 5 March 1929; *Educ* Rugby, Univ of London, St Thomas' Hospital Med Sch (BSc, MB BS, MD); *m* 29 Oct 1964, Fiona, da of Douglas C Love (d 1976), of Bristol; 3 s (Peter b 1965, Richard b 1967, Michael b 1970); *Career* flying offr and Flt Lt RAF 1956-58; res fell: MRC 1959-61, Johns Hopkins Univ Baltimore USA 1961-62; prof (former sr lectr and reader) St Thomas's Hosp 1962- (casualty offr 1955-56); author of over 315 articles and books; inaugral lectr Johns Hopkins Univ 1977 (elected lifetime memb Soc of Scholars 1970), Fogarty Scholar-in-Residence NIH Bethseda USA 1984-85, Theodore Badger visiting prof Harvard Univ Cambridge USA 1984, first Sawyer Scholar in Res Case Western Reserve Med Sch Cleveland USA 1985; pres: Int Epidemiological Assoc, Faculty of Community Med; vice chm W Lambeth Health Authy 1983-86, hon memb American Epidemiological Soc 1985; Hon DUniv Bordeaux 1981, Hon DUniv Free Univ of Berlin 1990; memb: RSM, Soc for Social Med, Royal Statistical Soc, Int Union Against Tuberculosis, Int Epidemiological Assoc; FFPHM, FRCPE, FRCP, FRCGP; *Clubs* Athenaeum; *Style*— Prof Walter Holland; Dept of Public Health Medicine, UMDS, St Thomas' Campus, London SE1 7EH (☎ 071 928 9292, fax 071 928 1468, telex 27913)

HOLLAND, Wright Henry (Harry); s of Joseph Holland (d 1942), of Glasgow, and Joan Rose, *née* Goddard; *b* 11 April 1941; *Educ* Rutlish Sch Merton, St Martin's Sch of Art (DipAD); *m* Maureen, da of Lucien Coulson; 2 da (Samantha Joan b 18 June 1964, Emma Corinna b 6 May 1967); *Career* artist; lectr 1969-78 (Coventry, Hull, Stourbridge, Cardiff); solo exhibitions: Roundhouse Gallery 1979, Oriel Gallery Cardiff 1979, Welsh Arts Cncl Touring Exhibition 1980, Mineta Move Gallery Brussels 1981, Robin Garton Gallery London 1982 and 1983, Arnold Katzen Gallery NY 1982, FIAC Paris (Mineta Move) 1983 and 1984, Ian Birksted Gallery 1984, Artiste Gallery Bath 1985, Edinburgh Demarcations (Garton & Cooke) 1985, Chicago Art Fair (Ian Birksted Gallery) 1986, New Drawings (Birksted Gallery) 1986, Andrew Knight Gallery Cardiff 1987, Bohun Gallery Henley 1987, 1989, Thumb Gallery 1988, 1990, Garton & Co 1988, Forum Art Fair Hamburg (Thumb Gallery) 1989; group exhibitions incl: Aspects of Realism 1976-78, From Wales 1977, Fruitmarket Gallery Edinburgh 1977, Nat Eisteddfod of Wales (prizewinner); 1978, Grandes et Jeunes d'aujourd'hui (Grand Palais Paris) 1979, Probity of Art (Welsh Arts Cncl touring exhibition) 1980, Br Art Show (Arts Cncl of GB) 1980, Art of the Eighties (Walker Art Gallery) 1981, Euro Print Biennale Heidelberg 1983, The Male Nude (Ebury Gallery) 1983, Bradford Print Biennale 1984, second Int Contemporary Art Fair 1985, Int Contemporary Art Fair LA (Thumb Gallery) 1986, 1987 and 1988, Bruton Gallery 1987, Self Portrait - A Modern View (touring) 1987, The Drawing Show (Thumb Gallery) 1988, Ways of Telling (Mostyn Gallery Wales) 1989, fourth Int Contemporary art Fair LA (Thumb Gallery) 1989; work in the collections of: Contemporary Art Soc, Tate Gallery, Newport Museum and Art Gallery, Glynn Yivian Art Gallery and Museum Swansea, Nat Museum of Wales Cardiff, Welsh Arts Cncl, Contemporary Arts Soc for Wales, Metropolitan Museum of Art NY, Heineken Collection Amsterdam, Euro Parly Collection, Belgian Nat Collection; *Clubs* Chelsea Arts; *Style*— Harry Holland, Esq; c/o Jill George, 38 Lexington St, London 31R 3HR (☎ 071 439 7319, fax 071 287 0478)

HOLLAND-HIBBERT, Hon Diana; MBE (1946); da of 4 Viscount Knutsford (d 1976); *b* 1914; *Career* Sr Cdr ATS, 1939-45 War; *Style*— The Hon Diana Holland-Hibbert; Munden, Watford, Herts (☎ 0923 672002)

HOLLAND-HIBBERT, Hon Henry Thurstan; er s and h of 6 Viscount Knutsford, *qv*; *b* 6 April 1959; *Educ* Eton, RAC Cirencester; *m* 1988, Katherine, da of Sir John Bruce Woolacott Ropner, 2 Bt; 1 da (Rosie b 1990); *Career* Coldstream Guards 1979-83; *Clubs* Boodles; *Style*— The Hon Henry Holland-Hibbert; 7 Walham Grove, London SW6

HOLLAND-MARTIN, (Robert) Robin George; s of Cyril Holland-Martin (d 1983), and Rosa, *née* Chadwyck-Healey; *b* 6 July 1939; *Educ* Eton; *m* 1976, Dominique, da of Maurice Fromaget; 2 da; *Career* Cazenove & Co 1960-74 (ptnr 1968-74), fin dir Paterson Products Ltd 1976-86, conslt Newmarket Venture Capital plc 1982-, dir Henderson Admin Group plc 1983-; memb: Cncl Met Hosp-Sunday Fund 1963- (chm 1977-), Homoeopathic Tst 1970-90 (vice-chm 1975-90) Advsy Cncl V & A Museum 1972-83, ctee Assocs of V & A 1976-85 (chm 1981-85), visiting ctee RCA 1982- (chm 1984-); tstee V & A 1983-85; hon dep treas Cons and Unionist Pty 1979-82; tstee Blackie Fndn Tst 1971- (chm 1987-); *Clubs* White's, RAC; *Style*— Robin Holland-Martin, Esq; 18 Tite St, London SW3 4HZ (☎ 071 352 7871)

HOLLAND-MARTIN, Dame Rosamund Mary; DBE (1983, OBE 1948), DL (Hereford & Worcester); da of Charles Harry St John Hornby (d 1946), and Cicely Rachel Emily, *née* Barclay (d 1971); *b* 26 June 1914; *m* 1951, Adm Sir Deric (Douglas Eric) Holland-Martin, GCB, DSO, DSC (d 1977), s of Robert Holland-Martin (d 1944), of Overbury Ct, Tewkesbury; 1 s (Benjamin), 1 da (Emma); *Career* memb CEC NSPCC 1947-, chm NSPCC 1969-88; pres: Sea Cadets, Friends of Worcester Cathedral; *Recreations* photography, needlework, collecting; *Style*— Lady Holland-Martin, DBE, DL; Bell's Castle, Kemerton, Tewkesbury, Glos GL20 7JW

HOLLANDS, Clive Thomas Patrick; s of Horace Patrick Hollands (d 1989), of London, and Ivy Louise Delane, *née* Faithfull (d 1967); *b* 26 April 1929; *Educ* St Clement Danes London, St Mary's Coll Liverpool; *m* 16 Dec 1950, Euphemia, da of William Erskine Garrett (d 1957), of Galloway; 1 s (Bruce b 1953), 1 da (Roberta b 1957); *Career* RN 1946-53 special serv engagement; chief petty offr writer Caltex for overseas tankship (UK) Ltd (dep marine personnel superintendent); dir Scot Soc for Prevention of Vivisection 1966-68, co sec St Andrew Animal Fund 1970, sec ctee for Reform of Animal Experimentation 1976, conslt 1989-; memb HM Govt Animal Procedures Ctee and Farm Animal Welfare Cncl; hon assoc Br Veterinary Assoc; *Books* Compassion is the Bugler - The Struggle for Animal Rights (1980), contrib: Animal Rights - A Symposium (1979), Humane Education - A Symposium (1981), In Defence of Animals (1985), Animal Experimentation - The Consensus Changes (1989), For the Love of Animals - True Stories from the Famous (1989); *Recreations* scouting; *Clubs* Royal Commonwealth House; *Style*— Clive Hollands, Esq; Burnbank Cottage, Soonhope, Peebles EH45 8BH (☎ 0721 22445); Queensferry Chambers, 10 Queensferry St, Edinburgh EH2 4PG (☎ 031 225 6039, fax 031 220 6377)

HOLLEDGE, Richard Antony; *b* 25 Oct 1946; *Educ* Hurstpierpoint Coll, Univ of Bristol; *Career* Mirror Group Training Scheme 1968-71, People Newspaper 1971-76, features ed Reveille 1976-77, dep chief sub Daily Mirror 1978-80; Sunday Mirror: dep chief sub ed 1977-78, chief sub ed 1980-82, asst ed 1982-87; night ed Today 1987-89, ed Wales on Sunday 1989-; *Recreations* skiing, gardening; *Style*— Richard Holledge, Esq; Wales on Sunday, Thomson House, Havelock St, Cardiff CF1 1WR (☎ 0222 223333)

HOLLENDEN, 3 Baron (UK 1912); Gordon Hope Hope-Morley; o s of Hon Claude Hope-Morley (d 1968, yr s of 1 Baron), and Lady Dorothy Edith Isabel Hobart-Hampden-Mercer-Henderson (d 1972), da of 7 Earl of Buckinghamshire; suc unc 1977; *b* 8 Jan 1914; *Educ* Eton; *m* 27 Oct 1945, Sonja, da of late Thorolf Sundt, of Bergen, Norway; 3 s; *Heir* s, Hon Ian Hampden Hope-Morley; *Career* served Black Watch 1939-45, Maj; alderman City of London 1954-58, former chm I and R Morley Ltd, ret; *Clubs* Brooks's, Beefsteak; *Style*— The Rt Hon the Lord Hollenden; Hall Place, Leigh, Tonbridge, Kent (☎ 0732 832255)

HOLLENDEN, Anne, Baroness; Violet Norris; da of Alfred Leverton, of Peterborough; *m* 1, Dr Frank Howitt, CVO (decd); *m* 2, 1963, as his 3 wife, 2 Baron Hollenden (d 1977); *Style*— The Rt Hon Anne, Lady Hollenden; Valley Farm, Duntisbourne Hill, nr Cirencester

HOLLEY, Rear Adm Ronald Victor; CB (1987); s of Lt Victor Edward Holley, BEM (d 1986), and Queenie Marion, *née* Watts (d 1989); *b* 13 July 1931; *Educ* Rondebosch SA, Portsmouth GS, RN Engrg Coll, RAF Tech Coll, NATO Def Coll, RCDS; *m* 21 Aug 1954, Dorothy Brierley, da of Lt James Brierley, MBE; 2 s (Jonathan b 1956, Matthew b 1957), 2 da (Rachel b 1959, Amanda b 1959); *Career* joined RN 1949, Cdr 1968, Capt and naval asst to controller of the Navy 1975, Cdre and dir helicopter projects Procurement Exec, Capt HMS Thunderer, Rear Adm staff RCDS 1984, dir gen aircraft, ret 1987; ADC 1984; tech dir Shell Aircraft 1987-; vice chm aerospace IMechE, sec Euro Helicopter Operators' Ctee; MIMechE 1958, MIEE 1988, FRAeS 1988; *Recreations* the bassoon, sailing, rowing; *Style*— Rear Adm Ronald Holley, CB;

55 Larksfield, Englefield Green, Surrey TW20 0RB (☎ 0784 435277); Shell Aircraft Ltd, Cardinal Point, Newall Road, London (Heathrow) Airport TW6 2HF (☎ 081 759 4531, fax 071 759 4582, telex 919651)

HOLLICK, Clive Richard; s of Leslie George and Olive Mary, *née* Scruton; *b* 20 May 1945; *Educ* Taunton's Sch Southampton, Univ of Nottingham (BA); *m* 1977, Susan Mary, *née* Woodford; 3 da; *Career* md MAI plc; dir subsids and other cos; *Recreations* reading, theatre, cinema, tennis, countryside; *Clubs* RAC; *Style—* Clive Hollick, Esq; c/o MAI plc, 8 Montague Close, London SE1 (☎ 071 407 7624)

HOLLICK, Peter Nugent; s of Dr Cyril Leslie Hollick, of Seaton, Devon, and Grace Helena, *née* Gibbins; *b* 23 Feb 1949; *Educ* Wycliffe Coll, Univ of Birmingham (LLB), barr Inns of Court Sch of Law, Brunel Univ (MEd); *Career* princ lectr Windsor and Maidenhead Coll 1983-85, head of Dept of Business Studies and Humanities Dunstable Coll 1985-; chm Beds Fedn Professional Assoc of Teachers, S Mids rep and chm Tertiary Educn Ctee Professional Assoc of Teachers, former moderator Business and Technician Educn Cncl (former sr examiner AEB), memb Cncl Coll of Preceptors (fell 1985); memb Hon Soc of the Middle Temple 1969; *Recreations* tennis, squash, cycling, photography, travel; *Style—* Peter Hollick, Esq; 1 Carlisle Close, Dunstable, Beds LU6 3PH; Dunstable Coll, Kingsway, Dunstable, Beds LU5 4HG (☎ 0582 696451)

HOLLIDAY, (Peter) David; s of Leslie John Holliday, *qv* of Berkhamsted, and Kathleen Joan Marjorie, *née* Stacey; *b* 20 July 1947; *Educ* Brixton Sch of Bldg, London Business Sch; *m* 1972, Diana Patricia, da of Philip Shirley Christian Aldred, of Surrey; 1 s (Michael Stuart b 1978), 2 da (Rebecca Louise b 1976, Amanda Alice b 1982); *Career* chm: Laing Homes 1983-88, Super-Homes 1983-88, John Laing Homes Inc (California) 1985-88; dir John Laing plc 1984-88, chief exec Admiral Homes 1988-; vice pres House Builders Fedn 1988-90; Freeman: City of London 1987, Worshipful Co of Plaisterers; FBIM, MCIOB, FInstD; *Recreations* sailing, golf; *Clubs* Royal Southern Yacht, Woburn Golf; *Style—* David Holliday, Esq; Dundry, Water End Rd, Potten End, Berkhamsted, Herts HP4 2SG (☎ 0442 86 5466)

HOLLIDAY, Prof Sir Frederick George Thomas; CBE (1975), DL (Co Durham 1985); s of Alfred Charles Holliday, of Scotland, and Margaret, *née* Reynolds; *b* 22 Sept 1935; *Educ* Bromsgrove Co HS, Univ of Sheffield (BSc, DSc); *m* 1957, Philippa Mary, da of Charles Davidson (d 1985), of Dunning, Scotland; 1 s (Richard John b 1964), 1 da (Helen Kirstin b 1961); *Career* Devpt Cmmn fisheries res student Aberdeen 1956-58, sci offr Marine Lab Aberdeen 1958-61, acting princ and vice chllr Univ of Stirling 1973-75 (prof and head Dept of Biology 1967-75, dep princ 1972-73), prof of zoology Univ of Aberdeen 1975-79 (lectr in zoology 1961-66), vice chllr and warden Univ of Durham 1980-90; chm: Nature Conservancy Cncl 1977-80 (memb 1975-80), Joint Nature Conservation Ctee 1990-; vice pres Scottish Wildlife Tst 1980-, tstee The Nat Heritage Meml Fund 1980-; non-exec memb Bd: Shell UK Ltd 1980-, BR Eastern Region Bd 1983-90 (chm 1986-90), Br Main Bd 1990-; chm ind review of Disposal of Radioactive Waste at Sea 1984; tstee The Scottish Civic Tst 1984-87; memb Bd: Northern Investors Ltd 1984-89, Lloyds Bank Northern Regnl Bd 1985- (chm 1986-89, dep chm 1989-), Leverhulme Tst Res Awards Advsy Ctee 1978- (chm 1987-); FRSE; kt 1990; *Recreations* hill walking, vegetable gardening; *Clubs* Cwlth Tst, Fettercairn Farmers'; *Style—* Prof Sir Frederick Holliday, CBE, DL, FRSE; Battleby, Redgorton, Perth PH1 3EW (☎ 0738 27921, fax 0738 30583)

HOLLIDAY, Hon Mrs (Jane); *née* Sinclair; yr da of 2 Baron Sinclair of Cleeve, OBE (d 1985); *b* 13 July 1955; *Educ* Sherborne Sch for Girls; *m* 1982, Robert Anthony John Holliday, s of R F Holliday, Holly Lodge, Ashwellthorpe, Norfolk; 1 s (James b 1984); 1 da (Fiona b 1987); *Style—* The Hon Mrs Holliday; Larkfield, Hanstead, Bury St Edmunds, Suffolk IP29 5NH

HOLLIDAY, Leslie John; s of John Holliday (d 1976), and Elsie May, *née* Hutchinson (d 1985); *b* 9 Jan 1921; *Educ* St John's Whitby; *m* 1943, Kathleen Joan Marjorie, da of Ernest Stacey (d 1963); 2 s (David b 1947, Philip b 1950); *Career* radio offr Merchant Navy 1940-45, Atlantic, Mediterranean and Indian Ocean; mgmnt conslt 1985-; non-exec dir: Decan Kelly Gp plc 1985-89, Robert M Douglas Hldgs plc 1986-89, chm and chief exec John Laing plc 1982-85; chm: Nat Contractors Gp, Nat Fedn of Bldg Trades Employers 1976-77, Laing Homes Ltd 1978-81, Super Homes Ltd 1979-81, Laing Mgmnt Contracting Ltd 1980-81, John Laing Construction Ltd 1980-84, John Laing Int Ltd 1981-82, Adm Homes Ltd 1989-; dir and chm Redrow Gp Ltd 1989-; Prince Philip Medal 1982; FCIOB, CBIM; *Recreations* golf; *Clubs* Porters Park, Berkhamsted; *Style—* Leslie Holliday, Esq; The White House, Frithsden Copse, Berkhamsted, Herts (☎ 04427 72563, fax 04427 74312)

HOLLIDAY, Hon Mrs ((Celia) Mary); *née* Bethell; da of 5 Baron Westbury, MC; *b* 5 March 1955; *m* 1980, L Brook Holliday; 2 da (Lucy b 10 Nov 1983, Serena b 30 Aug 1990); *Style—* The Hon Mrs Holliday; Mount St John, Felixkirk, Thirsk, N Yorks

HOLLIDGE, Ronald; *b* 28 Jan 1944; *m* 11 March 1967, Diana Margaret Rae, *née* Hermon; 1 s (Simon John b 1972), 1 da (Julie Ann b 1969); *Career* sr mangr Mincing Lane branch Lloyds Bank plc 1981-84 (various positions within Lloyds Bank plc 1963-81); md: Lloyds Devpt Capital Ltd 1984-, Lloyd's Merchant Bank Ltd 1990-; ACIB 1969; *Recreations* rugby football, squash, theatre, reading; *Clubs* Cornhill, Harvard, RAC; *Style—* Ronald Hollidge, Esq

HOLLIHEAD, Garry Stephen; s of Brian Clifford Hollihead, and Barbara Margaret, *née* Bodinnar; *b* 22 Feb 1960; *Educ* Ash Green HS Exhall Warwicks, Henley Coll Warwicks; *Career* chef; commis saucier Belfry Golf and Country Club 1980-81, commis soucier rising to sous chef 90 Park Lane 1981-84, chef L'Oasis La Napoule France 1984, saucier/larder Fourways Washington and premier sous chef Savoy (involved in promotional work for Savoy Group Florida) 1985-87, head chef Sutherlands Restaurant 1987-; *awards* Mouton Cadet Menu of the Year 1987, Good Food Guide Newcomer of the Year award 1989, Egon Ronay rosette 1989, 1990 and 1991, Ackerman Guide White Clover award 1989, Ackerman Guide Black Clover award 1990, Michelin Guide one star award; *Style—* Garry Hollihead, Esq; Sutherlands Restaurant, 45 Lexington Street, London W1

HOLLIMAN, (Henry) Raymond; s of Henry William Holliman (d 1964), of Croydon, Surrey, and Florence, *née* Oven (d 1978); *Educ* Croydon Coll; *m* 3 June 1964, Hazel Elsie, da of Bertram Higgs (d 1966); 2 s (Carl Henry b 20 May 1966, James Edward b 13 May 1973); *Career* Nat Serv REME E Africa; landowner and estate agent; princ Courciers Estate Agent (SE London estab 1912); md Professional Publication (printers & publishers) 1964-; memb Nat Assoc of Estate Agents; *Recreations* classic car meetings, golf, numismatist; *Clubs* Jaguar Drivers; *Style—* Raymond Holliman, Esq; 4 & 6 Station Rd, South Norwood, London SE25 5AJ (☎ 081 653 6333, fax 081 688 7041)

HOLLINGBERY, Michael John; s of George Henry Hollingbery (d 1958), and Mary Orovida Hammond (d 1984); *b* 16 April 1933; *Educ* Rossall; *m* 1962, Karen Jane, da of Edward Wells (d 1971); 2 s, 1 da; *Career* dir: Woolworth Hldgs plc, Wilson (Connolly) Hldgs plc, Hewetson plc; chm Comet Gp plc 1972-86 (dir 1958-86); chm: Humberside Industrialists Cncl 1981-87, Cons Northern Property Advsy Cncl 1986-90, Boothferry Constituency Patrons' Club 1987-90; memb: Cons Bd of Fin 1982-87, NEDO Sector Working Pty 1976-79; pres Humberside Youth Assoc; govr: Rossall Sch 1979-84, Queen Margaret's Sch (Escrick); Liveryman: Worshipful Co of Painter-Stainers 1980, Worshipful Co of Merchant Adventurers of City of York 1984; CBIM 1975; *Recreations* fishing, shooting; *Clubs* Brooks; *Style—* Michael Hollingbery, Esq

HOLLINGDALE, David John; *b* 19 June 1936; *Career* bd memb: J Smart and Co (Contractors) plc 1977-, Plean Precast Ltd 1982-, Kirkforthar Brick Co Ltd 1986-; *Style—* David Hollingdale, Esq; J Smart Co (Contractors) PLC, 28 Cramond Rd South, Edinburgh EH4 6AB (☎ 031 336 2181, fax 031 336 4037)

HOLLINGDALE, John Patrick; s of William George Hollingdale, of 375 Manford Way Chigwell Essex, and Mary Patricia, *née* Macmillan; *b* 20 April 1952; *Educ* Campion Sch, Hornchurch Essex, King's Coll London, Westminster Med Sch (MB BS); *m* 3 July 1976, Jane Susan, da of Dr Alwyn Kinsey, of Portman Chase Lodge, Priors Corner, Chalbury, nr Wimborne, Dorset; *Career* conslt orthopaedic surgn: Kettering Gen Hosp 1988-89, Central Middx Hosp 1989-; FBOA, FRCS, FRSM; *Books* contrib: Short Textbook of Surgery, Airds Companion to Surgical Studies; *Recreations* golf, skiing; *Clubs* Wellingborough Golf, Windsor Med Soc; *Style—* John Hollingdale, Esq; Central Middlesex Hospital, Acton Lane, Park Royal, London NW10 7NS (☎ 081 453 2416, 071 629 3763)

HOLLINGS, Hon Mr Justice; Sir (Alfred) Kenneth; MC (1944); s of Alfred Holdsworth Hollings (d 1941); *b* 12 June 1918; *Educ* Leys Sch Cambridge, Clare Coll Cambridge (MA); *m* 1949, Harriet Evelyn Isabella, da of W J C Fishbourne, OBE, of Brussels; 1 s, 1 da; *Career* serv WWII, Africa, Sicily and Italy, Maj RA (Shropshire Yeo); called to the Bar Middle Temple 1947; QC 1966, rec of Bolton 1968, co ct judge (Circuit 5) 1968-71, master of the bench Middle Temple 1971, judge of the High Ct of Justice (Family Div) 1971-, presiding judge of the Northern Circuit 1975-78; kt 1971; *Clubs* Garrick, Hurlingham, Tennis and Racquets (Manchester); *Style—* Hon Mr Justice Hollings, MC; Royal Courts of Justice, Strand, London WC2

HOLLINGS, Rev Michael Richard; MC (1943); s of Lt Cdr Richard Eustace Hollings, RN, and Agnes Mary, *née* Hamilton-Dalrymple; *b* 30 Dec 1921; *Educ* Beaumont Coll, St Catherine's Soc Oxford (MA), St Catherine's Sandhurst, Beda Coll Rome; *Career* Maj Coldstream Guards 1942-45, trained for priesthood Beda Coll Rome 1946-50, ordained Rome 1950, asst priest St Patrick's Soho Square London 1950-54, chaplain Westminster Cathedral 1954-58, asst chaplain London Univ 1958-59, chaplain to RCs at Oxford Univ 1959-70; parish priest: St Anselm's Southall Middx 1970-78, St Mary of the Angels Bayswater London 1978-, dean of North Kensington 1980-; religious advsr: ATV 1958-59, Rediffusion 1958-68, Thames Television 1968, advsr Prison Christian Fellowship 1983-; memb: Nat Catholic Radio and TV Cmmn 1968, Westminster Diocesan Schs Cmmn 1970-, Southall C of C 1971-78, Oxford and Cambridge Catholic Educn Bd 1971-78; exec Cncl of Christians and Jews 1971-79 and 1984-, lay memb Press Cncl 1969-75; memb: Nat Conf of Priests Standing Ctee 1974-76, Rampton Ctee 1979-81, Swann Ctee 1981-84; exec: Ealing Community Relations Cncl 1973-76, Notting Hill Social Cncl 1980-; chm N Kensington Action Gp 1980-81; memb: W London Family Service Unit 1981-, Portobello Tst Bd Christian Aid 1984-87; chaplain: SMOM 1957, Nat Cncl of Lay Apostolate 1970-74, Catholic Inst of Int Relations 1971-80; govr: St Charles Catholic VIth Form Coll 1990, Sion Manning Sch 1990; *Books* Hey, You! (1955), Purple Times (1957), Chaplaincraft (1963), The One Who Listens (1971), The Pastoral Care of Homosexuals (1971), It's Me, O Lord (1972), Day by Day (1972), The Shade of his Hand (1973), Restoring the Streets (1974), I Will be There (1975), You Must Be Joking, Lord (1975), The Catholic Prayer Book (1976), Alive to Death (1976), Living Priesthood (1977), His People's Way of Talking (1978), As Was His Custom (1979), St Thérèse of Lisieux (1981), Hearts not Garments (1982), Chaplet of Mary (1982), Path to Contemplation (1983), Go in Peace (1984), Christ Died at Notting Hill (1985), Athirst for God (1985), Prayers Before and after Bereavement (1986), By Love Alone (1986), Prayers for the Depressed (1986), You are not Alone (1988), Dying to Live (1990); *Recreations* reading, walking, people; *Style—* The Rev Michael Hollings, MC; St Mary of the Angels, Moorhouse Rd, Bayswater, London W2 5DJ (☎ 071 229 0487)

HOLLINGSWORTH, Elizabeth; da of Justin Brooke (d 1963), of Suffolk, and Doris Lascelles Brooke, *née* Mead (d 1981); *b* 20 Dec 1922; *Educ* Bedales Sch, Newnham Coll Cambridge (MA); *m* 11 June 1949 (m dis 1977), John Brian Hollingsworth, s of John Herbert Hollingsworth (d 1957), of Sussex; 1 s (John Christopher b 1955), 3 da (Elizabeth Mary b 1950, Rosamund Anna b 1953, Alice Camilla b 1957); *Career* dir and co sec: Justin Brooke Ltd (now Clopton Hall Farms Ltd) 1954- (chm 1977-87), Landowners Ltd 1970-76; marriage cnsllr 1962-87, chm Bury St Edmunds Branch Nat Farmers' Union 1985-87; churchwarden of St Andrew's Cotton Stowmarket 1980-87; *Style—* Mrs E Hollingsworth; 27 Northgate St, Bury St Edmunds, Suffolk; Clopton Hall Farms Ltd, Wickhambrook, Newmarket, Suffolk

HOLLINGSWORTH, Michael Charles; s of Albert George Hollingsworth, of Petersfield, Hampshire, and Gwendolen Marjorie; *b* 22 Feb 1946; *Educ* Reading Sch, Carlisle Sch; *m* 1, 10 Aug 1968 (m dis 1988), Patricia Margaret Jefferson Winn; 1 da (Rebecca b 7 Oct 1974); m 2, 1 Jan 1989, Anne Margaret Diamond; 2 s (Oliver b 12 July 1987, Jamie b 21 Dec 1988); *Career* prodr radio and TV BBC 1967-75; editor news and current affairs: Southern TV Ltd 1975-79, ATV Network Ltd 1979-82; sr prodr current affairs BBC 1982-84, dir of progs TV-am Ltd 1984-85, md Music Box Ltd 1985-88, chief exec Venture Broadcasting 1988-; dir: TV Production and Management Ltd, Good Morning Britain Ltd, New Era TV Ltd, Studio West Ltd, Venture Broadcasting; former dir TV-am Ltd and TV-am News Ltd (resigned 1986); memb Campaign for Freedom from the Press, editorial memb NUJ; *Recreations* polo, house renovation; *Clubs* RAC, Guards' Polo; *Style—* Michael Hollingsworth, Esq; 111 Albert St, London NW1 7NB (☎ 071 267 8737); 3 Route De La Poterie, Wimille, France; 67B Bedford Row, London WC1R 4HE

HOLLINGSWORTH, Thomas Henry; s of Thomas Henry Hollingsworth (d 1981), and Florence Beatrice, *née* Smith (d 1979); *b* 10 May 1932; *Educ* Clifton Coll and Kings Coll Cambridge (MA), LSE (PhD); *Career* asst in res Univ of Cambridge 1954-57, tech offr Alkali Div ICI Ltd 1957-60, Carnegie res fell then lectr then sr lectr then reader Univ of Glasgow 1963-88, UN advsr Manila Philippines 1969-70, visiting fell ANU Canberra 1970, visiting prof Univ of Cairo 1971-72, UN conslt Cairo 1972; former chm Historical Ctee Int Union for the Scientific Study of Population; FSS 1954; *Books* Demography of the Peerage (1964), Historical Demography (1969), Migration (1970); *Recreations* golf, real tennis, skiing, fine wines; *Clubs* Royal Cwlth Soc; *Style—* Thomas Hollingsworth, Esq; 8 Queen's Gardens, Glasgow G12 9DG (☎ 041 339 0046)

HOLLINGTON, Geoffrey Arnold (Geoff); s of Henry Cecil Hollington (d 1983), of West Wickham, Kent, and Eileen Caroline, *née* Fletcher; *b* 5 Feb 1949; *Educ* Beckenham GS Kent, Central Sch of Art and Design London (BA), RCA London (BA, MA); *m* 1, 1971 (m dis 1984) Judith Ann, da of Dennis Frederick Leonard Fox; 1 s (Simon James b 7 Feb 1979); m 2, 1984, Elizabeth Ann Beecham, da of Clement Joseph Lawton; 1 s (James Henry b 23 Sept 1986), 3 da (Gemma Beecham (adopted 1987) b 27 Oct 1977, Emily b and d 29 Feb 1985, Sophy Imogen b 18 July 1989); *Career* freelance interior designer 1974-76, visiting tutor Kingston Poly Surrey 1975-82, street furniture and landscape designer Milton Keynes Devpt Corp 1976-78, ptnr Glickman & Hollington (interior, furniture and product design) 1978-80, co-fndr Pointer Communication Ltd (communication design) 1979-80, princ Hollington Assocs (product and furniture design) 1980-; maj design projects incl: A WARE, B WARE (ceramics)

1976, Master Aerial (Milton Keynes) 1976, Bus Shelter System (Milton Keynes) 1977, Plexus (Furniture) PEL Ltd 1979, George Harvey (office furniture) GA Harvey Ltd 1982, Enterprise (home computer) Enterprise Computers Ltd 1983, Secta (seating) Gordon Russell plc 1984, Super Enterprise (chess computer) White & Alcock Ltd Hong Kong 1984, Basys (office chair) Syba Ltd 1987, Support Cabinets (office furniture) 1988, Hollington Chairs (office seating) 1989, Relay (office furniture) Herman Miller Inc USA 1990, Corporate Security Safes John Tann Ltd 1991; Gold award IBD (USA) 1988, Silver and Bronze awards IBD (USA) 1989, Silver award ARRIDO (Canada) 1990; FRSA 1988, memb Indust Design Soc of America 1991; *Publications* Hollington: Industrial Design (1990); *Style—* Geoff Hollington, Esq; Hollington Associates, The Old School House, 66 Leonard St, London EC2A 4QX (☎ 071 739 3501, fax 071 739 3549)

HOLLINGWORTH, John Harold; s of Harold Hollingworth (d 1978), of Birmingham, and Lilian Mary, *née* Harris (d 1982); *b* 11 July 1930; *Educ* King Edward's Sch Birmingham; *m* 1967 (m dis 1986), Susan Barbara, da of J H Walters (d 1984), of Isle of Man; *Career* MP (C) Birmingham All Saints 1959-64; chm Elmdon Tst (Stress Charity); govr Cambridge Symphony Orchestra Tst Ltd; dir Cambridge Connection Ltd (Support for young musicians); dir Thaxted Festival Fndn Ltd (Music Festival); *Recreations* walking, map reading, talking; *Clubs* Lansdowne; *Style—* John Hollingworth, Esq; 5 South Green, Widdington, Saffron Walden, Essex CB11 3SE (☎ 0799 40369)

HOLLINS, Rear Adm Hubert Walter Elphinstone; CB (1974); s of Lt-Col Walter Thorne Hollins (d 1956), and Ellen Murray, *née* Rigg (d 1974); *b* 8 June 1923; *Educ* Stubbington House, RNC Dartmouth; *m* 11 May 1963, Jillian Mary, da of Donald McAlpin, of Victoria, Australia; 1 s (Rupert Patrick b 1964), 1 da (Rachel Jane b 1965); *Career* RN 1940-76; in cmd HM Ships: Petard, Dundas, Antrim; flag offr Gibraltar; cmd Gib Med and Port Admiral Gibraltar 1972-74, Adm Cmdg Reserves 1974-76; gen mangr Middle East Navigation Aids Serv 1977-84; marine conslt 1984-; younger brother Trinity House, memb Trinity House Lighthouse Bd and assoc memb Corp of the Trinity House 1985-91; FBIM, MNI; *Recreations* fishing, gardening; *Clubs* RNVR YC; *Style—* Rear Adm Hubert W E Hollins, CB; Waunllan, Llandyfriog, Newcastle Emlyn, Dyfed SA38 9HB (☎ 0239 710456)

HOLLINS, Prof Sheila Clare; da of Capt Adrian M Kelly, of Bristol, and Monica Dallas, *née* Edwards; *b* 22 June 1946; *Educ* Notre Dame HS Sheffield, St Thomas's Hosp Med Sch London (MRCPsych); *m* 7 June 1969, Martin Prior Hollins, s of Harry Pryor Hollins (d 1985), of Cheadle Hulme; 1 s (Nigel b 1973), 3 da (Kathryn b 1971, Emily b 1976, Abigail b 1978); *Career* sr registrar in child psychiatry Earls Court Child Guidance Unit and Westminster Children's Hosp 1979-81, sr lectr and hon conslt in the psychiatry of mental handicap St George's Hosp Med Sch (prof 1990-), Wandsworth Health Authy and Richmond Twickenham and Roehampton Health Authy 1981-90, head Div of Psychiatry of Disability 1986-; regnl rep RCPsych; memb Steering Gp for Childrens Initiative Nat Devpt Team Advsy Gp on Disability Joseph Rowntree Meml Tst; FRCPsych 1988; *Books* Mental Handicap: A Multi Disciplinary Approach (ed with M Craft, J Bicknell, 1985), Going Somewhere - Pastoral Care for People with Mental Handicap (with M Grimer, 1988), When Dad Died and When Mum Died (2 books with L Sireling, 1990); *Recreations* family and music; *Style—* Prof Sheila Hollins; Department of Mental Health Science, St Georges Hospital Medical School, Cranmer Terrace, London SW17 0RE (☎ 081 672 9944 ext 55502)

HOLLIS, Hon Mr Justice; Hon Sir Anthony Barnard; s of Henry Lewis Hollis; *b* 11 May 1927; *Educ* Tonbridge, St Peter's Hall Oxford; *m* 1956, Pauline Mary, *née* Skuce; 1 step da; *Career* called to the Bar Gray's Inn 1951, bencher 1979; QC 1969, chm Family Law Bar Assoc 1974-76, Crown Court rec 1976-82, High Court judge 1982-; kt 1982; *Style—* The Hon Mr Justice Hollis; Royal Courts of Justice, Strand, London WC2

HOLLIS, Anthony John; s of Henry Clifford Hollis (d 1946), of Finchley, London, and Dora Elizabeth, *née* Mason (d 1957); *b* 31 Oct 1930; *Educ* King Edward VI GS Totnes; *m* 22 Oct 1960, Margaret Joyce, da of Percy Herbert Dennis (d 1979), of Radlett, Herts; 2 s (Richard b 1962, David b 1964), 2 da (Elizabeth b 1966, Catherine b 1969); *Career* Nat Serv 1953-55 RAPC, 2 Lt 1954, Lt; CA; sr ptnr: Hope Agar 1978-88 and 1990- (joined 1961), Kidsons 1988-90; tstee Finchley Charities, sec Old Totnesian Soc, treas Radlett Utd Free Church; Freeman City of London 1966, Liveryman Worshipful Co Fanmakers 1976; FCA 1964 (ACA 1953); *Recreations* gardening; *Style—* Anthony Hollis, Esq; Hope Agar, Epworthy House, 25 City Road, London EC1Y 1AR (☎ 071 628 5801); Briery Mead, 9 Gills Hill Lane, Radlett, Herts WD7 8DE (☎ 0923 856106)

HOLLIS, Arthur Norman; OBE (1985), DFC (1943); s of Egerton Clark Hollis (d 1967), of Eastbourne, Sussex, and Vera Lina, *née* Leigh (d 1944); *b* 11 Aug 1922; *Educ* Dulwich; *m* 2 Dec 1944, Elizabeth, da of Reginald Chase Edmunds (d 1986), of Westwell, nr Ashford, Kent; 1 s (Richard b 1953), 2 da (Jennifer b 1945, Sylvia b 1949); *Career* RAFVR 1941-46, Sqdn Ldr 1945-46; memb HAC 1978; CA; ptnr: Limebeer & Co 1953-75, Russell Limebeer 1975-88; sr ptnr based in City of London specialising in countries of W Europe; dir various cos; memb Mgmnt Ctee Yehudi Menuhin Sch 1964-88 (vice pres 1989), govr Live Music Now 1977-90, offr of various Cons Assocs; chm: Ashford Constituency 1980-83, Kent East Euro Constituency 1985-88 (vice pres 1988), Westwell Parish Cncl 1976-79; Master Worshipful Co of Woolmen 1982-83; FCA 1958, FRSA 1983; *Recreations* travel, shooting, country pursuits; *Clubs* Travellers', City of London, United and Cecil; *Style—* Arthur Hollis, Esq, OBE, DFC; Court Lodge, Westwell, nr Ashford, Kent TN25 4JX (☎ 023 371 2555)

HOLLIS, Eric Arthur; s of Arthur Thomas Hollis (d 1963), and May Annie, *née* Martin (d 1975); *b* 6 June 1918; *Educ* Addey and Stanhope; *m* 11 Nov 1944, Joan Helena, da of Alfred Gore (d 1946); 1 s (Keith b 1951), 1 da (Patricia b 1947); *Career* WWII Army served Africa, Italy, France 1939-45; CA; dir: Securicor Group plc 1958, Security Services plc 1974-; FCCA, FCT; *Recreations* golf, fishing; *Clubs* Arun YC; *Style—* Eric Hollis, Esq; Sutton Park House, 15 Carshalton Rd, Sutton, Surrey SM1 4LE (☎ 081 770 7000)

HOLLIS, John Charles; s of Charles Henry Hollis, and Audrey Cynthia, *née* Davis; *b* 16 June 1953; *Educ* Latymer Upper Sch, Univ of Bristol (BSc); *m* 22 July 1978, Clara Sian, da of Trevor Clement Tranter; 3 da (Emma b 1980, Lisa b 1981, Amy b 1983); *Career* Arthur Andersen: joined 1974, ptnr Andersen Consulting 1985, i/c Worldwide Financial Planning and Reporting Consulting Function 1985, i/c UK Consumer Servs Consulting Gp 1988, i/c UK Consumer Prods and Servs Sector 1990; memb IMA, FCA; *Books* Disappearing Financial Systems (1988), The Torturing and Dismembering of the Finance Function (1988); *Recreations* music, sports, interior design; *Clubs* RAC; *Style—* John Hollis, Esq; Andersen Consulting, 2 Arundel St, London WC2R 3LT (☎ 071 438 3832)

HOLLIS, John Denzil; s of Christopher Hollis (d 1977), of Mells, Somerset, and Margaret Madeleine, *née* King (d 1984); *b* 9 May 1931; *Educ* Stonyhurst, Trinity Coll Oxford (BA, MA); *m* 21 April 1960, Pauline Lorraine, da of Julian Janvrin (d 1988), of Vancouver, Canada; 1 s (Charles b 1962), 1 da (Katharine b 1961); *Career* Nat Serv cmmnd RB, active serv Kenya 1953-55, 2 i/c London RB Rangers TA 1955-66 (2 i/c 1965-66); Minnesota Mining and Mfrg Co 1955-59, head of PR Stock Exchange Cncl 1971-76 (memb staff 1959-76, head of Central Settlement Servs 1967-71); advsr to: Govt of Kuwait 1976-81, Eurokuwaiti Investmt Co 1981-85; dir of info Dewe Rogerson and Co Ltd 1985-; *Style—* John Hollis, Esq; 26 Westwood Rd, Barnes SW13 0LA (☎ 081 876 2027); 3 London Wall Bldgs, London Wall (☎ 071 638 9571)

HOLLIS, Prof Malcolm Richard Arthur; s of Arthur Edwin Hollis (d 1970), of 57 Hartwood Rd, Southport, Merseyside, and Esmé Muriel, *née* Pettit; *b* 17 March 1944; *Educ* King George V GS Southport, Univ of South Wales and Monmouth, Univ of London (BSc); *m* 11 Sept 1965, Andrea Joan, da of Sqdn Ldr John Edward Fuller (d 1989), of Challows, The Martlets, W Chiltington; 2 s (Richard b 1969, Gavin b 1976), 1 da (Tricia b 1970); *Career* chartered surveyor; ptnr Best Gapp & Ptnrs 1969, princ Malcolm Hollis Assoc 1972-80, ptnr Baxter Payne & Lepper (inc Malcolm Hollis Assocs) 1980-91 (dep chm 1986-88), ptnr Malcolm Hollis 1991-, Surveyor to the Fabric Worshipful Co Skinners 1982-, mangr professional servs Nationwide Anglia Estate Agents 1987-91, memb Cncl RICS Bldg Surveyors 1988-; cncllr London Borough Lambeth 1977-81; govr Woodmansterne Sch 1978-81 (chm 1979-81); over 100 appearances on TV and radio 1984-; prof Univ of Reading 1989; Freeman City of London 1983, Liveryman Worshipful Co Chartered Surveyors 1982; FSVA 1969, FIAS 1969, FRICS 1970, ACIARB 1974; *Books* Surveying Buildings (1983, 2 edn 1986, 3 edn 1989), Householders Action Guide (1984), Model Survey Reports (1985, 2 edn 1989), Surveying for Dilapidations (1988), Cavity Wall Tie Failure (1990), Surveyors Fact Book (1990); *Recreations* writing, photography, skiing, thinking; *Clubs* Hurlingham, Ski of GB; *Style—* Prof Malcolm Hollis; 6 Rydal Rd, London SW16 1QN (☎ 081 769 5092); 9 Brooks Court, London SW8 (☎ 071 622 9555, fax 071 630 0321, car 0860 350304)

HOLLIS, Richard George; s of George Edward Hollis (d 1981); *b* 19 Nov 1934; *Educ* Bancroft's Sch Essex; *m* 1967, Belinda Jacqueline, *née* Rose; 2 da; *Career* Nat Serv, ret Capt; fin dir HP Bulmer Holdings plc 1967-88; non-exec dir: Chloride Alcad Ltd (Chloride Gp) 1977-82, Alfred Preedy and Sons plc 1985-88; memb Consumers Ctees for GB and England and Wales 1979-84; FCA; *Recreations* fishing, music; *Clubs* Flyfishers'; *Style—* Richard Hollis, Esq; The Leys, Aston, Kingsland, Leominster, Herefordshire HR6 9PU (☎ 056 881 411)

HOLLIS OF HEIGHAM, Baroness (Life Peer UK 1990), of Heigham in the City of Norwich; Patricia Lesley Hollis; da of H L G Wells, of Norwich, and (Queenie) Rosalyn, *née* Clayforth; *b* 24 May 1941; *Educ* Plympton GS, Univ of Cambridge (BA, MA), Univ of California (Berkeley), Columbia Univ NY, Nuffield Coll Oxford (MA, DPhil); *m* 18 Sept 1965, (James) Martin Hollis, s of (Hugh) Mark Noel Hollis, of Oxted, Surrey; 2 s (Simon b 1969, Matthew b 1971); *Career* Harkness fell 1962-64, Nuffield scholar 1964-67, sr lectr (formerly lectr) modern history UEA 1967-89, dean Sch of English and American Studies UEA 1988-90; councillor Norwich City 1968- (ldr 1983-88); memb: E Anglia Economic Planning Cncl 1975-79, Regnl Health Authy 1979-83, BBC Regnl Advsy Ctee 1979-83, Norfolk CC 1981-85; dir Radio Broadland 1983; Parly candidate Gt Yarmouth 1974 and 1979; nat cmmr English Heritage 1988-, memb Press Cncl 1989-; FRHistS; cr a Life Peer 1990; *Books* The Pauper Press (1970), Class and Class Conflict 1815-50 (1973), Women in Public 1850-1900 (1979), Pressure from Without (1974), Ladies Elect: Women in English Local Govt 1865-1914 (1987); *Recreations* boating on the broads, domesticity; *Style—* The Rt Hon Baroness Hollis of Heigham; 30 Park Lane, Norwich (☎ 0603 621990); School of English and American Studies University of E Anglia, Norwich (☎ 0603 56161)

HOLLMAN, Dr Arthur; s of William Joseph Hollman (d 1968), of Bromley, Kent, and Isobel Rosson, *née* Sparrow (d 1987); *b* 7 Dec 1923; *Educ* Tiffin Boys Sch Kingston upon Thames, Univ of London (MB BS, MD); *m* 28 May 1949, Catharine Elizabeth, da of late Ferdinand Thomas Large, of Pett, Sussex; 4 da (Margaret b 1950, Susan b 1951, Anne b 1956, Barbara b 1957); *Career* sr registrar in cardiology Hammersmith Hosp 1957-62, hon sr lectr Dept of Med Middx Sch of Med 1962-, emeritus conslt UCH 1987- (house physician 1946, hon sr lectr Dept of Med 1962-, conslt cardiologist 1962-87), hon conslt Hosp for Sick Children Gt Ormond St London 1987- (conslt cardiologist 1970-87; fell of UCL 1983; memb Ctee of Mgmnt of Chelsea Physic Garden; Freeman: Worshipful Soc of Apothecaries 1980, City of London 1983; FRCP 1967, fell Linnean Soc 1983; *Recreations* gardening, especially medicinal plants; *Clubs* Athenaeum; *Style—* Dr Arthur Hollman; Seabank, Chick Hill, Pett, E Sussex TN35 4EQ (☎ 0424 81 3228)

HOLLOM, Sir Jasper Quintus; KBE (1975); s of Arthur Hollom (d 1954); *b* 16 Dec 1917; *Educ* King's Sch Bruton Somerset; *m* 1954, Patricia Elizabeth Mary Ellis; *Career* Bank of Eng: entered 1936, dep chief cashier 1956-62, chief cashier 1962-66, exec dir 1966-70, non-exec dir 1980-84, dep govr 1970-80; chm Eagle Star Gp 1985-87; chm: Cncl for Securities Industs 1985-86, Panel on Takeovers and Mergers 1980-87; non-exec dir: BAT Industries plc 1980-87, Portals Holdings plc 1980-88; *Style—* Sir Jasper Hollom, KBE; High Wood, Selborne, Alton, Hants GU34 3LA (☎ 042 050 317)

HOLLOWAY, Charles Henry Warner; s of Lt Adrian George Warner Holloway, of Boscobel, Minchinhampton, Glos, and Helen Pendrill, *née* Charles; *b* 2 Nov 1950; *Educ* Winchester, Univ Coll Oxford (BA, MA); *m* 20 Sept 1975, Georgina Alice, da of Maj Hon George Nathaniel Rous (d 1982), of Dennington Hall, Woodbridge, Suffolk; 2 s (George Henry Rous b 1983, Edward Charles b 1986), 2 da (Alice Victoria Pendrill b 1978, Lucinda Rose b 1980); *Career* admitted slr 1975; ptnr Daynes Hill & Perks Norwich; area cmmr for Breckland St John's Ambulance 1983-86; memb: Law Soc, Slrs Euro Gp; ACIArb; *Recreations* shooting, tennis; *Clubs* Norfolk, Vincent's; *Style—* Charles Holloway, Esq; The Old Rectory, Whissonsett, Dereham, Norfolk NR20 5TF (☎ 0328 700514); Daynes Hill & Perks, Holland Court, The Close, Norwich NR1 4DX (☎ 0603 611212, fax 0603 610535); Eversleds, 1 Gunpowder Sq, Printer St, London EC4 (☎ 071 936 2553, fax 071 936 2590)

HOLLOWAY, David Richard; s of William Edwyn Holloway (d 1952), and Margaret Boyd, *née* Schleselman (d 1979); *b* 3 June 1924; *Educ* Westminster, Birkbeck Coll London, Magdalen Coll Oxford; *m* 8 March 1952, Sylvia (Sally) Eileen, da of Douglas Arthur Gray; 2 s (Mark b 1954, Paul b 1956), 1 da (Pippa b 1958); *Career* RAF 1942, navigator 1944, served Middle East, Aden, Ceylon, India, PO 1945, sr welfare offr 2nd Indian Gp 1946; reporter: Middx Co Times 1940-41, Daily Sketch 1941-42, Daily Mirror 1949; News Chronicle: reporter and ldr writer 1950-53, asst literary ed 1953-58, book page ed 1958-60; lit ed Daily Telegraph 1968-88 (dep literary ed 1960-68); chm: Soc of Bookmen 1968-71, Booker Prize Judges 1969; registrar Royal Literary Fund 1981-; *Books* John Galsworthy (1968), Lewis and Clark on the Crossing of America (1971), Derby Day (1975), Playing The Empire (1979), Nothing So Became Them (with Michael Geare, 1987); *Clubs* Reform; *Style—* David Holloway, Esq; 95 Lonsdale Rd, London SW13 9DA (☎ 081 748 3711)

HOLLOWAY, Frank; s of late Frank Holloway; *b* 20 Oct 1924; *Educ* Burnage HS Manchester; *m* 1949, Elizabeth, *née* Beattie; 3 da; *Career* various sr fin appts in The Utd Steel Companies and later British Steel Corpn 1949-72; md: supplies and prodn control British Steel Corpn 1973-76, finance and supplies 1976-80, supplies and tport and bd memb 1978-; chm British Steel Corpn (Chemicals) Ltd; FCA, FBIM;

Recreations cricket, collecting books; *Style—* Frank Holloway, Esq; 11 Copperfield Way, Chislehurst, Kent (☎ 081 467 9559); BSC, Supplies and Transport Div, 9 Albert Embankment, London SE1 7SN (☎ 071 735 7654; telex 916061)

HOLLOWAY, Prof John Henry; s of William Henry Holloway (d 1983), of Coalville, and Ivy May, *née* Sarson; *b* 20 Dec 1938; *Educ* Ashby-de-la-Zouch Boys' GS, Univ of Birmingham (BSc, PhD, DSc); *m* 14 April 1962, Jennifer, da of Albert Burne, of Coalville; 1 s (Mark b 1969), 2 da (Sarah b 1964, Amanda b 1965); *Career* Univ of Aberdeen: asst lectr 1963-64, lectr 1964-70; Univ of Leicester: lectr 1971-78, sr lectr 1978-87, prof and head of chemistry 1987-; memb Inorganic Panel SERC; Royal Soc of Chemistry: chm Local Affairs Bd, memb Qualification & Educn Bd, memb External Rels Ctee, memb Membership Devpt Ctee, Careers Through Chemistry Ctee; CChem, FRSC; *Books* Noble-Gas Chemistry (1968); *Recreations* painting, drawing, sailing, classic car restoration; *Style—* Prof John Holloway; 43 Morland Ave, Stoneygate, Leicester LE2 2PF (☎ 0533 704701); Chemistry Department, The University, Leicester LE1 7RH (☎ 0533 522106, fax 0533 52200, telex LEICUL 347250)

HOLLOWAY, Julian Pendrill Warner; s of Adrian George Warner Holloway, of Boscobel, Minchinhampton, Glos, and Helen Pendrill, *née* Charles; *b* 6 May 1954; *Educ* Winchester, Univ of Durham (BA); *m* 4 Oct 1980, Emma Jane Caroline, da of Col Peter Charles Ormrod, MC, of Pen-y-Lan Ruabon, Wrexham, Clwyd; 2 s (James b 29 Sept 1986, Thomas b 14 March 1988), 1 da (Lavinia b 28 April 1984); *Career* articled clerk Messrs Denton Hall & Burgin 1979-81, admitted slr to the Supreme Ct 1981, asst slr Messrs Brecher & Co 1981-83, ptnr Messrs McKenna & Co 1988- (asst slr 1984-88); memb: Law Soc, Exec Ctee Centre for Dispute Resolution; *Recreations* tennis, skiing; *Style—* Julian Holloway, Esq; 64 Alderbrook Rd, London SW12 (☎ 081 675 0308); McKenna & Co, Mitre House, 160 Aldgate St, London EC1A 4DD (☎ 071 606 9000, fax 071 606 9100, telex 27251)

HOLLOWAY, Julian Robert Stanley; s of Stanley Augustus Holloway, OBE, the celebrated actor (d 1982), and Violet Marion, *née* Lane; *b* 24 June 1944; *Educ* Harrow, Royal Acad of Dramatic Art; *m* 1, (m dis 1977), Zena Cecilia Walker; 1 da (Sophie b 15 Sept 1977); *Career* actor; appearances on London Stage incl: When Did You Last See My Mother, Spitting Image, The Norman Conquests, Arsenic And Old Lace, Charley's Aunt, Pygmalion; theatre director: Play It Again Sam, When Did You Last See My Mother; film actor and producer: Carry On Films, The Spy's Wife, The Chairman's Wife, Loophole; TV appearances: The Importance of Being Earnest, An Adventure In Bed, Rebecca, The Scarlet And The Black, Ellis Island, The Endless Game, Michaelangelo; *Recreations* golf, cricket, racing; *Style—* Julian Holloway, Esq

HOLLOWAY, Laurence (Laurie); s of Marcus Holloway (d 1979), of Oldham, Lancs, and Annie, *née* Gillespie; *b* 31 March 1938; *Educ* Oldham GS; *m* 1, 31 March 1956, Julia Planck, da of Rufus Macdonald (d 1975), of Rothesay, Isle of Bute; 1 da (Karon b 1957); m 2, 16 June 1965, Marian Montgomery, singer, da of Forrest Marion Runnels (d 1966), of Atlanta, Georgia; 1 da (Abigail b 1967); *Career* pianist, composer, arranger; studio musician 1959-69; compositions incl: A Dream of Alice (BBC TV), pop preludes; musical dir: Engelbert Humperdinck 1969-74, Dame Edna Everage 1980-87; pianist for Judy Garland and Liza Minnelli London Paladium 1964; composer TV signature tunes incl Blind Date; *Recreations* golf, music; *Clubs* Middx CCC, Wig and Pen, Temple Golf; *Style—* Laurie Holloway, Esq; Elgin, Fishery Rd, Bray-on-Thames, Berkshire (☎ 0628 37715)

HOLLOWAY, Peter Henry Charles; s of Maj Frederick Charles Holloway, MC, and Kathleen Winifred, *née* Seear; *b* 12 Aug 1943; *Educ* Aldenham; *m* 1, March 1966 (m dis 1983), Patricia, *née* Monk; 2 s (Simon b 21 Feb 1970, Peter b 12 July 1971), 1 da (Penelope b 31 May 1968); m 2, 9 May 1984, Margaret Yvonne; 2 s (Frederick b 19 May 1984, Edward b 22 April 1987); *Career* dealer Joseph Sebag 1963-68, dir Slater Walker (Bahamas) 1968-71, Eurobond trader Samuel Montagu 1971-73, Eurobond mangr Banque Nationale de Paris 1973-74, mangr dealing ops Samuel Montagu 1974-79, int gilt sales mangr Laing & Cruickshank 1979-83, ptnr Wedd Durlacher Mordaunt & Co 1983-86; dir: Barclays de Zoete Wedd (Securities) 1986-, Barclays de Zoete Wedd Hldgs 1987-; md Barclays de Zoete Wedd Equity Trading & Global Princ Risk 1988-; memb Ctee Stock Exchange mkts; *Recreations* squash, swimming, walking; *Clubs* Gresham; *Style—* Peter Holloway, Esq; 523 Ben Jonson House, Barbican, London EC2Y 8DL; Churchgate Barn, Wood Dalling, Norfolk NR11 6SN; Ebbgate House, 2 Swan Lane, London EC4R 3TS (☎ 071 623 2323, fax 071 626 1753, telex 888221)

HOLLOWAY, Reginald Eric (Reg); CMG (1984); s of late Ernest and Beatrice Holloway; *b* 22 June 1932; *Educ* St Luke's Brighton, Brighton Tech Coll; *m* 1958, Anne Penelope, da of late Robert Walter, and Doris Lilian Pawley; 1 da; *Career* RAF 1953-55; apprentice reporter 1947-53, journalist in Britain and E Africa 1955-61, press offr Tanganyika Govt 1961-63, dir Br Info Br Guyana 1964-67, Info Dept FCO 1967-69 (Anguilla 1969), 2 later 1 sec chancery in Malta 1970-72, E African Dept FCO 1972-74, consul and head of Chancery Kathmandu 1974-77, asst head S Asian Dept FCO 1977-79 (cnsllr 1979, inspr 1979-81), consul gen Toronto 1981-85, sr Br trade cmmr Hong Kong 1985-89, consul gen Los Angles 1989-; *Style—* Reg Holloway, Esq, CMG; Br Consulate General, 3701 Wilshire Boulevard, Los Angeles; c/o Foreign and Commonwealth Office, London SW1A 2AH

HOLLOWAY, Dr Robin Greville; s of Robert Charles Holloway (d 1986), and Pamela Mary, *née* Jacob; *b* 19 Oct 1943; *Educ* St Paul's Cathedral Choir Sch, King's Coll Sch Wimbledon, King's Coll Cambridge, New Coll Oxford; *Career* lectr in music Univ of Cambridge 1975- (res fell 1969-75); wrote Scenes from Schumann (Cheltenham) 1970, Domination of Black (London) 1974, Second Concerto for Orchestra (Glasgow) 1979, Seascape and Harvest (Birmingham) 1986, Clarissa (Eng Nat Opera) 1989; *Books* Debussy and Wagner (1978); *Style—* Dr Robin Holloway; Gonville and Caius Coll, Cambridge CB2 1TA (☎ 0223 335424); 531 Caledonian Rd, London N7 9RH

HOLLOWS, Peter Twist; s of Samuel Hollows (d 1976), of Ribble Lodge, Lytham, Lancs, and Elizabeth, *née* Twist (d 1959); *b* 9 June 1921; *Educ* Silcoates Sch; *m* 19 Sept 1949, Joan Hurst, da of Arthur Smith (d 1965), of Cringles, Embsay, Skipton, Yorkshire ; 1 s (Jeremy b 1953), 1 da (Anne b 1951); *Career* RAF Coastal Cmd 1941-46 (despatches for work on airborne radar); stockbroker; memb: Manchester Stock Exchange 1948 (chm 1971-80), Manchester Stock Exchange Ctee 1966-80, Northern Stock Exchange Cncl 1971-73, Ctee of the Northern Unit of the Stock Exchange 1973-79; chm: Northern Stock Exchange 1972-73, Northern Unit of the Stock Exchange 1973-76; memb Cncl of the Stock Exchange 1973-79; treas property div Methodist Church 1967-91; memb: Fin Bd Methodist Church 1969-, Bd of Tstees for Methodist Church Purposes 1972-; *Recreations* travel, horticulture, classical music, cricket, rugby union; *Clubs* Rotary (pres Manchester) 1963-64; Lancashire CC, Flyde RUFC; *Style—* Peter Hollows, Esq; 11 Headroomgate Rd, St Annes-on-Sea, Lancs FY9 3BA (☎ 0253 722783)

HOLM, Dr Jessica Lynn; da of Ian Holm, MBE, and Lynn Mary, *née* Shaw; *b* 29 March 1960; *Educ* Putney HS for Girls, Royal Holloway Coll Univ of London (BSc, Phd); *m* 27 Feb 1988, Gavin Bernard Chappell, s of Lt-Col Robin Chappell, OBE; *Career* zoologist and broadcaster BBC Natural History Unit and others, presenter Radio 4 Natural History Progamme; films: The Case of the Vanishing Squirrel (1987), Daylight Robbery (1988), Badger Watch (1990); *Books* Whittet Squirrels (1987), The Red Squirrel (1989); contrib various articles on squirrels, foxes, badgers and parrots to wildlife and conservation magazines; *Recreations* drawing and painting, planning things I can't afford to do, wildlife, animals, dogs and hand reared captive bred parrots; *Style—* Dr Jessica Holm; c/o BBC Natural History Unit, Broadcasting House, Whiteladies Rd, Bristol BS8 2LR (☎ 0272 732211)

HOLM, Hon Mrs (Rosetta Mancroft); *née* Samuel; da of 1 Baron Mancroft (d 1942); *b* 1918; *m* 1, 1947, Alfred John Bostock Hill (d 1959, late puisne judge Malaya); m 2, 1966, Dr Cai Christian Holm (d 1983); *Style—* The Hon Mrs Holm; 12 Eaton Place, London SW1

HOLMAN, Lady; Adeline Betty; da of Sir Gilbert Fox, 1 Bt (d 1925); *b* 18 July 1906; *Educ* Heathfield Ascot; *m* 1, 1929 (m dis 1939), Capt Basil Allfrey; 2 s; m 2, 1940, as his 2 w, Sir Adrian Holman, KBE, CMG, MC (d 1974); Polish Cross of Merit 1972; *Recreations* waterfowl collecting, gardening; *Style—* Lady Holman; Bohunt Manor, Liphook, Hants

HOLMAN, Barry William; s of Ronald Cecil Holman, of Loughton, Essex, and Irene Winifred; *b* 7 July 1949; *Educ* Coopers Co GS; *m* 17 Aug 1974, Christine, da of Norman Thomas Richards; *Career* CA; own practice B W Holman & Co, Newman Harris & Co, Silver Altman & Co, Lewis Bloom, Macnair Mason; FCA; *Recreations* golf, horse riding, clay pigeon shooting, motor boat cruising, music, chess; *Clubs* ICAEW, Windsor Yacht, Abridge Golf and Country, Beldlam Golf Soc; *Style—* Barry W Holman, Esq; Brook House, Ongar Rd, Abridge, Essex RM4 1UH (☎ 0992 813 079); 309 High Rd, Loughton, Essex IG10 1AH (☎ 081 508 9228)

HOLMAN, Christopher Boot; s of Alexander McArthur Holman (d 1979), of Hyes, Rudgwick, Sussex, and Hon Margery Amy, *née* Boot (d 1987); *b* 8 Feb 1926; *Educ* Loretto Sch, Cirencester Agric Coll; *m* Hon Elizabeth Winifred Ponsonby, da of 5 Baron de Mauley (d 1962), of Langford House, Lechlade, Glos; 4 da (Sarah Charlotte, Serena Jane, Alice Elgiva, Catherine Rose); *Career* 1 Lt Royal Horse Gds 1944-47; Lloyds broker (underwriting name 1951-); farmer; High Sheriff of Warwickshire 1986-87; *Recreations* shooting, hunting, fishing; *Clubs* Boodles; *Style—* Christopher Holman, Esq

HOLMAN, David McArthur; s of Alexander McArthur Holman (d 1979), of Springland, Millbrook, Jersey, CI, and Hon Margery Amy, *née* Boot (d 1987); *b* 11 Dec 1928; *Educ* Rugby; *m* 1, 1952 (m dis 1965), Felicity Frances, da of Capt Rickard Donovan, CBE, RN (d 1956); 1 s (Mark Rickard b 1957 d 1987); m 2, 1966, Valerie Brythonig, *née* Pryor; 2 s (Michael Jesse b 1967, Andrew McArthur b 1968); *Career* Lt RHG 1946-49; chm and md: John Holman & Sons Ltd 1953-, David Holman & Co Ltd 1971-; chm Phyllis Holman Richards Adoption Soc 1970-; memb Lloyds 1954; *Recreations* field sports; *Clubs* Cavalry and Guards', City of London; *Style—* David Holman, Esq; Crundale House, Crundale, Canterbury, Kent CT4 7EH (☎ 0227 731020)

HOLMAN, Lady Diana Elizabeth Virginia Sydney; *née* Baird; o da of 12 Earl of Kintore (d 1989); *b* 22 June 1937; *m* 20 July 1957, John Francis Holman, OBE, eld s of Alexander McArthur Holman (d 1979), of Springland, Millbrook, Jersey, CI; 2 s, 2 da; *Style—* The Lady Diana Holman; Rickarton House, Stonehaven, Kincardineshire, Scotland AB3 2SU (☎ 0569 63236); 6 St Luke's St, London SW3 3RS(☎ 071 352 1475)

HOLMAN, Hon Mrs (Elizabeth Marjorie); *née* Plumb; er da of Baron Plumb (Life Peer), *qv*; *b* 1948; *m* 1, 1971 (m dis), Robin Arbuthnot; m 2, 1982, Maj Anthony Holman; 2 s (Thomas Henry b 1984, Charles Anthony b 1986); *Style—* The Hon Mrs Holman; 6B United Mansions, Shuifai Terrace, Hong Kong

HOLMAN, (Edward) James; s of Edward Theodore Holman, of Manaccan, Cornwall, and Mary Megan, *née* Morris, MBE; *b* 21 Aug 1947; *Educ* Dauntsey's, Exeter Coll Oxford (BA, MA); *m* 14 July 1979, Fiona Elisabeth, da of Ronald Cathcart Roxburgh, *qv*, of Wiggenhall St Mary, King's Lynn, Norfolk; 1 s (Edward b 1988), 1 da (Charlotte b 1984); *Career* called to the Bar Middle Temple 1971; memb Western Circuit in practice 1971-, standing counsel to the Treasury (Queen's Proctor); legal assessor UK Central Cncl for Nursing Midwifery and Health Visiting 1983-, asst recorder 1989-; sec Family Law Bar Assoc 1988-; memb: Cncl RYA 1980-83, 1984-87 and 1988-, Ctee Royal Ocean Racing Club 1984-87; *Recreations* sailing, skiing, music; *Clubs* Royal Yacht Sqdn, Royal Ocean Racing; *Style—* James Holman, Esq; 58 Grove Park, Camberwell, London SE5 8LG (☎ 071 274 0340); Queen Elizabeth Building, Temple, London EC4Y 9BS (☎ 071 583 7837, fax 071 353 5422)

HOLMAN, Richard Christopher; s of Frank Harold Homan (d 1984), and Joan, *née* Attrill (d 1988); *b* 16 June 1946; *Educ* Eton, Gonville and Caius Coll Cambridge (BA, MA); *m* 9 Aug 1969, Susan, da of George Amos Whittaker, of Wilmslow; 2 s (Nicholas b 12 Jan 1973, Simon b 26 May 1977); *Career* admitted slr 1971, dep dist registrar of High Court and dep registrar County Court 1982-88, asst rec 1988, managing ptnr Davis Wallis Foyster 1988-89 (ptnr 1973); memb Cncl Manchester Law Soc until 1990, memb Area Ctee NW Legal Aid, govr Parnall Hall Sch 1990-; *Recreations* golf, swimming, gardening, theatre; *Clubs* Wilmslow Golf; *Style—* Richard Holman, Esq; Davies Wallis Foyster, 37 Peter St, Manchester M2 5GB (☎ 061 228 3702, fax 061 835 2407, telex 668928)

HOLMAN, Hon Mrs ((Elizabeth) Winifred); *née* Ponsonby; da of 5 Baron de Mauley (d 1962), and Elgiva, da of Hon Cosparick Thomas Dundas (himself yr bro of 3rd Earl, later 1st Marquess of Zetland); *b* 1928; *m* 1950, Christopher Boot Holman (High Sheriff of Warwickshire 1986-87), s of Alexander MacArthur Holman (d 1979), and Margery Amy, da of 1 Lord Trent; 4 da; *Style—* The Hon Mrs Holman; Sheilbridge, Acharacle, Argyll (☎ 096 785 258); Foxcote, Shipston-on-Stour, Warwicks (☎ 060 882 240)

HOLME OF CHELTENHAM, Baron (Life Peer UK 1990), of Cheltenham in the County of Gloucestershire; Richard Gordon Holme; CBE (1983); s of J R Holme (d 1940), and E M Holme, *née* Eggleton; *b* 27 May 1936; *Educ* St John's Coll Oxford (MA); *m* 1958, Kay Mary, da of Vincent Powell; 2 s (Hon Richard Vincent b 1966, Hon John Gordon b (twin) 1966), 2 da (Hon Nicola Ann b 1959, Hon Penelope Jane b 1962); *Career* chm Constitutional Reform Centre 1984-, dir Avi Holdings 1987-, chm Threadneedle Publishing Group 1988-; sec Parly Democracy Tst 1979-, pres Lib Pty 1981; *Recreations* reading, walking, opera; *Clubs* Reform, Brooks's; *Style—* The Rt Hon Lord Holme of Cheltenham, CBE; 60 Chandos Place, London WC2N 4HG

HOLMES, Alan; MBE (1984); s of Thomas Henry Holmes (d 1985), and Margaret Holmes, *née* Plimley (d 1965); *b* 27 Feb 1940; *Educ* Grove Park GS Wrexham; *m* 5 Dec 1964, Patricia (Trish), da of Cecil Walsingham, ISO (d 1980); 1 s (Michael Alan b 8 June 1965), 1 da (Jane Diana b 20 May 1967); *Career* Miny of Housing and Local Govt 1958-64; joined FCO 1964: Kabul 1966, Paris 1968, Moscow 1970, Geneva 1971, FCO 1973, MECAS Beirut 1975, Tripoli 1976, Jeddah 1980, Al Khobar 1981, FCO 1984, Durban 1988; *Recreations* squash, tennis, music, walking; *Clubs* AA; *Style—* Alan Holmes, Esq, MBE; Highgate, Hophurst Lane, Crawley Down, Sussex RH10 4LJ (☎ 0342 714252); Foreign and Commonwealth Office, King Charles St, London SW1P 2AH (☎ 031 305 3041, fax 031 307 4661, telex 622428 SA)

HOLMES, Alan Wilson Jackson; s of Luke Jackson Holmes (d 1979); *b* 13 Sept 1945; *Educ* Portora Royal Sch Enniskillen, Cambridge Univ; *m* 1970, Frances-Maria, *née* Kadwell; 3 s, 1 da; *Career* dir Courage (Central) Ltd 1973-81, chm Courage (Scotland) Ltd 1979-81, dir Courage Ltd 1982-; *Recreations* golf, theatre; *Clubs* Royal and Ancient GC, Huntercombe GC; *Style*— Alan Holmes, Esq; The Copse, Ockham Road South, East Horsley, Surrey (☎ 04865-2396); Courage Ltd, Bridge St, Staines, Middx TW18 4TP

HOLMES, Andrew Jeremy; MBE (1987); s of Donald George Holmes (d 1986), of Uxbridge, Middx, and Janet Mary, *née* Hider; *b* 15 Oct 1959; *Educ* Latymer Upper, West London Inst (BA); *m* 18 Aug 1984, Pamela Anne, da of Derek Kent, of Portsmouth; 1 da (Aimée Elizabeth b 14 Nov 1987); *Career* oarsman; Olympic Games 1984 Gold medallist coxed fours; Cwlth Games 1986: Gold medallist coxed fours, Gold medallist coxless pairs; World Championships 1986, Gold medallist coxless pairs; World Championships 1987: Gold medallist coxless pairs, Silver medallist coxed pairs; Olympic Games 1988: Gold medallist coxless pairs, Bronze medallist coxed pairs; holder 2 World records, winner 9 Henley medals; *Recreations* classical music, antiques, interior design; *Clubs* Leander; *Style*— Andrew Holmes, Esq, MBE; Melfort Ave, Thornton Heath, Surrey CR4 7RH (☎ 081 684 0318, car tel 0836 527 469)

HOLMES, Anthony; CBE (1982); s of Herbert Holmes (d 1959), and Jessie, *née* Caffrey (d 1973); *b* 4 Sept 1931; *Educ* Calday Grange GS Wirral; *m* 1954, Sheila Frances, da of William Povall (d 1986); *Career* Sgt RAOC 1950-52; joined HM Customs and Excise 1949, transferred to Passport Office 1955; dep chief and passport offr 1977, chief passport offr 1980, head Passport Office; *Recreations* golf; *Clubs* Royal Liverpool GC, Cowdray Park GC; *Style*— Anthony Holmes, Esq, CBE; Passport Department, Clive House, Petty France, London SW1H 9HD (☎ 071 271 3000)

HOLMES, Barry Trevor; s of Edwin George Holmes (d 1977), and Marion Jones (d 1976); *b* 23 Sept 1933; *m* 15 Sept 1956 (m dis 1989), Dorothy, *née* Pitchforth; 3 da (Katharine b 1959, Alison b 1962, Joanne b 1967); *Career* Nat Serv Capt (temp) RA 1953-55; vice consul Br Embassy Quito 1958-62, second sec FO 1962-65 (memb 1950-53 and 1955-58), vice consul Br Consulate-Gen Vancouver 1965-68, first sec Br High Cmmn Nairobi 1972-75, first sec FCO 1975-80 (1968-72), commercial cnllr Br Embassy Helsinki 1980-85, consul-gen Br Consulate Gen Atlanta 1985-; dean Atlanta Consular Corps 1990-; *Recreations* chess, walking, reading spy stories; *Clubs* Atlanta Rotary; *Style*— Barry Holmes, Esq; British Consulate-General, 245 Peachtree Center Ave, Suite 2700, Atlanta, GA 30303, USA (☎ 404 524 8823, telex 240024 A/B BRITAIN, fax 404 524 3153)

HOLMES, Prof Brian; s of Albert Holmes (d 1966), of Folkestone, Kent, and Gertrude Maude, *née* Atkinson (d 1972); *b* 25 April 1920; *Educ* Salt HS Shipley, UCL (BSc), Univ of London Inst of Educn (PhD); *m* 1, 1945 (m dis 1971), Mary Isabel, *née* Refoy; 2 s (Nicholas Paul b 1947, Andrew Brian b 1950); m 2, 1971, Margaret Hon-Yin Wong; 1 da (Ruth Lin Wong b 1972); *Career* WWII Flt-Lt RAFVR served radar, CO RAF AME Stations in ME 1941-45; physics master: St Clement Danes 1946-51, King's Coll Sch Wimbledon 1949-51, lectr Univ of Durham 1951-53; Univ of London Inst of Educn: asst ed World Year Book of Educn 1953, lectr 1959, sr lectr 1963, reader 1964, prof 1975, prof of comparative educn and head dept 1975-85, pro-dir 1983-85, Charter fell 1979, dean and prof of educn Coll of Preceptors 1981-89; Dean Faculty of Educn Univ of London 1981-85; ed Educn Today; conslt: UNESCO, Int Bureau of Educn Geneva, OECD, Br Cncl, foreign govts; sr fellowship Japan Soc for Promotion of Sci 1987-88, visting lectr Nat Sci Cncl Republic of China 1988; visting prof: USA, Canadian and Japanese Univs; author of over 100 articles in jls and int periodicals; pres: Br Int and Comparative Educn Soc 1971, Comparative Educn Soc in Europe 1973-77 (sec treas 1961-73); chm World Congress Comparative Educn Socs 1974-77; annual professional visits USSR 1960-87; *Books* American Criticisms of American Education (1957), Problems in Education (1965), Educational Policy and the Mission Schools (ed, 1967), Comparative Education through the Literature (with T Bristow, 1968), International Guide to Educational Systems (1979), Comparative Education (1981), Diversity and Unity in Education (ed, 1980), Equality and Freedom in Education (ed 1985), The Curriculum (with M McLean 1989); *Recreations* collecting antique clocks; *Clubs* Royal Cwlth Soc; *Style*— Prof Brian Holmes; 110 Sumatra Road, London NW6 1PG (☎ 071 794 3835); University of London, Institute of Education, 20 Bedford Way, London WC1H OAL (☎ 071 636 1500)

HOLMES, David; CB (1985); s of George Archibald Holmes (d 1962), of Doncaster, and Annie, *née* Hill (d 1979); *b* 6 March 1935; *Educ* Doncaster GS, Christ Church Oxford (MA); *m* 1963, Ann, da of late John Chillingworth, of London; 1 s (Matthew b 1970), 2 da (Joanne b 1965, Elise b 1972); *Career* asst princ Miny of Tport and Civil Aviation 1957, princ HM Treasy 1965-68, princ private sec to Min of Tport 1968-70, asst sec DOE 1970, under sec 1976, dep sec Dept of Tport 1982-; *Style*— David Holmes, Esq, CB; Department of Transport, 2 Marsham St, London SW1P 3EB

HOLMES, Dr Geoffrey Kenneth Towndrow; s of Kenneth Geoffrey Holmes (d 1974), and Majorie, *née* Towndrow; *b* 15 Feb 1942; *Educ* Tupton Hall GS, Univ of Birmingham (BSc, MB ChB, MD); *m* 4 May 1970, Rosemary, da of Stanley Alfred Guy, MBE, of Derby; 1 s (Simon b 1973), 2 da (Rachel b 1971, Emma b 1976); *Career* res fell Birmingham Gen Hosp and Dept of Experimental Pathology Univ of Birmingham 1971-74, sr med registrar United Birmingham Hosps 1974-78, conslt physician and gastroenterologist Derbyshire Royal Infirmary 1978-, clinical teacher Univ of Nottingham 1980-; author various res papers on gastrointestinal disorders; memb Br Soc Gastro 1973, med advsr Derby and Dist Coeliac Soc 1980-, pres Derby and Burton Ileostomy Assoc 1986; memb BMA 1966, DRCOG 1969, MRCP 1970, FRCP 1984; *Books* Coeliac Disease Inflammatory Bowel Disease and Food Intolerance in Clinical Reactions to Food (1983), Coeliac Disease (1984), Coeliac Disease in Bockus Gastroenterology (1985); *Recreations* gardening, reading, theology; *Style*— Dr Geoffrey Holmes; 125 Whitaker Rd, Derby DE3 6AQ (☎ 0332 41005); Derbyshire Royal Infirmary, London Rd, Derby, Derbyshire (☎ 0332 47141)

HOLMES, Prof George Arthur; s of John Holmes (d 1949), of Aberystwyth, and Margaret, *née* Thomas (d 1977); *b* 22 April 1927; *Educ* Ardwyn Co Sch Aberystwyth, Univ Coll of Wales, St John's Coll Cambridge (MA, PhD); *m* 19 Dec 1953, (Evelyn) Anne, da of Dr John William Klein (d 1973), of Wimbledon; 2 s (Peter b 1955 d 1968, Nicholas b 1963), 2 da (Susan b 1957, Catherine (twin) b 1957); *Career* fell St John's Coll Cambridge 1951-54, tutor St Catherine's Soc Oxford 1954-62, fell and tutor St Catherine's Coll Oxford 1962- 89 (vice-master 1969-71), Chichele prof of medieval history and fell All Souls' Coll Oxford 1989-; memb Inst for Advanced Study Princeton 1967-68, delegate Oxford Univ Press 1982-, chm Victoria Co History Ctee of Inst of Historical Res 1978-89; FBA 1985; *Books* The Estates of the Higher Nobility in 14th Century England (1957), The Later Middle Ages (1962), The Florentine Enlightenment 1400-50 (1969), Europe: Hierarchy and Revolt 1320-1450 (1975), The Good Parliament (1975), Dante (1980), Florence, Rome and the Origins of the Renaissance (1986), The Oxford Illustrated History of Medieval Europe (ed, 1988), The First Age of the European City 1300-1500 (1990); *Style*— Prof George Holmes; Highmoor House, Bampton, Oxon (☎ 0993 850 408); All Souls College, Oxford (☎ 0865 279379)

HOLMES, George Dennis; CB (1979); s of James Henry Holmes (d 1960), of Gwynedd, N Wales, and Florence Jones (d 1978); *b* 9 Nov 1926; *Educ* John Bright's Sch Llandudno, Univ of Wales (BSc, DSc); *m* 1953, Sheila Rosemary, da of George Henry Woodger (d 1949), of Surrey; 3 da (Carolyn, Deborah, Nicola); *Career* dir gen Forestry Cmmn 1977-86; chm Scottish Cncl for Spastics 1986-; memb: E Bd Bank of Scotland 1987, Scottish Legal Aid Bd 1990-; FRSE; *Recreations* golf, fishing; *Style*— George Holmes, Esq, CB, FRSE; 7 Cammo Rd, Edinburgh EH4 8EF (☎ 031 339 7474)

HOLMES, Prof John Cameron; s of John Holmes (d 1982), and Susan Emily, *née* Cameron; *b* 3 April 1925; *Educ* Stirling HS, Univ of Edinburgh (BSc, PhD), Iowa State Univ (MS); *m* 23 Aug 1951, Ellen Miller Holmes, da of Capt William Hamilton, MC (d 1940); 1 s (Bill b 1960), 2 da (Patricia b 1955, Lesley b 1957); *Career* lectr then sr lectr Univ of Edinburgh 1949-74, head of Crop Prodn Advsy and Devpt Dept East of Scot Coll of Agric 1974-84, prof of crop prodn Univ of Edinburgh 1984-90; pres Euro Assoc for Potato Res 1987-90; *Recreations* reading, golf, skiing; *Style*— Prof John Holmes; 6 Alnwickhill Rd, Edinburgh EH16 6LF (☎ 031 664 3830)

HOLMES, Sir Maurice Andrew; s of Rev A T Holmes (d 1942); *b* 28 July 1911; *Educ* Felsted; *m* 1935, Joyce Esther Hicks; *Career* WWII serv RASC (despatches); called to the Bar Gray's Inn 1948; chm Tilling Gp 1960-65, London Tport Bd 1965-69; circuit admin SE circuit 1969-74; govr Felsted Sch; kt 1969; *Style*— Sir Maurice Holmes; The Limes, Felsted, nr Dunmow, Essex (☎ 0371 820352)

HOLMES, Sir Peter Fenwick; MC (1952); s of Gerald Hugh Holmes (d 1950), and Caroline Elizabeth, *née* Morris (d 1989); *b* 27 Sept 1932; *Educ* Malvern, Trinity Coll Cambridge (MA); *m* 19 March 1955, Judith Millicent, da of Brig Robert Fowler Walker, CBE, MC (d 1976); 3 da (Hermione b 1957, Josephine b 1958, Martha b 1961); *Career* Nat Serv Royal Leicestershire Regt 1950-52 (served Korea 1951-52); Royal Dutch/Shell Group of Companies 1956-; gen mangr Shell Markets ME 1965-68, chief rep Libya 1970-72, md Shell-BP Nigeria 1977-81, pres Shell International Trading 1981-83, md Royal Dutch/Shell Group 1982-, chm Shell Transport and Trading Co plc 1985-; tstee WWF UK 1989-; RIIA, FRGS; kt 1988; *Books* Mountains and a Monastery (1958), Nigeria, Giant of Africa (1985), Turkey, A Timeless Bridge (1988); *Recreations* mountaineering, skiing, travel to remote areas, photography, golf, 19th century travel books; *Clubs* Climbers', Himalayan, Alpine, Athenaeum, Sunningdale, Kandahar; *Style*— Sir Peter Holmes, MC; The Shell Transport and Trading Co plc, Shell Centre, London SE1 7NA (☎ 071 934 5611)

HOLMES, Peter Sloan; s of George Horner Gaffikin Holmes (d 1971), of 5 Tullybrannigan Rd, Newcastle, Co Down, and Anne Sloan, *née* Reid (d 1987); *b* 8 Dec 1942; *Educ* Rossall Sch Lancashire, Magdalen Coll Oxford (BA); *m* 14 April 1966, Patricia, da of Frederick Alexander McMahon (d 1984), of 2 Slievedarragh Park, Belfast; 2 s ((Christopher) Paul b 25 Jan 1967, Patrick Michael b 4 June 1969); *Career* Lt RNR 1965-68; teacher Eastbourne Coll 1965-68, head of English Grosvenor HS Belfast 1968-71, lectr and sr lectr Stranmillis Coll of Educn Belfast 1971-75; Dept of Educn: joined 1975, sr inspector 1980-82, staff inspector 1982-83, asst sec 1983-87, under sec 1987-; *Recreations* singing, sailing, classic cars; *Clubs* United Oxford & Cambridge University; *Style*— Peter Holmes, Esq; Department of Education for Northern Ireland, Rathgael House, Bangor, Co Down BT19 2PR (☎ 0247 27077)

HOLMES SELLORS, Patrick John; *b* 11 Feb 1934; *Educ* Rugby, Oriel Coll Oxford (BA, BM BCh, MA), Middx Hosp Med Sch (entrance scholar, state scholar, Douglas Cree prize in med); *m* ; 3 c; *Career* conslt ophthalmic surgn: Croydon Eye Unit, Royal Marsden Hosp, St Luke's Hosp for The Clergy; hon conslt ophthalmic surgn St George's Hosp, surgn-oculist to HM The Queen; author of various papers for presentation and jls and of chapters in med books; memb: Gen Optical Cncl, Cncl and Exec Ctee Coll of Ophthalmologists, Cncl Med Def Union; tstee: Dermot Pierse Lecture in Ophthalmology, Anne Allerton Tst for Ophthalmic Res; FRCS 1965, FCOphth 1990; *Books* An Outline of Ophthalmology (jtly, 1985); *Style*— Patrick J Holmes Sellors, Esq; High Burrows, The Drive, Behnont, Surrey SM2 7DP; 149 Harley St, London W1N 2DE

HOLMES-WALKER, Dr (William) Anthony; ERD (1971); s of Lt-Col William Roger Holmes Walker, TD (d 1967), of South Corner, Duncton, N Petworth, Sussex, and Katharine Grace, *née* Foote (d 1988); *b* 26 Jan 1926; *Educ* Westminster, Queen's Univ Belfast (BSc, PhD), Imperial Coll London (DIC); *m* 26 July 1952, Marie-Anne, da of Willy Eugene Russ (d 1959), of Villa Eugenie, 43 Evole, Neuchâtel, Switzerland; 2 da (Antonia b 1954, Katharine b 1957); *Career* RE: Belfast 1944, Lt 1945, Capt 1946, served ME; Lt-Col AER/TAVR 1960 (Maj 1956); tech offr ICI Ltd 1954-59, head of plastics R & D Metal Box Co Ltd 1959-66, prof of polymer sci & technol Brunel Univ 1966-74, dir Br Plastics Fedn 1974-81, visiting prof City Univ 1981-83, sec gen Euro Brewers Trade Assoc 1983-88, dir of industl liaison Univ of Reading 1988-90, assoc dir Inventions to Industry 1990-; memb Round Table Hemel Hempstead 1955-66, pres Villars Visitors Ski Club 1955-74, churchwarden St John's Boxmoor 1966-72; Freeman: City of London 1951, Worshipful Co of Skinners (Master 1980-81 and memb Ct); Liveryman Worshipful Co of Horners; FRSC 1966, FPRI 1969, FIM 1972; *Books* Polymer Conversion (1975); *Recreations* skiing, golf, music, genealogy; *Style*— Dr Anthony Holmes-Walker, ERD; Blue Cedars, Sheethanger Lane, Felden, Boxmoor, Herts HP3 0BG (☎ 0442 253117); Inventions to Industry, 346 High St, Northwood, Middx HA6 1BN (☎ 0923 835983)

HOLMPATRICK, 4 Baron (UK 1897), of HolmPatrick, Co Dublin; Hans James David Hamilton; eldest s of 3 Baron HolmPatrick (d 1991), and Anne Loys Roche, *née* Brass; *b* 15 March 1955; *m* 19 July 1984, Mrs Gill Francesca Anne du Feu, eldest da of Kenneth James Harding (d 1990), of Binisafua, Minorca; 1 s (Hon James Hans Stephen b 6 Oct 1982), 1 step s (Dominic Mark du Feu b 15 Jan 1975); *Heir* bro, Hon Ion Henry James Hamilton b 12 June 1956; *Style*— The Rt Hon Lord HolmPatrick; Kilbride, Trim, Co Meath, Republic of Ireland (☎ 0462 5138)

HOLNESS, Robert Wentworth John (Bob); s of Charles John Holness (d 1973), of Durban S Africa, and Ethel Eileen Holness (d 1972); *b* 12 Nov 1928; *Educ* Ashford GS Kent, Maidstone Coll of Art; *m* 16 April 1955, Mary Rose, da of Thomas Vernon Clifford; 1 s (Jonathan Clifford b 9 April 1966), 2 da (Carol Ann (Mrs Gibson) b 2 Feb 1956, Rosalind Mary b 23 Sept 1957); *Career* Nat Serv RAF 1947-49; apprentice in printing trade, memb repertory co Intimate Theatre (where met wife) S Africa 1953-55, radio actor, interviewer and presenter of music and magazine progs S Africa 1955-61, Granada TV Eng 1961-64 (host of quiz progs Take a Letter and Junior Criss Cross Quiz, worked on World in Action, What the Papers Say and Breakthrough, reporter, newsreader, interviewer and announcer), freelance 1964-68 (mainly with BBC in London), Thames TV 1968- (reporter and co presenter of Today news magazine prog), Radio 4 (presenter Top of the Form), Radio 2 (presenter Late Night Extra 1967-75), LBC (co-presenter AM Show 1975-86), freelance work incl voice-over commentary work and radio and tv tutoring, presenter Blockbusters (ITV) 1984-; *Awards* (jtly) Top News Presenter Nat Radio and Record Industs 1978, (for AM Show) Best Current Affairs Programming Local Radio awards 1979, Jt Ind Radio Personality Variety Club of GB 1979 and 1984, (for Blockbusters) Favourite Game Show on TV award TV Times 1985 and 1986 and four BAFTA nominations; Freeman City of London 1981, memb Worshipful Co of Glaziers; *Recreations* walking, gardening, listening to every type of music; *Style*— Bob Holness, Esq; c/o The Spotlight, 7 Leicester Place, London WC2H 7BP (☎ 071 437 7631)

HOLROYD, (William) Arthur Hepworth; s of Rev Harry Holroyd (d 1970), and

Annie Dodgshun Holroyd; *b* 15 Sept 1938; *Educ* Kingswood Sch Bath, Trinity Hall Cambridge (MA), Univ of Manchester (Dip); *m* 24 June 1967, Hilary; 3 s (Mark b 1968, Simon b 1970, Christopher b 1974); *Career* hosp sec: Crewe Meml Hosp 1963-65, Wycombe Gen Hosp 1965-67; seconded Dept Health 1967-69, dep gp sec Blackpool HMC 1969-72, regnl manpower offr Leeds RHB 1972-74, dist admin York Health Dist 1974-82, regnl admin Yorks RHA 1982-85, dist gen mangr Durham Health Authy 1985-; ed Hosp Traffic and Supply Problems 1969; memb: NHS Nat Staff Ctee 1973-82, Gen Nursing Cncl 1978-83, English Nat Bd Nursing Midwifery and Health Visiting 1980-87, NHS Trg Authy 1988-; FHSM 1972; *Recreations* classical music, walking, visiting Shetland Isles; *Style—* Arthur Holroyd, Esq; 3 Dunelm Court, South St, Durham DH1 4QX

HOLROYD, Air Marshal Sir Frank Martyn; KBE (1989), CB (1985); s of George Lumb Holroyd (d 1987), and Winifred Hetty, *née* Ford; *b* 30 Aug 1935; *Educ* Southend-On-Sea GS, RAF Tech Coll Henlow, Cranfield Inst Technol (MSc); *m* 1 Feb 1958, Veronica Christine, da of Arthur George Booth (d 1984); 2 s (Martyn Paul b 26 Jan 1959, Myles Justin b 9 Nov 1966), 1 da (Bryony Jane b 4 June 1961); *Career* RAF (initially Nat Serv cmmn) 1956, appt fighter stations RAF Leconfield and RAF Leeming, Blind Landing Experimental Unit RAE Bedford 1960-63, HQ Fighter Cmd 1965-67, OC electrical engrg sqdn RAF Changi Singapore 1967-69, Wing Cdr Staff Coll RAF Bracknell 1970, MOD 1970-72, OC engrg wing RAF Brize Norton 1972, Gp Capt 1974, Station Cdr No 1 Radio Sch RAF Locking 1974-76, sr engrg offr HQ 38 Gp 1976, Air Cdre dir Aircraft Engrg MOD 1977, RCDS 1981, Air Vice Marshal dir gen Strategic Electronic Engrg (former dir Weapons and Support Engrg) MOD, (PE) 1982, air offr engrg HQ Strike Cmd 1986, Air Marshal chief engr RAF 1988-, chief Logistics Support 1989-; memb: BBC Engrg Advsy Bd 1984-90, Advsy Cncl RMCS, Cncl Cranfield Inst Technol 1990- (Ct 1988-), Engrg Cncl; vice pres RAe Soc (pres elect 1991); CEng, FRAeS, FIEE, CBIM; *Recreations* gardening, maintaining 14th century house, sports; *Clubs* RAF; *Style—* Air Marshal Sir Frank Holroyd, KBE, CB; MOD, Neville House, Page St, London (☎ 071 218 5999)

HOLROYD, Michael de Courcy Fraser; CBE (1989); s of Basil de Courcy Fraser Holroyd, of Surrey, and Ulla, *née* Hall; *b* 27 Aug 1935; *Educ* Eton; *m* 1982, Margaret, da of John Frederick Drabble, QC (d 1983), of Suffolk; *Career* biographer; chm: Soc of Authors 1973-74, Nat Book League 1976-78; pres English PEN 1985-88; *Books* Lytton Strachey (1967-68), Augustus John (1974-75), Bernard Shaw (1988-91); *Recreations* listening to music and stories, watching people dance; *Style—* Michael Holroyd, Esq, CBE; 85 St Mark's Rd, London W10 6JS (☎ 081 960 4891)

HOLROYD, Lady Sheila Mary; da of late 4 Earl Cairns; *b* 1905; *m* 1930, Maj Charles Ivor Patrick Holroyd, late Rifle Bde; 2 s, 3 da; *Style—* The Lady Sheila Holroyd; Providence Cottage, Chute Cadley, Andover, Hants

HOLROYDE, Geoffrey Vernon; s of Harold Vincent Holroyde (d 1978), and Kathleen Olive, *née* Glover (d 1990); *b* 18 Sept 1928; *Educ* Wrekin Coll, Univ of Birmingham (BSc), Royal Coll of Organists (ARCO); *m* 20 Feb 1960, Elizabeth Mary, da of Rev Canon Ernest Oldham Connell (d 1986), of Edinburgh; 2 s (Nicholas b 22 Feb 1963, Timothy b 7 Nov 1968), 2 da (Jacqueline b 6 May 1962, Penelope b 5 May 1966); *Career* RN short serv cmmn 1949-54 1956-61; sch master and house tutor Welbeck Coll 1954-56, dir of studies and princ Eng Electric Staff Coll 1961-70, Br Leyland Central Trg staff 1970-71, head master Sidney Stringer Community Sch Coventry 1971-75, dir Coventry Poly 1975-87, advsr on higher educn Manpower Servs Cmmn 1987-88, dir GEC Mgmnt Coll 1988-; dir of music Collegiate Church of St Mary Warwick 1962-72; dir: Oken Singers 1972-78, Coventry Cathedral Chapter House Choir 1982-, Coventry and Warwickshire Young Organists Project 1978-84; hon life memb Royal Sch of Church Music 1970-, govr Mid Warwickshire Coll of Further Educn 1976-87; chm: Industl Links Advsy Gp of the CDP 1981-87, W Midlands RHA Non-Clinical Res Ctee 1986-90, Nat Forum for Performing Arts in Higher Educn 1987-90, Steering Ctee LET JMRT YTS Project 1988-90; memb: W Midlands Advsy Cncl for Further Educn 1975-86, Cncl of Higher Avon Navigational Tst 1980-, W Midlands RHA 1986-90, RSA Educn Indust Forum 1986-; *Books* Managing People (1968), Delegations (1968), Communications (1969), The Organs of St Mary's Warwick (1969), Enterprise in Higher Education (1988); *Recreations* Director of Coventry Cathedral Chapter House choir, organ playing, narrowboating; *Style—* Geoffrey Holroyde, Esq; 38 Coten End, Warwick CV34 4NP (☎ 0926 492329); GEC Management College, Dunchurch, Rugby, Warwickshire CV22 6QW (☎ 0788 810656, fax 0788 814451, telex 311879 DUNCOL G)

HOLT, Andrea Mary; da of Wilton Eric Holt, of 72 Victoria St, Ramsbottom, Bury, Lancs, and Maureen Margaret, *née* Rogers; *b* 11 Nov 1970; *Educ* St Gabriel's RC HS Bury, Bury Coll of Further Educn; *Career* professional table tennis player; Nat Jr champion 3 times, runner up English Championships 1989-90, semi finalist Italian Open 1990; England: first appearance aged 13, World and Euro Championships, over 60 appearances; memb GB training squad for Barcelona Olympics; currently ranked third in England; *Recreations* tennis, golf, watching football, listening to music; *Style—* Miss Andrea Holt; 72 Victoria St, Ramsbottom, nr Bury, Lancashire (☎ 0706 825197)

HOLT, Col (George) Anthony; s of George Denis Holt, of Bognor Regis, and Winifred, *née* Fletcher; *b* 4 July 1939; *Educ* Univ School Southport; *m* 15 April 1963, Monica, da of Maj Gordon Nuttall, of Camberley; 1 s (Mark b 1967, d 1986), 1 da (Amanda b 1965); *Career* Cmmnd RA 1959, served Cyprus 1960-62, Borneo 1966, NI 1970, CO 4 Field Regt RA 1980-82, divnl Col Staff Coll Camberley 1984-87, dep Cdr Sultan of Omans Artillery 1987-89; memb Hon Artillery Co 1958; FBIM 1986; *Recreations* golf, tennis, bridge; *Style—* Col Anthony Holt

HOLT, (Roma) Hazel Kathryn; da of Charles Douglas Young (d 1986), of Clearwell, Glos, and Roma, *née* Simpson; *b* 3 Sept 1928; *Educ* King Edward VI HS Birmingham, Newnham Coll Cambridge (BA); *m* Geoffrey Louis Holt; 1 s (Thomas Charles Louis, *qv*, b 13 Sept 1961); *Career* ed asst International African Institute 1950-79, feature writer and reviewer Stage and Television Today 1979-82; edited for publication the posthumous novels of Barbara Pym (Litarary executor): A Very Private Eye (with Hilary Pym 1984), Gone Away (1989), A Lot to Ask: A Life of Barbara Pym (1990), The Cruellest Month (1991); *Recreations* reading, writing and watching cats; *Clubs* Univ Womens; *Style—* Mrs Hazel Holt; Tivington Knowle, nr Minehead, Somerset TA24 8SX (☎ 0643 704707)

HOLT, Prof Sir James Clarke; s of Herbert Holt (d 1980), of Bradford, Yorks, and Eunice Holt, BEM, *née* Clarke (d 1974); *b* 26 April 1922; *Educ* Bradford Sch, Queen's Coll Oxford, Merton Coll Oxford (MA, DPhil); *m* 3 July 1950, (Alice Catherine) Elizabeth, da of David Suley (d 1962), of Bingley, Yorks; 1 s (Edmund b 7 Oct 1954); *Career* RA 1942-45, Capt 1943; prof of medieval history Univ of Nottingham 1962-66 (lectr 1949-62), dean of Faculty of Letters and Social Sciences Univ of Reading 1972-76 (prof of history 1966-78); Univ of Cambridge: prof of medieval history 1978-88, professorial fell Emmanuel Coll 1978-81, master Fitzwilliam Coll 1981-88; memb Advsy Cncl on Public Records 1974-81, chm of Cncl Pipe Roll Soc 1976-; vice pres: Selden Soc 1978-88, Br Acad 1987-89; pres: Royal Historical Soc 1980-84, Lincoln Record Soc 1987-; Hon DLitt Univ of Reading 1984; fell: Royal Historical Soc 1954, Br Acad 1978; Comendador de la Orden del Merito Civil 1988; kt 1990; *Recreations* music, mountaineering, fly-fishing; *Clubs* Utd Oxford and Cambridge, Nat Lib, MCC, Wayfarers (Liverpool); *Style—* Prof Sir James Holt; 5 Holben Close, Barton, Cambridge CB3 7AQ (☎ 0223 263074); Fitzwilliam College, Cambridge CB3 0DG (☎ 0223 332041)

HOLT, Joan Patricia; JP (1975); da of Edwin Charles Merrick Burrell (d 1950), of Gerrards Cross, Bucks, and Jane Burrell, OBE, *née* Martin (d 1983); *b* 15 Jan 1920; *Educ* Oakdene Sch Beaconsfield; *m* 12 June 1945, Brian Alfred Whittell Holt, s of Guy Whittell Holt (d 1966), of Wimbledon; 1 s (Richard b 1949), 1 da (Sarah b 1954); *Career* commnd WAAF 1942-45 admitted slr 1943, co dir and chm Ronaldsway Aircraft Co Ltd 1983; SSStJ 1989; *Clubs* English Speaking Union; *Style—* Mrs Joan Holt, JP; Balladoole House, Castletown, Isle of Man (☎ 0624 822620); Ronaldsway Aircraft Co Ltd, Ballasalla, Isle of Man (☎ 0624 822111)

HOLT, John Frederick; s of Edward Basil Holt (d 1984), and Monica, *née* Taylor; *b* 7 Oct 1947; *Educ* Ampleforth, Univ of Bristol (LLB); *m* 26 Sept 1970, Stephanie Ann, da of Peter Watson, of Belaugh, Norfolk; 3 s (Samuel John b 16 June 1973, Benjamin Alexander b 2 Sept 1974, Edward Daniel b 11 Oct 1980); *Career* called to the Bar Lincoln's Inn 1970, Co Ct Rules Ctee 1981-85, asst rec 1988-; *Recreations* cricket, restoring vintage motor cars; *Clubs* Twinstead Cricket; *Style—* John Holt, Esq; Wensum Chambers, 10a Wensum St, Norwich NR3 1HR (☎ 0603 617351, fax 0603 633589)

HOLT, Dr John Michael; s of Frank Holt (d 1977), and Constance Cora, *née* Walton; *b* 8 March 1935; *Educ* St Peter's Sch York, Univ of St Andrews (MB ChB, MD), Queen's Univ Ontario Canada (MSc), Univ of Oxford (MA); *m* 27 June 1959, Sheila Margaret, da of William Hood Morton (d 1968), of Harrogate; 1 s (Timothy b 8 May 1964), 3 da (Jane b 27 May 1960, Sally b 13 July 1962, Lucy b 30 July 1968); *Career* res fell Dept of Med and Biochemistry Queen's Univ Ontario Canada 1961-63, registrar lectr and med tutor Nuffield Dept of Med Radcliffe Infirmary Oxford 1963-74, conslt physician 1969-, dir of clinical studies Univ of Oxford 1972-77, fell Linacre Coll Oxford 1970-, chm med staff Oxford 1983-85; memb: Ctee on Safety of Med 1978-86, Oxford RHA 1984-88, Gen Bd of Faculties Univ of Oxford 1987-; examiner Univs of Oxford, London, Glasgow, Hong Kong; Liveryman Hall of Apothecaries, Freeman City of London; FRCP London 1974; *Recreations* sailing; *Clubs* Utd Oxford and Cambridge, Royal Cornwall Yacht; *Style—* Dr John Holt; Old Whitehill, Tackley, Oxon OX5 3AB; 23 Banbury Road, Oxford OX2 6NX; John Radcliffe Hosp, Headington, Oxford OX3 9DU (☎ 0865 817348, 0865 515036)

HOLT, (Stanley) John; s of Frederick Holt (d 1949), of Toot-Hill, nr Chipping Ongar, Essex, and May, *née* Abblett (d 1984); *b* 27 Sept 1931; *Educ* Chipping Ongar, Walthamstow; *m* 6 Aug 1959, Anne, da of Richard Catherall (d 1943); 3 da (Sarah b 30 May 1960, Ruth b 15 July 1962, Rachel b 13 April 1966); *Career* Nat Serv RAMC 1953-55; chm Isodan UK Ltd 1975-; formerly with: Rentokil Labs, Pilkington's Tiles, Bayer AG W Germany; ed The Liveryman; master Portsoken Ward Club; memb: Utd Ward Club, Royal Soc of St George, Cncl City Livery Club, Fellowship of Clerks; former chm Lunchtime Comment Club; Ct Asst Guild of Freemen, Freeman City of London 1983, Liveryman and Ct Asst Worshipful Co of Marketors 1983, Clerk Worshipful Co of Environmental Cleaners 1986; Asst Clerk Worshipful Co of Horners 1989; MCIM, MBIM, MIEx, FInstD; *Recreations* showering; *Clubs* Wig and Pen, City Livery; *Style—* John Holt, Esq; Whitethorns, Rannoch Rd, Crowborough, E Sussex TN6 1RA (☎ 0892 655 780); 102 Marlyn Lodge, Portsoken St, London E1 8RB (☎ 071 265 0753)

HOLT, Lady; Margaret; da of T S Lupton, formerly of Runswick, Cheadle Hulme, Cheshire; *m* 1931, Sir Edward Holt, 2 Bt (d 1968, when the title became ext); *Style—* Lady Holt

HOLT, Her Hon Judge Mary; da of Late Henry James Holt, and Sarah, *née* Chapman (d 1987); *Educ* Park Sch Preston, Girton Coll Cambridge (MA, LLB); *Career* called to the Bar Gray's Inn 1949 (Atkin Scholar 1949); practised at Chancery Bar on Northern Circuit 1949-77; MP (C) Preston N 1970-74, Parly candidate (C) Preston N Feb and OCt 1974; HM circuit judge 1977-; BRCS: vice pres Lancashire Branch 1976-, Badge of Hon 1989-; Freeman: City of Dallas Texas 1987, City of Denton Texas 1987; *Books* Benas and Essonhigh's Precedents of Pleading (ed 2 edn, 1956); *Recreations* walking; *Clubs* Royal Commonwealth Soc, Winckley (Preston); *Style—* Her Hon Judge Mary Holt; The Sessions House, Preston

HOLT, Nicholas John; s of Eric Holt and Eileen Patricia, *née* Macritchee; *b* 2 April 1958; *Educ* Manchester GS, Fitzwilliam Coll Cambridge (BA, MA); *m* 14 April 1984, Georgina Mary, da of Dr William Mann; 1 s (William b 1987), 1 da (Alexandra b 1989); *Career* articled clerk then asst slr Coward Chance 1980-84, asst slr then mangr Corp Legal Dept Jardine Matheson & Co Hong Kong 1984-87, legal and compliance dir Smith New Court plc 1989- (gp legal advsr 1987-89); memb Law Soc; *Recreations* football, squash, cricket; *Clubs* Reform; *Style—* Nicholas Holt, Esq; Smith New Court plc, Smith New Court House, PO Box 293, 20 Farringdon Rd, London EC1M 3NH (☎ 071 772 1349, fax 071 772 2900)

HOLT, Richard Anthony Appleby; s of Frederick Appleby Holt, OBE (d 1980), and Rae Vera Franz, *née* Hutchinson; *b* 11 March 1920; *Educ* Harrow, King's Coll Cambridge; *m* 6 Oct 1945, Daphne Vivien, da of Vice Adm Frank Henderson Pegram, CB, DSO (d 1944); 3 s (Christopher Appleby b 1947, Richard Frederick b 1956, Edward b 1960), 2 da (Harriet b 1949, Alice b 1954); *Career* Serv KRRC 1940-46, demobbed as Maj; slr 1949; dir Hutchinson Ltd 1952-80 (chm 1959, md 1978), chm Hutchinson Publishing 1965-80, dir Constable Publishing 1968-90; govr Harrow 1952-82 (chm Governing Body 1971-80); memb Ctee All England Lawn Tennis Club 1959-82; Liveryman Worshipful Co of Slrs 1960; *Clubs* All England Lawn Tennis, MCC; *Style—* Richard Holt, Esq; 55 Queen's Gate Mews, London SW7 5QN (☎ 071 589 8469)

HOLT, (James) Richard; MP (C) Langbaurgh 1983-; *b* 2 Aug 1931; *Educ* Wembley County GS, Hendon and Harrow Tech Colls; *m* 1959, Mary June Leathers; 1 s, 1 da; *Career* RN seaman; Parly candidate (C) Brent S Feb 1974; memb: Brent Borough Cncl 1964-74, Wycombe Borough Cncl 1976-; FIPM, MBIM; *Style—* Richard Holt, Esq, MP; House of Commons, London SW1

HOLT, Sarah Caroline; da of Brian Alfred Holt (d 1984), and Joan Patricia, *née* Burrell; *b* 25 Jan 1954; *Educ* Wycombe Abbey Sch, Girton Coll Cambridge (MA); *m* 18 Jan 1986, John Nicholas Sharman, s of Brig-Gen Ronald Llewellyn Sharman, RAMC (d 1974); 1 s (Thomas b 1988); *Career* slr; ptnr Norton Rose (specialising in shipping and aviation fin); *Recreations* history, music, aviation; *Style—* Miss Sarah Holt; Norton Rose, Kempson House, Camomile Street, London EC3A 7AN (☎ 071 283 2434, fax 071 588 1181, telex 883652)

HOLT, Thelma Mary Bernadette; da of David Holt (d 1941), and Ellan, *née* Finnagh Doyle (d 1969); *b* 4 Jan 1933; *Educ* St Anne's Coll for Girls, RADA; *m* 1, 31 March 1957 (m dis), Patrick Graucob; m 2, 6 Oct 1968 (m dis), David Pressman; *Career* actress 1955-68, jt art dir Open Space Theatre 1968-77, art dir Round House Theatre 1977-83, exec prodr Theatre of Comedy 1983-85, head of touring and commercial exploitation Nat Theatre 1985-88, exec prodr Peter Hall Co 1988; head: Int Theatre 89, Nat Theatre 1989-; Observer award for Special Achievement in Theatre 1987; dir: Thelma Holt Ltd, Vanessa Redgrave Enterprises Ltd, Theatre Investment Fund Ltd, Citizens' Theatre Glasgow, Petard Prodns Ltd; memb Cncl RADA; *Style—* Miss

Thelma Holt; Thelma Holt Ltd, Waldorf Chambers, 11 The Aldwych, London WC2B 4DA (☎ 071 379 0438, fax 071 836 9832)

HOLT, Thomas Charles Louis; s of Geoffrey Louis Holt, and (Roma) Hazel Kathryn Holt, *qv*, *née* Young; *b* 13 Sept 1961; *Educ* Westminster, Wadham Coll Oxford, Coll of Law Chancery Lane; *m* 6 Aug 1988, Kim Nicola, da of John Clifford Foster; *Career* author; publications incl: Poems by Tom Holt 1973, Lucia in Wartime (1985, US 1986), Lucia Triumphant (1986, US 1986), Expecting Someone Taller (1987, US 1988), Who's Afraid of Beowulf? (1988, US 1989), Goatsong (1989, US 1990), I Margaret (with Steve Nallon, 1989), The Walled Orchard 1990; *Recreations* numismatics, skeet shooting; *Style—* Thomas Holt, Esq; c/o James Hale, 47 Peckham Rye, London SE15 3NX (☎ and fax 071 732 6338)

HOLT, Vesey Martin Edward; DL (Shropshire 1986); s of Martin Drummond Vesey Holt (d 1956), of Mount Mascal, Bexley, Kent (d 1956), and Lady Phyllis Hedworth Camilla Herbert, sis of 5 and 6 Earls of Powis (d 1972); direct decendant of Lord Clive (Clive of India); *b* 28 March 1927; *Educ* Radley, RAC Cirencester; *m* 1955, Elizabeth Jane, da of John Geoffrey Sanger, of Prattenden, Bury, West Sussex; 1 s (Peter), 1 da (Amanda); *Career* farmer; ccncllr Shropshire 1968-74 and 1977-, govr Wrekin Coll 1968-, memb Shropshire Valuation Panel 1970- (dep chm 1984-), pres Shropshire CCC 1973-, pres Minor Counties Cricket Assoc 1983-; memb Agric Land Tbnl 1975-; High Sheriff Shropshire 1981, pres Wrekin Cons Assoc 1983-; *Recreations* shooting, cricket; *Clubs* Brooks's, MCC; *Style—* Vesey Holt, Esq, DL; Orleton Hall, Wellington, Telford, Shropshire (☎ 0952 242780); 42 Stanford Rd, London W8 (☎ 071 937 4970)

HOLTBY, Very Rev Robert Tinsley; s of William Holtby (d 1972), of Dalton, Thirsk, N Yorks, and Elsie, *née* Horsfield (d 1959); *b* 25 Feb 1921; *Educ* Scarborough Coll, St Edmund Hall Oxford (MA, BD), King's Coll Cambridge (MA); *m* 22 Nov 1947, Mary, da of Rt Rev Eric Graham, Bishop of Brechin (d 1964), of Forbes Court, Broughty Ferry, Dundee; 1 s (David b 1953), 2 da (Veronica b 1948, Caroline b 1951); *Career* ordained 1946, curate Pocklington Yorks 1946-48, chaplain to the Forces Catterick and Singapore 1948-52; chaplain and asst master: Malvern Coll 1952-54, St Edward's Sch Oxford 1954-59; canon residentiary Carlisle Cathedral and diocesan dir of educn 1959-67, gen sec Nat Soc for Religious Educn 1967-77, sec Schools Cncl C of E 1967-74, gen sec C of E Bd of Educn 1974-77, dean Chichester 1977-89, select preacher Oxford and Cambridge Univs, dean emeritus 1989-, visiting fell W Sussex Inst of Higher Educn; chm Cumberland Cncl of Social Servs 1962-67, memb Cumberland and Carlisle Educn Ctees, chaplain to High Sheriff of Cumberland; author of biographies, educnl and historical works; FSA; *Recreations* music, historical work; *Clubs* United Oxford and Cambridge, Yorkshire; *Style—* The Very Rev RT Holtby, FSA; 4 Hutton Hall, Huttons Ambo, York, N Yorks YO6 7HW (☎ 0653 696366)

HOLTON, Michael; s of George Arnold Holton (d 1950), of Hampstead Garden Suburb, and Ethel Maud, *née* Fountain (d 1976); *b* 30 Sept 1927; *Educ* Finchley Co GS, LSE (BSc); *m* 1, 14 July 1951 (m dis 1987), Daphne Elizabeth, da of Charles Stanley Bache (d 1950), of Gloucester; 1 s (Philip b 1960), 2 da (Alison b 1954, Rosemary b 1957); m 2, 11 April 1987, Joan Catherine, da of George Frederick Hickman (d 1984); *Career* Nat Serv RAF 1946-48; Civil Serv: Miny of Food 1949-54, Air Miny 1955-60, MOD 1961-68 and 1976-87, ret asst sec 1987; sec: Countryside Cmmn for Scotland 1968-70, Scottish Ctee Euro Conservation Year 1970, Carnegie UK Tst 1971-75, Royal Soc for Nature Conservation 1988- (cncl memb 1976-), RAF Mountaineering Assoc 1952-54, (organised RAF Himalayan Expedition 1954-55), Br Mountaineering Cncl 1955-59; dir Cairngorm Chairlift Co 1973-; FRGS 1952-68, FRSGS 1971-85; *Books* RAF Mountain Rescue Training Handbook (1953); *Clubs* Athenaeum, Alpine, Himalayan (Bombay); *Style—* Michael Holton, Esq; 4 Ludlow Way, Hampstead Garden Suburb, London N2 0LA (☎ 081 444 8582)

HOLWILL, Derek Paul Winsor; s of Frederick James Winsor Holwill (d 1967), and Brenda, *née* Wilks; *b* 25 Sept 1959; *Educ* Kings College Sch Wimbledon, Gonville and Caius Coll Cambridge (MA); *Career* called to the Bar Gray's Inn 1982; *Books* UK Law for The American Businessman (contrib, 1983); *Recreations* lindy hop, travel; *Style—* Derek Holwill, Esq; 4 Paper Buildings, Temple, London EC4Y 7EX (☎ 071 353 3366, fax 071 353 5778)

HOMAN, (Lawrence) Hugh Adair; s of Lawrence William Nicholson Homan (d 1981), of Harpenden, Herts, and Mary Graves, *née* Adair; *b* 26 June 1945; *Educ* Sherborne, Worcester Coll Oxford (MA); *m* 19 June 1971, Lyn Claudine, da of Lt Cdr Hubert John Douglas Hamilton (d 1975), of Deal, Kent; 1 s (Alexander b 1973), 1 da (Olivia b 1976); *Career* admitted slr 1970; asst slr Allen & Overy 1968-73, ptnr Berwin Leighton 1975-; memb Law Soc; *Recreations* sailing, golf; *Style—* Hugh Homan, Esq; Chantry Drift, Gedgrave Rd, Orford, Suffolk IP12 2NG; 21 Crescent Grove, London SW4 7AF; Berwin Leighton, Adelaide House, London Bridge, London EC4R 9HA (☎ 071 623 3144, fax 071 623 4416, telex 88642)

HOMAN, (Andrew) Mark; s of Philip John Lindsay Homan (d 1988), of Stokenham, Devon, and Elisabeth Clemency, *née* Hobson; *b* 27 June 1942; *Educ* Maidstone GS, Univ of Nottingham (BA); *m* 3 Oct 1970, Pamela Joan, da of George Lawson Robertson; 1 s (Andrew Thomas b 17 Sept 1977), 1 da (Sally Ann b 4 Aug 1974); *Career* Price Waterhouse: joined 1963, ptnr 1975, nat dir Corp Reconstruction & Insolvency Practice, chm Insolvency Advsy Gp Price Waterhouse World Firm Ltd; memb Accountants Advsy Panel Insolvency Law Review Ctee (Cork Ctee) 1979-81; memb Cncl: Insolvency Practitioners Assoc, Soc of Practitioners of Insolvency; chm Jt Insolvency Examination Bd; FCA (ACA 1966); *Recreations* cricket, gardening, chess, opera; *Clubs* MCC; *Style—* Mark Homan, Esq; Price Waterhouse, 1 London Bridge, London SE1 9QL (☎ 071 939 5620, fax 071 939 5566)

HOMAN, Hon Mrs (Mary Graham); *née* Buckley; da of 2 Baron Wrenbury (d 1940), and Helen Malise, *née* Graham; *b* 30 May 1929; *m* 8 April 1961, John Richard Seymour Homan, CBE, yr s of late Capt Charles Edward Homan, Elder Bro of Trin House; 1 s (Robert b 1964), 2 da (Frances b 1967, Rosalind b 1969); *Style—* The Hon Mrs Homan; 30 High St, Ticehurst, Sussex

HOMAN, (John) Richard Seymour; CBE (1985); s of Capt Charles Edward Homan (d 1936), of London and Hampshire, and Mary Muriel, *née* Hewetson (d 1979); *b* 7 Jan 1925; *Educ* Radley, ChCh Oxford (MA); *m* 7 April 1961, Hon Mary Graham, da of Rt Hon Lord Wrenbury (d 1940), of E Sussex and London; 1 s (Robert b 1964), 2 da (Frances b 1967, Rosalind b 1969); *Career* RNVR 1943, Sub Lt RNVR 1944-46; 2 Sealords Dept Admiralty London 1944, HMS Tracker 1944-45, Underwater Weapons Div 1945-46; corp internal mgmnt conslt Head Office ICI 1950-57, corp planner and export sales mangr ICI Metals/IMI 1957-64, dep head Computing and Mgmnt Servs Agric Div ICI 1964-68; NEDO: Br head Industl Div 1968-72, head Assessment Div 1972-74, asst industl dir 1974-77, acting industl dir 1977-79, dep industl dir 1979-83, industl dir 1984-85, chm Speciality Chemicals Sector Gp 1986-90; author of various NEDO reports incl Industrial Policies and Issues 1977-85, conslt CEGB and successor companies 1986-; chm Govrs Uplands Community Coll Wadhurst 1989-; Liveryman and memb Ct of Assts Worshipful Co of Salters, Freeman City of London (admitted to Livery 1957); *Recreations* walking, music, reading; *Clubs* Oxford & Cambridge (Pall Mall); *Style—* Richard Homan, Esq, CBE; 30 High St, Ticehurst, Wadhurst, E Sussex TN5 7AS (☎ 0580 200651)

HOMAN, Dr Roger Edward; s of Edward Alfred Homan, of Brighton, and Olive Florence, *née* Dent (d 1988); *b* 25 June 1944; *Educ* Varndean GS Brighton, Univ of Sussex (BA), Univ of Lancaster (PhD), LSE (MSc); *m* 4 Sept 1982, Caroline, da of Michael Arthur Baker, of Alfriston, East Sussex; *Career* lectr religious studies Brighton Coll Educn 1971-73 (lectr educn 1973-76), princ lectr educn Brighton Poly 1985- (lectr 1976-); memb: Prayer Book Soc (former nat vice-chm), Victorian Soc, Br Educnl Res Assoc; *Recreations* sweet peas and auriculas, church music, chapel hunting, poetry; *Style—* Dr Roger Homan; Crink View, Barcombe Mills, East Sussex BN8 5BJ (☎ 0273 400 238); Brighton Polytechnic, Falmer, East Sussex (☎ 0273 606 622)

HOME, Anna Margaret; da of James Douglas Home (d 1989), and Janet Mary, *née* Wheeler (d 1974); *b* 13 Jan 1938; *Educ* Convent of Our Lady St Leonards-on-Sea Sussex, St Anne's Coll Oxford (BA); *Career* joined: BBC Radio 1961, BBC TV 1964; res dir and prodr Children's Programmes 1964-70, exec prodr Children's Drama 1970-81; controller of programmes (later dep dir programmes) TVS 1981-86, head of Children's Programmes BBC TV 1986-; FRTS; *Recreations* reading, theatre, gardening; *Style—* Miss Anna Home; BBC Television, Television Centre, Wood Lane, London W12 7RJ (☎ 081 576 1875)

HOME, Sir David George; 13 Bt (NS 1671), of Blackadder, co Berwick; s of Sir John Home, 12 Bt (d 1938), and Hon Gwendolina Hyacinth Roma Mostyn (d 1960), sis of 7 Baron Vaux of Harrowden (d 1935); *b* 21 Jan 1904; *Educ* Harrow, Jesus Coll Cambridge; *m* 1933, Sheila, da of late Mervyn Campbell Stephen; 2 s (John b 1936, d 1988, Patrick b 1941), 2 da (Hermione b 1934, Anne b 1942, d 1986); *Heir* gs, William Dundas Home b 19 Feb 1968; *Career* Maj late Argyll and Sutherland Highlanders, memb Queen's Body Gd for Scotland (Royal Co of Archers); claims dormant Scottish Earldom of Dunbar (cr 1607); *Clubs* Brooks's, New (Edinburgh), Royal and Ancient (St Andrews); *Style—* Sir David Home, Bt; Winterfield, North Berwick, East Lothian EH39 4LY (☎ 0620 2962)

HOME, Dr Philip David; s of Philip Henry Home, and Kathleen Margaret, *née* Young; *b* 11 Jan 1948; *Educ* Birkenhead Sch, Univ of Oxford (BA, MA, DM, DPhil), Guys Hosp (BM BCh); *m* 27 Sept 1971, Elizabeth Mary, da of Sidney Thomas Broad; 1 s (Jonathan Paul b 1979), 1 da (Deborah Mary b 1976); *Career* Wellcome Tst sr res fell in clinical sci 1982-86, reader Univ of Newcastle upon Tyne 1986-, conslt physician Newcastle Health Authy 1986-, ed Diabetic Medicine 1987-; author of over 100 articles on aspects of diabetes med; memb Cncl Euro Assoc for Study of Diabetes (sec educn ctee), memb ctee Med and Scientific Section Br Diabetic Assoc, memb Assoc of Physicians of GB 1989-; FRCP 1989-; *Recreations* work; *Style—* Dr Philip Home; Department of Medicine, Framlington Place, Newcastle upon Tyne NE2 4HH (☎ 091 222 7149, fax 091 222 0723)

HOME OF THE HIRSEL, Baron (Life Peer UK 1974); Alexander Frederick Douglas-Home; KT (1962), PC (1951), DL (Lanarks 1960); s of 13 Earl of Home, KT, TD, JP, DL (d 1951) and Lady Lilian Lambton, da of 4 Earl of Durham; suc as 14 Earl of Home (S 1605), and also to titles Lord Home (S 1473), Lord Dunglass (S 1605, previously his title by courtesy), Baron Douglas (UK 1875); having disclaimed these peerages for life on becoming PM in 1963, he was created a life peer in 1974; *b* 2 July 1903; *Educ* Eton, ChCh Oxford; *m* 1936, Elizabeth Hester (d 1990), da of Very Rev Cyril Alington, DD (sometime Dean of Durham and Lord Home of the Hirsel's headmaster at Eton), by his w Hon Hester Lyttelton, da of 4 Baron Lyttelton; 1 s, 3 da; *Heir* (to all titles except Life Barony), s Hon David Douglas-Home (styled Lord Dunglass 1951-63); *Career* sits as Cons in House of Lords; Maj Lanark Yeo (TA Reserve), Brig Royal Co Archers (Queen's Body Gd for Scotland); MP (C) Lanark 1931-45 and 1950-51, Kinross and W Perth 1963-74; PPS to: chllr Exchequer 1936-37, PM (Neville Chamberlain) 1937-40; jt under sec of state for affrs May-July 1945, min State Scottish Office 1951-55, sec State Cwlth Rels 1955-60 (Lord pres Cncl Jan-Sept 1957 and Oct 1959-July 1960), ldr House of Lords 1957-60, foreign sec 1960-63, PM 1963-64, ldr oppn 1964-65, foreign sec 1970-74; chllr Order of Thistle 1973-, 1 chllr Heriot Watt Univ 1966-77, hon pres Cncl NATO 1974, pres Peace Through NATO; grand master Primrose League 1966, pres MCC 1966-67; Freedom of Edinburgh 1969, memb NFU 1964; *Clubs* Travellers', Carlton, Buck's, I Zingari (govr); *Style—* The Rt Hon Lord Home of the Hirsel, KT, PC, DL; The Hirsel, Coldstream, Berwicks (☎ 2345); Castlemains, Douglas, Lanarks (☎ 241); 28 Drayton Ct, Drayton Gardens, London SW10 9RH (☎ 071 373 4704); c/o House of Lords, London SW1

HOME ROBERTSON, John David; MP (Lab) East Lothian 1983-; s of Lt-Col John Wallace Robertson TD, JP, DL (d 1979), and Helen Margaret (d 1987), eld da of Lt-Col David Milne-Home (assumed additional name of Home by Scottish licence 1933); *b* 5 Dec 1948; *Educ* Ampleforth, West of Scotland Agric Coll; *m* 1977, Catherine Jean, da of Alex Brewster, of Glamis, Angus; 2 s (Alexander b 1979, Patrick b 1981); *Career* farmer; memb: NUPE, TSSA, Berwickshire Dist Cncl 1974-78, Borders Health Bd 1975-78; MP (Lab) Berwick and East Lothian (by-election) Oct 1978-83, memb Select Ctee Scottish Affrs 1979-83, chm Scottish Gp of Lab MPs 1983, Scottish Labour whip 1983-84; oppn spokesman: on Agric 1984-87 and 89-90 in Scotland 1987-89, Select Ctee on Defence 1990-; *Clubs* Prestonpans Labour, East Lothian Labour, Haddington Labour; *Style—* John Home Robertson, Esq, MP; House of Commons, London SW1 (☎ 071 219 4135)

HOMER, Peter Norman; s of Norman Homer, and Majorie Betty, *née* Sale; *b* 7 June 1939; *Educ* Moseley GS, Univ of Manchester (BSc, MSc); *m* 23 Aug 1961, Valerie Anne; 3 s (Mark b 1962, James b 1964, Michael b 1967); *Career* res scientist and corp planner 1961-73; dir: Simpson Lawrence Ltd 1973-74, subsids Grampian Holdings plc 1974-79; asst dir Scottish Devpt Agency 1979-84, chief exec IMD Hldgs Ltd 1984-86, dir James Finlay Bank Ltd 1986-; chm local Cons branch 1980-82; MBIM 1973; *Recreations* sailing, reading, wine, books; *Clubs* Royal Northern & Clyde Yacht (Commodore); *Style—* Peter Homer, Esq; James Finlay Bank Ltd, 10-14 West Nile St, Glasgow (☎ 041 204 1321, telex 777844, fax 041 204 4254)

HOMER, Dr Ronald Frederick; s of George Frederick Alexander Homer (d 1976), and Evelyn Partridge, *née* Chillington (d 1984); *b* 15 April 1926; *Educ* Dudley GS, Univ of Birmingham (BSc, PhD); *m* 1950, Audrey, *née* Adcock; 2 s (Richard b 1954, Peter b 1956); *Career* res chemist ICI 1948-59, gp mangr Nat Res Devpt Corp 1959-81, divnl dir Br Technol Gp 1981-82; conslt and writer on pewter and pewtering, ed Journal of the Pewter Society 1984-; numerous articles and part works on pewter; pres The Pewter Soc 1975-77; Leverhulme Tst Grant for Res on Pewtering 1983-85; Freeman of the City of London 1981, Liveryman Worshipful Co of Pewterers 1982 (archivist 1988-); FSA 1989; *Books* Five Centuries of Base Metal Spoons (1975), Provincial Pewterers (with DW Hall, 1985); *Recreations* gardening, DIY; *Style—* Dr Ronald Homer; Gorse Croft, West Hill Rd, West Hill, Ottery St Mary, Devon EX11 1TU

HON, Prof (Kwok Keung) Bernard; s of Chung Ki Hon, and Yuet Seen, *née* Shaw; *b* 16 Jan 1950; *Educ* Hong Kong Tech Coll, Univ of Birmingham (MSc, PhD); *m* 18 Dec 1976, Yuk Ching Metis, da of late Yat Chow Hui; 2 s (Chen Yue (Daniel) b 1979, Wai Yue (Adrian) b 1982); *Career* lectr: Univ of Bath 1979-81, Univ of Birmingham 1981-87; prof mfrg systems: Univ of Dundee 1987-1990, Univ of Liverpool 1990-; head Dept of Industrial Studies Univ of Liverpool 1990-; FIProdE 1990; *Recreations* badminton, music; *Style—* Prof Bernard Hon; Department of Industrial Studies,

University of Liverpool, PO Box 147, Liverpool L69 3BX (☎ 051 794 4681, fax 051 794 4693, telex 627095 UNILPL G)

HONDERICH, Prof Edgar Dawn Ross (Ted); s of John William Honderich (d 1956), and Rae Laura, *née* Armstrong (d 1952); *b* 30 Jan 1933; *Educ* Univ of Toronto (BA), Univ of London (PhD); *m* 1, 22 Aug 1964 (m dis 1976), Pauline da of Paul Goodwin (d 1976), of Dunlavin; 1 s (John Ruan b 1962), 1 da (Kiaran Aeveen b 1960); m 2, 8 Dec 1989, Jane, da of Maj Robert O'Grady, MC, of Midford Place, Bath; *Career* lectr in philosphy Univ of Sussex 1962-64, ed International Library of Philosophy And Scientific Method 1965-, advsy ed Penguin Philosophy 1965-, ed The Arguments of the Philosophers 1970-; visiting prof: Yale Univ 1970, City Univ of NY 1971; ed The Problems of Philosophy 1983-, Grote prof of philosphy of mind and logic UCL 1988- (lectr 1964-72, reader 1972-83, prof 1983-88); memb Lab Pty; memb: Mind Assoc, Aristotelian Soc; *Books* Punishment: The Supposed Justifications (1969), Essays on Freedom of Action (ed, 1973), Social Ends and Political Means (ed, 1976), Philosophy As It Is (ed with M Burnyeat, 1979), Violence for Equality: Inquiries in Political Philosophy (1980), Philosophy Through its Past (ed, 1984), Morality and Objectivity (ed, 1985), A Theory of Determinism: The Mind, Neuroscience and Life-Hopes (1988), Conservatism (1990); *Recreations* wine, music, cycling; *Clubs* Garrick, Beefsteak; *Style—* Prof Ted Honderich; 4 Keats Grove, London NW3 (☎ 071 435 2687); Dept of Philosophy, University College London, Gower St, London WC1 (☎ 071 380 7115)

HONE, Barry Nathaniel; s of Capt Thomas Nathaniel Hone, OBE (d 1946), of Bosbury House, nr Ledbury, Herefords, and Mary Eveline, *née* Byass (d 1982); *b* 15 Sept 1931; *Educ* Winchester; *m* 30 Sept 1955, Eva Agnarsdotter, da of Agnar August Hall (d 1969), of Alvesta, Sweden; 1 s (Rupert b 1966), 1 da (Joanna b 1963); *Career* rifleman 60 Rifles 1950, 2 Lt KSLI 1950 and 4 (Uganda) KAR 1951-52, 4 Bn KSLI TA 1952-62 (Maj 1958-62); dir Bosbury House Nurseries Ltd 1952-63, farmer and landowner Glentromie Inverness-shire 1964-75; dir: Graphic Systems Int Ltd 1976-77, employment dept The Offrs Assoc 1988- (recruitment conslt 1979-88); pres Kingussie Sheepdog Trials Assoc, sec West Grampian Deer Mgmnt Soc, chm Kingussle Cons and Unionist Assoc; *Recreations* shooting, fishing; *Clubs* Boodles, Army and Navy; *Style—* Barry Hone, Esq; 19 Bywater St, London SW3 4XD (☎ 071 584 3159); Glentromie Lodge, By Kingussie, Inverness-shire; The Officers Association, 48 Pall Mall, London SW1 (☎ 071 930 0125)

HONE, Maj-Gen Sir (Herbert) Ralph; KCMG (1951), KBE (1946, CBE (mil) 1943), MC (1918), TD (1946); s of Herbert Hone (d 1950); *b* 3 May 1896; *Educ* Varndean GS Brighton, Univ of London (LLB); *m* 1, 1918 (m dis 1945), Elizabeth Daisy Matthews; 1 s, 1 da; m 2, 1945, Sybil Mary, JP, da of A Collins (d 1941) and wid of Wing Cdr Geoffrey Simond (d 1942); 1 s; *Career* served WWI, Capt 1916, served WWII ME and S E Asia (despatches twice), Brig 1941, Maj-Gen 1943; called to the Bar Middle Temple 1924, registrar High Ct Zanzibar 1925-27, res magistrate Zanzibar 1927-28, crown counsel Tanganyika 1929-32; attorney-gen: Gibraltar 1933-36 (QC 1934), Uganda 1937-40 (QC 1938); sec gen to Govr Gen of Malaya 1946, dep cmmr gen for colonial affrs SE Asia 1948-49, govr and C-in-C N Borneo 1949-54, ret 1954; head Legal Div Cwlth Rels Office 1954-61; resumed practice at Bar 1961; constitutional advsr: Bahamas Govt, Kenya Conf 1962, Saudi Arabian Govt 1965, Bermuda Govt 1966; memb Chapter-Gen Order St John 1955-; GCStJ 1973; *Clubs* Athenaeun, Royal Cwlth Soc; *Style—* Maj-Gen Sir Ralph Hone, KCMG, KBE, MC, TD; 1 Paper Buildings, Temple, London EC4 (☎ 071 583 7355); 56 Kenilworth Court, Lower Richmond Rd, London SW15 (☎ 081 788 3367)

HONE, Richard Michael; s of Maj-Gen Sir Ralph Hone, KCMG, KBE, MC, TD, QC, and Sybil Mary, *née* Collins; *b* 15 Feb 1947; *Educ* St Paul's, (scholar) University Coll Oxford (MA); *m* 29 March 1980, Sarah, da of Col JWA Nicholl-Carne, of Guildford, Surrey; 2 s (Nathaniel b 1987, Rufus b 1989); *Career* called to the Bar Middle Temple 1970, asst rec Crown Ct 1986; GCStJ, OStJ 1972; *Recreations* reading, travel, wine, photography; *Clubs* Boodles, Pratts; *Style—* Richard Hone, Esq; 1 Shawfield St, Chelsea, London SW3 4BA (☎ 071 352 6999); 1 Paper Buildings, Temple, London EC4Y 7EP (☎ 071 583 7355, fax 071 353 2144)

HONER, Julian Anthony; s of John David Honer, of London, and Shirley, *née* Gerrish; *b* 19 Feb 1961; *Educ* Lewes Priory Sch, Univ of Stirling (BA), Univ of Birmingham, Barber Inst of Fine Arts (M Phil); *Career* researcher and cataloguer Dept of Modern Br Pictures Bonhams Fine Art Auctioneers Knightsbridge London 1986-88, fine art insur underwriter Eagle Star (Star Assurance Soc Ltd) 1988-89, co-fndr and account exec Frizzell Fine Art Insurance 1989-; author number of articles; friend Royal Acad of Arts, memb Br Sporting Arts Tst; *Recreations* travel, photography, music; *Style—* Julian Honer, Esq; Frizzell Fine Art Insurance, Frizzell House, 14-22 Elder St, London E1 6DF (☎ 071 247 6595, fax 071 377 9114, telex 8811077 FRILON G)

HONEY, William Andrew (Bill); *b* 19 Dec 1938; *Educ* Eastbourne GS; *m* 1963, Maureen, *née* McGrane; 2 s, 1 da; *Career* sr ptnr: Honey Barrett & Co (and assoc partnerships), WA Honey & Co, Cornfield Secretarial; dir: Investment Matters Ltd, Money Matters Ltd (and assoc cos), Cornfield Finance and Management Ltd, Eastbourne and District Managing Agency Ltd, Eastbourne and District Enterprise Agency Ltd, Honey Barrett and Co, Ocklynge Estates Ltd, Clipper Hotels Ltd, Hotel L'Horizon Ltd; memb: E Sussex CC 1977-81, Nat Cncl CBI 1982-87; chm E Sussex Family Practitioner Ctee 1988-90; Freeman City of London; ATII, FCA, FCIS, FCIArb, FBIM; *Recreations* family, home life; *Clubs* City Livery; *Style—* Bill Honey, Esq; Appledown, Old Willingdon Rd, Friston, E Dean, Eastbourne, E Sussex (☎ 0323 422022); Honeysuckle Cottage, Hill Bottom, Worth Matravers, Swanage, Dorset; 55 Gildredge Rd, Eastbourne, E Sussex BN21 4SF (☎ 0323 412277)

HONEYBORNE, Dr Christopher Henry Bruce; s of Henry Thomas Honeyborne, of Romsey, Hants, and Lily Margaret, *née* Fox; *b* 5 Dec 1940; *Educ* Cambridgeshire HS for Boys, St Catharine's Coll Cambridge (MA, DipAgSci), Univ of Reading (PhD); *m* 12 Oct 1968, (Anne) Veronica, da of Stephen Sullivan, of Guernsey; 1 s (James b 1970), 2 da (Clare b 1975, Katharine b 1986); *Career* res demonstrator Univ of Reading 1964-68, res scientist ARC Univ of Bristol 1968-70, mangr Cuprinol Ltd 1971-72, sr mangr Lazard Bros & Co Ltd 1972-77 (seconded to Dalgety Ltd 1976-77), Banque Paribas 1977-89 (dep gen mangr London Branch 1977-86, chief exec Quilter Goodison Co Ltd 1986-88); dir: Cartier Ltd 1979-, Modern Vitalcall Ltd 1983-, William Comyns & Sons Ltd 1990-, Comyns of London Ltd 1990-; chm: Lynne Stern Assocs 1987, Finotel plc 1989- (dir 1983), Cameron Richard and Smith (Holdings) Ltd 1989-; vice chm Wokingham & N Somerset Constituency Cons Assoc; memb Inst of Biology; *Recreations* gardening, shooting, tennis, viewing art; *Clubs* City of London, The Arts, United & Cecil; *Style—* Dr Christopher Honeyborne; Ashwick Court, Oakhill, Bath BA3 5BE (☎ 0749 840219, fax 0749 841007); Martins Cottage, Hovingham, York YO6 4LA

HONEYBOURNE, Dr David; s of Gerald George Honeybourne (d 1986), and Jean Beatrice, *née* Mapp; *b* 26 March 1951; *Educ* Redditch HS, Univ of Bristol Med Sch (MB ChB, MD); *m* 30 Aug 1980, Jane Elizabeth, da of Dr David John Rudman, of Whitton, London; 2 da (Laura Ann b 1982, Clare Louise b 1985); *Career* house physician Bristol Gen Hosp 1974, sr house offr Southmead Hosp Bristol 1975-76 (house surgn 1975) then Brook Hosp London 1976-77, registrar in med Kings Coll Hosp London 1977-78, res fell Kings Coll Hosp Med Sch London 1978-80, sr registrar in med Manchester 1980-85, conslt physician specialising in chest diseases Dudley Road Hosp Birmingham 1985-, post grad clinical tutor W Birmingham Health Authy, sr clinical lectr in med Univ of Birmingham; author books and pubns on chest diseases; memb: Br Thoracic Soc, Euro Respiratory Soc, American Thoracic Soc; MRCP 1977; *Recreations* photography; *Style—* Dr David Honeybourne; Priory Hospital, Priory Rd, Edgbaston, Birmingham B5 7UG (☎ 021 440 2323); Department of Thoracic Medicine, Dudley Road Hospital, Birmingham B18 7QH (☎ 021 554 3801, 021 551 1112)

HONEYCOMBE, (Ronald) Gordon; s of Gordon Samuel Honeycombe (d 1957), and Dorothy Louise Reid, *née* Fraser (d 1965); all the Honeycombes in the world (approx 350) are related, being descended from Matthew Honeycombe, of St Cleer, Cornwall, who died in 1728, the earliest Honeycombe is documented as John de Honyacombe of Calstock, Cornwall 1327; *b* 27 Sept 1936; *Educ* Edinburgh Acad, Univ Coll Oxford (MA); *Career* announcer Radio Hong Kong 1956-57, newscaster: ITN 1965-77, TV-am 1984-89; TV presenter: A Family Tree, Brass-Rubbing (1973), Something Special (1978), Family History (1979); TV narrator: Arthur C Clarke's Mysterious World (1980), A Shred of Evidence (1984); appeared in films: The Commuter, Ransom, The Medusa Touch, The Fourth Protocol, Castaway, Bullseye; appeared in plays: Playback 625 (1970), Paradise Lost (1975), Noye's Fludde (1978), and in various TV plays, charity and variety shows; writer, author and playwright; TV plays: The Golden Vision (1968), Time and Again (1974), The Thirteenth Day of Christmas (1985); radio plays: Paradise Lost (1975), Lancelot and Guinevere (1976); Royal Gala performances: God Save the Queen! (1977), A King shall have a Kingdom (1977); musicals: The Princess and the Goblins (1976), Waltz of my Heart (1980); stage plays: The Miracles (1960), The Redemption (1963), Paradise Lost (1975), Lancelot and Guinevere (1980); actor: Tomorrow's Audience 1961-62, RSC 1962-63, That Was The Week That Was 1964, Suspects 1989, Aladdin 1989, Run For Your Wife 1990, Aladdin 1990; *Books* Neither the Sea Nor the Sand (1969), Dragon under the Hill (1972), Adam's Tale (1974), Red Watch (1976), Nagasaki 1945 (1981), The Edge of Heaven (1981), Royal Wedding (1981), The Murders of the Black Museum (1982), The Year of the Princess (1982), Selfridges (1984), Official Celebration of the Royal Wedding (1986); *Recreations* brass-rubbing, bridge, crosswords; *Style—* Gordon Honeycombe, Esq; c/o Jon Roseman Associates, 103 Charing Cross Rd, London WC2H 0DT (☎ 071 439 8245)

HONEYCOMBE, Prof/Sir Robert William Kerr; s of William Honeycombe (d 1962), of Geelong, Victoria, Australia, and Rachel Annie (Rae), *née* Kerr (d 1952); *b* 2 May 1921; *Educ* Geelong Coll Australia, Univ of Melbourne (BSc, MSc, DSc), Univ of Cambridge (PhD); *m* 8 Dec 1947, June, da of Leslie Wilton Collins (d 1969); 2 da (Juliet Rae (Mrs Wilson) b 24 March 1950, Celia Alice b 1 Dec 1953); *Career* res offr Cwlth Scientific and Indust Res Orgn Aust 1942-47, ICI res fell Cavendish Laboratory Cambridge 1948-49, Royal Soc Armourers and Brasiers' res fell Cambridge 1949-51, prof of physical metallurgy Univ of Sheffield 1955-66 (sr lectr 1951-55), Goldsmiths' prof of Metallurgy Univ of Cambridge 1966-84 (now emeritus), pres of Clare Hall Cambridge 1978-80; pres: Inst of Metallurgists 1977-78, Metals Soc 1980-81; treas and vice pres The Royal Soc 1986-, memb Court Worshipful Co of Goldsmiths 1977 (prime warden 1986-87): Hon DApplied Sci Univ of Melbourne 1974, Hon DMet Univ of Sheffield 1983 Hon DMontan Wiss Leoben Univ 1990 hon fell Trinity Hall Cambridge 1974- (fell 1966-73); KT 1990; *Books* The Plastic Deformation of Metals (1968), Steels: Microstructure and Properties (1981); *Recreations* gardening, photography, walking; *Style—* Prof Sir Robert Honeycombe; 46 Main Street, Hardwick, Cambridge CB3 7QS (☎ 0954 210501); Department of Materials Science & Metallurgy, University of Cambridge, Pembroke St, Cambridge CB2 3QZ (☎ 0223 334300, fax 0223 334567, telex 81240 CAMSPL G)

HONIGSBERGER, Dr Leo Max; TD (1975); s of Max Honigsberger, of Chessetts Wood, West Midlands, and Lorna, *née* Mayell; *b* 20 Dec 1928; *Educ* Oundle, Univ of Capetown (MB ChB); *m* 21 Jan 1945, Joy, da of Melt de Kock (d 1968), of Paarl, Cape Province, SA; 2 da (Laura b 1957, Julia b 1959); *Career* conslt electroencephalographer Midland Centre for Neurosurgery 1964-71, conslt clinical neurophysiologist United Birmingham Hosps 1971-; chm Bromsgrove and Redditch DHA 1982-86, memb Bromsgrove DC 1980-82; FRPsych 1979; *Recreations* food and drink, sports cars; *Style—* Dr Leo Honigsberger, TD; Dept of Clinical Neurophysiology, The Central Birmingham District Health Authority (☎ 021 472 1311)

HONNYWILL, Godfrey Coleridge; s of John Honnywill (d 1984), of Tunbridge Wells, and Mary Rosalind, *née* Gair; ggggs of Samuel Taylor Coleridge; *b* 14 March 1934; *Educ* Sherborne; *m* 1962, Helen Newbery, da of Dudley Searle Freeman (d 1978), of Chiddingstone, Kent; 3 s (Charles b 1963, Thomas b 1965, David b 1967), 1 da (Alice (twin) b 1967); *Career* slr 1957; dir Crown Chemical Co (Hldgs) Ltd 1972-86; pres: Kent Law Soc 1974, Tunbridge Wells Law Soc 1980; memb Law Soc; *Recreations* travel, gardening; *Style—* Godfrey Honnywill, Esq; The Timberyard, Lamberhurst, Kent TN3 8DT (☎ 0892 890417); The Priory, Tunbridge Wells, Kent (☎ 0892 510222, fax 0892 510333)

HONORÉ, Prof Antony Maurice (Tony); QC (1987); s of Frédéric Maurice Honoré (d 1977), and Marjorie Erskine, *née* Gilbert; *b* 30 March 1921; *m* 1, 10 July 1948 (m dis), Martine Marie-Odette, da of Col Pierre Genouville (d 1976); 1 s (Frank Martin b 1952), 1 da (Veronique Martine b 1949); m 2, 28 June 1980, Deborah Mary, da of Sir Patrick Duncan; *Career* Union Def Forces 1940-45; cmmnd 1941, Lt Rand Light Infantry 1942, Mil Coll Vortrekkerhoogte 1943-45; asst lectr Univ of Nottingham 1948-49; Univ of Oxford: lectr Queen's Coll 1948-49, fell and praelector in law Queen's Coll 1949-64, Rhodes reader in Roman Dutch law 1958-70, fell New Coll 1964-70, regius prof of civil law 1971-88 (emeritus 1988-), fell All Souls Coll 1971-89 (emeritus 1989-), acting warden All Souls Coll 1987-89; Hon LLD: Univ of Edinburgh 1977, Univ of SA 1984, Univ of Stellenbosch 1988, Univ of Cape Town 1990; FBA 1972, hon bencher Lincoln's Inn 1971; *Books* The South African Law of Trusts (4 edn, 1991), Causation in The Law (2 edn with H L A Hart, 1986), Ulpian (1982), Emperors and Lawyers (1981), Gaius (1962), Tribonian (1978), Sex Law (1978), Making Law Bind (1987); *Style—* Prof Tony Honoré, QC; 94C Banbury Rd, Oxford OX2 6JT (☎ 0865 59684); All Souls College, Oxford OX1 4AL (☎ 0865 279379, fax 0865 279399)

HONYWOOD, Sir Filmer Courtenay William; 11 Bt (E 1660), of Evington, Kent; s of Col Sir William Wynne Honywood, 10 Bt, MC (d 1982), and Maud, yr da of William Hodgson-Wilson, of Hexgrave Park, Southwell, Notts; *b* 20 May 1930; *Educ* Downside, RMA Sandhurst, RAC Cirencester (MRAC Dip); *m* 1956, Elizabeth Margaret Mary Cynthia, 2 da of late Sir Alastair George Lionel Joseph Miller, 6 Bt; 2 s (Rupert Anthony b 1957, Simon Joseph b 1958), 2 da (Mary Caroline b 1961, Judith Mary Frances b 1964); *Heir* s, Rupert Honywood; *Career* 3 Carabiniers (Prince of Wales's Dragoon Gds); asst surveyor MAFF Maidstone 1966-73, surveyor Cockermouth Cumbria 1973-74, regnl surveyor and valuer 1978-88 Central Electricity Generating Bd 1974-88 (sr lands offr SE regn 1974-78) FRICS; *Style—* Sir Filmer Honywood, Bt; Greenway Forstal Farmhouse, Hollingbourne, Maidstone, Kent ME17 1QA (☎ 0622 880418)

HONYWOOD, Rupert Anthony; s and h of Sir Filmer Honywood, 11 Bt; *b* 2 March 1957; *Educ* Downside; *Career* systems' designer and md of Honywood Business

Consultancy Servs; *Style—* Rupert Honywood, Esq; 185 Primrose Lane, Shirley Oaks Village, Croydon, Surrey (☎ 081 763 1066)

HOOD *see also*: Fuller-Acland-Hood

HOOD, 7 Viscount (GB 1796); Sir Alexander Lambert Hood; 7 Bt (GB 1778); also Baron Hood (I 1782 and GB 1795); s of Rear Adm Hon Horace Hood, KCB (never invested due to death at Jutland 1916), MVO, DSO; suc bro, 6 Viscount 1981; Lord Hood is sixth in descent from 1 Viscount, the naval hero who captured Corsica 1793; *b* 11 March 1914; *Educ* RNC Dartmouth, Trinity Coll Cambridge (MA), Harvard Business Sch (MBA); *m* 1957, Diana Maud, CVO (1957, LVO 1952); *b* 1920; asst press sec to George VI 1947-52 (HM The Queen 1952-57), eldest da of Hon George Lyttelton (sometime asst master at Eton, 2 s of 8 Viscount Cobham, and yr bro of 9 Viscount), sister-in-law of two former house masters at Eton (Peter Lawrence and Robert Bourne), and sis of Humphrey Lyttelton, the jazz musician and journalist; 3 s; *Heir* s, Hon Henry Hood; *Career* Lt Cdr RNVR WWII; former chm: Continental and Industl Tst, Tanganyika Concessions Ltd; chm Petrofina (UK) 1982- (dir 1958-); dir: J Henry Schroder Wagg 1957-75, George Wimpey 1957-, Elbar (chm until 1983), Tanks Consolidated Investments (chm 1976-83), Union Minière SA Belgium, Abbott Laboratories Inc; former part time memb Br Waterways Bd; *Clubs* Brooks's; *Style—* The Rt Hon Viscount Hood; 67 Chelsea Square, London SW3 (☎ 071 352 4952); Loders Ct, Bridport, Dorset (☎ 0308 22983)

HOOD, (Hilary) David Richard; s of Maj Hilary Ollyett Dupuis Hood, RA (d 1982), and Mrs Patrick Reid, *née* Sampson; *b* 6 Feb 1955; *Educ* Dragon Sch Oxford, Radley, Millfield, King's Coll London (LLB); *Career* called to the Bar Inner Temple 1980; *Style—* David Hood, Esq; 4 King's Bench Walk, Temple, London EC4Y 7DL (☎ 071 353 0478)

HOOD, Eric Cochran; s of Harold Cochran Jellico Hood, of Scotland, and Catherine Cown Hood; *b* 2 Sept 1946; *Educ* Paisley GS, Paisley Coll of Technol (Bronze Medal, Full Tech City and Guilds Cotton Spinning), Outward Bound Sch Scotland; *m* 24 April 1979, Denise, da of Sidney Chapman, of Beds; 1 s (James William b 1976), 1 da (Carolyn Ann b 1986); *Career* dir Blue Arrow (UK) plc 1973, Flexglen Ltd 1976; previously with Marks and Spencer, Smith and Nephew, Coats Viyella; *Recreations* walking, music, reading, cooking; *Clubs* County Constitutional; *Style—* Eric Hood, Esq; 128 Clarence Rd, St Albans, Herts (☎ 0727 54094); Blue Arrow House, Camp Rd, St Albans, Herts AL1 5UA (☎ 0727 66266, fax (0727) 38064)

HOOD, Hon Lady (Ferelith Rosemary Florence); *née* Kenworthy; da of 10 Baron Strabolgi (d 1953), and his 1 w, Doris, *née* Whitley-Thomson (d 1988); *b* 31 May 1918; *Educ* Queen's Gate Sch London; *m* 30 April 1946, Sir Harold Joseph Hood, 2 Bt, TD; 2 s (John b 1952, Basil b 1955, also 1 s decd), 2 da (Josepha b 1953, Margaret b 1965); *Style—* The Hon Lady Hood; 31 Avenue Rd, St John's Wood, London NW8 (☎ 071 722 9088)

HOOD, Sir Harold Joseph; 2 Bt (UK 1922), of Wimbledon, Co Surrey, TD; s of Sir Joseph Hood, 1 Bt (d 1931); *b* 23 Jan 1916; *Educ* Downside; *m* 1946, Hon Ferelith Kenworthy, *see* Hon Lady Hood; 2 s, 2 da (and 1 s decd); *Heir* s, John Hood; *Career* 2 Lt 58 Middx Bn RE (AA) (TA) 1939, Lt RA 1941; ed The Catholic Who's Who 1952 edn, circulation dir Universe 1953-60, managing ed The Catholic Directory 1959-60, circulation dir Catholic Herald 1961-87; KCSG 1979, GCSG 1986, Kt of Sovereign Mil Order of Malta; *Clubs* Royal Automobile, MCC, Challoner; *Style—* Sir Harold Hood, Bt, TD; 31 Avenue Rd, St John's Wood, London NW8 6BS (☎ 071 722 9088, office: 071 588 3101)

HOOD, Hon Henry Lyttelton Alexander; s and h of 7 Viscount Hood; *b* 19 March 1958; *Style—* The Hon Henry Hood; 67 Chelsea Square, SW3 (☎ 071 352 4952)

HOOD, Hon John Samuel; 2 s of 7 Viscount Hood; *b* 16 Oct 1959; *Educ* Eton, Univ of NSW (BEng); *m* 1982, Melissa Anne, 2 da of Kerry D Bell, of Lane Cove, NSW, Australia; 1 s (Christian Alexander b 1989), 1 da (Gemma Kathryn b 1986); *Career* civil engr; *Clubs* Brooks's; *Style—* The Hon John Hood; 72 Thurleigh Rd, London SW12

HOOD, Prof Neil; s of Andrew Hood (d 1984), of Wishaw, Lanarks, and Elizabeth Taylor, *née* Carruthers; *b* 10 Aug 1943; *Educ* Wishaw HS, Univ of Glasgow (MA, MLitt); *m* 24 Aug 1966, Anna Watson, da of Alexander Clark, of Lesmahagow, Lanarks; 1 s (Cameron b 1970), 1 da (Annette b 1967); *Career* res fell and lectr Scottish Coll of Textiles 1966-68, lectr and sr lectr Paisley Coll of Technol 1968-78, prof of business policy Univ of Strathclyde 1979-, assoc dean and dean Strathclyde Business Sch Univ of Strathclyde 1982-87, dir Scottish Devpt Agency Scotland and Scottish Office 1987-89 (dir employment and special initiatives Scottish Devpt Agency 1989-90); visiting appts: Univ of Texas Dallas 1981, Stockholm Sch of Economics 1982-87, Euro Inst for Advanced Study in Mgmnt Brussels 1986; non-exec dir: Euroscot Meat (Holdings) Ltd 1981-86, Prestwick Holdings plc 1986-87, Lamberton (Holdings) Ltd 1989-, GA (Holdings) Ltd 1990-, Shanks and McEwan Group PLC 1990-, First Charlotte Assets Trust plc 1990-; investmt advsr Castleforth Fund Mangrs Ltd 1984-88, dir Scottish Devpt Fin Ltd 1984-90; advsr and consllt: Scottish Devpt Agency 1977-87, Sec of State for Scotland 1980-87, DTI 1981-83, Indust and Employment Ctee ESRC 1985-87; corp advsr S Scot Electricity Bd (Scottish Power plc) 1989, memb Bd Irvine Devpt Corp 1985-87, dir Lanarks Industrial Field Exec Ltd 1984-86; conslt to: Int Fin Corp Worldbank 1981-83, UN Centre of Transnational Corps 1982-83, ILO 1984-85; FRSE 1987; *Books* Chrysler UK - A Corporation in Transition (with S Young, 1977), The Economics of Multinational Enterprise (with S Young, 1979), Multinationals in Retreat: The Scottish Experience (with S Young, 1982), Multinational Investment Strategies in the British Isles (with S Young, 1983), Industry Policy and the Scottish Economy (co-ed with S Young, 1984), Foreign Multinationals and the British Economy (with S Young and J Hamill, 1988), Strategies in Global Competition (co-ed with J E Vahlne, 1988), The Scottish Financial Sector (with P Draper, 1 Smith and W Stewart, 1988); *Recreations* gardening, walking, reading, golf, writing; *Clubs* RAC, Glasgow; *Style—* Prof Neil Hood; Teviot, 12 Carlisle Rd, Hamilton ML3 7DB (☎ 0698 424870); Strathclyde Business Sch, University of Strathclyde, 193 Cathedral St, Glasgow G4 ORQ (☎ 041 552 4400, fax 041 552 2802, car 0831 503671)

HOOD, Dr Roger Grahame; s of Ronald Hugo Frederick Hood, of Aldridge, W Midlands, and Phyllis Eileen, *née* Murphy; *b* 12 June 1936; *Educ* King Edward's Sch Five Ways Birmingham, LSE (BSc), Downing Coll Cambridge (PhD); *m* 1, 15 June 1963 (m dis 1985), Barbara, da of Donald Waldo Smith (d 1979), of Washington, Illinois; 1 da (Catharine b 1964); m 2, 5 Oct 1985, Nancy Colquitt, da of Maj John Heyward Lynah (d 1984), of Charleston, S Carolina; 2 step da (Clare b 1964, Zoe b 1969); *Career* res offr LSE 1961-63, lectr in social admin Univ of Durham 1963-67, asst dir of res Inst of Criminology Univ of Cambridge 1967-73, fell Clare Hall Cambridge 1969-73, reader in criminology Univ of Oxford 1973, fell All Souls Coll Oxford 1973-; Sellin-Glueck Award for Int Contribs to Criminology 1986; memb: Parole Bd 1973, SSRC Ctee on Social Sci and Law 1975-79, Judicial Studies Bd 1979-85, Dept Ctee to Review the Parole System 1987-88; expert conslt UN Ctee on Crime Prevention and Control 1988, pres Br Soc of Criminology 1986-89; *Books* Sentencing in Magistrates Courts (1962), Borstal Re-Assessed (1965), Key Issues in Criminology (with Richard Sparks, 1970), Sentencing the Motoring Offender (1972), Crime, Criminology and Public Policy - Essays in Honour of Sir Leon Radzinowicz (ed, 1974), A History of English Criminal Law - Vol 5, The Emergence of Penal Policy (with Sir Leon Radzinowicz, 1986), The Death Penalty: A Worldwide Perspective (1989); *Recreations* cooking; *Style—* Dr Roger Hood; 63 Iffley Rd, Oxford OX4 1EF (☎ 0865 246084); All Souls Coll, Oxford OX4 1EF (☎ 0865 279347/274448)

HOOD, Stephen John; s of Leslie Gilbert Hood, of Canberra, Australia, and Margaret, *née* Vinnicombe; *b* 12 Feb 1947; *Educ* Brisbane Boys Coll, Univ of Queensland, Univ of London (LLM); *m* 1 Oct 1971, Maya, da of Leon Togonal (d 1984), of Paris; 4 s (Ludovic b 1973, William b 1974, Roderick b 1978, Frederick b 1980), 1 da (Victoria b 1985); *Career* ptnr Clifford Chance (formerly Coward Chance) 1978- (asst slr 1974-78), sr res ptnr Coward Chance Hong Kong 1981-86; chm: Royal Cwlth Soc in Hong Kong 1983-86, Fin Law Sub Ctee Law Soc Hong Kong 1984-86, Exec Ctee Sir Robert Menzies Meml Tst 1988-; memb Br Bd Euro Assoc for Chinese Law 1988-; cncl memb: Br Aust Soc 1981, Royal Cwlth Soc 1987-; Freeman City of London 1987; *Books* Equity Joint Ventures in The People's Republic of China (sr co-author 1985, second edn 1987), Technology Transfer in The People's Republic of China (1985, second edn 1988); *Clubs* Oriental, MCC, Hong Kong; *Style—* Stephen Hood, Esq; Royex House, Aldermanbury Sq, London EC2 (☎ 071 600 0808)

HOODLESS, Elisabeth Ann Marion Frost; da of Maj Raymond Evelyn Plummer, TD, of Shoreham House, Shoreham, Sevenoaks, Kent, and Maureen Grace, *née* Frost; *b* 11 Feb 1941; *Educ* Redland HS Bristol, Univ of Durham (BA), LSE (Dip); *m* 28 Aug 1965, Donald Bentley Hoodless, s of Ernest William Hoodless, of Weald Ridge, Ticehurst, E Sussex; 2 s (Christopher, Mark); *Career* CSV: asst dir 1963, dep dir 1972, exec dir 1975; cncllr London Borough of Islington 1964-68, JP Inner London 1969; chm: Westminster Juvenile Court 1985, Islington Juvenile Court 1988; memb Inst of Med Social Work 1963, Churchill Fellowship 1966, Sec of State's nominee to Personal Social Services Cncl 1972-79, Cwlth Youth Fellowship to Jamaica 1974, pres Volonteurope 1988, dep chm Speaker's Cmmn on Citizenship 1988-; *Recreations* ballet, gardening and travel; *Style—* Mrs Donald Hoodless; 17 Cross St, London N1 (☎ 071 359 0231); Weald Ridge, Ticehurst, E Sussex (☎ 0580 200256); CSV, 237 Pentonville Rd, London N1 9NJ (☎ 071 278 6601)

HOOK, Prof Andrew; s of Wilfred Thomas Hook (d 1964), and Jessie, *née* Dunnett (d 1984); *b* 21 Dec 1932; *Educ* Wick HS, Daniel Stewart's Coll Edinburgh, Univ of Edinburgh (MA), Princeton Univ New Jersey (PhD); *m* 18 July 1966, Judith Ann (d 1984), da of George Hibberd, of Comberton, Cambridge; 2 s (Caspar b 1968, Nathaniel b 1975), 1 da (Sarah b 1964); *Career* Nat Serv NCO Intelligence Corps 1954-56; lectr american lit Univ of Edinburgh 1961-70, sr lectr english Univ of Aberdeen 1970-79, Bradley prof of english literature Univ of Glasgow 1979-; CNAA: chm Ctee Humanities, memb Ctee Academic Affrs; chm Scottish Univ Cncl on Entrance English Panel memb Scottish Exam Bd; *Books* ed: Scott's Waverley (1972), Charlotte Brontë's Shirley (with Judith Hook, 1974), John Dos Passos Twentieth Century Views (1974); Scotland and America A Study of Cultural Relations 1750-1835 (1975), American Literature in Context 1865-1900 (1983), History of Scottish Literature Vol II 1660-1800 (1987); *Recreations* theatre, opera, reading; *Style—* Prof Andrew Hook; 5 Rosslyn Terrace, Glasgow G12 9NB (☎ 041 334 0113); Department of English Literature, University of Glasgow, Glasgow G12 8QQ (☎ 041 339 8855 ext 4226, fax 041 330 4601, telex 777070 UNIGLA)

HOOK, Brian Laurence; s of Laurence Hook, and Joan Brookes, *née* Read; *b* 31 Dec 1934; *Educ* Christ's Hosp Horsham, Oxford Sch of Architecture (Dip Arch); *m* 26 March 1960, (Thelma) Jill, da of Morton Griffiths Mathias (d 1974), of Deddington, Oxford; 3 da (Caroline, Sarah, Philippa); *Career* Nat Serv 2 Lt RE served Malta and N Africa 1958-60, Lt RE (TA) 1961-64; architect; assoc Peter Bosanquet & Ptnrs Oxford 1966-70, princ Brian Hook & Ptnrs (own practice) Abingdon and Oxford 1970-; co cncllr: Berks 1971-74, Oxfordshire 1973-81 and 1989-; chm: Oxfordshire Environmental Ctee 1979-81, govrs Sch of St Helen and S Katharine Abingdon 1985-90, Wantage Constituency Cons Assoc 1987-; ARIBA 1959; *Recreations* sailing, travel, water colour painting; *Clubs* Frewen (Oxford); *Style—* Brian Hook, Esq; The Forge, Kingston Bagpuize, Abingdon, Oxon OX13 5AG (☎ 0865 820377); St Simeon, Gorron, N Loire, France

HOOK, Hon Mrs (Edith Deirdre); *née* Handcock; da of late 7 Baron Castlemaine; *b* 1936; *m* 1, 1957 (m dis 1974), Keith Moss, BEM; 1 s; m 2, 1975, Terence Hook; *Style—* The Hon Mrs Hook

HOOK, Margaret; da of late Robert Barr, of Shadwell House, Yorks, and Edith Birkby Midgley; *b* 7 May 1918; *Educ* Calder Girls' Sch Seascale Cumberland, Univ of Leeds; *m* 12 July 1947, Sheriff William Thomson Hook, QC, s of late Peter Hook; 1 s (Christian b 1952); *Career* Jr Cdr ATS 1942-46, Staff Coll G3 staff duties Scot Cmd 1943-45, War Office Educn 1945-46; dir: Barr and Wallace Arnold Trust plc, TSB plc Scotland 1986-88, Edinburgh C of C 1980-83, Scottish Ballet 1983-84, Wallace Hotels Ltd 1987-; chm: Sibbald Travel, Arts and Indust Ctee Scot 1973-78, Scot IOD 1982-84; pres ABTA 1977-80; memb: Scot Econ Planning Cncl 1980-83, Nat Econ Devpt Cncl Hotel and Caterers 1978, Panel of Value Added Tax Tbnls for Scot 1980-90; CBIM; Lazo de Dama of the Order of Isabel la Catolica Spain; *Style—* Mrs William Hook; 33 Moray Place, Edinburgh EH3 6BX (☎ 031 225 5401); Kildavannan, Isle of Bute (☎ 0700 2455)

HOOK, Michael John; s of Frederick John Hook, and Eileen Naomi Louise, *née* Cox; *b* 3 July 1934; *Educ* Harrow GS; *m* 23 Aug 1958, Hazel, da of Geoffrey Rowling; 1 s (Philip Douglas b 12 Nov 1959), 1 da (Christine Vivien b 23 Dec 1961); *Career* Nat Serv 1952-54; Spottiswoode Advertising (now DDB/BMP) 1954-62, CPV International 1962-66, Ogilvy & Mather 1966-87 (md Ogilvy & Mather International Media 1981-87), Yershon Media Management 1987, fndr Media Mondiale 1989 (current clients incl: Alfa Laval, Lee Jeans, Barclays Bank, Bovis Abroad, Fred Perry, Nordisk Construction Co, Sanoma Corp, Abu Dhabi International Fair, Gamemakers International); writes for leading trade pubns and has spoken at seminars worldwide on topics related to int advtg, raised £12 million worth of donated space in int media for World Wildlife Fund 1978-87; memb Int Advtg Assoc (former dir UK Chapter), FIPA 1974 (MIPA 1960), chm Soc IPA 1971-72; *Recreations* umpiring hockey, and cricket, morris dancing, gardening, francophile; *Style—* Michael Hook, Esq; Media Mondiale, 17 Berners St, London W1P 3DD (☎ 071 636 7122, fax 323 1123)

HOOK, Rt Rev Dr Ross Sydney; MC (1946); s of Sydney Frank Hook (d 1959), of Cambridge, and Laura Harriet Hook (d 1973); *b* 19 Feb 1917; *Educ* Christ's Hosp, Peterhouse Cambridge (BA, MA); *m* 26 Aug 1948, Ruth Leslie, da of Rev Herman Masterman Biddell (d 1946), of Sandown, IOW; 1 s (Philip b 1950), 1 da (Deborah b 1956); *Career* chaplain RNVR 1943-46, 44 RM Commando 1943, Hldg Commando 1943-44, 2 Commando Bde 1944-46; curate Milton 1941-43, chaplain Ridley Hall Cambridge 1946-48, select preacher Univ of Cambridge 1948; rector: Chorlton-cum-Hardy Manchester 1948-52, St Luke's Chelsea 1952-61; rural dean 1952-61; chaplain: Chelsea Hosp for Women 1953-61, St Luke's Hosp 1955-61; canon residentiary Rochester 1961-65; examining chaplain to: Bishop of Rochester 1961-65, Bishop of Grantham 1965-72, Bishop of Lincoln 1965-72; dean of Stamford 1971-72, prebendary Lincoln Cathedral 1965-72, Bishop of Bradford 1972-80 (memb House of Lords 1975-80), chief of staff Archbishop of Canterbury 1980-84, asst Bishop Canterbury 1980-;

Freeman City of London 1981; Hon DLitt Univ of Bradford 1981; *Style—* The Rt Rev Dr Ross Hook, MC; Mill Rock, Newchurch, Romney Marsh, Kent TN29 0DN (☎ 0303 873 115)

HOOK, Susan Mary (Sue); da of Charles Ronald Bodger (d 1982), of Dorset, and Joan Bodger, *née* Ricketts; *b* 12 June 1944; *Educ* Totton Co GS, Winchester Coll of Art and Design (Intermediate Dip), Univ of Reading (BA); *m* 1977, Michael William, s of William George Hook, of Herts; *Career* ed dir Purnell Publishers Ltd 1982-83, md Colourmaster Ltd 1984-85, publishing dir (childrens books) Century Hutchinson Ltd 1985-86, publishing conslt (freelance) 1987-; *Recreations* gardening, tennis, painting, music (lapsed violinist), cooking, reading, skiing; *Style—* Mrs Sue Hook; Summer Cottage, Lurgashall, Petworth, West Sussex (☎ 042878 743)

HOOKER, David Symonds; s of Cdr John Joseph Symonds Hooker, RN, and Pamela Bowring, *née* Toms; *b* 9 Oct 1942; *Educ* Radley, Magdalene Coll Cambridge (MA), Royal Sch of Mines (MSc); *m* 16 Jan 1965, (Catharine) Sandra, da of Maurice Hilary Thornely Hodgson (d 1986); 2 s (Benjamin b 1969, Joshua b 1979), 1 da (Samantha b 1966); *Career* Pennzoil Co 1965-73, Edward Bates & Sons Ltd 1973-75; md: Candecca Resources plc 1978-82, Plascom Ltd 1982-85, Hurricane International Ltd 1985-87, Aberdeen Petroleum plc 1987-; *Style—* David Hooker, Esq; 29 Smith Terrace, London SW3 4DH; Ardura, Isle of Mull; 40 George St, London W1H 5RE

HOOKER, Dr Michael Ayerst; s of late Albert Ayerst Hooker (d 1989), of Broomsleigh Park, Seal Chart, Kent, and Marjorie Mitchell, *née* Gunson (d 1981); *b* 22 Jan 1923; *Educ* Marlborough, St Edmund Hall Oxford (MA), Univ of the Witwatersrand (PhD); *Career* HG 1940, Univ of Oxford Sr Trg Corps 1941 ACF TARO 1942-48; memb Br Cncl 1945-47, sch master 1947-51, WELLS Orgns in NZ and UK 1951-53, involved with visual aids and PR 1953-59; md: Hooker Craigmyle & Co Ltd 1959-72 (1 UK institutional fund-raising conslts), Michael Hooker and Assoc Ltd 1972-79 (has helped to raise some £70 million for good causes); chief exec govr Truman and Knightley Educnl Tst 1981-87, exec dir the Jerwood Award 1987-1991; sr educnl advsr The Jerwood Award 1991-; chm Fedn of Cons Students 1944, parly candidate (C) Coventry E 1955, various offices Cons Cwlth Cncl 1955-60; memb: Advsy Ctee on Charitable Fund Raising Nat Cncl of Social Serv 1971-73, Working Pty on Methodist Boarding Schs 1971-72; tstee: Ross McWhirter Fndn 1976-, Dicey Tst 1978-, Jerwood Oakham Fndn 1981-, Police Convalescence and Rehabilitation Tst 1985-, All Hallows Tst 1990-; govr Oakham Sch 1971-83, jt chm Routledge Soc 1986-90; FRSA 1990; *Books* The Charitable Status of Independent Schools (with C P Hill, 1969), School Development Programmes (1969), Counter Measures to Guard Against Loss of Charitable Status (1977); *Recreations* food and drink; *Clubs* Carlton, Royal Cwlth Soc; *Style—* Dr Michael Hooker; Carlton Club, 69 St James's St, London SW1

HOOKER, Prof Morna Dorothy; da of Percy Francis Hooker (d 1975), of High Salvington, Sussex, and Lily, *née* Riley (d 1988); *b* 19 May 1931; *Educ* Univ of Bristol (BA, MA), Univ of Manchester (PhD); *m* 30 March 1978, Rev Dr (Walter) David Stacey, s of Walter Stacey (d 1957); *Career* res fell Univ of Durham 1959-61, lectr in New Testament Kings Coll London 1961-70; Univ of Oxford: lectr in theology 1970-76, fell Linacre Coll 1970-76, lectr in theology Keble Coll 1972-76; Lady Margaret's prof of divinity Univ of Cambridge 1976-, fell Robinson Coll Cambridge 1977-; hon fell: Kings Coll 1979, Linacre Coll Oxford 1980; pres Studiorm Novi Testamenti Societas 1988-89 (memb 1959-); *Books* Jesus & The Servant (1959), The Son of Man in Mark (1967), What about The New Testament? (ed, 1979), Pauline Pieces (1979), Studying The New Testament (1979), Paul and Paulinism (ed, 1982), The Message of Mark (1983), Continuity and Discontinuity (1986), From Adam to Christ (1990), A Commentary on the Gospel According to St Mark (1991); *Recreations* molinology, music, walking; *Style—* Prof Morna Hooker; The Divinity Sch, St John's St, Cambridge CB2 1TW (☎ 0223 332 598)

HOOKER, Ronald George; CBE (1985); s of Alfred George Hooker (d 1956), and Gertrude, *née* Lane (d 1950); *b* 6 Aug 1921; *Educ* Mitcham GS, Wimbledon Tech Coll, Univ of London; *m* 26 June 1954, Eve, *née* Pigott; 1 s (Jonathan), 1 da (Jane); *Career* Philips Electrical Ltd 1938-50, special asst to Sir Norman Kipping Fedn of Br Indust 1948-50, Brush Group 1950-60, 600 Group 1960-65, Rolls Royce (1971) 1971-73; chm: Co-ordinated Land and Estates Ltd, Management and Business Services Ltd, Thos Storey (Engrs) Ltd, Warner Howard Group plc; dir: Airship Industrys Ltd, Computing Devices Holdings Ltd, GEI International plc, Hambros Industrial Management Ltd, The Top Management Partnership Ltd; fndr memb Engrg Cncl, memb Court of Cranfield Coll of Technol, former pres Engrg Employers' Fedn; hon fell Mfrg Engr (USA); Freeman City of London, memb Worshipful Co of Coachmakers' and Coach Harness Makers; FEng, hon life fell IPE, CBIM, FRSA; *Recreations* gardening, music, reading, travel; *Clubs* Athenaeum, City of London, Lansdowne; *Style—* Ronald Hooker, Esq, CBE; Loxborough House, Bledlow Ridge, nr High Wycombe, Bucks HP14 4AA; 6 Tufton Court, Tufton St, London; Hambros Bank, 41 Tower Hill, London EC3N 4HA (☎ 071 490 5000)

HOOKINS, Donald Henry; s of Henry Arthur Hookins (d 1922), and Lucy Helen, *née* Messenger (d 1978); *b* 19 March 1923; *Educ* locally in Henley and Reading; *m* 31 Jan 1951, Renée, da of James John Shefford; 2 da (Sara b 1955, Louise b 1959); *Career* Royal Berks Regt 1942-46; chm Gen Decorating Supplies Ltd 1961-88; pres: Henley and Dist Chamber of Trade, YMCA Henley Area 1973-, Henley Boys FC 1972-; chm Br Heart Foundation Henley area 1985-; *Recreations* charity work, amateur painter, fishing; *Clubs* Leander, Phyllis Court; *Style—* Donald Hookins, Esq; Ferry Cottage, Marlow Rd, Henley on Thames, Oxon RG9 3AX (☎ 0491 576328)

HOOKS, Kenneth John; s of Norman Henry Hooks, of Bangor, Co Down, N Ireland, and Florence Mary, *née* Wilson; *b* 1 Jan 1960; *Educ* Bangor GS, Queens Univ Belfast; *m* 9 Aug 1984, Lesley-Ann, da of Randal Young Black; 1 s (Gareth John b 3 Jan 1989); *Career* rugby union wing three quarter RFC and Ireland (6 caps); capt Bangor GS (winners Ulster Schs Cup 1978); memb: Irish Schs Athletics team 1976, Ulster Schs Rugby XV 1976-78, Irish Schs XV 1976-78; clubs: Queens Univ RFC 1978-83 (capt 1982-83), Ards RFC 1985-90 (capt 1989-90), Bangor RFC 1983-85 and 1990-; rep: Irish Univs 1979, Ulster 1979-, Ireland B (debut 1979, 2 caps); debut for Ireland v Scotland 1981; mathematics teacher Royal Sch Armagh 1983-; *Recreations* farming, gardening, hill walking, church youth work; *Style—* Kenneth Hooks, Esq; 32 Castle Gardens, Richhill, Co Armagh, Ireland (☎ 0762 870253)

HOOKWAY, Sir Harry Thurston; s of William Hookway (d 1982); *b* 23 July 1921; *Educ* Trinity Sch of John Whitgift, Univ of London (BSc, PhD); *m* 1956, Barbara, da of Oliver Butler; 1 s, 1 da; *Career* head Info Div Dept of Scientific and Industl Res 1964-65 (joined 1949), asst under sec DES 1969-73, dep chm and chief exec Br Library Bd 1973-84, pres Inst Info Scientists 1973-76; dir Arundel Castle Tstees 1976-, chm UNESCO Int Advsy Ctee on Documentation Libraries and Archives, govr Br Inst of Recorded Sound 1981-83, memb Royal Cmmn on Historical Monuments (Eng) 1981-88, pres Library Assoc 1985, chm LA Publishing Ltd 1986-89; pro chllr Univ of Loughborough 1987-; hon fell: Inst of Info Science, Library Assoc; Hon LLD Sheffield 1976, DLitt Loughborough 1980; kt 1978; *Style—* Sir Harry Hookway; 3 St James Green, Thirsk, North Yorkshire YO7 1AF

HOOLAHAN, Anthony Terence; QC (1973); s of Gerald Hoolahan (d 1961), and Doris Miriam Valentina, *née* Jackson; *b* 26 July 1925; *Educ* Dorset House Sussex, Framlingham Coll Suffolk, Lincoln Coll Oxford (MA); *m* 1949, Dorothy Veronica, da of Osmund Connochie (d 1963); 1 s (Mark b 1956), 1 da (Catriona b 1961); *Career* Sub Lt RNVR 1944, called to the Bar Inner Temple 1949; rec of the Crown Ct 1976-, bencher Inner Temple 1980, Social Security cmmr 1986, barr NI 1980, QC NI 1980; chm: Richmond Soc 1976-80, Tstees Richmond Museum 1983-; govr St Elizabeth's Sch Richmond 1989; *Recreations* swimming; *Clubs* RAC; *Style—* Anthony Hoolahan, Esq, QC; 83-86 Farringdon St, London EC4A 4BC (☎ 071 353 5145)

HOOLE, Sir Arthur Hugh; KB (1985); s of Hugh Francis Hoole (d 1947), of Surrey, and Gladys Emily, *née* Baker (d 1975); *b* 14 Jan 1924; *Educ* Sutton Co Sch, Emmanuel Coll Cambridge (MA, LLM); *m* 1945, Eleanor Mary, da of Frank Washington Hobbs (d 1931), of Sutton; 2 s (Philip b 1955, John b 1957), 2 da (Margaret b 1957, Elizabeth b 1961); *Career* Flying Offr RAFVR; admitted slr 1951; chm Govrs Coll of Law 1983-90, pres Law Soc 1984-85, memb Criminal Injuries Compensation Bd 1985-; govr: St Johns Sch Leatherhead 1987-, Sutton Manor HS 1987-; *Recreations* cricket, reading, music; *Clubs* RAC; *Style—* Sir Arthur Hoole, KB; Yew Tree House, St Nicholas Hill, Leatherhead, Surrey; Kings Shade Walk, High Street, Epsom, Surrey

HOOLE, Christopher John; s of Terence Kevin Hoole, of Malvern House, Sandringham Ave, Chorley, Lancs, and Lilian, *née* Hall; *b* 15 Feb 1948; *Educ* John Rigby GS, Orrel-Univ of Hull (BSc); *m* 21 Aug 1971, Jaqueline Francise Theresa, da of Joseph Smith, of Oban Crescent, Preston, Lancs; 2 s (James Benedict b 9 Nov 1979 Domonic John b 6 Aug 1990), 1 da (Caroline Anne b 26 Aug 1981); *Career* md: Cafe Inns plc 1986-, Northern Taverns plc 1988-, Third Avenue plc 1989, Vantage Inns 1990-; memb Subscription Club; *Recreations* art and design, food and drinks; *Style—* Christopher Hoole, Esq; Holm Lea Farm, Sandy Lane, Brindle, Preston, Lancs PR6 8NA (☎ 0772 313589); George House, 3 St Thomas' Rd, Chorley, Lancs PR7 1HP (☎ 02572 67777, fax 02572 60497, car 0836 379792)

HOOLE-LOWSLEY-WILLIAMS, Hon Mrs (Olivia); *née* Bootle-Wilbraham; da of late 6 Baron Skelmersdale and Ann, da of Percy Quilter (s of 1 Bt); *b* 1938; *m* 1961 (m dis 1975), Anthony John Hoole-Lowsley-Williams; 3 s (Richard Edward b 1962, Hugh Sebastian b 1964, Benjamin Christopher b 1968); *Style—* The Hon Mrs Hoole-Lowsley-Williams; 46 Haldane Road, Fulham, London SW6

HOOLEY, Paul James; JP; s of James Henry Hooley, of Bedford, and Vera Margory, *née* Foot; *b* 25 Aug 1941; *Educ* Ewell HS; *m* 4 Jan 1964, Helen Frances, da of Keith Richardson, of Bedford; 2 s (Simon b 1966, Benjamin b 1975), 1 da (Susan b 1964); *Career* chm and md Newnorth Burt Ltd 1966-89; dir CAEC Howard Group of Cos, local dir Cheltenham & Gloucester Building Society, propietor Paul Hooley & Assocs; Mayor N Beds 1978-79 (dep mayor 1977-78), chm Amenities Ctee 1983-87; pres: Kempston Cons Assoc, Riding for Disabled Bedford, Multiple Sclerosis Soc Bedford, St Raphael Assoc for Disabled Bedford; patron Cancer Relief Bedford, cmmr of taxes; Freeman City of London; FInstD; *Recreations* freemasonry, golf, local history, charitable work; *Clubs* Bedford, City Livery, IOD; *Style—* Paul J Hooley, Esq, JP; 29-33 Elstow Rd, Kempston, Bedford MK42 8HD (☎ 0234 851688, fax 0234 840671)

HOON, Geoffrey William; MEP (Lab) Derbyshire and Ashfield 1984-; s of Ernest Hoon, and June, *née* Collett; *b* 6 Dec 1953; *Educ* Jesus Coll Cambridge (MA); *m* 4 April 1981, Elaine Ann Dumelow; 1 s (Christopher b 15 May 1985), 2 da (Julia b 4 Nov 1987, Nathalie b 21 May 1990); *Career* lectr Univ of Leeds 1976-79, visiting prof of law Univ of Louisville 1979-80 barr 1982-84; *Recreations* sport, cinema, music; *Style—* Geoffrey Hoon, Esq, MEP; c/o 65A Nottingham Road, Derby DE1 3QS (☎ 0332 45636, 0332 295818)

HOOPER, Baroness (Life Peeress UK 1985); Gloria Hooper; da of Frederick Hooper, of Sparrow Grove, Shawford, Hants (d 1977), and Frances, *née* Maloney (d 1984); *b* 25 May 1939; *Educ* Univ of Southampton (BA); *Career* slr 1973, ptnr Taylor & Humbert 1974-85; MEP (C) Liverpool 1979-84; govt whip House of Lords 1985-87; Parly under sec of state: Dept Educn and Science 1987-88, Dept of Energy 1988-89, Dept of Health 1989-; *Style—* The Rt Hon Baroness Hooper; House of Lords, Westminster, London SW1A 0AA

HOOPER, John Charles; *b* 18 Nov 1940; *Educ* Wallington Co GS, Univ of Leeds (BA); *m* 2; 2 c, 2 step c; *Career* Procter & Gamble Ltd 1962-68 (copy supervisor, sr brand mangr), Glendinning Companies Inc 1968-72 (mktg conslt, head of 7 mfrg promotions, retail promotion conslt Westport Court, head of promotions Frankfurt Germany, md Danbury Mint), fin dir Scott International Marketing 1972-73, md Clarke Hooper plc 1974-; chm and fell The Mktg Soc (hon treas 1977-89), fell Inst of Sales Promotion; FRSA, FInstD; *Style—* John Hooper; Wychen, Beacon Hill, Penn, High Wycombe, Buckinghamshire HP10 8NJ (☎ 0494 813330); Clarke Hooper plc, 10 The Grove, Slough, Berks SL1 1QP (☎ 0753 77767, fax 0753 691951)

HOOPER, John Edward; s of William John Henry Hooper, and Noëlle Patricia Thérèse, *née* Lang (d 1979); *b* 17 July 1950; *Educ* St Benedict's Abbey London, St Catharine's Coll Cambridge (BA); *m* 19 July 1980, Hon Lucinda Mary Evans, da of 2 Baron Mountevans (d 1974); *Career* reporter BBC Current Affrs 1971-73, dip corr Independent Radio News 1973-74, corr Cyprus BBC, Guardian and Economist 1974-76; Guardian: corr Spain and Portugal 1976-79, reporter 1979-81, asst news ed 1981-84, energy and trade corr 1984-88; presenter Twenty Four Hours BBC World Service 1984-88, corr Spain and N Africa Guardian and Observer 1988-; winner Allen Lane award best first work of history or lit 1986; memb Soc of Authors; *Books* The Spaniards: a portrait of the new Spain (1986 and 1987); *Recreations* reading, travelling without having to write about it afterwards; *Style—* John Hooper, Esq; A/206-7 Calle Apolonio Morales 6, Madrid 28036, Spain (☎ 010 34 341 250 9748); c/o El Mundo Calle Sanchez Pacheco 61, Madrid 28036, Spain (☎ 010 34 341 586 4847, telex Spain 49353)

HOOPER, (William) John; s of William Guy Hooper (d 1981), of Wolverhampton, and Ruth, *née* Dutton; *b* 20 Oct 1931; *Educ* Wolverhampton GS; *m* 31 Aug 1958, Marguerite Elaine, da of Arthur McLachrie (d 1969), of Wolverhampton; 1 da (Emma Jane Louise b 1967); *Career* CA; dep chm and fin dir Banro Industries plc 1973-88, chm The Abbeygate Group Ltd 1989-; *Recreations* golf, gardening, family, overseas travel; *Style—* John Hooper, Esq; Lullington Court, Lullington, South Derbyshire DE12 8EJ

HOOPER, Sir Leonard James; KCMG (1967, CMG 1962), CBE 1951; s of James Edmund Hooper (d 1938), and Grace Lena Hooper (d 1968); *b* 23 July 1914; *Educ* Alleyn's Sch Dulwich, Worcester Coll Oxford; *m* 1, 1951 (m dis 1978), Ena Mary Osborn; m 2, 1978, Mary Kathleen Horwood, *née* Weeks; *Career* IDC 1953, dir Govt Communications HQ 1965-73 (joined 1938), dep sec Cabinet Office 1973-78, ret; *Style—* Sir Leonard J Hooper, KCMG, CBE; 9 Vittoria Walk, Cheltenham, Glos GL50 1TL (☎ 0242 511007)

HOOS, Hon Mrs (Sarah Marie Adelaide); *née* Cust; only surv da of 5 Baron Brownlow; *b* 3 Jan 1906; *m* 1930, Edward Jan Hoos (d 1962); 1 s (Peter), 1 da (Henrietta); *Style—* The Hon Mrs Hoos; The Wooden House, Manton, Oakham, Rutland, Leics LE15 8SZ

HOOSON, Baron (Life Peer UK 1979); (Hugh) Emlyn Hooson; QC (1960); s of Hugh Hooson, of Denbigh; *b* 26 March 1925; *Educ* Denbigh GS, Univ Coll of Wales; *m* 1950, Shirley Margaret Wynne, da of Sir George Hamer, CBE, of Powys; *Career* sits as Lib peer in House of Lords; called to the Bar Gray's Inn 1949, dep chm Merioneth QS 1960-67 (chm 1967-71), dep chm Flintshire QS 1960-71, rec Merthyr Tydfil 1971 and Swansea 1971, rec Crown Ct 1972-, ldr Wales & Chester circuit 1971-74, bencher Gray's Inn 1968 (vice-tres 1985, tres 1986); non-exec dir of Laura Ashley Hldgs Ltd 1985-; MP (Lib) Montgomeryshire 1962-79, ldr Welsh Lib Pty 1966-79, vice chm Political Ctee Atlantic Assembly 1976-79, vice pres Peace Through NATO 1985-, pres Llangollen Int Eisteddfod 1987-; hon professional fell Univ Coll of Wales 1971-; farmer; *Style*— The Rt Hon the Lord Hooson, QC; Summerfield, Llanidloes, Powys (☎ 055 12 2298); 1 Dr Johnson's Bldgs, Temple, London EC4 (☎ 01 353 9328): Sedan Ho, Stanley Place, Chester (☎ 0244 20480)

HOPCROFT, George William; s of Frederick Hopcroft (d 1952), and Dorothy Gertrude, *née* Bourne (d 1972); *b* 30 Sept 1927; *Educ* Chiswick GS, Univ of London (BCom), BNC Oxford, INSEAD Fontainebleau; *m* 31 March 1951, Audrey Joan, da of James Rodd (d 1963); 3 s (Terry b 1954, David b 1956, Martin b 1960), 1 da (Geraldine b 1958); *Career* sr underwriter Export Credits Guarantee Dept 1946-53 and 1957-65, asst UK trade cmmr Madras 1953-57, FCO 1965; first sec: (commercial) Amman 1965-69, (econ) Bonn 1969-71, (commercial) Kuala Lumpur 1971-75, FCO London 1975-77; cnsllr Br Embassy Bangkok 1977-81, fndr memb Export and Overseas Advsy Panel (EOTAP) 1982, advsr Govt of Belize 1982-83, underwriter Lloyd's 1981-, conslt on Int Affrs 1981-; vice pres Thames Valley Harriers (ex Civil Serv 880 yds champion); hon treas Hook Heath Residents Assoc; *Recreations* leisure and circumnavigation, sports, serendipity; *Clubs* Royal Cwlth Soc, British (Bangkok); *Style*— George Hopcroft, Esq; Frogs, Pond Rd, Hook Heath, Woking, Surrey GU22 0JT (☎ 0483 715121)

HOPE, Alan; JP (1962); George Edward Hope, of Sutton Coldfields, W Midlands, and Vera, *née* Emms; *b* 5 Jan 1933; *Educ* George Dixon GS; *m* 1960, Marilyn Margaret, da of Douglas Dawson; 1 s (Philip b 1961), 1 da (Caroline b 1973); *Career* Nat Serv RAF 1952-54; trained in printing ind chm of several cos in the printing ind and aluminium fabrication; Cons cncllr: Birmingham City Cncl 1962-74, W Midlands Co Cncl 1974- (chm: Trading Standards Ctee 1978-79, Fin Ctee 1979-80; ldr 1980-81, ldr cons oppn gp 1982-); chm Gen Servs Ctee AMA 1979-81, chm NMCU 1980-81, chm LACOTS 1980-81; magistrate 1974, chm Perry Barry Constituency Cons Assoc 1989-; govr: Birmingham Univ, Aston Univ; memb IBA Birmingham Advsy Ctee; *Clubs* Birmingham, Royal Commonwealth; *Style*— Councillor Alan Hope, Esq, JP; 7 Rosemary Drive, Little Aston Park, Streetly, Sutton Coldfield, West Midlands (☎ 021 353 3011); Renault Printing Co Ltd, Factory Centre, College Rd, Birmingham B44 8BS (☎ 356 0331)

HOPE, Bryan; s of Edward Sydney Hope (d 1959); *b* 27 July 1930; *m* 1964, Julia Anne, da of Aubrey Tearle (d 1989), of Eaton Bray, Beds; 2 da; *Career* dep chm Silver Collins & Co Ltd, vice chm Int Wine and Spirit Competition Ltd, dir Corkwise Ltd, conslt various publishing and printing cos; formerly: chm and chief exec Reed Business Publishing Ltd, pres Reed Exhibitions, chm Redwood Publishing, chief exec Racing Post Ltd; vice pres: Periodical Publishers Assoc (chm 1980-83), Barker Variety Club of GB; life memb Worcestershire CCC; *Recreations* fly fishing, cricket, rugby and other sports; *Clubs* RAC, IOD; *Style*— Bryan Hope, Esq; Ty Gobaith, Millbrook, Llangwm, Usk, Gwent NP5 1HP (☎ 02915 758)

HOPE, David D; s of Stanley D Hope (d 1976), and Anne, *née* Webber (d 1981); *b* 24 July 1958; *Educ* Christ's Hosp, St Edmund Hall Oxford; *m* Janet, da of O B E Brown, of Bolival, Missouri, USA; *Career* CA; qualified at Price Waterhouse; currently fin dir Ogilvy & Mather Direct (dir various gp cos); ACA 1984; *Clubs* Leander, Henley Royal Regatta, Petersfield Golf, IOD; *Style*— David Hope, Esq; 1 Meadow Cottages, West End Lane, Esher, Surrey KT10 8LE; Ogilvy & Mather Direct, Knightway House, 20 Soho Square, London W1V 6AD

HOPE, The Rt Hon Lord (James Arthur) David Hope; PC (1989); s of Arthur Henry Cecil Hope OBE, TD, WS (d 1986), of Edinburgh, and Muriel Ann Neilson, *née* Collie; *b* 27 June 1938; *Educ* Edinburgh Acad, Rugby, St John's Coll Cambridge (BA, MA), Univ of Edinburgh (LLB); *m* 11 Apr 1966, (Katharine) Mary, da of William Mark Kerr, WS (d 1985), of Edinburgh; 2 s (William b 1969, James (twin) b 1969), 1 da (Lucy b 1971); *Career* cmmnd Seaforth Highlanders 1957, Lt 1959; admitted Faculty of Advocates 1965, standing jr counsel in Scotland to Bd of Inland Revenue 1974-78, QC (Scotland 1978), advocate deputy 1978-82, chm Med Appeal Tbnls 1985-86, legal chm Pensions Appeal Tbnl 1985-86; memb Scottish Ctee on Law of Arbitration 1986-, elected dean of Faculty of Advocates 1986, senator of the Coll of Justice, a Lord of Session with the title of Lord Hope, Lord Justice General and Lord President of the Court of Session in Scotland 1989-; hon memb Canadian Bar Assoc 1987; *Books* Gloag and Henderson's Introduction to the Law of Scotland (jt ed 7 edn 1968, asst ed 8 edn 1980 and 9 edn 1987), Armour on Valuation for Rating (jt ed: 4 edn 1971, 5 edn 1985); *Clubs* New (Edinburgh); *Style*— The Rt Hon Lord Hope; Parliament House, Edinburgh EH1 1RQ (☎ 031 225 2595, fax 031 225 3642)

HOPE, Hon Mrs (Diana Lyall); *née* Mackie; da of Baron Mackie of Benshie (Life Peer); *b* 1946; *m* 1968, John Carlyle Hope; 4 da; *Style*— The Hon Mrs Hope; 3 St Bernard Cres, Edinburgh

HOPE, Emma Mary Constance; da of Capt John David Hope, of Poundhill Cottage, Bletchingly, Surrey, and Margaret Daphne, *née* Boutwood; *b* 11 July 1962; *Educ* Reigate Co Sch for Girls, Sevenoaks Sch, Cordwainers Coll (SIAD Dip); *Career* fndr own business 1984, opened own shop 1987; designer for: Laura Ashley, Betty Jackson, Jean Muir, Nicole Farhi; 5 Design Cncl Awards for Footwear 1987-88, Martini Style Award 1988, Harpers and Queens Awards for Excellence 1988; articles for Design magazine: Salvadore Ferragamo A review of his exhibition at the V & A 1988, Shoe Design: Tiptoeing into Industry - Review of College Shows 1988; memb Chartered Soc of Designers 1984-; *Recreations* exploring, riding; *Style*— Miss Emma Hope; Emma Hope's Shoes, 33 Amwell St, London EC1R 1UR (☎ 071 833 2367, fax 071 833 1796)

HOPE, Sir John Carl Alexander; 18 Bt (NS 1628), of Craighall, Co Fife; s of Gp Capt Sir Archibald Philip Hope, OBE, DFC, AE (d 1987), and Ruth (d 1986), da of Carl R Davis; *b* 10 June 1939; *Educ* Eton; *m* 1968, Merle Pringle, da of Robert Douglas, of Southside, Holbrook, Ipswich; 1 s, 1 da (Natasha Anne b 1971); *Heir* s, Alexander Archibald Douglas b 16 March 1969; *Style*— Sir John Hope, Bt; 9 Westleigh Ave, London SW15 6RF (☎ 081 785 7997)

HOPE, Hon Julian John Somerset; er s and h of 1 Baron Glendevon, PC; *b* 6 March 1950; *Educ* Eton, Christ Church Oxford; *Career* operatic prodr; resident prodr Welsh National Opera 1973-75; assoc prodr Glyndebourne Festival 1974-81; prodns incl: San Francisco Opera, Wexford and Edinburgh Festivals; *Style*— The Hon Julian Hope; 17 Wetherby Gdns, London SW5

HOPE, Sir (Charles) Peter; KCMG (1972, CMG 1956), TD (1945); s of George Leonard Nelson Hope (d 1973); *b* 29 May 1912; *Educ* Oratory Sch Reading, Univ of London, Univ of Cambridge (BSc, DSc); *m* 1936, Hazel Mary, da of George Turner (d 1920); 3 s; *Career* WWII RA (TA), Maj; entered WO 1938, transferred FO 1946, first sec Br Embassy Paris, asst head UN Dept FO 1950, cnsllr Bonn 1953-56, head news dept FO 1956-59, min Madrid 1959-62, consul gen Houston USA 1963-64, alternate del to UN 1965-68, ambass Mexico 1968-72, ret; memb Acad Int Law 1970, pres Br Assoc SMOM 1983-89, bailiff Grand Cross SMOM; Grand Cross of the Aztec Eagle, Grand Offr Merito Melitense, KStJ 1985; *Recreations* shooting, fishing; *Clubs* White's, Army and Navy; *Style*— Sir Peter Hope, KCMG, TD; North End House, Heyshott, Midhurst, Sussex (☎ 073 081 3877)

HOPE, (Edward Rowland) Peter; s of Edward Leach Hope (d 1929), of Bolton, and May, *née* Aspinall (d 1968); *b* 12 May 1928; *Educ* Bolton Co GS, Univ of Edinburgh (MA), Univ of Manchester (LLB); *m* 3 April 1959, Adeline Diana, da of Thomas Howarth Clarke; 3 da (Sarah b 7 Jan 1962, Janet b 7 Jan 1962, Victoria b 15 Oct 1963); *Career* served RA 1950-52, cmmnd 2 Lt 1951, 2 Lt TA 1953; slr of the Supreme Ct 1956, ptnr Porter Hope and Knipe, ret 1988, conslt 1988; pt/t chm Industl Tbnl 1975, registrar Dep Co Ct 1985; chm Bolton and Dist Civic Tst, memb and former pres Bolton Rotary Club, sec Mrs Lums Charity, tstee Queen St Mission; memb: The Law Soc, Bolton Inc Law Soc; *Recreations* golf, fell walking, sailing; *Style*— Peter Hope, Esq; Bodnant, 18 Regent Rd, Bolton, Lancashire BL6 4DJ (☎ 0204 40693); Rose Lea, Outgate, Ambleside, Cumbria (☎ 09666 537); 22 Bowkers Row, Bolton, Lancashire; 58 Market St, Westhoughton, Bolton, Lancashire (☎ 0204 386001, fax 0204 364168, telex 635109 CHAMCOMG)

HOPE, Sir Robert Holms-Kerr; 3 Bt (UK 1932), of Kinnettles, Co Angus; s of Sir Harry Hope, 1 Bt (d 1959); suc bro, Sir James Hope, 2 Bt, MM 1979; *b* 12 April 1900; *m* 1928, Margaret Eleanor, da of Very Rev Marshall Lang, DD, of The Manse, Whittingehame, East Lothian; *Heir* none; *Style*— Sir Robert Hope, Bt; Old Bridge House, Broxmouth, Dunbar, East Lothian

HOPE, (David) Terence; s of George Charles Oswald Hope (d 1988), and Lucy, *née* Bollom (d 1970); *b* 2 April 1946; *Educ* Rutherford GS Newcastle upon Tyne, Univ of Liverpool (MB ChB, ChM); *m* 28 Oct 1975, Vanessa Mary, da of Edwin Richardson, of W Sussex; 1 s ((Charles) Benjamin b 1976), 2 da (Lucy Alexandra b 1979, Victoria Mary b 1983); *Career* served in RNR; conslt neurosurgeon: Aberdeen 1982, Univ Hosp of Nottingham 1986; author of chapters in books on vascular neurosurgery; examiner RCS; memb Soc of British Neurological Surgeons, FRCS 1975; *Books* Chapters on Vascular Neurosurgery; *Recreations* fishing, shooting, gardening; *Style*— David Hope, Esq; The Nunnery, Hemington, Derby DE7 2RB (☎ 0332 811724); Dept of Neurosurgery, University Hospital, Queen's Medical Centre, Nottingham NG7 2UH (☎ 0602 709102)

HOPE, William Arthur; s of Peter Dorian Hope, and Elsie Mercy Thompson; *b* 6 Dec 1945; *Educ* Walpole GS; *m* 21 Sept 1968, Brenda June, da of Wilfred Leslie Charles Bond; 1 s (David b 1976), 1 da (Natalie b 1973); *Career* CA 1970; chm: Trilion plc 1983-87 (dir all subsidiary cos 1983-87), Sound Image Gp 1989-; dir: CSI Ltd 1989-, World Wide Soccer 1989-; FICA; *Recreations* sailing, tennis, soccer; *Clubs* The Groucho; *Style*— William Hope, Esq; Bois Cottage, Bridle Lane, Loudwater, Rickmansworth, Herts WD3 4JA

HOPE-DUNBAR, Sir David; 8 Bt (NS 1664), of Baldoon; o s of Maj Sir Basil Douglas Hope-Dunbar, 7 Bt (d 1961), and Edith Maud Maclaren, *née* Cross; *b* 13 July 1941; *Educ* Eton, RAC Cirencester; *m* 1971, Kathleen Ruth, yr da of late J Timothy Kenrick, of Birmingham; 1 s, 2 da; *Heir* s, Charles Hope-Dunbar b 5 March 1975; *Career* chartered surveyor; ARICS; *Recreations* fishing, tennis, shooting; *Style*— Sir David Hope-Dunbar, Bt; Banks House, Kirkcudbright (☎ 0557 30424)

HOPE-FALKNER, Patrick Miles; s of Robert E Hope-Falkner, and Diana, *née* Hazlerigg (d 1977); *b* 1 Dec 1949; *Educ* Wellington; *m* 17 June 1972, Wendy Margaret, da of Jack Douglas Mallinson (d 1966); 2 s (Timothy Douglas b 1980, James Edward b 1982); *Career* articles 1968-73, admitted slr 1973, Freshfields 1973-84, Lazard Brothers & Co Ltd 1985-90; dir: Lazard Investors Ltd 1985-90, Lazard Brothers & Co (Jersey) Ltd 1985-89, Crossman Block 1991-; memb Law Soc; *Clubs* Brooks; *Style*— Patrick Hope-Falkner, Esq; Crossman Block, Aldwych House, Aldwych, London WC2B 4HN (☎ 071 836 2000)

HOPE-MASON, David Gordon; s of Gordon Nisbett Hope-Mason (d 1987), and Gunnel Anna, *née* Schele; *b* 11 June 1940; *Educ* Haileybury, ISC; *m* 1, 15 June 1962 (m dis 1981), Maralyn Florence, da of Royce Gordon Martland, of St Brelades, Jersey, CI; 1 s (Justin b 1969), 1 da (Amanda b 1966); m 2, 9 May 1981; *Career* exec chm Lockwood Press Ltd, jt md Market Intelligence Ltd; govr Marlborough House Sch Hawkhurst Kent 1978-88; Liveryman Worshipful Co of Fruiterers 1973 (Master 1989, chm Awards Cncl); FIFP 1978; *Recreations* music, golf, skiing, computing; *Clubs* RAC, Royal Wimbledon Golf; *Style*— David Hope-Mason, Esq; Bounty House, Ropley, Hants SO24 0BY (☎ 0962 773601); Lockwood Press Ltd, Market Towers, London SW8 5NN (☎ 071 622 6677, fax 071 720 2047, telex 915149)

HOPE-MORLEY, Hon Ian Hampden; s and h of 3 Baron Hollenden, *qv*; *b* 23 Oct 1946; *Educ* Eton; *m* 1, 1972 (m dis), Béatrice Saulnier, da of Baron Pierre d'Anchald, of Paris; 1 s (Edward b 9 April 1981), 1 da (Juliette b 1974); m 2, 10 Oct 1988, Caroline N, da of Kim Ash, of Johannesburg, S Africa; *Style*— The Hon Ian Hope-Morley; Solinger, Great Hampden, Great Missenden, Bucks

HOPE-MORLEY, Hon Robin Gordon; s of 3 Baron Hollenden; *b* 9 June 1949; *Educ* Brickwall, Northiam; *Career* owner and dir London Phone Co Ltd; *Recreations* tennis, snooker; *Clubs* Brooks's, MCC; *Style*— The Hon Robin Hope-Morley; Flat 2, 159 Ebury St, London SW1

HOPE-STONE, Dr Harold Francis; s of Sidney Hope-Stone (d 1933), of Liverpool, and Doris, *née* Cohen (d 1943); *b* 20 Aug 1926; *Educ* The Liverpool Inst GS for Boys, Strathcona Acad Montreal, The London Hosp Medical Coll (MB BS, LRCP, MRCS); *m* 20 Aug 1954, Shelagh, da of Harold William Gallimore; 2 s (Rodney Alan b 5 July 1957, Hugh William b 10 Dec 1960), 1 da (Laura Doris b 16 Feb 1963); *Career* Capt RAMC RMO 13/18 Royal Hussars and King's African Rifles 1952-54; house surgn Poplar Hosp 1951; The London Hosp: house physician 1952, registrar Whitechapel Clinic 1955, registrar Radio Therapy Dept 1956-63, sr registrar Radio Therapy Dept 1963, conslt radiotherapist and oncologist 1963-, conslt in admin charge Dept of Radiotherapy and Oncology 1975-; hon conslt radiotherapist and oncologist: Whips Cross Hosp 1965-, Harold Wood Hosp Romford 1968-; lectr in radiotherapy and oncology Univ of London 1968-, advsr in radiation protection Queen Mary Coll London 1973-; chm: Medical Advsy Ctee The London Ind Hosp 1985-89, Regnl Advsy Ctee on Radiotherapy and Oncology NE Thames RHA 1970-79, Working Party Radiotherapy Servs NE Thames Region 1977-79; memb London Univ Bd Studies in Medicine 1970-, examiner RCR 1978-81, vice pres Section of Radiology RSM 1979-82 and 1986-88 (hon sec 1985-86), examiner for MD in radiotherapy Colombo Sri Lanka 1986-; The London Hosp: memb Adademic Bd 1971-74 and 1990-, chm Ctee Sch of Radiology and Radiotherapy 1976-80, chm Medical Records Sub Ctee Medical Cncl 1972-77, chm Div of Surgery 1980-84, chm Private Practice Sub Ctee of Medical Cncl 1977-85, Medical Cncl rep Final Medical Ctee 1978-80, memb Exec Ctee Scanner Appeal 1984-85, chm Medical Cncl 1988- (vice chm 1985-89); DMRT 1957, FRCR 1959; memb: BIR, Section of Radiology RSM, Section of Oncology RSM, Assoc Br Head and Neck Oncologists, Euro Soc of Therapeutic Radiology and Oncology, Br Oncological Soc; *Books* Tumours of the Testicle (jtly, 1970), Malignant Diseases in Children (contrib, 1975), Bladder Cancer (contrib, 1981), Urology I - Bladder Cancer (contrib, 1984), Radiotherapy in Clinical Practice (ed, 1986), Urological and Genital Cancer (co-ed, 1989); *Recreations* gardening, tennis, skiing, sailing, opera, ballet, theatre, travelling;

Style— Dr Harold E F Hope-Stone; 86 Harley St, London W1

HOPETOUN, Earl of; Andrew Victor Arthur Charles Hope; eldest s and h of 4 Marquess of Linlithgow, *qv*; *b* 22 May 1969; *Educ* Eton, Exeter Coll Oxford; *Career* Page of Honour to HM Queen Elizabeth The Queen Mother 1985-87; styled Viscount Aithrie 1969-87; *Style*— Earl of Hopetoun; c/o Hopetoun House, South Queensferry, West Lothian EH30 9SL

HOPKIN, Sir (William Aylsham) Bryan; CBE (1961); s of William Hopkin; *b* 7 Dec 1914; *Educ* Barry Co Sch, St John's Coll Cambridge, Univ of Manchester; *m* 1938, Renée Ricour; 2 s; *Career* joined Miny of Health 1938; dir Nat Inst of Econ and Social Res 1952-57, sec Cncl on Prices Productivity and Incomes 1957-58, dep dir Econ Dept Treasy 1958-65, Mauritius 1965, ODM 1966, dir-gen econ planning 1967-69, dir-gen Dept of Econ Affrs 1969; Treasy: dep chief econ advsr 1970-72, chief econ advsr and head Govt Econ Serv 1974-77; prof fell of econs Univ Coll Cardiff 1972-82; memb Cwlth Devpt Corp 1972-74, chm MSC Wales 1978-79; hon fell St John's Coll Cambridge 1982, hon prof Univ Coll Swansea 1988; kt 1971; *Style*— Sir Bryan Hopkin, CBE; Aberthin House, Aberthin, Cowbridge, S Glamorgan (☎ 0446 772303)

HOPKIN, Nicholas Buxton; s of Dr Geoffry Buxton Hopkin, of Littleton, Winchester, and Harriet, *née* Moxon; *b* 31 March 1944; *Educ* George Watson's Coll Edinburgh (MB ChB), Univ of Edinburgh (DLO); *m* 30 Sept 1966, Jennifer Margaret Bruce, da of Lt John MacPherson Ainslie, RN (ka 1944); 1 s (Tobias b 1976), 3 da (Lucy b 1967, Rosalind b 1970, Penelope b 1972); *Career* RN 1965-82, ret in rank of Surgn Cdr; conslt in otorhinolaryngology; formerly hon registrar Head and Neck Unit Royal Marsden Hosp 1979-80, currently conslt ENT Surgn W Dorset Health Authy; FRCS; *Recreations* travel, board-sailing, gardening; *Style*— Nicholas Hopkin, Esq; The Old Vicarage, Sydling St Nicholas, Dorchester, Dorset DT2 9PB; West Dorset Hospital, Dorchester (☎ 0305 251150 ext 4205)

HOPKIN, Raymond John; s of Hywel Raymond Hopkin (d 1970), of Farnborough, Hants, and Violette Madge Lorraine, *née* Lethaby; *b* 13 July 1944; *Educ* Farnborough GS, Imperial Coll London (BSc, ARCS); *m* 24 Nov 1967, Jeanette Graham, da of Robert William Clark (d 1990), of Sanquhar, Dumfriesshire; *Career* Equity & Law Life Assurance Society plc 1966-, dep gen mangr Equity & Law Assocs 1988-; chm Insur Servs Devpt Ctee BT 1988-89; memb Inst Mgmnt Servs 1975; *Recreations* bridge, golf, all music, Paradores, working; *Clubs* Phyllis Court (Henley-on-Thames); *Style*— Raymond Hopkin, Esq; Crawfordjohn, Upper Warren Ave, Caversham Heights, Reading RG4 7EB (☎ 0734 461 403); Equity & Law House, Amersham Rd, High Wycombe, Bucks HP13 5AL (☎ 0494 463 463, fax 0494 461 989, car 0860 613 628, telex 83385)

HOPKINS; *see*: Scott-Hopkins

HOPKINS, (Philip) Anthony; CBE (1987); s of Richard Arthur Hopkins (d 1981), and Muriel Annie Yeates; *b* 31 Dec 1937; *Educ* Cowbridge GS, RADA; *m* 1, 1968 (m dis 1972), Petronella; 1 da (Abigail b 1968); m 2, 1973, Jennifer Ann, da of Ronald Arthur Lynton; *Career* actor; first joined Nat Theatre 1965, Broadway debut Equus 1974; lived and worked (American films and TV) in USA 1975-84, returned to England 1984; films incl: The Lion in Winter 1967, The Looking Glass War 1968, Hamlet 1969, When Eight Bells Toll 1969, A Doll's House 1972, The Girl from Petrovka 1973, Juggernaut 1974, A Bridge Too Far 1976, Audrey Rose 1976, International Velvet 1977, Magic 1978, The Elephant Man 1979, The Bounty (Captain Bligh) 1983, The Good Father 1985, 84 Charing Cross Road 1984, The Dawning 1987, The Desperate Hours 1989, The Silence of the Lambs 1990; TV credits incl: A Heritage and Its History (ATV 1968), A Company of Five (ATV 1968), The Three Sisters (BBC TV 1969), The Peasants Revolt (ITV 1969), Dickens (BBC 1970), Danton (BBC 1970), The Poet Game (BBC 1970), Decision to Burn (Yorkshire 1970), War and Peace (BBC 1971, 1972), Cuculus Canorus (BBC 1972), Lloyd George (BBC 1972), QB VII (ABC 1973), Find Me (BBC 1973), A Childhood Friend (BBC 1974), Possessions (Granada 1974), All Creatures Great and Small (NBC TV 1974), The Arcata Promise (Yorkshire 1974), Dark Victory (NBC 1975), The Lindbergh Kidnapping Case (NBC 1975, Emmy award), Victory at Entebbe (ABC 1976), Kean (BBC 1978), The Voyage of the Mayflower (CBS 1979), The Bunker (CBS 1980, Emmy award), Peter and Paul (CBS 1980), Othello (BBC 1981), Little Eyolf (BBC 1981), The Hunchback of Notre Dame (CBS 1981), A Married Man (LWT Channel 4 1982), Strangers and Brothers (BBC 1983), The Arch of Triumph (CBS 1984), Mussolini and I (RAI Italy 1984), Hollywood Wives (ABC 1984), Guilty Conscience (CBS 1984), Across the Lake (BBC 1988), Heartland (BBC 1988), The Tenth Man (CBS 1988), Great Expectations (Magwitch, Disney Primetime TV USA 1988), To Be The Best (USA mini series); stage credits incl: A Flea in Her Ear, The Three Sisters, Dance of Death (Nat Theatre 1967), The Architect and The Emperor of Assyria, A Woman Killed with Kindness, Coriolanus (Nat Theatre 1971), The Taming of the Shrew (Chichester Festival Theatre 1972), Macbeth (Nat Theatre 1972), Equus (Plymouth Theatre NY 1974 and 1975, Huntington Hartford Theatre LA 1977), The Tempest (The Mark Taper Forum Theatre LA 1979), Old Times (Roundabout Theatre NY 1983), The Lonely Road (Old Vic Theatre London 1985), Pravda (Nat Theatre 1985), King Lear (1986), Antony and Cleopatra (1987), M Butterfly (Shaftesbury Theatre London 1989); *Recreations* piano; *Style*— Anthony Hopkins, Esq, CBE

HOPKINS, Dr Anthony Philip; s of Gerald Hopkins (d 1985), of London, and Barbara Isobel, *née* Summers (d 1988); *b* 15 Oct 1937; *Educ* Sherborne, Guy's Hosp Med Sch (MB), Univ of London, (MD); *m* 14 Aug 1965, Elizabeth Ann, da of Edward Wood; 3 s (Felix b 1968, Nicholas b 1971, Edward b 1973); *Career* physician i/c Dept of Neurological Sciences St Bartholomews Hosp 1976-88 (conslt neurologist 1972-76 and 1988-), dir Res Unit RCP 1988-; FRCP 1976; *Books* Epilepsy (1987), Measuring the quality of medical care (1990); *Recreations* reading, walking, theatre; *Clubs* Garrick; *Style*— Dr Anthony Hopkins; 149 Harley St, London W1N 2DE (☎ 071 935 4444)

HOPKINS, Antony; CBE (1976); *b* 21 March 1921; *Educ* Berkhamsted Sch, RCM; *m* Feb 1947, Alison; *Career* freelance composer of incidental music incl: Oedipus Rex (Old Vic 1945), Antony and Cleopatra (1945, 1953), Moby Dick (BBC 1947), The Oresteia (BBC 1956), twelve programmes on insects (BBC); films incl: Pickwick Papers, Decameron Nights, Billy Budd; operas incl: Lady Rohesia (1948), Three's Company (1953), Dr Musikus (1971); other works incl John and the Magic Music Man (1975, which won Grand Prix at Besançon Film Festival 1976); conductor of nearly all maj orchestras UK, also Hong Kong, Adelaide, Belgrade, Tokyo; pres numerous music clubs; medal of hon City of Tokyo 1973; doctorate Univ of Stirling, fell Robinson Coll Cambridge; Hon RAM, FRCM; *Books* Talking About Symphonies (1961), Talking About Concertos (1964), Music All Around Me (1967), Lucy and Peterkin (1968), Music Face to Face (with André Previn, 1971), Talking About Sonatas (1971), Downbeat Music Guide (1977), Understanding Music (1979), The Nine Symphonies of Beethoven (1981), Songs for Swinging Golfers (1981), Sounds of Music (1982), Beating Time (1982), Pathway to Music (1983), Musicamusings (1983), The Concertgoer's Companion (1984), The Concertgoer's Companion Vol 2 (1986), Exploring Music (1990); *Recreations* golf, motor sport; *Style*— Antony Hopkins, Esq, CBE; Woodyard, Ashridge, Berkhamsted, Herts (☎ 0442 842257)

HOPKINS, Clyde David Frederick; s of (Frederick) Paul Hopkins (d 1978), and Ivy May, *née* Hill; *b* 24 Sept 1946; *Educ* Barrow-in-Furness GS, Univ of Reading (BA); *m* 1969, Marilyn, da of Flt Lt James Ronald Hallam, of Wetherby, Yorks; *Career* painter; various occupations 1969-73 (incl printmaking demonstrator, gardener, visiting lectr and chief examiner; visiting pt/t and sessional lectr 1973-82 (incl Hull Coll of Art, Manchester Poly, Univ of Reading, Canterbury Coll of Art, Slade Sch, Chelsea Sch of Art, Cyprus Coll of Art), head of fine art Winchester Sch of Art 1987-90 (head of painting Chelsea Coll of Art 1990-); numerous solo and gp exhibitions in Great Britain and N America; Gtr London Arts Assoc award 1979, Arts Cncl of GB purchase award 1980, Mark Rothko Scholarship (USA) 1980-81; lectr on Joan Miro Whitechapel Gallery 1989; memb: Painting Faculty Br Sch at Rome 1985, The Edwin Austen Abbey Scholarship Cncl 1987-; *Recreations* music, extensive drinking, eating, travelling; *Style*— Clyde Hopkins, Esq; Francis Graham-Dixon Gallery, 17-18 Great Sutton St, London EC1V ODN (☎ 071 250 1962, fax 071 490 1069); Chelsea College of Art, Manresa Rd, London SW3 6LS (☎ 071 351 3844, fax 071 352 8721)

HOPKINS, Prof Colin Russell; s of Bleddyn Hopkins (d 1939), and Vivienne, *née* Jenkins; *b* 4 June 1939; *Educ* Pontypridd Boys GS, Univ of Wales (BSc, PhD); *m* Aug 1964, Hilary, da of Fredrick Floyd (d 1973); 1 s (Laurence b 1974), 1 da (Sally b 1971); *Career* dir MRC Inst for Molecular Cell Biology, prof Molecular biology Univ Coll London, Rank prof of physiological biochemistry Imperial Coll London, prof of med cell biology Univ of Liverpool Med Sch, assoc prof Rockefeller Univ New York; *Recreations* music; *Style*— Prof Colin Hopkins; Department of Biology, University College, Gower St, London WC1E 6BT

HOPKINS, Dr Colin Stirton; s of John Stirton Hopkins, of Beech Rise, Beech Lane, Macclesfield, and Dorothy Mary, *née* Blackhurst; *b* 24 Aug 1955; *Educ* Kings Sch Macclesfield, Liverpool Univ Med Sch (MB ChB); *m* 14 July 1984, Denise Elaine, da of Colin Cuthbertson; 2 da (Sarah Louise b 21 April 1987, Amy Jayne b 11 Feb 1990); *Career* jr anaesthetist Liverpool Health Authy 1980-88, conslt anaesthetist Mersey RHA 1989-; fell Coll of Anaesthetists 1982; *Recreations* mountaineering, driving; *Style*— Dr Colin Hopkins; Dept of Anaesthesia, Leighton Hospital, Leighton, Crewe (☎ 0270 255141 ext 2749)

HOPKINS, Daniel Robert; s of Kelvin Peter Hopkins, and Patricia Mabel, *née* Langley; *b* 29 Sept 1969; *Educ* Denbigh HS, Luton Sixth Form Coll, Univ of Birmingham; *Career* actor; Yakety Yak (Griffin Players) 1987, Hamlet (Luton Repertory Co) 1987, Hamlet (Luton Repertoy Co) 1987; Birmingham Univ Drama Dept: The Passion (Palace of the Young Pioneers Ukraine Soviet Union), Deathwatch 1990, The White Devil 1990; Nat Youth Theatre: Marat/Sade (Playhouse) 1989, Blitz (Playhouse) 1990; singer the Lazy Beat Big Band 1989-, songwriter/singer Headstack 1989-; John Staddon prize for citizenship 1988; *Recreations* music, theatre, swimming, squash, skiing; *Clubs* Stockwood Park Rugby Football, Birmingham Univ Jazz; *Style*— Daniel Hopkins, Esq; 1 Alexandra Ave, Luton, Beds LU3 1HE (☎ 0582 22913)

HOPKINS, David Rex Eugène; s of Frank Victor Densham Hopkins, of Somerset, and Vera Muriel Eugènie, *née* Wimhurst; *b* 29 June 1930; *Educ* Worthing HS for Boys, ChCh Oxford (MA); *m* 1955, Brenda Joyce, da of Cecil Thomas Phillips (d 1940), of London, and Irene Newcomb, *née* Briggs; 2 s (Mark b 1957, Jeremy b 1962), 2 da (Ruth b 1955, d 1985, Sarah b 1960); *Career* cmmnd RA 1952 Korea, asst princ WO 1953 (princ 1957), MOD 1964, asst sec 1967, HO 1969-70, RCDS 1971, def equipment secretariat 1972, dir HQ Security 1975, fin cnsllr UK delgn to NATO 1981, dir of quality assur (admin) 1983-90; *Recreations* church work, archaeological digging, fell walking, military history; *Style*— David Hopkins, Esq; 16 Hitherwood Drive, London SE19 1XB (☎ 081 670 7504)

HOPKINS, Capt David Sime Borrough; s of Thomas Wilfred Hopkins (d 1961), of Moorallerton Hall, Leeds, and Gladys Lilian Muir, *née* Douty (d 1955); *b* 24 Nov 1924; *Educ* Bradfield; *m* 26 Nov 1955, Jennifer Isabel, da of Sir John Cameron, of Cowsby Hall, Thirsk, N Yorks; 2 s (Stephen Borrough b 1956, Nicholas Martin b 1959), 2 da (Catherine Virginia b 1961, Sophie Anne b 1966); *Career* Capt KRRC 1943-47 NW Europe, Capt Yorks Hussars (TA) 1947-56; slr 1950; *Recreations* golf, gardening; *Clubs* Brooks's; *Style*— Capt David Hopkins; Galphay Manor, Ripon, N Yorks (☎ 076 583 205)

HOPKINS, Ian William; s of Keith Burne Hopkins, of Reigate, Surrey, and Laura Mary, *née* Dowie; *b* 23 April 1947; *Educ* Trinity Sch of John Whitgift; *m* 6 March 1971, Valerie Joan Frances, da of Ralph Hughes, of Horsham, Sussex; 1 s (Guy), 1 da (Kirsty); *Career* Arthur Young McClelland Moores & Co 1965-71, Citicorp Leasing International Inc 1971-72, London Multinational Bank Ltd and Chemical Bank International Ltd 1973-82, Charterhouse Japhet plc 1982-86, fin dir Baring Brothers & Co Ltd 1986-90 (head of treas 1991); FCA 1970, MICAS 1970; *Recreations* tennis, sailing, choral music; *Clubs* Riverside Racquets; *Style*— Ian Hopkins, Esq; 48 Glebe Rd, Barnes, London SW13 0ED (☎ 081 878 2227); Baring Brothers & Co Ltd, 8 Bishopsgate, London EC2N 4AE (☎ 071 280 1781, fax 071 283 7930, telex 883622)

HOPKINS, John Seddon; s of Alan Hopkins (d 1931), of Christchurch, NZ, and Adeline Mary, *née* Oates; *b* 4 March 1930; *Educ* St Bartholomew's Hosp London Univ (MB BS); *m* 26 Nov 1960, Carmel Rosemary, da of John Patrick McEvoy, of Tipperary; 2 s (Michael b 1963, Christopher b 1969), 3 da (Caroline b 1961, Louise b 1961, Rosalind (twin) b 1969); *Career* Capt RAMC Europe and Korea 1954-56; sr conslt orthopaedic surgn: Harlow Wood Orthopaedic, Mansfield and Newark Gen Hosp; clinical tutor Univ of Nottingham 1966; FRCS; *Recreations* theatre, travel, literary pursuits; *Clubs* New Bone; *Style*— John Hopkins, Esq; Northwood House, 15 North Park, Mansfield, Notts NG18 4PA (☎ 0623 25166)

HOPKINS, (Richard) Julian; s of Richard Robert Hopkins, CBE, of Harpenden, Herts, and Grace Hilda, *née* Hatfield (d 1973); *b* 12 Oct 1940; *Educ* Bedford Sch; *m* 1, 1961 (m dis 1969), Jennifer, *née* Hawkesworth; 1 s (Justin b 1962), 1 da (Julia b 1963); m 2, 6 Aug 1971, Maureen Mary, da of Norman George Hoye (d 1977), of London; 1 s (Benjamin b 1976); *Career* asst mangr London Palladium 1964-66, central servs mangr BBC 1966-70, exec dir RSPCA 1978-82 (admin and fin offr 1972-78), gen mangr Charity Christmas Card Cncl 1982-83, fin dir War on Want 1984-88, nat dir CARE Britain 1988-; fndr and memb Ctee Manor Theatre Gp W Sussex, dir and exec memb Ctee World Soc for Protection of Animals 1977-83, memb Farm Animal Welfare Cncl Miny of Agric 1979-83; FBIM 1976; *Recreations* music, particularly opera, theatre, travel; *Style*— J Hopkins, Esq; Rowan, 33 Needham Terrace, London NW2 6QL (☎ 081 452 4623); CARE Britain, 34-38 Southampton St, London WC2E 7HE (☎ 071 379 5247, fax 071 379 0543, telex 267239 CARE G)

HOPKINS, Keith Barrie; s of Clement Lawrence Hopkins (d 1979), of Coventry, and Beatrice Anne Roberts (d 1987); *b* 27 Oct 1929; *Educ* King Henry VIII Coventry, St John's Coll Oxford (MA); *m* April 1955, Madeline Ann, da of William George Gilbert; 3 s (Nicholas John b 26 Jan 1956, Rupert William b 1 July 1958, Matthew Thomas b 19 March 1963); *Career* trainee accountant Coventry Corp 1953, pub rels trainee Standard Motor Co 1955-58, overseas pub rels offr Standard Triumph 1958-62 (pub rels exec 1962-64), pub rels mangr Leyland Motor Corp 1964-68, dir pub rels British Leyland 1968-74, md Austin Morris Div British Leyland 1974-75, dir of sales and mktg Leyland Cars 1975-78, fndr Opus Public Relations Ltd (in partnership with Shandwick) 1978, sold shares in Opus to Shandwick 1984, fndr and md KBH Communications Ltd 1985-; MIPR, memb Pub Rels Consits Assoc; *Recreations* swimming, gymnastics, walking, reading, writing; *Clubs* RAC, Academy; *Style*— Keith Hopkins, Esq; 13

Carroll House, Gloucester Terrace, Lancaster Gate, London W2 3PP (☎ 071 723 0779); Redberry Cottage, 15 Market Square, Lower Heyford, Oxon (☎ 0869 40419); KBH Communications Ltd, 49/53 Kensington High St, London W8 5ED (☎ 071 938 3911, fax 071 938 4176)

HOPKINS, Rowland Rhys; s of David Verdun Hopkins, of Rugby, Warks, and Phyllis, *née* Dyson; *b* 19 Dec 1948; *Educ* Lawrence Sheriff Sch Rugby, UCL (LLB); *m* 12 Dec 1987, Elizabeth Ann, da of Ronald Williams (d 1980), of Church Stretton, Shrops; 1 da (Sarah Elizabeth b 24 Oct 1989); *Career* called to the Bar Inner Temple 1970; memb Gen Synod C of E 1985-90, chm House of Laity of Birmingham Diocesan Synod C of E 1988-; *Recreations* skiing, fell walking; *Style—* Rowland Hopkins, Esq; 108 Stanmore Rd, Edgbaston, Birmingham B16 0SX (☎ 021 429 8793); Victoria Chambers, 177 Corporation St, Birmingham B4 6RG (☎ 021 236 9900)

HOPKINS, Russell; OBE (1989); s of Charles Albert Hopkins (d 1948), of Sunderland, Co Durham, and Frances Doris, *née* Baldwin (d 1980); *b* 30 April 1932; *Educ* Barnard Castle Sch, Univ of Durham (BDS), Univ of London (MRCS, LRCP); *m* 24 April 1970, Jill Margaret, da of Dudley Frederick Pexton (d 1961); 2 s (Richard Jonathon b 6 May 1971, Robert Geoffrey Russell b 24 April 1979), 1 da (Claire Louise b 31 May 1972); *Career* gen dental practice Salisbury Rhodesia 1957-58 (Cambridge 1956-57), sr house offr (oral surgery) Nottingham Gen Hosp 1959, registrar (oral surgery) St Peters Hosp Chertsey 1959-61, house surgeon (surgery) Bolingbroke Hosp Wandsworth 1964, house physician (medicine) Mayday Hosp 1964, surgeon Union Castleline 1965, sr registrar (oral surgery) Royal Victoria Infirmary Newcastle-upon-Tyne 1965-68, gen mangr Unit 2 University Hosp of Wales 1985- (conslt oral maxillo and facial surgery 1968-); chm Hosp Dental Staff Ctee 1976-78, Hosp Med Staff Ctee and Med Bd 1980-82, chm Welsh Central Conslts Ctee 1990-, chm Gen Mangrs Gp BMA 1987-90; vice chm Welsh Cncl BMA 1990-; memb Joint Conslts Ctee 1980-, Central Ctee Hosp Med Services 1975-90; memb Cncl and hon treas BAOMS 1978-80, Llandudno Vase BAOMFS 1980; memb: BDA, BMA, BAOMS, BDS 1956; MRCS 1964, LRCP 1964, FDSRCS 1961; *Books* Atlas of Oral Preprosthetic Surgery (1986), Far Batlas Der Präprothelischen Chirurgie (1990), Mandibular Fractures in Maxillo Facial Injuries (1985), Preprosthetic Surgery in Surgery of Mouth & Jaws (1986), Bone Dysplasias in Clinical Dentistry (1986); *Recreations* golf, sea fishing, photography, walking North Pembrokeshire, work; *Style—* Russell Hopkins, Esq, OBE; 179 Cyncoed Rd, Cyncoed, Cardiff, South Glamorgan CF2 6AH (☎ 0222 752319); University Hospital of Wales, Heath Park, Cardiff (☎ 0222 747747, ext 2150)

HOPKINSON, Ven Barnabas John (Barney); s of Preb Alfred Stephan Hopkinson, of Dukes Watch, 2 St Swithun's Rd, Winchester, and Anne Cicely, *née* Fletcher (d 1988); *b* 11 May 1939; *Educ* Emmanuel Sch, Trinity Coll Cambridge (MA), Geneva Univ (Certificat d'Etudes Oecumeniques), Lincoln Theol Coll; *m* 27 July 1968, Esme Faith, da of Rev Cecil Wilson Gibbons (d 1985), of Cambridge; 3 da (Rachel b 1969, Sarah b 1971, Clare b 1974); *Career* asst curate: Langley 1965-67, Great St Mary's Cambridge 1967-70; asst chaplain Charterhouse 1970-75, rural dean Marlborough 1977-81 (team vicar 1976-81), rector Wimborne Minster 1981-86, canon Salisbury Cathedral 1983-, rural dean Wimborne 1985-86, archdeacon of Sarum 1986-, priest i/c Stratford-sub-Castle 1987-; *Recreations* walking, climbing, gardening; *Style—* The Ven the Archdeacon of Sarum; Russell House, Stratford-sub-Castle, Salisbury, Wilts SP1 3LG (☎ 0722 328756)

HOPKINSON, Brian Ridley; s of Rev EAE Hopkinson (d 1982), of Cheltenham, and May Olive, *née* Redding (d 1986); *b* 26 Feb 1938; *Educ* Univ of Birmingham (MB ChB, ChM); *m* 4 July 1962, Margaret Ruth, da of Percival Bull (d 1945), of Burton-on-Trent; 3 s (Nicholas b 1967, Adrian b 1968, Jonathan b 1969), 1 da (Susannah b 1971); *Career* RSO West Bromwich Hosp 1964 (house surgn 1962), lectr in surgery QE Hosp Birmingham 1968-73, conslt surgn Nottingham Gen Hosp 1973-, Hunterian prof RCS 1970; licenseed lay reader C of E 1961-, chm Trent Regnl Cncl BMA, memb: JCC Central Conslt Ctee BMA, memb Exec Ctee Vascular Surgical Soc of GB and Ireland; memb BMA, FRCS 1964; *Recreations* steam boating and motor caravaning at home & abroad; *Clubs* BMA; *Style—* Brian Hopkinson, Esq; Lincolnsfield, 18 Victoria Crescent, Private Rd, Sherwood, Nottingham NG5 4DA (☎ 06002 604117); 32 Regent St, Nottingham (☎ 0602 472860)

HOPKINSON, David Hugh Laing; CBE (1986), RD (1975), DL (1987); *b* 14 Aug 1926; *Educ* Wellington, Merton Coll Oxford (BA); *m* 1951, Prudence Margaret Holmes; 2 s (Adrian b 1953, Christopher b 1957), 2 da (Rosalind b 1955, Katherine b 1961); *Career* Lt Cdr RNVR 1944-65; clerk House of Commons 1949-59, chief exec M & G Group 1963-87, chm Harrisons and Crosfield plc, dep chm English China Clays plc, dir Wolverhampton and Dudley Breweries Merchants Trust; Church Cmmn 1973-; govr: Sherborne, Wellington; hon fell St Anne's Coll Oxford; tstee: West Dean Fndn, Paleant House Chichester, Royal Pavilion Brighton, Chichester Cathedral Devpt Tst; *Recreations* travel, opera; *Clubs* Brooks's; *Style—* David Hopkinson, Esq, CBE, RD, DL; St John's Priory, Poling, Arundel, W Sussex BN18 9PS (☎ 0903 882393)

HOPKINSON, Giles; CB (1990); s of Rev Arthur John Hopkinson, CIE (d 1953), of N Yorks, and Eleanor, *née* Richardson; *b* 20 Nov 1931; *Educ* Marlborough, Univ of Leeds (BSc); *m* 1956, Eleanor Jean, da of Leonard Harper Riddell (d 1984), of N Yorks; 3 da (Alison b 1958, Jane b 1959, Erica b 1962); *Career* E and J Richardson Ltd 1956, Forestal Land Timber and Rly's Co Ltd 1957; Civil Serv 1958, scientific offr Dept of Scientific and Industl Res (DSIR), princ Miny of Tport 1964, asst sec 1971, under sec personnel mgmnt DOE 1976, dir freight and ports Dept of Tport 1979, dir London Region Property Servs Agency DOE 1983-90, ret 1990; *Recreations* music, landscape gardening, restoration of antique furniture; *Clubs* Royal Cwlth Society; *Style—* Giles Hopkinson, Esq, CB; Digswell Water Mill, Digswell Lane, Welwyn Garden City, Herts AL7 1SW

HOPKINSON, Jeremy Stephen Frederick; s of John Gordon Hopkinson, of Crown House, Common Road, Kensworth, Dunstaple, and Edith, *née* Lord; *b* 28 Aug 1943; *Educ* Berkhamsted Sch; *m* 14 September 1968, Helle, da of Alfred Holter, of Brevik, Norway; step da of Frederick L Smidth; 1 s (Peter John b 18 Nov 1969), 2 da (Cecila Ann b 22 Feb 1972, Theresa Janet b 19 July 1974); *Career* articled clerk Robert H Marsh & Co CA 1961-68, Hillier Holls Frary & Co 1968-70; ptnr: Marsh Wood Drew & Co 1972-78 (joined 1970), Dearden Farrow 1978- (fellowing merger, chm Tax Ctee 1983-86), ptnr Binder Hamlyn; FCA 1976 (ACA 1966); *Recreations* golf, choir singing, marquetry; *Clubs* Woburn Golf & Country; *Style—* Jeremy Hopkinson, Esq; Lynghouse, 12 Heath Road, Great Brickhill, Milton Keynes, Buckinghamshire MK17 9AL (☎ 0525 261674); BDO Binder Hamlyn, 20 Old Bailey, London ECHM 7BH (☎ 071 489 6100, 071 489 6286)

HOPKINSON, Maj-Gen John Charles Oswald Rooke; CB (1984); s of Lt-Col John Oliver Hopkinson, and Aileen Disney, *née* Rooke; *b* 31 July 1931; *Educ* Stonyhurst, RMA Sandhurst; *m* 1956, Sarah Elizabeth, da of Maj-Gen (Matthew Herbert) Patrick Sayers, OBE; 3 s, 1 da; *Career* CO 1 Bn Queen's Own Highlanders 1972-74 (despatches), Dep Cdr 2 Armd Div and Cdr Osnabrück Garrison 1977-78, student RCDS 1979, dir Operational Requirements 3 (Army) 1980-82, COS HQ Allied Forces Northern Europe 1982-84, Col Queen's Own Highlanders 1983-; dir Br Field Sports Soc 1984-; *Recreations* shooting, fishing, sailing; *Clubs* Army and Navy; *Style—* Maj-Gen John Hopkinson, CB; Bigsweir, Gloucestershire; 59 Kennington Rd, London SE1 (☎ 071 928 4742)

HOPKINSON, Hon Nicholas Henry Eno; s (by 1 m) and h of 1 Baron Colyton, CMG, PC; *b* 18 Jan 1932; *Educ* Eton, Trinity Coll Cambridge; *m* 1957, Fiona Margaret, da of Sir (Thomas) Torquil Alphonso Munro, 5 Bt; 2 s; *Heir* s, Alisdair John, b 1958; *Career* engr and farmer; *Style—* The Hon Nicholas Hopkinson; Drumleys, Lindertis, Kirriemuir, Angus DD8 5NU (☎ 057 53 209)

HOPKINSON, Penelope Avril (Penny); da of Capt Brian Edward Hopkinson, of Kenilworth, Warwickshire, and Avril Frances Chandler, *née* Clark (d 1984); *b* 8 March 1949; *Educ* Lawnside Sch Great Malvern Worcs; *m* 23 Sept 1979 (m dis 1983), (Hans)-Jürgen Schäfer, s of late Hans-Schäfer, of W Germany; *Career* technical journalist 1969, ed Media International 1974, commerce and industry freelance journalist specialising in the emerging Gulf States for worldwide press, proprietor Manual Writers; memb Special Health Authy Maudsley and Bethlem Hosps 1988; *Books* The Gulf Handbook (ed, 1979), A Better World for Bahrain (1981); *Recreations* music, cookery, village cricket, Islam; *Style—* Mrs Penny Hopkinson; 26 Upper Addison Gardens, Holland Park, London W14 8AJ

HOPKINSON, Simon Charles; s of Frederick Bruce Hopkinson, of Pembrokeshire, and Anne Dorothie Mary, *née* Whitworth Trent Coll Derbyshire; *b* 5 June 1954; *Career* Normandie Hotel Birtle 1970-71, Hat & Feather Knutsford 1971-72, St Non's Hotel St Davids 1972-74, Druidstone Hotel Little Haven 1974-75, chef and proprietor: Shed Restaurant Dinas 1975-77, Hoppy's Restaurant 1977-78; inspr Egon Ronay 1978-80; chef: private house 1980-83, Hilare London 1983-89; chef and proprietor Bibendum 1989-; *Recreations* dining, losing at chess to Terence Conran, swimming, cooking; *Clubs* The Groucho, Colony Room; *Style—* Simon Hopkinson, Esq; Bibendum Restaurant Ltd, 81 Fulham Rd, London SW3 6RD (☎ 071 581 5817, fax 071 823 7925)

HOPKINSON, Rev (Alfred) Stephan; s of Ven John Henry Hopkinson (d 1960), of Cumbria, and Evelyn Mary, *née* Fountaine (d 1952); *b* 14 June 1908; *Educ* St Edward's Sch Oxford, Wadham Coll Oxford (MA); *m* 31 Dec 1935, Anne Cicely, da of Sir Walter Morley Fletcher, KBE, CB, (d 1933), of Kensington; 2 s (Barnabas b 1939, Simon b 1947), 4 da (Jennifer b 1937, Selina b 1941, Lucy b 1943, Elizabeth b 1945); *Career* former cnsllr and chaplain Winchester Coll; preb St Pauls Cathedral London, vicar St Mary Woolnoth, gen dir Industrial Christian Fellowship, anglican advsr to ATV, chaplain RNVR, hon curate The Univ Church Cambridge; *Recreations* gardening, travel; *Style—* The Rev Alfred S Hopkinson; 39 Madingly Rd, Cambridge CB3 0EL

HOPKIRK, (Margaret) Joyce; *née* Nicholson; da of late Walter Nicholson, of Newcastle, and late Veronica, *née* Keelan; *b* 2 March 1937; *Educ* Middle St Secdy Sch Newcastle; *m* 1, 1964, Peter Hopkirk; 1 da (Victoria b 11 April 1966); m 2, 9 Aug 1974, William James (Bill) Lear, s of Maj Cyril James Lear (d 1988), of Newick, Sussex; 1 s (Nicholas b 22 Nov 1975); *Career* women's ed (launch) Sun Newspapers 1969, ed (launch) Br Cosmopolitian 1970, asst ed Daily Mirror 1972-78, women's ed Sunday Times 1986, ed dir (launch) Br Elle 1987, ed She Magazine 1987-89, conslt ed TV Plus 1991-; *Style—* Mrs Joyce Hopkirk; Gadespring, Piccotts End, Hemel Hempstead, Herts (☎ 0442 245608)

HOPLEY, Damian Paul; *b* 12 April 1970; *Educ* Harrow, Univ of St Andrews; *Career* Rugby Unionplayer Wasps RFC; Eng Schs 1987-88; clubs: St Andrews Univ RFC 1988-90, Wasps RFC 1990-; rep: Eng Colts 1989 (3 caps), Scottish Univs 1988-90 (4 caps), Eng Students, London Division 1990, Eng B 1990 and 1991; England: memb squad, replacement v Wales 1991; Player of the Season St Andrews Univ Taverners Cricket Club 1989-90; *Recreations* blues and jazz piano, commuting, cricket, watersports, shooting, golf, touring; *Style—* Damian Hopley, Esq; Thorncote, Edgehill Rd, Ealing, London W13 8HW (☎ 081 998 9882); Wasps FC, Repton Avenue, Sudbury, nr Wembley, Middlesex HA0 3DW (☎ 081 902 4220)

HOPMEIER, George Alan Richard; JP (Inner London); s of Dr Lucian Hopmeier (d 1981), and Yolanda Hopmeier; *b* 23 Sept 1948; *Educ* Dulwich, UCL (BA); 1 da (Charlotte b 29 March 1981); *Career* md Martin Lucas Ltd 1981-, chief exec Culram International Ltd 1988-; Inner London Juvenile Cts Panel and W Central Div; memb: Inst for the Study and Treatment of Delinquency 1988, ISBA 1980, Buttle Tst 1989; *Recreations* boating, reading, flying; *Clubs* RAC; *Style—* George Hopmeier, Esq, JP; 31 Blenheim Gardens, London SW2 5EU (☎ 081 678 6060, fax 081 671 5134, telex 946072)

HOPPER, Andrew Christopher Graham; s of Hugh Christopher Hopper (d 1959), of Glamorgan, and Doreen Adele Harper (d 1976); *b* 1 Oct 1948; *Educ* Monkton Combe Sch Bath; *m* 6 Sept 1980, Rosamund Heather, da of Robert Nigel Towers, of Tiverton, Devon; *Career* HM dep coroner for S Glamorgan 1977-83 (retained to represent the Law Soc in disciplinary investigations and proceedings 1980-, retained by Continuing Educn Dept of the Law Soc to lecture on ethics and conduct 1986-), sr ptnr Adams and Black Cardiff 1982 (ptnr 1972), conslt Cartwrights Adams and Black 1988; *Recreations* claret, badminton; *Clubs* East India; *Style—* Andrew Hopper, Esq; Talygarn House, Talygarn, Pontyclun, Mid Glamorgan CF7 9JT; 36 West Bute St, Cardiff CF1 5UA (☎ 0443 237788, fax 0443 237410)

HOPPER, Brian Barnes; *b* 10 Jan 1926; *Educ* King George V Sch Southport, Univ of Liverpool (BEng); *m* 1952, Mavis Priscilla; 1 s, 2 da; *Career* formerly civil engr Shell-Mex and BP Ltd, CEGB and consulting engrs; projects mangr Unilever Ltd 1965-80, md Chester Waterworks Co 1980-90, conslt to Bd of dirs Unilever 1991-; memb Guild of Water Conservators (City of London), Freeman of City of London 1990; MICE, CEng, FBIM, MIWEM, MRSH; *Recreations* golf, tennis; *Clubs* Eaton Golf, Bickerton Tennis; *Style—* Brian B Hopper, Esq

HOPPER, Ian; s of John Frederick Hopper (d 1989), and Dora, *née* Lambert (d 1970); *b* 19 May 1938; *Educ* Dame Allans Sch Newcastle on Tyne, High Storrs GS Sheffield, Univ of Sheffield (MB ChB); *m* 19 Aug 1961, Christine Margaret, da of Tom Raymond Holroyd Wadsworth (d 1978); 1 s (Andrew b 1964), 1 da (Penny b 1962); *Career* sr ENT registrar Royal Infirmary Sheffield 1967-69, conslt ENT surgn Sunderland, Durham and S Tynewide Health Authys 1969-; memb Cncl Br Assoc of Otolaryngologists; FRCSEd 1967; *Recreations* travel, bowling; *Clubs* Sunderland; *Style—* Ian Hopper, Esq; 21 Beresford Park, Sunderland, Tyne and Wear (☎ 091 565 8865); Royal Infirmary, New Durham Rd, Sunderland (☎ 091 565 6256)

HOPPER, Lt-Col Patrick Desmond Leo; DL (Essex 1990); s of Brig Charles Reginald Leo Hopper (d 1959), and Daphne Elise, *née* Williams (d 1987); *b* 22 Nov 1930; *Educ* Monkton Combe Sch, RMA Sandhurst; *m* 28 March 1959, Gemma Felicity Bevan, da of Brig James Bevan Brown (d 1962); 1 s (Jonathan b 1962), 1 da (Joanna b 1960); *Career* cmmnd Suffolk Regt 1951, Platoon Cdr Malaya (despatches) 1951-53, served 3 Para 1953-57 (took part in Suez Op), Adj 1 Suffolk 1958-59, cmd 5 Bn Royal Anglian Regt 1973-75, Asst Adj-Gen Rhine Army 1975-78; ret from Regular Army 1978; sec East Anglia TA and VR Assoc 1986- (dep sec 1979-86), Dep Hon Col TA (Essex) Royal Anglian Regt 1987-; memb Ct Univ of Essex 1990-; *Recreations* fly fishing, sailing; *Clubs* Army and Navy; *Style—* Col Patrick D L Hopper, DL; St Crispins, Radwinter, Saffron Walden, Essex CB10 2TH (☎ 079 987 205); East Anglia TAVRA, 250 Springfield Rd, Chelmsford, Essex CM2 6BU (☎ 0245 354262)

HOPPER, Robert Thomas Cort; s of John Ronald Thomas Hopper, of The Old Vicarage, Church St, Langham, Rutland, and Joan Rosemary, *née* Thompson; *b* 26 June

1946; *Educ* Sedbergh, Univ of Manchester (BA); *m* 24 Aug 1972, Christine Anne, da of Bryan Christopher Ball; 1 s (Henry Oliver Charles b 25 April 1984), 2 da (Rebecca Clare Elizabeth b 19 Jan 1980, Sophie Anne Rosemary b 21 Oct 1982); *Career* art historian; articled clerk Messrs Pearless de Rougement (solicitors) Sussex 1964-68, dep princ keeper The Whitworth Art Gallery Univ of Manchester 1980-81 (asst keeper fine art 1973-80), dir Art Galleries and Museums City of Bradford Metropolitan DC 1981-88, dir Henry Moore Sculpture Tst 1988-, lectr Br Cncl lecture tour to India and Africa 1988; chm: Whitworth Arts Soc Univ of Manchester 1971-73, Visual Art Panel NW Arts Assoc 1979-81, Ctee of Mgmnt Yorkshire Sculpture Park Bretton Hall Wakefield 1981-, Advsy Panel Yorkshire and Humberside Museums Cncl 1985-, Photography Panel Yorkshire Arts Assoc 1985-86; memb: Sub Ctee Arts Cncl Exhibitions 1980-84, Photography Fellowship Ctee Nat Museum of Photography Film & Television W Yorks 1985-, Govrs Advsy Ctee Art and Design Bradford and Ilkley Community Coll 1985-; advsr to Art Recreation & Tourism Ctee Assoc of Metropolitan Authys 1986-88, dir Public Arts Ltd Wakefield 1986-89; exhibition selector and author of catalogue for Kettle's Yard Cambridge and Arts Cncl tour (titled True and Pure Sculpture - Frank Dobson 1886-1963) Preston, Hull and Birmingham 1981-82; Hon MA Univ of Bradford 1988; professional memb Museums Assoc 1981, FRSA 1982; *Recreations* walking, reading; *Style*— Robert Hopper, Esq; The Henry Moore Sculpture Trust, c/o Leeds City Art Gallery, Calverley St, Leeds (☎ 0532 462493, fax 0532 449689)

HOPPER, William Joseph; s of late Isaac Vance Hopper, and Jennie Josephine Black; *b* 9 Aug 1929; *Educ* Queen's Park Secdy Sch, Univ of Glasgow (BA); *m* 1959, Melisa; 1 da (Catherine b 1971); *Career* Flying Offr RAF; fin analyst W R Grace and Co New York 1956-59, London off mangr H Hentz and Co (memb NY Stock Exchange) 1960-66, gen mangr S G Warburg and Co Ltd 1966-69; dir: Hill Samuel and Co Ltd 1969-74, Morgan Grenfell and Co Ltd 1975-79; advsr Morgan Grenfell 1979-; dir: Wharf Resources Ltd (Calgary) 1984-, Manchester Ship Canal Co 1985-; fndr chm (now memb Exec Ctee) Inst for Fiscal Studies, treas Action Resource Centre 1985-; MEP (C) Greater Manchester W 1979-84; *Recreations* listening to music (records), gardening; *Clubs* St James's (Manchester); *Style*— William Hopper, Esq; 23 Great Winchester St, London EC2 (☎ 071 588 4545, telex 8953511)

HOPPS, Stuart Gary; s of Alec Hopps (d 1973), London, and Lucie, *née* Dombek; *b* 2 Dec 1942; *Educ* Stratford GS, Kings Coll London (BA), MFA Sarah Lawrence Coll; *Career* Dance Dept Dartington Coll of Art 1970-71, assoc dir Scottish Ballet 1971-76, fndr dir SB's movable Workshop, freelance choreographer; opera: The Cunning Little Vixen, Queen of Spades and Christmas Eve (ENO), Orfeo ed Euridice (Glyndebourne), Carmen (WNO), HMS Pinafore and The Merry Widow (Saddlers' Wells), The Cunning Little Vixen (Royal Opera), Macbeth (Metropoloitan Opera), Peter Grimes (Kent Opera); theatre work incl: A Midsummer Night's Dream, Salome, Candide (Edinburgh Festival), The Oresteia, Animal Farm (NT), Henry VIII and As You Like it (RSC), Oliver (Nat Youth Music Theatre); theatre in West End: Pal Joey, Girl Friends, The Rocky Horrow Show; fndr chm Dance Panel Gr London Arts, chm Br Assoc of Choreographers Steering Ctee, memb Dance Panel Arts Cncl of GB 1976-80, dir MA Studies Laban Centre, memb Accreditation Ctee Cncl for Dance Educn & Training, dep chm Choreographers' Ctee Equity; dir: Diversion Dance Co, Janet Smith Dancers; *Style*— Stuart Hopps, Esq; c/o Marina Martin Management, 6A Danbury St, London N1 8JU (☎ 071 359 3646, fax 071 359 7759)

HOPSON, David Joseph; s of Geoffrey Paul Hopson (d 1980), of Merryways, Newbury, and Nora Winifred, *née* Camp (d 1968); *b* 26 Feb 1929; *Educ* St Bartholomews GS Newbury; *m* 1 June 1957, Susan, da of Horace Caleb George Buckingham (d 1965); 2 s (Jonathan Joseph b 13 March 1960, Christopher Ian b 9 April 1963); *Career* RN 1946-49; chm: Camp Hopson & Co Ltd 1966- (dir 1961), Newbury Building Soc 1986- (dir 1963); pres Newbury and Dist Agric Soc 1991-; *Recreations* fly-fishing; *Clubs* Fly Fishers, Winnowing, Twenty; *Style*— David Hopson, Esq; Field Acre, Hoe Benham, Newbury, Berks; Camp Hopson & Co Ltd, 6-12 Northbrook St, Newbury, Berks RG13 1DN (☎ 0635 523 523, fax 0635 529 009)

HOPWOOD, Prof Anthony George; s of George Hopwood (d 1986), of Stoke-on-Trent, and Violet, *née* Simpson (d 1986); *b* 18 May 1944; *Educ* Hanley HS, LSE (BSc), Univ of Chicago (MBA, PhD); *m* 31 Aug 1967, Caryl, da of John H Davies (d 1981), of Ton Pentre, Mid Glam; 2 s (Mark b 1971, Justin b 1974); *Career* lectr in mgmnt accounting Manchester Business Sch 1970-73, sr staff Admin Staff Coll Henley-on-Thames 1973-75, visiting prof of mgmnt European Inst for Advanced Studies Mgmnt Brussels 1972-, professorial fell Oxford Centre for Mgmnt Studies 1976-78, ICA prof of accounting and fin reporting London Business Sch 1978-85, visiting distinguished prof of accounting Pennsylvania State Univ 1983-88, Ernst and Young prof of int accounting and fin mgmnt LSE 1985-; pres Euro Accounting Assoc 1977-79 and 1987-88, distinguished int lectr American Accounting Assoc 1981, John V Ratcliffe Meml lectr Univ of NSW 1988; accounting advsr to: Euro Cmmn 1989-90, OECD 1990-; memb: Mgmnt and Industl Rels Ctee SSRC 1975-79; Hon DEcon Turku Sch of Econs Finland 1989; *Books* An Accounting System and Managerial Behaviour (1973), Accounting and Human Behaviour (1974), Essays in British Accounting Research (with M Bromwich, 1981), Auditing Research (with M Bromwich and J Shaw, 1982), Accounting Standard Setting: An International Perspective (with M Bromwich, 1983), European Contributions to Accounting Research (with H Schreuder, 1984), Issues in Public Sector Accounting (with C Tomkins, 1984), Research and Current Issues in Management Accounting (with M Bromwich, 1986), Acccounting from the Outside (1989), International Pressures for Accounting Change (1989); *Style*— Prof Anthony Hopwood; Department of Accounting and Finance, London School of Economics and Political Science, Houghton St, London WC2A 2AE (☎ 071 405 7686, fax 071 242 0392, telex 24655 BLPES G)

HOPWOOD, Prof David Alan; s of Herbert Hopwood (d 1963), of Lymm, Cheshire, and Dora, *née* Grant (d 1972); *b* 19 Aug 1933; *Educ* Purbrook Park Co HS Hants, Lymm GS Cheshire, Univ of Cambridge (MA, PhD), Univ of Glasgow (DSc); *m* 15 Sept 1962, Joyce Lilian, da of Isaac Bloom (d 1964), of Hove, Sussex; 2 s (Nicholas Duncan b 1964, John Andrew b 1965), 1 da (Rebecca Jane b 1967); *Career* John Stothert bye-fell Magdalene Coll Cambridge 1956-58, univ demonstrator and asst lectr in botany Univ of Cambridge 1957-61, res fell St John's Coll Cambridge 1958-61, lectr in genetics Univ of Glasgow 1961-68, John Innes prof of genetics UEA and head Genetics Dept John Innes Inst 1968-; hon prof: Chinese Acad Med Sciences 1987, Chinese Acad of Sciences (Insts of Microbiology and Plant Physiology) 1987, Huazhong Agric Univ Wuhan China 1989; hon fell UMIST 1990; memb: Genetical Soc of GB 1957 (pres 1984-87), Euro Molecular Biology Orgn 1984, Academia Europaea 1988; hon memb: Spanish Microbiological Soc 1985, Hungarian Acad of Sciences 1990; for fell Indian Nat Sci Acad 1987; Hon Dr of Sci ETH Zürich 1989; FIBiol 1968, FRS 1979; *Recreations* fishing, gardening; *Style*— Prof David Hopwood, FRS; John Innes Inst, Colney Lane, Norwich NR4 7UH (☎ 0603 52571, fax 0603 56844, telex 975122); 244 Unthank Rd, Norwich NR2 2AH (☎ 0603 53488)

HORAM, John Rhodes; s of Sydney Horam, of Preston, Lancs; *b* 7 March 1939; *Educ* Silcoates Sch Wakefield, St Catharine's Coll Cambridge; *m* 1, 1977, Iris Crawley; m 2, 1987, Judith Jackson; *Career* former fin journalist: Financial Times, The Economist; Parly candidate (Lab) Folkestone and Hythe 1966, MP (Lab 1970-81, SDP 1981-83) Gateshead West; Parly under-sec Tport 1976-79, oppn spokesman econ affrs 1979-81, SDP econ spokesman 1981-83, joined Cons Pty Feb 1987; md: Commodities Res Unit Ltd 1983-87 (jt md 1968-70), CRU Holdings Ltd 1988-; *Style*— John Horam, Esq; 6 Bovingdon Rd, London SW6 2AP

HORDEN, Prof John Robert Backhouse; s of Henry Robert Horden (d 1950), of Warwicks, and Ethel Edith, *née* Backhouse (d 1970); *Educ* ChCh Oxford, Pembroke Coll Cambridge, Heidelberg, Sorbonne; *m* 10 Jan 1948, Aileen Mary, da of Col Walter John Douglas, TD (d 1949), of Warwicks and S Wales; 1 s (Peregrine b 1955); *Career* formerly: tutor and lectr ChCh Oxford; dir: Inst of Bibliography and Textual Criticism Univ of Leeds, Centre for Bibliographical Studies Univ of Stirling; Cecil Oldman Meml lectr 1971, Marc Fitch prize 1979, devised new academic discipline of publishing studies Univ of Leeds 1972, initiated first Br degree in PR Stirling Univ 1987; visiting prof: Pa State, Saskatchewan, Erlangen-Nürberg, Texas at Austin, Münster; Golf: represented England, Warwicks, Oxford, Cambridge and Br Univs; Doctor of Humane Letters honoris causa Indiana State Univ 1974; FSA, FRSL; *Books* Francis Quarles A Bibliography (1953), Quarles' Hosanna and Threnodes (1960), Art of the Drama (1969), English and Continental Emblem Books (22 vols 1968-74), Everyday Life in Seventeenth-Century England (1974), Techniques of Bibliography (1977), John Freeth (1985), Bibliographia (1991); *Recreations* golf, music, painting; *Clubs* Athenaeum; *Style*— Prof John Horden; Department of English, University of Stirling, Stirling FK9 4LA (☎ 0786 73171 ext 2362)

HORDER, Dr John Plaistowe; CBE (1980, OBE 1971); s of Gerald Morley Horder (d 1939), and Emma Ruth, *née* Plaistowe (d 1971); *b* 9 Dec 1919; *Educ* Lancing, Univ Coll Oxford (BA, MA), London Hosp Med Coll (BM BCh); *m* 20 Jan 1940, Elizabeth June, da of Maurice Wilson (d 1924); 2 s (Timothy John b 1943, William Morley b 1950), 2 da (Annabelle Mary b 1945, Josephine Elizabeth b 1953); *Career* GP London 1951-81, conslt to Expert Ctee WHO 1960-61, travelling fell 1964 and 1984, Jephcott visiting prof Univ of Nottingham; RCGP: chm Educn Ctee 1967-70, John Hunt fell 1973-76, pres 1979-82, Wolfson prof France and Belgium; RSM: pres section of gp, hon fell 1982, vice pres 1987-89; visiting fell King Edward's Hosp Fund 1983-86, visiting prof Royal Free Hosp Med Sch 1983-, pres Med Art Soc 1989-; hon fell Green Coll Oxford; Hon MD Free Univ Amsterdam 1985; hon memb The Canadian Coll of Family Practice 1981, visiting prof Univ of Zagreb Med Sch 1990- FRCGP 1970, FRCP 1972, FRCPsych 1980, FRCP (Ed) 1981; *Books* The Future General Practitioner (jtly and ed, 1972), 14 Prince's Gate (jtly, 1987); *Recreations* playing the piano, painting water-colours; *Style*— Dr John Horder, CBE; 98 Regent's Park Rd, London NW1 (☎ 071 722 3804); The Royal Free Hospital Medical School, Pond St, London NW3 (☎ 071 794 0500 ext 4294)

HORDER, 2 Baron (UK 1933); Sir Thomas Mervyn Horder; 2 Bt (UK 1923); s of 1 Baron Horder, GCVO, DL (d 1955); *b* 8 Dec 1910; *Educ* Winchester, Trinity Coll Cambridge; *m* 6 July 1946 (m dis 1957), Mary Ross, yr da of Dr William Scott McDougall, of Wallington, Surrey; *Heir* none; *Career* served WWII, RAF Fighter Cmd, Air HQ India and SEAC, Wing Cdr RAFVR; chm Gerald Duckworth and Co 1948-70; *Books* The Little Genius - a Memoir of the first Lord Horder (1966), Six Betjeman Songs (1967), On Their Own - Shipwrecks and Survivals (1988), Seven Shakespeare Songs (1988), Black Diamonds - Dorothy Parker Songs (1990); *Style*— The Rt Hon Lord Horder; c/o Gerald Duckworth and Co, 43 Gloucester Cres, London NW1 7DY

HORDERN, (Anthony) Christopher Shubra; s of Anthony Arthur Shubra Hordern (d 1981), of Jersey, CI, and Alison Mary, *née* Bigwood (d 1984); *b* 7 July 1936; *Educ* Malvern; *m* 1, 12 Sept 1959, Lucy (d 1988), da of Michael Pemberton Green; 1 s (Anthony Miles Shubra b 18 March 1965), 2 da (Catherine Anne b 2 June 1961, Josephine Alex b 21 Oct 1962); m2, 7 Oct 1989, Jane, da of David Moore Barlow; *Career* CA; articled clerk C Herbert Smith & Russell; Price Waterhouse: joined 1963 (on amalgamation with Howard Smith Thompson & Co), ptnr 1967-, int firm exchange Chicago 1967-68; pres: Birmingham CA's Students Soc 1976 (memb Ctee 1967-71, chm 1969-71), Birmingham and W Midlands Soc of CA's 1983-84 (memb Ctee 1970-85); memb Cncl Inst of CA's in England and Wales 1985-; govr: Alice Ottley Sch Worcester, Malvern Coll; tstee: Baron Davenport Charity Tst, Joseph Hopkins Charity (chm); Freeman City of London, memb Worshipful Co of Chartered Accountants 1987; FCA; *Recreations* walking, fly-fishing; *Clubs* RAC; *Style*— Christopher Hordern, Esq; Church House, North Piddle, Worcestershire WR7 4PR (☎ 0905 60847); Price Waterhouse, 169 Edmund St, Birmingham B3 2JB (☎ 021 200 3000, fax 021 200 2464)

HORDERN, Maj John Richard; s of Rev Richard Lynch Hordern (d 1969), and Nancy Letitia, *née* Travis; *b* 20 Jan 1941; *Educ* Hurstpierpoint Coll, RMA Sandhurst; *Career* army career 1959-85; Royal Regt of Fusiliers served: Hong Kong, BAOR, Aden, Canada, UN Cyprus, Ireland; emergency planning offr W Oxfordshire DC 1985-86; regnl organiser (West) Royal Cwlth Soc for the Blind; MBIM; *Style*— Maj John Hordern; 42 Cooper Rd, Westbury-on-Trym, Bristol, Avon B59 3RA (☎ 0272 629652)

HORDERN, Sir Michael Murray; CBE (1972); s of Capt Edward Joseph Calveley Hordern, CIE, RIN (d 1945), and Margaret Emily, *née* Murray (d 1933); *b* 3 Oct 1911; *Educ* Brighton Coll; *m* 27 April 1943, (Grace) Eveline, da of Dudley Mortimer; 1 da (Joanna); *Career* Nat Serv RNVR served Atlantic, Med, Indian and Pacific Oceans, Lt Cdr; actor; hon fell Queen Mary Coll Univ of London 1987; Hon DLitt: Univ of Exeter 1985, Univ of Warwick 1986: kt 1982; *Recreations* fishing; *Clubs* Garrick, Flyfishers'; *Style*— Sir Michael Hordern, CBE

HORDERN, Peter Maudslay; MP (C) Horsham 1983-, DL (Horsham 1983-); s of C H Hordern, MBE; *b* 18 April 1929; *Educ* Geelong GS Aust, Ch Ch Oxford; *m* 1964, Susan Chataway; 2 s, 1 da; *Career* former memb London Stock Exchange; chm: Petrofina UK, F & C Smaller Cos; dir Touche Remnant Technol; MP (C): Horsham 1964-74, Horsham and Crawley 1974-83; sec 1922 Ctee, chm Public Accounts Cmmn; *Style*— Peter Hordern, Esq, MP, DL; 55 Cadogan St, London SW3

HORE, Dr Brian David; s of William Harold Banks Hore, and Gladys Hilda, *née* Preedy; *b* 21 Sept 1937; *Educ* Lower Sch of John Lyon Harrow Middx, Bart's Hosp Med Coll, London Maudsley Hosp London (BSc, MB BS, MPhil); *m* Eva Elliot, da of George Elliot Shepherd (d 1955); 2 s (Ian b 19 March 1968, Andrew b 29 Jan 1971); *Career* house offr Bart's Hosp London 1963-65, registrar in psychiatry Maudsley Hosp 1967-70, sr registrar in psychological med Hammersmith Hosp 1970-71; conslt psychiatrist: Withington Hosp Manchester 1972-, Univ Hosp of S Manchester 1972-, hon lectr in psychiatry Univ of Manchester 1972- (lectr and hon conslt 1971-72); memb: Bd of Dirs ICAA Lausanne Switzerland, Exec Ctee and Jt Ctee Med Cncl on Alcoholism, Exec Ctee Substance Misuse section RCPsych; vice chm Turning Point, temp advsr WHO regnl Euro office; memb BMA 1963, FRCPsych 1981, FRCP 1983; *Books* Alcohol Dependence (1976), Alcohol Problems in Employment (jt ed and contrib, 1981), Alcohol and Health (jtly), Alcohol Our Favourite Drug (jtly, 1986); *Recreations* theatre, cinema, soccer (Manchester City FC); *Style*— Dr Brian Hore; 17 St John St, Manchester M3 4DR (☎ 061 834 5775)

HORLICK, Vice Adm Sir Edwin John (Ted); KBE (1981); s of late Edwin William Horlick; *b* 1925; *Educ* Bedford Modern Sch, RN Engrg Coll; *m* 1953, Jean Margaret, da of Herbert Covington; 4 s; *Career* Vice Adm 1979, Chief Naval Engr Offr 1981-83, dir-gen ships MOD (Navy) 1979-83, ret; FEng,FIMechE, MIMarE; *Recreations* golf, gardening; *Clubs* Army and Navy; *Style*— Vice Adm Sir Ted Horlick, KBE; Garden Apartment, 74 Gt Pulteney St, Bath BA2 4DL

HORLICK, James Cunliffe William; s and h of Sir John James Macdonald Horlick, 5 Bt; *b* 19 Nov 1956; *Educ* Eton; *m* 1985 Fiona Rosalie, *née* McLaren; 2 s (Alexander b 1987, Jack b 1989); *Career* co dir; *Clubs* Beefsteak; *Style*— James Horlick, Esq; Braelangwell House, Balblair, Dingwall, Ross-shire IV7 8LQ

HORLICK, Sir John James Macdonald; 5 Bt (UK 1914), of Cowley Manor, Gloucester; s of Lt-Col Sir James Nockells Horlick, 4 Bt, OBE, MC (d 1972); *b* 9 April 1922; *Educ* Eton, Babson Inst of Business Admin Wellesley Hills Mass USA; *m* 1948, June, da of Douglas Cory-Wright, CBE; 1 s, 2 da; *Heir* s, James Cunliffe William Horlick; *Career* served WWII, Capt Coldstream Gds; dep chm Horlicks Ltd 1968-72, ptnr Tournaig Farming Co 1973-, chm Highland Fish Farmers 1978-85; *Recreations* military history, model soldiers; *Clubs* Beefsteak, Highland (Inverness); *Style*— Sir John Horlick, Bt; Tournaig, Poolewe, Achnasheen, Ross-shire (☎ 044 586 250); Howberry Lane Cottage, Nuffield, nr Nettlebed, Oxon (☎ 0491 641454)

HORLOCK, Henry Wimburn Sudell; s of Rev Dr Henry Darrell Sudell Horlock (d 1953), and Mary Haliburton, *née* Laurie (d 1953); *b* 19 July 1915; *Educ* Pembroke Coll Oxford (MA); *m* 21 July 1960, Jeannetta Robin, da of Frederick Wilfred Tanner, JP (d 1958), of The Towers, Farnham Royal, Bucks; *Career* WWII Army 1939-42; civil serv 1942-60; fndr and dir Stepping Stone Sch 1962-87, memb Ct of Common Cncl 1969-, Sheriff City of London 1972-73, dep Ward of Farrington Within 1978-; chm: City of London Sheriffs' Soc 1985-, West Ham Park Ctee 1979-82, Police Ctee 1987-89; memb: Farringdon Ward Club 1970- (pres 1978-79), United Wards Club 1972- (pres 1980-81), City Livery Club 1969- (pres 1981-82), Guild of Freemen 1972- (Master 1986-87), Royal Soc of St George (City of London branch) 1972- (chm 1989-90); Freeman City of London 1937-; Liveryman Worshipful Co of: Saddlers 1937 (Master 1976-77), Parish Clerks 1966 (Master 1981-82), Plaisterers (1975), Fletchers 1977, Gardeners 1980; Cdr Order of Merit Federal Repub of Germany 1972, Cdr Nat Order of Aztec Eagle of Mexico 1973, Cdr Du Wissam Alouite of Morocco 1987; *Recreations* travel, country pursuits; *Clubs* Athenaeum, Guildhall, City Livery; *Style*— Wimburn Horlock, Esq; Copse Hill House, Lower Slaughter, Glos GL54 2HZ (☎ 0451 20276); 97 Defoe House, Barbican, London EC2Y 8DN (☎ 071 588 1602)

HORLOCK, Prof John Harold; s of Harold Edgar Horlock (d 1971), of Tonbridge, Kent, and Olive Margaret Horlock (d 1989); *b* 19 April 1928; *Educ* Edmonton Latymer Sch, St John's Coll Cambridge (MA, PhD, ScD); *m* 8 June 1953, Sheila Joy, da of Percy Kendolph Stutely (d 1980), of Hordle, Hants; 1 s (Timothy John b 4 Jan 1958), 2 da (Alison Ruth (Mrs Heap) b 20 April 1955, Jane Margaret (Mrs Spencer) b 28 Nov 1961); *Career* design engr Rolls Royce 1949-51; res fell St John's Coll Cambridge 1954-57, prof of mechanical engrg Univ of Liverpool 1958-67, prof of engrg Univ of Cambridge 1967-74; vice chllr: Univ of Salford 1974-80, Open Univ 1981-90 (fell 1990-); hon prof Univ of Warwick 1989-; dir: British Engine Insurance Ltd 1979-86, BL Technology Ltd 1979-87, National Grid co plc 1989-; memb: SRC 1974-77, Engrg Cncl 1982-84; chm: ARC 1979-80, Advsy Ctee on Safety of Nuclear Installations 1984-; vice pres Royal Soc 1982-84; Hon DSc: Heriot-Watt 1980, Salford 1981, Univ of E Asia 1985; Hon DEng Liverpool 1987; FRS 1976, FEng 1977, FIMechE; *Books* Axial Flow Compressors (1958), Axial Flow Turbines (1967), Actuator Disc Theory (1978), Cogeneration (1987); *Recreations* music, golf; *Clubs* Athenaeum, MCC; *Style*— Dr John Horlock; 2 The Ave, Ampthill, Beds MK45 2NR (☎ 0525 841307)

HORN, Hon Mrs (Angela Ierne Evelyn); *née* Dixon; da of late 1 Baron Glentoran; *b* 1907; *m* 1, 1929, Lt Cdr Peter Ross, RN (ka 1940), eldest s of Una Mary, Baroness de Ros, 26 holder of the peerage (d 1956) 2 da (incl late Georgina Angela, Baroness de Ros, *see* de Ros, 28 Baron); m 2, 1943 Lt Col Trevor Langdale Horn, MC, 16/5 Lancers (d 1966); 1 da (June Victoria Langdale b 1946); *Style*— The Hon Mrs Horn; Luckington Court, Chippenham, Wilts

HORN, Dr David Bowes; s of David Horn (d 1952), of Edinburgh, and Joan, *née* Milne (d 1989); *b* 18 Aug 1928; *Educ* Daniel Stewart's Coll Edinburgh, Heriot-Watt Univ Edinburgh (BSc), Univ of Edinburgh (PhD); *m* 5 Oct 1963, Shirley Kay, da of John Henry Riddell (d 1974), of Newcastle upon Tyne; 2 da (Kathryn b 1964, Jane b 1967); *Career* sr grade biochemist Western Infirmary Glasgow 1956-59 (with secondment to equip open and run new clinical chemical laboratory, Vale of Leven Hosp, Dunbartonshire), top grade biochemist Royal Victoria Infirmary Newcastle Upon Tyne 1964-66 (princ grade 1959-64), hon lectr in clinical biochemistry Univ of Newcastle 1963-66, head of Dept of Clinical Chemistry Edinburgh Northern Hosps Gp at Western Gen Hosp Edinburgh 1966-87, hon sr lectr in clinical chem Univ of Edinburgh 1966-87; memb Panel of Assessors for Top Grade Biochemist Appts Scot Home and Health Dept 1972-87, Lothian Health Bd: memb Area Scientific Servs Advsy Ctee 1974-79, Hepatitis Advsy Gp 1982-84, Advsy Gp on Genetic Servs 1985-87; CSTI: Registration Ctee of Scientists in Health Care 1979-86, Health Care Advsy Ctee 1985-88; memb: Dist Med Records Ctee 1975-83, Nat Consultative Ctee of Scientists in Professions Allied to Med 1975-79 (chm 1976-79), Computer Res Ctee of Chief Scientist Orgn 1976-83, Scientific Servs Advsy Gp 1977-79 (memb Sub Ctee in Clinical Chemistry 1973-79, chm Sub Ctee in Clinical Chemistry 1978-80), Assoc of Clinical Biochemists Cncl 1963-68 and 1978-80 (chm Scottish region 1978-80, hon treas 1964-68), Exam and Inst Ctee Royal Soc of Chemistry 1980-88 (rep on Jt Exam Bd for Mastership in Biochemistry 1973-88), Ethic Ctee Blood Transfusion Serv 1984-87; chm Div of Laboratory and Scientific Med N Lothian Dist 1975-79; FRSC 1961, FRCPath 1976, FRSE 1978, FIBiol 1989; *Recreations* walking, gardening; *Style*— Dr David B Horn; 2 Barnton Park, Edinburgh EH4 6JF (☎ 031 336 3444)

HORN, Donald Alexander; s of Alexander Henry Horn, of Invercargill, NZ, and Ruth Catherine, *née* Leonard; *b* 4 Jan 1944; *Educ* St Bedes Coll, Christ Church NZ; *m* 28 Dec 1967, Jean Ellen, da of Ernest Plumstead, of London; 3 da (Maria b 1969, Sarah b 1971, Julia b 1976); *Career* IBA 1965-: industl rels offr, dep head then head of personnel, head of personnel and admin, controller of admin 1991-; govr Barton Peveril Coll, external examiner Southampton Inst of Higher Educn; FIPM; *Recreations* music, theatre and travel; *Style*— Donald Horn, Esq; Independent Broadcasting Authority, 70 Brompton Rd, London SW3 1EY (☎ 071 584 7011, fax 071 584 3468, car 0836 207243)

HORN, Prof Gabriel; s of Abraham Horn (d 1946), of Birmingham, and Ann, *née* Grill (d 1976); *b* 9 Dec 1927; *Educ* Univ of Birmingham (BSc, MB ChB, MD), Univ of Cambridge (MA, ScD); *m* 1, 29 Nov 1952 (m dis 1979), Hon Anne Loveday Dean, da of Baron Soper (Life Peer), *qv*, of London, and Marie soper, *née* Dean; 2 s (Nigel b 1954, Andrew b 1960), 2 da (Amanda b 1953, Melissa b 1962); m 2, 30 Aug 1980, Priscilla, da of Edwin Victor Barrett (d 1976), of Cape Town, and Sarah Elizabeth, *née* McMaster (d 1989); *Career* Educn Branch RAF 1947-49; Univ of Cambridge: demonstrator and lectr in anatomy 1956-72, reader in neurobiology 1972-74, prof of zoology 1978-, head dept of zoology 1979-, fell King's Coll 1962-74 and 1978-; visiting prof Univ of California Berkeley USA 1963, visiting prof of zoology Makerere Univ Coll Uganda 1966, prof of anatomy and head of dept Univ of Bristol 1974-77, distinguished visiting prof Univ of Alberta 1988, visiting Miller prof Univ of California Berkeley 1989; memb: Biological Scis Advsy Panel and Ctee Scientific Res Cncl 1970-75, Res Ctee Mental Health Fndn 1973-78, Advsy Bd Inst of Animal Physiology Cambridge 1980-85; pubns in various scientific journals; FRS 1986, FInst Biology 1978; *Books* Memory, Imprinting and the Brain (1985), Short-term Changes in Neural Activity and Behaviour (jt ed 1970), Behavioural and Neural Aspects of Learning and Memory (jt ed 1991); *Recreations* riding, cycling, walking, listening to music, wine and conversation; *Style*— Prof Gabriel Horn; Jack of Clubs Barn, Fen Rd, Lode, Cambridgeshire CB5 9HE (☎ 0223 812 229), Univ of Cambridge, Department of Zoology, Downing St, Cambridge CB2 3EJ (☎ 0223 336 601, fax 0223 336 676, telex 81240 CAMSPL G)

HORN, Dr George; s of George Horn, MM (d 1937), of 5 Endcliffe Vale Ave, Sheffield, and Theodora, *née* Mason (d 1977); *b* 10 April 1928; *Educ* King Edward VII Sheffield, Univ of Sheffield (BSc, PhD, DSc); *m* 28 July 1951, Doreen, da of Edward Nash (d 1971), of Sheffield; 2 s (Christopher b 30 Oct 1954, Nicholas b 18 Jan 1957); *Career* 2 Lt 19 Air Formation Signal Regt Royal Signals 1948-49; res engr GEC Atomic Energy Div 1955-58, head of thermodynamics section CEGB Marchwood Engrg Laboratories 1958-65, head of engrg div GEGB Berkeley Nuclear Laboraties 1965-70, dep chm Ireland Alloys (Holdings) Ltd 1983 (gp tech dir 1970-89); author of over 40 scientific and tech papers; chm Advsy Ctee Dept of Chemical Engrg and Fuel Technol Univ of Sheffield 1989-; FInstE 1963, CEng 1968, MIMechE 1968, MInstMet 1975, AIME 1984, FIMechE 1990 (MIMechE 1968), EUR ING 1990, FRSA 1990; *Recreations* cricket, swimming, skiing; *Style*— Dr George Horn; 10 Fountain Craig, 1010 Gt Western Rd, Glasgow G12 0NR (☎ 041 334 1635); Ireland Alloys (Holdings) Ltd, P O Box 18, Hamilton, Scotland ML3 0EL (☎ 0698 822 246, fax 0698 825 167)

HORN, Hon Mrs (Mary Clare); *née* Douglas-Scott-Montagu; da of 2 Baron Montagu of Beaulieu, KCIE, CSI (d 1929); *b* 9 June 1928; *m* 1, 1953 (m dis 1968), David Bethune, Viscount Garnock (later 15 Earl of Lindsay) (d 1989); 1 s (16 Earl of Lindsay, *qv*), 1 da (Lady Caroline Wrey, *qv*); m 2, 1979, Timothy Charles Austin Horn; *Style*— The Hon Mrs Horn; Chapel House, Builth Wells, Powys (☎ 0982 560 236)

HORN, Trevor; s of Robert Horn, of Durham, and Elizabeth, *née* Lampton; *b* 15 July 1949; *Educ* Johnson GS; *m* 1980, Jill, da of David Sinclair; 1 s (Aaron b 15 Dec 1983), 2 da (Alexandra b 24 April 1982, Rebecca b 25 March 1990); *Career* record prodr; formerly vocalist of pop bands Buggles and Yes; fndr ZTT records, dir SPZ Group; past prodn credits incl: The Age of Plastic (Buggles 1980, Gold disc), Lexicon of Love (ABC 1982, Gold disc), Duck Rock (Malcolm McClaren 1983, Gold disc), 90125 (Yes, multi Platinum), Welcome To The Pleasure Dome (Frankie Goes To Hollywood, multi Platinum), Street Fighting Years (Simple Minds, Platinum disc), fndr memb and innovator Art of Noise; prodr of many other artists incl: Grace Jones, Spandau Ballet, Foreigner, Godley and Creme, Paul McCartney, Seal, Rod Stewart, Pet Shop Boys, Propaganda, Dollar; BPI Best Br prodr of the Year 1983 and 1985 (nominated 1983, 1984, 1985, 1986, 1987, 1988), Radio 1 award for contribution to pop music 1984; Ivor Novello awards: best recorded record for Owner of a Lonely Heart 1983, best contemporary song for Relax 1984, most performed work for Two Tribes 1984; BMI award for Owner of A Lonely Heart 1984, Grammy award best instrumental Cinema 90125; *Style*— Trevor Horn, Esq; Sarm Productions, 42-46 St Luke's Mews, London W11 1DG (☎ 071 221 5101, fax 071 221 3374)

HORNAK, Lady Patricia Sybil; *née* Douglas; da of 11 Marquess of Queensberry (d 1954); *b* 1918; *m* 1, 1938 (m dis 1950), Capt Count John Gerard de Bendern; 1 s, 2 da; m 2, 1954 (m dis 1960), Herman Hornak; 2 s; *Style*— Lady Patricia Hornak; 36 St James's Rd, Tunbridge Wells, Kent

HORNALL, Capt Robert William; DFC (1945); s of Archibald Hornall (d 1945), of Hamilton, Scotland, and Constance, *née* Troughton (d 1974); *b* 3 Nov 1922; *Educ* Hamilton Acad, Univ of Southampton; *m* 6 July 1945, Betty, da of Capt Sydney Arthur Farrow (d 1936), of Canvey Island, Essex; *Career* RAF 1940, awarded Wing's Moose Jaw Canada 1942, Fighter Cmd 1 Sqdn Acklington, Biggin Hill, Lympne, Martlesham Heath 1942-44, 245 Sqdn 2 TAF France, Belgium, Holland, Fl-Cdr 184 Sqdn 2 TAF Holland, Germany 1944-45, instr Ops Trg Unit 1945-46, demob 1946; Fl-Capt African routes Hunting-Clan 1947-55, sr vice-pres M East Airlines 1957-64 (ops mangr 1955-57), master air pilot 1965; memb: Bd of Dirs SITA 1958-64, Tech Ctee IATA 1959-64; special prod support exec Hawker Siddeley Aviation 1964-80, Br Aerospace 1980-86; tstee Amersham CC; memb; Amersham Soc, Thames & Chiltern C of C; Freeman City of London 1978, Liveryman Worshipful Co of Air Pilots and Air Navigators 1978; *Recreations* golf, rugby, racing, cricket; *Clubs* Bucks Co Rugby, Middx Co CC, RAF; *Style*— Capt Robert Hornall, DFC; 27 Whielden St, Old Amersham, Bucks HP7 OHU (☎ 0494 724728); Troika Consortium Ltd, 56 Abbey Gdns, London NW8 9AT (☎ 071 625 4597, fax 071 372 6056, telex 295528 FOSTAS G)

HORNBY, Sir Derek Peter; s of F N Hornby (d 1942), of Bournemouth, and Violet May, *née* Pardy; *Educ* Canford; *m* 20 Feb 1971, Sonia Margaret, da of Sidney Beesley (d 1985), of Birmingham; 2 s (Nicholas Peter John b 1957, Jonathan Peter b 1967), 2 da (Gillian Margaret b 1959, Victoria Jane b 1968); *Career* Mars Ltd 1960-64, Texas Instruments 1964-73, dir int operations Xerox Corp USA 1973-80, chm Rank Xerox UK Ltd 1984-90 (md Rank Xerox Servs Ltd 1980-84); chm: Br Overseas Trade Bd, ABSA, Savills, London & Edinburgh Insurance Group, Dixons plc, Astra Training; Liveryman Worshipful Co of Loriners; CBIM, FRSA, FIOD; kt; *Recreations* cricket, real tennis, theatre; *Clubs* Carlton, MCC, Leamington Real Tennis; *Style*— Sir Derek Hornby; Badgers Farm, Idlicote, Shipston on Stour, Warwickshire CV36 5DT (☎ 0608 61890); 11 St Catherines Mews, Milner St, London SW3 2PX (☎ 071 589 5765)

HORNBY, Derrick Richard; s of Richard Wittingham Hornby (d 1964); *b* 11 Jan 1926; *Educ* Southampton; *m* 1948, June, da of Nathaniel Steele (d 1963); *Career* md Edenvale (Express Dairy) 1968; chm: Carrington Viyella 1980, Spillers Foods Ltd 1973; *Recreations* golf, salmon fishing; *Style*— Derrick Hornby, Esq; 54 Cerne Abbas, The Avenue, Branksome Park, Poole, Dorset BH13 6HE

HORNBY, John Fleet; s of John Fleet Hornby, of Cumbria, and Marion, *née* Charnley (d 1981); *b* 23 Dec 1945; *Educ* Dowdales Co Sch Cumbria; *m* 1976, Elizabeth, da of John Chorley, of Cumbria; 1 s (Paul b 1978); *Career* CA; articled clerk R F Miller & Co 1963-68 (audit mangr 1968-69); James Fisher & Sons plc: accountant special duties 1969, asst co sec 1969-70, pa to MD 1970-71, group accountant 1971-78, divnl dir of fin 1978-81, fin dir 1981-86, commercial dir 1986-88, md 1988-89, chm and md 1989-; chm: Anchorage Ferrying Services Ltd, Shamrock Shipping Co Ltd, Westfield Shipping Co Ltd, R J Wood Newhaven Ltd, McArthur Morison & Co Ltd; dir: Anchorage Ferrying Services Ltd, Shamrock Shipping Co Ltd, Westfield Shipping Co Ltd, Onesimus Dorey (Shipowners) Ltd, Venisol Shipping Corp, Coe Metcalf Shipping Ltd, Mersey Offshore Services Ltd, R J Wood Newhaven Ltd, McArthur Morison & Co Ltd, Staria Shipping Inc (Panama); memb Cncl The Assoc of Employers of Members of The Former Registered Dock Workers Pension Fund; pres Barrow Chrysanthemum Soc, chm Governing Body Lindal & Marton Primary Sch, memb Governing Body Ulverston Victoria Sch; Freeman City of London, Liveryman Worshipful Co of Shipwrights (memb Charities Ctee); FCA 1968, FInstD; *Recreations* fell walking, fitness, travelling, reading; *Clubs* Royal Over-Seas; *Style*— John Hornby, Esq; Hillside, Guards Road, Lindal, nr Ulverston, Cumbria LA12 0TN (☎ 0229 65614); James Fisher and Sons plc, Fisher House, Barrow-in-Furness, Cumbria LA14 1HR (☎ 0229 22323, fax 0229 36761, telex 65163)

HORNBY, John Hugh; s of Richard Phipps Hornby, of Bowerchalke, Wilts, and Stella, *née* Hichens; *b* 23 Jan 1954; *Educ* Winchester, Univ of Exeter (BSc); *m* 18 June 1983, Anne Elizabeth Meredydd, da of George Hugh Kenefick Rae (d 1989); 2 s (David Hugh b 1988, Edward John b 1990); *Career* admitted slr 1980, ptnr Macfarlanes 1987 (joined 1977); *Recreations* most ball game sports, vocal classical music; *Clubs* Hurlingham; *Style—* John Hornby, Esq; 10 Norwich St, London EC4A 1BD (☎ 071 831 9222, fax 071 831 9607, telex 296381)

HORNBY, Richard Phipps; el s of Rt Rev Hugh Leyester Hornby, MC (d 1965), sometime Suffragan Bishop of Hulme (whose maternal grandmother Vere was da of Robert Gosling, DL, of Botley's Park Surrey, by Robert's w Georgina, da of Rt Hon John Sullivan and Lady Henrietta Hobart, 2 da of 3 Earl of Buckinghamshire), and Katherine Rebecca May (d 1979); *b* 20 June 1922; *Educ* Winchester, Trinity Coll Oxford (MA); *m* 1951, Stella, da of William Lionel Hichens, of North Aston Hall, Oxon; 3 s (John b 1954, Patrick b 1958, Simon b 1960), 1 da (Juliet b 1956); *Career* served WWII KRRC; asst master (history) Eton 1948-50; contested (C) Walthamstow W 1955 and 1956; MP (C) Tonbridge 1956-74, PPS to Duncan Sandys 1959-63, parly under-sec CRO and Cwlth Off 1963-64; with Unilever 1951-52; dir: J Walter Thompson 1974-81 (joined 1952), Cadbury Schweppes plc 1982-, McCorquodale plc 1982-; chm Halifax Bldg Soc 1983- (vice-chm 1981-83, dir 1976-); former memb: Gen Advsy Cncl BBC, Exec Ctee Br Cncl; *Recreations* most country pursuits, shooting, fishing, deer-stalking, hill walking, bird watching; *Clubs* Brooks's; *Style—* Richard Hornby, Esq

HORNBY, Sir Simon Michael; er s of Michael Charles St John Hornby (d 1987), of Pusey House, Faringdon, and Nicolette Joan, *née* Ward (d 1988); *b* 29 Dec 1934; *Educ* Eton, New Coll Oxford; *m* 15 June 1968, (Ann) Sheran, da of Peter Victor Ferdinand Cazalet, of Fairlawne, Tonbridge, Kent; *Career* 2 Lt Grenadier Gds 1953-55; W H Smith: joined 1958, merchandise dir 1968, retail dir 1974, retail md 1977, gp chief exec 1978, chm 1982; dir: Pearson plc 1978, Lloyds Bank plc 1988; tstee Br Museum 1975-85, chm Nat Book League 1978-80; memb: Property Ctee Nat Tst 1979-86 (Exec Ctee 1966-), RSA Cncl 1985-; chm: Design Cncl 1986-, Assoc of Business Sponsorship of the Arts 1988-; pres: Newsvendors' Benevolent Inst 1989, The Book Tst 1990; Freeman and Liveryman Worshipful Co of Goldsmiths 1955-; FBIM, FRSA; kt 1988; *Recreations* golf, gardening, music; *Clubs* Garrick; *Style—* Sir Simon Hornby; Lake House, Pusey, Faringdon, Oxon SN7 8QB; 8 Ennismore Gdns, London SW7 1NL; Strand House, 7 Holbein Place, London SW1W 8NR (☎ 071 730 1200, fax 071 730 1200 ext 5563, telex 887777 WHS G)

HORNBY PRIESTNALL, Cdr (Thomas) Keith; VRD (1963 and Clasp 1975); s of Rev Thomas Hornby Priestnall (d 1956), and Norah Hayward (d 1961); *b* 22 June 1925; *Educ* Burton Sch, Univ of Nottingham; *m* 2 Sept 1982, Gillian Christine, da of Police Supt William Edward Thomas Hinckley (d 1977), of Staffords; 1 da (Daniella b 1959); *Career* Cdr RNR, served WWII Midget Subs (X Craft); chm and md Salesprint and Display Ltd and Salesprint Temple Gp Ltd 1963-83, chm Peel House Publicity 1983-; vice pres E Midland Areas C of C; dir: Brewery Traders Pubns Ltd, Brewing and Distilling Int, Peel House Publicity Ltd; former chm and tstee Allied Brewery Traders' Assoc, chm Burton upon Trent & Uttoxeter SSAFA, pres Trg Ship Modwena Sea Cadet Corps; memb Inst of Brewing; *Recreations* riding, bird watching, sailing; *Clubs* Naval and Military, Army and Navy, The Burton, Inst of Dirs; *Style—* Cdr Keith Hornby Priestnall, VRD; The Old Rectory, Kedleston, Derbys (☎ 0332 841515); Peel House, Burton-upon-Trent, Staffs (☎ 0283 66784)

HORNE, Alistair Allan; s of late Sir (James) Allan Horne, and Auriol Camilla, *née* Hay; *b* 9 Nov 1925; *Educ* Jesus Coll Cambridge (MA), Le Rosey Switzerland, Millbrook USA; *m* 1, 1953 (m dis 1982), Renira Margaret, da of Adm Sir Geoffrey Hawkins, KBE, CB, MVO, DSC; 3 da; m 2, 1987, Sheelin Ryan Eccles; *Career* served RAF 1943-44, Coldstream Gds 1944-47, Capt attached to Intelligence Serv (ME); foreign corr Daily Telegraph 1952-55; founded Alistair Horne Res Fellowship in Modern History St Antony's Coll Oxford 1969 (supernumerary fell 1978-88, hon fell 1988-), fell Woodrow Wilson Centre Washington DC, USA 1980-81; contribs to a number of books and various periodicals; memb: Mgmnt Ctee Royal Literary Fund 1969-90, Franco-Br Cncl 1979-, Ctee of Mgmnt Soc of Authors 1979-81; tstee Imperial War Museum 1975-82; FRSL; *Publications* Back into Power (1955), The Land is Bright (1958), Canada and the Canadians (1961), The Price of Glory: Verdun 1916 (1962, Hawthornden Prize 1963), The Fall of Paris: The Siege and the Commune 1870-71 (1965), To Lose a Battle: France 1940 (1969), Death of a Generation (1970), The Terrible Year: The Paris Commune (1971), Small Earthquake in Chile (1972), A Savage War of Peace: Algeria 1954-62 (1972, Yorkshire Post Book of the Year Prize 1978, Wolfson Literary Award 1978), Napoleon Master of Europe 1805-07 (1979), The French Army and Politics 1870-1970 (1984), Macmillan 1894-1956, Vol I (1988), MacMillan 1957-86, Vol II (1989); *Recreations* skiing, gardening, painting, travel; *Clubs* Garrick, Beefsteak; *Style—* Alistair Horne, Esq; 21 St Petersburgh Place, London W2

HORNE, Barry; s of Clive Horne, of Clwyd, N Wales, and Mary, *née* Beal; *b* 18 May 1962; *Educ* Flint HS Clwyd, Univ of Liverpool (BSc, Football blue); *m* 1 July 1987, Lisa Ann, da of John Edwin Featherstone; *Career* professional footballer; amateur Rhyl 1983-84, 136 league appearances Wrexham 1984-87, 90 league appearances Portsmouth 1987-89, Southampton 1989-; 18 full caps Wales 1988-; Capt Liverpool Univ football team Univ Championships 1982; *Style—* Barry Horne, Esq; Southampton FC, The Dell, Milton Rd, Southampton, Hants S09 4XX (☎ 0703 220505)

HORNE, Christopher Malcolm; s of Gerald Fitzlait Horne (d 1970), and Dora, *née* Hartley; *b* 14 June 1941; *Educ* King Edward VI Chelmsford; *m* 12 Sept 1964, Christine Ann, da of Reginald Arthur Fradley (d 1985); 2 s (Darren James b 7 Feb 1968, Alec Gerald b 20 Jan 1970); *Career* Coutts & Co 1958-: head of personnel 1980-88, assoc dir 1980-89, sec of Bank 1988-, sr assoc dir 1989-; memb Vines Rochester URC; MInstD; *Recreations* golf, gardening, interest in most sports; *Clubs* Rochester & Cobham Park Golf; *Style—* Christopher Horne, Esq; Silver Birches, 151 Maidstone Rd, Chatham, Kent ME4 6JE (☎ 0634 847594); Coutts & Co, 440 Strand, London WC2R 0QS (☎ 071 379 6262)

HORNE, David Oliver; s of Herbert Oliver Horne, MBE (d 1946), and Edith Marion, *née* Sellers (d 1963); *b* 7 March 1932; *Educ* Fettes; *m* 6 June 1959, Joyce Heather, da of Lt-Col Gordon Bryson Kynoch, CBE, TD, of Skara Brae, Broomhill Rd, Keith, Banffshire, Scotland; 2 s (Richard b 24 July 1962, Douglas b 9 April 1970), 2 da (Angela b 17 May 1960, Susan b 2 June 1965); *Career* dir: S G Warburg & Co Ltd 1966-70, Williams & Glyns Bank 1970-78, Lloyds Bank Int 1978-85; chm and chief exec Lloyds Merchant Bank 1988- (md 1985-87); FCA 1958; *Recreations* golf; *Style—* David Horne, Esq; Four Winds, 5 The Gardens, Esher, Surrey KT10 8QF (☎ 0372 63510); 48 Chiswell St, London EC1Y 4XX (☎ 071 522 5000, fax 071 382 9803, car 0860 384430)

HORNE, Frederic Thomas; s of Lionel E Horne, JP (d 1953), of Moreton-in-Marsh, Glos, and Hilda Marsh, *née* Vaughan (d 1970); *b* 21 March 1917; *Educ* Chipping Campden GS; *m* 1944, Madeline, *née* Hatton; 2 s, 2 da; *Career* RAFVR 1939-55; admitted slr 1938; chief Taxing Master of the Supreme Ct, memb Lord Chancellors Advsy Ctee on Legal Aid; *Books* The Supreme Court Practice (co-ed, 1988), Atkins Court Forms (contrib 14 edn), Cordery on Solicitors (ed 8 edn); *Recreations* archaeology, cricket, grandchildren; *Clubs* MCC; *Style—* Frederic T Horne, Esq; Dunstall, 70 Quickley Lane, Chorleywood, Herts

HORNE, Geoffrey Norman; s of Albert Edward Horne (d 1982), of Berks, and Doris Irene, *née* Blackman; *b* 7 Feb 1941; *Educ* Slough GS, Open Univ (BA); *m* 1, 1967 (m dis 1977), Barbara Ann Mary; 1 s (Rupert b 1971); m 2, 1980, Davina Dorothy, da of David Lockwood London, of Dyfed; 2 s (Edward b 1984, Richard b 1986); *Career* in advertising; sr writer: CDP 1973-74, Davidson Pearce Berry and Spottiswoode 1974-77, Saatchi and Saatchi 1985-88; bd dir: KMP Partnership 1978-84 (creative dir 1977-84), Grandfield Rork Collins 1984-85 (creative gp head 1984-85), Saatchi and Saatchi 1985; over 60 advertising awards incl: Br Advertising Press awards, D and AD Assoc awards, NY One Show, Br Advertising TV awards, The Creative Circle; MIPA, MCAM; *Recreations* cooking, reading, travel; *Clubs* Phyllis Court; *Style—* Geoffrey Horne, Esq; Pine Ridge, 46 Altwood Rd, Maidenhead, Berks

HORNE, Sir (Alan) Gray Antony; 3 Bt (UK 1929), of Shackleford, Surrey; s of Antony Edgar Alan Horne (d 1954; only s of 2 Bt, Sir Alan Edgar Horne, MC, who died 1984), and Valentine Antonia, da of Valentine Dudensing, of Thenon, Dordogne, France and 55 East 57th St, New York City; *b* 11 July 1948; *m* 1980, Cecile Rose, da of Jacques Desplanche, of 5 rue de Cheverny, Romorantin, France; *Heir* none; *Style—* Sir Gray Horne, Bt; Château du Basty, Thenon, Dordogne, France

HORNE, Mark John Fraser; s of Maj Ian Hunter Horne, of Kelso, Roxburghshire, and Honor Nancy, *née* Humphries; *b* 5 Aug 1948; *Educ* The Oratory Sch, Heriot-Watt Univ Edinburgh; *m* 20 May 1976, Elizabeth Mary, da of Lt-Col Gwyn William Morgan-Jones (d 1964), and The Hon Lorraine, *née* Berry, of Tetbury, Gloucs; 1 s (Archie b 1985); *Career* owner of General Printing Co, previously dir M W Marshall (Int Money Brokers); *Recreations* racing (steward), tobogganing, shooting, fishing; *Clubs* White's, St Moritz Tobogganing; *Style—* Mark J F Horne, Esq; Laundry Hse, Adbury, Newbury, Berks; Midleton Est, Guildford, Surrey

HORNE, Dr Nigel William; s of Eric Charles Henry Horne (d 1963), and late Edith Margaret, *née* Boyd; *b* 13 Sept 1940; *Educ* Lower Sch of John Lyon Harrow, Univ of Bristol (BSc), Univ of Cambridge (PhD); *m* 30 Oct 1965, Jennifer Ann, da of William Henry Holton (d 1988); 1 s (Peter b 1970), 2 da (Catherine b 1967, Joanna b 1973); *Career* dir and gen mangr GEC Telecommunications Ltd 1976-81, md GEC Information Systems Ltd 1981-83; dir: Tech and Corp Devpt STC plc 1983-90, Abingworth plc 1985-1990; chm Info Technol Advsy Bd DTI 1988-; memb: Advsy Cncl on Sci and Technol, Cabinet Office, Esprit Advsy Bd Euro Cmmn; Freeman City of London; memb Guild of Info Technologists, FIIM 1979, FENG 1982, FRSA 1983, FIEE 1984; *Recreations* piano, music, gardening; *Clubs* United Oxford and Cambridge; *Style—* Dr Nigel Horne; IT Partner, KPMG Peat Marwick McLintock, 8 Salisbury Square, London EC4Y 8BB (☎ 071 236 8000)

HORNE, Robert Drake; s of Capt Harold Metcalfe Horne, RN (d 1960), and Dorothy Katharine, *née* Drake; *b* 23 April 1945; *Educ* Mill Hill Sch, Oriel Coll Oxford (BA); *m* 20 May 1972, Raymond Harold Gill, 3 da (Annabel Mary b 1974, Rachel Dorothy b 1977, Octavia Jane b 1981); *Career* DES: entered 1968, princ in Cabinet Office 1979-80, asst sec 1980-88, under sec and head Teachers' Pay and Gen Branch 1988-; *Recreations* entertaining Australians, running, gardening; *Style—* Robert Horne, Esq; Department of Education and Science, Elizabeth House, York Road, London SE1 7PH (☎ 071 934 9899, fax 071 934 9082)

HORNE, Prof (Charles Hugh) Wilson; s of Charles Hugh Wilson Horne (d 1977), and Jean, *née* Wells; *b* 13 Sept 1938; *Educ* Ardrossan Acad, Univ of Glasgow (MB ChB, MD), Univ of Aberdeen (DSc); *m* 5 Sept 1964, Agnes Irvine, da of Joseph Scott (d 1977); 1 s ((Charles Hugh) Wilson b 25 Oct 1969), 1 da (Glenda May b 16 Nov 1966); *Career* lectr in pathology Univ of Glasgow 1966-73, prof of immunopathology Univ of Aberdeen 1980-84 (sr lectr in pathology 1973-80), head of Sch of Pathological Sciences Univ of Newcastle upon Tyne 1988 (prof 1984-), and Novocastra Laboratories Newcastle upon Tyne 1989; author of numerous pubns on immunology and pathology; regnl advsr northern reg RCPath, memb Ctee Pathological Soc of GB and Ireland; FRCPath 1979; *Recreations* philately, golf; *Style—* Prof Wilson Horne; 7 Elmtree Grove, Gosforth, Newcastle upon Tyne NE3 4BG (☎ 091 284 8803); University Department of Pathology, Royal Victoria Infirmary, Queen Victoria Rd, Newcastle upon Tyne NE1 4LP (☎ 091 222 7144, fax 091 222 8100)

HORNE-ROBERTS, Jennifer; da of Frederick William Horne (d 1969), and Daisy Jessie Elizabeth, *née* Norman; *b* 15 Feb 1949; *Educ* State Schs NW London, Univ of Perugia (Dip Italian), Univ of London (BA); *m* 29 April 1987, Keith Michael Peter, s of Gerald Roberts (d 1962); 1 s (Harry Alexander b 29 June 1989), 1 da (Francesca Elizabeth b 24 July 1990); *Career* called to the Bar Middle Temple 1976, ad eundem memb Inner Temple; dir family Co; contrib pubns on: political issues, family law, employment law, human rights, literature; Parly candidate: (Lab) Fareham 1974, (Alliance) Medway 1987; cncllr Camden 1971-74; memb Bar Assocs: admin law, common law, family law; memb: Bar Euro Gp Justice and Amnesty Lawyers, Lib Democrats Lawyers Exec Ctee; former memb Young Bar Ctee chm Holborn and St Pancras Lib Democrats, prospective Parly candidate (Lib Democrats) Holborn and St Pancreas; *Books* Trade Unionists and the Law (1984); *Recreations* writing, visual and literary arts, politics (Liberal Democrat), travel; *Clubs* National Liberal, Highgate Golf, Arts, Dover Street; *Style—* Mrs Jennifer Horne-Roberts; 3 Paper Buildings, Temple EC4Y 7EU (☎ 071 583 1183, fax 071 583 2037, car 0831 251 390)

HORNER, Prof (Robert) Malcolm Wigglesworth; s of James William Horner (d 1986), and Emma Mary, *née* Wigglesworth (d 1977); *b* 27 July 1942; *Educ* Bolton Sch, UCL (BSc, PhD); *m* 21 March 1970, Beverley Anne, da of Ewart Alexander (d 1986); 1 s (Jonathan b 3 Oct 1980), 1 da (Victoria b 10 Sept 1977); *Career* Taylor Woodrow Construction Ltd: civil engr 1966-72, engrg rep W Germany 1972-74, site agent 1974-77; Univ of Dundee: lectr Dept Civil Engrg 1977-83, sr lectr 1983-86, head dept 1985-, prof engrg mgmnt 1986-; fndr chm Tayside branch Opening Windows on Engrg 1980-85, memb ICE Working Pty Strategy Construction Mgmnt Res 1987-89, chm Educn Ctee Engrg Cncl Regnl Orgn Mgmnt Ctee (E Scotland) 1988-; CEng, MICE, MBIM; *Recreations* gardening, amateur dramatics; *Clubs* Rotary; *Style—* Prof Malcolm Horner; Westfield Cottage, 11 Westfield Place, Dundee DD1 4JU, (☎ 0382 25933); Dept of Civil Engineering, The University, Dundee DD1 4HN, (☎ 0392 23181 ext 4350, telex 76293, fax 0382 201604)

HORNER, (William) Noel Arthur; s of William Arthur Horner, MBE (d 1984), of Derbys, and Kitty Barbara, *née* Tonkin; *b* 25 Dec 1942; *Educ* various GSs, Univ of Manchester (LLB); *m* 25 March 1967, Margaret Jean, da of Wilfred Teed Tayler (d 1978), of Exeter, Devon; 1 s (Julian b 1970), 3 da (Sally b 1968, Anna b 1978, Natasha b 1980); *Career* admitted slr 1969; ptnr: Amery Parkes and Co London 1969-72, Chellews St Ives 1973-77; princ Noel Horner 1977-; chllr Diocese of Damaraland-in-exile 1977-81; represented families of 2 decd lifeboatmen at Penlee Lifeboat Enquiry 1983; Ind Parly candidate St Ives 1983; *Recreations* music, history; *Clubs* Wig and Pen; *Style—* Noel Horner, Esq; c/o 73 Lemon St, Truro, Cornwall TR1 2PN (☎ 0872 71305)

HORNER, Stephen John; s of Harold Wallington Horner (d 1966), and Edith Harriet, *née* Spencer (d 1984); *b* 11 May 1944; *Educ* Radley; *m* 1968, Susanne Helen, da of John Basil Hancock (d 1983), 2 s (Simon Wallington b 1971, Edward John b 1975); *Career* fin dir Agar Cross & Co Ltd 1977-80, dir Westland Helicopters 1980-84, mangr aerospace div Midland Bank plc 1984-88, chief exec Kingsbridge Aviation 1988-90, dir Universal Aircraft Leasing Group; FCA, FBIM; MRAeS; *Recreations* fishing, farming, genealogy; *Clubs* Thames; *Style—* Stephen Horner Esq; Old Woodhayne Farm, Bishopswood, nr Chard, Somerset (☎ 046 034 342)

HORNER, Suzanne Jayne; da of Gordon Burgess, of 18 Newton Green, Leeds Rd, Wakefield, and Doreen, *née* Bolton; *b* 23 Feb 1963; *Educ* Wakefield Girls' HS, Loughborough Univ (BSc); *m* 19 Dec 1987, Richard Francis Horner, s of Francis Harold Horner, of 7 Reresby Crescent, Whiston, Rotherham, S Yorks; *Career* squash player; N of Eng open champion 1980-82, 1988 and 1989, Br Under 19 Champion 1982, world record for fastest official tournament victory 1986, semi finalist Br Closed Championships 1986 and 1987 (finalist 1989), quarter finalist Br Open Championships 1986 and 1987, (finalist 1990); open champion: Africa 1986 and 1987, Lee on Solent 1989, Swedish Open 1990, turned professional 1988, ranked 3 i England (7 in World), memb of three Eng World Championship Teams; *Clubs* Wakefield Squash, Huddersfield and Barnsley Squash; *Style—* Mrs Richard Horner

HORNSBY, Alan Kenneth; s of Harold Ernest Hornsby (d 1984), and Clarice Winifred Wilson (d 1979); *b* 17 Oct 1929; *Educ* Buckhurst Hill County HS; *m* 3 April 1954, Audrey Constance, da of Joseph Lister Brown (d 1967); 3 s (Trevor b 1957, Neil b 1958, Paul b 1961), 2 da (Julie b 1961, Alison b 1963); *Career* fin dir Smiths Industries plc 1976-89; FICA, fell Inst of Treasurers; *Recreations* tennis, golf; *Clubs* West Herts Tennis, West Herts Golf; *Style—* Alan Hornsby, Esq; Smiths Industries plc, 765 Finchley Rd, Childs Hill, Finchley, London NW11 8DS (☎ 081 458 3232, telex 925761)

HORNSBY, Dr Bevé; da of Lt Leonard William Hodges, RNAS (d 1917); *b* 13 Sept 1915; *Educ* St Felix Sch Southwold Suffolk, Univ of London (MSc, PhD), Univ Coll N Wales (M Ed); *m* 1, 14 July 1939, Capt Jack Myddleton Hornsby (d 1975), s of Maj Frederick Myddleton Hornsby, CBE (d 1931), of Millfield, Stoke D'Abernon, Surrey; 3 s (Michael b 1942, Peter b 1943, Christopher b 1948), 1 da (Julie b 1947); m 2, 21 Dec 1976 (m dis 1986), John Hillyard Tennyson Barley; *Career* ambulance driver FANY and Mechanised Tport Corps 1939-42, Pilot Civil Air Gd 1938-39; head of Speech Therapy Clinic Kingston 1969-71, head of remedial teaching St Thomas's Hosp 1970-71, teacher World Blind Clinic St Bartholomew's Hosp 1969-71, head Dyslexia Dept St Barts Hosp 1971-80, dir Hornsby Centre for Learning Difficulties 1980-, princ Hornsby House Sch 1987-; govr All Farthing Primary Sch Wandsworth, memb Wandsworth Common Mgmnt Ctee; hon fell: Coll of Speech Therapists, 1988, Br Dyslexia Assoc 1987; AFBPsS 1983, Chartered Psychologist; *Books* Alpha to Omega - The A to Z of Teaching Reading, Writing and Spelling (1974), Alpha to Omega Flash Cards (1975), Overcoming Dyslexia (1984), Before Alpha - A Pre-Reading Programme for the Under-Fives (1989), Alpha to Omega Activity Pack (1990); *Recreations* riding, sailing, golf, reading, walking, theatre, music; *Clubs* Royal Wimbledon Golf; *Style—* Dr Bevé Hornsby; The Hornsby Centre, 71 Wandsworth Common Westside, London SW18 2ED (☎ 071 871 2691/1092, fax 071 871 1092)

HORNSBY, Lady Elizabeth Anne Mary (Rufus); *née* Isaacs; da of 2 Marquess of Reading, GCMG, CBE, MC, TD, PC, QC, and Hon Eva Mond, CBE, JP, da of 1 Baron Melchett; *b* 11 Oct 1921; *m* 1945, Maj Derek Hornsby (d 1971), s of Maj Frank Hornsby (d 1935), and Hon Muriel Strutt, yst da of 2 Baron Belper, JP, DL; 2 s (Richard Gerald, m 1980, Maria Lara; 1 s (Simon b 1983, 1 da Rachael b 1982); David Julian, m 1975, Julie Ann Witford; 3 s (Alexander b 1977, Samuel b 1985 Michael b 1987)); *Career* Jr Cdr ATS WWII; *Style—* The Lady Elizabeth Hornsby; Flat K, 19 Warwick Square, London SW1 (☎ 071 821 7051)

HORNSBY, Timothy Richard; s of Harker William Hornsby (d 1973), and Agnes Nora Phillips; *b* 22 Sept 1940; *Educ* Bradfield, Ch Ch Oxford (MA); *m* 1971, Charmian Rosemary, da of Frederick Cleland Newton, of Weybridge; 1 s (Adrian b 1977), 1 da (Gabrielle b 1975); *Career* res lectr Christ Church Oxford 1964-65, HM Treasy 1971-73, dir ancient monuments historic bldgs and rural affrs DoE 1983-88, DG Nature Conservancy Cncl 1988-91; *Recreations* skiing; *Clubs* Athenaeum; *Style—* Timothy Hornsby, Esq; Nature Conservancy Council, Northminster House, Peterborough PE1 1UA (☎ 0733 340345)

HORNTVEDT, Kristoffer Charles (Kit); s of Lt Cdr Kjell Horntvedt, R Nor N, of Bergen, Norway, and Yvonne, *née* Carter; *b* 29 June 1946; *Educ* Barnstaple GS, Univ of Sussex (BA), Brandeis Univ Mass USA (Wien International Scholar); *m* 1970, Sally Ann, da of Shepherd Mead; *Career* advtg exec Lintas London 1969-76, dir of Ayer Barker (pt of Charles Barker Group) 1976-84, client service dir McAvoy Wreford Bayley (pt of Valin Pollen Group) 1984-86, fndr Horntvedt Associates 1986-; MIPR 1990; *Recreations* reading, church re-building, gardening, electric keyboard; *Clubs* Hurlingham; *Style—* Kit Horntvedt, Esq; Horntvedt Associates Ltd, The Power House, Alpha Place, Flood St, Chelsea, London SW3 5SZ (☎ 071 376 7611, fax 071 351 2951)

HORNYOLD, Antony Frederick; Marchese (of the Habsburg cr, and of the Papal cr) di Gandolfi (Emperor Charles V 1529, Pope Leo XIII 1895), Duca di Gandolfi (Pope Leo XIII 1899); s of Ralph Gandolfi-Hornyold (d 1938), s of Thomas Gandolfi-Hornyold, cr *Marchese* Gandolfi by Pope Leo XIII 1895 and *Duca* 1899, Thomas being in his turn s of John Vincent Gandolfi-Hornyold (12 *Marchese* di Gandolfi, of the cr of Emperor Charles V of 1529, according to Ruvigny), whose mother Teresa was sis of Thomas Hornyold, then sr male rep of the old Hornyold recusant family (Teresa and Thomas's aunt by marriage was Mrs Fitzherbert, whom George IV, when Prince of Wales, m in contravention of the Royal Marriages Act); *b* 20 June 1931; *Educ* Ampleforth, Trinity Coll Cambridge; *Heir* bro, Simon Hornyold (b 11 Feb 1933, educ Ampleforth, residence: 271 Sandycombe Rd, Richmond, Surrey); *Career* FO 1957-67 (1 sec Rawalpindi 1966-67), MOD 1967-90; Kt of SMOM; *Style—* Antony Hornyold, Esq; Blackmore House, Hanley Swan, Worcester WR8 0ES (☎ 0684 310202)

HORNYOLD-STRICKLAND, Angela Mary; *née* Engleheart; DL (Cumbria 1988); da of Francis Henry Arnold Engleheart (d 1963), and Filumena Mary, *née* Mayne (d 1983); *b* 31 May 1928; *Educ* New Hall Convent, St Mary's Convent Ascot; *m* 20 Jan 1951, Lt Cdr Thomas Henry Hornyold-Strickland, RN, 7 Count della Catena (d 1983), s of Henry Hornyold-Strickland (d 1975), of Kendal, Cumbria; 4 s (Henry b 1951, Robert b 1954, John b 1956, Edward b 1960), 2 da (Clare b 1953, Alice b 1959); *Career* pres: Br Red Cross Soc Westmorland 1972-74, Cumbria 1974-; vice pres Cumbria Assoc of Boys' Clubs 1975-, memb Bd Catholic Caring Servs (Diocese of Lancaster); *Clubs* Naval and Military; *Style—* Mrs Thomas Hornyold-Strickland (Dowager Countess della Catena, DL); Sizergh Castle, Kendal, Cumbria (☎ 05395 60285)

HORNYOLD-STRICKLAND, 8 Count Della Catena (Malta 1745) Henry Charles; s of Lt Cdr Thomas Henry Hornyold-Strickland, DSC, RN, 7 Count della Catena (d 1983), of Sizergh Castle, Kendal, Cumbria, and Angela Mary, *née* Engleheart; *b* 15 Dec 1951; *Educ* Ampleforth, Exeter Coll Oxford (BA), INSEAD Fontainebleau (MBA); *m* 1979, Claudine Thérèse, da of Clovis Poumirau, of Etche Churia, Av Des Piballes, Hossegor 40200, France; 2 s (Hugo b 1979, Thomas b 1985); *Career* ind mgmnt conslt 1984-; former mgmnt conslt Arthur D Little Ltd (1977-84), product support planning engr Rolls Royce Ltd (1973-76); dir: Allied Newspapers Ltd (Malta) 1988, Progress Press (Malta) 1988; Kt of Honour and Devotion SMOM 1977; *Style—* Henry Hornyold-Strickland, Esq (Count della Catena); 56 Ladbroke Rd, London W11 3NW (☎ 071 229 1949); Sizergh Castle, Kendal, Cumbria LA8 8AE (☎ 05395 60285)

HOROVITZ, Joseph; s of Dr Bela Horovitz (d 1955), and Lotte, *née* Beller; *b* 26 May 1926; *Educ* City of Oxford HS, New Coll Oxford (MA, BMus); *m* 16 Aug 1956, Anna Naomi, da of Frederic Moses Landau, of London; 2 da; *Career* WWII Army Educn Corps 1943-44; music dir Bristol Old Vic 1949-51, conductor Ballet Russes 1952, music staff Glyndebourne Opera 1956, prof of composition RCM 1961-, dir Performing Rights Soc 1969-, pres Conseil International des Auteurs de Musique 1981-89; winner: Cwlth Medal for Composition 1959, Ivor Novello Award 1976 and 1979; compositions incl: 16 ballets incl Alice in Wonderland, two one act operas, five string quartets, eight concertos, works for orchestra brass band and choirs incl Capt Noah and his Floating Zoo; Son et Lumière incl: St Paul's Cathedral, Canterbury Cathedral, Royal Pavilion Brighton, Chartwell; numerous TV scores incl: Search for the Nile, Lillie, The Tempest, Twelfth Night, Agatha Christie Series, Dorothy L Sayers series, Rumpole of the Bailey; memb: Royal Soc of Musicians 1968, Cncl Composers Guild of GB 1970; FRCM 1981; *Recreations* books; *Style—* Joseph Horovitz, Esq; The Royal College of Music, Prince Consort Rd, London SW7

HORRELL, John Ray; CBE (1979), TD (1960), DL (Hunts and Peterborough 1973); s of Harry Ray Horrell (d 1963), of Westwood, Peterborough, and Phyllis Mary, *née* Whittome; *b* 8 March 1929; *Educ* Wellingborough Sch; *m* 26 March 1951, Mary Elizabeth (Betty) Noëlle, da of Arthur Thomas Dickinson (d 1984), of Northorpe Hall, nr Gainsborough; 1 s (Peter Geoffrey Ray b 23 Feb 1952), 1 da (Judith Carolyn (Mrs Drewer) b 23 April 1954); *Career* Maj TA (ret); farmer; dir: Horrell's Farmers Ltd, Horrell's Dairies Ltd; memb Cambridgeshire (formerly Huntingdon and Peterborough) CC 1965- (chm 1971-77); chm: ACC 1981-83, E Anglia TA & VR Assoc 1986-, E of England Agric Soc 1984-87; memb Peterborough New Town Devpt Corp 1969-88, md East Anglia RHA 1986-; FRSA; *Recreations* country pursuits; *Clubs* Farmers'; *Style—* John Horrell, Esq, CBE, TD, DL; The Grove, Longthorpe, Peterborough, Cambs PE3 6LZ (☎ 0733 262618)

HORRELL, Roger William; CMG (1988), OBE (1974); s of William John Horrell (d 1980), and Dorice Enid, *née* Young; *b* 9 July 1935; *Educ* Shebbear Coll, Exeter Coll Oxford (MA); *m* 1970 (m dis 1975), Patricia Mildred Eileen Smith, *née* Binns; 1 s (Oliver b 1972), 1 da (Melissa b 1973); *Career* Nat Serv Devonshire Regt 1953-55; Overseas Civil Serv Kenya 1959-64; Dip Serv: FCO 1964, econ offr Dubai 1965-67, FCO 1967-70, Kampala 1970-73, FCO 1973-76, Lusaka 1976-80, cnsllr FCO 1980-; *Recreations* walking, bridge, reading, cricket spectator; *Clubs* Reform; *Style—* Roger Horrell, Esq, CMG, OBE; c/o FCO, King Charles St, London SW1 (☎ 071 270 3000)

HORROCKS, Peter Leslie; s of Arthur Edward Leslie Horrocks, of Beaconsfield, Bucks, and Phillis Margaret Chiene, *née* Bartholomew; *b* 31 Jan 1955; *Educ* Winchester, Trinity Hall Cambridge (MA); *Career* called to the Bar Middle Temple 1977 and Lincoln's Inn 1987, in private practice 1978-; memb Cncl: Sherlock Holmes Soc of London 1984-87 and 1990-, Royal Stuart Soc 1987-; Freeman City of London 1982; FRAS 1984; *Recreations* travel, real tennis, cricket, Sherlock Holmes, opera, collecting books, dancing the minuet; *Clubs* MCC, Royal Tennis Court; *Style—* Peter Horrocks, Esq; 22 Old Buildings, Lincoln's Inn, London WC2A 3UJ (☎ 071 831 0222, fax 071 831 2239)

HORROCKS, Raymond; CBE (1983); s of Cecil Horrocks (d 1933), and Elsie Horrocks; *b* 9 Jan 1930; *Educ* Bolton Municipal Secdy Sch, Wigan Technical Coll, Univ of Liverpool; *m* 1953, Pamela Florence, *née* Russell; 3 da (Susan, Lynn, Raina); *Career* HM Forces Army Intelligence Corps 1948-50; mgmnt trainee Textile Indust (Bolton and Manchester) 1950-51, sales rep Proctor and Gamble 1951-52, merchandiser Marks and Spencer 1953-58, buying controller Littlewoods Mail Order Stores 1958-63, mangr Ford Motor Co 1968-72 (depot mangr replacement parts 1963, mangr warranty and customer rels 1964, mangr car supply 1965, divnl mangr engine and special equipment operations 1966), regnl dir (Europe and ME) Materials Handling Gp 1972-77, chm and chief exec BL Cars Ltd 1981-82 (dep md 1977-78, chm and md Austin Morris Ltd 1978-80, md BL Cars 1980-81, bd of dirs BL Cars Ltd 1981-); chm: Unipart Gp Ltd 1981-86, Jaguar Cars Hldgs Ltd 1982-84; chm and chief exec ARG Hldgs Ltd 1981-, dir Nuffield Servs Ltd 1982-; non-exec dir: The Caravan Club 1983-, Jaguar plc 1984-85, Image Interiors (Wessex) Ltd 1985-; memb: CBI Cncl 1981-86, CBI Europe Ctee 1985-86; tstee Br Motor Ind Heritage Tst 1983-; chm: Exide Europe 1986-, Owen Ball Ltd 1987-; FIMI, CBIM, FRSA; *Recreations* fly fishing, steam trains, gardening, caravanning; *Style—* Ray Horrocks, Esq, CBE; Far End, Riverview Rd, Pangbourne, Reading, Berks RG8 7AU; BL plc, 106 Oxford Rd, Uxbridge, Middlesex UB8 1EH (☎ 0895 51177, telex 264654)

HORROX, Alan Stuart; s of Stanley Horrox, and Gudrun Horrox; *b* 3 Jan 1947; *Educ* St Johns Leatherhead, Christ's Coll Cambridge; *m* Viveka Britt Inger, da of Torsten Nyberg, of Fölinge, Sweden; 2 da (Anna Helga b 1981, Katarina b 1983); *Career* prodr-dir: childrens' progs BBC, educn progs, dramas and documentaries Thames TV (controller children's and educn dept 1986-); televised work incl: Our People, Small World, Accidental Death of an Anarchist, A Foreign Body, Voices in the Dark, The Belle of Amherst, Rose, The Gemini Factor, Catherine, Ingmar Bergman-The Magic Lantern, The Thief, Young Charlie Chaplin, The Green Eyed Monster, Brief Lives, Rosie The Great, Somewhere to Run, Handle with Care, Spatz, Lorna Doone, Forget About Me, Long Way Home, The Strangers, Sea Dragon, A Small Dance; Int Emmy 1987, Special Jury Award at the San Francisco Film Festival 1988, Valladolid Int Film Festival award 1988 (for best documentary), Special Prize for fiction at the Prix Europa 1988 and 1989, Prime Time Emmy Nomination 1989, BAFTA Nomination 1989, Chicago Int Film Festival Special Live Action Award 1990, BAFTA Nomination 1990, RTS Enid Love Award Nomination 1989/90, London Film Festival Screening 1990 (for Forget About Me); *Style—* Alan S Horrox, Esq; Thames TV, 149 Tottenham Court Rd, London W1 (☎ 071 387 9494)

HORSBRUGH, Ian Robert; s of Walter Horsbrugh (d 1973), and Sheila May, *née* Beckett-Overy; *b* 16 Sept 1941; *Educ* St Paul's, Guildhall Sch of Music and Drama, RCM; *m* 10 July 1965, Caroline Wakeling, da of Dr Alan Everett (d 1987); 2 s (Benedict b 1967, Matthew b 1972), 2 da (Lucy b 1968, Candida b 1970); *Career* head of music: St Mary's Sch Hendon 1969-72, Villiers HS Southall 1972-79; dep warden ILEA Music Centre 1979-85, vice dir RCM 1985-88, princ Guildhall Sch of Music and Drama 1988-; memb: Music Advsy Panel Arts Cncl of GB 1981-86, Music Ctee Br Cncl 1988-; Freeman City of London 1989; FRCM 1988, FGSM 1988, ISM 1981, FRSA; *Books* Leoš Janáček - The Field that Prospered (1981); *Recreations* watching sports, walking, reading; *Clubs* MCC; *Style—* Ian Horsbrugh, Esq; Guildhall School of Music and Drama, Barbican, London EC2Y 8DT (☎ 071 628 2571)

HORSBRUGH, Oliver Bethune; s of Archibald Walter Bethune Horsbrugh (d 1973), of Chelsea, Kensington and Richmond, and Sheila May, *née* Beckett-Overy; *b* 13 Nov 1937; *Educ* St Pauls; *m* 6 Oct 1962, Josephine Elsa, *née* Hall; 1 s (Edward b 8 Feb 1966), 1 da (Rebecca b 1 Feb 1969); *Career* Nat Serv RN 1956-58; TV 1958-: BBC TV staff dir 30 minute theatres Newcomers and Boy Meets Girl 1968-; freelance TV dir 1971- incl: Z Cars, The Brothers, Crown Court, Coronation Street, A Kind of Loving, Cribb, Fallen Hero, Bergerac, Juliet Bravo, The Gibraltar Inquest,

Birmingham 6 Appeal; dir: various corp videos, trg films, ITN bulletins; memb Dir's Guild of GB, BAFTA, GSM 1957; *Recreations* sport, photography, enjoying food and wine, visiting the cinema and theatre, history of cinema buildings; *Style—* Oliver Horsbrugh, Esq; 126 Hampton Rd, Twickenham, Middlesex TW2 5QR (☎ 081 894 6012)

HORSBRUGH, Prof Patrick Bethune; s of Charles Bethune Horsbrugh (d 1952), of Blessington House, Hillsborough, Co Down, NI, and Marion Rose, *née* McQueen (d 1959); *b* 21 June 1920; *Educ* Canford, AA Sch of Architecture (Dip), Univ of London (Dip), Harvard Univ Graduate Sch of Design; *Career* Nat Serv TA RA 1938-40, coastal cmd pilot RAF 1940-46; George Kadleigh Architects: designer High Paddington 1951, New Barbican Ctee Project, City of London co-designer 1954, Ministerial Appeal; federal capital proposals for Pakistan and Burma, Raglan Squire & Ptnrs 1956; visiting critic: Harvard Graduate Sch of Design 1956, Univ of Illinois, Univ of N Carolina 1957-58; dir Hamilton-Wentworth Planning Area Ontario Canada 1960 (dep dir 1959); prof of architecture: Univ of Nebraska 1961-65, Univ of Texas 1965-67, Univ of Notre Dame Indiana; memb AIA Ctee on Urban Regnl and Environmental Planning 1969-90; fndr Environic Fndn Int Inc 1970, memb Advsy Cncl Indiana State Bd of Educn 1986, memb VP Tunnel Assoc 1986; conslt in environic design, geotecture, thalatecture, syneotectural design and syneocopolitan planning; speaker at various int environmental and architectural conferences; memb: Soc for Preservation of Ancient Monuments, The Georgian Gp, The Irish Georgian Soc, Br Interplanetary Soc, Airship Assoc, Channel Tunnel Assoc, Inst for Earth Mysteries Studies, American Planners Assoc, American Soc of Landscape Architects, American Soc of Interior Designers, Nat Tst, Nat Tst for Historical Preservation, Environic Fndn Int Inc; memb RIBA, MRTPI, AICP, APA, FAIA, FRGS, FRSA, FBIS, Hon ASIP, Hon ASLA; *Books* High Building in the United Kingdom (1952), Pittsburgh Perceived, The Form, Features and Feasibilities of the Prodigious City (1963), Texas Conference on Our Environmental Crisis (ed, 1966); *Recreations* watercolour painting, music, literature, history, wildlife, travel, conviviality; *Clubs* Cosmos (Washington, DC); *Style—* Prof Patrick Horsbrugh; Environic Foundation International Inc, 916 St Vincent St, South Bend, Indiana 46617, USA (☎ 010 1 219 233 3357)

HORSBRUGH-PORTER, Sir John Simon; 4 Bt (UK 1902), of Merrion Sq, City and Co of Dublin; s of Col Sir Andrew Marshall Horsbrugh-Porter, DSO, 3 Bt (d 1986); *b* 18 Dec 1938; *Educ* Winchester, Trinity Coll Cambridge; *m* 18 July 1964, Lavinia Rose, 2 da of Ralph Meredyth Turton, of Kildale Hall, Whitby; 1 s (Andrew), 2 da (Anna b 1965, Zoe b 1967); *Heir* s, Andrew Alexander Marshall b 1971; *Career* served Nat Serv, 2 Lt 12 Lancers (Germany and Cyprus) 1957-59; schoolmaster; *Recreations* hunting, gliding, music, literature; *Style—* Sir John Horsbrugh-Porter, Bt; Bowers Croft, Coleshill, Amersham, Bucks HP7 0LS (☎ 0494 724596)

HORSBRUGH-PORTER, Mary, Lady; (Annette) Mary; *née* Browne-Clayton; o da of Brig-Gen Robert Clayton Browne-Clayton, DSO; *b* 28 April 1908; *Educ* Cheltenham Ladies Coll; *m* 21 April 1933, Col Sir Andrew Marshall Horsbrugh-Porter, 3 Bt, DSO and Bar (d 1986); 1 s (Sir John Simon, 4 Bt, b 1938), 2 da (Susan b 1936, Caroline Elaine, b 1940); *Recreations* gardening, writing; *Style—* Mary, Lady Horsbrugh-Porter; Lime Close, Lower Park St, Stow-on-the-Wold, Glos

HORSEMAN, Richard; s of Edward Victor Horseman (d 1963), and Helen Horseman (d 1964); *b* 2 Nov 1929; *Educ* Alcester GS (NDA, CDA); *m* 20 March 1954, Heather, da of Eric Winter, JP (d 1987); 4 da (Jane b 1955, Elizabeth b 1956, Dorothy b 1958, Wendy b 1961); *Career* experimental offr Agric Res Cncl 1964-66, mangr SW Area Fisons Gp 1966-78, md Int Furniture Agencies 1979-; Malaya Medal 1954; *Recreations* fishing, wine tasting, travel; *Style—* Richard Horseman, Esq; 63 Brontonfield Drive, Bridge of Farm, Perth PH2 9PP

HORSEY, Gordon; s of Edgar William Horsey, MBE, and Henrietta Victoria Horsey; *b* 20 July 1926; *Educ* Magnus GS, St Catharine's Coll Cambridge (BA, LLB); *m* 8 June 1951, Jean Mary, da of Harold Favill; 1 da (Rebecca Jane b 12 Dec 1957); *Career* WWII naval airman RN 1944-45, Capt RE 1946-48; slr in private practice 1953-70; registrar: Coventry County Ct 1971-73, Leicester County Ct 1973-90; rec Crown Ct 1978-84, dist judge 1991-; memb Law Soc; *Recreations* fly fishing; *Style—* Gordon Horsey, Esq; 23 The Ridgeway, Rothley, Leics LE7 7LE (☎ 0533 302545)

HORSEY, John Sebastian Norman James; s of Rev Frank Bokenham Horsey (d 1970), of Broadwindsor, Dorset, and Maria Luisa de Montezuma (d 1973); *b* 26 Nov 1938; *Educ* St John's Sch Leatherhead, City Univ London (Dip in Horology and Instrument Technol); *m* 1 (m dis); 3 s (Jonathan Charles b 25 Dec 1964, Guy Anthony b 29 July 1966, Mark Edward b 14 Sept 1968), 1 da (Charlotte Rosemary Louise b 23 June 1973), 1 step s (Thomas Duncan Stewart b 20 Feb 1972); m 2, 28 Oct 1978 (Eveline) Theresa Paton, da of Dr Edward Harry Stewart Weston (d 1978), of Charter Alley, Hampshire; 1 s (Oliver George Sebastian b 10 Dec 1979), 1 da (Natasha Annabel Clare b 13 April 1985); *Career* admitted slr 1966; memb Bd W Berkshire Housing Assoc, memb Parochial Church Cncl St Katharine's Savernake Forest; memb Law Soc 1966, memb IOD; *Recreations* music, skiing, tennis, shooting; *Style—* John Horsey, Esq; Durley House, Savernake, Marlborough, Wiltshire SN8 3AZ (☎ 0672 810217); 6 West Mills, Newbury, Berkshire (☎ 0635 523344, fax 0635 523444, car 0836 773251)

HORSFALL, Edward John Wright; s and h of Sir John Musgrave Horsfall, MC, TD, 3 Bt; *b* 17 Dec 1940; *Educ* Uppingham; *m* 1965, Rosemary, da of Frank N King, of East Morton, Keighley; 3 s; *Style—* Edward Horsfall Esq; Long Thatch, Uffington, Faringdon, Oxon SN7 7RP

HORSFALL, Sir John Musgrave; 3 Bt (UK 1909), MC (1946), TD (1949, and clasp 1951), JP (N Yorks 1959); s of Sir (John) Donald Horsfall, 2 Bt (d 1975); *b* 26 Aug 1915; *Educ* Uppingham; *m* 1940, Cassandra Nora Bernardine, da of late George Wright, of Brinkworth Hall, Elvington, York; 2 s, 1 da; *Heir* s, Edward Horsfall; *Career* late Maj Duke of Wellington's (W Riding) Regt, served 1939-45 war in Burma; Lloyds underwriter; gen cmmr of Taxes 1964-90; former dir: Skipton Building Society, John C Horsfall and Sons Ltd, Bradford Wool Exchange; dir Worsted Spinners Fedn 1954-80; memb: Bradford A Gp Hosp Mgmnt Ctee 1952-69, Skipton Rural DC 1952-74, Wool and Allied Textile Employer Cncl 1957-75, Wool Textile Delgn 1957-75; pres Skipton Div Cons Assoc 1966-79; *Style—* Sir John Horsfall Bt, MC, TD, JP; Greenfield House, Embsay, Skipton, N Yorks (☎ 0756 794560)

HORSFALL TURNER, Jonathan; s of Harold Horsfall Turner, CBE (d 1981), and Eileen Mary, *née* Jenkins; *b* 27 Nov 1945; *Educ* The Kings Sch Canterbury, Gonville and Caius Coll Cambridge (MA); *m* 25 Aug 1973, Yvonne Roberts, da of Angus Munro Thomson (d 1971); 1 da (Olivia Jane b 1980); *Career* admitted slr 1970; ptnr Allen and Overy 1973-; carried out res on Eng Mediaeval Graffiti of Canterbury Cathedral 1963-67 (manuscripts in cathedral library and results published by Canterbury Cathedral Chronicles); Freeman Worshipful Co of Slrs 1973; memb Law Soc 1970; *Recreations* architecture, antiques, opera, canals; *Clubs* Garrick; *Style—* Jonathan Horsfall Turner, Esq; Greenwich, London; Palace St, Canterbury

HORSFIELD, Maj-Gen David Ralph; OBE; s of Maj Ralph Beecroft Horsfield (d 1966), and Morah Susan Stuart, *née* Baynes (d 1980); *b* 17 Dec 1916; *Educ* Oundle, RMA Woolwich, Univ of Cambridge (MA); *m* 1948, Sheelah Patricia Royal, da of Thomas George Royal Eagan (d 1970); 2 s (Crispin b 1952, Hugo b 1955), 2 da (Antonia b 1954, Claudia b 1957); *Career* cmmnd Royal Signals 1936, WWII served in Egypt, Burma, Assam, India; cmd Burma Corps Signals 1942, instr Staff Coll Quetta 1944-45, cmd 2 Indian Airborne div Signals 1946-47, instr RMA Sandhurst 1950-53 (co cmd to HM King Hussein of Jordan), cmd 2 div Signal Regt 1956-59, princ Army Staff Offr MOD Malaya 1959-61, dir Telecommunications (army) 1966-68, ADC to HM The Queen 1968-69, dep Communications and Electronics SHAPE 1968-69, Maj-Gen 1969, chief Signal Offr BAOR 1969-72 (ret); dir Rollalong Ltd 1965-76, assoc conslt PA Management Consultants 1972-87; vice pres Nat Ski Fdn; MIOD; *Recreations* house and garden, skiing (Br Champion 1949); *Clubs* Ski Club of Great Britain, Hawks; *Style—* Maj-Gen David Horsfield, OBE; Southill House, Cranmore, Shepton Mallet, Somerset BA4 4QS (☎ 074 988 395)

HORSFIELD, Dr Dorothy; da of Cyril Gordon Horsfield (d 1968), and Mabel, *née* Berry (d 1981); *b* 24 Nov 1932; *Educ* Crossley and Porter Sch Halifax, Royal Free Hosp Sch of Med London (MB BS); *Career* sr house offr Royal Free Hosp 1960-61, registrar clinical pathology Guys Hosp 1963-66, lectr chemical pathology Nat Hosp for Nervous Diseases 1966-72, sr registrar chemical pathology Hammersmith Hosp 1975-76, conslt chemical pathologist Barnsley Dist Gen Hosp 1977-; memb CLA; conservation projects with: Countryside Cmmn, York Co Stand, York Racecourse, Yorks Agric Soc, NFU; FRSM 1961, ACP 1967, memb BMA 1979, FRCPath 1984; *Recreations* organic and compassionate farming, races, needlework, music; *Clubs* Naval; *Style—* Dr Dorothy Horsfield; Department of Chemical Pathology, Barnsley District General Hospital, Barnsley, S Yorks (☎ 0226 730000)

HORSFIELD, (John) Neil; s of John Clive Horsfield, of Newport, Gwent, and Alizon, *née* Hindle; *b* 7 Dec 1966; *Educ* Bassaleg Comprehensive Sch, Univ Coll Swansea (BEng); *Career* engr Ove Arup and Partners Cardiff 1990-; athlete; Silver medallist 1500m Euro Junior Championships 1985, AAA 1500m champion 1990, UK 1500m champion 1990, memb Br team Euro Championships Split Yugoslavia (1500m) 1990; Welsh Record holder at: 800m, 1500m, Mile; IStructE civil engineering prize; graduate memb ICE; *Clubs* Newport Harriers AC; *Style—* Neil Horsfield, Esq; 124 Tewkesbury St, Cathays, Cardiff, South Glamorgan CF2 4QS (☎ 0222 225247); Ove Arup and Partners, Cambrian Buildings, Mount Stuart Square, Cardiff CF1 6QP (☎ 0222 473727,fax 0222 472277)

HORSFIELD, Peter Muir Francis; QC (1978); s of Henry Taylor Horsfield, AFC, and Florence Lily, *née* Muir; *b* 15 Feb 1932; *Educ* Beaumont Sch, Trinity Coll Oxford (BA); *m* 1962, Anne Charlotte, da of late Sir Piers Debenham, 2 Bt; 3 s; *Career* RNR 1955-57 (Lt 1960); called to the Bar Middle Temple 1958, in practice at Chancery Bar 1958-, bencher 1984-; *Recreations* observational astronomy; *Clubs* Garrick; *Style—* Peter Horsfield, Esq, QC; Chambers, 8 Stone Buildings, Lincoln's Inn, London WC2A 3TA

HORSFIELD, (Thomas Norman) Roger; TD (1970, and three clasps 1976, 1982, 1988); s of Norman Horsfield (d 1968); *b* 21 Feb 1936; *Educ* Barrow GS, Univ of Manchester; *m* 1962, Ann, da of late James William Evans, of Wolverhampton; 1 s, 1 da; *Career* chm Condor Investmts Ltd, MIDPM, MPS, FBIM 1984; *Recreations* shooting; *Clubs* RAC, English XX Bisley; *Style—* Roger Horsfield, Esq, TD; 31 Fields Drive, Sandbach, Cheshire CW11 9EX

HORSFORD, Alan Arthur; s of Arthur Henry Horsford, and Winifred Horsford; *b* 31 May 1927; *Educ* Holt Sch, Univ of Liverpool (BA); *m* 1957, Enid Maureen, *née* Baker; 1 s (Jeffrey Alan b 1958), 1 da (Margaret Claire b 1963); *Career* gp chief exec Royal Insurance Holding plc 1985-89 (dir 1979), gen mangr Royal Insurance Canada 1974-79, dep chm Assoc of Br Insurers 1985-88; *Style—* Alan Horsford, Esq; 17 Darnhills, Radlett, Herts WD7 8LQ (☎ 0923 857277)

HORSFORD, Cyril Edward Sheehan; CVO (1984); s of Dr Cyril Arthur Bennett Horsford (d 1953), of 24 Harley St, London W1, and Edith Louise, *née* Sayers (d 1987); *b* 13 March 1929; *Educ* Marlborough, Clare Coll Cambridge (MA); *m* 31 Aug 1957, Susan Frances, da of Francis Randall Hugh Bolton (d 1937), of London; 1 s (Simon b 1958); *Career* 2 Lt RA 1948-49; called to the Bar Inner Temple 1953, clerk of arraigns Central Criminal Ct Old Bailey 1954-56, sr asst Inner London Sessions 1956-68, dep asst registrar of Criminal Appeals 1968-74, dep clerk Privy Cncl 1974-89, clerk Bar Disciplinary Tribunal 1990; vice pres Medico Legal Soc of London 1988, dir Int Inst of Space Law 1961-72; Andrew G Haley award for contrib to space law (Warsaw) 1964; Freeman City of London 1970; FBIS 1973; *Books* Assize and Quarter Sessions Handbook (1958); contrib: Halsbury's Laws of England (4 edn), Journal of Criminal Law, Criminal Law Review, Solicitors Journal; *Recreations* amateur theatre, flyfishing; *Style—* Cyril Horsford, Esq, CVO; 32 Prairie St, London SW8 3PP (☎ 071 622 5984)

HORSFORD, Maj-Gen Derek Gordon Thomond; CBE (1962, MBE 1953), DSO (1944, and bar 1945); s of Capt Harry Thomond Horsford (d 1963), of Crowborough, and Violet Edith, *née* Inglis (d 1989); *b* 7 Feb 1917; *Educ* Clifton, RMC Sandhurst; *m* 1948, Sheila Louise Russell, da of Capt Norman Stuart Crawford; 1 s (Ian b 1948), 1 step s (George b 1939), 2 step da (Joanna b 1942, Gail b 1945); *Career* cmmnd 8 Gurkha Rifles 1937, Cdr 4/1 Gurkha Rifles Burma 1944-45 (Lt Col), instr Staff Coll 1950-52, GSO1 2 Inf Div 1955-56, Cdr 1 Bn The Kings Regt 1957-59, AAG AG2 WO 1959-60 (Col), Cdr 24 Inf Bde Gp 1960-62 (Brig), IDC 1963, Brig Gen Staff HQ BAOR 1964-66, GOC 50 (Northumbrian) Div/Dist 1966-67 (Maj-Gen), GOC Yorks Dist 1967-68, GOC 17 Div Malaya Dist 1969-70, Dep Cdr land forces Hong Kong 1970-71, Col The Kings Regt 1965-70, Col The Gurkha Tport Regt 1973-78; ret 1972 (Maj-Gen); dir RCN Devpt Tst 1972-75, sec League of Remembrance 1978-90; *Recreations* travel; *Clubs* Army And Navy; *Style—* Maj-Gen Derek Horsford, CBE, DSO

HORSHAM, Archdeacon of; *see* Filby, The Ven William Charles Leonard

HORSHAM, Bishop of 1991-; Rt Rev John William Hind; s of Harold Hind, and Joan Mary, *née* Kemp (d 1976); *b* 19 June 1945; *Educ* Watford GS, Univ of Leeds (BA); *m* 16 April 1966, Janet Helen, da of David Hamilton Burns McLintock; 3 s (Dominic b 1967, Jonathan b 1969, Philip b 1971); *Career* asst master Leeds Modern Sch 1966-69, asst lectr King Alfred's Coll Winchester 1969-70, student Cuddesdon Theol Coll Oxford 1970-72; asst curate: St John the Baptist Church Catford Southend, Downham Team Ministry Doicese of Southwark 1972-76; vicar Christ Church Forest Hill Diocese of Southwark 1976-82, priest i/c St Paul's Forest Hill 1981-82, princ Chichester Theol Coll 1982-91, Bursalis prebendary and residentiary canon Chichester Cathedral 1982-91; *Books* contrib to: Stepping Stones (1987), Church, Kingdom, World (1986), Working for the Kingdom (1986); *Recreations* judo, languages; *Style—* The Rev Canon John Hind; Bishop's Lodge, Worth, Crawley, W Sussex RH10 4RT (☎ 0293 3883051)

HORSLEY, Adrian Mark; JP; s of Ian Mark Horsley, of Hayton, York, and Patricia Horsley, JP, *née* Farrell; *b* 12 April 1949; *Educ* Ampleforth, Leicester Sch of Architecture (DipArch); *m* 28 Sept 1974, Louise Jane, da of Peter Bentham Oughtred, JP, (qv) of Raby Lodge, Brough; 2 s (Adam b 1979, Luke b 1982); *Career* architect; with Gelder and Kitchen 1974- (ptnr 1978-); former pres N Humberside Soc of Architects, former chm Yorks Regn RIBA; memb: Disciplinary Ctee RIBA, Magistrates Assoc of E Yorks, Catholic Union of GB, Hull Civic Soc, Georgian Soc of E Yorks, The Company of Merchant Adventurers of the City of York 1978; ARIBA

1976, ACIArb 1980, FRSA 1984; *Recreations* shooting, tennis, gardening; *Style*— Adrian Horsley, Esq, JP; Gelder & Kitchen, Architects, Maister House, High St, Hull HU1 1NL (☎ 0482 24114, fax 0482 227003, car 0836 534607)

HORSLEY, Very Rev Dr Alan Avery; s of Reginald James Horsley, of Staffs, and Edith Irene, *née* Allen; *b* 13 May 1936; *Educ* Worcester Royal GS, Northampton GS, St Chad's Coll Durham (BA), The Queen's Coll at Birmingham Univ of Birmingham, Pacific Western Univ (MA, PhD); *Career* curate: Daventry 1960-63, St Giles Reading 1963-64, St Paul Wokingham 1964-66; vicar St Andrew Yeadon 1966-71, rector Heyford with Stowe-Nine-Churches 1971-78, rural dean Daventry 1976-78, vicar Oakham with Hambleton and Egleton 1978-86 (with Braunston and Brooke from 1980-), non-residentiary canon Peterborough 1979-86, canon emeritus 1986-, vicar Lanteglos-by-Fowey 1986-88, provost of St Andrew's Cathedral Inverness 1988-; p-in-c: St Mary-in-the Fields Culloden 1988-, St Paul Strathnairn 1988-; *Style*— The Very Rev Dr Alan Avery; The Cathedral Rectory, 15 Ardross St, Inverness IV3 5NS (☎ 0463 233535)

HORSLEY, Lady Angela Leslie; *née* Courtenay; da of late 16 Earl of Devon; *b* 1918; *Educ* Open Univ (BA); *m* 1947, Harold Cecil Moreton Horsley, MBE, Malayan Civil Service (ret) (d 1969); 2 s; *Style*— The Lady Angela Horsley; Marwood House, Offwell, Honiton, Devon EX14 9RW

HORSLEY, Christopher Peter Beresford; s of Air Marshal Sir Peter Horsley, KBE, LVO, AFC, and Lady (Phyllis) Horsley; *b* 12 Aug 1944; *Educ* Wellington, Inst of Science and Technol Univ of Manchester (BSc); *m* 18 June 1973, Simone Jane, da of James Wood, MBE; 1 s (James Peter b 1976), 3 da (Kate Louise b 1974, Joanna Marie b 1980, Camilla b 1985); *Career* RAFVR 1965-68; euro mktg mangr Bell Helicopter 1970-74, md Aerogulf Dubai 1975-78; chm: Arabian Aviation Corp Bahrain 1979-86, RCR Int Ltd 1986-; advsr Br Aerospace plc 1989; chm Tangmere Flight Spitfire Mk X1; *Recreations* skiing, fishing, flying; *Clubs* Oriental, RAF; *Style*— Christopher Horsley, Esq; RCR Int Ltd, RCR House, Segensworth West, Hants PO15 5TD

HORSLEY, Karin Elizabeth; da of Peter Edwin Horsley, of Peterborough, and Marjorie Pearl, *née* Jackson; *b* 24 Feb 1955; *Educ* Durham Girls GS, UCL (LLB); *Career* admitted slr 1979; slr: Simmons and Simmons 1979-82, Abbey Nat Bldg Soc 1982-84, Titmuss Sainer and Webb 1984-89, Middleton Potts 1989-; memb The City of London Slrs Co 1989; memb Law Soc; *Recreations* reading; *Style*— Ms Karin Horsley; Middleton Potts, 3 Cloth St, Long Lane, London EC1A 7LD (☎ 071 600 2333, telex 928357, fax 071 600 0108)

HORSLEY, Air Marshal Sir (Beresford) Peter Torrington; KCB (1974), CBE (1964), LVO (1956), AFC (1945); s of late Capt Arthur Beresford Horsley, CBE; *b* 26 March 1921; *Educ* Wellington; *m* 1, 1943 (m dis 1976), Phyllis Conrad Phinney; 1 s, 1 da; m 2, 1976, Ann MacKinnon, da of Gareth Crwys-Williams; 2 step s, 2 step da; *Career* joined RAF 1940, serv 2 TAF and Fighter Cmds; Equerry: to Princess Elizabeth and to the Duke of Edinburgh 1949-52, to HM The Queen 1952-53, to the Duke of Edinburgh 1953-56; Asst CAS Queen 1952-53, Equerry to the Duke of Edinburgh 1953-56; Asst CAS (Ops) 1968-70, AOC No 1 Bomber Gp 1971-73, Dep C-in-C Strike Cmd 1973-75, ret 1975; chm: ML Hldgs plc, Nat Printing Ink Co Ltd; dir: ML Aviation Co Ltd, Ml Aerospace and Def Ltd, ML Wallop Def Systems Ltd, IDS Aircraft Ltd, Horsley Hldgs Ltd, RCR Int Ltd; pres Yorkshire Skiing Ltd, memb Honeywell Advsy cncl; *Books* Journal of a Stamp Collector; *Style*— Air Marshal Sir Peter Horsley, KCB, CBE, LVO, AFC; c/o Barclays Bank Ltd, High St, Newmarket

HORSLEY-BERESFORD, Hon Mrs William; Ida Kaye; *m* 1941, as his 4 w, Hon William Arthur de la Poer Horsley-Beresford (d 1949), yst s of 3 Baron Decies d 1983; 1 s, 1 da; *Style*— The Hon Mrs William Horsley-Beresford; 53 Overstrand Mansions, Prince of Wales Drive, SW11

HORT, Andrew Edwin Fenton; s and h of Sir James Fenton Hort, 8 Bt; *b* 15 Nov 1954; *m* 15 Nov 1986, Mary, da of Jack Whibley, of Spalding, Lincs; 1 s (James b 1989), 1 da (Jennifer b 1987); *Style*— Andrew Hort, Esq; 100 Hertford Rd, London N2

HORT, Sir James Fenton; 8 Bt (GB 1767), of Castle Strange, Middx; s of Sir Fenton George Hort, 7 Bt (d 1960), and Gwendolene (d 1983), da of late Sir Walter Alcock, MVO; *b* 6 Sept 1926; *Educ* Marlborough, Trinity Coll Cambridge (BA, MB BChir); *m* 1951, Joan Mary, da of late Edward Peat, of Swallownest, Sheffield; 2 s, 2 da; *Heir* s, Andrew Hort; *Career* former med dir A H Robins Co Ltd; *Style*— Sir James Hort, Bt; Poundgate Lodge, Uckfield Rd, Crowborough, Sussex (☎ 0892 654470; office, 0293 560161)

HORTON, Brian; s of Richard Horton (d 1990), of Cannock, Staffs, and Irene, *née* Russell; *b* 4 Feb 1949; *Educ* Blake Secdy Modern; *m* Denise Andrea, da of John William Callaghan; 1 s (Matthew Brian b 27 April 1987), 1 da (Lucy Andrea (twin) b 27 April 1987); *Career* professional football manager; player: Walsall 1964-66, Hednesford Town 1966-70, Port Vale 1970-76 (236 appearances), Brighton & Hove Albion 1976-81 (218 appearances), Luton Town 1981-84 (118 appearances), Hull City 1984-88 (38 appearances); currently manager Oxford Utd; *Recreations* golf, badminton; *Style*— Brian Horton, Esq; Oxford United FC, Manor Ground, Headington, Oxford (☎ 0865 61503 fax 0865 741820)

HORTON, Clive Fielding; s of Frank Fielding Horton (d 1970), and Hilda Elizabeth, *née* Powell (d 1983); *b* 3 July 1931; *Educ* Dover Coll; *m* 4 April 1959, Wendy Bradley, da of Henry Jordan (d 1983), of Maidstone; 3 da (Jane b 1963, Susan b 1963, Katie b 1966); *Career* cmmnd RA 1954, served Malaya 1955-56; qualified CA 1954, sr ptnr Day Smith and Hunter 1979- (ptnr 1958); pres SE Soc of CAs 1972-73, memb Cncl ICAEW 1973-77; hon treas Kent Assoc for the Blind, memb Cncl Maidstone Hospice Appeal; *Recreations* golf; *Clubs* Royal St Georges Golf, Bearsted Golf (capt 1974); *Style*— Clive Horton, Esq; 14 Conway Rd, Maidstone, Kent ME16 0HD (☎ 0622 753695); Day Smith and Hunter, Star House, Maidstone, Kent ME14 1LT (☎ 0622 690666)

HORTON, Hon Mrs (Fiona Catherine); *née* Peake; da of 2 Viscount Ingleby; *b* 24 Jan 1955; *Educ* St Mary's Sch Wantage, Univ of Bristol (BA); *m* 23 July 1977, (Gavin) Tobias Alexander Winterbottom Horton, s of Alistair Winterbottom, of Crawley Grange, North Crawley, Newport Pagnell, Bucks; 2 s (George b 1983, Thomas b 1985), 2 da (Alice b 1978, Violet b 1980); *Career* on editorial staff Antique Collectors Magazine 1976-77; *Recreations* walking, gardening; *Style*— The Hon Mrs Horton; Whorlton Cottage, Swainby, Northallerton, N Yorks DL6 3ER (☎ 0642 700213); 12 Vicarage Gdns, London W8 4AH (☎ 071 229 3871)

HORTON, Gavin Tobias Alexander Winterbottom (Toby); s of Alistair Winterbottom, of Crawley Grange, N Crawley, Newport Pagnell, Bucks and formerly of Horton House, Northants, and Maria Kersti, n of Lord Winterbottom, *qv*; *b 18 Feb 1947*; *b* 18 Feb 1947; *Educ* Westminster, Ch Ch Oxford (MA); *m* 1977, Hon Fiona Catherine Peake, da of 2 Viscount Ingleby; 2 s (George William Arthur b 1983, Thomas Henry Ralph b 1985), 2 da (Alice Emily Rose b 1978, Violet Constance Lily b 1980); *Career* md Sound Broadcasting (Teesside) 1979-83, dir and head Corp Fin Dept Minster Trust Ltd 1984-90; Parly candidate (C) Sedgefield 1983, Parly agent (C) Bethnal Green and Stepney 1987, Euro Parly candidate (C) Yorkshire SW 1989, proposed housing debate motion Cons Conference 1989; chm Fndn for Def Studies; vice pres: Langbaurgh Cons Assoc, Yorks and Northern Branches Nat Soc of Cons and Unionist Agents; FBIM; *Books* Going to Market: New Policy for the Farming Industry (1985), Programme for Reform: a New Agenda for Broadcasting (1987); *Recreations* radio, country pursuits; *Clubs* Buck's, Northern Counties (Newcastle); *Style*— Toby Horton, Esq; Whorlton Cottage, Swainby, Northallerton, N Yorkshire DL6 3ER (☎ 0642 700213); 12 Vicarage Gdns, London W8 4AH (☎ 071 229 3871)

HORTON, Mark Anthony; s of Robert Anthony Horton, DFC, of Glanville, Tedburn St Mary, Exeter, and Hélène, *née* Dubois; *b* 30 Sept 1953; *Educ* Blundells, Univ of Birmingham (LLB); *m* 20 Dec 1986, Madeleine, da of Edward Hunter Curry, of Flat 56, Yola II, Marbella; 1 s (James Anthony b 1987); *Career* called to the Bar 1976, Albion Chambers S Bristol 1977-83, St Johns Chambers Bristol 1983-88; *Recreations* tennis, football; *Style*— Mark Horton, Esq; St Johns Chambers, Small St, Bristol (☎ 0272 213456, fax 294 821)

HORTON, Matthew Bethell; QC; s of Albert Leslie Horton, of Tunbridge Wells, Kent, and Gladys Rose Ellen, *née* Harding; *b* 23 Sept 1946; *Educ* Sevenoaks, Trinity Hall Cambridge (MA, LLM); *m* 1, 22 May 1972 (m dis 1983), Liliane, da of Henri Boleslawski, of Nice, France; 1 s (Jerome b 1971), 1 da (Vanessa b 1973); *Career* called to the Bar Middle Temple 1969; in private practice specialising in: commercial property law, local govt law, admin law, Parly law; memb: Admin Law Ctee of Justice, Ctee Parly Bar Mess, Ctee Jt Planning Law Conf; *Recreations* tennis, skiing, windsurfing; *Clubs* Tramp; *Style*— Matthew Horton, Esq, QC; 2 Mitre Court Buildings, Temple, London EC4Y 7BX (☎ 071 583 1380, fax 071 353 7772, telex 28916 REDBAG G)

HORTON, Dr Michael Anthony; s of Dr (John Anthony) Guy Horton, of Newcastle-upon-Tyne, and Margaret Louise, *née* Jenkins; *b* 6 May 1948; *Educ* Oundle, St Bartholomew's Hosp Med Coll Univ of London (BSc, MB BS); *m* 10 Aug 1968, Susan Geraldine Horton, JP, da of Capt Gerald Taylor, MBE (d 1973); 1 s (Benjamin b 1977), 1 da (Rachel b 1971); *Career* MRC fell UCL 1976-79, Imperial Cancer Res Fund St Bartholomews Hosp 1984- (Welcome Tst Clinical Res Fell 1979-84, sr lectr and conslt haemmetologist 1979-), author pubns on haematology and immunology; memb Lib Democrats, Scout Movement; MRCP, MRCPath; *Recreations* squash, archeology, family history; *Style*— Dr Michael Horton; 36 Roebuck Lane, Buckhurst Hill, Essex IG9 5QX (☎ 01 504 3931); Department of Haematology, St Bartholomew's Hospital, London EC1A 7BE (☎ 01 600 3965, fax 01 796 3907)

HORTON, Robert Baynes; s of W H Horton (d 1969), of Pangbourne; *b* 18 Aug 1939; *Educ* Kings Sch Canterbury, Univ of St Andrews (BSc), MIT (SM); *m* 1962, Sally Doreen, da of Edward Wells (d 1971), of Beverley, E Yorks; 1 s, 1 da; *Career* joined BP Co Ltd 1957, gen mangr BP Tanker Co 1975-76 and corp planning BP 1976-79, md and chief exec BP Chemicals Int 1980-83, md BP plc 1983-86 and 1988- (dep chm 1989-90, chm 1990-), chm Standard Oil Ohio 1986-88; non exec dir: ICL plc 1982-84, Pilkington Bros 1985-86, Emerson Electric 1987-; chancellor Univ of Kent at Canterbury 1990-; pres Chemical Industs Assoc 1982-84, memb SERC 1985-86, vice chm BIM 1985-; memb: Bd of MIT 1987-, Case Western Reserve Univ 1987-, Cleveland Orchestra 1987- Univ Funding Cncl 1989-; govr Kings Sch Canterbury 1983-, chm Tate Gallery Fndn 1988-; Hon LLD Dundee 1988, Hon DCL Kent 1990; *Recreations* music, country activities; *Clubs* Carlton, Leander, Union (Cleveland, Ohio); *Style*— Robert Horton, Esq; BP plc, Britannic House, 1 Finsbury Circus, London EC2M 7BA (☎ 071 496 4000, fax 071 920 8263, telex 888811)

HORTON, Hon Mrs (Susan Elizabeth); da of Baron Donovan (Life Peer, d 1971); *b* 1936; *m* 1960 (m dis 1984), Gerard Francis Horton; issue; *Style*— The Hon Mrs Horton; 27 Weemla Rd, Northbridge, NSW, Australia

HORTON-FAWKES, (George) Nicholas Le Gendre; er s of Maj Le Gendre George William Horton-Fawkes, OBE, DL (d 1982), and Sylvia, *née* Duckworth (d 1990), whose paternal grandmother was Hon Edina Campbell, sis of 2 and 3 Barons Stratheden and Campbell, and whose father's 1 cous was Gerald Duckworth, the half-bro of Virginia Woolf; *b* 20 Sept 1925; *Educ* Eton, Trinity Coll Cambridge; *m* 1954, Audrey, da of Welles Bosworth, of Marietta, Seine-et-Oise, France; 3 s (Francis b 1955, William b 1957, John b 1963); *Style*— Nicholas Horton-Fawkes, Esq; Farnley Hall, Otley, W Yorks (☎ 0943 462198)

HORWOOD, Maj Ellis George; MBE (1985); s of William Horwood, and Emma, *née* Binley; *b* 13 Oct 1911; *Educ* Bromley County GS; *m* Felicity Mary, da of Stanley Hodges; 3 s (Michael Ellis b 1944, Clive James b 1948, Mark William b 1972), 2 da (Susan Gay b 1943, Margaret Anne b 1950); *Career* Southern Provinces Mounted Rifles Madras 1930-39, Bromley Bn Home Gd 1940, 4 Bn 7 Gurkha Rifles 1941-46 (Maj 1946); publishing: Macmillan and Co Ltd London and Madras 1927-48, Hutchinson and Co London 1949-50, Cleaver-Hume Press 1950-57; fndr md and publisher Van Nostrand Co London 1957-72, fndr chm and publisher Ellis Horwood Ltd 1973-; Liveryman Worshipful Co of Blacksmiths, Freeman City of London; fell Royal Chem Soc 1950-; Silver medal for Int Cooperation Czechoslovakia (1978); *Books* Publishing (1983); *Recreations* Books, music, spectator sport, gardens; *Clubs* Hurlingham, Army and Navy, Sussex CC, Chichester Yacht; *Style*— Maj Ellis Horwood, MBE; Ellis Horwood Limited (Publishers), Market Cross House, Cooper St, Chichester, W Sussex (☎ 0243 789942, fax 0243 778855, telex 86516 (Cable: Elwood))

HORWOOD-SMART, John; s of late William Ogilvy Smart, and late Mabel Louisa Horwood; *b* 21 Oct 1924; *Educ* City of London Sch, Christ's Coll Cambridge (MA); *m* 3 Jan 1948, Sylvia, da of William Young Nutt (d 1926), of Cambridge; 1 s (Adrian Piers b 25 Sept 1953), 1 da (Rosamund (Mrs Blackford) b 21 Sept 1951); *Career* WWII Capt Intelligence Corps in SW Pacific and SE Asia; admitted slr 1951, Notary Public; hon fell Robinson Coll Cambridge, chm Anglo American Rels Ctee RAF Mildenhall Suffolk 1967-72; memb: Law Soc (former pres Cambridge and Dist), Prov Notary Soc; *Style*— John Horwood-Smart, Esq; Rutland Cottage, Cheveley, Newmarket (☎ 0638 730 236); Lushington House, Newmarket, Suffolk (☎ 0638 663571)

HORWOOD-SMART, Rosamund; da of John Horwood-Smart, of Cheveley, nr Newmarket, Suffolk, and Sylvia Nutt; *b* 21 Sept 1951; *Educ* Felixstowe Coll, Cambridgeshire HS for Girls, Inns of Court Sch of Law; *m* 16 July 1983, Richard Clive Blackford; 1 s (Frederick John b 3 Sept 1986), 1 da (Eleanor Kate b 30 Aug 1989); *Career* called to the Bar Inner Temple 1974, asst rec 1940-; memb: S Eastern Circuit, Criminal Bar Assoc, Bar European Gp; govr Int Students House London, tstee Prisoners of Conscience Fund; *Recreations* tennis, gardening, theatre; *Style*— Miss Rosamund Horwood-Smart; 5 Kings Bench Walk, Temple EC4 (☎ 071 353 4713, fax 071 353 5459)

HOSEASON, James William Nicholson; OBE (1990); s of William Ballantyne Hoseason (d 1950), of Lowestoft, and Jessie Mary Hoseason (d 1972); *b* 6 Nov 1928; *Educ* Lowestoft GS; *m* 20 March 1965, Lesley Jean, da of Leslie Charles Edmonds (d 1964), of Chedgrave, nr Norwich; 1 s (James Charles William b 6 Feb 1967); *Career* articled pupil then chartered civil engr and chartered structural engr Sir Owen Williams & Partners 1945-50; Hoseasons Holidays Ltd: trainee 1950, md 1952-64, chm and jt md 1964-; memb Inland Waterways Amenity Advsy Cncl 1972-80, govt appointed memb Anglian Water 1973-76, river cmmr Norfolk Broads 1982-88, past chm Br Hire Cruiser Fedn; Bd memb English Tourist Bd, memb Broads Authy (memb navigation ctee); FTS 1973, FBIM 1974, FCIM 1976; *Books* The Thousand Day Battle (1979, 2 edn 1987); *Recreations* sailing, writing, flying light aircraft, gardening; *Clubs* RAC,

Royal Norfolk & Suffolk Yacht; *Style*— James Hoseason, Esq, OBE; Hoseasons Holidays Ltd, Sunway House, Lowestoft, Suffolk NR32 3LT (☎ 0502 500 505, fax 0502 514 298, telex 975189-HOSEAS G)

HOSEGOOD, Charles Thomas Dennehy; s of Capt Thomas William Harold Hosegood (d 1939), and Nora Marie, *née* Dennehy (d 1946); *b* 4 Jan 1921; *Educ* King George V Hong Kong, Prior Park Coll Bath; *m* 9 Dec 1950, Jane, da of Norman Ernest Jacob (d 1969), of Weelsby Lodge, Weelsby Rd, Grimsby; 2 s (Nigel b 7 March 1953, Ian b 14 Jan 1958); *Career* WWII, Pilot Fleet Air Arm 1939-47; HMS Alcantara 1941-43, US Coast Guards Floyd Bennett Field NY 1944, RN memb jt servs Helicopter Experimental Unit AFEE RAF Beaulieu 1945-46; test pilot Br Aeroplane Co 1948-51 (chief helicopter test pilot 1951-60), chief test pilot Bristol Div Westlands Aircraft Ltd 1960-63, introduced helicopters to Electricity Indust 1963, offr-in-charge Jt Electricity Helicopter Unit 1963-83, ret 1983; maiden flights Bristol Helicopters: Bristol 173 tandem and first twin engine, Bristol 191, Bristol 192 (Belvedere); official air speed helicopter record 30 May 1961 and 2 June 1961 London-Paris-London; memb: Test Pilots Ctee SABC, Flying Ctee SBAC Farnborough Flying Display, Air Legislation Ctee for Helicopter Advsy Bd; GAPAN Master Pilot Certificate 1960; Freeman Worshipful Co of Air Pilots and Air Navigators 1964; Alan Marsh medal 1962; FRAeS 1976; Scroll of Bd of Fndn Flakkeese Gemeenschap 1953; *Recreations* cricket, squash, sailing, golf; *Clubs* Burnham and Berrow Somerset Golf, The Forty Cricket; *Style*— Charles Hosegood, Esq; The Hyall, Lye Hole, Wrington, Avon BS18 7RN

HOSELITZ, Steve; *b* 12 March 1947; *Career* editorial asst on ILIFFE trade magazine 1965, asst ed of a United Trade Press publication subsequently for Central Press Features until 1968; freelance journalist: UK 1968-69, India 1969-70; ed Indian and Eastern Engineer 1969-70, chief sub-ed West Lancashire Evening Gazette until 1977 (sub-ed 1970), ed South Wales Argus 1987- (dep ed 1977-87); *Style*— Steve Hoselitz, Esq; South Wales Argus, Cardiff Rd, Maesglas, Newport, Gwent NP9 1QW (☎ 0633 810000)

HOSFORD-TANNER, (Joseph) Michael; s of late Dr Hubert Hosford-Tanner, of London SW1, and Betty, *née* Bryce; *b* 8 Aug 1951; *Educ* Midleton Coll, Trinity Coll Dublin (BA, LLB); *Career* called to the Bar Inner Temple 1974, legal assessor Farriers Registration Cncl 1985; *Recreations* horses, cricket, travel; *Clubs* Chelsea Arts, Kildare Street and Univ; *Style*— Michael Hosford-Tanner, Esq; Queen Elizabeth Building, Temple, London EC4Y 9BS (☎ 071 583 7837, fax 071 353 5422)

HOSIE, David Paul; s of Dr C C Hosie, of The Cottage, Upton upon Severn, Worcs, and Madeleine, *née* Mallon; *b* 25 June 1962; *Educ* Williamwood HS Glasgow, Edinburgh Coll of Art (BA, Richard Ford award, Spanish Travelling scholarship, Andrew Grant major award for painting, G J Hutchinson award for painting); *m* ; 1 s (Samuel b 24 Jan 1986); *Career* artist; lectr in drawing and painting Edinburgh Coll of Art 1986-87, gallery artist RAAB Gallery London 1987, lectr in drawing and painting Glasgow Sch of Art 1987-90; solo exhibitions: RAAB Gallery London 1987, Roger Ramsay Gallery (Chicago) 1989, Hal Bromm Gallery (NY) 1990, Artisite Gallery (Bath) 1990, Fruitmarket Gallery (Edinburgh) 1990; gp exhibitions incl: Contemporary Arts Soc 1985 and 1986, New Generation Show (Compass Gallery Glasgow) 1986, Travelling Show (San Francisco) 1986, The Tron Gallery (Glasgow) 1986, Germinations (Centre de la Vielle Charité Marseilles, Breda, RCA London, Frauen Museum Bonn) 1986, The Rope of Europe (Galleria Gian Ferrari Milan, RAAB Gallery London) 1988, Metamorphosis (RAAB Gallery) 1989, Turning the Century: The New Scottish Painting (RAAB Gallery, Berlin, Ferrari Gallery Milan) 1990, Artecontemporanea (Milan, Berlin) 1990; most important works: Airport (1987), Beauty and the Beast (1987), Man the Unknown (1989), Orator (1989), The Night (1990), Father and Son (1990), New Territory (1990), Four Youths Isolated (1990), The Big Sin (1990); *Style*— David Hosie, Esq; 19 Balfour St, Leith, Edinburgh EH6 5DG (☎ 031 553 5347); RAAB Gallery, 6 Vauxhall Bridge Rd, Millbank, London SW1V 2SD (☎ 071 828 2588, fax 071 976 5041)

HOSKER, Gerald Albery; CB (1987); s of Leslie Reece Hosker (d 1971), and Constance, *née* Hubbard; *b* 28 July 1933; *Educ* Berkhamstead Sch; *m* 1956, Rachel Victoria Beatrice, da of Cdr Clifford Victor Middleton, RINVR (ret); 1 s (Jonathan Edward George b 1961), 1 da (Helen Bridget b 1958); *Career* admitted slr 1956, assoc Faculty of Secretaries and Admins 1964, legal asst Treasy Slrs Dept 1960; Treasy: sr legal asst 1966, asst slr 1973, princ asst slr 1980, dep 1982, slr DTI 1987-; FRSA (1964); *Clubs* Royal Cwlth Soc; *Style*— Gerald Hosker, Esq, CB

HOSKIN, Ernest Jabez; s of Jabez Edmund Hoskin (d 1957), of Elmside House, Elmside, Exeter, and Eva Maud, *née* Anstey; *b* 15 Sept 1920; *Educ* Heles Sch Exeter; *m* 14 Nov 1946, (Hilda) Joyce, da of William Arthur Mawhinney (d 1966), of Torquay and Belfast; 1 s (Peter b 17 Sept 1948); *Career* Gunner 163-55 LAA Regt TA 1939; served: France, Norway, Ceylon, cmmnd 1 Punjab Regt IA 1943, Lt 1944, Capt (Adj) 1944, Actg Maj 1945, served India and Burma, demob 1946; City Treasurer's Office Exeter 1938-49, sr inspr HM Customs and Excise 1949-79 (represented UK at Customs and Indirect Taxation Ctees of EEC 1974-79), led EEC delgn (indirect taxation) to Andean GP to promote a common market between Peru, Bolivia, Ecuador, Colombia and Venezuela 1979-80, registrar VAT Tbnls for the UK 1980-83, VAT conslt Coopers & Lybrand Deloitte 1983-, managing conslt ed VAT Intelligence 1985-89; memb Kent Dahlia Soc; Freeman: City of London 1980, Worshipful Co of Blacksmiths 1980; FTII 1986; *Books* Community Law and UK VAT (1988), Appealing to a VAT Tribunal (1989), VAT and Community Law (1989), Community Law Cases (1990); *Recreations* genealogy, golf, gardening; *Clubs* Chislehurst Golf; *Style*— Ernest Hoskin, Esq; Woodhayes, 76A The Ave, Beckenham, Kent BR3 2ES

HOSKING, Barbara Nancy; OBE (1985); da of William Henry Hosking (d 1963), and Ada Kathleen, *née* Murrish (d 1951); *b* 4 Nov 1926; *Educ* West Cornwall Sch for Girls, Hillcroft Coll; *Career* Civil Serv 1965-77, press offr 10 Downing St 1970-72, private sec to Parly Secs Cabinet Office 1973-75; controller info servs IBA 1977-86, former pres Media Soc, occasional broadcaster and writer, conslt Yorkshire TV; jt vice chm Nat Cncl of Voluntary Orgns; tstee: Charitees Aid Fndn, 300 Gp; FRSA 1984, FRTS 1988; *Recreations* opera, lieder, watching politics; *Clubs* Reform; *Style*— Miss Barbara Hosking, OBE; 8 Highgate Spinney, Crescent Rd, London N8 8AR (☎ 081 340 1853); Yorkshire Television, 32 Bedford Row, London WC1R 4HE (☎ 071 242 1666)

HOSKING, Prof Geoffrey Alan; s of Stuart William Stegall Hosking, of 7 Conway Rd, Maidstone, Kent, and Jean Ross, *née* Smillie; *b* 28 April 1942; *Educ* Maidstone GS, King's Coll Cambridge (BA), Moscow State Univ, St Anthony's Coll Oxford, Univ of Cambridge (MA, PhD); *m* 19 Dec 1970, Anne Lloyd Hirst; 2 da (Katya b 1974, Janet b 1978); *Career* lectr Univ of Essex: Dept of Govt 1966-71, Dept of History 1972-76, reader Dept of History 1976-80 and 1981-84; visiting prof: Dept of Political Sci Univ of Wisconsin USA 1971-72, Slavisches Inst Univ of Cologne 1980-81; prof of russian history Sch of Slavonic and E European Studies Univ of London 1984-; Reith lectr BBC 1988; memb: Cncl of Writers and Scholars Int 1985-, Cncl Keston Coll 1987-89, Bd of Govrs Camden Sch for Girls 1988-, Br Univs Assoc for Soviet and E Euro Studies; *Books* The Russian Constitutional Experiment: Government & Duma 1907-14 (1973), Beyond Socialist Realism: Soviet Fiction since Ivan Denisovich (1980), A History of The Soviet Union (1985, 2 edn 1990), The Awakening of The Soviet Union (1990); *Recreations* walking, music, chess; *Style*— Prof Geoffrey Hosking; School of Slavonic & East European Studies, University of London, Senate House, Malet St, London WC1E 7HU (☎ 071 637 4934 ext 4064)

HOSKING, John Everard; CBE, JP; s of J Everard Hosking, OBE (d 1978), and Eveline Margaret, *née* Shaxson; *b* 23 Oct 1929; *Educ* Marlborough, Wye Coll London (BSc); *m* 16 Sept 1953, Joan Cecily, da of John Wilfrid Whitaker, OBE (d 1980); 2 s (Julian Bernard b 1957, Bruce Adrian b 1960); *Career* farmer and landowner in Kent 1953-69; md Eastes and Loud Ltd 1965-69; dir: Ashford Corn Exchange Co 1965-69, Newgrain-Kent 1969-74, Agroup Ltd 1987-90, Bureau Europeen de Recherches SA 1987-, European Intelligence Ltd 1987-; chm Agra Europe (London) Ltd 1989- (chief exec 1974-89); chm: Ashford Magistrates' Court 1975-85, Centre for Euro Agric Studies Assoc 1977-83, Kent Magistrates' Courts Ctee 1984-88; vice pres Magistrates' Assoc (chm Cncl 1987-90); memb Royal Agric Soc 1960; *Books* Rural Response to the Resource Crisis in Europe (ed, 1981); *Recreations* the arts, the countryside; *Clubs* Farmers', Royal Overseas; *Style*— John Hosking, Esq, CBE, JP; Agra Europe (London) Ltd, 25 Frant Rd, Tunbridge Wells, Kent TN2 5JT (☎ 0892 33813, fax 0892 24593, telex 95114 AGRATW G)

HOSKINS, Arthur Henry James; CBE; s of Alfred George Hoskins; *b* 14 Jan 1923; *m* 1949, Margaret Lilian Rose, da of Albert Davis (d 1959); 1 child; *Career* certified accountant, chartered sec; md and dep chm Matthew Hall plc 1939-86; *Recreations* reading, walking; *Style*— Arthur Hoskins, Esq, CBE; 2 Acorn Close, Chislehurst, Kent BR7 6LD (☎ 081 467 0755)

HOSKINS, Prof Brian John; s of George Frederick Hoskins (d 1979), and Kathleen Matilda Louise, *née* Rattue; *b* 17 May 1945; *Educ* Bristol GS, Trinity Hall Cambridge (MA, PhD); *m* 25 May 1968, Jacqueline, *née* Holmes; 2 da (Brooke b 22 Sept 1972, Bryony b 7 Oct 1974); *Career* prof of meterology Univ of Reading 1981 (reader in atmospheric modelling 1976-81), conslt to Dept of Tport; memb Cncl Natural Environment Res Cncl; FRS 1988, FRMetS 1970; *Books* Large-Scale Dynamical Processes in the Atmosphere (1982); *Recreations* singing, gardening; *Style*— Prof Brian Hoskins, FRS; 32 Reading Rd, Wokingham, Berks RG11 1EH (☎ 0734 791015); Dept of Meterology, University of Reading, Whiteknights, Reading RG6 2AU (☎ 0734 318953, fax 0734 352604)

HOSKINS, Malcolm Geoffrey Ronald; s of Ronald Arthur Hoskins (d 1986), of Bath, and (Edith) Marjorie, *née* Caseley; *Educ* Felixstone Acad; *m* 21 Sept 1974, (Dorothy) Christine Naden; *Career* articled clerk Patterson & Thompson 1958-64, ptnr Touche Ross & Co 1971- (joined 1964); pres Manchester Soc of Chartered Accountants 1986-87, memb Cncl ICAEW 1988-; ACA 1963; *Recreations* cricket, racing, theatre; *Clubs* Lancashire CCC, Somerset CCC, Raceqoers; *Style*— Malcolm Hoskins, Esq; Touche Ross & Co, PO Box 500, Abbey House, 74 Mosley St, Manchester M60 2AT (☎ 061 228 3456)

HOSKINS, Robert (Bob); s of Robert Hoskins, and Elsie Lilian Hopkins; *b* 26 Oct 1942; *Educ* Stroud Green Sch; *m* 1 Jane Livesey; 1 s (Alexander b 8 Aug 1968), 1 da (Sarah b 30 Dec 1972); m 2, June 1982, Linda Banwell; 1 s (Jack Anthony b 5 March 1985), 1 da (Rosa Louise b 27 May 1983); *Career* actor; previously held numerous jobs incl accountant; theatre debut Unity Theatre London, early experience on tour with Ken Campbell's Road Show; film work incl: Foster in The National Health 1973, Royal Flash 1974, Big Mac in Inserts 1975, Colour Sergeant Major Williams in Zulu Dawn 1979-80, Harold Shand in The Long Good Friday 1979-80 (Evening Standard award for Best Actor, nominated for Best Actor award British Acad of Film & Television Arts), Rock and Roll manager in The Wall 1982, Colonel Perez in The Honorary Consul (titled Beyond The Limit in USA) 1982-83, Owney Madden in The Cotton Club 1984, Spoor in Brazil 1985-86, Stanley in Sweet Liberty 1985-86, George in The Woman Who Married Clark Gable 1985-86, George in Mona Lisa (nominated for Oscar award for best actor, won New York Critics and Golden Globe awards, Best Actor award Cannes Film Festival, also numerous English awards) 1985-86, The Priest in A Prayer For The Dying 1986-87, Eddie Valiant in Who Framed Roger Rabbit? 1986-87, Madden in The Lonely Passion of Judith Hearne 1986-87, Darky in The Raggedy Rawney (writer, dir and actor) 1988, Lou Landsky in Mermaids 1989, Jack Moony in Heart Condition 1990, Shatterd 1990, The Favour The Watch and The Very Big Fish 1990, The Projectionist 1990; tv work incl: Joe Gramaldi in Omnibus - It Must Be Something in the Water 1971-72, Knocker in Villians 1972-73, Woodbine in Her Majesty's Pleasure 1972-73, All Who Sail Around Her 1972-73, On the Road 1972-73, Crown Court 1972-73, New Scotland Yard 1972-73, Sexton in If there Weren't Any Blacks... 1972-73, Doobs in Thick as Thieves 1972-73, Schmoedius 1974, Shoulder to Shoulder 1974-75, Thriller -To Kill Two Birds 1975, Omnibus on Brecht 1975, Three Piece Suite 1977, In The Looking Glass 1977, Napoleon in Peninsular 1977, Arthur Parker in Pennies From Heaven (nominated BAFTA Best Actor) 1977 and re-run 1990, Chorus in Mycenae and Men 1980-81, Sheppey in Sheppey 1980-81, Arnie Cole in Flickers 1980-81, Iago in Othello 1981, Eddie Reed in You Don't Have to Walk to Fly 1982-83, The Beggars Opera 1983-84; Victoria Theatre Stoke-on-Trent 1968: Romeo and Juliet, Toad of Toad Hall, Christopher Pee in Heartbreak House; Century Theatre 1969: Marker in A View From the Bridge, Pinchwife in The Country Wife, Hiring in The Anniversary, Meneleus in The Trojan Women; other theatre work incl: Lenny in the Homecoming 1969 and Richard in Richard III 1970 (Hull Arts Theatre), Azdac in The Caucasian Chalk Circle and Lear (Royal Court Theatre) 1970-71, Bernie the Volt in Veterans (Royal Court Theatre) 1972, Sextus Pompeius in Anthony and Cleopatra (Bankside Globe Theatre) 1973, Lear in Lear (Dartington Hall) 1973, Mr Doolittel in Pygmalion (Albery Theatre) 1974, Common Man in A Man For All Seasons (Sixty Nine Theatre Company) 1974, Geography of a Horse Dreamer (Royal Court Theatre) 1974, Touchstone in As You Like It (Oxford Playhouse) 1975, Biu Cracker in Happy End (Lyric) 1975-76; The Royal Shakespeare Company 1976: Rocky in The Iceman Cometh, Seargeant in The Devil's Disciple, The World Turned Upside Down and Has Washington Legs? 1978, Lee in True West 1981, Nathan Detroit in Guys and Dolls 1982, Bosola in The Duchess of Malfi 1983; writer and actor The Bystander (Soho Poly Theatre) 1977; *Style*— Bob Hoskins, Esq; Hutton Management Ltd, 200 Fulham Rd, London SW10 9PN (☎ 071 352 4825, fax 071 351 4560)

HOSKINS, Stanley William; s of William Edward Hoskins (d 1953), and Rose, *née* Beatrice (d 1984); *b* 18 Oct 1913; *Educ* Latimer Upper Sch, Acton Poly; *m* Dorothy Emma Daisy, da of Louis Frederick Howard (d 1917); 1 da (Teresa Dorothy); *Career* TA Capt 2 Middx Aux Bomb Disposal Unit 1946; Bell Punch Co: chief tool draughtsman 1937-39, prodn engr 1939-41, chief draughtsman 1941-42, mechanical supt 1942-45; devpt engr Firestone Tyre & Rubber Co 1945-46, tech mangr Fluid Control GB Ltd 1945-50, md IV Pressure Controllers Ltd 1950-76; Freeman City of London 1961, Liverman Worshipful Co of Feltmakers; CEng, MIMechE, FIProdE, FIARB, Assoc RIMA, MIBE; *Clubs* City Livery; *Style*— Stanley Hoskins, Esq

HOSKYNS, Sir Benedict Leigh; 16 Bt (E 1676), of Harewood, Herefords; 3 s of Rev Sir Edwyn Clement Hoskyns, 13 Bt, MC, DD (d 1937), and Mary Trym, *née* Budden; suc bro, Sir John Chevallier Hoskyns, 15 Bt, 1956; *b* 27 May 1928; *Educ* Haileybury, Corpus Christi Cambridge (MB BChir), London Hosp; *m* 19 Sept 1953, Ann, da of Harry Wilkinson, of London; 2 s, 2 da; *Heir* s, Dr Edwyn Wren Hoskyns; *Career* Capt

RAMC (ret); in general practice 1958-; DObstRCOG 1958; *Style*— Sir Benedict Hoskyns, Bt; Harewood, Great Oakley, nr Harwich, Essex (☎ 0255 880341)

HOSKYNS, Edwyn Wren; s and h of Sir Benedict Leigh Hoskyns, 16 Bt; *b* 4 Feb 1956; *Educ* Nottingham Univ Med Sch (BM BS); *m* ; 1 s (Robin Chevallier b 5 July 1989); *Career* sr chorister King's Coll Cambridge 1969; *Style*— Edwyn Hoskyns Esq

HOSKYNS, Sir John Austin Hungerford Leigh; s of Lt-Col Chandos Benedict Arden Hoskyns (d of wounds after def of Calais 1940; gs of Rev Sir John Hoskyns, 9 Bt, JP), and Joyce Austin, *née* Taylor; *b* 23 Aug 1927; *Educ* Winchester; *m* 1956, Miranda Jane Marie, o da of Tom Mott, of W Bergholt, Essex; 2 s (Barnaby b 1959, Benedict b 1963), 1 da (Tamasine b 1961); *Career* Capt Rifle Bde; IBM (UK) 1957-64, fndr John Hoskyns and Co (later part of Hoskyns Gp, of which chm and md 1964-75), head of PM's Policy Unit 1979-82, special advsr to Sec State for Tport 1982, non-exec dir ICL 1982-84, dir-gen IOD 1984-89; dir: AGB Res 1983-88, Pergamon-AGB plc 1988-89, Clerical Medical and General Life Assurance Society 1983-, McKechnie 1983-: chm The Burton Group plc 1990-; Ferranti Int Signal 1986-; kt 1982; *Style*— Sir John Hoskyns; c/o Child & Co, 1 Fleet St, London EC4Y 1BD

HOSKYNS, Hon Mrs (Katharine Margaret); da of Baron Kaldor (Life Peer); *b* 1937; *m* 1958, Anthony Hungerford Hoskyns, s of Sir Chandos Wren Hoskyns, 14 Bt (ka 1945); 1 s, 2 da; *Style*— The Hon Mrs Hoskyns; 25 Hamilton Gdns, NW8

HOSKYNS, Mary, Lady; Mary Trym; da of late Edwin Budden, of Macclesfield; *m* 1922, the Rev Sir Edwyn Clement Hoskyns, MC, 13 Bt (d 1937); *Career* MA 1922, former Res fell of Newnham Coll Cambridge; *Style*— Mary, Lady Hoskyns; 25 Hamilton Gdns, NW8

HOSKYNS-ABRAHALL, (Anthony David) Wren; s of Rt Rev Anthony Leigh Egerton-Hoskyns-Abrahall (d 1982), former Bishop of Lancaster, and Margaret Ada, *née* Storey; *b* 19 May 1943; *Educ* St Johns Sch Leatherhead, Britannia RNC Dartmouth, London Graduate Sch of Business Studies; *m* 23 April 1965, Phyllis Penrose, da of Rear Adm Willian Penrose Mark-Wardlaw, DSO, DSC, ADC; 1 s (Mark b 22 July 1966) 1 da (Sarah b 18 April 1971); *Career* RNC Dartmouth 1961-63, HMS Tiger 1962-63, RN Trg then Staff Offr Ops Kenya Navy 1966-68, HMS Chichester 1969-70, HMS Rapid 1970, HMS Malcolm 1970-71, Flag Lt to FOSNI 1972-72; dir: Portsmouth & Sunderland Newspaper plc 1973-1977, Debenhams plc 1978-1982, Prontaprint 1982-; memb Southwark Diocesan Synod, ed Barnes In Common; cncllr Fareham BC 1974-76; HCIM 1979; *Recreations* fishing; *Style*— Wren Hoskyns-Abrahall, Esq; 20 Grange Rd, Barnes, London SW13 9RE (☎ 081 748 8455); 60 Wandsworth High St, London SW18 4ID (☎ 081 870 7672, fax 081 870 0056)

HOSTOMBE, Roger Eric; s of Eric Rudolf Hostombe, of Sheffield, and Irene, *née* Baxter; *b* 22 Dec 1942; *Educ* Sedbergh; *m* 20 Sept 1975, Susan Mary, da of Frank Ian Cobb, of Sheffield; 5 da (Clare b 1976, Natalie b 1979, Annabel b 1982, Lucinda b 1982, Sophie b 1989); *Career* CA 1968, exec chm HOSTOMBE GROUP LTD 1975-; underwriter Lloyds 1975-; regnl cncllr CBI Yorkshire and Humberside branch 1981-87; *Recreations* tennis, squash, skiing, gardening; *Clubs* The Sheffield, Annabels; *Style*— Roger E Hostombe, Esq; Fullwood Hall, Sheffield, Yorks S10 4PA (☎ 0742 302148); HOSTOMBE GROUP LTD, Minalloy House, Regent St, Sheffield S1 3NJ (☎ 0742 724324, telex 54213, fax 0742 729550)

HOTCHKIN, Neil Stafford; TD (1946), DL (1954); s of Col Stafford Vere Hotchkin, MC, DL, (d 1953), of The Manor House, Woodhall Spa, Lincs, and Dorothy Robinson, *née* Arnold, (d 1962); *b* 4 Feb 1914; *Educ* Eton, Trinity Coll Cambridge (BA); *m* 27 Feb 1954, Sallie, da of Hugh Sudell Bloomer (d 1964), of Gt Coates, Grimsby; 1 s (David Stafford b 3 Aug 1958), 1 da (Sarah Nicola b 1 Aug 1960); *Career* served Territorial 60 Field Regt RA 1938 (Capt 1940, Maj 1942), regt transferred to Chindits 1943, cmd 88 column in Burma 1944; memb London Stock Exchange 1938, pres English Golf Union 1972, patron Lincolnshire Union of Golf Clubs 1985; pres Woodhall Spa: Cricket Club, Football Club, Golf Club, Cons Club; pres Euro Golf Assoc 1989 (hon sec 1980-87); played cricket for Lincolnshire, Middlesex, Eton, and Univ of Cambridge; *Recreations* golf; *Clubs* R and A; *Style*— Neil Hotchkin, Esq, TD, DL; Womersley House, Woodhall Spa, Lincs LN10 6UY (☎ 0526 52127)

HOTHAM, Anthony; TD (1969); s of Edward Hotham (d 1985), and Freda Elizabeth, *née* Smith (d 1988); *b* 30 May 1933; *Educ* Warwick Sch; *m* 6 Nov 1954, Patricia Margaret, da of George Henry Day (d 1956); 2 s (Charles Anthony b 7 Sept 1959, Timothy Edward b 9 Oct 1961); *Career* Nat Serv 1952, cmmnd RASC 1953, TA 1954, Capt 1957, Maj 7 Bn Worcs Regt TA 1967, ret 1969; md Starr Roadways Ltd 1968-72; called to the Bar Middle Temple 1971, practised 1973-; memb CIT (until 1982), p/t pres Mental Health Review Tbnl; *Recreations* squash, golf, skiing; *Clubs* GB Ski; *Style*— Anthony Hotham, Esq, TD; 5 Fountain Court, Steelhouse Lane, Birmingham B4 6DR (☎ 021 236 5771, fax 021 236 2358, car 0836 636041)

HOTHAM, Capt (John) David Durand; s of John Beaumont Hotham (d 1924), and Gladys Mary, *née* Wilson (d 1972); *b* 5 Aug 1917; *Educ* Eton, New Coll Oxford (BA); *m* 11 Dec 1954, Marianne, da of Col Louis Pollak (d 1941), of Austria; *Career* Capt ret, serv M East, Italy, (Africa Star and Italian Campaign Medal); journalist and writer; corr The Times: Saigon 1955-57, Turkey 1958-66, Bonn 1966-69; *Books* The Turks (1972), Britain and Europe: Stay In Or Pull Out? (1975); *Recreations* music, golf, languages; *Clubs* New (Edinburgh); *Style*— Capt David Hotham; Milne Graden, Coldstream, Scotland (☎ 0289 82245)

HOTHAM, 8 Baron (I 1797); Sir Henry Durand Hotham; 18 Bt (E 1662), DL (Humberside 1981); 3 s of 7 Baron Hotham, CBE (d 1967), and Lady Letitia Cecil, da of 5 Marquess of Exeter; *b* 3 May 1940; *Educ* Eton; *m* 1972, Alexandra, 2 da of Maj Andrew Charles Stirling Home Drummond Moray; 2 s (Hon William, Hon George b 1974) 1 da (Hon Elizabeth b 1976); *Heir* s, Hon William Beaumont Hotham b 13 Oct 1972; *Career* former Lt Grenadier Gds; patron of 1 living; ADC to Gov Tasmania 1963-66; *Style*— The Rt Hon Lord Hotham, DL; Scorborough Hall, Driffield, Yorks; Dalton Hall, Dalton Holme, Beverley, Yorks

HOTHAM, Dowager Baroness; Lady Letitia Sibell Winifred; *née* Cecil; da of late 5 Marquess of Exeter, KG, CMG, TD and Hon Myra, *née* Orde-Powlett, da of 4 Baron Bolton, and Lady Algitha Lumley, da of 9 Earl of Scarbrough; *b* 1903; *m* 1937, 7 Baron Hotham (d 1967); 6 s (incl 8 Baron; 3 are decd); *Career* lady-in-waiting to HRH the Duchess of Gloucester 1935-37; *Style*— The Rt Hon The Dowager Lady Hotham; The School House, Dalton Holme, Beverley, Yorks

HOTHAM, Martin Patrick; only s of Lt Cdr The Hon David Hotham, DSC, RN (d 1962, bro of 7 Baron Hotham), and Aileen, *née* Coates; *b* 17 Aug 1941; *Educ* Stowe; *m* 2 Oct 1965, Erica Antoinette, da of Lt-Col Brian Maxwell Strang (d 1971), of N Wales; 2 s (Charles Beaumont David b 1969, Henry Ralph b 1974 d 1986), 2 da (Sophia Henrietta b 1967, Amelia Oriana Philadelphia b 1971); *Career* admitted slr 1966; *Recreations* shooting, racing, reading; *Clubs* Ipswich and Suffolk; *Style*— Martin Hotham, Esq; The Old Rectory, Drinkstone, Bury St Edmunds, Suffolk (☎ 0359 70834); 32 Lloyds Ave, Ipswich, Suffolk (☎ 0473 213311, fax 0473 257739)

HOTHAM, Maj Hon Peter; s of Capt Henry Edward Hotham (d 1912), and bro of 7 Baron (d 1967); raised to the rank of a Baron's son 1924; *b* 1904; *Educ* Winchester, RMC; *m* 1934, Margaret, da of Col Sir Robert Williams-Wynn, 9 Bt, KCB, DSO, TD (d 1951); 1 s, 2 da; *Career* Capt KOYLI 1936, Maj 1941, ret 1947; *Clubs* Buck's; *Style*— Maj The Hon Peter Hotham; Plas Newydd, Glascoed, Abergele, N Wales

HOTHERSALL, Dr (Thomas) Edward; s of Thomas Hothersall (d 1971), of Accrington, Lancashire, and Mary Alice, *née* O'Connor (d 1985); *b* 23 Sept 1939; *Educ* Thornleigh Coll Bolton, Univ of Edinburgh (MB ChB); *m* 4 April 1964, Pauline Ann, da of James Hepburn Waterston McMartin (d 1941); 4 s (Martin, James, Thomas, Duncan); *Career* res fell (diabetes) Royal Infirmary Edinburgh 1964-65, registrar Northern Gen Hosp Edinburgh 1966-69; conslt physician: Devonshire Royal Hosp 1969-79, N Staffs Health Authy 1969-; Midlands Rheumatology Soc: fndr sec 1972, pres 1979-82; chm Regnl Rheumatology Servs Ctee 1977-80 and 1983-85, pres Br Med Assoc N & Mid-Staff div 1978-79, dir of Depts of Rheumatology & Remedial Servs Staffs Rheumatology Centre 1981-; Br Soc Rheumatology: memb Cncl 1985-87, chm Clinical Affrs Ctee 1988-; Speciality Advsy Ctee (rheumatology) of Jt Ctee on Higher Med Trg: memb 1985-88, chm 1988-91; regnl advsr RCP of Edinburgh (W Midlands) 1982-, elected chm NW Rheumatology Club 1989-91, pres N Staffs Med Soc 1989-90, fndr chm Haywood Rheumatism Res & Devpt Fndn, pres Arthritis & Rheumatism Cncl (Potteries branch), chm N Staffs & Dist Cricket League, elected chm Med Advsy Ctee North Staffs Health Dist 1991-; memb: Ctee and hon med offr Staffordshire CCC, Stoke-on-Trent Rotary Club (sr vice pres 1991-92); *Style*— Dr Edward Hothersall; 540 Etruria Rd, Basford, Newcastle-under-Lyme, Staffs ST5 0SX (☎ 0782 614419, fax 0782 630270)

HOTHFIELD, 6 Baron (UK 1881), of Hothfield, Co Kent; Sir Anthony Charles Sackville Tufton; 7 Bt (UK 1851); s of 5 Baron Hothfield, TD, DL (d 1991), and Evelyn Margarette, *née* Mordaunt (d 1989); *b* 21 Oct 1939; *Educ* Eton, Magdalene Coll Cambridge (MA); *m* 1975, Lucinda Marjorie, da of Capt Timothy John Gurney, and formerly w of Capt Graham Morison Vere Nicoll; 1 s (Hon William Sackville b 1977), 1 da (Hon Emma b 1976); *Heir* s, Hon William Sackville Tufton b 14 Nov 1977; *Career* amateur tennis champion (singles 1964, doubles 1962, 1963 and 1964); CEng, MICE; *Style*— The Rt Hon Lord Hothfield; The Garden House, 11A High Street, Barkway, Royston, Herts SG8 8EA

HOUFE, Simon Richard; s of Eric Alfred Scholefield Houfe, and Kathleen, *née* Richardson (d 1983); *b* 13 Sept 1942; *Educ* Stowe, Italy; *Career* journalist and biographer; on staff V and A Museum 1963-65, working on art collection in Italy 1965, ed The Antique Collector 1970-74, antiques corr Homes and Gardens 1976-87, memb Projects Ctee Nat Art Collections Fund 1974-80; *Books* Old Bedfordshire (1975), The Birth of The Studio, 1893-1895 (1976), The Dalziel Family, Engravers and Illustrators (1978), The Dictionary of British Illustrators and Caricaturists, 1800-1914 (1978), Sir Albert Richardon - The Professor (1980), John Leech and The Victorian Scene (1984), Through Visitors Eyes, An Anthology (1990), Charles Keene, Catalogue (1991); contrib to: Apollo, Antiquarian Book Monthly Review, Country Life, A La Carte, Bedfordshire Magazine, Watercolours and Drawings; wrote chapter on antiques official programme book for Britain's entry to the EEC 1972; *Recreations* collecting; *Style*— Simon R Houfe, Esq; Avenue House, Ampthill, Beds MK45 2EH (☎ 0525 402115)

HOUGH, George Hubert; CBE (1965); s of late Wilfrid Hough; *b* 21 Oct 1921; *Educ* Winsford Verdin GS Cheshire, King's Coll London (PhD); *m* 1943, Hazel Ayrton, da of late Kenneth Russell; 1 s, 2 da; *Career* md Hawker Siddeley Dynamics Ltd 1977-78; memb: British Aerospace Bd, BAC Guided Weapons Div Bd 1977-78; chm and chief exec Br Smelter Constructions Ltd 1978-80, dir Programmed Neuro Cybernetics (UK Ltd) 1979-84, chm Forthstar Ltd 1980-; dir: Landis & Gyr UK 1978-84, Leigh Instruments Ltd (Canada) 1987-88; chm: Magnetic Components Ltd 1986-89, Abasec Ltd 1988-, Fernua Hldgs 1989-; *Books* The Anatomy of Major Projects (with P Morris); *Recreations* shooting, golf; *Clubs* St James's; *Style*— George H Hough, Esq, CBE; Trelyon, Rock, Wadebridge, Cornwall (☎ 0208 863454)

HOUGH, Prof James Richard; s of George Hough, of Brighton, Sussex, and Eileen Isobel, *née* Donovan; *b* 2 Aug 1937; *Educ* Xaverian Coll Brighton, Brighton GS, Univ of Keele (BA), Univ of London (MSc), Univ of Leicester (PhD); *m* 31 Aug 1968, Jane Louise, da of Vernon Blake Vincent (d 1982); 2 s (Steven David b 1972, Richard Martin b 1974), 1 da (Catherine Theresa b 1978); *Career* exec Lloyd's Underwriters 1953-65, sr lectr econ Huddersfield Poly 1971-72; Loughborough Univ of Technol: lectr 1972-77, sr lectr 1977-84, reader 1984-85, dean of educn and humanities 1985-88, prof 1988-; conslt on econs of educn for: World Bank, UNESCO, IIEP, The Br Cncl, ODA, TETOC; *Books* A Study of School Costs (1981), The French Economy (1982), Educational Policy (1984), Education and the National Economy (1987); *Recreations* walking, tennis, cycling, historical biography; *Style*— Prof James R Hough; Loughborough University, Loughborough, Leics LE11 3TU (☎ 0509 222752)

HOUGH, Richard; s of G S Hough (d 1970), of Brighton, and Margaret, *née* Esilman (d 1974); *b* 15 May 1922; *Educ* Frensham Heights; *m* 1, 17 July 1943 (m dis 1980), Helen Charlotte Woodyatt; 4 da (Sarah, Alexandra, Deborah, Bryony); m 2, 7 June 1980, Julie Marie (Judy) Taylor, MBE; *Career* Flt Lt RAF Pilot Fighter Cmd 1941-46; book publishing; mangr Bodley Head 1947-55, dir Hamish Hamilton 1955-70 (dir, fndr and md Hamish Hamilton Children's Books Ltd and Elm Tree Books); freelance writer 1955-; cncl memb and vice pres Navy Records Soc 1970-82, chm Auxiliary Hosps Ctee King Edward VII's Hosp Fund 1975-80 (cncl memb 1970-84); *Books* The Fleet That Had to Die (1958), Admirals in Collision (1959), The Potemkin Mutiny (1960), The Hunting of Force Z (1963), Dreadnought (1964), The Big Battleship (1966), First Sea Lord: an authorised life of Admiral Lord Fisher (1969), The Blind Horn's Hate (1971), Captain Bligh and Mr Christian (1972, Daily Express Best Book of the Sea Award), Louis and Victoria: the first Mountbattens (1974), One Boy's War: per astra ad ardua (1975), Advice to a Grand-daughter (Queen Victoria's letters, ed, 1975), The Great Admirals (1977), The Murder of Captain James Cook (1979), Man o' War (1979), Nelson (1980), Mountbatten: Hero of Our Time (1980), The Great War at Sea: 1914-1918 (1983), Edwina, Countess Mountbatten of Burma (1983), Former Naval Person: Churchill and the Wars at Sea (1985), The Ace of Clubs: a History of the Garrick (1986), The Longest Battle; the War at Sea 1939-45 (1986), Born Royal: the lives and loves of the the Windsors (1988), The Battle of Britain: the Jubilee History (with Denis Richards, 1989), Winston and Clementine, The Triumph of the Churchills (1990); *Clubs* Garrick, Beefsteak, MCC; *Style*— Richard Hough, Esq; 31 Meadowbank, Primrose Hill Road, London NW3 3AY (☎ 071 722 5663)

HOUGHAM, John William; s of William George Hougham, of Ash, Canterbury, Kent, and Emily Jane, *née* Smith; *b* 18 Jan 1937; *Educ* Sir Roger Manwood's Sch Sandwich Kent, Univ of Leeds (BA); *m* 26 Aug 1961, Peggy Edith, da of Ernest Grove (d 1972), of Hales Owen, Worcs; 1 s (Simon b 1967), 1 da (Elizabeth b 1965); *Career* Royal Regt of Artillery 1955-57 (2 Lt 1956), TA 1957-60 (Lt 1959); dir industl rels: Ford Espana SA Valencia Spain 1976-80, rels mfrg Ford of Europe Inc 1982-86; exec dir for personnel Ford Motor Co Ltd 1986-; memb: Cncl CRAC, Bd Personnel Mgmnt Servs Ltd, CBI Employment Policy Ctee, Engrg Indust Trg Bd, Cncl Engrg Trg Authy Ltd, IPM Ctee on Equal Opportunities, Trg and Employment Advsy Bd NI; FIPM 1980, CBIM 1986; *Recreations* walking, collecting books on Kent, fishing; *Style*— John Hougham, Esq; Ford Motor Co Ltd, Warley, Brentwood, Essex CM13 3BW (☎ 0277 253 000, fax 0277 262 066)

HOUGHTON, Dr John Theodore; CBE (1983); s of Sidney Maurice Houghton (d 1987), of Abingdon, and Miriam, *née* Yarwood (d 1974); *b* 30 Dec 1931; *Educ* Rhyl GS, Jesus Coll Oxford (MA, DPhil); *m* 1, 1962, Margaret Edith (d 1986), da of Neville

Broughton, of Colne, Lancs; 1 s (Peter b 1966), 1 da (Janet b 1964); m 2, 1988, Sheila, da of Sydney Thompson, of Bradford, Yorks; *Career* res fell Royal Aircraft Estab, lectr in atmospheric physics Oxford 1948 (reader 1962, prof 1976), official fell and tutor in physics Jesus Coll Oxford 1960-73 (prof fell 1973, hon fell 1983), visiting prof Univ of California LA 1969; developed: Selective Chopper Radiometer (for the Nimbus 4 and 5 satellites), Pressure Modulator Radiometer (flown on Nimbus 6) 1975, Stratospheric and Mesopheric Sounder (flown on Nimbus 7) 1978; Darton Prize (RMS) 1954, Buchan Prize (RMS) 1966, Charles Chree Medal of the Inst of Physics 1979, Glazebrook medal Inst of Physics 1989, jt winner Rank prize for oplo electronics 1989; fell Optical Soc of America; memb: American Meteorological Soc, American Geophysical Union; chm Jt Scientific Ctee for World Climate Res Programmes 1981-84, vice pres World Meteorological Orgn 1987-; FRS, FInstP, FRMets (pres 1976-78); *Books* Infra Red Physics (with S D Smith, 1966), The Physics of Atmospheres (1977, ed 1986), Remote Sensing of Atmospheres (with F W Taylor and C D Rodgers, 1984), The Global Climate (ed, 1984), Does God Play Dice? (1988); *Style—* Dr John Houghton, CBE, FRS; Chief Executive, Meteorological Office, London Road, Bracknell Berks RG12 2SZ

HOUGHTON, Raymond J (Ray); *b* 9 Jan 1962; *Career* professional footballer; 1 appearance West Ham Utd 1979-82, 129 league appearances Fulham 1982-85; Oxford Utd 1985-87: joined for a fee of £125,000, 83 league appearances, 10 goals; Liverpool 1987-; joined for a fee of £825,000, debut Oct 1987, over 100 appearances; 36 full caps Republic of Ireland 1986-90, represented Republic of Ireland in Euro Championships W Germany 1988 and World Cup Italy 1990; honours: League Cup 1986 (Oxford Utd), League Championship 1988 (Liverpool), FA Cup 1989 (Liverpool runners up 1988); *Style—* Ray Houghton, Esq; Liverpool FC, Anfield Road, Anfield, Liverpool L4 OTH (☎ 051 263 2361)

HOUGHTON, Maj-Gen Robert Dyer; CB (1962), OBE (1947), MC (1942), DL (1977); s of John Mayo Houghton, of Sarum, Dawlish, Devon (d 1947), and Lucy Evelyn, *née* Trotman (d 1973); *b* 7 March 1912; *Educ* Haileybury; *m* 1940, Dorothy Uladh, da of late Maj-Gen R W S Lyons, IMS; 2 s (John, Neill), 1 da (Lucy); *Career* RM Offr 1930-64, Maj-Gen 1961, Chief of Amphibious Warfare 1961, ADC to HM The Queen 1959-64; Col Cmdt RM 1973-75; gen sec Royal Utd Kingdom Beneficent Assoc 1968-78; *Recreations* gardening, model engrg; *Clubs* Army and Navy; *Style—* Maj-Gen Robert Houghton, CB, OBE, MC, DL; Vert House, Whitesmith, nr Lewes (☎ 0825 872451)

HOUGHTON OF SOWERBY, Baron (Life Peer UK 1974); Arthur Leslie Noel Douglas Houghton; CH (1967), PC (1964); s of John Houghton, of Long Eaton, Derbys; *b* 11 Aug 1898; *m* 1939, Vera, da of John Travis, of Southall; *Career* Lab whip in House of Lords; sec Inland Revenue Staff Fedn 1922-60, MP (Lab) Sowerby 1949-74, chllr Duchy of Lancaster 1964-66, min without portfolio 1966-67, chm PLP 1967-74; broadcaster BBC 1941-64, alderman LCC 1947-49; memb: Gen Cncl TUC 1952-60, Royal Cmmn on Standards of Conduct in Public Life; chm: Teachers' Pay Inquiry, Ctee on Finances of Political Parties, Ctee on Security of Cabinet Papers 1974-76, Ctee for Reform of Animal Experiments; vice pres: RSPCA 1978-82, Bldg Socs Assoc, League Against Cruel Sports; *Clubs* Reform; *Style—* The Rt Hon the Lord Houghton of Sowerby, CH, PC; Becks Cottage, Whitehill Lane, Bletchingley, Redhill, Surrey (☎ 0783 843340 3340); 110 Marsham Court, London SW1 (☎ 071 834 0602)

HOUISON CRAUFURD, Hon Mrs (Caroline Helen); *née* Berry; da of 2 Viscount Kemsley; *b* 1942; *m* 1965, John Peter Houison Craufurd of Craufurdland and Braehead; 2 s, 1 da; *Style—* The Hon Mrs Houison Craufurd; Craufurdland Castle, Kilmarnock, Ayrshire

HOULDEN, Prof Brian Thomas; s of Thomas Houlden, MBE, JP (d 1961), and Grace Ethel, *née* Webb (d 1989); *b* 23 April 1926; *Educ* Imperial Coll Univ of London (BSc, PhD, DIC, ARSM); *m* 2 Aug 1952, Margaret Joyce (d 1983), da of William Charles Douglas (d 1987); 2 s (Kim Peter b 1955, John Russell b 1959); *Career* scientist Br Non-Ferrous Metals Res Assoc 1949-51, dir of operational res NCB 1961-66 (scientist 1951-61), IOD prof of business studies Univ of Warwick 1966-; chm: Crofton Ltd, Bowker and Budd Ltd, Grass Concrete Ltd 1973-76; dir: MTG Ltd, Caird and Rayner Ltd 1977-79; chm Coventry Printers Ltd 1980-82; FInstD, memb Strategic Planning Soc, memb Operational Res Soc; *Books* Some Techniques of Operational Research (1962), Understanding Company Strategy (1990); *Recreations* golf; *Style—* Prof Brian Thomas Houlden; Inst of Directors' Professor Business Studies, Warwick Business School, University of Warwick, Coventry CV4 7AL (☎ 0203 523915)

HOULDSWORTH, Margaret, Lady; Margaret May; *née* Laurie; 4 da of Cecil Emilius Laurie, JP (d 1919; 3 s of Rev Sir Emilius Laurie, 3 Bt), and Helen Janet Douglas, *née* Campbell (d 1919); *b* 13 Jan 1908; *m* 30 April 1934, Lt-Col Sir Reginald Douglas Henry Houldsworth, 4 Bt, OBE, TD, DL (d 1989); 1 s, 2 da; *Style—* Margaret, Lady Houldsworth; Kirkbride, Maybole, Ayrshire (☎ 065 54 202)

HOULDSWORTH, Lady; Norah Clifford; *née* Halmshaw; da of Arthur Halmshaw, of Heckmondwike, Yorks; *m* 24 Sept 1946, Sir (Harold) Basil Houldsworth, 2 and last Bt (d 1990); 1 da ((Sarah) Belinda Clifford b 1949); *Style—* Lady Houldsworth; Shadwell House, Lundhill Rd, Wombwell, nr Barnsley, Yorks

HOULDSWORTH, Philippa Caroline (Pippy); da of Maj Ian George Henry Houldsworth, TD, JP (d 1963), of Dallas Lodge, Forres, Moray, and Clodagh, *née* Murray, JP; *b* 17 Aug 1957; *Educ* N Foreland Lodge, Sherfield on Loddon, Basingstoke; *Career* head buyer Children's Book Centre 1978-80, ed Childrens Book News 1981-82, mktg and PR consIt 1983-85, proprietor Houldsworth Fine Art 1987-; *Recreations* reading, tennis, riding, twentieth century painting and sculpture; *Style—* Miss Pippy Houldsworth; 46 Bassett Rd, London W10 6JL (☎ 081 969 8197, car 0836 66 44 84)

HOULDSWORTH, Sir Richard Thomas Reginald; 5 Bt (UK 1887), of Reddish, Manchester, Co Lancaster, and Coodham, Symington, Ayrshire; s of Sir Reginald Douglas Henry Houldsworth, 4 Bt, OBE, TD (d 1989), and Margaret May, *née* Laurie; *b* 2 Aug 1947; *Educ* Bredon Sch Tewkesbury; *m* 1970, Jane, o da of Alistair Orr, of Sydehead, Beith, Ayrshire; 2 s (Simon Richard Henry b 1971, Nicholas Peter George b 1975); *Heir* s, Simon Richard Henry Houldsworth b 1971; *Style—* Sir Richard Houldsworth, Bt; Kirkbride, Glenburn, Crosshill, Maybole, Ayrshire

HOULTON, (Arthur) Conrad Leighton; s of Arthur John Houlton (d 1951), of Marlborough Ave, Hessle, E Yorks, and Florence, *née* Thompson (d 1939); *b* 22 June 1908; *Educ* Hymers Coll Hull, Emmanuel Coll Cambridge (MA), St Bartholomew's Hosp Med Coll London (MA Oxon, MB BChir, DO, DOMS); *m* 12 June 1939, Edna Mary, da of Charles Pidsley (d 1956), of London; 3 s (John Leighton b 1944, Peter Godfrey b 1946, Michael Richard b 1947); *Career* ophthalmic surgn Oxford Eye Hosp 1938-73 (asst surgn 1938-42), clinical lectr in ophthalmology Univ of Oxford; chm Oxford Div BMA 1963, pres Oxford Med Soc 1966, vice pres and memb Cncl Section of Ophthalmology RSM, memb Prevention of Blindness Ctee RNIB; MRCS, LRCP, FCOphth; *Clubs* RSM, Rotary (Oxford); *Style—* Conrad Houlton, Esq; 1 Berrow Ct, Gardens Walk, Upton upon Severn, Worcs WR8 0JP (☎ 068 46 3407)

HOUNSFIELD, Sir Godfrey Newbold; CBE (1976); s of Thomas Hounsfield; *b* 28 Aug 1919; *Educ* Magnus GS Newark, Farady House Coll, City Coll London; *Career* consIt scientist central Res laboratories of Thorn EMI Hayes Middx (formerly sr staff scientist); kt 1981; *Style—* Sir Godfrey Hounsfield, CBE; 15 Crane Park Rd, Whitton, Middlesex TW12 6DF

HOUSE, Lt-Gen Sir David George; GCB (1977, KCB 1975), KCVO (1985), CBE (1967, OBE 1964), MC (1944); o s of Arthur George House, of 98 Wimpole Street, London W1; *b* 8 Aug 1922; *Educ* Regent's Park Sch London; *m* 25 Oct 1947, Sheila Betty Germaine, o da of Capt Robert Henry Darwin, Yorks Regt (d 1944); 2 da (Jennifer Rosamund b 18 July 1948, Elizabeth Mary b 2 Sept 1953); *Career* serv WWII Italy KRRC, dep mil sec MOD 1969-71, Maj-Gen 1971, COS HQ BAOR 1971-73, Lt-Gen 1973, dir of inf MOD 1973-75, GOC and Dir (Ops) NI 1975-77, ret; Col Cmdt: Small Arms Sch Corps 1974-77, The Light Div 1974-77; gentleman usher of the Black Rod House of Lords 1978-85; regnl dir Lloyds Bank Yorks and Humberside Regn 1985; *Style—* Lt-Gen Sir David House, GCB, KCVO, CBE, MC; Dormer Lodge, Aldborough, nr Boroughbridge, N Yorks YO5 9EP

HOUSE, Dr John Peter Humphry; s of (Arthur) Humphry House (d 1955), and Madeline Edith, *née* Church (d 1978); *b* 19 April 1945; *Educ* Westminster, New Coll Oxford (BA), Courtauld Inst of Art Univ of London (MA), Univ of London (PhD); *m* 31 Aug 1968, Jill Elaine, da of Ernest Sackville Turner, OBE, of Kew, Surrey; 2 s (Adam b 1973, Joseph b 1975); *Career* lectr: UEA 1969-76, UCL 1976-80, Courtauld Inst of Art Univ of London 1980-87; Slade prof of fine art Univ of Oxford 1986-87, reader Courtauld Inst of Art Univ of London 1987-, awarded Br Acad Res Readership 1988-90; organiser Impressionism exhibition Royal Acad of Arts 1974; co-organiser: Post-Impressionism exhibition Royal Acad of Arts 1979-80, Renoir exhibition Arts Cncl of GB 1985; *Books* Monet (1976, enlarged ed 1981), Monet; Nature into Art (1986), Impressionist and Post-Impressionist Masterpieces: The Courtauld Collection (co-author, 1987); *Recreations* second-hand bookshops; *Style—* Dr John House; Courtauld Inst of Art, Univ of London, Somerset House, The Strand, London WC2R ORN (☎ 071 872 0220)

HOUSE, Keren Ruth (Mrs John Hookway); s of Alan Sidney House, of 43 Russell Hill Road, Purley, Surrey, and Maureen Elizabeth Evelyn, *née* Atkinson; *b* 1 June 1951; *Educ* Purley Co GS for Girls, London Coll of Printing (BA), RCA (MA); *m* 9 Feb 1980, John Hookway, s of Leslie Hookway; 2 da (Jessica Rose b 27 Aug 1984, Eleanor Kate b 22 Oct 1987); *Career* lectr in graphic design Pennsylvania State Univ USA 1976-78; graphic designer: Bloomfield/Travis London 1978-79, Pentagram London 1979-81; pt/t lectr in graphic design Harrow Sch of Art 1981-82, fndr ptnr (with David Stuart) The Partnership London 1981-83, fndr ptnr and dir The Partners London 1983-87, art dir Glenn Travis Associates London 1988-90, external assessor BA course in graphic design Bath Coll of Higher Educn 1988-91, design dir the Design Bridge London 1990-; work accepted: D&ADA Annual and exhibition 1979, 1981, 1983, 1985, 1987 and 1989, Communication Art Annual (USA) 1982, 1986 and 1989; memb Jury Design & Art Direction: graphics 1986 and 1990, Illustration 1989; memb: D&ADA 1978, CSD 1982; *Recreations* my children, husband, house and garden; *Style—* Ms Keren House; The Design Bridge, 8-16 Cromer St, London WC1H 8LX (☎ 071 833 1311, fax 071 837 3084)

HOUSE, Hon Mrs (Susan Anne); *née* Irving; o da of Baron Irving of Dartford, PC, DL (Life Peer, d 1989); *b* 1946; *m* 1966, John House; *Style—* The Hon Mrs House; c/o The Lady Irving of Dartford, 10 Tynedale Close, Dartford, Kent

HOUSEGO-WOOLGAR, William Micheal; s of George Arthur Housego, of Brighton, and Irene Maureen, *née* Newman; *b* 3 July 1944; *Educ* Brighton Sch of Architecture, Leeds Sch of Town Planning, Brighton Mgmnt Coll (DipArch, DipTP, DMS); *m* 13 July 1968, Diana Lilian, da of William Woolgar (d 1971); 1 s (Alexis b 24 Nov 1970), 1 da (Isabella b 1 Oct 1972); *Career* Warr and King Hove 1966-67, architect and planner Leeds City Cncl 1969-72, asst borough planning offr and gp leader Brighton Cncl 1972-76, asst cmmr Sultanate Brunei Peranghan Bandar Dan Negara 1976-79, advsr Miny of Foreign Affrs Riyadh Dip Quartar Saudi Arabia 1980-83, sr architectural and planning advsr ODA 1983-; UK rep UN cmmn of human settlements 1984-89, Euro Bank for Reconstruction and Devpt 1991-; MRIBA 1972, MBIM 1975, FRSA 1976, MRIPA 1976, FRTPI 1988 (MRTPI 1975); *Recreations* tennis, philately, squash, ESP planning; *Clubs* Royale, Savage; *Style—* William Housego-Woolgar, Esq; ODA, Eland House, Stag Place, London SW1E 5DH (☎ 071 273 0406, telex 263907/8, fax 071 273 0652)

HOUSEMAN, Alexander Randolph; CBE (1984); s of Capt Alexander William Houseman (d 1962), and Elizabeth Maud, *née* Randolph (d 1986); *b* 9 May 1920; *Educ* Stockport GS, Stockport Coll; *m* 1942, Betty Edith (d 1990), da of Alfred G Norrington (d 1976); 1 da; *Career* apprenticed Crossley Motors Ltd and Fairey Aviation, prodn engr Ford Motor Co (aero engines) Ltd 1940-43, Saunders-Roe Ltd 1943-48, gen works mangr 1948-54, consIt (later dir, md and dep chm) P-E Int 1954-81; chm: W Canning Ltd 1975-80, NEDO EDC Gauge and Tool Indust 1978-85; dir: P-E Consulting Gp Ltd 1968-81, Record Ridgway Ltd 1978-81; dir and dep chm British Rail Engrg Ltd 1979-89; memb: Cncl Inst of Mgmnt Conslts 1968-80, industl advsy panel of Fellowship of Engrg 1980-; FEng, FIMechE, FIProdE (pres 1983-84), FIMC, CBIM, FRSA, life memb SME (USA), Hon Memb IIE (USA); various awards incl Nat Soc of Professional Engrs Distinguished Engrg Mgmnt Award (USA); *Recreations* DIY, walking, sailing, photography; *Clubs* Caledonian, RYA; *Style—* Alexander Houseman, Esq, CBE; 11 Kings Ave, Ealing, London W5 2SJ (☎ 081 997 3936)

HOUSLAY, Prof Miles Douglas; s of (Edwin) Douglas Houslay, of Wolverhampton, and Georgina Marie (Molly), *née* Jeffs; *b* 25 June 1950; *Educ* The Grammar Sch Brewood Staffs, UC Cardiff (BSc), Kings Coll Cambridge (PhD); *m* 29 July 1972, Rhian Mair, da of Charles Henry Gee, of Aberystwyth, Wales; 2 s (Thomas b 29 March 1981, Daniel b 21 Feb 1988), 1 da (Emma b 14 Feb 1978); *Career* res fell Queens' Coll Cambridge 1975-76 (ICI postdoctoral res fell Dept of Biochemistry 1974-76), reader in biochemistry UMIST 1982-84 (lectr 1976-82), Gardiner prof of biochemistry Univ of Glasgow 1984-; hon sr res fell: California Metabolic Res Fndn 1982-, Hannah Res Inst 1988-; Selby fell Aust Acad of Sci 1984; over 200 res pubns; Colworth medal Biochemical Soc GB 1985; FRSE, FIBiol, CBiol, FRSA; *Books* Dynamics of Biological Membranes (with K K Stanley, 1983); *Recreations* reading, hill walking, sailing, driving; *Style—* Prof Miles Houslay, FRSE; Molecular Pharmacology Group, Dept of Biochemistry, University of Glasgow, Glasgow G12 8QQ, Scotland (☎ 041 330 5903, fax 041 330 4620)

HOUSLEY, Dr Edward; s of Albert Edward Housley (d 1980), and Minnie, *née* Blagden (d 1934); *b* 10 Jan 1934; *Educ* Mundella GS, Univ of Birmingham (MB ChB); *m* 8 July 1956, Alma Mary, da of Harold Ferris (d 1968); 1 da (Lucy Elizabeth b 1962); *Career* short serv cmmn RAMC 1960-63; consIt physician Royal Infirmary Edinburgh 1970-, hon sr lectr in med Univ of Edinburgh 1970-, med specialist Armed Forces Scotland 1975-, dir Murrayfield plc 1982-; FRCPE 1975, FRCP 1979, FRSM 1986; *Recreations* tennis, skiing, crossword puzzles; *Style—* Dr Edward Housley; 16 Sunbury Place, Edinburgh EH4 3BY, (☎ 031 225 2040); Murrayfield Hospital, Edinburgh EH12 6UD, (☎ 031 334 0363)

HOUSLEY, Michael John Vernon; s of Ronald Housley, of Gorgys, High Rd, Chigwell, Essex, and Josephine Milne Housley (d 1988); *b* 15 March 1934; *Educ* Coopers' Company's Sch, King's Coll London; *m* 10 Sept 1960, Helen Russell, da of

Rex Ransom (d 1970), of 20 Blakehall Cres, London E11; 3 s (Russell b 15 March 1964, Richard b 12 March 1967, Matthew b 8 Oct 1970), 1 da (Catherine b 30 May 1962); *Career* Nat Serv RN 1954-56; dir Scott North & Co Ltd 1964-66 (joined as trainee 1956), sr ptnr Housley Heath & Co 1966-76; md: Hambro Housley Heath Ltd 1977-79, Michael Housley Ltd (insur broker) 1980-; memb Lloyds; gp scout ldr 1956, asst Co Cmmnr (Int) Essex 1984-; govr: Coopers Co and Coburn Educn Fdn, Coopers' Co Sch; Freeman City of London, Liveryman Worshipful Co of Coopers (memb Ct of Assts and treas), Liveryman Worshipful Co of Insurers; ACII 1960; *Recreations* walking, sailing, music; *Clubs* City of London East India; *Style*— MJV Housley, Esq; 4 Burnt House, Pudding Lane, Chigwell, Essex 1G7 6BY (☎ 081 500 3544); Barclays Bank Chambers, 99-101 Commercial St, London E1 6BG (☎ 071 247 3202, fax 071 375 1664, car phone 0836 230818, 0836 246 705, telex 265871 MONREF G Quote SJJ029 in First Line)

HOUSSEMAYNE DU BOULAY, Sir Roger William; KCVO (1982, CVO 1972), CMG (1975); s of Capt Charles Houssemayne du Boulay, RN; *b* 30 March 1922; *Educ* Winchester, Univ of Oxford; *m* 1957, Elizabeth, da of late Brig Francis Wyville Home, and Molly, Lady Pile (d 1988); 1 da, 2 step s; *Career* serv WWII, RAFVR Flt Lt, Pilot; Colonial Serv in Nigeria, joined FO 1959, Washington 1960-64, FO 1964-67; cnsllr Manila 1967-71, dir Asian Devpt Bank 1967-71 (alternate dir 1967-69), cnsllr and head chancery Paris 1971-73, resident cmmr New Hebrides 1973-75, Vice-Marshal Dip Corps 1975-82; *Recreations* bellringing, riding, gardening; *Clubs* Boodles; *Style*— Sir Roger Houssemayne du Boulay, KCVO, CMG; Anstey House, nr Buntingford, Herts

HOUSTON, Hon Mrs (Averil); *née* Vivian; JP (Herts); da of late 3 Baron Swansea, DSO, MVO, and Hon Winifred, *née* Hamilton, da of 1 Baron Holm Patrick, PC, and Lady Victoria, *née* Wellesley, sis of 3 and 4 Dukes of Wellington; *b* 1930; *m* 1953, Alexander William Houston; 2 s, 1 da; *Style*— The Hon Mrs Houston, JP; The Little House, Datchworth, Knebworth, Herts SG3 6ST

HOUSTON, Maj-Gen David; CBE (1975, OBE 1972), DL (Sutherland 1990); s of late David Houston, and Christina Charleson, *née* Dunnett; *b* 24 Feb 1929; *Educ* Latymer Upper Sch; *m* 1959, Jancis Veronica Burn; 2 s; *Career* cmmnd Royal Irish Fus 1949; cmd 1 Loyals then 1 QLR 1969-71, 8 Inf Bde 1974-75, Br Mil Attaché Washington 1977-79, BGS HQ UKLF 1979-80; pres Regular Cmmns Bd 1980-83, Col Queen's Lancs Regt 1983-; Hon Col Manchester & Salford Univ OTC 1985-90; *Style*— Maj-Gen David Houston, CBE, DL; c/o Bank of Scotland, Bonar Bridge, Sutherland IV24 3EB

HOUSTON, Prof Ian Briercliffe; s of Dr Walter Houston, and Nancy, *née* Briercliffe; *b* 11 Sept 1932; *Educ* Baines GS Poulton le Fylde, Univ of Manchester (MB ChB, MD); *m* 12 May 1956, Pamela Beryl, da of Leslie Rushton; 1 s (Andrew Ian b 9 Aug 1960), 2 da (Jacqueline Pamela b 7 Oct 1958, Fiona Elizabeth b 9 July 1963); *Career* Nuffield res fell Albert Einstein Coll of Med NY USA 1965-67, prof of child health Univ of Manchester 1974- (lectr 1963-69, sr lectr 1969-74), hon conslt in paediatrics Royal Manchester Childrens Hosp, dean of post grad med studies N Western Region; pres Assoc Of Clinical Profs Of Paediatrics, former pres Euro Soc For Paediatric Nephrology; memb: Br Paediatric Assoc 1968, Euro Soc For Paediatric Nephrology 1967, Assoc Of Clinical Profs and Heads Of Depts Of Paediatrics 1975; FRCP 1974; *Recreations* squash, gardening, walking; *Clubs* Northern Lawn Tennis; *Style*— Prof Ian Houston; Royal Manchester Children's Hospital, University Department of Child Health, Pendlebury, Manchester M27 1HA (☎ 061 794 ext 2231)

HOUSTON, James; s of Dr James Houston, of Warwick, and Joyce Graham, *née* Owens (d 1982); *b* 4 Oct 1946; *Educ* Oundle; *m* 9 Jan 1971, Edit Maria; 2 s (David James b 10 Jan 1975, Jonathan Matthew b 22 May 1981); *Career* articled clerk Russell Durie Kerr Watson (Birmingham office Spicer & Pegler, subsequently Spicer & Oppenheim, now Touche Ross) 1965-70; mangr Peat Marwick Mitchell Johannesburg 1971-76; Robson Rhodes: mangr and personal asst to the Midland Regnl Managing ptnr Birmingham 1977-80, ptnr Leicester 1981-, responsible for Corp Fin Servs East Midlands; memb Cncl Leicester C of C; *Recreations* golf, squash, tennis; *Clubs* Leicestershire (chm), Leicestershire Golf, Leicestershire Tennis, Leicester Squash; *Style*— James Houston, Esq; Robson Rhodes, 132 New Walk, Leicester LE1 7JA (☎ 0533 544 548)

HOUSTON, Dr James Caldwell; CBE (1982); s of David Houston (d 1955), and Minnie Walker Caldwell (d 1973); *b* 18 Feb 1917; *Educ* Mill Hill, Guy's Hosp Med Sch (MD); *m* 1946, Dr Thelma Cromarty, da of Prof John Cruickshank, CBE (d 1966), of Aberdeen; 4 s (Kenneth, Brian, Alan, Andrew); *Career* dean: Guy's Hosp Med and Dental Schs 1965-82, United Med and Dental Schs of Guy's and St Thomas's Hosps 1982-84; emeritus conslt physician Guy's Hosp, dir Clerical Med and Gen Life Assur Soc 1964-87, vice pres Med Def Union 1970-; FRCP; *Recreations* golf, gardening; *Clubs* Addington Golf; *Style*— Dr J Caldwell Houston, CBE; Discovery Cottage, St Katharine-by-the-Tower, London E1 9UG (☎ 071 481 8912); Cockhill Farm, Detling, Maidstone, Kent (☎ 0634 31395); Keats House, Guy's Hospital, SE1 9RT (☎ 071 955 5000)

HOUSTON, John; OBE (1990); s of Alexander Anderson Houston (d 1947), of Windygates, Fife, Scotland, and Alison Crichton, *née* McKelvie; *b* 1 April 1930; *Educ* Buckhaven HS Fife, Edingburgh Coll of Art (Dip Drawing and Painting, postgrad Dip, Andrew Grant travelling scholarship), Moray House Teachers Trg Coll (Teachers Trg Cert); *m* 1958, Elizabeth Violet, da of Thomas Blackader; *Career* dep head Sch of Drawing and Painting Edinburgh Coll of Art 1982-89 (teacher 1955-89); artist; works incl: Dusk (Scot Arts Cncl) 1971, Bathers (Carlsberg Breweries Copenhagen) 1966, Wisconsin Landscape (1969, Dune Sounds 1971, Lake Owen Wisconsin 1970-71, Summer In Fife (private collection Sweden) 1968, Low Tide, North Berwick 1982, Winter Walk 1985, Beach Party 1986-90, A Day By The Sea, Summer 1990; exhibits regularly with: Scot Gallery Edinburgh, Mercury Gallery London, Royal Scot Acad, Royal Acad, RGI; Awards incl: Guthrie award (Royal Scot Acad, 1964), Cargill prize (RGI, 1965 and 1988), Sir William Gillies prize (RSW, 1990); memb: SSA, RGI, RSW; RSA 1972; *Recreations* golf; *Clubs* Gullane Golf; *Style*— John Houston, Esq, OBE; 57 Fountainhall Rd, Edinbrugh EH9 2LH (☎ 031 667 3687)

HOUSTON, Robert Ian; s of Ivan Thomas Houston, of Gloucester (d 1985), and Joy, *née* Meehan (d 1987); *b* 18 Oct 1950; *Educ* Sebright Sch Worcestershire, Trent Poly Nottingham (BSc); *m* Gillian Duret, da of Frederick John Floyd; 2 s (Ian David b 8 July 1979, Andrew Robert b 6 May 1983), 1 da (Claire Alexandra b 10 March 1981); *Career* chartered surveyor; Richard Ellis 1972-80, chief exec Rowe & Pitman Property Services 1980-84, jt md Baring Houston & Saunders 1984-; FRICS; *Recreations* rugby, cricket; *Style*— Robert Houston, Esq; Winkford Lodge, Church Lane, Witley, nr Godalming, Surrey GU8 5PR (☎ 0428 683016); Baring, Houston & Saunders, Ellerman House, 12-20 Camomile St, London EC3A 7PT (☎ 071 621 1433, fax 071 623 8177)

HOUSTOUN, Lt-Col Andrew Beatty; OBE (1983), MC (1946), DL (Angus 1971); s of William McAulay Houstoun (d 1936), of Sachel Ct, Alfold, Surrey and Isobel Parke Irvine, *née* Beatty (d 1978); *b* 15 Oct 1922; *Educ* Harrow; *m* 14 Aug 1953, Mary Elizabeth, da of late Sir Douglas L Spencer-Nairn; 4 s (William, David, Alexander, Neil); *Career* Army 1941-56, 1 Royal Dragoons 1943-56, ret Maj 1956; joined Fife and Forfar Yeo Scottish Horse TA 1958, CO 1962-65, ret Lt-Col (& Brevet Col) 1965; farmer and landowner 1956-; memb Angus CC 1966-75 (vice chm Educn Ctee), vice pres Scot Landowner's Assoc 1983- (convener 1979-82), Scottish memb Euro Landowner's Orgn 1976-86, chllr's assessor Dundee Univ 1981-; Vice Lord Lt Angus 1987; *Recreations* country sports, gardening; *Clubs* Royal Perth Golfing Soc; *Style*— Lt-Col Andrew Houstoun, OBE, MC, DL; Lintrathen Lodge, Kirriemuir Angus DD8 5JJ (☎ 057 56 228)

HOUSTOUN-BOSWALL, Sir (Thomas) Alford; 8 Bt (UK 1836); s of Sir Thomas Houstoun-Boswall, 7 Bt (d 1982), by his 1 w (*see* Houstoun-Boswall, Margaret, Lady); *b* 23 May 1947; *m* 1971, Eliana Michele, da of Dr John Pearse, of NY; 1 s, 1 da (Julia Glencora b 1979); *Heir* s, Alexander Alford Houstoun-Boswall b 16 Sept 1972; *Style*— Sir Alford Houstoun-Boswall, Bt; 18 Rue Basse, Biot 06410, France (☎ 33 93 65 7244); 11 East 73rd St, New York City, NY 10021, USA (☎ 212 517 8057)

HOUSTOUN-BOSWALL, Margaret, Lady; Margaret; da of George Bullen-Smith, of Squirrels, Arlington, E Sussex; *m* 1945 (m dis 1970), as his 1 w, Sir Thomas Houstoun-Boswall, 7 Bt (d 1982); 1 s (Sir Alford H-B, 8 Bt, *qv*), 1 da (Georgina, m Alan Moore); *Career* Borough cncllr Eastbourne 1976-84; licentiate Guildhall Sch of Music; vice pres RELATE SE Sussex Marriage Guidance; *Style*— Margaret, Lady Houstoun-Boswall; 8 College Rd, Eastbourne, E Sussex (☎ 0323 32664)

HOVELL-THURLOW-CUMMING-BRUCE, Hon Roualeyn Robert; s and h of 8 Baron Thurlow, KCMG, *qv*; *b* 13 April 1952; *Educ* Milton Abbey; *m* 5 May 1980, Bridget Anne Julia, o da of (Hugh) Bruce Ismay Cheape, TD, of South Lodge, Craignure, Isle of Mull, Argyll; 2 s (Nicholas Edward b 1986, George Roualeyn Patrick b 1990), 1 da (Tessa Iona Bridget b 1987); *Clubs* Pratt's; *Style*— The Hon Roualeyn Hovell-Thurlow-Cumming-Bruce; 22 Hanover Sq, London W1R 0JL (☎ 071 493 6040, telex 23858)

HOW, Denzil Robert Onslow; s of Robert Boothby How (d 1990), of St Andrews, and Virginia, *née* Hughes-Onslow; *b* 3 Aug 1944; *Educ* Eton, Trinity Coll Cambridge; *m* 1, 1968 (m dis 1985), Sarah, da of John Collins, of Chetwode Manor, Buckingham; 4 da (Nicola b 1970, Antonia b 1975, Francesca b 1978, Georgina b 1981); m 2, 21 July 1989, Hon Catharine Gina Amita Vey, *née* Noble, eldest da of Baron Glenkinglass (Life Peer); *Career* chm: Rediweld Holdings plc 1972-, Mazer Wine Shippers plc 1985; *Recreations* stalking, shooting, skiing, golf, tennis, racing; *Clubs* Pitt (Cambridge), White's; *Style*— Denzil How, Esq; 23 Ladbroke Sq, London W11

HOW, Peter Cecil; s of Cecil How, of Lower Way, Upper Longdon, Rugeley, Staffs, and Dora, *née* Marshall (d 1960); *b* 27 June 1931; *Educ* Oundle, Open Univ (BA); *m* 21 Sept 1951, Jane, da of Thomas Erickson (d 1936); 2 s (Neil b 1952, Adam b 1954); *Career* dir Froggatt & Prior Ltd 1955-63; chm: How Group Ltd and assoc cos 1974-86 (dir 1963, chm How Group plc 1986-), Hansgross Estates plc 1986-, H & V Welfare Ltd 1974-90; pres: How Group Inc 1982-, Genie Climatique International 1986-88; memb W Midlands Regnl Cncl CBI 1979-85; memb Worshipful Co of Fan Makers 1975; *Recreations* travel, theatre, opera, music; *Clubs* East India, City Livery; *Style*— Peter How, Esq; 11 The Regents, Norfolk Rd, Edgbaston, Birmingham B15 3PP (☎ 021 454 4777); 5211 Everwood Run, Sarasota, Florida 34235, USA; How Group plc, Intersection House, West Bromwich, W Midlands B70 6RX (☎ 021 500 5000, fax 021 500 5159)

HOW, Ronald Mervyn; s of Mervyn Darvell How (d 1973), of Bucks, and Kathleen Dorothy, *née* Honour (d 1990); *b* 24 Dec 1927; *Educ* general schooling; *m* 30 June 1951, Brenda (d 1989), da of Harold Brown (d 1976), of Herts; 1 s (David b 1953), 1 da (Margaret b 1956); *Career* RAF AC1 1946-47; farmer; dir Br Poultry Fedn and Br Turkey Fedn 1978; treas: Chesham Rotary 1983-, Br Turkey Fedn 1984-88; pres Chesham Rotary 1981; ctee memb: Hawridge Commons Pres Soc 1970-, League of Friends Amersham and Chesham Hosps 1979- (now vice chm); Goodchild Trophy for Service to Turkey Indust 1987; *Recreations* tennis, computer programming, photography; *Clubs* Chesham Rotary, Amersham Photographic Soc; *Style*— Ronald How, Esq; Woodlands Cottage, The Vale, Chesham, Bucks (☎ 0494 782434); Woodlands Farm, The Vale, Chesham, Bucks (☎ 0494 783737)

HOWARD; *see*: Fitzalan Howard *or* Fitzalan-Howard

HOWARD, Hon Mrs Henry; Adèle le Bourgois Chapin; *née* Alsop; da of late Reese Denny Alsop, of New York City, USA; *b* 5 Nov 1914; *Educ* Bennington Coll (BA); *m* 1937, Lt-Col the Hon Henry Anthony Camillo Howard, CMG, Coldstream Gds (d 1977), 5 s of 1 Baron Howard of Penrith, GCB, GCMG, CVO (d 1939); 5 da (1 decd); *Recreations* carriage driving; *Style*— The Hon Mrs Henry Howard; Bushby House, Greystoke, Penrith, Cumberland (☎ 085 338 3302)

HOWARD, Anthony John; s of Peter Dunsmore Howard (d 1965, former Capt Eng Rugby Team), of Hill Farm, Brent Eleigh, Sudbury, Suffolk, and Doris Emily, *née* Metaxas (former winner Wimbledon Ladies Doubles); *b* 31 Dec 1937; *Educ* Cheam Sch, Eton, Trinity Coll Oxford; *m* 12 Oct 1963, Elisabeth Ann, da of Capt Roddie Casement, OBE, RN (d 1987); 1 s (Tom), 2 da (Katie, Emma); *Career* film res/prodr/dir for TV; 2000 films and progs for TV incl: Greece - The Hidden War, A Passage to Britain, A Full Life, Dick Barton - Special Agent, Country Ways, Every Night Something Awful, The Missa Luba; fndr Countryside Films Ltd (own film co) 1989-; *Books* nine books published on The English Countryside; *Recreations* walking, talking, reading, wood clearing; *Style*— Anthony Howard, Esq; Drove Cottage, Newbridge, nr Cadnam, Southampton, Hants, SO4 2NW (☎ 0703 813 233); Countryside Films Ltd, Production Office, TV Centre, Northam, Southampton, Hants S09 2HZ (☎ 0703 834 139)

HOWARD, Anthony Michell; s of late Canon Guy Howard, and Janet Rymer Howard; *b* 12 Feb 1934; *Educ* Westminster, Ch Ch Oxford; *m* 1965, Carol Anne Gaynor; *Career* formerly with Manchester Guardian and Sunday Times; ed The New Statesman 1972-78 (asst ed 1970-72, political corr 1961-64), ed The Listener 1979-81, dep ed The Observer 1981-88 (corr in Washington 1966-69, political columnist 1971-72), reporter BBC TV 1989-; *Books include* The Condensed Crossman Diaries (ed, 1979), RAB: The Life of R A Butler (1987), Crossman: The Pursuit of Power (1990); *Style*— Anthony Howard, Esq; 17 Addison Avenue, London W11 4QS (☎ 071 603 3749)

HOWARD, Hon Barnaby John; 2 s of 3 Baron Strathcona and Mount Royal (d 1959), and Hon Diana, *née* Loder (d 1985), da of 1 Baron Wakehurst; *b* 23 Nov 1925; *Educ* Eton, Trinity Coll Cambridge (MA), Harvard Univ; *m* 1, 19 Jan 1952 (m dis 1967), Elizabeth, yr da of Frank McConnell Mayfield, of St Louis, Missouri; 1 s, 2 da; m 2, 1970, Mrs F N H Bishop, da of late Ambrose Chambers, of NY; *Career* served WWII Sub Lt RNVR (Air Branch); cmmr S Rhodesian Forestry Cmmn 1957-63, chm Canadian American Investment and Management Services Ltd (Halifax NS Canada), gen ptnr Claflin Capital Management Inc (Boston Mass); *Clubs* Brooks's, Queen's, Mill Reef (Antigua); *Style*— The Hon Barnaby Howard; Pinebrook Rd, RR 2, Bedford, New York 10506, USA (☎ 914 234 3528); St Ann's Bay, Englishtown, Nova Scotia B0C 1H0, Canada (☎ 0101 902 929 2829)

HOWARD, Lady Carolyn Bridget Dacre; da of late 11 Earl of Carlisle; *b* 1919; *Career* Subaltern ATS, transfd to FANY Ambulance Corps 1939-45; *Style*— Lady Carolyn Howard; 16 Brunswick Rd, Penrith, Cumbria

HOWARD, (Thomas) Charles Francis; LVO (1968); s of Brig Thomas Farquharson Ker Howard, DSO (d 1962), of Southampton, and Anne Cuningham, *née* Scott; *b* 5 March 1937; *Educ* Winchester, Sandhurst; *m* 16 July 1969, Mary Henrietta, da of Capt

Hugh Dixon, DSC, RN (d 1960), of S Devon; 2 da (Jane b 1970, Philippa b 1971); *Career* 1 Queen's Dragoon Gds 1957-68, equerry to HM The Queen 1965-68, ret Hon Maj 1968; trainee in insur indust 1968-73, dir HA Outhwaite 1973-; *Recreations* gardening, silviculture, shooting; *Clubs* Army and Navy; *Style—* Charles Howard, Esq, LVO; Brunton House, Collingbourne Kingston, Marlborough, Wilts SN8 3SE (☎ 0264 850243); H A Outhwaite & Co Ltd, Regent House, 235 Regent St, London W1R 7AG (☎ 071 409 1630, fax 071 495 0267)

HOWARD, Hon David Francis; 3 s of 2 Baron Howard of Penrith; *b* 29 May 1949; *Educ* Ampleforth, Univ of Oxford; *m* 1981, Diana, da of late John S Radway, by Judith (subsequently 2 w of Lt-Col Esmond Baring, OBE (gs of 4 Baron Ashburtom) and since 1965 2 w of 3 Marquess of Linlithgow (d 1987); Diana was formerly w of Timothy L B Davis; 2 da (Rachel b 1982, Alice b 1983, Olivia b 1986, Frances b 1988); *Style—* The Hon David Howard

HOWARD, David Howarth Seymour; s and h of Sir (Hamilton) Edward de Coucey Howard, 2 Bt, GBE, *qv*; *b* 29 Dec 1945; *Educ* Radley, Worcester Coll Oxford (MA); *m* 6 June 1968, Valerie Picton, o da of late Derek Weatherly Crosse, of Chase House, Callis Court Rd, Broadstairs; 2 s, 2 da; *Career* Alderman City of London, Common Councilman City of London 1972-86; councillor London Borough of Sutton 1974-78; memb Stock Exchange; *Style—* David Howard, Esq; 25 Luke Street, London EC2

HOWARD, Cdr David Mowbray Algernon; s of Hon John Anthony Frederick Charles Howard (d 1971, s of 5 Earl of Effingham); hp of 6 Earl of Effingham; *b* 29 April 1939; *Educ* Fettes Coll; *m* 1964 (m dis 1975), Anne Mary, da of Harrison Sayer (d 1980), of Cambridge; 1 s (Edward b 1971); *Career* Offr RN; *Recreations* horseracing, squash, cricket, shooting, fishing; *Style—* Cdr David M A Howard, RN; 37 Purcell Crescent, London SW6 7PB (☎ 071 381 4176)

HOWARD, David Sanctuary; FSA; s of H Howard (d 1979); *b* 22 Jan 1928; *Educ* Stowe; *m* 1, 1952, Elizabeth, da of late Adm Sir Dudley North, GCVO; 1 s (Thomas), 3 da (Philippa, Sophie, Joanna); m 2, 1974, Anna-Maria, da of late Dante Bocci; m 3, 1989, Angela Mary, da of Robin Postlethwaite; *Career* Coldstream Guards 1946-48; co dir 1960-73, dir Heirloom and Howard Ltd 1973-; FSA; *Books* Chinese Armorial Porcelain (1974), China for the West (1978), New York and the China Trade (1984); *Clubs* Oriental; *Style—* David Howard, Esq, FSA; Heirloom & Howard Ltd, 12 Miles's Buildings, George Street, Bath BA1 2Q (☎ 0225 442544, fax 0225 442650)

HOWARD, Dennis; VRD (1965, and clasps 1975, 1985); s of Henry Thomas Howard (d 1938), and Henrietta, *née* Sturley (d 1969); *b* 24 March 1927; *Educ* Hymers Coll Hull, Univ Coll of Hull, Univ of London (BSc); *m* 10 July 1948, Hilda Mary, da of John Douglas Beeson (d 1931); 1 s (John Nigel b 1959), 2 da (Lorraine Alison b 1956, Lesley Ann b 1963); *Career* cmmnd RN 1945-50, RNR 1951-88, ret as Lt Cdr; HM Colonial Serv (Overseas Civil Serv) admin offr Western Region of Nigeria 1953-61; slr in private practice 1964-90, pt/t lectr in law Univ of Hull 1964-77; chm: Yorkshire Rent Assessment Ctee 1972-, Social Security Appeal Tbnl Hull 1978-, Med Appeals Tbnl Leeds 1987-; memb: Humberside FPC 1987-90, Humberside FHSA 1990-; memb Law Soc 1964; FFA 1982; *Style—* Dennis Howard, Esq, VRD; The White House, Middleton-on-the-Wolds, Driffield, E Yorks (☎ 037781 578)

HOWARD, Very Rev Donald; s of William Howard (d 1948), and Alexandra Eadie, *née* Buchanan (d 1979); *b* 21 Jan 1927; *Educ* King's Coll Univ of London (BA, AKC); *Career* design engineer: Blackburn Aircraft 1948-52, Hunting Percival Aircraft 1952-54, English Electric Company 1954-55; asst minister Saltburn-by-the-Sea Cleveland 1959-62, mission priest Diocese of Kimberley South Africa 1962-65; rector: St John's Church East London SA 1965-71, Holy Trinity Church Haddington East Lothian 1972-78; provost of St Andrew's Cathedral Aberdeen 1978-; *Style—* The Very Rev the Provost of St Andrew's; 15 Morningfield Rd, Aberdeen, Scotland AB2 4AP (☎ 0224 314765); Saint Andrew's Cathedral, King St, Aberdeen, AB2 3AX (☎ 0224 640290)

HOWARD, Hon Donald Alexander Euan; s (by 1 m) and h of 4 Baron Strathcona and Mount Royal; *b* 24 June 1961; *Educ* Gordonstoun, London Business Sch; *Career* cmmnd RN 1980-88; *Recreations* steam boats, sailing, shooting; *Clubs* Fishmongers; *Style—* The Hon D Alex Howard

HOWARD, Hon Edmund Bernard Carlo; CMG (1969), MVO (1961); s of 1 Baron Howard of Penrith, GCB, GCMG, CVO (d 1939); *b* 8 Sept 1909; *Educ* Downside, Newman Sch USA, New Coll Oxford; *m* 1936, Cécile Henriette, da of Charles Geoffroy-Dechaume, of Valmondois, France; 3 s, 1 da (and 1 da decd); *Career* served WWII KRRC (Italy), ret Maj; called to the Bar Middle Temple 1932, sec to tstees and mangrs of Stock Exchange 1937-39; Dip Serv: second sec (info) Rome 1947-51, FO 1951-53, first sec Madrid 1953-57, head of Chancery Bogota 1957-59, FO 1960, consul gen San Marino and consul Florence 1960-61, cnsllr Rome 1961-65, consul gen Genoa 1965-69, ret; Cdr Order of Merit Italy, 1973; *Books* Genoa, History and Art in an Old Seaport (1971); *Recreations* travel, gardening, walking; *Style—* The Hon Edmund Howard; CMG, MVO; Jerome Cottage, Marlow Common, Bucks SL7 2QR (☎ 0628 482129)

HOWARD, Sir (Hamilton) Edward (de Coucey); 2 Bt (UK 1955), of Great Rissington, Co Gloucester; GBE (1972); s of Sir (Harold Walter) Seymour Howard, 1 Bt, Lord Mayor of London 1954 (d 1967); *b* 29 Oct 1915; *Educ* Le Rosey, Radley, Worcester Coll Oxford; *m* 1943, Elizabeth Howarth, da of Maj Percy H Ludlow (d 1968); 2 s; *Heir* s, David Howard; *Career* serv WWII Flt Lt RAF (despatches); memb of Stock Exchange London 1946, sr ptnr Charles Stanley and Co (stockbrokers); chm: Eucryl 1946-71, LRC Int Ltd 1971-82; alderman City of London 1963, Sheriff City of London 1966, Lord Mayor of London 1971-72, HM Lt City of London 1976; Master Worshipful Co of Gardeners 1961; KStJ 1972; *Recreations* gardening; *Clubs* City of London, City Livery, United Wards; *Style—* Sir Edward Howard, Bt, GBE; Courtlands, Bishops Walk, Shirley Hills, Surrey CR0 5BA (☎ 081 656 4444); Charles Stanley and Co Ltd, Stockbrokers, 25 Luke St, London EC2A 4AR (☎ 071 739 8200)

HOWARD, Elizabeth Jane; da of David Liddon Howard (d 1962), and Katharine Margaret Somervell (d 1975); *b* 26 March 1923; *m* 1941 (m dis 1951), Peter Markham Scott (later Sir Peter Scott, CH, CBE, DSC, FRS; d 1989), s of Capt Robert Falcon Scott; 1 da (Nicola); m 2, James Douglas-Henry; m 3, 1965 (m dis 1983), Kingsley Amis, CBE, *qv*; *Career* novelist, playwright of 14 TV plays; *Books* The Beautiful Visit (1950), The Long View (1956), The Sea Change (1959), After Julius (1965), Something in Disguise (1969), Odd Girl Out (1972), Getting It Right (1982); books of short stories: Mr Wrong (1975), The Light Years (1990), Green Shades (1991); *Recreations* gardening, cooking, reading, music; *Style—* Miss Elizabeth Jane Howard; c/o Jonathan Clowes, Iron Bridge House, Bridge Approach, London NW1 8BD

HOWARD, Dr Frances Marianne (Mrs D Howard-Pearce); da of Vincent Joseph Howard, of South Norwood, and Dorothy Mary, *née* Newling; *b* 21 Aug 1946; *Educ* Coloma Convent, Royal Free Hosp Sch of Med (MB BS, MRCP, DCH, DRCOG); *m* 5 June 1982, David Ivan, s of Leonard Samuel Pearce, of Weir Quay, Devon; 1 da (Tamar Anne b 1984); *Career* RMO Middlesex Hosp 1973-74, hon sr registrar Hosp for Sick Children Gt Ormond St 1978-80, conslt paediatrician and geneticist Frimley Park Hosp 1981-, memb Academic Bd Br Paediatric Assoc 1989-; Dreamflight Doctor 1987-90; *Books* Catalogue of Unbalanced Translocations in Man (translation, 1984); *Recreations* lapidary, gardening, hedging and ditching; *Style—* Dr Frances Howard; Orchard House, Glaziers Lane, Normandy, Guildford, Surrey GU3 2DE (☎ 0483 810972); Frimley Park Hospital, Camberley, Surrey (☎ 0276 692777)

HOWARD, Francis John Adrian; s of Ewen Storrs Howard (d 1979), of Cape Town, S Africa, and Cynthia Beatrice, *née* Wallace; *b* 11 July 1935; *Educ* Michaelhouse, Natal SA, Univ of Natal SA; *m* 1961, Lynette, da of late John Ashford Mader, of S Africa; 2 s; *Career* dir: The Diamond Trading Co 1973-75, Beralt Tin and Wolfram Ltd 1977-86, Cape Industries plc 1977-86, Charter Consolidated plc 1978-87, Anderson Strathclyde Ltd 1980-87, Howard Perry Assocs Ltd 1987-, Nestor-BNA plc 1987-, Stream Resources Ltd 1988-, Hawtal Whiting plc 1988-, Consolidated Communications Mgmnt Ltd 1989-, I Hennig and Co Ltd 1990-; *Recreations* gardening, shooting, skiing; *Clubs* Country, Rand, Johannesburg, Boodles; *Style—* Francis Howard, Esq; 26 Chesson Rd, London W14 9QX (☎ 071 381 1814); Howard Perry Assocs Ltd, 1-5 Poland St, London W1V 3DG (☎ 071 287 3681)

HOWARD, (Cecil) Geoffrey; s of Arthur Cecil Howard (d 1965), of Tankerton, Kent, and Bessie, *née* Quinn (d 1919); *b* 14 Feb 1909; *Educ* St Christopher's Sch Letchworth Herts, Alleynes's Stevenage Herts; *m* 11 May 1935, Nora, da of Robert Alexander Le Plastrier (d 1947), of Bromley, Kent; 4 da (Frances b 7 March 1939, Joy b 25 Feb 1941, Ursula b 20 July 1946, Rosalind b 26 June 1948); *Career* 500 (Co of Kent) Sqdn Royal Auxiliary Air Force 1938-40, cmmnd RAF 1940, serv Air Rescue 1940-45; Martins Bank 1926-39; asst sec Surrey CCC 1946-48, sec Lancs CCC 1949-64, sec Surrey CCC 1965-75; mangr MCC tours: India, Pakistan and Ceylon 1951-52, Aust and NZ 1954-55, Pakistan 1955-56; hon treas Minor Counties Cricket Assoc 1975-84; UK agent: Bd of Control for Cricket in Pakistan 1952-70, Bd of Control for Cricket in India 1956-62; former Kent rugby player and Middx cricketer; memb Inst of Bankers; *Recreations* cricket, rugby football, dry stone-walling, gardening, reading; *Clubs* MCC, Surrey CCC (pres 1989), Lancs CCC; *Style—* Geoffrey Howard, Esq; The Barn, Windsoredge, Nailsworth, Gloucs

HOWARD, Greville Patrick Charles; s of Col Henry Redvers Greville Howard (d 1978), and Patience Nichol (d 1987); *b* 22 April 1941; *Educ* Eton; *m* 1, 4 March 1978 (decd); m 2, 20 Nov 1981, Mary Cortlandt, da of Robert Veitch Culverwell, of Chippenham, Wilts; 2 s (Thomas b 1983, Charles b 1986), 1 da (Annabel b 1984); *Career* landowner; dir Harvey and Thomson plc; *Recreations* hunting, tennis; *Style—* Greville P C Howard, Esq; Castle Rising, Kings Lynn, Norfolk

HOWARD, Dr James Griffiths; s of Joseph Griffiths Howard (d 1973), and Kathleen Mildred (d 1984); *b* 25 Sept 1927; *Educ* Raynes Park GS, Middx Hosp Med Sch, Univ of London (MB BS, PhD, MD); *m* 14 July 1951, Opal St Clair, da of John Harman Echalaz (d 1947); 1 s (Roger St Clair b 1956 d 1984), 2 da (Flavia Rosamund b 1954, Charmian Isabel b 1958); *Career* reader Depts of Zoology and Surgical Sci Univ of Edinburgh 1958-69; The Wellcome Research Laboratories 1969-86: dir biomedical res, head of Biological Res Div and head of experimental immunobiology; asst dir The Wellcome Tst 1986-90; FIBiol 1981, FRS 1984; *Recreations* fine arts, music, hillwalking, cooking; *Style—* Dr James Howard; c/o The Wellcome Trust, 1 Park Square West, London NW1 4LJ (☎ 071 486 4902)

HOWARD, Jane Alison; da of Mr Eric George Bullough, of Blackpool, Lancs, and Doreen Ruth, *née* Towers, of Thornton Cleveleys, Lancs; *b* 6 Feb 1956; *Educ* Blackpool Collegiate GS, LSE (BSc), Leeds Poly (Postgrad Mgmnt Dip); *Career* mgmnt trainee NHS 1978-79, dir Hospitality Servs AMI 1979-80, exec dir (later business devpt dir) The Rowland Co (Saatchi & Saatchi's PR Agency) 1982-91; won HCITB Travelling Scholarship award 1979; memb London Regn CBI; MHCIMA, MCFA; *Recreations* riding; *Clubs* RAC; *Style—* Mrs Jane Howard; 67-69 Whitfield St, London W1P 5RL (☎ 071 436 4060, fax 071 255 2131)

HOWARD, Jane Mary; da of Gilbert Edward Howard, of Yaxley, Suffolk, and Mary Teresa Howard, *née* Slater; *b* 20 Dec 1959; *Educ* Catherine McAuley Upper Sch Doncaster, Girton Coll Cambridge (BA); *Career* journalist: Thomson Regnl Newspapers 1982-84, Eveing Gazette Middlesbrough Cleveland; Journalists in Europe fellowship Paris 1985-86, chief sub-ed BBC World Serv 1986-88, Ankara correspondent for The Guardian and the BBC 1988-; NUJ 1981-; *Recreations* reading, theatre, TV, swimming, riding; *Style—* Miss Jane Howard; Cemal Nadir Sokak 21/2, Çankaya, Ankara, Turkey (☎ 010 904 138 2101, tlx 43462 EFTI TR, fax 010 904 138 9054)

HOWARD, Lady Jane Mary; *née* Waldegrave; resumed use of former married name, Lady Jane Howard, 1979; da of 12 Earl Waldegrave; *b* 1934; *m* 1, 1954 (m dis 1977), Donald Euan Palmer Howard, 4 Baron Strathcona and Mount Royal; 2 s, 4 da; m 2 (m dis 1979), Duncan McIntosh, OBE, AFC; *Career* guide, lectr, conslt Specialtours Ltd; *Style—* The Lady Jane Howard; 17 Durand Gdns, London SW9 0PS (☎ 071 582 9052)

HOWARD, Hon Mrs (Jean Margaret); *née* Parnell; da of 6 Baron Congleton (d 1932); *b* 4 June 1922; *m* 1952, as his 2 w, Frederick Henry, DSO, MC, s of Capt William Gilbert Howard, CBE, RN; 3 s (1 s decd), 1 da; *Career* hill farmer; *Style—* The Hon Mrs Howard; Isle of Ulva, Ulva Ferry, Mull, Argyll PA73 6LZ (☎ 068 85 243)

HOWARD, John Francis; s of William George Howard (d 1938), of London, and Frances Jane, *née* McLaren (d 1981); *b* 22 Oct 1918; *Educ* Merchant Taylors', King's Coll Univ of London (LLB); *m* 17 July 1948, Phyllis Morecroft, da of Bernard Horsford Heaver, MBE; 2 s (Charles John b 4 Aug 1949, Peter William Heaver b 8 Aug 1952), 1 da (Mary Catherine b 23 May 1960); *Career* WWII RA: militiaman 1939-40, Lt 1940-42, Pilot Offr to Flt Lt RAF (Pilot Fighter Cmd and 2 Tactical Air Force UK and Europe) 1942-46; called to the Bar Grays Inn 1949; GKN plc: gp sec 1960-73, dir, 1973-78, memb Mgmnt Ctee UK and Overseas; dir Birmingham Broadcasting Ltd 1973-89; chm: St John's Ambulance, New Forest Centre 1980-86; Freeman: City of London, City of Glasgow; Liveryman Worshipful Co of Coopers (memb Ct 1979, Master 1986); FCIS; *Recreations* gardening (rose growing), photography; *Clubs* RAF, Royal Lymington Yacht; *Style—* John Howard, Esq; Camera Principalis, The Old Deanery, 125 The Close, Salisbury, Wilts SP1 2EY (☎ 0722 332 129)

HOWARD, John Philip; s and h of Sir William Howard Lawson, 5 Bt; assumed by Royal Licence surname and arms of Howard 1962; *b* 6 June 1934; *m* 1960, Jean Veronica, da of late Col John Evelyn Marsh, DSO, OBE; 2 s (Philip William b 1961 (m 1988 Cara Margaret, da of Hon Martin Browne), Thomas John b 1963), 1 da (Julia Frances b 1964)); *Style—* John Howard, Esq; Corby Castle, Carlisle

HOWARD, Hon Jonathan Alan; s of 3 Baron Strathcona and Mount Royal (d 1959), and Hon Diana Evelyn, *née* Loder, da of 1 Baron Wakehurst; *b* 15 Nov 1933; *Educ* Eton, Trinity Coll Cambridge, Royal Inst of Tech Stockholm, Stockholm Univ; *m* 1, 1956 (m dis 1969), Hon Brigid Mary, *née* Westenra, da of 6 Baron Rossmore; 2 da; m 2, 1970, Cecilia Philipson; 1 s; *Career* former 2 Lt Coldstream Gds, Argyll and Sutherland Highlanders (TA); memb Nat Assoc of Swedish Architects; *Style—* The Hon Jonathan Howard; PACIM, Mindelo, Cape Verde

HOWARD, (James) Ken; s of Frank Howard (d 1974), of Mousehole, Cornwall, and Elizabeth Crawford, *née* Meikle (d 1987); *b* 26 Dec 1932; *Educ* Kilburn GS, Hornsey Coll of Art, Royal Coll of Art (ARCA); *m* 31 March 1961 (m dis 1974), Margaret Ann, da of Philip Popham, of Ickenham, Middx; *Career* Nat Serv RM 1953-55; artist; Br Cncl Scholarship Florence 1958-59, taught at various London Art Schs 1959-73, official artist Imperial War Museum NI 1978; painted for Br Army: NI, Germany, Cyprus, Hong Kong, Brunei, Nepal, Belize, Norway, Lebanon; one man exhibitions: Plymouth Art Centre 1955, John Whibley Gallery 1966-68, New Grafton Gallery 1971-, Oscar J

Peter Johnson 1986-, Duncalfe Gallery Harrogate 1987-, Jersey 1980, Hong Kong 1979, Nicosia 1982, Delhi 1983; works purchased by: Plymouth Art Gallery, Imperial War Museum, Guildhall Art Gallery, Ulster Museum, Nat Army Museum, Southend Art Gallery, HNC Art Gallery, Sheffield Art Gallery; portraits incl: Gerald Durrell, Gen Sir Martin Farndale; cmmns for: Drapers Co, Haberdashers Co, States of Jersey, HQ Br Army of the Rhine, HM Forces in Cyprus, The Stock Exchange, Lloyds of London, Royal Hosp Chelsea, Banque Paribas; Hon RBA 1988, Hon ROI 1988; NEAC 1962, RWA 1981, RWS 1983, ARA 1983; *Books* The War Artists (1986); *Style—* Ken Howard, Esq; 8 South Bolton Gardens, London SW5 0DH (☎ 071 373 2912); St Clements Hall, Paul Lane, Mousehole, Cornwall TR19 6TR (☎ 0737 731596)

HOWARD, Margaret; da of John Bernard Howard (d 1969), and Ellen Corwenna, *née* Roberts; *b* 29 March 1938; *Educ* St Mary's Convent Rhyl, St Teresa's Convent Sunbury-On-Thames, Guildhall Sch of Music and Drama (LGSM), Univ of Indiana USA; *Career* BBC announcer 1966-69; reporter: World This Weekend 1971-74, Pick of the Week 1974-91; female UK Personality of the Year Sony Awards 1984; memb LRAM; *Books* Margaret Howard's Pick of the Week (1984), Court Jesting (1986); *Recreations* riding, wine tasting; *Style—* Miss Margaret Howard; 215 Cavendish Rd, London SW12 (☎ 081 673 7336)

HOWARD, Dr Mary Elizabeth; da of William Joseph Howard (d 1974), and Mary, *née* Breaden (d 1979); *b* 17 April 1953; *Educ* Notre Dame HS Glasgow, Univ of Glasgow (MB ChB); *m* 14 July 1976, John Hilary Higgins, s of John Joseph Higgins, MBE (d 1972); 1 da (Louise Mary Anne b 1985); *Career* sr registrar in histopathology Gtr Glasgow Health Bd 1980-83 (house surgn and house physician 1976-77, registrar 1977-80), conslt histopathologist Lanarkshire Health Bd 1983-; memb: BMA, assoc Clinical Pathologists; FRCS 1976, MRCPath 1982; *Recreations* music, arts and crafts, reading; *Style—* Dr Mary Howard; Dept of Histopathology, Law Hospital, Carluke, Lanarkshire ML8 5ER (☎ 0698 351100)

HOWARD, Rt Hon Michael; PC (1990), QC (1982), MP (C) Folkestone and Hythe 1983-; s of late Bernard Howard, and Hilda Howard; *b* 7 July 1941; *Educ* Llanelli GS, Peterhouse Cambridge; *m* 1975, Sandra Clare, da of Wing Cdr Saville Paul; 1 s, 1 da, 1 step s; *Career* pres Cambridge Union 1962, called to the Bar Inner Temple 1964, chm Bow Gp 1970; contested (C) Liverpool Edge Hill 1966 and 1970, chm Coningsby Club 1972-73; memb: Cons Gp for Europe, Euro Movement eEec Ctee 1970-73; PPS to Slr-Gen 1984-85, Parly under sec of state for Consumer and Corporate Affrs 1985-87, min for Local Govt 1987-88; min for Water and Planning 1988-90; sec of state for Employment 1990-; *Recreations* watching sport, reading; *Clubs* Carlton; *Style—* The Rt Hon Michael Howard, QC, MP; House of Commons, London SW1

HOWARD, Sir Michael Eliot; CBE (1977), MC (1943); s of Geoffrey Eliot Howard (d 1956), of Dorset, and Edith Julia Emma Edinger (d 1977); *b* 29 Nov 1922; *Educ* Wellington, Christ Church Oxford (MA, DLitt); *Career* aerv Italian theatre with 2 & 3 Bns Coldstream Gds (Capt) 1943-45; prof war studies King's Coll London 1963-68, Chichele prof history of war Oxford 1977-80, pres Int Inst of Strategic Studies, Regius prof modern history Univ of Oxford 1980-, prof of history Yale Univ 1989-; *Books* The Franco-Prussian War (1961), Grand Strategy, Vol IV in UK Official History of World War II (1972), The Continental Commitment (1972), War in European History (1976); *Recreations* music; *Clubs* Athenaeum, Garrick; *Style—* Sir Michael Howard, CBE, MC; The Old Farm, Eastbury, Newbury, Berks RG16 7JN

HOWARD, Hon (Anthony) Michael Geoffrey; yst s of Baron Howard of Henderskelfe (d 1984); *b* 18 May 1958; *m* 1985, (Linda) Louise, yr da of Alexander McGrady, of Broughty Ferry, Angus; 2 da (Arabella Blanche Geneviee b 1986, Grania Alexandra Louise b 1988); *Style—* The Hon Michael Howard; Leyfield Farm, Coneysthorpe, York YO6 7DF

HOWARD, Michael Jonathan; s of Alec Howard (d 1960), and Marjorie Florence Taylor (d 1970); *b* 20 March 1927; *Educ* Bradfield Coll Berks; *m* 16 May 1953, Susan Mai, da of (George) Francis Pitt-Lewis (d 1966); 2 s (Roderic JP b 16 Oct 1959, Crispian MP b 26 March 1962); *Career* Nat Serv Sub Lt RNVR 1945-48; CA; Peat Marwick 1951, Unilever Gp 1952-82; dir gen Br Packaging Assoc 1983-87, sec gen Assoc Euro des Fabricants de Caisses en Carton Compact 1987-; memb Worshipful Co of Broderers; FCA, FCMA, MInst Packaging; *Recreations* following my wife to dressage competitions and my sons to horse trials; *Clubs* Naval; *Style—* Michael Howard, Esq; Purleigh Lodge, Purleigh, Chelmsford, Essex CM3 6PP (☎ 0621 828287); ASSCO Premier House, 10 Greycoat Place, London SW1P 1SB (☎ 071 232 8566, fax 071 222 0678, tlx 9413609)

HOWARD, Michael Newman; QC; s of Henry Ian Howard, and Tilly Celia, *née* Newman; *b* 10 June 1947; *Educ* Clifton Coll, Magdalen Coll Oxford (BA, MA, BCL); *Career* called to the Bar Gray's Inn 1974; lectr in law LSE 1970-74, in practice at the Bar 1972-, visiting prof of law Univ of Essex 1987-, memb Panel Lloyds Salvage Arbitrators 1988-, asst rec 1989-; *Books* Phipson on Evidence (jt ed, 12 edn 1976, 13 edn 1982, 14 edn 1990); *Recreations* books, music, sport; *Clubs* Oxford and Cambridge, RAC; *Style—* Michael Howard, Esq, QC; 2 Essex Court, Temple, London EC4Y 9AP (☎ 071 583 8381, fax 071 353 0998, telex 8812528 ADROIT G)

HOWARD, Michael Stockwin; s of Frank Henry Howard (d 1934), and Florence Mable, *née* Jones (d 1957); *b* 14 Sept 1922; *Educ* Ellesmere Coll, RAM; *Career* post war study with Marcel Dupré, organist and choirmaster Tewkesbury Abbey 1943-44, dir The Renaissance Singers 1944-64, organist and magister choristarum Ely Cathedral 1953-59, dir Cantores in Ecclesia 1964-83, asst BBC music presentation 1968-78, organist and rector Choir St Michael's Benedictine Abbey Farnborough 1984-86; int touring as recitalist and conductor Europe and Scandinavia: Prix Musical de Radio Brno 1967, Charpentier Academie Nationale Prix du Disque 1975; reg broadcasting BBC 1945- incl BBC promenade concerts and other princ festivals; recording incl work for: HMV, Argo, Oiseau Lyre, Time Life, Wealden and Herald; published various vocal and organ compositions; contrib incl: The Musical Times, The Monthly Musical Record, EMG Jnl, The Organists' Review; *Books* The Private Inferno (autobiography, 1975), A Tribute to Aristide Cavaillé-Coll (1986); *Recreations* steam railway traction and village fairgrounds; *Style—* Michael Howard, Esq; 9 Wallis Field, Groombridge, Sussex TN3 9SE (☎ 0892 863698)

HOWARD, Hon Nicholas Paul Geoffrey; s of Baron Howard of Henderskelfe (d 1984); *b* 1952; *Educ* Eton, Univ of Oxford; *m* 1983, Amanda Kate Victoria, only da of Derek Nimmo, actor, of Kensington; 1 s (George b 1985); *Style—* The Hon Nicholas Howard

HOWARD, Dr Norman; s of Philip Howard (d 1987), and Deborah Howard (d 1952); *b* 25 Nov 1926; *Educ* Haberdashers Aske's, Wadham Coll Oxford (MA, DM), UCH; *m* 26 June 1955, Anita, da of H Selby; 2 s (Anthony b 1956, David b 1959); *Career* registrar UCH 1954-56, registrar and sr registrar Royal Marsden Hosp 1956-63; conslt radiotherapy and oncology: Charing Cross Hosp 1963- (dir 1980-), Wembley Hosp 1965-, Royal Marsden Hosp 1970-; chm: Final Fellowship Bd RCR, Gunnar Nilsson Cancer Res Tst Fund, Med Staff Ctee Charing Cross Hosp 1974-79; dir Medical Insurance Agency Ltd; NW Thames RHA: memb Nuclear Accident working Pty, memb Breast Screening Div; DMRT 1956, FFR 1958, FRCR 1975; memb: BMA, RSM, BIR; Commendatore Order of Merit Republic of Italy 1976; *Books* Mediastinal Obstruction in Lung Cancer (1967), author of numerous chapters and papers on cancer; *Recreations* reading, theatre; *Style—* Dr Norman Howard; 5A Clarendon Rd, London W11 4JA, (☎ 071 229 6704); Old Malthouse Cottage, Shurlock Row, Reading RG10 0PL; 6 Devonshire Place, London W1; (☎ 071 487 5524) Charing Cross Hospital, London W6, (☎ 081 846 1732/1741, fax 081 846 1111); Cromwell Hospital, Cromwell Rd, London SW 5, (☎ 081 370 4233); 9 Beaumont Road, Windsor, Berks

HOWARD, Peter Reuben; s of Edward Reuben Howard (d 1966), of Battersea, and Ellen Ruth, *née* Carpenter (d 1979); *b* 18 Feb 1922; *Educ* Sir Walter St John's Sch, Univ of London (BSc, PhD); *m* 1945, Betty, da of Eakson Lee Morris (d 1972), of Norwich; 1 da (Suzanne); *Career* dir gen CEGB Transmission and Tech Servs Div 1977-85, vice pres IEE 1982-85, private conslt 1985-, dir ERA Technol Ltd 1985-91; Freeman City of London 1984, Liveryman of the Worshipful Co of Engineers 1984; FEng, FIEE; *Recreations* general engineering, photography, gardening; *Style—* Dr Peter R Howard; The Old Thatch, Blackmoor, Liss, Hants GU33 6BZ (☎ 0420 47 3642)

HOWARD, Hon Philip Esmé; s and h of 2 Baron Howard of Penrith, *qv*; *b* 1 May 1945; *Educ* Ampleforth, Ch Ch Oxford; *m* 1969, Sarah, da of late Barclay Walker; 2 s (Thomas Philip b 1974, Michael Barclay b 1984), 2 da (Natasha Mary b 1970, Laura Isabella b 1976); *Style—* The Hon Philip Howard; 45 Erpingham Rd, London SW15

HOWARD, Philip Nicholas Charles; s of Peter Dunsmore Howard (d 1965), and Doris Emily Metaxa; *b* 2 Nov 1933; *Educ* Eton, Trinity Coll Oxford (MA); *m* 1959, Myrtle Janet Mary, da of Sir Reginald Houldsworth, *qv*; 2 s, 1 da; *Career* Nat Serv Lt Black Watch; newspaper reporter, columnist and author; Glasgow Herald 1959-64, literary ed The Times 1978- (joined 1964), London ed Verbatim 1977-; FRSL; *Books* The Black Watch (1968), The Royal Palaces (1970), London's River (1975), New Words for Old (1977), The British Monarchy (1977), Weasel Words (1978), Words Fail Me (1980), A Word in Your Ear (1983), The State of the Language (1984), We Thundered Out, 200 Years of The Times 1785-1985 (1985), Winged Words (1988), Word-Watching (1988), A Word in Time (1990); *Recreations* reading, walking, talking; *Style—* Philip Howard, Esq; Flat 1, 47 Ladbroke Grove, London W11 3AR (☎ 071 727 1077)

HOWARD, (Ernest) Ronald; s of George Howard (d 1975), of Hammersmith, and Ethel Howard (d 1982); *b* 30 May 1925; *Educ* West Kensington Central Sch for Boys; *m* ; 2 s (Martin Andrew b 19 Nov 1953, Nicholas James b 15 Nov 1956); *Career* cameraman; started career as camera boy Harrods studio 1942, freelance cameraman BBC 1964- (worked on Top of the Pops for many years); ARPS, FBIPP 1982-; *Clubs* Hampshire House Photography Soc, London Portrait Group; *Style—* Ronald Howard, Esq; 20 Aldbourne Rd, Shepherds Bush, London W12 OLN (☎ 081 743 8194)

HOWARD, Ronald John Frederick; s of Frederick Percial Howard (d 1947), and Lydia Mary Howard (d 1976); *b* 1 Sept 1921; *Educ* Whitgift Middle Sch; *m* 1, 1944, (Sylvia) Betty (d 1974); m 2, 25 Sept 1976, (Ann) Veronica, da of Ward Turner Nicholson (d 1967); *Career* Metal Industries Ltd 1947-67 (dir 1959-67), dep gen mangr AEI/GEC 1967-68; chief exec dir: Plantation Holdings Ltd 1969-78, Phicom plc 1978-81 (chm 1981-84); non-exec dir: Cambridge Electronic Industries plc 1980-, Fothergill and Harvey plc 1973-87; dir: Cynanamid-Fothergill Ltd 1981-87, Infrared Associates Incorporated 1985-88; fndr memb of Bd and dep chm Chiltern Radio plc 1980-; chm: The Rank Phicom Video Group Ltd 1981-84, Technology Management Services Ltd 1981-, Baird UK Holdings Ltd 1982-89, Silver Chalice Productions International Ltd (Bermuda) and Silver Chalice Productions Ltd 1983-86, Reflex Holdings Ltd 1986-88, Commtel Consumer Electronics plc 1987-88, Synoptics Ltd 1988-, Universal Machine Itelligence Group Ltd 1989-90, Sy FA Data Systems plc 1990-; vice chm Spectros International plc (now Kratos Group plc) 1984-; Master Worshipful Co of Scientific Instrument Makers 1987; FInstnl 1981, CBIM 1984; *Recreations* sailing, photography; *Clubs* City of London, Savile, Royal Thames Yacht; *Style—* Ronald Howard, Esq; Springwood House, Ickwell Green, Beds SG18 9EE (☎ 076 727 348); Technology Management Services Ltd, P O Box 1775, London NW3 3EB (☎ 071 794 0606, car 0831 178 861)

HOWARD, Hon Simon Bartholomew Geoffrey; s of Baron Howard of Henderskelfe (d 1984); *b* 26 Jan 1956; *Educ* Eton, RAC Cirencester, Study Centre for Fine and Decorative Arts; *m* 1983, Annette Marie, Countess Compton, er da of Charles Antony Russell Smallwood, and formerly 2 w (m dis 1977), of Earl Compton (now 7 Marquess of Northampton); *Career* chm of estate co; landowner (10,000 acres); chm Yorkshire Regnl HHA; *Recreations* photography, wine, country sports; *Style—* The Hon Simon Howard; Castle Howard, York (☎ 065 384 444)

HOWARD, Terence; s of Thomas James Howard (d 1979), of Eastbourne, and Nora Emily, *née* Moore; *b* 31 Oct 1939; *Educ* St Pauls; *m* 1, 22 Aug 1969 (m dis), Venetia, da of Gordon Smith Cuninghame (d 1965); 2 s (Charles b 1974, Thomas b 1982), 2 da (Tara b 1964, Scarlett b 1973); m 2, 13 July 1983, Belinda Elizabeth, da of David Charlton Humphreys; *Career* creator and writer TV series The Other Arf 1979-83; chm: Cuninghame Howard Ltd 1979-89, Nowlan Howard Ltd 1989; exec creative dir Ayer Barker 1984-88; *Recreations* photography, tennis; *Clubs* Groucho; *Style—* Terence Howard, Esq; 1 Shalcomb St, London SW10 (☎ 071 352 2126); 171 Wardour St, London W1 (☎ 071 242 1111)

HOWARD, Timothy Charles Maxwell; s of Edward Maxwell Howard (d 1970), and Eleanor Monica Newsum; *b* 29 July 1947; *Educ* Uppingham, Univ of Dundee (LLB), Coll of Law; *m* 1970 (sep), Elizabeth Marion; 3 s (Andrew Oliver Maxwell b 30 April 1976, Edward William b 25 May 1978, Thomas Timothy b 26 May 1982); *Career* Norton Rose: joined 1970, asst slr 1973-78, ptnr 1978-, recruitment ptnr 1988-90, memb Mgmnt Ctee 1988-91; memb Editorial Bd: European Transport Law, Charterparty International, Maritime Focus; Liveryman City of London Slrs Co 1978; memb: Law Soc 1970, Baltic Exchange London, Maritime Arbitrators Assoc 1978; *Recreations* theatre, golf, DIY, travel; *Style—* Timothy Howard, Esq; Norton Rose, Kempson House, Camomile St, London EC3A 7AN (☎ 071 283 2434, fax 071 588 1181)

HOWARD, Hon William John; 4 s of 2 Baron Howard of Penrith; *b* 30 May 1953; *Educ* Ampleforth; *m* 1981, Alexandra Josephine, da of Maurice Graham; 2 da (Miranda b 1982, Elizabeth b 1984); *Career* concert pianist (debut at Wigmore Hall Dec 1981); *Style—* The Hon William Howard

HOWARD DE WALDEN, 9 Baron (E 1597); John Osmael Scott-Ellis; TD; also Baron Seaford (UK 1826); s of 8 Baron Howard de Walden (d 1946, gs of 1 Baron Seaford, whose w Elizabeth was gda of 4 Earl of Bristol (Lord Bristol's f's mother was maternal gda of 3 Earl of Suffolk, who also held the Barony of Howard de Walden) and Margherita Van Raalte CBE, da of Charles van Raalte, JP; *b* 27 Nov 1912; *Educ* Eton, Magdalene Coll Cambridge; *m* 1, 1934, Countess Irene Harrach (d 1975), yst da of Count Hans Albrecht Harrach, of Munich (of a Mediatised Sovereign House of the Holy Roman Empire; the title of Baron Harrach was conferred by Ferdinand I 1552 (and under the Hungarian crown 1563) and the title of Count Harrach was cr by Emperor Ferdinand II 1627); 4 da; m 2, 1978, Gillian, da of Cyril Buckley and formerly w of 17 Viscount Mountgarret; *Heir* all 4 da as coheiresses: Hon Mrs Czernin, Hon Mrs Buchan of Auchmacoy, Hon Mrs White, Hon Mrs Acloque; *Career* Maj Westminster Dragoons (TA); dir Howard de Walden Estates Ltd; *Clubs* Jockey (sr steward 1957, 1964, 1976), Turf, Whites; *Style—* The Rt Hon the Lord Howard de

Walden, TD; Avington Manor, Hungerford, Berks (☎ 0488 58229); Flat K, 90 Eaton Sq, London SW1 (☎ 071 235 7127)

HOWARD-DOBSON, Gen Sir Patrick John; GCB (1979, KCB 1974, CB 1973); s of Canon Howard Dobson; *b* 12 Aug 1921; *Educ* King's Coll Choir Sch, Framlingham Coll; *m* 1946, Barbara Mills; 2 s, 1 da; *Career* joined 7 QOH 1941, served Egypt, Burma, ME, Italy, Germany, CO QOH 1963-65, CO 20 Armd Bde 1965-67, COS Far East Cmd 1969-71, Cmdt Staff Coll Camberley 1972-74, MS 1974-76, QMG 1977-79, Vice CDS (personnel and logistics) 1979-81, ret; ADC Gen to HM The Queen 1978-81, Col Cmdt Army Catering Corps 1976-82; Nat Pres Royal Br Legion 1981-87; *Recreations* sailing, golf; *Clubs* Cavalry and Guards, Royal Cruising, Senior Golfers Soc; *Style—* Gen Sir Patrick Howard-Dobson, GCB; 1 Drury Park, Snape, Saxmundham, Suffolk IP17 1TA

HOWARD-HARRISON, Anthony; *b* 29 March 1946; *Educ* privately (Dip Child Psychology, Cert Residential Social Work); *m* (m dis); *Career* landowner; chm two sch governing bodies appointed by Devon CC 1974-85, voluntary social worker with the elderly and on drug-related problems, chm Howard-Harrison Charitable Tst 1985-, fndr Cloudsleigh Nursing Hospice 1984-, princ Ward House Sch Devon for Maladjusted and Handicapped Children 1974-78; memb: Br Psychological Soc, Assoc of Workers with Maladjusted Children, Plymouth Gen Hosp League Ctee, Plymouth and Dist Leukaemia Fund, St Luke's Hospice, Age Concern, Nat Fund for Res into Crippling Diseases (former chm), Moorhaven Hosp League of Friends; supporter: Broadreach House Drug Treatment Ctee, Dhaka BA Orphanage Bangladesh, Starlight Fndn, Third World Vol; *Recreations* flying (private pilot), rough shooting, antique collecting, foreign travel, eating good food constantly, visiting Third World; *Clubs* Royal Western Yacht, Ferrari Owners; *Style—* Anthony Howard-Harrison, Esq; Thorn Park Mews, Thorn Park, Mannamead, Plymouth PL3 4TG (☎ 0752 660811, fax 0752 6670); 217 Chelsea Cloisters, Sloane Avenue, Knightsbridge, London SW3

HOWARD-HIGGINS, Capt Bruce Arthur; s of Arthur Edward Howard-Higgins (d 1979), of Imperial Coll Field Station, Sunninghill, Berks, and Madeleine Agnes, *née* Stanley-Smith; *b* 31 May 1940; *Educ* Allhallows Sch; *m* 17 Aug 1966, Maureen Mary (Mo), da of Desmond Milton Whitehouse, TD, of Clifford Chambers, nr Stratford-upon-Avon, Warwicks; 2 s (Charles Milton, James Milton); *Career* Lt (previously 2 Lt) Army Air Corps 1965-71; served: UK, Germany, The Gulf; pilot BEA Viscount aircraft 1971-77; pilot British Airways: Boeing 707 1978-80 (also qualified as flt engr), Boeing 737 1981-83, seconded Air Mauritius 1984-86, B 737 1986-88, B 757 1989-; Gt Chesterford PCC, local Game conservancy branch; chm E Anglia Branch Army Air Corps Assoc; *Recreations* shooting, skiing, motoring, gourmet; *Style—* Capt Bruce Howard-Higgins; c/o British Airways, P O Box 10, London Heathrow Airport, Hounslow TW6 2JA, (☎ 081 759 5511)

HOWARD-JOHNSTON, Rear Adm Clarence Dinsmore; CB (1955), DSO (1942), DSC (1940); s of John Howard-Johnston, of Nice, Alpes Maritimes, France (d 1913), and Dorothy Florence, *née* Baird (m 2, 1914, Comte Pierre du Brueil St Germain, d 1971); his ancestor John Howard Johnston left sch prematurely in order to fight as a Drummer Boy for the North in American Civil War, subsequently entered Dartmouth Coll, USA, an engr, built Peruvian railroad through Andes; Silver Mine owner Casapalca, Peru; *b* 13 Oct 1903; *Educ* Royal Naval Colls Osborne & Dartmouth; *m* 1, 1928, Esmé (m dis 1940), yst da of late Philip John FitzGibbon of Poona, India; m 2, 1941 (m dis 1954), Lady Alexandra Henrietta Louisa Haig, da of 1 Earl Haig; 2 s, 1 da; m 3, 1955, Lise Rita Paulette, da of Paul César Helleu (d 1927); *Career* dir of studies Royal Hellenic Naval War Coll Athens 1938-40, dir Anti-U-Boat Div Naval Staff Admty 1943-45, Anti-Submarine Specialist to Cabinet Anti-U-Boat Meetings (under presidency of PM) 1943-45, cmd Cruiser HMS Bermuda, unit of Occupation Forces of Japan 1946-47, NA Paris 1947-50, Naval ADC to HM the Queen 1952; Cdr: Order of Phoenix of Greece (1940), American Legion of Merit (1945); *Recreations* fishing, pisciculture, hill walking, gardening; *Clubs* White's, Naval & Military, Royal Yacht Squadron (naval member), Jockey (Paris); *Style—* Rear Admiral Howard-Johnston, CB, DSO, DSC; 5 Avenue Jomini, 1004 Lausanne, 45 Rue Emile Ménier, 75116 Paris

HOWARD OF PENRITH, 2 Baron (UK 1930); Francis Philip Howard; DL (Glos 1960); 2 s of 1 Baron Howard of Penrith, GCB, GCMG, CVO (d 1939, 4 s of Henry Howard, n of 12 Duke of Norfolk), by his w Lady Isabella Giustiniani-Bandini, da of 8 Earl of Newburgh, Duca di Mondragone and Prince Giustiniani Bandini; *b* 5 Oct 1905; *Educ* Downside, Trinity Coll Cambridge; *m* 1 July 1944, Anne, da of John Beaumont Hotham (fifth in descent from Sir Beaumont Hotham, 7 Bt and f of 8, 9, 11 & 12 Bts, the last two being also 1 & 2 Barons Hotham); 4 s; *Heir* s, Hon Philip Howard; *Career* serv WWII, Capt RA (wounded); called to the Bar Middle Temple 1931; *Style—* The Rt Hon the Lord Howard of Penrith; Dean Farm, Coln St Aldwyns, Glos

HOWARD-SMITH, Hon Mrs (Patricia Ann); da of 1 Baron Lambury (d 1967); *b* 1929; *m* 1951 (m dis 1968) Capt Morfryn James Howard-Smith, RN; 1 s, 1 da; *Style—* The Hon Mrs Howard-Smith; Terrasses, 4 Chemin Romain, 06240 Beausoleil, France (☎ 93 78 35 94)

HOWARD-VYSE, Lt-Gen Sir Edward Dacre; KBE (1962, CBE 1955), CB (1958), MC (1941), DL (N Yorks 1974); s of Lt-Col Cecil Howard-Vyse, JP (d 1935), of Langton Hall, Malton, and Ethel Maud Elsmie, *née* Hast (d 1946); *b* 27 Nov 1905; *Educ* Wellington, RMA; *m* 1940, Mary Bridget, er da of Col Hon Claude Henry Comaraich Willoughby, CVO (d 1932); 2 s, 1 da; *Career* memb Br Olympic Equestrian Team 1936; 2 Lt RA 1925, Lt-Col 1941, served with BEF in Fr 1939-40, MEF 1941-44, cmd 1 RHA CMF 1944-45, Brig 1949, CRA 7 armd div BAOR 1951-53, cmdt Sch of Artillery 1953, Maj-Gen Artillery NAG 1956-58, Maj-Gen 1957, dir RA WO 1959-61, Lt-Gen 1961, GOC-in-C Western Cmd 1961-64, ret 1964; Col Cmdt: RA 1962-70, RHA 1968-70; vice pres ACF Assoc 1974-(chm 1964-73), vice pres Nat Artillery Assoc 1965-; DL East Riding and Kingston upon Hull 1964, Vice Lt 1968-74; *Recreations* country pursuits; *Clubs* Army and Navy; *Style—* Lt-Gen Sir Edward Howard-Vyse, KBE, CB, MC, DL; Langton House, Malton, North Yorks

HOWARTH, Alan Thomas; MP (C) Stratford-on-Avon 1983-, CBE (1982); *b* 11 June 1944; *Educ* Rugby, King's Coll Cambridge; *m* 1967, Gillian Martha, da of Arthur Chance, of Dublin; 2 s, 2 da; *Career* former head Chm's Office CCO (PS to Rt Hon William Whitelaw and Rt Hon Lord Thorneycroft as Pty Chm), dir Cons Res Dept 1979-81, vice chm Pty orgn 1980-81, PPS to Dr Rhodes Boyson 1985-87, appointed asst govt whip 1987; Lord Cmmr of the Treasy 1988, Parly under sec of state Dept of Educn and Sci June 1989; *Books* Changing Charity (jtly, 1984), Monty At Close Quarters (1985), Save Our Schools (1987), Arts: The Way Ahead; *Recreations* books, arts, running; *Style—* Alan Howarth, Esq, CBE, MP; House of Commons, London SW1

HOWARTH, David Armine; s of Osbert John Radcliffe Howarth (d 1954), of West Hill House, Downe, Kent, and Eleanor Katherine Paget (d 1965), of Vinesgate, Brasted Chart, Nr Sevenoaks, Kent; *b* 18 July 1912; *Educ* Tonbridge, Univ of Cambridge (MA); *m* 1, 1 Dec 1944 (m dis 1981), Nannette, da of William Russell Smith (d 1976), of Litlapund, Bigton, Shetland; 2 s (Stephen b 1952, Patrick b 1965), 4 da (Clare b 1946, Virginia b 1949, Joanna b 1955, Katherine b 1968); m 2, 10 April 1981 Joanna White; *Career* Lt Cdr RNVR 1940; BBC 1933-, war corr; FRSL, Norwegian Order of St Olav, Norwegian Cross of Freedom; *Books* The Shetland Bus (1951), We Die Alone (1955), The Sledge Patrol (1957), Dawn of D-Day (1959), The Shadow of the Dam (1961), My Land And My People (1962), The Desert King: A Life of Ibn Saud (1965), Panama: The Golden Isthmus (1966), Waterloo: A Near Run Thing (1968), Trafalgar (1969), Sovereign of the Seas (1974), The Greek Adventure (1976), Dhows (1977), 1066: The Year of The Conquest (1977), The Seafarers: Fighting Sail (1978), Men of War (1978), Dreadnoughts (1979), Pursued by a Bear: Autobiography (1986), The Story of P & O (with S Howarth, 1986), Nelson: The Immortal Memory (1988); *Recreations* cruising under sail; *Style—* David Howarth, Esq

HOWARTH, (James) Gerald Douglas; MP (C) Cannock and Burntwood 1983-; s of late James Howarth, of Berks, and Mary Howarth; *b* 12 Sept 1947; *Educ* Bloxham Sch Banbury, Univ of Southampton; *m* 1973, Elizabeth; 2 s, 1 da; *Career* gen sec Soc for Individual Freedom 1969-71, Bank of America International 1971-76, European Arab Bank 1976-81, Standard Chartered Bank plc 1981-83 (loan syndication mangr); conslt: Astra Hldgs plc, Standard Chartered Bank plc, Trade Indemnity plc, Br Cablemakers Confedn; memb Hounslow Borough Cncl 1982-83; PPS to: Michael Spicer MP Dept of Energy 1987-90 and DOE 1990-, Sir George Young MP DOE 1990-; hon sec Cons Parly Aviation Ctee 1983-87; fell Indust and Parly Tst; *Recreations* flying (Britannia Airways Parly Pilot of the Year 1988), walking, DIY; *Style—* Gerald Howarth, Esq, MP; House of Commons, London SW1

HOWARTH, Prof (Charles) Ian; s of Charles William Howarth (d 1972), of Jersey, and Violet, *née* Moore (d 1982); *b* 12 Nov 1928; *Educ* Manchester GS, Balliol coll Oxford (MA, DPhil); *m* 11 July 1951, (Sonia) Patricia (d 1981), da of William Young (d 1964), of Isle of Man; 3 s (Bill b 1954, James b 1956, Robert b 1972), 1 da (Kitty b 1958); *Career* pilot offr RAF Inst of Aviation Med 1954-56; res fell Miny of Aviation Oxford Univ 1956-58, lectr Univ of Hull 1958-64; Univ of Nottingham: prof of psychology and head of cept 1964-, dir Accident Res Unit 1970-, Blind Mobility Res Unit 1970-, dir Inst Applied Cognitive Sci 1986-; pres Br Psychological Soc, chm Human Factor Ctee MOD, memb Biological Sciences Ctee SERC; FBPsS 1987, C Psychol 1987; *Books* Structure of Psychology (with W E C Gillham, 1981), Studies of Selection Validation in British Industry (with C B T Cox J Watts and Lazzerini, 1981), Teaching and Talking with Deaf Children (with D Wood, H Wood, A Griffiths, 1986); *Recreations* sailing, several other sports, conversation; *Style—* Prof Ian Howarth; Department of Psychology, University of Nottingham, University Park, Nottingham NG7 2RD (☎ 0602 484848 ext 3185, fax 0602 590339)

HOWAT, Prof Henry Taylor; CBE (1971); s of Adam Howat, (d 1917), of Pittenweem, Fife, and Henrietta, *née* Taylor (d 1955); *b* 16 May 1911; *Educ* Cameron Public Sch, Madras Coll, Univ of St Andrews (MB ChB, MD); *m* 29 June 1940, Rosaline Green; 2 s (John Michael Taylor b 18 April 1945, Andrew Alexander Taylor b 12 Feb 1952), 1 da (Henrietta Mary Taylor b 23 July 1948); *Career* WWII cmmnd RAMC 1940-46; regtl MO UK, physician specialist MEF and Br Liberation Army, Lt-Col i/c Med Div BAOR, demobbed as Hon Lt-Col 1946; chief asst to Med Unit Manchester Royal Infirmary 1945-46 (previously 1936-38 and 1939-40); Ancoats Hosp Manchester: physician 1946-62, res MO 1938-40 , physician 1948-76, i/c Dept of Gastroenterology 1962-76; Univ of Manchester: reader in med 1969-72 (formerly lectr), prof of gastroenterology 1972-76 (now emeritus); chm: Med Exec Ctee Utd Manchester Hosps 1968-73, Faculty of Med Univ of Manchester 1968-72; first pres Euro Pancreatic Club 1965; pres: Br Soc of Gastroenterology 1968-69, Assoc of Physicians of GB and Ireland 1975-76, Pancreatic Soc of GB and Ireland 1978-79; Manchester Man of the Year 1973; Hon MD and medallist Faculty of Med Univ of Louvain Belgium 1945, Hon medallist JE Purkyne Czechoslovak Med Soc 1968, Hon MSc Univ of Manchester 1975, Hon Dip and Medallion Hungarian Gastroenterological Soc 1988; FRCP (London) 1948, FRCPE 1965; *Books* The Exocrine Pancreas (co-ed, 1979); *Recreations* golf; *Clubs* Athenaeum, Royal and Ancient Golf; *Style—* Prof Henry T Howat, CBE; 3 Brookdale Rise, 1 Hilton Rd, Bramhall, Cheshire SK7 3AG; 40 High St, Pittenweem, Fife KY10 2PL

HOWAT, John Michael Taylor; s of Henry Taylor Howat, CBE, of Bramhall, Cheshire, and Rosaline, *née* Green; *b* 18 April 1945; *Educ* Manchester Warehousemen and Clerks Orphan Sch Cheadle Hulme, Victoria Univ of Manchester (MB ChB, MD); *m* 16 July 1988, Dr Trudie Elizabeth Roberts, da of John Roberts, of Millbrook, Stalybridge; 1 da (Fiona Katherine b 17 Oct 1989); *Career* conslt surgn N Manchester gp of hosps 1982-, clinical dir of surgery N Manchester Gen Hosp; FRCS 1973; *Recreations* industrial archaeology, photography, clock restoration; *Style—* John Howat, Esq; Dept of Surgery, North Manchester General Hospital, Delauneys Rd, Manchester M8 6RB (☎ 061 795 4567 ext 2608)

HOWATSON, Dr (Susan) Rosalind; da of Gerald Bulmer, of 11 Capilano Park, Aughton, nr Ormskirk, Lancs, and Greta Lucy Bulmer, *née* Parkes; *b* 23 Dec 1947; *Educ* Univ of Aberdeen (BMedBiol, MB ChB); *m* 18 March 1978, Allan George, s of Allan Howatson, of 35 Park Drive, Leven, Fife; 1 s (Allan Gerald b 8 Feb 1980), 1 da (Victoria Anne b 23 Aug 1982); *Career* conslt pathologist Monklands Dist Gen Hosp 1983-; Freeman City of York 1983; memb BMA, IAP, ACP, SDS, SACC; FRCPath 1989, MRCPath 1978; *Style—* Dr Rosalind Howatson; 29 Braemar Crescent, Bearsden, Glasgow G61 1DE; Dept of Pathology, Monklands District General Hospital, Monkcourt Ave, Airdrie ML6 0J6 (☎ 0236 69344)

HOWDEN, Timothy Simon (Tim); s of Phillip Alexander Howden (d 1970), Irene Maud, *née* Thomas (d 1985); *b* 2 April 1937; *Educ* Tonbridge; *m* 20 Sept 1958 (m dis), Penelope Mary, *née* Wilmott; 2 s (Charles b 6 April 1959, Dominic b 12 Oct 1965), 1 da (Joanna b 4 April 1961); *Career* Nat Serv 2 Lt RA 1955-57; Reckitt and Colman 1959-73: sales mangr Industl Floor Care UK 1959-62, gen mangr Industl Floor Care France 1962-64, mktg mangr then dep md Germany 1964-70, dir Euro Div 1970-73; Ranks Hovis McDougall: dir Cereals Div 1973-75, md RHM Foods 1975-81, chm Bakery Div 1981-85, gp planning dir 1985-86, dep md 1987-, md 1989-; *Recreations* tennis, skiing, diving; *Clubs* Annabel's, Naval and Military; *Style—* Tim Howden, Esq; RHM plc, Alma Rd, Windsor, Berks SL4 3ST (☎ 0753 857123, fax 0753 846537, telex 847314)

HOWE, Charles Keith; s of Henry Beauclerk Howe (d 1948); *b* 11 March 1935; *Educ* Lancing, Trinity Hall Cambridge; *m* 1960, Carole, da of Alma Thomas Absalom, of Copthorne, Sussex; 1 s, 2 da; *Career* jt md Crystalate Hldgs 1978-83 (chief exec 1983-85), dir C H Resources Ltd 1985-, md Electra Holdings plc 1988-; *Recreations* cricket; *Clubs* MCC; *Style—* Charles Howe Esq; Billhurst, Lingfield Common, Lingfield, Surrey (☎ 0342 832848)

HOWE, Prof Christopher Barry; s of Charles Roderick Howe, and Patricia, *née* Creeden; *b* 3 Nov 1937; *Educ* William Ellis Sch Highgate London, St Catharine's Coll Cambridge (BA, MA), Univ of London (PhD); *m* 2 Dec 1967, Patricia Anne, da of L G Giles; 1 s (Roderick Giles b 1972), 1 da (Emma Claire b 1968); *Career* econ directorate Fed Br Industs 1961-63, res fell and lectr SOAS, reader in econs of Asia Univ of London 1972- (prof 1979-), head Contemporary China Inst 1972-78; memb Hong Kong Univ and Poly Grants Ctee 1974, UGC 1979-84; *Books* Employment and Economic Growth in Urban China (1971), Wage Patterns and Wage Policies in Modern China (1973), China's Economy: A Basic Guide (1978), Shanghai (1980), Foundations of the Chinese Planned Economy (1989); *Recreations* walking, swimming, cycling, antiquarian books, France, music, photography; *Style—* Prof Christopher Howe; 12

Highgate Ave, London N6 5RX; Rue Maurice Lithaire, Arromanches, Normandy, France; School of Oriental & African Studies, Thornaugh St, Russell Sq, London WC14 0XG (☎ 071 637 2388)

HOWE, Lady (Elspeth); JP (Inner London 1964-); *b* 8 Feb 1932; *Educ* Bath HS, Wycombe Abbey Sch, LSE (BSc); *m* Aug 1953, The Rt Hon Sir Geoffrey Howe, QC, MP, *qv*; 1 s (Alexander b 1959), 2 da (Caroline b 1955, Amanda (twin) b 1959); *Career* sec to princ of Architectural Assoc's Sch of Architecture 1952-55, dep chm Equal Opportunities Cmmn Manchester (chm Legal Ctee) 1975-79; chm Inner London Juvenile Cts: Southwark 1970-80, Greenwich 1980-83, Lambeth 1983-86, Wandsworth 1987-90; non-exec dir: Kingfisher (Holdings) plc (formerly Woolworth Hldgs plc) 1987-, United Biscuits (Holdings) Ltd 1988, Legal and General Group 1989-; pres: Peckham Settlement 1976-, Fedn of Recruitment and Employment Servs 1980-; chm: Business in the Community Women's Econ Decpt Initiative 1988-, NACRO Working Pty on Fine Enforcement 1980-81, NACRO drugs advsy gp 1988-; vice pres Pre-School Playgroups Assoc 1978-83; memb: Lord Chllr's Advsy Ctee on Legal Aid 1971-75, Parole Bd For England and Wales 1972-75; contrib articles to: The Times, Financial Times, Guardian, New Society; *Style—* Lady Howe, JP; c/o Barclays Bank, 4 Vere St, London W1

HOWE, Eric James; CBE (1990); s of Albert Henry Howe, and Florence Beatrice, *née* Hale; *b* 4 Oct 1931; *Educ* Stretford GS, Univ of Liverpool (BA); *m* 1967, Patricia Enid, *née* Schollick; 2 da; *Career* NCB 1954-59, Br Cotton Indust Res Assoc 1959-61, English Electric Computer Co 1961-66, memb Bd of Dirs Nat Computing Centre 1976-84 (joined 1966, dep dir 1975-84), Data Protection Registrar (responsible for implementing the Provisions of the Data Protection Act 1984) 1984-; chm: Nat Computer Users Forum 1977-84, Focus Ctee for Private Sector Users DOI 1982-84; memb: Cncl Br Computer Soc 1971-74 and 1980-83, NW Regnl Cncl CBI 1977-83, User Panel NEDO 1983-84; UK rep Confedn of Euro Computer Users' Assocs 1980-83; FBCS 1972, FIDPM 1990 (MIDPM 1981); *Recreations* local community work, gardening, piano; *Style—* Eric Howe, Esq; Data Protection Registrar, Springfield House, Water Lane, Wilmslow, Cheshire SK9 5AX

HOWE, 7 Earl (UK 1821); Frederick Richard Penn Curzon; also Baron Howe of Langar (GB 1788), Baron Curzon of Penn (GB 1794) and Viscount Curzon of Penn (UK 1802); s of Cdr (Chambré) George William Penn Curzon, RN (d 1976), and Enid Jane Victoria, da of late Malcolm Mackenzie Fergusson; suc cous, 6 Earl Howe, CBE (d 1984); *b* 29 Jan 1951; *Educ* Rugby, Christ Church Oxford (MA); *m* 1983, Elizabeth Helen, elder da of Capt Burleigh Edward St Lawrence Stuart, of Ickford, Bucks; 2 da (Lady Anna Elizabeth b 19 Jan 1987, Lady Flora Grace b 12 June 1989); *Heir* cous Charles Mark Penn Curzon (b 1967); *Career* banker and farmer; dir: Adam & Co plc 1987-90, Provident Life Assoc Ltd 1988-; pres: Nat Soc for Epilepsy, RNLI (Chilterns Branch), South Bucks Assoc for The Disabled, CPRE (Penn Country Branch); govr: King William IV Naval Fndn, Milton's Cottage Tst; hon treas The Trident Tst; *Recreations* words and music; *Style—* The Rt Hon the Earl Howe; Penn House, Amersham, Bucks HP7 0PS

HOWE, Prof Geoffrey Leslie; TD 1962 (bars 1969, 1974); s of Leo Leslie John Howe (d 1934), of Maidenhead, Berks, and Ada Blanche, *née* Partridge (d 1973); *b* 22 May 1924; *Educ* Royal Dental Hosp, Middx Hosps; *m* 8 April 1948, Heather Patricia Joan, *née* Hambly; 1 s (Timothy John b 31 May 1958); *Career* dental offr RADC 1946-49, Col RADC (V) 1972-75, Col RARO 1973- (hon Col Cmdt RADC 1975-90); prof oral surgery Univs of Durham and Newcastle upon Tyne 1959-67, dean Royal Dental Hosp London Sch of Dental Surgery 1973-78 (prof of oral surgery 1967-78), prof Univ of Hong Kong 1978-84 (fndr Dean of Dentistry 1978-83), dean Faculty of Dentistry Jordan Univ of Sci and Technol 1988- (prof of oral surgery 1986-); memb Cncl RCS 1977-78, vice pres Br Dental Assoc 1979 (vice chm 1971-73, chm cncl 1973-78); Liveryman Worshipful Co of Apothecaries, Int Freeman New Orleans USA, Freeman Louisville USA; hon fell: Philippine Coll of Oral and Maxillo-Facial Surgns 1979, Acad of Dentistry Int (USA) 1982; Fell Int Coll of Dentists, hon memb American Dental Assoc; LRCP, MRCS 1954, FDSRCS 1955 (LDSRCS 1946), MDS 1961, FFD RCSI 1964; OStJ; *Books* Extraction of Teeth (2 edn, 1980), Local Anaethesia in Dentistry (with F I H Whitehead, 2 edn, 1981), Minor Oral Surgery (3 edn, 1989); *Recreations* sailing, reading, music, club life; *Clubs* Savage, Hong Kong, Royal Hong Kong Yacht; *Style—* Prof Geoffrey Howe, TD; 70 Croham Manor Rd, S Croydon, Surrey CR2 7BF (☎ 081 686 0941); Villa 2-1, Marina de Casares, Sabinillas, Manilva, Andalucia, Spain; Flat 1A, Block 2, Southern Housing, Yarmouk University, Irbid, Jordan; University of Science and Technology, Irbid, Jordan (☎ 010962 2 295 111 ext 2087, fax 010962 2 295 123, telex 55545 JUST JO)

HOWE, Geoffrey Michael Thomas; s of Michael Edward Howe, and Susan Dorothy, *née* Allan; *b* 3 Sept 1949; *Educ* The Manchester GS, St John's Coll Cambridge (MA); *m* 14 Aug 1976, Alison Laura, da of Dr Raymond Bernard Sims; *Career* admitted slr 1973; ptnr Co Dept Clifford Turner 1980 (joined 1975), managing ptnr Clifford Chance 1989- (ptnr Co Dept 1987); memb Law Soc 1973; Freeman Worshipful Co of Slrs; *Recreations* tennis, flying, wine, antiques, opera; *Clubs* Oxford & Cambridge; *Style—* Geoffrey Howe, Esq; Clifford Chance, Royex House, Aldermanbury Square, London EC2 (☎ 971600 0808, telex 8959991, fax 071 726 8561)

HOWE, Rt Hon Sir (Richard Edward) Geoffrey; PC (1972), QC (1965), MP (C) E Surrey 1974-; er s of B Howe; *b* 20 Dec 1926; *Educ* Winchester, Trinity Hall Cambridge; *m* 1953, Elspeth Rosamund Morton Shand, JP, *qv*, da of Philip Shand; 1 s, 2 da; *Career* called to the Bar 1952; chm Bow Gp 1955, Parly candidate (C) Aberavon 1955 and 1959; memb Gen Bar Cncl 1957-61; md Crossbow 1957-60 (ed 1960-62); memb Cncl of Justice 1963-70; MP (C): Bebington 1964-66, Reigate 1970-74; oppn front bench spokesman Labour and Social Servs 1965-66, dep chm Glamorgan QS 1966-70, SG 1970-72, min Trade and Consumer Affrs 1972-74; oppn front bench spokesman: Social Servs 1974-75, Treasy and Econ Affrs 1975-79; Chllr Exchequer 1979-1983, lord cmmr Treasy 1979-83, chm IMF Policy-Making Interim Ctee 1982-1983; ldr team of Policy Gps preparing Cons Gen Election Manifesto 1982-83; sec state Foreign and Cwlth Affrs 1983-July 1989, Leader of the Commons and Lord Pres of the Cncl July 1989-Nov 1990, dep PM July 1989-Nov 1990; *Style—* The Rt Hon Sir Geoffrey Howe, QC, MP; c/o Barclays Bank, Cavendish Sq Branch, 4 Vere St, London W1

HOWE, Gordon James; s of Frank Ernest Howe (d 1979), of Colchester, Essex, and Jessie Smith, *née* Withycombe (d 1953); *b* 6 Jan 1932; *Educ* Royal Liberty Sch Romford Essex; *m* 28 April 1957, Dawn Angela, da of Albert Edward Diver (d 1969), of Banstead, Surrey; 1 s (Duncan b 1962, d 1964), 1 da (Fiona b 1966); *Career* RA 1954-56, Lt 1955; qualified CA 1954; Arthur Young (Ernst & Young): ptnr 1961, memb Exec Ctee 1977, chm Arthur Young Europe 1984, memb Int Cncl 1984, memb Exec Ctee 1990-; memb Int Mind Matter Charity; treas: Young Minds Charity, The Child Psychotherapy Tst; chm Centenany Conf Ctee ICAEW, non-exec memb SW Thames Regnl Health Authy 1990-, chm S Thames Blood Transfusion Service 1990; FCA 1964; *Recreations* swimming, travel, philately; *Clubs* RAC; *Style—* Gordon Howe, Esq; 31 Queen' Gate Gardens, London SW7 5RR (☎ 071 581 1637); Beckett House, 1 Lambeth Palace Rd, London (☎ 071 931 3100, fax 071 928 1345)

HOWE, John Francis; OBE (1974); s of late Frank Howe, OBE, of Devon, and Marjorie Alice, *née* Hubball; *b* 29 Jan 1944; *Educ* Shrewsbury, Balliol Coll Oxford (MA); *m* 1981, Angela Ephrosini, da of Charalambolos Nicolaides (d 1973), of Alicante and London; 1 da (Alexandra b 1983), 1 step da (Caroline b 1973); *Career* civil serv: princ MOD 1972 (asst princ 1967), civil advsr GOC NI 1972-73, asst sec MOD 1979 (private sec to Perm Under Sec 1975-78), seconded FCO, cnsllr UK Delgn to NATO 1981-84, head Def Arms Control Unit 1985-86, private sec to Sec of state for Def 1986-87, asst under sec of State (personnel and logistics) 1987-; *Books* International Security and Arms Control (contrib); *Recreations* travel, gardening; *Style—* John Howe, Esq, OBE; Ministry of Defence, Main Building, Whitehall SW1 (☎ 071 218 2762)

HOWE, Air Vice-Marshal John Frederick George; CB (1985), CBE (1980), AFC (1961); *b* 26 March 1930; *Educ* St Andrew's Coll Grahamstown S Africa; *m* 1961, Annabelle Gowing; 3 da; *Career* Cmdt-Gen RAF Regt and dir gen Security (RAF) 1983-85, ret; American DFC 1951, Air medal 1951; *Style—* Air Vice-Marshal J F G Howe, CB, CBE, AFC; c/o Barclays Bank plc, Oceanic House, 1 Cockspur St, London SW1

HOWE, The Rt Rev John William Alexander; s of Frederic Arthur (d 1979), and Elsie, *née* Garner (d 1975); *b* 14 July 1920; *Educ* Westcliff HS (Essex), St Chad's Coll, Durham Univ (BA, MA, BD); *Career* ordained 1943, dio of York, curate All Saints' Scarborough 1943-46; chaplain Adisadel Coll Ghana 1946-50; vice princ Edinburgh Theological Coll Scotland 1950-55; consecrated bishop of dio of Saint Andrews, Dunkeld and Dunblane 1955, bishop 1955-69; exec offr of the Anglican Communion 1969; first sec gen of Anglican Consultative Cncl 1971-82 (first research fell 1983-85, 1985 ret); asst bishop Dio of Ripon 1985-; sec Lambeth Conf 1978; hon degrees: STD General Theological Seminary, New York USA 1974, DD Lambeth 1978; *Books* Highways and Hedges: Anglicanism and the Universal Church (1985), various articles; presentation essays: Authy in The Anglican Communion; *Clubs* Royal Cwlth Soc; *Style—* The Rt Rev John Howe; 31 Scotton Drive, Knaresborough, N Yorks HG5 9HG (☎ 0423 866224)

HOWE, Leslie Clive; s of Alexander Leslie Howe, of 207 Turners Hill, Cheshunt, Herts, and Patricia Ann, *née* Lord; *b* 21 April 1955; *Educ* Cheshunt GS, Royal Dental Hosp Univ of London (BDS); *Career* house surgn Royal Dental Hosp 1979, sr house surgn London Hosp 1979-80; lectr in conservative dentistry: Royal Dental Hosp 1980-85, Guy's Dental Sch 1985-; Lunt Prize, Sounders scholarship, Baron Cornelius ver Heyden de Lancey award; memb: Br Soc for Restorative Dentistry, Br Soc for Dental Res; Accreditation in Restorative Denistry 1989; FDS 1983; *Style—* Leslie Howe, Esq; Conservation Department, Guys Hospital Dental School, London Bridge, London SE1 9RT (☎ 071 955 4533); 21 Wimpole St, London W1M 7AD (☎ 071 636 3101)

HOWE, Dr Martin; s of Leslie Wistow Howe (d 1979), and Dorothy Vernon, *née* Taylor-Farrell; *b* 9 Dec 1936; *Educ* High Storrs GS, Univ of Leeds (BCom), Univ of Sheffield (PhD); *m* 1959, Anne Cicely, da of Ernest Lawrenson, of Parbold; 3 s (Graeme Neil b 1963, Andrew b 1965, Robert b 1968); *Career* sr lectr Univ of Sheffield 1960-72 (formerly asst lectr and lectr), sr econ advsr MMC 1973-77, asst sec DTI 1980-84; OFT: sr economic advsr 1977-80, asst sec 1980-84, under sec dir Competition Policy Div 1984-; *Books* Equity Issues and The London Capital Market (with A J Merrett and GD Newbould, 1967); *Recreations* theatre, amateur dramatics, cricket, gardening; *Style—* Dr Martin Howe; Office of Fair Trading, Field House, Breams Buildings, London EC4A 1PR

HOWE, Martin Russell Thomson; s of Colin Thomson Howe (d 1988), of Kenley, Surrey, and Dr Angela Mary Brock (d 1977); *b* 26 June 1955; *Educ* Winchester, Trinity Hall Cambridge (MA); *m* 30 Dec 1989, Lynda Maureen, *née* Barnett; 1 s (Philip Anthony b 19 Oct 1990); *Career* called to the Bar Middle Temple 1978; specialising in: patents, copyright, trade mark, EEC law; jt ed Halsbury's Laws of England section Trade Marks, Trade Names and Designs; Parly candidate (Cons) Neath 1987, memb Hammersmith and Fulham Borough Cncl 1982-86 (chm Planning Ctee); *Recreations* flying gliders; *Style—* Martin Howe, Esq; Francis Taylor Building, Temple, London EC4Y 7BY (☎ 071 353 5657)

HOWE, Phillip; s of Roland Webster Howe, of Northallerton, N Yorks, and Monica Jean, *née* Sismey; *b* 18 Nov 1989; *Educ* Northallerton GS; *m* 23 Oct 1971, Dorothy Eleanor Howe; 1 s (Jonathan Webster b 23 March 1976), 1 da (Rachel Elizabeth b 13 April 1972); *Career* print prodn mangr Gestetner 1981-83; W H Houldershaw Ltd, Redlands Ltd, Insurance Printers Ltd: gen mangr 1983, md 1984-; *Style—* Phillip Howe, Esq; W H Houldershaw Ltd, 6 Totman Crescent, Brook Road Industrial Estate, Rayleigh, Essex SS6 7UY (☎ 0268 745511, fax 0268 747186)

HOWELL, Rt Hon David Arthur Russell; PC (1979), MP (C) Guildford 1966-; s of Col A H E Howell, DSO, TD, DL (d 1980), and Beryl Howell; *b* 18 Jan 1936; *Educ* Eton, King's Coll Cambridge (MA); *m* 1967, Davina, da of Maj David Wallace (ka 1944); 1 s, 2 da; *Career* serv Coldstream Gds 1954-56, 2 Lt; worked in Econ Section Treasy 1959-60, ldr writer Daily Telegraph 1960-64, chm Bow Gp 1961-62, ed Crossbow 1962-64, dir Cons Political Centre 1964-66, Parly candidate (C) Dudley 1964, lord cmmr Treasy 1970-71, Parly sec CSD 1970-72; Parly under sec: Employment 1971-72, NI March-Nov 1972; min of state: NI 1972-74, Energy 1974; sec of state Energy 1979-81, sec Transport 1981-83; chm House of Commons Foreign Affrs Ctee 1988- chm UK Japan 2000 Gp; dir: Trafalgar House plc, Queens Moat Hotels plc; memb Int Advsy Bd Swiss Bank Corporation; *Publications* A New Style of Government (1970), Time to Move On (1976), Freedom and Capital (1981), Blind Victory (1986); *Recreations* tennis, golf, writing, DIY; *Clubs* Buck's; *Style—* The Rt Hon David Howell, MP; House of Commons, London SW1

HOWELL, Rt Hon Denis Herbert; PC (1976), MP (Lab) Birmingham, Small Heath 1961-; s of Herbert and Bertha Howell; *b* 4 Sept 1923; *Educ* Gower St Sch, Handsworth GS; *m* 1955, Brenda Marjorie, da of Stephen Willson; 3 s, 1 da; *Career* MP (Lab): All Saints 1955-59, Small Heath 1961-; jt Parly under sec DES and Min for Sport 1964-70, min of state Housing and Local Govt 1969-70, oppn spokesman Local Govt and Sport 1970-74, min of state for the Environment and min for Sport 1974-79, oppn front bench spokesman Environment and Sport 1979-83, Home Affrs 1983-84, chm Labour Movement for Europe, Puer European Movement pres APEX 1971-83, memb Nat Exec 1982-83; former football league referee and memb Birmingham City Cncl, Silver medal Olympic Order 1981, vice pres Central Ctee of Physical Recreation; dir: Wembley Stadium Ltd, Birmingham Cable Authy, Denis Howell PR; Hon Freeman of City of Birmingham 1990; *Books* Soccer Referee Pelham (1969), Made in Birmingham (authobiography, 1990); *Recreations* sport, music, theatre; *Clubs* Reform, MCC, Warwickshire Cricket, Birmingham Press; *Style—* The Rt Hon Denis Howell, MP; 33 Moor Green Lane, Moseley, Birmingham B13 8NE

HOWELL, Air Vice-Marshal Evelyn Michael Thomas; CBE (1961); s of Sir Evelyn Berkeley Howell (d 1971), of Cambridge, and Laetitia Cecilia Campbell (d 1978); *b* 11 Sept 1913; *Educ* Downside, RAF Coll Cranwell; *m* 1, 1937, Helen Joan, da of Brig William Moring Hayes (d 1960); 1 s (Michael), 3 da (Jennifer, Mary, Philippa); m 2, 1972, Rosemary, da of Ian Alexander Cram, of Warwick; 1 s (Rupert b 1975), 1 da (Caroline b 1977); *Career* cmmnd RAF 1934, dir Air Armament Res & Devpt 1960-62, Cmdt RAF Tech Coll Henlow 1962-65, sr air staff offr Tech Trg Cmd 1966-67, ret 1967; Aircraft Indust 1967-79; *Recreations* gardening, conservation; *Clubs* RAF; *Style—* Air Vice-Marshal E M T Howell, CBE; Bank Farm, Lorton,

Cockermouth CA13 0RQ (☎ 090 085 617)

HOWELL, Prof John Bernard Lloyd (Jack); s of David John Howell (d 1978), of Ynystawe, Swansea, and Hilda Mary, *née* Hill (d 1943); *b* 1 Aug 1926; *Educ* Swansea GS, Middx Hosp Med Sch and Univ of London (BSc, MB BS, PhD); *m* 12 July 1952, Heather Joan, da of Lawrence Victor Rolfe (d 1939); 2 s (David b 1955, Peter b 1959), 1 da (Gillian b 1953); *Career* Nat Serv RAMC, Lt 1952, Capt 1953; Univ of Manchester: sr lectr and hon physician 1960-66, conslt physician and sr lectr 1966-69; Univ of Southampton: fndn prof of med 1969-, dean faculty of med 1978-83; memb GMC 1978-83, pres Thoracic Soc 1988-89, pres BMA 1989-90; chm Southampton & S W Hampshire Dist Health Authy 1983-; FRCP 1966, Hon FACP 1982; Hon Life Memb Canadian Thoracic Soc 1978; *Books* Breathlessness (1966); *Recreations* DIY, wine; *Style*— Prof Jack Howell, Esq; The Coach House, Bassett Wood Drive, Southampton SO2 3PT (☎ 0703 768878); Medicine I, Southampton General Hospital, Centre Block, Southampton (☎ 0703 777222)

HOWELL, John Frederick; s of Frederick John Howell, of Welwyn Garden City, and Glenys Griffiths (d 1990); *b* 16 July 1941; *Educ* Welwyn Garden GS, Univ Coll Swansea (BA), Univ of Manchester (MA), Univ of Reading (PhD); *Career* lectr Univ of Khartoum 1966-73, sr lectr Univ of Zambia 1973-77, dir ODI 1987- (res fell 1977-87), visiting prof Wye Coll Univ of London 1988-; pres UK Chapter Soc for Int Devpt, advsr All Pty Parly Gp on Overseas Devpt; *Style*— Prof John Howell; 11 St Marys Grove, London N1 2NT (☎ 071 226 9268); Overseas Development Institute, Regent's College, Regent's Park, London NW1 4NS (☎ 071 487 7413, fax 071 487 7590, telex 94082191 ODIUK)

HOWELL, Lisbeth Edna; da of Frederick Baynes, and Jessica Edna Baynes; *b* 23 March 1951; *Educ* Liverpool Inst HS for Girls, Univ of Bristol (BA); *m* ptnr common law husband, Ian Prowiewicz; 1 da (Alexandra b 19 Sept 1984); *Career* reporter BBC local radio 1972-77; Border TV: reporter presenter 1977-79, head of news 1986-88, dep dir of progs 1988-89; reporter presenter Tyne Tees TV 1981-84 (Granada TV 1979-81), currently managing ed Sky News; *Style*— Ms Lisbeth Howell

HOWELL, Maj-Gen Lloyd; CBE (1972); s of Thomas Idris Howell (d 1987), and Anne Howell (d 1964); *b* 28 Dec 1923; *Educ* Barry GS, UCW (BSc); *m* 1, 14 Feb 1945, Hazel (d 1974), da of Frank Edward Barker (d 1963); 5 s (Rhodri b 1945, d 1979, Geraint b 1948, Ceri b 1952, Dewi b 1956, Alwyn b 1959), 3 da (Carys b 1949, Eirlys b 1951, Sara b 1954); m 2, 19 April 1975, Elizabeth June Buchanan Husband, da of Archibald John Buchanan Atkinson (d 1966); *Career* Capt: regtl and staff appts RA 1943-47, instr RMA Sandhurst RAEC 1949-53, staff course RMCS 1953-54; Maj: TSO 2 Trials Estab RA 1954-57, SO 2 Educn Div HQ BAOR 1957-59, long GW Course RMCS 1959-60; Lt-Col: DS RMCS 1960-64, SEO Army Apprentices Coll 1964-67, headmaster and Cmdt Duke of York's Royal Mil Sch 1967-72 (Col 1970); Col educn MOD 1972-74, Brig chief educn offr UK Land Forces 1974-76; Maj-Gen: dir of Army Educn 1976-80, Col Cmdt RAEC 1982-86; conslt tech educn devpt UCW 1980-86; dir Bldg Trades Exhibitions Ltd 1980-; memb: Cncl City and Guilds of London Inst 1976-89, Ctee of Govrs UCW 1980-88; govr several schs 1980-; fell Univ Coll Cardiff 1981-; Hon MA Open Univ 1980; MRAeS 1963-80; *Recreations* golf, gardening; *Clubs* A & N; *Style*— Maj-Gen Lloyd Howell, CBE

HOWELL, Michael John; s of Jack Howell, and Emmie Mary Elizabeth Howell; *b* 9 June 1939; *Educ* Strodes, King's Coll London (LLB), Chigaco Univ (JD), Cape Town Univ; *m* 14 May 1966, Caroline Sarah Eifiona, da of Charles Herbert Gray; 2 da (Juliet b 1967, Lucy b 1973); *Career* admitted slr 1966; ptnr Clifford Chance (formerly Clifford-Turner) 1969- (joined 1964); Liveryman Worshipful Co of Coopers (Under warden 1988-89, Upper Warden 1989-90), Freeman Worshipful Co of Slrs; memb: Law Soc, Int Bar Assoc; assoc memb Chartered Inst of Patent Agents; *Clubs* City Livery; *Style*— Michael Howell, Esq; Wood Cottage, Dome Hill Park, London SE26 6SP (☎ 081 778 9763); Clifford Chance, Bow Bells House, Bread St, London EC4M 9BQ (☎ 071 600 0808, fax 071 956 0199, telex 887 847 LEGIS G)

HOWELL, Michael William Davis; s of Air Vice-Marshal Evelyn Thomas Howell, of Bank Farm, Lorton, Cumbria, and Helen Joan, *née* Hayes (d 1976); *b* 11 June 1947; *Educ* Charterhouse, Trinity Coll Cambridge, INSEAD and Harvard Business Sch (MBA); *m* 1975, Susan Wanda, da of Andrew Adie, (d 1986); 2 s (William b 1982, Andrew b 1988); *Career* gen mangr Gen Electric Co 1988-; vice pres: Cummins Engine Co Inc 1981-88, BL Truck & Bus Div 1969-74; *Recreations* aviation, sailing, motorcycling, singing; *Clubs* Royal Automobile; *Style*— Michael Howell, Esq; c/o Bank of Scotland, 38 Threadneedle St, London EC2P 2EH; 2901 E Lake Rd, Erie PA 16531 USA

HOWELL, Paul Frederic; MEP (EDG) Norfolk 1979-; s of Ralph Frederic Howell, MP, of Wendling Grange, Dereham, Norfolk, by his w Margaret Ellene; *b* 17 Jan 1951; *Educ* Gresham's, St Edmund Hall Oxford; *m* 23 May 1987, Johanna, *née* Turnbull; *Recreations* hunting, adventures; *Clubs* Farmers', Carlton; *Style*— Paul Howell Esq, MEP; The White House Farm, Bradenham Rd, Scarning, E Dereham, Norfolk NR20 3EY (☎ 036 287 239)

HOWELL, Paul Philip; CMG (1964), OBE (1955); s of Brig-Gen Philip Howell, CMG (ka 1916), and Rosalind Upcher, *née* Buxton (d 1968); *b* 13 Feb 1917; *Educ* Westminster, Trinity Coll Cambridge (MA, PhD), ChCh Oxford (MA, DPhil); *m* 1949, Bridgit Mary Radclyffe, da of Geoffrey Dundas Luard (d 1955), of Buckland Newton Place, Dorset; 2 s (Philip Luard b 1955, James Christopher Francis b 1960), 2 da (Rosalind Sabrina b 1951, Clare Lucinda b 1953); *Career* Sudan Political Serv 1938-55, Uganda Govt 1955-61; head of ME Devpt Div Beirut FO (later Miny of Overseas Devpt) 1961-69, fell and dir of devpt studies Wolfson Coll Cambridge 1969-83, emeritus fell 1983; *Books* Nuer Law (1954), The Jonglei Canal; Impact and Opportunity (ed, 1988); *Recreations* fishing, country pursuits; *Clubs* Royal Cwlth Soc, Norfolk (Norwich); *Style*— Paul P Howell Esq, CMG, OBE; Burfield Hall, Wymondham, Norfolk NR18 9SJ (☎ 0953 603389)

HOWELL, Peter Adrian; s of Lt Col Harry Alfred Adrian Howell, MBE (d 1985), of Chester, and Madge Maud Mary, *née* Thompson; *b* 29 July 1941; *Educ* Downside, Balliol Coll Oxford (BA, MA, MPhil); *Career* Univ of London: asst lectr then lectr Dept of Latin Bedford Coll 1964-85, lectr Dept of Classics Royal Holloway and Bedford New Coll 1985-; memb: Dept of Art and Architecture Liturgy Cmmn Roman Catholic Bishops; Conf for Eng and Wales 1977-84, Churches Ctee England Heritage 1984-88; chm Victorian Soc 1987- (memb Ctee 1968-), dep chm Jt Ctee Nat Amenity Socs 1991-; *Books* Victorian Churches (1968), Companion Guide to North Wales (with Elisabeth Beazley, 1975), Companion Guide to South Wales (with Elisabeth Beazley, 1977), A Commentary on Book I of the Epigramms of Martial (1980), The Faber Guide to Victorian Churches (ed with Ian Sutton, 1989); *Style*— Peter Howell, Esq; Department of Classics, Royal Holloway and Bedford New College, Egham Hill, Egham, Surrey TW20 0EX (☎ 0784 443211)

HOWELL, Ralph Frederic; MP (C) North Norfolk 1970-; s of Walter Howell, of Dereham, Norfolk; *b* 25 May 1923; *Educ* Diss GS; *m* 1950, Margaret, da of Walter Bone, of Gressenhall; 2 s, 1 da; *Career* RAF 1941-46; farmer; memb: Lloyd's, Mitford and Launditch RDC 1961-74; former local chm NFU, Parly candidate (C) N Norfolk 1966, memb Euro Parl 1974-79, former chm Cons Backbench Ctee Agric and Employment, memb Select Ctee on the Treasy and Civil Serv 1981-87, memb Cncl of Europe 1981-84 and 1987-; *Clubs* Carlton, Farmers'; *Style*— Ralph Howell, Esq, MP; Wendling Grange, Wendling, Dereham, Norfolk (☎ 036 287 247)

HOWELL, Dr Richard Stanley Charles; s of Rev Herbert Stanley Howell (d 1978), of Braceborough Rectory, Stamford Lincs, and Gwendolen Eleanor, *née* Davies; *b* 13 Aug 1945; *Educ* Stamford Sch, St Marys Hosp Med Sch London (MB BS); *m* 3 Jan 1976, Susan Katherine Veronica; *Career* res anaesthetist Mount Sinai Sch of Med NY 1971-72, sr registrar Addenbrookes Hosp Cambridge 1973-76; conslt anaesthetist: Walsgrave Hosp Coventry 1976, Warwickshire Private Hosp Leamington Spa 1980-; author of scientific papers on med gases and med gas systems; Coll of Anaesthetists regnl educnl advsr for W Midlands; DObstRCOG 1970, FFARCS 1973, FRSM 1984; *Recreations* church organist, railways, aviation; *Style*— Dr Richard Howell; Keppel Gate Cottage, Frankton, Rugby; Dept of Anaesthetics, Walsgrave Hospital, Coventry CV2 2DX (☎ 0203 602020)

HOWELL, Robert; s of Jim Howell, of Chesterfield, Derbys, and Gladys Mary, *née* Clayworth; *b* 18 April 1950; *Educ* Brunts' GS Mansfield, Univ of Manchester (BA); *m* 21 Sept 1984, Kathleen Mary, da of Richard John Rabey, of St Merryn, Cornwall; 1 s (Richard b 1987), 1 da (Nicola b 1984); *Career* asst treas Blue Circle Industries plc 1979-85, treas Tesco plc 1986-; ACMA 1979, MCT 1984; *Recreations* squash, various sports, fine wine; *Clubs* N London Squash; *Style*— Robert Howell, Esq; 51 Landrock Rd, Crouch End, London N8 9HR (☎ 081 348 2198); New Tesco House, Delamare Rd, Cheshunt, Herts EN8 9SL (☎ 0992 644137, fax 0992 35883)

HOWELL, Rupert Cortlandt Spencer; s of Lt-Col F R Howell, of New Mile House, Ascot, Berkshire, and Sheila Dorothy Lorne McCallum; *b* 6 Feb 1957; *Educ* Wellington, Univ of Warwick (BSc); *m* 4 Sept 1987, Claire Jane, da of Dr Nigel Ashworth; *Career* account exec Mathers Advertising (now Ogilvy and Mather Partners) 1979-80, account supervisor Grey Advertising 1982-83 (account mangr 1981); Young and Rubicam: account dir 1983-84, dir 1984-87, jt head of Account Mgmnt 1987; fndr ptnr Howell Henry Chaldecott Lury Ltd 1987-; MIPA 1989; *Recreations* cricket, soccer, golf, tennis (playing and spectating), rugby (spectating only!); *Clubs* MCC, London Rugby; *Style*— Rupert Howell, Esq; Howell Henry Chaldecott Lury Ltd, Kent House, 14-17 Market Place, Great Titchfield St, London W1N 7AJ (☎ 071 436 3333, fax 071 436 2677)

HOWELL, Dr Tudor Morgan; s of David John Howell; *b* 24 May 1924; *Educ* West Monmouth Sch, Univ of Cambridge; *m* 1953, Sara Margaret Janey, da of Rev Geoffrey Earle Raven; 2 s, 1 da; *Career* formerly temp Sub Lt RNVR; med practitioner; High Sheriff of Powys 1980; *Recreations* gardening; *Style*— Dr Tudor Howell; Ynyswen, Trefeglwys, Newtown, Powys (☎ 055 16 633)

HOWELL WILLIAMS, Peter; s of Rev Robert Howell Williams (d 1978), and Ellen Gwladys Howell Williams; *b* 22 June 1926; *Educ* Rydal Sch N Wales, Downing Coll Cambridge (MA, LLB); *m* 6 July 1954, Fiona Elizabeth, da of John Craig (d 1930); 1 s (Craig b 14 Sept 1957), 2 da (Rachel b 5 April 1955, Sian b 9 March 1960); *Career* mine sweepers RNVR 1944-47; admitted slr 1953, pres Law Soc Liverpool 1980-81, chm Mental Health Tbnl, sr ptnr Bell Lamb & Joynson Liverpool, ret 1990; Parly candidate 1964 and 1966, cncllr Wallasey Borough 1955-64; chm: Maritime Housing Assoc 1966-67, Merseyside Civic Soc 1966-71, Friends of Cleft Palate Unit 1971- (and co fndr), Everyman Theatre Liverpool 1983-; nat chm The Abbeyfield Soc 1985-90; memb: Law Soc, Solicitors Benevolent Assoc; cncllr N Wales Music Festival; *Books* Liverpolitana (1971), A Gentleman's Calling (1980); *Recreations* antiquarian books, conservation, golf; *Clubs* Athenaeum (Liverpool, pres 1980), Athenaeum (London); *Style*— Peter Howell Williams, Esq

HOWELLS, David John; s of Ivor Mervyn Howells, of Shrewsbury, and Veronica Carey, *née* Jones; *b* 14 March 1953; *Educ* London Hosp Med Coll (BDS), Univ Hosp of Wales (MScD); *m* 14 Feb 1981, Lisa Pauline, da of Peter Noble, of Esher, Surrey; 1 da (Lowri b 1989); *Career* postgrad training in orthodontics Welsh Nat Sch of Med, registrar Queen Alexandra Hosp Portsmouth 1982-84, sr registrar Birmingham Dental Hosp 1984-87, conslt in orthodontics W Glamorgan and E Dyfed Health Authys 1987-, currently engaged in private orthodontic practise; author of several academic papers in specialist jnls; LDS, DOrth, MOrth, FDS; *Recreations* scuba diving, hiking, photography; *Style*— David Howells, Esq; Dept of Orthodontics, Morriston Hospital, Swansea (☎ 0792 703101)

HOWELLS, Dr Kim Scott; MP (Lab) Pontypridd 1989-; s of Glanville James Howells, of 55 Erw Las, Penywaun, Aberdare, Mid-Glamorgan, and Glenys Joan, *née* Edwards; *b* 27 Nov 1946; *Educ* Mountain Ash GS, Hornsey Coll of Art, Cambridge Coll of Advanced Technol (BA), Univ of Warwick (PhD); *m* 22 Oct 1983, Eirlys, da of William Elfed Davies, of Bryncoch, Neath, West Glamorgan; 2 s (Cai James b 26 April 1984, Scott Aled b 20 Feb 1988), 1 da (Seren Rachel Morgans-Howells b 23 Dec 1976); *Career* steel worker 1969-70, coal miner 1970-71, lectr 1975-79; res offr: Univ of Wales 1979-82, NUM S Wales 1982-89 (also ed); tv presenter and writer 1986-89; memb House of Commons Select Ctee on the Environment; *Publications* various essays in collections dealing mainly with mining history, trade unionism, literature and the environment; *Recreations* mountaineering, cinema; *Clubs* Llantwit Fadre CC, Pontypridd CC, Hopkinstown CC; *Style*— Dr Kim Howells, MP; 30 Berw Road, Pontypridd, Mid-Glamorgan CF37 2AA (☎ 0443 402551, fax 0443 485628); House of Commons, Westminster, London SW1A 0AA (☎ 071 219 5813, fax 071 219 5526)

HOWELLS, Michael Sandbrook; s of Benjamin George Howells (d 1971), of Pembroke Dock, and Blodwen, *née* Francis (d 1978); *b* 29 May 1939; *Educ* Dean Close Sch, Cheltenham, Univ Coll London; *m* 18 June 1966, Pamela Vivian, da of Gordon Harry Francis, of Clandon, Surrey; 2 s (Luke b 1970, Toby b 1972); *Career* admitted slr 1966; sr ptnr Price and Kelway Slrs 1980 (ptnr 1971); HM Coroner Pembrokeshire 1980; memb: Cncl of Law Soc 1983, Supreme Ct Rule Ctee 1985, Cncl of Coroners Soc of England and Wales 1986; pres Milford Haven Civic Soc, vice chm Torch Theatre Milford Haven; *Recreations* theatre, bee keeping, messing about in boats; *Clubs* RAC, Waterloo, Milford Haven, Neyland Yacht; *Style*— Michael Howells, Esq; Glenowen, Mastlebridge, Milford Haven, Pembrokeshire SA73 1QS (☎ 0646 600 208); Price and Kelway, 17 Hamilton Terrace, Milford Haven, Pembrokeshire SA73 3JA (☎ 06465 69311, fax 06462 695848)

HOWELLS, Col (William) Peter; CBE (1988), OBE (Mil, 1976), TD (1964, 2 clasps 1970 and 1976), DL (Pembrokeshire (later Dyfed) 1973); s of Lt-Col Percy Rotherham Howells (d 1961), and Maggie May, *née* Jones, MBE, JP; *b* 17 Oct 1931; *Educ* Ellesmere Coll Shropshire; *m* 29 Aug 1956, Marlene Jane, da of Richard Stanley Scourfield (d 1966); 2 s (Paul b 1958, Philip b 1960); *Career* 1 Bn The Welch Regt 1950-52, 4 (V) Bn The Welch Regt 1952-69 (Hon Col 1982-); Pembroke Yeomanry 1967-69, 224 Sqdn RCT(V) 1969-71; CO 157 (Tport) Regt RCT (V) 1973-76, Col TA Wales 1977-80, Hon Col 4 (V) Bn Royal Regt of Wales 1982-; md and chm Howells (Jewellers) Ltd 1961-; ADC to HM The Queen 1978-82, High Sheriff of Dyfed 1980-81, OStJ (1988, SBStJ 1980); Wales Territorial Army Assoc: memb West Wales Ctee 1969-, memb 1973-, chm 1985, memb Cncl Reserve Forces 1985-; vice chm Tax Cmmrs for Haverfordwest Dist 1984- (tax cmmr 1977-); Nat Assoc of Round Tables: chm Tenby Branch 1955 (fndr vice chm 1954), pres Haverfordwest Branch 1979 (fndr chm 1957); pres: Haverfordwest Rotary Club 1969, Little and Broad Haven Lifeboat Ctee RNLI 1978-, St John Ambulance Bde Haverfordwest 1980-, Boys Bde Co

Haverfordwest 1982-83, Dyfed Ctee Duke of Edinburgh Award Scheme 1988-; Broad and Little Haven Branch Royal Br Legion: memb 1977-, vice pres 1978-81, pres 1981-, memb Ctee 1981-; chm Pembroke Yeomanry Dinner Club 1979-; Royal Br Legion: patron of Pembrokeshire Co Branch 1980-, elected vice pres for Wales 1988; Freeman Haverfordwest 1975; *Recreations* motoring, shooting, walking, music; *Clubs* Cardiff and County, Naval and Military; *Style—* Col Peter Howells, CBE, TD, DL; 2 Quay St, Haverfordwest, Pembrokeshire, Dyfed SA61 1BG (☎ 0437 762050, car 0860 845445)

HOWELLS, Roger Alan; s of Lt Col G E Howells, OBE, of Fleet, Hampshire, and Cecilia Doris May, *née* Pope; *b* 30 Oct 1943; *Educ* Farnborough GS; *m* 18 June 1982, (Edome) Rowena, da of late John Raymond Sharpe, of Earl Soham, Suffolk; 1 s (Christian Peter George b 1985) 1 da (Lucinda Chloe b 1983); *Career* Lt HAC 1968-74; dir: Howells Rawlings & Ward Ltd (industl fin advsrs) 1972-, Howells & Bingham Ltd (registered insur brokers) 1980-; memb Lloyd's; Freeman City of London 1978, Liveryman Worshipful Co of Makers of Playing Cards 1979; ACII 1969; *Recreations* tennis, golf, shooting, fishing; *Clubs* Hurlingham, Berkshire & Royal Wimbledon Golf; *Style—* R A Howells, Esq; 17 Nicosia Rd, London SW18 3RN (☎ 081 874 0299); 29 Bunhill Row, London EC1Y 8NE (☎ 071 638 8693, fax 071 638 1177)

HOWELLS, Roger Godfrey; s of Godfrey Frank Howells, of Bridgend, and Hilda, *née* Rogers; *b* 21 Oct 1954; *Educ* Bridgend Boys GS; *m* 20 March 1978 (m dis 1985), Susan Jean; *Career* CA; ptnr Cavells 1985-; dir Mutual Accountants Professional Indemnity Co Ltd, tutor Prince of Wales Business Initiative; ACA 1979; *Recreations* fishing, swimming, golf; *Style—* Roger Howells, Esq; Ross Cottage, Northwick Rd, Pilning, Bristol (☎ 04545 2438); Bridge House, 7-9 Church Rd, Lawrence Hill, Bristol (☎ 0272 558 414, fax 0272 558 407)

HOWERD, Francis Alick (Frankie); *b* 6 March 1922; *Career* WWII 1940-46, demob Sgt 1946; comedian and entertainer; worked in the London docks; started bottom of the bill in music-hall 1946, moved on to radio series Variety Bandbox; films incl: The Ladykillers, The Great St Trinians' Train Robbery, Carry on Doctor, The Runaway Bus; theatre: Bottom in a Midsummers Nights Dream (Old Vic), A Funny Thing Happened on the Way to the Forum; TV incl: Frankie Howerd Show, Frankie and Bruce Show, Francis Howerd's Tittertime, Up Pompeii, Frankie Howerd on Campus 1991; worldwide appearances for HM Forces Entertainment; *Recreations* theatre, walking, travelling, reading, music; *Style—* Frankie Howerd, Esq, OBE; c/o Tessa Le Bars Management, 18 Queen Anne St, London W1H 9LB (☎ 071 636 3191, fax 071 436 0229)

HOWERD, Frankie; *see*: Howard, Francis Alick

HOWES, Prof Christopher Kingston; s of Leonard Arthur Howes, OBE, of Norfolk, and Marion Amy, *née* Bussey; *b* 30 Jan 1942; *Educ* Gresham's, LSE, Coll of Estate Mgmnt (BSc), Univ of Reading (MPhil); *m* 1967, Clare, da of Gordon Edward Cunliffe (d 1987), of Sussex; 2 s (Robert b 1976, Ben b 1977), 2 da (Catherine b 1973, Rosaline b 1975 (decd)); *Career* GLC Planning & Valuation Depts 1965-67; ptnr (later sr ptnr) Chartered Surveyors & Planning Conslts 1967-79, dep dir Land Economy Directorate DOE 1979-80 (dir Land Economy 1981-84), dir Land and Property 1985-89, second Crown Estate cmmr and chief exec Crown Estate 1989-; visiting lectr Univs of: London, E Anglia (sr visiting fell 1973), Cambridge, Reading and Aberdeen 1966-; visiting prof UCL 1985-; memb Norwich Cncl 1970-74, magistrate for Norfolk 1973-79, memb Ct of Advsrs St Paul's Cathedral 1980-, steward and hon surveyor to Dean and Chapter Norwich Cathedral 1972-79, second cmmr and chief exec Crown Estate, memb Policy Review Ctee Royal Inst of Chartered Surveyors (Memb Planning & Devpt Divnl Cncl) 1984-, hon memb Cambridge Univ Land Soc 1989, memb HRH Prince of Wales's Cncl 1990; *Books* Value Maps: Aspects of Land and Property Values (1980), Economic Regeneration (1988), Urban Revitalization (1988); contributor to many books and articles in learned journals; *Recreations* music, art, sailing, fly fishing; *Clubs* Athenaeum, Norfolk (Norwich), Aldeburgh Yacht; *Style—* Prof Christopher Howes; Highfield House, Woldingham, Surrey; Roudham Lodge, Roudham, Norfolk; The Crown Estate, 16 Carlton House Terrace, London SW1Y 5AH (☎ 071 210 4231)

HOWES, Jacqueline Frances (Jaki); da of Frank Bernard Allen (d 1974), of Hardingstone, Northants, and Hilda Evelyn, *née* Bull; *b* 5 April 1943; *Educ* Northampton HS, Univ of Manchester (BA); *m* (m dis 1982), (Anthony) Mark, s of Anthony Cecil George Howes (d 1974); 1 da (Josephine); *Career* Guardian and Manchester Evening News Manchester 1969-71, Leach Rhodes and Walker 1971-72, sr lectr Sch of Architecture Huddersfield Poly 1972-89, conslt to Geoffrey Alsop Practice Manchester 1983-85, princ lectr in architecture Leeds Poly 1990-; numerous contrib to learned jls incl: Architects Journal, RIBA Journal, Yorkshire Architect; chair IT Working Gp RIBA; memb: Women Architects Gp, Cncl RIBA Yorks region; convenor IT Gp, ext examiner Portsmouth Poly, tstee Huddersfield Poly Fund for Students with Disabilities; ARCUK 1970, RIBA 1976; *Books* The Technology of Suspended Cable Net Structures (with Chaplin and Calderbank, 1984), Computers Count (1989); *Recreations* sailing, music, cartoons; *Style—* Mrs Jaki Howes; Leeds Polytechnic, School of the Environment, Brunswick Building, Leeds LS2 9BU (☎ 0532 832600)

HOWES, Prof Michael John; s of Lt Cdr Ernest Stanley George Howes (d 1984), of Lowestoft, Suffolk, and Louisa Anne, *née* Hart (d 1976); *b* 19 Jan 1941; *Educ* Lowestoft GS, Univ of Leeds (BSc, PhD); *m* 8 Oct 1960, Dianne Lucie, da of Rex Crutchfield, of Stevenage, Herts; 1 da (Emma); *Career* scientific offr MAFF 1957-62; Univ of Leeds: lectr 1967-78, sr lectr 1978-80, head of dept and prof of electronic engrg 1984-90; visiting prof Cornell Univ USA 1980-81, tech dir MM Microwave Yorks 1981-84; author of numerous engrg and scientific pubns; MInstP, FIEE, FIEEE; *Books* incl: Solid State Electronics (with D V Morgan, 1973), Microwave Devices (ed with D V Morgan, 1976), Optical Fibre Communications (ed with D V Morgan, 1980), Reliability and Degradation (ed with D V Morgan, 1982), Worked Examples in Microwave Subsystem Design (jtly, 1984), Reliability and Degradation (ed with D V Morgan, 1985); *Recreations* golf; *Clubs* Moortown Golf; *Style—* Prof Michael Howes; 32 West Park Drive, Leeds LS16 5BL (☎ 0532 752156); Dept of Electronic and Electrical Eng, The University, Leeds LS2 9JT (☎ 0532 332002, fax 0532 332032)

HOWGILL, Col Colin Humphrey Cowley; despatches 1977; s of Donald Robert Howgill, of Church Gate, Broadhembury, Nr Honiton, Devon, and Kathleen Isobel Queena, *née* Banks; *b* 8 June 1940; *Educ* Epsom Coll, Staff Coll Camberley (PSC(M)); *m* 9 July 1965, Pamela Mary, da of Cdr Alfred Marcus Hughes, OBE, RN, of The Red House, Clonway, Yelverton, Devon; 2 s (Michael Colin b 1968, David Charles b 1970), 1 da (Susan Rosemary b 1967); *Career* commissioned 2Lt RM 1958, Maj 1974, Lt Col 1979, Col 1983; CO 3 Commando Brigade Air Sqdn 1977-79, CO 42 Commando 1980-81 (Cdr for forces Vanuatu 1980), dir drafting and records 1982-84, Chief of Staff RM Commando Forces 1984-86, Chief of Staff Washington DC 1986-88 (asst def attaché and jt warfare attaché), aide-de-campe to HM The Queen 1988-89, ret 1989; int business conslt FoxCo Washington DC USA 1989-; Freeman City of Baltimor USA 1986; FBIM; New Hebrides medal of Honour 1980,Vanvatu Independence medal; *Recreations* fishing, shooting, skiing, diving; *Clubs* Farmers, Army and Navy, Tower (USA); *Style—* Col Colin Howgill; Fox International Investment Corporation (FoxCo), 144 Maple Ave, East Vienna, Virginia 22180, USA (☎ 703 281 7604/5, fax 703 759 2478)

HOWGRAVE-GRAHAM, Christopher Michael; s of Hamilton Stuart Howgrave-Graham, of The Old Farmhouse, Fulking, Henfield, Sussex, and Joyce Mary, *née* Rowlatt; *b* 18 Feb 1949; *Educ* Ardingly Coll, UEA (BA), Institut d'Etudes Politiques (distinction in d'etudes politiques); *m* 5 Aug 1972, Rossana, da of Giliande Mastroddi; 2 s (Jonathan b 7 Dec 1977, Matthew b 28 March 1981); *Career* NHS trainee (Winchester, Portsmouth, Kings Fund Coll London) 1971-73; planner: East Birmingham HMC 1973-74, South Birmingham Health Authy 1974-75; house governor St Stephen's Hosp 1975-80 (latterly sector admin Chelsea & Kensington), dep dist admin and acute servs mangr Redbridge Health Authy 1980-85, gen mangr Community & Mental Health Servs Barking Havering and Brentwood Health Authy 1986-88; dir acute servs: Bloomsbury 1989-90, Bloomsbury and Islington Health Authy; currently managing: The Middlesex Hosp and associated hosps, Univ Coll Hosp and associated hosps, Whittington and Royal Northern Hosps; sec Special Tstees of Middx Hosp, memb Inst of Health Serv Mangrs 1976; *Books* The Hospital in Little Chelsea (with Dr L Martin, 1978); *Recreations* squash, walking, gardening, seeing the family; *Style—* Christopher Howgrave-Graham, Esq; Director of Acute Services, Bloomsbury and Islington Health Authority, 25 Grafton Way, London WC1E 6DB (☎ 071 387 9300 ext 8160)

HOWICK OF GLENDALE, 2 Baron (UK 1960); Charles Evelyn Baring; s of 1 Baron Howick of Glendale, KG, GCMG, KCVO (d 1973; formerly Hon Sir Evelyn Baring, sometime govr Kenya and yst s of 1 Earl of Cromer), and Lady Mary Grey, da of 5 Earl Grey; *b* 30 Dec 1937; *Educ* Eton, New Coll Oxford; *m* 1964, Clare, yr da of Col Cyril Darby, MC, of Kemerton Court, Tewkesbury; 1 s, 3 da (Hon Rachel Monica b 1967, Hon Jessica Mary Clare b 1969, Hon Alice Olivia b 1971); *Heir* s, Hon David Evelyn Charles Baring b 26 March 1975; *Career* md Baring Bros & Co 1969-82, dir London Life Assoc 1972-82, dir Northern Rock Building Society 1988-; memb Exec Ctee Nat Art Collections Fund 1973-88; *Style—* The Rt Hon Lord Howick of Glendale; Howick, Alnwick, Northumberland NE66 3LB (☎ 066 577 624); 42 Bedford Gardens, London W8 (☎ 071 221 0880)

HOWICK OF GLENDALE, Mary, Baroness; Lady Mary Cecil Grey; da of 5 Earl Grey (d 1963); *b* 1907; *m* 1935, 1 Baron Howick of Glendale, KG, GCMG, KCVO (d 1973); 1 s (2 Baron), 2 da (Hon Lady Wakefield, Hon Mrs Gibbs); *Style—* The Rt Hon Mary, Lady Howick of Glendale; Howick, Alnwick, Northumberland

HOWIE, Hon Alisoun Mary Kyle; da of Baron Howie of Troon; *b* 2 April 1959; *Style—* The Hon Alisoun Howie; c/o 34 Temple Fortune Lane, London NW11

HOWIE, Hon Angus; s of Baron Howie of Troon; *b* 20 May 1963; *Style—* The Hon Angus Howie; c/o 34 Temple Fortune Lane, London NW11

HOWIE, Prof Archibald; s of Robert Howie, of Mayburn House, Clerk St, Loanhead, Midlothian, and Margaret Marshall, *née* McDonald (d 1971); *b* 8 March 1934; *Educ* Kirkcaldy HS, Univ of Edinburgh (BSc), California Inst of Technol (MS), Univ of Cambridge (PhD); *m* 15 Aug 1964, Melva Jean, da of Ernest Scott (d 1959), of Tynemouth, Northumberland; 1 s (David Robert b 9 Oct 1965, d 1986), 1 da (Helena Margaret b 14 July 1971); *Career* ICI fell Univ of Cambridge, res fell Churchill Coll 1960-61, demonstrator in physics Univ of Cambridge 1962-65, teaching fell in physics Churchill Coll 1962-86, lectr in physics Univ of Cambridge 1965-78 (reader 1978-86, prof 1986-, head Dept of Physics 1989-); visiting prof of physics: Aarhus 1974, Bologna 1984; pres Royal Microscopical Soc 1984-86; Hon Dr of Physics Bologna 1989; FRS 1978, FInstP 1978, Hon FRMS 1978; *Books* Electron Microscopy of Thin Crystals (jtly 1965, revised 1977), Electron Optical Imaging of Surfaces (jtly); *Recreations* winemaking; *Style—* Prof Archibald Howie, FRS; 194 Huntingdon Rd, Cambridge CB3 0LB (☎ 0223 276131); Cavendish Laboratory, Madingley Rd, Cambridge CB3 0HE (☎ 0223 337334, fax 0223 63263, telex 81292)

HOWIE, Ian Bryson; s of James Bryson Howie (d 1979), and Florence Augusta, *née* Bracey (d 1975); *b* 16 July 1928; *Educ* Alcester GS, Harper Adams Agricultural Coll (NDA); *m* 3 Nov 1951, Bridget Macbeth, da of John Bernard Field (d 1968); 3 s (David b 1954, Neil b 1956, Duncan b 1961); *Career* farm mangr to: Sir Edward Thompson 1954-57, GM Clive Whitfield Hereford 1958-; tstee Llangorse Sailing Club; memb: Cncl of NIAB, MAFF Priorities Bd for R & D; BGS Award 1988, CMA KFR Management Award 1989; FRAgS; *Recreations* hockey, sailing; *Clubs* Hereford CSC, Llangorse Sailing; *Style—* Ian Howie, Esq, OBE; Ryefield, Crizeley, Wormbridge, Hereford HR2 9DB (☎ 098 121 251)

HOWIE, Sir James William; s of James Milne Howie (d 1958); *b* 31 Dec 1907; *Educ* Robert Gordon's Coll Aberdeen, Univ of Aberdeen (MD); *m* 1935, Isabella Winifred Mitchell; 2 s, 1 da; *Career* Nat Serv WWII RAMC Nigeria and WO; prof of bacteriology Univ of Glasgow 1951-63, med dir Public Health Laboratory Serv 1963-73; QHP 1965-68; pres: RCPath 1966-69, BMA 1969-70 (Gold medal 1984); Hon LLD Univ of Aberdeen 1969; FRCP, FRCPGlas, FRCPEd, FRCPath, Hon ARCVS; kt 1969; *Books* Portraits From Memory (by British Medical Journal); *Recreations* golf, music, writing; *Style—* Sir James Howie; 34 Redford Ave, Edinburgh, Scotland EH13 0BU (☎ 031 441 3910)

HOWIE, Prof John Garvie Robertson; s of Sir James William Howie, *qv*, of 34 Redford Ave, Colinton, Edinburgh, and Lady Winifred Howie, *née* Mitchell; *b* 23 Jan 1937; *Educ* Univ of Glasgow (MD), Univ of Aberdeen (PhD); *m* 27 Dec 1962, Elizabeth Margaret (Margot), da of William Lochhead Donald, of Craigleith Rd, Edinburgh; 2 s (Alastair b 1963, Brian b 1965), 1 da (Claire b 1969); *Career* GP Glasgow 1966-70, sr lectr in gen practice (former lectr) Univ of Aberdeen 1970-80, prof of gen practice 1980-; FRCGP 1980, FRCPE 1989; *Books* Research in General Practice (2 edn, 1989); *Recreations* gardening, music, sport; *Style—* Prof John Howie; 4 Ravelrig Park, Balerno, Midlothian, Scotland EH14 7DL (☎ 031 449 6305); University of Edinburgh, Dept of General Practice, 20 West Richmond St, Edinburgh EH8 9DX (☎ 031 667 1011 ext 4412)

HOWIE, Prof John Mackintosh; s of Rev David Yuille Howie, of Aberdeen, and Janet Macdonald, *née* Mackintosh (d 1989); *b* 23 May 1936; *Educ* Robert Gordon's Coll Aberdeen, Univ of Aberdeen (MA, DSc), Balliol Coll Oxford (DPhil); *m* 5 Aug 1960, Dorothy Joyce Mitchell, da of Alfred James Miller, OBE (d 1980) of Aberdeen; 2 da (Anne b 1961, Katharine b 1963); *Career* asst in maths Univ of Aberdeen 1958-59, asst then lectr in maths Univ of Glasgow 1961-67, sr lectr in maths Univ of Stirling 1967-70, reagius prof of maths Univ of St Andrews 1970- (dean Faculty of Sci 1976-79); visiting appts: Tulane Univ 1964-65, Univ of Western Aust 1968, State Univ of NY at Buffalo 1969 & 1970, Monash Univ 1979, Northern Illinois Univ 1988; chm: Scot Central Ctee on Mathematics 1975-81, Dundee Coll of Educn 1983-87, Ctee to Review Fifth and Sixth Years (The Howie Ctee) 1990-; memb Ctee to Review Examinations (The Dunning Ctee) 1975-77, vice pres London Mathematical Soc 1984-86 and 1990-; FRSE 1971; *Books* An Introduction to Semigroup Theory (1976), and author of articles for various mathematical jls; *Recreations* music, gardening; *Style—* Prof John Howie, FRSE; Longacre, 19 Strathkinness High Rd, St Andrews, Fife KY16 9UA (☎ 0334 74103); Mathematical Institute, University of St Andrews, N Haugh, St Andrews, Fife KY16 9SS (☎ 0334 76161)

HOWIE, Paul Leonard; s of John Milford Howie (d 1988), of Adelaide, and Mary, *née* Victory; *b* 27 April 1944; *Educ* Sacred Heart Coll; *m* 1974, Lynne, da of Leslie

Franks; 1 s (Joshua Xavier b 22 Feb 1976), 1 da (Jessica Louise b 21 Jan 1978); *Career* fashion designer 1974-83, PR conslt then chief exec Lynne Franks Ltd 1983-; winner Knitwear Designer of the Year 1979; *Recreations* tennis, wine, the modern novel, theatre, wine, family, buddhism; *Clubs* RAC, Groucho's; *Style*— Paul Howie, Esq; Lynne Franks Ltd, 6-10 Frederick Close, Stanhope Place, London W2 2HD (☎ 071 724 6777, fax 071 724 8484, car 0831 432 719)

HOWIE, Prof Robert Andrew; s of Robert Howie (d 1959), of Rectory Farm, Emberton, Olney, Bucks, and Ruby, *née* Highet (d 1943); *b* 4 June 1923; *Educ* Bedford Sch, Trinity Coll Cambridge (MA, PhD, ScD); *m* 28 June 1952, (Honor) Eugenie, da of Robert Price Taylor, of Cardiff; 2 s (Robert Tremayne b 1956, Timothy Andrew b 1958); *Career* WWII 1941-46: Edinburgh Air Sqdn 1941-42, Pilots Wings and cmmn 1943, invalided out 1946 Flt Lt; asst lectr (later lectr) in geology Univ of Manchester 1953-62; King's Coll London: reader in geology 1962-70, prof of mineralogy 1970-85, fell 1980; Royal Holloway and Bedford New Coll London: Lyell prof of geology 1985-87, emeritus prof of mineralogy 1987-; Univ of London: memb Senate 1974, memb Ct 1984-89, chm Academic Cncl 1983-87; memb: Cwlth Scholarships Cmmn; Mineralogical Soc: sec 1965, ed Mineralogical Abstracts 1966-, managing tstee 1977-87, pres 1978-80; Geological Soc: vice pres 1973-75, Murchison medal 1976; *Books* Rock Forming Minerals (5 vols with W A Deer and J Zussman, 1962-63), An Introduction to the Rock Forming Minerals (1966); *Recreations* mineral collecting, writing abstracts; *Clubs* Geological Soc; *Style*— Prof Robert Howie; Department of Geology, Royal Holloway & Bedford New College, Egham, Surrey TW20 OEX (☎ 0784 434455)

HOWIE OF TROON, Baron (Life Peer UK 1978); William Howie; s of Peter Howie; *b* 2 March 1924; *Educ* Marr Coll Troon, Royal Tech Coll Glasgow; *m* 1951, Mairi, da of John Sanderson; 2 s, 2 da; *Career* civil engr, journalist and publisher; MP (Lab) Luton 1963-70, asst whip 1964-66, lord cmmr Treasy 1966-67, comptroller HM Household 1967-68, vice-chm PLP 1968-70, dir of internal rels Thos Telford Ltd; pro-chllr City Univ 1984- (memb Cncl 1968-); FICE, FRSA; *Style*— Rt Hon Lord Howie of Troon; 34 Temple Fortune Lane, London NW11 (☎ 081 455 0492)

HOWITT, Dr Geoffrey; s of Henry Howitt (d 1935), of Chadderton, Lancashire, and Alice, *née* Grisdale (d 1986); *b* 20 Sept 1926; *Educ* Chadderton GS, Univ of Manchester (MB ChB, MD); *m* 3 July 1953, Jean, *née* Sutcliffe; 3 s (Alistair John b 1955, Jeremy Paul b 1958, Christopher Mark b 1963); *Career* house offr med MRI 1951-52, sr house offr med MRI 1952-53, registrar med Glasgow RI 1955-58, sr registrar cardiology MRI 1958-60, conslt cardiologist MRI 1963-; sr lectr in cardiology Univ of Manchester 1966-67 (lectr 1960-66); memb: Assoc of Physicians of GB and Ireland, Br Cardiac Soc; FRCP, FRCPE; *Recreations* golf, opera; *Clubs* RAF, Wilmslow Golf; *Style*— Dr Geoffrey Howitt; Cardiology Dept, Manchester Royal Infirmary, Oxford Rd, Manchester (☎ 061 276 4144); Anson Medical Centre, 23 Anson Rd, Victoria Park, Manchester (☎ 061 224 1146)

HOWITT, Miriam; *née* Cooper; da of Charles Brodie Cooper (d 1978), of Broad Howe, Cumbria, and Lydia, *née* Peltzer (d 1984); *b* 1 Feb 1929; *Educ* St Leonard's Sch, St Andrews, AA Sch of Architecture (Dip Arch); *m* 8 Oct 1958, David Alan Howitt, s of Claude Elborne Howitt (d 1964), of Nottingham; 3 s (Nicholas b 1960, Mark b 1962, Paul b 1963), 1 da (Philipa b 1959); *Career* architect and designer; private practice with husband, work incl: airports, hotels, showrooms, offices, schools, clubs; winner Crown Inn Hotel Ampney Crucis Design competition 1975; Br Design in Japan Lighting 1988, former govr London Coll of Furniture, freedom to trade as citizen of City of London by virtue of birth on island of St Helena; MRIBA 1953, FCSD 1976 (formerly vice pres, memb Cncl, examiner, chm of Examiners); *Books* One Room Living (1972, Japanese edn, 1979); *Recreations* pottery, skiing, fell walking; *Style*— Mrs David Howitt; 33 Roehampton Gate, London SW15 5JR (☎ 081 878 0520, 081 878 0054)

HOWITT, Victor Charles; s of Sqdn Ldr Ronald Charles Howitt, DFC, of Flat 43, Rock Gdns, Bognor Regis, Sussex, and Ruby Frances Howitt (d 1976); *b* 13 July 1935; *m* 1, Dec 1956 (m dis 1977), Mary, da of Charles Langridge (d 1955); 2 s (Peter Charles b 28 Sept 1961, Stephen Jarvis Boughton b 7 Nov 1965), 1 da (Allison Mary b 13 Sept 1958); m 2, 17 June 1978, Elizabeth Anne (Betty), da of Charles Anthony Reghelini (d 1966); *Career* Nat Serv drill instr RAF 1953-55; articled CA 1951, trainee mangr 1952, locum dispensing optician R W Bradshaw 1960 (trainee 1956); dir Wigmores 1968, regnl md London and Home Counties D & A International 1974 (memb Devpt Team 1973); md 1982: Wigmores Ltd, Theodore Hamblin Ltd, Hamblin Wigmores Ltd; observer to Bd D & A Group Ltd 1983, dir of trg and chm Hamblin Wigmores 1983-85, dir D & A Group UK 1985-, md D & A Group Operations (gp ops dir 1985-89), Main Bd dir and UK Gp dir of retail devpt Dollond Aitchison Group plc 1989-; memb Cncl: Companies Ctee Gen Optical Cncl, Guild of Br Dispensing Opticians 1981-84, Fedn of Ophthalmic and Dispensing Opticians 1984-86; vice chm Abbey Park Resident Assoc 1986-87; Freeman: City of London 1988, Worshipful Co of Spectacle Makers 1988; FBDO 1961; *Recreations* photography, reading, gardening, old houses, travel, collecting cranberry glass and stamps; *Style*— Victor Howitt, Esq; On Spec, 46 Hither Green Lane, Bordesley, Near Redditch, N Worcs B98 9BW (☎ 0527 63568); Dollond & Aitchison Group (UK) plc, 1323 Coventry Rd, Yardley, Birmingham (☎ 021 706 6133, fax 021 708 1520, telex 339435, car phone 0836 729181)

HOWITT, William Fowler; s of Frederick Howitt, BEM (d 1976), and Isabel Strachan Fowler, *née* Howitt (d 1990); *b* 22 May 1924; *Educ* Perth Acad, Sch of Architecture Dundee (Dip Arch); *m* 21 July 1951, Ann Elizabeth, da of Archibald Joseph Hedges (d 1952); 3 s (Nicolas b 22 Dec 1952, William b 28 Nov 1957, James b 12 Feb 1961), 1 da (Anna b 20 Sept 1955); *Career* RM temp Lt 1943-46; architect St Thomas Hosp 1955-64, ptnr Cusdin, Burden and Howitt 1965-90 (specializing in hosps, med schs and univ work); princ works: Addenbrookes Hosp Cambridge, Royal Victoria Hosp Belfast, King Khaled Hosp Riyadh, St Thomas Medical Sch, Bart's Med Sch, Middlesex and UCL Med Sch, Univ of Cambridge, Univ of Durham, Univ of London, Univ of Hong Kong; conslt: Sharjah and Fujairah UAE, Tlemcen Algeria, King Fahd Med Centre Riyadh, teaching and paediatric hosps Nigeria, Tralee and Dublin Eire, Milan and Como; FRIBA 1968; *Recreations* reading, photography; *Style*— William Howitt, Esq; 32 Gloucester Rd, Teddington, Middlesex TW11 0NU (☎ 081 977 5772); ASFA Ltd, Woodcote Grove, Ashley Rd, Epsom, Surrey (☎ 0372 726140, fax 0372 743056, telex 266701 Atkins G)

HOWKER, Janni; da of Malcolm John Cookson Walker, of Kendal, Cumbria, and Mavis Nancy, *née* Bond; *b* 6 July 1957; *Educ* Monk's Dyke HS Louth Lincs, Kendal HS Cumbria, Univ of Lancaster (BA, MA); *m* 1 (m dis 1986), Ian Howker; m 2, 15 Oct 1988, Mick North, s of Tom North; 1 s (John Edward b 26 Jan 1990); *Career* author; various jobs 1976-84 (pt/t care asst hostel for mentally ill, invigilator for Open Univ, res asst, park attendant for Lancaster City Cncl, landlady for long distance lorry drivers), freelance author 1984-; TV work incl: Janni Howker-Storyteller (Thames TV) 1985, Dramarama (ITV) 1987, The Nature of the Beast (Channel 4) 1988; *Awards* Int Reading Assoc award 1985, Tom Gallon award Soc of Authors 1985, Burnley Express Children's Book of the Year 1985, Young Observer Teenage Fiction prize 1985, Whitbread award for Children's Fiction 1985, highly commended for Carnegie medal 1986 & 1987, Silver Pencil award (Holland) 1987, Somerset Maugham award 1987, Boston Globe Horn Book award 1987; memb: Soc of Authors, Arvon Fndn Cncl, Greenpeace, Green Pty; *Books* Badger on the Barge (1984), The Nature of the Beast (1985), Isaac Campion (1986); *Recreations* fell walking, silence, pubs, mending things, writing letters to friends, wishing I had time for recreations!; *Style*— Ms Janni Howker; The Cottage, Cumwhitton, Carlisle, Cumbria CA4 9EX (☎ 0228 60926)

HOWKINS, Ben Walter; s of Walter Ashby Howkins (d 1977), and Lesley Margaret, *née* Stops, of Olney, Buckinghamshire; *b* 19 Aug 1942; *Educ* Rugby, Amherst Coll Mass USA (Vintners scholar); *m* 6 Nov 1976, Clarissa Jane, da of Thomas John Fairbank, of Cambridge; 1 s (James b 1980), 1 da (Lucy b 1981); *Career* Lt Northamptonshire Yeomanry TA 1964-69; brand mangr IDV UK 1968-70, int sales and mktg dir Croft & Co 1970-80, md Morgan Furze 1980-89, dir Taylor Fladgate & Yeatman 1989-; chm Wine Devpt Bd 1990-; Freeman City of London 1986, Liveryman Worshipful Co of Vintners 1986; *Books* Rich, Rare and Red - A Guide to Port (1982, paperbook edn 1987); *Recreations* skiing, tennis, shooting; *Clubs* Brooks's; *Style*— Ben Howkins, Esq; 32 Westover Rd, London SW18 (☎ 081 870 3868); 9 Grosvenor Crescent Mews, London SW1 (☎ 071 823 2747, fax 071 245 6370)

HOWKINS, John Anthony; s of Col Ashby (Tim) Howkins (d 1977), and Lesley, *née* Stops; *b* 3 Aug 1945; *Educ* Rugby, Univ of Keele (BA), Architectural Assoc (AA Dip); *m* 1, 1971, Jill, da of Ian Liddington; m 2, 1977, Annabel, da of John Whittet; *Career* mktg mangr Lever Bros 1968-70, TV ed Time Out 1971-74, jt fndr TV4 Conf 1971, dir Whittet Books 1976-84, chm Pool Video Graz Austria 1976, TV columnist Illustrated London News 1981-83, ed Vision 1977-79, exec dir Int Inst of Communications 1984-89, conslt and dir ETR & Co 1989-, advisor Polish Radio and TV 1989-; exec ed Nat Electronics Review 1981-90, chm London Int Film Sch 1979-84; specialist advsr Select Ctee on Euro Communities House of Lords 1985; memb: Interim Action Ctee on the Film Indust DTI 1980-85, Exec Ctee Broadcasting Res Unit 1981-90, Br Screen Advsy Cncl (BSAC) DTI 1985-; vice chm New Media Assoc of Ind Producers 1984-85; *Books* Understanding Television (1977), Mass Communications in China (1982), New Technologies, New Policies (1982), Satellites International (1987); *Style*— John Howkins, Esq; 14 Balliol Rd, London W10 6LX (☎ 081 960 4023)

HOWL, (Oliver) Brian; s of Maj Clifford Howl (d 1962), of Maycroft, Ash Hill, Wolverhampton, and Doris, *née* Savill (d 1985); *b* 8 Oct 1922; *Educ* Shrewsbury, St John's Coll Cambridge (MA); *m* 16 June 1956, Dr Elizabeth Mary Caroline Dyke, da of Dr Sidney Campbell Dyke, of Wolverhampton; 1 s (Oliver Jonathan b 1960), 1 da (Julia Caroline b 1958); *Career* Nat Serv WWII Actg Sub Lt (E) RNVR 1943-46, Lt (E) RN 1946, served Med and Pacific Fleet; Lee Howl & Co Ltd (pump mfrs): mgmnt trainee 1947-48, jr mangr 1949-56, jt md 1956-62, sole md 1963-80, chm 1972-79; chm APE Lee Howl Ltd 1980-81; lectr in physics RMA Sandhurst 1948-49; dir: Bailey & Mackey Ltd 1963-87, Swiftfire Engineering Ltd 1979-, Villiers Ltd 1986-; pres W Bromwich W Cons and Unionist Assoc, tstee Ironbridge Gorge Museum Trust Ltd, fixture sec Greenflies CC, income tax cmmr 1986-; AMIMechE 1953, MIMechE 1972, CEng 1972; *Recreations* mountaineering, cricket, squash, beagling, rambling; *Clubs* Naval; *Style*— Brian Howl, Esq; 1 Merridale Grove, Finchfield, Wolverhampton (☎ 0902 27708)

HOWLAND, Lord; Andrew Ian Henry Russell; s and h of Marquess of Tavistock; *b* 30 March 1962; *Educ* Harrow, Harvard Univ (BA); *Recreations* racing, shooting; *Style*— Lord Howland; 6 Fairlawns, Dullingham Rd, Newmarket CB8 9JS; Tattersalls, Terrace House, Newmarket, Suffolk

HOWLAND JACKSON, Anthony Geoffrey Clive; s of Arthur Geoffrey Howland Jackson, and Pamela Foote, *née* Wauton; *b* 25 May 1941; *Educ* Sherborne; *m* 15 June 1963, Susan Ellen, da of Geoffrey Hickson, (d 1984); 1 s (James Geoffrey b 10 Feb 1965), 2 da (Anna Kate b 10 July 1968, Louisa Jane b 13 May 1971); *Career* md: Clarkson Puckle 1979-87, Bain Clarksons 1987; exec dir Gill & Duffus plc 1983-87; dep chm and md Hogg Group PLC 1987-; Freeman City of London, Liveryman Worshipful Co of Insurers; *Recreations* shooting, cricket, racing; *Clubs* Turf, City of London; *Style*— A G C Howland Jackson, Esq; Marks Gate, Fordham, Colchester, Essex CO6 3NR (☎ 0206 240 420); Lloyds Chambers, No 1 Portsoken St, London E1 8DF (☎ 071 480 4000, fax 071 480 4708, telex 884 633)

HOWLETT, Anthony Douglas; RD (1971); s of Ernest Robert Howlett (d 1968), of Lincs, and Catherine, *née* Broughton, of Lincs; *b* 30 Dec 1924; *Educ* King's Sch Rochester, Wellingborough, King's Sch Grantham, Trinity Coll Cambridge (MA, LLB); *m* 1952, Alfreda Dorothy, da of Arthur William Pearce (d 1976), of Sussex; *Career* Nat Serv RNVR 1942-46; RNVS 1951-60, RNR 1940-75, Lt Cdr 1968; called to the Bar Gray's Inn 1950, joined Govt Legal Serv 1951, i/c export credit guarantee branch 1972-75, i/c merchant shipping branch 1975-81; UK del: London Diplomatic Conf on Limitation of Liability for Maritime Claims 1976, Geneve Diplomatic Conf on Multi-Modal Tport 1980; vice chm Enfield Health Authy 1987-; memb Catenian Assoc 1987, fndr memb The Sherlock Holmes Soc (chm 1960-63 and 1986-89); Remembrancer of the City of London 1981-86, Freeman City of London 1981, Liveryman Worshipful Co of Scriveners 1981-; Order of King Abdul Aziz (II) Saudi Arabia 1981, Order of Oman (III) 1982, Cdr Order of Orange-Nassau Netherlands 1982, Offr Legion d'Honneur France 1984, Order of the Lion of Malawi 1985, Order of Qatar 1985; OStJ; *Books* author of numerous articles on Conan Doyle and Holmesiana; *Recreations* sailing, book browsing, Sherlock Holmes, opera, photography, foreign travel; *Clubs* Naval; *Style*— Anthony Howlett, Esq, RD; Rivendell, 37 Links Side, Enfield, Middx EN2 7QZ (☎ 081 363 5802)

HOWLETT, Gen Sir Geoffrey Hugh Whitby; KBE (1984, OBE 1972), MC (1952); s of Brig Bernard Howlett, DSO (ka 1943), and Joan, *née* Whitby; *b* 5 Feb 1930; *Educ* Wellington, RMA Sandhurst; *m* 1955, Elizabeth Anne, da of Sqdn Ldr Leonard Aspinal, of Speldhurst; 1 s, 2 da; *Career* cmmnd Queen's Own Royal West Kent Regt 1950, transfd Parachute Regt 1959, Mil Asst to C-in-C North (Oslo) 1969-71, cmd 2 Para 1971-73, RCDS 1973-75, cmd 16 Para Bde 1975-77, dir Army Recruiting 1977-79, GOC 1 Armoured Div (Lower Saxony, W Germany) 1979-82, Cmdt RMA Sandhurst 1982-83, GOC SE Dist 1983-85; C-in-C Allied Forces Northern Europe (Oslo) 1986-89; Col Cmdt: Army Catering Corps 1981-89, The Parachute Regt 1983-90; chm Serv Sound and Vision Corp 1990- (vice chm 1989); chm Leonard Cheshire Fndn 1990- (tstee 1988-); pres: CCF 1989-, Stragglers of Asia CC 1989-; cmmr Royal Hosp Chelsea 1989-, chm Reg Forces Employment Assoc 1990- (vice chm 1989); *Recreations* cricket, shooting; *Clubs* Naval & Military, MCC; *Style*— Gen Sir Geoffrey Howlett, KBE, MC; c/o Lloyds Bank, Tonbridge, Kent

HOWLETT, Neil Baillie; s of Terence Howlett (d 1975), of Storrington, W Sussex, and Margaret Marshall, *née* Baillie (d 1983); *b* 24 July 1934; *Educ* Trent Coll, King's Coll Cambridge (MA), Hochschule Für Musik Darstellende Kunst Stuttgart; *m* 1, 1962 (m dis 1988); 2 da (Alexander b 1971, Olivia b 1974); m 2, 1988, Carolyn, *née* Hawthorn; *Career* opera singer; Eng Opera Gp (Aldeburgh Festival, Soviet Union Tour) 1964; Glydebourne tour: L'Ormindo 1967, Idem 1968, Macbeth; Aix-en-Provence Festival: Don Giovanni 1970, Falstaff 1971; ENO 1972-89; guest appearances in: Cologne, Frankfurt, Hamburg, Royal Opera House Covent Garden, Athens Festival, Buenos Aires, Vichy Festival, Trieste, Netherlands Opera, Trondheim, ENO; concerts with: LPO, LSO, Oslo Philharmonic, Orquesta Nacional Madrid, Orquesta de Cataluna Barcelona, Radio Orch Katowice and Warsaw, Slovenian

Philharmonic, Maggio Musicale Firenze; recording Otello (with ENO 1984 and 1990); prof Guildhall Sch of Music 1974-, Kathleen Ferrier Meml Scholarship 1957; *Recreations* sport, history, philosophy, piano, gardening, theatre, reading; *Style—* Neil Howlett, Esq; Ingpen and Williams Ltd, 14 Kensington Court, London N8 (☎ 071 937 5158, fax 071 938 4175)

HOWLETT, Air Vice-Marshal Neville Stanley; CB (1982); s of Stanley Herbert Howlett (d 1981), and Ethel Shirley Pritchard (d 1934); *b* 17 April 1927; *Educ* Liverpool Inst HS, Peterhouse Cambridge; *m* 1952, Sylvia, da of James Foster (d 1982), of Lincs; 1 s (Michael), 1 da (Gillian); *Career* RAF pilot trg 1945-47, 32 and 64 (Fighter) Sqdns 1948-56, RAF Staff Coll Course 1957, Sqdn Cdr 229 (Fighter) OCU 1958-59, took part in London-Paris Air Race 1959, SO HQ Fighter Cmd 1959-61, OC Flying Wing RAF Coltishall 1961-63, RAF Coll of Air Warfare Course 1963, SO HQ Allied Forces Northern Europe 1964-66, OC Admin Wing RAF St Mawgan 1966-67, DS RAF Staff Coll 1967-69, Station Cdr RAF Leuchars 1970-72, RCDS Course 1972, Dir of Ops (Air Def and Overseas) MOD 1973-74, Air Attaché Washington DC 1975-77, Dir Mgmnt Support of Intelligence MOD 1978-80, DG RAF Personal Servs MOD 1980-82, ret; memb: Lord Chllr's Panel of Ind Inquiry Insprs 1982-, Homes Ctee Offrs' Assoc 1982, Pensions Appeal Tbnl 1988-; vice-pres RAF Assoc 1984-; *Recreations* golf, fishing; *Clubs* RAF, Phyllis Court (Henley-on-Thames), Huntercombe Golf; *Style—* Air Vice-Marshal Neville Howlett, CB; Milverton Bolney Trevor Drive, Lower Shiplake, Oxon RG9 3PG

HOWLETT, Dr Trevor Anthony; s of Ivan William Howlett, of Cambridge, and Daphne May, *née* Long; *b* 20 July 1952; *Educ* Perse Sch Cambridge, Gonville and Caius Coll Cambridge (BA, MA, MB BChir, MD, MRCP), King's Coll Hosp Med Sch London; *Career* house physician King's Coll Hosp 1977-78, sr house offr Central Middx Hosp London 1978-79, med registrar Frimley Park Hosp Surrey 1980-81, lectr in endocrinology Dept of Endocrinology Bart's 1985-88 (MRC trg fell 1981-85), conslt physician and endocrinologist Leicester Royal Infirmary Leicester 1988-, numerous scientific articles on clinical endocrinology and endogenous opioid peptides; FRSM, memb Soc for Endocrinology; *Recreations* gardening, cycling, skiing; *Style—* Dr Trevor Howlett; Leicester Royal Infirmary, Leicester LE1 5WW (☎ 0533 541414)

HOWLING, Richard John; s of Cecil Baden Howling, of Dorset, and Florence Irene Crowther, *née* Firth; *b* 22 Aug 1932; *Educ* Repton; *m* 4 April 1959, Shirley Maureen, da of Clifford Jackson (d 1964), of Lancs; 2 s (Rex b 1961, Philip b 1962), 1 da (Sally b 1964); *Career* Sub Lt RNVR 1956-58, serv Pacific, Malaya; chm Mediscus International Ltd and Mediscus Prods Ltd 1977-; ptnr Bird Potter & Co CAs 1961-68, dir Peter Robinson Ltd 1968-71, asst to Fin Dir Carreras Rothmans 1971-72, dir Rednor Ltd (and other subsids) 1972-74; chm: Actus Holdings Ltd 1988-90, The Schubert Group Ltd 1989-90, Wessex Export Club 1985-87, Dorset Indust Year Educn/Indust Ctee 1986; memb: Dorset Indust Matters Ctee 1987-, S West Regnl Cncl CBI 1985-, Fin and Econ Ctee (small firms) CBI 1985-87, Mktg and Consumer Affrs Ctee CBI 1987-; chm Dorset Co Gp CBI 1989-, memb Engrg Industs Assoc Nat Cncl 1985-87, Royal Warrant Holder as Organ Blower Manufacturer to HM The Queen (Watkins & Watson Ltd, a subsid of the Lingard Group) 1981-87; govr The Purbeck Sch 1988-; FCA, FRSA; *Recreations* sailing, tennis, golf, reading, photography, travel, walking; *Clubs* Royal Motor Yacht, Royal Over-Seas League, Poole Harbour Yacht; *Style—* Richard Howling, Esq; Roakham, Old Coastguard Rd, Sandbanks, Poole (☎ 0202 708976); Estepona, Spain; 10 Westminster Rd, Wareham, Dorset (☎ 09295 6311, telex 418496 MEDISC G, fax 09295 3967)

HOWMAN, Alastair Clive Ross; MBE (1967); s of Brig Ross Cosens Howman, CIE, OBE (d 1976), and Cecil Isabel Howman, of Pitlochry, Perthshire; *b* 8 July 1931; *Educ* Winchester, RMA Sandhurst; *m* 1, 22 May 1957, Elizabeth Ann, da of Adm Sir Richard Symonds-Tayler, KBE, CB (d 1971); 1 s (Charles Richard Ross b 1960), 1 da (Rosemary Ann Ross b 1962); m 2, 4 April 1980, Penny Lindsay, da of James Rankin; *Career* cmmnd The Argyll and Sutherland Highlanders 1952; serv: UK 1952-53, Guiana 1953-54, UK & BAOR (Berlin 1954-56), Cyprus 1958 (Co Cdr), BAOR 1960-62, serv as GSO 3 in HQ 1 Div; Staff Coll Camberley 1963, Malaya and Borneo (Co Cdr) 1964, GSO 2 Army Trg Directorate MOD 1965-67, Aden (Co Cdr and 2/c) 1967; dir Trade Coaters Ltd 1963, joined Manbré & Garton 1969, mktg dir Manbré Sugars 1972, md Gen Sugar Traders Ltd, Lochore & Ferguson Ltd 1979, established partnership Alastair Howman Agencies 1981; md: Craigtoun Meadows Ltd, Auchnahyle Farm & Crafts Ltd 1981; *Recreations* co sports, fly tying, tapestry; *Clubs* Royal Perth Golfing Soc; *Style—* Alastair Howman, Esq, MBE; Auchnahyle, Pitlochry, Perthshire (☎ 0796 2318, fax 0796 3657)

HOWMAN, Keith Cecil Ross; s of Brig Ross Howman, CIE, OBE (d 1977), and Cecil Isobel, *née* Elles; *b* 14 July 1935; *Educ* Winchester; *m* 8 Sept 1962, (Margaret) Jean Bruce, da of Ian Walker (d 1981); 1 s (Colin b 1968), 1 da (Susan b 1965); *Career* serv 1 Bn Argyll and Sutherland Highlanders Cyprus 1958-59; chm and md Trade Coaters Ltd 1966-; dir: Trade Coaters (Tradec) Ltd, Trade Coaters (Roofing) Ltd, Trade Coaters (Fabrication) Ltd, Auchnahyle Farm & Crafts Ltd, Ballechin Pheasantries Ltd, A B Incubators Ltd, Explorasia Ltd; chm World Pheasant Assoc (int conservation charity) 1985-; *Recreations* fishing, shooting, travel in Asia; *Style—* Keith Howman, Esq; Ashmere, Felix Lane, Shepperton, Middx (☎ 0932 225445); Trade Coaters Ltd, 34 Mead Lane, Chertsey, Surrey (☎ 09325 66591)

HOWORTH, Prof Jolyon Michael; s of Joseph Alfred Howorth (d 1966), and Constance, *née* Styles; *b* 4 May 1945; *Educ* Rossall and Henry Box Schs Witney Oxon, Univ of Manchester (BA), Univ of Reading (PhD), Univs of Lausanne and Geneva; *m* 1, 27 Aug 1966 (m dis 1982), Pauline, *née* Macqueen; 1 da (Stephanie Jeanne b 1974); m 2, 4 Jan 1985 (m dis 1987), Laura, *née* Levine; m 3, 5 Sept 1988, Dr (Kirstine) Mairi Maclean, da of Alexander Gordon Maclean, of Glasgow; 1 s (Alexander Boris b 1989), 1 da (Emily Kirstine b 1988); *Career* lectr: Univ of Paris III (Sorbonne Nouvelle) 1969-76, Ecole des Hautes Etudes Commerciales Paris 1970-76; visiting prof Univ of Wisconsin Madison USA 1974-75, sr lectr Univ of Aston 1979-85 (lectr 1976-79); visiting scholar Harvard Univ: 1981-82, 1984, 1985; prof of French civilisation Univ of Bath 1985-, dir Language Conslts for Indust Bath 1986-; conslt Univs Funding Cncl, fndr memb Assoc for Study of Modern and Contemporary France; memb: Royal Inst of Int Affrs, Int Inst for Strategic Studies, Soc for French Hist Studies, Institut Français d'Histoire Sociale; FRSA; *Books* with P Cerny: Elites in France: Origins, Reproduction and Power (1981), Edouard Vaillant et La Création de l'Unité Socialiste en France (1982), France: the Politics of Peace (1984); Defence and Dissent in Contemporary France (with P Chilton, 1984), Contemporary France: a review of interdisciplinary studies (with George Ross, vol 1 1987, vol 2 1988, vol 3 1989); *Recreations* numismatics, skiing, swimming, travel; *Style—* Prof Jolyon Howorth; 9 Chaucer Rd, Bath BA2 4QU (☎ 0225 335833); School of Modern Languages and International Studies, University of Bath, Bath BA2 7AY (☎ 0225 826490, fax 0225 826099 (gp 3), telex 449097)

HOWORTH, Michael John; s of Capt John Roger Howorth, of Highcliffe-on-Sea, Dorset, and Margaret Rhoda Howorth; *b* 21 Oct 1949; *Educ* HMS Conway Merchant Navy Trg Coll, Univ of Southampton; *m* 16 July 1977, Frances Rumney, da of Maj John Louis Rumney Samson (d 1988); 1 s (Charles William Samson b 4 May 1982), 1 da (Georgina Mary Rumney b 16 Dec 1979); *Career* RNR 1964-73; P and O Shipping Group 1967-76, formed Michael Howorth Associates 1976; dir: Copy King Group 1981, Samson Books Ltd 1982, Copyking Printing (from Ryman) 1990; ed dir Quick Print Publications Ltd 1991; memb Ctee Br Assoc of Printers and Copy Centres 1988; MIPR 1978, MInstM 1978; *Recreations* sailing, cruising, gastronomy; *Clubs* Hurlingham, Conway Cruising; *Style—* Michael Howorth, Esq; 47 Napier Ave, London SW6 3PS (☎ 071 731 7331, fax 071 736 5775); Michael Howorth Associates, 148 Sloane St, London SW1X 9BZ (☎ 071 736 3743, fax 071 736 2604, car 0836 250 992)

HOWSON, John Robert; s of Charles Howson (d 1981), and Grace Kershaw; *b* 9 June 1947; *Educ* Meols Cop HS Southport Lancs; *m* 15 June 1968, Glenys Susan, da of Kenneth George Turk, of Hampton Fields, Glos; 1 s (Adam b 1969), 1 da (Rebecca b 1972); *Career* retail mangr; founding chm Grafton Centre Retail Assoc Cambridge 1984-85, pres Portsmouth Dist Retail and Commercial Assoc 1986-87, vice pres SE Hants C of C and Indust 1987, memb Cambridge RFC 1984-85; *Recreations* golf, rugby union, early classic music; *Clubs* Cambridge Business and Prof, Royal Naval Club, Royal Albert Yacht; *Style—* John R Howson, Esq; C & A, Western Rd, Brighton; 86 Wicklands Ave, Saltdean, Brighton, E Sussex

HOWSON, Peter John; s of Tom William Howson, of 6 Fullarton Rd, Prestwick, Scotland, and Janet Rosemary, *née* Smith; *b* 27 March 1958; *Educ* Prestwick Acad, Glasgow Sch of Art (BA); *m* 1, 1983 (m dis 1984), Francis, *née* Nevay; m 2, 1989, Terry Jane, da of James Peter Cullen; 1 da (Lucie Elizabeth b 19 May 1986); *Career* RHF 1977; warehouseman Tesco Stores Ltd 1978, bouncer Caledonian Hotel 1978, shelf filler Safeway plc 1983, labourer 1983; painter: mural for Feltham Community Centre London (voluntary), The Boxer (series of etchings) 1985, Lowland Hero Spurns the Cynics 1986, Regimental Bath 1986, Saracen Heads (series of paintings), The Heroic Dosser 1987, The Noble Dosser 1987, Just Another Bloody Saturday 1987, A Wing and a Prayer 1987, The Fools of God 1989, The Wild Hunt 1989, The Sisters of Mercy 1989, Stairway to Heaven 1990, The Wrestlers 1990, Riding The Gauntlet 1990; pub collections: Tate Gallery, Museum of Modern Art NY, Met Museum of Modern Art NY, V & A, Oslo Museum of Modern Art, Scot Nat Gallery of Modern Art, Glasgow Art Galleries and Museum; Scot drawing prize 1985, Edwin Morgan prize 1987, first prize Euro Painters Sofia Bulgaria 1989, Henry Moore prize Bradford International Print Biennial; *Recreations* golf; *Style—* Peter Howson, Esq; Mathew Flowers, Flowers East, 199 Richmond Rd, London E8 (☎ 081 985 3333)

HOWSON, Roger Clive; s of Percy Clive Howson, of Leics, and Doris Clara Langham (d 1987); *b* 12 March 1943; *Educ* Gateway GS Leicester, King's Coll London (LLB); *m* 21 March 1968, Valerie Ann; 1 s (Daniel b 1972), 1 da (Nichola b 1969); *Career* slr 1967; dir and chief exec Buckley Investments Ltd 1985; dir and jt chief exec Rosehough plc and subsidiaries; *Recreations* rugby, cricket, golf; *Clubs* Oriental, Vipers RFC, Lutterworth Golf, Leics CC; *Style—* Roger Howson, Esq; 4 Spring Close, Lutterworth, Leics LE17 4DD (☎ 04555 2130); Rosehaugh plc, 53-55 Queen Anne St, London SW1M 0LJ (☎ 071 486 7100)

HOY, David Forrest; s of Peter Harold Hoy, of Bromley, Kent, and Helena Muriel, *née* Blackshaw; *b* 7 April 1946; *Educ* Leeds GS Yorks, Merchant Taylors' Sch Crosby Lancs; *m* 11 Sept 1971, Angela, da of John Piddock; 1 da (Susanne Mary b 4 April 1976); *Career* asst internal auditor Dunlop Co Ltd 1964-67, accountant Redwood Press Ltd 1967-68, gen mangr Guinness Superlatives Ltd 1974-76 (co accountant 1968-74), md Guinness Publishing Ltd 1976-88, project dir Guinness Enterprises Ltd 1989-90; vice pres: Gleneagles Gp Inc, Champneys Gp Inc 1991-; *Recreations* skiing, photography, philately; *Style—* David Hoy, Esq; 71 The Park, St Albans, Herts AL1 4RX; Guinness Enterprises Holdings Inc, 6 Landmark Square, Stamford, Connecticut, 06091, USA (☎ 203 359 7173, fax 203 359 7194)

HOY, Hon Ian Richard; s of Baron Hoy (Life Peer; d 1976), and Lady Hoy, *née* Nancy Hamlyn Rae McArthur; *b* 9 March 1945; *Educ* George Heriot's Sch, Edinburgh; *Career* memb: Edinburgh Corpn 1972-75, Lothian Regnl Cncl 1982-86, City of Edinburgh Dist Cncl 1988-; *Style—* The Hon Ian Hoy; 77 Orchard Road, Edinburgh EH4 2EX (☎ 031 332 5765)

HOY, Baroness; Nancy Hamlyn Rae; da of John McArthur; *m* 1942, Baron Hoy, PC (Life Peer d 1976); 1 s (Hon Ian Hoy); *Style—* The Rt Hon the Lady Hoy; 77 Orchard Rd, Edinburgh EH4 2EX (☎ 031 332 5765)

HOYER MILLAR, Hon Alastair James Harold; yr s of 1 Baron Inchyra, GCMG, CVO (d 1989); *b* 13 Nov 1936; *Educ* Eton; *m* 1974, Virginia Margaret Diana, da of William Perine Macauley, of Ballyward House, Manor Kilbride, Co Wicklow; 1 s (Mark Christian Frederick b 1975), 1 da (Martha Harriet Alice, b 1976); *Career* late Scots Gds; sec Pilgrim Tst 1980-; *Style—* The Hon Alastair Hoyer Millar; 16 Pembridge Villas, London W11

HOYER MILLAR, Hon Christian James Charles; o s and h of 2 Baron Inchyra, *qv*; *b* 12 Aug 1962; *Style—* The Hon Christian Hoyer Millar

HOYER MILLAR, Gurth Christian; s of Edward George Hoyer Millar, and Phyllis Edith Amy Wace (d 1956); *b* 13 Dec 1929; *Educ* Harrow, Oxford, Michigan Univ (LLM); *m* 17 March 1956, Jane Taylor, da of Harold John Aldington; 2 s (Christian b 1959, Luke b 1962), 1 da (Eliza b 1965); *Career* cmmnd Malaya 1949-50, cmmnd Reserve Bn SAS 1950-58; called to the Bar Middle Temple; main bd dir J Sainsbury plc: distribution 1966-, devpt 1974-; non-exec dir: Hudson Bay Co of Canada 1976-, London & Edinburgh Trust plc 1988-, Bunzl plc 1990-; chm: Homebase Ltd 1979-, J Sainsbury (Properties) Ltd 1988-, Bonhams (non-exec) 1988-; *Style—* Gurth Hoyer Miller, Esq; 27 Trevor Place, London SW7 1LD (☎ 071 584 3883); J Sainsbury plc, Stamford House, Stamford Street, London SE1 9LL (☎ 071 921 6785, telex 264241, car 0836 242659)

HOYES, Dr Thomas; s of Fred Hoyes, and Margaret Elizabeth Hoyes; *b* 19 Nov 1935; *Educ* Queen Elizabeth's GS Alford Lincs, Downing Coll Cambridge (BA, MA, PhD); *m* 27 Aug 1960, Amy Joan, da of Harry Bew Wood (d 1973), of Skegness, Lincolnshire; 2 da (Rebecca b 1963, Charlotte b 1966); *Career* conslt Hallam Brackett Chartered Surveyors Nottingham 1983-88 (ptnr 1963-83), prof of land mgmnt Univ of Reading 1983-88 (head of dept 1986-88), memb Lands Tbnl 1989; pres Cambridge Univ Land Soc 1973, govr Nottingham HS for Girls 1976-82; tstee Centre for Studies in Property Valuation City Univ 1989; memb: Rating Surveyors Assoc 1968, Gen Cncl RICS 1982-85 (pres Planning and Devpt Div 1983-84); Liveryman Worshipful Co of Chartered Surveyors 1980; ARICS 1964, FRICS 1969; *Recreations* adapting houses, gardening; *Clubs* Farmers; *Style—* Dr Thomas Hoyes; c/o The Lands Tribunal, 48-49 Chancery Lane, London WC2A 1JR (☎ 071 936 7200)

HOYLAND, John; *b* 12 Oct 1934; *Educ* Sheffield Coll of Art, Royal Acad Schs London; *m* 1958 (m dis 1968), Airi; 1 s (Jeremy b 1958); *Career* 1960s: taught at Hornsey, Oxford, Croydon, Luton and Chelsea Schs of Art; 1970s: taught at St Martin's Sch of Art and the Slade; solo exhibitions: Marlborough New London Gallery London 1964, Whitechapel Art Gallery London 1967, Waddington Galleries London 1970, Andre Emmerich Gallery NY 1972, Kingpitcher Contemporary Art Gallery Pittsburgh 1975, Waddington Galleries London (paintings 1966-68) 1976, Galeria Module Lisbon 1976-77, Serpentine Gallery London (retrospective) touring to Birmingham City Art Gallery and Mappin Art Gallery Sheffield 1979-80, Univ Gallery Univ of Melbourne touring to Art Gallery of S Aust Adelaide and Macquairie Galleries Sydney 1980; two man exhibitions: Biennial de Saô Paulo Brazil 1969, Leslie Waddington Prints London 1972,

Waddington Graphics London 1979, Van Straaten Gallery Chicago 1980, Hokin Gallery Miami 1981; gp exhibitions: RA Summer Exhibition 1956, 1957, 1958, 7th Tokyo Biennial Tokyo 1963, 4th Biennial Exhibition of Young Artists Musée d'Art Moderne de la Ville de Paris 1965, Documenta IV Kassel W Germany 1968, Gump's Gallery San Francisco 1981, Castlefield Gallery Manchester 1984, Erika Meyerovich Gallery San Francisco 1988, Waddington Galleries London 1990; set designs for Zansa Sadlers Wells; memb Rome Scholarship Ctee (printmaking) 1975; awards: prizewinner John Moores Liverpool Exhibition 1965 and Open Paintings Exhibition Belfast 1966; first prize: (with Robyn Denny) Edinburgh Open 100 Exhibition 1969, Chichester Nat Art Exhibition 1975, John Moores Liverpool Exhibition 1982, Korn Ferry Int Award Exhibition (with William Scott) 1986, Athena Art Awards Exhibition 1987; *Style—* John Hoyland, Esq

HOYLE, (Eric) Douglas Harvey; JP (1958), MP (Lab) Warrington North 1987-; s of late William Hoyle, and Leah Ellen Hoyle; *b* 17 Feb 1930; *Educ* Adlington Sch, Horwich and Bolton Tech Colls; *m* 1953, Pauline (d 1991), da of William Spencer; 1 s (Lindsay); *Career* sales engr; Parly candidate (Lab) Clitheroe 1964; MP (Lab): Nelson and Colne 1974-79 (contested same 1970 and 1974), Warrington (by-election) July 1981-1987; memb Manchester Regnl Hosp Bd 1968-74, pres ASTMS 1985-87 (memb 1958, vice pres 1981-85), pres MSF 1990- (jt pres 1988-90), memb Lab Pty NEC 1978-82 and 1983-85 (chm Home Policy Ctee 1983), chm Lab Parly Pty trade and indust ctee 1987-, memb House of Commons Trade and Indust Select Ctee 1985-; *Style—* Douglas Hoyle, Esq, JP, MP; 30 Ashfield Rd, Anderton, nr Chorley, Lancs

HOYLE, Prof Sir Fred; s of Benjamin Hoyle; *b* 24 June 1915; *Educ* Bingley GS, Emmanuel Coll Cambridge (MA); *m* 1939, Barbara Clark; 1 s, 1 da; *Career* fell St John's Coll Cambridge 1939-72, res in RADAR Admty 1940-45, Plumian prof of astronomy and experimental philosophy Cambridge Univ 1958-72, prof of astronomy Royal Inst 1969-72, Andrew D White prof-at-large Cornell Univ USA 1972-78, hon research prof Manchester Univ 1972-; fndr and dir Inst of Theoretical Astronomy Cambridge Univ 1967-72; foreign assoc US Nat Acad of Scis 1969, foreign memb American Philosophical Soc 1980; hon memb: American Acad of Arts and Scis 1964, Mark Twain Soc 1978, Royal Irish Acad in the Section of Sci 1977; hon fell: St John's Coll Cambridge 1973, Emmanuel Coll Cambridge 1983; FRS 1957; kt 1972; *Publications incl:* Man in the Universe (1966), From Stonehenge to Modern Cosmology (1973), Nicholas Copernicus (1973), The Relation of Physics and Cosmology (1973), Astronomy and Cosmology (1975), Ten Faces of the Universe (1977), On Stonhenge (1977), Energy or Extinction (1977), The Intelligent Universe (1983); with N C Wickramasinghe: Lifecloud (1978), Diseases from Space (1979), Space Travellers: The Bringers of Life (1981); *Novels incl:* The Black Cloud (1957), Ossian's Ride (1959), October the First is Too Late (1966), Element 79 (1967); with G Hoyle: Fifth Planet (1963), Rockets in Ursa Major (1969), Seven Steps to the Sun (1970), The Molecule Men (1971), The Inferno (1973), Into Deepest Space (1974), The Incandescent Ones (1977), The Westminster Disaster (1978), Comet Halley (1985); *Style—* Prof Sir Fred Hoyle, FRS; c/o The Royal Society, 6 Carlton House Terrace, London SW1Y 5AG

HOYLE, Rupert Felix; s of Stephen Thomas Hoyle (d 1971), of Bath, Avon, and Joan *née* Asher (d 1956); *b* 23 May 1939; *Educ* Ridge Sch Johannesburg, Hilton Coll, Univ of Cape Town (B Comm); *m* 1, 5 Sept 1964, Catherine, da of Reginald Albert Rawlings; 4 c (Caroline Joan b 20 January 1966, Audrey Lilian b 5 August 1967, Roger Stephen b 25 March 1970, Susan Olive b 24 March 1972); m 2, 11 Sept 1980, Janice Marie, da of A Herman Hutto; 1 s (Robert Herman b 11 Feb 1981); *Career* articled clerk Salisbury Rhodesia 1956-61, audit sr Turquand Young & Co London 1961-63, ptnr Deloitte Plender Griffiths Annan & Co Rhodesia 1969-77 (audit senior then manager 1963-69); Deloitte Haskins & Sells (now Coopers & Lybrand Deloitte): ptnr Johannesburg 1977-79, ptnr Cape Town 1979-86, audit ptnr London 1986-; FCA 1975 (ACA 1964), ACII 1988; *Recreations* golf, running; *Clubs* Horton Park Golf; *Style—* Rupert Hoyle, Esq; 4 Roeback Close, Ashtead, Surrey KT21 2DN (☎ 0372 272410); Coopers & Lybrand Deloitte, 128 Queen Victoria St, London EC4P 4JX (☎ 071 583 5000, fax 071 248 3623)

HOYLE, Susan; da of Roland Hoyle, and Joan, *née* Dickson; *b* 7 April 1953; *Educ* Nottingham HS for Girls, Univ of Bristol; *Career* educn offr Eng Nat Ballet (formerly London Festival Ballet) 1980-83, admin Extemporary Dance Theatre 1983-86, dance dir Arts Cncl 1989- (dance and mime offr 1986-89); *Style—* Ms Susan Hoyle; Arts Council of Great Britain, 14 Great Peter St, London SW1P 3NQ (☎ 071 333 0100, 071 973 6489, fax 071 973 6590)

HOYLES, Prof Celia Mary; da of Harold Gainsford French, of 17 The Heights, Loughton, Essex, and Elsie Florence, *née* Last; *b* 18 May 1946; *Educ* Univ of Manchester (BSc), Univ of London (MEd, PhD); *m* 25 July 1969, Martin, s of Arthur Hoyles; *Career* mathematics teacher in secdy schs 1967-72, sr lectr then princ lectr Poly of N London 1972-84, prof of mathematics educn Univ of London 1984-; presenter: Fun and Games YTV 1987-, several TV shows on gender and computing; *Books* Girls and Computing (1988), Logo Mathematics in the Classroom (with R Sutherland, 1989); *Recreations* tennis, swimming; *Style—* Prof Celia Hoyles; Institute of Education, University of London, 20 Bedford Way, London WC1 0AL (☎ 071 636 1500)

HOYOS, Hon Sir (Fabriciano) Alexander; s of Emigdio and Adelina Hoyos, of Peru; *b* 5 July 1912; *Educ* Harrison Coll, Codrington Coll, Durham Univ (MA); *m* 1, 1940, Kathleen Carmen (d 1970); 3 s, 1 da; m 2, 1973, Gladys Louise; *Career* leader-writer of Daily Advocate 1937-43, correspondent The Times London 1937-65; history teacher Barbados and Trinidad 1943-72; moderator and lectr Carribean History Survey Course Cave Hill University WI 1963-70; memb: Barbados Christian Cncl 1976-, Constitution Review Cmmn 1977-78, Privy Cncl for Barbados 1977-; Queen's Silver Jubilee Medal 1977; kt 1979; *Style—* Hon Sir Alexander Hoyos; Beachy Crest, Belair Cross Rd, St Philip, Barbados (☎ 36323)

HU, Eur Ing Sam Yu-Chai; s of Wei-Hsien Hu, of Malaysia, and Mary Yong; *b* 9 Feb 1956; *Educ* City Univ London (BSc), Loughborough Univ of Technol Leicestershire (MTech, Engrg Design Prize for Best Student 1986); *Career* plant and machine design engr Hume Far East Singapore 1980-82, design engr Philips Singapore 1982-85; sr design engr: Philips Electronics Hastings UK 1986-89, Moggridge Assocs London UK 1989-; MIMechE 1989, Eur Ing 1991; *Style—* Eur Ing Sam Hu; Moggridge Associates, 7/8 Jeffreys Place, Jeffreys St, London NW1 9PP (☎ 071 485 1170, fax 071 482 3970)

HUBBARD, (Richard) David Cairns; s of John Cairns Hubbard, of 6 Orchard Way, Esher, Surrey, and Gertrude Emilie, *née* Faure (d 1967); *b* 14 May 1936; *Educ* Tonbridge; *m* 7 Feb 1964, Hannah Neale, da of Arthur Gilbert Dennison (d 1988); 3 da (Katie-Jane b 1966, Juliet b 1970, Nicola b 1973); *Career* Nat Serv 2 Lt RA; Peat Marwick Mitchell & Co 1957-64; fin dir: Cape Industries plc 1972-74, Bache and Co (London) Ltd 1974-76; chm Powell Duffryn plc 1986- (fin dir 1976-85); chm Nat Fin Ctee Cancer Res Campaign 1986-89 (memb Cncl 1981-, chm Exec Ctee 1989-); Freeman City of London, Liveryman Worshipful Co of Skinners; FCA 1961; *Recreations* golf, skiing; *Clubs* Berks Golf (treas); *Style—* David Hubbard, Esq; Meadowcroft, Windlesham, Surrey GU20 6BJ (☎ 0276 721 98); Powell Duffryn House, London Rd, Bracknell, Berks RG12 2AQ (☎ 0344 531 01, fax 0344 505 99)

HUBBARD, Hon Frances Linden; da of 5 Baron Addington (d 1982); *b* 26 July 1962; *Educ* Southampton Univ (BA); *Career* journalist; *Clubs* National Liberal; *Style—* The Hon Frances Hubbard

HUBBARD, Jack; s of Arthur Fredrick Hubbard (d 1984), and Alice Mary, *née* Fairman (d 1985); *b* 11 Oct 1932; *Educ* Rochester Tech Sch, Univ of Cardiff (BSc); *m* 11 Sept 1960, Christine Lilian, da of Francis Held (d 1985); 2 s (Andrew b 14 June 1961, Peter b 30 Oct 1964); *Career* Nat Serv RAF 1953-55; Reed Int: central engrg 1956-57, head engrg res 1967-69, PA to Dep Chm 1969-71, md Timperley engrg 1971-73, divnl chief exec 1973-87; chief exec Medway Packaging Ncb Sweden 1987-, ret 1990; involved in church activities; Liveryman Worshipful Co of Horners; MIEE, MIMechE; *Recreations* rambling; *Style—* Jack Hubbard, Esq

HUBBARD, Jack Ernest; s of Frederick Ernest (d 1953), and Violet Frances, *née* Kerridge (d 1987); *b* 15 July 1925; *Educ* Braintree; *m* 6 Jan 1954, Cecily Susan, da of Cecil Mott Bowles (d 1985); 1 da (Susan Louise b 1969); *Career* sportsman; E of England Scrambles Champion, Jersey Sand Racing Champion; competed many int events in France, Holland, Ireland, Belgium; *Recreations* rifle shooting; *Clubs* Braintree (MC, LCC), Rifle; *Style—* Jack Hubbard, Esq; Hunters Roost, Church Rd, Bradwell, Braintree, Essex CM7 8EP (☎ 0376 62782); 135 High St, Aldeburgh, Suffolk

HUBBARD, John Michael; s of Leslie Leon Basil Hubbard, of W Midlands, and late Hilda Louise Hubbard; *b* 21 April 1943; *Educ* Tudor Grange GS Solihull; *m* 7 Sept 1969, Rosemary, da of Leslie Meeks, of Solihull; 2 s (James, Michael); *Career* CA; princ J Hubbard & Co; dir: Froude Engrg Ltd 1977-80, Worcester and Hereford Area C of C Trg Ltd 1985-87; FCA; *Style—* John M Hubbard, Esq; Cotsford, Old Malvern Rd, Powick, Worcester WR2 4RX (☎ 0905 830057)

HUBBARD, Joyce Mabel; da of Alexander George Liddle (d 1984), of Galashields, Scotland, and Doris Mabel, *née* Ingram (d 1987); *Educ* Kingsley Sch Hampstead, Holmewood Sch, Reimann Sch of Art, London Sch of Interior Design (DipAD); *m* 2, 1978, Anthony Francis Pearson Hubbard, s of Percy Francis Hubbard, MVO; *Career* previous work incl: designer in furniture indust Far East and Nigeria, mangr Exhibition Gallery Heal & Son, retail promotion offr Cncl of Industl Design, Design Advsy Serv Design Cncl 1979-82 (involved in all aspects of retail promotion and merchandising); lectr on design to numerous instns, fndr Joyce Hubbard Design Group 1982; FCSD, FRSA, MCIM; *Recreations* painting, reading; *Clubs* Arts, Caledonian; *Style—* Mrs Joyce Hubbard; Joyce Hubbard Design Group, 2 Milton Road, Cambridge CB4 1JY (☎ 0223 316770, fax 0223 350530)

HUBBARD, Hon Mrs (Julia Elizabeth); *née* Callaghan; yr da of Baron Callaghan of Cardiff, KG, PC (Life Peer), *qv*; *b* 1942; *m* 1967, Ian Hamilton Hubbard; 3 s (Tobin James Hamilton b 1970, Tom Ian b 1975, Sam Jonathan b 1976), 1 da (Joanna Jane b 1971); *Style—* The Hon Mrs Hubbard; Nettleslack Farm, Lowick Green, Cumbria

HUBBARD, Gp Capt Kenneth Gilbert; OBE (1952), DFC (1944), AFC (1957); s of Gilbert Claud Hubbard (d 1978), of 47 Gordon Ave, Norwich, Norfolk, and Florence, *née* Dack (d 1980); *b* 26 Feb 1920; *Educ* Norwich Tech Coll (Nat Cert, HNC); *m* 1, 1946 (m dis 1953), Daphne, da of Richard Taylor, of Norwich; m 2, Margaret Julia, *née* Grubbe; *Career* joined RAF 1940, Pilot 205 Gp ME and Italy, qualified flying instr A2; RAF Flying Coll: directing staff awarded PFC 1950-51, awarded PSA 1954; Wing Cdr and CO 49 Sqdn 1956-58, Capt Valiant XD818 dropped Britain's first hydrogen bomb at Christmas Island tests 1957, Gp Capt 1961, CO RAF E L Adam Libya 1961-62, CO RAF Scampton 1963-64, Gp Capt trg Transport Cmd 1964-66, ret 1966; memb Bd Hubbard Reader Group 1975-82, dir and memb Tst Bd Jubilee Theatre Tst Norwich; exec chm of all ATC Sqdn Civilian Ctees in S Suffolk, Blythburgh Parish cncllr, chm Local Review Ctee for parole HM Prison Blundeston (joined 1982); *Books* Operation Grapple (1984); *Recreations* horse riding, golf, writing; *Clubs* RAF, RAF Inominate; *Style—* Gp Capt Hubbard, OBE, DFC, AFC; The Priory, Blythburgh, Suffolk IP19 9LR (☎ 050 270 232)

HUBBARD, Leslie Antony Marcus; s of Gerald Jabez Hubbard, and Blanche Ivy May, *née* Turner; *b* 24 Jan 1936; *Educ* East Barnet GS, Northampton Coll of Advanced Technol (now City Univ); *m* 28 Sept 1958, Barbara, da of Leslie Norman Lunn (d 1988); 1 s (Geoffrey b 1961), 2 da (Julia b 1959, Carol b 1964); *Career* RAF 1958-63: sr optician RAF Hosp Halton 1958-60, sr optician RAF Hosp Changi Singapore 1960-63; optometrist 1963- (own practice High Wycombe 1966-); former chm: Bucks local optical ctee, Assoc of Optometrists Middle Thames Branch (former sec), Spectacle makers Soc; memb Oxford local optical ctee; memb Rotary Club of High Wycombe; Freeman City of London 1980, Liveryman Worshipful Co of Spectacle Makers 1981; FBCO 1980 (fndr fell); *Recreations* rambling, skiing; *Clubs* City Livery, Comrades (Wallingford); *Style—* Leslie Hubbard, Esq; Lima, 5 Beaconsfield Ave, High Wycombe, Bucks (☎ 0494 28 107); 55 West Wycombe Rd, High Wycombe, Bucks (☎ 0494 33 110)

HUBBARD, Michael Joseph; QC (1985); s of Joseph Thomas Hubbard, of Sussex, and Gwendoline Phyllis, *née* Bird (d 1957); *b* 16 June 1942; *Educ* Lancing; *m* 1967, Ruth Ann, da of John Logan, of Hants; 5 s (Mark b 1968, Duncan b 1970, Lucian b 1972, Angus b 1974, Quinten b 1976); *Career* slr 1966-72, called to the Bar Grays Inn 1972, joined Western Circuit; prosecuting counsel to Inland Revenue Western Circuit 1983-85; rec Crown Ct 1984; *Recreations* sailing; *Style—* Michael Hubbard, QC; Bartons, Stoughton, Chichester, Sussex; 1 Paper Buildings, Temple, London

HUBBARD, Hon Michael Walter Leslie; s of 5 Baron Addington (d 1982); hp of bro, 6 Baron Addington, *qv*; *b* 7 July 1965; *Educ* Hewett Sch Norwich, Univ of Manchester (BA), Leicester Polytechnic (PGD, MA); *Style—* The Hon Michael Hubbard

HUBBARD, Lady Miriam; *née* Fitzalan-Howard; da of 3 Baron Howard of Glossop, MBE, and Baroness Beaumont, OBE; sis of 17 Duke of Norfolk, *qv*; *b* 12 Dec 1924; *m* 19 April 1952, Lt Cdr Theodore Bernard Peregrine Hubbard, RN (ret), er s of late Theodore Stephen Hubbard; 2 s, 3 da; *Recreations* walking and dogs; *Style—* The Lady Miriam Hubbard; Thurston Croft, Bury St Edmunds, Suffolk

HUBBARD, Richard David Cairns; *b* 14 May 1936; *Educ* Tonbridge, Harvard Business Sch; *m* 1964, Hannah, *née* Dennison; 3 da; *Career* Nat Serv RA 1955-57; CA; Peat Marwick Mitchell & Co London 1957-64, sec and gp fin dir Cape Asbestos plc 1965-73, dir fin and admin Bache & Co London 1974-76, chm Powell Duffryn plc 1986- (gp fin dir 1976), non exec dir Southern Advsy Bd National Westminster Bank plc 1988-; non exec dir: Blue Circle Industries plc 1986-, London & Manchester Assurance Group plc 1989-, TR City of London Trust plc 1989-; Cancer Res Campaign (dep chm Bd, chm Exec Ctee), treas Berkshire Golf Club; Freeman City of London, Liveryman Worshipful Co of Skinners; *Recreations* golf, skiing, family; *Style—* Richard Hubbard, Esq; Meadowcroft, Windlesham, Surrey GU20 6BJ (☎ 0276 72198); Powell Duffryn House, London Rd, Bracknell, Berks RG12 2AQ (☎ 0344 53101, fax 0344 50599, telex 858906)

HUBBARD-RYLAND, Dr (Primrose) Anne; da of Benjamin John Hubbard, of London, and Sylvia Constance Kay; inventors of the 'Kay Loom'; *Educ* Univ of London, Univ of Liverpool; *m* 1, 16 July 1966, David Andrew Ryland, s of C Ryland, CBE, of Sussex; m 2, 4 June 1986, Paul John Starmer, s of Albert Edward Starmer (d 1982), of Northants; *Career* house physician Whittington Hosp London 1971-72, house surgn Northampton Gen Hosp 1973; dir Elizabethan Lace Co Ltd 1987; MRCS, LRCP; *Books* Condition of Geriatric Patients on Admission to Hospital (dental), Gerontologia Clinic (1973), Dental Care of the Elderly (Nursing Times, 1977); *Recreations* needlework, keep-fit, church choir; *Clubs* British Sub-Aqua; *Style*— Dr A Hubbard-Ryland; The Chapel House, Greens Norton, Northants NN12 8BS (☎ 0327 53663)

HUBER, Peter John; s of James Huber (d 1989), and Doris, *née* Fickling (d 1960); *b* 1 April 1940; *Educ* St Benedict's London, Columbia Univ NY USA; *m* Evelyn, da of William Hayhow; 2 da (Belinda b 13 Sept 1971, Gillian b 21 Jan 1974); *Career* advtg exec; J Walter Thompson: joined 1960, NY 1961-62, Amsterdam 1962-63, assoc dir London 1963-73, account dir 1973-79, Bd dir 1979-; MIPA 1985; *Clubs* MCC, Surrey CCC, Ealing Squash (chm 1976-); *Style*— Peter Huber, Esq; J Walter Thompson, 40 Berkeley Square, London W1X 6AD (☎ 071 499 4040, fax 071 493 8432)

HUCK, William Simpson; s of William Cecil Huck (d 1977), of Preston, Lancs, and Florence Ellen Davey, *née* Simpson (d 1982); *b* 24 June 1927; *Educ* Sedbergh; *m* 20 Aug 1955, Barbara Marion, da of Thomas Harold Berry (d 1943), of Chipping, Lancs; 2 s (Simon William John b 1958, Richard Anthony b 1959), 1 da (Kathryn Nancy b 1962); *Career* slr; pt/t chm Rent Tbnl and Rent Assessment Ctees (NW Area) 1965-75; chm Harris Charity Preston, treas Preston Grasshoppers RFC 1952-69 and sec 1969-71; pres: Preston Cricket and Hockey Club (Preston Sports Club) 1981-87, Preston Incorporated Law Soc 1985-86; *Recreations* cricket, rugby, shooting, gardening; *Style*— William S Huck, Esq; Withy Trees Barn, Cumeragh Lane, Preston PR3 2AN (☎ 0772 862711); 3 Ribblesdale Place, Preston PR1 3NA (☎ 0772 54048)

HUCKER, Michael; s of Lt-Col Ernest George Hucker, CBE (d 1986), of Willingdon, Sussex, and Mary Louise, *née* Jowett; *b* 25 Oct 1937; *Educ* St Dunstans Coll, LSE; *m* 7 Jan 1961, Hazel Zoë Hucker, JP, da of Alfred Roy Drake (d 1940), of Hampstead; 2 s (Nicholas b 1963, Rupert b 1967), 1 da (Sally (Mrs Ducker) b 1961); *Career* cmmnd RE 1957, served BAOR, W Africa, Malaysia, NI, MOD, Capt 1961, Maj 1967, ret 1976; called to the Bar Lincoln's Inn 1974; ALS prosecutor until 1976 (ret), in practice London 1976-, head of chambers 1978-, appointed by AG Counsel to Army Bd 1979, pt/t judge advocate 1983, asst rec 1988, represented soldiers in Gibraltar Inquest 1988, called to the Bar Gibraltar 1988; Freeman City of London 1978; MIRE 1957; *Recreations* music, English history, biography; *Style*— Michael Hucker, Esq; Hardwick Building, Lincolns Inn, London WC2 (☎ 071 242 2523, fax 071 831 6968)

HUCKER, Rev Michael Frederick; MBE (1970), QHC (1987); s of William John Hucker (d 1981), and Lucy Sophia, *née* Ashley; *b* 1 May 1933; *Educ* City of Bath Boys' Sch, Didsbury Coll Bristol, Univ of Bristol (MA), Univ of London (BD); *m* 13 May 1961, (Katherine) Rosemary, da of Sidney Cyril Parsons; 1 s (Martin William b 1963), 1 da (Rachel Mary b 1964); *Career* cmmnd chaplain RAF 1962, asst princ chaplain 1983; princ chaplain Church of Scotland and Free Churches 1987-90, sec Forces Bd of the Methodist Church 1990-; *Recreations* gardening, reading; *Style*— The Rev Michael Hucker, MBE, QHC; 1 Central Buildings, Westminster, London SW1H 9NU

HUCKERBY, Martin; s of George Wilcox Huckerby (d 1969), of Coulsdon Surrey, and Evelyn Agnes, *née* Martin; *b* 16 Aug 1945; *Educ* Emanuel Sch Wandsworth, Croydon Tech Coll, Univ of Keele (BA); *Career* journalist; news reporter Newcastle Evening Chronicle 1967-69, municipal reporter and music critic 1969-72; The Times: news reporter 1972-75, political reporter 1975-76, actg dep home news ed 1976-77, music and theatre reporter 1977-81, launched Arts Diary 1978-81, night news ed 1981-84, asst foreign news ed 1984-86l managing ed News on Sunday 1986-87, travelled round the world 1987-88, foreign news ed The Observer 1989-; *Recreations* travel, theatre, opera, books, wreaking occasional havoc; *Style*— Martin Huckerby, Esq; 272 Camberwell New Rd, London SE5 0RP (☎ 071 733 8324); The Observer, Chelsea Bridge House, Queenstown Road, London SW8 4NN (☎ 071 627 0700, fax 071 622 1571)

HUCKFIELD, Leslie John; s of Ernest Leslie Huckfield, and Suvla Huckfield; *b* 7 April 1942; *Educ* Prince Henry's GS Evesham, Keble Coll Oxford, Univ of Birmingham; *Career* contested (Lab) Warwick and Leamington 1966, MP (Lab) Nuneaton March 1967-83, PPS to Min of Public Bldgs and Works 1968-70, Parly under-sec for Industry 1976-79, oppn front bench spokesman on Industry 1979-81; memb: Lab NEC 1978-82, Lab W Midlands Regnl Exec Ctee 1978-82; political sec Nat Union Lab and Socialist Clubs 1979-82; former chm Lab Tport Gp 1974-76, ind advsr Cmmn of Tport Gp 1975-76; MEP (Lab) for Merseyside East 1984-89; pres Worcs Fedn of Young Socialists 1962-64; memb: Birmingham Regnl Hosp Bd 1970-72, Political Ctee Co-op Retail Soc 1981-; advertising mangr Tribune Pubns Ltd; currently princ offr of external resources St Helen's Coll Mersyside; *Publications* various newspaper and periodical articles; *Recreations* running marathons; *Style*— Leslie Huckfield, Esq; PO Box 200, Wigan, Lancashire WN5 0LU

HUCKIN, P(eter) Hugh; s of Albert Edward Huckin, OBE (d 1983), and Margaret, *née* Harris; *b* 17 Oct 1930; *Educ* Harrisons Coll Barbados, Haileybury & ISC, Royal Sch of Mines London Univ (BSc); *m* 5 Sept 1955, Anne Margaret, da of James Duncan Webster (d 1964); 2 da (Jennifer b 1960, Elizabeth b 1963); *Career* Lt RCS 1950-53; petroleum engr: Shell Int Holland and Columbia 1956-62, Texaco Trinidad 1962-63; chief petroleum engr: Iraq Petroleum Co 1964-73, ARCO 1973-75; md REMI (UK) Ltd 1975-76, chm Welldrill Gp Ltd 1977-; ARSM; *Recreations* work, garden, boats; *Style*— P Hugh Huckin, Esq; Haywards, Headley, Bordon, Hants GU35 8PX (☎ 0428 712224); Welldrill Ltd, Queen Anne House, Bagshot, Surrey GU19 5AT (☎ 0276 76666, fax 0276 76822)

HUCKLE, Sir (Henry) George; OBE (1969); s of George Henry and Lucy Huckle; *b* 9 Jan 1914; *Educ* Latymer Sch, Univ of Oxford; *Career* serv WWII bomber pilot (POW); Shell Gp 1945-70, md Shellstar Ltd 1965-70, ret; chm: Agric Trg Bd 1970-80, Home-Grown Cereals Authy 1977-83, Extrans Tech Servs Ltd 1980-89 (ret); kt 1977; *Recreations* competition bridge; *Clubs* Farmers'; *Style*— Sir George Huckle, OBE; Icknield House, Saxonhurst, Downton, Wilts

HUCKSTEP, Prof Ronald Lawrie; CMG (1971); s of Herbert George Huckstep, and Agnes, *née* Lawrie-Smith (d 1966); *b* 22 July 1926; *Educ* Cathedral Sch, Lester Inst, Aurora Univ Shanghai, Univ of Cambridge and Middlesex Hosp (MA, BCh, MD); *m* 2 Jan 1960, Margaret Ann, da of Dr Ronald Graeme Macbeth, of Meadow Close, Church Hanborough, Oxford; 2 s (Michael b 3 Sept 1963, Nigel b 19 Aug 1966), 1 da (Susan b 28 March 1961); *Career* Hunterian prof RCS 1959-60; prof of orthopaedic surgery Makerere Uni Kampala Uganda 1967-72; chm of orthopaedic surgery and dir of accident servs Prince of Wales and Prince Henry Hosps Sydney 1972-; Univ of NSW (current posts): prof of traumatic and orthopaedic surgery, chm Dept of Traumatic and Orthopaedic Surgery, rotating chm Sch of Surgery; author of numerous booklets and papers on orthopaedic surgery, trauma, rehabilitation and typhoid fever; vice pres Aust Orthopaedic Assoc 1982, pres Coast Med Assoc Sydney 1985-86, FTS, FRCS (Eng), FRCS (Edinburgh), FRACS; Irving Geist award Soc for the Rehabilitation of the Disabled 1967, LO Bett's Meml medal 1983, James Cook medal 1984, KL Sutherland medal 1985, Paul Harris medal Rotary Int 1987; Hon MD Univ of NSW 1988; *Books* Typhoid Fever and other Salmonella Infections (1962), A Simple Guide to Trauma (4 edn 1986, also in Italian and Japanese), Poliomeyelitis A Guide for Developing Countries (1975); *Recreations* photography, travel, swimming, designing orthopadeic implants and appliances; *Clubs* The Australian (Sydney); *Style*— Prof Ronald Huckstep, CMG; 108 Sugarloaf Crescent, Castlecrag, 2068, Sydney, NSW, Australia (☎ 010 61 2 958 1786); Department of Traumatic and Orthopaedic Surgery, University of New South Wales, Kensington, Sydney, NSW 2033, Australia (☎ 010 61 2 2666, fax 010 61 2 399 9774)

HUDD, Dr Nicholas Payne (Nick); s of Harold Payne Hudd (d 1977), of Essex, and Marguerita Eva, *née* Clarke; *b* 11 Oct 1945; *Educ* Palmer's Sch Essex, Sidney Sussex Coll Cambridge (MA, MB BChir, first boat colour), Westminster Hosp; *m* 11 Oct 1969, Gwendeleen Mary, da of John Johnstone, of Cardonald, Glasgow; 2 s (Alastair Payne b 28 Dec 1973, Robert Nicholas Harold b 23 June 1984); *Career* house surgn Westminster Children's Hosp 1970, house physician Princess Alexandra Hosp Harlow 1971, sr house offr Orsett Hosp 1972, med registrar St Andrew's Hosp Billericay and Basildon Hosp 1972-74, haematology registrar Orsett Hosp 1974-76; sr med registrar: Withington Hosp & Manchester Royal Infirmary 1976-78, Benenden Hosp 1977-79; conslt physician Benenden Hosp 1980-; memb: BMA, Br Diabetic Assoc, Historical Assoc, Royal Nat Rose Soc; chm Romney Marsh Historic Churches Tst 1988- (vice chm 1982-88), churchwarden St Mildred's Church Tenterden 1982-88, conductor Benenden Hosp Choir; MRCP 1976, FRSM 1978; *Recreations* golf music (singing and conducting), rose-growing, cricket, history, talking; *Clubs* Tenterden Golf, Kent CCC, The Historical Assoc, Royal National Rose Soc; *Style*— Dr Nick Hudd; 13 Elmfield, Tenterden, Kent TN30 6RE (☎ 0580 63704); Benenden Hospital, Cranbrook, Kent TN17 4AX (☎ 0580 240333, fax 0580 241877)

HUDD, Roy; s of Harold Hudd, of London, and Evelyn, *née* Barham; *b* 16 May 1936; *Educ* Croydon Secdy Tech Sch; *m* 25 Sept 1988, Deborah Ruth, da of Gordon Flitcroft (d 1986), of Warton, Lancashire; *Career* Nat Serv RAF 1956-58; comedian, playwright, author and actor; entered show business 1958; TV work incl: Not So Much a Programme More a Way of Life, The Malajusted Busker (winner Montreaux Pres Prize), Hudd, The Illustrated Weekly Hudd, Comedy Tonight, The 607080 Show, Movie Memories, Halls of Fame, The Puppet Man, Hometown, regular panelist on What's My Line?; theatre work incl: seasons at Richmond Theatre and The Young Vic, pantomine at Theatre Royal Bath, the clown in The Birth of Merlin (Theatre Clwyd), Fagin in Oliver!, Stanley Gardner in Run For Your Wife (Whitehall Theatre), The Fantasticks (Open Air Theatre) 1990, Babes in the Wood (Ashcroft Theatre, Croydon) 1990, Midsummer Night's Dream (Open Air Theatre) 1991; radio work incl: Workers Playtime, The News Huddlines, disc jockey Radio 2; writer of stage prodns: The Victorian Christmas, Roy Hudd's very own Music Hall, Just a Verse and Chorus, Beautiful Dreamer, While London Sleeps, Underneath the Arches (winner Best Actor in a Musical from Soc of West End Theatre); awards: Sony Gold award 1990 for outstanding contrib to radio, LWT Lifetime Achievement for Radio Comedy award 1990, King Rat of The Grand Order of Water Rats 1989; *Books* Music Hall (1970); *Recreations* walking, singing, napping; *Clubs* Green Room; *Style*— Roy Hudd, Esq; 652 Finchley Rd, London NW11 7NT

HUDDIE, Sir David Patrick; s of James Huddie (d 1936); *b* 12 March 1916; *Educ* Mountjoy Sch Dublin, Trinity Coll Dublin (MA); *m* 1941, Wilhelmina Betty, da of Dr John Booth (d 1940), of Cork; 3 s; *Career* engr; md Aero Engine Div Rolls-Royce Ltd 1965-70, chm Rolls-Royce Aero Engines Inc 1968-70; sr res fell Imp Coll London 1971-80 (hon fell 1981); Hon ScD Dublin; FIQA, FIMechE, FEng; kt 1968; *Recreations* music, reading, gardening; *Clubs* Athenaeum; *Style*— Sir David Huddie; The Croft, Butts Rd, Bakewell, Derbys (☎ 062 981 3330)

HUDDLESTON, The Most Reverend (Ernest Urban) Trevor; *b* 15 June 1913; *Educ* Lancing, ChCh Oxford (MA), Wells Theological Coll; *Career* ordained priest 1937; Community of Resurrection: joined 1939, priest i/c Sophiatown and Orlando Anglican Mission Dio of Johannesburg 1943, provincial in SA and supt St Peter's Sch 1949, guardian of novices Mirfield 1956, prior of London House 1958, bishop Dio of Masasi Tanganiyka 1960, suffragan bishop Stepney 1968, bishop of Mauritius 1978, archbishop of Anglican Province of Indian Ocean until 1983; Anti-Apartheid Movement: addressed founding meeting London 1959, vice pres 1961, pres 1981; chm Tstees Int Def and Aid Fund for SA 1983; addressed: UN Gen Assembly 1982, UN Special Ctee Against Apartheid 1984; initiated Nelson Mandela Int Reception Ctee 1990; provost Selly Oak Colls, patron Fair Play for Children, pres Nat Peace Cncl; Hon DD Aberdeen 1956, Hon DLit Lancaster 1972, Hon DD City of London 1987; UN Gold medal 1982; ANC Isitwalandwe 195 Zambian Order of Freedom (first class) 1984, Dag Hammerskjold award for peace 1984, Grand Cdr Nigerian Order of the Niger 1989; *Books* Naught for your Comfort (1956); *Style*— The Most Rev Trevor Huddleston, CR; House of the Resurrection, Mirfield, West Yorkshire WF14 0BN

HUDLESTON, Air Chief Marshal Sir Edmund Cuthbert; GCB (1963, KCB 1958, CB 1945), CBE (1943); s of Ven Cuthbert Hudleston (d 1944), Archdeacon of Perth, and Julia Marguerite, *née* Philips; *b* 30 Dec 1908; *Educ* Guildford Sch W Aust, RAF Coll Cranwell; *m* 1, 24 July 1936, Nancy (d 1980), da of Boyde Davis, of Rose Bay, Sydney, NSW; 1 s, 1 da; m 2, 1981, Brenda, da of A Whalley, of Darwen; *Career* joined RAF 1927, serv UK until 1933, India NWFP (despatches), RAF Staff Coll 1938, lent to Turkish Govt 1939-40, serv WWII ME and N Africa, Sicily, Italy 1941-43 (despatches 3 times), Gp Capt 1942, Air Cdr 1943, Sr Air SO Med Allied Tactical Air Forces 1943-44, AOC No 84 Gp 2 TAF Western Front 1944, IDC 1946, head UK Mil Delgn to Western Union Mil Staff Ctee 1948-50, AOC No 1 Gp Bomber Cmd 1950-51, dep COS Supreme HQ Allied Cmd Europe 1951-53, AOC No 3 Gp Bomber Cmd 1953-56, RAF instr IDC 1956-57, vice chief of Air Staff 1957-62, Air Marshal 1958, Air Chief Marshal 1961, AOC-in-C Tport Cmd 1962-63, Air Cdr Allied Air Forces Central Europe 1964-67, C-in-C Allied Forces Central Europe 1964-65; Air ADC to HM The Queen 1962-67, ret; dir Pilkington Bros (Optical Div) 1971-79; Cdr Legion of Merit (USA) 1944, Kt Cdr Order of Orange Nassau (Netherlands) 1945, Cdr Order of Couronne, Croix de Guerre (Belgium) 1945, Offr Legion of Honour 1956 and Croix de Guerre (France) 1957; *Clubs* RAF; *Style*— Air Chief Marshal Sir Edmund Hudleston, GCB, CBE; 156 Marine Court, St Leonards-on-Sea, East Sussex TN38 0DZ

HUDLESTON, James Wallace; s of Wilfrid Andrew Hudleston, of Cyprus, and Barbara Jeanne, *née* Robotham; *b* 14 July 1952; *Educ* Falcon Coll Essexvale Rhodesia; *m* 30 May 1979, Perronelle Jane, *née* Le Marchant; 1 s (Hugh Edward b 1983), 1 da (Tamara Avril b 1980); *Career* financier; dir The Hutton John Co Ltd; *Recreations* shooting, sailing, travel; *Clubs* Royal London Yacht; *Style*— James Hudleston, Esq; 252 Clapham Rd, London SW9 OPZ (☎ 071 735 2532)

HUDLICKA, Prof Olga; da of Jaroslav Hudlicky (d 1956), and Marie Hudlicka, *née* Babackova (d 1986); *b* 11 June 1926; *Educ* Charles Univ (MD), Czechoslovak Acad of Scis (PhD, DSc); *m* 24 June 1950, Dr Andrej Klein (d 1980), s of Majer Klein (d 1922); 1 s (Pavel b 1 Aug 1954), 1 da (Olga (Mrs Barochovsky) b 26 July 1951); *Career* scientist Institut of Physiology Czechoslovak Acad of Scis Prague 1950-69, visiting prof Goethe's Univ Frankfurt 1969, prof of physiology Univ of Birmingham 1987- (Dept of Physiology Med Sch 1969-); memb Br Physiological Soc 1972-, American Microcirculation Soc 1978, American Physiological Soc 1979-; hon sec Br Microcirculation Soc 1985-; *Books* Circulation in Skeletal Muscle (1968), Muscle Blood Flow (1973), Angiogenesis (1986), Muscle Ischaemia (1988); *Recreations* swimming, skiing; *Style*— Prof Olga Hudlicka; Dept of Physiology, The University of Birmingham

Medical School, Vincent Drive, Birmingham B15 2TJ (☎ 021 414 6908, fax 021 414 6924, telex 338938 SPAPHY G)

HUDSON, Mrs Jonathan; (Princess) Anna; *née* Obolensky; da of Prince Sergei Dimitrievitch Obolensky (of the Russian princely family descended from Mikhail Vsevolodovitch, Prince of Tchernigov (d 1368), 11 in descent from Rurik, founder of the Russian monarchy) and Patricia Olive, *née* Blake; *b* 2 Oct 1952, Windsor; *m* 26 Feb 1981, as his 2 wife, Jonathan Philip Hudson (b 19 Jan 1945, stockbroker), son of Philip Alexander Hudson and Loveday Catherine, *née* Gibbs, and bro of Martin Arthur Hudson (*qv*); *Style*— Mrs Jonathan Hudson; 11a Beauchamp Road, London SW11

HUDSON, Prof Anthony Hugh; s of Dr Thomas Albert Gibbs Hudson (d 1959), and Bridget, *née* Quinn (d 1979); *b* 21 Jan 1928; *Educ* St Joseph's Coll Blackpool, Pembroke Coll Cambridge, Univ of Manchester (PhD); *m* 10 Jan 1962, Joan Bernadette, da of Anthony O'Malley (d 1953); 1 s (Michael Hugh b 1963), 3 da (Mary Bridget b 1962, Margaret Mary Theresa b 1964, Catherine Agnes b 1965); *Career* called to the Bar Lincoln's Inn 1954, lectr Univ of Hull 1954-57 (asst lectr 1952-54); lectr in common Law Univ of Birmingham 1957-64; prof of common law Univ of Liverpool 1977- (sr lectr 1964-71, prof of law 1971-77, dean Faculty of Law 1971-78 and 1984-); *Books* jtly: Hood Phillips First Book of English Law (1977 and 1988), Pennington, Hudson & Mann Commercial Banking Law (1978), Stevens and Borrie Mercantile Law (1978); *Recreations* history, gardening, walking; *Style*— Prof Anthony Hudson; Univ of Liverpool, Faculty of Law, PO Box 147, Liverpool L69 3BX (☎ 051 794 2000, fax 051 708 6502, telex 627095)

HUDSON, (Norman) Barrie; s of William Hudson, of Coventry, and Lottie Mary, *née* Taylor; *b* 21 June 1937; *Educ* King Henry VIII Sch Coventry, Univ of Sheffield (BA), UCL (MSc); *m* 5 Oct 1963, Hazel, da of Capt Frederick Cotterill (d 1965); 2 s (Richard Jonathan b 12 March 1965, Mark William b 22 Jan 1974), 1 da (Catherine Jane b 13 Nov 1966); *Career* economist: Tube Investments Ltd 1960-62, Economist Intelligence Unit 1962-63; nat accounts advsr Govt of Jordan 1963-65, econ advsr Br Devpt Div Beirut 1967-72, sr econ advsr ODA 1973, head of Br Devpt Div Bangkok 1974-76, under sec (principal estabs offr) ODA 1981-85, under sec ODA (Africa) 1986-; *Recreations* theatre, reading, watching football and cricket; *Style*— Barrie Hudson, Esq; The Galleons, Sallows Shaw, Sole Street, Cobham, Kent DA13 9BP (☎ 0474 814419); Overseas Development Administration, Eland House, Stag Place, London SW1 (☎ 071 273 0549)

HUDSON, Brian Paige; s of Sir Edmund Hudson (d 1978), of Edinburgh, and Bodil Catherina, *née* Boschen; *b* 29 May 1945; *Educ* Marlborough, King's Coll Cambridge (MA); *m* 16 Jan 1971, Elisabeth Françoise, da of Jacques Cochemé (d 1971), of Rome; 2 da (Elodie Jacqueline b 16 Dec 1971, Emeline Elisabeth b 16 Sept 1973); *Career* princ HM Treasy 1970-76 (asst princ 1966-69, private sec to Head of Treasy 1969-70), sec Wilson Ctee on Fin Instns 1976-78; Den Norske Creditbank plc (formerly Nordic Bank): sr mangr 1978-79, assoc dir 1979-80, dep md 1981-88, md and chief exec 1989-; *Style*— Brian Hudson, Esq; Den Norske Creditbank plc, 20 St Dunstan's Hill, London EC3R 2HY (☎ 071 621 1111, fax 071 626 7400, telex 887654)

HUDSON, Hon Mrs (Carola); *née* Browne; er da of 6 Baron Kilmaine, CBE (d 1978); *b* 17 May 1932; *m* 30 April 1960, John Michael Carlyon Lowry Hudson, o s of late Herbert Hudson, of Gwavas, Tikokino, Hawkes Bay, NZ; 2 s, 1 da; *Style*— The Hon Mrs Hudson; Gwavas Station, Tikokino, Hawkes Bay, NZ

HUDSON, Lady Cathleen Blanche Lily; *née* Eliot; da of 6 Earl of St Germans, MC, and Lady Blanche Somerset, da of 9 Duke of Beaufort; through Lady Blanche she is co-heiress (with Samantha Cope and Alexandra Peyronel, *qqv*) to the Baronies of Botetourt and Herbert, which went into abeyance on the death of 10 Duke of Beaufort, KG, GCVO, PC (d 1984); *b* 29 July 1921; *m* 1, 1946 (m dis 1956), John Seyfried, of Kensington, RHG; 1 s, 1 da; m 2, 1957, Sir Havelock Hudson, *qv*; 1 s, 1 da; *Career* antique dealer; *Recreations* bridge; *Style*— The Lady Cathleen Hudson; The Old Rectory, Stanford Dingley, Berks (☎ 0734 744346)

HUDSON, Christopher John; s of John Augustus Hudson, of The Holt, Benenden, Kent, and Margaret Gwendolen, *née* Hunt; *b* 29 Sept 1946; *Educ* The King's Sch Canterbury, Jesus Coll Cambridge (MA); *m* 10 March 1978, (Margaret) Kirsty, da of Alexander Drummond McLeod, of The Garden House, Ticehurst, Sussex; 1 s (Rowland Alexander b 1983); *Career* ed Faber & Faber 1968-70, literary ed The Spectator 1971-73, Harkness Fell 1975-77, columnist The Evening Standard 1985-91 (leader writer 1978-81, literary ed 1982-85); memb Soc of Authors (PEN); *Books* Overlord (filmed 1975), The Final Act (1979), Insider Out (1981), The Killing Fields (1984), Colombo Heat (1986), Playing in the Sand (1989); *Style*— Christopher Hudson, Esq; 64 Westbourne Park Rd, London W2 5PJ (☎ 071 229 8586); Northcliffe House, 2 Derry St, London W8

HUDSON, Christopher Neville; s of Lovell Hudson, and Margaret, *née* Budden; *b* 19 July 1930; *Educ* Radley, Queens' Coll Cambridge (MA, MB MChir); *m* 2 Nov 1956, Caryl Marian, da of Wing Cdr Grenville Shaw (d 1942); 2 s (Grahame b 1960, Neil b 1969), 1 da (Jayne b 1963); *Career* reader in obstetrics and gynaecology Univ of London 1969-78, prof of obstetrics and gynaecology Univ of Sydney (Westmead) 1978-86, conslt obstetrician Bart's 1986-; FRCS, FRCOG, FRACOG; *Books* Shaw's Operative Gynaecology (1982), Ovarian Cancer (1986); *Recreations* wildfowling, fishing; *Clubs* Leander; *Style*— Christopher Hudson, Esq; St Bartholomew's Hospital, London EC1A 7BE

HUDSON, David Norman; s of Sir Edmund Peder Hudson (d 1978), of Edinburgh; *b* 29 May 1945; *Educ* Marlborough, Balliol Coll Oxford; *m* 1967, Rosemary McMahon, *née* Turner; 1 s (Stephen b 1969), 2 da (Isobel b 1971, Sarah b 1976); *Career* merchant banker, dir Samuel Montagu & Co Ltd 1974-81, asst gen mangr Arlabank 1981-84, ptnr and head of corporate fin James Capel & Co 1984-87, dep chm and chief exec Henry Ansbacher & Co Ltd 1987-89, dir and shareholder Campbell Lutyens Hudson & Co Ltd 1989; *Recreations* natural history, bridge, opera; *Style*— David Hudson, Esq; 37 Goldingham Ave, Loughton, Essex (☎ 081 508 4362)

HUDSON, Eric; s of John Wilden Hudson (d 1976), of W Yorks, and Ethel, *née* Burton (d 1981); *b* 31 Aug 1927; *Educ* GS in Yorks and Lancs; *m* 24 June 1954, Matilda (Biddy), da of Robert Francis Hutchison (d 1948), of Callander, Perthshire, Scotland; 1 s (Ian b 1958), 1 da (Mary b 1956); *Career* CA 1949, in practice 1958-, cncl memb Inst of CAs of England and Wales 1985-; lay preacher, memb various Methodist Church Ctees, chm Nat Children's Home Cleveland Ctee 1984-87; vice chm Teesside Stockton Cons Assoc 1972-74, treas Local Ecumenical Church 1988-; FCA; *Recreations* armchair cricket, walking, theatre; *Clubs* Lansdowne; *Style*— Eric Hudson, Esq; 22 Tunstall Ave, Hartlepool, Cleveland TS26 8NF (☎ 0429 231286); 114 Borough Road, Middlesborough, Cleveland TS1 2ES (☎ 0642 242365)

HUDSON, Felix Nettleton; s of Alfred Hudson (d 1950), of Dunfermline, and Anne Grace, *née* Nettleton (d 1950); *b* 11 Oct 1923; *Educ* St George's Bridlington; *m* 1 Sept 1948, Margarget Russell, da of Andrew Erskine (d 1950), of Dunfermline; 1 s (Alexander b 1955), 3 da (Anne (Mrs Lamont) b 1949, Susan (Mrs Dewar) b 1952, Jean (Mrs Boyling) b 1959); *Career* served WWII; Sgt 6 RTR (Egypt, Italy, Austria), 8 RTR (Austria, Italy, Palestine); md F Hudson Ltd (estab 1950); memb Dunfermline Rotary Club, pres Dunfermline Historical Soc, fndr pres Dunfermline Ski Club, fndr chm Scot Section Antiquarian Horological Soc; past pres: Edinburgh and E Scot Goldsmiths Assoc, Dunfermline Business Club, Dunfermline Civic Tst; author of various papers on horological subjects; memb Nat Assoc of Goldsmiths 1958; CMBHI 1954, FGA 1962, FSA Scot 1982; *Books* Scottish Longcase Clocks 1780-1870 (1976), Dunfermline Clockmakers (1982), Scottish Clockmakers - a brief History (1984); *Recreations* hill walking, skiing, writing, photography; *Style*— Felix Hudson, Esq, FSA; 5 Hunt Place, Crossford, Dunfermline, Fife (☎ 0383 724432); 2 Queen Anne St, Dunfermline, Fife KY12 7AY (☎ 0383 724311)

HUDSON, Francis Edward; TD; s of Edward Hudson (d 1945), of Bridge House, Harewood; *b* 10 June 1912; *Educ* Rugby; *m* 1944, Masha Violet, da of Col Murray Muirhead-Murray, DSO (d 1968); 1 s, 1 da; *Career* former Maj ME; former chm Yorkshire Post Newspapers (dep chm 1958, ret 1983), chm Doncaster Newspapers (ret 1981), dir United Newspapers (ret 1983); High Sheriff N Yorks 1981; *Recreations* fishing, shooting; *Style*— Francis Hudson, Esq, TD; Winterfield House, Hornby, Bedale, Yorks DL8 1NN (☎ 0748 811619)

HUDSON, Gaye; da of Sir Peter Emery, and Elizabeth, *née* Nicholson; *b* 14 Feb 1957; *Educ* Westonbirt Sch, Eastbourne Coll, Coll of Distributive Trade (CAM); *m* 2 Oct 1982, Jonathan Michael Hudson; 1 s (Charles Peter Meadows b 22 Dec 1989), 1 da (Holly Elizabeth b 13 Feb 1988); *Career* formerly with Young and Rubicam (advertising agency) and with int PR consultancies; currently main bd dir and head Creative Servs Gp Hill and Knowlton; *Recreations* total love of skiing; *Style*— Mrs Gaye Hudson; Hill and Knowlton, 5-11 Theobald's Rd, London WC1X 8SH (☎ 071 413 3000, fax 071 413 3111)

HUDSON, Prof George; s of George Hudson (d 1956), of Edenfield, and Edith Hannah, *née* Bennett (d 1956); *b* 10 Aug 1924; *Educ* Edenfield C of E Sch, Bury GS, Univ of Manchester (BSc, MB ChB, MSc), Univ of Bristol (MD, DSc); *m* 14 April 1955, Mary Patricia (d 1977), da of Frank Hibbert (d 1929), of Chester; 1 da (Elisabeth b 1961); *Career* Capt RAMC 1951-53, unit MO Green Howards Army Operational Res Gp; house offr Manchester Royal Infirmary 1949-50; Univ of Bristol: demonstrator in anatomy 1950-51, lectr then reader in anatomy 1953-68, pre-clinical dean 1963-68; visiting prof (Fulbright award) Univ of Minnesota 1959-60; Univ of Sheffield: admin dean 1968-83, hon clinical lectr in haematology 1968-75, prof of experimental haematology 1975-89, head Dept of Haematology 1981-89, postgrad dean 1984-88, regnl postgrad dean 1988-, emeritus prof of haematology 1989-; hon conslt in haematology Sheffield Health Authy 1969-89, chm Conf of Deans of prov Med Schs 1980-82, lay reader C of E 1953-; memb: Sheffield Regnl Hosp Bd 1970-74, Sheffield Health Authy 1974-84, Cncl for Med Postgrad Educn for England and Wales 1980-83; chm Ethical Ctee Northern Gen Hosp 1985-89; MRCPath 1970, FRCPath 1975, MRCP 1984, FRCP 1988; *Recreations* badminton, cavies, garden; *Style*— Prof George Hudson; The Medical School, Beech Hill Rd, Sheffield S10 2RX (☎ 0742 721747)

HUDSON, Gideon Dacre; s of John Hudson (d 1977), of High Wycombe Bucks, and Joan, *née* Lippold (d 1983); *b* 8 Nov 1944; *Educ* St Edward's Sch Oxford, Exeter Coll Oxford (MA); *m* 1, 30 May 1969 (m dis 1974), Elizabeth Janet, da of Cyril James Wells, of Bourne End, Bucks; m 2, 26 March 1976 (m dis 1986), Jane Bernice Martin, da of A F C Hann, of Finchley, London; 2 s (Piers b 18 Sept 1976, Jonathan b 14 Nov 1977), 1 step s (Nicolas Martin b 28 May 1971); *Career* admitted slr 1969; ptnr Allen and Overy 1974- (asst 1969-74); gen cmmr for taxes City of London; memb Law Soc; *Recreations* motor racing, cricket, golf; *Clubs* MCC, Free Foresters Cricket, Bucks CCC, BRSCC, Porsche GB; *Style*— Gideon Hudson, Esq; 9 Cheapside, London EC2V 6AD (☎ 071 248 9898, telex 8812801, fax 071 236 2191, car 08362 60197)

HUDSON, Gillian Grace; da of Brian Hudson (d 1985), of E Grinstead, Sussex, and Grace Iris, *née* Hill; *b* 23 March 1955; *Educ* Univ of Sussex (BA); *Career* press offr Eng Tourist Bd 1978-81, ed Home and County Magazine 1981-83, dep ed then ed Fitness Magazine 1984-85, ed Cook's Weekly 1986, dep ed then ed Company Magazine 1987-; BSME 1981, NUJ; *Recreations* cycling, reading, windsurfing, travel, walking, swimming; *Clubs* Groucho's; *Style*— Ms Gillian Hudson; Company Magazine, National Magazine House, 72 Broadwick St, London W1V 2BP (☎ 071 439 5000, fax 071 437 6886, telex 263879 NATMAG G)

HUDSON, Dr Harold Gaunt; s of Edwin Gaunt Hudson (d 1963), and Gertrude Elizabeth, *née* Jackson (d 1963); *b* 21 Feb 1912; *Educ* Repton, Clare Coll Cambridge (MA, PhD, DipAgric); *m* 1, 7 June 1937, Doreen (d 1987), da of Albert George Belben; 1 da (Ann b 14 April 1942); m 2, 18 Nov 1989, Ruth Helen, da of John Sidney Welford; *Career* offr Norfolk War Agric Ctee 1939-45, lectr in agric Univ of Cambridge 1945-47, farmer 1947-83; Alderman Norfolk CC 1955-72 (vice chm); chm: Educn Ctee Wymondham UDC 1963-72 (memb 1955-72), S Norfolk DC 1973-78, Shuttleworth Agric Coll, Norfolk Coll of Agric, Norfolk Coll Arts and Technol; govr Norwich Sch; govr Gresham Sch, tax cmmr and chm S Norfolk, memb cncl RVC, co pres Norfolk Young Farmers; pres: Norfolk Lawn Tennis Assoc, Norfolk Badminton Assoc; Silver Jubilee Medal 1977; FSS 1946, FRAgS 1975 (chm); *Recreations* tennis, bridge, sailing; *Clubs* Farmers; *Style*— Dr Harold G Hudson; St Marys, Vicar St, Wymondham, Norfolk NR18 OPJ (☎ 0953 603277)

HUDSON, Sir Havelock Henry Trevor; s of Savile Ernest Hudson (d 1952); *b* 4 Jan 1919; *Educ* Rugby; *m* 1, 1944 (m dis 1956), Elizabeth, da of Brig W Home; 2 s; m 2, Lady Cathleen, *qv*, da of 6 Earl of St Germans; 1 s, 1 da; *Career* serv WWII Europe; Lloyd's underwriter 1952-90; chm Lloyd's 1975-77 (dep chm 1969, 1971, 1973); memb Bd of Govrs: Pangbourne Coll 1976-89, Bradfield Coll 1978-89; pres City of London Outward Bound Assoc 1979-90; kt 1977; *Recreations* shooting, bridge; *Style*— Sir Havelock Hudson; The Old Rectory, Stanford Dingley, Berks (☎ 0734 744346)

HUDSON, Ian; s of Donald Pryce Hudson, of Hoylake, Wirral, Cheshire, and Emily Grandison, *née* Campbell (d 1969); *b* 27 April 1930; *Educ* Worksop Coll Notts, Univ of St Andrews (BSc); *m* 4 Sept 1965, Vivien Halliwell, da of Walter Marsden; 2 s (Andrew James b 28 July 1966, John Michael b 25 July 1968), 1 da (Joanne b 29 Dec 1971); *Career* Nat Serv RA 1952-54; Dyestuffs Div ICI 1954-60, Allied Colloids Ltd 1960-65, dir and princ BTI Chemicals Ltd 1966-71; various stockbroking roles in Jersey 1974-84 with: Kemp-Gee & Co, Sheppards & Chase, Laurie Milbank; investmt dir Morgan Grenfell (Jersey) Ltd 1984-88; memb Jersey branch IOD (ctee memb 1987-); *Recreations* golf; *Clubs* Royal and Ancient Golf, La Moye Golf; *Style*— Ian Hudson, Esq; Rosemount, Route des Genets, St Brelade, Jersey (☎ 0534 42560)

HUDSON, James Ralph; CBE (1976); s of William Shand Hudson (d 1967), and Ethel, *née* Summerskill (d 1953); *b* 15 Feb 1916; *Educ* King's Sch Canterbury, Middx Hosp Med Sch (MB BS, LRCP); *m* 29 June 1946, Margaret May Hunter, da of Paul Eugene Oulpe (d 1986); 2 s (James b 1949, Andrew b 1956), 2 da (Ann b 1948, Sarah b 1953); *Career* WWII RAFVR 1942-46: Flying Offr 1942-43, Flt Lt 1943-44, Sqdn Ldr 1944-46; civil conslt in ophthalmology to RAF 1970-82; res MO Tindal House Hosp Aylesbury 1939-42 house surgn and sr res offr Moorfields Eye Hosp; conslt ophthalmic surgn: W Middx Hosp 1950-56, Mount Vernon Hosp 1953-59, Moorfields Eye Hosp 1956-81, Guy's 1963-76; hon ophthalmic surgn: Hosp St John and St Elizabeth 1953-, King Edward VII Hosp for Offrs 1970-86; hon consulting surgn Moorfields Eye Hosp 1981-, conslt advsr in ophthalmology DHSS 1969-82; teacher: Inst of Ophthalmology Univ of London 1961-81, Guy's 1964-76; examiner Dip Ophthalmology Exam Bd of England 1960-65, memb Ct of Examiners RCS 1966-72; memb Soc Française d'Ophtal 1950-; membre déLégué Étranger 1970-, UK rep Union Européene des Médecins

Spécialistes Ophthalmology Section 1973- (pres 1982-86); hon steward Westminster Abbey 1972-88 (non-active list 1988-); Freeman City of London, Liveryman Worshipful Soc of Apothecaries 1953; DOMS, FRCS, Hon FCOphth 1990 (FCOphth 1988), Hon FRACO, FRSM; Ophthal Soc UK: memb 1948-, hon sec 1956-58, vice-pres 1969-71, pres 1982-84; Faculty Ophthalmologists: memb 1950-, memb Cncl 1960-81, hon sec 1960-70, vice pres 1970-74, pres 1974-77; Pilgrims of GB; *Recreations* motoring, travel; *Clubs* Garrick; *Style*— James Hudson, Esq, CBE; Flat 2, 17 Montagu Square, London W1H 1RD (☎ 071 487 2680); 8 Upper Wimpole St, London W1M 7TD (☎ 071 935 5038)

HUDSON, Lady Jane Catherine; *née* Leslie Melville; da of 14 Earl of Leven and Melville; *b* 5 May 1956; *m* 1977, Philip Mark Gurney Hudson; 2 da (Katherine b 1983, Susanna b 1986); *Style*— The Lady Jane Hudson; Southcott Lodge, Pewsey, Wilts SN9 5JF

HUDSON, John Lewis; s of Wilfred Hudson, and Edith Hudson; *Educ* Univ of Aston, Birmingham Poly (MSc); *m* 22 Sept 1973, Eileen Cornelia; 1 s (Mark Standring b 7 Feb 1975), 1 da (Vick Samantha b 24 Sept 1977); *Career* BSA Motorcycles Ltd 1960-71, Chrysler (UK) Ltd 1971-72, GEC Ltd 1971-72; md: Morphy Richards Ltd 1972-78, Sperryn & Co Ltd 1978-82; divnl md Fluid Controls Div Delta Group plc 1984-86 (joined 1978, divnl dir and gen mangr Gas Controls and Engrg Div 1982-84), gp chief exec Wagon Industrial Holdings 1986-; CEng, FIProdE, FIMechE, FBIM; *Recreations* walking, chess; *Style*— John Hudson, Esq; Wagon Industrial Holdings plc, Haldane House, Halesfield, Telford, Shropshire TF7 4PB (☎ 0952 680111, fax 0952 587811, car 0836 523160)

HUDSON, John Richard; s of Arthur Richard Hudson (d 1978), and Beryl Dorothy, *née* Brett; *b* 3 Sept 1944; *Educ* Ryde GS Ryde IOW, Thames Poly (HNC); *m* 12 Aug 1976, Kathleen Mary (Kate), *qv*, da of David Thomas Heckscher (d 1950), of Aust; *Career* recording engr and md Mayfair Recording Studios London, recorded more than 159 top ten records (studio voted top Br Recording Studio 1986); Grammy Award (USA) 1984, nominated for Br Acad Award 1985, Grammy Award Certificate for work on Tina Turner Live in Europe 1988; co-owner Millers Ct Birtsmorton Commercial Dairy Farm (home of the Millers Court Herd); ARPS; *Recreations* skiing, video filming and editing; *Style*— John Hudson, Esq; 2/1 Mayfair Mews, London NW1 8UU (☎ 071 586 7746); Millers Ct, Birtsmorton nr Malvern, Worcs WR13 6AP; Mayfair Recording Studios, 11A Sharpleshall St, London NW3 5NL (☎ 071 5867746, fax 01 586 9721)

HUDSON, Kathleen Mary (Kate); da of David Thomas Hecksher (d 1950), of Ipswich, Queensland, Aust, and Eileen Mary, *née* Downs; *b* 16 Aug 1944; *Educ* St Brigidine's Coll Scarborough, Queensland Aust; *m* 1 (m dis 1969), Raymond Douglas Geitz; m 2, 12 Aug 1976, John Richard Hudson, *qv*; *Career* telephonist Queensland Newspapers 1966-68, sec Leeds Music Sydney Aust 1968-73, PA Martin Coulter Music 1974-76, sec to Fin Dir Chrysalis Records London 1976-77, owner and md Mayfair Recording Studios 1977- (won Top Br Recording Studio 1986), co-owner Millers Ct Birtsmorton Commercial Dairy Farm (home of the Millers Court Herd); APRS; *Recreations* skiing; *Style*— Mrs Kate Hudson; 2-1 Mayfair Mews, London NW1 8UU (☎ 071 586 7746); Millers Ct, Birtsmorton, nr Malvern, Worcs WR13 6AP; Mayfair Recording Studios, 11A Sharpleshall St, London NW3 5NL (☎ 071 586 7746, fax 071 586 9721)

HUDSON, Kathryn Jane; da of Col Leslie Eric Hudson, OBE of, 365 Perth Rd, Dundee, Scotland, and Jacqueline Elizabeth Packard, *née* Bell; *b* 13 Feb 1959; *Educ* Univ of Bristol (LLB); *Career* called to the Bar Middle Temple 1981, tenant Chambers of Stewart Black 1983; awarded: Blackstone Entrance Exhibition 1978, Blackstone Pupillage 1983, Benefactors' Law Scholarship 1983; co-opted memb Young Barrister's Ctee; memb Hon Soc of Middle Temple 1978-; *Recreations* music, antiques, travel, the arts generally; *Style*— Miss Kathryn Hudson; 14 Gray's Inn Square, Gray's Inn, London WC1R 5JP (☎ 071 242 0858, fax 071 242 5434)

HUDSON, Prof Liam; s of Cyril Hudson (d 1985), and Kathleen Maud, *née* Shesgreen; *b* 20 July 1933; *Educ* Whitgift Sch, Univ of Oxford (MA), Univ of Cambridge (PhD); *m* 1, 8 Aug 1955 (m dis 1965), (Wendy) Elizabeth, da of Douglas Ward (d 1965); m 2, July 1965 (Claribel Violet) Bernadine, da of Bernard Louis Jacot de Boinod (d 1977); 3 s (Dominic b 1958, William b 1966, George b 1967), 2 da (Lucie b 1960, d 1965, Annabel b 1967); *Career* Nat Serv, 2 Lt RA 1952-54; fell King's Coll Cambridge 1966-68, prof educnl sciences Univ of Edinburgh 1968-77, memb Inst Advanced Study Princeton NJ 1974-75, prof psychology Brunel Univ 1977-87; memb Br Psychological Soc; *Books* Contrary Imaginations (1966), Frames of Mind (1968), The Cult of the Fact (1972), Human Beings (1975), The Nympholepts (1977), Bodies of Knowledge (1982), Night Life (1985); *Recreations* painting, photography, making things; *Style*— Prof Liam Hudson; Balas Copartnership, 34 North Park, Gerrards Cross, Bucks (☎ 0753 886 281)

HUDSON, Manley O (Jr); s of Judge Manley O Hudson (d 1960), of Cambridge, Mass, and Janet A Hudson, *née* Aldrich; *b* 25 June 1932; *Educ* Middx Sch Concord Mass, Harvard (AB), Harvard Law Sch (LLB); *m* 1 July 1971, Olivia, da of Count Olivier d'Ormesson, of Ormesson-sur-Marne, France; *Career* sec to Justice Reed Supreme Ct of the US 1956-57, ptnr Cleary Gottlieb Steen & Hamilton 1968- (assoc 1958-68); memb Cncl on Foreign Relations; memb: Assoc of the Bar City of NY, NY Co Lawyers Assoc, NY State Bar Assoc, American Bar Assoc, American Soc of Int Law, Union Internationale des Avocats; *Clubs* Century Assoc (NY), Knickerbocker (New York), Travellers (Paris), Turf; *Style*— Manley O Hudson, Jr, Esq; Cleary Gottlieb, Steen & Hamilton, 99 Bishopsgate, London EC2M 3YL (☎ 071 638 5291, fax 071 600 1698)

HUDSON, Mark Marshall; s of Tom Hudson, and Moira Catherine Hudson; *b* 29 March 1957; *Educ* Penarth GS, Esher GS, Chelsea Sch of Art, Winchester Sch of Art (BA, Hampshire travel award); *Career* travel writer; author of Our Grandmothers' Drums (1989); Thomas Cook award for best travel book 1990, Somerset Maugham award 1990; chm London Screenwriters Workshop 1983-85 (currently memb); memb Soc of Authors; *Recreations* music, travel; *Style*— Mark Hudson, Esq; Rogers Coleridge & White, 20 Powis Mews, London W11 1JN (☎ 071 221 3717, fax 071 229 9084)

HUDSON, Martin Arthur; s of Philip Alexander Hudson (d 1986), of Sussex, and Loveday Catherine, *née* Gibbs (d 1988); bro of Jonathan Philip Hudson (*see* Hudson, Mrs Jonathan); *b* 22 Jan 1947; *Educ* Eton; *m* 1975, Primrose Pearl, da of Hon Hugh de Beauchamp Lawson Johnston; 4 s (Hugh b 1977, Mark b 1978, Ian b 1979, Christopher b 1981); *Career* CA 1971; fin dir Houlder Offshore Ltd 1975-79 (non-exec dir 1979-85); chm: The Finsbury Secretariat Ltd 1983-, The Finsbury Business Centre Ltd 1988-; *Recreations* shooting, sailing, exercising 4 sons; *Clubs* Boodles; *Style*— Martin Hudson,Esq; 7 Grove Park Gardens, London W4 3RY (☎ 081 994 0245); First Floor, 262 Regent St, London W1R 5DA (☎ 071 631 0481)

HUDSON, (Anthony) Maxwell; s of Peter John Hudson, CB, of Haslemere, and Joan Howard Hudson, *née* Fitzgerald; *b* 12 April 1955; *Educ* St Paul's, New Coll Oxford (MA); *Career* admitted slr 1980; ptnr Frere Cholmeley 1987; *Recreations* wine and food, squash; *Clubs* United Oxford and Cambridge Univ; *Style*— Maxwell Hudson, Esq; Willow Court, Willow Place, London SW1; Frere Cholmeley, 28 Lincoln's Inn Fields, London WC2A 3HH (☎ 071 405 7878, fax 071 405 9056)

HUDSON, Lt-Gen Sir Peter; KCB (1977), CBE (1970, MBE 1965), DL (Berks 1984); s of Capt William Hudson (d 1964); *b* 14 Sept 1923; *Educ* Wellingborough Sch, Jesus Coll Cambridge; *m* 1949, Susan Anne, da of Maj Vernon Cyprian Knollys (d 1973); 1 da, 1 adopted s, 1 adopted da; *Career* cmmnd Rifle Bde 1944, served Mau Mau and Malaya Campaigns (despatches 2), CO 3 Royal Green Jackets 1966-67; GOC E Dist 1973-74, COS Allied Forces N Europe 1975-77, Dep C-in-C UKLF 1977-80; Col Cmdt Light Div 1977-80, Inspr-Gen TAVR 1978-80; sec gen Order St John 1981-88; Lt HM Tower of London 1986-89; chm: Green Jackets Club 1977-85, Rifle Brigade Museum Tstees 1979-85, Royal Sch Bath 1981-88 (govr 1976-), Rifle Bde Club and Assoc 1979-85, Eastern Wessex TAVRA 1980-, TAVR Cncl 1981-90; memb: Gen Advsy Cncl BBC 1981-84, Cncl Bradfield Coll 1983-, Cncl for Order of St John in Royal Berkshire 1988-; KStJ 1981; Hon Col Southampton UOTC 1979-85; pres RFA 1984-91, Fritsham PC 1989-; Hon Col 5RGJ 1985-; FBIM; *Recreations* travel, wildlife, watching most games and sports; *Clubs* Naval and Military, MCC, IZ, Greenjackets; *Style*— Lt-Gen Sir Peter Hudson, KCB, CBE, DL; Little Orchard, Frilsham, Newbury, Berks (☎ 0635 201266)

HUDSON, Brig Reginald Eustace Hamilton; DSO (1945); s of Edwin Hamilton Hudson (d 1951), of Rajpore, Budleigh Salterton, S Devon, and Grace Isobel, *née* Vaughan (d 1964); *b* 22 Aug 1904; *Educ* Haileybury, RMA Woolwich; *m* 1, 3 Oct 1930, (Gladys Mary) Maureen (d 1960), da of Capt Benjamin Henry Jones, CBE, RIM (d 1950), of Folkestone; m 2, 7 July 1962, Winifred Florence Isabel Vallentin, wid of Brig Claude Max Vallentin, MC, and da of Col Evelyn Fountaine Villiers, CMG, DSO (d 1955); *Career* cmmnd RA 1924, served in field, mountain and medium artillery units (UK and India) 1924-31, ADC to GOC Peshawar dist and in NWF campaign 1929-32, Asst-Adj Field Bde RA (UK) 1932-34, Instr RMA Woolwich 1935-38, student Staff Coll 1939, BM RA 4 Div BEF 1940 (incl Dunkirk evacuation), Instr Staff Coll 1941, CO Field Regt RA 1942-45 (inc BLA 1944-45), CRA 2 Div (Malaya and India 1945-47, Staff appt WO 1947-48, Cmd S Malaya 1949-50, Cmd AA Bde and 2 i/c AA Gp (UK) 1951-55, Cmd RA Depot and Woolwich Garrison 1955-57; (des 1945, 1949, 1950); ADC HM the Queen 1955-57; ret 1957; sec RA Inst Woolwich 1958-61, chm Ctee of Vol Welfare Work (BAOR) 1961-64; memb PCCs 1964-72; *Recreations* cricket, hockey, rackets, tennis, rugby; *Clubs* MCC, Free Foresters, IZ; *Style*— Brig Reginald Hudson, DSO; 38 Saffrons Ct, Compton Place Rd, Eastbourne, East Sussex BN21 1DX (☎ 0323 29601)

HUDSON, Richard Lawrence; s of Charles Percy Hudson, CBE (d 1982), of Equerry, Barrow Lane, Hessle, E Yorks, and Ethel Maud, *née* Howell (d 1991); *b* 24 March 1944; *Educ* Sedbergh, Grenoble Univ; *m* 1, Judith Bernadette Heaney; 2 s (Dominic William b 6 March 1972, Oliver Charles b 7 Jan 1974), 1 da (Emma Jane b 2 Oct 1969); m 2, 2 Dec 1978, Carol Sandra, da of Alan Megginson, of Beechwood, Driffield, E Yorks; 2 da (Annabel Juliet b 15 Dec 1979, Jennie Deborah b 21 Jan 1982); *Career* CA; Peat Marwick Mitchell & Co London 1963-70 (qualified 1968); ptnr: Hodgson Harris Hull 1975 (joined 1970), Price Waterhouse (following its merger with Hodgson IMPEY) 1990-; underwriting memb Lloyd's 1973-90; rugby formerly played for the 1st XV of Grenoble RFC and for Rosslyn Park RFC as well as playing cricket for numerous clubs; Freeman City of London 1979, memb Worshipful Co of CA's in England and Wales 1979; FCA 1973 (ACA 1968); *Recreations* shooting, cricket, tennis; *Clubs* Yorkshire Gentlemen's Cricket, Yorkshire County Cricket, Army and Navy; *Style*— Richard Hudson, Esq; 29 North Bar Without, Beverley, East Yorkshire HU17 7AG (☎ 0482 861382); Price Waterhouse, Queen Victoria House, Guildhall Road, Hull HU1 1HH (☎ 0482 224111, fax 0482 27479)

HUDSON, Prof Robert Francis; s of John Frederick Hudson (d 1966), and Ethel Lizzie, *née* Oldfield (d 1968); *b* 15 Dec 1922; *Educ* Brigg GS Lincs, Imperial Coll London (BSc, PhD, ARCS, DIC); *m* 3 Aug 1945, Monica Ashton, da of Charles Ashton Stray; 1 s (John Martin Edward b 1949), 2 da (Sarah Elizabeth b 1952, Mary Alexandra b 1952); *Career* asst lectr Imperial Coll 1945-47, conslt Wolsey Leicester 1945-50, lectr QMC London 1947-59, gp dir CERI Geneva 1960-66; prof of organic chemistry Univ of Kent 1966-85 (emeritus 1985-); visiting prof: Rochester USA 1970, Bergen 1971, CNRS Thiais Paris 1973, Calgary 1975, Mainz 1979, Queens Ontario 1983; memb: Chem Soc Cncl 1967-71; RSC: Dalton Cncl 1973-71, Perkin Cncl (RSC) 1980-83; FRSC, FRS; *Clubs* Athenaeum; *Style*— Prof Robert Hudson; 37 Puckle Lane, Canterbury, Kent (☎ 0227 61340); Univ of Kent, Canterbury

HUDSON, Prof Robin Lyth; s of Frederick Lyth Hudson, of Kidderminster, Worcs, and Enid, *née* Wright (d 1982); *b* 4 May 1940; *Educ* King Edward VI GS, Stockport GS, Univ of Oxford (BA, DPhil); *m* 22 July 1962, Geraldine Olga Margaret, da of Percival George Beak, MBE, of Dorchester on Thames; 3 s (Daniel b 1965,l Hugh b 1966, Michael b 1975), 1 da (Lucy b 1968); *Career* applied mathematics Univ of Nottingham: asst lectr 1964-66, lectr 1966-76, reader 1976-85, prof 1985-: head of mathematics dept Univ of Nottingham 1987-90; visiting prof Univ of: Heidelberg 1978, Denver 1980, Texas 1983; visiting prof Indian Statistical Inst 1987; memb Lab Pty, Amnesty Int, London Mathematical Soc, American Mathematical Soc; *Recreations* music, literature, walking; *Style*— Prof Robin Hudson; Mathematics Dept, Univ of Nottingham, Nottingham NG7 2RO (☎ 0602 484848, telex 37346 (UNINOT G), fax 0602 420 825)

HUDSON, Simon; s of Kenneth Hudson, of Winchester, Hants, and Mary, *née* Walker; *b* 17 Sept 1956; *Educ* Queen Mary's GS, Basingstoke Coll, LSE (BSc Econ); *m* 1983, Debra Susan, da of Albert Gail; *Career* investmt analyst and fund mangr Central Bd of Fin Church of England 1978-81; institutional equity salesman: James Capel & Co London 1981, James Capel Far East 1982-83; assoc dir Streets Financial 1983-86; jt md: Kingsway Financial 1986-88, Hudson Sandler Ltd 1988-; *Recreations* travelling, reading, film and theatre, skiing; *Style*— Simon Hudson, Esq; Hudson Sandler Limited, Cap House, 9-12 Long Lane, London EC1A 9HD (☎ 071 796 4133, fax 071 796 3480)

HUDSON, Thomas Charles; CBE (1975); s of Thomas Bingant Hudson (d 1972), and Elsie Elizabeth, *née* Harris (d 1973); *b* 23 Jan 1915; *Educ* Middleton HS Nova Scotia; *m* 1, 1944 (m dis 1973), Lois Alma Johnson, da of Crawford Johnson (d 1977), of Montreal; 2 s (Ronald b 1947, Peter b 1965), 1 da (Margo b 1951); m 2, 1986, Susan Gillian Van Kan, da of Albert William Gibb; *Career* serv WWII RCNVR (Lt) 1940-45; Nightingale Haymen & Co (CAs) 1935-40, sales rep IBM Canada 1946-51, md IBM London 1954-65 (sales mangr 1951-54), dir Plessey Co 1969-76, (fin dir 1967); chm: ICL 1971-79 (dir 1968), INFA Communications 1985-88; cncllr for Enfield GLC 1970-73, farmer in Devon 1979-; CA Canada; *Recreations* tennis, golf, skiing, gardening; *Clubs* Carlton, American; *Style*— Thomas Hudson, Esq, CBE; Hele Farm, North Bovey, Devon TQ13 8RW (☎ 0647 40249)

HUDSON, Tom; s of Michael John Hudson, and Jean Mary, *née* Overton; *b* 18 June 1963; *Educ* Dulwich, Univ of Oxford; *Career* copywriter Bartle Bogle Hegarty Ltd 1987-; *Clubs* Crystal Palace FC; *Style*— Tom Hudson, Esq; Bartle Bogle Hegarty Ltd, 24-27 Great Pulteney St, London W1R 3DB (☎ 071 734 1677)

HUE WILLIAMS, Charles James; s of Charles Anthony Hue Williams (d 1969), and Joan, *née* Winfindale; *b* 28 Sept 1942; *Educ* Harrow; *m* 14 March 1964, Joey Oriel Marie-Lou, da of Charles George Clover, of Fishponds, S Stoke, Goring on Thames, Oxon; 1 s (Mark b 29 Oct 1968), 1 da (Sarah b 27 June 1966); *Career* ptnr Wedd

Durlacher Mordaunt & Co 1970-85; dir: Kleinwort Benson Ltd 1986-, Kleinwort Benson Securities 1986-, Kleinwort Benson Holdings plc 1989-90; *Recreations* rackets, lawn tennis, real tennis, golf; *Clubs* Tennis and Rackets Assoc, Queen's, Royal St George's Sandwich, Royal and Ancient, MCC; *Style—* Charles Hue Williams, Esq; Headley Meadows, The Hanger, Headley, Hants (☎ 042 871 3232)

HUEBNER, Michael Denis; s of Dr Denis William Huebner, of Yarm, Cleveland, and Mary Irene Hargraves, *née* Jackson (d 1971); *b* 3 Sept 1941; *Educ* Rugby, St John's Coll Oxford (BA); *m* 18 Sept 1965, Wendy Ann, da of Brig Peter Crosthwaite, of Hove, Sussex; 1 s (Robin b 1971), 1 da (Clare b 1975); *Career* called to the Bar Gray's Inn 1965; Lord Chllrs Dept 1966: seconded Law Offrs Dept 1968-70, asst slr 1978, under sec 1985, circuit admin N Eastern Circuit 1985-88, princ estab and fin offr 1988-89, dep sec 1989-; *Recreations* looking at pictures, architecture; *Style—* Michael Huebner, Esq; Lord Chancellor's Dept, Trevelyan House, Great Peter Street, London SW1P 2BY

HUGGETT, Brian George Charles; MBE (1978); s of George William Huggett (d 1983), and Annie May, *née* Flower; *b* 18 Nov 1936; *m* 1962, Winifred, da of Griffith Hughes (d 1979); 2 da (Yvonne b 1968, Sandra b 1973); *Career* int professional golfer; 18 major wins incl: Dunlop Masters, PGA Match Play Champion, PGA Stroke Champion, Vardon Trophy winner, Welsh Nat Champion, second and third Br Open, Dutch Open, German Open, Portuguese Open, Algarve Open, Singapore Int; Ryder Cup player (6 appearances, former capt), Capt GB twice, World Cup player (9 appearances); golf course designer; dir; *Recreations* following sport generally; *Clubs* MCC, Royal Porthcawl Golf, Lord's Taverners; *Style—* Brian Huggett, Esq, MBE; Cherry Orchard, Weston-under-Penyard, Ross-on-Wye, Herefordshire HR9 7PH (☎ 0989 62634)

HUGGETT, Monica Elizabeth; da of Victor Lewis Huggett (d 1983), of Epsom, and Monica Germaine, *née* May; *b* 16 May 1953; *Educ* Green Sch for Girls, Isleworth, Royal Acad of Music London; *Career* ldr Amsterdam Baroque Orchestra 1979-87, ldr/dir The Hanover Bond 1983-86 (recordings incl Beethoven Symphonies), memb Trio Sonnerie with Sarah Cunningham and Mitzi Meyerson, signed Virgin Classics 1988; other recordings incl Bach sonatas with Ton Koopman, Vivaldi concertos with The Academy of Ancient Music; memb Musicians Union; *Recreations* gardening, motor cycling, non-business travel; *Style—* Ms Monica Huggett; c/o Francesca McManus, 71 Priory Rd, Kew Gardens, Surrey, TW9 3DH (☎ 01 940 7086)

HUGGINS, Sir Alan Armstrong; s of William Armstrong Huggins (d 1938); *b* 15 May 1921; *Educ* Radley, Sidney Sussex Coll Cambridge (MA); *m* 1, 1950 (m dis), Catherine Davidson, da of David Dick (d 1929); 2 s, 1 da; m 2, 1985, Elizabeth Low, da of Dr Christopher William Lumley Dodd (d 1973); *Career* serv WWII Admty; called to the Bar Lincoln's Inn 1947; resident magistrate Uganda 1951-53; Hong Kong: stipendiary magistrate 1953-58, dist judge 1958-65, puisne judge 1965-76, judicial cmmr Brunei 1966-87 and 1991-, justice of appeal 1976-80, vice pres Ct of Appeal 1980-87; justice of appeal: Gibraltar 1988, Br Antarctica 1988, Br Indian Ocean Territory 1988, Falkland Islands 1988, Bermuda 1989; hon life govr Br and Foreign Bible Soc, hon life memb American Bible Soc, Anglican reader; kt 1980; *Recreations* boating, archery, amateur theatre, tapestry, forestry; *Clubs* Royal Over-Seas League; *Style—* Sir Alan Huggins; Widdicombe Lodge, Widdicombe, Kingsbridge, Devon TQ7 2EF

HUGGINS, Hon Mrs (Jean Audrey); *née* Wigg; da of Baron Wigg, PC; *b* 1932; *m* 1955, Andrew Huggins; *Style—* The Hon Mrs Huggins; Ty Eiddew, Garndolbenmaen, Gwynedd, N Wales

HUGGINS, Rodney Philip; s of Maj Rowland Huggins (d 1961), of Reading, Berks, and Barbara Joan Trowbridge, *née* Hayter; *b* 26 Nov 1935; *Educ* Reading Sch, Lycée Lakanal Sceaux Paris; *m* 30 March 1959, José Rhoda, da of Charles Hatch; 1 s (Jeremy b 1963); *Career* Kenya advocate 1960-, fndr and sr ptnr RP Huggins and Co Slrs Reading 1961-85; chm: Nat Insur Local Tbnl 1975-84, Indust Tbnls 1981-84, Vaccine Damage Tbnl 1984-, VAT Tbnls 1988-; gen tax cmmr 1983-, regnl chm Social Security Appeals Tbnls 1984-, pres Nat Assoc of Round Tables of GB and I 1975-76, govr dist 109 of Rotary Int 1987-88, hon slr Nat Assoc Ex Tablers Clubs 1984-; Liveryman Worshipful Co of Arbitrators 1981-, Freeman City of London 1981-; FInst Arb; *Books* Guide to Procedure in Social Security Appeal Tribunals (1985), Guide to Procedure in Medical Appeal Tribunals; *Recreations* golf, singing, swimming, bridge; *Clubs* MCC, Leander, Royal Over-Seas League, Stoke Poges and Sonning Golf; *Style—* Rodney Huggins, Esq; The Quarries, 10 West Drive, Sonning-on-Thames, Berkshire (☎ 0734 693096); 22 Cerro Grand, Albufeira 8200, Algarve, Portugal; Office of the President of Social Security Appeal Tribunals, London South Region, Copthall House, 9 The Pavement, Grove Rd, Sutton, Surrey SM1 1DA (☎ 081 642 2226, car 0860 540822)

HUGH-JONES, Dr Kenneth; s of Evan Bonnor Hugh-Jones, CB (d 1978), and Elsie Muriel, *née* Iggulden (d 1950); *b* 21 Dec 1923; *Educ* Uppingham, St Mary's Hosp Univ of London (MB BS, MD); *m* 1, 1955, Denise (d 1986), da of Dr George Edward Hull (d 1965); 2 s (Simon b 1956, George b 1958), 2 da (Catherine, b 1963, Sarah b 1965); m 2, 1987, Ruth Theodora, wid of Richard Purdon Heppel, CMG, da of Dr Horatio Matthews (d 1970); *Career* conslt paediatrician: Westminster Children's Hosp, St Albans City Hosp; special interest in treating children with genetic diseases by bone marrow transplantation; FRCP, FRSM; *Style—* Dr Kenneth Hugh-Jones; The Heath, Redbourn, Herts AL3 7BZ (☎ 058 279 2347)

HUGH-JONES, Sir Wynn Normington; LVO (1961); s of Huw Hugh-Jones (d 1937), and May, *née* Normington (d 1979); *b* 1 Nov 1923; *Educ* Ludlow, Selwyn Coll Cambridge (MA); 1 s, 2 da; *Career* RAF 1943-46, Diplomatic Serv 1947-73: FO, Jeddah, Paris, Conakry, Rome (head of chancery), FCO, Zaire (Elizabethville), Ottawa (cnsllr and head of chancery) 1968-70, FCO 1971, Lord President's Office 1971, Cabinet Office 1972-73, dir gen English Speaking Union 1973-77; sec gen Lib Pty 1977-83; hon jt treas Lib Pty 1984-87; chm Avebury in Danger 1988-89; govr Queen Elizabeth Fndn for the Disabled 1985-, vice chm Eur-Atlantic Gp 1986-; FBIM; kt 1984; *Recreations* golf, gardening; *Clubs* Nat Lib; *Style—* Sir Wynn Hugh-Jones, LVO; Fosse House, Avebury, Wilts SN8 1RF

HUGH SMITH, Andrew Colin; s of Lt-Cdr Colin Hugh Smith, RN (d 1975); *b* 6 Sept 1931; *Educ* Ampleforth, Trinity Coll Cambridge; *m* 1964, Venetia, da of Lt-Col Peter Flower, of The Old Manse, Broughton, Stockbridge, Hants; 2 s; *Career* called to the Bar Inner Temple 1956, sr ptnr Capel-Cure Myers 1979-85, chm Holland & Holland plc 1987-; memb Stock Exchange 1970, chm Int Stock Exchange 1988-; *Recreations* reading, shooting, fishing, gardening; *Clubs* Brooks's, Pratt's; *Style—* Andrew Hugh Smith, Esq

HUGH SMITH, Col Henry Owen; LVO (1976); s of Lt Cdr Colin Edward Hugh Smith, RN (d 1975), and Hon Elizabeth Dulcie, *née* Hotham (d 1969), sister of 7 Baron Hotham; *b* 19 June 1937; *Educ* Ampleforth, Magdalene Coll Cambridge (BA 1961); *Career* cmmnd RHG (The Blues) 1957, The Blues and Royals 1969; served: Cyprus, Germany and NI (wounded), Egypt, Hong Kong, Kenya; Equerry to HRH the Duke of Edinburgh 1974-76, cmd The Blues and Royals 1978-80, GSO MOD 1980-83, ME and Hong Kong 1983-85, MOD 1985-87, def advsr to Br High Cmmr Nairobi Kenya 1987-; 4 class Order of the Lion of Finland 1976, 4 class Order of the Sacred Treasure of Japan 1975; *Recreations* sailing, photography, travel; *Clubs* Boodle's, Pratt's, Royal Yacht Sqdn; *Style—* Col Henry Hugh Smith, LVO; c/o National Westminster Bank plc, 1 Prince's St, London EC2P 2AH

HUGHES, Allan Berkeley Valentine; s of Capt Allan Gibson Hughes (d 1938), of Shrewsbury, and Kathleen Louise, *née* Paget (d 1973); *b* 27 Feb 1933; *Educ* Wellington; *m* 24 April 1964, (Gina) Ann, da of Alan Maconochie Stephen (d 1975), of St Brelades, Jersey; 2 s (Rupert b 18 April 1966, Oliver b 8 Aug 1968); *Career* Nat Serv 1951-53 (2 Lt QOH 1952-53), Lt Queen's Own Worcs Hussars 1953-57; admitted slr 1959, sr ptnr Payne Hicks Beach 1989- (ptnr 1960-89); dir Colonial Mutual Life Assurance 1990; chm: Iris Fund for Prevention of Blindness, Cncl of Govrs Heathfield Sch; memb Law Soc; *Recreations* gardening, shooting; *Clubs* Buck's, MCC, The Justinians; *Style—* Allan Hughes, Esq; Siddington Mill, Cirencester, Glos GL7 6EU; 10 Abbots House, St Mary Abbots Terrace, London; Payne Hicks Beach, 10 New Square, Lincoln's Inn, London WC2A 3QG (☎ 071 242 6041)

HUGHES, Aneurin Rhys; s of William Hughes, of Swansea, and Hilda Hughes; *b* 11 Feb 1937; *Educ* Swansea GS, Oregon City HS USA, UCW Aberystwyth (BA); *m* 1964, Jill Salisbury; 2 s; *Career* pres NUS 1962-64, res on Higher Educn in South America; HM Dip Serv FO London 1966-68; first sec: Political Advsr's Office (later Br High Cmmn) Singapore 1968-70, Br Embassy Rome 1971-73; Secretariat General of the Euro Community: head Div for Internal Coordination 1973-76, advsr to Spokesman and DG for Info 1977-80, chef de cabinet of Ivor Richard (memb Euro Cmmn) 1981-85, chm Selection Bd for Candidates from Spain and Portugal 1985-87, organiser Conf on Culture Econ New Technol (Florence) 1986-87, ambass and head of Delgn of the Euro Commn Oslo Norway 1987-; *Recreations* squash, golf, music, hashing; *Clubs* Travellers'; *Style—* Aneurin Hughes, Esq; European Commission Delegation, Haakon VII's Gate 6, PO Box 1643 Vika, 0119 Oslo 1, Norway (☎ 833583, fax 834055, telex 79967 COMEU N)

HUGHES, Anthony; s of Francis James Hughes (d 1983), and Mabel, *née* Hall; *b* 23 June 1938; *Educ* King Edward's Sch Birmingham; *m* 22 Sept 1973, Gillian Rose, da of Roger Hamilton Aitken, TD, of Birmingham; *Career* CA 1962-, sr ptnr J W Scrivens & Co 1967-; champion: Br Eton Fives nine times (a record) 1968-75, Br Rugby Fives Veterans 1986 and 1987; FCA; *Recreations* Eton Fives, travel; *Clubs* Edgbaston Priory; *Style—* Anthony Hughes, Esq; Imperial House, 350 Bournville La, Bournville, Birmingham, B30 1QZ (☎ 021 478 1431)

HUGHES, Dr Antony Elwyn; s of Ifor Elwyn Hughes, of 18 Fernhill Close, Mayals, Swansea and Anna Betty, *née* Ambler; *b* 9 Sept 1941; *Educ* Newport HS Gwent, Jesus College Oxford (Scott Prize in Physics); *m* 1963, Margaret Mary, Arthur James Lewis (d 1978); 2 s (Stephen Antony b 1963, James Elwyn b 1971), 2 da (Sarah Margaret b 1965, Joanna Mary b 1973); *Career* Harkness fell Cornell Univ USA 1967-69; UKAEA: scientific offr 1963-67, sr scientific offr 1969-72, princ scientific offr 1972-75, individual merit appt 1975-81, sr personal appt 1981-83, ldr Defects in Solids Gp 1973-78, ldr Solid State Scis Gp 1978-83, head Materials Physics Div 1983-86, dir Underlying Res and Non-Nuclear Energy Res 1986-87, chief scientist and dir Nuclear Res 1987-88; dir Laboratories SERC 1988-; memb ACORD Dept of Energy, chm Winterbrook Youth Club Harwell 1980-90, govr Didcot Girls Sch 1981-88; fell Inst of Physics (1972), CPhys; *Books* Real Solids and Radiation (1975), Defects and Their Structure in Non-Metallic Solids (ed 1976); *Recreations* walking, cycling, watching rugby & cricket, music, gardening; *Style—* Dr Antony E Hughes; Science and Engineering Research Council, Polaris House, North Star Avenue, Swindon, Wiltshire SN2 1ET (☎ 0793 411114, fax 0793 411099, 449466)

HUGHES, Prof Barry Peter; s of John Frederick Hughes (d 1987), of Wolverhampton, and Dorothy, *née* Elwell; *b* 29 Aug 1932; *Educ* Wolverhampton GS, Univ of Birmingham (BSc, PhD, DSc, DEng); *m* 21 Sept 1957, (Pamela) Anne, da of Joseph Sydney Barker, (d 1979) of Prestatyn; 1 s (Rowan b 29 Aug 1958), 2 da (Hilary b 6 Feb 1962, Sara b 8 March 1963); *Career* concrete engr in charge of site laboratory and concrete quality control Berkeley Nuclear Power Station 1956-58; Univ of Birmingham: lectr 1963-68, sr lectr 1968-71, reader 1971-73, prof of civil engrg 1974-; author of numerous res and tech pubns on concrete and concrete structures; chm: W Mids Region Concrete Soc 1974-75, Mids Branch Inst Structural Engrs 1976-77; memb: RSI Ctee CVCP7, Rilem Ctee TC-102 AFC; MICE 1961, FIStructE (memb 1969); *Books* Handbook for BS 5337 (1976), Limit State Theory for Reinforced Concrete Design (3 edn 1980); *Recreations* sailing, music, walking; *Clubs* Dale Sailing; *Style—* Prof Barry P Hughes; Long Barn, 8 Parkfields, Arden Drive, Dorridge, Solihull B93 8LL (☎ 0564 776584); Veronica Cottage, St Anne's Head, Dale, Pembrokeshire, Dyfed SA62 3RS; School of Civil Engineering, University of Birmingham, Edgbaston, Birmingham B15 2TT (☎ 021 414 5065, fax 021 414 3675)

HUGHES, (David) Brian; s of David Henry Hughes (d 1977), of Carmarthoneshire, S Wales, and Eirwen, *née* Thomas; *b* 29 Dec 1945; *Educ* Gwendraeth Valley GS Carmarthenshire, LSE (BSc); *m* 5 Oct 1968, Avis Mary, da of Henry William Good, of Bristol; *Career* prodn mangr Aquascutum Ltd 1967-70, personnel mangr J Sainsbury Ltd 1970-73, co personnel mangr Citröen Cars Ltd, dist personnel mangr Hammersmith Hosp and Charing Cross Hosp 1975-78, dep dist admin Northampton Health Authy 1982-85 (area personnel mangr 1978-82), gen mangr Northampton Gen Hosp 1985-; MIPM 1984, assoc Inst of Health Servs Mgmnt 1985; *Recreations* french food, medieval architecture, hill walking, cycling; *Style—* Brian Hughes, Esq; Bramley House, Hall Drive, Long Buckby, Northants NN6 7QU (☎ 0327 842740); Northampton General Hospital, Billing Rd, Northampton NN1 5BD (☎ 0604 235760, fax 0604 235674)

HUGHES, Brian Thomas; s of late Thomas Hughes; *b* 3 May 1937; *Educ* St Joseph's Coll, Univ of Glasgow; *m* 1962, Maureen Duignan, *née* Smyth; 3 s; *Career* dir and md Ranco Motors Ltd 1969-73, dir St Andrews Golf Hotel Ltd 1973-; *Recreations* golf, skiing; *Clubs* Murrayfield Golf, Edinburgh, New Golf, St Andrews; *Style—* Brian Hughes Esq; St Andrews Golf Hotel Ltd, 40 The Scores, St Andrews, Fife

HUGHES, Christopher Carl; s of Norman Alfred Hughes (d 1983), of Sheffield, and Betty, *née* Roebuck; *b* 19 Aug 1950; *Educ* Harrow Weald Co GS, Univ of Sheffield (BSc); *m* 26 Aug 1972, Julia Clare, da of Dr Maxwell Chapman Pennington, of Caerphilly; 1 s (Daniel Andrew b 13 Feb 1983); *Career* BBC: studio mangr World Serv 1971-73, prodr Radio Sheffield 1975-79 (station asst 1973-75), prodr Special Current Affrs Unit Radio 4 1979-80, md Radio Trent Ltd 1989- (prog controller 1980-89); memb Radio Acad; *Recreations* birdwatching, gardening; *Style—* Christopher Hughes, Esq; 3 Tow Court, Farndon, Newark, Notts NG24 3TT (☎ 0636 701015); Radio Trent Ltd, 29-31 Castlegate, Nottingham NG1 7AP (☎ 0602 581731, telex 37463 RAD TRENT, fax 0602 588614, car 0860 646725)

HUGHES, Christopher Wyndham; s of Dr John Philip Wyndham Hughes (d 1981), of Marsh Lock House, Henley-on-Thames, Oxfordshire, and Christine, *née* Jolley (d 1947); *b* 22 Nov 1941; *Educ* Manchester GS, King Edward's Sch Birmingham, UCL (LLB); *m* 31 Dec 1966, Gail, da of Percival Eric Ward (d 1957), of Cricklewood, London; 3 s (Christian Wyndham b 29 Feb 1968, Marcus Wyndham (twin) b 1968, Dominic Wyndham b 20 June 1974); *Career* slr 1966; articled clerk and slr until 1970 then ptnr Wragge & Co Birmingham 1970, Notary Public; Birmingham Law Soc: memb 1966, memb Cncl 1977-, jt hon sec 1977-84, vice pres 1988-89, pres 1989-90;

memb and later chm of Solihull Ctee of Cancer Res Campaign 1972-85, memb Bd Severn Trent Water Authy 1982-84, fndn govr of The Schs of King Edward VI Birmingham 1984-; memb: Law Soc 1966, The Provincial Notaries Soc 1979-; *Recreations* travel, theatre, sport, languages, old buildings; *Clubs* Warwickshire CCC; *Style—* Christopher Hughes, Esq; Cuttle Pool Farm, Cuttle Pool Lane, Knowle, Solihull, W Midlands B93 0AP (☎ 056477 2611); Wragge & Co, Bank House, 8 Cherry St, Birmingham B2 5JY (☎ 021 632 4131, fax 021 643 2417, telex 338728 WRAGGE G)

HUGHES, David Campbell; Trevor George Hughes (d 1988), of Herefordshire, and Flora Jean, *née* Britton; *b* 13 Dec 1953; *Educ* Millfield, King's College London (LLB); *Career* pres Union King's Coll London 1975-76; admitted slr 1979; ptnr Allen & Overy 1985-; Parly candidate (C) Bow and Poplar 1987; vice pres: Bow and Poplar Cons Assoc, City of London Solicitor's Co; memb Law Soc, MInstD; *Recreations* golf, riding, chess, cricket, gourmandising; *Clubs* RM Sherrin XI, Men of Principle; *Style—* David Hughes, Esq; 9 Cheapside, London EC2V 6AD (☎ 071 248 9898, tlx 8812801, fax 071 236 2192)

HUGHES, Sir David Collingwood; 14 Bt (GB 1773), of East Bergholt, Suffolk; s of Sir Richard Edgar Hughes, 13 Bt (d 1970), and Angela Lilian Adelaide, *née* Pell (d 1967); *b* 29 Dec 1936; *Educ* Oundle, Magdalene Coll Cambridge (MA); *m* 14 March 1964, Rosemary Ann, da of Rev John Pain, of Framfield Vicarage, Uckfield, Sussex; 4 s (Thomas b 1966, Timothy b 1968, Benjamin b 1969, Anthony b 1972); *Heir* s, Thomas Collingwood Hughes b 16 Feb 1966; *Career* heraldic sculptor, md Louis Lejeune Ltd 1978-; *Recreations* fishing; *Clubs* Flyfishers, Cambridge County; *Style—* Sir David Hughes, Bt; The Berristead, Wilburton, Ely, Cambs (☎ 0353 740770)

HUGHES, David Glyn; s of Richard Hughes (d 1959), and Miriam Hughes (d 1961); *b* 1 March 1928; *Educ* Darwin Street Secdy Modern Sch Northwich; *m* 11 Jan 1958, Mary, da of Harold Atkinson (d 1987); 1 da (Glynis Mary (Mrs Hughes-Broughton) b 13 Jan 1964); *Career* apprentice, later fitter and turner 1944-52; Labour Party: agent 1952-69 (Northwich, Bolton, Tonbridge, Portsmouth), regnl organiser Northern Region 1975-79 (asst regnl organiser 1969-75), nat agent 1979-88 (ret); *Recreations* gardening, walking; *Style—* David Hughes, Esq; 42 Langroyd Road, Tooting Bec, London SW17 7PL (☎ 081 672 2959)

HUGHES, David John; s of Glynn Hughes (d 1985), and Gwyneth Mary, *née* Jenkins; *b* 19 March 1955; *Educ* Wolverhampton GS, Jesus Coll Oxford (MA); *m* 4 Sept 1987, Linda Anne, da of Thomas Hunt, of Wolverhampton; 1 s (Richard b 1987), 1 da (Lisa b 1990); *Career* asst slr: Nabarro Nathanson 1980-82, Slaughter and May 1982-85; ptnr Pinsent & Co 1987- (asst slr 1985-87); memb Law Soc; *Recreations* music, theatre; *Style—* David Hughes, Esq; Post and Mail House, 26 Colmore Circus, Birmingham B4 6BH (☎ 021 200 1050, fax 021 200 1040)

HUGHES, David John; s of Gwilym Fielden Hughes (d 1989), and Edna Frances, *née* Cochrane; *b* 27 July 1930; *Educ* Eggar's GS, King's Coll Sch Wimbledon, ChCh Oxford (MA); *m* 1, April 1958 (m dis 1977), Mai Elisabeth, *née* Zetterling; m 2, Nov 1980, Elizabeth Jane, da of James Westoll, DL; 1 s (Merlin b 1984), 1 da (Anna Rose b 1981); *Career* Nat Serv RAF 1949-50, cmmnd PO 1949, Flying Offr (Res) 1951; ed asst London Magazine 1953-55, lit advsr Elek Books 1956, reader Rupert Hart-Davis Ltd 1957-60, screen writer of documentary and feature films 1960-, ed Town Magazine 1960-61, film critic The Sunday Times 1983-84, fiction critic The Mail On Sunday 1983-; FRSL 1986; *Books* A Feeling in the Air (1957), Sealed With a Loving Kiss (1958), J B Priestley an informal study (1958), The Horsehair Sofa (1961), The Major (1964), The Road to Stockholm (1964), The Seven Ages of England (1967), The Man Who Invented Tomorrow (1968), The Rosewater Revolution (1971), Evergreens (1976), Memories of Dying (1976), A Genoese Fancy (1979), The Imperial German Dinner Service (1983), The Pork Butcher (1984), But For Bunter (1985), Winter's Tales: New Series I (ed 1985), Best Short Stories (ed 1986, 1987, 1988, 1989, 1990); *Clubs* Savile; *Style—* David Hughes, Esq; c/o Anthony Sheil Associates Ltd, 43 Doughty Street, London WC1N 2LF (☎ 071 407 9351)

HUGHES, David Paul; s of William Thomas Lloyd Hughes (d 1979), of Newton-le-Willows, and Marjorie Helen, *née* Pamberton (d 1975); *b* 13 May 1947; *Educ* Newton-le-Willows GS; *m* 23 March 1973, Christine, da of late John Brooks; 1 s (James David b 22 July 1975); *Career* professional cricketer; Lancashire CCC: debut 1967, awarded county cap 1970, capt 1987-, benefit 1981; Tasmania 1975-77; tours: DH Robins' X1 SA 1972-73, England Cos W Indies 1974-75; Lancs tours: W Indies 1986 and 1987, Zimbabwe 1988, Aust 1989 and 1990; only fourth Lancs player to score over 10,000 runs and take over 500 wickets; 1 NatWest and 1 Benson & Hedges man of the match award, Wisden cricketer of the year 1987, Carphone capt of the year 1987; *Recreations* golf, rugby league; *Style—* David Hughes, Esq; Lancashire CCC, Old Trafford, Manchester M16 OPX (☎ 061 848 7021, fax 061 848 9021)

HUGHES, Dr David Treharne Dillon; s of Maj-Gen W D Hughes, CB, CBE, of Vine House, Summer Court, Tilford Rd, Farnham, and Kathleen Linda Elizabeth, *née* Thomas (d 1976); *b* 31 Oct 1931; *Educ* Cheltenham, Trinity Coll Oxford (BSc, MA), London Hosp Med Coll (BM BCh); *m* 11 Nov 1959, Gloria Anna; 1 s (David Edward Treharne b 29 April 1974), 2 da (Carly Anna b 22 Sept 1960, Mandy Lou b 19 Oct 1962); *Career* Capt RAMC 1959-61 (jr med specialist BMH Hong Kong); jr res fell MRC Univ of Oxford 1953-54, res fell Univ of California 1963-64, conslt physician London Hosp 1970- (jr appts 1957-68), head Dept of Clinical Investigation Wellcome Res Laboratories 1978-; memb: Hunterian Soc (former pres), Int Soc of Internal Med (former pres); Freeman City of London, Jr Warden Worshipful Soc of Apothecaries (memb Court 1981), memb RSM, FRCP; *Books* Tropical Health Science (1967), Human Biology and Hygiene (1969), Lung Function for the Clinical (1981); *Recreations* cricket, horseracing; *Clubs* Savage; *Style—* Dr David Hughes; The London Hospital, London E1 1BB (☎ 071 377 7417)

HUGHES, Hon Sir Davis; s of F Hughes; *b* 1910; *Educ* Launceston H S Tas; *m* 1940, Joan P, da of P Johnson; 1 s, 2 da; *Career* MLA NSW (Country Party) for Armidale 1950-53 and 1956-65, former ldr NSW Country Party, min for Public Works 1965-73, agent-gen for NSW in London 1973-78, chm Brambles Crouch Ltd 1980; kt 1975; *Style—* The Hon Sir Davis Hughes; 11 Sutherland Cres, Darling Point, NSW 2027, Australia

HUGHES, Air Vice-Marshal (Frederick) Desmond; CB (1972), CBE (1961), DSO (1945), DFC (and 2 bars 1941-43), AFC (1954), DL (Lincolnshire 1983); s of Frederick Cairns Hughes (d 1952), of Co Down, and Emily Hilda Kathleen, *née* Hunter (d 1977); *b* 6 June 1919; *Educ* Campbell Coll Belfast, Pembroke Coll Cambridge (MA); *m* 1941, Pamela Denton, da of Julius Harrison (d 1963), of Herts; 3 s (Patrick, Peter (decd), Michael); *Career* RAF 1939-74; WWII, Battle of Britain 1940; Night Fighters 1940-45: UK, Med, France, Germany; directing staff RAF Staff Coll Bracknell 1954-56, personal staff offr to Chief of Air Staff 1956-58, cmd RAF Station Geilenkirchen 1959-61; dir Air Staff Plans MOD 1962-64, Air Offr cmd 18 Gp 1968-70, AOC and Cmdt RAF Coll Cranwell 1970-72, dep cdr Br Forces Cyprus 1972-74; ADC to HM The Queen 1963; Hon Air Cdre 2503 Sqdn (Co of Lincoln) RAuxAF Regt 1982-; *Recreations* fishing, shooting, music; *Clubs* RAF; *Style—* Air Vice-Marshal Desmond Hughes CB, CBE, DSO, DFC, AFC, DL; c/o Midland Bank plc, Sleaford, Lincs

HUGHES, Rev Dr Edward Marshall; s of Edward William Hughes (d 1940), of Kent, and Mabel Frances, *née* Faggetter (d 1947); *b* 11 Nov 1913; *Educ* City of London Sch, King's Coll London, Cuddesdon Coll Oxford (MTh, PhD, AKC); *Career* warden St Peter's Coll Jamaica 1952-61, fell St Augustine's Coll Canterbury 1961-65, vicar of Dover 1971-84, chaplain to HM The Queen 1973-83; hon chaplain of the Co Assoc Men of Kent and Kentish Men 1979- (of which his father was a fndr memb 1897); *Recreations* gardening, exercising the dogs, computing; *Style—* The Rev Dr Edward Hughes; Woodlands, Sandwich Road, Woodnesborough, Sandwich, Kent CT13 0LZ (☎ 0304 617098)

HUGHES, Maj Francis Edward; s of Maj Edward O'Donovan Hughes (d 1966), of Asgard Hall, and Maud Georgina, *née* Maxwell (d 1976); *b* 24 Oct 1949; *Educ* Foyle Coll Londonderry, Portora Coll Queens Univ (BA) Trinity Coll (MA); *Career* memb: Ulster Arts Cncl, Londonderry Festival Ctee; chm Belfast Arts Club; *Recreations* hunting, sailing, climbing; *Clubs* Rossa (Londonderry); *Style—* Maj Francis Hughes; Asgand Hall, Co Londonderry; Boviel House, Maghan, Co Londonderry; New Buildings, Londondery (☎ 0504 22504)

HUGHES, George; s of Peter Hughes; *b* 4 May 1937; *Educ* Liverpool Collegiate, Gonville and Caius Coll Cambridge (MA), Harvard Business Sch (MBA); *m* 1963, Janet; 2 s (David b 1964, Edward b 1966); *Career* ski instr 1959; banker Paris 1960, IBM London 1960-69 (strategy unit mangr 1968-69), merchant banking London 1969-70, chm and chief exec Hughes International Ltd 1970-85, Willowbrook World Wide Ltd 1971-83, Castle Hughes Group Ltd 1975-87; landowner, author; chm Derbyshire CCC 1976-77, memb Test and Co Cricket Bd 1976-77; *Books* The Effective Use of Computers (1968), New Towns (1974), Economic Development as Strategic Choice (1978), Mobility: a basic human need (1979), Traffic Congestion in Capital Cities (1979), Getting Action and Making Things Happen (1979), Integrated Cattle Development (1980), Choosing the Best Way (1980), Control (1980), Scenario for the President (1981), Spare Parts Management (1981), Strategy for Survival (1982), Road to Recovery (1982), All the Meat and Milk China Needs (1984); *Recreations* travel, perception of visual patterns in thinking, historic buildings, shooting, soccer, tennis, squash; *Clubs* Carlton; *Style—* George Hughes, Esq; Xanadu, Matthews Green, Wokingham RG11 1JU

HUGHES, Gillian Mary; da of Reginald Frederick Hughes (d 1989), and Jean Mary, *née* Reid; *b* 12 Sept 1959; *Educ* Haywards Heath Coll, Bedford Coll Univ of London (BSc); *Career* ptnr Michael Allen Balfour, trainee accountant Spicer & Pegler CAs 1980-81, asst chief accountant Anzecs Executive Limited 1981-85; asst accountant: Fisons Scientific Equipment Division 1985-86, Continental Reinsurance Management Co Ltd 1986-89; fin accountant CCL Financial Group plc 1989-; memb: WWF, RSPB, Woodland Tst, Zoological Soc of London; ACCA 1985; *Recreations* spectating at equestrian events particularly racing and agricultural shows, gardening, zoology, travelling within Britain; *Style—* Ms Gillian Hughes; Penryn, off High St, Flimwell, East Sussex TN5 7PB (☎ 058 087 514); CCL Financial Group plc, 74 Shepherds Bush Green, London W12 8SD (☎ 081 740 7070, fax 081 749 2474)

HUGHES, Glyn Tegai; s of Rev John Hughes (d 1985), and Ketura, *née* Evans (d 1946); *b* 18 Jan 1923; *Educ* Newtown and Towyn Co Schs, Liverpool Inst, Manchester GS, Corpus Christi Coll Cambridge (MA, PhD); *m* 21 Aug 1957, Margaret Vera, da of Desmond Andrew Herbert, CMG (d 1976), of Brisbane, Queensland; 2 s (Alun b 1960, David b 1961); *Career* RWF 1942-46, temp Maj DAAG HQ Alfsea; lectr in eng Univ of Basel 1951-53, tutor to Faculty of Arts Univ of Manchester 1961-64 (lectr in comparative literary studies 1953-64), warden of Gregynog Univ of Wales 1964-89, BBC nat govr for Wales and chm Bdcasting Cncl for Wales 1971-79; memb Bd Channel 4 TV 1980-87, authy of S4C 1981-87; Lib Pty candidate W Denbign: 1950, 1955, 1959; memb Welsh Arts Cncl 1967-76, chm Undeb Cymru Fydd 1968-70, vice pres N Wales Arts Assoc 1977-, pres Private Libraries Assoc 1980-82, chm Welsh Bdcasting Tst 1988-, Methodist local preacher; *Books* Eichendorff's Taugenichts (1961), Romantic German Literature (1979), Thomas Olivers (ed, 1979), Williams Pantycelyn (1983); *Recreations* book collecting, shrub propagation; *Style—* Glyn Tegai Hughes, Esq; Rhyd-Y-Gro, Tregynon, Newtown, Powys SY16 3PR (☎ 0686 650 609)

HUGHES, Wing Cdr Gordon Edward; DSO, DFC (and bar), AEA; s of late Arthur Joseph Hughes, OBE, of Pages, Chigwell Row, Essex, and late Emma Elsie, *née* Grimwade; *b* 4 May 1918; *Educ* Kelly Coll Tavistock Devon, City and Guilds Coll, Imperial Coll London; *m* 5 July 1947, Elizabeth Jane, da of late Frank Kestrel Webb, of Constanzia, SA; 3 s (David Arthur b 26 July 1948, Sebastian Graham Francis b 30 March 1952, Richard Gordon Kelvin b 4 May 1954); *Career* Univ of London Air Sqdn 1937, joined RAF 1939, trg RAF Cranwell 1939, trained as armaments offr Manby Lincs 1940, 608A Sqdn Thornaby, pilot (Spitfires) No 1 photographic reconnaissance unit Benson Oxfordshire 1941, 336 Wing Photographic Reconnaissance Unit Italy (Mosquitoes) 1943, photographic duties 34 Wing Brussels 1944, shot down Germany 1945 (in hosp 1945-46), air cdr ATC Glasgow (Convalesence 1947, station cdr Turnhouse Scot 1947, demob 1947; joined 601 Sqdn (Vampires and Meteors) whilst test pilot for Kelvin Hughes Ltd, joined Kelvin Ltd sales and test pilot 1950, left firm to farm 1958; rep RAF Benevolent Fund Cyprus; RAgS, RHS, RAFA; *Recreations* gardening, farming, books; *Clubs* Royal Aero, English Speaking Union; *Style—* Wing Cdr Gordon E Hughes, DSO, DFC, AEA; Lemba, Paphos, Cyprus (☎ 010 357 06 241154, fax 010 357 60 233358, telex 6427 COLOR CY)

HUGHES, Dr Graham Robert Vivian; s of Robert Arthur Hughes, and Emily Elizabeth Hughes (d 1989); *b* 26 Nov 1940; *Educ* Cardiff HS For Boys, London Hosp Med Coll (MD); *m* 2 March 1966, Monica Ann; 1 s (Richard John Vivian b 7 July 1971), 1 da (Sarah Imogen b 19 Oct 1967); *Career* rheumatologist; trained London Hosp, res fell Columbia Presbytarian Hosp, reader in med and head of Dept of Rheumatology Royal Postgrad Med Sch London, conslt rheumatologist and head of the Lupus Arthritis Res Unit St Thomas' Hosp London, conslt rheumatologist RAF 1987, 600 pubns on arthritis res; chm LUPUS UK, tstee Br SLE (Lupus) Aid Soc; hon memb: Aust Rheumatology Soc, Scandinavian Rheumatology Soc, Hong Kong Rheumatology Soc Portugese Rheumatology Soc, Turkish Rheumatology Soc, memb: American Lupus Hall of Fame, Assoc of Physicians of GB & I; FRCP; *Books* Modern Topics in Rheumatology (1978), Systemic Lupus Erythematosus (1982), Connective tissue Diseases (3 edn, 1987), Lecture Notes in Rhematology (1987), Problems in The Rheumatic Diseases (1988), SLE: A Guide for Patients (1988); *Recreations* tennis, piano; *Style—* Dr Graham Hughes; Lupus Arthritis Research Unit, Rayne Institute, St Thomas' Hospital, London SE1 (☎ 071 928 9292 ext 2888)

HUGHES, Hon Harri Cledwyn; o s of Baron Cledwyn of Penrhos, CH, PC (Life Peer), *qv*; *b* 16 March 1955; *Educ* Holyhead Comprehensive, Davies's Tutorial London, Hammersmith and W London Coll; *m* 14 June 1986, Jennifer Meryl, da of R P Hughes, of Coedlys, Valley, Anglesey; 2 da (Anna Myra Jane b 12 June 1987, Sara Ellen b 20 Jan 1989); *Career* surveyor; *Recreations* water skiing, sailing, golf, photography; *Clubs* London Welsh Assoc; *Style—* The Hon Harri Cledwyn Hughes; 23 Lydford Road, Willesden Green, London NW2 5QY (☎ 071 451 5137); Penmorfa, Trearddur Bay, Anglesey, Gwynedd (☎ 0407 860 544)

HUGHES, Howard; s of Charles William Hughes (d 1969), of W Kirby, Cheshire, and Ethel May, *née* Howard; *b* 4 March 1938; *Educ* Rydal Sch; *m* 1, 20 June 1964, Joy Margaret (d 1984), da of Charles Francis Pilmore-Bedford (d 1966), of Keston, Kent;

2 s (Quentin b 1969, Edward b 1971), 1 da (Charlotte b 1974); m 2, 2 April 1988, Christine Margaret, da of Walter George Miles, of Tunbridge Wells, Kent; *Career* articled Bryce Hammer & Co Liverpool 1955-60; Price Waterhouse London: joined 1960, ptnr 1970-, memb Policy Ctee 1979-, dir London Office 1982-85, managing ptnr (UK) 1985, md Europe 1988-, memb World Bd 1988-; memb: Cncl Royal London Soc for Blind, Agric Wages Bd; FCA 1960; *Recreations* golf, music; *Clubs* Carlton, Wildernesse GC; *Style—* Howard Hughes, Esq; Witham, Woodland Rise, Seal, nr Sevenoaks, Kent TN15 0HZ (☎ 0732 61161), Price Waterhouse, Southwark Towers, 32 London Bridge St, London SE1 9SY (☎ 071 407 8989, fax 071 378 0647, telex 884657/8)

HUGHES, Hugh Kenneth (Ken); DFC; s of Thomas William Hughes (d 1951), and Louisa Maud, *née* Bond (d 1982); *b* 20 Feb 1920; *Educ* John Ruskin Sch Croydon; *m* 1, 14 July 1945, Joan Frances; 1 s (Nicholas b 1950), 2 da (Philippa b 1947, Penelope b 1951); m 2, 28 Feb 1987, Jane Elizabeth; 1 step s (Benjamin Edwards b 1980); *Career* learnt to fly No 19 E&RFTS Gatwick 1938; RAF 1939-45 serving Nos 79, 87, 3 Sqdns in: UK N Africa, Italy, Belgium, Holland, Germany; fighter tactics instr Milfield 1943; airline pilot 1946, fndr Aerocontracts Ltd 1947; currently chm Scoba Gp; *Recreations* flying; *Clubs* RAF, IOD, Annabel's; *Style—* Ken Hughes, Esq, DFC; c/o Gatwick House, Horley, Surrey RH6 9SU (☎ 0293 771133, telex 87116, fax 0293 774658)

HUGHES, Hugh Llewellyn; s of Dillwyn Hughes, 81 Daneland, Barnet, Herts, and Kathlyn Hughes; *b* 13 Feb 1952; *Educ* St Aloysius Coll Highgate; *m* Brigitte Marie-Cecile; 2 s (Marc b 10 Aug 1977, Simon b 9 Sept 1981); *Career* ptnr Wedd Durlacher Mordaunt, memb Exec Ctee Swiss Bank Corporation London; md: Savory Milln Int, Savory Milln, SBCI Savory Milln, Swiss Bank Corporation Equities; memb: Stock Exchange, TSA, Int Equity Markets Ctee; *Style—* Hugh Hughes, Esq; Asteys, 8 Camlet Way, Hadley Wood, Herts EN4 0LH (☎ 081 441 9002); Masjos, 213 Avenue Marechal Leclerc, 06210 Madelieu, France; Swiss Bank Corp, Swiss Bank House, 1 High Timber St, London EC4V 3SB (☎ 071 329 0329, fax 081 782 9043, telex 887434, car 0860 332904); Paribas Ltd, 33 Wigmore St, London W1H 0BN (☎ 071 355 2000, fax 071 895 2555, telex 296723)

HUGHES, Ian; s of David Aled Joseph Hughes, of Hecklebirnie, Sandilands, Lanark, and Sheila McKenzie Hughes; *b* 10 Dec 1958; *Educ* Lesmahagow HS, Lanark GS, Dundee Art Coll (Duncan of Drumfolk travelling scholar, Dip in Art, Ian Eadie Purchase prize); *m* 29 May 1987, Alison, da of John Wright; 1 s (Jacob John b 29 June 1988); *Career* artist; pt/t work: Kelvingrove Museum & Art Gallery Glasgow 1980, Art Therapy Dept Stobhill Hosp Glasgow 1981-82; artist-in residence Scottish Nat Gallery of Modern Art 1988-89; solo exhibitions: 369 Gallery Edinburgh 1985 and 1987, Thomas Clouston Clinic Edinburgh 1987, RAAB Gallery London 1988 (Berlin 1989), Scottish Nat Gallery of Modern Art 1989; group exhibitions incl: Mercury Gallery Edinburgh 1984, Collective Gallery Edinburgh 1984, The Smith Biennial Exhibition Stirling 1985 and 1987, Scottish Painting (Perth Museum & Art Gallery) 1986, MacLean Art Gallery & Museum Greenock (prize-winner) 1986, The Vigorous Imagination (Scottish Nat Gallery of Modern Art and Aberdeen Art Gallery) 1987, Open Exhibition (Fruitmarket Gallery, Edinburgh) 1988, Metropolis (RAAB Gallery, London and Berlin) 1988, Citac (Pasqualle Lucas Gallery Valencia, plus Spain and tour) 1989, Le Passion du Christ (Musée de L'Art Contemporain Paris, Dunkirk and tour) 1989, Obsessions and The Cityscape and Landscape (RAAB Gallery, London) 1990, Scottish Prints (Vanessa Devereux Gallery, London and NY and tour) 1990; work in collections of: Royal Coll of Physicians, Scottish Nat Gallery of Modern Art, The Contemporary Arts Soc, The Cole Porter Museum (USA), The Fine Arts Soc, Unilever Products plc, Dundee Art Coll, Musée de L'Art Contemporain à Dunkerque, Artspace Galleries (San Francisco), BBC Scotland, Pasqualle Lucas Gallery, Museum Nadwiślański (Poland), The Whitworth Museum & Art Gallery (Manchester); winner: Young Artists' Bursary Scottish Arts Cncl 1985, Inverclyde Biennial prize 1986; also registered staff nurse in psychiatry; *Recreations* jazz and classical music, painting; *Style—* Ian Hughes, Esq; 1 Roseburn Drive, Roseburn, Edinburgh EH12 5NR (☎ 031 337 7104); c/o Mr Bassam Boukamel, RAAB Gallery At Millbank, 6 Vauxhall Bridge Rd, London SW1V 2SD (☎ 071 828 2588, fax 071 976 5041)

HUGHES, Prof Ieuan Arwel; s of Arwel Hughes, OBE (d 1988), of Cardiff, and Enid Phillips, *née* Thomas; *b* 9 Nov 1944; *Educ* Univ of Wales Coll of Med (MB BCh, MD); *m* 27 July 1969, Margaret Maureen (Mac), da of William Edgar Davies; 2 s (Gareth Arwel, Wiliam Arwel), 1 da (Mari Arwel); *Career* reader in child health Univ of Wales Coll of Med 1985-89 (sr lectr 1979-85), prof of paediatrics Univ of Cambridge 1989-; sec Euro Soc of Paediatric Endocrinology; memb: Br Paediatric Assoc, RCP; *Books* Handbook of Endocrine Tests In Children (1989); *Recreations* music, travel, squash, cycling; *Style—* Prof Ieuan Hughes; University of Cambridge, Department of Paediatrics, Addenbrookes Hospital, Hills Rd, Cambridge CB2 2QQ (☎ 0223 336885, fax 0223 336709)

HUGHES, Sir Jack William; s of George William Hughes and Isabel Hughes, of Maidstone, Kent; *b* 26 Sept 1916; *Educ* Maidstone GS, London Univ (BSc); *m* 1939, Marie-Theresa (d 1987), da of Graham Parmley Thompson; *Career* Special Duties Branch RAF 1940-46, demobilised Sqdn Ldr; jt sr ptnr Jones Lang Wootton 1949-76, conslt Jones Lang Wootton Int Real Estate Advsrs 1976-86; chm Bracknell Devpt Corpn 1971-82; dir Housing Corpn (1974) Ltd 1974-78; dir: South Bank Estates 1960-, URPT 1961-86, Public Property Companies, MEPC 1971-86, Brighton Marina Co (rep Brighton Corpn) 1974-86, BR Property Bd 1976-86, BR Investmt Co 1981-83, TR Property Investmt Tst 1982-, Property and Reversionary Investmt 1982-86; chm Property Advsry Gp DOE 1978-82; memb: ctee Mercantile Credit Gp Property Div, ctee of mgmnt Charities Property Unit Tst 1967-74, Advsy Gp to DOE on Commercial Property 1974-78, DOE Working Pty on Housing Tenure 1976-77; chm South Hill Park Arts Centre Tst 1972-79; tstee New Towns Pensions Fund 1975-82; Freeman City of London, Liveryman Worshipful Co of Painter Stainers Guild 1960-; FRSA, FRICS; kt 1980; *Publications* (jtly) Town and Country Planning Act 1949 (RICS), The Land Problem: a fresh approach (chm RICS ctee); *Recreations* golf, travel, reading; *Style—* Sir Jack Hughes; Challoners, The Green, Rottingdean, East Sussex

HUGHES, Hon Janet Margaret; da of Baron Hughes, CBE, PC (Life Peer 1961), of The Stables, Ross, Comrie, Perthshire PH6 2JU, and Lady Hughes *née* Gordon; *b* 21 Feb 1956; *Educ* Dundee HS, Univ of Edinburgh (BSc); *Career* princ teacher of computing Forfar Acad 1984-; *Style—* The Hon Janet Hughes; Alltan, Tulloes, by Forfar, Angus (☎ 030 781 792)

HUGHES, John; s of Evan John Hughes, and Dellis, *née* Williams; *b* 28 April 1930; *Educ* Stationers' and Newspapermakers Sch London, Colby Coll; *m* 1, 20 Aug 1955 (m dis 1987), Vera Elizabeth Pockman; 1 s (Mark Evan), 2 da (Wendy, Elizabeth); m2, 1988, Peggy Janeane Chu; *Career* Natal Mercury Durban SA 1946-49 and 1952-54, Daily Mirror then Reuters London 1949-52; Christian Science Monitor Boston: joined 1954, corr Africa 1955-61, asst foreign ed 1962-64, corr Far East 1964-70, managing ed 1970, ed 1970-76, ed and mangr 1976-79 dir News Journal Co Wilmington 1975-78, broadcaster Westinghouse Broadcasting Co Boston 1962-70 (based Far East 1964-70), pres and publisher Hughes Newspapers Inc Orleans Mass 1977-81, assoc dir USIA Washington 1981-82, dir Voice of America 1982, public affairs sec Department of State 1982-84, syndicated columnist and TV commentator Orleans Mass 1985-89, pres Concord Communications Inc Rockland Maine 1989-; memb: American Soc of Newspaper Editors (dir 1972-80, pres 1978-79), Pulitzer Prize Bd 1975-81; Nieman fell Harvard 1961-62; Pulitzer prize for Int Reporting 1967, Overseas Press Club award 1970, Yankee Quill award (Sigme Detta Chi) 1977; The New Face of Africa (1961), Indonesian Upheaval (1967); *Clubs* Overseas Press, Hong Kong Country, Harvard, Army & Navy; *Style—* John Hughes, Esq; Box 1053, Orleans, Mass 02653, USA

HUGHES, Prof John Pinnington; s of Joseph Henry Hughes (d 1956), and Edith Annie Hughes; *b* 6 Jan 1942; *Educ* Mitcham Co GS, Chelsea Coll London (BSc), King's Coll London (PhD), Univ of Cambridge (MA); *m* (m dis 1981), Madeleine Carol; 1 da (Katherine b 1967); *Partner* Julie; 3 s (Joseph Francis b 1986, John Stephen b 1988, Tomas James b 1990), 1 da (Georgina Anne b 1984); *Career* sr lectr and dep dir Unit for Res on Addictive Drugs Univ of Aberdeen 1973-77 (lectr in pharmacology 1969-73), prof in pharmacological biochemistry Imperial Coll London 1979-83 (reader in biochemistry 1977-79), dir Parke-Davis Res Centre 1983-, fell Wolfson Coll Cambridge 1983-, vice pres of res Parke-Davis (Warner-Lambert Corp 1988-, hon prof of neuropharmacology Univ of Cambridge 1989-; jt chief ed Neuropeptides 1980-; memb: Substance Abuse Ctee, Mental Health Fndn, Scientific Ctee ABPI; sch govr Local Educn Authy Swaffham Prior Community Sch; Hon Dr of Med Univ Leige Belgium 1978; memb Biochemical Soc, MPS; *Books* Centrally Acting Peptides (1978), Opioid Peptides (1983), Opioids Past Present and Future (1984), The Neuropeptide Cholecystokinin (1989); *Recreations* gardening, dogs; *Style—* Prof John Hughes; Parke-Davis Research Univ, Addenbrooke's Hospital, Hills Rd, Cambridge CB2 2QB (☎ 0223 210 929, fax 0223 214534)

HUGHES, Prof Leslie Ernest; s of Charles Joseph Hughes (d 1975), of Parramatta, NSW, and Vera Dorothy, *née* Raines (d 1984); *b* 12 Aug 1932; *Educ* Parramatta HS, Univ of Sydney (MB BS); *m* 19 Dec 1955, Marian, da of James Edwin Castle (d 1956), of Sydney, NSW; 2 s (Graeme b 1964, Stephen b 1971), 2 da (Bronwyn b 1957, Gillian b 1960); *Career* reader in surgery Univ of Queensland 1964-71, Eleanor Roosevelt Int Cancer fell Roswell Park Meml Inst Buffalo NY 1969-70, prof of surgery Univ of Wales Coll of Med 1971-; visiting prof Albany Univ NY, Hong Kong, Benares, Sydney, Melbourne and Brisbane; FRCS 1959, FRACS 1959, DS (Queensland) 1974; *Books* Benign Disorders of the Breast (1988); *Recreations* music, walking; *Style—* Prof Leslie Hughes; Dept of Surgery, Univ of Wales, Coll of Medicine, Heath Park, Cardiff CF4 4XN

HUGHES, Dr Louis; s of Richard Hughes (d 1962), and Anne, *née* Green (d 1958); *b* 10 March 1932; *Educ* Holyhead County Sch, Univ Coll Cardiff, Welsh Nat Sch of Med (MB BCh, DObst); *m* 26 June 1959, Margaret Caroline Mary, da of Thomas Cyril Wootton, of Newport, Gwent; 1 s (Christopher b 1964), 1 da (Deborah b 1960); *Career* Capt RAMC (TA) 1964; pt/t MO (infertility): Royal Free Hosp 1972-, Queen Charlotte and Chelsea Hosp 1979-; conslt (infertility) Margaret Pyke Centre 1979-; author numerous papers on fertility; chm: Childless Tst 1980-83, Int Wine and Food Soc 1982-86 (memb Mgmnt Ctee); memb: Br Fertility Soc, Br Andrology Soc, American Fertility Soc; Freeman: City of London 1975, Worshipful Soc of Apothecaries 1974; MRCOG, MBMA, FRSM; *Books* Monographs on Wine; *Recreations* golf, wine and food, cricket, book collecting; *Clubs* MCC, Savile, Saintsbury, Denham Golf; *Style—* Dr Louis Hughes; Beechwood, Burton's Lane, Chalfont St Giles, Bucks HP8 4BA (☎ 0494 762297); 99 Harley St, London W1 (☎ 071 935 9004)

HUGHES, Malcolm Edward; *b* 22 July 1920; *Educ* Regional Coll of Art Manchester, RCA; *Career* artist; tutor: Sch of Architecture Polytechnic of Central London, Bath Acad, Chelsea Sch of Art; reader in fine art Sch of Postgraduate Studies The Slade Sch of Fine Art; co-fndr: The Systems Group 1969, Exhibiting Space 1984; numerous solo exhibitions; works in group exhibitions incl: Looking Forward (Whitechapel Art Gallery London) 1952, Four Artists: Reliefs, Constructions and Drawings (Victoria and Albert Museum) 1971, Systems (Whitechapel Art gallery and on tour with Arts Council) 1972, Basically White (ICA) 1974, Art as Thought Process for Arts Council (The Serpentine Gallery) 1974, New Work 2 (The Hayward Gallery London) 1975, Sculpture for the Blind (The Tate Gallery) 1976, British Artists of the Sixties (The Tate Gallery) 1977, British Painting 1952-77 (RA) 1977, Constructive Context (Warehouse Gallery London, Arts Cncl Tour) 1978, Arts Council Collection (Hayward Gallery) 1980, British Council Collection (Serpentine Gallery London) 1980, Systematic Constructive Work (The Ruskin Sch of Drawing and Fine Art Oxford) 1987, Modern British Sculpture (The Tate Gallery) 1988, Painting Space, Gallery Space (Annely Juda Fine Art) 1989; also numerous works in US, Euro and Br exhibitions; awarded: Arts Council award 1966, John Moores Exhibition prize 1967, Edwin Abbey premier scholarship 1973; hon res fell Univ Coll London 1982, emeritus reader in fine art Univ of London 1982, hon fell Univ Coll London 1991; memb: Arts Cncl Ctee, Rome and Abbey Scholarship Ctee; *Style—* Malcolm Hughes, Esq; Annely Juda Fine Art, 23 Dering Street, London W1R 9AA (☎ 071 629 7578, fax 071 491 2139)

HUGHES, (William) Mark; s of Prof Edward Hughes, of Univ of Durham (d 1965); *b* 18 Dec 1932; *Educ* Shincliffe Sch, Durham Sch, Balliol Coll Oxford (PhD); *m* 1958, Jennifer Mary, da of Dr G H Boobyer; 1 s, 2 da; *Career* res fell Newcastle 1958-60, staff tutor Univ of Manchester (Extra-Mural Dept), lectr Univ of Durham 1964-70, MP (Lab) Durham 1970-87, (did not seek re-election); memb Select Ctee on Expenditure 1970-74 and on Parly Cmmn 1970-75, PPS to Chief Sec to Treasy 1974-75, MEP 1975-79 when vice chm Agric Ctee and chm Fisheries Sub Ctee (both 1977-79), memb Delgn to Cncl of Europe Consultative Assembly and WEU 1974-75; vice chm Exec Ctee Br Cncl 1978- (memb 1974-); oppn front bench spokesman Agric Fish and Food 1981-; memb Gen Advsy Cncl BBC 1976-; hon vice pres Br Veterinary Assoc 1976-; memb Durham RDC 1968-70; *Style—* Dr Mark Hughes; Grimsdyke, Vicarage Rd, Potten End, Berkhamsted, Herts (☎ 044 27 73083)

HUGHES, Melvyn; s of Evan Llewellyn Hughes, of Newcastle upon Tyne, and Irene Kathleen, *née* Spires; *b* 18 Nov 1950; *Educ* Royal GS Newcastle upon Tyne, St Catherine's Coll Oxford (MA); *m* 6 July 1974, Diane, da of Percival Moffett (d 1987); 2 s (Richard b 2 Nov 1983, David b 9 March 1990), 1 da (Alexandra b 28 Oct 1980); *Career* personnel ptnr Slaughter and May 1989- (asst slr 1976-83, articled clerk 1974-76, ptnr 1983-); Freeman City of London; memb: City of London Slrs, Law Soc; *Recreations* reading, cars, sport; *Style—* Melvyn Hughes, Esq; Little Steading, Godden Green, Sevenoaks, Kent TN15 0JS (☎ 0732 61 610); Slaughter and May, 35 Basinghall St, London EC2V 5DB (☎ 071 600 1200, fax 071 726 0038/071 600 0289)

HUGHES, (Thomas) Merfyn; s of John Medwyn Hughes, of Beaumaris, Anglesey, and Jane Blodwen, *née* Roberts; *b* 8 April 1949; *Educ* Rydal Sch Colwyn Bay, Liverpool Univ (LLB); *m* 16 April 1977, Patricia Joan, da of John Edmund Talbot (d 1982), of Brentwood, Essex; 2 s (Thomas Jenkin Edmund b 14 Sep 1982, Joshua Edward Talbot b 7 Dec 1987), 1 da (Caitlin Mary b 19 Feb 1980); *Career* called to the Bar Inner Temple 1971, practising Wales and Chester circuit, asst recorder 1987; former Lab pty candidate Caernarfon; *Recreations* sailing, rugby; *Clubs* Royal Anglesey Yacht; *Style—* Merfyn Hughes, Esq; Plas Llanfaes, Beaumaris, Anglesey; 3 Stamford Court, Vicars Cross, Chester (☎ 0244 323 886); 40 King St, Chester

HUGHES, Michael; s of Leonard Hughes, of Clwyd and Gwyneth Mair, *née* Edwards; *b* 26 Feb 1951; *Educ* Rhyl GS, Univ of Manchester (BA), LSE (MSc); *m* 11 Feb 1978, Jane Ann, da of Percival Frederick Gosham, (d 1977) of Ipswich; 2 da (Sophie b 1979, Harriet b 1981); *Career* economist BP Pension Fund 1973-75, chief economist and ptnr de Zoete and Bevan 1976-86, dir Barclays de Zoete Wedd Ltd; BZW: Capital Markets 1986, exec dir Gilts Ltd 1986-, md Economics and Strategy 1989-; patron and chm fin ctee Cncl for Advancement of Communication with Deaf People; AMSIA 1977; *Recreations* horses; *Clubs* Gresham, National Liberal; *Style*— Michael Hughes, Esq; Ebbgate House, 2 Swan Lane, London EC4R 3TS (☎ 071 623 2323, fax 071 626 1753, telex 888221)

HUGHES, Dr (John) Michael Barton; s of Dr Stanley Barton Hughes (d 1963), of Helen's Bay, Co Down, and Dorothy Jane Augusta, *née* Tornblad; *b* 30 Nov 1936; *Educ* Lancing, Trinity Coll, Oxford (BM BCh, MA, DM); *m* 22 Feb 1963, Shirley Anne, da of Hedley Frank Stenning (d 1977); 2 da (Penelope Barton b 1971, Caroline Barton b 1975); *Career* house physician med unit London Hosp 1963-65, house physician and res fell Hammersmith Hosp 1965-65, MRC travelling fell Harvard Sch of Public Health 1968, reader in med Royal Postgrad Med Sch 1985- (lectr and sr lectr 1969-85), conslt physician Hammersmith Hosp 1974- (Cournand lectr 1975, Fleischner lectr 1989-); pubns incl chapters on: lung gas exchange, pulmonary circulation, radioisotopes, lung function; over a hundred sci articles on pulmonary physiology and lung disease; FRCP 1979; *Recreations* golf; *Clubs* Royal West Norfolk; *Style*— Dr Michael Hughes; Dept Medicine, Royal Postgraduate Medical School, Hammersmith Hospital, London W12 0HS (☎ 081 740 3269, fax 081 740 3169)

HUGHES, Michael John; s of Frank Miller Hughes, of Horsham, Sussex, and Jean Mary, MBE, *née* Allford; *b* 20 Nov 1949; *Educ* Collyer's GS Horsham, Oxford Poly, Univ of London (BEcon); *m* 10 Sept 1977, Elizabeth Charlotte Margaret Mary Antoinette Marie- Thérèse, da of Maj Leslie William Hutchins (d 1968), of Norwich; 2 da (Sophie b 1979, Caroline b 1982); *Career* gen mangr Anglia TV Ltd 1984-88; exec dir: Anglia TV Gp plc 1986, Anglia TV Ltd 1986; asst gp chief exec Anglia TV Gp plc 1988-90, dep gp chief exec Anglia TV Group plc 1990-; dir Anglia TV Telethon Tst 1987; chm Cinema and Television Benevolent Fund (CTBF) East of England ctee; *Recreations* tennis, squash, skiing, saxophone; *Clubs* East Anglian Lawn Tennis; *Style*— Michael Hughes, Esq; Hall Farmhouse, Stanfield, nr Wymondham, Norfolk NR18 9RL (☎ 0953 606199); Anglia Television Gp plc, Anglia House, Norwich (☎ 0603 615151, fax 0603 631032, telex 97424)

HUGHES, Nerys (Mrs Turley); da of Roger Edward Kerfoot Hughes (d 1974), of Rhyl, N Wales, and Annie Myfanwy, *née* Roberts; *Educ* Howells Sch Denbigh, Ross Bruford Coll; *m* 13 May 1972, (James) Patrick Turley, s of James Turley (d 1983), of Wednesbury, Staffs; 1 s (Ben b 1974), 1 da (Mari-Claire b 1978); *Career* actress; theatre work incl: BBC Rep Co, RSC, English Stage Co Royal Court; TV series incl: Diary of a Young Man, Liver Birds, District Nurse, Alphabet Zoo (children's TV); PYE Female Comedy Star Award 1974, Variety Club TV Actress of the Year 1984; vice pres Nat Children's Home; *Recreations* gardening, reading; *Style*— Miss Nerys Hughes (Mrs Turley); c/o Barry Burnett Organisation, Suite 42/43, Grafton House, 2/3 Golden Sq, London W1 (☎ 071 437 7048/9, fax 071 437 1098)

HUGHES, Nicholas Maxwell Lloyd; s of Glyn Hughes, of Brighton, and (Muriel) Joyce, *née* Hardaker; *b* 10 Oct 1955; *Educ* Univ of Sheffield (BA); *m* 8 June 1985, (Margaret) Ruth, da of Prof David Cornelius Morley, CBE, of Harpenden; *Career* admitted slr 1981; ptnr Barlow Lyde & Gilbert 1984-; author of articles on aviation law; Freeman City of London Slrs Co; memb: Int Bar Assoc, Royal Aeronautical Soc, Law Soc; *Recreations* viticulture, antique furniture, music, sailing; *Clubs* Wig and Pen, Marine; *Style*— Nicholas Hughes, Esq; Beaufort House, 15 St Botolph St, London EC3A 7NJ (☎ 071 782 8459, fax 071 782 8505, telex 913281 G)

HUGHES, Owain Arwel; s of Arwel Hughes (d 1988), of Cardiff and Enid Phillips, *née* Thomas; *b* 21 March 1942; *Educ* Howardian HS Cardiff, Univ Coll Cardiff, RCM London; *m* 23 July 1966, Jean Bowen, da of William Emlyn Lewis; 1 s (Geraint John b 15 Feb 1974), 1 da (Lisa Margaret b 25 Dec 1970); *Career* conductor; since 1970 has conducted all the UK symphony orchestras and their respective choirs, in particular The Hallé, London Philharmonic and The Royal Philharmonic; assoc conductor: BBC Welsh Symphony Orchestra 1980-86, Philharmonia Orchestra London 1985-90; musical dir Huddersfield Choral Soc 1980-86, fndr, artistic dir and conductor the Annual Welsh Proms 1986-; performances in: Holland, Denmark, Norway, Sweden, Finland, Iceland, Luxembourg, France, Germany, Portugal, Hong Kong and NZ; many TV appearances in concert or special projects incl Mahler Symphony no 8, Requiem series, Holy Week Series, Much Loved Music series; recordings incl: Music of Delius (Philharmonia Orchestra, ASV), London Symphony by Vaughan Williams (Philharmonia Orchestra, ASV), Music of Paul Patterson (London Philharmonic, EMI), Much Loved Music Vols I and II (Hallé Orchestra, EMI), Carols Album and Hymns Album (Huddersfield Choral Soc, EMI), St David by Arwel Hughes (BBC Welsh Orchestra and Choir, Chandos), African Sanctus by David Fanshawe (Ambrosian Chorus and Instrumentalists, Phillips); *awards* Gold medal Welsh Tourist Bd, Communicator of the year, 2 Gold discs BP1; memb Inst of Advanced Motorists, vice pres Nat Childrens Home; hon bard Royal Nat Eisteddfod of Wales; hon D Mus: CNAA London, Univ of Wales; *Recreations* rugby, cricket, golf, motoring, travel; *Clubs* Rugby Club of London, London Welsh Assoc, London Welsh Rugby; *Style*— Owain Arwel Hughes, Esq; c/o Peter Garvey, 32 Bigwood Avenue, Hove, East Sussex BN3 6FQ (☎ 0273 206623, fax 0273 208484)

HUGHES, Paul; s of James Henry Hughes (d 1986), of Dublin, and Mary, *née* O'Hanlon; *b* 22 June 1956; *m* 24 June 1983, Liliane Niederer; 1 s (Kean b 11 Sept 1990); *Career* knitwear designer for Cachaca shop King's Road 1976-70; own galleries: Textile Gallery NY 1979-81, Gallery of Ethnographic Textiles San Francisco 1981-82, Gallery of Antique and Ancient Textiles London 1983-; organiser of numerous historical, African and South American textile exhibitions; author of exhibition catalogues; conductor of ecological tours of Amazon, builder of Mississippi-style steamer boat from scratch to act as local field hosp for indigenous Indians of Bolivian/ Brazilian Amazon; *Style*— Paul Hughes, Esq; 3A Pembridge Square, London W2 4EW (☎ 071 243 8598, fax 071 221 8785)

HUGHES, (Robert) Peredur; s of Rev Robert Hughes (d 1938), of Coedlys, Valley, Anglesey, and Sidney, *née* Williams (d 1947); *b* 2 Aug 1916; *Educ* Holyhead GS, Univ Coll of Wales Aberystwyth (LLB); *m* 1946, Myra, da of John Bellis (d 1967), of Coedlys, Valley, Anglesey; 1 s (Robert Philip Hughes b 1947), 1 da (Jennifer Meryl Hughes b 1955); *Career* serv Inns of Ct Regt on Western Front; admitted slr 1946; clerk to cmmrs of taxes for Isle of Anglesey 1950-, sec of Lord Chllrs Advsy Ctee for Appt of Cmmrs for Income Tax 1950-, dep coroner for Isle of Anglesey 1957-77, clerk of justices for Isle of Anglesey 1960-85; *Recreations* cricket, sailing; *Style*— Peredur Hughes, Esq; Coedlys, Valley, Anglesey, Gwynedd (☎ 0407 740267); Stanley House, Holyhead, Anglesey (☎ 0407 2301)

HUGHES, (David Evan) Peter; s of Evan Gwilliam Forrest-Hughes, OBE (d 1983); *b* 27 April 1932; *Educ* St Paul's, St John's Coll Oxford (MA); *m* 8 Sept 1956, Iris, *née* Jenkins; *Career* Nat Serv 2 Lt 5 Regt RHA 1954-56; second master and head of sci Shrewsbury 1956-80, headmaster St Peter's Sch York 1980-84, head of sci Westminster 1984-89, dir Leverhulme Understanding Sci Project 1989-; *Style*— Peter Hughes, Esq; 14 Barton St, London SW1P 3NE (☎ 071 222 0868); Westminster Sch, 17 Dean's Yard, London SW1P 3PB (☎ 071 222 2831)

HUGHES, Peter Thomas; s of Peter Hughes, JP, of Old Sunfold Marine Drive, Rhos-on-Sea, Clwyd, and Jane Blakemore, *née* Woodward; *b* 16 June 1949; *Educ* Bolton Sch, Univ of Bristol; *m* 20 July 1974, Christine Stuart, da of Rex Taylor, of Abbeystone, Monks Way West Kirby, Wirral; 1 s (Richard b 12 July 1985), 1 da (Rosemary b 27 May 1982); *Career* called to the Bar Gray's Inn 1971, asst recorder Wales and Chester Circuit 1988-, chm Med Appeal Tbnl 1988-; chm: City of Chester Cons Assoc 1983-86, Euro Constituency Cncl 1984-87; memb Grays Inn 1967-; *Recreations* books, fell walking, gardening; *Style*— Peter Hughes, Esq; Kingsmead, Churton, Chester CH3 6LA (☎ 0829 271 231); Hause Gill Cottage, Seatoller, Borrowdale, Cumbria (☎ 07687 77603); 40 King St, Chester CH1 2AH (☎ 0244 323886)

HUGHES, Philip Arthur Booley; CBE (1982); s of Leslie Booley Hughes, and Elizabeth Alice, *née* Whyte; *b* 30 Jan 1936; *Educ* Bedford Sch, Univ of Cambridge (BA); *m* 21 Aug 1964, Psiche Maria Anna Claudia, da of Bertino Bertini (d 1971); 2 da (Francesca b 1966, Simona b 1968), 2 step da (Pauline b 1952, Carole b 1954); *Career* engr Shell International Petroleum Co 1957-61, computer conslt Scicon (formerly CEIR) 1961-69, dir Logics plc 1990- (co fndr chm and md 1969-72, chm 1972-90); artist with exhibitions: (with Beryl Bainbridge) Monks Gallery Sussex 1972, contemporary Br Painting Madrid 1983, contemporary painters Ridgeway Gallery Swindon 1986; one man exhibitions: Parkway Focus Gallery London 1976, Angela Flowers Gallery London 1977, Gallery Cance Manguin Vaucluse 1979 and 1985, Francis Kyle Gallery London 1979, 1982, 1984, 1987, 1989, Inverness Museum 1990; memb Cncl of RCA, dir Design Museum; *Style*— Philip Hughes, Esq, CBE; c/o Logica plc, 68 Newman St, London W1A 4SE

HUGHES, Richard; s of Lt Walter Cyril Hughes, RA (d 1947), of Cardiff, and Emily, *née* Palfrey (d 1941); *b* 15 April 1938; *Educ* Cardiff HS, Eaton Hall Offr Cadet Sch, Mons Offr Cadet Sch, Queens' Coll Cambridge (MA, LLM), Coll of Law Guildford Surrey; *m* 11 June 1963, Marie Elizabeth, da of William Rieb (d 1972), of Somerset West, Cape, SA; 1 s (David b 31 March 1964); *Career* cmmnd 2 Lt The Welch Regt 1958, serving Cyprus (GSM) and Libya 1958-59; legal advsr: Royal Insurance Group 1963-65, S African Mutual Life Assurance Society 1965-66; slr of the Supreme Ct 1969-91, sr ptnr Sprake and Hughes 1982- (ptnr in private practice 1969-91); literary critic and reviewer The Cape Times 1964-66; memb: Law Soc, Norfolk and Norwich Law Soc; *Recreations* travel, walking, reading, music; *Style*— Richard Hughes, Esq; Apple Acre, Low Rd, Norton Subcourse, nr Norwich, Norfolk NR14 6SA (☎ 050 846 316); Sprake and Hughes, Solicitors, 16 Broad St, Bungay, Suffolk; 8 Exchange St, Harleston, Norfolk

HUGHES, Prof Richard Anthony Cranmer; s of Dr Anthony Chester Cranmer Hughes, of Chester, and Lilian Mildred, *née* Crisp; *b* 11 Nov 1942; *Educ* Malborough Coll, Clare Coll Cambridge, Guy's Hosp Med Sch; *m* 17 Feb 1968, Coral Stephanie, da of James Albert Whittaker (d 1983); 1 s (Henry b 1975), 2 da (Polly b 1970, Romany b 1971); *Career* conslt neurologist Guys Hosp 1975, prof of neurology United Med and Dental Schs 1977, ed Journal of Neurology, Neurosurgery and Psychiatry 1979; govr Highgate Sch 1990-; FRCP 1980; *Books* Immunology of The Nervous System (1983), Guillain-Barrè Syndrome (1990); *Recreations* tennis, dinghy sailing, mountaineering, theatre; *Clubs* Royal Society of Medicine; *Style*— Prof Richard Hughes

HUGHES, Robert; MP (Lab) Aberdeen N 1970-; *b* 3 Jan 1932; *Educ* Robert Gordon's Coll Aberdeen, Benoni HS Transvaal, Pietermaritzburg Tech Coll; *m* 1957, Ina *née* Miller; 2 s, 3 da; *Career* formerly engrg apprentice in SA, chief draughtsman C F Wilson & Co 1932 Ltd (Aberdeen until 1970); contested N Angus and Mearns 1959, memb Aberdeen Town Cncl 1962-70 (convenor of Health and Welfare Ctee 1963-68 and Social Work Ctee 1969-70); memb: Standing Ctee on Immigration Bill 1971, Scot Affairs Select Ctee 1971; Parly under sec of state Scot Office 1974-75, jr oppn spokesman 1981-83; princ oppn spokesman: agriculture 1983-84, transport 1985-88; memb PLP Shadow Cabinet 1985-88; chm: Aberdeen City Lab Party 1961-69, Anti-Apartheid Movement (vice chm 1975-76) 1976-, Aberdeen CND (founder memb); memb AEU 1952-, Gen Med Cncl 1976-79, SA Ctee Movement for Colonial Freedom (now Liberation) 1955-, Scot Poverty Action Gp; *Recreations* fishing, golf; *Style*— Robert Hughes, Esq, MP; House of Commons, London SW1

HUGHES, Robert Charles; s of Clifford Gibson Hughes, of Walton-On-The-Hill, Surrey, and Elizabeth Joan, *née* Goodwin; *b* 20 Jan 1949; *Educ* Westminster, Emmanuel Coll Cambridge (MA); *m* 23 June 1973, Cynthia Rosemary (Cindy), da of Lionel Edward Charles Kirby-Turner (d 1986), of Guildford, Surrey; 3 da (Zoe b 1975, Emma b 1976, Sophie b 1980); *Career* Ernst & Young (formerly Barton Mayhew & Co): joined 1970, ptnr London 1978-81, ptnr Dubai UAE 1981-86, London 1986-; FCA; *Recreations* golf, squash, puzzles; *Clubs* Sutton Tennis and Squash; *Style*— Robert Hughes, Esq; Crazes, Heather Close, Kingswood, Surrey KT20 6NY (☎ 0737 832 256); Ernst & Young, Becket House, 1 Lambeth Palace Rd, London, SE1 7EU (☎ 071 928 2000, fax 071 928 1345, telex 885224)

HUGHES, Robert Gurth; MP (C) Harrow West 1987-; s of Gurth Martin Hughes, and Rosemary Dorothy, *née* Brown; *b* 14 July 1951; *Educ* Spring Grove GS, Harrow Coll of Technol; *m* 1986, Sandra Kathleen, da of James Vaughan; 3 da (Catherine b 1987, Elizabeth b 1988, Victoria b 1990); *Career* BBC TV news picture Ed until 1987; PPS to: Rt Hon Edward Heath MP 1988-90, Rt Hon Nicholas Scott 1990-; *Recreations* watching cricket, listening to music, photography; *Clubs* St Stephens & Constitutional, Harrow Borough Football; *Style*— Robert G Hughes, Esq; c/o House of Commons SW1A 0AA (☎ 071 219 6854)

HUGHES, Rodger Grant; s of Eric Hughes, of Rhyl, Clwyd, and Doreen, *née* Barnes; *b* 24 Aug 1948; *Educ* Rhyl GS, Queens' Coll Cambridge (MA); *m* 9 June 1973, Joan Clare, da of James Barker; 2 s (Marcus b 9 July 1979, Oliver b 2 Feb 1983); *Career* Price Waterhouse: joined 1970, ptnr 1982-, ptnr i/c Ind Business Gp 1988-; FCA 1973; *Style*— Rodger Hughes, Esq; Timbers, 3 Dempster Close, Long Ditton, Surrey; Price Waterhouse, Southwark Towers, 32 London Bridge St, London SE1 9SY (☎ 071 939 3000, fax 071 378 0647, telex 884657)

HUGHES, Dr Roger Llewellyn; s of Flt-Lt Clifford John Silke Hughes (d 1963), and Jean Christine Roger, *née* Stewart; *b* 2 June 1947; *Educ* The HS of Glasgow, Univ of Glasgow (MB ChB, MD); *m* 14 Oct 1971, Pamela Jane, da of Dr Finlay Finlayson (d 1983); 4 da (Vivienne b 1972, Caroline b 1974, Zoe b 1979, Jennifer b 1981); *Career* sr registrar Glasgow Royal Infirmary 1975 (sr house offr 1971-72, registrar of anaesthesia 1972-75), conslt in anaesthesia Stobhill Hosp Glasgow 1980-, currently hon clinical sr lectr Univ of Glasgow (lectr in anaesthesia 1975-80); author of papers on liver blood flow and baroreceptor reflex; chm of jr gp Assoc of Anaesthetists of GB and I 1977-79; memb: BMA, Intensive Care Soc; FRCP, FFARCS; *Recreations* gardening, walking; *Style*— Dr Roger Hughes; 7 Ballaig Ave, Bearsden, Glasgow GG1 4HA (☎ 041 942 5626); Stobhill Hospital, Glasgow G21 (☎ 041 558 0111); Glasgow Nuffield Hospital, Glasgow G12

HUGHES, Ronald Frederick (Ron); s of Harry Frederick James Hughes (d 1964), of Beccles, Suffolk, and Violet Kate, *née* Terry; *b* 21 Oct 1927; *Educ* Birmingham Central Tech Coll, Bradford Coll of Technol; *m* 21 Dec 1957, Cecilia Patricia, da of Maurice

Nunis (d 1957), of Sereemban, Malaysia; 2 s (Anthony b 1959, John b 1968), 1 da (Lesley -Ann b 1958); *Career* engrg cadet RE 1946, cmmnd RE 1950, SORE 3 Design HQ Malaya Cmd 1950, garrison engr Centl Malaya 1951, engr offr 22 SAS (Malayan Scouts) 1952, Adj CRE S Malaya 1953, SORE 3 Resources HQ Northern Cmd (UK) 1954; res asst BISRA 1954-55, civil engr (later md) HW Evans & Co Malayan 1955-59, civil engr WO Chessington 1959-63, works Gp Singapore 1963-66, area offr MPBW Malaya 1966-69, princ civil engr PO works MPBW 1969-76, area offr PSA Birmingham 1977-79, asst dir (later dir) civil engrg PSA 1979-87, conslt Mott MacDonald Conslt Engrs 1987-; memb: Standing Ctee for Structural Safety 1983-87, cncl Construction Indust res and info Assoc 1983-87, Parly Maritime Gp 1986-, cncl Steel Construction Inst 1986-88; govt del Permanent Int Assoc of Navigation Congresses 1983-, dir Construction Indust Computing Assoc 1982-87; FICE 1962 (memb bd Maritime Gp 1983), FIStructE 1987, MSIS (Fr) 1987; *Recreations* golf, squash, music, photography; *Clubs* Effingham (Surrey); *Style*— Ron Hughes, Esq; 9A The Street, West Horsley, Leatherhead, Surrey KT24 6AY (☎ 04 865 2182); Mott, MacDonald, Consulting Engineers, St Anne House, 20- 26 Wellesley Road, Croydon CR9 2UL (☎ 081 686 5041, fax 081 681 5706, telex 917 241)

HUGHES, Royston John; MP (Lab) Newport East 1983-; s of late John Hughes (coal miner), of Pontllanfraith, Mon; *b* 1925 June; *Educ* Pontllanfraith County GS, Ruskin Coll Oxford; *m* 1957, Florence Marion, da of John Appleyard, of Scarborough; 3 da; *Career* official TGWU 1959-66, memb Coventry City Cncl and sec Coventry Borough Lab Pty 1962-66; MP (Lab) Newport 1966-83; chm: PLP Sports Gp 1974-84, Welsh Lab Gp 1975-76, PLP Steel Gp 1975-86, Welsh Grantd Ctee 1982-84, Speaker's Panel 1982-84, Ctee of Selection 1982-84, front bench spokesman Welsh Affairs 1984-88, memb Exec Inter-Parly Union 1987 (treas 1990), jt chm All Party Motor Gp 1987; *Style*— Roy Hughes, Esq, MP; Chapel Field, Chapel Lane, Abergavenny, Gwent NP7 7BT

HUGHES, Prof Sean Patrick Francis; s of Dr Patrick Joseph Hughes, and Kathleen Ethel, *née* Biggs; *b* 2 Dec 1941; *Educ* Downside, St Mary's Hosp Med Sch Univ of London (MB BS, MS); *m* 22 Jan 1972, Dr Felicity Mary Anderson; 1 s (John Patrick b 3 Feb 1977), 2 da (Sarah Jane b 28 Nov 1972, Emily Anne b 25 July 1974); *Career* MO Save the Children Fund Nigeria, sr registrar in orthopaedics The Middx Hosp and Royal Nat Orthopaedic Hosp London, res fell Mayo Clinic USA, sr lectr/hon conslt orthopaedic surgn Royal Postgraduate Med Sch Hammersmith Hosp London, prof and head Dept Orthopaedic Surgery Univ of Edinburgh, hon conslt orthopaedic surgn Royal Infirmary Edinburgh and Princess Margaret Rose Orthopaedic Hosp Edinburgh, hon civilian orthopaedic conslt to RN; memb: Cncl RCS Edinburgh, Cncl Br Orthopaedic Assoc, Cncl Action Research, Ed Bd Jl of RCS Edinburgh; Fell Br Orthopaedic Assoc; FRSM; *Books* Musculoskeletal Infections, Short Textbook of Orthopaedics and Traumatology (4 ed), Orthopaedics: The Principles and Practice of Musculoskeletal Surgery; *Recreations* sailing, golf, lying in the sun; *Style*— Prof Sean Hughes; 9 Corrennie Gardens, Edinburgh EH10 6DG (☎ 031 447 1443); Univ Dept of Orthopaedic Surgery, Princess Margaret Rose Orthopaedic Hospital, Fairmilehead, Edinburgh EH10 7ED (☎ 031 445 4123)

HUGHES, Simon Henry Ward; MP (Lib) Southwark and Bermondsey 1983-; s of James Henry Annesley Hughes (d 1976), and Sylvia, *née* Ward; *b* 17 May 1951; *Educ* Christ Coll Brecon Wales, Selwyn Coll Cambridge (MA), Inns of Court Sch of Law, Coll of Europe Bruges; *Career* called to the Bar Inner Temple 1974; MP (Lib) Southwark, Bermondsey Feb-May 1983 and June 1983-; Lib Parly spokesman for the Environment July 1983- Jan'87, and June'87- March '88; Lib Democrat March 1988-, Alliance spokesman for Health Jan-June 1987; Lib Democrat spokesman for the environment March-Oct 1988 and for educn, sci, trg and youth Oct 1988-; *Style*— Simon Hughes, Esq, MP; 6 Lynton Rd, Bermondsey, London SE1; House of Commons, London SW1 (☎ 071 219 6256)

HUGHES, Simon Peter; s of Peter Clowe Hughes, and Erica Christine, *née* Brace; *b* 20 Dec 1959; *Educ* Latymer Upper Sch Hammersmith, Coll of St Hild & St Bede Durham Univ; *m* 31 March 1990, Jan Gillian, da of William E Rose; *Career* cricketer; played with: England Young Cricketers 1979, England A team v Sri Lanka 1981, Middlesex CCC 1980- (Beneficiary Year 1991, 320 appearances to date); Northern Transvaal SA 1982-83 (25 appearances); winner of (with Middlesex CCC) 4 County Championships (1980, 1982, 1985, 1990), 3 Nat West Trophies (1980, 1984, 1988), 2 Benson & Hedges Cups (1983, 1986), 1 Refuge League Cup (1990); author of: From the Inside (The Cricketer International) 1982-88, cricketers' Diary (The Independent) 1987-; presenter of sports features (BBC Breakfast News) 1989-, sports programmes (channel 4, BSB sports channel) 1989-, county Talk (Test Match Special BBC Radio 3) 1990-; *Recreations* silent movies, India & Indian Food, people, current affairs; *Style*— Simon Hughes, Esq; Middlesex CCC, Lords Cricket Ground, London NW8 8QN

HUGHES, Stephen Skipsey; MEP (Durham 1984); *b* 19 Aug 1952; *Educ* St Bede's Sch Lanchester, Newcastle Poly; *m* (m dis), Cynthia, 1 s, 2 da (twins); *Career* local govt offr; memb T&GWU; *Style*— S S Hughes, Esq, MEP; Room 4/74, County Hall, Durham DH1 5UR (☎ 091 384 9371, fax 091 386 0958 and 0325 384107)

HUGHES, Sir Trevor Poulton; KCB (1982, CB 1974); s of late Rev John Hughes, and Mary Grace, *née* Hughes; *b* 28 Sept 1925; *Educ* Ruthin Sch; *m* 1, 1950 (m dis), Mary Walwyn; 2 s; m 2, 1978, Barbara June Davison; *Career* serv RE, Capt 1945-48; former local govt engr; Miny of Transport 1961-62, Miny of Housing and Local Govt Engrg Inspectorate 1962-70; DOE: dep chief engr 1970-71, dir 1971-72, dir gen water engrg 1972-74, dep sec 1974-77; dep sec Dept of Tport 1977-80, perm sec Welsh Office 1980-85; chm Public Works and Municipal Servs Congress Cncl 1989-90 (vice chm 1975-89); a vice pres ICE 1984-86, memb Br Waterways Bd 1985-88, chm B & C E Holiday Mgmnt Co 1987-; Hon FIWEM, CEng, FICE; *Style*— Sir Trevor Hughes, KCB; Clearwell, 13 Brambleton Ave, Farnham, Surrey GU9 8RA (☎ 0252 714246)

HUGHES, Baron (Life Peer UK 1961); William Hughes; CBE (1965, OBE 1942), PC (1970), DL (Dundee 1960); s of Joseph Hughes (d 1962), and Margaret Ann, *née* Stott (d 1971); *b* 22 Jan 1911; *Educ* Balfour Street Public Sch Dundee, Dundee Tech, St Andrews Univ (hon LLD); *m* 1951, Christian Clacher, da of James Gordon; 2 da (Christian, Janet); *Recreations* gardening, travel; *Style*— The Rt Hon the Lord Hughes, CBE, PC, DL; The Stables, Ross, Comrie, Perthshire PH6 2JU (☎ 0764 70557); House of Lords (☎ 071 219 3207)

HUGHES, William Young; CBE (1987); s of Hugh Prentice Hughes, and Mary Henderson Hughes; *b* 12 April 1940; *Educ* Firth Park GS Sheffield, Univ of Glasgow (BSc), Univ of Strathclyde; *m* 1964, Anne MacDonald Richardson; 2 s, 1 da; *Career* lectr in Dept of Pharmacy Heriot-Watt Univ 1964-66, ptnr R Gordon Drummond Retail Chemists 1966-70, md MSJ Securities Ltd 1970-76, chm and chief exec Grampian Hldgs plc 1976-; dep chm Scottish Conservative Party 1989-, chm: Euro Summer Special Olympic Games 1990, CBI Scotland 1987-89; memb: Governing Cncl SCOTBIC, St Andrews Church Falkirk; *Recreations* golf; *Clubs* Glenbervie Golf; *Style*— William Hughes, Esq, CBE; The Elms, 12 Camelon Rd, Falkirk FK1 5RX; Grampian Hldgs plc, Stag House, Castlebank St, Glasgow G11 6DY (☎ 041 357 2000)

HUGHES-GAMES, Dr John Stephen; s of Guy Stephen Hughes-Games (d 1985), of Congresbury, nr Bristol, and Doris, *née* Munro-Smith (d 1989); *b* 26 May 1927; *Educ* King Williams Coll Isle of Man, Univ of Bristol (MB ChB), Faculty of Homoeopathy London (FF Hom); *m* 1, (m dis 1966), Hilary Cove; 1 s (Martin John b 16 April 1956), 1 da (Philippa b 3 May 1958); m 2, 26 July 1975, Susan Elizabeth, da of Tom Driver (d 1988), of Worthing; 2 s (Ben b 7 Oct 1977, Guy b 20 June 1982); *Career* Nat Serv Lt RA (Field) 1945-48; GP Knowle West Bristol 1959-; pres: Faculty of Homoeopathy Royal London Homoeopathic Hosp 1984-87, W Country Br Faculty of Homeopathy 1981-; chm Bristol Med Homoeopathic Gp, fndr memb W Country Flyfishers; *Recreations* fly fishing, sketching, family; *Clubs* Clifton (Bristol); *Style*— Dr John Hughes-Games; 22 Duchess Rd, Clifton, Bristol BS8 2LA (☎ 0272 735966); The William Budd Health Centre, Leinster Ave, Knowle, West Bristol 4 (☎ 0272 668404, car 0831 486222)

HUGHES HALLETT, Prof Andrew Jonathan; s of Vice Adm Sir Charles Hughes Hallett, KCB, CBE (d 1985), of Salisbury, Wilts, and Joyce Plumer, *née* Cobold; *b* 1 Nov 1947; *Educ* Radley, Univ of Warwick (BA), LSE (MSc), Nuffield Coll Oxford Univ (DPhil); *m* 22 July 1982, Claudia Ilse Luise, da of Karl Becker (d 1988), of Kassel, W Germany; 2 s (David b 1983, James b 1986), 1 da (Nicola b 1990); *Career* lectr in economics Univ of Bristol 1973-77, assoc prof of economics Erasmus Univ Rotterdam 1977-85, The David Dale Prof of Economics Univ of Newcastle upon Tyne 1985-89, Chair of Macro-economics Univ of Strathclyde 1989-; author papers: theory of economic policy, int economic policy, commodity markets and economic devpt, game theory, numerical analysis; fell Centre for Econ Policy Res; conslt to: UN, World Bank, EEC Cmmn, OECD, UNESCO, various govts; memb: Royal Econ Soc 1975, Euro Econ Assoc 1985; FRSA; *Books* Quantitative Economic Policies and Interactive Planning (1983), Applied Decision Analysis and Economic Behaviour (1984), Stabilising Speculative Commodity Markets (1987), Optimal Control, Expectations and Uncertainty (1989); *Recreations* hill walking, beer, jazz from the 30s, 40s and 50s, history; *Style*— Prof Andrew Hughes Hallett; Dept of Economics, University of Strathclyde, 100 Cathedral St, Glasgow G4 0LN (☎ 041 552 4400, telex 77472 UNSLIB G, fax 041 552 5589)

HUGHES-HALLETT, Michael Wyndham Norton; s of Lt-Col James Hughes-Hallett (d 1981), and Marjorie Eliza, *née* Collard; *b* 10 Nov 1926; *Educ* Eton; *m* 19 Oct 1948, Penelope Anne, da of Capt Sydney Fairbairn, MC (d 1943); 2 s (James b 1949, Thomas b 1954), 1 da (Lucy b 1952); *Career* WWII Lt Scots Gds 1943-46; pupil to Res Land Agent Sandringham Estate, res agent to OV Watney Esq, res agent and factor to Lord Dulverton and W Highland Woodlands Co, agent and sec Batsford Fndn; FRICS 1966; *Recreations* hunting, shooting, painting; *Clubs* Army & Navy, MCC; *Style*— Michael Hughes-Hallett, Esq; The Old Rectory, Barton on the Heath, Moreton-in-Marsh (☎ 0608 74349); Batsford Estate Office, Moreton in Marsh (☎ 0608 50722)

HUGHES-MORGAN, His Hon Judge; Sir David John; 3 Bt (UK 1925), of Penally, Pembroke; CB (Mil 1983), CBE (Mil 1973, MBE Mil 1959); s of Sir John Vernon Hughes-Morgan, 2 Bt (d 1969); *b* 11 Oct 1925; *Educ* RNC Dartmouth; *m* 1959, Isabel Jean Blacklock Gellatly Milne, da of John Milne Lindsay (d 1969), of Annan, Dumfriesshire; 3 s; *Heir* s, Parry Hughes-Morgan; *Career* Sub Lt RN, ret 1946; admitted slr 1950; cmmnd Army Legal Servs 1955, Brig Legal HQ UKLF 1976-78, dir Army Legal Servs BAOR 1978-80, dir Army Legal Servs (Maj Gen) MOD 1980-84; rec SE Circuit 1983-86, circuit judge 1986-; *Style*— His Hon Judge Sir David Hughes-Morgan, Bt, CB, CBE; c/o National Westminster Bank Ltd, 1 High St, Bromley, Kent BR1 1LL

HUGHES-MORGAN, (Ian) Parry David; s and h of Sir David John Hughes-Morgan, 3 Bt, CB, CBE; *b* 22 Feb 1960; *Style*— Parry Hughes-Morgan, Esq

HUGHES-ONSLOW, James Andrew; s of Andrew Hughes-Onslow (d 1979), and Betty Lee, half-sister of Lord Rossmore; gs of Capt Oliver Hughes-Onslow (d 1972), of Ayrshire; *b* 27 Aug 1945; *Educ* Castle Park Dublin, Eton; *m* 1982, Christina Louise, da of Peter Henry Hay, bro of Sir David Hay, of Aust; 1 s (Andrew b 1985), 2 da (Flora b 1988, Marina b 1990); *Career* sub ed and feature writer The Field 1968-70; reporter: Sunday Telegraph 1970-71, Daily Express 1971-73; columnist: The Spectator 1974-75, What's On in London 1976-82; columnist and feature writer London Evening Standard 1983-; articles and reviews in: Punch, The Times, The Field, Books and Bookmen, Business Traveller, The Spectator, Tatler, Country Times, Southside, The Illustrated London News, Country Living, The Melbourne Age, Sydney Morning Herald; *Recreations* travel; *Clubs* Boodle's; *Style*— James Hughes-Onslow, Esq; 42 Knatchbull Rd, Camberwell, London SE5 9QY (☎ 071 274 9347); The Evening Standard, 2 Derry St, London W8 5EE (☎ 071 938 8000)

HUGHES-PARRY, Thomas Antony; s of Maj Thomas Garrard Hughes-Parry, of Llangollen, Clwyd (d 1987), and Rachael Constance Luz, *née* Boger; *b* 9 Feb 1949; *Educ* Canford, Univ of Exeter (BSc); *m* 1 Jan 1976, Rosemary Constance, da of Robert James Foster; 2 s (Thomas David b 9 Sept 1981, Philip John b 19 Sept 1983); *Career* articled clerk Harmood Banner 1969-73, chartered accountant Investigation Dept Deloitte Haskins & Sells 1974-78, ptnr Beer Aplin 1979-; memb SW Soc Chartered Accountants Tech Advsy Ctee 1979- (delegate to London Ctee 1988-); Exeter District Soc of Chartered Accountants: careers advsr 1980-84, vice chm 1989-90, chm 1990-91; vice treas Exeter Cncl for Voluntary Service 1980-88, various offices Dawlish Round Table 1980-89, clerk to Govrs Maynard's Girls' Sch 1981, sec to Govrs Royal West of England Residential Sch for the Deaf 1986-, adult educn lectr 1986-, chm Exeter Voluntary Trading Enterprizes 1988-; FCA; *Recreations* squash, walking, gardening, yoga, windsurfing, classical music, reading; *Clubs* Exeter and County; *Style*— Thomas Hughes-Parry, Esq; Tregenna, 14 Longlands, Dawlish, Devon EX7 9NF (☎ 0626 863653); Beer Aplin, 17 Southernhay West, Exeter, Devon EX1 1PP (☎ 0392 77325, fax 0392 420927)

HUGHES-RECKITT, John Brian; s of Col Brian Holland Hughes-Reckitt, TD (d 1970), of Sproughton Hall, Ipswich, Suffolk, and Nancie Hughes-Reckitt (d 1979); *b* 16 Jan 1930; *Educ* Shrewsbury; *Career* Nat Serv 10 Royal Hussars (PWO) 1948-50; wine merchant Block Grey Block Ltd (London) 1950-72; hon treas Pedro Youth Club Hackney 1960-; memb Worshipful Co of Vintners; *Recreations* gardening, tennis, skiing; *Clubs* Cavalry and Guards'; *Style*— John Hughes-Reckitt, Esq; Pinswell Plantation, Colesbourne, Cheltenham, Glos GL53 9NP (☎ 024287 340); 32 Iffley Rd, London W6 0PA (☎ 081 741 1979)

HUGHES-WAKE-WALKER; *see*: Wake-Walker

HUGHESDON, Charles Frederick; AFC (1943); *b* 10 Dec 1909; *Educ* Raine's GS; *m* 1937, Florence Elizabeth (the actress Florence Desmond), wid of Capt Tom Campbell Black; 1 child; *Career* chm: Stewart Smith Group of Companies, Stewart Wrightson Group of Companies (until ret 1976), Tradewinds Helicopters Ltd, Charles Street Co; former chm and dir Tradewinds Airways Ltd; dir: Headington Brokers Ltd, Aeronautical Tst Ltd; hon treas Royal Aeronautical Soc 1969-85; FRAeS; kt of the Order of the Cedar (Lebanese Republic 1972); *Recreations* horse riding, shooting, water skiing, yachting, flying helicopters; *Clubs* RAF, Royal Thames Yacht; *Style*— Charles Hughesdon, Esq, AFC; Dunsborough Park, Ripley, Surrey GU23 6AL (☎ 0483 225366)

HUGHESDON, John Stephen; s of Eric Hughesdon, of Crowborough, Sussex, and Olive Mona, *née* Quirk (d 1980); *b* 9 Jan 1944; *Educ* Eltham Coll; *m* Mavis June, da of Charles Henry George Eburne, OBE; 1 s (Simon Charles b 18 Aug 1978), 1 da (b 22

Nov 1975); *Career* Peat Marwick Mitchell 1962-73 (articled 1962-66), ptnr Neville Russell 1977- (mangr 1973-77); sometime chm Practice Events Working Pty of LSCA, former memb Audit and Accountancy Advsy Ctee ICA, memb sub-ctee Auditing Practices Ctee, hon treas Girl's Bde Nat Cncl Eng & W 1979-; Freeman City of London, memb Guild of Freeman of City of London; FCA 1977 (ACA 1967); *Recreations* church, squash, golf; *Clubs* City Livery, Bishopsgate Ward; *Style—* John Hughesdon, Esq; 44 Christchurch Rd, Sidcup, Kent DA15 7HQ (☎ 081 300 6648); Neville Russell, 246 Bishopsgate, London EC2M 4PB (☎ 071 377 1000, fax 071 377 8931)

HUGHFF, Victor William; s of William Scott Hughff (d 1974), and Alice Doris, *née* Kerry (d 1988); *b* 30 May 1931; *Educ* City of Norwich; *m* 1955, Grace Margaret; 1 s (David), 1 da (Joanna); *Career* insur exec, chief gen mangr Norwich Union Insurance Group 1984-89; dir 1981-89: Norwich Union Life Insurance Society, Norwich Union Fire Insurance Society Ltd, Scottish Union & Nat Insurance Co, Maritime Insurance Co Ltd, Norwich Union Holdings plc, Norwich General Trust Ltd, Castle Finance Ltd, Norwich Union (Services) Ltd; dir Norwich Winterthur Holdings Ltd 1984-89; dir 1989-: Stalwart Assurance Group; plc, Congregational & General Insurance plc; memb Cncl Nat Assoc of Victim Support Schemes 1989-, chm Norwich and Dist Victim Support, elder United Reformed Church; FIA, CBIM; *Recreations* tennis, badminton; *Style—* Victor Hughff, Esq; 18 Hilly Plantation, Thorpe St Andrew, Norwich NR7 0JN (☎ 0603 34517)

HUGILL, John; QC (1976); s of John Alfred Hugill (d 1950), and Alice, *née* Clarke (d 1982); *b* 11 Aug 1930; *Educ* Fettes, Trinity Hall Cambridge (MA); *m* 1956, Patricia Elizabeth, da of Stanley Welton (d 1966), of Cheshire; 2 da (Gail b 1962, Rebecca b 1968); *Career* RA 1949-50 2 Lt, Capt RA (T); barr 1954, asst rec Bolton 1971 (rec 1972), rec 1972, bencher Middle Temple 1984; memb Senate of the Inns of Ct and the Bar 1984-86; memb Gen Cncl of the Bar 1987-89; chm: Darryn Clarke Inquiry 1979, Stanley Royd Inquiry 1985; *Recreations* sailing; *Style—* John Hugill, Esq, QC; 2 Old Bank St, Manchester M2 7PF (☎ 061 832 3791, car 0836 584211)

HUGO, Lt-Col Sir John Mandeville; KCVO (1969, CVO 1959), OBE (1947); s of R M Hugo (d 1921), and Marion, *née* Dickins (d 1942); *b* 1 July 1899; *Educ* Marlborough, RMA Woolwich; *m* 1952, Joan Winifred Hill; 2 da (Nicola-Jane, Tessa); *Career* WWI 2 Lt RFA 1917, appointed to RHA 1922, served WWII with 7 Light Cavalry (India), Lt-Col; cmd: Bombay Body Guard 1937-38, Bengal Body Guard 1938-39; mil sec to Govr Bengal 1939-40 and 1946-47; asst ceremonial sec CRO 1948-52, ceremonial and protocol sec 1952-69; gentleman usher to HM The Queen 1952-69 (extra gentleman usher 1969-); *Clubs* Army and Navy; *Style—* Lt-Col Sir John Hugo, KCVO, OBE; Hilltop House, Vines Cross, Heathfield, E Sussex (☎ 04353 2562)

HUHNE, Christopher Murray Paul; s of Peter Ivor Paul Huhne, and Margaret Ann Gladstone, *née* Murray; *b* 2 July 1954; *Educ* Westminster, Sorbonne, Magdalen Coll Oxford (BA); *m* 19 May 1984, Vicky, da of Nicholas Courmouzis (d 1987); 1 s (Nicholas b 1985), 1 da (Lydia b 1976), 2 step da (Georgia b 1976, Alexandra b 1979); *Career* freelance journalist 1975-76, graduate trainee Liverpool Daily Post 1976-77, Brussels corr The Economist 1977-80, economics ed The Guardian 1984- (economics leader writer 1980-84), business and economics ed The Independent on Sunday; author of various articles in academic jls; Parly candidate (SDP-Lib Alliance) Reading E 1983, Oxford W and Abingdon 1987; Freeman City of Osaka Japan 1985; memb: Royal Econ Soc, NUJ; *Books* Debt and Danger: The World Financial Crisis (with Lord Lever, 1985), Real World Economics (1990); *Recreations* cinema, gardening, family; *Style—* Christopher Huhne, Esq; 5 Crescent Grove, London SW4 7AHH (☎ 071 498 2618)

HULBERT-POWELL, Hon Mrs (Philippa Catherine); *née* St Aubyn; da of late 3 Baron St Levan and Hon Clementina, *née* Nicolson, da of 1 Baron Carnock; n of late Harold Nicolson, the writer, and 1 cous of Nigel Nicolson, the biographer; *b* 19 June 1922; *Educ* LSE; *m* 1948, Evelyn Charles Lacy Hulbert-Powell, (Lt Queen's Own Royal Regt, d 1985), only s of Rev Canon Charles Lacy Hulbert-Powell (d 1959), of Cambridge; 2 s, 3 da; *Recreations* gardening; *Style—* The Hon Mrs Hulbert-Powell; Park Farm, Rotherfield Lane, Mayfield, Sussex (☎ 0435 873222)

HULL, Prof Derek; s of William Hull (d 1974), of Blackpool, and Nellie, *née* Hayes (d 1958); *b* 8 Aug 1931; *Educ* Baines GS Poulton-Le-Fylde, Univ of Wales (BSc, PhD, DSc); *m* 5 Aug 1953, Pauline, da of Norman Scott (d 1950), of Halifax; 1 s (Andrew b 1956), 4 da (Sian b 1958, Karen b 1961, Beverley b 1965, Alison b 1967); *Career* section ldr AERE Harwell 1956-60; Univ of Liverpool: lectr 1960-62, sr Lectr 1962-64, prof 1964-84, dean of engrg 1971-74, pro vice chllr 1983-84; Goldsmiths prof Univ of Cambridge 1984-; Hon DTech Tampere Univ Finland 1987; FIM 1966, FPRI 1978, FEng 1986, FRS 1989; *Books* Introduction to Dislocations, An Introduction to Composite Materials; *Recreations* golf, fell walking, music; *Clubs* Gog Magog Golf, Heswall Golf; *Style—* Prof Derek Hull, FRS; 1 Chaucer Close, Cambridge CB2 2TS; Dept of Materials Science and Metallurgy, Univ of Cambridge, Pembroke St, Cambridge CB2 3QZ (☎ 0223 334305, fax 0223 334567)

HULL, Bishop of 1981; Rt Rev Donald George Snelgrove; TD (1973); s of William Henry Snelgrove (d 1956), of London and Plymouth, and Beatrice, *née* Upshall; *b* 21 April 1925; *Educ* Christ's Coll Finchley, Devonport HS, Queens' Coll Cambridge (MA); *m* 1949, Sylvia May, da of Charles Lowe (d 1962), of Derbyshire; 1 s (John b 1956), 1 da (Elizabeth b 1957); *Career* Sub Lt RNVR UK and Far East 1943-46; Royal Army Chaplains Dept 1960-74; ordained St Paul's Cathedral 1950; curate: St Thomas Oakwood 1950-53, St Anselm Hatch End 1953-56; vicar: Dronfield Derbyshire 1956-62, Hessle 1963-70; rural dean of Kingston upon Hull 1966-70, canon and prebendary of York 1969-81, archdeacon of the E Riding 1970-81, rector of Cherry Burton 1970-78; dir: Central Bd of Fin of C of E 1975-, Ecclesiastical Insurance Group 1978-, Church Schools Co Ltd 1981-, Yorks TV Telethon Trust Ltd 1987-; *Style—* The Rt Rev the Bishop of Hull, TD; Hullen House, Woodfield Lane, Hessle HU13 0ES (☎ 0482 649019)

HULL, Howard Antony; s of Michael Dias Hull (d 1982), and Phyllis Fairchild, *née* Proctor; *b* 26 Nov 1953; *Educ* Christ's Hospital Horsham, St Peter's Coll Oxford (MA); *m* 2 Aug 1977, Janet Elizabeth, da of Thomas Edward Lacy, of Lancs; *Career* schoolmaster Gordonstoun 1976-79, charity fund raising and devpt conslt 1980-, sr ptnr The Support Gp 1985-88; dir: China Challenge Ltd 1986-, devpt Acad of St Martin in the Fields 1988-90, devpt Liverpool Poly 1990-, dir The Liverpool Polytechnic Trust 1991-; tstee: Portland Sculptures Tst; memb: Advsy Cncl The Butler Tst, London Sketch Club; FRGS, MICFM; *Recreations* painting, kora music, the outdoors; *Clubs* Lansdowne; *Style—* Howard A Hull, Esq; 6 Sandlea House, Sandlea Park, West Kirby, Wirral (☎ 051 625 2098)

HULL, Janet Elizabeth; da of Thomas Edward Lacy (d 1989), of Southport, and Marjorie, *née* Forster; *b* 20 March 1955; *Educ* Southport HS for Girls, St Anne's Coll Oxford (BA), Napier Coll Edinburgh (DEML); *m* 1977 (m dis 1988), Howard Anthony Hull; *Career* advtg exec; account exec Ted Bates Ltd 1979-80, account mangr then account dir Abbott Mead Vickers SMS Ltd 1980-85, account dir then assoc dir Geer Gross Ltd 1985-86; Young & Rubicam Ltd 1986-: Bd account dir 1987, gp account dir 1988, head of account mgmnt 1990, memb Exec Ctee 1991; md Y & R Capital Image (Corporate Communications) 1990-; awarded numerous travelling scholarships and secondments; Hon MA Univ of Oxford 1989; memb Women's Advtg Club of London 1978, MInstD 1990; *Recreations* food and wine, classic cars, video film-making; *Clubs* Reform; *Style—* Ms Janet Hull; Young & Rubicam Ltd, Greater London House, Hampstead Rd, London NW1 7QP (☎ 071 380 6433)

HULL, John Folliott Charles; s of Sir Hubert Hull, CBE (d 1976), and Judith, *née* Stokes (d 1937); *b* 21 Oct 1925; *Educ* Downside, Jesus Coll Cambridge (MA); *m* 1951, Rosemarie Kathleen, da of Col Herbert Waring (d 1961); 1 s (Jonathan), 3 da (Judith-Rose, Charlotte, Victoria); *Career* Capt RA 1944-48, served with RIA 1945-48; called to the Bar Inner Temple 1952; dir: J Henry Schroder Wagg & Co Ltd 1961-72 and 1974-85 (md 1961-72, dep chm 1974-77, chm 1977-83), Schroders plc 1969-72 and 1974-85 (dep chm 1977-), Lucas Industries plc 1975-90, Legal & General Assurance Society 1976-79, Legal & General Group plc 1979-90, Goodwood Racecourse Limited 1987-; chm City Co Law Ctee 1976-79, dep chm Land Securities plc 1976-; memb cncl Manchester Business Sch 1974-86, lay memb Stock Exchange 1983-84; dep chm City Panel on Takeovers and Mergers 1987- (dir-gen 1972-74); *Recreations* reading political history, 19th century novelists; *Clubs* MCC; *Style—* John Hull, Esq; 33 Edwardes Square, London W8 6HH (☎ 071 603 0715); Little Norton, Norton sub Hamdon, Stoke sub Hamdon, Somerset (☎ 093 588 465); J Henry Schroder Wagg & Co Ltd, 120 Cheapside, London EC2V 6DS (☎ 071 382 6000, telex 885029)

HULL, John Grove; QC (1983); s of Tom Edward Orridge Hull (d 1957), and Marjorie Ethel Whitaker, *née* Dinsley; *b* 21 Aug 1931; *Educ* Rugby, King's Coll Cambridge (MA, LLB); *m* 1961, Gillian Ann, da of Leslie Fawcett Stemp (d 1968); 2 da (Katharine b 1965, Caroline b 1968); *Career* Nat Serv in RE 1954-56, 2 Lt; called to the Bar 1958; rec 1983; *Recreations* gardening, English literature; *Style—* John Hull, Esq, QC; Ravenshoe, 16 High Trees Rd, Reigate, Surrey RH2 7ES (☎ 0737 245181); Lamb Building, Temple, EC4Y 7AS (☎ 071 353 6381/2)

HULL, Hon Mrs (Patricia Ann); da of Baron Carron (Life Peer, d 1969); *b* 1945; *m* 1970, Victor Albert Hull and has issue; *Style—* The Hon Mrs Hull; c/o The Mrs Weidemann, The Gables, 27 Bromley Rd, London SE6 2TS

HULL, Paul Anthony; s of Cordell Benjamin Hull, and Eula Elizabeth, *née* Cargill; *b* 17 May 1968; *Educ* The Gordon Boy's Sch West End, Woking Surrey; *Career* Rugby Union fly half and centre Bristol FC; youth footballer Belmont Utd Harrow, Southampton trialist; clubs: RAF XV, Bristol FC; rep: Bucks Colts, RAF Colts and U21, Combined Servs Colts and U21, S and SW U21, S and SW Div, London Div, Eng Colts (3 caps at centre), Eng U21, Eng B (debut v Fiji 1990); England toured Argentina 1990; corpl and physical training instructor RAF 1989- (joined 1985); *Recreations* all sports, music (soul), good time (night life); *Style—* Paul Hull, Esq; Physical Education Flight, RAF Locking, Weston-super-Mare, Avon BS24 7AA (☎ 0934 822131 ext 435)

HULL, Robin; *b* 13 April 1934; *Educ* PCL (BSc), Imperial Coll of Sci and Technol London (MSc,DIC); *Career* RG Lewis Ltd 1972- (conslt 1978-), Rank Pullin Controls Ltd 1978-85, optical expert GEC Research Ltd 1985-86, optical designer and fndr Thin Film Coating Dept Lanarealm Ltd 1986-; author of paper Software for Thin Film Design and Production (1983); Williamson Res award 1978; ARPS, FBIPP, MInstP, CPhys; *Style—* Robin Hull, Esq; 11 Hulton Close, Boreham, Chelmsford, Essex CM3 3BU (☎ 0245 460117)

HULL, Rodney Stephen (Rod); s of Leonard Sidney Hull, of Hampstead Cottage Marina, Yalding, Kent, and Hilda Primrose, *née* Hughes (d 1975); *b* 13 Aug 1935; *Educ* Scheerness Tech Sch; *m* 1, 1959 (m dis 1973), Sandra Carter; 2 s (Deborah b 1961, Danielle b 1966); m 2, 1978, Cheryle Hylton; 2 s (Tobias James Leonard b 1977, Oliver Thomas Stephen b 1980), 1 da (Amelia Charlotte Primrose b 1979), 1 step da (Catrina Lee b 1969); *Career* elctrical apprentice 1951-56; emigrated to Aust 1958, TCN TV Channel 9 Sydney: prodr of children's progs, developed puppet Emu, writer and presenter of children's show; returned to UK 1970; performed as Rod Hull and Emu Royal Variety Show (Palladium) 1972, TV series with BBC and ITV; fndr Children's Royal Variety Show 1980; Freeman City of London; *Publications* poetry: The Reluctant Pote (1983); *Recreations* gardening, golf; *Clubs* Lords Taveners; *Style—* Rod Hull, Esq; Hilbou Productions, International Artistes, 235 Regent st, London W1 (☎ 071 439 8401)

HULLAND, Cdr Scott; s of Frederick Scott Hulland (d 1990), of Duffield, Derbyshire, and Ethel Vera Hulland (d 1973); *b* 13 March 1948; *Educ* Derby Sch, RN Engrg Coll (BSc), RNC Greenwich (MSc); *m* 16 Sept 1978, Deborah Margaret, da of Angus McKerrow Baird (d 1984), of Saltash Cornwall; *Career* RN Offr engrg specialization, currently serving in MOD(N); CEng, MIMechE, MINucE; *Recreations* gardening, singing, stamp collecting; *Style—* Cdr Scott Hulland

HULME, Geoffrey Gordon; CB (1984); s of Alfred Hulme, and Jessie Hulme; *b* 8 March 1931; *Educ* Kings Sch Macclesfield, CCC Oxford (MA); *m* 1951, Shirley Leigh, da of Herbert Cumberlidge (d 1980); 1 s (Andrew), 1 da (Alison); *Career* DHSS: joined min 1953, under sec 1974, dep sec and princ fin offr 1981-86; dir Public Expenditure Policy Unit 1986-; *Recreations* usual things, collecting edible fungi; *Clubs* Royal Automobile; *Style—* Geoffrey Hulme, Esq, CB; 163A Kennington Park Rd, London SE11; Stone Farm, Little Cornard, Sudbury, Suffolk; Public Finance Fndn, 3 Robert St, London WC2

HULME, Maj-Gen Jerrie Anthony; CB (1990); s of Stanley Hulme (d 1964), and Laurel, *née* Stockwin (d 1986); *b* 10 Aug 1935; *Educ* King Henry VIII Sch Coventry; *m* 1, Dec 1959 (m dis 1974), (Margaret May) Maureen, da of Godfrey Turton (d 1973); 2 s (Nicolas b 4 Oct 1961, Michael b 5 Oct 1965), 2 da (Katie b 2 Nov 1960, Sarah b 10 April 1963); m 2, Dec 1974, Janet Kathleen, *née* Mills; *Career* Nat Serv RAOC 1953-66, regtl appts Kenya Persian Gulf Aden 1956-66, Staff Coll Camberley 1966, staff appts 1967-70, Jt Servs Staff Coll Latimer 1970, Dir staff at Staff Coll 1971-74, cmd RAOC HQ 4 Div 1974-76, staff appt 1976-78, Col Staff Coll 1978-81, staff appt 1981-82, Dept Dir Gen of Ordnance Servs 1982-85, Dir logistic operations Army MOD 1985-88, Dir Gen ordnance servs 1988-; Freeman City of London 1986, Liveryman Worshipful Co of Gold and Silver Wyre Drawers 1990; FIPS 1987; *Clubs* Army and Navy, St James's; *Style—* Maj-Gen Jerrie Hulme, CB; c/o Lloyds Bank, 21-23 The Square, Kenilworth, Warks CV8 1EE

HULME, John; s of Arthur Hulme (d 1971), of Macclesfield, Cheshire, and Edith, *née* Bullock (d 1962); *b* 12 May 1933; *Educ* King's Sch Macclesfield, King's Coll Cambridge (BA, CertEd, MA); *m* 25 May 1957, Susanne, da of Dr Philipp Schwarz (d 1963), of Berlin, Germany; 1 s (Peter b 1965), 3 da (Caroline b 1958, Elizabeth b 1960, Nicola b 1962); *Career* Sqdn Ldr RAF Educn Branch 1957-72 (UK, Germany, Cyprus); asst educn offr London Boroughs of Barnet and Harrow 1972-88; writer, German interpreter and translator; *Books* Mörder Guss Reims (1981 and 1985), Les Oeuvres Complètes de Lord Charles (1984), Die Gesammelten Werke des Lord Charles (1984 and 1985), Guillaume Chèquespierre (1985), 1789 and All That (1988), De Inventione Nursery Rhymes (1990), De Cantus Volx (1990); *Recreations* travel, languages, writing, food and wine, squash, chess; *Style—* John Hulme, Esq; 27 Devereux Drive, Watford, Herts (☎ 0923 34560)

HULSE, Edward Jeremy Westrow; s and h of Sir (Hamilton) Westrow Hulse, 9 Bt; *b* 22 Nov 1932; *Educ* Eton; *m* 1957, Verity Ann, da of William Pilkington, of Ivywell, Routes des Issues, St John, Jersey; 1 s, 1 da; *Career* late Capt Scots Gds, High Sheriff of Hants 1978; *Style—* Edward Hulse, Esq, DL; Breamore House, nr

Fordingbridge, Hants (☎ 0725 22233)

HULSE, Richard Arthur Samuel; 2 s of Sir Westrow Hulse, 9 Bt; *b* 22 March 1936; *Educ* Eton; *m* 1963, Caroline Susan Joan, da of Sir George Tapps-Gervis Meyrick, 6 Bt, MC; 1 s (George Richard b 1967), 1 da (Frances Jacintha Caroline b 1968); *Career* 2 Lt Scots Guards Nat Serv in Germany; dir: Bain Dawes (Int) Ltd 1972-80, Robert Barrow Ltd 1980-84; chm Pitman & Co Ltd 1985-86, dir K C Webb & Co Ltd 1986-88, chm Willmead Ltd; *Recreations* shooting, fishing, gardening, backgammon, racing; *Clubs* White's; *Style*— Richard Hulse, Esq; Sherfield Mill, Sherfield English, nr Romsey, Hants (☎ 0794 22536)

HULSE, Sir (Hamilton) Westrow; 9 Bt (GB 1739), of Lincoln's Inn Fields; o s of Sir Hamilton John Hulse, 8 Bt (d 1931), and Estelle, *née* Campbell (d 1933); the 1 Bt was physician to Queen Anne, and to Kings George I and George II; *b* 20 June 1909; *Educ* Eton, ChCh Oxford; *m* 1, 7 Jan 1932 (m dis 1937), Philippa Mabel, yr da of late Arthur James Taylor, of Strensham Court, Worcs; 2 s; m 2, 3 June 1938, Ambrosine Nellie Orr (d 1940), o da of late Capt Herbert Stanley Orr Wilson, of Dunardagh, Blackrock, Co Dublin; m 3, 23 Oct 1945 (m dis 1954), Dorothy, da of late William Durran, and widow of James Anderson McKay Hamilton; m 4, 8 July 1954, Lucy Elizabeth Smitheyt, da of Col George Redesdale Brooker Spain, CMG, TD; *Heir* s, Edward Jeremy Westrow Hulse, *qv*; *Career* Wing Cdr RAF Vol Reserve, served WWII (despatches); called to the Bar Inner Temple 1932; *Clubs* Carlton, Leander; *Style*— Sir Westrow Hulse, Bt; Breamore, Hants (☎ 0725 22773)

HULTON, Sir Geoffrey Alan; 4 Bt (UK 1905), JP (Lancs 1955), DL (Greater Manchester 1974); s of Sir Roger Braddyll Hulton, 3 Bt (d 1956), and Hon Marjorie Evelyn Louise (d 1970), da of late 6 Viscount Mountmorres; *b* 21 Jan 1920; *Educ* Marlborough; *m* 1945, Mary Patricia, da of P A de Vere Reynolds, of Farnborough, Hants; *Heir* none; *Career* Capt RM (ret), Far East 1941-45 (POW); owner of Hulton Park Estate, pres Bolton West Constituency Cons Assoc, vice pres Lancs Co Cricket Club, memb Country Landowners' Assoc Lancs (former vice pres); Knight Cdr Order St Gregory The Great, Knight Cdr with Star Order of Holy Sepulchre; *Clubs* Victory; *Style*— Sir Geoffrey Hulton, Bt, JP, DL; The Cottage, Hulton Park, Over Hulton, Bolton BL5 1BE (☎ 0204 651324)

HUM, Christopher Owen; s of Norman Charles Hum (d 1950), and Muriel Kathleen, *née* Hines; *b* 27 Jan 1946; *Educ* Berkhamsted Sch, Pembroke Coll Cambridge (MA), Univ of Hong Kong; *m* 31 Oct 1970, Julia Mary, da of Sir Hugh Park *qv*, of London and Cornwall; 1 s (Jonathan b 1976), 1 da (Olivia b 1974); *Career* joined FCO 1967; Hong Kong 1968-70, Peking 1971-73, off of UK perm rep to the EEC Brussels 1973-75, FCO 1975-79, Peking 1979-81, Paris 1981-83; Hong Kong Dept FCO: asst head 1983, cnsllr 1985, head 1986-89; dep head Falkland Islands Dept FCO 1985-86, cnsllr and head of chancery UK Mission to the UN NYC 1989-; *Recreations* music (piano, viola), walking; *Style*— Christopher Hum, Esq; c/o Foreign and Commonwealth Office, King Charles Street, London SW1A 2AH; United Kingdom Mission to the United Nations, 845 Third Ave, New York NY 10022

HUMAN, (Henry) Robin John; s of Roger Henry Charles Human (d 1942), and Rosalind Mary, *née* Gepp; *b* 5 Oct 1937; *Educ* Repton Sch Derbyshire, Clare Coll Cambridge (BA); *m* 4 Nov 1961, Alison Phyllida, da of Dr Oliver Frederick Thompson; 1 s (Charles Robin Graham b 21 June 1963), 1 da (Joanna Alison b 7 April 1965); *Career* admitted slr 1965; ptnr Linklaters & Paines 1969 (joined 1962); memb: City of London Solicitors Co, Bd of Crown Agents 1986-; *Recreations* golf, shooting; *Clubs* MCC; *Style*— Robin Human, Esq; Linklaters & Paines, 59-67 Gresham St, London EC2V 7JA (☎ 071 606 7080, fax 071 606 5113)

HUMBLE, James Kenneth; s of Joseph Humble, and Alice, *née* Rhodes; *b* 8 May 1936; *m* 1962, Freda, da of George Frederick Holden, OBE (d 1964); 3 da (Josephine Clare b 1964, Rebecca Jane b 1965, Sarah Louise b 1966); *Career* dir Metrician Board 1978-80, chief Trading Standards Croydon 1967-73, supt metrology Nigeria 1962-66, dir Nat Metrological Coordinating Unit 1980-88; asst dir Office of Fair Trading 1973-78, chief exec Local Authy Coordinating Body on Trading Standards (Lacots) 1980-; memb: Methven Ctee 1976, Eden Ctee 1987, Cars Ctee 1984-; chm Euro Ctee of Experts 1976-; professional Rugby League 1958-62; DMS, DCA, FITSA; *Recreations* golf, bridge, opera; *Style*— James Humble, Esq; 153 Upperselsdon Rd, Croydon, Surrey (☎ 081 657 6170); PO Box 6, Token House, Croydon (☎ 081 688 1996)

HUME, Sir Alan Blyth; CB (1963); s of Walter Alan Hume (d 1937); *b* 5 Jan 1913; *Educ* George Heriot's Sch Edinburgh, Univ of Edinburgh (MA); *m* 1943, Marion Morton, da of William Garrett, QC; 1 s, 1 da; *Career* Scottish Office 1936-: asst under sec of state 1959-62, under sec Miny of Public Bldg and Works 1963-64, sec Scottish Devpt Dept 1965-73; chm: Ancient Monuments Bd Scotland 1973-81, Edinburgh New Town Conservation Ctee 1975-90; kt 1973; *Recreations* golf, fishing; *Clubs* New (Edinburgh), English Speaking Union; *Style*— Sir Alan Hume, CB; 12 Oswald Rd, Edinburgh, Scotland EH9 2HJ (☎ 031 667 2440)

HUME, Lady Catherine Mary Clementina; *née* Heathcote-Drummond-Willoughby; da of 2 Earl of Ancaster, GCVO, TD; co-heiress to Barony of niece, Baroness Willoughby de Eresby, *qv*; *b* 25 Sept 1906; *m* 1, 1935 (m dis 1947), John St Maur Ramsden (assas in Malaya 1948), s of Sir John Ramsden, 6 Bt; 1 da; m 2, 1948, Charles Wedderburn Hume (d 1974); *Style*— The Lady Catherine Hume; Hunting Ridge Farm, 2670 Ridge Rd, Charlottesville, Va 22901, USA

HUME, James Douglas Howden; CBE (1983); s of James Howden Hume (d 1981), and Kathleen Douglas, *née* Macfarlane (d 1973); *b* 4 May 1928; *Educ* Loretto, Royal Tech Coll, Univ of Glasgow (BSc), Univ of Strathclyde (LLD); *m* 1950, June Katharine, da of Sir Frank Spencer Spriggs, KBE (d 1969); 1 s (Duncan), 2 da (Evelyn (d 1989), Clare); *Career* chm: Howden Gp 1987 (dir 1957, md 1963, dep chm and md 1973), Drimard Ltd 1988; non exec dir: Cleaning Technol Ltd 1989, Ferrum Hldgs plc 1990; FIMechE; *Recreations* sailing; *Clubs* Royal Northern and Clyde Yacht, Royal Thames Yacht, Western; *Style*— J D H Hume, Esq, CBE; Drimard Ltd, 22 East Lennox Drive, Helensburgh, Dunbartonshire G84 9JD (☎ 0436 75132)

HUME, John; MP (SDLP) Foyle 1983-, MEP Socialist Group (EP) NI 1979-; *b* 18 Jan 1937; *Educ* St Columb's Coll, Nat Univ of Ireland; *m* 1951, Patricia Hone, 2 s, 2 da; *Career* pres Irish League of Credit Unions 1964-69; Derry civil rights leader 1968-70, Ind Stormont MP 1969-72; elected NI Assembly 1973, NI Convention 1975-76, special advsr to EEC Cmmr Burke 1977-79; memb: New Ireland Forum 1983-84, Irish TGWU (now SIPTU); fndr memb SDLP (dep ldr 1970-79, ldr 1979-), min for Commerce (in power-sharing exec) 1974; sponsor: Irish Anti-Apartheid Movement, Europeans for Nuclear Disarmament; memb Advsy Ctee on Protection of the Sea 1988-; Hon DUniv: Univ of Massachusetts 1985, Catholic Univ of America 1986, St Josephs University Philadelphia 1986, Tusculum Coll Tennesse 1988; assoc fell Center for Int Affrs Harvard 1976, res fell European studies Trinity Coll Dublin 1976-77; *Style*— John Hume, Esq, MP, MEP; 6 West End Park, Derry, Northern Ireland

HUME, Brig Richard Trevor Pierce; s of Capt Trevor Hume (d 1968), of Ongar, Essex, and Sybil Clare, *née* Lacy (d 1960); *b* 5 May 1934; *Educ* Ampleforth, RMA Sandhurst; *m* 1, 25 April 1962 (m dis), Gillian, da of Cdr Hodson, RN (d 1962); 1 da (Deirdre b 1963); m 2, 29 April 1971, Jane, da of Sir Eric Tansley, CMG, of London; 2 step s, 1 step da; *Career* cmmnd Irish Gds 1954, served Middle East, Far East, Europe, USA, Canada, Falklands, UK, NI; cmd: 1 Bn Irish Gds 1974-77, Irish Gds Regt 1979-81, 2 Inf Bde 1982-84 Fortress Gibraltar 1984-86; ret 1987; bursar St Catherine's Sch 1987-; res govr and dep constable Dover Castle, Dep Lord Warden Cinque Ports 1981-84; *Clubs* Army and Navy; *Style*— Brig Richard Hume; Little Orchard, Blackheath, Guildford, Surrey GU4 8QY (☎ 0483 892216); St Catherine's School, Bramley, Guildford, Surrey GU5 0DF (☎ 0483 892562)

HUME, Dr Robert; *b* 6 Jan 1928; *Educ* Ayr Acad, Bella Houston Acad, Univ of Glasgow (MB ChB, MD, DSc); *m* 1 June 1959, Kathleen Ann Ogilvie; 2 s (Robert, David), 1 da (Morag); *Career* Nat Serv Intelligence Corps, cmmnd Gordon Highlanders India and Germany 1946-48; Univ of Glasgow: Hutcheson Res Scholar 1955-56, Hall Fellowship 1956059, hon clinical lectr 1965, hon sub dean faculty of med 1988; conslt physician Southern Gen Hosp Glasgow 1965; author of numerous pubns on haemotological vascular disorders; memb BMA 1954, memb Scot Soc for Experimental Med 1955-, memb Br Soc for Haemotology 1960, memb Res Support Gp Gtr Glasgow Health Bd 1978, memb Intercollegiate Standing Ctee on Nuclear Med UK 1980-83, memb Scot cncl BMA 1980-83, chm Sub Ctee in med Gtr Glasgow Health Bd 1985, visitor and pres elect RCPSGlas 1988- (hon registrar in examinations 1971-83); memb Scot Soc of Physicians 1965, FRCPSGlas 1968 (Edinburgh 1969), memb Assoc of Physicians of GB and Ireland 1971; *Recreations* hillwalking, reading, opera, TV; *Clubs* Scott Royal Automobile, Cwlth Tst; *Style*— Dr Robert Hume; 6 Rubislaw Drive, Bearsden, Glasgow G61 1PR (☎ 041 942 5331); Southern General Hospital, Glasgow G51 4TF (☎ 041 445 2466)

HUME-WILLIAMS, Lady; Frances Mary; da of Edmond Arthur Hudson Groom, OBE, of Warham, Wells, Norfolk; *b* 4 Jan 1911; *m* 1949, as his 2 w, Sir Roy Ellis Hume-Williams, 2 and last Bt (d 1980), s of Rt Hon Sir William Ellis Hume-Williams, KBE, KC; *Recreations* flower arranging, gardening; *Style*— Lady Hume-Williams; Ardlui, The Highlands, East Horsley, Leatherhead, Surrey

HUMFREY, Lady Emma Mary Helena; *née* French; 3 da of 3 Earl of Ypres by his 1 w Maureen; *b* 8 Dec 1958; *Educ* private tutor; *m* 1980 (m dis 1989), Charles Geoffrey Humfrey, s of Charles Michael Humfrey, of Alderney; 1 s (Charles b 1986); *Style*— The Lady Emma Humfrey; Stow Bedon Hall, Attleborough, Norfolk

HUMM, Roger Frederick; s of Leonard Edward Humm, MBE (d 1964), and Gladys, *née* Prevotat (d 1986); *b* 7 March 1937; *Educ* Hampton Sch, Univ of Sheffield (BA); *m* 1966 (m dis), Marion Frances, *née* Czechman; *Career* md Ford Motor Co Ltd 1986-90 (div 1980-90); Liveryman Worshipful Co of Carmen; FIMI, CBIM, FID, FRSA; *Recreations* golf, scuba diving, writing, Harlequins; *Clubs* RAC, Variety of GB, Lord's Taverners; *Style*— Roger F Humm, Esq; c/o The Clock House, Kelvedon, Essex CO5 9DG

HUMMEL, Dr Frederick Cornelius; s of Cornelius Hummel, OBE (d 1972), and Caroline, *née* Riefler (d 1973); *b* 28 April 1915; *Educ* Humanistisches Gymnasium St Stephan Ausburg, Wadham Coll Oxford (MA, DPhil, BSc); *m* 1, 25 Jan 1941 (m dis 1961), Agnes Kathleen, *née* Rushforth; 1 s (Antony b 1941); m 2, 1961, Floriana Rosemary Silvia, da of William George Hollyer; 3 da (Anna b 1961, Silvia b 1963, Julia b 1964); *Career* Sgt and Lt KAR E African Forces 1939-43; dist forestry offr Uganda 1938-39 and 1943-45; Forestry Cmmn: mensuration offr 1946-61, controller of mgmnt servs 1966-68, cmmr of harvesting and mktg 1968-73; co dir Mexican Nat Forest Inventory 1961-66, head Forestry Div Cmmn of the Euro Communities 1973-80, ind conslt 1980-; Hon DUniv of Munich 1978; fell Inst Chartered Foresters 1982; *Books* Forest Policy - A Contribution to Resource Development (ed, 1984), Biomass Forestry in Europe - A Strategy for the Future (ed, 1988), Forestry Policies in Europe - an Analysis (1989); *Recreations* travelling off the beaten track; *Style*— Dr Frederick Hummel; 8 The Ridgeway, Guildford, Surrey GU1 2DG (☎ 0483 572 383)

HUMPHERY-SMITH, Cecil Raymond Julian; s of Frederick Humphery-Smith, MBE (d 1979), and Violet Agnes Humphery-Smith (d 1990); *b* 29 Oct 1928; *Educ* St John's Hurstpierpoint, Univ of London Sch of Hygiene and Tropical Med, Parma, Univ of Kent; *m* 1951, Alice Elizabeth Gwendoline, da of late Charles Thomas Cogle; 1 s, 5 da; *Career* mangr Consumer Servs Dept H J Heinz Co 1955-60, conslt De Rica Spa 1961-72, md Achievements Ltd 1961-81 (chm 1981); fndr princ and tstee Inst of Heraldic and Genealogical Studies, chm of Ct 1961-77, ed Family History 1963-; co-fndr fedn Family History Societies; lectr in extra mural studies: Univ of London 1951-, Univ of Oxford Delagacy 1960-65, Univ of Kent 1964-; visiting prof Univ of Minho 1970-72; designer of coats of arms; memb Cncl: Heraldry Soc 1953-, Manorial Soc of GB 1979-, Sub-Priory B Adrian Fortescue 1981-87, Domesday Nat Ctee 1984-85; Freeman and Liveryman Worshipful Cos of Broderers and Scriveners (hon historian); fell Heraldry Society; FSA, FSG; Academician l'Académie Internationale d'Héraldique 1976 (memb Cncl 1986-); memb: Confédération Internationale des Sciences Généalogique et Héraldique (vice pres 1980-86, pres 1986-90), UNESCO, ISSC, corr Int Archives Cncl; Knight of Obedience SMOM; *Publications* books incl: The Colour of Heraldry (jtly), General Armory Two, Heraldry in Canterbury Cathedral, Chronicles of Thomas Chough, Anglo-Norman Armory (2 volumes), An Atlas and Index of Parish Registers, A Genealogist's Bibliography, Our Family History, Introducing Family History, Sonnets of Life, Hugh Revel; author of numerous articles and lectures on subjects auxiliary to history and family history; *Recreations* writing sonnets, walking, listening to good music, enjoying the company of grandchildren; *Clubs* Challoner, Royal British, (Lisbon); *Style*— Cecil Humphery-Smith, Esq, FSA; Alcroft Grange, Hackington, Canterbury, Kent CT2 9NN (☎ 0227 462308); Fazarga, Moita-Fatima, 2495 Portugal

HUMPHRAYS, Rosemary; da of H W Davis (d 1970), and Janet, *née* Greening; *m* Harry Humphrays; 2 da (Louise (Mrs Rees), Julia (Mrs Sharp)); *Career* fndr memb Friends of GSMD 1980, elected to Common Cncl City of London Cripplegate Ward 1976 (chm Music Ctee 1981-85, chm Port & City Health and Social Servs Ctee 1990-), chm Cripplegate Fndn 1982-84 (govr 1977-), govr of Cripplegate Schs Fund (chm 1986-89); tstee: City Parochial Fndn 1984-, Tst for London 1987-; tstee: City Arts Tst, City of London Archeological Tst; memb Exec Ctee London Soc; Freeman City of London 1976; *Recreations* music, gardening, bridge; *Style*— Mrs Rosemary Humphrays; The Guildhall, London EC2P 2EJ (☎ 071 606 3030)

HUMPHREY, Albert S; s of Prof Albert Swartsindruver Humphrey, and Margaret Elizabeth Tomlinson, *née* Benton; *b* 2 June 1926; *Educ* Univ of Illinois (BSc), MIT (MSc), Harvard Sch of Business Admin (MBA); *m* 1, 6 Oct 1957 (m dis 1970), Virginia, da of Norman Potter (d 1976), of Cambridge, Mass; 2 s (Albert b 9 July 1959, Jonathon Benton Cantwell b 29 May 1962), 2 da (Virginia b 13 Sept 1960, Heidi b 10 Oct 1963); m 2, 20 Oct 1983, Myriam Alice Octaaf, da of Willy Petrus de Baere, of Lokeren, Belgium; 1 da (Stephania b 22 Sept 1986), 1 step s (Jonas Willems b 29 Aug 1974), 1 step da (Roosje Willems b 27 April 1972); *Career* staff engr Esso Standard Oil Co New Jersey 1948, chief of chemical and protective gp Office of the Chief Chemical Offr US Army Chemical Corp Washington DC 1952, asst to the Pres Penberthy Instrument Co Seattle 1955, chief of product planning Boeing Airplane Co Seattle 1956, mangr value analysis Small Aircraft Div GE Boston 1960, mangr of R & D planning P R Mallory & Co Inc Indianapolis 1961, head of mgmnt audit Gen Dynamics San Diego 1963, dir Int Exec Seminar in Business Planning Stanford Res Inst California and conslt NASA Office of Advanced Res and Technol Washington 1965, chief exec Business Planning and Devpt Kansas City 1969, currently chm and chief exec Business Planning and Devpt Inc (London); dir: Visual Enterprises Ltd (London), Sanbros Ltd (London), Candle Corporation of Europe Ltd (Huntingdon), Andrew Ltd (Bedford), Tower Lysprodukter a/s (Oslo Norway), Long Life Herbal Classics Inc (New Jersey USA), Petrochemische Anwendumgssysteme GmbH (Nurnberg Germany), Light Industry Ltd (London), Friborg Instruments Ltd; faculty memb: Extension Sch for Adult Educn Univ of Washington, US Naval Res Offrs Trg Sch; visiting prof Sch of Business and Mgmnt Newcastle Poly; assoc Blackwood Hodge Mgmnt Centre Nene Coll Northampton; memb English Speaking Union; frequent contrib to various business and mgmnt pubns; MInstM; memb: IOD, American Inst of Chemical Engrs, Harvard Alumni, MIT Alumni Assoc, Univ of Illinois Alumni Assoc; *Recreations* public service, seminars, lectures, writing, skiing, windsurfing, water skiing; *Clubs* East India, Devonshire Sports and Public Schools, Harvard (Boston); *Style—* Albert Humphrey, Esq; 34 Jellicoe House, 4 Osnaburgh St, London NW1 3AY (☎ 071 388 1838, fax 071 388 7030); 4030 Charlotte St, Kansas City, Missouri 64110, USA (☎ 816 753 0495); Sportlaan 6 W 22, 9100 Lokeren, Belgium (☎ 3291 488 666)

HUMPHREY, Ann Louise; da of John Frederick Wood (d 1989), of Selby, Yorkshire, and Brenda Elizabeth, *née* Simpson; *b* 24 July 1952; *Educ* Selby Girls' HS, Univ of Durham (BA), Kings Coll London (LLM); *m* 23 July 1977, s of Idwal Robert Humphrey, of Bosworth House, Woodbridge, Suffolk; *Career* stage Euro Cmmn 1974, admitted slr 1977, memb VAT Practitioners Gp 1982-, corp tax ptnr Richard Butler; memb Worshipful Co of Solicitors', memb Law Soc; *Books* Advanced Value Added Tax Planning (1988); *Recreations* golf, tennis, theatre, dance; *Style—* Mrs Ann Humphrey; Richards Butler, Beaufort House, 15 St Botolph St, London EC3A 7EE (☎ 071 247 6555, fax 071 247 5091, tlx 949494 RBLAW G)

HUMPHREY, Anthony Robert; s of Idwal Robert Humphrey, of Suffolk, and Mary Agnes, *née* Richards; *b* 12 Jan 1951; *Educ* Douai Sch, Univ of Durham (BA); *m* 24 July 1977, Ann Louise, da of John Drederick Wood (d 1989), of Yorkshire; *Career* Allen & Overy: joined 1973, ptnr 1981, specialises in fin and corp law; memb: Law Soc, Int Bar Assoc; *Recreations* golf, hunting, tennis, skiing; *Clubs* RAC; *Style—* Anthony Humphrey, Esq; Allen & Overy, 9 Cheapside, London EC2V 6AD (☎ 071 248 9898, telex 8812801, fax 071 236 2191)

HUMPHREY, (Frank) Basil; CB (1975); s of John Hartley Humphrey (d 1961), and Alice Maud, *née* Broadbent (d 1975); *b* 21 Sept 1918; *Educ* Brentwood Sch, St Catharine's Coll Cambridge (scholar, MA); *m* 1947, Olga, da of František Černý (d 1946), of Trenčín, Czechoslovakia; 2 s (Nicholas, Igor); *Career* served RA 1939-45, Adj 23 Mountain Regt and DAAG 4 Corps India and Burma; called to the Bar Middle Temple (Harmsworth scholar); Parly counsel office 1949-80, seconded as first Parly counsel fedn of Nigeria 1961-64 and counsel in charge at Law Cmmn 1971-72; *Recreations* gardening, mountain walking, music; *Style—* Basil Humphrey, Esq, CB; 1a The Ave, Chichester, W Sussex PO19 4PZ (☎ 0243 778783); Traverse des Rouvières, 83600 Bagnol's-en-Forêt, France (☎ 010 33 94 40 65 83)

HUMPHREY, Raymond John; s of Thomas Geoffrey Humphrey, and Mary Irene, *née* Warwick; *b* 4 Oct 1951; *Educ* St Joseph's GS Blackpool, Blackpool Sch of Technol & Art; *m* 1, 16 Aug 1975 (m dis); 1 s (Liam Jason b 4 Nov 1976); m 2, 26 May 1990, Lynne Roberta, da of Robert Fraser Andrews; *Career* professional photographer; formerly: industl photographer Winter & Kidson Preston, retinal photographer RPMS, commercial and advertising photographer Gordon Hammonds Photography Co Southampton, dir own co RHP Ltd Eastleigh 1982-; awards: Kitchenham Trophy (Industrial) 1979-80, Wessex Colour Plaque (Industl and Commercial) 1980-81, 1982-83 and 1984-86, Master Photographers industl award 1981-82, Master Photographers Pictorial Photography Gold certificate, 3M award Best Use of Colour in Industl and Commercial Photography 1981, Inst of Incorporated Photographers Industl and Commercial Photographer of the Year 1981-82, World Cncl of Professional Photographers Gold Certificate 1988; FBIPP; *Recreations* archery, pool, jogging; *Style—* Raymond Humphrey, Esq; RHP Ltd, Foxhills, 36 Ruskin Rd, Eastleigh, Hants SO5 4JS (☎ 0703 641237, car 0836 219617)

HUMPHREY OF DINNET, (James Malcolm) Marcus; DL (Aberdeenshire 1989); s of Lt Col James McGivern Humphrey, MC (d 1979), and Violet Joan, da of Col Sir Malcolm Barclay-Harvey of Dinnet, Govr of S Aust 1939-44 and for many years MP for Kincardine and W Aberdeenshire; *b* 1 May 1938; *Educ* Eton, ChCh Oxford (MA); *m* 15 Oct 1963, Sabrina Margaret, da of Lt Cdr Thomas Edward Pooley, RN (ret); 2 s (Edward b 1965, Simon b 1978), 2 da (Tania b 1966, Natasha b 1972); *Career* chartered surveyor; mangr own property; chm N of Scotland Bd Eagle Star Group 1971-91; memb: NFU of Scotland HQ Cncl 1968-73, Grampian Regnl Cncl 1974- (chm of fin 1974-78); Parly candidate (C) N Aberdeen 1966; chm of fin Aberdeen CC 1973-75, Grand Master Mason of Scotland 1983-88, memb Queens Bodyguard for Scotland 1969-; FRICS; OStJ 1970; DL (Aberdeenshire 1989); *Recreations* fishing, shooting, photography, philately; *Clubs* Boodle's, Royal Northern and Univ (Aberdeen); *Style—* Marcus Humphrey of Dinnet DL; Dinnet, Aboyne, Aberdeenshire; Estate Office, Dinnet, Aboyne AB34 5LL (☎ 03398 85341)

HUMPHREYS, Lt-Col Charles Andrew; MC; s of Brig Gen Gardiner Humphreys, CB, CMG, DSO (d 1942), and Lady Emily (d 1935), *née* Nugent, da of 10 Earl of Westmeath; *b* 9 April 1922; *Educ* Downside; *m* 21 Feb 1952, Phyllida Mary Delia, da of Capt Harold Pearce, RA (ka 1943); 3 s (Jasper Mark, Martin Charles, Toby James); *Career* cmmnd KRRC 1942, served 2 bn KRRC 1943-47, ADC to GOC 7 Armd Div 1948-49, Staff Coll Camberley 1951 (vc), Bde Maj 169 Green Jacket Bde (TA) 1955-56, 1 Bn KRRC 1957-60, Staff (GS02) HQ Afnorth (Oslo) 1961-63, Bde Adj Royal Greenjackets 1964-66, CO Oxfordshire and Bucks Lt (TA) 1967-68; defence attaché Helsinki 1969-71, ret 1975; sec Cncl for Voluntary Serv 1976-82; *Recreations* fishing, shooting; *Clubs* Army and Navy, MCC; *Style—* Lt-Col Charles Humphreys, MC; Berwick House, Berwick St James, Salisbury, Wiltshire (☎ 0722 790212)

HUMPHREYS, (David) Colin; CMG (1977); s of Charles Roland Lloyd Humphreys (d 1982), and Bethia Joan, *née* Bowie (d 1980); *b* 23 April 1925; *Educ* Eton, King's Coll Cambridge (MA); *m* 1952, Jill Allison, da of James Cranmer (d 1963); 2 s (David, Martin), 1 da (Camilla); *Career* Army Lt, served in UK and India 1943-46; civil servant Air Miny 1949, private sec to Sec of State for Air 1959-60; def cnsllr: UK Del to NATO 1960-63, Air Force Dept 1963-69, Imperial Def Coll 1970, dir Defence Policy Staff 1971-72, asst sec gen (Def Planning and Policy) NATO 1972-76, asst under sec (Naval Staff) 1977-79, dep under sec (Air) 1979-84, dir of devpt RIIA 1985-86; *Clubs* RAF, Wentworth; *Style—* Colin Humphreys, Esq, CMG; Rivendell, North Drive, Virginia Water, Surrey GU25 4NQ (☎ 0344 842180)

HUMPHREYS, Prof Colin John; s of Arthur William Humphreys, of Syston, Leicestershire; and Olive Annie Harton (d 1965); *b* 24 May 1941; *Educ* Luton GS, Imperial Coll London (BSc), Churchill Coll Cambridge (PhD), Jesus Coll Oxford (MA); *m* 30 July 1966, Sarah Jane, da of Henry Matthews, Cottingham, North Humberside; 2 da Katherine Jane Humphreys (b 1968), Elizabeth Mary Louise Humphreys (b 1971); *Career* Univ of Oxford: sr res offr 1971-80, lectr in metallurgy and sci of materials 1980-85, sr res fell Jesus Coll 1974-85; Henry Bell Wortley prof of materials engrg and head Dept of Materials Sci and Engrg Univ of Liverpool 1985-89: visiting prof: Arizona State Univ 1979, Univ of Illinois 1982-86; prof of materials sci Univ of Cambridge 1990-, professorial fell Selwyn Coll Cambridge 1990-; chm: Cmmn on Electron Diffraction Int Union of Crystallography 1984-87 (memb Cmmn on Int Tables), Materials Sci and Engrg Cmmn SERC 1988-91; memb Cncl: SERC 1988-92, Cncl Inst of Metals 1989-92, Ct Univ of Bradford 1990-; RSA medal 1963, Reginald Mitchell medal 1989, Rosenhain medal and prize 1989; C Eng (1980), FIM (1985), FInst P (1985); *Books* High Voltage Electron Microscopy (ed 1974), Electron Diffraction 1927-77 (ed 1978), Creation and Evolution, (1985, translated into Chinese 1988); *Recreations* chronology of biblical events, contemplating gardening; *Style—* Prof Colin Humphreys; Department of Materials Science and Metallurgy, University of Cambridge, Pembroke St, Cambridge CB2 3QZ (☎ 0223 334457, fax 0223 334437, telex 81240 CAMSPL G)

HUMPHREYS, Hon Mrs (Ella Zia); *née* Grimston; da of 1 Baron Grimston of Westbury (d 1979), and Sybil Rose (d 1977), da of Sir Sigmund Neumann, 1 Bt; *b* 4 May 1937; *m* 1972, Humphrey K Humphreys (d 1984); 1 da (Catherine Sybella b 1977); *Style—* The Hon Mrs Humphreys; Ferne Park Cottage, Berwick St John, Shaftesbury, Dorset (☎ 0747 828767)

HUMPHREYS, Emyr Owen; s of William Humphreys, of Prestatyn, Flints, and Sarah Rosina Humphreys; *b* 15 April 1919; *Educ* Univ Coll Aberystwyth, Univ Coll Bangor; *m* 1946, Elinor Myfanwy, da of Rev Griffith Jones, of Bontnewydd, Cairns; 3 s, 1 da; *Career* author; Somerset Maugham award 1953, Hawthornden prize 1959, Welsh Arts Cncl prize 1972, Soc of Authors Travelling award 1979, Welsh Arts Cncl Non Fiction prize 1984; hon prof of English Univ Coll of N Wales Bangor, hon fell: Univ of Wales Abeystwyth, Univ Coll Swansea; Gregynog Arts Fell 1974-75; Hon D Litt Univ of Wales; *Books* The Little Kingdom (1946), The Voice of a Stranger (1949), A Change of Heart (1951), Hear and Forgive (1952), A Man's Estate (1955), The Italian Wife (1957), Y Tri Llais (1958), A Toy Epic (1958), The Gift (1963), Outside the House of Baal (1965), Natives (1968), Ancestor Worship (1970), National Winner (1971), Flesh and Blood (1974), Landscapes (1976), The Best of Friends (1978), Penguin Modern Poets number 27 (1978), The Kingdom of Brân (1979), The Anchor Tree (1980), Pwyll a Riannon (1980), Miscellany Two (1981), The Taliesin Tradition (1983), Jones (1984), Salt of the Earth (1985), An Absolute Hero (1986), Darn o Dir (1986), Open Secrets (1988), Bonds of Attachment (1991); *Recreations* rural pursuits; *Style—* Emyr Humphreys, Esq; Llinon, Penyberth, Llanfairpwll, Ynys Môn, Gwynedd LL61 5YT

HUMPHREYS, Hon Mrs (Honor); *née* Byng; da of 10 Viscount Torrington (d 1961); *b* 29 Aug 1912; *m* 1937 (m dis 1951), Lisle Marles Humphreys; *Style—* The Hon Mrs Humphreys; 26 Swan Court, London SW3 5RT

HUMPHREYS, Sir (Raymond Evelyn) Myles; JP, DL (Belfast); s of Raymond and May Humphreys; *b* 24 March 1925; *Educ* Skegoneil Primary Sch, Londonderry HS, Belfast Royal Acad; *m* 1, 1963, Joan Tate (d 1979); 2 s (Ian, Mark); m 2, 1987, Sheila Clements-McFarland; *Career* res engr NI Road Tport Bd 1946-48, Ulster Tport Authy 1948-55, tport mangr Nestle's Food Prod (NI) Ltd 1955-59, dist tport offr St John Ambulance Bde 1946-66; memb: Belfast City Cncl 1964-81, NI Tport Hldg Co 1968-74, Nat Planning and Town Planning Cncl 1970-81 (chm 1976-77), NI Tourist Bd 1973-80, City Cncl Town Planning and Environmental Health Ctee 1973-75, NI Housing Exec 1975-78, May Ctee of Inquiry into UK Prison Servs 1978-79, bd of Abbey Nat Building Society 1981- (chm advsy bd NI 1981-); dir: Walter Alexander (Belfast) Ltd 1959-, Quick Service Stations Ltd 1971-86, Bowring Martin 1978-88; chm: Belfast Corp Housing Ctee 1966-69, NI Railways Co Ltd 1967-, Ulster Tourist Devpt Assoc 1968-78, City Cncl Planning Ctee 1973-75, Fin and Gen Purposes Ctee Belfast 1978-80, NI Police Authy 1976-86, Belfast Marathon Ltd 1981-85, NI Tport Holding Co 1988-; Belfast Harbour cmmr 1979-88; High Sheriff Belfast 1969, Lord Mayor 1975-77 (dep Lord Mayor 1970); sen Jr Chamber Int, NI rep Motability Int; pres: NI Polio Fellowship 1977-, City of Belfast Youth Orchestra 1980-; memb exec and former pres NI C of C and Indust, pres BIM (Belfast branch) 1983-; former pres Belfast Junior C of C; past chm: bd of mgmnt Dunlambert Secdy Sch, bd of visitors to HM Prison Belfast; memb: senate Queen's Univ Belfast 1975-77, ct Univ of Ulster 1985-; tstee Ulster Folk and Tport Museum 1976-81; memb cncl Queen's Silver Jubilee Appeal, dir Ulster Orchestra Soc 1980; Freeman City of London 1976; OStJ; FCIT, CBIM; kt 1977; *Clubs* Lansdowne; *Style—* Sir Myles Humphreys, JP, DL; Mylestone, 23 Massey Ave, Belfast BT4 2JT

HUMPHREYS, Nigel Craven; s of Gordon Stephen Humphreys (d 1985), of The Drive, Godalming, Surrey, and Joan Olive, *née* Mudditt; *b* 15 March 1938; *Educ* Sherborne, New Coll Oxford (MA); *m* 29 Sept 1962, Jennifer Nan, da of Maj Adrian Hugh Lovegrove, of West End House, Over Stratton, Somerset; 2 da (Julia b 1964, Annabella b 1966); *Career* RB 1956-58, cmmnd 1957, seconded to 3 Bn King's African Rifles Kenya; Courtaulds Ltd 1961-65, Andrews & Partners 1965-68, Chaucer Estates Ltd 1968-71, md Mitropa Group Brussels 1971-77; Tyzack & Partners Ltd: conslt 1977, ptnr 1978-84, managing ptnr 1984-; Vol Serv Housing Soc 1966-68, Cherwell Housing Tst 1968-71; Freeman City of London, memb Ct Worshipful Co of Glovers 1985; *Recreations* opera, shooting, distant uninhabited places; *Clubs* Boodles, Royal Green Jackets; *Style—* Nigel Humphreys, Esq; The Malt House, Chilton, Oxon OX11 0RZ (☎ 0235 834 409); 10 Hallam St, London W1N 6DJ (☎ 071 580 2924, fax 071 631 5317)

HUMPHREYS, Sir Olliver William; CBE (1957); s of late Rev J Willis Humphreys, of Bath; *b* 4 Sept 1902; *Educ* Caterham Sch, UCL (BSc); *m* 1933, Muriel Mary (d 1985), da of Charles John Hawkins, of Harrow; *Career* joined scientific staff GEC Res Laboratories 1925 (dir 1951-60); dir GEC 1953, vice-chm GEC Ltd 1963-67; pres: Inst of Physics 1956-58, Inst of Electrical Engrs 1964-65; fndr chm Conf of the Electronics Indust 1963-67; pres Caterham Sch 1972-; fell UCL 1963; kt 1968; *Style—* Sir Olliver Humphreys, CBE; Furze Hill Lodge, Furze Hill, Kingswood, Surrey KT20 6EP

HUMPHREYS, Col (Thomas) Victor; OBE (1958); s of Cdr Thomas Victor Humphreys (ka 1942), of Ballycastle, Co Antrim, and Anne Breakey, *née* Douglas (d 1967); *b* 26 May 1922; *Educ* Ballycastle HS Antrim, The Queens Univ of Belfast (MB BCh, BAO); *m* 18 Oct 1969, Elisabeth Penrose, da of Rev John Alfred Clarence Rogers (d 1984), vicar of Hindhead, Surrey; *Career* res hosp appts in med and surgery 1946-52, MO and second sec of legation HBM Legation Bucharest 1952-55, MO and first sec HBM Embassy Moscow 1955-57, surgn Royal Mail Line 1958-62; RAMC: entered 1963, Lt-Col 1969, Local Col 1977, Actg Col 1979, Col Staff 1980, sr specialist Army Community and Occupational Med 1980, regtl MO 2 Coldstream Gds and later Queen's Dragoon Gds; SMO: (UK) SHAPE Belgium 1971-74, HQ Allied Forces N Europe Oslo Norway 1974-77; CO Br Mil Hosp: Munster BAOR 1977-79, ADMS Berlin and CO BMH 1979-82; Cdr Army Med Servs: HQ Western Dist UK 1982-86, HQ London Dist Horse Gds 1986-87, ret 1987; pres emeritus Berlin Int Med Soc 1981-, a vice pres Coldstream Gds Assoc (Exeter) 1989-, Cdr Order of Polonia Restituta (govt in exile); OStJ 1981 (serving brother 1962); Lord of the Manor of Postcombe; *Publications:* author of articles in various professional med jls on medicine and surgery in Eastern Europe, various historical articles on European Monarchies (particularly the Habsburgs); *Recreations* european history, languages, genealogy, heraldry and all the vanished pomps of yesterday; *Style—* Col Victor Humphreys, OBE; Powderham House, Powderham, nr Exeter EX6 8JJ (☎ 0626 890 536)

HUMPHRIES, David Ernest; s of Ernest Augustus Humphries (d 1954), of Sussex, and Kathleen Humphries, *née* Keating (d 1986); *b* 3 Feb 1937; *Educ* Brighton Coll,

Corpus Christi Coll Oxford; *m* 1959, Wendy Rosemary, da of Thomas James Cook (d 1982), of Sussex; 1 s (Charles b 1969), 1 da (Sarah b 1965); *Career* RAE Farnborough 1961-81: materials dept 1961-66, avionics dept 1966-74, supt inertial navigation div 1974, supt weapon aiming systems div, supt flight systems dept 1975, head of systems assessment dept 1978-81; dir gen future projects Air Systems Controllerate MOD (PE) 1981-83, chief scientist RAF, dir gen res (C Sector) 1983-85, dir gen of res and technol Controllerate of Estab Res and Nuclear 1985-86, (asst chief scientific advsr projects and res); *Recreations* music, pipe organ (building and playing), reading; *Style*— David Humphries, Esq; 18 The Mount, Malton, North Yorks YO17 0ND (☎ 0653 693679); Miny of Defence, Main Building, Whitehall

HUMPHRIES, His Hon Judge; Gerard William; s of John Alfred Humphries (d 1980), and Marie Frances, *née* Whitwell (d 1980); *b* 13 Dec 1928; *Educ* St Bede's Coll Manchester, Univ of Manchester (LLB); *m* 1957, Margaret Valerie, da of William Woodburn Gelderd (d 1975), of Cumbria; 4 s (Stephen b 1961, Paul b 1962, David b 1966, Bernard b 1971), 1 da (Frances b 1967); *Career* Flying Offr RAF 1951-53; barr 1954-80, circuit judge 1980; Knight of the Holy Sepulchre (Vatican) 1986; *Recreations* tennis, gardening, music, sailing, golf, computers, caravanning; *Clubs* Lansdowne, Northern LT (Manchester); *Style*— His Hon Judge Humphries; Crown Court, Crown Square, Manchester

HUMPHRIES, John Anthony Charles; OBE (1980); s of Charles Humphries; *b* 15 June 1925; *Educ* Fettes, Peterhouse Cambridge; *m* 1951, Olga Jane, da of Dr Geoffrey Duckworth; 4 da; *Career* WWII RNVR 1943-46; admitted slr 1951, chm Evans of Leeds plc 1982-, memb London Bd Halifax Building Society 1985-; chm Water Space Amenity Cmmn 1973-83, vice pres Inland Waterways Assoc 1973- (chm 1970-73), memb Inland Waterways Amenity Advsy Cncl 1971-88, advsr to HM Govt on amenity use of water space 1972; memb: Nat Water Cncl 1973-83, Thames Water Authy 1983-87, Sports Cncl 1987-88; dep chm Environment Cncl 1985-, chm Southern Cncl for Sport and Recreation 1986-; *Recreations* inland waters, gardening; *Clubs* Naval, City; *Style*— John Humphries, Esq, OBE; 21 Parkside, Wimbledon, London SW19

HUMPHRIES, John Charles Freeman; s of Charles Montague Humphries (d 1963), of Newport, Gwent, and Lilian Mary Humphries (d 1968); *b* 2 Jan 1937; *Educ* St Julian's HS Newport Gwent; *m* 29 Aug 1959, Eliana Julia Paola, da of Joseph Mifsud (d 1970); 2 s (Mark Freeman b 16 Aug 1961, Owen John b 23 Oct 1963), 1 da (Rachel Julia b 19 Dec 1971); *Career* Nat Serv Aldershot 1958; dep ed Western mail 1973-80 (news ed 1965-73), London and city ed Thomson Regional Newspapers London 1985-88 (chief of Euro bureau Brussels 1980-85), ed Western Mail 1988-, launch ed Wales on Sunday 1989; fndr and tstee Br Bone Marrow Donor Appeal 1987-; memb Guild of Br Newspaper Eds; *Recreations* walking, opera, reading, rugby, cricket; *Style*— John Humphries, Esq; Fairfield, Ponthir Road, Caerleon, Gwent NP6 1NH (☎ 0633 420648); Western Mail Ltd, Thomson House, Havelock St, Cardiff, South Glamorgan (☎ 0222 223333)

HUMPHRIES, Peter John William; s of William Humphries, of Stratford, London, and Eileen Ethel Stevens, *née* Scannel; *b* 15 June 1935; *Educ* Stratford GS; *m* 18 June 1955, Kay, da of late Enoch Fowler, of Liverpool; 2 s (Peter b 1956, Kevin b 1964); *Career* served RAF 1952-59, Far East Air Force Cmd 3609 Sqdn; former automotive engr and tport mangr Miny of Tport GLC and Surrey CC, former chief engr Avon CC, dir Cromwell Engineering Inc (USA); fndr memb Inst of Municipal Tport, dir Bristol Packers (American Football Club); FBIM, MIRTE, MInstTA, MIMT; *Recreations* golf, rugby, american football, pub dominoes, putting the world to rights; *Clubs* Fosseyway Golf, Rosslyn Park FC, Bristol Packers AFC; *Style*— Peter Humphries, Esq; Nelson House, Pensford, Avon BS18 4AH; Cromwell Engineering Inc, PO Box 710055, San Jose, California, 95171 0055, USA

HUMPHRYS, John Desmond; s of Edward George Humphrys, and Winifred May Humphrys (d 1988); *b* 17 Aug 1943; *Educ* Cardiff HS; *m* 5 Sept 1964, Edna Wilding; 1 s (Christopher b 30 April 1967), 1 da (Catherine b 21 July 1969); *Career* BBC TV news: foreign corr in USA and SA 1970-80, dip corr 1980-81, presenter 1981-86; presenter of BBC Radio 4 Today Programme 1987-; memb Cncl Save the Children Fund; *Recreations* failed farmer; *Style*— John Humphrys, Esq; BBC, Broadcasting House, Langham Place, London W1A 1AA (☎ 071 927 5566)

HUMPHRYS, Lady (Eugénie) Pamela; *née* Wavell; da of 1 Earl Wavell, GCB, GCSI, GCIE, CMG, MC (d 1950); *b* 14 March 1918; *m* 14 March 1942, (Arthur) Francis Walter Humphrys, OBE, *qv*, s of Lt-Col Sir Francis Humphrys, GCMG, GCVO, KBE, CIE; 2 s, 1 da; *Style*— The Lady Pamela Humphrys; Marston Meysey Grange, nr Cricklade, Wilts (☎ 0285 810239)

HUNGERFORD, John Leonard; s of Leonard Harold Hungerford (d 1979), and Violet Miriam, *née* Bickerstaff; *b* 12 Oct 1944; *Educ* The Glyn Sch Epsom, Gonville and Caius Coll Cambridge, Charing Cross Hosp Med Sch (MA, MB BChir, DO); *m* 16 July 1987, Yvonne Carole, da of Sydney George Rayment (d 1962); 1 da (Miranda b 1988); *Career* conslt surgn Moorfields Eye Hosp 1983-, conslt ophthalmic surgn St Bartholomew's Hosp 1983-; memb Charged Particle Therapy Working Pty MRC, dir Proton Therapy Gp Imp Cancer Res Fund; FRCS 1978, FCOphth; *Recreations* travel, gardening, architecture; *Style*— John Hungerford, Esq; 114 Harley St, London W1N 1AG (☎ 071 935 1565, fax 071 224 1752)

HUNNICUTT, (Virginia) Gayle; da of Col S Hunnicutt, of Fort Worth, Texas, and Mary Virginia, *née* Dickenson; *b* 6 Feb 1943; *Educ* Pascal HS, UCLA (BA); *m* 1, 1968 (m dis 1974), David H Hemmings; 1 s (Nolan); m 2, 1 Sept 1978, Simon David Jenkins, *qv*, s of Rev Daniel Jenkins, of London; 1 s (Edward); *Career* actress; theatre: A Ride Across Lake Constance 1974, Twelfth Night 1975, The Tempest 1976, The Admiral Crichton 1977, A Woman of No Importance 1978, Hedda Gabler 1978, Peter Pan 1979, Macbeth 1980, Uncle Vanya 1980, The Philadelphia Story 1981, The Miss Firecracker Contest 1982, Exit The King 1983, The Doctor's Dilemma 1984, So Long On Lonely Street 1985, The Big Knife 1987; films: New Face in Hell 1967, Eye of the Cat and The Little Sisters 1968, Fragment of Fear 1969, Running Scared 1971, Scorpio 1972, Legend of Hell House 1973, L'Homme Sans Visage 1974, The Spiral Staircase 1976, Once in Paris 1977, Dream Lovers 1985, Target 1986, Silence Like Glass 1988; television: Man and Boy 1971, Humbolt's Gift 1971, The Golden Bowl 1972, The Ripening Seed 1973, Fall of Eagles 1974, The Ambassadors 1975, The Martian Chronicles 1978, A Man Called Intrepid 1979, Fantomas 1980, Tales of the Unexpected 1987, Taxi 1982, Dylan Thomas 1983, The First Modern Olympics 1984, Phillip Marlow 1984, Sherlock Holmes 1985, Privilege 1986, Strong Medicine 1986, Dream West 1987, Dallas 1989-90; memb Bd of Tstees The Theatre Tst, hon memb BFI 1980; memb: Acad of Motion Pictures Arts and Scis 1979, Br Theatre Assoc 1982; *Books* Health and Beauty in Motherhood (1984); *Recreations* travel; *Style*— Miss Gayle Hunnicutt; c/o The William Morris Agency, 31-32 Soho Square, London W1 (☎ 071 434 2191)

HUNNISETT, Dr Roy Frank; s of Frank Hunnisett, of Bexhill-on-Sea (d 1967), and Alice, *née* Budden (d 1979); *b* 26 Feb 1928; *Educ* Bexhill GS, New Coll Oxford (MA, DPhil); *m* 1, 7 Aug 1954 (m dis 1989), Edith Margaret, *née* Evans; m 2, 15 June 1989, Janet Heather, *née* Stevenson; *Career* Public Record Office 1953-88, pt/t lectr New Coll Oxford 1957-63; FRHistS 1961, FSA 1975; *Books* The Medieval Coroners' Rolls (1960), The Medieval Coroner (1961), Bedfordshire Coroners' Rolls (1961), Calendar of Nottinghamshire Coroners' Inquests 1485-1558 (1969), Indexing for Editors (1972), Editing Records for Publication (1977), Wiltshire Coroners' Bills 1752-1796 (1981), Sussex Coroners' Inquests 1485-1558 (1985); *Recreations* music, cricket; *Style*— Dr Roy Hunnisett; 23 Byron Gardens, Sutton, Surrey SM1 3QG (☎ 081 661 2618)

HUNSDON OF HUNSDON; *see*: Aldenham

HUNT, Alan Charles; CMG (1990); s of John Henry Hunt (d 1990), of Hounslow, and Nelly Elizabeth Hunt (d 1978); *b* 5 March 1941; *Educ* Latymer Upper Sch, UEA (BA); *m* 6 May 1978, Meredith Margaret, da of Reginald Claydon, of Sydney, Australia; 2 da (Charlotte Louise b 1980, Victoria Clare b 1982); *Career* clerical offr Miny of Power 1958; HM Dip Serv 1959-; vice consul Tehran 1962-63, third sec Jedda 1964-65, floating duties Latin America 1965-67, second later first sec FCO 1970-73; first sec: Panama 1973-76, Commercial Madrid 1977-81, FCO 1981-83; cnsllr (Economic) Oslo 1983-87, head Br Interests Section (later Chargé d'Affairs) Buenos Aires 1987-90; *Recreations* tennis, music, reading; *Style*— Alan Hunt, Esq, CMG; Foreign and Commonwealth Office, London SW1 (☎ 071 737 3375)

HUNT, Alannah Elizabeth; da of Humphrey Cecil Bowbeer Hunt (d 1965), of Curry Rivel, Somerset, and Molly Daphne Albury, *née* Hill (d 1979); *b* 22 March 1949; *Educ* Millfield, Taunton Tech Coll Somerset; *Career* selection conslt Webb Whitley Assoc Ltd 1975-82, dir Overseas Link Ltd 1982-84, head of exec selection Price Waterhouse 1984-, author of various articles on recruitment and selection; MBIM 1982, MPIM 1986, MIMC 1987; *Recreations* tennis, theatre, gardening; *Style*— Miss Alannah Hunt; Price Waterhouse Managment Consultants, No 1 London Bridge, London SE1 9QL (☎ 01 378 7200, fax 01 403 5265)

HUNT, Dr Albert Charles (Bill); s of Albert Edward Hunt (d 1944), of Bromley, Kent, and Ethel Olivia, *née* Sherborne (d 1984); *b* 26 Dec 1927; *Educ* Bromley GS, The London Hosp (MD, BS); *m* 1, 1950 (m dis 1974), Enid Watkins; 3 s (Matthew Sherborne b 1952, Paul Sherborne b 1954, Benjamin Sherborne b 1958); m 2, 1976 (m dis 1986), Faye Ann Mavius; m 3, 23 March 1987, Josephine Carol, da of Arthur Harold Whitney (d 1970), of W Mersea; *Career* pathologist to Home Office 1957-; reader in histopathology Univ of Bristol 1969-71 (reader in forensic pathology 1965-69), conslt histopathologist Plymouth 1971-; former vice-pres: RCP, World Assoc of Socs of Pathology; former chm cncl and pres Assoc of Clinical Pathologists; FRCP 1969; *Books* Pathology of Injury (1972); *Recreations* collecting all sorts of things; *Clubs* Savile; *Style*— Dr A C Hunt; 3 White Lane, The Barbican, Plymouth PL1 2LP (☎ 0752 662873); Dept of Histopathology, Derriford Hospital, Plymouth PL6 DH (☎ 0752 792241)

HUNT, Bernard Andrew Paul; s of Sir Joseph (Anthony) Hunt (d 1982), and Hilde, *née* Pollitzer; *b* 24 March 1944; *Educ* Oundle, Magdalene Coll Cambridge (MA); *m* 1973, Florence, da of Alan White, of W Sussex; 1 s (Andrew b 1977), 1 da (Susanna b 1975); *Career* architect, ptnr Hunt Thompson Assocs 1969-; *Recreations* cinema, theatre, reading, skiing; *Style*— Bernard Hunt, Esq; 34 Fitzroy Road, London NW1; 79 Parkway, London NW1 (☎ 01 485 8555, fax 01 485 1232)

HUNT, Dr Bernard Peter; s of William Branson Hunt, of Lincoln, and Ivy, *née* Hammond; *b* 30 July 1948; *Educ* Southend HS for Boys, St Catharine's Coll Cambridge (MA, MB); *m* 30 Sept 1972, June Elizabeth (Linda), da of George Syrnicki, of Buxton, Derbyshire; 2 s (Richard b 1976, Gareth b 1978), 1 da (Elizabeth b 1983); *Career* conslt rheumatologist Pilgrim Hosp Boston and Lincoln Acute Hosps 1982-; sec Boston Amateur Swimming Club, vice pres Lincoln Branch Arthritis and Rheumatism Cncl; MRCP 1976; *Recreations* swimming; *Style*— Dr Bernard Hunt; Saddlers Mead, Northlands, Sibsey, Boston, Lincs (☎ 0205 750165)

HUNT, Brian Norman; s of Norman Frederick Hunt (d 1970), and Irene Olive, *née* Brimble; *b* 1 July 1936; *Educ* Yeovil Tech Sch Somerset; *m* 20 Feb 1960, Norah Ann, da of Edward William Haynes (d 1972); 2 s (Timothy Andrew b 1962, Stephen Christopher b 1965); *Career* Nat Serv photographer RAF 1956-58, apprenticed to H Tilzey (photographer) 1952-56, chief photographer Cranfield Inst of Technol 1962- (joined as asst photographer 1958); pres Br Inst of Professional Photography 1979-80 (chm Industrial Ctee 1982-90); govr Salisbury Coll of Art 1984-; FRPS 1970 (memb 1967), FBIPP 1971 (memb 1958); *Recreations* charity work (chm church restoration appeal), caravanning, walking; *Style*— Brian Hunt, Esq; 16 Richmond Way, Newport Pagnell, Buckinghamshire MK16 0LF (☎ 0908 612875); Photography Dept, Cranfield Inst of Technology, Cranfield, Bedford MK43 OAL (☎ 0234 740111, fax 0234 750875)

HUNT, Dr the Hon Christopher Godfrey Evill; s of Baron Hunt of Fawley, CBE (Life Peer d 1987); *b* 1947; *Educ* London Univ (MA, MB BS); MRCS, LRCP, DObSt, RCOG; *m* 1979, Carol, *née* McDermott; 2 da; *Style*— Dr the Hon Christopher Hunt; 4455 West 2nd Avenue, Vancouver, Br Columbia V6R 1K6, Canada

HUNT, Rt Hon David James Fletcher; PC (1990), MBE (1973), MP (C) Wirral W 1983-; s of the late Alan Hunt, OBE; *b* 21 May 1942; *Educ* Liverpool Coll, Montpellier Univ, Univ of Bristol, Guildford Coll of Law; *m* 1973, Patricia Margery (Paddy), *née* Orchard; 2 s, 2 da; *Career* slr; ptnr Stanley Wasbrough and Co 1965-77, ptnr Beachcroft Stanleys 1977-; contested Bristol S 1970, Kingswood 1974; vice chm Nat Union Cons and Unionist Assocs 1974-76; chm: YC Nat Advsy Ctee 1972-73, Cons Gp for Europe 1981-82; vice chm Parly Youth Lobby 1978-80, pres Br Youth Cncl 1978-81 (chm 1971-74); PPS to: Trade Sec 1979-81, Def Sec 1981; jr Cons whip 1981-83, a lord cmmr of the Treasy (govt whip) 1983-84, MP (C) Wirral 1976-1983, vice chm Cons Party 1983-85, Parly under sec of state Dept of Energy 1984-87, dep govt chief whip 1987-89; treas HM Household 1987-89; minister for local Govt and Inner Cities 1989-90; appointed sec of state for Wales March 1990-; *Clubs* Hurlingham; *Style*— The Rt Hon David Hunt, MBE, MP; House of Commons, SW1A 0AA (☎ 071 219 3400)

HUNT, David Malcolm; s of Albert Francis Hunt (d 1990) of Southgate, London, and Winifred Helena, *née* Pearce; *b* 22 Dec 1941; *Educ* Owen's Sch, Univ of Warwick (MSc); *m* 24 Aug 1968, Betty, da of Maurice John Gifford Upchurch, of Huntingdon; 3 s (Jonathan) Mark b 5 Nov 1969, Patrick Simon b 26 March 1975, Wesley Paul (twin) b 26 March 1975); *Career* articled clerk Baker Sutton & Co 1961-68, auditor Arthur Anderson & Co 1968-70, Baker Sutton & Co 1971-75, ptnr and dir Human Resources Pannell Kerr Forster 1975-; non-exec memb Notts Family Health Servs Authy; dir and tstee: Pregnancy Advsy Servs Ltd, Family First Ltd Nottingham; FCA (ACA 1966), FITD 1979, FBIM 1972; On-The-Job Training (ICAEW, 1980), Business Briefing: Doctors Accounts (ICAEW, with G Littlewood, 1984); *Recreations* squash, music, theatre, working for charities; *Clubs* Royal Over-Seas League; *Style*— David Hunt, Esq; Pannell Kerr Forster Chartered Accountants, Harby Lodge, Pelham Road, Nottingham NG5 1AP (☎ 0602 606260, fax 0602 622229, car 0831 154134)

HUNT, David Roderic Notley; QC (1987); s of Dr Geoffrey Notley Hunt (d 1982), of Pembury, Kent, and Deborah Katharine Rosamund, *née* Clapham; *b* 22 June 1947; *Educ* Charterhouse, Trinity Coll Cambridge (MA); *m* 27 April 1974, Alison Connell, da of Lt-Col Arthur George Jelf (d 1958); 2 s (Thomas b 8 Feb 1976, Robert b 20 Feb 1979); *Career* called to the Bar Gray's Inn 1969, asst rec; *Recreations* sailing, golf, skiing; *Clubs* Bewl Valley Sailing, Nevill Golf; *Style*— David Hunt, Esq, QC; 2 Hare Court, Temple, London EC4Y 7BH (☎ 071 583 1770, fax 071 583 9269)

HUNT, Sir David Wathen Stather; KCMG (1963, CMG 1959), OBE (1943); s of

Rev Canon Bernard Hunt (d 1967), of Norwich, and Elizabeth, *née* Milner; *b* 25 Sept 1913; *Educ* St Lawrence Coll Ramsgate, Wadham Coll Oxford; *m* 1, 1948 (m dis 1967), Pamela Muriel, da of late Nicholas Medawar; 2 s; m 2, 1968, Iro, da of late John Myrianthousis; *Career* fell Magdalen Coll Oxford 1937; WWII Welch Regt Middle East, Balkans, N Africa, Sicily and Italy; Col Gen Staff Allied Force HQ 1945-46, Hon Col 1947; joined CRO 1947, private sec to PM 1950-52, dep UK high cmmr Pakistan 1954-56 (asst under-sec 1959), dep UK high cmmr Lagos 1960-62; high cmmr: Kampala 1962-65, Cyprus 1965-66, Nigeria 1967-69; ambass Brazil 1969-73; chm of govrs Cwlth Inst 1974-84; memb Appts Cmmn Press Cncl 1977-82, dir Observer 1982, visiting prof of int relations Univ of Edinburgh 1980; winner of TV Mastermind title 1977 and Mastermind Champions title 1982; pres Soc for Promotion of Hellenic Studies 1986-; US Bronze Star 1945; Grand Cross Order of Southern Cross Brazil 1985; *Publications* A Don at War (1966, revised edn 1990), On The Spot (1975), Footprints in Cyprus (ed, 1982), Gothic Art and the Renaissance in Cyprus (1987), Caterina Cornaro, Queen of Cyprus (ed, 1989); *Clubs* Athenaeum, Beefsteak; *Style—* Sir David Hunt, KCMG, OBE; Old Place, Lindfield, W Sussex RH16 2HU (☎ 044 47 2298)

HUNT, Cdr (Arthur) Douglas; RD (1948 and Bar 1966); s of Dr Arthur Douglas Hunt (d 1952, Capt RAMC), of Park Grange, Duffield Rd, Derby, and Mabel Sharpe, *née* Thomas; *b* 27 Sept 1919; *Educ* Derby GS, Brighton Coll, Nautical Coll Pangbourne, Southampton Coll of Nautical Studies; *m* 16 May 1942, Margaret Alison, da of Ernest William Sutcliffe (d 1947), of Carr Field, Carr Head Lane, Poulton-Le-Fylde, Lancs; 1 s (Christopher Douglas), 1 da (Jennifer Jane); *Career* RNR: Midshipman to Sub Lt 1939-42, Lt 1942-50, Lt Cdr 1950-56, Cdr 1956; MN (Union Castle Line) 1937-39, RN 1939-46, MN (Cunard Line) 1946-56, marine supt Cunard Line Southampton 1956-67, nautical surveyor and examiner of masters and mates 1977-83; sec RAF YC Hamble Hants 1968-70, chm Bursledon & Warsash Regatta Ctee 1970-73; Freeman City of London 1965, memb Hon Co of Master Mariners; *Recreations* sailing; *Clubs* Southampton Master Mariners (Capt 1977), Royal Southern Yacht Hamble; *Style—* Cdr Douglas Hunt, RD, RNR; Westward, Salterns Lane, Old Bursledon, Southampton, Hants SO3 8DH (☎ 042 121 2316)

HUNT, Dr Eric Millman; s of Arthur Millman Hunt (d 1951), and Irene Olive Cordwell (d 1981); *b* 30 April 1923; *Educ* Marling Sch Stroud, Univ of Leeds (BSc, PhD), UCL (Dip Chem Eng); *m* 1, 14 Dec 1957 (m dis 1971), Eve Sangster; 1 s (Trevor b 1959), 1 da (Cynthia b 1962); m 2, 15 July 1974, Phyllis Mary Charteris, da of Capt James Charteris Burleigh (d 1954); 1 s (Andrew b 1975), 1 da (Katrina b 1977); *Career* chief exec Akzo Chemicals Ltd 1967-81, chm Thomas Swan & Co Ltd 1982-, memb Merton and Sutton Health Authy 1990-; treas Plastics and Rubber Inst 1983- (chm 1981-83); chm N W Wimbledon Res Assoc 1982-88; memb Ct Univ of Surrey 1984-; Freeman City of London 1965, Clerk Worshipful Co of Horners 1982 (Liveryman 1965); FRSC, FIChemE, FPRI, FIOD; *Style—* Dr Eric Hunt; 37 Drax Avenue, Wimbledon, London SW20 (☎ 081 946 9767); 11 Hobart Place, London SW1 (☎ 071 245 9555, fax 071 823 1379)

HUNT, Lady; Esmé Jeanne; *née* Langston; da of Albert Edward Langston; *b* 31 Aug 1931; *m* 1960, as his 2 w, Sir Joseph Hunt, MBE (d 1982), chm Hymatic Engrg Co; 2 s, 2 da; *Recreations* reading, walking, gardening, music; *Style—* Lady Hunt; Field House, Huntington Lane, Ashford Carbonell, Ludlow, Shrops SY8 4DG

HUNT, (John) Frederick; s of Arthur Hunt (d 1942), and Beatrice, *née* May (d 1981); *b* 21 Oct 1925; *Educ* Scunthorpe GS, Queens Univ Belfast; *m* 17 Feb 1947, Maria, da of Ernesto Semenzato (d 1969); *Career* RA 1943-45, Intelligence Corps 1945-47, RAPC, Lt 1950-55; ptnr Stephenson Smart and Co Chartered Accountants Peterborough 1965-89; treas Cambridgeshire Assoc of Youth Clubs 1975-81, clerk Peterborough Almshouses Tst 1988-91, Florence Saunders Tst 1980-91; FCA 1950, ATII 1960, ACIArb 1989; *Recreations* travel, opera, bowls; *Clubs* City and Counties (Peterborough); *Style—* Frederick Hunt, Esq; 29 Audley Gate, Peterborough PE3 6PG (☎ 0733 262 900)

HUNT, Geoffrey Harman; s of Alan Harman Hunt, of Riverside, Thames St, Wallingford and Alma Joan Spence, *née* Anderson; *b* 14 Oct 1955; *Educ* High Wycombe, Royal GS, Univ of Exeter (LLB); *Career* admitted slr 1980, ptnr Cardales 1981-86, co slr Vickers plc 1986-88, co exec Fitch Lovell plc 1988-; *Recreations* hockey, tennis, skiing; *Style—* Geoffrey Hunt, Esq; 130 Wymering Mansions, Wymering Rd, London W9 2NF; Fitch Lovell plc, Market House, 85 Cowcross St, London EC1M 6LL (☎ 01 250 1559, fax 01 250 3334)

HUNT, (Henry) Holman; CBE (1988); s of Henry Hunt (d 1951); *b* 13 May 1924; *Educ* Queen's Park Sch Glasgow, Univ of Glasgow (MA); *m* 1954, Sonja, *née* Blom; 1 s, 2 da; *Career* mgmnt conslt; bd dir PA Consulting Group (formerly PA Management Consultants Ltd) 1970-83, md PA Computers and Telecommunications 1976-83; dep chm MMC 1985- (memb 1980-), pres Inst of Mgmnt Consltts 1974-75; *Recreations* music, reading, walking, travel, photography, gardening; *Clubs* Caledonian; *Style—* Holman Hunt, Esq, CBE; 28 The Ridings, Epsom, Surrey KT18 5JJ (☎ Epsom 720974); New Court, 48 Carey St, London WC2A 2JT (☎ 071 324 1446)

HUNT, (Patrick) James; QC (1987); s of Thomas Ronald Clifford Hunt, and Doreen Gwyneth Katarina, *née* Granville-George; *b* 26 Jan 1943; *Educ* Ashby de la Zouch Boys GS, Keble Coll Oxford (MA); *m* 20 July 1969, Susan Jennifer Goodhead, JP, da of Noel Allen Goodhead, of Swadlincote; 1 s (Thomas Miles Benjamin b 1973), 3 da (Victoria Katharine b 1971, Suzanna Elisabeth b 1980, Alexandra Emily b 1982); *Career* called to the Bar Gray's Inn 1968; rec of the Crown Ct 1982; memb Gen Cncl of the Bar 1989-, legal assessor to Disciplinary Ctee Royal Coll of Vet Surgns 1990-; *Recreations* singing, stonework; *Clubs* Northants County; *Style—* James Hunt, QC; Easton Hall, Easton on the Hill, Stamford, Lincs PE9 3LL; 1 King's Bench Walk, Temple, London EC4 (☎ 071 353 8436)

HUNT, James Simon Wallis; s of Wallis Glyn Eunthorpe Hunt, of Wiltshire, and Susan Noel Wentworth, *née* Davis; *b* 29 Aug 1947; *Educ* Wellington; *m* 1 (m dis), Suzy Miller; m 2, 17 Dec 1983, Sarah, da of Ian Lomax; 2 s (Tom, Freddie); *Career* racing driver Hesketh and McLaren teams 1973-79, World Motor Racing Champion 1976, commentator BBC TV Motor Racing 1980-; *Style—* James Hunt, Esq

HUNT, John Beresford; s of Alfred Stanley Hunt (d 1984), of Ilminster, Somerset, and Elma Nellie, *née* Stacey (d 1983); *b* 22 March 1935; *Educ* Taunton Sch; *m* 19 Sept 1964, Patricia Ann, da of William Hillier Taylor (d 1968), of Corsham, Wilts; 1 s (Charles Beresford b 13 Aug 1965), 1 da (Victoria Mary b 17 Oct 1967); *Career* Nat Serv RA cmmnd 1957-59, Somerset LI TA 1962-68 (Capt 1963); sr ptnr Albert Goodman & Co 1979- (ptnr 1962-79); chm Soc of CA 1982, pres SW Soc of CA 1988; memb: Somerset Assoc for the Blind, Taunton Ct Leet, Somerset Health Authy; FCA 1957; *Recreations* tennis, golf; *Clubs* Taunton Rotary; *Style—* John Hunt, Esq; Perris, Hatch Beauchamp, Taunton, Somerset TA3 6TH (☎ 0823 480 383); Messrs Albert Goodman & Co, Mary Street House, Mary Street, Taunton, Somerset (☎ 0823 286 096, fax 0823 286 096)

HUNT, John Brian; s of Peter Douglas Hunt, of Croxley Green, Herts, and Cynthia Mary, *née* Weatherilt; *b* 19 April 1951; *Educ* Rickmansworth GS, Harlow Tech Coll, Open Univ (BA); *m* 7 Feb 1986, Christine Elizabeth, da of Ronald Arthur Curl; 1 step s (Dean Keith Halls b 18 Feb 1970), 1 step da (Candice Margaret Halls b 30 Nov 1971); *Career* trainee journalist Doncaster Newspapers 1970-73, Sheffield Morning Telegraph 1973-79, dep chief sub ed Oracle Teletext 1979-84, scriptwriter and dep news ed 1984-89, sr news ed Channel Four News 1989-; memb NUJ Nat Exec 1979, vice chm NUJ Broadcasting Industl Cncl 1988-89, chm ITN Jt Shops' Ctee 1989-, tstee ITN Pension Fund; *Recreations* cricket, football, photography, travel; *Clubs* Watford FC; *Style—* John Hunt, Esq; 54 Valley Walk, Croxley Green, Rickmansworth, Hertfordshire WD3 3TG (☎ 0923 240814); Channel 4 News, 200 Gray's Inn Rd, London WC1 (☎ 071 430 4601)

HUNT, John Edward Francis; s of Thomas Francis Hunt, of Apt 28, Gosfield Hall, Gosfield, nr Halstead, Essex, and Norah Margaret, *née* Camps; *b* 25 April 1938; *Educ* Marlborough, Queen's Coll Oxford (MA); *m* 1 May 1965, Annabel Gillian, da of late Cdr Bradwell Talbot Turner, CVO, DSO, OBE, RN, 2 s (Mark b 1967, Justin b 1972), 2 da (Tamara b 1969, Fenella b 1977); *Career* admitted slr 1962, ptnr Hunt & Hunt 1965-; former vestry clerk St Michael's Cornhill with St Peter le Poer and St Benet Fink in City of London, former clerk to Cornhill Ward, memb Glebe Ctee Dio of Chelmsford, churchwarden St Peter's S Hanningfield; Freeman City of London 1967; memb Law Soc; *Recreations* reading, tennis, music, browsing; *Style—* J E F Hunt, Esq; Hunt & Hunt, Lambourne House, 7 Western Rd, Romford, Essex CM3 8YW (☎ 0708 764 433, fax 0708 762 915)

HUNT, Baron (Life Peer UK 1966); Sir (Henry Cecil) John Hunt; KG (1979), CBE (1945), DSO (1944); s of Capt Cecil Edwin Hunt, MC (d 1914), and Ethel Helen, *née* Crookshank; *b* 22 June 1910; *Educ* Marlborough, Sandhurst; *m* 3 Sept 1936, Joy, da of Dr Mowbray-Green; 4 da (Sally, Susan, Prudence, Jennifer); *Career* sits as SLD Peer in House of Lords; ldr Br Expedition to Mt Everest 1952-53; cmd 11 KRRC in Italy and Middle East 1943-44 and 11 Indian Inf Brigade in Italy and Greece 1944-46; post-war as GSO ALF Centl Europe, Planning Staff MELF, HQ (1) Br Corps, Asst Cmdt Staff Coll 1953-55, Cdr 168 Inf Bde TA 1955-56; rector Aberdeen Univ 1963-66; advsr to PM during Nigerian Civil War 1968-70; memb Royal Cmmn on Press 1973-77; chm: Inquiry into Police in NI 1969, Parole Bd England and Wales 1967-73, Intermediate Treatment Ctee 1980-85; pres: Alpine Club and Climbers' Club, Br Mountaineering Cncl, Nat Ski Fedn, Nat Assoc of Probation Offrs, Cncl for Volunteers Overseas, Rainer Fndn; pres: RGS 1977-80, Cncl Nat Parks 1980-86; hon degree's: Aberdeen, Durham, London, Leeds, City, Sheffield; kt 1953; *Style—* The Rt Hon the Lord Hunt, KG, CBE, DSO; Highway Cottage, Aston, Henley-on-Thames, Oxon

HUNT, Sir John Leonard; MP (C) Ravensbourne 1974-); s of William John Hunt (d 1968), of Keston, Kent, and Dora Maud Hunt; *b* 27 Oct 1929; *Educ* Dulwich; *Career* Bromley Borough Cncl: memb 1953-65, Alderman 1961-65, Mayor 1964; memb London Stock Exchange 1958-69; Parly candidate (C) Lewisham South 1959; MP (C) Bromley 1964-74; memb: Gen Advsy Cncl BBC 1975-87, Select Ctee on Home Affrs 1979-87 (memb chm's panel 1980-); jt chm Indo-British Parly Gp, memb UK Delgn to Cncl of Europe and Western Euro Union 1988-; kt 1989; *Style—* Sir John Hunt, MP; House of Commons, London, SW1A OAA

HUNT, Dr John Leslie; OBE (1987); s of Leslie Hunt (d 1963), of Christchurch, NZ, and Helen, *née* Clarke (d 1971); *b* 24 Jan 1924; *Educ* Christ's Coll Christchurch NZ, Canterbury Univ Coll, Otago Univ Med Sch Dunedin New Zealand (MB ChB, MRCP); *Career* med registrar Guy's Hosp London 1955-56, med advsr and mangr Med Dept British Drug Houses Ltd London 1957-60, lately princ (formerly sr) MO Dept of Health London; ed in chief of occasional official reports on health medicinal and social concerns for DHSS 1960-88; fndn ed: Prescriber's Journal 1961-89, Health Trends 1969-89; ed Annual Report on the State of Public Health 1962-88; ctee memb Australia and NZ Med and Dental Assoc; FFCM (formerly MFCM) 1979, FFPHM 1989; *Recreations* philology, reading, writing, travel; *Style—* Dr John Hunt, OBE; 109 Northcote Rd, Battersea, London SW11 6PN (☎ 071 738 0843)

HUNT, John Maitland; s of Richard Herbert Alexander Hunt (d 1978), and Eileen Mary Isabelle, *née* Witt; *b* 4 March 1932; *Educ* Radley, Wadham Coll Oxford (MA, BLitt); *m* 26 July 1969, Sarah, da of Lt-Gen Sir Derek Lang, KCB, DSO, MC, of W Lothian; 2 s (Jonathan Alexander b 1971, Richard Martin b 1973); *Career* sixth form tutor and head of Geography Dept Stowe Sch 1958-70; headmaster Roedean Sch 1971-84; FRGS; *Recreations* estate mgmnt, writing, travel; *Clubs* Royal Cwlth Soc; *Style—* John Hunt, Esq; Logie, Dunfermline, Fife KY12 8QN (☎ 0383 724357)

HUNT, Jonathan Charles Vivian; OBE (1983, 2nd clasp 1990), TD (1977, clasp 1983), DL (S Yorks 1981); s of Col George Vivian Hunt, OBE, TD (d 1979), of The Lodge, Woodvale Rd, Sheffield, and Sylvia Ann, *née* Tyzack (d 1985); *b* 6 March 1943; *Educ* Stowe; *m* 17 July 1971, Susan Aline, eld da of Francis Rawdon Crozier, of Thorpell House, Wickham Market, Woodbridge, Suffolk; 2 s (James b 14 Sept 1973, Edward 6 June 1976); *Career* TA: cmmnd Queen's Own Yorks Yeo 1963, transfd B (Sherwood Rangers Yeo) Sqdn Royal Yeo (OC 1975-78), cmd Royal Yeo 1979-82, Dep Cdr 49 Inf Bde 1983-87, Project Offr Fast Track (new TA compact commissioning course) 1987-91; Col TA: RMA Sandhurst 1988-91, Ind Units MOD 1991-; sr ptnr Wakesmith & Co Slrs Sheffield 1988- (ptnr 1967), dir Sheffield Training and Enterprise Cncl 1990-; chm: Sheffield Enterprise Agency Ltd 1986-, Rotherham Rural Div SSAFA; memb Law Soc 1966; *Recreations* sailing, walking, golf, TA; *Clubs* Sheffield, Lindrick Golf, Cavalry and Guards'; *Style—* Jonathan C V Hunt, Esq, OBE, TD, DL

HUNT, Dr the Hon Jonathan Philip Henderson; s of Baron Hunt of Fawley, CBE, (Life Peer d 1987); *b* 1947; *Educ* Charterhouse, Pembroke Coll Oxford (MA, BM, BCh), St Thomas's Hosp; *m* 1977, Monika, da of Dr Herbert Kuhlmann, of Schloss Urstein, Salzburg, Austria; 3 da; *Career* physician; *Style—* Dr the Hon Jonathan Hunt; 29 South Terrace, London SW7; 82 Sloane St, London SW7

HUNT, Brig Kenneth; OBE (1955), MC (1943); s of John Hunt (d 1952), and Elizabeth, *née* Sills (d 1974); *b* 26 May 1914; *Educ* Chatham House Sch Ramsgate, Army Staff Coll Camberley, IDC; *m* 28 Jan 1939, Mary Mabel, da of Charles Crickett (d 1962); 2 s (Timothy John Leigh b 30 July 1949, Jeremy Peter b 25 Sept 1950), 1 da (Sarah Elizabeth b and d 1948); *Career* cmmnd RA 1940, Africa, Italy, Austria with HAC, 1 RHA and 2 RHA 1942-46, Brevet Lt-Col 1955, CO 40 FD Regt 1958-60, Brig and CRA 51 Highland Div 1961-63, dep standing gp rep NATO Cncl 1964-66, resigned 1967; specialist advsr House of Commons Def Ctee 1971-84, dir Br Atlantic Ctee 1978-81; visiting prof: Fletcher Sch of Law Cambridge Mass 1975, Univ of Surrey 1978-86, Univ of Southern California 1979; res assoc Inst for Peace and Security Tokyo 1979-88, vice pres Int Inst for Strategic Studies 1988 (dep dir 1967-77); Freeman City of London 1977; Hon Dr political sci Korea Univ S Korea 1977; Order of the Rising Sun (3rd Class) Japan 1984; *Books* The Third World War (jtly, 1978), Europe in the Western Alliance (ed, 1988); *Recreations* fly fishing; *Clubs* Army & Navy; *Style—* Brig Kenneth Hunt, OBE, MC; 22 The Green, Ewell, Epsom, Surrey KT17 3JN (☎ 081 393 7906); Int Inst for Strategic Studies, 23 Tavistock St, London WC2E 7NQ (☎ 071 379 7676)

HUNT, Brig Malcolm Peter John; OBE (1984); s of Peter Gordon Hunt, of 2 Shilling St, Lavenham, Suffolk, and Rachel Margaret, *née* Owston; *b* 19 Nov 1938; *Educ* St John's Sch Leatherhead Surrey; *m* 22 Dec 1962, Margaret, da of Samuel Beadman Peat (d 1966); 2 s (James b 3 Dec 1964, John b 14 Dec 1966); *Career* joined RM 1957, 45 commando RM 1960-61 Malta, Aden, HMS Nubian 1966-68, Army Staff Coll Camberley 1971, Staff HQ 3 Commando Bde 1971-74, instr Army Staff Coll 1979-81,

CO 40 commando RM 1981-83 Falklands and NI, HQ NATO 1984-87, MOD 1987-90; *Recreations* reading, theatre, politics, all sport; *Style—* Brig Malcolm Hunt, OBE; c/o National Westminster Bank, 52 Royal Parade, Plymouth PL1 1ED

HUNT, Hon Martin John; s of Baron Hunt of Tanworth, GCB (Life Peer), and Hon Magdalen Mary (d 1971), da of 1 Baron Robinson; *b* 19 Nov 1962; *Educ* Worth Abbey, The City Univ; *Career* commodity broker, fund mangr Adam Harding Lueck Ltd; dir Futures Management Ltd 1985-89; *Recreations* skiing, motor racing, photography, shooting; *Style—* The Hon Martin Hunt; 24 Burnthwaite Rd, London SW6 5BE (☎ 071 381 4988); c/o Adam, Harding & Lueck Ltd, Willow House, Willow Place, London SW1P 1JH (☎ 071 931 8500)

HUNT, Maurice William; s of Maurice Hunt (d 1987), of London, and Helen, *née* Andrews; *b* 30 Aug 1936; *Educ* Selhurst GS Croydon Surrey, LSE (BSc); *m* 27 Aug 1960, Jean Mary, da of Herbert Ellis (d 1940); 1 s (Neil b 1965), 1 da (Claire b 1966); *Career* Nat Serv RAF 1955-57; ANZ Bank London 1953-66, Jt Iron Cncl 1967, Bd of Trade DTI 1968-84, RCDS 1982, sec and exec dir ops CBI 1984-85, dep dir gen AIB 1987-; *Clubs* RAC; *Style—* Maurice Hunt, Esq; 24 Fairford Close, Haywards Heath West Sussex (☎ 0444 452 916); Centre Point, New Oxford St, London WC1A IDU (☎ 071 379 7400, fax 071 240 1578, telex 21332)

HUNT, Hon Michael Anthony; s of Baron Hunt of Tanworth, GCB, and Hon Magdalen (d 1971), da of 1 Baron Robinson; *b* 1942; *m* 1963, Rosemary Ann, da of late Col Theodore Ernle Longridge, OBE; *Style—* The Hon Michael Hunt; 86 Foxhill, Olney, Bucks, MK46 5HF

HUNT, Dr Michael Ralph; s of Benjamin William Hunt (d 1975), and Marjorie Alice, *née* Atkinson; *b* 8 Jan 1939; *Educ* Haberdashers' Aske's, Univ of Bristol (BSc, PhD); *m* 8 June 1962, Catherine Claire, da of Sidney Jules Block (d 1974); 2 s (Graham b 1966, Stephen b 1968); *Career* postdoctoral fellowship Nat Res Cncl Ottawa Canada 1963-65, sci offr Central Electricity Res Labs 1965-70; Akzo Salt Chemical Div Holland: various positions 1970-81, res and devpt dir 1981-82, dir of chloralkali products 1982-86; md Akzo Chemicals Ltd 1986-; memb CBI SE cncl 1987-, memb CEFIC sector gp gen ctee 1982-86; author of six scientific papers, owner of one patent; *Recreations* music, art, sport, skiing, tennis; *Style—* Dr Michael Hunt; 1 Fife Way, Great Bookham, Surrey KT23 3PH (☎ 0372 58616); AKZO Chemicals Ltd, 1-5 Queens Rd, Hersham, Walton-on-Thames, Surrey KT12 5NL (☎ 0932 247891, fax 0932 231204, telex 21997)

HUNT, Adm Sir Nicholas John Streynsham; GCB (1987, KCB 1985), LVO (1961); s of Brig John Montgomerie Hunt (d 1980), of Godalming, Surrey, and Elizabeth, *née* Yates; *b* 7 Nov 1930; *Educ* RNC Dartmouth; *m* 1966, Meriel Eve, da of Maj Henry Cooke Givan; 2 s, 1 da; *Career* exec offr HMS Ark Royal 1969-71, RCDS 1974, dir of Naval Plans 1976-78, Flag Offr 2 Flotilla 1980-81, DG Naval Manpower and Trg 1981-83, Flag Offr Scot and NI 1983-85, C-in-C Fleet, Allied C-in-C Channel, C-in-C East Atlantic Area 1985-87; sometime asst private sec to HRH Princess Marina, Duchess of Kent; dep md (orgn and devpt) Eurotunnel; dir-gen Gen Cncl of British Shipping 1991-; chm: SW Surrey Dist Health Authy 1990-, Royal Navy Club of 1765 and 1785; cmmr Cwlth War Graves Cmmn, vice-pres English Speaking Union of Malta; CBIM; *Clubs* Boodle's, Woodroffes; *Style—* Adm Sir Nicholas Hunt, GCB, LVO; c/o Boodles, St James's, London

HUNT, (David) Peter; s of Rev Charles Christopher Hunt (d 1987), of Neasham, Co Durham, and Edna, *née* Clarke; *b* 25 April 1951; *Educ* Grangefield GS Stockton, Keble Coll Oxford (MA); *m* 1 June 1984, Cherryl Janet, da of Alexander Hubert Nicholson, of Pinner, Middx; 2 s (James b 1985, Nicholas b 1987); *Career* called to the Bar Gray's Inn 1974; memb Bar Cncl 1981-84, jr NE circuit 1982; *Books* Distribution of Matrimonial Assets on Divorce (1990); *Recreations* watching cricket, running; *Style—* Peter Hunt, Esq; 25 Park Square, Leeds LS1 2PW (☎ 0532 451, fax 0532 420 194)

HUNT, Sir Rex Masterman; CMG (1980); s of Henry William Hunt (d 1982), of Burnham, Bucks, and Ivy, *née* Masterman; *b* 29 June 1926; *Educ* Coatham Sch, St Peter's Coll Oxford (BA); *m* 22 Sept 1951, Mavis Amanda, da of George Arthur Buckland, MM, of Chingford, Essex; 1 s (Antony Paul Masterman b 29 June 1964), 1 da (Diana Molly Amanda (Mrs Thurman) b 2 May 1962); *Career* RAF 1944-48, Fighter Pilot Nos 5 and 26 Sqdns, Flt Lt; Hon Air Cdre RAuxAF No 2729 (City of Lincoln) Sqdn; Overseas Civil Service 1951: dist cmmr Uganda 1962, CRO 1963-64, first sec Kuching (Sarawak) 1964-65, Jesselton (Sabah) 1965-67, Brunei 1967, first sec (economic) Ankara 1968-70, first sec and head of chancery Jakarta 1970-72, M East Dept FCO 1972-74; cnsllr: Saigon 1974-75, Kuala Lumpur 1976-77; dep high cmmr 1977-79, high cmmr Br Antarctic Territory 1980-85; govr and C-in-C Falkland Islands 1980-82, temporarily forced to evacuate Islands owing to Argentinian invasion in April 1982, returned June 1982 as civil cmmr (govr 1985); pres Falkland Islands Assoc, vice pres World Ship Tst; vice pres Falkland Islands Fndn; Freeman of City of London 1979, Freedom of Stanley (Falkland Islands) 1985; kt 1982; *Recreations* golf, gardening; *Clubs* Wentworth; *Style—* Sir Rex Hunt, CMG

HUNT, Richard Bruce; s of late Percy Thompson Hunt; *b* 15 Dec 1927; *Educ* Christ's Hosp; *m* 1972, Ulrike Dorothea, *née* Schmidt; 2 da; *Career* md R B Hunt and Ptnrs Ltd 1966-, dir Baltic Exchange 1977-80 (re-elected 1981, chm 1985-87), dep chm Howe Robinson & Co Ltd 1990-; govr Christ's Hosp 1980-; Liveryman Worshipful Co of Shipwrights 1980; FICS 1955; *Recreations* golf, skiing; *Clubs* Royal Lymington Yacht, Royal Wimbledon Golf; *Style—* Richard Hunt, Esq; 77 Mansell Street, London E1 8AF

HUNT, Sir Robert Frederick; CBE (1974), DL (Glos 1977); s of Arthur Hunt, of Cheltenham; *b* 11 May 1918; *Educ* Pates G S Cheltenham, N Glos Tech Coll; *m* 1947, Joy (d 1984), da of Charles Harding; 4 da (of whom Jacqueline m Peter Heywood, *qv*); m 2, 1987, Joyce Baigent, da of Otto Leiske; *Career* WWII RAF Trg Cmd; joined Dowty Equipment as apprentice 1935; Dowty Gp: dir 1956-86, dep chm 1959-75, chief exec 1975-83, chm 1975-86; dir: Dowty Equipment of Canada 1949-86 (pres 1954-76, chm 1973-86), BL 1980-88 (dep chm 1982-88), Eagle Star Insur 1980-88, Dellfield Ltd 1983-86, Charter Consolidated 1983-; chm: gp mgmnt ctee Cheltenham Hosp 1959-74, Glos AHA 1974-81; Hon DSc Bath, Hon FRAes; FEng, FCASI; kt 1979; *Style—* Sir Robert Hunt, CBE, DL; Maple House, Withington, Glos GL58 4DA (☎ 0242 89344)

HUNT, Lady Rowena; *née* Montagu-Stuart-Wortley-Mackenzie; yr da of 4 Earl of Wharncliffe (d 1987), and Dowager Countess of Wharncliffe, *qv*; *b* 14 June 1961; *m* Oct 1986, John Hunt, s of Dr H G Hunt, of Greenwich; 1 s (Somerset Carlton Gerald b 9 Oct 1987); *Style—* The Lady Rowena Hunt; Minety House, Minety, nr Malmesbury, Wilts

HUNT, Terence William; s of William Herbert Hunt, (d 1983), and Audrey, *née* Austen; *b* 8 June 1955; *Educ* Royal Liberty GS, UEA (BA); *Career* teacher N Africa 1977-78, graduate trainee Macmillan Publishers 1978-79, copywriter Smith Bundy Partners 1979-83, bd dir DDM Advertising 1986 (creative dir 1983-86), chm Evans Hunt Scott 1990 (founding ptnr 1986); winner: over 40 creative and mktg awards, Most Creative Direct Marketer Campaign Poll 1989; *Books* Nationwide Book of Literary Quizzes (1979); *Recreations* Family, Running, Collecting Books; *Clubs* Groucho, Colony Rooms, Champneys; *Style—* Terry Hunt, Esq; 11 Granard Rd, London SW12 8UJ; Evans Hunt Scott/dma, New London House, 172 Drury Lane, London WC2B 5QR (☎ 071 242 2800, fax 071 831 3075)

HUNT, Terry; s of Thomas John Hunt (d 1976), of Taunton, Som, and Marie Louise, *née* Potter; *b* 8 Aug 1943; *Educ* Huish's GS Taunton; *m* 7 Jan 1967, Wendy Graeme, da of Dr Aldwyn Morgan George, MC, of Perranwell Cornwall; 1 s (Philip Benjamin (Ben) b 1968), 1 da (Nicola Jane b 1969); *Career* hosp admin: Tone Vale Hosp 1963-65, NE Som Hosps 1965-67, Winchester Hosps 1967-69, Lincoln Co Hosp 1969-70; hosp sec Wycombe Gen Hosp 1970-73, dep gp sec Hillingdon Hosps 1973-74, area gen admin Kensington & Chelsea and Westminster AHA (T) 1974-76, dist admin NW Kensington & Chelsea and Westminster 1976-82, dist admin Paddington & N Kensington Health Authy 1982-84; gen mangr NE Thames RHA 1984-; memb : Twyford & Dist Round Table 1975-84 (chm 1980-81, pres 1988), Ctee Reading Town Regatta 1983- (treas 1984-86, chm 1989-); memb Inst of Health Serv Mgmnt; *Recreations* sculling, rowing, cycling; *Style—* Terry Hunt, Esq; 36 Old Bath Road, Charvil, Reading, Berks (☎ 0734 341 062); 40 Eastbourne Terrace, London W2 (☎ 071 262 8011 ext 2037, fax 071 723 6623)

HUNT-DAVIS, Brig Miles Garth; CBE (1990, MBE 1977); s of Lt-Col Eric Hunt Davis, OBE, ED (d 1977), of Johannesburg, SA, and Mary Eleanor, *née* Boyce (d 1964); *b* 7 Nov 1938; *Educ* St Andrew's Coll Grahamstown SA; *m* 11 Jan 1965, (Anita) Gay, da of Francis James Ridsdale, of SA; 2 s (Justin b 11 Sept 1970, Benedict b 15 March 1972), 1 da (Joanna b 2 Jun 1968); *Career* cmmnd 6 Queen Elizabeth's Own Gurkha Rifles 1962, active serv Borneo and Malaya 1964-66, student Canadian Land Forces Cmd and Staff Coll 1969-70, Brig Maj 48 Gurkha Infantry Brigade 1974-76, Cmdt 7 Duke of Edinburgh's Own Gurkha Rifles 1976-79, Instr Staff Coll Camberley 1982-83; Cdr: Br Gurkhas Nepal 1985-87, Bde of Gurkhas 1987-90; hon pres Scout Assoc of Hong Kong, chm Gurkha Bd Assoc; FBIM 1983; *Books* Abridged History of the 6th Queen Elizabeth's Own Gurkha Rifles (1974); *Recreations* golf, Gurkha war medals; *Clubs* Johannesburg Country, Royal Hong Kong Golf, Commonwealth Trust, West Wilts Golf; *Style—* Brig Miles Hunt-Davis, CBE; Child and Co, 1 Fleet St, London EC4Y 1BD

HUNT OF TANWORTH, Baron (Life Peer UK 1980), of Stratford-upon-Avon; John Joseph Benedict; GCB (1977, KCB 1973, CB 1968); s of Maj Arthur L Hunt, MC (d 1959), of Hale House, Churt, Surrey, and Daphne Hunt (d 1956); *b* 23 Oct 1919; *Educ* Downside, Magdalene Coll Cambridge; *m* 1, 1941, Hon Magdalen Mary (d 1971), da of 1 Baron Robinson (d 1952); 2 s (Hon Michael, *qv*, Hon Martin b 1962, *qv*), 1 da (Hon Mrs H Gill b 1947); m 2, 1973, Madeleine Frances, da of Sir William Hume, CMG, and wid of Sir John Charles, KCB; *Career* RNVR 1940; Dominions Off 1946, attached office of High Cmmr for UK in Ceylon 1948-50, memb directing staff IDC 1951-52, office of High Cmmr for UK in Canada 1953-56, private sec to sec of Cabinet 1956-58, private sec to perm sec to Treasy and head of Civil Serv 1957-58, CRO 1958-60, Cabinet Off 1960-62, HM Treasy 1962, under-sec 1965-67, dep-sec 1968, first Civil Serv cmmr and dep sec CSD 1968-71, HM Treasy 1971, second perm sec Cabinet Off 1972, sec Cabinet 1973-79; chm Banque Nationale de Paris 1980-, dir IBM UK 1980-89, advsy dir Unilever 1980-90; chm: Disaster Emergency Ctee 1981-89, Govt Inquiry into Cable Expansion and Broadcasting Policy 1982, Ditchley Fndn 1983-, Tablet Publishing Co 1984-, Prudential Corp 1985-90 (dir 1980-, dep chm 1982-85); hon fell Magdalene Coll Cambridge; Officier Légion d'Honneur (France) 1987-; *Style—* The Rt Hon the Lord Hunt of Tanworth, GCB; 8 Wool Rd, Wimbledon, London SW20 (☎ 081 947 7640)

HUNTER, Hon Alan Marshall; s of Baron Hunter of Newington, MBE (Life Baron), *qv*; *b* 1946; *m* 1971, Elizabeth Goodall; *Style—* The Hon Alan Hunter; 31 Hillcrest Avenue, Nether Poppleton, York

HUNTER, Dr (James) Albert; TD (1965); s of John Nicolson Hunter (d 1958), of Annesville, Aith, Bixter, Shetland, and Mary Ann, *née* Tait (d 1950); *b* 2 May 1914; *Educ* Anderson Educnl Inst Lerwick, Royal Colls of Edinburgh Sch of Med; *m* 1, 21 July 1947 (m dis 1952), Helen, da of John Harrison (d 1961), of Woosung, 43 St Olaf St, Lerwick, Shetland; m 2, 21 Jan 1953, Helena Cathy (d 1977), da of Walter Fraser (d 1943), of Fairview, Whiteness, Shetland; 4 s (John Nicolson, Walter James Innes, Hamish Halcrow, Fraser Smith), 2 da (Christine Bryden Hunter, Eleanor Catherine Jane); *Career* Nat Serv Lt RAMC 1940, Capt 1941, Maj RAMC TA 1951-675; MO Sanatorium Unit Bridge of Earn Hosp Scot 1946 (Bangour Hosp Scot 1946), jr asst tuberculosis offr Edinburgh 1947, GP Voe Shetland 1962-78 (Bixter Shetland 1947-62); chm: RNLI Ctee Aith Shetland 1950-62, Social Work Ctee Shetland Is Cncl, Shetland Local Health Cncl 1979-91, Shetland Cons Assoc 1990; memb: Scot Thoracic Soc 1946, Shetland Is Cncl S Delting area 1978-90, Governing Body Northern Coll of Educn 1988-91; memb BMA 1939-, LRCPE, LRCSE, LRFP SG; *Recreations* angling, photography; *Style—* Dr Albert Hunter, TD; Kohima, Gott, Shetland ZE2 9SG (☎ 059 584 367)

HUNTER, Sir Alexander Albert; KBE (1976); s of Alexander Hunter, KSG; *b* 21 May 1920; *Educ* St John's Coll Belize, Regis Coll Denver USA, Queen's Univ Kingston Canada; *m* 1947, Araceli; 1 s, 2 da; *Career* served WWII RAF; joined James Brodie and Co 1947; co sec 1948, dir 1952-61, conslt 1975-82; Belize: MLA (PUP) 1961, min of Natural Resources Commerce and Industry 1961, MHR (PUP) 1965, min of Natural Resources and Trade 1965-69, min of Trade and Industry 1969-74; speaker of the House of Representatives of Belize 1974-79; rep of and conslt to: Auschutz Overseas Corp (Petroleum) Denver Colorado 1975-82, Pecten Belize Co (Shell Oil) Houston Texas 1982-; *Style—* Sir Alexander Hunter, KBE; 6 St Matthew St, Caribbean Shores, Belize City, Belize (☎ 44482)

HUNTER, Alexander Dudgeon; s of Ellis Dudgeon Hunter (d 1964), Monkscroft, Dunbar; *b* 5 Sept 1920; *Educ* Merchiston Castle Edinburgh, Heriot-Watt Univ Edinburgh; *m* 1944, Iris Patricia, da of William Grieve Reid Findlay (d 1963), of Felbrigg, Dunbar; *Career* chm, md and head brewer Belhaven Brewery Co Ltd 1972-82, dir Belhaven Brewery Gp 1972-82; brewing conslt 1983; *Recreations* swimming, gardening; *Clubs* Merchistonian, Scottish Wayfarers, Dunbar S and RFC; *Style—* Alexander Hunter, Esq; Monkscroft, Dunbar, East Lothian (☎ 0368 63309)

HUNTER, Air Vice-Marshal Alexander Freeland Cairns (Sandy); CBE (1982, OBE 1981), AFC (1978); s of Herbert Andrew Cairns Hunter (d 1948), and Lillian Edith Middleton, *née* Trail; *b* 8 March 1939; *Educ* Aberdeen GS, Univ of Aberdeen (MA, LLB); *m* 7 Nov 1964, Wilma Elizabeth, da of Howard Bruce-Wilson (d 1958); *Career* RAFVR 1957-62, RAF 1962-, 81 (PR) Sqdn FEAF 1964-67, Central Flying Sch 1967-68, Northumbrian Univs Air Sqdn 1968-69, Asst Air Attaché Moscow 1971-75, RAF Staff Coll 1974, Flt Cdr 230 Sqdn 1975-77, OC 18 Sqdn RAF Germany 1978-80, Air Warfare Course 1981, MOD (Air) Policy Div 1981, OC RAF Odiham 1981-83, Gp Capt Plans HQ Strike Cmd 1983-85, RCDS 1986, dir of PR for RAF 1987-88, Cmdt RAF Staff Coll 1989-90, admin of Sovereign Base Areas of Akrotiri and Dhekalia and cdr Br Forces Cyprus 1990-; *Recreations* shooting, fishing, hill walking, military history; *Style—* Air Vice-Marshall Sandy Hunter, CBE, AFC; Headquarters British Forces, Cyprus BFPO 53

HUNTER, Andrew Lorimer; s of Eric Newton Hunter (d 1982), of Gairloch, Wester Ross, Scotland, and Elizabeth Mary Anne, *née* Ewing; *b* 27 July 1946; *Educ* George Watson's Coll Edinburgh, Edinburgh Sch of Art; *m* 1, 1970 (m dis 1988), Patricia Thérèse O'Rourke; 1 s (Daniel b 1973), 1 da (Harriet b 1976); m 2, Alison Janet, da of Prof Ian Adair Silver, *qv*; *Career* packaging designer trainee William Thyne Ltd 1966-

70, dir Forth Studios 1973-79 (designer 1970-73), fndr and jt md Tayburn Design 1979-87, design dir McIlroy Coates Design Consultants 1987-; external assessor Scotvec Graphic Design courses 1987-, memb Advsy Bd Univ of Dundee for Duncan of Jordanstone Sch of Art 1990-; maj design projects incl: corporate indentity Murray Johnstone, identity and literature Glasgow Royal Concert Hall, corporate literature NCR Corp; fndr memb Creative Forum, memb D&ADA 1980, FCSD 1985 (MCSD 1966, chm Scot 1991-); *Recreations* skiing, hill walking, fishing, tennis, travel, gardening; *Style*— Andrew Hunter, Esq; Kinloch House, Market St, Haddington, East Lothian EH41 3JL (☎ 062 082 5981); McIlroy Coates Design Consultants, 10 Bernard St, Leith, Edinburgh EH6 6PP (☎ 031 555 1342, fax 031 555 1343)

HUNTER, Andrew Robert Frederick; MP (C) Basingstoke 1983-; s of late Sqdn Ldr Roger Edward Hunter, DFC, of Winchester, and Winifred Mary, *née* Nelson; *b* 8 Jan 1943; *Educ* St George's Sch Harpenden, Univ of Durham, Jesus Coll Cambridge; *m* 1972, Janet, da of Samuel Bourne, of Gloucester; 1 s, 1 da; *Career* Maj TAVR 1973- (resigned 1984); in indust 1969, asst master Harrow Sch 1971-83, parly candidate (C) Southampton Itchen 1979, sec Cons Environment Ctee 1984-85, memb Agric Select Ctee 1985, PPS to Lord Elton Min of State Dept of the Environment 1985-86, memb Environment Select Ctee 1986-, vice chm Cons Agric Ctee 1987-, fndr chm Parly Br/ Bophuthatswana Gp 1987-88 (sec 1988-), sec Cons NI Ctee 1990-, memb Land Usage Ctee CLA 1986-; memb Ct Univ of Southampton 1983-, vice pres Nat Prayer Book Soc 1987-; memb: NFU, Br Field Sports Soc (chm Falconry Ctee 1988-); Order of Polonia Restituta 1980; hon memb Soc of the Sealed Knot; *Recreations* cricket, field sports, model soldiers; *Clubs* MCC; *Style*— Andrew Hunter, Esq, MP; House of Commons, London SW1A OAA (☎ 01 219 5216)

HUNTER, Dr Anthony Rex (Tony); s of Ranulph Rex Hunter, of Bucksford Lodge, Great Chart, Ashford, Kent, and Nellie Ruby Elsie, *née* Hitchcock; *b* 23 Aug 1943; *Educ* Felsted, Gonville and Caius Coll Cambridge (BA, MD, PhD); *m* 1969 (m dis 1974), Philippa Charlotte Marrack; *Career* res fell Christ's Coll Cambridge 1968-71 and 1973-75; Salk Inst La Jolla: res assoc 1971-73, asst prof 1975-78, assoc prof 1978-82, prof 1982-; adjunct assoc prof Univ of Calif San Diego 1979-83, adjunct prof Univ of Calif 1983-; memb Editorial Bd: Molecular and Cellular Biology 1982-88 (ed 1989-), Jl of Virology 1982-, Molecular Endocrinology 1987-, Cancer Cells 1989-; assoc ed: Cell 1980-, Virology 1982-; Ludwig Inst for Cancer Res Scientific Review Ctee: chm Melbourne Branch 1987- (memb 1983-86), chm Middlesex Branch 1988-; memb: Advsy Ctee Frederick Cancer Res Facility 1985-89, Scientific Review Bd Howard Hughes Med Inst 1989-, Biology Panel AAAS Project 2061; vice chm Animal Cells and Viruses Gordon Conf 1988; FRS 1987, American Business Fndn for Cancer Res Award 1988; *Books* over 200 scientific pubns; *Recreations* white water rafting, exploring Baja peninsula; *Style*— Dr Tony Hunter, FRS; Molecular Biology and Virology Laboratory, The Salk Institute, PO Box 85800, San Diego, California 92186, USA (☎ 619 453 4100)

HUNTER, Brig (John) Antony; DSO (1944), OBE (1955, MBE 1943), MC 1942; s of Maj-Gen Sir Alan Hunter, KCVO, CB, CMG, DSO, MC (d 1942), and Hon Joan, *née* Adderley (d 1988), da of 5 Baron Norton; *b* 12 Jan 1991; *Educ* Stowe, RMC Sandhurst; *m* 1, 14 Feb 1944 (m dis 1971), Dauphine Laetitia Janet Colquhoun (d 1979), da of Nicholas Conyngham Simons Bosanquet (d 1955); 1 s (Antony b 1945), 1 da (Sarah (Mrs Ellson) b 1947); m 2, 1971, Carole, da of Dr David Reid Milligan (d 1985); *Career* cmmnd 60 Rifles 1934; regtl serv 1934-39: Ireland, Burma, Egypt; GSO3 (later GSO2) intelligence GHQ ME 1940-41, Co Cdr 1 KRRC Western Desert and Libya 1941-42, Bde Maj 4 Armd Bde El Alamein 1942, Staff Coll Haifa 1942-43, GSO2 ops HQ 13 Corps invasion of Sicily 1943, DSD Staff Coll Camberley 1943-44, CO 8 Bn The Rifle Bde Normandy to Germany 1944-45, GSO1 HQ 21 Army Gp Germany 1945-46, chief instr New Coll Sandhurst 1947-50, Jt Servs Staff Coll 1951, GSO1 6 Armd Div Germany 1952-55, CO 1 Bn Beds and Herts Regt 1955-57, Col GS ME ops WO Whitehall 1957-59, Cdr 11 Inf Bde Gp Germany 1960, ret 1960; Union Castle Line: 2 i/c Southampton 1960-63, dir staff Admin Staff Coll Henley 1963-64, area dir Southampton 1964-77 (also dir: Union Castle Line, Cayzer Irvine & Co, London & Southampton Stevedoring Co); regnl dir Lloyds Bank Salisbury region 1974-85, dir Red Funnel Gp 1977-85 (chm Vectis Tport Co), pres Ocean Sound Hldgs plc (dir 1984-), dir Southampton C of C 1966-75 (pres 1972-73); dir and dep chm Southern Radio Hldgs 1989-90; Freeman: City of London 1983, Worshipful Co of Bowyers 1983; FIOD 1966-85, MBIM 1966-77, MCIT 1966-77; *Recreations* fishing, shooting, archery, skiing; *Style*— Brig Antony Hunter, DSO, OBE, MC; The Wheelwrights, Warmington, Banbury OX17 1DB

HUNTER, (Charles) Christopher; s of Charles William Hunter (d 1972), of Nottingham, and Dorothy Mary, *née* Ward; *b* 2 Feb 1950; *Educ* High Pavement GS Nottingham, Guy's Hosp Univ of London (MB BS, Dip of Psychological Med); *Career* surgn Lt RN 1974-79 (med offr HMS Glamorgan 1974-76); conslt forensic psychiatrist and dep med dir Park Lane Hosp Liverpool 1982-89, conslt forensic psychiatrist and co-ordinator of the All Wales Forensic Psychiatric Service 1989-, advsr in forensic psychiatry to the Welsh Office 1989-; clinical teacher in forensic psychiatry Univ of Wales Coll of Med; memb BMA, MRCPsych 1980- (memb Exec Ctee forensic section), MRCS, LRCP; *Recreations* reading, theatre, travel; *Style*— Dr Christopher Hunter; Dept of Forensic Psychiatric Services, Whitchurch Hospital, Whitchurch, Cardiff, South Glamorgan (☎ 0222 693191, fax 0222 614799)

HUNTER, Doreen Eleanor Maude; da of James Wylie Hunter, of 9 Larch Hill Avenue, Craigavad, Holywood, Co Down, and Maude Elizabeth, *née* Warnock; *b* 14 Feb 1940; *Educ* Richmond Lodge Sch Belfast, Queen's Univ Belfast (BA), Univ of Reading (Dip Ed); *Career* headmistress: Princess Gardens Sch Belfast 1982-87, Hunterhouse Coll Belfast 1987-; govr Rockport Prep Sch Co Down 1987-, chm ptnrship NI Boarding Schs and Colls 1987-90, dir NI Railways 1987-; memb SHA 1982-; *Recreations* gardening, golf; *Clubs* Royal Belfast Golf, Malone Golf; *Style*— Miss Doreen Hunter; Hunterhouse Coll, Finaghy, Belfast BT10 0LE (☎ 0232 612293/612 588)

HUNTER, Geoffrey Martin; s of Albert Hunter, of Chester-le-Street, Co Durham, and Mary, *née* Martin; *b* 4 Jan 1956; *Educ* Chester-le-Street GS, Univ of Newcastle-upon-Tyne (LLB); *Career* called to the Bar Gray's Inn 1979, in practice NE circuit; *Recreations* motor sport, hot-air ballooning, ornithology; *Style*— G M Hunter, Esq; 73 Westgate Rd, Newcastle upon Tyne NE1 1SQ, (☎ 091 261 4407, 091 232 9785, fax 091 222 1845)

HUNTER, Sir Ian Bruce Hope; MBE (1945); s of William O Hunter; *b* 2 April 1919; *Educ* Fettes; *m* 1, 1949, Susan (d 1977), da of late Brig Alec Gaudie Russell; 4 da (Eugenie, Josephine, Serena, Catherine); m 2, 1984, Marie Sadie, da of Charles Golden, and wid of Sir Keith Showering (d 1982); 4 step s, 2 step da; *Career* dir numerous music festivals in UK and abroad: Bath 1948-68, Edinburgh 1950-55, City of London 1962-80, Brighton 1967-83, Hong Kong 1973-75; dir gen Cwlth Arts Festival 1965, pres and dir Harold Holt Ltd; chm: London Festival Ballet Tst 1984-89, Musicians Benevolent Fund 1987-; dir Euro Arts Fndn 1989-, vice chm Japan Festival Soc 1991-; Hon RCM 1984, FRSA (chm 1981-83); kt 1983; *Clubs* Garrick; *Style*— Sir Ian Hunter, MBE; Harold Holt Ltd, 31 Sinclair Rd, London W14

HUNTER, Hon Ian Thorburn; s of Baron Hunter of Newington, MBE, *qv*; *b* 1951; *m* 1974, Angela Hill; *Style*— The Hon Ian Hunter; 27 Affleck Gdns, Monikie, by Dundee

HUNTER, Ian William; s of William Gurnham Hunter, and Anna-Marie, *née* Faliescewska; *b* 17 March 1955; *Educ* Alleyn's Sch Dulwich, Univ of Surrey; *m* 8 Nov 1986, Susan, da of James Edward Morris; *Career* economist Bank of England 1975-79, fund mangr Swiss Bank Corp 1979-81, sr investmt mangr Lazard Bros 1981-87, dir Far E div Midland Montagu Asset Mgmnt 1987-; ACA; *Recreations* skiing, motor racing; *Style*— Ian Hunter, Esq; Hanelei, 11 Orchard End, Gt Bookham, Surrey (☎ 0372 459290); 10 Lower Thames St, London EC3R 6AE (☎ 071 260 9853, fax 071 260 9140, telex 8956886)

HUNTER, (Mary) Irene; *née* Durlacher; MBE (1956); da of Cyril Charles Henry Durlacher (d 1968), and Glady Caroline, *née* Armstrong (d 1946); *b* 27 Sept 1919; *Educ* Caledonia Sch Sussex, Queen Anne's Sch Reading; *m* 1, 16 Oct 1956, Jean Francois Clouët des Pesruches, OBE, MC (d 1957), s of Col Jean Clouët des Pesruches (d 1945); m 2, 13 Aug 1964, Antony Noel Hunter, MBE (d 1967), s of Noel Hunter (d 1954); *Career* WWII SOE served India and China 1941-45; Publicity Dept Imperial Airways 1937-41; PA: Jack Hylton 1946-47, Stuart Advertising 1947-49, HM Serv in Luxemberg, UN NY and Paris (Sir Gladwyn Jebb, now Lord Gladwyn in latter two posts) 1949-56, Baroness Jackson (Barbara Ward) 1968-81, Lord Gladwyn 1968-; memb Cncl Int Inst for Environment and Devpt; *Recreations* horse racing, cooking; *Style*— Mrs Irene Hunter, MBE; 21 Smith Terrace, London SW3 4DL (☎ 071 352 3289)

HUNTER, Jill; da of Robert Owen Hunter, of Sheffield, and Brenda Christine, *née* Johnson; *b* 14 Oct 1966; *Educ* Ryton Comp Monkwearmouth Coll (BTEC Nat Dip Business Studies); *Career* runner; placed ninth World Cross Country NZ 1988, placed seventh World Cross Country Norway 1989, placed sixth World Road 15km Brazil 1990, Br Olympian 3000m 1988, silver medal Cwlth Games 10 000m 1990, placed eighth Euro Championships 10 000m 1990, Top British ranked over 5000m and 10 000m 1990, ninth fastest in the world at 5000m 1990, tenth fastest in the world at 10 000m 1990; *Clubs* Valli Harriers; *Style*— Ms Jill Hunter; Fenwick Ltd, 39 Northumberland Street, Newcastle upon Tyne NE99 1AR (☎ 091 2325100 ext 2316)

HUNTER, Prof John Angus Alexander; s of Dr John Craig Alexander Hunter, of Holbeach, Lincolnshire, and Alison Hay Shand, *née* Alexander, MBE; *b* 16 June 1939; *Educ* Loretto, Pembroke Coll Cambridge (BA), Univ of Edinburgh (MB ChB, MD); *m* 26 Oct 1968, Ruth Mary, da of Douglas Verdun Farrow, of Spalding, Lincolnshire; 1 s (Hamish John Alexander b 2 July 1973), 2 da (Rebecca Jean Alexander b 13 Sept 1970, Abigail Ruth Alexander b 24 Jan 1972); *Career* med posts: Royal Infirmary Edinburgh, Inst of Dermatology London 1967, Univ of Minnesota USA 1968-69; Grant prof of dermatology Univ of Edinburgh 1981-, author dermatological papers in scientific jls; memb Med Appeal Tbnl; memb: BMA, Assoc of Physicians of GB and Ireland, Br Assoc of Dermatologists, Scottish Dermatological Soc, RSM; FRCPE 1978; *Books* Common Diseases of the Skin (with J A Savin, 1983), Clinical Dermatology (with J A Savin and M V Dahl, 1989); *Recreations* gardening, music, golf; *Clubs* Hon Co of Edinburgh Golfers, Hawks; *Style*— Prof John Hunter; Dept of Dermatology, University of Edinburgh, The Royal Infirmary, Edinburgh EH3 9YW (☎ 031 229 2477 ext 4128, fax 031 229 8769)

HUNTER, Judith Marylyn; da of Leslie Edward Palmer (d 1984), and Dorothy Edith, *née* Neave (d 1974); *b* 26 Jan 1938; *Educ* Blyth Sch Norwich, UCL (BSc); *m* 1 April 1961, Roy Leslie Hunter, s of William Henry Hunter (d 1951); 2 da (Fiona Louise Jane b 21 Jan 1961, Karen Teresa b 25 Dec 1963); *Career* adult educn tutor Univ of Oxford ESD and other educn 1969-, hon curator Royal Borough Collection Windsor 1977-, memb various cmmns for historical res 1981-; former vice chm and jl ed Berks Local History Assoc; memb: Consultative Ctee for Museums in Berkshire, Assoc of Local History Tutors 1986-; *Books* The Changing Face of Windsor (1977), The Story of a Village, Eton Wick 1217-1977 (1977), A Town in the Making: Slough 1851 (ed, 1980), The Story of Slough (1983), From Tudor Inn to Trusthouse Hotel (1984), Tough Assignment: A History of the Eton Wick Methodist Chapel 1886-1986 (1986), The George Inn, Southwark (1989), Victorian Childhood in Windsor (sch pack 1990), Slough: a pictorial history (1990); *Recreations* walking, gardening, theatre going; *Style*— Mrs Judith Hunter; 26 Wood Lane, Cippenham, Slough SL1 9EA (☎ 0753 25547)

HUNTER, Keith Robert; OBE (1981); s of Robert Ernest Williamson Hunter (d 1967), of Hull, and Winifred Mary, *née* Bradshaw (d 1987); *b* 29 May 1936; *Educ* Hymers Coll Hull, Magdalen Coll Oxford (MA), SOAS, Inst of Educn Univ of London; *m* 21 Dec 1959 (m dis 1989), Ann Patricia, da of Fredrick Fuller, of Eastbourne; 1 s (James b 1965), 2 da (Alisoun b 1961, Euphan b 1963); m 2, 16 Feb 1991, Victoria, da of George Solomonidis, of Athens; *Career* Nat Serv RAEC 1954-56; Br Cncl 1960-: Cambodia 1960-64, London 1964-66, Hong Kong 1967-69, Malaysia 1970-74, Algeria 1975-78, China 1979-82, controller Arts Div London 1985-90, dir Italy 1990-; *Recreations* music; *Style*— Keith Hunter, Esq, OBE; The British Council, 20 via Quattro Fontane, Rome 00184, Italy (☎ 06 4826641)

HUNTER, (James) Martin Hugh; s of Colin Boorer Garrett Hunter (d 1950), of IOW, and Barbara Anne Crawford, *née* Cavendish (d 1962); *b* 23 March 1937; *Educ* Shrewsbury, Pembroke Coll Cambridge (MA); *m* 21 Jan 1972, Linda Mary, da of Francis Kenneth Ernest Gamble (d 1971); *Career* admitted slr 1963; ptnr Freshfields 1967- (asst slr 1963); Freeman: City of London, Worshipful Co of Arbitrators, Worshipful Co of Slrs, Worshipful Co of Spectacle Makers; memb Law Soc, FCIArb; *Books* Law & Practice of International Commercial Arbitration (with Alan Redfern, 1986), Arbitration Title (ed), Butterworths Encyclopedia of Forms & Precedents (ed); *Recreations* cruising under sail, golf; *Clubs* Royal Cruising, Sunningdale Golf; *Style*— Martin Hunter, Esq; Freshfields, Whitefriars, 65 Fleet St, London EC4Y 1HT (☎ 071 936 4000, fax 071 248 3487/8/9, telex 889292)

HUNTER, Muir Vane Skerrett; QC (1965); s of Hugh Stewart Hunter (d 1980), and Bluebell Matilda, *née* Williams (d 1980); *b* 19 Aug 1913; *Educ* Westminster, Ch Ch Oxford (MA); *m* 1, 29 July 1939, Dorothea Verstone (d 1986), 1 da (Camilla b 7 April 1947); m 2, 4 July 1986, Gillian Victoria Joyce Petrie; *Career* WWII service enlisted RTR 1940, cmmnd 2 Lt RMA Sandhurst 1941, 2 Royal Gloucestershire Hussars, transferred 7 KOYLI (renamed 149 Regt RAC) 1941, Capt (Bde IO) 50 Indian Tank Bde India 1941, Staff Capt (GSO 3) Gen Staff Intelligence GHQ New Delhi 1942, Lt-Col (GSO 1) War and Legislative Depts Govt of India New Delhi (judge of Anti-Corruption Tbnl Lahore and Karachi) 1943, ret 1945, demobbed with rank of Hon Lt-Col 1946; called to the Bar Gray's Inn 1938 (Master of Bench 1975); fndr-chm N Kensington Neighbourhood Law Centre 1970, memb exec and Cncl Justice 1961-88, memb and int observer Amnesty Int, int observer Int Cmmn of Jurists; memb ctees DTI: Advsy Ctee on Draft EEC Bankruptcy Convention 1973-76, Insolvency Law Review Ctee 1977-82; govr RSC 1980-, memb Cncl Royal Shakespeare Theatre Tst 1970-; memb Gen Cncl of the Bar, MRI; *Books* Williams on Bankruptcy (later Williams & Muir Hunter on Bankruptcy, ed 1948, 1958, 1968, 1979), Muir Hunter on Personal Insolvency (sr author, 1988), Kerr on Receivers and Administrators (supervising ed, 1989); *Recreations* travel, theatre, music; *Clubs* Hurlingham, Union (Oxford); *Style*— Muir Hunter, Esq, QC; Hunterston, Donhead St Andrew, Shaftesbury, Dorset SP7 8EB (☎ 0747 828 779); 43 Church Rd, Barnes, London SW13 9HQ (☎ 081 748

6693); 3-4 South Square, Gray's Inn, London WC1R 5HP (☎ 071 696 9900)

HUNTER, (John) Murray; CB (1980), MC (1943); s of Rev John Mercer Hunter (d 1968), of Fife, and Frances Margaret, *née* Martin (d 1953); *b* 10 Nov 1920; *Educ* Kirkcaldy HS, Fettes, Clare Coll Cambridge (BA); *m* 1948, Margaret Mary Phyllis, da of Stanley Cursiter, CBE (d 1976); 2 s (Andrew, David), 3 da (Frances, Sunniva, Caroline); *Career* served Army 1941-45 W Desert, N Africa, Italy, Capt The Rifle Brigade; played rugby football Cambridge 1946, Scotland 1947; Dip Serv: consul gen Buenos Aires 1969-71, head of Latin America Dept FCO 1971-73; cmmnr for admin and fin Forestry Cmmn 1976-1981; Scottish tourist guide; chm Edinburgh W End Community Cncl 1983-86; *Recreations* music, curling; *Clubs* Scottish Tourist Guides Assoc, Nat Tst for Scotland, Hawks, Saltire Soc; *Style—* Murray Hunter, Esq, CB, MC; 21 Glencairn Cres, Edinburgh EH12 5BT (☎ 031 337 8785)

HUNTER, Dame Pamela; *née* Greenwell; DBE (1981); da of Col Thomas George Greenwell, TD, JP, DL (d 1967), of Whitburn Hall, Co Durham, and Mabel Winifred, *née* Catcheside (d 1967); *b* 3 Oct 1919; *Educ* Westonbirt Sch, Eastbourne Sch of Domestic Economy; *m* 1942, Gordon Lovegrove Hunter, s of Sir Summers Hunter, JP (d 1963), of Jesmond, Newcastle upon Tyne; 1 s (Mark), 1 da (Victoria); *Career* served WRNS 1942-45; memb: Northumbrian Water Authy 1973-77, Berwick-upon-Tweed Borough Cncl 1973-83; chm: Northern Area Cons Women's Advsy Ctee 1972-75 (vice-chm 1969-72), Cons Women's Nat Advsy Ctee 1978-81 (vice-chm 1974-75); vice-pres Nat Union of Cons and Unionist Assoc 1985- (memb Exec Ctee 1971-88, vice chm 1981-84, chm 1984-85), memb Cons Party Policy Ctee 1978-85; chm local ctees: Nat Soc of Prevention of Cruelty to Children, RNLI; elected Chatton Parish Cncl 1987; lay chm PCC; *Recreations* politics, antiques, the garden, crosswords; *Clubs* Lansdowne; *Style—* Dame Pamela Hunter, DBE; The Coach House, Chatton, Alnwick, Northumberland NE66 5PY (☎ 06685 259)

HUNTER, Paul Anthony; s of Gordon Nicholson Hunter (d 1985), of Leeds, and Kathleen Margaret, *née* Tyldesley; *b* 22 Nov 1944; *Educ* The Leys Sch Cambridge, Univ of Cambridge (MA, MB BChir), Middx Hosp Med Sch; *m* 10 July 1971, Elizabeth Alex, da of Wing Cdr Jack Granville Pearse, of Harston, Cambridgeshire; 1 s (Adam b 1978), 1 da (Rebecca b 1975); *Career* res surgical offr Moorfields Eye Hosp 1976-80, conslt ophthalmic surgn King's Coll Hosp 1982-, hon lectr King's Coll Hosp Med Sch Univ of London 1982-; hon sec Ophthalmological Soc of the UK 1987-88; FRCS 1977, FCOphth 1988; *Books* Atlas of Clinical Ophthalmology (jt ed 1985); *Recreations* gardening, travel, photography; *Style—* Paul Hunter, Esq; 94 Harley St, London W1N 1AF (☎ 071 9350777)

HUNTER, Peter Basil; s of Harry Norman Hunter, and Martha Rose, *née* Lloyd-Jones; *b* 19 Oct 1938; *Educ* Kingswood Sch Bath, Oxford Sch of Arch (Dip Arch); *Career* architect, ptnr Shepheard Epstein and Hunter 1962; involvement with: Univ of Lancaster, local authy housing, inner city devpts incl Salford Quays Manchester and Laganside Belfast, Lister City Bradford; former Civic Tst assessor; memb RIBA, FSAI; *Recreations* music; *Style—* Peter Hunter, Esq; 8 Golden Square, London W1R 3AF (☎ 01 287 3384, fax 01 287 3584)

HUNTER, Philip Brown; TD (1949); s of Charles Edward Hunter (d 1956), of Heswall, Wirral, and Marion, *née* Harper (d 1960); *b* 30 May 1909; *Educ* Birkenhead Sch, Univ of London (LLB); *m* 1 May 1937, Joyce Mary, da of John Holt (d 1969), of Hoylake, Wirral; 2 s (Charles b 1946, James b 1949), 2 da (Philippa b 1938, Katharine b 1955); *Career* WWII 1939-45: cmmnd TARA 1939 (Capt 1941, Maj 1942) served India and Burma; ptnr Laces & Co slrs 1946-60; chm: Cammell Laird 1966-70 (dir 1949-70), John Holt & Co (Liverpool) Ltd 1967-71 (dir 1957-71); dir: Guardian Assurance 1967-69, Guardian Royal Exchange 1969-79; memb Law Soc; *Recreations* sailing, gardening; *Clubs* Caledonian; *Style—* Philip Hunter, Esq, TD; Bryn Hyfryd, Holywell, Clwyd; Greystones, Trearddur Bay, Holyhead, Anglesey

HUNTER, Rita Nellie; CBE (1980); da of Charles Newton Hunter (d 1965), of Cheshire, and Lucy, *née* Parkinson-Davies (d 1973); *b* 15 Aug 1933; *Educ* Secdy Mod Sch; *m* 9 Dec 1960, John Darnley Thomas, s of Richard Thomas (d 1977), of Aberdare, S Wales; 1 da (Mairwyn Sarita b 30 Nov 1967); *Career* soprano; debut: Berlin 1970, Covent Garden 1972, Met NY 1972, Munich 1973; sang in first complete performance of Ring Cycle Sadler's Wells 1973; sang leading roles in: Aida, Il Trovatore, Masked Ball, Cavallria Rusticana, Lohengrin, Flying Dutchman, Idomeneo, Don Carlos, Isolda, Elektra, Sieglinda; recordings incl complete Siegfried and Götterdamerung, Walküre, Macbeth and solo CD Ritorna Vincitor; Hon DLitt Univ of Warwick 1978, Hon DMus Univ of Liverpool 1983, Hon RAM 1978; *Books* autobiography Wait Till The Sun Shines Nellie (1986); *Recreations* swimming, tapestry, cooking, oil painting; *Clubs* White Elephant, Royal Nat Rose Soc; *Style—* Miss Rita Hunter, CBE; 305 Bobbin Head Rd, North Turramurra, Sydney, NSW, Australia 2074 (☎ 02 44 5062, fax 02 488 7526)

HUNTER, Hon Robert Douglas; s of Baron Hunter of Newington, MBE (Life Baron), *qv*; *b* 1945; *m* 1969, Marion Mckenzie; *Style—* The Hon Robert Hunter; 2 Lindsay Ave, Cheadle Hulme, Cheshire, SK8 7BQ

HUNTER, William Hill; CBE (1971), JP (1970), DL (1987); s of Robert Dalglish Hunter (d 1942), of Ayrshire, and Margaret Walker, *née* Hill (d 1977); *b* 5 Nov 1916; *Educ* Cumnock Acad; *m* 22 March 1947, Kathleen, da of William Alfred Cole (d 1966), of Cardiff; 2 s (John b 1950, Robert b 1953); *Career* Private RASC 1940, cmmnd RA 1941, Severn Fixed Defences 1941-44, Staff Capt Middle East with Br Mil Govt Cyrenaica 1944-46; CA 1940; ptnr McLay McAlister and McGibbon Glasgow 1946-; pres Scot Young Unionist Assoc 1958-60, parly candidate (Unionist) S Ayrshire 1964 (1959), pres Scot Unionist Assoc 1964-65; dir: Abbey Nat Bldg Soc Scot advsy bd 1966-86, J and G Grant Glenfarclas Distillery 1966-; pres Renfrew West and Inverclyde Cons and Unionist Assoc 1972-; Quarrier's Homes: hon treas 1972-, acting chm 1989-; dir CBI Scot cncl 1978-84, pres City of Glasgow Friendly Soc 1980-88 (dir 1966-88), chm Salvation Army Advsy Bd in Strathclyde 1982- (chm Housing Assoc Scot Ltd), deacon convenor The Trades House of Glasgow 1986-87; *Recreations* gardening, golf, swimming, music; *Clubs* The Western (Glasgow), The Royal Scot Automobile (Glasgow); *Style—* William Hill Hunter, Esq, CBE, JP, DL; Armitage, Kilmacolm (☎ 050 587 2444); McLay McAlister and McGibbon CA, 53 Bothwell St, Glasgow G2 6TF (☎ 041 221 6516)

HUNTER, Dr William John; *b* 5 April 1937; *Educ* Westminster Hosp Med Sch London (MB BS, LRCP); *Career* Commission of the European Communities: princ admin 1974-83, head Div Industl Med and Hygiene 1983-88, dir Health and Safety Directorate 1988-; FFOM, MRCS; *Books* ed of several books and author of numerous articles on occupational safety and health; *Style—* Dr William Hunter; Commission of the European Communities, Health and Safety Directorate, Jean Monnet Building - Office C4/113, Plateau du Kirchberg-L-2920, Luxembourg (☎ 352 4301 2719, fax 352 4301 4511, telex COMEUR LU 3423 3446)

HUNTER BLAIR, Sir Edward Thomas; 8 Bt (GB 1786), of Dunskey; s of Sir James Hunter Blair, 7 Bt (d 1985), and Jean Galloway MacIntyre (d 1953); *b* 15 Dec 1920; *Educ* Eton, Univ of Paris, Balliol Coll Oxford (BA); *m* 21 April 1956, Norma (d 1972), er da of Walter S Harris (d 1983), of Bradford, Yorks; 1 adopted s (Alan Walter b 1961), 1 adopted da (Helen Cecilia b 1963); *Heir* bro, James Hunter Blair b 18 March 1926; *Career* served WWII 1939-41 with KOYLI, discharged; temp civil servant Miny of Info 1941-43; journalist London Evening News (asst foreign ed) 1944-49; mangr and dir own co in Yorks 1950-63, landowner and forester SW Scotland 1964-; memb Kirkcudbright CC 1970-71; memb: Scottish Countryside Activities Cncl, Timber Growers UK SW Scotland Ctee; *Books* Scotland Sings, A Story of Me (poems and autobiog, 1981), A Future Time, With An Earlier Life (poems, autobiog and prophecy), A Mission in Life (philosophy, religion, autobiog, poems, 1987), Nearing The Year 2000 (1990); *Recreations* gardening, hill walking; *Clubs* Western Meeting (Ayr), Royal Overseas League; *Style—* Sir Edward T Hunter Blair, Bt; Parton House, Castle Douglas, Kirkcudbrightshire DG7 3NB (☎ 064 47 234)

HUNTER BLAIR, James; s of Sir James Hunter Blair, 7 Bt (d 1985), and Jean, *née* McIntyre (d 1963); *b* 18 March 1926; *Educ* Eton, Balliol Coll Oxford (BA); *Career* Lt Scots Guards 1944-48; merchant banker London 1951-53, currently landowner family estate Ayrshire; former pres Royal Scot Forestry Soc, chm Historic Houses Assoc for Scotland, DL Ayrshire 1975; *Recreations* shooting, fishing, curling, going to the opera; *Style—* James Hunter Blair, Esq; Blairquhan, Maybole, Ayrshire (☎ 065 57 239)

HUNTER GORDON, Christopher Neil (Kit); s of Maj Patrick Hunter Gordon CBE, MC, JP, DL (d 1978), of Ballindoun, Beauly, Inverness, and Valerie Margaret Frances, *née* Ziani de Ferranti; *b* 8 June 1958; *Educ* Ampleforth, Trinity Hall Cambridge (MA); *m* 29 Sept 1984, Georgina Mary, da of Capt Owen Buckingham Varney, of Hill House, Dedham, Essex; 2 s (Sam William b 5 March 1988, Ivan b 20 Sept 1989); *Career* J Rothschild Holdings plc, md and Aurit Serv 1983-85, md and co fndr The Summit Gp plc 1985-, dir Comcap plc 1986; *Recreations* painting, architectural design, skiing, windsurfing; *Clubs* Brooks's, Chelsea Arts, United Oxford and Cambridge Univs; *Style—* Kit Hunter Gordon, Esq; 31 Alexander St, London W2 5NU (☎ 071 229 7566); The Summit Group plc, 84 St Katherine's Way, London E1 9YS (☎ 071 867 8400, fax 071 867 8667)

HUNTER GORDON, (John) Hugh; s of Maj Patrick Hunter Gordon, CBE, MC, JP, DL (d 1978), and Valerie Margaret Frances, *née* Ziani de Ferranti; *b* 7 June 1942; *Educ* Eton, Univ of St Andrews (BSc), Univ of Geneva (DiplAI); *m* 29 Oct 1966, Jillian Margaret, da of Richard Tredenham Fox-Carlyon (d 1979); 3 da (Alisa Carolyn b 1968, Tamsin Margaret b 1970, Kate Susanna b 1974); *Career* md: Ferranti Offshore Systems Ltd 1977-88, TRW Ferranti Subsea Ltd 1977-88, Ferranti Industl Electronics Ltd 1986-88, Murray-Johnstone Europe Ltd 1988-, Murray Universal SICAV; dir: Cairngorm Chairlift Co Ltd 1966-, Ferranti ORE Inc 1982-88; chm W Lothian Enterprise in Educn; FID, FBIM; *Recreations* skiing, sailing, shooting; *Clubs* Highland, Western, Scots; *Style—* Hugh Hunter Gordon, Esq; Murray Johnstone Ltd, 7 West Nile St, Glasgow G1 2PX (☎ 041 226 3131)

HUNTER GORDON, Nigel; s of Maj Patrick Hunter Gordon, CBE, MC, JP (d 1978), of Ballindoun House, Beauly, Inverness-shire, and Valerie Margaret Frances, *née* Ziani de Ferranti; *b* 2 Sept 1947; *Educ* Ampleforth, Univ of St Andrews (MA); *m* 16 April 1977, Linda Anne, da of Brendan Robert Magill, of Eastbourne; 2 s (Kim b 23 March 1981, Bret b 19 March 1983); *Career* trained as CA Coopers & Lybrand 1970-76, James C Pringle & Co CA Inverness 1977-79, tax ptnr Ernst & Young 1983 (joined 1979); Highland Area rep on Tax Practices Ctee, chm Highland Area Tax Ctee (memb Tech Sub Ctee); sec CBI Highland Area Gp; FCA 1975 (ACA 1973), ATII 1979 ACA 1977, FCA 1975, ATII 1979; *Recreations* skiing, windsurfing; *Clubs* Highland; *Style—* Nigel Hunter Gordon, Esq; Killearnan House, Muir of Ord, Ross-shire (☎ 0463 870002); Ernst & Young, Moray House, 16 Bank St, Inverness (☎ 0463 237581, fax 0463 226098, telex 75561)

HUNTER JONES, Col Hugh Edward; CBE (1980), MC (1942), TD (1946), JP (Essex 1965), DL (1961); s of Stanley Hunter Jones, of Marden Ash House, Ongar, Essex (d 1961); *b* 20 July 1915; *Educ* Rugby, Corpus Christi Coll Cambridge (MA); *m* 1947, Sheila Kathleen, da of Alfred Dickinson (d 1952), of The Lodge, Lanchester; 3 s (Nigel, Patrick, Nicholas), 1 da (Sarah); *Career* served Essex Yeo (CO 1959-62) 1938-43, MEF Staff Coll Haifa 1943, staff appts in Italy and Germany 1944-46, dep cdr RA 54 Div 1964-67 (cdr 1967), actg Brig; dir Charrington & Co until 1976, chm Hotel and Catering Indust Trg Bd 1973-85; pres: Br Inst of Innkeeping 1981-85, Friends of Essex Churches 1987-; chm E Anglian TAVR Assoc 1976-80; ADC to HM The Queen 1966-70; High Sheriff Essex 1963-64; Master Worshipful Co of Merchant Taylors 1976-77; *Recreations* country pursuits; *Clubs* Cavalry and Guards; *Style—* Col Hugh Hunter Jones, CBE, MC, TD, JP, DL; Church Farm, Langham, Colchester, Essex CO4 5PS (☎ 0206 322181)

HUNTER OF HUNTERSTON, Neil Aylmer; formerly Neil Aylmer Kennedy-Cochran-Patrick, officially recognised by the Lord Lyon in the name of Hunter of Hunterston 1969; 29 laird of Hunterston; recognised as chief of Clan Hunter by Lord Lyon 1983; s of William John Charles Kennedy-Cochran-Patrick, DSO, MC (k in airplane accident Johannesburg 1933), and Natalie Bertha, *née* Tanner (d 1966); *b* 5 May 1926; *Educ* Eton, Ridley Coll Ontario Canada, Trinity Coll Cambridge, Sorbonne; *m* 1952, Sonia Isabelle Jane, da of late Brig Dennis Walter Furlong, DSO, OBE, MC; 6 s (Charles b 1954, Robert b 1955, Nigel b 1957, John (twin) b 1957, Angus b 1960, Richard b 1962), 1 da (Pauline b 1953); *Career* served WWII RNVR; silver medallist (yachting) Olympic Games 1956; memb Royal Co of Archers (Queen's Body Guard for Scotland); OStJ; *Recreations* sailing, skiing, shooting, fishing; *Clubs* Royal Yacht Sqdn; *Style—* Hunter of Hunterston; Tour d'Escas, La Massana, Principat d'Andorra (☎ 010 33 628 35029, telex 590301 AB Hunter 301 AND)

HUNTER OF HUNTERSTON, YR, Charles Dennis; s and h of Hunter of Hunterston, *qv*; *b* 16 Feb 1954; *Educ* Eton, RAC Cirencester; *m* 1979, Joanna, da of Alistair Malcolm Morison Scottish Law Lord as Lord Morison, QC, of Edinburgh; 1 s (Ruaraidh b 1983); *Career* co dir; admin Clan Hunter Assoc; FRGS; *Recreations* sailing, shooting; *Clubs* Royal Yacht Sqdn, New (Edinburgh); *Style—* Charles Hunter of Hunterston, yr; Hunterston Castle, West Kilbride, Ayrshire, KA23 9QL; (telex 778373 HUNTER G); office: Central Cottage, PO Box 4, Hunterston Castle, West Kilbride, Ayrshire KA23 9QL (☎ 0294 823077)

HUNTER OF NEWINGTON, Baron (Life Peer UK 1978); Robert Brockie Hunter; MBE (1945), DL (1975); s of late Robert Marshall Hunter, of Edinburgh; *b* 14 July 1915; *Educ* George Watson's Coll, Univ of Edinburgh (MB ChB); *m* 1940, Kathleen Margaret, da of James Wilkie Douglas, master painter, of Perth; 3 s (Hon Robert, *qv*, Hon Alan, *qv*), 1 da (Hon Mrs Edward b 1948); *Career* WWII Lt-Col RAMC NW Europe and Egypt, personal physician to Field-Marshal Montgomery 1944-45; prof materia medica pharmacology and therapeutics: Univ of St Andrews 1948-67 (dean Faculty of Med 1958-62), Univ of Dundee 1967-68; vice-chllr and princ Univ of Birmingham 1968-81; memb: Advsy Ctee on Med Res (Scotland) 1955-60, GMC 1962-68, Clinical Res Bd MRC 1960-64, Ctee on Safety of Drugs Miny of Health 1963-68, W Midlands RHA 1974-80, Mgmnt Ctee King Edward's Hosp Fund for London 1980-84; chm: Clinical Trials Sub Ctee UGC 1964-68, Med Sub-Ctee UGC 1966-68, Med Advsy Ctee of Ctee of Vice-Chllrs and Princs, Working Pty on Med Admins in Health Serv DHSS 1970-72, Ind Sci Ctee on Smoking and Health DHSS 1973-80; advsr to Imperial Tobacco 1981-83; memb: House of Lords Select Ctee on Sci and Technol 1980-87, House of Lords Ctee on Euro Communities (Sub-Ctee C); Hon LLD: Univ of Dundee, Univ of Birmingham; Hon DSc Aston Univ; FRCP 1962, FRCPE, FIBiol, FACP, FFCM, FRSE; kt 1977; *Recreations* fishing; *Clubs* Oriental;

Style— The Rt Hon the Lord Hunter of Newington, MBE, DL, FRSE; 3 Oakdene Drive, Barnt Green, Birmingham B45 8LQ (☎ 021 445 2636)

HUNTER SMART, (William) Norman; s of William Hunter Smart (d 1960), and Margaret Thorburn, *née* Inglis (d 1966); *b* 25 May 1921; *Educ* George Watson's Coll Edinburgh; *m* 1, 9 Feb 1948, Bridget Beryl (d 1974), da of Dr Edward Philip Andreae (d 1975); 4 s (Alastair, Charles, James, Ian); m 2, 3 Dec 1977, Sheila Smith Stewart, da of Graham Mushet Speirs (d 1965), 1 step s (Robin); *Career* RAC Trg Centre 1941-42, cmmnd 1 Lothians and Border Horse 1943, 2 Lt Warwickshire Yeomanry, Capt (Adj) 1944 (despatches), served ME 1943-44, UK 1945, Germany 1946; CA 1948; ptnr Hays Akers and Hays 1950-86, sr ptnr Hays Allan 1984-86 (ret); chm C J Sims Ltd 1963-, Charterhouse Devpt Capital Fund Ltd 1987-; memb: The Gaming Bd of GB 1985-90, Scottish Legal Aid Bd 1987-89; pres Inst of CAs of Scotland 1978-79, chm Assoc of CAs London 1970-72, pres London Watsonian Club 1975-; *Recreations* gardening; *Clubs* The Caledonian; *Style—* Norman Hunter Smart, Esq; Lauriel House, Knowle Lane, Cranleigh, Surrey GU6 8JW (☎ 0483 273513)

HUNTER STEVENS, Michel; s of Aubrey Hunter Stevens, of Norfolk, and Odette Denise Nichols, *née* Malter, whose f was advsr to King of the Belgians on constitutional law; *b* 24 April 1946; *Educ* King's Sch Ely; *m* (m dis); 1 s (Marcus Hunter b 1974), 1 da (Philippa Rachel b 1976); *Career* CA 1974; with Tansley Witt and Co 1974-76, joined Price Waterhouse and Co Brussels 1976-77, Hunter Stevens CAs; *Recreations* skiing, tennis, walking, tree planting, music, racing; *Clubs* Chelsea; *Style—* Michel Hunter Stevens, Esq; Linden House, Abbots Ripton, Cambs PE17 2LJ (☎ 04873 365); 3 The Quay, St Ives, Cambridgeshire PE17 4BR (☎ 0480 67567)

HUNTER-TOD, Air Marshal Sir John Hunter; KBE (1971, OBE 1956), CB (1969); s of Hunter Finlay Tod (d 1923), of 11 Upper Wimpole St, London, and Yvonne Grace, *née* Rendall (who m 2, Cdr A P N Thorowgood, DSO, and d 1981); *b* 21 April 1917; *Educ* Marlborough, Trinity Coll Cambridge (MA), Coll of Aeronautics Cranfield (DCAe); *m* 12 Dec 1959, (Gwenith Ruth) Anne, da of late Thomas Chaffer Howard; 1 s (James Fredrik b 3 Dec 1960); *Career* cmmnd RAF 1940; served in night fighters Fighter Cmd and ME, HQME staff 1942, Actg Wing Cdr 1944, Air Miny 1945-46, Coll of Aeronautics Cranfield 1946-48, Guided Weapons Dept Royal Aircraft Estab 1949-55, HQ Fighter Cmd 1955-57, Br Jt Servs Mission Washington DC (as Gp Capt) 1957-60, dep dir radio Air Miny 1960-62, Air Cdre 1963, dir guided weapons (Air) Min of Aviation 1962-65, Air Offr Engrg RAF Germany 1965-67, AOC No 24 Gp RAF 1967-70, Air Vice-Marshal 1968, head of engrg and dir gen of Engrg RAF 1970-73, Air Marshal 1971, ret 1973; memb Ctee Sunninghill Cons Assoc, chm Ascot Branch RNLI; Hon DSc Cranfield Inst of Technol 1974; CEng; *Recreations* gardening; *Clubs* RAF; *Style—* Air Marshal Sir John Hunter-Tod, KBE, CB; 21 Ridge Hill, Dartmouth, Devon TQ6 9PE (☎ 0803 833130)

HUNTING, (Lindsay) Clive; s of Gerald Lindsay Hunting (d 1966), and Ruth, *née* Pyman (d 1972); *b* 22 Dec 1925; *Educ* Loretto, Trinity Hall Cambridge (MA); *m* 4 Oct 1952, Shelagh Mary Pamela, da of Capt A N V Hill-Lowe; 1 s (Peter), 1 da (Deborah); *Career* RN 1944-47; Hunting plc (formerly Hunting Group of Companies): joined 1950, dir 1952, vice chm 1962, chm 1975-; pres: Br Independent Air Tport Assoc 1960-62, Fedn Internationale de Transporte Aerien Privée 1961-63, Air Educn and Recreation Orgn 1970, Society of British Aerospace Companies Ltd 1985-86 (currently treas and memb Cncl); chm Air League 1968-71, memb cncl Cranfield inst of Technol 1989- (memb ct 1980-), former cdre Royal London YC; Nile Gold Medal for Aerospace Educn 1982; Freeman City of London 1982, former Master Worshipful Co of Coachmakers and Coach Harness Makers; CBIM 1980, CRAeS 1983, FRSA 1984; *Recreations* fishing, yachting, bird watching; *Clubs* Royal Yacht Sqdn, Royal London Yacht; *Style—* Clive Hunting, Esq; April Cottage, Alderbourne Lane, Fulmer, Slough SL3 6JB; Hunting plc, 3 Cockspur St, London SW1Y 5BQ (☎ 071 321 0123, fax 071 839 2072)

HUNTING, Richard Hugh; s of Charles Patrick Maule Hunting, CBE, and Diana Margaret, *née* Pereira; *b* 30 July 1946; *Educ* Rugby, Univ of Sheffield (BEng), Univ of Manchester (MBA); *m* 31 Oct 1970, Penelope Susan, da of Col L L Fleming, MBE, MC; 1 s (Rupert b 1974), 2 da (Joanna b 1976, Chloë b 1979); *Career* Hunting Group 1972-: Hunting Surveys and Consultants, Field Aviation, E A Gibson Shipbrokers, Hunting Oilfield Services, Hunting Engineering, chm Hunting Associated Industries 1989 (dir 1986-89), Hunting Petroleum Services 1989; memb Ct Worshipful Co of Ironmongers; *Recreations* skiing, board sailing, computing; *Clubs* Travellers'; *Style—* Richard Hunting, Esq; 3 Cockspur Street, London SW1Y 5BQ (☎ 071 321 0123, fax 071 839 2072)

HUNTINGDON, Bishop of 1980-; Rt Rev (William) Gordon Roe; s of William Henry Roe (d 1965), and Dorothy Myrtle, *née* Hayman (d 1975); *b* 5 Jan 1932; *Educ* Bournemouth Sch, Jesus Coll Oxford, St Stephen's House Oxford (MA, DPhil, DipTheol); *m* 1953, Mary Primrose, da of Nils Arthur Efram Andreén (d 1973); 2 s (Patrick b 1957, Michael b 1964), 2 da (Helen b 1955, Rachel b 1959); *Career* RAEC Sgt Instr; asst curate St Peter's Bournemouth 1958-61, priest i/c St Michaels Abingdon 1961-69, vice princ St Chad's Coll Durham 1969-74, vicar St Oswald's Durham and rural dean Durham 1974-80, hon canon Durham 1979-80, bishop Huntingdon 1980-; *Books* Lamennais and England (1966), J B Dykes, Priest and Musician (with Arthur Hutchings, 1976); *Recreations* French literature, painting; *Style—* The Rt Rev the Bishop of Huntingdon; 14 Lynn Rd, Ely, Cambs CB6 1DA (☎ 0353 662137)

HUNTINGDON, Countess of; Margaret; da of late H G Lane; *b* 23 June 1907; *Educ* St Stephen's Coll Folkestone, St Hugh's Coll Oxford (MA); *m* 1, 1934 (m dis 1939), Bryan Wallace, s of Edgar Wallace; m 2, 1944, 15 Earl of Huntingdon (d 1990); 2 da; *Career* novelist, biographer, journalist (as Margaret Lane); pres: Women's Press Club 1958-60, Dickens Fellowship 1959-61 and 1970, Johnson Soc 1971, Bronte Soc 1975-82, Jane Austen Soc; *Books* Faith, Hope, No Charity (Prix Femina-Vie Heureuse), Edgar Wallace: the Biography of a Phenomenon, Walk into My Parlour, Where Helen Lies, The Tale of Beatrix Potter, The Brontë Story, A Crown of Convolvulus, A Calabash of Diamonds, Life with Ionides, A Night at Sea, A Smell of Burning, Purely for Pleasure, The Day of the Feast, Frances Wright and the Great Experiment, Samuel Johnson and His World, Flora Thompson, The Magic Years of Beatrix Potter, (ed) Flora Thompson's A Country Calendar and other writings, The Drug-Like Bronte Dream; *Style—* The Rt Hon Margaret, Countess of Huntingdon; Blackbridge House, Beaulieu, Hants SO42 7YE

HUNTINGDON, 16 Earl of (E 1529); William Edward Robin Hood Hastings-Bass; s of Capt Peter Hastings-Bass (assumed additional name Bass 1954, d 1964), and Priscilla (b 1920, m 1947, dir Newbury Race Course, memb Jockey Club), da of Capt Sir Malcolm Bullock, 1 Bt, MBE, and Lady Victoria Stanley, da of 17 Earl of Derby; suc kinsman, 15 Earl of Huntingdon 1990; *b* 30 Jan 1948; *Educ* Winchester, Trinity Coll Cambridge; *m* 1989, Susan Mary Gavin, da of John Jellico Pelham Francis Warner, and gda of Sir Pelham Warner, MBE; *Heir* bro, Simon Aubrey Robin Hood Hastings-Bass b 1950; *Style—* The Rt Hon the Earl of Huntingdon; Hodcott House, West Ilsley, nr Newbury, Berks

HUNTINGFIELD, 6 Baron (I 1796); Sir Gerard Charles Arcedeckne Vanneck; 8 Bt (GB 1751); s of 5 Baron Huntingfield, KCMG, JP (d 1969), and his 1 w Margaret Eleanor, *née* Crosby (d 1943); *b* 29 May 1915; *Educ* Stowe, Trinity Coll Cambridge; *m* 27 Oct 1941, Janetta Lois, er da of Capt Reginald Hugh Errington, RN (ret); 1 s, 3 da (Hon Mrs Binney b 1944 d 1979, Hon Mrs Darell-Brown b 1946, Hon Mrs Bacon b 1954); *Heir* s, Hon Joshua Vanneck (twin) b 1954; *Career* served WWII Flt Sgt RAFVR; UN Secretariat 1946-75; *Style—* The Rt Hon Lord Huntingfield; 53 Barron's Way, Comberton, Cambridge CB3 7EQ

HUNTINGTON, Keith Graham; s of Nathaniel Huntington (Capt MN, d 1964), of 17 Pine View Drive, Heswall, Cheshire, and late Christina Louise, *née* Griffiths; *b* 22 Sept 1943; *Educ* Wirral GS Cheshire, Nat Coll of Heating Ventilation and Fan Engrg London, Liverpool Coll of Building; *m* 19 Aug 1967, Helen, da of John George McKay (d 1973), of 15 Eccleston Ave, Chester; 2 da (Georgina Louise b 14 April 1974, Nicola Jayne b 11 Dec 1975); *Career* sr heating and ventilation engr Husband & Co Conslt Engrs 1971-72, section ldr Edward A Pearce & Ptnrs Conslt Engrs Sheffield 1972-77; Edward A Pearce & Assocs (re-named Pearce Design Group 1988): assoc ptnr 1977-80, ptnr 1980-84, sr ptnr 1984-; CEng, MConsE, MASHRAE, FCIBSE; *Recreations* squash; *Clubs* Abbeydale Squash (Sheffield); *Style—* Keith Huntington, Esq; 35 Old Hay Close, Dore, Sheffield S17 3GP (☎ 0742 368156); Granby Croft, Matlock St, Bakewell, Derbys DE4 1ET (☎ 062981 3449, fax 062981 4741); 6 Marlborough Rd, Sheffield S10 1DB (☎ 0742 671188, fax 0742 671133)

HUNTINGTON-WHITELEY, Sir Hugo Baldwin; 3 Bt (UK 1918), of Grimley, Worcester, DL (Worcs 1972); s of Capt Sir Maurice Huntington-Whiteley, 2 Bt, RN (d 1975), and Lady (Pamela) Margaret (d 1976), 3 da of 1 Earl Baldwin of Bewdley, KG, PC; *b* 31 March 1924; *Educ* Eton; *m* 1959, Jean Marie Ramsay, JP, da of late Arthur Francis Ramsay Bock; 2 da (Sophie Elizabeth (Mrs Zdatny) b 1964, Charlotte Anne b 1965); *Heir* bro, (John) Miles Huntington-Whiteley, *qv*; *Career* RN 1942-47; ptnr Price Waterhouse 1963-83; High Sheriff of Worcs 1971; memb Ct of Assts Worshipful Co Goldsmiths' (Prime Warden 1989-90); FCA; *Recreations* music and travel; *Clubs* Brooks's; *Style—* Sir Hugo Huntington-Whiteley, Bt, DL; Ripple Hall, Tewkesbury, Glos (☎ 068 46 2431)

HUNTINGTON-WHITELEY, (John) Miles; VRD (two clasps); s of Capt Sir Maurice Huntington-Whiteley, 2 Bt (d 1975), and Lady (Pamela) Margaret (d 1976), 3 da of 1 Earl Baldwin of Bewdley, KG, PC; hp of bro, Sir Hugo Huntington-Whiteley, 3 Bt, *qv*; *b* 18 July 1929; *Educ* Eton, Trinity Coll Cambridge; *m* 1960, HIllH Countess Victoria Adelheid Clementine Luise, da of late HIllH Count Friedrich Wolfgang zu Castell-Rüdenhausen (ka 1940) *see* Debretts Peerage, Royal Family section; 1 s (Leopold Maurice b 1965), 2 da (Alice Louise Esther Margot b 1961, m 1985, Charles Percy Sewell, 3 s of the late Maj Geoffrey Richard Michael Sewell by his wife Joan, 3 da of Sir Watkin Williams-Wynn 8 Bt; Beatrice Irene Helen Victoria b 1962); *Career* Lt Cdr RNR; int investmt portfolio mangr James Capel & Co, on secondment to Coutts & Co; *Recreations* applied and fine arts, music, the paranormal; *Clubs* Naval; *Style—* Miles Huntington-Whiteley, Esq, VRD; 6 Matheson Rd, London W14 8SW (☎ 071 602 8484); Coutts & Co, 440 Strand, London WC2R OQS (☎ 071 753 1000)

HUNTLY, 13 Marquess of (S 1599) Granville Charles Gomer Gordon; Premier Marquess of Scotland, also Earl of Aboyne, Lord Gordon of Strathavon and Glenlivet (both S 1660), and Baron Meldrum of Morven (UK 1815); s of 12 Marquess of Huntly (d 1987), and his 1 w, Hon Pamela, *née* Berry, da of 1 Viscount Kemsley; *b* 4 Feb 1944; *Educ* Gordonstoun; *m* 1, 1972 (m dis 1990), Jane Elizabeth Angela, da of late Lt-Col Alistair Monteith Gibb and Hon Yoskyl, *née* Pearson, da of 2 Viscount Cowdray, DL; 1 s, 2 da (Lady Amy b 1975, Lady Lucy b 1979); m 2, 15 Feb 1991, Mrs Catheryn Millbourn; *Heir* s, Earl of Aboyne, *qv*; *Career* patron Inst of Commercial Management; chm: Hintlesham Hldgs Ltd, Windrush Hldgs Ltd; dir: Ampton Investments Ltd, Barsham Properties Ltd; *Style—* The Most Hon the Marquess of Huntly; Aboyne Castle, Aberdeenshire; Glassmill, 1 Battersea Bridge Rd, London SW11 9BG (☎ 071 738 1255)

HUNTLY, Pamela, Marchioness of; Hon (Mary) Pamela; *née* Berry; da of 1 Viscount Kemsley, GBE (d 1968); *b* 13 June 1918; *m* 15 March 1941 (m dis 1965), 12 Marquess of Huntly; 1 s (13 Marquess of Huntly), 1 da (Lady Lemina Lawson-Johnston); *Style—* Pamela, Marchioness of Huntly; 80 Old Church St, London SW3

HUNTON CARTER, Lt-Col (James) Anthony; OBE (1943); s of Arthur Hunton Carter (d 1961), and Winifred Ida, *née* Macmeikan (d 1947); *b* 12 Dec 1914; *Educ* Wells House Malvern Wells, Sedbergh; *m* 14 Oct 1942, Mae, da of John Christian Paulsen (d 1960), of Cape Town, SA; 1 s (Robert b 1952), 2 da (Susan b 1947, Jane b 1948); *Career* cmmnd King's Own Royal Regt 1937, served Palestine, Egypt, Libya, Tripolitania, Algeria, Sicily, Italy, France, Belgium, Holland, Germany (despatches 4 times), promoted Lt-Col 1943, ret 1948; author; dir and md (later chm) Ward Blenkinsop and Co Ltd; *Books* Maintenance in the Field; *Recreations* shooting, wood turning; *Style—* Lt-Col Anthony Hunton Carter, OBE; Casa Pelicanos, Colina Del Sol 62A, Calpe, Alicante, Spain

HUNTSMAN, Peter William; s of William Huntsman (d 1970), and Lydia Irene, *née* Clegg (d 1982); *b* 11 Aug 1935; *Educ* Hymers Coll Hull, Coll of Estate Mgmnt Univ of London (BSc), Cornell Univ USA; *m* 1, 30 Dec 1961 (m dis 1984), Janet Mary, da of William Albert Bell; 1 s (Mark William b 1965), 1 da (Fiona Mary b 1963); m 2, 21 June 1984, Cicely Eleanor Waymont, da of Robert Tamblin; *Career* MAFF: asst land cmmr 1961-66, sr asst land cmmr 1966-69, princ surveyor 1971-81; Kellogg Fndn Fellowship USA 1969-70, princ Coll of Estate Mgmnt Reading 1981-; Freeman: City of London, Worshipful Co of Chartered Surveyors; FRICS 1981, FAAV 1987; *Books* Walmsleys Rural Estate Management (contrib, 1978); *Recreations* golf, bridge, reading; *Clubs* Athenaeum, Farmers, Phyllis Ct (Henley); *Style—* Peter Huntsman, Esq; Coachmans Cottage, Bulmershe Rd, Reading; 3 Greystones, Burlington Rd, Swanage (☎ 0734 67426); College of Estate Management, Whiteknights, Reading (☎ 0734 861101, fax 0734 755344)

HUNWICKS, Trevor Alec; s of Alec Alfred Hunwicks, of Maldon, Essex, and Jean Hunwicks, *née* Brazier; *b* 22 Sept 1943; *Educ* Chislehurst and Sidcup GS; *m* 14 Dec 1968, Zara, da of Peter John Harris, of IOW; 1 s (William George b 7 Oct 1974), 1 da (Victoria Louise b 21 August 1971); *Career* Nationwide Anglia Building Soc (formerly Anglia Building Soc) 1968-: branch mangr 1968, dep London mangr 1970, London mangr 1971, London regnl mangr 1975, asst gen mangr mktg 1984, gen mangr mktg 1985, gen mangr corp devpt 1987-; md Incentives International plc 1990; chm of govrs Northampton Coll; FCIM 1981, FCBSI 1977, FBIM 1986; *Recreations* theatre, music, painting, tennis; *Clubs* RAC, Wig and Pen; *Style—* Trevor Hunwicks, Esq; The Old Barn, Ecton, Northampton, NN6 0QB (☎ 0604 406203); Incentives International plc, Greenlands Business Centre, Redditch, Worcestershire B98 7HD (☎ 0527/517766)

HUPPERT, Prof Herbert Eric; s of Leo Huppert (d 1957), and Alice, *née* Neuman (d 1967); *b* 26 Nov 1943; *Educ* Sydney Boys HS, Univ of Sydney (BSc), ANU (MSc), Univ of California San Diego (MS, PhD), Univ of Cambridge (MA, ScD); *m* 20 April 1966, Felicia Adina, da of Bernard David Ferster, of 72A Drumalbyn Rd, Bellevue Hill, NSW, Aust; 2 s (Julian b 1978, Rowan b 1982); *Career* Univ of Cambridge: fell King's Coll 1970-, asst dir of res 1970-81, lectr 1981-88, reader in geophysical dynamics 1988-89, prof of theoretical geophysics 1989-; prof of mathematics Univ of NSU 1991-, assoc ed Jl of Fluid Mechanics 1970-90, sr res fell BP Venture Unit 1983-89; co chm Scientist for the Release of Soviet Refusniks; FRS 1987; *Recreations* my children, playing squash, walking, dreaming of a less hassled life; *Style*— Prof Herbert Huppert, FRS; 46 De Freville Ave, Cambridge CB4 1HT, (☎ 0223 356071); Institute of Theoretical Geophysics, Depts of Applied Mathematics & Theoretical Physics and Earth Sciences, 20 Silver St, Cambridge CB3 9EW, (☎ 0223 337853, fax 0223 337918, tlx 81240 CAMSPL G)

HURD, Rt Hon Douglas Richard; CBE (1974), PC (1980), MP (C) Witney 1983-; eldest s of Baron Hurd, sometime MP Newbury and agric corr The Times (Life Peer, d 1966; himself er s of Sir Percy Angier Hurd, sometime MP Frome and Devizes, ed Canadian Gazette and London ed Montreal Star; Sir Percy was er bro of Sir Archibald Hurd, also a journalist (Daily Telegraph) and formerly chm Shipping World Co), and Stephanie Frances, *née* Corner (d 1985); *b* 8 March 1930; *Educ* Eton, Trinity Coll Cambridge (BA 1952, MA 1957); *m* 1, 10 Nov 1960 (m dis 1982), Tatiana Elizabeth Michelle, o da of (Arthur Charles) Benedict Eyre, MBE, of West Burton House, Bury, Sussex; 3 s (Nicholas Richard b 13 May 1962, Thomas Robert Benedict b 20 Sept 1964, Alexander Paul Anthony b 7 June 1969); m 2, 1982, Judy J, 2 da of Sidney Smart, of Oak Ash, Chaddleworth, Berks; 1 s (Philip Arthur b 1983), 1 da (Jessica Stephanie b 1985); *Career* Dip Serv 1952-66 (Peking, UK Mission to UN, Rome, also private sec to perm under sec FO); CRD 1966-68 (head Foreign Affrs Section 1968); MP (C) Mid Oxon Feb 1974-1983, private sec to Rt Hon Edward Heath as ldr of Oppn 1968-70, political sec to PM 1970-74, oppn spokesman Foreign Affrs (with special responsibility for EEC) 1976-79; min of State: FCO 1979-1983, Home Office 1983-84, Sec of State for NI 1984-85, Home Sec 1985-89, Sec of State for Foreign and Cwlth Affrs 1989-; visiting fell Nuffield Coll Oxford 1978; *Books* The Arrow War (1967), Truth Game (1972), Vote to Kill (1975), An End to Promises (1979); with Andrew Osmond: Send Him Victorious (1968), The Smile on The Face of the Tiger (1969), Scotch on the Rocks (1971), War Without Frontiers (1982); Palace of Enchantments (with Stephen Lamport, 1985); *Clubs* Beefsteak; *Style*— The Rt Hon Douglas Hurd, CBE, MP; c/o House of Commons, London SW1

HURD, Martyn Roy; s of (Bernard) Roy Hurd, and Marjorie Sheila, *née* Burton; *b* 28 Sept 1948; *Educ* Blatchington Court Seaford Sussex, Open Univ (BA); *m* 31 Aug 1976, Philippa Helen, da of (John) Angus Beckett, CB, CMG; 2 da (Jane b 6 May 1979, Helen b 21 July 1981); *Career* planning offr W Midlands Central Ind TV until 1983, mangr of prodn planning ITN 1983-; prodn mangr: General Election ITV 1987 and various Budget progs, televising House of Lords ITV 1987, Channel 4 Daily 1989, televising House of Commons ITV and Channel 4 1989; chm nat educational registered charity Norsuch (History and Dance) Ltd, memb RTS; *Recreations* walking, swimming, reading; *Style*— Martyn Hurd, Esq; 7 Roy Rd, Northwood, Middx HA6 1EQ (☎ 09274 26868); Independent Television News, 200 Grays Inn Road, London WC1X 8XZ (☎ 071 430 4495)

HURD, Mick; s of Norman Frank Hurd, of Hitchin, Herts, and Irene May, *née* Cook; *b* 18 Sept 1956; *Educ* Hitchin Boys' GS, Herts Coll of Art and design St Albans, Central Sch of Art (BA); *Career* design asst Palace Theatre Westcliff-on-Sea 1980-81; freelance designer of window displays and PR sets 1981-; window displays for shops incl: Barneys NY (5 sets incl Christmas 1988), Katherine Hamnett (temp shops and showroom), North Beach Leather Sloane St, Simpsons of Piccadilly, Browns South Molton St, Moschino at Italian Trade Centre, Hyper Hyper Kensington High St; PR Cos worked with incl: Lynne Franks (Ratners, Lamb's Rum, New York Seltzer, Cable & Co, Swatch Watches, Brylcream and Littlewoods), Shilland & Co (Levis), Marycia Woroneicka (Benetton); video art dir on various pop promos incl Cowboy Song and Do I Have To? (Inga); photographic backdrop designer for: Correspondent, BR, Independent on Sunday, Eurax; *Style*— Mick Hurd, Esq; 158 Essex Road, London N1 8LY (☎ 071 354 4826, fax 071 354 9805, mobile 0831 362 919)

HURD, Hon Stephen Anthony; JP (Wilts 1969); yr s of Baron Hurd (Life Peer, d 1966), and Stephanie Frances, *née* Corner (d 1985); bro Rt Hon Douglas Hurd *qv*; *b* 6 April 1933; *Educ* Winchester, Magdalene Coll Cambridge (BA, Dip Agric, MA); *m* 30 June 1973, Pepita Lilian, da of Lt-Col Walter Hingston, OBE, of The Old Vicarage, Ramsbury, Marlborough, Wilts; 2 s (William b 1976, Christopher b 1977); *Career* farmer; dir: North Wilts Cereals Ltd 1970-85, Gp Cereals Ltd 1970- 84, West of England Farmers Ltd 1968-1989 (chm 1988-89), West of England Building Soc (formerly Ramsbury Building Soc) 1973-90, Ramsbury Building Society 1973-86, Portman Building Society 1990, West Midland Farmers Assoc Ltd 1989-; tstee Duchess of Somerset Hosp Froxfield Wilts, chm Marlborough Petty Sessional Divn 1987-; *Style*— The Hon Stephen Hurd; Brown's Farm, Marlborough, Wilts SN8 4ND

HURDLE, Michael William Frederick; s of Maurice Frederick Hurdle, of Burton-on-Trent, and Mary Murielle Morton Wilson; *b* 3 June 1941; *Educ* Uppingham, Keele Univ (BA); *m* 1983, Jean Alicia, da of Frederick Ernest Savage (d 1975), of Burton-on-Trent; *Career* chm and md Marston Thompson and Evershed plc (Brewers); *Recreations* shooting, fishing, golf, tennis, horseracing; *Clubs* The Burton, Lloyds; *Style*— Michael Hurdle, Esq; Lower Stock Lane Farm, Marchington Woodlands, Uttoxeter, Staffs; Marston's plc, PO Box 26, Shobnall Rd, Burton-on-Trent DE14 2BW

HURFORD, Peter John; OBE (1984); *b* 22 Nov 1930; *Educ* Blundell's Sch, RCM, Jesus Coll Cambridge (MA, MusB); *m* 6 Aug 1955, Patricia Mary, da of Prof Sir Bryan Matthews, of Cambridge; 2 s, 1 da; *Career* organist; Master of the Music St Albans Cathedral 1958-78; fndr Int Organ Festival 1943; visiting prof: Univ of Cincinnati USA 1967-68, Univ of W Ontario 1974-77; visiting-artist-in-residence Sydney Opera House 1980-82, memb Cncl Royal Coll of Organists 1964- (pres 1980-82), conslt prof RAM 1988- (prof 1982-88), Memb Hon Cncl of Mgmnt Royal Philharmonic Soc 1983-87; frequent recital tours 1960- (America, Canada, Australia, New Zealand, E and W Europe, Japan and Far E); over 65 recordings incl: complete organ works of J S Bach, Couperin, Handel, Hindemith; radio appearances incl: 34 progs of Bach's complete organ music 1980 and 1982, 7 progs 1990; TV appearances incl Music in Time 1983; Hon DMus Baldwin-Wallace Coll Ohio 1981; Hon RAM 1981, HonFRSCM 1977, Hon FRCM 1987; *Books* Making Music on the Organ (1988), contrib to many Musical Magazines; *Recreations* walking, wine, silence; *Style*— Peter Hurford, Esq, OBE; Broom House, St Bernard's Rd, St Albans, Herts AL3 5RA

HURLEY, David Desmond; s of Frederick Desmond Hurley (d 1978), of Dublin, and Edith Duff Hurley (d 1976), of Toronto; *b* 8 Aug 1930; *Educ* Fettes; *m* 1955, Mary Cecil, da of William Moore, OBE, TD (d 1950); 2 s (Guy, Giles), 5 da (Caroline, Susanna, Alexandra, Sarah, Nicola); *Career* chm: Irish Exporters Assoc 1969-70, Visionhire Ltd 1978; md Electronic Rentals Gp plc 1982-88; dir: Atlantic Magnetics Ltd, Hoermann Electronics Ltd, CSO Brokers Ltd, Kintbury Ltd, F A Ewing & Co (London) Ltd, Euro Mercantile Exchange Ltd; chm Dorking Cons Assoc 1980-83, pres Mole Valley Cons Assoc 1983-86, memb Cons Bd of Fin 1985-86, govr The Mgmnt Coll Henley 1986-88; *Recreations* sailing (sea muffin), gardening; *Clubs* Royal Irish Yacht, Kobe Regatta and Athletic; *Style*— David Hurley, Esq; Ballydaheen, Portsalon, Co Donegal, Ireland

HURLEY, George Nevill; s of John Everard Hurley (d 1962), of Hawks Hill, Chobham, Surrey, and Mary, *née* Marchant (d 1991); *b* 21 May 1939; *Educ* Eton; *m* 1, 8 June 1964 (m dis 1989), Ann Elizabeth, da of J Dickinson (d 1982), of Ilford, Essex; 2 s (Andrew b 5 Oct 1971, Jonathan b 17 Sept 1975), m 2, 26 Oct 1990, Heather Yvonne Elizabeth; *Career* Nat Serv 1958-60: RB 1958-59, cmmnd KSLI 1959-60; TA serv Queen's Westminsters (later Queen's Royal Rifles) 1960-63; shipbroker; McGregor Gow & Holland 1961-62, Elder Smith & Co Ltd 1962-63, Elder Smith Goldsbrough Mort Aust 1963-66 (London 1966-81), mangr (chartering) Elders IXL Ltd 1981-83; dir: Elders Chartering Ltd 1983, Baltic Exchange Ltd 1983-88 and 1990-, Minerva Marine Hong Kong 1983-, Rimpacific Shipping (London) Ltd 1985-; *Recreations* shooting, gardening, music; *Style*— George Hurley, Esq; Elders Chartering Ltd, 40 Duke's Place, London EC3A 7LP (☎ 071 621 0757, fax 071 621 0167, telex 885 608)

HURN, Hon Mrs (Phillida Ann); da of late 9 Baron Walpole (d 1989); *b* 18 Jan 1950; *Educ* Abbots Hill Sch for Girls, Norwich HS for Girls; *m* 1, 1973 (m dis 1981), Clive Grainger Morgan-Evans; 2 s (Edward b 1973, Daniel b 1977); m 2, 1983, Antony Hurn, of Chop Lodge, Twyford, Norfolk; *Career* ptnr and worker of farm with husband; schools horses and rides in 3 day horse trials; *Recreations* keen supporter of Norwich City FC, riding in competitions; *Style*— The Hon Mrs Hurn; Beck Farm, Calthorpe, Norwich NR11 7NG

HURN, (Francis) Roger; s of Francis James Hurn, and Joyce Elsa, *née* Bennett; *b* 9 June 1938; *Educ* Marlborough; *m* 1980, Rosalind Jackson; 1 da; *Career* Nat Serv 1959-61; engrg appentice Rolls-Royce Motors 1956-58; Smiths Industries plc: export rep Automotive Business Europe and N America 1958-59 and 1961-65, export dir Motor Accessory Div 1969 (export mangr 1965-69), corp staff dir Overseas Ops 1969-74, md Int Ops 1974-76, exec dir 1976-78, chief exec and md 1981 - (md 1978-81); non-exec dir: Pilkington plc, SG Warbug Group plc; vice pres Engineering Employers Fedn; memb: Cncl Industl Soc, Economics and Fin Policy Ctee of CBI; dir Barnet Enterprise Tst Ltd; govr Henley Coll; Liveryman Worshipful Co of Coachmakers and Coach Harness Makers 1979; Young Business of the Year (The Guardian) 1980); *Style*— Roger Hurn, Esq; c/o Smith Industries plc, 765 Finchley Road, London NW11 8DS (☎ 081 458 3232)

HURN, Stanley Noel; s of Leonard Frederick Hurn (d 1973), of Colchester, and Kathleen Alice, *née* Frost (d 1984); *b* 24 Dec 1943; *Educ* Colchester Royal GS, Univ of Hull (BSc); *Career* mangr Standard Chartered Bank 1968-78, asst dir Orion Royal Bank Ltd 1978-82, dir Samuel Montagu & Co Ltd 1982-; ACIB; *Books* Syndicated Loans - A Handbook for Banker and Borrower (1990); *Style*— Stanley Hurn, Esq; 35 Durand Gardens, London SW9 0PS (☎ 01 735 8965); Samuel Montagu & Co Ltd, 10 Lower Thames St, London EC3R 6AE (☎ 01 260 9200)

HURRELL, Sir Anthony Gerald; KCVO (1986), CMG (1984); s of late William Hurrell, and Florence Hurrell; *b* 18 Feb 1927; *Educ* Norwich Sch, St Catharine's Coll Cambridge; *m* 1951, Jean, *née* Wyatt; 2 da; *Career* RAEC 1948-50, Miny of Lab 1950-53, Miny of Educn 1953-64, Miny of Overseas Devpt 1964, fell Center for Int Affrs Harvard 1969-70, head of SE Asia Devpt Div Bangkok 1972-74; under sec: Int Div ODM 1974-75, Central Policy Review Staff Cabinet Office 1976, Duchy of Lancaster 1977, Asia and Oceans Div ODA 1978-83, Int Div ODA 1983; ambass to Nepal 1983-86; *Style*— Sir Anthony Hurrell, KCVO, CMG; Lapwings, Dunwich, Saxmundham, Suffolk IP17 3DR

HURRELL, Air Vice-Marshal Frederick Charles; CB (1986), OBE (1970); s of Alexander John Hurrell (Lt, d 1933), and Maria Del Carmen, *née* Di Biedma (d 1968); *b* 24 April 1928; *Educ* Royal Masonic Schs Bushey, St Mary's Hosp Med Sch and Univ of London (MB BS); *m* 7 Oct 1950, Jay Ruby, da of Hugh Gordon Jarvis (d 1975); 5 da (Caroline b 1951, Rosemary b 1953, Katherine b 1956, Alexandra b 1959, Anne b 1960); *Career* cmmd RAF (Med Branch): flying offr 1953, sr med offr on flying stations in UK Aust and Far East 1954-67, Flt Lt 1954, Actg Sqdn Ldr 1954, Sqdn Ldr 1959, Wing Cdr 1965, various jr staff appts 1967-74, Gp Capt and dep dir of aviation med 1974-77, staff offr (aerospace med) Br Def Staff Washington 1978-80, Air Cdre and OC Princess Alexandra Hosp RAF Wroughton 1980-82, dir of health and res 1982-84, Air Vice-Marshal and princ med offr RAF Strike Cmd 1984-86, dir gen of med servs 1986-88, ret 1988; dir of appeals RAF Benelovent Fund 1988-; FRSM 1986, FRAeS 1987; CStJ 1986; *Recreations* photography, gardening, golf; *Clubs* RAF, Sports Club of London; *Style*— Air Vice-Marshal Frederick Hurrell, CB, OBE; Hale House, 4 Upper Hale Rd, Farnham, Surrey GU9 0NJ (☎ 0252 714 190); RAF Benevolent Fund, 67 Portland Place, London W1N 4AR (☎ 071 636 2654, fax 071 580 8343 ext 201)

HURREN, Kenneth Alwyn; s of Albert Arthur Hurren (d 1988), of Pinner, Middx, and Mary Pauline Bonar; *b* 14 Aug 1925; *Educ* Westminster, George Washington Univ USA; *m* 1, 1943 (m dis), Hopeton Lucille, da of Ernest Veale; 1 da (Hopeton Bonar (Bonnie) b 1944); m 2, 1972, Ruth Lilian Camlett, da of Samuel Hyman; *Career* freelance journalist 1947-, contribs to numerous newspapers and magazines incl: The Guardian, Baltimore Sun, Los Angeles Times, Telegraph Magazine, Radio Times, TV Times, Nova, Drama, Plays and Players; The Spectator 1970-76: assoc ed, arts ed, theatre critic; ed and theatre critic What's On In London 1976-82, theatre critic The Mail on Sunday 1983-; memb The Critics' Circle (chm Drama Section 1989-); *Books* Theatre Inside Out (1977); *Recreations* travel, reading, spectator sports; *Style*— Kenneth Hurren, Esq; 58 Paddenswick Rd, London W6 0UB (☎ 081 743 7913)

HURST, Lady Barbara; *née* Lindsay; 6 da of 27 Earl of Crawford and 10 of Balcarres, KT, PC (d 1940), and Constance (d 1947), da of Sir Henry Carstairs Pelly, 3 Bt, MP; *b* 31 Dec 1915; *m* 23 May 1939, Col Richard Lumley Hurst, Royal Sussex Regt TA, barr (d 1962), s of Sir Cecil James Barrington Hurst, GCMG, KCB; 1 s (Robert b 1945), 3 da (Elizabeth (Mrs Gilroy) b 1940, Cecilia (Mrs Goodlad) b 1944, Katharine (Mrs Gibbs) b 1948); *Style*— The Lady Barbara Hurst; Porters Farm, Rusper, Horsham, W Sussex RH12 4QA (☎ 0293 871593)

HURST, Geoffrey Charles (Geoff); s of Charles Hurst, of Chelmsford, Essex, and Evelyn May, *née* Hopkins; *b* 8 Dec 1941; *Educ* Rainsford Secdy Modern, Chelmsford, Essex; *m* 13 Oct 1964, Judith Helen, da of Jack Henry Harries; 3 da (Claire Helen b 30 Oct 1965, Joanne Louise b 16 March 1969, Charlotte Jane b 15 Feb 1977); *Career* former professional footballer and mangr; clubs: West Ham (500 apperances, 250 goals scored), Stoke City 1972-75 (128 appearances, 37 goals scored), West Bromwich Albion 1975-76 (12 appearances, 2 goals scored); mangr: Chelsea 1979-81, Kuwait 1982-84; England: debut v W Germany 1966, scored hat-trick in World Cup final 4-2 defeat of W Germany Wembley 1966, 49 caps, 24 goals; sales dir Motor-Plan Limited 1984-; *Books* World Game (1967); *Recreations* golf; *Style*— Geoff Hurst, Esq; Motor-Plan Ltd, Motor-Plan House, Kemp Road, Dagenham, Essex RM8 1SN (☎ 081 598 8761, fax 081 598 8813)

HURST, John Edward; s of Edward Gostling Hurst (d 1964), of Weston Longville, Norwich, and Grace, *née* Holder; *b* 10 Oct 1947; *Educ* Gresham's, Univ of London (LLB), Univ of Amsterdam (Post Grad Dip); *m* 19 Dec 1972, Julia, da of Hendrik Jan Engelbert van Beuningen, of Cothen (U), The Netherlands; 1 s (Robert Adriaan b 13 April 1979), 2 da (Olivia b 8 Sept 1974, Annette b 16 April 1977); *Career* admitted slr 1976; ptnr: Hurst van Beuningen (Farms) 1982-, Daynes Hill & Perks 1987-; nat chm Law Soc's Slr's Euro Gp 1987-88, lay chm Sparham Deanery Synod C of E; memb: Law Soc 1976, NFU 1982; *Books* Legal Issues of European Integration: Harmonisation of Company Law in the EEC (1974); *Recreations* swimming, stalking and country pursuits; *Clubs* Norfolk; *Style*— John Hurst, Esq; Daynes Hill & Perks, Holland Court, The Close, Norwich NR1 4DX (☎ 0603 660241, fax 0603 630588)

HURST, John George; s of John George Hurst, DSc (d 1972), of Artist's Cottage, Findon, Sussex; *b* 15 March 1926; *Educ* Steyning GS, RMA Sandhurst; *m* 1954, Angela Mary Ellen, da of Claude James Marsall (d 1958), of Butts Mead, Brockenhurst; 4 s; *Career* served 8 King's Royal Inf Hussars (NW Europe, Palestine, Korea), ret Maj; md S I Coolers Ltd, dir S I Group plc; memb of IOD; *Recreations* golf, tennis, equestrian activity, swimming, driving; *Clubs* Cavalry and Guards'; *Style*— John Hurst, Esq; 122 Cambridge St, Pimlico, London SW1 4QF (☎ office 01 686 4651)

HURST, Malcolm William; s of William Hurst, of 5 Dee Road, Rainhill, Liverpool, and Lily Hurst; *b* 26 June 1943; *Educ* St Helens GS, UMIST; *m* 16 Oct 1965, Patricia Margaret, da of Ernest Yates, of 57 Rivington Road, St Helens Merseyside; 2 s (Darly Malcolm b 7 April 1969, Simon Ashley b 15 Oct 1980), 1 da (Andrea Carol 22 Aug 1966); *Career* tech offr BICC Ltd 1959-64, quality control analyst Ford Motor Co Ltd 1964-68; Eaton Axles Ltd 1968-81: chief metallurgist, quality control mangr, mfrg engr mangr; sr mangr (consultancy) Peat Marwick McClintock 1981-86; shareholder/dir: Cunnington & Cooper Ltd 1986-, Glendale Furniture Co Ltd 1986-88, Bridgetest 1986-; owner/dir: Raven Int Aircraft Ltd 1987, Talhall Ltd 1987-, GFC Nominees Ltd, Funeral Payment Cover Ltd, MJM Investmts Ltd, Nuclear and General Engrg Ltd, Production 2000 Ltd, Project 2000 Ltd, Technology 2000 Ltd, Harmcatch Ltd; CEng, MIM, MIProdE, MBIM, FIQA, MIMC; *Recreations* flying, hand gliding, microlights, light aircraft, photography, electronics; *Style*— Malcolm Hurst, Esq; Cunnington & Cooper Ltd, Wall Hill, Dobcross, Oldham OL3 5RB (☎ 045787 3111, fax 045787 8781, telex 669851)

HURST, Paul Anthony (Tony); s of John William Hurst (d 1985), and Mildred Grace, *née* Smith (d 1984); *b* 19 July 1934; *Educ* Lancaster Royal GS; *m* 9 Nov 1957, Barbara, da of Robert Croft Woodhouse, of Lancaster, Lancashire; 2 s (Simon Jeremy b 1958, Timothy Paul b 1962), 1 da (Samantha Lee b 1976); *Career* chem and res chem: Lansil Ltd 1951-57, General Foods (Canada) Ltd 1957-60; trg offr personnel mangr: Nairn-Williamson Ltd 1960-69, Velmar Textiles Ltd 1960-69; gp personnel mangr Aerialite Ltd 1969-70, personnel mangr Knowles Electronic Inc 1970-74, mgmnt conslt Russell Ewbank & Ptnrs 1974; dir and ptnr: Barnet Keel International 1974-, Peter Dye Associates 1974-; FIPM, MBIM, MIIM, MIMC; *Style*— Tony Hurst, Esq; 4 Chyngton Place, Seaford, E Sussex BN25 4HQ (☎ 0323 899539); Peter Dye Associates, The Old Vicarage, Chiddingly, E Sussex BN8 6HE (☎ 0825 872703, fax 0825 872704)

HURST, Peter Thomas; s of Thomas Lyon Hurst (d 1981), of Cheshire, and Norah Mary, *née* Delaney (d 1977); *b* 27 Oct 1942; *Educ* Stonyhurst, Univ of London (LLB); *m* 1968, Diane, da of Ian George Irvine, of Cheshire; 1 s (Charles b 1975), 2 da (Elizabeth b 1970, Catherine b 1972); *Career* slr of Supreme Court 1967; ptnr: Hurst and Walker Slrs Liverpool 1967-77, Gair Roberts Hurst and Walker Slrs Liverpool 1977-81; Master Supreme Court 1981-; chm: Liverpool Young Slrs Gp 1979, NW Young Slrs Conf 1980; *Books* Butterworths Costs Service (1986), Costs in Criminal Cases, Solicitors' Remuneration, Cordery on Solicitors (contrib 8 edn, 1988), Supreme Court Practice 1991; *Style*— Peter Hurst, Esq; Supreme Court Taxing Office, Royal Courts of Justice, The Strand, London WC2

HURST, Dr Robert; CBE (1973), GM (1944); s of Percy Cecil Hurst (d 1960), of Nelson, NZ, and Margery, *née* Whitwell (d 1957); *b* 3 Jan 1915; *Educ* Nelson Coll NZ, Canterbury Univ NZ (BSc, MSc), Univ of Cambridge (PhD); *m* 28 Sept 1946, Rachael Jeanette, da of Charles Edward Marsh (d 1951), of Bexhill, Sussex; 3 s (Jonathan b 31 July 1949, Charles Edward b 8 Aug 1953, Nicholas Robert b 5 May 1956); *Career* demonstrator Chemistry Dept Canterbury Univ NZ 1938-39, experimental offr (bomb disposal res) HQ Miny of Supply 1940-45, gp ldr Transuranic Elements Gp Aere Harwell 1948-55, project ldr Homogeneous Reactor Project Aere Harwell 1956-57, chief chemist Res and Devpt Branch Industl Gp UKAEA 1957-58, dir Dounreay Experimental Reactor Estab UKAEA 1958-63; dir Br Ship Res Assoc 1963-77; JP (Caithness 1959-63); FRSC 1960-, companion RINA 1963-; *Books* Progress in Nuclear Engineering (ed, 1957); *Recreations* gardening, sailing; *Clubs* Athenaeum, Parkstone Yacht; *Style*— Dr Robert Hurst, CBE, GM; 15 Elms Ave, Parkstone, Poole, Dorset BH14 8EE (☎ 0202 733 109)

HURST-BROWN, Alan Dudley; s of Kenneth Hurst-Brown (d 1971), of Williamsburg, Virginia, and Dorothy Joan, *née* Pinhey (d 1957); *b* 27 Dec 1920; *Educ* Dragon, Wellington; *m* 9 Aug 1947, June Marcella, da of Cdr John Garrett Wood, RN (d 1982), of Aldeburgh, Suffolk; 2 s (David b 1949, Nigel b 1951, *qv*), 2 da (Marcella b 1954, Lucy b 1962); *Career* WWII Private Royal Berks Regt 1939-40, Lt The Rifle Bde 1940-46 (POW Italy and Germany 1941-45); sr ptnr: Read Hurst-Brown stockbrokers 1963-75 (ptnr 1949), Rowe & Pitman stockbrokers 1979-82 (ptnr 1975); ret 1982; non-exec dir Kingfisher plc 1982-, non-exec chm Whitburgh Investment Ltd 1982-90; Freeman City of London 1952, Liveryman Worshipful Co of Merchant Taylors 1952; *Recreations* fishing, golf, gardening; *Clubs* Boodle's; *Style*— Alan Hurst-Brown, Esq; The Mill House, Itchen Abbas, Winchester, Hants SO21 1BJ (☎ 096278 433)

HURST-BROWN, (Christopher) Nigel; s of Alan Dudley Hurst-Brown, *qv*, of Hants, and June Marcella, *née* Wood; *b* 11 July 1951; *Educ* Wellington, Univ of Bristol (BSc); *m* 1976, Candida Madeleine, da of Arthur George Bernard Drabble, of Surrey; 2 da (Annabella, Tania); *Career* dir: Hill Samuel Investment Management 1984-86, Mercury Ariel Management Group plc; md Lloyds Merchant Bank Ltd 1986-90; chm: Lloyds Investment Managers Ltd 1986-90, Warburg Ariel Management 1990-; *Recreations* golf, tennis, shooting, fishing; *Clubs* Berks GC; *Style*— Nigel Hurst-Brown, Esq; School Farm, Heckfield, nr Basingstoke, Hants (☎ 0734 326633); Mercury Ariel Management Group plc, 33 King William St, London EC4R 9AS (☎ 071 280 2800, fax 071 280 2820)

HURSTHOUSE, Roderick Henry; s of Henry Walter Hursthouse, of Portwey Close, Weymouth, and Joan, *née* Hanger; *b* 18 Nov 1952; *Educ* Broadway Sch, Coll of Law Guildford; *m* 19 April 1980, Joan, da of Thomas Emanuel Heath, of Hodge Hill, Birmingham; 2 s (Jonathan Roderick b 1982, Alexander James b 1984), 1 da (Bryony Jane b 1986); *Career* slr 1979-; fell Inst of Legal Execs 1978; *Recreations* shooting, swimming, arts, fishing; *Clubs* Royal Dorset YC; *Style*— Roderick Hursthouse, Esq; Rookside, Winters Close, Portesham, nr Weymouth, Dorset; 71 Fortuneswell Portland (☎ 0305 823111, fax 0305 820211), car (☎ 0836 249633)

HURSTHOUSE, Roger Stephen; *b* 20 June 1941; *Educ* Henry Mellish GS; *m* Janet; 2 s (James Roger b 1969, Andrew Stephen b 1972); *Career* articled Clerk Harold T Hooley & Co Nottingham 1957-62; Pannell Kerr Forster Nottingham: mangr 1962-68, ptnr 1968-, chm Nottingham Derby and Stoke Offices, memb Nat Bd of Mgmnt; pres: Nottingham Soc of CAs 1980-81, Nottinghamshire C of C and Indst 1988-90; memb: Bd Nottingham Devpt Enterprise, Bd Gtr Nottingham Trg and Enterprise Cncl, Ct of Univ of Nottingham; chm Nottinghamshire Business Venture, serving brother Order of St John, hon treas Cncl of Nottinghamshire; memb IOD; *Recreations* golf, cricket, music; *Clubs* 41; *Style*— Roger S Hursthouse, Esq; 24 Meadow Close, Turneys Quay, Nottingham NG2 3HZ (☎ 0602 860640)

HURT, John Vincent; s of Rev Father Arnould Herbert Hurt, and Phyllis, *née* Massey (d 1975); *b* 22 Jan 1940; *Educ* Lincoln Sch, St Martin's Sch of Art, RADA; *m* 1, 1984 (m dis 1990), Donna Lynn Peacock, da of Don Wesley Laurence (d 1986), of Texas USA; m 2, 1990, Jo Dalton; 1 s; *Career* actor, films: A Man for All Seasons (1966), 10 Rillington Place (1970), The Shout (1977), Midnight Express (1977) (Oscar nom, Br Acad Award), Alien (1978), Elephant Man (1980) (Oscar nom, Br Acad Award), Champions (1983), Nineteen Eighty-Four (1984), The Hit (1984); TV: The Naked Civil Servant (1975) (Br Acad Award, best actor TV), I Claudius (1976), Crime and Punishment (1977), King Lear (Fool) (with Olivier, 1982); theatre: Little Malcolm and His Struggle Against The Eunuchs (1966), Belcher's Luck (1966), The Caretaker (1971), Travesties (1973); *Recreations* cricket, conservation activity; *Clubs* MCC, TVRF; *Style*— John Hurt, Esq; Mt Kenya Game Ranch, PO Box 288, Nanyuki, Kenya; c/o Julian Belfrage Assts, 68 St James's St, London SW1 (☎ 01 491 4400)

HURWICH, (Bertram) David; s of Dr Jack Hurwich (d 1945), of Leicester, and Priscilla Evelyn, *née* Thomas (d 1977); *b* 26 July 1937; *Educ* Epsom Coll Surrey, Elland GS Yorks; *Career* David Hurwich & Co; fin conslt to the performing and visual arts incl: Théâtre de Complicité, Cheek by Jowl Theatre Co, Lindsay Kemp Dance Co, Cut and Thrust Theatre Co, Actors Touring Co (in association with Colin Essex & Associates); hon treas Inst for Study and Treatment of Delinquency; author on taxation, accountancy, artistic and travel subjects; FCA 1963, AInsET 1964; *Recreations* theatre, the arts, skiing, francophilia, crosswords; *Style*— David Hurwich, Esq; 26 Fir Lodge, 3 Gipsy Lane, Barnes SW15 5SA (☎ 081 878 6795)

HURWITZ, Emanuel Henry; CBE (1978); s of Isaac Hurwitz (d 1951), of 84 Bethune Rd, London, and Sarah Gabrilowitz (d 1966); *b* 7 May 1919; *Educ* RAM; *m* 3 Aug 1948, Kathleen Ethel, da of Reginald Samuel Crome, of Onslowe House, William St, Slough, Bucks; 1 s (Michael b 1949), 1 da (Jacqueline b 1942); *Career* musician band RAMC; concerts in: Eng, Ireland, Egypt, Palestine, Syria, Lebanon, Iraq, Iran, Germany, Italy; Ldr: Hurwitz String Quartet 1946-52, Goldsborough Orch 1947-57, London String Trio 1952-68, London Pianoforte Quartet 1952-68, Melos Ensemble of London 1956-74, English Chamber Orch 1957-69, New Philharmonia Orch 1969-71, Aeolian String Quartet 1970-81; prof RAM 1968-, visiting lectr RSAMD 1987-; recordings incl: Brandenburg Concerti, Handel Concerto Grossi, Schubert Octet, Beethoven Septet, Trout Quintet, Mozart and Brahms Clarinet Quintets, Complete Haydn String Quartets, Ravel, Debussy, Beethoven, etc; memb: Inc Soc of Musicians 1958, Euro String Teachers Assoc 1982; Gold Medal Worshipful Co of Musicians 1967; FRAM 1961, FRSAMD 1990; *Recreations* old violins and bows, swimming, walking, music of other instruments; *Style*— Emanuel Hurwitz, Esq, CBE; 25 Dollis Ave, London N3 1DA (☎ 081 346 3936)

HUSBAND, John; s of John Husband (d 1986), of Edgware, and Bridget Agnes Leahy; *b* 21 April 1945; *Educ* St Vincent's RC Sch Mill Hill, St James' RC HS Edgware, Univ of Hull (BSc); *m* 1, Hazel Mary; 1 s (James Alexander), 1 da (Alice Jane); m 2, Linda Mary, da of Noel Stephen O' Brien; 1 da (Laura Stephanie); *Career* Daily Mirror: trainee reporter 1966-68, fin reporter 1968-74, dep city ed 1974-90 (and Sunday Mirror 1975-90), city ed 1990- (and Sunday Mirror); Personal Fin Journalist of The Year 1990; memb NUJ 1966; *Books* Money Mirror (1980); *Recreations* music, record collecting, walking, history; *Style*— John Husband, Esq; Mirror Group Newspapers, 33 Holborn, London EC1P 1DQ (☎ 071 822 3323)

HUSBAND, Prof Thomas Mutrie (Tom); s of Thomas Mutrie Husband, and Janet, *née* Clark; *b* 7 July 1936; *Educ* Shawlands Acad Glasgow, Univ of Strathclyde (BSc, MA, PhD); *m* 1962, Pat Caldwell; 2 s; *Career* Weir Ltd Glasgow: apprentice fitter 1953-58, engr/jr mangr 1958-62, Sandwich degree student mech engrg 1958-61; various engrg and mgmnt positions ASEA Ltd (Denmark, UK, S Africa) 1962-65, teaching fell Univ of Chicago 1966-67, lectr Univ of Strathclyde 1969-70, sr lectr Univ of Glasgow 1970-73, prof of mfrg orgn Univ of Loughborough 1973-81, vice chllr Univ of Salford 1990-; Imperial Coll London: prof of engrg manufacture 1981-90, dir Centre for Robotics 1982-90, head Dept Mech Engrg 1983-90; memb: ACARD Working Gp on Advanced Mfrg Technol 1982-83, DTI/SERC Ctee on Advanced Mfrg Technol 1983; chm Mfrg Processes Ctee 1984-; FEng 1988, FIProdE, FIMechE; *Publications* Work Analysis and Pay Structure (1976), Maintenance and Terotechnology (1977), Education and Training in Robotics (1986), articles in various jls; *Recreations* watching Arsenal FC, music, theatre; *Style*— Prof Tom Husband; 34 Hawthorn Lane, Wilmslow SK9 5DG (☎ 0625 520519)

HUSKINSON, (George) Nicholas Nevil; s of Thomas Leonard Bousfield Huskinson (d 1974), of Triscombe House, Triscombe, Taunton, Somerset, and Helen Margaret, *née* Hales (d 1983); *b* 7 Dec 1948; *Educ* Eton, King's Coll Cambridge (MA); *m* 20 Dec 1972, Pennant Elfrida Lascelles, da of Thomas Lascelles Isa Shandon Valiant Iremonger, of Milbourne Manor, Malmesbury, Wilts; 2 s (Thomas b 1978, Charles b 1981); *Career* called to the Bar Grays Inn 1971, in practice 1971-; memb Local Govt and Planning Bar Assoc; *Books* Woodfall's Law of Landlord and Tenant (asst ed 28 edn, 1978); *Recreations* cooking, family life, wine and food; *Clubs* Beefsteak, MCC; *Style*— Nicholas Huskinson, Esq; 34 Cheyne Row, Chelsea, London SW3 5HL (☎ 071 352 6866); 4-5 Gray's Inn Square, Gray's Inn, London WC1R 5AY (☎ 071 404 5252, fax 071 242 7803, telex GRALAW 8953743)

HUSKISSON, Dr Edward Cameron; s of Edward William Huskisson, of Northwood, Middx, and Elinor Margot, *née* Gibson; *b* 7 April 1939; *Educ* Eastbourne Coll, King's Coll London and Westminster Hosp (BSc, MB BS, MD); *m* 2 s (Ian b 1971, Robert b 1990), 1 da (Anna b 1974); *Career* conslt physician St Bartholomew's Hosp London, conslt rheumatologist King Edward V11 Hosp for Offrs London; memb: BMA, RSM; MRCS, FRCP 1980 (MRCP 1967); *Books* Joint Disease All The Arthropathies (fourth edn 1988); *Style*— Dr Edward Huskisson; 14A Milford House, 7 Queen Anne St, London W1M 9FD, (☎ 071 636 4278)

HUSKISSON, Robert Andrews; CBE (1979); s of Edward Huskisson (d 1964), and Catherine Mary, *née* Downing (d 1964), of Buckhurst Hill; *b* 2 April 1923; *Educ* Merchant Taylors', St Edmund Hall Oxford; *m* 1969, Alice Marian Swaffin, da of William John Tuck; 2 step da; *Career* dep chief exec Shaw Savill and Albion Co Ltd 1971-72; pres: Br Shipping Fedn 1971-72, Int Shipping Fedn 1969-73; chm: Lloyd's Reg of Shipping 1973-83 (dep chm and treas 1972-73), Hotel and Catering Ctee 1975-79, Marine Technol Mgmnt Ctee SRC; dir: Smit International Group (UK) Ltd 1973-87, Lloyd's of London Press Ltd 1983-89, Harland and Wolff 1983-87, Chatham Historic Dockyard Tst 1984-; *Recreations* golf; *Clubs* Thorndon Park GC, Vincent's (Oxford); *Style*— Robert Huskisson, Esq, CBE; Lanterns, 3 Luppitt Close, Hutton Mount, Brentwood, Essex

HUSS, Lawrence John; s of Laurence Leslie Huss; *b* 16 March 1926; *Educ* Stirling HS, Univ of Glasgow (BSc); *m* 1952, Rita; 2 c; *Career* Flying Offr RAF, served UK and Germany; sub agent Holloway Bros (London) Ltd 1948-57; construction mangr: Shepherds Ltd York 1957-63, Clugston Constructions Ltd 1963-68; md Appleby Slag Co Ltd 1968-90; CEng, MICE; *Recreations* golf, fishing; *Style*— Lawrence Huss, Esq; Dunluce, 26 Town Hill Broughton, Brigg, S Humberside DN20 OHD (☎ Brigg 53424)

HUSSAIN, Nasser; s of Joe Hussain, of Brentwood, Essex, and Shireen, *née* Price; *b* 28 March 1968; *Educ* Highlands Sch Ilford, Forest Sch Snaresbrook, Univ of Durham (BSc); partner, Karen Birch; *Career* professional cricketer; former player Ilford Cricket Club, represented England Schs under 15 (capt 1 year) and Essex Sch; first class debut Essex CCC 1987, awarded county cap 1989; Young England: tour Sri Lanka 1987, Youth World Cup Aust 1988; England: memb tour India and W Indies

1990, 3 Test matches, 3 one-day Ints; Gold awards: Combined Univs v Somerset Benson & Hedges Cup, Young England v Aust; *Recreations* golf, football; *Style*— Nasser Hussain, Esq; c/o Essex CCC, County Ground, New Writtle Street, Chelmsford CM2 OPG (☎ 0245 252420)

HUSSEY, Anthony Laurence; s of Robert Edward Hussey (d 1947), and Veronica Antonia Maria, *née* Connolly; *b* 13 June 1937; *Educ* Beaumont Coll Old Windsor Berks; *m* Lorna Mary, da of James Cedric Ball; 2 s (Paul Alexander James b 20 April 1973, Charles Peter Anthony b 21 Feb 1975); *Career* Nat Serv 1 Bn Queens Royal Regt, 1 Bn Royal Sussex Regt served in Korea and Gibraltar 1956-58; dir Connolly Bros Ltd (Royal Warrant Holder on co behalf); Freeman City of London, Liveryman Worshipful Co of Furniture Makers; *Recreations* skiing, classic rallying, reading; *Clubs* Kanbahar Ski, RAC; *Style*— Anthony Hussey, Esq; 1 Pelhams Close, Esher, Surrey; Connolly Leathers Ltd, Wandle Bank, Wimbledon SW19 1DW (☎ 081 543 4611, fax 081 543 7455, car 0836 731176, telex 27495)

HUSSEY, Marmaduke James; s of Eric Robert James Hussey, CMG (d 1958), and Christine Elizabeth Justice, *née* Morley; *b* 29 Aug 1923; *Educ* Rugby, Trinity Coll Oxford; *m* 25 April 1959, Lady Susan Katharine, DCVO, *qv*, *née* Waldegrave; 1 s (James Arthur b 1961), 1 da (Katharine Elizabeth (Lady Brooke) b 1964); *Career* Lt Grenadier Gds 1942-45; joined Assoc Newspapers 1949 (dir 1964), md Harmsworth Pubns 1967-70, md and chief exec Times Newspapers Ltd 1971-80 when owned by Lord Thomson; dir: Thomson Orgn 1971-80, Times Newspapers Ltd 1982-86, Colonial Mutual Life Assur (Br Bd) 1982-, MK Electric Gp 1982-88, William Collins plc 1985-89; Rhodes tstee 1972-; chm: Royal Marsden Hosp 1985-, BBC 1986-; memb: Govt Working Pty on Artificial Limbs and Appliance Centres in England 1984-86, Br Cncl 1982-, Mgmnt Ctee, King Edward's Hosp Fund for London 1987-; hon fell Trinity Coll Oxford 1989; *Clubs* Brooks's; *Style*— Marmaduke Hussey, Esq; Waldegrave House, Chewton Mendip, nr Bath, Somerset (☎ 076 121 289); BBC Broadcasting House, Portland Place, London W1A 1AA (☎ 01 580 4468)

HUSSEY, Richard Alban; s of Sydney Frederick George Hussey (d 1949), and Doris Catherine Ellen, *née* Baker (d 1983); *b* 20 March 1940; *Educ* Colfe's GS; *m* 1967, Kay Frances, da of Albert Edward Povey England; 1 s (Paul Nicholas b 1977), 1 da (Erin Elizabeth b 1970); *Career* dir: Weidenfeld and Nicolson Ltd 1970, Weidenfeld (publishers) Ltd 1986; *Recreations* cricket and rugby football (played rugby for Kent on 5 occasions); *Clubs* Old Colfeians Rugby and Cricket; *Style*— Richard Hussey, Esq; Weidenfeld and Nicolson, 91 Clapham High St, London SW4 (☎ 071 622 9933)

HUSSEY, Lady Susan Katharine; *née* Waldegrave; DCVO (1984, CVO 1971); 5 da of 12 Earl Waldegrave, KG, GCVO; *b* 1 May 1939; *m* 25 April 1959, Marmaduke James Hussey, *qv*; 1 s (James Arthur b 1961, Page of Honour to HM The Queen 1975-76), 1 da (Katharine Elizabeth (Lady Brooke) b 1964); *Career* woman of the bedchamber to HM The Queen 1960-; *Style*— The Lady Susan Hussey, DCVO; Flat 15, 45-47 Courtfield Rd, London SW7 (☎ 071 370 1414); Waldegrave House, Chewton Mendip, nr Bath, Somerset (☎ 076 121 289)

HUSTLER, John Randolph; s of William Mostyn Collingwood Hustler (d 1976), and Angela Joan, *née* Hanson (d 1983); *b* 21 Aug 1946; *Educ* Eton; *m* 23 Sept 1978, Elizabeth Mary, da of Andrew George Hughes-Onslow (d 1979); 2 s (Charles b 1982, Frederick b 1986), 1 da (Willa b 1983); *Career* CA; ptnr Peat Marwick McLintock 1983- (joined 1965); FCA 1975; *Recreations* golf, gardening; *Clubs* Boodle's; *Style*— John Hustler, Esq; Ripsley House, Liphook, Hants GU30 7JH (☎ 0428 722 223); 1 Puddle Dock, Blackfriars, London EC4V 3PD (☎ 071 236 8000, fax 071 583 1938, telex 8811541)

HUSTON, Lady Margot Lavinia; 2 da of 6 Marquess of Cholmondeley, GCVO, MC (d 1990); *b* 27 Jan 1950; *m* 1978, (Walter) Anthony Huston, only s of John Huston, film dir (d 1987); 2 s (Matthew Alec, b 1979, Jack Alexander b 1982), 1 da (Laura Sybil b 1981); *Style*— The Lady Margot Huston; Village Farm, Houghton, King's Lynn, Norfolk

HUTCHEON, Dr Andrew William; s of George Hutcheon (d 1989), of 5 Devanha Gdns, E Aberdeen, and Elsie Sophia, *née* Murison (d 1983); *b* 21 May 1943; *Educ* Robert Gordon's Coll, Univ of Aberdeen (MB, ChB, MD); *m* 14 July 1966, Christine Gray, da of Francis Gray Cusiter, of Kiama, Berstane Rd, Kirkwall, Orkney; 1 s (Barry b 1970), 2 da (Louise b 1967, Wendy b 1973); *Career* house offr med and surgery Aberdeen Royal Infirmary 1968-69, sr house offr and registrar gen med Glasgow Western 1969-72, res fell Western Infirmary Glasgow 1972-75, sr registrar Western Infirmary Glasgow and Royal Marsden London 1975-78, conslt physician and conslt med oncologist Aberdeen Hosps 1978-, sr lectr in med Univ of Aberdeen 1978-; memb: Cancer Res Campaign, Imperial Cancer Res Fund, Br Assoc for Cancer Res; FRCP, FRCPE, MRCP; *Books* Textbook of Medical Treatment (contrib 1987); *Recreations* skiing, curling, marathon running; *Clubs* Rubislaw Curling, Aberdeen; *Style*— Dr Andrew Hutcheon; Moreseat, 159 Midstocket Rd, Aberdeen AB2 4LU (☎ 0224 637204); Ward 46, Aberdeen Royal Infirmary, Foresterhill, Aberdeen AB9 2ZB (☎ 0224 681818)

HUTCHESON, Karen; da of William Hutcheson, of Dunfermline, and Janet Millar, *née* Dickson; *b* 23 Sept 1965; *Educ* Queen Anne HS Dunfermline, Lauder Tech Coll Dunfermline; *Career* athlete; clubs Pitreavie 1981-83, Lochgelly & District 1983-85, Berry Hill Mansfield 1985- (hon memb); achievements at 1500m incl: WAAA intermediate indoor champion 1982 (third 1983), scot intermediate champion 1982, Scot champion 1987 (runner up 1988 and 1989), third UK Championships 1988, WAAA indoor champion 1989; achievements at 800m incl: third Scot Championships 1985, runner up Cosford Indoor Games 1986 and 1987, third WAAA Indoor Championships 1986 and 1987, Scot indoor champion 1989; runner up 3000m UK Championships 1989, fourth 3000m Cwlth Games 1990, winner Golden Mile Hong Kong 1991; represented GB and Scotland 1986- (under 21 int 1984-86); sports personality of the year Mansfield 1990; clerk CIS Insurance Ltd Dunfermline 1982-85, admin asst Area Benefit Office Dept of Employment Mansfield 1986-87 (typist 1986), admin offr Unemployment Benefit Office Dept of Employment Mansfield 1987-; *Clubs* International Athletes, British Milers; *Style*— Miss Karen Hutcheson; Karala, 8 Hermitage Lane, Mansfield, Notts NG18 5HA (☎ 0623 632393); Dept of Employment, Unemployment Benefit Office, Beech House, 58 Commercial Gate, Mansfield, Notts (☎ 0623 654822)

HUTCHESON, Robert Bennett; s of John Holden Hutcheson (d 1981), of Montreal, and Alice Bernadette, *née* Kinchsular (d 1985); *b* 23 July 1933; *Educ* Lower Canada Coll Montreal, McGill Univ Montreal (BA); *m* 30 Sept 1972 (m dis 1985), Nichola Caroline Pumphrey, da of Edward Laird, of Topsham, Devon; 4 da (Venetia b 1973, Sacha b 1974, Suki b 1976, Alice b 1977); *Career* sr registrar Hammersmith Hosp 1974-75, sr obstetrician and gynaecologist Gloucester Royal Hosp 1975-; FRCOG 1983; *Recreations* travel, photography, tennis; *Style*— Robert Hutcheson, Esq; 1 Burnet Close, Robinswood, Gloucester, Glos GL4 9YS (☎ 0452 305841); 9 College Green, Gloucester, Glos; Gloucester Maternity Hospital, Great Western Rd, Gloucester, Glos (☎ 0452 25512)

HUTCHINGS, Gregory Frederick; s of Capt Frederick Garside Hutchings, and Edna May, *née* McQueen; *b* 22 Jan 1947; *Educ* Uppingham, Univ of Aston (BSc), Aston Mgmnt Centre (MBA); *m* 14 June 1980, Caroline Jane; *Career* Hanson plc 1981-83, chief exec Tomkins plc 1984- (dir 1983-); *Recreations* sport, music, literature; *Style*— Gregory Hutchings, Esq; Tomkins plc, East Putney House, 84 Upper Richmond Rd, London SW15 2ST (☎ 081 871 4544)

HUTCHINGS, Dr Warwick; s of Hugh Hampden Hutchings (d 1978), and Olga, *née* Millar (d 1971); *b* 30 July 1928; *Educ* Wallingford GS, Loughborough Coll, Middx Hosp Med Sch; *m* 5 Aug 1961, Pamela, da of William Harry Edge (d 1954); 1 s (Craig b 1964), 2 da (Beverley b 1963, Alanah b 1969); *Career* registrar anaesthetist City Gen Hosp 1961-64, sr registrar anaesthetist Southend Gen Hosp 1964-66, conslt N Staffs Health Dist 1966-; memb: Coll of Anaesthetists 1965, Assoc Anaesthetists, Midland Soc of Anaesthetists, Hickman Anaesthetics Soc; *Recreations* model engineering, amateur radio, radio controlled model aircraft; *Style*— Dr Warwick Hutchings; Bitternsdale Farm, Lower Leigh, Stoke on Trent, Staffs ST10 4PE (☎ 0538 723262); Anaesthetic Department, New Surgical Development, City General Hospital, Newcastle Rd, Stoke on Trent, Staffs ST4 6QG (☎ 0782 621133 ext 2732)

HUTCHINS, Brig Peter Edward; s of Edward Stanley Hutchins (d 1976), and Afreda Beryl, *née* Newton-Davey (d 1985); *b* 11 Feb 1919; *Educ* St Dunstan's Coll London, UCL; *m* 1, 15 July 1944 (m dis), Cynthia Margaret, da of Gilbert Gaul Gross (d 1944), of Essex; 2 s (Jeremy b 1946, Miles b 1948), 1 da (Georgina b 1958); m 2, 28 July 1984, Barbara Patience, da of Frederick Dillon-Edwards (d 1952), of Bucks; *Career* WWII cmmnd RCS 1940, regtl cmmn 1944, eventually Brig GS MOD, ret 1970; attended Slade Sch of Fine Art 1937-39 (Alfred Rich Open Scholarship 1987, Slade scholar 1938-39), princ CS 1970-71, md London Press Centre 1971-88, memb and dir Int Press Centre 1971-88; chm and dir Greston Sch 1968-75, chm Armed Forces Art Soc 1976-90; FRSA, FBIM; *Recreations* painting, boats, gardening; *Clubs* Army and Navy, Press; *Style*— Brig Peter E Hutchins; 6 Yew Tree Court, Goring-on-Thames, Oxfordshire RG8 9HF (☎ 0491 874091)

HUTCHINSON, Frederick; MBE (1945); s of William Hutchinson (d 1950), and Margaret, *née* Kitching (d 1968); *b* 5 Dec 1915; *Educ* St Bede's Coll Manchester; *m* 5 Sept 1942, Edith, da of Arthur Nield (d 1953), of Oldham; 3 s (Michael b 1947, Nicholas b 1954, Stephen b 1957), 1 da (Denise Stephanie b 1945); *Career* TA 1938, Maj DAA and QMG 21 Army Gp 1939-46 UK and NW Europe (despatches twice); non-exec dir: Shiloh plc 1970- (sales dir 1970-81), sales mangr Elk Mill/Royton Spg Co Ltd 1954-70, mangr Shiloh Mills 1949-54, asst mangr Park and Sandy Lane Mills 1948-49; *Recreations* golf; *Style*— Frederick Hutchinson, Esq, MBE; 37 Broadway, Royton, Oldham OL2 5DD (☎ 061 626 4847)

HUTCHINSON, (Edward) Graham; s of Roger Hutchinson (d 1971), of Southport, Merseyside, and Katharine Norma, *née* Robinson (d 1984); *b* 11 Jan 1940; *Educ* Bryanston, King's Coll Cambridge (MA), Euro Inst of Business Admin Fontainebleau France (MBA); *m* 7 Nov 1970, Diana Fair, da of William Fair Milligan, of Heswall, Wirral, Merseyside; 1 s (Mark b 1974), 2 da (Camilla b 1972, Christina b 1977); *Career* md Dan-Air Servs Ltd 1981-; dir: Davies and Newman Holdings plc 1980-90, Bowater Europe 1977-80; dir and chief exec Neptun International Holding AG; *Recreations* leisure travel, music, family; *Clubs* Leander; *Style*— Graham Hutchinson, Esq; Silver Birches, Startins Lane, Cookham Dean, Berks SL6 9TS; Dan-Air Services Ltd, Newman House, Victoria Rd, Horley, Surrey RH6 7QG (☎ 0293 820700, telex 877677, fax 0293 774717)

HUTCHINSON, Prof John Neville; s of Frank Hutchinson (d 1978), and Elizabeth Helen, *née* Booth (d 1978); *b* 27 Dec 1926; *Educ* Bablake Sch Coventry, Univ of Birmingham (BSc), Univ of Cambridge (PhD), Univ of London (DSc); *m* 29 July 1961, Patricia, da of Frederick Hilton (d 1943); 1 s (Thomas b 8 April 1974), 2 da (Kristin b 15 Aug 1965, Julia b 23 Nov 1970); *Career* civil engr: Robert M Douglas (contractors) Ltd Birmingham 1947-50, Rendel Palmer & Tritton conslt engrs London 1950-57, Swedish Geotechnical Inst Stockholm 1957-58, Norwegian Geotechnical Inst Oslo 1958-61, soil mechanics Div Bldg Res Station Watford 1961-65; Dept Civil Engrg Imperial Coll: sr lectr 1965-70, reader in soil mechanics 1970-76, prof engrg geomorphology 1977-; FGS 1966, FICE 1983; *Recreations* gardening, music, painting, reading, mountaineering; *Style*— Prof John Hutchinson; Dept of Civil Engineering, Imperial College, Imperial College Rd, London SW7 2BU (☎ 071 589 5111 ex 4721, fax 071 823 8525, telex 918351)

HUTCHINSON, (Patrick) Lloyd; s of John Irvine Hutchinson, of Northern Ireland, and Adeleine, *née* Gibson; *b* 17 March 1967; *Educ* Antrim GS, Nat Youth Theatre, Ulster Youth Theatre, RADA (prize winner); *Career* actor; debut in Scout 1986, subsequent theatre work: Alain/Enrique in School for Wives (tour of Ireland) 1989, season with RSC 1990-91 (Costard in Love's Labours Lost, Ripio in Don Juan); Best Actor in Northern Ireland 1986 (for Ritual for Doll); *Recreations* skiing, squash, folk music; *Style*— Lloyd Hutchinson, Esq; Foxlodge, 2 Shanoguestown Rd, Muckamore, Antrim, Ireland BT41 4QL (☎ 08494 68212); Mayer Management, Suite 44, Grafton House, 2-3 Golden Square, London W1R 3AD (☎ 071 434 1242, fax 071 494 1547)

HUTCHINSON, Mark Bernard Michael; s of Andrew Hutchinson (d 1986), and Rosaleen Carmel, *née* Finnegan (d 1983); *b* 30 Sept 1959; *Educ* St Mary's Coll Comp Wallasey; *Career* actor; theatre work incl West End revivals of: Oklaoma! (1980), Mr Cinders (1983), Me and My Girl (1985), Eddie in Blood Brothers (1990-91); *Recreations* music, reading, eating, drinking, Sondheim & cream cakes; *Style*— Mark Hutchinson, Esq; Peter Browne Management, Pebro House, 13 St Martin's Road, London SW9 0SP

HUTCHINSON, (John) Maxwell; s of Frank Maxwell Hutchinson (d 1977), and Elizabeth Ross Muir, *née* Wright (d 1987); *b* 3 Dec 1948; *Educ* Scott Sutherland Sch of Architecture Aberdeen (Dip Arch), Architectural Assoc Sch of Architecture London; *Career* chm: Permarock Prodns Ltd Loughborough 1985-, Hutchinson and Ptnrs Architects (fndr 1972); RIBA: memb Cncl 1978-, sr vice pres 1988-89, pres 1989-; vice pres Industl Bldg Bureau 1988-; visiting prof in architecture Queen's Univ Belfast 1989-; Centenary fell Thames Poly assoc memb PRS 1988; Freeman City of London 1980, memb Ct of Assistance Worshipful Co of Chartered Architects 1988; AADipl, PRIBA, FBIM, FRSA; *Books* The Prince of Wales Right or Wrong? (1989); *Recreations* composing, recording, playing the guitar loudly, music of Edward Elgar, opera, ballet, theatre, riding, running, Rutland; *Clubs* Athenaeum; *Style*— Maxwell Hutchinson, Esq; 29 Pied Bull Court, Galen Place, London WC1; Cobblers Cottage, Empingham, Rutland; Hutchinson & Ptnrs, 401 St John St, London EC1

HUTCHINSON, Dr (Robert) Michael; s of Vivien Roy Owen Hutchinson (d 1969), and Iris May, *née* Moseley (d 1979); *b* 11 Sept 1939; *Educ* King Edward VI Sch Birmingham, Univ of Oxford (MA, BSc), St Mary's Hosp Med Sch (BM BCh); *m* 23 Sept 1967, Ann, da of Geoffrey Edward Milner (d 1979), of Hailsham, Sussex; 3 s (Jonathan Mark b 26 Aug 1970, Nicholas Paul b 19 May 1972, Andrew Simon James b 13 Dec 1976); *Career* registrar in clinical med and haematology Royal Postgrad Med Sch Hammersmith Hosp 1971-73, sr registrar in haematology United Bristol Hosps 1973-75, conslt haematologist Leicester AHA 1976-; author of numerous scientific pubns on related haematological disorders; memb: Br Soc of Haematology, MRC Working Party on Adult Leukemia and Related Disorders; tstee The Cope Childhood Oncology Fund, is actively involved in the church's miny of healing; FRCPath 1987, FRCP 1989; *Recreations* clarinet player in local orchestra and music group; *Style*— Dr Michael Hutchinson; Dept of Haematology, Leicester Royal Infirmary, Leicester LE1

5WW (☎ 0533 541414 ext 6611)

HUTCHINSON, Hon Nicholas St John; s of Baron Hutchinson of Lullington, QC (Life Peer); *b* 3 May 1946; *Style*— The Hon Nicholas Hutchinson

HUTCHINSON, Patricia Margaret; CMG (1981), CBE (1982); da of Francis Bernard Hutchinson (d 1982), and Margaret Evelyn Hutchinson (d 1980); *b* 18 June 1926; *Educ* abroad, St Paul's Girls Sch London, Somerville Coll Oxford; *Career* HM Dip Serv: FCO 1948-50, 3 sec Bucharest 1950-52, FCO 1952-55, 2 then 1 sec Berne 1955-58, 1 sec (commercial) Washington 1958-61, FCO 1961-64, 1 sec Lima 1964-67, dep vice-rep to Cncl of Europe 1967-69; councillor: Stockholm 1969-72, UK Perm Delgn to OECD 1973-75; consul gen Geneva 1975-80, ambass Montevideo 1980-83, consul gen Barcelona 1983-86; pres Somerville ASM 1988-91; *Recreations* travel, reading, music; *Clubs* Oxford and Cambridge; *Style*— Miss Patricia Hutchinson, CMG, CBE; c/o Nat Westminster Bank plc, 6 Tothill St, London SW1

HUTCHINSON, (George) Peter; CBE (1984); s of late Robert Hutchinson, and Eleanor Heath, *née* Moffitt; *b* 12 Dec 1926; *Educ* St Bees Sch Cumbria, Univ of Durham (BSc); *m* 7 June 1958, Audrey, da of late W O A Dodds; 1 s (Robert b 1959), 1 da (Katherine b 1962); *Career* chartered surveyor and land agent; sr ptnr J M Clark & Ptnrs; dir: Newcastle and Gateshead Water Co, Newcastle Int Airport; memb Northumberland CC 1973-, ldr Cons Gp 1985-, chm Educ Ctee 1988-; chm Northern Area Cons Cncl 1981-84; FRICS; *Recreations* gardening, travel; *Clubs* Northern Counties (Newcastle-upon-Tyne), Farmers'; *Style*— Peter Hutchinson, Esq, CBE; Low House, Hexham, Northumberland (☎ 043 473 237); J M Clark & Ptnrs, 5 Hencotes, Hexham, Northumberland (☎ 0434 602301)

HUTCHINSON, His Hon Judge Richard Hampson; s of John Riley Hutchinson (d 1958), of Leeds, and May, *née* Hampson (d 1959); *b* 31 Aug 1927; *Educ* Hull Univ Coll (LLB), St Bede's GS Bradford; *m* 1954, Nancy Mary, da of John William Jones Warrington (d 1983); 2 s (Christopher, Damian), 3 da (Paula, Hilary, Marie-Louise); *Career* Nat Serv 1949-51, Flying Offr RAF; called to the Bar Gray's Inn 1949, practised NE Circuit 1949-74; rec: Rotherham 1971, Crown Ct 1972-74; circuit judge 1974-, tech advsr Entral Cncl of Probation Ctees 1989-, memb County Ct Rules Ctee 1990-; *Recreations* reading, conversation; *Style*— His Hon Judge Hutchinson; Crown Court, Lincoln

HUTCHINSON, Thomas (Tom); s of Thomas Charles Hutchinson, of Sheffield, and Gladys, *née* Unsworth; *b* 22 May 1930; *Educ* Longley Cncl Sch Sheffield, City GS Sheffield, Univ of Sheffield (extra-mural dept); *m* Patricia; 2 s (Michael, Stephen), 1 da (Janetta); *Career* journalist; Sheffield Telegraph, Kinematograph Weekly, Picturegoer, Daily Cinema, ABC TV, Daily Express, Tyne Tees TV, ITN, Nova Magazine, Reveille, Evening Standard, Battle of Britain Film-Unit, Guardian; film critic: Sunday Telegraph , Now! Magazine, Scottish Sunday Standard, Mail On Sunday, Cinema 2 (BBC Radio 2), The Movie Quiz; sci fiction critic The Times, question setter Mastermind; Hon D Univ Sheffield; memb: Critics' Circle (chm), BAFTA; *Books* Horror and Fantasy In The Cinema, Marilyn Monroe, Elizabeth Taylor, Goddesses of The Cinema, Niven's Hollywood; *Recreations* walking to the cinema, worrying about my family, wondering why my wife puts up with me, books, crossword's, entertaining cats; *Clubs* Groucho; *Style*— Tom Hutchinson, Esq; 64 Southwood Lane, Highgate Village, London N6 5DY (☎ 081 340 8822)

HUTCHINSON OF LULLINGTON, Baron (Life Peer UK 1978); Jeremy Nicolas Hutchinson; QC (1961); o s of St John Hutchinson, KC (d 1943), and Mary, o da of Sir Hugh Barnes, KCSI, KCVO; *b* 28 March 1915; *Educ* Stowe, Magdalen Coll Oxford (MA); *m* 1, 1940 (m dis 1966), Dame Peggy Ashcroft, DBE, the actress *qv*; 1 s (Hon Nicholas St John, *qv*), 1 da (Hon Eliza b 14 June 1941); m 2, 1966, June Osborn; *Career* served WW II RNVR; barr 1939, recorder Bath 1962-72, Crown Court 1972-76; sat as Labour Peer in Lords till 1981/82 when joined SDP; vice-chm Arts Cncl 1977-79, chm Tstees Tate Gallery 1980-84 (tstee 1977-); prof of law RA 1988; tstee Chantrey Bequest 1987; *Clubs* MCC; *Style*— The Rt Hon Lord Hutchinson of Lullington, QC; 10 Blenheim Road, London NW8

HUTCHISON, David Alan; MBE (1976); s of Hector Donald Hutchison (d 1948), of Amberley Gardens, Bush Hill Park, Enfield, Middx, and Winifred, *née* Middlehurst (d 1986); *b* 13 Jan 1937; *Educ* Royal Masonic Sch Bushey Herts, Bartlett Sch of Architecture Univ Coll London (BA); *m* 3 April 1961 (m dis 1989), Helen Elizabeth, da of Arthur George Penn (d 1981), of High St Pembury, Tunbridge Wells, Kent; 2 s (Michael b 1 Nov 1963, Peter b 24 Dec 1966), 2 da (Gillian b 21 Jan 1962, Christine b 9 Aug 1965); m 2, 18 May 1990, Audrey, da of Horace Scott, of 19 Red Lion Road, Tolworth, Surrey; *Career* architect; worked with Powell & Moya 1960-64: chm: HLM (formerly Hutchison Locke & Monk) 1988- (fndr ptnr 1964), HLM Architects Ltd, HLM Planning Ltd, HLM Landscape Ltd; architect for major public sector cmmns in health and civic authys 1964-88; health projects (hosps) incl: Bournemouth, Cheltenham, Ealing, Whipps Cross, Lister, Sheffield Northern Gen, Medway, St James Dublin; civic projects: Surrey Heath Borough Cncl, Broxbourne Borough Cncl, Daventry Dist Cncl, Colchester Borough Cncl, Waltham Forest Cncl, Macclesfield Cncl Offices, Epsom and Ewell Cncl, Reigate and Banstead Cncl, Stoke-on-Trent Cncl; cmmns for Univs of Reading and Surrey; winner: int competition (architecture) Paisley Civic Centre 1964, 7 Civic Tst awards DOE Good Housing award, RIBA Architecture commendation, Redland Roof Tile award, RIBA Energy award; nat seat on Cncl RIBA 1987, assessor Civic Tst; Freeman: City of London 1977, Worshipful Co of Constructors 1977, Worshipful Co of Arbitrators 1987; RIBA, ARIAS, FIA, FFB, AInst(Hosp)E, FBIM, MIE, FRSA 1989; *Recreations* amateur theatre, local amenity soc; *Clubs* Camberley Soc (chm), Farnborough and RAE Operatic Soc, Camus Productions, Bath Light Operatic Gp; *Style*— David Hutchison, Esq, MBE; North House, 1 North Road, Bathwick, Bath, Avon BA2 6JB (☎ 0225 66915); HLM Architects Ltd, 2-4 Henry St, Bath, Avon BA1 1JT (☎ 0225 446551, fax 0225 445708, car 0831 407997)

HUTCHISON, Geordie Oliphant; s of Lt-Col R G O Hutchison (d 1934), and R G Hutchison, *née* Black (d 1985); *b* 11 June 1934; *Educ* Eton; *m* 1964, Virginia, da of Flt Lt Barbezat (d 1943); 2 s (James b 1966, Timothy b 1967), 1 da (Victoria b 1970); *Career* Lt RNVR 1957; md Calders and Grandidge Ltd 1974-, cmmr Forestry Cmmn 1981-89; chm: Meyer Timberframe Ltd 1985-, PDM Ltd 1987-; *Recreations* golf, shooting, skiing; *Clubs* Royal and Ancient Golf; *Style*— Geordie Hutchison, Esq; Bank of Scotland, Haymarket, Swallowfield House, Welby, Grantham, Lincs; Calders and Grandidge Ltd, London Rd, Boston, Lincs (☎ 0205 366660, fax 0205 352592, telex 378267)

HUTCHISON, Lt-Cdr Sir (George) Ian Clark; DL (Edinburgh 1958); s of Sir George A Clark Hutchison, KC, MP (d 1928); *b* 4 Jan 1903; *Educ* Edinburgh Acad, RNC Osborne, RNC Dartmouth; *m* 1926, Sheena Campbell (d 1966); 1 da; *Career* joined RN 1916, ret 1931, recalled 1939, served Naval Ordnance Inspection Dept 1939-43; MP (U) Edinburgh (West) 1941-59; memb Royal Co of Archers (Queen's Body Guard for Scotland); kt 1954; *Style*— Lt-Cdr Sir Ian Hutchison, DL; 16 Wester Coates Gdns, Edinburgh, Scotland EH12 5LT (☎ 031 337 4888)

HUTCHISON, Dr James Graham Pinney; s of Lt-Col Graham Seton Hutchison, DSO, MC (d 1946), of High Wycombe, Bucks, and Emile Beatrice, *née* Durham (d 1972); *b* 1 April 1923; *Educ* Edinburgh Acad, Guy's Hosp Med Sch (MB BS, MD); *m* 13 Sept 1952, Margaret Jane (Margot) *née* Price, da of late (Percy) Burr Price, of Scarsdale, New York; 2 s (Tom b 26 Sept 1953, Hugh b 14 June 1956), 5 da (Jean (Mrs Rowe) b 11 March 1955, Anne b 30 March 1958, Susan (Mrs Fothergill) b 8 Dec 1959, Eleanor (Mrs Strickson) b 10 Feb 1961, Sarah b 27 July 1964); *Career* Lt then Capt RAMC 1946-49; lectr and sr lectr dept of bacteriology Univ of Glasgow Western Infirmary 1957-65, dir regnl public health laboratory Birmingham 1965-89, conslt microbiologist E Birmingham Hosp; papers published in med and sci jls; FRCPG, FRCPath; *Recreations* literature (reading/writing), music, fine arts, gardening; *Clubs* Royal Overseas League; *Style*— Dr James Hutchison; 38 Chantry Rd, Moseley, Birmingham B13 8DJ (☎ 021 449 1535)

HUTCHISON, Sir Peter; 2 Bt (UK 1939), of Thurle, Streatley, Co Berks; s of Sir Robert Hutchison, 1 Bt (d 1960), of Thurle Grange, Streatley-on-Thames, nr Reading, and Laetitia Norah, *née* Ede (d 1963); *b* 27 Sept 1907; *Educ* Marlborough, Lincoln Coll Oxford (MA); *m* 16 July 1949, Mary-Grace, da of Very Rev Algernon Giles Seymour (d 1933, Rector and Provost of St Mary's Cathedral Glasgow); 2 s (Robert b 1954, Mark b 1960), 2 da (Elspeth b 1950, Alison b 1951); *Heir* s, Robert Hutchison, *qv*; *Career* Flt Lt RAFVR 1941-45, intelligence offr photographic reconaissance unit (PRU); admitted slr 1932; asst slr; Warwicks CC 1934-36, E Suffolk CC 1936-47; dep clerk of the peace of the CC E Suffolk 1947-70, clerk of the peace and county slr E Suffolk CC 1970-72; memb Suffolk Coastal Dist Cncl 1973-83; chm govrs Orwell Park Prep Sch Nacton nr Ipswich 1974-86; *Recreations* gardening, reading; *Style*— Sir Peter Hutchison, Bt

HUTCHISON, Sir Peter Craft; 2 Bt (UK 1956), of Rossie, Co Perth; s of Sir James Riley Holt Hutchison, 1 Bt, DSO, TD (d 1979), and Winefryde Eleanor Mayr (Anne) (d 1988); *b* 5 June 1935; *Educ* Eton, Magdalene Coll Cambridge (BA); *m* 1966, Virginia, da of John Millar Colville, of Gribloch, Kippen, Stirlingshire; 1 s; *Heir* s, James Colville Hutchison b 7 Oct 1967; *Career* former Lt Royal Scots Greys; chm Hutchison and Craft Ltd, dir Stakis plc and other cos; memb Bd Scottish Tourist Bd 1981-87, chm of tstees Royal Botanic Garden Edinburgh, currently vice chm Bd Br Waterways Bd (memb 1987-); *Style*— Sir Peter Hutchison, Bt; Milton House, Milton, by Dumbarton

HUTCHISON, Robert; s and h of Sir Peter Hutchison, 2 Bt, *qv*; *b* 25 May 1954; *Educ* Marlborough; *m* 7 Feb 1987, Anne Margaret, er da of Sir Michael Thomas, 11 Bt, *qv*; 2 s (Hugo Thomas Alexander b 16 April 1988, Guy Piers Giles b 30 April 1990); *Career* with J & A Scrimgeour Ltd 1973-78, financial adviser 1978-; *Recreations* tennis, watching association football, travelling, golf; *Clubs* Lansdowne, Hurlingham; *Style*— Robert Hutchison, Esq; 40 Averill St, London W6 8EB

HUTCHISON, Sidney Charles; CVO (1977, LVO 1967); s of Henry Hutchison (d 1979), and Augusta Rose, *née* Timmons (d 1912); *b* 26 March 1912; *Educ* Holloway Sch London, Univ of London (Dip History of Art); *m* 24 July 1937, Nancy Arnold (d 1985), da of Alfred Brindley (d 1962); *Career* Lt Cdr RNVR 1939-45; joined staff RA 1929, organist and choirmaster St Matthew's Westminster 1933-37, librarian RA 1949-68, lectr in history of art Univ of London 1957-67, sec RA 1968-82; gen cmmr of Taxes 1972-87; govr Holloway Sch 1969-81, tstee Chantrey Bequest 1982-; sec: E A Abbey Meml Tst Fndn 1960-87, Inc E A Abbey Scholarships 1965-, E Vincent Harris Fndn 1970-87, BR Inst Fndn 1968-82; pres Southgate Soc of Arts 1983-, hon archivist RA, memb ICOM, FRSA, FSA, FMA, FAAA; Offr Polonia Restituta 1971, Chevalier Belgian Order of the Crown 1972, Grand Decoration of Honour (silver) Austria 1972, Cavaliere Ufficiale al Merito della Repubblica Italiana 1980; *Books* The Homes of the Royal Academy (1956), The History of the Royal Academy 1768-1968 (1968; enlarged, updated edn 1768-1986, 1986); *Recreations* music, travel; *Clubs* Athenaeum, Arts; *Style*— Sidney Hutchison, Esq, CVO; 60 Belmont Close, Mount Pleasant, Cockfosters, Herts EN4 9LT (☎ 081 449 9821); Royal Academy of Arts, Piccadilly, London W1V 0DS (☎ 071 439 7438)

HUTCHISON, T O; s of late James Hutchison, and Thomasina, *née* Oliver; *b* 3 Jan 1931; *Educ* Hawick HS, Univ of St Andrews (BSc); *m* 1955, Frances Mary Ada; 3 s; *Career* dir: ICI Industries plc 1985-, ICI Australia 1985-91, Impkemix Investments Pty 1985-, Bank of Scotland 1985-, Cadbury Schweppes plc 1986-, Enterprise Oil plc 1987-90, Océ Finance Ltd 1977-79; chm Phillips-Imperial Petroleum Ltd 1982-85 (dir 1981-85); memb: Cncl British Plastics Fedn 1977-79, Advsy Ctee Energy International NV 1986-, Governing Cncl Scottish Business in the Community 1986; pres Assoc of Plastics Mfrs Europe 1980-82; CEFIC: memb Petrochemicals Advsy Gp 1982-85, memb Assembly of Corporate Assoc Membs and Ctee of Dirs 1986-; chm Europe Ctee CBI 1989-; *Recreations* tennis, fishing, music, golf; *Style*— T O Hutchison, Esq; c/o Imperial Chemical Industries plc, 9 Millbank, London SW1P 3JF

HUTCHISON, Prof William McPhee; s of William Hutchison (d 1956), of 18 Merryvale Ave, Giffnock, Glasgow, and Anne, *née* McPhee (d 1962); *b* 2 July 1924; *Educ* Eastwood HS, Univ of Glasgow (BSc, PhD), Univ of Strathclyde (DSc); *m* 15 March 1963, Rev Ella Duncan, da of James McLaughland, of 29 Fairway, Bearsden, Glasgow; 2 s (Bruce b 1964, Leslie b 1966); *Career* Univ of Strathclyde: asst lectr 1952-53, lectr 1953-68, sr lectr 1969-71, prof of parasitology 1971-86, res prof 1986-89 emeritus prof of parasitology 1989-; Fencing blue Glasgow Univ Athletic Club 1949, Scottish Epée Open Champion 1949, Ford Epée Cup 1949, Capt and Champion Glasgow Univ Fencing Club 1949-51; elder Church of Scotland; Robert Koch Fndn medal and prize 1970; FIBiol 1971, CBiol 1971, FRSE 1973, FLS 1974; *Recreations* gardening, woodwork, writing, music; *Style*— Prof William M Hutchison, FRSE; 597 Kilmarnock Rd, Newlands, Glasgow G43 2TH (☎ 041 637 4882); Biology Division, University of Strathclyde, Glasgow G1 1XW (☎ 041 552 4400)

HUTCHON, Dr David James Riddell; s of James Hutchon (d 1971), of Edinburgh, and Alice Mary, *née* McIntosh; *b* 17 April 1945; *Educ* George Watson's Boys Coll Edinburgh, Univ of Edinburgh (BSc, MB ChB); *m* 12 June 1971, Rosemary Elizabeth, da of Dr Ronald Caile (d 1978), of Southport, Lancs; 1 s (Christopher b 1978), 1 da (Fiona b 1979); *Career* govt med offr Grand Cayman BWI 1972-74, sr house offr Simpson Memorial Hosp Edinburgh 1974-76, registrar in obstetrics and gynaecology Ninewells Hosp Dundee 1976-78, res registrar Northwick Park Hosp London 1978-79, sr registrar in obstetrics and gynaecology Eastern Gen Hosp Edinburgh and clinical tutor Univ of Edinburgh 1979-81, conslt obstetrician and gynaecologist Darlington and Northallerton Health Authys 1981-; chm sr med staff ctee Memorial Hosp Darlington; FRCOG, fell Edinburgh Obstetrical Soc; *Recreations* golf, skiing, sailing; *Clubs* Blackwell Grange Golf; *Style*— Dr David Hutchon; 9 Farr Holme, Blackwell, Darlington, Co Durham DL3 8Q2 (☎ 0325 358134); Dept of Obstetrics and Gynaecology, Memorial Hospital, Darlington, Co Durham (☎ 0325 380100)

HUTLEY, Peter William; s of William Hutley (d 1976), and Dorothy Violet, *née* Abbott; *b* 24 Dec 1926; *Educ* Coll of Estate Mgmnt; *m* 19 June 1954, Ann Mary, da of Thomas Morris Cox (d 1974), 2 s (Nicholas Peter b 1959, Edward Thomas b 1962), 2 da (Charlotte Ann b 1956, Henrietta Frances Mary b 1965); *Career* Army Capt RE Br mil mission to Burma 1945-48; sr ptnr Pepper Angliss and Yarwood 1951-76, dep chm and md Property Growth Assurance Co Ltd 1968-76; chm: Shenley Trust Ltd 1973-76, Hutley Holdings plc 1976, Northbourne Developments Party Ltd 1983, Peter Hutley Investments Pty Ltd 1967, Hutley Rural Property Trust 1983, Pitt Street Securities Party Ltd 1983, Hutley Land (USSR) Ltd; memb Lloyds, FRICS; OStJ;

Clubs Bucks, Royal Thames Yacht; *Style*— Peter Hutley, Esq; Wintershall, Bramley, Surrey GU5 0LR

HUTSON, Maurice Arthur; s of William Arthur Hutson (d 1980), of S Yorkshire, and Ivy, *née* Roberts (d 1989); *b* 27 Jan 1934; *Educ* Gainsborough Tech Coll, Leeds Coll of Technol; *m* 1959, Janet, da of Arthur Edward Parkin, of S Yorkshire; 2 s (Mark Andrew b 1961, Jonathan Peter b 1970), 1 da (Helen Claire b 1963); *Career* chartered engr; devpt engr Tarmac Roadstone Ltd 1963-71 (prodn and engrg mangr 1965, staff offr 1970); chm and md: Seaham Harbour Dock Co 1971-81 (dir 1981-87), Mahcon Construction (Services) Ltd 1972-, Transport and Aggregates Ltd 1972-81, Wath Quarries Ltd 1977-, Allerton Engineering Ltd 1983-, Naylor Sportscars Ltd 1986-, Hutson Motor Company Ltd 1986-; chm and chief exec Parker Plant Ltd 1990-; dir: Neocast Ltd 1980-90, The Sundial Hotel Ltd Northallerton N Yorks, The Seaham Harbour Dock Co 1981-86; CEng, MIMechE, MIProdE, FIQ; *Recreations* motor sport, travel and walking, gardening; *Clubs* Rotary (Stokesley), 41 Club (Guisborough); *Style*— Maurice Hutson, Esq; South Hambleden, Morton Carr Lane, Nunthorpe, nr Middlesbrough, Cleveland TS7 0JU (☎ 0642 315077); Allerton Engineering Ltd, Romanby Road Works, Northallerton, N Yorks DL7 8NG (☎ 0609 774471/2, fax 0609 780364, telex 58102 ALLFAB)

HUTSON, Thomas Guybon; TD (1966); s of Guybon John Hutson (d 1963), of Kensington Mansions, and Diana Chisholm, *née* Davidson (d 1972); *b* 17 April 1931; *Educ* Morrison's Acad Crieff, St Paul's Sch Hammersmith; *m* 9 May 1959, (Ann) Rosemary, da of Arthur Cranfield Coltman (d 1981), of Westheath Close, Hampstead; 1 s (Charles b 1960), 3 da (Catherine b 1962, Anna b 1964, Fiona b 1970); *Career* Nat Serv: Private Gordon Highlanders 1949, cmmnd 2 Lt 1950; served Highland Bde Trg Centre, Fort George and Cameron Barracks Inverness 1951, 2 Lt 1 Bn London Scottish (TA) 1951, ret as Maj 1967; joined Bank of England 1948 (and after War Serv 1951), seconded Libya to establish Central Bank Tripoli 1957, mangr Exchange Control Dept Nat Bank Libya 1958, returned Bank of England 1959, Tozer Kemsley & Millbourn 1960 (who founded Int Factors), md Int Factors 1978- (dir 1967), pres Int Factors Gp 1985-87, chm Assoc Br Factors 1987-89; memb CBI South-Eastern Regional Council 1990-; FICM, FRPSL, memb Caledonian Soc London; *Books* Management of Trade Credit (1968); *Recreations* tennis, bridge, chess, opera, hill walking, philately, travel; *Style*— Thomas Hutson, Esq, TD; Ditchling Ct, Ditchling, Sussex BN6 8SP (☎ 07918 3558); Int Factors Ltd, Sovereign House, Church St, Brighton, Sussex (☎ 0273 21211, fax 0273 771501, telex 87382)

HUTT, Rev David Handley; s of Frank Handley Hutt, and Evelyn Violet Catherine, *née* Faarup; *b* 24 Aug 1938; *Educ* Brentwood, RMA Sandhurst, King's Coll London (AKC); *Career* Reg Army 1957-64; ordained: deacon 1969, priest 1970; curate: Bedford Park London 1969-70, St Matthew Westminster 1970-73; priest vicar and succentor Southwark Cath 1973-78, sr chaplain King's Coll Taunton 1978-82; vicar: St Alban and St Patrick Birmingham 1982-86, All Saints' St Marylebone 1986-; *Recreations* gardening, cooking, music, theatre; *Clubs* Athenaeum; *Style*— The Rev David Hutt; All Saints Vicarage, 7 Margaret St, London W1N 8JQ (☎ 071 636 1788, fax 071 436 4470)

HUTT, Peter Morrice; s of Sqdn Ldr Harry Morrice Hutt, of Caversham, Reading, Berks, and Joan Ethel Ludlaw, *née* Whitmore; *b* 15 April 1945; *Educ* Leighton Park Sch, Univ of Southampton (LLB); *m* 23 March 1974, Cynthia Anne, da of John Gauntlett Gubb (d 1988), of Uitenhage, SA; 1 s (Stephen b 1977); *Career* admitted slr 1969; ptnr Brain & Brain 1973-, Notary Public 1978; Rotherfield Peppard: chm Parish Cncl 1987-90, lay chm All Saints Parochial Church Cncl 1986-90; tstee Relief in Need Charity, tstee Mem/Hall, clerk Polehampton Charities Twyford, former memb Caversham Round Table; memb: Law Soc 1967, Slr Benevolent Assoc 1969, Provincial Notaries Soc 1978; *Recreations* music, walking, gardening, tennis; *Style*— Peter Hutt, Esq; Rushton House, Church Lane, Rotherfield Peppard, Henley-on-Thames RG9 5JR (☎ 049 17 335); Brain & Brain, Addington House, 73 London St, Reading RG1 4QB (☎ 0734 581 441, fax 0734 597 875, telex 847645)

HUTTON, Alasdair Henry; OBE (1990, MBE 1986), TD (1977); s of Alexander Hutton (d 1954), and Margaret Elizabeth, *née* Henderson; *b* 19 May 1940; *Educ* Gatehouse of Fleet Sch, Dollar Acad, Brisbane State HS Australia; *m* 1975, Deirdre Mary, da of Kenneth Alexander Hume Cassels, of Wimbish Green, Essex; 2 s (Thomas b 1978, Nicholas b 1982); *Career* journalist and broadcaster; MEP EDG 1979-89; tstee Community Service Volunteers 1985-; 2 i/c 15 Scottish (Volunteer) Bn The Parachute Regt 1979-86; memb Queen's Body Guard for Scotland, Royal Co of Archers 1987-; life memb John Buchan Soc, patron Volonteurop; elder Church of Scotland 1985-; *Style*— Alasdair Hutton, Esq, OBE, TD; Rosebank, Shedden Park Rd, Kelso TD5 7PX (☎ 0573 24369)

HUTTON, (Alan) Brian; s of Leslie Edward Hutton (d 1981), of Leeds, Yorks, and Annie Nora, *née* Browne; *b* 12 April 1937; *Educ* King Edward V GS; *m* 27 Aug 1965, Brenda, da of Francis Laidler; 1 da (Kate Frances b 29 July 1966); *Career* md: HS Fitter & Sons 1959-75, CR Barron Ltd 1975-85; own business Salford Meat Packers Ltd 1985-; Freeman: City of London 1983, Worshipful Co of Butchers 1982; *Recreations* soccer, horse racing, rugby league, cricket; *Style*— Brian Hutton, Esq; The Lodge, Ponsbourne Park, Newgate St Village, Hertfordshire SG13 8QT

HUTTON, Brian Gerald; s of James Hutton (d 1977), of Barrow-in-Furness, Cumbria, and Nora Hutton (d 1984); *b* 1 Nov 1933; *Educ* Barrow GS, Univ of Nottingham (BA), UCL (Dip in Archive Admin); *m* 23 May 1958, Serena Quartermaine, da of Charles Ernest May (d 1976), of Kingston Blount, Oxon; 1 s (Patrick James b 1964), 1 da (Katherine Mary b 1961); *Career* Nat Serv RN; Jt Servs Sch of Linguists 1955-57; asst archivist Herts County Record Office 1959-60; 1960-74: asst keeper and dep dir Public Record Office NI, administrator Ulster Historical Fndn, lectr archive admin Queen's Univ Belfast, princ Treas Div NI Civil Serv; sec and dep dir Nat Library Scotland 1974-88, archives conslt 1988-; Co sec Cncl for Protection of Rural England (Bucks); cmmnd Kentucky Col for services to archives 1982; *Recreations* walking in lake district, visiting art galleries, listening to music; *Clubs* Royal Commonwealth Soc, New (Edinburgh); *Style*— Brian Hutton, Esq; Elma Cottage, The Green, Kingston Blount, Oxon OX9 4SE (☎ 0844 54 173); 9 Wilton Rd, Edinburgh EH16 5NX (☎ 031 667 2145)

HUTTON, Deirdre Mary; da of Kenneth Alexander Home Cassels, of Wimbish Green, Essex, and Barbara Kathleen, *née* Alington; *b* 15 March 1949; *Educ* Sherborne Girls, Hartwell House; *m* 1 Nov 1975, Alasdair Henry Hutton, s of late Alexander Hutton; 2 s (Thomas Kennedy b 28 June 1978, Nicholas Alasdair b 27 Feb 1982); *Career* Anchor Housing Assoc Oxford 1973-75, res asst Glasgow C of C 1975-82, memb, treas, chm Brooklands Sch Bd 1984-, memb Music Ctee Scot Arts Cncl 1985-91, hon sec Kelso Music Soc 1985-; memb: Scot Consumer Cncl 1986-90, Scot Consultative Cncl on the Curriculum 1987-, Territorial Gp Borders Local Health Cncl 1988-, Ctee on Reporting 1989-; lay memb for Scot of Gen Dental Cncl and memb Professional Misconduct Ctee 1988-, memb Ctee to Review Curriculum Examinations in Fifth and Sixth Years of Scot Educn (Howie Ctee) 1990-, vice chm Scot Consumer Cncl 1990-91, memb Cncl Nat Consumer Cncl 1991-, chm Scot Consumer Cncl 1991-; *Recreations* gardening, music (particulary singing); *Style*— Mrs Deirdre Hutton; Scottish Consumer Council, 314 St Vincent St, Glasgow (☎ 041 226 5261)

HUTTON, His Hon Judge Gabriel Bruce; s of late Robert Crompton Hutton, of Gloucs, and late Elfreda, *née* Bruce; fourth successive generation of judges living in Gloucs; *b* 27 Aug 1932; *Educ* Marlborough, Trinity Coll Cambridge (BA); *m* 1965, Deborah Leigh, da of Vivian Leigh Windus (d 1950), of Sussex; 1 s (Alexander b 1972), 2 da (Joanna b 1966, Tamsin b 1968); *Career* called to the Bar Inner Temple 1956, dep chm Gloucs Quarter Sessions 1971, rec Crown Ct 1972-78, circuit judge 1978, liaison judge for Gloucs and res judge for Gloucester Crown Ct 1987; *Recreations* hunting (chm Berkeley), boating, shooting; *Style*— His Hon Judge Hutton; Chestal, Dursley, Gloucs (☎ 0453 543285)

HUTTON, Gordon White; s of Peter Young Hutton, and Elizabeth Edward, *née* Powrie; *b* 15 July 1933; *Educ* St Edward's Sch Oxford, Corpus Christi Coll Oxford (MA); *Career* broker Bray Gibb & Co Ltd 1957-60, underwriter and underwriting asst Miall Underwriting Agency 1961-70, chm and underwriter G W Hutton and Co Underwriting Agency Ltd 1970-; former memb Cncl and Ctee Lloyd's, Lloyd's Underwriters Assoc (chm 1979-80); memb NT Devpt Cncl; Freeman Worshipful Co of Curriers; chartered insurer Chartered Insur Inst; *Recreations* art, antiques, theatre, film; *Clubs* MCC; *Style*— Gordon Hutton, Esq; G W Hutton & Co (Underwriting Agency) Ltd, Lloyds, 1 Lime Street, London EC3M 7HL (☎ 071 327 3234, 071 626 2200)

HUTTON, Hon Mrs (Jacqueline Patricia); *née* Grant of Grant; da (by 1 m) of 5 Baron Strathspey; *b* 19 Jan 1942; *m* 30 April 1966, Malcolm Usheen Lingen Hutton; *Style*— The Hon Mrs Hutton; Kinsley, Banchory, Kincardineshire AB31 3RS

HUTTON, James Thomas; s of Thomas Hutton, of Glasgow, and Isobel, *née* Service; *b* 12 May 1923; *Educ* Provanside Secdy, Univ of Glasgow (BMus), RSAM (ARCM); *m* 14 Aug 1946, Anne Jamieson, da of Alexander Bowes (d 1972), of Paisley; 1 s (Richard b 1952); *Career* visiting specialist in music primary and secdy schs: Renfrewshire Educn Authy 1960-64, Lanarkshire Educn Authy 1964-88; composer: Symphony No 1 1948, Symphony No 2 1949, Helicon No 1 1950, Helicon No 2 1950, Movement for Septet 1958, Overture 1959, Consomme 1959, Apollo-Friday-Midway-Non Troppo, Integration 1971, A Movement 1971, Sextet 1971, Andante 1972, Synthesis 1972, Nucleus 1973, Sonus 1973, Brass 1974, Piano Concerto 1974, Scherzo 1974, Vox 1975, Renascence 1975, Overture-Braes 1976, Onyx 1976, Mobile 1976, Omega 1976, Hymn to David 1977, Juno 1978, Pax 1979, Diapason 1982, Xenium 1984; life memb EIS, fndr memb Scot Soc of Composers; *Recreations* improvising at the piano; *Style*— James Hutton, Esq; 88 Warwick, East Kilbride, Scotland G74 3PY (☎ 03552 25895)

HUTTON, John Christopher; s of John Francis Hutton, of Cranmer Ct, Llandaff, Cardiff, and Elizabeth Margery Ethel, *née* Pugh; *b* 7 June 1937; *Educ* Kingswood Sch Bath, Ch Ch Oxford (MA); *m* 5 Aug 1963, Elizabeth Ann, da of Prof Eric Evans (d 1967); 2 da (Catrin b 1965, Bethan b 1968); *Career* Nat Serv RA Cyprus 1956-58; methods engr Tube Investmts 1963-64 (graduate trainee 1961-63); Bristol and West Bldg Soc: PA to Gen Mangr 1964-67, res mangr 1967-76, asst gen mangr mktg and res 1976-86 (corporate info and analysis 1986-88), conslt fin mktg 1988-; conslt Money Which? 1971-; chm housing fin panel Bldg Socs Assoc 1973-84 (memb 1967-), co-chm Tech Sub Ctee of Jt Advsy Ctee on Mortgage Fin 1973-82; memb: Construction Industs Jt Forecasting Ctee NEDO 1978-89 (Housing Strategy Ctee 1975-77), Cncl Sub Ctee on Reserves and Liquidity BSA 1981 (ldr Netherlands Res Gp 1979), Fin Advertising Sub Ctee Advertising Standards Authy 1982-; dir: Bristol Bldgs Preservation Tst Ltd 1984-, The Wildscreen Tst 1987-; FSS 1968, assoc IMS 1968, memb Chartered Bldg Socs Inst; author of many articles for the nat press; *Recreations* antiques, wine, countryside, journalism; *Style*— John Hutton, Esq; Ferns Hill, Kingsweston Rd, Bristol BS11 0UX (☎ 0272 824 324); Wyevern, Aberedw, Builth Wells, Powys LD2 2UN

HUTTON, Matthew Charles Arthur; s of Capt Ronald David Hutton, MC (d 1984), of Langley Grange, Loddon, Norfolk, and Rhodanthe Winnaretta, *née* Leeds; *b* 10 Sept 1953; *Educ* Eton, Ch Ch Oxford (BA, MA); *m* 6 Oct 1984, Anne Elizabeth Caroline, da of Leslie James Leppard, DFC, of Cobb Cottage, Dalwood, Axminster, Devon; 1 s (David b 1988), 2 da (Victoria b 1986, Alexandra b 1990); *Career* tax conslt, ptnr Daynes Hill & Perks (Slrs) Norwich 1987-89; govr St Felix Sch Southwold 1987; AInstT 1980; *Recreations* family life, country pursuits; *Clubs* MCC, Norfolk (Norwich); *Style*— Matthew Hutton, Esq; Abbot's House, 25 White Hart St, Aylsham, Norfolk NR11 6HG (☎ 0263 734634, 0263 734849, fax 0263 734849)

HUTTON, Nicholas Robert Pardy; s of Benjamin Phillip Hutton, of 8 Portland Terrace, The Green, Richmond, Surrey, and Joan Reason, *née* Pardy; *b* 31 March 1944; *Educ* Kingston Sch of Art (Dip Arch); *m* 29 July 1966, Marie-Françoise Berthe Claudine, da of George Casimir Guy (d 1976), of Béziers, France; 1 s (Benjamin b 1971), 2 da (Pascale b 1967, Amy b 1972); *Career* worked in Béziers France for D Escorsa (former asst to Le Corbusier) 1966-67; Broadway Malyan: joined 1972, assoc 1980, equity ptnr 1984, opened London office 1986, promoting co in France 1989-; memb: Br Cncl of Shopping Centres, City Dialogue Luncheon Club; ARIBA 1971; *Recreations* travel, running a vineyard in France; *Style*— Nicholas Hutton, Esq; Broadway Malyan, 37 Soho Square, London W1V 5DG (☎ 071 437 0770, fax 071 437 1248)

HUTTON, (Hubert) Robin; s of Kenneth Douglas Hutton, and Dorothy, *née* de Wilde; *b* 22 April 1933; *Educ* Merchant Taylors', Peterhouse Cambridge (MA); *m* 1, 25 June 1956 (m dis 1967), Valerie, *née* Riseborough; 1 s (Andrew b 1958), 1 da (Sarah b 1960); m 2, 3 May 1969, Deborah, *née* Berkeley; 2 step da (Susan b 1957, Linda b 1959); *Career* Royal Tank Regt 1951-53; asst gen mangr Financial Corporation for Industry Ltd 1956-61, dir Hambros Bank Ltd 1961-70, special advsr HM Govt 1970-73, dir Fin Insts Commission of Euro Communities 1973-78, dir SG Warburg and Co Ltd 1978-82; dir gen: Accepting Houses Ctee, Issuing Houses Assoc 1982-87, Br Merchant Banking and Securities Houses Assoc 1988-; non-exec dir Northern Rock Building Soc, dir Investment Management Regulatory Organisation Ltd; memb Exec Ctee Br Bankers Assoc, chm English Nat Advsy Ctee on Telecoms; cricket, gardening, travel; *Clubs* MCC; *Style*— Robin Hutton, Esq; Church Farm, Athelington, nr Eye, Suffolk (☎ 072 876 361); 6 Frederick's Place, London EC2R 8BT (☎ 071 796 3606, fax 071 796 4345)

HUTTON, Lady; Virginia Jacomyn; JP; da of late Sir George Young, 4 Bt, MVO; *b* 1911; *Educ* England, Abroad; *m* 1936, Sir Noel Kilpatrick Hutton, CGB, QC (sometime First Parly Counsel; d 1984), s of William Hutton (d 1933); 2 s, 2 da; *Style*— Lady Hutton, JP; 8 Wyndham Way, Oxford OX2 8DF

HUTTON, Maj-Gen Walter Morland; CB (1964), CBE (1960), DSO (1943), MC (1936, Bar 1942); s of Walter Charles Stritch Hutton (d 1953), and Amy Mary, *née* Newton (d 1950); *b* 5 May 1912; *Educ* Allhallows Sch, Parkstone Sch, RMC Sandhurst, Staff Coll, Imperial Def Coll; *m* 1945, Peronelle Marie Stella, da of Cecil Arthur Stewart Luxmoore-Ball (d 1963); 2 s (David, Anthony), 1 da (Gillian); *Career* cmmnd 2 Lt RTC 1932, served in England, Egypt and Palestine 1936, 1 Class Army Interpreter in Arabic 1937; WWII cmdg: 5 RTR in Western Desert, Alamein and N Africa, 40 RTR in Italy; cmdt Sandhurst 1944-45, cmd Specialized Armour Devpt Unit 1946-47, Br liaison offr Kentucky and Virginia USA 1947-49, instr Staff Coll Camberley 1949-51, Col 1953, Brig 1955, BGS Arab Legion Jordan 1953-56, Imperial Def Coll

1957, Dep Cdr (Land) BFAP (Aden) 1957-59, dir Admin Plans War Office 1959-60, memb Jt Planning Staff 1959-60, Maj Gen 1961, dir gen Fighting Vehicles War Office 1961-64, Sr Army Directing Staff Imperial Defence Coll 1964-66, ret; home bursar Jesus Coll Oxford 1966 (fell 1967, MA 1967), examiner Military History Oxford 1968-69; memb Bd of Govrs Utd Oxford Hosps 1969-72; *Recreations* reading, chess; *Style*— Maj-Gen Walter Hutton, CB, CBE, DSO, MC

HUXLEY, Sir Andrew Fielding; OM (1983); s of Leonard Huxley (2 s of T H Huxley, the scientist and humanist), and his 2 w Rosalind, *née* Bruce; half-bro of Sir Julian Huxley, the biologist, and Aldous Huxley, the novelist; *b* 22 Nov 1917; *Educ* University Coll Sch Westminster, Trinity Coll Cambridge; *m* 1947, Jocelyn Richenda Gammell, JP, da of Michael Pease (whose paternal grandmother was Susanna, da of Joseph Fry, of the Bristol Quaker family of cocoa manufacturers, and 1 cous of Sir Theodore Fry, 1 Bt), and his w Hon Helen, *née* Wedgwood, JP, eldest da of 1 Baron Wedgwood; 1 s (Stewart Leonard b 1949), 5 da (Janet b 1948, Camilla b 1952, Eleanor b 1959, Henrietta b 1960, Clare b 1962); *Career* operational research for Anti-Aircraft Cmd and Admty WWII; fell Trinity Coll Cambridge 1941-60 and 1990- (dir of studies 1952-60), demonstrator Physiology Dept Cambridge 1946-50 (asst dir of research 1951-59, reader in experimental biophysics 1959-60), Jodrell prof of physiology and head of dept UCL 1960-69, Fullerian prof of physiology and comparative anatomy Royal Inst 1967-73, Royal Soc research prof Univ of London 1969-83 (emeritus prof of physiology 1983), Cecil H and Ida Green visiting prof Univ of BC 1980, master of Trinity Coll Cambridge 1984-90; chm British Nat Ctee for Physiological Sciences 1979-80, memb ARC 1977-81, pres British Assoc for Advancement of Science 1976-77; tstee: British Museum of Natural History 1981-91, Science Museum 1984-88; memb Nature Conservancy Cncl 1985-87, Animal Procedures Ctee (Home Office) 1987-; hon memb: Royal Inst 1981, Royal Irish Acad 1986, Japan Acad of Science 1988; Hon Fell: Inst of Biology, Darwin Coll Cambridge, Royal Soc of Canada, Royal Soc of Edinburgh, Univ Coll London, Imperial Coll, Fellowship of Engineering, Queen Mary Coll, Trinity Coll Cambridge; foreign assoc Nat Acad Sci USA, pres Int Union of Physiological Sciences 1986-; Nobel Laureate in Physiology or Medicine 1963, Copley Medal Royal Society 1973; Hon Dr of 21 Univs; FRS 1955 (memb cncl 1960-62 and 1977-79, pres 1980-85); kt 1974; *Books* Reflections on Muscle (1980); *Recreations* walking, designing scientific instruments; *Style*— Sir Andrew Huxley, OM, FRS; Manor Field, 1 Vicarage Drive, Grantchester, Cambridge CB3 9NG (☎ 0223 840207)

HUXLEY, Anthony Julian; s of Sir Julian S Huxley, FRS (d 1974), and Marie-Juliette, *née* Baillot; *b* 2 Dec 1920; *Educ* Dauntsey's Sch Wiltshire, Trinity Coll Cambridge (MA); *m* 1 Sept 1943 (m dis 1974), Ann, da of late Frederick Taylor; 3 da (Susanna b 1944, Lucinda b 1946, Victoria b 1948); m 2, Oct 1974, Alyson Ellen Vivien, *née* Archibald; 1 da (Zoe b 1979); *Career* sci offr: Operational Res RAF 1941-45, Historical Res Unit Miny of Aircraft Prodn 1945-46; Econ Res Unit BOAC 1947-48; ed Amateur Gardening 1967-71 (asst ed 1949-67); freelance writer photographer and ed 1971-, currently ed-in-chief RHS Dictionary of Gardening; vice pres RHS 1991 (memb Cncl 1979-91, memb various Ctees); pres: Horticultural Club, Saintpaulia and Houseplant Soc; former chm Int Dendrology Soc; *Books* ed or author 34 books incl: Flowers of the Mediterranean (with Oleg Polunin, 1965), Mountain Flowers of Europe (1967), Plant and Planet (1974), Flowers of Greece and the Aegean (with William Taylor, 1977), An Illustrated History of Gardening (1979), Success with Houseplants (gen ed, 1979), Penguin Encyclopedia of Gardening (1981), Wild Orchids of Britain and Europe (with P and J Davies, 1983), The Painted Garden (1988); *Recreations* photography, gardening, botanical travel; *Style*— Anthony Huxley, Esq; 50 Villiers Avenue, Surbiton, Surrey KT5 8BD (☎ 081 390 7983)

HUXLEY, Col Colin Wylde; s of Brig Christopher Huxley, CBE (d 1965), of London, and Edmée, *née* Ritchie; *b* 21 April 1928; *Educ* Bradfield, RMA Sandhurst; *m* 29 March 1958, Alison Barbour, da of George James Harris, MC (d 1958), of York; 1 s (Henry b 1962), 1 da (Annabel b 1960); *Career* cmmnd KOYLI 1948; served: Malaya, Germany, Aden, Cyprus, Berlin; instr RMA Sandhurst 1958-61, Staff GHQ FARELF Singapore 1961-63, MOD 1965-66, instr Sch of Infantry 1968-69, cmd LI Depot Shrewsbury 1969-72, AAG Light Div Winchester 1972-75, def advsr Br High Cmmn Nicosia 1976-79, Col Army HQ UKLF Wilton 1980-83, Dep Col LI (Yorks) 1980-85; tst dir Treloar Tst 1983-, govr Priors Field Sch Godalming 1983- (chm 1990-); *Recreations* pictures, picture framing, tennis, golf; *Style*— Col Colin W Huxley; Brook Lodge, Old Alresford, Hants SO24 9DH (☎ 0962 732582); Treloar Trust, Froyle, Alton, Hants (☎ 0420 22442)

HUXLEY, Elspeth Josceline; *née* Grant; CBE (1962); da of Maj Josceline Grant (d 1947), of Njoro, Kenya, and Hon Eleanor, *née* Grosvenor (d 1977); *b* 23 July 1907; *Educ* Univ of Reading; *m* 12 Dec 1931, Gervas Huxley, CMG, MC (d 1971), s of Dr Henry Huxley; 1 s (Charles b 1944); *Career* writer; author of 35 books incl: biography, autobiography, fiction, travel; most of these books relate to Africa and many to Kenya (her childhood home); two were semi-fictional autobiographical: The Flame Trees of Thika (TV Series) and The Mottled Lizard; Out in The Midday Sun (semi-travel, semi-autobiographical); freelance radio journalist; *Recreations* resting, gossip; *Style*— Mrs Elspeth Huxley, CBE; Green End, Oaksey, Malmesbury, Wiltshire (☎ 06667 252)

HUXLEY, Prof George Leonard; s of late Sir Leonard G M Huxley, and late Lady Huxley; *b* 23 Sept 1932; *Educ* Univ of Oxford (BA, Cromer Greek prize); *m* 1957, Davina Best; 3 da; *Career* Mil Serv cmmnd RE 1951; fell All Souls Coll Oxford 1955-61, asst dir Br Sch at Athens 1956-58, visiting lectr Harvard Univ 1958-59 and 1961-62, prof of Greek Queen's Univ of Belfast 1962-83, temp asst lectr St Patrick's Coll Maynooth 1984-85, hon res assoc Trinity Coll Dublin 1984-89, dir Gennadius Library American Sch of Classical Studies Athens 1986-89; hon prof of Greek Trinity Coll Dublin 1989-; memb: Exec NI Civil Rights Assoc 1971-72, Royal Irish Acad Dublin (sec for polite literature and antiquities 1979-86, sr vice pres 1984-85); chm Organising Ctee 8th Int Congress of Classical Studies Dublin 1984, sr vice pres Fédération Internationale des Sociétés d'Etudes Classiques 1984-89, Irish memb Standing Ctee for the Humanities Euro Sci Fedn Strasbourg 1978-86, memb Academia Europaea 1990, hon librarian Royal Irish Acad 1990, visiting prof of history Univ of Calif San Diego 1990; FSA; author of various articles on Hellenic and Byzantine subjects; *Books* Achaeans and Hittites (1960), Early Sparta (1962), The Early Ionians (1966), Greek Epic Poetry from Eumelos to Panyassis (ed with J N Coldstream, 1969), Kythera Excavations and Studies (1972), Pindar's Vision of the Past (1975), On Aristotle and Greek Society (1979), Homer and the Travellers (1988); *Clubs* Athenaeum; *Style*— Prof George Huxley, PSA; School of Classics, Trinity College, Dublin 2, Ireland (☎ 0001 772941, ext 1208)

HUXLEY, Hugh E; MBE (1948); s of Thomas Hugh Huxley (d 1967), and Olwen, *née* Roberts (d 1963); *b* 25 Feb 1924; *Educ* Park HS, Christ's Coll Cambridge (BA, MA, PhD, DSc), Mass Inst of Technol; *m* 12 Feb 1966, Frances, da of Glenway Maxon; 1 da (Olwen b 1970); *Career* radar offr RAF 1943-47; MRC 1954-87: Molecular Biology Unit Cambridge 1954-56, res assoc Dept of Biophysics London 1956-62, Laboratory of Molecular Biology Cambridge 1962-87 (dep dir 1978-, jt head Structural Studies Div 1975-); fell: Christ's Coll Cambridge 1953-56, King's Coll Cambridge 1961-67, Churchill Coll Cambridge 1967-87; dir Rosenstiel Basic Med Scis Res Center 1988-, prof of biol Brandeis Univ Waltham MA 1988-; memb editorial Bd: Jl of Cell Biology 1961-64, Jl of Molecular Biology 1962-70, 1978-87 and 1990-, Jl of Ultra-structure Research 1958-67, Jl of Cell Science 1966-70, Proceedings of the Royal Soc (B) 1969-71, Jl of Cell Motility and Muscle Research 1980-; jt ed Progress In Biographics and Molecular Biology 1964-67; memb: External Advsy Bd Rosenstiel Center 1971-77, Cncl Royal Soc 1973-75 and 1984-85, Sci Advsy Cncl European Molecular Biology Laboratory 1975-81 (currently memb Instrumentation Policy Planning Ctee, convenor Working Gp of Techniques and Instrumentation 1969-70), tstee Assoc Univs Inc 1987-90; awards: Feldberg prize for Experimental med res 1963, Hardy prize for Biological Research 1965, Louisa Cross Horwitz prize 1971, Feltrinelli Int prize for Med 1974, Gardner award 1975, Baly medal RCP 1975, E B Wilson award 1983, Albert Einstein World award of Sci 1987, Franklin medal 1990; hon foreign memb: Leopoldina Acad 1964, American Acad of Arts and Scis 1965, Danish Acad of Scis 1971; hon memb: American Assoc of Anatomists 1981, American Physiological Soc 1981, American Soc of Biological Chemists 1976; hon fell Christ's Coll Cambridge 1981, foreign assoc US Nat Acad of Scis 1978; Hon DSc: Harvard Univ 1969, Univ of Chicago 1974, Univ of Pennsylvania 1976; *Publications* various pubns in scientific jls; *Recreations* skiing, sailing; *Clubs* Oxford and Cambridge Univs; *Style*— Hugh Huxley, Esq, MBE; 349 Nashawtuc Rd, Concord, MA 01742, USA (☎ 508 369 4603); Rosenstiel Center, Brandeis Univ, 214 South St, Waltham, MA 02284, USA (☎ 617 736 2401, fax 617 736 2405)

HUXLEY, Prof Paul; s of Ernest William Huxley, of Derby, and Winifred Mary Huxley; *b* 12 May 1938; *Educ* Harrow Sch of Art, Royal Acad Sch; *m* 1, Sept 1957 (m dis 1972), Margaret Doris, da of James Perryman; 2 s (Mark b 1961, Nelson b 1963); m 2, May 1990, Susan Jennifer, da of Henry Francis Metcalfe; *Career* artist, prof of painting RCA 1986-; group exhibitions incl: Whitechapel Gallery London 1964, Marlborough Gerson NY 1965, Galerie Milano Milan 1965, Pittsburgh Int Carnegie Inst Pittsburgh 1967, UCLA Art Galleries Los Angeles 1968, Tate Gallery London 1968, Museum of Modern Art NY 1968, Museum am Ostwall Hanover 1969, Walker Art Gallery Liverpool 1973, Hayward Gallery London 1974, Royal Acad London 1977, Museo Municipal Madrid 1983, RCA London 1988, Mappin Art Gallery Sheffield 1988; solo exhibitions at galleries incl: Rowan Gallery London, Kornblee Gallery NY, Galleria da Emenda Lisbon, Forum Kunst Rotweil; cmmnd by London Tport to design 22 ceramic murals for King's Cross Underground Station 1984; works exhibited in public collections world-wide incl: Albright-Knox Gallery Buffalo NY, Art Gallery of NSW Aust, Leeds City Art Gallery, V & A Museum, Whitworth Art Gallery Manchester, Stuyvesant Fndn Holland, Ulster Museum Belfast, Art Gallery of Ontario Toronto, Centro Cultural Arte Contemporanes Mexico; memb: Ctee Serpentine Gallery 1971-74, Arts Panel Arts Cncl GB 1972-76; tstee Tate Gallery 1975-82; ARA 1987; *Books* Exhibition Road - Painters at The Royal College of Art (1988); *Style*— Prof Paul Huxley; 29 St Albans Ave, London W4 5LL (☎ 081 994 5111); Royal College of Art, Kensington Gore, London SW7 2EV (☎ 071 584 5020)

HUXTABLE, Gen Sir Charles Richard; KCB (1984, CB 1982), CBE (1976, OBE 1972, MBE 1961); s of Capt W R Huxtable; *b* 22 July 1931; *Educ* Wellington, RMA Sandhurst; *m* 31 March 1959, Mary, da of late Brig J H C Lawlor; 3 da; *Career* Col Cmdt The King's Div 1982-87 , Col Duke of Wellington's Regt 1982-90; Dir Army Staff Duties MOD 1982-83, Cdr Trg and Arms Directors 1983-86, Quartermaster Gen 1986-88, Cdr in Chief UK Land Forces 1988-90; ADC Gen 1988-90; *Clubs* Army and Navy; *Style*— Gen Sir Charles Huxtable, KCB, CBE; c/o Lloyds Bank, 23 High St, Teddington, Middx TW11 8EX

HYAM, His Hon Judge Michael Joshua; s of Isaac Joseph Hyam (d 1972), of Sussex, and Rachel Hyam; *b* 18 April 1938; *Educ* Westminster, Univ of Cambridge (MA); *m* 1968, Diana, da of Rupert Vernon Mortimer, of Yorks; 3 s; *Career* barr SE circuit 1962-84, rec Crown Ct 1983-84, circuit judge; memb: Cncl of Legal Educn 1980-85, Ethical Ctee Cromwell Hosp 1983-; govr Dulwich Coll Prep Sch 1986-; *Publications* Advocacy Skills (1990); *Recreations* book collecting, cricket, gardening; *Clubs* Garrick, Norfolk, MCC; *Style*— His Hon Judge Hyam; Combined Court, Norwich

HYATALI, Sir Isaac Emanuel; TC (1974); s of Joseph Hyatali (d 1938), and Esther Hyatali (d 1930); *b* 21 Nov 1917; *Educ* Naparima Coll Trinidad, Cncl of Legal Educn Gray's Inn London; *m* 1943, Audrey Monica, da of Stanislaus Joseph (d 1971) and Emily Joseph; 2 s, 1 da; *Career* Civil Serv 1939-44; called to the Bar Gray's Inn 1947; chm: Arima Rent Assessment Bd 1953-59, Agric Rent Bd Eastern Counties 1953-59, Bd of Inquiry Telephone Trade Dispute 1958, Bd of Inquiry Cement Trade Dispute 1959, Wages Cncl 1958-59, Oil and Water Bd 1959-62; judge Supreme Ct Trinidad and Tobago 1959-62, justice of appeal 1962-72, pres Industl Ct 1965-72, chief justice and pres of the Ct of Appeal Trinidad and Tobago 1972-83, justice of appeal Seychelles Republic 1983-86; chm: Election and Boundaries Cmmn 1983-, American Life and Gen Insur Co Ltd 1983-, Constitution Cmmn 1987; conslt Hyatali & Co (attorneys at law), memb Cncl of Mgmnt Br Inst of Int and Comparative Law 1982-, arbitrator and umpire of Int Civil Aviation Orgn 1980-; memb World Assoc of Judges; Ansa Fndn 1989-, McEneaney-Alston Fndn 1989; kt 1973; *Clubs* Royal Cwlth Soc, Union, Union Park Turf; *Style*— Sir Isaac Hyatali, TC; 8 Pomme Rose Ave, Cascade, St Ann's, Republic of Trinidad and Tobago (☎ 809 624 3049); chambers: 63 Edward St Port of Spain (☎ 809 623 4007), Salvatori Bldg, Frederick St, Port of Spain, Repub of Trinadad and Tobago (☎ 809 623 8733)

HYATT, Derek James; s of Albert James Hyatt (d 1972), of Ilkley, W Yorks, and Dorothy, *née* Sproat; *b* 21 Feb 1931; *Educ* Ilkley GS, Leeds Coll of Art (NDD), Norwich Coll of Art, RCA (ARCA); *m* 20 Feb 1960, Rosamond Joy, da of Sidney Rockey (d 1983), of Torquay; 1 da (Sally Jane b 27 June 1962); *Career* Nat Serv RAF fighter cmd 1952-54; artist writer and teacher; visiting lectr Kingston Sch of Art 1959-64, lectr Leeds Coll of Art 1964-68, sr lectr Leeds Poly 1968-84 (head of illustration studies), visiting prof Cincinnati Univ 1980; one man exhibitions incl: New Art Centre London 1960, 1961, 1963 and 1966, Thames Gallery Windsor 1964, Univ of York 1966, Arthur Gallery Tampa USA 1967, Scottish Gallery Edinburgh 1969, Compass Gallery Glasgow 1970, Waddington Gallery London 1975, Waddington and Tooths Gallery London 1977, Northern Arts Gallery 1980, Gillan Jason Gallery London 1988, Austin Desmond Gallery London 1989; public collections incl: Leeds Poly, City Gallery Carlisle, Nuffield Fndn London, Balliol Coll Oxford, Yorkshire Arts Assoc Bradford, Univ of Yale; life memb Nat Soc of Art Educn; *Books* The Challenge of Landscape Painting (1990), Ark Journal of RCA (ed nos 21, 22, 23); various pubns in jls incl: Arts Review, Modern Painters; *Recreations* tennis, badminton, walking, looking, drawing; *Style*— Derek Hyatt, Esq; Rectory Farm House, Collingham, Wetherby, Yorkshire LS22 5AS (☎ 0937 5 72265)

HYATT, Peter Robin; s of Maj Arthur John Roach Hyatt (d 1987), of 9 Kevan Drive, Send, nr Woking, Surrey, and Molly, *née* Newman (d 1983); *b* 12 May 1947; *Educ* Cheltenham; *m* 1 (m dis 1984), Julie Ann, *née* Cox; 1 s (Ralph James Roach b 1978), 1 da (Gabriella b 1975); m 2, 15 Jan 1988, Jenny Courtenay, da of Rt Rev John Bernard Taylor (Bishop of St Albans), *qv*; *Career* gp mangr Coopers and Lybrand 1964-80, div ptnr Neville Russell 1987- (sr mangr 1980-82, ptnr 1983-); dir: Care and Counsel, South American Missionary Soc; ACA 1971, FCA 1978; *Recreations* squash, golf, walking, watching cricket, rugby, running a pathfinder group; *Style*— Peter Hyatt, Esq; 3 Alderley Ct, Chesham Rd, Berkhamsted, Herts HP4 3AD (☎ 0442 873 191); Neville Russell, 246 Bishopsgate, London EC2 4PB (☎ 01 377 1000)

HYDE, Lt-Col (John) Anthony Wakeman; s of Lt-Col George Leslie Hyde, OBE (d 1978), of Ottershaw, Surrey, and Marjorie, *née* Halward (d 1961); *b* 19 Sept 1931; *Educ* Sherborne; *m* 12 Jan 1957, Felicity Anne, da of Maj James Leighton Breeds (d 1974), of Selsey, Sussex and Ngaturi, NZ; 1 s (James b 1959), 1 da (Lucy b 1963); *Career* cmmnd The Royal Sussex Regt 1952, Staff Coll Camberley 1962, HQ Land Forces Persian Gulf 1963-64, Co Cdr I R Sussex 1965-66, US Army Cmd & Gen Staff Coll (USACGSC) Leavenworth 1967, HQ Mobile Cmd Canada 1968-69, 2 i/c 1 RRF 1970-71, HQ DINF and HQUKLF 1972-77; ret 1978; ptnr (with wife) Bratton Antiques 1976-; *Recreations* goats, gardening; *Clubs* Army and Navy; *Style*— Lt-Col Anthony Hyde; Bratton Antiques, Market Place, Westbury, Wiltshire BA13 3DE (☎ 0373 823 021)

HYDE, Margaret Elizabeth; da of William Hyde (d 1972), of Bexley, Kent, and Betty Gwendolen Mary, *née* Haynes; *b* 5 March 1947; *Educ* Bexley HS Kent; *m* 18 April 1970, Stephen Geoffrey Noël, s of (Harry) Gordon Noël (d 1987), of Orpington, Kent; 1 da (Louisa b 1977); *Career* journalist Liverpool Echo and Daily Post 1970-73; BBC Radio Merseyside 1973-83: presenter and prodr, first woman news ed in English local radio 1979; BBC Radio Newsroom London 1983, head of progs Radio Lancashire 1984-86, chief asst BBC NW Regn TV and Radio 1986-87, managing ed BBC Radio Cambridgeshire 1987-; memb: bd of dirs Cambridge Symphony Orchestra, Assoc of Br Eds, Radio Acad; tstee Trustline (BBC Radio Cambridgeshire charity); *Recreations* music, theatre, criminology, naval history and talking!; *Style*— Miss Margaret Hyde; Staccato, 34 Hicks Lane, Girton, Cambridge CB3 0JS (☎ 0223 276886); BBC Radio Cambridgeshire, Broadcasting House, 104 Hills Rd, Cambridge CB2 1LD (☎ 0223 315970, fax 0223 464813)

HYDE, Michael Clarendon; s of Arthur Victor Hyde, MC (d 1944), of Coram St, London, and Winifred Florence, *née* Downton (d 1963); *b* 3 Sept 1923; *Educ* St John's Coll London; *m* 1, 3 Nov 1943, Irene Patricia, da of John Galliven (d 1943); 2 s (Nicholas b 1948, Philip b 1952); m 2, 14 April 1975, Shirley Audrey, da of George Mann, of Willoughby Close, Gt Barford, Beds; *Career* ed and publisher Chem Insight 1972-, md Hyde Chemical Publications Ltd 1977-; ed: Chemical Age 1958-71, Leather Trades Review 1956-58; vice pres Soc Of Chem Indust 1989-; *Recreations* swimming, fell walking, music, literature; *Clubs* Wig and Pen, IOD, Chemists', New York; *Style*— Michael Hyde, Esq; 6a West Grove, Greenwich, London SE10 8QT (☎ 081 691 6151, telex 297761, fax 081 692 7692); 12 Climping Court, Rackham Rd, Rustington (☎ 0903 783 749); Greyside Cottage, Underhill, Millon, Cumbria (☎ 0229 774833)

HYDE, Norman Vincent; JP (1970); s of Sidney Hyde, of Herts (d 1960), and Nellie, *née* Otter; *b* 28 April 1927; *Educ* Hitchin GS, UCL (BA); *m* 5 Sept 1953, Patricia Townsend, da of John Townsend Barker, JP, of Herts; 2 s (Jeremy b 1954, Christopher b 1955), 2 da (Theresa b 1959, Carolyn b 1963); *Career* RM 1944-47; architect self employed 1958-89, dep chm PSD 1987-89; chm: N Herts Licensing Ctee 1987, N Herts Betting and Gaming Ctee 1987-89; tax cmmr 1972 (chm 1984), memb Lord Chllrs Advsy Ctee 1984; Paul Harris fell 1989; FRSA 1984; *Recreations* restoring antique furniture, reading, DIY; *Style*— Norman V Hyde, Esq, JP; Windmill Hill House, Hitchin, Herts (☎ 0462 459617, fax 0462 454290, car ☎ 0860 350177)

HYDE, Peter John; s of Arthur Albert Hyde, of 1 Penshurst Close, Harpenden, Herts, and Eileen, *née* Smith; *b* 21 July 1941; *Educ* Aldenham; *m* 19 Feb 1971, Jennifer Anne, da of John Geoffrey Garrard Venables, of Hindleap, Maresfield Park, Uckfield, E Sussex; 1 s (Nicholas b 5 Jan 1976), 2 da (Henrietta b 24 May 1973, Gemma b 7 Nov 1979); *Career* WS Crawford Ltd 1960-64; Hyde and Ptnrs Ltd: dir 1966, md 1971, chm and chief exec 1976; memb: Cncl Inst of Practioners in Advertising 1974, membership Ctee Inst of Dirs 1977-88; pres Solus Club 1989 (hon treas 1983-), chm Bd of Govrs Epsom Sch of Art and Design 1989 (govr 1980); MCAM 1966, MIPA 1966, FIPA 1977; *Recreations* offshore sailing, skiing, tennis, swimming; *Clubs* Solus, Lymington Sailing, Ski Club of GB; *Style*— Peter Hyde, Esq; Elmet House, Brimpton, Berks RG7 4TB (☎ 0734 712977); Hyde & Partners Limited, Victoria Station House, 191 Victoria St, London SW1E 5NE (☎ 071 828 6771, telex 8954120, fax 071 828 6700, car 0836 777662)

HYDE PARKER, Sir Richard William; 12 Bt (E 1681); s of Sir William Stephen Hyde Parker, 11 Bt (d 1951); *b* 5 April 1937; *Educ* Millfield, RAC Cirencester; *m* 1972, Jean, da of late Sir Lindores Leslie, 9 Bt; 1 s (William), 3 da (twins Beata and Margaret b 1973, Lucy b 1975); *Heir* s, William John b 10 June 1983; *Style*— Sir Richard Hyde Parker, Bt; Melford Hall, Long Melford, Suffolk CO10 9AA

HYDE-THOMSON, Paul Cater; CBE, DL (Leicestershire 1986); s of Robert Hyde Hyde-Thomson (d 1970), of London, and Joan Perronet, *née* Sells (d 1972); *b* 17 March 1927; *Educ* Harrow, Ch Ch Oxford (MA); *m* 26 Oct 1950, Zoë Caroline Georgia, da of Robin Regis d'Erlanger, MC (d 1934); 1 s (Henry b 1954), 4 da (Catherine b 1952, Philippa b 1956, Eleanor b 1960, Lucy b 1971); *Career* Capt Oxon and Bucks LI; chm Ibstock Johnsen plc 1961- (dir 1951-); dir: McKechnie plc, TR Property Investment Trust plc, Simons Group Ltd; High Sheriff Leics 1965; pres Nat Cncl of Bldg Material Producers 1981-83, chm Blaby Cons Assoc 1986-89, memb Leics CC 1961-70; FCA 1954; *Recreations* music, art, travel, gardening; *Style*— Paul Hyde-Thomson, Esq, CBE, DL; The Stable House, North Kilworth, Lutterworth, Leics LE17 6JE (☎ 0858 880581); Flat 91, 55 Ebury St, London SW1 (☎ 071 730 5270); Ibstock Johnsen plc, Lutterworth House, Lutterworth, Leics LE17 4PS (☎ 0455 553071, fax 0455 553182, telex 341010)

HYDON, Kenneth John; s of John Thomas Hydon (d 1966); *b* 3 Nov 1944; *m* 1966, Sylvia Sheila; 2 c; *Career* fin dir: Racal Telecom plc, Orbitel Mobile Communications (Holdings) Ltd, Martin Dawes Communications Ltd; *Recreations* badminton, sailing; *Style*— Kenneth Hydon, Esq

HYLAND, Paul Robert; s of Kenneth George Hyland (d 1979), and Hetta Grace, *née* Tilsley, of Umberleigh, Devon; *b* 15 Sept 1947; *Educ* Canford, Univ of Bristol (BSc); *m* 1, 21 Aug 1971 (m dis 1988), Noëlle Jean, da of James Houston Angus; m 2, 8 Dec 1990, Margaret Ann, da of Thomas William Ware; *Career* writer; teacher of creative writing Arvon Fndn and other centres, chm Orchard Theatre Company; memb: Cncl Beaford Arts Centre, Soc of Authors; broadcast work incl: plays, drama-documentaries, features, poetry; *Books* Purbeck: The Ingrained Island (1978), Poems of Z (1982), Wight: Biography of an Island (1984), The Stubborn Forest (1984), The Black Heart: A Voyage into Central Africa (1988); *Style*— Paul Hyland, Esq; David Higham Associates Ltd, 5-8 Lower John St, Golden Square, London W1R 4HA (☎ 071 437 7888, fax 071 437 1072)

HYLAND, (Henry) Stanley; s of Harry Hugh Hyland (d 1943), and Annie, *née* Rhodes (d 1974); *b* 26 Jan 1914; *Educ* Bradford GS, Birkbeck Coll, London Univ (BA); *m* 20 April 1940, Nora, da of Harold Hopkinson (d 1968); 2 s (Jeremy b 1944, Henry b 1951); *Career* WWII Lieut (special branch) RNVR 1940-46; librarian Br Scientific Instruments Res Assoc 1946-47, res librarian House of Commons 1947- 51; BBC: successively news sub ed, reporter, programme organiser, producer (radio), producer (tv), chief asst Current Affrs Gp (tv) 1951-70; fndr dir Hyvision Ltd 1970-; chm Gt Bardfield Historical Soc 1977-87; *Books* Curiosities from Parliament (1955), Who Goes Hang (1958), Green Grow the Tresses-O (1965), Top Bloody Secret (1969); *Style*— Stanley Hyland, Esq; Cage Cottage, Great Bardfield, Braintree, Essex CM7 4ST (☎ 0371 810 413); Hyvision Ltd, 20 Bowling Green Lane, London EC1R 0BD (☎ 01 490 4943, fax 01 490 4908)

HYLANDER, Dennis; s of Bert Hylander (d 1981), of Glasgow, and Sybil Rosenberg; *b* 1 Oct 1933; *Educ* Giffnock Sch Glasgow, Christchurch School Southport, UCLA USA; *m* 18 Jan 1962, Simone, da of Joseph Swieca; 1 s (Phillip Simon b 29 July 1968), 1 da (Myriam Sophia b 14 Feb 1964); *Career* photographer; former proprietor of studios in Canada and Aust; lectr in photography; memb Kodak Gold circle (award for outstanding work), memb Professional Photographers of America; fell: Royal Photographic Soc (memb Qualifications Panel), Br Inst of Professional Photographers (chm N W Mgmnt Ctee), MPA; FRSA; *Recreations* golf, swimming, snooker; *Style*— Dennis Hylander, Esq; The Dennis Hylander Studios, 31 Church Rd, Gatley, Cheshire (☎ 061 428 2939, 061 491 0605)

HYLTON, 5 Baron (UK 1866); Sir Raymond Hervey Jolliffe; 5 Bt (UK 1821); s of Lt-Col 4 Baron Hylton (d 1967, whose mother was Lady Alice Hervey, da of 3 Marquess of Bristol) and Lady Perdita Asquith (sis of 2 Earl of Oxford and Asquith and gda of 1 Earl, better known as HH Asquith, the Lib PM, by his 1 w); *b* 13 June 1932; *Educ* Eton, Trinity Coll Oxford (MA); *m* 1966, Joanna, da of Andrew de Bertodano, himself eldest s of 8 Marques de Moral (cr by King Charles III of Spain 1765), by Andrew's m to Lady Sylvia Savile (3 da of late 6 Earl of Mexborough, and sis of Lady Agnes Eyston and Lady Sarah Cumming-Bruce); 4 s (Hon William b 1967, Hon Andrew b 1969, Hon Alexander b 1973, Hon John b 1977), 1 da (Hon Emily b 1975); *Heir* s, Hon William Jolliffe; *Career* Lt Coldstream Gds Reserve; asst priv sec to Govr-Gen Canada 1960-62; sits as Independent peer House of Lords; previously chm: Catholic Housing Aid Soc, Nat Federation of Housing Associations, Housing Assoc Charitable Tst, Help the Aged Housing Tst; pres: NIACRO, Hugh of Witham Foundation; govr Ammerdown Study Center, tstee Acorn Christian Healing Tst; hon treas Project on Human Rights and Responsibilities in Britain and Ireland; ARICS; *Style*— The Rt Hon the Lord Hylton; Ammerdown, Radstock, Bath BA3 5SH

HYLTON-FOSTER, Baroness (Life Peer UK 1965); Hon Audrey Pellew Hylton-Foster; *née* Clifton-Brown; DBE (1990); da of 1 and last Viscount Ruffside, PC, DL (d 1958); *b* 19 May 1908; *Educ* St George's Ascot; *m* 1931, Rt Hon Sir Harry Hylton-Foster, QC, MP, speaker House of Commons 1959-65 (d 1965), s of Harry Braustyn Hylton-Foster; *Career* dir Chelsea div London Branch BRCS 1950-60, pres London Branch British Red Cross 1960-83, appointed to Nat BRCS HQ consultative panel 1984-86, pres Prevention of Blindness Research Fund 1965-76; memb cncl BRCS 1967-80; convenor Cross Bench Peers 1974-; *Recreations* fishing, gardening; *Style*— The Rt Hon the Baroness Hylton-Foster, DBE; 54 Cranmer Court, Whitehead Grove, London SW3 3HW (☎ 071 584 2889); The Coach House, Tanhurst, Leith Hill, Holmbury St Mary, Dorking, Surrey RH5 6LU (☎ 0306 711975)

HYMAN, Howard Jonathan; s of Joe Hyman, of 24 Kingston House, London SW7 and Corrine Irene, *née* Abrahams; *b* 23 Oct 1949; *Educ* Bedales Sch, Univ of Manchester (BA); *m* 21 Sept 1972, Anne Moira, da of Capt Harry Sowden, of 3 Goodwood, Owler Park Rd, Middleton, Ilkley, Yorks; 2 s (Daniel b 1977, Sam b 1979), 1 da (Hannah b 1982); *Career* Price Waterhouse: ptnr 1984-, specialist advsr on privatisation HM Treasy 1984-87, ptnr i/c Privatisation Servs Dept 1987-90, head Corporate Fin Europe 1990-; FCA; *Recreations* walking, classical music, cricket, gardening; *Clubs* Reform, MCC; *Style*— Howard Hyman, Esq; 30 Sheen Common Drive, Richmond, Surrey (☎ 081 878 2618); Price Waterhouse, Southwark Towers, 32 London Bridge St, London SE1 9SY (☎ 071 939 2048, 071 939 3000, fax 071 378 0647, telex 884657/8)

HYMAN, Hon Mrs (Laura Alice); *née* Boyd; da of 6 Baron Kilmarnock, MBE (d 1975); *b* 10 June 1934; *Educ* Langford Grove, Barcombe Mills nr Lewes; *m* 1962, (Robert) Anthony Hyman; 2 s, 1 da; *Style*— The Hon Mrs Hyman; 38a Downshire Hill, Hampstead, London NW3 1NU (☎ 071 794 4529)

HYMAN, Robin Philip; s of Leonard Albert Hyman (d 1964), of London, and Helen, *née* Mautner; *b* 9 Sept 1931; *Educ* Henley GS, Univ of Birmingham (BA); *m* 17 April 1966, Inge, *née* Neufeld; 2 s (James b 29 May 1967, Peter b 23 Nov 1968), 1 da (Philippa 13 March 1971); *Career* Nat Serv RAF 1949-51; ed Mermaid 1953-54, md Evans Bros Ltd 1972-77 (dep md 1967, dir 1964), chm Bell and Hyman Ltd 1977-86, chm and chief exec Unwin Hyman Ltd 1989- (md 1986-88); memb Ed Bd World Yearbook of Educn 1969-73, treas Educnl Publishers Cncl 1972-75 (memb Exec Ctee 1971-76), memb 1 Br Publishers Delegn to China 1978, pres Publishers Assoc 1989- (memb Cncl 1975-, treas 1982-84, vice pres 1988-89); *Books* A Dictionary of Famous Quotations (1962), Boys and Girls First Dictionary (with John Trevaskis 1967); with Inge Hyman: Barnabas Ball at the Circus (1967), Runaway James and the Night Owl (1968), The Hippo Who Wanted to Fly (1973), The Greatest Explorers in the World (1978), The Treasure Box (1980); *Clubs* Garrick, MCC; *Style*— Robin Hyman, Esq; 101 Hampstead Way, London NW11 7LR (☎ 081 455 7055)

HYND, Ronald; s of William John Hens, of London, and Alice Louisa, *née* Griffiths; *b* 22 April 1931; *Educ* Holloway Co Sch, Rambert Sch of Ballet; *m* 24 June 1957, Annette, da of James Lees Page (d 1979); 1 da (Louise b 20 April 1968); *Career* ballet dancer, dir and choreographer; Ballet Rambert 1949-51, Royal Ballet 1951-70, danced all major classical roles and many dramatic and romantic ballets; dir Bavarian State Ballet 1984-86 (1970-73); choreographed full length ballets: The Nutcracker (London Festival Ballet) 1976, Rosalinda (Festival Ballet Johannesburg, Houston, Ljubljana, Santiago, Cincinnati) 1978, Papillon (Houston, Sadlers Wells Royal Ballet, Johannesburg, Munich, Santiago) 1980, Le Diable a Quatre (Johannesburg Santiago) 1984, Coppelia (Festival Ballet) 1985, The Merry Widow (Canada) 1986 (Australia) 1975, Ludwig II (Munich) 1986, Hunchback of Notre Dame (Houston) 1988; one act ballets incl: Dvorak Variations, Le Baiser de la Fee, Mozartiana, Pasiphaë, La Chatte, Wendekriese, Das Telefon, Charlotte Bronte, Liaisons Amoureuses, Marco Polo, Scherzo Capriccioso, The Seasons, The Sanguine Fan, Les Valses, In a Summer Garden, Fanfare; *Recreations* music, travel, gardens; *Style*— Ronald Hynd, Esq

HYNES, Dermott Francis; s of John Joseph Hynes (d 1975), of Kilrickle, Loughrea, Co Galway, Republic of Ireland, and Mary, *née* Byrnes (d 1926); *b* 2 July 1924; *Educ* St Columb's Coll Derry NI, Univ of London (LLB, LLM); *m* 2 Jan 1952, Theresa, da of Joseph Jordan, PC (d 1950); 2 s (Shane Joseph b 24 April 1954, Eamonn Francis b 21 March 1956); *Career* called to the Bar Inner Temple; vice chm of govrs St Gregory's Sch Ealing; *Recreations* reading, fishing, theatre; *Clubs* Nat Liberal, Irish (Council memb); *Style*— Dermott Hynes, Esq; 61 Castlebar Park, Ealing, London W5 1BA (☎ 081 997 0197); 9 Kings Bench Walk, Temple, London EC4 (☎ 071 353 9564)

HYPHER, David Charles; s of Harold Eldric Hypher, MBE (d 1971), of Byfleet, Surrey, and Marcia Evelyn, *née* Spalding; *b* 24 July 1941; *Educ* Weybridge Tech Coll; *m* 1, March 1966 (m dis 1971), Jenifer da of Robert Ingle; m 2, 17 July 1978, Pamela Alison, da of Peter Rowland Craddock; 2 da (Nicola, Emma); *Career* stockbroker 1958-82; dir: INVESCO MIM Management Ltd (Britannia Asset Mgmnt) 1983-, MIM Britannia Unit Trust Managers Ltd 1984-, various INVESCO MIM Britannia International (offshore) Jersey fund cos 1985-, MIM International Management 1987-, London Wall Britannia 1989-; tstee and govr Rydes Hill Prep Sch Guildford; memb: Stock Exchange 1972-83, ASIA 1965-; *Recreations* collecting antiques and cars; *Style*—

David Hypher, Esq; Comptons Farmhouse, Frog Grove Lane, Wood St Village, nr Guildford, Surrey (☎ 0483 234938); 8 La Fustera, Benisa, Alicante, Spain; c/o INVESCO MIM Management Ltd, 11 Devonshire Sq, London EC2 (☎ 071 454 3150)

HYPHER, Terence Joseph; s of Dr Noel Charles Hypher (d 1979), of Slough, Berks, and Winifreda Mary, *née* Filmer; *b* 24 March 1932; *Educ* St Edmund's Coll Ware Herts, Nat Univ of Ireland (MB BCh, BAO); *m* Valerie Jane, da of Henry Percy Walker (d 1961); 3 s (Austen b 1965, Duncan b 1966, Marcus b 1967); *Career* ophthalmic surgn; asst surgn St John Ophthalmic Hosp Jerusalem 1965-66, lectr Ophthalmology Univ of Liverpool 1974-79, hon sr registrar St Paul's Eye Hosp Liverpool 1974-79, conslt ophthalmologist West Glamorgan Health Authy 1979-88; FRCSEd, FCOphth; OStJ 1969; *Recreations* machine knitting, music, literature, art; *Style*— Terence Hypher, Esq; 46 Hendrefoilan Rd, Sketty, Swansea SA2 9LT

HYTNER, Benet Alan; QC (1970); s of Maurice Hytner (d 1978), of Manchester, and Sarah, *née* Goldberg (d 1988); *b* 29 Dec 1927; *Educ* Manchester GS, Trinity Hall Cambridge (MA); *m* 19 Dec 1954 (m dis 1980), Joyce Hytner, *qv*, da of Maj Bernard Myers (d 1979), of Cheshire; 3 s (Nicholas b 1956,*qv*, Richard b 1959, James b 1964), 1 da (Jennifer b 1958); *Career* Nat Serv Lt RASC 1949-51; called to the Bar Middle Temple 1952, rec Crown Ct 1970-, bencher 1977-, judge of appeal Isle of Man 1980-, ldr Northern Circuit 1984-88; memb: Gen Cncl of the Bar 1969-73 and 1984-88, Senate of Inns of Ct and Bar 1977-81; *Recreations* walking, reading, theatre; *Clubs* MCC; *Style*— Benet Hytner, Esq, QC; 5 Essex Court Temple, London EC4Y 9AH; 25 Byrom St, Manchester M3 4PF

HYTNER, Joyce Anita; da of Bernard Myers (d 1979), of Altrincham Cheshire, and Vera Myers, *née* Classick (d 1974); *b* 9 Dec 1935; *Educ* Withington Girls' Sch Manchester; *m* 19 Dec 1954 (m dis 1980), Benet Hytner, QC, *qv*; 3 s (Nicholas b 1956, *qv*, Richard b 1959, James b 1964), 1 da (Jennifer b 1958); *Career* mangr external rels Granada Television; *Recreations* theatre, music; *Style*— Mrs Joyce Hytner; 1A Shepherd Market, London W1Y 7HS (☎ 071 491 0312); Granada Television, 36 Golden Square, London W1R 4AH (☎ 071 734 8080)

HYTNER, Nicholas Robert; s of Benet Alan Hytner, QC, *qv*, of London, and Joyce Hytner, *qv*, *née* Myers; *b* 7 May 1956; *Educ* Manchester GS, Trinity Hall Cambridge (MA); *Career* theatre dir; prodns at Northcott Theatre Exeter and Leeds Playhouse; assoc dir Royal Exchange Theatre Manchester 1985-88 (prodns incl As You Like It, Edward II, Schiller's Don Carlos); prodr: The Scarlet Pimpernel (Chichester & West End) 1985, Measure for Measure (RSC) 1987, The Tempest (RSC) 1988, King Lear (RSC) 1990, Miss Saigon (Drury Lane Theatre and Broadway) 1989-91; assoc dir NT: Ghetto 1989-, Wind in the Willows 1990-; operatic prodns incl: King Priam (Kent Opera) 1984, Rienzi (ENO) 1983, Xerxes (ENO) 1985, The Magic Flute (ENO) 1988, Julius Caesar (Paris Opéra) 1987, Nozze di Figaro (Opéra de Genève) 1989; awards incl: Laurence Olivier award for Best Opera Prodn (Xerxes), Evening Standard Opera award (Xerxes), Evening Standard Best Director award, Critics' Circle Best Director award 1989; *Style*— Nicholas Hytner, Esq; National Theatre, South Bank, London SE1 (☎ 071 928 2033)

I

IBBOTSON, (George) Derek; s of John Robert Ibbotson, of 9 Lady House Lane, Berry Brow, Huddersfield, and Mabel, *née* Heeley; *b* 17 June 1932; *Educ* Berry Brow Cncl Sch, Almondbury GS, Huddersfield Tech Coll; *m* 1, 6 Nov 1956 (m dis), Madeline Wooller; 3 da (Christina b 15 June 1957, Nicola b 23 April 1960, Georgina b 25 April 1967); m 2, 26 March 1976, Ann Parmenter, da of Victor Sheldon; 1 da (Joanna Dee b 8 June 1978), 1 step s (Mark David Parmenter b 6 July 1962), 1 step da (Mandy Ann Parmenter b 20 June 1964); *Career* athlete; debut Eng Amateur Athletics Assoc team 1952, debut GB Athletics team 1955 (represented GB on fifty occassions, indoors, outdoors and cross country); significant achievements incl: Yorkshire jr 1 mile champion 1949-50 and 1951, Northern counties champion, AAA 3 mile champion 1955 and 1956, Olympic Bronze medallist 5000m Melbourne 1956, World record holder for 1 mile in 3 minutes 57.2 seconds (White City Stadium London) 1957, World record holder for 4 x 1 mile relay 1957, Cwlth 1 mile and 3 mile record holder 1956 and 1957, Yorkshire Veterans Squash title 1975, No 1 for Yorkshire Mens Vintage Team (over 55); Nat Serv 1954-56; sales mangr in electrical trade 1957-67, Puma 1967-; AIEE; *Recreations* golf and squash; *Style*— Derek Ibbotson, Esq; Weatherhill House, 19 Weatherhill Road, Lindley, Huddersfield, Yorkshire HD3 3LD (☎ 0484 647 310); Puma UK, Grange Road, Batley Yorkshire WF17 6PU (☎ 0924 442200)

IBBOTSON, Eva Maria Charlotte Michele; da of Berthold Wiesner (d 1973), of London and Anna, *née* Gmeyner (d 1991); *b* 21 Jan 1925; *Educ* Dartington Hall Devon, Bedford Coll London (BSc); *m* 1948, Alan Ibbotson; 3 s (Tobias b 1951, Piers b 1954, Justin b 1959), 1 da (Lalage b 1949); *Career* lectr Univ of London 1945-48; author 1953-; *books* for children: The Great Ghost Rescue (1975), Which Witch (1979), The Haunting of Hiramc Hopgood (1987), The Worm and The Toffee Nosed Princess (1989), Not just a Witch (1989); for adults: Countess Below Stairs (1981), Magic Flutes (1983), A Glove Shop in Vienna (1984), A Company of Swans (1985), Madensky Square (1988); awarded: Carnegie Commendation (for Which Witch) 1979 Romantic Novel of the Year award 1983; *Recreations* travel, music; *Style*— Mrs Eva Ibbotson; Curtis Brown, 162-168 Regent St, London W1R 5TB (☎ 071 872 0331)

IBBOTSON, Peter Stamford; s of Capt Arthur Ibbotson, of Cranleigh, Surrey, and Ivy Elizabeth, *née* Acton (d 1988); *b* 13 Dec 1943; *Educ* Manchester GS, St Catherine's Coll Oxford (BA); *m* 13 Dec 1975, Susan Mary, da of Capt Peter Eric Fyers Crewdson, of Summerhow, Kendal, Cumbria; 2 s (John William Stamford b 1977, James Francis Peter b 1978), 1 da (Jane Elizabeth Phillippa b 1980); *Career* ed: Panorama 1983-85, Newsweek 1978-82; dep dir of progs BBC TV 1987-89, corp conslt Channel 4 TV 1989-91; dir: FTC plc, UK Radio Developments Ltd; *Books* The Third Age of Broadcasting (co-author, 1978); *Recreations* silviculture, photography; *Clubs* RAC; *Style*— Peter Ibbotson, Esq; Newnham Farm House, Wallingford, Oxon OX10 8BW (☎ 0491 33111); FTC plc, Munro House, King St, London WC2 (☎ 071 836 3091, fax 071 497 0516)

IBBOTT, Alec; CBE (1988); s of Francis Joseph Ibbott (d 1976), of Croydon, Surrey, and Madge Winifred, *née* Graham (d 1976); *b* 14 Oct 1930; *Educ* Selhurst GS Croydon; *m* 4 April 1964, Margaret Elizabeth, da of Rev Ernest Alfred Brown (d 1968), of Sompting, Sussex; 1 s (Jonathan b 1971), 1 da (Elizabeth b 1969); *Career* Nat Serv Intelligence Corps 1949-51; joined FO 1949, ed FO list 1951, studied at MECAS 1955-56, second sec and vice consul Br Embassy Rabat 1956 , FO 1960, second sec (inf) Br Embassy Tripoli 1961, second sec Br Embassy Benghazi 1961, first sec (inf) Br Embassy Khartoum 1965, FCO 1967, asst political agent Dubai 1971, first sec, head of chancery and consul Br Embassy Dubai 1971 and Abu Dhabi 1972, first sec and head of chancery Br High Cmmn Nicosia 1973, first sec FCO 1975, first sec and head of chancery Br Embassy Caracas 1977, cnsllr and head of chancery Br Embassy Khartoum 1979, seconded to Int Mil Serv Ltd 1982, HM ambass and consul gen Monrovia 1985, Br high cmmr Banjul 1988-90; *Books* Professionalism: Problems and Prospects in Liberia (1986), One Hundred Years of English Law in the Gambia: Whither Gambian Law (1988); *Recreations* reading, walking, bird watching, Scottish dancing; *Style*— Alec Ibbott, Esq, CBE

IBBS, Sir Robin John; KBE (1988); o s of late Prof T L Ibbs, MC, and Marjorie, *née* Bell; *b* 21 April 1926; *Educ* Toronto Univ, Trinity Coll Cambridge (MA); *m* 1952, Iris Barbara, da of late S Hall; 1 da; *Career* called to the Bar Lincoln's Inn; head CPRS Cabinet Office 1980-82 (seconded from ICI, of which dir 1976-80 and 1982-88, having joined 1952), dep chm Lloyds Bank plc 1988-; Prime Minister's advsr on efficiency in govt 1983-88; chm cncl UCL 1989-; Hon DSc Univ of Bradford 1986; kt 1982; *Style*— Sir Robin Ibbs, KBE; Lloyd's Bank plc, 71 Lombard St, London EC3P 3BS

IDDESLEIGH, Dowager Countess of; Elizabeth; da of late Frederic Sawrey Archibald Lowndes, of 9 Barton St, Westminster, SW1; *m* 1930, 3 Earl of Iddesleigh (d 1970); 2 s (4 Earl, Hon Edward Northcote), 2 da (Lady Catherine Northcote; Lady Hilda Swan, w of York Herald); *Style*— The Rt Hon the Dowager Countess of Iddesleigh; Iddesleigh, Pynes, Exeter EX5 5EF

IDDESLEIGH, 4 Earl of (UK 1885); Sir Stafford Henry Northcote; 11 Bt (E 1641), DL (Devon 1979); also Viscount St Cyres (UK 1885); s of 3 Earl of Iddesleigh (d 1970, gs of 1 Earl, better known as Sir Stafford Northcote, a confidant of Gladstone in his youth and of Disraeli in maturity); *b* 14 July 1932; *Educ* Downside; *m* 1955, Maria Luisa (Mima) Alvarez-Builla y Urquijo, Condesa del Real Agrado (Spain CR of 1771), DL (Devon 1987), da of Don Gonzalo Alvarez-Builla y Alvera and Maria Luisa, Viscountess Exmouth; 1 s, 1 da; *Heir* s, Viscount St Cyres; *Career* late 2 Lt Irish Gds; chm S W TSB 1981-83, trustee of England and Wales TSB 1983-86, chm S W region TSB 1983-; dir: Westward TV 1981-82, Television South West 1982-, TSB Group plc 1987-, United Dominions Trust Ltd 1983-87, TSB Commercial Holdings Ltd 1987-; *Recreations* shooting; *Clubs* Army & Navy; *Style*— The Rt Hon the Earl of Iddesleigh, DL; Shillands House, Upton-Pyne-Hill, Exeter, Devon EX5 5EB (☎ 0392 58916)

IDDON, Michael Ian; s of Harold Edgar (d 1971), and Edna Iddon, *née* McTear (d 1981); *b* 18 Oct 1938; *Educ* Arnold Sch Blackpool, Harris Technical Coll Preston; *m* 1963, Rhona, da of Robert Paul (d 1972), of Chorley; 2 s (Michael James b 1965, David Robert b 1966), 1 da (Katherine Michelle b 1971); *Career* chm and jt md Iddon Bros Ltd 1971, dir engr and Marine Applications Ltd 1980, non-exec dir RAPRA Technology Ltd 1985; vice pres Engrg Employers Fedn NW; holder of The Plastics and Rubber Inst Nelton award Gold medal 1985, Hancock medal 1988; CEng, MIMechE, FPRI; *Recreations* fishing, golf, classic cars, stamps; *Clubs* Shaw Hill Golf and Country (Chorley); *Style*— Michael Iddon, Esq; The Crest 2 Kingsway, Penwortham, Preston, Lancs PR1 0AP (☎ 0772 742416); Iddon Bros Ltd, Quin Street, Leyland PR5 1TB (☎ 0772 421258)

IDE, Christopher George; s of George Frederick Ide, of West Wickham, Kent, and Edith Harty, *née* Good; *b* 25 Sept 1950; *Educ* Howard Sch Croydon, Heath Clark GS, Imperial Coll London (BSc); *m* 21 Oct 1978 (m dis 1989), Elizabeth Mary Miller; 1 s (Edward Christopher b 30 Nov 1983); *Career* actuarial student The English Insurance Company Ltd 1972-73; The Swiss Life Group: joined 1973, asst actuary 1975-81, dep actuary 1982-86, UK actuary (incl resp of appointed actuary) 1987-89, gen mangr Swiss Life (UK) plc 1989-, chm Swiss Life (UK) Services Ltd 1989-, chm Swiss Life Unit Trust Management Co Ltd 1989-; Freeman City of London 1982, Liveryman Worshipful Co of Actuaries 1982; FIA 1975, ASA 1985; *Recreations* hockey, piano playing, opera going, the works of Anthony Trollope; *Clubs* Reform; *Style*— Christopher Ide, Esq; Swiss Life (UK) plc, PO Box 127, Swiss Life House, 101 London Rd, Sevenoaks, Kent TN13 1BG (☎ 0732 450161, fax 0732 463801, car 0831 147019)

IEVERS, Rear Adm John Augustine; CB (1962), OBE (1945); s of Eyre Francis Ievers (d 1958), of Kent, and Catherine Lilian, *née* Macbeth (d 1941); *b* 2 Dec 1912; *Educ* RNC Dartmouth; *m* 1937, Peggy Garth, da of James Marshall, of Lancs; 1 s (Michael b 1948), 2 da (Carolyn b 1938, Maxine b 1945); *Career* joined RN 1926, served WWII in HMS Glasgow (Norwegian Campaign) and HMS Hermes (Indian Ocean and Ceylon), Capt 1951, cmmnd HMS Burgmead Bay (American and West Indies), RN Air Station Lossiemouth 1952-54, dep dir Air Warfare 1954-57, Capt Air Mediterranean 1957-60, promoted Rear Adm 1960, dep controller Aircraft, Miny of Aviation 1960-64; *Recreations* golf; *Style*— Rear Adm John Ievers, CB, OBE; 3 Hollywood Court, Hollywood Lane, Lymington, Hants (☎ 092575 77268)

IGGLESDEN, Alan Paul; s of Alan Trevor Igglesdon, of Westerham, and Gillian Catherine, *née* Relf; *b* 8 Oct 1964; *Educ* Churchill Sch Westerham; *m* 20 Jan 1990, Hilary Moira, da of William Henry Middleton; *Career* professional cricket player; cricket coach in townships of Cape Town SA 1985-89, represented Western Province and Avendale CC Cape Town SA 1987-88; Kent CCC 1986- (awarded county cap 1989); England: 1 Test match v Aust 1989, A team tour Kenya and Zimbabwe 1990; leading wicket-taker CCC 1989; *Recreations* Crystal Palace FC, golf, music, most sports, spending time with my wife; *Style*— Alan Igglesden, Esq; Kent CCC, St Lawrence Ground, Old Dover Rd, Canterbury CT1 3NZ (☎ 0227 456886, fax 0227 76168)

IKERRIN, Viscount; David James Theobald Somerset Butler; s and h of 9 Earl of Carrick; *b* 9 Jan 1953; *Educ* Downside; *m* 1975, Philippa, da of Wing Cdr L V Craxton, RAF; 3 s (Hon Arion Thomas Piers Hamilton, Hon Piers Edmund Theobald Lismalyn b 1979, Hon Lindsay Simon Turville Somerset (twin) b 1979); *Heir* s, Hon Arion Thomas Piers Hamilton Butler b 1 Sept 1975; *Style*— Viscount Ikerrin

ILCHESTER, 9 Earl of (GB 1756), Maurice Vivian de Touffreville Fox-Strangways; Lord Ilchester of Ilchester, Somerset, and Baron Strangways of Woodford Strangways, Dorset (GB 1741), and Lord Ilchester and Stavordale, Baron of Redlynch, Somerset (GB 1747); s of 8 Earl of Ilchester (d 1970), and Laure Georgine Emilie, *née* Mazaraki; the 1 Earl was unc of Charles James Fox and brother of 1 Lord Holland; from 1889 Holland House reverted to the Earls of Ilchester before being bombed in WWII; it is now a Youth Hostel; *b* 1 April 1920; *Educ* Kingsbridge Sch; *m* 29 Nov 1941, Diana Mary Elizabeth, da of George Frederick Simpson, of Cassington, Oxford; *Heir* bro, Hon Raymond Fox-Strangways, *qv*; *Career* RAF 1936-76 (ret Gp Capt); vice chm Nottingham Building Society 1985-87 (dir 1982-90); md: Biggin Hill News Ltd, Bromley Borough News Ltd, County Border News Ltd 1983-; pres: Soc of Engrs 1974-75, Edenbridge Town Band 1976-, Biggin Hill Branch RAFA 1976-, 2427 (Biggin Hill) Sqdn ATC 1977-, SE Area RAFA 1978-, Inst Nuclear Engrs 1982-84; vice chm Biggin Hill Airport Consultative Ctee 1976-86 and 1989-, chm of Govrs Cannock Sch 1978-, memb House of Lords Select Ctee on Sci and Technol 1984-89; Freeman City of London, Liveryman Guild of Air Pilots and Air Navigators; CEng, MRAeS, FINucE, Hon FSE, FBIM, FInstD, FRSA; *Recreations* outdoor activities, passive enjoyment of the arts; *Clubs* RAF; *Style*— The Rt Hon the Earl of Ilchester; Farley Mill, Westerham, Kent TN16 1UB (☎ 0959 62314); Biggin Hill News Ltd, Winterton House, Westerham, Kent TN16 1AJ (☎ 0959 64766)

ILES, Adrian; s of Arthur Henry Iles, of Loughton, Essex, and Joan, *née* Williams; *b* 19 Sept 1958; *Educ* Buckhurst Hill Co HS Essex, Jesus Coll Cambridge (MA); *m* 16 March 1985, Helen Marie, da of Frederick James Singleton, of Layer Breton, nr Colchester, Essex; 1 da (Rosemary b 30 Aug 1989); *Career* called to the Bar Inner Temple 1980, memb SE Circuit; memb Panel of Chm Disciplinary Ctee Milk Marketing Bd 1990-; *Recreations* cricket; *Clubs* High Beach Cricket, Essex County Cricket; *Style*— Adrian Iles, Esq; 5 Paper Buildings, Temple, London EC4Y 7HB (☎ 071 583 9275, fax 071 583 1926, telex 8956431 ANTON G)

ILEY, Geoffrey Norman; s of (Henry) Norman Iley (d 1975), of Stratford-upon-Avon, and Winifred Lalla, *née* Bowman (d 1988); *b* 24 Sept 1928; *Educ* Oakham Sch, Univ of London (BSc), Univ of Birmingham; *Career* asst gen mangr MG Car Co Abingdon 1955-58, prodn mangr Morris Motors Ltd Cowley 1958-61, dep to dir of supplies British Motor Corporation 1961-65 (dir prodn, paint, trim, assembly 1965-68); md: Triplex Safety Glass Co Birmingham 1968-72, Pilkington ACI Ltd Aust 1972-77; dir Pilkington plc 1977-90, non-exec dir Wellman plc 1989-; non-exec chm Wellman plc 1990-; Freeman City of London 1984, Liveryman Worshipful Co of Spectaclemakers 1986; FBIM, CEng, MIMechE, MIProdE; *Recreations* golf, walking, motoring, theatre, reading; *Clubs* East India, Australian, Melbourne; *Style*— Geoffrey Iley, Esq; Wellman plc, Cornwall Rd, Smethwick, West Midlands B66 2LB (☎ 021 555 5464, fax 021 558 2446)

ILIFFE, Hon Mrs Richard; Christine Marie; da of Alfred Baton Baker, of Hastings, Sussex; *m* 1940, Hon (William Henry) Richard Iliffe (d 1959); 2 s; *Style*— The Hon Mrs Richard Iliffe; Church Cottage, Aldworth, Reading, Berks; 11 Evelyn Gardens, London SW7 3BE

ILIFFE, 2 Baron (UK 1933); Edward Langton Iliffe; s of 1 Baron Iliffe, GBE (d 1960), and Charlotte, *née* Gilding (d 1972); *b* 25 Jan 1908; *Educ* Sherborne, France, Clare Coll Cambridge; *m* 8 Dec 1938, Renée (dep pres London Branch Br Red Cross Soc), da of René Merandon du Plessis, of Chamarel, Mauritius; *Heir* nephew, Robert Iliffe; *Career* WWII RAFVR (despatches), vice chm Birmingham Post and Mail Ltd 1957-74; former chm: Coventry Evening Telegraph, Cambridge News; tstee Shakespeare's Birthplace; High Sheriff Berks 1957; Hon Freeman City of Coventry; *Clubs* Brooks's, Carlton, Royal Yacht Squadron; *Style*— The Rt Hon the Lord Iliffe; 38 St James's Place, London SW1 (☎ 071 493 1938); Basildon Park, Lower Basildon, nr Reading, Berks RG8 9NR (☎ 0734 844409)

ILIFFE, Robert Peter Richard; s of Hon William Henry Richard Iliffe (d 1959; yr s of 1 Baron Iliffe, GBE); hp of uncle, 2 Baron Iliffe; *b* 22 Nov 1944; *Educ* Eton, Ch Ch Oxford; *m* 1966, Rosemary Anne, da of Cdr Arthur Grey Skipwith, RN; 3 s, 1 da; *Career* chm Yattendon Investment Trust Limited (parent co of Cambridge Newspapers Ltd, The Burton Daily Mail Ltd, West of England Newspapers Ltd); dir: Bemrose Corporation plc, Marina Developments plc, British Air Transport (Holdings) Ltd, Ralston Investment Trust plc, The Highland Printing & Publishing Group Ltd, Ingersoll Publications Ltd (parent co of The Birmingham Post & Mail Ltd, Coventry Newspapers Ltd); High Sheriff of Warks 1983-84, memb Cncl Royal Agric Soc of England; *Style*— Robert Iliffe, Esq; The Old Rectory, Ashow, Kenilworth, Warwickshire CV8 2LE

ILLINGWORTH, Dr David Gordon; CVO (1987, LVO 1980); s of Sir Cyril Gordon Illingworth (d 1959), and Grace Margaret Illingworth; *b* 22 Dec 1921; *Educ* George Watson's Coll, Univ of Edinburgh (MD, MB ChB); *m* 1946, Lesley Anderson, da of George Beagrie (d 1937), of Peterhead; 2 s (Lawrence, Stephen), 1 da (Susan); *Career* Surgn Lieut RNVR 1944-46, served in Atlantic and Northern Waters (2 Escort Group); various medical appts Edinburgh Northern Hosps 1947-80, travelling fell Nuffield Fndn 1966, surgn apothecary HM Household Palace of Holyrood House 1970-87, sr lectr Dept of Rehabilitation Studies Univ of Edinburgh 1975-80; FRCP; *Publications* papers in learned jls on cancer diagnosis and preventive medicine; *Recreations* golf, gardening; *Clubs* Univ of Edinburgh Staff, Bruntsfield Links Golfing Society; *Style*— Dr David Illingworth, CVO; 19 Napier Rd, Edinburgh EH10 5AZ (☎ 031 229 8102)

ILLINGWORTH, Hon Mrs (Katherine Elliott); da of Baron Foot (Life Peer); *b* 1937; *m* 1, 1955, David Stavely Gordon; 2 s, 1 da; m 2, David Illingworth (d 1976); 1 s; *Style*— The Hon Mrs Illingworth; 36 Albert Park Place, Montpelier, Bristol

ILLINGWORTH, Lady Margaret Cynthia; *née* Lindsay; da of late 27 Earl of Crawford and 10 of Balcarres, KT, PC, and Constance, da of Sir Henry Carstairs Pelly, MP, 3 Bt; *b* 27 June 1902; *m* 1928, Lt-Col Henry Cyril Harker Illingworth, MC, JP (d 1979), King's Royal Rifle Corps (Offr of Order of Crown of Romania); *Career* ARRC; *Style*— The Lady Margaret Illingworth; Headon Lodge, Brompton-by-Sawdon, Scarborough, Yorks (☎ 0723 85928)

ILLINGWORTH, Richard Keith; s of Keith Illingworth, of Bradford, W Yorkshire, and Margaret, *née* Hill; *b* 23 Aug 1963; *Educ* Salts GS Saltaire Bradford; *m* Anne Louise, da of George Bentley, 2 s (Miles Jonathan b 28 Aug 1987, Thomas Lynden b 20 April 1989); *Career* professional cricketer Worcestershire CCC 1982- (awarded county cap 1986); close seasons: Whitbread Scholarship with Colts CC Brisbane 1982-83, Wisden Cricket X1 to Barbados 1983, St Heliers Univ Auckland 1986-87 and 1987-88, Zingari CC Pietermaritzburg and Natal 1988-89; England A tour: Zimbabwe 1990, Pakistan and Sri Lanka 1991; civil servant 1981, buyer Golding Pipework Services close season 1989-90; *Recreations* playing golf and soccer, watching Leeds Utd FC; *Style*— Richard Illingworth, Esq; Worcestershire CCC, New Rd, Worcester WR2 4QQ

ILLIS, Dr Léon Sebastian; s of Sacha Illis (d 1933), of London, and Rebecca Magyar (d 1976); *b* 4 March 1930; *Educ* UCH London (BSc, MB BS, MD, FRCP); *m* 14 Oct 1967, Oonagh Mary, da of Lt-Col Derek Lewton-Brain, of Sevenoaks, Kent; 3 s (Max b 13 Jan 1970, Ben b 11 Apr 1973, Sebastian b 30 Dec 1974); *Career* RAC and RA 1948-50; RMO Nat Hosp Queen Sq London 1963-67 (registrar, sr registrar), conslt neurologist Wessex Neurological Centre Southampton 1967-, clinical sr lectr neurology Univ of Southampton Med Sch 1967-; visiting prof: Univ of Sri Lanka 1972 and 1977, Univ of Wisconsin 1984, numerous papers in scientific jls; tstee Int Spinal Res Tst, chm Scientific Ctee Int Spinal Res Tst; pres: S of Eng Neurosci Assoc, Int Neuromodulation Soc; FRCP 1975; *Books* Rehabilitation of the Neurological Patient (ed, 1982), Herpes Simplex Encephalitis (1973), Viral Diseases of the Central Nervous System (1976), Spinal Cord Dysfunction (1988), Disorders of the Spinal Cord in Current Opinion (ed, 1988-89), Numerous Papers in Scientific Journals; *Recreations* skiing, sailing, walking; *Clubs* RSM Royal Lymington Yacht; *Style*— Dr Léon Illis; Pond House, Sowley, Lymington, Hampshire SO41 5SQ (☎ 059 065 351); Wessex Neurological Centre, Southampton, Hampshire (☎ 0703 777222)

ILLMAN, (Charles) John; s of Henry Alfred Charles Illman, of Kirkby Fleetham, Northallerton, Yorks, and Margaret Moorhouse (d 1975); *b* 22 Sept 1944; *Educ* King's Sch Ely; *m* 1975, Elizabeth Mary, da of Ronald Stamp; 2 s (James David Charles b 21 Dec 1979, Christopher George John b 12 June 1982); *Career* student actor Nottingham Playhouse 1963, asst stage mangr Southwold Repertory Company 1963; trainee reporter Hertfordshire Express 1964, reporter The Journal Newcastle upon Tyne 1968, features ed General Practitioner 1971; ed: New Psychiatry 1974, General Practitioner 1975; freelance journalist 1976-83, med corr Daily Mail 1983-88, health ed The Guardian 1989-; columnist Woman magazine; special award Medical Journalists Assoc 1978 for work in The Sunday Times and World Medicine; memb Medical Journalists Assoc 1977, RSM 1987; *Books* Body Machine (jtly, 1981); *Recreations* family, cricket, running, reading, scuba diving; *Style*— John Illman, Esq; The Guardian, 119 Farringdon Rd, London EC1R 3ER (☎ 071 278 2332, fax 071 837 2114)

ILLSLEY, Eric; MP (Lab) Barnsley Central 1987-; s of John Illsley, of S Yorks, and Maud, *née* Bassett; *b* 9 April 1955; *Educ* Barnsley Holgate GS, Univ of Leeds (LLB); *m* 1978, Dawn, da of Robert Charles Webb, of Barnsley; 2 da (Alexandra b 1980, Rebecca b 1982); *Career* chief offr Yorks Area NUM 1985-87; memb: House of Commons Select Ctee on Energy, House of Commons Select Ctee on Televising Proceedings of House of Commons; jt chm All Party Parly Glass Gp, treas Yorks Gp of Labour MPs; *Recreations* squash, jogging; *Clubs* Barnsley Squash; *Style*— Eric Illsley, Esq, MP; House of Commons, Westminster, London SW1 (☎ 071 219 3501); 18B Regent St, Barnsley S75 1DY (☎ 0226 730692)

IMAIZUMI, Yokichi; s of Tokujiro Imaizumi, and Chiyoko Imaizumi; *b* 22 Feb 1928; *Educ* Tokyo Univ of Commerce Japan, Univ of Chicago USA; *m* Toyoko; 1 s (Junri b 1963), 1 da (Mariko (Mrs Watanabe)); *Career* Mitsubishi Bank Tokyo 1952, dir Japan International Bank London 1971-72, dep chief mangr Int Div Mitsubishi Bank Tokyo 1973-74, dir and gen mangr Japan International Bank London 1975-76, dep chief mangr Business Div Mitsubishi Bank Tokyo 1977, asst chief mangr Credito Italiano Spa Tokyo Branch, advsr Int HQ The Nikko Securities Co Ltd Tokyo 1986, advsr The Nikko Securities Co (Europe) Ltd London 1986-87, co-chm The Nikko Bank (UK) plc 1987-; *Recreations* golf, reading; *Clubs* Overseas Bankers, Highgate Golf; *Style*— Yokichi Imaizumi; 17 Godliman St, London EC4V 5BD (☎ 071 528 7070, fax 071 528 7077, telex 928703)

IMBERT, Sir Peter Michael; QPM (1980); s of William Henry Imbert, and Frances May, *née* Hodge (d 1985); *b* 27 April 1933; *Educ* Harvey GS Folkestone Kent; *m* 1956, Iris Rosina, da of Christopher Thomas Charles Dove (d 1984), of London; 1 s (Simon), 2 da (Elaine, Sally); *Career* asst and dep constable Surrey Constabulary 1976-79, chief constable Thames Valley Police 1979-85; Met Police: joined 1953, detective chief supt until 1976, dep cmmr 1985-87, cmmr 1987-; *Recreations* golf, gardening; *Style*— Sir Peter Imbert, QPM; New Scotland Yard, London SW1H 0BG (☎ 071 230 1212)

IMBERT-TERRY, Sir Michael Edward Stanley; 5 Bt (UK 1917); s of Maj Sir Edward Henry Bouhier Imbert-Terry, MC, 3 Bt (d 1978), and Lady Sackville, *née* Garton, of Knole, Kent; suc bro, Sir Andrew Imbert-Terry, 4 Bt (d 1985); *b* 18 April 1950; *Educ* Cranleigh; *m* 1975, Frances, 3 da of Peter Scott (d 1978), of Ealing; 2 s (Brychan b 1975, Jack b 1985), 2 da (Song b 1973, Bryony b 1980); *Heir* s, Brychan Edward; *Style*— Sir Michael Imbert-Terry, Bt; Little Hennowe, St Ewe, St Austell, Cornwall (☎ 0726 843893)

IMESON, Michael David; s of Terence Imeson, of Allerton, Bradford, Yorks, and Marian, *née* Glasby; *b* 26 Oct 1955; *Educ* Hanson GS Bradford, Univ of Bradford (BSc), LSE (MPhil); *Career* ed Export Times 1983-84; reporter: The Times Diary 1986, London Daily News 1987; ed Maxwell Consumer Publishing and Communications 1987-90; *Recreations* running, photography, travel; *Style*— Michael Imeson, Esq; 17-18 Westbourne St, London W2 2TZ (☎ 071 402 1508); Greater London House, Hampstead Rd, London NW1 (☎ 071 377 4633, fax 071 383 7570)

IMPALLOMENI, Mario Giuseppe; s of Prof Col Rosario Impallomeni (d 1983), and Ada, *née* Ascarelli, of Genoa Italy; *b* 19 July 1937; *Educ* Scuole Pie Fiorentine Florence Italy, Faculty of Med Univ of Florence Italy (MD); *m* 10 March 1973, Madeleine Clare, da of Hugh Edward Blackburn (d 1964); 1 s (Tommaso Fergus b 11 Oct 1979), 1 da (Laura Chiara b 18 July 1982); *Career* jr lectr Dept of Clinical Med Univ of Florence Italy 1961-66, registrar Queen's Hosp Croydon 1966-69, conslt physician Italian Hospital London 1969-, sr registrar Central Middlesex Hosp & St Thomas' Hosp 1969-78, conslt geriatrician N Middlesex Hosp & St Anne's Hosp 1972-78, conslt geriatrician and sr lectr Hammersmith Hosp 1978-; contrib to several books on geriatric med, memb ed bd of several med jls; chm NE branch Br Geriatrics Soc 1985-89; MRCP 1969, FRCP 1985; *Recreations* history, chess, cycling, fell walking, classic music; *Style*— Mario Impallomeni, Esq; Geriatric Unit, Department of Medicine, Royal Postgraduate Medical School, Hammersmith Hospital, Du Cane Road, London W12 0HS (☎ 081 743 2030, fax 081 740 3169)

IMPEY, Gerald Lawrence; s of Lt-Col Lawrence Impey, CSI, CIE, CBE (d 1944), of Mastrick Hall, 3 The Ave, Bournemouth, and Frances Mary, *née* Cassidy; *b* 6 Dec 1921; *Educ* Repton; *m* 31 Oct 1946, Monica Violet, da of Samuel Reginald Beechey (d 1962), of Whatley Hall Florence Rd, Bournemouth; 1 s (Lawrence Hastings b 23 Oct 1951), 1 da (Joy Frances b 24 May 1954); *Career* radio offr Merchant Navy 1940-45; company dir 1946-54; called to the Bar Middle Temple 1954; in practice 1945-, barr and slr Fed Supreme Ct Nigeria 1957-, Nigerian Bar Cncl 1961-64, ed-in-chief Lawtel Database (Prestel) 1980-; memb Nigerian Red Cross Lagos 1957-66, chm Lagos Flying Club 1966-76; FInstD 1969; *Clubs* Royal Automobile, Inst of Dirs; *Style*— Gerald Impey, Esq; Ikeja House, 14 Majestic Drive, Onchan, Isle of Man (☎ 0624 75828, fax 0624 24344); All Saints Chambers, 2 All Saints Court, Bristol BS1 1JN (☎ 0624 75828, fax 0624 24344)

IMPEY, John Edward; s of Capt L A Impey; *b* 4 March 1931; *Educ* Eton; *m* 1, 1959 (m dis 1981), Patricia, *née* Creery; 1 s, 2 da; m 2, 1985, Antonia, da of O J G McMullen; *Career* Nat Serv Coldstream Guards; dir County Bank Ltd 1967-79, vice chm Capper Neill plc 1979-1983; exec Williams de Broe 1983; MICAS; *Recreations* winter sports, country pursuits; *Style*— John Impey, Esq; 5 Ladbroke Walk, London W11

IMRAY, Colin Henry; CMG (1983); s of Henry Gibbon Imray (d 1936), and Frances Olive, *née* Badman; *b* 21 Sept 1933; *Educ* Highgate and Hotchkiss USA, Balliol Coll Oxford; *m* 1957, Shirley Margaret, da of Ernest Matthews (d 1972); 1 s (Christopher), 3 da (Frances, Elizabeth, Alison); *Career* Nat Serv 2 Lt Seaforth Highlanders (Royal W African Force) 1952-54; CRO 1957, third (later second) sec UK High Cmmn Canberra 1958-61, first sec Nairobi 1963-66, Br Trade Cmmn Montreal 1970-73, cnsllr head of Chancery, consul gen Islamabad 1973-77, RCDS 1977, commercial cnsllr Tel Aviv 1977-80, dep high cmmr Bombay 1980-84, dep chief clerk and chief inspr FCO 1984-85, Br high cmmr to the Utd Republic of Tanzania 1986-89, Br high cmmr to the People's Republic of Bangladesh 1989-; *Recreations* travel, walking; *Clubs* Travellers', Royal Cwlth Soc; *Style*— Colin Imray, Esq, CMG; c/o FCO Heads of Mission, King Charles St, London SW1A 2AH

IMRIE, Prof Derek Charles; s of Charles Imrie (d 1970), of Montrose, Angus, and Margaret Ellen, *née* Patching (d 1955); *b* 22 Jan 1939; *Educ* RGS Guildford, Bishophalt Sch Hillingdon, UCL (BSc, PhD); *m* 24 Aug 1963, Sandra Veronica, da of Albert Best, BEM (d 1977), of Ruislip; 2 da (Alison b 1968, Claire b 1970); *Career* res fell Harvard Univ 1966-68, lectr UCL 1968-81, reader physics Univ of London 1981-84 (ICI res fell 1963-66), dean of sci Brunel Univ 1988- (prof physics 1984-, head physics 1985-); memb Nuclear Physics Bd SERC; FInstP 1973, C Phys, FRSA 1989; *Recreations* travel, DIY; *Style*— Prof Derek Imrie, Brunel Univ, Dept of Physics, Uxbridge, Middx UB8 3PM (☎ 0895 74000 fax 0895 72391 telex 2611739); Brunel Univ, Dept of Physics, Uxbridge, Middx UB8 3PH (☎ 0895 74000, fax 0895 72391, telex 261173 G)

IMRIE, Frazer Keith Elliott; s of William Alexander Richie Imrie (d 1941), and Lily Patience, *née* Taylor (d 1988); *b* 4 Dec 1932; *m* 17 Aug 1957, Janice Margaret, da of Albert Edward Molloy (d 1975); 1 s (Andrew Keith Elliott b 1961), 3 da (Judith Meryl (Mrs Bliss) b 1964, Elizabeth Anne b 1964, Sarah Jane b 1964); *Career* private conslt microbiologist and food technologist 1956-59 (pub analyst for Watford and St Albans), dir of res Manbre & Garton UK Ltd 1959-68, head Fermentation Dept Philip Lyle Memorial Res Laboratory Univ of Reading 1968-71, fell Leverhulme Indust Res Univ of Aston-in-Birmingham 1971-73, gp devpt mangr and div md of New Ventures Tate & Lyle plc 1973-82; Sempernova plc 1982- (fndr, exec chm, chief exec), fndr and md PPRD Ltd 1982-; author of 30 scientific papers, contrib to scientific text books, sometime broadcaster on biological topics; former chm Microbiology Panel Food Res Assoc, advsr on Codex Alimentarius Miny of Agric; former memb UK Govt Advsy Ctee on Energy; memb Tech Ctee Int Sugar Res Fndn, assoc referee Int Cmmn for Unification of Methods of Sugar Analysis, past chm OECD Ctee on Energy Resources, memb CENTO Travelling Working Gp on Res and Devpt in Developing Countries, conslt OECD on Molasses Utilisation in Greek Sugar Indust; co organiser and princ lectr on industl fermentation, UNESCO, UNEP, ICRO Regional Trg Course 1976, memb Br Govt Tech Mission to USSR 1974, former tech cnslt Nat Fedn of Fruit and Potato Trades; guest lectr: Conference on Post-harvest Physiology of Pineapples Inst de Recherches sur Les Fruits et Agrumes Montpellier France 1986, Guangdong Acad of Agric Sci Guangzhou China 1986, South China Agric Univ 1985, Miny of Agric Trg Course on Post-Harvest Technol Beijing China 1989 and 1990; FRSA, fell IOD; *Recreations* travel, reading, gardening; *Style*— Frazer Imrie, Esq; Sempernova plc, 106

London St, Reading, Berks RG1 4SJ (☎ 0734 504531, fax 0734 509289, telex 846027 SEMPER G)

INCE, David Henry Gason; DFC; s of Maj Douglas Edward Ince, MC (d 1966), and Isobel, *née* Warren (d 1976), of Devonshire Lodge, Copthorne, Sussex; *b* 23 March 1921; *Educ* Cheltenham, Univ of Glasgow (BSc); *m* 1954, Anne, da of Archer Robert Burton, CBE (d 1961), of The Causey, Westgate, Old Town, Bridlington, Yorks; 2 da (Virginia b 1955, Rosalind b 1964); *Career* mangr Guided Weapons Div Elliott Bros (London) Ltd 1958-60, asst gen mangr Elliott Flight Automation Ltd 1960-65; md: Bryans Aeroquipment Ltd (former sales dir) 1965-70, LSM Controls and Seltronic Group 1968-70; gp dir Gascoigne Group Ltd 1971-82, ptnr Dynamic Relations 1983-; *Recreations* gliding, writing, woodworking, gardening; *Style—* David Ince, Esq, DFC; Church Cottage, Church Lane, Easton, Winchester, Hants SO21 1EH (☎ 096 278 372)

INCE, Nigel Valentine; s of Capt Norman Sedgwick Ince, MC (d 1962), and Angela Isobel, *née* Yorke (d 1984); *b* 18 April 1930; *Educ* Cheltenham, Radley; *m* 15 Aug 1959, Pamela Mary, da of Herbert Crewe Horobin (d 1959); 1 s (Robin Charles Crewe b 1969), 2 da (Camilla Jane b 1962, Sarah Elizabeth b 1964); *Career* dir: ABC Travel Guides 1975, ABC International 1984, General & Executive Travel Ltd 1985-90; *Recreations* shooting, fishing, photography; *Style—* Nigel Ince, Esq; The Lodge, Chenies, Nr Rickmansworth, Herts WD3 6ER (☎ 0923 282562)

INCH, Sir John Ritchie; CVO (1969), CBE (1958), QPM (1961); s of James Inch (d 1973); *b* 14 May 1911; *Educ* Hamilton Academy, Glasgow Univ (MA, LLB); *m* 1941, Anne Ferguson Shaw; 1 s, 2 da; *Career* chief constable: Dunfermline City Police 1943, combined Fife Constabulary 1949, Edinburgh City Police 1955-75; OStJ 1964; kt 1972; *Recreations* shooting, fishing, golf; *Clubs* Royal Scots (Edinburgh); *Style—* Sir John Inch, CVO, CBE, QPM; Fairways, 192 Whitehouse Rd, Barnton, Edinburgh EH4 6DA (☎ 031 336 3558)

INCHBALD, Denis John Elliot; s of Rev Christopher Chantrey Elliot Inchbald, CF (d 1976), and Olivia Jane, *née* Mills (d 1975); *b* 9 May 1923; *Educ* Oswestry Sch, Jesus Coll Cambridge; *m* 1955, Jacqueline Hazel, *née* Jones; *Career* Lt RNVR; head of publicity Br Industs Fair 1954-56; dir PR Foote Cone & Belding Ltd 1959-68, chm and md Welbeck PR Ltd 1968-84, chm Welbeck PR 1985-88; independent PR conslt 1988-; pres Inst PR 1969-70, chm PRCA 1975-78, memb Cncl Int PR Assoc 1989-; *Recreations* reading, gardening, photography, travel; *Clubs* Reform, Naval, MCC; *Style—* Denis Inchbald, Esq; 10 Shardeloes, Amersham, Bucks HP7 0RL (☎ 0494 726781)

INCHBALD, Michael John Chantrey; s of Maj Geoffrey Herbert Elliot Inchbald (d 1982), and Rosemary Evelyn, *née* Ilbert (d 1958); *b* 8 March 1920; *Educ* Sherborne, Architectural Assoc Sch of Architecture; *m* 1, 31 July 1955 (m dis 1964), Jacqueline Anne Bromley; 1 s (Courtenay Charles Ilbert b Dec 1958), 1 da (Charlotte Amanda b Feb 1960); m 2, June 1964 (m dis 1969), Eunice Haymes; *Career* designer; co fndr Inchbald Sch of Design, dir Michael Inchbald Ltd 1953-; Freeman Worshipful Co of Clockmakers 1984; FCSD; *Recreations* arts, travel, antiques, walking; *Style—* Michael Inchbald, Esq; Stanley House, 10 Milner St, London SW3 2PU (☎ 071 584 8832)

INCHBALD, Stephen Charles Elliot; s of Ralph Mordaunt Elliot Inchbald, da of Gertrude Elizabeth, *née* Ferres; *b* 16 Dec 1940; *Educ* Downside; *m* 16 Dec 1968, Elizabeth Mary, da of Bryan Frank Pocock (d 1979); 2 s (Charles b 1972, Alexander b 1974), 1 da (Louise b 1978); *Career* chartered surveyor, auctioneer and estate agent; md TSB Property Servs Ltd 1988; FIOD, FRICS; *Recreations* shooting, gardening, travel; *Clubs* IOD, Beaconsfield Golf; *Style—* Stephen Inchbald, Esq; TSB Property Services Ltd, 21 Victoria St, Windsor, Berks SL4 1HB (☎ 0753 831323, fax 0753 830271)

INCHCAPE, 3 Earl of (UK 1929); Kenneth James William Mackay; also Baron Inchcape (UK 1911), Viscount Inchcape (UK 1924), and Viscount Glenapp (UK 1929); s of 2 Earl of Inchcape (d 1939), and his 1 w, Joan (d 1933), da of Rt Hon John Francis Moriarty, Lord Justice of Appeal in Ireland; *b* 27 Dec 1917; *Educ* Eton, Trinity Coll Cambridge (MA); *m* 1, 12 Feb 1941 (m dis 1954), Aline Thorn, da of Sir Richard Arthur Pease, 2 Bt, and widow of Patrick Claude Hannay, FO AAF; 2 s (Viscount Glenapp, *qv*, Hon James b 1947), 1 da (Lady Lucinda b 1941); m 2, 13 Feb 1965, Caroline Cholmeley, da of Cholmeley Harrison, of Emo Court, Co Leix; 2 s (Hon Shane b 1972, Hon Ivan b 1976), and 1 adopted s (Anthony b 1967); *Heir* s, Viscount Glenapp; *Career* served WWII Maj 12 Royal Lancers, 27 Lancers (Europe); chm and chief exec Inchcape plc 1958-83 (now life pres); chm P&O Steam Navigation Co 1973-83 (chief exec 1978-81); former dir: Standard Chartered Bank Ltd, Guardian Royal Exchange, National Provincial Bank, Burmah Oil, British Petroleum, BAII plc; pres Cwlth Soc for the Deaf, pres Gen Cncl British Shipping 1976-77; Freeman and Lieut City of London; Prime Warden: Worshipful Co of Shipwrights 1967, Worshipful Co of Fishmongers 1977-78; *Recreations* field sports, farming; *Clubs* White's, Cavalry and Guards', Brooks's, Buck's, Oriental, City; *Style—* The Rt Hon the Earl of Inchcape; Addington Manor, Addington, Bucks MK18 2JR (☎ 029 671 4545); Carlock House, Glenapp Estate, Ballantrae, By Girvan, Ayrshire (☎ 046 583 224)

INCHIQUIN, 18 Baron (I 1543); Sir Conor Myles John O'Brien; 10 Bt (I 1686); s of Hon (Fionn) Myles Maryons O'Brien (yst s of 15 Baron Inchiquin); suc unc, 17 Baron Inchiquin, 1982; Lord Inchiquin is 13 in descent from the 3 s of 1 Baron Inchiquin, the latter being cr Earl of Thomond for life; The descendants of the eldest s of the 1 Baron held the Marquessate of Thomond 1800-55; The O'Briens descend from Brian Boroimhe, Prince of Thomond and High King of Ireland in 1002, who was k at the moment of victory against the Danes in the Battle of Clontarf 1014; *b* 17 July 1943; *Educ* Eton; *m* 1988, Helen O'Farrell, da of Gerald Fitzgerald Farrell, of Newtown Forbes, Co Longford; 1 da (Hon Slaney Alexandra Anne b 7 July 1989); *Heir* father's 1 cous, Maj Murrough O'Brien; *Career* late Capt 14/20 King's Hussars; *Clubs* Kildare Street and University (Dublin); *Style—* The Rt Hon the Lord Inchiquin; Thomond House, Dromoland, Newmarket-on-Fergus, Co Clare, Republic of Ireland (☎ 061 71304)

INCHIQUIN, Baroness; Vera Maud; da of Rev Clifton Samuel Winter; *m* 1945, Maj 17 Baron Inchiquin (d 1982); *Career* FANY, WTS (EA) 1940-45; *Style—* The Rt Hon The Lady Inchiquin; Winton House, Dawlish, Devon; Hanway Lodge, Richards Castle, Ludlow, Salop

INCHYRA, Elizabeth, Baroness; (Anna Judith) Elizabeth; o da of Jonkheer Reneke de Marees van Swinderen, GCVO (d 1955), Netherlands Min in London 1913-37, and Elizabeth Linsey (d 1950), da of Charles Carroll Glover, of Washington, DC; *m* 15 April 1931, 1 Baron Inchyra, GCMG, CVO (d 1989); 2 s (2 Baron Inchyra, Hon Alastair James Harold Hoyer Millar, *qqv*), 2 da (Hon Mrs Wallace, Hon Mrs Whitehead, *qqv*); *Style—* The Rt Hon Elizabeth, Lady Inchyra; Inchyra House, Glencarse, Perthshire

INCHYRA, 2 Baron (UK 1962), of St Madoes, Co Perth; Robert Charles Reneke Hoyer Millar; er s of 1 Baron Inchyra, GCMG, CVO (d 1989), and (Anna Judith) Elizabeth, da of Jonkheer Reneke de Marees van Swinderen, sometime Netherlands Min in London; *b* 4 April 1935; *Educ* Eton, New Coll Oxford; *m* 1 Aug 1961, Fiona Mary, yr da of Edmund Charles Reginald Sheffield (d 1977), of Normanby Park, Scunthorpe, Lincs; 1 s (Hon Christian James Charles Hoyer), 2 da (Hon Henrietta Julia Hoyer (Hon Mrs Villanueva Brandt) b 21 Sept 1964, Hon Louisa Mary Hoyer b 26 April 1968); *Heir* s, Hon (Christian) James Charles Hoyer Millar b 12 Aug 1962; *Career* late Scots Gds; banker; local dir Barclays Bank Newcastle upon Tyne 1967-75, regnl gen mangr Barclays Bank 1976-81, dep chm Barclays Bank Tst Co Ltd 1982-85, gen mangr Barclays Bank plc 1985-87; dir UK Fin Services 1987-88; sec gen British Bankers Assoc and Ctee of London and Scottish Banks 1988-; memb Queen's Body Guard for Scotland (Royal Co of Archers); *Clubs* White's, Pratt's; *Style—* The Rt Hon the Lord Inchyra; Rookley Manor, King's Somborne, Stockbridge, Hants SO20 6QX (☎ 0794 388319); British Bankers Assoc, 10 Lombard St, London EC3V 9EL (☎ 071 626 1567)

IND, Jack Kenneth; s of Rev William Price Ind (d 1956), of Harlington, Beds, and Doris Maud, *née* Cavell (d 1990); *b* 20 Jan 1935; *Educ* Lichfield Cathedral Choir Sch, Marlborough, St John's Coll Oxford (MA), Univ of London (PGCE); *m* 2 Sept 1964, Elizabeth Olive, da of Gordon Edgar Toombs (d 1956), of Wokingham, Berks; 2 s (Mark Alexander b 1967, Hugh Timothy b 1969), 2 da (Rebecca Jane b 1965, Katharine Elizabeth b 1972); *Career* Nat Serv 2 Lt RA 1953-55; asst master Wellingborough Sch 1960-63, housemaster Tonbridge Sch 1970-81 (asst master 1963-81), headmaster Dover Coll 1981-; memb: HMC, Governing Body Gt Walstead Sch W Sussex, Jt Assoc of Classics Teachers 1960; reader C of E 1963-; vice pres: Dover Opera and Dramatic Soc, Dover Soc; *Recreations* music, reading; *Clubs* Public Schools'; *Style—* Jack K Ind, Esq; Headmaster's House, Dover College, Dover, Kent CT17 9RH (☎ 0304 205 905); Dover College, Dover, Kent CT17 9RH (☎ 0304 205 969, fax 0304 242 208)

IND, Dr Philip Waterloo; s of John Waterloo Ind, of San Juan, Spain, and Marjorie, *née* Hesketh; *b* 17 Feb 1950; *Educ* Haberdashers' Aske's, Gonville and Caius Coll Cambridge (BA, MA), UCL (MB ChB); *m* 30 June 1973, Dr Sally Ind, da of Dr Charles Hutcheon Thomson (d 1962), of Low Fell, Co Durham; 1 s (Robert b 3 Oct 1977), 2 da (Sarah b 25 April 1980, Kathryn b 28 Oct 1982); *Career* med registrar Edgeware Gen Hosp 1975, hon sr registrar Hammersmith Hosp 1981 (registrar 1977), hon sr lectr and conslt physician Hammersmith and Ealing Gen Hosp 1985-; multiple academic papers and book chapters; MRCP 1977; *Recreations* reading, windsurfing, bridge, squash, tennis; *Style—* Dr Philip Ind; Respiratory Med Clinical Investigation Unit, Royal Postgrad Med Sch, Hammersmith Hosp, Ducane Rd, London W12 0HS (☎ 081 740 3077)

INFIELD, Paul Louis; s of Gordon Mark Infield, of 23 Trinity Court, 170A Gloucester Terrace, and Roda Molca, *née* Lincoln; *b* 1 July 1957; *Educ* Haberdashers' Aske's, The Peddie Sch Hightstown New Jersey USA, Univ of Sheffield (LLB); *m* 6 Feb 1987, Catharine Grace, da of Ancrum Francis Evans, of Harpley House, Clifton on Teme, Worcs, 1 s (Samuel b 1988); *Career* called to the Bar Inner Temple 1980; memb Bd of Deps of Br Jews; Freeman City of London 1979, Liveryman Worshipful Co of Plaisterers 1979; *Recreations* photography, running; *Clubs* RAC; *Style—* Paul Infield, Esq; 34 Hillier Rd, London SW11 6AV (☎ 071 228 1055); 5 Paper Bldgs, Temple, London EC4Y 7HB (☎ 071 583 9275/4555, 071 353 8494, fax 071 583 1926/2031)

ING, Dr Brian Stuart; s of Denis Wilfred Ing, of 53 Boundstone Lane, Lancing, Sussex, and Christine Joyce Elenor, *née* Austin; *b* 23 Aug 1947; *Educ* Steyning, Sidney Sussex Coll Cambridge (BA, MA), Cavendish Lab Cambridge (PhD); *m* 5 Sept 1970, Ann Maureen Elaine, da of Reginald Ambrose Bennidict Lambert (d 1977); 1 s (James b 1981), 2 da (Julie-Ann b 1972, Victoria b 1974); *Career* Inter Bank Res Organisation, Anglia Water Authy, Scicon, managing conslt Arthur Young 1977-82, gp mangr CACI 1983-85, dir Clark Whitehill Consultants 1985-87, assoc ptnr Clark Whitehill 1987-; FCCA, FIMC; *Style—* Dr Brian Ing; 24 Woodcock Close, Impington, Cambridge CB4 4LD (☎ 0223 234 291); Clark Whitehill Consultants, 25 New Street Square, London EC4A 3LN (☎ 071 353 1577, fax 071 583 1720, telex 887422)

ING, David Newson; MBE (1986); s of Gilbert Newson Ing (d 1975), of Hull, E Yorks, and Edith Mary, *née* Adamson (d 1982); *b* 30 May 1934; *Educ* Pocklington Sch York; *m* 15 Sept 1962, Penelope Ann, da of Basil Charles William Hart, of Cranleigh, Surrey; 2 s (Richard b 1965, William b 1967); *Career* Nat Serv cmmnd RAF 1957-59 (Sword of Honour); admitted slr 1957; sr ptnr Downs Slrs Dorking 1985- (joined 1961, ptnr 1963); lay chm Dorking Deanery Synod 1970-73; chm: Mgmnt Ctee Dorking and Dist CAB 1966-85, Surrey Building Soc 1981- (dir 1969-); hon slr Fire Servs Nat Benevolent Fund 1975-, The Lutyens Tst 1984-; Master Worshipful Co of Woolmen 1988-89 (Liveryman 1967-); memb Law Soc; *Recreations* reading, walking, gardening, cricket, theatre, opera; *Clubs* The Law Soc, MCC; *Style—* David N Ing, Esq, MBE; Ravenspur, Sutton Place, Abinger Hammer, Dorking, Surrey RH5 6RN (☎ 0306 730260); 156 High Street, Dorking, Surrey RH4 1BQ (☎ 0306 880110, fax 0306 76577, car 08313 28966, telex 859905 DOWNS G)

ING, Simon Burton; JP (1979); s of Cyril Henry Ing (d 1977); *b* 23 May 1938; *Educ* St Edward's Sch, Imperial Coll London; *m* 1962, Hazel Diana, da of Leonard Clare (d 1971); 1 s (Jason b 1972), 1 da (Sophie b 1974); *Career* ptnr Coopers & Lybrand Deloitte; dir King's Lynn Festival 1989- (chm 1989-90), chm of Govrs Beeston Hall Sch 1982-89; Freeman City of London 1984; FCA; *Recreations* golf, swimming, gardening; *Clubs* IOD; *Style—* Simon Ing, Esq, JP; 15 King St, King's Lynn, Norfolk PE30 1ET (☎ 0553 774810); 11 King St, King's Lynn, Norfolk PE30 1ET (☎ 0553 761316, telex 817843, fax 0553 766454)

INGAMELLS, John Anderson Stuart; s of George Harry Ingamells (d 1988), and Gladys Lucy, *née* Rollett (d 1979); *b* 12 Nov 1934; *Educ* Hastings and Eastbourne GS, Univ of Cambridge (BA); *m* 30 May 1964, Hazel, da of George William Wilson (d 1985); 2 da (Ann b 1965, Clare b 1969); *Career* 2 Lt RASC 1956-58, serv Cyprus; art asst York City Art Gallery 1959-63, asst keeper Nat Museum of Wales Cardiff 1963-67, curator York City Art Gallery 1967-77, dir Wallace Collection 1978- (asst to dir 1977-78); catalogues of pictures produced incl: The Davies Collection of French Art 1967, The English Episcopal Portrait 1981, Wallace Collection vol 1 1985 vol II 1986 vol III 1989; author of articles in: The Burlington Magazine, Apollo, The Walpole Soc, Journal of Aesthetics, La Revue du Louvre; tstee Dulwich Picture Gallery 1988, memb Cncl Paul Mellon Centre for Studies in Br Art London; FRSA 1988; *Style—* John Ingamells, Esq; The Wallace Collection, Hertford House, Manchester Square, London W1M 6BN (☎ 071 935 0687)

INGE, Gen Sir Peter Anthony; KCB (1988); s of Raymond Inge, and Grace Maud Caroline, *née* Du Rose (d 1962); *b* 5 Aug 1935; *Educ* Wrekin Coll, RMA Sandhurst; *m* 26 Nov 1960, Letitia Marion, da of Trevor Thornton Berry (d 1967), of Swinithwaite Hall, Leyburn, N Yorks; 2 da (Antonia b 17 May 1962, Verity b 12 Oct 1965); *Career* cmmnd Green Howards 1954; served: HK, Malaya, Germany, Libya and N Ireland, ADC to GOC 4 Div 1960-61, Adj 1 Green Howards 1963-64, student Staff Coll 1966, MOD 1967-69, Co Cdr 1 Green Howards 1969-70, student JSSC 1971, BM 11 Armd Bde 1972, instr Staff Coll 1973-74, CO 1 Green Howards 1974-76, Cmdt Jr Div Staff Coll 1977-79, Cdr Task Force C/4 Armd Bde 1980-81, Chief of Staff HQ 1 (Br) Corps 1982-83, GOC NE Dist/2 Inf DN 1984-86, DGLP (A) MOD 1986-87, cdr 1 (Br) Corps 1987-89, C-in-C BAOR and Cdr NAG 1989-; Col The Green Howards 1982, Col Cmdt RMP 1987, APTC 1988; *Recreations* cricket, walking, music, reading (especially military history); *Style—* Gen Sir Peter Inge, KCB; c/o Barclays Bank, Leyburn, N Yorks; HQ, British Army of the Rhine, BFPO 140

INGE-INNES-LILLINGSTON, George David; CBE (1986), DL (Staffs 1969); s of Cdr Hugh William Innes-Lillingston, RN (d 1953); *b* 13 Nov 1923; *Educ* Stowe, Merton Coll Oxford (MA); *m* 1, 1946, Alison Mary (d 1947), da of late Rev Canon Frederick Green; 1 da; m 2, 1955, Elizabeth Violet Grizel, da of Lt-Gen Sir William Montgomerie Thomson, KCMG, CB, MC (d 1963); 2 s, 1 da; *Career* WWII served Lt RNVR 1942-45; Lt Cdr RNR 1966; memb Agric Land Tbnl 1962-72; chm: N Birmingham & Dist Hosps 1968-74, Agric and Horticultural Ctee BSI 1980-86, Sail Trg Assoc (Midland Region) 1983-; dir Lands Improvement Gp of Co 1983-; Crown Estate Cmmr 1974-; pres: Staffs Agric Soc 1970-71, CLA 1979-81 (chm 1977-79, pres Staffs Branch 1983-); High Sheriff Staffs 1966; JP 1967-75; FRAgS 1986; *Recreations* growing trees; *Clubs* Boodle's, Royal Thames Yacht, Royal Highland Yacht (Oban), Farmers'; *Style*— George Inge-Innes-Lillingston, Esq, CBE, DL; The Old Kennels, Thorpe Constantine, Tamworth, Staffs (☎ 0827 830224/5)

INGHAM, Sir Bernard; s of Garnet Ingham (d 1974), of Hebden Bridge, W Yorks; *b* 21 June 1932; *Educ* Hebden Bridge GS; *m* 1956, Nancy Hilda, da of Ernest Hoyle (d 1944), of Halifax, W Yorks; 1 s; *Career* journalist: Hebden Bridge Times 1948-52, The Yorkshire Post and Yorkshire Evening Post 1952-59, The Yorkshire Post (northern industl corr) 1959-62, The Guardian 1962-67; civil servant: press advsr Nat Bd for Prices and Incomes 1967-68, head info Dept Employment and Productivity 1968-72; dir of info: Dept of Employment 1973, Dept of Energy 1974-78, under sec (energy conservation div) Dept of Energy 1978-79, chief press sec to Prime Minister 1979-90, visiting fell Dept of Politics Univ of Newcastle upon Tyne; kt 1990; *Recreations* walking, gardening, reading; *Clubs* Reform; *Style*— Sir Bernard Ingham; 9 Monahan Ave, Purley, Surrey CR8 3BB (☎ 087 660 8970)

INGHAM, (George) Bryan; s of George William Ingham (d 1990), and Alice May, *née* Mitchell (d 1989); *b* 11 June 1936; *Educ* St Martins Sch of Art, Royal Coll of Art, Academmia Britannica Rome; *Career* artist; two man exhibitions: Lords Gallery London (with David Hall) 1963, Ashgate Gallery (with Elizabeth Frink) 1965, Ashgate Gallery (with Anthony Gross) 1968, Wills Lane Gallery St Ives (with Anthony Gross) 1970; solo exhibitions: Kunsthalle Bremen, Kunsthalle Wordspede Germany, Francis Graham Dixon Gallery 1989, 1990 and 1991; working on restoration programme of Stobhall by Perth for The Earl of Perth 1966-; John Murray travelling scholarship, Italian Govt travelling scholarship, Leverhulme post graduate res award; former memb: Penwith Soc St Ives, Royal Soc of Painter-Etcher and Engravers; *Clubs* Blue Anchor (Helston); *Style*— Bryan Ingham, Esq; c/o Francis Graham-Dixon Gallery, 17-18 Great Sutton St, London EC1V ODN (☎ 071 250 1962)

INGHAM, Prof Derek Binns; s of George Arthur Ingham (d 1967), and Fanny Walton, *née* Binns (d 1965); *b* 7 Aug 1942; *Educ* Univ of Leeds (BSc, PhD, DSc); *m* 22 Aug 1964, Jean, da of Tom Hirst (d 1963); 1 s (Mark Andrew b 10 July 1967), 1 da (Catherine Gail b 30 Dec 1965); *Career* Univ of Leeds: lectr in mathematics 1968-78 (1964-66), sr lectr 1978-83, reader 1983-86, prof 1986-, head of Dept of Applied Mathematical Studies 1988-; CLE Moore instr Mass Inst of Technol Boston Mass USA 1966-68, FIMA 1988; *Books* Boundary Integral Equation Analyses of Singular, Potential and Biharmonic Problems (1984), The Mathematics of Blunt Body Sampling (1988); *Recreations* all forms of sport; *Style*— Prof Derek Ingham; 3 Fairfax Ave, Menston, Ilkley, W Yorks LS29 6EP (☎ 0943 75810); Dept of Applied Mathematical Studies, University of Leeds, Leeds, W Yorks LS2 9JT (☎ 0532 335113, fax 0532 429925, telex 0532 556473)

INGHAM, Graham; s of Alan Ingham, of 34 Tunstead Rd, Stacksteads, Bacup, Lancs, and Marjorie, *née* White; *b* 30 Sept 1953; *Educ* Bacup and Rawtenstall GS, Thames Poly (BA), LSE (MSc); *Career* HM Treasy 1975-84: private sec to Sir Kenneth Couzens 1978-80, princ monetary policy 1980-81, princ Euro monetary affrs 1982-84; visiting fell and Fulbright scholar Princeton Univ 1981-82, econs specialist BBC World Serv 1984-88, econs corr BBC TV news and current affrs 1988-; *Books* Contributor To Romance of the Three Empires (contrib, 1988); *Recreations* opera, travel, reading; *Clubs* Reform; *Style*— Graham Ingham, Esq; BBC Television Centre, Room 7090, Wood Lane, London W12 7RJ (☎ 081 576 7485, fax 081 746 0787, car 0860 389436)

INGHAM, Dr John Bernard; s of Sir Bernard Ingham, *qv*, of Purley, Surrey, and Lady Nancy Ingham, *née* Hoyle; *b* 16 Feb 1958; *Educ* John Fisher GS Purley Surrey, Univ of Durham (BA, Fulbright scholar, PhD), Bowling Green State Univ of Ohio USA (MA); *m* 7 Sept 1985, Christine, da of James Yendley; *Career* visiting researcher Georgetown Univ Washington DC USA 1982-83, asst ed then dep ed BNFL News house jl British Nuclear Fuels plc 1984-87, ed Sellascene house jl Sellafield Site 1986-87, freelance sports reporter Sunday Express 1986-89; reporter 1987-89: Northern Correspondent, Building Magazine, Chartered Surveyor Weekly; defence and dip corr Daily Express London 1990- (news reporter Manchester 1989-90); winner: Philip Wigley Memorial prize Br Assoc for Canadian Studies 1984, Br Assoc for Industl Eds award (Sellascene Magazine) 1987; memb NUJ 1985; *Recreations* travel, birdwatching, following cricket and soccer; *Style*— Dr John Ingham; Defence Correspondent, The Daily Express, Ludgate House, 245 Blackfriars Rd, London SE1 9UX (☎ 071 922 7106, fax 071 620 0654)

INGHAM, Maj (Francis) Roger; TD (and bar); s of Maj Joshua Lister Ingham (d 1963), of Wighill Park, Tadcaster, Yorks, and Violet Warburton, *née* Warburton-Lee (d 1980), (*see* Burke's Landed Gentry, 1952 edn); *b* 18 May 1914; *Educ* Eton, RAC Cirencester; *m* 26 June 1943, Edna Maud, da of Frederick Hynde Fox, JP, DL (d 1988), of Inglewood, Ledsham, Wirral, Cheshire; 1 s (Philip William b 1947), 1 da (Sarah Jane b 1944); *Career* 2 Lt Queens Own Yorkshire Dragoons 1935, Maj 1942, served in WWII in Palestine, Syria and Western Desert (ret 1956); dir Ingham's Thornhill Collieries Ltd 1937-47 (nationalised 1947); dir and chm: Croft & Blackburn Ltd, Harold Nickols Ltd, Kirkstall Fin Ltd 1947-80; High Sheriff Yorks 1956, chm Cncl OStJ for S and W Yorks 1966-80; FLAS; KStJ 1976; *Recreations* lawn tennis, shooting, skiing; *Clubs* Naval and Military; *Style*— Maj Roger Ingham, TD; Bellwood Hall, Ripon, N Yorks (☎ 0765 2005)

INGILBY, Diana, Lady; Diana; da of Brig-Gen Sir George Lethbridge Colvin, CB, CMG, DSO (d 1962); *m* 1948, Maj Sir Joslan William Vivian Ingilby, 5 Bt (d 1974); 1 s, 2 da; *Career* rural dist cncllr Nidderdale RDC to 1973; dist cncllr Harrogate Borough Cncl 1973-86 (hon alderman 1986); *Style*— Diana, Lady Ingilby; Ripley Castle, Ripley, Harrogate, N Yorks HG3 3AY (☎ 0423 770186)

INGILBY, Sir Thomas Colvin William; 6 Bt (UK 1866), of Ripley Castle, Yorkshire; s of Maj Sir Joslan William Vivian Ingilby, 5 Bt, JP, DL (d 1974); *b* 17 July 1955; *Educ* Eton, RAC Cirencester (MRAC); *m* 25 Feb 1984, Emma Clare Roebuck, da of Maj Richard R Thompson, of Whinfield, Strensall, York; 3 s (James William Francis b 1985, Joslan Richard Ryland b 1986, Jack Henry Thomas b 1990), 1 da (Eleanor Jane Pamela b 1989); *Heir* s, James William Francis b 15 June 1985; *Career* teacher Springvale Sch Rhodesia 1973-74; asst land agent: Stephenson & Son York 1978-80, Strutt and Parker Harrogate 1981-83; mangr Ripley Castle Estates 1983-; lecture tours USA 1978 and 1979; int hon citizen New Orleans 1979; tstee Cathedral Camps (reg charity) 1983; pres: Harrogate and Dist Talking Newspaper 1978-, Nidd Valley Evening NADFAS 1986-, Harrogate Gilbert and Sullivan Soc 1987-, Nidderdale Amateur Cricket League 1979-; govr Ashville Coll Harrogate 1985-; fndr and coordinator Nat Stately Home Hotline (a stately home and museum neighbourhood watch scheme) 1988; dir: Party Spirit Ltd 1988-, N York Trg and Enterprise Cncl 1989-; memb Cncl Yorks Agric Soc 1989-; ARICS, FAAV; landowner (1800 acres); *Recreations* cricket, tennis, walking, historical research, reading; *Style*— Sir Thomas Ingilby, Bt; Ripley Castle, Ripley, nr Harrogate, N Yorks HG3 3AY (☎ 0423 770053, 0423 770152)

INGLE, Dr Stephen James; s of James Ingle, of London, and Violet Grace, *née* Stephenson; *b* 6 Nov 1940; *Educ* The Roan Sch, Univ of Sheffield (BA, MA, DipEd), Victoria Univ of Wellington NZ (PhD); *m* 5 Aug 1964, Margaret Anne, da of Henry James Hubert Farmer (d 1979), of Sutton Bridge, Lincs; 2 s (Jonathan James Stuart b 11 Oct 1970, Benedict John Stephen b 13 April 1972), 1 da (Cassie Louise b 8 June 1979); *Career* Cwlth scholar in NZ 1964-67, head of Dept Univ of Hull 1985- (lectr in politics 1967-80, sr lectr 1980-); memb E Yorkshire Health Authy, sec Political Studies Assoc UK 1987-88; *Books* Socialist Thought in Imaginative Literature (1979), Parliament and Health Policy (1981), British Party System (2 edn 1989); *Recreations* music, theatre, hill walking; *Style*— Dr Stephen Ingle; Downs Hall, Cottingham, East Yorkshire HU16 5SD (☎ 848154); 3 Norse Longhouse, Hurst, Richmond, North Yorkshire DL11 7NW; University of Hull, Hull, Yorkshire HU6 7RX (☎ 0482 465749, fax 0482 466366)

INGLEBY, 2 Viscount (UK 1956); Martin Raymond Peake; s of 1 Viscount Ingleby (d 1966), and Joan, Viscountess Ingleby, *qv*; *b* 31 May 1926; *Educ* Eton, Trinity Coll Oxford; *m* 1952, Susan, da of Capt Henderson Landale, of Ewell Manor, W Farleigh, Kent; 1s (decd) 4 da; *Heir* none; *Career* late Lt Coldstream Gds; called to the Bar Inner Temple 1956; dir Hargreaves Gp Ltd 1960-80, CC N Riding Yorks 1964-67; landowner; *Recreations* forestry; *Style*— The Rt Hon the Viscount Ingleby; Snilesworth, Northallerton, N Yorks DL6 3QD; Flat 1, 61 Onslow Square, London SW7 3LS

INGLEFIELD; *see*: Crompton-Inglefield

INGLEFIELD, David Gilbert Charles; s of Sir Gilbert Inglefield, GBE, TD, of 6 Rutland House, Marloes Rd, London, and Barbara, *née* Thompson; *b* 19 Nov 1934; *Educ* Eton, Trinity Coll Cambridge (MA); *m* 31 Oct 1970, Jean Mary, MBE, da of Col Sir Alan Gomme-Duncan, MC (d 1963), of Dunbarney, Bridge of Earn, Perthshire; 1 s (Charles b 1977), 1 da (Mary b 1974); *Career* Nat Serv 1953-55, 2 Lt 12 Royal Lancers; serv: Malaya, BAOR; advsr to the Tstees of the Police Fndn; memb Overseas Ctee Save the Children Fund 1969-80, chm Prevention of Blindness Res Fund 1969-72, tstee Order of Malta Homes Tst 1975-; memb Chapter-Gen OstJ 1979-, Sheriff City of London 1980-81, memb Ct of Assts Worshipful Co of Haberdashers; OStJ 1973, Sovereign and Mil Order of Merit 1978, Order of Gorkha Dakshina Bahu (Nepal) Class III 1980, Order of King Abdul Aziz (Saudi Arabia) 1981; *Recreations* travel, shooting, military history; *Clubs* Boodles; *Style*— David Inglefield, Esq; The Old Rectory, Staunton-In-The-Vale, Orston, Notts NG13 9PE

INGLEFIELD, Sir Gilbert Samuel; GBE (1968), TD; s of Adm Sir Frederick Inglefield, KCB; *b* 13 March 1909; *Educ* Eton, Trinity Coll Cambridge; *m* 1933, Laura Barbara Frances, DStJ, da of Capt Gilbert Thompson, of the Connaught Rangers; 2 s, 1 da; *Career* served WWII Sherwood Foresters (France, Far East); Br Cncl: asst rep Egypt 1946-49, London 1949-56; chm Barbican Ctee 1963-66, Lord Mayor London 1967-68 (Alderman Aldersgate Ward 1959-79, Sheriff 1963-64), one of HM's Lieuts City of London, chm City Arts Tst 1968-76, chllr Order St John of Jerusalem 1969-78, dep kt princ Imperial Soc Kts Bachelor 1972-88, govr Fedn Br Artists 1972-, former DL Beds 1973, tstee LSO, govr Royal Shakespeare Theatre, memb Redundant Churches Fund; former: church cmmr for Eng, memb Royal Fine Arts Cmmn, tstee London Festival Ballet Tst, provincial grand master Beds Freemasons; Master: Worshipful Co of Haberdashers 1972, Worshipful Co of Musicians' 1974; asst Worshipful Co of Painter Stainers'; Hon DSc City Univ 1967; Hon GSM; hon memb RBA, Hon FCLM, ARIBA, AADipl, FRSA; GCStJ; kt 1965; *Clubs* Athenaeum; *Style*— Sir Gilbert Inglefield, GBE, TD; 6 Rutland House, Marloes Rd, London W8 5LE (☎ 071 937 3458)

INGLEFIELD, Timothy John Urquhart (Tim); s of William John Inglefield, DFC, of Dorset, and Mabel Dorothy Chattel; *b* 3 Nov 1946; *Educ* Harrow, Imperial Coll London (BSc); *m* 1975, Felicity Mary, da of Sqdn Ldr Edward Lawrence McMullen, MBE (ret); 2 da (Theresa b 1978, Kirstin b 1981); *Career* merchant banker; *Recreations* sailing, shooting, Normandy fish restaurants; *Clubs* Carlton; *Style*— Tim Inglefield, Esq; Grove House, Manor Close, Penn, Bucks HP10 8HZ

INGLEFIELD-WATSON, Lt-Col Sir John Forbes; 5 Bt (UK 1895); s of Sir Derrick William Inglefield-Watson, 4 Bt (d 1987), by his 1 w, Margrett Georgina (now Mrs Savill), da of Col Thomas Stokes George Hugh Robertson Aikman, CB; *b* 16 May 1926; *Educ* Eton; *Heir* 2 cous Simon Conran Hamilton Watson b 11 Aug 1939; *Career* RE 1945-81: cmmnd 1946, ret as Lt-Col 1981; *Recreations* philately, football refereeing (FA staff referee instr 1978-); *Style*— Lt-Col Sir John Inglefield-Watson, Bt; The Ross, Hamilton, Lanarkshire, ML3 7UF (☎ 0698 283734)

INGLEFIELD-WATSON, Lady; Therese; *née* Bodon; late Prof Charles Bodon, of Budapest; *m* 1946 (as his 2 w), Sir Derrick Inglefield-Watson, 4 Bt (d 1987); *Style*— Lady Inglefield-Watson; Ringshill House, Wouldham, nr Rochester, Kent ME1 3RB (☎ 0634 61514)

INGLETON, Diana Margaret; da of John Harston (d 1981), of Norfolk, and Freda Mary, *née* Boulton; *b* 7 Dec 1957; *Educ* Havant GS, Havant Sixth Form Coll, Winchester Sch of Art, Norwich Sch of Art (BA); *m* 17 May 1976, William Simon Luke Ingleton, s of Richard William John Ingleton; *Career* designer Interface Design 1980-84; sr designer: John Nash & Friends 1984-86, Nucleus Design Ltd 1986- (extensive work for London Sinfonietta 1986-88); DBG 1989; *Recreations* horse riding, conservation, golf, tennis; *Style*— Ms Diana Ingleton; Nucleus Design Ltd, John Loftus House, Summer Road, Thames Ditton, Surrey KT7 ORD

INGLEWOOD, 2 Baron (UK 1964); (William) Richard (Fletcher-)Vane; MEP (C) Cumbria and Lancashire North 1989-; s of 1 Baron Inglewood, TD, DL (d 1989); *b* 31 July 1951; *Educ* Eton, Trinity Coll Cambridge (MA), Cumbria Coll of Agric and Forestry; *m* 29 Aug 1986, Cressida Rosa, yst da of late (Alan) Desmond Frederick Pemberton-Pigott, CMG, of Fawe Park, Keswick; 1 s (Henry William Frederick b 24 Dec 1990), 2 da (Miranda Mary b 19 May 1987, Rosa Katharine b 25 July 1989); *Heir* s, Hon Henry William Frederick (Fletcher-)Vane b 24 Dec 1990; *Career* called to the Bar Lincoln's Inn 1975; contested (C): Houghton and Washington Gen Election 1983, Durham Euro-Election 1984; memb: Lake Dist Special Planning Bd 1984-90, Regnl Land Drainage Ctee NWWA 1985-89, Ct Univ of Lancaster 1985, NWWA 1987; ARICS; *Clubs* Travellers', Pratt's; *Style*— The Rt Hon Lord Inglewood, MEP; Hutton-in-the-Forest, Penrith, Cumbria CA11 9TH (☎ 085 34 500); Flat 4, 111 Alderney St, London SW1 (☎ 071 821 8127)

INGLIS, Prof (James) Alistair MacFarlane; CBE (1984); s of Alexander Inglis (d 1948), and Dr Edith Marion Douglas, *née* Smith (d 1960); *b* 24 Dec 1928; *Educ* Fettes, Univ of St Andrews (MA), Univ of Glasgow (LLB); *m* 18 April 1959, (Mary) Elizabeth, da of John Ronald Howie, JP, (d 1982); 2 s (Alexander b 1960, Ronald b 1973), 3 da (Elspeth b 1962, Morag b 1963, Marion b 1966); *Career* Nat Serv RCS 1952-54, ret Capt TA; sr ptnr McClure Naismith Anderson and Gardiner Glasgow (ptnr 1956-), prof of professional legal practice Univ of Glasgow 1984- (prof of conveyancing 1979-); contrib to various jls; pres Rent Assessment Panel Scotland

1976-87, memb Gtr Glasgow Health Bd 1975-83, dean Royal Faculty of Procurators Glasgow 1989-; memb Law Soc Scotland 1952-; *Recreations* golf, gardening; *Clubs* Western (Glasgow); *Style*— Prof Alistair Inglis, CBE; 292 St Vincent St, Glasgow G2 5TQ (☎ 041 204 2700, telex 779233, fax 041 248 3998); University of Glasgow, Glasgow G12 8QQ

INGLIS, Brian St John; s of Sir Claude Cavendish Inglis (d 1974), and Vera Margaret St John (d 1972), elder da of late John Redmond Blood, of Malahide, Co Dublin; *b* 31 July 1916; *Educ* Shrewsbury, Magdalen Coll Oxford (BA), Trinity Coll Dublin (PhD); *m* 1958 (m dis), Ruth Langdon; 1 s (Neil), 1 da (Diana); *Career* Sqdn Ldr Coastal Cmd RAF 1944-45; ed Spectator 1959-62; writer and presenter: What the Papers Say 1956-, All our Yesterdays 1962-73; *Books* The Story of Ireland (1956), West Briton (1962), Fringe Medicine (1964), Abdication (1967), Poverty and the Industrial Revolution (1971), Roger Casement (1973), The Forbidden Game (1975), The Opium War (1976), Natural and Supernatural (1977), Natural Medicine (1978), The Diseases of Civilisation (1981), Science and Parascience (1984), The Paranormal (1985), The Hidden Power (1986), The Unknown Guest (1987), The Power of Dreams (1987), Trance (1989), Downstart (1990), Coincidence (1990); *Style*— Brian Inglis, Esq; Garden Flat, 23 Lambolle Rd, London NW3 4HS (☎ 071 794 0297)

INGLIS, George Bruton; s of Cecil George Inglis (d 1968), and Ethel Mabel, *née* Till (d 1987); *Educ* Winchester, Pembroke Coll Oxford (MA); *m* 16 Nov 1968, Patricia Mary, da of Archibald Christian Forbes (d 1967); 3 s (James b 1970, Robert b 1972, Jonathan b 1974); *Career* sr ptnr Slaughter and May 1986- (ptnr 1966-86); memb Law Soc; *Recreations* gardening; *Style*— George Inglis, Esq; 35 Basinghall St, London EC2V 5DB (☎ 071 600 1200)

INGLIS, George Harrison; *b* 25 Nov 1927; *Educ* Univ of Durham (BSc MechEng); *Career* apprentice CA Parsons & Co Ltd, nuclear indust 1952- (initially on design of Calder Hall reactors), chief mechanical engr NPPC 1955- 60 (consortium constructing power stations Bradwell, Latina and Dungeness A), chief engr fuel Prodn Gp UKAEA 1960; transferred to BNFL: divnl chief engr 1973, dir Fuel Div 1976, memb Bd 1976-84; md and memb Bd Urenco Ltd 1984-, chm Bd of dirs Urenco Inc USA, chm of Mgmnt Centec Gmb H Germany 1984-; FIMechE, FEng 1983; *Style*— George Inglis, Esq; Urenco Ltd, Oxford Rd, Marlow, Bucks SL7 2NL

INGLIS, Lt-Col John Charles; s of Maj Harold John Inglis, DSO, MC (d 1967), of Llansantffraed House, Bwlch, Brecon, and Elsie, *née* Tower (d 1958); *b* 18 March 1925; *Educ* Winchester; *m* 16 May 1959, Rosaleen Marjory Florinda, da of Capt Hubert Henry de Burgh, DSO, RN (d 1960), of Oldtown, Naas, Co Kildare, Ireland; 2 s (Charles b 1965, James b 1968); *Career* joined RAC 1943, cmmnd Grenadier Gds 1944, 2 Lt 4 Tank Bn NW Europe campaign 1945, transferred 15/19 The Kings Royal Hussars, served Palestine campaign 1945, Capt 1951, Malaya campaign 1954-57, Maj NI 1958, Staff Coll 1959, Lt-Col 1967, CO 15/19 The Kings Royal Hussars 1968-70, ret 1972; nat field sec The Salmon and Trout Assoc 1972-86, regnl sec Game Conservancy Tst 1988-90; *Recreations* shooting, fishing; *Clubs* Farmers; *Style*— Lt-Col John Inglis; Hope Bowdler Hall, Church Stretton, Shropshire (☎ 0694 722 041)

INGLIS, (James Craufuird) Roger; WS; s of Lt-Col John Inglis (d 1967); *b* 2 June 1925; *Educ* Winchester, Cambridge, Univ of Edinburgh; *m* 1952, Phoebe Aeonie, da of Edward Mackenzie Murray-Buchanan; 2 s, 4 da; *Career* dir: Scottish Provident Institution for Mutual Life Assurance 1962-, Royal Bank of Scotland plc 1967-89, Selective Assets Trust plc 1988-; ptnr Shepherd & Wedderburn WS 1976-89; chm: Br Assets Tst plc 1978- (dir 1957-78), Investors Capital Tst plc 1985-, Ivory & Sime Optimum Income Tst plc 1989-, Euro Assets Tst NV 1972-; *Recreations* golf; *Clubs* R & A, Army and Navy, New (Edinburgh), Hon Co of Edinburgh Golfers; *Style*— Roger Inglis, Esq, WS; Inglisfield, Gifford, East Lothian EH41 4JH (☎ 062 081 339)

INGLIS-JONES, Nigel John; QC (1982); s of Maj John Alfred Inglis-Jones (d 1977), and Hermione, *née* Vivian (d 1958); *b* 7 May 1935; *Educ* Eton, Trinity Coll Oxford (BA); *m* 1, 1965, Lenette (d 1986), o da of Lt Col Sir Walter Bromley-Davenport, of Cheshire; 2 s (James b 1968, Valentine b 1972), 2 da (Imogen b 1966, Cressida b 1967); m 2, 1987, Ursula Jane Drury, y da of the late Captain G D and Mrs Culverwell (now Lady Pile), of Sussex; *Career* served as Ensign (Nat Serv) with Grenadier Gds 1953-55; rec of the Crown Ct 1977, bencher Inner Temple 1981; *Books* The Law of Occupational Pensions Schemens; *Recreations* fishing, gardening, collecting early English glass; *Clubs* MCC; *Style*— Nigel Inglis-Jones, Esq, QC; 4 Sheen Common Drive, Richmond, Surrey TW10 5BN (☎ 081 878 1320); Lamb Building, Temple, London EC4Y 7AS (☎ 071 353 6381)

INGLIS OF GLENCORSE, Sir Roderick John; 10 Bt (NS 1703), of Glencorse, Midlothian (formerly Mackenzie of Gairloch, Ross-shire); s of Sir Maxwell Ian Hector Inglis, 9 Bt (d 1974); *b* 25 Jan 1936; *Educ* Winchester, Edinburgh Univ (MB ChB); *m* 1, 1960 (m dis 1975), Rachel Evelyn, da of Lt-Col N M Morris, of Dowdstown, Ardee, Co Louth; 2 s (Ian b 1965, and Alexander (twin) b 1965, and 1 s decd), 1 da (Amanda b 1963); m 2, 1975 (m dis 1977), Geraldine, da of R H Kirk, of Thaxted, Essex; 1 da (Harriet b 1976); m 3, 1986, Marilyn, da of A L Irwin, of Glasgow; 1 s (Harry b 1986); *Heir* s, Ian Richard Inglis of Glencorse, yr, b 1965; *Clubs* Country (Pietermaritzberg); *Style*— Sir Roderick Inglis of Glencorse, Bt; 18 Cordwalles Rd, Pietersmaritzburg, Natal, S Africa

INGMAN, David Charles; s of Charles Ingman (d 1983), of Torquay, and Muriel, *née* Bevan (d 1974); *b* 22 March 1928; *Educ* Univ of London (BSc), Univ of Durham (MSc); *m* 29 Dec 1951, Joan Elizabeth Walker; 2 da (Heather b 26 Dec 1953, Suzanne b 20 July 1957); *Career* ICI 1949-85: works mangr Polyolefines Wilton 1972-75, div dir for Prodn and Engrg 1975-78, div res dir 1978, dep chm Plastics Div 1978, gp dir Plastics and Petrochemical Div 1981-85; dir Engrg Servs Ltd 1975-78, alternative dir ACCI Ltd SA 1978-82, non-exec dir Negretti-Zambra 1979-81, chm and chief exec Bestobell plc 1985-86, chm Br Waterways Bd 1987-; memb Nationalised Industs Chm's Gp 1987-; *Recreations* golf, painting, gardening, travel; *Style*— David Ingman, Esq; British Waterways Board, Greycaine Rd, Watford WD2 4JR (☎ 0923 226422, fax 0923 226081, car 0836 521 163)

INGMIRE, David Richard Bonner; s of Gordon Ingmire, and Dorothy Edith, *née* Bonner; *b* 29 Sept 1940; *Educ* Chatham House Sch, Kings Coll London (BA); *m* ; 2 s (James b 20 June 1968, Charles b 29 Sept 1971); *Career* articled clerk Blackburns Robson Coates & Co 1962-65, qualified CA 1965, Neville Russell 1967-69, corporate tax offr Binder Hamlyn 1970-72, corporate tax mangr Arthur Young McClelland Moores & Co 1972-74, corporate tax ptnr Neville Russell 1974-; Freeman City of London, memb Worshipful Co of Glaziers and Painters of Glass; FCA, ATII; *Recreations* music, theatre, travel, long distance walking; *Style*— David Ingmire, Esq; Neville Russell Chartered Accountants, 246 Bishopsgate, London EC2M 4PB (☎ 071 377 1000, fax 071 377 8931)

INGRAM, Adam Paterson; MP (Lab) East Kilbride 1987-; s of Bert Ingram, of Glasgow, and Louisa, *née* Paterson; *b* 1 Feb 1947; *Educ* Cranhill Secdy Sch; *m* 20 March 1970, Maureen, da of Leo McMahon, of Glasgow; *Career* systems analyst SSEB 1970-77, trade union official NALGO 1977-87; memb: Lab Pty, Co-op Pty; *Recreations* fishing, cooking, reading; *Style*— Adam Ingram, Esq, MP; 129 Teal Crescent, East Kilbride G75 8UT (☎ 035 52 35343); House of Commons, Westminster, London SW1A 0AA (☎ 071 219 4093, fax 035 52 65252)

INGRAM, Christopher John; s of Thomas Frank Ingram, of Southwick, Sussex, and late Gladys Agnes, *née* Louttid; *b* 9 June 1943; *Educ* Woking GS Surrey; *m* 10 Oct 1964, Janet Elizabeth, da of late Charles Rye; 1 s (Jonathan Devereux b 25 June 1969), 1 da (Kathryn Elizabeth b 30 March 1967); *Career* Collett Dickenson Pearce 1960-62 (messenger, voucher clerk, media asst), media planner and buyer Greenlys 1962-64, press planner and buyer then TV time buyer Grey Advertising 1964-65, media planner and buyer then media gp head KMP 1965-68, media gp head Dorland 1969-70, media mangr then media dir KMP 1970-72, md TMD 1972-76, chm and md Chris Ingram Associates 1976-, chm and chief exec CIA Group plc 1976-; memb Assoc of Media INds, hon patron of Young Vic, sponsor Royal Acad of Arts; *Recreations* jogging, watching athletics and football, art, music, history, the business of business; *Clubs* Solus, English Speaking Union, Guildford & Godalming Athletic; *Style*— Christopher Ingram, Esq; CIA Group plc, 1 Paris Garden, Stamford St, London SE1 8NU (☎ 071 633 9999, fax 071 261 1226)

INGRAM, Dr David John Edward; CBE (1991); s of John Evans Ingram (d 1967), of Ships Lantern, Bexhill-on-Sea, and Marie Florence, *née* Weller (d 1965); *b* 6 April 1927; *Educ* King's Coll Sch Wimbledon, New Coll Oxford, Clarendon Lab Oxford (MA, DPhil, DSc); *m* 4 July 1952, (Ruth) Geraldine Grace, da of Donald McNair (d 1975), of The Old Grammar School, Cirencester, Glos; 2 s (Jonathan b 1953, Bruce b 1960), 1 da Marion b 1956); *Career* lectr and reader Dept of Electronics Univ of Southampton 1952-59, dep vice chllr Univ of Keele 1964 and 1968-71 (prof and head of physics 1959-73), princ Chelsea Coll Univ of London 1973-80, vice chllr Univ of Kent 1980-; memb Governing Body: SPCK 1985-, South Bank Poly 1988-, King's Coll Med Sch 1984-; treas Ctee of Vice Chllrs and Princs 1988-; memb: Enterprise Agency of E Kent, Kent C C Educn Ctee; vice chm Canterbury-Reims Twinning Assoc, pres Kent Fedn of Amenity Socs 1986-87; chm: Chaucer Hosp Community Advsy Bd, Kent Co Consultative Ctee for Industry Year 1986, Nat Unit on Staff Devpt for Univs 1988-, Br Cncl Ctee on Europe 1989-; tstee Canterbury Cathedral Appeal Tst; memb Bd of Govrs: King's Sch Canterbury, Cobham Hall Sch; Hon DSc: Univ of Clermont-Ferrand 1960, Univ of Keele 1983; fell: Roehampton Inst 1988, King's Coll London; FInstP; *Books* Spectroscopy at Radio and Microwave Frequencies (1955, 2 edn 1967), Free Radicals as Studied by Electron Spin Resonance (1958), Biological and Biochemical Applications of Electron Spin Resonance (1969), Radiation and Quantum Physics (1973), Radio and Microwave Spectroscopy (1976); *Recreations* sailing, DIY; *Clubs* Athenaeum; *Style*— Dr David J E Ingram, CBE; 22 Ethelbert Rd, Canterbury, Kent CT1 3NE (☎ 0227 65855); The Registry, The University, Canterbury, Kent CT2 7NZ (☎ 0227 764 000, fax 0227 451 684, telex 965449)

INGRAM, Dr David Stanley; s of Stanley Arthur Ingram, of Berrow, Somerset, and Vera May, *née* Mansfield (d 1973); *b* 10 Oct 1941; *Educ* Yardley GS Birmingham, Univ of Hull (BSc, PhD), Univ of Cambridge (MA, ScD); *m* 28 July 1965, Alison Winifred, da of Spencer Thomas Graham (d 1975); 2 s (Michael b 27 Aug 1967, Jonathan b 14 Aug 1969); *Career* res fell: Univ of Glasgow 1966-68, Univ of Cambridge 1968-69; sr scientific offr Agric Res Cncl Cambridge 1969-74; Univ of Cambridge: lectr in botany 1974-88, fell of Downing Coll 1974-90 (dean, tutor and dir of studies in biology), reader in plant pathology 1988-90; regius keeper Royal Botanic Garden Edinburgh 1990-; memb: Grants Bd AFRC, Governing Body IPSR Cambridge Laboratory; chm Sci Cncl Sainsbury Laboratory, ed bds of various scientific jls; scientific advsr Gatsby Charitable Fndn; tstee of various Gardens and Charities; FIBiol 1988; *Books* Plant Tissue Culture (1974), Tissue Culture Methods for Plant Pathologists (1980), Cambridge Encyclopaedia of Life Sciences (1985), Advances in Plant Pathology (vols I-VII, 1982-90); *Recreations* literature, music, art, ceramics, gardening, travel, strolling around capital cities; *Style*— Dr David Ingram; Royal Botanic Garden Edinburgh EH3 5LR (☎ 031 552 7171, fax 031 552 0382)

INGRAM, David Vernon; s of (Harold) Vernon Ingram, OBE, TD (Col RAMC, d 1980), of Ferndown, Dorset, and Bessie Mary, *née* Montauban; *b* 13 Nov 1939; *Educ* Rugby, St Johns Coll Cambridge, Middx Hosp Med Sch (MA, MB BChir), Royal Coll of Surgns London; *m* 13 May 1967, Stella Mary, da of (Alan) Howard Cornes (d 1974), of Stockton Brook, Staffs; 1 s (Matthew b 1969), 2 da (Harriet b 1970, Catherine b 1972); *Career* sr resident offr Moorfields Eye Hosp London 1969-70, sr ophthalmic registrar St George's Hosp London 1970-73; conslt ophthalmic surgn: Sussex Eye Hosp Brighton 1973-, Cuckfield and Crawley Health Dist 1973-; pres Brighton and Sussex Medico Chirurgical Soc 1988; Liveryman Worshipful Soc of Apothecaries of London 1970, Freeman City of London 1971; FRCS 1969, FRSM 1971, FCOphth 1988; *Recreations* yacht cruising, photography, DIY; *Clubs* Cruising Assoc; *Style*— David Ingram, Esq; 4 Tongdean Rd, Hove, E Sussex BN3 6QB (☎ 0273 552 305); Sussex Eye Hosp, Eastern Rd, Brighton (☎ 0273 606 124)

INGRAM, Sir James Herbert Charles; 4 Bt (UK 1893), of Swineshead Abbey, Lincolnshire; s of (Herbert) Robin Ingram (d 1979, only s of Sir Herbert Ingram, 3 Bt, who d 1980), by his first w, Shiela, only da of late Charles Peczenik; *b* 6 May 1966; *Educ* Eton, Cardiff Univ; *Heir* half bro, Nicholas Ingram *qv*; *Recreations* golf, shooting, skiing, tennis; *Style*— Sir James Ingram, Bt; 8 Pitt St, London W8 4NX (☎ 071 937 8287)

INGRAM, Martin Alexander; s of late George Ingram, of The Old Rectory, Folkington, Sussex, and late Joyce Mercia, *née* Jones; *b* 1 July 1945; *Educ* Charterhouse, Kings Coll Univ of London (LLB); *m* 28 Feb 1970, Amanda Susanna, da of Stephen Alexander Lockhart, CMG, OBE (d 1989), of 10 Shelley Court, Tite Street, London SW3; 1 s (Bruce Richard b 14 July 1972), 1 da (Antonia Mary b 11 Aug 1976); *Career* Heseltine Moss & Co 1976-88, chm and md Brown Shipley Stockbroking Ltd 1988-; ASIA, memb Int Stock Exchange; *Recreations* painting, tennis; *Clubs* Brooks's, St Moritz Tobogganing; *Style*— Martin Ingram, Esq; Brown Shipley Stockbroking Ltd, Founders Court, Lothbury, London EC2 (☎ 071 726 4059, fax 071 726 2896, telex 918975)

INGRAM, Michael Warren; OBE (1986), JP (1949), DL (Glos 1978); 2 s of Sir Herbert Ingram, 2 Bt (d 1957); *b* 20 June 1917; *Educ* Winchester, Balliol Coll Oxford; *m* 1944, Auriol Blanche, da of Lt-Gen Sir Arthur Francis Smith, KCB, KBE, DSO, MC (d 1978, whose mother was Lady Blanche Keith Falconer, herself 2 da of 8 Earl of Kintore), and Hon Lady Smith (d 1990), da of 1 Baron Somerleyton; 1 s, 3 da; *Career* dir private manufacturing company; chm National Star Centre for Disabled Youth; *Recreations* tennis, golf, shooting, collecting English watercolours; *Clubs* Lansdowne; *Style*— Michael Ingram, Esq, OBE, JP, DL; The Manor House, South Cerney, Cirencester, Glos (☎ 0285 861902)

INGRAM, Nicholas David; s of (Herbert) Robin Ingram (d 1979, only s of Sir Herbert Ingram, 3 Bt, who d 1980), by his 2 w, Sallie Willoughby, da of Frank Hilary Minoprio; hp of half-bro, Sir James Ingram, 4 Bt; *b* 12 June 1975; *Style*— Nicholas Ingram Esq; Southridge House, nr Streatley, Berks RG8 9SJ

INGRAM, Paul; s of John Granville Ingram, (d 1971), of Manchester, and Sybil, *née* Johnson; *b* 20 Sept 1934; *Educ* Manchester Central HS, Univ of Nottingham (BSc); *m* 10 Aug 1957 (m dis 1988), Jennifer Gillian, da of Eric Morgan (d 1978), of Castletown, IOM; 1 s (David) Mark b 3 Aug 1960), 1 da (Susan Elizabeth b 2 July 1959); *Career* conservation offr and gp conservation offr Govt of the Fedn of Rhodesia and Nyasaland 1956-63, advsy offr Nat Agric Serv 1965-88; MAFF: memb Long Term Policy

Planning Unit 1969-72, chief agric offr 1986-87, dir farm and countryside serv and commercial dir 1987-88; head Agric Servs Dept Barclays Bank plc 1988-; *Recreations* sailing; *Clubs* Farmers, Civil Service; *Style*— Paul Ingram, Esq; Barclays Bank plc, Juxon House, St Pauls Churchyard, London EC4M 8EH (☎ 071 248 9155)

INGRAM, Paul Anthony Michael; s of Bruce Courtney Maynard Ingram (d 1973), and Brenda Lilian, *née* Wright; *b* 7 Aug 1947; *Educ* Barkers Butts Sch; *m* 9 July 1988, Hilary Jean, da of Raif Godfrey, JP, of Gelliwelltog, Crucorney, Powys; *Career* md systems resources Rover - BL Cars 1973 - (former systems programmer responsible online communications systems), fndr dir Systems Resources Ltd; memb Computing Serv Assoc, rep IBM Computer Users Assoc; *Recreations* motor racing; *Clubs* British Racing and Sports Car, Jaguar Drivers; *Style*— Paul Ingram, Esq; Systems Resources Ltd, Systems House, 27 Spon St, Coventry CV1 3BA (☎ 0203 630630, fax 0203 220246, car 0836 235064, telex 317165)

INGRAM, Dr Robert Meynell; s of George Ingram (d 1972), of Ashton-on-Mersey, Cheshire, and Winifred Mabel, *née* Kay (d 1983); *b* 11 July 1929; *Educ* Shrewsbury, New Coll Oxford, St Thomas's Hosp Med Sch London; *m* 7 Jan 1956, Beryl Evelyn, da of Charles Herbert, of Hill Farm, Goodrich, Ross-on-Wye; 1 s (Richard George b 8 Feb 1957), 2 da (Jillian Mary b 15 May 1958, Sheila Ann b 30 May 1961); *Career* RAMC 1947-49; house surgn St Thomas's Hosp London 1954-57, out patient offr Moorfields Eye Hosp London 1957-61, registrar Manchester Royal Eye Hosp 1961-64, visiting instr Univ of Oregon Med Sch Portland Oregon 1965, sr registrar Manchester Royal Eye Hosp 1966-67, conslt ophthalmologist Kettering Gen Hosp 1967-; former pres Kettering Rotary Club; FCOphth 1988; *Style*— Dr Robert Ingram; 118 Northampton Rd, Kettering, Northants (☎ 0536 514196); General Hospital, Rothwell Road, Kettering (☎ 0536 410666)

INGRAMS, Hon Caspar David; s and h of Baroness Darcy de Knayth *qv*; *b* 5 Jan 1962; *Style*— The Hon Caspar Ingrams

INGRAMS, Leonard Victor; OBE (1980); s of Leonard St Clair Ingrams, OBE (d 1953), and Victoria Susan Beatrice, *née* Reid; *b* 1 Sept 1941; *Educ* Stonyhurst, Munich Univ, Corpus Christi Oxford (MA); *m* 19 Sept 1964, Rosalind Ann, da of Antony Ross Moore, CMG, of Tonchbridge, Brill; 1 s (Rupert b 23 Aug 1967), 3 da (Lucy b 3 Dec 1965, Elizabeth b 9 Feb 1971, Catherine b 30 Nov 1976); *Career* Baring Bros 1967, Eurofinance 1968-69, mangr and dir London Multinat Bank 1970-73, md Baring Bros 1975-81 (mangr 1973-74), chief advsr to the Govr Saudi Arabian Monetary Agency 1981-84 (sr advsr 1975-79); dir: Robert Fleming Holdings Ltd, Robert Fleming & Co Ltd, Robert Fleming Investment Management; chm: Deutschland Investment Corp, Garsington Opera Ltd; *Publications* author of contribs to the Oxyrhynchus Papyri (various vols), Bond Portfolio Mgmnt (1989); *Recreations* music, gardening; *Clubs* Beefsteak; *Style*— Leonard Ingrams, Esq, OBE; 25 Copthall Ave, London EC2 (☎ 071 638 5858, fax 071 588 7219); Garsington Manor, Garsington, Oxford OX9 9DH

INGRAMS, Richard Reid; s of Leonard St Clair Ingrams (s of Rev William Smith Ingrams, MA), and Victoria Susan Beatrice, da of Sir James Reid, 1 Bt, GCVO, KCB, MD, LLD, who was successively physician to Queen Victoria, to King Edward VII and to King George V; *see also* Darcy de Knayth, Baroness; *b* 19 Aug 1937; *Educ* Shrewsbury, Univ Coll Oxford; *m* 1962, Mary Joan Morgan; 1 s, 1 da (and 1 s decd); *Career* editor Private Eye 1963-86; *Style*— Richard Ingrams Esq; Forge House, Aldworth, Reading, Berks

INGREY-SENN, Dr Ronald Charles; s of Charles Senn (d 1938), of Westcliff-on-Sea, Essex, and Florence May, *née* Henderson (d 1975); *b* 24 Dec 1920; *Educ* Fairfax High Sch Westcliff-on-Sea, Univ of Leeds (MB ChB, DMJ, DPM); *m* 29 April 1944, (Louisa) Jean, da of Alexander Algar Ingrey; 1 s (Andrew b 1947), 1 da (Annette b 1951); *Career* RAF Med Branch 1940-46; gen med practice NHS 1957-69, Med Civil Serv 1969; Home Office: asst under-sec 1981, dir of prison med serv 1981-83 (dep dir 1976-81); conslt psychiatrist memb Parole Bd of England and Wales 1985-89; cmmr Mental Health Act 1983-85; memb: St Albans Rotary Club, Medico-Legal Soc London 1969; co dir St John Ambulance Herts 1987-90; Freeman City of London, Liveryman Worshipful Soc of Apothecaries; FRCPsych; *Recreations* water colour, calligraphy; *Style*— Dr Ronald Ingrey-Senn; 26 Battlefield Rd, St Albans, Herts (☎ 0727 860785)

INGROW, Baron (Life Peer UK 1982), of Keighley, W Yorkshire; John Aked Taylor; OBE (1960), TD (1951), JP (Keighley, Yorks 1949), DL (W Yorks, formerly West Riding 1971); s of Percy Taylor, of Knowle Spring House, Keighley, and Gladys, *née* Broster (who m 2, Sir Donald Horsfall, 2 Bt); *b* 15 Aug 1917; *Educ* Shrewsbury; *m* 1949, Barbara Mary, da of Percy Wright Stirk, of Crestmead, Keighley; 2 da (Hon Anne Elizabeth (Hon Mrs Dent) b 1951, Hon Diana Mary (Hon Mrs Dent) b 1953); *Career* served WWII Duke of Wellington's Regt and Royal Signals (Norway, Middle East, Sicily, NW Europe, Far East), Maj; chm and md Timothy Taylor and Co Ltd, Mayor Keighley 1956-57; Keighley Town Cncl: chm Educn Ctee 1949-61, chm Fin Ctee 1961-74, memb 1946-67; memb: Keighley Cons Assoc 1952-56 and 1957-67; gen cmmr Income Tax 1965; chm Yorks Area Nat Union Cons and Unionist Assocs 1966-71, pres Ctee Nat Union Cons and Unionist Assocs 1982-83 (memb Exec Ctee 1971-76), Lord Lieut W Yorks 1985- (Vice Lord Lieut 1976-85); chm Yorks W Cons Euro Constituency Cncl 1978-84, hon treas Magistrates' Assoc 1976-86 (memb Cncl 1957-86); kt 1972; *Style*— The Rt Hon Lord Ingrow, OBE, TD; Fieldhead, Keighley, W Yorks (☎ 0535 603895)

INKIN, Geoffrey David; OBE (1974, MBE 1971), DL (Gwent 1983); s of Noel David Inkin (d 1983), of Cardiff, and Evelyn Margaret Inkin; *b* 2 Oct 1934; *Educ* Dean Close Sch, RMA Sandhurst, RAC Cirencester; *m* 1961, Susan Elizabeth, da of Lt-Col Laurence Stewart Sheldon (d 1988), of East Coker; 3 s (Piers b 1965, Charles b 1967, Edmund b 1971); *Career* cmmnd Royal Welch Fusiliers 1955-74, Malaya 1956-57, Cyprus 1958-59 (despatches), cmd 1 Bn 1972-74; Parly candidate (Cons) Ebbw Vale 1977-79, memb Gwent CC 1977-83, chm Cwmbran Devpt Corpn 1983-87 (memb Bd 1980-83), memb Bd Welsh Devpt Agency 1984-87; High Sheriff of Gwent 1987; chm: Land Authy for Wales 1986-, Cardiff Bay Devpt Corp 1987-; memb Cncl UWIST 1987-88, memb Ct Univ Coll of Wales of Cardiff 1988-; *Clubs* Brooks's, Cardiff and County, Ebbw Vale Cons; *Style*— Geoffrey Inkin, Esq, OBE, DL; Court St Lawrence, Llangovan, Monmouth NP5 4BT (☎ 0291 690 279)

INKSON, Prof John Christopher; s of George William Inkson, and Catherine Cynthia, *née* Laing (d 1988); *b* 18 Feb 1946; *Educ* Gateshead GS, Univ of Manchester (BSc), Univ of Cambridge (MA, PhD, ScD); *m* 26 Feb 1966, Pamela *née* Hepworth, da of William Henry Hepworth (d 1971); 1 s (Jonathan Allen b 17 March 1972), 2 da (Andrea Louisa b 11 Aug 1966, Beverley Jane b 5 March 1969); *Career* res physicist English Electric 1966-69, res fell Jesus Coll Cambridge 1972-85, demonstrator and lectr Univ of Cambridge 1975-85, prof of theoretical physics Univ of Exeter 1985- (head Dept of Physics 1989-); conslt: MOD, Plessey Research; FInstP; *Books* Many Body Theory of Solids (1984); *Recreations* reading, walking; *Style*— Prof John Inkson; 8 Betony Rise, Exeter EX2 5RR (☎ 0392 54774); Department of Physics, University of Exeter, Exeter EX4 4QL (☎ 0392 264148, tlx 42894 EXUNIV G, fax 0392 264111)

INMAN, Edward Oliver; s of John Inman, of Cumnor, Oxford, and Peggy Florence, *née* Beard; *b* 12 Aug 1948; *Educ* King's Coll Sch Wimbledon, Gonville and Caius Coll Cambridge (MA), Sch of Slavonic and E European Studies London (MA); *m* 1, 3 April 1971 (m dis 1982), Elizabeth Heather Winifred, da of Ian Douglas, of Scotland; 1 s (James b 29 Dec 1974), 1 da (Louise b 10 Nov 1977); m 2, 27 June 1984, Sherida Lesley, da of John Brooks Sturton, of Biddenham, Bedford; 1 da (Isabel b 20 Aug 1986), 2 step da (Rachel b 23 Aug 1978, Harriet b 2 April 1980); *Career* Imperial War Museum: joined as res asst Dept of Documents 1972, asst Central Directorate 1974, dir Duxford Airfield 1988 (keeper 1978); *Style*— Edward Inman, Esq; Imperial War Museum, Duxford Airfield, Cambridge CB2 4QR (☎ 0223 833963, fax 0223 837267)

INMAN, Stephen Eric; s of John Eric Inman (d 1978), and Vera Alice, *née* Willis (d 1985); *b* 14 Oct 1935; *Educ* All Saints Sch Bloxham, St Thomas's Hosp Med Sch Univ of London (MB BS); *m* 1 July 1961, Ione Elizabeth Jill, da of Maurice Scott Murdoch (d 1963); 2 s (Paul b 1966, Dominic b 1973), 1 da (Nicola b 1962); *Career* resident med offr: Queen Charlotte's Hosp 1965-66, Chelsea Hosp for Women 1966-67; lectr St Thomas's Hosp 1968-70, sr registrar St Thomas's Hosp 1970-74, conslt obstetrician and gynaecologist W Surrey/NE Hants Health Dist 1974, chm Div of Obstetrics, Gynaecology and Paedriatrics at Frimley Park Hosp; memb Hosp Conslts and Specialists Assoc 1974; FRCOG 1981; *Recreations* sailing, swimming, squash, tennis; *Clubs* Royal Aldershot Officers'; *Style*— Stephen E Inman, Esq; Folly Hill House, Farnham, Surrey (☎ 0252 713389)

INMAN, Prof William Howard Wallace; s of Wallace Mills Inman (d 1971), and Maude Mary, *née* Andrews (d 1973); *b* 1 Aug 1929; *Educ* Ampleforth, Caius Coll Cambridge (MA); *m* 21 July 1962, June Evelyn, da of Stewart Arthur Maggs (d 1970), of Doncaster; 3 da (Stella b 1955 (adopted), Rosemary b 1963, Charlotte b 1966); *Career* med advsr ICI Ltd Pharmaceuticals Div 1959-64, princ med offr DHSS Ctee on Safety of Medicines 1964-80, dir Drug Safety Res Unit 1980-, prof of pharmacoepidemiology Univ of Southampton 1985-; author of Monitoring for Drug Safety (1980), ed of Prescription-Event Monitoring News, advsr to drug regulatory agencies & pharmaceutical indust worldwide; FRCP, FFPHM, FFPM; *Recreations* fishing, gardening; *Style*— Prof William Inman; Southcroft House, Botley, Southampton (☎ 0703 692631); Drug Safety Research Unit, Bursledon Hall, Southampton

INNERDALE, John Hamilton; JP; s of Hamilton Innerdale (d 1982), of Eastbourne, E Sussex, and Margaret, *née* Cameron (d 1981); *b* 11 Feb 1933; *Educ* Cheadle Hulme Sch (BA, DipArch), Univ of Manchester; *m* 22 Aug 1959, Diana Grace, da of Sidney Herbert Mould (d 1982), of E Dean, E Sussex; 3 s (Jonathan Hamilton, James Cameron, Michael John); *Career* CA; dir: Careform Ltd, Triumph Build Ltd; FRIBA 1967 (ARIBA 1960); *Recreations* tennis, mountaineering, beekeeping, painting, sailing; *Style*— John Innerdale, Esq, JP; 15 Denton Rd, Eastbourne, E Sussex (☎ 0323 326 00); Wordsworth House, Sockbridge, Cumbria (☎ 0768 68322); Innerdale Hudson Architects, Chartered Architects, 25 Lushington Rd, Eastbourne (☎ 0323 410421, fax 0323 410621)

INNES, Andrew Ross; s of Sir Andrew Lockhart Innes, KBE, CB, QC (d 1960), and Irene Campbell, *née* Ross (d 1979); *b* 3 March 1944; *Educ* Eaton House PS, Pierrepont House Sch Farnham; *m* 22 June 1968, Sheila Maire, da of Brian Grazier Phips McKechnie, of Worcester; 1 s (Jamie Lockhart b 25 April 1973), 1 da (Penny Alexandra b 24 May 1971); *Career* stockbroker 1963-75; bldg contractor 1975-; memb local Village Hall Ctee; *Recreations* gardening, TV; *Style*— Andrew R Innes, Esq; Easter Calzeat House, Broughton, Biggar ML12 6HQ (☎ 08994 359)

INNES, Callum; s of Donald Innes, of Edinburgh, and Christina Dow, *née* Charmichael (d 1968); *b* 5 March 1962; *m* 20 Sept 1990, Hyjdla Jadwiqa Paula Kosaniuk; *Career* artist; solo exhibitions: Artspace Gallery 1986, 369 Gallery Edinburgh 1988, Frith St Gallery London 1990, Jan Turner Gallery LA 1990; selected gp exhibitions: Scottish Young Contemporaries 1985, Smith Biennial Stirling 1985 and 1989, Greenock Biennial Scotland 1988, 369 Gallery 1988 and 1989, Scatter (Third Eye Centre Glasgow) 1989, The Fruitmarket Gallery Edinburgh 1989, The Br Art Show 1990, Hayward Gallery London 1990, Resumé (Frith Street Gallery London) 1990, Painting Alone (The Pace Gallery NY) 1990; *Style*— Callum Innes, Esq; Jane Hamlyn, Frith Street Gallery, 60 Frith St, London W1V 5TA (☎ 071 494 1550, fax 071 287 3733)

INNES, Christian, Lady; (Elizabeth) Christian; eldest da of Lt-Col Charles Henry Watson, DSO, IMS (d 1954), of Cheltenham, Glos; *Educ* Cheltenham Ladies Coll, Royal Sch Bath; *m* 27 May 1961, as his 2 w, Lt-Col Sir (Ronald Gordon) Berowald Innes of Balvenie, 16 Bt (d 1988); *Career* WWII WRNS 1942-46, served SEAC (under Lord Louis Mountbatten); sec to the late Clifford Ellis (fndr and princ Bath Acad of Art) 1946-53, sec to Prof of Educn Makerere Coll Uganda 1958-61; *Style*— Christian, Lady Innes; The Loom House, Aultgowrie, Muir of Ord, Ross-shire IV6 7XA

INNES, David Archibald; s of Lt-Col J A Innes, DSO, (d 1948), of Horringer Manor, Bury St Edmunds, Suffolk, and Evelyn Adelaide, *née* Dawnay (d 1985); *b* 1 May 1931; *Educ* Eton, Magdalene Coll Cambridge (MA); *m* 10 June 1955, Philippa, da of Maj Sir Alastair Penrose Gordon Cumming, MC (d 1939); 2 s (Guy b 1956, John b 1959), 1 da (Davina b 1957); *Career* ptnr Rowe and Pitman 1958-84, memb Stock Exchange Cncl 1979-83; farmer 1976- (breeder of Limpsfield Herd of Pedigree Friesians); memb: Bd of Tstees Chevening Estate 1983-, Kent Ctee CLA 1989-, Kent and E Sussex Ctee Nat Tst 1989-; tstee Kent Gdns Tst 1987-; *Recreations* shooting, golf, gardening; *Clubs* Boodle's, Cavalry and Guards', Rye Golf; *Style*— David Innes, Esq; Hensill House, Hawkhurst, Kent TN18 4QH (☎ 0580 752162)

INNES, (Alexander) Guy Berowald; s and h of Sir Peter Innes of Balvenie, 17 Bt, *qv*; *b* 4 May 1960; *Educ* Queen Mary Coll Basingstoke; *Career* financial conslt; *Style*— Guy Innes, Esq; Storkgate House, Baydon Road, Lambourn, Berkshire

INNES, Lt-Col James; s of Lt-Col James Archibald Innes, DSO (d 1948), and Lady Barbara, *née* Lowther (d 1979); *b* 7 June 1915; *Educ* Eton; *m* 14 Jan 1941, Hon (Veronica Wenefryde) Nefertari, da of Capt the Hon Richard Bethell (d 1929); 2 s (James R, Peter D), 1 da (Elizabeth M (Mrs Nicholl)); *Career* 2 Lt Coldstream Gds 1935, served France and Germany 1939-45 (despatches twice), Capt 1945 (temp Lt-Col), ret as Hon Lt-Col 1949; chm of Tstees John Innes Fndn 1961-90, vice chm John Innes Inst 1961-90, dir and chm Univ Life Assur Soc, memb Ct UEA 1969-, vice pres BOA 1980- (treas 1964-80); JP: Berks 1955-73, Inner London 1973-74; Liveryman Worshipful Co of Clothworkers 1936 (memb Ct 1971, Master (excused serv) 1983-84), Hon DCL UEA 1989; memb Royal Inst GB, memb London Stock Exchange 1955-80; *Recreations* gardening, game shooting; *Clubs* Turf, All England Lawn Tennis and Croquet; *Style*— Lt-Col James Innes; 25 Beaufort Close, London SW15 3TL (☎ 081 785 6614)

INNES, Prof (Norman) Lindsay; s of Norman James Mackay Innes (d 1945), and Catherine Mitchell, *née* Porter; *b* 3 May 1934; *Educ* Webster's Seminary Kirriemuir, Univ of Aberdeen (BSc, PhD), Univ of Cambridge, Univ of Birmingham (DSc); *m* 18 April (1960), Marjory Niven, da of William Farquhar (d 1938); 1 s (Neil b 1962), 1 da (Helen b 1964); *Career* sr cotton breeder Cotton Res Corpn: Sudan 1958-66, Uganda 1966-71; head Cotton Res Unit Uganda 1972, head Plant Breeding Section Nat Vegetable Res Station 1973-84 (dep dir 1977-84), hon prof Univ of Birmingham 1973-84 (former hon lectr), head Plant Breeding Div Scot Crop Res Inst 1984-89 (dep dir 1986-); hon prof: Univ of St Andrews 1985-, Univ of Dundee 1988; memb Governing Bd Int Crop Res Inst for Semi-Arid Tropics India 1982-88 (chm prog Ctee 1984-88), sec to Governing Bd Int Potato Centre Peru 1989- (memb 1988); author of numerous pubns in sci jls on agriculture, horticulture, plant breeding, genetics; chm Br Assoc of Plant Breeders 1982-84; memb: Oxfam Cncl of Tstees 1982-84, Bd of Euro

Assoc of Plant Breeders 1981-86; vice pres Assoc of Applied Biology 1990-; Freeman City of Antigua and Guatemala 1989; FBiol 1979, FIHort 1986, FRSE 1989; *Recreations* golf, photography, travel; *Clubs* Carnoustie Golf; *Style—* Prof Lindsay Innes, FRSE; Scottish Crop Research Institute, Invergowrie, Dundee, Scotland DD2 5DA (☎ 0382 562731, fax 0382 562426)

INNES, Lady Lucy Buchan; *née* Sinclair; da of late 18 Earl of Caithness; *b* 1902; *m* 1928, Sir Thomas Innes of Learney, GCVO, LLD (d 1971); 2 s, 1 da; *Style—* The Lady Lucy Innes; The Laigh Riggs, Torphins, Aberdeenshire

INNES, Peter David; s of Lt-Col James Innes, of 25 Beaufort Close, Putney, and Hon Veronica Winefryde Nefertari, *née* Bethell; *b* 25 Aug 1952; *Educ* Eton; *m* 9 Aug 1980, Carolyn Ann Darley, da of Julian Blackwell, of Ossefield, Appleton, Oxford; 1 s (James b 1982), 2 da (Clemmie b 1984, Laura b 1987); *Career* Coldstream Gds 1972-78; Capt 1976; *Recreations* hunting, racing, fishing; *Clubs* Cavalry & Guards'; *Style—* Peter Innes, Esq; Boon House, Lauder, Berwickshire TD2 6SB

INNES, Sheila Miriam; da of Dr James McGregor Innes, of Purton Court, Farnham Royal, Bucks, and Nora Elizabeth Amelia, *née* Wacks; *b* 25 Jan 1931; *Educ* Talbot Heath Sch Bournemouth, Lady Margaret Hall Oxford (MA); *Career* prodr BBC Radio World Serv 1955-61; BBC TV: prodr family programmes 1961-65, exec prodr Further Educn TV 1973-77, head BBC Continuing Educn TV 1977-84, controller BBC Educnl Broadcasting 1984-87; currently dep chm The Open College (formerly chief exec); memb: Gen Bd Alcoholics Anonymous 1980-83, Bd of Govrs Centre for Info on Language Teaching and Res 1981-84, Cncl for Educnl Technol 1984-86, Cncl Open Univ 1984-87, City & Guilds of London Inst, Educn Ctee RSA 1989-; chm: Br Gas Trg Awards 1989-, BTEC Product Devpt Ctee 1989-; pres (Educn Section) Br Assoc for the Advancement of Sci 1989-; govr Talbot Heath Sch Bournemouth; hon memb Standing Conf on Schools Sci and Technol; memb RTS 1984, CBIM 1987, FRSA 1987, FITD 1987; *Books* author of numerous articles in educn jls; *Recreations* music (classical & jazz), swimming, photography, travel, languages, country pursuits; *Clubs* Reform; *Style—* Miss Sheila Innes; The Knowle, Seer Green Lane, Jordans, Bucks HP9 2ST (☎ 02407 4575); The Open College, 101 Wigmore St, London W1H 9AA (☎ 071 935 8088, fax 071 935 0415, telex 24483 OCOLGE G)

INNES, Simon Alexander; s of Brian Stanley Innes, of London, and Felicity, *née* McNair-Wilson; *b* 10 Dec 1958; *Educ* St Christopher Sch, Univ of Warwick (LLB); *m* 14 July 1984, Emma Jane, da of Malcolm McIndoe; 1 s (Jack b 1988), 1 da (Harriet b 1987); *Career* RA Woolwich 1977-78, RMA Sandhurst Queen's Royal Irish Hussars 1978-79; barr Middle Temple, ed Reader's Digest 1987-88, co dir Consumer Legal Servs 1988-; chm Holland Park Harriers; memb: Hon Soc Middle Temple, Royal United Serv Inst, Inst of Strategic Studies; *Books* The Middle East Wars 1949-80 (1984); *Recreations* racing, skiing, hunting; *Style—* Simon Innes, Esq; 2 Royal Crescent Mews, Kensington, London W11 (☎ 071 376 1050); Consumer Legal Serv, London House, Kensington, London W8 4PF

INNES, Hon Mrs (Veronica Wenefryde Nefertari); *née* Bethell; da of Hon Richard Bethell (d 1929), and Evelyn Lucia Milicent, *née* Hutton (d 1956); sis of 4 and 5 Barons Westbury; *b* 15 July 1917; *m* 1941, Lt-Col James Innes, Coldstream Gds, s of Lt-Col James Innes, DSO (d 1948), by Lady Barbara Lowther, da of 6 Earl of Lonsdale, OBE, JP, DL; 2 s, 1 da; *Style—* The Hon Mrs Innes; 25 Beaufort Close, London SW15 3TL (☎ 081 785 6614)

INNES-KER, Lord Robert Anthony (Robin); 2 s of 9 Duke of Roxburghe (d 1974); *b* 28 May 1959; *Educ* Gordonstoun; *Career* short service cmmn Royal Horse Gds/ Dragoons (Blues & Royals): 2 Lt 1979-81, Lt 1981-, cmd Blues and Royals detachment in Falkland Islands 1982 (despatches); stockbroker 1983; *Recreations* fishing, hunting, shooting and all ball games; *Clubs* Turf, Queen's Vanderbilt; *Style—* Lord Robert Innes-Ker; 6 Fawcett Street, London SW10 9PA

INNES OF BALVENIE, Sir Peter Alexander Berowald; 17 Bt (NS 1628), of Balvenie, Banffshire; s of Lt-Col Sir Berowald Innes of Balvenie, 16 Bt (d 1988), and his 1 w Elizabeth Haughton, *née* Fayle (d 1958); *b* 6 Jan 1937; *Educ* Prince of Wales Sch Nairobi, Bristol Univ (BSc); *m* 18 July 1959, Julia Mary, yr da of late Alfred Stoyell Levesley, of Burlington Road, Bristol; 2 s (Alexander Guy Berowald b 1960, Alastair John Peter b 1965), 1 da (Fiona Julie b 1963); *Heir* s, Alexander Guy Berowald Innes, *qv*; *Career* conslt civil engr; ptnr Scott Wilson Kirkpatrick & Ptnrs; FICE; *Recreations* travel, pointers; *Style—* Sir Peter Innes of Balvenie, Bt; The Wheel House, Nations Hill, Kings Worthy, Winchester SO23 7QY

INNES OF COXTON, Sir David Charles Kenneth Gordon; 12 Bt (NS 1686), of Coxton, Co Moray; o s of Sir Charles Kenneth Gordon Innes of Coxton, 11 Bt (d 1990), and Margaret Colquhoun Lockhart, *née* Robertson; *b* 17 April 1940; *Educ* Haileybury, London Univ (BSc Eng); *m* 1969, Marjorie Alison, da of Ernest W Parker; 1 s (Alastair Charles Deverell b 1970), 1 da (Dione Elizabeth Colquhoun b 1974); *Heir* s, Alastair Charles Deverell Innes b 17 Sept 1970; *Career* ACGI; *Style—* Sir David Innes of Coxton, Bt; 28 Wadham Close, Shepperton, Middx

INNES OF EDINGIGHT, Malcolm Rognvald; KCVO (1990, CVO 1981), WS (1964); s of Sir Thomas Innes of Learney, GCVO, LLD (d 1971), and Lady Lucy Buchan, 3 da of 18 Earl of Caithness; *b* 25 May 1938; *Educ* The Edinburgh Acad, Edinburgh Univ (MA, LLB); *m* 19 Oct 1963, Joan, da of Thomas D Hay, CA, of Edinburgh; 3 s (John Berowald Innes of Edingight, yr b 1965, Colin William Innes of Kinnairdy b 1967, Michael Thomas Innes of Crommey b 1970); *Career* Lord Lyon King of Arms 1981- (Falkland Pursuivant Extraordinary 1957-58, Carrick Pursuivant 1958-71, Marchmont Herald 1971-81, Lyon Clerk and Keeper of the Records 1966-81); sec to Order of Thistle 1981-; pres Heraldry Soc Scotland; KStJ 1981; FSA (Scot); Grand Offr Merit SMO Malta; memb Royal Co of Archers (Queen's Body Guard for Scotland); *Recreations* reading; *Clubs* New (Edinburgh), Puffin's (Edinburgh); *Style—* Sir Malcolm Innes of Edingight, KCVO, WS, FSA, Lord Lyon King of Arms; Edingight, Grange, Keith, Banffshire AB5 3TD (☎ 046 686 270); Court of the Lord Lyon, HM New Register House, Edinburgh EH1 3YT (☎ 031 556 7255, fax 031 556 7255)

INNES-SMITH, Robert Stuart; s of Stuart William Innes-Smith, MM, MRCS, LRCP (d 1953), of Bedmonton Manor, Sittingbourne, Kent, and Florence Constance, *née* Green (d 1977); *b* 10 March 1928; *Educ* abroad, Univ of Sheffield, Lincoln's Inn (LLB); *m* 5 June 1954, Elizabeth Greta, da of Bertram John Lamb (d 1938), of Chestfield, Kent; 1 s (James Stuart Tenison b 1966), 2 da (Victoria (Mrs Simon Keeble) b 1957, Augusta Sibyl b 1961); *Career* asst Burke's Peerage 1953-54, sr asst librarian Reuters News Agency 1954-56, ed-in-chief then ed dir Illustrated County Magazine Gp 1960-69, ed Edinburgh Tatler and Glasgow Illustrated 1961-67, dir and ed Tatler and Bystander 1968-69, in charge of publications for English Life Publications Ltd, Pilgrim Press Ltd and Derbyshire Countryside Ltd 1969-; *Books And Monographs* An Outline of Heraldry in England and Scotland (1973, 6 edn 1990), Notable Derbyshire Houses (1972), The Dukeries (1953), The Dukeries and Sherwood Forest (1974), Windsor Castle, St George's Chapel and Parks (with foreword by Sir Sacheverell Sitwell, Bt, CH), Notable Derbyshire Churches (1976), Castleton and its Caves (1976), Wellington (1970), Marlborough (1974), The Derbyshire Guide (ed, 1982), Glamis Castle (1983), Jervaulx Abbey (1972), Whitehall (1978), Pembroke Castle (1990), Matlock Bath (1978), Bakewell (1977), St Mildred's, Whippingham (with foreword by Countess Mountbatten of Burma, 1989), The House of Innes (1990) contributor to: The Sunday Telegraph, Country Life, The Lady, Derbyshire Life, Debrett's Best of Britain; *Clubs* Beefsteak; *Style—* Robert Innes-Smith, Esq; The Old Vicarage, Swinburne Street, Derby DE1 2HL (☎ 0332 383510); English Life Publications Ltd, Lodge Lane, Derby DE1 3HE (☎ 0332 47087)

INNES-WILKIN, David; s of Charles Wilkin (d 1978), and Louisa Jane, *née* Innes; *b* 1 May 1946; *Educ* Lowestoft GS, Liverpool Univ Sch of Architecture (BArch, MCD); *m* 1, 10 April 1968, Beryl; 2 s (Dylan b 1972, Matthew b 1974), 1 da (Thomasine b 1971); m 2, 25 April 1987, Sarah, da of Rev Prof Peter Runham Ackroyd; 1 da (Emma Jane b 1990); *Career* chartered architect; princ Innes-Wilkins Associates, chm SW Housing Assoc 1986-87, pioneered tenant participation in new housing estates designed 1979-; memb: RIBA Regnl Ctee, Community Architecture Gp 1983; visiting lectr Univs of Liverpool, Cardiff, Manchester and Bristol; memb Int Congress of Architects; design awards: RTPI Commendation 1983, Housing Centre Tst Jubilee award for Good Design in Housing 1983, Times/RIBA Community Enterprise awards 1986/87 (three); *Publications include* A Common Language (The Architects Jl, 1984), Among The Grass-Roots (RIBA Jl, 1983), Cuba: Universal Home Ownership (Roof, 1987), Shelter and Cities (Int Congress of Architects, 1987), Community Schools (Educn Res Unit, 1972); *Recreations* offshore sailing, music, writing, the Renaissance; *Clubs* The Clifton (Bristol); *Style—* David Innes-Wilkin, Esq; Regent Chambers, 24 Regent St, Clifton, Bristol BS1 4HB

INNISS, Sir Clifford de Lisle; s of Archibald de Lisle Inniss (d 1957), and Lelia Emmaline, *née* Springer (d 1963); *b* 26 Oct 1910; *Educ* Harrison Coll Barbados, Queen's Coll Oxford (BA, BCL); *Career* called to the Bar Middle Temple 1935, KC Tanganyika 1950, QC Trinidad and Tobago 1953; legal draftsman: Barbados 1938, Tanganyika 1947; slr gen Tanganyika 1949, attorney gen Trinidad and Tobago 1953, chief justice Br Honduras (later Belize) 1957-72, judge of the Cts of Appeal of Bermuda, the Bahamas and the Turks and Caicos Islands 1974-75; judge of the Ct of Appeal of Belize 1974-81; chm of Integrity Cmmn of Nat Assembly of Belize 1981-87; memb of Belize Advsy Cncl 1985; kt 1961; *Recreations* cricket, tennis, gardening; *Clubs* Barbados Yacht, Pickwick CC Barbados; *Style—* Sir Clifford Inniss; 11/13 Oriole Ave, Belmopan, Belize

INNOCENT, Harold Sidney; s of Harry William Harrison (d 1932), and late Jennie Henry; *Educ* Broad St Secondary Modern Coventry, Churchfield HS Coventry; *Career* Nat Serv RAF; actor; appeared with: NT, RSC, Old Vic Theatre Co, Chichester Festival Theatre, The Young Vic; West End: The School for Scandal, The Importance of Being Earnest, Pericles, Dear Antoine, The Magistrate, Donkey's Years, Henry IV (Pirandello) 1990; The Grace of Mary Travers at Royal Court, Rocket to the Moon and Ascent of Mount Fiji at Hampstead Theatre Club; Sir Despard in Ruddigore for New Sadler's Wells Opera Co, Cayley Drummle in the Second Mrs Tanquerey NT (Clarence Derwent award Best Supporting Actor 1982), Boniface in The Beaux Stratagem NT 1989-90; films incl: Casanova, The Tall Guy, Buster, Henry V, Little Dorritt, The Big Steal, The Yellow Dog, Without a Clue, Prince of Thieves; TV incl: An Englishman Abroad, Porterhouse Blue, Paradise Postponed, Tale of Two Cities, Killing Time, May to December; American TV incl: Have Gun - Will Travel, Gun Smoke, Ben Casey, Alfred Hitchcock Presents, The New Breed, Sea Hunt, Adventures in Paradise; *Recreations* reading, travel, music (particulary opera), letter writing; *Style—* Harold Innocent, Esq; c/o Susan Angel, Susan Angel Associates Ltd, 12 D'Arblay St, London W1V 3FP (☎ 071 439 3086)

INSALL, Donald W; OBE (1981); s of William R Insall (d 1966), of Bristol, and Phyllis Irene, *née* Hill (d 1987); *b* 7 Feb 1926; *Educ* Bristol GS, Univ of Bristol; *m* 13 June 1964, Libby, da of Malcolm H Moss, of Nanpantan, Loughborough, Leics; 2 s (Robert b 1965, Christopher b 1968), 1 da (Hilary b 1972); *Career* WWII Coldstream Gds (Regtl HQ Staff); dir Donald W Insall & Assocs Ltd architects and planning conslts specialising in architectural conservation and conservation conslts City of Chester 1970-87 (princ 1958-); awards incl: Queen's Silver Jubilee medal 1977, Europa Nostra medals, Euro Architectural Heritage awards; visiting lectr RCA 1964-69, adjunct prof Univ of Syracuse 1971-81, visiting prof Coll of Europe Catholic Univ of Leuven Belgium 1980-, conslt architect Worshipful Co of Goldsmiths; academician and memb Selection/Hanging Ctee Royal West of England Acad, fell Soc of Antiquaries of London; memb: UK Cncl Int Cncl of Monuments and Sites 1968-85, Cncl RSA 1976-78, RA Reynolds Club, Historic Bldgs Cncl for England 1971-83, Ancient Monuments Bd for England 1980-83; cmmr Historic Bldgs and Monuments Cmmn for England 1984-89, memb Advsy Ctee Getty Grants Programme 1988-; life memb: SPAB (and memb Cncl), Georgian Gp, Victorian Soc, Royal Photographic Soc, Nat Tst; hon memb Bath Preservation Tst, vice chm Conf on Trg in Architectural Conservation 1989- (hon sec 1959-89); FRSA 1948, FRIBA 1948, FRTPI 1973, RWA 1985; *Books* The Care of Old Buildings Today (1973), Chester: A Study in Conservation (1968), Conservation in Action (1982), Historic Buildings: Action to Maintain the Expertise for their Care & Repair (1974); contrib to: Encyclopaedia Britannica, Buildings - Who Cares? (Arts Council Film for ITV); *Recreations* visiting, photographing, enjoying places, appreciating craftsmanship; *Clubs* Athenaeum; *Style—* Donald Insall, Esq, OBE; 73 Kew Green, Richmond, Surrey; Donald W Insall & Associates Ltd, 19 West Eaton Place, London SW1 8LT (☎ 071 245 9888, fax 071 235 4370)

INSCH, Brian Douglas; s of James Ferguson Insch, CBE, of Barnt Green, nr Birmingham, and Jean, *née* Cunningham; *b* 2 Feb 1942; *Educ* Fettes, Aston Univ; *m* 1 June 1968, Susan Jane, da of Kenneth Hal Harper, of East Bridgford, Notts; 2 s (Mark Harper b 1975, Andrew Ferguson b 1977); *Career* GKN plc: joined 1963, commercial dir Salisbury Transmission (subsid co) 1972 (md 1974), sales dir Hardy Spicer Ltd (subsid co) 1973, gen commercial mangr 1979, corporate mgmnt dir 1982, dir 1986, human resources dir 1987; FCIS 1966; *Recreations* golf; *Style—* Brian Insch, Esq; GKN plc, PO Box 55, Redditch, Worcs B98 0TL (☎ 0527 517715, fax 0527 517715, telex 3366321)

INSCH, Dr Gordon McConochie; s of James Gordon Insch (d 1977), and Alice Helen Goulding McConochie (d 1963); *b* 18 June 1927; *Educ* Morrison's Acad Crieff, Univ of St Andrews, Univ of Glasgow (BSc, PhD); *m* 1954, Audrey Keith, da of George Keith Drew (d 1957); 1 s (Keith), 1 da (Lindsay); *Career* dir Br Nuclear Design & Construction Ltd 1969-75, conslt Atomic Power Constructions Ltd 1989- (dir 1971-89); CEng, FIMechE, FInstP; *Recreations* golf; *Clubs* Centro Español de Londres; *Style—* Dr Gordon Insch; National Nuclear Corp Ltd, Risley, Warrington, Cheshire WA3 6BZ (☎ 0925 51291, telex 627727); Woodlands 50 Leigh Rd, Prestbury, Macclesfield, Cheshire SK10 4HX (☎ 0625 829505)

INSKIP, Hon Mrs (Clare Elizabeth Anne); *née* Buxton; da of 2 Baron Noel-Buxton (d 1980); *b* 1954; *m* 1977, Owen Hampden Inskip; *Style—* The Hon Mrs Inskip

INSKIP, Henry Thurston; JP; s of Geoffrey May Inskip, JP (d 1959), and Lily Ethel, *née* Thurston (d 1979); *b* 2 April 1934; *Educ* Bedford Sch; *m* 9 May 1959, Margaret Vera, da of William James Topping, of Saffron Walden, Essex; 1 s (Charles b 1962), 2 da (Elizabeth b 1963, Amanda b 1963); *Career* chartered surveyor; sr ptnr E H C Inskip & Son architects and surveyors (fnded by gf in 1900); FRICS; *Recreations* history, photography, genealogy; *Style—* Henry Inskip, Esq, JP; 8 Rothsay Gardens, Bedford MK40 3QB (☎ 0234 266784); E H C Inskip and Son, 47 Goldington Rd, Bedford MK40 3LG (☎ 0234 261266)

INSKIP, His Hon Judge John Hampden Inskip; QC (1966); s of Sir John Hampden Inskip, KBE, sometime Lord Mayor of Bristol (yr bro of 1 Viscount Caldecote), by his w Hon Janet, *née* Maclay, 2 da of 1 Baron Maclay; *b* 1 Feb 1924; *Educ* Clifton, King's Coll Cambridge; *m* 1947, Ann Howell, yr da of late Lt-Col Owen Stanley Davies, DSO, MC, TD, RE, by his w, subsequently Lady Gueterbock; 1 s (Owen b 1953), 1 da (Diana b 1950); *Career* barr Inner Temple 1949, dep chm Hants QS 1967-71, rec 1970-82, memb Criminal Law Revision Ctee 1973-82, pres Transport Tbnl 1982-, circuit judge (Western) 1982-; *Style—* His Hon Judge Inskip, QC; Clerks, Bramshott, Liphook, Hants

INSKIP, Hon Piers James Hampden; s and h of 2 Viscount Caldecote; *b* 20 May 1947; *Educ* Eton, Magdalene Coll Cambridge; *m* 1, 1970 (m dis 1981), Susan Bridget, da of late W P Mellen, of Hill Farm, Gt Sampford, Essex; m 2, 1984, Kristine Elizabeth, da of Harvey Holbrooke-Jackson, of 12 Abbots Close, Ramsey, Cambs; 1 s (Thomas James b 22 March 1985); *Career* associate dir Carlton Communications; *Recreations* golf, tennis; *Style—* The Hon Piers Inskip

INSOLE, Douglas John; CBE (1979); s of John Herbert Insole (d 1975), and Margaret Rose, *née* Moore (d 1988); *b* 18 April 1926; *Educ* Sir George Monoux GS, St Catharine's Coll Cambridge (MA); *m* 18 Sept 1948, Barbara Hazel (d 1982), da of James Ridgway (d 1981); 3 da (Susan Carole b 1950, d 1979, Anne Barbara b 1953, Gwenda Elizabeth b 1958); *Career* Special Communications Unit Royal Signals 1944-46; capt: Univ of Cambridge CC 1949, Essex CCC 1950-60, England (9 appearances), vice capt S African tour 1956; chm England Selectors 1964-68, mangr England tour to Australia 1978-79 and 1982-83; chm: Essex CCC, TCCB; tstee MCC; JP Chingford Bench 1962-74; Town & City Properties 1970-75, Fosroc Int 1975-85, Trollope & Colls Holdings 1975-; memb FA Cncl; Freeman City of London; *Recreations* cricket, soccer, jazz; *Clubs* MCC, Essex CCC, East India & Sports; *Style—* Douglas Insole, Esq, CBE; 8 Hadleigh Court, Crescent Rd, Chingford, London E4 6AX (☎ 081 529 6546); Trocoll House, Wakering Rd, Barking, Essex IG11 8PD (☎ 081 591 1199, fax 081 594 8242)

INSTANCE, David John; s of Horace Arthur Instance, and Ellen Rosina, *née* Perkins; *b* 15 Dec 1938; *Educ* Woolwich Poly (HNC Engineering), LSPGA (Dip Printing Mgmnt); *m* 19 Oct 1963, Lydia Fiamma, da of Carlo Lago (d 1984); 2 s (Simon David, Andrew Edward); *Career* Nat Serv Lt RE, served Malaya; chm and md Instance Gp of Cos; holder of many patents covering engrg/printing application; dir of numerous subsidiary cos incl: Ditchling Press Ltd, Inprint Systems Italy, Inprint Systems France, Inprint Systems USA, Inprint Systems Germany, Cybertet USA; *Recreations* reading, opera, skiing, walking; *Style—* David Instance, Esq; Guinea Hall, Sellindge, nr Ashford-Kent TN25 6EG (☎ 030 381 3115); David J Instance Ltd, T/A Inprint Systems, Foster Road, Ashford Business Park, Ashford, Kent TH24 0LQ

INSTONE, Jeffrey Patrick Robert (Jeff); *b* 2 April 1941; *Educ* Peter Symonds' Sch Winchester, Royal Naval Sch Malta, Winchester Sch of Art, Inst of Educn Univ of London, Central St Martin's, London Inst; *m* 1, 1966, Bonita Giovanna Noelle Boella; 1 s (Jacob Valentine b 1968); m 2, 1977, Geraldine Anne Manby; 1 da (Lucy Kate b 1978); *Career* artist; exhibitions incl: Wordprints (Galleri Grafikhuset Stockholm) 1974, Whitechapel Open 1975-79 and 1987, The Terre Verte Venus Probe (Serpentine Gallery) 1976, Script (Galeria Akumulatory 2 and House Gallery) 1979, The English Artist and the Word (Sao Paolo Biennal, Br Cncl) 1979, 69,000 Words on a Brick Wall (Matt's Gallery) 1980, 970 Numbers on a Tiled Floor (Riverside Studios) 1980, Script (Galeria Akumulatory 2, Poznan and Gallery x Wrodaw) 1981, Retrospective (Winchester Gallery) 1982, 6 Artists (Penwith Galleries) 1982, Casts (Matt's Gallery) 1983, Transfers (AIR Gallery) 1984, Echoes (Matt's Gallery) 1987, Staff (Oxford Poly) 1988, Critics' Space (AIR Gallery) 1989, Forever Amber at Zebra Crossing and A Brush with Time (Poznań Acad for Visual Arts) 1990; *Awards* Gtr London Authy and Br Cncl awards 1979 and 1981, Elephant Tst and Br Cncl awards 1990; pubns incl: various articles 1987-90, The Terre Verte Venus Probe 1975, Script 1980, Echoes 1987; work in Br Cncl collection; *Style—* Jeff Instone, Esq; 38 Yeldham Rd, Hammersmith, London W6 (☎ 081 741 4521); Space Studios, 7 Winkley St, Bethnal Green, London E2 6PY (☎ 071 739 1147)

INSTONE, Peter Duncan; s of Geoffrey Charles Instone, of Plaistow, W Sussex, and Kathleen Marjorie, *née* Hawkeswood (d 1960); *b* 31 Oct 1942; *Educ* Uppingham; *m* 6 May 1966, Anne Mary, da of Maurice Dennis Pannell, of Findon, W Sussex; 1 s (Dominic b 1969), 1 da (Amanda b 1966); *Career* slr; ptnr Masons; sec St Bride's St Worldwide Media Tst, tstee St Bride's Restoration Fund Tst, dep chm Bd of Govrs St Bride's Fndn; memb Law Soc; *Recreations* travel, gardening, visiting battlefields; *Clubs* Lansdowne; *Style—* Peter Instone, Esq; Little Coopers, Hermongers, Rudgwick, West Sussex RH12 3AL; 30 Aylesbury St, London EC1R 0ER (☎ 071 490 400, fax 071 490 2545, telex 8811117)

INSTONE, Ralph Bernard Samuel; s of Capt Alfred Instone, JP (d 1957), and Phyllis Hilda, *née* Goldberg (d 1971); *b* 27 July 1918; *Educ* Westminster, Ch Ch Oxford; *m* 11 March 1941 (m dis 1973), Sybil Esther, da of Jack Palca (d 1920); 3 s (Daniel b 1947, Stephen b 1954, Simon b 1957), 1 da (Sara b 1946, d 1969); *Career* Army 1939-46, Inf 1939-41, GCHQ 1941-44, ret Capt; educn offr Notts and Derby 1945-46; called to the Bar Inner Temple 1945, in practice Lincoln's Inn 1946-, numerous articles on co law in legal and accountancy jls; *Recreations* lawn tennis, bridge; *Clubs* Roehampton; *Style—* Ralph B S Instone, Esq; 18 Fairacres, Roehampton Lane, London SW15 5LX; 7 New Sq, Lincoln's Inn, London WC2A 3QS

INVERARITY, James Alexander (Sandy); OBE; s of William Inverarity (d 1978), and Alexina, *née* Davidson (d 1978); *b* 17 Sept 1935; *Educ* Loretto; *m* 8 March 1960, Jean Stewart, da of James Rae Gellatly (d 1979); 1 s (Graeme b 1964), 2 da (Catherine b 1960, Alison b 1962); *Career* farmer, CA and co dir; pres NFU of Scot 1970-71; memb: Eggs Authy 1971-74, Governing Body E of Scot Coll of Agric 1974-, Farm Animal Welfare Cncl 1978-88, Panel of Agric Arbiters 1983-, Governing Body Scot Crop Res Inst 1984- (chm 1989-), Dairy Produce Quota Tbnl for Scot 1984-85; dir: Scot Agric Securities Corp plc 1983- (chm 1987-), Utd Oilseeds Prodrs Ltd 1985- (chm 1987-); *Recreations* shooting, curling; *Clubs* Farmers', Royal Scottish Automobile; *Style—* Sandy Inverarity, Esq, OBE; Cransley Liff, by Dundee DD2 5NP (☎ 0382 580327)

INVERFORTH, 4 Baron (UK 1919); Andrew Peter Weir; only s of 3 Baron Inverforth (d 1982), and Jill Elizabeth Inverforth, *née* Thornycroft, *qv*; *b* 16 Nov 1966; *Educ* Marlborough; *Heir* unc, Hon John Vincent Weir; *Style—* The Rt Hon the Lord Inverforth; 27 Hyde Park St, London W2 2JS (☎ 071 262 5721)

INVERFORTH, Iris, Baroness; Iris Beryl; da of late Charles Vincent, 4 Bn The Buffs; *m* 26 June 1929, 2 Baron Inverforth (d 1975); 2 s (late 3 Baron, Hon (John) Vincent Weir, *qv*); *Style—* The Rt Hon Iris, Lady Inverforth; 24 Clarence Terrace, Regent's Park, London NW1 4RD

INVERFORTH, Baroness; Jill Elizabeth; o da of John Ward Thornycroft, CBE (d 1989), of Bembridge, IOW; *m* 26 Jan 1966, 3 Baron Inverforth (d 1982); 1 s (4 Baron *qv*), 1 da (Hon Clarinda Weir b 22 May 1968); *Style—* The Rt Hon Lady Inverforth; 27 Hyde Park St, London W2 2JS (☎ 071 262 5721)

INVERURIE, Lord; James William Falconer Keith; Master of Kintore; s and h of 13 Earl of Kintore, *qv*; *b* 15 April 1976; *Educ* Gordonstoun; *Style—* Lord Inverurie

INVEST, Clive Frederick; s of Frederick Arthur Invest (d 1986), of Toddington, Bedfordshire, and Daphne Mary, *née* Bice; *b* 6 Oct 1940; *Educ* Southgate County GS, Royal Dental Hosp London (BDS, LDS, RCS); *m* 19 March 1966, Kirsten Elizabeth, da of Alfin Isaksen (d 1986), of Oslo; 2 s (James Clive Frederick b 27 Feb 1972, Robin Julian b 21 March 1975); *Career* pilot offr RAF 1963, qualified as dental surgn 1965, Flt Lt RAF Dental Branch 1965-70; in private practice: Geelong Aust 1970-71, Chichester Sussex 1971-74, Harley St London 1974-; teacher and clinical asst Guy's Hosp 1978-83; memb: BDA, Br Soc of Restorative Dentistry, Br Endodontic Soc; Former memb Cncl Endo Soc; *Books* contrib one chapter in General Dental Practitioner's Handbook; *Recreations* skiing, windsurfing, waterskiing, swimming, photography, art, reading; *Clubs* Royal Air Force; *Style—* Clive Invest, Esq; 21 Hill Road, Haslemere, Surrey GU27 2JN (☎ 0428 653457); 90 Harley St, London W1N 1AF (☎ 071 935 5400, fax 071 935 4185)

IPSWICH, Archdeacon of; *see*: Gibson, The Ven Terence Allen

IRANI, Dr Mehernoosh Sheriar; s of Sheriar Ardeshir Irani, of London, and Banoo Sheriar; *b* 24 Aug 1949; *Educ* Chiswick County GS for Boys, KCH (BSc, MB BS); *m* 19 Sept 1987, Susan Clare, da of Air Cdre Philip David Mallilieu Moore, of Farnborough, Hampshire; 1 da (Jasmine b 1989); *Career* house physician KCH 1974, house surgn Kent and Sussex Hosp Tunbridge Wells 1974, registrar in nephrology and gen med Canterbury Hosp Kent 1977 (sr house offr 1975-76), registrar in rheumatology and gen med Radcliffe Infirmary Oxford 1977-79, hon sr registrar and res fell Dept of Rheumatology and Biochemical Pharmacology KCH 1979-81, sr registrar Westminster and Charing Cross Hosp 1981-85, conslt rheumatologist Ashford Hosp Middx; visiting physician: Princess Margaret Hosp Windsor, Royal Masonic Hosp, Lister Hosp; MO Br Olympic team: Los Angeles 1984, Seoul 1988; MO Br Cwlth games team: Edinburgh 1986, Auckland NZ 1990; MO: Br Amateur Weightlifters Assoc 1986-, BCU 1986-, Eng Badminton Team World Championships Beijing China 1987, Br Dragon Boat Racing Assoc 1988-; sec gen Int Assoc of Olympic Med Offrs 1988-; memb: Br Aeromedical Practitioners Assoc, Br Soc for Rheumatology, BOA; MRCS, MRCP, LRCP; *Books* contrib to Rheumatology and Rehabilitation (1984); *Recreations* family, cricket; *Clubs* Riverside; *Style—* Dr Mehernoosh Irani; 20 Devonshire Gardens, Chiswick, London W4 3TN (☎ 081 994 0119); Dept of Rheumatology, Ashford Hospital, London Rd, Ashford, Middlesex TW15 3AA (☎ 0784 251188, fax 0784 64488)

IRBY, Charles Leonard Anthony; s of The Hon Anthony P Irby (d 1986), of Osborne House, South Bolton Gardens, London SW5, and Mary, *née* Apponyi (d 1952); *b* 5 June 1945; *Educ* Eton; *m* 23 Sept 1971, Sarah Jane, da of Col David G Sutherland, MC, of 51 Victoria Road, London W8; 1 s (Nicholas Charles Anthony b 10 July 1975), 1 da (Caroline Sarah b 21 May 1977); *Career* dir Baring Brothers & Co Ltd 1984-; FCA; *Recreations* travel, photography, skiing; *Clubs* City; *Style—* Charles Irby, Esq; 125 Blenheim Crescent, London W11 2EQ (☎ 071 221 2979); The Old Vicarage, Chieveley, Newbury, Berks, RG16 8UX (☎ 0635 248 117); Baring Bros & Co Ltd, 8 Bishopsgate, London EC2N 4AE (☎ 071 280 1000, fax 071 283 2224)

IRBY, (George Anthony) Peter; s of Hon Anthony Peter Irby (d 1986), and Mary, *née* Apponyi (d 1952); *b* 3 June 1942; *Educ* Eton; *m* 10 Oct 1981, Ginger Kay, da of Frank E Wallace (d 1977), of Texas, USA; 2 s (Edward b 1986, Richard Peter Anthony Wallace b 1988, d 1989), 2 da (Mary (decd), Katharine b 1984); *Career* Maj Royal Green Jackets 1961-79; advertising mangr (Europe & ME) New York Times 1981-; *Recreations* golf; *Style—* Peter Irby, Esq; Hill House, 64 Honor Oak Road, London SE23 3RZ; The New York Times, 76 Shoe Lane, London EC4A 3JB (☎ 071 353 2174/3472, fax 071 583 1458, telex 263317 NYKTMS G)

IREDALE, (John) Martin; s of John Leslie Iredale (d 1988), of 44 Whitehouse Rd, Woodcote, Reading, and Hilda, *née* Palfry; *b* 10 June 1939; *Educ* Abingdon Sch; *m* 14 Sept 1963, (Margaret) Anne, da of Reginald Walter Jewell (d 1968), of 15 Winser Drive, Reading; 3 s (Edward b 1 May 1965, Mathew b 3 Oct 1966, William b 18 May 1976), 1 da (Hannah b 30 March 1973); *Career* CA and licensed insolvency practitioner; ptnr: Cork Gully 1971-, Coopers Lybrand and Deloitte 1983-; sec Royal Shakespeare Theatre Tst 1970-, govr Royal Shakespeare Theatre 1981-, memb Hodgson Ctee On Profits of Crime and Their Recovery 1981-82, pres Old Abingdonian Club 1982-84, chm Cornhill Club 1985-86; Freeman City of London 1973, Liveryman Worshipful Co of Carmen 1978; FCA 1963, FIPA 1985; *Books* Receivership Manual (with C J Hughes, 1987); *Recreations* waiting on my family; *Clubs* Leander, Cornhill, Reading Abbey Rotary; *Style—* Martin Iredale, Esq; Holybrook Farm House, Burghfield Bridge, Reading RG3 3RA (☎ 0734 575 108); Cork Gully, Shelley House, 3 Noble St, London EC2V 7DQ (☎ 071 606 7700, fax 071 606 9887, car 0860 522 370)

IREDALE, Dr Peter; s of Henry Iredale (d 1965), of Brownhills, Staffordshire, and Annie, *née* Kirby; *b* 15 March 1932; *Educ* King Edward VI GS, Univ of Bristol (BSc, Phd); *m* 11 April 1957, Judith Margaret, da of John Herod Marshall (d 1976), of Long Eaton, Nottingham 1 s (John b 1960), 3 da (Susan b 1962, Helen b 1964, Alison b 1966); *Career* AERE Harwell: res on nuclear instrumentation 1955-69, non-destructive testing 1969-70, computer storage 1970-73, head of Nuclear Instrumentation Gp 1975-77, head of Mktg and Sales Dept 1977-79 (prev 1973-74), head of Marine Technol Support Unit 1979-81, dir engrg 1981-86, dep dir Harwell 1986-87, dir Harwell Laboratory 1987-90, dir Culham and Harwell Sites 1990-; pubns and scientific papers on high energy physics and nuclear instrumentation; visiting fell Wolfson Coll; FInstP, FIEE; *Books* publications on high energy physics and nuclear instrumentation (scientific papers); *Recreations* family, music, working with wood, gardening, walking; *Style—* Dr Peter Iredale; The Harwell Laboratory, Harwell, Didcot, Oxfordshire (☎ 0235 432831)

IREDALE, Dr Roger Oliver; s of Fred Iredale (d 1978), of Sussex, and Elsie Florence, *née* Hills (d 1990); *b* 13 Aug 1934; *Educ* Harrow Co GS, Univ of Reading (BA, MA, PhD), Peterhouse Cambridge; *m* 1968, Mavis, da of Charles Frederick Bowtell, of York; 1 s (Simon Crispian b 1974), 1 da (Rachel Samia b 1971); *Career* teacher Hele's Sch Exeter 1959-61, lectr (later sr lectr) Bishop Otter Coll Chichester 1962-70, Br Cncl offr and maitre de conferences Univ of Algiers 1970-72, lectr Chichester Coll of Further Educn 1972-73, Br Cncl offr Madras 1973-75, lectr in educn Univ of Leeds 1975-79, chief educn advsr Overseas Devpt Admin FCO 1983- (educn advsr 1979-83); memb Cwlth Scholarship Cmmn 1984-, cmmr Sino-Br Friendship Scholarship Scheme 1986-; govr: SOAS 1983-, Queen Elizabeth House Oxford 1986-87, The Cwlth of Learning 1988-; writer of poems for BBC Radio 3 and in anthologies and jls; *Publications* Turning Bronzes (poems, 1974), Out Towards the Dark (poems, 1978); articles in Comparative Education and other jls; *Recreations* sailing, poetry, writing, restoring the discarded; *Style—* Dr Roger Iredale; Overseas Development Administration, Eland House, Stag Place, London SW1E 5DH (☎ 071 273 0125)

IRELAND, Adrian William Velleman; *b* 1 March 1945; *Educ* Stowe; *m* 19 July 1975, (Victoria) Jane, da of Maj Myles Harry Cooper (d 1986), of Bideford, Devon; 2 s (Rupert b 1977, Frederic b 1979); *Career* with Akroyd and Smithers stock jobbers until 1986, dir S G Warburg Securities 1986-; *Recreations* travel, cricket, food; *Clubs* City of London, Boodle's, MCC; *Style—* Adrian Ireland, Esq; 7 Dalebury Rd, London SW17; 1 Finsbury Ave, London EC2 (☎ 071 606 1066)

IRELAND, Norman Charles; s of Charles Ireland (d 1980), and Winifred Alice Ireland (d 1962); *b* 28 May 1927; *Educ* UK, USA, India; *m* 18 Aug 1953, Gillian Margaret (Gill), da of William James Harrison (d 1976); 1 s (David Alistair b 30 April 1958), 1 da (Jennifer Fiona b 11 Nov 1955); *Career* RAF 1945-48; Avon Rubber 1954-65, chief accountant Utd Glass 1965-67, fin dir BTR 1967-87 (ret as exec 1987); chm: London & Met plc 1986-, Bowater Industries plc 1987-, The Housing Finance Corp 1988-, Intermediate Capital Group Ltd; non-exec dir 1987-: BTR plc, Meggitt Holdings plc, Scottish Heritable Tst plc; MICAS, memb Inst of Cost and Mgmnt Accountants; *Recreations* gardening, watching and listening to music, ballet, opera; *Style*— Norman Ireland, Esq

IRELAND, Richard Henry; s of George Thomas Ireland (d 1970), of Fulham, and Irene Edith, *née* Lunt; *b* 30 April 1946; *Educ* London Tech Sch; *m* 30 Sept 1967, Joan Florence, da of William Thomas Smith (d 1958), of Lewisham; 1 s (Robert b 1972), 1 da (Suzanne b 1975); *Career* admitted slr 1978; Slaughter and May 1978; ptnr: Eaton & Burley 1982, Rowe & Maw 1984; memb Law Soc 1978; *Recreations* fly fishing, walking, reading; *Style*— Richard Ireland, Esq; Verdon, Old Perry St, Chislehurst, Kent BR7 6PP (☎ 071 248 4282); Rowe & Maw, 20 Black Friars Lane, London EC4V 6HD (☎ 071 248 4282, fax 071 248 2009, telex 262787)

IRELAND, Sheriff Ronald David; QC (1964); s of William Alexander Ireland (d 1969), and Agnes Victoria Brown (d 1958); *b* 13 March 1925; *Educ* Watson's Coll Edinburgh, Balliol Coll Oxford (MA), Univ of Edinburgh (LLB); *Career* advocate of the Scottish Bar 1952, prof of Scots law Univ of Aberdeen 1958-71 (dean of the Faculty of Law 1964-67); Sheriff of Lothian and Borders 1972-88, dir Scottish Cts Admin 1975-78, Sheriff Princ of Grampian Highland and Islands 1988-; *Clubs* New (Edinburgh), Royal Northern and Univ (Aberdeen), Highland (Inverness); *Style*— Sheriff Ronald Ireland, QC; 6a Greenhill Gardens, Edinburgh; The Castle, Inverness

IRELAND, Hon Mrs (Sheila Marian); *née* Poole; da of 1 Baron Poole, CBE, TD, PC; *b* 1940; *m* 1, 1966 (m dis), Cob Stenham, *qv*; m 2, 1980, George Ian Kenneth Ireland; *Style*— The Hon Mrs Ireland; 9 Albert Place, London W8

IREMONGER, (William) John; s of Rev William George Iremonger, (d 1964), and Ruth Ida, *née* Gascoigne (d 1964); *b* 10 April 1912; *Educ* Hurstpierpoint, Keble Coll Oxford, Grenoble Univ France; *m* 8 Nov 1947, Christine Margaret, da of Lewis Gottwaltz (d 1928), of The Nook, Southern Down, S Wales; 2 s (Jonathan b 19 March 1953, Robert b 16 July 1962), 4 da (Susan b 24 July 1949, d 1950, Penelope b 15 Nov 1950, Joanna b 20 July 1955, Nicola b 1 April 1958); *Career* WWII Flying Offr RAF 1940-46; started own business (hotel and property) 1947, underwriting memb Lloyd's 1974-, vice chm Dorset CC (memb 1968-); *Recreations* walking, music, photography; *Clubs* Lansdowne; *Style*— John Iremonger, Esq; The Choughs, 95 Golf Links Rd, Ferndown, Dorset BH22 8BU (☎ 0202 874 325); Breton, Loubes Bernac, 47120 Duras, France; 55 Kensington Court, London W8 (☎ 071 937 8922)

IREMONGER, Pennant Elfrida Lascelles; da of Thomas Lascelles Isa Shandon Valiant Iremonger, of Milbourne Manor, Malmesbury, Wilts SN16 9JA, and Lucille d'Oyen, *née* Parks (d 1989); *b* 6 Oct 1943; *Educ* Westonbirt Sch Tetbury Glos; *m* 20 Dec 1972, (George) Nicholas Nevil Huskinson, s of (Thomas) Leonard Bousfield Huskinson (d 1974), of Triscombe House, Bishops Lydeard, Somerset; 2 s (Thomas b 12 Oct 1978, Charles b 14 Aug 1981); *Career* admitted slr 1967, legal asst Slr's Dept Cmmrs Met Police New Scot Yard 1968-72, called to the Bar Inner Temple 1972; memb: Inner Temple, Br Acad of Forensic Sci; *Recreations* family life, friendship, gardening; *Style*— Miss Pennant Iremonger; Francis Taylor Building, Temple, London EC4Y 7BY (☎ 071 353 7786, fax 071 353 0659)

IRISH, John George Augustus; CBE (1989); s of Albert Edwin Irish, of Hinton St George, Somerset (d 1986), and Rosa Anna Elizabeth, *née* Norris (d 1963); *b* 1 Aug 1931; *Educ* Crewkerne Sch, LSE (BSc); *m* 1, 1953 (m dis 1967), Joan, *née* Hall; 1 s (Timothy b 1964), 1 da (Nicola b 1962); m 2, 1968, Isabel Josephine, o da of late Bernhard Berenzweig, of Harrow-on-the-Hill, Middx; 4 s (Jonathan b 1970, Nicholas b 1972, Hugo b 1979, Charles b 1981); *Career* cmmnd Nat Serv 1952-54; exec Marks and Spencer 1954-65, retail dir David Greig 1965-70; chm: Eight Till Late Ltd 1981-, Spar UK Ltd 1983- (md 1981-); dir IGT (Amsterdam based trading co of Int Spar) 1983-, vice chm Spar Guild of Grocers 1984-; chief exec: Spar Foods Distributors, Landmark Cash and Carry Ltd, Spar Landmark Services 1985-; dep chm Retail Consortium, non-exec dir NAAFI 1990-; chm: Voluntary Gp Assoc, Cncl Inst of Grocery Distribution; memb: NEDC Distributive Trades, Cncl and Fund Raising Ctee Nat Grocers' Benevolent Fund 1983-90; Supermarketing Man of the Year 1986, Independent Grocer Gold award 1987; govr Orley Farm Sch Middx; FIGD 1985; *Recreations* history, conservation, education; *Clubs* IOD; *Style*— John Irish, Esq, CBE; Fourbuoys House, Georgian Way, Harrow-on-the-Hill, Middx HA1 3LF (☎ 081 864 6953); Spar (UK) Ltd, 32-40 Headstone Drive, Harrow, Middx HA3 5QT (☎ 081 863 5511, telex 923215 SPARHA)

IRISH, Sir Ronald Arthur; OBE (1963); s of Arthur Irish (d 1968); *b* 26 March 1913; *Educ* Fort St HS; *m* 1960, Noella Jean Austin, da of Leslie Stuart Fraser; 3 s; *Career* former: sr ptnr Irish Young and Outhwaite CA's, chm Rothmans of Pall Mall (Australia) Ltd; pres Inst of CA's Aust 1956-58, chm Manufacturing Industs Advsy Cncl 1966-72, pres Tenth Int Congress of Accountants 1972; life memb: Australian Soc of Accountants 1972, Inst of CA's in Australia 1974; hon fell Univ of Sydney 1986; FCA; kt 1970; *Books* Auditing; *Clubs* Union and Australian (Sydney); *Style*— Sir Ronald Irish, OBE; 2803/85 Spring St, Bondi Junction, NSW 2022, Australia

IRONS, Jeremy John; s of Paul Dugan Irons (d 1983), and Barbara Anne Brereton Brymer, *née* Sharpe; *b* 19 Sept 1948; *Educ* Sherborne, Bristol Old Vic Theatre Sch; *m* 23 March 1978 (m dis), Sinead Mary, da of Cyril James Cusack, actor; 2 s (Samuel b 16 Sept 1978, Maximilian b 17 Oct 1985); *Career* actor; joined Bristol Old Vic Theatre Co 1971; stage appearances incl: A Winter's Tale, What the Butler Saw, Hayfever, Godspell 1971, Wild Oats RSC 1975, Simon Gray's Rear Column (Clarence Derwent Award) 1976; TV: Brideshead Revisited (TV Times Best Actor Award) 1982; Films: French Lieutenant's Woman (Variety Club Best Actor Award), Moonlighting 1982, The Captain's Doll (BBC TV film) 1982, The Wild Duck (Australian film of Ibsen play) 1983, Betrayal 1983, Swann in Love 1983, The Mission 1985, Dead Ringers (Best Actor NY Critics Award) 1988, Chorus of Disapproval 1988, Danny Champion of the World 1988, Australia 1989, Reversal of Fortune (Golden Globe Best Actor award) 1990; Broadway: The Real Thing (Tony Award Best Actor, Drama League Distinguished Performance Award) 1984; RSC 1986-87 A Winter's Tale, The Rover, Richard II; *Recreations* sailing, riding, skiing, flying; *Style*— Jeremy Irons, Esq; c/o Hutton Mangement, 200 Fulham Rd, London SW10

IRONSIDE, Hon Charles Edmund Grenville; s and h of 2 Baron Ironside; *b* 1 July 1956; *m* 17 Aug 1985, Hon Elizabeth Mary Law, eldest da of 2 Baron Coleraine; 2 da (Emily Charlotte b 23 Oct 1988, another b 12 March 1990); *Style*— The Hon Charles Ironside; 25 Patience Rd, London SW11

IRONSIDE, 2 Baron (UK 1941); Edmund Oslac Ironside; s of Field Marshal 1 Baron Ironside, GCB, CMG, DSO (d 1959); *b* 21 Sept 1924; *Educ* Tonbridge; hon CGIA 1986; *m* 1950, Audrey Marigold, da of late Col the Hon Thomas George Breadalbane Morgan-Grenville, DSO, OBE, MC (3 s of Lady Kinloss in her own right); 1 s, 1 da; *Heir* s, Hon Charles Ironside; *Career* Lt RN 1943-52; Marconi Co 1952-59, English Electro Leo Computers 1959-64, Cryosystems Ltd 1964-68, International Research and Development Co Ltd 1968-84, NEI plc 1984-; memb: Organising Ctee Br Library 1972-74, Select Ctee European Communities 1974-; chm Sci Reference Library Advsy Ctee 1975-85; pres: Electric Vehicle Assoc of Great Britain 1975-83, European Electric Road Vehicle Assoc 1980-82 (vice-pres 1978-80), Sea Cadet Corps Chelmsford 1959-88; vice-pres: Inst of Patentees and Inventors 1976-, Parly and Scientific Ctee 1977-80 and 1983-86 (dep chm 1974-77); treas All Pty Energy Studies Gp 1979-; memb Privy Cncl of Ct City Univ 1975- (memb Cncl 1986-88); memb Ct Univ of Essex 1982- (memb Cncl 1984-87); Master Worshipful Co of Skinners 1981-82; *Books* Highroad to Command (1972); *Clubs* Royal Ocean Racing; *Style*— The Rt Hon the Lord Ironside; Priory House, Old House Lane, Boxted, Colchester Essex CO4 5RB

IRONSIDE, Hon Mrs (Elizabeth Mary); *née* Law; da (by 1 m) of 2 Baron Coleraine; *b* 4 Feb 1961; *m* 17 Aug 1985, Hon Charles Edmund Grenville Ironside, only s of 2 Baron Ironside; 1 da (Emily Charlotte b 23 Oct 1988); *Style*— The Hon Mrs Ironside; 25 Patience Road, London SW11

IRONSIDE, Graham; s of James Mackie Ironside (d 1981), of Aberdeen, Scotland, and Nan, *née* Thomson; *b* 12 Sept 1989; *Educ* Robert Gordon's Coll Aberdeen; *m* 25 July 1963, Sheena Jane Simpson, da of Cathy Carstairs, of Auchterarder, Perthshire, Scotland; 1 da (Gillian); *Career* head of regnl progs Yorkshire TV 1982- (news ed 1971, ed Calendar 1974); *Recreations* golf, gardening, grandson; *Style*— Graham Ironside, Esq; Yorkshire TV, The TV Centre, Kirkstall Rd, Leeds, Yorks LS16 9AN (☎ 0532 438283, fax 0532 433655, telex 0532 557232)

IRONSIDE WOOD, Timothy Swaington; s of Lt-Col F D I Wood, RA (ret) (d 1986), and Olga Madeleine, *née* Mills-Browne; *Educ* Wellington, Univ of Manchester (BA); *m* 28 May 1978, Jane Elizabeth Ursula, da of Ian Alexander Ross Peebles (d 1980); 2 s (Robert b 1980, Nicholas b 1982); *Career* theatre and TV actor 1970-72; BBC TV: prodr and dir music and arts 1976-79, assoc prodr drama 1978-82, prodr plays and films 1983-; prodns incl works by: Edward Bond, David Hare, Graham Reid, Christopher Hampton; series incl: Ties of Blood 1985, The Ginger Tree 1989; memb BAFTA; *Recreations* cricket, snooker, fishing; *Style*— Timothy Ironside Wood, Esq; BBC Films, Television Centre, Wood Lane, London W12 7RJ (☎ 081 576 1275, fax 081 576 7054)

IRVIN, Albert Henry Thomas; s of Albert Henry Jesse Irvin (d 1947), of London, and Nina Lucy, *née* Jackson (d 1944); *b* 21 Aug 1922; *Educ* Holloway Co Sch, Northampton Sch of Art, Goldsmith's Coll Sch of Art London (NDD); *m* 1947, Beatrice Olive, da of John Wagner Nicolson; 2 da (Priscilla Jane b 24 July 1949, Celia Ann b 26 Feb 1959); *Career* artist; pt/t teacher Spencer Park Comp Sch 1959-62, evening class teacher Wandsworth Prison 1959-63, princ lectr in painting Goldsmith's Coll Sch of Art London 1962-83; solo exhibitions incl: 57 Gallery Edinburgh 1960, New Art Centre London 1963, 1965, 1971 and 1973, Exe Gallery Exeter 1969, Galerie Folker Skumma Berlin 1972 and 1978, Städtishe Kunstsammlungen Ludwsigshafen 1974, Galerie Klaus Lüpke Frankfurt 1972 and 1976, Berlin Opera House 1975, Aberdeen Art Gallery 1976, Acme Gallery London 1980, Gimpel Fils Gallery London 1982, 1984, 1986 and 1990, Aberdeen Art Gallery 1983, Ikon Gallery Birmingham 1983, Jersey Arts Cncl Gallery 1984, Kilkenny Castle 1985, Hendriks Galery Dublin 1986, Carine Campo Gallery Antwerp 1987 and 1989, Talbot Rice Gallery Edinburgh 1988, Gimpel and Weitzenhoffer New York 1988, Serpentine Gallery London 1990, Spacex Gallery Exeter 1990, Gallery Monochrome Brussels 1990, Welsh Arts Cncl 1990, Gimpel Fils ARCO Madrid 1991; gp exhibitions incl: London Group 1951, British Painting 74 (Hayward Gallery) 1974, British Art Show tour 1979, Home and Abroad (Serpentine Gallery) 1985, Coventry Gallery Sydney 1985, Int Print Biennale Bradford (prize winner) 1986, Royal Acad Summer Exhibition 1987-90 (prize winner 1987 and 1989), Hoyland Beattie Irvin (Sunderland) 1988, Int Print Biennale Ljubljana 1989, Great British Art Show (Glasgow) 1990; works in the collections of: The Tate Gallery, Arts Cncl of GB, Br Cncl and private and public collections throughout Britain and abroad; commissions incl painting for Maternity Wing Homerton Hosp Hackney 1987; awards: from Arts Cncl (for visit to USA 1968, Major award 1975, Purchase award 1980), Gulbenkian Print award 1983, Giles Bequest prize from V & A Museum and Br Museum at Int Print Biennale Bradford 1986; memb London Gp 1965; *Recreations* music, reading, football; *Clubs* Chelsea Arts; *Style*— Albert Irvin, Esq; 19 Gorst Rd, London SW11 6JB (☎ 071 228 2929); 71 Stepney Green, London E1 3LE; c/o Gimpel Fils, 30 Davies St, London W1Y 1LG (☎ 071 493 2488, fax 071 629 5732)

IRVIN, Thomas Thoburn; s of Thomas Thoburn Irvin (d 1969), of Aberdeen, Scotland, and Catherine, *née* Argo (d 1985); *b* 14 Sept 1940; *Educ* Aberdeen GS, Univ of Aberdeen (MB ChB, PhD, ChM); *m* 7 Aug 1965, Joan Marr, da of James Reid (d 1980), of Aberdeen, Scotland; 2 s (Thomas b 1970, Simon b 1974), 1 da (Rachel b 1968); *Career* lectr in surgery Univ of Leeds 1970-73 and 1974, res surgn Univ of California San Francisco 1973-74, reader in surgery Univ of Sheffield (sr lectr in surgery 1974-78), conslt surgn Royal Devon and Exeter Hosp 1978-; memb: Br Soc of Gastroenterology, Int Coll of Surgns; chm med staff Exeter Health Authy; memb Assoc of Surgns GB 1974; FRCSEd 1968; *Books* Wound Healing! Principles and Practice (1981); *Recreations* music, squash; *Style*— Thomas Irvin, Esq

IRVINE, Brian Alexander; s of William Irvine, of Airdrie, and Isobel, *née* Garden; *b* 24 May 1965; *Educ* Airdrie Acad, Glasgow Tech Coll; *m* 27 May 1988, Donna Frances, da of Donald Rennie Main; 1 da (Hannah Danielle b 25 Sept 1990); *Career* professional footballer; Falkirk 1984-85 (debut v Morton 1984, 44 appearances), Aberdeen 1985- (over 180 appearances); Scotland: full cap v Romania 1990, 2 semi-professional caps 1985; Scottish Cup Winner's medal 1990 v Celtic (scored winning penalty in penalty decider), Skol Cup Winner's medal 1990 v Rangers (Loser's medal 1988 and 1989); Clydesale Bank 1981-84; *Recreations* committed Christian; *Style*— Brian Irvine, Esq; Aberdeen Football Club, Pittodrie Stadium, Aberdeen AB2 1QH (☎ 0224 632328)

IRVINE, Rt Hon Sir Bryant Godman; PC (1982); s of William Henry Irvine, and Ada Mary, *née* Bryant, of Toronto; *b* 25 July 1909; *Educ* Upper Canada Coll Toronto, St Paul's, Magdalen Coll Oxford (MA); *m* 1945, Valborg Cecilie (d 1990), da of late Peter Frederick Carslund, of Fyn, Denmark; 2 da; *Career* WWII serv Lt-Cdr RNVR, at sea and on staff C-in-C Western Approaches, Cdr US Naval Forces Europe; called to the Bar 1932; farmer, memb Exec Ctee NFU (E Sussex) 1947-84 (branch chm 1956-58); chm: SE Agric Land Tbnl 1954-56, YCs' Union 1946-47; Parly candidate (C) Wood Green and Lower Tottenham 1951, MP (C) Rye 1955-83; PPS to: min Educn and Parly sec Miny Educn 1957-59, fin sec Treasy 1959-60; chm: Cons Horticulture Sub Ctee 1960-62, All Pty Tourist and Resort Ctee 1964-66; vice chm Cons Ctee on Agric 1964-70, memb Select Ctee Agric 1967-69, jt sec 1922 Ctee 1965-68 (hon tres 1974-76), jt sec and vice chm Cons Cwlth Affrs Ctee 1957-66, memb Exec Ctee Cwlth Parly Assoc UK branch 1964-76 and 1982-83 (memb Gen Cncl and hon treas 1970-73), chm British-Canadian Parly Gp 1964-83, vice chm Cons Foreign and Cwlth Affrs Ctee 1973-76 (jt sec 1967-73), memb Speaker's Panel Chairmen 1965-76, dep chm Ways and Means Ctee House of Commons and dep speaker 1976-82, represented Mr Speaker at the Millenium of Tynwald IOM 1979, Cwlth Speakers Conf Ottawa 1981, 150 Anniversary of Parly Govt Cayman Islands 1982, ldr Parly Delgn to UNO 1982; pres: Br Resorts Assoc 1962-80, Southern Counties Agric Trading Soc 1983-86;

CInstCE 1938-74; kt 1986; *Clubs* Carlton, Pratt's, Naval; *Style*— The Rt Hon Sir Bryant Godman Irvine; Flat 91, 24 John Islip St, London SW1 (☎ 071 834 9221); Great Ote Hall, Burgess Hill, W Sussex (☎ 044 423 2179)

IRVINE, David Patrick; s of John Irvine (d 1956), of Kendal, and Elizabeth, *née* Patrick; *Educ* Kendal GS; *Career* Nat Serv RAF 1957-58; news reporter Lancashire Evening Post 1953-56, ldr writer Coventry Evening Telegraph 1966-69 (rugby union and cricket corr 1959-66), tennis and rugby union corr Guardian 1976- (northern cricket and rugby union corr 1969-76); memb Lawn Tennis Writers' Assoc 1976- (chm 1986-87); *Books* The Joy of Rugby (1978), Lawn Tennis Association Yearbook (fndr ed, 1980-87); *Recreations* walking, classical music; *Style*— David Irvine, Esq; The Guardian, 119 Farringdon Rd, London EC1R 3ER

IRVINE, Dr Donald Hamilton; CBE (1987, OBE 1979); s of late Dr Andrew Bell Hamilton Irvine, and Dorothy Mary, *née* Buckley; *b* 2 June 1935; *Educ* King Edward VI GS Morpeth, Med Sch Univ of Newcastle upon Tyne (MB BS, MD); *m* 1, 16 July 1960 (m dis 1985), Margaret Mary, da of late Francis McGuckin of Ponteland, Northumberland; 2 s (Alastair b 1962, Angus b 1968), 1 da (Amanda b 1966); m 2, 28 June 1986, Sally, da of Stanley Arthur Day, of Bellingen, NSW; *Career* princ GP Lintonville Med Gp Northumberland 1960-, regnl advsr GP Regnl Postgrad Inst for Med and Dentistry Univ of Newcastle upon Tyne 1973-; memb Gen Med Cncl 1979- (chm of Ctee of Standards and Med Ethics); RCGP: memb Cncl 1968-, hon sec 1972-78, chm of Cncl 1982-85 ; memb: Jt Ctee on Postgrad Trg for GP 1976- (chm 1988-), UK Central Cncl for Nursing Midwifery and Health Visiting 1983-, Bd of govrs MSD fndn 1983-89, The Audit Cmmn 1990-; MRCGP 1965; fell: BMA, RSM; FRCGP 1972; *Books* The Future General Practioner - Learning and Teaching (jtly, 1972), Managing for Quality in General Practice (1990); *Recreations* gardening, bird watching, going to the theatre; *Style*— Dr Donald Irvine, Esq, CBE; Mole End, Fairmoor, Morpeth, Northumberland (☎ 0670 515746); 11 Cedarland Ct, Roland Gardens, London SW7 3RW (☎ 071 373 5234); Lintonville Med Gp, Lintonville, Old Lane, Ashington, Northumberland (☎ 0670 812772, fax 0670 510046)

IRVINE, His Honour Judge James Eccles Malise; yr s of Brig-Gen Alfred Ernest Irvine, CB, CMG, DSO, DLI (d 1962), of Wotton under Edge, Glos, and Katharine Helen, *née* Graham (d 1984); *b* 10 July 1925; *Educ* Stowe, Merton Coll Oxford (MA); *m* 24 July 1954, Anne, eld da of Col Geoffrey Egerton-Warburton, DSO, TD, JP, DL (d 1961); ggs of Rev Rowland Egerton-Warburton, bro of 8 and 9 Bts Grey-Egerton), of Grafton Hall, Malpas, Cheshire, and Hon Georgiana Mary Dormer, MBE (d 1955), eld da of 14 Baron Dormer; 1 s (David Peter Gerald b 1963), 1 da (Susan Caroline Jane b 1961); *Career* WWII served Grenadier Gds 1943-46 (Hon Capt 1946); called to the Bar Inner Temple 1949 (Poland Prize in Criminal Law), prosecuting counsel for inland revenue on Oxford circuit 1965-71, dep chm Glos QS 1967-71, circuit judge 1972-; Lay Judge of Ct of Arches for Province of Canterbury and of Chancery Ct of York for Province of York 1981-; *Books* Parties and Pleasures: the Diaries of Helen Graham 1823-26 (1954); *Style*— His Honour Judge Irvine; c/o Oxford Combined Crown and County Court Centre, St Aldates, Oxford OX1 1TL

IRVINE, John Ferguson; CB (1983); s of Joseph Ferguson Irvine (d 1980), of Scotland, and Helen Dick, *née* Gardner (d 1985); *b* 13 Nov 1920; *Educ* Ardrossan Acad, Univ of Glasgow (MA); *m* 1, 1945, Doris, da of Thomas Partidge (d 1952), of Birmingham; 1 s (Graham b 1946), 1 da (Gwyneth b 1949); m 2, 1980, Christine Margot, da of Thomas Tudor, of Staffs; 2 s (Thomas b 1982, William b 1983), and 2 step s (Richard b 1970, John b 1977); *Career* Flt Lt flying boat capt Atlantic, North Sea, Indian Ocean; administrative civil servant: Scottish Office 1946, N Ireland civil servant 1948, asst sec 1959, under sec 1971, permanent sec 1976, ret 1983 as permanent sec Dept of Environment for N Ireland; seconded chief exec Ulster Transport Authy and N Ireland Transport Hldg Co 1976-78; chief exec Indust Therapy Organisation (Ulster) Ltd 1983-; *Recreations* distance running, soccer, Mallorca; *Style*— John F Irvine, Esq, CB; Industrial Therapy Organisation, Downpatrick, Co Down BT30 6HG (☎ 0396 2647)

IRVINE, Lucy; *Educ* checkered, left conventional educn and home early; 3 c; *Career* author; *Books* Castaway, Runaway, One is One; *Clubs* Chelsea Arts; *Style*— Lucy Irvine; A P Watt, 20 John Street, London WC1 4HL (☎ 071 405 6774)

IRVINE, Prof (John) Maxwell; s of John MacDonald Irvine (d 1977), of Edinburgh, and Joan Paterson, *née* Adamson (d 1982); *b* 28 Feb 1939; *Educ* George Heriot's Sch, Univ of Edinburgh (BSc), Univ of Michigan (MSc), Univ of Manchester (PhD); *m* 14 Sept 1962, Grace Irvine, da of Edward Ritchie, of Edinburgh; 1 s (Ritchie b 26 April 1971); *Career* res assoc Univ of Cornell 1966-68, head Nuclear Theory Gp SERC Daresbury Lab 1974-76; Univ of Manchester: asst lectr 1964-66, lectr 1968-73, sr lectr 1973-76, reader 1976-82, prof 1983-, dean sci 1989; vice pres IOP 1983-87 (memb Cncl 1981-87 and 1988-), chm SERC Nuclear Structure Ctee 1984-88; memb Cncl EPS 1989; FInstP 1971, FRAS 1986; *Books* Basis of Modern Physics (1967), Nuclear Structure Theory (1972), Heavy Nuclei, Super Heavy Nuclei and Neutron Stars (1975), Neutron Stars (1978); *Recreations* tennis, hill walking; *Style*— Prof Maxwell Irvine; Physics Dept, The Univ, Manchester M13 9PL (☎ 061 275 4210, fax 061 273 5867, telex 36149 JODREL G)

IRVINE, Michael Fraser; MP (C) Ipswich 1987-; s of Rt Hon Sir Arthur James Irvine, QC, MP (d 1978) of London, and Eleanor, *née* Morris; *b* 21 Oct 1939; *Educ* Rugby, Oriel Coll Oxford (BA); *Career* barr 1964-; Parly candidate (C) Bishop Auckland 1979; *Recreations* hill walking in Scotland; *Style*— Michael Irvine, Esq, MP; 1 Crown Office Row, Temple, London EC4Y 7HH (☎ 071 583 9292, telex 8953152, fax 071 353 9292)

IRVINE-COLE, Paul Frederick; s of Maj N W Cole, and Agnes, *née* Irvine; *b* 11 Sept 1942; *Educ* King's Coll Taunton; *m* 13 Feb 1976, Vanessa, da of Capt Edward Dorian Dudley-Ryder; 3 s (Alexander b 10 Nov 1977, Oliver b 18 Oct 1979, Mark b 1 Feb 1987); *Career* race horse trainer; *Recreations* tennis; *Clubs* Turf Club; *Style*— Paul Frederick Irvine-Cole, Esq; Whatcombe, nr Wantage, Oxfordshire OX12 9NW (☎ 04882 433, fax 04882 609, car 0831 475388)

IRVINE OF LAIRG, Baron (Life Peer UK 1987), of Lairg, District of Sutherland; Alexander Andrew Mackay Irvine; QC (1978); s of Alexander Irvine and Margaret Christina, da of late Alexander Macmillan; *b* 23 June 1940; *Educ* Inverness Royal Acad, Hutchesons' Boys' GS Glasgow, Glasgow Univ (MA, LLB), Christ's Coll Cambridge (BA, LLB); *m* 1974, Alison Mary, yst da of Dr James Shaw McNair, MD; 2 s (Hon David b 1974, Hon Alastair b 1976); *Career* called to the Bar Inner Temple 1967, bencher 1985, rec 1985-88; lectr LSE 1965-69; *Recreations* collecting paintings, reading, theatre, cinema; *Clubs* Garrick; *Style*— Baron Alexander Irvine of Lairg, QC; 11 King's Bench Walk, Temple, London EC4Y 7EQ (☎ 071 583 0610, fax 071 583 9123 3690, telex 884620 BARLEX)

IRVING, Barrie Leslie; s of Herbert Leslie Irving, of Jersey, CI, and Joan Fletcher, *née* Robinson (d 1976); *b* 6 Oct 1942; *Educ* Stowe, Pembroke Coll Cambridge (BA), Graduate Sch of Univ of California at Berkeley (MA); *m* 1, 11 July 1964 (m dis 1982), (Pamela) Jane, da of Capt Ronald Leese (ka 1943); 1 s (Dominic Paul b 25 May 1972), 1 da (Samantha Jane b 15 May 1968); m 2, Susan Margaret, da of Alec John Davey (d 1971); 1 s (Benjamin Alec James b 16 March 1985); *Career* psychologist and criminologist; res staff Inst of Human Devpt Univ at California Berkeley 1965-66, professional staff (later memb Mgmnt Ctee) Tavistock Inst of Human Relations London 1966-79, dir The Police Fndn 1980-; special assignments incl: conslt to the official slr for Sir Henry Fisher's Inquiry into the Murder of Maxwell Confait 1977, res conslt to the Royal Cmmn on Criminal Procedure 1979; exec cmmr and cnsllr Nat Step Families Assoc; *Books* The Psychological Dynamics of Smoking (1968), Tied Cottages in British Agriculture (1975), Police Interrogation (1980), Regulating Custodial Interviews (1988), Police Interrogation (1989); *Recreations* tennis, golf, fencing, piano; *Clubs* Naval and Military; *Style*— Barrie Irving, Esq; The Police Foundation, 314-316 Vauxhall Bridge Rd, London SW1Y 1AA (☎ 071 828 1438/9)

IRVING, Dr (John) Bruce; s of Edward James Bruges Irving (d 1976), of Balgownie, Kirkintilloch, and Marjorie Olive, *née* Dumbleton; *b* 19 June 1942; *Educ* Lenzie Acad, Univ of Glasgow (BSc, PhD), Univ of Stirling (MSc); *m* 14 June 1969, Margaret Anne, da of James Elgin McWilliam (d 1976), of Uphall, W Lothian; 2 s (Christopher b 1971, Peter b 1973), 1 da (Anna b 1978); *Career* researcher Nat Engrg Lab E Kilbride 1969-78, info systems mangr (formerly project coordinator) Chloride Tech Ltd Manchester 1978-85, dir info technol Dumfries and Galloway Regnl Cncl 1986-; Laird of Bonshaw; former pres: Ayrshire Philatelic Soc, Dumfries Philatelic Soc; FBIM 1988, FSAS 1989; *Recreations* outdoor pursuits, family history, philately; *Style*— Dr Bruce Irving; Bonshaw Tower, Kirtlebridge, Lockerbie, Dumfriesshire DG11 3LY (☎ 046 15 256)

IRVING, Sir Charles Graham; MP (C) Cheltenham Oct 1974-; s of Charles Graham Irving, of Cheltenham, and Ethel Maude, *née* Collett (d 1957); *b* 6 May 1923; *Educ* Cheltenham GS, Lucton Sch Herefordshire; *Career* chm: Irving Hotels Ltd Cheltenham and London 1964-75, Western Travel Co 1986-90 (now dir), House of Commons Catering Ctee 1979-, All Pty Gp Mental Health; conslt public affairs Dowty Gp plc 1986- (dir public relations 1964-86); treas All Pty Gp Penal Affairs; memb: Cheltenham Borough Cncl 1948- (chm of fin and policy 1959-84 and 1987-90), Gloucestershire CC 1948-81 (chm of social servs 1975-81, hon alderman 1981); Mayor of Cheltenham 1958-60 and 1971-72; chm: Stonham Housing Assoc Ltd 1974-, SW Midlands Soc; fndr memb Nat Victims' Support Schemes 1973-, vice chm NACRO 1975-, fndr pres Cheltenham and Dist Housing Assoc, pres Cheltenham and N Cotswolds Eye Therapy Tst; Freeman Borough of Cheltenham 1976; kt 1990; *Books* After-care in the Community, Case of the Meter Victims, House of Commons Cookery Book; *Recreations* antiques, social work; *Clubs* St Stephen's Constitutional, St James's; *Style*— Sir Charles Irving, MP; The Grange, Malvern Rd, Cheltenham, Glos (☎ 0242 523083); Constituency Office: Douglas House, Vittoria Walk, Cheltenham (☎ 0242 522958); House of Commons, London SW1A OAA (☎ 071 219 4095)

IRVING, (Edward) Clifford; CBE 1981; s of William Radcliffe Irving (d 1950), of Peel, IOM, and Mabel Henrietta, *née* Cottier (d 1920); *b* 24 May 1914; *Educ* Douglas HS, Chatham and Oshawa Collegiates Canada; *m* 11 Oct 1941, Norah Constance, da of Harold Page (d 1960), of Luton, Beds; 1 s (Paul Julian b 1949), 1 da (Caroline b 1953); *Career* cmmnd RA 1940, later at War Office responsible for economic matters in ex-Italian colonies under mil govt; dir Irvings Ltd 1950-84; chm: Bank of Wales (IOM) Ltd 1985-87, Etam (IOM) Ltd 1985-, Bank of Scotland (IOM) Ltd 1987-, Refuge (IOM) Ltd 1988-; memb House of Keys 1955-61, 1966-81 and 1984-87 (actg speaker 1971-81); memb IOM Govt Depts 1955-: Airports 1955-58, Assessment 1955-56, Social Security 1956, Local Govt 1956-62, Harbours 1985-87, Indust Advsy Cncl 1961-62 and 1971-81, Civil Serv Cmmn 1976-81, Indust Dept 1988-; memb: Exec Cncl IOM Govt 1968-81, Legislative Cncl IOM 1987-; chm: Exec Cncl 1977-81, IOM Tourist Bd 1971-81, IOM Sports Cncl 1971-81, IOM Harbours Bd 1985-87, IOM Govt TT Race Ctee 1971-81; pres: Douglas Angling Club, IOM Angling Assoc, Manx Parascending Club, Manx Nat Powerboat Club, Wanderers Male Voice Choir, Douglas Branch RNLI; *Recreations* powerboating, angling; *Style*— Clifford Irving, Esq, CBE; Highfield, Belmont Road, Douglas, IOM (☎ 0624 73652)

IRVING, Dr Henry Charles; s of Dr Gerald Ian Irving, of Leeds, and Sonia Carol, *née* Sinson; *b* 6 Oct 1950; *Educ* Leeds GS, King's Coll and Westminster Med Sch London Univ (MB BS); *m* 8 July 1973, (Alison) Jane, da of Peter Brackup, of Leeds; 2 da (Juliet b 1975, Georgina b 1978); *Career* conslt radiologist and head Ultrasound Dept St James's Univ Hosp Leeds 1979-, sr clinical lectr radiodiagnosis Univ of Leeds 1979-, dir radiology Seacroft Hosp Leeds 1985-; memb Cncl and hon treas Br Med Ultrasound Soc, memb specialist advsy gps on interventional radiology and ultrasound RCR; FRCR 1978; *Books* chapters in: Ultrasound in Inflammatory Diseases (1983), A Text Book of Radiology, Vol 4, The Alimentary Tract (1988), Practical Ultrasound (1988); *Recreations* golf, tennis; *Clubs* Moor Allerton Golf, Chapel Allerton Lawn Tennis; *Style*— Dr Henry Irving; 20 Clarendon Rd, Leeds LS2 9PF (☎ 0532 452232)

IRVING, Hon Stephen John; o s of Baron Irving of Dartford, PC, DL (Life Peer, d 1989), and Mildred, *née* Weedy; *b* 11 Nov 1959; *Educ* Dartford GS; *m* 11 Aug 1984, Lesley Anne, yr da of Richard Neil Herbert (d 1987), of Wilmington, Kent; 1 da (Emily Rebecca b 30 Oct 1990); *Career* banker; membership sec Dartford & District Twinning Assoc, treas Dartford Football Club Supporters Assoc; *Recreations* travel, theatre, football; *Style*— The Hon Stephen Irving; 25 Princes Ave, Dartford, Kent DA2 6NF (☎ 0322 229041)

IRVING, (James) Wyllie; TD; s of John Irving, MBE (d 1931), and Jessie Howatson Mitchell Wyllie (d 1925); *b* 21 April 1914; *Educ* Fettes, Univ of Glasgow; *m* 31 March 1937, Henrietta Mary, da of Henry Purcell (d 1940), of Co Dublin; 2 da (Christine b 1946, Pamela b 1948); *Career* Maj Cheshire Regt 1939-45; KOSB (TA) 1948-59; controller SW Scot Civil Def Gp 1960-68; slr; ptnr Primrose and Gordon Dumfries 1937-; memb Bd Mgmnt Dumfries and Galloway Hosps 1965-71 (chm 1968-71); chm: Bd of Mgmnt Dumfries and Galloway and Crichton Royal Hosps 1972-74, Dumfries and Galloway Health Bd 1973-80; sec: County of Dumfries Valuation Appeal Ctee 1956-72, SW Scot Local Employment Ctee 1960-74, Local Bd of Dirs Scot Union & Nat Insur Co 1973-85; dir Dumfries Trading Estate Ltd 1961-89; SSC, Hon Sheriff South Strathclyde Dumfries and Galloway 1963-, Notary Public; *Recreations* reading, gardening; *Style*— J Wyllie Irving, Esq, TD; Kirkbrae (The Old Manse), Lochrutton, Nr Dumfries DG2 8NH (☎ 038 773 301); 92 Irish St, Dumfries (☎ Dumfries 67316)

IRVING OF DARTFORD, Baroness; Mildred; *née* Weedy; da of Charlton Weedy, of Morpeth; *m* 1942, Baron Irving of Dartford, PC, DL (Life Peer, d 1989); 1 s (Hon Stephen John, *qv*), 1 da (Hon Susan Anne (Hon Mrs House), *qv*) (and 1 s decd); *Style*— The Rt Hon the Lady Irving of Dartford; 10 Tynedale Close, Dartford, Kent (☎ 0322 225105)

IRWIN, Basil William Seymour; MC (1945), TD (1946 2 Clasps), DL (Greater London 1967); s of Maj William James Irwin (d 1960); *b* 27 May 1919; *Educ* Tonbridge; *m* 1949, Eleanor Ruth, da of Edwin Burgess; *Career* Brevet Col, served Europe and ME; TAVR, ADC to HM The Queen 1968-73; former merchant banker, vice chm Ionian Bank Ltd until 1978; dir: Archimedes Investment Trust plc, Grahams Rintoul Investment Trust plc; *Clubs* Special Forces; *Style*— Basil Irwin, Esq, MC, TD, DL; The Thatch, Stansted, Essex (☎ 0279 812207)

IRWIN, Maj-Gen Brian St George; CB (1975); s of Lt-Col Alfred Percy Bulteel Irwin, DSO (d 1976), of Maumfin, Moyard, Co Galway, and Eileen, *née* Holberton (d 1974); *b* 16 Sept 1917; *Educ* Rugby, RMA Woolwich, Trinity Hall Cambridge (MA); *m* 23 Dec 1939, Audrey Lilla, da of Lt-Col Hugh Barkley Steen, IMS (d 1951), of

Dunboe, Shepperton-on-Thames, Middx; 2 s (Michael St George b 1940, (Brian) Christopher b 1946); *Career* cmmnd 2 Lt RE 1937; WWII served: Western Desert 1941-43 (despatches), Sicily and Italy 1943-44 (despatches), Greece 1944-45; Cyprus 1956-59 (despatches) and 1961-63, dir of mil survey MOD 1965-69, Maj-Gen 1969-74, dir gen Ordnance Survey 1969-77, ret Army 1974; under sec Civil Serv 1974-77; Col Cmdt RE 1977-82; FRICS 1949- (memb Cncl 1969-70 and 1972-76), FRGS 1960- (memb Cncl 1966-70, vice pres 1974-77); *Recreations* golf, fishing, genealogy; *Clubs* Army and Navy; *Style*— Maj-Gen Brian Irwin, CB; 16 Northerwood House, Swan Green, Lyndhurst, Hampshire SO43 7DT (☎ 0703 283499)

IRWIN, Christopher Conran; s of John Conran Irwin, of Petersfield, Hants, and Helen Hermione, *née* Fletcher; *b* 2 April 1948; *Educ* Bedales Sch, Univ of Sussex; *m* Stephanie Jane, da of Hilary Noble Ball (d 1972); 1 s (John) Phineas Hilary b 1978), 2 da (Bryony b 1972, Tamsin b 1974); *Career* freelance broadcaster BBC Radio Brighton 1968-69, Fed Tst for Educn and Res 1969-75, sr visiting fell Univ of Sussex 1972-73, current affrs prodr BBC 1975, sec BBC Scot 1978-80, head of radio Scot 1980-82, gen mangr DBS Devpt 1982-85, fndr promoter Br Satellite Bdcasting Ltd and gen mangr New Media Pearson plc 1986-87, special advsr to DG BBC 1988-89, controller of resources and admin BBC World Serv 1989-; memb: Tport Users Consultative Ctee for W of England, Bd John Logie Baird Inst; dir Caribbean Relay Co; *Books* The Security of Western Europe (with Sir Bernard Burrows, 1972), Electing the European Parliament (1973); *Recreations* industrial archaeology, walking, timetables, music; *Style*— Christopher Irwin, Esq; Bourton House, Bourton, Bishops Cannings, Devizes, Wiltshire (☎ 0380 86 252); BBC World Service, Bush House, London WC2B 4PH (☎ 071 257 2551, 071 379 6841, telex 265781)

IRWIN, Prof David George; s of George Archibald Raven Irwin (d 1973), of London, and Doris, *née* Tetlow (d 1988); *b* 24 June 1933; *Educ* Holgate GS Barnsley, Queen's Coll Oxford (MA, open exhibitioner, winner the Laurence Binyon prize), Courtauld Inst of Art Univ of London (PhD); *m* 26 March 1960, Francina Mary, da of Richard Kaikhrusru Sorabji (d 1950), of Oxford; 1 s (Dickon b 1966), 1 da (Saskia b 1963); *Career* Nat Serv 1951-53, Capt RAEC 1952-53; lectr in history of fine art and asst keeper of univ art collections Univ of Glasgow 1959-70, prof of history of art and head of Dept Univ of Aberdeen 1970-; memb Ed Bd of British Journal for Eighteenth Century Studies, pres Br Soc for Eighteenth Century Studies; memb Ctee: Aberdeen Art Gallery, Architectural Heritage Soc of Scotland; memb: Art Panel of Scottish Arts Cncl, Cncl of Walpole Soc, Cncl of Europe Exhibition Ctee 1972; FSA 1968, FRSA 1974; *Books* English Neoclassical Art (1966), Paul Klee (1968), Visual Arts, Taste and Criticism (1969), Winckelmann: Writings on Art (1972), Designs and Ornaments of the Empire Style (1974), Scottish Painters: At Home and Abroad 1700 to 1900 (jtly with Francina Irwin, 1975), John Flaxman: Sculptor, Illustrator, Designer (1979); *Recreations* swimming, aerobics, walking, gardening, travel; *Style*— Professor David Irwin, FSA

IRWIN, (Frederick George) Ernest; s of George Irwin, and Margaret Irwin; *b* 19 Nov 1933; *Educ* Trinity Coll Dublin (BA, BAI), Univ of Iowa State (MSc); *m* 11 Sept 1964, Juliet Faith, da of Antony Alexander Fitzgerald Tatlow; 1 s (George b 14 April 1972), 2 da (Katharine b 19 March 1969, Aisling b 31 May 1966); *Career* area engr DuPont Construction 1958-61; Ove Arup and Ptnrs: design engr London 1961-64, chief engr Ghana 1964-68, regnl assoc 1968-75, dir 1975- (head of Birmingham office responsible for: engrg design of Int Convention Centre Birmingham, Nat Exhibition Centre extension, land reclamation projects); dir Ove Arup Partnership 1989; chm: ICE Res Sub-Ctee 1985-87, ICE Research Focus, ICE Structures and Bldg Bd, ICE report construction res and devpt (published 1987); memb: ICE Cncl 1985-87 and 1989-, Ctee Birmingham Good Design Initiative; tstee Lench's Tst; FICE, FIStructE; *Recreations* golf, drawing; *Clubs* Edgbaston Golf; *Style*— Ernest Irwin, Esq; 46 Selly Wick Rd, Selly Park, Birmingham B29 7JA; Ove Arup & Ptnrs, 3 Duchess Place, Edgbaston, Birmingham, B16 8NH (☎ 021 454 6261, fax 021 454 8853, telex 339468)

IRWIN, Felicity Ann; JP (Poole 1985); da of Lt-Col Arthur Thomas Begg Green, ED (d 1982), and Doris, Lady Pechell, *qv*; *b* 7 June 1947; *Educ* Queen Margaret Coll Wellington NZ; *m* 12 March 1969, (Alastair) Giles Irwin, s of Dr Desmond Irwin, of Clarendon House, Woodford Green, Essex; 3 da (Charlotte Ann b 26 Aug 1970, Candida Jane b 21 Dec 1973, Claudia b 14 Dec 1976); *Career* regnl exec Television South 1987-; hon sec Wessex Branch IOD; chm: Dorset Family Conciliation Serv, Poole and East Dorset Branch NSPCC; MInstD 1977, MIPR 1988; *Recreations* royal tennis, lawn tennis, water skiing; *Style*— Mrs Giles Irwin, JP; Stanbridge House, Stanbridge, Wimborne, Dorset BH21 4JD (☎ 0258 840129); TVS, Poole Art Centre, Poole, Dorset (☎ 0202 684375, fax 0202 682263)

IRWIN, (David) Gwyther Broome; s of Gwyther William Powell (d 1960), and Barbara Ethel, *née* Dallimore; *b* 7 May 1931; *Educ* Bryanston, Central Sch of Art & Design; *m* 10 April 1960, Elizabeth Anne, da of Robert Gowlett; 2 s (Brom Gwyther Giles b 1 Oct 1962, Capel Robert Powell b 10 April 1967), 1 da (Charlotte Alicia Estelle b 26 Dec 1963); *Career* artist; lectr: Bath Acad of Art 1963, Hornsey Coll of Art 1966, Chelsea Sch of Art 1967-69; head of fine art Brighton Poly 1969-84; designed and cut Rectangular Relief for BP House 1965-68; solo exhibitons: Gallery One 1957, AIA Gallery 1957, ICA 1958, Gimpel Fils (various years 1959-87), New Art Centre 1973, 1975, 1977, Newcastle Poly Gallery 1978, Kettle's Yard Cambridge 1981; group exhibitions incl: Young Contemporaries 1953, Paris Biennale 1960, Collage (Museum of Modern Art NY) 1961, John Moores Liverpool Exhibitions 1961, 1963, 1978, British Kunst Denmark 1963, XXXII Venice Biennale 1964, Recent British Painting (Tate) 1967, Contemporary British Painting (Albright Knox Art Gallery USA) 1974, Three Decades of Artists (Royal Acad) 1983, Recalling the 50s (Serpentine Gallery) 1985, Print 86 (Barbican) 1986, Summer Show (Royal Acad) 1986; works in public collections incl: Tate, Arts Cncl of GB, DOE, Peggy Guggenheim Venice, Yale; works incl: *paper collages* Room at the Top, The Springer, Pinky I and II; *constructions* String-gent, Rise and Fall; *acrylic on canvas* The Avid Aviator, Double Torque; *watercolours* Bird of Fate, Close-up, Study for Portrait; memb Cncl of Nat Academic Awards 1971-78; Greater London Arts Assoc Award 1978; *Recreations* poker, chess, golf, wind-surfing; *Clubs* Chelsea Arts, Stenodoc Golf; *Style*— Gwyther Irwin, Esq; 21 Hillbury Rd, London SW17 8JT (☎ 081 673 7930); 2 The Glyddins, Rock, Wadebridge, Cornwall (☎ 0208 863186)

IRWIN, Ian Sutherland; CBE (1982); s of Andrew Campbell Irwin (d 1967), of Glasgow, and Elizabeth Ritchie, *née* Arnott; *b* 20 Feb 1933; *Educ* Whitehill Sr Secdy Sch Glasgow, Univ of Glasgow (BL); *m* 2 May 1959, (Margaret Miller) Maureen, da of John Scoullar Irvine (d 1990), of Edinburgh; 2 s (Graeme Andrew b 1961, Derek John b 1965); *Career* Nat Serv Sgt RAPC attached to 1 Bn Seaforth Highlanders 1957-59; Hon Col 154 Regt RCT (V) 1986-; accountant Kirkcaldy Linoleum Market 1959-60, commercial mangr Scottish Omnibuses Ltd 1960-64; Scottish Transport Group: gp accountant 1965-68, gp sec 1969-75, dir and md 1975-86, chm and chief exec 1987-; non-exec dir Scottish Mortgage & Trust 1986-, dir Scottish Business in the Community; memb Cncl CBI and CBI Scotland, hon vice pres Int Union Public Tport, pres Bus and Coach Cncl 1979-80, vice pres Inst of Tport 1984-87; ACA, CIPFA, FCIT, CBIM, FInstD; *Recreations* golf, foreign travel, reading; *Clubs* Caledonian, MCC; *Style*— Ian Irwin, Esq, CBE; 10 Moray Place, Edinburgh (☎ 031 225 6454); Scottish Tport Gp, 114/116 George St, Edinburgh EH2 4LX (☎ 031 226 7491)

IRWIN, Lord; James Charles Wood; s and h of 3 Earl of Halifax; *b* 24 Aug 1977; *Style*— Lord Irwin; Garrowby, York YO4 1QD

IRWIN, Dr Michael Henry Knox; s of William Knox Irwin, FRCS, MD (d 1973), of Watford Heath, Herts, and Edith Isabel Mary, *née* Collins; descendant of John Knox; *b* 5 June 1931; *Educ* Merchant Taylors' Sch, St Bart's Hosp London (MB BS), Columbia Univ NY (MPH); *m* 1, 1958 (m dis 1982), Elizabeth Miriam, *née* Naumann; 3 da (Christina, Pamela, Diana); m 2, 1983, Frederica Todd, da of Frederick Gordon Harlow, of Savannah, Ga, USA; *Career* physician; joined UN 1957, UN medical dir 1969-73, dir of personnel UN Devpt Programme 1973-76, UNICEF rep in Bangladesh 1977-80, sr advsr UNICEF 1980-82, medical dir UN, UNDP and UNICEF 1982-89, dir Health Servs Dept World Bank 1989-90; conslt American Assoc of Blood Banks 1984-90, advsr Action Cncl 1990-91; Offr Cross Int Fedn of Blood Donor Organisations 1984; *Books* Overweight: a Problem for Millions (1964), What Do We Know About Allergies? (1972), Nuclear Energy: Good or Bad? (1984), The Cocaine Epidemic (1985), Can We Survive Nuclear War? (1985), Talpa (1990); *Recreations* travelling, bicycling, writing; *Clubs* Royal Soc of Medicine (London); *Style*— Dr Michael Irwin; 15 Hovedene, 95 Cromwell Rd, Hove, Sussex BN3 3EH

ISAAC, David Ward; s of Augustus William Isaac, of Westmead, Willoughby, Boston, Lincs, and Jessica Doreen, *née* Beaulah; *b* 23 June 1933; *Educ* Bootham Sch York; *m* 14 Sept 1957, Eileen Mary, da of Reginald Lennard Victor Hayman (d 1972); 2 s (Martin b 1961, Stephen b 1972), 2 da (Jennifer b 1959, Heather b 1965); *Career* Nat Serv RMP 1950-52; md: GN Beulah Ltd 1961, Thomas Linnell (Boston) Ltd 1972 (main dir Bd Thomas Linell & Sons Ltd Northampton 1976), Appleby & Sons Ltd Bristol 1983, Appleby Westward Ltd 1984 (and for gp 1988); regnl dir Amalgamated Foods Ltd 1980, regnl chm Nat Guild of Spar Grocers; *Recreations* tennis, swimming, walking; *Clubs* Tavistock and Whitchurch Tennis, Tavistock GC; *Style*— David Isaac, Esq; Appleby Westwald GP plc, PO Box 3, Callington Rd, Saltash, Cornwall PL12 6LT (☎ 0752 843171, telex 45106)

ISAACS *see also*: Rufus Isaacs

ISAACS, Dame Albertha Madeline; DBE (1974); da of late Robert Hanna, and Lilla, *née* Minns; *b* 18 April 1900; *Educ* Cosmopolitan HS and Victoria HS Nassau; *m* ; 3 s, 1 da; *Career* memb Progressive Liberal Party, senator 1968-72, memb of PLP's Nat Gen Cncl and of Cncl of Women; *Style*— Dame Albertha Isaacs, DBE; c/o Progressive Liberal Party, Head Office, Nassau, Bahamas

ISAACS, Dr Anthony Donald; s of David Isaacs, of London, and Rosa, *née* Hockman; *b* 18 Jan 1931; *Educ* Univ of London, Charing Cross Hosp London Univ (MB BS, DPM); *m* 15 Dec 1963, Elissa, da of Isaac Cedar (d 1977), 1 s (Timothy b 13 Sept 1967), 1 da (Catharine b 28 Oct 1964); *Career* Nat Serv RAMC Lt to Capt 1955-57; conslt psychiatrist: Bethlem Royal and Maudsley Hosp 1963-90, Charter Nightingale Hosp (serv dir Adult Psychiatry); sub dean Inst of Psychiatry Univ of London 1982-90; vice chm Grants Ctee King Edward's Hosp Fund for London; Freeman City of London 1962; FRCP, FRCPsych, FRSM; *Books* Studies in Geriatric Psychiatry (1978), Psychiatric Examination in Clinical Practice (1981, 3 edn 1990); *Style*— Dr Anthony Isaacs; 138 Harley St, London W1H 1AH (☎ 071 935 1963/0554)

ISAACS, Anthony Hyman; s of Eric Hyman Isaacs (d 1985), and Marjorie Josephine, *née* Solomon (d 1983); *b* 9 Aug 1934; *Educ* Cheltenham Coll, Pembroke Coll Cambridge (BA); *m* 31 March 1964, Jennifer Irene, JP, da of Sir James Cameron, CBE, TD, *qv*; 3 s (Roderick b 1968, Matthew b 1972, Oliver b 1976), 2 da (Jessica b 1966, Diana b 1970); *Career* RN 1952-54, Sub Lt RNVR; Stephenson Harwood (formerly Stephenson Harwood & Tatham): articled to Sir Anthony Lousada 1957-60, ptnr 1964, sr ptnr 1987; dir: Thornton & Co Limited, Andrew Weir & Company Limited; co-opted memb Co Law Ctee of the Law Soc; memb: Slr's Disciplinary Tbnl 1988, Cncl Peper Harow Fndn, Advsy Ctee The Rehearsal Orchestra, Law Soc; *Recreations* music, gardening, reading, theatre; *Clubs* Garrick; *Style*— Anthony Isaacs, Esq; One St Paul's Churchyard, London, EC4M 8SH (☎ 071 329 4422, fax 071 606 0822, telex 886789 SHSPC G)

ISAACS, Dr Anthony John; s of Benjamin H Isaacs, of Finchley, and Lily, *née* Rogol; *b* 22 Oct 1942; *Educ* Wanstead County HS, Hertford Coll Oxford (BA), Westminster Med Sch (MA, BM BCh); *m* 1, 12 Dec 1971 (m dis), Jill, da of Paul Elek (d 1976), of Highgate; q s (Jeremy b 1973, Adrian b 1976, Nicholas (twin b 1976); m 2, 24 Oct 1986, Edie Lynda, *née* Friedman; 1 da (Anna b 1988); *Career* Dept of Health: SMO Meds Div 1984-5, PMO Meds Div and assessor Ctee on Safety of Meds 1985-86, sr PMO, under sec and head of Med Manpower and Educn Div 1986-;hon conslt endocrinologist Middx Hosp and UCH 1986-; memb steering gps for the implementation of achieving a balance and on undergraduate med and dental educn, memb Ministerial Group on Jr Doctors' Hours; parent govr Hendon Sch; MRCP 1971; *Books* Anorexia Nervosa (with P Dally and J Gomez, 1979); *Recreations* table tennis, music, cinema; *Clubs* Royal Society of Medicine; *Style*— Dr Anthony Isaacs; Department of Health, Portland Court, 158-176 Great Portland St, London W1N 5TB (☎ 071 872 9302)

ISAACS, Prof Bernard; CBE (1989); s of Louis Isaacs (d 1972), of Glasgow, and Rosine Naomi, *née* Lion (d 1958); *b* 20 July 1924; *Educ* Kilmarnock Acad, Glasgow Univ (MB ChB, MD); *m* 27 Aug 1957, Dorothy Beulah, da of Abe Berman (d 1959), of Glasgow; 4 s (Lionel b 1959, Aubrey b 1962, Michael b 1962, Alick b 1968); *Career* Capt (formerly Lt) RAMC 1948-50; conslt physician in geriatric med: Forest Hall Hosp Glasgow 1961-64, Glasgow Royal Infirmary 1964-74; Charles Hayward prof of geriatric med Univ of Birmingham 1975-89; dir Centre for Applied Gerontology Univ of Birmingham 1989-; memb: S Birmingham Health Authy 1981-85, Br Geriatric Soc 1957-89, Chest Heart and Stroke Assoc, Age Concern, Centre for Policy on Ageing; FRCP (Glasgow 1961, Edinburgh 1974, London 1986); *Books* Introduction to Geriatrics (1969), Survival of the Unfittest (1971), Giants of Geriatrics (1989); *Style*— Prof Bernard Isaacs, CBE; 33 Greville Drive, Birmingham B15 2UU (☎ 021 440 3418); Centre for Applied Gerontology, Hayward Building, Selly Oak Hospital, Birmingham B29 6JL (☎ 021 472 5313, ext 4109)

ISAACS, Geoffrey Lewis; s of Laurence Isaacs (d 1955), of 8 Pembroke Rd, Moor Park, Northwood, Middx, and Gladys Rachel, *née* Jacobs (d 1982); *b* 29 Sept 1935; *Educ* Merchant Taylors', Coll of Law; *m* 23 Sept 1960, (Barbara) Jane, da of Charles Stanley Catlow, of 66 Church Rd, Weston Favell, Northampton; 2 s (Mark b 1961, Tom b 1968), 1 da (Caroline b 1964); *Career* admitted slr 1958, ptnr Tarlo Lyons 1960; dir: Kerax Ltd, Whippendell Electrical Manufacturing Co (Watford) Ltd, Soil Structures International Ltd, OH1 UK Ltd, Servequip Ltd, Broadoak Flexible Packaging Ltd, Packaging Ltd, Ralvin Pacific Properties Inc California; Freeman: City of London 1979, Worshipful Co of Painter Stainers 1979; memb Law Soc 1958; *Recreations* golf, travel, theatre, walking; *Clubs* City Livery, Moor Park Golf, Old Merchant Taylors'; *Style*— Geoffrey Isaacs, Esq; Benthills, 1 Kings Farm Rd, Chorleywood, Herts WD3 5HF (☎ 092328 3340); High Holborn House, 52/54 High Holborn, London WC1V 6RU (☎ 071 405 2000, fax 071 405 3976, telex 267572)

ISAACS, Jeremy Israel; s of Isidore Isaacs, and Sara, *née* Jacobs; *b* 28 Sept 1932; *Educ* Glasgow Acad, Merton Coll Oxford (MA, pres Oxford Union); *m* 1, 1958, Tamara (d 1986); 1 s, 1 da; m 2, 1988, Gillian Mary; *Career* television prodr; prodr:

Granada TV 1958-63 (progs incl What the Papers Say, All Our Yesterdays), Associated-Rediffusion 1963-65 (This Week), BBC 1965-67 (Panorama); Associated-Rediffusion (renamed Thames Television 1968): controller of features 1967-74, dir of progs 1974-78, prodr The World at War 1974, conslt Hollywood series; ind prodr: A Sense of Freedom (Scottish TV), Ireland - A Television History (13 part series BBC TV); chief exec Channel 4 1981-87, gen dir Royal Opera House 1988- (dir 1985-88); awarded: Desmond Davis award for outstanding contrib to TV 1972, George Polk Meml award 1973, Cyril Bennett award for outstanding contrib to TV programming (RTS) 1982; govr BFI 1979, memb Bd Open Coll 1986-; Hon DLitt: Univ of Strathclyde 1984, Univ of Bristol 1988; Cdr Order of Arts and Letters France 1988; *Recreations* walking, reading; *Style—* Jeremy Isaacs, Esq; Royal Opera House, 45 Floral St, London WC2

ISAAMAN, Gerald Michael; s of Asher Isaaman (d 1975), and Lily Finklestein; *b* 22 Dec 1933; *Educ* Dame Alice Owens GS; *m* 1962, Delphine, da of Arnold Bertram Walker, of Whitby, Yorks; 1 s (Daniel); *Career* journalist; N London Observer Series 1950, gen mangr Hampstead and Highgate Express 1990- (joined 1955, ed 1968-); chm: Mgmnt Bd Camden Arts Tst 1970-82, Exhibitions Ctee Camden Arts Centre 1971-82, Russell Housing Soc 1976-82, Tstees King's Cross Disaster Fund 1987-89; memb: Camden Festival Tst 1982-, Bd Assoc of Br Eds 1985-; fndr tstee Arkwright Arts Tst 1971; *Recreations* listening to jazz, collecting postcards, pontificating; *Style—* Gerald Isaaman, Esq; 9 Lyndhurst Rd, Hampstead, London NW3 5PX (☎ 071 794 3950); Hampstead and Highgate Express, Marlborough House, 179/189 Finchley Rd, London NW3 6LB (☎ 071 794 5691)

ISDELL-CARPENTER, Peter; s of Richard Isdell-Carpenter, OBE (d 1986), and Rosemary, *née* Ashworth; *b* 18 Nov 1940; *Educ* Marlborough, St John's Coll Oxford (BA); *m* 28 Sept 1966, Antoinette, da of Louis Cass (d 1952); 1 s (Simon b 1968), 2 da (Katherine b 1968, Nicola b 1970); *Career* Birds Eye Foods Ltd 1964-69, Grey Advertising 1969-70, dir Young and Rubicam Advertising Ltd 1970-78, md Sea Tack Ltd 1978-81, dir of mktg Young and Rubicam (Europe) Ltd 1981-; *Recreations* sailing, skiing, music; *Clubs* Boodle's, Sloane; *Style—* Peter Isdell-Carpenter, Esq; The Manor House, Newton Valence, nr Alton, Hants (☎ 0420 58295); Young and Rubicam Europe Ltd, Greater London House, Hampstead Rd, London NW1 (☎ 071 387 9366, car 0836 253 800)

ISHAM, Sir Ian Vere Gyles; 13 Bt (E 1627), of Lamport, Northamptonshire; s of Lt-Col Vere Arthur Richard Isham, MC (d 1968), and suc to kinsman Sir Gyles Isham, 12 Bt (d 1976); *b* 17 July 1923; *Educ* Eton, Worcester Coll Oxford; *Heir* bro, Norman Isham (*qv*); *Career* marketing analyst and cartographer; *Clubs* Overseas; *Style—* Sir Ian Isham, Bt; 40 Turnpike Link, Croydon, Surrey (☎ 081 686 1256)

ISHAM, Norman Murray Crawford; OBE; s of late Lt-Col Vere Arthur Richard Isham, MC; hp of bro, Sir Ian Isham, 13 Bt; *b* 28 Jan 1930; *Educ* Stowe, Univ of Cape Town (B Arch); *m* 1956, Joan, da of late Leonard James Genet, of Umtali, Zimbabwe; 2 s, 1 da; *Career* architect, civil serv; memb RIBA; *Style—* Norman Isham, Esq, OBE; 5 Langton Way, Park Hill, Croydon, Surrey CRO 5JS

ISHIGURO, Kazuo; s of Shizuo Ishiguro, and Shizuko Michida; *b* 8 Nov 1954; *Educ* Woking Co GS, Univ of Kent (BA), Univ of East Anglia (MA); *m* Lorna Anne, da of Nicol Mackechnie MacDougall; *Career* author; novels: A Pale View of the Hills (1982, Winifred Holtby award 1983), An Artist of the Floating World (1986, Whitbread Book of the Year 1987), The Remains of the Day (1989, Booker prize 1989); TV plays: A Profile of Arthur J Mason (broadcast 1984), The Gourmet (broadcast 1987); work translated into 22 foreign languages; memb: Soc of Authors 1989, PEN 1989, RSL 1989, Royal Soc for the Encouragement of Arts, Manufactures and Commerce 1990; *Recreations* playing musical instruments; *Style—* Kazuo Ishiguro, Esq; Rogers, Coleridge and White Ltd, 20 Powis Mews, London W11 1JN (☎ 071 221 3717, fax 071 229 9084)

ISLES, Maj-Gen Donald Edward; CB (1978), OBE (1968), DL (Lincs 1990); s of Harold Isles (d 1956), and Kathleen, *née* Trenam (d 1979); *b* 19 July 1924; *Educ* Roundhay Sch Leeds, Univ of Leeds, RMCS, Jt Serv Staff Coll; *m* 1948, Sheila Mary, *née* Thorpe; 3 s, 1 da; *Career* cmmnd Duke of Wellington's Regt 1943; CO 1 DWR 1965-67, Col GS Royal Armaments Res and Devpt Estab 1971-72, dir of Munitions Br Def Staff Washington 1972-75, dir-gen of Weapons MOD 1975-78, Col DWR 1975-82, ret; dir and dep mangr British Manufacturing & Research Co Ltd Grantham 1979-89, def advsr Astra Holdings plc London 1989-; *Recreations* squash, tennis, shooting; *Clubs* MCC, Army and Navy; *Style—* Maj-Gen Donald Isles, CB, OBE, DL; c/o Lloyds Bank plc, Cox's & King's Branch, 7 Pall Mall, London SW1Y 5NA (☎ office 071 495 3747)

ISRAEL, Rev Dr Martin Spencer; s of Elie Benjamin Israel (d 1980), of Johannesburg, SA, and Minnie, *née* Israel (d 1957); *b* 30 April 1927; *Educ* Parktown Boys HS Johannesburg SA, Univ of the Witwatersrand SA (MB ChB); *Career* RAMC 1955-57, Capt; registrar in pathology Royal Hosp Wolverhampton 1953-55; RCS: res fell in pathology 1957-60, lectr in microbiology 1961-66, sr lectr in pathology 1967-81, hon lectr 1982; curate St Michael Cornhill London 1974-76, asst priest Holy Trinity with All Saints S Kensington 1977-82 (priest i/c 1983); pres Churches' Fellowship for Psychical and Spiritual Studies; MRCP 1952, FRCPath 1975; *Books* General Pathology (with J B Walter, 1963), Summons to Life (1974), Precarious Living (1976), Smouldering Fire (1978), The Pain that Heals (1981), Living Alone (1982), The Spirit of Counsel (1983), Healing as Sacrament (1984), The Discipline of Love (1985), Coming in Glory (1986), Gethsemane (1987), The Pearl of Great Price (1988), The Dark Face of Reality (1989), The Quest for Wholeness (1989), Creation (1989), Night Thoughts (1990), A Light on the Path (1990); *Style—* The Rev Dr Martin Israel; Flat 2, 26 Tregunter Rd, London SW10 9LH

ISSA, Moneim; s of Mustapha Issa (d 1987), of Alexandria, Egypt, and Zakeya, *née* Zaky; *b* 21 Aug 1939; *Educ* Abbesseya HS Alexandria, Univ of Alexandria (BChD); *m* 1962, Christa Sylvia, da of Balthasar Sima (d 1973), of Marquartstein, Germany; 1 s (Thomas b 1963), 1 da (Alexandra b 1971); *Career* lectr Univ of Alexandria 1961-62, clinical asst Eatman Dental Hosp 1964-65, sr house surgn Leicester Royal Infirmary 1966, sr registrar Bart's Hosp 1969-73 (registrar 1966-68), conslt oral and maxillofacial surgn and postgrad tutor W Middx Univ Hosp 1973-79, conslt oral and maxillofacial surgn to Oxford RHA and E Berks Dist 1973-, conslt to BA in oral and maxillofacial surgery 1986-; former chm BDA Windsor Section, memb Windsor Med Soc; FFD RCSI 1968, FDS RCS 1969, fell Br Assoc of Oral and Maxillofacial Surgns 1973, memb Hosp Conslts and Specialists Assoc 1974; *Books* Oral Surgery Section: Hamlyn Medical Encyclopaedia (1978), Maxillo Facial Injuris Section: Operative Plastic & Reconstructive Surgery (1980); *Recreations* tennis, skiing, waterskiing, chess; *Style—* Moneim Issa, Esq; St Bernards, Oak End Way, Gerrards Cross, Bucks SL9 8DB (☎ 0753 888123); Consulting Rooms: Alma Medica, 47 Alma Rd, Windsor; Hospitals: King Edward VII, Windsor, Wrexham Park Hospital, Slough, St Mark's Hospital, Maidenhead, Princess Margaret Hospital, Windsor, Mount Vernon Hospital, Northwood, Middlesex (☎ 0753 868754, fax 0753 886633, telex 846246 ISSA)

ISSERLIS, Steven John; s of George Isserlis, and Cynthia Saville; *b* 19 Dec 1958; *Educ* City of London Sch, Int Cello Centre, Oberlin Coll Ohio; *m* Pauline Anne Mara; 1 s (Gabriel Mara b 26 April 1990); *Career* cellist; recitals and concerts all over Europe, N America and USSR; invited by: all maj Br orchs, Chicago Symphony, Minnesota Orch, Montreal Symphony, Boston Symphony, various important Euro and Scandinavian orchs; played with: Eng Baroque Soloists, London Classical Players; works with conductors incl: Edo de Waart, Christoph Eschenbach, Andre Previn, Roger Norrington, Richard Hickox, John Eliot Gardiner, Oliver Knussen, Andrew Litton; has played a leading role in many prestigious chamber music projects incl his own festival Schumann and his Circle (Wigmore Hall London), gave string section masterclass BBC Young Musician of the Year 1990; recordings incl: Elgar Cello Concerto Opus 85, Bloch Schelomo (with LSO, conductor Richard Hickox, Virgin Classics, 1989), Kabalevsky Concerto No 2, Prokofiev Concertino Opus 132 and Andante Opus 133 (with London Philharmonic Orch, conductor Andrew Litton, Virgin Classics, 1989), Debussy, Poulenc, Frank Sonatas (with Pascal Devoyon, Virgin Classics, 1989), Tchaikovsky works for cello and orchestra (with Chamber Orchestra of Europe, conductor John Eliot Gardiner, Virgin Classics, 1990), works by Brahms, Fauré Martinu (Hyperion, 1985-89); *Recreations* sleeping, eating, talking, generally wasting time (my own and others'); *Style—* Steven Isserlis, Esq; Harrison & Parrott Ltd, 12 Penzance Place, London W11 4PA (☎ 071 229 9166, fax 071 221 5042)

ISTED, Barrington James (Barry); s of James William Isted (d 1978), of Croydon, and Gwendolyne Irene, *née* Fleetwood; *b* 12 July 1935; *Educ* Wallington County GS Surrey, Univ of Nottingham (BA); *m* 31 May 1963, Glenda Jeanne, da of Thomas Leonard Bunyan, of Broxbourne, Herts; 2 s (Jonathan b 1964, Daniel b 1965); *Career* corporate ed: Pyrene Ltd 1957-58, Formica Ltd 1958-59; dir of personnel: Potterton Int Ltd 1968-72, De La Rue Gp 1977-88 (corp ed 1960-63, pubns mangr 1963-65, trg offr 1965-67, manpower controller 1973-77); co sec De La Rue Co plc 1985-88; pres Br Assoc of Ind Eds 1989- (nat chm 1967-68, chm of Senate 1981-84, vice-pres 1984-89), govr London Business Sch 1984-87 (chm Business Liason Ctee); memb: Industl Tribunals for Eng and Wales 1984-, London Bd of Crimestoppers 1987-88; Freeman: City of London 1987, Worshipful Co of Makers of Playing Cards 1987; fell Br Assoc of Industl Eds 1968, FBIM 1980; Fedn of Euro Industl Eds Assoc Dip of Honour 1975; *Books* British Industry's Editors and Their Views (1981); *Recreations* writing, travel, food and drink; *Clubs* Reform; *Style—* Barry Isted, Esq; Pinnacles, Hatfield Broad Oak, Bishops Stortford, Hertfordshire CM22 7HS (☎ 027970 397)

IVANOVIĆ, Vane Ivan Stevan; s of Dr Ivan R Ivanović (d 1949), of Zagreb, and Milica, *née* Popović (d 1969); *b* 9 June 1913; *Educ* Westminster, Peterhouse Cambridge (BA, MA); *m* 1939, June Veronica, da of Rev John L Fisher, Canon of Colchester (d 1970); 2 s (Ivan Božidar, Andrija), 1 da (Milica); *Career* serv WWII, Middle E & Italy, Maj; chm: Yugoslav Shipping Ctee 1941 (memb 1941-45), Assoc of Free Yugoslavs 1949-69, Ivanovic & Co 1949-67; consul gen Monaco in London 1967-89; Offr Order of Grimaldi (Monaco) 1975; *Recreations* diving and spear fishing, track and field athletics, jogging, sailing; *Clubs* White's, MCC, Brooks's; *Style—* Vane Ivanović, Esq; 1 Ruelle Ste Barbe, Monaco (☎ 93300996); 4 Audley Square, London W1Y 5DR (☎ 071 629 0734)

IVEAGH, 3 Earl of (UK 1919); Sir Arthur Francis Benjamin Guinness; 3 Bt (UK 1885); also Baron Iveagh (UK 1891), Viscount Iveagh (UK 1905), Viscount Elveden (UK 1919); s of Maj Arthur Onslow Edward Guinness, Viscount Elveden (ka 1945 - 2 s of 2 Earl), and Lady Elizabeth Hare (d 1990), da of 4 Earl of Listowel (d 1931); suc gf, 2 Earl of Iveagh, KG, CB, CMG 1967; 1 cous of Rt Hon Paul Channon, MP; *b* 20 May 1937; *Educ* Eton, Trinity Coll Cambridge, Univ of Grenoble; *m* 1963 (m dis 1984), Miranda Daphne Jane, da of Maj Charles Michael Smiley, of Castle Fraser, Aberdeenshire; 2 s (Viscount Elveden, Hon Rory Michael Benjamin b 12 Dec 1974), 2 da; *Heir* s, Viscount Elveden; *Career* memb Irish Senate 1973-77; pres Guinness Group; *Clubs* White's, Royal Yacht Sqdn, Kildare St and Univ (Dublin); *Style—* The Rt Hon the Earl of Iveagh; Guinness Ireland Ltd, St James's Gate Brewery, Dublin 8 (☎ 0001 533645)

IVENS, Michael William; CBE (1983); s of Harry Guest Ivens, and Nina Ailion; *b* 15 March 1924; *Educ* Quinton Sch London; *m* 1, 3 March 1951, Rosalie Joy, da of Bertrand Turnbull (d 1943); 3 s, 1 da; m 2, 17 July 1971, Katherine Patricia, da of John Kellock Laurence; 2 s; *Career* mangr Communications Dept ESSO 1955-68, jt ed Twentieth Century 1967-72, dir Standard Telephone 1970-71; dir: Fndn for Business Responsibilities 1968-, Aims of Indust 1971-; jt fndr & vice pres Freedom Assoc 1982-, jt fndr & tstee Res Fndn for Study of Terrorism 1986-, memb Cncl Poetry Soc 1989 (hon treas 1989); *Books* The Practice of Industrial Communication (1963), Case Studies in Management (1964), The Case for Capitalism (1967), Industry and Values (1970), Prophets of Freedom & Enterprise (1975); Bachman Book of Freedom Quotes (jt ed, 1978); *poetry* Another Sky (1963), Last Waltz (1964), Private and Public (1968), Born Early (1975), No Woman is an Island (1983), New Divine Comedy (1989); *Recreations* dog walking, reading, campaigning; *Clubs* Carlton; *Style—* Michael Ivens, Esq, CBE; Aims of Industry, 40 Doughty St, London WC1 (☎ 071 405 5195)

IVENS-FERRAZ, Lady Almary Bridget; *née* Coke; da of 6 Earl of Leicester; *b* 1938; *m* 1963, Peter Ivens-Ferraz; 4 da; *Style—* The Lady Almary Ivens-Ferraz; 19 Lady Smith St, Dan Pienaat, Bloemfontein, Orange Free State, S Africa; 33 Sixth Ave, Parktown N, Johannesburg, S Africa

IVERSEN, Leslie Lars; s of Svend Iversen, and Anna Caia Iversen; *b* 31 Oct 1937; *Educ* Heles Sch, Trinity Coll Cambridge (BA, MA, PhD, prize fellowship); *m* 1961, Susan Diana; 1 s, 1 da (and 1 da decd); *Career* Nat Serv Educn Branch RN 1956-58; Harkness fell of the Cwlth Fund Nat Inst of Mental Health Harvard Med Sch 1964-66, res fell Trinity Coll and Dept of Pharmacology Cambridge 1966-71, Locke res fell Royal Soc London 1967-71, dir MRC Neurochemical Pharmacology Unit Cambridge 1971-83, vice pres Neuroscience Research Centre Merck Sharp & Dohme Research Laboratories Harlow 1987- (exec dir 1983-87); assoc of neurosciences Res Prog MIT USA 1975-84, foreign hon memb American Acad of Arts and Sciences 1981, Rennebohm lectr Univ of Wisconsin USA 1984, visiting prof Inst of Psychiatry Univ of London 1985, assoc memb Royal Coll of Psychiatrists UK 1986, foreign assoc memb Nat Acad of Sciences USA 1986, hon prof Beijing Med Univ China 1988; memb: Academia Europaea, American Coll of Neuropsychopharmacology, Assoc of Br Pharmacautrical Industs Scientific Ctee, Bayliss and Starling Soc, Biochemical Soc UK, BBC Science Consultative Gp, Br Pharmacological Soc, Collegium Internationale Neuro-Psychopharmacologicum, Euro Molecular Biology Orgn, Feldberg Fndn 1989, Int Brain Res Orgn, Int Soc for Neurochemistry, Physiological Soc UK, Royal Acad of Med Belgium, Royal Soc of Med London, Save Br Science, Soc for Drug Res UK, Soc for Neuroscience USA; pres Euro Neuroscience Assoc 1980-82 (vice pres 1978-80); FRS 1980; *Books* The Update of Storage of Noradrenaline in Sympathetic Nerves (1967), Behavioural Pharmacology (with S D Iversen, 1975), author of numerous articles in learned jls; *Style—* Leslie Iversen, Esq, FRS; Merck Sharp & Dohme Neuroscience Research Centre, Terlings Park, Eastwick Road, nr Harlow, Essex CM20 2QR

IVES, Prof Eric William; s of Frederick Henry Ives (d 1981), of Trowbridge, and Ethel Lily, *née* Hall; *b* 12 July 1931; *Educ* Brentwood Sch, Queen Mary Coll (BA, PhD); *m* 1 April 1961, Christine Ruth, da of Norman Henry Deham (d 1971), of Dewsbury; 1 s (John b 1967), 1 da (Susan b 1963); *Career* Univ of Birmingham: memb History of Part Tst 1957, fell Shakespeare Inst 1958-61, sr lectr mod history 1972-83 (lectr 1968-72), prof English history 1987- (reader 1983-87), dean Faculty of Arts 1987-89 (dept dean 1982-84), pro vice-chllr 1989-; lectr mod history Univ of Liverpool 1962-68 (asst lectr 1961-62); memb Cncl Hist Assoc 1968-77, govr Warwick Schs Fndn 1980-, chm Ctee Govrs Warwich Sch 1985, govr Coventry Sch 1985-88; memb: Academic Bd Spurgeons Coll 1987-, Cncl Regents Park Coll Oxford 1988-, Ct Univ of Warwick 1989-; chm Stratford-upon-Avon Choral Soc 1985-; FRHist 1963, FSA 1984; *Books* Letters & Accounts of William Bereton (1976), God in History (1979), Faction in Tudor England (1979, 2nd ed 1986), The Common Lawyers of Pre-Reformation England (1983), Anne Boleyn (1986); *Recreations* sailing, choral singing, lay preaching; *Style—* Prof E W Ives, FSA; Sch of History, Univ of Birmingham, Birmingham B15 2TT (☎ 021 414 3344, fax 021 414 4534)

IVES, Kenneth Ainsworth; s of Lawrence George Ives (d 1956), and Margaret, *née* Walker (d 1979); *b* 26 March 1934; *Educ* Queen Mary's GS Walsall, Pembroke Coll Oxford (BA, MA), RADA (Leverhulme scholar); *m* 1, Anne Brown; m 2, Imogen Hassall; m 3, Marti Caine; *Career* Mil Serv Lieut RN; director: over fifty plays for BBC TV, NT and West End, seven plays by Harold Pinter; currently directing The Philanthropist for theatre (by Christopher Hampton, with Edward Fox in leading role); *Recreations* cricket, opera, reading, walking; *Clubs* Garrick, MCC; *Style—* Kenneth Ives, Esq

IVES, Prof Kenneth James; s of Walter Leslie Ives (d 1966), of London, and Grace Amelia, *née* Curson (d 1983); *b* 29 Nov 1926; *Educ* William Ellis GS London, UCL (BSc, PhD, DSc); *m* 29 March 1952, Brenda Grace, da of Rev Frederick Walter Tilley (d 1987), of Leatherhead, Surrey; 1 s (Matthew b 1962), 1 da (Cherrill (Mrs Theobald) b 1953); *Career* asst engr Metropolitan Water Bd London 1948-55; UCL: prof lectr and reader 1955-84, Chadwick Prof 1984-; res fell Harvard Univ USA 1958-59, visiting assoc prof Univ of N Carolina USA 1964, visiting prof Univ of Delft Netherlands 1977; expert advsr on environmental health WHO 1966-, hon exec ed Int Assoc on Water Pollution Res and Control 1984-; author of numerous articles in jls; FICE 1952, MASCE 1959, FEng 1986; *Books* The Scientific Basis of Filtration (1975), The Scientific Basis of Flocculation (1978), The Scientific Basis of Flotation (1984); *Recreations* squash, ballroom dancing; *Style—* Prof Kenneth Ives; Department of Civil and Municipal Engineering, Univ Coll London, Gower St, London WC1E 6BT (☎ 071 380 7224, fax 071 380 0986, telex 296273 UCLENG G)

IVES, William Leonard; OBE (1959); s of Alfred Leonard Ives (d 1962), and Ada Smith (d 1968); *b* 20 April 1906; *Educ* Alleynes GS, King's Coll London (LLB); *m* 1935, Margaret Joyce, da of James Antony (d 1980); *Career* Wing Cdr RAF 1940-45 (despatches), sr offr i/c Danube Allied Cmd for Austria 1944-45; called to the Bar Middle Temple 1930; dep Parly offr Met Water Bd 1930-34, dep chm Br Waterways 1955-62, chm Nat Jt Cncl for Inland Waterways Indust 1955-62, chm Tendring Hundred Water Works Co 1966-90; memb: Cncl Water Companies Assoc 1965-90, Chartered Inst of Tport 1978-; *Recreations* bridge, foreign travel, RAF; *Style—* William Ives, Esq, OBE; North Down, Upper Stoneborough Lane, Budleigh, Salterton (☎ 039 54 2077)

IVISON, David Malcolm; s of John Ivison (d 1979), of Lichfield and Ruth Ellen *née* Summerfield; *b* 22 March 1936; *Educ* King Edward VI Sch Lichfield; *m* 4 April 1961, Lieselotte, da of Johannes Verse, of Germany; 1 s (Marcel b 1963), 1 da (Nicola b 1965); *Career* RMA Sandhurst 1954-55, RASC 1955-58, Gurkha Tport Regt 1958-80; serv Malaya and Borneo, Army Staff Coll Camberley 1967-68, Lt-Col NATO HQ Belgium 1980-83; distribution mangr Tate and Lyle 1984-85, chief exec Inst of Road Tport Engrs 1985-88; MBIM 1969, FCIT 1976, MILDM 1979, MIRTE 1986; *Recreations* swimming, languages, reading; *Style—* David Ivison, Esq; 1 Dundaff Close, Camberley, Surrey, GU15 1AF (☎ 0276 27778)

IVORY, (James) Angus; s of Basil Gerritsen Ivory (d 1973), of Jamaica, and Joan Mary, *née* White; *b* 31 July 1932; *Educ* Eton, Toronto Univ Canada (BA); *m* 26 Oct 1956, Nancy Ann, da of William Park, of Toronto, Canada; 2 s (Gavin b 1957, Colin b 1959), 1 da (Gillian b 1964); *Career* md Brown Brothers Harriman Ltd, previously dir Clark Dodge & Co Inc 1960-74; chm Wall Street Int Corpn 1967-70; memb: Cncl US Investmt Community 1967-70, UK Assoc of New York Stock Exchange; chm Cncl Securities Indust 1980-82; *Recreations* hunting, farming; *Clubs* White's, Lansdowne, Toronto; *Style—* J Angus Ivory, Esq; Greenway Farm, Tockenham, Swindon SN4 7PP (☎ 079385 2367); 11F Warwick Square, London SW1 (☎ 071 834 5968); Brown Bros Harriman Ltd, Garden House, 18 Finsbury Circus, London EC2M 7BP

IVORY, Brian Gammell; s of Eric James Ivory (d 1988), and Alice Margaret Joan, *née* Gammell (d 1984); *b* 10 April 1949; *Educ* Eton, Magdalene Coll Cambridge (MA); *m* 21 Feb 1981, Oona Mairi Macphie, da of Archibald Ian Bell-MacDonald (d 1987); 1 s (Euan b 1986), 1 da (Roseanna b 1989); *Career* CA; dir: The Highland Distilleries Co plc 1978- (md 1988-), Matthew Gloag & Son Ltd 1987-; Scottish Arts Cncl: memb Cncl 1983-, chm Combined Arts Ctee 1984-88, memb Policy and Resources Ctee 1984-, vice chm Cncl 1988-; memb Arts Cncl of GB 1988-; *Recreations* the arts, farming, hillwalking; *Clubs* New (Edinburgh), RSAC (Glasgow); *Style—* Brian Ivory, Esq; Brewlands, Glenisla, by Blairgowrie, Perthshire PH11 8PL; 12 Ann St, Edinburgh EH4 1PJ; The Highland Distilleries Company plc, 106 West Nile St, Glasgow G1 2QY (☎ 041 332 7511, fax 041 332 8532)

IVORY, James Francis; s of Capt Edward Patrick Ivory, US Army (d 1967), of Dinuba, California, and Hallie Millicent, *née* De Loney (d 1963); *b* 7 June 1928; *Educ* Univ of Oregon (BA), Univ of Southern California (MA); *Career* fdnr Merchant Ivory Productions (with Ismail Merchant and Ruth Prawer Jhabvala) 1963; films incl: Shakespeare Wallah (1965), Savages (1972), Autobiography of a Princess (1975), Roseland (1977), Hullabaloo Over Georgie and Bonnie's Pictures (1978), The Europeans (1979), Quartet (1981), Heat and Dust (1983), The Bostonians (1984), A Room with a View (1986, nominated best dir Acad Awards 1987), Maurice (1987, Silver Lion Venice Film Festival), Slaves of New York (1989), Mr and Mrs Bridge (1990); Guggenheim fell 1975; memb: Dirs Guild of America, Writers Guild of America; *Recreations* looking at pictures; *Style—* James Ivory, Esq; Patroon St, Claverack, NY 12513, USA (☎ 0101 518 851 7808); Merchant Ivory Productions, 46 Lexington St, London W1R 3LH (☎ 071 437 1200/071 439 4335)

IZAT, (Alexander) John Rennie; JP; s of Sir James Rennie Izat (d 1962), of Balliliesk, and Lady (Eva Mary Steen) Izat, *née* Cairns (d 1984); *b* 14 July 1932; *Educ* Trinity Coll Glenalmorld, Oriel Coll Oxford (MA); *m* 12 April 1958, Frederica Ann, da of Colin Champness McNiel, of Hants; 1 s (Alexander b 1960), 2 da (Davina b 1959, Rosanna b 1963); *Career* stockbroker; ptnr Williams de Broe & Co London 1955-75; John Izat & Ptnrs: Balliliesk and Naemoor 1961-87, High Cocklaw 1987-; dir: United Auctions (Scotland) Ltd, Holiday Cottages (Scotland) Ltd, Cromlix Estates, C Champness & Co, Shires Investment plc, Wiston Investment Co, Glasgow Investment Managers Ltd; chm: U A Properties Ltd, U A Forestry Ltd; farmer; past pres Fife-Kinross NFU & Kinross Agric Assoc, dir Royal Highland Agric Assoc 1985-; chm: Scottish Woods and Forest Awards, Sch Shield Competition; chm Ctee of Glenalmond Coll; *Recreations* shooting, Suffolk sheep; *Style—* John Izat, Esq, JP; High Cocklaw, Berwick upon Tweed TD15 1UZ (☎ 0289 86591)

J

JACK, Sir Alieu Sulayman; *b* 14 July 1922; *Educ* St Augustine's Sch; *m* 1946, Yai Marie Cham, 4 s, 4 da (and 1 da decd); *Career* md Gambia Nat Trading Co 1948-, speaker House of Representatives Gambia 1962-72 and 1977-83, min of works and communications The Gambia 1972-77; Grand Cdr of the Nat Order of the Republic of The Gambia; kt 1970; *Style*— Sir Alieu Jack; PO Box 376, Banjul, The Gambia (☎ office: 28431, residence 92204); 166 Mosque Rd, Serekunda, The Republic of The Gambia

JACK, Janet Marie; da of Albert Frederick Kaye (d 1951), and Ida, *née* Hancock (d 1951); *b* 5 June 1934; *Educ* Sutton HS, Architectural Assoc Sch of Architecture (AADipl), UCL (LD), Thames Poly (Dip LD); *m* 8 Feb 1963, William Jack, s of Col Frank Weaver Jack, TD (d 1984); 1 s (Angus b 1963, d 1990), 1 da (Amy b 1965); *Career* architect; Architects Co-Ptnrship 1957-58, Harry Weesse Assocs Chicago 1958-59, IM PEI NY 1960, Planning and Devpt Ltd 1960-63, Dame Sylvia Crowe 1965-66, own landscape practice 1967-81; Building Design Partnership: joined 1981, ptnr 1986, sr ptnr 1988; Landscape Inst: publicity offr 1984-88, memb External Affrs Ctee 1984-; memb Landscape Advsy Ctee on Trunk Roads Dept of Tport 1987, chm Signing Sub Ctee 1990; RIBA 1961, ALI 1973, FRSA 1987; *Books* The Design of Atria (contrib, 1983), The Design of Shopping Centres (contrib, 1989); *Recreations* yoga, opera, art, architecture, the environment; *Style*— Mrs Janet Jack; Building Design Partnership, 16 Gresse St, London W1A 4WD

JACK, (John) Michael; MP (C) Fylde 1987-; s of Ralph Niven, of York, and Florence Edith, *née* Reed; mothers family Hewish of Devon said to have arrived with William the Conqueror; *b* 17 Sept 1946; *Educ* Bradford GS, Bradford Tech Coll, Univ of Leicester (BA, MPhil); *m* 1976, Alison Jane, da of Cncllr Brian Rhodes Musgrave; 2 s (Edmund b 1979, Oliver b 1981); *Career* sales dir L O Jeffs Ltd 1980-87; formerly: with Marks & Spencer and Procter & Gamble, PPS to Rt Hon John Gummer MP Min of Agric Fisheries and Food, sec Cons NW Membs Gp; currently Parly under sec Miny of Social Security; *Recreations* motor sport, dinghy sailing, Boule player; *Style*— Michael Jack, Esq, MP; House of Commons, Westminster, London SW1A 0AA

JACK, Raymond Evan; QC (1982); s of Evan Stuart Maclean Jack, and Charlotte, *née* Fry; *b* 13 Nov 1942; *Educ* Rugby, Trinity Coll Cambridge (MA); *m* 1 Oct 1976, Elizabeth Alison (Liza), da of Canon James Seymour Denys Mansel, KCVO; 1 s (Alexander b 1986), 2 da (Katherine b 1979, Lucy b 1981); *Career* called to the Bar Inner Temple 1976; SE Circuit; rec Crown Ct 1989; *Publications* Documentary Credits (1991); *Style*— Raymond Jack, Esq, QC; 1 Hare Court, Temple, London EC4Y 7BE (☎ 071 353 3171, fax 071 583 9127, telex 8814348)

JACK, Prof Robert Barr; CBE; s of Robert Hendry Jack (d 1966), of Largs, Ayrshire, and Christina Alexandra, *née* Barr (d 1961); *b* 18 March 1928; *Educ* Kilsyth Acad, Glasgow HS, Univ of Glasgow (MA, LLB); *m* 1958, Anna Thorburn, da of George Harris Thomson, of Glasgow; 2 s (Robert Thomson Barr b 1961, David George b 1963); *Career* slr; sr ptnr McGrigor Donald Glasgow Edinburgh and London, prof of mercantile law Univ of Glasgow author of various articles on aspects of company law; memb: Co Law Ctee Law Soc of Scotland 1971- (convener 1978-85), Scot Law Cmmn 1974-77, Advs Panel Co Law DOT 1980-83, Cncl of the Stock Exchange 1984-86, Ind Bd of The Securities Assoc 1986-, UK Panel of Arbitrators Int Centre for Settlement of Investment Disputes 1989-; lay memb Cncl for the Securities Indust 1983-85, Scot observer Insolvency Law Review Ctee DOT 1977-82; chm: Joseph Dunn (Bottlers) Ltd 1983-; Brownlee plc 1984-86, Review Ctee on Banking Servs Law 1987-89; dir: Scottish Met Property plc 1980-, Clyde Football Club Ltd 1980-, Bank of Scotland 1985-, Scottish Mutual Assur Soc 1987-, chm Scottish Nat Cncl of YMCAs 1966-73 (pres 1983-), govr Hutchesons' Educnl Tst Glasgow 1978-87 (chm 1980-87), chm The Turnberry Tst 1983-, memb Bd Govrs Beatson Inst for Cancer Res Glasgow 1989-; *Publications* author of papers on various aspects of company law and the statutory regulation and self regulation of the City; *Recreations* golf, football; *Clubs* Caledonian, Western (Glasgow), Pollok Golf, Shiskine Golf and Tennis (Isle of Arran); *Style*— Prof R B Jack, CBE; 39 Mansewood Road, Glasgow G43 1TN (☎ 041 632 1659); McGrigor Donald, Pacific House, 70 Wellington St, Glasgow G2 6SB (☎ 041 248 6677)

JACK, Roland Maclean; s of Evan Stuart Maclean Jack, and Charlotte Ellen, *née* Fry; *b* 22 July 1948; *Educ* Oundle; *m* 24 June 1978, Hon Fiona Georgina, da of Lord Ironside; 1 s (Oliver Edmund Maclean b 7 Nov 1983), 1 da (Anthea Audrey Charlotte b 30 March 1985); *Career* dir: Turner Porter Assocs 1984-85, McCann Consultancy 1986-88; managing ptnr Dark Horse Design 1988-; *Recreations* running, photography; *Style*— Roland Jack, Esq; The Old Vicarage, Lyford, nr Wantage, Oxfordshire OX12 0EF; The Old Vicarage Studio, Lyford, nr Wantage, Oxfordshire OX12 0EF (☎ 0235 868036, fax 0235 868084)

JACK, Prof Ronald Dyce Sadler; s of Muirice Jack (d 1982), of Ayr, and Edith Emily Sadler (d 1984); *b* 3 April 1941; *Educ* Ayr Acad, Univ of Glasgow (MA, DLitt), Univ of Edinburgh (PhD); *m* (Christabel) Kirsty Margaret, da of Rev Maj Angus Macdonald Nicolson, TD (d 1975), of Ayr; 2 da (Fiona b 1968, Isla b 1972); *Career* Dept of English Lit Univ of Edinburgh: lectr 1965, reader 1978, assoc dean 1971-73, prof Scot and medieval lit 1987; visiting prof Univ of Virginia 1973-74; govr Newbattle Abbey Coll 1984-88, memb Scot Consultative Ctee on the Curriculum 1987-89, dir UCCA 1989-; *Books* incl: The Italian Influence on Scottish Literature (1972), Scottish Prose 1550-1700 (ed, 1978), Choice of Scottish Verse 1560-1660 (ed, 1978), The Art of Robert Burns (co-ed, 1982), Alexander Montgomerie (1985), Scottish Literature's Debt to Italy (1986), Patterns of Divine Comedy (1989); *Recreations* golf; *Style*— Prof Ronald Jack; 54 Buckstone Rd, Edinburgh EH10 6UN (☎ 031 443 3498); Department of English Literature, University of Edinburgh, David Hume Tower, George Square, Edinburgh EH8 9JX (☎ 031 667 1011 ext 6259)

JACK, Dr Timothy Michael; s of Michael Henry Fingland Jack (d 1990), of Teignmouth, S Devon, and Margaret Joyce, *née* Baker (d 1978); *b* 5 July 1947; *Educ* King Edward's Sch Birmingham, Guy's Hosp (MB BS); *m* 20 Oct 1979, (Veronica) Jane, da of Richard Christopher Warde (d 1953), of Orpington, Kent; 2 s (Benjamin b 1983, Jonathan b 1986); *Career* anaesthetist Shanta Bhawan Hosp Kathmandu Nepal 1974-76, sr registrar Nuffield Dept of Anaesthetics Radcliffe Infirmary Oxford 1978-82, conslt anaesthetist Leeds Gen Infirmary and hon lectr Univ of Leeds 1982-90, conslt in pain relief and clinical servs mangr Oxford Regnl Pain Relief Unit Oxford; memb: Exec Ctee Christian Med Fellowship, Personnel Ctee Interserve (UK); FFARCS 1977; *Recreations* sailing, mountain-walking, gardening, bird-watching; *Style*— Dr Tim Jack; 46 Eaton Rd, Appleton, Abingdon, Oxon OX13 5JA

JACK, William; s of Col Frank W Jack, TD, JP (d 1984), of Aberdeenshire, Scotland, and Edith Margaret, *née* Forsyth (d 1974); *b* 12 Dec 1933; *Educ* Aberdeen GS, Aberdeen Coll of Architecture, Cornell Univ (MArch); *m* 8 Feb 1963, Janet Marie, da of Albert Frederick Kaye (d 1951); 1 s (Angus b 31 Dec 1963), 1 da (Amy Frances b 28 July 1965); *Career* Building Design Ptnrship: joined 1961, ptnr 1966, sr ptnr 1968, chm 1990; designer of many projects in UK and overseas; MRIBA; *Recreations* opera, theatre, architecture, golf; *Style*— William Jack, Esq; 1 1/2 Southern Rd, London N2 9LH (☎ 071 444 0260); Building Design Partnership, 16 Gresse St, London W1A 4WD (☎ 071 631 4733, fax 01 631 0393, telex 25322)

JACK, Dr William Logan; JP (Herefordshire); s of Dr Robert Lockhart Jack, DSC (d 1964), of 52 Clowes St, Melbourne, Aust, and Frances Augusta, *née* Marr (d 1963); *b* 25 Dec 1907; *Educ* St Peter's Coll Adelaide, Univ of Adelaide (MB BS); *m* 15 May 1940, Dorothy Margaret, da of Lt-Col G W Dryland, of Pitfour, Kington, Hereford; 3 s (Robert Logan b 1941, William Logan b 1946, Ian Logan b 1948), 2 da (Felicity Logan (Mrs Hutchings) b 1943, Veronica Logan (Mrs Allen) b 1948); *Career* surgn Kington Hosp 1933-78; chm: KUDC 1947-52 (memb 1945), Kington Horse Show 1951-72; govr Lady Hawkins Sch Kington 1952-, fndr memb and currently pres Llangorse Sailing Club 1952-, vice pres (formerly chm) N Hereford Cons Assoc, vice chm Hereford & Worcs branch Magistrates Assoc 1972-77; *Style*— Dr W Logan Jack, JP; Huntington Court, Huntington Kingdon, Hereford (☎ 0544 230330)

JACKAMAN, Timothy John; s of Walter Edward John Jackaman, of Kent, and Valerie May, *née* Roberts; *b* 1 Feb 1958; *Educ* Dulwich, Goldsmiths Coll London (BA); 1 s; *Career* journalist Westminster Press (Kentish Times Group) 1979-81, freelance journalist Ferrari Press Agency 1981-82, account exec City & Commercial Communications Ltd 1982-83, dir City Marketing Ltd 1983-86, head fin PR Div Hill & Knowlton London 1987-89 (Hong Kong 1986-87), md Square Mile Communications 1989-; *Recreations* rugby football; *Style*— Timothy Jackaman, Esq; 21 The Woodlands, Clapham Common Northside, 52-54 Carter Lane, London EC4V 5EA (☎ 071 622 9956); Square Mile Communications Ltd, Glade House, 52-54 Carter Lane, London EC4 5EA (☎ 071 329 4496, fax 071 329 0310)

JACKLIN, Anthony (Tony); CBE (1990, OBE 1970); s of Arther David Jacklin, of Bottesford, South Humberside, and Doris Lillian Jacklin; *b* 7 July 1944; *Educ* Doncaster Road Secdy Modern Scunthorpe S Humberside; *m* 1, 1966, Vivian (d 1988); 5 c (Bradley Mark b 12 Nov 1969, Warren b 10 Sept 1972, Tina b 27 March 1975, Anna-May b 17 Feb 1979, Alistair James b 11 Aug 1981); m 2, Dec 1988, Astrid May, da of Tormod Waagen; *Career* professional golfer 1962-85; began playing golf 1953, Lincolnshire jr champion 1959-61, Lincolnshire Open champion 1961, memb Br Boys team 1960, turned professional 1962, Br Asst champion 1964, Coombe Hill Asssts champion 1964; winner of 24 tournaments worldwide incl: Jacksonville Open 1968 and 1972, Br Open 1969, US Open 1970, Br PGA 1972 and 1982, Italian Open 1973, Dunlop Masters 1973, German Open 1979; played in 7 Ryder Cup matches 1967-79; capt Euro Ryder Cup team: 1983, 1985 (won), 1987 (won), 1989 (drawn); dir of golf San Roque Club Cadiz Sapin 1988-, currently golf course designer; life vice pres PGA 1970 (hon life memb Euro Tournament Players Div); *Recreations* shooting; *Style*— Tony Jacklin, Esq, CBE; Quothquhan Lodge, nr Biggar, Strathclyde, Scotland

JACKLIN, Robert Arthur; s of Frederick Arthur Jacklin (d 1978), of Colchester, Essex, and Edith Emily, *née* Howard (d 1982); *b* 10 April 1934; *Educ* Culford Sch Bury St Edmunds, Emmanuel Coll Cambridge (MA); *m* 20 April 1967, Penelope Grace, da of Charles Arthur Godwin Lywood (d 1970); 1 s (Michael b 1969), 2 da (Annabel b 1970, Rosamond b 1975); *Career* Nat Serv 2 Lt RA 1953-55, Capt Essex Yeo (TA) 1955-65; admitted slr 1962; sr ptnr Sparling Benham & Brough 1984 (ptnr 1967-); pres Suffolk and N Essex Law Soc 1990-91, vice chm Age Concern Colchester, hon sec Abbeyfield Colchester Soc; memb Law Soc 1962; *Recreations* sailing, music, fell walking; *Clubs* Colchester Garrison Officers, Royal Harwich Yacht; *Style*— Robert Jacklin, Esq; 3 West Stockwell St, Colchester, Essex, CO1 1HQ (☎ 0206 577767, fax 0206 564551)

JACKLIN, Walter William (Bill); s of Harold Jacklin (d 1964), of London, and Alice Mary, *née* Jones (d 1988); *b* 1 Jan 1943; *Educ* Walthamstow Sch of Art, Royal Coll of ARt (MA, ARA); *m* 1979, Lesley Sarina, da of Monty Berman; *Career* artist; teaching at various art colls 1967-75; solo exhibitions incl: Nigel Greenwood Inc London 1970, 1971 and 1975, Hester Van Royen Gallery London 1973 and 1977, Marlborough Fine Art London 1980, 1983 and 1988, Marlborough Gallery New York 1985, 1987 and 1990; included in numerous int gp exhibitions; pub collections incl: Art Gallery of Sydney Aust, Arts Cncl of GB, Br Cncl London, Br Museum, Govt Arts Collection GB, Metropolitan Museum of Art, NY, Tate Gallery, V & A Museum, Yale Centre for Br Art Newhaven USA; ARA; *Recreations* running, planting trees; *Clubs* Chelsea Arts; *Style*— Bill Jacklin, Esq; c/o Marlborough Fine Art, 6 Albermarle St, London W1 (☎ 212 541 4900, fax 212 541 4948)

JACKMAN, Cassandra; da of Michael John Jackman, of 14 Yarmouth Rd, North Walsham, Norfolk, and Patricia Anne, *née* Loades; *b* 22 Dec 1972; *Educ* North Walsham HS; *Career* professional squash player; clubs represented: North Walsham Ladies and Mens, Barnham Broom Ladies and Men, Pontefract Mens (Yorkshire League), Colets Ladies (Nat Super league); 30 jr England caps under 16 and under 19, 7 sr England caps; tournament wins: various Norfolk jr titles, Norfolk Ladies champion 1987-, E Anglian Jr Open under 19 1987-90, Euro under 19 1989, Br Open under 16 1988, Br Open under 19 1990-91, Br Open under 23 1989, Br Doubles 1987, N of England Ladies 1990; memb England under 19 team winning: Euro Championships 1988 and 1990, World Championships Auckland 1989; ranked England number 8 and England under 19 number 1; Squash Player Magazine player of the year 1985, Avia girl of the year award 1987-88; *Recreations* cinema, tv, music, reading, nightclubs, animals; *Style*— Ms Cassandra Jackman; The Limes, 14 Yarmouth Rd, North Walsham, Norfolk NR28 9AT (☎ 0692 402621); Barnham Broom Country Club, Horingham Rd, Barnham Broom, Norfolk (☎ 060545 741)

JACKMAN, Frederick Charles; s of Stanley Charles Jackman (d 1978), of Brentwood, Essex, and Lilian May, *née* Brassett; *b* 29 Feb 1944; *Educ* Warren Sch Dagenham, Barking Coll of Technol, Borough Poly (HNC); *m* 14 June 1969, Zarene, da of Karim Gulam Husain (d 1973), of London; *Career* Stinton Jones & Ptnrs 1960-64, Costain Construction 1964-66, T P Bennett & Son 1966-69, Arup Assocs 1969-73, Upton Assoc Bldg Servs Consulting Engrs 1973- (resident Dubai 1976, sr ptnr 1979-); MConsE, FCIBSE, FIHospE; *Recreations* travel, walking, fishing; *Clubs* Phyllis Court (Henley); *Style—* Frederick Jackman, Esq; New House, Holyport Rd, Maidenhead, Berks (☎ 0628 34102); Upton Associates, Pilot House, West Wycombe Rd, High Wycombe, Bucks HP12 3AB (☎ 0494 450931, fax 0494 31464)

JACKOWSKI, Andrzej Aleksander; s of Henryk Soplica Jackowski (d 1978), and Anne Biernaczak; *b* 4 Dec 1947; *Educ* Holland Park Sch, Camberwell Coll of Art, Falmouth Sch of Art (Dip AD), Royal Coll of Art (MA); *m* 1, 1 May 1970 (m dis 1989), Nicolette Tester; 1 da (Laura b 3 Feb 1972); ptnr Eve Ashley; 1 s (Louis b 5 Oct 1990); *Career* artist; lectr 1977-86 (Royal Coll of Art, Byam Shaw Sch of Art Brighton); solo exhibitions: Univ of Surrey 1978-79, Moira Kelly Fine Art 1982, Bluecoat Gallery Liverpool (touring) 1984, Marlborough Fine Art 1986, 1989 and 1990, Gardner Centre Gallery Brighton 1989, Castlefield Gallery Manchester transfd Nottingham Castle Museum 1989; group exhibitions incl: John Moores Exhibitions (Walker Art Gallery Liverpool) 1976, 1980-81 and 1982-83, Narrative Painting (Arnolfini Bristol, travelling) 1979-80, Inner Worlds (Arts Cncl of GB, travelling), Eight in the Eighties (Britain Salutes New York Festival, NY) 1983, Interiors (Anne Berthoud Gallery) 1983-84, New Works on Paper (Br Cncl Travelling Exhibition) 1983-85, House and Abroad (Serpentine) 1984, The Image as Catalyst (Ashmolean Oxford) 1984, Human Interest, Fifty Years of British Art About People (Cornerhouse Manchester) 1985; Introducing with Pleasure: Star Choices from the Arts Cncl Collection (travelling exhibition, Gardner Centre Brighton) 1987; An Anthology: Artists who studied with Peter de Francia (Camden Arts Centre 1987; Cries and Whispers: New Works for the Br Cncl Collection (travelling exhibition Aust NZ) 1988; 150 Anniversary Exhibition, Exhibition Road Painters at the Royal Coll of Art (RCA) 1988; Object and Image: Aspects of British Art in the 1980s (City Museum and Art Gallery, Stoke on Trent) 1988; The New British Painting (The Contemporary Arts Centre Cincinnati, travelling exhibition) 1988, The Tree of Life (South Bank Centre travelling exhibition Cornerhouse Gallery Manchester) 1989, School of London Words on Paper (Odette Gilbert Gallery) 1989, Now for the Future (The South Bank Centre) 1990, Picturing People (Br Cncl travelling exhibition, Not Art Gallery Kuala Lumpur, Hong Kong Museum of Art, The Empress Palace Singapore) 1990, On View (Marlborough) 1990, Tribute to Peter Fuller (Beaux Arts Bath) 1990; work in public collections of: Arts Cncl of GB, Br Cncl, Contemporary Arts Soc, Euro Parly, RCA, SE Arts, Univ of Liverpool, Univ of Surrey; SE Arts fell Univ of Surrey 1978-79, Tolly Cobbold/ Eastern Arts Major prize 1981; *Style—* Andrzej Jackowski, Esq; Marlborough Fine Art, 6 Albermarle St, London W1X 4BY (☎ 071 629 5161, fax 071 629 6338)

JACKSON, Alan Francis; *b* 25 April 1935; *Educ* Westminster; *m* Jean Elizabeth; 1 da (Kate); *Career* J H Minet & Co Ltd 1955-58, worked in Canada 1958-62, underwriter Robert Bradford Ltd 1962-78, Alan Jackson Underwriting Agencies Ltd 1979- (merged with Wren Underwriting Agencies Ltd 1986, presently dep chm); sr dep chm Cncl of Lloyds; Freeman Worshipful Co of Goldsmiths; FIIC, memb ACII; *Recreations* golf; *Style—* Alan Jackson, Esq; Lloyd's of London, 1 Lime St, London EC3M 7HL (☎ 071 623 7100 Ext 4145, fax 071 623 8698, telex 987321 LLOYDS G)

JACKSON, Andrew Graham; s of Thomas Armitage Geoffrey Jackson (d 1985), and Hilda Marion Jackson; *b* 5 May 1937; *Educ* Denstone Coll, Jesus Coll Cambridge (MA); *m* 1964, Christine Margaret, da of Charles Edward Chapman, of Oundle; 1 s (Matthew b 1971), 2 da (Sarah b 1967, Claire b 1969); *Career* Nat Serv Lt served Suez 1956; Stewarts & Lloyds Corby 1960-67; Denco Holdings Ltd: joined 1967, sales mangr 1967-69, sales dir dep md 1972-77, gp md 1977-85; dir AMEC Projects Ltd 1985-86, md Keg Services Ltd 1986-, Lloyds underwriter; pres Hereford Dist Scouts Assoc; Liveryman: Worshipful Co of Carmen, Worshipful Co of Engrs (asst); CEng, FIMechE, FBIM; *Recreations* squash, water skiing, scuba diving; *Clubs* RAC; *Style—* Andrew Jackson, Esq; The Orchard, Lyde, Hereford (☎ 0432 272 830); Keg Services Ltd, Twyford Rd, Hereford HR2 6JR (☎ 0432 353 300, fax 0432 268 141)

JACKSON, Andrew Malcolm; s of Douglas MacGilchrist Jackson, of 17 Milford Court, Milford on Sea, and Mabel Pauline, *née* Brand; *b* 4 May 1945; *Educ* Marlborough Coll, Middx Hosp Med Sch Univ of London (MB BS); *m* Anne Marie, da of Joseph Lucas, of 38 Regency Drive, Silksworth, Sunderland; 2 s (Charles b 1979, Adam Stuart b 1981); *Career* conslt orthopaedic surgn: UCH 1981, Hosp for Sick Children Gt Ormond St 1981; hon conslt Royal Nat Orthopaedic Hosp 1983; Freeman City of London 1981, Liveryman Worshipful Soc of Apothecaries; FRCS 1979, memb RSM; *Recreations* sailing, fishing; *Style—* Andrew Jackson, Esq; 107 Harley St, London W1 (☎ 071 935 9521)

JACKSON, Andrew Michael; s of Anthony Hargreaves Jackson, of Boughton, Northampton (d 1990), and Evelyn Mary, *née* Anson (d 1987); *b* 27 Feb 1940; *Educ* Sedbergh; *m* 1 April 1967, Jillian Felicity, da of Denys Gordon Parfitt, of Shalford, Guildford, Surrey; 1 s (David Richard Anthony b 5 March 1968); *Career* admitted slr 1965; ptnr Hutson Poole 1984, Notary Public 1986; memb Guildford Rotary Club, cncl memb Guildford and Dist C of C, chm Surrey C of C; memb: Law Soc 1965, Notaries Soc 1986; *Recreations* inland cruising, carriage driving; *Clubs* The County (Guildford); *Style—* Andrew Jackson, Esq; Tangley Field, Wonersh, Guildford, Surrey GU5 0PY (☎ 0483 65719); Hutson Poole Williamson Solicitors, 17 & 18 Quarry St, Guildford, Surrey GU1 3XA (☎ 0483 65244, fax 0483 575 961)

JACKSON, Anthony James; JP (1980); s of Harold Samuel Jackson, of Green End Cottage, The Green, Cavendish, Suffolk, and Delta Patricia Smith (d 1986); *b* 22 Oct 1938; *Educ* St Paul's; *m* 16 Oct 1965, (Gillian) Barbara, da of Nevil Maurice Ernest Proes (d 1982); 2 s (Andrew William Ernest Anthony Jackson Proes b 7 May 1969, Richard Douglas Campbell Jackson Proes b 11 Aug 1972), 1 da (Alexandra Claire Campbell Jackson Proes b 22 Oct 1967); *Career* dir Zodiac Office Products (Pty) Ltd Australia 1982, dep md Kores Nordic Holdings A/S Copenhagen 1983-88; dir: Arenson Group plc 1988-, Channel Express Group plc 1988-89, Keymax International Ltd, M & W Mack Ltd; chief exec Kores UK Ops 1989-; Tax Cmmr; Freedom City of London 1987, Liveryman Worshipful Co of Stationers' and Newspaper Makers' 1989; FInstD 1980; *Recreations* shooting, fishing, sailing, riding/hunting, tennis; *Clubs* Aldeburgh Yacht, Hon Artillery Co Saddle

JACKSON, Ashley Norman; s of Norman Valentine Jackson (POW Malaya, executed 1944/45), and Dulcie Olga, *née* Scott (Mrs Haigh); *b* 22 Oct 1940; *Educ* St Joseph's Singapore, Holyrood Barnsley S Yorks, Barnsley Coll of Art; *m* 22 Dec 1962, (Patricia) Anne, da of Donald Hutchinson, of Barnsley, S Yorks; 2 da (Heather b 11 Nov 1968, Claudia b 15 Sept 1970); *Career* artist; exhibited: RI, RBA, RWS, Britain in Watercolour, UA; one man shows: Upper Grosvenor Gallery, Mall Gallery, Christina Foyle Gallery, Spanish Inst of Culture, London, New York, Chicago, San Francisco, Washington, Dallas, one-man exhibition in Huddersfield opened by HRH The Prince of Wales 1987; works in the collections of: MOD, RN, NCB, British Gas, NUM; own tv series on: Yorkshire TV (A Brush with Ashley), BBC 1, Channel 4 and PBS in America; tstee Barnsley Coll, chm Yorks Watercolour Soc, memb Bd and chm Appeals Prince's Youth Business Tst W Yorks; chm FRSA 1964; *Books* My Own Flesh and Blood (1981), The Artist's Notebook (1985), Ashley Jackson's World of Art 1 and 2 (1988); *Style—* Ashley Jackson, Esq; Ashley Jackson Galleries, 13-15 Huddersfield Rd, Holmfirth, Huddersfield (☎ 0484 686460)

JACKSON, Barbara Amy Bridget; da of Walter Dumolo Jackson (d 1979), and Vera Joan, *née* Pepper (d 1990); *b* 10 July 1936; *Educ* Bredenbury Court Herefordshire, Gardenhurst Burnham-on-Sea; *Career* co sec and dir P F Jackson Ltd Birmingham 1975-85; int golfer; Br Girls Champion 1954; Staffs Ladies Champion: 1954, 1956-59, 1963-64, 1966-69, 1976; Midland Ladies Champion: 1954, 1956-60, 1969; toured Aust and NZ with Br Jr Team 1955, Eng Ladies Champion 1956, German Ladies Champion 1956, Canadian Ladies Champion 1967; represented GB and I v USA: 1958, 1964, 1968; represented GB and I v Euro: 1959, 1963, 1965, 1967 (non playing capt 1973, 1975); represented GB in Cwlth tournament 1959 and 1967; represented Eng in home int: 1955-59, 1963-66 (non playing capt 1973-74); int and nat selector 1983-88; tstee Rhodes Almshouses Birmingham 1983-; pres: Midlands Div Eng Ladies Golf Assoc 1988-91, Staffs Ladies Golf Assoc 1988-89; *Recreations* embroidery, golf, watching other sports; *Clubs* Edgbaston and Royal St David's Golf, Handsworth Hunstanton and Killarney Golf (hon life memb); *Style—* Miss Bridget Jackson

JACKSON, Barry Trevor; s of late Arthur Stanley Jackson, of Chingford, and Violet May, *née* Fry; *b* 7 July 1936; *Educ* Sir George Monoux GS, King's Coll London, Westminster Med Sch (entrance scholar, MB MS); *m* 1962, Sheila May, *née* Wood, of Bollington Cheshire; 2 s (Simon, James), 1 da (Sarah); *Career* surgn to HM's Household 1983-; conslt surgn: St Thomas' Hosp 1972-, Queen Victoria Hosp East Grinstead 1977-, King Edward VII Hosp for Offrs 1983-; hon sec Assoc Surgn of GB and Ireland 1986-91, hon conslt surgn to the Army 1990-; memb: Ct of Examiners RCS England 1983-89, Cncl RSM 1987 - (pres elect Section of Coloproctology 1990-91), Cncl Assoc of Coloproctology of GB and Ireland 1990-; asst ed Annals RCS England 1984-; FRCS; *Recreations* book collecting, reading, opera, the arts generally; *Clubs* Athenaeum; *Style—* Barry Jackson, Esq; Mapledene, 7 St Matthew's Ave, Surbiton, Surrey KT6 6JJ; St Thomas' Hosp, London SE1 7EH; The Consulting Rooms, York House, London SE1 7EH

JACKSON, Betty (Mrs David Cohen); MBE (1987); da of Arthur Jackson (d 1977), of Lancs, and Phyllis Gertrude, *née* Rains (d 1983); *b* 24 June 1949; *Educ* Bacup and Rawtenstall GS Lancs, Birmingham Coll Art and Design; *m* 14 Jan 1986, David Cohen, s of Mansour Cohen (d 1977), of Marseille, France; 1 s (Oliver Mansour b 1987), 1 da (Pascale Phyllis b 1986); *Career* chief designer Quorum 1973, fndr Betty Jackson Ltd 1981, launched Betty Jackson for Men 1986; Cotton Designer of the Year 1983, Br Designer of the Year 1985, Fil D'Or award by International Linen 1985 and 1989, Viyella award by Coates Viyella 1987; hon fell: Univ of Birmingham 1988, RCA 1989; RDI 1988; *Clubs* Moscow, Grouchos; *Style—* Miss Betty Jackson, MBE; 33 Tottenham St, London W1P 9PE (☎ 071 631 1010, fax 071 323 0609, telex 25663 Betty J G)

JACKSON, Very Rev Brandon Donald; s of Herbert Jackson (d 1977), and Millicent, *née* Haddock (d 1980); *b* 11 Aug 1934; *Educ* Stockport Sch, Univ of Liverpool, Univ of Oxford (LLB); *m* 1958, Mary Lindsay, da of John Philip; 2 s (Timothy Philip b 1959, Robert Brandon b 1961), 1 da (Sarah Lindsay b 1964); *Career* curate: Christ Church New Malden Surrey 1958-61, St George Leeds 1961-65; vicar St Peters Shipley 1965-77, provost Bradford Catholic 1977-89, dean of Lincoln 1989-; memb: Gen Synod of the C of E 1970-77 and 1980-89, Gen Synod Marriages Cmmn 1974-78; church cmmr 1971-73; memb: Cncl of Wycliffe Hall Oxford 1971-85, St John's Coll Nottingham 1986-89; govr: Harrogate Coll 1974-84, Bradford GS 1977, Bishop Grossteste Coll Lincoln 1989-, Lincoln Christ's Hosp Sch 1989-; scriptwriter conslt: Stars on Sunday, Emmerdale Farm; Hon DLitt Univ of Bradford 1990; *Recreations* sport, cricket, squash, fell-walking, fishing, reading; *Style—* The Very Rev the Dean of Lincoln; The Deanery, Eastgate, Lincoln, LN2 1QG

JACKSON, Calvin Leigh Raphael; s of Air Cdre John Arthur George Jackson, CBE, DFC, AFC, of Somerset Road, Wimbledon Common, London, and Yolanda Jackson; *b* 13 Aug 1952; *Educ* Douai Sch, King's Coll London (LLB, LLM), Corpus Christ Coll Cambridge (MPhil); *Career* called to the Bar Lincoln's Inn 1975, practice at Bar 1981-83, govt legal serv 1983-85, sr compensation conslt William M Mercer Fraser Ltd 1985-87, princ Coopers & Lybrand Deloitte 1987-; memb Hon Soc of Lincoln's Inn; *Clubs* Utd Oxford and Cambridge; *Style—* Calvin Jackson, Esq; c/o Coopers & Lybrand Deloitte, International and Executive Compensatial Division, Plumtree Court London EC4A 4HT (☎ 071 822 4885, fax 071 822 4488, telex 887470)

JACKSON, Dr Caroline Frances; MEP (C) Wiltshire 1984-; *b* 5 Nov 1946; *Educ* Sch of St Clare Penzance, St Hugh's Coll Oxford (MA), Nuffield Coll Oxford (DPhil); *m* 1975, Robert Victor Jackson; 1 s (decd); *Career* res fell St Hugh's Coll 1972, memb Oxford City Cncl 1970-73, Parly candidate (C) Birmingham Erdington 1974; EDG: secretariat Luxembourg 1974-76, Brussels 1976-78, head London Office 1979-84; dir: Peugeot Talbot UK Ltd 1987-, Inst Euro Environment Policy; memb: Nat Consumer Cncl 1982-84, UK Nat Ctee for Euro Environment Year 1987; *Books* A Student's Guide to Europe (1985), Europe's Environment: A Conservative Approach (1989); *Recreations* walking, painting, tennis, golf; *Style—* Dr Caroline Jackson, MEP; 74 Carlisle Mansions, Carlisle Place, London SW1P 1HZ (☎ 071 828 6113)

JACKSON, Charles Vivian; s of Louis Charles Jackson, MC, of E Sussex, and Sylvia, *née* Kerr; *b* 2 July 1953; *Educ* Marlborough, Magdalen Coll Oxford (MA), Stanford (MBA); *m* 12 Feb 1982, Frances Miriam, da of Frederick Schwartzstein (d 1982), of NJ; 1 s (David b 1985), 1 da (Rebecca b 1983); *Career* dir: Warburg Investment Management 1985-, Mercury Bond 1985-, Munich London 1986-; md Mercury Asset Management Holdings 1987- (dir 1986-87); *Clubs* Travellers'; *Style—* Charles Jackson, Esq; 33 King William St, London EC4R 9AS (☎ 071 280 2800)

JACKSON, Christopher Murray; MEP (C) Kent East 1979-; s of Rev Howard Murray Jackson (d 1955), and Doris Bessie Jackson; *b* 24 May 1935; *Educ* Kingswood Sch Bath, Magdalen Coll Oxford (MA), Univ of Frankfurt, LSE; *m* 1971, Carlie Elizabeth, da of Bernard Sidney Keeling; 1 s, 1 da; *Career* Nat Serv cmmd Pilot RAF; former dir of corp devpt Spillers Ltd, sr mangr Unilever Ltd; Cons pty spokesman on: co-operation with developing countries 1981-1986, agric 1987-89; elected dep ldr Br's Cons MEPs and dep chm Euro Democratic Gp 1989; *Style—* Christopher Jackson Esq, MEP; 8 Wellmeade Drive, Sevenoaks, Kent TN13 1QA (☎ 0732 456688)

JACKSON, Daphne Diana; da of Maj Thomas Casey MC, (d 1958), of Nairobi, Kenya, and Agnes Nora, *née* Gradden (d 1989); *b* 8 Oct 1933; *Educ* Folkestone GS; *m* 18 July 1953, John Hudleston Jackson, s of Henry John Huddlestone Jackson, (d 1945), of Newcastle, Staffs; *Career* personnel and central servs offr Borough Engr and Surveyor's Dept London Borough of Hounslow 1968-86, asst personnel offr City Engrs Dept City of Birmingham 1986-; chairperson Gen Advsy Ctee IBA 1985- (memb 1980-); memb: Nat Employment Ctee, Nat Assoc for the Care and Rehabilitation of Offenders 1984-86, WI and Soroptimist Int; govr Cleeve Prior CP School 1989-; Freeman City of London 1980, memb Worshipful Co of Chartered Secs and Admins 1980; ACIS; *Recreations* bereavement cnsllr, reading, embroidery, learning about antiques; *Style—* Mrs John Jackson; 3 Manor Ct, Cleeve Prior, Evesham, Worcs

WR11 5LQ (☎ 0789 772817); Personnel Div, City Engineer's Department, 1 Lancaster Circus, Queensway, Birmingham (☎ 021 300 7842)

JACKSON, Prof David Cooper; s of Rev James Jackson (d 1983), and Mary Emma Jackson; *b* 3 Dec 1931; *Educ* Ashville Coll Harrogate, Brasenose Coll Oxford (BCL, MA); *m* 1967, Roma Lilian, da of late William Pendergast; *Career* called to the Bar Inner Temple 1957, pt/t prof of law Univ of Southampton (prof of law 1971-84, dean 1972-75 and 1978-81, dep vice chllr 1983-84); dir Inst of Maritime Law Southampton 1983-84 and 1987-89, conslt Shipping Legislation UNCTAD 1979-80 and 1983-84; vice pres Immigration Appeal Tbnl; visiting prof: QMC London 1969, Arizona State Univ 1976; Sir John Latham prof of law Monash Univ Aust 1966-70; *Books* Principles of Property Law (1967), The Conflicts Process (1975), The Enforcement of Maritime Claims (1985), World Shipping Laws (gen ed, 1979), Civil Jurisdiction and Judgments: Maritime Claims (1987); *Recreations* travel; *Style*— Prof David Jackson; office: 231 Strand, London (☎ 071 353 8060)

JACKSON, Dr David Edward Pritchett; s of Reginald Robert George Pritchett Jackson, of Bridge Farm, Norwell Woodhouse, Newark on Trent, Notts, and Dorothy Elizabeth, *née* Hodgson (d 1989); *b* 9 Dec 1941; *Educ* Rossall Sch, MECAS Shemlan Lebanon, Pembroke Coll Cambridge (BA, MA, PhD, Judo half blue); *m* 9 July 1982, Margaret Letitia, da of Melville Brown, of 6 Bruce St, St Andrews, Fife; *Career* Lt-Cdr RNR 1972-82; res fell Pembroke Coll Cambridge 1967-70, sr lectr in Arabic studies Univ of St Andrews 1984- (asst lectr in Arabic language and lit 1967-68, lectr in Arabic studies 1968-84, chm dept 1979-86, dir Sch of Abbasid Studies 1979-), ed occasional papers Sch of Abbasid Studies; memb RNA St Andrews and NE Fife branch (memb Ctee 1984-86); fell Br Soc for Middle Eastern Studies 1974-; *Books* Saladin, the Politics of the Holy War (with MC Lyons, 1982); *Recreations* the river, music, food, golf; *Clubs* Hawks, Leander, Oriental, Royal and Ancient Golf (St Andrews); *Style*— Dr David Jackson; 5 River Terrace, Guardbridge, by St Andrews, Fife KY16 0XA (☎ 033483 561); Department of Arabic Studies, The University, St Andrews, Scotland KY16 9AL

JACKSON, Dominique; da of Fred Jackson, of W Yorks, and Christina, *née* Sands (d 1975); *b* 6 Jan 1962; *Educ* Assumption Convent Richmond N Yorks, Magdalen Coll Oxford (BA, scholar); *Career* Reuters News Agency 1984-88; assignments incl Hong Kong, Amsterdam, London, Rio de Janeiro; Financial Times London 1988-90, dep features ed The European 1990-; *Style*— Miss Dominique Jackson; The European, Orbit House, 5 New Fetter Lane, London EC4A 1AP (☎ 071 822 2020, fax 071 377 4773)

JACKSON, Douglas; s of Bernard Jackson (d 1953), of Walbrook House, Aylmer Road, London N2, and Johanna Jackson (d 1966); *b* 1 Sept 1916; *Educ* Guy's Hosp London (LDS); *Career* dental surgn 1938-71; numerous Violin and Piano recordings; Freeman City of London 1967, memb Guild of Freemen 1978; memb: BDA, BASCA FRCS; *Recreations* music (composer operas and classical music, surround sound, videos, charity concerts), inventing, photography, travel; *Style*— Douglas Jackson, Esq; 1 Broad Walk, Winchmore Hill, London N21 3DA (☎ 081 882 1100)

JACKSON, Sir (John) Edward; KCMG (1984, CMG 1977); *b* 21 June 1925; *Educ* Ardingly, Corpus Christi Coll Cambridge; *m* 1952, Eve Stainton, *née* Harris; 2 s, 1 da; *Career* Sub Lt, RNVR 1943-46; Dip Serv FO 1947-49, Br Embassy Paris 1949-52, Br Embassy Bonn 1956-59, NATO Def Coll 1969, cnsllr and political advsr Br Mil Govt Berlin 1969-73, head Def Dept FCO 1973-75, ambass to Havana 1975-79, head UK Delgn on Mutual and Balanced Reduction of Forces in Central Europe (ambass) 1980-82, ambass to Brussels 1982-85; chm Brecon Beacons Natural Waters - Spadel Ltd 1985-; dir Armistice Festival 1985-89; tstee Imperial War Museum 1985-, chm Anglo-Belgian Soc, dep chm Belgo-Luxembourg C of C; *Recreations* tennis, the arts; *Clubs* Anglo-Belgian, Hurlingham; *Style*— Sir Edward Jackson, KCMG

JACKSON, Enid, Lady; Enid; da of Stanley Hugh Groome (d 1965), of Kingston-upon-Thames; *m* 1, 1937 (m dis 1950), as his 2 w, (Alfred) Chester Beatty (d 1983); m 2, 1953, Sir John Montrésor Jackson, 6 Bt (d 1980); *Style*— Enid, Lady Jackson; Rose Cottage, Charing, Kent TN27 0EN

JACKSON, Graeme; s of Lewis Reginald Jackson, and Winifred Ivy Jackson; *b* 13 March 1943; *Educ* Brighton Coll; *m* 1, 22 Nov 1963, Elizabeth (decd); 1 s (Richard Andrew St John b 22 April 1964); m 2, 10 Aug 1972 (m dis 1980), Janet, da of Robert Tyndall; *Career* jr surveyor Ibbet Moseley Card 1959-61, surveyor Donaldson & Co 1961-64, dir Central of Dist Properties plc 1966-71 (surveyor 1964-66), chm London and Manchester Securities plc 1971-83, chm and chief exec Warringtons plc 1986-; *Recreations* ocean racing, real tennis, opera; *Clubs* RORC, Island SC, Queens (Royal Berkshire); *Style*— Graeme Jackson, Esq; 56 Grosvenor Hill, London W1X 2JE (☎ 01 499 2997); Burnside Cottage, Isle-of-Harris, Western Isles, Scotland; 12 Commandore Club, Punta Gorda, Florida, USA; 74 Grosvenor St, London W1X 9DD (☎ 071 491 2768, fax 071 499 0589, car 0860 344539)

JACKSON, Ina, Lady; Ina; da of James Leonard Joyce, FRCS, of Reading; *m* 1966, as his 2 w, Sir William Jackson, 7 Bt (d 1985); *Style*— Lady Jackson; 8 West View, Brampton, Cumbria CA8 1QC

JACKSON, Isaiah Allen III; s of Isaiah Allen Jackson Jr, MD (d 1983), and Alma, *née* Alverta Norris; *b* 22 Jan 1945; *Educ* Putney Sch, Harvard Univ (BA), Stanford Univ (MA), Juilliard Sch (MS, DMA); *m* 6 Aug 1977, Helen Caroline, da of Olaf Elert Tuntland; 1 s (Benjamin b 1980), 2 da (Katharine b 1982, Caroline b 1984); *Career* fndr and conductor Juilliard String Ensemble 1970-71; asst conductor: American Symphony (Stokowski) 1970-71, Baltimore Symphony (Comissiona) 1971-73; assoc conductor Rochester Philharmonic (Zinman) 1973-87; music dir: Flint Symphony 1982-87, Royal Ballet 1987-90 (princ conductor 1986), Dayton Philharmonic 1987-; *Style*— Isaiah Jackson, Esq; The Royal Ballet, Covent Garden, London WC2E 9DD (☎ 071 240 1200, fax 071 497 9220)

JACKSON, Brig John Albert; MBE (1971), GM (1974); s of John Albert Jackson (d 1982), and Evelyn Florence Kate, *née* Pinkney; *b* 18 Dec 1935; *Educ* Middlesbrough HS, RMC of Science Shrivenham; *m* 19 Nov 1960, Monica Beatrice Elizabeth, da of Frederick Shepherd (d 1983); 2 da (Fiona, Jane); *Career* RMA Sandhurst, Staff Coll Camberley, Army 1954-89, ret Brig; sec Bookmakers' Ctee Horse Race Betting Levy Bd 1989, memb local Cons Pty and church, selector C of E Advsy Cncl for Churchs Ministry; Liveryman Worshipful Co of Gold and Silver Wyre Drawers, Freeman City of London; FBIM 1971, FILDM 1987, MIPS 1987; *Recreations* choral singing; *Clubs* Army and Navy; *Style*— Brig John Jackson, MBE, GM; Horse Race Betting Levy Board, 52 Grosvenor Gardens, London SW1W 04U (☎ 071 730 4540, fax 071 823 5007, telex 9419514 LEVYBD G)

JACKSON, John David; s of Cecil Jackson (d 1986), and Gwendoline Jackson (d 1976); *b* 7 Dec 1933; *Educ* Oundle, McGill Univ Montreal (BComm, LA); *m* 11 Dec 1966, Hilary Anne, da of Sir Rudolph Lyons, QC, of Leeds; 4 da (Johanna b 1971, Julie b 1974, Jenny b 1976, Janie (twin) b 1976); *Career* chm: and md Centaur Clothes Manufacturing Ltd, JR Clothes Ltd, Alexandre of England 1988 Ltd, Leeds Western Health Authy; dir: William Baird plc, Leeds City Development Co Ltd, Nidd Vale Motors Ltd; memb Bd Leeds Development Corporation (UDC); pres Leeds Chamber of Commerce and Indust 1990-, chm Yorkshire and Humberside Region Br Clothing Industl Assoc (memb Exec Cncl); memb Inst of Chartered Accountants Quebec Canada; *Recreations* tennis, sailing, skiing (water & snow); *Style*— John Jackson, Esq; Red Oaks, Manor House Lane, Leeds LS17 9JD; Centaur Clothes (Manufacturing) Limited, 91 Great George St, Leeds, LS1 3BS

JACKSON, John Edgar; s of Wilfred Jackson JP (d 1965), of Burnley, and Sarah, *née* Duckworth (d 1956); *b* 11 Dec 1939; *Educ* Burnley GS, Kansas City CHS; *m* 1, 1963 (m dis 1987), Marilyn Cooper Jackson; 1 s (Jonathan b 1967), 1 da (Rebekah b 1965); m 2, 30 Sept 1988, Kathryn Lesley, da of Roland H Hughes, BEM, of Manchester; *Career* called to the Bar Middle Temple 1970; chm Burnley FC 1981-84 (dir 1976-84); *Recreations* soccer, horse racing; *Style*— John Jackson, Esq; Far Laithe, Lower Chapel Lane, Grindleton, Lancs BB7 4RN (☎ 0200 41561); 40 King St, Manchester (☎ 061 832 9082)

JACKSON, (Henry) John; s of James William Jackson, and Annie Margaret, *née* Best; *b* 10 Sept 1937; *Educ* Hackney Downs GS, Pitman's Coll; *m* 17 Aug 1972, Jill Yvonne, da of Albert Horace Ireson, OBE, of Seaford, E Sussex; *Career* served: 67 Trg Regt RAC 1955, 1 King's Dragoon Gds 1956-58, 28 Cwlth Inf Bde, 17 Gurkha Div Malaya; telephone typist Press Assoc Sport 1952-54, sub ed The Scotsman 1954-55, racing reporter and sub ed Press Assoc Sport 1958-62, racing sub ed Daily Telegraph Sport 1962-66, reporter Ilford Pictorial 1966-67, educn and Parly corr London Evening News 1967-75, Parly rep Press Assoc 1975-76, freelance 1976-79, reporter Saudi Press Agency 1979-80, publishing dir Municipal Jl 1989-90 (ed 1980, dir 1986-89), ed Public Money 1990-; memb: Cromwell Assoc, Br Horse Soc, Br Field Sports Soc, Redbridge LBC 1968-74; Parly candidate (cons) Erith Crayford 1970 and Hornchurch 1974; Freeman City of London; memb Worshipful Co of Loriners; *Recreations* horseriding, cricket, English Civil War history; *Clubs* MCC; *Style*— John Jackson, Esq; Wingfield Farm, Wing, Leighton Buzzard LU7 0LD (☎ 0296 688 972); Public Money, 50 Poland St, London W1V 4AX (☎ 071 287 9800, fax 071 287 8873)

JACKSON, Judith Margaret (Mrs John Horam); da of Ernest Jackson, MBE (d 1970), and Lucy Margaret Jackson (d 1990); *b* 1 May 1936; *Educ* Dartington Hall Sch, Univ of London (BA, LGSM), Univ of Paris (Dip Civ Fr); *m* 6 June 1963 (m dis 1976), Peter Jopp, s of George Jopp (d 1969); 2 s (Fraser b 1965, Lincoln b 1968); m 2, John Rhodes Horam *qv*; *Career* TV presenter Associated Rediffusion 1961-65 and BBC 1965-80; motoring ed: The Sunday Times 1970-84, The Guardian 1987-; dir: UK 2000 1987-, Dartington Int Summer Sch 1984-; hon treas Woman on the Move Against Cancer; *Books* Man and the Automobile (1979); *Recreations* music, cookery; *Style*— Miss Judith Jackson; 6 Bovingdon Rd, London SW6 2AP (☎ 071 736 8521)

JACKSON, Keith Arnold; s of late John Keith Jackson and hp of kinsman, Sir Robert Jackson, Bt; *b* 1921; *m* Pauline Mona, da of B P Climo, of Wellington, NZ; 4 s, 1 da; *Style*— Keith Jackson, Esq; Coast Rd, Wainuiomata, New Zealand

JACKSON, Keith Ian; s of Herbert George Jackson (d 1971), of Leicester, and Betty Edith Jackson; *Educ* Guthlaton GS Wigston Leicester, Univ of Sheffield (BA); *m* 22 Oct 1983, Jacqueline Mary, da of Kenneth John Pink, of Little Plumstead, Norfolk; *Career* called to the Bar Middle Temple 1975; in practice Midland and Oxford Circuit 1976-; *Recreations* gardening, listening to music, food and wine; *Style*— Keith Jackson, Esq; Romsey House, Main St, Newton, Notts NG13 8HN; King Charles House Chambers, Standard Hill, Notts NGL 6FX (☎ 0602 418851, fax 0602 414169)

JACKSON, Keith William; s of William Henry Jackson (d 1979), of Liverpool, and Elsie May, *née* Cockburn; *b* 21 Nov 1942; *Educ* Liverpool Coll, Univ of Liverpool (LLB); *m* 1, 21 June 1969 (m dis 1979), Janet Mary, da of George Cecil Lees, of The Wirral; 2 da (Sarah Ann b 1974, Louise Claire (twin) b 1974); m 2, 16 June 1989, Diana Georgina, da of Prof Roger Arthur Burgess, of Wirral; *Career* slr; ptnr Philip Jones Hillyer & Jackson of Chester and Bebington; hockey: English Univs, Lancs (capt 1975-76), North of England and England B, pres Lancs Hockey Assoc 1986-88; cricket: rep Liverpool competition winners Steiner Cup 1975, capt Neston CC 1974-75; *Recreations* golf, cricket, squash, gardening; *Clubs* Eaton Park Golf, Neston Cricket, Northern Hockey; *Style*— Keith Jackson, Esq; Parry's Well, The Rake, Burton, South Wirral, Cheshire (☎ 051 336 2735); Bell Tower Walk, Chester (☎ 0244 45551, fax 0244 42824)

JACKSON, Kenneth (Ken); s of Joseph Henry Jackson (d 1965), of Dewsbury, and Ada, *née* Smith (d 1981); *b* 23 Sept 1939; *Educ* Dewsbury Wheelwright GS, Batley Tech and Art Coll, Harvard Business Sch; *m* 25 Aug 1962, Elisabeth Joyce, da of David William Wilks (d 1975), of Dewsbury; 1 s ((Stephen) David b 8 Feb 1970); *Career* md Spencer & Halstead Ltd 1971 (personnel dir 1968-); vice pres: Bonded Abrasives Europe Carborundum & Co USA 1978, (sales and mktg) Abrasives Carborundum Div Sohio 1981; gp md Carborundum Abrasives plc (became Carbo plc 1984); *Recreations* travel, gardening; *Style*— Ken Jackson, Esq; Savile Ings Farm, Holywell Green, Halifax, W Yorks HX4 9BS (☎ 0422 372608); Carbo plc, Lakeside, PO Box 55, Trafford Pk, Manchester M17 1HP (☎ 061 872 2381, fax 061 872 1471, telex 667344 CARBOM G)

JACKSON, Very Rev Lawrence; s of Walter Jackson (d 1947), and Edith, *née* Gray (d 1955); *b* 22 March 1926; *Educ* Alderman Newton's Sch Leicester, King's Coll London (AKC); *m* 1955, Faith Anne, da of Philip Henry Seymour, of Suffolk; 4 da (Charlotte b 1955, Deborah b 1957, Rachel b 1961, Lucy b 1966); *Career* asst curate St Margaret's Leicester 1951-54; vicar of: Wymeswold 1955-59, St James The Greater Leicester 1959-65, Coventry 1965-73; canon of Coventry Cathedral 1967-73, provost of Blackburn 1973-; memb Gen Synod of the C of E 1974-, church cmmr 1981-, sr chaplain ACF Leics, Rutland and Warwick 1955-70; Liveryman Worshipful Co of Fruiterers; *Recreations* music, architecture, theatre, countryside, after dinner speaking; *Clubs* Carlton, Eccentric, Lord's Taverners, Forty, Lighthouse; *Style*— The Very Rev Lawrence Jackson; The Provost's House, Preston New Rd, Blackburn BB2 6PS (☎ 0254 52502); Provost's Office, Cathedral Close, Blackburn BB1 5AA (☎ 0254 51814)

JACKSON, Marilyn; da of Alfred Thomas Wilson (d 1988), of 26 Appletree Gdns, Walkerville, Newcastle Upon Tyne, and Mary Wilhelmina, *née* Liddie; *b* 27 Jan 1945; *Educ* Stephenson Meml HS Wallsend, Coll of Further Educn Whitley Bay; *m* 15 Oct 1966, David Henry Jackson, s of Henry Jackson (d 1983); 2 da (Peta b 1969, Trudi b 1973); *Career* fashion model 1966-79, TV hostess Opportunity Knocks 1967-68, admin Jeanette McNamee Model Agency 1977-78, personnel offr Co-op Laundry Soc Wallsend 1978-80, asst to indust dir T Crossling and Co Ltd 1980-87, co sec Regional Engineers Distributors Group Ltd 1982-90, memb Bd G & AE Slingsby Ltd Hull 1988- (admin mangr 1987); sec Battle Hill Townswomen Guild 1975-78 (chm 1972-75); *Recreations* housework!; *Style*— Mrs Marilyn Jackson; 82 Montagu Ave, Gosforth, Newcastle Upon Tyne NE3 4SB (☎ 091 285 3752); G & A E Slingsby Ltd, Leads Rd, Hull HU8 0DD (☎ 0482 838 880, fax 0482 878 827)

JACKSON, Brig Michael David (Mike); MBE (1979); s of Maj George Michael Jackson (d 1982), of Camberley, Surrey, and Ivy, *née* Bower; *b* 21 March 1944; *Educ* Stamford Sch, Univ of Birmingham (BSoc Sc), RMA Sandhurst; *m* 2, 4 May 1985, Sarah Carolyn, da of Col Brian Jackson Coombe, GM, of Dormy House, Wood's Hill, Limpley Stoke, Wilts; 2 s (Mark b 1973, Thomas b 1990), 1 da (Amanda b 1971); *Career* bde maj Berlin Inf Bde 1977-78, co cdr 2 Para 1979-80, directing staff Staff Coll 1981-83, CO1 Para 1984-86, sr directing staff Jt Serv Def Coll 1986-88, serv fell Wolfson Coll Cambridge 1989, cdr 39 Inf Bde 1989-; memb MENSA; Freeman City of

London 1988; *Books* Central Region vs Out-of-Area: Future Commitments, Tri-Service Press, 1990 (contrib, 1990); *Recreations* skiing, tennis, music; *Style—* Brig Mike Jackson, MBE; Regtl HQ, The Parachute Regt, Browning Barracks, Aldershot, Hants GU11 2BU

JACKSON, Michael Edward Wilson; s of Sqdn Ldr Edward Grosvenor Jackson, of The Field House, E Rigton, Yorks, and Yvonne Brenda Jackson, OBE, *née* Wilson; *b* 16 March 1950; *Educ* The Leys Sch, Cambridge Univ (LLB); *m* 1, 19 April 1980 (m dis), Prudence Elizabeth Robinson, da of Michael John Boardman, of White Howe, Norfolk; m 2, 18 Nov 1989, Harriet Leigh, da of Air Cdre Denis Wilson; *Career* dir The Guidehouse Gp plc 1983-; FCA 1986; *Recreations* tennis; *Clubs* The Vanderbilt Tennis, Royal Automobile, Annabel's; *Style—* Michael Jackson, Esq; 80 Deodar Rd, Putney, London SW15 (☎ 081 874 4564); Vestry House, Greyfriars Passage, Newgate St, London EC1R 7BA (☎ 071 606 6321)

JACKSON, (Richard) Michael; CVO (1983); s of Richard William Jackson (d 1979), of Bexhill, and Charlotte, *née* Wrightson (d 1978); *b* 12 July 1940; *Educ* Darlington GS, Paisley GS, Univ of Glasgow (MA); *m* 27 Dec 1961, Mary Elizabeth (Mollie), da of Dr Andrew Symington Kitchin (d 1978), of Skelmorlie, Ayrshire; 1 s (Andrew b 1968), 1 da (Dorothy b 1963); *Career* SO 1961-72, The Hague 1972-75, transferred to Dip Serv 1975, Euro Integration Dept FCO 1975-76, Panama City 1976-79, Arms Control and Disarmament Dept FCO 1979-81, Buenos Aires 1981-82, Falkland Islands Dept FCO 1982, Stockholm 1982-87, Seoul 1987-; Cdr of Order of Northern Star Sweden 1983; *Recreations* bird-watching, real ale; *Style—* R M Jackson, Esq, CVO; c/o FCO (Seoul), King Charles Street, London SW1 2AH

JACKSON, Sir Michael Roland; 5 Bt (UK 1902), of Stansted House, Stansted, Essex; s of Sir (Walter David) Russell Jackson, 4 Bt (d 1956), and Kathleen, *née* Hunter (d 1975); *b* 20 April 1919; *Educ* Stowe, Clare Coll Cambridge (MA); *m* 1, 1942 (m dis 1969), (Hilda) Margaret, da of Cecil George Herbert Richardson, CBE (d 1976); 1 s, 1 da; m 2, 1969, Hazel Mary, da of Ernest Harold Edwards (d 1981); *Heir* s, Thomas Jackson; *Career* WWII, Flt Lt RAFVR; engr ret 1979; CEng, MIEE, FIQA; *Style—* Sir Michael Jackson, Bt; Jolliffe's House, Stour Row, Shaftesbury, Dorset SP7 0QW

JACKSON, Sir Nicholas Fane St George; 3 Bt (UK 1913), of Eagle House, Wimbledon, Surrey; s of Sir Hugh Nicholas Jackson, 2 Bt (d 1979), and Violet, Lady Jackson, *qv*; the 1 baronet, Sir T G Jackson, Bt, was the architect responsible for many buildings in Oxford incl Examination Schools Brasenose, Hertford and Trinity Coll Oxford; *b* 4 Sept 1934; *Educ* Radley Coll, Wadham Coll Oxford, Royal Acad of Music; *m* 1, 1961 (m dis 1968), Jennifer Ann, da of F A Squire, of 8 Marylebone St, Wondon W1; m 2 1972, Nadia Francoise Genevieve, da of Georges Michard, of St Etienne, France; 1 s; *Heir* s, Thomas Graham St George Jackson b 5 Oct 1980; *Career* organist, harpsichordist and composer; organist: St Anne's Soho 1963-68, St James's Piccadilly 1971-74, St Lawrence Jewry 1974-77; organist and master of the choristers St David's Cathedral 1977-84, musical dir and fndr St David's Cathedral Bach Festival 1979; concert tours: USA, France, Germany, Spain, Japan, Belgium; dir Festival Bach at Santes Creus Spain 1987; dir Concertante of London 1987-; jr Warden Worshipful Co of Drapers 1985-86; LRAM, ARCM; compositions published by Boosey & Hawkes, Cardiff Univ Press, Anglo-American Publishers; *Recreations* travel, writing; *Style—* Sir Nicholas Jackson, Bt

JACKSON, Hon Mrs (Pamela); *née* Freeman-Mitford; 2 da of 2 Baron Redesdale, JP (d 1958), and Sydney, *née* Bowles (d 1963), and sis of Nancy, Jessica, and Unity Mitford, Hon Lady Mosley, and (Debo) Duchess of Devonshire; *b* 25 Nov 1907; *m* 1936 (m dis 1951), Wing Cdr Prof Derek Ainslie Jackson, OBE, DFC, AFC, RAFVR, s of Sir Charles Jackson; *Style—* The Hon Mrs Jackson; Woodfield House, Caudle Green, Cheltenham, Glos (☎ 028 582 300)

JACKSON, (Kevin) Paul; s of T Leslie Jackson, of 22 Welsby Court, Eaton Rise, London W5, and Jo, *née* Spoonley; *b* 2 Oct 1947; *Educ* Gunnersbury GS, Univ of Exeter (BA); *m* 21 Aug 1981, Judith Elizabeth, da of John Charles Cain, DSO, of The Old Bakery, Cowden, Kent; 2 da (Amy b 1981, Katie b 1984); *Career* stage mgmnt: Marlowe Theatre Canterbury 1970, Thorndike Theatre Leatherhead 1971; prodn work BBC TV: Two Ronnies, 3 of a Kind, Carrott's Lib, The Young Ones, Happy Families 1971-82; freelance prodr and dir: Canon and Ball, Girls on Top 1982-84; prodr and chm Paul Jackson Productions: Red Dwarf, Don't Miss Wax, Saturday Live 1984-86; exec prodr Appointments of Dennis Jennings (Oscar Best Live Action Short 1989); md NGTV 1987; Guardian columnist 1988, chm Comic Relief 1987-, vice chm Charity Projects 1990-; memb IPPA Cncl 1987-88; BAFTA 1983 and 1984; *Recreations* theatre, rugby, travel, food and wine, friends and family; *Style—* Paul Jackson, Esq; 24 Denmark St, London WC2H 8NJ (☎ 071 379 5953, fax 071 379 0831, telex 21760 RANGO G)

JACKSON, Paul Mervyn; s of Brian Mervyn Jackson (d 1979), and Margaret Irene, *née* Sythes; *b* 12 July 1947; *Educ* Cranleigh Sch; *m* 15 June 1974, Nina Ann, da of Robert Ferdinand Delliére; 2 da (Portia b 12 June 1977, Olivia b 19 April 1979); *Career* surveyor; fndr Victory Land Ltd 1983; Freeman City of London 1972, Liveryman Worshipful Co of Merchant Taylors 1978; FRICS 1970; *Recreations* golf, running, Formula 1 motor racing; *Style—* Paul Jackson, Esq; The Old Farm, 6 Fife Rd, London SW14 7EP; Victory Land Ltd, 46/47 Pall Mall, London SW1Y 5JG (☎ 071 408 1067, fax 071 493 8633, car 0836 292 562)

JACKSON, Peter Grayling; *Career* publisher and md of News International Hachette Ltd (publishers of Elle Magazine in Britain and SKY Magazine throughout Europe), formerly ed of Sunday Times Magazine, and SUNDAY (News of the World's magazine); twice winner of Editor of the Year award (presented by Br Soc of Magazine Editors) for work on: TV Times 1974, and SUNDAY 1981; *Clubs* RAC, Steering Wheel; *Style—* Peter Jackson, Esq; c/o News International Hachette Ltd, 4-12 Lower Regent Street, London SW1 (☎ 01 930 9050)

JACKSON, Peter Guy; s of Edwin Arthur Jackson (d 1953), of 13 North St, Ashford, Kent, and Grace Marion, *née* Rudd (d 1942); *b* 5 Nov 1921; *Educ* Ashford GS, Herne Bay Coll; *m* 1, 26 April 1943, Joan Dorothy (d 1951), da of Wilfred Abraham Caton (d 1980), of Essex; 2 s (Richard Peter Caton b 1945 d 1947, James Edwin Caton b 1947), 1 da (Anne b 1949); m 2, 17 May 1952 (m dis 1984), Barbara Eveline Caton; 2 da (Jane b 1955, Gillian b 1958); m 3, 2 Feb 1985, Janice Wager; *Career* Cadet Br India Steam Navigation Co 1939-42; RNR: Sub Lt 1943-45, Lt 1945-63, Lt Cdr 1963-66; E C Harris & Ptnrs chartered quantity surveyors: joined 1952, ptnr 1962, conslt 1978-; studying for Lay Miny Anglican Church; Freeman City of London, Liveryman Worshipful Co of Needlemakers; ARICS 1949, FRICS 1962; *Recreations* gardening, DIY, model making; *Style—* Peter Jackson, Esq; Richmond Cottage, Fambridge Rd, Althorne, Chelmsford, Essex CM3 6BZ (☎ 0621 741 022); c/o E C Harris Partners, The Old Rectory, Church Rd, Bowers Gifford, Basildon, Essex (☎ 0268 559 666, fax 0268 858 153)

JACKSON, Peter John Edward; s of David Charles Jackson (d 1977), of Kent, and Sarah Ann, *née* Manester; *b* 14 May 1944; *Educ* Brockley County GS, Sprachen und Dolmetscher Inst Hamburg, Univ of London (LLB), Tübingen Univ W Germany (Dr Jur); *m* 23 Sept 1967, Ursula Henny, da of Paul Schubert (d 1945), and Henny Schubert (d 1980), of Hamburg; 2 da (Philippa b 1972, Pia b 1984); *Career* called to the Bar Middle Temple, and N Ireland, dep circuit judge 1979-81, asst rec 1982-83, rec of Crown Ct 1983-; *Recreations* horse riding, German language, German law; *Style—* Dr Peter Jackson; 3 Pump Court Temple, London EC4Y 7AJ (☎ 071 353 0711, fax 071 353 3319); D 7000 Stuttgart 50, Seelbergstrasse 8 (☎ 0711 561465, fax 0711 552407)

JACKSON, Peter Maitland; s of Leonard Edward Jackson (d 1988), of Shanklin House, Loughborough Rd, Rothley, Leics, and Contance Mary, *née* White; *b* 13 June 1949; *Educ* Loughborough GS; *m* 20 Oct 1984, Jacqueline Mary, da of Frederick Harrison, of 43 Westfield Drive, Loughborough, Leics; 2 s (Matthew b 15 Dec 1986, Samuel b 2 March 1990); *Career* chm L E Jackson (Coachworks) Ltd 1988- (md 1981-); memb: Nat Mfrs Cncl GB 1983, Rotary Club of Loughborough; IOTA 1980; *Recreations* music, fly fishing; *Style—* Peter M Jackson, Esq; L E Jackson (Coachworks) Ltd, Vehicle Body Centre, Queens Road, Loughborough, Leicester LE11 1HD (☎ 0509 230811, fax 0509 216117); Charnwood Lodge, 148 Swithland Lane, Rothley, Leicestershire LE7 7SF

JACKSON, Dr Peter Warren; s of Dr Robert Edward Jackson, and Rosina Kathleen, *née* Warren; *b* 7 Feb 1935; *Educ* St Bees Sch Cumbria, Victoria Univ Manchester (MB ChB); *m* 1, 23 April 1960 (m dis 1980), Ann, da of Sydney James Wrigglesworth (d 1965); 3 s (Nicholas b 1961, David d 1963, Michael b 1964), 1 da (Susan b 1964); m 2, 30 May 1980, Susan Evelyn, da of Peter John Tyndall (d 1987); *Career* conslt anaesthetist Manchester Royal Infirmary 1968; fell Manchester Med Soc (pres Section of Anaesthetics 1988-89); memb: BMA, HCSA; fell Coll of Anaesthetists; *Books* Practical Anaesthesia for Surgical Emergencies (ed); *Recreations* golf, fishing, shooting, bowls; *Clubs* Wilmslow Golf, Ollerton Gun; *Style—* Dr Peter Jackson; Fortingall, 88 Hollin Lane, Styal, Wilmslow, Cheshire SK9 4JJ (☎ 0625 523815); Dept of Anaesthetics, Royal Infirmary, Manchester (☎ 061 276 4551, car 0860 615921)

JACKSON, Air Vice-Marshal Sir Ralph Coburn; KBE (1973), CB (1963); s of Ralph Jackson (d 1937), and Phillis Cooper, *née* Dodds (d 1964); *b* 22 June 1914; *Educ* Oakmount Westmorland, Guy's Hosp; *m* 1939, Joan Lucy, da of Lewellin de Sidnia Crowley (d 1952); 2 s, 2 da; *Career* joined RAF 1938, WWII served France, Russia, W Africa (despatches, served MO 46 Gp for Br Casualty Air Evacuation 1944-45); consIt in med RAF Hosps 1946-66: Aden, Halton, Wegberg; gp capt 1957, MacArthur lectr Univ of Edinburgh 1959, Air Cdre 1961, consIt advsr in med RAF 1966-74, advsr in med CAA 1966-75, Air Vice-Marshal 1969, QHP 1969-75, sr consIt RAF 1971-75; chm Def Med Servs Post Grad Cncl 1973-75; med referee to various life insur cos 1976-88; hon civil consIt in med to RAF 1975-, hon med consIt RAF Benevolent Fund 1975-, dir and med advsr French Hosp Rochester 1986-; Lady Cade medal RCS 1960; Freeman City of London, Liveryman Worshipful Soc of Apothecaries; FRCP, FRCPE, MRCS; *Recreations* bird and wildlife watching, genealogy; *Clubs* RAF; *Style—* Air Vice-Marshal Sir Ralph Jackson, KBE, CB; Cherry Trees, Ball Rd, Pewsey, Wilts SN9 5BL (☎ 0672 62042)

JACKSON, Raymond Allen (Jak); s of Sgt Maurice Jackson (d 1960), and Mary Ann, *née* Murphy; *b* 11 March 1927; *Educ* Clipstone Road Sch London, Lyulph Stanley Central, Willesden Sch of Art (Nat Cert in Drawing, Dip in Illustration); *m* Claudie Sidonie, da of Henri Grenier (d 1974); 1 s (Patrick b 1 Oct 1959), 2 da (Dominique b 20 Sept 1957, Nathalie b 5 Feb 1965); *Career* Nat Serv Sgt RAOC 1945-48 (attached Educn Corps); Link House Group 1950-51, Keymers Advertising 1951-52, cartoonist Evening Standard 1952-; *Books* JAK Annuals 1971-; *Recreations* judo; *Clubs* Judokan; *Style—* Raymond Jackson, Esq; Northcliffe House, 2 Derry St, Kensington W8 5EE (☎ 071 938 7556)

JACKSON, Richard Anthony; s of Harold Reginald Jackson (d 1948), of Harrogate, N Yorks, and Irene Dallas, *née* Nelson (d 1968); *b* 31 March 1932; *Educ* Cheltenham; *Career* Nat Serv RE 1950-52; salesman Henry A Lane & Co Ltd 1953-56, merchandising asst Walt Disney Productions Ltd 1956-59, dir Richard Jackson Personal Management Ltd (actors representation); produced plays in London West End and on Fringe incl: Madame de Sade (Kings Head) 1975, Charles Trenet in concert (Royal Albert Hall) 1975, The Bitter Tears of Petra Von Kant (New End) 1976, An Evening with Quentin Crisp (Duke of Yorks and Ambassadors) 1978, The Singular Life of Albert Nobbs, Alterations, Tribute to Lili Lamont (New End) 1978, Flashpoint (New End and Mayfair) 1978, A Day in Hollywood, A Night in The Ukraine (New End and Mayfair, Evening Standard Award for Best Musical and Plays and Players Award for Best Comedy) 1979, The Square, La Musica, Portrait of Dora (New End) 1979, Appearances (Mayfair) 1980, A Galway Girl (Lyric Studio) 1980, Bar and Ger (Lyric Studio) 1981, Latin (Lyric Studio) 1983, The Human Voice (with Susannah York, performed world-wide since 1984) Swimming Pools at War (Offstage) 1985, Matthew, Mark, Luke and Charlie (Latchmere) 1986, I Ought to be in Pictures (Offstage) 1986, Pier Pasolini (Offstage) 1987, Creditors, Latin (New End) 1989 Beached (Old Red Lion) 1990, Hamlet (Howarth Festival U.S.A.) 1990; memb BAFTA; *Recreations* table tennis, crosswords; *Clubs* Green Room; *Style—* Richard Jackson, Esq; 48 William Mews, London SW1X 9HQ (☎ 071 235 3759); 59 Knightsbridge, London SW1X 7RA (☎ 071 235 3671)

JACKSON, Maj Richard Francis Laidlay; TD (1945); s of Francis Crichton Jackson (d 1947), and Frances Isobel, *née* Laidlay (d 1963); *b* 19 July 1917; *Educ* Tonbridge, Wye Coll London; *m* 30 Dec 1944, Anne Kythe Mackenzie, da of Walter Lee (d 1940), of India; 3 da (Jacqueline (Mrs Scott) b 23 April 1947, Penelope (Mrs Shaw) b 4 Oct 1949, Frances (Mrs Geoghegan) b 29 Nov 1951); *Career* cmmnd RA (TA) 1939, AA Cmd 1939-42, served Ceylon 1942-43, Burma 1943-44 (DAQMG); ptnr Wood Hanbury Rhodes & Jackson 1945-66, chm Morris Hanbury Jackson 1980 (ptnr and dir 1966-81); memb: Pony Club 1965-68, Cons Assoc 1965-70; *Recreations* croquet, gardening; *Style—* Maj Richard Jackson, TD; Shipley Hall, Brooks Green, Horsham, W Sussex (☎ 0403 741 409)

JACKSON, Richard Peter; s of Richard Charles Jackson (d 1982), of Newlands, Fowlmere, Cambs, and Allison Mary Clare, *née* Hicks; *b* 21 March 1944; *Educ* Bishop's Stortford Coll Herts, City Univ London (BSc); *m* 1, 30 April 1966 (m dis 1986), Rosemary Phyllis Choat Stickels, da of Samuel Harry Choat Jenkins, of Rougham Hill, Bury St Edmunds, Suffolk; 2 s (Piers b 1970, Giles b 1972); m 2, 24 July 1987, Annabel Gemma Jane (formerly Mrs Gunn), da of Maj Rodney Charles Hitchcock (d 1969), of Branch Hill, Hampstead, London; *Career* indentured engr George Wimpey & Co London 1963-69, structural engr Firth Cleveland Jamaica 1969-71, sec engr Bullen & Ptnrs Croydon 1971-73, assoc John Powlesland & Assoc Colchester 1973-76, sr ptnr Richard Jackson Partnership Hadleigh Ipswich Suffolk and London Docklands 1976-; memb Ctee E Anglian branch Faculty of Bldg (former chm), memb Ctee E Anglian branch Lighthouse Club; CEng 1969, MICE 1971, MConsE 1983, FIStructE 1983; *Recreations* tennis, skiing; *Clubs* Placemakers, Lighthouse; *Style—* Richard Jackson, Esq; Hill Barn, Hitcham, Ipswich, Suffolk (☎ 0449 741 399); Richard Jackson Ptnrship, Consulting Civil & Structural Engineers, 26 High St, Hadleigh, Ipswich, Suffolk IP7 5AP (☎ 0473 823 939, fax 0473 823 226)

JACKSON, Sir Robert; 7 Bt (UK 1815), of Arlsey, Bedfordshire; s of Maj Francis Gorham Jackson (d 1942, 2 s of 4 Bt); suc kinsman, Sir John Montrésor Jackson, 6 Bt 1980; *b* 16 March 1910; *Educ* St George's Coll; *m* 1943, Maria E Casamayou, of Montevideo, Uruguay; 2 da; *Heir* kinsman, Keith Jackson; *Clubs* English

(Montevideo); *Style—* Sir Robert Jackson, Bt; Bulevard Artigas 266, Flat 601, Montevideo, Uruguay (☎ 010 598 2 71 5032)

JACKSON, Robert Kenneth; s of John Kenneth Jackson (d 1977), of Kendal, Cumbria, and Laura Theresa, *née* Rankin (d 1976); *b* 26 Feb 1933; *Educ* Heversham GS, Clare Coll Cambridge (MB BCh, MA), St Thomas's Hosp Med Sch; *m* 21 June 1967, Margaret Elizabeth, da of Norman Dixon, of Aycliffe, Co Durham; 1 s (Robert Andrew b 2 April 1970), 1 da (Emma Jane b 20 Feb 1968); *Career* Surgn Spec RAF 1960-64; chief asst Orthopaedic Dept St Thomas' Hosp London 1966-71, conslt orthopaedic surgn Southampton Gen Hosp 1971-; exec memb Br Scoliosis Soc, conslt memb Southampton Health Authy; FRCS 1964, fell Br Orthopaedic Assoc; *Books* More Dilemmas in the Management of the Neurological Patient (1987); *Recreations* fishing, orienteering, mountaineering; *Clubs* RAF; *Style—* Robert Jackson, Esq; 12 Brookvale Rd, Southampton, Hants (☎ 0703 555047); Southampton General Hospital, 4 Hulse Rd, Soythampton SO1 2JX (☎ 0703 224229)

JACKSON, Robert Victor; MP (C) Wantage 1983-; *b* 24 Sept 1946; *Educ* Falcon Coll S Rhodesia, St Edmund Hall Oxford, All Souls Coll Oxford; *m* 1975, Caroline Frances, DPhil, MEP (C) Wilts 1984-, da of G H Harvey; 1 s decd; *Career* memb Oxford City Cncl 1969-71, political advsr to Employment sec 1973-74, Parly candidate (C) Manchester Central Oct 1974, memb Cabinet of Sir Christopher Soames (now Lord Soames, *qv*), EEC Cmmn 1974-76, chef de cabinet to Pres EEC Econ and Social Ctee Brussels 1976-78, MEP (C) Upper Thames 1979-84, special advsr to Lord Soames as Govr Rhodesia 1979-80, rapporteur European Parl Budget Ctee 1982-; Parly under sec of state: DES with responsibility for higher educn and sci 1987-90, Dept of Employment with responsibility for training and the Employment Serv 1990-; former ed The Round Table and Int Affrs (Chatham House); author of several books; *Style—* Robert Jackson, Esq, MP; New House, Southmoor, Oxfordshire OX13 5HR (☎ 0865 821243); 74 Carlisle Place, London SW1P 1HT (☎ 01 828 6113)

JACKSON, (Michael) Rodney; s of John William Jackson, of N Humberside, and Nora, *née* Phipps (d 1984); *b* 16 April 1935; *Educ* Queen Elizabeth GS Wakefield, Queens' Coll Cambridge (MA, LLM); *m* 1968, Anne Margaret, da of Prof Eric William Hawkins, CBE, of N Humberside; 2 s (Nicholas b 1969, Richard b 1972); *Career* admitted slr 1962; rec of the Crown Ct 1985-; Notary Public 1967; *Recreations* fell walking; *Clubs* Royal Cwlth Soc; *Style—* Rodney Jackson, Esq; 11 The Paddock, Swanland, North Ferriby, North Humberside HU14 3QW (☎ 0482 633278); PO Box 47, Victoria Chambers, Bowlalley Lane, Hull HU1 1XY (☎ 0482 25242, telex 592419, fax 0482 212974)

JACKSON, Dr (William) Roland Cedric; s and h of Sir Thomas Jackson, 8 Bt, *qv*; *b* 9 Jan 1954; *Educ* Wycliffe Coll, St Peter's Coll Oxford (MA), Exeter Coll Oxford (DPhil); *m* 1977, Nicola Mary, yr da of Prof Peter Davis, of St Mawes, Cornwall; 3 s (Adam William Roland b 1982, James Anthony Foljambe b 1984, Oliver Thomas Peter b 1990); *Career* head of science Backwell Sch 1986-89; educn advsr ICI 1989-; *Style—* Dr Roland Jackson; Summer Hill, 14 Glebe Rd, Welwyn, Herts AL6 9PB (☎ 0438 840255)

JACKSON, Rupert Matthew; QC (1987); s of George Henry Jackson (d 1981), and Nancy Barbara, *née* May; *b* 7 March 1948; *Educ* Christ's Hosp, Jesus Coll Cambridge (MA, LLB); *m* 20 Sept 1975, Claire Corinne, da of Harry Potter (d 1979); 3 da (Corinne b 1981, Chloe b 1983, Tamsin b 1985); *Career* called to the Bar Middle Temple 1972, practising SE Circuit, rec 1990; FRSA; *Books* Professional Negligence (jtly, 2 edn 1987); *Style—* Rupert Jackson, Esq, QC; 2 Crown Office Row, Temple, London EC4Y 7HJ (☎ 071 583 8155, fax 071 583 1205)

JACKSON, Hon Mrs Edward (Susannah Albinia); *née* Chaytor; yst da of late (Alfred) Drewett Chaytor, of Spennithorne Hall, Leyburn, Yorks; *b* 13 Nov 1939; *m* 1971, as his 2 w, Capt Hon Edward Lawies Jackson, RHG (d 1982), o son of 3 Baron Allerton, *qv*; 2 da (Olivia Susannah b 1975, Katharine Elizabeth b 1978); *Career* photographer; *Style—* Hon Mrs Edward Jackson; The Old Rectory, Cottisford, Brackley, Northants NN13 5SW

JACKSON, Thomas St Felix; s and h of Sir Michael Roland Jackson, 5 Bt; *b* 27 Sept 1946; *Educ* Stowe, Southampton Univ (BA); *m* 1980, Georgina Victoria, da of George Harold Malcolm Scatliff, of Springlands Farm, Wineham, Sussex; 2 da (Lucy Harriet b 1982, Charlotte Dare b 1986); *Career* md Billington Jackson Advertising Ltd; *Recreations* golf, cricket, photography, reading; *Clubs* Royal Wimbledon Golf, Naval and Military, MCC; *Style—* Thomas Jackson, Esq; 30 Westover Road, London SW18 (☎ 01 874 3550); Billington Jackson Advertising Ltd, 219 King's Road, London SW3 5EJ (☎ 01 351 0006)

JACKSON, Sir (William) Thomas; 8 Bt (UK 1869), of The Manor House, Birkenhead; s of Sir William Jackson, 7 Bt (d 1985), and his 1 w, Lady Ankaret Cecilia Caroline Howard (d 1945), da of 10 Earl of Carlisle; *b* 12 Oct 1927; *Educ* Mill Hill, RAC Cirencester; *m* 1951, Gilian Malise, eld da of John Stobart, MBE, of Farlam Ghyll, Brampton, Cumbria; 3 s (Roland b 1954, Piers Anthony b 1955, Jolyon Thomas b 1957); *Heir* s, (William) Roland Cedric, *qv*; *Style—* Sir Thomas Jackson, Bt; Fell End, Mungrisdale, Penrith, Cumbria CA11 0XR

JACKSON, Violet, Lady; Violet Marguerite Loftus; yr da of Loftus St George (d 1952) and Marguerite Isabel Clifford, *neé* Borrer (d 1956); *b* 11 March 1904; *m* 15 July 1931, Sir Hugh Nicholas Jackson, 2 Bt (d 1979); 1 s (Nicholas, 3 Bt, *qv*), 1 da (Louise, Mrs M Taraniuk); *Style—* Violet, Lady Jackson; 38 Oakley St, London SW3 5HA

JACKSON, William Clifford Maurice; s of Arthur Newton Jackson (d 1986), and Helen Monica, *née* Maurice; *b* 23 Jan 1943; *Educ* Bedales Sch Petersfield Hampshire, Univ of Perugia; *m* 30 Sept 1967, Carol Janet, da of John Patterson; 1 s (Alexander William Maurice b 12 March 1970), 1 da (Amy Fiona Gibb b 10 Nov 1968); *Career* PA to md J Davey & Son 1963-68; Aitken Dott Ltd the Scottish Gallery (formerly Aitken Dott & Son): PA to sole proprietor William J Macaulay 1968-72, jr ptnr 1971-72, sr ptnr 1975-84, md Edinburgh 1984-88, md Edinburgh and London (Aitken Dott plc) 1988-91; md: William Jackson Gallery 1991-; writer lectr and broadcaster on Scot art; pubns: Herdsmans Liverpool (1966), A Patron of Art (managing ed and contrib, 1990-); MInstD; memb: Ctee Scot Crafts Centre 1970-73, Mgmnt Ctee Arts Educn Tst 1983-86, Selection Ctee of Art 1989-, Business Design Centre Islington 1989-; *Recreations* music, opera, cinema, classic cars; *Clubs* The Arts, Citroen Maserati, Lasham Gliding; *Style—* William Jackson, Esq; William Jackson Gallery, 28 Cork Street, London W1X 1HB (☎ 071 287 2121, fax 071 287 2018)

JACKSON, Gen Sir William Godfrey Fothergill; GBE (1975), OBE (1958), KCB (1971), MC (1940, and bar 1943); s of Col Albert Jackson (d 1956), and Eleanor Mary Fothergill (d 1978), of Ravenstonedale, Cumbria; *b* 28 Aug 1917; *Educ* Shrewsbury, RMA Woolwich, King's Coll Cambridge (MA); *m* 1946, Joan Mary, da of Capt C P Buesden, of Bournemouth; 1 s, 1 da; *Career* cmmnd RE 1937; served WW II: Norway, N Africa, Sicily, Italy, Far East; dep dir Staff Duties W O 1962-64, IDC 1965, dir CDS's Unison Planning Staff 1966-68, asst CGS Op Requirements MOD 1968-70, GOC-in-C Northern Cmd 1970-72, QMG 1973-76, mil historian Cabinet Off 1977-88, govr and C-in-C Gibraltar 1978-82; ADC Gen to HM The Queen 1974-76; Col Cmmdt: RE 1971-81, Gurkha Engrs 1971-76, RAOC 1973-78; Kermit Roosevelt Exchange exchange lectr to USA 1975, Hon Col Engr and Rlwy Staff Corps RE TAVR 1977-; KStJ 1978; *Books* Attack in the West (1953), Seven Roads to Moscow (1957), Battle for Italy (1967), Battle for Rome (1969), Alexander of Tunis (1971), The North African Campaigns (1975), Overlord: Normandy 1944 (1978), Vol VI British Official History of the Mediterranean and Middle East Campaigns (Pt 1 1984, Pt 2 1987, Pt 3 1988), Withdrawal from Empire (1986) Rock of the Gibraltarians (1987), Alternative Third World War (1987), Britains Defence Dilemmas (1990), The 'Chiefs'; A history of the British Chiefs of Staff (1991); *Clubs* Army and Navy; *Style—* Gen Sir William Jackson, GBE, KCB, MC; Royal Bank of Scotland, Holt Branch, Whitehall, London SW1

JACKSON, Dr William Thomas; s of William Thomas Jackson (d 1967), of 49 Commercial Rd, Bulwell, Nottingham, and Elizabeth, *née* Martin (d 1950); *b* 22 Aug 1926; *Educ* Henry Mellish GS, Glasgow Vet Coll, Univ of Edinburgh (DVSM), Univ of Berne, Coll of Law; *m* 11 July 1953, Anthea June, da of Capt Robert Richard Gillard (d 1950), of Sholing, Southampton; 2 da (Elizabeth Helen Anthea b 1954, Barbara Ann (Mrs Partridge) b 1956); *Career* asst vet surgeon 1948-53; vet offr Miny of Agric 1953; stationed: Worcs 1959, Birkenhead Port 1964, Beverley E Yorks 1971; DVO Lewes E Sussex 1987 (Animal Welfare Section Tolworth 1977); called to the Bar Lincoln's Inn 1975; nat del and local treas IPCS 1964-71; memb Cncl Br Inst of Agric Conslts, Boy Scout Cmmr 1969-71, legal assessor and memb Cncl Soc for Veterinary Ethology 1986- (sec 1977-86), pres Sussex BVA 1985-87, dir Raystede Animal Welfare Centre 1987-; memb: BVA, RCVS, ClArb; *Recreations* violin, sailing, cycling, walking, cross country skiing, swimming, english literature; *Style—* Dr William Jackson; 19 Ravens' Croft, Eastbourne, East Sussex BN20 7HX (☎ 0323 33589); Westgate Chambers, 144 High St, Lewes, East Sussex BN7 1XT (☎ 0273 480510, DX 50250 LEWES 2, fax 0273 480475)

JACKSON, William Unsworth (Bill); CBE (1985); s of William Jackson (d 1959), and Margaret Esplen, *née* Sunderland (d 1984); *b* 9 Feb 1926; *Educ* Alsop HS Liverpool; *m* 27 Sept 1952, Valerie Annette, da of Robert Henry Llewellyn (d 1966); 1 s (Philip Robert b 1957), 1 da (Deborah Ann b 1954); *Career* slr; dep co clerk Kent CC 1970-73, chief exec Kent CC 1973-86; dir Kent Econ Devpt Bd 1982-86; pres Soc of Local Authy Chief Execs 1985-86, memb Tunbridge Wells DHA 1986-, tstee Charity Aid Fndn 1986-, chm UK Steering Ctee on Community Tsts 1988-, adjudicator on political restrictions in local govt Engand Wales 1989-; *Recreations* gardening; *Clubs* Royal Over-Seas; *Style—* Bill Jackson, Esq, CBE; 34 Yardley Park Rd, Tonbridge, Kent TN9 1NF (☎ 0732 351078)

JACKSON OF BURNLEY, Baroness; Mary Elizabeth; da of Dr Robert Oliphant Boswall (d 1977); *m* 1938, Baron Jackson of Burnley (Life Peer, d 1970); 2 da (Hon Mrs Freeston, Hon Mrs Moffatt); *Style—* The Rt Hon the Lady Jackson of Burnley; Flat 6, Ritchie Court, 380 Banbury Rd, Oxford

JACKSON-STOPS, Timothy William; s of Anthony Ashworth Briggs (d 1987, who assumed by deed poll the surnmane of Jackson-Stops 1949), and Jean Jackson, *née* Jackson-Stops; *b* 20 Aug 1942; *Educ* Eton; *m* 27 June 1987, Jenny; *Career* chm Jackson-Stops & Staff; FRICS (1975); *Recreations* skiing, shooting, fishing, sailing; *Clubs* Buck's; *Style—* Timothy Jackson-Stops, Esq; Wood Burcote, Towcester, Northants NN12 7JP (☎ 0327 50443); 14 Curzon St, London W1Y 7FH (☎ 071 499 6291, fax 071 495 2936)

JACOB, Lt-Gen Sir (Edward) Ian Claud; GBE (1960, KBE 1946, CBE 1942), CB (1944); s of Field Marshal Sir Claud Jacob, GCB, GCSI, KCMG (d 1948); *b* 27 Sept 1899; *Educ* Wellington, RMA Woolwich, King's Coll Cambridge (BA); *m* 1924, Cecil Bisset (d 1991), da of Maj-Gen Sir Francis Treherne (d 1955); 2 s (*see* Jacob, Cdr John C); *Career* 2 Lt RE 1918, Bde Maj Canal Bde Egypt 1936-38, Maj 1938, mil asst sec Ctee of Imperial Def 1938-39, serv WWII, mil asst sec War Cabinet 1939-46, Col 1942, Brig 1943, Temp Maj-Gen 1945, ret with hon rank of Maj-Gen 1946; recalled to be Chief Staff Offr to Min Def with temp rank of Lt-Gen 1952; BBC: controller Euro serv 1946-48, dir external serv 1948-51, dir gen 1952-60; dir: Fisons 1960-70, EMI Ltd 1960-73; chm: Covent Garden Market Authy 1961-66, Blyth Breeding Co 1968-85, Matthews Holdings 1970-76; tstee Imperial War Museum 1970-76; cncllr: E Suffolk 1960-70, Suffolk 1974-77; JP Suffolk 1961-69, Alderman 1970-74, DL Suffolk 1964-85; *Recreations* golf; *Clubs* Army & Navy (chm 1959-67); *Style—* Lt-Gen Sir Ian Jacob, GBE, CB; The Red House, Woodbridge, Suffolk IP12 4AD (☎ 039 43 2001)

JACOB, Sir Issac Hai (Jack); QC (1976); s of Jacob Isaiah Jacob (d 1936), of Shanghai, China; *b* 5 June 1908; *Educ* Shanghai Public Sch for Boys, LSE, UCL (LLB); *m* 1940, Rose Mary Jenkins, da of John William Samwell (d 1918); 2 s; *Career* Nat Serv WWII RAOC, Staff Capt WO 1943-45; called to the Bar Gray's Inn 1930 (hon bencher 1978); sr master Supreme Ct Queen's Bench 1975-80 (master 1957-75), Queen's Remembrancer 1975-80; hon lectr in law UCL 1959-74 (fell 1966, visiting prof English law 1974-87); visiting prof: Univ of Sydney NSW 1971, Osgoode Hall Law Sch, York Univ Toronto 1971; dir of Inst of Advanced Legal Studies Univ of London 1986-88; memb Lord Chllr's Dept Ctees on: (Pearson) Funds in Ct 1958-59, Revision of Rules of Supreme Ct 1960-65, (Payne) Enforcement of Judgement Debts (Payne) 1965-69, Winn Ctee on Personal Injuries Litigation 1966-68, (Kerr) Foreign Judgements 1976-80, chm Working Pty on Form of Writ of Summons and Appearance 1978; advsy ed Court Forms 1962-, ed Annual Practice 1961-66; gen ed: Supreme Court Practice 1967-, Civil Justice Quarterly 1982-; pres Bentham Club UCL 1986 (chm 1965-85), pres Assoc of Law Teachers; vice pres: Selden Soc (cncl memb), Inst of Legal Execs, Industl Law Soc; memb Gen C tee Bar Assoc for Commerce Fin and Indust; memb Senate of Inns of Ct and the Bar 1975-78; memb: Ct of Govrs Poly of Central London 1970-88, Broderers' Co 1977; Freeman: City of London 1976; hon memb: Cncl of Justice 1987, Soc of Public Teachers of Law, Int Assoc of Procedure Law; hon fell Poly of Central London 1988, Hon LLD: Birmingham 1978, London 1981; Dr Juris hc (Würzburg, Bavaria) 1982; kt 1979; *Books* The Fabric of English Civil Justice (1986); *Style—* Sir Jack Jacob, QC; 16 The Park, Golders Green, London NW11 7SU (☎ 081 458 3832)

JACOB, Cdr John Claud; DL (Suffolk 1988); s of Lt-Gen Sir Ian Jacob, GBE, CB, *qv*, and Cecil Bisset, *née* Treherne (d 1991); *b* 9 June 1925; *Educ* Sherborne; *m* 1948, Rosemary Elizabeth, da of Leonard Shuter (d 1960); 2 s; *Career* entered RN 1943, served WWII Home and East Indies Stations, served Suez 1956, Cdr 1957, ret 1962; farmer; chm Radio Orwell 1971-89, joined with Saxon Radio (founded 1981) as wholly owned subsid of Suffolk Group Radio (chm 1981-87); treas Aldeburgh Fndn 1980-, chm Organic Farmers and Growers Ltd 1975-86; *Clubs* Farmers'; *Style—* Cdr John Jacob, DL; c/o Aldeburgh Foundation, High Street, Aldeburgh, Suffolk (☎ 0473 216971); 74 Lee Rd, Aldeburgh, Suffolk IP5 5EY (☎ 0728 452491)

JACOB, (John) Peter; s of William Thomas Jacob (d 1960), and Doris Olwen, *née* Llewellyn; *b* 13 May 1942; *Educ* Sir William Borase's Sch, Univ of Durham (BA), Univ of Newcastle (BArch); *m* 21 July 1982, Lesley Diana, da of Alfred Charles Thomas James, of Maidenhead, Berkshire; 1 da (Katharine b 1985); *Career* Kingston Poly Sch of Architecture: princ lectr 1972-83, dep head 1983-87, head of sch 1987-; chm Kingston Chapter RIBA 1980-82, memb Cncl RIBA 1983-89, memb Bd of Architectural Educn Architect's Registration Cncl 1987-, chm RIBA Pubns Ltd 1989-; RIBA 1967, FRSA 1988; *Recreations* reading, riding, motoring; *Style—* Peter Jacob, Esq; 8 The Poplars, South Ascot, Berkshire (☎ 0344 20894); School of Architecture, Kingston Poly, Knights Park, Kingston-upon-Thames, Surrey (☎ 081 549 6151, fax

081 547 1450)

JACOB, Robin Raphael Hayim; QC (1981), QC (NSW 1989); s of Sir Jack I H Jacob, of London, and Rose Mary, *née* Samwell; *b* 26 April 1941; *Educ* Mountgrace Comp Sch, St Paul's, Trinity Coll Cambridge, (MA), LSE (LLB); *m* 1967, Wendy, da of Leslie Huw Thomas Jones; 3 s (Sam b 1970, Matthew b 1972, Oliver b 1975); *Career* called to the Bar 1965, jr counsel to Treasy in patent matters 1976-81; *Style—* Robin Jacob Esq, QC; Francis Taylor Building, Temple, London EC4

JACOB, Rev Canon Dr William Mungo; s of John William Carey Jacob (d 1982), of Ringstead, Hunstanton, Norfolk, and Mary Marsters, *née* Dewar (d 1959); *b* 15 Nov 1944; *Educ* King Edward VII Sch Kings Lynn, Univ of Hull (LLB), Linacre Coll Oxford (BA, MA), Univ of Edinburgh (Dip), Univ of Exeter (PhD); *Career* asst curate Wymondham Norfolk 1970-73, asst chaplain Univ of Exeter 1973-75, dir of pastoral studies Salisbury and Wells Theol Coll 1975-80 (vice princ 1977-80), sec Ctee for Theol Educn Advsy Cncl for Church's Miny 1980-86, warden Lincoln Theol Coll and prebendary of Gretton in Lincoln Cathedral 1986-; *Style—* The Rev Canon Dr William Jacob; The Warden's House, Drury Lane, Lincoln LN1 3BP (☎ 0522 5258 79); Lincoln Theological Coll, Lincoln LN1 3BP (☎ 0522 5388 85)

JACOBS, Prof Arthur David; s of Alexander Susman Jacobs (d 1972), and Estelle, *née* Isaacs (d 1981); *b* 14 June 1922; *Educ* Manchester GS, Univ of Oxford (MA); *m* 4 Nov 1953, Betty Upton Hughes; 2 s (Julian b 1957, Michael b 1960); *Career* served WWII 1942-46; music critic Daily Express 1947-52, freelance writer on music 1953-, prof RAM 1964-79, head music dept Huddersfield Poly 1979-84, fndr ed British Music Yearbook 1972, memb Bd Eds Opera magazine 1962-; *Books* incl: Music Lover's Anthology (1948), Gilbert and Sullivan (1951), Choral Music (1963), Libretto of Opera One Man Show by Nicholas Maw (1964), Pan Book of Opera (with Stanley Sadie, expanded edn 1984), A Short History of Western Music (1972), The New Penguin Dictionary of Music (new edn 1991), Arthur Sullivan: a Victorian musician (1984), Pan Book of Orchestral Music (1988), The Penguin Dictionary of Musical Performers (1990), many opera translations incl Berg's Lulu; *Style—* Prof Arthur Jacobs; 10 Oldbury Close, Sevenoaks, Kent TN15 9DJ (☎ 0732 884006)

JACOBS, Brian David Lewis; s of John Barry Lewis Jacobs, of Pennypot Cottage, Pennypot Lane, Chobham, Surrey, and Elizabeth, *née* Menzies; *b* 14 Dec 1949; *Educ* Charterhouse; *m* 26 Nov 1983, Rosalind Mary, da of late Leslie Jory; 2 da (Katherine Alice (Katie) b 3 Sept 1985, Emily Rose b 13 Dec 1988); *Career* Horniblow Cox-Freeman 1968-71 (messenger rising to res asst), media and market res exec Southern TV 1971-74, market res exec Access 1974, media res mangr Davidson Pearce 1974-80; Leo Burnett: assoc media dir 1980, media dir 1985, exec media dir 1986, vice chm and exec media dir 1990-; memb CAM, FIPA 1982; *Books* Spending Advertising Money (with Dr Simon Broadbent, 1984); *Recreations* golf, family, reading books on media and advertising, viewing ads; *Clubs* Sunningdale Golf; *Style—* Brian Jacobs, Esq; 61 Woodlawn Road, London SW6 6PS (☎ 071 731 3854); Leo Burnett Advertising, 48 St Martins Lane, London WC2N 4EJ (☎ 071 836 2424, fax 071 829 7049)

JACOBS, David Lewis; DL (Gtr London 1983); s of late David Jacobs and late Jeanette Victoria, *née* Goldsmid; *b* 19 May 1926; *Educ* Belmont Coll, Strand Sch; *m* 1, 15 Sept 1949 (m dis 1972), Patricia Bradlaw; m 2, 1975 Caroline Munro (d 1975); m 3, 1979, Mrs Lindsay Stuart Hutcheson; 1 s (Jeremy decd), 3 da (Carol, Joanna, Emma), 1 step s (Guy); *Career* RN 1944-47; radio/tv broadcaster; first broadcast Navy Mixture 1944; announcer: Forces Broadcasting 1944-45 (chief), Radio SEAC Ceylon 1945-47 (asst station dir 1947); freelance, BBC and Radio Luxembourg top disc-jockey 1947-53; radio credits incl: Housewive's Choice, Journey into Space, BBC Jazz Club, Pick of the Pops, Any Questions, Any Answers, Melodies for You, David Jacobs show; TV credits incl: 6 Royal Command Performances, Juke Box Jury, Top of the Pops, Little Women, What's my Line, Miss World, Eurovision Song Contest, Come Dancing, Questions, Primetime, and many others; dir: Duke of Yorks Theatre 1979-85, Man in the Moon UK Ltd 1986-, Kingston Theatre Tst 1990-, Video Travel Guides; rep DL Royal Borough of Kingston Upon Thames; chm Think Br Campaign 1985 (dep chm 1983-85); pres Royal Br Legion (Kingston); vice pres: Stars Orgn for Spastics (past chm), Wimbledon Girls Choir; awards: RSPCA Richard Martin award, Variety Club, BBC TV Personality 1960, BBC Radio Personality 1975, Sony Gold Award Outstanding Radio Contribs 1985, Sony Hall of Fame 1988; *Books* Jacobs Ladder (1963), Caroline (1978), Any Questions? (with Michael Bowen, 1981); *Recreations* talking and listening, hotels; *Clubs* Garrick, St James's, Helford River Sailing; *Style—* David Jacobs, Esq, DL; 203 Pavilion Rd, London SW1X 0BJ

JACOBS, David Michael; s of Arthur Jacobs (d 1955), and Eileen Mai, *née* Salanson; *b* 4 June 1930; *Educ* Clifton, St Edmund Hall Oxford; *m* 29 Sept 1974, Marion Sally, da of Louis Davis (d 1987); *Career* Nat Serv 1948-50; Eng language announcer Voice of Israel Jerusalem 1962-64, ed Valentine Mitchell London 1965-69, PRO Zionist Fedn London 1969-74, gen sec Anglo-Jewish Assoc London 1974-82, involved in tourist industry 1985-, fndr with Paul Mallier Britain from the Inside 1988; chm: Chiltern Progressive Synagogue (formerly Beds-Herts) 1978-84, St Albans branch UN Assoc 1979-85; memb Exec Anglo-Jewish Assoc 1984-, hon vice pres Chiltern Synagogue 1986-; *Books* Israel (World in Colour Series, 1968), princ contrib The Jewish Communities of the World (1989); *Recreations* gardening, reading history and literature; *Style—* David M Jacobs, Esq; 23 Worley Rd, St Albans, Herts AL3 5NR (☎ 0727 58454)

JACOBS, Donald; s of Harry Jacobs (d 1980), of London, and Hetty, *née* Lands; *b* 21 April 1931; *Educ* Grocers Co Sch; *m* 8 Oct 1958, Jeanette, da of Bert Conway (d 1967), of Croydon; 2 s (Jonathan b 1962, Simon b 1965); *Career* CA; dir: Walker Bros Civil Engrg Ltd, Disjay Ltd, Metropolis Fin Ltd 1987; *Recreations* tennis, music, theatre, travel; *Style—* Donald Jacobs, Esq; 20 Cheyne Walk, London NW4 3QJ (☎ 081 202 5708); 47 St Johns Wood, High St, London NW8 7NJ

JACOBS, Godfrey Frederick; s of Frederick George Jacobs (d 1963), of Woodford, Essex, and Louise Lily, *née* Phipps; *Educ* South West Essex Tech Coll, Wansfell Coll Essex; *m* Hazell Thirza, *née* Robertson; 2 da (Lorne Alison b 10 June 1958, Clare Morag b 13 April 1960); *Career* Nat Serv Tport Cmd RAF 1949-51; dir (overseas) English Property Corporation 1968-75, gen property mangr MTRC Hong Kong 1976-79; 1979-86: exec dir US Assets Ltd, dir and pres AMP Property Services, Inc of San Francisco, chm Copthorn Holdings Ltd (Toronto); chm Suncrest Developments plc 1986-; memb: World Wildlife Fund of Canada, Community Assoc for Riding for Disabled (Canada), 200 Canadians for Wildlife, Utd Wards Club of London; Freeman City of London 1964 (renter warden 1990-91), Liveryman Worshipful Co of Painter Stainers 1964, former Master Hon Co of Freemen of the City of London in N America; FSVA 1963, ABIM 1966, FCIArb 1977, FInstD 1961; *Recreations* charity work; *Clubs* Naval, City Livery; *Style—* Godfrey Jacobs, Esq

JACOBS, Prof Howard Saul; s of Flt Lt Joseph Jacobs, of 79 Marlborough Mansions, Cannon Hill, London NW6, and Florence Jacobs (d 1950); *b* 9 June 1938; *Educ* Malvern, Gonville and Caius Coll Cambridge (BA), Middx Hosp Med Sch (MB BChir), Univ of London (MD); *m* 15 July 1962, Sandra Rose, da of Mark Garelick; 3 da (Caroline, Susanna, Amber); *Career* asst prof UCLA 1969-74, sr lectr St Mary's Hosp Med Sch 1974-81, prof Univ Coll London and Middx Sch of Medicine 1983- (reader gynaecological endocrinology 1981-83), civilian conslt endocrinology RAF 1985-; memb Ctee on Safety of Medicines 1983-, former memb MRC Advsy Ctee on Oral Contraception 1983-88; *Recreations* tennis, music, reading, theatre; *Style—* Prof Howard Jacobs; 169 Gloucester Ave, London NW1 8LA (☎ 071 722 5593); Middx Hosp, Mortimer St, London W1N 8AA (☎ 071 380 9451, fax 071 636 9941)

JACOBS, John Arthur; s of Arthur George Jacobs (d 1949), and Elfrida Malvine Beck (d 1952); *b* 13 April 1916; *Educ* Dorking HS, Dorking County Sch, Univ Coll London (BA, MA, PhD, DSc); *m* 1, 1942, Daisy Sarah Ann Montgomerie (d 1974); 2 da (Coral Elizabeth b 1942, Margaret Ann b 1948); m 2, 1974 (m dis 1981), Margaret Jones; m 3, 24 June 1982, Ann Grace Wintle, da of Albert James Wintle (d 1990); *Career* instructor Lt RN 1941-46; lectr in mathematics Royal Holloway Coll Univ of London 1946-51, assoc prof of geophysics Univ of Toronto 1951-57, prof of geophysics Univ of British Columbia 1957-67, dir Inst of Earth Sciences Vancouver 1961-67, Killam Memorial prof of earth science Univ of Alberta 1967-74, dir Inst Earth & Planetary Physics Univ of Alberta 1970-74, prof of geophysics Univ of Cambridge 1974-83, emeritus prof of geophysics Univ of Cambridge 1983-, Hon Prof Inst Earth Studies Aberystwyth 1988-; memb many nat and int ctees on geophysics, vice master Darwin Coll Cambridge 1978-83; Hon DSc Univ of British Columbia Vancouver; FRSC 1958, FRAS 1951, fell American Geophysical Union 1975; Centennial medal of Canada 1967, Gold medal Canadian Assoc Physicists, J Tuzo Wilson Medal Canadian Geophysical Union 1982; *Books* Physics & Geology (with R D Russell and J T Wilson, 1959 and 1974), The Earths Core and Geomagnetism (1963), Geomagnetic Micropulsations (1970), A Textbook on Geonomy (1974), The Earth's Core (1975 and 1987), Reversals of the Earths Magnetic Feild (1984); *Recreations* walking, music; *Style—* Prof John Jacobs; 4 Castell Brychan, Aberystwyth SY23 2JD (☎ 0970 623 436); Institute of Earth Studies, University College of Wales, Aberystwyth SY23 3DB (☎ 0970 622646, fax 0970 622659)

JACOBS, John Robert Maurice; s of Robert Jacobs (d 1934), and Vivian Jacobs (d 1978); *b* 14 March 1925; *Educ* Maltby GS; *m* 25 Jan 1949, Rita, da of Joseph Wragg (d 1957), of Woodsetts, Worksop, Notts; 1 s (Johnathan b 1960), 1 da (Joanna b 1957); *Career* Sgt Flt Engr 1944; golfer and golf course architect; Br Int professional golfer 1954-58; Ryder Cup: player 1955, non playing capt 1979 and 1981; dir Euro Tour 1971-76; *Books* Golf (1960), Play Better Golf (1969), Practical Golf (1973), Golf Doctor (1979), Jacobs Impact on Golf (1987); *Recreations* fishing, shooting, golf; *Clubs* Brockenhurst, Bramshaw, Sandy Lodge, Lake Nona (USA), John O' Gaunt; *Style—* John Jacobs, Esq; Stable Cottage, Chapel Lane, Lyndhurst, Hamps (☎ 042 128 2743)

JACOBS, Hon Sir Kenneth Sydney; KBE (1976); s of Albert Sydney Jacobs; *b* 5 Oct 1917; *Educ* Knox GS NSW, Sydney Univ Aust (BA, LLB); *m* 1952, Eleanor Mary Neal; 1 da; *Career* barr NSW 1947, QC 1958, Supreme Court of NSW Australia: judge 1960, judge of appeal 1966, pres Court of Appeal 1972, justice of High Ct of Aust 1974-79; *Style—* The Hon Sir Kenneth Jacobs, KBE; Crooks Lane Corner, Axford, Marlborough, Wilts SN8 2HA

JACOBS, Rabbi Prof Louis; CBE (1990); s of Harry Jacobs (d 1968), of Manchester, and Lena, *née* Myerstone (d 1956); *b* 17 July 1920; *Educ* Manchester Central HS, UCL (BA, PhD); *m* 28 March 1944, Sophie, da of Israel Lisagorska (d 1945), of London; 2 s (Ivor b 1945, David b 1952), 1 da (Naomi b 1947); *Career* rabbi: Central Synagogue Manchester 1948-1954, New West End Synagogue London 1954-60; tutor Jews' Coll London 1959-62, dir Soc Study of Jewish Theology 1962-64, rabbi New London Synagogue 1964-; visiting prof: Harvard Divinity Sch 1985-86, Univ of Lancaster 1988-; hon fell: UCL 1988, Leo Baeck Coll London 1988; former pres London Soc for Study of Religion, pres Assoc for Jewish Studies; hon citizen: Texas 1961, New Orleans 1963; Hon DHL: Spertus Coll 1987, Hebrew Union Cincinnati 1989, Jewish Theological Seminary New York 1989; *Books* We Have Reason To Believe (1957), Studies in Talmudic Logic (1961), Principles of the Jewish Faith (1964), A Jewish Theology (1973), Hasidic Prayer (1977), Jewish Mystical Testimonies (1977), The Talmudic Argument (1985), Helping With Inquiries: An Autobiograph (1989), Holy Living: Saints and Saintliness in Judaism (1990), God Torah Israel (1990); *Recreations* hillwalking, theatre, cinema; *Style—* Rabbi Prof Louis Jacobs, CBE; 27 Clifton Hill, St John's Wood, London NW8 0QE (☎ 071 624 1299); The New London Synagogue, 33 Abbey Rd, London NW8 (☎ 071 328 1026/7)

JACOBS, Michael Edward Hyman; s of Harry Ronald Jacobs (d 1966), of London, and Edmonde, *née* London; *b* 21 May 1948; *Educ* St Paul's, Univ of Birmingham (LLB); *m* 5 March 1973, Ruth; 2 s; *Career* admitted slr 1972; ptnr Nicholson Graham & Jones 1976-, ed Trust Law International (formerly Trust Law and Practice) Frank Cass & Co Ltd 1989-; author of articles on corporate and personal taxation; fndr memb Share Scheme Lawyers Gp 1989-; Freeman City of London 1983, Liveryman Worshipful Co of Solicitors' 1987; memb Law Soc, Int Bar Assoc; FBIM 1983; *Books* Tax on Takeovers (1989, 1990), Tolley's Tax Planning (1989, 3 edn 1991); *Style—* Michael Jacobs, Esq; Nicholson Graham & Jones, 25-31 Moorgate, London EC2R 6AR (☎ 071 628 9151, fax 071 638 3102, telex 8811848)

JACOBS, Norman Nathaniel; ERD (1964); s of Abram Gershon Jacobs (d 1953), of London, and Deborah, *née* Nabarro (d 1969); *b* 8 Aug 1930; *Educ* Christ's Hosp Horsham, Exeter Coll Oxford (MA); *m* 11 July 1957, Elizabeth Rose, da of Dr Raphael Shaffer (d 1965), of Cheltenham; 2 s (Simon Anthony b 1962, David Raphael b 1968), 2 da (Ruth Helen b 1960, Susan Naomi b 1965); *Career* 2 Lt Army 1949-51, Capt AER 1957-64; admitted slr 1958; ptnr Slaughter & May 1973-90; dir Sports Aid Fndn (London and SE), govr Christs Hosp, steward Br Boxing Bd of Control, memb Sports Cncl, chm Football Licensing Authy; Freeman City of London 1970; FRSA 1989; *Recreations* walking, trekking, music, spectating; *Clubs* MCC; *Style—* Norman Jacobs Esq, ERD; 64 Moss Lane, Pinner, Middx HAS 3AU (☎ 081 866 0840)

JACOBS, Paul Granville; s of Thomas Granville Jacobs, of London, and Marjorie Rosina, *née* Walters; *b* 15 Feb 1946; *Educ* The Leys Sch Cambridge, Exeter Univ (LLB); *Career* admitted slr 1970; commercial property ptnr: Clifford Turner 1978-86, Clifford Chance 1986-; Freeman City of London; *Recreations* horse racing, the arts; *Clubs* RAC; *Style—* Paul Jacobs, Esq; Clifford Chance, Blackfriars House, 19 New Bridge Street, London EC4V 6BY (☎ 01 353 0211, fax 489 0046, telex 887847 LEGIS G, car 0836 743698)

JACOBS, Paul Martin; s of Colin Alfred James Jacobs, of Ruthin, Clwyd, and Betty Mary, *née* Rowse; *b* 11 Dec 1951; *Educ* Oundle, The Queen's Coll Oxford (MA), Univ of Liverpool (MB ChB); *m* 11 Feb 1989, Deborah Clare Josephine, da of Arthur Ernest Smith, of Haslemere, Surrey; *Career* resident surgical offr Moorfields Eye Hosp 1982-85, conslt ophthalmic surgn Univ Hosp Nottingham 1988-; memb Ophthalmic Gp Ctee BMA; FRCS Glasgow 1984, FCOphth 1988; *Recreations* music, skiing, angling; *Clubs* Royal Soc of Med; *Style—* Paul Jacobs, Esq; University Hospital, Nottingham NG7 2UH (☎ 0602 421421)

JACOBS, Peter; s of Bertram Jacobs (d 1982), and Phyllis Jacobs (d 1982); *b* 26 Sept 1938; *Educ* Merchant Taylors, Queen's Coll Cambridge (MA); *m* 21 Dec 1974, Susan Frances, da of Eric Simeon Boyes; 2 da (Sarah b 1977, Helen b 1978); *Career* 2 Lt 1958-59, Royal Hampshire Regt 1957-59; mktg res; fencing: Br Epée Champion (1962, 1964, 1970), Br Olympic Teams (1964, 1968), Cwlth Team (1962, 1966, 1970), mangr Br Olympic Team (1972, 1976), World Univ Epée Champion 1963; vice pres Amateur Fencing Assoc, memb Exec Ctee Int Fencing Fedn 1985-88 (memb Statutes Ctee

1977-); Liveryman Worshipful Co of Weavers 1971; *Style—* Peter Jacobs, Esq

JACOBS, Peter Alan; s of Cyril Jacobs (d 1973), and Sybil, *née* Jones (d 1976); *b* 22 Feb 1943; *Educ* Univ of Glasgow (BSc), Univ of Aston (Dip Mgmnt Studies); *m* 31 May 1966, Eileen Dorothy, da of Dr Leslie Naftalin; 2 s (Andrew Mark b 1969, Michael Henry (twin) b 1969), 1 da (Katrina Ruth b 1972); *Career* prodn mangr tube investmts Raleigh Cycles 1966-70, commercial mangr and prodn mangr Pedigree Petfood (Mars Inc) 1970-83, sales dir Mars Confectionery 1983-86, chief exec Br Sugar Berisford Int 1989- (main bd dir and md 1986-89); MInstD; *Recreations* tennis, music, theatre; *Style—* Peter Jacobs, Esq; Berisford International, 1 Prescot St, London E1 8AY (☎ 071 481 9144)

JACOBS, Sir Piers; KBE (1989, OBE 1981); s of Selwyn Jacobs, and Dorothy, *née* Fredman; *b* 27 May 1933; *Educ* St Paul's; *m* 13 April 1964, Josephine Lee; 1 da (Isobel Lee b 9 July 1966); *Career* Army Legal Serv 1955-57; Hong Kong Govt slr 1962-65, 1965-68, asst registrar gen 1968-76, registrar general 1976-82, sec for econ serv 1982-86, fin sec 1986-; hon pres: Hong Kong PHAB Assoc, Soc for Child Health & Devpt, hon vice pres Hong Kong Girl Guides Assoc, memb: Law Soc Eng and Wales and Hong Kong; *Recreations* walking, swimming and reading; *Clubs* Hong Kong, Royal Hong Kong Jockey, Oriental; *Style—* Sir Piers Jacobs, KBE; 45 Shouson Hill Rd, Hong Kong; Central Government Offices, Main Wing, 5/F Lower Albert Rd, Hong Kong (☎ 810 2589)

JACOBS, Sqdn Ldr Vivian Kenneth; s of Frederick Charles Jacobs (d 1959), of Auckland, NZ, and Jane Ellen, *née* Ransley (d 1954); *b* 18 Sept 1918; *Educ* Mount Albert GS Auckland, Auckland Teachers Trg Coll (Teachers' C Primary Sch Cert), Auckland Univ Coll, Royal Scot Acad of Music Glasgow; *m* 19 April 1945 (m dis 1963), 1 s (Martin Julian b 1951), 1 da (Louisa Fan b 1956); *Career* RNZAF 1940, cmmnd 1941, 136 Fighter Sqdn 1941, Sqdn Ldr OC Wingate Clandestine Airfield, RAF Broadway N Burma 1944, Personal Staff Offr to Air Marshal Sir Victor Goddard AOA SE Asia Air Cmd, cmmnd RAF 1947, graduate RAF Staff Coll Bracknell 1949; Air Miny 1950-52 OC 45 Sqdn FEAF, Singapore, Butterworth, Malaya 1953-56, Cadet Staff Liason 61 Gp 1956-57; outside sales rep Russell & Somers Travel Agents Auckland 1958-61, mangr own travel agency Auckland 1962-66, sales mangr S Pacific US Travel Services (US Govt Dept of Commerce) Sydney Aust 1967-69, S Pacific sales dir Kneisel Travel Portland, Oregon 1970-74, own agency 1975-82; chorus master for NZ Opera Co 1959-60, choir master NSW Police Choir Sydney 1968, estab Jubilee Theatre Arts Soc Norwich 1985, developed project to create music theatre acad for full trg in music theatre for youngsters 16-25 years (now a registered charity), produced series of Gilbert & Sullivan operettas for 10-17 year olds 1985-88 in Norwich; nominee Unsung Hero of 1987 Award Norwich; *Recreations* music theatre and working with young people in musical prodns; *Clubs* RAF; *Style—* Sqdn Ldr Vivian K Jacobs; 31 Cuckoofield Lane, Mulbarton, Norfolk NR14 8AY; General Director, Jubilee Theatre Arts Soc Ltd (☎ 0508 70072)

JACOBSON, Hon Colin; s of Baron Jacobson (Life Peer, d 1988); *b* 1941; *m* 1972, Josephine, da of John William Gates; *Style—* The Hon Colin Jacobson; 48 Parkway, NW1

JACOBSON, Howard; s of Max Jacobson, of Manchester, and Anita, *née* Black; *b* 25 Aug 1942; *Educ* Stand GS Whitefield, Downing Coll Cambridge (BA, MA, Table Tennis half blue); *m* 1, 1964 (m dis 1972), Barbara, *née* Starr; 1 s (Conrad b 1968); m 2, 1978, Rosalin Joy, da of Alan Sadler, of Balnarring, Aust; *Career* lectr in Eng lit Univ of Sydney 1965-67, Eng tutor Selwyn Coll Cambridge 1969-72, sr lectr Wolverhampton Poly 1974-81, novelist and critic 1981-; *Books* Shakespeare's Magnanimity (with Wilbur Sarders, 1978), Coming From Behind 1983, Peeping Tom 1984, Redback 1986, In The Land of Oz 1987; reg reviewer The Observer and TLS, own column The Late Show BBC 2, TV critic Sunday Correspondent; reg contrib Modern Painters 1988- (currently memb editorial Bd); *Recreations* appearing on television; *Style—* Howard Jacobson, Esq; Peters Fraser & Dunlop, 503-4 The Chambers, Chelsea Harbour, London SW10 0XF (☎ 071 376 7676, 071 352 7356, fax 071 351 1756)

JACOBSON, Ivor Julian; s of Harry Jacobson (d 1980), and Rae, *née* Tatz (d 1950); *b* 6 May 1940; *Educ* King Edward VII Sch Johannesburg, Univ of Witwatersrand S Africa (BComm); *m* 23 Dec 1963, Joan Yocheved, da of Isiah Adelson (d 1974); 1 s (Russell b 1965), 2 da (Lauren b 1968, Amanda b 1970); *Career* articled clerk Levitt Kirson Gross & Co 1963-65, trainee mangr and dir Brown Bros Shipping Co (Pty) Ltd 1966-67, fndr and md Int Shipping Co (Pty) Ltd 1968-87, chief exec Trade and Indust Gp (with subsids in many countries incl: S Africa, UK, USA, Singapore, Aust, Belgium, The Netherlands) 1973-; *Recreations* squash, horse riding; *Clubs* The Transvaal Automobile; *Style—* Ivor Jacobson, Esq; 200 North St, Harrison, New York 10528, USA (☎ 914 667 7299); 31 Brookside Drive, Greenwich Ct, 06830 NY, USA (☎ 010 1 203 661 5813, fax 010 1 203 661 5833)

JACOBSON, Julian; s of Herbert Lawrence Jacobson, of San Jose, Costa Rica, and Fiora, *née* Ravasini; *b* 13 April 1953; *Educ* Coll Mellerio Rosmini Domodossola Italy, Univ De Geneve Switzerland; *Career* Du Pont de Nemours Int SA Geneva Switzerland 1974-76, Kidder Peabody (Suisse) SA Geneva Switzerland 1976-79, md Kidder Peabody Int Ltd 1985- (joined 1980), dir Pasfin Servizi Finanziari SPA Milan Italy 1988-; *Recreations* tennis, skiing, basketball; *Style—* Julian Jacobson, Esq; 7 Lincoln House, Basil St, London SW3 1AN (☎ 071 589 2237); Kidder Peabody Int Ltd, 107 Cheapside, London EC2V 6DD (☎ 071 480 8115, fax 071 726 2796, car 0836 203 333, telex 884694)

JACOBSON, Hon Philip; s of Baron Jacobson (Life Peer, d 1988); *b* 1938; *m* 1967, Ann, da of late Gilbert Mathison; *Style—* The Hon Philip Jacobson; 29 Carmalt Gdns, London SW15

JACOBSON, Baroness; Phyllis June; da of late Frank S Buck; *m* 1938, Baron Jacobson, MC (Life Peer, d 1988); 2 s (Hon Philip b 1938, Hon Colin b 1941), 1 da (Hon Pamela b 1944); *Style—* The Rt Hon Lady Jacobson; 6 Avenue Road, St Albans, Herts

JACOBSON, Ronald Terry (Ronnie); s of Michael Wolfe Jacobson (d 1943) of Leeds and Fay, *née* Schloss (d 1979); *b* 13 June 1938; *Educ* Grocers Co Sch; *m* 8 Jan 1961, Sandra Rosalind; 2 s (Michael Jonathan b 15 Sept 1966, Murray Robert b 8 June 1971); *Career* ptnr: Zorn and Leigh-Hunt 1968-76, Astaire & Co 1970-76; sr ptnr Jacobson Townsley & Co 1976-91; memb Br Boxing Bd of Control; *Style—* Ronnie Jacobson, Esq; Jacobson Townsley & Co, 44 Worship St, London EC2A 2JT (☎ 071 377 6161, fax 071 895 8128)

JACOBSON, Prof Werner Ulrich (Jacob); s of Dr Otto Jacobson (d 1968), of San Francisco California, and Paula Margaret, *née* Masur; *b* 4 Jan 1906; *Educ* Momsen Gymnasium Berlin, Univ of Heidelberg (MD), University of Cambridge (PhD, ScD); *m* 14 Feb 1934, Gertrude Elena (d 1969), da of Prof Eric Ebler (d 1925); *Career* Home Guard 1940-45; Univ of Cambridge: academic assistance grant 1933-34, Rockefeller grant 1934-35, Sir Halley Stewart prof of med res 1978- (res fell 1935-78); visiting sr res assoc Galveston Univ of Texas Med Branch 1948-49, Harvard Med Sch 1949-54, visiting prof Harvard Med Sch 1969-70 and 1972; contrib to various med books and publications; memb: Physiological Soc, Int Soc of Haematology; fell Cambridge Philosophical Soc; FRCP 1986, FRCPath 1986, FRSM, FRSTM; *Recreations* gardening, classical music, Limoges enamel; *Style—* Prof W Jacobson; Dept of Paediatrics University of Cambridge, Level 8, Addenbrooke's Hospital, Cambridge CB2 2QQ (☎ 0223 217544)

JACOBY, Hans Gert; *b* 7 July 1926; *Educ* Taplow GS, Westminster Tech Coll, Imperial Coll London, City and Guilds (BSC Eng); *m* 1955, Patricia Rose; 1 s; *Career* chm Br Mantle Mfrs Assoc 1973-77 (memb Exec Bd), fndr memb and current chm (1977-) Clothing Export Cncl, md Jacoby & Bratt and Assoc Cos, chm Export Advsy Gp for Clothing (economic devpt ctee of clothing indust); *Style—* Hans Jacoby Esq; 7 Kingwood Pk, Hendon AV, Finchley, London, N3 (☎ 01 346 3763)

JACOMB, Sir Martin Wakefield; s of Hilary Jacomb, and Félise Jacomb; *b* 11 Nov 1929; *Educ* Eton, Worcester Coll Oxford (MA); *m* 1960, Evelyn Helen, *née* Heathcoat-Amory; 2 s, 1 da; *Career* called to the Bar Inner Temple 1955, practised at bar 1955-68; dep chm Barclays Bank plc 1985, chm Barclays de Zoete Wedd 1986; dir: Bank of England 1986-, Christian Salvesen plc 1974-87, Commercial Union Assurance Co plc 1984- (dep chm 1987), British Gas plc 1981-87, Royal Opera House Covent Garden Ltd 1987-, The Daily Telegraph plc 1986-, Rio Tinto Zinc Corporation plc 1987-; external memb Fin Ctee Oxford Univ Press 1971-; tstee Nat Heritage Meml Fund 1982-; *Style—* Sir Martin Jacomb; Barclays de Zoete Wedd, PO Box 188, Ebbgate House, 2 Swan Lane, London EC4R 3TS (071 623 2323)

JACOMB-HOOD, Edward Wykeham; s of Canon Francis Edward Shaw Jacomb-Hood (d 1960), of Chichester, and Margaret Irene, *née* Chilver (d 1963); *b* 18 March 1920; *Educ* Lancing, King's Coll London (BSc); *m* 25 June 1955, Honor Margaret, da of Sidney Edward Jones (d 1942), of London; 1 s (Anthony Wykeham b 1959), 2 da (Anna Margaret b 1956, Julia Honor b 1957); *Career* WWII Capt Royal Bombay Sappers and Miners RE; ptnr Livesey and Henderson Consulting Engineers 1959-66, conslt Dobbie and Partners 1967-90; memb: Synod Diocese of Chichester, Mid-Sussex NADFAS; Liveryman City of London 1984 (Freeman 1986); memb Assoc of Consulting Engrs 1966-90; FICE 1963; *Recreations* gardening, photography, walking, skiing, bridge; *Clubs* Athenaeum; *Style—* Edward Jacomb-Hood, Esq; Backwoods, Lindfield, Haywards Heath, Sussex RH16 2EN (☎ 0444 483310)

JACQUES, Hon Cecil Philip; er s of Baron Jacques (Life Peer); *b* 20 Sept 1930; *Educ* Univ Coll London (BSc); *m* 1, 1960 (m dis 1977), Rita Ann Florence Hurford; 2 s (John b 1962, Neil b 1963); m 2, 1983, Mrs Carrine Royston, *née* Johnson; *Career* sr staff engr Lockhead Missiles and Space Co Inc Sunnyvale California 1960-; *Clubs* Br American of Northern California Inc; *Style—* The Hon Cecil Jacques; 873 Somerset Drive, Sunnyvale, CA 94087; work (☎ 408 742 1669, 408 742 1932, 408 742 1933)

JACQUES, Baron (Life Peer UK 1968), of Portsea Island, Co Southampton; John Henry Jacques; JP (Portsmouth); s of Thomas Dobson Jacques (d 1941), of Ashington, Northumberland, and Annie Bircham (d 1972); *b* 11 Jan 1905; *Educ* Victoria Coll Jersey, Univ Manchester (BCom), Co-op Coll Manchester; *m* 1, 1929, Constance (d 1987), da of Harry White (d 1950), of Bournville, Birmingham; 2 s (Hon Cecil Philip b 1930, Hon Paul b 1932), 1 da (Hon Anne b 1941); m 2, 1989, Violet Jacques; *Career* sits as Labour Peer in Lords; chief exec Portsea Island Co-op Soc Ltd Portsmouth 1945-65, pres Co-op Congress 1961, chm Co-op Union 1964-70, pres Retail Trades Educn Cncl 1971-75, a lord in waiting (Govt whip) 1974-77 and 1979, a dep chm of Ctees 1977-85; *Clubs* Co-operative (Portsmouth); *Style—* The Rt Hon the Lord Jacques, JP; 23 Hartford House, Pembroke Park, Portsmouth PO1 2TN (☎ 0705 738111)

JACQUES, Dr Martin; s of Dennis Arthur Jacques, of 11 Hardwick Lane, Bury St Edmunds, Suffolk, and Dorothy *née* Preston (d 1989); *b* 1 Oct 1945; *Educ* King Henry VIII Sch Coventry, Univ of Manchester (BA, MA), King's Coll Cambridge (scholar, PhD); *m* 1969-75, Brenda Simson; ptnr, 1978- Philippa Anne, da of Sqdn Ldr Lloyd Norman Langton, RAF Ret; *Career* lectr in econ and social history Univ of Bristol 1971-77, ed Marxism Today 1977-; columnist: Sunday Times 1988-, The Times 1990-, L' Unità (Rome) 1990-; occasional contrib: The Guardian, The Independent, La Stampa, Le Monde Diplomatique; reg broadcaster tv and radio; memb Exec Ctee Communist Pty 1967-90 (memb Political Ctee 1978-80 and 1982-90); memb Econ History Soc 1971-77, FRSA 1991-; *Books* Forward March of Labour Halted (co-ed and contrib, 1981), The Politics of Thatcherism (co-ed and contrib, 1983), New Times (co-ed and contrib, 1989); contrib to various other publications; *Recreations* squash, tennis, skiing, running, motor racing, reading, cooking; *Style—* Dr Martin Jacques; 31 Sussex Way, London N7 6RT (☎ 071 272 0885, fax 071 281 2402); Marxism Today, 6-9 Cynthia St, London N1 9JF (☎ 071 278 4430, fax 071 278 4427)

JACQUES, Dr the Hon Paul; yr s of Baron Jacques (Life Peer); *b* 8 Jan 1932; *Educ* Edinburgh Univ (MB ChB); *m* 20 Sept 1958, Nina Mollie, da of James MacKenzie, of Leigh-on-Sea, Essex; 1 s, 3 da; *Style—* Dr the Hon Paul Jacques; Pinestead, 1B Twentylands Drive, East Leake, Loughborough, Leics

JACQUES, Peter Roy Albert; CBE (1990); s of George Henry Jacques (d 1984), and Ivy Mary, *née* Farr (1988); *b* 12 Aug 1939; *Educ* Archbishop Temple's Sch, Newcastle upon Tyne Poly (BSc), Univ of Leics; *m* 21 Aug 1965, Jacqueline Anne, da of Robert George Sears, of Worthing; 1 s (Jonathan Peter), 1 da (Tamsin Eleanor); *Recreations* yoga, gardening, walking, golf, reading; *Style—* Peter Jacques, Esq; TUC, Congress House, Gt Russell St, London WC1B 3LS (☎ 071 636 4030)

JAFFAR, Fouad Khaled; s of Khalid Mohammed Jaffar, ambassador to UK 1963-65, head of Diplomatic and Political Dept, and Miriam Abdullah Al-Askar; *b* 24 Nov 1945; *Educ* Wittleberry Sch Northants, Concord Coll Tunbridge Wells, Leeds Univ (BA); *m* 11 Aug 1971, Elizabeth Jane, da of Herbert Vaughan Burke (d 1981); 1 s (Khaled b 15 Sept 1978), 1 da (Sara b 16 June 1975); *Career* UK directorships: Kuwait Investment Office (dep chm and gen mangr), Autobar Group Ltd (dep chm 1982-), Autobar Industries Ltd (chm 1983-), Hays Group Ltd (chm 1983-87), Hays Holdings Ltd (vice chm 1980-87), St Martin's Holdings Ltd (chm 1974-), St Martins (Industry) Ltd (dir 1980-), St Martin's Property Corporation Ltd and St Martins Property Investment Ltd (vice chm 1974- and 1975-), Timeregal Ltd (chm 1980-); German directorships: Zach AG and Westend Industl GMBH (md 1984-); Dutch directorships: Autobar Group BV (md 1981-), Univend BV (memb Supervisory Bd); Spanish directorships: Industs del Papel y de la Celulosa Sa (pres 1984-), Prima Inmobilaira Sa and Torras Hostench Sa (vice pres 1987-), Cros Sa (dir 1987-); Singapore directorships: Overseas Union Bank Centre (dir 1984-), Sassoon Holdings Pte Ltd (vice chm 1986-); dir United Plantations Berhad (Malaysia) 1982-; Hong Kong directorships: Dao Heng Bank and Duo Heng Holdings (dep chm 1984-); *Recreations* walking, cycling, swimming; *Style—* Fouad Jaffar, Esq; Kuwait Investment Office, St Vedast House, 150 Cheapside, London EC2V 6ET (☎ 071 606 8080, fax 071 606 1605/2561, telex LONDON 886301)

JAFFÉ, Prof (Andrew) Michael; CBE; s of Arthur Daniel Jaffé, OBE, of 59 Putney Hill, London SW15, and Marie Marguerite, *née* Strauss; *b* 3 June 1923; *Educ* Eton (King's Scholar), King's Coll Cambridge (MA, DLitt), Courtauld Inst of Art, Harvard, NY Inst of Fine Arts; *m* Patricia Ann Milne Henderson, da of Alexander Roy Henderson; 2 s (Daniel, Benjamin), 2 da (Deborah, Dorothea); *Career* served RNVR, Lt Cdr ret; dir Fitzwilliam Museum Cambridge 1973-90 (prof of history of western art 1973-90), fell King's Coll Cambridge 1952-, fell Cwlth Fund Harvard and NY Univ 1951-53, asst lectr in fine arts Univ of Cambridge 1956 (lectr 1961), prof of renaissance art Washington Univ 1960-61, visiting prof Harvard 1961 (and 1968-69), head Dept of Hist of Art Univ of Cambridge 1969-73 (reader in history of western art 1968), organiser Jordaens Exhibition Ottawa 1968-69; memb Cambridge Festival Bd, memb Bd Eastern Arts Assoc; Nat Tst: Regnl Ctee (Wessex), Art Panel; govr Br Inst of Florence (representing vice-chllrs and princs); Nat Art Collections Fund Award for Life Service to the Arts 1989; FRSA 1969; Officier Ordre de Léopold Belgium, Ordre des Arts et Lettres France, hon foreign memb American Acad of Arts and Sciences; *Books* Van Dyck's Antwerp Sketchbook (1966), Rubens (1967), Jordaens (1968), Rubens and Italy (1977), author of articles and reviews (art historical) in various Euro and N American jls; *Recreations* viticulture; *Clubs* Brooks's, Beefsteak, Turf; *Style—* Prof Michael Jaffè, CBE; Clifton Maybank, Yeovil, Somerset BA22 9UZ

JAFFERJEE, Aftab Asger; s of Asger A Jafferjee, of 51/1 DS Fonseka Rd, Colombo 3, Sri Lanka, and Tara H, *née* Kajiji; *b* 25 June 1956; *Educ* St Paul's Sch Darjeeling India, Rugby, Univ Coll Durham (BA); *Career* called to the Bar Inner Temple 1980, specialist in criminal law; *Recreations* theatre, travel; *Style—* Aftab Jafferjee, Esq; 2 Harcourt Buildings, Temple, London EC4Y 9DB (☎ 071 353 2112)

JAFFRAY, Anne, Lady; Anne; only da of Capt John Otho Paget, MC (d 1934), of Thorpe Satchville Hall, Leics; *Educ* Langford Grove, Schs: France, Germany; *m* 1, 1942 (m dis 1950), Sir John Godfrey Worsley-Taylor, 3 Bt (d 1952); 1 da (Annette Pamela, *qv*); m 2, 1950, Col Sir William Edmund Jaffray, 4 Bt, TD, JP, DL (d 1953); 1 s (William Otho, 5 Bt, *qv*); *Career* memb Hants CC 1964-79; *Recreations* tennis, fishing, field-sports; *Style—* Anne, Lady Jaffray; Haydown House, Weston Patrick, Basingstoke, Hants

JAFFRAY, Nicholas Gordon Alexander; s and h of Sir William Jaffray, 5 Bt, *qv*; *b* 1 Nov 1951; *Style—* Nicholas Jaffray, Esq

JAFFRAY, Sir William Otho; 5 Bt (UK 1892), of Skilts, Studley, Warwickshire; s of Lt-Col Sir William Edmund Jaffray, 4 Bt, TD, JP, DL (d 1953); *b* 1 Nov 1951; *Educ* Eton; *m* 9 May 1981, Cynthia Ross Corrington, da of William M Geering, of Montreal, Quebec, Canada; 3 s (Nicholas b 1982, Jack Henry William b 3 Aug 1987, William Lawrence Paget b 5 March 1990), 1 da (Alexandra Marina Ross b 1984); *Heir* s, Nicholas Gordon Alexander b 18 Oct 1982, *qv*; *Career* property conslt; *Style—* Sir William Jaffray, Bt; The Manor House, Priors Dean, Petersfield, Hants (☎ 073 084 483)

JAFFREY, Saeed; s of Dr Hamid Hussain Jaffrey (d 1984), of Lucknow UP India, and Hadia Imam (d 1987); *Educ* Wynberg-Allen Sch and St George's Coll Mussoorie Uttar Pradesh India, Univ of Allahabad Uttar Pradesh India (MA), RADA, The Catholic Univ of America Washington DC USA (Fulbright scholar, MA); *m* 1, 1958 (m dis 1966), Madhur Jaffrey; 3 da (Zia b 1959, Meera Shameem b 1960, Sakina b 1962); m 2, 1980 Jennifer Irene, da of William Edward Sorrell, of Rustington, W Sussex; *Career* actor; formed own Eng theatre co Delhi, became first Indian actor to tour and perform Shakespeare across the US; joined Actor's Studio NY where he played leads in: Lorca's Blood Wedding, Rashomon, Twelfth Night; Broadway debut as Prof Godbolé in A Passage to India, toured US in Brecht on Brecht, produced wrote and narrated the NY radio programme Reflections of India, recorded The Art of Love - a reworking with music of the Kama Sutra; West End theatre incl: Brahma in Kindly Monkeys, On a Foggy Day (St Martin's Theatre), Captain Brassbound's Conversion (Cambridge Theatre), My Giddy Aunt (Churchill Theatre, Bromley), A Touch of Brightness (Royal Court), The Mother Country (Riverside Studios), Oberon in A Midsummer Night's Dream (Regent's Park), Ibrahim in White Chameleon (Royal Nat Theatre); tv incl: Jimmy Sharma in Tandoori Nights (Channel Four), Nawab in Jewel In The Crown (Granada), Frankie Bhoolabhoy in Staying On, Biju Ram in The Far Pavilions, leading role in A View From The Window (BBC 2), three maj roles in Partition (Channel Four), Rafiq in Gangsters (BBC TV), Minder, Tales of the Unexpected, Callan, Destiny (Play for Today), Love Match (BBC 2), A Killing on the Exchange (Anglia TV), Hard Cases (Central), Rumpole of the Bailey (Thames TV); film work incl: Billy Fish in The Man Who Would Be King, The Guru, Hullabaloo Over Georgie and Bonnie's Pictures, Courtesans of Bombay, Hussain in The Deceivers, The Wilby Conspiracy, Nasser in My Beautiful Laundrette, Patel in Gandhi, Hamidullah in A Passage To India, three lead roles in Masala, lead in Walk of Life, first film in India was The Chessplayers; writer and broadcaster hundreds of scripts in Hindi, Urdu and English, actor numerous plays for BBC Radio Four incl most notably The Pump where he played nine roles, other radio work incl the Rajah in In The Native State (BBC Radio 3) and Village By The Sea (BBC Radio) where he played all 39 characters; *awards* nominated for BAFTA award for Best Supporting Actor in My Beautiful Laundrette, winner Filmfare and Film World awards (India) for Best Actor in The Chessplayers, winner a dozen awards (India) for Best Actor in Ram Teri Ganga Maili, winner awards for Dil and Khudgarz; *Recreations* snooker, cricket, languages, cartooning, cooking, building cultural bridges; *Clubs* Union (Stratford-upon-Avon), Gerry's (Soho), Ealing Snooker, The Br Legion; *Style—* Saeed Jaffrey, Esq; Derek Webster, Associated International Management, 5 Denmark St, London WC2H 8LP (☎ 071 836 2001)

JAGGARD, Anthony John Thorrold; JP (1976); s of Rev Arthur William Percival Jaggard (d 1967), of Guilsborough Vicarage, Northamptonshire, and Isabel Louise May, *née* Capell (d 1972); *b* 5 June 1936; *Educ* Bedford Sch, Liverpool Sch of Architecture Univ of Liverpool; *m* 29 April 1961, (Elizabeth) Jane, da of Col Sir Joseph William Weld, OBE, TD (former Ld-Lt Dorset 1964-84), of Lulworth Manor, Dorset; 2 s (Oliver b and d 3 April 1970, Simon (twin) b 3 April 1970), 3 da (Victoria (Mrs Nigel Beer) b 14 Jan 1962, Charlotte b 27 Jan 1964, Sarah b 5 March 1968); *Career* Cheshire (Earl of Chester's) Yeomanry 1958-67 (Capt 1964, Adj 1967), RARO 1967-86; ptnr John Stark and Partners architects 1965-; projects incl consultation on: Callaly Castle Northumberland, Hoddam Castle Dumfries, Ince Castle Cornwall, Lulworth Castle Dorset, Wardour Castle Wiltshire; designed or remodelled new houses at Gaston Grange Bentworth Hants, Longford House Sydling St Nicholas Dorset, Lulworth Castle House Dorset, Oakfield Park Mortimer Berks; contrib Archaeological Journal; memb Exec Cncl S Dorset Cons Assoc 1965-81; cncl memb: Dorset Nat Hist and Archaeological Soc 1969-, Dorset Cncl of St John 1978-81; dir Dorset Bldgs Preservation Tst 1984-89, cncl memb Royal Archaeological Inst 1987-; Liveryman Worshipful Co of Painter Stainers 1975; FRSA 1986; FSA 1990; *Recreations* old buildings, gardening, shooting; *Clubs* Cavalry and Guards'; *Style—* Anthony Jaggard, Esq, JP, FSA; Winfrith Court, Winfrith Newburgh, Dorset DT2 8JR (☎ 0305 852 800); John Stark and Partners, 13 and 14 Princes St, Dorchester DT1 1TW (☎ 0305 262636, fax 0305 260960)

JAGGER, Cedric Sargeant; s of Charles Sargeant Jagger, MC (d 1934), of London, and Violet Constance, *née* Smith (d 1964); *b* 14 June 1920; *Educ* Westminster; *m* 1, 22 March 1952 (m dis 1972), Jane Angela, da of James Hynds (d 1975); 1 s (Christopher b 18 May 1958), 1 da (Lindsay b 19 Sept 1954); m 2, 5 April 1972, Christine, da of James Fergus Brown, of Sevenoaks, Kent; *Career* WWII RA 1940-46, served 8 Army ME 1942, then N Africa, Sicily and Italy, WO at end of war; perm staff ICI 1938-72, pt/t memb and chm of selection bds CS Cmmn 1973-86, pt/t asst curator then first keeper of the Clockmakers' Co Collection, Guildhall, London 1974-88; JP Hampshire 1975; horological historian and author 1968-; memb: The Stables Theatre Tst, Soc of Authors 1987; life memb Hastings and St Leonards Museums Assoc, Friend of Rye Harbour Nature Reserve; Liveryman Worshipful Co of Clockmakers' 1980 (Freeman 1975); *Books* Clocks (1973), The World's Great Clocks and Watches (1977), Royal Clocks - The British Monarchy and its Timekeepers 1300-1900 (1983), The Artistry of the English Watch (1988); *Recreations* principally work - also photography and music; *Clubs* The Arts; *Style—* Cedric Jagger, Esq

JAGGS, Michael Richard Moore; s of Rev Arthur Ernest Jaggs (d 1975), of Tilford Vicarage, Tilford, Surrey, and Mary Enid, *née* Moore; *b* 7 Nov 1937; *Educ* Wells Cathedral Sch, Pierrepont Sch, City Univ (FBDO, PhD); *m* 1, 15 Sept 1962 (m dis), Gillian, da of (Francis) Allen Eyre, MBE (d 1969); 2 s (Richard, Alexander), 2 da (Sarah, Sophie); m 2, 30 Aug 1980, Janet Elizabeth, *née* Talbot; *Career* qualified dispensing optician 1956, in private practice 1961-, practice merged with Dollond & Aitchison 1988, hosp appt Odstock Hosp Salisbury; in control of: Moore Jaggs Ltd, Crofting Ltd (investmt co), Paxhill plc; chm Bd of Govrs Pierrepont Sch Surrey, past chm Assoc of Contact Lens Manufacurers; Freeman City of London, Liveryman Worshipful Co of Spectacle Makers; fell: Assoc of Br Dispensing Opticians, Royal Soc of Health, Br Contact Lens Assoc (past pres); *Books* Scleral lenses - a clinical guide (1980); *Recreations* skiing, sailing, swimming; *Style—* Michael Jaggs, Esq; Turnpike Field, Hartley Wintney, Hampshire RG27 8HY (☎ 025126 2658); 19 Duchess Mews, London W1 (☎ 071 580 9192)

JAIN, Dr Virendra Kumar; s of Trilok Chandra Jain (d 1974), and Roop Wati Jain; *b* 3 Aug 1935; *Educ* Agra (BSc, MB BS); *m* 23 Nov 1960, Kamlesh, da of Jagdish Prashad Jain (d 1944); 1 s (Sanjiv b 1965), 2 da (Angela b 1964, Meena b 1977); *Career* sr registrar in psychiatry Powick Hosp Worcester 1966-68, lectr in psychiatry and sr registrar Professorial Unit Univ of Liverpool 1968-70, conslt psychiatrist Barnsley District Gen Hosp 1970-; chm: Barnsley Div Br Med Assoc (memb Yorks Regnl Cncl), Barnsley Div Overseas Doctors' Assoc; memb: Standing Conference of Asian Organisation UK Nat Cncl, BMA, Br Soc of Med and Dental Hypnosis, Br Assoc of Psychopharmacology; FRC Psych, DPM, MRCP, MRCS; *Books* A Short Introductory Guide to Clinical Psychiatry (1984); *Recreations* entertaining, playing tennis, listening to Indian classical music; *Clubs* Sandal Lawn Tennis, Walton Hall Country; *Style—* Dr Virendra Jain; Shantiniketan, 17 Beechfield, Sandal, Wakefield, West Yorkshire WF2 6AW (☎ 0924 255207); Department of Psychological Medicine, Barnsley District General Hospital, Gawber Road, Barnsley, South Yorkshire S75 2EP (☎ 0226 730000)

JAINE, Tom William Mahony; s of William Edwin Jaine (d 1970), and Aileen, *née* Mahony (d 1943); *b* 4 June 1943; *Educ* Kingswood Sch Bath, Balliol Coll Oxford (BA); *m* Sally Caroline, da of Andrew Agnew, of Crowborough; 4 da (Harriet b 1974, Elizabeth b 1976, Matilda b 1985, Frances b 1987); *Career* restaurateur 1973-84; ed: Good Food Guide 1989-, Journal of the International Wine and Food Society 1989-; *Recreations* baking; *Style—* Tom Jaine, Esq; Allaleigh House, Blackawton, Totnes, Devon TQ9 7DL (☎ 080 421 269)

JAKES, Clifford Duncan; s of Ernest Thomas Jakes (d 1963), of Leigh on Sea, Essex; *b* 29 Dec 1942; *Educ* Westcliff HS Southend-on-Sea, Aston Univ; *Career* articled Wilkins Kennedy & Co London 1960-65, mgmnt trainee Tube Investments Ltd 1966-67, fin dir Raleigh Cycles (Malaysia) 1968-71, fin controller (Overseas Div) Raleigh Industries Ltd Nottingham 1971-73, fin dir and md Warren Plantation Holdings London 1974-81, mgmnt conslt 1982, gp md Link House Publications 1983-; FCA; *Recreations* theatre, sport, preservation of wild life; *Clubs* City, Selangor (Malaysia), Bengal (Calcutta); *Style—* Clifford Jakes, Esq; 10 Harley St, Leigh on Sea, Essex (☎ 0702 75758); Link House Publications plc, Robert Rogers House, New Orchard, Poole, Dorset (☎ 0202 671171)

JAKEWAY, Sir (Francis) Derek; KCMG (1963, CMG 1956), OBE (1948); s of Francis Edward Jakeway; *b* 6 June 1915; *Educ* Hele's Sch Exeter, Exeter Coll Oxford (MA); *m* 1941, Phyllis Lindsay Watson; 3 s; *Career* entered Colonial Service (Nigeria) 1937, sec to Seychelles Govt 1946-49, chief sec: Br Guiana 1955-59, Sarawak 1959-63, govr and C-in-C Fiji 1964-68, ret; chm Devon Area Health Authy 1974-82; KStJ 1964; *Style—* Sir Derek Jakeway, KCMG, OBE; 78 Douglas Ave, Exmouth, Devon (☎ 039 582 271342)

JAKOBOVITS, Baron (Life Peer UK 1988), of Regent's Park in Greater London; Sir Immanuel Jakobovits; s of Rabbi Dr Julius Jakobovits, of Konigsberg, Germany; *b* 8 Feb 1921,Konigsberg, Germany; *Educ* Univ of London (PhD), Jews' Coll London, Yeshivah Etz Chaim London (DD), City Univ (DLitt), DD (Lambeth); *m* 1949, Amélie, da of Rabbi Dr Elie Munk; 2 s (Dr Hon Julian b 1950, Rabbi Hon Samuel b 1951), 4 da (Esther (Hon Mrs Pearlman) b 1953, Jeanette (Hon Mrs Turner) b 1956, Aviva (Hon Mrs Adler) b 1958, Elisheva (Hon Mrs Homburger) b 1966); *Career* minister of three London synagogues 1941-49, chief rabbi of Ireland 1949-58, rabbi Fifth Ave Synagogue (New York) 1958-67, chief rabbi of The United Hebrew Congregations of Br Cwlth of Nats 1967-; pres Conf on Euro Rabbis; kt 1981; *Books* Jewish Medical Ethics (1959), Jewish Law Faces Modern Problems (1965), Journal of a Rabbi (1966), The Timely and the Timeless (1977), 'If Only My People..'.Zionism in My Life (1984); co-author of The Jewish Hospital Compendium (1963), etc; *Style—* The Rt Hon Lord Jakobovits, Chief Rabbi; Adler House, Tavistock Square, London WC1H 9HN (☎ 071 387 1066)

JAMAL, Dr Goran Atallah; s of Atallah Jamal (Al-Talabani), of Iraq, and Nusrat Jamal (d 1987); *b* 19 July 1953; *Educ* Baghdad Univ (MB ChB), Univ of Glasgow (PhD, MD); *m* 15 Dec 1983, Vian, da of Maj-Gen Mohamad Salih Anber (ret), of Iraq; 1 da (Lazia b 23 May 1986); *Career* sr registrar in neurology Bart's Med Sch 1986-88, conslt Dept of Neurology and sr clinical lectr Univ of Glasgow 1988- (res fell in neurology 1981-86), sr lectr in neurosciences Dept of Educn Strathclyde Region 1988-; memb: Assoc of Br Neurologists, The EEG Soc, Assoc of Br Clinical Neurophysiologists, Scottish Assoc of Neurosciences, New York Acad of Sci, American Assoc of Electrodiagnostic Med, American EEG Soc; MRCP (Glas); *Clubs* The Pond Leisure (Glasgow); *Style—* Dr Goran Jamal; 241 Milngavie Rd, Bearsden, Glasgow G61 3DQ (☎ 041 942 8687); Glasgow University Dept of Neurology, Institute of Neurological Sciences, Southern General Hospital, Glasgow G51 4TF (☎ 041 445 2466)

JAMAL, Mahmood; s of Maulana Jamal Mian, of Firangi Mahal, and Kaniz Fatima Asar; *Educ* St Joseph's Sch Dacca, SOAS, Univ of London (BA); *Career* poet, prodr and dir; poems broadcast on Radio 3 and published in various magazines incl London Magazine; prodr of TV films; co fndr Retake Film and Video Collective (winner BFI Independent Film and TV award 1988), co ed Black Phoenix Magazine 1979-, lit advsr and vice chm Steering Ctee Roundhouse Arts Centre 1984, winner Minority Rights Gp award for poetry and translation 1985, lit advsr to Gtr London Arts 1986-, advsr and memb Editorial Bd Third Text Quarterly 1987-, participant in poetry in festivals throughout the country incl Arts Cncl Festival Southbank; memb Assoc of Admin Accountants; *Books* Coins for Charon (1976), Silence Inside A Guns Mouth (1984), Penguin Book of Modern Urdu Poetry (ed and translator, 1986); *Recreations* tennis, squash, cricket; *Clubs* South Hampstead Lawn Tennis; *Style—* Mahmood Jamal, Esq; 69 Dartmouth Rd, London NW2 4EP (☎ 081 452 8170); 19 Liddell Rd, London NW6 (☎ 071 328 4676)

JAMAL, Patricia Barbara; da of Lt Cdr John Enda Bernard Healy, RNVR (d 1967), and Barbara Maud, *née* Taylor; *b* 3 Sept 1943; *Educ* St Maur's Convent Weybridge,

Ursuline Convent Wimbledon, Brooklands Coll Weybridge; *m* 16 Dec 1971, (Nizar) Ahmed Jamal, s of Abdulmalek Ahmed Jamal, of Vancouver, Canada; 3 da (Jenna b 1977, Sarah b 1980, Isabel b 1982); *Career* business devpt offr Bank of Montreal London 1983-87, chief dealer GTS Corp Servs Barclays Bank 1987-; dir Aston Charities Tst Ltd 1978-; *Recreations* family, reading, music, swimming; *Style—* Mrs Patricia Jamal; 8 St Margaret's Cres, Putney, London SW15 6HL (☎ 081 785 7165); Barclays Bank plc, Global Treasy Servs, Murray House, 1 Royal Mint Court, London EC3 N4HH (☎ 071 283 0909)

JAMES, Prof Alan Morien; s of Willie James (d 1983), of Newport, Gwent, and Martha, *née* John d (1990); *b* 20 Jan 1933; *Educ* Newport HS, LSE (BSc); *m* 1, 18 Aug 1956 (m dis 1980), Jean Valerie, da of Ernest Hancox, of Newport, Gwent; 4 s (Morien b 1958, Gwyn b 1962, Gareth b 1964, David b 1965), 3 da (Helen b and d 1959, Nesta b 1961, Ceri b 1969); m 2, 19 March 1981, Lorna, da of Frank Eric Lloyd, of Chester; *Career* LSE: asst lectr, lectr, sr lectr, reader 1957-73; Rockefeller res fell Inst of War and Peace Studies Univ USA 1968, prof and head of Dept of Int Rels Univ of Keele 1974-90 (res prof 1990-); visiting prof: Dept of Int Rels Univ of Ife Nigeria 1981, Sch of Int Studies Jawaharial Nehru Univ New Delhi 1983; chm Br Int Studies Assoc 1979-83, memb Soc Studies Sub Ctee Univ Grants Ctee 1983-89, advsr in politics and int studies Univ Funding Cncl 1989-; *Books* The Politics of Peacekeeping (1969), The Bases of International Order (ed 1973), Sovereign Statehood: The Basis of International Society (1986), Peacekeeping in International Politics (1990); *Recreations* hill and coast walking, supporting Port Vale FC, music, food, theatre; *Clubs* Commonwealth House; *Style—* Prof Alan James; 23 Park Lane, Congleton, Cheshire CW12 3DG (☎ 0260 271801); Dept of International Relations, University of Keele, Keele, Staffordshire ST5 5BG (☎ 0782 621111, fax 0782 613847, telex 36113 UNKLIB G)

JAMES, Alan Murray; s of Harold Birkett James (d 1961), of Sutton, Surrey, and Nellie Beatrice, *née* Covington (d 1981); *b* 24 Feb 1925; *Educ* Sutton Valence, Univ of Birmingham (RE army course), Clare Coll Cambridge (MA); *m* 7 June 1952, Janette Mary, da of Harold Pridmore Lack (d 1974); 3 da (Linda b 1954, Susan b 1956, Mandy b 1961); *Career* WWII RE 1943-47, cmmnd 1945, KGVO Bengal Sappers and Miners 1945-47, Capt 1947, served Indonesia and Malaysia; md and chm Tate and Lyle Technical Services 1961-75, dir Sugar Industry Technologists Inc 1965-78, md Tate and Lyle Enterprises 1969-75, chm Sugar Knowledge International 1981-; underwriting memb Lloyds 1982-; pres Sugar Processing Res 1972-74; Freeman: City of London 1948, Worshipful Co of Loriners; *Recreations* tennis, squash, travel; *Clubs* RAC, Bromley Cricket, Middleton, Richmond Football, Cambridge Univ Rugby Union Football; *Style—* Alan James, Esq; 12 Shornefield Close, Bickley, Kent BR1 2HX (☎ 081 467 4579, telex 934968); 16 Crossbush Rd, Felpham, W Sussex PO22 7LS

JAMES, Albert (Alby); s of Albert Samuel James (d 1982), of London, and Florence Cassetta Renalda, *née* Thomas (d 1989); *Educ* St David's C of E Sch London, Southgate Technical Coll London, Univ of E Anglia (BA), Univ of London; *m* 5 Jan 1980, Vanessa Mary, da of Capt Christopher Simmonds; 2 s (William Marcus b 17 March 1980, Benjamin Andrew b 16 April 1982), 1 da (Eloïse Sarah b 4 Aug 1988); *Career* theatre director; econ researcher Middle East Economic Digest Consultants 1977-78, artistic dir Stopgap Theatre Company 1978-79, arts cncl trainee asst dir English Stage Company 1979-80, freelance dir 1980-82, asst dir Royal Shakespeare Company (Barbican) 1982-83, freelance dir 1983-84, artistic dir and chief exec Temba Theatre Company 1984-; productions incl: Verdict (Stopgap Theatre) 1976, Mr Wilberforce, MP (Westminster Theatre) 1980, Meetings (Hampstead Theatre) 1982, Light up for Life (RSC One Year On Barbican Festival) 1983, The Boot Dance (Temba) 1984, Porgy and Bess (assoc dir, Glyndebourne Festival Opera) 1986 and 1987, Fences (Liverpool Playhouse and The Garrick London) 1990, Avé Afrika (RADA) 1990, Ghosts (Temba tour) 1991; specialist advsr for performing arts CNAA; memb: BBC Gen Advsy Cncl, Arts Centre Gp Productions, Dirs Guild of GB; *Recreations* listening to music, reading, photography, squash, swimming, religion and politics, film-making, foreign travel, tennis; *Style—* Alby James, Esq; Temba Theatre Co, Dominion House, 101 Southwark Street, London SE1 0JH (☎ 071 261 0991, fax 071 261 9715)

JAMES, Hon Anthony Christopher Walter Paul; 2 s of 5 Baron Northbourne; *b* 14 Jan 1963; *Style—* The Hon Anthony James; 11 Eaton Place, London SW1

JAMES, Charles Edwin Frederic; s of Frederic Crockett Gwilym James (d 1970), formerly treas of the Great Universal Stores Ltd, and Marjorie Peggy, *née* Peace (d 1976); *b* 17 April 1943; *Educ* Trent Coll Derbyshire, Selwyn Coll Cambridge (MA); *m* 1968, Diana Mary Francis, da of James Francis Thornton (d 1977), formerly chm and md William Thornton & Sons Ltd; 2 s (Daniel b 1971, Philip b 1973); *Career* barr 1965, barr-at-law practising Northern Circuit, rec of the Crown Ct 1982-; *Recreations* family pursuits; *Clubs* Cambridge Univ Cricket, Royal Liverpool Golf, Royal Mersey Yacht; *Style—* Charles James, Esq; Broomlands, 38 Vyner Road South, Birkenhead, Merseyside L43 7PR (☎ 051 652 1951); Refuge Assurance House, Derby Square, Liverpool L2 1TS (☎ 051 709 4222)

JAMES, Hon Charles Walter Henry; eldest s & h of 5 Baron Northbourne, qv; *b* 14 June 1960; *Educ* Eton, Magdalen Coll Oxford; *m* 3 Oct 1987, Catherine Lucy, o da of W Ralph Burrows, of Prescot, Lancs; 1 s (Henry Christopher William b 3 Dec 1988); *Career* dir: Rede Investments Ltd, Redesdale Investments Ltd, Betteshanger Farms Ltd, Kent Salads Holdings Ltd; *Style—* The Hon Charles James; Northbourne Court, Northbourne, Kent CT14 0LW (☎ 0304 374617); Home Farm, Betteshanger, Kent CT14 0LW (☎ 0304 611281, fax 0304 614512)

JAMES, Christopher John; s of John Thomas Walters James, MC (d 1978), of Monmouth, and Cicely Hilda, *née* Purton (formerly Motteram) (d 1970); *b* 20 March 1932; *Educ* Clifton, Magdalene Coll Cambridge (MA); *m* 20 Sept 1958, Elizabeth Marion Cicely, da of Thomas Finlayson Thomson (d 1977), of Winchester; 1 s (Timothy b 10 Dec 1959), 1 da (Caroline b 10 Oct 1962); *Career* Nat Serv cmmn RA 1951-52, TA 1952-60; admitted slr 1958, sr ptnr Martineau Johnson 1989-, chm Birmingham Midshires Building Society 1990-; pres Birmingham Law Soc 1983-84, chm Cncl Edgbaston HS for Girls 1987-90; *Clubs* Little Aston Golf, the Birmingham; *Style—* Christopher James, Esq; Martineau Johnson, St Philip's House, St Philip's Place, Birmingham B3 2PP (☎ 021 200 3300, fax 021 200 3330, telex 339793)

JAMES, His Honour Judge Christopher Philip; s of Herbert Edgar James, CBE (d 1977); *b* 27 May 1934; *Educ* Felsted, Magdalene Coll Cambridge (MA); *Career* cmmnd RASC 1953; barr Gray's Inn 1959, rec Crown Ct 1979, circuit judge 1980-; *Clubs* United Oxford and Cambridge Univ; *Style—* His Honour Judge James

JAMES, Clare Veronica; yr da of Baron Saint Brides, GCMG, CVO, MBE, PC (Life Peer; d 1989), and his 1 w, Elizabeth Margaret Roper, *née* Piesse (d 1966); *b* 14 Sept 1950; *Educ* Wycombe Abbey, Univ of London (BSc), RSA Dip in Teaching English as a Foreign Language; *m* 10 Jan 1970 (m dis 1978), Dr Patrick Duncan, s of Patrick Baker Duncan (d 1967); 1 s (Patrick b 1973); *Career* teacher of English as a foreign language International Business Colleges Ltd London 1977-80 and Stockholm 1980-; freelance translator from Swedish to English 1982-; authorised by Swedish Bd of Trade as pub translator from Swedish into English 1987; employee of own company The Word Shop (Sprakverkstan AB) 1986-; conslt on English language work; *Recreations* reading, travel; *Style—* Ms Clare James; Köpenhamnsgatan 24, 2 tr, S-164 42 Kista, Sweden (☎ 010 46 8 750 8846, fax 010 46 8 751 5001)

JAMES, Clive (né Vivian Leopold); s of Albert Arthur James, and Minora May, *née* Darke; *b* 7 Oct 1939; *Educ* Sydney Tech HS, Univ of Sydney, Pembroke Coll Cambridge (pres footlights); *Career* TV presenter and entertainer: record lyricist for Pete Atkin; albums incl: Beware of Beautiful Strangers, Driving through the Mythical America, A King at Nightfall, The Road of Silk, Secret Drinker, Live Lible, The Master of the Revels; song-book A First Folio (with Pete Atkin); feature writer The Observer 1972- (TV critic 1972-82); presenter TV series: Cinema, Up Sunday, So It Goes, A Question of Sex, Saturday Night People, Clive James on Television, The Late Clive James, The Late Show with Clive James, Saturday Night Clive, The Talk Show with Clive James; TV documentaries: Shakespeare in Perspective Hamlet 1980, The Clive James Paris Fashion Show 1981, Clive James and the Calendar Girls 1981, The Return of the Flash of Lightning 1982, Clive James in Las Vagas 1982, Clive James meets Roman Polanski 1984, The Clive James Great American Beauty Pageant 1984, Clive James in Dallas 1985, Clive James meets Katherine Hepburn 1986, Clive James on Safari 1986, Clive James and the Heroes of San Francisco 1987, Clive James in Japan 1987, Postcard from Rio 1989, Postcard from Chicago 1989, Postcard from Paris 1989, Clive James meets Jane Fonda, Clive James on the 80s 1989, Postcard from Miami 1990, Postcard from Rome 1990, Postcard from Shanghai 1990, Clive James meets Ronald Regan 1990; non-fiction publications incl: The Metropolitan Critic 1974, The Fate of Felicity Fark in the Land of the Media 1975, Peregrine Prykke's Pilgrimage through the London Literary World 1976, Britannia Bright's Bewilderment in the Wilderness of Westminster 1976, Visions Before Midnight 1977, At the Pillars of Hercules 1979, First Reactions 1980, Charles Charming's Challenges on the Pathway to the Throne 1981, Crystal Bucket 1981, From the Land of Shadows 1982, Glued to the Box 1982, Flying Visits 1984, Snakecharmers in Texas 1988; fiction publications: Brilliant Creatures 1983, The Remake 1987; verse: Fan-mail 1977, Poem of the year 1983, Other Passports: poems 1958-85; autobiographies incl: Unreliable Memoirs 1980, Falling Towards England: Unreliable Memoirs II 1985, May Week Was in June: Unreliable Memoirs III 1990; *Style—* Clive James, Esq; c/o AD Peters & Co, 5th Floor, The Chambers, Chelsea Harbour, Lots Rd, London SW10 0XF

JAMES, Sir Cynlais Kenneth Morgan; KCMG (1985, CMG 1976); s of Thomas and Lydia James; *b* 29 April 1926; *Educ* Trinity Coll Cambridge; *m* 1953, Mary, da of Richard Désiré Girouard and Lady Blanche Maud de la Poer Beresford, da of 6 Marquess of Waterford, KP, and Lady Beatrix Fitzmaurice, da of 5 Marquess of Lansdowne, also sis of the architectural historian Mark Girouard, *qv*; 2 da; *Career* served RAF 1944-47; FO (now FCO) 1951: former 1 sec Moscow, head W Euro Dept FCO and min Paris; ambass to Poland 1981-83, under sec of state FCO 1983, ambass to Mexico 1983-86; DG Canning House 1987-; dir Thomas Cook; dir chm Br Inst Paris; Order of the Aztec Eagle (First Class), Order of Andreas Bello (Venezuala); (First Class); Dr HC of the Mexican Acad of Int Law; *Clubs* Brooks's, Pratt's, Travellers' (Paris), Beefsteak; *Style—* Sir Cynlais James, KCMG; Canning House, 2 Belgrave Square, London SW1

JAMES, Prof David Edward; s of Charles Edward James (d 1982), of Eastleigh, Hants, and Dorothy Hilda, *née* Reeves (d 1984); *b* 31 July 1937; *Educ* Peter Symonds Sch Winchester, Univ of Reading (BSc), Univ of Oxford (Dip Ed), Univ of London (Dip Further Ed), Univ of Durham (MEd); *m* 30 March 1963, Penelope Jane, da of Lt Cdr Edward J Murray, of Bradford-on-Avon, Wilts; 2 s (Philip b 1966, Christopher b 1969), 1 da (Lucy b 1964); *Career* lectr in zoology and psychology City of Bath Tech Coll 1961-63, lectr in sci and psychology St Mary's Coll of Educn Newcastle upon Tyne 1963-64; Univ of Surrey: lectr in educnl psychology 1964-68, res lectr in educn 1968-69, dir of adult educn 1969-80, prof of adult educn 1980-81, prof and head of Dept of Educnl Studies 1981-; chm Br Assoc for Educnl Gerontology, vice chm Br Assoc for Services to the Elderly, Preretirement Assoc of GB and NI; memb: Bd of Educn Royal Coll of Nursing, Educn Ctee Royal Coll of Midwives, Governing Body Centre for Int Briefing, Moor Park Tst for Christian Adult Educn, Surrey County Educn Ctee, Gen Nursing Cncl 1972-80, UK Central Cncl for Nursing Midwifery and Health Visiting 1980-83, English Nat Bd for Nursing Midwifery and Health Visiting 1983-88; CBiol, MIBiol 1963, CPsych, AFBPsS 1966, FRSH 1974, FRSA 1974; *Books* A Students guide to Efficient Study (1966), Introduction to Psychology (1968); *Recreations* farming; *Style—* Prof David James; Dept of Educational Studies, University of Surrey, Guildford GU2 5XH (☎ 0483 571281 ext 3122, fax 300803, telex 859331)

JAMES, Hon Mrs (Deborah Katherine Louise); *née* Suenson-Taylor; 2 da of 2 Baron Grantchester, QC; *b* 9 April 1957; *Educ* Cheltenham Ladies' Coll; *m* 1977, Michael James; *Style—* The Hon Mrs James; The Old Rectory, Earnley, nr Chichester, W Sussex

JAMES, Derek Claude; OBE (1989); s of Cecil Claude James (d 1987), and Violet, *née* Rudge (d 1974); *b* 9 March 1929; *Educ* King Edward's GS Birmingham, Open Univ (BA); *m* 16 Oct 1954, Evelyn, *née* Thomas; 1 s (Stephen b 1955), 1 da (Kathryn (Mrs Dawson) b 1956); *Career* RA 1947-49; local govt 1946-69: Birmingham, Coventry, Bradford; Leeds City Cncl: princ offr 1969-73, dep dir of social servs 1973-78, dir of social servs 1978-89; pres Nat Assoc of Nursery and Family Care 1988-; chm Nightstop Leeds (scheme to assist homeless young people); memb: St Anne's Shelter & Housing Action Ltd Leeds 1976-89, Yorks RHA 1976-82, Nat Advsy Cncl for Employment of Disabled People 1985-89; memb: Panel of Experts Registered Homes Tribunal 1990-, Health Advsy Serv 1990-, Assoc of Dirs of Social Servs; *Recreations* gardening, watching sport; *Style—* Derek James, Esq, OBE; Hill House, Woodhall Hills, Calverley, Pudsey, West Yorkshire LS28 5QY (☎ 0532 578 044)

JAMES, Air Vice-Marshal Edgar; CBE (1966), DFC (1945, AFC 1948 and bar 1959); s of Richard George James (d 1967), and Gertrude, *née* Barnes (d 1942); *b* 19 Oct 1915; *Educ* Neath GS; *m* 1941, Josephine, da of John Steel (d 1980), of Harrogate; 2 s (Stephen b 1945, David b 1949); *Career* RAF 1939-, cmmnd 1940, 305 and 107 Sqdns NW Europe (King's Commendation for Meritorious Service in the Air 1943 and 1944), CO 68 Sqdn 1954-55 Germany (Queen's commendation 1956), chief instr and asst Cmdt Central Flying Sch 1959-61, dir operational regts MOD 1962-65, Cdr Br Forces Zambia 1966, Air Vice-Marshal 1967, dep controller Miny of Technol 1967-69, ret 1969; aviation conslt 1970-86; FRAeS 1971; *Recreations* sailing, golf; *Clubs* RAF, Royal Western Yacht; *Style—* Air Vice-Marshal James; Low Mead, Traine Paddock, Modbury, Devon PL21 0RN (☎ 0458 830 492)

JAMES, Edwin Kenneth George; s of Edwin Percy (d 1956), and Jessie Marion, *née* Clarke; *b* 27 Dec 1916; *Educ* Latymer Upper Sch, Univ of London (BSc); *m* 1941, Dorothy Margaret, da of Arthur Pratt (d 1961), of London; 1 da (Carolyn Margaret b 1943); *Career* WO 1938, Chemical Def Exploration Station 1942, Austral Field Exploration Station 1944-46, Operational Res Gp US Army MD USA 1950-54, dir Biological and Chemical Def MOD 1961, HM Treasy 1967, chief scientific offr Civil Serv Dept 1970; chief exec PAG Ltd 1977-87, chm Photon plc and Pagsolar Technology Ltd 1986-89; Silver medal of Operational Res Soc 1979; FRCS, FOR; *Clubs* Athenaeum; *Style—* Kenneth James, Esq; 5 Waterseet Rd, Harnham, Salisbury, Wilts (☎ 0722 334099)

JAMES, Rev Canon Eric Arthur; s of John Morgan James, and Alice Amelia James; *b*

14 April 1925; *Educ* Dagenham County HS, King's Coll London (MA, BD, FKC); *Career* asst curate St Stephen with St John Westminster 1951-55, chaplain Trinity Coll Cambridge 1955-59, select preacher to Univ of Cambridge 1959-60, vicar St George Camberwell and warden Trinity Coll Mission 1959-64, dir Parish and People 1964-69, canon residentiary and precentor Southwark Cathedral 1966-73, proctor in convocation 1964-72, canon residentiary and missioner Diocese of St Albans 1973-83, hon canon 1983-, preacher to Gray's Inn 1978-; commissary to: Bishop of Kimberley 1965-67, Archbishop of Melanesia 1969-; examining chaplain to: Bishop of St Albans 1973-83, Bishop of Truro 1983-; hon dir Christian Action 1979-; chaplain to HM The Queen 1984-; *Books* The Double Cure (1957, 2 edn 1980), Odd Man Out (1962), Spirituality for Today (ed, 1968), Stewards of the Mysteries of God (ed, 1979), A Life of Bishop John A T Robinson, Scholar, Pastor, Prophet (1987), Where Three Ways Meet (ed, 1987), God's Truth (ed, 1988), Judge Not: A Selection of Sermons Preached in Gray's Inn Chapel 1978-88 (1989), Collected Thoughts: Fifty Scripts for BBC's Thought For The Day (1990), A Last Eccentric: A Symposium concerning the Revd Canon F A Simpson, Historian, Preacher and Eccentric; *Recreations* music; *Clubs* Reform, Royal Cwlth Soc; *Style—* The Rev Canon Eric James; 11 Denny Crescent, Kennington, London SE11 4UY; Christian Action, St Peter's House, 308 Kennington Lane, London SE11 5HY (☎ 071 735 2372)

JAMES, Dr (David William) Francis; OBE (1989); s of Thomas Martin James (d 1962), of Harefield, Middx, and Margaret Anne, *née* Francis (d 1984); *b* 29 March 1929; *Educ* Cyfarthfa GS, Univ of Wales (BSc), Univ of London (PhD); *m* 4 April 1953, Elaine Maureen, da of Thomas Hewett (d 1955); 2 da (Rosalind b 1955, Heather b 1958); *Career* Flying Offr RAF 1954-56 (educn offr); res offr ICI Ltd 1956-60, lectr and sr lectr Univ of Wales Bangor 1960-71, dep princ Glamorgan Poly 1971-72, dir Poly of Wales 1972-78, dir and chief exec Br Ceramic Res Ltd; chm Leek and Dist Camera Club; memb: Methodist Church, Cncl Nat Academic Awards (CNAA) 1975-82; chm Ctee for Res Degrees (CNAA) 1980-86 (memb 1976-82), SERC Polys Ctee 1975-78, Trg Ctee Wales Cncl for Disabled 1974-78; hon fell Poly of Wales 1986; FRSA 1976, FICeram 1985 (pres 1989); *Recreations* photography, DIY; *Clubs* Royal Cwlth; *Style—* Dr Francis James, OBE; Fairways, Birchall, Leek, Staffs (☎ 0538 373311); British Ceramic Res Ltd (Ceram Research), Queen's Road, Penkhull, Stoke-on-Trent, Staffs (☎ 45431, fax 0782 412331, telex 36228 BCRA G)

JAMES, (Christopher) Garth; s of Howell Gywn James (d 1951), and Winifred, *née* Fugler (d 1990); *b* 25 March 1947; *Educ* Epsom Coll, Univ of Southampton (BSc); *Career* investmt analyst Hoare Govett 1969, res dir Hoare Govett (Far East) based in Hong Kong 1972-78, corp fin dir Hoare Govett Corporate Finance 1978-; *Recreations* skiing, sailing, tennis, eating; *Style—* Garth James, Esq; Hoare Govett Corporate Finance, Security Pacific House, 4 Broadgate, London EC2M 7LE (☎ 071 601 0101)

JAMES, Dr (David) Geraint; s of David James (d 1928), of Treherbert, Wales, and Sarah, *née* Davies (d 1978); *b* 2 Jan 1922; *Educ* Pontypridd Co Sch, Jesus Coll Cambridge (MA, MD), Middx Hosp Univ of London (MRCS, LRCP, MRCP), Columbia Univ NY; *m* 15 Dec 1951, Prof Dame Sheila Patricia Violet Sherlock, DBE; 2 da (Amanda b 15 Sept 1958, Auriole b 7 Dec 1963); *Career* Surgn-Lt RNVR 1946-48; serv: HMS Halcyon, HMS Theseus; conslt physician RN 1972-85; dean of studies Royal Northern Hosp London 1968-88 (conslt physician 1959-), prof med Univ of London and Miami, conslt ophthalmic physician St Thomas' Hosp London; pres: Harvey Soc London 1963, Osler Club London, Med Soc London 1980; fndr London Med Ophthalmology Soc 1964, organising soc World Congress History of Med 1972; cncl memb: RCP 1983, Hunterian Soc 1984; pres London Glamorganshire Soc 1971-75, fndr pres World Assoc of Sarcoidosis 1987, ed International Journal Sarcoidosis, vice pres Post Grad Med Fedn; hon corr Thoracic Soc of: France, Italy, Portugal, French Nat Acad of Med; white robed memb Bardic Circle of Wales 1984; Freeman: Worshipful Co of Apothecaries 1960-, City of London; Hon LLD Univ of Wales 1982; FRCP 1964, Hon FACP 1990; *Books* Textbook of Infections (1957), Colour Atlas of Respiratory Diseases (1981), Sarcoidosis (1985), W B Saunders; *Recreations* tennis, rugby, international Welshness; *Clubs* Athenaeum; *Style—* Dr D Geraint James; 41 York Terrace East, Regent's Park, London NW1 4PT (☎ 071 486 4560); 149 Harley St, London W1N 1HG (☎ 071 935 4444)

JAMES, Gerald Reaveley; s of Capt William Gilbert Ferdinand James (d 1965), of Deer Orchard House, Cumberland, and Annie, *née* Rydiard (d 1985); *b* 7 Sept 1937; *Educ* Sedbergh; *m* 5 Dec 1964, Gisela, da of Erich Christian Hess (ka 1943); 3 s (Christian Gilbert Furnival b 22 July 1967, Andrew Francis Reaveley b 17 Oct 1968, Alexander Gerald Reaveley b 11 Feb 1981); *Career* RA 1955, 16 Ind Parachute Bde 1956-58; CA; Peat Marwick Mitchell 1958-64, Hill Samuel & Co Ltd 1964-68, Baring Bros & Co Ltd 1968-72, dir Henry Ansbacher & Co Ltd 1972-76, conslt Singer & Friedlander 1976-78; dir: Belhaven Brewery & Co Ltd 1978-82, Norton Telecoms Group plc 1978-82, VW Thermax plc 1982-83; chm: Astra Holdings plc 1981-, Astra Holdings Corporation (USA) 1986-, Astra (Canada) 1986-, Kilgore Corporation USA 1987-, Walters Group USA 1988-, Accudyne Corporation USA 1988-, Astra Defence Systems Ltd 1988-, PRB sa (Belgium) 1989-, Hayley and Weller Ltd 1989; Freeman City of London 1989, Liveryman Worshipful Co of Gunmakers 1989 (Freeman 1988); FCA 1964, FIOD 1984, MBIM 1980; *Recreations* shooting, fishing, cricket, rugby, tennis; *Clubs* Naval and Mil, East India, Roehampton; *Style—* Gerald James, Esq; 2 Laurel Road, Barnes, London SW13 0EE (☎ 071 876 1436); Deer Orchard House, Cockermouth, Cumbria; 6 St James's Place, London SW1 (☎ 071 495 3787, fax 071 495 0493, telex 295279)

JAMES, Geraldine; da of Gerald Thomas (d 27 May 1987), of Cornwall, and Annabella, *née* Doogan (d 6 May 1987); *b* 25 Oct 1955; *Educ* Downe House Sch Newbury, Drama Centre London; *m* 28 June 1986, Joseph Sebastian Blatchley, s of John Blatchley; 1 da (Eleanor b 20 June 1985); *Career* actress; worked in repertory theatre 1972-75 at: Chester, Exeter, Coventry; roles incl: Miss Julie, Desdemona, Raina, Annie Sullivan; fringe theatre in London incl: Almost Free 1976, Little Theatre 1976, Bush 1983, Man in the Moon 1986; other works incl: The White Devil Oxford Playhouse 1981, When I was a Girl I Used to Scream and Shout Whitehall Theatre 1987, Cymbeline Nat Theatre 1988, Portia in The Merchant of Venice Peter Hall Co 1989; Merchant of Venice Broadway (Tony award nomination) 1990; TV incl: Dummy 1977 (BAFTA Best Actress nomination), Love Among The Artists 1978, The History Man 1980, Jewel In The Crown (BAFTA Best Actress nomination), Blott on the Landscape 1984, Echoes 1987; films incl: Sweet William 1978, Night Cruiser 1978, Gandhi 1981, Wolves of Willoughby Chase 1988, The Tall Guy 1988, She's Been Away 1989 (Vencie Film Festival Best Actress Award), If Look's Could Kill 1990, The Bridge 1990; *Recreations* music; *Style—* Miss Geraldine James; Julian Belfrage Assoc, 68 St James Street, SW1 (☎ 071 491 4400)

JAMES, Glen William; s of Clifford Vizetelly James, of Long Ashton, Bristol, and Kathleen Mary Flora, *née* Doull; *b* 22 Aug 1952; *Educ* King's Coll Sch Wimbledon, New Coll Oxford (MA); *m* 15 Aug 1987, Amanda Claire, da of Phillip Dorrell, of Worcester; *Career* admitted slr 1976, ptnr Slaughter and May 1983-; Freeman Worshipful Co of Solicitors; memb Law Soc; *Recreations* music, reading, various sports; *Clubs* RAC; *Style—* Glen James, Esq; Slaughter and May, 35 Basinghall St, London EC2V 5DB (☎ 071 600 1200, fax 071 600 0289, telex 883486/888926)

JAMES, Helen; *née* Shaw; da of Peter Shaw, and Joan Mary, *née* Turner; *b* 29 March 1951; *Educ* Cheadle Hulme Sch, Girton Coll Cambridge (MA); *m* 30 August 1976, Allan James, s of Thomas Raymond James; 1 s (Peter Thomas b 26 March 1979), 2 da (Clare Elizabeth b 21 Oct 1980, Sarah Linda b 29 Sept 1985); *Career* actuary; trainee Equity and Law 1972-74, ptnr Clay & Ptnrs 1977- (joined 1975); *Style—* Mrs Helen James; 15 Church Ave, Ruislip, Middx HA4 7HX (☎ 0895 631 758); Clay & Partners 61 Brook St, London W1 (☎ 071 408 1600)

JAMES, Henry Leonard; CB (1979); s of Leonard Mark James (d 1967), of Birmingham, and Alice Esther, *née* Jones (d 1971); *b* 12 Dec 1919; *Educ* King Edward VI Sch Birmingham; *m* 26 Mar 1949, Sylvia Mary (d 1989), da of Rupert John George Bickell (d 1952), of Bournemouth; *Career* ed The Window Miny Nat Insur 1947-51, press offr Miny Pension and Nat Insur 1951-55, head films radio and tv Admlty 1955-61, dep chief info offr Miny of Educn 1961-64, dep press sec to PM 1964-69 (press sec 1970-71 and 1979), chief info offr Miny of Housing 1969-70, dir of info DOE 1971-74, dir gen COI 1974-78, PRO Vickers Ltd 1978, dir gen Nat Assoc of Pension Funds 1980-86; assoc dir Godwins Ltd 1987-, editorial conslt Tolleys Ltd 1987-, dir Pielle Ltd 1989-; memb: BOTB 1980-84, Cncl RSPCA 1980-83; FIPR (pres 1979), FCAM (vice pres 1984-), FRSA; *Recreations* literary and visual arts; *Style—* Henry James, Esq, CB; 53 Beaufort Rd, London W5 3EB (☎ 081 997 3021); Godwins Ltd, Briarcliff House, Kingsmead, Farnborough, Hampshire GU14 (☎ 0252 544 484, fax 0252 522 206, telex 858241)

JAMES, Dr (Richard) Hugh; s of Rev Peter Heppell James, of 57 Tynedale Rd, Loughborough, Leicester, and (Patience) Eve, *née* Carrick (d 1982); *b* 21 Dec 1945; *Educ* St Lawrence Coll Ramsgate, King's Coll Hosp Univ of London (MB BS, DA, DRCOG), Liverpool Sch of Tropical Medicine (DTMH); *m* 15 April 1967, Vivien Mary, da of Frank Reginald Hills, JP, of 5 Farm Close, Littlethorpe, Leicester; 2 s (Alasdair b 1970, Joel b 1979), 1 da (Liesl b 1972); *Career* worked with Ruanda mission CMS 1970-74 (later med dir Hôpital De Matana), sr house offr and registrar anaesthesia KCH (house offr 1968-69); sr registrar anaesthesia: KCH, Bromley Hosp, Sydenham Childrens' Hosp, Brook and Queen Victoria E Grinstead Hosps, conslt anaesthetist and hon clinical teacher Univ Med Sch Leicester and Leicester Royal Infirmary 1980; memb: Trent Regnl Conslts and Specialists Ctee, Leicester Diocesan Synod, Leicester S Deanery Synod; govr Brocks Hill Sch; FFARCS 1977; *Books* author of chapter on Day Case Anaesthesia in Textbook of Anaesthesia (2 edn, jtly ed G Smith and A R Aitkenhead, 1990), What Happens When series (med advsr, 1985); *Recreations* travel, camping, DIY; *Style—* Dr Hugh James; 36 Ridge Way, Oadby, Leicester LE2 5TN (☎ 0533 714596); Dept of Anaesthesia, Leicester Royal Infirmary, Infirmary Sq, Leicester LE1 5WW (☎ 0533 541414)

JAMES, Dr Ian Meurig; s of Thomas John James, of Norton, Swansea, and Margery, *née* Bennett; *b* 15 Feb 1937; *Educ* Gowerton GS, UCH Med Sch London (MB BS), Gonville and Caius Coll Cambridge (PhD); *m* 1, 16 Nov 1968 (m dis 1986), Margery Lia; 2 da (Alice Margery b 25 Aug 1969, Emily Angela b 19 Jan 1971); m 2, 28 March 1987, Jane Elizabeth, da of Hugh Faulkner, of Bucks; 1 s (Jeremy Rhidian b 24 Aug 1990); *Career* MacKenzie MacKinnan-Streatfield res fell RCP and RCS held at Univ of Cambridge 1965-68; Royal Free Hosp: conslt physician 1972-, sr lectr RFH Med Sch 1972-, reader clinical pharmacology 1984-; dir Cambridge Symphony Orch, chm Br Performing Arts Medicine Tst, former chm Int Soc for Study of Tension in Performance; FRCP 1975, FRSA 1988; *Recreations* music and the arts; *Style—* Dr Ian James; 12 Dawes Lane, Sarratt, Rickmansworth, Herts WD3 6BB (☎ 0923 265066) Section of Clinical Pharmacology, Dept of Academic Med, Royal Free Hosp, Pond St, Hampstead, London NW3 2QG (☎ 071 794 0500)

JAMES, Prof Ioan Mackenzie; s of Reginald Douglas James (d 1966), of Norwood, Broad Oak, Heathfield, Sussex, and Jessie Agnes, *née* Surridge (d 1982); *b* 23 May 1928; *Educ* St Paul's, Queen's Coll Oxford; *m* 1 July 1961, Rosemary Gordon, da of William George Stewart (d 1953); *Career* Cwlth fund fell: Princeton, Berkeley, Inst for Advanced Study 1954-55; Tapp res fell Gonville and Caius Coll Cambridge 1956, reader in pure mathematics Oxford 1957-69, sr res fell St John's Coll Oxford 1959-69, Savilian prof of geometry Oxford 1970-; hon fell St John's Coll Oxford 1987, professorial fell New Coll Oxford 1987, pres London Mathematical Soc 1985-86 (treas 1969-79), govr St Paul's Sch and St Paul's Girls' Sch 1970; hon prof Univ of Wales 1989; FRS 1968; *Books* The Topology of Stiefel Manifolds (1976), General Topology and Homotopy Theory (1984), Topological and Uniform Spaces (1987), Fibrewise Topology (1988), Introduction to Uniform Spaces (1990); *Style—* Prof Ioan James, FRS; Mathematical Institute, 24-29 St Giles, Oxford OX1 3LB (☎ 0865 273 541)

JAMES, Prof James Roderick; s of James Henry James (d 1933), and Muriel May, *née* Trueman; *b* 20 June 1933; *Educ* Headlands GS Swindon, Univ of London (external student, BSc, PhD, DSc); *m* 5 March 1955, Pamela Joy, da of William Henry Frederick Stephens; 1 s (Julian Maxwell b 8 May 1962), 1 da (April Louise b 24 Feb 1956); *Career* Nat Serv RAF 1952-54; AERE Harwell 1950-52, radar devpt engr E K Cole Ltd 1954-58, applications engr Semiconductors Ltd 1958-61, demonstrator RMCS 1961-65, sr scientific offr AERE 1966; RMCS: sr lectr 1967, sr princ scientific offr and res prof 1976, dep chief scientific offr 1982, currently prof of electromagnetic systems engrg dip Electromagnetic Engrg Res Gp, dir Wolfson RF Engrg Centre, chm Sch of Electrical Engrg and Science 1989; chm: Inst of Electronic and Radio Engrs Papers Ctee 1973-76, IEE Professional Gp on Antennas and Propagation 1980-83, IEE Int Conf on Antennas and Propagation 1983, Electronics Div IEE 1988-89; memb IEE Electronics Divnl Bd, pres Inst of Electronic and Radio Engrs 1984-85 (rep on Ctees of Engrg Cncl); FIEE, FIMA, FEng 1987; *Style—* Prof J R James; Royal Military College of Science (Cranfield), Shrivenham, Swindon, Wilts SN6 8LA

JAMES, Hon Mrs (Jaquetta Mary Theresa); da of 11 Baron Digby, KG, DSO, MC, TD (d 1964); *b* 28 Oct 1928; *Educ* Sherborne Sch for Girls; *m* 1950, David Pelham Guthrie-James, MBE, DSC (d 1986), s of Wing-Cdr Sir Archibald James, KBE, MC (d 1979); 4 s, 2 da; *Career* memb: Mid-Sussex Hosp Mgmnt Ctee 1960-68, Dorset Area Health Authority 1974-81; chm Hamilton Lodge Sch for Deaf Children Brighton 1962-80; *Recreations* gardening; *Style—* The Hon Mrs James; Torosay Castle, Craignure, Isle of Mull, Argyll PA65 6AY (☎ 068 02 421)

JAMES, Jeremy Edward; s of Herbert Edward James, of Beckenham, Kent, and Edith Marjorie, *née* Day; *b* 6 June 1941; *Educ* Dulwich; *m* 1 (m dis 1978), Suzanne; 1 s (Richard David b 1964), 1 da (Tanya b 1968); m 2, 7 June 1980, Jacqueline, da of Thomas Walter Latter (d 1975); 1 da (Alison b 1982); *Career* controller Air Hldgs 1964-69; dir: Williams Hudson 1970-79, Sungate Resources 1980-83, Inoco plc 1986-, Gulf Resources & Chem Corpn 1989-; FCA; *Recreations* golf, sailing; *Clubs* Langley Park Golf; *Style—* Jeremy James, Esq; Gaiters, Bishops Walk, Croydon, Surrey CR0 5BA (☎ 081 654 4213); Inoco plc, 21 Hertford St, London W1Y 7DA (☎ 071 491 2686, fax 071 930 9613, telex 295899, car 0836 280176)

JAMES, John Anthony; s of Charles Thomas James (d 1979), of Sutton Coldfield, and Gwenith Aylwin, *née* Jones; *b* 15 July 1945; *Educ* King Edward VI GS Lichfield, Univ of Bristol (LLB); *m* 10 Sept 1973, Gwyneth Jane, da of Ambrose Elwyn Evans (d 1975), of Altrincham; 2 da (Harriet Lucy b 24 Sept 1975, Emily Jane b 22 Nov 1977); *Career* slr: admitted to Supreme Ct of Judicature 1969, ptnr Edge & Ellison 1974-; sr jt hon sec Cncl Birmingham Law Soc 1987-91, sec W Midlands Assoc of Law Soc

1991-; memb Editorial Advsy Bd of the Law Soc's Gazette, chm Environment and Infrastructure Ctee Birmingham City 2000, memb Ctee Midlands Branch IOD, former memb Exec Ctee Nat Confedn of Parent-Teacher Assoc; FInstD 1985-; memb: Law Soc 1970, Birmingham Law Soc 1970 (memb Cncl 1986-); *Recreations* reading, writing, theatre, opera; *Clubs* Midlands Sporting, Belfry Sporting, Avenue Bowling, Warwickshire Co Cricket; *Style—* John James, Esq; Edge & Ellison, Rutland House, 148 Edmund St, Birmingham B3 2JR (☎ 021 200 2001, fax 021 200 1991, telex 336370, car 0836 505748)

JAMES, John Arthur William; s of Dr Peter Michael James (d 1971), and Eileen Mary, *née* Walters; *b* 7 Jan 1942; *Educ* Douai Sch Berks; *m* 5 Aug 1967, Barbara, da of Maj William Nicholls (d 1955); 1 s (John-Leo b 1982), 2 da (Jessica b 1968, Alice b 1970); *Career* admitted slr 1967, sr ptnr Hand Morgan & Owen Stafford 1988; under sheriff Staffs and W Midlands 1983, dep coroner S Staffs 1987, clerk to Cmmrs of Taxes Stafford and Cannock 1987, adjudicator on immigration 1986; memb Bd Stafford Prison 1975- (chm 1983-86); *Recreations* walking, shooting; *Clubs* Stafford County; *Style—* John James, Esq; Presford House, Butterbank, nr Seighford, Stafford, Staffs (☎ 0785 282530); 17 Martin St, Stafford, Staffs (☎ 0785 211411, fax 0785 48573)

JAMES, John Christopher Urmston; s of John Urmston James (d 1964), of Llandeilo, Dyfed, and Ellen Irene, *née* Walker; *b* 22 June 1937; *Educ* Hereford Cathedral Sch; *m* 1, (m dis 1982), Gillian Mary, *née* Davies; m 2, 20 Nov 1982, Patricia Mary, da of Arthur Leslie Walter White (d 1984), of Peckham, London; 2 s (David Henry Urmston b 3 Feb 1960, Christopher Hammond Urmston b 1 Jan 1961); *Career* trainee buyer Harrods 1954; rep: Jaeger 1961, Pringle 1972; sec LTA 1981- (asst sec 1973-81); memb: Nat Tst, Friends of the Earth, Trinity Hospice, Ealing Nat Tst; churchwarden St Paul's Ealing; *Recreations* tennis, rugby union, walking, architecture, topography, the countryside; *Clubs* Queen's, Questors, London Welsh, West Hants; *Style—* John James, Esq; c/o Lawn Tennis Association, The Queen's Club, West Kensington, London W14 9EG (☎ 071 385 2366, fax 071 381 5965, telex 895 6036)

JAMES, John Denis; s of Kenneth Alfred James, of Alvechurch, Worcestershire, and Pauline Audry, *née* Haymen; *b* 30 Aug 1950; *Educ* Bridley Moor GS Redditch; *m* 3 Sept 1975, Barbara Elizabeth, da of John Thorpe, of Birmingham; 1 s (Christopher John b 1975), 1 da (Emma Louise b 1978); *Career* trainee photographer Redditch Indicator 1965, sr photographer Birmingham Post and Mail 1972, Midland Photographer of the Year 1981 and 1987, Midland News Photographer of the Year 1987, Nat Br Press Award Photographer of 1987, Kodak News Photographer of 1987; memb Inst of Journalists; *Recreations* off road buggy racing; *Style—* John James, Esq; 2 Boultons Lane, Crabbs Cross, Redditch, Worcs B97 5NY (☎ 0527 44797); Birmingham Post and Mail, Colmore Circus, Birmingham (☎ 021 236 3366)

JAMES, John Henry; step s of George Arthur James (d 1975), and Doris May, *née* Peachey (d 1973); *b* 19 July 1944; *Educ* Ludlow GS, Keble Coll Oxford (exhibitioner, BA, Dip in Econ & Political Sci, graduate scholar); *m* 1, 1966 (m dis 1976), Bonita Mary, *née* Woolsey; m 2, 1976 (m dis 1986), Hedwig, *née* Walter; m 3, 25 April 1987, Anita Mary Stockton, da of Leonard Bryan Scarth QPM; *Career* Civil Serv: joined 1966, asst princ Ministry Pensions and Nat Insurance then Ministry Social Security DHSS 1968, private sec to First Permanent Sec 1969-71, princ 1971-78, seconded HM Treasury 1974-76, asst sec 1978-86, under sec 1986-91, dir Health Authy Fin 1986-90, memb NHS Mgmnt Bd 1986-89, non-exec dir Laing Homes 1987-89; district gen mangr: Harrow Health Authy 1990-, Parkside Health Authy 1991-; memb Kings Fund Inst Advsy Cncl 1990-; licentiate Inst Health Services Mgmnt 1989; *Books* contrib author Oxford Textbook of Public Health (1985); *Recreations* playing chess and cricket, food, wine, travel; *Style—* John James, Esq; Harrow District Health Authority Northwick Park Hospital, Watford Rd, Harrow Middx HA1 3UJ; Parkside District Health Authority, Bays 6 & 7, South Wharf Rd, London W2 1PF (☎ 081 869 2686, fax 081 423 0046, car 0836 569424, telex 923410)

JAMES, Jonathan Elwyn Rayner; (QC 1988); s of Basil James, of Brockham, Surrey, and Moira Houlding, *née* Rayner; *b* 26 July 1950; *Educ* King's Coll Sch Wimbledon, Christ's Coll Cambridge (MA, LLM), Univ of Brussels Licencié Spécial en Droit Européen; *m* 3 Jan 1981, Anne, da of Henry McRae (d 1984); 1 s (Daniel Charles Rayner b 23 Dec 1981); *Career* called to the Bar Lincoln's Inn 1971; *Books* EEC Anti Trust Law (jt ed, 1975), Copinger and Skone James on Copyright (jt ed 1980, 1991); *Recreations* DIY, squash, opera, travel; *Style—* Jonathan James, Esq, QC; 5 New Square, Lincoln's Inn, London WC2A 3RJ (☎ 071 404 0404)

JAMES, (David) Keith Marlais; s of James Lewis James, of 9 The Mount, Dinas Powis, S Glamorgan, and Margaret Evelyn James; *b* 16 Aug 1944; *Educ* Cardiff HS, W Monmouth Sch, Queens' Coll Cambridge (BA, MA); *m* 4 Aug 1973, Kathleen Linda, da of Wilfred Lawson Marrs, OBE (d 1981), of Cyncoed, Cardiff; 1 s (Thomas b 1983), 2 da (Alys b 1978, Elizabeth b 1980); *Career* slr; ptnr Phillilps and Buck 1969-; dir: various cos in Hamard Gp 1977-86, Bank of Wales plc 1988-; chm: Welsh Exec of UN Assoc 1977-80, Welsh Centre for Int Affrs 1979-84; memb: UK Mgmnt Ctee Freedom from Hunger Campaign 1978-87, Welsh Mgmnt Ctee IOD 1985-, Ct UWIST 1985-88, Cncl UWIST 1985-88, Advsy Panel Cardiff Business Sch 1986-, Cncl Univ of Wales Coll of Cardiff 1988; vice pres Cardiff Business Club 1987-, dep chm Inst of Welsh Affrs 1987-; memb: Law Soc, IOD; *Recreations* golf, skiing; *Clubs* Cardiff and County, Royal Porthcawl Golf; *Style—* Keith James, Esq; Trehedyn Cottage, Peterston-Super-Ely, S Glamorgan; Phillips and Buck, Fitzalan House, Fitzalan Court, Cardiff (☎ 0222 471147, fax 0222 463447, telex 497625 FILBUK G DX 33016)

JAMES, Keith Royston; s of William Ewart Gladstone James (d 1990), of Birmingham, and Lilian Elizabeth James (d 1966); *b* 22 Aug 1930; *Educ* King Edward VI Camp Hill Sch Birmingham, Univ of Birmingham; *m* 6 May 1961, Venice Imogen, da of Maj Henry St John Murray Findlay (d 1954); 1 s (William b 1964), 3 da (Rohaise b 1966, Selina b 1968, April b 1971); *Career* admitted slr 1954, sr ptnr Needham & James; dir: Technology and Law 1980, A E Westwood Ltd 1969, Turley Sheet Metal Products 1969; author articles on the application of technology to the law; chm Soc for Computers and Law 1988-90; *Books* A Guide to the Electronic Office for Practising Solicitors; *Recreations* shooting, walking, tennis; *Clubs* Athenaeum, Birmingham; *Style—* Keith R James, Esq; Norton Curlieu, nr Warwick CV35 8JR (☎ 092 684 2372); Needham & James, Windsor House, Temple Row, Birmingham B2 5LF (☎ 021 200 1188, fax 021 236 9228, telex 338460 NEEJAM G, car 0860 513882)

JAMES, Kevan David; s of David Henry James (d 1987), of Enfield, N London, and Helen Shepherd, *née* Adams; *b* 18 March 1961; *Educ* Edmonton Co Secdy Sch N London; *m* 1987, Deborah Elaine, da of William Reginald Mays; *Career* Middlesex CCC: debut 1980, 9 first class appearances, 18 one day appearances; Hampshire CCC: debut 1985, 72 first class appearances, 90 one day appearances; Wellington Province NZ: 12 first class appearances, 8 one day appearances; Eng Young Cricketers tour W Indies 1980-81 (Aust 1979-80); ptnr KK Wines 1980-; *Style—* Kevan James, Esq; Hampshire CCC, County Cricket Ground, Southampton SO9 2TY (☎ 0703 333788, fax 0703 330121)

JAMES, Mark Hugh; s of Roland Malcolm Dennis James, of Stamford, Lincolnshire, and Doreen Vivien Eugenia Bayard, *née* Wace; *b* 28 Oct 1953; *Educ* Stamford Sch; *m* 18 Oct 1980, Jane Anne; *Career* professional golfer; winner English Amateur Championships 1974, runner up Br Amateur Championships 1975; turned professional 1976, winner 14 maj Euro tournaments and various others worldwide; int appearances: Ryder Cup 1977, 1979, 1981 and 1989 (winners), Hennessy Cup 1978, 1980, 1982 and 1984, Dunhill Cup 1988, 1989 and 1990, World Cup 1978, 1980, 1982, 1984, 1987, 1988 and 1990; Rookie of the Year 1976; *Recreations* American football, gardening, science; *Style—* Mark James, Esq; c/o PGA European Tour, Wentworth Club, Virginia Water, Surrey (☎ 0344 842881)

JAMES, Martin Jonathan; s of Kenneth Charles James, of Christchurch, NZ, and Beatrice Rose, *née* Dickson; *b* 22 Sept 1961; *Educ* NZ Sch of Dance; *m* 8 Feb 1985, Adrienne Jane Terehunga, da of Flt Lt James Matheson, DFC, of Christchurch, NZ; *Career* Royal NZ Ballet 1981, awarded Queen Elizabeth II Arts Cncl Grant for study in America 1982, promoted princ dancer, first one man graphic arts exhibition Molesworth Gallery NZ 1984, gained int recognition fourth World Ballet competition Japan 1984, English Nat Ballet 1985- (princ dancer 1987-); roles incl: Albrecht and Hilarion in Giselle, Franz in Coppelia, Prince in The Nutcracker (with Lynn Seymour), Toreador in Petit's Carmen, Romeo and Paris in Ashton's Romeo and Juliet, Blackamoor in Petrushka, world premiere Christopher Bruce's Symphony in 3 movements, Three Preludes (choreographer Ben Stevenson); Paris summer season 1987 incl: Kevin Haigen's Meditation (with Natalia Makarova created role), Spectre de la Rose, Le Corsaire, Makarova's Swan Lake, title role in Cranko's Onegin (and with Ekaterina Maximova), Oedipus in Sphinx (Glen Tetley), title role Apollo (Balanchine), Symphony in C (Balanchine), Napoli (Bournonville), Land (Christopher Bruce), Bull in Cruel Garden (Christopher Bruce and Lyndsey Kemp); guest appearances: London, Hong Kong, Paris, Le Creusot, Genée Awards dancing Le Corsaire 1988 and dancing Flower Festival of Genzano 1989; film and TV performances incl: Gillian Lynne's Look of Love (princ role as Eros) 1989, Natalia Makarova's Swan Lake; memb Educn Dept London Festival Ballet, yearly engagements Ilkley Seminar Summer Sch; ARAD 1979, Solo Seal 1980; *Recreations* tennis, painting, rugby, swimming, therapeutic massage; *Clubs* Elmwood Tennis; *Style—* Martin James, Esq; New Zealand (☎ 010 64 581 1245); English Nat Ballet, 39 Jay Mews, London SW7 2ES

JAMES, Michael; s of Aubrey Charles James (d 1986), of Chilcompton, Somerset, and Ada Emily, *née* Milsom (d 1938); *b* 19 Feb 1925; *Educ* Wells Cathedral Sch, RWA Sch of Architecture; *m* 4 April 1953, Margaret Rose (d 1984), da of George Brazier; 1 adopted da (Sarah Nicola b 12 May 1959); *Career* WW11 1943-1946, Lt 18 Cavalry Indian Army 1945-46, Capt SSO Razmak NW Frontier 1946; architect and town planner in private practices 1952-, chm Elsworth Sykes Ptnrs Ltd 1985-90; magistrate Highgate Ct 1967-84; FRIBA 1950, MRTPI 1954, ACIArb 1980; *Recreations* golf, painting; *Clubs* Reform; *Style—* Michael James, Esq; The Coach House, 49a Maresfield Gardens, London NW3 5TE (☎ 071 435 5501); Elsworth Sykes Partnership, 27 Queen Anne St, London W1M 9FB (☎ 071 580 5886)

JAMES, Michael Leonard; s of late Leonard James, of Portreath, Cornwall; *b* 7 Feb 1941; *Educ* Latymer Upper Sch, Christ's Coll Cambridge (MA); *m* 1975, Jill Elizabeth, da of George Tarján, OBE, of Budapest; 2 da (Ruth b 1978, Susanna b 1980); *Career* entered Br Govt Serv (GCHQ) 1963, private sec to Rt Hon Jennie Lee MP Min for the Arts 1966-68, DES 1968-71, planning unit of Rt Hon Margaret Thatcher MP Sec of State for Educn & Sci 1971-73, asst sec 1973, DCSO 1974, advsr to OECD Paris and UK govr Int Inst for Mgmnt of Technol (IIMT) Milan 1973-75, int negotiations on non-proliferation of nuclear weapons 1975-78, dir Int Atomic Energy Agency Vienna 1978-83, advsr on int rels Cmmn of the Euro Communities Brussels 1983-85, chm The Hartland Press Ltd 1985-; govr: E Devon Coll of Further Educn Tiverton 1985-, Colyton GS 1985-90, Sidmouth Community Coll 1988-; chm: Bd of Govrs Axe Vale Further Educn Unit Seaton 1987- (memb 1985-), Civil Serv Selection Bds 1983-90; memb: Exeter Social Security Appeal Tbnl 1986-, Exeter and Taunton VAT Appeal Tbnl 1987-; hon fell Univ of Exeter; FRSA; *Books* Internationalization to Prevent the Spread of Nuclear Weapons (1980), articles on int relations and nuclear energy, five novels under a pseudonym (SW Arts Literary award 1984); *Clubs* Athenaeum, United Oxford and Cambridge University, Int PEN, Devon and Exeter Institution; *Style—* Michael James, Esq; Cotte Barton, Branscombe, Devon EX12 3BH

JAMES, Dame Naomi Christine; DBE (1979); da of Charles Robert Power, of Rotorua, New Zealand; *b* 2 March 1949; *Educ* Rotorua Girls' HS NZ; *m* 1, 1976, Robert A James (d 1983), of Andover, Hants, s of J S James; 1 da (Lois Anne b 1983); m 2, 4 Sept 1990, Eric G Haythorne, o s of G V Haythorne, of Ottawa, Canada; *Career* former language teacher and hairdresser; yachtswoman: winner Binatone Round Br and Ireland Race in trimaran Colt Cars GB 1982, NZ Yachtsman of the Year 1978, recipient RYS Chichester Trophy 1978, winner Ladies' prize Observer Transatlantic Race 1980 (women's record for solo crossing), circumnavigated world as first woman solo via Cape Horn Sept 1977-June 1978; tstee Nat Maritime Museum, memb Cncl Winston Churchill Memorial Tst; writer and presenter BBC Documentary Polynesian Triangle (Great Journeys Series) 1989; *Books* Women Alone (1978), At One With the Sea (1979), At Sea on Land (1981), Courage at Sea (1987); *Recreations* tennis, golf, skiing; *Clubs* Royal Lymington Yacht, Royal Dart Yacht, Royal Western Yacht; *Style—* Dame Naomi James, DBE

JAMES, Noel David Glaves; OBE (1964), MC (1945), TD (1946); s of Rev David Taliesin Robert James (d 1935), and Gertrude Ethel Ellen, *née* Glaves (d 1963); *b* 16 Sept 1911; *Educ* Haileybury, RAC Cirencester; *m* 29 Dec 1949, (Laura) Cecilia (d 1970), da of Sir Richard Winn Livingstone (d 1960); 3 s (Timothy b 1952, Alastair b 1954 d 1960, Jeremy b 1961); *Career* cmmnd 2 Lt RA TA 1933; WWII 1939-46 served: France (Dunkirk), Belgium, Persia, Iraq, Palestine, Syria, Italy (despatches); land agent 1933-39, bursar CCC Oxford 1946-51, land agent Univ of Oxford and estates bursar BNC Oxford 1951-61, agent for Lord Clinton and The Clinton Devon Estates 1961-76; fell: Corpus Christi Coll, Brasenose Coll; pres: Chartered Land Agents Soc 1957-58, Royal Forestry Soc 1962-64; FRICS 1950; *Books* Working Plans for Estate Woodlands (1948), Notes on Estate Forestry (1949), An Experiment in Forestry (1951), The Trees of Bicton (1969), The Arboriculturalists Companion (2 edn, 1990), A Book of Trees Anthology (1973), Before the Echoes Die Away (1980), A History of English Forestry (1981), A Forestry Centenary (1982), Gunners at Larkhill (1983), Plain Soldiering (1987), The Foresters Companion (4 edn, 1989); *Recreations* forestry, shooting, country life; *Clubs* Army and Navy; *Style—* N D G James, Esq, OBE, MC, TD; Blakemore House, Kersbrook, Budleigh Salterton, Devon EX9 7AB (☎ 03954 3886)

JAMES, Prof the Hon Oliver Francis Wintour; o s of Baron James of Rusholme (Life Peer), *qv*, and Cordelia Mary, *née* Wintour; *b* 23 Sept 1943; *Educ* Winchester, Balliol Coll Oxford (MA, BM BCh); *m* 4 Sept 1965, Rosanna, er da of Maj Gordon Bentley Foster (d 1963), of Sleightholme Dale, Fadmoor, York; 1 s (Patrick Esmond b 4 May 1967), 1 da (Helen b 26 Jan 1970); *Career* landowner (170 acres); prof of geriatric med Univ of Newcastle upon Tyne 1985-; memb Cncl: RCP, Br Geriatric Soc; sec Br Assoc for Study of the Liver; tstee Sir James Knott Tst; FRCP 1981; *Books* Ageing Liver and Gastrointestinal Tract (ed 1987); *Recreations* golf, gardening; *Style—* Prof the Hon Oliver James; Sleightholmedale Lodge, Kirbymoorside, York YO6 6JG; Medical Unit 1, Freeman Hospital, Newcastle upon Tyne NE7 7DN (☎ 091 2843111, extension 3244)

JAMES, (William) Paul; s of Sir Frederick Seton James, KCMG, KBE (d 1934), and

Lady Doris Francis James (d 1956); *b* 22 Aug 1921; *Educ* Haileybury, PCL (Dip Arch); *m* 4 Jan 1947, (Florence) Peggy, da of Josephy Harvey; 1 s (Julian Paul b 1958), 3 da (Jennifer b 1948, Fenella b 1952, Caroline b 1954); *Career* WWII RAF 1940-45; architect on staff of Lord Holford 1950-60, princ in private practice 1960-67, seconded planning conslt DHSS 1967-68, fndr ptnr and chm Hosp Design Partnership (London, Leeds and Birmingham) 1968-79, int conslt in hosp planning 1979-; author of numerous articles in professional jls 1970-85; chm Royal Turnbridge Wells Civic Soc; FRIBA 1970 (ARIBA 1950); *Books* Hospitals - Designs and Development (1986); *Recreations* lawn tennis, walking, reading, travel, writing; *Clubs* Sloane; *Style—* Paul James, Esq; Lawnside, 3 Hungershall Park, Tunbridge Wells, Kent (☎ 0892 25726)

JAMES, Dr Peter Charles; *b* 15 Jan 1943; *Educ* Magdalen Coll Oxford (MA), UCL (PhD), Univ of London (BSc); *m* 12 June 1971, Vivien Elizabeth, *née* Ball; 1 s (Christian Stuart b 1974), 2 da (Charlotte Magdalen b 1976, Catherine Eleanor b 1982); *Career* OECD Paris 1968-73, N Carolina Nat Bank 1973-, md Carolina Bank Ltd 1978-87, gp chief exec Panmure Gordon Bankers Ltd 1987-; *Recreations* music, reading, sports; *Clubs* Hurlingham; *Style—* Dr Peter James; 15 Hobury St, London SW10; Robins, Upper Wardley, Milland, Liphook, Hants; Panmure Gordon Bankers Ltd, 14 Moorfields, Highwalk, London EC2

JAMES, Dr Peter David; s of Thomas Geraint Illtyd James, 1 Freeland Road, Ealing Common, London W5 3HR, and Dorothy Marguerite, *née* John; *b* 20 Aug 1943; *Educ* Mill Hill, Middlesex Hosp Med Sch, Univ of London (MB BS); *m* 14 Sept 1968, Angela Judith, da of William Robert Hearn, of Stonegarth, Hovingham, North Yorks; *Career* lectr in pathology: Makerere Univ Kampala Uganda 1970-72, Bland-Sutton Inst Middx Hosp London 1972-73 (asst lectr 1967-70); conslt and hon sr lectr in histopathology Univ Hosp Nottingham 1973-; memb: BMA, Br Soc of Gastroenterology, Br Div Int Acad of Pathology; *Recreations* squash, shooting, horse riding; *Style—* Dr Peter James; Histopathology Dept, University Hospital, Nottingham NG7 2UH (☎ 0602 709175)

JAMES, Peter John; s of John Burnett James, and Cornelia, *née* Kates; *b* 22 Aug 1948; *Educ* Charterhouse, Ravensbourne Coll of Art and Design; *m* 21 April 1979, Georgina Valerie James, da of T D Wilkin, of Hove, Sussex; *Career* dir: Quadrant Films Toronto 1972-75, Yellowbill Ltd 1977, Cornelia James Ltd; currently md: Cornelia James Contracts Ltd, Cornelia James Neckwear Ltd; film prodr: Dead of Night 1973, Spanish Fly 1976, Biggles 1985 (assoc prodr); Royal Warrant Holder Queen's Warrant for Glove Mfrs; memb Soc of Authors, Soc for Psychical Res, Crime Writers' Assoc; Freeman City of London 1980, Worshipful Co of Glovers; author; *Books* Dead Letter Drop (1981), Atom Bomb Angel (1982), Billionaire (1983), Possession (1988), Dreamer (1989), Sweet Heart (1990), Twilight (1991); *Recreations* golf, tennis, skiing, classic sports cars, wine, food; *Clubs* Tramp, The Academy; *Style—* Peter James, Esq; Cornelia James Ltd, 123 Havelock Rd, Brighton BN1 6GS (☎ 0273 508 866, fax 0273 541 656, telex 877057)

JAMES, Prof Peter Maunde Coram; VRD (1964); s of Capt Vincent Coram James (d 1972), of London, and Mildred Ivy, *née* Gooch (d 1982); *b* 2 April 1922; *Educ* Westminster, Univ of London (LDS, RCS, MDS), Univ of St Andrew's (DPD); *m* 27 Nov 1945, Denise Mary, da of John Waring Bond (d 1948), of Gravesend; 4 s (Nicholas, John, Martin, Richard); *Career* Surgn Lt RNVR 1945-48, demobbed 1948, continued in RNVR (later RNR) until ret as Surgn Lt Cdr 1963; registrar res asst and hon lectr Inst of Dental Surgery Univ of London 1949-55; Royal Dental Hosp: sr lectr Dept of Children's Dentistry 1955, asst dean 1958-66, hon conslt dental surgn 1961, dir Dept of Childrens' Dentistry 1962; reader in preventive dentistry Univ of London 1965; Univ of Birmingham: John Humphreys prof of dental health and head of Dept of Dental Health 1966-87, dir Dental sch 1978-82, postgrad advsr in dentistry 1983-86; emeritus prof 1987-; conslt advsr in community dentistry DHSS 1977-82, W Mids regnl advsr Faculty of Dental Surgery RCS 1976-82, chm Specialist Advsy Ctee in Community Dental Health and memb Jt Ctee for Higher Trg in Dentistry RCS 1981-86; ed Community Dental Health; pres Br Dental Assoc Central Counties Branch 1981-82; memb: Birmingham AHA 1979-82, Birmingham Central DHA 1982-85; fndr pres and hon life memb Br Soc for the Study of Community Dentistry, hon life memb BDA, former pres and hon life memb Br Paedodontic Soc; *Recreations* walking, reading, music, messing about in boats; *Clubs* RSM; *Style—* Prof Peter James, VRD; The Pump House, Bishopton Spa, Stratford-upon-Avon, Warwickshire CV37 9QY (☎ 0789 204 330)

JAMES, Prof Philip Seaforth; s of Dr Philip William James, MC (d 1934), of Croydon, Surrey, and Muriel Lindley, *née* Rankin (d 1971); *b* 28 May 1914; *Educ* Charterhouse, Trinity Coll Oxford (MA), Yale Law Sch; *m* 4 Jan 1954, Wybetty, da of Claus Pieter Gerth (d 1968), of Enschede, Holland; 2 s (Nicholas b 1955, Edward b 1958); *Career* WWII RA 1940-45, serv Burma, Maj (despatches); called to the Bar Inner Temple 1939, fell and tutor Exeter Coll Oxford 1946-49, in bar practice 1949-52, prof of law and head of dept Univ of Leeds 1952-75, prof and chm of Law Faculty Univ of Buckingham 1975-81 (emeritus prof 1988); visiting prof: Yale Univ and Univ of Louisville USA 1960-61, Univ of S Carolina 1972-73, NY Law Sch 1981-83; pres Soc of Public Teachers of Law 1971, chm Yorks Rent Assessment Ctee 1966-75, govr Swinton Con Coll 1970-81, assessor to Co Ct on Race Rels 1972-; Freeman of Madison Indiana 1961; hon memb Mark Twain Soc 1979; Hon LLD Univ of Buckingham 1987; *Books* Introduction to English Law (1950), General Principles of the Law of Torts (1958); *Recreations* gardening; *Clubs* Nat Lib; *Style—* Prof Philip James; Chestnut View, Whitfield, nr Brackley, Northants NN13 5TQ (☎ 02805 246); Walk Mill Cottage, Duddon Bridge, Broughton-in-Furness, Cumbria LA20 6EU (☎ 06576 788)

JAMES, Prof (William) Philip Trehearne; s of Jenkin William James (d 1944), and Lilian Mary, *née* Shaw; *b* 27 June 1938; *Educ* Ackworth Sch Pontefract Yorks, UCL (BSc), UCH (MB, BSc, MD), Cambridge Univ (MA), London Univ (DSc); *m* 1961, Jean Hamilton, da of James Lingford Moorhouse (d 1977); 1 s (Mark), 1 da (Claire); *Career* asst dir MRC Dunn Nutrition Unit Cambridge 1974-82, dir Rowett Res Inst Aberdeen 1982-, hon res prof Univ of Aberdeen; memb: Applied Food and Nutrition Res Ctee MAFF, DHSS Ctee on Medical Aspects of Food Policy Irradiated and Novel Foods; formerly chm Working Pty on Nat Advsy Ctee of Nutrition Educn, vice chm FAO/WHO/UNU Expert Consultation on Energy and Protein Requirement of Man 1981-85; chm: FAO Expert Consultation on Nat Energy Needs 1987, UK Nat Food Alliance 1987-90, pres Coronary Prevention Group 1990- (chm 1988-); memb Nutrition Advsy Ctee WHO Euro Reg 1985-, chm consultation on Nutrition and Health WHO 1989-91, special advsr to WHO DG 1989-, advsr FAO on Sixth World Food Survey 1989-; meml lectures: Cuthbertson 1979, Ames 1985, Middleton 1986, Davidson 1987, Minshull 1989, Mehta Oration India 1985, Peter Beckett Dublin 1983; FRCP 1978, FRS(E) 1986,FIBiol 1987; *Books* on European Food Policy 1989, Manual for Calculating Energy Requirements (1989); papers on nutrient absorption, energy and protein metabolism, health policy and food labelling; *Recreations* talking, writing government reports, eating; *Clubs* Athenaeum (London); *Style—* Prof Philip James; Wardenhill, Bucksburn, Aberdeen, Scotland AB2 9SA (☎ 0224 712623); The Rowett Research Institute, Greenburn Rd, Bucksburn, Aberdeen, Scotland AB2 9SB (☎ 0224 712751, fax 0224 715349, telex 739988)

JAMES, Richard Austin; CB, MC (1945); s of Thomas Maurice James (d 1962), of Kent, and Hilda Joan, *née* Castle (d 1987); *b* 26 May 1920; *Educ* Clifton, Emmanuel Coll Cambridge; *m* 1948, Joan Betty, da of Albert Malcolm Boorer (d 1932); 2 s (Thomas, Andrew), 1 da (Sally); *Career* RE 1939-41, Queen's Own Royal West Kent Regt 1941-46 served in ME and Europe (despatches); Home Office 1948, private sec to Chllr of the Duchy of Lancaster (the late Lord Hill and the late Mr Iain Macleod) 1960 (asst sec 1961), receiver Met Police Dist 1977-80 (dep receiver 1970-73), dep under sec of state Home Office 1980 (asst under sec 1974-76); memb Cncl of Mgmnt of Distressed Gentlefolk Aid Assoc 1982-88 (gen sec 1981-82), memb Ctee of Mgmnt Sussex Housing Assoc for the Aged 1985-90; pres The Brunswick Boys' Club Tst 1990-; Freeman City of London; *Recreations* cricket, garden construction; *Clubs* Athenaeum, MCC; *Style—* Richard James, Esq, CB, MC; 5 Gadge Close, Thame, Oxfordshire OX9 2BD

JAMES, Richard Daniel; *Educ* King's Coll; 3 s, 1 da; *Career* health authority administrator; charge nurse: Harris Hosp Texas 1973-74, Central middlesex Hosp 1975-77; nursing offr: Harefield Hosp 1975-77, Hammersmith Hosp 1977-79; sr nursing offr Ham Green Hosp and Clevedon Hosp 1979-82, dir Nursing Services Hosp and Community Bristol and Weston Health Authy 1983-85, unit gen mangr (gen) Salisbury Health Authy 1989- (unit gen mangr (community) 1986-89); SRN 1972, RCNT 1975, NDN 1983; *Style—* Richard James, Esq; Providence Cottage, Gutch Common, Semley, Shaftesbury, Dorset SP7 9AZ

JAMES, Hon Roderick Morrice; o s of Baron Saint Brides, GCMG, CVO, MBE, PC (Life Peer; d 1989), and his 1 w, Elizabeth Margaret Roper, *née* Piesse (d 1966); *b* 1956; *Educ* Emmanuel Coll Cambridge; *m* 24 Oct 1981, Harriet Sophie, yst da of Lt Cdr John Benians, RN, of Westfield, Headley, Hants; 2 s (Caspian b 1985, Pasco b 1987); *Style—* The Hon Roderick James; Hopkiln Cottage, Gracious Street, Selborne, Hants

JAMES, Hon Sebastian Richard Edward Cuthbert; 3 and yst s of 5th Baron Northbourne; *b* 11 March 1966; *Educ* Eton, Magdalen College Oxford; *Career* assoc conslt Bain UK Ltd; *Recreations* skiing, sailing, travel; *Clubs* The Lily, Ronnie Scott's; *Style—* The Hon Sebastian James

JAMES, Lady Serena Mary Barbara; *née* Lumley; JP (Richmond); da of late 10 Earl of Scarbrough, KG, GBE, KCB, TD; *b* 1901; *m* 1923, as his 2 w (he m 1 Lady Evelyn Wellesley, da of 4 Duke of Wellington; 1 s), Hon Robert James, s of late 2 Baron Northbourne; 2 da (*see Baron Westbury*); *Career* DStJ; *Style—* The Lady Serena James, JP; St Nicholas, Richmond, Yorks

JAMES, Simon Robert; s of Alan William James, and Dorothy Denise James; *b* 1 April 1952; *Educ* LSE (BSc), Univ of London (MSc); *Career* res asst LSE 1974-76, sr lectr in economics Univ of Exeter 1988- (lectr 1976-88); Books include: Self Assessment for Income Tax (with N A Barr and Prof A R Prest, 1977), The Economics of Taxation (with Prof CW Nobes, 1978), A Dictionary of Economic Quotations (1981), Pears Guide to Money and Investment (1982), A Dictionary of Sexist Quotations (1984), A Dictionary of Legal Quotations (1987), The Comprehensibility of Taxation (1987), A Dictionary of Business Quotation (1990); *Recreations* cooking, rambling, quotations; *Style—* Simon James, Esq; Department of Economics, University of Exeter, Amory Building, Rennes Drive, Exeter EX4 4RJ (☎ 0392 263204, fax 0392 263108, telex 42894 EXUNIV G)

JAMES, Stephen Lawrence; s of Walter Amyas James (d 1978), of Clifton, Bristol, and Cecile Juliet, *née* Hillman (d 1970); *b* 19 Oct 1930; *Educ* Clifton, St Catharine's Coll Cambridge (BA); *m* 1955 (m dis 1986), Patricia Eleanor Favell, da of Reginald Cave (d 1968), of Bristol; 2 s (Oliver, Benedict), 2 da (Gabrielle, Miranda); *Career* admitted slr 1959; sr ptnr Simmons & Simmons 1980; dir: Horace Clarkson plc, Sofipac (London) Ltd; memb Worshipful Co of Glaziers 1964; memb Law Soc 1959; *Recreations* yachting (yacht 'Jacobite'), gardening; *Clubs* Royal Yacht Sqdn, Royal Thames Yacht, Royal Lymington Yacht, Royal Ocean Racing; *Style—* Stephen James, Esq; Widden, Shirley Holms, Lymington, Hants SO41 8NL (☎ 0590 682226); 20 Queen's Gate Gardens, London SW7 5LZ (☎ 071 581 4953); Simmons and Simmons, 14 Dominion Street, London EC2M 2RJ (☎ 071 628 2020, fax 071 588 4129, telex 888562 SIMMON G, car 0831 391420)

JAMES, Terence (Terry); s of Robert Joseph James (d 1986), of Long Stratton, Norfolk, and Nellie Wallis, *née* Beare; *b* 6 June 1935; *Educ* Paston Sch, Magdalene Coll Cambridge (MA); *m* 12 Aug 1958, Julie Estelle, da of Charles Anderson Robson (d 1953), of Shelford, Cambs; 1 s (Michael b 1962), 1 da (Linda b 1961); *Career* Nat Serv RAF 1953-55; dir Fisons plc 1976-80; chm: FBC Ltd 1980-86, Chlor-Chem 1982-90, Schering Holdings Ltd 1986-90 (non-exec dir 1990-); dep chm Anglia HEC 1989-, non-exec dir Berol-Nobel (UK) Ltd 1990-; memb CBI Regnl Cncl, tstee Cambridge Fndn 1989-; FID 1984; *Recreations* golf, contemplative indolence; *Clubs* John O'Gaunt Golf; *Style—* Terry James, Esq; 215 Wimpole Road, Barton, Cambridge CB3 YAE (☎ 0223 262 070, fax 0223 263 776)

JAMES, Thomas Garnet Henry (Harry); CBE (1984); s of Thomas Garnet James (d 1956), and Edith, *née* Griffiths (d 1958); *b* 8 May 1923; *Educ* Neath GS, Exeter Coll Oxford (BA, MA); *m* 15 Aug 1956, Diana Margaret, da of Harold Lancelot Vavasseur Durell (d 1929); 1 s (Stephen Garnet Vavasseur b 1958); *Career* WWII cmmnd RA served NW Europe 1942-4 5; keeper Egyptian & Assyrian antiquities Br Museum 1974-88 (dep keeper and asst keeper, joined 1951); Laycock student Worcester Coll Oxford 1954-60, Wilbour fell The Brooklyn Museum NY 1964, visiting prof Coll de France Paris 1983; hon chm Bd of Govrs Inst of Egyptian Art & Archaeology Memphis State Univ 1985- (visiting prof 1990); vice pres Egypt Exploration Soc 1990 (chm 1983-89), chm Advsy Ctee Freud Museum 1986-; FBA 1976; *Books* The Mastaba of Khentika (1953), Hieroglyphic Texts in the Br Museum (I 1961, IX 1970), The Hekanakhte Papers (1962), Corpus of Hieroglyphic Inscriptions in The Brooklyn Museum (I 1974), Pharaoh's People (1984), Ancient Egypt (1988); *Recreations* music, cooking; *Clubs* United Oxford and Cambridge; *Style—* T G H James, Esq, CBE; 14 Turner Close, London NW11 6TU (☎ 081 455 9221)

JAMES, Prof Vivian Hector Thomas; s of William Percy James (d 1970), of London, and Alice May James (d 1936); *b* 29 Dec 1924; *Educ* Latymer's Upper Sch, Univ of London (BSc, PhD, DSc); *m* 20 April 1958, Betty Irene, da of Frederick Pike (d 1941), of London; *Career* joined RAF 1942, served as cmmnd pilot in UK and M East, released Fl Lt 1946; sci staff Nat Inst for Med Res 1952-56, reader in chemical pathology St Mary's Hosp Med Sch 1962-67 (lectr 1956-62), prof of chemical endocrinology Univ of London 1967-73, prof and head of Dept of Chemical Pathology St Mary's Hosp Med Sch Univ of London 1973-, chm Div of Pathology St Mary's Hosp 1981; ed Clinical Endocrinology 1972-74; memb Herts AHA 1967-72, sec Clinical Endocrinology Ctee MRC 1976-82, chm Human Pituitary Collection MRC, pres Section of Endocrinology RSM 1976-78, gen sec Soc for Endocrinology 1979-83 (treas 1983-), dep sec gen Int Soc of Endocrinology 1986-, sec gen Euro Fedn of Endocrine Socs 1987-; Freedom of Haverfordwest; FRCPath, Hon MRCP, Fiorino D'Oro City of Florence 1977; *Books* Hormones in Blood (1983), The Adrenal Gland (1979); *Recreations* languages; *Clubs* RSM; *Style—* Prof Vivian James; Dept of Chemical Pathology, St Mary's Hospital Medical School, London W1 1PG (☎ 071 725 1353)

JAMES, Prof Walter; CBE (1977); s of George Herbert James, and Mary Kathleen, *née* Crutch; *b* 8 Dec 1924; *Educ* Royal GS Worcester, St Luke's Coll Exeter, Univ of

Nottingham (BA); *m* 21 Aug 1948, Joyce Dorothy, da of Frederick George Allan Woollaston (d 1975); 2 s (Alan b 1962, Andrew b 1965); *Career* lectr adult educn Univ of Nottingham 1948-69, prof educnl studies Open Univ 1969-84 (dean and dir 1969-77); UK rep Cncl of Europe working parties on: Devpt of Adult Educn 1973-81, Adult Educn for Community Devpt 1982-87, Adult Educn for Change 1988- (project dir 1982-87); chm: Nat Cncl for Voluntary Youth Servs 1970-76, Review of Trg p/t Youth and Community Workers 1975-77, Religious Advsy Bd, Scout Assoc 1977-82, In Serv Trg and Educn Panel for Youth and Community Work 1978-82, Cncl for Educn and Trg in Youth and Community Work 1982-85, Nat Advsy Cncl for the Youth Serv 1986-88; tstee: Trident Educnl Tst 1972-86, Young Volunteer Force Fndn 1972-77, Community Projects Fndn 1977-90, Community Devpt Fndn 1990-; pres Inst of Playleadership 1972-74, Fair Play for Children 1979-82; *Books* The Standard of Living (with F J Bayliss, 1964), Virginia Woolf Selections from her Essays (ed, 1966); contrib: Encyclopaedia of Education (1968), Teaching Techniques in Adult Education (1971), Mass Media and Adult Education (1971); The Development of Adult Education (with H Janne and P Dominice, 1980), The 14 Pilot Experiments Vols 1-3 (1984), Handbook on Co-operative Monitoring (1986), Role of Media in Adult Education and Community Development (1988); *Recreations* living; *Style—* Prof Walter James, CBE; 25 Kepplestone, Staveley Road, Eastbourne BN20 7JZ (☎ 0323 23376)

JAMES, William Stirling; s of Wing Cdr Sir Archibald William Henry James, KBE, MC (d 1980), and Eugenia, *née* Morris (d 1991); *b* 20 Nov 1941; *Educ* St George's Coll Rhodesia, Stonyhurst, Magdalene Coll Cambridge (MA); *Career* Morgan Grenfell & Co Ltd 1964-65, Touche Ross & Co London 1965-68 (NY 1968-69), Hill Samuel & Co Ltd 1969-(dir 1980-); farmer; external memb Lloyd's; ACA 1968, FCA 1978; *Recreations* shooting, bridge; *Clubs* Boodle's, Pratt's, Annabel's; *Style—* William James, Esq; 12 Godfrey St, London SW3 3TA (☎ 071 352 4097); Champions Farm, Pulborough, Sussex RH20 3EF; 100 Wood St, London EC2P 2AJ (☎ 071 628 8011)

JAMES DUFF OF HATTON, David Robin Millais; s of Capt Christopher Alexander James, RN (d 1969), and Cynthia Swire (d 1970); *b* 29 May 1945; *Educ* Trinity Coll Glenalmond, RAC Cirencester; *m* 1, 14 March 1970 (m dis 1982), Monica Jean, da of Thomas G Browne; 1 s (Rory b 1978), 3 da (Fiona b 1971, Tania b 1973, Nicola b 1980); m 2, 20 Feb 1988, Jayne Elizabeth, da of James Bryce, of Coupar Angus; *Career* chm BFSS in Scotland 1990- (former vice chm), coordinator for Operation Raleigh Grampian Region; memb Queen's Bodyguard for Scotland (The Royal Co of Archers); *Recreations* golf, cricket, tennis, field sports; *Clubs* Royal and Ancient, St Andrews, MCC; *Style—* David James Duff of Hatton; Hatton Castle, Turriff, Aberdeenshire (☎ 0888 62279); Estate Office, Hatton Estates, Turriff (☎ 0888 63624)

JAMES OF HOLLAND PARK, Phyllis Dorothy James (P D James); OBE (1983); da of late Sydney Victor James, and late Dorothy May Amelia, *née* Hone; *b* 3 Aug 1920; *Educ* Cambridge HS for Girls; *m* 8 Aug 1941, Connor Bantry White (decd), s of Harry Bantry White, MC; 2 da (Clare Bantry (Mrs Flook) b 1942, Jane Bantry (Mrs McLeod) b 1944); *Career* admin NHS 1949-68, princ Serving Police and Criminal Policy Dept Home Office 1968-79; novelist; chm: Soc of Authors 1984-86, Booker Prize Judges 1987; memb Bd Br Cncl 1988, chm Lit Advsy Panel and memb Arts Cncl 1988, govr BBC 1988; assoc fell Downing Coll Cambridge; fell: RSL, RSA; cr a Life Peer 1991; *Books* Cover her Face (1962), A Mind to Murder (1963), Unnatural Causes (1967), Shroud for a Nightingale (1971), The Maul and the Peartree (with T A Critchley, 1971), An Unsuitable Job for a Woman (1972), The Black Tower (1975), Death of an Expert Witness (1977), Innocent Blood (1980), The Skull Beneath the Skin (1982), A Taste for Death (1986), Devices and Desires (1989); *Recreations* reading, exploring churches, walking by the sea, television; *Clubs* The Detective; *Style—* Miss P D James, OBE; Elaine Greene Literary Agent, 31 Newington Green, London N16 9PU (☎ 071 249 2971)

JAMES OF RUSHOLME, Baron (Life Peer UK 1959), of Fallowfield, Co Palatine of Lancaster; Sir Eric John Francis James; s of Francis William James (d 1945), of Parkstone, Dorset, and Lilian, *née* Taylor (d 1961); *b* 13 April 1909; *Educ* Taunton's Sch Southampton, Queen's Coll Oxford (BA, BSc, MA, DPhil); *m* 11 April 1939, Cordelia Mary, da of Maj-Gen FitzGerald Wintour, CB, CBE; 1 s (Hon Oliver Francis Wintour b 23 Sept 1943); *Career* high master Manchester GS 1945-62, vice chllr Univ of York 1962-72; chm: Headmasters' Conf 1953-54, Communications Res Ctee in Building Indust 1963, Inquiry into Teacher Trg 1971, Personal Social Servs Cncl 1973-76, Royal Fine Art Cmmn 1973-79; Hon LLD McGill York (Toronto), Hon DLitt New Brunswick, DUniv York, Hon FRIBA 1979, Hon Fell Queen's Coll Oxford; kt 1956; *Books* Science and Education, An Essay on the Content of Education, Education and Leadership; *Style—* The Rt Hon the Lord James of Rusholme; Penhill Cottage, West Witton, Leyburn, N Yorks

JAMESON, Andrew David; s of Stanley Jameson, of Liverpool, and Diane Selina, *née* Cook; *b* 19 Feb 1965; *Educ* Chesterfield HS Crosby, Kelly Coll Tavistock, Arizona State Univ (BSc, BA); *Career* investmt banking Banque Indosuez London 1989; swimmer; Cwlth Games 1986 Gold medallist 100m Butterfly (Cwlth record holder), World Championshipss 1986 Bronze medallist 100m Butterfly, Euro Championshipss 1987 Gold medallist 100m Butterfly, World Univ Games 1987 (Capt Br team) Gold medallist 100m Freestyle and 100m Butterfly, Aust and American Open 1988 Champion 100m Butterfly, Olympic Games 1988 Bronze medallist 100m Butterfly; Br Swimmer of the Year 1985; swimming commentator: BBC 1989-91, Eurosport 1990-91; *Style—* Andrew Jameson, Esq; 26 Thames Village, Hartington Rd, Chiswick, London W4 3UE (☎ 081 994 9057); Banque Indosuez, 52-62 Bishopsgate, London EC2N 4AR (☎ 071 638 3600, fax 071 628 4724, telex 892967 INDOSU G)

JAMESON, Derek; s of Mrs E Barrett; *b* 29 Nov 1929; *Educ* elementary schs East London; *m* 1, 1948, Jacqueline Sinclair (decd); 1 s, 1 da; m 2, 1971 (m dis 1977), Pauline Tomlin; 2 s; m 3, 1988, Ellen Petrie; *Career* Reuters 1944-60; ed: London American 1960-61, Daily Express 1961-63, Sunday Mirror 1963-75; northern ed Daily Mirror 1975-76, managing ed Daily Mirror 1976-77; ed: Daily Express 1977-78, Daily Star 1978-80, News of the World 1981-83; TV and Radio commentator; *Style—* Derek Jameson, Esq; BBC Radio 2, Broadcasting House, London W1A 1AA (☎ 071 927 4652)

JAMESON, Julian Richard Musgrave; yr s of Thomas Ormsby Jameson (d 1965), and Joan Moira Maud (d 1953), da of Sir Richard John Musgrave, 5 Bt, JP, DL; *b* 6 June 1928; *Educ* St Colomba's; *m* Ann Dwyer; 1 s, 1 da; *Career* memb Stock Exchange 1962; former dir Goodbody James Capel (stockbrokers); *Style—* Julian Jameson, Esq; Garretstown, Dunshaughlin, Co Meath, Republic of Ireland

JAMESON, Air Cdre Patrick Geraint (Jamie); CB (1959), DSO (1943), DFC (1940, and bar 1941); s of Robert Delvin Jameson (d 1952), of Delvin Lodge, and Katherine Lenora Jameson, *née* Dick (d 1965); *b* 10 Nov 1912; *Educ* Hutt Central, Hutt Valley HS; *m* 1941, Hilda Nellie Haiselden, da of Bertie Fitzherbert Webster, of NZ; 1 s (John), 1 da (Suzanne); *Career* joined RAF 1936, No 8 FTS Montrose 1936, posted to No 46 Fighter Sqdn Norwegian Campaign 1940, cmd 266 Spitfire Sqdn (Battle of Britain), 12 Gp Wing Leader based at Wittering 1941-42, (Dieppe Operation) Wing Leader North Weald leading Norwegian Spitfire Wing 1942, HQ No 11 Gp 1943, planning fighter ops 1944, Cdr 122 Mustang Wing in Normandy Beach-head, Belgium, Holland, Germany, Denmark, Staff Coll 1946, Air Miny Fighter Operational Trg, 1949 OC Day Fighter Leaders Sch & Gp Capt Ops Central Fighter Estab, OC RAF Station Wunstorf Germany 1952, SASO HQ No 11 Gp 1954, Air Cdre 1956, apptd SASO of 2nd TAF RAF Germany, Task Force Cdr Operation Grapple (Christmas Island) 1959; ret 1960; mentioned in despatches 5 times; Norwegian War Cross with Swords, Cdr Order of Orange-Nassau, American Silver Star; *Recreations* fishing, shooting, golf; *Clubs* RAF, Hutt, Hutt Golf; *Style—* Air Cdre Jamie Jameson, CB, DSO, DFC; 70 Wai-iti Crescent, Lower Hutt, New Zealand (☎ 010 644 697693)

JAMESON, (Arthur) Roy; s of Arthur Jameson (d 1945), and Jessie, *née* Wright (d 1947); *b* 27 Dec 1930; *Educ* Hutton GS, Univ of London (LLB, LMRTPI); *m* 5 Aug 1961, Pauline, da of John Charles Crook (d 1966); 1 s (Andrew Roy b 1965), 2 da (Caroline Judith b 1963, Alison Claire b 1968); *Career* slr and NP; clerk Fulwood UDC 1968-74; hon sec Preston Incorporated Law Soc 1976-80 (pres 1986-87), pres Assoc of North Western Law Socs 1988-89, local rep Slrs' Benevolent Assoc, memb Cncl Notaries' Soc 1987-; clerk to: Bd of Mgmnt Royal Cross Sch for the Deaf Preston 1969-90, Withnell Parish Cncl 1974-77; govr Hutton GS, chm Gt Manchester and Lancashire Rent Assessment Ctee 1989-; *Recreations* fencing, amateur dramatics; *Style—* Roy Jameson, Esq; 11 Regent Drive, Fulwood, Preston, Lancashire PR2 3JA (☎ 0772 719312); 69 Friargate, Preston, Lancashire PR1 2LD (☎ 0772 555616)

JAMESON, Susan Catherine (Sue); da of Harold Donald Davis, and Elizabeth, *née* Foulds; *b* 3 July 1955; *Educ* Surbiton HS, Univ of Liverpool (BA); ; 1 s (Oliver Rupert Linton Mills b 26 Oct 1984); *Career* trainee then reporter and news reader Radio City Liverpool 1976-78; LBC Radio London: presenter LBC Reports 1978-80, arts corr 1980-89, Moscow corr 1989-; Moscow corr London Evening Standard 1989-; winner Radio Arts Journalist of the Year (BP Arts Journalism awards) 1989; *Books* Themes in Drama (contrib 1980, 1988); *Recreations* UK: yoga, dance, transforming houses, Moscow: tobogganing and killing cockroaches; *Style—* Ms Sue Jameson; LBC Radio, Crown House, 72 Hammersmith Rd, London W14 8YE (☎ 071 973 1152, fax 071 371 2300)

JAMIESON, Andrew Thomas; s of Alexander Jamieson (d 1960), and Catherine Elizabeth, *née* MacDonald (d 1977); *b* 16 Feb 1928; *Educ* George Heriot's Sch Edinburgh, Univ of Edinburgh (BSc); *m* 18 March 1953, Evelyn Hall, da of James Andrew Hiddleston (d 1983); 1 s (Alexander James Andrew b 1958), 1 da (Elizabeth Helen Hall b 1956); *Career* Nat Serv 1950-52; dir Panmure Gordon Ltd 1986- (ptnr 1964-86, fin dir 1986-); chm Hemel Hempstead Cons Assoc 1972-74; Freeman City of London, Liveryman Worshipful Co of Actuaries; FFA 1951, AIA, FSS 1956; *Books* Investment Management (with J G Day, 1974); *Recreations* hill walking, cattle rearing; *Clubs* Caledonian, Actuaries; *Style—* Andrew Jamieson, Esq; Rookwoods, Sible Hedingham, Essex; 14 Moorfields Highwalk, London EC2; Château de la Commorderie, St Siffret, 30700 France

JAMIESON, Crawford William; s of Crawford John Baird Jamieson (d 1979), and Elizabeth, *née* McAulay; *b* 28 Sept 1937; *Educ* Dulwich, Univ of London Guy's Hosp (MB BS, MS); *m* 18 Nov 1961, Gay Jane, da of Brig Albert Gillibrand, DSO, TD (d 1942); 1 s (Crawford Philip b 1966); *Career* res fell Tulane Univ New Orleans 1968, Hunterian prof RCS of England 1970, asst dir Surgical Unit St Mary's Hosp 1970-72, conslt surgn St Thomas' Hosp, hon conslt surgn Hammersmith Hosp, sr lectr Royal Postgrad Med Sch; chm: Br Jl of Surgery, Vascular Advsy Ctee Vascular Surgical Soc; memb: Surgical Res Soc, Vascular Surgical Soc; FRCS; *Books* Surgical Management of Vascular disease (1982), Current Operative Surgery: Vascular Surgery (1985), Vascular Surgery: Issues in Current Practice (1987), Limb Salvage & Amputation for Vascular disease (1988); *Recreations* fishing, shooting, gun dog training; *Clubs* Bishopstoke Flyfishers'; *Style—* Crawford Jamieson, Esq; Hydgegate, Long Sutton, Odiham, Hants RG25 1TA (☎ 0256 862320); 19 Gladstone St, London SE1 6EY (☎ 071 928 9834); The Consulting Rooms, York House, 199 Westminster Bridge Rd, London SE1 7UT (☎ 071 928 3013)

JAMIESON, Maj David Auldjo; VC (1944), CVO (1990); s of Sir Archibald Jamieson, KBE, MC; *b* 1 Oct 1920; *Educ* Eton; *m* 1, 1948, Nancy (d 1963), da of Robert Elwes, JP; 1 s, 2 da; m 2, 1969, Joanna, da of Edward Woodall; *Career* 2 Lt Royal Norfolk Regt 1939, Capt 1940; dir: Australian Agriculture Co 1949-78 (govr 1952-76), Australian Mutual Provident Soc (UK) 1963-89 (dep chm 1973-89), National Westminster Bank plc 1983-87; Lt HM Body Guard of Hon Corps of Gentlemen at Arms 1986-90 (memb 1968-90); High Sheriff Norfolk 1980; *Style—* Maj David Jamieson, VC, CVO; The Drove House, Thornham, Hunstanton, Norfolk (☎ 048 526 206)

JAMIESON, Wing Cdr Harold Clive (Jamie); OBE (1967, MBE 1966); s of Harold Jamieson (d 1968), of 33 Cornwall Ave, Welling, Kent, and Hannah Marie, *née* Mathias (d 1981); *b* 31 March 1930; *Educ* Godalming Co GS, Guildford Tech Coll, Univ of London (HNC), SW London Coll (HND); *m* 24 March 1951, Gwendoline May, da of Edward Hunt (d 1957), of 15 Teignmouth Rd, Welling, Kent; 1 s (Martin b 1957), 4 da (Nicola b 1954, Lynne b 1957, Edwina b 1960, Tracy b 1960); *Career* Electronic Offrs' Course RAF Henlow 1952, OC Electronic Trg RAF Halton 1952-57, Univ Grad Electronic Course 1957 (Flt Lt), Flying Course 1958, OC Ground Electronics RAF Wyton 1959-62, OC Special Signals Unit Berlin, Sqdn Ldr 1962-67, OC Special Signals HQSC RAF Medmenham, Wing Cdr EN HQ 90 Gp RAF Medmenham 1969-72; commendations 1963 and 1965; divnl mangr Perkin- Elmer (UK) Ltd 1972-76, prod dir Richard Garrett Engineering Ltd 1976-79 (md 1979-80), dir AFA Minerva (EMI) Ltd 1980-82, md Oceanics SPL Ltd 1982-, conslt Sovereign Services; treas CMS Farnham and Aldershot Deanery Assoc; CEng MRAES 1964, CEng MIERE 1965; *Recreations* antiques, church, travel; *Style—* Wing Cdr H C Jamieson, OBE; Jayview, Shortheath Rd, Farnham, Surrey GU9 8RZ (☎ 0252 723965, fax 0252 734366)

JAMIESON, James McAulay; s of Crawford John Baird Jamieson (d 1978), of Blackheath, London, and Elizabeth, *née* McAulay; *b* 5 June 1939; *Educ* St Dunstan's Coll; *m* 12 Dec 1964, (Frances) Vivian, da of Col Francis Alan Forman (d 1980), of Eltham; 2 s (Alan b 3 Feb 1970, William b 3 Oct 1972); *Career* Everett Morgan and Grundy 1958-64, qualified CA 1964; Price Waterhouse: Jamaica 1964-68, NY 1968-72, London 1972-; FCA 1964; *Recreations* golf; *Clubs* The Royal St George's Golf, Royal Blackheath Golf, Littlestone Golf; *Style—* James Jamieson, Esq; 23 Morden Rd, Blackheath, London SE3 OAD (☎ 081 852 0050); 16 Aynsley Court, Strand St, Sandwich, Kent (☎ 0304 615093); Price Waterhouse, Southwark Towers, 32 London Bridge St, London SE1 9SY (☎ 071 407 8989, fax 071 407 0545)

JAMIESON, Maj Lenox Harvey; s of Lt-Col Harvey Morro Harvey-Jamieson, OBE, TD, DL, WS, *qv*, and Maude Frances Wilmot Ridout; ggf: James Wilcocks Carrall created hon Mandarin and order of Double Dragon 1900 (1849-1902); ggf: Maj Gen Sir Robert Murdoch-Smith, KCMG (1835-1900) late RE excavated sites of antiquity in Med and Persia 1854-85, many artefacts now in Br Museum; gggf: John Hayter, painter in ordinary to Queen Victoria (1800-85); gguncle: Sir George Hayter (1792-1871), painter; *b* 23 Feb 1937; *Educ* The Edinburgh Acad, Univ of Edinburgh; *m* 8 May 1981, Audrey Mackay, da of David Mackay Paterson (d 1981), late of Woodcliff, Kilmacolm, Renfrewshire; *Career* cmmnd RE 1959-90, served in Far East, Middle East, UK, attached RN HMS Fearless 1965-67, sr personnel offr Scotland 1982-90 (ret), Recruiting and Lia Staff Scotland 1990-; memb Queen's Body Guard for Scotland

(Royal Co of Archers) 1971-; *Recreations* archery, gardening, model engineering, vintage motor cars; *Clubs* Army and Navy, 20 Ghost; *Style—* Maj Lenox Jamieson; c/o Army and Navy Club, Pall Mall, London

JAMIESON, Lady Mariegold Magdalene; *née* Fitzalan Howard; da of 3 Baron Howard of Glossop, MBE (d 1972), and Baroness Beaumont, OBE (d 1971); sis of 17 Duke of Norfolk, KG, CB, CBE, MC, DL; *b* 1919; *Educ* private; *m* 1957, Gerald James Auldjo Jamieson, s of Sir Archibald Auldjo Jamieson, KBE, MC; 2 s; *Style—* The Lady Mariegold Jamieson; 17 Elvaston Place, London SW7; Yarrow House, Elmham, Dereham, Norfolk

JANAS, Ludovic Joseph; s of Wojciech Janas (d 1938), and Apolonia, *née* Tengowska (d 1945); *b* 31 Aug 1926; *Educ* Univ Coll Cork (BA), Birkbeck Coll London; *Career* computer conslt; statistician N Br and Mercantile Insur Co Ltd 1952-60; chief programmer: Commercial Union Assur Co Ltd 1960-64, Wiggins Teape Ltd 1964-72 (data processing mangr 1966-70, gp systems mangr 1970-72); dir computing and mgmnt servs King's Coll Hosp London 1972-73, data processing mangr Phoenix Assur plc Bristol 1973-85, mgmnt servs mangr Phoenix Assur 1985-86, computer mangr Sun Alliance Gp 1985-86, PA to chm IBM Computer Users' Assoc 1986-87; served on Computer Res Ctee of: Br Insur Assoc, Data Protection Ctees, CBI; fell: Br Computer Soc, Royal Statistical Soc; memb Royal Inst of Philosophy; *Recreations* badminton, mountaineering; *Style—* Ludovic Janas, Esq; Wint Hill House, Wint Hill, Banwell, Avon BS24 6NN

JANCAR, Dr Joze; s of Josip Jancar (d 1971), of Zalna, and Marija, *née* Tomlje; *b* 23 May 1920; *Educ* Real Gymnasium Ljubljana, Ljubljana Univ, Graz Univ, Galway Univ, Dublin Univ (MB BCh, BAO, DPM); *m* 18 Oct 1945, Marija, da of Anton Hribar (d 1968), of Ponova Vas; 2 s (Joseph b 1953, Martin b 1956), 1 da (Sonja b 1950); *Career* asst MO Ballinasloe 1952, registrar Mercer's Hosp Dublin 1954; Stoke Park Hosp Bristol: jr hosp MO 1956-59, sr hosp MO 1959-61, conslt psychiatrist 1961-85, hon conslt psychiatrist 1985; clinical lectr in mental health Univ of Bristol 1961-85; Blake Marsh lectr awarded Burden res gold medal and prize 1971, 1974; distinguished achievement award for scientific literature IASSMO New Delhi 1985, vice pres RCPsych 1981-83, pres Bristol Medico-Chirurgical Soc 1985-86, memb Bristol Medico-Historical Soc; med memb: Mental Health Review Tbnl, 1963-89 Mental Health Act Cmmn 1983-87; cncl memb Burden Inst Bristol; hon offr Cncl Int Assoc for the Scientific Study of Mental Deficiency 1988; Freeman City of London 1980, Liveryman Worshipful Soc of Apothecaries 1980; memb BMA 1952, FRSM 1969, FRCPsych 1971 (hon 1988); *Books* Stoke Park Studies - Mental Subnormality (1961), Clinical Pathology in Mental Retardation (jtly 1968); *Recreations* history, travel, languages; *Clubs* Savages (Bristol); *Style—* Dr Joze Jancar ; Emona, Beaufort Place, Frenchay, Bristol BS16 1PE (☎ 0272 567 891); Stoke Park Hospital, Stapleton, Bristol BS16 1QU (☎ 0272 655261)

JANES, (John) Douglas Webster; CB (1975); s of John Arnold Janes (d 1949), and Maud Mackinnon, *née* Webster (d 1938); *b* 17 Aug 1918; *Educ* Trinity Acad Edinburgh, Southgate Co Sch Middx, City and Guilds Coll Univ of London (BScEng, DIC); *m* 1943, Margaret Isabel, *née* Smith (d 1978); 1 s, 2 da; m 2, 1986, Joan Walker; *Career* princ fin offr Miny of Housing and Local Govt DOE 1968-73 (dep sec 1973), chief exec Maplin Devpt Authy 1973-74, dep sec NI Office 1974-79; various mgmnt orgn reviews 1979-81; memb Home Grown Timber Advsy Ctee 1979-81 (chm 1981-); sec Bach Choir 1981-89; ACGI; *Recreations* singing in choirs, using my hands; *Style—* Douglas Janes Esq, CB

JANION, Rear Adm Sir Hugh Penderel; KCVO (1981); s of Capt Ralph Penderel Janion, RN (d 1963), and Winifred Derwent, *née* Craig (d 1983); *b* 28 Sept 1923; *Educ* RNC Dartmouth; *m* 1956, Elizabeth Monica, da of Col Cecil Leonard Ferard (d 1970); 1 s, 1 da; *Career* joined RN 1937, served WWII Russian convoys, invasions of Sicily and Italy, served Korean War Inchon landing, Cdr 1958, cmd HMS Jewel, exec offr HMS Ark Royal, Capt 1966, cmd HMS Aurora, cmd HMS Bristol, Rear Adm 1975, ADC to HM The Queen 1975, Flag Offr Royal Yachts 1975-81; extra equerry to HM The Queen 1975-; yr bro Trinity House 1976-; *Recreations* golf, sailing, gardening; *Clubs* Naval and Military, Royal Yacht Sqdn, Royal Naval and Royal Albert, Imperial Poona Yacht, Sherborne Golf; *Style—* Rear Adm Sir Hugh Janion, KCVO; King's Hayes, Batcombe, Shepton Mallet, Somerset BA4 6HF (☎ 074 985 300)

JANMAN, Timothy Simon (Tim); MP (C) Thurrock 1987-; s of J Janman, of Banbury, and Irene, *née* Frith; *b* 9 Sept 1956; *Educ* Sir William Borlase GS, Univ of Nottingham (BSc); *m* 29 Sept 1990, Shirley Buckingham; *Career* Ford Motor Co 1979-83 (industl rels), IBM UK Ltd 1983-87 (sales); sec: Cons Backbench Employment Ctee 1987-88 (vice chm 1988-), Cons Backbench Home Affairs Ctee 1989-; vice pres: Jordan is Palestine Ctee, Selsdon Gp; memb Employment Select Ctee 1989-; *Recreations* theatre, restaurants, reading; *Style—* Tim Janman, MP; House of Commons, London SW1A 0AA (☎ 071 219 4001)

JANNER, Baroness; Elsie Sybil; CBE (1968), JP (Inner London 1936); da of Joseph Cohen, and Henrietta, *née* Nathansohn; *Educ* Centl Newcastle HS, S Hampstead HS, Switzerland; *m* 1927, Baron Janner (Life Peer, d 1982); 1 s (Greville, *qv*), 1 da (Lady Morris of Kenwood); *Career* CC candidate (Lab) Mile End LCC 1947; pres Brady Clubs and Settlement; former chm: Inner London Juvenile Cts Panel, Stonham Housing Assoc Advsy Bd 1975-83, Thames Bench Magistrates 1975; pres: Stonham Housing Assoc, Brady Clubs and Settlement Whitechapel; vice pres (former hon treas) Magistrates Assoc, tstee and former vice chm Mitchell City of London Charity and Educnl Fndn 1986-, chm Stonham Meml Tst, tstee Barnett Janner Charitable Tst; Fell Inst of Advanced Motorists (dep chm 1981-85); hon vice pres Fedn of Women Zionists, pres Brady-Maccabi Youth and Community Centre Edgware, vice pres Assoc Jewish Youth; Freeman City of London; *Books* Barnett Janner - A Personal Portrait (1984); *Style—* The Rt Hon the Lady Janner, CBE, JP; 45 Morpeth Mansions, Morpeth Terrace, London SW1P 1ET (☎ 071 828 8700)

JANNER, Hon Greville Ewan; QC (1971), MP (Lab) Leicester West 1974-; s of Baron Janner (Life Peer, d 1982) and Baroness Janner, *qv*; *b* 11 July 1928; *Educ* Bishop's Coll Sch Canada, St Paul's Sch, Trinity Hall Cambridge, Harvard Law Sch USA; *m* 1955, Myra Louise, *née* Sheink; 1 s, 2 da; *Career* called to the Bar 1955, author, journalist, broadcaster; contested (Lab) Wimbledon 1955, MP (Lab) Leicester North West 1970-74, memb Select Ctee on Employment, chm All Pty Safety Gp, vice chm All Pty Parly Ctee for Release of Soviet Jewry; pres Retired Exec's Action Clearing House (REACH) 1980-; vice pres World Jewish Congress 1981-86; former dir Jewish Chronicle Newspaper Ltd, dir Ladbroke plc 1986-; pres Bd of Deputies British Jews 1979-85, first pres Cwlth Jewish Cncl 1982-; FIPM 1976; *Recreations* Magic Circle; *Style—* The Hon Greville Janner, QC, MP; House of Commons, London SW1 0AA (☎ 071 219 4469)

JANNEY, Rodney Turnbull; s of Robert Turnbull Janney (d 1968), of Sutton Coldfield, and Edna Ruth, *née* Goodwin (d 1974); *b* 18 March 1940; *Educ* Trinity Coll of Music (LTCL); *m* 29 July 1968, Jennifer Maureen, da of Thomas Charles Roderick (d 1952); *Career* oboe and cor anglais reedmaker 1971-; *Recreations* hill walking, classical music, interior design, drawing; *Style—* Rodney T Janney, Esq; Bearnock Lodge, Glenurquhart, Inverness-shire

JANSEN, Cletus Patrick; *Career* md: GEC Projects and Automation Gp (all subsidiary cos of GEC plc), GEC Electrical Projects Ltd (gained Queen's Award for Export in 1982 and 1983), GEC Industl Controls Ltd, GEC Mechanical Handling Ltd, GEC Robot Systems Ltd, GEC Automation Projects Inc (USA), GEC Machines Ltd, GEC Small Machines and GEC Marine & Industl Gears Ltd; *Style—* Cletus Jansen, Esq; GEC Electrical Projects Ltd, Boughton Rd, Rugby, Warwicks CV21 1BU (☎ 0788 2144)

JANSON, Hamish Timothy Warren; s of Capt Rex Tarbutt Janson URD, RNVR (d 1962), and Kirsteen Elizabeth Russel, *née* Workman (d 1980); *b* 16 Nov 1940; *Educ* Gordonstoun, Grenoble Univ, Trinity Coll Cambridge (BA); *m* 28 Nov 1964, (Frances) Belinda, da of Maj-Gen J M L Gavin, of Slathurst Farm, Milland, Sussex; 2 da (Sophie b 1968, Emma b 1970); *Career* CA; Aran Dexter 1963-67, William Brandt & Co 1968-69, Provincial Insurance 1970-90, non-exec dir Columbus Trust Group; FCA; *Recreations* sailing, skiing, shooting; *Clubs* RYS, Royal Thames Yacht, Bembridge Sailing; *Style—* Hamish Janson, Esq; 22 Hans Place, London SW1X 0EP (☎ 071 589 0156, fax 071 584 0174)

JANSZ, Dr Clifford Cyril Arthur; s of Sir Herbert Eric Jansz, CMG (d 1976), of Fortis House, Hammers Lane, Mill Hill, London, and Beatrix, *née* Van Langenberg (d 1954); *b* 13 Jan 1924; *Educ* St Peter's Coll Colombo Sri Lanka, Univ of Ceylon (MB BS), Great Ormond Street Hosp for Sick Children (DCH), Inst of Public Health Gt Portland Place London (DPH), Birkbeck Coll London; *m* 19 April 1949, Margaret (Peggy) Louise, da of Stanley Studholm Wallbeoff (d 1957), of The Park, Lady McCallums Drive, Kandy, Sri Lanka; 1 s (Richard), 4 da (Ann, Sabrina, Litza, Natania); *Career* MO Govt Health Serv Sri Lanka 1949-54, asst MO Essex CC 1959-63, sr asst MO Middx 1963-64, sr MO London Borough Brent 1964-66, princ MO London Borough Greenwich 1966-69, chief health servs offr London Borough Hammersmith 1969-72, dir of health servs London Borough Harrow 1973-74, dist community physician and MO of environmental health 1974-89, ret 1989; tstee CJ Ward Tst Harrow 1973-89; memb BMA 1955, FFCM 1982 (memb 1973); *Recreations* tennis, photography, model railways; *Style—* Dr Clifford Jansz; Fortis House, Hammers Lane, Mill Hill, London NW7 4DJ (☎ 081 959 1565)

JANTET, Georges Henry; s of Auguste Jantet (d 1955), and Renée, *née* Jacob (d 1978); *b* 5 Oct 1927; *Educ* Lycée Français de Londres, St Benedict's Sch Ealing, St Mary's Hosp Med Sch London (MB BS, Martin John Turner prize); *m* 4 June 1955, Alice, da of Jean-Francôis Moulin, of St Etienne, France; 1 s (Bruno b 16 April 1957), 3 da (Martine (Mrs Cremer) b 4 March 1956, Blandine (Mrs Maniere) b 24 March 1959, Nadine b 16 March 1963); *Career* Mil Serv with Serv de Santé des Armées Paris and Lyon 1952-53; house surgeon St Mary's Hosp then The Miller Hosp 1951-52, res surgical offr Hôpital Français London 1953-54, sr house offr Royal Marsden Hosp 1954-55; St Mary's Hosp: prosector in anatomy and demonstrator Dept of Anatomy Med Sch 1953, res casualty surgeon 1954, surgical registrar Surgical Professorial Unit 1955-57, sr registrar in surgery 1959-66 (also Regnl Hosp Bd NW Thames), assoc teacher Med Sch 1970-; lectr in surgery and res fell Surgical Professorial Unit St Thomas' Hosp and Med Sch 1957-59, res fell and asst in surgery Dept of Surgery Peter Bent Brigham Hosp Harvard 1961-62, conslt in gen and vascular surgery The Ealing Hosp and Assoc Hosps 1966-; hon conslt surgeon: Dispensaire Fraņais London 1967-, The Italian Hosp London 1967-, Hammersmith Hosp and Royal Postgrad Med Sch 1974- (also sr lectr in surgery); RCS: surgical tutor 1973-77, regnl advsr 1977-88, memb Manpower Advsy Panel 1987-, memb Euro Gp 1989-, chm Ct of Examiners 1986-87; memb numerous ctees NW Thames Regnl Health Authy (chm Surgeons Ctee 1989-); FRCS 1955 (MRCS 1951), FRSM 1966; memb: BMA 1960, Cncl Assoc of Surgeons of GB & Ireland 1987- (fell 1966), Vascular Surgical Soc of GB & Ireland, Cncl Hunterian Soc 1975-90 (fell 1966, pres 1986-87), Société Clinique Française 1985- (pres 1987-90), Br Lymphology Interest Gp 1987-; memb Editorial Bd various learned jnls; *Books* New Trends In Basic Lymphology (co-ed, 1967), Phlebology 1985 (co-ed, 1986); author of chapters in various books; *Recreations* family and social life, tennis, sailing, fishing, skiing, travelling, history, current affairs, music; *Clubs* Surgical Specialists Soc, Roehampton; *Style—* Georges Jantet, Esq; 41 Audley Rd, London W5 3ES (☎ 081 997 2485); 82 Harley St, London W1N 1AE (☎ 071 580 9784, 081 967 5611, fax 081 574 0185)

JANVRIN, Vice Adm Sir (Hugh) Richard Benest; KCB (1969, CB 1965), DSC (1940); s of Rev Canon Claud William Janvrin (d 1965), of Fairford, Glos, and Irene Monica, *née* Turner (d 1981); *b* 9 May 1915; *Educ* RNC Dartmouth; *m* 1938, Nancy, da of late F B Fielding, of Gloucester; 2 s; *Career* joined RN 1929, Lt 1937, served WWII, Capt 1954, dir Tactics and Weapons Policy Admty 1962-63, Rear Adm 1964, Flag Offr Aircraft Carriers 1964-66, Dep Chief of Naval Staff 1966-68, Vice Adm 1967, Flag Offr Naval Air Cmd 1968-70, ret 1971; *Style—* Vice Adm Sir Richard Janvrin, KCB, DSC; Allen's Close, Chalford Hill, Stroud, Glos GL6 8QJ (☎ 0453 882336)

JANVRIN, Robin Berry; LVO (1983); s of Vice Adm Sir Richard Janvrin, KCB, DSC, and Nancy Edyth, *née* Fielding; *b* 20 Sept 1946; *Educ* Marlborough, BNC Oxford; *m* 22 Oct 1977, Isabelle, da of Yann de Boissonneaux de Chevigny; 1 s, 2 da; *Career* RN: RNC Dartmouth 1964, HMS Devonshire 1965, HMS Lynx 1970, HMS Ganges 1973, HMS Royal Arthur 1974; Dip Serv: FCO 1975, 1978 and 1984, first sec UK Delgn NATO 1976, New Delhi 1981, cnsllr and dep head Personnel Dept 1985-87; asst private sec to HM The Queen 1990- (press sec 1987-90); *Style—* Robin Janvrin, Esq, LVO; Buckingham Palace, London SW1 1AA

JAQUES, John Michael; MBE (1988); s of William Edward Jaques, of La Providence, Rochester, Kent, and Gertrude, *née* Scott (d 1980); *b* 29 Sept 1930; *Educ* Cambridge HS; *m* 27 Jan 1962, Caroline, da of Philip Reddie Knapman, of Stanton Drew, Avon; 2 s (Rupert b 1962, Matthew b 1964); *Career* architect; sr ptnr Jaques Muir & Ptnrs chartered architects; practice cmmns incl: housing schemes, banks, religious bldgs, sports centres, museums, theatres, laboratories and med bldgs, telecommunication centres, planning studies; 1989 Civic Tst Commendation for the restoration of the Palace Theatre London; architect for major restoration work to Church of the Holy Sepulchre Jerusalem; memb Cncl The Anglo Jordanian Soc 1980-86; memb Ctee Friends of St John Ophthalmic Hosp Jerusalem 1982-86; OStJ 1985, Order of El Istiqlal (Jordan) 1977; RIBA, FRSA; *Recreations* shooting, hunting, fishing, painting, glass engraving, visiting ancient antiquities; *Clubs* Arts; *Style—* John M Jaques, Esq, MBE; 8 Vine Yard, Sanctuary St, London SE1 1QL (☎ 071 357 7428, fax 071 357 7650)

JARDINE, Sir Andrew Colin Douglas; 5 Bt (UK 1916), of Godalming, Surrey; er s of Brig Sir Ian Liddell Jardine, 4 Bt, OBE, MC (d 1982), and Priscilla, *née* Scott-Phillips; *b* 30 Nov 1955; *Educ* Charterhouse; *Heir* bro, Michael Ian Christopher Jardine b 4 Oct 1958; *Career* served Royal Green Jackets 1975-78; C T Bowring & Co 1979-81, Henderson Admin Gp plc 1981-; *Style—* Sir Andrew Jardine, Bt; 99 Addison Rd, London W14 8DD (☎ 071 603 6434)

JARDINE, Sheriff James Christopher Macnaughton; s of James Jardine (d 1952), of Glasgow, and Jean Paterson, *née* Stuart (d 1966); *b* 18 Jan 1930; *Educ* Glasgow Acad, Gresham House Sch Ayrshire, Univ of Glasgow (BL); *m* 1955, Vena Gordon, da of Daniel Gordon Kight (d 1973), of Renfrewshire; 1 da (Susan); *Career* slr; princ Nelson & Mackay 1955-56, ptnr McClure Naismith Brodie & Co Slrs Glasgow 1956-69; Sheriff: Stirling Dunbarton and Clackmannan (later N Strathclyde) at Dumbarton 1969-79, Glasgow and Strathkelvin 1979-; *Recreations* boating, music, theatre, ballet, opera; *Style*— Sheriff James Jardine; Sheriff's Chambers, Sheriff Court of Glasgow and Strathkelvin, 1 Carlton Place, Glasgow G5 9DA

JARDINE, Michael Ian Christopher; s of late Brig Sir Ian Liddel Jardine, 4 Bt, OBE, MC (d 1982), and Priscilla, Lady Jardine, *qv*; hp of bro, Sir Andrew Jardine, 5 Bt, *qv*; *b* 1958; *m* (Maria) Milky; 2 s; *Style*— Michael Jardine, Esq; 12 Graham Ave, Ealing, London W13 9TQ

JARDINE, Stewart; s of John Douglas Jardine, of 14 Cecil Street, Newton Park, Port Elizabeth, South Africa, and Marion Fletcher, *née* Campbell; *b* 24 Dec 1965; *Educ* Kingswood Coll Grahamstown SA, Cardiff Inst of HE (HNC, BA); *Career* Rugby Union scrum half Glamorgan Wanderers RFC and Scotland; memb Eastern Province Schs Squad SA 1983-84; clubs: Telford RFC 1986-87, S Glamorgan Inst RFC 1987-90, Glamorgan Wanderers RFC 1990-; rep: Shropshire 1986-87, Welsh Colleges 1987-90, Scottish Students 1987-91 (tour students World Cup 1988, capt 1988-91), GB students 1989 (capt), Anglo-Scots 1988-91, Scotland B 1989- (debut v Ireland 1990); Scotland: toured Japan 1989; cricket: memb Wellington CC XI 1985-87, memb Shropshire CC Squad 1987; asst Pentwyn Leisure Centre Cardiff; *Recreations* golf, windsurfing, water skiing, cricket and squash; *Style*— Stewart Jardine, Esq; 73 Glenroy St, Roath, Cardiff, Wales CF2 3JY (☎ 0222 488187); c/o Gordon Alston, Scottish Rugby Union, Murrayfield, Edinburgh EH12 5PJ

JARDINE OF APPLEGIRTH, Sir Alexander Maule; 12 Bt (NS 1672), of Applegirth, Dumfriesshire; 23 Chief of Clan Jardine; s of Col Sir William Edward Jardine of Applegirth, 11 Bt, OBE, TD, JP, DL (d 1986), and Ann Graham Maitland; *b* 24 Aug 1947; *Educ* Gordonstoun; *m* 9 Oct 1982, Mary Beatrice, posthumous only child of Hon John Cross (yst s of 2 Viscount Cross), and Sybil Anne, *née* Murray, who m subsequently Lt Cdr James Parker-Jervis, RN (ggs of Hon Edward Parker-Jervis, 2 s of 2 Viscount St Vincent); 1 s (William Murray b 1984), 2 da (Kirsty Sybil b 1986, Jean Maule b 1988); *Heir* s, William Murray; *Career* farmer; memb Queen's Body Guard for Scotland (Royal Co of Archers); *Recreations* shooting, fishing, curling; *Style*— Sir Alexander Jardine of Applegirth, Bt; Ash House, Thwaites, Millom, Cumbria LA18 5HY (☎ 0229 716331)

JARMAN, David Alexander Elijah; JP (Surrey 1983); s of Lt Cdr Alexander William Jarman, RNVR (d 1985), and Ivy L Jarman (d 1989); *b* 16 Jan 1936; *Educ* Tiffin Sch Kingston-upon-Thames; *m* 22 Dec 1962, Brenda Mary, da of Dr Douglas Arthur Blount (d 1966), of Dunstable, Beds; *Career* mangr Road Tport Indust until 1969, called to the Bar Inner Temple 1969; practiced SE circuit 1969-81, legal advsr British Aerospace plc 1981; memb: Magistrates Assoc, Bar Assoc for Commerce Fin and Indust; *Recreations* yachting, gardening, genealogy and local history; *Clubs* Middle Thames Yacht; *Style*— David Jarman, Esq, JP; c/o British Aerospace plc, Company Headquarters, PO Box 87, Royal Aerospace Establishment, Farnborough, Hants GU14 6YU

JARMAN, Michael Charles; JP (1978); s of Charles Bertram Jarman; *b* 12 June 1936; *Educ* Rossall; *m* 1965, Helen Barbara, da of Cecil Charles Robinson; 1 s, 3 da; *Career* md: Avenue Farms Ltd 1964-, Midon Properties Ltd 1964-; chm The Wipac Gp of Cos 1977-88 (dir 1964-77); govr Agric Soc; MInstM, gen cmmr of income tax 1984, memb Mktg Soc 1979, FID, FCA; *Recreations* salmon fishing, equestrian sports, farming; *Clubs* Farmers'; *Style*— Michael Jarman, Esq, JP; Castle Fields, Buckingham (☎ 0280 812127)

JARMAN, Nicolas Francis Barnaby; QC (1985); s of Archibald Seymour Jarman (d 1982), of Brighton, and Helen Marie Klenk; *b* 19 June 1938; *Educ* Harrow, ChCh Oxford (MA); *m* 1, 1973 (m dis 1977), Jennifer Michelle, da of Michael Lawrence Lawrence-Smith (d 1988), of Suffolk; 1 da (Jemima b 1975); m 2, Julia Elizabeth, da of Leonard Owen John, of Swansea; *Career* JVO Mons Offr Trg Sch 1957, cmmnd RA 1957, served Cyprus; called to the Bar Inner Temple 1965-, in practice Midlands & Oxford circuit, rec Crown Ct 1982-; *Recreations* flyfishing, France; *Style*— Nicolas Jarman, Esq, QC; 13 Blithfield St, London W8 6RH (☎ 071 937 0982); 4 King's Bench Walk, Temple, London EC4 (☎ 071 353 3581)

JARMAN, Roger Whitney; s of Reginald Cecil Jarman (d 1989), and Marjorie Dix, *née* Whitney (d 1970); *b* 16 Feb 1935; *Educ* Cathays HS Cardiff, Univ of Birmingham (BSocSc); *m* 1959, Patricia Dorothy, da of Trevor Henry Odwell (d 1977); 1 s (Christopher b 1960); *Career* instr in Lib studies Vauxhall Motors 1960-62, recruitment offr Vauxhall Motors 1962-64, asst sec Appt Bd Univ of Bristol 1964-68, princ Civil Serv Cmmn 1968-72, princ Welsh Office Euro Div 1972-74, asst sec Devolution Div 1974-78, asst sec Perm Sec Div 1978-80, under sec Land Use Planning Gp 1980-83, under sec Tport Highways and Planning Gp Welsh Office 1983-88, under sec Housing Health and Social Servs Policy Gp; *Recreations* reading, cooking, walking; *Clubs* Civil Serv; *Style*— Roger Jarman, Esq; Welsh Office, Cathays Park, Cardiff (☎ 0222 825257)

JARMAN-PRICE, Russell; s of Robert Eustace Price, JP, and Redena Mary, *née* Stockdale; *b* 18 May 1954; *Educ* Priory GS Shrewsbury, Univ of Loughborough (BSc); *m* 1 Sept 1988, Amanda Jayn, da of Maj Roy Longden Rozier; *Career* account exec Benton and Bowles (London) 1976-78, account mangr TBWA (London) 1976-80, account dir Gold Greenlees Trott 1980-81, bd account dir Hedger Mitchel Stark 1981-84; md: Still Price Court Twivy De Souza, Lintas Ltd 1985-;IPA; *Recreations* riding, painting, driving, walking, cinema; *Clubs* Burkes; *Style*— Russell Jarman-Price, Esq; 84 Eccleston Square, London SW1V 1PX (☎ 071 932 8888, fax 071 932 8412, car 0836 228 970, 0860 305 093)

JARRATT, Sir Alexander Anthony (Alex); CB (1968); s of Alexander Jarratt (d 1943), and Mary Jarratt (d 1970); *b* 19 Jan 1924; *Educ* Royal Liberty GS Essex, Univ of Birmingham (BCom); *m* 1946, Mary Philomena, da of Louis Keogh (d 1932); 1 s, 2 da; *Career* Petty Offr Fleet Air Arm, served Far East; civil servant: Miny of Power 1949-64, seconded Treasy 1953-54, Cabinet Office 1964-65, sec Prices and Incomes Bd 1964-68, dep under sec Dept of Employment and Productivity 1968-70, dep sec Miny of Agric 1970; chief exec IPC and IPC Newspapers 1970-73, chm and chief exec Reed Int 1974-85 (dir 1970-), dir ICI 1975-, dep chm Midland Bank 1980-, chm Smith's Industries plc 1985-, dep chm Prudential Corporation 1987-; pres Advertising Assoc 1979-83, former memb NEDC; former chm CBI Econ Policy Ctee and Employment Policy Ctee, former memb President's Ctee CBI; chm: Industl Soc 1975-79, Henley Admin Staff Coll 1976-89, Centre for Dispute Resolution 1990-; govr Ashridge Mgmnt Coll, chllr Univ of Birmingham (Hon LLD) 1983-; Hon DSc Cranfield, DUniv Brunel; FRSA; kt 1979; *Recreations* the countryside, reading; *Clubs* Savile; *Style*— Sir Alex Jarratt, CB; Smiths Industries plc, 765 Finchley Rd, Childs Hill, London NW11 8DS (☎ 081 458 3232, telex 928761)

JARRATT, Dr John Anthony; s of Leslie Jarratt (d 1958), and Lily, *née* Tweedie (d 1977); *b* 26 Dec 1939; *Educ* Spalding GS, Univ of Sheffield Med Sch (MB ChB); *m* 21 Feb 1970, Patricia Anne, da of Jack Madin, of Alford, Lincolnshire; 2 s (Mark b 24 Nov 1971, Paul b 5 Aug 1975); *Career* Nat Hosp for Nervous Diseases London: academic registrar 1969-70, MRC res fell 1970-72, registrar in clinical neurophysiology 1972; registrar in neurology Middx Hosp 1972, sr registrar Dept of Clinical Neurophysiology Rigshospitalet Copenhagen 1973, conslt in clinical neurophysiology Sheffield AHA 1976-, hon lectr in neurology Univ of Sheffield 1976-; author of numerous scientific pubns; sec Assoc of Br Clinical Neurophysiologists 1984-88 (pres 1990-), memb Jt Neurosciences Ctee 1984-88, chm Jt Ctee on Higher Med Trg in Clinical Neurophysiology RCP 1988- (memb 1984-88), memb Expert Panel EEC 1989, assoc memb EEG Soc 1975, memb Assoc of Br Neurologists 1978; FRCP 1981; *Recreations* golf, photography, music, travel, technical innovation; *Style*— Dr John Jarratt; Department of Clinical Neurophysiology, Royal Hallamshire Hospital, Sheffield S10 2JF (☎ 0742 766222)

JARRATT, Prof Peter; s of Edward Jarratt (d 1988), and Edna Mary Eliza, *née* Pearson (d 1976); *b* 2 Jan 1935; *Educ* Bingley GS, Univ of Manchester (BSc), Univ of Bradford (PhD); *m* 1 June 1971, Jeanette, da of Lucien Adrian Debeir (d 1946); 1 s (Robin Alexander Debeir b 1972), 1 da (Sophie Amanda Debeir b 1978); *Career* sr lectr Univ of Bradford 1963-72, dir of Computing Laboratory 1972-75; Univ of Birmingham: prof of computer sci 1975-, dir of Computer Centre 1975-90, dean of Faculty of Sci 1985-88, exec vice chm for info technol 1990-, devpt advsr to Vice Chllr 1985-; dir: TV and Film Unit 1983-, Birmingham Res Park 1985-88; govr Royal Nat Coll for the Blind; memb Exec Ctee Lunar Soc of Birmingham, tstee Nat Fndn for Conductive Educn; FIMA 1968, FBCS 1968, FSS 1972, CEng 1990; *Recreations* gardening, mountain walking, opera, chess; *Style*— Prof Peter Jarratt; 42 Reddings Road, Moseley, Birmingham B13 8LN (☎ 021 449 7160); The University of Birmingham, Edgbaston, Birmingham B15 2TT (☎ 021 414 4775, fax 021 414 3971)

JARRETT, Dr (Boaz) Antony; s of Frank Jarrett (d 1963), of Cox Corner, Ockley, Surrey, and Ethel Mary, *née* Budden; *b* 24 July 1923; *Educ* Windsor Co Boys' Sch, Imperial Coll London (BSc, PhD, DIC, ACGI); *m* 2 Oct 1948, Patricia Eveline, da of Arthur White (d 1976), of Forest Row, Sussex; 2 da (Lianne b 6 Sept 1951, Naomi b 11 Sept 1955); *Career* Sub Lt (A) RNVR air engr 1943-46; res contract Imperial Coll 1946-48, gen factory mangr Lucas Cav Ltd 1949-63, md Eaton-Env Ltd 1963-66, tech dir Lucas Cav Ltd 1966-81, gp dir prodn technol Lucas Industries plc 1981-86; pres Old Centralians (Engrs' Alumnus Assoc of Imperial Coll) 1986-87, memb Tech Ctee RAC, former govr Claremont Fan Ct Sch Esher (chm CDT Ctee); Freeman City of London 1984, Liveryman Worshipful Co of Engrs 1984; FIMechE 1965, MSAE 1978, FCGI 1981, FEng 1983, FRSA 1984, Eur Ing 1989; *Clubs* RAC; *Style*— Dr Antony Jarrett; c/o Royal Automobile Club, 85 Pall Mall, London SW1Y 5HS

JARRETT, Sir Clifford George; KBE (1956, CBE 1945), CB (1949); s of George Jarrett; *b* 1909; *Educ* Dover Co Sch, Sidney Sussex Coll Cambridge; *m* 1, 1933, Hilda Goodchild (d 1975); 1 s, 2 da; m 2, 1978, Mary, da of C Beacock; *Career* Home Office 1932, perm sec Admty 1961-64 (joined 1934, dep sec 1950-61), perm under sec Miny of Pensions and Nat Insur (later DHSS) 1964-70; tstee Nat Maritime Museum 1969-81; chm: Dover Harbour Bd 1971-80, Tobacco Res Cncl 1971-78; memb Civil Serv Security Appeals Panel until 1982; *Style*— Sir Clifford Jarrett, KBE, CB; 1 The Coach House, Derry Hill, Menston, Ilkley, W Yorks

JARRETT, Denis William; s of William Antoine Jarrett (d 1965), and Edith Jessie, *née* Williams (d 1936); *b* 9 April 1924; *Educ* City of London Sch; *m* 1952, Celia Mary, da of Albert Samuel Otten (d 1942); 1 s (Stephen Howard b 1957), 1 da (Elisabeth Mary b 1954); *Career* RAF 1942-47; City of London Corporation 1940-42 and 1947-55, in advertising and direct mail 1955-87 (creative servs mangr Allen & Hanburys Ltd and Glaxo Operations (UK) Ltd, conslt for UK and overseas markets); memb Advertising Standards Bd of Finance Ltd, life vice pres Br Direct Mktg Assoc (chm 1975-85); former memb: Cncl of Advertising Assoc, Code of Advertising Practice Ctee (Mail Order Ctee), Direct Mail Servs Standards Bd, Mailing Preference Ltd, Int Ctee Direct Mktg Assoc of USA, Ctee Direct Mktg World Congress; John Dickinson Award for personal servs to direct mail/mktg 1977; memb Br Direct Mktg Assoc 1965; *Recreations* boating, travel, concerts, walking, reading, theatre, antiques, Suffolk conservation RNLI; *Style*— Denis Jarrett, Esq; 10 Drury Park, Snape, Saxmundham, Suffolk IP17 1TA (☎ 072 888 8133)

JARRETT, Paul Eugene Marcus; s of Dr Maurice Eugene Decimus Jarrett (d 1987), of Woking, Surrey, and Doris Mabel Lake, of Cobham, Surrey; *b* 18 Feb 1943; *Educ* Queen Elizabeth's GS Blackburn Lancs, Downing Coll Cambridge (MA), St Thomas's Hosp London (MB BChir, DObstRCOG); *m* 1 April 1966, Ann, da of George Wilson (d 1982), of Blackburn Lancs; 1 s (Michael b 1972); *Career* med dir Bioplan Holdings plc Chertsey Surrey 1986-, dir of med servs Kingston Hosp Kingston-upon-Thames Surrey 1987- (conslt surgn 1978-); tstee The Princess Alice Hospice Esher Surrey, chm The Br Assoc of Day Surgery; FRCS 1972; *Recreations* medical antiques, golf; *Style*— Paul Jarrett, Esq; Langleys, Queens Drive, Oxshott, Surrey KT22 0PB (☎ 0372 842259); Kingston Hospital, Wolverton Ave, Kingston-upon-Thames, Surrey KT2 7QB (☎ 081 546 7711); Bioplan Holdings plc, Eldridge House, 25 Windsor St, Chertsey, Surrey KT16 8AY (☎ 0932 569166, fax 0932 568229, car 0860 320062)

JARVI, Neeme; s of August Järvi (d 1960), and Elss Järvi (d 1984); musical family, bro Vallo Järvi conductor, theatre 'Estonia' Tallinn Estonia; *b* 7 June 1937; *Educ* Tallinn Music Sch Leningrad, Conservatory of Music Rimski-Korsakov (post grad); *m* 1961, Lillia Järvi; 2 s (Paavo, Kristjan), 1 da (Maarika); *Career* music dir Estonian Radio Symphony Orchestra, theatre opera and ballet Estonia 1960-73, Estonian State Symphony Orchestra 1973-80, concerts and tours with Leningrad and Moscow Orchestras, emigration to USA 1980; music dir Gothenburg Symphony Orchestra Sweden 1980-, musical dir and chief conductor The Scottish Nat Orchestra 1984-; concerts and opera performances: Met New York, Philadelphia, Boston, Chicago, San Francisco, Los Angeles, German Orchestra, London Orchestra (Philharmonic LPO, LSO), Canada, Mexico, Brazil; recordings with: EMI, Philips, DG, BIS, Chandos; *Style*— Neeme Järvi, Esq; c/o Columbia Artists Management Inc, 165 West 57th Street, New York, NY 10019, USA

JARVIS, David; s of Harold Jarvis (d 1945), and Phyllis Emma, *née* Hart; *b* 9 March 1941; *Educ* Gillingham GS, Maidstone Coll of Tech; *m* 9 Feb 1963, Williamina Bell, da of William Herbert Colby; 1 s (Julian David b 1966), 2 da (Andrea Claire b 1968, Nicola Emma b 1976); *Career* Anderson Clayton: controller and treas Milne and Cosa 1963-68, fin admin Peru 1968-70, gen mangr Consumer Prods Div Mexico 1970-78; gen mangr Int Business Devpt The Pillsbury Co USA 1978-81, vice chm and chief fin offr Norwest Corp USA 1981-86, md Salomon Bros USA UK 1986-, chm The Northgate Corp; voyageur Outward Bound Sch Minnesota, ex tstee Fin Accounting Standards Bd USA; ACMA 1960; *Recreations* tennis, golf; *Clubs* Canning, Riverside; *Style*— David Jarvis, Esq; 64 Cadogan Sq, London SW1 (☎ 071 584 2007); The Small House, Great Rissington, Glos (☎ 0451 21727); Salomon Bros Int, Victoria Plaza, 111 Buckingham Palace Rd, London SW1W OSB (☎ 071 721 3974, fax 071 736 5773, telex 886441)

JARVIS, David William; s of George Harry Jarvis, and Doris Annie, *née* Mabbitt; *b* 25 April 1947; *Educ* City of London Sch, Univ of Exeter (BA); *m* 1972, Elizabeth Ann Rowena, da of Fergus Ferguson (d 1969); 1 s (John David George b 1982), 2 da (Rowena Gilliam b 1978, Katherine Elizabeth b 1980); *Career* dir of fin Harvey of Bristol Ltd 1984-88; former dir: John Harvey & Sons Ltd, John Harvey & Sons (Espana) Ltd, Jhesa, Fernando A De Terry Sa, A Delor & Cie Sa, Commercial Agencie (Spain), Commercial Agencies (Tenerife), John Harvey & Sons (Portugal) Ltd, Palomino & Vergara SA; md Allied Distillers Ltd 1988-; chm: George Ballantine and Son Ltd, William Teacher and Sons Ltd; dir Hiram Walker-Allied Vintners Ltd 1990-; FCCA; *Recreations* sports, walking, reading, current affairs; *Style*— David Jarvis, Esq; Harveys of Bristol, Harvey House, Whitechurch Lane, Whitchurch, Bristol (☎ 0272

836161)

JARVIS, Gerald Joseph; s of Maurice Jarvis (d 1956), and Sarah, *née* Brown (d 1964); *b* 4 Jan 1947; *Educ* Pembroke Coll Oxford (BA), Univ of Oxford Sch of Med (BM, BCh); *m* 1 Oct 1977, Elizabeth Honor, da of Gordon Wilson Izatt, of Chapel Green, Earlsferry, Fife, Scotland; 2 s (Thomas Edward Maurice b 11 Sept 1979, Alexander James Patric b 11 Dec 1984), 1 da (Emma Elizabeth b 25 Feb 1982); *Career* conslt obstetrician and gynaecologist St James Univ Hosp Leeds 1981-, hon lectr in med Univ of Leeds 1981-; author of various publications on obstetrics and gynaecology; examiner RCOG 1989-, convenor of Nat Course on the Treatment of Female Urinary Incontinence; Freemason (Pilgrim Lodge No 7728); FRCSEd 1975, FRCOG 1989; *Books* Female Urinary Incontinence (1990); *Recreations* playing piano, egyptology; *Clubs* United Oxford & Cambridge Univ; *Style—* Gerald Jarvis, Esq; Beechwood House, Raby Park, Wetherby LS22 4SA (☎ 0937 62218); BUPA Hospital, Roundhay Hall, Jackson Ave, Leeds LS8 1NT (☎ 0532 693939)

JARVIS, John Manners; QC; s of Donald Edward Manners Jarvis, TD, of Rockbourne, Hants, and Theodora Brixie, *née* Bryant; *b* 20 Nov 1947; *Educ* Kings Coll Sch Wimbledon, Emmanuel Coll Cambridge (MA); *m* 5 May 1972, Janet Rona, da of Eric Cresswell Kitson, OBE (d 1975), of Mersham, Kent; 2 s (Christopher b 1974, Fergus b 1976); *Career* called to the Bar Lincoln's Inn 1970; practice at Commercial Bar, asst rec; govr Kings Coll Sch Wimbledon; *Recreations* tennis, sailing, skiing, cycling, music; *Clubs* Hurlingham; *Style—* John Jarvis, Esq, QC; 3 Gray's Inn Place, Gray's Inn, London WC1R 5EA (☎ 071 831 8441, fax 071 831 8479)

JARVIS, Martin; s of Denys Jarvis, and Margot Jarvis; *b* 4 Aug 1941; *Educ* Whitgift Sch, RADA; *m* 1; 2 s; m 2, 1974, Rosalind Ayres; *Career* actor; first appearance Nat Youth Theatre 1960-62 (played Henry V Sadler's Wells 1962); theatre work incl: Manchester Library Theatre 1962-63, Poor Bitos (Duke of York's) 1963, Man and Superman (Vaudeville) 1966, The Bandwagon (Mermaid) 1970, The Rivals (USA) 1973, title role in Hamlet (Festival of Br Theatre) 1973, The Circle (Haymarket) 1976, She Stoops to Conquer (Canada and Hong Kong Arts Festivals) 1977, Caught in the Act (Garrick) 1981; National Theatre: Importance of Being Earnest 1982, Victoria Station 1983, The Trojan War Will Not Take Place 1983; later theatre work incl: Woman in Mind (Vaudeville) 1986, The Perfect Party (Greenwich) 1987, Jerome in Henceforward (Vaudeville) 1989, Viktor in Exchange (Vaudeville) 1990, Sir Andrew Agnecheek in Sir Peter Hall's revival Twelfth Night (Playhouse); TV work incl: The Forsythe Saga 1967, Nicholas Nickleby 1968, David Copperfield 1975, Rings on their Fingers 1978, Breakaway 1980, The Black Tower 1985, Chelworth 1988, Rumpole of the Bailey 1988-89, Countdown 1990, You Say Potato (LA) 1990-, guest star Inspector Morse (Greeks Bearing Gifts, feature length TV film) 1991; films incl: The Last Escape, Ike, The Bunker, Taste the Blood of Dracula, Buster; numerous radio performances incl: Charles Dickens in The Best of Times, one-man series Jarvis' Frayn; adapted and read over 40 of Richmal Crompton's William stories for radio TV and cassette, all voices in children's animated series Huxley Pig 1989; cassette recordings incl: Just William, David Copperfield 1991; pres Croydon Histrionic Soc 1984-; contrib Comic Relief and Children in Need; *Books* Bright Boy (1977), short stories for radio, articles in The Listener, Punch, Evening Standard, High Life, commentaries for TV film documentaries and arts programmes; *Recreations* Indian food, Beethoven, Mozart, people-watching; *Clubs* BBC; *Style—* Martin Jarvis, Esq; c/o Michael Whitehall Ltd, 125 Gloucester Rd, London SW7 (☎ 071 224 8466)

JARVIS, Paul William; s of Malcolm Jarvis, of Caldicot, Gwent, and Marjorie, *née* Lofthouse; *b* 29 June 1965; *Educ* Bydales Comp Sch Marske-by-Sea Cleveland; *m* 3 Dec 1988, Wendy Jayne; 1 s (Alexander Michael b 13 June 1989); *Career* professional cricketer; debut Yorkshire CCC 1981-, awarded county cap 1986; England under 19 v W Indies 1982 and Aust 1983; 6 test matches: v NZ (2) 1988, v W Indies (2) 1988, v Aust (2) 1989; 5 one day Ints: v Aust 1988, v NZ (4) 1988; memb Mike Gatting tour to SA 1990; youngest player to represent Yorkshire aged 16; *Recreations* fishing, golf, drinking in the local pub; *Style—* Paul Jarivs, Esq; c/o Yorkshire CCC, Headingley, Leeds, LS6 3BU (☎ 0532 787394)

JASKEL, Martin Stephen; s of David Jaskel (d 1956), and Fanny Jaskel (d 1981); *b* 3 June 1946; *Educ* St Marylebone GS, Univ of Manchester (BA); *m* 13 May 1976, Antone Sheila; 1 da (Felicity b 1981); *Career* gilt edged salesperson Phillips & Drew 1967-72, gilt edged exec Capel Cure Myers 1972-75, ptnr W Greenwell & Co 1981-86 (gilt edged exec 1976-81), dir Greenwell Montagu Gilt Edged 1986-88, treasy sales dir Midland Montagu 1988-90; dir of global sales NatWest Gp Treasy and Capital Mkts 1990-; Freeman City of London 1980, memb Guild of World Traders 1987; memb Stock Exchange 1972; *Recreations* cricket, opera, books, travel; *Clubs* MCC; *Style—* Martin Jaskel, Esq; 26 Loudoun Road, London NW8 0LT (☎ 081 483 2328); National Westminster, 135 Bishopsgate, London EC2M 3UR (☎ 071 375 4906, fax 071 334 1611, car 0836 701248)

JASON, David; s of Arthur White, and Olwen, *née* Jones; *Educ* Northside Secdy Sch; *Career* actor; first professional job with Bromley Repertory 1965; early work incl: 3 months in Crossroads, tour with Ron Moody in Peter Pan, summer seasons with Bob Monkhouse and Dick Emery; TV: Do Not Adjust Your Set 1967, Top Secret Life of Edgar Briggs (LWT), Lucky Fella (LWT), with Ronnie Barker in His Lordship Entertains, with Ronnie Barker in Open All Hours, A Bit of a Do (Yorkshire TV), Only Fools and Horses (BBC1); theatre: No Sex Please We're British (Strand Theatre) 1972, Look No Hands (Strand Theatre), Norman Conquest (Oxford Playhouse), The Relapse (tour with Cambridge Theatre Company); voice of many cartoon characters incl Dangermouse, Count Duckula and Toad in Wind in the Willows; awards: BAFTA Best Actor, Radio Times Funniest Actor, Variety Club Personality of the Year, Sony Radio award, Water Rats Personality of the Year, TV Times Actor of the Year, TV Times Funniest Actor; *Recreations* skin diving, gliding, restoration of old machines, work; *Style—* David Jason, Esq; Richard Stone Partnership, 25 Whitehall, London SW1A 2BS (☎ 071 839 6421)

JASON, Gillian Brett; da of Anthony Romney Francis Bosworth (d 1963), of London, and Joan Lena, *née* Brett; *b* 30 June 1941; *Educ* Dominican Convent Staffs, Ely House Sch for Girls Wolverhampton, Royal Ballet Sch London, London Opera Centre; *m* 21 March 1961, Neville Jason; 1 s (Alexander b 1970), 1 da (Elinor b 1967); *Career* gallery director, singer and ballerina; work incl: Fairy Cobweb in A Midsummer Night's Dream (Old Vic) 1957, Eng Nat Opera Ballet 1959, London's Festival Ballet 1959-60, Schubert and Schumann lieder rêcital (Wigmore Hall) 1962, title role in Cinderella (Richmond Theatre) 1964, Moses and Aaron (Royal Opera House) 1965, Karl Ebert Master Class (BBC TV) 1967, alto solos and arias in St John Passion and St Matthew Passion (Bad) for Southern Opera, Handel Opera Soc and concert in Queen Elizabeth Hall, concert of Mahler Symphony No 2 and three songs 1969; curator Campbell and Franks (Fine Arts) London 1973-79, private dealer 1980-, md Gillian Jason Gallery 1981-; *awards* Br Ballet Orgn award (for Royal Ballet Sch) 1957, Vaughan-Williams Tst bursary (for London Opera Centre) 1966, Countess of Munster Tst award (for further singing studies) 1966, finalist Kathleen Ferrier Meml scholarship (RAM) 1966; memb: Soc of London Art Dealers 1990-, Ctee for 20th Century Br Art Fair 1990-; *Recreations* music, yoga, tennis, riding, roadrunning; *Style—* Mrs Gillian Jason; 42 Inverness St, London NW1 7HB (☎ 071 267 4835, fax 071 284 0614)

JASPAN, Andrew; s of Mervyn Aubrey Jaspan (d 1974), and Helen, *née* Wright; *b* 20 April 1953; *Educ* Beverley GS, Marlborough, Univ of Manchester (BA); *Career* founding ed New Manchester Review 1975-77; sub ed: Daily Telegraph 1978-80, Daily Mirror 1981; reporter journalists in Europe (Paris) 1982, sub ed and reporter The Times 1983-85, asst news ed The Sunday Times 1985-88; ed: The Sunday Times Scotland 1988, Scotland on Sunday 1989-; *Recreations* reading, squash, psychology; *Clubs* Glasgow Art; *Style—* Andrew Jaspan, Esq; Scotland on Sunday, 20 North Bridge, Edinburgh EH1 1YT (☎ 031 243 3475)

JAUNCEY, Hon James Malise Dundas; er s of Baron Jauncey of Tullichettle (Life Peer) and his 1 w Jean, *née* Cunninghame Graham (now Lady Polwarth); *b* 29 Sept 1949; *Educ* Radley, Univ of Aberdeen (LLB); *m* 1, 26 April 1980 (m dis 1986), Caroline Elizabeth, da of Charles Ede, of The Garden House, Hollington, Newbury, Berks; 2 da (Sophie Jean Elizabeth b 1980, Eleanor Fleur b 1983); m 2, 10 Sept 1988, Sarah Jacqueline, da of Lt-Col (David Ludovic) Peter Lindsay, DSO (d 1971), of Meribel Les Allues, Savoie, France; *Career* journalist, publisher and author; *Books* The Albatross Conspiracy (1990); *Recreations* skiing, music; *Style—* The Hon James Jauncey; c/o Tullichettle, Comrie, Perthshire (☎ 0764 70349)

JAUNCEY, Hon Simon Helias; yr s of Baron Jauncey of Tullichettle (Life Peer), and his 1 w Jean, *née* Cunninghame Graham (now Lady Polwarth); *b* 8 Oct 1953; *Educ* Radley, Univ of Bristol (BA); *m* 1979, Aurora, da of Juan de Jesus Castaneda, of Apartado Aereo 33394, Bogota, Colombia; 2 s (Jeremy Cunninghame b 1984, Thomas Charles b 1987); *Style—* The Hon Simon Jauncey; 128 Cavendish Drive, London E11

JAUNCEY OF TULLICHETTLE, Baron (Life Peer UK 1988), of Comrie in the District of Perth and Kinross; Charles Eliot Jauncey; PC (1988); o s of Capt John Henry Jauncey, of Tullichettle, DSO, RN (d 1958), and Muriel Charlie, eldest da of Adm Sir Charles Dundas of Dundas, KCMG, 28 Chief of Dundas; *b* 8 May 1925; *Educ* Radley, Ch Ch Oxford (MA, hon student 1990), Univ of Glasgow (LLB); *m* 1, 1948 (m dis 1969), Jean, o da of late Adm Sir Angus Edward Malise Bontine Cunninghame Graham, KBE, CB, of Ardoch, Cardross, Dunbartonshire; 2 s (Hon James Malise Dundas b 1949, Hon Simon Helias b 1953), 1 da (Hon Arabella Bridget Rachel b 1965); m 2, 1973 (m dis 1977), Elizabeth, da of Capt R H V Sivewright, DSC, RN, and wid of Maj John Ballingal, MC; m 3, 1977, (Sarah) Camilla, da of late Lt-Col Charles Frederick Cathcart, DSO (ggs of 2 Earl Cathcart); 1 da (Hon Cressida Jane b 1981); *Career* served WWII Sub Lt RNVR; advocate 1949; Kintyre Pursuivant of Arms 1955-71; QC 1963; Sheriff Principal Fife and Kinross 1971-74, judge Cts of Appeal Jersey and Guernsey 1972-79, senator Coll of Justice Scotland 1979-88, Lord of Appeal in Ordinary 1988-, Hon Master of Bench of Middle Temple 1988; memb Royal Co Archers (Queen's Bodyguard for Scotland); *Recreations* shooting, fishing, genealogy, bicycling; *Clubs* Royal (Perth); *Style—* The Rt Hon Lord Jauncey of Tullichettle, PC; Tullichettle, Comrie, Perthshire (☎ 0764 70349); 1 Plowden Buildings, Temple, London EC4 (☎ 071 583 4246)

JAVER, Monique Alicia; da of Jerold Milton Javer, and Anne Heather, *née* Clark; *b* 22 July 1967; *Educ* St Matthew's Episcopal Sch, Crocker Sch Hillsborough Calif, San Diego Univ; *Career* tennis player; professional debut 1988; represented GB: debut Maureen Connolly Brinker Cup under 21 1988, Wightman Cup 1988, Federation Cup Atlanta 1990, Euro Cup 1990 (finalist); achievements incl: winner Jr Orange Bowl under 21 Amateur Championships Calif 1984 and 1985, winner Singapore Open 1988 (semi-finalist 1989), semi-finalist Br Nats 1989, semi-finalist Virginia-Slims Arizona 1990; competed at various Grand Slam events; number one ranked collegiate player USA 1986 and 1987, number one ranked player GB 1990; *Recreations* ballet, figure skating, theatre, animals; *Style—* Miss Monique Javer; Flat 21, Buckingham Gate, London SW1 (☎ 071 828 9338); 60 Knightwood Lane, Hillsborough, Calif 94010, USA (☎ 415 344 7562, fax 415 692 4675)

JAVERI, Ratnakar Madhusudan; s of Madhusudan Vinayakrao Javeri (d 1959), of Bombay, and Shalini Madhusudan Javeri (d 1952); *b* 5 Sept 1932; *Educ* Dip Arch; *m* 20 Feb 1960, Shubhangi Ratnakar, da of Pandurang Hari Vaidya (d 1975), of Bombay; 1 s (Bharat b 1961), 1 da (Nutan b 1963); *Career* architect; lectr and prof in Bombay 1960-70, paper setter and examiner for Indian Univs 1965-68, chief architectural asst Newmarket UDC 1970-72; asst architect: Sir William Halcrow and Partners 1972-73, John Whisson and Partners Newmarket 1973-74; architect's asst Coop Soc 1975-81, practising architect Sole Principal Ilford 1982-; ARIBIA 1960, FIIA 1985, FFB 1986, FRSA 1987; *Recreations* travel, drawing, photography, music; *Style—* Ratnakar Javeri, Esq; 32 Duke Road, Barkingside, Ilford, Essex IG6 1NL (☎ 081 551 3495

JAWARA, Hon Sir Dawda Kairaba; Hon GCMG (1974); *b* 16 May 1924; *Educ* Muslim Primary Sch, Methodist GS, Achimota Coll (Vet Sch), Univ of Glasgow; *Career* princ vet offr for The Gambia govt 1957-60 (vet offr 1954-57); ldr People's Progressive Party The Gambia 1960, min of Educn 1960-61, premier 1962-63, PM 1963-70, pres The Republic of Gambia 1970-; Grand Cross Order of Lebanon 1966, Nat Order of Republic of Senegal 1967, Order of Propitious Clouds of China (Taiwan) 1968, Nat Order of Republic of Guinea 1973, Grand Offr Order of Islamic Republic of Mauritania 1967, Grand Cordon of Most Venerable Order of Knighthood Pioneers of Republic of Liberia 1968, Grand Commander Nat Order of Federal Republic of Nigeria 1970, Grand Master Order of the Republic of The Gambia 1972, Commander of Golden Ark (Netherlands) 1979, Peutinger Gold medal Peutinger-Collegium Munich 1979, Agricola medal 1980; DSc: Ife Univ, Colorado State Univ; kt 1966; *Books* Sir Dawda Speaks (1971), Sunrise in the Sahel (forthcoming); *Recreations* golf, gardening; *Style—* Hon Sir Dawda Jawara, GCMG; State House, Banjul, The Gambia

JAY, Allan Louis Neville; MBE (1970); s of Capt Lionel Stanley Goldstone, MC (ka 1943), and Vera Rebecca, *née* Esterman; *b* 30 June 1931; *Educ* Cheltenham, St Edmund Hall Oxford (BA); *m* 18 Jan 1959, Carole Patricia, da of Harry Monk; 2 da (Georgina b 1961, Felicity b 1963); *Career* sr ptnr Allan Jay & Co slrs; fencer; World Foil champion 1959, double Olympic Silver medalist at epée Rome 1960, Cwlth Foil champion 1966, non playing capt GB fencing team 1982-, many times nat champion at foil and epée; vice pres Amateur Fencing Assoc; memb Law Soc 1959; *Recreations* fencing; *Style—* Allan Jay, Esq, MBE; 17 Gurney Drive, London N2 0DF (☎ 081 455 9034)

JAY, Sir Antony Rupert; s of Ernest Jay (d 1957), of London, and Catherine Mary, *née* Hay (d 1981); *b* 20 April 1930; *Educ* St Paul's, Magdalene Coll Cambridge (BA, MA); *m* 15 June 1957, Rosemary Jill, da of Leslie Watkins, of Stratford upon Avon; 2 s (Michael b 1959, David b 1972), 2 da (Ros b 1961, Kate b 1964); *Career* Nat Serv Royal Signals 1952-54 (2 Lt 1953), Lt TA 1954; BBC 1955-64: ed Tonight 1962-63, head talks features 1963-64; ed A Prime Minister on Prime Ministers 1977; writer: Royal Family (1969), Yes Minister (3 series with Jonathan Lynn, 1980-82), Yes Prime Minister (2 series, 1985 and 1987); BAFTA Writers Award 1988; memb Annan Ctee on Future of Broadcasting 1974-77; Hon MA Sheffield 1987, Hon DBA Int Mgmnt Centre Buckingham 1988; *Books* Management and Machiavelli (1967), To England with Love (with David Frost, 1967), Effective Presentation (1970), Corporation Man (1972), The Complete Yes Minister (with Jonathan Lynn, 1984), Yes Prime Minister (1986, vol II 1987); *Style—* Sir Antony Jay; Video Arts Ltd, Dumbarton House, 68 Oxford St, London W1N 9LA (☎ 071 637 7288)

JAY, Prof Barrie Samuel; s of Maurice Bernard Jay (d 1959), of London, and Julia, *née* Sterling (d 1965); *b* 7 May 1929; *Educ* Perse Sch Cambridge, Gonville and Caius Coll Cambridge (MB BChir, MA, MD); *m* 19 Jan 1954, Marcelle Ruby, da of Alan Byre (d 1968), of Paris; 2 s (Robert b 1959, Stephen b 1961); *Career* conslt ophthalmic surgn London Hosp 1965-79, conslt surgn Moorfields Eye Hosp 1969-; dean Inst of Ophthalmology London 1980-85, conslt advsr in ophthalmology DHSS 1982-88, prof of clinical ophthalmology Univ of London 1985-; pres Faculty of Ophthalmologists 1986-88, vice pres Coll of Ophthalmologists 1988-; Liveryman: Worshipful Soc of Apothecaries (memb Ct 1985-), Worshipful Co of Barbers; FRCS 1962, FRPSL 1986, FCOphth 1988; *Books* System of Ophthalmology vol XI (jtly 1969), Postal History of Great Britain and Ireland (jtly 1981); British County Catalogue of Postal History, vols 1-5 (jtly 1978-90); *Recreations* postal history, gardening; *Style*— Prof Barrie Jay; 10 Beltane Drive, London SW19 5JR (☎ 081 947 1771)

JAY, Baron (Life Peer UK 1987), of Battersea in Greater London; Douglas Patrick Thomas Jay; PC (1952); s of Edward Aubrey Hastings Jay, OBE (d 1950), of Hampstead, London NW3; *b* 23 March 1907; *Educ* Winchester, New Coll Oxford; *m* 1, 1933 (m dis 1972), Margaret Christian, eld da of late James Clerk Maxwell Garnett, CBE; 2 s (Hon Peter b 1937, Hon Martin b 1939), 2 da (Hon Helen (Hon Mrs Pennant-Rea) b 1945, Hon Catherine (Hon Mrs Boyd) b 1945); m 2, 1972, Mary Lavinia, da of Maj Hugh Lewis Thomas, of 12 Woodlands Park, Merrow, Guildford; *Career* memb staff The Times 1929-33 and The Economist 1933-37, city ed Daily Herald 1937-40; MP (Lab): Battersea N 1946-74, Wandsworth Battersea N 1974-83; asst sec Miny of Supply 1940-43, princ asst sec BOT 1943-45; PA on econ affrs to PM 1945-46, econ sec Treasy 1947-50, fin sec Treasy 1950-51, pres BOT 1964-67; chm: Common Mkt Safeguards Campaign 1970-77, London Motorway Action Gp 1968-80; dir: Courtaulds 1967-70, Trade Union Unit Tst 1967-80; fell All Souls Coll Oxford 1968- (and 1930-37); *Books* The Socialist Case (1937), Socialism in the New Society (1962), After the Common Market (1968), Change and Fortune (1980), Sterling, A Plea for Moderation (1985); *Style*— The Rt Hon the Lord Jay, PC; Causeway Cottage, Minster Lovell, Oxford OX8 5RN (☎ 0993 775 235)

JAY, John Philip Bromberg; s of Alec Jay and (Helena) June Jay; *b* 1 April 1957; *Educ* UCS, Magdalen Coll Oxford (BA); *m* 15 Aug 1987, Susy, da of Donald Streeter; *Career* reporter Western Mail 1979-81; city reporter: Thomson Regnl Newspapers 1981-83, Sunday Telegraph 1984-86; city ed Sunday Times 1986 (dep business ed 1988), city & business ed Sunday Telegraph 1989; *Recreations* walking, cinema, theatre; *Style*— John Jay, Esq; The Sunday Telegraph, 2nd Floor, Salters Hall, 4 Fore St, London EC2Y 5DT (☎ 071 538 7901, fax 071 638 0180)

JAY, Hon Mrs (Margaret Ann); *née* Callaghan; er da of Baron Callaghan of Cardiff, KG, PC (Life Peer), *qv*; b 1939; *m* 1961 (m dis 1986), Hon Peter Jay, *qv*; 1 s, 2 da; *Career* dir Nat Aids Tst; memb and vice chm Parkside Health Authy; *Style*— The Hon Mrs Jay; 44 Blomfield Road, London W9 2PF; National Aids Trust, Euston Tower, 286 Euston Rd, London NW1 3DN

JAY, Hon Martin; yr s of Baron Jay, PC (Life Peer), *qv*; *Educ* Winchester, New Coll Oxford (BA); *m* 1969, Sandra, *née* Williams; 1 s (Adam b 1976), 2 da (Claudia b 1971, Tabitha b 1972); *Career* industrialist; chief exec Yosper Thornycroft (Holdings) plc; *Style*— The Hon Martin Jay; Bishop's Court, Bishop's Sutton, Alresford, Hants

JAY, Hon Peter; er s of Baron Jay, PC (Life Peer), *qv*; *b* 7 Feb 1937; *Educ* Winchester, ChCh Oxford (MA); *m* 1, 1961 (m dis 1986), Hon Margaret Ann Callaghan, er da of Baron Callaghan of Cardiff, KG, PC (Life Peer), *qv*; 1 s (Patrick James Peter b 1971), 2 da (Tamsin Margaret b 1965, Alice Katharine b 1968); m 2, Emma Bettina, da of Peter Kai Thornton; 2 s (Thomas Hastings b 1987, Samuel Arthur Maxwell b 1988); issue by Jane Tustian; Nicholas James Tustian b 1980; *Career* Midshipman and Sub Lt RNVR 1956-57; former pres Oxford Union; economics ed The Times 1967-77, assoc ed Times Business News 1969-77, presenter Weekend World ITV 1972-77; ambass to USA 1977-79, conslt Economist Gp 1979-81; dir Econ Intelligence Unit 1979-83; chm Nat Cncl for Voluntary Orgns 1981-; chm and chief exec TV AM 1980-83, presenter A Week in Politics 1983-86, ed Banking World 1983-86; HM Treasy: asst princ 1961-64, private sec to Jt Perm Sec 1964, princ 1964-67, economics ed: The Times 1967-77, BBC 1990-; dir: New Nat Theatre Washington DC 1979-81, Landen Press Ltd 1983-; visiting scholar Brookings Inst 1979-80, Wincott Meml lectr 1975, Copland Meml lectr 1980; COS to Robert Maxwell 1986-89; chm United Way (UK) Ltd 1982-83 and various United Way subsids; memb Cncl Cinema and TV Benevolent Fund 1982-83, govr Ditchley Fndn 1982-; holds various broadcasting honours and TV awards; *Recreations* sailing (yacht 'Norvantes'); *Clubs* Garrick; *Style*— The Hon Peter Jay; 39 Castlebar Rd, London W5 2DJ (☎ 081 998 3570)

JAY, Peter Alfred; s of Edgar Jay (d 1949), of Lancing, Sussex, and Edith, *née* Marks (d 1974); *b* 24 June 1930; *Educ* Cheltenham, Oriel Coll Oxford (BA); *m* 18 Oct 1966, Jane Ohna Campbell, da of Maj Gordon Logan Miller (d 1959), of Troon, Ayrshire; *Career* Nat Serv Sub Lt RNVR, trained Russian interpreter, later Lt Seaman Branch RNVR; fndr Peter Jay and Partners electrical conslts 1956 (later conslt engrs on bldg servs 1966), advsr to Nat Tst on electrical installation, advsr on electrical installations and lighting to Central Cncl for the Care of Churches; author of various papers and articles on lighting; chm Paddington Waterways and Maida Vale Soc 1974-88, vice pres Illuminating Engr Soc 1974-77; MInstP 1972, FIOA 1976, FCIBSE 1978, FRSA 1989; *Books* Electrical Installations (with J Hemsley, 1962); *Recreations* music; *Style*— Peter Jay, Esq; 1 Penfold Place, London NW1 6RJ (☎ 071 262 3147, fax 071 723 1559)

JAYACHANDRA, Dr Chickaballapur Reddiyappa; s of Chickaballapur Reddiyappa (d 1931), and Lakshmamma, *née* Kempaiah (d 1979); *b* 21 Nov 1928; *Educ* in India (MB BS); *m* 6 Sept 1961, Sujaya, da of Nanjunda Gowda (d 1977); *Career* paediatric registrar Walton Hosp and Childrens Hosp Liverpool 1961-67, conslt paediatrician NW RHA 1968-; memb Oldham Health Authy 1977-87; memb BPA 1969, FRCPE 1986; *Books* Child Management: Five Universal Basic Principles (1988); *Recreations* gardening, tennis, badminton; *Style*— Dr Chickaballapur Jayachandra; The Royal Oldham Hospital, Oldham, Lancs (☎ 061 624 0420)

JAYAWANT, Prof Bhalchandra Vinayak; s of (Rao Saheb) Vinayak Laxman Jayawant (d 1971), of Nagpur, India, and Indira Jayawant (d 1948); *b* 22 April 1930; *Educ* Univ of Bombay (BE), Univ of Bristol (PhD), Univ of Sussex (DSc); *m* 3 Sept 1960, (Elizabeth) Monica, da of George William Bowdler (d 1985); 1 s (Richard Anthony b 4 April 1962), 1 da (Frances Rachael b 12 Aug 1964); *Career* jr engr Metropolitan Vickers Manchester 1956-60, lectr in electrical engrg Queen's Univ Belfast 1960-65, dean Sch of Engrg Univ of Sussex 1985- (reader electrical engrg 1965-72, prof of electrical engrg 1972-); IEE: chm Sussex Centre, chm Computing and Control Div, memb Cncl; Sir Harold Hartley Medal 1988; FIEE, FInstMC; *Books* Induction Machines (1968), Electromagnetic Suspension and Levitation Techniques; *Recreations* walking on the Downs, French wines; *Style*— Prof Bhalchandra Jayawant; School of Engineering and Applied Sciences, University of Sussex, Falmer, Brighton BN1 9QT (☎ 0273 606755, fax 0273 678 399, telex 878358 ENGINE G)

JAYES, Anthony Peter; s of Grayson Jayes (d 1982), of Walsall, and Doris Ada, *née* Green (d 1985); *b* 11 May 1939; *Educ* Elmore Green HS Bloxwich Walsall, Univ of London (LLB); *m* 4 June 1966, Mary Patricia, da of Thomas Donaghy, of Aldridge, W Midlands; 1 s (Stephen Charles b 12 Feb 1968), 1 da (Ursula Frances b 2 Jan 1972); *Career* articled clerk Ridsale Cozens & Purslow CAs Walsall 1956-62, Peat Marwick Mitchell & Co 1962-64, Cooper Bros 1962-64, princ lectr in taxation Sandwell Coll 1964-; practising CA then ptnr Jayes Scriven & Co Rugeley Staffs; hon auditor: Beaudesert Tst 1965-75, Rugeley CAB 1984-87; treas local branch Cons and Unionist Pty 1974-88; hon auditor Colwich and Little Haywood Village Hall 1982-; qualified MCC coach 1983; FCA 1962, ATII 1965; *Recreations* village cricket club; *Clubs* Uttoxeter Golf; *Style*— Anthony Jayes, Esq; Pennycroft, The Orchard, Coley Lane, Little Haywood, Stafford ST18 0UJ (☎ 0889 882 641); Jayes Scriven & Co, Chartered Accountants, Crossley Stone, Rugeley, Staffs (☎ 08894 577743)

JAYSON, Prof Malcolm Irving Vivian; *b* 9 Dec 1937; *Educ* Middx Hosp Sch, Univ of London (MB BS), Univ of Bristol (MD, MRCP); *m* 1 July 1962, Judith; 2 s (Gordon b 1963, Robert b 1966); *Career* lectr and sr lectr in med (rheumatology) Univ of Bristol and Royal Nat Hosp for Rheumatic Disease Bath 1967-77, prof of rheumatology and dir of Rheumatism Res Laboratories Univ of Manchester 1977-; sec gen Int Back Pain Soc; FRCP 1969, RSM; *Books* Total Hip Replacement (1971), Stills Disease: Juvenile Chronic Polyarthritis (1976), Collagen In Health and Disease (1982), Locomotor Disability In General Practise (1983), Lumbar Spine and Back Pain (1987), Back Pain - The Facts (1987), Rheumatism and Arthritis (1991); *Recreations* antiques, music, trout fishing; *Style*— Prof Malcolm Jayson; The Gate House, 8 Lancaster Rd, Didsbury, Manchester M20 8TY (☎ 061 445 1729); Rheumatic Diseases Centre, Hope Hospital, Eccles Old Rd, Salford M6 8HD (☎ 061 787 4369, fax 061 787 7432)

JEANNERET, Hon Mrs (Marian Elizabeth); da of Baron Hobson (Life Peer, d 1966); *b* 1942; *Educ* Newnham Coll Cambridge (MA, PhD); *m* 1968, Michel Jeanneret; *Style*— The Hon Mrs Jeanneret; 18 South Vale, London SE19 (☎ 081 771 5094)

JEANS, Michael Henry Vickery; s of Henry Tendron Wilson Jeans, of Bullaven, 24 Woodside Ave, Walton-on-Thames, Surrey, and Joan Kathleen, *née* Vickery; *b* 14 March 1943; *Educ* St Edward's Sch Oxford, Univ of Bristol (BA); *m* 1, 27 June 1970 (m dis 1981), Iris Carla, da of Franco Dell'Acqua, of Milan, Italy; m 2, 12 Jan 1987, Paula Wendy, da of David Arthur Spraggs, of Thorpe Bay, Essex; 1 s (James b 25 Aug 1987), 1 da (Rebecca (twin) b 25 Aug 1987); *Career* CA; trainee accountant Peat Marwick McLintock (formerly Peat Marwick Mitchell) 1964-67, asst accountant Blue Circle Group 1967-70, ptnr KPMG Peat Marwick McLintock 1981- (conslt 1970-); govr Haberdashers' Aske's Sch Elstree, memb St Matthews Bayswater PCC; Freeman City of London 1965; Liveryman: Worshipful Co of Haberdashers 1965 (memb Ct 1985), Worshipful Co of CAs 1991; pres Inst of Mgmnt Conslts 1990-91 (fell 1970); FCMA 1971, FCA 1967, MMS 1984; *Recreations* tennis, opera, theatre, Italy; *Clubs* Kingston Rowing, Mensa, Soc of London Ragamuffins; *Style*— M H V Jeans, Esq; 36 Bark Place, Bayswater, London W2 4AT (☎ 071 229 7303); KPMG Peat Marwick McLintock, 8 Salisbury Square, Blackfriars, London EC4Y 8BB (☎ 071 236 8000, fax 071 248 6552, telex 8811541 PMMLON G)

JEAPES, Maj Gen Anthony Showan (Tony); CB (1987), OBE (1977), MC (1959); s of Stanley Arthur Bernard (d 1971), and Dorothy Irene, *née* Showan (d 1979); *b* 6 March 1935; *Educ* Raynes Park GS, RMA Sandhurst, Staff Coll Camberley, NDC Latimer; *m* 1959, Jennifer Clare, da of Lt-Col O G W White, DSO, OBE (d 1975); 1 s (Benjamin Patrick b 1965), 1 da (Antonia Clare b 1968); *Career* enlisted 1953, cmmnd Dorset Regt 1955, joined 22 Special Air Serv Regt Malaya 1958; serv: Oman and Trucial States, India, Kenya, USA, Malaysia; DS Army Staff Coll 1972-74, CO 22 SAS Regt 1974-77, BMAT Bangladesh 1977-79, dep cmdt Sch of Inf 1979-81, cmd 5 Airborne Bde 1982-85, cmd LF NI 1985-87, GOC SW Dist 1987-90 (ret); *Books* SAS: Operation Oman (1981); *Recreations* offshore sailing, country pursuits; *Clubs* Army and Navy; *Style*— Maj Gen Tony Jeapes, CB, OBE, MC; c/o National Westminster Bank, 80 Market Place, Warminster

JEBB, Lionel Richard; s of Richard Lewthwaite Jebb (d 1961), of The Lyth, Ellesmere, and Marjorie Joy, *née* Jacobs; *b* 21 Dec 1934; *Educ* Shrewsbury, Merton Coll Oxford (MA); *m* 28 May 1960, Corinna Margaret, da of late Charles Peter Elmhirst Hawkesworth, of Aldborough House, Boroughbridge, N Yorks; 2 s (Richard b 1961, Andrew b 1966), 1 da (Sophie b 1963); *Career* farmer and landowner; memb: Shropshire CC 1970-81 (chm Resources Sub Ctee 1978-81), Cncl CLA 1975-88; chm Shropshire: Branch CLA 1985-88, Ctee of COSIRA 1982-, Rural Devpt Forum 1985-, Conservation Devpt Tst 1981-88; lay chm Ellesmere Deanery Synod 1970-74 and 1980-85, vice chm Walford Coll of Agric 1981-88, chm Adcote Sch Shrewsbury 1989-; memb: Rural Voice 1981-88, Rural Employment Gp, NEDC Agric Sector Gp 1987-89, Shropshire Trg and Enterprise Cncl 1990-, Shropshire Regnl Bd Prince's Youth Business Tst 1989; *Recreations* conservation, shooting; *Clubs* Royal Overseas League; *Style*— L R Jebb, Esq; The Lyth, Ellesmere, Shropshire SY12 0HR

JEBB, Hon Miles Alvery Gladwyn; s and h of 1 Baron Gladwyn, GCMG, GCVO, CB, qv; *b* 3 March 1930; *Educ* Eton, Magdalen Coll Oxford (MA); *Career* 2 Lt Welsh Gds, Pilot Offr RAFVR; sr mgmnt with British Airways until 1983; *Books* The Thames Valley Heritage Walk (1980), A Guide to the South Downs Way (1984), Walkers (1986), A Guide to the Thames Path (1988), East Anglia, an Anthology (1990); *Recreations* long distance walking; *Clubs* Brooks's, Beefsteak; *Style*— The Hon Miles Jebb; E1 Albany, Piccadilly, London W1V 9RH

JEBB, Dom (Anthony) Philip; s of Reginald Douglas Jebb, MC (d 1977), of King's Land, Shipley, Horsham, Sussex, and Eleanor Philippa (d 1979), da of Hilaire Belloc; *b* 14 Aug 1932; *Educ* Downside, Christ's Coll Cambridge (MA); *Career* clothed as a monk of Downside 1950, ordained priest 1956, curate Midsomer Norton 1960-62, headmaster Downside Sch 1980-91 (teacher 1960-, housemaster 1962-75, dep headmaster 1975-80), prior Monastic Community of Downside 1991-; archivist and annalist English Benedictine Congregation 1972-; memb: Cncl Somerset Records Soc 1975-, Univ of Bath 1983-87, Ctee area 7 Secdy Heads Assoc 1984-87, HMC, SHA; Chaplain Magistral Obedience Br Assoc SMOM 1978; chm: EBC Theol Cmmn 1979-82 (memb 1969-82), SW Div HMC 1988; del to Gen Chapter EBC 1980-; vice pres SW Amateur Fencing Assoc, princ speaker AGM of W1 in The Albert Hall 1988; *Books* Missale de Lesnes (ed, 1964), Religious Education (ed, 1968), Widowed (1973), Consider Your Call (contrib, 1978), A Touch of God (contrib, 1982), By Death Parted (ed 1986); *Recreations* fencing, archaeology, cosmology, canoeing; *Clubs* East India, Stratton-on-the-Fosse Cricket (pres); *Style*— Dom Philip Jebb; Downside Abbey, Stratton-on-the-Fosse, Bath BA3 4RJ (☎ 0761 232 206)

JEEPS, Richard Eric Gautrey; CBE (1977); s of Francis Herbert Jeeps, MC, of Willingham, Cambridge, and Mildred Mary Eileen Jeeps; *b* 25 Nov 1931; *Educ* Bedford Modern Sch; *m* 1, 1954 (m dis), Jean; 3 da (Deborah Margaret (Mrs Jarvis) b 1956, Caroline Anne b 1958, Louise Elizabeth b 1963); m 2, 1985 (m dis), Janet; m 3, 1989, (Charmaine) Jennifer; *Career* chm Sports Cncl of GB 1978-84; rugby career: Cambridge City 1948-49, Northampton 1949-62 and 1964, Eastern Counties 1950-62, England 1956-62 (24 caps), Barbarians 1958-62, British Lions (13 caps: SA 1955 and 1962, NZ 1959); pres R F U Twickenham 1976-77 (memb Ctee 1962-); *Recreations* golf; *Clubs* Newmarket Golf, Cambridge Rugby; *Style*— Richard Jeeps, Esq, CBE; Stocks Restaurant, 78 High St, Bottisham, Cambridge (☎ 0223 811202)

JEEVES, Prof Malcolm Alexander; s of Alexander Frederic Thomas Jeeves (d 1977), and Helena May, *née* Hammond (d 1975); *b* 16 Nov 1926; *Educ* Stamford Sch, St John's Coll Cambridge (BA, MA, PhD), Harvard; *m* 7 April 1955, Ruth Elisabeth, da of Oscar Cecil Hartridge (d 1983); 2 da (Sarah b 1958, Joanna b 1961); *Career* Army 1945-48, cmmnd Royal Lincs Regt, served 1 Bn Sherwood Foresters BAOR; lectr Dept of Psychology Univ of Leeds 1956-59, fndn prof and head of Dept of Psychology Univ of Adelaide S Aust 1959-69 (dean Faculty of Arts 1963-64), fndn prof of psychology Univ of St Andrews 1969- (vice princ 1981-85); ed in chief Neuropsychologia 1990-; pres: Int Neuropsychological Symposium 1985-, Psychology Section Br Assoc for the Advancement of Sci 1988-89; memb: Cncl Sci and Engrg Res Cncl 1985-89, Neuroscience and Mental Health Bd MRC 1985-89; vice pres Royal Soc Edinburgh 1990- (memb Cncl 1986-89); Hon Sheriff E Lothian and Tayside; memb Experimental Psychology Soc, FRSE 1980, FBPsS 1958; *Books* Thinking in Structures (with Z P Dienes, 1965), The Effects of Structural Relations upon Transfer (with Z P Dienes, 1968), The Scientific Enterprise and Christian Faith (1969), Experimental Psychology: an Introduction For Biologists (1974), Psychology and Christianity: the view both ways (1976), Analysis of Structural Learning (with G B Greer, 1983), Free to be Different (with R J Berry and D Atkinson, 1984), Behavioural Sciences: A Christian Perspective (1984), Psychology - Through the Eyes of Faith (with D G Myers, 1987); *Recreations* fly-fishing, music, walking; *Style*— Prof Malcolm Jeeves; 7 Hepburn Gardens, St Andrews, Fife, Scotland (☎ 0334 73545); Department of Psychology, University of St Andrews, St Andrews, Fife, Scotland KY16 9JU (☎ 0334 76161 ext 7173, fax 0334 77441)

JEEWOOLALL, Sir Ramesh; s of Shivprasad Jeewoolall; *b* 20 Dec 1940; *Educ* Mauritius Inns of Court Law Sch; *m* 1971, Usweenee Reetoo; 2 s; *Career* called to the Bar Middle Temple 1968, magistrate 1971-72; chm Mauritius Tea Devpt Authy 1972-76; memb Mauritius Parl 1976-, speaker House of Assembly 1979-; kt 1979; *Style*— Sir Ramesh Jeewoolall; Q1, Farquhar Ave, Quatre Bornes, Mauritius (☎ 4 5918)

JEFFARES, Prof Alexander Norman (Derry); s of Cecil Norman Jeffares (d 1950), and Agnes, *née* Fraser (d 1970); *b* 11 Aug 1920; *Educ* HS Dublin, Trinity Coll Dublin (BA, MA, PhD), Oriel Coll Oxford (MA, DPhil); *m* 29 July 1947, Jeanne Agnes, da of Emil Calembert (d 1932), of Brussels; 1 da (Felicity Anne b 1 Jan 1949); *Career* lectr in classics Trinity Coll Dublin 1943-44, lectr in Eng Groningen Univ 1946-48, lectr Univ of Edinburgh 1949-51, Jury prof of Eng Univ of Adelaide S Aust 1951-56, prof of Eng lit Univ of Leeds 1957-74, prof of Eng studies Univ of Stirling 1974-86; md Academy Advisory Services Ltd 1970-, dir Colin Smthe Ltd 1978-; vice pres Film & TV Cncl S Aust 1951-56; vice chm: Muckhart Community Cncl 1976-86, Scottish Arts Cncl 1978-84; pres PEN Scotland 1986-89, chm Book Tst Scotland 1985-88, vice pres The Royal Soc of Edinburgh 1988-90; memb ACGB 1980-84, life fell Assoc for Cwlth Lit and Language Studies (chm 1966-68), hon life pres Int Assoc for the Study of Anglo-Irish Lit 1973-; FAHA 1970, FRSL 1965, FRSE 1981, FRSA 1963, AM 1988; *Books* W B Yeats: Man and Poet (1949, 1966), A Commentary on the Collected Poems of Yeats (1968), The Circus Animals (1970), A Commentary on the Collected Plays of Yeats (with A S Knowland, 1975), Restoration Drama (4 vols, 1974), A History of Anglo-Irish Literature (1982), Poems of Yeats: A New Selection (1984, 1987), Brought Up in Dublin (poems, 1987), Brought Up to Leave (poems 1987), W B Yeats, A New Biography (1988), Yeats's Poems (1989), W B Yeats, A Vision (1990), W B Yeats, The Love Poems (1990); *Recreations* drawing, motoring, restoring old houses; *Clubs* Athenaeum, Royal Cwlth Soc; *Style*— Prof Derry Jeffares, FRSE; Craighead Cottage, Fifeness, Crail, Fife (☎ 0333 50898)

JEFFCOATE, Sir (Thomas) Norman Arthur; s of Arthur Jeffcoate (d 1914), of Nuneaton; *b* 25 March 1907; *Educ* King Edward VI Sch Nuneaton, Univ of Liverpool (MB ChB, MD); *m* 1937, Josephine Lindsay (d 1981); 4 s; *Career* conslt obstetrician and gynaecologist Royal Liverpool Utd Hosp 1932-72, prof of obstetrics and gynaecology Univ of Liverpool 1945-72, emeritus prof 1972-; pres RCOG 1969-72; kt 1970; *Books* Principles of Gynaecology (1957, 5 edn 1987, renamed Jeffcoate's Principles of Gynaecology); *Style*— Sir Norman Jeffcoate; 6 Riversdale Rd, Liverpool, Merseyside LI9 3QW (☎ 051 427 1448)

JEFFCOATE, Dr William James; s of Prof Sir Norman Jeffcoate; *b* 31 May 1947; *Educ* Liverpool Coll, St John's Coll Cambridge (MA), Middx Hosp Med Sch (MB BChir); *Career* conslt physician and endocrinologist City Hosp Nottingham 1979-; FRCP; *Style*— Dr William Jeffcoate; Nottingham City Hospital, Hucknall Rd, Nottingham NG5 1PB (☎ 0602 691169)

JEFFCOCK, David Philip; s of William Philip Jeffcock (d 1963), of Worlingham Grove, Suffolk, and Margaret Renée, *née* Cayley (d 1975); *b* 8 July 1933; *Educ* Ampleforth, Trinity Coll Cambridge (BA); *m* 14 Dec 1963, Josephine Anne, da of Maj Harold George Warde-Norbury (d 1974), of Hooton Pagnell Hall, Doncaster; 2 s (John b 1968, George b 1970), 2 da (Venetia b 1964, Cordelia b 1965); *Career* Parly candidate 1964; co-author various pubns on tax and law reform for Sir Alec Douglas-Home 1965; patron Court Jeffcock AOF; memb: The Stock Exchange 1971-, The Securities Assoc 1990-; *Recreations* books, history, music, racing; *Style*— David Jeffcock, Esq; Wellington House, Captains Row, Lymington, Hampshire SO41 9RR (☎ 0590 672237, fax 0590 673592); c/o Greig Middleton & Co Ltd, 66 Wilson St, London EC2A 2BL (☎ 071 247 0007, fax 071 377 0353)

JEFFERIES, David George; CBE; s of George Jefferies (d 1981), of Upminster, Essex, and Emma, *née* Braybrook (d 1979); *b* 26 Dec 1933; *m* 12 Dec 1959, Jeanette Ann (Jean); *Career* chief engr Southern Electric 1972-74, dir NW Region CEGB 1974-77, dir of personnel CECB 1977-81, chm LEB 1981-86, dep chm Electricity Cncl 1986-90; chm: National Grid Co plc 1990-, Electricity Supply Pension Ltd; Freeman City of London 1982, Liveryman Worshipful Co of Wax Chandlers; FEng, FIEE, CBIM, FInstE; *Recreations* golf, gardening, music; *Clubs* Athenaeum, RAC, Foxhills; *Style*— David Jefferies, Esq, CBE; The National Grid Company plc, National Grid House, Sumner St, London SE1 9JU (☎ 071 620 8323)

JEFFERIES, James (Jim); s of James Jefferies, of Wallyford, Midlothian, and Helen, *née* Johnstone; *b* 22 Nov 1950; *Educ* Musselburgh GS; *m* 24 June 1972, Linda, da of Joseph Sidonio; 1 s (Calum b 10 March 1983), 1 da (Louise b 19 Nov 1980); *Career* professional football manager; player Heart of Midlothian 1967-81: professional 1969, debut v East Fife 1972, latterly capt; mangr: Berwick Rangers 1988-90 (player 1981-84), Falkirk 1990-; honours with Hearts: runners up Scot Cup 1976, Scot Div 1 Championship 1980 (capt); mangr of the month Dec 1990; insurance sales mangr 1984-90; *Recreations* golf (club champion 9 times); *Style*— Jim Jefferies, Esq; Brockville Park, Cooperage Lane, Hope St, Falkirk (☎ 0324 24121, fax 0324 612418)

JEFFERIES, Col Patrick Hugh Mostyn; s of Norman Jefferies (d 1952), and Anne Isobel, *née* Lucas (d 1974); *b* 22 Sept 1919; *Educ* Bromsgrove, RMC Sandhurst; *m* 6 Oct 1945, (Adelaide) Elizabeth (d 1970), da of Daniel Edward Buckney (d 1964), of Seaford, Sussex; 2 s (Hugh b 1948, Paul b 1953), 1 da (Clare b 1951); *Career* WWII cmmnd Worcs Regt 1939, India 1939-44, BAOR 1945-50, Staff Coll Camberley 1951, GHQ Middle East 1952-55, MOD 1956-59, cdr 4 Bn Queen's Own Nigeria Regt 1960-62, HQ Allied Mobile Force NATO 1963-66, mil attaché Tehran and Kabul 1967-70, HQ Northern Army Gp NATO 1970-73; *Recreations* growing vines and making wine; *Clubs* Army and Navy; *Style*— Col Patrick Jefferies; Puck's Hill, Lulsley, Knightwick, Worcestershire WR6 5QW (☎ 0886 21665)

JEFFERIES, Patrick Vernon; s of Lt-Col Frederick William, of 35 Kings Rd, Barnet, Herts, and Barbara Millicent, *née* Short; *b* 12 June 1935; *Educ* Haileybury, Law Socs Sch of Law; *m* 26 May 1962, Angela Margaret, da of Capt George Francis Hounslow Blunt, of The Priory, Abbotskerswell, Newton Abbot, Devon; 2 da (Margo b 1966, Anna b 1969); *Career* Nat Serv 2 Lt RA 1958-60; admitted slr 1958, sr ptnr Merton Jones Lewsey & Jefferies 1979-; memb Law Soc, veteran memb HAC 1965; Freeman City of London 1966, Liveryman Worshipful Co of Merchant Taylors 1976; *Recreations* sailing, DIY; *Clubs* HAC Mess, Bosham Sailing; *Style*— Patrick Jefferies, Esq; Shamrock Cottage, Bosham Lane, Bosham, Chichester, W Sussex PO18 8HG; 13 Finchley Lodge, Gainsborough Rd, London N12 8AL; 753 High Rd, London N12 8LG (☎ 081 446 4301, fax 081 446 5117)

JEFFERIES, Roger David; s of George Edward Jefferies, of Tetbury, Glos, and Freda Rose, *née* Marshall; *b* 13 Oct 1939; *Educ* Whitgift Sch Croydon, Balliol Coll Oxford (BA, BCL); *m* 1, 1962 (m dis 1974), Jennifer Anne, da of Leslie Ernest Southgate (d 1984), of Rowhedge, Essex; 1 s (William b 1965), 2 da (Sophie b 1967, Polly b 1970); m 2, 1974 (m dis 1984), Margaret Sealy, *née* Pointer; m 3, 1984, Pamela Mary Elsey, da of Benjamin Arnet Holden, of Harpenden, Herts; 1 s (Harry b 1986); *Career* articled clerk to Sir Charles Barratt town clerk Coventry 1961-64, admitted slr 1965, asst slr Coventry City Cncl 1965-68, asst town clerk Southend Co Borough Cncl 1968-70, dir Ops London Borough of Hammersmith 1970-75, chief exec London Borough of Hounslow 1975-90; chief exec London Borough of Croydon 1990-; clerk: Mortlake Crematorium Bd 1973-90, W London Waste Authy 1986-90; under-sec (on secondment) DOE 1983-85; sec Hounslow Arts Tst 1975-90; memb: Cncl RIPA 1982-88, Bd of Pub Fin Fndn 1987-, Regnl Advsy Ctee Arts Cncl 1984-88; tstee South African Advanced Educn Project 1989-, dir Extemporary Dance Co 1989-91, pres Soc of Local Authy Chief Execs 1990-91; memb Law Soc 1975; *Books* Tackling the Town Hall (1982); *Recreations* theatre, cooking, growing vegetables; *Style*— Roger Jefferies, Esq

JEFFERIES, Sheelagh; CBE (1987); da of Norman Jefferies (d 1944), and Vera, *née* Bradley (d 1954); *b* 25 Aug 1926; *Educ* Harrogate GS, Girton Coll Cambridge (MA), Smith Coll Northampton Mass USA (MA); *Career* archivist RIIA 1947-50 and 1951-52; info offr: COI 1953-60, Office of the Chllr of the Duchy of Lancaster 1960-61; press offr PM's Office 1961-67, princ info offr Privy Cncl Office 1967-69, chief press offr Miny of Housing of Local Govt 1969-71, head of Parly liaison then head of news Dept of the Environment 1971-74, chief info offr Dept of Prices & Consumer Protection 1974-77; COI: dir of overseas press and radio 1977-78, controller (Home) 1978-83, dep dir gen 1983-86, actg dir gen Jan-June 1987; media conslt WRVS HQ 1988-; FIPR 1986, FCAM 1989; *Style*— Ms Sheelagh Jefferies, CBE; 6 Eversfield Rd, Richmond, Surrey TW9 2AP (☎ 081 940 9229)

JEFFERIES, Stephen; s of George Frederick Jefferies, of Birmingham, and Kitty Barbara, *née* Salisbury; *b* 24 June 1951; *Educ* Royal Ballet Sch (Upper); *m* 1972, Rashna, da of Homi B Minocher Homji; 1 s (Christopher b 1985), 1 da (Lara b 1982); *Career* all maj roles with the Royal Ballet & Nat Ballet of Canada, 22 roles created; ARAD Hons; *Recreations* golf; *Style*— Stephen Jefferies, Esq; Royal Opera House, Covent Garden, London WC2 (☎ 071 240 1200)

JEFFERISS, Christopher David; s of Cdr Derek Jefferiss, TD (d 1987), and Vivien Margaret, *née* Hodges (d 1983); *b* 18 Nov 1940; *Educ* Sherborne, Middx Hosp Univ of London (MB BS); *m* 16 April 1966, Madlen Elizabeth Prys, da of William Prys Roberts, of Old Abbey Court, Exeter; 1 s (Frederic b 1968), 2 da (Elizabeth b 1970, Emily b 1974); *Career* SHO Middx and Central Hosps 1964-66, surgical registrar W Dorset Hosps 1966-69, registrar and sr registrar Southwest RHA 1970-76, conslt orthopaedic surgn Exeter 1976-; articles in med and legal press on: orthopaedics, hand surgery, med litigation; memb: BMA, BSSH, BOA, Medicolegal Soc; FRCS 1970; *Style*— Christopher Jefferiss, Esq; 15 Southernhay East, Exeter, Devon EX1 (☎ 0392 54515)

JEFFERS, Prof John Norman Richard; s of Lt-Col J H Jeffers, OBE (d 1980), of Woodhall Spa, Lincs, and Emily Matilda Alice, *née* Robinson (d 1974); *b* 10 Sept 1926; *Educ* Portsmouth GS, Benmore Forestry Sch Dunoon; *m* 25 July 1951, Edna May, da of Earnest Reginald Parratt (d 1973), of Farnham, Surrey; 1 da (Ysanne b 11 July 1963); *Career* Forestry Cmmn: res forester 1944-53, princ statistician 1953-68, dir Merlewood Res Station Nature Conservancy 1968-73; Inst of Terrestrial Ecology (NERC): dep dir 1973-75, dir 1976-86; visiting prof: Dept of Chemical and Process Engineering Univ of Newcastle 1990-, Maths Inst Univ of Kent 1988-; hon prof Cmmn for Integrated Survey of Nat Resources Academia Sinica Peoples Republic of China; memb Grange and Dist Concert Club, memb PCC; DSc (honouris causa) Univ of Lancaster; memb Biometric Soc; FIS, FRSS, FIBiol, FCHIFOR; *Books* Experimental Design and Analysis in Forestry (1953), An Introduction to Systems Analysis: with ecological examples (1978), Modelling (1982), Practitioner's handbook on the modelling of dynamic change in ecosystems (1988); *Recreations* military history; *Clubs* Athenaeum; *Style*— Prof John Jeffers; Ellerhow, Lindale, Grange-over-Sands, Cumbria LA11 6NA (☎ 05395 33731)

JEFFERS, Raymond Jackson; s of George Dennis Jeffers, of Albany, Ipswich, Suffolk, and Jeannine, *née* Jacquier; *b* 5 Aug 1954; *Educ* Stanwell Sch Penarth, Aberystwyth Univ Coll of Wales (LLB), Wadham Coll Oxford (BCL); *m* 4 Sept 1982, Carol Elizabeth, da of John Bernard Awty, of Freshwater, IOW; *Career* admitted slr 1980, ptnr Corporate Dept Linklaters & Paines 1986-; memb Employment Law Sub-Ctee City of London Slrs Co 1987 (memb Commercial Law Sub-Ctee 1986); memb Law Soc 1980; *Recreations* ornithology, badminton, golf, tennis; *Style*— Raymond Jeffers, Esq; Barrington House, 59-67 Gresham St, London EC2V 7JA (☎ 071 606 7080, fax 071 606 5113, telex 884349/888167)

JEFFERSON, (John) Bryan; CB (1989), CBE (1983); s of John Jefferson (d 1940), of Sheffield, Yorks, and Marjorie, *née* Oxley; *b* 26 April 1928; *Educ* Lady Manners Sch Bakewell Derbyshire, Univ of Sheffield (Dip Arch); *m* 26 July 1954 (m dis 1965), Alison Mary, da of Basil Gray (d 1960); 3 s (Timothy b 1955, David b 1958, Peter b 1960); *Career* Nat Serv RAF 1948-50; asst Morrison and Partners Derby 1956-57, estab practice Sheffield 1957, Jefferson Sheard and Partners (London, Sheffield, Peterborough) 1960-84; DOE 1984-: dir gen Design Property Servs Agency, chief architectural advsr to Sec of State for Environment; pres Sheffield Soc of Architects 1973-74, chm RIBA Yorks Region 1974-75, pres Concrete Soc 1977-78, pres RIBA 1979-81; Freeman City of London 1982; Hon Doctorate in Civil Engrg Univ of Bradford 1987; RIBA 1954, RSA 1983, hon FRAIC 1981; *Recreations* sailing, music, skiing; *Clubs* Royal Western Yacht; *Style*— Bryan Jefferson, Esq, CB, CBE; 6 St Andrews Mansions, Dorset St, London W1H 3FD (☎ 071 486 6219); Department of Environment, 2 Marsham St, London SW1P (☎ 071 276 3625)

JEFFERSON, David John; s of Edward Hemmings Jefferson (d 1959), of Maidenhead, Berks, and Margaret Agatha, *née* Young (d 1977); *b* 14 June 1932; *Educ* Windsor GS, Coll of Law; *m* 6 Jan 1962, Barbara Anne, da of Richard Bevington Cooper, of Arnside, Cumbria, 1 s (Peter b 1968), 2 da (Sarah b 1963, Lucy b 1970); *Career* 2 Lt Intelligence Corps 1957-58; sr ptnr Maxwell Batley Slrs 1985- (ptnr 1963-); memb Cncl Law Soc 1968-, chm Incorporated Cncl of Law Reporting for England and Wales 1987-; memb: Datchet Parish Cncl 1965-83 (chm 1971-73), Eton RDC 1967-74, Royal Borough of Windsor and Maidenhead Cncl 1974-83; chm Church Adoption Soc 1977-88; Freeman City of London 1969, Liveryman Worshipful Co of Slrs 1969; memb Law

Soc 1957; *Recreations* conversation, music, ballet, opera, theatre, swimming, skiing, collecting books, drawings and water colours; *Clubs* Special Forces, Royal Thames Yacht, City of London, Leander; *Style—* David Jefferson, Esq; The Vyne, Deep Field, Datchet, Berks SL3 9JS (☎ 0753 43087); Maxwell Batley, 27 Chancery Lane, London WC2A 1PA (☎ 071 405 7888, fax 071 242 7133, telex 28717)

JEFFERSON, Sir George Rowland; CBE (1969); s of Harold Jefferson, and Eva Elizabeth Ellen; *b* 26 March 1921; *Educ* Dartford GS; *m* 1943, Irene, da of Frederick Watson-Browne; 3 s; *Career* REME; dir: Br Aerospace (former chm and md Dynamics Gp), Br Scandinavian Aviation, Hawker Siddeley Dynamics; memb NEB 1979-80; dep chm Post Office 1980, dir Babcock Int 1980-87, chm BT 1981-87, non exec dir Lloyds Bank plc 1986-, chm Matthew Hall plc 1987-88; memb: NEDC 1981-84, NICG 1980-84; Freeman City of London; Hon DSc Univ of Bristol 1984, Hon DUniv of Essex 1985; FEng, Hon FIMechE, FIEE, FRAeS, FRSA, CBIM, FCGI; kt 1981; *Style—* Sir George Jefferson, CBE

JEFFERSON, Joan Ena; da of William Jefferson, and Ruth Ena, *née* Leake; *b* 15 Aug 1946; *Educ* Univ of Newcastle (BA), Westminster Coll Oxford (DipEd); *Career* head of history Scarbrouogh Girls HS 1970-73 (asst mistress 1968-70), head of humanities Graham Sch Scarborough 1973-75; headmistress: Humanby Hall Sch Filey 1979-86 (dep headmistress 1975-79), St Swithun's Sch Winchester 1986-; dep chm Common Entrance Bd; memb: Cncl GSA, Bloxham Project Steering Ctee; *Recreations* drama, theatre, reading, cooking, photography; *Clubs* Royal Commonwealth Soc; *Style—* Miss Joan Jefferson

JEFFERY, Brian Maurice; s of Maurice Frank Jeffery (d 1968); *b* 24 June 1941; *Educ* Northampton GS, Univ of Birmingham; *m* 1963, Susan, *née* Fearn; 1 s, 1 da; *Career* chm and md Swift and Co Ltd 1978-81, chief exec Alfred Marks Gp 1981-; *Recreations* sport, music; *Clubs* RAC, Durrant's; *Style—* Brian Jeffery, Esq; The Tumbles, Hersham, Bude, Cornwall (☎ 028 882 251); Alfred Marks Bureau Ltd, ADIA House, 84-86 Regent St, London W1R 5PA (☎ 071 437 7855, telex 298240)

JEFFERY, David John; s of Stanley John Friend Jeffery (d 1972), and Sylvia May, *née* Mashford; *b* 18 Feb 1936; *Educ* Sutton HS Plymouth, RNC Greenwich, Croydon Coll of Technol, RCDS; *m* 28 March 1959, Margaret, da of George Yates (d 1983); 1 s (Christopher b 6 Aug 1968), 2 da (Karen b 6 Sept 1962, Susan b 27 July 1964); *Career* Nat Serv RAOC 1954-56; Admty dir Stores Dept 1956-66 (Devonport, Risley, Singapore, London), MOD 1968-70, princ Treasy Centre for Admin Studies 1970-72, mgmnt sci trg advsr Malaysian Govt Kuala Lumpur 1972-74, princ Civil Serv Dept 1974-76, sr princ MOD 1976-80, asst sec 1980-84, dir Armaments and Mgmnt Servs RN Supply and Tport Serv 1984-86; chief exec river and bd memb Port of London Authy 1986-; chm PLACON Ltd 1987-; tstee dir Pilots Nat Pension Fund 1988-; dir: Br Ports Fedn Ltd 1988-, Estuary Servs Ltd 1988- (chm 1988-90); memb: Mgmnt Ctee Br Ports Assoc 1986-88, Int Assoc of Ports and Harbours 1986-; Freeman: City of London 1987, Worshipful Co of Watermen and Lightermen of River Thames 1987-; *Style—* David Jeffery, Esq; The Old Coach House, Nunney, Frome, Somerset BA11 4LZ; Flat 4, 91 Lansdowne Way, London SW8; Port of London Authority, Europe House, World Trade Centre, London E1 9AA (☎ 071 481 8484, fax 071 481 0313, telex 941 3062 PLALON G)

JEFFERY, Duncan Charles; s of Henry C Jeffery, of Gt Yarmouth, and Ada E Jeffrey; *b* 15 Dec 1952; *Educ* Gt Yarmouth GS; *m* 11 Aug 1979, Mary Elizabeth, da of William John Hayden, TD; *Career* Euro corr Press Assoc 1976, asst ed Eastern Daily Press 1984, ed Southern Evening Echo 1986; memb Guild of British Newspaper Eds; *Recreations* golf, sailing, cookery, antiquarian books; *Clubs* Farmers; *Style—* Duncan Jeffery, Esq; 45 Above Bar, Southampton, Hants (☎ 0703 634134, fax 0703 630428)

JEFFERY, Edgar Charles; s of Edred Fleetwood Jeffery (d 1953), of The Parade, Epsom, and Grace, *née* Friston (d 1977); *b* 6 Aug 1922; *Educ* Tiffin Sch Kingston upon Thames, Architectural Assoc; *m* 18 May 1963, Barbara Joyce, da of Maj Frank Herbert Briggs (d 1981), of Silvretta, Torquay; 1 da (Fiona Jane b 1964), 1 s (David William b 1966); *Career* architect, chartered surveyor, county architect Northumberland 1973-85; chm Timber Res and Devpt Assoc N Region; maj works: Queen's Hall Arts Centre Hexham 1983, County Hall Morpeth 1983, Duchess High Sch Alnwick 1980; ARIBA, ARICS, FRSA; *Recreations* water colours, water sports, walking, working; *Style—* Edgar Jeffery, Esq; Lea House, Fladbury, Worcs WR10 2QW

JEFFERY, Keith Howard; s of James Walter Jeffery (d 1959), and Ruth, *née* Auld (d 1977); *b* 10 April 1926; *Educ* Merchant Taylors', Pembroke Coll Oxford (MA); *Career* Lt RHA 1946, served: Italy, Austria, Middle East (despatches Palestine 1948); admin Civil Serv 1950, Air Miny 1950-61, Cabinet Office 1961-63, sec Robbins' Ctee on Higher Educn 1963-64, Office of the Min for the Arts 1964-70, Arts Cncl of GB 1970-82; London Rep of the FVS Fndn of Hamburg 1970-; Monteverdi tstee 1988-; FRSA 1978; *Recreations* music, theatre; *Clubs* Garrick; *Style—* Keith Jeffery, Esq; North Grange, Langley Park, Buckinghamshire

JEFFERY, Very Rev Robert Martin Colquhoun; s of Norman Clare Jeffery (d 1972), and Gwenedd Isabel, *née* Field; *b* 30 April 1935; *Educ* St Paul's, King's Coll London (BD, AKC); *m* 4 May 1948, Ruth Margaret, da of Everard Tinling (d 1978), of Surrey; 3 s (Graham b 1969, Hilary b 1971, Charles b 1975), 1 da (Phillipa b 1975); *Career* asst curate: St Aidan Grangetown 1959-61, St Mary Barnes 1961-63; asst sec Missionary and Ecumenical of Church Assembly 1964-68, sec Dept of Mission and Unity Br Cncl of Churches 1968-71, vicar St Andrew Headington 1971-78, rural dean Cowley 1972-78, Lichfield diocesan missioner 1978-80, memb Gen Synod of C of E 1982, archdeacon of Salop 1980-87, dean of Worcester 1987-; *Books* Unity in Nigeria (1964), Christian Unity and the Anglican Community (with D M Paton, 1965 and 1968), Areas of Ecumenical Experiment (1968), Ecumenical Experiments: A Handbook (1971), Case Studies in Unity (1972), By What Authority (1987); *Recreations* local history, cooking; *Style—* The Very Rev the Dean of Worcester; 10 College Green, Worcester (☎ 0905 27821, office 0905 28854)

JEFFERY, Timothy Arthur Rodney; s of Rodney Albert Jeffery, of 2 Bingham Drive, Lyminston, Hants, and Edith Rosina, *née* Meeks; *b* 13 June 1956; *Educ* The Methodist Coll Belfast, Univ of Kent at Canterbury (BA); *m* 14 April 1984, (Margaret) Jennifer, da of Harold Gibson; 1 da (Kate Elizabeth Rosina b 4 Dec 1987); *Career* features ed Yachting World 1978-88, yachting corr The Daily Telegraph 1988-; former chm UKC Sports Fedn, memb Yachting Journalists Assoc 1977; *Books* Sail of the Century (1983), Practical Sailing (1986), Sailing Year (1987), Royal Ocean Racing; *Recreations* sailing, windsurfing, tennis; *Clubs* Royal Ocean Racing; *Style—* Timothy Jeffery, Esq; The Daily Telegraph, Peterborough Court at South Quay, 181 Marsh Wall, London E14 9SR (☎ 071 538 5000, fax 071 538 1332)

JEFFORD, Barbara Mary; OBE (1965); da of Percival Francis Jefford (d 1961), and Elizabeth Mary Ellen, *née* Laity (d 1979); *b* 26 July 1930; *Educ* Weirfield Sch Taunton, Eileen Hartly-Hodder Studio Bristol (LGSM), RADA London (Bancroft Gold medal); *m* 1, (m dis 1961), Terence Longdon; m 2,13 May 1967, John Arnold Turner, s of William John Turner; *Career* actress; Shakespeare debut as Viola in Twelfth Night (Dolphin Theatre Brighton) 1949, worked at Shakespeare Meml Theatre 1950 1951 and 1954, led co with Anthony Quayle on Australasian Tour 1953, leading lady at Old Vic 1956-62 (incl tours of UK, USA, Europe and USSR), led HM Tennant Co with Ralph Richardson on tour of S America and Europe to mark Shakespeare's Quartercentenary 1964, roles in West End and with regnl cos (incl Oxford Playhouse) 1960s 70s and 80s, int tours for Br Cncl (The Labours of Love, two-handed show with husband, John Turner), Prospect Productions and Bristol Old Vic; leading roles with: NT 1976 and 1987, RSC 1967 and 1989-90; film debut as Molly Bloom in Ulysses; subsequent films incl: The Shoes of The Fisherman, And The Ship Sails On, Where Angels Fear to Tread; extensive radio and tv work throughout career; *Recreations* music, swimming, gardening; *Style—* Ms Barbara Jefford, OBE; c/o Fraser & Dunlop Ltd, The Chambers, Chelsea Harbour, Lots Rd, London SW10 0XF (☎ 071 376 7676, fax 071 352 7325, 071 351 1756)

JEFFREY, Gordon Boyd Buchanan; s of William Barclay Boyd Jeffrey (d 1982), of Southport, Lancs, and Jean Ross, *née* Macgregor; *b* 12 April 1935; *Educ* Merchant Taylors Sch Crosby, Univ of Liverpool (LLB); *m* 11 May 1963, Jill Virginia, da of William Frederick Baker (d 1980), of Southport; 3 s (Andrew b 20 April 1965, Robert b 4 April 1967, Jonathan b 22 Aug 1973), 1 da (Sarah Jane b and d 1970); *Career* Nat Serv cmmnd Royal Artillery 1958-60, served with 2 Field Regt RA and 17 Gurkha Div during terrorist emergency in Malaya; admitted slr 1958; ptnr Laces & Co (now Lace Mawer) 1963-; jt chm World Amateur Golf Cncl; memb Law Soc; *Recreations* golf, fishing; *Clubs* Royal & Ancient Golf (St Andrews, chm Gen Ctee), The Royal Birkdale Golf (tstee); *Style—* Gordon Jeffrey, Esq; Lace Mawer, Solicitors, Castle Chambers, 43 Castle St, Liverpool L2 9SU (☎ 051 236 2002, fax 051 236 2585, telex 627229)

JEFFREY, Ian Nelson; s of John Nelson Jeffrey, of St Boswells, Roxburghshire, Scotland, and Alice Ogle (d 1980); *b* 8 Jan 1942; *Educ* The Duke's Sch Alnwick, Univ of Manchester (BA), The Courtauld Inst (MA); *m* 1965, Christina Mary, da of Frederick Harry Booth; 2 da (Catherine Mary b 1968, Laura Anne b 1973); *Career* pt/t lectr Brighton Coll of Art 1967-69, lectr and princ lectr Goldsmiths Coll of Art 1969-87; freelance writer and critic 1988-; essays and criticism in: London Magazine, Studio International, Creative Camera; organiser and collaborator exhibitions for Arts Council: The Real Thing (Hayward Gallery) 1974, Cityscape (Royal Acad) 1978, The Thirties (Hayward Gallery) 1980, Landscape in Britain 1850-1950 (Hayward Gallery) 1983, La France - Images of Woman and Ideas of Nation 1789-1989 (Hayward Gallery) 1989; memb Advsy Ctee: Br Cncl (memb Fine Arts Ctee 1982-87), Arts Cncl; *Books* Photography: A Concise History (1981), The British Landscape 1920- 50 (1984); *Recreations* gardening; *Style—* Ian Jeffrey, Esq

JEFFREY, John; s of James Jeffrey, and Margaret Lambie, *née* Young; *b* 25 March 1959; *Educ* Merchiston Castle Sch Edinburgh, Univ of Newcastle (BSc); *Career* Rugby Union flanker RFC and Scotland (33 caps); represented: English Univs, British Univs; Clubs: Kelso RFC (capt 1987/88 and 1988/89, twice Scottish champions), South of Scotland 1982- (capt 1988-), Barbarians RFC; 3 caps Scotland B; Scotland: debut v Aust 1984, Five Nations debut v Ireland 1985, tour Romania 1984, tour USA 1985, France 1986, memb World Cup Squad 1987, tour NZ 1990, Championship and Grand Slam winners 1990, record 9 tries scored by a forward; British Lions: IRB celebration team 1986, tour Aust 1989; farmer Kersknowe and Frogden farms; *Recreations* golf, sailing, water skiing; *Clubs* MENSA; *Style—* John Jeffrey, Esq; Kersknowe, Kelso, Roxburghshire, Scotland TD5 8AA (☎ 057 34 212)

JEFFREY, John Christopher; s of Cyril Henry Jeffrey (d 1985), and Mary Elizabeth, *née* Jones; *b* 21 July 1942; *Educ* Clifton Coll Bristol; *m* 27 Sept 1974, Diana Lisa, da of Cecil Raymond (d 1988), of Messiter-Tooze; 2 s (Justin b 1971, Nicholas b 1975); *Career* CA 1965-; Deloitte Haskins & Sells: ptnr Zambia 1970-75, ptnr i/c Kitwe Zambia 1975-78, managing ptnr Lusaka Zambia 1978-84, ptnr i/c Leeds Bradford 1984-85, managing ptnr N Region Manchester Liverpool Newcastle Leeds; FCA 1965; *Recreations* golf, skiing; *Clubs* St James', Manchester-Prestbury Golf; *Style—* John C Jeffrey, Esq; Greenbank, Chelford Road, Prestbury, Cheshire SK10 4PT (☎ 0625 828 979); Coopers & Lybrand Deloitte, Richmond House, 1 Rumford Place, Liverpool L3 9QS (☎ 051 227 4242, fax 051 227 4575, car 0860 612 082, telex 628724)

JEFFREY, Capt John Robert (Ian); OBE (1965); s of James Jeffrey (d 1964), of Glenpatrick, Renfrewshire, and Mina Sadler, *née* Ferguson (d 1949); *b* 1 Dec 1922; *Educ* Johnstone HS Renfrewshire; *m* 1, 25 Sept 1948, Elizabeth Comfort (d 1989), da of Roger Newton Goode (d 1926), of Des Moines, Iowa, USA; 1 s (J Stuart b 1951), 2 da (Sandra (Mrs Cleaver) b 1949, Wendy (Mrs Tobi) b 1955); m 2, 1990, Faith Garland, da of Errol Barraclough, of Shanghai, China, and West Byfleet, Surrey; *Career* WWII: RAFVR 1941, serv No 53 and No 86 Sqdns Coastal Cmd 1942-45 (despatches); seconded to BOAC 1945, Capt 1947; Cdr flying: Liberator, Constellation 049, Stratocruiser, DC Seven Seas, Boeing 707, Boeing 747; BOAC trg Capt, instrument rating examiner 1959, Master Air Pilot, sr Capt first class 1959, ret 1977; dir ECG Consultants Ltd 1966-; memb exec ctee BALPA 1960-66 (fin chm 1960-62, chm central bd 1962-66); memb: Nat Jt Cncl for Civil Air Tport 1962-66, Air League Cncl 1967-79; assessor Fay Inquiry into Munich Air Crash 1968-69; chm Frimley and Camberley UDC 1963-65 (memb 1959-65), Parly candidate (Cons) Coventry SW 1974 (twice), JP 1966-86; Freeman City of London 1957, Liveryman Guild of Air Pilots and Navigators 1965; FCIT 1970, MRAEs 1966; *Clubs* RAF; *Style—* Capt Ian Jeffrey, OBE; 15 Billing Rd, London SW10 (☎ 071 351 2165); 1 Park Place, Canary Wharf, London E14 4HJ (☎ 071 352 0760, car 0836 205 401)

JEFFREY, Nicholas; s of Manfred Jeffrey, of Essex, and Doris MacKay, *née* Spouge; *b* 6 June 1942; *Educ* Ecclesfield GS, Univ of Sheffield (LLB); *m* 1965, Dianne Michelle, da of Cyril Cantor (d 1985); 2 s (Alexander b 1966, David b 1969), 2 da (Danya b 1968, Miranda b 1971); *Career* chief exec Cantors plc and all subsidiary companies 1980- (dir 1967-), dep chm Hallamshire Investments plc 1989; *Recreations* shooting, sailing; *Style—* Nicholas Jeffrey, Esq; Riley Croft, Eyam, Derbyshire; Cantors plc, 164-170 Queens Rd, Sheffield S2 4DY (☎ 0742 766461, fax 0742 769070, telex 547037)

JEFFREY, Hon Mrs (Oonagh Elizabeth); *née* Gibson; da of 3 Baron Ashbourne; *b* 1935; *m* 1963, John William Jeffrey; 1 s, 1 da; *Style—* The Hon Mrs Jeffrey; Alding, Grayswood Rd, Haslemere, Surrey

JEFFREY-COOK, John; *b* 5 Jan 1936; *Educ* Whitgift Middle Sch Croydon; *m* 12 May 1962, Gillian Audrey, da of Ronald Albert Kettle (d 1982), of Croydon; 2 s (Richard Daniel b 1964, Malcolm John b 1970 d 1981), 1 da (Fiona Elizabeth b 1966); *Career* managing ed of taxation books Butterworth Law Publishers 1966-77, dir of pubns Deloitte Haskins & Sells 1977-85, ptnr Moores Rowland 1985-; ed Moores Rowland's Yellow and Orange Tax Guides 1987-; memb: Ctee London & Dist Soc of CAs 1966-77, Cncl Inst of Taxation 1977-90 (treas 1981-88), Cncl Assoc of Taxation Technicians 1989-; Freeman City of London 1980, memb Worshipful Co of CAs 1980; FCA 1958, FCIS 1959, FTII 1964, ATT 1989; *Books* Simon's Tax (ed, 1970), de Voil's Value Added Tax (1973), Simon's Taxes Intelligence and Cases (1973), Butterworths Orange Tax Handbook (1976), Foster's Capital Taxes Encyclopaedia (1976), Moores Rowland's Taxation of Farmers and Farming (1989); *Recreations* genealogy, cinema; *Style—* John Jeffrey-Cook, Esq; 32 Campion Close, Croydon, Surrey CRO 5SN (☎ 081 688 3887); Moores Rowland, 9 Bedford Park, Croydon, Surrey CRO 2AP (☎ 081 686 9281, fax 081 760 0411)

JEFFREYS, Prof Alec John; s of Sydney Victor Jeffreys, of Corton, Lowestoft, Suffolk, and Joan, *née* Knight; *b* 9 Jan 1950; *Educ* Luton GS, Luton Sixth Form Coll,

Merton Coll Oxford (BA, MA, DPhil); *m* 28 Aug 1971, Susan, da of Frederick Charles Robert Miles (d 1975), of Luton, Beds; 2 da (Sarah Catherine b 1979, Elizabeth Jane b 1983); *Career* postdoctoral res fell Euro Molecular Biology Orgn Univ of Amsterdam 1975-77, prof of genetics Univ of Leicester 1987- (lectr 1977-72, Lister Inst res fell 1982-, reader 1984-87), devpt genetic fingerprinting system 1984-; Wolfson res prof of Royal Soc 1991-; memb: EMBO, HUGO, Genetical Soc, Biochemical Soc; hon fell Merton Coll Oxford; fell Forensic Sci Soc of India; FRS; *Recreations* swimming, walking, postal history; *Style*— Prof Alec Jeffreys, FRS; Dept of Genetics, Adrian Building, Univ of Leicester, Univ Rd, Leicester LE1 7RH (☎ 0533 523435, fax 0533 523489)

JEFFREYS, Annie-Lou, Lady Jeffreys; Anne Louise (Annie-Lou); da of His Hon Judge Sir (William) Shirley Worthington-Evans, 2 Bt (d 1971, when Btcy became extinct); *b* 1934; *m* 1967 (m dis 1981), 2 Baron Jeffreys, *qv*; 1 da (Sophie Louise); *Style*— Annie-Lou, Lady Jeffreys; The Cottage, Willesley, Tetbury, Glos

JEFFREYS, 3 Baron (UK 1952); Christopher Henry Mark Jeffreys; s of 2 Baron Jeffreys (d 1986), and Mrs Alexander Clarke, of Foxhill House, Hawling, Glos; *b* 22 May 1957; *Educ* Eton; *m* 22 Aug 1985, Anne Elisabeth, da of Antoine Denarie, and Mrs Derek Johnson, of Boden Hall, Scholar Green, Cheshire; 1 s (Hon Arthur Mark Henry b 1989), 1 da (Hon Alice Mary b 1986); *Heir* s, Hon Arthur Mark Henry Jeffreys b 18 Feb 1989; *Career* futures broker; *Recreations* country sports, skiing; *Clubs* Whites, Annabels; *Style*— The Rt Hon the Lord Jeffreys; Bottom Farm, Eaton, Grantham, Lincolnshire NG32 1ET

JEFFREYS, Hon George Christian Darell; raised to the rank of a Baron's son 1961; s of Capt Christopher John Darell Jeffreys, MVO (ka 1940, only s of 1 Baron Jeffreys), and Lady Rosemary Beatrice, *née* Agar (d 1984), da of 4 Earl of Normanton; *b* 2 Dec 1939; *Educ* Eton, RMA Sandhurst; *m* 3 April 1967, (Karen) Elizabeth Mary, da of Col Hugo Meynell, MC, JP, DL (d 1960), of Hollybush Park, Newborough, Burton-on-Trent; 1 s (Christopher George Hugo b 1984), 2 da (Zara Serena b 1972, Susannah Elizabeth b 1975); *Career* Capt Grenadier Gds 1964, ret 1966; with C T Bowring & Co Ltd 1966-68; Seccombe Marshall & Campion plc: joined 1968, co sec 1974, dir 1976, md 1978-87; with RIM Fund Management Ltd 1987-88, Hill Samuel Investment Services Ltd 1989-; *Recreations* hunting, shooting, golf, cricket; *Clubs* Boodle's; *Style*— The Hon George Jeffreys; The Green Farm, Tidmington, Shipston-on-Stour, Warwicks CV36 5LR (☎ 0608 61423)

JEFFREYS, Martyn Edward; s of William Herbert Jeffreys (d 1961), of Ealing, and Nora Emilie, *née* Crane; *b* 20 Jan 1938; *Educ* St Clement Danes, Univ of Bristol (BSc); *m* 29 Oct 1960, Carol, da of Marcel Faustin Boclet (d 1964), of Twickenham; 2 s (Andrew b 1962, Adam b 1968), 1 da (Katy b 1965); *Career* operational res scientist BP 1961-63, sr mathematician and mangr Mathematical Programming Div SD-Scicon (formerly CEIR Ltd) 1964-67, chief mgmnt scis conslt and head professional servs SIA Ltd 1968-70, sr ptnr Wootton Jeffreys & Ptnrs 1971-84, exec chm Wootton Jeffreys Systems Ltd 1985-86, chm Jeffreys Systems plc 1987-; FBCS 1973, CEng 1990; *Style*— Martyn Jeffreys, Esq; 196 Epsom Road, Merrow, Guildford, Surrey GU1 2RR (☎ 0483 39598); Jeffreys House, 21 Normandy Street, Alton, Hampshire GU34 1DD (☎ 0420 541541, fax 0420 541640, car 0836 283850)

JEFFREYS, Dr Roy Arthur; s of Arthur Thomas George Jeffreys (d 1981), and Elsie Clara, *née* Pegler (d 1976); *b* 7 April 1926; *Educ* Kilburn GS, King's Coll London (BSc, AKC, MSc, PhD); *m* 1 Dec 1951, Joyce Margaret Dorothy, da of Stanley Holloway, DCM, MM (d 1963); 3 s (Paul Robert b 1956, Charles Francis b 1960, Timothy b 1964); *Career* co dir Res Div Kodak Ltd 1981- (dir of res 1978-88), ret 1988; conslt R & D Mgmnt 1989-; hon treas Royal Soc Chemistry, chm Personnel Policy Ctee Royal Soc of Chem, sr fell Brunel Mgmnt Prog, industl assoc Royal Holloway Coll, vice chm Special Health Authy, memb Exec Ctee R and D Soc 1990; Progress medal RPS; FBIM, FInstD, FRSocChem, CChem, Hon FRPS; *Recreations* marathon running; *Style*— Dr Roy Jeffreys; 2 Hillview Rd, Hatch End, Pinner, Middx (☎ 081 428 4173); Brunel Management Programme, B10SS, Brunel University,Uxbridge, Middx UB8 3PH

JEFFRIES, Lionel Charles; s of Bernard Jackson, and Elsie Jackson; *b* 19 June 1926; *Educ* Queen Elizabeth's GS Wimborne Dorset, RADA (Dip, Kendal Award 1947); *m* 30 June 1951, Eileen, da of William Walsh (d 1963); 1 s (Timothy), 2 da (Elizabeth, Martha); *Career* War Serv 1939-45, Capt Oxford and Bucks LI Burma, RWAFF (Burma Star); actor (stage and film) 1949-, film prodr, dir, screen writer; appeared in: 7 West End plays, over 100 feature films, Broadway (Pygmalion 1987); writer and dir: The Railway Children 1972, The Amazing Mr Blunden, The Water Babies 1979; TV films: Danny, Chorus of Disapproval 1988, Ending Up 1989, The Wild Duck (Phoenix, West End) 1990; *Recreations* oil painting, swimming; *Clubs* St James; *Style*— Lionel Jeffries, Esq; c/o ICM, 388-396 Oxford St, London W19 HE (☎ 071 629 8080)

JEFFRIES, Michael Makepeace Eugene; s of William Eugene Jeffries (d 1975), of Port of Spain, Trinidad, and Margaret, *née* Makepeace; *b* 17 Sept 1944; *Educ* Queens Royal Coll Port of Spain Trinidad, Poly of North London (Dip Arch); *m* 10 Sept 1966, Pamela Mary, da of Sir Gordon Booth, KCMG, CVO, of Walton-on-the-Hill, Surrey; 2 s (Andrew b 1969, Simon b 1973), 2 da (Kathryn b 1971, Victoria b 1975); *Career* John Laing and Sons Ltd 1963-67, Deeks Bousell Ptnrship 1968-73, Bradshaw Gass and Hope 1973-75; ASFA Ltd (WS Atkins Gp) 1975-: dir 1978, chm and md 1979; dir WS Atkins Conslts 1979; chm Banstead Round Table 1980, memb Cncl London C of C; RIBA 1973, FRSA 1987; *Recreations* golf, sailing, skiing, water colours, antiquarian horology; *Style*— Michael Jeffries, Esq; Sixways, Court Rd, Banstead, Surrey SM7 2NQ (☎ 0737 359 518); Woodcote Grove, Ashley Rd, Epsom, Surrey KT18 5BW (☎ 03727 23 555, fax 03727 43 006, car 0860 366 251, telex 266701 ATKINS G)

JEFFS, Cyril Raymond (Ray); OBE (1988); s of George James Horatio Jeffs, CVO, OBE, of Pixham Firs Cottage, Pixham Lane, Dorking, Surrey, and Phyllis Rosina, *née* Bell; *b* 6 April 1922; *Educ* Wallington GS; *m* 2 March 1946, Beatrice Elizabeth (Betty), da of Capt Walter Lawrence Evelyn Gordon (d 1964); 3 da (Anne b 29 May 1947, Susan b 16 June 1949, Diana b 17 Sept 1950); *Career* Fleet Air Arm: pilot 1941-46, awarded wings 1941, cmmnd 1941, (despatches); RNVR Air Div 1946-50, Lt; Br Aviation Insur Co Ltd: Underwriting Dept 1939-40 and 1946-54, underwriter's asst 1955-56; Aviation & Gen Insur Co Ltd: asst underwriter 1957-58, gen mangr & chief underwriter 1959-87; aviation underwriter: The Prudential Assur Co Ltd 1967-87, Pearl Assur Co Ltd 1970-87; chm and md CRJ Insur Conslts (Aviation) Ltd 1987-; Order of Merit Guild of Air Pilots and Air Navigators 1988 (warden 1973-75); cncl memb Air Registration Bd 1960-72, chm Aviation Insur Offices Assoc 1965-67, pres Int Union of Aviation Insurers 1968-70, vice chm Airworthiness Requirements Bd CAA 1972-89, chm Underwriting Ctee Int Union Aviation Insurers 1980-87; Freeman City of London 1967; Liveryman: Guild of Air Pilots and Air Navigators, Worshipful Co of Insurers; assoc MRAeS, hon memb Int Union of Aviation Insurers; *Recreations* walking, swimming; *Clubs* City of London, Naval and Military, Royal Aero; *Style*— Ray Jeffs, Esq, OBE; 6 Killock, Martello Park, Canford Cliffs, Poole, Dorset BH13 7BA (☎ 0202 700788); CRJ Insurance Consultants (Aviation) Ltd, 400 Capability Green, Luton, Bedfordshire LU1 3LU

JEFFS, Julian; QC (1975); s of Alfred Wright Jeffs (d 1974); *b* 5 April 1931; *Educ* Mostyn House Sch, Wrekin Coll, Downing Coll Cambridge; *m* 1966, Deborah, *née* Bevan; 3 s (Daniel b 1968, Alexander b 1970, Benjamin b 1972); *Career* called to the Bar Grays Inn 1958; rec 1975, bencher Gray's Inn 1981, chm Patent Bar Assoc 1981-89; memb Ctee of Mgmnt Int Wine and Food Soc 1965-67 and 1971-82, gen cmmr of Income Taxes 1983-; memb: Senate of the Inns of Ct and Bar 1984-85, Bar Cncl 1988-89; vice pres Circle of Wine Writers (chm 1970-72); gen ed Faber's Wine Series; *Books* Sherry (1961, 3 edn 1982), Clerk & Lindsell on Torts (co-ed, 13 edn 1969 - 16 edn 1989), The Wines of Europe (1971), Little Dictionary of Drink (1973), Encyclopedia of United Kingdom and European Patent Law (jtly, 1977); *Recreations* wine, walking, old cars, Iberian things; *Clubs* Beefsteak, Garrick, Reform, Saintsbury; *Style*— Julian Jeffs, Esq, QC; Francis Taylor Bldg, Temple, London EC4 (☎ 071 353 5657); Church Farm House, East Ilsley, Newbury, Berks (☎ 063 528 216)

JEFFS, Dr Nicholas Graham; s of John Grahame Jeffs (d 1974), and Evelyn Maude, *née* Cattermole; *b* 20 Nov 1950; *Educ* Lycee Victor Hugo Marrakesh Morocco, Nottingham HS, Middx Hosp Med Sch (MB BS); *m* 18 Jan 1975, Jennifer Mary, da of Robert Herbert Rogers, of 9 Gainsborough Rd, Colchester, Essex; 2 s (Richard b 1978, Thomas b 1983); *Career* anaesthetist; registrar London Hosp 1976-78, lectr Univ of London 1978-79, sr registrar St Mary's Hosp 1981-82, conslt and dir intensive care unit Luton and Dunstable Hosp 1982-; FFARCS 1978, fell Coll of Anaesthetics, memb Intensive Care Soc; *Recreations* model engineering, pistol shooting; *Style*— Dr Nicholas Jeffs; 28 Ludlow Ave, Luton, Bedfordshire LU1 3RW (☎ 0582 451504); Luton and Dunstable Hospital, Luton, Bedfordshire LU4 0DZ (☎ 0582 491122 ext 2395)

JEGER, Baroness (Life Peer UK 1979), of St Pancras in Greater London; Lena May Jeger; da of Charles Chivers (d 1971), of Yorkley, Glos, and Eugenie Alice James (d 1969); *b* 19 Nov 1915; *Educ* Southgate Co Sch Middx, Birkbeck Coll London Univ (BA); *m* 1948, Dr Santo Wayburn Jeger, MP (d 1953); *Career* sits as Labour peer in House of Lords; on London staff Manchester Guardian 1951-54 and 1961-; MP (Lab): LCC 1951-54, Holborn and St Pancras South Nov 1953-1959 and 1964-74, Camden Holborn and St Pancras South 1974-79; memb Nat Exec Ctee Labour Party 1968-80 (vice chm 1978-79, chm 1979-80); UK rep Status of Women Cmmn UN 1967, memb Consultative Assembly of Cncl of Europe and Western Euro Union, memb Chm's Panel House of Commons 1971-79; oppn spokesman (Lords) Social Security 1983-; *Style*— The Rt Hon the Lady Jeger; 9 Cumberland Terrace, Regent's Park, London NW1

JEHANGIR, Sir Hirji Cowasji; 3 Bt (UK 1908), of Bombay; s of Sir Cowasji Jehangir, 2 Bt, GBE, KCIE, OBE (d 1962); *b* 1 Nov 1915; *Educ* St Xavier's Sch Bombay, Magdalene Coll Cambridge; *m* 10 Aug 1952, Jinoo, er da of Kakushroo H Cama; 2 s (Jehangir, Adi b 1956); *Heir* s, Jehangir Hirji Jehangir, b 23 Nov 1953, m 21 March 1988, Jasmine, da of Beji Billimoria (1 s, Cowasji b 28 March 1990); *Career* merchant and landlord; chm: Jehangir Art Gallery Bombay, Cowasji Jehangir Charity Tst; pres Parsi Public Sch Soc; *Clubs* Willingdon (Bombay), Royal Over-Seas League, English Speaking Union; *Style*— Sir Hirji Jehangir, Bt; Readymoney House, 49 Nepean Sea Rd, Bombay-400 036, India; 24 Kensington Court Gdns, Kensington Court Place, London W8

JEJEEBHOY, Sir Jamsetjee; 7 Bt (UK 1857), of Bombay; s of Rustamjee J C Jamsetjee (d 1947), n of 4 Bt; suc kinsman Sir Jamsetjee Jejeebhoy 1968, when he assumed the name of Jamsetjee Jejeebhoy in lieu of Maneckjee Rustamjee Jamsetjee; *b* 19 April 1913; *Educ* Univ of Bombay (BA); *m* 1943, Shirin Jehangir Cama; 1 s (Rustomjee b 16 Nov 1957), 1 da (Ayesha); *Heir* s, Rustomjee Jejeebhoy; *Career* chm: Sir Jamsetjee Jejeebhoy Charity Fund, Sir J J Parsee Benevolent Instn, Zoroastrian Bldg Fund, Seth Rustomjee Jamsetjee Jejeebhoy Gujarat Sch Fund, M F Cama Athornan Instn & M M Cama Educn Fund, Bombay Panjrapole, HB Wadia Atash-Behram Funds, Parsee Dhandha Rojgar Fund, Iran League; vice chm K R Cama Oriental Inst; tstee: A H Wadia Charity Tst, Byramjee Jeejeebhoy Parsi Charitable Instn, Cowasji Behramji Divecha Charity Tst, Parsee Surat Charity Fund, Framjee Cowasjee Inst, Eranee Charity Funds and Dharamhala; memb Exec Ctee Bomanjee Dinshaw Petit Parsee Gen Hosp, created Special Exec Magistrate 1977; *Clubs* Willingdon Sports, WIAA, Royal Western India Turf, Poona; *Style*— Sir Jamsetjee Jejeebhoy, Bt; Beaulieu, 95 Worli Seaface, Bombay 400 025, India (☎ 4930955); Maneckjee Wadia Building, 127 Mahatma Gandhi Rd, Fort, Bombay 400 001, India (☎ 273843)

JEJEEBHOY, Rustomjee; s and h of Sir Jamsetjee Jejeebhoy, 7 Bt, of Bombay, and Shirin Jamsetjee Jejeebhoy; *b* 16 Nov 1957; *Educ* Bombay Univ (BCom, LLM); *m* 1984, Delara Jal Bhaisa, da of Jal Nariman Bhaisa, of Bombay; 1 s (Jehangir b 20 Jan 1986); *Career* tstee: Sir Jamsetjee Jejeebhoy Parsee Benevolent Instn, Sir Jamsetjee Jejeebhoy Charity Fund, M F Cama Athornan Instn & M M Cama Educn Fund, Parsee Dhandha Rojgar Fund, Eranlee Charity Funds and Dharamshala; service legal executive, TATA Exports Ltd Bombay 1983; dir: Beaulieu Inv Pvt Ltd 1975, Dawn Threads Pvt Ltd 1984, Palmera Inv Pvt Ltd 1984; *Recreations* sports, music, reading; *Clubs* Willingdon Sports, Royal Western India Turf; *Style*— Rustomjee Jejeebhoy, Esq; Beaulieu 95 Worli Seaface, Bombay 400 025 (☎ 4938517); Block A, Shivsagar Estates, Dr Annie Besant Rd, Worli, Bombay 400018 (☎ 494 8573)

JELF, Maj-Gen Richard William; CBE (1947, OBE 1944); s of Sir Ernest Arthur Jelf (d 1950, King's Remembrancer and Master of the Supreme Ct), of Pinner, Middx, and Rose Frances, *née* Reeves (d 1923); *b* 16 June 1904; *Educ* Cheltenham, RMA Woolwich; *m* 23 July 1928, Nowell, da of Maj Nowell Sampson-Way (d 1948), of Manor House, Henbury, Bristol; 3 s (Timothy b 1929, Nicholas b 1932, Jeremy b 1943), 1 da (Jan b 1943); *Career* cmmnd RA 1924, Staff Coll Quetta 1936-37, memb directing staff Staff Coll Camberley 1942, GSO1 49 Div 1942-44, CO Northumberland Hussars 1944-45, Col GS 8 Corps 1945, cdr Cologne Dist CCG 1946, dep dir staff duties WO 1946-47, IDC 1948, cdr RA 2 Div 1948-49, dep dir RA WO 1949, dep chief orgn and trg SHAPE 1950-52, COS Eastern Cmd 1955-57, cmdt Police Coll 1957-63, regnl dir Civil Def 1963-68; ADC to HM The Queen 1952; hon sec RNLI Lyme Regis 1972-84; *Style*— Maj-Gen Richard Jelf, CBE; 10 Hills Place, Guildford Rd, Horsham, W Sussex RH12 1XT (☎ 0403 217 071)

JELLICOE, (Patricia) Ann; OBE (1984); da of Maj John Andrea Jellicoe (d 1975), and Frances Jackson Henderson; *b* 15 July 1927; *Educ* Polam Hall Sch Darlington, Queen Margaret's Sch Castle Howard York, Central Sch of Speech & Drama; *m* 1962, David Roger Mayne; 1 s (Tom b 1969), 1 da (Katkin b 1966); *Career* theatre director, playwright and actress; fndr Cockpit Theatre Co to experiment with Open Stage 1952-54, taught acting and directed plays Central Sch of Speech and Drama 1954-56, literary mangr Royal Court Theatre 1972-74, set up first community play Lyme Regis 1978, fndr and dir Colway Theatre Tst (to produce and develop community plays); Elsie Fogarty prize 1947, 3rd prize Observer Playwriting Competition 1956; pres Colway Theatre Tst; *Books* Some Unconscious Influences in the Theatre (1967), The Shell Guide to Devon (with Roger Mayne, 1975), Community Plays-How to Put Them on (1987); *Plays* The Sport of My Mad Mother (1958), The Knack (1962), Shelley (1965), The Giveaway (1969), Flora and the Bandits (1975), The Bargain (1979); *Plays for children* The Rising Generation (1967), You'll Never Guess! (1973), Clever Elsie, Smiling John, Silent Peter (1974), A Good Thing or a Bad Thing (1974); *Translations and Adaptations* Rosmersholm (1959), The Lady From the Sea (1961), The Seagull

(1964), Der Freischutz (1964); *Community Plays* incl The Reckoning (1978), The Tide (1980), The Western Women (1984), Money & Land (1988), Under the God (1989); *Recreations* reading theatrical biography; *Style—* Ms Ann Jellicoe, OBE; Colway Manor, Lyme Regis, Dorset DT7 3HD

JELLICOE, Sir Geoffrey Alan; CBE (1961); s of George Edward Jellicoe; *b* 8 Oct 1900; *Educ* Cheltenham, Architectural Assoc; *m* 1936, Ursula, da of Sir Bernard Pares, KBE, DCL; *Career* former sr ptnr Jellicoe & Coleridge Architects; former pres Inst Landscape Architects, hon pres Int Fedn Landscape Architects; former memb Royal Fine Art Cmmn, former tstee Tate Gallery; FRIBA, PPILA, FRTPI; kt 1979; *Style—* Sir Geoffrey Jellicoe, CBE; 14 Highpoint, North Hill, Highgate, London N6 4BA (☎ 081 348 0123)

JELLICOE, 2 Earl (UK 1925); George Patrick John Rushworth Jellicoe; KBE (1986), DSO (1942), MC (1944), PC (1963); also Viscount Jellicoe of Scapa (UK 1917), and Viscount Brocas of Southampton (UK 1925); s of Adm of the Fleet 1 Earl Jellicoe, GCB, OM, GCVO (d 1935); *b* 4 April 1918; *Educ* Winchester, Trinity Coll Cambridge; *m* 1, 23 March 1944 (m dis 1966), Patricia Christine, o da of Jeremiah O'Kane, of Vancouver, Canada; 2 s (Viscount Brocas, Hon Nicholas Charles b 1953), 2 da (Lady Alexandra Patricia Gwendoline b 1944, Lady Zara Lison Josephine b 1948); m, 2, 1966, Philippa Ann, da of late Philip Dunne, of Gatley Park, Leominster; 1 s (Hon John Philip b 1966), 2 da (Lady Emma Rose b 1967, Lady Daisy b 1970); *Heir* s, Viscount Brocas; *Career* page of honour to HM King George VI; WWII: ME Lt-Col Coldstream Gds, 1 SAS Regt, Special Boat Serv Regt (wounded, despatches thrice, Legion of Honour, French Croix de Guerre, Greek War Cross); Dip Serv 1947-58 (served Washington, Brussels and Baghdad); lord-in-waiting to HM The Queen Feb-June 1961; Parly under-sec Miny of Housing and Local Govt 1961-62, min of state Home Office 1962-63, first Lord of the Admty 1963-64; Lord Privy Seal, min in charge Civil Service, Leader of House of Lords 1970-73; chm: MRC 1982-90, E Euro Trade Cncl 1986-90, Davy Corp 1985-90, Greece Fund 1987-, Booker Tate 1988-; dir: Tate & Lyle plc (chm 1978-83), Sotheby's Holdings 1973-, S G Warburg & Co 1973-88, Morgan Crucible 1974-88, Smiths Industries 1973-86; pres London C of C 1980-83; chm: Br Overseas Trade Bd 1983-86, Parly & Scientific Ctee 1980-83, Prevention of Terrorism Act Review 1982-83, Cncl of King's Coll London 1974-83; chllr Southampton Univ 1984-; FRS 1990; *Recreations* travel, skiing; *Clubs* Brooks's, Special Forces; *Style—* The Rt Hon the Earl Jellicoe, KBE, DSO, MC, PC, FRS; Tidcombe Manor, Tidcombe, nr Marlborough, Wilts (☎ 026 489 225); 97 Onslow Square, London SW7 (☎ 071 584 1551)

JELLICOE, Dr Jillian Ann; da of George Molyneux Jellicoe (d 1972), of Liverpool, and Ellen, *née* Fitzsimmons; *b* 28 June 1947; *Educ* Holly Lodge HS for Girls Liverpool, KCH Med Sch; *m* 29 Sept 1973, Alan Fitzgerald, s of Raymond Charles Fitzgerald, of Brockenhurst, Hants; *Career* house surgn and house physician Hereford hosps 1970-71; sr house in offr: obstetrics Royal Victoria Hosp Bournemouth 1972, anaesthetics Whiston Hosp Lancs 1972-73; GP Bournemouth 1973-77, registrar Liverpool RHA 1978-80, sr registrar Wessex Region 1981-84, conslt anaesthetist Shackleton Dept of Anaesthetics Southampton Gen Hosp 1985-, clinical sub-dean Faculty of Med Univ of Southampton 1989-, tutor Coll of Anaesthetists Southampton Hosp; memb: BMA, Assoc of Anaesthetists, Assoc of Cardio-Thoracic Anaesthetists; LRCP, MRCS 1970, DObstRCOG 1972, DA 1973, FFARCS 1980; *Recreations* reading, watching cricket, cats; *Style—* Dr Jillian Ann Jellicoe; Shackleton Dept of Anaesthetics, Southampton General Hospital, Tremona Road, Southampton (☎ 0703 777222)

JELLICOE, Hon Nicholas Charles Joseph John; s of 2 Earl Jellicoe, KBE, DSO, MC, PC; hp of bro, Viscount Brocas; *b* 23 March 1953; *Educ* Eton, Univ of York; *m* 29 Dec 1982, Patricia, da of Count Arturo Ruiz de Castilla, of Madrid, Spain, and Lima, Peru; 1 da (Zoë Anaya b 15 June 1988); *Style—* The Hon Nicholas Jellicoe; 2 Villas on the Heath, Vale of Heath, Hampstead, London NW3 1BA (☎ 071 794 2026)

JELLICOE, Lady Zara Lison Josephine; has resumed maiden name; da of 2 Earl Jellicoe, DSO, MC, PC; *b* 24 Sept 1948; *m* 9 May 1983 (m dis 1987), Bruce Gilliam, s of Alvin Bruce Gilliam, of Houston, Texas, and of Mrs Robert Wright, of Carmel, Calif; *Style—* The Lady Zara Jellicoe; 219 Villa Garden Drive, Mill Valley, California 94941, USA

JEMSON, Nigel Bradley; s of Christopher William Jemson, of Preston, and Susan Elaine, *née* Randle; *b* 10 Aug 1969; *Educ* Hutton GS Preston; *Career* professional footballer; Preston North End: joined as apprentice 1985, debut 1986, 35 appearances, 13 goals; Nottingham Forest 1988-: joined for a fee of £250,000, debut 1989, over 50 appearances, 15 goals; on loan to Bolton Wanderers and Preston North End (12 appearances, 3 goals); England under 21 cap v Wales 1990; youngest first team player in history of Preston North End aged 16, Barclays Young Eagle of the month Jan 1990, Littlewoods Cup Winner's medal 1990 (scored winning goal in final v Oldham Athletic); *Recreations* golf, cricket; *Style—* Nigel Jemson, Esq; Nottingham Forest FC, City Ground, Nottingham (☎ 0602 822202)

JENCKS, Charles Alexander; s of Gardner Platt Jencks (d 1989), and Ruth Dewitt, *née* Read; *b* 21 June 1939; *Educ* Brooks Sch, Harvard Univ (BA, MA), Univ of London (Fulbright scholar, PhD); *m* 1, Pamela Balding; 2 s (Ivor Cusimo b 1969, Justin Alexanda b 1972); m 2, 1978, Maggie, *née* Keswick; 1 s (John Keswick b 1979), 1 da (Lily Clare b 1980); *Career* writer on architecture 1966-, lectr and prof 1969-, tv writer and sometime participant 1971-, architect and designer 1976-, writer on art 1985-, garden designer 1989-, writer on non architectural subjects 1989-; author of numerous books and articles on the subject of modern architecture and its successors; furniture and drawings exhibited at over 40 int univs; memb: AA, RSA; *Style—* Charles Jencks, Esq; Academy Editions, 42 Leinster Gardens, London W2 (☎ 071 402 2141, fax 071 723 9540)

JENKALA, Adrian Aleksander; s of Georgius Ihorus Jenkala, and Olena, *née* Karpynec; *b* 21 May 1957; *Educ* Latymer Upper Sch, Univ of London (BSc, LLB); *Career* called to the Bar Middle Temple 1984; practising barr 1984-, lectr in law City of London Poly 1985-; legal sec to Int Cmmn of Inquiry into 1932-33 Famine in Urkaine 1987-90 (report presented to UN in 1990); Freeman City of London; ACIArb; *Recreations* squash, skiing, ski instructing; *Style—* Adrian Jenkala, Esq; 2 Temple Gdns, London EC4Y 9AY (☎ 071 353 4636, fax 071 583 3455)

JENKIN, Hon Bernard Christison; yr son of Baron Jenkin of Roding, PC, *qv*; *Educ* Highgate, William Ellis Sch, Corpus Christi Coll Cambridge; *m* 24 Sept 1988, Anne Caroline, da of late Hon Charles Strutt, and sis of 6 Baron Rayleigh, *qv*; 1 s (Robert Patrick Christison b 13 May 1989); *Style—* The Hon Bernard Jenkin; 116 Kennington Rd, London SE11 6RE

JENKIN, Rev the Hon Charles Alexander Graham; er s of Baron Jenkin of Roding, PC, *qv*; *Educ* Highgate, UCL, Westcott House Cambridge; *m* 1984, Susan, da of Roy Collins; 1 da (Alexandra Emily b 21 Feb 1989); *Career* ordained 1984; *Style—* The Rev the Hon Charles Jenkin; St Anne's House, 51 St Anne's Rd, Canvey Island, Essex SS8 7LS

JENKIN, Rear Adm (David) Conrad; CB (1983); s of C O F Jenkin; yr bro of The Rt Hon Lord Jenkin of Roding *qv*; *b* 25 Oct 1928; *Educ* RNC Dartmouth; *m* 1958, Jennifer Margaret Nowell; 3 s, 1 da; *Career* RN 1942, flag offr First Flotilla 1981-82, cmdt Jt Servs Def Coll 1982-84; *Style—* Rear Adm Conrad Jenkin, CB; Knapsyard House, West Meon, Hants GU32 1LF (☎ 073 086 227)

JENKIN, David Chellew; s of Col Frederick Charles Jenkin, DSO (d 1959), and Dorothy Tryphosa, *née* Bromley (d 1982); *b* 6 June 1927; *Educ* King's Sch Canterbury, EMI Instit, Southall Tech Coll; *m* 20 Sept 1952, Elsie May, da of Thomas Roberts (d 1961); 3 s (Christopher b 1955, Michael b 1959, Nicholas b 1966), 1 da (Ann b 1954); *Career* Lance Corpl wireless RAC instr 1944-48; Tech Section EMI Factories Ltd 1950, sr engr Associated Reddifusion TV London 1958, station engr and chief engr Westward TV Plymouth 1961, dir of engrg TSW Broadcasting Ltd (formerly TSW Television South West Ltd) Plymouth 1981-; memb Inst of Engrg, MIEE 1966, FRTS 1987; *Recreations* moor walking, hill scaling; *Style—* David Jenkin, Esq; TSW Broadcasting Ltd, Derrys Cross, Plymouth PL1 2SP (☎ 0752 663322, telex 81: ITA113-9312130252, car 0836 591 894)

JENKIN, Ian Evers Tregarthen; OBE (1984); s of late Henry Archibald Tregarthen Jenkin, OBE (d 1951), of The Firs, Norton, Worcs, and Dagmar, *née* Leggott (d 1969); *b* 18 June 1920; *Educ* Stowe, Slade Sch of Fine Art, Camberwell Sch of Art and Crafts, Trinity Coll Cambridge (MA); *Career* Mil Serv RA 1940-46; dir and co-fndr (with Lord Young of Dartington) Open Coll of The Arts 1986-89 (pres 1989-91, vice pres 1991-), curator Royal Acad Schs 1985-86, princ Camberwell Sch of Art and Crafts 1975-85, ret; sec and tutor Slade Sch of Fine Art UCL 1949-75; memb: Art Panel Arts Cncl 1979-82 (also vice chm), Crafts Cncl 1981-84, Educn Ctee 1981-84 (also chm), Nat Advsy Body for Public Sector Higher Educn Art and Design Working Gp 1982-85, Nat Conservation Advsy Ctee 1984-86, Arts Ctee RSA 1989-; chm: Painting Faculty Br Sch at Rome 1977-86, Fine Arts Faculty 1986-90 (memb Cncl 1981-90); Gulbenkian Fndn Craft Initiative Working Pty 1985-89; govr: Hounslow Borough Coll 1976-81, W Surrey Coll of Art and Design 1975-, Wimbledon Sch of Art 1985-90, Loughborough Coll of Art and Design 1985-, Norfolk Inst of Art and Design 1988-90; memb Exec Ctee Arts Servs Grants Ltd 1977 (vice chm 1983-90), fndr and tstee Camberwell Residential Academic and Fellowship Tst, pres Dulwich Decorative and Fine Arts Soc 1984-; memb: Exec Ctee and Restoration Advsy Ctee City and Guilds of London Art Sch 1985-, Fine Art Advsy Bd Amersham Coll of Further Educn 1990-, Arts Consultative Ctee Langley Co 1991-; vice pres The Nine Elms Group of Artists 1991; tstee: Sir Stanley Spencer Meml Tst 1982-, Birgit Skiöld Meml Tst 1988-; memb Advsy Ctee Paintings in Hospitals 1982-, memb Cncl Edwin Austin Abbey Scholarships 1985-; dir Guild of St George 1986- (companion 1984-); Hon Dr Arts CNAA 1987; FRSA 1975; *Publications* Disaster Planning and Preparedness, A Survey of Practices and Procedures, Br Library R & D Report (1986), An Outline Disaster Control Plan, Br Library Information Guide (1987), William Johnson, His Contribution to Art Educn (1981); *Recreations* painting, gardening, farming; *Clubs* Athenaeum, Bucks, Arts; *Style—* Ian Tregarthen Jenkin, Esq, OBE; Grove Farm, Fifield, Maidenhead, Berks SL6 2PF (☎ 0628 24486)

JENKIN OF RODING, Baron (Life Peer UK 1987), of Wanstead and Woodford in Greater London; (Charles) Patrick Fleeming Jenkin; PC (1973); s of Charles O F Jenkin (d 1939), of Gerrards Cross, Bucks; er bro of Rear Adm David Conrad Jenkin, *qv*; *b* 7 Sept 1926; *Educ* Clifton, Jesus Coll Cambridge; *m* 1952, Alison Monica, eldest da of late Capt Philip Skelton Graham, RN; 2 s (Rev Hon Charles Alexander Graham b 1954, Hon Bernard Christison b 1959), 2 da (Hon Nicola Mary b 1956, Hon Flora Margaret b 1962); *Career* Queen's Own Cameron Highlanders 1945-48; called to the Bar Middle Temple 1952-57, Distillers Co Ltd 1957-70; memb Hornsey Borough Cncl 1960-63; govr Westfield Coll Univ of London 1964-70; MP (C) Wanstead and Woodford 1964-87, jt vice chm Cons Parly Trade and Power Ctee 1966, oppn front bench spokesman on Treasy, Trade and Econ Affrs 1965-70, fin sec to Treasy 1970-72, chief sec to Treasy 1972-74, min for Energy Jan-March 1974, memb Shadow Cabinet and shadow spokesman on Energy 1974-76 and on Social Servs 1976-79; sec of State for: Social Servs 1979-81, Indust 1981-83, DOE 1983-85; chm: Friends' Provident Life Office, Lamco Paper Sales Ltd; dir Nat Econ Res Assocs Inc (UK office); advsr: Arthur Andersen & Co, Sumitomo Tst and Bank Ltd; chm: UK-Japan 2000 Gp 1986-90, Taverner Concerts Tst, Target Finland, Westfield Coll Tst; vice pres: Nat Assoc of Local Cncls, Assoc of Metropolitan Authorities; pres: Greater London Area Conservatives, British Urban Regeneration Assoc, Friends of Wanstead Hosp; memb Cncl Guide Dogs for The Blind Assoc; *Recreations* gardening, music, bricklaying, sailing, DIY; *Clubs* West Essex Cons; *Style—* The Rt Hon the Lord Jenkin of Roding, PC; Home Farm, Matching Rd, Hatfield Heath, Bishop's Stortford, Herts CM22 7AS; 703 Howard House, Dolphin Sq, London SW1 3LX; 15 Old Bailey, London EC4M 7AP (☎ 071 329 4454)

JENKINS, Alan Dominique; s of Ian Samuel Jenkins, of Dorset, and Jeannette Juliette; *b* 27 May 1952; *Educ* Clifton Coll, New Coll Oxford (BA); *m* 30 June 1979, Caroline, da of Paul Treverton Jones (d 1983), of Gwent; 1 s (Mark b 30 May 1982), 2 da (Claire b 13 April 1984, Alice 17 Oct 1989); *Career* admitted slr 1977, ptnr Frere Cholmeley 1983-; memb: Law Soc, Holborn Law Soc, Int Bar Assoc, UK Environmental Law Assoc; *Recreations* tennis, skiing, golf, swimming, music, theatre; *Clubs* Roehampton; *Style—* Alan Jenkins, Esq; Frere Cholmeley, 28 Lincoln's Inn Fields, London WC2A 3HH (☎ 071 405 7878, fax 071 405 9056, telex 27623 FRERESG)

JENKINS, Prof Aubrey Dennis; s of Arthur William Jenkins (d 1982), and Mabel Emily, *née* Street (d 1970); *b* 6 Sept 1927; *Educ* Dartford GS, Sir John Cass Tech Inst, King's Coll London (BSc, PhD, DSc); *m* 29 Dec 1987, Jitka, da of Josef Horský (d 1975); *Career* res chemist Courtaulds Fundamental Res Laboratory 1950-60, res mangr Gillette Fundamental Res Laboratory 1960-64, Univ of Sussex 1964- (prof of polymer sci 1971-); Heyrovský Gold medal for chemistry from Czechoslovak Acad of Scis 1990; sec Macromolecular Div Int Union of Pure and Applied Chemistry, memb Brighton Health Authy 1938-90; FRSC 1957; *Books* Kinetics of Vinyl Polymerization (1958), Reactivity Mechanism and Structure in Polymer Chemistry (1974), Polymer Science (1972); *Recreations* music, travel; *Clubs* G B, E Europe Centre; *Style—* Prof Aubrey Jenkins; Shoe Box Cottage, 115 Keymer Road, Hassocks, W Sussex BN6 8QL (☎ 07918 5410); School of Chemistry and Molecular Sciences, Univ of Sussex, Brighton, Sussex BN1 9QJ (☎ 0273 678321)

JENKINS, Brian Garton; s of Owen Garton Jenkins (d 1963), and Doris Enid, *née* Webber (d 1986); *b* 3 Dec 1935; *Educ* Tonbridge, Trinity Coll Oxford (MA); *m* 2 Jun 1967, (Elizabeth) Ann, da of John Philip Manning Prentice (d 1981), of Suffolk; 1 s (Charles b 1973), 1 da (Julia b 1971); *Career* 2 Lt RA 1955-57, served Gibraltar; CA; head of Audit Coopers & Lybrand Deloitte 1986- (ptnr 1969-, joined 1960); pres ICAEW 1985-86, govr Royal Shakespeare Theatre 1981-, memb Cmmn for New Towns 1990-; Alderman City of London 1980- (Sheriff 1987-88); Liveryman: Worshipful Co of CAs 1980- (Master 1990), Worshipful Co of Merchant Taylors 1984- (memb Ct 1989-); ACA 1963, FCA 1974, FRSA 1980; *Books* An Audit Approach to Computers (jtly, 1978, 1986); *Recreations* garden construction, old books, large jigsaw puzzles, ephemera; *Clubs* Brooks's, City of London, City Livery; *Style—* Brian Jenkins, Esq; Plumtree Court, London EC4A 4HT (☎ 071 583 5000, fax 071 822 4652)

JENKINS, Brian Stuart; s of Harold Griffith Jenkins (d 1970), of Christleton, Chester, and Ida Lily, *née* Stuart (d 1986); *b* 26 May 1934; *Educ* Shrewsbury; *m* 5 Sept 1959, Teresa Sheelagh, da of Stephen George Ronan (d 1980), of Wigfair Isaph, St Asaph, N Wales; 2 s (Nicolaus Stuart b 13 March 1961, Simon Spencer b 26 March 1962), 1 da (Vanessa Stephanie b 7 July 1965); *Career* RN 1952-54, Midshipman 1953 (served HMS Surprise, fleet despatch vessel Med Fleet), Mersey Div RNR, ret Lt 1960; CA; sr ptnr Haswell Bros 1970-; chm Wrexham and East Denbighshire Water Co 1987- (dir 1969-), former memb Wales Regnl Bd TSB Gp plc; FCA 1966; *Recreations* sailing, shooting, travel; *Clubs* Royal Yacht Sqdn; *Style—* Brian Jenkins, Esq; Beeston House, Tarporley, Cheshire (☎ 0829 260 326)

JENKINS, Catrin Mary; da of Charles Bryan Jenkins, of Gorwelion, 2 Croft Lane, Southerndown, Mid Glamorgan, and Anne, *née* Davies-Jones; *b* 22 Dec 1958; *Educ* Llanelli Girls GS, Univ Coll Cardiff (LLB); *Career* admitted slr 1983; ptnr Philips & Buck 1988-; *Style—* Miss Catrin Jenkins; 15 Hollybush Rise, Cyncoed, Cardiff, Wales (☎ 0222 733695); Fitzalan House, Fitzalan Rd, Cardiff, Wales CF2 1XZ (☎ 0222 471147, telex 792331)

JENKINS, Hon Charles Arthur Simon; s of Baron Jenkins of Hillhead (Life Peer), *qv*; *b* 25 March 1949; *Educ* Winchester, Holland Park Sch, New Coll Oxford; *m* 11 Sept 1971, Ivana Alexandra, da of Ing Ivo Vladimir Sertic (d 1986), of Zagreb, Yugoslavia; 2 da (Alexandra Dorothea b 14 March 1986, Helena Harriet b 13 May 1988); *Career* Euro ed Economist Intelligence Unit 1975-, ed Euro Trends (quarterly magazine on Euro affrs); memb Clapham Soc Planning and Tport Ctee; *Style—* The Hon Charles Jenkins; Economist Intelligence Unit, 40 Duke Street, London W1A 1DW (☎ 071 493 6711)

JENKINS, Clive Ferguson; s of Merlyn Jenkins (d 1975), and Annie Elizabeth, *née* Davies (d 1970); *b* 19 Oct 1936; *Educ* Dynevor Secdy Sch Swansea, Welsh Sch of Architecture Cardiff (Dip Arch); *m* 11 Aug 1962, Pauline Helen, da of William George Sutton (d 1974), of Swansea; 1 s (Craig Warren b 1969), 1 da (Kimberley Sian b 1967); *Career* chartered architect private practice, dir PM Devpts Ltd 1987; fndr sec Welsh Water Ski Ctee 1963, Welsh Water Ski Jumping Champion 1970 (overall runner up 1970); RIBA; *Recreations* snow skiing, golf, scuba diving; *Style—* Clive F Jenkins, Esq; 8 Northway, Bishopston, Gower, W Glam (☎ 044 128 2210); 42 Newton Rd, Oystermouth, Swansea (☎ 07920 361830)

JENKINS, Prof David; s of Alfred Thomas Jenkins (d 1960), and Doris Cecelia, *née* Hutchings; *b* 1 March 1926; *Educ* Marlborough, RVC, Univ of Cambridge (MA), Univ of Oxford (PhD, DSc); *m* 8 April 1961, Margaret, da of James Wellwood Johnston (d 1958); 1 s (Gavin b 1969), 1 da (Fenella b 1967); *Career* vertebrate ecologist Nature Conservancy 1956-72; asst dir res: Scotland NC 1966-72, Inst of Terrestrial Ecology 1972-86; head Banchory Res Station; hon prof Aberdeen 1986-; chm Sci Advsy Ctee World Pheasant Assoc 1976-; FRSE, MRCVS; *Books* Population Control in Protected Partridges (1961), Social Behaviour in the Partridge (1963), Population Studies on Red Grouse in N E Scotland (with A Watson and G R Miller, 1963), Population Fluctuations in the Red Grouse (with A Watson and G R Miller, 1967), Structure and Regulation of a Shelduck Population (with M G Murray and P Hall, 1975), Ecology of Otters in Scotland and Otter Breeding and Dispersion in Mid-Deeside Aberdeenshire in 1974-79 (1980); *Recreations* natural history, gardening; *Style—* Prof David Jenkins, FRSE; Whitewalls, Aboyne, Aberdeenshire AB3 5JB

JENKINS, Dr David Anthony Lawson; s of Phillip Ronald Jenkins (d 1969), of Leigh on Sea, Essex, and Olive Lilian, *née* Lear; *b* 5 Dec 1938; *Educ* Dauntseys Sch Wilts, Clare Coll Cambridge (BA, DPhil); *m* 13 Feb 1963, Evanthia, da of Spirithonos Nicolopoulou, of Patras; 2 s (Charles David b 19 June 1969, Anthony Phillip b 8 Aug 1970); *Career* BP 1961-: chief geologist Exploration 1979-82, sr vice pres Exploration and Prodn Canada 1983-84, gen mangr Exploration 1985-88, Devpt, chief exec Technol Exploration 1988-, dir Exploration 1989-, dir Canada 1989-; fell Geological Soc, AAPG; *Recreations* tennis, theatre, gardening, current affairs, travel; *Style—* Dr David Jenkins; Ardennes, East Rd, St George's Hill, Weybridge; D'Arcy House, 146 Queen Victoria St, London EC4V 4BY (☎ 071 489 6565, fax 071 489 6626, telex 888811)

JENKINS, Edward Victor; s of Ernest Victor Jenkins (d 1977), of Hedd Wyn, Chandag Rd, Keynsham, Bristol, and Winifred Agnes, *née* Capron (d 1983); *b* 17 Aug 1932; *Educ* Frays Coll Uxbridge, Ealing GS, Northampton Engrg Coll (BSc), Imperial Coll London (DIC); *m* 5 Sept 1959, Elisabeth, da of Hubert Deacon Harrison, OBE, MC (d 1987), of Victoria, Vancouver, BC, Canada; 1 s (Christopher b 1965), 1 da (Victoria b 1968); *Career* Nat Serv RE 1956-58; engrg pupil 1951-55, Holland and Hannen & Cubitts Ltd 1958-66; G Maunsell & Ptnrs: section and resident engr 1966-72, sr engr 1972-73, assoc 1973-75, project ptnr seconded to Maunsell Consultants Asia Hong Kong 1978-81, md 1987-; dir Guy Maunsell International Ltd; FICE, MConsE; *Recreations* sailing, rugby football, choral singing; *Clubs* Army & Navy, Royal Hong Kong Yacht; *Style—* Edward Jenkins, Esq; Yeoman House, 63 Croydon Rd, London SE20 7TP (☎ 081 778 6060, fax 081 659 5568, telex 946 171)

JENKINS, Dr Elizabeth; da of George Woodward Turner (d 1962), of Anglesey, and Elsie Aggie, *née* Fox; *b* 15 Feb 1922; *Educ* Withington Girls' Sch Manchester, Victoria Univ of Manchester (MB ChB); *m* 25 March 1944, Sqdn Ldr Richard John Jenkins, s of the late Rev John Jenkins; 1 s (Simon b 1947), 2 da (Anne Elizabeth (Mrs Rees-Jenkins) b 1949, Diana Margaret (Mrs Gray-Buchanan) b 1952); *Career* MO Govt of Aden 1954-56; assoc specialist in psychiatry St John's Hosp Lincoln 1964- (prev med asst and clinical asst); memb: Lincoln City Cncl 1976-, Lincolnshire CC (chm Social Serv 1983-89); dir Family Policy Studies Centre 1988-, dep chm Lincoln Cons Assoc 1983-86; SSStJ 1972; *Recreations* local community, gardening; *Style—* Dr Elizabeth Jenkins

JENKINS, Very Rev Frank Graham; s of Edward Jenkins (d 1961), of Glamorgan, and Miriam Martha Jenkins, *née* Morse (d 1978); *b* 24 Feb 1923; *Educ* Cyfarthfa Castle Sch Merthyr Tydfil, Port Talbot Secdy GS, St Davids Coll Lampeter (BA), Jesus Coll Oxford (BA, MA), St Michael's Coll Llandaff; *m* 1 Aug 1950, Ena Doraine, da of Eardley Morgan Parry (d 1970), of Port Talbot; 2 s (Timothy b 1955, Peter b 1958), 1 da (Caroline b 1951); *Career* cmmnd Welsh Regt 1944-46 (Capt), CF (TA) 1956-61; curate of Llangeinor 1950-53, minor canon Llandaff Cathedral 1953-60, vicar of Abertillery 1960-64, vicar of Risca 1964-75, vicar of Caerleon 1975-76, dean of Monmouth 1976-90; *Style—* The Very Rev the Dean of Monmouth; Rivendell, 209 Christchurch Road, Newport, Gwent NP9 7QL (☎ 0633 255278)

JENKINS, Prof George Charles; s of John Robinson Jenkins (d 1969), of Stoneygate, Leics, and Mabel Rebecca, *née* Smith (d 1985); *b* 2 Aug 1927; *Educ* Wyggeston Leics, St Bartholomew's Hosp Med Coll, Univ of London (MB BS, PhD); *m* 28 April 1956, Elizabeth Claire, da of Cecil Joseph Welch (d 1963), of Carlton Rd, Ealing; 1 s (Mark Andrew b 15 Nov 1957), 2 da (Nicola Claire b 11 April 1961, Camilla Anne b 3 Jan 1963); *Career* Sqdn Ldr RAF (Med Branch) 1952-54, civilian conslt haematologist RN 1978-; conslt haematologist: N Middx Hosp 1963-65, Royal London Hosp 1965-; reader in haematology Univ of London 1971-74, prof of haematology Univ of London at London Hosp Med Coll 1974-; vice pres RCPath 1981-84, pres Br Soc for Haematology 1988-89, pres Br Acad of Forensic Sci 1990- (chm Exec Cncl 1985-89), memb Ctee on Dental and Surgical Materials (Ctee of Safety of Meds of DOH) 1990-; patron Home Farm Tst; Freeman City of London 1961, memb Worshipful Co of Spectacle Makers 1961; FRCPath 1975, FRCPE 1990; *Books* Advanced Haematology (jt ed and author); *Recreations* fishing, music, theatre going; *Style—* Prof George Jenkins; 19 Bush Hill, London N21 2DB (☎ 081 360 1484); London Hosp Medical College, Whitechapel, London E1 2AD (☎ 071 377 7178)

JENKINS, Graeme James Ewers; s of Kenneth Arthur Jenkins, of London, and Marjorie Joyce, *née* Ewers; *b* 31 Dec 1958; *Educ* Dulwich, Gonville and Caius Coll Cambridge (MA), RCM London; *m* 19 July 1986, Joanna, da of Christopher Charles Cyprian Bridge, ERD, of E Sussex; 1 da (Martha Nancy b 18 May 1989); *Career* conductor; music dir: Glyndebourne Touring Opera 1985-91, Glyndebourne Festival Opera, English Nat Opera, Scottish Opera, Kent Opera, Opera North, Geneva Opera, Netherlands Opera, Canadian Opera, Australian Opera, princ Br orchestras; Freeman Worshipful Co of Goldsmiths 1989; ARCM; *Recreations* reading, cooking; *Clubs* Savile; *Style—* Graeme Jenkins, Esq; Pond Cottage, Friston, Nr Eastbourne, E Sussex BN20 0AG (☎ 0323 423400)

JENKINS, Prof Harold; s of Henry Jenkins (d 1932), of Shenley Church End, Bucks, and Mildred, *née* Carter (d 1959); *b* 19 July 1909; *Educ* UCL (BA, MA); *m* 23 Jan 1939, Gladys Grace (d 1984), da of Albert George Victor Puddifoot (d 1960), of London; *Career* William Noble fell of Liverpool 1935-36; Univ of Witwatersrand SA: jr lectr in English 1936-38, lectr 1938-44 (DLitt 1944), sr lectr 1945; reader in English UCL 1946-54 (lectr 1945-46), prof of English Westfield Coll London 1954-67, visiting prof Duke Univ USA 1957-58, Regius prof of rhetoric and English literature Univ of Edinburgh 1967-71 (emeritus 1971-), visiting prof Univ of Oslo 1974; gen ed The Arden Shakespeare 1958-82; memb Ed Bd: Shakespeare Survey 1964-72, Studies in English Literature 1961-78; contrib: Modern Language Review, Review of English Studies, The Library, Studies in Bibliography, Shakespeare Survey; pres Malone Soc 1989- (cncl memb 1955-89); awarded Shakespeare Prize Stiftung FVS Hamburg 1986; Hon DLitt Iona Coll New Rochelle NY USA 1983; FBA 1989; memb: Int Shakespeare Assoc, Int Assoc of Univ Profs of English; *Publications* The Life and Work of Henry Chettle (1934), Edward Benlowes (1952), The Structural Problem in Shakespeare's Henry IV (1956), The Catastrophe in Shakespearean Tragedy (1969), Hamlet (ed, 1982); *Clubs* Athenaeum; *Style—* Prof Harold Jenkins; 22 North Crescent, Finchley, London N3 3LL

JENKINS, Howard Max Lewis; s of Sqdn Ldr Lewis Max Jenkins, MBE (d 1981), of Bournemouth, and Georgina Ann, *née* Beasant (d 1989); *b* 30 July 1947; *Educ* Bournemouth Sch, Univ of London Middx Hosp (MB BS); *m* 20 Nov 1971, Carol Ann, da of Christopher Downs Hankinson (d 1958), of Southampton; 2 da (Catherine b 1976, Sarah b 1979); *Career* house surgn Middx Hosp 1972, registrar Professorial Unit Nottingham 1976-79, conslt obstetrician and gynaecologist Derby City Hosp 1985-, clinical teacher Univ of Nottingham 1985- (med res fell 1979-81, clinical lectr in obstetrics and gynaecology 1981-85); author of many papers in professional jls and chapters in books; memb Examination Ctee and examiner RCOG, examiner Univ of Nottingham; memb: Nuffield Visiting Soc, Birmingham and Midland Obstetrics and Gynaecology Soc; DM Univ of Nottingham 1984; DObst RCOG 1973, FRCOG 1990 (MRCOG 1977); *Recreations* family and home, any machinery (mechanical, electrical and electronic); *Style—* Mr Howard Jenkins; Derby City Hospital, Uttoxeter Rd, Derby DE3 3NE (☎ 0332 40131); 15 Vernon St, Derby DE1 1FT (☎ 0332 47272)

JENKINS, Hugh Royston; s of Hubert Graham (d 1977), of Llanelli, S Wales, and Violet, *née* Aston; *b* 9 Nov 1933; *Educ* Llanelli GS; *m* (m dis); *Career* LCC 1956-63, md CIN Properties Ltd 1969-73 (asst property controller 1963-69), dir gen NCB Pension Funds 1973-85, chief exec Heron Fin Corpn LA 1985-86, gp investmt dir Allied Dunbar Assur plc 1986-, chm and chief exec Allied Dunbar Asset Mgmnt plc 1986-, chm Dunbar Bank plc 1986-; formerly: lay memb Int Stock Exchange, memb City Capital Markets Ctee, vice chm Nat Assoc of Pension Funds and chm of the Investmt Ctee, non-exec dir Stock Conversion plc, non-exec dir London and Manchester Assur plc; currently non exec dir: Heron Int NV, Unilever Pensions Ltd, IBM Pension Tst Co Ltd, Property Advsy Ctee DOE; FRICS, FPMI, memb Anglo-American Real Estate Inst; *Recreations* theatre; *Clubs* Garrick; *Style—* Hugh Jenkins, Esq; 3 Christchurch Terrace, Chelsea SW3; Sackville House, 9-15 Sackville St, London W1 (☎ 071 434 3211, fax 071 494 3067, car 0850 359088)

JENKINS, Ian David Pearson; s of Norman Marsden Jenkins, of Emsworth, and Beryl Margaret Andrews, *née* Pearson; *b* 24 Aug 1946; *Educ* Denstone Coll, King's Coll London (LLB); *m* 6 Jan 1973, Judy Mary, da of John Ernest Middleton Rogers (d 1971), of Salisbury, Rhodesia; 2 s (Peter b 27 June 1979, David b 22 March 1982); *Career* sr ptnr Barlow Lyde & Gilbert 1989-; *Recreations* sailing; *Clubs* Royal Thames Yacht, Royal Southern Yacht, Ocean Cruising; *Style—* Ian Jenkins, Esq; 39 Sheen Common Drive, Richmond, Surrey TW10 5BW (☎ 081 876 6905); Beaufort House, 15 St Botolph St, London EC3A 7NJ (☎ 071 247 2277, fax 071 782 8500, telex 913281)

JENKINS, Dr Ivor; CBE (1970); s of Thomas Jenkins (d 1955), of Gwynfryn, Kingsbridge, Gorseinon, Swansea, and Mary Emily Ellen, *née* Evans (d 1959); *b* 25 July 1913; *Educ* Gowerton GS, Univ Coll Swansea (BSc, MSc, DSc); *m* 19 April 1941, Caroline Wijnanda, da of William John James (d 1961), of 47 Roxeth Hill, Harrow, Middx; 2 s (Brian James b 4 April 1944, Peter Anthony b 15 Feb 1947); *Career* chief metallurgist GEC Hirst Res Centre 1952-61; dir for res: Manganese Bronze Holdings Ltd 1961-69, Delta Metal Co Ltd 1969-78; Williams prize Iron and Steel Inst 1946, Platinum medal The Metals Soc 1978; fell UC Swansea 1986, pres Onehouse Harleston and Shelland (Suffolk) Community Cncl 1974-80; FEng 1979, FIM 1948 (pres 1965-66 and 1968-69); fell American Soc of Metals; *Books* Controlled Atmospheres for the Heat Treatment of Metals (1946); *Recreations* walking, swimming; *Clubs* Athenaeum, Anglo-Belgian; *Style—* Dr Ivor Jenkins, CBE; 31 Trotyn Croft, Aldwick Felds, Aldwick, Bognor Regis, W Sussex PO21 3TX (☎ 0243 828749)

JENKINS, John George; CBE; s of George John Jenkins, and Alice Maud, *née* Prickett; *b* 26 Aug 1919; *Educ* Winchester, Univ of Edinburgh; *m* 1948, Chloe Evelyn, da of John Kenward; 1 s (Martin), 3 da (Alison, Penelope, Jocelyn); *Career* farmer landowner (694 acres); dir Agric Mortgage Corpn 1969-90, chm Utd Oilseeds Ltd 1983-87; pres NFU of Scotland 1960-61; *Recreations* tennis, bridge; *Clubs* Farmers; *Style—* John Jenkins, Esq, CBE

JENKINS, Hon Mrs (Judith Catharine Dean); 3 da of Baron Soper (Life Peer); *b* 25 Oct 1942; *Educ* BSc; *m* 1970, Alan Jenkins, BEd; *Style—* The Hon Mrs Jenkins

JENKINS, Maurice; s of David Jenkins (d 1978), and Josephine Lily Jenkins; *b* 9 July 1925; *Educ* Acklam Sch Middlesborough, Univ of Manchester, Univ of London; *m* 1951, Dorothy, *née* Tait; 1 s, 2 da; *Career* admin offr HM Overseas Civil Serv Nigeria 1951-62; chm Rugby Portland Cement Co plc 1984- (dep chm 1976-84, md 1968-84), chm and dir of assoc cos Cockburn Cement Ltd W Aust 1974-; memb London Bd Norwich Union Insur Gp 1974-80, dir AP Bank Ltd 1981-; vice pres Nat Cncl of Bldg Material Prodrs 1976-; memb Nat Econ Devpt Ctee for Civil Engrg 1972-82; cncl memb CBI 1984-; *Recreations* business, family; *Style—* Maurice Jenkins, Esq; 5 Bilton Rd, Rugby, Warwicks (☎ 0788 65547); Rugby Portland Cement Co plc, Crown House, Rugby CV21 2DT (☎ 0788 2111, telex 31523)

JENKINS, Michael Nicholas Howard; OBE (1991); s of Maj Cyril Norman Jenkins (d 1985), and Maud Evelyn Sophie, *née* Shorter; *b* 13 Oct 1932; *Educ* Tonbridge, Merton Coll Oxford (BA); *m* 28 Sept 1957, Jacqueline Frances, da of Francis Jones (d

1979); 3 s (Howard Michael Charles b 1958, (Edward) Hugo b 1961, Oliver John b 1966); *Career* Nat Serv 2 Lt RA 1951-53; Shell-Mex and BP 1956-61, IBM UK 1961-67, ptnr Robson Morrow Management Consultants 1967-71, tech dir The Stock Exchange 1971-77, md European Options Exchange Amsterdam 1977-80, chief exec London International Financial Futures Exchange 1981-; FBIM; *Recreations* games, music, woodworking; *Clubs* Wilderness (Sevenoaks); *Style—* Michael Jenkins, Esq, OBE; The London International, Financial Futures Exchange, The Royal Exchange, London EC3V 3PJ (☎ 071 623 0444, fax 071 588 3624, telex 893893 LIFFE G)

JENKINS, HE Sir Michael Romilly Heald; KCMG (1990, CMG 1984); s of Romilly James Heald Jenkins (d 1969), and Celine Juliette, *née* Haeglar; *b* 9 Jan 1936; *Educ* King's Coll Cambridge (BA); *m* 1968, Maxine Louise, da of Dudley Hodson (d 1982); 1 s (Nicholas b 1975), 1 da (Catherine b 1971); *Career* HM Dip Serv (Paris, Moscow, Bonn) 1959-; dep sec-gen of Euro Cmmn 1981-83, asst under-sec of state FCO 1983-85, min HM Embassy Washington 1985-87; Br ambass The Hague 1988-; contrib to History Today; *Books* Arakcheev, Grand Vizir of the Russian Empire (1969); *Clubs* Athenaeum, MCC; *Style—* HE Sir Michael Jenkins, KCMG; c/o Foreign & Commonwealth Office, London SW1

JENKINS, Nicholas Garratt; s of Edward Adam (d 1965), and Betty, *née* Warburton; *b* 16 Feb 1939; *Educ* Bradfield, Byam Shaw Sch of Art, St Martins Sch of Art; *m* 1, 1960, Marie France Aries; 2 da (Nathalie b 1961, Carolyn b 1964); m 2, 1981, Jane Hiller; 2 da (Alys b 1986, Lucy b 1988); *Career* display designer Simpson's Piccadilly 1961-62, art dir New English Library 1963-64, sr tutor RCA 1965-75, co-fndr Guyatt/Jenkins (now renamed the Jenkins Group) 1975, currently sr dir TJG and Nicholas Jenkins & Associates; chm Design Week awards 1990 and 1991, co-fndr Design Business Assoc, significant achievements incl: two solo exhibitions of poster designs (RCA and Univ of Marseilles), design of corporate identities for W H Smith, The Nat Gallery, Queen's Silver Jubliee, CIMA, PRS; Fell RCA, FCSD (former vice pres), FRSA; award winner first prize Israel Museum Book Design; *Books* photographics, David Hicks Living With Design, The Monarchy Book; *Recreations* writing and jazz; *Style—* Nicholas Jenkins, Esq; The Jenkins Group, 9 Tufton Street, London SW1 (☎ 071 799 1090, fax 071 222 6751)

JENKINS, Nicholas Stephen; s of Walter Walker Jenkins (d 1982), of Tanglewood, Pyrford, Surrey, and Teresa Davis, *née* Callens; *b* 8 Feb 1954; *Educ* Salesian Coll Chertsey, Harlow Coll; *m* 25 Oct 1974, Marion Joanne, da of Henry Alexander Findlay (d 1966), of Chatham, Kent; 2 s (Joel, Jordan); *Career* PR conslt; formed Jenkins Group 1975-; MIPR; *Recreations* tennis, helicopters, historic aircraft; *Clubs* Castle (Rochester), Roffen, Helicopter Club of GB; *Style—* Nicholas Jenkins, Esq; Castle Chambers, Castle Hill, Rochester, Kent; Berkeley House, 186 High St, Rochester, Kent ME1 1EY (☎ 0634 408 325, fax 0634 830 930, car 0860 414285, telex 94015848 JORG G)

JENKINS, (Graham) Nicholas Vellacott; s of Gwynne Jenkins (d 1988), of Radlett, Herts and Irene Lillan, *née* Vellacott; *b* 15 Dec 1945; *Educ* Radley; *m* 23 April 1977, Margaret Alice, *née* Bailey; 4 s (Nicolas Edward Vellacott b 9 May 1978, Jonathan William Vellacott b 16 July 1980, Edward Henry Vellacott b 20 March 1984, William Alexander Vellacott b 7 April 1987); *Career* CA; Whinney, Smith & Whinney (now Ernst & Young): articled clerk (London) 1964, Cardiff office 1968, London 1969; ptnr Moores Rowland 1974 (formerly Rowland & Co) (joined 1970); Freeman City of London, Liveryman Worshipful Co of Barbers; FCA (ACA 1969); *Recreations* fishing, golf; *Clubs* Hon Artillery Co, Flyfishers, Ashridge Golf, Royal Porthcawl Golf; *Style—* Nicholas Jenkins, Esq; Moores Rowland, Clifford's Inn, Fetter Lane, London EC4A 1AS (☎ 071 831 2345)

JENKINS, Sir Owain Trevor; s of Sir John Lewis Jenkins, KCSI (d 1912); bro of Rt Hon Lord Jenkins (d 1967), and of Sir Evan Meredith Jenkins, GCIE, KCSI (d 1985); *b* 20 Feb 1907; *Educ* Charterhouse, Balliol Coll Oxford; *m* 1940, Sybil Léonie, da of Maj-Gen Lionel Herbert, CB, CVO (d 1929); *Career* served WWII 45 Cavalry IA, Maj; md Balmer Lawrie & Co (Calcutta) 1948-59 (joined 1929); dir: Calcutta Electric Supply Corpn, MacLeod Russel & Co Ltd, and other cos 1960-82; pres: Bengal C of C and Indust 1956-57, Assoc C of Cs of India 1956-57, UK Citizens Assoc 1957-58; kt 1958; *Books* The Dark Horse (with Rumer Godden, 1981), Merchant Prince, Memoirs (1987); *Clubs* Oriental; *Style—* Sir Owain Jenkins; Boles House, East St, Petworth, W Sussex GU28 0AB (☎ 0798 42531)

JENKINS, Peter George James; s of Kenneth E Jenkins, of Norfolk, and Joan, *née* Croger (d 1981); *b* 11 May 1934; *Educ* Culford Sch, Trinity Hall Cambridge (BA, MA), Univ of Oxford (MA), Univ of Wisconsin USA; *m* 1, 1960, Charlotte (d 1970), da of John Strachey; 1 da (Amy b 20 Oct 1963); m 2, 28 Dec 1970, Mary Louisa (Polly), da of Philip Toynbee; 1 s (Nathaniel b 10 Jan 1985), 2 da (Milly b 5 Dec 1971, Flora b 17 Dec 1976); *Career* journalist; Financial Times 1958-60; The Guardian 1960-85: lab corr 1963-70, Washington corr 1972-74, political commentator and policy ed 1974-85; theatre critic The Spectator 1978-81, political columnist The Sunday Times 1985-87, assoc ed The Independent 1987-; first stage play Illuminations (1980), TV series Struggle (1983); Granada TV Journalist of the Year 1978; *Books* The Battle of Downing Street (1970), 1987 Mrs Thatcher's Revolution - The Ending of the Socialist Era (1987); *Clubs* Garrick; *Style—* Peter Jenkins, Esq; 1 Crescent Grove, London SW4 7AF (☎ 071 622 6492); The Independent, 40 City Rd, London EC1Y 2DB (☎ 071 253 1222)

JENKINS, Peter Sefton; s of John Harry Sefton Jenkins (d 1978), of Croft Lodge, Bramley, Northants, and Helen Summers, *née* Staveley; *b* 9 Feb 1948; *Educ* King's Sch Canterbury, St Edmund Hall Oxford (MA); *m* 8 June 1972, Jacqueline, da of John Mills (d 1976); 2 s (Benjamin b 13 June 1975, Christopher b 7 April 1979); *Career* HM Customs and Excise 1969-86: private sec to chm 1972-74, Cabinet Office 1974-77, involved in EC negotiations on customs duty harmonisations 1977-79, private sec to Chllr of Exchequer 1979, asst sec VAT Admin 1983-86; ptnr VAT and Customs Gp Ernst & Whinney 1986-; memb VAT Practioners Gp 1988; *Recreations* squash, music (violin, singing), opera, walking; *Clubs* Reform; *Style—* Peter Jenkins, Esq; 63 Guibal Road, London, SE12 (☎ 081 857 1548), Ernst Whinney, Becket House, 1 Lambeth Palace Road, London, SE1 7EU (☎ 071 928 2000, fax 071 928 1345)

JENKINS, (William Martyn) Peter; s of Cyfaude Glyndwr Jenkins, of Swansea, and Helen Phillips, *née* Frew; *b* 4 Feb 1954; *Educ* Bishop Gore GS Swansea, King's Coll Cambridge (MA), London Business Sch (MBA); *m* 18 Dec 1976, Deborah Jenkins, da of Maj Ronald Jarman, of Whitstable; 2 s (Matthew b 5 June 1985, Eliot b 18 Aug 1988); *Career* princ Booz Allen and Hamilton 1981-86, md Spicer and Oppenheim Conslts 1986-; *Style—* Peter Jenkins, Esq; Friary Court, 65 Crutched Friars, London EC3N 2NP (☎ 071 480 7766, fax 071 480 6958)

JENKINS, Dr Rachel; da of Peter Osborne McDougall, of Durham, and Beryl, *née* Braddock; *b* 17 April 1949; *Educ* Monmouth Sch for Girls, St Paul's Girls Sch, Girton Coll Cambridge (BA, MA, MB BChir, MD); *m* 6 July 1974, (David) Keith Jenkins, s of Lt Cdr David Edward Jenkins, of Chesterfield; 1 s (Benjamin b 1983), 1 da (Ruth b 1979); *Career* registrar Maudsley Hosp 1975-77, conslt psychiatrist and sr lectr Bart's 1985-88, hon sr lectr Inst of Psychiatry 1985- (res worker and Wellcome fell 1977-82, sr lectr 1982-85), princ MO Mental Health Div Dept of Health 1988-; 45 pubns in res jnls; memb: BMA Mental Health Ctee, Mental Health Fndn Res Ctee, RCPsych Res Ctee; MRCPsych 1978; *Books* Sex Differences in Minor Psychiatric Morbidity (1985), The Classification of Psychosocial Problems in Primary Care (1987), Post Viral Fatigue Syndrome (1990); *Recreations* wild orchids, needlework, swimming, walking, reading; *Style—* Dr Rachel Jenkins; 68 Clapham Common Northside, London SW4 9SB (☎ 071 228 4283); Le Fresse, Palluaud, St Severin, Charente, France; Mental Health Division, Department of Health, Alexander Fleming House, Elephant and Castle, London SE1 6BY (☎ 071 972 4334)

JENKINS, Simon David; s of Dr Daniel Jenkins and Nell Jenkins; *b* 10 June 1943; *Educ* Mill Hill Sch, St John's Coll Oxford (BA); *m* 1978, Gayle Hunnicutt, *qv*, the actress; 1 s (Edward Lloyd b 24 Feb 1982), 1 step s (Nolan); *Career* journalist; Country Life 1965, news ed Times Education Supplement 1966-68, columnist Evening Standard 1968-74, Insight ed Sunday Times 1974-75, ed Evening Standard 1976-78 (dep ed 1975-76), political ed The Economist 1979-86, columnist Sunday Times 1986-90, ed The Times 1990-; *Books* A City at Risk (1971), Landlords of London (1974), Insight on Portugal (ed, 1975), Newspapers: The Power and The Money (1979), The Companion Guide to Outer London (1981), The Battle for the Falklands (with Max Hastings, 1983), Images of Hampstead (1983), With Respect Ambassador (with Anne Sloman, 1985), The Market for Glory (1986); *Style—* Simon Jenkins, Esq; The Times, 1 Virginia St, London E1 9BD (☎ 071 782 5000)

JENKINS, Dr (Bernard) Stephen; s of Bernard Pizzy Terence Jenkins (d 1952), and Jane, *née* Webb; *b* 21 Dec 1939; *Educ* Christ's Coll Cambridge (MA, MB, BChir); *m* 4 July 1964 (m dis 1983), Diana, da of Edward Farmer (d 1985), of Henley-on-Thames; *Career* conslt cardiologist St Thomas Hosp 1971, dist gen mangr West Lambeth Health Authy 1985; memb Br Cardiac Soc, FRSA, FRCP; *Recreations* music; *Style—* Dr Stephen Jenkins; 15a Cleveland Square, London W2 (☎ 071 262 4159); St Thomas Hospital, Lambeth Palace Rd, London SE1 (☎ 071 928 9292, fax 071 261 9690)

JENKINS-MCKENZIE, Dulcibel Edna; da of Brig Ralph Alexander Broderick (d 1971), and Dulcie Broderick, *née* Lunt (d 1982); *b* 1 Aug 1918; *Educ* Badminton Sch Bristol, Univ of Birmingham (BA), Birkbeck Coll London, Maria Grey Coll, Coll of Law; *m* 1, 1944, John Rickatson Jenkins, s of Harold Carnegie Jenkins (d 1947); 2 s (Brian Harold Broderick b 1945, David Christopher Broderick b 1947); m 2, 1973, William McKenzie, s of Daniel McKenzie (d 1981); *Career* teacher and lawyer, HM Inspr of Factories 1941-44, lectr West London Coll 1964-68, practising barr 1967-69, sr legal asst Dept of Trade 1969-82; chm Rent Assessment Ctee 1982-89; publisher Greengates Press; art exhibition Burgh House London 1984; befriender Charing Cross Hosp; memb: Itchenor PPC, Ind Publishers Guild 1987-; Freeman City of London; *Books* Chronicles of John R Jenkins, Steps to the Bar, Moonshine Lands; *Recreations* travelling, painting, languages, swimming; *Clubs* Itchenor SC, Hurlingham; *Style—* Mrs Dulcibel E Jenkins-McKenzie; 89 Cornwall Gdns, London SW7 4AX (☎ 071 584 7674); Greengates, Itchenor, Chichester (☎ 0243 512 411)

JENKINS OF HILLHEAD, Baron (Life Peer UK 1987), of Pontypool in the Co of Gwent; Roy Harris Jenkins; PC (1964); o s of Arthur Jenkins (d 1946); MP (Lab) Pontypool 1935-46, Parly sec Miny Town and Country Planning then Educn 1945 and pps to Rt Hon Clement Attlee (later 1 Earl Attlee) 1940-45, and Hattie Jenkins; *b* 11 Nov 1920; *Educ* Abersychan GS, Balliol Coll Oxford (hon fell 1969); *m* 1945, Dame (Mary) Jennifer, DBE (chm Nat Tst 1986-; former chm: Historic Bldg Cncl for England 1975-85, Consumers' Assoc; tstee The Wallace Collection), da of Sir Parker Morris (d 1972 expert on housing after whom Parker Morris standards are named); 2 s (Hon Charles Arthur Simon b 1949, Hon Edward Nicholas b 1954), 1 da (Hon Cynthia Delanie (Hon Mrs Crosthwait) b 1951); *Career* RA 1942-44, special intelligence 1944-46 (Capt); ICFC 1946-48, contested (Lab) Solihull 1945; MP (Lab): Southwark Central 1948-50, Birmingham Stechford 1950-76; former chm and memb Exec Fabian Soc; pps to Cwlth Relations Sec 1949-50, memb UK Delgn to Cncl of Europe 1955-57; memb Ctee of Mgmnt Soc of Authors; dir John Lewis Partnership 1962-64; min of aviation 1964-65, home sec 1965-67, chllr of the Exchequer 1967-70, dep ldr Lab Party 1970-72; awarded Charlemagne and Robert Schuman prizes for services to Euro unity 1972; former govr Br Film Inst; vice pres Inst Fiscal Studies 1970-; home sec 1974-76; pres Br in Europe (EEC membership referendum) 1975; dep chm Common Market Campaign; pres Lab Ctee for Europe; chm Lab Euro Ctee; pres UK Cncl Euro Movement, pres UWIST 1975-81; tstee Pilgrims Tst 1973-; pres European Cmmn 1977-81; dir Morgan Grenfell Holdings 1981-82; fndr memb: Cncl for Social Democracy Jan 1981, SDP March 1981; contested (SDP) Warrington 1981; MP (SDP) Glasgow Hillhead (by-election) 1982-87; elected first SDP ldr 1982, resigned 1983, having led Alliance with Rt Hon David Steel into June 1983 Election; chllr of Oxford Univ 1987-; pres Royal Soc of Literature 1988-; *Publications inc* Mr Attlee: An Interim Biography, Pursuit of Progress, Mr Balfour's Poodle, Sir Charles Dilke, Asquith, Afternoon on the Potomac, What Matters Now, Nine Men of Power, Partnership of Principle, Truman, Baldwin, Gallery of Twentieth Century Portraits European Diary 1977-81; *Clubs* Brooks's, Athenaeum, Reform, Beefsteak, Pratt's, Utd Oxford and Cambridge Univ; *Style—* The Rt Hon Lord Jenkins of Hillhead, PC; St Amand's House, East Hendred, Oxon; 2 Kensington Park Gdns, London W11; House of Lords, London SW1 (071 219 6661)

JENKINS OF PUTNEY, Baron (UK 1981), of Wandsworth, Greater London; Hugh Gater Jenkins; s of Joseph Walter Jenkins (d 1955), and late Florence, *née* Gater; *b* 27 July 1908; *Educ* Enfield GS; *m* 1936, Marie Ethel (d 1989), da of Sqdn-Ldr Ernest Christopher Crosbie, RAF; *Career* sits as Lab Peer in House of Lords; served WWII, Flt-Lt RAF, UK, Burma, Pacific; with Prudential Assurance Co 1930-40; head English Programmes Rangoon Radio 1945, research offr National Union of Bank Employees (editor The Bank Officer) 1946-50; asst gen-sec Actors Equity 1950-64; MP (Lab) Wandsworth (Putney) 1964-79, min of Arts 1974-76; memb: Arts Cncl 1968-71, Drama Panel 1972-74, National Theatre Bd 1976-80; dir Theatres Trust 1977-86 (now conslt), writer and broadcaster; vice pres Theatres Advsy Cncl 1980-, pres Battersea Arts Centre 1985-88, vice pres CND 1981- (chm 1979-81, Aldermaston Marcher); *Books* The Culture Gap (1979), Rank and File (1980); *Recreations* reading, writing (radio plays), listening, talking, looking, avoiding retirement; *Style—* The Rt Hon the Lord Jenkins of Putney; House of Lords, London SW1 (☎ 071 219 6706, 071 836 8591)

JENKINSON, Dermot Julian; s of Julian Charles Lewis Jenkinson, and Diana Catherine Baird; *b* 2 Dec 1954; *Educ* Eton, Eurocentre (Lausanne and Cologne); *m* 2 May 1979, Miranda Jane, da of John Maxwell Menzies; 1 s (Oliver John Banks), 1 da (Emily Lavinia); *Career* dir: John Menzies plc 1985, Frank Smythson Inc 1985, Telegroup (Holdings) Ltd 1983; chm Early Learning Centres Inc 1986; *Clubs* Turf, New; *Style—* Dermot J Jenkinson, Esq; Philpstoun House, Linlithgow, West Lothian, Philpstoun (☎ 050 683 4287); 108 Princes Street, Edinburgh (☎ 031 225 8555)

JENKINSON, Frances, Lady; Frances; da of Harry Stremmel, of New York, USA; *m* 9 Oct 1943, Sir Anthony Banks Jenkinson, 13 Bt (d 1989); 1 s (Sir John Banks, 14 Bt, *qv*), 2 da (Jennifer Ann b 26 Nov 1947, Emily Frances Joan b 2 Sept 1953); *Style—* Frances, Lady Jenkinson; 491 South Church Street, Georgetown, Grand Cayman, British West Indies

JENKINSON, Dr James Lawrence; s of William Sinclair Jenkinson (d 1973), of

Haddington, and Eleanora Cree, *née* Lawrie; *b* 9 Jan 1939; *Educ* Edinburgh Acad, Univ of Edinburgh (MB ChB); *m* 7 Aug 1963, (Isabella) Annette Livingstone, da of Rev Alexander Downie Thomson, of Gifford; 3 da (Sheila b 1965, Fiona b 1969, Clare b 1972); *Career* conslt anaesthetist 1972, pt/t sr lectr Univ of Edinburgh 1987; examiner: RCS(Ed) 1971-, RCS 1986-, Univ of Glasgow 1987-90; pres N Br Pain Assoc 1985-88, memb Cncl Intractable Pain Soc of GB & I 1986-89; FFARCS 1969; memb fell: Assoc ANAES 1965-, Standing Ctee in Scotland Coll of Anaesthetists 1988-; RSM 1988; *Recreations* music, hill walking; *Style—* Dr James Jenkinson; Dept of Clinical Neurosciences, Western Gen Hosp, Crewe Rd, Edinburgh EH4 2XU (☎ 031 332 2525)

JENKINSON, Sir John Banks; 14 Bt (E 1661), of Hawkesbury, Co Gloucester; o s of Sir Anthony Banks Jenkinson, 13 Bt (d 1989); *b* 16 Feb 1945; *Educ* Eton, Univ of Miami USA; *m* 1979, Josephine Mary Marshall-Andrew; 1 s, 1 da; *Heir* s, George Samuel Anthony Banks Jenkinson b 8 Nov 1980; *Style—* Sir John Jenkinson, Bt; Hawkesbury Home Farm, Hawkesbury, Badminton, Avon GL9 1AY

JENKINSON, Valerie Robertson; da of late William Mar Erskine, and Flora Ernestine, *née* Robertson; *b* 16 March 1934; *Educ* St Paul's; *m* 1 March 1962, Eric Reginald Jenkinson, s of Percy Jenkinson; *Career* qualified SRN 1960; various posts Medway Health Authy 1960-79, registered clinical nurse tutor 1973, commissioning nurse New Maidstone Dist Gen Hosp Maidstone Health Authy 1973-83, dir Nursing Servs Canterbury Gen Unit Canterbury and Thanet Health Authy 1983-89; *Recreations* cooking, gardening, music; *Style—* Mrs Eric Jenkinson; Invermar, 26 Richdore Rd, Waltham, nr Canterbury, Kent CT4 5SJ (☎ 0227 70 477)

JENKS, (Maurice Arthur) Brian; s and h of Sir Richard Atherley Jenks, 2 Bt; *b* 28 Oct 1933; *Educ* Charterhouse; *m* 1962, Susan, da of Leslie Allen, of Glenside, Star Lane, Hooley, Surrey; 1 da; *Career* CA; *Recreations* wine, racing; *Style—* Brian Jenks Esq

JENKYNS, Richard Henry Austen; s of Henry Leigh Jenkyns (whose mother Winifred was gda of the Rev James Austen-Leigh, himself n of Jane Austen), of Aldeburgh; *b* 18 March 1949; *Educ* Eton, Balliol Coll Oxford; *Career* writer and classicist; fell All Souls Oxford 1972-81, lectr in classics Univ of Bristol 1978-81, fell Lady Margaret Hall Oxford 1981-; *Books* The Victorians and Ancient Greece (1980, winner of Arts Cncl Nat Book Award 1981 and Yorkshire Post Book Award 1981), Three Classical Poets (1982); *Recreations* playing the piano, looking at buildings; *Style—* Richard Jenkyns, Esq; Lady Margaret Hall, Oxford (☎ 0865 274300)

JENNER, Ann Maureen; da of Kenneth George Jenner, of GB, and Margaret Rosetta Jenner; *b* 8 March 1944; *Educ* Royal Ballet Sch; *m* 16 Jan 1980, Dale Robert Baker; 1 s (Dale Anthony Baker b 1982); *Career* Royal Ballet Co: joined 1961, soloist 1967, princ dancer 1970-78; Aust Ballet Co 1978-80; roles incl: Giselle, Sleeping Beauty, Romeo and Juliet, Cinderella, Coppelia, Anna Karenina, Don Quixote, Mayerling, La Fille Mal Gardée, Les Sylphides, Firebird, Midsummer's Night Dream, Symphonic Variations; dir Nat Theatre Ballet Sch Aust 1989-; guest teacher: Aust Ballet Co, San Francisco Ballet Co, San Francisco Ballet Sch, Queensland Ballet Co, Sydney Dance Co; *Style—* Ms Ann Jenner; National Theatre Ballet Sch, c/r Carlisle and Barkly Street, St Kilda, Melbourne, Vic 3182,, Australia (☎ 534 0221)

JENNER, Prof Frederick Alexander (Alec); s of late Frederick James Henry Jenner, and late Marion Wilson, *née* Young; *b* 15 March 1927; *Educ* Queen's Coll Taunton, Univ of Sheffield (MB ChB, PhD); *m* 21 July 1951, Barbara Mary, da of Francis Langford Killick (d 1983); 2 da ((Margaret) Anne, Mary Elizabeth); *Career* petty offr and radar mechanic RN 1945-48; dir Phoenix House Ltd 1984-; memb Ctee on Safety of Medicines 1976-83; memb RSM, FRCPsych 1972, FRCP 1980; *Recreations* gardening, music, reading, poultry-rearing; *Style—* Prof Alec Jenner; Mannor Farm, Brightholmlee Lane, Wharncliffe Side, Sheffield S30 3DB (☎ 0742 862546); University Department of Psychiatry, Royal Hallamshire Hospital, Glossop Road, Sheffield S10 2JF (☎ 0742 766222 ext 2644)

JENNER, Michael Eugene; s of Eugene Jenner (d 1945), and Beatrice Jenner (d 1976); *b* 7 Jan 1936; *Educ* St George's Coll Surrey; *m* 9 June 1962, Jane Elizabeth, da of Harold Goodhew Turner, CMG (d 1978); 1 s (Mark Eugene b 1963), 2 da (Clare Elizabeth b 1967, Lucy Jane b 1972); *Career* CT Bowring 1952-: asst dir 1967, dir Marine Div 1969, dep chief exec 1971, chief exec 1974; jt dep chm CT Bowring (Insurance Hldgs) Ltd 1976, chief exec CT Bowring Insurance 1979, dir Parent Bd CT Bowring & Co 1979; dir: Bowring Tyson, CTB Offshore Oil UK, Terra Nova Insurance Brokers; fndr and chm: Jenner Fenton Slade Ltd 1980, JFS Reinsurance Brokers 1981; chm LIBC 1987; ACII; *Recreations* golf, racehorse owner; *Clubs* Piltdown Golf, Royal St George's Golf, Royal Cinque Port Golf, Annabels; *Style—* Michael Jenner; Moons Farm, Barcombe Rd, Piltdown, nr Uckfield, E Sussex (☎ 082 2037); 42 Cadogan Lane, London SW1 (☎ 071 235 5832); Jenner Fenton Slade Ltd, Knollys House, 47 Mark Lane, London EC3R 7QH (☎ 071 929 4500)

JENNER, Prof Peter George; s of George Edwin Jenner, of Gravesend, Kent (d 1948), and Edith, *née* Hallett; *b* 6 July 1946; *Educ* Gravesend GS, Chelsea Coll London (BPharm, PhD, DSc); *m* 1 Dec 1973, Katherine Mary Philomena, da of Hilary David Harrison Snell (d 1958); 1 s (Terence Martin b 19 Oct 1977); *Career* postgrad fell Dept of Pharmacy Chelsea Coll London 1970-72; Univ Dept of Neurology Inst of Psychiatry: lectr biochemistry 1972-78, sr lectr 1978-85, reader in neurochemical pharmacology 1985-89; reader in neurochemical pharmacology KCH 1985-89 (hon sr lectr 1983-85), hon sr lectr Inst of Neurology 1988-, dir Parkinson's Disease Soc Experimental Res Laboratories 1988-, prof of pharmacology and head of dept King's Coll London 1989-; memb: Royal Pharmaceutical Soc, Br Pharmacological Soc, Drug Res Soc, Euro Neurochemistry Soc, Brain Res Assoc, Euro Neuroscience Assoc, Int League Against Epilepsy; *Books* Drug Metabolism: Chemical & Biochemical Aspects (with B Testa, 1976), Concepts in Drug Metabolism (co-ed B Testa, pt A 1980, pt B 1981), Approaches to the Use of Bromocriptine in Parkinson's Disease (co-ed, 1985), Recent Developments in Parkinson's Disease (co-ed, 1986), Neurological Disorders (co-ed, 1987), Neurotoxins and their Pharamcological Implications (ed, 1987), Disorders of Movement (co-ed, 1989); *Recreations* gardening, driving; *Style—* Prof Peter Jenner; Pharmacology Group, Biomedical Sciences Division, King's College London, Manresa Road SW3 6LX (☎ 071 351 2488 ext 2501, fax 071 376 4735)

JENNER, Victor John; JP (Hants 1975); s of Leonard Jenner (d 1954), and Daisy Beatrice, *née* Dormer (d 1939); *b* 20 March 1926; *Educ* Portsmouth Northern GS; *m* 15 May 1945, Ann Lilian May, da of Frank Godfrey Welch (d 1955), of Portsmouth; 1 s (John Colin b 1946), 1 da (Linda Ann b 1947); *Career* Oxford and Bucks LI 1945, 2 Bn Hants Regt 1945, 8 Bn Suffolk Regt 1946-47; Wadham Bros Ltd 1947-50, Harris & Parkin Ltd 1950-52, md Harbottle-Leeson Ltd 1952-, chm EMMA Ltd (consortium of 26 cos) 1976-, dep chm Juvenile Panel Portsmouth 1982-; chm: Freight Tport Assoc (Portsmouth Area) 1962-65, Hants & Dorset Branch Electrical & Electronic Industs Benevolent Assoc 1972-77 (pres 1977), Tstees St Petroc Community 1972-, Licensing Justices Ports 1976-, Licensing Ctee 1978-, Hants Standing Conf of Licensing 1982, Portsmouth Poly Govrs 1985-, Fin & Gen Purposes Ctee 1985-; memb: Portsmouth Cathedral Businessmens Ctee 1955-, Electricity Consultative Cncl (Southern Area) 1972-90, Manpower Servs Bd (Southern Area) 1980-84; pres: Portsmouth Incorp C of C 1972-, UK Commercial Traveller Assoc (Portsmouth and Southsea) 1965-; Freeman City of London 1973, Liveryman Worshipful Co of Carmen 1973; FIOD 1967, FBIM 1980, MITA 1985; *Recreations* gardening; *Clubs* 1664, MCC; *Style—* Victor J Jenner, Esq, JP; Vannic, Well Hill, Hambledon Rd, Denmead, Hants PO7 6HB (☎ 0705 255919); Harbottle-Leeson Ltd, Asquith House, 22 Middle St, Portsmouth, Hants PO5 4BJ (☎ 0705 820535, fax 0705 295655, car tel 0836 617623)

JENNETT, Prof (William) Bryan; s of Robert William Jennett, of 285 Waldegrave Rd, Twickenham (d 1956), and Jessie Pate, *née* Loudon (d 1975); *b* 1 March 1926; *Educ* King's Coll Sch Wimbledon, King George VI Sch Southport, Univ of Liverpool (MB ChB, MD); *m* 15 Sept 1950, Sheila Mary, da of Herbert Pope, of Liverpool (d 1966); 3 s (Peter Dennis b 1953, Martin Robert b 1954, John Duncan b 1964), 1 da (Hilary Anne b 1957); *Career* Maj RAMC 1951-53; conslt neurosurgeon Glasgow 1963-68, prof of neurosurgery Inst Neurological Sci 1968-, memb Court Univ of Glasgow 1986- (dean Faculty of Med 1981-86); pres Section of Neurology RSM 1986-87; memb: MRC 1979-83, Chief Scientist Ctee Scotland 1984-; *Books* Epilepsy After Non-Missile Head Injuries (2 edn, 1975), Introduction to Neurosurgery (4 edn, 1983), Management of Head Injuries (with G Teasdale, 1981), High Technology Medicine: Benefits and Burdens (1984); *Recreations* writing, sailing; *Clubs* RSM; *Style—* Prof Bryan Jennett; 83 Hughenden Lane, Glasgow G12 9XN (☎ 041 334 5148); Department of Neurosurgery, Institute of Neurological Sciences, Glasgow G51 4TF (☎ 041 445 2466, fax 041 425 1583)

JENNETT, Frederick Stuart; CBE (1985); s of Horace Frederick Jennett (d 1948), of Balgownie, Wenallt Rd, Rhiwbina, Glam, and Jenny Sophia Hall (d 1969); *b* 22 April 1924; *Educ* Whitchurch GS, Welsh Sch of Architecture UWIST (DipArch); *m* 9 July 1948, Nada Eusebia, da of George Allan Phillips (d 1968), of Sherbourne, Hawthorn, Pontypridd, Glam; 2 da (Sara Elizabeth b 9 June 1950, Claire Katy b 21 Feb 1955); *Career* Lt RS 1942-46, served Far East; architect: Alwyn Lloyd & Gordon Cardiff 1949-51; architect and planner: Cwmbran Devpt Corp 1951-55, Lois de Soissons & Ptnrs Welwyn Garden City 1955-56; assoc S Colwyn Foulkes & Ptnrs 1956-62, chm and sr ptnr Percy Thomas Partnership Bristol 1971-89 (assoc 1962-64, ptnr 1964-70); conslt architect: Frederick S Jennet (and town planner), Studio BAAD (architects) West Yorks; author papers on: hosp planning, fast constructs, refurbishment of historic bldgs; memb: Br Conslts Bureau, Br Healthcare Export Cncl; FRIBA 1949, MTPI 1955, FRSA 1985; *Recreations* hill walking, watercolour painting, running; *Clubs* Reform; *Style—* Frederick Jennett, Esq, CBE; Portland Lodge, Lower Almondsbury, Bristol BS12 4EJ (☎ 0454 615175)

JENNINGS, Alex Michael; s of Michael Thomas Jennings, of Shenfield, Essex, and Peggy Patrica, *née* Mahoney; *b* 10 May 1957; *Educ* Abbs Cross Tech HS Hornchurch Essex, Univ of Warwick (BA), Bristol Old Vic Theatre Sch; partner, Lesley Moors; 1 s (Ralph Jennings Moors b 23 March 1990); *Career* actor; theatre work incl: Toad of Toad Hall (Leeds Playhouse), Dandy Dick (Cambridge Theatre), Hay Fever (Theatre Royal York), Can't Pay Won't Pay (Bristol Old Vic), The Scarlet Pimpernel (Her Majesty's) 1985, The Country Wife (Royal Exchange Manchester), Too Clever By Half (Old Vic, Drama Magazine Best Actor award 1988, Plays and Players Actor of the Year award 1988, Oliver award for Comedy Performance of the Year) 1988, Ghetto (NT), The Liar (Old Vic), The Wild Duck (Peter Hall Co); work for the RSC: Hyde Park, The Taming of the Shrew, Measure For Measure, Richard II; work for TV: Smiley's People (BBC TV), The Franchise Affair (BBC TV), Alfonso Bonzo (BBC TV), The Kit Curran Radio Show (Thames TV), Shelley (Thames TV), Ashenden (BBC TV/Kelso Films); film: War Requiem (dir Derek Jarman); *Style—* Alex Jennings, Esq

JENNINGS, Prof Barry Randall; s of Albert James Jennings (d 1981), of Worthing, Sussex, and Ethel Victoria Elizabeth, *née* Randall (d 1983); *b* 3 March 1939; *Educ* St Olaves and St Saviours GS Tower Bridge, Univ of Southampton (BSc, PhD, DSc); *m* 1 Sept 1964, Margaret Penelope (Penny), da of Lionel Wall (d 1977), of Newport, Gwent; 2 da (Carolyn b 1966, Samantha b 1969); *Career* res fell Strasbourg Univ 1964-65, ICI fell Univ of Southampton 1965-66, lectr in physics Queen Elizabeth Coll London 1966-71, head of physics Brunel Univ 1982-84 (reader 1971-77, prof of experimental physics 1977-84), estab prof of physics Univ of Reading 1984-89, currently res dir ECC International Ltd and visiting prof of physics Univ of Reading; author of 200 scientific articles and holder of ten patents; former memb Scientific Ctee Assoc for Int Cancer Res; memb: Ctee Standing Conf of Profs of Physics, Cncl Minerals Inst Res Orgn (ed journal Polymer); chm Int Ctee for Mol Electro-optics, past pres Br Biophys Soc, past chm Br Polymer Phys Soc, hon ed Jl of Physics D (Applied); Cowan-Keedy prize Southampton Univ (1961), Soc of Chemical Indust Polymer prize 1969; visiting prof Univ of San Luis and Santa Rosa Argentina 1979; FInstP 1970, CPhys 1985; *Books* Atoms in Contact (with V J Morris, 1974), Electro-optics and Dielectric of Macromolecules (1979); *Recreations* swimming, long cased clocks, church activities; *Style—* Prof Barry Jennings; Luney Barton House, Lower Sticker, St Austell, Cornwall PL26 7JH (☎ 0726 882219); ECC International Ltd, John Keay House, St Austell, Cornwall PL25 4DJ (☎ 0726 624025)

JENNINGS, Hon Mrs (Catherine Frances); *née* Donaldson; yr da of Baron Donaldson of Kingsbridge, OBE (Life Peer), *qv*; *b* 18 Nov 1945; *m* 1973, G Mark Jennings; children; *Style—* The Hon Mrs Jennings; 57 Winsham Grove, London SW11 6NB

JENNINGS, Charles James; s of Douglas Vivian Jennings, MC, Witley Manor, Witley, Surrey, and Virginia, *née* Turle; *b* 27 Oct 1951; *Educ* Harrow, Durham Univ (BA); *m* 8 May 1976, Julia Frances, da of Philip Whiffen, of Mole End, Oxshott, Cobham, Essex; 1 s (Simon Charles b 1980), 1 da (Anna Francis b 1978); *Career* Freshfields 1980-82, ptnr Wilde Sapte 1986-; memb: Law Soc, City of London Solicitors Co; *Recreations* tennis, gardening; *Clubs* City of London; *Style—* Charles Jennings, Esq; Kingsdown Farm, Burwash Common, Etchingham, Sussex; Queensbridge House, 60 Upper Thames St, London EC4 (☎ 071 236 3050)

JENNINGS, Prof David Harry; s of Harry Jennings (d 1982), of Cirencester, and Doris, *née* Hewitson (d 1961); *b* 30 March 1932; *Educ* Merchant Taylors' Crosby, Univ of Cambridge (BA), Univ of Oxford (MA, DPhil); *m* Ruth Mary, da of Capt Gerald Hope Sworder (d 1959), of St Teath, Cornwall; 2 da (Alison b 1960, Hilary b 1962); *Career* King George VI meml fell Univ of Rochester 1956-57; Leeds: ICI fell 1957-60, lectr in botany 1960-66, reader in plant physiology 1966-68; Univ of Liverpool: prof of botany 1969-, head of Dept of Botany 1975-85, dean Faculty of Sci 1977-80 and 1988-, pro-vice chllr 1981-84; pres Br Mycological Soc 1986; memb: Cncl Marine Biological Assoc, Cwlth Scholarships Cmmn; dir: Liverpool Playhouse, Merseyside Innovation Centre; FIBiol 1971; *Books* The Absorption of Solutes by Plant Cells (1963); *Recreations* architecture, painting, walking, exploring cities; *Style—* Prof David Jennings; 40 Garth Drive, Liverpool L18 6HW (☎ 051 724 3273); Department of Genetics & Microbiology, The University, PO Box 147, Liverpool L69 3BX (☎ 051 794 5118, fax 051 708 6502, telex 627095 UNILPL G)

JENNINGS, Hon Mrs (Deanna Christine); *née* Layton; o da of 2 Baron Layton (d 1989); *b* 19 Oct 1938; *Educ* St Paul's Girls' Sch, St Bartholomew's Hosp Med Sch London (MB BS); *m* 1964, Melvin Calverley Jennings, s of Dr Calverley Middlemiss Jennings (d 1985); 3 s (Andrew Melvin, Simon, Robert); *Career* med practitioner; princ in gen practice Reigate; MRCS, LRCP, DSMA; *Style—* The Hon Mrs Jennings; Barn

Ridge, 18 High Trees Rd, Reigate, Surrey RH2 7EJ (☎ 0737 240847)

JENNINGS, Elizabeth Joan; da of Dr Henry Cecil Jennings, of Oxford, and Mary Helen, *née* Turner; *b* 18 July 1926; *Educ* Oxford HS, St Anne's Coll Oxford (BA); *Career* poet: asst Oxford City Library 1950-58, reader for Chatto & Windus Ltd 1958-60; poetry incl: Poems (1953, Arts Cncl prize), A Way of Looking (1955, Somerset Maugham award 1956), A Sense of the World (1958), The Batsford Book of Children's Verse (ed, 1958), Song for a Birth or a Death (1961), Michelangelo's Sonnets (trans, 1961), Recoveries (1964), The Mind Has Mountains (1966, Richard Hillary prize 1966), The Secret Brother (for children 1966), Collected Poems (1967), The Animals' Arrival (1969, Arts Cncl Bursary 1969), A Choice of Christina Rosetti's Verse (ed, 1970), Lucidities (1970), Relationships (1972), Growing Points (1975), Consequently I Rejoice (1977), After The Ark (for children, 1978), Selected Poems (1980), Moments of Grace (1980), The Batsford Book of Religious Verse (1981), Celebrations and Elegies (1982), In Praise of Our Lady (anthology, 1982), Extending the Territory (1985), A Quintet (for children, 1985), Collected Poems 1953-86 (1986, W H Smith award 1987), Tributes (1989); prose incl: Let's Have Some Poetry (1960), Every Changing Shape (1961), Robert Frost (1964), Christianity and Poetry (1965), Seven Men of Vision (1976); also poems and articles in: New Statesman, New Yorker, Botteghe Oscure, Observer, Spectator, Listener, Vogue, The Independent; *Recreations* theatre, cinema, looking at pictures, collecting dolls houses and miniatures; *Clubs* Soc of Authors; *Style—* Miss Elizabeth Jennings; c/o David Higham Associates Ltd, 5-8 Lower John St, London W1R 4HA

JENNINGS, James; JP (Cunninghame 1969); s of Mark Jennings (d 1977), and Janet, *née* McGrath (d 1977); *b* 18 Feb 1925; *Educ* St Palladius Sch Dalry, St Michael's Coll Irvine; *m* 1, 1943, Margaret Cook, *née* Barclay; 3 s (Daniel Mark, David Mark, James), 2 da (Janette Matilda, Marie Elizabeth); m 2, 18 Oct 1974, Margaret Mary (Greta), *née* Hughes, JP; 2 da (Frances, Jaqueline); *Career* RAF 1942-46; involved Steel Ind 1946-79; memb: Ayr CC 1958, Police Cncl GB, Police Cncl UK 1978-79, LACSAB 1986-88; chm: Ayr CC Police and Law Ctee 1964-70, Ayrshire Jt Police Ctee 1970-75, N Ayreshire Crime Prevention Panel 1970-82, Cunninghame Justices Ctee 1975-, Police and Fire Ctee, Strathclyde Regnl Cncl 1978-82; convener Strathclyde Regnl Cncl 1986- (memb 1974, vice convener 1982-86), memb Police Negotiating Bd (official side) 1988 (vice chm then chm 1984-88), chm Garnock Valley Devpt Exec 1988-, dir Euro Summer Special Olympic Games 1990 (Strathclyde) Ltd 1988-; Parly Candidate (Lab) Perth and E Perthshire 1966; jt patron Mayfest Ltd, vice pres St Andrew's Ambulance Assoc; hon pres: Scottish Retirement Cncl, Princess Louise Scottish Hosp (Erskine Hosp); hon vice pres: SNO Chorus, Royal Br Legion Scotland (Dalry and Dist Branch); patron Assoc Youth Clubs Strathclyde; chm Police and Fire Strathclyde Regnl Cncl 1990; Hon Sheriff Strathclyde 1990; *Recreations* local community involvement; *Clubs* Royal Scottish Automobile (Glasgow), Garnock Lab (chm), St Andrew's Sporting (hon life patron); *Style—* James Jennings, Esq, JP; 4 Place View, Kilbirnie, Ayrshire KA25 6BG (☎ 0505 3339); Strathclyde Regnl Cncl, India St, Glasgow G2 4PF (☎ 041 204 2900, fax 041 227 2870, telex 77428)

JENNINGS, John Southwood; CBE (1985); s of George Southwood Jennings (d 1978), of Crowle, Worcs, and Irene Beatrice, *née* Bartlett; *b* 30 March 1937; *Educ* Oldbury GS, Univ of Birmingham (BSc), Univ of Edinburgh (PhD), London Business Sch; *m* 1961, Gloria Ann, da of Edward Albert Griffiths (d 1985), of Hope Cove, Devon; 1 s (Iain), 1 da (Susan); *Career* geologist; chief geologist Shell UK Exploration and Production Ltd London 1968-70, exploration mangr Petroleum Development Oman Ltd 1971-75 (prodn mangr 1975-76), gen mangr and chief rep Shell Group of Companies Turkey 1976-79, md exploration and prodn Shell UK Ltd London 1979-84, exploration and prodn co-ordinator Shell International Petroleum Maatschappij BV The Hague 1984-89, md Royal Dutch-Shell Group 1987-; FGS; *Recreations* flyfishing, shooting, photography, travel; *Clubs* Flyfishers', Brooks's; *Style—* John Jennings, Esq, CBE; 32 Eaton Terrace, London SW1; Lange Viyverberg 6B, 2513 AC, The Hague, The Netherlands (☎ 070 365 18 97); office: Carel Van Bylandtlaan 30, The Hague, The Netherlands (☎ 070 377 3710, telex 36000)

JENNINGS, The Very Rev Kenneth Neal; s of Reginald Tinsley Jennings (d 1976), and Edith Dora, *née* Page (d 1982); *b* 8 Nov 1930; *Educ* Hertford GS, Corpus Christi Coll Cambridge (BA), Cuddesdon Theological Coll; *m* 9 Sept 1972, Wendy Margaret, da of Sir John Arthur Stallworthy, of 8 College Green, Gloucester; 1 s (Mark Nicholas b 1976), 1 da (Katharine Rachel b 1975); *Career* Nat Serv RA 1950-51; asst curate Holy Trinity Ramsgate 1956-59; vice princ: Bishop's Coll Calcutta 1961-66 (lectr 1959-61), Cuddesdon Coll Oxford 1967-73; vicar St Mary's Hitchin 1973-76, team rector Parish of Hitchin 1977-82, dean of Gloucester 1983-; *Recreations* fell walking, music; *Style—* The Very Rev the Dean of Gloucester; The Deanery, Miller's Green, Gloucester GL1 2BP (☎ 0452 524167)

JENNINGS, Dr Kevin; s of Kevin Jennings, and Bridget, *née* Flynn; *b* 9 March 1947; *Educ* Downside, St Bart's Med Sch (MB BS); *m* 24 June 1978, Heather Joanne, da of Ray Wolfenden; 2 s (Mark b 1979, Thomas b 1981), 1 da (Debra b 1987); *Career* registrar: King's Coll London 1976-78, London Chest Hosp 1978-80; sr registrar Freeman Hosp Newcastle 1980-83, conslt cardiologist Aberdeen Royal Infirmary 1983-; FRCP 1988; *Books* several articles on ischaemic heart disease and cardiac imaging; *Style—* Dr Kevin Jennings; Dept of Cardiology, Royal Infirmary, Foresterhill, Aberdeen AB9 2ZB (☎ 0224 681818, fax 0224 208402)

JENNINGS, Marie Patricia; da of Harold Robert Jennings, and Phyllis Hortense; *b* 25 Dec 1930; *Educ* Presentation Convent Coll Srinagar Kashmir; *m* 1 (m dis), Michael Keegan; 1 s (Michael Geoffrey b 18 July 1962); m 2, 3 Jan 1976, (Harry) Brian, s of Harry Locke; *Career* md The Roy Bernard Co Ltd 1960-65; special advsr: Stanley Tools 1961-89, The Unit Trust Association 1976-, The Midland Bank Group 1978-; dir: Lexington Ltd (JWT) 1971-75, The PR Consultants Association 1979-84 (conslt), Cadogan Management Ltd 1984-; Woman of the Year 1969, hon treas Nat Assoc Womens Clubs (memb Fin and Gen Purposes Ctee) 1977-87; memb: Cncl Fin Int Mangrs and Brokers Regnl Assoc 1986-, Insur Ombudsman Bureau 1988-; Exec Ctee Wider Share Ownership Cncl 1987-; memb: RSA, IOD, Inst of PR, NUJ, Br Acad of Experts; *Books* The Money Guide (1983), Getting the Message Across (1988), Women and Money (1988), Money Go Round (1977), Moneyspinner (1985), A Guide to Good Corporate Citizenship (1990); *Recreations* reading, writing; *Clubs* IOD; *Style—* Ms Marie Jennings; 57 Cadogan St, Sloane Square, London SW3 2QJ (☎ 071 589 9778); The Old Toll House, Stancombe, Stroud, Glos; The Court House, Bisley, Stroud, Glos GL6 7AA (☎ 071 930 4241/0452 770003, fax 071 930 6993/0452 770058)

JENNINGS, Patrick Thomas; s of Charles Thomas Jennings (d 1983), of Witham, Essex, and Helen Joan, *née* Scorer; *b* 23 Feb 1948; *Educ* Forest Sch; *m* Jayne, da of Ronald Stanley Green; 1 s (Edward Thomas Patrick b 16 Aug 1990), 3 da (Victoria Anne b 3 June 1977, Joanna Emily b 6 Oct 1979, Charlotte Joy b 16 Oct 1984); *Career* articled clerk H Kennard & Son 1967-72; Slaughter and May: joined 1973, ptnr 1979, currently property group ptnr; chm Building Contracts Ctee of the Construction Law Ctee Int Bar Assoc 1985-89; memb: Law Soc, Anglo-American Real Property Inst; author of various articles and papers on construction law; *Style—* Patrick Jennings, Esq; Slaughter and May, 35 Basinghall St, London EC2V 5DB (☎ 071 600 1200, fax 071 600 0289)

JENNINGS, Percival Henry; CBE (1953); s of Canon Henry Richard Jennings (d 1951), and Susan, *née* Milton (d 1952); *b* 8 Dec 1903; *Educ* Christ's Hosp; *m* 23 June 1934, Margaret Katharine Musgrave, da of late Brig Gen Hugh Stuart Rogers, CMG, DSO (d 1951), 3 da (Penelope b 1938, Margaret b 1940, Josephine b 1947); *Career* overseas audit service: asst auditor Northern Rhodesia 1927-31, asst auditor Mauritius 1931-35, auditor Br Honduras 1935-38, dep dir Gold Coast 1938-45, dep dir Nigeria 1945-48; dir of audit Hong Hong 1948-55 (dep DG 1955-60, DG 1960-63); *Recreations* gardening; *Clubs* Royal Cwlth Soc, Royal Over-Seas League; *Style—* Percival Jennings, Esq, CBE; Littlewood, Lelant, St Ives, Cornwall (☎ 0736 753407)

JENNINGS, Rev Peter; s of Robert William Jennings, of Sale, Cheshire, and Margaret Irene, *née* Rogerson; *b* 9 Oct 1937; *Educ* Manchester GS, Keble Coll Oxford (MA), Univ of Manchester (MA); *m* 28 Dec 1963, Cynthia Margaret, da of Thomas Widdop Leicester, of Llandudno, Gwynedd; 2 s (Timothy Howard b 4 May 1965, Nicholas Andrew b 8 May 1967); *Career* asst min Swansea Methodist Circuit 1963-67, tutor warden Youth Centre for Social and Community Studies London Mission (East) Circuit 1967-74, gen sec Cncl of Christians and Jews 1974-81, assoc min Wesley's Chapel City Road 1976-81, asst min Walthamstow and Chingford Methodist Circuit 1981-82; supt: Whitechapel Methodist Mission 1982-91, Ilford Methodist Circuit 1991-; actively involved with Cncl of Christians and Jews; *Recreations* photography, travel; *Clubs* Stepney Rotary (former pres); *Style—* The Rev Peter Jennings; Whitechapel Methodist Mission, 212 Whitechapel Rd, London E1 1BJ (☎ 071 247 8280)

JENNINGS, Sir Raymond Winter; QC (1945); s of Sir Arthur Oldham Jennings, MBE (d 1934); *b* 12 Dec 1897; *Educ* Rugby, RMC Sandhurst, Oriel Coll Oxford (MA, BCL); *m* 1930, Sheila Helen Grant (d 1972); 1 s, 1 da; *Career* serv WWI Lt Royal Fusiliers; called to Bar Inner Temple 1922, bencher Lincoln's Inn 1951, master of the Ct of Protection 1956-70; kt 1968; *Clubs* Athenaeum; *Style—* Sir Raymond Jennings, QC; 14c The Upper Drive, Hove, East Sussex BN3 6GN (☎ 0273 773361)

JENNINGS, Prof Sir Robert Yewdall; QC (1969); s of Arthur Jennings, of Idle, Yorks; *b* 19 Oct 1913; *Educ* Belle Vue G S Bradford, Downing Coll Cambridge (LLB, hon fell 1982), Harvard; *m* 1955, Christine Dorothy, da of late H Bernard Bennett, of Lydd, Kent; 1 s, 2 da; *Career* served WWII Intelligence Corps Maj; asst lectr law LSE 1938-39, fell Jesus Coll Cambridge 1939- (sr tutor 1949-55, then pres, hon fell 1982), called to the Bar Lincoln's Inn 1943 (hon bencher 1970), Whewell prof of int law Univ of Cambridge 1955-81, reader in int law Cncl of Legal Educn 1959-70, judge Int Ct of Justice The Hague 1982-; jt ed: International and Comparative Law Quarterly 1955-61, British Year Book of International Law 1960-, vice pres Inst of Int Law 1979-81 (pres 1981-83, hon memb 1985); Hon LLD Univ of Hull 1987, Hon Dr Juris Univ of Saarland 1988, Hon LLD Univ of Rome 1990; kt 1981; *Clubs* Utd Oxford and Cambridge Univ, Haagsche Plaats Royaal (The Hague); *Style—* Prof Sir Robert Jennings, QC; Jesus College, Cambridge (☎ 0223 68611); Peace Palace, 2517 KJ The Hague, Netherlands

JENNISON, Prof Roger Clifton; s of George Robert Jennison (d 1948), of Morningside, 28 Park Drive, Grimsby, Lincolnshire, and Elsie Grace, *née* Clifton (d 1959); *b* 18 Dec 1922; *Educ* Clee GS Grimsby, Hull Tech Coll, Univ of Manchester (BSc, PhD); *m* 7 Nov 1952, Jean Gordon, da of Douglas George Gordon Gray (d 1967), of Newton Cottage, Arduthie Rd, Stonehaven, Kincardineshire; 2 s (Michael b 1956, Timothy b 1963), 2 da (Heather b 1960, Jacqueline b and d 1962); *Career* RAF aircrew 1943-47, cmmnd 1946; Mackinnon res student of The Royal Soc 1951-53, sr lectr in physics Univ of Manchester 1965 (lectr in radio astronomy 1954-60, sr lectr 1960-64), dep master of Eliot Coll 1966-75, personal chair in radio astronomy Univ of Kent at Canterbury 1981- (fndn chair in electronics 1965-, dir Electronic Laboratories 1966-80); pres Inst of Electronics, govr Medway and Maidstone Colls Of Technol 1966-76, memb ct City Univ 1967, acting chm Canterbury Arts Cncl 1987-88; FRAS 1960, PPIE 1963, FInstP 1965, FIEE 1967, FRSA 1973, CEng 1985; *Books* Fourier Transforms And Convolutions (1961), Introduction to Radio Astronomy (1965), over 100 scientific papers in learned jls; *Recreations* painting, sculpture, tennis, sailing, DIY; *Style—* Prof Roger Jennison; Wildwood, Nackington, Canterbury, Kent CT4 7AY (☎ 0227 61430); The Electronics Laboratories, The University, Canterbury, Kent (☎ 764000 ext 3222)

JENRICK, William John; s of Sidney Thomas Jenrick, of Dukinfield, Cheshire, and Ivy Jenrick, *née* Barret; *b* 23 Nov 1940; *Educ* Ducie H S; *m* 1975, Jennifer Ann, da of Eric Alexander Robertson (d 1979); 1 s (Robert b 1982), 1 da (Jane b 1979); *Career* md: Cannon (Holdings) Ltd, Cannon Industries Ltd; chm: Charlton & Jenrick Ltd, Grate Ideas (Midlands) Ltd; pres Round Table 1981 (chm 1980); capt Shropshire Minor Co Chess Team 1982-83; chm and chief exec Ctee Soc of British Gas Industry 1985; ACMA; *Recreations* chess, sailing; *Style—* William Jenrick Esq; Lark Rise, Haughton Lane, Shifnal, Shropshire (☎ 0952 461311; office 0902 43161)

JENSEN, Michael Harold; s of Eric Axel Jensen (d 1964); *b* 24 Oct 1942; *Educ* St Lawrence Coll; *m* 1969, Linda, da of Ernest Edwards; 2 da; *Career* md: Eden Ct Property Co Ltd 1968-79, HL Thomson Ltd 1976-81, HL Thomson (E Anglia) Ltd 1977-81, Hogg Robinson Gardner Mountain International Ltd 1977-81; exec dir Willis Faber & Dumas Ltd (insurance brokers) 1981-87; chm: Jensen Dickens Ltd (insurance brokers), Thamesgate Holdings Ltd, D F Prockter Ltd; Freeman: Worshipful Co of Carmen 1978, City of London 1978; memb Lloyd's 1980; *Recreations* shooting, sailing (yacht, MY Cheoy Lin); *Clubs* Lloyd's Yacht, Haven Ports Yacht, Deben Yacht; *Style—* Michael Jensen, Esq; Oaken, Falconers Park, Sawbridgeworth, Herts; Moorings, Navere Meadows, Woodbridge, Suffolk; Jensen Dickens Ltd, Lloyd's Ave House, 6 Lloyd's Ave, London EC3N 3AX (☎ 071 480 6474)

JENSEN, Thomas George; s of Thomas Swensen Jensen (d 1963), and Ruth Ordell, *née* Ford; *b* 20 Jan 1948; *Educ* Nederland Opliedings Instituut Voor Het Buitenland (BA); *m* 1 March 1971, Miki Hotta, da of Kuniyoshi Hotta, of Japan; 1 da (Katura Renia b 1972); *Career* vice pres Seattle First Nat Bank 1973-83, asst gen mangr Saudi Investmt Bank 1983-86, dir IBJ Int Ltd 1986-; *Recreations* tennis; *Style—* Thomas Jensen, Esq; 5 Brasenose House, 35 Kensington High St, London W8 5BA (☎ 071 937 2516); IBJ International, Bucklersbury House, 3 Queen Victoria St, London EC4N 8HR (☎ 071 236 1090)

JEPHCOTT, Sir (John) Anthony; 2 Bt (UK 1962), of East Portlemouth, Co Devon; s of Sir Harry Jephcott, 1 Bt (d 1978), and Doris, da of Henry Gregory; *b* 21 May 1924; *Educ* Aldenham, St John's Coll Oxford, LSE (BCom); *m* 1, 1949 (m dis 1978), Sylvia Mary, da of Thorsten F Relling, of Wellington, NZ; 2 da; m 2, 1978, Josephine Agnes, da of Philip Sheridan, of Perth, WA; *Heir* bro, Neil Jephcott; *Career* 1939-45 war with REME, later RAEC; formerly manufacturer of anaesthesia equipment; md: Penlon Ltd 1952-73, Pen Medic Ltd NZ 1973-78; contrib to scientific journals; Hon FFARACS 1990; *Books* A History of Longworth Scientific Instrument Co Ltd (1988); *Style—* Sir Anthony Jephcott, Bt; 21 Brilliant St, St Heliers, Auckland 5, New Zealand

JEPHCOTT, Neil Welbourn; s of Sir Harry Jephcott, 1 Bt (d 1978), and hp of bro, Sir Anthony Jephcott, 2 Bt; *b* 3 June 1929; *Educ* Aldenham, Emmanuel Coll Cambridge (MA); *m* 1, 1951, Mary Denise (d 1977), da of Arthur Muddiman, of Abbots Mead, W Clandon, Surrey; m 2, 1978, Mary Florence, da of James John Daly (d 1950); *Career* professional engr; *Recreations* sailing; *Clubs* Royal Ocean Racing; *Style—* Neil Jephcott, Esq; Thalassa, East Portlemouth, Salcombe, S Devon

JEREMIAH, Melvyn Gwynne; s of Bryn Jeremiah (d 1967), of Gwent, and Fanny Evelyn Mary, *née* Rogers (d 1987); *b* 10 March 1939; *Educ* Abertillery County Sch; *m* 1960 (m dis 1970), Clare, da of William Bailey, of Devon; *Career* civil servant; appt HO 1958, Customs and Excise 1963, Cabinet Office 1975, Treasy 1976, Welsh Office 1979; Dept of Health 1987-; dir Ashley Gardens Freeholds Ltd 1986-89; chief exec Disablement Servs Authy 1987-91; sec Assoc of First Div Civil Servants 1967-70; *Recreations* work, people; *Clubs* Reform; *Style—* Melvyn Jeremiah, Esq; 110 Ashley Gardens, Thirleby Road, London SW1P 1HJ (☎ 071 828 1588); Bwthyn Llon, St Harmon Road, Rhayader, Powys LD6 5LS (☎ 0597 810286)

JERRAM, Maj-Gen Richard Martyn; CB (1984), MBE (1960); s of Brig R M Jerram, DSO, MC (d 1974), and Monica, *née* Gillies (d 1975); *b* 14 Aug 1928; *Educ* Marlborough, RMA Sandhurst; *m* Feb 1987, Susan, *née Roberts*, wid of Mr John Naylor; *Career* cmmnd RTR 1948, instr Staff Coll Camberley 1964-67, CO 3 RTR 1969-71, Brig 1976, Maj-Gen 1981, dir RAC MOD 1981-84, Col Cmdt RTR 1982-88; *Clubs* Army & Navy; *Style—* Maj-Gen Richard Jerram, CB, MBE; Trehane, Trevanson, Wadebridge, Cornwall PL27 7HB (0208 81 2523)

JERROM, Michael George Lindsay; s of late Maj Michael Francis Jerrom, and Irene Edith, *née* Fry; *b* 14 April 1942; *Educ* Sherborne, Oxford Univ (MA); *m* 1, 1 June 1968 (m dis), Rosalind Mary, da of late Dr Bernard James Sanger, of Fairhaven, Leveretts Lane, Walberswick, Suffolk; 1 s (Charles Lindsay b 11 May 1973), 1 da (Amanda Suzanne b 25 Aug 1970); m 2, 8 Sept 1979, Dorothy Fay Allgood; *Career* audit mangr Thornton Baker & Co London 1968-70 (accountancy articles 1964-67), section leader Overseas Containers Ltd 1971-72, co sec Int Caledonian Assets Ltd and Argyle Sercurities Ltd 1972-73; dir: Jardine Properties Ltd 1973-75, Norwest Holst Int Ltd 1975-77, CCL Fin Servs Ltd 1977-, Axis Property Mgmnt Ltd; md: Selective Construction Projects plc 1984, CCL Devpts plc 1986; chm The Vector Collection plc 1988-90, dir Look at Languages Communications Experts Ltd 1989; memb Pubns Review Panel ICAEW; ctee memb (former capt): Old Shirburnian Golfing Soc, Wrotham Health Golf Club; memb Oxford and Cambridge Golfing Soc; FCA 1968; *Recreations* golf, local affairs, ex chairman conservative branch; *Clubs* East India, Thorpe Hall, Wrotham Heath, Royal Cinque Ports, Oxford Soc; *Style—* Michael Jerrom, Esq; 107 Jermyn St, London SW1Y 6EE (☎ 071 930 8367, fax 071 839 4598)

JERVIS, Hon Edward Robert James; s and h of 7 Viscount St Vincent; *b* 12 May 1951; *Educ* Radley; *m* 1977, Victoria Margaret, da of Wilton Joseph Oldham, of Jersey; 1 da (Emma Margaret Anne b 1980); *Career* co dir; *Recreations* skiing, water sports, chess, backgammon; *Style—* The Hon Edward Jervis; Colinas Verdes 26, Bensafrim, Lagos 8600, Algarve, Portugal

JERVIS, Hon (Ronald Nigel) John; s of 7 Viscount St Vincent; *b* 1954; *Educ* Eton, Univ of Durham; *m* 1983, Gillian Lois, *née* Sharp; 1 s (David Stephen), 1 da (Sarah Francis); *Career* software engr; *Recreations* books, music, gardening, foreign travel; *Style—* The Hon John Jervis

JERVIS, Roger David; s of David William Jervis, of Northampton, and Ada Ellen, *née* Barker; *b* 1 May 1942; *Educ* Northampton GS; *m* 11 March 1967, Carole Margaret, da of George Coles Ashton, of Northampton; 1 s (Guy b 1972), 1 da (Katie b 1969); *Career* articled accountant Dutton and Co Northampton 1959-65, co sec and dep to gp accountant Wilson plc property co's 1965-69, fndr Jervis and Ptnrs 1970-; Kingsthorpe Golf Club Northampton: hon treas 1974-82, capt 1982, tstee 1974-88; hon treas Northants Golf Union 1982-, pres Soc of Northants Golf Capts 1990-; govr: Northampton Sch for Boys, Abington Vale Middle Sch; FCA 1965; *Recreations* golf, horse racing; *Clubs* Northampton Co, Kingstorpe Golf; *Style—* Roger Jervis, Esq; 38 Thorburn Rd, Northampton NN3 3DA (☎ 0604 408 277); 20-22 Harborough Rd, Northampton (☎ 0604 714 600, fax 0604 719 304)

JERVIS, Simon Swynfen; s of Capt John Swynfen Jervis (ka 1944), and Diana Elizabeth, *née* Marriott (now Mrs Christopher Parker); *b* 9 Jan 1943; *Educ* Downside, Corpus Christi Coll Cambridge; *m* 19 April 1969, Fionnuala, da of Dr John MacMahon (d 1961); 1 s (John Swynfen b 25 June 1973), 1 da (Thalia Swynfen b 5 Jan 1971); *Career* student asst, asst keeper of art Leicester Museum and Art Gallery 1964-66; V & A: asst keeper Dept of Furniture 1966-75, deputy keeper 1975-89, acting keeper 1989, curator 1989-90; guest scholar J Paul Getty Museum 1988-89, dir Fitzwilliam Museum Cambridge 1990; ed Furniture History Society 1987-; memb: Exec Cncl Soc of Antiquaries 1987-90 (memb Cncl 1986-88), Properties Ctee NT 1987- (Arts Panel 1982-, chm 1987-); FSA 1983, FRSA 1990; *Books* Victorian Furniture (1968), Printed Furniture Designs Before 1650 (1974), High Victorian Design (1983), Penguin Dictionary of Design and Designers (1984), Furniture from Austria and Hungary in the Victoria and Albert Museum (1986); *Recreations* tennis; *Style—* Simon Jervis, Esq, FSA; Fitzwilliam Museum, Cambridge CB2 1RB (☎ 0223 332922)

JERVOIS, David Reginald Warren; s of Reginald Charles Warren Jervois (d 1978), and Hettie Florence, *née* Clark; *b* 4 Dec 1928; *Educ* Marlborough, Peterhouse Cambridge (BA); *m* 20 Sept 1958, Pamela Joan, da of Stanley James Hill (d 1979); 1 da (Jane Elizabeth b 1969); *Career* admitted slr 1957, Notary Public 1979; ptnr Woollcombe Watts & Co 1963-; clerk to Cmmrs of Income Tax Newton Abbot Teignbridge Div 1973-89, chm Torquay Supp Benefit Appeal Tribunal 1982-, fndr memb Bovey Tracey Rotary Club (pres 1981); hon sec: S Devon CC 1964-, Torbay Hockey Club 1969-, Devon Co Hockey Assoc 1987-; *Recreations* cricket, hockey, golf, model railways, philately; *Clubs* S Devon Cricket, MCC, Dragons Cricket, Torbay Hockey, Stover Golf; *Style—* David R W Jervois, Esq; Lower Close, Chapple Rd, Bovey Tracey, Devon TQ13 9JX (☎ 0626 833292); Church House, Queen St, Newton Abbot, Devon (☎ 0626 331199)

JERVOISE, John Loveys; s of Capt John Loveys, MC (d 1974), of Chudleigh, Devon, and Barbara Tristram Ellis, o da of Arthur Tristram Ellis Jervoise (d 1942); descended maternally from Sir Thomas Jervoise, MP (d 1654), who acquired Herriard through his marriage to Lucy, eldest da of Sir Richard Powlet (*see* Burke's Landed Gentry, 18 edn, vol I, 1965); *b* 16 July 1935; *Educ* Hardye's Sch Dorchester, MacDonald Coll McGill Univ (Dip Agric), Seale-Hayne Agric Coll (Dip Farm Mgmnt); *m* 12 Aug 1961, Jane Elizabeth, eldest da of James Henry Lawrence Newnham (d 1975), of Stokelake, Chudleigh, Devon; 2 s (John Tristram b 3 May 1962, Anthony Richard b 2 Aug 1964), 2 da (Sarah Jane b 18 Nov 1965, Anne Elizabeth (twin) b 18 Nov 1965); *Career* Nat Serv Lt Devonshire Regt 1953-56, Capt 4/5 Bn Royal Hampshire Regt TA 1960-68; farmer and landowner; Basingstoke Rural DC 1964-74 (chm Planning Ctee 1970-74), Basingstoke and Deane Borough Cncl 1974-78 (chm Planning Ctee 1977-78); dir Mid Southern Water Co 1974-, chm Hampshire Branch Country Landowners Assoc 1986-88, pres Black Welsh Mountain Sheep Breeders Assoc 1980-82; High Sheriff of Hampshire 1989-90; MInstPet; *Recreations* hunting, shooting, walking; *Clubs* Naval and Military, RAC, Devon and Exeter Inst (Exeter); *Style—* John Loveys Jervoise, Esq; Herriard Park, Basingstoke, Hampshire RG25 2PL (☎ 0256 83252); Estate Office, Herriard Park, Basingstoke, Hants (☎ 0256 83275)

JESNICK, Ian Jeffrey; s of Hyman, of London, and Alma Sheila, *née* Rosenberg (d 1990); *b* 14 Jan 1953; *Educ* Grocers GS, Lanchester Poly (BA), Coll of Distributive Trades London (CAM); *m* July 1987, Vivienne Pauline, da of Ian Saxton; 1 s (Mark Saxton b 5 Feb 1989), 1 da (Leah Georgina Davida b 23 Nov 1990); *Career* Cable & Wireless Ltd 1974-76, Wellcome Foundation Ltd 1976-79, Daniel J Edelman 1979-80, Leslie Bishop Company/Media Relations Ltd 1980-86, dir Richmond Towers Limited 1986-; *Style—* Ian Jesnick, Esq; 3 Aldred Road, West Hampstead, London NW6 1AN (☎ 071 794 9582); Richmond Towers Public Relations Limited, 26 Fitzroy Square, London W1P 6BT (☎ 071 388 7421, fax 071 388 7761)

JESS, Digby Charles; s of Ronald Ernest Jess, of Cornwood, Devon, and Betty Cordelia Brookes, *née* Cundy; *b* 14 Nov 1953; *Educ* Plymouth Coll, Univ of Aston (BSc), Univ of Manchester (LLM); *m* 4 Aug 1980, Bridie Ann, da of Bartholomew Connolly, of Galway, Eire; 1 s (Piers b 1988); *Career* barr Grays Inn, in practice Manchester 1981-, lectr in law (pt/t) Univ of Manchester 1986-87; ctee memb: N W branch CIArb, Manchester Inc Law Library; ACIArb 1981; *Books* The Insurance of Professional Negligence Risks: Law and Practice (1 edn 1982, 2 edn 1989), The Insurance of Commercial Risks: Law and Practice (1986), vol on Insurance in The Encyclopaedia of Forms and Precedents (vol 20, 1988), many articles for legal jls; *Recreations* fencing, walking, squash, theatre; *Style—* Digby C Jess, Esq; 26 Carlton Ave, Wilmslow, Cheshire SK9 4EP (☎ 0625 536191); 8 King St, Manchester M2 6AQ (☎ 061 834 9560, fax 061 834 2733); 2 Pump Court, Temple, London (☎ 071 353 5597)

JESSEL, Hon Mrs (Amelia Grace); *née* FitzRoy; da of 2 Viscount Daventry (d 1986); *b* 26 March 1930; *Educ* East Haddon Hall Sch 1946; *m* 1950 (m dis 1978), as his 1 wife, Capt David Charles George Jessel (d 1985), Coldstream Gds (s of late Sir Richard Hugh Jessel); 1 s, 1 da; *Career* gun dog trainer, field trial and int show judge; memb Council for Guide Dogs for the Blind Assoc; pres: South and West Counties Field Trial Soc, Meon Valley Working Spaniel Club; chm Kennel Club Field Trial Cncl; *Recreations* stalking, fishing, sailing; *Style—* The Hon Mrs Jessel; Bridge Cottage, Stoke Charity, Winchester, Hants (☎ 0962 760259)

JESSEL, Betty, Lady; (Joan) Betty; *née* Ewart; da of late Dr David Ewart, OBE, of Chichester; *m* 1, 1933 (m dis 1946), 2 Baron Russell of Liverpool, CBE, MC (d 1981); 1 da; m 2, 1948, as his 2 w, Sir George Jessel, MC, 2 Bt (d 1977); *Recreations* gardening; *Clubs* Army and Navy; *Style—* Betty, Lady Jessel; Ladham House, Ladham Lane, Goudhurst, Kent TN17 1DB (☎ 0580 211203)

JESSEL, Hon Camilla Edith Mairi Elizabeth; *née* Jessel; elder and only surv da of 2 and last Baron Jessel (d 1990), and his 1 w, Lady Helen Maglona Vane-Tempest-Stewart (d 1986), da of 7 Marquess of Londonderry; *b* 17 April 1940; *m* 1 Nov 1960 (m annulled 1972), Don Juan Carlos del Prado y Ruspoli, 11 Marques de Caicedo (cr Spain 1712); b 30 June 1934, succession to title recognised 28 Sept 1966; 2 s (Miguel Angel b 1961, Alfonso Segundo b 1966); resumed maiden name; *Style—* The Hon Camilla Jessel; Calle Lope de Vega 29, Madrid, Spain

JESSEL, Sir Charles John; 3 Bt (UK 1883), of Ladham House, Goudhurst, Kent; s of Sir George Jessel, MC, 2 Bt (d 1977); *b* 29 Dec 1924; *Educ* Eton, Balliol Coll Oxford; *m* 1, 1956, Shirley Cornelia (d 1977), da of John Waters, of Northampton; 2 s, 1 da; m 2, 1979 (m dis 1983), Gwendolyn Mary, da of late Laurance Devereux, OBE, and widow of Charles Langer; *Heir* s, George Jessel; *Career* Lt 15/19 Hussars (despatches) WWII; Northampton Inst of Agric 1951-52, Inst of Optimum Nutrition, farmer 1953-85, in ptnrship with son 1985-, nutrition conslt 1987-; JP Kent 1960-78; chm: Ashford NFU 1963-64, Canterbury Farmers Club 1972; pres: Kent Branch Men of the Trees 1979-83, Br Soc of Dowsers 1987-; hon fell Psionic Med Soc 1977; memb Inst of Allergy Therapists 1990; *Books* An Anthology of Inner Silence (1990); *Recreations* gardening, planting trees; *Clubs* Cavalry and Guards; *Style—* Sir Charles Jessel, Bt; South Hill Farm, Hastingleigh, nr Ashford, Kent (☎ 023 375 325)

JESSEL, George Elphinstone; s and h of Sir Charles Jessel, 3 Bt, and Shirley Cornelia, *née* Waters (d 1977), of South Hill Farm, Hastingleigh, Ashford, Kent; *b* 15 Dec 1957; *Educ* Milton Abbey, RAC Cirencester; *m* 10 Dec 1988, Rose Amila Coutts-Smith; *Career* cmmnd Lt 15/19 Royal Hussars, Germany, Canada and Cyprus 1978-82; farmer (ptnr with father) 1985-; *Recreations* skiing, travelling; *Clubs* Cavalry & Guards, Farmers; *Style—* George Jessel, Esq; Stoakes Cottage, Hastingleigh, Ashford, Kent TN25 5HG (☎ 023 375 216); South Hill Farm, Hastingleigh, Ashford, Kent TN25 5HL (☎ 023 375 325)

JESSEL, Baroness; Jessica Marian Jessel; *née* de Wet; da of late William de Wet, of Rondebosch, Cape Town, S Africa, and Mrs H Taylor; *m* 20 Dec 1960, as his 2 w, 2 and last Baron Jessel, CBE (d 1990); *Style—* The Rt Hon the Lady Jessel; 4 Sloane Terrace Mansions, London SW1X 9DG

JESSEL, Oliver Richard; s of Cdr Richard Frederick Jessel, DSO, OBE, DSC (d 1988), of Marden, Kent; er bro of Toby Jessel, MP; *b* 24 Aug 1929; *Educ* Rugby; *m* 1950, Gloria Rosalie Teresa, *née* Holden; 1 s, 5 da; *Career* chm: many cos in Jessel Group 1954-89, Charles Clifford Industs (non-ferrous metals gp) 1978-81; former chm London Australian & General Exploration Co; fndr: New Issue Unit Trust, Castle Communications plc; *Clubs* Garrick; *Style—* Oliver Jessel Esq; Merrington Place, Rolvenden, Cranbrook, Kent TN17 4PJ (☎ 0580 241428)

JESSEL, Toby Francis Henry; MP (C) Twickenham 1970-; yr s of Cdr Richard Jessel, DSO, OBE, DSC, RN (d 1988), and Winifred May (d 1977), da of Maj Walter Levy, DSO, and Hon Mrs Levy (later Hon Mrs Ionides), da of 1 Viscount Bearsted; *b* 11 July 1934; *Educ* RNC Dartmouth, Balliol Coll Oxford; *m* 1, 1967 (m dis); 1 da (decd); m 2, 1980, Eira Heath; *Career* Sub Lt RNVR 1954; Parly candidate (Cons):Peckham 1964, Hull N 1966; chm: Anglo-Belgian Parly Gp, Cons Arts and Heritage Ctee; memb Cncl Europe 1976-, GLC memb Richmond 1967-73; Liveryman Worshipful Co of Musicians; Chev de l'Ordre de la Couronne Belgium; *Recreations* piano, gardening, skiing, swimming; *Clubs* Garrick, Hurlingham; *Style—* Toby Jessel Esq, MP; Old Court House, Hampton Court, E Molesey, Surrey KT8 9BW

JESSUP, Graham Marcus; s of Basil Graham Jessup (d 1979), of Ash Platt, Kent, and Jessie Laura, *née* Chappell (d 1979); *b* 14 Feb 1947; *Educ* Sevenoaks Sch, Univ of Bristol (BSc); *m* 17 Aug 1967, Susan Janet Melland, da of Peter William Gilpin (Gp Capt ret), of Culvers Close, Oxon; 2 s (Simon b 1972, Richard b 1974); *Career* client servs dir Newton & Godin Ltd; dir: Newton & Godin Ltd 1982-, Promotional Campaigns Ltd 1982-, Dowton Advertising Ltd 1980-82; *Recreations* golf, sailing; *Clubs* Knole Park Golf; *Style—* Graham M Jessup, Esq; Parksland Cottage, 7 Weald Rd, Sevenoaks, Kent; Newton & Godin Ltd, Union House, The Pantiles, Tunbridge Wells, Kent (☎ 0892 510520, car ☎ 0860 325 374)

JEUNE, Senator Reginald Robert; OBE (1979); s of Reginald Valpy Jeune (d 1974), and Jessie Maud, *née* Robinson (d 1945); *b* 22 Oct 1920; *Educ* De La Salle Coll Jersey; *m* 1946, Monica Lillian, da of Hedley Charles Valpy, of Jersey; 2 s (Richard Francis Valpy b 1949, Nicholas Charles b 1954), 1 da (Susan Elizabeth b 1958); *Career* slr Royal Ct of Jersey 1945-; ret sr ptnr Mourant du Feu & Jeune (now conslt); Sen of States of Jersey (pres Policy and Resources Ctee); chm: Cwlth Parly Assoc (Exec Jersey Branch), Jersey Electricity Co Ltd, TSB Channel Islands Ltd; memb Bd TSB Group plc; OStJ, Chevalier of the Order of Orange Nassau, Offr of the Ordre de Merite Nationale; *Recreations* golf; *Clubs* Carlton, RAC, MCC, Victoria (Jersey), United, Royal Jersey Golf, La Moye Golf; *Style—* Senator Reginald R Jeune, OBE; Messrs Mourant du Feu & Jeune, 18 Grenville St, St Helier, Jersey, CI (☎ 0534 74343, fax 0534 79064, telex 4192064)

JEWEL, Jimmy Arthur Thomas; s of James A Jewel, and Gertrude, *née* Driver; *b* 4 Dec 1912; *m* Aug 1939, Belle Bluett; 1 s (Kerry James b 11 Feb 1947), 1 adopted da

(Piper Belle b 21 July 1955); *Career* made debut at age of four in Robinson Crusoe (Alhambra Theatre Barnsley), stage mangr for family show until age of eighteen, then solo act-; extensive radio theatre and tv work as half of Jewel & Warris until 1967; later tv work incl: Spanner & Dearest, Spring & Autumn, Funny Man, numerous plays; theatre work incl: Neil Simon's Sunshine Boys (Piccadilly Theatre), Trevor Griffith's Comedians (Royal Nat Theatre), You Can't Take It With You (Royal Nat Theatre); Variety Club lunch in his honour 1976 and special award for contribution to entertainment 1984; *Style—* Jimmy Jewel, Esq; Rupert Prior, Howes & Prior, 66 Berkely House, Hayhill, London W1 (☎ 071 493 7270/7655)

JEWELL, David John; s of Wing Cdr John Jewell, OBE (d 1985), of Porthleven, Cornwall, and Rachel, *née* Miners (d 1962); *b* 24 March 1934; *Educ* Blundell's, St John's Coll Oxford (MA, MSc); *m* 23 Aug 1958, Katharine Frida, da of Prof Hans Sigmund Heller (d 1974), of Bristol; 1 s (John Edward), 3 da (Rachel Susannah, Sarah Josephine, Tamsin Mary Katharine); *Career* Nat Serv Pilot Offr RAF 1952-54; head of Sci Dept: Eastbourne Coll 1958-62, Winchester Coll 1962-67; dep head Lawrence Weston Sch Bristol 1967-70; head master: Bristol Cathedral Sch 1970-79, Repton 1979-87; master Haileybury and Imperial Serv Coll 1987-; nat rep and chm HMC sub ctees, chm HMC 1990; FRSA 1981; *Recreations* music, cricket, Cornwall; *Clubs* East India, MCC, Bristol Savages; *Style—* David Jewell, Esq; The Master's Lodge, Haileybury, Hertford SG13 7NU (☎ 0992 462 352)

JEWELL, Dr Derek Parry; s of Ralph Parry Jewell, of 24 Hillcrest, Thornbury, Glos, and Eileen Rose, *née* Champion; *b* 14 June 1941; *Educ* Bristol GS, Pembroke Coll Oxford (MA, DPhil, BM BCh); *m* 6 July 1974, Barbara Margaret, da of Leonard Pearson Lockwood, of 5 Stowford Court, Bayswater Rd, Oxford; 1 s (Christopher b 1979), 1 da (Carolyn b 1981); *Career* visiting asst prof Stanford Univ Sch of Med 1973-74, sr lectr in med Royal Free Hosp 1974-80, conslt physician and univ lectr Oxford 1980-; memb Res Ctee RCP 1978-87; memb Ed Bds: Gut, Clinical Science, European Journal of Gastroenterology and Hepatology; ed Topics in Gastroenterology 1973 and 1984-89; FRCP 1979 (MRCP 1970); *Books* Clinical Gastrointestinal Immunology (1979); *Recreations* music, gardening; *Style—* Dr Derek Jewell; 4 The Green, Horton-cum-Studley, Oxon OX9 1AE (☎ 0865 735 315); Radcliffe Infirmary, Oxford (☎ 0865 816829, fax 0865 790 792)

JEWELL, Prof Peter Arundel; s of Percy Arundel Jewell (d 1960), of Bude, Cornwall, and Ivy Dorothea, *née* Ennis (d 1962); *b* 16 June 1925; *Educ* Wandsworth Sch, Univ of Reading (major open scholar, BSc), St John's Coll Cambridge (BA, Wright's prizeman, MA, Gedge Prizeman, PhD, ARC postgrad scholar, Wellcome res scholar); *m* 26 June 1958, Juliet, da of Alan Clutton-Brock (d 1970); 3 da (Sarah Abigail b 1959, Vanessa Topsy b 1961, Rebecca Tamsin b 1963); *Career* lectr RVC 1951-61, res fell Zoological Soc 1961-66, prof biology and dir Div Biological Sci Univ of Nigeria 1966-67, sr lectr Zoology UCL 1966-72 (dir MSc course in Conservation 1968-70), prof zoology Royal Holloway Coll London 1972-77, Mary Marshall and Arthur Walton prof of physiology of reproduction 1977-; fndr memb Rare Breeds Survival Tst, vice pres Zoological Soc, chm Mammal Soc; memb: Cambridge Ctee Flora and Fauna Preservation Soc, Gloucester Cattle Soc; fell and memb Cncl St John's Coll Cambridge; CBiol (1985), FIBiol (1960); *Books* Island Survivors: The Ecology of the Soay Sheep of St Kilda (1974), Problems in Management of Locally Abundant Wild Mammals (1987), Large African Mammals in their Environment (1989); *Recreations* paintings and sculptures, pottery, pets, Cornish history; *Style—* Prof Peter Jewell; University of Cambridge, Research Group in Mammalian Ecology and Reproduction, Physiological Laboratory, Downing St, Cambridge CB2 3EG (☎ 0223 333891, fax 0223 222840)

JEWISS, John E; s of John W Jewiss (d 1978), and Marjorie Jewiss Bailey; *b* 4 April 1944; *Educ* Selhurst Grammar Sch; *m* 1966, Sandra, da of Gerald A J Peacock; 2 da (Paula b 1968, Kerry b 1970); *Career* chm Hartley Cooper Gp Hldgs 1982-83; dir: C E Heath Gp 1973-77, Hartley Cooper Gp 1977-81; md Gibbs Hartley Cooper 1983-85; independent mgmnt conslt 1985-; *Recreations* cricket, badminton, music, drama, art; *Clubs* Les Ambassadeurs, Wellington; *Style—* John Jewiss, Esq; Hoddydodd Hall, Spains Hall Rd, Willingale, Essex CM5 0QD

JEWITT, Anthony John; s of John Jewitt, and Ellen, *née* Tatlock; *b* 7 Oct 1935; *Educ* Chingford GS, Harvard Business Sch; *m* 26 July 1958, Janet Julia, *née* Smith; 3 da (Marie Julia Anne b 28 June 1960, Jennie Anne Louise b 15 July 1962, Catherine Jane b 8 April 1965); *Career* served in army Capt 1958-60; gp chm ICC Information Group Ltd; dir: SI Management Ltd, Mar-Com Systems Ltd; BIM, MInstM, MICSA; *Recreations* skiing, tennis, horse racing; *Clubs* St James's; *Style—* Anthony Jewitt, Esq; Majenca, Pelling Hill, Old Windsor, Berks SL4 2LL (☎ 0753 865289); ICC Information Group Ltd, Field House, 72 Oldfield Rd, Hampton, Middx TW12 2HQ (☎ 081 783 1122, fax 081 783 0049, telex 296090)

JEWITT, Cdr Dermod James Boris (Toby); DSC; s of Capt Reuben James Charles Jewitt (d 1958), and Enid Alice, *née* Bagot; *b* 13 Oct 1908; *Educ* RNC; *m* 1, March 1941 (m dis 1951), Pamela Mary Scrutton; 2 da (Sarah Mary (Mrs Best) b 1943, Penelope Anne (Mrs Allanson-Bailey) b 1946); m 2, 19 Sept 1960, Emma Jane, da of Reginald Martin Vick, OBE; 1 s (Charles James Bagot b 1965); *Career* RNC Dartmouth 1922-25; HMS: Valiant 1926-28, Seraph 1930-32, Amazon 1932-33, Keith 1933-34, Sussex 1934-35, Wolsey 1935-36, Ivanhoe 1936-39; Cdr HMS: Northern Spray 1939-40, Vimy 1940-41, Winchester 1941-42, Meteor 1942-44, Hasdrubal 1945, President 1945-47 Nereide 1947-49; Jt Serv Staff Coll 1949-50, invalided 1950 (despatches twice); Scruttons Ltd: master stevedores 1950, indust dir; chm London Ocean Trade Employers 1971-72; *Recreations* country pursuits, golf; *Style—* Cdr Toby Jewitt, DSC; Penton Lodge, Penton Lane, Crediton, Devon EX17 1ED (☎ 036 32 3827)

JEWITT, John James; OBE (1979), JP (1966); s of John James Jewitt, MBE (d 1984), of Sheffield, and Edna May, *née* Hobson; *b* 28 Feb 1924; *Educ* Firth Park GS; *m* 1, 27 Aug 1948, Dorothy Allice (d 1974), da of Lawrence Dungworth (d 1965), of Derby; 1 s (Christopher b 1951), 1 da (Alison b 1958 d 1974); m 2, 20 March 1976, Meinir Constance, da of Sydney Thomas Bailey (d 1987), of Sheffield; 1 s (Marc b 1978), 1 da (Claire b 1976); *Career* dir: J C H Castings 1974-83, Radio Hallam 1974-; chm Thos C Hurdley 1978-86, md Footprint Tools Ltd 1970- (chm 1984); pres Sheffield Junior Chamber of Commerce 1959-60; chm: Selection Ctee Sheffield Outward Bound Tst 1965-72, Cncl of S Yorkshire and Hallamshire Boys Clubs 1976-, Mgmnt Ctee and chm Hillsborough Boys Club Sheffield 1969-, Sheffield Light Trades Employers Assoc 1974-77; pres Cncl of Hand Tools for Europe (14 countries) 1988-90, pres Fedn of Br Hand Tools Manufacturers 1985-87; memb: Nat Cncl of Assoc of Boys Clubs 1964-, Local Affairs Ctee Chamber of Commerce 1978-; Freeman Worshipful Co of Cutlers in Hallamshire; *Recreations* sailing, wind surfing, squash, skiing; *Clubs* Sheffield, Lansdowne; *Style—* John Jewitt, Esq, OBE, JP; The Homestead, Pinfold Hill, Curbar, via Sheffield S30 1YL (☎ 0433 31500); Footprint Tools Ltd, PO Box 19, Hollis Croft, Sheffield S1 3HY (☎ 0742 753200)

JEWITT, Ronald William; s of Cyril George Jewitt (d 1982), of Newport, Gwent, and Hilda Laura Jewitt (d 1972); *b* 25 Jan 1942; *Educ* Newport HS, Newport and Mon Tech Coll, Brunel Coll of Advanced Tech; *m* 30 March 1963, June Rose, da of Reginald Barley (d 1982), of Newport, Gwent; 2 s (Peter Ronald b 1964, David Charles b 1965), 1 da (Penelope Anne b 1967); *Career* asst chemist Monsanto Chemicals Ltd 1958-62, dep analyst Expandite Ltd 1962-64, res and devpt chemist Burt Boulton and Haywood Ltd 1964-66, analytical chemist London Transport 1966; pres: Caversham and Mapledurham Royal Br Legion, Reading Mid-Week Assoc Cricket League, Royal Berks Sports and Social Club; chm Caversham Cons Assoc; memb: Reading Borough Cncl 1973-91 (housing chm 1979-84, Mayor 1984-85, Dep Mayor 1985-86), Berks CC 1977- (ldr 1986-90); *Recreations* walking, swimming; *Style—* Ronald Jewitt, Esq; 98 Chiltern Road, Caversham, Reading, Berkshire RG4 0JD (☎ 0734 481147); 55 Lot's Road, London SW10 (☎ 071 352 3727 ext 37)

JEWKES, Sir Gordon Wesley; KCMG (1990, CMG 1980); s of Jesse Jewkes (d 1943), and Anne Plumb (d 1983); *b* 18 Nov 1931; *Educ* Barrow in Furness GS; *m* 1954, Joyce, da of John Lyons (d 1975); 2 s (Nigel, Stephen); *Career* Nat Serv and Army Emergency Reserve (AER), Capt RAOC 1968; Home Civil Serv 1948-68; first sec Cwlth Office later FCO, consul (commercial) Chicago 1969-72, dep high cmmr Port of Spain 1972-75, head of Fin Dept FCO, fin offr Dip Serv 1975-79; consul gen: Cleveland 1979-82, Chicago 1982-85; govr Falkland Islands and high cmmr Br Antarctic Territory 1985-88; consul gen NY and dir gen Trade and Investmt USA 1989-; *Recreations* music, walking, travel; *Clubs* Travellers'; *Style—* Sir Gordon Jewkes, KCMG; c/o Foreign & Commonwealth Office, King Charles St, London SW1A 2AH

JEWSON, Richard Wilson; s of Charles Boardman Jewson (d 1981), of Norfolk, and Joyce Marjorie, *née* Laws; *b* 5 Aug 1944; *Educ* Rugby, Pembroke Coll Cambridge (MA); *m* 1965, Sarah Rosemary, da of Henry Nevill Spencer, of Kenilworth; 1 s (William b 1968), 3 da (Henrietta b 1966, Charlotte b 1970, Camilla b 1976); *Career* md Jewson Ltd 1974-86, non-exec dir Eastern Counties Newspaper Group Ltd 1982, md Meyer International plc 1986, non-exec dir Anglican Water plc 1991-; memb Cncl Univ of E Anglia 1980-; CBIM; *Recreations* gardening, tennis; *Clubs* Boodle's, Royal W Norfolk Golf, RSA; *Style—* Richard Jewson, Esq; Dades Farm, Barnham Broom, Norfolk NR9 4BT (☎ 060 545237); Villiers House, The Strand, London (☎ 071 839 7766)

JEYNES, Edward Raymond (Ted); s of Albert Edward Jeynes (d 1977), and Florence Kate, *née* White (d 1990); *b* 23 June 1922; *Educ* Central GS; *m* Jacqueline Mary, da of Ralph Parsons, of Scotland; 1 s (Matthew Simon b 1988), 3 da (Susan Carole b 1958, Deborah Ruth b 1966, Catherine Tamsin b 1986); *Career* CA; sr ptnr West Midlands Price Waterhouse until 1982; dir: Wheway plc, Centrax Ltd, Noel Penny Turbines Ltd; chm Eliza Tinsley Gp plc, dep chm Healey Mouldings Ltd, vice chm Heart of England Building Soc; *Style—* Ted Jaynes; The Woodlands, Dunley, nr Stourport-on-Severn, Worcs DY13 0TZ (☎ 029 93 2001)

JHABVALA, Ruth Prawer; da of Marcus Prawer (d 1948), and Eleaonora, *née* Cohn (d 1983); *b* 7 May 1927; *Educ* Hendon Co Sch London, London Univ (MA); *m* 16 June 1951, Cyrus Jhabvala, s of Shiavakshah Jhabvala (d 1973); 3 da (Renana b 1952, Ava b 1955, Firoza b 1957); *Career* authoress; films: Shakespeare Wallah 1964, Autobiography of a Princess 1975, The Bostonians 1985, Room With A View 1986; Hon DLitt London; FRSL; *Books* To Whom She Will (1955), The Nature of Passion (1956), The Householder (1960), Heat and Dust (1975), Out of India (1986), Three Continents (1987); *Style—* Mrs Ruth Jhabvala; 400 East 52nd St, New York, NY 10022, USA; c/o John Murray, 50 Albemarle St, London W1

JIP, Dr James; s of Joseph Wing Jip (d 1980), of 43 West Derby Rd, Liverpool 6, and Lai Jip (d 1977); *b* 10 July 1949; *Educ* Liverpool Collegiate Sch, Liverpool Univ Med Sch (MB ChB); *m* 20 Nov 1972, Margaret Victoria Ann, da of Victor Matthew Boulton (d 1970), of 3 Broadgate Ave, St Helens, Merseyside; 2 s (Edward James b 5 Jan 1976, Paul Francis b 13 Dec 1977), 1 da (Caroline Ann b 20 Aug 1981); *Career* house physician Whiston Hosp Merseyside 1972-73, house surgn St Helen's Hosp Merseyside 1973, registrar pathology Walton Hosp Merseyside 1974-75 (sr house offr pathology 1973-74), sr registrar pathology Mersey RHA 1975-80, conslt haematologist Bolton Gen Hosp 1980-; memb: Br Med Assoc, Br Soc Haematology, Br Blood Transfusion Soc, NW Regnl Haematology Sub-Ctee; MRCPath 1980; *Recreations* foreign travel, chess, piano; *Clubs* Bolton Chess (2 team capt); *Style—* Dr James Jip; The Dept of Haematology, Bolton Gen Hosp, Minerva Rd, Bolton, Lancs BL4 0JR (☎ 0204 22444)

JIRICNA, Eva Magdalena; da of Josef Jiricny (d 1973), and Eva, *née* Svata; *b* 3 March 1939; *Educ* Tech Univ of Prague, Prague Acad of Fine Arts; *Career* architect; seconded to GLC's Sch Division 1968-69, Lois de Soissons Partnership 1969-78 (laterly project architect), in practice with David Hodges 1978-82, freelance working from Richard Rogers Partnership 1982-84, fndr ptnr own practice with Kathy Kerr 1984-86, reformed co as Eva Jericna Architects 1986-; interior work for clients incl: Lloyds Headquarters Buildings, Harrods, Joseph, Legends, Joan & David; lectr various venues; MRIBA, memb Cncl AA; Hon Fell RCA 1990; *Style—* Ms Eva Jiricna; Eva Jericna Architects, 7 Dering Street, London W1R 9AB (☎ 071 286 1653)

JOACHIM, Dr Margaret Jane; *née* Carpenter; da of Reginald Carpenter, DSO, of Pensilva, Cornwall, and Joyce Margaret, *née* Howard (d 1977); *b* 25 June 1949; *Educ* Brighton & Hove HS, St Hugh's Coll Oxford (MA), W Midlands Coll of Educn, Univ of Birmingham (PhD); *m* 2 July 1970, Paul Joseph Joachim, s of Joseph Joachim, of Marlborough, Wilts; *Career* Vol Serv WRNR, served HMS Sussex 1965-67, offr cadet OTC Univ of Oxford 1967-70; teacher Stourbridge Girls HS 1971-73 (pt/t 1973-76), pt/t lectr Univ (extramural) and WEA 1972-77, post doctoral res fell in geology Univ of Birmingham 1976-79; programmer BOC Datasolve 1979-80, programmer and conslt IP Sharp Associates 1980-84, futures database mangr Rudolf Wolff & Co Ltd 1984-87, sales exec (UK Insurance Services) EDS Ltd 1988-; fndr: Univ of Oxford Gilbert & Sullivan Soc, The Steam Apprentice Club, chm Working Gp (Int) to establish women's lobby in Brussels, friend Ironbridge Gorge Museum; Parly candidate: (Lib) W Glos 1979, (Alliance) Finchley 1983, (Alliance) Epsom and Ewell 1987; chm Fawcett Soc 1984-87 (memb Exec Ctee 1990-), pres elect Woman's Lib Fedn 1988, memb Exec Ctee 300 Gp 1988-, jt co-ordinator WIPL 1987-88, chair LD Woman's Orgn 1989 (vice chair 1990-); FRES 1977, AMIGeol 1978; *Recreations* reading, sailing, walking, singing, visiting traction engine rallies, making jam; *Clubs* Reform, IOD; *Style—* Dr Margaret Joachim; 8 Newburgh Rd, London W3 6DG (☎ 081 993 0936); EDS Ltd, 4 Roundwood Avenue, Stockley Park, Uxbridge, Middlesex UB11 1BQ

JOB, Rev Canon (Evan) Roger Gould; s of Thomas Brian Job (d 1985), of Ipswich, and Elsie Maud Gould (d 1987); *b* 15 May 1936; *Educ* The Kings Sch Canterbury, Magdalen Coll Oxford (BA, MA), Cuddesdon Theol Coll; *m* 4 July 1964, Rose Constance Mary, da of Lt Col Stanley Gordon, MC, TD (d 1982), of Hooton, Wirral; 2 s (Jonathan b 1967, Christopher b 1971); *Career* Nat Serv RN 1955-57; ordained: deacon 1962, priest 1963 in Liverpool Cathedral; asst curate Liverpool Parish Church 1962-65, vicar St John New Springs Wigan 1965-70, minor canon and precentor Manchester Cathedral 1970-74, precentor and sacrist Westminster Abbey 1974-79, canon residentiary precentor and sacrist Winchester Cathedral 1979-; Winchester area chm Royal Sch of Church Music 1984-, local pres Save the Children Fund 1981-, chm Winchester and Dist Christian Cncl 1986-87; *Recreations* gardening, piano; *Style—* The Rev Canon Roger Job; 8 The Close, Winchester SO23 9LS (☎ 0962 853137)

JOBSON, Anne Margaret; da of Colin Thomas Figgins Bell, of Fareham, Hants, and

Margaret, *née* Porter; *b* 12 Jan 1952; *Educ* Purbrook Park Co GS, City of London Poly (BA); *m* 10 July 1976, (Stephen) Andrew Jobson, s of Norman Jobson, of Walkden, Manchester; *Career* barr at law as Anne Bell, fndr memb of chambers 1977-; memb Harrow Cons Assoc; *Recreations* gardening, walking, theatre, watching cricket, keeping fit; *Style*— Mrs Anne Jobson; 24 Parkfield Crescent, North Harrow, Middx HA2 6JZ (☎ 081 428 5868); 1st Floor, 2 Kings Bench Walk, Temple, London EC4Y 7DE (☎ 071 353 9276, fax 071 353 9949, car 0831 424983)

JOBSON, Lady Lavinia Anne; *née* Brabazon; yr da of 14 Earl of Meath; *b* 1945; *m* 1969, John Ernest Baron Jobson; 1 s, 3 da; *Style*— The Lady Lavinia Jobson; Barnacullia, Kilmacanogue, Co Wicklow, Republic of Ireland

JOBSON, Timothy Akers; s of Maj E O A Jobson (d 1965), and Joan, *née* Webb (d 1991); *b* 16 July 1944; *Educ* Bromsgrove, Keble Coll Oxford (MA); *m* 1, 27 July 1970 (m dis 1980), Lee Bazeley; 1 s (Simon b 1973), 1 da (Annie b 1974); m 2, 7 April 1982, Susan F Jeavons; *Career* admitted slr 1968; ptnr: Lyon Clark & Co W Bromwich 1970-84, Keely Smith & Jobson Lichfield 1985-; co sec Barnt Green Waters Ltd; dep chm W Bromwich & Dist YMCA; *Recreations* sailing, swimming; *Clubs* Barnt Green Sailing (hon sec 1981-86); *Style*— Timothy Jobson, Esq; c/o Keely Smith & Jobson, 16 Bore Street, Lichfield, Staffs WS13 6LL

JOCELYN, Viscountess; Ann Margareta Maria; *née* Henning; da of Dr Gunnar Henning (d 1948), and Mrs Kerstin Magnusson; *b* 5 Aug 1948; *Educ* Lund Univ Sweden (BA); *m* 13 Feb 1986, as his 2 w, Viscount Jocelyn, *qv*; 1 s (Shane Robert Henning b 1989); *Career* author and literary translator (Swedish/English); translations incl: Love's Gravity by Per Wästberg, The Silk Road by Jan Myrdal, Mitt Liv by Ingrid Bergman; *Books* (as Ann Henning) Modern Astrology (1984), The Connemara Whirlwind (1990); *Recreations* riding, pony breeding, reading; *Style*— Viscountess Jocelyn; 4 The Boltons, London SW10 9TB (☎ 071 373 8303)

JOCELYN, Dr Henry David; s of John Daniel Jocelyn (d 1956), and Phyllis Irene, *née* Burton (d 1977); *b* 22 Aug 1933; *Educ* Canterbury Boys' HS NSW, Univ of Sydney (BA), St John's Coll Cambridge (MA, PhD); *m* 22 Oct 1958, Margaret Jill , da of Bert James Morton (d 1984); 2s (Luke b 1962, Edmund b 1968); *Career* memb academic staff Univ of Sydney 1960-73, Hulme prof Latin Univ of Manchester 1973-; FBA 1982; *Style*— Dr Henry D Jocelyn; 4 Clayton Ave, Manchester M20 0BN (☎ 061 434 1526); Department of Greek and Latin, University of Manchester, M13 9PL (☎ 061 275 3022)

JOCELYN, Hon James Michael; s of 9 Earl of Roden; *b* 12 April 1943; *Educ* Stowe, Trinity Coll Dublin; *Style*— The Hon James Jocelyn; Glynsk, Cashel, Connemara, Co Galway, Eire

JOCELYN, Viscount; Robert John Jocelyn; eldest s and h of 9 Earl of Roden; *b* 25 Aug 1938; *Educ* Stowe; *m* 1, 1970 (m dis 1982), Sara Cecilia, da of late Brig Andrew Dunlop, of Que Que, Zimbabwe; 1 da (Cecilia Rose b 1976); m 2, 1986, Ann Margareta Maria, da of Dr Gunnar Henning, of Goteborg, Sweden; 1 s (Shane Robert Henning b 9 Dec 1989); *Heir* s, Hon Shane Robert Hanning Jocelyn b 9 Dec 1989; *Career* insurance broker; *Style*— Viscount Jocelyn; 4 The Boltons, London SW10 9TB (☎ 071 373 8303)

JOCELYN, Hon Thomas Alan; 2 s of 9 Earl of Roden; *b* 4 Oct 1941; *Educ* Stowe, RNC Dartmouth; *m* 1966 (m dis 1983), Fiona, da of Capt Rudland Dallas Cairns, DSC, RN, of Co Wexford; 2 da, 1 s; *Career* Lt-Cdr RN (ret 1979); *Style*— Lt Cdr The Hon Thomas Jocelyn, RN

JODRELL, Michael Francis Mostyn Owen; s of Col Herbert Lewis Mostyn-Owen (d 1972), and Susan Dorothy, *née* Ramsden-Jodrell (d 1965); *b* 9 Dec 1935; *Educ* Eton; *m* 25 April 1964, Veronica Mary, da of Lt-Col Oscar Leslie Boord, MC (d 1967); 2 s (Henry b 28 April 1967, William b 8 Oct 1969); *Career* Lt Grenadier Gds; ptnr Rowe & Pitman 1972-86, dir Mercury Mgmnt plc 1989, vice chm Mercury Asset Mgmnt Private Investors Gp Ltd 1988; Liveryman Worshipful Co of Fishmongers; *Recreations* photography, gardening, shooting; *Clubs* Pratts; *Style*— Michael M O Jodrell, Esq; Leigh Court, Shaftesbury, Dorset (☎ 074 7828 261); 33 King William St, London EC4 (☎ 071 280 2800)

JOEL, Victoria Lynne Roberts (Vicky); da of Llywellyn James Roberts Joel (d 1970), of Gravesend, Kent, and Nora, *née* Bagshaw (d 1981); *b* 18 July 1952; *Educ* Ashford Sch for Girls Kent, Univ of Manchester (BA); *partner*, Stephen Bobasch; *Career* mktg asst Taylor Law & Co Ltd 1973-75, prod mangr Lyons Maid Ltd 1975-77, gp prod mangr Book Club Associates 1977-80; DDM Advertising Ltd: account mangr 1980-85, account dir 1985-87, client servs dir 1987-88; Eng area mangr and vice pres for Euro Time-Life Books 1989-; memb Cncl and dir BDMA 1989-, memb Mktg Soc 1989-; *Style*— Ms Vicky Joel; Time-Life books (Europe) Inc, Time & Life Building, 153 New Bond St, London W1Y 0AA (☎ 071 499 4080, fax 071 499 9377)

JOELSON, Stephen Laurance Robert; s of Maurice Joelson, of London, and Maureen Michelle, *née* Wien; *b* 28 Feb 1956; *Educ* Latymer Upper Sch, Univ of Reading (LLB); *Career* called to the Bar Gray's Inn 1980, attorney at law admitted to the Bar of California USA 1989; *Recreations* skiing, football; *Clubs* Holmes Place, The Bank, The Globe; *Style*— Stephen Joelson, Esq; 3 New Square, Lincoln's Inn, London, WC2A 3RS (☎ 071 242 2523, fax 071 831 6968)

JOFFE, Joel Goodman; s of Abraham Michael Joffe (d 1984), of Johannesburg, and Dena, *née* Idelson (d 1984); *b* 12 May 1932; *Educ* Univ of Witwatersrand Johannesburg (BCom, LLB); *m* 1 Nov 1962, Vanetta, da of François Pretorius (d 1975), of Port Elizabeth, S Africa; 3 da (Deborah b 11 June 1963, Lisa b 13 Aug 1964, Abigail b 4 Sept 1969); *Career* lawyer SA 1954-65; admin dir Abbey Life Assur plc 1966-70, dep chm (formerly dir and md) Allied Dunbar Assur plc 1971-; chm: Swindon Cncl of Voluntary Servs 1973-80, Oxfam 1980- (tstee, hon sec and chm of exec ctee), Swindon Health Authy 1988-; *Recreations* tennis, squash, cycling; *Style*— Joel Joffe, Esq

JOFFRE, Hugues; s of Bernard Joffre, of Paris, and Muriel, *née* Robert; *b* 7 July 1958; *Educ* Lycée Champollion Grenoble, Lycée Edouard Herriot Lyon, Univ of Grenoble; *m* Nazan, da of late Ismail Agar; 1 step da (Lara Stoby b 4 July 1980); *Career* Contemporary Art Dept Sotheby's: expert 1982-86, dep dir 1986-88, dir 1988-91, sr dir 1991-; *Style*— Hugues Joffre, Esq; Sotheby's Contemporary Art Department, 34-35 New Bond Street, London W1 (☎ 071 408 5400, fax 071 355 4398)

JOHANSEN, Hon Mrs (Jane); *née* Blyton; eldest da of Baron Blyton, Life Peer (d 1987); *b* 1920; *m* 1943, John Johansen (d 1955); children; *Style*— The Hon Mrs Johansen; 139 Brockley Ave, S Shields, Tyne and Wear

JOHANSEN-BERG, Rev John; s of John Alfred Johansen-Berg, of Middlesbrough, Cleveland, and Caroline, *née* Gettings; *b* 4 Nov 1935; *Educ* Acklam Hall GS, Univ of Leeds (BA, BD), Univ of Cambridge (MA); *m* 17 July 1971, Joan Scott, da of James Parnham, of Leeds, Yorks; 2 s (Mark b 1973, James (Jake) b 1977), 1 da (Heidi b 1974); *Career* tutor Westminster Coll Cambridge 1961-62, ordained 1962, min St Ninian's Presbyterian Church Luton Beds 1962-70, fndr min St Katherine of Genoa Church Dunstable Beds 1966-70, frontier mission work in Everton Liverpool resulting in the bldg of the Rock Church Centre 1970-77, min St Andrew's United Reformed Church Ealing 1977-86, fndr Community for Reconciliation 1984 (pastoral ldr Birmingham 1986-); moderator: United Reformed Church 1980-81, Free Church Federal Cncl 1987-88; memb: Br Cncl of Churches Assembly 1987-90, SA Advsy Ctee, Namibia Advsy Gp, Forum of Churches Together in England 1990-; fndr Christian Concern for SA; memb and former chm: Christian Fellowship Tst, Namibia Christian Exchange; chm: Clergy Against Nuclear Arms, Church and Soc Dept of URC 1972-79, BCC Working Party which produced Non-Violent Action: A Christian Appraisal (SCM 1973) and Violence, Non-Violence and Social Change (BCC 1977), URC Gp which produced Good News the Poor: New Enterprise in Mission (URC 1982); fndr: Ecumenical Order of Miny 1990, Romania Concern 1990; jt ed The Journal of the Presbyterian Historical Soc 1964-70; *Books* Arian or Arminian? Presbyterian Continuity in the Eighteenth Century (1969), Prayers of The Way (1987), Prayers of Pilgrimage (1988), Prayers of Prophecy (1990); *Recreations* walking, mountain climbing/walking, badminton, tennis, golf; *Style*— The Rev John Johansen-Berg; Barnes Close, Chadwich Manor, nr Bromsgrove, Worcs B61 ORA (☎ 0562 710231); Community for Reconciliation, Barnes Close, Chadwich Manor, nr Bromsgrove, Worcs B61 ORA

JOHANSON, Capt Philip; s of Stanely Theodore Johanson, of 66 Patrington Garth, Bransholme, Hull, North Humberside, and Betty Johanson (d 1984); *b* 10 April 1947; *Educ* Alderman Cogan C of E Sch Kingston upon Hull; *Career* Church Army: head of missions 1975-83, dir of evangelism 1983-90, chief sec 1990-; chm African Pastor Fund, memb C of E Advsy Cncl on the Churches, Ministry (ACCM) Lay Ministry Ctee; *Recreations* theatre, music, travel, reading; *Style*— Capt Philip Johanson; Church Army Headquarters, Independents Rd, Blackheath, London SE3 9LG (☎ 081 318 1226, fax 071 318 5258)

JOHN, (Richard) Alun; s of Thomas Guy John (d 1969), and Edith, *née* John (d 1979); *b* 7 April 1948; *Educ* Whitchurch GS; *m* 14 June 1980, (Elizabeth) Sara, da of Denis W Kent, of Beaconsfield, Bucks; 1 s (Guy b 7 Oct 1985), 1 da (Lucy b 5 April 1989); *Career* photographer South Wales Echo and Western Mail 1966, photographer The Press Assoc 1977, ed The Associated Press; dep picture ed: Evening Standard 1981, Mail on Sunday 1982; picture ed The Independent 1986, gp picture ed Mirror Group Newspapers 1989-, exec vice chm Syndication International 1989-; external examiner Univ of Sheffield, selector RPS Exhibitions 1988-89, conslt picture ed Thomson Fndn; Gerald Barry award from What the Papers Say 1987; *Books* Newspaper Photography (1988); *Recreations* travel, writing, shooting; *Style*— Alun John, Esq; Randall Mead, Binfield Berks RS12 5EL; Mirror Group Newspapers, Holborn Circus, London (☎ 071 353 0246, fax 071 404 0787)

JOHN, Arthur Walwyn; CBE (1967, OBE 1945); s of Oliver Walwyn John (d 1953), of Cardiff, and Elsie Maud, *née* Davies (d 1980); *b* 1 Dec 1912; *Educ* Marlborough; *m* 1, 24 Sept 1949, Elizabeth Rosabelle (d 1979), yr da of Ernest David Williams, of Radyr, Cardiff; 1 s (Oliver b 1961), 2 da (Ann b 1952, Sarah b 1953); m 2, 30 May 1986, Bonita Lynne, da of Sebastian Maritano; *Career* joined army 1939, cmmnd 1940, War Office 1941, DAQMG First Army 1942, HQ Allied Armies in Italy 1942, AQMG Allied Forces HQ 1944 (despatches 1943 and 1945); asst to commercial mangr (collieries) Powell Duffryn Assoc Collieries Ltd 1936, chief accountant John Lewis & Co Ltd 1945, chm Coal Prods Div NCB 1962-68 (dep dir gen of fin 1946, dir gen 1955, memb Bd 1961-68); dir: Unigate Ltd 1969-75, Property Holding and Investment Trust Ltd 1976-87 (chm 1982-84), Stenhouse Holdings plc 1976-87 (chm 1983-87), Reed Stenhouse Companies Ltd Canada 1977-84, J H Sankey & Son Ltd 1965-86, Schroder Property Fund 1971-88, Chartered Accountants Trustees Ltd 1982-87, Wincanton Contracts Finance Ltd 1983-85; chm: Teamdale Distribution Ltd 1982-, Chale Property Holdings plc 1986-87; memb Price Cmmn 1976-77; memb Ct: Univ of Wales Aberystwyth, City Univ; Freeman City of London, Memb Ct Worshipful Co of Chartered Accountants 1977 (Master 1981-82); CA 1934 (memb Cncl 1965-81); *Recreations* gardening, golf, walking; *Clubs* Army and Navy; *Style*— Arthur John, Esq, CBE; Limber, Top Park, Gerrards Cross, Bucks SL9 7PW (☎ 0753 884811)

JOHN, Daniel; s of Michael Hanlon John, of London, and Patricia Ann, *née* Hawkes; *b* 6 June 1961; *Educ* Archbishop Tenison's GS London; *Career* trainee journalist West London Observer 1979-83, sr reporter West Kent Extra Series 1983-84, former reporter and sub ed Kent Evening Post, industl reporter 1984-86, fin reporter Birmingham Post 1986-88, freelance reporter 1988-89 (The Guardian, Mail on Sunday, Daily Star), fin corr The Guardian 1989-; received Proficiency Test Cert from Nat Cncl for Trg of Journalists; NEC memb NUJ 1986-87; memb: Charter 88, Friends of the Earth; *Recreations* reading, current affairs, music, cooking, entertaining, cricket; *Clubs* Fleet Street Strollers Cricket; *Style*— Daniel John, Esq; The Guardian, 119 Farringdon Road, London EC1R 3ER (☎ 071 278 2532)

JOHN, Elton Hercules (born Reg Dwight); s of Stanley Dwight, and Sheila, *née* Sewell; *b* 25 March 1947; *Educ* Pinner GS, RAM; *Career* pop singer and pianist; keyboard player with R & B band Bluesology 1965, first album Empty Sky released 1969, US debut at Troubadour Folk Club 1970, single Your Song first UK and US Top 10 record 1971, renowned during 1970s for outlandish costumes and ludicrous spectacles, albums Goodbye Yellow Brick Road, Captain Fantastic and The Brown Dirt Cowboy and Blue Moves confirmed worldwide stardom, toured Communist Block (first Western pop star to play eight sell-out dates in Leningrad), album A Single Man 1978 and subsequent tour stripped away razzmataz of early seventies shows, album Two Low for Zero 1983 provided four worldwide hits, broadcast of Live in Australia album viewed by record Australian TV audience of six million 1987, stage costumes and memorabilia sold by Sotheby's 1988, 34th album Sleeping with the Past released 1989, No 1 in UK Album Charts July 1990, over 3 million copies sold worldwide, double A-Sided single Sacrifice/Healing Hands No 1 five weeks in UK (first UK No 1, all proceeds donated to AIDS related charities); No 1 double album The Very Best of Elton John released Dec 1990; significant achievements: record seven sell-out shows Madison Square Gardens, first artist to enter Billboard US Album chart at No 1, seven consecutive No 1 US albums, writer of over 200 songs, more weeks spent in UK chart than any other recording artist during 1970s, winner Best Male Artist Brit award 1991; chm Watford FC 1979-90; involved in many charities incl: Nordoff Robbins Music Therapy, Terence Higgins Tst, Body Positive, London Lighthouse; *Recreations* Watford FC (life pres); *Style*— Elton John, Esq; John Reid Enterprises, 32 Galena Rd, London W6 0LT (☎ 081 741 9933, fax 081 741 3938)

JOHN, Hon Mrs (Jane Lesley); *née* Nicol; da of Alexander Douglas Ian Nicol, by his w, Baroness Nicol (Life Peeress); *m* 1984, Edward John, only s of J E John, of Margam, Port Talbot, W Glam; *Style*— The Hon Mrs John

JOHN, Hon Mrs ((Mary) Joan Fenella Hope); *née* Hope-Morley; da of 2 Baron Hollenden, JP (d 1977); *b* 1915; *m* 1, 1941 (m dis 1965), David Babington Smith, s of late Sir Henry Babington Smith, GBE, CH, KCB, CSI; 1 da; m 2, 1966, Geoffrey John; *Style*— The Hon Mrs John; Lime House, Kintbury, Newbury, Berks

JOHN, Dr Joshy; s of Prof P V Ulahannan Mapilla, of Changanachery, Kerala, India, and Mary, *née* Joseph; *b* 9 Oct 1940; *Educ* St Berchmans' HS, Kerala Univ (BSc, MB BS), Univ of Sheffield (MD); *m* 25 Jan 1970, Tresa, da of K J Jacob, of Kerala, India; 2 s (Jason Joseph b 30 June 1974, James George b 7 Nov 1983), 1 da (Mary Anne b 14 March 1979); *Career* conslt physician genito-urinary med: St Mary's Hosp Luton, St Alban's City Hosp Herts; hon conslt (HIV and AIDS Unit) Kobler Centre, St Stephen's Clinic Fulham and Westminster Hosp; former conslt physician venereology: Derby Royal Infirmary, Derby and Chesterfield Royal Hosp; hon lectr Med Div Univ of

Sheffield; memb: Int Union Against VD and Treponematoses, Med Soc Study of VD, American VD Assoc, Indian Assoc Study of Sexually Transmitted Diseases, Int Soc for AIDS, AIDS Task Force St Mary's Hosp Luton, AIDS Action Gp St Alban's City Hosp, VD Advsy Sub-Ctee NW Thames RHA; FRSM; *Books* papers on non-gonococcal urethritis therapy, asymptomatic gonorrhoea in male and abnormal forms of trichomonas vaginalis; *Recreations* tennis, swimming, reading; *Style—* Dr Joshy John; St Mary's Hospital, Dunstable Rd, Luton (☎ 0582 21261); St Albans City Hospital, Normandy Road, St Albans (☎ 0727 866122); 139 Harley St, London W1N 1DJ (☎ 071 224 3303)

JOHN, Maldwyn Noel; s of Thomas Daniel John (d 1944), of Pontypridd, Glamorgan, and Beatrice May, *née* Clare (d 1971); *b* 25 Dec 1929; *Educ* Pontypridd GS, Univ Coll Cardiff (BSc); *m* 27 June 1953, Margaret, *née* Cannell; 2 s (Steven Thomas b 1959, Paul David b 1962); *Career* Metropolitan Vickers Electrical Co Manchester 1950-59, Atomic Energy Estab UKAEA Winfrith 1959-63, chief engr and divnl mangr AEI/GEC Manchester 1963-69; Kennedy & Donkin Consulting Engrs: chief electrical engr 1969-72, ptnr 1972-87, chm 1987-; pres Inst of Electrical Engrs 1983-84; memb: Ct UWIST 1984-88, Overseas Projects Bd 1987-; dir Nat Inspection Cncl for Electrical Installation Contractors (NICEIC) 1988-, govr Broadwater County Secdy Sch Godalming Surrey; Freeman: City of London 1987, Worshipful Co of Engrs 1987; CEng 1966, FIEE 1969, MConsE 1973, FEng 1979, FIEEE 1985; *Books* Practical Diakoptics for Electrical Networks (jtly, 1969), Power Circuit Breakers Theory & Design (jtly, 1 edn 1975, 2 edn 1982); *Recreations* golf; *Clubs* Bramley Golf (Surrey); *Style—* M N John, Esq; Kennedy & Donkin Group Ltd, Westbrook Mills, Godalming, Surrey GU7 2AZ (☎ 0483 425900, fax 0483 425136, telex 859373 KDHO G)

JOHN, Sir Rupert Godfrey; s of Donelley Westmore John (d 1951); *b* 19 May 1916; *Educ* St Vincent GS, London Univ (BA, DipEd), New York Univ; *m* 1937, Hepsy, da of Samuel Norris; 3 s (and 1 s decd), 1 da; *Career* called to the Bar Gray's Inn; first asst master St Kitts and Nevis GS 1943, asst master St Vincent GS 1944-52, private law practice St Vincent 1952-58, magistrate Grenada WI 1958-60, acting attorney gen Grenada 1960-62, human rights offr UN 1962-70, memb int team of observers Nigeria 1969-70, sr human rights offr 1970, govr St Vincent 1970-76; memb: Barclays Bank Int Ltd Policy Advsy Ctee (St Vincent) 1977-85, West India Ctee, special fellow to UN Inst of Trg and Res 1978-85, founded Assoc of Sr Citizens of St Vincent and The Grenadines, pres Caricare, Caribbean Inst for observance and protection human rights and democratic and humanitarian principles 1987-88; Caricare Human Rights Awards 1988; KStJ 1971; kt 1971; *Recreations* reading, walking, swimming; *Clubs* Royal Commonwealth Soc; *Style—* Sir Rupert John; PO Box 677, Cane Garden, St Vincent, West Indies (☎ 809 4561500)

JOHN, Stewart Morris; s of Ivor Morgan John (d 1989), of Shepperton, Middx, and Lilian, *née* Morris (d 1989); *b* 28 Nov 1938; *Educ* Porth Co GS, N Staffs Tech Coll, Southall Tech Coll (HNC); *m* 3 July 1961, Susan Anne, da of William Alfred Cody; 1 s (Philip Andrew b 23 May 1964), 1 da (Sarah Margaret b 10 Nov 1967); *Career* BOAC apprentice aeronautical engr 1955-60, seconded as station engr to Kuwait Airways 1961-65, seconded as chief engr Borneo to Malaysia-Singapore Airlines E Malaysia 1965-67 (gen inspr and project engr Singapore 1963-66), engr Avionics Devpt London Airport 1967-70, asst to Gen Manager Maintenance 1970-71, works supt Mechanical Workshops 1972-73, aircraft maintenance supt 1973-74, maintenance mangr American Aircraft 1975-77, engrg dir Cathay Pacific Airways 1980- (dep dir engrg and maintenance Hong Kong 1977-80); dir Thompson Aircraft Tires Co Asia 1985-; Ground Support Engineering Pty Aust 1989-; dep chm Hong Kong Aircraft Engineering 1987- (dir 1982-), chm Assoc Engineers Ltd Hong Kong 1990-; chm Exec Ctee and vice pres Far East Int Fedn of Airworthiness 1975-, chm Hong Kong Branch Royal Aeronautical Soc 1984; Gold medal Br Assoc of Aviation Cnslts 1991; FEng, FHIE, FRAeS; *Recreations* folf, classic cars, rugger; *Clubs* The Hong Kong, Shek-o Country, Hong Kong Aviation, Bentley Drivers; *Style—* Stewart John, Esq; Treetops, 7 Customs Pass, Lot 31 D D 228, Fei Ngo Shan Road, Kowloon, Hong Kong (☎ 010 852 351 6747); Cathy Pacific Airways Ltd, Engineering Dep, 9th Floor, Technical Building, 88 Concorde Rd, Hong Kong International Airport, Hong Kong (☎ 010 852 747 8747, fax 010 852 764 6579)

JOHN, Vivien (Mrs John White); da of Augustus E John, OM (d 1969), of Fryern Court, Fordingbridge, Hants, and Dorelia, *née* McNeill; *b* 8 March 1915; *Educ* privately at home, Slade Sch of Art, Euston Road Sch of Art, Chelsea Sch of Art, Academic de la Grande Chaumiere; *m* June 1945, Dr John Cosby White; 1 s and 1 s decd; *Career* artist; solo exhibitions: Walker's Galleries London 1953, Pollocks Toy Museum 1961, Univ of Liverpool 1967, Upper Grosvenor Galleries 1971, Chester Beatty Res Inst 1971, Halesworth Gallery Suffolk 1973, Editions Graphiques 1977, Port Moresby 1982-84, Holland Gallery 1987; gp exhibitions: Cooling Galleries 1935, Royal Acad Summer Exhibition 1945, 1953, 1956 and 1965, United Soc of Artists 1946, Norrland London 1951, O'Hanna Gallery 1959-60, Brighton Art Gallery's Autumn Exhibition 1964-65, Hampstead Artists' Cncl 1967, Michael Parkin Gallery Summer Exhibition 1987, Sally Hunter 1987, Michael Parkin Gallery Winter Exhibition 1988, Bloomsbury Workshop 1988; *Recreations* walking, riding; *Style—* Ms Vivien John

JOHN-MACKIE, Baron (Life Peer UK 1981), of Nazeing, Co Essex; John Mackie; s of Maitland Mackie, OBE, farmer, and Mary, *née* Yull; er bro of Baron Mackie of Benshie and Sir Maitland Mackie, Lord-Lt of Aberdeenshire; *b* 24 Nov 1909; *Educ* Aberdeen GS, N of Scotland Coll of Agric; *m* 1934, Jeannie Inglis, da of Robert Milne; 3 s (Hon James Alexander b 1935, Hon John Maitland b 1944, Hon George Yull b 1949), 2 da (Hon Jean Simpson (Hon Mrs Fairweather) b 1937, Hon Mary Yull b 1940); *Career* sits as Lab Peer in Lords; farmer in Essex; MP (Lab) Enfield E 1959-74, jt parly sec Miny of Agric 1964-70; chm Forestry Cmmn 1976-79; oppn forestry spokesman; *Style—* The Rt Hon the Lord John-Mackie; Harold's Park, Nazeing, Waltham Abbey, Essex (☎ 099 289 2202)

JOHNS, Alan Wesley; CMG (1990), OBE (1973); s of Harold Wesley Johns (d 1971), and Catherine Louisa, *née* James; *b* 27 March 1931; *Educ* Farnborough GS Hants, Univ of London (BSc), Univ of Southampton (Cert Ed); *m* 17 April 1954, Joan Margaret, da of Leslie Charles Wheeler, of Westbury, Wilts; 1 s (Mark b 1963), 1 da (Emma b 1966); *Career* teacher various secdy schs Wiltshire LEA 1953-61, educn offr Govt St Helena 1961-68 (chm Educn Bd 1962-68, exec and legislative cncllr 1963-68); dir educn: Govt Seychelle Islands 1968-74 (chm Educn Ctee 1968-74), Govt Gibraltar 1974-78 (memb Pub Serv Cmmn 1974-78); exec dir Royal Cwlth Soc for the Blind 1984- (dep dir 1978-83); chm Int Non Govt Orgns Partnership Ctee in Blindness Prevention 1983-, pres Int Agency for the Prevention of Blindness 1990- (vice pres 1986-90), chm Consultative Gp NGOS to WHO programme for Prevention of Blindness 1986-90; *Recreations* travel in developing countries, house maintenance, sailing; *Clubs* Rotary (Haywards Heath); *Style—* Alan Johns, Esq, CMG, OBE; Grosvenor Hall, Bolnore Rd, Haywards Heath, W Sussex RH16 4YF (☎ 0444 412424, fax 0444 415866, telex 87167 COMBLD); Royal Commonwealth Society For the Blind, Norris House, Burrell Rd, Haywards Heath, W Sussex RH16 3AZ (☎ 0444 412424, fax 0444 415866, telex 87167 COMBLD)

JOHNS, Prof Allan Thomas; s of William George Johns, of Exeter, Devon, and Ivy Maud, *née* Camble; *b* 14 April 1942; *Educ* St Lukes Sch Exeter, Univ of Bath (BSc, PhD, DSc); *m* 23 Sept 1972, Marion, da of Charles Franklin (d 1952); 2 da (Louisa Anne b 1979, Victoria Helen b 1981); *Career* asst dist engr S W Electricity Bd 1963-68, reader in power systems Univ of Bath 1976-84 (res fell 1968-69, lectr in electrical engrg 1969-76), head of Electrical Electronic and Information Engineering Dept and dir of Power and Energy Systems Research Centre City University 1988-91 (prof of electrical and electronic engineering 1984-88), prof of electrical engineering Univ of Bath 1991-; chm SERC Electricity Research Co-Funding Ctee 1989-; conslt: GEC, CEGB, British Technol Group; ed: IEE Power Engineering Series 1984-, IEE Power Engineering Journal 1989-; author of over 120 res papers, awarded 3 learned soc premiums (1968, 1982, 1988); FIEE 1981, FRSA 1988, CEng; *Recreations* ice skating, bowls, walking, piano, singing (professional concert tenor); *Clubs* Swindon Ice Dance, Swindon NE Bowling (pres 1990-); *Style—* Prof Allan T Johns; School of Electronic and Electrical Engineering, Univeristy of Bath, Claverton Down, Bath, Avon BA2 7AY (☎ 0225 826826, fax 0225 826305)

JOHNS, David John; *b* 29 April 1931; *Educ* St Brendan's Coll Bristol, Univ of Bristol (BSc, MSc), Loughborough Univ of Technol (PhD, DSc); *m* 27 March 1954, Sheila Jean, *née* Read; 1 da (Susan Mary Ann (Mrs Butler)); *Career* student apprentice (later tech offr section ldr) Br Aeroplane Co Ltd 1949-57, sr tech offr Sir W G Armstrong Whitworth A/C Ltd 1957-58, lectr Cranfield Inst of Technol 1958-63; Loughborough Univ of Technol 1964-83: reader, prof, head of Dept of Tport Technol, dean of Sch of Engrg, sr pro vice chllr; dir City Poly Hong Kong 1983-89; vice chllr and princ Univ of Bradford 1989-; memb: Aeronautical Res Cncl Dynamics Ctee (later chm) 1970-80, (later vice pres and pres elect) Cncl Inst of Acoustics 1979-83, Environmental Pollution Advsy Ctee Hong Kong (later chm) 1984-88, Vocational Trg Cncl (Hong Kong) 1984-89, Hong Kong Productivity Cncl 1984-89, Cncl Hong Kong Inst of Engrs 1984-89; CEng 1968, FRAeS 1969, FIOA 1977, FCIT 1977, FHKIE 1984, FAeSI 1986, FEng 1990; *Books* Thermal Stress Analyses (1965); *Recreations* walking, bridge, music; *Clubs* Athenaeum, Hong Kong, Royal Hong Kong Jockey; *Style—* Prof David Johns; Vice Chancellor's Office, University of Bradford, W Yorks BD7 1DP (☎ 0274 733 466, fax 0274 305 340)

JOHNS, Michael Alan; s of Mr John William Johns, of Sevenoaks, Kent, and Kathleen Eva, *née* Hummerston (d 1982); *b* 20 July 1946; *Educ* Judd Sch Tunbridge, Queens' Coll Cambridge (BA, MA); *Career* Inland Revenue 1967-79, Central Policy Review Staff 1979-80, Inland Revenue 1980-84, seconded Orion Royal Bank 1985, Inland Revenue 1986- (dir Oil and Fin Div 1988-); *Recreations* skiing, teaching (adults), moral philosophy; *Style—* Mr Michael Johns, Esq; Bd of Inland Revenue, Somerset House, Strand, London WC2R 1LB (☎ 071 438 7739, fax 071 4389 6148)

JOHNS, Michael Charles; s of Arthur Charles Johns, of Crediton Devon, and Margaret Mary (d 1986); *b* 20 Dec 1974; *Educ* Tiffin Sch, St Edmund Hall Oxford (BA, Cross Country blue 1967 and 1968), Law Soc Finals (New Inn prize); *m* Sept 1970, Lucy Mary; 2 da (Kathryn Helen b 23 Oct 1973, Clare Louise b 16 April 1976); *Career* ptnr: Withers 1974-87 (joined 1970), Ashurst Morris Crisp 1987-; dir: London Forfaiting Company plc 1984-, Exco International plc 1985-; *Style—* Michael Johns, Esq; Ashurst Morris Crisp, Broadwalk House, 5 Appold St, London EC2 (☎ 071 638 1111, fax 071 972 7990)

JOHNS, Michael Stephen Mackelcan; s of Jack Elliott Mackelcan Johns (d 1968), of Starvacres, Radlett, Herts, and Janet, *née* Price; *b* 18 Oct 1943; *Educ* Marlborough; *m* 1, 20 Sept 1968 (m dis 1975), Joanna Turner, *née* Gilligan; 2 s (Alexander b 16 Sept 1971, Toby b 1 Sept 1973); m 2, 10 March 1979, Gillian, da of Geoffrey Duckett White, of Perth, Western Aust; 1 da (Sophie b 2 Feb 1984); *Career* slr; managing ptnr Nicholson Graham & Jones 1987- (ptnr 1973-), non-exec dir Merchant Retail Group plc 1979-; memb: Law Soc, IOD; *Recreations* golf, cricket, gardening; *Clubs* MCC, Hurlingham, St Georges Hill Golf; *Style—* Michael Johns, Esq; 22 Bowerdean St, London SW6 3TW (☎ 071 731 7607); 25-31 Moorgate, London EC2R 6AR (☎ 071 628 9151, fax 071 638 3102, telex 8811848)

JOHNS, Rev Patricia Holly (Pat); da of W A H Harris, and V F Harris, *née* Chinnery; *b* 13 Nov 1933; *Educ* Blackheath HS, Girton Coll Cambridge (BA, MA), Hughes Hall Cambridge (Cert Ed); *m* 2 Aug 1958, Michael C B Johns (d 1965), s of Alfred S Bedford Johns, of Exeter; 1 s (Paul b 1961), 1 da (Sarah b 1964); *Career* mathematics teacher: Cheltenham Ladies Coll 1957-58, Macclesfield HS 1958-60; St Albans HS: mathematics teacher 1966-70, head of mathematics and dir of studies 1970-75; sr mistress Gordonstoun Sch 1975-80, headmistress St Mary's Sch Wantage 1980-; lay reader 1979-, ordained deacon 1990; memb: SHA, GSA; *Recreations* singing, corgis, travel; *Style—* The Rev Pat Johns; 3 Post Office Lane, Wantage, Oxon; St Mary's School, Wantage, Oxon (☎ 021 57 3571)

JOHNS, Patrick (Paddy); s of R M Johns, and F W Johns; *b* 19 Feb 1968; *Educ* Royal Sch Dungannon, Armagh Coll of Further Educn, Univ of Newcastle, Trinity Coll Dublin; *Career* Rugby Union lock forward Dublin Univ FC and Ireland (1 cap); clubs: Dungannon RFC 1986-87, Newcastle Univ RFC 1987-88, Newcastle Gosford RFC 1988-89, Dublin Univ FC 1989-; rep: Irish Schoolboys (4 caps), Ireland U21 (1 cap), Ireland U25 (3 caps), Ireland B (debut v Scotland 1989), Irish Univs, Irish Students, Ulster (10 caps, Inter-Provincial series winners 1988, 1989, 1990); debut Ireland v Argentina 1990; final year dental student Trinity Coll Dublin; *Recreations* painting, reading, music, food; *Style—* Paddy Johns, Esq; c/o Trinity Rugby Rooms, Trinity Coll Dublin, Dublin 1

JOHNS, Peter Andrew; s of Lt John Francis, DSC, RNVR, of Porthcawl, and Megan, *née* Isaac; *b* 31 Dec 1947; *Educ* Bridgend GS, UCL (BSc); *m* 12 Aug 1985, Rosanne Helen Josephine, da of Capt William John Howard Slayter, RA, of Oxted, Surrey; 2 s (Jack b 1987, Robert b 1989); *Career* non-exec dir Merchant Bank of Central Africa 1985-, dir NM Rothschild & Sons Ltd 1987-; ACIB 1975; *Recreations* golf, tennis, books; *Clubs* RAC; *Style—* Peter Johns, Esq; 56 Canonbury Park South, London N1 2JG (☎ 071 354 3570); New Court, St Swithins Lane, London EC4P 4DU (☎ 071 280 5000, fax 071 280 5400, telex 888031)

JOHNS, Air Vice-Marshal Richard Edward; CBE (1985 OBE 1978), LVO (1972); s of Lt-Col Herbert Edward Johns, RM (d 1977), of Emsworth, Hants, and Marjory Harley, *née* Everett; *b* 28 July 1939; *Educ* Portsmouth GS, RAF Coll Cranwell; *m* 23 Oct 1965, Elizabeth Naomi Anne, da of Air Cdre Frederick John Manning (d 1988), of Eynsham, Oxford; 1 s (Douglas b 1972), 2 da (Victoria b 1970, Harriet b 1974); *Career* RAF, No 64 (F) Sqdn 1960-63, No 1417 (FR) Flt Aden 1965-67, flying instr duties 1968-71 (including tuition of HRH The Prince of Wales 1970-71), Staff Coll 1972, PSO/CINC NEAF 1973, No 3 (F) Sqdn as CO 1975-77, MOD Air Staff 1978-81, Stn Cdr and Harrier Force Cdr RAF Gutersloh 1982-84, RCDS 1985, SASO HQ RAF Germany 1986-88, SASO HQ Strike Cmd 1989-; *Recreations* military history, rugby, cricket; *Clubs* RAF; *Style—* Air Vice-Marshal Richard Johns, CBE, LVO; c/o Lloyds Bank, Cox's & Kings Branch, PO Box 1190, 7 Pall Mall, London SW1

JOHNSON; *see*: Campbell-Johnson

JOHNSON, Prof Alan Godfrey; s of Dr Douglas Johnson, of Pulborough, Sussex, and Dorothy Middleton, *née* James; *b* 19 Jan 1938; *Educ* Epsom Coll, Trinity Coll Cambridge (MA, MB MChir); *m* 7 July 1962, Esther Caroline, da of James Millner Vellacott (d 1983); 2 s (Paul b 1964, Andrew b 1966), 1 da (Fyona b 1970); *Career* house physician and surgn UCH 1963-64, sr house offr and surgical registrar Redhill

Gen Hosp 1965-67, res fell and lectr Charing Cross Hosp (surgical registrar 1967-68), sr lectr then reader in surgery Univ of London 1971-79, prof of surgery Univ of Sheffield 1979-; Hunterian prof RCS 1973-74; memb: Specialist Advsy Ctee in Gen Surgery, Nat Confidential Enquiry into Perioperative Deaths Steering Ctee, Editorial Ctee of British Journal of Surgery, Surgical Res Soc, Br Soc of Gastroenterology, Surgical Travellers; chm Christian Med Fellowship, dir James IV Assoc of Surgns, govr Birkdale Sch; memb Assoc of Surgns of GB and Ireland; FRCS; *Books* Aims and Motives in Clinical Medicine (1975), Techniques of Vagotomy (1979), Liver Disease and Gallstones - The Facts (1987), Pathways in Medical Ethics (1990); *Recreations* ornithology, hill walking, music (organ), painting (watercolour); *Style*— Prof Alan Johnson; University Surgical Unit, Royal Hallamshire Hosp, Glossop Rd, Sheffield S10 2JF (☎ 0742 766 222 ext 2025, fax 0742 700876)

JOHNSON, Alan Michael Borthwick; s of Dennis Daniel Borthwick Johnson, OBE (d 1976), of Calderstones, Liverpool, and Nora, *née* MacLeod; *b* 7 June 1944; *Educ* Liverpool Coll 1951-63, CCC Oxford (MA); *Career* called to the Bar Middle Temple (Harmsworth scholar) 1971; ad eundem Gray's Inn 1973; memb Criminal Bar Assoc; *Clubs* Oxford Society; *Style*— Alan Johnson, Esq; 1 Farm Place, London W8 7SX; 1 Gray's Inn Square, Gray's Inn, London WC1R 5AA (☎ 071 405 8946/8, fax 071 405 1617)

JOHNSON, Air Vice Marshal Alan Taylor; s of Percy Johnson (d 1988), and Janet, *née* Taylor (d 1990); *b* 3 March 1931; *Educ* Mexborough GS, Univ of Sheffield (MB ChB, Dip Av Med, MFOM, MFCM, Sir Arthur Hall trophy 1956); *m* 24 Aug 1954, Margaret Ellen, da of Albert Mee (d 1983); 3 s (Simon Rusell b and d 1957, Adrian Robert Alexander b 1959, Matthew William Edward b 1964), 3 da (Deborah Anne b 1955, Bridget Louise b 1958, Lisa Charlotte b 1962); *Career* RAF: Cmmnd 1957, MO RAF Gaydon 1957-59, Princess Mary's RAF Hosp Akrotiri Cyprus 1959-61, No 1 Parachute Trg Sch RAF Abingdon 1961-65, RAF Changi Singapore 1965-67, RAF Inst of Aviation Med 1967-71, RAF Bruggen Germany 1971-74, Med S O (Air) HQ RAF Support Cmd 1974-77, RAF Brize Norton 1977-78, chief aerospace med HQ SAC Offutt AFB USA 1978-91, dep dir health and res (aviation med) 1981-84, OC Princess Alexandra Hosp RAF Wroughton 1984-86, asst surgn gen (environmental med and res) MOD 1986, PMO HQ RAF Germany 1986-88, PMO HQ Strike Cmd 1988-; QHS 1986; hon med advsr Br Parachute Assoc 1967-71, chm Safety and Trg Ctee BPA 1968-71, head Br Delgn World Parachuting Championships 1970, 1972 and 1974, hon memb Assoc of Mil Surgns (USA) 1980; pres Adastrian Cricket Club 1986-91, vice pres RAF Cricket Assoc 1990-; FRAeS 1983; *Recreations* music, cricket, sport parachuting; *Clubs* Royal Air Force; *Style*— Air Vice-Marshal Alan Johnson; c/o Lloyds Bank, 99 High St, Huntingdon, Cambs PE18 6DU

JOHNSON, Hon Mrs (Anne); *née* Robbins; da of Baron Robbins, CH, CB (Life Peer, d 1984), and Baroness Robbins, *qv*; *b* 16 Oct 1925; *Educ* UCL; *m* 1958, Christopher Johnson, *qv*; 1 s, 3 da; *Style*— The Hon Mrs Johnson; 39 Wood Lane, London N6 (☎ 081 340 4970)

JOHNSON, Prof Barry Edward; s of Edward Johnson (d 1964), of Burgess Hill, Sussex, and Evelyn May, *née* Bailey (d 1980); *b* 1 Aug 1937; *Educ* Epsom Co GS, Hobart State HS, Univ of Tasmania (BSc), Univ of Cambridge (PhD); *m* 1 Nov 1961 (m dis 1979); 2 s (Martin b 1963, Adrian b 1966), 1 da (Susan b 1964); *Career* instr Univ of California Berkeley 1961-62, lectr Univ of Exeter 1963-65; Univ of Newcastle-upon-Tyne: lectr 1965-68, reader 1968-69, prof pure mathematics 1969-, dean Faculty of Sci 1986-89, visiting prof Univ of Yale New Haven USA 1970-71 (visiting lectr 1962-63); pres London Mathematical Soc 1980-82 (memb Cncl 1975-78), govr Royal GS Newcastle 1987-; FRS 1978; *Books* Cohomology in Banach Algebras (1970); *Recreations* reading, travel; *Style*— Prof Barry Johnson, FRS; 12 Roseworth Crescent, Gosforth, Newcastle upon Tyne NE3 1NR (☎ 091 284 5363); Dept of Mathematics and Statistics, The Univ, Newcastle upon Tyne NE1 7RU (☎ 091 222 6000, fax 091 261 1182)

JOHNSON, (Alexander) Boris de Pfeffel; s of Stanley Patrick Johnson, of Nethercote, Winsford, Minehead, Somerset, and Charlotte Mary Offlow, *née* Fawcett; *b* 19 June 1964; *Educ* Eton, Balliol Coll Oxford (Brackenbury scholar, BA); *m* 1987, Allegra, da of William Mostyn-Owen; *Career* reporter; LEK Management Consultants 1987; trainee reporter The Times 1987, reporter Wolverhampton Express & Star 1988; The Daily Telegraph: leader writer 1988, Euro community corr Brussels 1989-; appearances on radio and TV; *Books* The Oxford Myth (contrib, 1988); *Recreations* painting, writing, deep sea diving, all games, kung fu; *Style*— Boris Johnson, Esq; 29 Petite Rue de L'Eglise, Brussels 1150, Belgium (☎ 010 322 772 1057); 75 Sinclair Rd, London W14; 13 Square Marie-Louise, Brussels 1040, Belgium (☎ 010 322 230 6956, fax 010 322 230 6220)

JOHNSON, Brian Michael; s of Frederick William Johnson, of Woking, and Helen Josephine, *née* Whitmarsh; *b* 1 May 1939; *Educ* Finchley GS, Univ of Sheffield (BEng); *m* 1, 24 Aug 1963 (m dis 1973), Jennifer Ann, da of Thomas Kenneth Derham (d 1989), of Earsham Hall, Norfolk; 3 s (Arawn b 1964, Jess b 1971, James b 1973), 2 da (Fiona b 1965, Emily b 1974); m 2, 31 March 1973, Maureen Patricia, *née* Haines (d 1981); m 3, 10 July 1982, Diana Victoria, *née* Armstrong; *Career* trainee engr Balfour Beatty & Co Ltd 1961-64, site agent Costain Civil Engrg 1964-70, contracts mangr Tilbury Gp 1970-73, chm and md Anglo Dutch Dredging Co Ltd 1973-; papers on engrg subjects and contract law; memb Central Dredging Assoc 1980-, assoc memb Hydraulics Res 1985-, chm Fedn of Dredging Contractors 1989-90 (memb 1973-, chm 1981-82), memb Code of Practice Maritime Structures BSI (chm 1989-90); author papers on engrg subjects and contract law; CEng 1967, FICE 1988 (MICE 1967); *Recreations* music, violin (Windsor & Maidenhead Symphony Orch), art-antiques, classic cars, tennis, cycling; *Clubs* Athenaeum; *Style*— Brian Johnson, Esq; Old Thatch, Tittle Row, Maidenhead, Berks SL6 4PZ (☎ 0628 23963); Anglo-Dutch Dredging Co Ltd, Highway House, London End, Beaconsfield, Bucks HP9 2HN (☎ 0494 675646, telex 837042, fax 0494 678628, car 0860 381387)

JOHNSON, Carole Ann; da of Dr David Langridge, of Ramsey Abbey, Ramsey, Cambridgeshire, and Patricia Marion, *née* Johnson; *b* 17 June 1964; *Educ* Ramsey Abbey Sch, St Hugh's Coll Oxford (MA, pres Law Soc); *m* 1 Aug 1987, Richard Anthony Johnson, s of Tony Albert Johnson; *Career* Arthur Young CA 1985-89, tutor in law and taxation BPP Holdings 1989-; chm Nat Students Liaison Ctee, memb Educ & Training Directorate ICAEW; ACA 1989; *Recreations* Fulham & Hammersmith Choral Soc; *Style*— Mrs Carole Johnson

JOHNSON, Prof Charles Edward; s of Charles Montague Johnson (d 1980), of Watford, Herts, and Margaret Joyce, *née* Cordy (d 1982); *b* 21 Oct 1928; *Educ* Watford GS, Balliol Coll Oxford (MA, DPhil); *m* 1, 27 July 1957 (m dis 1980), Anne-Grete, da of Dr Arne Gorm Lauritzen, of Seattle, USA; 3 s (Paul b 1960, Ian b 1962, Michael b 1964); m 2, 29 July 1983, Jacqueline Anne, da of Brian Birch, of Southport; 2 s (William b 1987, Benjamin b 1988), 1 da (Lisa b 1984); *Career* Nat Serv RAF 1947-49; DSIR res fell Clarendon Laboratory Oxford 1955-57, Fulbright fell Univ of California Berkeley 1957-59, res assoc Argonne Nat Laboratory Univ of Chicago 1962-63, princ scientific offr AERE Harwell 1963-70 (sr res fell 1959-62), Royal Soc/NSERC visiting prof Univ of Toronto 1986-87, Lyon Jones prof of physics Univ of Liverpool 1987- (prof experimental physics 1970-86); contrib to books and scientific jls; served on Ctees SERC, pres of STEM (Sci and Technol Educn on Merseyside); FInstP; *Books* Mössbauer Spectroscopy and its Applications (1985); *Recreations* walking, reading; *Style*— Prof Charles Johnson; 17 Nicholas Rd, Liverpool L23 6TS (☎ 051 924 0162); Oliver Lodge Laboratory, Univ of Liverpool, PO Box 147, Liverpool L69 3BX (☎ 051 794 3359, fax 051 794 3444, telex 627095 UNILPL G)

JOHNSON, Christopher Edmund; s of Christopher Joseph Johnson, of Victoria Drive, Bognor Regis, W Sussex, and Phyllis, *née* Cox; *b* 17 Jan 1934; *Educ* Salesian Coll Chertsey, Collyers Sch Horsham; *m* 12 Jan 1956, Janet Yvonne, da of (Henry) James Wakefield, of Guildford Rd, Horsham, W Sussex; 8 s (Simon b 1958, Guy b 1959, Rupert b 1961, Max b 1965, Crispin b 1969, Roderick b 1972, Quentin b 1974, Tristan b 1977), 3 da (Nicola b 1957, Philippa b 1963, Clare b 1967); *Career* RN 1952-54, Sub Lt RNVR; MOD: princ Prog and Budget Div 1966-70, princ Gen Staff Div 1970-71, UK jt cmd sec Singapore 1971-74, asst sec Gen Staff Div 1975-76, Gen Fin Div 1976-79, asst sec Civilian Mgmnt Div 1979-84, dir gen Def Accounts 1985-89; *Recreations* gardening, reading; *Style*— Chris Johnson, Esq; Southcot House, Lyncombe Hill, Bath BA2 4PQ (☎ 0225 314247); Palmeras Beach, Puerto del Carmen, Lanzarote

JOHNSON, Christopher Louis McIntosh; s of Donald McIntosh Johnson, MP for Carlisle 1955-64 (d 1978); *b* 12 June 1931; *Educ* Winchester, Magdalen Coll Oxford; *m* 1958, Hon Anne, *qv*; 1 s, 3 da; *Career* Capt RAEC; Financial Times: foreign ed 1965-67, managing ed 1967-70, dir Business Enterprises Div 1971-72 dir 1972-76; econ advsr Lloyds Bank 1976-, visiting prof in econs Univ of Surrey 1986-89; *Books* Anatomy of UK Finance, North Sea Energy Wealth, Measuring the Economy; *Recreations* sailboarding, music; *Clubs* Overseas Bankers; *Style*— Christopher Johnson Esq; 39 Wood Lane, London N6 (☎ 081 340 4970)

JOHNSON, Colin Trevor; s of Richard Johnson (d 1986), of Eccles, Manchester, and Annie Evelyn, *née* Breakell; *b* 11 April 1942; *Educ* Worsley Tech Coll, Salford Sch of Art, Manchester Coll of Art; *Career* artist; solo exhibitions incl: Monks Hall Museum and Art Gallery Eccles 1961, 1963, 1969, 1972 and 1978, N W Arts Centre Manchester 1974, Victoria Gallery Harrogate 1975 and 1977, Granada TV 1968, 1969, 1973 and 1976, RNCM 1974, 1978 and 1987, Theatre Royal York 1976, Derby City Art Gallery 1980, Salt House Gallery St Ives Cornwall 1981 and 1984, Liberty's London 1983, Barbican 1984, Guildhall Art Gallery London 1985, Harrogate Gallery 1986, Brewhouse Art Centre Tauton 1987, Falmouth Art Gallery 1987 and 1990, Buxton Art Gallery 1988, Bridgewater Art Centre 1989, Swinton Art Gallery 1969, 1972 and 1989, St Giles Cripplegate London 1990, Maclaurin Art Gallery Ayr 1990, Univ of Salford 1990; mixed exhibitions incl: Park Sq Gallery Leeds 1972-74, Manchester Acad and Manchester City Art Gallery 1976 (1982-91), Royal Acad Business Galleries 1983-85; public collections incl: BBC TV, Derby City Art Gallery, Lancs Libraries, Univ of Manchester, Univ of Salford, City of London, City of Manchester; artist-in-residence: Manchester Festival 1980, City of London Festival 1984, Wigan Int Jazz Festival 1986 and 1987, Int Nuclear Physics Conf 1986; cmmns: Granada TV 1968, BBC NW 1975, Royal Exchange Theatre Manchester 1978; dir: Swinton & Pendlebury Festival 1973, Bolton Festival 1979; memb Ctee Friends of St Ives Cornwall, assoc memb Penwith Soc of Arts, hon friend Manchester Camerata Orchestra; memb Manchester Acad of Fine Arts; *Recreations* travelling, collecting books, tiles, jugs; *Style*— Colin Johnson, Esq; 27 Bedford Rd, St Ives, Cornwall TR26 1SP (☎ 0736 794 622)

JOHNSON, Colpoys Guy (Matt); s and h of Sir Peter Johnson, 7 Bt; *b* 13 Nov 1965; *Educ* Winchester, Kings Coll London; *m* 1990, Marie-Louise, da of John Holroyd, of Guildford, Surrey; *Career* Samuel Montagu and Co Ltd 1990-; FRGS; *Recreations* yachting, fly-fishing; *Clubs* Royal Ocean Racing, Royal Lymington Yacht; *Style*— Colpoys Johnson, Esq; Dene End, Buckland Dene, Lymington, Hants SO41 9DT (☎ 0590 675921); 40 Mossbury Road, London SW11 2PB (☎ 071 223 2408)

JOHNSON, David Gordon; s of Sidney Burnup Johnson, of Newcastle upon Tyne, and Pearl, *née* Jenkinson; *b* 13 Dec 1951; *Educ* Dame Allan's Boys' Sch Newcastle Upon Tyne, Univ of Manchester (BSc); *m* 1, Lesley Annis Johnson (m dis 1986); 2 s (James Scott b 1981, Mark David b 1983); m 2, 17 May 1988, Judith Ann, da of Gerald Arthur Vernon Leaf, of Leeds; 1 s (Edward Matthew b 1989), 1 da (Jessica Aimée b 1991); *Career* ptnr Duncan C Fraser and Co 1977, dir William M Mercer Fraser Ltd 1986; pres Soc of Pension Conslts; Freeman: City of London 1989, Worshipful Co of Actuaries 1989; FIA 1976; *Recreations* private aviation, motor racing; *Clubs* Reform; *Style*— David G Johnson, Esq; 2 Aldenham Grove, Radlett, Herts; William M Mercer Fraser Ltd, Telford House, 14 Tothill St, London (☎ 071 222 9121, fax 071 222 6140)

JOHNSON, David John Crump; s of Stanley Charles Johnson (d 1983), of Little Knoll, Dunsley Kinver, Stourbridge, West Midlands, and Mary, *née* Blunsom; *b* 10 March 1938; *Educ* King Edward VI GS Stourbridge, Univ of Bristol; *m* 25 Aug 1962, Valerie Margaret, JP, da of Arthur Henry Heathcock, of Englefield, 9 Walker Ave, Wollescote, Stourbridge; 3 da (Katherine Jane b 1966, Victoria Louise b 1968, Kirsty Valerie b 1972); *Career* CA 1962; articled clerk Agar Bates Neal & Co (now Coopers & Lybrand Deloitte) Birmingham 1958-62, Stanley C Johnson & Son Stourbridge 1962-; High Sheriff of W Midlands 1989-90; former pres: Wollaston Lawn Tennis Club 1977-85, Stourbridge Rotary Club 1978-79; memb Inst of Taxation; FCA; *Recreations* lawn tennis, walking, literature; *Style*— David Johnson, Esq; Yew Tree House, Shenstone, Kidderminster, Worcs DY10 4BY (☎ 056 777 464); 22 Worcester St, Stourbridge, West Midlands DY8 1BH (☎ 0384 395380/372008, fax 0384 440468)

JOHNSON, David Leonard; s of Richard Lewis Johnson, of Las Palmas, Canary Islands, and Olive Mary, *née* Bellamy; *b* 2 Feb 1956; *Educ* Wellington, Univ of Durham; *m* 13 Dec 1986, Susan, da of James Fitzjohn, of Carlton in Lindrick, Nr Worksop, Notts; 1 s (Edward James b 1988), 1 da (Caroline Francesca b 1990); *Career* admitted slr 1981; Rowe & Maw 1979-87, ptnr D J Freeman & Co 1988- (slr 1987-88); memb Law Soc 1981, ACIArb 1987; *Style*— David Johnson, Esq; D J Freeman & Co, 43 Fetter Lane, London EC4A 1NA

JOHNSON, Hon Mrs (Diana Gillian Amanda); *née* Pritchard; da of Baron Pritchard (Life Peer); *b* 1948; *Educ* Georgetown Univ USA (BA) 1974; *m* 1, 1969 (m dis 1977), David Huntington Williams; 2 s; m 2, 1984, Harry, s of Henry Leslie Johnson, of Offchurch Bury, Warwicks; 2 da; *Career* writer, equestrian mangr, farmer; *Clubs* Lyford Cay (Bahamas), Pytchley Hunt, Offchwch Bury Polo, Warwicks Hunt; *Style*— The Hon Mrs Johnson; Red House Farm, Campion Hills, Royal Leamington Spa, Warwicks

JOHNSON, Donal Keith; s of Edmund Donald Johnson (d 1971), and Jean Marion, *née* Chapter (d 1970); *b* 11 June 1928; *Educ* Magdalen Coll Sch Oxford; *m* 8 Aug 1955, Hilary Anita, da of Capt Frank Smith (d 1938), of Stanhope Farm, Stanwell, Middx; 1 s (Neil b 1960), 1 da (Sarah b 1958); *Career* CA; sr ptnr Bryden Johnson and Co 1970- (ptnr 1958); FCA 1953; Liveryman Worshipful Co of Needlemakers 1969, Freeman City of London 1968; FCA 1953; *Recreations* golf; *Clubs* RAC; *Style*— Donal Johnson, Esq; The Downe House, Ricketts Hill, Tatsfield, Westerham, Kent (☎ 0959 77318); Bryden Johnson and Co, Kings Parade, Lower Coombe St, Croydon CRO 1AA (☎ 081 686 0255, fax 081 688 5620, telex 928110 BJCO G)

JOHNSON, Dr Donald Arthur Wheatley; s of Arthur Edwin Johnson (d 1982), of London, and Ellen Victoria, *née* Wheatley (d 1983); *b* 18 April 1934; *Educ* Nat Univ of Ireland (MD), Univ of Manchester (MSC, DPM); *m* 3 Aug 1957, Dr Sheila MacDonald

Johnson, da of Dr Hector MacDonald Walker (d 1969), of Manchester and Banff Scotland; 2 s (Ian James b 23 Nov 1960, Angus Howard b 9 June 1964); *Career* Capt RAMC 1960-63; lectr Univ of Manchester 1969-, res fell Oxford, conslt psychiatrist: N Manchester Gen Hosp 1971-74, Univ Hosp of S Manchester 1974-; magistrate in Manchester 1977-88, chm NW Div RCPsych 1986- (past sec, convener and exec memb), regnl advsr in psychiatry N W Health Authy 1987-, clinical dir Dept of Psychiatry Univ Hosp of S Manchester, former chm of N Manchester Med Soc, former sec and pres Psychiatry Section Manchester Med Soc, fndr memb Br Assoc for Psychopharmacology; DRCOG 1963, FRCPsych 1977 (MRCPsych 1972); *Books* New Perspectives in Treatment of Schizophrenia (1985), Causes and Management of Depression in Schizophrenia (1985), Maintenance Treatment of Chronic Schizophrenia (1989); *Recreations* walking, shooting, fishing; *Clubs* Lancashire Cricket; *Style*— Dr Donald Johnson; Lyndhurst, Warrington Road, Mere, Cheshire WA16 0TE (☎ 0565 830 188); Lavina Cottage, Greenhead, Sidbury, Sidmouth, Devon; Dept of Psychiatry, University Hospital of South Manchester, West Didsbury, Manchester M20 8LR (☎ 061 445 8111)

JOHNSON, Hon Mrs (Elizabeth Ann Cynlais); *née* Evans; da of Baron Evans of Claughton (Life Peer); *b* 1957; *Educ* BEd; *m* 18 March 1989, Ian Frederick Johnson; *Clubs* Oxton Cricket (tennis section), Bebington Oval Ski; *Style*— The Hon Mrs Johnson

JOHNSON, Emma Louise; da of Roger George Johnson, of Petts Wood, Kent, and Mary, *née* Froud; *b* 20 May 1966; *Educ* Newstead Wood Sch, Sevenoaks Sch, Pembroke Coll Cambridge; *Career* clarinettist; debuts: London (Barbican Centre) 1985, Austria (Konzerthaus Vienna) 1985, France (Montpellier Festival with the Polish Chamber Orch) 1986, Africa (tour of Zimbabwe) 1986, USA (Newport Festival) 1989, Tokyo 1990, USSR 1990; tours with: Royal Philharmonic Orch, Bournemouth Sinfonietta, Eng Chamber Orch; concerts with Royal Liverpool Philharmonic, City of London Sinfonia, Halle, New Japan Philharmonic; Netherlands Radio Symphony, Warsaw Sinfonia (with Sir Yehudi Menuhin), LSO, London Mozart Players, Schubert Festival Hohenems (with Arleen Auger); various tv appearances; recordings for ASV: Mozart Clarinet Concerto with the Eng Chamber Orch under Leppard (1985), Crusell Clarinet Concerto number 2, Weber, Baermann, Rossini with the Eng Chamber Orch with Eco/Groves (1986), Weber Clarinet Concerto number 1, Crusell, Tartini, Debussy with the Eng Chamber Orch under Tortelier (1987), La Clarinette Francaise (1988), Weber Concerto no 2, Crussell Concerto no 3, Spohr Concerto no 1 with Eco/Schwartz, A Clarinet Celebration (1990), Emma Johnson plays Weber (1991), Crusell Concerto no 1, Krommer Concerto, Kozeluh Concerto with RPO under Gunther Herbig (1991); composed Variations on a Hungarian Folk Tune (for solo clarinet) 1988; winner BBC Young Musician of the Year 1984, Eurovision Young Musician of the Year Bronze award 1984, Wavenden award 1986, USA Young Concert Artists award 1991; *Recreations* learning languages, literature, theatre, writing about music; *Style*— Ms Emma Johnson; Artists' Management International, 12/13 Richmond Buildings, London W1V 5AF (☎ 071 439 7515, fax 071 439 8021)

JOHNSON, Hon Mrs (Frances Ann); *née* Guest; da of 2 Viscount Wimborne, OBE, JP, DL; *b* 18 Nov 1942; *m* 1971, Ernest Johnson; *Style*— The Hon Mrs Johnson; 420 E 86th St, NYC, New York, USA

JOHNSON, Frank Robert; s of Ernest Johnson, and Doreen, *née* Skinner; *b* 20 Jan 1943; *Educ* Chartesey Secdy Sch Shoreditch, Shoreditch Secdy Sch; *Career* reporter: Walthamstow Post 1960-61, Walthamstow Guardian 1961-65, North Western Evening Mail 1965-66, Nottingham Evening Post and Guardian Journal 1966; asst lobby corr Liverpool Daily Post 1966-68, lobby corr Liverpool Echo 1968-69, political staff Sun 1969-72, parly sketch writer and ldr writer Daily Telegraph 1972-79, columnist Now! Magazine 1979-81; The Times: parly sketch writer 1981-83, Paris diarist 1984, Bonn corr 1985-86, parly sketch writer 1986-87, assoc ed 1987; princ assoc ed Sunday Telegraph 1988; awards: Parly Sketch Writer of the Year 1977, Granada What the Papers Say 1977, Columnist of the Year 1981, British Press 1981; *Recreations* opera, ballet; *Clubs* Beefsteak, Garrick; *Style*— Frank Johnson, Esq; 12 Battishill St, London N1 1TE; Sunday Telegraph, Peterborough Court at South Quay, 181 Marsh Wall, London E14 9SR (☎ 071 538 5000, fax , 071 538 1330, telex 22874 TELLDNG)

JOHNSON, Frederick Duncan John; OBE (1986); s of Frederick Johnson, BEM (d 1964), of Oak Hurst, Waterworks Rd, Otterbourne, Hants, and Agnes Paton, *née* MacAlpine (d 1964); *b* 24 Sept 1932; *Educ* Peter Symonds' Sch Winchester, Univ of Southampton (BSc); *m* 11 Aug 1956, Ann Margaret, da of Bernard Bradley Bond Smyth (d 1986), of Duneside, Church Lane, Sutton on Sea, Lincs; 1 s (Stirling Duncan Arthur b 4 Jan 1958), 1 da (Sally Ann b 21 Aug 1962); *Career* motorway engr Surrey CC 1965-68, supt engr SE Rd Construction Unit Dept of Tport 1968-70, ret; Co Surveyor Somerset CC 1975-89 (dep 1970-75); former sec Co Surveyors' Soc (centenary pres 1985-86); memb Street Works Advsy Ctee Dept of Tport; FBIM 1970, FIHT 1982, FICE 1985, CEng; *Recreations* golf, sports, landscape gardening; *Clubs* RAC; *Style*— Frederick D J Johnson, Esq, OBE; Kingfisher Cottage, Williton, Somerset

JOHNSON, Lt-Gen Sir Garry Dene; KCB (1990), OBE (1978, MBE 1971), MC (1965); *b* 20 Sept 1937; *Educ* Christ's Hosp; *m* 20 Aug 1962, Caroline Sarah, *née* Frearson; 2 s (Charles b 1963, Nicholas b 1969); *Career* Cmmnd 1956, I Bn Royal Green Jackets 1976-79, cmd 11 Armoured Bde 1981-82, Asst Chief of Def Staff (NATO UK) 1985-87, Col 10 Princess Mary's Own Gurkha Rifles 1985-, cmd Br Forces Hong Kong, Maj-Gen Bde of Gurkhas 1987-89, cmd Training and Arms Dirs 1989-, Col Cmdt Light Div 1990; *Books* Brightly Shone the Dawn (1980); *Recreations* travel; *Clubs* Army and Navy; *Style*— Lt-Gen Sir Garry Johnson, KCB, OBE, MC; Headquarters United Kingdom Land Forces, Erskine Barracks, Wilton, Salisbury, Wilts SP2 0AG

JOHNSON, Geoffrey Leslie Stephen; s of Owen Arthur Johnson, of Canterbury, and Eileen Ethel, *née* Watson; *b* 7 June 1945; *Educ* Sir Roger Manwoods Sandwich; *m* 7 Oct 1967, Toni, da of Hughie Greenwood, of Worthing; 2 da (Lesley b 1969, Susannah b 1972); *Career* Provincial Insurance Co Ltd 1965-74, Excess Insurance Gp 1974-86, Shearson Lehman and Hutton 1987-90; tech resources mangr Kingston & Sutton Jt Computer Ctee; AMBIM 1984, MBCS 1988; *Recreations* athletics, music; *Style*— Geoffrey Johnson, Esq; Kingston & Sutton JCC, 104 Green Lane, Worcester Park, Surrey KT4 8AS (☎ 081 770 4161)

JOHNSON, Graham Rhodes; s of John Edward Donald Johnson (d 1986), and Violet May, *née* Johnson; *b* 10 July 1950; *Educ* Hamilton HS Bulawayo Zimbabwe, Royal Acad of Music London; *Career* concert accompanist; accompanied Elisabeth Schwarzkopf, Victoria de Los Angeles, Peter Shreier, Margaret Price, Dame Janet Baker, Felicity Lott, Ann Murray, Sarah Walker, Anthony Rolfe Johnson, Stephen Varcoe, Philip Langridge, Elly Ameling; fndr The Songmakers' Almanac 1976, writer of BBC series for TV and radio, has taught classes throughout the world, has produced many recordings incl a complete Schubert Lieder series for Hyperion beginning 1988, prof of accompaniment at Guildhall Sch of Music; FRAM 1985, FGSM 1988; *Books* The Unashamed Accompanist by Gerald Moore (contrib, 1984), The Britten Companion (contrib, 1984), Song on Record (contrib, 1986); *Recreations* restaurants and fine wine, book collecting; *Style*— Graham Johnson, Esq; 83 Fordwych Rd, London NW2 3TL (☎ 081 452 5193, fax 081 452 5081)

JOHNSON, Harold Graham; s of Harold Johnson (d 1979), of Chatteris, Cambs, and Irene Hetherington, *née* Clowes (d 1988); *b* 11 Dec 1933; *Educ* March GS, QMC London (BSc), Imperial Coll London (DIC); *m* 5 Nov 1966, Jennifer Mary, da of Leonard Victor Harold Hazelton (d 1959), of St Albans, Herts; 2 s (Adrian b 1970, Philip b 1972); *Career* Nat Serv Lt RE 1956-58; asst engr Miny of Works Aldermaston 1954-56, engr Balfour Beatty (Tanzania and Nigeria) 1961-63, exec engr Govt of Uganda 1964-66, dir Sir William Halcrow and Ptnrs 1982 (asst engr 1958-61, engr 1966-67, assoc 1977); ptnr: Halcrow Int Partnership 1983, The Halcrow Partnership 1988-; former memb : PCC (Holy Trinity Brompton, St Mary Beaconsfield, St Helen Abingdon), Abingdon Deanery Synod; former sec UNA Beaconsfield; cuidadano honorario San Pedro Sula Honduras 1975; CEng, FICE, FIWEM, CDipAF, FRSA; *Recreations* sailing, walking, gardening; *Style*— H Graham Johnson, Esq; Caledon, 23 Picklers Hill, Abingdon, Oxon OX14 2BB, (☎ 0235 520907); Burderop Park, Swindon, Wilts SN4 OQD, (☎ 0793 812479, fax 0793 812089, telex 44844 Halwil G)

JOHNSON, Hugh Eric Allan; s of Maj Guy Francis Johnson, CBE (d 1969), of London, and Grace Enid Marian, *née* Kittel; *b* 10 March 1939; *Educ* Rugby, King's Coll Cambridge (BA, MA); *m* 13 March 1965, Judith Eve, da of Col Antony Gibbons Grinling, MBE, MC (d 1982), of Dyrham, Glos; 1 s (Redmond b 1970), 2 da (Lucy b 1967, Kitty-Alice b 1973); *Career* staff writer Vogue and House & Garden 1960-63, ed Wine & Food (sec Wine & Food Soc 1963-65), travel ed Sunday Times 1967 (wine corr 1962-67), ed Queen 1968-70, pres Sunday Times Wine Club 1973-, ed dir The Garden 1975-, gardening corr New York Times 1985-86; chm: Winestar Productions Ltd, The Movie Business, The Hugh Johnson Collection Ltd; dir Société Grile de Château Latour (Coldstream Hills Pty); wine conslt: Jardines Wine and Br Airways; films: How to Handle A Wine (video 1984), Wine - A Users Guide, Vintage - A History of Wine (with W G B H Boston and Channel 4, 1989); churchwarden St James Great Saling 1974-; *Books* Wine (1966 ,revised 1974), The World Atlas of Wine (1971, revised 1987, 1985), The International Book of Trees (1973, revised 1984), The California Wine Book (with Bob Thompson, 1976), Hugh Johnson's Pocket Wine Book (annually 1977-), The Principles of Gardening (1979, revised 1984), Understanding Wine (1980), Hugh Johnson's Wine Companion (1983, revised 1987), The Atlas of German Wines (1986), The Hugh Johnson Cellar Book (1986), The Wine Atlas of France (with Hubrecht Duijker, 1987), The Story of Wine (1989); many articles on gastronomy, gardening, travel; *Recreations* gardening, travel, pictures; *Clubs* Garrick, Saintsbury; *Style*— Hugh Johnson, Esq; Saling Hall, Great Saling, Essex CM7 5DT; 73 St James's St, London SW1

JOHNSON, Hugh Nicholas Tysilio; s of Basil Tysilio Johnson, of Suncourt, Chalvington, nr Hailsham, E Sussex, and Stella Gwendolen Johnson (d 1987); *b* 7 June 1957; *Educ* Lancing, Eastbourne Coll of Art (Dip Photography); *m* 21 Dec 1983, Hazel, da of Ian Francis and Ann Digby; 1 s (Frederick Charles Tysilio b 19 March 1989), 1 da (Camilla Henrietta b 18 March 1985); *Career* photographer; asst to James Cotier and Terence Donovan 1979-80, began career as advertising and editorial photographer (specialising in still life, location, people, animials, cars) 1980; clients incl: BP, Sony, VW, Volvo, IBM, Texaco, Br Govt, Benson & Hedges, World of Interiors, Vogue, Silk Cut, ICI, Carling Black Label; Grand Prize at NY Festival of Arts and Advertising; awards from: AFAEP, Campaign Posters, Campaign Press, D&ADA, Creative Circle; work selected for special mention by George Roger (fndr of Magnum), work selected for V & A exhibition Photography Now; memb: AFAEP; *Books* many pictures in various books; *Recreations* travelling, art, wildlife, sports; *Style*— Hugh Johnson, Esq; Hugh Johnson Studio, 1A Chance St, London E1 6JT (☎ 071 729 1989, fax 071 729 1504)

JOHNSON, Hugh Stringer; s of Richard Stringer Johnson, CBE, TD (d 1981), of Medbourne Manor, Market Harborough, Leics, and Isabel Alice, *née* Hezlett; *b* 24 May 1939; *Educ* Sherborne, Gonville and Caius Coll Cambridge (MA, LLB); *m* 4 March 1967, Marie-Odile, da of Comte Antoine Tillette De Clermont-Tonnerre, of 5 Rue De Mouchy, Versailles; 2 s (Antony b 1967, Charles b 1971), 1 da (Marie-Caroline b 1969); *Career* admitted slr 1966, ptnr Biddle & Co London 1966-; Freeman City of London 1970, Liveryman Worshipful Co of Ironmongers 1970 (memb Ct 1988); *Style*— Hugh Johnson, Esq; 5 Lichfield Rd, Kew, Richmond, Surrey TW9 3JR (☎ 081 948 4518); Hauranne, 1 Allee Adrienne, Bois De La Chaize, Noirmoutier-En-L'Ile, France; 1 Gresham St, London EC2 (☎ 071 606 9301)

JOHNSON, Ian Frederick; s of Alan Frederick Johnson, of 1 Broomhall Close, Oswestry, Shropshire, and Betty, *née* Edwards; *b* 10 March 1960; *Educ* Oswestry Boys HS, Univ of Reading (LLB); *m* 18 March 1989, The Hon Elizabeth Anne Cynlais, da of Lord Evans of Claughton, of 69 Bidston Rd, Claughton, Birkenhead; *Career* called to the Bar Gray's Inn 1982; memb Northern Circuit, practising out of Liverpool specialising in chancery 1983-; *Recreations* golf, sports cars, skiing; *Clubs* Wirral Ladies Golf, The Oval Ski; *Style*— Ian Johnson, Esq; 1 Oaklea Road, Irby, Wirral L61 3US (☎ 051 648 7645); 20 North John St, Liverpool (☎ 051 236 6757)

JOHNSON, Air Vice-Marshal James Edgar; CB (1965), CBE (1960), DSO (and two Bars 1943, 1944), DFC (1941, and Bar 1942); s of Alfred Edward Johnson (d 1953), and Beatrice May Rossell (d 1978); *b* 9 March 1915; *Educ* Loughborough GS, Univ of Nottingham; *m* 14 Nov 1942 (m dis), Pauline Ingate; 2 s (Michael James Barrie b 1944, Christopher b 1945); *Career* Air Offr cmd Middle East 1963-60 (ret 1966); DL Leicestershire; dir: Aircraft Equipment (International) Ltd, Westminster Scaffolding Ltd; Legion of Merit (USA), DFC (USA), Air Medal (USA), Legion d'Honneur (France), Order of Leopold (Belgium), Croix de Guerre (Belgium); *Recreations* fishing and writing; *Clubs* RAF; *Style*— Air Vice-Marshal James Johnson, CB, CBE, DSO, DFC; The Stables, Hargate Hall, Buxton, Derbyshire SK17 8TA (☎ 0298 871522)

JOHNSON, Prof James Henry; s of James William Johnson (d 1955), of Belfast, and Martha Moore, *née* Linton (d 1983); *b* 19 Nov 1930; *Educ* Belfast Royal Acad, Queen's Univ Belfast (BA), Univ of Wisconsin (MA), Univ of London (PhD); *m* 31 March 1956, Jean, da of Dr John James McKane (d 1969), of Salford; 2 s (David b 1969, Owen b 1971), 2 da (Ruth b 1957, Kathleen b 1958); *Career* Whitbeck fell Univ of Wisconsin 1953-54, reader UCL 1965-74 (lectr 1954-65), princ Lonsdale Coll 1982-87, dean of grad studies Univ of Lancaster 1985- (prof 1974-); pres Inst of Br Geographers 1989; FRGS; *Books* Urban Geography (1967), Trends in Geography (co-ed, 1969), Housing and Geographical Mobility of Labour (jtly, 1974), Urbanisation (1980), Suburban Growth (ed, 1974), Labour Migration (co-ed, 1990); *Recreations* walking, photography; *Style*— Prof James H Johnson; The Coach-House, Wyreside Hall, Dolphinholme, Lancaster LA2 9DH (☎ 0524 791046); Dept of Geography, University of Lancaster, Lancaster LA1 4YB (☎ 0524 65201, fax 0524 63806, telex 65111 LANCUL G)

JOHNSON, Sir John Rodney; KCMG (1988, CMG 1980); s of Edwin Done Johnson, OBE (d 1967), of Kendal, Cumbria, and Florence Mary, *née* Clough (d 1980); *b* 6 Sept 1930; *Educ* Manchester GS, Univ of Oxford (BA, MA); *m* 11 Sept 1956, Jean Mary, da of Ernest Lewis (d 1949), of Manor Farm, Eyton; 3 s (Nicholas b 1957, Charles b 1962, Edward b 1967), 1 da (Julia b 1959); *Career* Nat Serv 2 Lt RA 1949-51; HM Overseas Civil Serv 1955-64, dist offr later dist cmmr Kenya; HM Diplomatic Serv 1966-90, 1 sec FCO 1966-69, head of Chancery British Embassy Algiers 1969-72, dep high cmmr Barbados 1972-74, political cnsllr Br High Cmmn Nigeria 1975-78, ambass to Chad and head of W African Dept FCO (concurrently) 1978-80, Br high cmmr to Zambia 1980-84, asst under sec of state Africa 1984-86; Br high cmmr to Kenya 1986-90; sr admin asst ctee of Vice Chllrs and Princs of UK Univs 1964-65, dir Univ of Oxford Foreign Serv Prog 1990-, special elect fell Keble Coll Oxford 1990-, chm Countryside Cmmn for Eng 1991, memb Cncl Royal African Soc; *Recreations* walkling mountains, travel in remote places; *Clubs* Travellers', Climbers'; *Style—* Sir John Johnson, KCMG

JOHNSON, Kathryn Louise; da of Robert Henry Edwards (the former professional footballer), 73 Lynn Rd, Grimston, King's Lynn, and Benita, *née* Langdon; *Educ* Springwood HS; *m* 7 July 1990, Peter George Johnson, s of George Henry Johnson; *Career* hockey player; Pelicans Ladies Hockey Club 1980-89, Leicester Ladies Hockey Club 1989-; represented Norfolk and East: under 18 under 21, sr; England: under 18, under 21, 37 full caps, played at World Cup Sydney 1990; computer operator and clerical asst; *Recreations* all sports; 8 Loke Road, Kings Lynn, Norfolk PE30 2AB (☎ 0553 766686)

JOHNSON, Kenneth Walford; s of Edward Stanley Johnson (d 1974), and Esma Vera May Johnson (d 1982); *b* 21 Nov 1921; *Educ* Merchant Taylors', London Univ (LLB); *m* 15 Oct 1952, Nerys Gwendolen (d 1985), da of Dr Richard Tudor Edwards (d 1971), of Stanmore; 2 da (Janet b 1955, Katharine b 1958); *Career* WWII Flying Offr RAF 1941-46; taxation specialist (ret); dir cos in: Robert Luff Ltd 1968-, Moor Park (1958) Ltd 1981-; CA; *Recreations* golf, bridge, listening to music; *Clubs* Moor Park Golf, Sandy Lodge Golf; *Style—* Kenneth Johnson, Esq; 97 Wolsey Road, Moor Park, Northwood, Middx HA6 2ER (☎ 09274 24367)

JOHNSON, Michael Francis George; s of Dr Walter James Johnson (d 1979), of Great Witley, Worcester, and Phyllis Lucy, *née* Hayward (d 1979); *b* 26 March 1942; *Educ* Shrewsbury, INSEAD, Fontainebleau (MBA); *m* 1, 10 April 1971 (m dis 1983), Jose Marie Lucie Simone, da of Dr Alfred Viau (d 1968), of Port Au Prince, Haiti; 2 s (Benjamin b 1974, Jeremy b 1982), 1 da (Alix b 1976); m2, 1 Feb 1984, Jane Elizabeth, da of John Merrick, of Stedham, Midhurst, W Sussex; 1 s (Oliver b 1985); *Career* CA 1966, md Synkin SA Brussels 1973-78; dir: ERA Gp plc 1981-87, Surfachem Gp plc 1987-; fin dir Broad Street Gp plc 1986-88; chm: Chiltern Engrg Ltd 1986-, W Notting Ltd 1988, Dudes Clothing Ltd 1988; vice chm Octavia Hill & Rowe Housing Assoc; *Recreations* tennis, cross country running; *Style—* Michael Johnson, Esq; Bassett House, Claverton, Bath; 9 Needham Rd, London W11 (☎ 071 229 5423); 44 Hanover St, Liverpool L1 4AA (☎ 051 708 7323, fax 051 708 5381, car 0860 338 187)

JOHNSON, Michael Ross; s of Myron Johnson (d 1972), of Delphi, Indiana, USA, and Eileen Rahilly Johnson (d 1975); *b* 23 Nov 1938; *Educ* San Jose State Coll (BA), Columbia Univ NY; *m* 28 May 1966, Jacqueline, da of Joseph Zimbardo; 3 da (Stephanie, Raphaëlle, Delphine); *Career* editorial staff Hayward Daily Review 1960-61; The Associated Press: corr Charleston W Virginia 1962-63, ed NY 1964-66, corr Moscow 1967-71; bureau chief McGraw-Hill World News Paris 1971-76, dir McGraw-Hill World News NY 1976-82, ed in chief Int Mgmnt 1982-; memb: American Soc of Magazine Editors, Paris America Club, Overseas Press Club; *Recreations* piano, weight lifting, juggling flaming torches; *Clubs* Wig and Pen; *Style—* Michael Johnson, Esq; International Management, 7-11 St John's Hill, London SW11 1TE

JOHNSON, Michael Sloan; s of Maj Harold Bell Johnson, TD, TA (d 1975), and Jean Louise, *née* Sloan; *b* 3 June 1947; *Educ* Upper Canada Coll Toronto, St Andrews Scots Sch Buenos Aires Argentina, Trinity Coll Cambridge (BA, LLB, MA, LLM); *m* 27 July 1972, Judith Mary, da of Arthur Lawton, of Crewe, Cheshire; 1 s (Matthew Richard b 7 Sept 1979), 1 da (Rosalind Mary b 5 Nov 1980); *Career* called to the Bar Lincoln's Inn 1971, memb Northern circuit 1972-, Chancery practitioner Manchester 1972-; churchwarden St Mary's Parish Church Hawkshaw Bury Lancs 1986-, pres Cambridge Univ Law Soc 1969, memb Ecclesiastical Law Soc 1988-; *Recreations* music, modern languages, wine; *Clubs* Portico Library Manchester; *Style—* Michael Johnson, Esq; 7 Troutbeck Close, Hawkshaw, Bury, Lancs BL8 4LJ (☎ 020 488 4088); Crown Sq Chambers, 1 Deans Ct, Crown Sq, Manchester M3 3HA (☎ 061 833 9801, fax 061 835 2483, DX 14326 Manchester)

JOHNSON, Col Neil Anthony; OBE (Mil 1989), TD (1986); s of Anthony Johnson, of Glamorganshire, and Dilys Mabel Vera, *née* Smith; *b* 13 April 1949; *Educ* Canton Sch Cardiff, RMA Sandhurst; *m* 1971, Judith Gail, da of Dr Ian Ferguson (d 1978), of Cardiff; 3 da (Sarah b 1973, Amanda b 1975, Victoria b 1977); *Career* CO 4 Bn The Royal Green Jackets 1986-89, Dep Cdr 160 (Welsh) Inf Bde; exec dir Br Leyland Ltd 1977-82; dir: Jaguar Cars Ltd 1982-86, Euro Ops Rover Gp BAe 1989-; ADC to HM Queen 1990; Freeman City of London, Liveryman Worshipful Co of Coach Makers and Coach Harness Makers; FIMI, MInstM, MBIM; *Recreations* shooting, reading, riding, farming; *Clubs* Army and Navy, RAC, Royal Green Jackets; *Style—* Col Neil Johnson, OBE, TD; c/o Lloyds Bank, Teme St, Tenbury Wells, Worcestershire; Military HQ Wales, The Barracks, Brecon

JOHNSON, Nevil; s of Geoffrey Enoch Johnson (d 1962), of Darlington, and Doris, *née* Thompson, MBE; *b* 6 Feb 1929; *Educ* Queen Elizabeth GS Darlington, Univ Coll Oxford (BA, MA); *m* 29 June 1957, Ulla, da of Dr Peter van Aubel, Distinguished Serv Cross of Fed Repub of Germany (d 1964), of Dusseldorf; 2 s (Peter b 4 June 1961, Christopher b 3 Oct 1964); *Career* Nat Serv Army REME 1947-49; admin class Home Civil Serv 1952-62 (princ minys: supply, housing, local govt); lectr in politics Univ of Nottingham 1962-66, sr lectr in politics Univ of Warwick 1966-69; reader comparative study of insts and professorial fell Nuffield Coll Univ of Oxford 1969-, hon ed Pub Admin Journal of Royal Inst Pub Admin 1967-81, memb Econ and Social Res Cncl 1981-87, pt/t memb Civil Serv Cmmn 1982-85; chm: Bd Faculty of Social Studies Univ of Oxford 1976-78, Study of Parl Gp 1984-87; town cncllr Abingdon 1976-78; memb Political Studies Assoc; *Books* Parliament & Administration: the Estimates Ctee 1945-65 (1966), Government in the Federal Republic of Germany (1973 and 1983), In Search of the Constitution (1977 and 1980), The Limits of Political Science (1989); *Recreations* walking, gardening; *Clubs* United Oxford and Cambridge Univ; *Style—* Nevil Johnson, Esq; 2 Race Farm Cottages, Race Farm Lane, Kingston Bagpuize, Oxon (☎ 0865 820777); Nuffield Coll, Oxford

JOHNSON, Nigel Derrick Marson; s of Grosvenor Marson Johnson (d 1981), and Diana Margery Joan, *née* Webb (d 1972); *b* 8 Dec 1942; *Educ* Oakmount Sch, Epsom Coll; *m* 26 Sept 1970, Dr Wendy Jane Johnson, da of Frank William Higlett; *Career* articled clerk Woolley and Waldron Southampton 1960-65, qualified chartered accountant 1966; ptnr: Woolley & Waldron 1969-76, Whinney Murray & Co 1976-81, Ernst & Whinney 1981-89, Ernst & Young 1989-; FCA 1977 (ACA 1966); *Recreations* cricket, golf, skiing; *Clubs* MCC, Hampshire Hogs CC, Rioteers CC, Hockley Golf; *Style—* Nigel Johnson, Esq; Summerhill, Fairfield Rd, Shawford, nr Winchester, Hampshire (☎ 0962 713115); Ernst & Young, Wessex House, 19 Threefield Lane, Southampton SO1 1TW (☎ 0703 230230)

JOHNSON, Norman McIntosh; s of Dr Donald McIntosh Johnson (d 1978), of Sutton, Surrey, and Betty Muriel, *née* Plaisted (d 1979); *b* 1 Feb 1948; *Educ* Westminster, Bart's (MB BS, MD); *m* 22 July 1972, Penelope Norah, da of Dr Trevor Alan Morris Johns; 2 s (Daniel b 22 Aug 1975, William b 14 Oct 1978), 2 da (Claire b 23 Dec 1973, Alice b 10 Feb 1981); *Career* sr lectr in med and undergrad sub dean Univ Coll and Middx Hosp Med Sch (formerly post grad sub dean and clinical tutor), conslt physician Middx and Whittington Hosps; course organiser: RSM, Br Postgrad Med Fndn, Br Journal of Hospital Medicine; FRCP 1987; *Books* Pocket Consultant in Respiratory Medicine (1989); *Recreations* family and DIY; *Style—* Dr Norman Johnson; 146 Burbage Rd, London SE21 7AG; 19 Wimpole St, London W1 (☎ 071 637 8760)

JOHNSON, Hon Mrs (Patricia Mary); *née* French; da of late 6 Baron De Freyne; *b* 1917; *m* 1941, Reginald Johnson (d 1958); 1 s, 1 da; *Style—* The Hon Mrs Johnson; 4 Linley Court, Rouse Gardens, London SE21

JOHNSON, Paul; s of Donald Edward Johnson, of 8 Fairfield Avenue, Balderton, Newark, Notts, and Joyce, *née* Edwards; *b* 24 April 1965; *Educ* Grove Comp Sch; *m* (m dis 1989), Hazel Katrina Lynam; *Career* professional cricketer; Nottinghamshire CCC 1981-: Sunday League debut 1981, Championship debut 1982, awarded county cap 1986, currently vice capt; represented: English Schs Cricket Assoc 1980, Young England under 19 v W Indies 1981 and Aust 1982, TCCB XI v India 1990; *Recreations* truffle hunting, watching most sports, red wine; *Style—* Paul Johnson, Esq; Nottinghamshire CCC, Trent Bridge, Nottingham NG2 6AG (☎ 0602 821525)

JOHNSON, Paul Bede; s of William Aloysius Johnson (d 1943), and Anne, *née* Hynes (d 1982); *b* 2 Nov 1928; *Educ* Stonyhurst, Magdalen Coll Oxford; *m* Marigold Edgerton Gigneac, da of Dr Thomas Hunt, of Upper Harley St, London W1 (d 1983); 3 s (Daniel Benedict b 1957, Cosmo James Theodore b 1958, Luke Oliver b 1961), 1 da (Sophie Jane Louise b 1963); *Career* Nat Serv Capt Army 1949-51; asst exec ed Realities Paris 1952-55, ed New Stateman London 1964-70 (asst ed then dep ed 1955-64), memb Bd New Statesman Publishing Co 1964-76; contrib: London Times, Daily Telegraph, Daily Mail, Wall Street Journal, New York Times, Washington Post, and various other newspapers and periodicals; frequently involved in broadcasting and the prodn of TV documentaries, int lectr to academic govt and business audiences; De Witt Wallace Prof of Communications American Inst for Public Policy Res Washington 1980; memb: Royal Commission on the Press 1974-77, Cable Authority 1984-90; winner numerous literary prizes incl: Yorkshire Post Book of the Year award 1975, Francis Boyer award for servs to pub policy 1979, Krug award for excellence (literature) 1982; *Books* A History of Christianity (1976), A History of the Modern World (1983), A History of the Jews (1987), Intellectuals (1988); *Recreations* hill walking, painting; *Clubs* Beefsteak; *Style—* Paul Johnson, Esq; The Coach House, Over Stowey, nr Bridgewater, Somerset (☎ 0278 732 393); 29 Newton Rd, London W2 5JR (☎ 071 229 3859, fax 071 792 1676)

JOHNSON, Paula Joan; da of Maj Grosvenor Marson Johnson (d 1981), and Diana Margery Joan, *née* Webb (d 1972); *b* 12 Sept 1953; *Educ* Atherley C of E Church Sch Southampton, Univ of Exeter (BA); *m* 20 April 1985, Lance Hamilton, s of John Harold Poynter, of Castillon Du Gard, Remoulins, Gard, France; *Career* asst literary ed: Now! Magazine 1979-81, Mail on Sunday 1982-83, literary ed Mail on Sunday 1983-; *Clubs* Royal London Yacht, Lansdowne; *Style—* Miss Paula Johnson; Donnington, nr Newbury, Berks; Billing Place, London; Northcliffe House, 2 Denny St, London W8 5TS (☎ 071 938 6000, fax 071 937 3745)

JOHNSON, Peter Alec Barwell; s of Oscar Ernest Johnson (d 1968), of Rippington Manor, Gt Gransden, Cambridgeshire, and Marjorie, *née* Barwell; *b* 26 July 1936; *Educ* Uppingham; *m* 3 July 1965, Gay Marilyn, da of Douglas Bennington Lindsay, of 27 Ave de Bude, Geneva, Switzerland; 2 da (Juliet b 1966, Annabel b 1970); *Career* tstee and fndr: The Br Sporting Art Tst, Ctee of the World of Watercolours and Drawing Fair, East Anglian Ctee of the Historic Houses Assoc; chm and md Oscar & Peter Johnson Ltd, vice chm Cromwell Museum, patron of the Art Project for Addenbrooke's Hosp; memb Cncl: Br Antique Dealers Assoc 1970-80, Kensington & Chelsea C of C, Ctee of West London Family Serv Unit; guide Chelsea Physic Garden; chm: Cleaner Royal Borough, Hans Town Ward Cons 1969-72; Br delegate Conseil Internationale de la Chasse; *Books* The Nasmyth Family (with E Money, 1977); *Recreations* gardening, riding, reading; *Clubs* Bucks, Hurlingham; *Style—* Peter Johnson, Esq; 1 The Little Boltons, London SW10 (☎ 071 373 7038); Rippington Manor, Great Gransden, Cambridge; Oscar & Peter Johnson Ltd, Lowndes Lodge Gallery, 27 Lowndes St, London SW1X 9HY (☎ 071 235 6464, fax 071 823 1057, car 0860 335980)

JOHNSON, Peter Charles; s of William Arthur Johnson, of 55 Norrice Lea, London N2, and Suzanne Renee, *née* Roubitschek; *b* 12 Nov 1950; *Educ* Merchant Taylors' Sch Crosby, Pembroke Coll Cambridge (MA); *m* 27 July 1974, Judith Anne, da of Vincent Larvan of Oxford Court, Trafalgar Road, Southport; 2 s (Matthew b 1980, Elliot b 1982), 2 da (Charlotte b 1987, Sophie (twin) b 1987); *Career* Herbert Smith and Co 1973-75, admitted slr 1975, sr ptnr Alexan Johnson; Freeman City of London, Liveryman Worshipful Co of Distillers 1978-; memb Law Soc; *Recreations* sailing; *Clubs* United Oxford and Cambridge Univ, Wig and Pen; *Style—* Peter Johnson, Esq; 12 Wallace Road, London N1; 11 Lanark Sq, Glengall Bridge, Isle of Dogs, London E14 (☎ 071 538 5621, fax 071 538 2442)

JOHNSON, Sir Peter Colpoys Paley; 7 Bt (GB 1755), of New York, North America; s of Lt-Col Sir John Johnson, 6 Bt, MBE (d 1975); *b* 26 March 1930; *Educ* Wellington, RMC of Science Shrivenham; *m* 1, 1956, (m dis 1972), Clare, da of Dr Nigel Bruce; 1 s, 2 da; m 2, 1973, Caroline Elisabeth, da of Wing Cdr Sir John Hodsoll, CB (d 1971); 1 s; *Heir* s, Colpoys Guy Johnson; *Career* RA 1949-61 (Capt); publisher; dir Nautical Publishing Co Ltd 1971-81, publisher nautical books Macmillan London Ltd 1981-86, author and consultant editor 1986-; Hon Col King's Royal Regt of New York (Canadian); *Books* Ocean Racing and Offshore Yachts (1970 and 1972), Boating Britain (1973), Guinness Book of Yachting Facts and Feats (1975), Guinness Guide to Sailing (1981), This is Fast Cruising (1986), Encyclopedia of Yachting (1989), and 3 reference works; *Recreations* sailing, DIY; *Clubs* Royal Yacht Squadron, Royal Ocean Racing, Royal Lymington Yacht; *Style—* Sir Peter Johnson, Bt; Dene End, Buckland Dene, Lymington, Hampshire SO41 9DT (☎ 0590 75921, fax 0590 72885)

JOHNSON, Brig Peter Dunbar; s of Dr P Dunbar Johnson (d 1984), of Tapshaw, Male Hill, St Leonards-on-Sea, Sussex, and Barbara Leigh, *née* Hutton; *b* 15 April 1931; *Educ* Sherborne, RMA Sandhurst, Staff Coll (psc), Jt Servs Staff Coll (jssc), Royal Coll of Defence (RCDS); *m* 1961, Marthe Marie Eugenie, da of Marquis Yvés de Simon de Palmas (d 1975), of La Raterie, Corbery, Loches, France; 3 s (Mark, Stephen, Paul); *Career* cmmnd Royal Sussex Regt 1951, CO 5 Queens 1971-73; dep dir Manning 1981-84; ADC to HM The Queen 1983-; gen sec Offr Assoc 1984-; *Recreations* golf, skiing, gardening; *Clubs* Army & Navy, Royal St George's (Sandwich); *Style—* Brig P D Johnson; Homestall, Doddington, Kent ME9 0HF (☎ 079 586 212); Officers Association, 48 Pall Mall, London SW1

JOHNSON, Peter Lincoln; s of Lincoln Ernest Johnson (d 1949), of Birstall, Leics, and Lilian Gertrude, *née* Pearce; *b* 12 June 1943; *Educ* Loughborough GS; *m* 1 June 1982, Lynne Marie, da of Harry Westwell, of Lanzarote, Canary Islands; *Career* creative direction on advertising campaigns: Jensen Motor Cars 1964, Schweppes 1966-68, Jaeger 1968-70, Bally Shoes 1968-70, Barratt Devpts 1971-83, Dixons 1984-86, NE Electricity 1984-87, English Estates 1988-90, Cameron Hall Devpt 1988-90, Rush & Tomkins Contractor/Developer 1988-90, Northern Devpt Co 1989-90, Yuill Group (Heritage Homes) 1988-, Braathens SAFE Airlines 1990-, Electrolux Klippan

(Kangol) Auto Safety 1990-; *Recreations* music, walking, cookery; *Clubs* The Sloane; *Style—* Peter Johnson, Esq; The Mill, Black Hall Mill, Steel, Hexham, Northumberland NE47 OLF (☎ 043473 432); Martin Tait Redheads Ltd, Buxton House, Buxton St, Newcastle upon Tyne NE1 6NJ (☎ 091 232 1926)

JOHNSON, Prof Peter Malcolm; s of Ronald John Johnson (d 1968), and Beryl Mary, *née* Donaldson; *b* 20 April 1950; *Educ* Dulwich, Jesus Coll Oxford (BA, MA, DSc), Univ of London (PhD); *m* 11 Nov 1972, Wendy Susan, da of James Macer Wright, of London; 2 da (Katherine b 1976, Nicole b 1978); *Career* Royal Soc visiting fell Rikshospitalet Univ Hosp Oslo 1975-76, prof Dept of Immunology Univ of Liverpool 1985- (lectr 1977-80, sr lectr 1980-82, reader 1982-85); memb Steering Ctee and co-ordinator trophoblast vaccine prog WHO Birth Control Vaccine Task Force, cncllr and treas Int Soc Immunology of Reproduction, co-fndr and chm Br Materno-Fetal Immunology Gp; chm: Sci Ctee Clatterbridge Cancer Res Tst, Med Advsy Panel Nat Eczema Soc, Res Ctee Univ of Liverpool Med Sch; MRCPath 1981; *Books* 150 papers and reviews concerning human immunology, notably the immunology of pregnancy; *Recreations* sailing, squash, football; *Clubs* West Kirby Sailing; *Style—* Prof Peter Johnson; Dept of Immunology, University of Liverpool, PO Box 147, Liverpool L69 3BX (☎ 051 706 4354, fax 051 708 6502, telex 627095 UNILPL G)

JOHNSON, Philip Robert; s of Robert Johnson, of Stockport, and Cicely, *née* Swalwell; *b* 12 Oct 1946; *Educ* Dialstone Sch Stockport; *m* 27 Aug 1969, Janette Anne, da of Arthur Gowling; 2 da (Clare Louise b 6 May 1976, (Nicola) Kate b 23 Sept 1978); *Career* articled clerk Pitt & Co Manchester 1964-69, qualified chartered accountant 1969, firm merged to become Mann Judd & Co 1970; ptnr: Mann Judd 1977, Touche Ross 1979 (following merger); currently ptnr i/c Manchester Audit and memb UK Bd of Ptnrs Touche Ross; ACA 1970; *Recreations* travel, watching all forms of sport; *Style—* Philip R Johnson, Esq; Arden House, Coppice Lane, Disley, Stockport, Cheshire SK12 2LT; Touche Ross & Co, Abbey House, 74 Mosley St, Manchester (☎ 061 228 3456)

JOHNSON, Dr Ralph Hudson; s of Sydney R E Johnson; *b* 3 Dec 1933; *Educ* Rugby, St Catharine's Coll Cambridge (Lord Kitchener scholar, Draper's Co scholar, MA, MB BChir, MD), Worcester Coll Oxford (MA, DM, DPhil), Univ of Glasgow (DSc); *m* 1970, Gillian Sidney, *née* Keith; 1 s, 1 da; *Career* house physician and surgn UCH 1958-59, sr house surgn Radcliffe Infirmary Oxford 1960-61, fell Nat Fund for Res into Crippling Diseases 1961-63; Univ of Oxford: Schorstein med res fell 1963-65, MRC scientific staff and asst to Regius Prof of Medicine 1964-67, dean St Peter's Coll 1965-68, lectr in neurology 1967-68; sr lectr in neurology Univ of Glasgow 1968-77, hon conslt neurologist Inst of Neurological Sciences Glasgow 1968-77, warden Queen Margaret Hall Univ of Glasgow 1968-77, prof of medicine Wellington Sch Med Univ of Otago NZ 1977-87 (dean 1977-86), conslt neurologist Wellington Hosp Bd 1977-87, NZ-All India visiting fell 1979, dir post grad med educn and training Univ of Oxford 1987-, professional fell Wadham Coll Oxford 1987-, conslt physician and neurologist Oxford RHA and Oxford Health Authy 1987-; memb: Med Faculty Bd Univ of Glasgow 1973-76, Med Faculty Bd Univ of Otago 1977-86, Med Educn Ctee NZ Med Assoc 1980-84, Awards Ctee MRC (NZ) 1984-87, Cncl and Bd of Mgmnt Wellington Med Res Fndn 1977-87, Oxford Health Authy 1989-90, Gen Med Cncl 1989-; chm: Med Advsy Ctee Multiple Sclerosis Soc NZ 1978-87, Jt Planning and Advsy Ctee Oxford RHA 1988-; tstee Malaghan Inst of Med Res 1987, dir Appeal and devpt offr Wadham Coll Oxford 1989-; Wyndham Deedes scholar 1963, BMA res award 1984, Arris and Gale lectr RCS Eng 1965, EG Fearnsides scholar Univ of Cambridge 1966-67, TK Stubbins sr res fell RCP 1968; FRSE, FRACP, FRCPG; *Books* Disorders of the Autonomic Nervous System (with J M K Spalding, 1974), Living with Disability (with Gillian S Johnson, 1978), Neurocardiology (with D G Lamble and J M K Spalding, 1984), numerous contribs to learned scientific jls; *Recreations* book collecting, sailing; *Style—* Dr Ralph Johnson; Wadham College, Oxford OX1 3PN (☎ 0865 221517)

JOHNSON, Rex Sutherland; s of Adam Sutherland Johnson (d 1950), and Grace Elizabeth, *née* Bedwell (d 1988); *b* 24 Aug 1928; *Educ* Royal HS Edinburgh, George Heriot's Sch Edinburgh, Northern Poly Sch of Architecture (Dip Arch); *m* 24 Aug 1957, Betty Elsie, da of Herbert Charles Manning (d 1974), of Witham, Essex; 2 s (Mark Sutherland b 1958, Michael Charles b 1960); *Career* RN 1947-48; sr architect TP Bennett & Son London 1946-61, jr ptnr Oliver Law & Partners London 1961-63, ptnr Ronald Ward & Partners London 1963-89; dir: Ronald Ward International Ltd 1980-89, QE Design Ltd 1989-; ptnr RWP 1989-; memb Cncl London C of C and Indust 1976-, former chm Platt Cons Soc Kent 1976-79, pres United Ward Club of the City of London 1989, former pres and rotarian Westminster and Pimlico Rotary Club, memb Br Acad of Experts 1989; Freeman City of London 1969, Sr Warden Guild of Freeman City of London 1990; Liveryman: Worshipful Co of Carmen, Worshipful Co of Woolmen (memb Court); FRIBA 1968, FCIArb 1971; *Recreations* golf, photography, architecture, travel; *Clubs* City Livery, Caledonian; *Style—* Rex Johnson, Esq; Whitepines, Longmill Lane, Crouch, nr Sevenoaks, Kent TN15 8QB; RWP, The Pump House, Jacob's Well Mews, George St, London W1H 5PD (☎ 071 224 4788)

JOHNSON, Richard Keith; s of Keith Holcombe Johnson (d 1972), of Essex, and Frances Louisa Olive, *née* Tweed (d 1962); *b* 30 July 1927; *Educ* Parkfield Sch, Felsted, RADA; *m* 1, 9 Feb 1957 (m dis 1964), Sheila, da of Herbert Sweet (d 1988), of London; 1 s (Jervis b 1959), 1 da (Sorel b 1961); m 2, 15 March 1965 (m dis 1966), (Marilyn Pauline) Kim Novak, of USA; m 3, 2 July 1982, Marie Louise, *née* Norlund, of London; 1 s (Nicholas b 1979), 1 da (Jennifer b 1984); *Career* served RN (supply asst HM Yacht Victoria and Albert) 1945-48; actor and producer; first stage appearance Hamlet (Opera House Manchester) 1944; major roles incl: Marius Tertius in The First Victoria 1950, Pierre in The Madwoman of Chaillot 1951, Demetrius in A Midsummers Night's Dream 1951, George Phillips in After my Fashion 1952, Beauchamp Earl of Warwick in The Lark 1955, Laertes in Hamlet 1955, Jack Absolute in The Rivals 1956, Lord Plynlimmon in Plaintiff in a Pretty Hat 1956; RSC 1957-62 roles incl: Orlando in As You Like It, Mark Anthony in Julius Caesar, Leonatus in Cymbeline, Ferdinand in The Tempest, Romeo in Romeo and Juliet, Sir Andrew Aguecheek in Twelfth Night, title role in Pericles, Don John in Much Ado About Nothing; National Theatre 1975-78 roles incl: Charles in Blithe Spirit, Pinchwife in the Country Wife, Pilate in The Passion, title role in The Guardsman; UK tour Death Trap 1982, first film appearance in Captain Horatio Hornblower 1950; films incl: Never So Few 1959, The Haunting 1963, The Pumpkin Eater 1964, Operation Crossbow 1965, Khartoum 1966, Deadlier than the Male 1966, Hennessy 1975; first TV appearance 1949; leading roles in TV prodns incl: Rembrandt, Anthony and Cleopatra, Claudius in Hamlet, The Member for Chelsea, Cymberline; recent TV films incl A Man for All Seasons and Voice of the Heart 1988; prodr of films incl: The Biko Inquest, Serjeant Musgrave's Dance, The Playboy of the Western World, Old Times, Turtle Diary, Castaway, The Lonely Passion of Judith Hearne; fndr chm and jt chief exec United Br Artists 1982- memb Cncl BAFTA 1976-78; *Books* Hennessy (original story for film 1974); *Recreations* gardening, music, travel; *Style—* Richard Johnson, Esq; 2 Stokenchurch St, London SW6 3TR (☎ 071 736 5920)

JOHNSON, Hon Mr Justice; Sir Robert Lionel; s of Edward Harold Johnson (d 1986), and Ellen Lydiate Johnson (d 1989); *b* 9 Feb 1933; *Educ* Watford GS, LSE (LLB); *m* 1957, Linda Mary, da of Charles William Bennie (d 1975), of Durham; 1 s (Robert b 1968), 2 da (Melanie b 1961, Edwina b 1962); *Career* served 5 Royal Iniskilling Dragoon Gds 1955-57 (Capt), ADC to GOC Northern Cmd 1956-57, Inns of Court Regt 1957-64; called to the Bar Gray's Inn 1957, rec Crown Ct 1977-89, QC 1978, bencher 1986, judge High Court (Family Div) 1989-; jr counsel to Treasury in probate matters 1975-78, legal assessor GNC 1977-82; chm: Bar Fees Legal Aid Ctee 1984-86, Family Law Bar Assoc 1984-86; memb: Bar Cncl 1981-88 (vice chm 1987, chm 1988), Supreme Ct Procedure Ctee 1982-87, Law Soc Legal Aid Ctee 1981-87, Judicial Studies Bd 1989-; memb Nat Exec Ctee and tstee Cystic Fibrosis Res Tst 1964-, hon sec Int Cystic Fibrosis (Muscoviscidosis) Assoc 1984-90; kt 1989; *Recreations* gardening, charitable work; *Style—* Hon Mr Justice Johnson; Royal Courts of Justice, Strand, London WC2A 2LL

JOHNSON, Robert William Greenwood; s of Robert William Johnson (d 1960), and Susan, *née* Mills (d 1980); *b* 15 March 1942; *Educ* Licensed Victuallers' Sch Slough Berks, Univ of Durham (MB BS, MS); *m* 30 July 1966, Dr Carolyn Mary Johnson, da of John Edmund Vooght, of Guilton Ash, Woolton Hill, Newbury, Berks; 1 s (Julian Robert Greenwood b 20 Aug 1972), 1 da (Melanie Jane b 16 June 1969); *Career* asst prof of surgery Univ of California 1973-74, conslt surgn Manchester Royal Infirmary 1974-, hon reader in surgery Univ of Manchester, Hunterian prof RCS 1980, memb Transplant Advsy Panel UK Transplant Mgmnt Ctee Dept of Health; chm Med Exec Ctee Central Manchester Health Authy; Freeman Worshipful Co of Innholders 1965; FRCS 1970; *Recreations* golf, tennis, skiing; *Style—* Robert Johnson, Esq; Evergreen, Chapel Lane, Hale Barns, Cheshire WA15 0AJ (☎ 061 980 8840); Renal Transplant Unit, Royal Infirmary, Manchester M13 9WL (☎ 061 276 4413)

JOHNSON, Sir Robin Eliot; 7 Bt (UK 1818), of Bath; s of Maj Percy Eliot Johnson (d 1962), and kinsman of Sir Victor Johnson, 6 Bt (d 1986); *b* 1929; *Educ* St John's Coll Johannesburg; *m* 1954, Barbara Alfreda, da of late Alfred T Brown, of Germiston, Transvaal; 1 s, 2 da; *Style—* Sir Robin Johnson, Bt

JOHNSON, Sir Ronald Ernest Charles; CB (1961), JP (Edinburgh 1972); s of Ernest Johnson (d 1965); *b* 3 May 1913; *Educ* Portsmouth GS, St John's Coll Cambridge (MA); *m* 1938, Elizabeth Gladys Nuttall; 2 s (and 1 s decd); *Career* Nat Serv WWII: Sub Lt (special) RNVR, Eastern Theatre; entered Scot Office 1935; sec: Scot Home and Health Dept 1963-72 (under-sec 1956-62), Cmmns for Scot 1972-78; memb: Scot Records Advsy Cncl 1975-81, Ctee on Admin of Sheriffdoms 1981-82; chm Fire Serv Res and Trg Tst 1976-89; pres: Edinburgh Bach Soc 1973-86; kt 1970; *Recreations* church organ; *Style—* Sir Ronald Johnson, CB, JP; 14 Eglinton Crescent, Edinburgh, Scotland EH12 5DD (☎ 031 337 7733)

JOHNSON, Roy Arthur; s of Leonard Arthur Johnson (d 1974), of Hove, Sussex, and Cicely Elsie, *née* Turner; *b* 3 March 1937; *Educ* Lancing; *m* 31 July 1965, Heather Campbell, da of Alfred John Heald, of Hove, Sussex; 2 s (Mark b 1967, Paul b 1968); *Career* CA 1960; ptnr: Coopers & Lybrand 1966-, Cork Gully 1981-; Inst of CAs of Scotland: moderator of examination bd 1975-87, memb Cncl 1984-90, convenor of Fin and Gen Purposes Ctee 1986-90; dir Glasgow C of C; Deacon of the Incorporation of Cordiners of Glasgow 1976 (memb 1968), Deacon Convener of the Trades House of Glasgow 1990; MIPA 1986; *Recreations* golf, photography, gardening; *Clubs* Caledonian, Western (Glasgow); *Style—* Roy Johnson, Esq; 8 Hillcrest Drive, Newton Mearns, Glasgow G77 5HH (☎ 041 639 3800); Coopers & Lybrand Deloitte, Kintyre House, 209 West George St, Glasgow (☎ 041 248 2644, fax 041 221 8256, telex 779396)

JOHNSON, Stanley Patrick; s of Wilfred Johnson, and Irene Johnson; *b* 18 Aug 1940; *Educ* Sherborne, Exeter Coll Oxford (MA); *m* 1, 1963 (m dis 1979), Charlotte Offlow Fawcett; 3 s (Alexander, Leo, Joseph), 1 da (Rachel); m 2, 1981, Mrs Jennifer Kidd; 1 s (Maximilian), 1 da (Julia); *Career* on staff of Int Planned Parenthood Fedn London 1971-73, conslt to UN Fund of Population Activities 1971-73, head of Prevention of Pollution and Nuisances Div EEC 1973-77, advsr to head of Environment and Consumer Protection Service EEC 1977-79, MEP (EDG) IOW and E Hants 1979-84, environmental advsr to EEC Cmmn Brussels; Newdigate prize for Poetry 1962, RSPCA Richard Martin award, Greenpeace prize 1984; *Books* Life Without Birth (1970), The Green Revolution (1972), The Population Problem (1973), The Politics of the Environment (1973), Antarctica - Last Great Wilderness (1984), World Population and the United Nations (1988); *Novels* Gold Drain (1967), Panther Jones for President (1968), God Bless America (1974), The Doomsday Deposit (1980), The Marburg Virus (1982), Tunnel (1984), The Commissioner (1987), Dragon River (1989); *Recreations* writing, travel; *Clubs* Savile; *Style—* Stanley Johnson, Esq, MEP; West Nethercote, Winsford, Minehead, Somerset

JOHNSON, Timothy Charles; s of John Arthur Johnson, of Wakefield, and Louis Jessie, *née* Hewitt; *b* 10 Nov 1945; *Educ* Fakenham GS; *m* 25 March 1972, Elizabeth Mary, da of Ben Blake (d 1977); 1 s (William Timothy b 12 March 1978); *Career* architect; own practice 1971-88; property developer; dir Mand Developments Ltd, sole proprietor Jexin Properties, ptnr Kenwood Devpts, ptnr JLS Financial Services, dir Kenwood Construction (East Anglia) Ltd; past chm Holt Round Table; *Recreations* game shooting, squash, swimming, skiing, wine; *Clubs* Holt 41, Aylsham Squash; *Style—* Timothy C Johnson, Esq; Branksome House, 166 St Clements Hill, Norwich, Norfolk NR3 4DG (☎ 0603 415068); Les Beaux Pins, Saint Dizant du Gua, France; 35 Whiffler Rd, Norwich, Norfolk NR3 2AW (☎ 0603 415068, 485376, fax 0603 787496, car tel 0860 200994); JLS Financial Consultants, 1 Riverside Rd, Norwich Norfolk NR1 1SQ (☎ 0603 762650, fax 0603 762651)

JOHNSON, Trevor William; s of Rene Frank Albert Johnson (d 1952), of Moseley, Birmingham, and Felicia, *née* Gibbs (d 1953); *b* 22 Nov 1928; *Educ* Woodroughs Sch Cheltenham, King Edwards Sch Birmingham, Univ of Durham, Univ of Oxford; *m* 1, 26 May 1953 (m dis 1971), Anne, da of Frederick Link (d 1939), of Birmingham; 2 s (Rupert Merlin b 20 Jan 1961, (William) Eustace Basil b 17 Feb 1964), 2 da (Amanda Louise (Mrs Farr) b 5 March 1954, Hannah Morgan b 29 Aug 1957); m 2, 21 May 1977, Jan Mary Brookes, da of Frederick Jones (d 1939), of Wrexham; 1 s (Christopher Ewen Brockhouse), 2 da (Sally Ann Brockhouse (Mrs Spray) b 2 Feb 1955, Susan Brockhouse b 9 March 1958); *Career* Nat Serv Army 1947-49; plays: The Bishopton Letter (BBC Radio) 1961, Funny Thing About Einstein (CBC) 1961, Fair For The Fair 1962; md Royds Midland 1970-74, dir Royds Advertising Gp, C D Harrison Cowley 1977-81, md and chief exec H B Johnson Woodier 1981-; memb Birmingham Chamber of Commerce; *Recreations* music; *Clubs* Anglo-Belgian; *Style—* Trevor Johnson, Esq; 1 Shrewsbury Rd, Much Wenlock, Shropshire (☎ 0952 727844); H B Johnson Woodier Ltd, 95 Hagley Rd, Edgbaston, Birmingham B16 8LA (☎ 021 454 9390, fax 021 454 9935)

JOHNSON, Victor Horace (Johnnie); s of late Herbert Johnson; *b* 14 May 1920; *Educ* Handsworth GS, Birmingham Sch of Architecture; *m* 1972, Gillian Margaret, *née* Longmore; 2 s, 1 da, 2 step s, 1 step da; *Career* chartered builder; md Herbert Johnson Ltd 1946-61; chm: Page-Johnson Builders Ltd 1961-72, West European Building Corporation Ltd 1969-78; dir Bovis Ltd 1972-74, chm Page Johnson Homes Ltd 1972-; fndr: The Johnnie Johnson Tst 1961-, The Johnnie Johnson Adventure Tst/ Youth Afloat 1972-; *Recreations* flying, sailing (yacht 'British Maid'), forestry, farming; *Clubs* RAF, Lloyd's Yacht, Royal Dart Yacht, Royal Perth Yacht (W Australia); *Style—* Victor Johnson, Esq; Elmdon House, Elmdon Park, Solihull, West Midlands (☎ 021

742 3157); Farthings, Beacon Rd, Kingswear, Dartmouth, Devon (☎ 080 425 577); 5 Vervain Way, Riverton, Perth, WA 6155 (☎ 457 4789)

JOHNSON, Prof William (Bill); s of James Johnson (d 1968), and Elizabeth, *née* Riley (d 1968); *b* 20 April 1922; *Educ* Manchester Central High GS, Manchester Coll of Technol (now UMIST) (BSc), Univ of London (BSc), Univ of Manchester (DSc); *m* 6 April 1946, Heather Marie, da of John B Thornber; 3 s (Philip James b 5 May 1948, Christopher John b 19 July 1951, Jeremy William b 16 June 1954), 2 da (Helen b 23 April 1953, Sarah b 6 Feb 1959); *Career* HM Forces 1943-47: cmmnd REME 1944, served UK, Italy and Austria; admin grade Civil Serv 1948-50; lectr in mechanical engrg: Northampton Poly (now City Univ) 1950-51, Univ of Sheffield 1952-56, sr lectr Univ of Manchester 1956-60; prof and head of Dept of Mechanical Engrg UMIST 1960-75, prof of mechanics Univ of Cambridge 1975-82; visiting prof Industrial Engrg Dept Purdue Univ USA 1983-85, United Technologies Distinguished Prof of Engrg 1988 and 1989; IMechE: T Bernard Hall Prize 1965 and 1966, James Clayton Fund prize 1972 and 1977, James Clayton prize for Educn and Res 1987, Silver medal Inst Sheet Metal Engrg; Hon DTech Univ of Bradford 1976, Hon DEng Univ of Sheffield 1986, fell Univ Coll London 1981, Foreign fell Acad of Athens 1982; FIMechE 1960, FRS 1982, FEng 1983; *Books* Mechanics of Metal Extrusion (with H Kudo, 1962), Engineering Plasticity (with PB Mellor, 1967 and 1973), Impact Strength of Materials (1972), the Crashworthiness of Vehicles (with AG Mamalis 1978), Engineering Plasticity: Metal Forming Processes (with AG Mamalis); *Recreations* walking, travel, gardening; *Style—* Prof William Johnson, FRS; Ridge Hall, Chapel-en-le-Frith, via Stockport, Cheshire SK12 6UD (☎ 0298 812441)

JOHNSON, Capt William Jefferson; OBE (1965), MVO (1962); s of Lancelot Johnson (d 1953), of Workington, Cumbria, and Janet, *née* Muir (d 1959); *b* 13 Aug 1909; *Educ* Workington GS; *m* 1, 29 Dec 1938 (m dis 1950), Marjorie Claire, *née* Wigglesworth; 2 s (Graeme b 1941, Neil b 1946); m 2, 21 Sept 1950, Wendy Mhairi, da of John McNicol (d 1954); 1 da (Jean b 1953); *Career* Pilot III (F) Sqdn 1931-35, flying instr No 4 FTS 1936-38, transfer to reserve 1939, recalled with VR cmmn as flying instr Desford and Kingstown Carlisle 1940, test pilot RAF Silloth, released to civil aviation 1942; assoc Airways Jt Ctee Liverpool 1942; Scottish Airways: Capt and flight mangr 1946-53, mangr flight ops trg 1953-74, chm IATA Flight Crew Trg Ctee 1967-74, cmd Royal flight to S America 1962; Master Air Pilot Certificate 1953; memb: Rotary 1966-87, London Diocesan Synod 1976-80, Malcolm Sargent Festival Choir, Woking Choral Soc; sec Samaritans Weybridge Branch 1977-81, steward and guide Guildford Cathedral 1986-; Freeman City of London, Liveryman Worshipful Co Air Pilots and Air Navigators 1957; FCIT 1964; *Recreations* mountaineering, music, choral singing; *Clubs* Royal Air Force; *Style—* Capt William Johnson, OBE, MVO; Rivey Lodge, 94 Old Woking Rd, West Byfleet, Surrey KT 14 6HU (☎ 09323 43 164)

JOHNSON-FERGUSON, Ian Edward; s and h of Sir Neil Johnson-Ferguson, 3 Bt, TD, JP, DL, *qv*; *b* 1 Feb 1932; *Educ* Ampleforth, Trinity Coll Cambridge (BA), Imperial Coll London (DIC); *m* 9 April 1964, Rosemary Teresa, yr da of Cecil John Whitehead, of The Old House, Crockham Hill, Edenbridge, Kent; 3 s (Mark Edward, b 14 Aug 1965, Paul Duncan b 20 Aug 1966, Simon Joseph b 23 July 1967); *Style—* Ian Johnson-Ferguson, Esq; Copthall Place, Upper Clatford, Andover SP11 7LR

JOHNSON-FERGUSON, Lt-Col Sir Neil Edward; 3 Bt (UK 1906), of Springkell, Co Dumfries, Kenyon, Newchurch-in- Culcheth, Co Palatine of Lancaster, and Wiston, Co Lanark; TD, JP (Dumfriesshire 1954), DL (Dumfriesshire 1957); s of Col Sir Edward Alexander James Johnson-Ferguson, 2 Bt, TD, JP, DL (d 1953), and Hon Elsie Dorothea, *née* McLaren (d 1972), da of 1 Baron Aberconway; *b* 2 May 1905; *Educ* Winchester, Trinity Coll Cambridge (BA); *m* 20 Jan 1931, Sheila Marion (d 1985), er da of Col Herbert Swynfen Jervis, MC (d 1965), of Tilford, Surrey; 4 s (Ian Edward, *qv*, Christopher Charles b 14 April 1933, Michael Herbert, JP b 27 Sept 1934, Nicholas Swynfen b 28 Dec 1938); *Heir* s, Ian Edward Johnson-Ferguson, *qv*; *Career* RAE Farnborough 1928-39, UKAE Seascale 1949-56, Maj Lanarkshire Yeo, Lt Col RCS (TA); memb Dumfries CC, vice-lt Co of Dumfries 1956-80; Legion of Merit (USA); *Recreations* shooting, forestry, photography; *Style—* Sir Neil Johnson-Ferguson; Springkell, Lockerbie, Dumfrieshire (☎ 046 16 230)

JOHNSON-GILBERT, Christopher Ian; s of Thomas Ian Johnson-Gilbert, of St John's Wood, London, and Gillian June, *née* Pool; *b* 28 Jan 1955; *Educ* Rugby, Worcester Coll Oxford (BA); *m* 25 July 1981, Emma Davina Mary, da of Hon C M Woodhouse, DSO, OBE; 3 da (Cordelia b 14 June 1983, Jemima b 24 July 1985, Imogen b 11 Jan 1990); *Career* admitted slr 1980; ptnr Linklaters & Paines 1986-; memb: City of London Slrs Co, Int Bar Assoc; *Clubs* MCC, RAC, Vincent's, Grannies; *Style—* Christopher Johnson-Gilbert, Esq; House A-5, 200 Victoria Rd, Hong Kong (☎ 855 1744); Linklaters & Paines, 14th Floor Alexandra House, Chater Rd, Central, Hong Kong (☎ 8424888, fax 8108133)

JOHNSON-GILBERT, Ronald Stuart; OBE (1977); s of Sir Ian Anderson Johnson-Gilbert, CBE, JP, DL (d 1974), of Edinburgh, and Rosalind Sybil, *née* Bell-Hughes (d 1977); *b* 14 July 1925; *Educ* Edinburgh Acad, Rugby, BNC Oxford (MA); *m* 10 March 1951, Ann Weir, da of Capt Thomas Weir Drummond, RNVR, TD (d 1953), of Greenock; 3 da (Clare Chevalier, Emma, Lydia Smith); *Career* Intelligence Corps 1943-46; sec: Royal Coll of Surgeons of England 1951-88 (formerly asst sec), Int Fedn of Surgical Colls 1962-72; hon sec (later hon treas) Med Cmmn on Accident Prevention 1980-, tstee Hunterian Tst 1990; memb Court of Patrons RCS 1990; Hon FFARCS 1983, Hon FRCS 1987, Hon FDSRCS 1987, Hon FRCSI 1989; *Recreations* literature, golf, music; *Style—* Ronald Johnson-Gilbert, Esq, OBE; Home Farm, Castle Rising, King's Lynn, Norfolk (☎ 0553 631 720)

JOHNSON-GILBERT, Thomas Ian; s of Sir Ian Anderson Johnson-Gilbert, CBE, JP, DL (d 1974), and Rosalind Sybil, *née* Bell-Hughes (d 1977); *b* 2 June 1923; *Educ* Edinburgh Acad, Rugby, Trinity Coll Oxford (MA); *m* 25 Nov 1950, Gillian June, da of Gordon Desmond Pool (d 1942), of London; 1 s (Christopher), 1 da (Catherine); *Career* Flt Lt VR 1943-46; admitted slr 1950; sr ptnr Coward Chance 1980-87 (ptnr 1954-), jt sr ptnr Clifford Chance 1987-89; Freeman Worshipful Co of Slrs; memb: Law Soc (Cncl 1970-88), Int Bar Assoc; *Recreations* reading, arts, travel, spectator sport; *Clubs* Athenaeum; City of London, MCC; *Style—* Thomas Johnson-Gilbert, Esq; c/o Clifford Chance, Royex House, Aldermanbury Square, London EC2 (☎ 071 600 0808, fax 01 726 8561, telex 895 9991)

JOHNSON-HILL, Nigel; s of Kenelm Clifton Johnson-Hill, JP (d 1977), and Joyce Wynne, *née* Booth; *b* 8 Dec 1946; *Educ* Rugby; *m* 23 Oct 1971, Catherine, da of Edward Sainsbury, TD; 1 s (Sam b 1978), 2 da (Chloe b 1976, Anna b 1981); *Career* bank offr Hong Kong & Shanghai Banking Corp 1965-73, stockbroker WI Carr (Overseas) 1973-78, md Hoare Govett 1978-87; stockbroker and chief exec Hoenig & Co Ltd 1988-; memb: Stock Exchange 1979, The Securities Assoc 1988; *Recreations* wine, skiing, tennis; *Clubs* Oriental, Hong Kong; *Style—* Nigel Johnson-Hill, Esq; Park Farm, Milland, Liphook, Hampshire, GU30 7JT; c/o Hoenig & Co Ltd, 5 London Wall Bldgs, Finsbury Circus, London EC2M 5NT (☎ 071 588 6622, fax 071 588 6497)

JOHNSON-LAIRD, Dr Philip Nicholas; s of Frederick Ryberg Johnson-Laird (d 1962), of Middlesborough, and Dorothy, *née* Blackett (d 1947); *b* 10 Oct 1936; *Educ* Culford Sch, Univ Coll London (BA, PhD); *m* 1 Aug 1959, Maureen Mary Bridget, da of John Henry Sullivan (d 1948); 1 s (Benjamin b 1966), 1 da (Dorothy b 1971); *Career* asst lectr in psychology Univ Coll London 1966-67 (lectr 1967-73), visiting memb The Inst for Advanced Study Princeton New Jersey 1971-72, reader in experimental pyschology Univ of Sussex, 1973-78 (prof 1978-82), visiting fell Cognitive Sci Prog Stanford Univ spring 1980; visiting prof in psychology: Stanford Univ Spring 1985, Princeton Univ spring 1986 and 1987; asst dir MRC Applied Psychology Unit Cambridge 1983-89; fell Darwin Coll Cambridge 1986-89; memb: Experimental Psychology Soc, Br Psychology Soc; Doctorate Göteborg Sweden 1983, FBA 1986; *Books* Pyschology of Reasoning (with P C Wason, 1972), Language and Perception (with G A Miller, 1976), Mental Models (1983), The Computer and the Mind (1988); *Style—* Dr Philip Johnson-Laird; Department of Psychology, Princeton University, NJ 08540, USA (☎ 609 258 4432)

JOHNSON-MARSHALL, Prof Percy Edwin Alan; CMG (1975); s of Felix William Norman Johnson-Marshall (d 1957), and Kate Jane, *née* Little (d 1975); *b* 20 Jan 1915; *Educ* Queen Elizabeth Sch Kirkby Lonsdale Liverpool, Univ of Edinburgh (MA); *m* 1944, April Phyllis Trix, da of Harold Bridger, of Argentina; 3 s (William, Stirling, Nicholas), 4 da (Mary, Katherine, Caroline, Ursula); *Career* Nat Serv RE in India and Burma 1942-46, Maj; asst regnl planning offr LCC i/c of London's reconstruction areas incl: Stepney, Poplar (Lansbury), S Bank, City (incl Barbican); sr lectr, reader and prof Univ of Edinburgh 1964-85 (emeritus prof), planning conslt 1960-; memb RTPI, DistTP; *Books* Rebuilding Cities (1966); *Recreations* reading, writing, photography, travelling, hill walking; *Clubs* Univ of Edinburgh Staff; *Style—* Prof Percy Johnson-Marshall, CMG; Bella Vista, Duddingston Village, Edinburgh (☎ 031 661 2019); Percy Johnson Marshall Partners, 64 The Causeway, Duddington, Edinburgh

JOHNSON SMITH, Sir Geoffrey; DL; MP (C) Wealden 1983-; s of J Johnson Smith; *b* 16 April 1924; *Educ* Charterhouse, Lincoln Coll Oxford; *m* Jeanne Pomeroy; 2 s, 1 da; *Career* WWII Capt RA 1942-47; served: UK, Belgium, India; BBC TV 1953-54 and 1955-59; memb LCC 1955-58; MP (Cons): Holborn and St Pancras South 1959-64, East Grinstead 1965-1983; PPS BOT and Miny Pensions 1960-63, opposition whip 1965, vice chm Cons Party 1965-71, Parly under sec of state for Def 1971-72, Parly sec CSD 1972-74; former memb IBA Gen Advsy Cncl; chm Select Ctee Membs Interests 1979-; memb: Exec 1922 Ctee 1979- (vice chm 1988), Mil Ctee N Atlantic Assembly 1981- (chm 1985, ldr of Br Delgn to NAA 1987-, vice pres 1990-), memb Bd LWT (Holdings) 1982-, govr British Film Inst 1981-87, chm Cons Defence Ctee 1988-, chm Thames Salmon Tst 1987; kt 1982; *Recreations* fishing, tennis; *Clubs* Travellers'; *Style—* Sir Geoffrey Johnson Smith, DL, MP; House of Commons, London SW1 (☎ 071 219 4158)

JOHNSTON, Alan Charles MacPherson; QC (1980); s of Hon Lord Dunpark, *qv*, and Katherine Margaret, *née* Mitchell (d 1982); *b* 13 Jan 1942; *Educ* Loretto, Jesus Coll Cambridge (BA), Univ of Edinburgh (LLB); *m* 30 July 1966, Anthea Jean, da of John Blackburn (d 1985); 3 s (Alexander b 1969, Charles b 1971, Nicholas b 1974); *Career* advocate 1967, standing jr counsel Scottish Home and Health Dept 1972-78, dean Faculty of Advocates 1989- (treas 1978-89, advocate depute 1979-82); chm: Industl Tbnl 1982-88, Med Appeal Tbnl 1984-89; *Recreations* fishing, golf, shooting; *Clubs* New (Edinburgh), Univ Pitt Cambridge; *Style—* Alan Johnston, Esq, QC; 3 Circus Gardens, Edinburgh EH3 6TN (☎ 031 225 1862); Parkend, Stichill, Roxburghshire; Advocate Library, Parl House, Edinburgh (☎ 031 226 5071)

JOHNSTON, Alastair John Carmichael; OBE (1990); s of Harry Scott Johnston (d 1973), of Tayport, Fife, and Jean Carmichael (d 1966); *b* 16 Sept 1928; *Educ* Harris Academy Dundee, Univ of St Andrews (BSc); *m* 7 Sept 1953, Morag Elizabeth, da of Robert Campbell (d 1956), of Tayport, Fife; 2 s (Malcolm b 1957, Scott b 1963); *Career* North British Rubber Co Edinburgh 1953-59, plant mangr Armstrong Cork Co Gateshead 1960-70, dir Wm Briggs & Sons Ltd Dundee 1970-74; md: Permanite Ltd Essex 1974-77, Trident Equipment Ltd Herts 1977-81; dir Uniroyal Ltd Dumfries 1982-85, md The Gates Rubber Co Ltd Edinburgh and Dumfries 1986-; memb Scottish Cncl CBI 1983-, dep chm Dumfries and Galloway Enterprise Co 1990-; CEng, FIProdE, FBIM; *Recreations* hill walking; *Style—* Alastair Johnston, Esq, OBE; 8 Ravelston Park, Edinburgh EH4 3DX (☎ 031 332 8409); Mill of Camserney, Aberfeldy PH15 2JF; The Gates Rubber Co Ltd, NCR House, 2 Roseburn Gardens, Edinburgh EH12 5NJ (☎ 031 337 4007, fax 031 337 4042)

JOHNSTON, Sir Alexander; GCB (1962, CB 1946), KBE (1953); s of Alexander Simpson Johnston (d 1960); *b* 27 Aug 1905; *Educ* George Heriot's Sch Edinburgh, Univ of Edinburgh; *m* 1947, Betty Joan, CBE, *qv*; 1 s, 1 da; *Career* civil servant: Home Office, Cabinet Office, Treasy; chm Bd of Inland Revenue 1958-68; dep chm: Monopolies Cmmn 1969-76, Takeover Panel 1970-83, Cncl for the Securities Indust 1978-83; Hon DSc London Univ 1977; Hon LLD Univ of Leicester 1986; *Recreations* gardening; *Clubs* Reform; *Style—* Sir Alexander Johnston, GCB, KBE; 18 Mallord St, London SW3 6DU (☎ 071 352 6840)

JOHNSTON, Alexander David; s of Sir Alexander Johnston, GCB, KBE, of 18 Mallord St, London SW3, and Lady Johnston, CBE, *née* Harris; *b* 3 Sept 1951; *Educ* Westminster, Corpus Christie Coll Cambridge (MA); *m* 14 March 1980, Jackie Barbara, da of Ernie Stephenson; 2 s (Mark Edward b 29 June 1987, George Frederic b 1 March 1990); *Career* dir Lazard Bros 1973-; *Recreations* skiing, walking, reading; *Style—* Alexander Johnston, Esq; Lazard Brothers, 21 Moorfields, London EC2P 2HT (☎ 071 588 2721)

JOHNSTON, Hon Mrs (Anne Rosalinde); *née* Tedder; da of 2 Baron Tedder; *b* 1963; *m* 1989, Euan Angus Johnston, s of David Johnston, of Leuchars, Fife; *Style—* The Hon Mrs Johnston

JOHNSTON, Arthur Robert Court; s of William Court Johnston, MC (d 1946), of Carlisle, and Mabel Caroline, *née* Tucker; *b* 22 July 1924; *Educ* St Bees Sch, Univ of Liverpool Sch of Architecture (BArch); *m* 13 June 1953, (Sylvia) Fay, da of George Lionel Spencer Lightfoot, OBE (d 1972), of Carlisle; 2 s (Richard b 1955, Adrian b 1961), 1 da (Sarah b 1963); *Career* served Queen's Royal and Border Regts 1943-46; architect; dir: Johnston and Wright Architects 1950-, Romead Ltd 1989-; fndr chm Cumbrian Best Kept Village Competition 1957-; FRIBA 1958; *Recreations* arts, sport, travel; *Clubs* Border and County (Carlisle); *Style—* Arthur Johnston, Esq; Hill Crest, Beaumont, Carlisle, Cumbria CA5 6EF (☎ 0228 576277); 15 Castle Street, Carlisle, Cumbria, CA3 8TD (☎ 0228 25161, fax 0228 515 559)

JOHNSTON, Barrie Colin; s of Alfred John Johnston, OBE (d 1964); *b* 7 Aug 1925; *Educ* Epsom Coll; *m* 1952, Cynthia Anne, *née* Clark; 1 s (Alastair John), 1 da (Nicola Mary); *Career* Lt RM Far East; merchant banker (ret); dir: Charterhouse Japhet Ltd 1973-84, T H White Ltd 1981-87, Mountleigh Gp Ltd plc 1983-89, Mornington Bldg Soc 1988-; memb: Mgmnt Ctee The Pension Fund Property Unit Tst 1966-69, Mgmnt Ctee Charities Property Unit Tst 1967-88, Cncl Barnardos 1980-, Cncl King George's Fund for Sailors 1982-, (hon treas 1985-); fin advsr Charities Aid Fndn 1976-; Fin Ctee Spastics Soc 1984-88; tstee Charities Aid Fndn 1989- (chm Investment Ctee 1976-); FPMI, FRSA; AMSIA; *Recreations* sport, travel; *Style—* Barrie Johnston, Esq; Yew Cottage, 8 The Green, Ewell, Surrey (☎ 081 393 2920)

JOHNSTON, Lady; Betty Joan; CBE (1989); da of Edward Harris; *Educ* Cheltenham Ladies' Coll, St Hugh's Coll Oxford; *m* 1947, Sir Alexander Johnston, GCB, KBE, *qv*; 1 s, 1 da; *Career* called to the Bar Gray's Inn 1940; JP Inner London 1966; dep Parly counsel Law Cmmn 1975-83, standing counsel General Synod 1983-88; chm: Girls'

Public Day Schs Tst 1975-, Francis Holland (C of E) Schs Tst 1978-, Governing Bodies Girls' Schs Assoc 1979-89, Independent Schs Jt Cncl 1983-86; memb Cncl Queen's Coll London; *Clubs* University Women's; *Style*— Lady Johnston, CBE; 18 Mallord St, London SW3 6DU (☎ 071 352 6840)

JOHNSTON, Brian Alexander; CBE (1991, OBE 1983), MC (1945); s of Lt-Col C E Johnston, DSO, MC (d 1922), and Pleasance, *née* Alt (d 1957); *b* 24 June 1912; *Educ* Eton, New Coll Oxford (BA); *m* 22 April 1948, Pauline, da of Col William Tozer, CBE, TD (d 1971); 3 s ((Charles) Barry b 22 April 1949, (William) Andrew b 27 March 1954, (Philip) Ian b 2 May 1957), 2 da (Clare Eileen b 14 Sept 1951, Joanna Jane b 28 Nov 1965); *Career* WWII: 2 Bn Grenadier Gds 1940-45 (demobbed as Maj), served Normandy Campaign, capture of Brussels and Nijmegen Bridge, crossing the Rhine; broadcaster and commentator BBC: memb of staff 1946-72, cricket commentator TV 1946-70, cricket commentator on radio Test Match Specials 1970-, BBC cricket corr 1963-72; freelance: In Town tonight, Down Your Way, ceremonial and royal occasions; *Books* Let's Go Somewhere (1952), Armchair Cricket (1957), Stumped for a Tale (1965), The Wit of Cricket (1968), All About Cricket (1972), Its Been A Lot of Fun (1974), Its a Funny Game (1978), Rain Stops Play (1979), Chatterboxes (1983), Now Heres a Funny Thing (1984), Brian Johnston's Guide to Cricket (1986), Its Been a Piece of Cake (1989), The Tale of Billy Bouncer (1990), Down Your Way (1991); *Recreations* cricket, golf, theatre; *Clubs* MCC; *Style*— Brian Johnston, Esq, CBE, MC; 43 Boundary Rd, St John's Wood, London NW8 OJE (☎ 071 286 2991)

JOHNSTON, Daniel (Dan); OBE (1974); s of Daniel Johnston (d 1961), of Colne, Lancashire , and Elizabeth, *née* Johnson (d 1957); *b* 20 March 1912; *Educ* Colne GS, UMIST (BSc); *m* 20 Dec 1944, Helen, da of Frederick J Thornber; 2 s (Roger b 1947, Peter b 1948); *Career* mil serv E Lancs Regt and RASC (becoming Maj Staff GHQ India) 1942-46; designer mangr and dir in various E Lancs textiles firms 1935-42 and 1947-54, memb of industl liaison staff then head Industl Design The Design Cncl 1954-75, pres Chartered Soc of Designers 1973-74, design conslt 1976-; author numerous articles for design and trade press; enterprise cnsllr DTI; ATI, FCSD; *Books* Design Protection (3 edn, 1989); *Recreations* in younger years - football, cricket, tennis; *Style*— Dan Johnston, Esq, OBE; Forest Cottage, 5 Sunnybank, Hawkhurst Rd, Flimwell, Wadhurst, Sussex TN5 7QR (☎ 058 087 472)

JOHNSTON, David Lawrence; s of Herbert David Johnston (d 1983), and Hilda Eleanor, *née* Wood, of Chichester, Sussex; *b* 12 April 1936; *Educ* Lancastrian Sch Chichester, King's Coll Univ of Durham (BSc); *m* 7 July 1959, Beatrice Ann, da of John Turnbull Witten (d 1973); 3 da (Fiona b 1960, Pauline b 1961, Kate b 1970); *Career* Lt RN 1959-62, electrical offr HMS Eastbourne 1960-62; MOD: overseeing Wallsend 1962-63, design Bath 1963-66, prodn and project mgmnt Devonport Dockyard 1966-73, dockyard policy Bath 1973-76, design Bath 1976-79, prodn and planning Portsmouth Dockyard 1979-81, asst under sec of state and md Devonport Dockyard 1984-87; chm DDL (mgmnt buy out co) 1985-87, dep chm DML 1987, mgmnt conslt 1988, dir gen Nat Inspection Cncl for Electrical Installation Contracting (NICEIC) 1989-; dir: NICQA Ltd 1989-, NSCIA Ltd 1989-90, NACOSS Ltd 1990-; FIEE 1980, FBIM 1982, RCNC; *Recreations* walking, gardening, modernizing houses; *Clubs* Army and Navy; *Style*— David Johnston, Esq; The Old Orchard, Harrowbeer Lane, Yelverton, Devon PL20 6DZ (☎ 0822 854 310); Vintage House, 37 Albert Embankment, London SE1 7UJ (☎ 071 582 7746, fax 071 820 0831)

JOHNSTON, David Tucker; OBE (1980); s of William Court Johnston, MC (d 1945) of Scotby, Carlisle, and Mabel Caroline, *née* Tucker; *b* 1 April 1927; *Educ* St Bees Sch Cumbria, AA London (AADIP); *m* 4 Sept 1954, Jane Medeleine, da of Neil Grant Mackilligin, JP (d 1984), of Froxfield, Petersfield, Hants; 1 s (Andrew b 1955), 1 da (Caroline b 1957); *Career* Lt RE 1944-47; dir: Johnston and Wright architects 1971- (ptnr 1953-71); Johndyke Ltd 1989-; govr St Bees Sch; FRIBA 1966 (ARIBA 1953); *Recreations* fishing, golf, painting, sketching; *Clubs* Border and Co Lansdowne, Southerness Golf, Silloth on Solway Golf, Royal and Ancient Golf; *Style*— David Johnston, Esq, OBE; Longburgh Head, Burgh-by-Sands, Carlisle CA5 6AF (☎ 0228 76381); Johnston and Wright architects, 15 Castle St, Carlisle CA3 8TD (☎ 0228 25161, fax 515559)

JOHNSTON, Dr Derek Iain; s of John Johnston, and Anna, *née* Howitt; *b* 31 May 1943; *Educ* Collyers Sch, Queens' Coll Cambridge (MA, MD, BChir); *m* 19 April 1969, Heather Christine, da of Donald Stuart; 3 s (Andrew b 1971, Robert b 1976, James b 1979), 1 da (Emily b 1972); *Career* conslt paediatrician and endocrinologist 1976-; MRCP 1970, FRCP 1982; *Books* Essential Paediatrics (1981); *Recreations* sailing; *Style*— Dr Derek Johnston; Children's Department, University Hospital, Queens Medical Centre, Nottingham NG7 2UH (☎ 0602 421421)

JOHNSTON, Edward Alexander; KBE (1989) CB (1975); s of Prof Edward Hamilton Johnston (d 1942), and Iris, *née* May; *b* 19 March 1929; *Educ* Groton Sch USA, Marlborough, New Coll Oxford (BA); *m* 1, 2 June 1956 (m dis 1981), Veronica Mary *née* Bernays 2 s (Philip b 1960, Paul b 1965), 2 da (Sara b 1958, Anna b 1963); m 2, 21 July 1981, Christine Elizabeth Nash, *née* Shepherd; *Career* actuary; Equity and Law Life Assur Soc 1952, Govt Actuary's Dept 1958, appointed Govt Actuary 1973-89 (ret), dir Noble Lowndes Actuarial Services 1989-; tstee Occupational Pensions Advsy Serv, Cncl Inst of Actuaries 1973-88, pres Pensions Mgmnt Inst 1985-87 (Cncl 1983-88); FIA 1957, FPMI 1976; *Clubs* Reform; *Style*— Sir Edward Johnston, KBE, CB; Noble Lowndes & Partners Ltd, Norfolk House, Wellesley Rd, Croydon CR9 3EB (☎ 081 666 8228)

JOHNSTON, Edward Ingram; s of Samuel William Johnston (d 1954); *b* 27 May 1930; *Educ* Portora Royal Sch; *Career* dir: Securicor (Ulster) Ltd, Citron Estates (Belfast) Ltd; FCA; *Recreations* reading, music, sport; *Style*— Edward Johnston, Esq; 89 Whiterock Rd, Killinchy, Co Down, NI

JOHNSTON, Hon Lady (Elizabeth Rosemary); JP (Berks); da of 2 Baron Hardinge of Penshurst, GCB, GCVO, MC, PC (d 1960) and Helen, Lady Hardinge of Penshurst (d 1979); *b* 3 April 1927; *m* 1949, Lt-Col Sir John F D Johnston, GCVO, MC, *qv*; 1 s, 1 da; *Career* formerly WRNS; professional photographer; *Style*— The Hon Lady Johnston, JP; Stone Hill, Newport, Dyfed; The Great Park, Windsor, Berks SL4 2HP

JOHNSTON, Frederick Patrick Mair; s of Frederick Mair Johnston (d 1973), of Falkirk, and Muriel Kathleen, *née* Macbeth; the Johnston family have had a continuous controlling interest in Johnston Press plc and its predecessor since 1767; *b* 15 Sept 1935; *Educ* Lancing, New Coll Oxford (MA); *m* 1961, Elizabeth Ann, da of Robert Thomas Jones, of Montgomery, Wales; 2 s (Michael b 1962, Robert b 1964); *Career* cmmnd Royal Scots Fusiliers, served East Africa 4 Uganda Bn KAR 1955-56; dir: Johnston press plc (F Johnston & Co Ltd until 1988) 1962-; chm: Johnston Newspaper Group 1973-, Dunn & Wilson Group 1976-; pres: Young Newspapermen's Assoc 1968-69, Forth Valley C of C 1972-73, Scottish Newspaper Proprietors' Assoc 1976-78; memb Press Cncl 1974-88, chm Central Scot Manpower Ctee 1976-83; treas: Soc of Master Printers of Scotland 1981-86, Cwlth Press Union 1987-; pres Newspaper Soc 1989-90; *Recreations* reading, travelling; *Clubs* New (Edinburgh), Caledonian, Royal Cwlth Soc; *Style*— Frederick P M Johnston, Esq; 1 Grange Terrace, Edinburgh EH9 2LD (☎ 031 667 9201); 53 Manor Place, Edinburgh EH3 7EG (☎ 031 225 3361)

JOHNSTON, Geoffrey Edward Forshaw; s of Ronald Douglas Graham Johnston (d 1985), of Hallhouse, Fenwick, Ayrshire, and Nancy Forshaw, *née* Price; *b* 20 June 1940; *Educ* Loretto, Univ of St Andrews (LLB 1961); *m* 21 Dec 1964, Elizabeth Anne, da of Maj William C Lockhart, of Irvine; 2 da (Susanna b 12 May 1968, Victoria b 14 Aug 1969); *Career* apprentice CA then qualified asst with Wilson Stirling & Co 1959-65; dir: Arbuckle Smith (Holdings) Ltd 1967-68 (mgmnt trainee 1965-67), Arbuckle Smith Group 1968-69; md: Arbuckle, Smith & Co Ltd 1972-, Cambria Investments Ltd 1972-; dir: Petrasco Services Ltd Aberdeen, Onward Baylis Ltd Wolverhampton, Partners in Distribution Ltd, Lomond Sch Helensburgh; dir Glasgow C of C 1980-; memb Scot Valuation Advsy Cncl 1982-; nat chm BIFA (formerly IFF) 1990-91; memb Merchants' House City of Glasgow; Belgian Consul for Glasgow, W of Scot and Northern Isles; fellIFF, FILDM, MBIM, CA; *Recreations* sailing, skiing, hillwalking, gardening, golf, DIY; *Clubs* Royal Northern and Clyde Yacht, Royal Western Yacht, Scottish Ski, RNVR; *Style*— Geoffrey Johnston, Esq; Arbuckle, Smith & Co Ltd, 91 Mitchell St, Glasgow G1 3LS (☎ 041 248 5050, fax 041 248 5631, telex 778212)

JOHNSTON, Gilbert; s of David Kidd Johnston, of Dundee (d 1953), and Agnes Penman, *née* Neish (d 1957); *b* 11 March 1932; *Educ* Harris Acad Dundee; *m* 24 April 1957, Aileen, da of John Brown, of Dundee (d 1955); 2 s (Scott b 1959, Derek b 1962); *Career* Nat Serv 2 Lt Army 1956-58; CA 1956; worked ICI and Rolls Royce, gp chief exec J C Bamford Excavators Ltd 1977- (dealer dept mangr 1964, gp planning dir 1972); memb Midland Indust Cncl; CBIM; *Recreations* swimming, golf, gardening, music, reading; *Style*— Gilbert Johnston, Esq; J C Bamford Excavators Ltd, Rocester, Uttoxeter, Staffs ST14 5JP (☎ 0889 590312, fax 0889 590769, telex 36 372)

JOHNSTON, Sheriff (Alexander) Graham; WS (1971); s of Hon Lord Kincraig, *qv*, and Margaret Joan, *née* Graham; *b* 16 July 1944; *Educ* Edinburgh Acad, Strathallan Sch, Univ of Edinburgh (LLB), Univ Coll Oxford (BA, Golf Blue); *m* 1, 1972 (m dis 1982), Susan Gay Horne; 2 s (Robin Graham b 30 Nov 1973, Paul Mark b 20 Oct 1975); m 2, 6 Feb 1982, Dr Angela Astrid Synnove Anderson, da of Mayer Olsen, of Newport-on-Tay; *Career* ptnr Hagart & Burn-Murdoch WS 1972-82; Sheriff: Grampian Highlands & Islands Aberdeen 1982-85, Glasgow & Strathkelvin at Glasgow 1985-; ed Scottish Civil Law Reports 1987-; hon fell Inst of Professional Investigators 1979; hon pres Family Law Assoc; memb Cncl Strathclyde Conciliation Service; memb Incorporation of Barbers (Glasgow); *Books* Scottish Civil Law Reports (ed 1987-); *Recreations* golf, puzzles, bridge, cooking; *Clubs* Elie Golf House, Vincent's (Oxford); *Style*— Sheriff Graham Johnston, WS; 3 North Dean Park Ave, Bothwell, Lanarkshire G71 8HH (☎ 0698 852177); Prospect Cottage, Ferry Road, Elie, Fife (☎ 0333 330184); Sheriff Court House, 1 Carlton Place, Glasgow (☎ 041 429 8888)

JOHNSTON, Lady; Helen Torrey; *née* Du Bois; da of Benjamin Franklin Du Bois; *m* 1941, Sir Thomas Alexander Johnston, 13 Bt (d 1984); 1 s (Sir Thomas Alexander, 14 Bt), 2 da (Helen Du Bois b 1944: m 1969, Phillip Thomas Sargent; Leslie Sheldon b 1951: m 1972, David Charles Krempa); *Style*— Lady Johnston; 350 W Delwood Drive, Mobile, Alabama 36606, USA

JOHNSTON, Dr Ian Alistair; s of Donald Dalrymple Johnston (d 1985), and Muriel Joyce Johnston; *b* 2 May 1944; *Educ* Royal GS High Wycombe, Univ of Birmingham (BSc, PhD); *m* 1973, Mary Bridget, da of Francis Patrick Lube (d 1985); 1 s (Donald b 1979), 1 da (Claire b 1981); *Career* asst princ Dept of Employment 1969 (princ 1973, asst sec 1978, under sec 1984); private sec to Sir Denis Barnes 1972-74, first sec Br Embassy Brussels 1975-78; Advsy Conciliation Serv 1978-84; dir Planning and Resources MSC 1984-85 (chief exec VET Gp 1985-87), dep dir-gen Dept of Employment Trg 1987-; *Recreations* bird watching, skiing, tennis; *Style*— Dr Ian Johnston; Dept of Employment Training, Moorfoot, Sheffield 1 (☎ 0742 594108)

JOHNSTON, Ian Andrew Hill; s of John Hill Johnston (d 1962), of Bearsden, Glasgow, and Ethel, *née* Andrew (d 1987); *b* 9 July 1926; *Educ* Jordan Hill Coll Sch, Univ of Glasgow (BSc); *m* 4 Feb 1956, Gwenyth Claire, da of John Lloyd (d 1981), of Glasgow; 1 s (Ian Lloyd b 2 April 1959), 1 da (Sally Eve b 2 Oct 1957); *Career* dir: Trusthouse Forte plc, Gen Accident Life; co cncllr N Yorks 1970-77; *Recreations* skiing, shooting; *Clubs* Caledonian; *Style*— Ian Johnston, Esq; THF plc, 166 High Holborn, London WC1V 6TT (☎ 071 836 7744)

JOHNSTON, Cdr Ian Edgar; OBE (1981); s of Maj Alan Robert Charles Johnston (d 1970), of Emsworth, Hants, and Evelyn Beatrice, *née* Edgar (d 1961); *b* 17 May 1929; *Educ* RNC Dartmouth; *m* 6 Aug 1955, Marcia Elaine, da of Douglas Sioda Macnamara Faulkner (d 1970), of Melbourne, Australia; 2 da (Sara b 1956, Marguerite b 1960); *Career* entered RNC Dartmouth 1943, served at sea 1946-67, Naval Staff Washington DC 1968-70, jt servs Staff Coll Latimer 1970, MOD 1971-73, 2i/c RNAS Yeovilton 1973-75, Queen's Harbourmaster and Cdr Dockyard Gibraltar 1975-78, Naval Liaison Offr London 1978-82; Br Diabetic Assoc 1982-, cross country commentator Br Horse Soc; Hon Sheriff Monterey Cal (1969); Freeman City of London 1980; FBIM 1982, ICFM 1986; *Recreations* field sports, horse trials; *Clubs* Oriental, Anchorites; *Style*— Cdr Ian Johnston, OBE, RN; Holbrook, Yetminster, Sherborne, Dorset DT9 6HQ; British Diabetic Association, 10 Queen Anne St, London W1M OBD (☎ 071 323 1531)

JOHNSTON, Prof Ivan David Alexander; s of David Johnston, and Mary, *née* Clarke; *b* 4 Oct 1929; *Educ* Royal Belfast Acad, Queen's Univ Belfast (MB Bch, MCH); *m* 1, 3 Sept 1959, Elizabeth (d 1987); 2 s (Stephen Robert David b 29 Nov 1961, Philip Ivan b 11 Dec 1962); m 2, 16 Dec 1989, Annette, *née* Elphinstone; *Career* lectr in surgery Queen's Univ 1954-59, res asst Mayo Clinic USA 1959-61, sr lectr and conslt surgn Royal Post Grad Med Sch London 1963-66, prof and head of Dept of Surgery Univ of Newcastle 1966-, sr surgn Royal Victoria Infirmary 1966-; Hon Col 201 NGen Hosp RAMC 1989; memb: Northumberland Health Authy, Cncl RCS; FRSM, FRCS 1959, non FACS 1985, FRCSEd 1987; *Books* Metabolic Basis Surgical Care (1968), Advances in Parenteral Nutrition (1980), Modern Trends in Surgical Endocrinology (1986); *Recreations* gardening, photography; *Clubs* RSM, 1942, Grey Truner Surgical; *Style*— Prof Ivan Johnston; Dept of Surgery, Medical School University of Newcastle, Framlington Place, Newcastle upon Tyne (☎ 091 222 7067)

JOHNSTON, Sir John Baines; GCMG (1978, KCMG 1966, CMG 1962), KCVO (1972); s of Rev Andrew Smith Johnston (d 1966); *b* 13 May 1918; *Educ* Banbury GS, Queen's Coll Oxford (MA); *m* 1969, Elizabeth Mary, da of John Foster Crace (d 1960); 1 s (John b 1970); *Career* served WWII Maj Gordon Highlanders; Colonial Office 1947-57, dep high cmmr S Africa 1959-61; Br high cmmr: Sierra Leone 1961-63, Rhodesia 1963-65, Malaysia 1971-74, Canada 1974-78, ret; chm the ARELS Examination Tst, govr BBC 1978-85, memb Disasters Emergency Ctee; *Style*— Sir John Johnston, GCMG, KCVO; 5 Victoria Rd, Oxford OX2 7QF (☎ 0865 56927)

JOHNSTON, John Douglas Hartley; s of Dr John Johnston (d 1982), and Rhoda Margaret, *née* Hartley (d 1990); *b* 19 March 1935; *Educ* Manchester GS, Univ of Cambridge (MA, LLB, PhD), Harvard Law Sch (LLM); *Career* called to the Bar Lincoln's Inn 1963; princ asst slr Inland Revenue 1986- (legal asst 1968, sr legal asst 1971, asst slr 1976); sidesman Great St Mary's Church Cambridge; *Recreations* walking, gardening, listening to music; *Style*— J D H Johnston, Esq; Solicitor's Office, Inland Revenue, Somerset House, London, WC2, (☎ 071 438 7265, fax 071 438 6246)

JOHNSTON, Lt-Col Sir John Frederick Dame; GCVO (1987, KCVO 1981, CVO 1977, MVO 1971), MC (1945); s of Frederick Horace Johnston (d 1935), and Winifred Emily, *née* Dame (d 1983); *b* 24 Aug 1922; *Educ* Ampleforth; *m* 4 Nov 1949, Hon Elizabeth Rosemary, *qv*, da of 2 Baron Hardinge of Penshurst, GCB, GCVO, MC, PC (d 1960); 1 s (Christopher Michael b 1951), 1 da (Joanna Elizabeth b 1953); *Career* Grenadier Gds 1941-64 (cmd 1 Bn 1962-64); comptroller Lord Chamberlain's Office 1981-87 (asst comptroller 1964-81); pres King George's Pension Fund for Actors and Actresses; chm Combined Theatrical Charities Appeals Cncl; dir: Theatre Royal Windsor, Claridge's Hotel; pres Hearing Dogs for the Deaf; Freeman City of London 1985; recipient of 32 foreign orders and decorations; *Recreations* gundogs, golf; *Clubs* Boodle's, Pratt's, Swinley Forest Golf; *Style—* Lt-Col Sir John Johnston, GCVO, MC; Stone Hill, Newport, Dyfed; Studio Cottage, The Great Park, Windsor, Berks SL4 2HP

JOHNSTON, Capt John Richard Cox (Johnnie); CBE (1976); s of John Samuel Cox Johnston (d 1929), of Elm Bank, Worplesdon, nr Guilford, Surrey, and Florence, *née* Knight (d 1957); *b* 29 Aug 1923; *Educ* RNC Dartmouth; *m* 22 Jan 1949, Audrey Margaret, da of Gordon Johnston Humbert (d 1974), of Budleigh Salterton, Devon; 1 s (Colin b 5 March 1954), 1 da (Vivien b 31 Jan 1950); *Career* Midshipman Durban, Dorsetshire and King George V 1941-42, Sub-Lt 59 LCA Flotilla 1942-44, Lt flying trg 1944-49, qual as Air Weapons Offr 1949, Gp Air Weapons Offr Theseus and Glory Off Korea 1950-51, Lt Cdr Indefatigable 1951-53, Warrior (for H Bomb tests) 1956-57, Directorate of Air Warfare 1957-59, Cdr Ulster 1960-61, JSSC 1962, DSD RN Staff Coll 1963-64, Fleet Ops Offr to CinC HF 1964-66; Capt: Tartar 1967-68, MOD 1969-72, Osprey 1972-74, Bulwark 1974-76; chief exec Nat Smallbore Rifle Assoc 1977-80; vice chm S Dorset Cons Assoc; FRAeS, FBIM; *Recreations* fishing, shooting, gundog training; *Style—* Capt Johnnie Johnston, CBE, RN; Old Barn Cottage, Affpuddle, Dorchester, Dorset DT2 7HH (☎ 0305 848268)

JOHNSTON, Leslie; s of John Bruce Johnston (d 1935), of Hillside, Belfast, and Emma Belinda, *née* Atkinson (d 1933); *b* 15 Feb 1909; *Educ* Royal Belfast Academical Inst, Queen's Univ Belfast (BCom), Open Univ (BA); *m* 10 June 1938, Dorothy Jane, da of Capt Thomas Matthews Wright (d 1939); 2 da (Janet Bruce b 1939, Vivien Louise b 1943); *Career* md Ulster Bank Tst Co 1970-; cncllr Heath Ward S Kesteven DC 1977-87, hon treas and later vice chm NI Mental Health Assoc until 1975; OStJ; *Recreations* bridge, walking, gardening; *Clubs* Grantham Cons, Sleaford Golf, St John House; *Style—* Leslie Johnston, Esq; Laburnum Cottage, Frieston, Caythorpe, Grantham, Lincs NG32 3BY (☎ 0400 72563)

JOHNSTON, Mark Steven; s of Ronald Johnston, of Gartmore, by Stirling, Scotland, and Mary Woods, *née* Nicol; *b* 10 Oct 1959; *Educ* M'Laren HS Calander Stirlingshire, Univ of Glasgow; *m* 8 June 1985, Deirdre Munro, da of Dr Duncan Ferguson, of 14 Cromarty Cres, Bearsden, Glasgow; *Career* veterinary practice 1983-86; race horse trainer; trainer's license 1987; horses trained incl: Hinari Televideo, Craft Express, Lifewatch Vision; races won incl: Portland Handicap 1989, Cock of the N Stakes 1989, William Hill Sprint Handicap Ascot 1989; MRCVS 1983; *Style—* Mark Johnston, Esq; Kingsley House, Middleham, Leyburn, N Yorks (☎ 0969 22237, fax 0969 22484, car 0836 748820)

JOHNSTON, Lt-Gen Sir Maurice Robert; KCB (1981), OBE (1971), DL (1990); s of Brig Allen Leigh Johnston, OBE; *b* 27 Oct 1929; *Educ* Wellington, RMA Sandhurst; *m* 1960, Belinda Sladen; 1 s, 1 da; *Career* cmmnd RA 1949, transferred Queen's Bays 1954, Mil Asst to CGS 1968-71, CO 1 Queen's Dragoon Gds 1971-73, Cdr 20 Armd Bde 1973-75, Brig Gen Staff HQ UK Land Forces 1977-78, Sr Directing Staff RCDS 1979-80, Asst CGS 1980, Dep Chief Def Staff 1981-83; ret 1984; co dir; chm Secondary Resources plc 1988-; *Style—* Lt-Gen Sir Maurice Johnston, KCB, OBE, DL; Ivy House, Worton, Devizes, Wilts (☎ 0380 723727)

JOHNSTON, Richard Arthur; s of Arthur Robert Court Johnston, of Beaumont, Carlisle, Cumbria, and Sylvia Fay, *née* Lightfoot; *b* 10 April 1955; *Educ* St Bees Sch Cumbria, Ealing Tech Coll; *m* 1 April 1989, Julia Mary, da of Anthony John Harvey, of Birmingham; 1 s (William Richard b 14 March 1990); *Career* theatre dir Birmingham Hippodrome Theatre 1980-88, chief exec Contemporary Dance Tst 1988-90; dep chm and chief exec Stoll Moss Theatres Ltd 1990-; *Recreations* environment, sport, theatre; *Style—* Richard Johnston, Esq; 14 Dagmar Terrace Islington London N1 2BN (☎ 071 226 3279); Stoll Moss Theatres Ltd, 21 Soho Square, London W1V 5ED (☎ 071 437 2274)

JOHNSTON, Sir (David) Russell; MP (Lib Dem) Inverness 1964-83, Nairn and Lochaber 1983-; s of David Knox Johnston (d 1972); *b* 1932; *Educ* Portree HS Isle of Skye, Univ of Edinburgh (MA); *m* 1967, Joan Graham, da of Donald Menzies; 3 s; *Career* Nat Serv cmmnd Intelligence Corps 1958; history teacher Liberton Secdy Sch Edinburgh 1961-63; memb Exec Scottish Lib Pty 1961-, res asst Scottish Lib Pty 1963-64; Lib MP: Inverness 1964-83, Inverness Nairn and Lochaber 1983-88; Lib spokesman on foreign and cwlth affrs 1970-75 and 1979-85, Lib spokesman on Scotland 1970-73, 1975-83 and 1985-87, Alliance spokesman on Scotland and Euro Community Affrs 1987; Lib Dem spokesman; foreign and cwlth affrs 1988-89, Euro Community and East Euro affrs 1989-; first UK Lib memb of Euro Parl 1973-75 and 1976-79 (vice pres Political Ctee 1976-79), stood at first Euro direct election 1979 and 1989; pres Scottish Lib Dems 1988- (chm 1970-74, ldr 1974-88); dep ldr Lib Dems (1989); memb: Royal Cmmn on Scottish Local Govt 1966, Western Euro Union Assembly (Rep to Cncl of Europe 1984-86 and 1987); vice pres Euro Liberal Democractic and Reform Parties; winner of debating trophies: The Scotsman 1956 and 1957, The Observer Mace 1961; kt 1985; *Publications* : Highland Development, To be a Liberal, Scottish Liberal Party Conference Speeches 1971-78 and 1979-86; *Clubs* Scottish Liberal; *Style—* Sir Russell Johnston, MP; House of Commons, London SW1A 0AA

JOHNSTON, Dr Sheila; *Educ* Univ of Southampton (BA), Univ of London (PhD); *Career* film writer and critic The Independent 1986-; *Style—* Dr Sheila Johnston; The Independent, 40 City Rd, London EC1Y 2DB (☎ 071 253 1222, fax 071 956 1894)

JOHNSTON, Thomas; OBE (1982); s of John Watson Johnston (d 1970), of Skelmorlie; *b* 27 June 1927; *Educ* Royal Tech Coll, Glasgow Univ (BSc); *m* 24 Dec 1949, Gwendoline Jean, *née* Bird; 1 s, 3 da; *Career* md Barr & Stroud Ltd 1977-, chm Pilkington Electro-Optical Materials Ltd 1986 dir: Pilkington Electro-Optical Div 1979, W Bd Bank of Scotland 1984-, Scottish Amicable Life Assur Soc 1987-; memb: Scottish Industl Devpt Advsy Bd, Scottish Engrg Employers Assoc, Ct of Strathclyde Univ; FIProdE, FRSA; *Recreations* high hills, grand opera, cottage garden; *Clubs* Western; *Style—* Thomas Johnston, Esq, OBE; 43 Strathblane Rd, Milngavie, Glasgow G62 8HA; Barr & Stroud Ltd, Anniesland, Glasgow G13 1HZ (☎ 041 954 9601, fax 041 954 2380)

JOHNSTON, Sir Thomas Alexander; 14 Bt (NS 1626); only s of Sir Thomas Alexander Johnston, 13 Bt (d 1984); *b* 1 Feb 1956; *Heir* none; *Style—* Sir Thomas A Johnston, Bt; 350 West Delwood Drive, Mobile, Alabama 36606, USA

JOHNSTON, Dr Thomas Lothian (Tom); DL (City of Edinburgh 1987); s of Thompson Braidford Johnston (d 1981), and Janet Bell, *née* Lothian (d 1969); *b* 9 March 1927; *Educ* Hawick HS, Univ of Edinburgh (MA, PhD), Univ of Stockholm; *m* 20 July 1956, Joan Winifred, da of Ernest Chalmers Fahmy, FRCSE, FRCPE, FRCOG (d 1983), of Edinburgh; 2 s (David b 1961, Andrew b 1963), 3 da (Caroline b 1959, Christine b 1967, Katharine b 1967); *Career* Sub Lt RNVR 1944-47; lectr in political economy Univ of Edinburgh 1953-65; prof of economics Heriot-Watt Univ 1966-76, chm MSC Scot 1977-80, economic conslt to Sec of State for Scot 1977-81, princ and vice chllr Heriot-Watt Univ 1981-88 (now princ emeritus); arbitrator and mediator; memb: Scottish Milk Marketing Bd 1967-72, Scottish Telecommunications Bd 1977-81; dir: First Charlotte Assets Tst 1981-, Scot Life Assurance Co 1989-, Hodgson Martin Ltd 1989-; visiting academic: Univ of Illinois 1962-63, Queen's Univ Canada 1965, Int Inst of Labour Studies Geneva 1973, Western Australia Inst of Technol 1979; head of Inquiry into Water Strike 1983; Hon DUniv Edinburgh 1986, DEd, CNAA 1989, FEIS 1989, Hon LLD Univ of Glasgow 1989, Hon DUniv Heriot-Watt 1989; foreign memb Royal Swedish Acad of Engrg Sciences; FRSE 1979, CBIM 1983, FRSA 1983, FIPM 1985; Cdr Royal Swedish Order of the Polar Star 1985; *Recreations* walking, gardening; *Style—* Dr Tom Johnston, DL, FRSE; 14 Mansionhouse Rd, Edinburgh EH9 1TZ (☎ 031 667 1439)

JOHNSTON, William Bryce; s of William Bryce Johnston, ISO (d 1963), of Edinburgh, and Isabel Winifred Chester, *née* Highley (d 1953); *b* 16 Sept 1921; *Educ* George Watson's Coll Edinburgh, Edinburgh Univ (MA, BD); *m* 9 Oct 1947, Ruth Margaret, da of Rev James Arthur Cowley (d 1960), of Edinburgh; 1 s (Iain Arthur Bryce b 19 Dec 1950), 2 da (Fiona Margaret b 6 Nov 1952, Rosemary Swan (Mrs McCulloch) b 18 Feb 1958); *Career* Chaplain to the Forces 1945-49; minister: St Andrew's Church Bo'ness 1949-55, St George's Church Greenock 1955-64, Colinton Parish Church 1964-; Chaplain HM Prison Greenock 1959-64; convenor Gen Assembly Ctees: Church and Nation 1972-76, Inter-Church Relations 1979-81; moderator of the Gen Assembly 1980-81, Chaplain-in-Ordinary to HM The Queen in Scotland 1981-; chm Judicial Commn 1986-, visiting lectr in Social Ethics Heriot-Watt Univ 1966-87, tstee Scottish Nat War Memorial 1981-, memb Bdcasting Cncl for Scotland 1983-87; Hon DD Aberdeen Univ 1980, Hon DLitt Heriot-Watt Univ 1989; *Books* translation: Karl Barth, Dogmatics (1960), John Calvin: Epistle To The Hebrews (1963); Ethics and Defence (ed 1987); *Recreations* organ-playing, bowls; *Clubs* New (Edinburgh); *Style—* The Very Rev William Johnston; The Manse of Colinton, Edinburgh EH13 0JR (☎ 031 441 2315)

JOHNSTON, William James; s of Thomas Hamilton Johnston (d 1951), of Enniskillen, Co Fermanagh, and Mary Kathleen, *née* Bracken (d 1977); *b* 3 April 1919; *Educ* Portora Royal Sch Enniskillen Co Fermanagh; *m* 6 Dec 1943, Joan Elizabeth Nancye, da of Rev William John Young (d 1927), of Newtownbutler, Co Fermanagh; 2 da (Heather b 1945, Janet (Mrs Moore) b 1948); *Career* qualified CA 1942; dep sec Antrim CC 1944-68, dep town clerk Belfast Corpn 1968-73, town clerk and chief exec Belfast City Cncl 1973-79, sec Assoc of Local Authorities NI 1979-82; memb: NI Advsy Bd Abbey Nat Bldg Soc 1982-89, BBC NI Advsy Cncl 1965-69, Bd of Arts Cncl of NI 1974-80, Local Govt Staff Cmmn 1974-84, NI Tourist Bd 1980-85, NI Australian Bicentennial Ctee; chm: Public Serv Trg Cncl 1974-83, Nat House Bldg Cncl (NI) 1989-; FCA; *Recreations* golf, live theatre, travel; *Clubs* Royal Portrush Golf, Cushendall Golf, Malone Golf; *Style—* William Johnston, Esq; 47 Layde Rd, Cushendall, Ballymena, Co Antrim BT44 0NQ; Flat 4, 29 Windsor Ave, Belfast BT9 6EJ (☎ 02667 71 211, 0232 660 793)

JOHNSTON-JONES, David Ranald; s of Lt-Col Kenneth Charles Johnston-Jones, MBE, MC (d 1970), and Stella Margaret, *née* Sharvill (d 1988); *b* 14 Oct 1926; *Educ* Bedford Sch, New Coll Oxford (MA); *m* 24 April 1954, Millicent Elspeth, da of Reginald Douglas Gibbs (d 1987); 1 s (Nicholas b 1963), 3 da (Virginia b 1956, Vivienne b 1957, Valerie b 1960); *Career* Capt RM and Intelligence Corps 1945-48; active service in Palestine; civil asst WO 1951-58, serv in London, Egypt, Cyprus; sch master 1958-86; rector of Morrison's Acad (Crieff) 1974-78; headmaster of Merchant Taylor's Sch (Crosby) 1979-86; *Books* The Deathless Train, The Life and Work of R S Surtees (1974), The Cambridge Guide to Literature in English (contrib, 1988); *Recreations* writing, lecturing, C19 literature; *Style—* David R Johnston-Jones, Esq; 12 Ferry Path, Cambridge CB4 1HB (☎ 0223 358916)

JOHNSTON OF ROCKPORT, Baron (Life Peer UK 1987), of Caversham, Co Berks; Sir Charles Collier Johnston; TD; s of Capt Charles Moore Johnston (ka Battle of Somme 1916), and Muriel Florence Edmeston, *née* Mellon (d 1963); *b* 4 March 1915; *Educ* Tonbridge; *m* 1, 15 June 1939 (m dis 1979), Audrey Boyes, da of late Edgar Monk; 2 s (Hon Michael Charles b 20 Oct 1942, Hon Timothy Courtenay b 29 May 1945); m 2, 1 Sept 1981, Mrs Yvonne Shearman, da of late Reginald Marley; *Career* chm Standex International Ltd 1951-77 (formerly Roehlen-Martin Ltd, md 1948-76), engravers and engrs, of Cheshire; Bredbury, Cheshire; chm: Thames and Kennet Marina Ltd 1982-, James Burn International 1986- (dir 1983), Standex Hldgs Ltd 1986-, Macclesfield Constituency Cons Assoc 1961-65; hon treas NW Cons, memb Cons Bd of Finance 1965-71, chm NW Area Cons 1971-76, memb Exec Ctee Nat Union of Cons and Unionist Assocs 1965-88 (chm 1976-81), pres Nat Union of Cons and Unionist Assocs 1986-87, Nat chm Cons Friends of Israel 1983-86, memb Boyd Cmmn as official observers of elections held in Zimbabwe/Rhodesia April 1980; *Recreations* spectator sports, travelling, gardening; *Clubs* Royal Over-Seas League; *Style—* The Rt Hon the Lord Johnston of Rockport, TD; of Rockport, TD; House of Lords, London SW1

JOHNSTONE, Adam; s of Maj Richard Johnstone (d 1919), of Fulford Hall, Wythall, Worcs, and Florence Catherine May, *née* Harris (d 1957); *b* 28 Aug 1912; *Educ* Gresham's; *m* 1, 24 March 1946, Ella Mary (d 1971), da of Maj Godfrey Edmonds, of Kingsbridge, Devon; 2 da (Laurelie b 4 March 1947, Janet b 22 Sept 1949); m 2, 3 June 1972, Monica Katharine Mary, da of Wilfred Hodsoll; *Career* RASC 1939-47, Maj 1942 (POW Japan 1942-45); Kleinwort Son & Co and subsids 1947-54: jt md Fendrake Ltd, pres Drake America Corp USA; chm: Mark Cross USA, Sales Audits Ltd 1954-64; visiting prof of mktg INSEAD Fontainebleau France 1958-64, chief exec Motherwell Bridge Contracting & Trading Co Ltd 1964-67, dep chm Gallaway Mechanical Servs 1973-79, chm J Broadwood & Sons Ltd 1974-83; pres of appeal RAM, chm Broadwood Charitable Tst, pres PMA, memb Cons Assoc; Hon FRAM 1989; MInstM 1948, charter memb American Inst Mgmnt 1949; *Recreations* gardening, travel, photography, wine; *Clubs* Naval and Military, Wig and Pen, Ebury Court; *Style—* Adam Johnstone, Esq; Temple Wood, Capel, Surrey

JOHNSTONE, Air Vice-Marshal Alexander Vallance Riddell; CB (1966), DFC (1940), AE, DL (Glasgow); s of Alexander Lang Johnstone (d 1950), and Daisy, *née* Riddell; *b* 2 June 1916; *Educ* Kelvinside Acad; *m* 1940, Margaret, da of James T Croll, of Glasgow; 1 s, 2 da; *Career* RAF 1935-68; fndr and first CAS Royal Malayan Air Force 1957-58, dir of personnel Air Miny 1962-64, Cdr Air Forces Borneo 1964-65, Air Offr Scotland 1965-68, Cdr Air N Atlantic 1965-68; vice chm Cncl TA and VRA 1969-79, chm Climax Cleaning Co Ltd 1980-; *Recreations* golf; *Clubs* RAF; *Style—* Air Vice-Marshal Alexander Johnstone, CB, DFC, AE, DL; 36 Castle Brooks, Framlingham, Woodbridge, Suffolk IP13 (☎ 0728 723770)

JOHNSTONE, David William Robert; s of William Johnstone (d 1948), and Elizabeth Hankin, *née* Hedley; *b* 20 Nov 1936; *Educ* St Bees Sch, Clare Coll Cambridge (MA); *m* 1962, Penelope Susan, da of Dr David Robert Sloan, of Blagdon, Bristol; 3 da (Penelope Harriet b 1964, Jessica Lucy b 1966, Bryony Aileen b 1969); *Career* CA; ptnr Thomson McLintock & Co 1969; dir: JT Group Ltd 1979-, TSW TV South West plc 1980-, Praxis plc 1989-; chm Dartington & Co Ltd 1990 (fndr 1979); FCA; *Recreations* gardening, walking, theatre, music; *Style—* David Johnstone, Esq; Lake House, Grib Lane, Blagdon, Bristol BS18 6SA (☎ 0761 62533); Dartington & Company, 70 Prince St, Bristol BS1 4QD (☎ 0272 213206)

JOHNSTONE, Hon Francis Patrick Harcourt (Vanden-Bempde-); s and h of 5 Baron Derwent, LVO, *qv*; *b* 23 Sept 1965; *Educ* Eton, Edinburgh Univ; *m* 6 Oct 1990, Cressida E, o da of Christopher Bourke, of 61 Kingsmead Road, London SW2; *Style—* The Hon Francis Vanden-Bempde-Johnstone; Hackness Hall, Scarborough, N Yorks

JOHNSTONE, Sir Frederic Allan George; 10 Bt (NS 1700), of Westerhall, Dumfriesshire; s of Sir George Frederic Thomas Tankerville Johnstone, 9 Bt (d 1952); *b* 23 Feb 1906; *Educ* Imperial Service Coll; *m* 1, 1933 (m dis 1941), Gladys Hands; m 2, 1946, Doris, da of late W L Shortridge, of Blackheath, SE; 2 s; *Heir* s, (George) Richard Douglas Johnstone; *Style—* Sir Frederic Johnstone, Bt; Urry's Cottage, Freshwater, Isle of Wight

JOHNSTONE, Ian Temple; s of John Johnstone (d 1976), of Edinburgh, and Kate, *née* Ramply (d 1989); *b* 25 Feb 1923; *Educ* Edinburgh Acad, Corpus Christi Coll Cambridge (MA), Univ of Edinburgh (LLB); *m* 29 March 1958, Frances Helen, da of Campbell Ferenbach, of Edinburgh; 3 da (Gillian b 1959, Alison b 1961, Sara b 1964); *Career* cmmnd 79 Field Regt RA 1943, mountain artillery course India 1945, transfd Movement Control HQ Burma Cmd, appointed Staff Capt Q Movements (Air) 1946-47; ptnr Baillie Gifford Writers to the Signet Edinburgh 1950; dir: Friends Provident Life Office 1964, Inch Kenneth Kajang Rubber plc 1970; chm Baillie Gifford Shin Nippon plc 1985; sr ptnr Biggart Baillie and Gifford WS slrs Edinburgh and Glasgow 1985-88, memb Cncl Lawn Tennis Assoc 1967-77, pres Scottish Lawn Tennis Assoc 1968-70, treas Soc of Writers to HM Signet 1974-84, govr St Margaret's Sch Edinburgh 1978-91 (chm 1981-91), gen cmmr of Income Tax, memb Cncl Edinburgh Festival Soc 1989; *Recreations* listening to music, watching sport, gentle hill walking, photography, world travel, 1930s films; *Clubs* New Edinburgh; *Style—* Ian Johnstone, Esq; 45 Moray Place, Edinburgh EH3 6BQ (☎ 031 225 2021)

JOHNSTONE, (John) Raymond; CBE (1988); o s of Capt Henry James Johnstone, RN, of The Myretoun, Menstrie, Clackmannanshire (d 1947, fourth in descent from John Johnstone, who commanded the artillery at the Battle of Plassey, to which victory he substantially contributed, and who was s of Sir James Johnstone, 3 Bt), and Margaret Alison McIntyre (d 1984); *b* 27 Oct 1929; *Educ* Eton, Trinity Coll Cambridge (BA); *m* 1979, Susan Sara, da of Christopher Gerald Gore (d 1955), widow of Peter Quixano Henriques (d 1974), and of Basil Ziani de Ferranti; 5 step s , 2 step da; *Career* chm: Murray Johnstone Ltd 1984- (md 1968-88), Dominion Insurance Ltd 1978, Scottish Amicable Life Assurance Soc 1983-85 (dir 1971-), Scottish Fin Enterprise 1989-, Glasgow Cultural Enterprise Ltd, Summit Group plc 1989-, Forestry Commission 1989-, Yamaichi-Murray Johnstone Ltd, Landel Insurance Holdings; hon pres Scottish Opera (chm 1983-86), memb, Scottish Econ Cncl; *Recreations* fishing, music, farming; *Clubs* Western (Glasgow); *Style—* Raymond Johnstone, Esq; Wards, Gartocharn, Dunbartonshire G83 8SB (☎ 038 983 321, fax 038 883 493)

JOHNSTONE, (George) Richard Douglas; s and h of Sir Frederic Johnstone, 10 Bt; *b* 21 Aug 1948; *Educ* Magdalen Coll Oxford; *m* 1976, Gwyneth, da of Arthur Bailey, of Hastings; 1 s (Frederic Robert Arthur b 1981), 1 da (Caroline b 1983); *Career* dir DBI Assocs Ltd, mgmnt conslts; *Style—* Richard Johnstone, Esq

JOHNSTONE, Prof William; s of Rev Thomas Kennedy Johnstone (d 1981), of Ashburn, New Galloway, and Evelyn Hope, *née* Murray (d 1987); *b* 6 May 1936; *Educ* Hamilton Acad, Univ of Glasgow (MA, BD), Univ of Marburg; *m* 25 June 1964, Elizabeth Mary, da of Thomas Ward, of Oswaldtwistle, Lancs; 1 s (Adam Ward b 14 Feb 1969), 1 da (Anna b 15 Nov 1970); *Career* prof of Hebrew and Semitic languages Univ of Aberdeen 1980- (lectr 1962-72, sr lectr 1972-80, dean Faculty of Divinity 1984-87); memb Soc Old Testament Study (pres 1990); *Recreations* gardening, travel; *Style—* Prof William Johnstone; 37 Rubislaw Den South, Aberdeen AB2 6BD; King's Coll, University of Aberdeen, Old Aberdeen, AB9 2UB (☎ 0224 272378)

JOHNSTONE, William Neill (Bill); s of Harry McCall Johnstone (d 1985), of Forfar, and Ethel Mary Neill; *b* 16 May 1938; *Educ* Forfar Acad, Edinburgh Acad, Univ of Edinburgh, Scottish Coll of Textiles, RCA; *m* (m dis), 2 da (Catriona Mhairi b 14 Dec 1964, Lilian MacDonald b 14 March 1966); *Career* designer then design dir R G Neill & Son 1961-70, md and design dir Neill of Langholm 1970-85, design dir Illingworth Morris Group and co-ordinator trg programme 1982-85, fndr: Neill Johnstone Ltd 1986 (specialises in providing seasonal collections for int apparel fabric markets), Fabric Design Consultants International Ltd 1989-; IWS design conslt 1978-; memb C B W T Steering Ctee 1981-85 (chm 1982-85); indust on selection panel S D A/S W I Designer Graduate Attachment Scheme; selected to be a Royal Designer 1989; *Recreations* climbing, hill walking, collecting inuit carvings; *Style—* Bill Johnstone, Esq; Neill Johnstone Ltd, William St, Langholm, Scotland DG13 OBN (☎ 03873 81122, fax 03873 81106)

JOICEY, Hon Andrew Hugh; yr s of 4 Baron Joicey, *qv*; *b* 24 Dec 1955; *Educ* Eton, ChCh Oxford; *Career* farmer; *Style—* The Hon Andrew Joicey

JOICEY, Hon James Michael; s and h of 4 Baron Joicey; *b* 28 June 1953; *Educ* Eton, ChCh Oxford; *m* 16 June 1984, Harriet, da of Rev William Thompson, of Oxnam Manse, Jedburgh, Roxburghshire; 1 s (William James b 21 May 1990), 1 da (Hannah Elisabeth b 25 June 1988); *Style—* The Hon James Joicey; East Flodden Farmhouse, Milfield, Wooler, Northumberland NE71 6JF

JOICEY, 4 Baron (UK 1906); Sir Michael Edward Joicey; 4 Bt (UK 1893), DL (Northumberland 1985); s of 3 Baron Joicey (d 1966), and Lady Joan Lambton, da of 4 Earl of Durham; through his mother Lord Joicey is 1 cous to Lord Home of the Hirsel and (6) Duke of Sutherland; *b* 28 Feb 1925; *Educ* Eton, ChCh Oxford; *m* 1952, Elisabeth, da of Lt-Col Hon Ian Melville, TD, yst s of 11 Earl of Leven and Melville; 2 s, 1 da; *Heir* s, Hon James Joicey; *Career* served WWII Capt Coldstream Gds; MFH The N Northumberland 1954-74; *Recreations* shooting, stalking, fishing; *Clubs* Kennel, Lansdowne, N Counties (Newcastle); *Style—* The Rt Hon the Lord Joicey, DL; Etal Manor, Berwick-on-Tweed TD15 2PU (☎ 089082 205); Loch Choire Lodge, Kinbrace, Sutherland KW11 6UD (☎ 043 13 222)

JOICEY-CECIL, James David Edward; s of late Edward Wilfrid George Joicey-Cecil (d 1985), gs of 3 Marquess of Exeter, and Rosemary Lusia, *née* Bowes-Lyon (d 1989), gd of 14 Earl of Strathmore and Kinghorne, and of 5 Earl of Portarlington; *b* 24 Sept 1946; *Educ* Eton; *m* 1975, Jane Susanna Brydon, da of Capt P W B Adeley (d 1968); 2 da (Katherine Mary b 1978, Susanna Maud b 1981); *Career* memb Stock Exchange 1978-, ptnr James Capel & Co 1978-; FCA; *Clubs* Annabel's, City; *Style—* James Joicey-Cecil, Esq; 49 Clapham Common South Side, London SW4 9BX (☎ 071 622 0576)

JOINER, Dr Charles Louis; s of Maj C A Joiner (d 1952), of Whyteleafe, Surrey, and Kathleen, *née* O'Malley (d 1978); *b* 21 Jan 1923; *Educ* Tonbridge, Guy's Hosp Med Sch (MB BS,MD); *m* 9 Dec 1947, Helen Mary, da of Basil Reginald Lovell, MBE (d 1984), of Littleton, Hants; 1 s (David b 1961), 1 da (Sarah b 1958); *Career* RAMC 1946-48; physician to Guy's Hosp, Bromley Gp of Hosps 1959-88, hon physician to the Army 1974-88, chief conslt physician Sun Alliance Insurance Co; FRCP, FRSM; *Books* Short Text Book of Medicine (1969); *Recreations* shooting, English lit and history, antique porcelain; *Clubs* Athenaeum; *Style—* Dr Charles Joiner; Ashton, Mead Rd, Chislehurst, Kent (☎ 081 467 4060); Suite 302, Emblem House, 27 Tooley St, London SE1 (☎ 071 407 0292)

JOLL, Christopher Andrew; s of Sqdn Ldr Ian K S Joll, DFC, AE, RAuxAf (d 1978), and Eileen Mary Sassoon Sykes; *b* 16 Oct 1948; *Educ* Oundle, RMA Sandhurst (Armorers and Braziers Co young offrs prize), Mansfield Coll Oxford (MA); *Career* served Br Army: joined RMA Sandhurst 1966, cmmnd 2 Lieut Life Gds 1968, served NI 1969, 1970, 1972 and 1974 ret 1976; gen mangr Michael Peters & Ptnrs Ltd 1978 (joined 1977), dir corp affrs United Scientific Holdings 1988 (joined 1978), chief exec Charles Barker City Ltd 1989 (dir 1988), dir Charles Barker Ltd 1989; memb: Queen's Silver Jubilee Appeal (chm Ideas Ctee) 1976-77, Mansfield Coll Oxford Appeal 1978, Mktg Ctee ENO 1986-89; co prodr Jose Carreras And Friends concert in aid of Jose Carreras Int Leukaemia Fndn 1990-91; MIPR; *Recreations* field sports, bridge, charity fund raising and sponsorship; *Clubs* Garrick; *Style—* Christopher Joll, Esq

JOLL, Prof James Bysse; s of Lt-Col Harry Haweis Joll, DSO, MC (d 1950), and Alice Muriel, *née* Edwards (d 1955); *b* 21 June 1918; *Educ* Winchester, Univ of Bordeaux New Coll Oxford (MA); *Career* served WWII The Devonshire Regt and SOE 1939-45; fell and tutor in politics New Coll Oxford 1946-51, fell and sub warden St Antony's Coll Oxford 1951-67, emeritus prof of int history Univ of London 1981- (Stevenson prof 1967-81); visiting memb Inst for Advanced Study Princeton 1954 and 1971; visiting prof of history: Stanford Univ Calif 1958, Univ of Sydney 1979, Univ of Iowa 1980; visiting lectr in history Harvard Univ 1962, Benjamin Meaker visiting prof Univ of Bristol 1985; hon prof of history Univ of Warwick 1981-87, hon fell LSE 1985; Hon DLitt Warwick 1988; FBA 1977; *Books* The Second International 1889-1914 (1955, 2 edn, 1974), Intellectuals in Politics (1960), The Anarchists (1964, 2 edn, 1979), Europe since 1870 (1973, 4 edn, 1990), Gramsci (1977), The Orgins of the First World War (1984); *Style—* Prof James Joll; 24 Ashchurch Park Villas, London W12 9SP (☎ 081 749 5221)

JOLL, Hon Mrs (Katharine (Kate) Mary); *née* Howard; 2 da (by 1 m) of 4 Baron Strathcona and Mount Royal; *b* 11 Sept 1956; *Educ* Sherborne, Clare Coll Cambridge; *m* 1, 17 Aug 1976 (m dis 1981), Gavin Michael Strachan, of Edinburgh; m 2, 30 March 1982 (having resumed her maiden name), William Evelyn Hinton Joll, s of Evelyn Joll, of Pelham Place, S Kensington; 1 s (Harry b 30 Nov 1983), 2 da (Flora b 17 Aug 1985, Hannah b 8 June 1988); *Recreations* cooking, reading; *Style—* The Hon Mrs Joll; 17 Durand Gdns, London SW9 0PS (☎ 071 582 7280)

JOLLES, Dr Alicia (Mrs M G G Herbert); da of Dr Benjamin Jolles (d 1985), of Northampton, and Miriam, *née* Blake; *b* 24 Dec 1947; *Educ* Northampton HS, Westfield Coll London, (BA, PhD); *m* 10 June 1981, Martin Geoffrey Greenham Herbert, s of Geoffrey Basil Herbert (d 1974); 1 s (Edward b 21 Jan 1987), 2 da (Susannah b 20 Oct 1982, Katharine b 8 Aug 1985); *Career* Coward Chance: slr 1977, ptnr 1981 (known as Clifford Chance 1987-); Freeman City of London, memb: Law Soc, City of London Slrs Co; *Recreations* family, sailing, gardening; *Style—* Dr Alicia Jolles; 23 Alwyne Rd, London N1 2HN (☎ 071 226 8159); The Gables, East Bergholt, Suffolk; Clifford Chance, 19 New Bridge St, London EC4V 6BY (☎ 071 353 0211, fax 071 489 0046, telex 887847)

JOLLES, Bernard Nathan; s of Dr Benjamin Jolles (d 1985), of Northampton, and Miriam, *née* Blake; *b* 23 Aug 1949; *Educ* Bedford Sch, St John's Coll Cambridge (MA), Balliol Coll Oxford (MSc), London Business Sch (MSc); *m* 1 Dec 1986, Pamela, da of Horace Knight (d 1973), of Hastings; 1 da (Antonia Sarah b 21 Jan 1989); *Career* merchant banker; dir: Samuel Montagu & Co Ltd 1982-87, Henry Ansbacher & Co Ltd 1988-; *Recreations* flying, golf, skiing, tennis; *Style—* Bernard N Jolles, Esq; 110 Regent's Park Rd, London NW1 8UG (☎ 071 722 5522)

JOLLIFFE, Sir Anthony Stuart; GBE (1982), JP (City of London); s of Robert Jolliffe; *b* 12 Aug 1938; *Educ* Porchester Sch Bournemouth; *m* 1962, Anne Elizabeth Phillips; 1 s, 2 da; *Career* Lord Mayor London 1982-83 (Sheriff 1980-81, alderman Candlewick Ward 1975-, hon treas Sheriff's & Recorder's Fund, pres Candlewick Ward Club); memb: Governing Body Utd Wards Club, Guild of Freemen, Court Painter Stainers' Co, Court Chartered Accountants in England & Wales, Wheelwrights' Co, Cncl Operation Drake Fellowship, Heritage of London Tst Special Ctee, Variety Club of GB; tstee Police Fndn; vice chm St John Ambulance Assoc City of London Branch, OStJ 1981; vice pres European League for Economic Cooperation, hon treas Britain in Europe Residual Fund; chartered accountant 1964- and sr ptnr Jolliffe Cork & Co, also int chm Jolliffe Cork Ingram; dir: E Fogarty & Co, SAS Catering, Nikko Trading UK, Capital for Industry, Erskine House Investments, Marlborough Property Hldgs (Devpts) & subsids, Albany Commercial & Industl Devpts, Gantry Railing, Specialweld; FCA, FRSA, ATII; *Recreations* classic cars, theatre, sailing (yacht 'Kleen Sweeps'); *Clubs* City Livery, Royal London Yacht, Thames Motor Yacht; *Style—* Sir Anthony Jolliffe, GBE, JP; c/o Thornton Baker & Co, Fairfax House, Fulwood Place, London WC1; Oakwood, 2 Park Close, Batchworth Heath, Rickmansworth, Herts (☎ 092 74 29877); c/o Jolliffe Cork & Co, Elvian House, 18/20 St Andrew St, London EC4A 3AE

JOLLIFFE, John Anthony; s of Donald Norman Jolliffe (d 1967), of Dover, Kent and Edith Constance Mary, *née* Lovegrove; *b* 1 Aug 1937; *Educ* Dover Coll; *m* 1, 5 June 1965 (m dis 1983), Jacqueline Mary, *née* Smith, 1 s (Jeffrey b 1968), 1 da (Jenny b 1966); m 2, 3 Aug 1984 (m dis 1986), Irmgard Elizabeth, *née* Melville; 1 s (Andrew b 1985); m 3, 11 Aug 1990, Dorothy Jane, *née* Sane; *Career* Nat Serv RAF 1955-57; ptnr R Watson & Sons 1967- (joined 1957); examiner in pension funds Inst of Actuaries 1970-75 (tutor 1965-70), memb UK Steering Ctee for Local Govt Superannuation 1975-, chm ACA Local Govt Superannuation Ctee 1975-, treas Assoc Consulting Actuaries 1980-84, dir London Aerial Tours Ltd 1983-, memb Cncl Nat Assoc of Pension Funds 1983-; chm: NAPF Int Ctee 1986-88, Euro Fedn of Retirement Provison 1988-, pres Sarl Joke Berek France 1990-; Freeman City of London, Liveryman Worshipful Co of Actuaries; FIA 1964, ASA (USA) 1971, FPMI 1977; *Recreations* flying, tennis, travel; *Clubs* Reform; *Style—* John Jolliffe, Esq; Sunhurst, Clay Lane, South Nutfield, Redhill, Surrey, RH1 4EG (☎ 0737 762441); Watson House, London Rd, Reigate, Surrey RH2 9PQ (☎ 0737 241144, fax 0737 241496, telex 946070)

JOLLIFFE, Hon John Hedworth; s of 4 Baron Hylton (d 1967), and Perdita, da of Raymond Asquith, e s of 1 Earl of Oxford and Asquith; *b* 1935; *Educ* Eton, Ch Ch Oxford (MA); *m* 1965, Hon Victoria Elizabeth Catherine, *née* Eden, da of 7 Baron Henley (d 1977); *Career* dir: Constable Publishers 1967-75, Bain Clarkson (insurance brokers) 1979-; Kt SMO Malta; *Books* Raymond Asquith, Life and Letters; *Clubs* Brooks's, Beefsteak, Pratt's, Polish Hearth; *Style—* The Hon John Jolliffe; Church House, Chesterblade, Shepton Mallet, Somerset BA4 4QX, (☎ 0749 88413)

JOLLIFFE, Robert St John; s of Robert Jolliffe, of Firs Lodge, Troutstream Way, Loudwater, Rickmansworth, Herts, and Vi Dorothea, *née* Crumbleholme; *b* 26 June 1943; *Educ* Watford GS; *m* 12 July 1968, Sarah Anne, da of Maj W N Spraggs (d 1988), of 16 Gatehill Rd, Northwood, Middx; 2 s (James b 1973, Charles b 1976); *Career* CA; ptnr: Fryer Whitehill (resigned 1975), Jolliffe Cork & Co 1975-82, Grant Thornton (resigned 1988); gp fin dir: Automagic Hldgs plc 1988-, non-exec dir CP Carpets (Kidderminster) Ltd 1988; pres Bishopsgate Ward Club 1988-89; Freeman City of London 1969, Liveryman Worshipful Co of Painter-Stainers 1969; FCA 1979; *Recreations* golf, music, sailing; *Clubs* Moor Park Golf, Edgbaston Priory Birmingham, Royal Soc of St George, IOD; *Style—* Robert Jolliffe, Esq; Cobblers, Rooks Hill, Loudwater, Rickmansworth, Herts WD3 4HZ (☎ 0923 771 834); AM House,

Coldharbour Lane, Harpenden, Herts (☎ 0582 460 960, fax 05827 64547, car 0860 318 662)

JOLLIFFE, Hon William Henry Martin; s and h of 5 Baron Hylton, DL; *b* 1 April 1967; *Educ* Ampleforth, Univ of York, RAC Cirencester; *Style—* The Hon William Jolliffe; Ammerdown House, Radstock, Bath, Somerset BA3 5SH (☎ 0761 32227)

JOLLY, Lt Cdr Edward John; s of Thomas Alfred Jolly, of Stubbington, and Kate Aline Mary, *née* Attle; *b* 11 March 1941; *Educ* Glendale GS London, Loughborough Univ (MSc); *m* 1, 18 Sept 1965, Sally Russ; 1 s (Leslie James b 1966); m 2, 3 May 1986, Patricia Elizabeth Jolly; *Career* entered Mil Serv 1957, trained in med laboratory sci, cmmnd 1970, RNC Greenwich (trained in radiological protection for appts in nuclear submarine support), Inst of Naval Medicine Alverstoke (submarine environmental res), RN Staff Coll 1981, MOD 1981-85, ret; safety and security mangr The Stock Exchange 1985-; *Recreations* walking, badminton; *Style—* Lt Cdr Edward Jolly; 164 Teg Down Meads, Winchester, Hants (☎ 0962 65583); The Stock Exchange, London EC2N 1HP (☎ 071 588 2355)

JOLLY, Michael Gordon; *b* 21 Sept 1952; *Career* exec dir Madame Tussaud's and The London Planetarium 1987-; *Style—* Michael Jolly, Esq; The Tussauds Group Limited, York Court, Allsop Place, London NW1 5LR (☎ 071 935 686, fax 071 465 0864)

JOLLY, Peter Stanley; s of Stanley Kenyon Jolly, and Gertrude Ethel May, *née* Scott (d 1977); *b* 11 Nov 1941; *Educ* Fairfax HS, Coll of Technol Southend; *m* 9 Sept 1967, Barbara Olive, da of William Arthur Warren (d 1945); 3 s (Martin Peter b 1969, Adrian Stanley b 1978, Christopher William b 1984); *Career* Spicer & Pegler (now Spicer & Oppenheim) 1966-68; Consolidated Gold Fields Gp: mgmnt accountant 1968, chief accountant 1977, gp internal auditor and admin mangr 1980, operations fin gp exec 1986, fin dir CGF Euro Sales Ltd 1987-89; conslt Hanson Gp 1989-90, chief exec designate Enterprises Devpt & Trg Ltd 1989-90, gp internal review exec Smith & Nephew plc 1990-; memb: Scout Movement 1983-85, Info Technol Ctee Inst CA; FCA 1966, ATII 1966; *Recreations* scouting (Queen Scout), swimming, tennis, genealogy; *Clubs* Scout Movement, IOD; *Style—* Peter Jolly, Esq; 167 Hadleigh Rd, Leigh-on-Sea, Essex SS9 2LR (☎ 0702 76912)

JOLLY, (Arthur) Richard; s of late Arthur Jolly, and Flora Doris, *née* Leaver; *b* 30 June 1934; *Educ* Brighton Coll, Magdalene Coll Cambridge (BA, MA), Yale Univ (MA, PhD); *m* 1963, Alison Bishop; 2s, 2da; *Career* community devpt offr Baringo Dist Kenya 1957-59, res fell E Africa Inst of Social Res Makerere Coll Uganda 1963-64, res offr Dept of Applied Econs Univ of Cambridge 1964-68 (seconded as advsr on manpower Govt of Zambia 1964-66), fell Inst of Devpt of Studies 1968 (dir 1972-81), professional fell Univ of Sussex 1971, advsr on manpower aid ODM 1968, sr economist Miny of Devpt and Fin Zambia 1970, advsr Parly Select Ctee on Overseas Aid and Devpt 1974-75, ILO advsr on planning Madagascar 1975-, memb Triennial Revue Gp Cwlth Fund for Tech Co-operation 1975-76; memb: UK Cncl on Int Devpt 1974-78, UN Ctee for Devpt Planning 1978-81, dep exec dir UNICEF NY 1982-; special conslt in N-S Issues to Sec Gen OECD 1978, sometime memb and chief of ILO and UN Missions and conslt to various govts and int orgns, sec Br Alpine Hannibal Expedition 1959; memb: Founding Ctee Euro Assoc of Devpt Insts 1972-75, Governing Cncl 1976-85, N-S Round Table 1976- (vice pres 1982-85, chm 1988-), Editorial Bd World Devpt 1973-, master Worshipful Co of Curriers 1977-78; Hon DLitt Univ of E Anglia 1988 Cuba: the economic and social revolution (jtly, 1964), Planning Education for African Development (1969), Redistribution with Growth (jtly, 1974), The Impact of World Recession on Children (ed jtly, 1984), The Poverty of Progress (contrib, 1982), author various articles in professional jls; *Recreations* billiards, crowuet, nearly missing trains and planes; *Style—* Richard Jolly, Esq; Institute of Development Studies, University of Sussex, Brighton, Sussex BN1 9RE (☎ 0273 606261); Unicef, Unicef House, 3 United Nations Plaza, NY 10017, USA (☎ 212 326 7017)

JOLLY, Air Cdre Robert Malcolm; CBE (1969); s of Robert Imrie Jolly (d 1940), and Ethel Thompson, *née* Elliott (d 1967); *b* 4 Aug 1920; *Educ* Skerry's Coll Newcastle; *m* 1946, Josette Jacqueline, da of Gabrielle Baindeky (d 1934); *Career* served in RAF 1940-75; Malta 1941-1945 and 1946-49, Egypt 1945, Iraq 1945-1946, dir Personnel Servs RAF 1970-75, ret as Air Cdre; md Leonard Griffiths and Assocs 1975-77, vice pres MWS Consultants Inc 1978-80, computer advsr to Cyprus Govt 1981; gen mangr & dir of Diebold Research Program 1984-85; *Recreations* boating, gardening, DIY; *Clubs* RAF; *Style—* Air Cdre Robert Jolly, CBE; Villa Gray Golf, Trig Galata, High Ridge, St Andrews, Malta SC (☎ 010 356 333083)

JOLOWICZ, Prof John Anthony (Tony); s of Prof Herbert Felix Jolowicz (d 1954), of London and Oxford, and Ruby Victoria, *née* Wagner (d 1963); *b* 11 April 1926; *Educ* Oundle, Trinity Coll Cambridge (MA); *m* 8 Aug 1957, Poppy, da of Norman Stanley; 1 s (Nathaniel Herbert b 20 July 1963), 2 da (Kate (Mrs Little) b 4 May 1959, Sophie b 26 June 1961); *Career* Lt RASC 1944-48; called to the Bar 1952, master of the bench Gray's Inn 1978; Univ of Cambridge: asst lectr 1955, lectr 1959, reader 1972, prof of comparative law 1976-, chm faculty of law 1984-86, (fell Trinity Coll 1952-); prof associè Univ de Paris II 1976-, Lionel Cohen lectr Univ of Jerusalem 1983; pres SPTL 1986-87, ed of various law jls and author of various legal works; HonD Universidad Nacional Autónoma de México 1985; *Recreations* reading, music, travel; *Clubs* Leander, RAC; *Style—* Prof J A Jolowicz; West Green House, Barrington, Cambridge CB2 5SA (☎ 0223 870 495); La Truffière, 47120 St Jean-de-Duras, France; Trinity College, Cambridge CB2 1TQ (☎ 0223 338 400, 0223 338 461, fax 0223 338 564)

JOLY, Hon Mrs (Diana Olive); *née* Newall; da of 1 Baron Newall, GCB, OM, GCMG, CBE, AM (d 1963); *b* 1927; *m* 1956 (m dis 1967), John Leonard Joly; 1 da (Harriet Diana b 1960); *Style—* The Hon Mrs Joly; Tower House, 8 Reybridge, Lacock, Chippenham, Wilts

JOLY DE LOTBINIERE, Lt-Col Sir Edmond; s of Brig-Gen Henri Gustave Joly de Lotbinière, DSO, JP (descended from Michel, Marquis de Lotbinière, sole French subject of Canadian birth to be created a Marquis, thus honoured by Louis XVI in 1784), and Mildred, da of Charles Seymour Grenfell (first cous of Field Marshal 1 Baron Grenfell, GCB, GCMG, PC); *b* 17 March 1903; *Educ* Eton, RMA Woolwich; *m* 1, 1928 (m dis 1937), Hon Elizabeth Jolliffe (da of 3 Baron Hylton); 2 s (Thomas and Michael, *qqv*); m 2, 1937, Helen (d 1953), da of Dr Hartley Ferrar, of NZ; m 3, 1954, as her 2 husb, Evelyn Adelaide (b 1904, d 1985), er da of Nigel Dawnay, s of Hon William Dawnay, JP, DL, 6 s of 7 Viscount Downe, widow of Lt-Col James Innes, DSO (*see* Hall, Sir John Bernard, 3 Bt); *Career* cmmnd RE 1921, ret 1928; RARO 1928-45, served Abyssinia, E Africa (despatches), Lt-Col 1943; pres Bury St Edmunds Conservative Assoc 1972-79 (chm 1953-72), chm and md building material companies; chm Eastern Provincial Area Cons Assoc 1961-65 (pres 1969-72); kt 1964; *Clubs* Naval and Military; *Style—* Lt-Col Sir Edmond Joly de Lotbinière; Horringer Manor, Bury St Edmunds, Suffolk (☎ 028 488 208); Lignacite (Brandon) Ltd, Victoria Works, Brandon, Suffolk (☎ 0842 810 678)

JOLY DE LOTBINIERE, Michael Edmond; 2 s of Lt-Col Sir Edmond Joly de Lotbinière, *qv*, by his 1 w, Hon Elizabeth Jolliffe, da of 3 Baron Hylton; *b* 3 Feb 1932; *Educ* Eton, Downing Cambridge; *m* 1956, Angela, yr da of Col Eugene St John Birnie, of Belgravia, by Lady Kathleen Courtenay, 3 da of 16 Earl of Devon; 2 s, 1 da; *Career* former tobacco farmer (Rhodesia); dir building materials-manufacturing cos; *Style—* Michael Joly de Lotbinière, Esq; Rougham House, Bury St Edmunds, Suffolk

JOLY DE LOTBINIERE, Thomas Henry; s of Lt-Col Sir Edmond Joly de Lotbinière, *qv*, by his 1 w, Hon Elizabeth Jolliffe, da of 3 Baron Hylton; *b* 18 July 1929; *Educ* Eton, Trinity Coll Cambridge (BA); *m* 15 Sept 1953, Prudence Mary, da of Thomas Richard Bevan (d 1970), of Hadlow Down; 1 s (Nicholas b 1955), 2 da (Lucy b 1957, Henrietta b 1960); *Career* sr ptnr Grenfell & Colegrave (stockbrokers) 1978-86, vice pres Canadian Imperial Bank of Commerce 1986-, chm CIBC Investment Ltd 1989; memb Stock Exchange 1959; *Recreations* gardening, shooting; *Clubs* City of London; *Style—* Thomas Joly de Lotbinière, Esq; Cottons Centre, Cottons Lane, London SE1 2QL (☎ 071 234 6000, fax 071 407 4127, telex 28902)

JONAS, Christopher William; s of Philip Griffith Jonas, MC (d 1982), of Oxted, Surrey, and Kathleen Marjory, *née* Ellis; *b* 19 Aug 1941; *Educ* Charterhouse, Coll of Estate Mgmnt, London Business Sch; *m* 30 Nov 1968, (Jennifer Susan) Penny, da of Bernard Leslie Barker (d 1976), of Fulbeck, Grantham; 3 s ((Leslie) Peter b 16 April 1970, Toby Philip b 10 Nov 1971, Max Christopher b 2 Feb 1977), 1 da (Freya Josephine Wendy b 4 Feb 1981); *Career* TA Inns of Ct Regt 1959-66; Jones Lang Wootton 1959-67; Drivers Jonas: ptnr 1967-82, manging ptnr 1982-87, sr ptnr 1987-; vice pres RICS, property advsr Staffs CC 1982-; memb Bd: Port of London Authy 1985-, The Securities Assoc 1988-; chm Econs Res Assoc (USA), memb: Urban Land Inst USA, American Soc of Real Estate Cnsllrs; tstee Property Centre City Univ; Liveryman: Worshipful Co of Clothworkers 1962, Worshipful Co of Chartered Surveyors 1978 (asst 1990); FRICS 1975, FRSA, FIOD; *Recreations* Wagner, other music, skiing, golf, tennis; *Clubs* Naval and Military, Toronto (Toronto); *Style—* Christopher William Jonas, Esq; Drivers Jonas, 16 Suffolk St, London SW1Y 4HQ (☎ 071 930 9731, fax 071 930 3690, telex 917080)

JONAS, George Siegfried; s of George Jonas (d 1942), and Frieda, *née* Glaser (d 1942); *b* 2 Jan 1928; *Educ* Barnton Brunner Sr Sch, LSE (LLB); *m* 23 Dec 1951, Frieda, da of the late Marcus Reinert; 1 s (Steven Michael b 1956), 1 da (Helen Ann b 1959); *Career* slr; sr ptnr George Jonas & Co; Cncl memb Birmingham Law Soc 1965- (pres 1979-80, vice pres 1978-79, hon life memb 1985-) and chm Litigation and Legal and Ctee 1972-79; chm No 6 Regnl Duty Slr Ctee 1984-87; chm Bd of Mgmnt City of Birmingham Symphony Orch 1974- (dep chm 1971-74, memb 1966-); memb Birmingham City Cncl 1959-65 and 1966-69, chm Public Library Ctee 1962-65; Lab pty candidate Hall Green 1966; fndr tstee Cannon Hill Tst, chm The Margery Fry Memorial Tst 1970-85, pres W Midlands Campaign for Abolition of Capital Punishment 1990 (former chm); awarded Gold medal of the Birmingham Civic Soc (1986); *Recreations* music, cricket, modern transport; *Clubs* The Birmingham; *Style—* George S Jonas, Esq; 1b Burke Ave, Birmingham B13 9XB (☎ 021 777 3773); 190 Corporation St, Birmingham B4 6RD (☎ 021 212 4111, fax 021 2121770)

JONAS, Peter; s of Walter Adolf Jonas (d 1965), of Hamburg and London, and Hilda May, *née* Ziadie; *b* 14 Oct 1946; *Educ* Worth Sch, Univ of Sussex (BA), Royal Northern Coll of Music (LRAM), Royal Coll of Music (CAMS), Eastman Sch of Music, Univ of Rochester USA; *m* 22 Nov 1989, Lucy, da of Christopher Hull; *Career* Chicago Symphony Orch: asst to music dir 1974-76, artistic admin 1976-85; dir of artistic admin Orchestral Assoc of Chicago 1977-85 (Chicago Symphony Orch, Civil Orch of Chicago, Chicago Symphony Chorus, Allied Arts Assoc, Orchestra Hall), gen dir ENO 1985-; memb: Bd of Mgmnt Nat Opera Studio 1985-, Cncl of Mgmnt London Lighthouse 1990-; FRCM 1989 (memb Cncl 1988), FRSA 1989; *Recreations* music, theatre, cinema, architectural models, Eastern Europe; *Clubs* Athenaeum; *Style—* Peter Jonas, Esq; 18 Lonsdale Place, Barnsbury Street, London N1 1EL (☎ 071 609 9427); English National Opera, London Coliseum, St Martins Lane, London WC2N 4ES (☎ 071 836 0111)

JONDORF, Dr Werner Robert; s of Wilhelm Jondorf (d 1957), and Irmgard Jondorf (d 1937); *b* 2 Dec 1928; *Educ* King Henry VIII GS Abergavenny, Univ Coll Cardiff (BSc), St Mary's Hosp Med Sch London (PhD); *m* 25 July 1963, Gillian, da of Roy Digby Moore (d 1975), of Oakington, Cambs; 4 da (Harriet b 1964, Sarah b 1965, Miranda (twin) b 1965, Alice b 1969); *Career* visiting scientist: Dept of Chemical Pharmacology Nat Heart Inst, Nat Insts of Health Bethesda Md USA 1957-60; special lectr Chester Beatty Res Inst London 1961-, special res fell Dept of Biochemistry Univ of Glasgow 1962-63; guest worker: Nat Cancer Inst, Nat Insts of Health Bethesda (md 1964-65); assoc res prof Dept of Pharmacology The George Washington Univ Med Center Washington DC USA 1968-71 (asst res prof 1963-68), Leverhulme res fell Dept of Pharmacology Univ of Glasgow 1971-73, res fell Dept of Biochemistry Univ of Cambridge 1973-74, res scientist RSS Labs Newmarket Suffolk 1974-79, Swiss Nat Fund supported Guest Faculty, Inst of Pharmacology Univ of Berne Switzerland 1979-81, memb scientist Endocrinology Section Bourn Hall Clinic Bourn Cambridge 1982-85, guest faculty memb Inst of Pharmacology Univ of Berne Switzerland 1986-, visiting res fell Mayo Clinic Rochester MN 55905 USA 1988; numerous scientific pubns incl: Mechanism of Action of Drugs, Evolution, Species, Age and Hormone Dependence on Response to Drugs and Toxic Agents; *Books* Signals to Noise (1963), Messages from Planet Earth (1978), Through the Gates of Time (1987); *Recreations* chess, motorcycling, civic affairs, study of Central and S American civilisations, photography, poetry; *Style—* Dr W Robert Jondorf; 3 Gough Way, Cambridge CB3 9LN

JONES, Adrian Nicholas; s of William Albert Jones, of 8 Silver Lane, Billingshurst, Sussex, and Emily Doris Jones; *b* 22 July 1961; *Educ* Seaford Coll; *m* 1 Oct 1988, Elizabeth Antoinette, da of Derek Thomas Aspen; 1 da (Amy Elizabeth b 2 May 1990); *Career* professional cricketer; Sussex CCC 1980-86 and 1990-, awarded county cap 1986, Somerset CCC 1987-90, awarded county cap 1987; represented: Sussex Schs Eleven 1978-80, Young England 1981-82; record wickets in John Player League match for Sussex (7 for 42 v Notts) 1986, record 17 wickets in a season Benson & Hedges Cup for Somerset; employment during off-seasons: player and coach overseas until 1984, Crown Financial Management 1984-86, Hughes & Hughes Ltd 1989-91, Jarvis-Allen Ltd 1989-91; *Recreations* most sports, history; *Style—* Adrian Jones, Esq; Sussex CCC, County Ground, Eaton Rd, Hove BN3 3AN (☎ 0273 732161)

JONES, Adrianne Shirley (Ann); MBE; da of Adrian Arthur Haydon (d 1973), and Doris, *née* Jordan (d 1986); *b* 17 Oct 1938; *Educ* Kings Norton GS; *m* 1962, Philip Frank Jones; 2 s (Michael Andrew b 1973, Christopher Haydon b 1978), 1 da (Philippa Ann (Pippa) b 1971); *Career* former international table tennis and lawn tennis player; *table tennis career* 66 England caps 1954-58, memb English Corbillon Cup Team 1954-58, singles finalist World Championships Stockholm 1957, winner 10 Euro Nat Singles Championships; *tennis career* memb Br Wightman Cup Team 1957-67, 1970 and 1975, winner Wimbledon singles and mixed doubles 1969; finalist: Wimbledon singles 1967, Forest Hills USA 1961 and 1967, semi-finalist Wimbledon singles 1958, 1960, 1962, 1963, 1966 and 1968; holder Nat Singles Championships 1966: GB (hard courts), France, Italy, Russia; indoor champion: GB, France, Germany; world rankings: No3 1961, No5 1962 and 1963, No8 1964, No5 1966, No2 1967, No1 1968, No2 1969; capt: Br Fedn Cup Team 1963-66 and 1971, Wightman Cup Team 1971 and 1972; capt for Br Team 1988: Wightman Cup, Fedn Cup, Euro Cup, Maureen Connelly Trophy; chm Women's Int Tennis Cncl 1977-84, Euro dir of ops Women's Tennis Assoc 1978-84, dir Women's Int Tennis 1991-, tennis commentator BBC, referee Women's Tennis

Tournament circuit; BBC Sports Personality of The Year 1969; *Books* Tackle Table Tennis My Way (1958), A Game to Love (1971); *Recreations* most sports, foreign languages and travel, most books, psychology, astronomy; *Clubs* Edgbaston Priory Lawn Tennis, All England Lawn Tennis; *Style—* Mrs Ann Jones, MBE; 85 Westfield Rd, Edgbaston, Birmingham B15 3JF (☎ 021 454 4964)

JONES, Alan Martin; s of John Edward Jones (d 1977), and Ina Marjorie, *née* Hartshorne (d 1987); *b* 27 Sept 1941; *Educ* Brewood GS; *m* 5 Sept 1964, Valerie, da of Edward Mitchell, of Wolverhampton; 1 s (Sean b 1966); *Career* fin dir: D F Bevan (Hldgs) plc 1974-86, Wheway Distribution Ltd 1986-87; md Wheway Secretarial Services Ltd 1987-; FCCA, ACMA; *Style—* Alan M Jones, Esq; 5 Firsway, Wightwick, Wolverhampton, WV6 8BJ (☎ 0902 762051); 214 Hagley Rd, Edgbaston, Birmingham B16 9PH (☎ 021 456 3634, car 0860 523820)

JONES, (Robert) Alan; s of William Arthur Jones (d 1967), of London, and Nellie Catherine, *née* Swinnerton (d 1980); *Educ* Eltham Coll; *m* 20 March 1954, Brenda, da of Gerald Charles Candish Dixon (d 1986); 1 s (Haydn b 1966), 2 da (Persephone b 1964, Anneliese b 1968); *Career* Nat Serv 1948-50, cmmnd 2 Lt (served in Libya); md Crown House Eng Ltd (formerly FH Wheeler Ltd) 1967, chm CHE Ltd 1974-79, md Balfour Kilpatrick 1989 (dir 1979); Liveryman Worshipful Co of Glaziers and Painters of Glass 1970; CEng, FIEE, FCIBSE, CBIM; *Recreations* golf, literature, gardening; *Clubs* Betchworth Park Golf, RAC; *Style—* R Alan Jones, Esq

JONES, Alan Wingate; s of Gilbert Victor Jones (d 1971), of Kingswood, Surrey, and Isobel Nairn Wilson; *b* 15 Oct 1939; *Educ* Sutton Valence, Kings Coll Cambridge (MA); *m* 6 July 1974, Judith Ann, da of George William Curtis (d 1952); 1 s (Mark b 1975), 1 da (Sophie b 1980); *Career* md Plessey Electronic Systems, former dir Plessey Co plc; chief exec Westland Group plc; *Recreations* skiing, opera; *Clubs* RAC; *Style—* Alan W Jones, Esq; The Grange, North Cadbury, Somerset BA22 7BY (☎ 0963 40269); Westlands, Yeovil BA20 2YB

JONES, Allen; s of William Jones, and Madeline, *née* Aveson; *b* 1 Sept 1937; *Educ* Ealing GS for Boys, Hornsey Sch of Art, RCA; *m* 1964 (m dis 1978), Janet, *née* Bowen; 2 da (Thea b 1967, Sarah b (twin) 1967); *Career* teacher of lithography Croydon Coll of Art 1961-63, teacher of painting Chelsea Sch of Art 1966-68; painter; first int exhibition Paris Biennale 1961; one man exhibitions incl: Arthur Tooth & Sons (London), Neundorf (Hamburg), Zwirner (Cologne), Galeria Milano (Milan), Crispolti (Rome), Aschofberger (Zurich), Ariadne (Vienna), Von Wentzel (Cologne), Springer (Berlin), Thorden Wetterling (Gothenburg), Helland Wetterling (Stockholm), C Conles (NY), Richard Feigen Gallery (NYC, Chicago and Los Angeles), Marlborough Fine Art (London), Waddington Galleries (London), James Corcoran Gallery (Los Angeles), Galerie Patrice Trigano (Paris); museum group exhibitions incl: ICA Graphic Retrospective 1978, Graphic Retrospective UCLA 1978, Retrospective of Painting Walker Art Gallery (Liverpool, touring England and Germany) 1979, Young Contemporaries Paris Biennale, British Art Today, San Francisco Touring Exhibition, Decade Painting and Sculpture Tate Gallery; cmmns incl: Liverpool Int Garden Festival 1984, sculpture for Cottons Atrium London Bridge City 1987; designer of sets for TV and stage in UK and Germany (incl sets and costumes for Rambert Dance Co 1989); RA; *Books* Allen Jones Figures (1969), Allen Jones Projects (1971), Waitress (1972), Sheer Magic (1979); *Recreations* gardening; *Clubs* Zanzibar, Garrick; *Style—* Allen Jones, Esq; c/o Waddington Galleries, 11 Cork St, London W1X 1PD (☎ 071 437 8611, fax 071 734 4146)

JONES, Dr Alun Denry Wynn; s of Thomas D Jones (d 1982), of Penygroes, Dyfed, and Ray, *née* Morgan; *b* 13 Nov 1939; *Educ* Amman Valley GS Ammanford, ChCh Oxford (MA, DPhil); *m* 22 Aug 1964, Ann, da of Brinley Edwards (d 1955), of Betws, Dyfed; 2 da (Helen b 1966, Ingrid b 1969); *Career* sr student Cmmn for the Exhibition of 1851 1964-66, sr res fell UKAEA 1966-67, Lockheed Missiles and Space Co California 1967-70, tutor Open Univ 1971-82, dep ed Nature Macmillan Jls 1972-73 (joined 1971), British Steel Corporation 1974-77, British Steel Overseas Services 1977-81, asst dir Tech Change Centre 1982-85, dir and sec Wolfson Fndn 1987-90 (dep dir 1986-87), chief exec Inst of Physics 1990-; Br Assoc for Advancement of Sci: sec Working Pty on Social Concern and Biological Advances 1972-74, memb Section X Ctee 1981-; Br Library: memb Advsy Cncl 1983-85, Document Supply Centre Advsy Ctee 1986-89; memb Cncl Nat Library of Wales 1987- (govr 1986-), govr Univ Coll of Wales Aberystwyth 1990-; FInstP 1973, CDipAF 1977, CPhys 1987; *Books* Our Future Inheritance: Choice or Chance (jtly, 1974); *Recreations* Welsh culture, gardening, theatre; *Style—* Dr Alun Jones; 4 Wheatsheaf Close, Woking, Surrey GU21 4BP; 47 Belgrave Square, London SW1X 8QX (☎ 071 235 6111)

JONES, Andrew Bryden; s of David Jones, of 1 Sheriffmuirlands Rd, Causewayhead, Stirling, Scotland, and Ellen Milne, *née* Rennie (d 1983); *b* 31 March 1948; *Educ* HS of Stirling; *m* 9 Feb 1974, Rosemary Ann, da of Norman Thomas Clarke, of 7 Ardmore Lane, Buckhurst Hill, Essex; 2 s (Alasdair David b 1975, Douglas Ian b 1976); *Career* CA apprentice Dickson Middleton & Co Stirling 1965-70, qualified 1970, sr accountant in tax Arthur Andersen Glasgow 1970-71, mangr in tax Edward Moore & Co London 1971-74, supervisor to mangr Whinney Murray London 1974-79; Ernst & Whinney: ptnr 1979, ptnr i/c tax London 1984-88, nat tax ptnr 1988, coordinating ptnr of firms exec 1988; Ernst & Young: ptnr i/c int tax 1989-90, nat tax ptnr 1990-; MICAS 1970; *Recreations* watching sons play sport, golf, reading; *Style—* Andrew B Jones, Esq; Chipleys, 9 Pishiobury Drive, Sawbridgeworth, Herts CM21 0AD (☎ 0279 723135); Ernst & Young, Rolls House, 7 Rolls Buildings, Fetter Lane, London EC4A 1NH

JONES, Anne; da of Sydney Joseph Pickard (d 1987), and Hilda Everitt, *née* Bird; *b* 8 April 1935; *Educ* Harrow Weald Co Sch, Westfield Coll London (BA), King's Coll London (PGCE); *m* 9 Aug 1958 (m dis 1988), Cyril Gareth Jones, s of Lyell Jones (d 1936); 1 s (Christopher Lyell b 24 July 1962), 2 da (Catherine Rachel b 8 Aug 1963, Rebecca Madryn b 15 March 1966); *Career* asst mistress: Malvern Girls Coll 1957-58, Godolphin and Latymer Sch 1958-62, Dulwich Coll 1964; sch cnsllr Mayfield London 1965-71, dep head Thomas Calton Sch London 1971-74; head: Vauxhall Manor Sch 1974-81, Cranford Community Coll 1981-87, dir of educn programmes, Training Agency Employment Dept 1987-; visiting prof of educn Univ of Sheffield; former chm Area Manpower Bd London SW; memb Cncl CRAC; FRSA (memb Cncl), hon memb City and Guilds Inst; *Books* Counselling Adolescents: School and after (1986), Leadership for Tomorrows Schools (1987); *Recreations* walking, dining, swimming, boating; *Style—* Mrs Anne Jones; 8 Southerton Road, London W6 0PH (☎ 081 748 6399)

JONES, (Albert) Arthur; s of Frederick Henry Jone (d 1918), of Bedford, and Emma Elizabeth, *née* Shreeves (d 1935), of Bedford; *b* 23 Oct 1915; *Educ* Bedford Modern Sch; *m* 15 Feb 1939, (Peggy) Joyce Jones, da of Arthur Wingate (d 1972), of Bedford; 1s (Peter b 1942), 1 da (Alison (Mrs Rice) b 1946); *Career* Bedfordshire Yeomanry RA (territorial) 1938, WWII 1 armoured div, served ME (captured Alamein 1942, escaped POW 1943), demobilised as captain; memb Bedford Rurual Dist Cncl 1946-49, Bedford Borough Cncl 1949-74: alderman 1957-74, mayor 1957-58 and 1958-59; memb: Housing Ctee of the Assoc of Municipal Corps 1951-66, Governing Body of Harpur Charity Bedford 1953-89, Bedfordshire Co Cncl 1956-67, Central Housing Ctee 1959-62; MP for Daventry 1962-79, chm Local Govt Nat Advsy Ctee Conservative Party 1963-73; memb of select ctees: Immigration and Race Relations 1968-70, Expenditure 1971-79, chm Enviromental Sub-Ctee 1974-79; memb Speaker's Panel of Chairmen, UK rep to Consultative Assembly of Cncl of Europe and Assembly of WEU 1971-73, fndr memb UK Housing Assoc 1972-82; memb: Anglian Water Authy 1980-82, Cmmn for the New Towns 1980-88 (dep chm 1982-88), dep chm St Andrews Hosp Northampton 1984-91 (govr 1979-), memb Int Union of Local Authys UK Branch; FSVA; *Books* Future Housing Policy (1960), War on Waste (1965), Local Governors at Work (1968), For the Record, Bedford 1945-74 Land Use & Financial Planning (1981), Britain's Heritage (1985); *Style—* Arthur Jones, Esq; Moor Farm, Pavenham, Bedfordshire MK43 7NU; 6 Mill St, Bedford MK40 3HD (☎ 0234 51301, fax 0234 269147)

JONES, Arthur Edward; s of Arthur Albert Jones, DCM (d 1963), of Bulwer, Daleside Gdns, Chigwell, Essex, and Mary Alice, *née* Clements (d 1987); *b* 20 Feb 1922; *Educ* Leyton Co HS; *m* 28 June 1947, (Hannah) Elizabeth, da of Albert Storey (d 1933); 1 s (Stephen Arthur b 1950), 1 da (Jill Elizabeth b 1952); *Career* WWII RN 1941-46; dir A & M Jones & Sons Ltd 1946-85; vice pres Essex Co Badminton Assoc 1973-, chm Br Badminton Olympic Ctee 1986-90; Badminton Assoc of Eng: memb Cncl 1956-73, vice pres 1973-86, chm 1975-84, pres 1986-90; Int Badminton Fedn: memb Cncl 1976-84, vice pres 1984-90, pres 1990-; *Recreations* philately, swimming, golf; *Style—* Arthur Jones, Esq; 2 Broadstrood, Loughton, Essex IG10 2SE (☎ 081 508 7218, fax 081 508 3146)

JONES, Prof Arthur S; s of John Jones (d 1986), of Newcastle upon Tyne, and Anne, *née* Hamilton (d 1938); *b* 17 May 1932; *Educ* Gosforth GS, Kirkley Hall Farm Inst Northumberland, King's Coll Univ of Durham (BSc), Univ of Aberdeen (PhD); *m* 6 January 1962, Mary Margaret, da of George Smith (d 1974), of Aberdeen; 3 s (Graeme Angus b 19 Nov 1962, Roland Philip b 17 May 1964, Nathan Mark b 13 Oct 1966), 1 da (Camilla Anne b 10 March 1970); *Career* cmmnd Army 2 Lt 1955-57, pilot offr RAF Vol Res 1958-62; Rowett Res Inst: scientific offr Applied Biochemistry Dept 1959, sr scientific offr Applied Biochemistry Dept and head of Pig Section Applied Nutrition Dept 1961, princ scientific offr head of Applied Nutrition Dept 1966, sr princ scientific offr head of Applied Nutrition Dept 1971, sr princ scientific offr and chm Applied Sciences Div 1975, dep chief scientific offr and dep dir 1983; princ North of Scotland Coll of Agric, holder of Strathcon Fordyce Chair of Agric Univ of Aberdeen; chm of Scottish Beef Development Ltd; govr: Rowett Res Inst, Aberdeen Centre for Land Use 1986; princ Royal Agric Coll Cirencester; author of numerous scientific pubns in the field of agric; FIBiol 1968, FBIM 1978, FRSA 1989; *Recreations* yachting; *Style—* Prof Arthur Jones; Barley Lodge, Strand Rd, Cirencester, Gloucestershire GL7 6JS (☎ 0285 653578); Royal Agricultural Coll, Cirencester, Gloucestershire 6L7 6JS (☎ 0285 652531, fax 0285 680219)

JONES, Rt Hon Aubrey; PC (1955); s of Evan and Margaret Aubrey Jones; *b* 20 Nov 1911; *Educ* Cyfartha Castle Secdy Sch Merthyr Tydfil, LSE; *m* 1948, Joan, da of G Godfrey-Isaacs; 2 s; *Career* editorial and foreign staff The Times 1937-39 and 1947-48; contested SE Essex 1945 and Heywood and Radcliffe 1946; MP (Unionist) Birmingham Hall Green 1950-65, PPS to Min of State Econ Affrs 1952 and to Min of Materials 1953; min of fuel and power 1955-57, min of supply 1957-59; chm Prices and Incomes Bd 1965-70; pres Oxford Energy Policy Club 1976-88, sr research assoc St Antony's Coll Oxford 1979-82, fellow commoner Churchill Coll Cambridge 1972 (1982-86); dir: Black & Decker 1977-83, Thomas Tilling 1970-82 and formerly GKN and Courtaulds; chm: Cornhill Insurance 1971-74 (dir 1971), former chm Staveley and Laporte Industs; visiting fell Science Policy Res Unit Univ of Sussex 1986; hon fellow LSE 1959 (memb Court of Govrs 1964), Hon DSc Bath; *Style—* The Rt Hon Aubrey Jones; Arnen, Limmer Lane, Felpham, Bognor Regis, W Sussex (☎ 0243 582722)

JONES, Prof (Norman) Barrie; s of Lesley Robert Jones, of Bebington, Merseyside, and Edith, *née* Morris; *b* 3 Jan 1941; *Educ* Liverpool Inst, Univ of Manchester (BSc), McMaster Univ (MEng), Univ of Sussex (DPhil); *m* 13 July 1963, Sandra Mary, da of George Albert Potts (d 1981), of Liverpool; 1 s (Geoffrey Stephen b 7 May 1967), 1 da (Victoria Mary b 21 Oct 1965); *Career* Univ of Sussex: lectr 1968-73, reader 1973-84, dir Centre for Med Res 1982-84; Univ of Leicester: prof of engrg 1985-, head Dept of Engrg; sec Biomedical Section Br Assoc; memb Biological Engrg Soc 1969; CEng 1978, FIEE 1984; *Style—* Prof Barrie Jones; Department of Engineering, The University, Leicester LE1 7RH (☎ 0533 522550, telex 347250, fax 0533 522619)

JONES, Prof Barry Edward; s of Frederick Edward Jones, of Winchcombe, Glos, and Margaret Alice, *née* Redwood (d 1975); *b* 11 March 1940; *Educ* Cheltenham GS, N Gloucestershire Tech Coll, Univ of Manchester (BSc, MSc, PhD, DSc); *m* 7 Dec 1963, Julie, da of William Pritchard, of Torquay, Devon; 2 da (Ruth Gillian Sarah b 1966, Jennifer Claire b 1969); *Career* scientific asst Govt Communications Headquarters Cheltenham 1956-60, lectr in electrical engrg Univ of Manchester 1964-81, pt/t tutor Faculty of Technol The Open Univ 1972-84, sr lectr Dept of Instrumentation and Analytical Sci UMIST 1981-86; Brunel Univ: Hewlett Packard prof of mfrg metrology 1986-, dir The Brunel Centre for Mfrg Metrology 1986-; chm IEE Professional Gp on Fundamental Aspects of Measurement 1980-81, hon ed Jl of Physics E Sci Inst 1983-87, memb CNAA 1983-85; CEng 1970, FInstMC 1979, FInstP 1982, FIEE 1984, CPhys 1986; *Books* Instrumentation, Measurement and Feedback (1977), Instrument Science and Technology, (ed and contrib Vol 1 1982, Vol 2 1983, Vol 3 1985), Current Advances in Sensors (ed and contrib, 1987); *Recreations* music, gardening, Methodist local preacher; *Style—* Prof Barry Jones; The Brunel Centre for Manufacturing Metrology, Brunel Univ, Uxbridge, Middlesex UB8 3PH (☎ 0895 74000 ext 2514, fax 0895 32806, telex 261173 G)

JONES, Barry Malcolm; s of Albert George Jones (d 1980), and Margaret Eileen, *née* Clark; *b* 4 April 1951; *Educ* Battersea GS, Charing Cross Hosp Med Sch Univ of London (MS, MB BS, LRCP); *m* 12 May 1973, Janine Diane, da of Laurence Henry Gilbey, of London; 1 s (Huw b 1984), 1 da (Georgina b 1986); *Career* sr registrar in plastic surgery Mount Vernon Hosp 1982-85, fell in craniofacial surgery Hôpital des Enfants Malades Paris 1985, currently conslt plastic and cranio-facial surgn The Hosp for Sick Children Gt Ormond St London and UCH Gower St London; memb: Br Assoc Plastic Surgns, Br Assoc Aesthetic Plastic Surgns, Euro Assoc Plastic Surgns, Int Microsurgical Soc, Euro Craniofacial Soc, Hand Soc, Int Soc of Craniomaxillofacial Surgns, Craniofacial Soc of GB; Freeman: City of London 1982, Worshipful Soc of Apothecaries; FRCS (MRCS); *Recreations* exercise, golf, literature, culinary arts, oeneology; *Clubs* RAC, Moor Park Golf; *Style—* Barry M Jones, Esq; 48 Wimpole St, London W1M 7DG (☎ 071 224 1892, car 0860 449616); The Hospital for Sick Children, Great Ormond St, London WC1; University College Hospital, Gower St, London W1

JONES, Dr (Richard) Barry; s of Richard Humphrey Jones (d 1973), and Catherine Ann, *née* Herbert; *b* 27 Jan 1935; *Educ* Haberdashers' Aske's, BNC Oxford, Guy's Med Sch (MA, BM BCh); *m* 20 July 1962, Dorothee, da of Bernhard Franz Siebel, of W Germany; 5 s (Llewellyn b 1960, Alexander b 1963, Robert b 1965, Michael b 1968, Peter b 1975), 3 da (Deborah b 1960, Rebecca b 1963, Katherine b 1966); *Career* ed Child Care Health and Development 1974, conslt developmental paediatrician Moorfields Eye Hosp and Hosp for Sick Children London 1975-, hon sr lectr in developmental paediatrics Insts of Ophthalmology and Child Health Univ of London 1975, dir Donald Winnicott Centre 1975; hon paediatrician: RNIB, Sense (memb Cncl

Mgmnt Educn Ctee, chm Family Advsy Ctee; FRCP, fell Coll of Ophthalmologists; *Recreations* philosophy of medicine, walking; *Style—* Dr Barry Jones; 17 Dartmouth Row, London, SE10 8AW (☎ 081 692 7989); Moorfields Eye Hospital, City Rd, London EC1V 2PD (☎ 081 253 3411); Donald Winnicott Centre, Queen Elizabeth Hospital For Children, Hackney Rd, London E2 8PS

JONES, (Stephen) Barry; MP (Lab) Alyn and Deeside 1983-; s of Stephen Jones by his w Grace; *b* 1937; *m* Janet Davies; 1 s; *Career* MP (Lab) Flint E 1970-1983, parly under sec Wales 1974-79, oppn front bench spokesman: Employment 1981-Nov 1983, Wales and memb shadow cabinet Nov 1983-87; *Clubs* Connah's Quay Labour; *Style—* Barry Jones, Esq, MP; 30 Paper Mill Lane, Oakenholt, Flint, Clwyd (☎ 035 26 3430)

JONES, Brenda; da of Edward Jones (d 1950), and Margaret Jones, *née* Thomas (d 1981); *b* 20 Oct 1938; *Educ* Blackburne House Liverpool, Univ Coll of N Wales Bangor; *m* 1973, Roger Houghton, s of Geoffrey Houghton; 1 s (Geoffrey b 1966), 2 da (Jane b 1968, Daisy b 1975); *Career* Kenya corr The Guardian, dep prodn ed Sunday Times Business News, dep ed Cosmopolitan, woman's ed Sunday Times Magazine; *Books* Cosmopolitan's Guide to Getting Ahead (1981); *Style—* Ms Brenda Jones; Sunday Times Magazine (☎ 071 833 7188)

JONES, Brian Christopher; s of George Jones, of 39 Talbot Rd, Isleworth, Middx, and Doreen Jones; *b* 13 Jan 1955; *Educ* Spring Grove Central Sch Middx, Maidenhead Tech Coll, Twickenham Tech Coll (ONC, HNC); *m* 26 April 1959, Sian Jones; 1 s (Ben b 6 Aug 1988), 1 da (Jemma b 14 Feb 1986); *Career* student apprentice SEB 1971-79, electrical engr James R Briggs 1979-81, dir Aukett Associates 1988- (joined 1981); memb Inst of Electrical and Electronic Inc Engrg; *Style—* Brian Jones, Esq; Aukett Associates, 13 Chelsea Embankment, London SW3 4LA (☎ 071 352 0142, car 0836 204760)

JONES, Brian Robert; s of Charles Robert Jones (d 1973), and Ellen Elsie Walker (d 1990); *b* 7 Jan 1946; *Educ* Wallington GS; *m* 1968, Sandra Thirlwall, da of William Davies (d 1953); 1 da (Elaine b 1969); *Career* gen mangr and actuary Royal London Mutual Insur Soc Ltd 1987- (dir 1985-); chm Royal London Unit Tst Mangrs Ltd 1987- (dir 1981-); FIA; *Recreations* gardening, opera, reading, enjoyment of the countryside; *Style—* Brian Jones, Esq; Tarkwa, Daisy Green, Groton, Boxford, nr Colchester, Essex CO6 5EN (☎ 0787 210814); Royal London House, Middleborough, Colchester, Essex CO1 1RA (☎ 0206 761761, fax 0206 578449, telex 987723)

JONES, Dr (Robert) Brinley; s of John Elias Jones, and Mary Ann, *née* Williams; *b* 27 Feb 1929; *Educ* Tonypandy GS, Univ Coll Cardiff (BA, DipEd, Fell), Jesus Coll Oxford (DPhil); *m* 1971, Stephanie Avril Hall; 1 s; *Career* educn offr RAF Kidlington and Bicester 1955-58 (cmmd 1955); asst master Penarth GS 1958-60, lectr Univ Coll Swansea 1960-66, asst registrar Univ of Wales 1966-69, dir Univ of Wales Press 1969-76, Warden Llandovery Coll 1976-88, memb Broadcasting Standards Council 1988-; memb: Literature Ctee Welsh Arts Cncl 1968-74 and 1981-87, Bd Br Cncl 1987- (chm Welsh Advsy Ctee 1987), Court and Cncl Nat Library of Wales 1974-82, Cncl St David's Univ Coll Lampeter 1977- (hon fell 1987), Governing Body Church in Wales 1981-, Court Univ Coll Swansea 1983-, Cncl Trinity Coll Carmarthen 1984-, Welsh Acad 1981-; chm Dinefwr Tourism Gp 1988-, managing tstee St Micheal's Theol Coll 1982-, hon memb Druidic Order Gorsedd of Bards 1979-, vice pres Llangollen Int Musical Eisteddfod 1989-; ed The European Teacher 1964-69; FSA 1971, FCP 1982, FRCS 1988; *Books* The Old British Tongue (1970-), Anatomy of Wales (contrib and ed, 1972), Writers of Wales (ed with M Stephens, 1970), Astudiaethau ar yr Hengerdd: studies in old Welsh poetry (ed with R Bromwich, 1978), Introducing Wales (1978), 3 edn 1988), Certain Scholars of Wales (1986); *Recreations* walking, farming, music; *Style—* Dr R Brinley Jones, FSA; Drovers Farm, Porthyrhyd, Llanwrda, Dyfed SA19 8DF (☎ 055 85 649)

JONES, (Martin) Bruce; s of Edward Stanley Jones (d 1955), and Elvia Hinton, *née* Bloomer; *b* 28 Aug 1940; *Educ* Cheltenham, Oriel Coll Oxford (BA); *m* 1 Jan 1971, Gillian Ruth, da of Harold Eardley Moxon (d 1974); 1 s (Crispin b 1974), 2 da (Abigail b 1972, Isabelle b 1980); *Career* market res exec Market Investigations Ltd 1962-70, investmt analyst Strauss Turnbull & Co 1970-77, sr investmt analyst WI CARR/CARR SEBAG 1977-82, dir investmt res Kitcat & Aitken 1982-; AMSIA; *Recreations* antiques; *Style—* Bruce Jones, Esq; Whitworth Lane, Loughton, Milton Keynes, Beds MK5 8EB (☎ 0908 670 393); Kitcat & Aitken, 71 Queen Victoria St, London EC4V 4DE (☎ 071 489 1966, fax 071 329 6150, telex 888297)

JONES, Bryan Sydney Powell; s of Leonard Stanley Jones (d 1946), and Ethel, *née* Angle (d 1981); *b* 20 Feb 1932; *Educ* Watford Boys' GS, Jesus Coll Cambridge (MA, LLM); *m* 18 Aug 1962, Jennifer Marion, da of Claude Gilbert Betts (d 1984); 1 s (Christopher b 1968), 2 da (Catherine b 1964, Alison b 1966); *Career* Nat Serv Pilot Offr RAF 1950-51, Flt Lt Royal Aux AF 1960; admitted slr 1957, ptnr JW Ward & Son 1963-; memb Bath CC 1963-72, chm Govrs Bath Coll Higher Educn 1967-74, pres Bath Law Soc 1977-79, vice chm Avon CC 1988-89 (memb 1985-89); charter memb Bath Lions Club 1963-; memb Law Soc; *Recreations* walking; *Style—* Bryan Jones, Esq; 92 High St, Marshfield SN14 8LS (☎ 0225 891 053); 52 Broad St, Bristol BS1 2EP (☎ 0272 292 811, fax 0272 290 6863)

JONES, Bryn; s of Gwilym Jones, of Northampton, and Winifred Ivy, *née* Fuller; *b* 25 Oct 1947; *Educ* Harold Hill GS, Brighton Poly, Sch of Architecture (Dip Arch); *m* 25 July 1970, Caroline Anne Mary, da of Alfred John Lamb (d 1982); 1 s (Evan Rhys b 30 June 1977), 1 da (Sarah Louise b 12 Dec 1975); *Career* G Wimpey & Co Ltd: asst area architect Maidstone 1973-74, regnl architect Luton 1974-78, princ architect London 1978-79; asst chief architect Wilcon Homes 1979-80; Woods Harwidk Ltd: architect, assoc, dir 1981-; RIBA 1974; *Recreations* private pilot; *Style—* Bryn Jones, Esq; 17 Goldington Rd, Bedford, Beds MK40 3NH (☎ 0234 268862, fax 0234 53034, car 0831 30784)

JONES, Carey (Frederick); s of Clifford William Jones (d 1990), of Bonvilston, S Glam, and Mary Gwendoline, *née* Thomas; *Educ* Llandovery Coll Univ of Wales Aberystwyth (BSc), Selwyn Coll Cambridge (MA); *m* 2 Dec 1979, Bernadette Marie, da of Anthony Fulgoni; 1 s (Alexander Anthony b 10 Feb 1985), 1 da (Mariclare Dominique b 2 July 1981); *Career* graduate surveyor MAFF 1975-79, surveyor Mid Glam CC 1979-80, sr surveyor Cardiff City Cncl 1980-82 (surveyor 1980-81), sole princ Crown & Co Chartered Surveyors 1982; chief exec Royal Life Estates West 1988-; ARICS 1979; *Recreations* skiing, squash, classic cars; *Clubs* Pitt; *Style—* Carey Jones, Esq; Royal Life Estates West, 364-372 Cowbridge Road West, Ely, Cardiff CF5 5BY (☎ 0222 596025, fax 0222 597985)

JONES, Prof Charles; s of Charles Jones (d 1962), of Glasgow, and Margaret, *née* Fagan; *b* 24 Dec 1939; *Educ* St Aloysius Coll Glasgow, Univ of Glasgow (MA, BLitt); *m* 12 Aug 1966, Isla, da of Alexander Shennan (d 1989); *Career* lectr Dept of English: Univ of Hull 1964-67, Univ of Edinburgh 1967-78; prof Sch of English Univ of Durham 1978-90, Forbes prof of English language Univ of Edinburgh 1990-; *Books* Introduction to Middle English (1973), Phonological Structure and The History of English (1974), Grammatical Gender in English (1988), A History of English Phonology (1989); *Recreations* breeding Soay sheep; *Clubs* Edinburgh Arts; *Style—* Prof Charles Jones; Laggan Cottage, Faladam, Midlothian EH37 5SU (☎ 0875 33 652); Dept of English Language, University of Edinburgh, David Hume Tower, George Square, Edinburgh EH8 9JX (☎ 031 667 1011)

JONES, Christopher Kenneth; s of William Henry Jones (d 1942), and Dorothy Irene, *née* Tonge; *b* 22 March 1939; *Educ* Sir Roger Manwood's GS Sandwich, Univ of Southampton Sch of Navigation; *m* 29 June 1963, (Moira) Jane, da of Gp Capt David Fowler McIntyre, AFC (d 1957), of Lochgreen House, Troon, Ayrshire; 2 s (Mark b 1964, Neil b 1965), 1 da (Amanda b 1967); *Career* third offr Union-Castle Mail SS Co Ltd 1959-62, merchandise dir Peter Robinson/Top Shop Ltd 1964-72, dep md Richard Shops Ltd 1972-76, md Bally London Shoe Co Ltd 1976-80, chief exec Lillywhites Ltd 1980-84, md retail activities Seaco Inc 1984-86, The Windsor Mktg Partnership Ltd 1989; Freeman City of London; FRSA 1974; *Recreations* skiing, golf; *Style—* Christopher Jones, Esq; 12 Hamilton Drive, Sunningdale, Berkshire SL5 9PP (☎ 0344 21837, fax 0344 23371)

JONES, Christopher Michael Stuart; s of Flt Lt Richard Leoline Jones, RAFVR, of Witney, Oxon, and Elizabeth Margaret, *née* Cook; *b* 1 Jan 1944; *m* 1 Sept 1966, Jennifer Amy, da of Leonardus Franciscus Aarts, of Wolverhampton, Mids; 1 s (Richard b 3 June 1970), 1 da (Victoria b 16 Oct 1973); *Career* sales mangr RH Macy NY USA 1964; James Beattie: buyer Wolverhampton 1965, gen mangr Birkenhead 1972; James Beattie Solihull: gen mangr 1974, gp merchandise controller 1977, merchandise dir 1979, jt md 1984; memb Steering Ctee Wolverhampton Ptnrs in Progress; *Recreations* gardening, DIY, collecting antique clocks; *Clubs* Rotary, 41 (Tettenhall); *Style—* Christopher Jones, Esq; Woodbury, Wergs Rd, Tettenhall, Wolverhampton WV6 8TD (☎ 0902 759 200); James Beattie plc, Victoria St, Wolverhampton WV1 (☎ 0902 22 311, fax 0902 28 144)

JONES, (Robert Miles) Christopher; s of Rev Richard Ebenezer Jones (d 1937), of Whittington Rectory, nr Cheltenham, Glos, and Mary Helen, *née* Jenkins (d 1967); *b* 9 July 1922; *Educ* Haileybury, Royal Agric Coll; *m* 6 June 1952, Sandra Mary (d 1986), da of Lt-Col William Franklin Beavan, OBE, DL (d 1985), of Halkyn Castle, Flint; 2 s (Richard b 1953, David b 1956), 1 da (Susan b 1954); *Career* RAF 1940-46, cmmnd 1941, serv ME 1941-44, Europe 1944-46; land agent to Duke of Westminster 1950-84, Tstees of Grosvenor Estate 1950-84; FLAS, FAI, FRICS; *Recreations* shooting and fishing; *Style—* R M C Jones, Esq; Langstone Court, Llangarron, Ross-on-Wye, Herefordshire HR9 6NR (☎ 098 984 254)

JONES, (John) Clement; CBE (1972); only s of Clement Daniel Jones (d 1916), of Haverfordwest; *b* 22 June 1915; *Educ* Ardwyn, Aberystwyth, Open Univ (BA); *m* 1938, Marjorie, da of George Gibson, of Llandrindod Wells; 3 s; *Career* journalist and broadcaster; ed and dir Express and Star Wolverhampton 1960-75; media consIt Cwlth and UNESCO 1975-, exec dir Beacon Radio (programming) 1974-78, pres Guild Br Newspaper Editors, govr Br Inst of Human Rights 1971-85; FRSA; *Recreations* gardening, beekeeping, writing, broadcasting; *Clubs* Athenaeum; *Style—* J Clement Jones, Esq, CBE; 7 South View Drive, Walton on the Naze, Essex CO14 8EP

JONES, Clive Hugh; s of David John Jones, of Harrow, Middx and Marjorie Viola, *née* Hobbs (d 1981); *b* 25 Aug 1958; *Educ* Merchant Taylor's, St John's Coll Oxford (BA); *m* 23 July 1988, Judith Helen, da of Gwynfryn George Bond, of Sabden, Lancashire; *Career* called to the Bar Middle Temple 1981; Freeman: City of London 1984, Worshipful Co of Merchant Taylors; MCIA 1986; *Recreations* golf, the arts and travel; *Clubs* Sudbury Golf; *Style—* Clive H Jones, Esq; Strand Chambers, 218 Strand, London WC2 R1AP (☎ 071 353 7825, fax 071 483 2073)

JONES, Clive Lawson; s of John Lawson Jones (d 1986), and Gladys Irene, *née* Daines; *b* 16 March 1937; *Educ* Cranleigh Sch, Univ of Wales (BSc); *m* 4 April 1961, Susan Brenda, da of late Walter Angus McLeod; 1 s (Robin b 26 Dec 1964), 1 da (Tracy b 28 Dec 1966); *Career* with: BP 1957-61, Texaco Trinidad 1961-68; princ DTI 1968-73, asst sec Dept of Energy 1973-77, energy cnsllr Br Embassy Washington DC 1977-81, under sec Dept of Energy 1981-82, dir energy policy EC 1982-86, dep dir-gen for energy EC Cmmn 1987-; *Style—* Clive Jones, Esq; CEE DGXVII, 200 Rue De La Loi, 1049 Brussels, Belgium (☎ 010 32 2235 7096)

JONES, Clive William; s of Kenneth David Llewellyn Jones, of Pontllanfraith, Gwent, S Wales, and Joan Muriel, *née* Withers; *b* 10 Jan 1949; *Educ* Newbridge GS, Gwent S Wales, LSE (BSc Econ); *m* 1, 1971 (m dis 1987), Frances Jones; 2 s (Paul Dafydd b 24 Oct 1973, Samuel Alun b 7 Sept 1975), 1 da (Angharad Elizabeth Louisa b 7 May 1979); m 2, 12 Nov 1988, Fern Mary Philomena, da of Tony Britton, of London; *Career* journalist Yorkshire Post Group 1970-73, news ed and asst ed Morning Telegraph 1973-78, prodr Yorkshire TV 1978-82, ed (former managing ed) TV AM 1982-84; TV South 1984-: dep dir of progs, controller of news current affrs and sport, dir TVS Productions Ltd and TVS TV Ltd; memb: Cncl Mgmnt Artswork Ltd youth arts charity), film and video panel Southern Arts Assoc; *Recreations* books, films, rugby; *Style—* Clive Jones, Esq; Television South, TV Centre, Southampton SO9 5HZ (☎ 0703 634211, fax 0703 834122)

JONES, Courtney John Lyndhurst; MBE (1980), OBE (1989); s of Reginald Claude Jones, and Inez Mary, *née* Willsher; *b* 30 April 1933; *Educ* Ringwood GS, Bournemouth Sch of Art (NDD); *Career* Nat Serv RAF 1955-57; Brice dance champion, Euro ice dance champion, world ice dance champion with June Markham 1957-58 (with Doreen Denny 1958-61); design dir Clifton Slimline Ltd 1964-74, freelance design consIt 1974-; int judge and referee of ice skating and ice dancing, pres and chm of bd Nat Skating Assoc of GB 1987- (chm of cncl 1977-86); *Recreations* skating, reading, music, the arts; *Style—* Courtney Jones, Esq, OBE; 9 Kings Ave, Parkstone, Poole, Dorset BH14 9QF

JONES, David Alan Freeborn; s of Daniel Edward (d 1966), of King's Norton, Birmingham, and Winnifred Kate, *née* Freeborn (d 1990); *b* 28 March 1943; *Educ* King's Norton GS, Univ of Nottingham (LLB); *m* 15 Feb 1969, Mavis, da of John Douglas (d 1961), of Northumbria; 1 s (Nicholas 1971), 2 da (Rachel b 1973, Hannah b 1980); *Career* called to the Bar Gray's Inn 1967, in practice Birmingham 1969-, head of chambers 1985, organiser deliverer and publisher Annual Lecture to the Birmingham Bar and Midland and Oxford Circuit on Criminal Law, law lectr Birmingham Coll of Commerce 1965-68; Criminal Bar Assoc; *Recreations* cricket, golf, ornithology, gardening, tennis; *Clubs* Alvechurch CC, Fulford Heath and Aberdovey Golf, RSPB; *Style—* David Jones, Esq; 12 Cherry Hill Avenue, Barnt Green, Birmingham B45 8LA (☎ 021 445 1935); 3 Fountain Court, Steelhouse Lane, Birmingham B4 6DR (☎ 021 236 5854, fax 021 236 7008)

JONES, David Alwyn; s of late Trefor Jones, of London, and Marion Edna, *née* Miles; *b* 23 June 1934; *Educ* St John's Sch Leatherhead, Corpus Christi Coll Cambridge (BA), Magdalen Coll Oxford (DPhil); *m* 29 Aug 1959, Hazel Cordelia, da of Dan Lewis, FRS, of London and Berks; 2 s (Edmund b 6 June 1963, Hugh b 2 Sept 1965), 1 da (Catherine b 26 Dec 1961); *Career* lectr in genetics Univ of Birmingham 1961-73, prof in genetics Univ of Hull 1973-89, prof and chm Dept of Botany Univ of Florida 1989-; memb: Br Assoc for the Advancement of Science, Ctees of Sections D and K 1974-89; chm: Membership Ctee Inst of Biology 1982-87, Co-ordinating Ctee for Cytology and Genetics 1974-87; pres Int Soc of Chemical Ecology 1987-88; FIBiol 1974; *Books* Variation and Adaptation in Plant Service (with D A Wilkins, 1971), Analysis of Populations (with T J Crawford, 1976); *Style—* Prof David Jones; Pleione Cottage, 83 Freehold Street, Lower Heyford, nr Bicester, Oxon OX5 3NT (☎ 0869 47619); USA (☎ 0101 904 338 0680); Department of Botany, 220 Bartram Hall, University of Florida, Gainesville, FL 32611 USA (☎ 0101 904 392 1175, fax 0101 904

392 3993)

JONES, Dr David Arthur; s of Eric Langley Jones (d 1973), of Liverpool, and Loris Edith, *née* Cook (d 1969); *b* 31 May 1927; *Educ* Roundhay Sch Leeds, Univ of Leeds (BSc, PhD); *m* 17 Sept 1955, Heather Ann St Clair, da of Humphrey St Clair Gilby (d 1979), of Perth Australia; 1 s (Robin b 1959); *Career* British Thompson-Houston Co Ltd 1950-52; Brush Electrical Engineering Co Ltd: joined 1952, PA to tech dir 1953-55, res mangr 1960-64; lectr Univ of Leeds 1955-60, asst dir of engrg The English Electric Co Ltd 1964-69, dir: Ewbank Consulting Ltd 1969-82, Old Ship Hotel Brighton Ltd 1980-87, Ewbank Preece Group Ltd 1982-87; chm Cncl Brighton Poly 1983-87 (dep chm Bd of Govrs), pres Inst of Electrical Engrs 1990-91, sr conslt Ewbank Preece Group Ltd, judge of Prince of Wales award for Industl Innovation; hon fell Brighton Poly; FIEE 1968, FBIM 1984, FRSA 1987, FEng 1987; *Recreations* boating, photography, computers; *Clubs* IEE Council Dining, Dynamicables; *Style—* Dr David Jones; Thatchcroft, 18 Clayton Avenue, Hassocks, W Sussex BN6 8HD (☎ 07918 6469, fax 07918 6469), Ewbank Preece Group Ltd, Prudential House, North St, Brighton BN1 1RZ (☎ 0273 724533, fax 0273 200483, telex 878102 (EPLBTN G))

JONES, Rev David Ian Stewart; s of Rev John Milton Granville Jones (d 1986), and Evelyn Moyes Stewart, *née* Chedburn (d 1965); *b* 3 May 1934; *Educ* St John's Sch Leatherhead, Selwyn Coll Cambridge (MA); *m* 19 Aug 1967, Susan Rosemary, da of Eric Arthur Hardy-Smith (d 1958); 1 s (Benedict b 12 Sept 1970), 1 da (Katherine (twin) b 12 Sept 1970); *Career* RCS 1952-54; ordained priest Manchester Cathedral 1960, curate Oldham Parish Church 1959-62, vicar All Saints Elton Bury Lancs 1962-66, conduct and sr chaplain Eton 1970-74 (asst conduct and chaplain 1966-70), headmaster Bryanston 1974-82, rector Bristol City Parish 1982-85; dir Lambeth Charities 1985-, hon priest vicar of Southwark Cathedral 1985-, govr Forest Sch 1987-; *Recreations* reading, walking, music; *Clubs* East India, Devonshire, Sports and Public Schools; *Style—* The Rev David Jones; 127 Kennington Road, London SE11 6SF (☎ 071 735 2531, office 071 735 1925)

JONES, (John) David; s of John Trevor Jones, of The Orchard, 5 Allerton Beeches, Liverpool, and Mair Eluned Jones; *b* 11 Oct 1955; *Educ* Liverpool Coll, Univ of Oxford (MA), Univ of London (PhD); *Career* insur analyst L Messel & Co 1981-83, asst dir and head of French res E B Savory Milln & Co 1983-86, divnl dir and head of French res Warburg Securities 1986-, dir Bacot-Allain (head of French res); registered rep Stock Exchange 1987, memb Société Francaise des Analystes Financiers 1988; *Recreations* classical music, theatre, cinema, reading; *Clubs* United Oxford and Cambridge University, Oxford Soc, Bow Group; *Style—* David Jones, Esq; 147 Boulevard St Michel, 75005, Paris (☎ 010 331 4633 8480); 17 Hale House, Bessborough Gardens, 7 Drummond Gate, London SW1 V2HS; Warburg Securites, c/o Bacot-Allain, 65 Rue de Courcelles, 75008, Paris, France (☎ 010 331 48 88 3306)

JONES, David Martin; *b* 14 Aug 1944; *Educ* Univ of London (BSc, B Vet Med); *Career* The Zoological Soc of London: vet offr Whipsnade Park Zoo 1969-75, sr vet offr and head Dept of Vet Sci 1975-84, asst dir of zoos 1981-84, dir of zoos 1984-; overseas conslt, fund-raiser, author of scientific papers and articles; chm: Fauna and Flora Preservation Soc, Conservation Review Gp World Wide Fund for Nature (UK), Brooke Hosp for Animals; tstee World Wide Fund for Nature (UK), memb Bd of Studies Zoology Univ of London; MRCVS, FIBiol; *Style—* David Jones, Esq; Zoological Society of London, Regent's Park, London NW1 4RY (☎ 071 722 3333, fax 071 483 4436, telex 265247)

JONES, David Morris; s of Capt Morris Jones, MN (ka 1941) of Beaumaris, Anglesey, and Menna Lloyd, *née* Evans; *b* 24 March 1940; *Educ* Beaumaris GS, Univ Coll Bangor (BA, Dip Ed); *m* 3 Dec 1971, Patricia; 2 da (Sian b 24 Nov 1976, Eira b 17 Feb 1980); *Career* journalist Liverpool Daily Post and Echo Ltd 1962-63; BBC Wales: news asst 1963-64, sr news asst 1964-67, chief news asst 1967-71, TV news prodr 1971-82, managing ed news and current affrs 1982-85, ed Wales news and current affrs 1985-; currently: memb Radio TV News Dirs Assoc (USA), head of news TVS, contractor for S and SE Eng ITV; memb RTS; *Recreations* sailing; *Style—* David Morris Jones, Esq; TVS Television Centre, Northam, Southampton (☎ 0703 834050); TVS Television Centre, Vinters Park, Maidstone (☎ 0622 684682/684442)

JONES, Hon Mrs (Deborah Katherine Louise); *née* Suenson-Taylor; 2 da of 2 Baron Grantchester, CBE, QC; *b* 9 April 1957; *Educ* Cheltenham Ladies' Coll; *m* 1977, Michael Paul Jones; 1 s (Christopher Michael b 1987); *Style—* The Hon Mrs Jones; Windsor, Church Road, W Wittering, W Sussex

JONES, Della Louise Gething; da of Cyril Vincent Jones (d 1982), and Eileen Gething Jones; *Educ* Neath Girls GS, Royal Coll of Music (LRAM, ARCM, GRSM); *m* 2 April 1988, Paul Anthony Hooper Vigars, s of Norman Vigars; *Career* mezzo-soprano; soloist ENO 1977-82, Sung with all maj Br opera cos and at opera houses and concert halls throughout Europe, USA and USSR (specializing in Rossini, Handel and Mozart); Dido in Les Troyens (WNO) 1987, Ramiro in Finta Giardinera and Cecilio in Lucio Silla (Mostly Mozart Festival NY), Sorceress in Dido and Aeneas (Buckingham Palace tercentenary celebration of William and Mary 1988), Rosina in Il Barbier di Suviglia (Covent Gqarden) 1990; Laurence Olivier Award nomination for Rosina in The Barber of Seville ENO 1988; extensive recordings (incl Recital of Rossini arias 1990), frequent radio and tv broadcasts; *Recreations* collecting elephants, visiting Venice for Bellini, writing cadenzas, animal welfare; *Style—* Miss Della Jones; Music International, 13 Ardilaun Rd, Highbury, London N5 2QR (☎ 071 359 5183)

JONES, Dennis; s of Dennis Jones, and Emily, *née* Buckley; *b* 17 Feb 1950; *Educ* Urmston GS; *m* 25 Aug 1984, Joan, da of Norman Bernard Cronshaw (d 1983); 3 s (Gary b 1958, Mark b 1960, Simon b 1967), 1 da (Johanna b 1968); *Career* dir: Hazlewood Foods plc 1975-, Irishwire Products plc 1986-; FCA; *Recreations* golf; *Clubs* Club de Golfe Las Brisas; *Style—* Dennis Jones, Esq; Hazlewood Foods plc, Rowditch, Derby DE1 1NB (☎ 0332 295295)

JONES, Donald Keith; s of David Burne Jones (d 1965), of Handsworth, Birmingham, and Peggy, *née* Lane (d 1930); *b* 29 March 1930; *Educ* Handsworth Coll Birmingham; *m* 20 March 1956, Barbara, da of Sidney Hinchcliffe, of Wakefield, Yorks; 1 da (Amanda Louise b 28 Aug 1958); *Career* Pilot Offr RAF: flying trg 1951, 20 Sqdn 1953; ESSO UK plc: div dir industl/consumer 1970 (planning and econ 1973), dir int and specialties 1975-85; dir Br Road Fedn 1983-88; chm Mid Surrey Health Authy 1986-; *Recreations* golf, walking, music and dining out; *Clubs* RAF, Betchworth Park Golf; *Style—* Donald Jones, Esq; Latchetts, Park Lane, Reigate, Surrey RH2 8JX (☎ 07372 46 016); West Park Hospital, Horton Lane, Epsom, Surrey KT19 8PB (☎ 03727 27 811)

JONES, Prof Douglas Samuel; MBE (1945); s of Jesse Dewis Jones (d 1932), and Bessie *née* Streather; *b* 10 Jan 1922; *Educ* Wolverhampton GS, CCC Oxford (MA, hon fell 1980), Univ of Manchester (DSc); *m* 23 Sept 1950, Ivy, da of Henry Styles (d 1932); 1 s (Philip b 1960), 1 da (Helen b 1958); *Career* WWII Flt Lt RAFVR 1941-45; fell Cwlth Fund MIT 1947-48; Univ of Manchester (asst lectr, lectr, sr lectr) 1948-57, res prof NY Univ 1955, prof of mathematics Univ of Keele 1957-64, visiting prof Courant Inst 1962-63, Ivory Prof of mathematics Univ of Dundee 1964-; memb: Mathematical Sci Sub Ctee 1971-86 (chm 1976-86), Cncl Royal Soc 1973-74, UGC 1976-86, Computer Bd 1977-82, Visiting Ctee OU 1982-87, Cncl Inst of Mathematics and its Applications 1982 (pres 1988-89); Keith prize Royal Soc of Edinburgh 1974, van der Pol gold medal of Int Union of Radio Sci 1981, Naylor prize of London Mathematical Soc 1987; hon DSc Univ of Strathclyde 1975; CEng, FIMA 1964, FRSE 1967, FRS 1968, FIEE 1989; *Books* Electrical and Mechanical Oscillations (1961), Theory of Electromagnetism (1964), Generalised Functions (1966), Introductory Analysis Vol 1 (1969, Vol 2 1970), Methods in Electromagnetic Wave Propagation (1979, reissued as 2 volumes in 1987), Elementary Information Theory (1979), The Theory of Generalised Functions (1982), Differential Equations and Mathematical Biology (1983), Acoustic and Electromagnetic Waves (1986), Assembly programming and the 8086 Microprocessor (1988); *Clubs* Oxford and Cambridge; *Style—* Prof Douglas Jones, MBE, FRSE, FRS; Department of Mathematics and Computer Science, The University, Dundee, DD1 4HN (☎ 0382 23181)

JONES, Edward Bartley; s of Meurig Bartley Jones, of 6 Pound Close, Yarnton, nr Oxford, and Ruby, *née* Morris; *b* 24 Dec 1952; *Educ* Cardiff High Sch, Balliol Coll Oxford (BA); *Career* called to the Bar Lincoln's Inn 1975, chancery and commercial barr in Liverpool 1976-, pt/t lectr Univ of Liverpool 1977-81; *Recreations* horse riding, hunting, opera, skiing; *Clubs* Oxford & Cambridge, Racquet Liverpool; *Style—* Edward Jones, Esq; Church Farmhouse, Dodleston, Cheshire CH4 9NN (☎ 0244 660905), 2nd Floor, 7 Queen Avenue, Liverpool 2 (☎ 051 2368240, fax 051 2773005, car 0836 720459)

JONES, Rt Hon Lord Justice; Rt Hon Sir Edward Warburton Jones; PC (1979), PC (N Ireland 1965); s of Hume Riversdale Jones, LLD, Resident Magistrate, and Elizabeth Anne Phibbs; yr bro of Gen Sir Charles Jones, GCB, CBE, MC (d 1988); *b* 3 July 1912; *Educ* Portora Royal Sch Enniskillen N Ireland, Trinity Coll Dublin (LLB); *m* 1, 1941, Margaret Anne Crosland (d 1953), da of William Smellie (d 1955); 3 s (Graham, Peter, Hume); m 2, 1953, Ruth Buchan (d 1990), sis of his 1 w; 1 s (Charles); *Career* serv WWII Royal Irish Fusiliers, Hon Lt-Col 1946; MP (U) Londonderry 1951-68 (NI Parl); barrister NI 1936 and Middle Temple 1964, QC (NI) 1948, jr crown counsel Belfast 1945-55, attorney-gen NI 1964-68, High Court judge NI 1968-72, Lord Justice of Appeal NI 1972-84, hon master of Bench Middle Temple 1982-; vice pres College Historical Soc Trinity Coll Dublin; kt 1973; *Books* Jones L J His Life and Times an autobiography; *Recreations* golf, sailing; *Clubs* Army and Navy, Royal Portrush Golf (Capt 1956-58), Ulster Reform, Royal Co Down; *Style—* The Rt Hon Lord Justice Jones; Craig-y-Mor, Trearddur Bay, Anglesey (☎ 0407 860406); Amesbury Abbey, Amesbury, Wilts

JONES, Sir (Charles) Edward Webb; KCB (1989), CBE (1985); s of late Gen Sir Charles Jones, GCB, CBE, MC (d 1988), of Amesbury Abbey, Amesbury, Wilts, and Ouida Margaret Jones; *b* 25 Sept 1936; *Educ* Portora Royal Sch Enniskillen NI; *m* 20 Feb 1965, Suzanne Vere, da of G R P Leschallas, of Little Canon, Wateringbury, Kent; 2 s (Hume b 1967, Benjamin b 1978), 1 da (Jemma b 1971); *Career* cmmnd Oxford and Bucks LI 1956, Green Jackets 1958, Royal Green Jackets 1967, Maj DAA and QMG HQ 7 Armd Bde 1968, Lt-Col dir of staff Staff Coll 1973, CO 1 Bn Royal Green Jackets 1974, Col MO4 MOD 1976, RCDS 1980, Brig Cdr 6 Armd Bde 1981, Cdr Br Military Advsy and Trg Team Zimbabwe 1983, Maj-Gen Dir Gen TA and Orgn 1985, Col Cmdt Royal Army Educnl Corps 1986, Cdr 3 Armd Div 1987, Lt-Gen QMG 1988, Col Cmdt Royal Green Jackets 1988; *Recreations* fishing, golf; *Clubs* Army and Navy; *Style—* Sir Edward Jones, KCB, CBE

JONES, Emlyn Bartley; MBE (1975); s of Ernest Jones, MM (d 1955), of Buckley, Clywd, and Sarah Jones (d 1982); *b* 9 Dec 1920; *Educ* Alun GS Mold Clywd, Normal Coll Bangor N Wales (Cert Ed), Loughborough Coll (Dip Physical Ed); *m* 27 March 1944, (Constance) Inez, da of Richard William Jones, of Mold, Clwyd; 1 da (Madeleine Bartley (Mrs Ward) b 11 Oct 1946); *Career* Flt Lt Radar Branch 1941-46, cmmnd Flt Lt 1943, demobbed 1946; teacher history and physical educn Flint Modern Secdy Sch Clwyd 1946, tech rep CCPR N Wales 1947-51, tech advsr CCPR London HQ 1951-62, tv sports commentator ITV 1955-, dir Crystal Palace Nat Sports Centre 1962-78, dir gen The Sports Co 1978-83, self employed conslt sport and leisure 1983-; pres Br Assoc Nat Sports Admins, vice pres Nat Assoc of Boys' Clubs, individual memb CCPR, govr Dulwich Coll, fndr co memb London Sports Med Inst; FBIM 1984; *Books* Learning Lawn Tennis (1960), Sport in Space (1985); *Recreations* golf, skiing, watching sport, reading, walking; *Clubs* Royal Air Force; *Style—* Emlyn Jones, Esq, MBE; Chwarae Teg, 1 B Allison Grove, Dulwich, London SE21 7ER (☎ 081 693 7528)

JONES, Prof Emrys; s of Samuel Garfield Jones (d 1969), and Annie, *née* Williams (d 1983); *b* 17 Aug 1920; *Educ* Aberdare Boys' GS, Univ Coll of Wales Aberystwyth (BSc, MSc, PhD); *m* 7 Aug 1948, Iona Vivien, da of Richard Hywel Hughes (d 1972); 2 da (Catrin b 1955, Rhianon b 1958, d 1980); *Career* asst lectr in geography Univ Coll London 1947-50, lectr and sr lectr Queen's Univ Belfast 1950-58, reader and prof LSE 1959-84, emeritus 1984; conslt in planning and urbanisation; Royal Geographical Soc: fell 1947, chm Regnl Studies 1968-70, memb Cncl 1972-78, vice pres 1978-83; pres Hon Soc of Cymmrodorion 1989- (memb Cncl 1978-, chm 1983-89), memb Govt Ctee of Enquiry into Allotment 1969; Royal Geographical Soc Victoria medal 1977; fell: Univ of Wales 1946-47, Rockefeller Fndn NY; Hon DSc Queen's Univ Belfast 1978, Hon DUniv Open Univ 1990; *Books* Social Geography of Belfast (1960), Introduction to Human Geography (1964), Towns and Cities (1965), Atlas of London (1970), Cities (with E Van Zandt, 1974), Introduction to Social Geography (with J Eyles, 1977), Metropolis (1990); *Recreations* books, music; *Clubs* Athenaeum; *Style—* Prof Emrys Jones; 2 Pine Close, North Rd, Berkhamsted, Herts HP4 3BZ (☎ 0442 875 422)

JONES, Prof Emrys Lloyd; s of Peter Jones (d 1984), and Elizabeth Jane, *née* Evans; *b* 30 March 1931; *Educ* Neath GS, Magdalen Coll Oxford (BA, Violet Vaughan Morgan scholarship, Charles Oldham Shakespeare prize); *m* 1 Sept 1965, Barbara Maud, da of Leonard Everett; 1 da (Hester b 1967); *Career* Univ of Oxford: fell and tutor Magdalen Coll 1955-77, reader in Eng 1977-84, Goldsmiths' prof of Eng lit 1984, fell New Coll 1984; FBA 1982; *Books* Scenic Form in Shakespeare (1971), The Origins of Shakespeare (1977), Poems of Henry Howard, Earl of Surrey (ed 1964), Antony and Cleopatra (1977); *Recreations* looking at buildings, opera; *Style—* Prof Emrys Jones; New College, Oxford (☎ 0865 79522)

JONES, Sir (William) Emrys; s of late William Jones; *b* 6 July 1915; *Educ* Llandovery GS, Univ Coll of Wales; *m* 1, 1938 (m dis 1966), Megan Ann Morgan; 3 s; m 2, 1967, Gwyneth George; *Career* MAFF: chief agric advsr 1967-71, dir-gen agric devpt and advsy serv 1971-73; princ Agric Coll Cirencester 1973-78, emeritus 1978-85; dir Lloyds Bank (N and E Midlands Region) 1978-86, chm Velcourt Mgmnt Servs 1983-84; kt 1971; *Clubs* Farmers'; *Style—* Sir Emrys Jones; The Draey, 18 St Mary's Park, Louth, Lincs

JONES, Dr Emyr Wyn; s of Evan Walter Jones, of Bodelen, Ffordd Caerdydd, Pweeheli, Gwynedd, and Buddug Morwenna Jones; *b* 23 Feb 1950; *Educ* Pweeheli GS, Univ of Nottingham (DM), Univ of Liverpool (MB ChB); *m* 19 April 1974, Patricia Anne, da of Crowley Hammond (d 1989), of 99 Kirby Rd, Walton on Naze, Essex; 1 s (Dafydd Benjamin b 28 Nov 1981), 3 da (Anne-Mair b 11 May 1976, Rhiannon Clare b 27 July 1978, Sioned Patricia b 17 March 1980); *Career* registrar in med Royal Liverpool Hosp 1976-78, clinical res fell and hon sr registrar Dept of Med Univ Hosp Queen's Med Centre Nottingham 1979-86, conslt physician specialising in diabetes mellitus and endocrinology 1986-; author of papers on: platelets, thrombosis, diabetes; clinical tutor Doncaster Postgrad Med Fedn, memb Med and Scientific Section Br

Diabetic Assoc; memb BMA, MRCP 1978; *Recreations* playing guitar in a rock'n roll band, all sorts of music, ornithology; *Style—* Dr Emyr Jones; 16 St Eric's Rd, Bessacarr, South Yorkshire DN4 6NG (☎ 0302 531059); Doncaster Royal Infirmary, Armthorpe Rd, Doncaster, S Yorks DN2 5LT (☎ 0302 366666)

JONES, Ernest Edward (Ted); s of William Edward (Ted) Jones (d 1976), of 25 Rose Crescent, Scawthorne, Doncaster, and Eileen, *née* Gasser (d 1986); *b* 15 Oct 1931; *Educ* Sheffield De La Salle Coll, Hopwood Hall Coll of Educn, Univ of Manchester, Sheffield Poly (Cert Ed, DipSci, DEM); *m* 27 Dec 1955, Mary Ellen, da of (Joseph) Rennison Armstrong (d 1955); 1 s (Peter Edward b 22 Nov 1956), 1 da (Elizabeth Mary b 1 Feb 1958); *Career* Nat Serv RAF (lectr in radar systems); sch master 1953-; memb Doncaster Met Borough Cncl 1980- (vice chm Educn Ctee 1983-, chm Further Educn Ctee 1983-); chm: Doncaster Community Health Cncl 1981-, Trent Regnl Assoc of Health Cncls 1988-, Assoc Yorks and Humberside Educn Authy 1988, S Yorks Int Archaeological Ctee 1987-; memb: Exec Yorks Art Assoc 1983, Yorks and Humberside Museums Cncl 1983-, Cncl Nat Museums Assoc, Ct Univ of Hull 1983-, Cncl Univ of Sheffield 1983-, Cncl Univ of Bradford 1986-; memb Doncaster Co Borough Cncl 1962-74, S Yorks CC 1973-77 (dep chm 1973-75, chm 1975-76); FRSA 1983, FRSH 1989 (MRSH 1974); *Recreations* music, fine arts, caravanning; *Style—* Ted Jones, Esq; 11 Norborough Rd, Doncaster, S Yorks (☎ 0302 366122); Mansion House, Doncaster (☎ 0302 734444)

JONES, Dr Eurfron Gwynne; da of William Gwynne Jones (d 1967), and Annie, *née* Harries (d 1975); *b* 24 Sept 1934; *Educ* Aberdare Girls' GS, Univ Coll Cardiff, Univ of Wales (BSc, Phd); *m* 13 Sept 1968, Michael John Coyle; 1 s (David Michael Gwynne b 17 Sept 1975); *Career* joined BBC as gen trainee 1959; prodr educn programmes for sch and adults 1959-75, freelance writer and broadcaster, media conslt for Int Childrens Centre and Educn Cmmn of the States 1975-83, asst head of Sch BBC Radio 1983-84, BBC head of Sch TV 1984-87, controller educn broadcasting; memb Cncl: Royal Inst, Open Univ, fell Smallpeice Tst; Hon LLD Exeter 1990; memb Royal Television Soc; *Books* Children Growing UP (1973), The First Five Years (1975), Television Magic (1978); *Recreations* photography; *Style—* Dr Eurfron Jones; BBC, Villiers House, The Broadway, Ealing, London W5 2PA (☎ 081 991 8033, telex 265781, fax 081 840 6720)

JONES, (John) Evan; s of Flt Lt Oliver Jones, of Great Waldingfield, Sudbury, Suffolk, and Susannah, *née* McCartney-Murray; *b* 12 Feb 1959; *Educ* Sudbury GS, Hatfield Coll, Univ of Durham (BA); *Career* called to the Bar Inner Temple 1982; *Recreations* fencing, reading, motor racing and cars; *Clubs* Nat Lib; *Style—* J Evan Jones, Esq; 3 Kings Bench Walk, Inner Temple, Fleet St, London EC4Y 7DQ (☎ 071 353 2416, fax 071 353 2941)

JONES, Sir Ewart Ray Herbert; s of William Jones (d 1924); *b* 16 March 1911; *Educ* Grove Park Sch Wrexham, Univ Coll of N Wales Bangor, Univ of Manchester (MA, DSc, PhD); *m* 1937, Frances Mary Copp; 1 s, 2 da; *Career* Sir Samuel Hall prof of chemistry Manchester Univ 1947-55, Waynflete prof of chemistry Oxford Univ 1955-78, emeritus prof 1978-; hon fell Magdalen Coll Oxford (fell 1955-78); chm Anchor and Guardian Housing Assoc 1979-84; FRS; kt 1963; *Style—* Sir Ewart Jones, FRS; 6 Sandy Lane, Yarnton, Oxford OX5 1PB (☎ 086 75 2581)

JONES, Frederick Charles (Freddie); s of Charles Edward Jones, from Stoke-on-Trent, and Ida Elizabeth, *née* Goodwin; *b* 12 Sept 1927; *Educ* Longton HS, Rose Bruford Coll of Speech & Drama (acting prize, radio prize); *m* Jennifer Elizabeth, da of Reginald Heslewood (d 1990); 3 s (Toby Edward b 7 Sept 1966, Rupert Frederick b 6 July 1968, Caspar Boyd b 16 Nov 1971); *Career* actor; worked in repertory at: Stockton on Tees, Bridlington, Lincoln, Bristol Old Vic, The Flora Robson Playhouse, University Theatre Newcastle upon Tyne, The Royal Exchange Theatre; stage performances in London incl: Mister (Duchess Theatre), Dear Janet Rosenberg (Hampstead Theatre), The Cloud (Hampstead Theatre), The Dresser (Queens Theatre), Tramway Road (Lyric Hammersmith), One Man Show Called John Clare (Lyric Hammersmith), Sunset and Glories (The Playhouse Leeds); performed with RSC in: The Marat Sade, Birthday Party, Afore Night Come, The Lower Depths, also toured Venice and Dublin with Touch of the Poet and Hong Kong with Death of a Salesman; TV credits incl: Secret Orchards, Brensham People, Germinal, Uncle Vanya, Nana, Sword of Honour, Sweeney Todd, The Caesars, Pennies from Heaven, Joe's Ark, Ghosts, John Clare Omnibus, Tiny Revolutions, The Last Evensong, Vanity Fair, Kremlin Fairwell, Mashenka, Shoot the Revolution, Vaclav Havel's The Interview and Inspector Morse; film credits incl: The Bliss of Mrs Blossom, Anthony and Cleopatra, Far From The Madding Crowd, Accident, Juggernaut, Zulu Dawn, The Elephant Man, Fire Fox, Krull, Dune, Fellini's E la Nave va (and The Ship Sails On), Erik the Viking, Karel Kachyna's The Last Butterfly; numerous radio performances incl: Look Here Old Son, John Clare in a Song in the Night, Gogol, Skelton - The Winking Goose and Peter Barnes' People; winner Monte Carlo Golden Nymph best actor for Claudius in The Caesars; *Recreations* gardening, cooking, golf; *Clubs* Garrick; *Style—* Freddie Jones, Esq; Crinan House, Charlbury, Oxfordshire (☎ 0608 811014); Bluethorn Ltd, 7 High Park Rd, Kew, Richmond

JONES, Dr (Cyril) Gareth; s of Lyell Jones (d 1937), and Ceridwen, *née* Jenkins; *b* 28 May 1933; *Educ* Nantyglo GS, Christ's Coll Cambridge (MA), Birkbeck Coll London (PhD); *m* 1, 9 Aug 1958 (m dis 1988), Anne, da of Sidney Pickard (d 1987), of Bampton, Oxfordshire; 1 s (Christopher b 24 July 1962), 2 da (Katy b 8 Aug 1963, Becky b 15 March 1966); m 2, 7 April 1989, Helen Patricia Rahming; *Career* RAF 1954-56; Stationers' Company's Sch 1957-59, Dulwich Coll 1959-63, Esso Petroleum Co 1963-69, Booz Allen and Hamilton mgmnt conslts 1969-85 (vice pres 1973, managing ptnr UK 1974); dir Booz Allen & Hamilton Inc 1981-84, managing ptnr Ernst & Whinney mgmnt conslts 1985-89; memb: Arthritis and Rheumatism Cncl 1973-86, Bd Welsh Water Authy 1981-85, Strategic Options Ltd, Welsh Health Planning Forum 1989-, Bd of Mgmnt Secdy Housing Assoc for Wales 1979-; non-exec dir Gwent Health Authy 1990-, dir Welsh Nat Opera 1990-; FIAM 1987; *Books* Strategy for Schools (jtly, 1964), Perspectives in Manpower Planning (jtly, 1967); *Recreations* travel, walking, opera; *Clubs* Reform, IOD; *Style—* Dr Gareth Jones; Tre Graig House, Tre Graig Road, Bwlch, Powys LD3 7SJ (☎ 0874 730 650)

JONES, Prof (David) Gareth; s of William John Jones (d 1973), of Cray, Powys, and Katie Blodwen, *née* Jones; *b* 7 March 1934; *Educ* Priory GS Shrewsbury, Univ Coll of Wales Aberystwyth (BSc, PhD, DSc); *m* 25 June 1960, Anita Mary, da of Kenneth Joseph John (d 1982), of Neath, W Glamorgan; 3 s (Richard Huw, Philip Alun Rhys, Justin Gareth); *Career* RAF aircrew Coastal Cmd 1952-54; microbiologist Welsh Plant Breading Station 1959-65, head of Dept Univ Coll Wales 1987- (lectr 1965-68, sr lectr 1968-81, reader 1981-85, prof 1985-); sec Fedn of Br Plant Pathologists 1971-76, pres Assoc of Applied Biologists 1990 (memb 1973, sec 1976-86, pres elect 1989); memb: Soc of Applied Bacteriology 1960, Br Mycological Soc 1966; *Books* Cereal Diseases - Their Pathology and Control (1978), Plant Pathology - Principles and Practices (1978); *Recreations* rugby refereeing, surfing, fishing, travel; *Style—* Prof Gareth Jones; 65 Maeshendre, Waunfawr, Aberystwyth, Dyfed SY23 3PS (☎ 0970 623802), Department of Agricultural Sciences, Univ College of Wales, Aberystwyth, Dyfed SY23 3DD (☎ 0970 622215)

JONES, Prof Gareth Hywel; QC (1986); s of Benjamin Thomas Jones (d 1967), and Mabel Jane Jones (d 1977); *b* 10 Nov 1930; *Educ* Porth Co GS, VCL (LLB), St Catherines Coll Cambridge (MA, LLD), Harvard Univ (LLM); *m* 21 March 1959, Vivienne Joy, da of Colin Edward Packridge (d 1983); 2 s (Christopher b 1960, Steven b 1961), 1 da (Alisa b 1965); *Career* Vice Master Trinity Coll Cambridge 1986- (fell 1961-, Downing prof of the Law of England 1975-); fell UCL 1988; FBA 1982; *Clubs* Beafsteak; *Style—* Prof Gareth Jones, QC; Trinity Coll, Cambridge CB2 1TQ (☎ 0223 338 473)

JONES, George Briscoe; CBE (1988); s of Arthur Briscoe Jones (d 1975), and Mary Alexandra, *née* Taylor (d 1982); *b* 1 June 1929; *Educ* Caldy Grange GS, Wallasey GS; *m* 26 March 1955, Audrey Patricia, da of Thomas Arthur Kendrick (d 1976); 2 da (Christine Jennifer (Mrs Hawkins) b 22 May 1958, Deborah Ann (Mrs Campbell) b 4 July 1961); *Career* Army 1947-49; clerk to commercial mangr and co sec BEC Ltd 1949-67, planning mangr Agric Div Unilever 1967-71, chm Unitrition International Ltd 1976-82; dir: BOCM Silcock 1974-82 (corp planning mangr 1971-74), Cooperative Devpt Agency 1982-90, Job Ownership Ltd 1984-, Ptnrship in Business Ltd 1988-, Chrisamer Ltd 1989-; pres Pavillon Theatre Gp Basingstoke; *Recreations* reading, drama, painting, sculpture, metalwork, chess, bridge; *Clubs* Farmers; *Style—* George Jones, Esq, CBE; 3 Beverley Close, Basingstoke, Hants (☎ 0256 282 39)

JONES, George Quentin; s of John Clement Jones, of Walton on Naze, Essex, and Marjorie, *née* Gibson; *b* 28 Feb 1945; *Educ* Highfield Sch Wolverhampton; *m* 1, April 1972 (m dis 1989), Diana, *née* Chittenden; 1 s (Timothy Edward b 13 Jan 1979), 1 da (Jennifer Lucy b 2 Jan 1976); m 2, 29 Dec 1990, Teresa Grace, da of John Lancelot Rolleston; *Career* trainee journalist Eastern Daily Press 1963-67, journalist South Wales Argus and Western Mail 1967-69, Reuters London 1969, Parly staff The Times 1969-73, Parly and political corr The Scotsman 1973-82; political corr: The Sunday Telegraph 1982-85, The Sunday Times 1985-86, The Daily Telegraph 1986-88; political ed The Daily Telegraph 1988-; chm Journalists Parly Lobby 1987-88; FRSA 1987; *Clubs* Athenaeum; *Style—* George Jones, Esq; Daily Telegraph, 181 Marsh Wall, London E14 9SR (☎ 071 538 5000)

JONES, Prof George William; s of George William Jones (d 1973), of Wolverhampton, and Grace Annie, *née* Cowmeadow (d 1982); *b* 4 Feb 1938; *Educ* Wolverhampton GS, Jesus Coll Oxford (BA, MA), Nuffield Coll Oxford (DPhil); *m* 14 Sept 1963, Diana Mary, da of Henry Charles Bedwell (d 1982), of Kidlington; 1 s (Maxwell b 1969), 1 da (Rebecca b 1966); *Career* lectr Univ of Leeds 1965-66 (asst lectr 1963-65); LSE: lectr 1966-71, sr lectr 1971-74, reader 1974-76, prof of govt 1976-; memb Layfield Ctee on Local Govt Fin 1974-76, vice chm Political Sci and Int Rels Ctee of Social Sci Res Cncl 1978-81 (memb 1977-81); FRHist 1980, memb RIPA 1963 (memb Cncl 1984-90); *Books* Borough Politics (1969), Herbert Morrison (co-author, 1973), Political Leadership in Local Authorities (jt ed, 1978), New Approaches to the Study of Central-Local Government Relationships (ed, 1980), The Case for Local Government (jt author, 1985), Between Centre and Locality (jt ed, 1985); *Recreations* cinema, eating, reading, dancing; *Clubs* National Film; *Style—* Prof G W Jones; Dept of Govt, London School of Economics and Political Science, Houghton St, London WC2A 2AE (☎ 071 955 7179, fax 071 831 1707, telex 24655 BLPES G)

JONES, Geraint Martyn; s of Robert Kenneth Jones, of Luton, and Frances Elizabeth, *née* Mayo; *b* 15 July 1948; *Educ* St Albans Sch, Christ's Coll Cambridge (MA, LLM), Inns of Court Sch of Law; *m* 29 July 1978, Caroline Mary Jones, da of Lt Peter Edwin Cecil Eyres, RNVR (d 1975); 1 s (Robert b 1980), 1 da (Louisa b 1982); *Career* called to the Bar Gray's Inn 1972; practised: London 1972-74, S E Circuit mainly in Cambridge 1974-; principally commercial, property and planning law; chm Rent Assesment Ctees 1985-; chm Madingley Sch Tst 1988-; memb: RYA, RNLI, OGA, Cruising Assoc; *Recreations* sailing, golf, jazz, carpentry, reading; *Clubs* Cambs Rugby, Toft Red Lion Rowing, Royal Norfolk and Suffolk Yacht; *Style—* Geraint Jones, Esq; Fenners Chambers, 3 Madingley Rd, Cambridge CB3 OEE (☎ 0223 68761, fax 0223 313007); Lamb Building, Temple, London EC4

JONES, Geraint Stanley; s of Rev David Stanley Jones (d 1974); *b* 26 April 1936; *Educ* Pontypridd GS, UCNW Bangor (BA, DipEd); *m* 1961, Rhiannon, da of Emrys Williams (d 1971); 2 da (Sioned b 1965, Siwan b 1966); *Career* served RAEC, Sgt; BBC Wales: studio mangr 1960-62, prodn asst Current Affrs (TV) 1962-65, TV prodr Current Affrs 1965-69, prodr Features and Documentaries 1969-73, asst head of progs Wales 1973-74, head of progs Wales 1974-81, controller BBC Wales 1981-85, dir Public Affrs 1986-87; md Regnl Bdcasting BBC 1987-89, chief exec S4C (Welsh Fourth Channel Authy) 1989-; hon fell UCNW, memb Court and Cncl Univ Coll Wales Aberystwyth; chm: Welsh Coll of Music and Drama, Euro Bdcasting Union TV Prog Ctee, Ryan Davies Tst; memb UK Freedom from Hunger Ctee; FRSA; *Recreations* music, painting, horse riding; *Clubs* Cardiff and County; *Style—* Geraint Stanley Jones, Esq; c/o S4C, Parc Tyglas, Llanishen, Cardiff (☎ 0222 747444)

JONES, Dr Gerald; s of John Jones, and Gladys *née* Roberts; *b* 25 Jan 1939; *Educ* Swansea GS, Merton Coll Oxford, London Hosp Med Coll (BA, BM BCh, PhD); *m* 1, 1 Aug 1964, (m dis 1988), Anne, da of Walter Heatley Morris (d 1977); 1 s (Jonathan Robert b 1976), 2 da (Paula Caroline b 1969, Katharine Helen b 1970); m 2, 19 Oct 1990, Dr Julia Friese; *Career* Hosp appts 1965-69, med res 1969-74, private indust 1974-75, sr princ med offr Dept of Health; FRCP; *Recreations* music, reading; *Style—* Dr Gerald Jones; Eileen House, 80-94 Newington Causeway, London SE1 6EF (☎ 071 972 2838)

JONES, (Robert) Gerallt Hamlet; s of Rev Richard Emrys Jones (d 1969), of Ynys Môn, and Elizabeth Ellen (d 1988); *b* 11 Sept 1934; *Educ* Denstone Coll, VCNW (BA, MA, Dip Ed); *m* 15 Sept 1962, Susan Lloyd, da of Richard Heber Lloyd Griffith (d 1975), of Borth-y-Gest; 2 s (Rhys Gerallt b 1969, Dafydd Gerallt b 1972), 1 da (Ceri Rhiannon b 1964); *Career* lectr in educn Univ of Wales 1960-65, princ Mandeville Teachers Coll Jamaica 1965-67, warden and headmaster Llandovery Coll 1967-76, sr tutor Extra- Mural Dept UW 1979-88, warden Gregynog Hall UW 1988-; author of TV documentaries and series incl Joni Jones; winner: Prose Medal Nat Eisteddfod 1977 and 1979, Hugh McDiarmid Trophy 1987, Welsh Arts Cncl Poetry Award 1990; ed Taliesin 1986-; memb Broadcasting Cncl Wales 1967-72, chm Welsh Acad 1982-87, dir Aberystwyth Devpt Studies Course 1986-, memb Welsh Arts Cncl 1987-; memb Yr Academi Cymreig (the Welsh Acad) 1964; *Books* author of 35 vols in Welsh lang incl: Ymysg y Drain (1959), Cwlwm (1962), Y Foel Fawr (1962), Poetry of Wales 1930-70 (1972), Jamaican Landscape (1969), Jamaican Interlude (1972), Triptych (1977), Cafflogion (1979), Tair Drama (1988), Seicoleg Cardota (1989), Cerddi 1959-89 (1989); *Recreations* cricket, hill-walking; *Style—* Gerallt Jones, Esq; Leri, Dolybont, Borth, Dyfed (☎ 0970 871 525); Gregynog Hall, University of Wales, Newtown, Powys (☎ 0686 87 224)

JONES, Prof Glanville Rees Jeffreys; s of Benjamin Jones (d 1977), of 23 Glen Rd, Neath, and Sarah, *née* Jeffreys (d 1955); *b* 12 Dec 1923; *Educ* Neath Intermediate Sch, UCW Aberystwyth (BA, MA); *m* 1 (m dis 1958), Margaret Rosina Ann Stevens; m 2, 12 Sept 1959, Pamela, da of Frank Winship (d 1985), of Welford Rd, Filey; 1 s (David), 1 da (Sarah); *Career* Nat Serv Sapper Trigonometrical Survey RE 1943-44, 2 Lt RWF 1944-45, Lt RWF 1945-46; Univ of Leeds: asst lectr in geography 1949-52, lectr 1952-65, sr lectr 1965-69, reader in historical geography 1969-74, prof 1974-89, emeritus prof 1989-; O'Donnell lectr Univ of Wales 1975, Hywell Dda prize 1974; chm

Area Advsy Ctee for Rescue Archaeology Dept of Environment for Yorks-Humberside 1975-79, pres anthropology and archaeology section Br Assoc for the Advancement of Sci 1982-83; FSA 1978; *Books* Geography as Human Ecology (author and ed with S R Eyre, 1966), Leeds and its Region (author and ed with M W Beresford, 1967), Post-Roman Wales in the Agrarian History of England and Wales (1972); *Recreations* gardening, military history, observing politics; *Style—* Prof Glanville Jones, FSA; 26 Lee Lane East, Horsforth, Leeds LS18 5RE (☎ 0532 582968); School of Geography, The University of Leeds, Leeds LS2 9JT

JONES, (Thomas) Glanville; s of Evan James Jones (d 1981), of London, and Maggie, *née* Evans (d 1972); *Educ* Clement Danes GS, Univ Coll London (LLB), Inns of Ct Sch of Law; *m* 29 Aug 1964, Valma Shirley, da of Ivor Jones, of Swansea; 3 s (Aled Prydderch b 1966, Dyfan Rhodri b 1968, Geraint Islwyn b 1971); *Career* called to the Bar 1956, rec Crown Ct; chm The Guild for the Promotion of Welsh Music 1970-; *Recreations* music, rugby, reading; *Clubs* Ffynone (Swansea); *Style—* T Glanville Jones, Esq; "Gelligron", 12 Eastcliff, Southgate, West Glamorgan SA3 2AS (☎ 044 128 3118); Angel Chambers, 94 Walter Rd, Swansea SA1 5QA (☎ 0792 464623)

JONES, Sir Glyn Smallwood; GCMG (1964, KCMG 1960, CMG 1957), MBE (1944); s of Gwilym Ioan Jones (d 1942); *b* 9 Jan 1908; *Educ* King's Sch Chester, St Catherine's Coll Oxford (MA); *m* 1942, Nancy Madoc Featherstone; 1 da (and 1 s decd); *Career* entered Colonial Serv (N Rhodesia) 1931, min for native affrs and chief cmmr N Rhodesia 1959, chief sec Nyasaland 1960-61, govr Nyasaland 1961-64, govr-gen and C-in-C Malawi 1964-66; advsr on govt admin to PM of Lesotho 1969-71; Br Govt observer Zimbabwe elections 1980; dep chm Lord Pearce Cmmn for test of Rhodesian opinion 1971-72; hon fell St Catherine's Coll Oxford; KStJ; *Recreations* fishing, golf; *Clubs* MCC, Athenaeum, Royal Commonwealth Soc; *Style—* Sir Glyn Jones, GCMG, MBE

JONES, Prof (Walton) Glyn; s of Emrys Jones, and Dorothy Ada, *née* North; *b* 29 Oct 1928; *Educ* Manchester GS, Pembroke Coll Cambridge (BA, MA, PhD); *m* 1, 12 June 1953 (m dis 1981), (Karen) Ruth, da Vilhelm Olaf Fleischer; 2 s (Stephen b 1 Dec 1956, Olaf b 11 June 1958), 2 da (Monica b 9 June 1962, Anna b 29 June 1965); m 2, 30 Nov 1981, Kirsten, da of Christen Gade; *Career* reader in Danish UCL 1966-73 (Queen Alexandra lectr in Danish 1956-66), visiting prof of Danish Univ of Iceland 1971, prof of Scandinavian studies Newcastle upon Tyne 1973-86, prof of lit Faroese Acad 1979-81, prof of euro lit UEA 1986-; memb Cncl Anglo-Danish Soc, hon memb Swedish Lit Soc Finland 1985, fell Royal Norwegian Acad of Sciences 1988; corresponding memb Danish Soc of Authors 1989; *Books* Johannes Joørgensens modne AÅr (1963), Johannes Joørgensen (1969), Denmark (1970), William Heinesen (1974), Faero Kosmos (1974), Danish: A Grammar (1981), Tove Jansson (1984), Vägen Fran Mumindalen (1984), Denmark: A Modern History (1986); *Recreations* Music, Danish church architecture; *Style—* Prof Glyn Jones; School of Modern Languages and European History, University of East Anglia, Norwich NR4 7TJ (☎ 0603 56161)

JONES, Rev Canon Glyndwr; s of Bertie Samuel Jones (d 1965), of Birchgrove, Swansea, and Elizabeth Ellen Jones; *b* 25 Nov 1935; *Educ* Dynevor Sch Swansea, St Michael's Theol Coll Llandaff Univ of Wales (Dip Theol); *m* 1, 13 Dec 1961, Cynthia Elaine Jenkins (d 1964); m 2, 23 July 1966, (Marion) Anita, da of David Morris (d 1969), of Plasmarl, Swansea; 1 s (Robert b 11 Aug 1970), 1 da (Susan b 30 June 1968); *Career* Nat Serv 1954-56, RAPC attached 19 Field Regt RA, served Korea, Hong Kong, demobbed Sgt AER; ordained Brecon Cath: deacon 1962, priest 1963; curate: Clydach 1962-64, Llangyfelach 1964-67, Sketty 1967-70; rector: Bryngwyn with Newchurch and Llanbedr, Painscastle with Llandewi Fach 1970-70; Missions to Seamen port chaplain Swansea and Port Talbot 1972-76, sr chaplain Port of London 1976-81, aux ministries sec Central Office 1981-85, asst gen sec Central office 1985-90, gen sec 1990-; memb Cncl: Marine Soc 1990-, Ptnrship for World Mission 1990-, Int Christian Maritime Assoc 1990-, Merchant Navy Welfare Bd 1990-; Hon Chaplain Royal Alfred Seafarers Soc 1987, hon canon St Michael's Cathedral Kobe Japan 1988; Chaplain: Co of Information Technologists 1989, Worshipful Co of Innholders 1990, Worshipful Co of Farriers 1990, Worshipful Co of Carmen 1990; Freeman City of London 1990; chaplain to HM The Queen 1990; *Recreations* sport, music, reading, theatre, travel; *Clubs* Royal Commonwealth Soc; *Style—* The Rev Canon Glyndwr Jones; The Missions to Seamen, St Michael Paternoster Royal, College Hill, London EC4R 2RL (☎ 071 248 5202, fax 071 248 4761)

JONES, Sir Gordon Pearce; s of Alun Pearce Jones (d 1979), of Swansea, and Miriam Jones; *b* 17 Feb 1927; *Educ* Swansea GS, Univ of Wales (BSc); *m* 15 Dec 1951, Gloria Stuart, da of Stuart Carr Melville, of Edinburgh; 2 s (Huw b 3 Feb 1960, Hywel (twin) b 3 Feb 1960), 1 da (Elspeth b 14 July 1957); *Career* Lt RN 1947-51; scientist: Br Iron and Steel Res Assoc 1951-56, raw material planning Iron and Steel Indust 1956-64, UK sales mangr Esso Petroleum Co Ltd 1961-64, mktg/sales dir English Steel Corp 1964- 68, dir-gen mangr Murex 1968-70, md Rotherham Tinsley Steels 1970, md Firth Vickers 1974-79, dir TW Ward plc 1979-82; chm: Yorkshire Water 1983-, Water Authys Assoc 1987-89; memb Pres Ctee CBI 1988-89; memb BIM, hon fell IWEM; kt 1990; *Recreations* reading, music, opera, railway history, travel; *Clubs* Naval and Military; *Style—* Sir Gordon Jones; Yorkshire Water plc, 2 The Embankment, Sovereign Street, Leeds LS1 4BG (☎ 0532 343 234, fax 0532 342 332)

JONES, (David) Graham; *b* 16 June 1951; *Educ* Queen Elizabeth GS Wakefield, Keble Coll Oxford (MA), Univ of Wales Coll of Cardiff; *m* 23 March 1977, Lynne Francis; *Career* leader writer Glasgow Herald 1973-74; reporter: Sheffield Star 1973, The Sun 1974-79; Now! Magazine 1979-81 (reporter, dep foreign ed), Foreign Desk Daily Mail and Mail On Sunday 1981-83, Daily Telegraph 1983-89 (reporter, political staff, asst news ed, chief asst news ed, dep news ed), news ed Daily Star 1989-; *Books* Forked Tongues (1984), Own Goals (1985), The Forked Tongues Annual (1985), Plane Crazy (1986), I Don't Hate Men But.../I Don't Hate Women But... (1986), Boat Crazy (1987), The Official Candidate's Book of Political Insults (1987), I Love Sex/I Hate Sex (with Lynne Jones, 1989), The Book of Total Snobbery (with Lynne Jones 1989); *Recreations* writing, photography, gardening; *Style—* Graham Jones, Esq; Daily Star, Express Newspapers plc, 245 Blackfriars Rd, London SE1 9UX (☎ 071 922 7373, fax 071 922 7960)

JONES, Graham Edward; s of Edward Thomas Jones (d 1980), and Dora Rachel, *née* Hughes; *b* 22 Sept 1944; *Educ* Birkenhead Sch, Fitzwilliam Coll Cambridge (MA); *m* 29 Oct 1976, Vanessa Mary Heloïse; *Career* asst master Charterhouse 1961 (later head of economics and politics and housemaster), awarder in economics Oxford and Cambridge Examination Bd 1979-, reviser in economics JMB 1981-, seconded to BP 1981, headmaster Repton 1987-; FRSA; *Recreations* painting, walking, music, cooking, the classics; *Style—* Graham Jones, Esq; The Hall, Repton, Derby DE6 6FH (☎ 0283 702375)

JONES, His Hon Judge Graham Julian; s of David John Jones, CBE (d 1974), and Edna Lillie Jones, *née* Marshall; *b* 17 July 1936; *Educ* Porth Co GS, Univ of Cambridge (MA, LLM); *m* 30 Aug 1961, Dorothy, da of James Smith Tickle (d 1980), of Abergavenny; 2 s (Nicholas David Julian b 1963, Timothy James Julian b 1968), 1 da (Sarah Elizabeth b 1965); *Career* ptnr Morgan Bruce & Nicholas (slrs Cardiff) 1961-85; dep circuit judge 1975-78, recorder 1978-85, circuit judge Wales & Chester circuit 1985-; pres Assoc Law Soc of Wales 1982-84; memb Lord Chllr Legal Aid advsy ctee 1980-85; *Recreations* golf, boats; *Clubs* Cardiff and County, Radyr Golf (Cardiff), Royal Porthcawl Golf; *Style—* His Hon Judge Graham Jones; Cardiff Crown Court, Cathays Park, Cardiff

JONES, Gwilym Haydn; MP (C) Cardiff North 1983-; s of Evan Haydn Jones, and Mary Elizabeth Gwenhwyfar, *née* Moseley; *b* 1947; *Educ* London and S Wales; *m* 1974, Linda Margaret, da of David Mathew John (d 1980), of Cardiff; 1 s (Grant), 1 da (Fay); *Career* insur broker, dir Bowring Wales Ltd; memb Cardiff City Cncl 1969-72 and 1973-83, Parly election agent SE Cardiff 1974, memb The Select Ctee on Welsh Affrs 1983-; sec Welsh Cons Backbenchers 1984-; PPS to Min of State for Transport 1991-; sec All Party Parly Gp for the Fund for the Replacement of Animals in Med Experiments; *Recreations* golf, model railways; *Clubs* County Conservative, Cardiff & County, Rhiwbina Rugby, United Services Mess; *Style—* Gwilym Jones, Esq, MP; House of Commons, London SW1 (☎ 071 219 3000)

JONES, Rev Gwilym Henry; s of John Lloyd Jones (d 1971), and Jennie, *née* Roberts (d 1973); *Educ* Univ Coll of N Wales Bangor (BA, PhD, DD), Jesus Coll Oxford (MA); *m* 28 March 1959, Mary Christabel, da of Owen Trevor Williams (d 1972); 2 s (Rhys b 18 May 1966, Huw b 24 Jan 1969), 1 da (Ruth b 13 April 1975); *Career* min Presbyterian Church of Wales 1956-61, prof of Hebrew Theological Coll Aberystwyth 1961-66, prof of religious studies Univ Coll of N Wales Bangor 1987- (lectr 1966, sr lectr 1979, reader 1984); dean: of divinity Univ of Wales 1987-90, of arts Univ Coll of Northern Wales 1988-91; *Books* Arweiniad I'r Hen Destament (1966), Gwirionedd y Gair (1974), Cerddi Seion (1975), Gramadeg Hebraeg y Beibl (1976), Diwinyddiaeth Yr Hen Destament (1979), Y Gair Ddoe a Heddiw: Eseia o Jerwsalem (1988), 1 and 2 Kings (New Century Bible) (1984), The Nathan Narratives (1990); *Recreations* walking, gardening, music; *Style—* Rev Gwilym Jones; Coed Gadlys, Llansadwrn, Menai Bridge, Gwynedd LL59 5SE (☎ 0248 712226), Dept of Religious Studies, University Coll of North Wales, Bangor, Gwynedd LL57 2DG (☎ 0248 351151 ext 2078)

JONES, Dr Gwyn Miah Gwynfor; s of Robert Jones (d 1979), of Porthmadog, and Jane Irene, *née* Evans (d 1981); *b* 2 Dec 1948; *Educ* Univ of Manchester (BSc), Univ of Essex (PhD); *m* 10 Jan 1976, Maria Linda, Kenneth Johnson; 2 da (Victoria b 1980, Holly b 1982); *Career* various appts ICL until 1981, chm and chief exec Corporate Technol Gp PLC 1981-87, chm Welsh Devpt Agency 1988-, dir Apricot Computers PLC 1989-; memb: Cncl Univ of Wales, Ct Univ Coll of Swansea, Prince of Wales Ctee Prince's Youth Business Tst; FBCS 1987; *Recreations* skiing, golf, tennis; *Style—* Dr Gwyn Jones; Welsh Developement Agency, Pearl Assurance House, Greyfriars Road, Cardiff (☎ 0222 222666)

JONES, Dame Gwyneth; DBE (1986, CBE 1976); da of late Edward George Jones, and late Violet, *née* Webster; *b* 7 Nov 1936; *Educ* Townpath Secdy Modern Sch Pontipool, RCM, Academia Chiqiana Siena, Zurich Int Opera Studio; *m* Till Haberfield; 1 da; *Career* opera singer; principal dramatic soprano: Royal Opera House Covent Garden 1963-, Vienna State Opera 1966-, Bavarian State Opera 1966-; guest artiste: Vienna, London, Paris, The Met NY, La Scala Milan, Berlin, Munich, Hamburg, Barcelona, Buenos Aires, Tokyo, San Francisco, Bayreuth Festival, Salzburg Festival, Verona Festival, Edinburgh Festival; roles incl: Strauss (Salome, Helen of Egypt, Ariadne, The Dyer's Wife and Marschallin in Rosenkavalier), Wagner (Sieqlinde, Eva, Senta, Kundry), Beethoven (Fidelio), Lady Macbeth, Desdemona, Tosca, Madame Butterfly; film & TV roles: Isolde, Aida, Turandot, Senta, Vennis, Merry Widow, marschallin, Fidelio, Elizabeth, Brunnhilde, Dyers Wife, Poppea, La Voix Humaine; Hon DMus Wales, Kammersangerin Austria and Bavaria, Shakespeare Prize FRG 1987, Bundsverdienskreuz FRG 1988; FRCM, Hon memb Vienna State Opera; *Style—* Dame Gwyneth Jones, DBE, CBE; PO Box 8037, Zurich, Switzerland

JONES, Gwyneth Ann; da of Desmond James Jones, and Mary Rita, *née* Dugdale; *b* 14 Feb 1952; *Educ* Notre Dame Convent Sch Manchester, Univ of Sussex (BA); *m* 1976, Peter Wilson Gwillian; 1 s (Gabriel Jimi Jones b 4 Sept 1987); *Career* author; children's books under own name: Water In The Air (1977), The Influence of Ironwood (1978), The Exchange (1979), Dear Hill (1980); children's books under name of Ann Halam: Ally Ally Aster (1981), The Alder Tree (1982), King Death's Garden (1986), The Daymaker (1987), Transformations (1988), The Skybreaker (1990); novels under own name: Divine Endurance (1984), Escape Plans (1986), Kairos (1988), The Hidden Ones (1988); memb: SE Arts Literature Panel 1988-, Science Fiction Foundation 1986-; *Recreations* weight training, walking, gardening, DIY, book reviewing; *Clubs* The Zap, Shape; *Style—* Ms Gwyneth Jones; c/o Toby Eady Assoc, 18 Park Walk, London SW10 0AQ (☎ 081 948 1010)

JONES, Sir Harry Ernest; CBE (1955); s of Harry Charles Ofield Jones (d 1947); *b* 1 Aug 1911; *Educ* Stamford Sch, St John's Coll Cambridge (BA); *m* 1935, Phyllis Eva, da of Alfred Dixon (d 1963); *Career* entered NI Civil Serv 1934, perm sec Miny of Commerce 1955, agent in GB for NI 1970-76; *Recreations* fly-fishing; *Clubs* Stowe Fly-Fishing, Willowbrook Fly-Fishers; *Style—* Sir Harry Jones, CBE; Homelea, Nassington, Peterborough (☎ 0780 782675)

JONES, Dr (John) Howel; s of John Emrys Jones (d 1969), and Mary, *née* Edwards (d 1972); *b* 4 March 1928; *Educ* Ardwyn GS Aberystwyth, Wrekin Coll Wellington Shropshire, Sidney Sussex Coll Cambridge (MA, MD), St George's Hosp Med Sch; *m* 27 June 1953, Sheila Mary, da of Thomas Forster (d 1982); 2 s (Hugh, David), 1 da (Elizabeth); *Career* RAMC Capt in UK and Far East 1954-56; house offr and registrar posts: St George's Hosp London, Brompton Hosp, Queen Elizabeth Hosp Birmingham 1952-61; sr med registrar St George's Hosp and Central Middx Hosp 1961-66, conslt physician W Midlands RHA Coventry and Rugby 1966-; MO: GB Olympic Team 1976-84, England Cwlth Games Team 1978-82; hon med advsr Cwlth Games Fedn 1982-90; memb Br Soc of Gastro-enterology 1964, FRCP 1973; *Recreations* gardening, reading; *Style—* Dr Howel Jones; 5 Davenport Rd, Earlsdon, Coventry CV5 6QA (☎ 0203 677838)

JONES, Ven (Thomas) Hughie; s of Edward Teifi Jones (Battery Sgt RA, d 1973), of Aberystwyth, and Ellen, *née* Jones (d 1978); *b* 15 Aug 1927; *Educ* William Hume's Sch Manchester, Univ of Wales (Cardiff, BA), Univ of London (BD), Univ of Leicester (MA); *m* 26 Dec 1949, Beryl Joan, da of late Robert William Henderson (Corpl RAMC), of Chepstow; 2 da (Susan b 1951, Christine b 1954); *Career* volunteered Fleet Air Arm 1944, deferred, never served; warden Bible Trg Inst Glasgow 1949-57, minister John St Baptist Church Glasgow 1951-54, teacher and lectr Leicester & Leicestershire Educn Authorities 1955-75, princ Hind Leys Coll Shepshed Leics 1976-81, rector The Langtons Leics 1981-86, adult educn offr Diocese of Leicester 1981-84, archdeacon of Loughborough 1986-; memb: Welsh Soc, Ecclesiastical Law Soc (vice chm) Crime Prevention Panel, Local Educn Authy; FBIM 1974, FRAS 1977; *Recreations* gardening, bee keeping, entomology, genealogy, literature, Welsh affairs; *Clubs* Carlton, Leicestershire, Leics Co Cricket, Leicester Boxing and Sporting; *Style—* The Ven the Archdeacon of Loughborough; The Archdeaconry, Church Rd, Glenfield, Leicester LE3 8DP (☎ 0533 311 632); Church House, 3-5 St Martins East, Leicester LE1 5FX (☎ 0533 27445)

JONES, Hywel Francis; s of Brymor Jones (d 1957), of Morriston, Swansea, and Maggie Beatrice, *née* Francis (d 1987); *b* 28 Dec 1928; *Educ* Swansea GS, St John's Coll Cambridge (BA, MA); *m* 10 March 1959, Marian Rosser, da of Sidney Craven (d

1951), of Morriston, Swansea; 1 da (Sharon); *Career* Nat Serv RAPC 1953-55; dep co treas Breconshire CC 1956-59, asst co treas Carmarthenshire CC 1959-66, borough treas Port Talbot Borough Cncl 1966-75, cmmr Local Admin in Wales 1975- (sec 1975-85), local ombudsman 1985-; memb Public Works Loan Bd 1971-75, fin advsr AMC 1972-74; treas Royal Nat Eisteddfod of Wales 1975-, memb Gorsedd of Bards 1977; CIPFA 1953; *Recreations* music, reading, gardening; *Style*— Hywel F Jones, Esq; Godre'r Rhiw, 1 Lon Heulog, Baglan, Port Talbot SA12 8SY (☎ 0639 813 822); Derwen House, Court Rd, Bridgend CF31 1BN (☎ 0656 661 325)

JONES, Hywel Glyn; s of Thomas Glyndwr Jones (d 1984), and Anne, *née* Williams (d 1978); *b* 1 July 1948; *Educ* Whitchurch GS Cardiff, Trinity Coll Cambridge (MA); *m* 1 Aug 1970, Julia Claire, da of Lionel Davies; *Career* lectr in economics Univ of Warwick 1971-73, lectr in economics of the firm Univ of Oxford 1973-77 (fell Linacre Coll, lectr Worcester Coll 1973-77), dir and chief exec the Henley Centre 1981-85 (dir of int forecasting 1977-81); chm: Hywel Jones & Assocs 1985-, Fixpoint Ltd 1988-; *Books* Second Abstract of British Historical Statistics (with B R Mitchell, 1970), An Introduction to Modern Theories of Economic Growth (1974), Full Circle into the Future?, Britain into the 21st Century (1984); *Recreations* conversation, walking, military history, boating; *Style*— Hywel Jones, Esq; 59 Yarnells Hill, Oxford OX2 9BE (☎ 0865 240 916); Fixpoint Ltd, Euston House, 81-103 Euston St, London NW1 2ET (☎ 071 387 0019, fax 071 872 0095)

JONES, Ian; s of Reginald Sampson Jones (d 1977), of Birmingham, and Florence, *née* Lees; *b* 3 July 1947; *Educ* Queensbridge Sch Birmingham, Hall Green Tech Coll Birmingham, Birmingham Poly Sch of Fine Art (BA), RCA (MA); *m* 2 July 1966, Carole Ann, da of Albert Percival Holmes; 2 s (Antony Ian b 27 Dec 1966, Stuart Timothy b 12 Oct 1968); *Career* artist; apprentice toolmaker W H Doherty Co Ltd 1963-69; toolmaker: Aero Coldform Co Ltd 1969-72, Producit Co Ltd 1972-75; teacher of art at: Limerick Coll of Art & Design, Birmingham Sch of Fine Art, St Martin's Coll of Art London, Kingston Poly, Canterbury Art Coll, Brighton Poly Sch of Fine Art; major works: Head (Father) 1982, Drinking & Smoking 1982, The Engineer 1982, The Life Raft 1985, Tightrope Walker 1986, A Quick Trip to Ireland 1987, Hi Heel Sneakers 1987, There'll Be a Bit of a Breeze Tonight 1987, The Wedding 1988, Shoes on a Custard Carpet 1989, Celebrating the Buff Envelope 1989, The Karin B 1989, brummagem 1989, Sweet Smell of Success 1989, Reflections 1989, Money Talks 1990; solo exhibitions: chapter Art Centre Cardiff 1984, 21 Days Work (Leamington Spa 1985, Stratford upon Avon 1986), Recent Paintings and Drawings (Consort Gallery, ICST) 1987, Some New York (Vortex Gallery London) 1987, Recent Paintings (Camden Arts Centre, London) 1988, Anderson O'Day Gallery 1989-91; gp exhibitions incl: Drawings (Foyle Gallery, Birmingham) 1975, 5 Painters (Consort Gallery) 1981, New Contemporaries (ICA Gallery) 1982, New Blood on Paper (MOMA, Oxford) 1983, Gallery 24 London 1984, Open Studios (Fish Island Artists, London) 1985, Print Show (The Grannery, Limerick) 1986, Mead Gallery Warwick Univ 1987, Athena Awards (Barbican) 1988, Images of Paradise (Harewood House, Yorks) 1989, Contemporary London (Transart Cologne) 1989, Salon de la Jeune Peinture Grand Palais Paris 1990; works in the public collections of: Unilever, Nordstern Cologne, WEA, Guiness Brewing Worldwide, Pepsi Cola; awards: Whitworth Wallis prize 1976, John Minton award 1982, major award Greater London Arts award 1983, short list prize Athena Awards 1988, Unilever prize Portobello Festival 1989; *Recreations* music; *Style*— Ian Jones, Esq; Anderson O'Day Gallery, 255 Portobello Rd, London W11 1LR

JONES, (Charles) Ian McMillan; s of Wilfred Charles Jones (d 1986), of Wroxham, Norfolk, and Bessie, *née* McMillan; *b* 11 Oct 1934; *Educ* Bishop's Stortford Coll, St John's Coll Cambridge (MA, PGCE, Capt Camb Univ Hockey XI 1958/59); *m* 9 Aug 1962, Jennifer Marie, da of Alec Potter (d 1980), of Hertford; 2 s (William Ian b 18 Jan 1964, Robert Andrew b 28 Jan 1970); *Career* Nat Serv 1953-55, cmmnd RA, Subalt 45 Field Regt in BAOR, regtl motor tport offr, TA 1955-57, Lt Herts Yeomanry; head Geography Dept Bishop's Stortford Coll 1960-70 (asst to Headmaster 1967-70), vice princ King William's Coll IOM 1971-75, Headmaster Bedford Sch 1975-86, dir Studies Britannia RNC Dartmouth 1986-88, project dir The Centre for Br Teachers Negara Brunei Darussalam 1988-, Malaysia 1990-, educnl advsr Kolej Tuanku Ja'afar Malaysia 1988-; played for: England Hockey XI 1959-64, GB Hockey XI 1959-64; competed in Rome and Tokyo Olympics, mangr/coach England Hockey XI 1967-69; English Schoolboy Hockey Assoc: chm 1976-86, pres 1980-88; mangr England Schoolboy Hockey XI 1967-77; memb: Ctee of Headmasters' Conf 1981-83, IOM Sports Cncl 1972-75; chm ISIS Central 1981-83; FBIM 1981, FRSA 1981; contributed feature articles on hockey to The Guardian 1969-72; *Recreations* hockey, cricket, squash, golf; *Clubs* MCC, Hawks, Pantai Mentiri Golf (Brunei); *Style*— Ian Jones, Esq; Riverain, Staitheway Rd, Wroxham, Norwich, Norfolk NR12 8TH (☎ 0603 782307); The Centre for British Teachers, Quality House, Gyosei Campus, London Road, Reading RG1 5AQ (☎ 0734 756200, fax 0734 756365)

JONES, Ian Quayle; WS; s of Arnold Bates Jones (d 1977), of Poynton, Cheshire, and Lilian Quayle Jones (d 1989); *b* 14 July 1941; *Educ* Strathallan Sch, Univ of Edinburgh (MA, LLB); *m* 24 Feb 1968, Christine Ann, da of Kenneth Macrae, WS (d 1984), of Edinburgh; 2 s (Simon Quayle b 1977, Richard Ian b 1980), 1 da (Stephanie Margaret b 1974); *Career* ptnr Cowan and Stewart WS 1968-72, fund mangr Ivory & Syme 1972-74, dir Br Linen Bank Ltd 1974-83 (mangr, asst dir), jt md Quayle Munro 1983-, non-exec chm Nevis Range Devpt Co plc 1989-; govr Strathallan Sch; *Recreations* golf, skiing, fishing; *Clubs* Hon Co of Edinburgh Golfers; *Style*— Ian Jones, Esq, WS; The Stone House, 1 Pentland Road, Edinburgh (☎ 031 441 3034); 42 Charlotte Square, Edinburgh EH2 4HQ (☎ 031 226 4421, fax 031 225 3391)

JONES, Iddon Lloyd; JP (1979); s of Morris Jones (d 1963), of Harlech, and Dorothy Lloyd, *née* Roberts (d 1986); *b* 1 Nov 1933; *Educ* Barmouth GS, UCW Swansea (BSc); *m* 7 Sept 1968, Ann, da of Harry Trefor Jones, of Criccieth; 1 s (Huw Lloyd b 22 May 1972), 1 da (Nia Lloyd b 29 Sept 1970); *Career* Nat Serv 1955-57, cmmnd Flying Offr RAF (airfield construction branch); ptnr NW office James Williamson & Ptnrs cnslt engrs 1957-89, currently dir Mott MacDonald Structural & Industrial Ltd; work incl: Ffestiniog pumped storage project, Wylfa nuclear power station, Dinorwig pumped storage project, N Sea oil related work offshore Shetlands; md Merz Rendel Williamson Ltd, dir Mott MacDonald Wales & Power Divs; former capt Penmaenmawr Golf Club; CEng, FICE, FIHT, MConsE; *Recreations* golf; *Clubs* RSAC, Penmaenmawr Golf; *Style*— Iddon Jones, Esq, JP; Treflys, Conwy Old Road, Penmaemawr, Gwynedd LL34 6RD (☎ 0492 623 622); 11 Wynnstay Road, Colwyn Bay, Clwyd LL29 8NB (☎ 0492 531 833)

JONES, Ieuan; s of David Edward Humphries Jones, of Mathrafal, Meifod, Powys, Wales, and Beryl Elizabeth Mary, *née* Proudlove; *b* 24 Jan 1963; *Educ* Llanfair Caereinion Sch, RCM (Most Distinguished Student award, Tagore Gold medal, Winner Royal Overseas League music competition, runner up Israel Harp contest); *Career* harpist; appointed harpist to the House of Commons 1984, London debut Purcell Room 1985, Wigmore Hall debut 1987; recitals: Dusseldorf 1986 and 1990, Amsterdam 1987, Ireland 1987, Vienna 1987, Holland 1987, Valencia Spain 1987 and 1988, Mid West tour USA 1989, Wigmore Hall 1990, Paris 1990, St David's Hall Cardiff 1988 and 1990; tours with: Bournemouth Sinfonietta 1986, 1987 and 1988, Welsh Chamber Orch 1988, London Festival Orch 1989 and 1990; tv and radio appearances incl: Wogan 1986, Daytime Live 1988, AVRO tv Holland 1987, Billy Butler Show 1988 and 1990, Derek Jameson 1988, Gloria Hunniford 1988 and 1990; appearances at many festivals in the UK and abroad; private appearance before HRH Queen Elizabeth the Queen Mother at the Royal Lodge Windsor 1986, guest appearance St James' Palace 1988 and Holyrood House 1989; recordings: The Uncommon Harp (1987), The Two Sides of Ieuan Jones (1988), ...In The French Style (1990), Mozart in Paris (1990); ARCM 1981; *Recreations* health & fitness, travel; *Style*— Ieuan Jones, Esq; c/o Neil Chaffey, 8 Laxton Gardens, Baldock, Herts SG7 6DA (☎ 0462 895094, fax 0462 491378)

JONES, Ieuan Wyn; MP (Plaid Cymru) Ynys Mon 1987-; s of Rev John Jones (d 1977), of Gwynedd, and Mair Elizabeth Jones, *née* Pritchard; *b* 22 May 1949; *Educ* Pontardawe GS Ysgol-Y-Berwyn, Y Bala & Liverpool Poly (LLB); *m* 1974, Eirian Llwyd, da of John Nefydd Jones, of Clwyd; 2 s (Gerallt b 1975, Owain b 1978), 1 da (Gwenllian b 1977); *Career* slr 1973, ptnr William Jones & Talog Davies Ruthin Clwyd 1974 (ptnr Llangefni Branch 1985-); *Recreations* sport, local history; *Style*— Ieuan Jones, Esq, MP; Ty Newydd Rhosmeirch, Llangefni (☎ 0248 72261, 0248 723599); House of Commons (☎ 071 219 5021)

JONES, Jack Anthony; s of Jack Jones (d 1973), and Patricia, *née* Hackett (d 1989); *b* 12 Oct 1957; *Educ* Chatham House GS Ramsgate, Univ of Nottingham (BSc), Imperial Coll of Sci & Technol (MSc); *m* 30 May 1981, Bridget Jane, da of Peter Linington, of Somali Farm, Birchington, Kent; 1 s (Christopher Peter b 24 Sept 1987), 1 da (Katherine Patricia b 20 Sept 89); *Career* mining engr: Gold Fields of SA 1979-80, Shell (SA) 1980-82, Shell (Botswana) 1982-83; stockbroker UBS Phillips & Drew 1984-; MIMM 1985, CEng 1986; *Style*— Jack Jones, Esq; Conyers, 18 Woodside Rd, Sevenoaks, Kent TN13 3HE (☎ 0732 453740); UBS Phillips & Drew, 100 Liverpool St, London EC2M 2RH (☎ 071 901 1319)

JONES, Jack James Larkin; CH (1978), MBE (1950); s of George Jones (d 1969), of Liverpool, and Ann Devoy (d 1963); *b* 29 July 1913; *Educ* Elementary Sch Liverpool, Toxteth Tech Sch Liverpool; *m* 1938, Evelyn Mary, da of Joseph Taylor (d 1954), of Knutsford; 2 s (Jack, Michael); *Career* served Spanish Civil War (wounded Ebro Battle 1938); first employed in engrg and docks industs, dep chm Nat Ports Cncl 1967-79, gen sec TGWU 1969-78, vice pres Int Tport Workers Fedn 1972-, memb Bd ACAS 1974-78, chm Int Ctee Nationalised Industs and Tport Ctees of TUC; pres EFTA Trade Union 1972-74, Royal Cmmn on Criminal Procedure 1978-80, chm Pensioners Liaison forum 1988-, vice chm Nat Pensioners Convention 1980-; Hon DLitt Warwick 1978; FCIT; *Books* The Incompatibles (1967), A to Z of Trades Unionism and Industrial Relations (with Max Morris, 1982), Union Man (autobiography, 1986); *Recreations* walking; *Clubs* Tom Mann Trades (Coventry); *Style*— Jack Jones, Esq, CH, MBE; 74 Ruskin Park House, Champion Hill, London SE5 8TH; (☎ 071 274 7067)

JONES, James; s of James Bertram Jones (d 1969); *b* 1 March 1925; *Educ* Kelvinside, Royal Tech Coll, West of Scotland Commercial Coll; *m* 1953, Janet Young Mitchell, *née* Lockhart; 1 s (Stephen b 1960), 1 da (Carol b 1961); *Career* mgmnt conslt; md: David Scott & Co Ltd 1960-68, L Sterne & Co Ltd 1968-71, J Jones (Glasgow) Ltd 1971-, Blairs Ltd 1974-; *Recreations* golf; *Clubs* Reform, Naval and Military, Royal Aero, Caledonian; *Style*— James Jones Esq; 97 Kelvin Ct, Glasgow G12 0AH (☎ 041 221 1715)

JONES, Janet Eveline; JP (1979); da of Edward Leslie Coppack, JP (d 1981), of Colherne, Bryn Arnold, Connah's Quay, Clwyd, and Agnes Jamieson, *née* McRae; *b* 27 June 1930; *Educ* Hawarden GS, The Froebel Educn Inst (dip); *m* 21 Aug 1954, Thomas Mathias Jones, s of David Elwyn Jones (d 1971), of Bryn Arnold, Connah's Quay, Clwyd; 2 s (Christopher Thomas b 1960 David Edward b 4 Jan 1962), 1 da (Helen Lesley (Mrs Byrne) b 9 Jan 1958); *Career* head teacher Astmoor Infants Sch 1971-81, disability retirement 1981; author of various reports and submissions to select ctees on educn, writer of reports for Womans Nat Ctee; pres: NAHT Halton South 1975-76, Runcorn and Dist Soroptimists 1985-86 and 1990-91; nat chm Br Assoc for Early Childhood Educn 1986-89 (chm Cheshire Branch 1979-80), sch govr, fndr memb Cheshire Woman of the Year Steering Ctee, co-chm Womans Nat Cmmn 1987-89, memb Standing Ctee Social Servs SEAC 1989-91; borough cncllr (Lib Dem) Halton Cheshire 1990-; patron Prix de Femmes d' Europe; *Recreations* reading, swimming, photography; *Clubs* The Soroptimist; *Style*— Mrs Janet Jones, JP; 8 Kenilworth Ave, Runcorn, Cheshire WA7 4XQ (☎ 0928 574 223); BAECE, 111 City House, 463 Bethnal Green Rd, London E2 9QH (☎ 071 739 7594)

JONES, Hon Jeffrey Richard; CBE (1979); s of Rev Thomas Jones (d 1962), and Winifred, *née* Williams; *b* 18 Nov 1921; *Educ* Grove Park Wrexham, Denstone Coll Staffs, Keble Coll Oxford (MA); *m* 1955, Ann Rosaleen, da of Michael Carberry (d 1963), of Derbys; 1 s (Thomas), 1 da (Philippa); *Career* Flt Lt (Pilot) RAFVR 1941-46; art master Mountgrace Comp Sch Middx 1953-54, called to the Bar Middle Temple 1954, ed Law Reports Northern Nigeria 1968-75; chief justice: Kano State Nigeria 1975-80, Repub of Kiribati 1980-85; pres Ct of Appeal Kiribati 1981-85; memb Ct of Appeal: 1983, Solomon Islands 1984; pres Rotary Club Kano 1977; *Publications* Some Cases on Criminal Procedure and Evidence (1967 and 1968), Criminal Procedure of the Northern States of Nigeria (1975); *Recreations* duck shooting, sea fishing, golf, art; *Style*— Hon Jeffrey Jones, CBE; Bradley Cottage, Bradley Lane, Holt, Wilts (☎ 0225 782004)

JONES, Hon Mrs (Jennifer Margaret); da of Baron Pilkington (Life Peer, d 1983) by 1 w, Rosamond Margaret Rowan (d 1953); *b* 1933; *m* 1958, Dennis Jones; children; *Style*— The Hon Mrs Jones; Swallow Cottage, Burbage, Leics

JONES, Prof (William) Jeremy; s of Thomas John Jones (d 1975), of Llandeilo, Dyfed, and Margaret Jeremy (d 1958); *b* 15 Aug 1935; *Educ* Llandeilo GS, UCW Aberystwyth (BSc, MSc), Trinity Coll Cambridge (PhD); *m* 29 June 1963, (Margaret) Anne, da of Dr Frederick Greystock Robertson, of Cobourg, Ontario, Canada; 2 s (Jeremy b 18 May 1964, d 1987, Michael b 28 March 1968), 1 da (Suzanne b 19 June 1970); *Career* Univ of Cambridge: external res student Trinity Coll 1958-60, title A res fell Trinity Coll 1960-64, demonstrator in physical chemistry 1965-70, lectr 1970-78, tutor Trinity Coll 1973-78 (fell and dir studies 1964-78); res student Courtaulds 1958-61, fell Nat Res Cncl of Canada 1962-64, prof and head Dept of Chemistry UCW Aberystwyth 1978-88, prof of chemistry Univ Coll Swansea 1988-; memb Optical Soc of America 1978; FRSC 1978; *Recreations* golf, gardening, walking; *Style*— Prof Jeremy Jones; 2 Knoll Ave, Uplands, Swansea SA2 0JN (☎ 0792 298149); Department of Chemistry, University College of Swansea, Singleton Park SA2 8PP (☎ 0792 295507)

JONES, Hon Mrs (Joanna Catherine); *née* Grant; da of Maj Sir Arthur Lindsay Grant, 11 Bt (ka 1944), and Baroness Tweedsmuir of Belhelvie (Life Peeress, d 1978); *b* 1935; *m* 1954 (m dis 1966), Dominick Jones, s of Sir (George) Roderick Jones, KBE; 1 s; *Style*— The Hon Mrs Jones; c/o Romily Jones, 162 Elborough Street, London SW18 5DL

JONES, John Bannister; s of Harry Bannister Jones (d 1956), of Bebington, and Ruth, *née* Dunn (d 1958); *b* 7 Dec 1929; *Educ* Birkenhead Sch, Univ of Liverpool (Bcom); *m* 3 May 1975, (Winifred) Jonquil, da of Stanley Hanson (d 1978), of Didsbury, Manchester; 2 (Christopher b 5 Aug 1960, Michael b 23 Feb 1965); *Career*

Nat Serv 2 Lt RAPC 1954-56; CA; nat vice chm Pannell Kerr Forster Manchester 1980-85 (ptnr 1961, sr ptnr 1978); FCA; *Recreations* music, travel, walking; *Style*— John Jones, Esq; 3 Goodrington Rd, Handforth, Wilmslow, Cheshire SK9 3AT; Sovereign House, Queen St, Manchester M2 THR (☎ 061 832 5481, fax 061 832 3849, telex 669417 PANKER

JONES, John Elfed; CBE (1987), DL; s of Urien Maelgwyn Jones (d 1978); *b* 19 March 1933; *Educ* Blaenau Ffestiniog GS, Denbighshire Tech Coll, Heriot-Watt Coll; *m* 1957, Mary Sheila, da of David Thomas Rosser; 2 da (Bethan, Delyth); *Career* Flying Offr RAF; chartered electrical engr CEGB 1949-1969, dep md Anglesey Aluminium Metal Ltd 1969-79, under sec (indust) Welsh Office 1979-82, chm Welsh Water Authy 1982-; chm Bwrdd Yr Iaith Gymraeg (Welsh Language Bd) 1988-; CEng, FIEE, FRSA, CBIM; *Recreations* fishing (salmon and trout), attending Eisteddfodau; *Style*— John Elfed Jones Esq, CBE, DL; Ty Mawr, Coety, Penybontarogwr, Morgannwg Ganol CF35 6BN (☎ 0656x 653039); Welsh Water PLC, Cambrian Way, Brecon, Powys LD3 7HP (☎ 0874 3181)

JONES, (Henry) John Franklin; s of late Lt-Col James Walker Jones, DSO, and Doris Marjorie, *née* Franklin; *b* 6 May 1924; *Educ* Blundell's, Merton Coll Oxford; *m* 10 Dec 1949, Jean Verity, da of Samuel Robinson, CMG (d 1973), of London; 1 s, 1 da; *Career* WWII serv Ordinary Seaman RN 1943, Intelligence Staff Eastern Fleet 1944; Univ of Oxford: fell and tutor jurisprudence 1949-56, univ sr lectr 1956-62, fell and tutor in Eng lit 1962-79, prof of poetry 1979-84; Dill Meml Lectr Queen's Univ Belfast 1983; football corr The Observer 1956-59; tv appearances incl The Modern World 1988; pubns incl: The Egotistical Sublime (1954, fifth edn 1978), The British Imagination (contrib 1961), on Aristotle and Greek Tragedy (1965, fifth edn 1980), Dickens and the Twentieth Century (contrib 1962), John Keats' Dream of Truth (1969, second edn 1980), The Morality of Art (1969), The Same God (1971), Dostoevskey (1983, second edn 1985); *Style*— John Jones, Esq; Holywell Cottage, Oxford (☎ 0865 247 702); Yellands, Brisworthy, Shaugh Prior, Plympton, Devon (☎ 075 539 310)

JONES, Sir John Lewis; KCB (1983), CMG (1972); *b* 17 Feb 1923; *Educ* Christ's Coll Camb (MA); *m* 1948, Daphne Nora (*née* Redman); *Career* RA 1942-46, Sudan Govt 1947-55, MOD 1955-85; *Clubs* United Oxford and Cambridge; *Style*— Sir John Jones, KCB, CMG

JONES, John Maurice; s of Maurice Parry Jones, of Llwynderw, Bala, N Wales, and Armorel Winifred, *née* Adams; *b* 6 March 1943; *Educ* Llandovery Coll, Middx Hosp Univ of London (MB BS); *m* 17 Feb 1968, Valerie Patricia; 1 s (Richard b 1973), 2 da (Katie b 1970, Vanessa b 1971); *Career* surgical registrar Edinburgh 1970-74, orthopaedic registrar St George's Hosp London 1974-76, sr registrar Cardiff 1976-80, orthopaedic conslt Leicester 1980-; fell Presbyterian St Luke's Chicago; memb: BSSH; FBOA, FRCSEd; *Style*— John Jones, Esq; 8 Knighton Dr, Leics LE2 3HB (☎ 0533 706961); BUPA Hospital, Gartree Rd, Leics LE2 2FF (☎ 0533 720888, fax 0533 720666, car 0860553135)

JONES, Prof John Richards; s of William Jones (d 1972), of Tregaron, and Mary Ann, *née* Richards; *b* 27 Dec 1937; *Educ* Tregaron GS, UCW (BSc 1958, PhD 1961, DSc 1977); *m* 28 Dec 1963, Eirlys Williams, da of Trevor Thomas (d 1966), of Pontlliw; 2 da (Carys b 1964, Siân b 1965); *Career* Battersea Coll of Advanced Technol: asst lectr physical chemistry 1961-63, lectr physical chemistry (and Univ of Surrey) 1963-82, reader 1982-88, head of Chemistry Dept 1984-85, personal chair radiochemistry 1988-; fell Royal Soc of Chem; *Books* The Ionisation of Carbon Acids, (1973), Handbook of Tritium NMR Spectroscopy and Applications (with E A Evans, D C Warrell and J A Elvidge 1985); *Recreations* cricket, gardening; *Style*— Prof John Jones; Heatherdale, New Park Rd, Cranleigh, Surrey GU6 7HJ (☎ 0483 273483); Chemistry Department, University of Surrey, Guildford, Surrey GU2 5XH (☎ 0483 571281 ext 2581, fax 0483 300803)

JONES, Kay Mary; da of John Victor Jones (d 1972), of Birkenhead, Merseyside, and Barbara Mary Imogen Jones, BEM; *b* 2 Sept 1945; *Educ* Wycombe Abbey Sch, Univ of Sussex, Univ of Aix Marseilles; *Career* called to the Bar Grays Inn 1974; specialises in int family law, assoc memb American Bar Assoc, ptnr IVP Lectures; contrib New Law Journal; ABA 1986; *Recreations* theatre, arts, sailing, writing; *Clubs* Reform, Network; *Style*— Miss Kay Jones; 63 Brent Terrace, London NW2 1BY (☎ 071 458 8498); 4 Veruwam Buildings, Gray's Inn, London WC1R 5LW (☎ 071 405 6114, fax 071 831 6112, car 0860 341674)

JONES, Sir Keith Stephen; s of S W Jones; *b* 7 July 1911; *Educ* Newington Coll Univ of Sydney; *m* 1936, Kathleen, da of A E Abbott; 3 s; *Career* memb Newington Coll Cncl 1951-70, CMO NSW State Emergency Servs 1968-74, memb NSW Med Bd 1971-81, pres Aust Med Assoc 1973-76; chm: Australasian Med Publishing Co 1976-82, Nat Specialist Qualifications Advsy Ctee 1979-82, Blue Cross Assoc of Aust 1983-85; pres MBF of Aust 1983-86; emeritus conslt surgn Manly Dist Hosp 1982-; Gold Medal Aust Med Assoc 1976; FRCS, FRACS, FRACGP, FACEM; kt 1980; *Style*— Sir Keith Jones; 123 Bayview Village, Cabbage Tree Rd, Bayview, NSW 2104 Australia (☎ 02 997 2876)

JONES, Hon Sir Kenneth George Illtyd; s of late Richard Arthur Jones; *b* 26 May 1921; *Educ* Brigg GS, Univ Coll Oxford (MA); *m* 1, 1947, Dulcie Thursfield (d 1977); 1 s, 2 da; m 2, 1978, June Patricia, da of late Leslie Arthur Doxey; *Career* served WWII RA; called to the Bar Gray's Inn 1946, QC 1962; rec: Shrewsbury 1964-66, Wolverhampton 1966-71; bencher 1969, rec of the Crown Ct 1972, circuit judge 1972, judge of the High Court of Justice (Queen's Bench Div) 1974-88, treas Gray's Inn 1987; kt 1974; *Style*— The Hon Sir Kenneth Jones; c/o Coutts & Co, 188 Fleet St, London EC4A 2HT

JONES, Sir (John) Kenneth Trevor; CBE (1956), QC (1976); s of John Jones; *b* 11 July 1910; *Educ* King Henry VIII GS Abergavenny, Univ Coll of Wales, St John's Coll Cambridge; *m* 1940, Menna Jones; 2 s; *Career* served WWII RA; called to the Bar Lincoln's Inn 1937; entered Home Office 1945, legal advsr Home Office 1956-77; memb Standing Ctee on Criminal Law Reform 1959-80; kt 1965; *Clubs* Athenaeum; *Style*— Sir Kenneth Jones, CBE, QC; 7 Chilton Court, Walton on Thames, Surrey KT12 1NG (☎ 0932 226890)

JONES, Kevin Anthony; s of Kenneth Jones, of W Yorks, and Erica, *née* Boxall; *b* 13 May 1960; *Educ* Ossett Sch, Wakefield Coll of Technol & Arts; *Career* advertising art dir; Wasey Campbell-Ewald 1978, The KMP Partnership 1981, Lowe Howard Spink 1983, Wight Collins Rutherford Scott Matthews Marcantonio 1987, The Leagas Delaney Partnership 1988, Lowe Howard Spink 1989-; winner numerous advtg awards; *Recreations* cinema, reading; *Style*— Kevin Jones, Esq; Lowe Howard Spink, Bowater House, 68-114 Knightsbridge, London SW1 (☎ 071 584 5033)

JONES, Laurance Aubrey; s of Aubrey Joseph Goldsmid Jones (d 1990), of The Chestnuts, Godmanchester, Huntingdon, and Frances Laura, *née* Ward; *b* 7 April 1936; *Educ* King's Sch Rochester; *m* 8 July 1961, Joan, da of Douglas Stanley Sargeant, of 6 Jeffery Close, Staplehurst, Kent; *Career* Nat Serv RAF 1954-56; Royal Insurance Group 1953-54 and 1956-57, National Employers Mutual General Insurance Association Ltd 1957-58, co sec Marchant & Tubb Ltd 1959-67, jt sec Tollemache & Cobbold Group Cambridge 1967-70, dep sec International Timber Corporation Ltd 1970-77, gp sec Land Securities plc 1977-; Cncl memb Chartered Secs East Anglian Branch; Freeman: Maidstone 1957, City of London 1981, Liveryman Worshipful Co of Chartered Secs and Administrators 1981; FCIS 1972 (assoc 1968); *Recreations* tennis, skiing, golf, travel, bridge; *Clubs* City Livery; *Style*— Laurance Jones, Esq; Florus House, Widdington, Saffron Walden, Essex CB11 3SB; 99 Le Panoramic, Thollon Les Memises, 74500 Evian Les Bains, France; 95 John Trundle Court, Barbican, London EC2 (☎ 071 353 4222, fax 071 353 7871, telex 934019)

JONES, Air Marshal Sir Laurence Alfred; KCB (1984), AFC (1971); s of Benjamin Howel Jones and Irene Dorothy Jones; *b* 18 Jan 1933; *m* 1956, Brenda Ann Jones; 2 da; *Career* RAF Coll Cranwell 1951-53, served ME and Germany; Rcds, jssc, psc; SASO Strike Cmd 1982-84, ACAS (ops) 1984, ACDS (progs) 1985-86, ACAS 1986-87, Air Memb for Personnel 1987-89, ret 1990; currently Lt Govr Isle of Man; *Style*— Air Marshal Sir Laurence Jones, KCB, AFC

JONES, Lucy Katharine; da of Anthony Tom Brett-Jones, CBE, and Ann, *née* Fox; *b* 21 Feb 1955; *Educ* Cheyne Spastic Centre, King Alfred's Sch Hampstead, Byam Shaw Sch of Drawing and Painting, Camberwell Sch of Art (BA), RCA (MA, Cubitt award for painting, Anstruther award for painting), Br Sch in Rome (The Rome scholar in painting); *m* Peter Leach; *Career* self employed artist and painter; visiting tutor at various art colls incl: Ruskin Sch of Art, Byam Shaw Sch of Art, West Surrey Coll of Art and Design, Winchester Sch of Art; pt/t tutor at Chelsea Coll of Art; solo exhibitions: Spitalfields Health Centre in assoc with Whitechapel Art Gallery 1987, Angela Flowers Gallery London 1987 and 1989, Drumcroon Art Educn Centre Wigan 1990, Flowers East London 1991; gp exhibitions incl: Royal Acad Summer Exhibition 1981, The Pick of Graduate Art (Christies Inaugural) 1982, 10 Artisti della Accademia Britannica (Palazzo Barberini, Rome) 1984, Canvas-New British Painters (John Hansard Gallery and Milton Keynes City Art Gallery) 1986, Artist of the Day (Angela Flowers Gallery) 1986, Young Masters (The Solomon Gallery, London) 1986, Whitechapel Open (Whitechapel Art Gallery, London) 1987, Passage West (Angela Flowers Ireland, Co Cork) 1987, The Subjective City (The Small Mansion Arts Centre, London) 1988, London Glasgow NY: New Acquisitions (Metropolitan Museum of Art, USA) 1988, Contemporary Portraits (Flowers East, London) 1988, Big Paintings (Flowers East) 1989, XXI International Festival of Painting Cagnes-sur-Mer-France 1989, Flowers at Moos (Gallery Moos, NY) 1990, The Subjective City (Cleveland Gallery, Middlesborough and tour) 1990, Rome 1980-90 (RCA) 1990, Rome scholars 1980-90 (RCA) 1990, Drumcroon The First Ten Years (Drumcroon Educn Art Centre) 1990; works in the public collections of: Sheffield City Art Gallery, Univ of Reading, Arts Cncl, Security Pacific, Metropolitan Museum of Art, Rugby Museum, Drumcroon Education Art Centre Wigan, Unilever plc, Contemporary Art Soc; awards: Oppenheim-John Downes Meml Tst 1986, Daler-Rowney award (best work in oil) Royal Acad Exhibition 1987; *Recreations* swimming, music, opera, cooking, sailing; *Style*— Ms Lucy Jones; Angela Flowers Gallery plc, Flowers East, 199-205 Richmond Rd, London E8 3NJ (☎ 081 985 3333, fax 081 985 0067)

JONES, Malcolm; s of Absalom Lewis Jones (d 1973), and Winnifred Mary, *née* O'Brien (d 1980); *b* 22 Oct 1932; *Educ* Luton GS, LSE (BSc); *m* 12 April 1954, Patricia Yvonne, da of Trevor Emery; 1 s (Michael Barry b 29 March 1963), 2 da (Beverly Shân b 20 Nov 1956, Elizabeth Lynne b 29 March 1963); *Career* sr fin exec: Vauxhall Motors 1957-67, John Laing & Son 1968-71; chief accountant guided weapons British Aircraft Co Ltd 1971-75, Westland Group plc 1975-87 (gp business dir, gp programme dir, fin dir, commercial dir), fin controller AAA/BAAB 1987-; FCMA, FCCA, FBIM; *Recreations* sport, literature; *Style*— Malcolm Jones, Esq; 11 Evertons Close, Millers Lodge, Droitwich Spa, Worcs WR9 8AE (☎ 0905 779666)

JONES, Prof Malcolm Vince; s of Reginald Cross Jones (d 1986), and Winifred Ethel, *née* Vince; *b* 7 Jan 1940; *Educ* Cotham GS Bristol, Univ of Nottingham (BA, PhD); *m* 27 July 1963, Jennifer Rosemary, da of Frederick Walter Durrant (d 1987); 1 s (Alexander b 30 May 1967), 1 da (Helen b 5 Dec 1968); *Career* asst lectr in Russian Sch of Euro Studies Univ of Sussex 1965-67, prof Dept of Slavonic Studies Univ of Nottingham 1980- (lectr 1967-73, sr lectr 1973-80), dean Faculty of Arts Univ of Nottingham 1982-85 (vice dean 1976-79), pro-vice chllr Univ of Nottingham 1987-; memb Ed Bd: Birmingham Slavonic Monographs 1976-, Renaissance and Mod Studies 1977-; gen ed Cambridge Studies In Russian Literature; hon pres: Assoc of Teachers of Russian 1985-86, Br Universities Assoc of Slavists 1986-88 (hon sec 1974-76); hon vice pres Br Assoc For Soviet Slavonic And E Euro Studies 1988-, hon vice pres Coordinating Cncl for Area Studies Assoc 1988-; *Books* Dostoyevsky The Novel of Discord (1976), New Essays On Tolstoy (ed, 1978), New Essays On Dostoyevsky (jt ed, 1983), Dostoyevsky after Bakhtin (1990); *Recreations* painting; *Clubs* University, Nottingham; *Style*— Prof Malcolm Jones; Univ of Nottingham, Dept of Slavonic Studies, Univ Park, Nottingham NG7 2RD (☎ 0602 484848 ext 2554)

JONES, Martyn David; MP (L) Clwyd South West 1987-; s of Vernon Pritchard Jones, of Wrexham, and Violet Gwendoline Jones, *née* Griffiths; *b* 1 March 1947; *Educ* Grove Park GS Wrexham, Trent Poly; *m* 1974, Rhona, da of Roger Bellis, of Wrexham; 1 s (Nicholas b 1984), 1 da (Linzi b 1974); *Career* co cncllr 1981-89, opposition whip 1988-; memb Agric Select Ctee; MIBiol; *Recreations* backpacking, target shooting, sailing; *Clubs* Wrexham Lager Sports & Soc, Wrexham British Rail; *Style*— Martyn Jones, Esq, MP; 5 Maes yr Haf, Smithy Lane, Wrexham (☎ Wrexham 263236); House of Commons London SW1A 0AA (☎ 071 219 3417)

JONES, Maude Elizabeth; CBE (1973); 2 da of Edward William Jones (d 1953), of Dolben, Ruthin, N Wales; *b* 14 Jan 1921; *Educ* Brynhyfryd Sch for Girls Ruthin; *Career* joined Foreign Rels Dept Joint War Orgn BRCS and Order of St John 1940, dir Jr Red Cross 1960 (dep dir 1949), dep dir gen for branch affrs BRCS 1966, memb Jt Ctee Order of St John and BRCS 1966-77, dep dir gen Br Red Cross Soc 1970-77; memb: Nat Cncl of Social Serv 1966-77, FANY 1966-77; govr St David's Sch Ashford Middx; SSStJ 1959; *Recreations* music, gardening, reading; *Clubs* New Cavendish; *Style*— Miss Maude Jones, CBE; Dolben, Ruthin, N Wales (☎ 082 42 2443)

JONES, (Christopher) Maurice; DL (Hants 1984); s of Sydney Edward Jones (d 1942), of Evelyn Gardens, London SW7, and Margaret Jesse, *née* Collis-Sandes (d 1956); *b* 17 May 1919; *Educ* Rugby, Trinity Coll Cambridge (MA); *m* 3 May 1947, Isobel Gwyn, da of William Reginald Bown; 1 s (Nicholas b 1952), 2 da (Susannah (Mrs Lyle) b 1948, Caroline b 1950); *Career* Nat Serv WWII cmmnd RA POW Singapore (worked on Siam-Burma railway) 1939-45; md John Lewis Partnership; 4,000 Acre estate Hants 1946-81; memb Hants CC 1965- (chm 1984-86 and 1989-); chm: Glebe ctee Winchester Diocese 1974, Test and Itchen Fishing Assoc 1972-81; pres Romsey Show 1981; *Recreations* NH racing, country pursuits, visiting old churches; *Style*— Maurice Jones, Esq, DL; One, The Grange, Longstock, Stockbride, Hants

JONES, Medwyn; s of Capt Ieuan Glyn Du Platt Jones, of Llandbedr Duffryn, Clwyd, N Wales, and Margaret, *née* Owen; *b* 13 Sept 1955; *Educ* Scorton Sch, Chester GS, Univ of Sheffield (LLB), The Coll of Law; *Career* slr Theodore Goddard 1980-81 (articled clerk 1978-80), ptnr Walker Martineau 1983- (slr 1981-83); Freeman City of London; memb: City of London Solicitor's Company 1988, Law Soc 1980; *Recreations* skiing; *Style*— Medwyn Jones, Esq; Walker Martineau Stringer Soul, 64 Queen St, London EC4R IAD (☎ 071 236 4232, fax 071 236 2525)

JONES, Miah Gwynfor (Gwyn); s of Robert Jones (d 1979), of Porthmadog, Gwynedd, and Jane Irene, *née* Evans (d 1981); *b* 2 Dec 1948; *Educ* Ysgol Eifionydd

Porthmadog Univ of Manchester (BSc), Univ of Essex (PhD); *m* 10 Jan 1976, Maria Linda, da of Kenneth Johnson (d 1984), of Swansea; 2 da (Victoria Rachel Sian b 1980, Holly Alexandra Jane b 1982); *Career* British Steel 1975-77, ICL 1977-81, chm and chief exec Corporate Technology Group plc 1981-87, chm Welsh Devpt Agency 1988-; non-exec dir: ACT Group plc 1989-, Welsh Water Enterprises Ltd 1990-; memb Advsy Ctee Assoc of MBAs, Cncl Univ of Wales, Bd of Euro Business Sch Univ of Swansea, Prince of Wales Ctee, Prince's Youth Business Tst; FBCS; *Recreations* golf, tennis, skiing, travel; *Style*— Dr Gwyn Jones; Welsh Development Agency, Pearl House, Greyfriars Rd, Cardiff (☎ 0222 222666, fax 0222 238849)

JONES, Michael Abbott; s of Ronald Edgar Jones (d 1980), and Irene Gertrude, *née* Abbott; *b* 3 May 1944; *Educ* Felsted, Magdalen Coll Oxford (BA, DipEd); *m* 13 June 1973, Wendy Christine, da of Stanley Saward; 2 da (Cressida b 14 Nov 1976, Miranda (twin) b 14 Nov 1976); *Career* jt Sec The Life Offices' Assoc 1982 (joined 1968), chief exec ABI 1987- (mangr Legislation Dept 1985-87); *Style*— Michael Jones, Esq; 51 Forest Side, London E4 6BA; Association of British Insurers, Aldermary House, 10-15 Queen St, London EC4N 1TT (☎ 071 248 4477, fax 071 489 1120)

JONES, Michael Frederick; s of Glyn Frederick Jones, of Glos, and Elizabeth, *née* Coopey; *b* 3 July 1937; *Educ* Crypt Sch Glos; *m* 28 Feb 1959, Sheila Joan, da of Charles Dawes, of Chaldon, Surrey; 3 s (Edward b 1966, John b 1968, Richard b 1970); *Career* reporter; Maidenhead Advertiser 1956-59, Northern Echo 1959-61, Manchester Evening News 1961-64; lab reporter: Financial Times 1964-65, The Daily Telegraph 1965-67; news ed asst ed The Times Business News 1967-70, managing ed The Asian Hong Kong 1971; The Sunday Times: assoc news ed 1972-75, political corr 1975-84, political ed 1984-; chm Parly Press Gallery 1989-91; memb Inst of Journalists 1987; *Recreations* recovering; *Style*— Michael Jones, Esq; The Sunday Times, 1 Pennington St, Wapping, London E1 (☎ 071 782 5834, telex 262139 TIMES G)

JONES, Michael Lynn Norman; s of Lynn Daniel Jones, of, Rhiwbina, Cardiff, and Mary Hannah, *née* Edwards; *b* 14 Jan 1943; *Educ* Neath Boys GS, Jesus Coll Oxford (BA, MA), Coll of Law; *m* 16 April 1974, Ethni, da of Gwynfryn Morgan Daniel (d 1960), of Llys-y-Coed, West Orchard Cres, Llandaff, Cardiff; 1 s (Garmon b 1975), 3 da (Mererid b 1976, Gwenfair b 1979, Rhiannon b 1982); *Career* slr; ptnr C Hugh James & Ptnrs Cardiff 1966, sr ptnr Hugh James Jones & Jenkins Cardiff 1970-; memb: Wales and Chester Circuit Advsy Ctee 1971-77, Curriculum Cncl Wales 1988-; asst sec Cardiff and Dist Law soc 1969-; govr: Coed-y-G of Welsh Primary Sch 1985-, Glantaf Welsh HS 1988; elder Salem Presbyterian Church of Wales Canton Cardiff 1988; memb: Law Soc 1966, CIArb 1987; *Recreations* gardening, walking; *Clubs* Cardiff & County, Oxford Union; *Style*— Michael Jones, Esq; Allt-y-Wennol, Peterston-super-Ely, Cardiff (☎ 0446 760 383); Hugh James, Jones & Jenkins, Arlbee Ho, Greyfriars Rd, Cardiff (☎ 0222 224 871, fax 0222 388 222)

JONES, (Philip) Michael Thyer; s of Philip Emlyn Thyer Jones, DFC (d 1974), of Gorseinon, S Wales, and Elizabeth Vivien Thyer, *née* Fannon; *b* 21 April 1914; *Educ* Roan Sch Blackheath; *m* 21 May 1965, Barbara Mary, da of George Johnstone, of Thornhill, Dumfriesshire, Scotland; 3 da (Fiona b 1968, Alison b 1970, Katey b 1974); *Career* Int Stock Exchange 1959-63; Capel-Cure Myers: various posts 1959-63, head investmts 1969-70, ptnr fin and admin 1970-85; tech servs dir Capel-Cure Myers Capital Management; MInstAM 1970; *Recreations* flying, rock climbing, deep sea fishing, skiing, shooting; *Style*— Michael Jones, Esq; The Registry, Royal Mint Court, London EC3N 4EY (☎ 071 488 4000, fax 071 481 3798)

JONES, Nicholas (John); s of John Sterry Jones, and Ann Margaret, *née* Dunand; *b* 18 July 1958; *Educ* Malvern Coll, Royal Scottish Acad of Music, Int Cello Centre (ARCM); *m* 17 Dec 1983, Isobelle Lillian, da of John McGuinness, of Strabane, N Ireland; *Career* concert cellist and musical dir; given concerts at major festivals and regular Purcell Room recitals; founded Johannes Piano Trio with Michael Bochmann and Iwan Llewelyn Jones; principal cello English String Orchestra; *Recreations* walking, reading, looking at art, theatre, opera, conversation, humour; *Style*— Nicholas Jones, Esq; Tanybryn, Rhydypennan, Bow Street, Dyfed SY24 5AD (☎ 0970 820 300); Arts Centre, Penglais, Aberystwyth, Dyfed SY23 3DE (☎ 0970 4277)

JONES, Nicholas Graham; s of Albert William Jones, and Gwendolen Mary Muriel Taylor-Jones, *née* Phillips; *b* 13 Aug 1948; *Educ* Latymer Upper Sch, St Catherine's Coll Oxford (MA); *m* 25 Sept 1976, Shelagh Ann, da of Robert Maitland Farror; 1 s (Benjamin Nicholas Farror b 1986); *Career* film ed and prodr BBC 1969, called to the Bar 1975 Inner Temple, asst rec S Eastern Circuit 1990; memb Criminal Bar Assoc; *Recreations* sailing, walking, music; *Clubs* Royal Ocean Racing, Bar Yacht (racing capt), Frensham Pond Sailing; *Style*— Nicholas Jones, Esq; 4 Brick Court, Temple, London EC4Y 9AD (☎ 071 583 8455, fax 071 353 1699)

JONES, Nicholas Michael Houssemayne; s of Henry J E Jones, of Kitsbury Orchard, nr Moreton-in-Marsh, Glos, and Patricia Rose, *née* Holland; *b* 27 Oct 1946; *Educ* Winchester, London Business Sch (MSc); *m* 25 March 1971, Veronica Anne, da of Brig The Hon R G Hamilton-Russell, DSO, LVO, *qv*; 1 s (Oliver Mark b 5 April 1977), 1 da (Rowena Rose b 5 Sept 1975); *Career* Peat Marwick Mitchell 1965-73, dir J Henry Schroder Wagg & Co 1975-87, md Lazard Brothers & Co 1987-; FCA 1969; *Recreations* racing, tennis, stalking, bridge, painting; *Style*— Nicholas Jones, Esq; Rectory Farmhouse, Church Enstone, Oxfordshire OX7 4NN; 12 Paulton's St, London SW3 5DR; Lazard Brothers & Co, Limited, 21 Moorfields, London EC2P 2HT (☎ 071 588 2721)

JONES, Nigel Michael; s of Ralph Michael Jones, of Wolverhampton, and Patricia May, *née* Phelps; *b* 23 Sept 1960; *Educ* Wolverhampton GS, Keble Coll Oxford (exhibitioner, BA); *m* 27 June 1987, Gillian Hazel, da of Eric Keith Philpot; *Career* advertising exec; Bd dir BMP DDB Needham 1988- (joined as graduate trainee 1984); accounts worked on: Quaker Cereals, Schering-Plough, Alliance & Leicester Building Society, Scottish Amicable Life Assurance, Courage, ICI Dulux, AIDS Health Education Authy, Birds Eye; winner of: US TV and Radio Commercials Festival Mobius award 1987, 1st prize IPA Advertising Effectiveness Awards 1988, 1st prize and grand prix IPA Advertising Effectiveness Awards 1990, various chess championships 1971-83; *Recreations* music, bonsai, walking, chess, Wolverhampton Wanderers; *Style*— Nigel Jones, Esq; BMP DDB Needham, 12 Bishops Bridge Rd, London W2 6AA (☎ 071 258 3979)

JONES, Prof Norman; s of Edward Valentine Jones, and Mary Alice, *née* Collins; *b* 18 March 1938; *Educ* Liverpool Poly (ordinary Nat Cert), UMIST (BScTech, MScTech, PhD, DSc), Univ of Manchester (DSc); *m* 11 July 1964, Jenny, da of Fred Schofield (d 1946); 2 da (Alison Elizabeth b 29 Aug 1967, Catherine Ann b 8 March 1971); *Career* pt/t lectr Dept of Mech Engrg Manchester Coll of Sci and Technol 1961-63, James Clayton fell IME 1962-63, asst lectr Faculty of Technol Univ of Manchester 1963-65; asst prof: Dept of Mech Engrg Georgic Inst of Technol USA 1965-66, Dept of Engrg Brown Univ USA 1966-68; Dept of Ocean Engrg MIT USA: asst prof 1968-70, assoc prof 1970-77, prof 1977-79; head of Dept of Mech Engrg Univ of Liverpool 1982-90 (prof 1979); memb: Safety in Mines Res Advsy Bd 1985-, Ductile Collapse Ctee 3.1 Int Ship Structures Congress 1985-88, Hull and Machinery Ctee Def Scientific Advsy Cncl 1989-, Man-made Hazards Ctee Inter-Engrg Inst Hazards Forum 1990-, Solid Mechanics Conf Ctee Euro Mechanics Cncl 1990-; memb: ASME 1966, P Eng Massachusetts 1972, FIMech E 1980, FRINA 1980; *Books* Structural Crashworthiness (1983), Structural Failure (1989), Structural Impact (1989); *Recreations* walking, music; *Style*— Prof Norman Jones; Department of Mechanical Engineering, The University of Liverpool, PO Box 147, Liverpool L69 3BX (☎ 051 794 4858, fax 051 794 4848, telex 627095 UNILPL G)

JONES, Dr Norman Fielding; s of William John Jones (d 1968), of Aberbeeg, Gwent, and Winifred, *née* Evans (d 1974); *b* 3 May 1931; *Educ* Christ Coll Brecon, King's Coll Cambridge (MA, MD), St Thomas's Hosp Med Sch (B Chir), Univ of N Carolina; *m* 15 March 1958, Ann Pye, da of Dr Charles Cecil Howard Chavasse (d 1971), of Alcester, Warwicks; 3 s (Christopher b 1960, Richard b 1963, Michael b 1967); *Career* Nat Serv 1949-50; conslt physician St Thomas's Hosp London 1967-, physician King Edward VII's Hosp for Offrs 1977-, chm Dist Mgmnt Team and Staff Ctee St Thomas's Hosp 1977-78, conslt physician Met Police 1980-, hon conslt physician Army 1980-; RCP: chm Ctee on Renal Disease 1980-, chm Ctee on Legal Aspects of Med 1989-, sr censor and vice pres 1989-90, chief med offr Equitable Life Assur Soc 1985-, hon conslt physician Royal Hosp Chelsea 1987-, vice chm W Lambeth Health Authy 1989-90, special tstee St Thomas' Hosp 1989-; FRCP 1970, memb Nat, European and Int Socs of Nephrology; *Books* Recent Advances in Renal Disease (ed 1975), Renal Disease (ed with Sir Douglas Black, 1979), Recent Advances in Renal Medicine (ed with D K Peters, 1982); *Recreations* iconology, modern English literature; *Style*— Dr Norman Jones; 1 Annesley Rd, London SE3 0JX (☎ 081 856 0583); St Thomas's Hosp, London SE1 7EH (☎ 071 928 9292)

JONES, Norman Henry; QC (1985); s of Warrant Offr Henry Robert Jones, DFM, of Hillview, Myrtle Street, Appledore, Bideford, N Devon, and Charlotte Isabel Scott, *née* Davis; *b* 12 Dec 1941; *Educ* Bideford GS, North Devon Tech Coll, Univ of Leeds (LLB, LLM); *m* 28 March 1970, Trudy Helen, da of Frederick George Chamberlain (d 1974), of Werrington, Peterborough; 2 s (Gareth b 22 Dec 1977, Nicholas b 14 April 1981), 1 da (Helena b 6 April 1983); *Career* called to the Bar Middle Temple 1968, rec 1987; govr Guiseley Sch; *Recreations* boating, walking; *Style*— Norman Jones, Esq, QC; Danehurst, Greenfield Lane, Guiseley, Leeds LS20 9HF (☎ 0943 781 92); Park Court Chambers, 40 Park Cross St, Leeds LS1 2QH (☎ 0532 433 277, fax 0532 421 285, telex 666135)

JONES, Maj Norman Leslie; TD (1986); s of Dudley Frederick Saville Jones (d 1967), of Birkenhead, Wirral, and Margaret, *née* Thompson; *b* 15 Jan 1948; *Educ* St Hugh's RC Secondary Sch Birkenhead, Liverpool Coll of Commerce, Chester Coll of Law; *m* 8 Sept 1973, Maria Teresa, da of John Cubells (d 1988), of Higher Bebington, Wirral; 1 s (Daniel b 1985), 2 da (Rebeca b 1978 (d 1979), Stephanie b 1983); *Career* TA 1968-, 208 (Merseyside) Gen Hosp RAMC (V) Liverpool, cmmnd Unit Paymaster 208 (Merseyside) Gen Hosp RAMC (V) 1978, Capt 1980, Maj 1990; slr Supreme Ct 1976; civil claims specialist; legal advsr Radio Merseyside Helpline; fell Inst of Legal Execs 1973; memb Law Soc 1976; *Recreations* writing, gardening, furniture restoration; *Style*— Maj Norman Jones, TD; 9 Reservoir Rd North, Prenton, Birkenhead, Wirral (☎ 051 608 4723); 27 Hamilton Square, Birkenhead, Wirral (☎ 051 647 7001, fax 051 647 7004)

JONES, Norman William; CBE (1984), TD (1962); s of James William Jones (d 1957), and Mabel, *née* Pyewell (d 1972); *b* 5 Nov 1923; *Educ* Gravesend Sch; *m* 1950, Evelyn June, da of Gilbert Hall (d 1977); 2 s; *Career* served HM Forces 1942-47, Maj Airborne Forces Europe and Burma; Lloyds Bank plc: dir 1976-, gp chief exec 1978-83, dep chm 1984-89, vice chm 1989-; dir Lloyds Abbey Life plc 1989-; chm Aust & NZ Trade Advsy Ctee (BOTB) 1985-88; FIB; *Recreations* sailing, photography; *Clubs* Overseas Bankers'; *Style*— Norman Jones, Esq, CBE, TD; Rowans, 21 College Ave, Grays, Essex RM17 5UN (☎ 0375 373101); Lloyds Bank plc, 71 Lombard St, London EC3P 3BS (☎ 071 626 1500)

JONES, Paul Adrian; né Pond; s of Norman Henry Pond, of Worthing, W Sussex, and Amelia Josephine, *née* Hadfield; *b* 24 Feb 1942; *Educ* Portsmouth GS, Edinburgh Acad, Jesus Coll Oxford; *m* 1, 1963, Sheila MacLeod; 2 s (Matthew b 21 Oct 1963, Jacob b 10 Jan 1965); m 2, Fiona Jayne, da of Hugh Holbein Hendley); *Career* singer, musician, composer, actor, writer and presenter, *Music* gp lead singer Manfred Mann 1962-66 (composer The One in the Middle, 5-4-3-2-1 for TV pop show Ready Steady Go! and others), solo singer 1966-71, memb The Blues Band 1979-; songs recorded by numerous artists incl Helen Shapiro and Eric Clapton, has played harmonica for other recording artists, TV and advertisements; composer of theme music incl: BBC TV series The Wednesday Play and Fighting Back, films Privilege, The Committee and Intimate Reflections, BBC documentary The Last Vacation, *Theatre* incl: Jack Argue in Muzeeka (debut, Open Space Theatre) 1969, Conduct Unbecoming (Queen's Theatre) 1969-70 and Ethel Barrymore Theatre NY) 1970-71, The Banana Box (Apollo Theatre) 1973, Pippin (Her Majesty's Theatre) 1973-74, Joseph and the Amazing Technicolour Dreamcoat tour 1976, Drake's Dream (Shaftesbury and Westminster Theatres) 1977-78, Cats (New London Theatre) 1982, Guys and Dolls (Nat Theatre) 1982-83, The Pyjama Game (Leicester Haymarket and tour) 1985-86, Kiss Me Kate (RSC, Stratford tour and Old Vic) 1987, Julius Caesar (Ludlow Festival) 1989; Films Privilege 1966, The Committee 1968, Demons of the Mind 1971, The Blues Band 1980, *TV* incl: Top of the Pops, Ready Steady Go! (and other pop shows), A Bit of Descretion (Yorkshire TV) 1968, Square One (LWT) 1971, Z-Cars (BBC) 1972, The Protectors 1973, A Different Kind of Frost, Jackanory, The Sweeney, Space 1999, Great Big Groovy Horse, Twiggy Show (BBC), A Matter of Taste (BBC), The Songwriters (BBC) 1978, The Beggar's Opera (Channel 4) 1983, Weekend (Granada) 1983-84, A Plus 4 (Thames and Channel 4) 1984-85, Beat the Teacher 1985-86, John Lennon - A Journey in the Life 1985, A Royal Celebration 1985, Lyrics by Time Rice 1985, Live from the Palladium 1988, Hudson and Halls 1990, Uncle Jack scenes 1990; author They Put You Where You Are (play, BBC) 1966, *Radio* Paul Jones on Music (Radio 4) 1983, Counterpoint (BBC World Serv) 1982-85, GLR 1988-90, Jazz FM 1990-; UK Male Vocalist Br Blues Connection Awards 1990; memb: Br Actors Equity, Musicians Union, Br Academy of Songwriters Composers and Authors; *Recreations* music, books, walking, food, conversation; *Style*— Paul Jones, Esq; Chattow and Linnit, Prince of Wales Theatre, Coventry St, London W1V 7FE (☎ 071 930 6677, fax 071 930 0091)

JONES, Brig Peter; CBE (1988, MBE 1975); s of Trevor Jones, of Stoud, and Mona Mary, *née* Bishop (d 1975); *b* 17 Aug 1938; *Educ* Cheshunt GS, UCL (LLB); *m* 13 April 1966, Margaret Ann, da of Edward Lea (d 1976); *Career* served RA 1960-: 2 Lt TA 1960-63, Lt 42 Med Regt UK and BAOR 1963-66, Capt (adj) 324 HYAD Regt TA UK 1966-67, Capt (adj) 101 Med Regt TA UK 1967-68, Capt (adj) 25 Lt Regt UK and Hong Kong 1968-71, Maj (DAA & QMG) 8 Inf Bde NI 1971-75, Maj (battery cmd) 3RHA UK NI Cyprus Belize 1975-77, Lt Col (GSOI) Staff Coll UK 1977-80, CO 49 FO Regt 1980-82, Col (Chief instr) Royal Sch Artillery UK 1982-84, Col (ACOS) HQ BRIT Forces Falkland Islands 1984-85, Col (ACOS) HQ NI 1984-88, Col (co ops) HQ AFNORTU Norway 1988-89; *Recreations* hockey, squash, industrial archeology; *Clubs* Army & Navy; *Style*— Brig Peter Jones, CBE; c/o MOD, Whitehall, London SW1

JONES, Peter Boam; s of Cecil Walley Jones, of Cheshire, and Dorothy, *née* Boam; *b* 11 June 1930; *Educ* Nantwich and Acton GS; *m* 1960, Patricia Ann, da of Tom Dewhurst, JP, of Worcestershire; 1 s (Anthony b 1963), 1 da (Victoria b 1967); *Career* Nat Serv 1953-55, cmmnd Lt RAOC 1954; ptnr Touche Ross & Co Birmingham

1965-82, dep chm Maxim Investmt Gp, chm Time Craft Designs Ltd; dir: Saracens Cycles Ltd, Aquarian Hldgs Gp; pres: Birmingham and W Midland Soc of Chartered Accountants 1980-81, Birmingham CA Students Soc 1979-80; Freeman City of London, Liveryman Worshipful Co of Chartered Accountants; FCA; *Recreations* gardening, tennis, travelling; *Clubs* Birmingham; *Style—* Peter Jones, Esq; The Heath, Longdon Heath, Upton upon Severn, Worcestershire (☎ 06846 4495)

JONES, Peter Eldon; s of Wilfrid Eldon Jones (d 1985), of Kingston upon Thames, and Jessie Meikle, *née* Buchanan (d 1970); *b* 11 Oct 1927; *Educ* Surbiton GS, Kingston Poly, UCL (DipTP); *m* 1, 1954 (m dis 1984), Gisela Marie, da of Maj Landforstmeister Karl Heinrich von Arnswaldt (d 1985) of Celle, Germany; 2 s (Christopher b 1955, Andrew b 1958), 1 da (Hella b 1962); m 2, 1985, Claudia Ann Mary Milner-Brown, da of John Alan Laurence, of Gt Waltham, Essex; *Career* sr asst architect Powell and Moya 1950-54, joined Arch Dept LCC 1954, dep of sch architecture LCC 1960-65, town devpt architect/planner GLC 1965-71, tech policy architect GLC 1971-74, acting dir of architecture GLC 1980-82 (educn architect 1974-82), dir architecture and superintending architect Met Bldgs GLC/ILEA 1982-86, dir Watkins Gray Peter Jones Ltd 1986-; conslt: Watkins Gray Int, DES; chm: Abbeyfield and Pirbright Bldg Ctees; pres Soc Chief Architects of Local Authys 1983-84, memb EEC Advsy Ctee on Educn & Trg of Architects 1986-90; Freeman: City of London 1968, Worshipful Co of Chartered Architects 1988; vice pres RIBA 1985-86, FRIBA, FRTPI, FRSA, FCSD; *Books* Good House Design (1956); *Recreations* photography, travel, bridge, golf; *Clubs* Woking Golf; *Style—* Peter Jones, Esq; Watkins Gray Peter Jones Ltd, Alexander House, 1a Spur Rd, Orpington, Kent (☎ 0689 36141, fax 0689 35152)

JONES, Peter George Edward Fitzgerald; CB (1985); s of Dr John Christopher Jones (d 1960), of Sussex, and Emily Isabel Howell (d 1954); *b* 7 June 1925; *Educ* Fairfield Sch Birmingham, Dulwich, Croydon Tech, Battersea Poly (BSc); *m* 1, 8 July 1950, Gwendoline Iris (d 1964), da of George Edwin Humphreys (d 1952), of London; 2 s (Graham b 1951, Laurence b 1956 (decd)); m 2, 17 June 1967, Jacqueline Angela, da of Clifford Meyer Gilbert, of Newbury; 2 s (Christopher b 1968, Jason b 1971), 1 da (Tracey b 1969); *Career* pilot F/O RAF 1943-47 (India, Malaya, China); sr scientist GEC Res Labs Wembley 1951-54; UKAEA 1954-73 and MOD 1973-87: sr sci offr 1954-58, princ 1958-63, supt electronics res 1964-66, sr supt warhead electronics 1966-68, sr supt special systems 1968-74, chief of warhead devpt 1974-76, dep dir 1976-80, princ dep dir 1980-82, dir AWRE 1982-87 (ret 1987); conslt MOD on nuclear safety 1987-; thermonuclear tests Christmas Island 1957-58, participation with USA under mutual def agreement 1958-87 (with underground tests 1974-87), devpt of Chevaline and Trident 1968-87; FInstP; *Recreations* motoring, flying; *Style—* Peter Jones, Esq; Rhyd-y-Felin, Upper Llanover, Abergavenny, Gwent NP7 9DD

JONES, Peter Henry Francis; s of Eric Roberts Jones, MBE, of Swansea, and Betty Irene, *née* Longhurst (d 1981); *b* 25 Feb 1952; *Educ* Bishop Gore GS Swansea, Newport HS Gwent, Balliol Coll Oxford (MA); *m* 3 June 1978, Anne Elizabeth, da of David Jones, DFC, of Cheadle; 2 da (Clare b 14 May 1980, Eleanor b 14 July 1982); *Career* admitted slr 1977; ptnr: Darlington & Parkinson 1979-87, John Howell & Co Sheffield 1987-; memb Law Soc's Family Law Ctee; chm Legal Servs Conf 1986-; memb: Lord Chllr's Advsy Ctee on Legal Aid 1983-, Children Act Procedure Advsy Gp; *Recreations* cricket, tennis, rugby, reading; *Clubs* Dethreau Boat, Scorpions Cricket, Fulwood Lawn Tennis; *Style—* Peter Jones, Esq; 427/431 London Rd, Sheffield S2 (☎ 0742 501 000)

JONES, Prof Peter Howard; s of Thomas Leslie Jones (d 1963), of London, and Hilda Croesora, *née* Parkinson (d 1982); *b* 18 Dec 1935; *Educ* Highgate Sch, Queens' Coll Cambridge; *m* 8 Oct 1960, (Elizabeth) Jean, da of Robert James Roberton, JP (d 1972), of Morebattle, Roxburghshire; 2 da (Rachel b 1964, Laura b 1969); *Career* Br Cncl 1960-61, res scholar Univ of Cambridge 1961-63, asst lectr in philosophy Univ of Nottingham 1963-64; visiting prof of philosophy: Rochester Univ NY 1969-70, Dartmouth Coll New Hampshire 1973 and 1983, Carleton Coll Minnesota 1974, Oklahoma Univ 1978, Baylor Univ 1978; visiting fell Humanities Res Centre Australian Nat Univ 1984, prof of philosophy Univ of Edinburgh 1984- (lectr then reader 1964-84), dir Inst for Advanced Studies in the Humanities 1986-; tstee: Nat Museums of Scotland, Univ of Edinburgh Development Tst; govr Morrison's Acad; FRSE, FRSA; *Books* Philosophy and the Novel (1975), Hume's Sentiments (1982), A Hotbed of Genius (1986), Philosophy and Science in The Scottish Enlightenment (ed, 1988), The Science of Man in the Scottish Enlightenment (ed, 1989), Adam Smith Reviewed (ed, 1991), Rousseau and Liberty (ed, 1991); *Recreations* opera, chamber music, architecture, arts, travel; *Clubs* New (Edinburgh); *Style—* Prof Peter Jones; Institute for Advanced Studies, University of Edinburgh, Hope Park Square, Edinburgh EH8 9NW (☎ 031 662 4174, fax 031 668 2252)

JONES, Peter Ivan; s of Glyndwr Jones, of Bridport, and Edith Evelyn, *née* Whittaker; *b* 14 Dec 1942; *Educ* Gravesend GS, LSE (BScEcon); *m* 1 (m dis 1969), Judith, *née* Watson; 1 s (Nicholas Francis Marham b 1968), 1 da (Claire Amanda Markham b 1964); m 2, 15 Aug 1970, Elizabeth, da of Raymond Gent; 1 s (Matthew Alexander b 1978), 1 da (Victoria Louise b 1975); *Career* dir Boase Massimi Pollitt Partnership 1968-75, non-exec dir Boase Massimi Pollitt plc 1983-88, chief exec 1989; dir Omnicom Inc 1989, chm BBDO Ltd 1989-90, chief exec UK Omnicom UK plc 1989-; pres Racehorse Owners Assoc 1990-92; MIPA 1971; *Books Publications* Trainers Record (1973-87); *Recreations* horse racing; *Style—* Peter Jones, Esq; Melplash Farmhouse, Melplash, Bridport, Dorset DT6 3UH (☎ 030 888 383); 38A Rossetti Garden Mansions, Flood St, London SW3 5QX (☎ 071 352 6510); Omnicom UK plc, 54 Baker St, London W1M 1DJ (☎ 071 486 7200)

JONES, Dr Philip Edward; s of Edward Thomas Jones (d 1946), and Stella Mary, *née* Coen; *b* 5 Oct 1945; *Educ* Manchester GS, Univ of Birmingham Med Sch (MRCP); *m* 2 Sept 1972, Bernadette Catherine, da of John Terence Cain (d 1978); 3 da (Nina Jones b 1980, Stephanie Jones b 1984, Sarah Jones b 1988); *Career* house physician Dudley Rd Hosp Birmingham 1968-69, registrar Univ Coll Hosp and Whittington Hosp 1972-75, registrar and res fell Hammersmith Hosp 1975-77, sr registrar Manchester Royal Infirmary 1977-82, conslt physician Wythenshawe Hosp 1982-; memb: Br Soc Gatroenerology, N W Gastroenterology Soc, Manchester Med Soc; FRCP 1989; *Recreations* swimming, music; *Style—* Dr Philip Jones; Wythenshawe Hosp, Dept of Gastroenterology, Southmoor Rd, Wythenshawe, Manchester M23 9LT (☎ 061 946 2394)

JONES, Philip Mark; CBE (1986, OBE 1977); s of John Jones (d 1957), and Mabel, *née* Copestake (d 1980); *b* 12 March 1928; *Educ* RCM (ARCM); *m* 1 Aug 1956, Ursula, da of Walter Strebi (d 1981); *Career* princ trumpet with all maj orchestras London 1949-72, fndr and dir Philip Jones Brass Ensemble 1951-86; dir Wind and Percussion Dept: RNC Manchester 1975-77, Guildhall Sch Music and Drama City of London 1983-88; ed Just Brass Series Chester Music London 1975-89, princ Trinity Coll of Music London 1988-; created over fifty gramophone records with Philip Brass Ensemble; memb: Arts Cncl GB 1984-88, Royal Soc Musicians 1951-; memb Worshipful Co of Musicians 1987-, Freeman City of London 1988; FRNCM 1977, FRCM 1983, FRSA 1983, FGSM 1984, hon FTCL 1988; *Recreations* mountain walking, skiing; *Style—* Philip Jones, Esq, CBE; 14 Hamilton Terrace, London NW8 9UG (071 286 9155)

JONES, Sir (Thomas) Philip; CB (1978); *b* 13 July 1931; *Educ* Cowbridge GS, Jesus Coll Oxford (MA); *m* 1955, Mary; *Career* asst princ MOS 1955, princ Miny of Aviation 1959, on loan to HM Treasy 1964-66, PPS to min of Aviation 1966-67, asst sec Miny of Technol subsequently Miny of Aviation Supply 1967-71; under sec: DTI 1971, Dept of Energy 1974; dep sec Dept of Energy 1976-83; chm Total Oil Marine plc, Dames & Moore Barry Ltd; dir IVO Energy Ltd, Gas Transmission Ltd; memb Br Nat Oil Corp 1980-82, chm Electricity Cncl 1983-90; kt 1986; *Style—* Sir Philip Jones, CB; Total Marine Oil plc, Berkeley Square House, Berkeley Square, London W1X 6LT (☎ 071 499 6080)

JONES, (William) Quentin; s of William Stephen Jones (d 1981), and Joan Constance, *née* Reach; *b* 18 Nov 1946; *Educ* Bradfield, Coll of Estate Mgmnt London; *m* 1, 4 Oct 1970 (m dis 1982), Jane Elizabeth; 4 s (Richard b 1973, Gregory Chamberlain b 1973, Russell Chamberlain b 1975, Edward b 1976); m 2, 5 April 1984, Diana Mary, da of Maj Albert Henry Hilton; *Career* chm JM Jones & Sons (Holdings) Ltd 1981-90 (dir 1970), Landform Properties Ltd 1990; Freeman City of London, Liveryman Worshipful Co of Masons; FRICS 1969; *Recreations* tennis, swimming; *Style—* Quentin Jones, Esq; Greenacres, Lambridge Wood Rd, Henley on Thames, Oxon RG9 3BP (☎ 0491 573 200)

JONES, Ralph Godfrey; s of William Ewart Jones (d 1971), of Ammanford, Wales, and Emily Frances (d 1969); *b* 6 April 1926; *Educ* Amman Valley GS, Swansea Univ (BSc); *m* 27 Sept 1947, Dorothy Lilian, da of Leonard Heath (d 1955), of Syston, Leics; 3 s (Vincent b 7 June 1948, David b 22 March 1953, Godfrey (twin) b 1953); *Career* fndr Preci-Spark Ltd (sub contractor to the aero-space indust) 1960; Freeman City of London 1974, Liveryman Worshipful Co of Fanmakers 1974; *Recreations* equestrian activities; *Style—* Ralph Jones, Esq; Sandhills Cottage Farm, Newtown, Linford, Leics (☎ 0530 242 275) Preci-Spark Ltd, Syston, Leics (☎ 0533 607 911, fax 0533 609 461, telex 342125 PRECI G)

JONES, Raymond John (Ray); s of late Hubert Clarence Eric Jones, of Staffs, and Florence Evelyn, *née* Bettles; *b* 31 Dec 1934; *Educ* Queen Elizabeth GS Staffs; *m* 1958, Margaret Heather (d 1988), da of George Clamp (d 1976), of Staffs; 2 da (Helen Susan b 1964, Claire Elizabeth b 1967); m 2, 1989, Joan Mary, da of S Bridgewater (d 1976); *Career* dir The Tamworth Herald Co Ltd Newspaper Publishers and Printers 1989; md Herald Promotions Ltd 1989; *Recreations* music, gardening; *Clubs* Rotary (Tamworth Anker, fndr pres); *Style—* Ray Jones, Esq; 9 Moor Lane, Bolehall, Tamworth, Staffs (☎ 0827 54800); 10 Aldergate, Tamworth, Staffs (☎ 0827 60741)

JONES, Prof Reginald Victor; CB (1946), CBE (1942); s of Harold Victor Jones (d 1953), and Alice Margaret, *née* May (d 1978); *b* 29 Sept 1911; *Educ* Alleyn's Sch Dulwich, Wadham Coll Oxford, Balliol Coll Oxford (MA, DPhil); *m* 21 March 1940, Vera Margaret, da of Charles Cain (d 1920); 1 s (Robert Bruce b 11 Feb 1944), 2 da (Susan Primrose (Mrs Addison) b 10 Feb 1941, Rosemary Ann (Mrs Forsyth) b 21 July 1950); *Career* dir intelligence res Air Miny 1946 (asst dir 1941-46), prof of natural philosophy Univ of Aberdeen 1946-81, dir scientific intelligence MOD 1952-53, hon memb Electronic Security Cmd USAF 1981-; author of numerous papers on scientific and def topics; chm: Infra-Red Ctee Miny of Supply and Aviation 1950-64, Br Tport Common Res Advsy Cncl 1954-55, Safety in Mines Res Advsy Bd 1956-60 (memb 1950-56); pres Crabtree Fndn 1958, chm Inst of Physics Ctee on Univ Physics 1961-63, memb Carriers Panel 1962-63, chm Paul Fund Ctee Royal Soc 1962-84 (vice pres 1971-72), chm Air Def Working Pty 1963-64, memb Scientific Advsy Cncl War Office 1963-66, chm Electronics Res Cncl Miny of Aviation and Technol 1964-70, govr Dulwich 1965-79, jt ed Notes and Records of the Royal Soc 1969-, rapporteur Euro Convention on Human Rights 1970, chm Br Nat Ctee for History of Sci Med and Technol 1970-78, pres Section A Br Assoc 1971, life govr Haileybury 1978, hon fell Coll of Preceptors 1978, visiting prof Univ of Colorado 1982, companion Operational Res Soc 1983, visitor RMCS 1983; hon fell Inst of Measurement and Control 1984, Br Horological Inst 1985, Wadham Coll Oxford, Balliol Coll Oxford; memb other various ctees on electronics, scientific res, measurement, def and educn; Hon Mayor San Antonio Texas 1982, Hon Freeman Clockmaker's Co 1984, hon memb American Soc of Precision Engrg 1990; Hon DSc: Univ of Strathclyde 1969, Univ of Kent 1980; Hon DUniv: Univ of York 1976, Open Univ, Univ of Surrey 1979; Hon LLD Univ of Bristol 1979, Bailie of Benachie 1980; FRSE 1949, FRS 1965, Hon FIEE 1983, CPhys, CEng; BOIMA Prize Inst of Physics 1934, US Medal of Freedom with Silver Palm 1946, US Medal for Merit 1947, Duddell Medal Physical Soc 1960, Parsons Medal 1967, Hartley Medal Inst of Measurement and Control 1972, Mexican Miny of Telecommunications Medal 1973, Rutherford Medal USSR 1 977, RG Mitchell Medal 1979, Old Crows Medal 1980; *Books* Most Secret War (1978), Instruments and Experiences (1988), Reflections on Intelligence (1989); *Recreations* history, fishing; *Clubs* Athenaeum, Special Forces, Royal Northern and Univ (Aberdeen); *Style—* Prof Reginald Jones, CB, CBE, FRS, FRSE; 8 Queen's Terrace, Aberdeen (☎ 0224 648184); The White House, Corgarff, Aberdeenshire (☎ 09756 51406)

JONES, Rhidian Huw Brynmor; s of Rev Preb Ivor Brynmor Jones, RD (d 1982), of Sutton Coldfield, Warwickshire, and Elizabeth Mary, *née* Morris; *b* 13 July 1943; *Educ* Queen Mary's GS Walsall, Keble Coll Oxford (MA); *m* 8 Aug 1970, Monica Marianne, da of Bror Eric Sjunne Sjöholm (d 1957), of Halmstad, Sweden; 1 s (Gavin b 1982), 1 da (Anna b 1978); *Career* trainee sec asst Selection Tst Ltd 1966-68, legal asst Total Oil GB Ltd 1968-69, co sec J E Lesser (Hldgs) Ltd 1969, asst sec Granada Group Ltd 1970-76, articled clerk and asst slr Herbert Smith and Co 1976-80, sr asst slr Kenneth Brown Baker 1980-81, ptnr Turner Kenneth Brown 1981-; vice pres Ealing FC (RU), cncl memb Anglo Swedish Soc; Freeman City of London Slrs' Co 1979; FCIS 1976, memb Law Soc 1978, FBIM 1987, MInstD 1987; *Recreations* rugby, Scandinavian studies; *Clubs* Wig and Pen; *Style—* Rhidian Jones, Esq; Roseleigh, 80 Elers Road, Ealing, London W13 9QD (☎ 081 579 9785); Turner Kenneth Brown, Slrs, 100 Fetter Lane, London EC4A 1DD (☎ 071 242 6006, fax 071 242 3003, telex 297696 TKBLAW G, car 0831 175744)

JONES, Rev Dr Richard Granville; s of Henry William Jones (d 1955), previously of Polzeath, later of Rock, Cornwall and then of Totnes, Devon, and Ida Grace, *née* Wintle (d 1947); *b* 26 July 1926; *Educ* Truro Sch Cornwall, St Johns Coll Cambridge, Univ of Manchester (BD); *m* 9 Aug 1955, Kathleen, da of Alfred Stone, of Manchester; 3 da (Nichola Grace b 1957, Stephanie Clare b 1959, Hilary Faith b 1964); *Career* Instr Lt RN 1947-49, HMS Drake; SCM staff sec E Midlands 1953-55; min: Sheffield 1955-64, Birkenhead 1964-69; tutor/sr tutor/princ Hartley Victoria Coll 1969-82, lectr in social and pastoral theol Univ of Manchester 1969-82, minister Holt Norfolk 1982-83, chm E Anglia dist Methodist Church 1983-, pres Methodist Conf 1988-89; chm: St Martins Housing Tst Norwich 1984-, Norfolk Ecumerical Cncl 1989-; Hon DD Univ of Hull 1988; *Books* Worship for Today (ed, 1968), Towards a Radical Church (1970), How goes Christian Marriage (1978) Groundwork of Worship & Preaching (1980), Groundwork of Christian Ethics (1984); author of numerous hymns; *Recreations* walking, reading; *Style—* The Rev Dr Richard Jones; 24 Townsend Road, Norwich NR4 6RG

JONES, Robert; s of John Idris Jones (d 1970), and Eleanor Myfanwy, *née* Williams; *b* 8 Dec 1946; *Educ* Rhymney GS Gwent, Tredegar GS Gwent, Sir John Cass Coll London (BSc); *m* June 1976, Elsa, da of James Basil Robinson (d 1946); 1 s (Timothy

Robert b 14 July 1978); *Career* graduate trainee Unilever 1969-70; account mangr: S H Benson & Co 1970-71, Young & Rubica 1971-73; account dir: McCann Erickson 1973-75, Counter Products Marketing 1975-79; md Imbibers Wines 1979-87, business devpt dir VAP Advertising and Marketing Group 1987-; developed Taggards (the nat mountaineering safety scheme) 1988; Compagnon of Confrerie St Etienne Alsace 1976, memb Circle of Winewriters 1984; *Books* The Imbibers Guide to Wine Pronunciation (1980), European Rulers (1981), Snowdon (1991); *Recreations* music, wine, cycling, bird watching, mountain walking, designing games; *Style—* Robert Jones, Esq; VAP Advertising & Marketing Group, Langford Lane, Kidlington, Oxon OX5 1LL (☎ 0865 842800, fax 0865 841678)

JONES, Robert Brannock; MP (C) West Herts 1983-; s of Ray Elwin and Iris Pamela Jones; *b* 26 Sept 1950; *Educ* Merchant Taylors', Univ of St Andrews (MA); *m* 1989, Jennifer Anne, da of late Lewis Sandercock; *Career* memb: St Andrews Borough Cncl 1972-75, Fife CC 1973-75, Chiltern DC 1979-83; contested (C): Kirkcaldy Oct 1974, Teesside Stockton 1979; *Style—* Robert Jones Esq, MP; House of Commons, London SW1

JONES, Robert Henry; TD (1967); s of George Samuel Jones (d 1986), and Gertie Gladys Nash; *b* 10 April 1933; *Educ* Rendcomb Coll Cirencester (Open Scholarship), Bristol Business Sch, London Business Sch; *m* 18 July 1973, Valerie Ann, da of Edmund Norman Underwood (d 1982); 1 s (Paul Harris b 1963), 1 da (Caroline b 1975); *Career* Nat Serv Offr in Devonshire Regt Active Service (Mau Mau Campaign) Kenya 1953-54, TA Service (Glosters) 1954-67, final rank Maj; ind professional chm, non-exec dir and advsr; md Lonsdale Printing and Packaging 1969-76; chm: Howard Jones Group Ltd 1980-88, CWF Contractors 1980-85, Dataforms Ltd 1981-84, Blatchford Ltd 1987-, W of Eng Branch IOD 1984-89 (memb Cncl), A J Charlton and Sons 1990-, FTP Broadcasting Plc01990-; hockey Southgate 1 XI 1960-61, W Gloucester 1961-69, represented TA 1957-58; *Recreations* tennis, shooting, music of the 1920s and 1930, trumpet playing, sailing hockey, skiing; *Clubs* Clifton, Institute of Directors, Bristol Commercial; *Style—* Robert H Jones, Esq, TD; 26 Duchess Rd, Clifton, Bristol BS8 2LA (☎ 0272 737801)

JONES, Prof Robert Maynard; s of Sydney Jones (d 1956), of Cardiff, and Edith Jones (d 1981); *b* 20 May 1929; *Educ* Univs of Wales and Ireland (MA, PhD, DLitt); *m* 27 Dec 1952, Anne Elizabeth, da of John James (d 1979), of Clunderwen; 1 s (Rhodri Siôn), 1 da (Lowri Dole); *Career* head of Dept of Welsh Language and Lit Univ of Wales Aberystwyth 1980- (lectr and sr lectr 1955-77, reader 1978; memb: Arts Cncl Wales, ed Bd Welsh Nat Dictionary, Bd Celtic Studies; memb Yr Academi Gymreig 1965; *Books* incl: Nid Yw Dŵr yn Plygu (1958), I'r Arch (1959), Cyflwyno'r Gymraeg (1964), Ci Wrth y Drws (1968), System in Child Language (1970), Traed Prydferth (1973), Tafod y llenor (1974), Llen Cymru a Chrefydd (1977), Casgliad o Gerddi (1988); *Clubs* Y Bedol (Aberystwyth); *Style—* Prof Robert Jones; Tandderwen, Heol Llanbadarn, Aberystwyth, Dyfed SY23 1HB (☎ 0970 623603)

JONES, Robert Nicholas; s of Cliff Jones, and Marian Jones; *b* 10 Nov 1965; *m* 8 August 1987, Megan, da of Clive Rowlands, OBE; *Career* Rugby Union scrum-half Swansea RFC and Wales (34 caps); clubs: Swansea RFC (capt), Barbarians RFC; rep Wales B (debut 1985); Wales: debut v England 1986, memb World Cup squad 1987 (5 appearances), memb Triple Crown winning team 1988 (capt 1990), tour NZ 1988 (1 test appearance), partnered Jonathan Davies, *qv*, 22 times; Br Lions tour Aust 1989 (3 test appearances); rep Wales in cricket on three age levels; fin exec; *Recreations* golf, cricket; *Style—* Robert Jones, Esq; c/o Swansea RFC, St Helen's Ground, Swansea, West Galmorgan (☎ 0792 464918/466593)

JONES, (James) Roger; s of Albert James Jones, and Hilda Vera, *née* Evans (d 1989); *b* 30 May 1952; *Educ* Shrewsbury, St Catharine's Coll Cambridge (sr scholar, MA); *Career* called to the Bar Middle Temple 1974 (Lloyd Jacob Meml exhibitioner, Astbury scholar), practised Oxford and Midland Circuit 1975-83, sr asst Office of the Parliamentary Counsel 1988- (joined 1983), memb Law Commission 1988-91; *Recreations* walking the dog; *Clubs* Travellers'; *Style—* Roger Jones, Esq; Office of the Parliamentary Counsel, 36 Whitehall, London SW1

JONES, (Owen Griffith) Ronald (Ron); s of William Tascar Jones, of Brynaman, Dyfed, and Bronwen Eirlys, *née* Jenkins; *b* 11 Dec 1948; *Educ* Amman Valley GS, Univ Coll Cardiff (BSc); *m* 1970, (Elizabeth) Cheryl; 1 da (Nia Mair b 1983); *Career* ptnr Arthur Andersen & Co 1983; chm Agenda Productions Ltd 1989-; dir Theatr Dalier Sylw, memb Welsh Language Bd, memb Cncl Inst of Welsh Affrs, treas Glamorgan CCC; FICA 1974; *Clubs* Reform; *Style—* Ron Jones, Esq; 43A Hollybush Rd, Cardiff (☎ 0222 762 351); Agenda Television, The Television Centre, St Davids Square, Swansea (☎ 0792 470470)

JONES, Ronald Fitzgerald (Ron); OBE (1989); s of Henry Fitzgerald Jones (d 1941), of Liverpool, and Margaret Chisholm, *née* Mackenzie (d 1964); *b* 16 Feb 1926; *Educ* Skerry's Coll Liverpool, Wallasey Catering Coll (CGLI Diplomas 150 and 151); *m* 1, 1951, Jeanette Pamela (d 1975), da of Samuel Wood; 2 s (Graham Stuart b 1955, Russell Brent b 1959); m 2, 1978, Eve Helen Hunter Macpherson, da of David Warren; *Career* WWII RN 1944-46; trainee hotel mangr 1946-53, gen mangr Dornoch Hotel Scotland 1956-57, sr asst mangr Midland Hotel Manchester 1957-58; gen mangr: Turnberry Hotel Ayrshire 1958-61, Station Hotel Hull 1961-64, Queen's Hotel Leeds 1964-67, Central Hotel Glasgow 1967-69, Royal Garden Hotel London 1969-72, Athenaeum Hotel London 1972-84; dir and gen mangr Claridge's London 1984-; Master Innholder 1979, Hotelier of the Year 1988; Freeman City of London 1979, Hon Citizen City of New Orleans 1979, Liveryman Worshipful Co of Distillers 1987, Freeman Worshipful Co of Innholders 1990; FHCIMA 1979 (memb 1969); *Recreations* painting, music, travel, theatre; *Style—* Ron Jones, Esq, OBE; Roosters, Todenham, Gloucestershire; Director & General Manager, Claridge's, Brook Street, London W1A 2JQ (☎ 071 629 8860, fax 071 499 2210)

JONES, Prof Ronald Mervyn; s of Cdr Glyn Owen Jones, MBE (d 1987), and Doris, *née* Woodley (d 1983); *b* 24 April 1947; *Educ* Devonport HS Plymouth, Univ of Liverpool (MB ChB); *m* 1, 1970 (m dis 1988), Angela Christine, *née* Parsonage; 1 s (Alex b 1979), 1 da (Emily b 1976); m 2, 22 Sept 1989, Caroline Ann, da of Dr Neil L Wordsworth Marshall; *Career* memb Faculty: Karolinska Inst Stockholm 1978, Univ of Michigan USA 1979-80; conslt Nottingham Hosps 1981-82, sr lectr and conslt Guys Hosp 1982-90, prof of anaesthetics Imperial Coll London and conslt anaesthetist St Mary's Hosp 1990- academican Euro Acad of Anaesthesiology; hon life memb Aust Soc of Anaesthetists; FFARCS; *Books* Current European Anaesthesiology Vols I II III (1986,1987,1988), Medicine for Anaesthetists (1989); *Recreations* music, history, architecture; *Clubs* Royal Naval Sailing Association, London Flotilla; *Style—* Prof Ronald Jones; St Mary's Hospital, London W2 (☎ 071 725 1681)

JONES, Prof Ronald Samuel; s of Samuel Jones (d 1974), of Chapel House, Old Racecourse, Oswestry, Shropshire, and Gladys Jane, *née* Philips (d 1953); *b* 29 Oct 1937; *Educ* Oswestry Boys HS, Univ of Liverpool (BVSc); *m* 21 April 1962, Pamela, da of Wilfred Evans, of Rock Cottage, Pant Oswestry, Shropshire; 2 da (Rachel Mary Patricia B 1963, Alison Jane b 1966); *Career* Univ of Glasgow: house surgn 1960-61, univ asst 1961-62; Univ of Liverpool: lectr 1962-77, sr lectr 1977-86, reader 1986-89, prof 1990-; magistrate City of Liverpool; MRCVS 1960, FRCVS 1981, FIBiol 1988; *Recreations* gardening, horse racing, philately; *Style—* Prof Ronald S Jones; 7 Birch Road, Oxton, Birkenhead, Merseyside L43 5UF (☎ 051 653 9008), University Department of Anaesthesia, Royal Liverpool Hospital, University of Liverpool, PO Box 147, Liverpool L69 3BX (☎ 051 706 4006)

JONES, Rupert James Livingston; s of Walter Herbert Jones (d 1982), and Dorothy Jocelyn, *née* Dignum (d 1989); *b* 2 Sept 1953; *Educ* Kings Coll Sch, Wimbledon, Univ of Birmingham (LLB); *m* 24 June 1978, Sheila Carol, da of Andrew Kertesz, of Penderyn, Mid Glam; 2 s (Oliver b 10 June 1984, Stephen b 13 Sept 1989), 1 da (Philippa b 31 Jan 1987); *Career* admitted slr 1978, ptnr Allen and Overy 1985- (articled clerk 1976-78, asst slr 1978-85); chm London Young Solicitors Gp 1987-88 (Ctee 1984-89); memb: Nat Ctee of Young Solicitors Gp 1986-89, Whittington Ctee of City of London Solicitors Company 1988-; memb Worshipful Co of Slrs 1985-; memb Law Soc 1976; *Recreations* gardening, cinema, motoring; *Style—* Rupert Jones, Esq; Allen & Overy, 9 Cheapside, London EC2V 6AD (☎ 071 248 9898, fax 071 236 2192, telex 8812801)

JONES, Samuel; s of Rev Samuel Jones, of The Manse, Thurlow Rd, Nairn, Scotland, and Sarah Johnston, *née* McCulloch; *b* 27 Dec 1939; *Educ* Morpeth GS, Univ of Manchester (LLB), Univ of Kent (MA); *m* 17 Oct 1964, Jean Ann, da of Frank Broadhurst, of 66 Buckfast Close, Macclesfield, Cheshire; 2 da (Allison b 1 March 1967, Tracey b 16 Oct 1970); *Career* chief exec Leics CC 1976-91, clerk of Lieutenancy Leics 1976-91, sec Lord Chancellor's Advsy Ctee for Leics 1976-91; town clerk designate City of London (May 1991-); hon sec Soc of Local Authy Chief Execs (SOLACE) 1988-; memb Law Soc; *Style—* Samuel Jones, Esq; 16 Wimborne Road, Leicester LE2 3RP (☎ 0533 705395); Chapel Knoll, 26 Hobbs Hill, Croyde, Devon EX33 1LZ (☎ 0271 890210); County Hall, Glenfield, Leicester LE3 8RA (☎ 0533 656000, fax 0533 656260, telex 341478, car 0860 257792)

JONES, Dr Schuyler; s of Schuyler Jones, of Wichita, Kansas, USA, and Ignace, *née* Mead; *b* 7 Feb 1930; *Educ* Wichita HS, Univ of Edinburgh (MA), Univ of Oxford (MA, DPhil); *m* 20 Dec 1955, Lis Margit Sondergaard, da of Malling Rasmussen, of Karlby, Denmark; 1 s (Peter Rasmussen b 2 Aug 1956), 1 da (Hannah Lis b 3 Oct 1962); *Career* lectr in ethnology Univ of Oxford 1970-71, curator Pitt Rivers Museum 1985- (asst curator 1971-85), head Dept of Ethnology and Prehistory 1985-; anthropological expeditions: N Africa, The Sahara, W Africa 1951, French Equatorial Africa, Belgian Congo, E Africa 1952, S Africa, The Zambezi and Congo Rivers 1953, French W Africa, The Sahara 1954, Eastern Med 1956, Greek Is 1957, Turkey, Iran, Afghanistan, Pakistan, India, Nepal 1958, Pakistan, Kashmir, Afghanistan 1959, Nuristan 1960-70, Central China, Gobi Desert, Chinese Turkestan 1984, E Africa 1985, Central China, Tibet, Gobi Desert 1986, S China, Chinese Turkestan, Hunza, Gilgit 1988; cncl memb RAI 1986-90, tstee Horniman Museum London 1989-; *Books* Sous le Soleil Africain (1955), Under the African Sun (1956), Annotated Bibliography of Nuristan (Kafiristan) & the Kalash Kafirs of Chitral (1966), The Political Organization of the Kam Kafirs (1967), Men of Influence in Nuristan (1974), Nuristan (with Lennart Edelberg, 1979), Hunting and Trading on the Great Plains 1859-1875, (ed, 1986); *Style—* Dr Schuyler Jones; Pitt Rivers Museum, Univ of Oxford, South Parks Rd, Oxford OX1 3PP (☎ 0865 270 924)

JONES, Sir Simon Warley Frederick Benton; 4 Bt (UK 1919), of Treeton, West Riding of Yorks, JP (Lincs 1971); s of Lt-Col Sir Peter Fawcett Benton Jones, 3 Bt, OBE (d 1972), and Nancy, *née* Pickering; *b* 11 Sept 1941; *Educ* Eton, Trinity Coll Cambridge; *m* 14 April 1966, Margaret Fiona, eldest da of David Rutherford Dickson; 3 s, 2 da; *Heir* s, James Peter Martin Benton Jones b 1 Jan 1973; *Career* farmer; High Sheriff Lincs 1977-78; *Recreations* shooting, fishing; *Style—* Sir Simon Benton Jones, Bt, JP; Irnham Hall, Grantham, Lincs (☎ 047 684 212); Sopley, Christchurch, Dorset

JONES, (John) Stanley; s of George White Jones (d 1958), of Wigan, Lancs, and Elizabeth Jones; *b* 10 June 1933; *Educ* Wigan GS, Wigan Art Sch (NDD), Slade Sch of Art UCL (Slade Dip in Fine Art), Ecole des Beaux Arts Paris; *m* 18 March 1961, Jennifer Francis, da of Lawrence Frederick Stone; 1 s (Matthew b 4 June 1965), 1 da (Liza b 17 Dec 1962); *Career* lectr in lithography Slade Sch of Fine Art UCL 1958, co fndr Curwen Studio London 1958; dir: Curwen Prints Ltd 1962-, Curwen Chilford Prints; pres Printmakers Cncl, memb Royal Soc of Painter Etchers; *Books* Lithography for Artists (1963); *Recreations* walking, appreciation of music; *Style—* Stanley Jones, Esq; Curwen Prints Ltd, 4 Windmill St, London W1 (☎ 071 636 1459); Curwen Chilford Prints, Chilford Hall, nr Linton, Cambridgeshire (☎ 0223 89354)

JONES, Stewart Elgan; s of Gwilym John Jones (d 1987), of Flecknoe, Warwickshire, and Elizabeth, *née* Davies; *b* 20 Jan 1945; *Educ* Cheltenham, Queen's Coll Oxford (MA); *m* 21 July 1979, Jennifer Anne, da of Maj James Ian Leonard Syddall (d 1963), of Riseley, Berks; 2 da (Eleanor b 1980, Clementine b 1981), 1 step s (James b 1971), 1 step da (Katherine b 1969); *Career* barr Gray's Inn 1972, memb of Western Circuit, recorder Crown Ct 1990; *Recreations* home, hearth, the great outdoors; *Clubs* MCC; *Style—* Stewart E Jones, Esq; 3 Paper Buildings, Temple, London, EC4Y 7EU (☎ 071 583 8055, fax 071 353 6271)

JONES, Stuart Kingston; s of Peter Jones (d 1990), and Barbara Ann Jones; *b* 26 May 1951; *Educ* Shrewsbury, Hotchkiss Sch USA (Winston Churchill scholarship, 3 Dips); *Career* sub editor and writer The Field Magazine 1972-74; The Times Newspaper: sub editor 1974-80, asst sports editor 1980-81, football corr 1981-; *Recreations* sport (especially golf, tennis and cricket), photography, reading; *Style—* Stuart Jones, Esq; The Times Newspaper, 1 Pennington St, London E1 (☎ 071 782 5944)

JONES, Terence Graham Parry (Terry); s of late Alick George Parry Jones, and Dilys Louise, *née* Newnes (d 1971); *b* 1 Feb 1942; *Educ* Royal GS Guildford, St Edmund Hall Oxford; *m* 20 June 1970, Alison, da of James Veitch Telfer; 1 s (William George Parry b 1976), 1 da (Sarah Louise Parry b 1974); *Career* writer and performer Monty Python's Flying Circus BBC TV 1969-75; film dir: Monty Python and the Holy Grail 1974, Monty Python's Life of Brian 1978, Monty Python's Meaning of Life 1981, Personal Services 1986, Erik the Viking 1989; *Books* Chaucer's Knight (1980), Fairy Tales (1981), The Saga of Erik the Viking (1983), Nicobobinus (1986), The Curse of the Vampire's Socks (1988), Attacks of Opinion (1988); *Style—* Terry Jones, Esq; 68A Delancey St, London NW1 (☎ 071 284 0242)

JONES, Thomas Henry (Tom); s of Cadwaladr Jones (d 1986), and Olwen Ellyw, *née* Humphreys; *b* 8 Feb 1950; *Educ* Tywyn Sch Merioneth, Univ Coll of Wales Aberystwyth (BA); *m* 20 Sept 1980, Dr Margaret Elizabeth Jones, da of John Wyn Jones, of Plas Gwyn, Llangyniew, Welshpool, Powys; 1 s (Owain b 1 Sept 1985) 1 da (Siwan b 12 Jan 1988); *Career* farmer; former vice-pres Farmers Union of Wales; memb: S4C Authy, Countryside Cmmn Ctee Wales, Miny Agric Hill Farm Advsy Ctee, Countryside Council for Wales, National Parks Review Panel; ASSO Royal Agric Socs; *Books* Brain Yn Y Brwyn (1976), Dyddiadur Ffarmwr (1985); *Style—* Tom Jones, Esq; Plas Coch, Dolanog, Welshpool, Powys (☎ 0938 810553)

JONES, Timothy Arthur; s of Canon Idwal Jones, *qv*, of Leam Cottage, Birdingbury, Warwicks, and Jean Margaret, *née* Shuttleworth; *b* 20 April 1951; *Educ* Christ's Hosp Horsham, Jesus Coll Cambridge, LSE, Coll of Law Chancery Lane; *m* 1979 (m dis 1988); 1 da (Harriet b 1980); *Career* called to the Bar: Inner Temple 1975, Kings Inns Dublin 1990; practising Midland and Oxford Circuit, specialising in commercial, landlord and tenant, planning and administrative law, dep head of Irish Chambers; Parly candidate (Lib later Lib Democrat): Warwick and Leamington 1974, Mid Staffordshire 1983 and 1987, Mid Staffordshire 1990; pres Cambridge Univ Liberal Club 1970; memb Standing Ctee Cambridge Union 1971, vice chm League of Friends Rugeley Hosp 1985-89; memb: Lib Democrat Federal Policy Ctee, Lib Democrats Federal Appeals Panel, Local Govt and Planning Bar Assoc, Admin Law Bar Assoc; *Recreations* theatre, walking, ornitholoogy; *Style—* Timothy Jones, Esq; 25 Kingsley Wood Rd, nr Rugeley, Staffs WS15 2UF; St Ive's Chambers, 9 Fountain Court, Steelhouse Lane, Birmingham B4 6DR (☎ 021 236 0863/0929/8952, fax 021 236 6961)

JONES, Timothy Duncan; s of Robert Walter Jones, and Doreen, *née* Price; *b* 16 Jan 1967; *Educ* Dartmouth HS, Great Barr Birmingham; *Career* memb GB swimming team for: Olympic Games 1988, Euro Championships 1989, Cwlth Games 1986 and 1990; holder Br record 200m butterfly, ranked number 1 in GB 1988, 1989 and 1990; finalist in Euro Championships 1989; *Recreations* golf, electronic music, travelling; *Style—* Timothy Jones, Esq; 2 George Road, Great Barr, Birmingham B43 6LG (☎ 021 3586438)

JONES, Trevor Courtney; s of William Jones (d 1979), of Hereford, and Edith Frances, *née* Webb (d 1963); *b* 14 Aug 1929; *Educ* Newport HS, Cardiff Univ (MM); *m* 24 Oct 1975, Rosemary Morley, da of Henry Vaughan Lowndes (d 1951), of Cheshire; 1 s (Simon Geoffrey b 30 Oct 1977); *Career* master mariner Union Castle Mail Steamship Co 1952-60, theatre mangr Royal Opera House 1971- (asst theatre mangr 1960-71); memb Covent Garden Forum; memb Hon Co of Master Mariners 1970; *Recreations* sailing, music, opera, ballet, theatre, reading; *Style—* Trevor Jones, Esq; 132 Tachbrook St, London SW1 (☎ 01 834 5273); The White Lodge, The Warren, Caversham, Berks; 42 Rue Des Lingots, Honfleur, Calvados, France 14600; Royal Opera House, Covent Garden, London WC2E 9DD (☎ 071 240 1200, fax 071 836 1762, telex 27988 COVGAR G)

JONES, Prof Trevor Mervyn; s of Samuel James Jones, of Edinburgh, Scotland, and Hilda May, *née* Walley (d 1981); *b* 19 Aug 1942; *Educ* Wolverhampton Sch, Kings Coll, Univ of London (BPharm, PhD); *m* 9 April 1965, Verity Ann, da of Richard Bates (d 1963), of Emsworth; 1 s (Timothy Damian b 1970), 1 da (Amanda Melissa b 1968); *Career* lectr Univ of Nottingham, head of devpt The Boots Co Ltd, dir res devpt and med Wellcome plc, visiting prof Kings Coll London and Univ of Strathclyde, author various pubns; memb UK Medicines Cmmn; Freeman Worshipful Soc of Apothecaries 1988; FPS, CChem, FRCS, MCPP; *Books* Drug Delivery to the Respiratory Tract (1987); *Recreations* gardening; *Clubs* Atheneum; *Style—* Prof Trevor Jones; Wellcome Research Laboratories, Langley Court, Beckenham, Kent BR3 3BS (☎ 081 658 2211)

JONES, Sir (Owen) Trevor; s of Owen and Ada Jones, of Dyserth; *b* 1927; *Career* memb Liverpool City Cncl 1968, Liverpool District Cncl 1973-, ldr Liverpool City Cncl; memb Merseyside Devpt Corpn 1981-; pres Liberal Party 1972-73, contested (Lib) Liverpool Toxteth 1974; kt 1981; *Style—* Sir Trevor Jones; Town Hall, Liverpool L2 3SW

JONES, Prof Tudor Bowden; s of Idris Jones (d 1961), of Ystradgynlais S Wales, and Tydvil Ann, *née* Bowden (d 1978); *b* 8 Nov 1934; *Educ* Univ of Wales, Univ Coll Swansea (BSc, PhD, DSc); *m* 16 Aug 1960, Patricia (Pat); 2 s (Owen Bowden b 14 Jan 1968, Hywel Bowden b 11 Sept 1970); *Career* sr res assoc US Nat Acad of Sci 1971-72, conslt on ionospheric radiowave propogation to UK US and Canadian Govt Agencies, prof of ionospheric physics Univ of Leicester 1980 (former lectr sr lectr and reader); memb various ctees SERC; FInstP, FIEE, CEng, FRAS; *Books* Ionospheric Radiowave Propagation (1969); *Recreations* classical music, rugby football; *Style—* Prof Tudor Jones; 4 Covert Close, Oadby, Leicester LE2 4HB (☎ 0533 713118), Physics Dept, The University, Leicester LE1 7RH (☎ 0533 523561, fax 0533 523555)

JONES, Dr William George (Bill); s of Arthur Constable Jones (d 1987), of Widnes, Cheshire, and Edna May, *née* Rickart (d 1981); *b* 26 Dec 1945; *Educ* Wade Deacon GS Widnes, Univ of Birmingham (MB ChB), Univ of London (DMRT); *m* 28 June 1969, Anthea Jane, da of Arie Heesterman, of Leeds, W Yorks; 2 da (Penny b 1972, Karen b 1975); *Career* registrar and sr registrar Central Birmingham Hosps 1970-75, conslt radiotherapist and oncologist W Glamorgan Health Authy Swansea 1975-78, lectr then sr lectr in radiotherapy Univ of Leeds, hon conslt in radiotherapy and oncology: Leeds Western DHA, Leeds Eastern DHA, Pontefract DHA, Yorkshire RHA; memb: Rotary Int (Leeds Elmete), working parties on urological tumours and testicular tumour Med Res Cncl, Urological Gp Euro Organisation for Res on Treatment of Cancer, Trout and Salmon Assoc; FRCR 1974, FRSM 1976, memb Br Inst of Radiology 1978; *Books* Germ Cell Tumours (ed with C K Anderson and A Millford Ward, 1981), Germ Cell Tumours II (ed with C K Anderson and A Millford Ward, 1985), Prostrate Cancer and Testicular Cancer (ed with D W W newling, 1990); *Recreations* game fishing, gardening, reading; *Style—* Dr Bill Jones; 32 Adel Towers Court, Adel, Leeds, W Yorks LS16 8ER (☎ 0532 610330); University of Leeds, Department of Radiotherapy, Tunbridge Building, Cookridge Hospital, Leeds LS16 6QB (☎ 0532 673411, fax 0532 611507)

JONES, William George Tilston; s of Thomas Tilston Jones (d 1976), and Amy Ethel, *née* Millar; *b* 7 Jan 1942; *Educ* Portsmouth GS, Portsmouth Poly (BSc); *m* 18 Dec 1965, Fiona Mary; 1 da (Zoë Samantha b 1966); *Career* PO: exec engr 1965-69, head of gp 1969-75, head of section 1975-78, head of div system x devpt 1978-80; BT: dep dir system x 1980-83, dir system evolution and standards 1983-84, chief exec technol 1984-86, dir technol studies 1988-90, consIt 1990-; exec in residence Int Mgmnt Inst Geneva 1987; hon fellowship Portsmouth Poly 1989; FIEE; *Recreations* theatre, debating society, camping; *Style—* William Jones, Esq; 1a The Drive, Radlett, Herts WD7 7DA (☎ 0923 854 448)

JONES, (Gwilym) Wyn; CBE (1977); s of Rev John Jones (d 1943), and Elizabeth, *née* Roberts (d 1929); *b* 12 July 1926; *Educ* Llanrwst GS, UCNW (BA), Univ of London; *m* 2 June 1951, Ruth, da of the late John Henry Thomas; 1 s (Gareth Wyn b 28 Sept 1964), 1 da (Nerys Wyn b 25 Feb 1956); *Career* WWII served RN 1944-47; colonial admin Gilbert & Ellice Island, Tarawa, Phoenix Island & Ocean Island 1950-61, memb Treas Bd Solomon Islands 1961, sec to Chief Min Cncl of Mins Solomon Islands 1974-77 (asst sec 1961, sr asst sec 1967, dep chief sec 1974), govr Montserrat 1977-80; admin Cwmni Theatr Cymru (Welsh Nat Theatre) 1982-85, memb Gwynedd Health Authy 1982-90, assoc memb 1990-; *Recreations* walking arthritically alone; *Style—* Wyn Jones, Esq, CBE; Y Frondeg, 13 Warren Drive, Deganwy, Gwynedd LL31 9ST (☎ 0492 5833 77)

JONES, (Ieuan) Wyn; JP 1972; s of Tom Jones (d 1978), of Haverfordwest, and Dilys Vaughan Jones, *née* Williams (d 1959); *b* 8 Dec 1928; *Educ* Ellesmere Coll, Univ of London (BA), Univ of Liverpool (Dip CD); *m* 11 July 1959, Elfrida Mary, da of Michael Ionides (d 1978), of Surrey; 1 s (Gareth b 1962), 1 da (Emma b 1960); *Career* architect; dep architect MOD Iraq 1956-59; ptnr: Hirst & Jones, Moore Simpson & Ptnrs 1959-68, Wyn Jones, Paul Andrews & Associates 1968; cmmns incl numerous domestic & commercial buildings in West Wales, PCC Admin Building Texaco Refinery; also numerous restorations incl St Mary Haverfordwest; Picton Castle & Pembroke Castle; awarded: 3 Civic Tst Awards 1968, 1970 and 1982 Welsh Office Housing Medal 1968; architect to St Davids Diocesan Bd of Finance, FRIBA 1969; *Recreations* hunting, gardening, sketching, historical buildings; *Style—* Wyn Jones, Esq, JP; Blaencilgoed House, Ludchurch, Narberth, Dyfed (☎ 083 483 605); 22 High Street, Haverfordwest, Dyfed (☎ 0437 765156)

JONES, Dr (Richard) Wyn; s of Thomas Jones (d 1964), of Bagillt, Clwyd, and Eva, *née* Bloor; *b* 16 Dec 1944; *Educ* Holywell GS, Univ of Liverpool (MBChB, MPsyMed, DPM); *m* 16 Feb 1973, Margaret, da of Harry Green (d 1976), of Southport; 2 da (Helen b 1975, Susan b 1977); *Career* Capt RAMC (V) 1969-74; consIt psychiatrist Fazakerly and Walton Hosps 1977-, hon clinical lectr Univ of Liverpool 1977-; memb: Mersey Mental Health Review Tbnl 1983-, BMA; *Recreations* skiing, walking, travel; *Style—* Dr Wyn Jones; Danefield, Alt Road, Hightown, Liverpool (☎ 051 9292821), Department of Psychiatry, Fazakerley Hosp, Longmoor Lane, Liverpool L9 7AL (☎ 051 5293555)

JONES, Wynn Rees; s of Iorwerth Jones of Machynlleth, Powys, and Catherine Jane, *née* Rees; *b* 18 Feb 1941; *Educ* Machynlleth GS; *m* 28 April 1962, Eira, da of Trevor Jones (d 1962); 2 da (Karen Wynn b 18 Sept 1963, Nia Wynn b 16 Nov 1967); *Career* Barclay's Bank: mangr Port Talbot 1978-81, gen mangr asst Lombard St 1982-83, local dir S Wales Regnl Office 1984-87, retail dir Shrewsbury Regnl Office 1988-; memb Cncl Nat Museum of Wales; ACIB; *Recreations* antiques, motoring, all sport; *Style—* Wynn Jones, Esq; South Lodge, Norton, Shifnall, Shropshire TF11 9EE; Barclays Bank Plc, Regional Office, St Marys Place, Shrewsbury, SY1 1DU (☎ 0743 232901, fax 0743 231630)

JONES, Wynne Melville; s of Rev John Melville Jones (d 1972), and Eirlys, *née* Davies; *b* 7 Aug 1947; *Educ* Co Secondary Sch Tregaron, Swansea Coll of Art, Trinity Coll Camarthers; *m* 1971, Linda Rees, da of John Verdun Rees; 2 da (Meleri Wyn, Manon Wyn); *Career* head of PR Welsh League of Youth 1975 (co organiser Camarthenshire 1969, publicity offr headquarters 1971), fndr Strata Public Relations & Advertising Aberystwyth 1979, exec dir Strata Matrix 1989- (result of merger between Strata and Cardiff Design & Advertising Co); chm: Nat Cncl Welsh League of Youth, Bd of Dirs Golwg (Welsh language current affrs magazine); memb Ct and Cncl Univ Coll of Wales, fndr and memb Welsh PR Assoc; *Recreations* art appreciation, swimming, rural activities; *Style—* Wynne Jones, Esq; 23/25 North Parade, Aberystwyth, Dyfed SY23 2JN (☎ 0970 625552, fax 0970 612774); 1 Talbot St, Cardiff CF1 9BW (☎ 0222 231231, fax 0222 372798)

JONES-LEE, Prof Michael Whittaker; s of Lt-Col Walter Whittaker Jones-Lee (d 1977), of Leybourne, Kent, and Christina, *née* Hamilton (d 1985); *b* 3 April 1944; *Educ* Prince Rupert Sch Wilhelmshaven, Bishop Wordsworth's Sch Sailsbury, Univ of Sheffield (BEng), Univ of York (DPhil); *m* 20 Dec 1969, Hazel, da of Arthur Stephen Knight; 2 s (Rupert 1974, Ben 1976), 1 da (Sarah b 1979); *Career* sr lectr Dept of Political Econ Univ of St Andrews 1971-72; Univ of York: Esmée Fairbairn lectr in fin 1967-71, sr lectr Dept of Econs 1972-76, reader Dept of Econs 1976-77; Univ of Newcastle upon Tyne: prof Dept of Econs 1977-, head Dept of Econs 1984-, dean Faculty of Social Sci 1984-88; consIt Dept of Tport and HSE; *Books* The Value of Life: An Economic Analysis (1976), The Value of Life and Safety (ed, 1982), The Economics of Safety and Physical Risk (1989); *Recreations* shopping and old sportscars; *Style—* Prof Michael Jones-Lee; Dept of Economics, University of Newcastle upon Tyne, Newcastle-upon-Tyne NE1 7RU (☎ 091 2226000, telex 53654, fax 091 2226548)

JONES-PARRY, Sir Ernest; s of John Parry (d 1958); *b* 16 July 1908; *Educ* St Asaph Sch, Univ of Wales (MA), Univ of London (PhD); *m* 1938, (Marjorie Elizabeth) Mary, da of Hugh Garfield Powell (d 1926); 2 s (Rupert, Tristram); *Career* lectr in history Univ Coll of Wales 1935-40; Miny of Food 1941, Miny of Agric Fisheries and Food 1954 (under sec 1957-64); exec dir: Int Sugar Cncl 1965-67, Int Sugar Orgn 1968-78; kt 1978; *Publications* The Spanish Marriages 1841-46 (1936), The Correspondence of Lord Aberdeen and Princess Lieven 1832-1854 (2 vols Royal Historical Soc 1938-39); *Recreations* reading, watching cricket; *Clubs* Athenaeum; *Style—* Sir Ernest Jones-Parry; Flat 3, 34 Sussex Sq, Brighton, Sussex BN2 5AD (☎ 0273 688894)

JONZEN, Karin; da of Uno Lowenadler, and Gerda Munck, *née* Fulkila; *b* 22 Dec 1914; *Educ* Wimbledon HS, Slade Sch of Art, Royal Acad Stockholm; *m* 1, 26 Feb 1944, Basil Jonzen (d 1969), s of Birger Jonzen; 1 s (Martin b 1948); m 2, 1972, Ake Sucksforff; *Career* Ambulance Serv 1941-45; artist; extra mural lectr in art appreciation 1965-71, lectr Camden Arts Centre 1968-72; works in municipal galleries incl: The Tate, Glasgow, Liverpool, Brighton, Bradford, Southend, Doncaster, Melbourne Aust, White Museum Cornell Univ USA, Nat Portrait Gallery; works in public: over life size bronze gp Guildhall forecourt, life size bronze London Wall Moorgate, life size youth New Delhi WHO Bldg, life size torso bronze WHO Bldg Geneva, over life size bust of Samuel Pepys Seething Lane, young girl Lower Sloan St; work in churches: carving on Guildford Cathedral, Madonna and Child Pieta Swedish Church, Madonna and Child St Mary le Bow, Madonna and Child St Saviours Church Warwick Ave, Madonna and Child St Mary and St Gabriel S Harting, St Michael St Michaels Church Golders Green, Acension Gp Selwyn Coll Chapel Cambridge, St Ann and St Mary gp St Ann and St Mary Church Lewes; Prix de Rome 1939, Theodorn Glelchen award 1947, Gold medal Academia della Arte e Lavore Parma, Gold medal Int Parly for Safety and Peace USA, Silver medal RBS; memb London Gp; FRBS; *Books* Karin Jonzen Sculptor (1976); *Style—* Mrs Karin Jonzen; The Studio, 6A Gunter Grove, London SW10 0UJ (☎ 071 351 0594)

JOPLIN, Prof Graham Frank; s of Frank Joplin (d 1984), of Wellington, NZ, and Mary Victoria, *née* Feist (d 1984); *b* 11 May 1927; *Educ* Wellington Coll NZ, Univ of Victoria NZ, Univ of Otago Med Sch NZ (MB ChB), Univ of London (PhD); *m* 24 Jan 1959, Helen Agnes, da of James Stanley Logan (d 1958), of Lockerbie, Scotland; 2 da (Pamela Mary b 1960, Anne Helen (Mrs Youlton) b 1963); *Career* jr clinical appts in: NZ hosps 1952-54, London hosps 1955-63; sr lectr then reader then prof of clinical endocrinology and hon consIt physician Royal Postgrad Med Sch and Hammersmith Hosp London 1967-89 (Wellcome sr clinical res fell and lectr 1963-67), author and co author over 300 scientific articles on endocrinology calcium metabolism, contrib overseas, reg advsr RCP 1981-83; FRCP 1970 (MRCP 1956); *Books* Dynamic Studies of Metabolic Bone Disease (jt ed, 1964), A Report on Diabetic Blindness in the UK (jtly, 1969); contrib: Modern Trends in Radiotherapy (1967), Hospital Medicine (1968), Carbohydrate Metabolism and its Disorders (1968), Symposium on Advanced Medicine (1968); *Recreations* gardening, music; *Style—* Prof Graham Joplin

JOPLING, Rt Hon (Thomas) Michael; PC (1979), MP (C) Westmorland and Lonsdale 1983-; s of late Mark Bellerby Jopling; *b* 10 Dec 1930; *Educ* Cheltenham, King's Coll Newcastle; *m* 1958, Gail, da of late Ernest Dickinson; 2 s; *Career* farmer; contested (C) Wakefield 1959, memb Nat Cncl NFU 1962-64, MP (C) Westmorland 1964-1983, PPS to Min Agric 1970-71, asst govt whip 1971-73, Lord Cmmr Treasy 1973-74, oppn whip 1974, oppn spokesman Agric 1974-79, shadow min Agric 1975-76, parly sec to Treasy and govt chief whip 1979-1983, min Agric Fishery and Food 1983-87; pres EEC Cncls of Agric and Fishery Ministers 1986; hon sec Br and American Parly Gp 1987-; memb: Foreign Affrs Select Ctee 1987-, Int Exec Cwlth Parly Assoc 1988-89 (memb UK Exec 1974-79 and 1987, vice chm 1977-79); pres Auto Cycle Union 1989-; *Style—* The Rt Hon Michael Jopling, MP; Ainderby Hall, Thirsk, N Yorks YO7 4HZ (☎ 0845 567 224); Clyder Howe Cottage, Windermere, Cumbria (☎ 096 62 2590)

JORDAN, (Leslie) Alan; DL (Essex 1988); s of Dr Leslie Jordan (d 1930), and Ellen Florence, *née* Holmes; *b* 10 Oct 1930; *Educ* Kings Sch Ely, RAC; *m* July 1957 (m dis

1972), Elizabeth; 1 da (Rebecca Elizabeth b 13 June 1961); *Career* cmmnd Royal Norfolk Regt 1948-51; currently bd dir and chm Eastern Region Savills; High Sheriff of Essex; chm Essex Scout Cncl; Freeman: City of London, Worshipful Co of Farmers; memb RICS; *Recreations* fishing, shooting, gardening; *Clubs* Farmers; *Style*— Alan Jordan, Esq, DL; Great Lodge, Great Bardfield, Braintree, Essex CM7 4QD (☎ 0371 810776), Savills House, 24 Hills Rd, Cambridge CB2 1JW (☎ 0223 322955, car 0836 275599)

JORDAN, Andrew; s of Andrew Jordan, of Belfast, and Bessie, *née* Gray (d 1977); *b* 12 March 1950; *Educ* Queen's Univ Belfast (BSc), Darwin Coll Cambridge (Dip in Mathematical Statistics), Cranfield Sch of Mgmnt (MBA); *Career* statistician Unilever Res Ltd 1974-77 (statistician Overseas Devpt Admin 1977-79), investmt controller 3i 1980-84; ptnr Coopers & Lybrand (now Coopers & Lybrand Deloitte) 1985-; fell Royal Statistical Soc; *Recreations* squash, diving, skiing; *Style*— Andrew Jordan, Esq; 8A Belvedere Drive, London SW19 7BY (☎ 081 947 0183); Coopers & Lybrand Deloitte, Plumtree Ct, London EC4A 4HT (☎ 071 822 8573, fax 071 822 8500)

JORDAN, Andrew Kevin (Andy); s of William John Jordan, and Elsa, *née* Brewer; *b* 10 June 1950; *Educ* Univ of Bristol (BA), St Mary's Coll Southampton (Dip in Drama); *Career* theatre dir; fndr Bristol Express Theatre Co 1978, fndr assoc dir Playfair Film and TV Productions Ltd 1980; Scotsman Fringe First Awards: A Respectable Family by Maxim Gorki Edinburgh 1977, Lunatic and Lover by Michael Meyer Edinburgh 1978; radio drama prodr BBC 1988-; memb: CND, Friends of the Earth, Greenpeace, Antiapartheid Movement, Labour Pty; memb: Directors' Guild GB, Equity, BETA; *Recreations* travel, reading, cinema, theatre; *Style*— Andy Jordan, Esq; 20 Mocatta House, Brady St, Whitechapel, London E1 5DL (☎ 071 247 4156), BBC Christchurch Studios, 38 Portland St, Bristol BS8 4JB (☎ 0272 732211 ext 2458)

JORDAN, Dr Carole; da of Reginald Sidney Jordan, and Ethel May, *née* Waller; *b* 19 July 1941; *Educ* Harrow Co GS for Girls, UCL (BSc, PhD); *Career* res assoc Jt Inst for Laboratory Astrophysics Univ of Colorado USA 1966, post doctoral appt UKAEA Culham Lab 1966-69; SRC's Astrophysics Res Unit Culham Laboratory: post doctoral res asst 1969-71, sr scientific offr 1971-73, princ scientific offr 1973-76; univ lectr Dept of Theoretical Physics Univ of Oxford, fell and tutor in physics Somerville Coll Oxford 1976-; sec RAS 1981-, memb SERC 1985-; FRAS 1966, memb IAU 1967, FInstP 1973, FRS 1990; *Recreations* gardening; *Style*— Dr Carole Jordan, FRS; Dept of Theoretical Physics, Univ of Oxford, 1 Keble Rd, Oxford OX1 3NP (☎ 0865 273 980, fax 0965 273 418, telex 83245 NUCLOX)

JORDAN, Cyril George; s of George Henry Jordan (d 1985), of High Wycombe, and Rose Mabel, *née* Liddon (d 1963); *b* 23 July 1929; *Educ* Mill End Secdy Modern High Wycombe, Sch of Photography Regent St London (BIPP preliminary and intermediate certificates, City and Guilds intermediate and final certificates); *m* 1961, Edna Mary, da of late Cyril Henry Smith, of Lane End, High Wycombe; 1 s (Ross Henry b 11 Jan 1968); *Career* Nat Serv RAF; trainee under the late Cyril Roberts 1945-52, photographic techician Hulton Press Picture Post Library 1952-54, sr photographer Hector Smith Studios Chesham Bucks 1954-58; Colour Centre Limited: technician 1958, fndr and mangr branch in Regent St, md 1966, gp md 1969; fndr CJ Products 1982; fell Assoc of Photographic Technicians 1971, FBIPP 1974, ASIAD 1976, MCSD 1978; *Books* The Manual of the Etch Bleach and Dye Process (1989); *Recreations* gardening, classical music, active part in local organisation, chairman of Village Hall Management Committee, president of Local Horticultural Society; *Clubs* The Tuesday; *Style*— Cyril Jordan, Esq; Larkfield, Bledlow Ridge, High Wycombe, Bucks HP14 4AL (☎ 024 027 352); C J Products, West Yard Industrial Estate, Saunderton, High Wycombe, Bucks (☎ 024 024 4174, fax 024 024 4175)

JORDAN, Francis Leo (Frank); CBE (1989), QPM (1982); s of Leo Thomas Jordan (d 1967), of Stone, Staffs, and Mary, *née* Moloney (d 1982); *b* 15 June 1930; *Educ* St Joseph's Coll; *m* 1951, Ruth, da of James Ashmore (d 1970), of Cheshire; 1 s (Francis b 1958), 2 da (Karen b 1957, Diane b 1962); *Career* joined Staffs Police 1950 attaining rank of Chief Superintendent, seconded to Cyprus Police during EOKA emergency 1956-58, staff offr to HO Police Inspectorate 1975, asst chief constable W Midlands 1976, dep chief constable of Kent 1979, chief constable of Kent 1982-89; chm Kent Children's House Soc 1979-81 (hon patron), vice pres Assoc of Kent CCs 1982-89; memb: Kent Co Ctee SSAFA 1986-89, Kent Agric Soc, Assoc Men of Kent and Kentish Men, Band of Brothers; appointed to Parole Bd 1990; CBIM 1985, FRSA 1990; OStJ 1988; *Recreations* shooting, walking, old buildings, travel; *Clubs* Royal Over-Seas League, Hopper's Tie; *Style*— Frank Jordan, Esq, CBE, QPM; c/o Police Headquarters, Sutton Rd, Maidstone, Kent ME15 9BZ (☎ 0622 690690, telex 96132)

JORDAN, Gayton (Gay); da of Stafford Walter Beckett (d 1985), of Shaldon, South Devon, and Catharine Barbara, *née* Marshall (d 1982); *b* 26 Feb 1951; *Educ* Convent of Notre Dame Teignmouth Devon, UCL (LLB, LLM); *m* 19 April 1976, David Jordan, s of William Henry Jordan; *Career* asst sec The Chartered Assoc of Certified Accountants 1978-86 (former asst professional educn sec), dir Inst of Trading Standards Admin 1987-; fell RSPB (memb Enfield Local Gp); *Recreations* reading, hill walking, travel and camping in Africa, bird and animal watching; *Style*— Mrs Gay Jordan; Flat 2, 6 Warwick Rd, New Southgate, London N11 2TU (☎ 081 368 8122); 4-5 Hadleigh Business Centre, 351 London Rd, Hadleigh, Essex SS7 2BT (☎ 0702 559922, fax 0702 559902)

JORDAN, Gerard Michael; s of Arthur Thomas Jordan (d 1971), of Upton, Wirral, Cheshire, and Ruby Eveline, *née* Charlton (d 1979); *b* 25 Sept 1929; *Educ* Grange Sch Birkenhead, Univ of Liverpool (BEng); *m* 26 March 1955, Vera Maud, da of George Peers (d 1967), of Bidston, Cheshire; 1 s (Paul Charlton b 1966), 1 da (Nichola Lesley b 1961); *Career* engr offr Mercantile Marine, gp engr Proctor & Gamble UK 1955-59; UKAEA: princ professional and tech offr 1959-72, asst dir 1972-75, dep dir 1975-84, dir of engrg 1984-87, dir of Dounreay Estab 1987-; conslt (ex officio) Highlands Regnl Cncl and Highland and Islands Devpt Bd, indust rep to CBI Highlands Region Cncl memb Thurso Tech Coll; MIMechE; *Recreations* golf, sailing, DIY; *Style*— Gerard Jordan, Esq; The Cottage, Reay, Caithness, Scotland KW14 7RE (☎ 0847 81202); Dounreay Nuclear Power Development Establishment, Thurso, Caithness, Scotland KW14 7TZ (☎ 0847 62121)

JORDAN, John Oliver Philip; s of Arther Oliver Jordan (d 1976), of Southampton, and Daisy Gertrude, *née* Jerrim (d 1980); *b* 4 Feb 1936; *Educ* Barton Peverel GS; *m* 30 April 1960, Ann Lochhead, da of Maj Donald Robert Daniels (d 1988), of Southampton; 2 s (Peter John 1961, Andrew b 1966), 2 da (Elizabeth b 1963, Alison b 1968); *Career* Nat Serv cmmnd RAPC, 6 years Army Emergerncy Reserve RAPC (Capt/pay-master); CA 1957; currently sr ptnr Jordan Brookes & Co; FCA 1966, ATII; *Style*— John Jordan, Esq; Parmenter House, Tower Rd, Winchester SO23 8TD (☎ 0962 852263, fax 0962 841 197)

JORDAN, Joseph (Joe); *b* 15 Dec 1951; *Educ* St Aidens Sch Wishaw; *m* 27 June 1977, Judith Maria, da of Harold Joseph Smith; 4 c (Lucy Elizabeth b 27 Oct 1978, Andrew Joseph b 14 Dec 1979, Thomas Michael b 24 May 1981, Caroline Laura b 27 Sept 1984); *Career* professional football manager; former player: Morton, Leeds Utd, Manchester Utd, AC Milan Italy, Verona Italy, Southampton; Bristol City: player, asst mangr and coach, mangr 1988-90; mangr Heart of Midlothian 1990-; Scotland caps: 1 under 23, 52 full 1973-82; represented Scotland in World Cup: W Germany 1974, Argentina 1978, Spain 1982; honours: League Championship Leeds Utd 1974 (European Cup Winners Cup 1973, European Cup finalist 1975), FA Cup finalist (Man Utd) 1979, Seria B Championship (AC Milan) 1983, Italian Cup finalists (Verona) 1984, promotion to Div 2 Bristol City 1990; *Recreations* walking dogs, children; *Style*— Joe Jordan, Esq; Heart of Midlothian FC, Tynecastle Park, Gorgie Road, Edinburgh EH11 2NL (☎ 031 337 6132)

JORDAN, Michael Anthony; s of Charles Thomas Jordan (d 1956), of The Ferns, Duffield, Derbys, and Florence Emily, *née* Golder (d 1977); *b* 20 Aug 1931; *Educ* Haileybury; *m* 1, 9 Dec 1956 (m dis 1989), Brenda Elizabeth, *née* Gee; 1 s (Mark b 1959), 1 da (Fiona b 1961); m 2, Feb 1990, Dorothea, *née* Coureau; *Career* joined RH March Son & Co 1958 (ptnr 1959-68); ptnr: Saker & Langdon Davis 1968, WH Cork Gully & Co 1968-80, Coopers and Lybrand 1980- (now Coopers and Lybrand Deloitte) sr ptnr Cork Gully 1983-; High Ct of Justice Isle of Man (jt inspr into affairs of The Savings and Investment Bank Ltd 1979); govr Royal Shakespeare Theatre 1979; FCA; *Recreations* opera, DIY; *Style*— Michael Jordan, Esq; Ballinger Farm, Ballinger, nr Great Missenden, Bucks HP16 9LQ (☎ 02406 3298); Shelley House, 3 Noble St, London EC2V 7DQ (☎ 071 606 7700, fax 071 606 9887, telex 884 730 CORKGY G)

JORDAN, Dr Michael John; s of Dr John Jordan (d 1963), of Kidderminster, Worcs, and Margaret Tuer, *née* Harper, MBE; *b* 26 May 1949; *Educ* Malvern, Trinity Hall Cambridge, St Thomas's Hosp Med Sch; *m* 12 May 1984, (Gena) Rosamund, da of Alan Rigby Horler; 2 da (Camilla b 1986, Olivia b 1988); *Career* Anaesthetics Dept St Thomas's Hosp: sr house offr 1976, registrar 1977, sr registrar 1979; visiting asst prof of anaesthesiology Univ of Texas Dallas USA 1981-82, conslt anaesthetist Bart's 1983-; FFARCS 1978; memb: Anaesthetic Res Soc, BMA, Assoc of Anaesthetists; *Recreations* photography, music, cinema, theatre; *Clubs* Hurlingham, RSM; *Style*— Dr Michael Jordan; 29 Acfold Rd, London SW6 2AJ (☎ 071 731 4356); Department of Anaesthesia, St Bartholomew's Hospital, London EC1A 7BE (☎ 071 601 7518, car 0860 533423)

JORDAN, Philip Spencer; s of Frank William Jordan, and Morfydd Enid, *née* Thomas; *b* 24 Feb 1953; *Educ* Swavesey Village Coll, Leicester Poly (Dip Arch); *m* 28 Oct 1989, Marilyn, da of Fred Longden; 2 s (Paul David b 1980, Keir Richard b 1982), 1 da (Emily Keziar b 1988); *Career* architect: Cound Page Cambridge 1980-82, Covell Matthews Wheatley Architects 1982-85; ptnr Philip Jordan Architects 1985-87, md Forum Architects (London) Ltd 1989- (ptnr 1987-89); dir: Jordan & Bateman Architects Ltd, Domicile Design Ltd, exhibitor Int 40 under 40 exhibition RIBA; vice pres RIBA 1987-89 (memb and memb Cncl), fndr memb Building Experiences Tst; *Recreations* family, sport, gardening and painting; *Clubs* 5 Iron; *Style*— Philip Jordan, Esq; Colon, 113 High St, Trumpington, Cambridge CB2 2JD (☎ 0223 841908, car 0836 690213)

JORDAN, Air Marshal Sir Richard Bowen; KCB (1956, CB 1947), DFC (1941); s of Alfred Ormand Jordan (d 1942); *b* 7 Feb 1902; *Educ* Marlborough, RAF Coll Cranwell; *m* 1932, Freda Monica Minton Haines (d 1985), da of Mrs Miles Bruton (d 1950); 1 da; *Career* joined RAF 1921, served WWII, Gp Capt 1941, Air Cdre 1947, Air Vice-Marshal 1951, Air Marshal 1956, dir-gen orgn Air Miny 1953-55, AOC-in-C Maintenance Cmd 1956-58, ret 1958; Polonia Restituta 1942, Orange Nassau 1948; *Recreations* shooting, gardening; *Style*— Air Marshal Sir Richard Jordan, KCB, DFC; 4 Stonegate Court, Stonegate, Wadhurst, East Sussex TN5 7EQ

JORDAN, Dr Stephen Christopher; s of Cyril Arthur Jordan (d 1989), and Kathleen May, *née* Brook (d 1985); *b* 8 May 1933; *Educ* Queen Elizabeth's Hospital Bristol, Univ of Bristol (MB ChB, MD); *m* 6 Nov 1965, Linda Helen, da of Edward Wright (d 1982); 1 s (Neil Alexander b 1969), 1 da (Louise Helen b 1967); *Career* registrar: Royal Berks Hosp Reading 1959-61, Radcliffe Infirmary Oxford 1959-61, Gen Infirmary Leeds 1961; sr registrar Bristol Royal Infirmary 1966-, conslt cardiologist Bristol Royal Infirmary 1969- (Bristol Children's Hosp); memb Br Cardiac Soc, memb Br Med Assoc; FRCP 1972 (MRCP 1962), Nat Heart Hosp London 1963, Hosp for Sick Children Gt Ormond St London 1964; *Books* Heart Disease in Paediatrics (1979), Synopsis of Cardiology (1981); *Recreations* industrial archaeology; *Style*— Dr Stephen Jordan; 5 Leigh Rd, Clifton, Bristol BS8 2DA (☎ 0272 736589); Bristol Royal Infirmary, Bristol BS2 8HW (☎ 0272 230000)

JORDAN, Terence; s of late Thomas William Jordan, and Elsie Elizabeth, *née* Davies; *b* 29 July 1936; *Educ* Hazeltine Sch Lower Sydenham; *m* 1, 17 March 1955 (m dis), Margaret Route; 1 s (Barry John b 1957), 1 da (Karen b 1960); m 2, 7 Sept 1964 (m dis), Valerie Ann Eustace; 1 s (Neil b 1966); m 3, 10 March 1986, Herchel Maclear-Williams (*née* Maclear-Morris); 1 step da (Charlotte Rachael Maclear b 1975); *Career* md Terrys Jewellers Ltd 1979-, dir Ratners Jewellers plc 1984-, md Ernest Jones Ltd 1988-, md Zales Jewellers 1988-; *Recreations* golf, travel, philately; *Clubs* Flackwell Heath Golf; *Style*— Terence Jordan, Esq; Ratners HQ, 25 Great Portland Street, London W1

JORDAN, Terence Frank; s of Frank William Jordan, of Papworth Everard, Cambridge, and Morfydd Enid Jordan; *b* 16 Oct 1941; *Educ* Leicester Coll of Art and Design (Dip Arch); *m* 1, 1963 (m dis 1976), Christine Ann; 1 s (Simon David b 23 April 1972), 1 da (Elizabeth Ann b 25 March 1964); m 2, 7 April 1978, Anita Lesley, da of Douglas Richard Reed, of Cambridge; 1 s (Daniel Thomas b 24 Nov 1981), 1 da (Sarah Louise b 7 Sept 1986); *Career* fndr ptnr Clark and Jordan 1973-76, md Covell Matthews Wheatley 1985- (fndr dir 1976); Cambridge Preservation Soc: memb Mgmnt Ctee, former chm Fin and Property Ctee 1978-84; MRIBA; FRSA; *Recreations* music, golf, gardening; *Style*— Terence Jordan, Esq; Grove Cottage, 40 Church St, Haslingfield, Cambridge CB3 7JE (☎ 0223 872346); Covell Matthews Wheatley, 19 Bourdon Place, London W1X 9HZ (☎ 071 409 2444, fax 071 491 8661)

JORDAN, William Brian; s of Walter Jordan (d 1974), and Alice, *née* Heath; *b* 28 Jan 1936; *Educ* Barford Rd Secdy Modern Birmingham; *m* 8 Nov 1958, Jean Ann, da of Ernest Livesey; 3 da (Pamela, Lisa, Dawn); *Career* pres AEU 1986; memb: TUC Gen and major ctees, NEDC, Engrg Indust Trg Bd, Advsy ACAS; pres Euro Metalworkers (EEC), Br Section Int Metalworkers Fedn; govr: LSE, Manchester Business Sch; memb: BBC Bd of Govrs 1988, Winston Churchill Meml Tst; City & Guilds Insignia award in Technol (Honoris Causa); *Recreations* reading, most sports; *Clubs* E57 Working Man's Club Birmingham, Austin Sports & Social Club; *Style*— William Jordan, Esq; 110 Peckham Rd, London, SE15 5EL (☎ 071 703 4231, fax 071 701 7862)

JORDAN-MOSS, Norman; CB (1972), CMG (1965); s of Arthur Moss, and Ellen, *née* Jordan Round; *b* 5 Feb 1920; *Educ* Manchester GS, St John's Coll Cambridge (MA); *m* 1, 1965, Kathleen, *née* Lusmore (d 1974); 1 s, 1 da; m 2, 1976, Philippa Rands; 1 da; *Career* Miny of Econ Warfare 1940-44; HM Treasy 1944-80: asst rep ME 1945-48 (princ 1948), first sec (econ) Belgrade 1952-55, fin cnsllr Washington 1956-60, asst sec 1956-68, cnsllr UK Perm Delgn to OECD Paris 1963-66, under sec 1968-71, dep sec 1976-80; dep under sec of state DHSS 1971-76; dir 1928 Investment Tst 1980-85, conslt Hambros Bank 1981-83; dir: Crown Life Assurance Co 1980-84, Crown Life Pensions 1980-90, Crown Life Mgmnt Servs 1980-, Crown Fin Mgmnt 1984-; *Recreations* music, theatre; *Clubs* Travellers'; *Style*— Norman Jordan-Moss, Esq, CB, CMG; Milton Way, Westcott, Dorking, Surrey

JOSCELYNE, Richard Patrick; s of Dr Patrick Joscelyne (d 1963), of Westbury-on-Trym, Bristol, and Rosalind Effie, *née* Whitcombe; *b* 19 June 1934; *Educ* Bryanston,

Queen's Coll Cambridge (MA); *m* 1, 5 Feb 1961 (m dis 1988), Vera Lucia Melo; 1 s (Richard b 1964), 1 da (Patricia b 1963); m 2, 1988, Rita Irangani, *née* Dias; *Career* Br Cncl: Montevideo 1962-67, Moscow 1967-69, Madrid 1969-73, dir N and Latin America Dept 1973-77, rep Sri Lanka 1977-80, controller Asia and America Div 1980-82, fin controller 1982-87, Spain 1987-; Encomienda De La Orden De Merito Civil (Spain 1988); *Style—* Richard Joscelyne, Esq; c/o British Council, 10 Spring Gardens, London SW1A 2BN (☎ 071 930 8466)

JOSÉ, (Thomas) Leonard; JP; s of William José (d 1967), of Penzance, and Jessie, *née* Brown Wark (d 1974); *b* 11 May 1926; *Educ* schs in Cornwall, Scotland and England; *m* 29 March 1952, Gwendoline Joyce, da of Archibald Butler (d 1945), of Hounslow; 1 s (Alan), 2 da (Karen, Miranda); *Career* London Scottish (Gordon Highlanders) TA 1948-52: Lance-Corpl 1949, Corpl 1950, Sgt 1951; pt/t res inspr Kenya Polic 1953-55, Lloyd's 1944-87 (memb 1977), HP Motor Policies 1944-48, Hogg Robinson & Capel Cure Ltd 1948-49, Arbon Langrish & Co Ltd 1949-55, Ernest A Notcutt & Co Ltd 1955-87 (later Eastern Produce Holdings, Clarkson Puckle, now Bain Clarkson), dir Telecommunications Network Ltd 1990-; registered insur broker; magistrate Bromley Bench 1979, ed Bromley Business, PR exec Bromley Borough C of C; govr: Valley Primary Sch Shortlands, Princess Plain Primary Bromley, The Emily Dowling Fndn; sidesman and chm Rooms Ctee Bromley Parish Church; life memb: Nat Tst for Scotland, Cornwall Naturalists Tst; memb: Guild of Freeman, The Hon Soc of Knights of the Round Table, (fndr) Uxbridge Round Table 1948-52, E Africa Round Table No 1 Nairobi 1953, Ruislip Round Table 1956-57, London Cornish Assoc, Royal Cornwall Agric Assoc, Kent Co Agric Soc, Bd Kent Business Fedn, Chartered Insur Inst; friend St George's Chapel Windsor, hon memb Ruislip '41' Ctee 1970; vice chm W Kent Cornish Assoc; Freeman City of London 1959, Liveryman Worshipful Co of Carmen 1982; *Books* Road Transport Safety and Security Handbook (contrib, 1982); *Recreations* cooking, golf, reading, walking; *Clubs* Bromley Conservative, City Livery, Chelwood, Shortland Golf; *Style—* Leonard José, Esq, JP; 14 The Glen, Shortlands, Bromley, Kent BR2 0JB (☎ 081 464 3548)

JOSEPH, Bernard Michael; s of Harry Toby (d 1989), of London, and Esther, *née* Markson; *b* 27 Sept 1948; *Educ* Bede GS for Boys; *m* 12 Oct 1980, Ruth Lesley-Ann, *née* Trent; 1 s (Darren Paul b 2 Sept 1985), 1 da (Danielle Natasha b 20 May 1983); *Career* CA; trainee Jennings Johnson 1971-75, Peat Marwick & Mitchell 1957-77, Nash Broad & Co 1977-79, sole practitioner 1979-88, ptnr Johnsons 1988-90, sr ptnr Greaves Joseph & Co 1990-; treas Voluntary Action Westminster; Freeman: City of London, Worshipful Co of CAs; FICA 1975, MInstD, memb Nat Fedn of Self Employed; *Clubs* 41; *Style—* Bernard Joseph, Esq; 3 Hillersdon Ave, Edgware, Middx, HA8 7SG (☎ 081 958 5746); No 3 Pride Court, 80 White Lion St, London N1 (☎ 071 278 6129, fax 071 278 6264)

JOSEPH, Jack Michael; s of Joseph Joseph (d 1918), of London, and Catherine Joseph (d 1932); *b* 3 April 1910; *Educ* Essex Co HS, Westham Tech Coll; *m* 2 Sept 1934, Bertha, da of Moss Harris (d 1936); *Career* Nat Serv RAF LAC fitter 1942-43, Flying Offr ops navigator 1943-45, Flying Offr educnl and vocational trg offr 1945-46; jr clerk Sedgwick Collins Ltd 1926-27, branch mangr Barclays Bank Ltd Bow 1954-70 (served in various branches 1927-54), estate mgmnt C Henry Bond & Co 1971-73; dir: Honourgold Ltd, Bryanston Square Res Assoc Ltd; chm Bryanston Square Tst, govr Coopers Co & Coborn Educnl Fndn 1968-88, former pres Rotary Club of Bow 1970, memb Rotary Club of Bethnal Green; former hon treas: Br Czechoslovak Friendship League, Br Hosp in Vietnam; former Nat Exec memb Banking Insur & Fin Union; hon treas: Local Branch Br Red Cross 1961-70, Local Branch Air Trg Corps 1969-70; chm local Nat Savings Ctee 1954-70, former Tbnl memb Miny of Lab 1960-69; Freeman City of London 1962, Liveryman Worshipful Co of Coopers 1967; *Recreations* painting, photography, walking, watching cricket and football, campaigning for social justice; *Clubs* Royal Automobile, Cricketers of London; *Style—* Jack Joseph, Esq; 8 Bryanston Sq, London W1H 7FF (☎ 071 262 0353)

JOSEPH, Jenny; da of Louis Joseph (d 1979), and Florence Ethel, *née* Cotton (d 1989); *b* 7 May 1932; *Educ* Badminton Sch, St Hilda's Coll Oxford (scholar, BA); *m* late Charles Anthony Coles; 1 s (Martin Louis b 1961), 2 da (Penelope Clare b 1963, Rebecca Ruth b 1965); *Career* journalist: Bedfordshire Times, Oxford Mail; broadcaster and lectr; *Books for children* (with Katherine Hoskyns): Boots (1966), Wheels (1966), Wind (1967), Water (1967), Tea (1968), Sunday (1968); other books incl: The Unlooked-for Season (1960, Gregory award), Rose in the Afternoon and Other Poems (1974, Cholmondeley award), The Thinking Heart (1978), Beyond Descartes (1983), Persephone: A Story (1985, James Tait Black award), The Inland Sea (1989), Beached Boats (with photographs by Robert Mitchell, 1991); *Style—* Miss Jenny Joseph; 17 Windmill Road, Minchinhampton, Gloucester GL6 9DX; agent: John Johnson Ltd, Clerkenwell House, 45-47 Clerkenwell Green, London EC1R 0HT

JOSEPH, Joe; *b* 20 May 1955; *m* Jane Louise, *née* Winterbotham; 1 s (Thomas Daniel b 20 Nov 1989); *Career* formerly with Reuters News Agency (London, NY), currently Tokyo corr The Times; *Style—* Joe Joseph, Esq; The Times, 1 Pennington St, London E1 9XN (☎ 071 782 5000)

JOSEPH, Baron (Life Peer UK 1987), of Portsoken, in the City of London; Sir Keith Sinjohn Joseph; 2 Bt (UK 1943), CH (1986), PC (1962); o s of Sir Samuel George Joseph, 1 Bt (d 1944), and Edna Cicely, *née* Phillips (d 1981); *b* 17 Jan 1918; *Educ* Harrow, Magdalen Coll Oxford; *m* 1, 6 July 1951 (m dis 1985), Hellen Louise, yr da of Sigmar Guggenheimer, of NY; 1 s (James), 3 da (Emma Catherine Sarah b 1956, Julia Rachel b 1959, Anna Jane Rebecca b 1964); m 2, 16 Aug 1990, Mrs Yolanda V Sheriff, of Connecticut, USA; *Heir* (to baronetcy) s, Hon James Samuel Joseph b 27 Jan 1955; *Career* served WWII in Italy as Capt RA (wounded, despatches); called to the Bar Middle Temple 1946, common councilman of City of London for Ward of Portsoken 1946, alderman 1946-49; Parly candidate (C) Baron's Ct 1955, MP (C) Leeds NE 1956-87, PPS to Parly Under Sec of State CRO 1957-59, Parly under-sec Miny of Housing and Local Govt 1959-61, min of state BOT 1961-62, min for Housing and Local Govt and min for Welsh Affrs 1962-64; sec of state for: Social Services DHSS 1970-74, Industry 1979-81, Educn 1981-86; dep chm Bovis Holdings Ltd 1964-70; pt/t conslt: Cable & Wireless plc 1986-, Trusthouse Forte 1986-89, Bovis Ltd 1986-89 (dir 1989-); co-fndr and first chm Fndn for Mgmnt Educn 1959, fndr and chm Mgmnt Ctee Centre for Policy Studies Ltd 1974-79, chm Cons Pty Advsy Ctee on Policy, fndr and first chm Mulberry Housing Tst 1965-69; Liveryman Worshipful Co of Vintners; fell All Souls' Coll Oxford; *Style—* The Rt Hon the Lord Joseph, CH, PC; House of Lords, London SW1A 0PW

JOSEPH, Sir (Herbert) Leslie; DL (Mid Glam 1982); s of late David Ernest Joseph, and Florence Joseph; *b* 4 Jan 1908; *Educ* King's Sch Canterbury; *m* 1, 1934, Emily Irene, da of late Dr Patrick Murphy, of Aberdare; 2 da (decd); m 2, 4 Nov 1989, Christine Jones; *Career* served WWII RE, Major, Abyssinia, Sudan and Egypt; vice chm Trusthouse Forte 1970-80; former pres Assoc Amusement Parks Proprietors; former chm: Nat Amusements Cncl, Amusement Caterers' Assoc, Housing Production Bd for Wales; govr King's Sch Canterbury 1968-; High Sheriff Mid-Glam 1975-76; kt 1952; *Style—* Sir Leslie Joseph, DL; Coedargraig, Newton, Porthcawl, Mid-Glamorgan (☎ 065 671 2610)

JOSEPH, Neville Anthony; s of Jack Joseph (d 1985), of Stanmore, Middx, and Lily Joseph, *née* Libo; *b* 27 Feb 1937; *Educ* Ilfracombe GS, Bancrofts Sch; *m* 10 Oct 1962, Elna; 1 s (Philip Michael b 1964), 2 da (Viola Elna b 1966, Alexandra Louise b 1968); *Career* chartered accountant 1959-; md private bankers; FCA, FCIS, FTII; *Recreations* computers; *Style—* Neville A Joseph, Esq; Marlowe House, Hale Road, Wendover, Bucks HP22 6NE (☎ 0296 62 3167)

JOSEPH, Richard Lewis; s of Alfred Joseph (d 1967), of London, and Rose Sarah, *née* Melzack; *b* 24 July 1949; *Educ* Algernon Road Sch, Haberdashers' Aske's Sch; *m* March 1974, Linda Carol, da of Frank Hyams; 1 s (Mark Alan b Nov 1981), 1 da (Danielle Frances b July 1978); *Career* articled clerk: Lewis Bloom, Blick Rothenberg & Noble; qualified chartered accountant 1972, Stoy Hayward & Co 1972, Elliott Woolfe & Rose 1977-78, fin controller Unit Tst Gp 1978-, private practice 1978-; fndr Micro Computer Gp of N London, chm Ctee N London Soc of CAs, 1990- (joined 1986), chm Edgware & Burnt Oak Business Club, memb Ctee Edgware & Burnt Oak C of C; FCA (ACA 1972); *Recreations* golf, music, cricket, football, guitarist with Apex Corner (60's rolk revival band); *Clubs* Elstree Golf; *Style—* Richard Joseph, Esq; 2nd Floor, 65 Station Rd, Edgware, Middlesex HA8 7HX (☎ 081 952 5407, fax 081 951 0779)

JOSEPH, Roger Vanhava Anthony; s of Vanhava Anthony Joseph, and Margaret, *née* Paul; *b* 24 Dec 1965; *Educ* St Mary's RC Sch, Cardinal Hinsley HS; *m* ; 2 da (Kelisha b 8 June 1986, Keisha (twin) b 8 June 1986); *Career* professional footballer; 107 first team appearances Brentford 1983-87, transferred to Wimbledon 1987- (memb Football League team v Army FA 1989), over 50 appearances; Most Improved Player awards Brentford and Wimbledon; involved with property and fashion; *Recreations* badminton, pool, socialising; *Style—* Roger Joseph, Esq; c/o Ambrose Mendy, 49 Durnsford Rd, Wimbledon, London SW19 (☎ 081 946 6311)

JOSEPHS, Dr Wilfred; s of Philip Isaac Josephs (d 1955), and Rachel, *née* Block; *b* 24 July 1927; *Educ* Rutherford GS Newcastle upon Tyne, Univ of Durham (BDS); *m* 2 Sept 1956, Valerie Gloria (sep); 2 da (Philippa b 1961, Claudia b 1963); *Career* Capt RADC 1952-53 (Lt 1951); composer in residence: Univ of Wisconsin Milwaukee 1970-, Roosevelt Univ Chicago 1972-; music conslt London Int Film Sch 1988-, lectr film and TV music Dartington Int Summer Sch of Music; important works: requiem, 10 symphonies, 18 concertos, 10 overtures, 4 string quartets, chamber works, ballets including Equus and Cyrano de Bergerac, Rebecca (opera); written music for 115 TV prodns incl: The Great War, I Claudius, Horizon, Art of the Western World; 26 feature and 33 documentary films; memb: Cncl Performing Rights Soc, Exec Cncl Composer Guild, Jt Consultative Ctee BAFTA, Ctee Friends of LIFS; Assoc Professional Composers, Assoc Ind Prodrs; Jon DMus Univ of Newcastle upon Tyne 1978; *Recreations* cinema, video, music, swimming; *Clubs* 7 Dials; *Style—* Dr Wilfred Josephs; 15 Douglas Court, Quex Rd, London NW6 4PT (☎ 071 625 8917); The Old Manor Cottage, Poffley End, Hailey, Oxon (☎ 0993 702422)

JOSIPOVICI, Prof Gabriel David; s of Jean Josipovici, of Italy, and Sacha Elena, *née* Rabinovitch; *b* 8 Oct 1940; *Educ* Victoria Coll Cairo Egypt, Cheltenham Coll, St Edmund Hall Oxford; *Career* prof Univ of Sussex 1963- (former lectr and reader); author; plays for the stage incl: Dreams of Mrs Fraser (Theatre Upstairs) 1972, Flow (Edinburgh Lyceum) 1973, Marathon (ICA) 1978; radio plays incl: Playback 1972, AG 1977, Vergil Dying 1980, Mr Vee 1989; *Books* The Inventory (1968), The World and The Book (1971), Mobius the Stripper (1975), Migrations (1977), Conversations in Another Room (1984), Contre-Jour (1986), The Book of God: A Response to the Bible (1988), Steps: Selected Fiction and Drama (1990), The Big Glass (1991); *Style—* Prof Gabriel Josipovici; Univ of Sussex, Arts Building, Falmer, Brighton, Sussex (☎ 0273 606755)

JOSLIN, Paul; s of Edgar Alfred (d 1958), and Mary Elizabeth Elsie, *née* Buckeridge; *b* 20 Nov 1950; *Educ* City of Portsmouth Tech HS, Royal Coll Music (GRSM, LRAM, ARCM); *m* 2 August 1975, Gwenllian Elfyn, da of Rev Ifor Elfyn Ellis, of Rhuddlan, North Wales; *Career* organist and dir of music St Paul's Onslow Sq London 1972-; Holy Trinity Brompton London: associate dir of music 1977-79, organist and dir 1979-; asst conductor Brompton Choral Soc 1977-81; solo and organ accompanist; continuo work with London Bach Orchestra and Thames Chamber Orchestra, concerto soloist with and memb of Eng Chamber Orchestra, choral and orchestral conductor BBC Radio and TV; memb Br Inst of Organ Studies; *Recreations* architecture, swimming, 35mm photography, collection 78rpm classical records; *Style—* Paul Joslin, Esq; 109 Hanover Rd, London NW10 3DN (☎ 081 459 5547); Holy Trinity Brompton, Brompton Rd, London SW7 (☎ 071 581 8255)

JOSLIN, Chief Constable Peter David; QPM (1983); s of Frederick William Joslin, of Essex, and Emma, *née* Smith (d 1979); *b* 26 Oct 1933; *Educ* King Edward VI GS Chelmsford, Univ of Essex (BA); *m* 26 Oct 1933, Kathleen Josephine, da of Patrick Monaghan, of Eire; 2 s (Russell b 1961, Stephen b 1964), 1 da (Angela b 1972); *Career* police offr; police constable to supt Essex Police 1954-74, asst chief constable (ops) Leics Constabulary 1976 (chief supt 1974), currently chief constable Warks Constabulary (dep chief 1977); *Recreations* cricket, football, golf, swimming, gardening, house renovation, after dinner speaking, good wines; *Clubs* Royal Over-Seas League; *Style—* Chief Constable Peter Joslin, QPM; Warwickshire Constabulary, PO Box 4, Leek Wootton, Warwick CV35 7QB (☎ 0926 415 000, telex 31548, fax 0926 50362)

JOSLING, Frederick John; s of John Frederick Josling (d 1975), and Emily Esther, *née* Baker (d 1987); *b* 22 Sept 1930; *Educ* St Albans Sch; *m* 1 April 1961, Elisabeth Mary, da of Thomas Reginald Harrison (d 1970); 2 s (Nicholas b 1966, William b 1970), 1 da (Emma b 1963); *Career* dir Lopex plc 1980-83, dep chm Kirkwoods 1981-86, md Interlink 1973-80 (chm 1981); chm: ASL Central 1986-88, Alliance International Ltd 1987-; FIPA, FCAM; *Recreations* cricket, gardening; *Clubs* MCC, Lord's Taverners (chm 1976-78), Reform; *Style—* F J Josling, Esq; Badger's Holt, Caddington, nr Luton, Beds LU1 4AD (☎ 0582 23797); Alliance International Ltd, 30 Gray's Inn Rd, London WC1X 8HR (☎ 071 242 4444, fax 071 404 4165)

JOSSE, Dr (Silvain) Edouard; OBE (1983); s of Albert Josse, of London, and Charlotte, *née* Karolicki; *b* 8 May 1933; *Educ* Highgate Sch, Middx Hosp Med Sch and Univ of London (MB BS, MA, LRCP); *m* 15 May 1960 (m dis 1983), Lea, da of Alter Majer Ber (d 1977); 2 s (David b 22 July 1961, Jeremy b 14 July 1968), 1 da (Ann b 19 Sept 1964); *Career* gen med practitioner 1962, sr forensic med examiner Metropolitian Police 1964, regnl advsr in gen practice NE Thames Region Br Postgrad Med Fedn Univ of London 1976, former GP memb NE Thames RHA; memb Standing Ctee on Postgrad Med Educn, former memb Enfield and Haringey Family Practitioners' Ctee, sec gen UEMO 1982-86; chm Enfield and Haringey Local Med Ctee; MRCS, FRCGP 1977, DMJ, FZS, APSGB, MLS, BAFS; memb: BMA 1956, RSM 1978; *Recreations* skiing, gardening, history, good wine tasting; *Clubs* MCC, Middx Cricket; *Style—* Dr Edouard Josse, OBE; 2 Willowside Court, 31 Waverley Road, Enfield EN2 7DP (☎ 081 323 6271); British Postgraduate Med Fedn, West Wing, Nurses Home, N Middx Hosp, Sterling Way, Edmonton, London N18 1QX (☎ 081 803 5313, fax 081 884 2773, car 0836 243330)

JOST, Dr H Peter; CBE (1969); s of Leo Jost (d 1941); *b* 25 Jan 1921; *Educ* Liverpool Tech Coll, Manchester Coll of Technol; *m* 1948, Margaret Josephine, da of Michael Kadesh (d 1952); 2 da; *Career* co dir; chm: K S Paul Group, Associated Technology Group; Lord President's nominee for Ct of Univ of Salford 1970-87, first pres Int

Tribology Cncl 1973-, chm Manchester Technol Assoc in London 1976-; memb: Parly and Scientific Ctee 1976-, Steering Ctee 1983- (hon sec 1990), Cncl Engrg Instns 1977-84 (chm Home Affrs Ctee 1980-84); pres: Inst Prodn Engrs 1977-78, Manchester Technol Assoc 1984-85; vice pres Inst Mech Engrs 1987; hon industl prof Liverpool Poly, hon prof Univ of Wales; Hon DSc Univ of Salford 1970, Hon DTech Cncl for Nat Academic Awards 1987, Hon DSc Slovak Univ 1987, Hon DEng Univ of Leeds 1989, Hon DSc Univ of Bath 1990; Liveryman Worshipful Co of Engrs, Freeman City of London; State Legislative Commendation of State of California (USA) 1978, Gold Insignia of Order of Merit of Polish People's Republic 1986; *Recreations* music, gardening; *Clubs* Athenaeum; *Style—* Dr H Peter Jost, CBE; Hill House, Wills Grove, Mill Hill, London NW7 1QL (☎ 081 959 3355); K S Paul Products Ltd, Eley Rd, Eley Estate, London N18 3DB (☎ 081 345 5566)

JOST, Hon Mrs (Marylyn Jane); *née* Macdonald; da of Rt Hon Lord MacDonald of Gwaenysgor, 2 Baron McDonald of Gwaenysgor and Leslie Margaret; *b* 10 Oct 1951; *m* 1977, Peter Ronald, s of Ronald Jost of 5 Manor Grove, Fifield, Maidenhead, Berks; 2 s (Edward b 1980, Thomas b 1983), and 1 s (decd); *Style—* The Hon Mrs Peter Jost

JOUGHIN, Michael; CBE (1971), JP (County of Moray); s of John Clague Joughin (d 1960), and May, *née* Hocken (d 1957); *b* 26 April 1926; *Educ* Kelly Coll Tavistock Devon; *m* 1, 1948, Lesley; 1 s (James), 1 da (Gail); m 2, 1981, Anne; *Career* Lt RM 1944-52, seconded Fleet Air Arm 1946-49, ditched off Malta 1949, invalided 1952, Capt 11 Bn (TA) Seaforth Highlanders 1952-53; chm: N of Scotland Hydro-Electric Bd 1983-90, Scottish Hydro-Electric plc 1990-, N of Scotland Milk Mktg Bd Inverness 1974-83, Grassland and Forage Ctee JCC, Scottish Agric Devpt Cncl 1971-80, Govrs of N of Scotland Coll of Agric Aberdeen 1969-72, Govrs of Blairmore Prep Sch nr Huntly 1966-72, NEDC's Working Party on Livestock, N of Scotland Grassland Soc 1970-71, Elgin Mkt Green Auction Co 1969-70; pres Nat Farmers' Union of Scot 1964-66; govr: Animal Diseases Res Assoc Edinburgh 1969-74, Scottish Plant Breeding Station Pentlandfield 1969-74, Rowett Res Inst Aberdeen 1968-74; memb: NE Bd Bank of Scotland 1989-, Awards Ctee the Massey-Ferguson Nat Award for Servs to UK Agric, Scottish Constitutional Ctee (Douglas-Home Ctee) 1969-70, Intervention Bd for Agric Produce London 1972-76, NEDC for Agric 1967-70, Agric Mktg Devpt Exec Ctee London 1965-68, Br Farm Produce Cncl London 1965-66, Selection Ctee Nuffield Farming Scholarships; fndr presenter Farming Programme Country Focus Grampian TV 1961-64 and 1967-69; farmer 700 acres 1952-90; FRAS, CBIM; DL County of Moray 1974-80; *Recreations* sailing; *Clubs* New (Edinburgh), RNSA, RMSC, Goldfish; *Style—* Michael Joughin, Esq, CBE, JP; Elderslie, Findhorn, Moray (☎ 0309 30277); Scottish Hydro Electric plc, Rothesay Terrace, Edinburgh (☎ 031 225 1361)

JOURDAIN, James William; s of Henry James Jourdain (d 1966); *b* 28 Feb 1928; *Educ* Radley; *m* 1953, Molly Elizabeth, da of Paul Gustavus Arthur Anthony, OBE; 2 s (Richard, Michael), 2 da (Diana, Nicola); *Career* served RNVR 1946-48; md Blyth Greene Jourdain & Co Ltd 1969-; dir: Ireland Blyth & Co Ltd (Mauritius) 1972-, Bank of Mauritius 1967-69; chm Blyth Bros & Co Ltd Mauritius 1964-69, md Swire Blyth & Co Ltd London 1980-; *Recreations* sport, music, travel; *Clubs* City of London, MCC; *Style—* James Jourdain Esq; Tazar, Whiteman's Green, Cuckfield, Sussex (☎ 0444 454723)

JOURDAN, Martin Hubert Thomas; s of Charles Henry Hans Jourdan; *b* 22 Nov 1940; *Educ* Mill Hill Sch, Harvard Business Sch; *m* 1963, Enid Valerie; 3 children; *Career* chairmaker; chm: Parker Knoll plc (renamed Cornwell Parker plc 1988) 1976- (furniture and fabrics), Southern Region CBI 1977-88 (chm 1981-83), Lambert Howarth Gp plc 1985-90; *Recreations* walking, golf; *Clubs* Old Millhillians; *Style—* Martin Jourdan Esq; The Courtyard, Frogmoor, High Wycombe, Bucks (☎ 0494 21144)

JOWELL, Prof Jeffrey Lionel; s of Jack Jowell, of Cape Town, SA, and Emily, *née* Katzaenellenbogen; *b* 4 Nov 1938; *Educ* Univ of Cape Town (BA, LLB), Hertford Coll Oxford (BA, MA), Harvard Law Sch (LLM, SJD); *m* 8 Dec 1963, Frances Barbara, da of Dr Moses Suzman, of Johannesburg; 1 s (Daniel b 11 June 1969), 1 da (Joanna b 2 Sept 1967); *Career* called to the Bar Middle Temple 1965; res asst Harvard Law Sch 1966-68, fell Jt Centre Urban Studies Harvard and MIT 1967-68, assoc prof of law and admin studies York Univ Toronto 1968-71; LSE: Leverhulme fell urban legal studies 1972-74, lectr in law 1974-75; SSRC: chm Social Sci and Law Ctee 1981-84, vice chm Govt and Law Ctee 1982-84; memb Nuffield Ctee Town and Country Planning 1983-86, chm Ctee of Heads Univ Law Schs 1984-86; Faculty of Law UCL: prof of public law 1975, dean 1979-89, head of Dept 1982-89; Lionel Cohen lectr in hebrew Univ of Jerusalem 1986, visiting prof Univ of Paris 1991; Hon DJur Athens 1987, Hon LLD Ritsumeikan 1988; *Books* Law and Bureaucracy (1975), Lord Denning: The Judge And The Law (jt ed, 1984), The Changing Constitution (jt ed, 1985 and 1989); *Recreations* tennis, exploring Exmoor and London; *Clubs* Garrick; *Style—* Prof Jeffrey Jowell; 7 Hampstead Hill Gardens, London NW3 2PH (☎ 071 794 6645); Hantons, Exford, Somerset TA24 7LY; UCL, Gower St, London WC1 (☎ 071 380 7014)

JOWETT, (Edward) Ian; s of Eddie Jowett (d 1966), of 145 Moore Ave, Bradford, W Yorks, and Maud Alberta, *née* Holmes (d 1974); *b* 23 July 1928; *Educ* Bradford GS, Queen's Coll Oxford (MA, BCL); *m* 20 Oct 1962, Eileen Elizabeth, da of Stanley James Adamson (d 1969), of 94 Ashingdon Rd, Rochford, Essex; 2 da (Susan b 1964, Carolyn b 1967); *Career* Nat Serv in Army served: Palestine, Egypt, Libya 1947-49; called to the Bar Middle Temple 1952; asst to Co Sec Richard Thomas and Baldwins Ltd 1955-62, legal mangr Total Oil (GB) Ltd 1962-74, dir legal affairs Ford Motor Credit Co Ltd 1974-78, dir legal affairs Euro Credit Operations Ford of Europe Inc 1978-; fndr memb Bar Assoc of Commerce Fin and Indust; elder Utd Reform Church; memb Bar Cncl 1955; *Books* author articles in learned jls and law review article in Title Retention Clauses (1980); *Recreations* cricket, ornithology, travelling; *Clubs* RCS; *Style—* Ian Jowett, Esq; 10 Arundel Gardens, Westcliff-on-Sea, Essex SSO OBJ (☎ 0702 344 182); 1 Hubert Road, Brentwood, Essex CM14 4QL (☎ 0277 224 400, fax 0277 231 649, telex 995184 FMCCBWG

JOWETT, Richard Lund; s of Harry Jowett (d 1975), of Ryedale, 43 The Moorway, Tranmere Park, Guiseley, nr Leeds, Yorks, and Vera Millicent, *née* Gent; *b* 29 April 1937; *Educ* Bradford GS, Magdalen Coll Oxford, Middlesex Hosp Med Sch (MA); *m* 27 Aug 1966, (Catherine) Louise, da of Maj Robert Pitts Heaton (d 1985); 3 s (Andrew b 1971, James b 1972, Charles b 1978); *Career* conslt orthopaedic surgn Wessex RHA 1974-; FRCS 1968; *Recreations* golf, cricket; *Clubs* Parkstone Golf, Medical Golfing Soc, MCC, Oxford and Cambridge Golfing Soc, County Cricketers' Golfing Soc; *Style—* Richard Jowett, Esq; Sandecotes Lodge, 34 Sandecotes Rd, Parkstone, Poole, Dorset BH14 8NZ (☎ 0202 740696)

JOWITT, Juliet Diana Margaret; *née* Brackenbury; da of Lt-Col Robert Henry Langton Brackenbury, OBE (d 1978), and Eleanor Trewlove, *née* Springman (d 1971); *b* 24 Aug 1940; *Educ* Hatherop Castle, Switzerland and Spain; *m* 1963, (Frederick) Thomas Benson Jowitt; 1 s, 1 da; *Career* assoc shopping ed House & Garden and Vogue 1966-69, proprietor Wood House Design (interior design) 1971-; memb: Interior Decorators' and Designers' Assoc (memb Cncl 1989), IBA 1981-86, Domestic Coal Consumers' Cncl 1985-, Potato Mktg Bd 1986-90; dir: Yorkshire TV Ltd 1987, Yorkshire TV Holdings plc 1989; JP N Yorks 1973; *Style—* Mrs Thomas Jowitt; Thorpe Lodge, Littlethorpe, Ripon, N Yorks HG4 3LU; 11 St George Sq, London SW1V 2HX

JOWITT, Prof Paul William; s of Stanley Jowitt, of Thurcroft, Yorks, and Joan Mary, *née* Goundry; *b* 3 Aug 1950; *Educ* Maltby GS, Imperial Coll London (BSc, PhD); *m* 11 Aug 1973, Jane Catriona, da of Lt Ronald George Urquhart, of Romford, Essex; 1 s (Christopher b 17 Feb 1978), 1 da (Hannah b 29 June 1980); *Career* lectr in civil engrg Imperial Coll 1974-86 (warden Falmouth Hall 1980-86), chm Tynemarch Systems Engrg Ltd 1984-86 (dir 1984-), ed Journal of Civil Engineering Systems 1985-, head of Dept of Civil Engrg Heriot Watt Univ 1989- (prof 1987-); author of various specialist tech pubns and jl articles; memb various nat and local assoc ctees ICE; MICE 1988, CEng 1988; *Recreations* painting, Morgan 3-wheelers, restoring old houses; *Clubs* Chaps, Links; *Style—* Prof Paul Jowitt; 22 Fountainhall Rd, The Grange, Edinburgh EH9 2LW (☎ 031 667 5696); Department of Civil Engineering, Heriot Watt University, Edinburgh EH14 4AS (☎ 031 449 5111, fax 031 451 3170)

JOWITT, Peter John Russell; s of Harold John Duncan Mackintosh Jowitt, of Burgage Paddock, Southwell, Notts, and Kathleen Joyce, *née* Clark; *b* 30 July 1942; *Educ* Bryanston, Univ of Nottingham (BEd); *Career* asst master Cheltenham Coll 1979-82, dep headmaster Cokethorpe Sch 1982-84, head of modern languages Claire's Court Sch 1985-89; dir Monksoft Ltd 1988-, researcher Language Centre Univ of Buckingham 1989-; memb Ctee Nat Sch's Regatta 1973-, selector GB Jr Rowing Team 1974-76, chm Jr Rowing Ctee and memb Exec Ctee Amateur Rowing Assoc 1978-79, memb Jr Cmmn FISA 1979-84 (holder umpire's licence 1971-); chef de mission Moscow 1979, chm Kitchin Soc 1989- (sec 1986-89), memb Physical Educn Assoc; *Recreations* ocean racing, rowing administration, computer assisted language learning; *Clubs* Lloyd's YC, Leander; *Style—* Peter Jowitt, Esq; Burgage Mews, Southwell, Notts NG25 0ER (☎ 0636 813545, car 0836 507861)

JOY, David Anthony Welton; s of Richard Clapham Joy (d 1964), of York, and Annie Doreen, *née* Welton; *b* 14 June 1942; *Educ* St Peter's Sch York; *m* 28 March 1967, Judith Margaret, da of Wilfrid Agar (d 1963), of York; 2 s (Richard b 10 March 1970, Thomas b 1 Aug 1975), 1 da (Fiona b 6 March 1968); *Career* gen reporter Yorkshire Post 1962-65, books ed Dalesman Publishing Co 1970-88 (ed asst 1965-70), ed The Dalesman 1988-; sec Craven Branch CPRE, ed Cumbrian railways assoc; *Books* Settle-Carlisle Railway (with W R Mitchell, 1966), Main Line Over Shap (1967), Cumbrian Coast Railways (1968), Whitby-Pickering Railway (1969), Railways in the North (1970), Traction Engines in the North (1970), George Hudson of York (with A J Peacock, 1971), Steamtown (1972), Railways of the Lake Counties (1973), Regional History of the Railways of Great Britain: South and West Yorkshire (1975, 2 edn 1984), Railways in Lancashire (1975), Settle-Carlisle Centenary (with W R Mitchel, 1975), Railways of Yorkshire: The West Riding (1976), North Yorkshire Moors Railway (with Peter Williams, 1977), Steam on the North York Moors (1978), Yorkshire Railways (with A Haigh, 1979), Steam on the Settle and Carlisle (1981), Yorkshire Dales Railway (1983), Settle-Carlisle in Colour (1983), Regional History of the Railways of Great Britain: The Lake Counties (1983), Portrait of the Settle-Carlisle (1984), The Dalesman: A Celebration of 50 Years (1989), Life in the Yorkshire Coalfield (1989); *Recreations* photography, walking, modelling; *Style—* David Joy, Esq; Hole Bottom, Hebden, Skipton, North Yorkshire BD23 5DL (☎ 0756 752369); Dalesman Publishing Co, Clapham, Lancaster LA2 8EB (☎ 046 85 225)

JOYCE, Christoper; s of Ernest Joyce, and Kathleen, *née* Boyle; *b* 19 Sept 1943; *Educ* Cranbrook Sch Kent, Brighton Coll of Art; *m* Jakki, da of John Caunce; 1 s (James b 15 Feb 1983), 1 da (Sophie b 15 Jan 1970); *Career* photographer; self taught and self employed 1961-, runs own studio 1967-, numerous solo exhibitions; judge for photographic awards and scholarships; memb The Photographers Assoc (former chm and vice chm); *Recreations* photography and film making; *Style—* Christoper Joyce, Esq; Christopher Joyce Studio, 14A Dufours Place, London W1 (☎ 071 287 6118, fax 071 287 0126)

JOYCE, Michael Herbert; JP (1981); s of Tom Joyce, and Mary Jackson; *b* 5 April 1933; *Educ* King Edward VII Sch Lytham St Anne's Lancs, St Bees Sch Cumbria; *m* 8 Sept 1956, Sheila, da of Hubert Taylor; 2 s (Nicholas Tom b 14 Oct 1959, Andrew Michael b 15 Oct 1960); *Career* Nat Serv 5 RTR 1958-60; ptnr McKeith Dickinson & Ptnrs 1970-83, md Omn's Devpts 1983-; *Recreations* golf; *Clubs* St Anne's Old Link S, Aloha (Marbella); *Style—* Michael Joyce, Esq; 6 Lindsay Court, New Road, St Annes-On-Sea (☎ 0253 465 96); 4 South King St, Blackpool (☎ 0253 20 016)

JOYCE, William Jesson (Bill); CBE (1968); s of Geoffrey Joyce (d 1937), of Blackfordby, Burton-on-Trent, and Dorothy Lilian, *née* Jesson (d 1983); *b* 5 Dec 1917; *Educ* Ashby-de-la-Zouch GS; *m* 28 April 1946, Isabel Mary (d 1985), da of late James Keir Simpson, of Christchurch, NZ; 2 da (Marianne b 26 April 1952, Margaret b 11 June 1956); *Career* WWII guardsman Coldstream Gds, Maj Royal Leics Regt, served N Africa and Italy (despatches); with FW Woolworth & Co Ltd at Taunton Exeter Bristol and Plymouth 1936-39; Elder Dempster Lines Ltd: joined 1946, Ghana mangr 1962-65, Nigeria mangr 1965-66; dir and West Coast mangr: Elder Dempster Agencies Ltd, Sierra Leone Shipping Agencies, Liner Agencies (Ghana) Ltd, Elder Dempster Agencies (Nigeria) Ltd, West Africa Properties (Nigeria) Ltd, Elder Dempster Agencies (The Gambia) Ltd 1966-72, ret 1973; *Style—* Bill Joyce, Esq, CBE; 3 Upton Close, Upton, Wirral, Merseyside L49 6NA (☎ 051 677 3827)

JOYNER, Prof Richard William; s of Stanley William Joyner, of Carrickfergus, Co Antrim, and Jenny Kane, *née* Hagan; *b* 20 Dec 1944; *Educ* Belfast HS, Queen's Univ Belfast (BSc, DSc), Univ of Bradford (PhD); *m* 1 Sept 1967, (Ann) Jenepher, da of George Wilson Grange, of Belfast; 2 da (Clare b 24 July 1970, Carol b 9 Dec 1974); *Career* res fell Univ of California Berkeley 1970-71, memb Staff Chemistry Dept Univ of Bradford 1971-80, head Fundamentals of Catalysis Res Gp and Res Assoc BP Res Sunbury-on-Thames 1980-87, dir Leverhulme Centre for Innovative Catalysis and prof of chemistry Univ of Liverpool 1987-; chm Br Vacuum Cncl; memb: Cncl Int Union Vacuum Sci Technol and its Applications, Int Advsy Bd Faraday Transactions, Editorial Bd Catalysis Letters; chm and memb Ctee Surface Reactivity and Catalysis Gp Royal Soc Chemistry (sec 1982-86); FRSC 1989; *publications* about 110 scientific publications in international journals, including several book chapters; *Recreations* music, biographies; *Style—* Prof Richard Joyner; 10 West Close, Noctorum, Birkenhead L43 9RR (☎ 051 677 5924); Leverhulme Centre for Innovative Catalysis, Chemistry Department, University of Liverpool, PO Box 147, Liverpool L69 3BX (☎ 051 794 3582, fax 051 794 3588, telex 627095)

JOYNSON, (George) Colin Whittell; s of George Whittell Joynson (d 1965), and Joan Lily, *née* Heyworth (d 1951); *b* 9 April 1929; *Educ* Stowe; *m* 3 April 1954, Jean Emilia Hilda, da of Ralph Wicksteed (d 1962); 1 s (Richard b 1959), 1 da (Nicola b 1955); *Career* aircraftsman RAF; former commodity broker and memb of leading UK exchanges; dir Richard Joynson Ltd 1965-; chm: London Wool 1965, Coffee Terminal Mkt of London 1970; business broker 1971-; memb Business Search Unit 1979-; memb Olympic Bobsleigh Team 1948; *Clubs* Gresham, RAC, St Moritz Tobogganing; *Style—* Colin Joynson, Esq; Portland House, Kettering, Northamptonshire NN15 7HL (☎ 0536 83015)

JOYNSON, Dr David Huw Malcolm; s of David Cyril Joynson (d 1989), of High

Cross, Newport, Gwent, and Rosetta, *née* Gough; *b* 4 Oct 1943; *Educ* Bassaleg GS, Univ of Wales Coll of Med (MB BCh), Univ of London (DipBact); *m* 15 July 1967, Menna Bennett, da of Emrys Bennett Owen (d 1988); 1 s (Owain Bennett), 2 da (Nia Bennet, Heledd Bennett); *Career* conslt med microbiolotist W Glamorgan Health Authy 1975-, dir Pub Health Laboratory Swansea and head of Toxoplasma Reference Laboratory; MRCP 1971, MIBiol 1980; *Recreations* golf , skiing, watching rugby; *Style*— Dr David Joynson; Public Health Laboratory, Singleton Hospital, Sgeti, Swansea, Wales SA2 8QA (☎ 0792 205666, fax 0792 202320)

JOYNSON, Kenneth Mercer; s of Edgar Hilton Joynson (d 1974), and Nellie, *née* Clausey (d 1943); *b* 8 Oct 1926; *Educ* Lymn GS Cheshire, Wolverhampton Tech Teachers Coll (Cert Ed); *m* 22 Sept 1951, Ruth Madeleine, da of Cyril Bentley Jackson (d 1931); 1 s (Richard b 25 Jan 1956); *Career* CA; asst accountant Bell & Nicholson Ltd Birmingham 1951-57, accountant Newey Eyre Ltd Birmingham 1957-59, sr audit mangr Impey Cudworth Co Birmingham 1959-62, princ Joynson & Co Sutton Coldfield 1963-66, sr lectr and head accounting studies Peterborough Regnl Coll 1967-80, lectr and examiner Chartered Building Socs' Inst 1972-86, princ Joynson & Co Peterborough 1981-; disabled through Polio 1931, vice chm (later chm) Polio Fellowship Birmingham 1953-65, chm Age Concern Deeping and Dist Lincolnshire 1972-; various offices 1958-67: W Midland Lib Pty, Rutland and Stamford Lib Assoc, Stamford and Spalding Lib Assoc; now memb SLD; parish cncllr Deeping St James Parish Cncl 1979-83, cncllr South Kesteven Dist Cncl 1983-89; ACA 1951, FCA 1961; *Recreations* marathon running, association football; *Clubs* Peterborough Athletics, Stamford Town FC; *Style*— Kenneth Joynson, Esq; 39 Manor Way, Deeping St James, Peterborough PE6 8PS (☎ 0778 343 506); Cushing Fairbairn Wardle & Co, 73 Park Rd, Peterborough PE1 2JN (☎ 0733 313 600)

JOYNSON, Peter Assheton; JP (1976); s of Maj Will Joynson (d 1970), of Perths, and Mary Hamilton Clegg (d 1971); *b* 9 May 1928; *Educ* Eton, RAC Cirencester; *m* 14 May 1955, Catherine Hilda Douglas, BEM, 2 da of Lt-Col A V C Douglas (d 1977), of Mains; 1 s (Michael William b 1959), 1 da (Theresa Cicely b 1961); *Career* land agent; fndr ptnr Managed Estates Stirling; memb: Justice Ctee, Justices' Prison Ctee 1980, Forth Valley Health Bd 1989-, Queen's Bodyguard for Scotland (The Royal Co of Archers) 1965-; MRAC, QALAS; *Recreations* shooting, fishing, hill walking; *Clubs* New (Edinburgh), Flyfishers'; *Style*— Peter A Joynson, Esq, JP; Laraich, Aberfoyle, By Stirling (☎ 08772 232); Managed Estates, 18 Maxwell Place, Stirling FK8 1JU (☎ 0786 62519)

JUDA, Annely; da of Dr Kurt Brauer (d 1951), of London, and Margaret, *née* Goldmann (d 1971); *b* 23 Sept 1914; *Educ* High Sch, Reimann Sch of Art and Design London; *m* 1939, Paul Juda; 1 s (David b Feb 1946), 2 da (Carol b April 1942, Susan b May 1951); *Career* admin Eric Estorick's art collection 1956-58, with Kaplan Gallery London 1958-60, dir and fndr Molton Gallery London 1960, Hamilton Galleries London 1963; opened own gallery Annely Juda Fine Art with son David Juda 1968 (merged with Rowan Gallery 1982 to form Juda Rowan Gallery before reverting to former name and status 1987); exhibitions administered incl: Russian Works (Tokyo Gallery Japan) 1983, Dada-Constructivism: The Janus Face of the Twenties Sept-Dec 1984, Dada and Constructivism (The Seibu Museum of Art Tokyo) Oct-Nov 1988, The Seibu Tsukashin Hall Amagaski Nov-Dec 1988, The Museum of Mordern Art Kamakura Jan-Feb 1989, Centro de Arte Sofia Madrid March-May 1989; memb Art Dealers' Assoc; *Style*— Mrs Annely Juda; Annely Juda Fine Art, 23 Dering St, London W1R 9AA (☎ 071 629 7578, fax 071 491 2139)

JUDA, David; s of Paul Juda, and Annely Juda; *Educ* Ibstock Place Froebel Sch, John Kelly Secdy Modern, Kilburn Poly; *m* March 1983, Yuko Shiraishi, da of Masahiro Shinoda; *Career* ptnr Annely Juda Fine Art 1978 (joined 1967); memb Exec Ctee Fine Art and Antiques Export Ctee 1971-, vice chm Soc of London Art Dealers 1986- (memb 1970-); *Recreations* skiing; *Clubs* Groucho's; *Style*— David Juda, Esq; Annely Juda Fine Art, 23 Dering Street, London W1R 9AA (☎ 071 629 7578, fax 071 491 2139)

JUDAH, Nigel Leopold; s of Edward Joseph Judah (d 1966), and Sylvia Sarah, *née* Frank (d 1970); *b* 6 Dec 1930; *Educ* Charterhouse, Univ of Lausanne; *m* 24 Aug 1970 (m dis 1989), Phoebe Ann; 1 s (Samual b 8 July 1978), 2 da (Henrietta b 10 July 1972, Hannah b 24 Aug 1975); *Career* CA; fin dir and sec Reuters Holdings plc 1981 (joined 1955, sec and chief accountant 1960, sec and asst gen mangr 1967); dir: Reuters Ltd, Visnews Ltd; govr Charterhouse Sch, memb Devpt Cncl National Theatre, memb of the Senate Inst of Chartered Accountants, chm Reuter Fund; Order of Merit (Italy); FCA; *Recreations* opera, wine, collecting pictures; *Clubs* Brooks's, Garrick; *Style*— Nigel Judah, Esq; 1 Hans Place, London SW1X 0EU (☎ 071 581 3799); Reuters Ltd, 85 Fleet St, London EC4P 4AJ (☎ 071 324 7007, fax 071 324 5400, telex 929785)

JUDD, Allan Frederick; s of Frederick James Judd (d 1950), of Surbiton, Surrey, and Ruth Emma, *née* Mansell (d 1967); *b* 17 Aug 1911; *Educ* Kingston GS, Wimbledon Tech Coll, Law Soc Sch of Law; *m* 1, Dorothy Frances Judd (d 1968); 1 s (Richard Allan Follett b 1942); m 2, Violet Muriel Bell, da of Joseph George Follett, of Hove, Sussex; 1 step s (David John Bell b 1942); *Career* joined RA 1940, cmmnd 1941; served: 2 Army France and Germany, Belsen liberation and rehabilitation of camp inmates, mil govt Minden, legal section judge intermediate; admitted slr 1934, ptnr and conslt Simmonds Church Smiles 1946-89; clerk General Cmmr of Taxes: West Brixton Div 1949-86, First East Brixton Div 1971-86; sec Lord Chllr Advsy Ctee 1960-89, former hon legal advsr Offrs' Assoc (Br Legion); memb Met Water Bd 1956-59; pres: Holborn Law Soc (fndr memb) 1963-64, Rotary Club Wandsworth 1975-76; Mayor Holborn Borough Cncl 1959-60 and 1963-64 (memb 1950-64), JP, Alderman 1961; memb Utd Ward Club City of London; Freeman City of London, memb Worshipful Co of Fruiterers; MInstD; *Clubs* Carlton, Kingston Rowing, Luxembourg Soc; *Style*— Allan Judd, Esq; 13 Bedford Row, London WC2

JUDD, Clifford Harold Alfred; CB (1987); s of Alfred Ernest Judd (d 1966), and Florence Louisa, *née* Peacock; *b* 27 June 1927; *Educ* Christ's Hosp, Keble Coll Oxford; *m* 9 Aug 1951, (Elizabeth) Margaret, da of late Albert William Holmes; 2 da (Caroline b 1969, Rosemary b 1970); *Career* Nat Serv 2 Lt RA 1947-48 (invalided out); HM Treasy: exec offr 1948, through ranks princ 1964, sr princ 1969, asst sec 1973, under sec to Treasy Offr of Accounts 1981-87; memb Royal Patriotic Fund Corp 1987-; *Recreations* cricket, golf, DIY; *Clubs* Sevenoaks' Vine Cricket, Knole Park Golf; *Style*— Clifford Judd, Esq, CB; 4 Colets Orchard, Otford, Sevenoaks, Kent TN14 5RA (☎ 09592 2398)

JUDD, Frank Ashcroft; s of Charles W Judd, CBE (d 1974), of Surrey, and Helen Osborn Judd, JP, *née* Ashcroft (d 1982); *b* 28 March 1935; *Educ* City of London Sch, LSE (BSc); *m* 1961, Christine Elizabeth Louise, da of Frederick Ward Willington (d 1966), of Kent; 2 da (Elizabeth b 1967, Philippa b 1969); *Career* F/O RAF 1957-59; gen sec Int Voluntary Serv 1960-66; MP 1966-79; PPS to: Min of Housing and Local Govt 1967-70, Ldr of Oppn 1970-72; jr oppn def spokesman 1972-74, Parly under sec of state for Def RN 1974-76, min for Overseas Devpt 1976-77, min of state FCO 1977-79; assoc dir Int Defence & Aid Fund for Southern Africa 1979-80, dir VSO 1980-85, dir Oxfam 1985-; hon fell Portsmouth Poly; memb: Cncl of Overseas Devpt Inst, Governing Body Queen Elizabeth House, Univ of Oxford, Exec Ctee Int Cncl of Voluntary Agencies; govr LSE; Hon DLitt; FRSA; *Books* Radical Future (jtly, 1967), Fabian International Essays (1970), Purpose in Socialism (1973); *Recreations* hill walking, family holidays; *Clubs* Royal Cwlth Soc; *Style*— Frank Judd, Esq; Belmont, 21 Mill Lane, Old Marston, Oxford OX3 0PY (☎ 0865 721 447); Oxfam, 274 Banbury Rd, Oxford OX2 7DZ (☎ 0865 56777)

JUDD, James Hubert; s of Capt Leslie A Judd (d 1967), of Stewkley Grange, Leighton Buzzard, and Enid, *née* Crichton (d 1974); *b* 27 March 1933; *Educ* Eton; *m* 19 March 1982, Lady Zinnia Rosemary, *née* Denison, da of 4 Earl of Londesborough (d 1937); *Career* 2 Lt Irish Gds 1952-53; chm and md Walter Judd Ltd 1971-; MIPA; *Recreations* hunting, shooting, skiing, farming; *Clubs* City of London, MCC, White's; *Style*— James Judd, Esq; 1A Bow Lane, London EC4M 9EJ (☎ 071 236 4541, fax 071 248 8139)

JUDD, Lionel Henry; s of John Basil Thomas Judd (d 1983), and Cynthia Margaret Georgina, *née* White-Smith; *b* 24 Oct 1945; *Educ* The Leys Sch Cambridge, Downing Coll Cambridge (MA); *m* 19 Sept 1970, Janet Elizabeth, da of Arthur Boyton Fraser (d 1966), of The Limes, Stansted, Essex; 1 s (Edward b 1972), 1 da (Alexandra b 1975); *Career* admitted slr 1972; ptnr Darley Cumberland (now Cumberland Ellis Piers) 1975-; *Recreations* rowing, country pursuits, travel; *Clubs* Leander; *Style*— Lionel Judd, Esq; Little Coombe, Wendover, Bucks HP22 6EQ; Columbia House, 69 Aldwych, London WC2B 4RW (☎ 071 242 0422, fax 071 831 9081)

JUDD, Vincent Sydney; s of Sydney Arthur Judd, of 9 Manor Rd, Wheathampstead, Herts, and Hilda Lillian Judd; *b* 15 April 1944; *Educ* St Albans Sch; *m* 16 Sept 1968, Betty, da of James Humphrey, of 60 Larke Way, Leagrave, Beds; 4 da (Christine b 1971, Eve b 1972 d 1973, Sally b 1976, Fiona b 1978); *Career* qualified CA 1966, insolvency practitioner; memb ICAEW; *Recreations* transport, photography, gardening; *Style*— Vincent Judd, Esq; 7 High St, Harpenden, Herts (☎ 0582 762649, 0582 768936, fax 0582 460674)

JUDD, Lady Zinnia Rosemary; *née* Denison; da of 4 Earl of Londesborough (d 1937); *b* 1937,(posthumously); *m* 1, 1957 (m dis 1961), Peter Comins; 1 s (Timothy b 1958, changed name to Pollock after 1968); m 2, 1961 (m dis 1964), John David Leslie Melville (only s of Hon David Leslie Melville, MBE, 3 s of 11 Earl of Leven and Melville); m 3, 1964 (m dis 1967), Maj Hugh Cantlie, Scots Gds; 1 s (Charles); m 4, 1968 (as his 3 w), Ralph John Hamilton Pollock, publisher (d 1980, gggs of Rt Hon Sir Frederick Pollock, 1 Bt); m 5, 1982, James (Jamie) H Judd; *Style*— The Lady Zinnia Judd; Stewkley Grange, Leighton Buzzard, Beds

JUDGE, David Leslie; s of Harry Judge, MC, of Islington, London, and Joan Beryl, *née* Tomey (d 1978); *b* 23 May 1942; *Educ* Malvern, Merton Coll Oxford (MA); *m* 19 Sept 1964, Angela Monica, da of Col Edward Douglas Lawson Whatley, OBE, TD, DL, (d 1981), of Malvern, Worcs; 1 s (Edward b 1971), 1 da (Joanna b 1969); *Career* slr 1969, sec Abbeyfield (Malvern) Soc Ltd, hon slr and memb Ctee Malvern CAB, church warden St John's, Clerk to Malvern Hills Conservators 1979-; memb Law Soc 1967-; *Recreations* field sports, fishing, shooting, stalking; *Style*— David Judge, Esq; Shuttifield Cottage, Birchwood, Storridge, Malvern, Worcs WR13 5HA (☎ 08864 243); Priors Croft, Grange Rd, Malvern, Worcs (☎ 0684 892298)

JUDSON-RHODES, Hon Dr (Pamela); *née* Rhodes; da of Baron Rhodes, KG, DFC, PC, DL, and Anne, da of John Henry Bradbury; *b* 1 May 1927; *Educ* Manchester Univ (BA), Univ of Pennsylvania (PhD); *m* 1953 (m dis 1969), Walter Leaman Hemphill, s of late Wesley Hemphill; 2 s, 2 da; m 2, 1990, S Sheldon Judson Jr; *Career* prof emeritus in art history; *Style*— The Hon Dr Judson-Rhodes; 18 Aiken Ave, Princeton, New Jersey 08540, USA

JUKES, John Andrew; CB (1968); s of Capt (Andrew) Munro Jukes (d 1918), and Gertrude Elizabeth, *née* King (d 1957); *b* 19 May 1917; *Educ* Shrewsbury, St John's Coll Cambridge (MA), LSE (BSc); *m* 19 June 1943, Muriel, da of Frederick James Child; 2 s (Andrew b 1946, David b 1952), 2 da (Margaret (Mrs Condick) b 1944, Rosemary (Dr Fowler) b 1950); *Career* on cmmn RAF 1940; econ advsr: Econ Section Cabinet Office and Treasy 1948-54, UK Atomic Energy Authy 1954-64; dep dir gen and dep sec Dept of Econ Affrs 1964-69, dep sec Miny of Tport 1969-71; dep sec DOE: econs and resources 1970-72, environmental protection 1972-74; dir Gen Highways Dept of Tport 1974-77, memb Exec Bd CEGB 1977-80; memb: SDP 1981-87, Merton and Sutton DHA 1986, pres Lib Democrats 1990- (memb 1988-); London Borough of Sutton: rep on Cncl for Social Democracy 1982-86, cncllr 1986-90, chm Fin Sub Ctee and Resources Sub Ctee; *Recreations* gardening; *Style*— John Jukes, Esq, CB; 38 Albion Rd, Sutton, Surrey SM2 5TF (☎ 081 642 5018)

JUKES, Paul Francis; s of Frederick Jukes (d 1987), of London, and Mary, *née* Galloway (d 1980); *b* 23 Aug 1952; *Educ* St Ignatius Coll North London, Middlesex Poly; *m* 6 April 1974, Geraldine, da of James Fahey (d 1989), of London; 4 s (Adam b 1975, Christopher b 1978, Jeremy b 1981, Daniel b 1984); *Career* Cooper Lancaster CAs 1971-76, The Br CECA Co Ltd 1976- (appointed md 1982); sch govr St Paul's RC First Sch, memb Parish Pastoral Cncl Sacred Heart Cobham; FCA 1981, FInstD, FBIM; *Recreations* running (particularly road running); *Clubs* RAC, Cobham Catholic Boys Football; *Style*— Paul Jukes, Esq; The British CECA Co Ltd, Rowan Ct, 56 High St, Wimbledon Village, London SW19 5EE (☎ 081 946 7774, fax 081 947 3873, telex 928041)

JULIAN, Prof Desmond Gareth; s of Dr Frederick Bennett Julian, MC (d 1958), and Jane Frances, *née* Galbraith (d 1956); *b* 24 April 1926; *Educ* Leighton Park Sch, St John's Coll Cambridge (MA, MD), Middx Hosp London; *m* 1, 8 July 1956, Mary Ruth (d 1964), da of John Jessup (d 1968); 1 s (Paul Richard b 1962), 1 da (Claire Frances b 1960); m 2, 10 Dec 1988, Claire, da of Frederick Bolam Marley; *Career* RNVR 1949-51; conslt cardiologist Sydney Hosp Aust 1961-64, conslt cardiologist Royal Infirmary Edinburgh 1964-74, prof of cardiology Univ of Newcastle upon Tyne 1975-86, conslt med dir Br Heart Fndn 1986-; second vice pres RCP 1990; MD Gothenburg 1986; FRCP: London, Edinburgh, Aust; *Books* Cardiology (1970, 5 edn 1988); *Recreations* skiing, walking; *Clubs* Athenaeum; *Style*— Prof Desmond Julian; Flat 1, 7 Netherhall Gardens, London NW3 5RN (☎ 071 435 8254); British Heart Foundation, 14 Fitzhardinge St, London W1H 4DN (☎ 071 935 0185)

JULIEN, Michael Frederick; *b* 22 March 1938; *Educ* St Edward's Sch Oxford; *m* Ellen; 1 s (Mark), 2 da (Heidi, Christine); *Career* gp fin dir: BICC Ltd 1976-83, Midland Bank 1983-86; md fin and admin Guinness plc 1987-, gp chief exec Storehouse plc 1988-, non-exec dir Guinness plc 1988-; Liveryman Worshipful Co of Barber-Surgeons; vice pres Br Digestive Fndn; FCA, FCT; *Clubs* City Livery Club; *Style*— Michael F Julien, Esq; Storehouse plc, The Heal's Building, 196 Tottenham Court Road, London W1P 9LD (☎ 071 631 0101, fax 071 436 4236, telex 296475)

JULIUS, Dr DeAnne; da of Marvin G Julius, of Iowa, USA, and Maxine M, *née* Meeske; *b* 14 April 1949; *Educ* Iowa State Univ (BSc), Univ of California (MA, PhD); *m* 21 Nov 1976, Ian Alexander Harvey, s of Dr Alexander Harvey (d 1987), of Cardiff; 1 s (Ross b 9 Dec 1980), 1 da (Megan b 28 March 1979); *Career* lectr Univ of California 1972-75, economic advsr The World Bank 1975-82, md Logan Associates Inc 1982-86, dir of economics RIIA 1986-89, chief economist Shell International Petroleum Co Ltd 1989-; memb Bd of Mgmnt LSHTM; hon fell UCL 1986; *Books* Global Companies and Public Policy: The Growing Challenge of Foreign Direct Investment (1990), The Economics of Natural Gas (1990), The Monetary Implications of the 1992 Process (1990); *Clubs* IOD; *Style*— Dr DeAnne Julius; Shell Centre, London SE1 7NA (☎ 071 9342661, telex 919651 Shell G, fax 071 9348060)

JUNGELS, Dr Pierre; s of Henri Jungels, former pres of Labaz; *b* 18 Feb 1944; *Educ* Univ of Liege (Ing Civ), California Inst of Technol (PhD); *m* 2, 1988, Caroline, da of Dr S R G Benc, of Worcester; 2 children; *Career* ben mangr and chief exec Petrangol (Angola) 1977-80, md and chief exec Petrofina (UK) 1981-89, chm/dir various Petrofina subsidiaries in UK, Belgium and France, elected to Main Bd of Petrofina SA Brussels; pres The Inst of Petroleum 1986-88, md Petrofina SA 1989; *Recreations* tennis, skiing; *Clubs* Anglo-Belgian; *Style—* Dr Pierre Jungels; L'Hurlimpré, 21 rue de Chaumont, B 5980 Longveville, Belgium (☎ 010 32 10 888680); Petrofina SA, Rue de L'Industrie, 52, B 1040 Brussels, Belgium (☎ 010 322 233 9111)

JUNGIUS, Vice Adm Sir James George; KBE (1977), DL (Cornwall 1982); s of Maj E Jungius, MC; *b* 15 Nov 1923; *Educ* RNC Dartmouth; *m* 1949, Rosemary Frances Turquand Matthey; 3 s; *Career* RN: served WWII Atlantic and Med, Commando Ops Adriatic, asst naval attaché Washington 1968-70, asst chief Naval Staff Operational Requirements 1972-74, Rear Adm 1972, Vice-Adm 1974, Dep Supreme Allied Cdr Atlantic 1975-77, Supreme Allied Cdr Atlantic's Rep Europe 1978-80, ret; navigation specialist; fell Wood Corp (Western Div); OStJ (chm Cncl for Cornwall); CBIM (pres Cornwall Branch); *Recreations* sailing, fishing; *Clubs* Pilgrims, RN Club of 1765 and 1785, Royal Over-Seas League; *Style—* Vice Adm Sir James Jungius, KBE, DL; c/o National Westminster Bank, 26 Molesworth St, Wadebridge, Cornwall PL27 7DL

JUNIPER, Richard Pudan; s of Leonard Alfred Vey Juniper (d 1988), of London, and Edna Amy, *née* Pudan; *b* 11 April 1938; *Educ* Highgate Sch London, Guy's Hosp London (MB BS, BDS); *m* 19 Feb 1971, Honor Murray, da of Denis Fargher Glass, of Charing, Kent; 1 s (Matthew b 1973), 1 da (Zoe b 1975); *Career* sr registrar in oral and maxillo facial surgery Queen Victoria Hosp E Grinstead 1970-72; conslt oral and maxillo-facial surgn: Brighton Health Dist 1972-82, Oxford Health Authy 1982-; clinical lectr Oxford Univ Med Sch 1982-; hon sec: Odontological Section RSM 1979, Br Assoc of Oral and Maxillo Facial Surgns 1983-86; memb Bd of Faculty of Dental Surgery RCS 1989-; Freeman City of London, memb Ct Worshipful Co of Poulters 1982-; Hon MA Univ of Oxford; FDS RCS 1968, FRSM 1968, fell BAOMS 1982; memb: BMA, BDA, Intractable Pain Soc, Craniofacial Soc 1986; *Books* Emergencies in Dental Practice (with B Parkins, 1990); *Style—* Richard Juniper, Esq; Dept of Oral and Maxillo Facial Surgery, John Radcliffe Hospital, Oxford OX3 9DU

JUNKIN, John Francis; s of Detective Inspector John Junkin (d 1972), and Elizabeth, *née* Cavanagh; *b* 29 Jan 1930; *Educ* Aylesbury GS, Holy Cross Acad Edinburgh, West Ham GS, St Mary's Coll Twickenham; *m* 16 Sept 1977, Jennifer, da of George Henry (Harry) Claybourn (d 1965), of Goole, Yorks; 1 da (Annabel b 1978); *Career* actor; over 1,000 tv appearances, theatre work incl 12 months with Joan Littlewood's Theatre Workshop and four West End appearances; writer and co-writer of approximately 1,500 tv and radio shows; memb: Star Orgn for Spastics, Variety Club GB; Freeman City of London 1985; *Recreations* crosswords, board games, reading; *Style—* John Junkin, Esq; c/o Richard Grenville, London Management, Regent St, London, W1 (☎ 071 493 1610)

JUNOR, Brian James Ross; s of Donald Junor, MBE (d 1986), of Dundee, and Ann Russell, *née* Mackie (d 1985); *b* 10 Feb 1946; *Educ* Dundee HS, Univ of St Andrews (MB ChB), Univ of Dundee (MD); *m* 1, 4 Feb 1972, Sheena MacLeod (d 1972), da of Sir Donald Douglas, of White House, Nevay Newtyle; m 2, 19 Jan 1979, Elizabeth Jane, da of John Fotheringham, OBE, of St Helen's, Elie, Fife; 1 s (Malcolm b 1980), 1 da (Katherine b 1982); *Career* sr registrar of medicine Aberdeen Royal Infirmary 1976-78, Aust Kidney Res Fndn fell Univ of Melbourne 1978-79, hon clinical lectr Univ of Glasgow 1979-, conslt nephrologist Gtr Glasgow Health Authy 1979-; memb Jt Ctee for Higher Med Training, sec Specialist Advsy Ctee in Renal Diseases; memb BMA 1970, FRCPS 1982, FRCPE 1987; *Recreations* skiing, gardening, golf; *Style—* Brian Junor, Esq; The Barn, Ballagan, Stathblane, Glasgow (☎ 0360 70767); Renal Unit, Western Infirmary, Dunbarton Rd, Glasgow (☎ 041 339 8822)

JUNOR, Sir John; s of Alexander Junor, of Black Isle; *b* 15 Jan 1919; *Educ* Univ of Glasgow (MA); *m* 1942, Pamela Welsh; 1 s, 1 da; *Career* served WWII RNVR; Parly candidate (Lib): Kincardine and W Aberdeen 1945, Edinburgh E 1948, Dundee W 1951; journalist; dir Express Newspapers (formerly Beaverbrook Newspapers) 1960-86, chm Sunday Express 1968-86 (ed 1954-86); dir Fleet Holdings 1982-85; kt 1980; *Books* The Best of JJ (1981), Listening for a Midnight Tram (memoirs, 1990); *Recreations* golf; *Clubs* Royal and Ancient, Walton Heath; *Style—* Sir John Junor; c/o Bank of Scotland, 16 Piccadilly, London W1

JUPP, Hon Sir Kenneth Graham Jupp; MC (1943); s of Albert Leonard Jupp, shipbroker; *b* 2 June 1917; *Educ* Perse Sch Cambridge, Univ Coll Oxford (MA); *m* 1947, Kathleen Elizabeth, da of Richard Owen Richards, farmer, of Morton Hall, Morton, Salop; 2 s, 2 da; *Career* Maj, served WWII, Europe and N Africa 1939-43, on WO Selection Bd 1943-46; called to the Bar Lincoln's Inn 1945, dep chm Cambs and Isle of Ely QS 1965-71, QC 1966, rec Crown Ct 1972-75, judge High Ct (Queen's Bench) 1975-90, presiding judge NE Circuit 1977-81; chm Ind Schs Tbnl 1964-67, chm Public Enquiry into Fire at Fairfield Home Nottingham 1975; kt 1975; *Recreations* music, language, reading; *Clubs* Garrick; *Style—* The Hon Sir Kenneth Jupp, MC; Royal Courts of Justice, Strand, London WC2

JURKIEWICZ, Hon Mrs (Enid Aughard); *née* Jones; da of Baron Maelor (Life Peer); *m* E Jurkiewicz; *Style—* The Hon Mrs Jurkiewicz; 16 Snowdon Drive, Wrexham, Denbighshire

JURY, Capt Peter Charles Cotton; s of Col Edward Cotton Jury, CMG, MC (d 1966); *b* 30 Aug 1919; *Educ* Rugby, King's Coll Cambridge; *m* 1953 (m dis), (Ursula Joan) Sally, da of Maj-Gen Sir William Abraham, CBE (d 1980); 2 da (Sophie, Polly); *Career* Capt 13/18 Royal Hussars: BEF 1939-40, BLA 1944-45; md: Shelbourne Hotel Ltd Dublin 1947-60, Trust Houses Ireland Ltd 1960-72; dir Trust House Hotels 1967-71, chm Trusthouse Forte Ireland Ltd 1972-80, pres Int Hotel Assoc 1977-78, dir Minibar (UK) Ltd 1986-90; *Clubs* Army & Navy; *Style—* Capt Peter Jury; The Old Vicarage, Beadlam, Nawton, York YO6 5ST (☎ 0439 71220)

JUSTHAM, David Gwyn; s of John Farquhar Richard Justham (d 1948), and Margaret Anne, *née* John (d 1969); *b* 23 Dec 1923; *Educ* Bristol GS; *m* 31 March 1950, Isobel Thelma, da of George Gordon Thomson, MC (d 1968); 1 s (Jamie b 1951), 1 da (Julia b 1954); *Career* Flt Lt (pilot) RAF 1941-46; slr 1949, various appts with ICI plc 1955-65 and IMI plc 1965-85; dir: IMI plc 1968-85, Nat Exhibition Centre Ltd 1979-89 (chm 1982-89), H Samuel plc 1981-84, Central Ind TV plc 1981- (chm 1986-); chm Birmingham Hippodrome Theatre Tst Ltd 1979-89, memb Cncl of Mgmnt CBSO 1984-88, pres Birmingham Chamber of Indust and Commerce 1974-75, gen cmmr of Income Tax 1972-77; High Sheriff W Midlands 1981-82; hon life memb Ct of Govrs 1986- (memb 1976-); dep pro-chllr Univ of Birmingham 1966-88; *Recreations* opera, theatre; *Style—* David Justham, Esq; 9 Birch Hollow, Edgbaston, Birmingham B15 2QE (☎ 021 454 0688)

JUSTICE, Nicholas Alexander; *b* 17 Aug 1945; *Educ* Christ's Coll Christchurch NZ, Univ of Canterbury NZ (BE, ME); *m* 28 Dec 1968, Patricia; 1 s (Andrey b 1981), 2 da (Emma b 1976, Anetta b 1982); *Career* chief engr Hawker Siddeley Dynamics Engrg Ltd 1981, md Strategic Systems Technol Ltd 1983-; memb Inst of Measurement & Control; *Style—* Nicholas A Justice, Esq; 14 Landons Close, London E14 9QQ (☎ 071 538 8228, fax 071 515 3887)

K

KABERRY, Hon Andrew Murdoch Scott; 2 s of Baron Kaberry of Adel, TD (Life Peer), *qv*; *b* 22 Sept 1946; *Educ* Repton, East Anglia Univ (BA); *Career* FCA 1972, chartered accountant; *Style*— The Hon Andrew Kaberry; Thorp Arch Hall, Boston Spa, W Yorks

KABERRY, Hon Christopher Donald; s and h (to baronetcy only) of Baron Kaberry of Adel, TD, DL (Life Peer); *b* 14 March 1943; *Educ* Repton; *m* 25 March 1967, Gaenor Elizabeth Vowe, yr da of Cecil Vowe Peake, MBE, of Redbourn, St Albans, Herts; 2 s (James Christopher b 1 April 1970, Angus George b 1972), 1 da (Claire Elizabeth b 1974); *Career* chartered accountant; *Style*— The Hon Christopher Kaberry; The Croft, Rookery Lane, Wymondham, Melton Mowbray, Leics LE14 2AU (☎ 057 284 663)

KABERRY, Hon Simon Edward John; 3 and yst s of Baron Kaberry of Adel, TD (Life Peer); *b* 14 Dec 1948; *Educ* Repton; *Career* admitted solicitor 1974; *Style*— The Hon Simon Kaberry; Adel Willows, Otley Rd, Leeds

KABERRY OF ADEL, Baron (Life Peer UK 1983), of Adel, City of Leeds; Sir Donald Kaberry; 1 Bt (UK 1960), of Adel cum Eccup, City of Leeds; TD (1947), DL (W Yorks 1976); s of Abraham Kaberry (d 1954), of Leeds, and Lily, *née* MacKenzie; *b* 18 Aug 1907; *Educ* Leeds GS, Univ of Leeds; *m* 3 Sept 1940, Lily Margaret, da of late Edmund Scott, of Morley, W Yorks; 3 s (Hon Christopher Donald b 1943, Hon Andrew Murdoch Scott b 1946, Hon Simon Edward John b 1948); *Heir* to baronetcy only, s, Christopher Donald Kaberry, *qv*; *Career* sits as Cons Peer in House of Lords; served WWII, RA, Dunkirk and NW Europe (despatches 2), Actg Col, chief legal offr to Mil Govr of Hamburg 1945; slr 1930; memb Leeds City Cncl 1930-39 and 1946-50; MP (C) Leeds NW 1950-83; asst govt whip 1952-55, parly sec BOT 1955; memb: Select Ctee Nationalised Industries 1961-83 (chm Sub-Ctee), Speaker's Panel of Chairmen 1974-83; chm Select Ctee Industry and Trade 1979-83; vice chm Cons Pty 1955-61, chm Assoc of Cons Clubs 1961-88 (now patron), pres York Area Cncl of Cons Pty 1966- (chm 1951-55, dep pres 1956-65); former chm: Yorkshire Chemicals Ltd, W H Baxter Ltd, E Walker & Co Ltd; Nat Pres Dunkirk Veterans Assoc 1988-; life pres Headingley Royal British Legion 1960-; chm Leeds Teaching Hosps 1961-75 (chm Special Tstees 1975-86); *Clubs* Carlton, St Stephen's, Constitutional; *Style*— The Rt Hon the Lord Kaberry of Adel TD, DL; 1 Otley Rd, Harrogate, N Yorkshire HG2 0DJ

KADOORIE, Baron (Life Peer UK 1981), of Kowloon in Hong Kong and of the City of Westminster; Sir Lawrence Kadoorie; CBE (1970), JP (1936); s of Sir Elly Kadoorie, KBE (d 1944), of Marble Hall, Shanghai, China, and 6 Princes Gate, London SW7, and Laura, *née* Mocatta; *b* 2 June 1899; *Educ* Cathedral Sch Shanghai, St Vincent's Eastbourne, Clifton; *m* 1938, Muriel, da of D S Gubbay, of Hong Kong; 1 s (Hon Michael David b 1941), 1 da (Hon Rita Laura McAulay b 1940); *Career* joint proprietor Sir Elly Kadoorie & Sons; chm: China Light and Power, Schroders Asia Ltd, Nanyang Cotton Mill Ltd; dir: Sir Elly Kadoorie & Sons Ltd, and various other companies; kt 1974; *Recreations* sports cars, photography, Chinese works of art; *Clubs* Hong Kong, Jewish Recreation; *Style*— The Rt Hon the Lord Kadoorie, CBE, JP; 24 Kadoorie Ave, Kowloon, Hong Kong (☎ 7116129)

KADOORIE, Hon Michael David; o s of Baron Kadoorie, CBE (Life Peer); *b* 19 July 1941; *Educ* King George V Sch Hong Kong, Le Rosey Switzerland; *m* 1984, Betty, da of Juan E Tamayo, of Coral Gables, Florida, USA; 2 da (Natalie b 1986, Bettina b 1987); *Career* chm: The Hongkong & Shanghai Hotels Ltd, Heliservices (HK) Ltd, Rotair Ltd; dir China Light & Power Co Ltd and other cos; *Recreations* world travel, flying, motor cars, boats, skiing, water skiing, photography; *Clubs* Hong Kong, American (Hong Kong), Eagle Ski (Gstaad), Vintage Sports Car, Hong Kong Aviation, Royal Hong Kong Jockey; *Style*— The Hon Michael Kadoorie; No 68 Deep Water Bay Road, Hong Kong; 24th Floor, St George's Building, No 2 Ice House Street, Central, Hong Kong (☎ 010 852 524 9221, fax 010 852 845 9133)

KADRI, Sibghatullah; QC (1989); s of Alhaj Maulana Firasatullah Kadri (d 1990), and Begum Tanwir Fatima, *née* Hamidi (d 1986); *b* 23 April 1937; *Educ* Christian HS Budaun UP India, SM Sci Coll Karachi Univ Pakistan, Inns of Court School of Law London; *m* 1963, Carita Elisabeth da of Ole Idman (d 1973), of Helsinki; 1 s (Sadakat b 1964), 1 da (Maria Fatima b 1965); *Career* BBC External Serv 1965-68, prodr and presenter BBC Home Serv, visiting lectr in Urdu Holborn Coll 1966-68; called to the Bar Inner Temple 1969, head of chambers 1973-, Pakistan Students Fedn in Br: gen sec 1961-62, vice pres 1962-63; pres Inner Temple Students Assoc 1968-69; Standing Conference of Pakistani Orgn: gen sec 1975-78, pres 1978-84; convener Asian Action Ctee 1976, vice chm Jt Ctee Against Racism, chm Soc of Black Lawyers 1981-83, sec Br Lawyers Ctee for Human Rights and Justice in Pakistan 1984-, chm Asian Lawyers Conference, memb Bar Cncls Race Rels Ctee 1989 (1982-85, 1988); *Style*— Sibghatullah Kadri, Esq, QC; 100 Girdwood Rd, London SW18 5QT (☎ 081 789 1941); 6 Kings Bench Walk, Temple, London EC4Y 7DR (☎ 071 353 4931/2, 071 583 0695/8, fax 071 353 1726)

KAFETZ, Dr Kalman Meir; s of Vivian Kafetz, of Regent's Park, London (d 1969), and Rose, *née* Gilbert (d 1982); *b* 3 Dec 1947; *Educ* Eton, St Thomas' Hosp Med Sch (BSc, MB BS); *m* 11 Oct 1972, Marion Linda, da of Gerald Singer, of Mill Hill, London; 2 s (Alexander b 1976, Sebastian b 1980), 1 da (Cordelia b 1983); *Career* conslt physician Dept of Medicine for Elderly People Whipps Cross Hosp London 1982-, hon lectr Med Coll St Bartholomews Hosp 1987-, teacher Univ of London 1987-; memb Br Geriatrics Soc; MRCP (UK) 1976; *Books* Clinical Tests - Geriatric Medicine (1986); *Recreations* Cornish history; *Style*— Dr Kalman Kafetz; 22 Offham Slope, London N12 7BZ (☎ 081 445 5119); Old Court Cottage, Kenegie Manor, Gulval, Penzance, Cornwall TR10 8YW; Connaught Day Hospital, Whipps Cross Hospital, London E11 1NR (☎ 081 539 5522)

KAGAN, Baron (Life Peer UK 1976), of Elland, Co of West Yorkshire; Joseph Kagan; s of Benjamin Kagan (d 1988, aged 109), of Leeds; *b* 6 June 1915; *Educ* High Sch Kaunas Lithuania, Leeds Univ; *m* 1943, Margaret, da of George Strom; 2 s (Hon Michael George b 1950, Hon Daniel b 1953), 1 da (Hon Anne Eugenia b 1965); *Career* dir Kagan Textiles, chm Gannex Gp of Cos (founded 1951); kt 1970 (annulled 1981); *Style*— The Rt Hon the Lord Kagan; 15 Fixby Rd, Huddersfield, Yorks (☎ 0484 25202); Barkisland Hall, Barkisland, Halifax, W Yorks (☎ 0422 74121)

KAGAN, Hon Michael George; s of Baron Kagan (Life Peer); *b* 1950; *Style*— The Hon Michael Kagan

KAHAN, George; s of Joseph Kahan (d 1979), and Xenia, *née* Kirschner; *b* 11 June 1931; *Educ* St Paul's; *m* 26 May 1959, Avril Pamela, *née* Cooper; 1 s (Adam b 1960); *Career* dir Park Royal Woodworkers Ltd 1960-74 (joined 1951), asst sec Dept of Employment 1980-88 (princ 1975-76), Health and Safety Exec 1976-80, dir of conciliation and arbitration ACAS 1988-; *Recreations* listening to music, reading; *Style*— George Kahan, Esq; 2 Abbotsbury Close, Kensington, London W14 8EG (☎ 071 603 6752); Advisory Conciliation and Arbitrarion Service, 27 Wilton St, London SW1X 7AZ (☎ 071 210 3650, fax 071 210 3708)

KAHRMANN, Rainer Thomas Christian; s of Dr Johannes Wilhelm Karl Kahrmann, of W Germany, and Therese, *née* Gillrath; *b* 28 May 1943; *Educ* Neusprachliches Gymnasium Erkelenz W Germany, Univ of Fribourg (LIC RER Pol, Dr RER Pol); *m* 8 Dec 1972, Christiane Jeanne Maria, *née* De Muller; 2 da (Louise b 27 Sept 1979, Alice b 19 Nov 1981); *Career* apprenticeship Commerzbank AG W Germany 1963-64, Dow Chemical Co (Dow Banking Corp) 1969-88, md EBC Amro Bank Ltd 1974-89, chm EBC Amro Int Investment Management Ltd 1989-; memb Nat Liberal Club; *Recreations* work, family, antiquarian horology; *Clubs* Nat Liberal; *Style*— Rainer Kahrmann, Esq; EBC Amro Asset Management Ltd, 10 Devonshire Sq, London EC2M 4HS (☎ 071 621 0101, fax 071 626 7915, telex 8811001)

KAKKAD, Sunil Shantilal; s of Shantilal Kalyanji Kakkad, of London, and Usha Shantilal, *née* Kanani; *b* 19 May 1959; *Educ* Alder Sch Finchely, Barnet Coll, Univ of Hull (LLB); *m* 23 Aug 1984, Darshna Sunil, da of Kantilal Vithaldas Hindocha, of Harrow, Middx; 1 s (Rajiv Sunil b 1990); *Career* admitted slr 1984; Hill Dickinson & Co 1984-89, ptnr Hill Taylor Dickinson 1989-; memb Law Soc; *Recreations* reading, music; *Style*— Sunil Kakkad, Esq; Hill Taylor Dickinson, Irongate House, Duke's Place, London EC3A 7LP (☎ 071 283 9033, 071 283 1144, telex 888470)

KALDERON, Dr David; OBE (1987); s of Prof Solomon Kalderon (d 1968), of Belgrade, Yugoslavia, and Diana, and, *née* Konforti (d 1989); *b* 24 Nov 1928; *Educ* Univ of Vienna (Dipl ing), City and Guilds Coll Univ of London (DIC), Univ of London (PhD); *m* 12 June 1955, Eva Suzanne, da of Fritz B Hoffmann (d 1983), of London; 2 s (Mark Adam b 1 March 1957, Daniel David b 1 Aug 1959); *Career* dep chief turbine engr GEC 1961-65, turbine plant design engr GEGB 1965-70, asst md GEC Turbine Generators Ltd 1980-89 (Engrg dir 1970-89), tech dir and asst md Electromechanical Div GEC Alsthom 1989-; author of various tech articles; FI MechE 1970, FEng 1979; *Recreations* music, visual arts, theatre; *Style*— Dr David Kalderon, OBE; 86 Tiddington Rd, Stratford upon Avon, Warwickshire CV37 7BA (☎ 0789 293804); GEC Alsthom, Electromechanical Divison, Steam Turbines, Newbold Rd, Rugby, Warwickshire CV21 2NH (☎ 0788 531315, fax 0788 531986, telex 31463)

KALDOR, Hon Mary Henrietta; da of Baron Kaldor (Life Peer, d 1986); *b* 1946; *Books* The Baroque Arsenal (1982); *Style*— The Hon Mary Kaldor; c/o André Deutsch Ltd, 105 Great Russell St, WC1 (☎ 071 580 2746)

KALETSKY, Anatole; s of Jacob Kaletsky (d 1989), and Esther, *née* Feinsilber; *b* 1 June 1952; *Educ* King's Coll Cambridge (hon sr scholarship, BA, Dip Econ), Harvard Univ Graduate Sch (Kennedy memorial scholarship, MA); *m* 5 Dec 1985, Fiona Elizabeth, da of Christopher Murphy; 1 s (Michael b 10 Dec 1988), 1 da (Katherine b 2 Nov 1986); *Career* fin writer The Economist 1976-79; The Financial Times: ldr and feature writer 1979-81, Washington corr 1981-84, int econs corr 1984-86, chief New York Bureau 1986-90, Moscow corr 1990, sr features writer April-Sept 1990; econs ed The Times 1990-; Specialist Writer of the Year Br Press Award 1980; conslt: UN Devpt Ctee, UN Conf on Trade and Devpt, Twentieth Century Fund; numerous television and radio appearances; *Books* The Costs of Default (1985); *Style*— Anatole Kaletsky, Esq; The Times, 1 Pennington St, London E1 9XN (☎ 071 782 5000, fax 071 782 5112)

KALISHER, Michael David Lionel; QC (1984); s of Samuel Kalisher (d 1966), and Rose, *née* Chester (d 1970); *b* 24 Feb 1941; *Educ* Hove Co GS, Univ of Bristol (LLB); *m* 1967, Helen, da of Albert Edward McCandless, of N Ireland; 1 s (Jason b 1972), 2 da (Justine b 1969, Natasha b 1973); *Career* slr 1965-69, called to the Bar Inner Temple 1970, rec Crown Ct 1985, bencher Inner Temple; memb: Crown Ct Rules Ctee 1989, Efficiency Cmmn 1989; vice chm Criminal Bar Assoc 1989; *Recreations* squash, tennis, reading; *Clubs* Roehampton; *Style*— Michael Kalisher, Esq, QC; 1 Hare Court, Temple, London EC4 (☎ 071 353 5324, fax 071 353 0667)

KALKHOF, Peter Heinz; s of Heinz Emil Kalkhof (d 1945), and Kate Ottilie, *née* Binder (d 1976); *b* 20 Dec 1933; *Educ* Sch of Arts and Crafts Braunschweig, Acad of Fine Art Stuttgart, Slade Sch of Fine Art London, École des Beaux Arts Paris; *m* 1962, Jeanne The Soen Nio; 1 s (Peter T L b 1964); *Career* artist; lectr in painting Univ of Reading 1970- (pt/t lectr in lithography and etching 1964-70); one man exhibitions: Galerie in der Garage Stuttgart 1964, Oxford Gallery 1970, Annely Juda Fine Art London 1970, 1974, 1977, 1979 and 1990, Wellmann Galerie Dusseldorf 1973, Galerie HS Erkelenz 1974, Royal Shakespeare Theatre 1975, Oliver Dowling Gallery Dublin 1976, Kulturgeschichtliches Museum Osnabruck 1977, Hertfordshire Coll of Art and Design St Albans 1978, Kunstverein Marburg 1979, Goethe Inst London 1981, Juda Rowan Gallery London 1983, Galerie Altes Rathaus Worth am Rhein 1987, Landesmuseum Oldenburg 1988, Camden Arts Centre London 1989, Ostpreussisches Landesmuseum Luneburg 1989; mixed exhibitions incl: Spectrum 1971 (Alexandra Palace London) 1971, International Biennale of Drawing (Middlesbrough) 1973 and 1979, British Painting 74 (Hayward Gallery London) 1974, Celebrating 8 Artists (Kensington and Chelsea Arts Cncl Exhibition) 1977, Six Painters (Univ of Reading Art Gallery) 1984, Three Decades of Contemporary Art (Juda Rowan Gallery) 1985, From Prism to Paint Box (Welsh Arts Cncl touring exhibition) 1989-90; awards: travel grant for Br Isles Slade Sch 1961, artist in residence Osnabruck Germany 1985; memb: Br Museum Soc, Soc for Anglo-Chinese Understanding; friend Royal Acad; *Recreations* travelling, reading, listening to music, seeing films, visiting museums exhibitions art galleries etc; *Style*— Peter Kalkhof, Esq; c/o Annely Juda Fine Art, 23 Dering St, London W1R 9AA

KALMS, (Harold) Stanley; s of Charles Kalms (d 1978), and Cissie, *née* Schlagman (d 1990); *b* 21 Nov 1931; *Educ* Christ's Coll Finchley; *m* 28 Feb 1954, Pamela Audrey, da of Morris Jimack (d 1968), of London; 3 s (Richard b 10 March 1955, Stephen b 3 Dec 1956, Paul b 6 March 1963); *Career* chm Dixons Gp plc; non-exec dir Br Gas plc 1987-; Hon City and Guilds Insignia Award in Technol (Hon CGIA) 1988; *Recreations* communal educnl activities, sailing, opera; *Style—* Stanley Kalms, Esq; Dixons Gp plc, 29 Farm St, London W1X 7RD (☎ 071 499 3494, fax 071 629 1410, telex 923427)

KAMDAR, Batookrai Anopchand; s of Anopchand Keshavlal Kamdar, and Lilavati, *née* Shah; *b* 29 Oct 1939; *Educ* Gujarat Univ (MB BS), MRCS (tutor); *m* 27 May 1964, Dr Beni Kamdar, da of Dr Chandulal Chhotalal Shah, of Baroda, India; 1 s (Neel b 1965), 1 da (Sujata b 1967); *Career* orthopaedic registrar: Hammersmith Hosp 1970-71, Heatherwood Hosp Ascot Berks 1971-72; sr orthopaedic registrar Royal Free Hosp London 1973-75, conslt orthopaedic surgn Dartford and Gravesham Health Dist 1975-; memb: RSM, BMA, Br Orthopaedic Assoc; FRCSEd; *Pubns:* Complications Following Total Knee Replacement (1974), Soft Tissue Calcification Following Total Hip Replacement (1976), Early Soft Tissue Release in CTEV (1977); *Recreations* reading, music, philately, cricket; *Clubs* MCC; *Style—* Batookrai Kamdar, Esq; 7 Liskeard Close, Chislehurst, Kent BR7 6RT (☎ 081 467 9851); West Hill Hospital, Dartford, Kent; Blackheath Hospital, Blackheath, London; Fawkham Manor Hospital, Fawkham, Kent (☎ 0322 23223)

KAMIL, Geoffrey Harvey; s of Peter Kamil of Princess Court, Harrogate Road, Leeds, and Sadie, *née* Morris; *b* 17 Aug 1942; *Educ* Leeds GS, Univ of Leeds (LLB); *m* 17 March 1968, Andrea Pauline, da of Gerald Ellis, of Leeds; 2 da (Sharon b 1969, Debra b 1971); *Career* slr of Supreme Ct of Judicators 1968-, ptnr J Levi Leeds 1974-87; stipendiary magistrate W Midlands 1987-90 (dep 1985), W Yorkshire 1990; asst rec of Crown Ct 1986-; memb: Ctee of Leeds Law Soc 1982-87, Leeds Cts Ctee 1983-87, Leeds Duty Slr Ctee 1985-87; sec Stonham's Kirkstall Lodge Leeds 1974-87; *Recreations* golf, sailing, swimming, collectors' cars; *Clubs* Shirley Park Golf, Moor Allerton Golf; *Style—* Geoffrey Kamil, Esq

KAMINSKI, Stanislaw Aloyz; s of Walenty Kaminski (d 1975), of Toruñ, Poland, and Marta, *née* Kulczyk (d 1974); *b* 8 May 1925; *Educ* Polish Accountancy Sch for ex-soldiers Glasgow; *m* 1, 1949, Joan, da of John Marshall; 1 s (Michael b 2 Sept 1952), 1 da (Anne b 21 May 1950); m 2, Ceinwen Mary, da of William Morris; 1 s (Mark b 29 Jan 1962); *Career* WWII Polish Army 1941-45; trainee 1946-50: Hyde Park Hotel, Nell Gwyn House, RAC Pall Mall; gen asst Grand Hotel Harrogate 1950-54, asst mangr Seabank Hotel Porthcawl 1954-57, mangr Belgrave Hotel Tenby Wales 1957-64; Davies Hotels: gen mangr Ivy Bush Royal Hotel 1967 (md 1965-67, mangr 1964-65); Ivy Bush Royal Hotel (Corm) Ltd: mangr 1967-75, md Dyfed Outside Caterers 1967-75; gen mangr: Falcon Inns Ltd 1975-77, Trust House Forte Hotel Ltd 1977-80; md Landrise Hotels Ltd (Inn on the Avenue) Cardiff 1980-85; Gold Medalion award Welsh Tourist Bd 1985, Chevaliers du Testevin 1974, Master Innholder award 1978; Freeman City of London 1978, memb Worshipful Co of Innholders; memb: Carmarthenshire Tourist Ctee 1964-69, SW Wales Tourist Assoc 1964-69, Exec Ctee SW Tourist Cncl 1969-76, Mktg and Promotion Panel S Wales Tourist Cncl 1969-74, E Midland Div BHRCA 1969-74, Welsh Div BHRCA 1975-76; assoc memb S Wales Tourism Cncl 1969-76; FHCIMA 1976 (MHCIMA 1965); *Style—* Stanislaw Kaminski, Esq; San Amaro 2, 38400 Puerto de la Cruz, Tenerife, Canary Islands (☎ Tenerife 387264)

KAMINSKY, (Roman) David; s of Orist Kaminsky (d 1963), and Marion, *née* Jones; *b* 28 Dec 1950; *Educ* Stockland Green Bi-Lateral Sch, Manchester Coll of Art; *m* 24 May 1975, Elizabeth Louise, da of Albert Edward Walter Morley (d 1975); 1 s (Jonathan David b 27 Oct 1982), 1 da (Lydia Rose Marion b 7 Aug 1981); *Career* prodn mangr Constantine Colour Finishing Ltd 1980-87 (hand printer 1972-80), fndr Kaminski Photographic Labs Ltd 1987-; memb BIPP Fellowship and Associateship Selection Panel (sector 3) 1989-90; BIPP: licentiate 1978, assoc 1985, fell 1986; *Recreations* fly fishing, photography; *Style—* David Kaminsky, Esq; Kaminski Professional Photographic, Laboratories Ltd, 112-116 Park Hill Rd, Harborne, Birmingham B17 9HD (☎ 021 427 1160, fax 021 428 1442)

KAMLANA, Sikandar Hayat; s of Mehr Allah Dad Khan Kamlana Sial, and Saleh, *née* Bibi (d 1964); *b* 12 Sept 1946; *Educ* Nishtar Med Coll Multan Pakistan (MB BS), Conjoint Bd of London (DPM), Univ of Sheffield (Dip Psychotherapy); *m* 10 Oct 1971, Misbah Sultana, da of Chaudhry Qamar Dean (d 1989); 1 s (Ameen b 23 Aug 1981), 1 da (Shehneela b 7 Aug 1972); *Career* W Cumberland Hosp: sr house offr in psychiatry 1972-73, registrar 1974-77, sr registrar 1978-81, conslt 1982-; author of pubns on psychotherapy and related topics; MRCPsych 1977; *Recreations* tennis, badminton; *Style—* Dr Sikandar Kamlana; Balcraig, 33 Stainburn Rd, Workington, Cumbria CA14 1SW (☎ 0900 60 2618); West Cumberland Hosp, Hensingham, Whitehaven, Cumbria (☎ 0946 69 3181)

KAN, Sir Yuet-Keung; GBE (1979, CBE 1967, OBE 1959), JP; s of Kan Tong Po, JP; *b* 26 July 1913; *Educ* Hong Kong Univ, London Univ (BA); *m* 1940, Ida; 2 s, 1 da; *Career* slr; chm Hong Kong Trade Devpt Cncl 1979-83; pro chllr Chinese Univ of Hong Kong; Hon LLD: Hong Kong Univ, Chinese Univ; kt 1972; *Style—* Sir Yuet-Keung Kan, GBE, JP; Swire House, 11 Floor, Chater Rd, Hong Kong (☎ 010 852 238181)

KANABUS, Annabel; da of Sir Robert Sainsbury, and Lisa, *née* Van den Bergh; *b* 22 Jan 1948; *Educ* Francis Holland Sch, Univ of East Anglia (BSc); *m* 13 March 1975, Peter John Kanabus, s of Edward Kanabus; 2 s (Jason b 9 June 1976, Adrian b 15 Feb 1978); *Career* fndr and tstee of the charity Avert 1986-; tstee: St Thomas' Youth Centre, Sainsbury Unit Fund Univ of East Anglia; *Recreations* cycling, watching television; *Style—* Mrs Annabel Kanabus; Avert, PO Box 91, Horsham, West Sussex RH13 7YR (☎ 0403 864010, fax 0403 864235)

KANAKARATNAM, Dr Gunaseelan; s of Dr Arumugam Kanakaratnam, of Canberra, Australia, and Pathmawathy Pichamuttu (d 1985); *b* 20 April 1933; *Educ* Royal Coll Colombo Sri Lanka, Univ of Ceylon (MB BS), RCS (DPM); *Career* registrar Fairfields Hosp Hitchin Herts 1965, conslt psychiatrist Fairfields Hosp and Bedford Gen Hosp 1971; FRCPsych 1971; *Recreations* cricket, swimming, gardening, travel; *Style—* Dr Gunaseelan Kanakaratnam; Fairfield Hospital, near Stotfold, Hitchin, Herts SG5 4AA (☎ 0462 730123)

KANDER, Nadav; *b* 1961; *Career* photographic asst London 1981-85, established own studio in London and worked freelance on numerous major advertising campaigns 1986-; awards incl: AFAEP Gold award for landscape Photography 1989, award from Art Directors Club of NY 1989, Silver award for Best Photography for Creative Circle Honours 1990, 2 Awards of Excellence from Communications Arts 1990, winner Eurobest Photography 1990, 4 finalists' positions in Press Photography Eurobest Competition, AFAEP Silver award for landscape photography; exhibitions or publications of work incl: Selections of 1987 Image Magazine, Photographers Gallery London 1987, Special Photographers Co London 1987 and 1990, D & AD Annual 1988, 1989 and 1990, Lurt's Archive 1988, V & A 1988, New Tate Gallery, Communication Arts Photography Annual 1989 and 1990, Creative Circle Annual 1990; articles in various pubns incl: British Journal of Photography 1987, Direction Magazine 1988, SLR Magazine 1989, Campaign Press 1989, Graphis Magazine 1989, Conde Nast's Traveler Magazine; memb: AFAEP 1986, D & AD Assoc 1988, Judging Ctee of Photography Assoc of the Netherlands 1991; *Style—* Nadav Kander, Esq; c/o Nadav Kander Photography, 1/7 Britannia Row, London N1

KANE, (David) John; s of Harry Fitchet Kane (d 1987), and Mary, *née* Gordon Philip (d 1988); *b* 27 Oct 1945; *Educ* Brechin HS, Arbroath HS, Glasgow Acad of Music and Drama; *m* 1, 5 Jan 1965 (m dis 1972), Rosemary Rimmer; 1 da (Alice Tiffany b 17 Aug 1965); m 2, 14 Oct 1972, Alison Mary Hope Robine, *née* Warner; 1 s (Simon Leplastrier b 3 Nv 1974), 1 da Susanna Mary Louise b 27 Aug 1976); *Career* actor; characters played in RSC prodns: Puck in A Midsummer Night's Dream and Prince Myshkin in Subject to Fits 1965-72, Caliban in The Tempest 1988-89, Bob in Outside Edge at Hampstead and The Globe; writer or creator of TV series incl: Black Beauty, Dick Turpin, Son of The Bride, The Vamp, Cloppa Castle, The Feathered Serpent, Four Idle Hands, Smuggler, A Little Touch of Wisdom, Happy Ever After, Me and My Girl, Terry and June, Never the Twain, All in Good Faith; stage plays incl: The Rise and Fall of Rumplestiltskin, Murder Dear Watson, Plastic Birthday, The Scarlet Blade, Jack and the Beanstalk, Wizard of Oz, The Other Side of Paradise, Jumpin' Jehovah; *Recreations* reading, music, old films; *Style—* John Kane, Esq

KANE, Martin Christopher; s of Bernard Kane, of Milngavie, Glasgow, and Rosina, *née* Maguire; *b* 3 June 1958; *Educ* St Andrew's HS Clydebank Glasgow, Edinburgh Coll of Art (BA); *Career* artist; solo exhibitions: Artist of the Day (Angela Flowers Gallery) 1988, Memory and Imagination (Jill George Thumb Gallery London) 1990; gp exhibitions incl: student annual exhibition (Royal Scottish Acad) 1986 and 1987, New Generation (Compass Gallery Glasgow) 1987, Obsessions (Raab Gallery London) 1987, Two Scottish Artists (Boundary Gallery) 1988, Int Art Fair (LA with Thumb Gallery) 1989 and 1990, Art 90 (Design Centre London) 1990, London to Atlanta (Thumb Gallery, Atlanta USA) 1990; public collections: Glasgow District Cncl, Cleveland Museum Middlesborough, CBS Collection, Scottish Devpt Agency Glasgow; semi professional popular music bass guitarist; *Style—* Martin Kane, Esq; Thumb Gallery, 38 Lexington St, Soho, London (☎ 071 439 7319, fax 071 287 0478)

KANE, Richard George; s of Charles Edward Wright (d 1974), of Lincoln, and Mary Kathleen Wright; *b* 17 Sept 1938; *Educ* City Sch London, Univ of Leeds, RADA; *m* 1, 1967 (m dis 1972), Jean Hastings; m 2, 1975, Jenny Lee; 1 s (Tom b 1977); *Career* actor; theatre repertory work incl: Dundee, Glasgow Citizens, Bristol Old Vic, Oxford Playhouse, Manchester Stables, Chichester Festival Theatre, Edinburgh Lyceum; London Fringe: Royal Court, Hampstead Theatre Club, Greenwich Theatre, Bush, Open Space; West End roles incl: Mark Gertler in Bloomsbury (Phoenix) 1974, Nightingale in Vieux Carré (Piccadilly) 1978, Roger Dervish in Outside Edge (Queens) 1979, Leslie Bainbridge in Taking Steps (Lyric) 1980, Sir Benjamin Backbite in The School for Scandal (Duke of York) 1983, Ben Weeks in The Normal Heart (Albany) 1985, William Featherstone in How The Other Half Loves (Duke of York) 1988, Sidney Hopcroft in Absurd Person Singular (Whitehall) 1990; TV work incl: two series of Hot Metal (LWT) 1984 and 1986, The Insurance Man, Blind Justice (BBC), Inspector Morse (Zenith); film work incl: Col Weaver in A Bridge Too Far 1976, Gen Jaruselski in Squaring The Circle 1982; radio work incl: Kenrio Watanabe in Sweet Dreams (BBC) 1984, Henry in Henry And The Dogs 1986, Branston in The Event of The Season (BBC) 1987; wrote play Sweet Dreams (performed Colchester Mercury Theatre 1982, King's Head Theatre Club 1982, BBC Radio 1984); *Awards* Scottish Television Theatre award 1969, nominated Most Promising Newcomer of the Year 1968; *Recreations* football, reading; *Style—* Richard Kane, Esq; William Morris Agency (UK) Ltd, 31 Soho Square, London W1V 5DG (☎ 071 434 2191)

KANIS, Dr John Anthony; s of Max Kanis (d 1957) of London, and Elizabeth Mary, *née* Mees; *b* 2 Sept 1944; *Educ* Univ of Edinburgh (MB ChB); *m* 1, 11 April 1966 (m dis 1984), Patricia Sheila, *née* Mclaren; 4 da (Lisa b 13 Dec 1967, Emma b 24 Sept 1969, Sarah b 4 July 1971, Rebecca b 2 Jan 1975); m 2, 19 June 1989, Monique Nicole Christiane, da of Georges Marie Benéton, of Route du Moulinet 45290 Varennes-Changy, France; *Career* Welcome sr res fell Univ of Oxford 1976-79; conslt: Royal Hallamshire Hosp 1979-, Miny Health France 1981-; reader human metabolism Univ of Sheffield 1982-, pres Euro Fndn for Osteoporosis and Bone Disease 1987-, advsr osteoporosis WHO 1988-; ed Osteoforum, author of 400 scientific pubns on bone disease; FRCP 1984, FRCPE 1986, MRCPath 1982; *Books* Paget's Disease of the Bone; *Recreations* antiques restoration, genealogy; *Style—* Dr John Kanis; Park Elms, 3 Park Lane, Broomhall Park, Sheffield S10 2DU (☎ 0742 661242); Dept of Human Metabolism & Clinical Biochemistry, University of Sheffield Medical School, Beech Hill Rd, Sheffield S10 2RX (☎ 0742 739 176, fax 0742 726 938, tlx 547216 UGSHEF G)

KANTOROWICZ TORO, Donald; s of Rodolph Kantorowicz, and Blanca Livia, *née* Toro; *b* 4 Aug 1943; *Educ* Jesuit Sch Cali Colombia, Hochschule für Welthandel Vienna (MBA), LSE, Faculté de Droit et Sciences Economiques Paris (DEconSc); *m* 12 Sept 1973 (m dis 1986), Chantal, *née* Lancrenoa; 2 da (Melanie b 1976, Johana b 1978); *Career* Banque de L'Union Européenne Paris 1969-71, asst mangr Bank of Amercia Paris 1972-77, asst vice pres Bank of America Madrid 1977-78, vice pres and mangr Bank of America Barcelona 1979-80, md and chief exec Consolidado UK Ltd 1980-; memb French Fin Assoc Paris; *Recreations* skiing, sailing, classical music, history; *Clubs* Overseas Bankers, Interallie Paris; *Style—* Donald Kantorowicz Toro, Esq; 11 South Terrace, London SW7 (☎ 071 584 8185); Consolidado UK Ltd, Vestry House, Laurence Pountney Hill, London EC4R OEH (☎ 071 283 0801, fax 071 283 0875, telex 291109)

KAO, Prof Charles K; s of Chun-Hsian Kao, of Hong Kong, and Sin-Fang, *née* King (d 1976); *b* 4 Nov 1933; *Educ* St Joseph's Coll Hong Kong, Univ of London (BSc, PhD); *m* 19 Sept 1959, Gwen May-Wan da of Ping-Sum Wong (d 1946), of UK; 1 s (Simon b 1961, Amanda b 1963); *Career* Standard Telephones and Cables Ltd 1957-60, Standard Telecommunications Laboratories Ltd 1961-70, Chm Dept Electronics The Chinese Univ of Hong Kong 1970-74, chief scientist and dir engrg Electro-Optical Products Div ITT Roanoke Va, USA 1974-82, exec scientist and corp dir res ITT Advanced Technology Centre Connecticut USA 1982-87, vice chancellor The Chinese Univ of Hong Kong 1987-; Freeman City of Genoa Italy; Hon DSc: The Chinese Univ of Hong Kong 1985, Univ of Sussex 1990; memb Nat Acad of Engrg USA, foreign memb Royal Swedish Academy of Engrg Sciences Sweden; FIEE, FIEEE, FEng, fell Royal Soc for the encouragement of Arts, Manufactures and Commerce; *Books* author of Optical Fiber Systems: Technology, Design and Applications (1982), Optical Fibre (IEE Materials and Devices Series 6, 1988); *Recreations* tennis, hiking, gourmet cooking; *Clubs* Royal Hong Kong Jockey, The Hong Kong Country, World Trade Centre (Hong Kong); *Style—* Prof Charles Kao; Vice-Chancellor's Office, The Chinese University of Hong Kong, Shatin, N T, Hong Kong (☎ 010 852 603 6333, fax 010 852 603 6197, telex 50301 CUHK HX)

KAPLAN, Hon Mrs (Edwina); *née* Sandys; da (by 1 m) of Baron Duncan-Sandys, CH, PC; *b* 1938; *m* 1, 1960 (m dis 1973), Pierson John Shirley Dixon, MP, s of late Sir Pierson John Dixon, GCMG, CB; 2 s; m 2, 1985, Richard D Kaplan; *Style—* The Hon Mrs Kaplan; 210 E 46th St, NY 10017, USA

KAPOOR, Anish; *Educ* Hornsey Coll of Art London, Chelsea Sch of Art; *Career* artist, sculptor; teacher Wolverhampton Poly 1979, artist in res Walker Art Gallery Liverpool 1982; one person exhibition incl: Patrice Alexandre Paris 1980, Lisson Gallery 1983, 1985, 1988 and 1989-90, Walker Art Gallery Liverpool 1982 & 1983, Barbara Gladstone Gallery NY 1984, 1986 and 1989-90, Stedelijk Van Abbermuseum

Erndhoven 1986, Ray Hughes Gallery 1987, Br Pavilion Venice 1990, Palacio de Velazguez Madrid 1991, Feuerle Koln 1991; gp exhibitions incl: Art Into Landscape 1 (Serpentine Gallery London) 1974, Young Contemporaries (Royal Academy London) 1975, London/New York 1982 (Lisson Gallery London) 1982, Paris Biennale (Paris) 1982, India: Myth and Reality (Museum of Modern Art Oxford) 1982, Finland Biennale (Helsinki) 1983, Sculpture 1983 (Van Krimpen Gallery Amsterdam) 1983, New Art (Tate) 1983, An International Survey of Recent Painting and Sculpture (Museum of Modern Art NY) 1984, Nouvelle Biennale de Paris (Paris) 1985, Europa oggi/Europe now (Museo d'Arte Contemporanea Italy) 1988, Starlit Waters, British Sculpture: An International Art 1968-88 (Tate Gallery Liverpool) 1988, Heroes of Contemporary Art (Galerie Saqqarah Switzerland) 1990-91, British Art Now (touring) 1990-91; *Style*— Anish Kapoor, Esq; Lisson Gallery (London) Ltd, 67 Lisson St, London NW1 5DA (☎ 071 724 2739, fax 071 724 7124)

KAPP, Carlo David; s of Robert Scope Kapp (d 1975), of Hayling Is, Hants, and Paola Luisa, *née* Putoto; *b* 31 July 1947; *Educ* Ladybarn Sch Manchester; *m* 1, 28 March 1970 (m dis 1978), Jean Gillian, da of Aubrey Charles Overington (d 1980), of Richmond, Surrey; 1 da (Kelli Anne b 4 July 1977); m 2, 30 Oct 1979, Basia Evelyn, da of Dr Abraham Seinwel Bardach (d 1988), of London; 1 s (Daniel Joseph Scope b 5 Oct 1980), 1 da (Pippa Luisa b 25 Feb 1983); *Career* jt display mangr Marshal & Snelgrove Manchester 1966-67, design dir Kempthorns Richmond 1967-68, interior display mangr Debenham & Freebody 1968-70, display mangr Swears & Wells Group, overseas sabbatical 1971-74, creative servs mangr Estee Lauder Group (UK) 1974-81; chm and md: Dawson Kapp Overseas 1981-88, The DKO Group plc 1988-; govr RNLI; memb: The Little Ship Club, Greenpeace; *Recreations* shooting, golf, skiing, marathon running, sailing; *Clubs* RAC, Les Ambassadors, LSC, Wimbledon Park Golf; *Style*— Carlo Kapp, Esq; Kiln House, 210 New King's Rd, London SW6 (☎ 071 384 1941, fax 071 384 1874)

KARA, Peter Bhupatsingh; s of Bhimsingh Kara (d 1968), of S Africa; *b* 5 July 1944; *Educ* Damelin Coll S Africa; *m* 1969, Gita, da of Gulabsingh Parmar, of India; 1 s, 1 da; *Career* fin dir Arthur Woollacott Holdings Ltd; dir: Wrappings & Packings (Engineering) Ltd, R Peters (London) Ltd, Eulatimex Ltd, Gwelo Manufacturing Co Ltd, Charles Pretzlik & Son Ltd, Jolly Bags Ltd, Interactive Educational Services Ltd, Lowfield Securities Ltd (md), EP Packaging Ltd, Lobbyglen Ltd; memb Assoc of Certified Accountants, MInstD; *Style*— Peter Kara, Esq; 11 Fitzroy Sq, London W1 (☎ 071 388 9591); 73 Windmill Hill Drive, Bletchley, Bucks

KARAT, David Spencer; s of Lt Rene Karat, and Frances, *née* Levy; *b* 1 Aug 1951; *Educ* Merchant Taylors, Univ of Leicester (LLB); *m* 1 Sept 1976, Shirley Lessels, da of Capt Edward Addison Williams; 2 da (Florence Louisa b 22 Sept 1980, Emma Rachel b 21 May 1985); *Career* slr Slaughter & May 1976, gp counsel Royal Bank of Canada 1980; md: Merrill Lynch 1989 (assoc dir 1984, exec dir 1986), Salomon Brothers International Limited 1990; memb Fin Advsy Ctee Save The Children, memb Law Soc; *Recreations* tennis, running, theatre, jazz and classical music; *Clubs* RAC; *Style*— David S Karat, Esq; Victoria Plaza, 111 Buckingham Palace Rd, London SW1W 0SB (☎ 071 721 3805, fax 071 736 5773)

KARK, Austen Steven; CBE (1987); s of Maj Norman Kark, and Ethel, *née* Goldberg (d 1980); *b* 20 Oct 1926; *Educ* Upper Canada Coll Toronto, Nautical Coll Pangbourne, RNC, Magdalen Coll Oxford (MA); *m* 1, 1949 (m dis 1954), Margaret Solomon, da of S Schmahmann, of S Africa; 2 da (Catherine b 1950, Teresa b 1953); m 2, 1954, Nina Mary (novelist Nina Bawden, *qv*), da of Cdr Charles Mabey (d 1976), of Herne Bay; 1 da (Perdita b 1957), 2 step s (Nicholas Bawden (d 1983), Robert Bawden); *Career* Midshipman RIN 1944-46, E Indies Flt, HMS Nelson, HMS London; dir first prodn of Sartre's The Flies Oxford 1948; BBC: joined 1954, head S Euro Serv 1964, E Euro and Russian Serv 1972, ed World Serv 1973, controller Eng Servs 1974, advsr the late Lord Soames on election broadcasting Rhodesia, chm Harare Govt Report on Radio and TV Zimbabwe, md external broadcasting 1984-86 (dep md 1981-84), ret 1986; chm: seminar in American Studies UK Alumni Salzburg 1979-85, CPC Guide books 1987; UK del CSCE London Info Forum 1989; *Recreations* real tennis, travelling, mosaics; *Clubs* Oriental, MCC, Royal Tennis Ct; *Style*— Austen Kark, Esq, CBE; 22 Noel Rd, London N1 8HA

KARLWEIS, Georges Joseph Christophe; s of Oskar Karlweis, and Ferdinanda Gabrielle, *née* Coulon; *b* 25 Jan 1928; *Educ* Univ of Paris (LLB); *m* 6 June 1986, Brigitte, da of Robert Camplez; *Career* economical corr AGEFI Paris 1946-52, sec gen Société Industrielle des Huiles au Marac Casablanca Morocco 1952-55, with Baron Edmond de Rothschild's gp 1955- (currently on the bd of numerous int gp cos); *Clubs* Golf of Geneva, Golf du Domaine Impérial de Gland (Switz), Golf of Cannes-Mougins, Golf of Mortefontaine (France), Maxim's Business (Paris); *Style*— Georges Karlweis, Esq; La Petite Pommeraie, 3 Chemin Palud, 1292 Pregny-Geneva, Switzerland, 199 Bd St Germain, 75007 Paris (☎ 022 758 2479); Banque Privée Edmond de Rothschild S A 18 rue de Hesse, 1204 Geneva, Switzerland (☎ 022 21 91 11, car 077 24 98 82, fax 022 21 16 77)

KARN, Prof Valerie Ann; da of Arthur Frederick Thomas Karn (d 1968), and Winnifred Alice Whisson; *b* 17 May 1939; *Educ* Newquay Co GS, Lady Margaret Hall Oxford (BA), Univ of the Punjab Lahore Pakistan, Grad Sch of Design Harvard Univ; 1 da (Jacqui b 1974); *Career* res fell inst of social and econ res York Univ 1964-66, sr lectr centre for urban and regnl studies Birmingham Univ (formerly res assoc, lectr) 1966-84, res fell Urban Inst and advsr to the Dept of Housing and Urban Development Washington DC USA 1979-80, prof of environmental health and housing Salford Univ and dir Salford Centre for Housing Studies 1984-; memb: NW Regnl Ctee Anchor Housing Assoc 1986-88, Ctee of Inquiry into Glasgow's Housing 1986-88; chm Supervisory Gp of the feasibility study for Hulme Estate Manchester 1986-88, memb Academic Bd Salford Coll of Technol 1987-(formerly chm Special Projects Ctee Copec Housing Tst Birmingham); res offr to the Central Housing Advsy Ctee 1967-69 (memb Sub Ctee housing mgmnt The Cullingworth Ctee 1967-69), memb Housing Servs Advsy Gp DOE 1976-79, memb Duke of Edinburgh's Inquiry into Br Housing 1984-85, special cmmr Cmmn for Rural Equality (on an inquiry into Liverpool City Cncl'c housing allocations), chm Res Steering Gp Nat Fedn Housing Assocs 1988-(memb 1984-), external advsr Inst of Housings professional qualification, chm Editorial Bd Roof (Shelter's housing jl 1986); memb Assoc of the Inst of Housing; *Books* various articles and books incl: Retiring to the Seaside (1977), The Consumers Experience of Housing (ed with C Ungerson, 1980), Home Ownership in the Inner City (with P Williams and J Kemeny, 1985), Race, Class and Public Housing (with J Henderson, 1986); *Recreations* gardening; *Style*— Prof Valerie Karn; 71 Barton Rd, Worsley M28 4PF (☎ 061 794 7791); Environmental Health and Housing, Telford Building, Univ of Salford, Salford M5 (☎ 061 736 5843 ext 7308)

KARNEY, Andrew Lumsdaine; s of Rev Gilbert Henry Peter Karney, and Celia Finch Wigham, *née* Richardson; gf Rt Rev Arthur B L Karney, First Bishop of Johannesburg; *b* 24 May 1942; *Educ* Rugby, Trinity Coll Cambridge; *m* 1969, Beryl Fleur, da of late Louis Goldwyn, of Australia; 1 s (Peter John b 1972); *Career* staff memb UN Relief and Works Agency Beirut and Gaza Strip 1963-64, devpt engr for Standard Telephones and Cables London and Paris 1965-68, sr scientist General Electric Co Hirst Res Centre 1968-71, planning engr communications Br Gas Corp 1972-73, conslt Logica plc 1973-, chm Logica Communications Ltd 1984-; dir: Cable London plc 1984-86, Logica General Systems Spa Italy 1984-, Logica Technol Services Ltd Hong Kong 1986-, Logica plc 1986-, Logica Data Architects Inc USA 1988-90, Logica Aerospace and Defence Ltd 1989-; corp devpt dir Logica plc 1989-; memb Ctee Nat Electronics Cncl 1989-; *Recreations* travel, photography; *Style*— Andrew Karney, Esq; 16 Kemplay Rd, London NW3 1SY; Logica, 68 Newman St, London W1A 4SE (☎ 071 637 9111, fax 071 387 3578)

KARSLAKE, Brig Antony Edward Kent; s of Edward Kent Haliburton Karslake (d 1988), of George Nympton, N Devon, and Eleanor Paget Musgrave, *née* Harvey; *b* 9 Sept 1932; *Educ* Eton, ChCh Oxford (MA); *m* 31 Aug 1956, June Pauline, da of Henry William Harris Eastwood (d 1981), of Long Mynd, Hexham, Northumberland; 2 s (John, William), 2 da (Caroline, Sarah); *Career* cmmnd Kings Royal Rifle Corps 1955, seconded Capt 4 King's African Rifles 1957-60, NATO Staff Allied Land Forces Central Europe 1961-63, tech staff course RMCS 1964-66, Royal Green Jackets 1966, Lt-Col Ecole Superieure de Guerre Paris 1973-75, Col-Brig MOD 1980-88, ret 1988; *Recreations* shooting, travel; *Clubs* Army and Navy; *Style*— Brig Antony Karslake; Nymert St George House, George Nympton, South Molton, N Devon; Parsonage House, Watchfield, Oxon

KARSTEN, Ian George Francis; QC (1990); s of Dr Frederick Karsten, and Edith Karsten; *b* 27 July 1944; *Educ* William Ellis Sch Highgate, Magdalen Coll Oxford (MA, BCL); *m* 25 May 1984, Moira Elizabeth Ann, da of Wing Cdr Laurence O'Hara; 2 da (Lucy Caroline Jane b 9 Oct 1985, Emma Catherine Louise b 17 June 1988); *Career* called to the Bar Grays Inn 1967; Midland and Oxford Circuit; in practice 1970-; lectr in law: Univ of Southampton 1966-70, LSE 1970-88; delegate to Hague Conf on Private Int Law 1973-77 (Convention on the Law Applicable to Agency, appointed rapporteur), ldr UK Delegation to Unidroit Conf (Convention on Agency in the Int Sale of Goods) Bucharest 1979 and Geneva 1983, legal assessor UK Cncl for Nursing Midwifery and Health Visiting 1989-; diplomé of Hague Acad of Int Law; *Books* "Conflict of Laws" Halsbury's Laws of England (co-author 4 edn, 1974); *Recreations* opera, travel, chess; *Style*— Ian Karsten, Esq, QC

KARTEN, Ian Herman; s of Israel Karten (d 1945), and Helen, *née* Baron (d 1976); *b* 14 Dec 1920; *Educ* private, Univ of London (BSc); *m* 9 Dec 1968, Mildred Elizabeth, da of Selim Laurence Hart (d 1973); *Career* RAF cmmnd (technical branch) Pilot Offr 1942, serv HQ Bomber Cmd, Air Disarmament Denmark (despatches 1946), demobilised Flt Lt 1946; Multitone Electronics plc (formerly Multitone Electric Co Ltd): joined 1947, mfrg mangr, export mangr, gen mangr, md 1961, chm and chief exec offr 1978-; *Recreations* reading, music; *Clubs* Athenaeum; *Style*— Ian Karten, Esq; The Mill House, Newark, Ripley, Surrey GU23 6DP (☎ 0483 225 020); Multitone Electronics plc, 12 Underwood St, London N1 7JT (☎ 071 253 7611, fax 071 253 8409, telex 266518)

KASER, Michael Charles; s of Charles Joseph Kaser (d 1983), of St Albans, Herts, and Mabel Lucina, *née* Blunden (d 1976); *b* 2 May 1926; *Educ* Gunnersbury Catholic GS, Wimbledon Coll, Kings Coll Cambridge (BA, MA), Univ of Oxford (MA); *m* 13 May 1954, Elizabeth Ann Mary, da of Cyril Gascoigne Piggford (d 1956), of Springs, SA; 4 s (Gregory b 1955, Matthew b 1956, Benet b 1959, Thomas b 1962), 1 da (Lucy b 1968); *Career* economist; chief sci advsr Dept Miny of Works 1946-47, Economic Intelligence Dept FO 1947-51, second sec HM Embassy Moscow 1949, economic affrs offr UN Economic Cmmn for Europe Geneva 1951-63, visiting prof Graduate Inst of Int Studies Univ of Geneva 1959-63; Univ of Oxford: Leverhulme res fell St Antony's Coll 1960-62, faculty fell St Antony's Coll 1963-72, faculty lectr in Soviet economics 1963-72, govr Plater Coll 1968-, professorial fell St Antony's Coll 1972-, reader in economics 1972-, assoc fell Templeton Coll 1983-, dir Inst of Russian Soviet and East Euro Studies 1988-, chm Advsy Cncl for Adult Educn Oxford 1972-78, Latin preacher Univ Church of St Mary the Virgin 1982; visiting fell Henley Mgmnt Coll 1986-; sec Cwlth Assoc of Geneva 1956-63; memb: Cncl Royal Economic Soc 1976-86 and 1987-90, Royal Inst of Int Affrs 1979-85 and 1986-, Exec Ctee Int Economic Assoc 1974-83 and 1986- (gen ed 1986-), Int Social Sciences Cncl (UNESCO) 1980-, Advsy Bd Inst for East-West Security Studies NY 1989-90; chm: Coordinating Cncl of Area Studies Assocs 1986-88, Wilton Park Acad Cncl (FCO) 1986-; pres Br Assoc for Soviet Slavic and East Euro Studies 1988- (previously first chm and then memb Ctee Nat Assoc for Soviet and East Euro Studies 1964-); sec Br Acad Ctee for S E Euro Studies 1988-; KSG 1990; *Books* Comecon: Integration Problems of the Planned Economies (1965 and 1967), Soviet Economics (1970), Planning in Eastern Europe (jtly 1970), The New Economic Systems of Eastern Europe (1975), The Soviet Union since the Fall of Khrushchev (1975), Health Care in the Soviet Union and Eastern Europe (1976), Soviet Policy for the 1980's (1982); gen ed: The Cambridge Encyclopedia of Russia and the Soviet Union (1982-), The Economic History of Eastern Europe 1919-75 (3 vols 1985-86); *Recreations* walking; *Clubs* Reform; *Style*— Michael Kaser, Esq; 7 Chadlington Rd, Oxford OX2 6SY (☎ 0865 515 581); St Antony's Coll, Oxford OX2 6JF (☎ 0865 596 51, fax 0865 310 518)

KASKET, Esther; *née* Laredo; da of Joseph Solomon Laredo (d 1972), and Allegra, *née* Maratchi; both families mentioned in histories of Moroccan, Gibraltarian, Spanish and Mancunian Jewry; the Laredos (Christians and Jews) granted coat of arms in 1254 by Don Alfonso VIII; *b* 16 March 1930; *Educ* Mrs Pratt's Private Eng Sch Mazagan Morocco, Lycée de Jeunes Filles Casablanca, Manchester HS for Girls, Newnham Coll Cambridge (BA, MA); *m* 20 April 1958, Harold Kasket, s of Maurice Kasket (d 1969); 1 s (Alan Joseph b 1963), 1 da (Anna Caroline b 1962); *Career* exec with Mullens & Co govt brokers 1951-59, pt/t teaching 1959-68, returned to stockbroking James Capel & Co 1968-76; joined Laurence Prust & Co (later ptnr) 1976, ptnr Laurence Prust & Co Ltd 1985-86, memb Exec Bd Laurence Prust Broking Securities Ltd 1987-90 (dir 1986-90), investment conslt National Provident Institution 1990-; memb Ctee Woman of the Year Assoc; exhibited paintings and drawings at Hampstead Arts Club and Stock Exchange Art Soc; *Recreations* painting, horse-riding, gardening, theatre, music; *Clubs* Parrot; *Style*— Mrs Esther Kasket; 7 Lymington Rd, London NW6 1HX (☎ 071 794 5251); 48 Gracechurch St, London EC3P 3HH

KASMIN, Aaron Augustus; s of John Kasmin, of London, and Jane, *née* Nicholson; *b* 23 Aug 1963; *Educ* Bousfield London, Ashfold Bucks, Port Regis Dorset, David Game Tutors London, Hogarth Tutors London, Chelsea Sch of Art; *m* 30 Sept 1988, Sarah Elizabeth, da of David Patrick Shane; *Career* artist; solo exhibitions: Gallery 24 1986, Albermarle Gallery 1987 and 1988; gp exhibitions: Artist of The Day (Angela Flowers Gallery) 1985, Albermarle Gallery 1987 and 1991, Contemporary Art Soc Art Market 1988-89; *Recreations* collecting tribal art, carpet croquet, travelling; *Style*— Aaron Kasmin, Esq; 20 Ifield Rd, London SW10 (☎ 071 352 0746)

KASSEM, Tarek Jamal Hamid; s of Jamal Hamid Kassem, and Nadida Saeed, *née* Fahoum; *b* 28 Aug 1946; *Educ* City of London Poly; *m* 1 (m dis 1984), Salma Rayes; 1 s (Khaled Tarek b 1975); m 2, 28 June 1985, Susan Wendy Mary Kassem, JP, da of Harold James Boylet, of Guildford, Surrey; *Career* trainee: Arabian American Oil Co Dahran Saudi Arabia, Electro-Components Holdings Ltd 1969-70; asst sec George Wills & Co Holdings Ltd 1970-73, Vickers de Costa London 1973-74, Arab Bank Investment Co Ltd 1974-87, Quanta Group Holdings Ltd 1987-; chm R & G Fin Consultants Ltd 1988, non-exec dir Walker Crips Weddle Beck plc 1989; memb Arab

Bankers Assoc London; *Recreations* tennis, photography, reading; *Style*— Tarek Kassem, Esq; Empire House, 8-14 St Martin's-le-Grand, London EC1A 4AD (☎ 071 606 7491, fax 071 606 9827, telex 886318 QUANTA G)

KATIN, Peter Roy; s of Jerrold Katin, and Gertrude May Katin (d 1975); *b* 14 Nov 1930; *Educ* RAM; *Career* pianist; musical talent evident at age of four, admitted to RAM at age of twelve; debut: Wigmore Hall 1948, Henry Wood Promenade Concert (with Tchaikovsky's second Concerto) 1952; first postwar Br artist to make a solo tour of the USSR 1958; early influences incl: Clifford Curzon, Claudio Arrau and Myra Hess; recordings incl: the complete Mozart Sonatas, the Chopin Nocturnes and Impromptus, the complete Grieg Lyric Pieces, pieces by Schubert, Tchaikovsky, Schumann, Rachmaninov, Brahms, Scarlatti and Mendelssohn; composer of various piano pieces and songs, the song cycle Sequence (words by Charlotte Morrow) and various cadenzas to Beethoven and Mozart Concertos; series of subscription recitals and master classes for young artists 1968-78, prof RAM 1956-60, visiting prof Univ of W Ontario 1978-84; *Awards* Eric Brough meml prize 1942, Chopin arts award 1977; ARCM 1952, FRAM 1960; *Recreations* theatre, literature, writing, photography, record collections; *Style*— Peter Katin, Esq; Helen Sykes Management, West End House, 33 Lower Richmond Rd, London SW14 7EZ (☎ 081 876 8276, fax 081 876 8277)

KATO, Takashi; *b* 1 Feb 1935; *Educ* Hitotsu Bashi Univ (BA); *m* 31 Oct 1965, Sonoko; 1 s (Daisaku), 1 da (Yukiko); *Career* The Nikko Securities Co Ltd Tokyo: joined 1959, mangr for Securities Dept 1971, seconded and exec vice-pres United Chase Merchant Bankers Singapore 1978, returned Tokyo 1981, gen mangr Int Fin Div 1982, gen mangr Int Planning Div 1983; md The Nikko Bank (UK) plc 1989 (dep md 1988); *Recreations* antiques, reading, music; *Clubs* Overseas Bankers; *Style*— Takashi Kato, Esq; The Nikko Bank (UK) plc, Nikko House, 17 Godliman St, London EC4V 5BD (☎ 071 528 7070, 071 528 7077, telex 928703 NIKOBK, car 0836 285 778)

KATZ, Sir Bernard; s of Max Katz (d 1971); *b* 26 March 1911; *Educ* Univ of Leipzig (MD), Univ of London (PhD, DSc); *m* 1945, Marguerite Penly; 2 s; *Career* served WWII Flt Lt RAAF; prof and head of Biophysics Dept UCL 1952-78, emeritus prof 1978-; Nobel prize (jtly) for Physiology and Medicine 1970; FRS 1952; kt 1969; *Style*— Sir Bernard Katz, FRS; University College, London WC1E 6BT (☎ 071 387 7050)

KAUFFMANN, Prof C Michael; s of Arthur Kauffmann (d 1983), and Tamara, *née* Karp (d 1977); *b* 5 Feb 1931; *Educ* St Paul's, Merton Coll Oxford, Warburg Inst Univ of London (jr res fell, PhD); *m* 1954, Dorothea, *née* Hill; 2 s (Francis b 1957, Martin b 1962); *Career* asst curator Photographic Collection Warburg Inst 1957, keeper Manchester City Art Gallery 1958-60; V&A Museum: asst keeper 1960-75, asst to the Dir 1963-66, keeper Dept of Prints & Drawings and Paintings 1975-85, prof of history of art and dir Courtauld Inst of Art Univ of London 1985-; pubns: The Baths of Puzzuoli: medieval illuminations of Peter of Eboli's poem 1959, An Altar-piece of the Apocalypse 1968, Victoria & Albert Museum Catalogue of Foreign Paintings 1973, British Romanesque Manuscripts 1975, Catalogue of Paintings in the Wellington Museum 1982, John Varley 1984; FBA 1987, FMA, FSA; *Style*— Prof C M Kauffmann; Director, Courtauld Institute of Art, Somerset House, Strand, London WC2R 0RN (☎ 071 872 0220)

KAUFMAN, Rt Hon Gerald Bernard; PC (1978), MP (Lab) Manchester Gorton 1983-; s of Louis Kaufman, and Jane Kaufman; *b* 21 June 1930; *Educ* Leeds GS, Queen's Coll Oxford; *Career* political staff Daily Mirror 1955-64, political corr New Statesman 1964-65, Lab Parly press liaison offr 1965-70, MP (Lab) Manchester Ardwick 1970-83, Parly under sec Environment 1974-75, Parly under sec Indust 1975, min of state Dept of Indust 1975-79; oppn front bench spokesman and memb Shadow Cabinet: Environment 1980-83, Home Affrs 1983-87, Foreign and Cwlth Affairs 1987-; *Style*— The Rt Hon Gerald Kaufman, MP; 87 Charlbert Court, Eamont St, London NW8 (☎ 071 722 6264)

KAUKAS, Bernard Aloysius; MBE (1984); s of Joseph Kaukas (d 1964), of Tottenham, and Ethel Mary, *née* Morgan-Adlam (d 1979); *b* 30 July 1922; *Educ* St Ignatius Coll Stamford Hill, Northern Poly London (DipArch); *m* 23 May 1945, Pamela Dora, da of David Widdowson, MBE (d 1980), of Hampstead Garden Suburb; 1 s (Christopher David b 6 Sept 1946), 1 da (Amanda Mary (Mrs Burroughs) b 18 June 1954); *Career* RN 1941-46; BR: planning offr 1946-68, chief architect 1968-74, devpt dir Property Bd 1974-77, dir of environment 1977-84; planning conslt to Michael Burroughs Assoc 1984-; memb Int Cncl on Monuments and Sites; ARIBA 1952, FRSA 1977; *Recreations* painting, writing, collecting; *Clubs* Savage; *Style*— Bernard Kaukas, Esq, MBE; 13 Lynwood Road, Ealing, London W5 1JQ (☎ 081 998 1499)

KAVANAGH, Prof Dennis Anthony; s of Patrick Joseph Kavanagh, and Agnes, *née* Campbell; *b* 27 March 1941; *Educ* St Anselm's Coll, Univ of Manchester (BA, MA); *m* 13 Aug 1966, Monica Anne, *née* Taylor; 1 s (David b 20 Nov 1970), 3 da (Jane b 24 July 1968, Catherine b 4 Nov 1972, Helen b 3 Jan 1981); *Career* currently prof politics Univ of Nottingham; *Books* books incl: The British General Election of February 1974 (with David Butler), The British General Election of 1979 (with David Butler), British Politics Today (with W Jones), New Trends in British Politics (ed, with Richard Rose), The Politics of the Labour Party (ed), Political Science and Political Behaviour, The British General Election 1983 (with David Butler), Thatcherism and British Politics, The British General Election of 1987 (with David Butler), Consensus Politic from Attlee to Thatcher (with Peter Morris), The Thatcher Effect (ed, with Anthony Seldon), Comparative Government and Politics, Personalities and Politics; *Recreations* running, tennis; *Style*— Prof Dennis Kavanagh; 4 Florence Boot Close, University Park, Nottingham; Politics Dept, Nottingham University, University Park, Nottingham NG7 2RD (☎ 0602 484848)

KAVANAGH, Patrick Joseph; s of H E (Ted) Kavanagh (d 1958), and Agnes O'Keefe (d 1985); *b* 6 Jan 1931; *Educ* Douai Sch, Lycée Jaccard, Merton Coll Oxford (MA); *m* 1, 1956, Sally (d 1958), da of Hon Mrs R N Philipps (Rosamond Lehmann), and Lord Milford; m 2, 1964, Catherine, da of Sir John Ward, GCMG, of St Margaret's Bay, Kent; 2 s (Cornelius b 1966, Bruno b 1969); *Career* actor 1959-70; writer, columnist The Spectator 1983-; *Poems* One and One (1960), On the Way to the Depot (1977), About Time (1970), Edward Thomas in Heaven (1974), Life Before Death (1979), Selected Poems (1982), Presences (1987); *novels* A Song and Dance (1968, Guardian Fiction Prize), A Happy Man (1972), People and Weather (1979), Only by Mistake (1986), The Perfect Stranger (autobiography, Richard Hillary Prize 1966); *for children* Scarf Jack (1978), Rebel for Good (1980); *edited* Collected Poems of Ivor Gurney (1982), The Essential G K Chesterton (1985), Oxford Book of Short Poems (with James Michie); *essays* People and Places (1988); *travel* Finding Connections; *Style*— P J Kavanagh, Esq; Peters Fraser & Dunlop, 5th Floor, The Chambers, Chelsea Harbour, Lots Rd, London SW10 0XT

KAVANAGH, Peter Richard Michael; s of Patrick Bernard Kavanagh, CBE, QPM, of Epsom, and Beryl Annie, *née* Williams (d 1984); *b* 20 Feb 1959; *Educ* Wimbledon Coll, Gonville and Caius Coll Cambridge (BA, MA); *m* 16 Nov 1985, Vivien Mary, da of Gordon Samuel Hart, of Bromham, Bedfordshire; 1 da (Emma b 1988); *Career* admitted slr 1984; ptnr Theodore Goddard 1989; memb Law Soc; *Style*— Peter Kavanagh, Esq; Theodore Goddard, 150 Aldersgate St, London EC1A 4EJ (☎ 071 606 8855, fax 071 606 4390)

KAVANAGH, Susan (Sue) (Mrs Michael Kavanagh); da of Leslie Simon Koppenhagen (d 1962) of London, and Bella, *née* Pollitzer (d 1953); *b* 8 Feb 1935; *Educ* The Grove Sch Surrey, Byam Shaw Sch of Art, Putney Sch of Art; *m* 1959, Michael Kavanagh, s of Jack Kavanagh; 2 s (Simon James b 1962, Julian Gavin b 1970), 1 da (Amanda Isabella b 1960); *Career* artist; freelance artist 1955; asst to John Ryan 1956-60 (drawing cartoons incl Harris Tweed for Eagle comic and Lettice Leaf for Girl, assisting in animations for Captain Pugwash); freelance illustration and greeting cards; solo exhibitions: Montpelier Studio Gallery London 1987 and 1990, Grapelane Gallery York 1990; gp exhibitions incl: Royal Acad Summer Exhibitions 1977-85, The Soc for Rural Britain 1981, Nat Soc of Painters Sculptors & Printmakers (Mall Gallery) 1983, The Royal Soc Exhibition of Flowers & Gardens (Mall Gallery) 1984, The Royal Soc of Painters in Water Colours (Mall Gallery 1984 and 1985, Bankside Gallery 1985), Bath Festival 1985, Evening Standard Campaign for London 1984, World of Water Colours (Fulham) 1986 and 1987, Sunday Times Exhibition for English Landscape and Seascape (Mall Gallery) 1987, pictures for New Wing St George's Hosp 1987, Mixed Exhibition Water Colours (Fulham Gallery) 1988, 20th Century Contemporary Arts Fair 1988, Open exhibition for watercolours (Bankside Gallery) 1988 and 1990, New English Club open exhibition 1988; assoc memb Nat Soc of Painters Etchers & Sculptors 1983, World of Watercolours 1987-88 (Park Lane Hotel); *Recreations* opera, concerts, theatre, music, travelling; *Clubs* Chelsea Arts; *Style*— Ms Sue Kavanagh; 29 Edwardes Square, Kensington, London W8 6HH; Oak House, Four Elms, Kent; Studio 7 Pembroke Mews (☎ 071 603 8559, 071 938 2486)

KAVANAGH, Trevor Michael Thomas; s of Bernard George Kavanagh (d 1978), and Alice Rose, *née* Thompson; *b* 19 Jan 1943; *Educ* Reigate GS; *m* 1967, Jacqueline Gai, da of John Swindells; 2 s (Benjamin b 14 June 1969, Simon John b 20 March 1971); *Career* currently political ed The Sun London; chm The Lobby House of Commons Westminster 1990-91; *Recreations* golf, swimming; *Clubs* RAC, Pall Mall; *Style*— Trevor Kavanagh, Esq; The Sun, PO Box 481, Virginia St, London E1 9BD (☎ 071 782 4000, telex 262135)

KAY, Sir Andrew Watt; s of David Watt Kay; *b* 14 Aug 1916; *Educ* Ayr Acad, Univ Glasgow (MD, ChM, DSc); *m* 1943, Janetta Main Roxburgh; 2 s, 2 da; *Career* served WWII Maj RAMC; prof of surgery Univ of Sheffield 1958-64, regius prof of surgery Univ of Glasgow 1964-81, pt/t chief scientist Scottish Home and Health Dept 1973-81, chm Scottish Hosp Endowments Res Tst 1982-89; FRCS, FRSE, Hon DSc, FRACS, FACS, FCM (S Africa), FRCSI, FRCS (Canada); kt 1973; *Books* Textbook of Surgical Physiology; *Recreations* gardening; *Style*— Sir Andrew Kay, FRSE; 14 North Campbell Ave, Milngavie, Glasgow G62 7AA (☎ 041 956 3378)

KAY, Brian Muir; s of Dr Herbert Kay, of Nunthorpe, Middlesborough, and Jean, *née* Kerr; *b* 15 Sept 1957; *Educ* St Peter's Sch York, Bristol Univ (BA); *Career* journalist; Yorkshire Evening Post 1980, Yorkshire Post 1986, Argos Consumer Journalist of the Year 1987, Campaigning Journalist of the Year British Press Awards 1988; *Recreations* travel, skiing, champagne, slow cars; *Style*— Brian Kay, Esq; Headingley, Leeds (☎ 05362 758 849); Yorkshire Post, Wellington St, Leeds LS1 1RF (☎ 0532 432 701 ext 347)

KAY, Brian Wilfrid; s of Wilfrid Ernest Kay (d 1953), of Chester, and Jessie Ashby Howe (d 1947); *b* 30 July 1921; *Educ* Kings Sch Chester, Univ Coll Oxford (MA); *m* 5 April 1947, Dorothea Sheppard, da of Rev Eric John Lawson; 2 da (Sarah b 1948, Elizabeth b 1951); *Career* asst master in classics Birkenhead Sch 1947-59, head of classics Liverpool Collegiate Sch 1959-64, HM chief inspr of Schs 1977-81 (inspr 1964-81, staff inspr 1971-77), sr res fell Culham Coll Inst 1982-; *Recreations* music, gardening, architectural history; *Style*— Brian Kay, Esq; Pond Cottage, Botolph Claydon, Buckingham MK18 2NG (☎ 029 671 3477)

KAY, Ernest; s of Harold Kay, and Florence Kay; *b* 21 June 1915; *Educ* Spring Bank Central Sch Darwen Lancs; *m* 1941, Marjorie, *née* Peover (d 1987); 2 s (John Michael b 1943, Richard Andrew b 1945), 1 da (Belinda Jean (Mrs Wilson) b 1950); *Career* reporter: Darwen News 1931-34, Ashton-under-Lyne Reporter 1934-38; industl corr Manchester Guardian and Evening News 1938-41, reporter The Star London 1941-47; managing ed: Wolverhampton Express and Star 1952-54 London Evening News 1954-57; ed and publisher John O'London's 1957-61, managing ed Time and Tide 1961-67, fndr and dir gen Int Biographical Centre Cambridge 1967- (dir gen NY 1976-86); chm: Kay Sons and Daughter Ltd 1967-77, Dartmouth Chronicle Gp Ltd 1968-77; pres Melrose Pres Ltd 1970-77; chm: Cambridge and Newmarket Radio Ltd 1981-, Cambridge Symphony Orchestra Tst 1979-83; Emperor Haile Selassie Gold medal 1971; Key to City of: Las Vegas 1972, NY 1975, Miami 1978, New Orleans 1978 (and hon citzen), Beverly Hills 1981; Staff Col and ADC to Govr of Louisiana 1979, Hon Sen State of Louisiana 1986; Hon DLitt Karachi 1967, Hon PhD Hong Kong 1976; FRSA 1967, FRGS 1975; Gold medal Ordre Supreme Imperial Orthodoxe Constantinian de Saint-Georges Greece; *Books* incl: Great Men of Yorkshire (1956 and 1960), Isles of Flowers: the Story of the Isles of Scilly (1956, 3 edn 1977), The Wit of Harold Wilson (1967); ed: Dictionary of International Biography (1967-), International Who's Who in Poetry (1970-), International Youth in Achievement (1981-); *Recreations* reading, writing, music, watching cricket, travel; *Clubs* Surrey CCC, Lancashire CCC, National Arts (NY); *Style*— Ernest Kay, Esq; International Biographical Centre, Cambridge CB2 3QP (☎ 0353 721839, fax 0353 721839, car 0836 250959, 0860 359018)

KAY, John William; QC (1984); s of Christopher Herbert Kay (d 1970), of Blundellsands, nr Liverpool, and Ida Muriel, *née* Harper; *b* 13 Sept 1943; *Educ* Denstone Coll, Christ's Coll Cambridge (MA); *m* 13 Aug 1966, Jeffa, da of Maj Graham Bourke Connell, MBE (d 1968); 1 s (Benedict b 1975), 2 da (Amanda b 1969, Tiffany b 1971); *Career* called to the Bar Gray's Inn 1968; tutor in law Univ of Liverpool 1968-69, in practice Northern Circuit 1968-, rec of the Crown Ct 1982-, memb Gen Cncl of the Bar 1988-; *Recreations* gardening, genealogy, horse racing; *Clubs* Athenaeum (Liverpool), Racquet (Liverpool); *Style*— John Kay, Esq, QC; Markhams, 17 Far Moss Rd, Blundellsands, Liverpool L23 8TG (☎ 051 924 5804); Exchange Chambers, Pearl Assurance House, Derby Square, Liverpool LS 9XX (☎ 051 236 7747, fax 051 236 3433)

KAY, Jolyon Christopher; s of Colin Mardall Kay (d 1950), and Gertrude Fanny Kay (d 1983); *b* 19 Sept 1930; *Educ* Charterhouse, St John's Coll Cambridge (BSc); *m* 19 May 1956, Shirley Mary, *qv*, da of Thomas John Clarke (d 1983); 2 s (Tim b 1957, Toby b 1969), 2 da (Gigi b 1959, Katherine b 1965); *Career* design engr Albright and Wilson 1954-58, sr scientific offr AERE and UKAEA 1958-61, Battelle Inst Geneva 1961-64; FCO 1964-90, HM consul gen Dubai UAE 1985, Gulf Consultancy 1990; *Recreations* skiing, croquet, acting; *Style*— Jolyon Kay, Esq; Little Triton, Blewbury, Didcot, Oxon OX11 9PE (☎ 0235 850 010)

KAY, Maurice Ralph; QC; s of Ralph Kay (d 1981), of Knutsford, and Hylda Jones; *b* 6 Dec 1942; *Educ* William Hulmes GS Manchester, Univ of Sheffield (LLB, PhD); *m* 24 July 1968, Margaret Angela, da of Joseph Bernard Alcock, of Formby (d 1985); 4 s (Jonathan b 1969, Dominic b 1971, Oliver 1975, Tristan b 1982); *Career* lectr: Univ of Hull 1967-72, Univ of Manchester 1972-73; prof of law Univ of Keele 1973-83; called to the Bar Gray's Inn 1975-; memb Grays Inn, Wales and Chester circuit, asst rec

1987-, rec 1988-; *Books* ed and contrib legal text books; *Recreations* music, theatre, sport; *Clubs* Reform; *Style*— Maurice Kay, Esq, QC; 3 Paper Buildings, Temple, London, EC4Y 7EU, (☎ 071 583 8055, 0244 323070, fax 071 353 6271, 0244 42930, 0270 626736)

KAY, Neville Rupert Mason; TD; s of Hubert Maurice Kay, of Highgate, London, and Moira Fredricka, *née* Mason (d 1985); *b* 22 June 1934; *Educ* High Pavement GS Nottingham, Univ of Sheffield (LRCMPS); *m* 14 Nov 1958, Josephine, da of late Horace Alcock, of Pocklington; 1 s (Christopher b 1962), 2 da (Suzanne b 1959, Sarah b 1978); *Career* MO Flt Lt RAF 1980-84, currently Lt-Col RAMC (TA); conslt orthopaedic surgn: Royal Hallamshire Hosp, King Edward VII Orthopaedic Hosp Rivelin, Claremont Hosp Sheffield; hon lectr in orthopaedics Univ of Sheffield; former pres S Yorks Medico-Legal Soc 1984; fell Br Orthopaedic Assoc, FRCS; *Books* Complications of Total Joint Replacement (1985); *Recreations* skiing, hill walking; *Style*— Neville Kay, Esq, TD; Westwood House, 11 Brocco Bank, Sheffield S11 8RQ (☎ 0742 662988)

KAY, Philip Bruce; *b* 13 Nov 1955; *Educ* Dulwich, Wadham Coll Oxford (open scholarship, BA, The Second De Paravicini Prize, The Second Craven Scholarship); *Career* asst mangr Banking Div J Henry Schroder Wagg & Co Ltd 1979-84, mangr Institutional Sales Schroder Asia Securities Ltd 1984-85, Schroders plc (London) 1979-85, head of Japanese equity sales De Zoete & Bevan (London 1985-86, dir Smith New Court plc 1986- (head of Asia/Pacific stockbroking, chm Smith New Court Far East Ltd Hong Kong); memb Stock and Share Advsy Ctee Peterhouse Coll Cambridge 1986-90; *Style*— Philip Kay, Esq; 46 Grove Lane, London SE5 8ST (☎ 071 701 0480)

KAY, Philip Haworth; s of John Winder Kay, of Poole, Dorset, and Freda, *née* Haworth; *b* 30 July 1949; *Educ* Poole GS, Univ of Oxford (BA, MA), Guy's Hosp Med Sch (BM BCh); *m* 8 Feb 1975, (Sheila) Janis, da of John Bellingham, of Torquay, Devon; 1 s ((John) Edward Bellingham b 12 Feb 1982), 1 da (Emily Jane b 8 May 1979); *Career* sr conslt cardiothoracic surgn Gen Infirmary at Leeds 1987-; FRCS 1979; *Recreations* keep fit, photography, music, theatre; *Clubs* Bramhope Health and Fitness, Headingly Golf; *Style*— Philip Kay, Esq; The General Infirmary at Leeds, Great George St, Leeds LS1 3EX (☎ 0532 432799)

KAY, Shirley; da of Thomas John Clarke (d 1983), of Hackleton House, Northants, and Jessie, *née* McColl (d 1963); *b* 13 May 1933; *Educ* Northampton HS, Girton Coll Cambridge (BA); *m* 19 May 1956, Jolyon Christopher Kay, *qv*, s of Colin Mardall Kay (d 1950), of West Thurrock, Essex; 2 s (Tim b 1957, Toby b 1969), 2 da (Gigi b 1959, Katharine b 1964); *Career* writer and TV presenter; *Books* The Arab World (1967), Morocco (1980), Emirates Archaeological Heritage (1986); *Recreations* skiing, camping, gardening; *Style*— Mrs Shirley Kay; Little Triton, Blewbury, Didcot, Oxon OX11 9PE (☎ 0235 850 010); Dubai TV, Dubai, UAE

KAY, Susan Elaine; da of Donald Jackson Hodgson, of Manchester, and Joyce, *née* Martyn; *b* 24 June 1952; *Educ* Brookway HS Manchester, Mather Coll of Educn (Cert in Teaching), Univ of Manchester (BEd); *m* 1974, Norman Kay, s of Norman Kay (d 1975); 1 s (Tristan Andrew b 18 Feb 1979), 1 da (Sarah Elizabeth b 23 April 1982); *Career* author; infant sch teacher until 1979; books: Legacy (1985, Historical Novel prize in memory of Georgette Heyer 1985, Betty Trask award for a first novel 1985), Phantom (1990, short-listed Romantic Novel of the Year award 1991); *Recreations* theatre, craft work, writing; *Style*— Mrs Susan Kay; c/o Heather Jeeves, 15 Campden Hill Square, London W8 7JY (☎ 071 727 1699)

KAY, Thomas David; s of Martin Robert Kay, of 8 The Pastures, Downley, High Wycombe, Bucks, and Anne Jaqueline, *née* Schlegel; *b* 22 May 1969; *Educ* The John Hampden GS High Wycombe, Nottingham Poly; *Career* oarsman; began rowing Marlow Rowing Club 1979, Nottinghamshire County Rowing Assoc 1988-; 6 int caps: Bronze medal Piediluco 1989, Silver medal Duisburg 1989, fourth place Lucerne 1989, Silver medal Lucerne 1990, Gold medal Ottensheim 1990 (under 23), Bronze medal Tasmania 1990; achievements incl: Gold and Silver medal Nat Championships 1985, Silver and Bronze Nat Championships 1986, Ladies Plate Henley Royal Regatta 1989, Thames Cup Henley Royal Regatta 1990, winner Match des Seniors under 23 World Championships 1990, Bronze medal World Championships 1990; nat heavyweight and lightweight eights record 1990; Sgt Sarèchal de Logis 7 Regt de Chasseurs French Army 1987-88; *Style*— Thomas Kay, Esq; c/o Amateur Rowing Association, 6 Lower Mall, Hammersmith, London W6 9DJ

KAYALI, Nuha Zaki Mohammed; da of Zaki M Aboul Hammed (d 1965), of West Bank, Jordan, and Akifah Tawfeek, *née* Lutfi; *b* 21 April 1946; *Educ* in Kuwait, Ein Shams Med Sch (MB Bch); *m* 1 Feb 1971, Zaid Kayali, s of Yahia Kayali (d 1980), of Jordan; 1 s (Hazem b 1973), 2 da (Tala b 1974, Haifa b 1980); *Career* conslt ophthalmic surgn: Whipps Cross Hosp, Newham Gen Hosp, Holly House Private Hosp, Roding Hosp; FRCSEd, fell Coll of Opthalmologists; *Recreations* reading, swimming, gardening; *Style*— Mrs Nuha Kayali; Whipps Cross Hospital, Leytonstone, E11; Newham General Hospital, Plaistow, London; Holly House Private Hospital, Buckhurst Hill, Roding Hospital, Woodford Green

KAYE; *see*: Lister-Kaye

KAYE, Alan; s of Wallace Kaye (d 1978), of Horwich, and Nellie Elizabeth, *née* Cookson; *b* 24 June 1936; *Educ* Rivington and Blackrod GS; *m* 21 June 1958, Betty, da of Ernest Rainford (d 1970), of Adlington, Lancs; 1 s (Andrew b 1960), 1 da (Janet b 1961); *Career* dep gen mangr Filter Div Automotive Products plc 1969-70; Dobson Park Industries plc: chief exec Mining Equipment Div 1974-80 (fin dir 1970-74), dep chief exec 1984, chief exec 1985; *Recreations* gardening, music, reading, walking; *Style*— Alan Kaye, Esq; Mill Hill Farm, Mill Lane, Goosnargh, Preston, Lancs PR3 2JX (☎ 0722 865014); Dobson Park Industries plc, Dobson Park House, Manchester Rd, Ince, Wigan, Lancs WN2 2DX (☎ 0942 31421, telex 67355, fax 0942 47058)

KAYE, Sir David Alexander Gordon; 4 Bt (UK 1923), of Huddersfield, Co York; s of Sir (Henry) Gordon Kaye, 2 Bt (d 1956); suc bro, Sir Stephen Kaye, 3 Bt, 1983; *b* 26 July 1919; *Educ* Stowe, Cambridge Univ (BA); *m* 1, 10 Oct 1942 (m dis 1950), Elizabeth Rosemary, only da of Capt Malcolm Hurtley, of Baynards Manor, Horsham, Sussex; m 2, 15 June 1955, Adelle Frances, da of Denis Lionel Thomas, of Brisbane, Qld; 2 s, 4 da; *Heir* s, Paul Henry Gordon Kaye; *Career* MRCS Eng, LRCP London; *Style*— Sir David Kaye, Bt; Yerinandah, Moggill Rd, The Gap, Brisbane, Queensland, Australia

KAYE, David Raymond; s of Michael Kaye (d 1981), and Elizabeth, *née* Wasserman; *b* 29 March 1932; *Educ* Nottingham HS, St Pauls, Univ of Cambridge (MA), Univ of Michigan USA, Oxford (Dip Stats); *m* 15 Oct 1966, Sara Frances, da of Edwyn Lyte (d 1979); 2 s (James b 1970, George b 1972), 1 da (Sophie b 1967); *Career* 2/Lt RA 1952; Shell International Petroleum 1958-62, ptnr Andersen Consltg (Arthur Andersen & Co) 1967-90 (joined 1962); memb: Cncl of Amadeus Scholarship Fund, Exec Working Gp of Programme of Information and Communication Technol (ESRC), Audit Ctee Roehampton Inst; chm Tree of Life Appeal (N London Hospice); tstee Charities Effectiveness Review Tst; FSS, FOR, FIMC; *Books* Gamechange: the impact of information technology on corporate strategies and structures: a boardroom agenda (1989); *Recreations* walking, sculpture; *Clubs* Athenaeum; *Style*— David Kaye, Esq; 37 Wood Lane, London N6 5UD (☎ 081 340 1624); Office: 2 Arundel St, London WC2R 3LT (☎ 071 438 3606, fax 071 438 5649)

KAYE, Col Douglas Robert Beaumont; DSO (1942, bar 1945); s of Robert Walter Kaye, JP (d 1957), of Great Glen Manor, Leics, and Marian, *née* Robinson (d 1946); *b* 18 Nov 1909; *Educ* Harrow; *m* 16 Nov 1946, (Florence) Audrey Emma, da of Henry Archibald Bellville (d 1930), of Tedstone Court, Bromyard, Hereford; 1 s (John b 1951), 1 da (Sarah (Mrs Gilbert) b 1947); *Career* 2 Lt Leics Yeo 1928, 10 Royal Hussars 1931, DAPM Jerusalem 1939-41, APM Cairo HQ 30 Corps 1941-43, Lt-Col cmdg 10 Royal Hussars N Africa, Italy 1943-46, wounded (despatches twice), psc 1946, Bde Maj 30 Lowland Ind Armd Bde TA 1947-49, Lt-Col cmdg 16/5 Queens Royal Lancers 1949-51, AA and QMG 56 London Armd Div TA 1952-54, Col, Cmdt and chief instr Gunnery Sch RAC Centre 1954-56; hon sec: Newmarket and Thurlow Hunt 1959-70 (MFH 1957-59), Puckeridge and Thurlow 1970-88; JP Cambs 1961, DL 1963, High Sheriff Cambs and Isle of Ely 1971, chm Newmarket DC 1972-74 (cncllr 1958-74), memb E Cambs DC 1974-83; Lord of the Manor of Brinkley; *Recreations* hunting, shooting; *Clubs* Cavalry; *Style*— Col Douglas Kaye, DSO; Brinkley Hall, Newmarket, Suffolk (☎ 0638 507202)

KAYE, Sir Emmanuel; CBE (1967); *b* 29 Nov 1914; *Educ* Richmond Hill Sch, Twickenham Tech; *m* 1946, Elizabeth, *née* Cutler; 1 s, 2 da; *Career* jt fndr chm Lansing Bagnall Ltd 1943-89, fndr chm The Kaye Organisation Ltd 1966-80, Kaye Steel Stockholders Ltd 1978-, Conference Booking Centre 1986-, Hart Ventures plc 1989-, pres Lansing Linde Ltd 1989-, fndr chm Kaye Enterprises Ltd 1989-, Elvetham Hall Ltd, Pool & Sons (Hartley Whitney) Ltd; memb Econ and Fin Policy Ctee CBI 1985-; chm Thrombosis Res Tst and Thrombosis Res Inst; FBIM, FRSA; *Clubs* Brooks's; *Style*— Sir Emmanuel Kaye, CBE

KAYE, Dr Georges Sabry; s of Dr Georges Kaye, of Beirut, The Lebanon, and Claire, *née* De las Case; *b* 21 May 1949; *Educ* Villa St Jean, Fribourg, Ratcliffe, King's Coll London (BSc), Westminster Hosp Med Sch (MB BS); *m* 18 Dec 1982, Georgina Margaret, da of Simon Harold John Arthur Knott, of Hammersmith, London; 1 s (Charles Edwin Georges b 20 June 1985), 2 da (Alice Georgina Claire b 1 Jan 1987, Olivia Sarah Louise b 25 Oct 1988); *Career* physician i/c occupational health dept Cromwell Hosp 1982-; co physician to: Gen Electric, Salomon Bros International, Air France; memb International Commission on Occupational Health; memb BMA 1974; *Books* La Soif (The Thirst) (1976); *Recreations* french literature, lute playing; *Clubs* The Reform; *Style*— Dr Georges Kaye; 2 Pennant Mews, London W8; 2nd Braco Castle, Perthshire; Cromwell Hospital, Cromwell Road, London SW5 (☎ 071 370 4233)

KAYE, Jeremy Robin; s of Kenneth Brown Kaye (d 1985), of Doncaster, and Hannah Eleanor Christabel, *née* Scott; *b* 25 Sept 1937; *Educ* Eastbourne Coll, Worcester Coll Oxford (BA, MA); *Career* Nat Serv Bombardier RA 1956-58; called to the Bar Inner Temple 1962; asst sec Limmer and Trinidad Lake Asphalt Co Ltd 1962-67, chief legal offr and asst sec Limmer Hldgs Ltd 1967-72; sec: Arbuthnot Latham Holdings Ltd 1975-81, Dow Scandia Holdings Ltd 1982-86, Secure Trust Group plc 1987-; dir Arbuthnot Latham Bank Ltd 1984- (sec 1973-); lay chm East Grinstead Deanery 1977-87 (sec 1967-77), memb Chichester Diocesan Synod 1970-73 and 1988-; FCIS; *Recreations* gardening, cricket, golf; *Clubs* MCC, Holtye Golf; *Style*— Jeremy Kaye, Esq; 64 Blount Ave, East Grinstead, West Sussex RH19 1JW (☎ 0342 321 294); 131 Finsbury Pavement, Moorgate, London EC2A 1AY (☎ 071 280 8514, fax 071 638 1545, telex 885970)

KAYE, Laurence Martin; s of Moss Kaye, and Beatrice, *née* Herman; *b* 1 Sept 1949; *Educ* Haberdashers' Aske's, Sydney Sussex Coll Cambridge (BA, MA); *m* 1 July 1976, Lauren Merrill, *née* Shaymow; 1 s (David Benjamin b 22 Sept 1978), 1 da (Debra Ann b 16 Oct 1981); *Career* articled clerk to Brecher & Co 1972; admitted slr 1975; ptnr at Brecher & Co 1977, ptnr Saunders Sobell Leigh & Dobin 1980-; former chm Mount Vernon Cleft Lip and Palate Assoc Ltd, chm Meher Babe Assoc Ltd; memb Law Soc; *Recreations* tennis, golf, theatre, yoga; *Clubs* Radlett Lawn Tennis; *Style*— Laurence Kaye, Esq; Saunder Sobell Leigh & Dobin, 20 Red Lion St, Holborn, London WC1R 4AE (☎ 071 242 2525, fax 071 405 4202, telex 21762)

KAYE, Mary Margaret (Mollie); da of Sir Cecil Kaye, CSI, CIE, CBE (d 1935), and late Margaret Sarah (Daisy), *née* Bryson; *Educ* The Lawn Sch Clevedon Somerset; *m* Maj-Gen Goff Hamilton, CB, CBE, DSO (d 1985); 2 da; *Career* author; books: Six Bars at Seven (1939), Potter Pinner Meadow (1937), Strange Island (1940, reprinted as Death in the Andamans, 1985), Death Walks in Kashmir (1953, reprinted as Death in Kashmir, 1984), Death Walks in Berlin (1955, reprinted at Death in Berlin, 1985), Death Walks in Cyprus (1956, reprinted as Death in Cyprus, 1984), The House of Shade (1959, reprinted as Death in Zanzibar, 1983), Later Than You Think (1958, reprinted as Death in Kenya, 1983), Shadow of the Moon (1957, reprinted 1979), Trade Wind (1963, reprinted 1981), The Far Pavilions (1978), The Golden Calm (ed diary of Emily Metcalf, 1980), The Ordinary Princess (children's Book, 1980), Thistledown (1981), Moon of Other Days (ed selection of Kipling's poems, 1988), The Sun In The Morning (1990); illustrator of other books for children; FRSL 1990; *Recreations* painting; *Clubs* Army & Navy; Northbrook, Near Farnham, Surrey GU10 5EU (☎ 0420 23251); c/o David Higham Associates Ltd, 5-8 Lower John St, Golden Square, London W1R 4HA (☎ 071 437 7888, fax 071 437 1072)

KAYE, Col Michael Arthur Chadwick Porter; TD (1948), DL (W Yorks 1974-); s of Col Harold Swift Kaye, DSO, MC (d 1953), of St Johns Lodge, Wakefield, Yorks, and Dora Margaret, *née* Porter (d 1968); *b* 11 Jan 1916; *Educ* Harrow, Pembroke Coll Cambridge (MA); *m* 21 June 1941, Betty (d 1973), da of Maj-Gen EA Sutton, CB, CBE, MC (d 1964), of Highcliffe, Hants; 2 s (Colin b 20 July 1943, Patrick b 3 Feb 1945), 1 da (Anne b 23 March 1942); *Career* 4 KOYLI 1935-47, Lt-Col 1947-51, Col 1951-55, Hon Col 1955- 66, Cmdt West Riding ACF 1955-59; ADC to HM The Queen 1969-71; chm Marshall Kaye & Marshall Ltd 1953-68; memb exec ctee ACF Assoc 1956- 88, chm Yorks TA & VR Assoc 1968-73, Yorks regnl organiser Br Heart Fndn 1968-82, memb bd of visitors New Hall Detention Centre 1970-86, cmmr of taxes Wakefield Dist 1977-90; DL W Riding and City of York 1960-74; *Recreations* cricket, travel; *Clubs* Yorkshire, MCC, I Zingari; *Style*— Col Michael Kaye, TD, DL; 224, Mount Vale, York YO2 2DL (☎ 0904 36760)

KAYE, Michael Kaye; s of Harry Kaye (d 1973), and Annie, *née* Steinberg (d 1943); *b* 27 Feb 1925; *Educ* West Ham Secdy Sch; *m* 1, 28 March 1950 (m dis 1959), Muriel, da of Barnet Greenberg (d 1973), of London; 1 da (Ann b 9 July 1952); m 2, 6 Sept 1962, Fay, da of Morris Bercovitch (d 1950), of London; *Career* REME 1943-45, Intelligence Corps 1945-47; journalist and PR 1947-53, PR and mktg tobacco indust 1953-61, PR mangr Rothmans Ltd 1961-74, PR dir Carreras Rothmans Group 1974-76, dir Peter Stuyvesant Fndn 1963-76, gen admin Rupert Fndn 1972-76, md LSO 1976-80; arts dir GLC 1980-83; gen admin: South Bank Concert Halls 1980-83, Young Concert Artists Tst 1983-; festival dir City of London Festival 1984-; Whitechapel Art Gallery 1964-75: tstee, fin chm, Gen Purposes Ctee; tstee Youth & Music 1970-78; memb: Exec Ctee Carl Flesch Int Violin Competition 1989-, Cncl Centre for Jewish Studies and Jewish-Christian Relations 1989-; FRSA 1986; *Recreations* music, photography; *Style*— Michael Kaye, Esq; 3 Coppice Way, London E18 2DU (☎ 081 989 1281); City Arts Trust, 230 Bishopsgate, London EC2 (☎ 071 377 0540, fax 071 377 1972)

KAYE, Capt Paul Henry Gordon; s (by 2 m) and h of Sir David Alexander Gordon

Kaye, 4 Bt, *qv*; *b* 19 Feb 1958; *m* 1984, Sally Ann Louise; *Career* cmmnd RAE 1982, Capt; memb National Party; *Recreations* rugby union, scuba diving; *Style—* Capt Paul Kaye; Lot 4 Basin Rd South, Samsonville, Queensland 4520, Australia

KAYE, Roger Godfrey; TD (1980, 1985), QC (1989); s of Anthony Harmsworth Kaye (d 1971), and Heidi Alice, *née* Jordy (d 1984); *b* 21 Oct 1946; *Educ* Kings Sch Canterbury, Univ of Birmingham (LLB); *m* 15 April 1974, Melloney Rose, da of The Rev Harry Martin Westall; *Career* called to the Bar Lincoln's Inn 1970; jr Treasy Counsel in Insolvency Matters 1978-89, dep High Ct Bankruptcy registrar 1984, vice chm Bar Cncl Fees Collection Ctee 1989, chm Bristol and Cardiff Chancery Bar Assoc; dep High Ct Judge 1990; *Recreations* going home; *Clubs* RAC, Army and Navy, Special Forces; *Style—* Roger Kaye, Esq, TD, QC; 24 Old Buildings, Lincoln's Inn, London WC2A 3UJ (☎ 071 4040946, fax 071 4051360, telex 940 14909 BROD G)

KAYE, Simon; s of Isaac Kaye (d 1964), of 20 Rutland Park Gdns, London, and Dora, *née* Liborvitch (d 1964); *b* 22 July 1935; *Educ* Wycombe Sch; *m* 8 Sept 1957, Sylvia Adrienne, da of Michael Kagan (d 1982); 2 s (Jeremy b 22 Oct 1959, Trevor b 6 May 1966), 1 da (Elaine b 24 Sept 1962); *Career* entered film indust 1953, sound mixer 1962, dir Siren Sound 1967-, recorded over sixty Br and American films; winner of Oscar for Platoon; 3 BAFTA Awards for: Oh! What a Lovely War, A Bridge too Far, Cry Freedom; 9 Br Acad Nominations for: Charge of the Light Brigade, Lion in Winter, Oh! What a Lovely War, Sunday, Bloody Sunday, A Bridge too Far, Reds, Ghandi, Indiana Jones and the Temple of Doom, Cry Freedom; 3 Oscar Nominations: Reds, Ghandi, Platoon; *Style—* Simon Kaye, Esq; 39 Bellfield Ave, Harrow Weald, Middx HA3 6ST (☎ 081 428 4823)

KAYE, William; s of Henry Kaye (d 1958), of Wakefield, and Alice Kaye (d 1964); *b* 26 Feb 1914; *Educ* Thornes House Sch; *m* 21 June 1937, (Emma) May (d 1947), da of Rowland Harrison, of Wakefield; m 2, June 1949, (Elizabeth) Branwen (d 1982), da of Rev Thomas Elwy-Williams, of Trefriw, N Wales; *Career* served RAF 1942-44; civil servant, ret 1970; memb Governing Cncl Fedn of Environment Socs 1968-70, patron Nat Domesday Celebrations 1986, memb Manorial Soc of GB, Lord of the Manor of Hulland Derbyshire; *Recreations* music, gardening, golf, studies in medieval history; *Clubs* Civil Service, Betws-y-Coed Golf; *Style—* William Kaye, Esq; Minffordd, Capel Garmon, Llanrwst, Gwynedd (☎ 069 02 483)

KAZANTZIS, Prof George; s of Constantine Kazantzis (d 1981), of Ealing, London, and Andromache, *née* Karamanolis; *b* 18 Sept 1924; *Educ* Univ of London (MB BS, PhD); *m* 24 June 1973, Virginia Iphegenia, da of George Valassis (d 1977), of Thessaloniki, Greece; 1 s (Alexander b 1976), 1 da (Ariadne b 1974); *Career* appts in med and surgery St Bartholomews and London Hosps 1950-58, clinical scientific staff MRC 1958-65, prof of occupational med London Sch of Hygiene 1986-89 (sr lectr then reader 1979-86), hon consIt physician The Middx Hosp 1986-89 (lectr then sr lectr Med Professorial Unit 1965-78); 120 pubns on occupational and environmental med in int jnls; memb: Bd of Mgmnt Slough and Milton Keynes Occupational Health Servs, Study Gp on pollution control priorities The Royal Soc; pres section in occupational Med RSM 1984-85; FRCS 1957, FRCP 1979, FFCM (RCP) 1979, FFOM (RCP) 1979; *Books* contrib: Oxford Companion To Medicine (1986), Handbook On The Toxicology of Metals (1986), Oxford Textbook of Medicine (1987); *Recreations* music, being with family; *Clubs* The Athenaeum; *Style—* Prof George Kazantzis; 35 Mount Park Crescent, Ealing, London W5 2RR (☎ 081 997 3287); Environmental Geochemistry Research, Royal School of Mines, Imperial College, Prince Consort Rd, London SW7 2BP (☎ 071 589 5111 ext 5546, fax 071 225 8544, telex 929484), Dept of Medicine, The Middlesex Hospital, London W1N 8AA

KAZANTZIS, (Lady) Judith Elizabeth; *née* Pakenham; does not use style of Lady; da of 7 Earl of Longford, KG, PC; *b* 1940; *Educ* Somerville Coll Oxford; *m* 1963 (m dis 1982), Alexander John Kazantzis, s of Constantine Kazantzis (d 1981); 1 s, 1 da; partner, Irving Weinman, US novelist; *Career* poet, short story writer and watercolourist; *Style—* Ms Judith Kazantzis; 32 Ladbroke Grove, London W11 3BQ; The Foreman's, nr Glynde, Sussex

KEABLE-ELLIOTT, Dr Robert Anthony (Tony); OBE; s of Robert Keable (d 1927), and Jolie, *née* Buck (d 1924); *b* 14 Nov 1924; *Educ* Sherborne, Guys Hosp London (MB BS); *m* 9 May 1953, Gilian Mary, da of Brig Colin Ross Marshall Hutchison, DSO, MC (d 1943); 4 s (David b 1954, Ian b 1956, Trevor b 1958, Simon b 1960); *Career* GP 1948-88; BMA: memb 1949-, memb Cncl 1964-, chm Gen Med Servs Ctee 1964-68, treas 1981-86; memb Fin Corp of Gen Practice 1974-79, dir BMA Services Ltd, chm Jl Ctee BMA 1988-; fndr memb Chiltern Med Soc 1956 (pres 1964); chm Ibstone Parish Cncl, memb Gen Med Cncl 1989-; Freeman: City of London 1986, Soc of Apothecaries of London 1986; FRCGP 1964, Fell BMA 1987; *Recreations* golf, sailing, gardening; *Style—* Dr Tony Keable-Elliott, OBE; Peels, Ibstone, High Wycombe, Bucks

KEAL, Anthony Charles (Tony); s of Maj Kitchener Keal, of Thornton Dale, Yorkshire, and Joan Marjorie, *née* Ayling; *b* 12 July 1951; *Educ* Stowe, New Coll Oxford (BA); *m* 24 Nov 1979, (Janet) Michele, da of John Charles King, of Javea, Spain; 4 s (Julian Charles b 1982, Jonathan David b 1986, Christopher James b 1987, Alexander Anthony b 1988); *Career* slr Allen & Overy 1976, slr and co sec Libra Bank plc 1976-78, ptnr Allen & Overy 1982- (slr 1978-82); memb Worshipful Co of Slrs; memb Law Soc; *Recreations* sailing, travel, family; *Clubs* Thames Sailing, Twickenham Yacht; *Style—* Tony Keal, Esq; 9 Cheapside, London EC2V 6AD (☎ 071 248 9898, fax 071 236 2192, telex 8812801/2)

KEANE, Desmond St John; QC (1981); *b* 21 Aug 1941; *Educ* Downside, Wadham Coll Oxford (MA); *Career* called to the Bar Middle Temple 1964; rec 1979-; QC: Hong Kong 1982, NSW and Cwlth of Aust 1987; *Recreations* cricket; *Clubs* Utd Oxford and Cambridge Univ, Kildare St and Univ (Dublin), Hong Kong; *Style—* Desmond Keane, Esq, QC; 2 Paper Buildings, Temple, London EC4Y 7ET (☎ 071 936 2611, fax 071 583 3423)

KEANE, Dillie; da of Dr Francis Keane, of Portsmouth, and Miriam, *née* Slattery; *b* 23 May 1952; *Educ* Covent of the Sacred Heart Woldingham, Trinity Coll Dublin, LAMDA; *partner* Dr Sam Hutt (stage Hank Wangford); *Career* fndr memb Fascinating Aida with Marilyn Cutts and Adele Anderson (dir Nica Burns), now solo comedienne, columnist Punch Magazine, London corr Showbusiness; recordings: Sweet FA and A Load of Old Sequins (with Fascinating Aida); one woman show Single Again nominated for Perrier award 1990, winner City Limited Most Popular Cabaret Act 1985; *Books* Fascinating Who? (1987); *Recreations* walking, windsurfing, shopping in foreign capitals, tapestry, shopping anywhere, more shopping; *Clubs* Willesden Sports Centre; *Style—* Ms Dillie Keane

KEANE, Sheriff Francis Joseph; s of Thomas Keane (d 1967), of W Lothian, and Helen Flynn; *b* 5 Jan 1936; *Educ* Blairs Coll Aberdeen, Gregorian Univ Rome (PHL), Univ of Edinburgh (LLB); *m* 19 April 1960, Lucia Corio, da of John Morrison (d 1983), of Glasgow; 2 s (Paul b 1963, Mark b 1965), 1 da (Lucy b 1961); *Career* slr; ptnr McCluskey Keane & Co Edinburgh 1959; deputy procurator fiscal: Perth 1961, Edinburgh 1963; sr deputy procurator fiscal Edinburgh 1971, sr legal asst Crown Office Edinburgh 1972, procurator fiscal Airdrie 1976, regnl procurator fiscal S Strathclyde Dumfries and Galloway 1980; pres Procurators Fiscal Soc 1982-84; Sheriff Glasgow and Strathkelvin 1984; *Recreations* music, tennis, painting; *Style—* Sheriff Francis Keane; Sheriffs Chambers, Sheriff Court of Glasgow and Strathkelvin, PO Box 23, 1 Carlton Pl, Glasgow G5 9DA (☎ 041 429 8888)

KEANE, (Mary) Georgina; da of Dr Henry Anthony Keane, of Eire and S Wales, and Patricia Josephine, *née* Nolan; *b* 3 Feb 1954; *Educ* Convent of the Sacred Heart Woldingham Surrey; *m* 21 Dec 1978, Dr Saad Al-Damluji, s of Prof Salem Al-Damluji, of Abu Dhabi, United Arab Emirates; 2 s (Salem b 1981, Hassan b 1982); *Career* barr 1975-84 (chambers in London, Colchester Ipswich and Norwich), legal advsr Employment Affrs Directorate CBI 1984-86, conslt barr Titmuss Sainer and Webb 1986-88; admitted slr 1988; ptnr and head employment unit Titmuss Sainer and Webb 1988-; memb: Exec Ctee Industl Law Soc, Employment Ctee Fawcett Soc; *Recreations* horse-riding, theatre, avoiding domestic chores; *Style—* Miss Georgina Keane; Titmuss Sainer & Webb, 2 Serjeants' Inn, London EC4Y 1LT (☎ 071 583 5353, fax 071 353 3683, telex 23823 ADVICE G)

KEANE, John Charles; s and h of Sir Richard Keane, 6 Bt; *b* 16 Sept 1941; *Educ* Eton, Ch Ch Oxford; *Style—* John Keane Esq; c/o Cappoquin House, Cappoquin, Co Waterford, Ireland

KEANE, John Granville Colpoys; s of Granville Keane (d 1990), and Elaine Violet Meredith Doubble; *b* 12 Sept 1954; *Educ* Cheam Sch Newbury Berks, Wellington, Camberwell Sch of Art (BA); *Career* artist; solo exhibitions incl: Peking, Moscow, Milton Keynes (Minsky's Gallery London) 1980, Some of it Works on Paper (Centre 181 London) 1982, War Efforts (Pentonville Gallery London) 1984, Conspiracy Theories (Angela Flowers Gallery London) 1985, Perspective '85 (Basel Art Fair Switzerland) 1985, Work Ethics (Angela Flowers Gallery London) 1986, Bee Keeping in the War Zone (Angela Flowers Gallery) 1988, Against the Wall (Turnpike Gallery Leigh Gtr Manchester) 1988, The Accident (cmmnd painting and screenprint for Greenpeace, Flowers East London) 1988, Divided States (Terry Dintenfass Gallery NY, Forum Hamburg Germany) 1989, The Other Cheek? (Flowers East London) 1990; gp exhibitions incl: Whitechapel Open (Whitechapel Art Gallery London) 1983, 1984 and 1987, Art for Schools (Wells Centre Norfolk) 1983, Artists Against Apartheid (Royal Festival Hall London) 1986, Athena Art Award (Barbican Art Gallery London) 1987, Self Portrait (Artiste Gallery Bath) 1987, State of the Nation (Herbert Art Gallery Coventry) 1987, Art for the City (Lloyd's Building London) 1987, The Print Show (Angela Flowers Gallery London) 1988, Nutidskunst Silkesborg (Kunstmuseum Copenhagen) 1988, 4th International Young Artists Competition (Union of Fine Artists Sofia Bulgaria) 1989, The Thatcher Years - an Artistic Retrospective (Flowers East London) 1989, Flowers at Moos (Gallery Moos NY) 1990, Where There is Discord (Cleveland Gallery Middlesborough) 1990, Angela Flowers Gallery 1990 (Barbican Concourse Gallery London) 1990; work in several public collections incl: Imperial War Museum, The Economist, The Guardian; artist in residence Whitefield Sch London 1985-86; official Br war artist Gulf Crisis 1991; *Style—* John Keane, Esq; Flowers East, 199-205 Richmond Road, London E8 3NJ (☎ 081 985 3333, fax 081 985 0067)

KEANE, Mary Nesta (Molly); da of Walter Clermont Skrine, and Agnes Shakespeare, *née* Higginson; *b* 20 July 1904; *Educ* privately; *m* 19 Oct 1938, Robert Lumley (Bobbie) Keane, s of Lt-Col Richard Henry Keane, CBE; 1 da (Adele Sara b 1940); *Career* novelist and playwright; plays incl: Spring Meeting (with John Berry) Ambassadors Theatre and in NY 1938, Ducks and Drakes Apollo Theatre 1941, Guardian Angel Gate Theatre Dublin 1944, Treasure Hunt Apollo Theatre 1949, Dazzling Prospects; books written as M J Farrell: The Knight of Cheerful Countenance, This Angel Knight, Young Entry, Taking Chances, Mad Puppets Town, Conversation Piece, Devoted Ladies (1934), Full House (1935), The Rising Tide (1937), Two Days in Aragon (1941), Loving Without Tears (1951), Treasure Hunt (1952); books written as Molly Keane incl: Good Behaviour (1981, televised 1983), Time After Time 1983 (televised 1986), Nursery Cooking (1985), Loving and Giving (1988); Hon DLitt 1989: Univ of Ireland, Univ of Ulster; FRSL 1985; *Recreations* gardening, reading; *Clubs* The Groucho; *Style—* Mrs Molly Keane; c/o Munnay Pollinger Literary Agency, 4 Garrick St, London WC2 9BH

KEANE, Philip Vincent; s of Bernard Vincent Keane (d 1983), of London, and Brenda Ellen Margaret, *née* Ford; *b* 11 Aug 1940; *Educ* Wimbledon Coll GS, LSE (BSc); *m* 18 Sept 1965, (Kathleen) Winifred, da of William Aloysius Thomson (d 1987), of London; 2 da (Angelina Teresa b 14 Sept 1968, Noelle Francesca b 16 Dec 1969); *Career* Tstee Dept Lloyds Bank 1964-66, sr investmt analyst Esso Pension Tst 1967-71, head of investmt res Mercantile & Gen Reinsurance 1971-75, equity fund mangr Prudential Pensions 1976-77, investmt mangr Rea Bros Ltd 1977-81; dir: Wardley Investmt Mgmnt Ltd, HK Unit Tst Mangrs Ltd 1981-82, Rea Bros (Investmt Mgmnt) Ltd 1982-89, CS Investmt Mgmnt Ltd 1989-; AMSIA; *Recreations* travel, photography, skiing, literature; *Style—* Philip Keane, Esq; 70 Pine Grove, off Lake Rd, Wimbledon, London SW19 7HE; CS Investment Management Ltd, 125 High Holborn, London WC1V 6PY (☎ 071 242 1148)

KEANE, Sir Richard Michael; 6 Bt (UK 1801), of Cappoquin, Co Waterford; s of Lt-Col Sir John Keane, 5 Bt, DSO (d 1956), and Lady Eleanor Hicks-Beach (d 1960), da of 1 Earl St Aldwyn; *b* 29 Jan 1909; *Educ* Sherborne, Ch Ch Oxford; *m* 1939, Olivia Dorothy, da of Oliver Hawkshaw, TD; 2 s, 1 da; *Heir* s John Charles Keane; *Career* served with Co of London Yeo and 10 Royal Hussars 1939-44, liaison offr (Maj) with HQ Vojvodina Yugoslav partisans 1944, attached British Military Mission Belgrade 1944-45; diplomatic corr: Reuters 1935-37, Sunday Times (also asst to editor) 1937-39; publicity conslt to ICI Ltd 1950-62; farmer; *Recreations* fishing, farming; *Clubs* Cavalry and Guards'; *Style—* Sir Richard Keane, Bt; Cappoquin House, Cappoquin, Co Waterford, Ireland (☎ 058 54004)

KEAR, Graham Francis; s of Richard Walter Kear (d 1976), and Eva, *née* Davies (d 1967); *b* 9 Oct 1928; *Educ* St Julien's HS Newport, Balliol Coll Oxford (BA); *m* 9 Oct 1978, Joyce Eileen, da of Frank Bartram Parks (d 1973); *Career* Nat Serv RAF 1947-49; Civil Serv: Miny of Supply 1951-52 and 1954-57, UK Delg to Euro Coal and Steel Community 1953-54, Miny of Aviation 1957-59 and 1960-63, NATO Maintance and Supply Agency 1959-60, MOD 1963-65, Cabinet Office 1968-71, Miny of Aviation DTI 1971-72, under sec Dept of Energy 1974-80; assoc fell Harvard Univ 1972-73, asst sec Abbeyfield Richmond Soc 1984-; *Recreations* reading; *Style—* Graham Kear, Esq; 28 Eastbourne Rd, Brentford, Middx (☎ 081 560 4746); Abbeyfield, 4 Ennerdale Rd, Kew, Richmond, Surrey (☎ 081 948 3977)

KEARLEY, Chester Dagley Hugh; s of late Hon Mark Hudson Kearley (s of 1 Viscount Devonport); kinsman and hp of 3 Viscount Devonport; *b* 29 April 1932; *m* 1974, Josefa Mesquida; *Style—* Chester Kearley, Esq; S Patos, 466 Denia, Alicante, Spain

KEARLEY, Hon Marilyn Whitson; da of late 2 Viscount Devonport; *b* 1939; *Style—* Ms Marilyn Kearley

KEARNEY, Prof Hugh Francis; s of Hugh Kearney (d 1973), and Martha Louisa, *née* Thomas (d 1971); *b* 22 Jan 1924; *Educ* St Francis Xaviers Coll Liverpool, Peterhouse Cambridge (scholar, MA), French Govt scholar, NU1 (PhD); *m* 1956, Catherine Murphy; 2 s (Hugh b 1959, Peter b 1960), 1 da (Martha b 1957); *Career* Mil Serv Queen's Royal Regt 1943-45; Manchester Univ Press 1948-50, lectr Univ Coll Dublin 1950-62, reader in history Univ of Sussex 1962-70, Richard Pares prof of history Univ of Edinburgh 1970-75, Amundson prof of Br history Univ of Pittsburgh

1975-; visiting fell: Univ Coll Aberystwyth 1985, Peterhouse Cambridge 1985; visiting prof: Univ of Calif Berkeley 1967, Concordia Univ Montreal 1979; memb: Soc for British Studies (USA), American Ctee for Irish Studies; *Books* Strafford in Ireland (1959, 3 edn 1989), Origin of the Scientific Revolution (1964), Scholars and Gentlemen: Universities and Society in Pre-Industrial Britain 1500-1700 (1970), Science and Change 1500-1700 (1971, 5 edn 1986), The British Isles: A History of Four Nations (1989); *Recreations* walking, travel, reading, theatre, opera, sailing; *Style*— Prof Hugh Kearney; Ellwood Cottage, School Lane, Bardwell, Suffolk IP31 1AD (☎ 0359 50713); History Department, University of Pittsburgh, Pittsburgh PA15260 (☎ 421 7479)

KEARNEY, Hon Sir William John Francis; CBE (1976); s of W J K Kearney; *b* 8 Jan 1935; *Educ* Wolstanton CGS, Sydney GS, Sydney Univ, Univ Coll London; *m* 1959, Jessie, da of L Yung; 3 da; *Career* dormant cmmn as admin of PNG 1973, high cmmr of PNG 1973-75, judge Supreme Ct PNG 1976-82, dep chief justice 1980-82, judge Supreme Ct Northern Territory 1982-, Aboriginal Land cmmr 1982-; kt 1982; *Style*— The Hon Sir William Kearney, CBE; Judges' Chambers, Supreme Court, Darwin, NT 5790, Australia

KEARNS, Lady; Betty; *née* Broadbent; da of Newton Broadbent, of Burnley; *m* 1946, Sir Frederick Matthias Kearns, KCB, MC (d 1983); 1 da; *Style*— Lady Kearns; 26 Brookway, Blackheath, London SE3 (☎ 081 852 0747)

KEAST, Roger John; s of Horace Keast, of Gwellyets, Truro, Cornwall, and Margaret, *née* Legard; *b* 4 Dec 1942; *Educ* Truro Sch, Univ of Exeter (LLB); *m* 1, 25 March 1970 (m dis 1975), Anne Elizabeth, da of Norman Samuel Cross, of Lanteague, Goonhavern, Truro, Cornwall; m 2, 9 July 1976, (Elizabeth) Ann, da of Albert John Folland (d 1982), of W Forde, Stockleigh, Pomeroy, Devon; 1 s (Paul Edward John b 15 Nov 1977), 2 step da (Sarah Annette Radford b 14 July 1966, Carole Suzanne Radford b 20 Nov 1967); *Career* Stephens and Scown St Austell Exeter 1963-: articled clerk 1963-66, slr 1966-70, ptnr 1970-, dep sr ptnr 1986-91, sr ptnr 1991-; memb Exeter City Cncl 1968-81, Mayor City of Exeter 1977-78; hon slr: Devon Young Farmers Club 1968-, Somerset and Dorset Railway Club 1982-, Exeter and District Hoteliers Assoc 1989-; pres Exeter Male Voice Choir 1979-; memb Cncl Exeter Univ 1979-90, Privy Cncl's appointee Ct of Exeter Univ 1980-, fndr memb Exeter Castle Rotary Club 1985-; hon alderman; Hon MA Univ of Exeter 1978; memb Law Soc 1966; *Style*— Roger Keast, Esq; Arroya House, Mount Rise, Kenn, nr Exeter, Devon (☎ 0392 832889); 27-28 Southernhay East, Exeter (☎ 0392 210700, fax 0392 74010)

KEAT, Alan Michael; s of Ernest Frank Keat, of Liphook, Surrey, and Joyce Evelyn, *née* Curtis; *b* 12 May 1942; *Educ* Charterhouse, Merton Coll Oxford (MA); *m* 9 July 1966, Lorna Marion, da of Horace Henry Wilson, of Chesterfield, Derbys; 3 da (Anna b 19 Oct 1968, Jane b 18 Sept 1972, Rebecca b 22 June 1975); *Career* admitted slr 1966, ptnr Travers Smith Braithwaite 1970-, non-exec dir Beazer plc 1986-89; *Style*— Alan Keat, Esq; 10 Snow Hill, London EC1A 2AL (☎ 071 248 9133, fax 071 236 3728, telex 887117)

KEATING, Caron Louisa; *Educ* Univ of Bristol (BA); *Career* as a teenager appeared in Radio and TV commercials and presented several religious and youth oriented progs in NI incl Green Rock and Channel One, co-presenter of BBC TV's Blue Peter 1986-, has filmed in Russia 1987 and USA 1988 for Blue Peter Summer Assignments, filmed in Kampuchea for Blue Peter famine appeal and later fronted the appeal incl and interview with Mrs Thatcher, co-presenter BBC TV's The Garden Party; recent TV appearances incl: Wogan, The Six O'Clock Show and Top to the Pops; *Recreations* scuba diving, absailing, skiing, motor racing; *Style*— Ms Caron Keating; BBC Television Centre, Wood Lane, London W12 7RJ (☎ 01 743 8000)

KEATING, Donald Norran; QC (1972); *b* 24 June 1924; *Educ* Roan Sch, Kings Coll London (BA); *m* 1, 1945, Betty Katharine (d 1975); 2 s (Giles b 1956, Roland b 1961), 1 da (Jenny b 1951); m 2, 2 Dec 1978, (Kay) Rosamond, *née* Blundell Jones; 1 s (Oliver b 1981), 1 step da (Natasha b 1966); *Career* Flt Lt RAFVR 1943-46; called to the Bar Lincoln's Inn 1950, bencher 1979, rec Crown Ct 1972-87, int arbitrator in construction disputes, memb Dept of Trade study team on Prof Liability Review 1988-89; FCIArb; *Books* Building Contracts, (edns 1955, 1963, 1969, 1978 & Supps 1982, 1984); *Recreations* theatre, music, travel, walking; *Clubs* Garrick; *Style*— Donald Keating, Esq, QC; c/o D N Keating QC, 10 Essex St, Outer Temple, WC2R 3AA (☎ 071 240 6981, fax 071 240 7722, telex 8955650 IIKBWG)

KEATING, Frank; s of Bryan Keating, of Cheltenham, Glos, and Monica, *née* Marsh; *b* 4 Oct 1937; *Educ* Belmont Abbey, Douai; *m* 1987, Jane A Sinclair; 1 s, 1 da; *Career* prodr Independent Television 1963-74; columnist: The Guardian 1975-, Punch 1982-89, The Spectator 1989-; TV series incl: Maestro (BBC 1), Italy, My Italy (ITV); Sportswriter of Year 1978, 1980 and 1988; Magazine Writer of Year 1987; *Books* Bowled Over, Another Bloody Day in Paradise, High, Wide and Handsome, Gents and Players; *Recreations* Channel 4, Radio 4, gardening; *Clubs* Chelsea Arts; *Style*— Frank Keating, Esq; Church House, Marden, Hereford; The Guardian, London (☎ 071 278 2332)

KEATING, Henry Reymond Fitzwalter (Harry); s of John Hervey Keating (d 1950), and Muriel Margharita, *née* Clews (d 1986); *Educ* Merchant Taylors' Sch, Trinity Coll Dublin (BA); *m* 3 Oct 1953, Sheila Mary, da of William Ford Mitchell, ISO (d 1968); 3 s (Simon b 1955, Piers b 1960, Hugo b 1964), 1 da (Bryony b 1957); *Career* Army 1945-48; journalist 1952-63; chm: Crime Writers Assoc 1970-71, Soc of Authors 1982-84; pres The Detection Club 1986-; *Books* Death and the Visiting Firemen (1959), The Perfect Murder (1964), The Murder of the Maharajah (1980), The Lucky Alphonse (1982), Under A Monsoon Cloud (1986), Dead on Time (1988), Inspector Ghote His Life and Crimes 1989), The Iciest Sin (1990); *Style*— H R F Keating, Esq; 35 Northumberland Place, London W2 5AS (☎ 071 229 1100)

KEATING, John David; s of Peter Steven Keating (d 1944, war casualty), of York, and Muriel Emily Alice Lamport; *b* 18 June 1943; *Educ* Dorset Inst of HE, Highbury Coll Portsmouth; *m* 28 Aug 1970, Linda Margaret, da of Sidney Reginald Hall, of Blackheath, London SE12; 1 s (Matthew b 1971), 1 da (Sarah b 1973); *Career* seagoing purser with P & O 1960-70, Lt reserve serv RN 2 Submarine Div 1970-71; asst to md CWS 1972-74, UK divnl accountant Borden Chemical Corp 1975-81, fndr dir and proprietor WRA Ltd 1982-; dir: WRA Holdings Ltd 1984-, WRA (Offshore) Ltd (Sub-Sea Devpt) 1985-; md Wessex Resins & Adhesives Ltd; elected memb for Ringwood South Ward of New Forest Dist Cncl 1987-; FCCA 1977, MHCIMA, ACCA; *Recreations* sailing, skiing; *Clubs* Naval, Royal Naval Sailing Assoc; *Style*— John Keating, Esq; Greenways, Hightown Hill, Ringwood, Hampshire (☎ 0425 475 446); Wessex Resins & Adhesives Ltd, Wessex House, 189-193 Spring Rd, Southampton (☎ 0703 444 744, telex 47388, fax 0703 431 792)

KEATING, (Kay) Rosamond Blundell; da of Geoffrey Blundell Jones, and Avis Marguerite, *née* Dyer; *b* 3 Oct 1943; *Educ* Maynard Sch Exeter, St Hughs Coll Oxford (MA); *m* 1, 18 Dec 1965, Edmund Anthony Deighton (d 1974); 1 da (Natasha b 9 June 1966); m 2, 2 Dec 1978, Donald Norman Keating, QC; 1 s (Oliver Sebastian b 19 June 1981); *Career* called to the Bar Grays Inn 1966; metropolitan stipendiary magistrate 1987; *Recreations* travel, opera, riding, walking; *Style*— Mrs Rosamond Keating; Greenwich Magistrates Court, 9 Blackheath Rd, London SE8 8PG

KEATINGE, Sir Edgar Mayne; CBE (1954); s of Gerald Francis Keatinge, CIE (d 1965); *b* 3 Feb 1905; *Educ* Rugby, South Africa; *m* 1930, Katharine Lucile (d 1990), da of Reginald John Burrell (d 1948); 1 s (Bill), 1 da (Bridget); *Career* joined Suffolk Yeo 1937, Cmdt School of Artillery W Africa 1942-43, Lt-Col RA; MP (C) West Suffolk Bury St Edmunds Div 1944-45; memb Panel Land Tbnl SW Area 1948-74, chm Wessex Area Nat Union of Cons Assocs 1951-54, govr Sherborne Sch 1951-74; memb Cncl Royal African Soc 1970-80; kt 1960; *Clubs* Carlton, Boodle's; *Style*— Sir Edgar Keatinge, CBE; Teffont, Salisbury, Wilts SP3 5RG (☎ 072 276 224)

KEATINGE, Richard Arthur Davis; *b* 30 Aug 1947; *Educ* Portora Royal Sch, Trinity Coll Dublin (BA), University Coll Dublin (MBA), Wharton Business Sch (AMP); *m* 1970, Athene; 2 s (Benjamin b 17 Aug 1973, Douglas b 5 May 1976), 1 da (Rebecca b 4 Sept 1979); *Career* fin journalist: Reuters Ltd 1969-71, The Irish Times 1971-78; Bank of Ireland: dir and corp fin exec 1978-83, head of gp strategy 1983-86, chief exec UK 1986-90, exec dir Britain 1990-; *Recreations* golf, fishing, cricket; *Clubs* Royal Mid Surrey, Overseas Bankers'; *Style*— Richard Keatinge, Esq; Bank of Ireland, 36 Queen St, London EC4R 1BN (☎ 071 329 4500, fax 071 489 1886, telex 8812635, car 0836 620731)

KEATINGE, Prof William Richard; s of Sir Edgar Keatinge, of Teffont Evias, Salisbury, Wilts, and Katherine Lucille; *b* 18 May 1931; *Educ* Upper Canada Coll, Rugby, Univ of Cambridge (MA, MB BChir, PhD); *m* 15 Oct 1955, Margaret Ellen Annette, da of David Hegarty (d 1973); 1 s (Richard), 2 da (Claire, Mary); *Career* RNVR seconded for res at Univ of Cambridge 1956-58; dir of studies in med and jr res fell Pembroke Coll Cambridge 1958-60, fell Cardiovascular Res Inst San Francisco 1960-61, MRC post and fell Pembroke Coll Oxford 1961-68; head of Physiology Dept: London Hosp Med Coll 1981-90 (reader 1968-71, prof 1971-), Queen Mary and Westfield Coll 1990-; memb: Physiological Soc 1959, RSM; MRCP 1984; *Books* Survival In Cold Water, Local Mechanisms Controlling Blood Vessels; *Recreations* archaeology, sailing; *Style*— Prof William Keatinge; Dept of Physiology, Queen Mary and Westfield Coll, Mile End Rd, London E1 4NS (☎ 071 982 6365)

KEATLEY, (Robert) Bryan; TD (1961); s of James Walter Stanley Keatley (d 1978), of Royston, and Helen Rankin Thompson; *b* 21 March 1930; *Educ* Aldenham, St Catharine's Coll Cambridge (MA); *m* 14 Sept 1957, Diana, da of Frank Harvey, of Bishops Stortford; 2 s (Robert b 1967, Richard (twin) b 1967), 2 da (Georgina b 1960, Rebecca b 1962); *Career* chartered surveyor and land agent; conslt Humberts London 1990- (ptnr 1962-90, sr ptnr 1980-85); underwriting memb of Lloyds; reg army 1949-50, TA Cambs Regt (16 Airborne Div), Maj & OC Herts Regt; Nat Tst: Fin Ctee 1983, Estates Panel 1983, Enterprise Bd 1984; dir: Landplan Ltd 1974, Glen Rinnes Ltd 1990-; chm Formfield (BES) 1984, dir Rural Assets 1987 (chm 1990); cmmr of taxes 1960, chm Herts (Hadhams Branch) Royal Br Legion 1984; Freeman City of London 1978, Liveryman Worshipful Co of Farmers; FRICS, FRSA; *Recreations* shooting, conservation, gardens, browsing; *Clubs* Boodle's, Farmers'; *Style*— Bryan Keatley, Esq, TD; Hadham Park, nr Bishops Stortford, Herts CM23 1JH (☎ 0279 652040); Estate Office (☎ 0279 506626, fax 0279 504761); Humberts, 25 Grosvenor Street, London (☎ 071 629 6700, telex 27444, fax 071 493 4346)

KEATLEY, John Rankin Macdonald; s of James Walter Stanley Keatley (d 1978), of Royston, and Helen Rankin Thompson; *b* 20 Aug 1933; *Educ* Aldenham, RAC Circencester; *m* 1964 (m dis 1980), Carolyn Margaret, da of Rodney Telford Morell, of Melbourne, Australia; 1 s (James b 1965), 1 da (Arabella b 1967); *Career* 2 Lt Duke of Wellington's Regt Korea 1952-53, Capt Hertfordshire Regt TA; Parly candidate (C) Hemsworth 1964; leader Cambridge CC 1967-69; chm Applied Botanics plc 1984, dir REA Holdings plc 1978; tstee: Cambridge Museum of Technol 1970, Decorative Arts Soc 1990; pres: SW Cambridgeshire Cons Assoc 1987, Arts Cncl of North Hertfordshire 1991; memb: Ctee Contemporary Art Soc 1989, Syndicate Fitzwilliam Museum Cambridge 1990; hon fell Guild of Designer Book Binders 1989; *Clubs* Lansdowne; *Style*— J R M Keatley, Esq; Melbourn Lodge, Royston, Herts SG8 6AL (☎ 0763 260680)

KEATLEY, William Halliday; TD (1970); s of James Walter Stanley Keatley (d 1978), of Royston, and Helen Rankin, *née* Thompson; *b* 22 Sept 1935; *Educ* Aldenham, St Catharine's Coll Cambridge (MA); *m* 3 Sept 1965, (Elizabeth) Jane, da of Capt Thomas Abdy Combe (d 1984); 2 da; *Career* 2 Field Batty Gold Coast RWAFF 1954-56, Cambs Regt and Suffolk and Cambs Regt 1956-72; ptnr Prust & Co 1965-71 (joined 1959), Laurence Prust & Co 1971-85 (dep sr ptnr 1983-85), sr ptnr Laurence Keen & Co 1986-, non-exec dir Pershing Ltd; memb Int Stock Exchange; *Style*— W H Keatley, Esq, TD; Heddon Hall, Parracombe, N Devon EX31 4QL (☎ 059 83 409); Laurence Keen & Co, 49-51 Bow Lane, Cheapside, London EC4M 9LX (☎ 071 489 9493)

KEATS, Louis Maurice; s of Samuel Keats, of Middx and Brussels, and Betty, *née* Young; *b* 23 Feb 1944; *Educ* Preston Manor GS; *m* 10 Sept 1967, Helen, da of Fred Grant, of Middx; 2 da (Tara b 1968, Sara b 1972); *Career* sr ptnr Keats Poulter (CAs) 1972, chm Data Servs Gp 1987 (dir 1984), dir Nat Youth Jazz Orchestra 1984, chm Ben Uri Art Soc 1988; FCA 1969, FCCA 1982, FBIM 1981; *Recreations* art, music, classic motor cars; *Style*— Louis M Keats, Esq; 21 Lonsdale Road, London SW13 9JP; 33 Cork Street, London W1X 1HB (☎ 071 439 1986, fax 071 734 3106)

KEAY, Dr Ronald William John; CBE (1977, OBE 1966); s of Harold John Keay (d 1962), of Richmond Surrey, and Marion Lucy, *née* Flick (d 1971); *Educ* King's Coll Sch Wimbledon, St John's Coll Oxford (BSc, MA, DPhil); *m* 18 Aug 1944, Joan Mary, da of Rev Alfred Edward Walden; 1 s (Martin John b 1951), 2 da (Alison Marion (Mrs Eldridge) b 1946, Hilary Ruth (Mrs Kinnell) b 1948); *Career* Colonial Forest Serv 1942-62; dir forest res 1960-62, exec sec The Royal Soc 1977-85 (dep exec sec 1962-77), visiting prof Univ of Essex 1990-; numerous papers on: tropical african plant ecology and taxonomy, sci policy; pres: Sci Assoc Nigeria 1961-62, African Studies Assoc 1971-72; vice pres Nigerian Field Soc 1987- (chm UK branch 1985-91), pres Inst of Biology 1988-90 (hon fell), treas Linnean Soc of London 1989- (vice pres 1961-65, 1971-73, 1974-76); church warden St Martin-in-the-Fields 1981-87; hon fell RHS; *Books* Flora of West Tropical Africa Vol 1 (1954-58), Nigerian Trees (1960-64), Trees of Nigeria (1989); *Recreations* gardening; *Clubs* The Athenaeum; *Style*— Dr Ronald Keay, CBE; 38 Birch Grove, Cobham, Surrey KT11 2HR (☎ 0932 865677)

KEBLE-WHITE, (Arthur) James; s of Capt Geoffrey Meredith Keble-White, RN (d 1961), of Hants and Violet Gertrude Alice, *née* Preston (d 1963); *b* 29 May 1930; *Educ* Winchester, Trinity Coll Cambridge (MA); *m* 7 May 1955, Penelope Mary, da of John Newsam McClean (d 1986), of Cirencester, Glos; 3 da (Caroline b 1957, Julia b 1959, Diana b 1964); *Career* chartered engr; dir Ove Arup & Partners, md Carrier Engineering Co Ltd (resigned 1974); FIMechE, FCIBSE; *Style*— James Keble-White, Esq; Burdocks, Wisborough Green, Billingshurst, Sussex RH14 0HA (☎ 0403 700276); Ove Arup & Partners, 13 Fitzroy St, London W1P 6BQ (☎ 071 636 1531)

KEE, Hon Mrs (Catherine Mary); OBE (1977); da of Baron Trevelyan (Life Peer; d 1985); *b* 1943; *m* 10 Dec 1990, Robert Kee; *Career* gen mangr The Burlington Magazine 1980-; *Style*— The Hon Mrs Kee, OBE

KEE, Robert; s of Robert Kee (d 1958), and Dorothy Frances, *née* Monkman (d 1964); *b* 5 Oct 1919; *Educ* Rottingdean Sch Sussex, Stowe, Magdalen Coll Oxford (MA); *m* 1, 1948, Janetta, da of G H J Woolley; 1 da (Georgiana); m 2, 1960, Cynthia Charlotte, da of Edward Judah; 2 s (Alexander, Benjamin (decd)), 1 da (Sarah); m 3, 1990, The Hon Catherine Mary, da of Lord Trevelyan; *Career* author and broadcaster, TV interviewer, presenter, TV documentary maker 1958-; Richard Dimbleby Award 1976, Jacobs Award (Dublin) for BBC Ireland 1981; memb: ACTT, Equity; *Publications* A Crowd is not Company (1948), The Impossible Shore (1949), A Sign of the Times (1956), Broadstrop in Season (1959), Refugee World (1961), The Green Flag (1972), Ireland: A History (1981), 1939 (1984), 1945 (1985), Trial and Error (1986), Munich: The Eleventh Hour (1988), The Picture Post Album (1989); *Style*— Robert Kee, Esq; Rogers Coleridge and White, 20 Powis Mews, London W11 1JN (☎ 071 221 3717)

KEE, His Hon William; s of Robert Kee (d 1958), and Dorothy Frances, *née* Monkman (d 1964); *b* 15 Oct 1921; *Educ* Stowe; *m* 1953, Helga Wessel, da of Erling Christian Haneborg Eckhoff (d 1980), of Oslo, Norway; 1 s (Peter William b 1960), 3 da (Christine Frances b 1954, Susanna Helga b 1957, Karen Mary b 1964); *Career* Army 1941-46, Orkneys and India, attached 9 Gurkha Rifles, Staff Capt; called to the Bar Inner Temple 1948; jt chm Ind Sch Tbnl 1971-72; circuit judge 1972-90, princ judge for Co Courts in Kent 1985-90; *Books* Divorce Case Book (1950), Encyclopaedia of Court Forms and Halsbury's Laws of England (contrib); *Recreations* walking, listening to music; *Style*— His Hon William Kee

KEEBLE, Sir (Herbert Ben) Curtis; GCMG (1982, KCMG 1978, CMG 1970); s of Herbert Keeble (d 1949), of Walton on the Naze, and Gertrude Keeble, BEM, *née* Hardy (d 1969); *b* 18 Sept 1922; *Educ* Clacton Co HS, Univ of London; *m* 2 April 1947, Margaret Ellen Stephenson Stuart, da of John Fraser, of Edinburgh; 3 da (Dr Suzanne (Richardson) b 1949, Sally b 1951, Jane b 1955); *Career* served HM Forces 1942-47; Dip Serv: served Berlin, Washington, Jakarta; former cnsllr and head Euro Econ Orgns Dept FCO, commercial cnsllr Berne 1965-68, min Canberra 1968-71, asst under sec of state FCO 1971-73, ambass German Democratic Republic 1974-76, dep under sec FCO (chief clerk) 1976-78, ambass to USSR 1978-82, ret; conslt to FCO 1984-; advsr to House of Commons Foreign Affairs Ctee 1985-86; govr BBC 1985-90; memb Cncl: Royal Inst of Int Affairs 1984-90, Sch of Slavonic and East European Studies 1984-; chm GB and USSR Assoc 1985-; *Books* The Soviet State (ed, 1985), Britain and the Soviet Union 1917-89 (1990); *Recreations* sailing; *Clubs* Naval; *Style*— Sir Curtis Keeble, GCMG; Dormers, St Leonards Rd, Thames Ditton, Surrey KT7 0RR (☎ 081 398 7778)

KEEBLE, Donovan Horace Leslie; MC (1945), TD (1975); s of Horace Keeble (d 1967), and Dorothy Lesley, *née* de Caux (d 1938); *b* 11 Jan 1912; *Educ* Thornton Heath Sch, King's Coll London (BSc), Battersea Poly; *m* 12 June 1937, Joan Florence, da of Edwin John Tessier (d 1960); 2 da (Domini b 20 Feb 1939 d 1987, Hulda b 19 July 1943); *Career* cmmnd 2 Lt RE TA 1938, Lt 226 Field Co 48 S Midland Div 1939, Capt 1940, Maj 53 SW Div 1941, SO2 (RE) with CE 21 Army Gp, released from embodied serv 1946, ret hon Maj 1975; engr Croydon London CC and Reading 1932-39; asst md 1946-51: Cheecol Processes Ltd, Permacem Paint Co Ltd; chief engr Nat Bldg and Housing Bd S Rhodesia 1951-53; fndr ptnr Maggs and Keeble Conslt Engrs S Rhodesia 1953-62; fndr dir: and chm BMMK and Ptnrs (consulting engrs) 1962-81, Southern Testing Laboratories Geotechnical Conslts 1962-; fndr and first chm Assoc of Consltg Engrs S Rhodesia, former chm Borrowdale Rd Cncl S Rhodesia, former pres E Grinstead Rotary Club, chm Borrowdale constituency under PM S Rhodesia 1961; FICE 1938, FIHT 1947, MConsE; *Recreations* pottery and ceramics, swimming, walking, travelling; *Clubs* RAC; *Style*— Donovan Keeble, Esq, MC, TD; Regency Cottage, Fairwarp, E Sussex TN22 3BE (☎ 08257 2940); Keeble House, Stuart Way, E Grinstead, W Sussex RH19 4QA (☎ 0342 313 156, fax 0342 410 321, telex 95637 TELSER)

KEEBLE, Giles; s of Thomas Whitfield Keeble, and Ursula, *née* Scott-Morris; *b* 12 Nov 1949; *Educ* The King's Sch Canterbury, St John's Coll Cambridge (MA); *m* 1981 (m dis 1988), Gillian, *née* Perry; 2 s (Nicholas, Sam); *Career* account handler JWT 1971-73, account mangr BMP 1973-75, sr account mangr and account planner FGA 1975-76; copywriter: FGA 1976-77, Abbott Mead Vicker 1978-81, WCRS 1981-88 (dir 1984); creative dir Leo Burnett 1988-; winner various advertising indust awards; *Recreations* sport, music, children; *Clubs* Hawks, Groucho; *Style*— Giles Keeble, Esq; Leo Burnett, 48 St Martins Lane, London WC2 4EJ (☎ 071 836 2424, fax 071 829 7026/7)

KEEBLE, John Francis; s of Frank Edward Keeble (d 1989), and Lilith Louise Keeble; *b* 26 April 1933; *Educ* Slough GS, Acton Tech Coll (BSc); *m* 29 March 1958, Vivienne, da of Reginald William Anderson; 1 s (Peter b 1960), 1 da (Elizabeth b 1964); *Career* 2 Lt RCS 1954-56; methods study asst Pharmaceutical Co 1956-60 (res asst 1950-54), sr admin BBC TV 1968-83 (orgn and methods conslt 1960-66, asst to head TV drama 1966-68), sr admin dir business admin and dep chief exec BBC Enterprises Ltd 1983-; dir: BBC Telecordiale 1988-, BBC Sub tv Ltd 1990-, Twin Network Ltd 1990-; vice pres: Broadcasting Support Servs, Nat Aids Helpline; FRTS (memb 1970-); *Recreations* theatre, ballet travel; *Style*— John Keeble, Esq; 4 Turner Rd, Slough Berks SL3 7AN (☎ 0753 33850); BBC Enterprises, Woodlands, 80 Wood Lane, London WC12 0TT (☎ 081 576 2276, fax 081 749 0538, tlx 934678)

KEEFE, Prof Terence (Terry); s of Wilfrid Patrick Keefe (d 1979), and Laura Clara, *née* Mitchell; *b* 1 Feb 1940; *Educ* Five Ways GS Birmingham, Univ of Leicester (BA, MA), Univ of London (BA); *m* 30 June 1962, Sheila Roberta, da of John Parkin (d 1975), of Gt Yarmouth; 1 s (Simon Patrick b 24 Dec 1968), 1 da (Rosanna Jancis b 24 April 1971); *Career* asst master Lincoln City GS 1963-65, asst lectr then lectr then sr lectr in French Univ of Leicester 1965-88, prof of French studies Univ of Lancaster 1988-; memb: Exec Ctee French Studies Soc, Assoc of Univ Professors of French; *Books* Simone De Beauvoir: A Study of Her Writings (1983), French Existentialist Fiction (1986), Zola and the Craft of Fiction (co-ed, 1990); *Recreations* golf; *Style*— Prof Terry Keefe; Dept of Modern Languages, Lonsdale College, University of Lancaster, Lancaster LA1 4YN (☎ 0524 65201 ext 2667)

KEEFFE, Barrie Colin; s of Edward Thomas Keeffe, and Constance Beatrice, *née* Marsh; *b* 31 Oct 1945; *Educ* East Ham GS; *m* 1, 1969 (m dis 1979), Dee Sarah Truman; m 2, 1981, Verity Eileen Proud, *née* Bargate (d 1981); 2 step s; m 3, 1983, Julia Lindsay; *Career* actor Nat Youth Theatre, journalist, writer-in-residence Shaw Theatre, resident playwright Royal Shakespeare Co 1978, assoc writer Theatre Royal Stratford East 1986-; memb Bd of Dirs: Soho Theatre Co 1978-, Theatre Royal Stratford 1989-; Theatre plays: Only a Game 1973, A Sight of Glory 1975, Scribes 1975, Here Comes the Sun 1976, Gimme Shelter 1977, A Mad World My Master 1977, Barbarians 1977, Gotcha 1977, Frozen Assets 1978, Sus 1979, Bastard Angel 1980, She's So Modern 1980, Black Lear 1980, Chorus Girls 1981, Better Times 1985, King of England 1988, My Girl 1989, Not Fade Away 1990, Wild Justice 1990; TV Plays: Nipper 1977, Champions 1978, Hanging Around 1978, Waterloo Sunset 1979, King 1984; TV Series No Excuses 1983; Film: The Long Good Friday 1981; French Critics Prix Revelation 1978, Giles Cooper Best Radio Plays 1980, Mystery Writers of America Edgar Allan Poe Award 1982; *Novels* Gadabout (1969), No Excuses (1983); *Recreations* origami; *Style*— Barrie Keeffe, Esq; 110 Annandale Rd, Greenwich, London SE10 0JZ

KEEGAN, John Desmond Patrick; s of Francis Joseph Keegan (d 1975), of London, and Eileen Mary, *née* Bridgman; *b* 15 May 1934; *Educ* King's Coll Taunton, Wimbledon Coll, Balliol Coll Oxford (BA, MA); *m* 10 Dec 1960, Susanne Ingeborg, da of Dr Thomas Everett, of Horsington, Somerset (d 1974); 2 s (Thomas b 1963, Matthew b 1965), 2 da (Lucy Newmark b 1961, Rose Keegan b 1965); *Career* sr lectr in war studies RMA Sandhurst 1960-86, defence ed Daily Telegraph 1986-; visitor Sexey's Hosp Bruton Somerset; FRHistS, FRSL; *Books* The Face of Battle (1976), World Armies (1978), Six Armies in Normandy (1982), The Mask of Command (1987), The Price of Admiralty (1988), The Second World War (1989); *Clubs* Garrick, Beefsteak, The Brook (NY); *Style*— John Keegan, Esq; The Manor House, Kilmington, Warminster, Wilts BA12 6RD (☎ 09853 574); The Daily Telegraph, 181 Marsh Wall, London E14 9SR (☎ 071 538 5000)

KEEGAN, William James Gregory; s of William Patrick Keegan, of Wimbledon, and Sheila Julia, *née* Buckley (d 1976); *b* 3 July 1938; *Educ* Wimbledon Coll, Trinity Coll Cambridge (MA); *m* 7 Feb 1967 (m dis 1982), Tessa, *née* Young (wid of late John Ashton); 2 s, 2 da; *Career* Nat Serv 5 Royal Tank Regt RASC (cmmnd 1958) 1957-59; journalist: Financial Times 1963-64, Daily Mail 1964-67; economics corr Financial Times 1967-76, worked Econ Intelligence Dept Bank of England 1976-77, economics ed The Observer 1977- (assoc ed 1982-); memb: BBC Advsy Ctee on Business and Industl Affrs 1981-88, Cncl Employment Inst 1987-, Advsy Bd Dept of Applied Economics Univ of Cambridge 1988-; visiting prof of journalism Univ of Sheffield 1989- (hon res fell 1990-), memb CNAA (Ctee for Social Sci 1991-); *Books* fiction: Consulting Father Wintergreen (1974), A Real Killing (1976); non-fiction: Who Runs The Economy (jtly, 1978), Mrs Thatcher's Economic Experiment (1984), Britain Without Oil (1985), Mr Lawson's Gamble (1989); *Clubs* Garrick; *Style*— William Keegan, Esq; The Observer, Chelsea Bridge House, Queenstown Rd, London SW8 4NN (☎ 071 627 0700)

KEELING, Christopher Anthony Gedge; s of Sir Edward Keeling, MC, MP, DL (d 1954), of 20 Wilton Street, London SW1, and Martha Ann, *née* Darling; *b* 15 June 1930; *Educ* Eton, RMA Sandhurst; *m* 1, 20 Sept 1955 (m dis 1972), Veronica, da of Alec Waugh, writer (d 1980), of Edrington, Silchester, Berks; 2 s (Simon Alexander Edward d 1982, Julian James), 1 da (Nicola Sara); m 2, 1974, Rachael Macdonald; *Career* Capt Grenadier Gds 1948-56; chm Fenchurch Underwriting Agencies Ltd, dir Fenchurch Insur Hldgs Ltd; dir: Jago Venton Underwriting Agencies Ltd, Castle Underwriting Agencies Ltd, Burton Rowe & Viner Ltd; chm Venton Underwriting Agency Ltd; Freeman City of London, Liveryman Worshipful Co of Fishmongers 1955; *Recreations* shooting, reading, watching cricket; *Clubs* White's, MCC, Beefsteak; *Style*— Christopher Keeling, Esq; Leyden House, Thames Bank, London SW14 7QR (☎ 081 876 7375); 136 Minories, London EC3N 1QN (☎ 071 488 2388, fax 071 481 9467, telex 884442 LOQOTE G)

KEELING, Frank; s of George Basil Keeling (d 1966), and Lily, *née* Bate; *b* 10 April 1929; *Educ* Queen Mary's GS Walsall, Selwyn Coll Cambridge (exhibitioner, MA); *m* 1955, Gillian Margaret Sansome (d 1990); 1 s (Adrian Francis b 1967), 1 da (Judith Ann b 1964); *Career* stock broker; Godefroi Bros (membs London Stock Exchange) 1953-55, F H Finney & Co, Fyshe Horton Finney & Co, Fyshe Horton Finney Ltd (membs Stock Exchange) 1955-; *Style*— Frank Keeling, Esq; Fyshe Norton Finney Ltd, Charles House, 148-149 Great Charles St, Birmingham B3 3HT (☎ 021 236 3111, fax 021 236 4875)

KEELING, Surgn Rear Adm John; CBE (1978); *b* 28 Oct 1921; *Educ* Queen Elizabeth's Sch Hartlebury, Univ of Birmingham; *m* 1948, Olwen Anne; 2 s (1 decd); *Career* RN 1946; Fleet Air Arm until 1975, dir of environmental med 1975-77, dep med dir-gen (Naval) 1977-80, dir of med policy and plans MOD 1980-83, chm NATO Jt Civil/ Mil Med Gp 1981-83; QHP 1977-83; MFOM; *Recreations* caravanning, microcomputers; *Clubs* Army and Navy; *Style*— Surgn Rear Adm John Keeling, CBE; Merlin Cottage, Brockhampton, Hereford HR1 4TQ (☎ 098986 649)

KEELING, John Arthur Bernard; DFC (1943); s of Sir John Henry Keeling (d 1978); *b* 31 Oct 1922; *Educ* Eton, Ch Ch Oxford (MA); *m* 1961, Mary Jocelyn, da of Eric Heseltine Wenham (d 1959); 2 s; *Career* serv RAF 1941-45, Flt Lt, NW Europe, Malta and Italy; CA 1949; chm: London & Yorks Tst Hldgs Ltd 1965-88 (dir 1952-88), W Riding Worsted & Woollen Mills Ltd 1968-75 (dir 1959-75), Close Bros Gp plc 1975-87 (dir 1959-87); dir: Bowater Industs plc 1968-88, RIT and Northern plc 1968-85; farmer 1967-: advsr Br Airways Pension Fund 1959-85, chm St Michael's Hospice Hastings 1988-; *Recreations* travel, gardening; *Clubs* White's; *Style*— John Keeling Esq, DFC; 48 Melton Court, Old Brompton Rd, London SW7 3JH (☎ 071 584 0333); Hurst House, Sedlescombe, E Sussex TN33 0PE (☎ 0424 870340)

KEELING, John Nevill; s of Canon John Nevill Keeling, Vicar of Brighton, (d 1987), and Beryl, *née* Lloyd; *b* 17 March 1939; *Educ* High Wycombe Royal GS, Regent St Poly, Poly of Photography (Dip in Cinematography); *m* 1967, Sonia Nancy, da of Thomas Jesse Wood; 2 da (Emma Isobel b 1970, Philippa Nancy b 1972); *Career* film cameraman Film Dept BBC TV London 1962-66; Keeling Film Prodns (servicing BBC TV and commercial TV) estab 1966; set up camera & lighting facilities for Euston Films; mktg conslt for independent schs 1976-, estab Euro-One Productions Ltd (prodr films/video for corporate presentation) 1982-; winner BIPP Woodstock Trophy for Video Prodn 1985; FBIPP 1985; *Style*— John Keeling, Esq; Euro-One Productions, Field House, Poyntington, Sherborne, Dorset DT9 4LF (☎ 096 322 251)

KEELING, Richard Geoffrey; s of Lt Cdr Geoffrey Philip Keeling, of Pear Tree Cottage, Garboldisham, Diss, Norfolk, and Marcena, *née* Orcutt; *b* 4 Sept 1947; *Educ* All Hallous Sch; *m* 7 May 1983, Frederika, da fo Frederick Joseph Wassell, of 154 Worcester Rd, Hagley, Worcs; 2 s (Frederick b 1984, Henry b 1988); *Career* ptnr Elliot Son & Boyton Surveyors and Valuers 1975-; Royal Ocean Racing Club: memb Ctee 1982-84, Rear Cdre 1985-86, Vice Cdre 1988-89, memb Cncl Royal Yachting Assoc 1985-87; fell: RGS 1985, RICS 1987, Rating and Valuation Assoc 1987; *Recreations* sailing, skiing, tennis; *Clubs* Royal Yacht Squadron, Royal Ocean Racing; *Style*— Richard Keeling, Esq; 71 Deodar Rd, Putney, London SW15 2NU (☎ 081 874 7784); 15 Cavendish Square, London W1 (☎ 071 323 3007, car 0836 508589)

KEELING, Robert William Maynard; s of Dr George Sydney Keeling (d 1957), of Attleborough, Norfolk, and Florence Amy Maynard (d 1951); *b* 16 Dec 1917; *Educ* Uppingham, Corpus Christi Coll Cambridge; *m* 1942, Kathleen Busill, da of Herbert Busill-Jones, JP (d 1955), of Walsall, Staffs; 1 s (Jonathan b 1952), 2 da (Anne b 1945, Karen b 1948); *Career* Army 1939-46, Maj RASC; served: Western Desert, Libya, Palestine, Trans-Jordan, Egypt, Italy, Greece, Berlin (despatches 1944); GSO 2, Control Cmmn for Germany 1945; FO (German Econ Dept) 1946-47, admitted slr 1950; ptnr Monier-Williams & Keeling 1956-80, slr to the Vintners Co 1953-79 rec Crown Ct 1980-89; diplôme de grande médaille d'argent Corporation des Vignerons de Champagne 1988; Kt Cdr Order of Civil Merit of Spain 1967; *Recreations* travel, painting; *Style*— Robert Keeling, Esq; Vale Bank, Chadlington, Oxford

KEEN, Charles William Lyle; s of Harold Hugh Keen (d 1974), and Catherine Eleanor Lyle, *née* Cummins; *b* 4 July 1936; *Educ* Winchester, New Coll Oxford (MA); *m* 21 July 1962, Lady (Priscilla) Mary Rose, *qv*, da of 6 Earl Howe, CBE (d 1984); 1 s (William b 1970), 3 da (Laura b 1963, Eleanor b 1965, Alice b 1966); *Career* Lt The Royal Dragoons; local dir Barclays Bank: Reading 1967-71 (sr local dir 1974-81), Nottingham 1971-74; dir: Barclays Unicorn Gp Ltd 1978-81, Barclays Merchant Bank 1981-87, Barclays de Zoete Wedd Hldgs Ltd 1986-87; regnl dir Barclays Bank 1987-;

AIB 1964; *Books* The Mondragon Experience (1977); *Recreations* rural sports and pastimes; *Style—* Charles Keen, Esq; St Mary's Farm House, Beenham, Reading, Berks (☎ 0734 713705); 2 Circus Place, London Wall, London EC2

KEEN, Frank William Ernest; s of Frederick Henry Ernest Keen (ka 1945), and Elsie Dora, *née* Muckett (d 1977); *b* 28 Jan 1929; *Educ* Prices GS Fareham Hants; *m* 4 March 1950, Doreen May, da of George Charles Salmon (d 1977); 2 da (Sandra Anne (Mrs Meggs) b 1952, Rossalyn (Mrs Watchorn) b 1955); *Career* Nat Serv RE 1947-49; local govt offr (engr and surveyor) 1944-60, princ own firm of surveyors 1960-83; former memb Bognor Regis Round Table and Rotary Club, memb W Sussex CC 1968- (chm Educn Ctee), vice chm Sussex Police Authy 1982-85 and 1988- (memb 1977-, chm 1985-88); Freeman City of London, Liveryman Worshipful Co of Painter Stainers; MICE, FRICS, FSVA, FIHT; *Recreations* golf; *Style—* Frank Keen, Esq; 4 St Richard's Drive, Bognor Regis, West Sussex PO21 3BH (☎ 0243 263 350)

KEEN, Lady (Priscilla) Mary Rose; *née* Curzon; da of 6 Earl Howe, CBE; *b* 12 Feb 1940; *Educ* Lawnside Worcs, Lady Margaret Hall Oxford; *m* 1962, Charles William Lyle Keen, *qv*; 1 s, 3 da; *Books* The Garden Border Book, The Glory of the English Garden; *Recreations* gardening; *Style—* The Lady Mary Keen; St Mary's Farm, Beenham, Reading, Berks (☎ 0734 713705)

KEEN, Maurice Hugh; s of Harold Hugh Keen (d 1974), and Catherine, *née* Cummins; *b* 30 Oct 1933; *Educ* Winchester (scholar), Balliol Coll Oxford (BA); *m* 20 July 1968, Mary Agnes, da of Francis Keegan; 3 da (Catherine b 1969, Harriet b 1971, Clare b 1973); *Career* Nat Serv 2 Lt Royal Ulster Rifles 1952-54; jr res fell The Queen's Coll Oxford 1957-61, fell and tutor medieval history Balliol Coll Oxford 1961-; govr Blundell's Sch 1970-89, fell Winchester Coll 1989-; FSA 1987, FBA 1990; *Books* The Outlaws of Medieval Legend (1961), The Laws of War in the Later Middle Ages (1965), Pelican History of Medieval Europe (1968), England in the Later Middle Ages (1973), Chivalry (1984), English Society in the Later Middle Ages (1990); *Recreations* fishing, shooting; *Style—* Maurice Keen, Esq, FSA; Balliol College, Oxford OX1 3BJ (☎ 0865 277777)

KEEN, Robert Victor; s of Hedley Victor Keen (d 1978), and Elsie Frances, *née* Bush (d 1976); *b* 1 Jan 1934; *Educ* Simon Langton Sch Canterbury; *m* 1 (m dis 1966), Christine, *née* Brind; 1 s (Justin Robert b 19 July 1958), 1 da (Naomi Theresa b 30 May 1961); m 2, 30 Nov 1966, Pamela Rosina, da of Ralph Knight; 1 s (James Thomas b 6 April 1971); *Career* Nat Serv Cmmn The Buffs 1954-56; PT mangr (plastics/ chemicals) Distillers Co 1956-64, account gp dir J Walter Thompson 1964-68, md Interpublic PR 1968-74, dir (int corp affairs) Rank Xerox 1974-80, chm Charles Barker Consulting Group 1980-; JP 1984-88; MIPR; *Recreations* sailing; *Clubs* Royal Lymington Yacht; *Style—* Robert Keen, Esq; Rivendell, Ridgeway Lane, Lymington, Hants (☎ 0590 673030); 44 Andrewes House, Barbican, London EC2; 30 Farringdon St, London EC4A 4EA (☎ 071 634 1000, fax 071 236 0170, telex 883588/887928)

KEEN, Dr Timothy Frank; s of Frank Keen, MBE (d 1986), of Keensacre, Burnham Beeches, Bucks, and Lillian, *née* Hooley (d 1976); *b* 9 Nov 1953; *Educ* St Paul's, Univ of Nottingham (BSc, PhD); *m* 6 Aug 1983, Victoria Ann, da of Jeffrey James Brandon, of Keyworth, Notts; 1 s (Henry b 20 Feb 1986), 1 da (Lucinda b 15 June 1987); *Career* md Keen Computers Ltd 1978-84, gen mangr Intelligence Research Ltd 1985, chm and chief exec Keen Ltd 1985-89, mktg mangr Keen Networks (part of Willaire Group plc) 1990-; chm and cncl memb Computer Retailers Assoc 1978-83, cncl memb Parly Info Ctee 1983-86, dir Nottingham Info Technol Ctee 1983-84, pres Britwell Carnival Charity; FBIM 1981, FIOD 1981, MBCS 1982; *Recreations* fly fishing, shooting, breeding highland cattle; *Clubs* RAC; *Style—* Dr Timothy Keen; Keensacre, Burnham Beeches, Bucks SL2 3TA (☎ 0753 64 4404); Keen, Matrix House, Lincoln Rd, Cressex Industrial Estate, High Wycombe, Bucks HP12 3RD (☎ 0494 472707, fax 0494 33757)

KEENE, Bryan Richard; s of Edward Stanley William Keene (d 1963), of Weybridge, and Sybil White, *née* Holmes; *b* 14 Sept 1937; *Educ* St James' Boys Sch Weybridge; *Career* Securities Agency Ltd/Drayton Corporation Ltd 1963-74, asst dir Samuel Montagu & Co Ltd 1974-84, dir and co sec Invesco MIM Management Ltd 1984-, dir Invesco MIM Capital Ltd 1984-, Elliot Assocs Ltd 1984-, Anglo-Scottish Securities Ltd 1986-, Staple Investmt Trust Ltd 1986-; co sec: MIM Britannia Ltd 1986-, MIM Britannia Unit Trust Mangrs Ltd 1986-; FCIS 1968, ATII 1977; *Style—* Bryan Keene, Esq; Woodside, Winterbourne Grove, Weybridge, Surrey (☎ 0932 841708); 11 Devonshire Sq, London EC2M 4YR (☎ 071 626 3434)

KEENE, David Wolfe; QC (1980); s of Edward Henry Wolfe Keene (d 1987), and Lilian Marjorie, *née* Conway; *b* 15 April 1941; *Educ* Hampton GS, Balliol Coll Oxford (Eldon scholar, BA, BCL, Winter Williams prize), Inner Temple (Public Int Law prize); *m* 1965, Gillian Margaret, da of Geoffrey Lawrance; 1 s (Edward Geoffrey Wolfe b 1970), 1 da (Harriet Margaret b 1968); *Career* called to the Bar Inner Temple 1964, bencher 1987-, rec The Crown Court 1989-; chm Examination-in-Public Cumbria Structure Plan 1980, inspector County Hall (London) Public Inquiry 1987, vice chm Local Govt and Planning Bar Assoc 1990-, sometime memb Final Selection Bd Planning Inspectorate DOE; memb Exec Ctee Amnesty International (Br section) 1965-68; *Books* The Adult Criminal (co-author 1967); *Clubs* Athenaeum; *Style—* David Keene, Esq, QC; 4-5 Gray's Inn Square, Gray's Inn, London WC1R 5AY (☎ 071 404 5252, fax 071 242 7803)

KEENE, Gareth John; s of Victor Horace Keene, of Kent, and Muriel Olive, *née* Whitehead; *b* 31 March 1944; *Educ* Tonbridge, St John's Coll Cambridge (MA, LLM); *m* 1, 1969 (m dis 1983), Georgina, da of David Walter Patrick Thomas, of Cambs; 3 s (Timothy b 1973, David b 1975, Jonathan b 1979); m 2, 1983, Charlotte Louise, da of Peter Frank Lester (d 1985), of Devon; *Career* called to the Bar Gray's Inn 1966; sec Allen & Hanburys Ltd 1968-73, admin Dartington Coll of Arts 1973-78 (later govr), sec The Dartington Hall Tst 1978-83, int legal conslt and dir TSW TV SW Holdings plc 1980-; sec Euro Community Chamber Orchestra Tst, chm Beaford Arts Centre; Freeman City of London 1971, Liveryman Worshipful Co of Skinners' 1974; *Books* Sacred and Secular (with Adam Fox, 1975); *Recreations* music; *Clubs* RSM; *Style—* Gareth Keene, Esq; Buttermead, Manaton, Newton Abbot, Devon TQ13 9XG (☎ 064722 208, fax 064722 410)

KEENE, Mac Frederick Turner; s of FFH Keene, of Roxburn Way, Ruislip, Middx, and Constance Eileen Keene (d 1971); *b* 14 March 1932; *Educ* John Lyon Sch Harrow; *m* 2 May 1953, Margaret, da of Herbert Lomas; 3 s (Vincent Simon b 1953, Mark Richard b 1955, Paul Malcolm b 1960), 1 da (Helen Thérèse (Mrs Smith) b 1958); *Career* journalist; Middlesex County Press Uxbridge 1952-59, Westminster Press London 1959-60, Daily Sketch 1960-61, 1962-66 and 1970-71, Daily Express 1961, IPC Sun 1966-70; Daily Mail: joined 1971, features ed 1976-83, assoc managing ed 1983-87, exec ed (leisure) 1987-; *Recreations* skiing, travel, gardening, eating and drinking well; *Style—* Mac Keene, Esq; The Old House, Croxley Green, Hertfordshire (☎ 0923 720598); Daily Mail, Northcliffe House, 2 Derry St, Kensington, London W8 5TT (☎ 071 938 6161, fax 071 937 3251, car 0860 220 893)

KEENE, Raymond Dennis; OBE (1985); s of Dennis Arthur Keene, of Worthing, and Doris Anita, *née* Leat (d 1969); *b* 29 Jan 1948; *Educ* Dulwich, Trinity Coll Cambridge (MA); *m* 1974, Annette Sara, da of Walter Goodman; *Career* chess corr: The Spectator 1977-, The Times 1985-, Thames Television 1986-; author of over 70 books; memb Eng Olympic chess team 1966, 1968, 1970, 1972, 1974, 1976, 1978, 1980, Br Chess Champion 1971, Olympic Bronze medal 1976, chess grandmaster 1976 (life title); fell Royal Soc of Arts and Commerce; *Recreations* attending ballet, theatre, opera; *Clubs* Athenaeum, RAC; *Style—* Raymond Keene, Esq, OBE; 23 Hyde Park Place, London W2 2LP (☎ 071 262 5348); Times Newspaper, News International, 1 Virginia St, London E1 (fax 071 402 6183)

KEENLYSIDE, Brig Richard Headlam (Dick); CBE (1957), DSO (1946); s of Capt Guy Francis Headlam Keenlyside (ka France 1914), and late Rose Margaret, *née* Knyvett; *b* 13 May 1909; *Educ* Charterhouse, RMA Woolwich; *m* 1, 1937, Aileen Evelyn D'Auvergne (d 1960), da of Capt Nigel Hogg (ka 1916); 2 da (Susan (Mrs Lionel Vale) b 1939, Jane (Mrs John Jacob) b 1940); m 2, 28 April 1962, Ann Christian (d 1988), wid of Maj-Gen F N Mitchell, da of Maj Nigel Livingstone-Learmonth (ka 1915); 3 step da (Mona Mitchell, CVO, Josephine (Mrs John Robinson), Marion (Mrs Ian Weston)); *Career* cmmnd 2 Lt 1929, served England 1929-34, India (now Pakistan) 1935-39, (Capt) France 1939, (Maj) France, Belgium, Dunkirk, England 1940; Egypt, Sudan, Eritrea, Palestine 1940-42; Lt-Col Tripoli, Algeria, Normandy, Belgium, Holland, Germany 1943-45; Regtl Cdr and WO England 1945-50, SO Germany 1950-53, Regtl Cdr England 1953-54, SO Singapore 1954-57, Cdr RA 56 (London) Div 1958-61, ret 1961; dir CLA Game Fair 1963-74; *Recreations* shooting, golf, playing the piano; *Clubs* Army and Navy; *Style—* Brig R H Keenlyside, CBE, DSO; Valley Farm, Blackford, Yeovil, Somerset BA22 7EF (☎ 0963 40304)

KEEPING, Bryan Edward; s of Douglas William Joseph Keeping (d 1967), of Poole, and Ena Anne, *née* Coombes; *b* 23 March 1936; *Educ* Poole GS, Balliol Coll Oxford (MA); *m* 19 Oct 1963, Christine Margaret, da of Arthur Ivor Brown (d 1973), of Newport, Gwent; 1 s (David b 1965), 1 da (Jennifer b 1968); *Career* Nat Serv RAF 1955-57; sr ptnr Trevanions slrs 1980- (ptnr 1965-); memb Poole Rotary Club; *Recreations* golf, boating; *Clubs* Parkstone Golf, RM Yacht; *Style—* Bryan Keeping, Esq; 20 Greenwood Ave, Poole, Dorset, BH1 48QD (☎ 0202 709 608); Trevanions, 15 Church Road, Parkstone, Poole, Dorset BH1 48UF (☎ 0202 715 815, fax 0202 715 511)

KEER, Colin John Gordon; s of Maj Martin Cordy Keer, MC, of Violet Cottage, Blockley, Gloucs, and Leila Lorna, *née* Troup; *b* 19 April 1950; *Educ* Radley, Magdalene Coll Cambridge (MA); *Career* asst mangr Price Waterhouse 1976 (joined 1972), dir Samuel Montagu & Co Ltd 1984-86 (joined 1976), md Bankers Tst Co 1986-; *Recreations* tennis, gardening; *Style—* Colin Keer, Esq; Bankers Trust Co, 1 Appold St, Broadgate, London EC2A 2HE (☎ 071 982 2505, fax 071 982 2256)

KEEVIL, (Ambrose) Clement Arthur; s of Col Sir Ambrose Keevil, KBE, MC, DL (d 1973); *b* 21 Sept 1919; *Educ* Tonbridge, Queen's Coll Oxford (BA); *m* 1945, Olwen Marjorie Enid, da of John Gibbins; 2 s (Philip, Julian), 1 da (Harriet); *Career* served Middx Regt, RA Adj, GSO 2 (AIR) AFHQ Italy (despatches); a fndr dir Fitch Lovell plc (dep chm until ret 1983), fndr memb and former chm Fish Farming Branch NFU; Master Worshipful Co of Poulters 1966-67, Freeman City of London; FRSA; *Recreations* painting; *Clubs* Army and Navy; *Style—* Clement Keevil, Esq; Buckwell Place, Herstmonceux, East Sussex BN27 4JT

KEEVIL, Philip Samuel; s of Arnold Herbert Keevil (d 1965), of Lewes, Sussex, and Gladys Cecilia, *née* Haydon (d 1982); *b* 24 Sept 1937; *Educ* Brockenhurst County HS; *m* 27 Feb 1960, Joan Kathleen, da of Wallace Henry Brown, of S Wigston, Leicester; 1 s (Andrew b 1960), 1 da (Vicky b 1963); *Career* conslt architect in private practice; md Applied Cad Services Ltd Computer Graphics 1984-, fndr chm Autocad User Group UK; former pres Nene Valley Rotary Club; *Recreations* painting, music; *Clubs* Northampton and County; *Style—* Philip Keevil, Esq; The Bungalow, 1 Sandringham Rd, Northampton; Applied Cad Services Ltd, Ashton House, Kent Rd, Northampton NN5 6XB (☎ 0604 587921)

KEEYS, Geoffrey Foster; s of Richard Kipling Foster Keeys, and Joan, *née* Anderson; *b* 29 Oct 1944; *Educ* Abingdon Sch, Univ of Manchester (LLB); *m* 4 April 1970, Christine Mary (Donna), da of Henry Albert Lavers, of Newbury; 1 s (Henry Foster b 16 April 1976), 1 da (Georgia Ellen b 22 May 1974); *Career* graduate trainee Mobil Oil 1966-68, various personnel positions to dir personnel and ind relations (Euro and world export) Massey Ferguson 1968-82, dir gp personnel Chubb & Son plc 1982-84, gen mangr Personnel and Business Servs Prudential Corporation plc 1984-; memb advsy bds: Personnel Management (Magazine Inst Personnel Mgmnt), Centre Strategic Mgmnt and Change Univ of Warwick; memb Nat Ctee Nat Assoc Boys Clubs; FIPM; *Recreations* golf, cricket; *Clubs* RAC; *Style—* Geoffrey Keeys, Esq; Prudential Corporation, 1 Stephen St, London W1P 2AP (☎ 071 548 3777)

KEFFER, John W; s of James Morgan Keffer (d 1935), and Dove, *née* Douglas (d 1934); *b* 5 June 1923; *Educ* Texas Technol Univ (BA), The Univ of Texas (JD), Johns Hopkins Univ (MA); *m* 25 Aug 1954, Natalia, da of Baron Giulio Blanc (d 1978), of Le Chateau, Tolochenaz, Switzerland; 2 s (Charles b 1955 d 1959, John b 1957); *Career* ensign USNR 1943; served Europe 1944-45: Normandy Invasion 1944, Invasion Southern France 1944, Lt (JG); served Pacific 1945-46: Okinawa, Philippines, Occupation of Japan; lawyer 1950-53: Schuster & Davenport NY, Travieso Paul Caracas Venezuela; gen counsel: Esso Standard Oil Havana Cuba 1954-60, Coral Gables Florida 1960-63, Creole Petroleum Corp Caracas Venezuela 1964-73, Esso Europe London 1973-85, Counsel Fulbright & Jaworski London 1986-; chm tstees American Museum in Br 1982- (tstee 1979-), memb advsy bd Royal Acad 1987-; memb: Int Bar Assoc, American Bar Assoc, Texas Bar; *Recreations* photography, collecting paintings, drawings, watercolours, antiques; *Clubs* Garrick, Brooks's, Univ (NY), Circolo Della Caccia (Rome); *Style—* John Keffer, Esq; Fulbright & Jaworski, 2 St James's Place, London SW1A 1NP (☎ 01 629 1207, fax 01 493 8259, telex 28310)

KEFFORD, Anthony John Roland; s of Harry Roland Kefford, of 6 The Leys, Basildon, Essex, and Joyce, *née* Reeves; *b* 18 Jan 1954; *Educ* City of London Sch, QMC (BSc), Poly of Central London (Dip Law); *m* 21 Nov 1981, Janet Maureen, da of Douglas Malcolm Grant of 92 Castledon Rd, Wickford, Essex; 1 da (Edith b 20 July 1983); *Career* called to the Bar Middle Temple 1980; in practice Norwich 1981-; *Style—* Anthony Kefford, Esq; Wensum Chambers, 10A Wensum St, Norwich NR3 1HR

KEIGHTLEY, Maj-Gen Richard Charles; CB (1987); s of Gen Sir Charles F Keightley, GCB, GBE, DSO (d 1974), and Joan Lydia, da of Brig-Gen G N T Smyth-Osbourne, CB, CMG, DSO (d 1942); *b* 2 July 1933; *Educ* Marlborough, RMA Sandhurst; *m* 21 Oct 1958, Caroline Rosemary, da of Col Sir Thomas Butler, 12 Bt, DSO, OBE, MVO, *qv*; 3 da (Charlotte (Mrs Jenkinson) b 21 March 1961, Arabella (Mrs O'Connell) b 31 July 1962, Victoria b 3 Dec 1965); *Career* cmmnd 5 Royal Inniskilling Dragoon Gds 1953; served Suez Canal Zone, Far East, Libya, NI, Germany, Cdr 1972-75; Cdr: Task Force E 1978-79, Western Dist 1982-83, Cmdt RMA Sandhurst 1983-87, Col 5 Royal Inniskilling Dragoon Gds 1986-91; chm: Combined Servs Polo Assoc 1982-87, W Dorset Health Authy 1988-; *Recreations* equitation, field sports, cricket, farming; *Clubs* Cavalry and Guards'; *Style—* Maj-Gen Richard Keightley, CB; Kennels Cottage, Tarrant Gunville, Blandford, Dorset DT11 8JQ (☎ 025889 418); Somerleigh Gate, Dorset County Hospital, Dorchester, Dorset (☎ 0305 63123)

KEIL, Charles George; *b* 7 March 1933; *Educ* St Bartholomew's GS Newbury, QMC

London; *m* 23 April 1960, Janette Catherine; 2 s (Duncan b 1963, Ewan b 1964), 1 da (Fiona b 1962); *Career* fighter pilot RAF 1951-55, Flt Lt; served Canada, Germany, France, Cyprus; ed of monthly aviation journal Aircraft Engineering 1959-65, dir John Fowler & Ptnrs Ltd (PR consltS) 1971-73, md Hall Harrison Cowley PR Birmingham Ltd 1974-; dir: Harrison Cowley Advty (Midlands) Ltd 1975-89, Harrison Cowley Photographic Ltd 1978-90; chm: Hall Harrison Cowley Bristol Ltd 1988-, Hall Harrison PR Gp (Birmingham, Bristol, Cardiff, Edinburgh, Maidenhead, Manchester and Southampton) 1988-; *Recreations* reading, dog walking, painting, activity holidays; *Clubs* RAF; *Style*— Charles Keil, Esq; Illyria, 536 Streetsbsrook Rd, West Midlands B91 1RD (☎ 021 705 0773); Hall Harrison Cowley Public Relations Birmingham Ltd, 154 Great Charles St, Birmingham B3 3HU (☎ 021 236 7532)

KEILL, (William Richard) Ian; s of Cdre W J D Keill (d 1980), and Annie Mavis, *née* Dash; *b* 11 May 1937; *Educ* Liverpool Coll, RADA (Dip); *m* 1963 (m dis 1977), Carole Ann, *née* Bishop; 1 s (Jeremy William Richard b 8 Oct 1964); m 2, Enid Averil, *née* Musson; *Career* actor then dir prodr and writer; BBC TV: prodr and dir Up Sunday 1971-73, 30 revues inc One Mans Weeks 1971-74, The End of the Pier Show 1974; pioneered electronic fantasy on TV with: The Snow Queen 1976, The Light Princess 1978, The Ghost Downstairs 1982; prodr strip cartoon Jane, dir and prodr two schoolgirl dramas 1982-83, prodr History of Westerns 1987, dir childrens ghost serial 1988, prodr Lucinda Lambton in Desirable Dwelling Forty Minutes 1988, prodr Frederic Raphael in Frontiers 1989; *Recreations* collecting books and recorded music, photography; *Style*— Ian Keill, Esq; 4 Boyn Hill Close, Maidenhead, Berks SL6 4JD (☎ 0628 31978)

KEIR, Prof Hamish Macdonald; s of Esme Charles Robson Keir (d 1967), of Ayr, Scotland, and Mabel Munro, *née* Blackstock (d 1979); *b* 5 Sept 1931; *Educ* Ayr Acad, Univ of Glasgow (BSc, PhD, DSc); *m* 1, 15 July 1958, Eleanor Louise, da of Ivor Campbell (d 1974), of Oban, Scotland; 1 s (Kenneth James Macdonald b 1962), 2 da (Catriona Louise b 1959, Deirdre Jean b 1961); m 2, Lindsay Margaret, da of William A G Gerrie, of Aberdeen, Scotland; 1 da; *Career* Univ of Glasgow: asst lectr in biochemistry 1956-59, lectr 1960-66, sr lectr 1966-68; James Hudson Brown res fell in pharmacology Yale Univ USA 1959-60, vice princ Univ of Aberdeen 1982-84 (Macleod-Smith Prof of biochemistry and head of dept 1968-); govr Rowett Res Inst 1968- (chm 1989), pres Fedn of Euro Biochemical Socs 1981-83, memb Br Nation Ctee for Biochemistry Royal Soc 1986-; chm: Jt Purchasing Consortium Univs of Scotland 1986-89, The Biochemical Soc 1986-; govr Macaulay Land Use Res Inst 1987-, pres Euro Union of Socs for Experimental Biology 1989-; govr Longridge Towers Sch 1987-; FRSE 1969; *Recreations* piano, travel, golf; *Clubs* Conservative Club, Aberdeen; *Style*— Prof Hamish Keir, FRSE; 9 Westholme Cres South, Aberdeen AB2 6AF (☎ 0224 324515); Department of Biochemistry, University of Aberdeen, Marischal College, Aberdeen AB9 1AS (☎ 0224 273121, telex UNIABN G 73458, fax 0224 273144)

KEIR, James Dewar; QC; s of Lt-Col David Robert Keir, DSO (d 1947), of Edinburgh, and Elizabeth Lunan, *née* Ross (d 1975); *b* 30 Nov 1921; *Educ* Edinburgh Acad, ChCh Oxford (MA); *m* 7 July 1948, Jean Mary, da of Rev Edward Percival Orr (d 1970), of Diss, Norfolk; 2 s (Robert b 17 Sept 1954, Simon b 29 March 1957), 2 da (Alison b 22 Aug 1950, Caroline b 11 Feb 1952); *Career* Capt Black Watch RHR served: ME, Italy, Austria; called to the Bar Inner Temple 1949, legal advsr Utd Africa Co Ltd 1954, head of legal servs Unilever Ltd 1973, jt sec Unilever NV and Unilever plc 1976-84; dir Open Univ Education Enterprises Ltd 1983-88; pres E Grinstead RFC 1969-88; chm: City and E London Family Practitioner Ctee 1985-89, Pharmacists Review Panel 1986-, E Grinstead Decorative and Fine Arts Soc 1987-; memb Monopolies and Mergers Cmmn 1987-; *Recreations* watching rugby, opera, reading; *Clubs* Caledonian; *Style*— James Keir, Esq, QC; The Crossways, 1 High St, Dormansland, Lingfield, Surrey RH7 6PU (☎ 0342 834621)

KEIR, Dr Michael Ian Stenhouse; s of Sir David Lindsay Keir (d 1973), of Hillsborough, Lincombe Lane, Boars Hill, Oxford, and Anna Clunie, *née* Dale; *b* 16 May 1934; *Educ* Charterhouse, New Coll Oxford (MA, BM BCh); *m* 14 Jan 1961 (m dis 1986), Maria Grazia, da of Gen Joseph Piana (d 1969), of Rome; 2 s (Mark Robert b 1961, Thomas Joseph b 1968); *Career* conslt dermatologist: Kent and Canterbury Hosp 1969-77, Whipps Cross Hosp London 1980-; hon lectr Bart's Med Coll 1987-; memb Dermatological Section RSM, BMA, Br Assoc of Dermatologists, Huntarian Soc; memb fell Royal Soc of Tropical Med and Hygiene; FRCPE 1977; *Recreations* swimming, travelling; *Style*— Dr Michael Keir

KEIR, Lady (Elizabeth) Sophia Rhiannon; *née* Paget; da of 7 Marquess of Anglesey, DL; *b* 14 May 1954; *m* 1983, Robert Keir, s of James Dewar Keir, QC, *qv*; *Style*— The Lady Sophia Keir

KEIR WATSON, Robin; s of Robert Keir Watson (d 1929); *b* 12 Sept 1915; *Educ* Hillhead HS Glasgow, Univ of Glasgow; *m* 1950, Veronica Josephine Yolande (d 1979); *Career* chartered engr and accountant; chm Associated Engineering Ltd 1970-80; recipient of Cncl of Inst of Petroleum award in recognition of servs to the Inst 1983; Freeman City of London, Liveryman Worshipful Co of Shipwrights 1972; *Recreations* educnl res in energy subjects, walking, voluntary work of educnl nature; *Clubs* Caledonian, Western (Glasgow); *Style*— Robin Keir Watson, Esq; 18 Kelvin Court, Glasgow G12 OAB (☎ 041 334 8763)

KEIRLE, David Alan; s of Alan George Keirle, of St Albans, Hertfordshire, and Frances, *née* Windsor (d 1966); *b* 19 Oct 1955; *Educ* Borehamwood GS, Poly of the South Bank (BA), RIBA (postgrad Dip Arch); *m* 1982, Lesley Anne, da of Charles Edwards, 2 s (Matthew Alan b 1968, Simon Alexander b 1988); *Career* Newan Levinson Ltd: joined 1977, chartered architect 1983, ptnr 1986, dir 1987; md: Newman Levinson Ltd 1989, DM & M Newman Levinson Ltd; ARIBA 1983; *Recreations* family, flying (PPL) in UK & Europe, skiing; *Style*— David Keirle, Esq; Newman Levinson, Northumberland House, 155-157 Great Portland Street, London W1N 6NU (☎ 071 637 8511, fax 071 636 8408)

KEITH, Hon Alastair James; s of Baron Keith of Castleacre (Life Peer); *b* 1947; *Educ* Eton, Harvard Univ (BA, MBA); *m* 1983, Jayne Will, yr da of late Walter C Teagle, Jr; 1 s (Alexander b 1984), 1 da (Serena b 1986); *Career* banker; *Style*— The Hon Alastair Keith; 150 East 73, New York City, New York, USA

KEITH, Lady Ariel Olivia Winifred; *née* Baird; CVO; 2 da of 1 Viscount Stonehaven, PC, GCMG, DSO (d 1941), and Countess of Kintore (d 1974); *b* 16 Aug 1916; *m* 25 April 1946 (m dis 1958), Sir Kenneth Alexander Keith (now Lord Keith of Castleacre); 1 s, 1 da; *Career* lady-in-waiting to HRH Princess Alice, Countess of Athlone 1940; *Style*— The Lady Ariel Keith, CVO; Flat B, 9 Cadogan Square, London SW1X 0HT (☎ 071 235 5343)

KEITH, Brian Richard; QC(1989); s of Alan Keith, OBE and Pearl, *née* Rebuck; *b* 14 April 1944; *Educ* UCS, Lincoln Coll Oxford (BA), Harvard Law Sch; *m* 16 Nov 1978, Gilly Mary, da of Air Cdre Ivan James de la Plain, CBE; 1 s (Benjamin b 15 March 1982), 1 da (Joanna b 22 Oct 1980); *Career* called to the Bar Inner Temple 1968, in practice 1969-; *Recreations* playing tennis, stamp collecting; *Style*— Brian Keith, Esq, QC; 11 Kings Bench Walk, Temple, London EC4Y 7EQ (☎ 071 583 0610)

KEITH, Ian Douglas; s of Leonard Douglas Keith, and Bertha Kent, *née* Straghan; *b* 13 Oct 1929; *Educ* Strathallan Forgandenny Perth; *m* 5 Sept 1959, Rosemary Enriqueta, da of Col William Herbert Treays, RE (d 1960), of Treetops, Orpington, Kent; 3 da (Sophie Henrietta b 1963, Sarah Louise b 1965, Fiona Mary b 1967); *Career* admitted slr 1960, ptnr Whitley Hughes & Luscombe 1963 (amalgamated with Donne Mileham & Haddock 1986); Notary Public 1963; chm govrs Handcross Prep Park Sch 1976-87, sole clerk to NHSS Tbnl for Eng and Wales; memb Law Soc; *Recreations* sailing, tennis, gardening; *Clubs* Bosham Sailing; *Style*— Ian Keith, Esq; 25 Queens Sq, Crawley, West Sussex, RH10 1EU (☎ 0293 545971, fax 0293 543760)

KEITH, Penelope Anne Constance; OBE (1989); da of Frederick Hatfield, and Constance Mary Keith; *Educ* Webber Douglas Acad; *m* 1978, Rodney Timson; *Career* actress; worked in repertory Chesterfield, Lincoln, Manchester, Salisbury; seasons with RSC; *roles played* Maggie Howard in Suddenly at Home (Fortune Theatre) 1971, Sarah in The Norman Conquests (Greenwich and Globe Theatre) 1974, Lady Driver in Donkey's Years 1976, Orinthia in The Apple Cart (Chichester and Phoenix Theatre) 1977, Epifania in the Millionairess (Haymarket) 1982, Sarah in Moving (Queen's) 1981, Maggie in Hobson's Choice (Haymarket) 1982, Lady Cicely Waynflete in Captain Brassbound's Conversion (Haymarket) 1982, Judith Bliss in Hayfever (Queen's) 1983, The Dragon's Tail (Apollo) 1985, Miranda (Chichester) 1987, The Deep Blue Sea (Haymarket) 1988, Dear Charles, Yvonne Arnaud (Guildford) 1990, The Merry Wives of Windsor (Chichester) 1990; *TV appearances* Six Shades of Black, Kate, The Pallisters, Jackanory, Saving it for Albie, The Morecambe and Wise Christmas Show, Tickle on the Tum, Woof, The Good Life, To the Manor Born, Sweet Sixteen, Executive Stress, No Job for a Lady; former presenter: What's My Line, Capability Brown, Growing Places; *film* The Priest of Love 1980; *awards* BAFTA 1976 and 1977, SWET 1976, Variety Club of GB 1976 and 1979, Pye Female Comedy Star 1977, Radio Industries 1978 and 1979, Daily Express 1979/80/81/82, BBC TV Swap Shop 1977-78 and 1979-80, TV Times 1976, 1977-78, 1979-80, 1983 and 1988, United States TV and Radio Mobius 1988; pres Actors Benevolent Fund 1989; *Style*— Miss Penelope Keith, OBE; c/o London Management, Regent Street, London W1R 7AG

KEITH, Capt (James) Robin Glyn; s of Col Norman Alistair Keith (d 1983), and Monica Margaret, *née* Price, (d 1988); *b* 13 March 1944; *Educ* Tonbridge; *m* 8 Jan 1979, Wendy Gay, da of Wing Cdr Harvey Heyworth (d 1957); 1 s (James b 1979); *Career* 14/20 Kings Hussars 1962-68, attended Army Wings Course Middle Wallop (later attached to Army Air Corps) 1964-68; commercial helicopter pilot Bristow Helicopters Ltd 1968-74 (S American Basin, Ghana, Dahomey, Indonesia, Malaysia, Singapore, West Aust); md and fndr McAlpine Helicopters 1974-87 (fndr McAlpine Helicopters Servs NZ 1984), fndr European Helicopters Ltd 1988-; memb Br Assoc for Shooting and Conservation; Upper Freeman of Guild of Air Pilots and Navigators 1984; MRAeS 1988; *Recreations* shooting, deer stalking, fishing; *Clubs* Cavalry and Guards; *Style*— Capt Robin Keith; Kingfisher's Cottage, Nelson Close, Stockbridge, Hants (☎ 0264 810 300, fax 0264 810 260, car 0836 275 143)

KEITH, Hon Thomas Hamilton; 2 s of Baron Keith of Kinkel (Life Peer); *b* 30 April 1961; *Educ* Magdalen Coll Oxford; *Career* barr; *Style*— The Hon Thomas Keith; Fountain Court Chambers, Temple, London EC4Y 9DH

KEITH-LUCAS, Prof Bryan; CBE (1983); s of Dr Keith Lucas, FRS (ka 1916), and Alys, *née* Hubbard (d 1955); *b* 1 Aug 1912; *Educ* Gresham's, Pembroke Coll Cambridge (MA), Univ of Kent at Canterbury (DLitt); *m* 24 Oct 1946, Mary Ross Keith-Lucas, MBE (Sheriff of Canterbury 1971), da of Dr J Hardwicke (d 1940), of Woolpit, Suffolk; 1 s (Peter b 1950), 2 da (Jane (Mrs Bird) b 1948, Polly (Mrs Dangerfield) b 1950); *Career* enlisted Buffs 1939; Sherwood Foresters: cmmnd 1940, Adj 2/5 Bn 1941, serv N Africa and Italy 1942-44, (despatches 1943), Maj DAAG Cyprus 1945-46; admitted slr 1937; asst slr: Royal Borough of Kensington 1937-46, Nottingham 1946-48; sr lectr Univ of Oxford 1948-65, bursar Nuffield Coll 1957-65 (fell 1950-65), prof of govt Univ of Kent at Canterbury 1965-77, Master Darwin Coll 1970-74; parish cncllr Cumnor 1950-56, city cncllr Oxford 1950-65; chm: Cmmn on Elections Sierra Leone 1954, Cmmn on Elections Mauritius 1955-56, Nat Assoc of Parish Cncls 1964-70, Canterbury Soc 1972-75; memb: Roberts Ctee on Public Libraries 1957-59, Mallaby Ctee on Staffing in Local Govt 1964-67, Local Govt Cmmn for England 1965-66, Royal Cmmn on Elections in Fiji 1975; pres: Kent Assoc of Parish Cncls 1976-81, Kent Fedn of Amenity Socs 1976-81, Stour Valley Soc 1982-, Kent Soc 1985-88; hon fell Inst of Local Govt Studies Birmingham Univ 1973; *Publications*: The English Local Government Franchise (1952), English Local Government in the 19th and 20th Centuries (1977), History of Local Government in the 20th Century (with P G Richards, 1978), The Unreformed Local Government System (1979), Parish Affairs (the Government of Kent under George III) (1986); *Recreations* walking; *Clubs* Nat Lib; *Style*— Prof Bryan Keith-Lucas, CBE; 7 Church St, Wye, Ashford, Kent TN25 5BN (☎ 0233 812 621)

KEITH-LUCAS, Prof David; CBE (1973); s of Keith Lucas (d 1916), and Alys Hubbard (d 1955); *b* 25 March 1911; *Educ* Greshams, Gonville & Caius Coll Cambridge (BA, MA); *m* 1, 25 April 1942, Dorothy De Bauduy (d 1979), da of Leslie S Robertson (d 1916); 2 s (Michael b 1944, Christopher b 1949), 1 da (Mary (now Mrs Benjamin) b 1943); m 2, 11 July 1981, Phyllis Marion Everard, da of Bertram William Whurr (d 1939); *Career* Short Bros & Harland Ltd: chief designer 1949-58, tech dir 1958-65; Cranfield Inst of Tech: prof of aircraft design 1965-72, chm Coll of Aeronautics 1972-76, pro vice chllr 1970-73, prof emeritus 1976; pt/t dir John Brown & Co 1970-77, chm N I Assoc of Boy's Clubs 1952-65; memb: Senate Queens Univ Belfast 1955-65, Roskill Cmmn on Third London Airport 1968-70; pres Royal Aeronautical Soc 1968-69 (Gold medal 1975), memb Bd CAA 1972-80, chm Airworthiness Requirements Bd 1973-81; Hon DSc: Queens Univ Belfast 1968, Cranfield 1975; FIMechE 1949, hon FAIAA 1974, FEng 1978, hon FRAeS 1979; *Books* The Shape of Wings to Come (1952); *Recreations* vintage car, vintage cabin cruiser; *Style*— Prof David Keith-Lucas, CBE; Manor Close, Emberton, Olney, Bucks MK46 5BX (☎ 0234 711552)

KEITH-MURRAY, Maj Peter; s of David Keith-Murray (d 1968), and Nancy Mai, *née* Gautschi; hp of kinsman, Sir Patrick Murray of Ochtertyre, 12 Bt; *b* 12 June 1935; *m* 15 June 1960, Judith Anne, da of William Andrew Tinsley (d 1962); 1 s (Andrew b 7 Dec 1965), 1 da (Leslie Lascelle b 30 Jan 1961); *Career* RCAF 1954-91 (ret); Canadian Forces Decoration with 2 clasps (long service and good conduct); *Style*— Maj Peter Keith-Murray; 895 Brentwood Heights, Bentwood Bay, BC VOS 1AO, Canada (☎ 604 652-0574)

KEITH OF CASTLEACRE, Baron (Life Peer UK 1980), of Swaffham, Co Norfolk; Kenneth Alexander Keith; s of Edward Charles Keith (d 1972), naturalist and writer, of Swanton Morley House, Dereham, Norfolk; *b* 30 Aug 1916; *Educ* Rugby; *m* 1, 25 April 1946 (m dis 1958), Lady Ariel Olivia Winifred Baird, 2 da of 1 Viscount Stonehaven, GCMG, DSO, PC, and (Ethel) Sydney, Countess of Kintore; 1 s, 1 da; m 2, 1962 (m dis 1972), Mrs Nancy (Slim) Hayward, *née* Mary Raye Gross (d 1990), formerly w of (1) Howard Hawks, the film dir, and (2) Leland Hayward, theatre and film agent; m 3, 1973, Marie-Luz, da of Capt Robert Peel Dennistoun-Webster, RN, and formerly wife of (1) Adrian Donald Henderson and (2) James Robert Hanbury; *Career* 2 Lt Welsh Gds 1939, Lt-Col 1945, served in N Africa, Italy, France and Germany (despatches, Croix de Guerre with Silver Star), asst to Gir-Gen Political

Intelligence Dept FO 1945-46, merchant banker and industrialist; vice chm BEA 1964-71, chm Hill Samuel Group Ltd 1970-80, dir British Airways 1971-72, chm and chief exec Rolls-Royce Ltd 1972-80, Beecham Group Ltd (dir 1949-87, vice chm 1956-65 and 1974-87, chm Beecham Group 1985-86); dir: Eagle Star Insurance Co 1955-75, National Provincial Bank 1967-69, Standard Telephones and Cables Ltd (chm 1985-89); chm Arlington Securities 1982-90; pres: Royal Norfolk Agricultural Assoc 1989, Br Standards Inst 1989-, ROSPA 1989-; hon companion Royal Aeronautical Soc; FRSA, FBIM; kt 1969; *Recreations* farming, shooting, golf; *Clubs* White's, Pratt's, Links (NY); *Style—* The Rt Hon the Lord Keith of Castleacre; 9 Eaton Sq, London SW1W 9DB (☎ 071 730 4000); The Wicken House, Castle Acre, Norfolk (0760 755225)

KEITH OF KINKEL, Baron (Life Peer UK 1976), of Strathtummel in District of Perth and Kinross; Hon Henry Shanks Keith; PC (1976); o s of Baron Keith of Avonholm (Life Peer, d 1964), and Jean Maitland, *née* Bennett; *b* 7 Feb 1922; *Educ* Edinburgh Acad, Magdalen Coll Oxford (Hon Fell 1977), Univ of Edinburgh; *m* 17 Dec 1955, Alison Hope Alan, yr da of Alan Brown, of Fairways, St Andrews; 4 s (Hon James Alan b 1959, Hon Thomas Hamilton b 1961, Hon Hugo George b 1967, Hon Alexander Lindsay (twin) b 1967), 1 da (Hon Deborah Jane b 1957); *Career* Scots Gds 1941-45 (despatches); advocate Scottish Bar 1950, called to the Bar Gray's Inn 1951, bencher 1976, QC (Scot) 1962, Sheriff of Roxburgh, Berwick and Selkirk 1970-71; dep chm Parly Boundary Cmmn for Scotland 1971; senator of College of Justice in Scotland with judicial title of Lord Keith 1971-77, Lord of Appeal in Ordinary 1977-; memb Ctee on Law of Defamation 1970-73, chm Ctee on Powers of the Revenue Depts 1980-83; *Clubs* Flyfishers'; *Style—* The Rt Hon the Lord Keith of Kinkel, PC; House of Lords, London SW1

KELBIE, Sheriff David; s of Robert Kelbie, of Plymouth, and Monica Eileen Pearn; *b* 28 Feb 1945; *Educ* Inverurie Acad, Univ of Aberdeen (LLB); *m* 1966, Helen Mary, da of William Ross Smith, of Aberdeen; 1 s (Alasdair David b 1975), 1 da (Catriona Helen b 1972); *Career* advocate 1968; Sheriff: North Strathclyde at Dumbarton 1979-86, Grampian, Highland and Islands, Aberdeen, Stonehaven 1986-; *Recreations* sailing; *Style—* Sheriff David Kelbie; 38 Earlspark Drive, Bieldside, Aberdeen (☎ 0224 868237); Aberdeen Sheriff Ct (☎ 0224 572780)

KELL, Richard Alexander; s of Rev George Kell (d 1970), of Lisburn, and Florence Irene, *née* Musgrave; *b* 1 Nov 1927; *Educ* Methodist Coll Belfast, Wesley Coll Dublin, Univ of Dublin (BA); *m* 31 Dec 1953, Muriel Adelaide (d 1975), da of Oscar Nairn (d 1950); 2 s (Colin b 1955, Timothy b 1958), 2 da (Carolyn b 1957, Shelagh b 1962); *Career* poet, composer and teacher; performances by various soloists and ensembles incl: Royal Liverpool Philharmonic Orchestra, Northern Sinfonia Orchestra; teacher of Eng Lit: Isleworth Poly 1960-70, Newcastle upon Tyne Poly 1970-83; *Books* Control Tower (1962), Differences (1969), The Broken Circle (1981), In Praise of Warmth (1987); *Recreations* fell walking, swimming; *Style—* Richard Kell, Esq; 18 Rectory Grove, Gosforth, Newcastle upon Tyne NE3 1AL

KELLAND, John William; LVO (1977), QPM (1975); s of William John Kelland (d 1976), of Devon, and Violet Ethel, *née* Olsen (d 1983); *b* 18 Aug 1929; *Educ* Sutton HS, Plymouth Poly; *m* 1, 14 May 1963, Brenda Nancy (d 1985), da of Edward Foulsham (d 1948), of London; 2 s (Michael John b 1950, Andrew b 1953); m 2, 17 May 1986, Frances Elizabeth, da of Thomas Byrne (d 1953), of Ireland; 1 step da (Jean Margaret McDonald b 1963); *Career* Nat Serv RAF Pilot Offr 1947-49; inspr Plymouth City Police 1950-67, supt Devon and Cornwall Constabulary 1968-72 Sr Cmd Course Police Staff Coll 1972, asst chief constable Cumbria Constabulary 1972-74, cmmr Royal Fiji Police 1975-78, dir sr cmd trg Police Staff Coll UK 1978-80, ret; fndr Mgmnt Consultancy 1981; 1981-85: chm Civil Serv Selection Bds, sr conslt Royal Inst of Public Admin, sr lectr Business Studies Cornwall Coll of Higher Educn, facilitator Interpersonal Skills Seminar; overseas police advsr and inspr gen of Dependent Territories Police FCO 1985-; FBIM 1972; *Recreations* sport, wild life, travel, choral singing; *Clubs* Royal Overseas, Civil Serv; *Style—* John Kelland, Esq, LVO, QPM; Foreign and Commonwealth Office, Room 2/105, Old Admiralty Building, Whitehall (☎ 071 210 6330)

KELLAR, David Crawford; s of Prof Robert James Kellar (d 1980), of Edinburgh, and Gertrude Crawford, *née* Aitken (d 1980); *b* 30 March 1932; *Educ* Rugby, Univ of Edinburgh (MA, LLB); *m* 25 June 1960, Agnes Gilchrist, da of Leslie James Hastie, of Dumfries; 1 s (Ewen b 1962), 1 da (Gail b 1966); *Career* slr, Notary Public estate agent; sec Faculty of Procurators of Dumfriesshire 1968-88, pres Scottish Law Agents Soc 1984-86; *Recreations* photography, cookery, jazz piano; *Style—* David Kellar, Esq; Woodlea, Shawhead, Dumfries (☎ 0387 73 324); 135 Irish St, Dumfries DG1 2NT (☎ 0387 55351, fax , 0387 57306)

KELLAS, Arthur Roy Handasyde; CMG (1963); s of Henry Kellas (d 1923), of Aberdeen, and Mary, *née* Brown (d 1956); *b* 6 May 1915; *Educ* Aberdeen GS, Univ of Aberdeen (MA), Balliol Coll Oxford (BA), Ecole des Sciences Politiques Paris; *m* 27 Aug 1952, (Katharine) Bridget, da of Sir John Le Rougetel, KCMG, MC (d 1975), of Alton, Hants; 2 s (Ian b 1955, Roger b 1958), 1 da (Miranda b 1953); *Career* WWII 2 Lt 7 Bn Border Regt 1939-40 (10 Ind Company 1940), Lt 1 Bn Parachute Regt 1941-43, Capt SOE 1943-44; Dip Serv; third sec 1939, third sec Tehran Embassy 1944-47; first sec: Helsinki Legation 1949-51, Cairo Embassy 1951-52, Baghdad Embassy 1954-58; cnsllr: Tehran Embassy 1958-62, Tel Aviv Embassy 1964-65; ambass: Kathmandu 1966-70, Aden 1970-72; high cmmr Tanzania 1973-75; FRGS 1960; Pahlavi Order (Taj) Iran 1960; *Clubs* United Oxford and Cambridge Univ; *Style—* Arthur Kellas, Esq, CMG; Inverockle, Achateny, Acharacle, Argyll, Scotland (☎ 097 23265); 59 Cockburn St, Edinburgh (☎ 031 2262398)

KELLAWAY, Prof Ian Walter; s of Leslie William Kellaway, (d 1975), and Margaret Seaton, *née* Webber; *b* 10 March 1944; *Educ* King Edward VI GS Totnes, Univ of London (BPharm, PhD, DSc); *m* 2 Aug 1969, Kay Elizabeth, da of Raymond Cyril Downey, of Ystrad Mynach; 1 s (Robert b 5 July 1972), 1 da (Jane b 21 May 1974); *Career* lectr in pharmaceutics Dept of Pharmacy Univ of Nottingham 1969-79, prof of pharmaceutics Welsh Sch of Pharmacy Univ of Wales Coll Cardiff 1979-; memb Welsh Scheme for the Devpt of Health and Soc Res, Welsh Ctee for Postgrad Pharmaceutical Educn; fell Royal Pharmaceutical Soc 1969; *Recreations* gardening, travel; *Style—* Prof Ian Kellaway; 9 Dan-Y-Bryn Ave, Radyr, S Glamorgan, Wales (☎ 0222 842427); Welsh School of Pharmacy, UWCC, PO Box 13, Cardiff CF1 3XF (☎ 0222 874159)

KELLAWAY, Richard James; s of Francis Percival Hamley Kellaway (d 1979), of Reading, and Mildred Alice, *née* Neal; *b* 30 May 1945; *Educ* Presentation Coll Reading, Pembroke Coll Cambridge (MA); *m* 18 Oct 1970, Marie-Louise Anne, da of Vincent Michael Franklin (d 1955), of Beckenham; 2 s (Nicholas Franklin b 7 March 1975, Christopher Michael b 4 Aug 1984), 1 da (Antonia Helen b 4 Oct 1972); *Career* commercial mangr Paktank Storage Co Ltd 1968-73, dir Tankfreight Co Ltd 1973-77; md: Felixstowe Tank Development Ltd 1975-77, GATX Terminals Ltd 1979- (joined 1977); chm: Tees Storage Co Ltd, Manchester Jetline Ltd; dir: Wymondham Oil Storage Co Ltd, Unitank Pencol Ltd; cncllr London Borough of Bromley 1971-74, parly candidate (C) Bristol South 1974; FInstPet; *Recreations* music, golf; *Clubs* Carlton; *Style—* Richard Kellaway, Esq; Somerley, Startins Lane, Cookham Dean, Berks SL6 9TS (☎ 06284 2605); GATX Terminals Ltd, Nicholson House, High St, Maidenhead, Berks SL6 1LQ (☎ 0628 771 242, fax 0628 771 678, telex 847862)

KELLEHER, Brig Dame Joan Evelyn; DBE (1965); da of Kenneth George Henderson; *b* 24 Dec 1915; *m* 1970, Brig M F H Kelleher, OBE, MC, late RAMC; *Career* joined ATS 1941, cmmnd 1941, WRAC 1949, dir WRAC 1964-67; Hon ADC to HM The Queen 1964-67; *Recreations* golf, gardening; *Style—* Brig Dame Joan Kelleher, DBE; c/o Midland Bank, 123 Chancery Lane, London WC2A 1QH

KELLER, Hon Mrs (Susan Henriette); er da of Baron Schon (Life Peer); *b* 23 Oct 1941; *Educ* Badminton Sch Bristol, Ecole Hotelière Switzerland; *m* 1964, Richard Henry Keller, s of Arthur Keller; 2 s (Philip Henry b 1965, Nicholas Frank b 1970), 1 da (Annabel Jane b 1967); *Career* fitness instructor; *Recreations* aerobics, tennis, antiques; *Clubs* Annabel's; *Style—* The Hon Mrs Keller; Hillmorton, Wills Grove, Mill Hill Village, London NW7 (☎ 081 959 4442)

KELLETT, Anthony; s of Albert Kellett (d 1980), and Lilian, *née* Holroyd; *b* 24 Sept 1937; *Educ* Batley GS, Leeds Sch of Architecture (Dip Arch); *m* 4 Sept 1964 (m dis 1984); 2 s (Anthony John b 1967, Martin James b 1970); *Career* CA; ptnr: Davidson Marsh & Co 1971-79, Kellett & Robinson 1980-; former pres IOM Soc of Architects and Surveyors; FASI, ACIArb, RIBA; *Recreations* choral singing, painting; *Clubs* Ellan Vannin, Rotary of Rushen and Western Mann; *Style—* Anthony Kellett, Esq; 32 Birch Hill Ave, Onchan, Douglas, IOM (☎ 0624 672255); Sydney Mount, Bucks Rd, Douglas, IOM (☎ 0624 628141)

KELLETT, Audrey, Lady Kellett; Audrey Margaret; *née* Phillips; *m* 1938, Sir Stanley Everard Kellett, 6 Bt (d 1983); 1 s (Sir Stanley, 7 Bt, *qv*), 1 da; *Style—* Audrey, Lady Kellett; 33 Caroma Avenue, Kyeemagh, NSW 2216, Australia

KELLETT, Sir Brian Smith; s of Harold Lamb Kellett (d 1935) and Amy Elizabeth, *née* Smith (d 1984); *b* 8 May 1922; *Educ* Manchester GS, Trinity Coll Cambridge; *m* 1947, Janet Lesly Street; 3 da; *Career* civil servant with Admty, Miny of Tport 1942-48, Sir Robert Watson-Watt & Partners 1948-49, Pilkington Bros 1949-55; former chm British Aluminium Company; chm: Tube Investments (TI Group) 1976-84 (md 1968-82), Port of London Authy 1985-, Br Ports Fedn 1990-; dir: Unigate 1974-, Nat Westminster Bank 1981-, Lombard North Central 1985-, Investmt Mgmnt Regulatory Orgn 1987-90; govr: Imperial Coll 1979-, London Business Sch 1976-84; kt 1979; *Style—* Sir Brian Kellett; The Old Malt House, Deddington, Banbury, Oxon OX15 0TG

KELLETT, Caroline Anne; da of John Luce Kellet, of The Mount, Cookham Dean, Berks, and Gillian Hazel, *née* Ripley; *Educ* Convent of the Nativity of our Lord Berks, Wycombe Abbey Sch, Wadham Coll Oxford (BA); *Career* fashion features ed Vogue 1981-86, contributing ed W 1987-88; fashion ed: Evening Standard 1988-89, Tatler Magazine 1989-90; TV presenter BSB 1990; *Recreations* botany, travel, art, 19 century French literature, cinematography; *Style—* Miss Caroline Kellett; 21 Wilton St, London SW1

KELLETT, Ida, Lady; Ida Mary Grace Weaver; *m* 7 May 1952, Sir Henry de Castres Kellett, 5 Bt (d 1966); *Style—* Ida, Lady Kellett

KELLETT, Peter; s of Milton Hampden Kellett (d 1966), and Margaret Mary, *née* Hart; *b* 29 Aug 1927; *Educ* Cotton Coll N Staffs, Univ of St Andrews (BSc); *m* 5 Sept 1949, Jean Mcintosh, da of Robert Fulcar Browning (d 1936); 2 s (Michael b 1954, David b 1965), 2 da (Jane b 1950, Sarah b 1962); *Career* head of computing and res (later gen mangr) Elliott Automation Computers Ltd 1967, fndr Lamerholm Ltd 1975; currently chm and md: Lamerholm Fleming Ltd, Lamerholm Ltd, Fleming Instruments Ltd; FIEE, CEng; *Recreations* hill walking, woodworking, eighteenth and nineteenth century literature; *Style—* Peter Kellett, Esq; Fife House, Graveley, Herts (☎ 0438 352175); Lamerholm Fleming Ltd, Caxton Way, Stevenage, Herts SG1 2DE (☎ 0438 728844, fax 0438 742326, telex 82385)

KELLETT, Sir Stanley Charles; 7 Bt (UK 1801), of Lota, Cork; s of Sir Stanley Everard Kellett, 6 Bt (d 1983), and Audrey Margaret, *née* Phillips; *b* 5 March 1940; *m* 1, 1962 (m dis 1968), Lorraine May, da of F Winspear; m 2, 1968, Margaret Ann, da of James W Bofinger; m 3, 1982, Catherine Lorna, da of W J C Or; 1 da (Leah Catherine Elizabeth, b 1983); *Style—* Sir Stanley Kellett, Bt; 58 Glad Gunson Drive, Eleebana, NSW Australia

KELLETT-BOWMAN, Edward Thomas; JP (Middx 1966), MEP (EDG) Hants Central 1988-; s of Reginald Edward Bowman (d 1934), and Mabel Bowman; *b* 25 Feb 1931; *Educ* Reed's Sch, Slough Coll of Technol (DMS), Cranfield Inst of Technol (MBA); *m* 1, 1960, Margaret Blakemore (d 1970); 3 s, 1 da; m 2, 1971, (Mary) Elaine Kellett (Dame Elaine Kellett-Bowman, MP, *qv*); *Career* MEP (EDG) Lancs E 1979-84; FBIM; *Recreations* shooting, tennis, swimming; *Style—* Edward Kellett-Bowman, Esq, JP, MEP; Naishes Barn, Newnham, Hampshire RG27 9AF

KELLETT-BOWMAN, Dame (Mary) Elaine; *née* Kay; DBE (1989), MP (C) Lancaster 1970-; da of late Walter Kay; *b* 8 July 1924; *Educ* Queen Mary's Sch Lytham, The Mount Sch York, St Anne's Coll Oxford; *m* 1, 1945, Charles Norman Kellett (d 1959); 3 s, 1 da; m 2, 1971, Edward Thomas Kellett-Bowman, MEP, JP, *qv*; 3 step s, 1 step da; *Career* farmer; welfare worker London and Liverpool; called to the Bar Middle Temple 1964, in practice 1968-74; contested (C): Nelson and Colne 1955, S W Norfolk 1959 and 1959 by-election, Buckingham 1964 and 1966; memb Press Cncl 1964-68; Alderman Camden Boro 1968-74, chm Welfare Ctee 1969; MEP (EDG) Cumbria 1979-84; *Clubs* English Speaking Union; *Style—* Dame Elaine Kellett-Bowman, DBE, MP

KELLEY, Malcolm Percy; s of Percy William Alfred Kelley (d 1978), and Gladys Beatrice Kelley (d 1986); *b* 21 July 1931; *Educ* Thames Valley GS; *m* 24 Aug 1957, Pamela, da of John Ernest Conway (d 1968); *Career* sales dir: Penguin Books Ltd 1970-72, Ladybird Books Ltd 1972-73; md Ladybird Books Ltd 1973-; dir: Longman Group UK 1981-, Pickwick Group plc 1988-; chm: Ladybird Books Inc 1985-, Sunbird Publishing Ltd 1986-; *Recreations* following rugby football, reading, cooking, jogging; *Clubs* Rosslyn Park RFC, Leicester RFC; *Style—* Malcolm Kelley, Esq; 50 Outwoods Rd, Loughborough, Leics LE11 3LY; Ladybird Books Ltd, Beeches Road, Loughborough, Leics (fax 234672, telex 341347)

KELLOCK, His Hon Judge Thomas Oslaf; QC (1965); s of Thomas Herbert Kellock (d 1922), and Margaret Brooke (d 1972); *b* 4 July 1923; *Educ* Rugby, Clare Coll Cambridge (BA); *m* 18 March 1967, Jane Ursula, da of Arthur George Symonds (d 1944), of Dorset; *Career* RNVR (special branch) 1944-46; called to the Bar Inner Temple 1949, bencher 1973, dir Legal Div Cwlth Secretariat 1969-72, circuit judge 1976-; *Recreations* travelling; *Clubs* Reform; *Style—* His Hon Judge T O Kellock, QC; 8 Huntingdon Drive, The Park, Nottingham NG7 1BW (☎ 0602 418304); 8 Kings Bench Walk, Inner Temple, London EC4Y 7DU

KELLY, Alan Keith; s of Julius Israel Kelly, DSO (d 1964), of Hove, East Sussex, and Gladys, *née* Goldstone; *b* 18 Aug 1941; *Educ* Brighton Coll; *m* 24 Oct 1970, Christine Barbara, da of Lewis Henry Weller, of Faversham, Kent; 1 s (Julian b 1971, Amanda b 1973); *Career* CA; sr personal fin ptnr Chantry Vellacott 1991-, course dir and princ speaker Inst CA's introductory course Investment and Financial Planning for the Individual (chm advanced course); FCA 1965; *Books* Financial Planning for the Individual (1986, 3 edn 1989); *Recreations* tennis, theatre, travel, music; *Clubs* Weald Tennis; *Style—* Alan Kelly, Esq; Kyrenia House, 12 Deanway, Hove, East Sussex BN3 6DG (☎ 0273 504989); Chantrey Vellacott, Russell Square House, 10-12 Russell Square, London WC1B 5LF (☎ 071 436 3666, fax 071 436 8884)

KELLY, Anthony; CBE (1988); *b* 25 Jan 1929; *Educ* Presentation Coll Reading, Univ of Reading (scholar, BSc), Trinity Coll Cambridge (PhD, ScD); *m* Christina Margaret, *née* Dunleavie; 4 c; *Career* scientist and engr; researcher Illinois Univ, ICI res fell Univ of Birmingham, asst prof then assoc prof metallurgy and materials science Technological Inst of North Western Univ Chicago, lectr in metallurgy Univ of Cambridge 1958, founding fell and dir studies in natural sciences Churchill Coll Cambridge until 1967, dep dir Materials Gp National Physical Laboratory 1969-74 (supt Div of Inorganic and Metallic Structure 1967-69), seconded to ICI 1974, vice chancellor Univ of Surrey 1975- (prof 1988); former visiting prof: Univ of Göttingen, Carnegie-Mellon Univ, Ecole Polytechnique Federale de Lausanne; dir British Non-Ferous Metals Research Association 1970-72; chm: Engineering Materials Requirements Bd Dept of Indust 1976-80, Standing Ctee on Structural Safety (estab by Inst of Civil and Structural Engrs) 1987-; Fndr Euro Assoc for Composite Materials 1984, currently dir Johnson Wax and chm Surrey Satellite Technology; Extraordinary fell Churchill Coll Cambridge 1985, Medal of Excellence Univ of Delaware USA 1984; foreign assoc Nat Acad of Engrg of USA 1986, FRS 1973, FEng; author of numerous scientific papers and five books; *Style*— Prof Anthony Kelly, CBE, FRS; Univ of Surrey, Guildford, Surrey GU2 5XH (☎ 0483 509249, fax 0483 572480)

KELLY, Barbara Mary; da of John Maxwell Prentice, JP, of Dalbeattie, Stewartry of Kirkcudbright, and Barbara Bain, *née* Adam (d 1989); *b* 27 Feb 1940; *Educ* Dalbeattie HS, Kirkcudbright Acad, Moray House Edinburgh; *m* 28 July 1960, Kenneth Archibald Kelly, s of Thomas Archibald Grant Kelly (d 1960); 2 s (Neil Grant b 1963, Jonathon Ormiston b 1965, d 1985), 2 da (Joanna Barbara b 1970, Christian Maxwell b 1972); *Career* freelance journalist with the BBC, ptnr in mixed farming enterprise; chm Scottish Consumer Cncl 1985-, memb Nat Consumer Cncl 1985-, chm Rural Forum Scotland 1988-, memb Scottish Enterprise; former chm: Dumfries and Galloway Area Manpower Bd, Scottish Advsy Ctee Duke of Edinburgh Award (memb UK Advsy Ctee 1981-85); tstee Scottish Silver Jubilee Tst; *Recreations* family, cooking, walking, gardening of necessity; *Style*— Mrs Barbara Kelly; Barncleugh, Irongray, Dumfries, Dumfries and Galloway DG2 9SE (☎ 0387 73210); Scottish Consumer Council, 314 St Vincent St, Glasgow G3 8XW (☎ 041 226 5261

KELLY, Bernard Noel; s of Sir David Kelly, GCMG, MC (d 1959), of Tara House, Co Wexford, and Comtesse de Vaux; *b* 23 April 1930; *Educ* Downside; *m* 11 July 1952, Lady Mirabel Magdalene Fitzalan Howard, sister of 17 Duke of Norfolk, *qv*; 7 s, 1 da; *Career* Capt 8 Queen's Royal Irish Hussars incl reserves 1948-60; slr 1956; ptnr Simmons and Simmons 1958-62; banker; dir: S G Warburg & Co 1963-76, Barnes Gp Inc (USA) 1975-, Investment AB Ostermalm (Sweden) 1976-, Lazard Bros and Co Ltd 1980-90 (vice-chm and md 1981-85), Highcross plc 1988, Phoenix Re (USA) 1988, Stockholm and London plc 1990, Societe Generale Investissement (LUX) 1990; chm: International Select Fund Ltd 1988, First Equity Services Ltd 1987, Campell Lutyens Hudson & Co Ltd 1990; *Clubs* Athenaeum, Brooks's, Kildare and University (Dublin); *Style*— Bernard Kelly, Esq; 4 Clifford St, London W1 (☎ 071 439 7191)

KELLY, Air Vice-Marshal (Herbert) Brian; CB (1983), LVO (1960); s of Surgn Capt James Cecil Kelly, DSC (d 1961), of Clonmore, Charing, Kent, and Meta Matheson, *née* Fraser (d 1971); *b* 12 Aug 1921; *Educ* Epsom Coll, St Thomas's Hosp London Univ (MB BS MD, DCH, MRCP); *Career* registered med practitioner; med offr RNVR 1945-48; conslt in med RAF Hosps: Aden, Ely, Nocton Hall, Singapore, Cyprus, Germany; med branch RAF 1953-83, sr conslt to RAF 1979-83 (formerly conslt advsr in med), ret; conslt med advsr to PPP Medical Centre, conslt advsr to CAA; QHS 1978-83; Liveryman Worshipful Soc of Apothecaries, Freeman City of London; MFOM 1982, FRSM 1948, FRCP 1968, fell Med Soc of London 1959; *Recreations* choral singing, DIY; *Clubs* RAF; *Style*— Air Vice-Marshal Brian Kelly, CB, LVO; 32 Chiswick Quay, Hartington Rd, London W4 3UR (☎ 081 995 5042)

KELLY, Brian Owen; s of George Alfred Kelly (d 1983), and Delia, *née* Cafferkey (d 1983); *b* 9 Jan 1943; *Educ* Presentation Coll Reading, Farnborough Coll of Technol; *m* 17 Oct 1970, (Anne) Christine, da of Fred Payne (d 1985); *Career* scientific asst Service Electronics Res Laboratory 1959-64, experimental offr Admty Compass Observatory 1964-70, sr engr Bendix Aerospace Michigan USA 1970-73, vice pres United Detector Technology LA 1973-78, gen mangr Centronic Optical Systems Ltd Croydon 1978-85, md Centronic Ltd 1985-; chm: Dosimeter Corporation of America USA, Mini Instruments Ltd Essex, Centronic Inc USA; memb Cncl Def Mfrs Assoc, govr Addington HS Croydon; MIERE 1975, MInstP 1979, FBIM 1980, CPhys; *Recreations* golf, bridge, chess; *Style*— Brian Kelly, Esq; Green Roofs, Dower House Crescent, Tunbridge Wells, Kent TN4 0TT; Centronic House, King Henry's Drive, Croydon CR9 0BG (☎ 0689 42 121, fax 0489 43 053, telex 876 474 CENTRO G)

KELLY, Charles Henry; CBE (1986), QPM (1978), DL (Staffs 1979); s of Charles Henry Kelly (d 1984), and Phoebe Jane Kelly (d 1948); *b* 15 July 1930; *Educ* Douglas HS for Boys IOM, London Univ (LLB); *m* 1952, Doris; 1 s (Kevin), 1 da (Lynne); *Career* asst chief constable Essex 1972-76, dep chief constable Staffordshire 1976-77, chief constable Staffordshire 1977-; assoc prof Criminal Justice Dept Michigan State Univ 1990-; chm: ACPO Communications Ctee 1983-, No 3 ACPO Regnl Conf 1985-; memb Ct Keele Univ 1990; CStJ 1983; *Recreations* music, cricket, reading; *Clubs* Special Forces; *Style*— Charles Kelly, Esq, CBE, QPM, DL; Baswich House, Cannock Rd, Stafford ST17 0QG (☎ 0785 57717)

KELLY, Christopher Aliaga; s of Ambrose Aliaga Kelly (d 1953); *b* 28 Sept 1920; *Educ* St Mary's Coll Dublin; *m* 1948, Cynthia Averill, da of Lt-Col the Hon Thomas George Breadalbane Morgan-Grenville DSO, OBE (d 1965); 1 s, 1 da; *Career* jt md: Cookson Group; dir: Allied Irish Banks Ltd; chm: Goodlass Wall Ltd, Alexander Fergusson Ltd, dir: Fry's Diecastings, Goodlass Nerolac Paints India, Valentine Varnish & Lacquer; past pres Confedn of Irish Industry; *Clubs* Stephens Green (Dublin); *Style*— Christopher Kelly, Esq; 10 Rawlings St, London SW3 (☎ 01 584 1155)

KELLY, Christopher Michael; s of Patrick Joseph Kelly, and Una Kelly; *b* 29 Oct 1945; *Educ* Downside; *m* 30 March 1970, Margaret; 1 s (Timothy b 7 June 1979), 1 da (Samantha 27 Sept 1975); *Career* mktg trainee Shell Mex & BP Ltd 1963-65, account dir Cogent Elliott Advertising 1965-75, sales and mktg dir Hertz Europe Ltd 1975-79; md: Hertz UK Ltd 1979-84, Reed Executive plc 1984-; *Style*— Christopher Kelly, Esq; 33 Dukes Ave, London W4 2AA; Reed Executive plc, 140 The Broadway, Tolworth, Surrey KT6 7JE (☎ 081 399 5221, fax 081 399 2185)

KELLY, Christopher William; s of Dr Reginald Edward Kelly (d 1990), and Peggy Kathleen, *née* Stone; *b* 18 Aug 1946; *Educ* Beaumont Coll, Trinity Coll Cambridge (MA), Univ of Manchester (MA); *m* 1970, Alison Mary Collens, da of Dr Henry Durant (d 1982), and Peggy Durant; 2 s (Jake b 1974, Toby b 1976), 1 da (Rachel b 1980); *Career* asst princ HM Treasy 1970, private sec to fin sec 1971-73, sec to Wilson Ctee of Inquiry into Fin Insts 1978-80, asst sec HM Treasy 1981, under sec Pay and Industl Relations Gp in Treasy 1987; *Recreations* narrow boating; *Style*— Christopher Kelly, Esq; HM Treasury, Parliament St, London SW1 3PAG (☎ 071 270 4500)

KELLY, David; s of Bernard Myrddin Kelly (d 1977), and Mabel Elizabeth, *née* Beard (d 1981); *b* 29 Oct 1936; *Educ* Stonyhurst, Lincoln Coll Oxford (MA); *Career* E Lancs Regt 1955-57 (served Royal W Africa Frontier Force 1957); TA E Lancs Regt; called to the Bar 1962, ICI 1962-67, Amalgamated Metal Corporation and British Metal Corporation 1967-72, Woodall-Duckham Group 1972-74, B Elliott plc 1974-84, The Ogilvy Gp (Holdings) 1985-; *Recreations* tennis, golf, skiing; *Clubs* United Oxford & Cambridge; *Style*— David Kelly, Esq; 19 Kingslawn Close, Howards Lane, Putney, London SW15 6QJ (☎ 081 789 3344); Brettenham House, Lancaster Place, London WC2E 7EZ (☎ 071 836 2466, fax 071 836 5938)

KELLY, Dr David Roy; s of Roy Alfred Kelly, and Marie Rose Kelly; *b* 16 April 1955; *Educ* Univ of Salford (BSc, PhD), Univ of Waterloo Canada, Univ of Maryland, Univ of Oxford; *m* 13 Sept 1980, Judith Wendy, da of Eric Hadfield, of Marston, Yorkshire; 1 da (Lauren Rachael Olivia b 14 July 1990); *Career* post doctoral fell: Univ of Waterloo 1979-80, Univ of Maryland 1980- 81, Univ of Oxford 1981-84; New Blood lectr in organic chem Univ Coll Cardiff 1984-, speaker The Chemistry of Sexual Attraction, over 30 pubns in jls; sec: Euro Symposium on Bioorganic Chemistry 1986-90 (memb Ctee 1986-), Gregynog Symposium for Young Br Chemists 1987-; memb: ACS, SCI; MRSC (C Chem) 1979, ECLAIR 209; *Books* Biotransformations in Preparative Organic Chemistry (with S M Roberts H G Davies and R H Green, 1989); *Recreations* cabinet maker; *Style*— Dr David Kelly; School of Chemistry and Applied Chemistry, University of Wales, College of Cardiff, PO Box 912, Cardiff CF1 3TB (☎ 0222 874063, fax 0222 874056, telex 0222 498635, mobile tel 0831 231465)

KELLY, Dr Desmond Hamilton Wilson; s of Norman Wilson Kelly, OBE (d 1976), and Anne Elizabeth, *née* Megarry (d 1976); *b* 2 June 1934; *Educ* King's Sch Canterbury, St Thomas' Hosp Univ of London (Crawford Exhibitioner, MB BS, MRCP, Plank Prize in psychiatry); *m* 6 Feb 1960, Angela Marjorie, da of Stuart Way Shapland; 2 s (Jonathan Desmond b 6 Jan 1963, Simon James 16 Nov 1965); *Career* St Thomas' Hosp: med casualty offr 1958, house surgn 1959, psychiatric house physician 1959; RAMC 1960-63; St Thomas' Hosp: res registrar 1963-65, sr registrar 1965-67, chief asst psychiatry 1968-69; registrar The Maudsley Hosp 1965, Nuffield Fndn Medical Fellowship Johns Hopkins Hosp USA 1967-68, conslt psychiatrist St George's Hosp 1971-79 (sr lectr and hon conslt 1969-71), med dir The Priory Hosp 1980-; lectr in USA & ME; Pavlovian Award and Medal Soc of N America 1971, physician of the year 1981; chm the Priory Hosps Gp 1988 (dir 1981); memb: Assoc of Univ Teachers of Psychiatry 1970, Int Ctee for the Prevention and Treatment of Depression UK (chm 1976), Cncl Psychiatric Section of RSM 1977-80; pres: UK Branch Int Stress and Tension Control Soc 1985-88, Int Stress Mgmnt Assoc 1988-; FRSM 1963, DPM 1961, MD 1965, MRCPsych 1971, FRCPsych 1975, FRCP 1977; *Books* Anxiety and Emotions: physiological basis and treatment (1980), A Practical Handbook for the Treatment of Depression (co-ed,1987), author of over 50 papers; *Recreations* tennis, skiing, windsurfing, gardening; *Clubs* Roehampton; *Style*— Dr Desmond Kelly; The Priory Hospital, Priory Lane, London SW15 5JJ (☎ 081 876 8261, fax 081 392 2632)

KELLY, Desmond Hugh; s of Fredrick Henry Kelly (d 1973), of Harare, Zimbabwe, and Mary Josephine, *née* Bracken; *b* 13 Jan 1942; *Educ* Christian Brothers Coll Buiawayo Zimbabwe, Elaine Archibald Ballet Sch Buiawayo Zimbabwe, Ruth French Dance Acad London; *m* 4 Jan 1963, Denise Jeanette, da of Henri Charles le Comte; 1 s (Joel Henry b 1 June 1973), 1 da (Emma Louise b 30 Dec 1970); *Career* dancer; princ London Festival Ballet 1964 (joined 1959), Zurich Ballet 1966-67, ballet master teacher and princ dancer New Zealand Ballet 1967-68, Nat Ballet of Washington 1968-70 (most notable role James in La Sylphide with Margot Fonteyn), The Royal Ballet 1970-76 (ballets incl Swan Lake, Giselle and Romeo and Juliet); Sadler's Wells Royal Ballet: princ dancer 1976-78, ballet master 1978-,asst to dir 1988, currently asst dir; recent roles incl: Thomas in La Fille Mal gardee, Dr Coppelius in Coppelia Dago in Facade, Mr Hobson in David Bintley's Hobson's Choice; various TV appearances; *Recreations* theatre, gardening, cooking, reading; *Style*— Desmond Kelly, Esq; Birmingham Royal Ballet, Birmingham Hippodrome, Thorp St, Birmingham B5 HAU (☎ 021 622 2555, fax 021 622 5038)

KELLY, (Reay) Diarmaid Anthony; s of Capt Edward Raymond Anthony Kelly, of 4A Belgrave Mews North, London SW1, and Bridget Ramsay, *née* Hornby; *b* 8 July 1959; *Educ* Ampleforth; *Career* sales exec Henderson Crosthwaite & Co 1981-84, dir Baring Securities Ltd 1984-; *Recreations* racing; *Clubs* Boodle's, Pratt's, Turf; *Style*— Diarmaid Kelly, Esq; 11 Markham Square, London SW3; c/o Baring Securities Ltd, Lloyds Chambers, 1 Portsoken St, London E1 (☎ 071 621 1500, fax 071 623 1873)

KELLY, Dominic Noel David Miles Charles; s of Bernard Noel Kelly, *qv*, and Lady Mirabel Magdalene Fitzalan Howard, sis of 17 Duke of Norfolk; *b* 24 June 1953; *Educ* Worth Abbey; *m* 3 Oct 1982, Miranda Rita, da of Lance Macklin; 3 da (Sabine b 21 April 1983, Alice b 9 March 1985, Celina b 24 Oct 1987); *Career* cmmnd Queen's Royal Irish Hussars 1971, resigned 1977; *Recreations* tennis; *Clubs* Pratt's; *Style*— Dominic Kelly, Esq; 17/19 Shellwood Road, London SW11 5BJ (☎ 071 228 1109); 50 Sullivan Road, London SW6 3DX (☎ 071 731 1303, fax 071 731 5644, car 0836 638893 or 212874)

KELLY, Prof Donald Francis; s of John Francis Kelly (d 1963) of Chelmsford, Essex, and Blanche Helen, *née* Murphy; *b* 20 July 1933; *Educ* King Edward VI GS Chelmsford Essex, Univ of Bristol (BVSc), Univ of Cambridge (MA, PhD); *m* 13 Oct 1962, Patricia Ann, da of William Septimus Holt (d 1965) of Bolton, Lancs; 3 s (Andrew b 1964, Ian b 1966, David b 1972); *Career* Nat Serv 2 Lt RASC 1951-53, RAVC (RARO); demonstrator in animal pathology Univ of Cambridge 1965-66 (demonstrator in pathology 1965-66), assoc prof of pathology Sch Vet Med Univ of Pennsylvania 1966-70, sr lectr in vet pathology Univ of Bristol, 1970-79, prof and head Dept of Vet Pathology Univ of Liverpool 1979-; MRCVS 1957, FRCPath 1980; *Books* Notes on Pathology for Small Animal Clinicians (with V M Lucke and C J Gaskell, 1982); *Recreations* photography, reading, walking, house maintenance; *Clubs* Backwell Working Mens; *Style*— Prof Donald Kelly; Dept of Veterinary Pathology, University of Liverpool, PO Box 147, Liverpool L69 3BX (☎ 051 794 4264, fax 051 708 6502, telex 627095 UNILPL G)

KELLY, Dr Francis Patrick (Frank); s of Francis Kelly, and Margaret, *née* McFadden; *b* 28 Dec 1950; *Educ* Van Mildert Coll Durham (BSc), Emmanuel Coll Cambridge (PhD); *m* 1972, Jacqueline Pullin; 2 s; *Career* operational res analyst Scicon Ltd, conslt and examiner computing Open Univ 1976-81 (pt/t tutor 1973-76); Univ of Cambridge: lectr in Statistical Lab 1978-86, Fell Christ's Coll 1976- (variously dir of studies, tutor, memb Coll Cncl, memb Investmts Ctee), Nuffield Fndn Sci Res Fell 1986-87, Reader in Mathematics of Systems 1986-90, Prof of the Mathematics of Systems 1990-; Rollo Davidson prize 1979, Guy medal in Silver (RSS 1989); assoc ed: Stochastic Models 1983-86, Annals of Probability 1984-, Jl of the Royal Statistical Soc 1986-, Probability in the Engineering and Informational Scis 1986-; FRS 1989; *Books* Reversibility and Stochastic Networks 1979, numerous articles in mathematical & Statistical jls; *Style*— Dr Frank Kelly, FRS; Statistical Laboratory, 16 Mill Lane, Cambridge CB2 1SB (☎ 0223 337963, fax 0223 337956)

KELLY, (Robert Henry) Graham; s of Thomas John Kelly (d 1960); *b* 23 Dec 1945; *Educ* Baines GS Pulton-Le-Fylde; *m* 18 July 1970, Elizabeth Anne, *née* Wilkinson; 1 s (Stephen b 1974), 1 da (Alison b 1972); *Career* Barclays Bank 1964-68, sec Football League 1979-88, chief exec FA 1989-; tstee: Football Grounds Improvement Tst 1985-88, Football Tst 1989-; FCIS 1974; *Style*— Graham Kelly, Esq; 16 Lancaster Gate, London W2 3LW (☎ 071 402 7151, fax 071 402 0486, telex 261110)

KELLY, John Anthony Brian; RD (1974); s of Lt Cdr Brian James Parmenter Kelly,

DSC, of Bangor, Co Down, N Ireland, and Ethne Mary, *née* Ryan (d 1977); *b* 21 Aug 1941; *Educ* Bangor GS N Ireland, Fort Augustus Abbey Sch Scotland, Queen's Univ Belfast (LLB); *m* 28 March 1973, Denise Anne, da of Richard James Circuit, of St Albans; 2 s (Christopher b 1977, Nicholas b 1982), 2 da (Katrina b 1973, Joanna b 1975); *Career* Lt Cdr RNR 1959-84; Price Waterhouse and Co 1963-68 (qualified 1967), exec Old Broad St Securities 1968-70, exec and assoc Laurie Milbank and Co 1970-78, dir Brown Shipley and Co Ltd 1982- (mangr 1978), non-exec dir Cosalt plc 1986; memb PCC St Teresa's Church Beaconsfield 1983-, memb Cncl of Cooperation Ireland; Liveryman Worshipful Co of Founders; FICA; *Recreations* walking, reading, poetry, tennis; *Clubs* The Naval, Royal Ulster Yacht; *Style—* John Kelly, Esq, RD; Cherrytrees, Penn Rd, Beaconsfield, Bucks HP9 2LW; c/o Brown Shipley & Co Ltd, Founders Court, Lothbury, London EC2R 7HE (☎ 071 606 9833, fax 071 796 4875)

KELLY, Rt Hon Sir John William (Basil); PC (1984); s of Thomas William Kelly (d 1955), of NI, and Emily Frances, *née* Donaldson (d 1966); *b* 10 May 1920; *Educ* Methodist Coll Belfast, Trinity Coll Dublin (BA, LLB); *m* 1957, Pamela, da of Thomas Colmer Colthurst (d 1960), of Aldershot; *Career* called to the Bar: NI 1944-, Middle Temple 1970; MP NI 1964-72, attorney gen NI 1968-72, judge of High Ct NI 1973-85, Lord Justice of Appeal Supreme Ct of Judicature NI 1984-; kt 1984; *Recreations* golf, travel, music; *Style—* Rt Hon Sir Basil Kelly, PC; Royal Courts of Justice, Belfast BT1 3JF

KELLY, Laurence Charles Kevin; s of Sir David Kelly, GCMG, MC (d 1959); *b* 11 April 1933; *Educ* Downside, New Coll Oxford (MA); *m* 1963, Linda, da of Maj R G McNair Scott, and Hon Mrs Scott, of Huish House, Old Basing, Hants; 1 s, 2 da; *Career* Lt Life Gds 1949-52; served F O 1955-56, Guest Keen and Nettlefolds 1956-72; dir: GKN Int Trading 1972, Morganite Int Ltd 1984-, KAE Ltd 1985-88; chm Queenborough Steel Co 1980-89; vice chm: British Steel Consumers' Cncl 1974 (res 1985), Helical Bar 1986-88 (dir 1972-, chm 1984-); memb: bd N Ireland Devpt Agency 1972-78, Monopolies and Mergers Cmmn 1982-; sr assoc memb St Antony's Coll Oxford 1985; FRGS; *Books* Lermontov: Tragedy in the Caucasus (1978), St Petersburg (1981), Moscow (1983), Travellers' Companion Istanbul (1987), Proposals (with D L Kelly); *Recreations* swimming; *Clubs* Brooks's, Turf, Beefsteak, University (Dublin); *Style—* Laurence Kelly, Esq; 44 Ladbroke Grove, London W11 2PA (☎ 071 727 4663); Lorton Hall, Low Lorton, nr Cockermouth, Cumbria CA13 9UP (☎ 0900 85252)

KELLY, Lady; (Renée) Marie-Noële Ghislaine; *née* de Jourda de Vaux; da of Comte de Jourda de Vaux, and Baronne Snoy; *b* 25 Dec 1901; *Educ* abroad; *m* 1929, as his 2 w, Sir David Kelly, GCMG, MC (d 1959); a Knight of Malta and ambassador successively to Berne, Argentina, Turkey (USSR); 2 s; *Career* writer: numerous articles in: Times, Connoisseur, Country Life; Friend of St John and St Elizabeth's Hosp; vice-pres: Anglo-Turkish Assoc, Anglo-Belgian Cncl; Dame of Hon and Devotion SMO Malta; *Books* Turkish Delights (1951), Mirror to Russia (1952), Picture Book of Russia (1952), This Delicious Land Portugal, Dawn to Dusk (1956); *Recreations* swimming, walking; *Style—* Lady Kelly; 27 Carlyle Sq, London SW3 (☎ 071 352 9186)

KELLY, Martyn Alexander; s of Donald Frederick Kelly (d 1971), and Joan Mayne, *née* Townsend; *b* 1 May 1947; *Educ* Bassaley GS Gwent, Univ of Oxford (MA); *m* 14 Aug 1976, Susan Jane, da of Dr Aneurin Williams; 3 s (Alexander b 2 June 1977, Tristram b 12 Dec 1978, Henry b 11 May 1982); *Career* called to the Bar Inner Temple 1972; memb Wales and Chester Circuit; *Recreations* sport; *Clubs* Leander; *Style—* Martyn Kelly, Esq; 34 Park Place, Cardiff (☎ 382731)

KELLY, Matthias John; s of Ambrose Kelly, of Dungannon, Co Tyrone, N Ireland, and Anne, *née* McKiernan (d 1973); *b* 21 April 1954; *Educ* St Patrick's Secdy and St Patrick's Acad Dungannon Co Tyrone, Trinity Coll Dublin (BA, LLB), Cncl of Legal Educn London; *m* 5 May 1979, Helen Ann, da of Peter Joseph Holmes (d 1974), of Longford, Ireland; 1 s (Peter b 1986), 1 da (Anne b 1987); *Career* called to the Bar: Gray's Inn 1979, N Ireland 1983, Republic of Ireland 1983; admitted attorney: New York 1986, USA Federal Bar 1987; hon life memb Br Soc of Criminology 1986; FLBA 1981, CLBA 1987, memb Soc of Labour Lawyers 1979; *Recreations* squash, walking, cycling, reading; *Style—* Matthias Kelly, Esq; 33 Langbourne Ave, Highgate, London N6 6PS (☎ 081 348 0208); 14 Gray's Inn Sq, Gray's Inn, London WC1R 5JB (☎ 071 242 0858, fax 071 242 5434)

KELLY, Dr Michael; CBE (1983), JP (Glasgow 1973), DL (1983); s of David Kelly (d 1972); *b* 1 Nov 1940; *Educ* Univ of Strathclyde (BSc, PhD); *m* 1965, Zita, da of Hugh Harkins; 3 c; *Career* economics lectr Univ of Strathclyde 1967-84; Lord Provost of Glasgow (and ex officioB Lord-Lieut) 1980-84, Lord Rector Univ of Glasgow 1984-87; chm RSSPCC 1987-, pres Inst of Mktg (Strathclyde Branch) 1986- (fell 1989), dir Celtic FC 1990-; memb Scot ABSA 1986-90, Scot Ctee Nat Arts Collection Fund 1990-; Hon LLB Univ of Glasgow 1983; OStJ 1984; *Recreations* football, photography, philately, phillumeny (collecting match books & boxes); *Style—* Dr Michael Kelly, CBE, JP, DL; 50 Aytoun Rd, Glasgow G41 5HE

KELLY, Prof Michael Howard; s of Kenneth Howard Kelly, of Hull, and Kathleen Mary, *née* Lucas; *b* 19 Nov 1946; *Educ* Hull GS, Univ of Warwick (BA, PhD); *m* 3 Jan 1975, Josephine Ann, da of Patrick Joseph Doyle, of Dublin; 2 s (Thomas Doyle b 1980, Paul Doyle b 1983); *Career* lectr in French Univ Coll Dublin 1972-86, prof French Univ of Southampton 1986-; pres Assoc Univ Profs of French, former chm Irish Cncl Civil Liberties; *Books* Pioneer of the Catholic Revival: Emannuel Mounier (1979), Modern French Marxism (1982), Formes et Enjeu du Roman (1986); *Recreations* football, swimming, cinema; *Style—* Prof Michael Kelly; Dept of French, The University, Southampton SO9 5NH

KELLY, Cmmr Owen; QPM (1987); s of Owen Kelly (d 1943), and Anna Maria, *née* Hamill; *b* 10 April 1932; *Educ* St Modan's HS, St Ninians Stirling Scotland; *m* 8 Aug 1957, Sheila Ann, da of Dennis McCarthy (d 1981); 5 s (Rupert Owen b 2 Aug 1960, Owen b 17 July 1963, Noel b 14 March 1967, Christopher b 13 Nov 1970, Robert Finlay b 14 Nov 1979); *Career* joined Met Police 1953, cmmr City of London Police 1985- (asst cmmr 1982); pres City of London Leukaemia Res Fund 1985-, hon sec Chief Constables' Club 1989; CStJ 1987 (OStJ 1986); Freeman City of London 1982; memb Assoc Chief Police Office 1981; Order of Civil Merit Spain 1986, Ordre du Wissam Alouite Class III Morocco 1987, Commandeur Ordre du Mérite Senegal 1988; *Recreations* walking, horse riding, reading, DIY, house and car maintenance; *Clubs* Guildhall; *Style—* Cmmr Owen Kelly, QPM; City of London Police HQ, 26 Old Jewry, London EC2R 8DJ (☎ 071 601 2001, fax 071 601 2260, telex 887074)

KELLY, Rt Rev Patrick Altham; *see*: Salford, Bishop of

KELLY, Peter David; s of Major Joseph Kelly, MBE (d 1949), and Doris *née* Connely (d 1987); *b* 13 Aug 1944; *Educ* Lord Wandsworth Coll, London Hosp (MB BS); *m* 29 July 1978, Andrea Gillian, da of Francis Eric Holmes, of The Mill House, Latton, Cricklade, Wilts; 2 s (Matthew b 1981, David b 1984); *Career* conslt to accident and emergency dept Lister Hosp Herts 1978-; magistrate div of Stevenage county of Hertford 1983-, parish cncllr 1988-; FRCSEd, FRCS; *Recreations* gardening, presidigitation; *Style—* Peter Kelly, Esq; The White House, High St, Graveley, Hitchin, Herts SG4 7LA (☎ 0438 355546); The Lister Hospital, Stevenage, Herts (☎ 0438 314333)

KELLY, Philip John; s of William Kelly (d 1979), of Crosby, Merseyside, and Mary Winifred, *née* Ellison; *b* 18 Sept 1946; *Educ* St Mary's Coll Crosby, Univ of Leeds (BA); *m* 12 Nov 1988, Dorothy Margaret Jones; 2 s (Matthew b 1980, Robert b 1986); *Career* freelance jounalist and PR conslt 1970-87; co-fndr: Leveller 1976, State Research 1977; ed Tribune 1987-; chm London Freelance Branch NUJ 1983; cncllr (Lab) London Borough of Islington 1984-86 and 1990-; *Recreations* railways, model railways; *Clubs* Red Rose; *Style—* Philip Kelly, Esq; 56 Windsor Rd, London N7 6JL; Tribune, 308 Grays Inn Rd, London WC1X 8DY (☎ 071 278 0911)

KELLY, Dr William Francis; s of William Francis Kelly (d 1951), of Wolverhampton, and Lilian Rose, *née* Foister (d 1986); *b* 16 June 1942; *Educ* Royal Wolverhampton Sch, Univ of London (BSc), St Mary's Med Sch London (MB BS, MD); *m* 21 Aug 1971, Miranda Jane, da of Leonard Oscar Goddard, of Wonersh, Surrey; 1 s (Adam John William b 1974), 1 da (Juliet Miranda b 1977); *Career* qualified CA 1964 (resigned 1972); conslt physician S Tees Health Authy 1983, hon clinical tutor Charing Cross and Westminster Med Schs 1987, clinical lectr Univ of Newcastle 1988; author of 30 articles in endocrine and diabetic jnls' editorial asst Clinical Endocrinology; MRCP 1975; memb: Br Diabetic Assoc 1976 (pres S Tees Branch), Endocrine Section RSM 1978, FRCP 1989; *Recreations* walking, literature, photography; *Style—* Dr William Kelly; Diabetes Care Centre, Middlesbrough General Hospital, Ayresome Green Lane, Middlesbrough, Cleveland TS5 5AZ (☎ 0642 850222)

KELMAN, Alistair Bruce; s of James Bruce Edward Kelman (d 1983), of London, and Florence Gwendoline, *née* Cutts (d 1987); *b* 11 Aug 1952; *Educ* Haberdasher's; Askes', Univ of Birmingham (BSc); *m* 2 Sept 1978, Diana Elizabeth, da of Prof Joseph Tinsley, of Aberdeen, Scotland; *Career* called to the Bar Middle Temple 1977, specialist in computer law 1979-; fndr memb Parly Info Technol Ctee House of Parl (resigned 1983); AMBCS 1982, ACIArb 1986; *Books* The Computer in Court (with R Sujer, 1982), Computer Fraud in Small Businesses (1985); *Recreations* writing, piano playing and composing, horseriding and hacking; *Style—* Alistair Kelman, Esq; New Court, Temple, London EC4Y 9BE (☎ 071 353 0517, fax 071 583 5885)

KELSALL, Prof Malcolm Miles; s of Alec James Kelsall, and Hetty May, *née* Miles; *b* 27 Feb 1938; *Educ* William Hulme's GS Manchester, Brasenose Coll Oxford (MA, BLitt); *m* 5 Aug 1961, Mary Emily, da of George Hurley IVES (d 1978); *Career* advsy ed The Byron Journal, memb Mgmnt Ctee Welsh Nat Drama Co 1976-77; *Books* Sarah Fielding's David Simple (ed, 1969), Thomas Otway's Venice Preserved (ed, 1969), William Congreve's Love for Love (ed, 1969), Joseph Trapp's Lectures on Poetry (ed, 1973), JM Synge's The Playboy of the Western World (ed 1975), Christopher Marlowe (1981), Congreve: The Way of the World (1981), Joseph Trapp's The Preface of the Aneis (ed 1982), Studying Drama (1985), Byron's Politics (1987), Literature and Criticism (ed, 1990), The Great Good Place: The Country House and English Literature (1991); *Recreations* theatre, long distance running; *Style—* Prof Malcolm Kelsall; Ashbrook, Cae Rex, Cowbridge, S Glamorgan CF7 7JS (☎ 04463 2627); University of Wales, PO Box 94, Cardiff CF1 3XE (☎ 0222 874244)

KELSEY, Alan Howard Mitchell; s of Emanuel Kelsey (d 1985), of London, and Dorothy Mitchell, *née* Smith; *b* 10 April 1949; *Educ* Kings Coll Sch Wimbledon, Oriel Coll Oxford (BA, MA); *m* 12 March 1977, Sarah D'Oyly, da of Robin Carlyle Sayer, of Little Walsingham, Norfolk; 2 s (Guy b 21 Feb 1980, William b 29 July 1981), 1 da (Keziah b 19 Jan 1978); *Career* Kitcat & Aitken: tport investmt analyst 1975-88, head of res 1987-89, head of corp fin 1989-90; dir: RBC Dominian Securities International 1988-, RBC Dominian Securities Inc 1989-; chm local cons Assoc 1985-88; memb: cncl of The Society of Investmt Analysts 1986-88, Int Stock Exchange; memb Chartered Inst of Tport; *Recreations* rowing; *Clubs* Brooks's; *Style—* Alan Kelsey, Esq; The Priory, Little Waldingfield, Suffolk CO10 0SW; Flat 90, Marlborough, Walton St, London SW3 (☎ 071 584 4238); RBC Dominian Securities International Ltd, RBC Centre, 71 Queen Victoria St, London EC4V 4DE (☎ 071 489 1966, fax 071 329 6150, telex 888297)

KELSEY, Maj-Gen John; CBE (1968); s of Benjamin Richard Kelsey and Daisy, *née* Powell; *b* 1 Nov 1920; *Educ* Royal Masonic Sch, Emmanuel Coll Cambridge, Royal Mil Coll of Sci (BSc), UCL (BSc); *m* 1, 1944, Phyllis Margaret, da of Henry Smith, of Chingford; 1 s, 1 da; *Career* RE 1940 (N Africa and Europe), Mil Survey Units in UK, North Africa, West Indies and Germany; sr instr Geodsy Sch of Mil Survey 1951-53; offr Ordnance Survey 1954-59, dir of field survey 1969-72, dir of mil survey MOD 1972-77, sec Western Euro Sub Cmmn of Int Cmmn for Artificial Satellites 1967-71 (pres 1971-75); chm: Working Party Satellite Geodsy 1975-86, Survey and Mapping Conference Steering Gp 1981-87; non-exec dir Wild Heerburg UK Ltd, cnslt to Wild Heerburg Ltd and Ernst Leitz Wetzlar GmbH; memb RGS 1977-88, MRICS; *Style—* Maj-Gen John Kelsey, CBE

KELSEY TESTORF, Linda; da of Maj Samuel Cohen, and Rhona, *née* Fox; *b* 15 April 1952; *Educ* Woodhouse GS, Univ of Warwick; *m* 16 March 1972 (m dis 1981); 1 s (Thomas C b 19 May 1988); *Career* ed: Cosmopoliton Magazine 1985-89, She magazine 1989; Periodical Publishers Assoc Ed of the Year 1989; chm Br Soc of Magazine Editors 1987; Br Soc of Magazine Editors Women's Magazine Editor of the Year 1990; *Clubs* Groucho; *Style—* Ms Linda Kelsey Testorf; 72 Broadwick St, London W1V 2BP (☎ 071 437 6886)

KELTON, Michael John St Goar; s of Gerald St Goar Kelton (d 1972), and Beatrice Millicent, da of J B Body (md S Pearson & Co, responsible for many engrg devpts in Mexico *ca* 1900 incl: draining of Valley of Mexico, construction of Vera Cruz harbour, founding Mexican Eagle Oil Co); *b* 25 March 1933; *Educ* Stowe, Queens' Coll Cambridge (MA); *m* 19 June 1958, Joanna Elizabeth, da of Sir (William) John Peel, MP (C) Leicester SE 1957-74; 3 s (Jeremy b 1960, Andrew b 1961, Simon b 1966); *Career* Capt 3 Carabiniers (now Royal Scots Dragoon Gds); merchant banker Lazard Bros and Co Ltd 1957-, dir Lazard Securities until 1971; stockbroker: late Scott, Goff Hancock, Raphael Zorn Hemsley Ltd 1976-; *Recreations* shooting, fishing, golf; *Clubs* Cavalry and Guards', Flyfishers', Hankley Common Golf; *Style—* Michael Kelton, Esq; Pipers Well, Churt, Farnham, Surrey GU10 2NT (☎ 042 871 3194); Raphael Zorn Hemsley Ltd, 10 Throgmorton Ave, London EC2 (☎ 071 628 4000)

KEMBALL, Christopher Ross Maguire; MBE (Mil 1973); s of John Patrick Gerard Kemball, of Vila Praia De Ancora, Portugal, and Rachel Lucy, *née* Vernon; *b* 29 Dec 1946; *Educ* Ampleforth, Pembroke Coll Cambridge (BA); *m* 3 Feb 1979, Frances Maria, da of Flt Lt Richard Peter Monico, RAF (d 1945); 1 s (Charles b 1983); *Career* Regular Army Capt (actg Maj) Royal Green Jackets 1968-75, Sultan's Armed Forces, Maj Northern Frontier Regt 1972-73; dir Kleinwort Benson Ltd 1975-86, vice chm Kleinwort Benson Hldgs Inc 1984-86, md Dillon Read & Co Inc 1986-, exec md and co-head Dillon Read Ltd 1987-; *Recreations* opera, swimming, skiing, shooting; *Clubs* Royal Green Jackets, Brooks's, Royal Automobile; *Style—* Christopher Kemball, Esq, MBE; Dillon Read Ltd, Devonshire House, Mayfair Place, London W1X 5FH (☎ 071 493 1239)

KEMBALL, Air Marshal Sir John; KCB (1990), CBE (1981); s of Richard Charles Kemball (d 1983), of Colchester, and Margaret James, *née* Robson (d 1987); *b* 31 Jan 1939; *Educ* Uppingham, Open Univ (BA); *m* 1962, Valerie Geraldine, da of Maj Albert John Webster, RA, of Sussex; 2 da (Katherine b 1964, Samantha b 1966); *Career* cmmnd RAF 1957, served France, Middle East, USA, cmd No 54 Sqdn RAF Laarbruch, Cmdt RAF Central Flying Sch 1983-85, Cdr Br Forces Falkland Islands

1985-86, Chief of Staff and dep C-in-C Strike Cmd 1989; *Recreations* field sports, cricket, tennis, skiing; *Clubs* RAF; *Style*— Air Marshal Sir John Kemball, KCB, CBE; c/o Midland Bank, 46 Market Hill, Sudbury, Suffolk CO10 6ES

KEMBALL-COOK, Lt-Col Brian Hartley; s of Sir Basil Alfred Kemball-Cook, KCMG, CB (d 1949), and Nancy Annie, *née* Pavitt (d 1959); *b* 12 Dec 1912; *Educ* Shrewsbury Sch, Balliol Coll Oxford (BA, MA); *m* 2 Aug 1947, (Gladys) Marian, da of Robert Charles Reginald Richards, OBE (d 1979); 3 s (David b 1952, Oliver b 1955, Geoffrey b 1955), 1 da (Jessica b 1948); *Career* Intelligence Corps 1940-46; UK Port Security Control 1941-44, Supreme HQ, Allied Expdn Force 1944-45, G2 30 Corps Germany 1945-46, regnl intelligence offr and political advsr to Regnl Cmmr Hanover 1946 (despatches 1945); princ Miny of Tport 1946-47, sr classics master Repton 1947-56 (sixth form classics master 1936-40); headmaster: Queen Elizabeth's GS Blackburn 1956-65, Bedford Modern Sch 1965-77; chm Beds Music Festival 1966-77, tutor Workers' Educnl Assoc 1972-77, lectr Womens' Insts 1983-; contrib to Education; memb HMC 1956; *Books* Shakespeare's Coriolanus (ed, 1955), Threatened Standards (1972), Homer's Odyssey (trans into English hexameters); *Recreations* mountaineering, music; *Clubs* Climbers Club; *Style*— Lt-Col Brian Kemball-Cook; 12 Francis Close, Hitchin, Herts SG4 9EJ (☎ 0462 438862)

KEMBER, Anthony Joseph; s of Thomas Kingsley Kember (d 1968), and May Lena, *née* Pryor (d 1972); *b* 1 Nov 1931; *Educ* St Edmund Hall Oxford (MA); *m* 3 Aug 1957, Drusilla Mary, da of Geoffrey Lionel Boyce, of Broad Oak, Cambridge Park, Twickenham, Middx; 1 s (Julian James Kingsley b 18 May 1960), 2 da (Selina May b 28 April 1962, Perdita Jane b 15 Jan 1965); *Career* dep house govr and sec to Bd of Govrs Westminster Hosp 1961-69, gp sec Hillingdon Gp Hosp Mgmnt Ctee 1969-73, area admin Kensington and Chelsea and Westminster AHA (teaching) 1973-78, gen mangr SW Thames RHA 1978-89, currently communications advsr Dept of Health Whitehall; tstee Disabled Living Fndn 1981- (vice chm 1989-); AHSM 1963; *Recreations* royal tennis, lawn tennis, painting, golf; *Clubs* Roehampton, Exiles, Royal Tennis Court Hampton Court Palace; *Style*— Anthony Kember, Esq; 16 Orchard Rise, Richmond Upon Thames, Surrey TW10 5BX (☎ 080 876 5192); Department of Health, Richmond House, 71 Whitehall, London SW1A 2NS

KEMBERY, John Philip; s of Alec George Kembery, of Keynsham, Somerset; *b* 6 Oct 1939; *Educ* Queen Elizabeth's Hosp Bristol, Univ of Surrey; *m* 1964, Marjorie Carolyn, da of Gilbert James Bowler, of Bridge End House, Much Cowarne, Herefordshire; 2 s; *Career* md: Alcan Extrusions 1975-80, Alcan Metal Centres 1980-81; chm: McKechnie Metals (non ferrous metal mfrs) (md 1981-87), PSM Int plc; dir and chm metals and engrg divs McKechnie plc 1986-; pres Br Non Ferrous Metals Fedn 1988-; fell Inst of Metals, FInstD; *Recreations* golf, shooting, good food; *Style*— John Kembery, Esq; 37 Broad Oaks, Solihull, W Midlands (☎ 021 705 3214); McKechnie plc, Leighswood Rd, Aldridge, Walsall, W Midlands WS9 8DS (☎ 0922 743887)

KEMBLE, Bruce Charles James; s of Harold James Kemble (d 1983), and Dorothea Grace Finley (d 1989); *b* 15 Sept 1938; *Educ* Dulwich, Downing Coll Cambridge (MA); *m* 1, 1963 (m dis 1983), Helen, da of Sven Vanem, of Nordberg, Olso, Norway; 1 s (Boyd Sven b 1966), 2 da (Marianne b 1971, Sally Clare b 1973); m 2, Susan Odette Reid; 1 s (Harry Reid-Kemble b 1988); *Career* journalist; Cambridge News Service 1961-62, BBC Norwich 1962-63, educn corr Daily Express 1964-81 (joined 1963), chief home affairs corr The Sun 1981-86; educn corr: The Sunday Times 1986-88, The Evening Standard 1988-; *Books* Give Your Child A Chance (1970, 2 edn 1989), How to Pass Exams (1974), How to Choose a School (1979); *Recreations* National Hunt racing; *Style*— Bruce Kemble, Esq; Evening Standard, Northcliffe House, 2 Derry St, Kensington W8 5EE (☎ 071 938 7528/9, fax 071 937 3193)

KEMBLE, James (Victor) Harvey; s of James Kemble (d 1978), of Putney, London, and Dorothy Eleanor, *née* Wright; *Educ* Charterhouse, King's Coll Cambridge (MA, MB BChir); *m* 1965, Deirdre Margaret Fender, da of Herbert Lockhart Latta (d 1966), of Castlecomer, Eire; 1 s (Ian b 1971), 1 da (Nicola b 1968); *Career* surgical registrar The Middx Hosp 1968-70, sr registrar Salisbury and Hammersmith Hosp 1972-77; conslt plastic surgn 1977-: Bart's, NE Thames Regnl Plastic Surgery, Burns Centre St Andrews Hosp Essex; author of numerous articles on surgery of the hand, skin cancer and burns; memb: Essex Archaeological Tst, Essex Soc for Archaeology and History, Br Soc for Surgery of the Hand; treas Journal of Hand Surgery; memb Br Assoc of Plastic Surgns, MRCS, FRCS, LRCP; *Books* Plastic Surgical and Burns Nursing (with BE Lamb, 1984), Practical Burns Management (with BE Lamb 1987); *Recreations* skiing, archeology, landscape history, topography; *Style*— James Harvey Kemble, Esq; 6 Upper Harley St, London NW1 4PS (☎ 071 935 3070)

KEMMIS, Hon Mrs (Bridget Mary Dean); 2 da of Baron Soper (Life Peer); *b* 17 Dec 1933; *m* 15 Sept 1956, Owen Henry Kemmis, MA (decd), o s of late Hubert Beresford Kemmis; 1 s; *Style*— The Hon Mrs Kemmis; Garden Flat, Parliament Hill, Hampstead NW3

KEMP, Alan Scott; s of Alexander Scott Kemp (d 1968), of Edinburgh, and Christina Margaret, *née* Stocks (d 1965); *b* 2 April 1944; *Educ* George Heriots Sch Edinburgh; *m* 9 Dec 1967, June, da of John Christie (d 1986), of Edinburgh; 2 s (Graeme, Martin); *Career* dep mangr The Edinburgh Investmt Trust plc 1974-84, investmt dir Dunedin Fund Mangrs Ltd 1985-, dir Edinburgh Sports Club Ltd; memb Murrayfield and Cramond Rotary Club; MICAS; *Recreations* golf, squash; *Style*— Alan Kemp, Esq; 65 Whitehouse Rd, Edinburgh EH4 6PE (☎ 031 312 7182); Dunedin Fund Mangers Ltd, Dunedin Ho, 25 Ravelston Tce, Edinburgh EH4 3EX (☎ 031 315 2500, fax 031 315 2222, telex 72229)

KEMP, Arnold; s of Robert Kemp (d 1968), of Edinburgh, and Meta Elizabeth, *née* Strachan; *b* 15 Feb 1939; *Educ* Edinburgh Acad, Univ of Edinburgh (MA); *Career* sub ed: The Scotsman 1959-62, The Guardian 1962-65; The Scotsman: prodn ed 1965-70, London ed 1970-72, dep ed 1972-81; ed Glasgow Herald 1981-; *Clubs* Caledonian, Glasgow Arts; *Style*— Arnold Kemp, Esq; Glasgow Herald, 195 Albion St, Glasgow G1 1QP (☎ 011 552 6255, fax 041 552 2288

KEMP, Brian Richard Calvert; s of Brian Richard Kemp, and Kathleen Mary Kemp; *b* 21 Oct 1943; *Educ* Bradfield, Univ of Loughborough (BTech), Stanford Graduate Sch of Business (MBA); *m* (Diana) Judith Scott; *Career* mktg offr Associated Electrical Industries 1966-68, mktg cnslt P E Consulting Group; Tube Investments: commercial planning exec Steel Tube Div 1972-74, mktg dir Tube Products 1974-76, md T I Silencers Distributuion cos 1976-78; British Alcan Aluminium plc: mktg dir Finished Products Div 1978-79, business devpt dir Alcan Sheet Ltd 1979-80, dir and gen mangr Foils Div 1980-82, md Rolled Products Div 1982-86; exec dir Parkfield Group plc 1986; dep chief exec Simon Engineering plc 1988 (md Mfrg Div 1987), chief exec Simon Engineering plc 1989-; *Style*— Brian Kemp, Esq; Simon Engineering plc, PO Box 31, Stockport, Cheshire SK3 0RT (☎ 061 428 3600, fax 061 491 2472, telex 665923 SIMENG G, car 0831 206624)

KEMP, Brian William; s of William Kemp (d 1984), of Solihull, and Muriel Beatrice, *née* Taylor; *b* 29 Jan 1939; *Educ* Moseley GS Birmingham; *m* 1, 15 Feb 1964 (m dis 1988), Mary Christine, da of Harry Hughes, of Birmingham; 2 s (Andrew b 1970, Jonathan b 1973), 1 da (Alison b 1967); m 2, 20 May 1988, Sheila Margaret, da of Walter Patrick, of Birmingham; *Career* sr ptnr Allenbrooke Kingsley Mills (formerly R Kingsley Mills and Co) 1986- (ptnr 1970-); FCA 1962, ATII 1965; *Recreations* yachting; *Clubs* Salcombe Yacht; *Style*— Brian Kemp, Esq; Allenbrooke Kingsley Mills, 614 Stratford Rd, Birmingham B11 4BE (☎ 021 777 6762, fax 021 777 2319)

KEMP, Charles James Bowring; s of Capt Michael John Barnett Kemp, ERD (d 1982), of Winchcombe, Glos, and Brigid Ann Vernon-Smith, *née* Bowring; *b* 27 April 1951; *Educ* Shrewsbury, UCL (LLB); *m* 21 Dec 1974, Fenella Anne, da of Harry Herring, of Cropwell Butler, Nottingham; 1 s (Marcus b 28 Feb 1979), 1 da (Sophie b 11 Feb 1977); *Career* called to the Bar Gray's Inn 1973, asst rec 1987; parish cncllr Chailey PC; *Recreations* tennis, swimming, golf, country pursuits; *Style*— Charles Kemp, Esq; Keepers, Cinder Hill, Chailey, nr Lewes, East Sussex BN8 4HP (☎ 082 572 3168, fax 082 572 4106); 1 King's Bench Walk, Temple, London EC4Y 7DB (☎ 071 583 6266, fax 071 583 2068)

KEMP, David Michael; s of John David Kemp, of 26 Parkfield Ave, North Harrow, Middx, and Irene Florence, *née* Cross; *b* 20 Feb 1953; *Educ* Blackwell Secdy Modern, Newlands Park Coll; *m* 15 Oct 1982, Debbi Jean, da of John Drake, of Huntington Beach, California; *Career* professional footballer: debut Crystal Palace 1975 (44 appearances), Portsmouth (70 appearances), Carlisle (44 appearances), Plymouth (100 appearances), Edmonton Drillers USA, Seattle Sounders USA; *Recreations* reading, travel, sports; *Style*— David Kemp, Esq; c/o Plymouth Argyle Football Club, Home Park, Plymouth, Devon (☎ 0752 562561, fax 0752 606167)

KEMP, David Stephen; s of Stephen Nicholas Kemp (d 1967), of Bromley, Kent, and Mary Grace, *née* Gibbs (d 1976); *b* 14 Dec 1928; *Educ* Tonbridge, Brasenose Coll Oxford (MA); *m* 16 April 1966, Marion Elizabeth, da of Dr Maurice Sibley Blower (d 1982), of Rake, Hants; 3 s (Anthony David b 1967, William James Stephen b 1971, Peter John b 1973); *Career* 2 Lt Duke of Wellington's Regt 1948; articled clerk E F Turner & Sons 1952; admitted slr 1955; Tonbridge Sch: asst master 1956, housemaster 1969, second master 1971, actg headmaster 1990; played hockey for Kent; Mental Health Act mangr Leybourne Grange Hosp, chm Govrs Marlborough House Sch, govr Claremont Sch, memb Ctee Kent CCC; Liveryman Worshipful Co of Skinners 1954; *Recreations* cricket, golf, reading; *Clubs* Vincents, MCC, Bude & N Cornwall Golf; *Style*— David Kemp, Esq; Summerlands, Portman Park, Tonbridge, Kent TN9 1LW (☎ 0732 350 023)

KEMP, Rt Rev Eric Waldram; *see*: Chichester, Bishop of

KEMP, Harry Vincent; s of Alfred Vincent Kemp (d 1959), of Pinner, Middx, and Lucy Edith, *née* Tomkins (d 1946); *b* 11 Dec 1911; *Educ* Stowe, Clare Coll Cambridge (BA, MA), Univ of London Inst of Educn (DipEd); *m* 1, 9 July 1941 (m dis 1952), (Lilian) Alix (d 1966), da of Herr Eiermann, of Nuremburg; 1 s (Hugh McDowell b 31 July 1953); m 2, 5 Oct 1957 (m dis 1976), Eunice Ellen, *née* Frost; *Career* WWII RA 1940-41, cmmnd RAOC 1941, released Capt EME 1946; teacher 1935-71, ret 1971; poet; *Books* poetry: Epilogue III (contrib, ed with Laura Riding and Robert Graves, 1937), The Left Heresy (with Laura Riding and Robert Graves, 1939), Poems as of Now (1969), Poems as of Then (1972), Poems in Variety (1977), Ten Messengers (with Witold Kawalec, 1977), Verses for Heidi (with Harry Gordon, 1978), Collected Poems (1985), Poems for Erato (1990); *Recreations* cricket, travel, mathematical logic; *Clubs* MCC, Cryptics, Stowe Templars; *Style*— Harry Kemp, Esq; 6 Western Villas, Western Rd, Crediton, Devon EX17 3NA (☎ 03632 3502)

KEMP, Hubert Bond Stafford (Hugh); s of John Stafford Kemp (d 1966), of Cardiff, and Cecillia Isabel, *née* Bond (d 1964); *b* 25 March 1925; *Educ* Cardiff HS, Univ of South Wales, St Thomas' Hosp and Univ of London (MB BS, MS); *m* 22 June 1967, Moyra Ann Margaret, da of William Arthur Odgers (d 1951), of Johannesburg; 3 da (Siân b 16 Jan 1961, Sarah b 10 Oct 1962, Louise b 4 June 1975); *Career* hon consIt Royal Nat orthopaedic Hosp London and Stanmore 1965-74, hon sr lectr of Orthopaedics 1974-90 (sr lectr 1965-74), conslt Royal Nat Orthopaedic Hosp London and Stanmore 1974-90, Hunterian prof RCS 1969; visiting prof VII Congress of Soc Latino America de Orthopedia y Traumatologica 1971; chm London Bone Tumour Unit 1985-; memb MRC working parties: Tuberculosis of the Spine 1974-, Osteosarcoma 1985-; MRCS 1947, LRCP 1947, FRCSE 1960, FRCS 1970; *Books* Orthopaedic Diagnosis (jtly 1984), A Postgraduate Textbook of Clinical Orthopaedics (contrib 1983), Bailliere's Clinical Oncology (contrib 1987), Butterworth's Operative Surgery (contrib, 1991); *Recreations* fishing, painting; *Style*— Hugh Kemp, Esq; 55 Loom Lane, Radlett, Herts WD7 8NX (☎ 0923 854265); 107 Harley St, London W1N 1DG (☎ 071 935 2776)

KEMP, (Edmund) Jeremy James; s of Edmund Reginald Walker, of Felixstowe, Suffolk, and Elsa May, *née* Kemp (d 1983); *b* 3 Feb 1935; *Educ* Abbotsholme Sch Staffs, Central School of Speech and Drama (Dip Dramatic Art); *Career* Nat Serv 1953-55, served Duke of Wellington Regt, cmmnd 2 Lt 1 Bn Gordon Highlanders; actor; Old Vic 1958-60; TV incl: Z-Cars (Bob Steele original cast), Colditz (Sqdn Ldr Shaw), Peter the Great, Winds of War, War and Remembrance (US TV); plays incl: St Joan (Warwick), The Winters Tale (Leontes), Henry VIII (Norfolk); over thirty films incl: Operation Crossbow, The Blue Max, Darling Lili; memb of Br Actors Equity Cncl for last 5 years; *Recreations* course games, cricket, golf, skiing, walking, natural history; *Style*— Jeremy Kemp, Esq; 29 Britannia Rd, London SW6 2HJ (☎ 071 736 4059); 8749 Wonderland Avenue, Los Angeles, California 90046, USA (☎ 010 1 213 654 7920); Marina Martin, 6A Danbury St, London NI8 JU (☎ 071 359 3646)

KEMP, Prof Martin John; s of Frederick Maurice Kemp, of Watton, Norfolk, and Violet Anne, *née* Tull; *b* 5 March 1942; *Educ* Windsor GS, Downing Coll Cambridge (BA, MA), Courtauld Inst of Art Univ of London; *m* 27 Aug 1966, Jill, da of Dennis William Lightfoot, of Bisham, Marlow, Bucks; 1 s (Jonathan b 1976), 1 da (Joanna b 1972); *Career* lectr in history of western art Dalhousie Univ Nova Scotia Canada 1965-65, lectr in fine arts Univ of Glasgow 1966-81, prof of fine arts Univ of St Andrews 1981- (memb Univ court 1988-), memb Inst for Advanced Study Princeton 1984-85, Slade prof Univ of Cambridge 1987-88, Benjamin Sonenberg visiting prof Inst of Fine Arts NY Univ; dir St Andrews Festival plc, hockey coach Univ of St Andrews and Madras Coll (ladies), pres Scottish Univs sports fedn (Mens Hockey); tstee Nat Galleries of Scotland 1982-87, Victoria and Albert Museum 1986-89; hon prof of history Royal Scottish Acad 1985-, chm Assoc of Art Historians 1989-, memb Exec Scottish Museums Cncl 1990-, dir and chm Graeme Murray Gallery 1990-; FRSA 1983, HRSA 1985, HRIAS 1988; *Recreations* sport especially hockey; *Style*— Prof Martin Kemp; Orillia, 45 Pittenweem Rd, Anstruther, Fife, Scotland; Dept of Fine Art, Univ of St Andrews, St Andrews, Fife

KEMP, Michael Alfred Lawrence; s of Alfred Lawrence Kemp (d 1968), and Margaret, *née* Smith; *b* 19 March 1941; *Educ* Greenwich Central Sch; *m* 1, 1965, Janet Anne, da of Charles Blogg, OBE; 1 s (Lawrence Michael b 1968); m 2, Patricia Deborah, da of Jack Kitching (d 1986); 1 s (Paul Lawrence Michael b 1971), 1 da (Lindsey b 1974); *Career* md: G & L Ralli Investment & Trustee Co Ltd 1977 (dir 1973-), G & L Ralli Finance Co Ltd 1977- (dir 1972-), Ralli Investment Co Ltd 1976-; dir Frowds Ltd 1983-, chm Ralli Bondite Ltd 1989- (dir 1981-); AMSIA; *Recreations* gardening, rugby union supporter, horseracing; *Clubs* City of London; *Style*— Michael A L Kemp, Esq; 5 Westott Close, Bickley, Kent BR1 2TU (☎ 081 468 7347)

KEMP, Michael Cedric; s of Thomas Alfred Kemp (d 1979) of Rollesby, Norfolk, and Rosemary Anne Rydon (d 1979); *b* 31 March 1930; *Educ* Tottenham Poly; *m* 1, 1951,

Olive Ruth (d 1980), da of William Alison; 1 s (Nigel Adrian b 1960), 3 da (Lynette Jacqueline b 1952, Gillian Ruth b 1954, Alison Jane b 1966); m 2, Frances Merle, *née* Skilling 1982; *Career* Mil Serv RE 1948-50; jr librarian Daily Telegraph 1948, jr Manchester Guardian 1948, jr reported Norfolk News Co 1950-52 (Eastern Daily Press, Eastern Evening News, Yarmouth Mercury, in charge dist Swaffham office Dereham & Fakenham Times); cts and gen reporter: North West Evening Mail 1952-53; Halifax Daily Courier 1953-54, dep news Sunday Chronicle 1954, tech reporter Daily Express 1954-56, Daily Sketch 1957-71 (tech reporter, dep motoring corr, motoring corr), motoring corr Daily Mail 1971-; broadcaster: BBC, IRN, Br Forces Bdcasting Servs; conslt: Universal News Servs, Ospray motoring books; founded: Motoring Braodcasts Lts (recorded motoring info serv) 1968, Radio Motor Show (service now run by BBC); ldr of major unleaded petrol campaign 1989-90, winner Carl Hoepner Environmental trophy 1989; memb Guild of Motoring Writers 1971-; *Books* AA Book of the Car (contrib); *Recreations* motoring, walking; *Style*— Michael Kemp, Esq; Daily Mail, 2 Derry St, Kensington, London W8 5TT (☎ 071 938 6108, fax 071 937 3251, car 0831 346130)

KEMP, (Bernard) Peter; s of William Gordon Kemp, of Chorley, Lancashire, and Teresa, *née* Howarth; *b* 16 Oct 1942; *Educ* Thornleigh Coll Bolton, King's Coll Univ of London (BA, MPhil); *Career* lectr in English Middx Poly 1968-88; reg book reviewer: The Listener 1978-91, TLS 1980- (weekly TV and radio column 1982-86), Sunday Times (fiction) 1987-; theatre reviewer The Independent 1986-90, reg bdcasting on Kaleidoscope, Critics' Forum, Meridian; *Books* Muriel Spark (1974), H G Wells and The Culminating Ape (1982); *Recreations* travel, art galleries, music, gardening; *Style*— Peter Kemp, Esq

KEMP, Peter Mant MacIntyre; DSO (1945); s of Sir Norman Wright Kemp (d 1937), and Olivia Maria, *née* Martin (d 1946); *b* 19 Aug 1915; *Educ* Wellington, Trinity Coll Cambridge (MA); *m* 20 Nov 1946 (m dis 1958), Cynthia Margaret, da of Col Vivian Henry CB (d 1930); *Career* cmmnd 1940, Capt 1940, Maj 1943, Lt-Col 1946; author; life assur underwriter Imperial Life of Canada; *Books* Mine Were of Trouble (1957), No Colours or Crest (1958), Aims for Oblivion (1961), Br Glin Vietnam (jtly, 1969); *Recreations* tavern talk and travel; *Clubs* White's, Pratt's, Special Forces, Chelsea Arts; *Style*— Peter Kemp, Esq, DSO; 24 Radnor Walk, London SW3 4BN (☎ 071 352 9356)

KEMP, (Charles) Richard Foster; s of (Charles) Ian Taggart Kemp, of Gerrards Cross, Bucks, and Jean Maisie, *née* Foster; *b* 5 Jan 1957; *Educ* Bedford Sch, Queen's Coll Cambridge (MA, rugby fives team); *Career* mangr Chemical Bank London and NY 1978-84; dir: Charterhouse Development Capital Ltd London 1984-87, Brown Shipley Venture Managers London 1988-, Brown Shipley & Co Ltd 1988-; memb Br Venture Capital Assoc 1987; *Recreations* golf, squash, skiing; *Style*— Richard Kemp, Esq; Brown Shipley Venture Managers Ltd, Founders Court, Lothbury, London EC2R 7HE (☎ 071 606 9833, fax 071 600 2279)

KEMP, Robert Thayer; s of Robert Kemp (d 1968), and Ada, *née* Thayer; *b* 18 June 1928; *Educ* Bromley GS, Univ of London (BA); *m* 1951, Gwendolyn Mabel, da of Rev Charles Stanley Minty (d 1930); *Career* former dir International Group Export Credits Guarantee Dept 1985-88 (asst 1970-75, under sec 1975-85), export credit conslt and non-exec dir Sedgwick James Credit Ltd 1989-; *Publications* Review of Future Status Options for ECGD (1989); *Recreations* gardening, theatre, music; *Clubs* Overseas Bankers; *Style*— Robert Kemp, Esq; 294 Tubbenden Lane South, Farnborough, Orpington, Kent BR6 7DN (☎ 0689 853924)

KEMP, Hon St John Durival; s and h of 1 Viscount Rochdale, OBE, TD, DL; *b* 15 Jan 1938; *Educ* Eton; *m* 1, 1960 (m dis 1974), Serena Clark-Hall; 2 s, 2 da; m 2, 1976, Elizabeth Anderton; *Style*— The Hon St John Kemp; Rosetrees, Portinscale, Keswick, Cumbria CA12 5TZ

KEMP, (Athole) Stephen Horsford; LVO (1983), OBE (1958, MBE 1950); s of Sir Joseph Horsford Kemp, CBE, KC (d 1950), and Mary, *née* Stuart (d 1954); *b* 21 Oct 1917; *Educ* Westminster, ChCh Oxford (MA); *m* 3 Aug 1940, (Marjorie) Alison, da of Geoffrey Rowley Bostock (d 1961); 2 s (Richard b 27 Oct 1948, Charles b 29 Aug 1952), 1 da (Katherine b 27 Nov 1950); *Career* cmd RA 1939-46; Malayan CS: appointed on secondment from RA 1940 (recalled to RA 1941, POW Singapore and Thailand Burma Railway 1942-45), reverted to Malayan CS 1946, sec to Govt Fedn of Malaya 1955-57, dep perm sec PM's Dept Malaysia 1957-61; Royal Cwlth Soc: dep sec gen 1964-67, sec gen 1967-83 (ret), hon sec Library Tst 1984-90, hon chief examiner Cwlth Essay Comp 1986-; memb Rights of Way Ctee CPRE Oxon 1983-; Oxford Fieldpaths Soc: memb Exec Ctee 1983, vice chm 1985; Open Spaces Soc: local corr W Oxon 1983, clerk Langford Parish Cncl 1987-; Freeman City of Winnipeg Manitoba Canada 1969; JMN (Johan Mangku Negara) Malaysia 1958; *Recreations* gardening, rights of way, wine; *Clubs* Royal Cwlth Soc; *Style*— Stephen Kemp, Esq, LVO, OBE; Lockey House, Langford, Lechlade, Glos GL7 3LF (☎ 036 786 239); Commonwealth House, 18 Northumberland Ave, London WC2N 5BJ (☎ 071 930 6733)

KEMP, Prof Terence James; s of Thomas Brynmor Kemp (d 1978), and Emily Maud, *née* Spriggs (d 1982); *b* 26 June 1938; *Educ* Cardiff HS, Watford GS, Jesus Coll Oxford (MA, DPhil, DSc); *m* 8 April 1961, Sheila Therese, da of Henry Francis Turner (d 1972); 1 s (Jeremy b 1964), 2 da (Celia b 1966, Penelope b 1969); *Career* Univ of Warwick: asst lectr 1965, lectr 1966, sr lectr 1970, reader 1974, prof 1980-, pro-vice chllr 1983-89; CChem, FRSC 1969, FRSA 1986; OM Polish Repub 1985; *Books* Introductory Photochemistry (1971); *Recreations* philately, cinema, walking; *Style*— Prof Terence Kemp; 93 Leamington Rd, Coventry CV3 6GQ (☎ 0203 414735); Department of Chemistry, University of Warwick, Coventry CV4 7AL (☎ 0203 523235, telex 31406 COVLIB, fax 0203 524112)

KEMP, Timothy; s of Capt Maurice Kemp, TD, of Walton-on-the-Hill, Surrey, and Gwendoline, *née* Atkinson (d 1979); *b* 16 April 1948; *Educ* Cranleigh; *m* 12 Jan 1974, Susan Elouise, da of Graham Cox (d 1982), of Chipstead, Surrey; 1 s (Robert b 20 March 1980), 1 da (Katie b 27 March 1978); *Career* Hon Artillery Co TA 1967-74; insur broker; elected memb of Lloyd's 1979, dir Gibbs Hartley Cooper Ltd 1985 (joined 1971); ACII 1971; *Recreations* golf, gardening; *Clubs* HAC, Lloyd's GC, Royal Ashdown Forest GC; *Style*— Timothy Kemp, Esq; Rush Green, Forest Row, E Sussex; Gibbs Hartley Cooper Ltd, Bishops Court, 27-33 Artillery La, London E1 7LP (☎ 071 247 5433)

KEMP-GEE, Hon Mrs (Lucy); *née* Lyttelton; 3 da of 10 Viscount Cobham (d 1977); *b* 1954; *m* 1980, Mark Norman Kemp-Gee; 3 s; *Style*— The Hon Mrs Kemp-Gee; Beech Tree Cottage, Preston Candover, Basingstoke, Hants RG25 2EJ

KEMP-GEE, Mark Norman; s of Bernard Kemp-Gee, and Ann, *née* MacKilligin; *b* 19 Dec 1945; *Educ* Marlborough, Pembroke Coll Oxford (MA); *m* 26 July 1980, The Hon Lucy Lyttelton, 3 da of late Viscount Cobham KG; *Career* chm Greig Middleton & Co Ltd (stockbrokers); *Recreations* tennis, skiing; *Style*— Mark Kemp-Gee, Esq; Greig Middleton & Co Ltd, 66 Wilson St, London EC2A 2BL (☎ 071 247 0007, fax 071 377 0353)

KEMP-WELCH, John; s of Peter Wellesbourne Kemp-Welch, OBE (d 1964), and Peggy Penelope, *née* Hunter; sr rep of the family descended from Martin Kemp-Welch (1772-1837), who assumed, by Royal Licence, 1795, the additional name of Welch, in compliance with the testamentary injunctions of his maternal unc, George Welch, banker and fndr of the banking house of Welch Rogers Olding and Rogers; *b* 31 March 1936; *Educ* Winchester; *m* 1964, Diana Elisabeth, da of Dr A W D Leishman (d 1978); 1 s, 3 da; *Career* memb Stock Exchange 1959, jt sr ptnr Cazenove & Co (stockbrokers); dir: Lowland Investment Co plc, Updown Investment Co plc, Garrows Farm Ltd 1964, Savoy Hotel plc 1985-; govr Ditchley Fndn, memb Courtauld Inst of Art Tst; tstee: Kings Medical Res Tst, Game Conservancy Tst; govr North Foreland Lodge Sch; CBIM, FRSA; *Recreations* shooting, farming, the hills of Perthshire; *Clubs* White's, City of London, MCC; *Style*— John Kemp-Welch, Esq; Little Hallingbury Place, Bishop's Stortford, Herts; Garrows, Amulree, Dunkeld, Perthshire; Cazenove & Co, 12 Tokenhouse Yard, London EC2R 7AN (☎ 071 588 2828, telex 886758)

KEMPE, John William Rolfe; CVO (1979); s of William Alfred Kempe (d 1922), of Nairobi, and Kunigunda, *née* Neville-Rolfe (d 1959); *b* 29 Oct 1917; *Educ* Stowe, Clare Coll Cambridge (MA); *m* 21 Dec 1957, Barbara Nan Stephen, da of Dr Charles Reginald Ralston Huxtable, MC (d 1980), of Sydney, NSW, Australia; 2 s (Nicholas Charles b 5 May 1959, Clive William Rolfe b 26 May 1961), 1 da (Penelope Jane b 21 April 1964); *Career* WW11 serv RAF 1939-45: RAFVR Trg and Fighter Cmd, flying Spitfires (602 Sqdn), Beaufighters, Mosquitoes, N Africa and Med, Wing Cdr 153 and 255 Night Fighter Sqdns 1943-44; BOT 1945-47, John Brown & Thos Firth (Overseas) Ltd 1947-48, head Maths Dept Gordonstoun 1948-51, princ Hyderabad Public Sch Deccan India 1951-54; headmaster: Corby GS 1955-67, Gordonstoun 1968-78; ret 1979; mountaineering in Alps, India and Peru; memb: Everest Fndn Ctee 1956-62, Brathay Exploration Ctee 1964-73; vice Pres Euro Atlantic Movement Team 1989-, chm Round Square Int Serv 1980-88, govr Stamford Sch 1979-89; tstee Kurt Hahn Tst 1986-88, Thornton Smith Tst, Plevins Charity; FRGS; *Recreations* one time mountaineering, reading, writing, walking, travel; *Clubs* Alpine, RGS; *Style*— John Kempe, Esq, CVO; Maple Tree Cottage, 24 Old Leicester Rd, Wansford, nr Peterborough PE8 6JR (☎ 0780 782618)

KEMPSELL, John Douglas (Jake); s of Alfred Kempsell (d 1986), of Dumfries, and Elizabeth Agnes, *née* Ashmore; *b* 24 March 1940; *Educ* Dumfries Acad, Edinburgh Coll of Art (Andrew Grant Bequest and post-dip scholarships, DA, postgrad dip); *m* 1, 1961 (m dis 1982), Elizabeth Wilma, da of Gavin Gordon Lennox; 1 s (Gavin Lennox Ashmore b Jan 1968), 1 da (Karen Elizabeth b July 1962); m 2, April 1984, Elizabeth Anne, da of Robert Wood; *Career* lectr in sculpture Edinburgh Coll of Art 1965-75, dir of sculpture Duncan of Jordanstone Coll of Art 1975-; sculptor; seminal works: Eve Figure (1962), Celtic Harpy (1967), Archaic Sunrise (1976), Squaring the Circle (Almost) (1979), Glasgow Sheriff Ct Houses Cmmn 1985-86, Luminous and Cool (1990); exhibitions incl: The British Art Show (Mappin Gallery Sheffield, Hatton Gallery Univ of Newcastle, Arnolfi Gallery Bristol) 1979-80, Wood (Royal Botanical Gardens, Edinburgh Festival) 1980, Sculpture at Margam Maquettes for Public Sculpture (Welsh Sculpture Tst) 1982, Sculpture in a Country Park (Welsh Sculpture Tst) 1983-84, Built in Scotland (travelling exhibition) 1983-84 Touching on Nature (Arts in Fife Travelling Exhibition) 1987-88, Art in the Garden (Glasgow Garden Festival) 1988; first one-man show (Richard Demarco Gallery) 1970; Scottish Arts Cncl Sculpture Cmmn 1978, major cmmn for Dundee Public Arts Programme 1984-85; visiting lectr numerous art schs; external assessor: Univ of London Goldsmith's Coll 1982-84, Edinburgh Coll of Art and Univ of Edinburgh MA courses 1983-87, memb various professional ctees 1967-; *Recreations* previously gliding, small bore rifle, presently golf; *Clubs* Broughty Golf; *Style*— Jake Kempsell, Esq; Duncan of Jordanstone College of Art, Perth Rd, Dundee (☎ 0392 23261 ext 228)

KEMPTON, Paul William; s of Ronald Arthur Kempton, and Jill Rosemary, *née* Weston; *b* 2 May 1957; *Educ* Berkhamsted Sch for Boys, Lanchester Poly (BA); *m* 21 Feb 1981, Christine Ann, da of Robert William Lee, of New House Barn, Marlborough, Devon; 2 s (Peter William b 1984, Robert Anthony b 1986); *Career* legal advsr Thorn EMI Screen Entertainment 1983-85, head of legal and business affrs The Music Channel Ltd 1985-87, gen mangr Super Channel Ltd 1988-89 (dir of business affrs 1987-88), PW Kempton Assoc 1989-; *Recreations* rugby, hockey, cricket, films and cinema; *Style*— Paul Kempton, Esq; 9-13 Grape St, London WC2H 8DR (☎ 071 240 3422, telex 28622 CHIL G, fax 071 497 9113)

KEMSLEY, Arthur Joseph; s of Joseph Alfred Kemsley (d 1966), of Stepney, East London, and Ivy Elizabeth Everet; *b* 21 May 1936; *Educ* Nicholas Gibson Secdy Sch; *m* 1967, Maureen (d 1989); 1 da (Gemma Louise b 29 Sept 1983); *Career* SAC RAF 1953-58; photographer; copy boy Advertising Dept Kemsley Newspapers 1951-52, gen asst Pathe Pictorial 1952-53, prodn mangr BAA 1989- (formerly Heathrow Airport Ltd, joined 1958, chief photographer 1965-89); 2 Gold and 3 Silver medals World Airports Photographers competition 1988, Bronze medallion USAF (for photographing the space shuttle Discovery; memb Professional Photographers of America; MBKS, FRPS, FBIPP; *Recreations* research and development in new visual imaging, bringing up daughter; *Style*— Arthur Kemsley, Esq; Building 224, Norwood Crescent, Heathrow Airport, Hounslow, Middlesex (☎ 081 745 7461, fax 081 745 7099)

KEMSLEY, Viscountess; Lady Hélène Candida; *née* Hay; da of 11 Marquess of Tweeddale (d 1967); *b* 1913; *m* 1933, 2 Viscount Kemsley; 4 da; *Career* DStJ; *Style*— The Rt Hon the Viscountess Kemsley; Field House, Thorpe Lubenham, Market Harborough, Leics

KEMSLEY, Viscount (UK 1945); Sir (Geoffrey) Lionel Berry; 2 Bt (UK 1928), DL (Leics 1972); Baron Kemsley (UK 1936); s of 1 Viscount Kemsley, GBE (d 1968); *b* 29 June 1909; *Educ* Marlborough, Magdalen Coll Oxford; *m* 1933, Lady Hélène Hay, *qv*; 4 da; *Heir* nephew, Richard Gomer Berry, b 1951, s of late Hon Denis Gomer Berry, TD; *Career* served WW II as Capt Grenadier Gds (invalided out 1942); dep chm Kemsley Newspapers Ltd 1938-59, MP (C) Buckingham 1943-45; Master Worshipful Co of Spectacle Makers 1949-51 and 1959-61; CC Northants 1964-70; High Sheriff Leics 1967; chm St Andrew's Hosp Northampton 1973-84, pres Assoc of Independent Hosps 1976-83, memb Chapter Gen of OStJ; FRSA; KStJ; *Clubs* Turf, Pratt's, Royal Over-Seas League; *Style*— The Rt Hon the Viscount Kemsley, DL; Field House, Thorpe Lubenham, Market Harborough, Leics (☎ 0858 462816)

KENCH, Eric Arthur; s of Joseph Peter Kench, of Oxfordshire, and Ethel Catherine, *née* Younger; *b* 30 Sept 1952; *Educ* Henley GS; *m* 20 July 1974, Kathleen Jennifer, da of Philip Hague (d 1980); 1 s (David b 1979), 2 da (Caroline b 1981, Sarah b 1982); *Career* CA; formed E A Kench & Co 1982, past chm Thames Valley Young CA Gp, Thames Valley rep ICA EW, Smaller Practitioners Ctee 1984-90, memb ICA Changing Environment Gp 1984-87, pres Thames Valley Soc of CAs 1987-88, memb ICAEW Gen Practitioner Bd 1990-; FCA; *Recreations* squash, flying (private pilot), reading, working; *Style*— Eric Kench, Esq; 5 All Hallows Rd, Caversham, Reading RG4 0LP (☎ 0734 475624); E A Kench & Co, 8 Station Rd, Henley-on-Thames RG9 1AY (☎ 0491 578207)

KENDAL, Felicity Anne; da of Geoffrey Kendal, of Swan Court, Chelsea, London, and Laura, *née* Liddell; *Educ* convents in India; *m* 1, 1969 (m dis 1976), Drewe Henley; 1 s (Charles b 23 Jan 1973); m 2, 1983 (m dis 1991), Michael Edward Rudman, s of Duke Rudman, of Dallas, Texas; 1 s (Jacob Henry b 1 Oct 1987); *Career* grew up touring and acting with parents theatre co in India and Far East, London debut in Minor Murder (Savoy) 1967; plays: Henry V and The Promise (Leicester)

1968, Back to Methuselah (NT) 1969, A Midsummer Night's Dream and Much Ado About Nothing (Regents Park) 1970, Kean (Oxford) 1970 and (London) 1971, Romeo and Juliet, 'Tis Pity She's a Whore 1972, The Three Arrows 1972, The Norman Conquests (Globe) 1974, Once Upon a Time (Bristol) 1976, Arms and the Man (Greenwich) 1978, Clouds (Duke of York's) 1978, Amadeus (NT) 1979, Othello (NT) 1980, On the Razzle (NT) 1981, The Second Mrs Tanqueray (NT) 1981, The Real Thing (Strand) 1982, Jumpers (Aldwych) 1985, Made in Bangkok (Aldwych) 1986, Hapgood (Aldwych) 1988, Much Ado About Nothing and Ivanov (Strand) 1989, Hidden Laughter (Vaudeville) 1990; TV: The Good Life 1975-77, Twelfth Night 1979, Solo 1980 and 1982, The Mistress 1985; films: Shakespeare Wallah 1965, Valentino 1976; awards: Variety Club Most Promising Newcomer 1974, Best Actress 1979, Clarence Derwent award 1980, Variety Club Woman of the Year Best Actress award 1984; Evening Standard Best Actress award 1989; *Recreations* golf; *Clubs* RAC, Royal Mid Surrey Golf, Dyrem Pk Golf; *Style—* Miss Felicity Kendal; Chatto & Linnit, Prince of Wales Theatre, Coventry St, London W1 (☎ 071 930 6677, fax 071 930 0091)

KENDALL, Dr David; s of Guy Kendall (d 1960), of Witley, Surrey, and Ada, *née* Sampson (d 1958); *b* 13 Feb 1924; *Educ* Westminster, Oriel Coll Oxford (Theodore Williams scholar in anatomy, MA, DM), St Thomas' Hosp (Murchison scholar); *m* 1 (m dis), Wilfrida, da of Arthur Lawson, of Canada; 1 s (Martin b 1944), 1 da (Linda b 1940); m 2 (m dis), Sally, da of Col Stanley Purkis; *Career* St Thomas' Hosp (res anaethetist, casualty offr, house physician to Med Unit, sr med casualty offr, first sec Neurology Dept), The National Hosp for Nervous Diseases (res med offr, registrar), estab Regnl Neurological Centre at Guildford 1948-65, assoc prof of Neurology Dalhousie Univ Halifax Canada 1966; conslt neurologist: Atkinson Morleys (St George's) Hosp, St Helier Hosp, Epsom Hosp; ret 1983; conslt neurologist in mainly medico-legal practice, publication in various med jls; fndr memb Res Advsy Ctee Multiple Sclerosis Soc; FRCP, FRSM 1938, memb Assoc of Br Neurologists 1953; *Recreations* music, calligraphy; *Style—* Dr David Kendall; 8 Bushey Shaw, Ashtead, Surrey KT21 2HP; 9 Devonshire Place, London W1N 1PB (☎ 071 487 4447)

KENDALL, Rev Frank; s of Norman Kendall (d 1976), of Ripon, Yorkshire, and Violet, *née* Bloor; *b* 15 Dec 1940; *Educ* Bradford GS, Corpus Christi Coll Cambridge (MA), London Univ (Dip in Religious Studies); *m* 20 Feb 1965, Brenda, da of Walter Isaac Pickin (d 1982), of Royston; 1 s (Andrew b 1970), 1 da (Angela b 1969); *Career* Civil Serv; asst princ then princ Miny of Public Building and Works 1962-70, princ Dept of Economic Affairs 1967-68, princ and asst sec DOE 1970-84, under sec and NW regnl dir Depts of the Environment and Tport 1984-89, chief exec St Helens Met Borough Cncl; ordained: deacon 1974, priest 1975; hon curate: Lingfield 1974-75 and 1978-82, Limpsfield 1982-84 (Diocese of Southwark), Sketty 1975-78 (Diocese of Swansea and Brecon); licensed preacher Diocese of Manchester 1984-89, Diocese of Liverpool 1989-; FRSA 1990; *Recreations* painting, DIY; *Style—* The Rev Frank Kendall; Cromwell Villa, 260 Prescot Road, St Helens, Merseyside WA10 3HR (☎ 0744 27626); St Helens MBC, Town Hall, Victoria Square, St Helens, Merseyside WA10 1HP (☎ 0744 24061, fax 0744 33337, telex 627813)

KENDALL, George Langton; JP (1966 Bucks); s of Gordon Kendall (d 1972), of Leics, and Elsie Winifred, *née* Breeze (d 1989); coat of arms 1448 confirmed under seal by Clarenceux King of Arms; John Kendall, sec to Richard III, killed at Bosworth Leics; *b* 19 June 1927; *Educ* Haileybury; *m* 13 June 1959, Elizabeth Jane, da of W G E Shand, of NZ; 1 s (Angus b 1960), 1 da (Mary-Anne b 1962); *Career* Sub Lt RNVR, served Far East; chartered surveyor; chm and sr ptnr Raffety Buckland 1980-89 (ret 1989); memb: Bow Gp 1955-65, Cncl RICS 1956-59, Wycombe Borough Cncl 1966-69, Cncl Univ of Buckingham 1986-; memb and chm Personnel Ctee Bucks CC 1970-77; gen cmmr of taxes 1983-; High Sheriff Bucks 1986-87; life memb Primrose League; Liveryman Worshipful Co of Chartered Surveyors; FIOD (ret); *Recreations* golf, shooting, sailing, crew memb Taiseer IV (first winner Britannia Cup Cowes 1951); *Clubs* Naval, MCC; *Style—* George Langton Kendall, Esq, JP; c/o 30 High St, High Wycombe, Bucks (☎ 0494 21234, fax 0494 36362)

KENDALL, Howard; s of John James Kendall, and May, *née* Atkinson; *b* 22 May 1946; *Educ* Washington GS; *m* Cynthia Ruth; 1 s (Simon), 2 da (Hayley, Lisa); *Career* professional football manager; player: Preston North End 1961-67, Everton 1967-74, Birmingham City 1974-77; player-coach Stoke City 1977-79, player-mangr Blackburn Rovers 1979-81; mangr: Everton 1981-87 and 1990-, Athletic Bilbao Spain 1987-89, Manchester City 1989-90; England caps: schoolboy, youth, under 23; achievements as mangr Everton: League Championships 1985 and 1987, FA Cup 1984, Euro Cup-Winners' Cup 1985; *Recreations* golf, cricket; *Style—* Howard Kendall, Esq; Everton FC, Goodison Park, Liverpool L4 4EL (☎ 051 521 2020, fax 051 523 9666)

KENDALL, John Melville; s of Capt Charles Edward Kendall (d 1978), of Great Nineveh, Benenden, Kent, and Cara Honoria, *née* Pelly; *b* 1 Sept 1931; *Educ* Ampleforth; *m* 23 Feb 1971, Anthea Diana, da of Col T D Partridge; 1 s (Mark b 12 Jan 1972), 1 da (Sophia b 4 July 1973); *Career* Lt RN 1952-56; chm Charles Kendall Gp of Cos 1978-; Order of Sultan Qaboos Sultanate of Oman; *Recreations* sailing, skiing, hunting; *Clubs* Brooks's; *Style—* John Kendall, Esq; Coombe Priory, Shaftesbury, Dorset; 7 Albert Ct, Prince Consort Rd, London SW7 2BJ (☎ 071 589 1256, fax 071 581 5761, telex 919060)

KENDALL, Lady; Kathleen Ruth (Whitfield); da of Roland Abel Phillipson (d 1925), of Bournemouth; *b* 20 Nov 1904; *Educ* Bournemouth Collegiate Sch, Les Allières Lausanne, Switzerland; *m* 1947, as his 2 w, Sir Maurice George Kendall (d 1983), s of John Roughton, of Derby, prof of statistics Univ of London 1949-61, dir World Fertility Survey 1972-80, chm Scientific Control Systems; *Recreations* languages, reading; *Style—* Lady Kendall; c/o Barclays Bank, 117 Dulwich Village, Dulwich, London SE21 7BD

KENDALL-TAYLOR, Prof Pat; da of Kendall-Taylor, CBE, of Wimbledon, and Dorothy, *née* Lawton (d 1958); *b* 17 Feb 1937; *Educ* RCM (ARCM), Royal Free Hosp Univ of London (MD); *Career* lectr med Univ of Sheffield 1968-74, prof endocrinology Univ of Newcastle upon Tyne 1985- (sr lectr and reader med in 1980-85), conslt physician Royal Victoria Infirmary Newcastle upon Tyne; memb Assoc Physicians 1973, FRCP; *Books* Casebook in Endocrinology (1987), numerous chapters and papers on endocrinology/medicine; *Recreations* fell-walking, gardening, bird watching, music; *Style—* Prof Pat Kendall-Taylor; Royal Victoria Infirmary, Newcastle on Tyne NE1 4LP (☎ 091 232 5131)

KENDELL, Prof Robert Evan; s of Robert Owen Kendell (d 1954), and Joan, *née* Evans (d 1986); *b* 28 March 1935; *Educ* Mill Hill Sch, Peterhouse Cambridge (BA, MA, MB BChir, MD), King's Coll Hosp Med Sch London; *m* 2 Dec 1961, Dr Ann Whitfield, da of Dr Gerald Whitfield (d 1972), of Lindfield, Sussex; 2 s (Patrick b 1968, Harry b 1970), 2 da (Katherine b 1965, Judith b 1966); *Career* registrar then sr registrar The Maudsley Hosp London 1962-66, visiting prof Univ of Vermont Coll of Med USA 1969-70, reader in psychiatry Inst of Psychiatry London 1970-74, (res worker 1966-70), dean Faculty of Med Univ of Edinburgh 1986-90 (prof of psychiatry 1974-), Gaskell Gold Medal RCPsych 1967, Paul Hoch Medal American Psychopathological Assoc 1988; WHO: chm Expert Ctee on Alcohol Consumption 1979, memb Expert Advsy Panel on Mental Health 1979-; memb MRC 1984-88; FRCP 1974, FRCPE 1977, FRCPsych 1979; *Books* The Classification of Depressive Illnesses (1968), The Role of Diagnosis in Psychiatry (1975), Companion to Psychiatric Studies (ed, 4 edn, 1988); *Recreations* overeating, walking up hills; *Clubs* Climbers; *Style—* Prof R E Kendell; 3 West Castle Rd, Edinburgh EH10 5AT (☎ 031 229 4966); University Dept of Psychiatry, Royal Edinburgh Hospital, Edinburgh EH10 5HF (☎ 031 447 2011)

KENDRA, Rev Kenneth Ernest; OBE (1966); s of Ernest Kendra (d 1938), of Newton upon Derwent, Yorks, and Emily, *née* Lister; *b* 27 Oct 1913; *Educ* Wilberforce Sch York, Univ of Leeds (BA, MA), Scholae Cancellarii Lincoln; *m* 14 July 1951, Kathleen, da of Alderman Charles W Whatley, OBE (d 1960), of Burderop, Chiseldon, Marlborough, Wilts; 2 da (Emily Jane, Judith Anne Morse); *Career* chaplain to the forces 1945, 6 Airborne Div 1946; sr chaplain 3 Inf Div 1953, chaplain RMA Sandhurst 1954, sr chaplain 5 Inf Bde 1958, dep asst chaplain Gen BAOR 1963, asst chaplain gen HQ Far East 1968, hon chaplain to HM The Queen 1970, ret 1971; ordained: deacon 1942, priest 1943; curate Pocklington Yorks 1943-45, vicar of Lee on the Solent Hants 1971-80; pres Mere and Dist Hist Soc; *Style—* The Rev Kenneth Kendra, OBE; Highfields, Castle Hill Lane, Mere, Wilts BA12 6JB, (☎ 0747 860823)

KENDREW, Sir John Cowdery; CBE (1963); s of Wilfrid Kendrew; *b* 24 March 1917; *Educ* Clifton, Trinity Coll Cambridge (ScD, PhD); *Career* served WWII Miny of Aircraft Prodn, Hon Wing Cdr RAF ME and SE Asia; dep chm MRC Laboratory of Molecular Biology Cambridge 1946-74, dir gen Euro Molecular Biology Laboratory 1975-82; jt winner Nobel prize for Chemistry 1962, Royal Soc Royal medal 1965; chm Governing Cncl UN Univ 1983-85 (memb 1980-86); pres: St John's Coll Oxford 1981-87, Br Assoc for the Advancement of Sci 1974, Int Cncl of Scientific Unions 1983-88; hon fell: Peterhouse and Trinity Coll Cambridge, St John's Coll Oxford; Hon DSc: Reading, Keele, Exeter, Buckingham, Madrid, Siena; Hon DUniv Stirling, Hon Prof Univ of Heidelberg 1982; FRS; kt 1974; *Clubs* Athenaeum; *Style—* Sir John Kendrew, CBE, FRS; The Old Guildhall, 4 Church Lane, Linton, Cambridge CB1 6JX (☎ 0223 891 545)

KENDRICK, Clinton Jansen; *b* 2 Aug 1943; *Educ* Phillips Acad, Yale Univ (BA Eng Lit), New York Univ Graduate Sch; *m* 11 Oct 1970, Mary Claudell Jallande; 1 s (Nicholas b 1974), 1 da (Charlotte Fortier b 1977); *Career* pres Alliance Capital Mgmnt Corp New York, chm Alliance Capital Mgmnt Int Inc London; *Style—* Clinton Kendrick, Esq; 1345 Avenue of the Americas, New York 10105 (☎ 212 969 1030); 43 Upper Grosvenor Street, London W1X 9PG

KENEFICK, John Stanislaus; s of Thomas Kenefick (d 1972), and Margaret, *née* O'Mahony; *b* 10 Feb 1937; *m* Erica Ann; 2 s (Nicholas b 16 June 1971, Timothy b 3 Oct 1972), 2 da (Susanna b 6 June 1976, Elizabeth b 3 April 1979); *Career* MB BCh 1960, N Middlesex Hosp 1963-66, Royal Free Hosp 1966-75, conslt surgn Barnet Gen Hosp 1975-; FRSM, FRCS, FRCS Ed; *Recreations* golf, fishing, shooting; *Style—* John Kenefick, Esq; 72 Harley St, London W1N 1AE (☎ 071 636 6756)

KENILOREA, Rt Hon Sir Peter; KBE, PC (1979); *b* 23 May 1943; *Educ* Univ and Teachers' Coll NZ; *m* 1971, Margaret Kwanairara; 2 s, 2 da; *Career* PM Solomon Islands 1978-81, chief min 1976-78; MLA Solomon Islands 1976-; *Style—* The Rt Hon Sir Peter Kenilorea, KBE, PC; Legislative Assembly, Honiara, Guadalcanal, Solomon Islands

KENILWORTH, Jacqueline, Baroness; Jacqueline Paulette; *née* Gelpi; da of late Robert Gelpi, of Lyon, France; *m* 28 Aug 1948, 3 Baron Kenilworth (d 1981); 1 s (4 Baron), 1 da (Hon Mrs McCarraher); *Style—* The Rt Hon Jacqueline, Baroness Kenilworth; 2 Lexham Walk, London W8 (☎ 071 370 6805)

KENILWORTH, 4 Baron (UK 1937); (John) Randle Siddeley; only s of 3 Baron Kenilworth (d 1981); *b* 16 June 1954; *Educ* Northease Manor, London Coll of Furniture; *m* 1983, Kim, only da of Danie Serfontein, of Newcastle upon Tyne; *Style—* The Rt Hon the Lord Kenilworth; 52 Hartismere Rd, London SW6

KENNAIR, William Brignall; s of Joseph Terry Kennair, of Newcastle upon Tyne, and Nancy, *née* Neasham; *b* 6 June 1956; *Educ* Royal GS Newcastle upon Tyne, UCL (LLB); *m* 2 Aug 1980, Karen Elizabeth, da of Keith John Williams, of Cardiff; *Career* ptnr John Venn & Sons London 1986- (articled clerk 1978-83, assoc 1983-86), Notary Public (John Venn & Sons, Notaries and Translators); Freeman City of London 1983-, Liveryman Worshipful Co of Scriveners 1983-; memb Assoc Int De Jeunes Avocats 1985-; *Recreations* cuisine, wine, travel; *Style—* William Kennair, Esq; John Venn & Sons, Imperial House, 15-19 Kingsway, London WC2B 6UU (☎ 071 836 9522, fax 071 836 3182, telex 262582 VENLEX G, modem 071 240 5350)

KENNARD, Sir George Arnold Ford; 3 Bt (UK 1891), of Fernhill, co Southampton; s of late Sir Coleridge Kennard, 1 Bt; suc bro, Sir Laurence Ury Charles Kennard, 2 Bt, 1967; *b* 27 April 1915; *Educ* Eton; *m* 1, 1940 (m dis 1958), Cecilia Violet Cokayne, da of Maj Cecil John Cokayne Maunsell, JP; 1 da; m 2, 1958 (m dis 1974), Mrs Molly Jesse Rudd Miskin, da of late Hugh Wyllie, of Fishbourne, Sussex; m 3, 1985, Nicola, da of Capt Peter Gawan Carew (d 1966) and formerly w of Charles Louis Breitmeyer; *Heir* none; *Career* WWII 1939-45 (despatches twice, Pow), Lt-Col (cmdg) late 4 Queen's Own Hussars; Midland rep for Cement Marketing Co; *Books* Loopy (autobiography, 1990); *Clubs* Cavalry and Guards'; *Style—* Sir George Kennard, Bt; Gogwell, Tiverton, Devon (☎ 0884 253153)

KENNARD, Michael Frederick; s of Julius Kennard (d 1986), and Phyllis, *née* Swyers; *b* 2 Feb 1927; *Educ* Univ Coll Sch London, Northampton Eng Coll, Univ of London (BSc); *m* Sept 1955, Ruth, 2 da (Elaine b 1958, Emma b 1964); *Career* civil engr; Sir William Halcrow and Partners 1948-52, Cubitts Ltd 1953-54, Sandeman Kennard and Partners 1954-70 (ptnr 1955-70), sr ptnr Rofe Kennard and Lapworth 1985- (ptnr 1970-85), conslting engr specialising in dams, geotech engrg and water engrg; appt by Min of Agric to Flood Defence Ctee Nat Rivers Authy Thames Regn, chm Br Section of Int Cmmn of Large Dams 1977-80; FIWEM, FICE 1952; *Books* author of tech papers on dams and water engrg; *Style—* Michael Kennard, Esq; 25 Talbot Crescent, London NW4 4HS; Rofe Kennard and Lapworth; 2/4 Sutton Court Road, Sutton, Surrey SM1 4SS (☎ 081 643 8201, fax 081 642 8469, telex 946688)

KENNARD, Nigel Robert; s of Herbert Edward Kennard (d 1971), of Guernsey, and Esther Mary, *née* Plummer; *b* 23 July 1944; *Educ* Lancing; *m* 15 March 1969, Anne Jane, da of Kenneth Embden Archer, of Sussex; 2 s (Edward b 1973, James b 1976); *Career* CA in own practice 1978; dir Kesgrave Hall Sch Ltd 1984, fin chm English Guernsey Cattle Soc (bred champion Guernsey cow RASE 1987); FCA; *Recreations* cattle breeding, hockey; *Style—* Nigel R Kennard, Esq; Instead Manor, Weybread, Diss, Norfolk IP21 5UH (☎ 0379 852350)

KENNARD, Prof Olga; OBE (1988); da of Joir Weisz, and Catherina, *née* Sternberg (d 1988); *b* 23 March 1924; *Educ* Prince Henry VIII GS, Univ of Cambridge (ScD); *m* 1948 (m dis 1961), Dr David William Kennard; 2 da (Susanna Clare b 1955, Julia Sarah b 1958); *Career* res asst Cavendish Laboratory Cambridge 1944-48; MRC: memb Scientific Staff Vision Res Unit 1948-51, Nat Inst for Med Res 1951-61, Chem Laboratory Univ of Cambridge 1961-, special appt 1971-89; scientific dir Cambridge Crystallographic Data Centre 1965-, visiting prof Univ of London 1988-; author of scientific papers and books on scientific data; memb numerous ctees of scientific socs; FRS 1987; *Recreations* swimming, cooking, reading; *Style—* Prof Olga Kennard, OBE, FRS; Crystallographic Data Centre, University Chemical Lab, Lensfield Rd, Cambridge CB2 1EW (☎ 0223 336408, fax 0223 332288)

KENNAWAY, Prof Alexander; s of Dr Noah Barou (d 1955), and Mrs Sophie Barou (d 1956); *b* 14 Aug 1923; *Educ* St Paul's, Pembroke Coll Cambridge (MA); *m* 1, 1947 (m dis 1970), Xenia Rebel; 1 s (Igor b 1947), 1 da (Nadia b 1950); m 2, 1973, Jean Simpson, da of Stanley Church (d 1982); *Career* WWII Lt Cdr RN served: Med, East Indies, Pacific; consulting engr 1966-; dir: BTR Industries 1960-66, Lankro Chemicals 1970-77, Thomas Jourdan Group 1976-82; chm Terrafix Ltd 1983-90; visiting prof of chemical (now mechanical) engrg Imperial Coll 1976-; memb bd Civil Aviation Authy 1979-82, sometime memb Standing Advsy Ctee on Artificial Limbs DHSS; *Books* contrib: Plastics in Surgery (1956), Polythene, Its Technology and Uses (1958), The British Malaise (1982); sole author: Engineers in Industry, A Management Guide to Self Improvement (1981); *Recreations* sailing, chess, music, self-education, thinking; *Clubs* Royal Naval Sailing Assoc; *Style—* Prof Alexander Kennaway; 12 Fairholme Cres, Ashtead, Surrey KT21 2HN (☎ 0372 277 678); Imperial College of Science, Technology and Medicine, Exhibition Rd, London SW7

KENNAWAY, John-Michael; s and h of Sir John Kennaway, 5 Bt, and Christina Veronica, *née* Urszenyi; *b* 17 Feb 1962; *Educ* King Edward's Sch Bath, Hampshire Coll of Agriculture; *m* 22 Oct 1988, Lucy Frances, yr da of Dr Jeremy Houlton Bradshaw- Smith, of Ottery St Mary, Devon; *Career* ornamental fish farmer, landowner (1200 acres); *Recreations* shooting, scuba diving; *Style—* John-Michael Kennaway, Esq; Escot, Ottery St Mary, Devon EX11 1LU (☎ 0404 822 188)

KENNEDY, Dr Alexander; s of late Alexander Kennedy, and Florence Edith, *née* Callin; *b* 20 April 1933; *Educ* Merchant Taylors', Univ of Liverpool (MB ChB, MD); *m* 6 Aug 1960, Marlene Joan Campbell, da of Alfred Beveridge (d 1939), of Edinburgh; 1 s (Alistair b 1969), 1 da (Fiona b 1963); *Career* RAF Med Branch, Flt Lt pathologist RAF Hosp Wroughton 1958-61; lectr pathology Univ of Liverpool 1961-67, visiting asst prof Dept of Pathology Univ of Chicago 1968, sr lectr Dept of Pathology Univ of Sheffield 1968-77, hon conslt pathologist Sheffield Area Health Authy 1969-77, currently conslt histopathologist Northern Gen Hosp Sheffield, hon clinical lectr Univ of Sheffield; memb: Pathological Soc of GB and Ireland, British Soc for Clinical Cytology, Sheffield Medico-Chirurgical Soc, British Thoracic Soc, Trent Regnl Thoracic Soc, Pulmonary Pathology Club; FRCPath 1985 (MRCPath 1966); *Books* Essentials of Surgical Pathology: A Programmed Instruction Text (with A C Daniels and F Strauss, 1974), Basic Techniques in Diagnostic Histopathology (1977); *Recreations* cycling, walking, music, gardening; *Style—* Dr Alexander Kennedy; Dept of Histopathology, Northern Gen Hosp, Herries Rd, Sheffield S5 7AU (☎ 0742 434343 ext 4849)

KENNEDY, Andrew David; s of Maj Denis George Kennedy (d 1970), of London, and Catherine Clementina, *née* MacGregor; *b* 20 May 1943; *Educ* Downside, Gonville and Caius Coll Cambridge (MA); *m* 3 Jan 1970, Mary Frances, da of Frank Turnbull (d 1981), of Lancs; 2 s (James Andrew b 21 Sept 1970, Mark Richard b 4 Nov 1972); *Career* admitted slr 1965; sr ptnr Beachcroft Stanleys 1988-; dir E Surrey Water Plc 1979, chm Sutton District Water Plc 1988, dir Ludgate Insurance Co 1989; govr: Wimbledon Coll, St Margaret's Sch; Freeman: Worshipful Co of Slrs 1988, City of London 1989; memb Law Soc 1965 (memb cncl 1986); *Recreations* golf, cricket; *Clubs* MCC, City Law, Royal Wimbledon Golf; *Style—* Andrew Kennedy, Esq; Friars Croft, 19 Wool Rd, Wimbledon, London SW20 OHN (☎ 081 946 3208); Beachcroft Stanleys, 20 Furnival St, London EC4R 1BN (☎ 071 242 1011, telex 264607, fax 071 831 6630)

KENNEDY, Dr Cameron Thomas Campbell; s of Thomas Kennedy (d 1981), and Dorian, *née* Talbot; *b* 30 Jan 1947; *Educ* Forest Sch Snaresbrook, Queens' Coll Cambridge and UCH (MA, MB BChir); *m* 19 May 1973, Dr Rosalind Penolope, da of Raymond Whittier Baldwin, of Penn, Macclesfield Rd, Alderley Edge, Cheshire; 3 s (Nicholas b 5 June 1979, Thomas b 3 March 1981, Stephen b 29 Jan 1984); *Career* registrar in dermatology London Hosp 1973-75, sr registrar St George's Hosp 1975-80; Bristol Royal Infirmary: conslt dermatologist 1981-, postgraduate clinical tutor 1985-89; conslt dermatologist: Southmead Hosp Bristol 1981-, Bristol Children's Hosp 1981-; memb Br Assoc of Dermatologists, non-res fell American Acad of Dermatology; FRCP 1986, FRSM; *Recreations* gardening, reading; *Clubs* Bristol Savages; *Style—* Dr Cameron Kennedy; 16 Sion Hill, Clifton, Bristol BS8 4AZ (☎ 0272 741935); Bristol Royal Infirmary, Dept of Dermatology, Marlborough St, Bristol BS2 8HW (☎ 0272 230000)

KENNEDY, Charles Peter; MP (Lib Democrat) Ross, Cromarty and Skye 1987-; s of Ian Kennedy and Mary MacVarish, *née* MacEachen, of Fort William; *b* 25 Nov 1959; *Educ* Lochaber HS Fort William, Glasgow Univ (MA), Indiana Univ USA (Fulbright Scholarship, Masters Degree 1990); *Career* broadcaster and journalist BBC Highland Inverness 1982; graduate student/lecturer (speech communications and British politics) Indiana Univ USA 1982-83; MP (SDP) Ross, Cromarty and Skye 1983-87, chm SDP Cncl for Scotland 1983, Lib Democrat spokesman on Health 1989-; *Recreations* music, reading, writing; *Clubs* National Liberal; *Style—* Charles Kennedy, Esq, MP; House of Commons, London SW1

KENNEDY, Prof Clive Russell; s of Thomas Kennedy (ka 1941), of Paisley, Renfrewshire, and Victoria Alice, *née* Russell; *b* 17 June 1941; *Educ* Liverpool Coll, Univ of Liverpool (BSc, PhD, DSc); *m* 23 Feb 1963, Beryl Pamela (d 1978), da of David Redvers Jones (d 1979), of Portargothi, Nantgaredig, Carmarthen; 1 s (Aidan b 1970), 1 da (Kate b 1971); m 2, 5 May 1979, Margaret Hilary, da of Bernard Wise (d 1973), of Oxford; *Career* asst zoology Univ Coll Dublin 1963-64, asst lectr zoology Univ of Birmingham 1964-65; Univ of Exeter: lectr biological sci 1965-76, reader in zoology 1976-86, prof parasitology 1986-, dean of sci 1990-; visiting prof King's Coll London 1986-; memb: Ctee NERC 1984-88, Regional Fisheries Advsy Ctee, Nat Rivers Authy, Br Soc Parasitology 1968, Fisheries Soc Br Isles 1969; *Books* Ecological Animal Parasitology (1975), Ecological Aspects Parasitology (1976), numerous papers in sci jls; *Recreations* walking, churches, glass; *Style—* Prof Clive Kennedy; Dept of Biological Sciences, The University, Exeter EX4 4PS (☎ 0392 263757, fax 0392 263700, telex 42894 EXUNIVG)

KENNEDY, Sir Clyde David Allen; s of late D H Kennedy; *b* 20 Nov 1912; *Educ* Mount Albert GS, Univ of Auckland; *m* 1937, Sarah Stacpoole; 2 s, 1 da; *Career* co dir Aust Casing Co Pty Ltd 1939-82, chm Sydney Turf Club 1972-77 and 1980-83 (dir 1964-83, vice chm 1967-72); memb Totalizator Agency Bd of NSW 1965-82, chm Spinal Res Fndn; kt 1973; *Style—* Sir Clyde Kennedy; 13A/23 Thornton St, Darling Point, NSW 2027, Australia

KENNEDY, Dr David Duncan; s of Capt Alan Robert Kennedy (d 1967), and Mary Gertrude, *née* Simpson (d 1968); *b* 20 April 1937; *Educ* Quarry Bank HS Liverpool, King Edward's GS Stourbridge, Univ of Bristol (MB ChB); *m* 10 April 1965, (Janet) Lesley, da of Leslie Rupert Middleton (d 1986); 1 s (Christopher b 1969), 2 da (Katherine b 1967, Fiona b 1972); *Career* sr registrar chem pathology United Liverpool Hosps 1966-69; conslt chem pathologist: Fife Area Authy 1969-79, Yorkshire RHA (Grimsby, Scunthorpe, Goole and Louth) 1979-; memb: Assoc Clinical Biochemists, Assoc Clinical Pathologists, Yorks Regn Scientific Ctee, Yorks Regn Med Ctee; FRCPath 1980 (MRCPath 1968); *Recreations* gardening, woodwork, photography, walking; *Style—* Dr David Kennedy; 1 Utterby Drive, Grimsby, S Humberside DN34 4UA (☎ 0472 355880); Pathology Dept, Grimsby Gen Hosp, Scartho Rd, Grimsby, S Humberside DN33 2BA (☎ 0472 74111 ext 7390)

KENNEDY, Lord David Thomas; s of 7 Marquess of Ailsa, OBE, DL; *b* 3 July 1958; *Educ* Strathallan Sch, Berks Coll of Ag; *Career* farmer; *Recreations* shooting, fishing, vintage car restoration, travel; *Clubs* New (Edinburgh); *Style—* The Lord David Kennedy; Morriston Farm, Maidens, Maybole, Ayrshire

KENNEDY, Ambassador Eamon; s of Luke William Kennedy (d 1980), of Dublin, and Ellen Stafford (d 1955); maternal gf, Matthew Stafford, memb of Irish Senate (late 1930's); both gfs participated in 1916 Rising in Dublin; *b* 13 Dec 1921; *Educ* UC Dublin (MA, BComm), Nat Univ of Ireland (PhD); *m* 1960, Barbara Jane, da of William Black (d 1980), pres of Chock Full Coffee Corpn, of NY; 1 s (Mark b 1970) 1 da (Helen b 1967); *Career* entered Dept Foreign Affrs 1943; consul NY 1947; second sec Ottawa 1947; first sec: Washington 1949, Paris 1950, (actg chief of protocol), Dept Foreign Affairs 1954; cncllr Perm Mission UN NY 1956; ambass: Fedn Rep Nigeria 1961, Fedn Rep Germany 1964, France 1970; perm rep to UN 1974; ambass: Britain 1978, Italy, Turkey and Libya 1983-; Grand Cross of Merit of France 1974, Grand Cross of Merit of Federal Republic of Germany 1970; *Recreations* golf, theatre, music; *Clubs* Acquasanta (Rome), Old Collegians Rowing (Dublin); *Style—* His Excellency Mr Eamon Kennedy; Via Valle delle Camene 3, 00184 Roma, Italy (☎ 778035); Embassy of Ireland, Largo del Nazareno 3, 00187 Roma, Italy

KENNEDY, Sir Francis; KCMG (1986), CBE (1977, MBE 1958); s of James Kennedy (d 1961), and Alice, *née* Bentham (d 1978); *b* 9 May 1926; *Educ* Preston Catholic Coll, Univ of Manchester (BA), Univ of London (BA); *m* 4 March 1957, Anne O'Malley; 2 s (Mark b 1960, Jonathan b 1966), 2 da (Sarah b 1958, Ruth b 1965); *Career* RN 1944-46; HM Colonial Serv Nigeria 1953-64, Dip Serv 1964-86: served Kuching, Dar es Salaam, Istanbul, Atlanta, Lagos; ambass to Angola and ambass non-resident to São Tomé and Principe 1981-83, HM consul-gen at NY and DG Br Trade Devpt USA 1983-86; BA 1986- (bd memb 1987-); dir: Global Analysis Systems Ltd 1986-, Fluor-Daniel 1986- (chm 1989-), Hambourne Devpt Co Ltd 1987-, Smith & Nephew 1988-, Fleming Overseas Investmt Tst 1988-; memb: Bd of Inward 1986-90; Bd of Govrs: Br Liver Fndn 1990-, Lancs Poly; *Recreations* watching cricket, golf, gardening; *Clubs* Brooks's; *Style—* Sir Francis Kennedy, KCMG, CBE; c/o British Airways, London Airport (☎ 01 093 4915)

KENNEDY, Geoffrey Farrer; s of Sir John MacFarlane Kennedy, OBE (d 1954), of Shalford, Surrey, and Dorothy, *née* Farrer (d 1974); *b* 30 Oct 1908; *Educ* Oundle, Trinity Coll Cambridge (BA, MA); *m* 1, 1938 (m dis 1948), Daska, *née* Ivanovic; 1 s (John Alexander b 1942), 3 da (Tessa Georgina b 1939, Marina Milica b 1939, Caroline Bella b 1944); m 2, 6 June 1950, Daphne, da of Graham Sinclair Summersell (d 1951), of Oxshott; 2 s (Christopher Michael Graham b 1954, Anthony Geoffrey Richard b 1957); *Career* student apprentice BTH Rugby 1930-32, sr ptnr Kennedy & Donkin 1964-75 (asst engr 1932-34, ptnr 1934-64), sr conslt Kennedy & Donkin Group and Kennedy & Donkin International Consulting Engineers 1975-; chm: Br Conslts Bureau 1969-72, Assoc of Consulting Engrs 1972-73; Hon FIEE, FInstCE, Hon MConsE, FIMechE, memb ASME, FCIT; Order of Merit First Class Egypt 1959; *Books* A History of Kennedy & Donkin 1889-1989 (1989); *Recreations* yachting, walking; *Clubs* Royal Yacht Squadron, Royal Thames Yacht; *Style—* Geoffrey Kennedy, Esq; Lowsley House, Liphook, Hants (☎ 0428 723120); Kennedy & Donkin Group, Westbrook Mills, Godalming, Surrey (☎ 04898 25900)

KENNEDY, Graham Norbert; *b* 21 Oct 1936; *Career* dir James Capel & Co; memb: Stock Exchange 1974, Cncl of Stock Exchange; jt chm Cncl's Quotations Ctee, chm Cncl's Primary Markets Division Bd; *Recreations* golf, shooting, music; *Clubs* Boodle's, City of London; *Style—* Graham Kennedy, Esq; Hatchetts, Church Lane, Worting, Basingstoke, Hants (☎ 0256 21764); James Capel & Co, James Capel House, 6 Bevis Marks, London EC34 7JQ (☎ 071 621 0011, telex 888866)

KENNEDY, Iain Manning; s of William Stanley Kennedy (d 1983), and Pamela Ellen, *née* Manning; *b* 15 Sept 1942; *Educ* Glenalmond, Pembroke Coll Cambridge (MA); *m* 18 Aug 1971, Ingrid Annette, da of Andersson Holgar Adolf Herr (d 1986); 2 da (Lucy Gunilla b 1974, Anna Ingrid b 1976); *Career* dir Church & Co plc 1974-; *Recreations* golf, philately; *Style—* Iain Kennedy, Esq; 3 Townsend Close, Hanging Houghton, Northampton NN6 9HP (☎ 0604 880755); office (☎ 0604 751251)

KENNEDY, Ian Philip; s of Maj Algernon Thomas Kennedy, TD (d 1990), and Marie Dolores, *née* Dorté (d 1984); *b* 22 July 1932; *Educ* Downside, Guildford Tech Coll (BSc); *m* 17 Sept 1960, Sheila Veronica, da of Arnold Albert Crook (d 1961); 1 s (Andrew b 10 Dec 1964), 1 da (Carole b 26 July 1961); *Career* Nat Serv cmmnd 2 Lt RAOC 1951-53, TA 1953-55 (Lt 1954); Wiggins Teape Group Ltd 1953-90: sales and mktg dir of industl papers 1964-70, gen mangr Stoneywood Paper Mill Aberdeen 1970-78, divnl gen mangr of printings writings and carbonless papers 1979-81, divnl gen mangr of printing and writing papers, photographic and drawing office papers 1981-84, chief exec fine papers (also gp Bd dir) 1984-89; chm Bd of Tstees Wiggins Teape Pension Fund 1987, md the Wiggins Teape Group 1989, dir Wiggins Teape Appleton Plc 1990, former pres Eupagraph, former chm NE Scot Productivity Assoc; Br Paper and Board Indust Fedn: former chm Commercial Ctee, former memb Industl Rels Ctee, pres 1989; Freeman: City of London 1954, Worshipful Co of Grocers 1954; MInstM 1970; *Recreations* gardening, reading, photography, music; *Style—* Ian Kennedy, Esq; Tudor House, Cricket Hill Lane, Yateley, Surrey; The Wiggins Teape Group Ltd, Gateway House, Basing View, Basingstoke, Hants (☎ 0256 842 020)

KENNEDY, James; OBE (1976); s of Alexander Milroy Kennedy (d 1951), of Edinburgh, and Mary Augusta Raeburn Inches (d 1944); *b* 2 Aug 1907; *Educ* Glenalmond Coll, Jesus Coll Cambridge (BA); *m* 1941, Horatia Bedford, da of Thomas Bedford Franklin (d 1960), of Edinburgh; *Career* RAF 1940-45 (UK and Egypt), Sqdn Ldr 1945; chm Jenners Ltd Edinburgh 1951-82 (jt md 1946-73, pres 1987); dir: Edinburgh C of C 1954-57, Scottish Provident Inst 1959-81; Master of the Company of Edinburgh Merchants 1957-59; memb Bd of Mgmnt Edinburgh Savings Bank 1946-75 (chm 1969-75); chm: Tstee Savings Bank of South Scotland 1975-79; DL City and County of the City of Edinburgh 1963-84, memb Queens Body Guard for Scotland (The Royal Co of Archers) 1936; *Recreations* deer stalking, salmon fishing, golf, gardening; *Clubs* New (Edinburgh), Muirfield, Gullane; *Style—* James Kennedy, Esq, OBE; 19 Clarendon Crescent, Edinburgh EH4 1PU (☎ 031 332 3400)

KENNEDY, Joanna Alicia Gore; *née* Ormsby; da of Capt Gerald Anthony Gore Ormsby, DSC, DSO, RN (ret), of Stoke Row, Oxfordshire, and Nancy Mary (Susan), *née* Williams (d 1974); *b* 22 July 1950; *Educ* Queen Anne's Sch Caversham, Lady Margaret Hall Oxford (MA); *m* 21 July 1979, Richard Paul Kennedy; 2 s (Peter b 1985, David b 1988); *Career* sr engr Ove Arup & Ptnrs 1979- (design engr 1972, asst resident engr (Runnymede Bridge) 1977), project admin Arup Assocs 1987; memb: Engrg Cncl 1984-86 and 1987-, Cncl Inst of Civil Engrs 1984-87, advsy cncl RNEC Manadon 1988-; govr Downe House Sch; FRSA 1986, CEng, MICE, ACIArb; *Style—* Mrs Joanna Kennedy; Ove Arup & Partners, 13 Fitzroy St, London W1P 6BQ (☎ 071 636 1531, fax 071 580 3924)

KENNEDY, Rt Rev Monsignor John; s of James Kennedy (d 1961), and Alice, *née* Bentham (d 1978); *b* 31 Dec 1930; *Educ* St Joseph's Coll Upholland, English Coll Rome (PhL, STL), Campion Hall Oxford (MPhil); *Career* curate: St John's Wigan 1956-64, St Austin's St Helens 1964-66, St Edmund's Waterloo Liverpool 1966-68; lectr Christ's Coll Liverpool 1968-83 (head Dept of Theology 1975-), rector English Coll Rome 1984-; *Books* Priest & People (contrib, 1968); *Recreations* golf, cricket;

Clubs Royal Birkdale Golf (Southport), Royal Over-Seas League; *Style—* The Rt Rev Monsignor Kennedy; 45 Via Monserrato, Roma 00186, Italy (☎ 686 4185)

KENNEDY, John Gvozdenovic; s of Danilo Gvozdenovic, and Daphne, *née* Kennedy; *b* 18 June 1965; *Educ* Royal Russell Sch Addington Surrey; *Career* dir Pin Point Int (UK) Ltd 1987-, Parly conslt various cos, PA to The Rt Hon John Moore, MP 1987-; selected as prospective parly candidate (Cons) for Barking 1989; *Recreations* shooting, skiing, travel, photography; *Clubs* Landsdowne; *Style—* John Kennedy, Esq; 9 Cork St, London W1 (☎ 071 231 4740) 2-26 Norman Shaw North Building, House of Commons, London SW1A 0AA (☎ fax 071 232 1088, car 0860 301 703)

KENNEDY, Dr (Allan) Laurence; s of William Kennedy, of Lisburn Co Antrim, and Marie, *née* Midgley; *b* 24 Jan 1948; *Educ* Methodist Coll Belfast, Queen's Univ Belfast (MB BCh, MD); *m* 21 July 1978, Sarah Louise, da of George McElnea (d 1979), of Mullaghmore, Co Monaghan; 2 s (Christopher b 1981, Jonathan b 1985); *Career* res fell Univ of Florida 1978-80, conslt physician Royal Victoria Hosp Belfast 1980-; chm: N Down Cons Assoc 1988-89 (fndr memb), NI Area Cncl (Cons) 1989-90; memb Nat Union Exec Ctee of Cons Pty; Cons Cncllr N Down Borough Cncl 1989; memb: Nat Exec Cncl Br Diabetic Assoc, Cons Med Soc; chm: NI Ctee Br Diabetic Assoc, NI Cons Area Cncl; MRCP 1975, memb Assoc Physicians of GB and Ireland 1988, FRCPEd 1989, FRCP 1990; *Books* contrib International Textbook of Diabetes Mellitus (1989); *Recreations* family life, listening to music, golf; *Clubs* Royal Belfast Golf, RSM; *Style—* Dr Laurence Kennedy; 3 My Lady's Mile, Holywood, Co Down BT18 9EW (☎ 02317 2427); Royal Victoria Hospital, Belfast BT12 6BA (☎ 0232 240503 ext 3480)

KENNEDY, Ludovic Henry Coverley; s of Capt Edward Kennedy, RN (ka 1939; ggs of Hon Robert Kennedy, bro of 1 Marquess of Ailsa and 3 s of 11 Earl of Cassillis), and Rosalind, da of Sir Ludovic Grant, 11 Bt of Dalvey; *b* 3 Nov 1919; *Educ* Eton, Ch Ch Oxford; *m* 1950, Moira Shearer (formerly ballerina with Sadler's Wells Ballet, actress (including The Red Shoes), and lecturer), da of Harold King; 1 s, 3 da; *Career* Lt RNVR; contested (Lib) Rochdale 1958 and 1959; writer and broadcaster; West German Cross of Merit First Class; *Publications inc* 10 Rillington Place, Pursuit, The Airman Carpenter, On My Way to the Club (autobiography); *Clubs* Brooks's, Army and Navy, Beefsteak; *Style—* Ludovic Kennedy; c/o Rogers, Coleridge & White, 22 Powis Mews, London W11 1JN

KENNEDY, Sir Michael Edward; 8 Bt (UK 1836), of Johnstown Kennedy, Co Dublin; s Lt-Col Sir (George) Ronald Derrick Kennedy, 7 Bt, OBE (d 1988); *b* 12 April 1956; *Educ* Rotherfield Hall Sussex; *m* 1984, Helen Christine Jennifer, da of Patrick Lancelot Rae, of Nine Acres, Halstead, Kent; 2 da (Constance b 1984, Josephine b 1986); *Heir* uncle, Mark Gordon Kennedy b 3 Feb 1932; *Style—* Michael Kennedy, Esq; Johnstown Kennedy, Rathcoole, Co Dublin; c/o Noelle, Lady Kennedy, Harraton Square Church Lane, Exning, Suffolk

KENNEDY, Neil Richard; s of Walter Kennedy (d 1988), and Vera Nancy Kennedy; *b* 6 March 1946; *Educ* Uppingham; *m* 1, Georgina Theresa, *née* Tolhurst (d 1979); 2 s (Angus b 19 Jan 1973, James b 7 Sept 1978), 2 da (Caroline b 28 Oct 1971, Elizabeth b 8 Oct 1976); m 2, 28 Nov 1980, Johanna, da of Gert Woudstra, of Holland; *Career* Colman Prentis & Valley Ltd 1963-65, dep md Childs-Greene Associates Ltd 1965-76, md Brunnings plc 1976-78, vice chm BSB Dorland Ltd 1978-; tstee Royal Burnham Yacht Club (former cdre); *Books* Retail Handbook (1988); *Recreations* skiing, sailing, shooting; *Clubs* Royal Burnham Yacht, Royal Thames Yacht; *Style—* Neil Kennedy, Esq

KENNEDY, Nigel Paul; s of John Kennedy, and Scylla, *née* Stoner; *b* 28 Dec 1956; *Educ* Yehudi Menuhin Sch, Juillard Sch of Performing Arts; *Career* solo violinist; debut at Festival Hall with Philharmonia Orch 1977, Berlin debut with Berlin Philharmonia 1980, Henry Wood Promenade debut 1981, New York debut with BBC Symphony Orch 1987, tour of Hong Kong and Aust with Hallé Orch 1981; recordings incl: Tchaikovsky, Sibelius, Vivaldi (Double Platinum Disc), Elgar Violin Concerto (Record of the Year 1985, Gold Disc), Bruch and Mendelssohn (Gold Disc), Walton Violin and Viola, and Let Loose; *Style—* Nigel Kennedy, Esq; John Stanley, 28 Nottingham Place, London W1M 3FD (☎ 071 935 1640)

KENNEDY, Noelle, Lady; Noelle Mona; *née* Green; da of Charles Henry Green, of Hunworth, Melton Constable, Norfolk; *m* 1949, Lt-Col Sir (George) Ronald Derrick Kennedy, 7 Bt, OBE, RA (d 1988); 1 s (Sir Michael, 8 Bt, *qv*), 1 da (Carolyn Phyllis (Mrs Jan Blaauw) b 1950); Harraton Square, Church Lane, Exning, Suffolk

KENNEDY, Hon Mr Justice; Hon Sir Paul Joseph Morrow Kennedy; QC (1973); s of late Dr Joseph Morrow Kennedy, of Sheffield, and Bridget Teresa Kennedy; *b* 12 June 1935; *Educ* Ampleforth, Gonville and Caius Coll Cambridge; *m* 1965, Hon Virginia, *qv*, da of Baron Devlin; 2 s, 2 da; *Career* called to the Bar Gray's Inn 1960; rec 1972, bencher 1982, High Court Judge 1983-, presiding judge NE Circuit 1985-89; kt; *Style—* The Hon Mr Justice Kennedy; Royal Courts of Justice, Strand, London WC2A 2LL

KENNEDY, Prof Peter Graham Edward; s of Philip Kennedy, of London, and Gertrude Sylvia, *née* Summer; *b* 28 March 1951; *Educ* Univ Col Sch London, UCL and UCH (MB BS, MD, PhD, MRCP); *m* 6 July 1983, Catherine Ann, da of Christopher King; 1 s (Luke b 1988); *Career* hon res asst MRC Neuroimmunology Project UCL 1978-80, sr registrar (formerly registrar) in neurology Nat Hosp London 1981-84, asst prof of neurology John Hopkins Univ Sch of Med USA 1985, Burton prof and head of Dept of Neurology Univ of Glasgow 1987 (sr lectr in neurology and virology 1986-87), conslt neurologist Inst of Neurological Sciences Glasgow 1986; memb Med Res Advsy Ctee Multiple Sclerosis Soc; memb Editorial Bds: Neuropathology and Applied Neurobiology, the Journal of Neuroimmunology, Postgraduate Medical Jl and Seminars in the Neurosciences Guarantor of Brain; lectr The Fleming Lecture 1990 (Royal Coll of Physicians and Surgns of Glasgow); patron cancer res charity QUEST, chm Med Res Advsy Ctee Scot Motor Neurone Disease Assoc; BUPA Med Fndn Doctor of the Year Res award 1990; FRCP London 1988, MRCPath 1988, FRCP Glasgow 1989, FRSM; memb: Assoc Br Neurologists, American Neurological Assoc, Soc for Gen Microbiology, Assoc Clinical Profs of Med, Br Soc Study of Infection, Euro Neurological Soc, Scottish Assoc Neurological Sciences, Scottish Soc Physicians, Royal Medico-Chirurgical Soc Glasgow, Assoc of Physicians GB and I; fell: Fellowship of Postgrad Med, Br Astronomical Assoc; *Books* Infections of the Nervous System (ed with R T Johnson, 1987); *Recreations* astronomy, walking in country, tennis, music; *Style—* Prof Peter Kennedy; 23 Hamilton Ave, Pollokshields, Glasgow G41 4JG (☎ 041 427 4754); Glasgow University Department of Neurology, Institute of Neurological Sciences, Southern General Hospital, Glasgow G51 4TF (☎ 041 445 2466 ext 4028)

KENNEDY, Richard Paul; s of David Clifton Kennedy, of Southampton, and Evelyn Mary Hall, *née* Tindale; *b* 17 Feb 1949; *Educ* Charterhouse (foundation scholar), New Coll Oxford (exhibitioner, BA, MA); *m* 21 July 1979, Joanna Alicia Gore, *qv*, da of Capt Gerald Anthony Gore Ormsby, DSC, DSO, RN (ret), of Stoke Row, Oxfordshire; 2 s (Peter Michael Andrew b 1985, David Anthony James b 1988); *Career* asst master: Shrewsbury Sch 1971-77, Westminster Sch 1977-84; dep headmaster Bishop's Stortford Coll 1984-89, headmaster Highgate Sch 1989-; GB int athlete 1973-76, memb Acad of St Martin-in-the-Fields Chorus 1977-, govr The Hall Sch Hampstead 1989-; *Recreations* choral music; *Clubs* East India, Devonshire, Sports and Public Schs, Vincent's (Oxford); *Style—* Richard Kennedy, Esq; Highgate School, North Rd, London N6 4AY (☎ 081 340 1524, fax 081 340 7674)

KENNEDY, Terence Leslie; s of Charles Matheson Kennedy, MBE (d 1948), of Plymouth, and Mabel Maud, *née* Hore (d 1971); *b* 12 Dec 1919; *Educ* St Edward's Sch Oxford, London Hosp Med Coll (MB BS, MS); *m* 21 June 1949, Bridget Frances, da of William Walker (d 1954), of Bromley Rd, London; 1 s (Peter), 2 da (Helen, Penelope); *Career* Surgn Lt RNVR 1942-46; surgical registrar London Hosp 1946-50, conslt surgn Royal Victoria Hosp 1950-; numerous articles on gastric surgery in jls and chapters in textbooks; Hon MD Queen's Univ Belfast 1981; memb: Br Soc of Gastroenterology, Br Soc of Endocrine Surgns, BMA, Ulster Med Soc, Assoc of Surgns of GB and I (memb Cncl 1970-76, pres 1981); FRCS (memb Cncl 1981-89); *Recreations* sailing, gardening; *Style—* Terence Kennedy, Esq; Blackwater Rocks, 47 Saintfield Rd, Killinchy, Co Down BT23 6RL (☎ 0238 541470)

KENNEDY, Tessa Georgina (Mrs Elliott Kastner); da of Geoffrey Farrer Kennedy, of Lowsley House, Liphook, Hants, and Daska McLean, *née* Ivanovic; *b* 6 Dec 1938; *Educ* Oak Hall Haslemere Surrey, Ecole de Beaux Arts Paris; *m* 1, 27 Jan 1958 (m dis 1969), Dominick Evelyn Bede Elwes, s of Simon Elwes (d 1975); 3 s (Cassian b 1959, Damian b 1960, Cary b 1962); m 2, 26 June 1971, Elliott Kastner; 1 s (Dillon b 1970), 1 da (Milica b 1972); *Career* interior designer; former clients incl: John Barry, Sam Spiegel, Richard Burton, Stanley Kubrick, Viscount Hambleden, De Beers, BUPA Hosps, HM King of Jordan, Michael Winner, Candice Bergen, Rudolf Nureyev, George Harrison; currently Claridges; pres UK Chapter ISID; *Recreations* tennis, movies, watching American football; *Style—* Miss Tessa Kennedy; 2 Hyde Park Gdns, London W2 2LT (☎ 071 723 4686); 1 East 62nd St, New York, NY 10021; Studio 5, 91/97 Freston Rd, London W11 4BD (☎ 071 221 4546, fax 071 229 2899, car 0836 201 980)

KENNEDY, Air Chief Marshal Sir Thomas Lawrie; GCB (KCB 1980, CB 1978), AFC (1953, and Bar 1960); s of James Domoné Kennedy and Margaret Henderson, *née* Lawrie; *b* 19 May 1928; *Educ* Hawick HS, RAF Coll Cranwell; *m* 1959, Margaret Ann Parker; 1 s, 2 da; *Career* cmmnd RAF 1949; Dep C-in-C RAF Strike Cmd 1979-81, C-in-C RAF Germany and Cdr Second Allied Tactical Air Force 1981-83; air memb for personnel, Air Force Bd 1983-; Air ADC to HM 1983-; *Style—* Air Chief Marshal Sir Thomas Kennedy, GCB, AFC, ADC; c/o MOD, Whitehall, London SW1

KENNEDY, Hon Lady (Virginia); yr (twin) da of Baron Devlin, PC (Life Peer); *b* 2 March 1940; *m* 1965, Hon Sir Paul Kennedy, a Judge of the High Court of Justice, *qv*; 2 s (Christopher b 1966, John b 1969), 2 da (Joanna b 1968, Brigid b 1971); *Career* memb Press Cncl 1987-90; *Style—* The Hon Lady Kennedy; c/o The Hon Mr Justice Kennedy, Royal Courts of Justice, Strand, London WC2A 2LL

KENNEDY, William Michael Clifford; s of Dr Clifford Donald Kennedy, and Isobel Sinclair Kennedy (d 1984); *b* 29 Oct 1935; *Educ* Rugby, Merton Coll Oxford (BA); *m* 1962, Judith Victoria, da of Kenneth Fulton Gibb, of Fife; 1 s (Niall b 1964), 1 da (Tessa b 1965); *Career* CA; dir: The Scottish Life Assurance Co 1976-, Venture Assocs SA 1978-, Martin Currie Inc 1978-, Martin Currie Investment Management Ltd 1978-, Martin Currie Pacific Tst 1985-; md Martin Currie Ltd 1989-; fin advsr Royal Scottish Acad; *Recreations* shooting, fishing, golf, gardening, music; *Clubs* New (Edinburgh); Hon Co of Edinburgh Golfers; *Style—* Michael Kennedy, Esq; Oak Lodge, Inveresk, Midlothian EH21 7TE (☎ 031 665 8822); 29 Charlotte Square, Edinburgh EH2 4HA (☎ 031 225 3811, telex 72505)

KENNEDY-SANIGAR, Patrick; s of William Adrian George Sanigar, of Aldreth, Cambridgeshire, and Patricia Ann, *née* Kay; *b* 27 Sept 1957; *Educ* Soham GS Cambs, Soham Village Coll Cambs, Gordonstoun, Canterbury Coll of Art Sch of Architecture (BA, DipArch); *m* 12 Oct 1989, Melena Kay, da of Alan Mark Kennedy; *Career* head of design Townscape Homes Ltd 1981 (site agent 1979); fndr: Townscape Designs Ltd (dir and head of design) 1982, Townscape Interiors Ltd 1984, Harbour Studios 1986 (having resigned all directorships of the Townscape gp); set up Faithdean Interiors (office of Harbour Studios) Chatham Dockyard 1991; projects inc: The Tube shoe retail chain 1985 (featured Designers Journal 1986), restoration in assoc with Lionel March The How House (LA) 1986; memb Visiting Bd Panel RIBA 1987-89; FCSD 1988 (co chm of Interiors Gp and memb Cncl 1990), fell Br Inst of Interior Design 1988; *Recreations* qualified open water scuba diver, qualified gymnasium instr, swimming, motor racing, earth sheltered housing; *Style—* Patrick Kennedy-Sanigar, Esq; 7 Little Meadow, Upper Harbledown, Canterbury, Kent CT2 9BD (☎ 0227 767967); Harbour Studios, Harbour Buildings, Sea St, Whitstable, Kent CT5 1AF (☎ 0227 265556, fax 0227 276190)

KENNERLEY, Prof James Anthony Machell (Tony); s of William James Kennerley, of Bankhall Lane, Hale, Cheshire, and late Vida May, *née* Machell (d 1984); *b* 24 Oct 1933; *Educ* Altrincham GS, Rhyl GS, Univ of Manchester (BSc), Imp Coll London (MSc); *m* 12 Jan 1978, Dorothy Mary, da of George Paterson Simpson; 1 s (David James b 20 Nov 1978), 1 da (Elizabeth Lindsay (twin) b 20 November 1978); *Career* PO RAFVR 1952-57, Flying Offr RCAF 1959-62; aerodynamicist: AV Roe & Co Manchester 1955-58, Pratt & Whitney USA 1958-59; asst prof of mathematics Univ of New Brunswick Canada 1962-67, dir of studies Manchester Business Sch 1967-69, assoc prof of business admin Columbia Univ Business Sch NY 1969-70, sr lectr in mktg and quantitative methods London Business Sch 1970-73, dir Strathclyde Univ Business Sch 1973-83 (prof 1973-83); dir S Scotland Electricity Bd 1977-84; chm: Arbitration Panel Scottish Milk Mktg Bd 1981-83, W Surrey and NE Hants Health Authy 1986-, Cncl for Professions Supplementary to Medicine 1990-; arbitrator ACAS 1976-; dir First Step Housing Co Waverley Borough Cncl 1990-; memb Bridgegate Tst Glasgow 1982-85; AFIMA, MIMechE, AFRAeS, FBIM; *Books* Guide To Business Schools (1985); *Recreations* flying, travelling; *Clubs* Reform, Caledonian; *Style—* Prof Tony Kennerley; 5 Old Rectory Gdns, Busbridge, Godalming, Surrey GU7 1XB (☎ 04868 28108); West Surrey and North East Hampshire Health Authority, Abbey House, 282 Farnborough Rd, Farnborough, Hants GU14 7NE (☎ 0252 548 881)

KENNERLEY, Peter Dilworth; TD (1989); s of John Dilworth Kennerley, and Margery, *née* Dugard (d 1977); *b* 9 June 1956; *Educ* Collyers Sch, Sidney Sussex Coll Cambridge (MA); *m* 1989, (Anne Marie) Ghislaine du Roy, da of late Hon Sir Thomas Galbraith, KBE, MP; 1 da (Sarah b 30 Jan 1991); *Career* TA Maj Royal Yeo 1986; Simmons & Simmons: joined 1979, admitted slr 1981, ptnr 1986; sec Panel on Takeovers and Mergers 1986-88; memb Law Soc; *Clubs* Cavalry and Guard's; *Style—* Peter Kennerley, Esq; 112 Streathbourne Rd, London SW17 8QY (☎ 081 672 7305); Simmons & Simmons, 14 Dominion St, London EC2M 2RJ (☎ 071 628 2020, fax 071 588 4129, telex 888562)

KENNET, 2 Baron (UK 1935); Wayland Hilton Young; s of 1 Baron Kennet, GBE, DSO, DSC, PC (d 1960), and Kathleen, da of Rev Canon Lloyd Stewart Bruce (3 s of Sir James Bruce, 2 Bt) and widow of Capt Robert Falcon Scott, CVO, RN, the Antarctic explorer; Lady Kennet was a sculptor whose works include the statue of her first husband in Waterloo Place; *b* 2 Aug 1923; *Educ* Stowe, Trinity Coll Cambridge (MA), Univ of Perugia; *m* 24 Jan 1948, Elizabeth Ann, da of Capt Bryan Fullerton Adams, DSO, RN; 1 s, 5 da; *Heir* s, Hon Thoby Young; *Career* Sits as Lab peer in House of Lords; RN 1942-45, FO 1946-47 and 1949-51, del Parly Assemblies WEU and Cncl of Europe 1962-65, Parly sec Miny of Housing and Local Govt 1966-70, Labour oppn spokesman Foreign Affrs and Science Policy 1971-74; chm: Advsy Ctee on Oil Pollution of the Sea 1970-74, CPRE 1971-72, Int Parly Conferences on the Environment 1972-78; MEP 1978-79, SDP Whip in House of Lords 1981-83, SDP spokesman on Defence and Foreign Affrs 1981-90; Hon FRIBA; author and journalist; *Recreations* sailing, walking; *Style—* The Lord Kennet; House of Lords, London SW1

KENNETT-BROWN, David; JP (Willesden 1975-); s of Thomas Kennett Brown (d 1979), and Vanda, *née* Low; *b* 29 Jan 1938; *Educ* Durston House Ealing, Monkton Combe Sch Bath, Lincoln Coll Oxford (MA), London Univ (Dip Crim); *m* 1966, Wendy Margaret, da of Frederick Gordon Evans (d 1984); 1 s (Neil b 1969), 2 da (Kathryn b 1967, Alison b 1971); *Career* churchwarden St John's Church W Ealing 1973-86, dep chm Juvenile & Domestic Cts Panel 1979-82, chm London Rent Assessment Panel 1979-82, pres Central & South Middx Law Soc 1982-, chm Inner London Juvenile Cts 1983-, Metropolitan stipendiary magistrate 1983-, asst Crown Ct recorder 1984-; FCIArt; *Recreations* walking, gardening, family life; *Style—* David Kennett-Brown, Esq, JP; 34 The Mall, Ealing, London W5; Inner London Magistrates Ct Service, Bush House, NW Wing, Aldwych, Strand, London WC2

KENNEY, Anthony; s of Eric Alfred Allen Kenney, of 1 Cross Way, West Mersea, Essex, and Doris Winifred, *née* Dollwood; *b* 17 Jan 1942; *Educ* Brentwood Sch, Caius Coll Cambridge (MA), The London Hosp Med Coll (MB BChir); *m* 1, 1966 (m dis 1973), Elizabeth Dain Fielding; 2 s (Christopher Julian b 1967, Nicholas Charles b 1970); m 2, 17 March 1973, Patricia Clare, da of Maj Rafe Trevor Newbery, MBE (d 1981); 2 s (Alexander William b 1974, Simon Rafe b 1977), 1 da (Louise Clare b 1980); *Career* formerly: sr registrar Westminster and Kingston Hosps, sr house surgn Queen Charlotte's and Chelsea Hosp for Women, res accoucheur The London Hosp; currently conslt obstetrician and gynaecologist St Thomas's Hosp London; examiner: Univ of Cambridge, Univ of London, Royal Coll of Obstetricians and Gynaecologists; FRCS 1970, FRCOG 1987 (MRCOG 1972); *Recreations* canal cruising, foreign travel; *Clubs* RSM, Med Soc of London; *Style—* Anthony Kenney, Esq; 17 Wimpole St, London W1M 7AD (☎ 081 942 0440)

KENNEY, Antony Reginald; s of Herbert Howard Kenney (d 1976), of Carshalton, and Winifred Charlotte, *née* Wilson (d 1980); *b* 23 Feb 1931; *Educ* John Fisher Sch Purley, Christ's Coll Cambridge (MA), Birkbeck Coll London (BSc); *m* 31 July 1970, Carol Jane, da of Thomas Noel Charles Izod, of Leamington Spa; 2 s (James Benedict Thomas b 11 Feb 1973, Benedict Antony b 15 July 1987), 1 da (Louise Mary b 29 Nov 1971); *Career* St Benedict's Sch Ealing 1956-59, St Mary's Coll Twickenham 1959- (currently vice princ); tstee and memb mgmnt bd Prince's Tst; *Books* incl a variety of educnl works; *Recreations* wooodcarving, DIY; *Style—* Antony Kenney, Esq; St Mary's College, Twickenham, Middlesex TW1 4SX (☎ 081 892 0051, fax 081 744 2080)

KENNEY, Edward John; s of George Kenney, and Emmy Carlina Elfrida, *née* Schwenke; *b* 29 Feb 1924; *Educ* Christ's Hospital, Trinity Coll Cambridge (Craven scholar, Craven student, MA, Chancellor's medallist); *m* 18 June 1955, (Gwyneth) Anne, da of late Henry Albert Harris; *Career* served WWII: Royal Signals UK and India 1943-46, cmmnd 1944, Lt 1945; asst lectr Univ of Leeds 1951-52; Univ of Cambridge: res fell Trinity Coll 1952-53, asst lectr 1955-60, lectr 1966-70, reader in Latin lit and textual criticism 1970-74, Kennedy prof of Latin 1974-82; Peterhouse Cambridge: fell 1953-91, dir of studies in classics 1953-74, librarian 1953-82, tutor 1956-82, sr tutor 1962-65, Perne librarian 1987-91, domestic bursar 1987-88; jt ed Classical Quarterly 1959-65, Sather prof of classical lit Berkley 1968, Care Newell Jackson lectr Harvard Univ 1980 (James C Loeb fell in classical philology 1967-68); author of articles and reviews in classical jls; pres: Jt Assoc of Classical Teachers 1977-79, Classical Assoc 1982-83; foreign memb Royal Netherlands Acad of Arts and Scis 1976, treas and chm Cncl of Almoners Christ's Hospital 1984-86; *Books* P Ouidi Nasonis Amores (ed, 1961), Ovidiana Graeca (ed with Mrs P E Easterling, 1965), Appendix Vergiliana (ed with W V Clausen, F R D Goodyear, J A Richmond, 1966), Lucretius De Rerum Natura III (ed, 1971), The Classical Text (1974), Cambridge History of Classical Literature II (ed, 1982), The Ploughman's Lunch (1984), Ovid Metamorphoses (introduction and notes, 1965), Ovid, The Love Poems (introduction and notes, 1990), Apuleius Cupid & Psyche (1990); *Recreations* cats, books; *Style—* Prof E J Kenney; Peterhouse, Cambridge CB2 1RD

KENNY, Dr Anthony John Patrick; s of John Kenny, and Margaret, *née* Jones; *b* 16 March 1931; *Educ* St Joseph's Coll Upholland, Gregorian Univ Rome, St Benet's Hall Oxford (DPhil); *m* 2 April 1966, Nancy Caroline, da of Henry T Gayley Jr, of Ithaca, NY, USA; 2 s (Robert b 1968, Charles b 1970); *Career* master Balliol Coll Oxford 1978-89, pro vice chllr Univ of Oxford 1985-, warden and sec Rhodes Tst Oxford 1989-; fell Br Acad 1974 (vice pres 1986-88, pres 1989-); Hon DLitt Bristol 1982, Hon DHumLitt Denison Ohio 1986, Hon DCL Oxon 1987, Hon DLitt: Liverpool 1988, Glasgow 1990, Lafayette Pennsylvania 1990; *Books* Descartes (1968), Wittgenstein (1973), Will, Freedom and Power (1975), Freewill and Responsibility (1978), The God of the Philisophers (1979), A Path from Rome (1986), The Road to Hillsborough (1986), The Heritage of Wisdom (1987), Reason and Religion (1987), The Metaphysics of Mind (1989); *Clubs* United Oxford and Cambridge Univ, Athenaeum; *Style—* Dr Anthony Kenny; Rhodes House, Oxford

KENNY, His Hon Judge Anthony Marriott; s of Noel Edgar Edward Marriott Kenny, OBE (d 1972), of Zimbabwe and Zambia, and Cynthia Margaret Seton, *née* Melville; *b* 24 May 1939; *Educ* St Andrew's Coll, Christ's Coll Cambridge (MA); *m* 1969, Monica, da of Hector Bennet Grant Mackenzie, of S Africa; 3 s (Julian Hector Marriott b 1972, Christian Edward Mackenzie b 1977, Nicholas William Mackenzie b 1983); *Career* called to the Bar Gray's Inn 1963; rec of the Crown Ct 1980-87, circuit judge 1987, princ judge in civil matters Reading and Thames Valley Gp of Courts 1990 designated family judge 1990; *Recreations* travelling, skiing, music, reading, tennis; *Style—* His Hon Judge Kenny; Melbury Place, Wentworth, Surrey GU25 4LB

KENNY, Gen Sir Brian Leslie Graham; KCB (1985), CBE (1979); s of Brig James Wolfenden Kenny, CBE (d 1978); *b* 18 June 1934; *Educ* Canford; *m* 1958, Diana Catherine Jane, da of Brig Felton Arthur Hamilton Mathew, OBE, MC (d 1977); 2 s; *Career* CO Queen's Royal Irish Hussars 1974-76, Col GS HQ 4 Armd Div 1976-78, Brig 1978, cmd 12 Armd Bde 1978-80, Maj-Gen 1982, GOC 1 Armd Div 1982-83, dir Army Staff Duties MOD 1983-85, Col Cmdt Royal Army Veterinary Corps 1983-, Col QRIH 1985, cmd (BR) Corps 1985-87, C-in-C BAOR/CImd NORTHAG 1987-89, Col Cmdt RAC 1989, D SACEUR 1990; govr Canford Sch; *Recreations* cricket, tennis, skiing; *Clubs* MCC, IZ, Free Foresters, Cavalry and Guards'; *Style—* Gen Sir Brian Kenny, KCB, CBE; c/o Lloyds Bank plc, 19 Obelisk Way, Camberley, Surrey GU15 3SE

KENNY, Michael James; s of James Kenny, of Blackburn, Lancashire, and Ellen, *née* Gordon; *b* 10 June 1941; *Educ* St Francis Xavier's Coll Liverpool, Liverpool Coll of Art, Slade Sch of Fine Art; *m* 1, July 1962 (m dis), Gillian Wainwright; m 2, June 1968 (m dis), Rosemary Flood; m 3, 20 Dec 1978, Angela Helen, da of Maj Anthony Smith of Dorset; 1 s, 2 da; *Career* visiting lectr Slade Sch of Fine Art 1970-82, dir of fine art studies Goldsmith's Coll London 1983-88; works in collections of: Tate Gallery, V & A Museum, British Museum; numerous one-man exhibitions in: Paris, Milan, Tokyo, Frankfurt; public sculptures in: Scotland (Lumsden), Paris (Parc de la Courneuve), Cambridge and England (Addenbrookes Hosp), Japan (Yotohama Business Park); memb Cathedrals Advsy Ctee; ARA 1976, RA 1986; *Recreations* ornithology; *Clubs* Chelsea Arts, Arts; *Style—* Michael Kenny, Esq; 71 Stepney Green, London E1 3LE (☎ 071 790 3409); Annely Juda Fina Art, 23 Dering St, London W1R 9AA (☎ 071 629 7578, fax 071 491 2139)

KENNY, Prof Phillip Herbert; s of Robert Kenney, of King's Lynn, and Moira, *née* Davies; *b* 9 Aug 1948; *Educ* Univ of Bristol (LLB), Univ of Cambridge (Dip Crim), Univ of Columbia (LLM); *m* 7 Aug 1970, Ann Mary, da of Harold Langley (d 1970), of Winchester; 1 s (Stephen b 1982), 3 da (Julia b 1975, Angharad b 1977, Helen b 1979); *Career* slr; head of Law Dept Newcastle Poly 1980-, former univ and poly lectr, legal dir Educn Assets Bd; conslt Messrs Dickinson Dees Slrs Newcastle upon Tyne; *Recreations* pigeon racing, walking, sailing; *Clubs* North of England Homing Union; *Style—* Prof Phillip Kenny; 105 Kenton Rd, Gosforth NE3 4NL; Newcastle upon Tyne Polytechnic, Newcastle upon Tyne

KENNY, Thomas; s of John Kenny (d 1944), and Lucy, *née* O'Dea (d 1960); *b* 3 June 1919; *Educ* Univ Sch Dublin, Nat Univ of Ireland; *m* 1944, Blanche, da of Frank Aubrey Blanche, of Surrey; 1 s, 1 da; *Career* chm: GEI International plc, Sheffield Forgemasters plc, CDB Investments Ltd, Industrial Funding Trust Ltd, Campden Hill Gate Ltd; FCA; *Recreations* fly fishing, racing; *Clubs* Arts, City of London, Flyfishers'; *Style—* Thomas Kenny, Esq; Brettenham House, Lancaster Place, London WC2E 7EN (☎ 071 379 7555); 10 Campden Hill Gate, Duchess of Bedford's Walk, London W8

KENRICK, Martin John; s of William Edmund Kenrick (d 1981), of Birmingham, and Elizabeth Dorothy Magdalen, *née* Loveday; family non-conformists who settled with others in Midlands, family firm run by sixth generation; *b* 5 Feb 1940; *Educ* Newlands, Rugby, Trinity Coll Dublin (MA, BComm), Cranfield Inst of Tech (MSc); *m* 21 Feb 1970, Christine Mary, da of Charles Ronald Wingham (d 1972), of St Albans, Herts; 1 s (Hilgrove b 1977), 2 da (Tanya b 1972, Helen b 1973); *Career* guardian Birmingham Assay Office 1971-, cmmr of Taxes 1972, chm Archibald Kenrick & Sons Ltd 1978- (md 1973-78), dir Birmingham R & D Ltd 1985-(chm 1985-87); Univ of Birmingham: hon life memb Ct of Govrs 1978, memb Cncl 1981-, memb Fin and Gen Purpose Ctee 1987-88; memb Mgmnt Ctee W Mids Regnl Mgmnt Centre 1978-82; Birmingham Chamber of Indust and Commerce: memb Cncl 1981-, memb Gen Purposes Ctee 1982-, chm Educn Ctee 1985-89 (pres 1990-91), memb Working Pty for Indust Year 1985-86, vice pres 1988-90; dir: Birmingham Chamber Training Ltd 1986-87, Black Country Museum Tst 1987-; chm: Policy Gp Birmingham Local Employer Network 1987-89, W Mids Region Indust Matters 1987-90, Birmingham Educn Ptnrship 1989-; *Recreations* ornithology, skiing, tennis, squash, hockey, gardening; *Style—* Martin J Kenrick, Esq; The Mount, 37 Richmond Hill Rd, Edgbaston, Birmingham B15 3RR (☎ 021 454 4720); Archibald Kenrick & Sons Ltd, PO Box 9 West Bromwich, West Midlands B70 6DB (☎ 021 553 2741, fax 021 500 6332, telex 336470 KENRIC G)

KENROY, James Royston; s of Ronald Victor Kenroy, of Hampshire, and Marjorie Barbara, *née* Hughes (d 1987); *b* 10 Jan 1932; *Educ* Tonbridge; *m* 25 June 1966, (Margaret) Deirdre, da of Rev (Gordon) Ronald Paterson, MBE; 2 da (Vanessa b 17 Aug 1967, Rebecca b 15 Oct 1968); *Career* admitted slr 1956, sr ptnr Glanvilles 1983-; pres Hants Inc Law Soc 1985-86, fndr chm Portsmouth and S E Hants Conveyancing Protocol 1986-, int rel offr RTBI 1968-70, ed World Cncl of Young Mens' Serv Clubs 1970-72; dep coroner City of Portsmouth 1984-, coroner Portsmouth and S E Hants 1989-; pt/t chm Soc Sec Appeal Tbnls 1987-; memb Coroners Soc; *Recreations* family life; *Clubs* RN and Royal Albert Yacht; *Style—* James Kenroy, Esq; 16 Landport Terr, Portsmouth (☎ 0705 827231)

KENSINGTON, 8 Baron (I 1776 and UK 1886); Hugh Ivor Edwardes; s of Capt Hon Owen Edwardes (d 1937, 2 s of 6 Baron Kensington, CMG, DSO, TD, JP, DL); suc unc, 7 Baron, 1981; *b* 24 Nov 1933; *Educ* Eton; *m* 1961, Juliet Elizabeth Massy, da of Capt Alexander Massy Anderson (d 1943); 2 s (Hon Owen b 21 July 1964, Hon Rupert b 25 Jan 1967), 1 da (Hon Amanda, *qv*); *Heir* s, Hon (William) Owen Alexander Edwardes; *Career* farmer and thoroughbred breeder; *Recreations* horse breeding, shooting; *Clubs* Boodle's, Durban; *Style—* The Rt Hon the Lord Kensington; Friar Tuck, PO Box 549, Mooi River, 3300 Natal, S Africa (☎ 0333 36323)

KENSINGTON, Bishop of 1987-; Rt Rev John George Hughes; s of Joseph Ernest Hughes (d 1969), of Darlaston, S Staffs, and Florence Amy, *née* Fisher; *b* 30 Jan 1935; *Educ* Wednesbury Boys' HS, Queens' Coll Cambridge (MA), Univ of Leeds (PhD), Cuddesdon Theol Coll; *m* 3 Aug 1963, Maureen, da of Percy Harrison (d 1977), of Huncoat, Lancs; 2 s (David John b 11 Jan 1965, Jonathan Harrison b 16 Oct 1968); *Career* ordained: deacon 1960, priest 1961; curate Brighouse Wakefield 1960-63, vicar Clifton 1963-70; ACCM: selection sec 1970-73, sr selection sec 1973-76; warden St Michael's Coll Llandaff 1976-87, hon canon Llandaff Cathedral 1980-87, bishop of Kensington 1987-; lectr in church history Univ of Wales 1976-88; memb: Governing Body of the Church in Wales 1977-87, Cncl of Churches for Wales Theol Educn Ctee 1981-87 (chm Subject Bd 1984-87); dean Univ Sch of Theol Cardiff 1984-87; *Style—* The Rt Rev the Lord Bishop of Kensington; 19 Campden Hill Square, London W8 7JY (☎ 071 727 9819)

KENSWOOD, 2 Baron (UK 1951); John Michael Howard Whitfield; s of 1 Baron Kenswood (d 1963); *b* 6 April 1930; *Educ* Trinity Sch Ontario, Harrow, Grenoble Univ, Emmanuel Coll Cambridge; *m* 1951, Deirdre Anna Louise, da of Colin Malcolm Methven, of Errol, Perthshire; 4 s (Hon Michael b 1955, Hon Anthony b 1957, Hon Steven b 1958, Hon Benjamin b 1961), 1 da (Hon Anna Louisa b 1964); *Heir* s, Hon Michael Whitfield; *Style—* The Rt Hon the Lord Kenswood; Domaine de la Foret, 31340 Villemur sur Tarn, France

KENT, Brian Hamilton; s of Clarence Kent (d 1946), of 17 Mottram Rd, Hyde, Cheshire, and Edyth Kent (d 1963); *b* 29 Sept 1931; *Educ* Hyde GS, Univ of Salford (BSc); *m* 15 May 1954, Margery, da of Laurence Foulds (d 1974), of Vernon Rd, Bredbury, Cheshire; 1 s (Peter Hamilton b 15 April 1958), 2 da (Wendy Susan (Mrs Matin) b 13 July 1960, Linda Anne b 10 Oct 1961); *Career* Lt RN 1954-57; mangr Mather and Platt Contracting Ltd 1960, marketing dir Morganite Carbon Ltd 1965, and Alfa Laval UK Ltd 1970, chm Staveley Industries plc 1987 (chief exec and gp md 1980); chm Industry and Parliamentary Tst, cncl memb CBI; FIMechE, FIEE; *Recreations* boating, bridge, tennis; *Clubs* RAC, Directors; *Style—* Brian Kent, Esq; Collingwood, 16 Woodlands Rd, Surbiton, Surrey KT6 6PS (☎ 01 390 2232); Staveley House, 11 Dingwall Rd, Croydon, Surrey CR9 3DB (☎ 01 688 4404, fax 01 760 0563, telex 915855, car 0860 364853)

KENT, Geoffrey Charles; s of Percival Whitehead Kent, and Madge Kent; *b* 2 Feb 1922; *Educ* Blackpool GS; *m* 1955, Brenda Georgine; *Career* WWII, Coastal Cmd RAF; joined Imperial Group 1958: chm and md John Player 1975-78 (jt md 1969), memb Bd 1975-86; chm and chief exec: Courage Ltd 1978-81, Imperial Gp plc 1981-86; dir: Lloyds Bank plc 1981-, Lloyds Bank Int 1983-85, Lloyds Merchant Bank Hldgs 1985-87;dep chm: Coral plc 1986-89, John Howitt Gp Ltd 1988-, chm Mansfield Brewery plc 1989-; memb Lloyds of London 1985-; FCIM, CBIM; *Recreations* flying (full instrument rating), skiing; *Clubs* RAF; *Style—* Geoffrey Kent, Esq; Hill House, Gonalston, Notts NG14 7JA (☎ 0602 663303)

KENT, Sir Harold Simcox; GCB (1963, KCB 1954, CB 1946), QC (1973); s of Percy Horace Braund Kent, OBE, MC (d 1963), of Clavering, Cooden, Sussex, and Anna

Mary, *née* Simcox; *b* 11 Nov 1903; *Educ* Rugby, Merton Coll Oxford; *m* 14 April 1930, Zillah (d 1987), da of Henry Rees Lloyd; 1 s, 1 da (decd); *Career* called to the Bar Inner Temple 1928; Parly Cncl 1940-53; HM procurator-gen and Treasy slr 1953-63; slr: Bank Rate Tribunal 1957, Vassall Tribunal 1962; standing counsel to Church Assembly and Gen Synod 1964-72; memb Security Cmmn 1967-72; vicar-gen Province of Canterbury 1970-76, dean of Arches Ct of Canterbury and auditor of Chancery Ct of York 1972-76, commissary to Dean and Chapter of St Paul's Cathedral 1976-; *Books* In on the Act (1979); *Clubs* United Oxford and Cambridge Univ; *Style*— Sir Harold Kent, GCB, QC; Alderley, Calf Lane, Chipping Campden, Glos (☎ 0386 840421)

KENT, Dr John Philip Cozens; s of John Cozens Kent, DCM (d 1990), and Lucy Ella, *née* Binns (d 1984); *b* 28 Sept 1928; *Educ* Minchenden Co GS, UCL (BA, PhD); *m* 21 Oct 1961, Patricia Eleanor, da of Lionel Maldwyn Bunford (d 1961); 1 s (Philip b 1962), 1 da (Hilary b 1965); *Career* Nat Serv 1951-53, 2 Lt RASC 1952; Br Museum Dept of Coins and Medals: asst keeper 1953-74, dep keeper 1974-83, keeper 1983-90; pres: Br Assoc of Numismatic Socs 1974-78, Royal Numismatic Soc 1984-89, London and Middx Archaelogical Soc 1985-88, Barnet and Dist Local Hist Soc 1980-; FRNS 1948, FSA 1961, FBA 1986, FMA 1988; memb International Numismatic Commission 1986-91, memb Instituto de Sintra 1986, medal Royal Numismatic Soc 1990; *Books* Late Roman Bronze Coinage (jtly 1960), Wealth of the Roman World (with K S Painter, 1977), Roman Coins (1978), 2000 Years of British Coins and Medals (1978), Roman Imperial Coinage Vol VIII, The Family of Constantine I 337-364 (1981), A Selection of Byzantine Coins in the Barber Institute of Fine Arts (1985), British Museum Catalogue of Celtic Coins Vol I (with M R Mays, 1987), Catalogue of Silver Coins of the East Celts and other Balkan Peoples (1987); Vol II: Silver Coins of North Italy, South and Central France, Switzerland and South Germany (1990); *Recreations* local history and archaeology, mediaeval music, railway history; *Style*— Dr John Kent; 16 Newmans Way, Hadley Wood, Barnet, Herts EN4 OLR

KENT, John Sutcliffe; s of John Kent (d 1970), of Essex, and Elsie, *née* Sutcliffe; *b* 27 Jan 1930; *Educ* Pangbourne Nautical Coll Berks; *m* 3 June 1958, Jean Margaret, da of James Lennox (d 1982), of Essex; 2 da (Elizabeth Ann b 1960, Hilary Alison b 1964); *Career* Lt RNVR 1951-53; dir: Guild of Architectural Ironmongers, Kent Blaxill & Co Ltd; *Recreations* golf, bowling; *Clubs* Colchester Garrison Officers, Colchester Golf; *Style*— John Kent, Esq; Hill House, Gravel Hill, Nayland, Colchester CO6 4JB; Kent Blaxill & Co Ltd, PO Box 17, Colchester CO2 9SY

KENT, Dr Paul Welberry; JP (1972); s of Thomas William Kent (d 1975), of Doncaster, and Marion, *née* Cox (d 1954); *b* 19 April 1923; *Educ* Doncaster GS, Univ of Birmingham (BSc, PhD), Jesus Coll Oxford (MA, DPhil, DSc); *m* 23 Aug 1952, Rosemary Elizabeth Boutflower, da of Maj Charles Herbert Boutflower Shepherd, MC, TD (d 1980), of Oxford; 3 s (Anthony b 1955, Richard b 1961, Peter b 1964), 1 da (Deborah b 1957); *Career* asst lectr subsequently ICI fell Univ of Birmingham 1946-50, visiting fell Princeton Univ NJ 1948-49, demonstrator in biochemistry Univ of Oxford 1950-72, tutor and Dr Lees reader Ch Ch Coll Oxford 1955-72 (emeritus student 1972-), master Van Mildert Coll Univ of Durham 1972-82 (res dir 1972-82); biochemical conslt and visiting prof Windsor Univ Ontario 1971 and 1980; memb: Oxford City Cncl 1964-72, Ctee Biochemical Soc 1963-67, Chemical Cncl 1965-70, Advsy Ctee Cystic Fibrosis Res Cncl 1977-82; govr: Oxford Coll of Technol (subsequently Oxford Poly) 1964-72 and 1983 (vice chm 1966-69, chm 1969-70), St Chad's Coll Durham 1976-88, Pusey House Oxford 1983-; memb Oxford Poly Higher Educn Corp 1988- (currently dep chm); hon fell Canterbury Coll Ontario 1974, Hon DLitt Drury Coll USA 1973, Verdienstkreuz (Bundes Republik) 1970; author of articles in scientific jls and jt author of scientific monographs; FRSC 1950; *Books* Biochemistry of the Amino Sugars (with M W Whitehouse, 1955), International Aspects of the Provision of Medical Care (1976); *Recreations* travel, flute and organ music; *Clubs* Athenaeum; *Style*— Dr Paul Kent, JP; Bricoe Gate, Baldersdale, Barnard Castle, Co Durham DL12 9UL; 18 Arnolds Way, Cumnor Hill, Oxford OX2 9JB (☎ 0865 862087)

KENT, Roderick David; s of Dr Basil Stanley Kent, of Wheat House, Wheathold, Ramsdell, Hants, and Vivien Margaret, *née* Baker; *b* 14 Aug 1947; *Educ* King's Sch Canterbury, CCC Oxford (MA); *m* 12 Aug 1972, Belinda Jane, da of W H Mitchell (d 1983), of Francheville, Grouville, Jersey; 3 da (Sophie b 1974, Nicola b 1976, Tiffany b 1978); *Career* with J Henry Schroder Wagg & Co Ltd 1969-71, Banque Blyth (Paris) 1971, Institut Européen d'Administration des Affaires (INSEAD) 1971-72, Triumph Investment Tst 1972-74; Close Bros 1974- (md 1975-); Liveryman of Worshipful Co of Pewterers; MBA 1972; *Recreations* sport; *Style*— Roderick Kent Esq; Close Brothers Ltd, 36 Great St Helens, London EC3A 6AP (☎ 071 283 2241, fax 071 623 9699, telex 8814274); Wolverton Cottage, Wolverton, nr Basingstoke, Hants RG26 5SX (☎ 0635 298 276)

KENT, Brig Sidney Harcourt; OBE (1944); s of Maj Geoffrey Harcourt Kent (d 1979), of Hindhead, and Muriel Hutton, *née* Potts (d 1981); *b* 22 April 1915; *Educ* Wellington Coll, RMC Sandhurst; *m* 5 March 1945, Nina Ruth, da of Gen Sir Geoffry Allen Percival Scoones, KCB, KBE, CSI, DSO, MC (d 1975), of Ashdon, Essex; 1 s (Simon b 1948), 1 da (Susan b 1946); *Career* 2 Lt KOYLI, Lt-Col 1944, Brig 1944; GSO1 8 Army 1944, BGS Allied Land Forces SE Asia 1944; cmd 128 Inf Bde (TA) 1960-63; mangr and sec Turf Bd 1965, gen mangr and chief exec Jockey Club 1969, advsr Royal Horse Soc Teheran 1978, tech advsr Nicosia Race Club 1979, conslt steward Jamaica Racing Cmmn 1984-86; dir racing Macao Jockey Club 1989; *Recreations* farming, travel, vintage cars; *Style*— Brig Sidney H Kent, OBE; The Old Vicarage, Kingsey, Aylesbury, Bucks (☎ 0844 291 411); Maroni Village, Larnaca, Cyprus (☎ 0433 2614)

KENT, Trevor Lincoln; s of Ernest George Kent (d 1987), of Gerrards Cross, Bucks, and Evelyn Gertrude Mary, *née* Fuller; *b* 28 March 1947; *Educ* Denstone Coll, London Coll of Commerce; *m* 7 July 1979, Angela Christine, da of Gp Capt John Thornhill Shaw, DSO, DFC, AFC (d 1975), of Worplesdon, Surrey; 4 s (Toby d 1980, Lincoln b 1982, Warwick b 1983, Leicester b 1987); *Career* sr ptnr Trevor Kent & Co estate agents auctioneers 1971-; regular contrib on radio TV and in the press on residential property matters, co-presenter Moving and Improving; dist cncllr South Bucks DC 1978-82; pres Nat Assoc of Estate Agents 1989-90 (media spokesman 1991-), memb Inter Professional Working Pty on the transfer of residential property 1989, licenced asst CoE, fell Nat Assoc of Estate Agents; *Recreations* playing cricket, watching the garden grow, separating the boys, not dieting; *Clubs* Middlesex and Bucks County Cricket; *Style*— Trevor Kent, Esq; The Nat Assoc of Estate Agents, 21 Jury St, Warwick CV34 4EH (☎ 0926 496800, fax 0926 400 953)

KENTISH, Lt Cdr William; VRD (1968, and clasp 1974); s of Capt William Kentish (d 1954), of 41 Amesbury Rd, Moseley, Birmingham, and Florence Gladys Louise Kentish (d 1963); *b* 14 Sept 1918; *Educ* King Edward's Sch Birmingham, Cambridge Univ (MA, LLM); *m* 1, 1952 (m dis 1954), Daphne, *née* Cunynghame; m 2, 1957 (m dis 1967), Sylvia Mary, *née* Abbotts; 2 s (William David b 10 Jan 1958, Miles Adrian b 20 April 1959); *Career* Sub Lt RNVR trg HMS King Alfred 1939, served with Naval ASDIC trawlers in Bristol Channel 1939-40, HMS Arethusa 1940-42, drafted to HMS Carnarvon Castle 1942, Lt 1942, served in HMS Rockrose and as gunnery offr HMS Artic Explorer in convoys from Cape Town to Durban and back 1943, CO HM Fairmile Motor Launch 857 1944-45, active serv in Burma 1945, demob 1946; re-joined RNVR 1950, Navigating Pilotage Certificate 1955 served in HMS Truelove and HMS Sheffield, Lt Cdr 1956, trained as Naval Control of Shipping Offr 1960-74; admitted slr 1948; ptnr: James Kentish & Atkins, Kentish & Co, Cottrell & Co, Cottrell Son & Wm Kentish, Cottrell Kentish & Bache, Haynes Duffell Kentish & Co; Notary Public 1965; cncl memb Birmingham Law Soc 1980-84, hon sec Cons Political Gp; memb Law Soc; *Recreations* golf, swimming; *Clubs* MCC, Birmingham, Edgbaston GC; *Style*— Lt Cdr William Kentish, VRD; 88 Salisbury Rd, Moseley, Birmingham B13 8JY (☎ 021 449 3933); Essex House, 27 Temple St, Birmingham B2 5RQ (☎ 021 643 1235, fax 021 643 1314)

KENTON, Jeremy Martin; s of Dr Ralph J Kenton (d 1988), of Westcliff on Sea, Essex, and Veronica Maisie, *née* Field; *b* 11 Dec 1955; *Educ* Chigwell Sch, Br Coll of Naturopathy and Osteopathy (Dip in Osteopathy, Dip in Naturopathy); *m* Sharon Anna, da of Reginald Calder; 1 da (Katrina Anna); *Career* lectr Br Coll of Naturopathy and Osteopathy London 1979-, private osteopath London and Essex 1979-; regular broadcaster on nat and local radio and TV 1980-, author numerous of articles in newspapers and magazines; Br Naturopathic and Osteopathic Assoc: memb Cncl 1980-, vice pres 1986, pres 1987-; Br delegate to Euro Osteopathic Liaison Ctee Brussels 1985, memb Ctee Cncl for Complimentary and Alternative Med 1986-88, sr clinician Br Coll of Naturopathy and Osteopathy Teaching Clinic 1986-, pres Gen Cncl and Register of Naturopaths 1988-89, memb Cncl Gen Cncl and Register of Osteopaths 1988-; MRO; *Recreations* horse riding, skiing, offshore power boat racing, theatre, music; *Clubs* East India; *Style*— Jeremy Kenton, Esq; 121 The Ave, Highams Park, London E4 9RX (☎ 081 531 0055); 2 Ceylon Rd, Westcliff on Sea, Essex (☎ 0702 341297); 10 Harley St, London W1 (☎ 071 636 6054, car 0836 771151)

KENTRIDGE, Sydney; QC (1984); s of Morris Kentridge (d 1964), of Johannesburg, and May, *née* Shafner (d 1971); *b* 5 Nov 1922; *Educ* King Edward VII Sch Johannesburg, Univ of Witwatersrand (BA), Univ of Oxford (MA); *m* 15 Jan 1952, Felicia, da of Max Geffen, of Johannesburg (d 1977); 2 s (William, Matthew), 2 da (Catherine, Elizabeth); *Career* WWII Lt SA Forces served E Africa, Sicily, Italy; memb: Johannesburg Bar 1949-, sr counsel SA 1965; called to the Bar Lincoln's Inn 1977, bencher Lincoln's Inn, hon fell Exeter Coll Oxford, Roberts lectr Univ of Pennsylvania 1979, Granville Clark prize (USA) 1978; judge of the Cts of Appeal of Jersey, Guernsey and Republic of Botswana; Hon LLD: Leicester 1985, Cape Town 1987, Seaton Hall, New Jersey 1978, Natal 1989; *Recreations* opera-going; *Clubs* Athenaeum; *Style*— Sydney Kentridge, Esq, QC; Brick Court Chambers, 15-19 Devereux Court, London WC2 (☎ 071 583 0777, 071 583 9401)

KENWARD, Elizabeth; MBE (1986); da of Brian Charles Durant Kemp-Welch (d 1950), of Kineton, Warwicks, and Verena, *née* Venour (d 1968); *b* 14 July 1906; *Educ* privately and Les Tourelles Brussels; *m* 22 June 1932 (m dis 1942), late Capt Peter Trayton Kenward, s of late Edward Kenward, of Mill Farm House, Tenterden, Kent; 1 s (Jim Trayton b 1933); *Career* social ed; Jennifer of Jennifer's Diary (Tatler 1944-59, Queen Magazine 1959-70, Harpers & Queen 1970-); Official Sister of St John 1986; *Recreations* flat racing, theatre, flying (quickest trip Caracas and back for a dinner party by Air France Concorde); *Clubs* Annabel's; *Style*— Mrs Elizabeth Kenward, MBE; Harpers & Queen, 72 Broadwick St, London W1V 2BP

KENWORTHY, Hon Basil Frederick de la Pole; TD (1958); 3 s of 10 Baron Strabolgi (d 1952), and his 1 w, Doris (d 1988), da of Sir Frederick Whitley Whitley-Thomson, JP, MP; *b* 24 March 1920; *Educ* Oundle, Lincoln Coll Oxford (BA, MA); *m* 18 March 1948 (m dis 1965), Chloë, 2 da of Henry Gerard Walter Sandeman and Hon Phyllis Leigh, da of 2 Baron Newton, PC; 3 da (Mrs William Healey b 1949, Mrs John Vincent b 1950, Mrs Sebastian Kent b 1958); *Career* Capt RA (TA Reserve), served Norway, India, Palestine, Western Desert, Greece, Crete and Germany; FInstPet, MInstT, memb BFSS; *Recreations* shooting, music; *Clubs* Hurlingham, Anglo-Turkish Assoc, Turco-British Assoc, Istanbul Club, Lincoln Soc, Oxford Union Soc; *Style*— The Hon Basil Kenworthy, TD; c/o The Hurlingham Club, Ranelagh Gardens, London SW6 3PR

KENWORTHY, Joan Margaret; da of Albert Kenworthy (d 1984), and Amy, *née* Cobbold (d 1965); *b* 10 Dec 1933; *Educ* GS for Girls Barrow-in-Furness, St Hilda's Coll Oxford (BLitt, MA); *Career* temp tutorships: St Hugh's Coll Oxford 1958-59, Bedford Coll London 1959-60; sr lectr Univ of Liverpool 1973-77 (asst lectr 1960-63, lectr 1963-73); warden: Salisbury Hall 1966-77, Morton House 1974-77; memb Geography Assoc, Br Ecological Soc, African Studies Assoc; memb Inst of Br Geographers, FRGS, FRMetS; *Books* contrib to several books on climatology and Africa; *Clubs* Royal Cwlth Soc; *Style*— Miss Joan M Kenworthy; 1 Elvet Garth, South Rd, Durham DH1 3TP (☎ 091 384 3865); St Mary's Coll, University of Durham, Durham DH1 3LR (☎ 091 374 2700)

KENWORTHY, (Frederick) John; s of Rev Fred Kenworthy, MA, BD (d 1974), and Ethel Kenworthy, *née* Radcliffe; *b* 6 Dec 1943; *Educ* William Hulme's GS Manchester, Univ of Manchester (BA); *m* 1968, Diana, da of Reginald Flintham (d 1948); 1 da (Hannah Frances b 1983); *Career* asst princ MOD (Navy) 1966, Treasy centre for Admin Studies 1968-69, Br Steel Corp Sheffield 1969; princ MOD 1972, asst sec Royal Cmmn on the Press Secretariat 1974, dir Weapons Resources and Progs (Naval) MOD 1979-83; head of RN Size and Shape Policy Div MOD 1983-86; DHSS: dir of ops Disablement Servs Div 1986-87, dir ops Disablement Servs Authy 1987-88; DSS: under sec 1989, chief Info Technology Servs Agency 1990-; *Recreations* music, sport, photography; *Clubs* Lansdown Tennis and Squash, Racquets (Bath); *Style*— F John Kenworthy, Esq

KENWORTHY, Rev the Hon Jonathan Malcolm Atholl; s of late 10 Baron Strabolgi, by his 1 w, Doris, da of Sir Frederick Whitley Whitley-Thomson, JP, MP; hp of bro, 11 Baron, *qv*; *b* 16 Sept 1916; *Educ* Oundle, Pembroke Coll Cambridge (MA), Ridley Hall Cambridge; *m* 1, 1943, Joan Marion (d 1963), da of late Claude Gilbert Gaster, of Tunbridge Wells; 2 da (Mrs D Brown b 1944, Mrs G Collins b 1946); m 2, 1963, Victoria Hewitt; 2 s (Andrew b 1967, James b 1971), 1 da (Penelope (Mrs S Bass) b 1964); *Career* served WWII, CF NW Europe 1944, NE India 1945-47; rector St Clement's Oxford 1947-54; vicar: Hoddesdon 1954-63, All Saints' Burton on Trent 1963-65; chaplain St John's Bangalore 1965-66, vicar Christ Church Penge 1966-75, rector Yelvertoft and Lilbourne 1975-82; *Style*— The Rev the Hon Malcolm Kenworthy; 37 North Rd, Combe Down, Bath (☎ 0225 835447)

KENWORTHY-BROWNE, Dr (James) Michael; s of Bernard Evelyn Kenworthy-Browne (d 1979), of Herts; bro Peter Kenworthy-Brown, *qv*; *b* 22 March 1936; *Educ* Ampleforth, Oriel Oxford (MA, BM, BCh, MRCP (UK), FRCGP); *m* 1, 1962, Anne (d 1983), da of Vernon Mayer (d 1982); 1 s (Nicholas b 1971), 3 da (Joanna b 1966, Frances b 1966, Michelle b 1966); m 2, 1985, Elizabeth Mary, da of John Hassell; *Career* Nat Serv 2 Lt Cyprus 1956-57; med practitioner Oxford City and Univ, past gen med and cardiac registrar Radcliffe Infirmary 1967-79, past course organizer Gen Practice Training Oxford City and County 1975-83; *Recreations* travel, wine appreciation; *Clubs* Vincents; *Style*— Dr Michael Kenworthy-Browne, Esq; Heron Hill, Harberton Mead, Oxford OX3 0DB (☎ 0865 66568); The Jericho Health Centre, Walton Street, Oxford OX2 6NW (☎ 0865 52971)

KENWORTHY-BROWNE, (Bernard) Peter Francis; s of Bernard Evelyn Kenworthy-Browne (d 1979), formerly of Wellbury, nr Hitchin, Herts, and Margaret

Sibylla (d 1985), da of late Sir George Hadcock, KBE, FRS; bro Dr Michael Kenworthy-Browne, *qv*; *b* 11 May 1930; *Educ* Ampleforth, Oriel Coll Oxford (MA); *m* 1, 1975 (m dis 1982), Jane Elizabeth, da of late Denis Malcolm Mackie; m 2, 1989, Elizabeth Anne, da of late Dr J A Bowen-Jones; *Career* Nat Serv 2 Lt Irish Guards 1949-50; called to the Bar Lincoln's Inn 1955, Oxford and Midland and Oxford circuits 1957-82, rec of the Crown Ct 1981-82, registrar of the Family Div of High Ct of Justice 1982-91, district judge 1991-; *Recreations* music, shooting, photography, gardening, field sports; *Clubs* Cavalry and Guards; *Style—* Peter Kenworthy-Browne, Esq; 30 Dewhurst Rd, London W14 0ES (☎ 071 602 9580); Principal Registry, Family Div, Somerset House, Strand, London WC2R 1LP

KENYON, Antony Howard; s of Frank Kenyon (d 1987), and Kathleen, *née* Richards; *b* 1 Oct 1954; *Educ* St Albans GS for Boys, Univ of Manchester (BSc); *m* 6 Sept 1985, Linda, da of John Burke; 1 s (James b 6 Dec 1986), 2 step da (Nicola West b 24 April 1974, Samatha West b 12 May 1975); *Career* trainee Benton & Bowles 1977-78, media buyer Allen Brady & Marsh 1978-80, media mangr McCann-Erickson 1980-83, exec media dir Dorland Advertising 1983-88, jt md IDK Media Ltd 1988-; *Recreations* flyfishing; *Style—* Antony Kenyon, Esq; IDK Media Ltd, 1 Wardour St, London W1V 3HE (☎ 071 734 3444, fax 071 734 8164)

KENYON, Sir George Henry; JP (Cheshire 1959), DL (Chester 1969), DL (Manchester 1983); s of George Henry Kenyon; *b* 10 July 1912; *Educ* Radley, Manchester Univ (LLD); *m* 1938, Christine Dorey, *née* Brentnall; 2 s, 1 da; *Career* chm: William Kenyon & Sons Ltd 1961-82 (dir 1942-), Williams and Glyn's Bank Ltd 1978-83 (dir 1972-83), S Tameside Bench 1974-82, Cncl Manchester Univ 1972-80; dir: Manchester Ship Canal 1972-, Royal Bank of Scotland 1979-83; kt 1976; *Style—* Sir George Kenyon, JP, DL; Limefield House, Hyde, Cheshire (☎ 061 368 2012)

KENYON, Guy Stuart; s of Horace Stuart Kenyon, of Ringstead Hunstanton Norfolk, and Katherine Mary, *née* Chapman; *b* 6 Jan 1948; *Educ* Perse Sch Cambridge, Univ of Edinburgh (BSc, MB ChB, MD); *m* 30 Sept 1989, Judith Elizabeth, da of Edward Meirion Morgan, of Pine Tops, Kettering, Northants; 1 s (James Edward Stuart b 1 Feb 1991); *Career* RNR 1979-88, Surgn Lt Cdr; training in gen surgery United Bristol and Royal Northern Hosps 1977-80, registrar and sr registrar in otolaryngology London Hosp, Royal Free Hosp and Royal Surrey County Hosp Guildford 1981-84; conslt surgn in otolaryngology London Hosp and Hosps for Sick Children London 1987-, conslt surgn St Luke's Hosp for the clergy 1987-; contrib papers on neuro-otology and head and neck cancer; memb: Med Soc of London, The Otorhinolaryngological Res Soc 1983, The Joseph Soc 1987; FRCSEd 1980, FRCS 1982; *Books* Hutchinson's Clinical Examination (1984), Textbook of Otolaryngology (contrib, 1988), many articles in medical journals; *Recreations* skiing, swimming, music, reading; *Clubs* RSM, Royal Naval Medical, Blizzard; *Style—* Guy Kenyon, Esq; 12B Ellington Road, Muswell Hill, London N10 3DG (☎ 081 883 6215, fax 081 442 0551); 18 Upper Wimpole Street, London W1M 7TB (☎ 071 486 0853)

KENYON, Col John Frederick; OBE (1970), MC (1944); s of Lt-Col Herbert Edward Kenyon, DSO (d 1958), of Pradoe, Oswestry, Shropshire, and Gwendoline Ethel Graham, *née* Ommanney (d 1958); *b* 30 Dec 1921; *Educ* Marlborough, Staff Coll Camberley, Jt Servs Staff Coll Latimer; *m* 1, 8 Aug 1947 (m dis 1960), Jean Molyneux, da of Howard Godfrey, MC (d 1964), of Wilts; 2 s (John b 24 Oct 1948, Richard b 3 Dec 1951); m 2, 5 Aug 1960 (m dis 1981), Margaret Bowker Remington; m 3, 20 July 1982, Janet Mary, da of Fisher Maddicott, of Devon; *Career* cmmnd RA: India 1942, Burma 1943-46, NWFP and Hazara ops India 1946-47; instr in Gunnery 1948-50, Staff Coll Camberley 1951, Suez Canal 1952-54, Jt Servs Staff Coll 1959, cdr Chestnut Troop RHA 1960-61, mil asst to C-in-C Far E Land Forces 1962-64, GSO 1 Ops, Intelligence and Security HQ 1 Br Corps 1966-69, Def Naval Mil Attaché Brussels 1971-73; pres Freemen of England and Wales, chm Shrewsbury Abbey Heritage Project, govr Derwen Trg Coll for the Disabled, patron Br Torch Delegation; co cncllr Shropshire CC 1977-85; conducted successful campaign to restore the county name of Shropshire, raplacing Salop; Freeman City of London 1983, Grand Master Freemen of Shrewsbury; Offr Order of Leopold Belgium 1989; *Recreations* conservation on estates, fighting bureaucracy, shooting, tennis; *Clubs* Farmers; *Style—* Col John Kenyon, OBE, MC; Pradoe, Oswestry, Shropshire SY11 4ER (☎ 0691 88218)

KENYON, 5 Baron (GB 1788); Sir Lloyd Tyrell-Kenyon; 5 Bt (GB 1784), CBE (1972), DL (Flint 1948); s of 4 Baron Kenyon (d 1927); *b* 13 Sept 1917; *Educ* Eton, Magdalene Coll Cambridge; *m* 1946, Leila Mary, da of Cdr John Wyndham Cookson, RN (ret), by the Cdr's w Mary (da of Sir Alan Colquhoun, 6 Bt, KCB, JP, DL, and Aunt of Countess of Arran); Leila was wid of Hugh William Jardine Ethelston Peel; 3 s (Hon Lloyd b 1947, Hon Richard b 1948, Hon Thomas b 1954), 1 da (Hon Katharine b 1959); *Heir* s, Hon Lloyd Tyrell-Kenyon; *Career* 2 Lt Shrops Yeo 1937, Lt RA (TA), ret 1943 with hon rank of Capt; dir Lloyds Bank Ltd 1962-85 (chm NW Bd 1962-88); pres Univ Coll of N Wales Bangor 1947-82; chm Nat Portrait Gallery 1966-88 (tstee 1953-88); memb: Royal Cmmn on Historical MSS 1966-, Bd Ancient Monuments for Wales 1979-87, Flint CC 1946 (chm 1954-55); Hon LLD Univ of Wales 1958; *Clubs* Brooks's, Cavalry & Guards, Beefsteak; *Style—* The Rt Hon the Lord Kenyon, CBE, DL; Cumbers House, Gredington, Whitchurch, Salop SY13 3DH (☎ 094 874 330)

KENYON, Philip Stephen (Phil); s of Richard Bernard Kenyon, of Lancashire, and Vera Daphne Kenyon; *b* 7 May 1956; *Educ* Montgomery Secdy Modern Sch, Blackpool Coll of Food Research (HND); *m* 1984, Charmaine; 1 s (Peter b 1988), 1 da (Pascale b 1986); *Career* professional squash player; began playing ICI Sports Club Thornton Lancs 1971, competitive debut St Annes Tennis & Squash Club 1972 (winner), full time amateur player 1978 (formerly pt/t), professional 1979-; England: 30 under 19 cups (capt 1976), 52 full caps (capt World Championships 1987); honours incl: Br jr champion 1973-75, world jr champion 1974-75, Lancs sr champion 1974-78 (jr champion 1973-76), Br under 23 champion 1975 and 1978-79, Swiss Open winner 1976, Dutch Open winner 1977, Br closed champion 1977, 1981, 1983, 1985, NZ Open winner 1978, World Amateur runner up 1979, Irish Open winner 1979, Jamaican Open winner 1979, 1981 and 1990, GB world team champions 1979, Singapore Open champion 1986, Hong Kong Open champion 1986; highest World ranking of number four 1985-86 (most succesful Br squash player over past decade); Personality of the Year awards: Squash Rackets Assoc 1976-77, Observer 1984; former employment: food research Chorley Wood Herts 1975-76, jt designer first aluminium squash racket Elite Sports 1976-77; *Recreations* water skiing, windsurfing, golf, tennis, motoring, fast cars, swimming; *Style—* Phil Kenyon, Esq; c/o Squash Rackets Association, Westpoint, 33-34 Warple Way, Acton, London W3 0RQ (☎ fax 0222 228185)

KEOGH, Andrew John; s of George Augustine Keogh (d 1961), of Bolton, Lancs, and Flora Theresa Furt Keogh, JP, *née* Angler (d 1981); *b* 9 Jan 1938; *Educ* Salesian Coll Bolton, Univ of Glasgow (MB ChB); *m* 19 Jan 1967, Mary Ruth, da of Frederic Newman, of Sidcup, Kent; 2 s (Edward John b 25 Feb 1972, George b 25 May 1977), 2 da (Emma Louise b 25 Feb 1969, Amy Victoria b 28 Jan 1970); *Career* serv TA; SHO and registrar in orthopaedics Bromley Gp Hosps 1964-65; registrar: in surgery Lewisham 1967-69, in neurosurgery Woolwich 1969-72, sr registrar and lectr in neurosurgery Univ of Sheffield 1972-78, conslt neurosurgn NW Regnl Health Authy 1978-; FRCS 1969; memb: Soc of Br Neurological Surgns 1972, BMA 1980; *Style—* Andrew Keogh, Esq; Grantham House, 21 Beech Grove, Ashton, Preston PR2 1DX (☎ 0772 726475); Royal Preston Hospital, Sharoe Green Lane, Preston (☎ 0772 716 565)

KEOGH, Colin Denis; s of John Denis Keogh, and Hillary Joan, *née* Campbell; *b* 27 July 1953; *Educ* St John's Coll SA, Eton, Univ Coll Oxford (MA), INSEAD (MBA); *m* 26 Aug 1978, Joanna Mary Martyn, da of John Frederick Leapman; 2 s (Thomas b 27 March 1983, William b 6 May 1987), 2 da (Kate b 6 Nov 1984, Georgina b 10 Aug 1990); *Career* Arthur Andersen & Co 1978-82, INSEAD 1982-83, Saudi Int Bank 1983-85, dir Close Bros Ltd 1986-; memb Inst Taxation; *Recreations* sport, theatre; *Style—* Colin Keogh, Esq; 66 Manville Rd, London SW17 8JL (☎ 081 672 1340); Close Brothers Ltd, 36 Great St Helen's, London EC3A 6AP (☎ 071 283 2241, fax 071 623 9699)

KEOGH, Eddie Patrick; s of Edward Keogh, of 9 Vincent Gardens, Dollis Hill, London, and Elizabeth, *née* Kelly; *b* 6 Nov 1962; *Educ* St Benedict's Sch Ealing, Paddington Coll, Richmond Coll (NCTJ course in photography); *m* 8 Sept 1990, Cathy, da of James Stimpson; *Career* sports photographer; Mercury Press Agency Liverpool 1983-84, Fleet St News Agency (sport & general) 1984-85 (covered the Los Angeles Olympics), freelance photographer 1985-86 (Mail on Sunday, Daily Mirror, Today), sports photographer Today newspaper 1986-; *Clubs* St Andrews FC, Today FC; *Style—* Eddie Keogh, Esq; 28 Alder Grove, Dollis Hill, London NW2 7DB (☎ 081 452 5784); Today Newspaper, 70 Vauxhall Bridge Rd, London SW1V 2RP (☎ 071 630 1300, car 0836 242015)

KEOGH, Malcolm Christopher; s of Ronald Keogh, of Bowdon, Cheshire, and Dorothy, *née* Bulley; *b* 13 April 1944; *Educ* Stonyhurst, Coll of Law London, Liverpool Poly; *m* 30 Aug 1969, Marie-Catherine, da of Henri Pouplard, of Angers, France; *Career* admitted slr 1969; sr ptnr Ronald Keogh & Co Altrincham 1974-87, appointed consular agent of France for Manchester 1985, ptnr Pannone March Pearson Manchester (formerly Pannone Blackburn Manchester) 1987-, dir Pannone De Backer EEIG (int grouping of lawyers) 1987-; chm: Northern Chamber Orch 1984-89, Franco Br Business Club Manchester 1988-; pres Franco Br Cultural Assoc Manchester 1990-; memb: Law Soc 1969- (Int Promotion Ctee 1989-), Manchester Law Soc 1969-; *Books* (part author) Daily Telegraph Guide to Buying Property in France (1990); *Recreations* flying, languages, international affairs, wine, electronics, DIY; *Clubs* Franco-British Business; *Style—* Malcolm Keogh, Esq; Pannone March Pearson, 41 Spring Gardens Manchester M2 2BB (☎ 061 832 3000, fax 061 832 2655, telex 668172)

KEOGH, (Anthony) Patrick; s of Arthur Wilfrid Keogh (d 1947), of Enfield, Middlesex, and Vere Alberta, *née* Stock (d 1981); *b* 10 Aug 1929; *Educ* St Ignatius Coll London, Univ of London (MA, LLB, LLM); *m* 3 May 1952, Eileen, da of Michael Lynch (d 1964), of Farran, County Cork; 3 s (Kevin b 8 Feb 1953, Dominic b 5 July 1955, Benedict (twin) b 5 July 1955), 2 da (Angela b 16 March 1959, Fiona b 2 May 1962); *Career* Flying Offr RAF 1949-51; admitted slr 1959, pres N Middlesex Law Soc 1972-73, admin Highgate Duty Slr Scheme 1985-90; Grand Knight (Edmonton) Knights of St Columbia May 1964; chm: Edmonton Freedom from Hunger Campaign 1964, Hornsey Round Table 1969-70; pres Southgate Catenian Assoc 1974-75 and 1984-85; Freeman City of London 1963, Liveryman Worshipful Co of Slrs 1963; memb: Law Soc, Br Legal Assoc; Knight of St John of Jerusalem 1978; *Recreations* my family, walking, skiing, swimming; *Style—* Patrick Keogh, Esq; St Thomas More's, 28 Methuen Park Road, Muswell Hill, London N10 2JT (☎ 081 444 6900), Attorneys' Bench, 335 Muswell Hill Broadway, Muswell Hill, London N10 1BW (☎ 081 883 4412, fax 081 883 6278)

KEOHANE, Desmond John; s of William Patrick Keohane (d 1971), of Sheerness, Kent, and Mabel Margaret, *née* Coleman; *b* 5 July 1928; *Educ* Borden GS Sittingbourne Kent, Univ of Birmingham (BA), Univ of London (PGCE); *m* 13 Aug 1960, Mary, da of Patrick Kelliher, of Northampton; 2 s (Jeremy b 1961, John b 1968), 2 da (Ann b 1963, Clare b 1964); *Career* Nat Serv Flying Offr Educn Branch RAF 1950-52; schoolteacher and coll lectr 1953-64; vice princ Havering Tech Coll 1969-71 (head of Dept of Soc and Academic Studies 1964-68); princ: Northampton Coll of Further Educn 1971-76, Oxford Coll of Further Educn 1976-90; govr: St Mary's Sch Northampton 1972-90, Thomas Becket Sch Northampton 1973- (chm 1983-), Oxford Area Arts Cncl 1980-85, Oxford Sch 1982-86, Oxford Poly 1983-87; memb: Southern Regnl Cncl for Further Educn 1977-, Cncl Secdy Examinations 1983-86, Bd Berks and Oxon Area Manpower 1985-89, Special Employment Measures Advsy Gp (MSC) 1986-89; educn and trg conslt 1991-; FBIM 1981; *Recreations* watching cricket, walking; *Style—* Desmond Keohane, Esq; 14 Abington Park Crescent, Northampton NN3 3AD (☎ 0604 38829); Oxford College of Further Education, Oxpens Rd, Oxford OX1 1SA (☎ 0865 245871, fax 0865 248871)

KEOHANE, Prof Kevin William; CBE (1976); s of William Patrick Keohane (d 1971), and Mabel Margaret, *née* Coleman; *b* 28 Feb 1923; *Educ* Borden GS, Univ of Bristol (BSc, PhD); *m* 26 Feb 1949, Mary Margaret Patricia, da of Charles Ashford (d 1938); 1 s (Stephen b 1964), 3 da (Elizabeth b 1952, Katharine b 1953, Hilary b 1957); *Career* served WWII RAF 1943-46 (Far East); prof of sci educn Univ of London 1968-76 (prof of physics 1964-68), rector Roehampton Inst of Higher Educn 1976-88; dir and exec vice chm Taylor & Francis Ltd 1974-, chm Nuffield Chelsea Curriculum Tst 1976- (dir Nuffield Fndn Sci Teaching Projects 1966-76), Royal Soc Leverhulme prof to Brazil 1971, vice chm Int Advsy Panel Chinese Prov Univs Project 1985-; memb: Richmond Twickenham and Roehampton Health Authy 1987-90, Merton Local Educn Authy 1988-90, Cncl Univ of Surrey 1988-; visiting hon prof King's Coll London 1989-; Hon DUniv Surrey 1987; Bragg medallist Inst of Physics 1990; FInstP 1960; KSG 1983; *Recreations* rugby (spectator), bee keeping; *Clubs* Roslyn Park RFC, Athenaeum; *Style—* Dr Kevin Keohane, CBE; 3 Thetford Rd, New Malden KT3 5DN (☎ 081 942 6861)

KER, David Peter James; s of Capt David John Richard Ker, MC, DL, JP, of Fayleys Border House, Aldworth, Reading, Berks, and Virginia Mary Eloise, *née* Howard; *b* 23 July 1951; *Educ* Eton; *m* 27 June 1974, Alexandra Mary, da of Vice Adm Sir Dymock Watson, KCB, CBE, DL (d 1987), of Trebinshwyn, nr Brecon, Powys; 2 s (David Edward Richard b 18 Dec 1979, d 17 March 1980, David Humphry Rivers b 11 Oct 1982), 1 da (Claire Rose b 23 Nov 1977); *Career* fndr and sole proprietor David Ker Fine Art 1980-; dir: Parc St Roman SA 1977-79, Oceanic Development Co (Bahamas) Ltd 1979-80, Ker Management Ltd 1980-, Belgrave Frames Ltd 1986-, John Paravicini Ltd 1988; memb Soc of London Art Dealers 1986; *Recreations* shooting, fishing, collecting fine art, racing; *Clubs* Whites, Turf, Beefsteak, Pratts, The Brook (NY); *Style—* David Ker, Esq; 85 Bourne St, London SW1W 8HF (☎ 071 730 8365, fax 071 730 3352, car 0860 385 769)

KER-LINDSAY, Hon Mrs (Anne Bradbury); da of 2 Baron Bradbury; *b* 19 Sept 1947; *m* 1970, Alastair James Ker-Lindsay; 4 s (James b 4 May 1972, Mark b 21 June 1973, John Alexander b 10 Aug 1977, Adam Ronald b 28 Feb 1979), 1 da (Laura Anne b 27 April 1985); *Style—* The Hon Mrs Ker-Lindsay; Manor House, 26 St John's Wood Park, London NW8 6QP

KERBY, John Vyvyan; s of Dr Theo Rosser Fred Kerby (d 1947), and Constance Mary, *née* Newell (d 1954); *b* 14 Dec 1942; *Educ* Eton, ChCh Oxford (MA); *m* 23

June 1978, Shirley Elizabeth, da of Sydney John Pope (d 1970); 1 step s, 1 step da; *Career* temp asst princ Colonial Office 1965-67, asst princ Miny of Overseas Devpt 1967-70, private sec to Parly Under Sec FCO 1970-71, memb Civil Serv Selection Bd 1974-75, head Br Devpt Div in SA 1983-86, under sec and princ estabs offr ODA 1986- (princ 1971-74 and 1975-77, asst sec 1977-83); *Recreations* gardening, entomology, cricket; *Style—* John Kerby, Esq; Overseas Development Administration, Eland House, Stag Place, London, SW1 (☎ 071 273 0380)

KERDEL-VEGAS, HE Dr Francisco; hon CBE (1973); s of Oswaldo Kerdel, and Sofia Vegas; *b* 3 Jan 1928; *Educ* Liceo Andres Bello Caracas (BSc), Universidad Central de Venezuela Caracas (MD), Harvard, Univ of NY (MSc); *m* Martha Ramos; 2 s (Francisco, Martin), 4 da (Margaret, Maria Isabel, Luisa Sofia, Ana Luisa); *Career* prof of dermatology Universidad Central de Venezuela 1961-77 (asst prof 1954-58, assoc prof 1958-61), visiting scientist Dept of Experimental Pathology ARC Inst of Animal Physiology Cambridge GB 1966-67, memb Trinity Coll Cambridge 1966-67, scientific attaché Venezuelan Embassy London 1966-67, academic vice chllr Simon Bolivar Univ 1969-70, memb bd of the Univ Metropolitana Caracas 1970-, prosser of the White Oration RCP 1972; fell: Venezuelan Acad of Med 1967-, Venezuelan Acad of Sciences 1971-; memb Natural Resources Cncl 1969-79, pres of FUDENA 1974; Venezuelan ambass to the Court of St James's 1987-; numerous pubns in sci jls; contrib to various dermatology textbooks; nat Venezuelan Ctee United World Colls 1974-80, FUDENA 1974; exec dir Panamerican Fedn of Faculties of Med 1977-78; hon degree of doctor in sci California Coll of Podiatric Med 1975; fell Royal Soc of Tropical Med and Hygiene London 1966, Huguenot Soc of London, Int Assoc of Allergology, American Coll of Physicians 1982, RGS 1981, Coll of Physicians of Philadelphia 1981, memb: Br Assoc of Dermatologists, RSM, West German Assoc of Dermatologists; memb Socs of Dermatology: France, Austria, Spain, Portugal, Brazil, Argentina, Mexico, Colombia, Ecuador, Peru, Central America, Cuba, Israel, S Africa; Order of Andres Bello Venezuela 1970, Order Cecilio Acosta Venezuela 1976, Order Francisco de Miranda Venezuela 1978, Order Diego de Losada Venezuela 1985, Order El Libertador 1986, Chevalier de la Legion de'Honneur France 1972; *Books* Tratado de Dermatologia (1959); *Recreations* travelling, swimming, photography; *Clubs* United Oxford & Cambridge University, Caracas Country, Camüri Grande (Venezuela), New York Univ; *Style—* HE Dr Francisco Kerdel-Vegas, CBE; 25 Melbury Rd, London W14 (☎ 071 602 3234); 1 Cromwell Rd, London SW7 (☎ 071 584 5375, telex 264186, fax 071 589 8887, car 0860 227291)

KEREVAN, Austin James (Jim); s of James Kerevan (d 1983), of Lincoln, and Olive, *née* Stroud; *b* 18 May 1935; *Educ* City Sch Lincoln; *m* 14 May 1966, Yvonne, da of John Burns (d 1985); 2 s (Mark James b 22 July 1968, Thomas James b 19 Sept 1984), 1 da (Emily Jane b 4 Nov 1971); *Career* RAF 1959-61; qualified CA 1959; KPMG Peat Marwick McLintock: joined Peat Marwick Mitchell 1961, London office 1961-75, Reading 1975-, currently sr ptnr Thames Valley practice; FCA (ACA 1959), MInstD; *Recreations* family, golf, reading (all sorts), bridge, studying railways; *Clubs* West Hill Golf, Huntercombe Golf, Trevose Golf; *Style—* Jim Kerevan, Esq; Springfield, The Street, Mortimer, Berkshire RG7 3PE (☎ 0734 333305); KPMG Peat Marwick McLintock, Abbots House, Abbey St, Reading, Berkshire RG1 3BG (☎ 0734 505555, fax 0734 589285)

KERNICK, Robert (Robin) Charles; s of John Wilson Kernick, OBE (d 1974), and Myrth Gwendoline, *née* Whittall (d 1989); *b* 11 May 1927; *Educ* Blundell's, Sidney Sussex Coll Cambridge (MA); *m* 1, 1951, Gillian, da of late Brig John Burne; 1 s (Mark Robert John b 1957), 1 da (Georgina Mary b 1954); m 2, Elizabeth, da of Surgn Rear Adm Sir Henry White, KCVO, CBE (d 1976); *Career* Capt Queen's (late King's) Dragoon Gds: (serv Palestine and N Africa); dir Grand Metropolitan Ltd 1972-75, md IDV Ltd 1972-75, chm Corney and Barrow Ltd 1981-88; Clerk of The Royal Cellars 1978-; *Recreations* golf, shooting, skiing; *Clubs* Cavalry & Guards, MCC, Huntercombe Golf, Swinley Forest Golf; *Style—* Robin Kernick, Esq; 12 Helmet Row, London EC1V 3QJ (☎ 071 251 4051, fax 071 608 1373)

KERR; *see*: Blair-Kerr

KERR, Allan Marshall; s of Dr Hugh Findlay Kerr (d 1967), of Greenock, Scotland, and Dorothy Mary Allan, *née* Martin (d 1978); *b* 25 Nov 1934; *Educ* Greenock Acad, HS of Glasgow, Paisley Tech Coll Combined (S&M Dept of T Cert); *m* 1, 2 Aug 1961, Joan Sorbie (d 1988), da of Thomas Millar (d 1961), of Glasgow; 2 s (Allan Thomas b 1963, David Marshal b 1966); m 2, 31 Dec 1988, Barbara Judith, *née* Nairn; 1 step s (Adam Johnathon Crosthwaite b 1967), 2 step da (Phillipa Jill (Mrs MacLean) b 1963, Belinda Kate Crosthwaite b 1964); *Career* engr offr Merchant Navy, Furness Withy Ltd 1958-62, Union Castle Line 1963-64; apprentice Scotts S&E Co Ltd Greenock 1953-58, engr mangr Ardossan Dockyard 1962-63, superintendent engr Clyde Shipping Co Ltd Glasgow 1964-75, dir and gen mangr Forth Tugs Ltd Grangemouth 1975-86, md Tees Towing Co Ltd 1986-; chm: Firth of Forth Shipowners Assoc 1982-84, Br Tug Owners Assoc 1984-86; vice chm Tees Wharf Operators Assoc 1988-; Fell Inst Marine Engrs 1961; *Recreations* golf, DIY, rough gardening; *Clubs* Naval, Middlesbrough Golf; *Style—* Allan M Kerr, Esq; Rook House, Skutterskelfe, Hutton Rudby, Yarm, Cleveland TS15 0JP (☎ 0642 700855); Cory Towage (Tees) Ltd, Tees Wharf, Dockside Rd, Middlesbrough, Cleveland TS3 6AB (☎ 0642 247273, fax 0642 224693)

KERR, Andrew Mark; s of William Mark Kerr, WS (d 1985), of Edinburgh, and Katharine Marjorie Anne, *née* Stevenson (d 1989); *b* 17 Jan 1940; *Educ* Edinburgh Acad, Univ of Cambridge (BA), Univ of Edinburgh (LLB); *m* 23 Sept 1967 (Jane) Susanna, da of James Cumming Robertson, CBE, of Oldhamstocks House, Cockburnspath, Berwickshire; 1 da (Elizabeth Louise b 1971); *Career* slr; British Petroleum 1961-62, apprentice Davidson & Syme WS (now Dundas & Wilson CS) 1964-67; Bell & Scott Bruce & Kerr WS (now Bell & Scott WS): joined 1967, ptnr 1969, sr ptnr 1987-; clerk Soc of Writers to HM Signet 1983-; RNR 1961-76; sec Edinburgh Festival Fringe Society Ltd 1969-, vice chm Edinburgh New Town Conservation Ctee 1972-76, chm Edinburgh Solicitors' Property Centre 1976-81; memb: Cncl Edinburgh Int Festival 1978-82, Cncl St George's Sch for Girls Edinburgh 1985-, Scottish Arts Cncl 1988- (chm Drama Ctee 1988-91); *Recreations* architecture, hill walking, music, ships, skiing, theatre; *Clubs* New (Edinburgh); *Style—* Andrew Kerr, Esq; 16 Ann Street, Edinburgh EH4 1PJ (☎ 031 332 9857); Bell & Scott WS, 16 Hill St, Edinburgh EH2 3LD (☎ 031 226 6703, fax 031 226 7602)

KERR, Colin Alan Lincoln; s of William Kerr (d 1967), of London, and Emily Jessica Kerr (d 1984); *b* 15 June 1929; *Educ* Bristol GS, Regent St Poly, Coll of Estate Mgmnt; *m* 17 Oct 1958, Françoise Marie Jeanne Marcelle (d 1990), da of George Govin (d 1986), of Paris; 2 s (Anthony Marc George Lincoln b 6 April 1971, Stephane Pierre Lincoln b 11 Nov 1961), 1 da (Delphine Marie Ingrid b 28 May 1974); *Career* cmmnd RA 1952-54; Edward Erdman: joined 1949-51, rejoined 1954, jt sr ptnr 1976, sr ptnr 1986; chm Commercial Prop Ctee RICS 1983-86, dir Fin Devpt Bd NSPCC 1983-; Freeman City of London, Liveryman Worshipful Co of Chartered Surveyors 1979; AAI 1951, FRICS 1962; *Recreations* sailing, golf, skiing; *Clubs* Oriental, Royal Lymington Yacht, Little Ship, Highgate Golf; *Style—* Colin Kerr, Esq; Blue Orchard, Courtenay Ave, Highgate, London N6 4LP; Hammeux Des Piste, Megeve, France; 6 Grosvenor St, London W1 (☎ 071 629 8191, fax 071 409 2757, telex 28169)

KERR, David Alexander; MC (1945), TD (1952); s of Alexander Smith Kerr (d 1967), and Teresa, *née* Andrews (d 1960); *b* 30 Sept 1916; *Educ* Canford Sch; *m* 23 April 1949, (Elizabeth) Phoebe Coxwell, da of Herbert Pinkney Cresswell, MBE, (d 1963), of Charingworth Manor, Chipping Campden, Gloucestershire; 1 s (David Robert Creswell b 1950), 1 da (Diana Juliet b 1953); *Career* Maj Argyll and Sutherland Highlanders TA 5/6 Bn 1936-52 (despatches); Westburn Sugar Refineries Ltd Greenock: tech dir 1949, refinery dir 1955, jt md 1960, md 1967, chm 1972-79; dir Manbre & Garton 1972-76, md Manbre Sugars 1972-76, dir Tate & Lyle Renfineries 1976-79; JP Renfrewshire 1959 (DL 1962); chm Renfrewshire Scout Assoc 1971-73; (co cmmr 1964-70); pres Renfrew and Inverclyde Area Scout Cncl 1976-, hon chief cmmr Scout Assoc Scotland 1981- (chief cmmr 1977-81); vice chm ACF League (Ayshire and Renfrewshire) 1989; *Recreations* garden, philately, photography, donkeys; *Style—* David Kerr, Esq, MC, TD, JP, DL; Whitefarland, 88 Octavia Terrace, Greenock, Renfrewshire PA16 7PY

KERR, Prof David James; s of Robert James Andrew Kerr, and Sarah, *née* Pettigrew; *b* 14 June 1956; *Educ* Eastwood HS Glasgow, Univ of Glasgow (BSc, MB ChB, MSc, MD, PhD); *m* 12 July 1980, Anne Miller, da of William Young, of 74 Beechwood Drive, Glasgow; 1 s (Stewart b 26 Oct 1981), 2 da (Sarah b 6 Dec 1982, Fiona b 9 Dec 1985); *Career* sr lectr in med oncology and hon conslt physician Beatson Oncology Centre Western Infirmary Glasgow 1989-; visiting prof Univ of Strathclyde Glasgow 1990-; memb: Cancer Res Campaign, Br Assoc for Cancer Res, Assoc of Cancer Physicians, Euro Orgn for Cancer Treatment and Res; MRCP; *Books* Advances in Oncology (1990), Oxford Textbooks of Oncology (1991); *Recreations* football, busking; *Clubs* Partick Thistle Supporter's; *Style—* Prof David Kerr; 7 Alder Rd, Mansewood, Glasgow (☎ 041 637 3110); Beatson Oncology Centre, Western Infirmary, Glasgow (☎ 041 339 8822)

KERR, Prof David Nicol Sharp; s of William Sharp Kerr (d 1972), and Elsie May Ransted (d 1989); *b* 27 Dec 1927; *Educ* George Watson's Boys Sch Edinburgh, Univ of Edinburgh (MB ChB), Univ of Wisconsin (MSc); *m* 2 July 1960, Mary Eleanor Jones, da of Capt John Roberts, of Plas Meilw, Plas Rd, Holyhead, Gwynedd; 2 s (Gordon b 1963, Ian b 1965), 1 da (Jane b 1961); *Career* RNVR Surgn Lt 1953-55, RNR Surgn Lt Cdr 1963; prof of med Univ of Newcastle upon Tyne 1968-83, dean Royal Postgraduate Med Sch 1984-, prof of renal med Univ of London 1986-; RCP: Goulstonian lectr 1968, Lumleian lectr 1983, censor 1982-84, sr censor 1990-91; formerly: pres Renal Assoc UK, conf pres Euro Renal Assoc, memb MRC Systems Bd; memb: Cncl Br Heart Fndn, Cncl Int Soc of Nephrology; FRCP 1968 (memb 1955), FRCPE 1967 (memb 1955); *Books* Short Textbook of Renal Disease (1968), Sections in med textbooks; *Recreations* fell walking, jogging; *Clubs* Athenaeum; *Style—* Prof David Kerr; 22 Carbery Ave, London W3 9AL (☎ 081 992 3231); 12 Brundholme Gardens, Keswick, Cumbria CA12 4NZ (☎ 07687 74382); Royal Postgraduate Med Sch, Du Cane Rd, London W12 ONN (☎ 081 740 3200, fax 081 740 3203)

KERR, Dr Graeme Douglas; s of Douglas Kirkland Kerr (d 1963), and Louie Ellen, *née* Stevens; *b* 1 Jan 1933; *Educ* Waitaki Public Sch, University of Otago (MB ChB); *m* 1960, Annette, da of George Denney; 1 s (Iain b 1966), 1 da (Jane b 1963); *Career* res fell Morrow Dept of Gastroenterology Royal Prince Alfred Hosp Sydney, Australia 1966; conslt gastroenterologist: Waikato Hosp 1967-71, Royal Shrewsbury Hosp 1972-; memb: Br Soc of Gastroenterology, Med Equestrian Soc, Aust Gastroenterological Soc, NZ Gastroenterological Soc; FRACP 1973, FRCP 1978; *Recreations* horse trials, scuba diving; *Clubs* BHS Horse Trials Gp, British Sub-aqua Gp; *Style—* Dr Graeme Kerr; Chaney Plough, Exfordsgreen, Longden, Shrewsbury SY5 8HH (☎ 074373 651); Royal Shrewsbury Hospital, Mytton Oak Rd, Shrewsbury, Shropshire SY3 8XZF (☎ 0743 231122 ext 3299)

KERR, Dr Ian Hamilton; s of Dr James Henry Kerr, of Balnastraid, Duthil, Carrbridge,ld, Inverness, and Margaret, *née* Hunter (d 1988); *b* 17 Aug 1927; *Educ* Oundle, Clare Coll Cambridge, Guy's Hosp Med Sch (MA, MB BChir, MRCP); *m* 3 May 1952, Esther Selkirk, da of Thomas Tyson (d 1961), of Urmston, Lancs; 2 s (Andrew b 1955, Mark b 1958); *Career* MO Flt Lt RAF Stafford 1953-55, instr in radiology Yale Univ Med Sch USA 1962-63; conslt radiologist: St Georges Hosp London 1963-72, Brompton Hosp London 1968-89; hon sr lectr Nat Heart and Lung Inst Univ of London 1968-88, conslt radiologist King Edward VII Hosp Midhurst 1969-90; hon med sec Br Inst of Radiology 1969-72 (memb Cncl 1968-73), vice pres RCR 1987-89 (memb editorial Bd 1976-83, examiner 1981-84, ed 1983-87); FRCP 1972, FFR 1962, FRCR 1975; *Books* Clinical Atlas of Respiratory Diseases (jtly, 1989); *Recreations* golf, bridge; *Clubs* Royal Air Force; *Style—* Dr Ian Kerr; Balnastraid, Duthil, Carrbridge, Inverness PH23 3ND (☎ 047984 321)

KERR, Jill; da of Eric David Kerr, MC, of Barn Cottage, Cryers Hill Lane, Widmer End, High Wycombe, Bucks, and Betty, *née* Knight; *b* 2 July 1949; *Educ* Univ of York (BA, MA); *Career* Dept MSS and Early Printed Books Trinity Coll Dublin 1971-72, Photo-Archives Courtauld Inst Univ of London 1973-75, Dean and Chapter Canterbury Cathedral (estab system for recording the restoration of the stained glass) 1975, Radcliffe Tst Scheme for the Crafts 1974-75, sec Corpus Vitrearum Medii Aevi GB (Br Acad) 1975-84, inspr Historic Bldgs and Monuments Cmmn for England (English Heritage) 1984-88, head Western Region Historic Bldgs Div English Heritage 1988-91, head SW Region (Cons) English Heritage 1991-; various contribs specialist lit; memb: Br Soc of Master Glass Painters 1969- (Cncl memb and hon jt ed of the soc's jl 1983-86), Br Archaeological Assoc 1972- (Cncl memb 1981-85), Assoc for Studies in the Conservation of Historic Bldgs 1984- (visits sec 1988-), Stained Glass Advsy Ctee Cncl for the Care of Churches of the C of E 1984-; hon sec to the tstees Ely Stained Glass Museum 1978-84; Freeman City of London 1984, Liveryman Worshipful Co of Glaziers Painters and Stainers of Glass; *Recreations* talking, travelling; *Style—* Miss Jill Kerr; Historic Buildings and Monuments Commission for England, Fortress House, 23 Savile Row, London W1X 2HE (☎ 071 973 3000, fax 071 973 3001)

KERR, Lord John Andrew Christopher; s of late Capt Andrew William Kerr, RN (gs of 7 Marquess of Lothian) and bro of 12 Marquess of Lothian; raised to the rank of a Marquess's son 1941; *b* 1927; *Educ* Ampleforth, Christ Church Oxford; *m* 1949, Isabel Marion, da of Sir Hugh Gurney, KCMG, MVO, and Mariota, da of Rt Hon Sir Lancelot Carnegie, GCVO, KCMG (d 1933); 3 s (William b 1950, David b 1952, Andrew b 1955), 2 da (Marion b 1960, Catherine b 1965); *Career* late Capt Scots Guards; chm Bloomsbury Book Auctions 1983- (formerly mangr book dept of Sotheby's); *Style—* The Lord John Kerr; Holly Bank, Wootton, Woodstock, Oxford

KERR, John Michael Bryan Leslie; s of James Leslie Kerr (d 1983), of Bedford, and Norah Kathleen Mary, *née* Walker (d 1974); *b* 28 Nov 1942; *Educ* Bedford Sch, Magdalen Coll Oxford (exhibitioner, BA); *m* 1963, Julia Laureen Barbara, da of F W P Thorne; 2 da (Madeleine b 1964, Alison b 1966); *Career* accountant Nat Coal Bd 1966-71 (admin trainee 1964-66); Ibstock Johnsen plc: mgmnt accountant 1971-75, fin dir Ibstock Building Products 1976-80, pres USA subsid 1981-82, corp devpt mangr 1983; md Sumit Equity Ventures 1985- (joined 1984); assoc Chartered Inst of Mgmnt Accountants 1974; *Recreations* theatre, road-running, reading; *Style—* John Kerr, Esq; Sumit Equity Ventures Limited, 12 Newhall Street, Birmingham B3 3ER (☎ 021 200 2244, fax 021 233 4628, car 0831 393148)

KERR, Sir John Olav; KCMG (1991, CMG 1987); s of Dr J D O Kerr (d 1987), and J

C Kerr; *b* 22 Feb 1942; *Educ* Glasgow Acad, Pembroke Coll Oxford; *m* 1965, Elizabeth Mary, da of Wilfrid George Kalaugher, of Newcastle; 2 s, 3 da; *Career* HM Dip Serv: joined 1966, served FO Moscow Rawalpindi and FCO, private sec to Permanent Under Sec FCO 1974-79, head DM1 Div HM Treasury 1979-81, princ private sec to Chancellor of the Exchequer 1981-84, head of Chancery Washington 1984-87, asst under sec of state FCO 1987-90, ambass and UK perm rep to EC 1990-; *Style—* Sir John Kerr, KCMG; c/o Foreign & Commonwealth Office, King Charles St, London SW1A

KERR, Rt Hon Sir John Robert; AK (1976, AC 1975), GCMG (1976, KCMG 1974, CMG 1966), GCVO (1977), PC (1977), QC (1953); s of Harry Kerr (d 1962), and Laura May, *née* Cardwell (d 1972), of Sydney; *b* 24 Sept 1914; *Educ* Fort St Boys' HS Sydney, Univ of Sydney (LLB); *m* 1, 1938, Alison (d 1974), da of Frederick Worstead, of Sydney; 1 s, 2 da; m 2, 1975, Anne Dorothy Robson, DStJ, da of late John Taggart; *Career* 2 AIF 1942-46 (Col); barr in practice 1938-66; first princ Aust Sch of Pacific Admin 1946-48, organising sec S Pacific Cmmn 1946-47; Federal Judge 1966-72, Chief Justice of NSW 1972-74, lt-govr NSW 1973-74, govr-gen Australia 1974-77; pres: NSW Bar Assoc 1964, Law Cncl of Australia 1964-66, Law Assoc for Asia and Western Pacific 1966-70; presided at Third Cwlth and Empire Law Conf Sydney 1965, hon life memb Law Soc of England and Wales 1965-, hon memb American Bar Assoc 1967-; KStJ 1974 *see Debretts Handbook of Australia and New Zealand*; *Clubs* Union (Sydney); *Style—* The Rt Hon Sir John Kerr, AK, GCMG, GCVO QC; Suite 2, 11th Floor, Norwich House, 6-10 O'Connell St, Sydney, NSW, 2000, Australia

KERR, Rt Hon Lord Justice; Rt Hon Sir Michael Robert Emanuel; PC (1981); s of Alfred Kerr; *b* 1 March 1921; *Educ* Aldenham, Clare Cambridge; *m* 1, 1952 (m dis 1982), Julia (actress, played Mrs Dale's da-in-law in Mrs Dale's Diary on BBC radio), da of Joseph Braddock; 2 s, 1 da; m 2, 1983, Diana Sneezum, yr da of H Neville Sneezum, of Gothic House, E Bergholt, Suffolk; 1 da; *Career* served WWII Fl-Lt RAF; barr 1948, QC 1961, dep chm Hants QS 1961-71, Lord Justice of Appeal 1981-, High Ct Judge (Queen's Bench) 1972-81, chm Law Commission 1978-81, Lord Justice of Appeal 1981-, first chm Supreme Ct Procedure Cncl 1982-; pres Chartered Inst of Arbitrators 1983-; pres Br German Tourists Assoc 1985-; memb cncl mgmnt Br Inst Int and Comparative Law 1973-, chm Lord-Chllr's Inter Deptl Ctee on EEC Judgements Convention 1974-, vice pres Br Maritime Law Assoc 1977-, memb Inst Advanced Legal Studies 1979-85; chm ctee mgmnt Centre Commercial Law Studies QMC 1980-; kt 1972; *Style—* The Rt Hon Lord Justice Kerr, PC; Royal Courts of Justice, Strand, London WC2A 2LL

KERR, Lord Ralph William Francis Joseph; s of 12 Marquess of Lothian, KCVO; *b* 7 Nov 1957; *Educ* Ampleforth; *m* 1, 1980 (m dis 1987), Lady Virginia Mary Elizabeth, *qv*, da of 11 Duke of Grafton, KG; m 2, 5 March 1988, Marie-Claire, yr da of Donald Black, MC, of Edenwood, Cupar, Fife; 2 s (John Walter Donald Peter b 8 Aug 1988, Frederic James Michael Ralph b 23 Oct 1989); *Career* political res, composer; currently estate mangr, songwriter, Sotheby's rep; *Recreations* playing the piano; *Style—* The Lord Ralph Kerr; 20 Upper Cheyne Row, London SW3 (☎ 071 352 7017); Melbourne Hall, Melbourne, Derby (☎ 0332 862163)

KERR, The Rt Rev Robert (Ray); *see*: Bradford, The Bishop of

KERR, Rose; da of William Antony Kerr, of The Old Vicarage, Almeley, Herefordshire, and Elizabeth, *née* Rendell; *b* 23 Feb 1953; *Educ* Convent of Sacred Heart Hammersmith, Belmont Abbey Hereford, SOAS Univ of London (BA), Languages Inst of Beijing; *m* Stephen Charles Lord; *Career* fell Percival David Fndn of Chinese Art 1976-78; V&A Far Eastern Dept: res asst 1978, asst keeper 1979, keeper 1987; memb: Exec Cncl GB - China Assoc 1989, Cncl Oriental Ceramic Soc, Br Assoc for Chinese Studies; *Books* Kiln Sherds of Ancient China (with P Hughes-Stanton, 1980), Guanyin A Masterpiece Revealed (with John Larson, 1985), Chinese Ceramics - (Porcelain of the Qing Dynasty) (1986), Later Chinese Bronzes (1990); *Recreations* walking, reading, gardening; *Style—* Ms Rose Kerr; Far Eastern Dept, Victoria & Albert Museum, London SW7 2RL (☎ 071 938 8263, fax 071 938 8341, tlx 268831 VICART G)

KERR, Thomas Henry; CB (1983); s of Albert Edward Kerr, of Westborough, Newark (d 1963); *b* 18 June 1924; *Educ* Magnus GS Newark, Univ Coll Univ of Durham (BSc); *m* 1946, Myrnie Evelyn Martin, da of Edward Hughes, of Newark, Notts (d 1965); *Career* Flt Lt, served Europe and Africa, pilot RAFVR 1942-53, Aero Flight RAE 1949-55, head Supersonic Flt Gp 1955-59, sci advsr to C-in-C Bomber Cmd High Wycombe 1960-64, head Assessment Div Weapons Dept RAE 1964-66, dep dir and dir Def Operational Analysis Estab 1966-70, head Weapons Res Gp Weapons Dept RAE 1970-74; dir: Nat Gas Turbine Establishment 1974-80, Royal Aircraft Establishment 1980-84, Hunting Engineering 1988- (tech dir 1986-88); R & D dir Royal Ordnance plc 1984-85; pres RAS; *Recreations* bridge, water-skiing, tennis, badminton; *Style—* Thomas Kerr, Esq, CB; Bundu, 13 Kingsley Ave, Camberley, Surrey GU15 2NA (☎ 0276 25961); Hunting Engineering, Ampthill, Bedford (☎ 0525 841000)

KERR, Lady Virginia Mary Elizabeth; *née* FitzRoy; da of 11 Duke of Grafton, KG; *b* 1954; *m* 1980 (m dis 1987), Lord Ralph Kerr, *qv*; *Style—* The Lady Virginia Kerr; c/o His Grace the Duke of Grafton, KG, Euston Hall, Thetford, Norfolk

KERR-DINEEN, Michael Norman Colin; s of Frederick George Kerr-Dineen (d 1988), and Hermione Iris, *née* Macdonald; *b* 14 July 1952; *Educ* Marlborough, Univ of Edinburgh (MA); *m* 1, 1976 (m dis 1981), Catharine, da of Alexander McCrindle; 1 s (Robert Crockford b 4 Oct 1979); m 2, 1988, Sally, da of Raymond Leonard; 1 s (Luke Giles b 26 Feb 1989); *Career* Economic Intelligence Dept Bank of England 1975-79, PA to chm and chief exec British National Oil Corporation 1979-81, exec Alastair Morton & Co 1981-82; md: Guinness Peat Group 1982-88, Cambridge International Partners NY 1988-89; chief-exec: Laing & Cruickshank Investment Management 1989-, Credit Lyonnais Laing 1990, Credit Lyonnais Securities 1990; Freeman City of London, memb Worshipful Co of Woolmen; *Recreations* horse racing, golf, skiing, opera; *Clubs* MCC, St Mellion; *Style—* Michael Kerr-Dineen, Esq; 67 Onslow Gardens, London SW7 (☎ 071 835 1452); Credit Lyonnais Securities, Broadwalk Hoause, 5 Appold Street, London EC2A 2DA (☎ 071 588 4000, fax 071 588 0290)

KERRIGAN, Gervase Niall William; s of William John Kerrigan (d 1983), of Louth, Lincs, and Eileen Josephine, *née* Martin; *b* 7 April 1939; *Educ* King Edward VI GS Louth, Caius Coll Cambridge (MA, MB BChir), St Bart's; *m* 20 Feb 1971, Angela Rosemary, da of Alan George Stuart Cobb, MBE (d 1972), of Maidstone, Kent; 1 s (Thomas b 1976), 2 da (Julia b 1972, Philippa b 1974); *Career* conslt physician W Suffolk 1976; FRCP 1982; *Recreations* beagling, reading, wine; *Clubs* Travellers'; *Style—* Gervase Kerrigan, Esq; The Old Manor, Dalham, Newmarket, Suffolk CB8 8TF (☎ 0638 500395)

KERRISON, Roger Edmund Fulke; yr s of Roger Fulke Kerrison, JP (d 1976), of Burgh Hall, Aylsham, Norfolk, and Cecil Scott, *née* Craft (d 1983); descended from Matthias Kerrison, of Seething, Norfolk, b 1650 (*see* Burke's Landed Gentry, 18 edn, vol II, 1969); *b* 21 Jan 1920; *Educ* Eton, Trinity Coll Cambridge; *m* 21 Sept 1942, (Edith) Anne Edmonstone, o da of Maj Lewis Aloysius Macdonald Hastings, MC, late RFA (d 1966); 1 s (Philip Roger Stephen b 18 Feb 1950, d 1978), 2 da ((Caroline) Felicity (Mrs Sandford Cox) b 19 Sept 1943, Theresa Mary (Mrs Marlborough Pryor) b 2 April 1948); *Career* served WWII as Lt Cdr RNVR (FAA) 1940-45; md A R Taylor & Co Ltd 1951-76, dir Olympia Ltd; Lloyd's Underwriting Name 1965-; farmer; Freeman City of Norwich; *Recreations* fishing, shooting; *Style—* Roger Kerrison, Esq; Sloley Lodge, nr Norwich, Norfolk (☎ 069 269 253)

KERRUISH, Sir (Henry) Charles; OBE (1964); *b* 23 July 1917; *Educ* Ramsey GS; *m* 1, 1944, Margaret Gell; 1 s, 3 da; m 2, 1975, Kay Warriner; *Career* farmer; speaker House of Keys 1962-90 (memb 1946-90), regnl cncllr Br Isles & Med Cwlth Parly Assoc 1975-77, pres Cwlth Parly Assoc (vice pres 1983), pres of Tynwald (and Legislative Cncl) 1990-; memb Ct Univ of Liverpool 1974-; Hon LLD Univ of Lancaster 1990; kt 1979; *Style—* Sir Charles Kerruish, OBE; Ballafayle, Maughold, IOM (☎ 0624 812293)

KERRY, Francis Robert; s of Francis Kerry (d 1935); *b* 24 Oct 1914; *Educ* Burton-on-Trent GS; *m* 1965, Zena Pamela, da of Ewart Illsley (d 1972); 6 children; *Career* pres Fine Art Developments plc and assoc cos, dir Mayflower Finance (Burton) Ltd; *Recreations* yachting; *Style—* Francis Kerry, Esq; Drakelow House, Burton-on-Trent, Staffs (☎ 0283 68106); Casa Drakelow, 60 Urbanizaciones, Playa Fotges, Muro, Mallorca

KERRY, 23 Knight of (first recorded use of title 1468; The Green Knight); Maj Sir George Peter Maurice FitzGerald; 5 Bt (UK 1880), of Valentia, Co Kerry, MC (1944); the title Knight of Kerry was conferred upon his son Maurice by John Fitz Thomas FitzGerald, Earl of Decies and Desmond, by virtue of his royal seigniory as a Count Palatine and his descendants have ever since been so styled in Acts of Parliament, patents under the Great Seal and other documents; the first baronet was 19 Knight of Kerry; 2, but only surviving, s of Capt 22 Knight of Kerry (Sir Arthur Henry Brinsley FitzGerald, 4 Bt, d 1967), and Mary, *née* Forester; *b* 27 Feb 1917; *Educ* Harrow, RMC Sandhurst; *m* 1939, Angela Dora, da of late Capt James Rankin Mitchell; 1 s, 1 da (Rosanna, m Count Richard Gurowski); *Heir* s, Adrian James Andrew Denis FitzGerald; *Career* 2 Lt Irish Gds cmmnd 1937, served Palestine 1938 (despatches), and Norway, N Africa, Italy 1939-45, Maj 1943, ret 1948; *Style—* Major the Knight of Kerry, Bt, MC; Colin's Farm House, 55 High Street, Durrington, Salisbury, Wilts SP4 8AQ (☎ 0980 52242)

KERRY, Sir Michael James; KCB (1982, CB 1976), QC (1984); s of Russell Kerry (d 1948), and Marjorie, *née* Kensington (d 1967); *b* 5 July 1923; *Educ* Rugby, St John's Coll Oxford (MA); *m* 1952, Sidney Rosetta Elizabeth, *née* Foster; 1 s, (Patrick b 1965), 2 da (Lucy, Frances); *Career* called to the Bar Lincoln's Inn 1949, joined BOT as legal asst 1951, slr DTI 1973-80 (princ asst slr 1972), HM procurator gen and treasy slr 1980-84, bencher Lincoln's Inn 1984, dep chm Lautro Ltd 1987; hon fell St John's Coll Oxford 1986; *Recreations* golf; *Style—* Sir Michael Kerry, KCB, QC; S Bedales, Lewes Rd, Haywards Heath, W Sussex (☎ 044 4831 303)

KERSEN, Mark; s of Harry Kersen (d 1967), and Ann Kersen (d 1985); *b* 23 Oct 1935; *Educ* Strodes GS Egham Surrey; *m* 8 Sept 1962, Ann Jeanette; 1 s (Timothy b 1969); *Career* Nat Serv 1958-59; copy boy Manchester Guardian 1952; journalist: Windsor, Slough and Eton Express 1952-56, Slough Express, Express & Star Wolverhampton 1959- (feature writer, dep news ed); ed: Shropshire Star 1970-72, Express & Star 1972 (dir 1973, gen mangr 1978, md 1981); dir and jt md Midland News Assoc; memb: Newspaper Panel, Monopolies Cmmn; pres W Midlands Newspaper Soc 1985; *Style—* Mark Kersen, Esq; Express & Star Ltd, 50-51 Queen St, Wolverhampton WV1 3BU (☎ 0902 313 131, fax 0902 772415, car tel 0860 837973, telex 335490)

KERSH, Cyril; s of Hyman Kersh (d 1929), of London, and Leah, *née* Miller (d 1962); *b* 24 Feb 1925; *Educ* Westcliff HS; *m* 25 June 1956, Suzanne; *Career* RN 1943-47; reporter then news and features ed The People 1943-54, features ed Illustrated 1954-59, features staff London Evening Standard 1959-60; ed: Men Only 1960-63, Reveille 1976-79; asst ed then managing ed Sunday Mirror 1979-85 (ed then sr features exec 1963-76); Duke of Redonda 1960; *Books* The Aggravations of Minnie Ashe (1970), The Diabolical Liberties of Uncle May (1973), The Soho Summer of Mr Green (1974), The Shepherd's Bush Connection (1975), Minnie Ashe at War (1979), A Few Gross Words (1990); *Recreations* walking, reading, talking; *Clubs* Our Society; *Style—* Cyril Kersh, Esq

KERSHAW, Sir (John) Anthony; MC (1943), DL; s of Judge John Felix Kershaw (d 1927); *b* 14 Dec 1915; *Educ* Eton, Balliol Coll Oxford (BA); *m* 1939, Barbara, da of Harry Mitton Crookenden (d 1953); 2 s, 2 da; *Career* WWII: 16/5 Lancers, Reserve Forces 1946-56, CO Royal Gloucs Hussars 1953-56, (C) psc; barr 1939; City of Westminster cnllr 1946-49, cnllr LCC 1948-51, MP (C) Stroud 1955-87, Parly sec Miny of Public Building and Works 1970, Parly under sec of state FCO 1970-73, Parly under sec of State for Def (RAF) 1973-74, chm House of Commons Select Ctee on Foreign Affrs 1979-87, vice chm British Cncl 1975-87; kt 1981; *Recreations* field sports; *Clubs* White's; *Style—* Sir Anthony Kershaw, MC, DL; West Barn, Didmarton, Badminton, Glos GL9 1DT (☎ 045 423 630)

KERSHAW, Cissie, Baroness; Cissie Burness; da of Charles E Smyth, of Friern Barnet; *m* 1933, 2 Baron Kershaw (d 1961); *Style—* The Rt Hon Cissie, Lady Kershaw; 45 Glamis Rd, Newquay, Cornwall

KERSHAW, David Robert; s of Noel Ernest Kershaw, TD, and Dorothy Anne, *née* Cheyne, b 1953; *Educ* Urmston GS, Trinity Coll Cambridge (MA); *m* 1978, Christine Anne, da of late John Spear Sexton; 3 s (Oliver James b 1979, Toby Thomas b 1984, Charles Henry Alexander b 1986), 1 da (Isabelle Alice Katharine b 1989); *Career* admitted slr 1978; specialist in corporate fin, mergers and acquisitions and banking; ptnr Ashurst Morris Crisp 1986-; *Recreations* classical guitar, windsurfing, tennis, literature; *Style—* David Kershaw, Esq; Ashurst Morris Crisp, Broadwalk House, 5 Appold St, London EC2A 2HA (☎ 071 638 1111, fax 071 972 7990)

KERSHAW, Hon Donald Arthur; JP (Richmond Upon Thames); s of 1 Baron Kershaw, OBE (d 1961); *b* 1915; *m* 1942, Barbara Edith, da of Lt-Col Cecil Graham Ford (d 1945), of Richmond, Surrey (d 1986); 2 s (Ian, Mark); *Career* RAF 1940-45; admitted slr 1939; *Style—* The Hon Donald Kershaw, JP; 32 Hans Rd, London SW3 (☎ 071 581 2627)

KERSHAW, His Hon Judge Henry Aidan; s of Rev Henry Kershaw (d 1970), and Hilda Shaw, *née* Brooker-Carey; *b* 11 May 1927; *Educ* St John's Leatherhead, Brasenose Coll Oxford (BA); *m* 31 March 1960, Daphne Patricia, wid of Dr C R Cowan, da of George Egerton Howlett (d 1960); 2 s (Michael b 1961, Nicholas b 1963), 2 step s (Charles b 1951, Richard b 1956); *Career* RN 1946-48; called to the Bar Inner Temple 1953, practised Northern Circuit 1953-76; asst rec Oldham Quarter Sessions 1970-71, rec Crown Ct 1972-76, circuit judge 1976; cncllr Bolton Co Borough Cncl 1954-57, dep chm Agric Land Tbnl 1972-76, chm (later vice pres) Lancs Sch Golf Assoc 1981, vice pres Eng Sch Golf Assoc, exec memb Lancs Union of Golf Clubs 1985-89; *Recreations* golf, skiing, oil painting, music; *Clubs* Royal and Ancient Golf (St Andrews), Bolton Golf (Capt 1983-84), West Hill Golf; *Style—* His Hon Judge Kershaw; Broadhaven, 54 St Andrew's Rd, Lostock, Bolton (☎ 0204 47088)

KERSHAW, Joseph Anthony; s of Joseph Henry Kershaw, of Preston; *b* 26 Nov 1935; *Educ* Ushaw Coll Univ of Durham, Preston Catholic Coll SJ; *m* 1959, Ann, da of John Whittle (d 1964), of Preston; 3 s, 2 da; *Career* short serv cmmn RAOC, Lt; Unilever Ltd 1958-67, gp mktg mangr Co-Op Wholesale Soc (CWS) 1967-69; md:

Underline Ltd 1969-71, Merchant Div Reed International Ltd 1971-73; head of mktg (non-foods) CWS 1973-75, first dir Nat Consumer Cncl 1975, ind mgmnt conslt 1975-; assoc dir Foote Cone & Belding Ltd 1979-84; dir: John Stork & Partners Ltd 1980-84, Allia (UK) Ltd 1984; chm: Antonian Investment Ltd 1985-87, Organised Business Data Ltd 1987-89; memb CPRE; *Recreations* fishing, shooting, cooking, balloon pilot; *Style*— Joseph Kershaw, Esq; Westmead, Meins Rd, Blackburn, Lancs BB2 6QF (☎ 0254 55915)

KERSHAW, Katharine, Baroness; Katharine Dorothea; da of Charles H Staines, of Clapham; *m* 1935, 3 Baron Kershaw (d 1962); 1 s (4 Baron), 1 da (Mrs David Pickett b 1943); *Style*— The Rt Hon Katharine, Lady Kershaw; 2 Coombe Court, 84b Worcester Rd, Sutton, Surrey SM2 6QH

KERSHAW, His Hon Judge (Philip) Michael; QC (1980); s of His Honour Philip Charles Stones Kershaw (d 1986), and Michaela, *née* Raffael; *b* 23 April 1941; *Educ* Ampleforth, St John's Coll Oxford (BA, MA); *m* 30 Dec 1980, Anne; 1 s (Francis Edward b 23 Aug 1984); *Career* called to the Bar Gray's Inn 1963, rec 1980, circuit judge Northern Circuit 1990-; ACIArb; *Style*— His Hon Judge Michael Kershaw, QC; The Crown Court, Crown Square, Manchester

KERSHAW, Hon Peter John; s of 1 Baron Kershaw, OBE (d 1961); *b* 19 July 1924; *Educ* Queen Elizabeth's GS Barnet, King's Coll London (BSc); *m* 1948, Brenda Margaret, da of James Austin Smith (d 1966), of Brighton; 1 s (Michael b 1951); *Career* Sub Lt RNVR 1945-46; chartered civil engr; dir and chief engr of Sir Robert McAlpine & Sons Ltd 1977- (ret 1987); FEng, FICE; *Style*— The Hon Peter Kershaw; 22 Orchard Rise, Richmond, Surrey TW10 5BX (☎ 081 876 2660)

KERSHAW, Richard Ruegg; s of Raymond Newton Kershaw, CMG, MC (d 1981), of Warren Row, Berks, and Hilda Mary, *née* Ruegg (d 1989); *b* 16 April 1934; *Educ* Cheltenham, Clare Coll Cambridge, Univ of Virginia Grad Sch; *m* 22 April 1962 (m dis 1967), Venetia, da of Basil Murray (d 1938); 1 da (Sophy Charlotte b 1963), 1 step s (Rupert Sylvester b 1959); *Career* Nat Serv 2 Lt RA 1952-54, served BAOR; asst princ Cwlth Rels Office 1958-59, features writer Financial Times 1959-60, dip corr The Scotsman 1960-63, ed Africa Confidential 1963-68, memb BBC Panorama reporting team 1965-75; presenter: Newsday then Newsweek BBC 1975-80, World Tonight BBC 1980-, Nationwide BBC 1980-83, Business Programme Channel Four 1988-89; pres Dip and Cwlth Writers Assoc 1965-67; memb cncl: Overseas Devpt Inst 1975-, Minority Rights Gp 1975-, Cheltenham Coll 1977-, RGS 1979-82; first Eisenhower fell from UK to USA 1963; FRGS 1978; *Recreations* cricket, skiing; *Clubs* Brooks's, Beefsteak, MCC, Hurlingham; *Style*— Richard Kershaw, Esq; 82 Prince of Wales Mansions, Prince of Wales Drive, London SW11 4BL (☎ 071 622 3453)

KERSHAW, (John) Stephen; s of Raymond Newton Kershaw, CMG, MC (d 1981), and Hilda Mary (d 1989); *b* 21 Dec 1931; *Educ* Cheltenham, New Coll Oxford; *Career* investmt mgmnt, incl in developing countries of Br Cwlth; former dir: Bandanga Tea Plantations Ltd, Henckell du Buisson & Co Ltd, Plantation Tst Co plc; author of various articles in investment jls and newspapers; fndr memb Stock Exchange Sailing Assoc 1961; memb: Bow Group 1961-76 (memb Corp Taxation Res Gp 1967-69, memb Overseas Devpt Res Gp 1974-76), Cons Cwlth and Overseas Cncl 1972-76; *Publications* Referendum (jtly, 1975); *Recreations* travel, reading, vintage cars; *Clubs* Oriental; *Style*— Stephen Kershaw, Esq; 139 Pavilion Rd, London SW1X 0BL; Puerto Sotogrande, Spain

KERSHAW, Walter; s of Walter Kershaw, of Ashford, Middx, and Florence, *née* Ward; *b* 7 Dec 1940; *Educ* De La Salle Coll Salford, Univ of Durham (BA); *Career* war artist Kings Regt NI 1976; artist and pioneer large external mural painting; UK work: Manchester Trafford Park, Sci Museum, Manchester United FC, CEGB, Univ of Salford 1979-89, Br Aerospace and Granada TV 1984-88, Wensum Lodge Norwich 1985; work abroad: Brazil, São Paulo and Recife 1983-88; works exhibited: V and A, Tate Gallery, Nat Portrait Gallery, Gulbenkian Fndn and Arts Cncl Berlin and Brazil; in conversation BBC Radio Four with Sue MacGregor 1984; *Recreations* travel, cricket, photography; *Clubs* Littleborough Cricket; *Style*— Walter Kershaw, Esq; Studio, Todmorden Rd, Littleborough, Lancashire OL15 9EG (☎ 0706 79653)

KERSLAKE, Dennis David; s of Denis Henry Kerslake, and Doreen Mary, *née* Carl; *b* 30 June 1957; *Educ* Whitgift Sch S Croydon, Univ of Exeter (BA, hockey blue), represented Eng Univs Cricket and Surrey Young Cricketers); *m* 13 Aug 1983, Jacqueline Ann, da of Brian Anthony Murphy; 1 s (Benjamin Thomas b 17 June 1989); *Career* asst product mangr Beecham Group 1980 (graduate mktg trainee 1979), account mangr International Marketing and Promotions 1982 (account exec 1981), brand mangr Courage Ltd 1984, dir Purchasepoint Group 1986 (account dir 1985), md LGM 1989 (dir 1987); hockey player Full Surrey Hockey XI; *Awards* winner Annual Int Sledge Race Bormio 2000 Italy 1989; *Recreations* music, theatre, wine, travel; *Clubs* Purley Hockey, Poisoned Dwarfs, Soho Strollers; *Style*— Dennis Kerslake, Esq; LGM Marketing Services Ltd, 16 Bedford Square, London WC1B 3JA (☎ 071 631 4544, fax 071 323 1169)

KERSLEY, Dr Jonathan Bernard; s of Edward Kersley (d 1976), of London, and Hilda, *née* Stone; *b* 4 March 1942; *Educ* Christ's Coll Finchley London, St Bartholomew's Hosp Med Coll Univ of London (MB BS), FRCS (Eng), DObstRCOG); *m* 13 April 1969, Susan Esther, da of Prof William W Mushin, CBE, of Cardiff; 1 s (Benjamin Alexander b 8 Aug 1973), 2 da (Deborah Anne b 26 March 1971, Sarah Rebecca b 16 Dec 1976); *Career* sr house offr Luton and Dunstable Hosp 1971-72, registrar in surgery St Bartholomew's Hosp 1973 (house surgn to professorial surgical unit 1967 and thoracic unit 1968), registrar in surgery Portsmouth Hosp 1972-74 (house physician 1967), sr orthopaedic registrar Addenbrookes Hosp Cambridge 1974-78, conslt orthopaedic surgn E Birmingham Hosp 1978-; memb: Int Arthroscopy Assoc, Euro Soc for Surgery of the Knee; Br Assoc for Surgery of the Knee, fell Br Orthopaedic Assoc; FRCS, memb BMA; *Recreations* gardening, aviculture; *Style*— Dr Jonathan B Kersley; Treverven, 41 Moor Green Lane, Moseley, Birmingham B13 8NE (☎ 021 449 1707); East Birmingham Hospital, Bordesley Green East, Birmingham B9 5ST (☎ 021 766 6611)

KERTESZ, Lady Gillian Moyra Katherine; *née* Cecil; da of 6 Marquess of Exeter, KCMG (d 1981), and his 1 w, Lady Mary, *née* Montagu Douglas Scott (d 1984), da of 7 Duke of Buccleuch; *b* 8 March 1935; *m* 1, 23 Nov 1954 (m dis 1978), Sir Giles Henry Charles Floyd, 7 Bt; 2 s (David, Henry); *m* 2, 24 April 1979, George Michael Kertesz, s of Zoltan Kertesz (d 1975), of Budapest and Nagyvard; *Career* Coronation Medal 1953; *Style*— The Lady Gillian Kertesz; 57 Peel St, London W8 7PA (☎ 071 727 5898); Holly House, Northchapel, nr Petworth, W Sussex (☎ 042 878 580)

KESSELER, Dr Michael Edward; s of Sydney Joseph Kesseler (d 1989), and Edith Maud, *née* Smith (d 1978); *b* 18 Dec 1946; *Educ* King Edward's Sch Five Ways Birmingham, Univ of Birmingham (MB ChB); *m* 15 April 1978, Gale, da of Clifford Narbett, of Snitterfield, Warwickshire; *Career* sr registrar in dermatology Royal S Hants Hosp 1978-83, conslt dermatologist Rotherham Dist Gen Hosp and hon lectr in dermatology Univ of Sheffield 1983-; memb exec ctee Rotherham BMA; MRCP 1978, FRCP 1989, FRSM; *Recreations* walking, wine, theatre; *Style*— Dr Michael Kesseler; The Beeches, Doncaster Rd, Thrybergh, Rotherham S65 4NU (☎ 0709 850307); Rotherham District General Hospital, Moorgate Rd, Oakwood, Rotherham, S Yorks S60 2UD (☎ 0709 820000)

KESSLER, George Bernard; s of William Kessler, of London, and Joanna, *née* Rubner; *b* 17 Aug 1953; *Educ* City of London Sch, Univ of Nottingham (BSc); *m* 25 Oct 1986, Deborah Susan, da of Beni Baltfried Jaffe, of London; 2 da (Madeleine b 1987, Flora b 1988); *Career* conslt Logica 1976-77, prodn dir Kesslers International 1984-87, operations dir Kesslers Group 1987-, md Kesslers Manufacturing 1989-; memb: Bd London East TEC, Newham Compact Employers Mgmnt Gp; jt chm Newham Compact Steering Ctee, chair London East TEC Educn Advsy Gp, dir Newham Educn Employer Ptnrship, chair of govrs Newham Community Coll; *Recreations* contemporary art, reading, theatre; *Clubs* Savile; *Style*— George Kessler, Esq; 22 Tanza Rd, Hampstead, London NW3 2UB; Kesslers International Ltd, 1 Warton Rd, Stratford, London E15 2NF (☎ 081 534 0106, fax 081 519 6695, telex 897731)

KESTELMAN, Morris; s of Joseph Kestelman (d 1973), of Chicago, and Sarah, *née* Platz (d 1977); *b* 5 Oct 1905; *Educ* Central Fndn Boys Sch, Central Sch of Art and Craft, RCA; *m* 1935, Dorothy Mary, da of Capt James Creagh; 1 da (Sara b 1944); *Style*— Morris Kestelman, Esq; 74b Belsize Park Gardens, London NW3 4NG (☎ 071 722 0569); Boundary Gallery, 98 Boundary Rd, London NW8 0RH

KESTER, Ralph Charles; s of John David Kester, of Toronto, Canada, and Christine Petronella, *née* Miller; *b* 16 Feb 1938; *Educ* Univ of Cape Town (MB ChM); *m* 19 Sept 1964, Ilse Helga, da of John Phillip Meyer (d 1969), of Knysna, Cape Province, SA; 1 s (Bruce b 1967), 1 da (Anthea b 1966); *Career* sr surgical registrar Dundee Teaching Hosps 1970-74, sr Fulbright travel scholar and res fell Univ of California San Diego 1971-72, sr surgical lectr Univ of Leeds 1974-80, hon surgn St James's Univ Hosp Leeds, Hunter prof of surgery 1982, Arris and Gale lectr RCS 1984, currently conslt gen and vascular surgn St James' Univ Hosp Leeds; hon surgn to Yorkshire Rugby Union; memb: Surgical Res Soc, Vascular Surgical Soc of GB and I, Assoc of Surgns of GB and I; FRCS 1965; *Books* A Practice of Vascular Surgery (1981); *Recreations* rugby union football; *Style*— Ralph Kester, Esq; Dept of Surgery, St James's University Hospital, Beckett St, Leeds, West Yorks LS9 7TF (☎ 0532 433144)

KESTEVEN, Dr Patrick James Layton; s of Dr Geoffrey Layton Kesteven, and Mona, *née* Scott; *b* 7 Nov 1949; *Educ* Geelong GS, Univ of Sydney (MB BS), Univ of London (PhD); *m* 4 Dec 1971, Maureen Anne, da of Patrick Maloney; *Career* conslt haematologist Freeman Hosp, clinical lectr Newcastle Univ Med Sch 1986-, med dir Haemocell plc 1988-; FRACP 1980, FRCPA 1984, assoc memb RCP, memb BMA; *Style*— Dr Patrick Kesteven; Dept of Haematology, Freeman Hospital, Freeman Rd, High Heaton, Newcastle upon Tyne NE7 7DN (☎ 091 284 3111 ext 3271, fax 091 213 1968)

KESWICK, Hon Mrs (Annabel Térèse); *née* Fraser; yr da of 15 Lord Lovat; *b* 15 Oct 1942; *m* 1, 1964 (m dis 1978), 14 Lord Reay; 2 s, 1 da; m 2, 1985, Henry Neville Lindley Keswick, eld s of Sir William Johnston Keswick (d 1990); *Style*— The Hon Mrs Keswick; 28 Arlington House, Arlington St, London SW1

KESWICK, (John) Chippendale Lindley; s of Sir William Johnston Keswick (d 1990), and Mary, *née* Lindley; *b* 2 Feb 1940; *Educ* Eton, Univ of Aix Marseilles; *m* 1966, Lady Sarah Ramsay *qv*, da of 16 Earl of Dalhousie, KT, GCVO, GBE, MC, *qv*; 3 s (David b 1967, Tobias b 1968, Adam b 1973); *Career* ahm Hambros Bank Ltd; jt dep chm Hambros plc 1990; dir: Persimmon plc 1984, Hunters & Frankau Group Ltd 1986-, Charter Consolidated plc 1988-; memb Cncl Cancer Res Campaign 1978-; hon treas Children's Co Holidays Fund; memb Royal Co of Archers; *Recreations* bridge, field sports; *Clubs* White's, Portland (chm); *Style*— Chippendale Keswick, Esq; c/o Hambros Bank Ltd, 41 Tower Hill, London EC3N 4HA (☎ 071 480 5000, telex 883851, fax 071 702 4424)

KESWICK, Lady; (Celia) Clare Mary Alice; da of Gervase Elwes (d 1921), and Lady Winifride, *née* Feilding (d 1959), 4 da of 8 Earl of Denbigh and Desmond; *b* 13 Jan 1905; *m* 1940, Sir John Keswick, KCMG (d 1982), sometime chm and dir Jardine Matheson & Co; 1 da; *Style*— Lady Keswick; Portrack House, Holywood, Dumfries (☎ 0387 276); Flat 5, 56 Holland Park, London W11 3RS

KESWICK, Henry Neville Lindley; s of Sir William Johnston Keswick (d 1990), and Mary, *née* Lindley; *b* 29 Sept 1938; *Educ* Eton, Trinity Coll Cambridge (BA); *m* 1985, Annabel Térèse (Tessa), da of 15 Lord Lovat, *qv*; *Career* Nat Serv cmmn Scots Guards 1956-58; dir Jardine Matheson & Co Ltd 1967 (chm 1972-75); dir: Sun Alliance & London Insurance 1975-, Robert Fleming Hldgs; chm: Matheson & Co Ltd 1975-, Jardine Matheson Hldgs Ltd, Jardine Strategic Hldgs Ltd, Hong Kong Assoc; dir: Mandarin Oriental Ltd, Dairy Farm Int Ltd, Rothmans Int plc, Hongkong & Shanghai Banking Corpn (London Ctee), United Racecourses; *Recreations* country pursuits; *Clubs* White's, Turf, Third Guards; *Style*— Henry Keswick, Esq; Matheson & Co Ltd, 3 Lombard St, London EC3V 9AQ (☎ 071 528 4000, fax 071 623 5024)

KESWICK, Lady Sarah; *née* Ramsay; da of 16 Earl of Dalhousie, KT, GCVO, GBE, MC; *b* 1945; *m* 1966, Chippendale Keswick, *qv*; 3 children; *Style*— The Lady Sarah Keswick; 1a Ilchester Place, London W14 (☎ 071 603 2873); Auchendolly House, Old Bridge of Urr, Castle Douglas, Kirkcudbrightshire (☎ 055 665 265)

KESWICK, Simon; s of Sir William Johnston Keswick (d 1990), and Mary, *née* Lindley; the firm of Jardine Matheson was founded in 1832 by William Jardine and James Matheson; the Keswicks of Dumfries married into the Jardine family in the mid-nineteenth century; *Educ* Eton, Trinity Coll Cambridge; *Career* dir Jardine Matheson (chm 1983-89); *Style*— Simon Keswick, Esq; Jardine Matheson & Co, 3 Lombard St, London EC3

KETT, George Anthony; s of George Robert Kett, and Lilian Hester, *née* Groves (d 1987); *b* 15 Feb 1943; *Educ* Christ's Coll Blackheath; *m* 23 May 1970, Margaret Anne; 1 s (Nicholas George b 1 June 1973), 1 da (Georgina Anne b 14 Sept 1978); *Career* subst underwriter of Red Star Policies Lloyd's 1960-65, underwriter of Corinthian Motor Policies Lloyd's 1977 (dep underwriter 1965-77); dep chm Rose Thomson Young Ltd 1990 (dir 1982); govr Christ's Coll Blackheath; *Recreations* golf, gardening, reading; *Style*— George Kett, Esq

KETT-WHITE, John Roderick; s of Sqdn-Ldr Cyril Thomas (Jack) White, MBE (d 1953), of Exeter and Singapore, and Frances Ada, *née* Lean (later Mrs Johnny Johnson d 1979); *b* 2 Jan 1938; *Educ* privately, at public and state GS, Guy's Med and Dental Sch Univ of London; *m* 16 May 1964, Elizabeth Anne, da of Frederick Sidney Kett (d 1981), of Weycroft Manor, Axminster, Devon; 2 s (Charles Rupert b 1966, Tho b 1967), 1 da (Anna Sophia b 1965); *Career* landowner; dental surgn Wilton Place SW1 1962-64, sr house offr Bristol Dental Hosp 1969; gen practice 1964-: Devon, Somerset, Avon; dist cncllr Wansdyke 1981-, ldr and chm Policy and Resource Ctee Wansdyke Cncl 1987-89; former memb Bristol Health Authy, chm Bathavon Div N Somerset Cons Assoc; author of various papers incl: Management of Change of Local Government, A New Way of Treating the Patient, Wansdyke Experience, Origin of a New Species; *Recreations* the arts, the countryside; *Clubs* Bath Clinical Soc; *Style*— John Kett-White, Esq; Iford Park, Hinton Charterhouse, Nr Bath (☎ 0225 72 32 28); Wansdyke Cncl, The Hollies, Midsomer Norton, Bath (☎ 0761 417785)

KETTELEY, John Henry Beevor; s of John Joseph Beevor Ketteley (d 1975), and Violet, *née* Robinson; *b* 9 Aug 1939; *Educ* Brentwood Sch Essex, Hackley Sch Tarrytown NY USA; *m* 15 April 1967, Susan Elizabeth, da of Robert Charles Jay

Gordon, of Great Wakering, Essex; 2 s (Stephen b 13 Nov 1973, Thomas b 20 Aug 1985), 2 da (Sara b 11 July 1969, Alexandra b 15 Nov 1970); *Career* exec dir S G Warburg & Co Ltd 1972-81, non-exec dir (dep chm) BTP plc 1978-, md Rea Bros plc 1981-83, exec dir Barclays De Zoete Wedd Ltd 1983-87; non-exec dir: Fairholt plc 1987-89, Boosey & Hawkes plc 1987-; Freeman City of London 1978, Liveryman Worshipful Co of CAs 1978; FCA 1970; *Recreations* sailing, golf, tennis, squash; *Clubs* Royal Burnham YC, Royal Corinthian YC; *Style*— John Ketteley, Esq; Keeway, Ferry Rd, Creeksea, Burnham on Crouch, Essex CMO 8PL (☎ 0621 783748, fax 0621 784966, car 0860 252941); Clos Beausoleil, Quartier Garigouille, 30670 Aigues Vives, France

KETTLE, Martin James; *b* 7 Sept 1949; *Educ* Leeds Modern Sch, Balliol Coll Oxford; *m* Alison Hannah; 2 s; *Career* journalist and writer; ed Guardian Europe; *Books* Policing the Police (with Peter Hain 1980), Uprising (with Lucy Hodges 1982); *Style*— Martin Kettle, Esq; 29 East Bank, London N16 5QS (☎ 081 802 8484); The Guardian, 119 Farringdon Rd, London EC1R 3ER (☎ 071 278 2332)

KETTLEWELL, Cmdt Dame Marion Mildred; DBE (1970, CBE 1964); da of George Wildman Kettlewell, and Mildred Frances, *née* Atkinson; *b* 20 Feb 1914; *Educ* Godolphin Sch Salisbury, St Christopher's Coll Blackheath; *Career* worked for Fellowship of Maple Leaf Alta Canada 1935-38, worked for local cncl 1939-41; joined WRNS 1941, cmnd as Third Offr 1942, Supt WRNS on staff of Flag Offr Air 1961-64, Supt Trg and Drafting 1964-67, dir WRNS 1967-70, gen sec GFS 1971-78, pres Assoc of Wrens 1981-; *Recreations* needlework, walking, ornithology; *Style*— Cmdt Dame Marion Kettlewell, DBE; Flat 2, 9 John Islip St, London SW1P 4PU

KETTLEWELL, Capt Nigel Ion Charles; JP (Salisbury 1989); s of Cdr Charles Robert Kettlewell (d 1963); *b* 19 March 1934; *Educ* Allhallows Sch, RNC Dartmouth; *m* 1964, Lady Serena Jane, *qv*, *née* Dundas, da of 3 Marquess of Zetland (d 1989); 1 s (Robert James b 1965), 2 da (Melissa Jane b 1968, Charlotte Rose b 1970); *Career* qualified in Signals 1960, served HM Yacht Britannia 1957-58 and 1963-64, Staff Coll 1965, in command HM Ships Rhyl 1974-75, Brighton 1975-76, MOD 1976-86, Capt RN 1979, chief naval signal offr 1983-86, ADC to HM The Queen 1986-88, Cdre Cmdg HMS Drake 1986-88; ret 1988; yr bro of Trinity House 1978, companion IERE 1986; co cncllr Wiltshire 1989; *Recreations* gardening, industrial archaeology; *Clubs* Naval and Military; *Style*— Capt Nigel Kettlewell, JP, RN; The Old Rectory, Newton Toney, Salisbury, Wilts (☎ 098 064 311)

KETTLEWELL, Lady Serena Jane; *née* Dundas; o da of 3 Marquess of Zetland, ED, DL (d 1989); *b* 10 Sept 1940; *m* 1964, Capt Nigel Ion Charles Kettlewell, RN, *qv*; 1 s, 2 da; *Style*— The Lady Serena Kettlewell; The Old Rectory, Newton Toney, Salisbury, Wilts (☎ 098 064 311)

KEULS, Peter Hans; s of Cdr Hans Agathus Keuls (d 1985), of Hursterpoint, Sussex, and Pauline Mary, *née* MacGuire; *b* 24 May 1952; *Educ* Worth Sch Turners Hill Sussex; *m* 12 May 1979, Caroline Arabella Margaret, da of Dr Anthony Barket, of Sandford, Devon; 2 da (Clair Anthonia b 12 Jan 1983, Hannah Alexandra b 30 July 1985); *Career* admitted slr 1977; ptnr: Hamlins Grammar & Hamlin 1982-87, Trower Still & Keeling 1986-87 (articled clerk 1973-77), Trowers & Hamlin 1987-; seminar speaker on assured tenancies and related matters to local govt gp Law Soc and SW Housing Gp Trg Scheme; memb Law Soc; *Recreations* drawing, painting, cycling, classic cars; *Style*— Peter Keuls, Esq; 8 Southernham West, Exeter, Devon EX1 1JG (☎ 0392 217466, fax 0392 221047)

KEVILL-DAVIES, Christopher Evelyn (Kit); CBE (1973); s of William A S H Kevill-Davies, JP (ka 1915), of Croft Castle, Hereford, and Dorothy Mortlock, *née* Lacon (d 1965); *b* 12 July 1913; *Educ* Radley; *m* 23 June 1938, Virginia Louisa, da of Adm Ronald Arthur Hopwood, CB (d 1949), of 7 Sloane Gardens, London SW1; 1 s (Rev Christopher Charles b 1944), 1 da (Anne Margaret (Mrs Bartholomew) b 1939); *Career* served WWII Suffolk Yeo 1939-43 and Grenadier Gds 1943-45 in France, Belgium and Germany, Capt; memb Gt Yarmouth Borough Cncl 1946-53; chm Norfolk Mental Deficiency HMC 1950-69, vice chm E Anglian Regnl Health Authy 1974-82, chm E Lacon & Co (brewers) Gt Yarmouth 1963-75 (dir 1936, vice chm 1946), memb Gen Cncl King Edward Hosp Fund for London 1972; JP 1954-82, High Sheriff of Norfolk 1965, DL (Norfolk 1974-82); Liveryman Worshipful Co of Fishmongers 1967; *Clubs* Cavalry and Guards', RAC, Norfolk; *Style*— Christopher Kevill-Davies, CBE; 11 Hale House, 34 de Vere Gardens, London W8 5AQ (☎ 071 937 5066)

KEVILLE, Sir (William) Errington; CBE (1947); s of William Edwin Keville (d 1941); *b* 3 Jan 1901; *Educ* Merchant Taylors'; *m* 1928, Ailsa Sherwood McMillan; 3 s, 2 da; *Career* memb Cncl Chamber of Shipping 1940- (vice pres 1960, pres 1961); memb: Bd Port of London Authority 1943-59, Ctee Lloyds Register of Shipping 1957-68; dir: Shaw Savill & Albion Co Ltd 1941-68 (former dep chm), Furness Withy & Co Ltd 1950-68 (chm 1962-68); chm: Gen Cncl of Br Shipping 1961, Int Chamber of Shipping 1963-68, Ctee of European Shipowners 1963-65, Ctee of European Nat Shipowners' Assocs 1963-65; dir Nat Bank of NZ 1946-75; kt 1962; *Recreations* walking, gardening; *Style*— Sir Errington Keville, CBE; c/o Bunts End, Leigh, Surrey RH2 8NS

KEY, Anthony Henry Lawrence (Tony); s of Harry Joseph Lawrence Key (d 1987), of Worthing, Sussex, and Lillian Coke (d 1982); *b* 22 June 1936; *Educ* Stanley Tech Coll, Croydon Poly; *m* 1958, Josephine Ann, da of Edward J Becket; 3 da (Joanne b 1963, Bridget b 1965, Belinda b 1973); *Career* qualified mech engr; designer: in precision engrg of teleprinters and fax machines, of domestic appliances Morphy Richards; designer and engr Seiscom geophysical exploration, industl offr Design Council until 1984, design mangr British Airports 1984-87, corp head of design British Telecom 1987-; award for design mgmnt 1990, Engr of the Year Inst of Engrg Designers 1976; Freeman City of London 1984; FRCA, MIED, FCSD; *Recreations* game fishing, golf; *Style*— Tony Key, Esq; British Telecommunications plc, 81 Newgate St, London EC1A 7AJ (☎ 071 356 5397, fax 071 356 6227)

KEY, Brian Michael; MEP (Lab) S Yorks 1979-; s of Leslie Granville Key, and Nora Alice, *née* Haylett; *b* 1947,Sept; *Educ* Darfield Primary Sch, Wath upon Dearne GS, Liverpool Univ (BA); *Career* offr W Riding County Cncl 1970-73, sr admin offr S Yorks County Cncl 1973-79; MEP 1979; *Style*— Brian Key, Esq, MEP; 25 Cliff Road, Darfield, Barnsley, Yorks; office: 36 Nelson St, Rotherham S65 1EX (☎ 0709 75944)

KEY, Geoffrey George Bamford; s of George Key (Sgt RA, d 1967), of Manchester, and Marion, *née* Bamford; *b* 13 May 1941; *Educ* Manchester High Sch of Art, Manchester Regnl Coll of Art (Nat Dip of Design, Dip of Associateship of Manchester, Postgrad in Sculpture); *Career* major exhibitions: Salford Art Gallery 1966, Univ of Manchester 1969, Erica Bourne Gallery London 1974, Salon d'Automne Clermont Ferrand France 1974, Nancy France 1974, Gallery Tendenz Germany 1977, Lausanne Switzerland 1980, Madison Avenue NY 1980, Solomon Gallery Dublin 1983, Solomon Gallery London 1985, Damme Belgium 1990; work incl in the collections of: Salford Art Gallery, Manchester City Art Gallery, Bolton Art Gallery, NW Arts Assoc, Univ of Manchester, Wigan Corp, Granada TV, Chateau de St Oven France; cncl memb: Friends of Salford Art Gallery, Manchester Acad of Fine Art (memb 1970); *Books* G Key A Book of Drawings and Interview (1975), Daydreams (1981); *Recreations* collecting 16th & 17th century works of art; *Style*— Geoffrey Key, Esq; 59 Acresfield Rd, Pendleton, Salford 6, Lancashire (☎ 061 736 6014)

KEY, (Simon) Robert; MP (C) Salisbury 1983-; s of Rt Rev John Maurice Key (d 1984), and Agnes Joan (Dence); Rt Rev John Key (d 1984) was Bishop of Sherborne (1946-60) and Bishop of Truro (1960-73); *b* 22 April 1945; *Educ* Salisbury Cathedral Sch, Sherborne, Clare Coll Cambridge (MA), Cert Ed; *m* 1968, Susan Prisilla Bright, da of Very Revd Thomas Thurstan Irvine, former Dean of St Andrews; 2 s (James (decd), Adam b 1974), 2 da (Sophy b 1977, Helen b 1979); *Career* MP (C) Salisbury 1983-; memb Commons Select Ctee on Educn Sci and the Arts 1983-86; chm Cncl for Educn in the Cwlth 1984-87; memb UK Nat Cmmn for UNESCO 1985-86; PPS to: Rt Hon Edward Heath, MP 1984-85, Min of State for Energy 1985-87, Rt Hon Chris Patten, MP (at Miny of Overseas Devpt and Dept of the Environment 1987-90); Parly under sec of state DOE 1990-; memb MRC 1989-90; *Clubs* Athenaeum; *Style*— Robert Key, Esq, MP; 12 Brown St, Salisbury, Wilts (☎ 0722 333141); House of Commons, London SW1

KEYDEN, James Aitken; s of John Keyden (d 1969); *b* 15 May 1909; *Educ* Glasgow HS; *m* 1940, Doris Margaret, *née* Crawford; 2 s (and 1 decd), 3 da (and 1 decd); *Career* CA; dir: Pressed Steel Co Ltd 1953-63, Scottish United Investors Ltd 1961-80, George Blair plc 1963-89, Scottish Gas Board 1964-73, Brown Shipley & Co Ltd 1979-84, Volvo Trucks (GB) Ltd 1966-84; chm Rowan & Boden Ltd 1968-71; *Recreations* golf, fishing; *Clubs* Royal Scottish Automobile; *Style*— James Keyden, Esq; Craigie Burn, Glencairn Rd, Kilmacolm, Renfrewshire (☎ 050 587 2478)

KEYES, Hon Charles William Packe; s and h of 2 Baron Keyes, *qv*; *b* 8 Dec 1951; *m* 1, 1978 (m dis), Sadiye Yasmin, da of Mahir Coskun, of Istanbul; m 2, 1984, Sally, da of Thomas Jackson; 1 da (Anne Merula b 1985); *Style*— The Hon Charles Keyes

KEYES, Hon Elizabeth Mary; da of Adm of the Fleet 1 Baron Keyes, GCB, KCVO, CMG, DSO (d 1945), and Eva Mary Salvin (d 1973), da of Edward Salvin Bowlby, DL, of Gilston Park, Herts and Knoydart, Inverness (whose er s was awarded a posthumous VC for leading Commando raid on Gen Rommel's HQ at Sidi Rafa, Libya 1941); *b* 10 May 1915; *Educ* Westonbirt; *Career* WWII 1939-45 with VAD (RN); smallholder (ret), former breeder of Anglo-Arabs (Working Hunter of the Year 1960), beef, cattle and geese; *Books* Geoffrey Keyes, VC, of the Rommel Raid (1956); *Recreations* writing leaflets on local and national topics, conservation; *Clubs* Nat Farmers' Union, VAD (RN) Assoc; *Style*— The Hon Elizabeth Keyes; Wood Lane Cottage, Tingewick, Buckingham MK18 4QS (☎ 02804 303)

KEYES, 2 Baron (UK 1943); Sir Roger George Bowlby Keyes; 2 Bt (UK 1919); s of Adm of the Fleet 1 Baron Keyes, GCB, KCVO, CMG, DSO (d 1945), and Eva Mary Salvin, *née* Bowlby (d 1973); *b* 14 March 1919; *Educ* King's Mead Sch Seaford, RNC Dartmouth; *m* 6 Dec 1947, Grizelda Mary, da of late Lt-Col William Packe, DSO; 3 s (Hon Charles, *qv*, Hon John, Hon Adrian), 2 da (Hon Mrs Crompton 1950, Hon Mrs Young b 1958); *Heir* s, Hon Charles Keyes; *Career* WWII serv RN, N Sea and Med 1939-45, ret 1949; co dir, conslt; author; *Books* Outrageous Fortune (1984),Un Règne Brisé (1985), Echec au Roi (1986), Een Beproeft Koning (1986), Complot Tegen de Koning (1988); *Clubs* Anglo-Belgian; *Style*— The Rt Hon the Lord Keyes; Elmscroft, Charlton Lane, West Farleigh, nr Maidstone, Kent ME15 0NY (☎ 0622 812477)

KEYNES, Hon Mrs (Anne Pinsent); *née* Adrian; da of 1 Baron Adrian, OM (d 1977), and Hester, *née* Pinsent, DBE, BEM (d 1966); *b* 27 May 1924; *Educ* Downe House, Somerville Coll Oxford (MA); *m* 1945, Richard Keynes, CBE, FRS, s of Sir Geoffrey Keynes (d 1982), and Margaret, da of Sir George Darwin, KCB, FRS, of Newnham Grange, Cambridge; 3 s (Randal b 1948, Roger b 1951, Simon b 1952), and 1 s decd; *Style*— The Hon Mrs Keynes; 4 Herschel Rd, Cambridge (☎ 0223 353107); Primrose Farm, Wiveton, nr Holt, Norfolk (☎ 0263 740317)

KEYS, David Chaloner; s of John Henry Keys (d 1982), of Sussex, and Jean Winifred, *née* Glover (d 1970); *b* 12 Feb 1934; *Educ* Merchant Taylors' Sch, St John's Coll Oxford (MA); *m* 20 June 1959, Pamela Helen, da of Philip Henry Megson (d 1984), of Cheshire; 3 da (Charlotte b 1962, Harriet b 1965, Rebecca b 1973); *Career* flying offr RAF 1953-55; private sec to Dep Govr Bank of Eng 1963 (joined 1958), seconded to UK Treasy Delgn Washington 1964-66, seconded as md Bank of Mauritius 1968-70, with Morgan Grenfell 1971; dir: MG and Co Ltd 1973-88, A De Gruchy and Co Ltd 1982-(chm 1988-), MG Group 1987-88, Norwich Union Insurance Group 1988-, Robert M Douglas Holdings plc 1989-; chm HFC Bank plc 1989- (dir 1982-); non-exec dir: Maples Holdings Ltd (later chm) 1975-80, Thomas Borthwick and Sons plc 1981-84, Target Group plc 1986-87; chm E Surrey Health Authy 1988-90; *Recreations* reading, travelling, ornithology; *Style*— David Keys, Esq; Tower Hill House, Tower Hill, Dorking, Surrey RH4 2AP (☎ 0306 885625); 23 Great Winchester St, London EC2P 2AX (☎ 071 588 4545); Cley Old Hall, Cley-Next-The-Sea, Norfolk NR25 7RY (☎ 0263 740549)

KEYS, Richard John; s of Henry John Keys, of Rustington, Sussex, and Bessie, *née* Taylor; *b* 10 April 1951; *Educ* Lewes Co GS for Boys; *m* 5 Dec 1974, Helen Kathryn, da of Alan Herbert Jackson; 2 da (Emily Sarah b 19 Feb 1986, Letitia Mary b 2 March 1990); *Career* articled clerk Singleton Fabian Derbyshire 1969-75; Coopers & Lybrand Deloitte: joined Cooper Bros & Co 1973, ptnr Coopers & Lybrand 1984-, chm Energy Water and Tport Sector Gp 1989-; memb Tech Ctee ICAEW 1988-90; FCA (ACA 1973); *Recreations* shooting, opera, gardening; *Style*— Richard Keys, Esq; Coopers & Lybrand Deloitte, Plumtree Court, London EC4A 4HT (☎ 071 583 5000, fax 071 822 4476)

KHAMBATA, Ardeshir Shiavax; s of Shiavax Savabjee Khambata (d 1969), of Bombay, India, and Coomi, *née* Lam; *b* 13 Oct 1935; *Educ* Cathedral Sch Bomay India, Univ of Bombay (MB BS); *Career* conslt ENT surgn and laryngologist 1973-; memb: RSM, The Harveian Soc, Med Soc London; FRCS; *Books* contrib: Music And the Brain (1977), Diseases of the Ear, Nose and Throat (1979), Voice (1983); *Recreations* music, singing, opera; *Style*— Ardeshir Khambata, Esq

KHAN, (Mohammed) Ilyas; s of Mahammed Yasin Khan (d 1970), of Gillingham, Kent, and Hafiza, *née* Begum; *b* 14 Oct 1945; *Educ* Duke of Gloucester Sch Nairobi Kenya; *m* 14 April 1972, Amtul Naseer, da of Abdul Rehman Qureshi (d 1965); 1 da (Maham Hina b 1988); *Career* Cncl of Legal Educn 1965-68, called to the Bar Lincoln's Inn 1969, res magistrate Kenya 1977-80; memb exec UK Ahmadinyya Muslin Assoc (pres Birmingham branch); *Recreations* cricket, squash; *Style*— Ilyas Khan, Esq; 7 Fountain Court, Steelhouse Lane, Birmingham B4 6DR (☎ 021 236 8531, fax 021 236 4408)

KHAN, Dr Jameel Ullah; s of Amanat Ullah Khan, of Tonk, Rajasthan, India, and Rafi Un, *née* Nisa (d 1986); *b* 30 Sept 1942; *Educ* Government HS India, Maharja's Coll Jaipur India, Aligarh Muslim Univ Aligarh India, Med Coll Srinigarludia (univ football and badminton player); *m* 5 April 1979, Nicoliades Desporella (now Mrs Nikhat Jameel Khan), da of Nicholas Nicholiades of Cyprus; 2 s (Talat Jameel b 8 Oct 1981, Zubeen Jameel b 15 March 1985); *Career* Sir Gianga Ram Hosp India 1971-72, Birkenhead Gen Hosp Merseyside 1972-73, Gp trg Salop 1973-74, Southend Gen Hosp Essex 1974-76, princ gen practitioner 1976-, private practice Harley St; memb: Enfield and Harringay Med Ctee, Cons Pty Southgate and Palmers Green, Masonic Temple London; *Recreations* Dysham Park Country Golf, David Lloyd's Tennis, Mayfield Tennis; *Style*— Dr Jameel Khan; Clare House, 109 North Circular Rd, London N13 5EL (☎ 081 803 8605, surgery 081 807 2045); 100 Harley St, London W1 (☎ 071 487 5564)

KHAN, Dr Kamaluddin; s of Fida Husain Khan (d 1945), and Jameelunisa, *née* Begum; *b* 5 July 1937; *Educ* Univ of Liverpool (PhD); *m* 1963, Ghazala Parveen, da of Hamid Husain Khan, of Gorakhpur, India; 3 s (Dr Salahuddin Khan b 17 June 1965, Asif Kamal b 27 March 1972, Yousuf Kamal b 22 Sept 1982); *Career* conslt psychiatrist Clatterbridge and Arrowe Park Hosp 1977-, hon clinical lectr in psychiatry Univ of Liverpool 1979-, med advsr to Br Memb Cncl of World Veterans Fedn 1984-, pt/t lord cllrs med visitor for Wales 1989-; memb: Unit Mgmnt Bd for Community and Support Hosps Wirral, World Fed of Mental Health; chm Joint Care Planning for the Mentally Ill Wirral; *Recreations* travelling, chess, bridge; *Style—* Dr Kamaluddin Khan; Department of Psychiatry, Arrowe Park Hospital, Arrowe Park Rd, Upton, Wirral L49 5LN (☎ 051 678 5111)

KHAN, Dr Saeed Ahmad; s of Muhammed Khawas Khan (d 1976), of Peshwar, NW Frontier, Pakistan, and Khudija, *née* Ahmad (d 1965); *b* 1 Nov 1936; *Educ* Islamia Coll, Peshwar Univ; *m* 25 Oct 1965, Selma Mubaraka, da of Wilfred Benjamin Reynolds (d 1971), of Ackworth, W Yorks; 3 s (Khalid b 1968, Karim b 1969, Imran b 1973), 1 da (Tahira b 1966); *Career* resident house physician Dw Med Coll Civil Hosp Karachi 1960-61; sr house offr: Manchester and Salford Skin Hosp 1962-63, St Johns Hosp for the Diseases of the Skin 1963-64, gen med Middleton Hosp Ilkley 1964, gen med and dermatology Pinderfields Hosp Wakefield 1964-65; locum conslt dermatologist The Royal Infirmary Edinburgh 1968 (registrar dept of dermatology 1965-67, hon lectr and sr registrar dept of dermatology 1967-71); conslt dermatologist: Wakefield and Dewsbury Dist Hosps 1971-87, Wakefield Dist Hosps 1987); pres Ahmaddiya Muslim Assoc Spen Valley; memb: Br Assoc of Dematologists, N of England Dermatological Soc; MB BS Karachi Univ 1961, DTM and H London 1962; memb BMA, MRCPE 1965, FRCP 1985; *Books* contrib incl: Scottish Medical Journal (1968), British Medical Journal (1970), British Journal of Dermatology (1971), Archives of Dermatology (1972), Practitioner (1978), Practitioner (1981); *Recreations* walking, bee keeping, charity work; *Style—* Dr Saeed Khan; Firdene, Fusden Lane, Off Spen Lane, Gomersal, West Yorkshire (☎ 0274 873907); Pinderfields General Hospital, Aberford Rd, Wakefield, W Yorkshire WF1 4DG (☎ 0924 375217 ext 2273)

KHANGURA, Jagpal Singh; s of Joginder Singh Khangura (d 1978), of Latala, Punjab, India, and Harnam Kaur Khangura (d 1942); *b* 12 May 1937; *Educ* Punjab Univ (BA); *m* 17 Sept 1960, Gurdial Kaur Khangura; 2 s (Jasbir Singh b 1963, Satbir Singh b 1967); *Career* sub-postmaster 1963-81, hotelier 1981-86, chief exec Premier Hotel Gp 1986-; vice chm Hounslow Community Relations Cncl 1982-87, gen sec Indian Workers Assoc 1987-; cncllr London Borough of Hounslow 1986-; *Recreations* gardening; *Style—* Jagpal Khangura, Esq; 85 Byron Ave, Cranford, Middx (☎ 081 897 8508); Premier Hotels, West End Rd, Ruislip, Middx (☎ 0895 621000, fax 0895 621635, telex 892514)

KHASRU, (Mohammed) Ameer; s of Abdur Rahman Khasru, of Bangladesh, and Saleha Khasru; *b* 28 Jan 1942; *Educ* Collegiate Sch Chittagong, Univ of Dhaka (BCom); *m* 4 March 1965, Chantal Berthe, da of Andre Faucher (d 1979), of France; 1 s (Stephane Reza b 1966), 1 da (Ambreen Joy b 1970); *Career* sr ptnr Khasru & Co London; chief accountant: Burmah Eastern Ltd, Chittagong Bangladesh 1968-71; sr lectr Business Studies SW London Coll 1971-74, trg mangr 1974-78; FCA; *Recreations* swimming, tennis, theatre, reading, good food; *Clubs* Asian City (treas); *Style—* Ameer Khasru, Esq; 236 Linen Hall, 162 Regent Street, London W1R 5TB (☎ 071 437 5401)

KHOO, Francis Kah Siang; s of Teng Eng (decd), and Swee Neo, *née* Chew; *b* 23 Oct 1947; *Educ* Univ of Singapore (LLB), Univ of London (MA); *m* 29 Jan 1977, Dr Swee Chai, da of Peng Liat Ang; *Career* advocate and slr Singapore 1971-77; business and political journalist London 1980-87; gen sec War on Want London (Br Devpt Aid Agency) 1988-89; vice chm and fndr memb Medical Aid for Palestinians 1984-; memb: NUJ 1979-, Singapore Law Soc 1971-; *Books* Bungaraya Blooms All Day; *Recreations* hill walking, swimming; *Style—* Francis Khoo, Esq

KHOURY, Dr Ghassan George; s of George Sammaan Khoury, of Amman, Jordan, and Margaret, *née* Rizik; *b* 14 July 1954; *Educ* Bryanston, UCL, UCH; *m* 7 Aug 1984, Sonia, da of Jubran Khoury, of Jifna, Ramallah, Israel; 1 s (George Ghassan b 1986); *Career* lectr in radiotherapy and oncology Univ of Leeds 1986-89, conslt in radiotherapy and oncology Portsmouth 1989-; memb radiotherapy co-op gp EORTC; MRCP 1981, FRCR 1985; memb: BMA 1978, British Oncological Assoc 1987; *Recreations* swimming, squash; *Style—* Dr Ghassan Khoury; St Marys Hospital, Milton Rd, Portsmouth PO3 6AD (☎ 0705 822331)

KIBAZO, Joel Serunkuma; s of Godfrey Serunkuma Lule, and Margaret Mary, *née* Namusisi; *b* 24 June 1961; *Educ* HS for Boys Swindon, Kingsbury HS London, Sunderland Poly (BA), Univ of Reading (MA), Univ of Bradford (MBA); *Career* trainee reporter New Life 1986-87, political corr The Voice 1987-88, stockmarkets reporter Financial Times 1989- (gen reporter 1988-89); co fndr: Black Journalists Assoc 1989, Br Uganda soc (current chm); memb Assoc of MBAs; *Recreations* squash, swimming, African history, Third World development issues; *Style—* Joel Kibazo, Esq; Financial Times, 1 Southwark Bridge, London SE1 9HL (☎ 071 873 3227, fax 071 407 5700)

KIBBEY, (Sidney) Basil; s of Percy Edwin Kibbey (d 1939), of Mickleover, and Winifred, *née* Garratt (d 1968); *b* 3 Dec 1916; *Educ* Derby Sch, Admin Staff Coll Henley; *m* 3 June 1939, (Violet Gertrude) Jane, da of John George Eyre (d 1956), of Lincs; 1 s (Paul b 1943), 1 da (Anna (twin) b 1943); *Career* princ Miny of Nat Insur 1951, sec Nat Insur Advsy Ctee 1960-62, asst sec Miny of Pensions and Nat Insur 1962, under-sec DHSS 1971-76, visiting lectr Civil Serv Coll 1976-; *Recreations* photography, gardening; *Clubs* English-Speaking Union; *Style—* Basil Kibbey, Esq; 29 Beaulieu Close, Datchet, Berks SL3 9DD (☎ 0753 49 101)

KIDBY, Robert James; s of James Clarence Kidby, of Vixenlaw, Warninglid, Sussex, and Myrtle Eileen, *née* Wright; *b* 27 Feb 1951; *Educ* Steyning GS, Univ of London (LLB); *m* 3 Dec 1977, Stephanie Elizabeth Mary, da of Morris Shipley, of Hook, Basingstoke, Hants; 1 s (Samuel Robert b 4 Aug 1985), 1 da (Harriet Elizabeth Cynthia b 6 Nov 1988); *Career* admitted slr 1977; ptnr: Durrant Piesse 1985-88, Lovell White Durrant 1988-; Freeman Worshipful Co of Slrs 1984; memb Law Soc 1978; *Recreations* electric guitar, Antarctic memorabilia; *Style—* Robert Kidby, Esq; Lovell White Durrant, 65 Holborn Viaduct, London EC1A 2DY (☎ 071 236 0066)

KIDD, Jean Buyers; da of James William Olson, MBE (d 1978), and Helen Henderson, *née* Ingram (d 1953); *b* 10 May 1925; *Educ* Findochty Sch, Buckie HS, RSAM (DipMusEd RSAM, LRAM, ARCM), BA; *m* 12 April 1952, David Hughes Kidd (d 1953), s of David Kidd; *Career* music dir SNO Junior and Youth Choruses 1978-; performances with: SNO, LSO, LPO, BBC, SSO, Scottish Opera, English Nat Opera, on radio and television, at Edinburgh Int Festival; works performed incl: Berlioz Requiem and Te Deum, Mahler Symphonies 2, 3 and 8, Liszt Dante Symphony, Bach St John and St Matthew Passions, Peter Maxwell Davies' The Peat Cutters (World Premiere), Gordon Crosse's Sea Psalms (first performance), Stephen Clemes' Up Your Street (first performance); sec Scottish Certificate of Educn Examination Bd 1979-81, fndr Bellahouston Music Soc; *Style—* Mrs Jean Kidd

KIDD, John Edward Aitken; s of Maj Edward Daltrey Kidd (d 1979), and Hon Janet Gladys, *née* Aitken (d 1988), da of 1 Baron Beaverbrook; *b* 12 Dec 1944; *Educ* Harrow; *m* 2 April 1973, Wendy Madeleine, da of Sir John Rowland Hodge, MBE; 1 s (Jack Edward b 1973), 2 da (Jemma Madeleine b 1974, Jodie Elizabeth b 1978); *Career* Jr Euro Individual Showjumping Champion 1962, represented GB in Europe, USA and Africa 1964-72, represented England 11 v The Commonwealth (Polo) on Int Day at Windsor 1972; dir: London United Investmts plc 1977-81, Aitken Home plc 1982-86, Careplus Inc USA 1987-, All England Jumping Course Hickstead 1989-; chm Columbia Laboratories Inc USA 1987-; *Books* Reins In Our Hands (1966), Take Off (1974), Biographies On Showjumping Career; *Recreations* polo; *Clubs* Buck's; *Style—* John Kidd, Esq; Hilliers, Petworth, West Sussex; Holders House, St James, Barbados; Suite 1809, 745 Fifth Ave, New York City, NY, USA

KIDD, Richard; *Educ* Univ of Newcastle, British Sch Rome; *Career* artist; teacher: Trent Poly and Univ of Reading 1975-76, Univ of Newcastle 1976-80; Harkness fell San Francisco 1980, moved to NY 1981, returned to UK 1987; solo exhibitions: Sunderland Arts Centre 1976, Rowan Gallery 1977, 1979, 1980, Turnpike Gallery Leigh 1978, Armand Bartos NY 1983, Alexander Milliken Gallery NY 1983, Juda Rowan Gallery 1983, Mayor Rowan Gallery 1990; group exhibitions incl: Northern Painters and Sculptors (Peter Stoyvesant Fndn Sunderland Arts Centre) 1974, John Moores Liverpool Exhibition 9 and 10 1974 and 1976, Mostra 75 (Rome) 1975, Growing up with Art (Leics Collection Whitechapel Gallery) 1980, Br Artists in NY (Newhouse Gallery NY) 1983, New Works on Paper (Br Cncl tour) 1984-86; work in the collections of incl: Arts Cncl of GB, Kunsthaus Zurich, Museum of Modern Art Rio de Janeiro, Sanisbury Centre Norwich, Ulster Museum Belfast, Clare Coll Cambridge; equal first prize Peter Stuyvesant Fndn 1974, prize John Moores Liverpool Exhibition 9 1974, Abbey major scholar Rome 1974, Arts Cncl award 1976, N Arts fell 1976; *Style—* Richard Kidd, Esq; c/o Mayor Rowan Gallery, 31a Bruton Place, London W1X 7AB (☎ 071 499 3011, fax 071 355 3486)

KIDD, Sir Robert Hill; KBE (1979), CB (1975); s of Andrew Kidd (d 1947), and Florence, *née* Hill (d 1963); *b* 3 Feb 1918; *Educ* Royal Belfast Academical Inst, Univ of Dublin (BA, BLitt); *m* 1942, Harriet Moore, da of Rev E H Williamson, BLitt, PhD, of Ballina and Tralee, Eire; (3 s, 2 da); *Career* Actg Maj SEAC, cmmnd 1942, RUR, later attached to Intelligence Corps; NI Civil Serv 1947-79 (head of NICS 1976-79); dir Allied Irish Banks Ltd 1979-85, chm Belfast Car Ferries Ltd 1983-88, NI chm of Cooperaton North 1982-86; pro chancellor and chm of Cncl New Univ of Ulster 1980-84; tstee: Scot Irish Tst, 1980-, chm Ulster Historical Fndn 1988-; dir Irish American Partnership 1988-; Hon DLitt Univ of Ulster 1985; *Recreations* gardening, photography; *Clubs* Civil Serv; *Style—* Sir Robert Kidd, KBE, CB; 24 Massey Court, Belfast BT4 3GJ (☎ 0232 768694)

KIDDY, Dennis; s of Thomas William Kiddy (d 1987), and Violet, *née* Snead; *b* 6 Dec 1951; *Educ* Blackpool GS, Worcester Coll Oxford (MA); *Career* musician; organ scholar Worcester Coll Univ of Oxford 1970-73; dir of music: Beaudesert Park 1974-75, Repton Prep Sch 1975-83, Wymondham Coll 1983-84; devpt offr St Edmund's Sch Canterbury 1984-; hon sr memb Darwin Coll Univ of Kent 1986, dir of music Lambeth Conf 1988; *Recreations* cooking; *Style—* Dennis Kiddy, Esq; St Edmund's Sch, Canterbury, Kent CT2 8HU (☎ 0227 454 575)

KIDNER, David Hudson; OBE (1985); s of Clifford Hudson Kidner (d 1970), and Elspeth Mary, *née* Creeke (d 1973); *b* 13 March 1931; *Educ* Burnley GS; *m* 1954, (Elizabeth) Alison, da of Austin Marshall (d 1969), of Mawgan Porth Cornwall; 3 s (Paul, Alan, Brian); *Career* asst clerk Burnley Borough Magistrates Ct 1947, princ clerk Wallington Magistrates' Ct 1953; slr 1964; clerk to the Justices for Five Petty Sessional Divs Isle of Ely Cambs 1966, clerk to the Justices Coventry 1973, hon sec Justices' Clerks Soc 1976-81, pres Justices' Clerks' Soc 1983-84; chm Coventry Diocesan Social Responsibility Ctee 1980-; hon LLM Univ of Birmingham 1986; *Recreations* walking, rugby (spectator); *Style—* David Kidner Esq, OBE; Magistrates Courts, Little Park St, Coventry CV1 2SQ (☎ 0203 630666 ext 2114)

KIDNER, Michael James; s of Norman William Kidner (d 1931), of Kettering, and Kathleen Kidner (d 1976); *b* 11 Sept 1917; *Educ* Bedales Sch, Univ of Cambridge (MA); *m* 24 Feb 1951, Marion, da of Morton Frederick (d 1975), of NY, USA; 1 s (Simon Morton b 15 Sept 1962, d 10 March 1982); *Career* Nat Serv Royal Canadian Signal Corps 1942-46; artist and sculptor; one man shows incl: ACGB Expo Serpentine Gallery London 1984, Museum of Contemporary Art Lodz Poland 1985, Joszefvarosi Kaillito Teerem Gallery Budapest Hungary 1986, Amos Anderson Museum Helsinki Finland 1987, The Wave: Concepts in Construction Galerie Hubert Winter Vienna Austria 1990, At-tension to the Wave CIGA NYC 1990; numerous gp expos worldwide; public collections incl: Tate Gallery, Museum of Mod Art NY, Nat Gallery of Aust Canberra, Amos Anderson Museum Helsinki, Manchester City Art Gallery, Victoria and Albert Museum; recent cmmns: sculpture for the Museo Internazionale di Scultura all'Aperto Citta di Portofino Italy 1988, sculpture in Vissingen Holland 1989; *Books* Elastic Membrane (1980); *Style—* Michael Kidner, Esq; 18 Hampstead Hill Gardens, London NW3 2PL (☎ 071 435 9630)

KIDSON, Capt Ian Harold; s of Capt Harold Brookes Kidson (d 1969), of 7 Clifton Rd, Tettenhall, Wolverhampton, and Dorothea, *née* Johnston (d 1975); *b* 8 Feb 1920; *Educ* Malvern; *m* 1 Sept 1954, Anne Augusta, da of Leonard Dudley Braithwaite (d 1970), of Fosse House, Stourbridge Rd, Wombourn, Wolverhampton; 3 s (Jonathan b 1956, Bruce b 1958, Paul b 1962), 3 da (Elena b 1955, Suzanne b 1964, Annabel b 1974); *Career* cmmnd 2 Lt 2/6 S Staffs Regt (TA) 1939, Capt (co cdr) 6 Bn KOYLI 1942, 4/6 Bn KAR Serv overseas (E Africa, Ceylon, India, Burma) 1943-46; articled clerk to CA 1937-39 and 1946-48, sales rep agric engrs 1948-50, co sec and dir Multiple Retail Grocers 1950-61 (md 1961-62); JW Braithwaite & Son Ltd (bookbinders) 1962-: co sec 1965-70, chm and md 1970-; chm Church Eaton Branch Stafford Cons Assoc 1971-87, church warden Church Eaton Stafford 1983-86, pres Glebelands Sports Assoc 1983-; memb: Bd Govrs PNEU Sch 1958-78 (chm 1975-78), Bd Visitors HM Prison Featherstone Staffs 1979-88, Br Printing Industs Fedn (pres Midland Region 1974); *Recreations* tennis, shooting, gardening; *Style—* Capt Ian Kidson; Little Onn Hall, Church Eaton, Stafford ST20 OAU (☎ 0785 840 154); J W Braithwaite & Son Ltd, PO Box 20, Pountney St, Wolverhampton, W Midlands WV2 4HY (☎ 0902 52209, fax 0902 352918)

KIDSTON, Hon Mrs (Patricia Anne); *née* Manners; da of 4 Baron Manners, MC (d 1972); *b* 1927; *m* 1946, John Bonham Kidston (d 1968), gs Sir George Bonham, 2 Bt; 2 s (Francis b 1947, Jonathan b 1951), 1 da (Virginia b 1953); *Style—* The Hon Mrs Kidston; Pluscarden, Elgin, Morayshire

KIDSTON-MONTGOMERIE OF SOUTHANNAN, Col George Jardine; DSO (1942), MC (1941), DL (Wilts 1960); s of Richard Logan Kidston (d 1920), of Beenham Court, Newbury, and Sophia Egidia Gwendolin Montgomerie; recognised by Lord Lyon King of Arms upon his succession to feudal barony of Southannan, Ayrshire through his maternal grandmother Lady Sophia Montgomerie, co-heiress to her father 14 Earl of Eglinton and Winton; *b* 8 March 1907; *Educ* Eton, RMC Sandhurst; *m* 26 July 1932, Lydia Cecelia, da of Maj P Mason, DSO (ka 1915); 1 s (Robert Alexander b 1937), 1 da (Philippa Sophia b 1935); *Career* joined 12 Royal Lancers 1926, cmd 12 Royal Lancers 1942-43, cmd 4 Hussars 1947-49, Col QRIH 1965-69; memb Royal Co of Archers (Queen's Body Guard for Scot); one of HM's Hon Corps of Gentlemen-at-Arms; *Recreations* hunting, shooting, fishing; *Clubs* White's, Cavalry and Guards'; *Style—* Col George Kidston-Montgomerie of Southannan, DSO, MC, DL; Longbottom,

Biddesden, Andover, Hants (☎ 026 470 226)

KIDWELL, Raymond Incledon; QC (1968); s of Montague Ernest Kidwell (d 1988), and Dorothy, *née* Incledon (d 1980); *b* 8 Aug 1926; *Educ* Whitgift Sch, Magdalen Coll Oxford (BCL, MA); *m* 1, 1951 (m dis) Enid, *née* Rowe; 2 s (Barry Gerard b 1956, Nicholas Justin b 1958); m 2, 1976, Dr Carol Evelyn Beryl Maddison; *Career* Nat Serv RAFVR 1944-48; called to the Bar Gray's Inn 1951, rec 1972, bencher 1978; *Recreations* travel, photography; *Clubs* United Oxford and Cambridge Univ; *Style*— Raymond Kidwell, QC; Sanderstead House, Rectory Park, Sanderstead, Surrey CR2 9JR (☎ 081 657 4161); 2 Crown Office Row, Temple, London EC4Y 7HY (☎ 071 353 9337, fax 071 583 0589 (GPS 2/3), telex 8954005 TWOCOR G)

KIELY, Dr David George; s of George Thomas Kiely (d 1964), of Ballynahinch, Co Down, and Susan, *née* Wolfenden (d 1972); *b* 23 July 1925; *Educ* Down HS Downpatrick, Queen's Univ Belfast (BSc, MSc), Sorbonne (DSc), Royal Naval Staff Coll; *m* 17 Aug 1956, Dr Ann Wilhelmina, da of John William Kilpatrick (d 1961), of Kilwarlin House, St James's, Hillsborough, Co Down; 1 s (Patrick b 1964), 1 da (Fiona b 1961); *Career* Civil Serv (MOD); RNS Serv: joined 1944, head of Electronic Warfare Div ASWE 1965-68, head of Communications and Sensor Dept ASWE 1968-72, under sec 1972, dir gen Telecommunications PE MOD 1972-74, dir gen Strategic Electronic Systems PE MOD 1974-76, dir gen Electronics Res 1976-78, dir Naval Surface Weapons ASWE 1978-83, the Chief Naval Weapon Systems Engr 1983-84; chm R & D Policy Ctee of the Gen Lighthouse Authys of the UK and Eire 1974-; conslt engr Chemring plc 1985- (gp chief exec 1984-85); govr Portsmouth Coll of Technol 1965-69, chm Cncl Chichester Cathedral 1985-89 (memb 1982-89); CEng, FIEE, CPhys, FInstP; *Books* Dielectric Aerials (1953), Marine Navigational Aids for Coastal Waters of the British Isles (1987), Naval Electronic Warfare (1988), Naval Surface Weapons (1988), Defence Procurement (1990); *Recreations* fly fishing, gardening, aviculture; *Clubs* Naval and Military; *Style*— Dr D G Kiely; Cranleigh, 107 Havant Rd, Emsworth, Hampshire PO10 7LF (☎ 0243 372250)

KIENDL, Hon Mrs (Judith Caroline); *née* Ross; yr da of Baron Ross of Newport (Life Peer), *qv*; *b* 1 Nov 1952; *m* 1983, Theodore Kiendl; *Style*— The Hon Mrs Kiendl; 65 Tyrwhitt Road, Brockley, London SE14

KIER, Michael Hector; s of Mogens Kier, and Birthe, *née* Andreasen; *b* 22 Oct 1946; *Educ* Repton, King's Coll London; *m* 15 May 1971, Jane Elizabeth, da of J R Childs; *Career* jt md: Fielding Juggins Money & Stewart 1981-86, Heath Fielding Insur Broking Ltd 1986-89; chm C E Heath Latin America Ltd 1986-, gp md C E Heath plc 1989- (insur broker 1968-77, dir 1986-); *Style*— Michael H Kier, Esq; C E Heath plc, 150 Minories, London EC3N 1NR (☎ 071 488 2488, fax 071 481 3606, telex 8813001)

KIERNAN, Michael Joseph; s of James Andrew Kiernan, of 1 Barnstead Ave, Blackrock, Cork, and Angela, *née* Lane; *b* 17 Jan 1961; *Educ* Presentation Brothers Coll, Cork; *m* 30 June 1988, Anne Patricia, da of Dr Thomas Christopher O'Connor; 1 da (Alison May b 11 Dec 1989); *Career* Rugby Union centre and wing threequarter Dolphin RFC and Ireland (43 caps); Munster Schs: Jr Cup medallist 1976, Sr cup medallist 1979; memb Irish Schs team 1979; Irish 200m Champion 1981, memb Irish Int Athletics team v Scotland and Denmark 1981; clubs: Dolphin RFC 1980-, Landsdowne RFC 1983-85, Barbarians RFC; rep: Munster (record 51 appearances); Ireland: toured SA 1981, debut v Wales 1982, won Triple Crown 1982 and 1985, Five Nations Champions 1983 (shared with France), memb World Cup squad 1987, toured USA and Canada 1989, Most points scored by an Ireland player in internationals (currently 308); Br Lions: toured NZ 1983 (3 test appearances); Cork Supreme Sports Star award 1985; dir fin servs co; *Recreations* golf, tennis, swimming, music; *Style*— Michael Kiernan, Esq; 35 Wainsfort, Rochestown Rd, Cork, Ireland (☎ 021 364187)

KIKANO, Khalil Naoum; *b* 20 Aug 1938; *m* 22 Nov 1959, Hanne, 1 s (Naoum b 1960), 2 da (Margo b 1964, Lara b 1969); *Career* Banque Sabbag SAL Beirut 1956-63, mangr of audit Whinney Murray & Co 1964-68; The Royal Bank of Canada: mangr (Middle E) SAL Beirut 1969-77, regnl offr (Middle E and Africa) Montreal 1977, gen mangr (Middle E and Africa) London 1982, vice-pres (Middle E and Africa) 1983, vice-pres of lending 1988; memb Centre of Arbitration and Concilliation Union of Arab Banks; *Clubs* RAC; *Style*— Khalil Kikano, Esq; 6 Cornwall Mansions, 33 Kensington Court, London W8 5BG (☎ 071 937 9346); The Royal Bank of Canada, 71 Queen Victoria St, London EC4V 4DE (☎ 071 489 1188, fax 071 329 6065, telex 929111)

KILBORN, Dr John Robert; s of Charles James Kilborn, of Desborough, Northants, and Winifred Jane, *née* Fenton; *b* 22 April 1939; *Educ* Kettering GS, Univ of Durham, Univ of Newcastle-upon-Tyne (BSc, PhD, MB BS); *m* 3 July 1965, Jean Margaret (Jan), da of Stewart Allen (d 1966), of Newcastle-upon-Tyne; 3 s (David John b 1970, Andrew James b 1973, Christopher Richard b 1975); *Career* physician Royal Victoria Infirmary Newcastle 1969-71, clinical res physician Hoffman la Roche 1971-73, SMO Glaxo Gp 1973-77, cardiovascular clinical res leader then med dir UK Laboratories d'Etudes et de Recherche Synthélabo Paris and London 1977-83; md: Lorex Pharmaceuticals Ltd 1983-88, Eurocetus UK Ltd 1988-; FFPM 1989; *Books* International Symposium (with D Harrison P L Morselli, 1983); *Recreations* tennis, skiing; *Clubs* Harpenden Lawn Tennis; *Style*— Dr John Kilborn; Eurocetus UK Ltd, Salamander Quay West, Park Lane, Harefield, Middx UB9 6NY (☎ 0895 824955)

KILBRACKEN, 3 Baron (UK 1909); John Raymond Godley; DSC (1945); s of 2 Baron Kilbracken, CB, KC (d 1950), and his 1 w, Elizabeth, *née* Hamilton; bro of Prof Hon Wynne Godley, the economist, and gs of 1 Baron who was Gladstone's private sec and a perm under sec for India; *b* 17 Oct 1920; *Educ* Eton, Balliol Coll Oxford (MA); *m* 1, 1943 (m dis 1949), Penelope, da of Rear Adm Sir Cecil Reyne, KBE (d 1958); 1 s (Hon Christopher b 1945; and 1 s decd Simon); m 2, 1981 (m dis 1989), Susan, da of late Norman Hazlewood; 1 s (Hon Seán b 1981); *Heir* s, Hon Christopher Godley; *Career* sits as Lab peer in House of Lords; serv WWII RNVR Fleet Air Arm, Lt Cdr; journalist and author; winner of Times Educnl Supplement Information Book Award 1982 for books for children aged 10-16; *Books* Tell Me The Next One (1950), The Master Forger (1951), Living Like A Lord (1954), A Peer Behind The Curtain (1959), Shamrocks and Unicorns (1962), Van Meegeren (1967), Bring Back My Stringbag (1979), The Easy Way to Bird Recognition (1982), The Easy Way to Tree Recognition (1983), The Easy Way to Wild Flower Recognition (1984); *Recreations* bird watching; *Style*— The Rt Hon Lord Kilbracken, DSC; Killegar, Cavan, Rep of Ireland (☎ 010 353 49 34309)

KILBY, Michael Leopold; MEP; s of Guy Kilby (d 1972), and Grace Kilby; *b* 3 Sept 1924; *Educ* Coll of Technol; *m* 21 March 1952, Mary, da of Eric Sanders (d 1981); 3 s (Guy, Marcus, Robert); *Career* General Motors Corporation: head of Euro planning, govt and trade relations 1972-79, mktg and serv mangr Euro Sales, plant mangr 1966-71; author; novels incl: Man at the Sharp End, Mammon Inc; *Recreations* cricket; *Clubs* Beds CC, Dunstable Town CC, Luton CC; *Style*— Michael Kilby Esq, MEP; Grange Barn, Haversham Village, Milton Keynes, Bucks MK19 7DX (☎ 0908 313 613); Nat-West, High Street, Stony Stratford, Bucks

KILDARE, Marquess of; Maurice FitzGerald; s and h of 8 Duke of Leinster by his 2 w, Anne, *née* Smith; *b* 7 April 1948; *Educ* Millfield; *m* 1972, Fiona Mary Francesca, da of late Harry Hollick, of Sutton Courtenay, Abingdon; 1 s, 2 da (Lady Francesca b 6 July 1976, Lady Pollyanna b 9 May 1982); *Heir* s, Earl of Offaly b 12 Jan 1974; *Career* landscape gardener and designer Maxwell Communications Corpn plc, Headington, Oxon; pres Oxfordshire Dyslexia Assoc 1978-; *Recreations* shooting, fishing, riding, squash, sailing; *Style*— Marquess of Kildare; Courtyard House, Oakley Park, Frilford Heath, Oxon OX13 6QW

KILFEDDER, James Alexander; MP (Ulster Popular Unionist Pty 1980-, Down N 1970-); s of Robert Kilfedder (d 1964), of Eastonville, Millisle, Co Down; *b* 16 July 1928; *Educ* Portora Royal Sch Enniskillen, Univ of Dublin; *Career* Irish barr 1952, Gray's Inn 1958, MP (UU) Belfast W 1964-66, Official Unionist memb: NI Assembly 1973-74, NI Convention 1975-76, second NI Assembly 1982-86, resigned from Official Unionist Pty 1979 to stand as UU, fndr memb and ldr Ulster Popular Unionist Pty 1980-, speaker NI Assembly 1982-86; *Style*— James Kilfedder, Esq, MP; 96 Seacliff Rd, Bangor, Co Down BT20 5EZ, Northern Ireland (☎ 0247 451690)

KILGOUR, Dr John Lowell; CB (1987); s of Ormonde John Lowell Kilgour (d 1946), of Aberdeen, Scot, and Catherine, *née* MacInnes (d 1925); *b* 26 July 1924; *Educ* St Christopher's Hove Sussex, Aberdeen GS, Univ of Aberdeen (MB ChB); *m* 24 Oct 1955, Daphne, da of Walter Tully (d 1958), of Otterburn, Northumberland; 2 s (Alastair Hugh Lowell, Simon Walter Lowell); *Career* Lt RAMC 1947-48, Capt RAMC 1948-50; Maj: 26 Field Ambulance Korea 1950-52, Depot and Trg Estab RAMC 1953-54; Lt-Col CO 23 Parachute Field Ambulance 1954-57 (served Suez, Cyprus), registrar Queen Alexandra Mil Hosp 1957-59, Gen Staff Coll Camberley 1959-60, DADG WO 1960-61, ADMS GHQ FARELF (Singapore, Brunei) 1961-64, JSSC 1964-65, Cmdt RAMC Field Trg Sch 1965-66; gen mangr WF Schlesinger 1966-68; joined Med Civil Serv 1968, med offr in med manpower postgrad med educn implementation of Todd Report, sr med offr 1970-71, princ med offr head of Int Health Div DHSS 1971-73, chief med advsr and under sec Miny of Overseas Devpt 1973-78, seconded dir of coordination (D2) WHO Geneva until 1983, dir and under sec Prison Med Serv Home Office 1983-89, chm science recruitment Civil Serv Cmmn and Med Bds, assessor for Dept of Social Servs and various commercial consultancies 1989-; ldr of UK delgns to WHO and Cncl of Euro Public Health Ctees 1971-78; chm: Ctee for Surveillance of Communicable Diseases 1976, EPHC 1976; govr London Sch of Tropical Med and Hygiene 1986-89 (visiting lectr 1973-89); memb: UN Advsy Ctee on Coordination 1978-83, Exec Ctee Royal Cwlth Soc of the Blind 1983-89, Cncl Liverpool Sch of Tropical Med 1973-87; Cons Speaking Prize (London and SE) 1967; MRCGP 1961, FFCM 1974, FFPHM 1989; *Books* Medical Migration (1971), Global Impact of AIDS (1988), plus numerous contributions to med and general publications; *Clubs* Athenaeum, Hurlingham, Royal Windsor Racing; *Style*— Dr John L Kilgour, CB; Stoke House, 22 Amersham Road, Chesham Bois, Bucks HP6 5PE (☎ 0494 726100)

KILKENNY, Bernard Crook; s of William Kilkenny (d 1985), of Branksome Park, Poole, Dorset, and Lilian, *née* Crook; *b* 6 Sept 1928; *Educ* Beaumont Coll, New Coll Oxford (BA, BSc, DPhil, MA); *m* 1 Feb 1958 (m dis 1985), Patricia Ann, da of Thomas William Howard, of Northwood, Middx; 2 s (Charles b 1965, Neville b 1966), 2 da (Elizabeth b 1959, Caroline b 1961); *Career* RHA 1952-54, HAC 1954-62; dir: Allied Breweries 1969-78 (jt md (UK) Ltd 1973-88, dep chm (UK) Ltd, chm (UK) Ltd & subsid Cos 1975-88); dir Scottish & Newcastle Breweries plc (ret 1988); chm: Thistle Hotels, William Younger & Co, Home Brewery, Waverley Vintners Ltd; dir Invergordon Distillers Group plc 1989, chm Innsite International Ltd 1990; former Master Worshipful Co of Brewers; *Recreations* golf, sailing, skiing, shooting, bridge; *Clubs* Royal Thames Yacht, Moor Park Golf, Hon Co of Edinburgh Golfers, New (Edinburgh); *Style*— Bernard Kilkenny, Esq; 45 Heriot Row, Edinburgh EH3 6EX (☎ 031 225 7729); 17 Eaton Mansions, Cliveden Place, London (☎ 071 730 0036)

KILLALA, Neal John Patrick; s of Ernest Killala (d 1978), and Joan Lambert, *née* Evans; *b* 20 Jan 1945; *Educ* Dulwich, St John's Coll Cambridge (MA, MB BChir); *m* 3 Feb 1973, Jennifer Ann, da of Norman Francis Lee (d 1986); 2 s (Stewart b 18 March 1975, James b 14 Aug 1986), 5 da (Anne b 1 June 1978, Helen b 3 Feb 1980, Lucy b 17 Nov 1981, Janet b 26 June 1984, Fiona b 13 Aug 1986); *Career* DCH 1973, Dip Obs RCOG 1973, DPM 1975, MRCPsych 1978; psychiatric registrar: Belmont Hosp Surrey 1974-76, Maudsley Hosp London 1978-80; sr registrar N Middlesex Hosp 1981-, conslt psychiatrist Runwell Hosp Essex 1981-, hon conslt psychiatrist St Luke's Hosp for the Clergy; co-opted probation ctee Essex CC; memb: NE Thames Regnl Conslts and Hosp specialists Ctee, NE Thames Regnl Advsy Ctee, NE Thames Regnl Drug Advsy Ctee, Regnl Drug Team, Mgmnt Ctee Fair Havens Christian Hospice Southend-on-Sea, BMA, Soc for Study for Addiciton, Med Cncl on Alcoholism, New Directions in the Study of Alcohol Gp; *Recreations* reading, music, walking, swimming; *Style*— Dr Neal J P Killala; 16 Drake Rd, Westcliff-on-Sea, Essex SS0 8LP (☎ 0702 354819); Roche Unit, Union Lane, Rochford, Essex SS4 1RB (☎ 0702 541100)

KILLANIN, 3 Baron (UK 1900); Sir Michael Morris; 3 Bt (UK 1885); MBE (1945), TD (1945); s of Lt-Col Hon George Morris, Irish Gds (ka 1914, yr bro of 2 Baron) by his w Dora Wesley Hall; gs of 1 Baron, formerly Lord Chief Justice of Ireland and later Lord of Appeal in Ordinary; suc unc 1927; *b* 30 July 1914; *Educ* Eton, Sorbonne, Magdalene Coll Cambridge (MA); *m* 1945, Sheila Mary, MBE, da of late Rev Canon Douglas Dunlop, of Co Galway; 3 s, 1 da; *Heir* s, Hon Redmond Morris; *Career* serv WWII KRRC, Bde Maj 30 Armd Bde, (Normandy Landing); journalist on Daily Express, then Daily Mail (reported on Chinese/Japanese War 1937-); formerly dir: Irish Shell Ltd, Beamish & Crawford Ltd, Ulster Bank Ltd, Syntex (Ireland) Ltd; formerly chm: Northern Telecom (Ireland) Ltd, Gallaher (Dublin) Ltd, Chubb Ireland Ltd, Hibernian Life Assoc Ltd, Ulster Investmt Bank Ltd, Lombard & Ulster Banking Ireland Ltd; pres Olympic Cncl of Ireland 1950-73; Int Olympic Ctee: memb 1952, memb Exec Bd 1967, vice pres 1968, pres 1972-80, hon life pres 1980-; memb (nominated by Irish Govt): Cultural Relations Ctee 1947-72, Nat Monuments Advsy Cncl 1947-80, Central Cmm Irish Red Cross Soc 1947-72, Irish Sailors and Soldiers Land Tst 1955-; chm: Irish Govt Nat Heritage Cncl 1988-, Irish Govt Cmmn on Thoroughbred Breeding and Racing 1982-; steward of Turf Club 1973-75 and 1981-83; memb: Irish Nat Hunt Steeplechase Ctee, Royal Irish Academy 1952, French Acad of Sports 1974; hon life memb Royal Dublin Soc 1981; Hon LLD Nat U of Ireland 1975, Hon DLitt New U of Ulster 1977; decorations include: Kt of Honour and Devotion SMOM 1943, Medal Miroslav Tyrs (Czech) 1970, Cdr Grand Cross (FDR) 1972, Star of Sacred Treasure (2 class, Japan) 1972, Grand Offr Order of Merit (Italy) 1973, Grand Cross Order of Civil Merit (Spain) 1976, Grand Offr Order of Republic (Tunisia) 1976, Grand Offr Order of Phoenix (Greece) 1976, Order of Madara Rider (Bulgaria), Cdr Legion of Honour (Fr) 1980, Olympic Order of Merit (gold) 1980; *Books* Four Days (1938), Sir Godfrey Kneller (1952), The Shell Guide to Ireland (with Prof Michael Duignan, 1962), The Olympic Games (with John Rodda, 1975/1983), The Olympic Games - Moscow - Lake Placid (with John Medoc, 1979/1983), My Olympic Years (autobiography, 1983), My Ireland (1987); *films* (with John Ford) The Quiet Man (1952), The Rising of the Moon, The Playboy of the Western World, Gideon's Day, Young Cassidy; *Clubs* Garrick, County (Galway), Stephen's Green (Dublin); *Style*— The Rt Hon the Lord Killanin, MBE, TD; 9 Lower Mount Pleasant Ave, Dublin 6; St Annins, Spiddal, Co Galway

KILLEARN, 2 Baron (UK 1943); Sir Graham Curtis Lampson; 4 Bt (UK 1866); s of 1 Baron Killearn, GCMG, CB, MVO, PC (d 1964), sometime envoy to China and Egypt (s of Norman George Lampson who was yst s of Sir Curtis Miranda Lampson, 1 Bt, dep chm of Atlantic Telegraph Co which laid the first Atlantic telegraph cable

1865), by his 1 w, Rachel Mary Hele (d 1930), da of William Wilton Phipps and Dame Jessie, DBE, JP, da of William Butler Duncan, of 1 Fifth Ave, New York; suc 1 cous once removed, Sir Curtis George Lampson, 3 Bt, 1971; *b* 28 Oct 1919; *Educ* Eton, Magdalen Coll Oxford (MA); *m* 15 May 1946, Nadine Marie Cathryn, o da of Vice Adm Cecil Horace Pilcher, DSO; 2 da (Hon Mrs Meynell, Hon Lady Bonsor *qqv*); *Heir* half-bro, Hon Victor Lampson, *qv*; *Career* formerly Maj Scots Gds, served ME, Italy; Bronze Star (USA); *Style—* The Rt Hon the Lord Killearn; 58 Melton Court, Old Brompton Rd, London SW7 3JJ (☎ 071 584 7700)

KILLEARN, Dowager Baroness; Jacqueline Aldine Leslie; da of Marchese Senator Sir Aldo Castellani, KCMG, FRCP, FACP; *m* 1934, as his 2 w, 1 Baron Killearn, GCMG, CB, MVO, PC (d 1964); *Style—* The Rt Hon the Dowager Lady Killearn; 23 Harley St W1; Haremere Hall, Etchingham, E Sussex

KILLICK, Elizabeth Audrey; da of George Wellstead Killick (d 1976), of Rhodes Minnis, Kent, and Winifred Rose, *née* Baines (d 1941); *b* 10 Sept 1924; *Educ* Streatham Hill HS, Altrincham Co HS, Univ of St Andrews (BSc, DSc); *Career* radar mechanic LACW WAAF 1943-46, lab asst RAF Inst of Aviation Med 1947, res and devpt Admiralty Signal and Radar Estate 1951, Admiralty Underwater Weapons Estate 1969-84 (head Submarine Sonar Systems Div 1969-75, head Weapons Dept 1975-84); memb Bd Marine Technology Directorate Ltd 1986-; FIEE 1980, FEng 1982; *Recreations* skiing, sailing, local history; *Style—* Miss Elizabeth Killick

KILLICK, Sir John Edward; GCMG (1979, KCMG 1971, CMG 1966); s of Edward William James Killick (d 1972); *b* 18 Nov 1919; *Educ* Latymer Upper Sch, UCL (fell), Univ of Bonn; *m* 1, 1949, Lynette du Preez, da of William Oxenham Leach (d 1984); m 2, 1985, Irene Monica Harries Easton, OBE, da of Malcolm Henry Easton; *Career* WWII Capt (Army) W Africa and W Europe; Dip Serv 1946-; asst under sec of state 1968-71, ambass USSR 1971-73, dep under sec of state 1973-75, ambass and perm UK rep to NATO 1975-79, ret; dir Dunlop SA 1980-85; pres Br Atlantic Ctee, chm Southborough Soc; *Recreations* golf; *Clubs* Brooks's, Garrick, East India Devonshire, Sports and Public Schs; *Style—* Sir John Killick, GCMG; Challoner's Cottage, 2 Birchwood Ave, Southborough, Kent TN4 0UE

KILLICK, Dr Stephen Robert; s of Herbert Percy Killick, of Poulton-le-Fylde, Lancs, and Lois Margaret, *née* Richardson (d 1985); *b* 30 Dec 1952; *Educ* Univ of London Guys Hosp Med Sch (BSc, MB BS, MD); *m* 25 May 1985, Diane, da of George Hall Billings (d 1980); 2 da (Georgina b 15 Oct 1987, Harriet b 10 Nov 1990); *Career* SE England jr hosp doctor 1976-79, surgical registrar Soweto SA 1979-80, SE England jr hosp doctor qualifying in gynaecology 1980-82, res fell Univ of Manchester 1982-88, conslt obstetrician and gynaecologist and sr lectr Univ of Manchester 1988-, numerous articles in med pubs; pres Withington Hosp Obstetric Fund; MRCOG; *Recreations* rugby, badminton, gardening; *Style—* Dr Stephen Killick; 34 Eagle Brow, Lymm, Cheshire WA13 0LY (☎ 092 575 2851); Department of Obstetrics and Gynaecology Withington Hospital, Nell Lane, Manchester M20 8LR (☎ 061 447 3810)

KILLINGBECK, Bernard Richard; s of Robert William Killingbeck, of Norfolk, and Gertrude Edith (d 1981); *b* 20 Aug 1950; *Educ* St Joseph's Coll, Ipswich; *m* 21 July 1979, Catherine Margaret, da of George Gibson Cargill (d 1969), of Norfolk; 1 s (Thomas); *Career* dir of private food, soft drinks and cosmetic co; *Recreations* golf; *Clubs* Royal West Norfolk Golf; *Style—* Bernard R Killingbeck, Esq; Abbey Farm, Guestwick, Norfolk N0R 20QW (☎ 036 284242)

KILMAINE, 7 Baron (I 1789); Sir John David Henry Browne; 13 Bt (NS 1636); s of 6 Baron Kilmaine, CBE (d 1978); *b* 2 April 1948; *Educ* Eton; *m* 1982, Linda, yr da of Dennis Robinson; 1 s, 1 da (Alice b 1985); *Heir* s, Hon John Francis Sandford Browne b 4 April 1983; *Career* dir: Fusion (Bickenhill) Ltd 1969-, Whale Tankers Ltd 1974-; *Style—* The Rt Hon the Lord Kilmaine

KILMARNOCK, 7 Baron (UK 1831); Alastair Ivor Gilbert Boyd; s of 6 Baron Kilmarnock, MBE, TD (d 1975), and of Hon Rosemary Guest (d 1971), da of 1 Viscount Wimborne. Lord Kilmarnock's f (6 Baron) changed his family name from Hay to Boyd 1941, having succeeded his bro, the 22 Earl of Erroll (in the UK Barony only) the same year; 5 in descent from the 18 Earl of Erroll cr 1 Baron Kilmarnock who m (1820) Elizabeth FitzClarence, a natural da of William IV by the actress Mrs Jordan; *b* 11 May 1927; *Educ* Bradfield, King's Coll Cambridge; *m* 1, 1954 (m dis 1969, she d 1975) Diana Mary, da of D Grant Gibson; m 2, 1977, Hilary Ann, da of Leonard Sidney Bardwell; *Heir* bro, Hon Robin Jordan Boyd; *Career* Lt Irish Gds, serv Palestine 1947-48; joined SDP 1981; vice-pres Inst Sales & Mktg Mgmnt 1981-; chief of Clan Boyd, page to Lord High Constable of Scotland at Coronation of HM King George VI; *Books* Sabbatical Year (1958), The Road from Ronda (1969), The Companion Guide to Madrid and Central Spain (1974); *Clubs* Pratt's; *Style—* The Rt Hon the Lord Kilmarnock; 1 Bridge St, Thornborough, Bucks MK18 2DN; Apartado 12, Ronda, Malaga, Spain

KILMISTER, (Claude Alaric) Anthony; s of Dr Claude Emile Kilmister (d 1951), of Swansea, S Wales, and Margaret E Mogford, *née* Gee; *b* 22 July 1931; *Educ* Shrewsbury; *m* 24 May 1958, Sheila, da of Lawrence Harwood (d 1984), of Hyde, Cheshire; *Career* Nat Serv 1950-52, cmmnd Army; NCB 1952-54, and with (C) Pty Orgn 1954-60; gen sec Cinema and TV Benevolent Fund 1962-72 (asst sec 1960-61), chm of Prayer Book Soc 1989- (fndr memb and dep chm BCP Action Gp (its forerunner) 1972-79), exec dir Parkinson's Disease Soc 1972-, fndr memb Ctee Action for Neurological Diseases 1987-; *Books* The Good Church Guide (1982), When Will Ye be Wise? (1983), My Favourite Betjeman (1985); *Recreations* writing, walking; *Clubs* Athenaeum; *Style—* Anthony Kilmister, Esq; 36 The Drive, Northwood, Middx HA6 1HP (☎ 092 74 24278)

KILPATRICK, Dr Ann Wilhelmina; da of John William Kilpatrick (d 1961), of Kilwarlin Ho, St James's, Hillsborough, Co Down, N I, and Anna Maria, *née* Brereton (d 1973); *b* 14 May 1924; *Educ* The Methodist Coll Belfast, Queen's Univ Belfast (MB BCh, BAO, DPH), Univ of London (DCH); *m* 17 Aug 1956, Dr David George Kiely, s of George Thomas Kiely (d 1964), of Ballynahinch, Co Down, NI; 1 s (Patrick b 1964), 1 da (Fiona b 1961); *Career* med paediatric registrar Alder Hey Childrens' Hosp Liverpool 1951; asst med offr of health: Walsall 1952, Downpatrick 1954, Portsmouth 1956 (sr clinical med offr 1978-89); specialist in assessing devpt of young children (from birth to five years) by interactive testing until 1990-; current chm of govrs East Shore Special Sch Portsmouth, govr Cliffdale First and Middle Special Schs Portsmouth; memb BMA 1948, MFCM 1974, assoc memb BPA 1982; *Recreations* flyfishing, gardening, foreign travel; *Style—* Dr Ann W Kilpatrick; Cranleigh, 107 Havant Rd, Emsworth, Hants PO10 7LF (☎ 0243 372 250); The School Clinic, Battenburg Ave, Portsmouth, Hants (☎ 0705 664 235, 0705 611 398)

KILPATRICK, Sir Robert; CBE (1979); s of Robert Kilpatrick (d 1974), of 4 Plantation Row, Coaltown of Wemyss, Fife, and Catherine Sharp, *née* Glover (d 1944); *b* 29 July 1926; *Educ* Buckhaven HS, Univ of Edinburgh (MB ChB, MD); *m* 28 Oct 1950, Elizabeth Gibson Page, da of Alexander Sharp Forbes, of The Barn, 12 Mill Lane, Smeeton Westerby, Leics; 2 s (Neil b 25 March 1956, John b 28 May 1959), 1 da (Katherine b 9 Aug 1951); *Career* Univ of Sheffield: lectr 1955-56, prof of clinical pharmacology and therapeutics 1966-75, dean Faculty of Med 1970-73; Univ of Leicester: dean Faculty of Med 1975-89, prof and head Dept of Clinical Pharmacology and Therapeutics 1975-83, prof of med 1984-89; pres GMC 1989-; Hon DUniv Edinburgh 1987; FRCPE 1963, FRCP 1975, memb Physiological Soc 1960; kt 1986; *Recreations* idling; *Clubs* Reform, Royal and Ancient; *Style—* Sir Robert Kilpatrick, CBE; The Barn, 12 Mill Lane, Smeeton Westerby, Leics LE8 0QL (☎ 0533 79 2202); General Medical Council, 44 Hallam St, London W1N 6AE (☎ 071 580 7642, fax 071 436 1384)

KILPATRICK, Prof (George) Stewart; OBE (1986); s of Hugh Kilpatrick (d 1951), of Edinburgh, and Annie Merricks, *née* Johnstone Stewart (d 1972); *b* 26 June 1925; *Educ* George Watson's Coll Edinburgh, Univ of Edinburgh Med Sch (MB ChB, MD); *m* 11 May 1954, Joan, da of Martin Askew (d 1970), of Cornwall; *Career* Nat Serv Maj RAMC 1949-51; Univ of Wales Coll Med 1963-90: dean of clinical studies 1970-87, vice provost 1987-90, prof and head Dept of Tuberculosis and Chest Diseases; conslt physician S Glam Health Authy; chm: Assoc of Med Deans of Europe, Cncl for the Assoc of the Study of Med Educn, Scientific Ctees of Int Union Against Tuberculosis and Lung Disease; MRCPE 1952, FRCPE 1966, FRCP 1972; memb: Assoc of Physicians of GB and Ireland, Br Thoracic Soc, Soc of Physicians in Wales; *Recreations* foreign travel, photography, reading; *Style—* Prof Stewart Kilpatrick, OBE; 14 Millbrook Rd, Dinas Powys, South Glamorgan CF6 4DA (☎ 0222 513149); University of Wales College of Medicine, Heath Park, Cardiff, CF4 4XN (☎ 0222 755944, fax 0222 766208)

KILROY, Patrick Canice; s of Thomas Kilroy (d 1976), and Mary, *née* Devine (d 1977); *b* 12 Oct 1929; *Educ* St Kieran's Coll Kilkenny, Univ Coll Dublin; *m* 1958, Dorothy, da of Michael Donnelly, of Dublin (d 1958); 2 s (Mark, Stephen), 3 da (Aisling, Helen, Cliona); *Career* slr; chm Gowan Group Ltd; dir: Waterford Wedgwood plc, Irish Distillers Group plc, Banque Nationale de Paris (Ireland) Ltd, Irish Life Assurance Co plc; chm: Church & Gen Insurance Co plc, Union Camp Ireland; Chev de l'Ordre Nat du Mérite; *Recreations* golf, tennis; *Clubs* Miltown Golf, Fitzwilliam Lawn Tennis; *Style—* Patrick Kilroy, Esq; Anerley, 45 Cowper Rd, Dublin 6 (☎ 975283); office: 69 Lower Leeson St, Dublin 2 (☎ 766166, fax 767823)

KILROY, Thomas; s of Thomas Kilroy, of Callan, Co Kilkenny, Ireland, and Mary, *née* Devine; *b* 23 Sept 1934; *Educ* St Kieran's Coll Kilkenny, Univ Coll Dublin; *m* 1, 1963 (m dis 1980), Patricia, *née* Cobey; 3 s; m 2, 1981, Julia Lowell, *née* Carlson; 1 da; *Career* lectr in Eng Univ Coll Dublin 1965-73, prof of modern Eng Univ Coll Galway 1979-89; writer; novel The Big Chapel 1971; plays: The Death and Resurrection of Mr Roche 1968, Tea and Sex and Shakespeare 1976, Talbot's Box 1977, Double Cross 1986, The Madame MacAdam Travelling Theatre 1991; Guardian fiction prize 1971, short list Booker prize 1971, Heinneman award for literature 1972, AIB literary prize 1972, American - Irish Fndn award 1975; memb: AOSDANA, Irish Acad of Letters; FRSL; *Style—* Thomas Kilroy, Esq; Kilmaine, County Mayo, Ireland (☎ 010 353 93 33361); Margaret Ramsay Ltd, 14A Goodwins Court, St Martins Lane, London WC2N 4LL (☎ 071 240 0691, fax 071 836 6807)

KILROY-SILK, Robert; s of William Silk (d 1943); *b* 19 May 1942; *Educ* Secdy Modern Sch, Sparkhill Commercial Sch, Saltley GS, LSE; *m* 1963, Jan, da of William Beech; 1 s, 1 da; *Career* lectr Univ of Liverpool 1966-74, govr Nat Heart and Chest Hosp 1974-77; MP (Lab): Ormskirk Feb 1974-1983, Knowsley North 1983-86; PPS to Min of Arts 1975-76, memb Select Ctee on Race Relations and on Wealth Tax 1974-75, vice chm PLP Home Affrs Gp 1976-79, chm PLP Civil Liberties Gp 1979-84, chm Parly Penal Affrs Gp 1979-86, memb Select Ctee Home Affrs 1979-84, chm PLP Home Affrs Gp 1983-84, frontbench spokesman Home Affrs 1984-86; TV presenter Kilroy! 1986-, columnist: Times 1987-90, Daily Express 1990-; chm The Kilroy Television Co 1989-; *Publications* Socialism since Marx (1973), The Ceremony of Innocence (novel 1984), Hard Labour: The Political Diary of Robert Kilroy-Silk (1986); *Recreations* gardening; *Style—* Robert Kilroy-Silk, Esq; Kilroy! BBC TV, Lime Grove, London (☎ 081 576 7821)

KIM, Young Tae; s of Jong Chul Kim, of Seoul, Korea, and Youn Sik Kim; *b* 23 April 1954; *Educ* Shinil HS Seoul Korea, Univ of Seoul (LLB); *m* 1981, Soohyun; 1 da (Kyung Eun b 1982); *Career* res mangr and fund mangr Korea Investment Trust Co Ltd 1978-87 (trained with Lazard Bros, Vickers da Costa, Yamaichi International (Europe) 1982-83), currently head of Korea team Schroder Securities (joined 1988); winner awards from Minister of Finance Korea 1985; memb Korean Securities Analysts Assoc 1984; *Recreations* golf; *Clubs* Gatton Manor Golf; *Style—* Young Kim, Esq; Schroder Securities, 120 Cheapside, London EC2V 6DS (☎ 071 382 3229)

KIMBALL, Baron (Life Peer UK 1985), of Easton, Co Leics; Marcus Richard Kimball; DL (Leics 1984); s of late Maj Lawrence Kimball, JP, DL, sometime MP Loughborough, by his 1 w, Kathleen Joan, only surviving da of Richard Ratcliff, of Stanford Hall, Loughborough, by his w Christine, 3 da of Vaughan Hanning Vaughan-Lee, JP, DL, sometime MP W Somerset; *b* 18 Oct 1928; *Educ* Eton, Trinity Coll Cambridge; *m* 1956, June Mary, only da of Montagu John Fenwick (whose mother Millicent was da of Rt Hon Lord Robert Montagu, 2 s of 6 Duke of Manchester), of Great Stukeley Hall, Huntingdon; 2 da (Hon Mrs Gibbs, Hon Mrs Straker *qqv*); *Career* Lt Leics Yeo (TA) 1947, Capt 1952, Maj 1955; MP for Gainsborough Div of Lincs (C) 1956-83, CC Rutland 1955-, PC rep Cncl of RCVS 1969-82 (Hon ARCVS 1982); external memb Cncl Lloyds 1982-91; dir: Royal Tst Bank 1970-, South East Assured Tenancies 1984-; chm: BFSS 1966-82, Fire Arms Consultation Ctee 1989, Univ of Cambridge Vet Sch Tst 1989; pres Hunters Improvement Soc 1989; kt 1981; *Recreations* fox hunting, past jt master of FitzWilliam and Cottesmore; *Clubs* White's, Pratt's; *Style—* Rt Hon Lord Kimball, DL; Great Easton Manor, Market Harborough, Leics LE16 8TB (☎ 0536 770333); Altnaharra, Lairg, Sutherland IV27 4AE (☎ 054 981 224)

KIMBER, Sir Charles Dixon; 3 Bt (UK 1904); s of Sir Henry Dixon Kimber, 2 Bt (d 1950); *b* 7 Jan 1912; *Educ* Eton, Balliol Coll Oxford; *m* 1, 1933 (m dis 1950), Ursula, da of late Ernest Roy Bird, MP; 3 s; m 2, 1950 (m dis 1965), Margaret, da of Francis John Bonham; 1 da; *Heir* s, Timothy Kimber *qv*; *Style—* Sir Charles Kimber, Bt; No 2 Duxford, Hinton Waldrist, nr Faringdon, Oxon (☎ Longworth 820004)

KIMBER, Derek Barton; OBE (1945); s of George Kimber, and Marion, *née* Barton; *b* 2 May 1917; *Educ* Bedford Sch, Imp Coll London (MSc, DIC), Royal Naval Coll Greenwich (RCNC); *m* 1943, Gwendoline Margaret Maude Brotherton; 2 s, 2 da; *Career* Royal Corps of Naval Constructors 1939-49, conslt Unwick Orr & Ptnrs Ltd 1950-54; Fairfield Shipbuilding & Engrg Co Ltd: mangr 1954, dir 1961, dep md 1963-65; dir Harland & Wolff Ltd 1966-69, dir gen Chemical Industries Assoc 1970-73; chm: Austin & Pickersgill Ltd 1973-83, Bartram & Sons 1973-83, Sunderland Shipbuilders Ltd 1980-83, Govan Shipbuilders Ltd 1980-83, Smiths Dock Ltd 1980-83; dir: A & P Appledore International Ltd 1974-77, British Ship Research Association (Tstees) Ltd 1973-81, R S Dalgliesh Ltd 1978-80, Equity Capital for Industry Ltd 1977-86, Essar Forrester (Holdings) Ltd 1983-, Wilks Shipping Co Ltd 1986-, AMARC (TES) Ltd 1986; chm: London & Overseas Freighters plc 1984-, Short Sea Europe plc 1989-; Glasgow C of C 1962-65; chm C & G Jt Advsy Ctee for Shipbuilding 1968-70, pres Clyde Shipbuilders Assoc 1964-65; memb Shipbuilding Indust Trg Bd 1964-69; Lloyds Register of Shipping: Scottish Ctee 1964-65, Gen Ctee 1973, Tech Ctee 1976-80, Exec Bd 1978-84; memb Res Cncl Br Ship Res Assoc 1973-81, chm Br Tech Ctee American Bureau of Shipping 1989- (memb 1976-); memb: Standing Ctee Assoc of W Euro Shipbuilders 1976-89 (chm 1983-84), Ctee of EEC Shipbuilders Assoc 1985-89;

underwriting memb Lloyds 1985-, chm Mgmnt Bd Shipbuilders & Repairers Nat Assoc 1974-76 (vice pres 1976-77); memb: Jt Indust Consultative Ctee (SRNA/CSEU) 1966-76, EDC Chem Indust 1970-72, Process Plant Working Party (NEDO) 1970-72, CBI Central Cncl 1970-72 and 1975-84, N Reg Cncl CBI (chm 1975-77), Steering Ctee Int Maritime Industs Forum 1981-, Cncl RINA (pres 1977-81), Cncl Welding Inst 1959-74 and 1976-82, Bd CEI 1977-81 (Exec Ctee 1978-80), G & G Sr Awards Ctee 1970-81, Cncl NE Coast Inst of Engrs and Shipbuilders 1974- (pres 1982-84); vice pres Br Maritime League 1985-87, tstee AMARC Fndn 1986-, govr Imp Coll London 1967-87; memb: Ct City Univ, City of London Br Royal Soc of St George 1985-, Smeatonian Soc 1984-; pres Old Centralians 1985-86; Liveryman: Worshipful Co of Shipwrights 1967 (asst to Ct 1974, Prime Warden 1986-87), Worshipful Co of Engrs 1984-; Gold medal RINA 1977; Hon FRINA 1981, FEng 1976, FCGI, FIMechE, FIMarE, FNECInst, FRSA; *publications* contrib on shipbuilding in various learned jls; *Recreations* DIY, golf, rough gardening; *Clubs* Brook's, Caledonian, City Livery, Aldgate Ward, Anchovites, MCC, Den Norske, Yacht Club of Greece; *Style*— Derek Kimber, Esq, OBE; Broughton, Monk's Rd, Virginia Water, Surrey GU25 4RR

KIMBER, Timothy Roy Henry; s and h of Sir Charles Dixon Kimber, 3 Bt; *b* 3 June 1936; *Educ* Eton; *m* 1, 1960 (m dis 1974), Antonia Kathleen Brenda, da of Sir Francis John Watkin Williams, 8 Bt, QC; 2 s; m 2, 1979, Susan Hare, da of late J K Brooks, and widow of Richard Coulthurst North, of Newton Hall, Lancs; *Career* banker; dir Lazard Bros & Co Ltd; *Clubs* Boodle's, Royal Lytham St Anne's Golf; *Style*— Timothy Kimber, Esq; Newton Hall, via Carnforth, Lancashire (☎ 0468 71232, work 05242 72146)

KIMBER-SMITH, Geoffrey; s of Alan Harold Kimber-Smith, of Wilts, and Dorothy Coulthard, *née* Wood; *b* 15 April 1950; *Educ* Glasgow Acad, Royal GS High Wycombe, Derby Poly; *m* ; 2 s (Mathew b 1974, Thomas 1984); *Career* accountant; Lion Oil Tool Ltd 1985-, Motors Wokingham Ltd 1976-85; DP Media Services Ltd 1983-85, Gramak (Engineering) Ltd 1984-85, D Cooper (Engineering) Ltd 1985-86, Lion Engineering Services Ltd 1989-, ES Exhibitions Ltd 1989-, Townsin Teece Evans Ltd 1989-; FICM, ACE; *Recreations* motor racing; *Style*— Geoffrey Kimber-Smith, Esq; 26 Mill Close, Wokingham, Berks; Admiralty Rd, Gt Yarmouth, Norfolk (☎ 0493 856414, telex 975210)

KIMBERLEY, 4 Earl of (UK 1866); Sir John Wodehouse; 11 Bt (estab 1611); also 6 Baron Wodehouse (GB 1797); s of 3 Earl of Kimberley, CBE, MC (d 1941) and Frances Margaret Irby, niece of Lord Boston; *b* 12 May 1924; *Educ* Eton, Magdalene Coll Cambridge; *m* 1, 1945 (m dis 1948), Diana Evelyn, da of late Lt-Col the Hon Sir Piers Walter Legh, GCVO, KCB, CMG, CIE, OBE (yr s of 2 Baron Newton); m 2, 1949 (m dis 1952), Carmel June (Dunnett), da of late Michael Maguire, of Melbourne, Aust; 1 s; m 3, 1953 (m dis 1960), Mrs Cynthia Abdy Westendarp, da of E Abdy Collins, FRCS, MRCP, of The Chantrey, Saxmundham, Suffolk; 2 s; m 4, 1961 (m dis 1965), Margaret, da of Alby Simons; 1 s; m 5, 1970 (m dis 1982), Gillian, da of Col Norman Ireland-Smith, and formerly w of John Raw; m 6, 1982, Jane, da of Lt-Col Christopher d'A P Consett, DSO, MC, of The Bawn, Osgodby, Thirsk, N Yorks; *Heir* Lord Wodehouse b 1951; *Career* served as Lt Gren Gds in Gds Armd Div 1943-45; Br Bobsleigh Team 1950-58, Cresta Rider 1948-58; former Lib spokesman on aviation and aerospace, def, voluntary community servs; expelled from Lib Pty May 1979, has since sat as Cons Peer in House of Lords; delegate to N Atlantic Assembly 1981-; memb: House of Lords All Pty Def Study Gp (Hon Sec 1978-), Air League Cncl 1981, Assoc Cons Peers, Br Maritime League Cncl, Royal Utd Services Inst, Int Inst for Strategic Studies, Br Atlantic Ctee; vice pres World Cncl on Alcoholism, chm National Cncl on Alcoholism 1982-85; ARAeS; *Recreations* fishing, shooting, racing, gardening, bridge; *Clubs* White's, MCC, Naval and Military, House of Lords Yacht, House of Lords Fly Fishing, Falmouth Shark Angling (pres); *Style*— The Rt Hon the Earl of Kimberley; Hailstone House, Cricklade, Wilts SN6 6JP (☎ 0793 750344, fax 0793 752078)

KIMMINS, Malcolm Brian Johnston; s of Lt-Gen Sir Brian Kimmins, KBE, CB, DL (d 1979); *b* 12 Feb 1937; *Educ* Harrow, Grenoble Univ; *m* 1968, Jane, da of Thomas Douglas Pilkington; 1 s, 2 da; *Career* chm Corney & Barrow Group plc; *Recreations* horse racing, golf, shooting; *Clubs* White's, Jockey; *Style*— Malcolm Kimmins Esq; Corney & Barrow Ltd, 12 Helmet Row, London EC1V 3NN (☎ 071 251 4051)

KIMMINS, Robert; s of James Kimmins, of Wigan, and Hilda, *née* Beddows; *b* 28 Jan 1962; *Educ* Cansfield HS, Wigan Coll of Technol; *m* 19 July 1986, Julie Ann, da of late Brian John Davies; 1 s (Stephen William b 16 July 1990); *Career* Rugby Union lock forward Orrell RUFC; clubs: Wigan RLFC Colts 1976-78, Lancs RUFC Colts 1979-80, Orrell RUFC 1981- (300 appearances), Barbaricans RFC 1989-; rep: Lancs 1983- (over 20 appearances), North of England 1987-, Eng B (debut 1985, 8 caps) 1985-90; England: tour Argentina 1990; bricklayer 1981- (apprentice 1978-81); *Recreations* railway, photography, travel; *Style*— Robert Kimmins, Esq; Orrell RUFC, Edgehall Rd, Orrell, Wigan WN5 8TL (☎ 623193)

KINAHAN, Sir (Robert George Caldwell) Robin; ERD (1946), JP (1950); s of Henry Kinahan (d 1958); *b* 24 Sept 1916; *Educ* Stowe; *m* 1950, Coralie Isabel, da of Capt Charles de Burgh, RN (d 1968); 2 s, 3 da; *Career* Capt RA 1939-45, served France and Far East; cllr and alderman Belfast Corpn 1949-64; High Sheriff: Belfast (1955), Co Antrim (1969); MP (NI) Clifton 1958-59, Lord Mayor of Belfast 1959-61; dir: Gallaher Ltd 1967-81, National Westminster Bank 1973-83, Eagle Star Insurance Co (local) to 1981, STC (NI) Ltd, Abbey Life (Ireland) Ltd 1981-87; chm: Bass Ireland Ltd 1958-78, Inglis & Co Ltd 1962-82, E T Green Ltd 1964-82, Ulster Bank Ltd 1970-82 (dep chm 1964-70), Abbeyfield Belfast Soc 1983-, Cheshire House (NI) 1983-87; Lord Lt Co Borough of Belfast 1985- (DL 1962); kt 1961; *Recreations* gardening, farming; *Style*— Sir Robin Kinahan, ERD, JP; Castle Upton, Templepatrick, Co Antrim, N Ireland (☎ 08494 32466)

KINCADE, Dr James; CBE (1988); s of George Kincade (d 1965), and Rebecca Jane, *née* Lyons (d 1983); *b* 4 Jan 1925; *Educ* Foyle Coll Londonderry, Trinity Coll Dublin (MA), Oriel Coll Oxford (MA, BLitt), Univ of Edinburgh (PhD); *m* 26 Aug 1952, (Elizabeth) Fay, da of James Anderson Piggot, OBE, JP, DL (d 1961); 1 s (James Anderson b 26 Aug 1953), 1 da (Ruth b 20 Feb 1956); *Career* RAF 1943-47 (cmmnd 1944); head of English Merchiston Castle Sch 1955-61 (teacher 1952-61), visiting prof of philosophy Indiana Univ 1959; headmaster: Dungannon Royal Sch 1961-74, Methodist Coll Belfast 1974-88; Queen's Univ Belfast: memb Senate, chm External Relations Ctee, memb Standing Ctee; cncl memb Cncl of Catholic Maintained Schs, memb educn ctee UTV 1979-85, nat govr for NI BBC 1985-, dir Design Cncl NI 1990-; SHA 1961-88, HMC 1974-88; *Recreations* gardening, walking; *Style*— Dr James Kincade, CBE; Harry's Rd, Culcavy, Co Down BT26 6HJ (☎ 0846 683865)

KINCAID, Col John William Martin (Bill); s of Maj John Brian Shortt Kincaid (d 1944), and Stella May, *née* Martin (d 1980); *b* 1 July 1940; *Educ* Cheltenham Coll, RMA Sandhurst, Fitzwilliam Coll Cambridge (BA, MA); *m* 17 June 1965, Hilary Jane, da of Elmore Cooper (d 1989); 2 s (John b 2 April 1966, Charles b 27 Aug 1968), 1 da (Rebecca b 28 Dec 1972); *Career* regtl duty RA 1961-72, army staff course Shrivenham and Camberley 1973-74, MOD 1977-79, cdr 50 Missile Regt 1977-79, Maj MGO Secretariat MOD 1979-81, NDC 1981, Lt Col MOD LSOR 6 1981-84, Lt Col MOD MLRS 1984-87, Col MOD LSOR 6 1987-; *Recreations* cricket, hockey, choral singing, gardening; *Clubs* Royal Artillery Cricket, Stragglers of Asia Cricket, Sunbury Cricket (capt); *Style*— Col Bill Kincaid; MOD (LSOR 6), Neville House, Page St, London SW1 (☎ 071 218 4386)

KINCRAIG, Hon Lord; Robert Smith Johnston; s of William Turner Johnston, of Glasgow; *b* 10 Oct 1918; *Educ* Strathallan, St John's Coll Cambridge, Univ of Glasgow; *m* 1943, Margaret Joan, da of Col A Graham, of Glasgow; 1 s, 1 da; *Career* advocate 1942, QC 1955, Sheriff princ Roxburgh & Berwick 1964-70, senator Coll of Justice and Lord of Session 1972-87, with title of Lord Kincraig; dean Faculty of Advocates 1970-72; *Recreations* gardening; *Clubs* Hon Co Edinburgh Golfers, RSAC (Glasgow); *Style*— The Hon Lord Kincraig; Westwood Cottage, Longniddry, E Lothian (☎ 0875 53583)

KINDER, John Russell; s of Herbert Kinder, of Leicester, and Kathleen Margaret, *née* Sarson; *b* 10 Nov 1937; *Educ* Wyggeston GS Leicester, Corpus Christi Coll Oxford (MA in PPE); *m* 1964, Diana Christine, da of Frederick Gordan Evans (d 1984); 4 s (Mark Russell b 1966, Andrew John b 1967, Stephen James b 1970, Jonathan Charles b 1974); *Career* RAF 1956-58; dir: William Brandts Sons & Co Ltd 1975-77; jt md Warwick Engineering Investmts Ltd 1978-80; md CH Industrials plc 1980-; dir: Aston Martin Lagonda 1980-83, Aston Martin Tickford 1981-; FICA; *Recreations* tennis, sailing, christian youth work; *Style*— John Kinder, Esq; 23 Woodville Gardens, Ealing, London W5 2LL (☎ 997 1207); CH Industrials, 33 Cavendish Square, London W1 (☎ 491 7860)

KINDERSLEY, Christian Philip; s of Hon Philip Leyland Kindersley, of The Coach House, Northwick Park, Blockley, Gloucs, and Violet Valerie Gwendolen, *née* French; *b* 19 March 1950; *Educ* Eton; *m* 5 May 1973, Hilary Luise, da of David Radcliffe Guard (d 1979); 1 s (Alexander), 2 da (Vanessa, Davina); *Career* ptnr Cazenove & Co 1982-(joined 1970); Freeman City of London 1983, Liveryman Worshipful Co of Fishmongers 1983; *Recreations* shooting, tennis, reading; *Clubs* White's, City of London, MCC; *Style*— Christian Kindersley, Esq; 12 Tokenhouse Yard, London EC2R 7AN (☎ 071 588 2828, fax 071 606 9205, car 0860 289439, telex 886758)

KINDERSLEY, Gay; s of Hon Philip Kindersley (4 s of 1 Baron Kindersley, GBE) by his 1 w, Oonagh, yst da of Hon Arthur Guinness (2 s of 1 Earl of Iveagh), who m 2, 4 Baron Oranmore and Browne and 3, Miguel Ferreras; *b* 2 June 1930; *Educ* Eton; *m* 1, 1956 (m dis 1976), Margaret, da of Hugh Wakefield, of Mount St, Mayfair; 2 s, 2 da; m 2, 1976, Philippa Harper; 2 s; *Career* gentleman rider (amateur jockey) and trainer; *Clubs* Turf; *Style*— Gay Kindersley, Esq; Parsonage Farm and Stables, East Garston, Newbury, Berks (☎ Great Shefford (048 839) 301/279)

KINDERSLEY, Hon Philip Leyland; s of 1 Baron Kindersley, GBE (d 1954); *b* 11 March 1907; *Educ* Eton, Christ Church Oxford; *m* 1, 1929 (m dis 1936), Oonagh, da of Hon (Arthur) Ernest Guinness (d 1949, 2 s of late 1 Earl of Iveagh); 1 s, 1 da (decd); m 2, 1936, Valerie Violet (formerly w of late 4 Baron Brougham and Vaux), da of Hon Gerald French, DSO (2 s of late 1 Earl of Ypres, KP, GCB, OM, GCVO, KCMG, PC) 1 s, 2 da; *Career* serv WWII in N Africa (wounded, POW); Capt Coldstream Gds; stockbroker, ret 1977; chm Lingfield Racecourse, ret 1982; *Recreations* hunting; *Clubs* White's; *Style*— The Hon Philip Kindersley; The Coach House, Northwick Park, Blockley, Glos

KINDERSLEY, Lt-Col (Claude) Richard Henry; DSO (1944), MC (1943); s of Lt-Col Archibald Ogilvie Littleton Kindersley, CMG, DL (d 1955), and Edith Mary, *née* Craven (d 1936); *b* 11 Dec 1911; *Educ* Wellington, Trinity Coll Cambridge (MA); *m* 5 Oct 1933, Vivien Mary, da of Sqdn Ldr Charles John Wharton Darwin, DSO (d 1941); 3 da (Gloria b 1940, Avril b 1944, Susan b 1948); *Career* cmmnd HLI 1933, served 2 Bn HLI (NW Frontier, Palestine, ME 1936-43), 1 Bn HLI (France and Germany) 1944-45, Cdr 1 Bn HLI 1945, Inf Boys Bn 1953-54, ret 1955; dir The Trade Counter Ltd; DL 1962-74, IOW High Sheriff 1974, Vice Lord-Lt 1979-86; *Recreations* sailing; *Clubs* Royal Yacht Sqdn, Royal Solent YC; *Style*— Lt-Col Richard Kindersley, DSO, MC, DL; Hamstead Grange, Yarmouth, Isle of Wight (☎ 0983 760230)

KINDERSLEY, The Rt Hon the Lord Robert Hugh Molesworth Kindersley; s of 2 Baron Kindersley, CBE, MC (d 1976), and Nancy Farnsworth (d 1977); *b* 18 Aug 1929; *Educ* Eton, Trinity Coll Oxford, Harvard Business Sch; *m* 1, 4 Sept 1954 (m dis 1989), Venice Marigold (Rosie), da of late Capt Lord (Arthur) Francis Henry Hill, (yr s of 6 Marquess of Downside); 3 s (Rupert John Molesworth b 11 March 1955, Hugh Francis b 22 June 1956 (d 6 March 1991), Dickon Michael b 9 Feb 1962), 1 da (Anna Lucy b 19 June 1965); m 2, 1989, Patricia Margaret (Tita), o da of late Brig Hugh Ronald Norman, DSO, MC, of St Clere, Kemsing, Kent, and former w of Henry Colum Crichton-Stuart; *Career* Lt Scots Gds served Malaya 1949; dir: London Assurance 1957-, Witan Investment Co Ltd 1958-85, Steel Co of Wales 1959-67, Lazard Bros and Co Ltd 1960-, Marconi Co Ltd 1963-68, Sun Alliance & London Insurance Group 1965-, English Electric Co Ltd 1966-68, GEC Ltd 1968-70, British Match Corporation Ltd 1969-73, Swedish Match Co 1973-85, Maersk Co Ltd 1986-; chm: Cwlth Devpt Corpn 1980-89, Siam Selective Growth Trust 1990-, Brent Walker Group plc 1991-; dep chm Advsy Cncl ECGD 1975-80; fin advsr Export Gp for the Constructional Industs 1961-85; chm BBA 1976-78, pres Anglo-Taiwan Trade Ctee 1976-86; memb Inst Int d'Etudes Bancaires 1971-85; memb Ct Worshipful Co of Fishmongers 1973- (Prime Warden 1989-90); *Recreations* all sports, deer, gardening; *Clubs* All England Lawn Tennis and Croquet (memb Ctee), Queen's, MCC, Pratt's; *Style*— The Rt Hon The Lord Kindersley; West Green Farm, Shipbourne, Kent TN11 9PU (☎ 0732 810293); 25 Grafton Square, London SW4 0DB (☎ 071 622 1198); 21 Moorfields, London EC2P 2HT (☎ 071 588 2721, fax 071 628 2485)

KINDERSLEY, Hon Rupert John Molesworth; s and h of 3 Baron Kindersley; *b* 11 March 1955; *Educ* Eton; *m* 2 Aug 1975, Sarah Anne, da of late John D Warde; 1 s (Frederick b 1987), 1 da (Rebecca b 1985); *Career* Freeman of City of London, Liveryman Worshipful Co of Fishmongers 1990; FIMBRA 1987; *Style*— The Hon Rupert Kindersley; c/o The Daniels Group, 6-10 Bruton St, London W1X 7AG (☎ 071 629 6669, fax 071 629 0450)

KINDERSLEY, Hon Mrs Philip; Violet Valerie; *née* French; da of Lt-Col Hon Gerald French, DSO (2 s of 1 Earl of Ypres and an author); *m* 1, 1931 (m dis 1934), 4 Baron Brougham and Vaux (d 1967); 1 s decd ; m 2, 1936, as his 2 w, Hon Philip Kindersley, 4 s of 1 Baron Kindersley, GBE; 1 s (Christian Philip), 2 da (Mrs Robert Philipson-Stow, Hon Mrs Peregrine Fairfax); *Style*— The Hon Mrs Kindersley; High Paddocks, Lye Green, Crowborough, Sussex (☎ 0892 3127)

KING, Sir Albert; OBE (1958), JP; s of George King (d 1915); *b* 20 Aug 1905; *Educ* Primrose Hill Leeds; *m* 1928, Pauline Riley; 1 da; *Career* full-time offr AUEW 1942-70: sec Leeds Div 1942-52, div organiser 1952-70, TUC regnl sec 1958-70, ret; ldr Labour Gp Leeds Met DC 1959-78; kt 1975; *Recreations* walking, reading; *Clubs* Beeston WMC; *Style*— Sir Albert King, OBE, JP; 25 Brookhill Ave, Leeds LS17 8QA (☎ 0532 684684)

KING, Dr Alexander Hyatt (Alec); s of Thomas Hyatt King (d 1945), of London, and Mabel Jessie, *née* Brayne (d 1947); *b* 18 July 1911; *Educ* Dulwich, King's Coll Cambridge (MA); *m* 15 May 1943, Evelyn Mary (Eve), da of David Arthur Davies (d 1951), of Purley, Surrey; 2 s (David Hyatt b 29 April 1946, Edmund Mervyn Bellamy b 29 April 1949); *Career* Br Museum: Dept of Printed Books 1934, supt Music Room 1944-73, dep keeper 1959-76; music librarian Br Library 1973-76; hon sec Br Union Catalogue of Early Music 1948-57, chm Exec Ctee Br Inst of Recorded Sound 1948-

62, Sandars reader in bibliography Univ of Cambridge 1962; pres Int Assoc of Music Libraries 1955-59, hon memb Int Assoc of Music Libraries 1968, hon librarian Royal Philharmonic Soc 1969-82, pres Royal Music Assoc 1970-74, tstee of Hinrichsen Fndn 1976-82; Hon Dr Univ of York 1979, Hon D Mus Univ of St Andrews 1981; *Books* Chamber Music (1948), Four Hundred Years of Music Printing (1964), Handel and His Autographs (1967), Mozart Wind and String Concertos (1978), The New Oxford History of Music Vol 8 (contrib, 1982), Musical Pursuits, Selected Essays (1987); *Recreations* opera, cricket (watching), exploring Suffolk; *Clubs* MCC; *Style*— Dr Alec Hyatt King; 37 Pier Ave, Southwold, Suffolk IP18 6BU (☎ 0502 72 4274)

KING, Prof Anthony Stephen; s of Harold Stark King (d 1949), and Marjorie Mary, *née* James (d 1982); *b* 17 Nov 1934; *Educ* Queen's Univ Kingston Ontario Canada (BA), Univ of Oxford (BA, DPhil); *m* 1, 1965, Vera Korte (d 1972); m 2, Janet Frances Mary, da of Adm of the Fleet Sir Michael Pollock, KGCB, DSO, *qv*, of The Ivy House, Churchstoke, Montgomery, Powys; *Career* fell Magdalen Coll Oxford 1961-65; Univ of Essex 1966-: sr lectr in govt 1966-67, reader 1967-69, prof 1969-, academic pro vice chllr 1986-89; fell Center for Advanced Study in the Behavioral Scis Stanford California 1977-78, visiting prof of pub int affrs Princeton Univ 1984; *Books* Westminster and Beyond (with Anne Slaman, 1973), British Members of Parliament (1974), Why is Britain Becoming Harder to Govern? (ed, 1976), Britain Says Yes: The 1975 Referendum on the Common Market (1977), The British Prime Minister (ed, second edn 1985), The New American Political System (ed, 2 edn 1990); *Recreations* music, holidays, walking; *Clubs* Royal Cwlth Soc; *Style*— Prof Anthony King; Dept of Govt, University of Essex, Wivenhoe Park, Colchester, Essex CO4 3SQ (☎ 0206 873393)

KING, Barbara Sarah; da of John Henry Otty (d 1978), of Yorks, and Florence Harriet, *née* Robinson (d 1985); *b* 14 June 1946; *Educ* Secdy Modern Otley, privately; *m* 21 July 1962, James King; 1 s (James Martin b 1964, d 1964), 1 da (Sarah Jane b 1972); *Career* md Slimming Magazine Clubs Ltd 1988- (exec dir 1985-); dir: Argus Consumer Magazine Division 1988, Argus Press Group; contrib to health and diet pubns; MInstD MInstM; *Recreations* reading, writing, wine making; *Style*— Mrs Barbara King

KING, Brian Maurice; s of Maurice James King, and late Grace Mary, *née* Escott; *b* 8 Aug 1933; *Educ* Westcliff HS, Southend Sch of Architecture; *m* 23 Aug 1958, Joan, da of Arthur Rouse; 2 s (Andrew James b 1961, Daniel John b 1963); *Career* architect and landscape architect; formed own practice 1982; chm Wells Housing Assoc, served in Friends Ambulance Unit Int Serv 1956-58; ARIBA; *Recreations* dinghy sailing, painting, drawing, walking; *Clubs* Wilsonian; *Style*— Brian King, Esq; 67 Kingswood Rd, Bromley, Kent BR2 0NL (☎ 081 460 7658); 34 Hill Rise, Richmond, Surrey TW10 6UA (☎ 081 948 8191)

KING, Col Bryan Arthur George; TD (1972); s of George Henry King (d 1966), of Wallasey, and Ethel, *née* Hughes (d 1990); *b* 29 April 1930; *Educ* Birkenhead Sch; *m* 21 May 1960, Elizabeth, da of late Jack Oddy, of Chester; 2 da (Jane b 1962, Julia b 1967); *Career* TA 1959-79, 4 Bn Cheshire Regt, Mercian Vols and Cheshire ACF, Col 1978, memb Regtl Cncl Cheshire Regt, vice chm NW Eng TAVR; sr ptnr Wayman-Hales Slrs Chester, hon slr Cheshire Regt; memb Cncl Law Soc 1982-; govr The Queen's Sch Chester, pres Deeside Ramblers Hockey Club; *Recreations* travel, gardening; *Clubs* Army and Navy, Chester City; *Style*— Col Bryan King, TD; Taluca, Church Lane, Upton By Chester, Cheshire (☎ 0244 381 436); 12 White Friars, Chester (☎ 0244 321 122, fax 0244 343642)

KING, Christopher John; s of Kavan John King, of 5 Roebuck Court, 29 Rooney Road, New Malden, Surrey and Gwendoline June, *née* Kent (d 1985); *b* 15 Oct 1959; *Educ* Kings Coll Sch Wimbledon, Univ of Edinburgh; *m* 1989, Gayle Shiona, da of John Thomson, of 17 White Wisp Gardens Dollar, Clackmannanshire; 1 s (James Alexander b 4 Oct 1990); *Career* cmmnd Royal Regt of FUS 1978-; brand mangr Proctor and Gamble Limited 1982-84, account supervisor Ted Bates Advertising 1984, account dir grey Advertising Limited 1985-87, Bd dir Jenner Keating Becker Reay 1989-91 (acc dir 1987-88), Bd dir Reay Keating Hamer 1991-; MIPA; *Style*— Christopher King, Esq; 75 Santos Road, London SW18 1NT; Reay Keating Hamer, 65-66 Frith St, London N1V 5TA

KING, Prof David Anthony; s of Arnold Tom Wallis King, of Johannesburg, SA, and Patricia Mary Bede, *née* Vardy; *b* 12 Aug 1939; *Educ* St John's Coll Johannesburg, Univ of Witwatersrand SA (BSc, PhD), UEA (ScD); *m* 5 Nov 1983, Jane Margaret Lichtenstein (uses maiden name), da of Hans Lichtenstein, of Llandrindod Wells, Wales; 3 s (Benjamin Tom b 11 Nov 1973, Tobias Alexander b 15 Sept 1975, Zachary Adam b 17 Sept 1986), 1 da (Emily Sarah b 20 Feb 1984); *Career* Shell scholar Imp Coll London 1963-66, lectr in chemical physics UEA Norwich 1966-74, Brunner prof of physical chemistry Univ of Liverpool 1974-88, 1920 prof of physical chemistry Univ of Cambridge 1988- (fell St John's Coll); pres AUT 1976-77; memb: Leverhulme Tst Res Awards Advsy Ctee 1980-, Direction Ctee Fritz Haber Inst Berlin 1981-; ed Chemical Physics Letters 1989-, chm Kettle's Yard (House and Art Gallery) Cambridge 1989-; MInstP 1967, FRSC 1974 (medal and award for surface chem 1978, Tilden Lectr 1988-89); Br Vac Cncl medal and award for research 1991; *Books* numerous scientific pubns on The Chemical Physics of Solid Surfaces and Gas/Surface Interactions; *Recreations* art, photography; *Style*— Prof David King; 28 Bateman St, Cambridge CB2 1NB (☎ 0223 315629); Dept of Chemistry, Lensfield Rd, Univ of Cambridge, Cambridge; St John's College, St John's St, Cambridge (☎ 0223 336338, fax 0223 336332)

KING, Gp Capt Dennis; MBE (1970); s of Arthur Lawrence King (d 1971), of Liversedge, Yorks, and Ada, *née* Brook (d 1972); *b* 2 March 1934; *Educ* Knaresborough and Heckmondwike GS, Kings Coll London, RAF Staff Coll, Nat Defence Coll; *m* 1, 10 June 1960 (m dis 1975), (Sylvia) Ann, da of Stanley Ormond Roch (d 1960), of Kingswear, Devon; 2 da (Annabelle b 1963, Jennifer b 1964); *Career* RAF: PO 1957, Sqdn Ldr 1968, Wing Cdr 1974, Gp Capt 1980-84; bursar Froebel Inst London 1984-85, sec Nat Small Bore Rifle Assoc 1985-; *Recreations* sport, small bore rifle shooting (Eng rep 1955, GB rep 1964, GB champ 1956), gardening, music; *Style*— Gp Capt Dennis King, MBE, RAF; National Small Bore Rifle Association, Lord Roberts House, Bisley Camp, Brookwood, Woking, Surrey GU24 0NP

KING, Diana Mary; da of Robin Garnett Milton Bull, of Nesscliffe, Shropshire, and Phyllis Rosemary, *née* Hill; *b* 22 June 1953; *Educ* Sutton Coldfield Girls GS, Univ of Sheffield (BA); *m* 23 May 1981, Philip Adrian King, s of Harry King, OBE (d 1984); *Career* Univ of Sheffield OTC 1972-75, 3 Bn Yorks Vol 1975-80, ret with rank of Capt; admitted slr 1979, private practice as litigation slr 1979-85, chief exec Eng Ski Cncl 1985-; memb: Exec Ctee Br Gliding Assoc, CBSO chorus; *Recreations* gliding, music, gardening; *Clubs* Midland Gliding; *Style*— Mrs Diana King; English Ski Council, Area Library Building, Queensway Mall, The Cornbow, Halesowen, West Midlands B63 4AJ (☎ 021 501 2314)

KING, Hon Mrs (Elizabeth Patricia); *née* White; da of 4th Baron Annaly, MC, and Lady Lavinia Spencer, da of 6th Earl Spencer, KG, GCVO, VD, PC; is 1 cous once removed of HRH Princess of Wales; *b* 5 Nov 1923; *m* 1945, Lt Cdr Osborne King, DSC, DL, RNVR, *qv*; 1 s (James b 1952, m 1981 Sally, da of Alan Walker-Gray), 2 da (Elizabeth Lavinia Sara b 1946, m 1969, David Hugh Montgomery; Patricia Rose b 1947, m 1970, Antony Douglas North); *Style*— The Hon Mrs King; Rademon, Crossgar, Co Down, N Ireland (☎ 0396 830214)

KING, Elizabeth Rosalind; da of Graham George King, of 24 Willifield Way, Hampstead Garden Suburb, London NW11, and Margaret Elizabeth, *née* Mitchell; *b* 28 Oct 1969; *Educ* Weydon Comp Sch, Farnham Sixth Form Coll, Bath Coll of Higer Educn; *Career* singer, actress; roles incl: title role in Annie (Redgrave Theatre Farnham) 1985, The Wife in Lorca's Blood Wedding (Bloomsbury Theatre) 1988, Raissa Filipovna in The Suicide (Bloomsbury Theatre) 1989, Elsie in Blitz (Playhouse Embankment London) 1990; sang as solo cabaret artist Annual Nat Youth Theatre Charity of GB Ball (Grosvenor House Hotel Park Lane) 1989 and 1990, played cabaret artist in a film documentary for CASIO with Jools Holland 1989; *Style*— Ms Elizabeth King; Storeys, Old Compton Lane, Farnham, Surrey GU9 8EG (☎ 0252 726027)

KING, Francis Henry; CBE (1985); s of Eustace Arthur Cecil King (d 1937), and Faith Mina, *née* Read; *b* 4 March 1923; *Educ* Shrewsbury, Balliol Coll Oxford (MA); *Career* Br Cncl Offr 1950-63; lectr: Florence Italy 1950-51, Salonica and Athens Greece 1951-57; asst rep Finland 1957-58, regnl dir Kyoto Japan 1958-63; drama critic Sunday Telegraph 1976-88; Int pres PEN 1986-89; FRSL 1958-; *Books* The Dividing Stream (1951, Somerset Maughan Award), The Man on the Rock (1957), The Custom House (1961), The Needle (1975), Act of Darkness (1983), Voices in an Empty Room (1984), The Woman Who Was God (1988), The Ant Colony (1991); *Recreations* mountaineering and pot-holing; *Style*— Francis King, Esq, CBE; 19 Gordon Place, London W8 4JE (☎ 071 937 5715)

KING, Gen Sir Frank Douglas; GCB (1976, KCB 1972, CB 1971), MBE (1953); s of Arthur King; *b* 9 March 1919; *Educ* Wallingford GS; *m* 1946, Joy Emily; 1 s, 2 da; *Career* joined Army 1939, serv WWII, cmd Parachute Bn Gp Cyprus 1960-62, cmd Inf Bde Gp Germany 1962-64, Brig 1965, Maj-Gen 1966, dir Land/Air Warfare MOD (Army) 1966-68, Cmdt RMCS 1969-71, GOC-in-C Strategic Cmd 1971, dep C-in-C UKLF 1972-73, GOC NI 1973-75, Gen 1976, Cdr Northern Army Gp and C-in-C BAOR 1976-78, ADC Gen to HM The Queen 1977-78, ret; chm: John Taylor Tst 1978-88, Assets Protection International Ltd 1981-86; mil advsr Short Bros Ltd Belfast 1979-84; dir: Control Risks Ltd 1979-86, Kilton Properties, Springthorpe Property Co, PLAZA Fish Ltd, Airborne Forces Charitable Devpt Tst 1988; tstee Airborne Forces Security Tst 1981-, memb Cncl Air League 1982-89; *Clubs* Ashridge Golf, Berks Golf, Army & Navy; *Style*— Gen Sir Frank King, GCB, MBE; Royal Bank of Scotland, Columbia House, 69 Aldwych, London WC2

KING, Henry Edward St Leger; s of Robert James King, and Dorothy Louisa Marie *née* Wickert; *b* 11 Oct 1936; *Educ* Whitgift Middle Sch, Fitzwilliam Coll Cambridge (MA, LLB); *m* 1, 10 April 1964, Kathleen Bridget, da of William Wilcock (d 1971); 1 s (Simon b 1969, d 1984), 1 da (Alexandra b 1966); m 2, 27 Jan 1990, Susie Amy, da of Gerson Goldsmith; *Career* Nat Serv 2 Lt 1959-61; admitted slr 1964; ptnr Denton Hall Burgin & Warrens 1967-; dir: City Centre Restuarants plc, Rentokil Gp plc, Gulf & Western Gp Ltd, Capital Equipment Leasing Ltd, GKN Chep Ltd, Brambles UK Ltd, Brambles Euro Ltd, DMR UK Ltd; *Recreations* travel, theatre, music; *Style*— Henry King, Esq; 5 Chancery Lane, Clifford's Inn, London EC4A 1BU (☎ 071 242 1212)

KING, Ian Ayliffe; s of Jack Edward King (d 1990), of Henley on Thames, and Hilda Bessie King; *b* 25 April 1939; *Educ* Bromsgrove Sch; *m* 1963, Rosemary Frances, da of Sir Gordon Wolstenholme, OBE; 4 c (Joanna Susan b 24 Aug 1965, Giles Edward Ayliffe b 12 Nov 1966, Oliver Charles Ayliffe b 2 Jan 1972, Philippa Rosemary b 1 Sept 1977); *Career* Lawn Tennis Assoc: memb Cncl 1981- (representing Hereford & Worcester County Lawn Tennis Assoc), memb County and Club Ctee 1983-87 (chm 1984-87), memb Finance Ctee 1983-87, Loans and Special Projects 1983-87, memb Bd of Mgmnt 1984-, dep pres 1988-90, pres 1991-; Wimbledon: memb Ctee of Mgmnt of the Championships 1987-, memb Ticket Ctee 1987-90, memb Media Ctee 1990, memb Royal Box Ctee 1991-; Hereford & Worcester County Lawn Tennis Assoc: memb Ctee 1969-, chm 1980-; CA 1962-; ptnr Kidsons Impey (formerly Chalmers Impey/ Hodgson Impey) 1968-; dir: E Walters (Ludlow) Ltd 1968-85, Baker & Sons (Margate) 1975-, All England Ground Ltd 1991-, LTA Trust Ltd 1991-, LTA Nominees Ltd 1990; tstee Sir Barry Jackson Tst; *Recreations* tennis, cricket, theatre, travel; *Clubs* Birmingham Tennis, Buckland Tennis, Barnt Green Tennis, Edgbaston Priory Tennis, West Hants Tennis; *Style*— Ian King, Esq; The Mount, Stoke Prior, Bromsgrove, Worcestershire B60 4JU (☎ 0527 31281)

KING, Ian Charles; *b* 28 Dec 1934; *Educ* Univ Coll Sch Hampstead, Bartlett Sch of Achitecture Univ of London (Dip Arch); *m* 1, (m dis); m 2, 5 Feb 1980, Nathalie Wareham, *née* Singh; *Career* architect in private practice 1964-, chm Ian C King Ltd Chartered Architects; govr Univ Coll Sch Hampstead London, hon treas Architects Benevolent Soc; Freeman City of London 1981; Liveryman: Worshipful Co of Glass Sellers 1982, Worshipful Co of Chartered Architects 1988; MRIBA 1960; *Recreations* lawn tennis, theatre, veteran cars; *Clubs* All England Lawn Tennis and Croquet, Hurlingham, Athenaeum; *Style*— Ian C King, Esq; 214 Ashley Gardens, Emery Hill St, London SW1; 77-83 Upper Richmond Rd, London SW15 2DT (☎ 081 785 3408, fax 081 780 1949)

KING, Jack Naisbitt; s of John George King (d 1944), and Grace, *née* Naisbitt (d 1989); *b* 19 Sept 1928; *Educ* Emmanuel Coll Cambridge (BA, MA), Univ of Adelaide (MA); *m* 4 s, 3 da; *Career* Wolfson Coll: founding fell 1965-, bursar and sec of tstees 1968-79, dir course and programme 1979- (vice pres 1984-88), sr fell 1984-; Univ pro-proctor 1990-91; memb: Cambridge Police Authy 1980-89, Ctee Drinking Fountain Assoc 1990- chm Fairleigh Dickinson Fndn New Jersey 1981-; tstee: Cluff Fndn, Gosnold UK Tst, Royal Opera House Tst 1985-89, Royal Opera House Endowment Tst 1985-; Freeman City of London; memb: Worshipful Co of Blacksmiths, Co of Waterman and Lightermen of River Thames; Yates Medallion 1980, Hon DHL William Jewell Coll Missouri; FRSA; *Clubs* Leander, RAF, City Livery, Beefsteak; *Style*— Jack King, Esq; Wolfson College, Cambridge, Cambs CB3 9BB (☎ 0223 335 900)

KING, James Archibald; s of John Howard King (d 1973), of Ballater, and Margaret Whyte Smail, *née* Bannatyne; *b* 25 May 1951; *Educ* Melville Coll Edinburgh, Univ of Strathclyde (BA); *m* 1, 8 Oct 1977 (m dis 1982), Amanda Jane, da of Alan Lea Ferrand, of Woodside, Minshull Vernon, Cheshire; m 2, 29 Jan 1983, Katharine Stein, da of Henry Stein McCall, of High Auchengare, Rhu, Dunbartonshire; *Career* account exec Grey Advertising 1972-74; account dir: French Gold Abbott 1974-79, Abbott Mead Vickers 1979-81; dir Ogilvy & Mather (Scotland) 1981-87, client servs dir Hall Advertising 1987-89, dir James Kings Consultancy 1989-, chm Central New Town Assoc of Edinburgh 1990-; MIPA 1982; *Recreations* sailing, shooting, skiing, photography; *Clubs* RORC (memb Ctee 1980-81), Royal Northern & Clyde YC (memb Ctee 1981-83), Annabels; *Style*— James King, Esq; 7 Royal Circus, Edinburgh EH3 6TL (☎ 031 225 2882)

KING, Jennifer Hilary Laura; da of Rev Thomas Symmons Magson, of Highworth, Wilts, and Rita, *née* Carter; *b* 7 Nov 1947; *Educ* Commonweal Sch Swindon, Queenswood, Univ of Bristol (LLB); *m* 11 July 1977 (m dis 1985); 2 s (Alan b 17 Sept 1977, John b 20 June 1980); *Career* admitted slr 1973, ptnr Bevan Ashford, specialist in family law; memb Law Soc Child Care Panel; legal advsr: RELATE, The Samaritans; *Style*— Mrs Jennifer King; Bevan Ashford, 6 High St, Swindon, Wilts SN1 3ES (☎ 0793 511111, fax 0793 511258)

KING, John Arthur Charles; *b* 7 April 1933; *Educ* Sir Joseph Williamson's Mathematical Sch Rochester Kent, Univ of Bristol (BSc); *m* ; 2 s; *Career* IBM 1956-70, UK md Telex Computer Products 1971-73, dir UK Data Processing Div Metra Consulting 1974-75, UK dir of Mktg rising to Euro Dir of Business and Market Devpt Business Systems and Communications Group 1976-81, commercial dir Philips International Business Communications Systems 1981-83, dir Main Bd and md Overseas Div BT 1983-88, chm Quotron International Citicorp Information Business 1989; CBIM, FBCS, fell IOD; *Recreations* sport (tennis), bridge, music (piano, orchestral, opera); *Style—* John King, Esq; 1 Washington Close, Beech Road, Reigate, Surrey RH2 9LT; Quotron, 5 Roundwood Ave, Stockley Park, Uxbridge, Middlesex UB11 1AX (☎ 071 971 2600, fax 071 971 2608)

KING, Sir John Christopher; 4 Bt (UK 1888), of Campsie, Stirlingshire; s of Sir James Granville Le Neve King, 3 Bt, TD (d 1989); *b* 31 March 1933; *Educ* Eton; *m* 1, 3 Oct 1958 (m dis 1972), Patricia Monica, o da of late Lt-Col Kingsley Osbern Nugent Foster, DSO, OBE; 1 s, 1 da; m 2, 1984, Mrs (Aline) Jane Holley, er da of Col Douglas Alexander Brett, GC, OBE, MC; *Heir* s, James Rupert King b 24 May 1961; *Career* Sub Lt RNVR, 1 Lt Berkshire Yeo TA; memb Stock Exchange 1958-73; *Recreations* sailing, shooting; *Clubs* Brooks's; *Style—* Sir John King, Bt; c/o Messrs C Hoare & Co, 37 Fleet St, London EC4

KING, John Edward; s of late Capt Albert Edward King, and Margaret King; *b* 30 May 1922; *Educ* Penarth Co Sch, SOAS London; *m* 1, 1948 (m dis), Pamela, *née* White; 1 da; m 2, 1956, Mary Margaret, *née* Beaton; 2 da; *Career* WWII 1941-47: Rifle Bde, RWF, Nigeria Regt RWAFF; Capt served Chindit campaign Burma (despatches); Overseas Civil Serv: cadet Colonial Admin Serv N Nigeria 1947, permanent sec Fed Govt of Nigeria 1960, ret 1963; CRO 1963, Navy Dept MOD 1966-69, private sec to Sec of State for Wales 1969-71, asst sec Welsh Office 1971-77, princ estab offr and under sec Welsh Off 1977-82, conslt Dept of Educn and dir China Studies Centre Univ Coll Cardiff 1984-87; civil serv memb Civil Serv Cmmn Final Selection Bd 1977-82 (external memb 1982-86); chm: Insole Ct Action Gp 1989-, Friends of the Welsh Coll of Music and Drama 1990-; *Recreations* books, swimming, tennis, watercolour painting; *Clubs* Civil Service, Llandaff Inst, Cardiff Lawn Tennis; *Style—* John King, Esq; Fairfields, Fairwater Road, Llandaff, Cardiff CF5 2LF (☎ 0222 562825)

KING, John Keeley; s of George Frederick John King (d 1965), and Winifred Florence, *née* Hayes; *b* 24 June 1938; *Educ* Hove Coll; *m* 23 March 1968, Susan Ann, da of Lt-Col Harry Loe, OBE, RASC (d 1968), of Hampshire; 2 da (Alison Jane b 8 May 1972, Joanna Emily, b 11 March 1977); *Career* chm G J King Gp Devpt and Construction Co 1975, dir Southern Radio Hldgs 1989- (chm Southern Sound plc 1989-); ACIOB 1980, FInstD 1987; *Recreations* motor sport, classic car collector, boating, golf; *Clubs* RSRN Yacht, Dyke Golf, AMOC, Rotary (Brighton), Brighton & Hove MC (pres), HSCC; *Style—* John King, Esq; 110 Woodland Dr, Hove, Sussex BN3 6DE (☎ 0273 508486); G J King Business Centre, Reeds Lane, Sayers Common, Hassocks, Sussex BN6 9LS (☎ 0273 832577, fax 0273 832892, car 0836 705668)

KING, (Kenneth George) Jonathan; s of George Farquhar Jones King and Ailsa King; *b* 6 Dec 1945; *Educ* Trinity Coll Cambridge (BA); *Career* entertainer; entered tv indust 1964, recording artist Everyone's Gone To The Moon 1965; tv: presenter and creator Entertainment USA and No Limits (BBC 2), columnist Sun Newspaper; *Books* The Polish Boy and the Pope, Bible II, Adventures of Tim; *Style—* Jonathan King, Esq; 1 Wyndham Yard, Wyndham Place, London W1H 1AR (☎ 071 402 7433, fax 071 402 2866, telex 298976)

KING, Julian Rex; Sqdn Ldr Arthur Herbert Edward King (d 1977), of Esher, Surrey, and Ada Marion, *née* Algar (d 1986); *b* 31 March 1944; *Educ* St John's Sch Leatherhead, Kingston Poly; *m* 1 March 1969, Gillian Mary, da of Stanley James Hemmett (d 1988), of Sherborne, Dorset; 2 s (Matthew b 1976, Thomas b 1981), 1 da (Sarah b 1973); *Career* mgr Regency Bookshop Surbiton Surrey 1964-66, mgr and fndr College Bookshop Kingston Surrey 1966-69, co proprietor and co fndr Centre Bookshop Croydon Surrey 1969-73, co proprietor, co fndr (with Colin Spooner) and md Prism Press Book Publishers Ltd Bridport Dorset, New York and Sydney 1974-; *Recreations* reading; *Style—* Julian King, Esq; Prism Press Book Publishers Ltd, 2 South St, Bridport, Dorset DT6 3NQ (☎ 0308 27022, fax 0308 421015)

KING, Hon Mrs (Madeleine Coleman); da of Baron Cohen of Brighton (Life Peer, d 1966); *b* 11 July 1946; *Educ* Univ of London (BA); *m* 1978, Ross King, s of Kenneth King (d 1958); 1 s, 1 da; *Career* called to the Bar Inner Temple 1971, barr and slr in Alberta Canada 1983, sr memb Acad of Family Mediators; *Style—* The Hon Mrs King; 3222, 3rd St SW, Calgary, Alberta T2S 1V3, Canada (☎ 403 243 4899)

KING, Malcolm James Geoffrey; s of Douglas James Edward King; of Hadley Wood, Herts, and Betty Alice, *née* Martin; *b* 10 April 1945; *Educ* Harrow, Coll of Estate Mgmnt, Univ of Western Ontario (MBA); *m* 6 June 1970, Jennifer Kate, da of Arthur Charles Rose; 1 s (Oliver James b 25 March 1975), 1 da (Annabel Kate b 11 Jan 1973); *Career* chartered surveyor Gerald Eve 1963-68; King & Co: joined 1968, head Investment Dept 1970, assoc 1972-75, ptnr 1975-88, jt sr ptnr 1988-; Freeman City of London, memb Worshipful Co of Wheelwrights; FRICS; *Recreations* fly fishing, golf, shooting, stalking, helicopter flying, gardening; *Clubs* Flyfishers, Wentworth, Hadley Wood, Moretons; *Style—* Malcolm King, Esq; King & Co, 7 Stratford Place, London W1N 9AE (☎ 071 493 4933, fax 409 0676)

KING, Prof Mervyn Allister; s of Eric Frank King, and Kathleen Alice, *née* Passingham; *b* 30 March 1948; *Educ* Wolverhampton GS, King's Coll Cambridge (BA, MA); *Career* jr res offr Dept of Applied Econs (memb Cambridge Growth Project) 1969-73, Kennedy Scholarship Harvard Univ 1971-72; Univ of Cambridge: fell and dir studies St John's Coll 1972-77, res offr Dept of Applied Econs 1972-76, lectr Faculty of Econs 1976-77, visiting prof of econs Harvard Univ 1982, Esmée Fairbairn prof of investmt Univ of Birmingham 1977-84, visiting prof of econs MIT 1983-84, prof of econs LSE 1984-; memb: Meade Ctee on Taxation (sec) 1975-78, Prog Ctee Econometric Soc Congress 1974, 1979, 1985, Econs Ctee ESRC 1980-82, Res Ctee ENSAE Paris 1985, Exec Ctee IFS 1985, Econ Policy Panel 1985-86, CLARE Gp 1976-85, Ed Bd Jl of Industl Economics 1977-83, Cncl and Exec Ctee Royal Econ Soc 1981-86, Bd The Securities Assoc 1987-89, City Capital Markets Ctee 1988-; co dir ESRC Res Prog on Taxation Incentives and Distribution of Income LSE 1979-; res assoc NBER 1978-, fell Centre for Econ Policy Res 1984-; co dir (with C Goodhart) Fin Mkts Gp LSE 1987-, dir Bank of England 1991-; asst ed Economic Journal 1974-75, assoc ed Journal of Public Economics 1982-, managing ed Review of Economic Studies 1978-83, memb Ed Bd American Economic Review 1985-, chm Soc of Econ Analysis; Walras-Bowley lectr Econ Soc, Review of Econs lectr Cambridge, assoc memb Inst of Fiscal and Monetary Policy Miny of Fin Japan; conslt: NZ treasy 1979, OECD 1982, Royal Cmmn on Distribution of Income and Wealth; res fell INSEE Paris 1977, hon res fell UCL; Helsinki Univ medal 1982; *Books* Public Policy and the Corporation (1977), The British Tax System (with J A Kay, 1978, 5 edn 1990), Indexing for Inflation (ed with T Liesner, 1975), The Taxation of Income from Capital: A Comparative Study of the US, UK, Sweden and West Germany (with D Fullerton et al, 1984), author of numerous articles; *Style—* Prof Mervyn King; Lionel Robbins Building, London School of Economics, Houghton St, London WC 2AE (☎ 071 955 7275)

KING, (Denys) Michael Gwilym; CVO (1989); s of William James King, and Hilda May; *b* 29 May 1929; *Educ* St Edmund's Sch Canterbury, Simon Longton Sch Canterbury, Battersea Poly, Univ of London (BSc); *m* 1, 1956 (m dis 1973), Monica Helen; 2 da; m 2, 1985, Ann Elizabeth; *Career* Nat Serv RE, design and site engr George Wimpey & Co Ltd 1951-55, design and product engr Ontario Paper Co 1956-58, chief Civil engr and produce mangr Humphries & Glas (Canada) Ltd 1958-61, dir industl engrg John Laing and Son 1971-74 (sr engr rising to commercial mangr 1961-71); Br Airports Authy: engrg dir 1974-77, dir Heathrow 1977-86, chm and md Heathrow Airport Ltd 1986-88, md Airports Division 1988-91; chm: Gatwick Airport Ltd, Stansted Airport Ltd, Scottish Airports Ltd; dir: BAA Trust Co Ltd, Lynton plc; chm: Airport Operators Cncl Int 1986-87, Airport Assocs Co-ordinating Cncl 1987; CEng, FICE 1977, MIMechE 1966; *Recreations* yachting, squash; *Clubs* Foxhill's County (Ottershaw), Mid Surrey Squash; *Style—* Michael King, Esq, CVO; c/o BAA plc, 130 Wilton Rd, London SW1V 1LQ

KING, Prof Michael Stuart; s of Edward Roy King (d 1963), of Thornham, Norfolk, and Jessie Margaret, *née* Davis; *b* 2 June 1931; *Educ* St Edwards Sch Oxford, Univ of Glasgow (BSc), Univ of California (MS, PhD); *m* 1, 9 June 1962 (m dis 1983), Margaret Helen Hoeschen, da of Theodore de Vassily Bujila (d 1979), of Montreal Canada; 2 s (Bernard John Edward b 1967, David Matthew Stuart b 1971), 1 da (Sarah Bernadine Margaret b 1966); m 2, 21 Oct 1989, (Shirley) Georgina, da of Dr the Hon Walter Symington Maclay (d 1963), of Newbury Berks; *Career* prof of geological engrg Univ of Saskatchewan Canada 1966-81, prof of mechanical engrg Univ of California Berkeley USA 1981-86, Phoebe Apperson Hearst Distinguished prof 1986, oil indust prof of petroleum engrg Imperial Coll 1986-; FIMechE 1985, FGS 1985, FRSA 1990; *Recreations* foxhunting, shooting, music; *Style—* Prof Michael King; Cedar House, Hellidon, nr Daventry, Northamptonshire NN11 6LG (☎ 0327 61919); Royal School of Mines, Imperial College of Science, Technology and Medicine, London SW7 2BP (☎ 071 225 8746, fax 071 589 6806, telex 929484)

KING, Michael William; s of Alfred William King (d 1983), and Jessie, *née* Carter; *b* 31 Aug 1934; *Educ* Univ of London (BA); *m* 5 March 1960, Teresa, da of Ben Benjamin (d 1965); 1 s (Russell William b 1963), 1 da (Sarah Elizabeth b 1961); *Career* Nat Serv Royal West Kent Regt 1956-57; mgmnt trainee then leading buyer Ford Motor Co 1958-64, AEI Hotpoint 1964-68: purchasing mangr 1964, prodn mangr 1965, central ops mangr 1966; Lake and Elliot 1968-72: main bd dir and div chief 1968, gp devpt dir 1971; gp chief exec Heatrae Sadia International 1972-84, business conslt 1984-, various directorships and consultancies incl chief exec East Anglian Regnl Health Authy (three year project); Freeman City of London, Liveryman Worshipful Co of Coopers; MBIM, MIOD; *Recreations* tennis, skiing, music, antiques; *Style—* Michael King, Esq; Moat Cottage, Pleshey, Essex CM3 1HG (☎ 0245 37 202, fax 0245 37 242)

KING, Mike; *b* 22 Sept 1962; *Educ* St Benedict's Ealing; *Career* photographer; jr small sports photographic agency, Allsports agency, currently chief sports photographer The Observer; Sports Cncl Black and White Photographer of the Year 1989, Nikon Sports Photographer of the Year 1989 and 1990; memb Ctee Professional Sports Photographers Assoc; *Recreations* cycling; *Style—* Mike King, Esq; 115 Palace Rd, London SW2 3LB (☎ 081 674 4275); The Observer, Chelsea Bridge House, Queenstown Rd, London SW8 4NN (☎ 071 627 0700)

KING, Nicholas Geoffrey; s of Geoffrey Thomas King, of Cross Cottage, Barford St Martin, Salisbury, Wiltshire, and Rita Mary, *née* Bull; *b* 21 July 1951; *Educ* Canford Sch Dorset; *m* 1, 12 Oct 1974 (m dis 1983), Lillian Amanda Rosemary da of John Langrigg Kirconel; 2 da (Julia b 1978, Abigail b 1982); m 2, Jane Carol, da of Gywnvor Nicholas; *Career* Charles Church Developments Ltd: chief accountant 1976-78, gp fin dir 1978-87, gp md 1987-; fundraiser and supporter Cons Pty; FCA 1974, memb Lloyd's 1985-; *Recreations* shooting, farming; *Style—* Nicholas King, Esq; Hughenden Chase, Denner Hill, Gt Missenden, Buckinghamshire (☎ 024024 2384); Charles Church Developments plc, Charles Church House, Knoll Rd, Camberley, Surrey (☎ 0276 62299, fax 0276 62712)

KING, Vice Adm Sir Norman Ross Dutton; KBE (1989); s of Sir Norman King, KCMG (d 1963), and Mona, *née* Dutton (d 1982); family name which was adopted from town of Dutton in Cheshire can be traced back to Sir Thomas Dutton of Dutton, Sheriff of Cheshire in 1226; *b* 19 March 1933; *Educ* Fonthill Sch, RNC Dartmouth; *m* 1967, Patricia Rosemary, da of Dr Lionel Brian Furber (d 1981); 2 da (Annabelle b 1970, Melissa b 1978); *Career* CO HMS Leopard 1967-68, XO HMS Intrepid 1972-73, NA to Second Sea Lord 1975-77, RCDS 1978, CO HMS Newcastle 1979-80, Dir of Naval Offr Appts (Seamen Offrs) 1983-84, Cmdr Br Navy Staff Washington, Br Naval Attaché Washington, UKNLR to SACLANT 1985-86, Naval Sec 1987, COS to Cdr Allied Naval Forces S Europe 1988-; *Recreations* tennis, music, chess; *Clubs* Royal Navy of 1765 and 1785; *Style—* Vice Adm Sir Norman King, KBE; c/o Lloyds Bank, Faversham, Kent

KING, Lt-Cdr (James) Osborne; DSC (1945), DL (Co Down); s of James King (d 1943); *b* 8 Oct 1914; *Educ* Campbell Coll; *m* 1945, Hon Elizabeth (*see* Hon Mrs (E P) King); *Career* Lt Cdr RNVR, serv WWII; dir/sec Rademon Dvpts Ltd, dir Rademon Properties Ltd; chm: Montgomery Hldgs, Charleston Partnership; *Recreations* shooting; *Clubs* Kildare St (Dublin); *Style—* Lt Cdr Osborne King, DSC, DL; Rademon, Crossgar, Co Down, N Ireland (☎ 0396 830214)

KING, Patrick Thomas Colum; s of Patrick William King (d 1978), Pro Ecclesia Et Pontifice, and Agnes Norah King, MBE, *née* Lynch; *b* 27 May 1938; *Educ* St George's Coll Weybridge, LSE, (LLB, LLM); *Career* admitted slr 1962, ptnr Herbert Smith 1968- (asst slr 1962-65, assoc 1965-68); capt: Blackheath FC 1964-66, capt Hampshire RFU 1965-67, Barbarian 1965, Munster Interprovincial 1966, Ireland Trials 1966; pres Hants RFU 1983-86 (treas 1971-82), hon vice pres London Div RFU 1988 (sec 1979-86) memb City of London Slrs Co; La Medaille de la Ville de Paris 1980; memb Worshipful Co of Scriveners; *Recreations* rugby union football, racing, historical res, opera; *Clubs* Reform, Barbarians Rugby Football, MCC, City of London Catenians; *Style—* Patrick King, Esq; 14 Regents Court, St George's Avenue, Weybridge KT13 0DQ (☎ 0932 847013); Exchange House, Primrose St, London EC2A 2HS (☎ 071 374 8000, fax 071 496 0043)

KING, Penelope, Lady; Penelope Charlotte; *née* Cooper-Key; o da of Capt Edmund Moore Cooper Cooper-Key, CB, MVO, RN (d 1933), of Landford, Fleet, Hants, and Florence Margaret Penelope, *née* Wigram; *b* 16 May 1901; *m* 21 Nov 1928, Sir James Granville Le Neve King, 3 Bt, TD (d 1989); 1 s (Sir John Christopher, 4 Bt, *qv*), 2 da (Susan Penelope b 1929, Diana Bridget b 1935); *Style—* Penelope, Lady King; Church Farm House, Chilbolton, Stockbridge, Hants

KING, Air Vice-Marshal Peter Francis; CB (1987), OBE (1964); s of William George King, MBE (d 1968), of Huntingdon, and Florence Margaret, *née* Sell (d 1955); *b* 17 Sept 1922; *Educ* Framlingham Coll, King's Coll London, Charing Cross Hosp London, Univ of Edinburgh (DLO); *m* 1945, Doreen Maxwell, da of Jorgen Hansen-Aarøe (d 1960), of Northwood; 1 s (Nigel), 1 da (Suzanne); *Career* cmmnd RAF 1945, serving offr and conslt in otolaryngology, specialist in otorhinolaryngology, employed in Cosford, Ely, Fayid, Halton and CME, conslt in otorhinolaryngology 1955, Hunterian prof RCS 1964, conslt advsr in otorhinolaryngology 1966-83, Air Cdre 1976, reader in aviation med Inst of Aviation Med 1977-79, Whittingham prof in aviation med IAM and RCP 1979-83, Air Vice-Marshal 1983-, dean RAF Med 1983-85, sr conslt RAF 1985-87; conslt: Herts Health Authy 1963-, CAA 1973-, King Edward VII Hosp Midhurst 1987; hon surgn to HM The Queen 1979-87, examiner for Dip in Aviation Med RCP 1980-, pres section of otology RSM 1977-78, chm Br Soc of Audiology 1979-81, vice-chm RNID 1980-88 (vice-pres 1990-); memb Cncl Br Assoc of Otolaryngologists 1960-89; memb Ed Bd Br Jl of Audiology 1980-89; CStJ (1987); FRCSE; *Recreations* sculpture, looking at prints; *Clubs* RAF; *Style*— Air Vice-Marshal Peter King, CB, OBE; 5 Churchill Gate, Woodstock, Oxon OX7 1QW (☎ 0993 813115)

KING, Hon Philip James Stephen; s of Baron King of Wartnaby (Life Peer); twin with Rupert *qv*; *b* 1950; *Educ* Harrow; *m* 27 June 1989, Caroline, da of E G A Hillesley, of Gillingham, Kent; 1 da (Charlotte Kathleen Rachel b 27 March 1990); *Style*— The Hon Philip King; 77 Stanhope Mews East, London SW7 5QT

KING, Prof Phillip; CBE (1974); s of Thomas John King (d 1973), of UK, France and N Africa, and Gabrielle Laurence, *née* Liautard (d 1975); *Educ* Mill Hill Sch, Univ of Cambridge (MA); *m* (m dis); 1 s (Anthony Thomas b 1965 d 1984); *Career* emeritus prof of sculpture RCA 1990- (prof 1981-80); memb Visual Arts Ctee Arts Cncl, tstee Tate Gallery 1967-69; RA 1987 (ARA 1977); *Recreations* travelling, swimming, music, wind surfing; *Style*— Prof Phillip King, CBE; 26 Savernake Rd, London (☎ 071 482 3039); c/o Mayor Rowan Gallery, 31a Bruton Place, London W1X 7AB (☎ 071 499 3011, fax 071 355 3486)

KING, Prof Preston Theodore; s of Clennon King (d 1975), of Albany, GA, USA, and Margaret, *née* Slater (d 1990); *b* 3 March 1936; *Educ* Fisk Univ (BA), Oberlin Coll, Univ of Atlanta, Univ of Vienna, Univ of Strasbourg, Univ of Paris, LSE (MSc, PhD); *m* 1 s (Slater b 1969), 1 da (Oona b 1967); *Career* tutor LSE 1958-60, Univ of Maryland 1961, and lectr Univ of Keele 1961-62, lectr Univ of Ghana 1963-66, lectr Univ of Sheffield 1966-68, reader Univ of E Africa Nairobi 1968-70, sr res assoc Acton Soc Tst 1970-72; Univ of Nairobi: prof 1972-76, chm dept 1972-74, founded Diplomacy Training Prog for anglophone Africa 1972-73, dir DTP 1973-74; prof of political sci Univ of NSW 1976- (head of sch 1978-81), prof of politics Univ of Lancaster 1986- (head of dept 1986-87); external examiner: Makerere Univ 1973, Univ of Khartoum 1974-75, Univ of the S Pacific Fiji 1977-83, Univ of Liverpool 1988-91; visiting prof: Univ of Dar es Salaam 1973, Institut des Relations Internationales Univ of Cameroun 1976, McGill Univ 1981, LSE Philosophy Dept 1983 (politics dep 1979); gen ed Aust Nat Univ Monograph Series in Social and Political Thought 1977-80, gen ed Int Series in Social and Political Thought 1980-; author of numerous articles and reviews on socio-political related topics published in nat and int jls; broadcaster; memb: Exec Ctee Conference for the Study of Political Thought, Advsy Ctee Centre for Res in Ethnic Relations Univ of Warwick, Policy and Fin Ctee Northwest Arts, Ed Advsy Bd New Community 1989-; involvement in various int political orgns and conferences; *Books* incl: Fear of Power (1967), The History of Ideas (1983), The Ideology of Order (1974), Toleration (1976), Federalism (1982), An African Winter (1986); *Style*— Prof Preston King; Department of Politics, University of Lancaster, Lancaster LA1 4YF (☎ 0524 65201 ext 4282, fax 0524 63806, telex 65111 Lancul G)

KING, Sir Richard Brian Meredith; KCB (1975, CB 1970), MC (1944); s of Bernard King (d 1968), of Claygate, Surrey, and Dorothy, *née* Scrivener (d 1974); *b* 2 Aug 1920; *Educ* Kings Coll Sch Wimbledon; *m* 24 Dec 1944, (Blanche) Phyllis, da of Edward Owen Roberts (d 1975), of Shalbourne, Wilts; 2 s (Hilary b 1949, Julian b 1956), 1 da (Pauline b 1946); *Career* cmmnd N Irish Horse 1941, Capt 1944, Maj 1945, served N Africa and Italy; Civil Serv: Air Miny 1939-41, Miny of Works 1946, seconded to HM Treasy 1953-55, PPS to Min of Works 1956-57, seconded to Cabinet Secretariat 1958-61, sec gen of independence constitutional conferences for Malta 1959 (Kenya 1960, W Indies Fedn 1960, Fedn for Rhodesa, N Rhodesia and Nyasaland 1961), asst sec Dept of Tech Cooperation 1961, perm sec Miny of Overseas Devpt 1973 (under sec 1964, dep sec 1968), exec sec World Bank/IMF Jt Devpt Ctee 1976-80, sr advsr to S G Warburg & Co Ltd 1980-85, devpt fin conslt 1985-; *Books* Planning the British Aid Programme (1971), Criteria for Europe's Development Policy to the Third World (1974); *Recreations* music, lawn tennis, gardening; *Clubs* All-England Lawn Tennis; *Style*— Sir Richard King, KCB, MC; Woodlands Farm House, Woodlands Lane, Cobham, Surrey KT11 3PY (☎ 0372 843 491)

KING, Hon Richard John Rodney; s of Baron King of Wartnaby (Life Peer); *b* 1943; *Educ* Le Rosey (Switzerland); *m* 1985, Monica, da of Erich Boehm, of Boca Raton, Fla, USA; 1 s (b 1986); *Style*— The Hon Richard King; 7612 Covey Chase, Charlotte, North Carolina 28210, USA

KING, Robert John Stephen; s of Stephen King, of Wolverhampton, and Margaret Digby; *b* 27 June 1960; *Educ* Radley, St John's Coll Cambridge (MA); *Career* conductor and harpsichordist; dir: The King's Consort (baroque orch), Consort Records; conductor and dir on over two dozen record on: Hyperion, Pickwick, Erato, Meridian, Consort, Collins Classics; guest dir: Nat Youth Music Theatre, Choir of New Coll Oxford, Euro Baroque Orchestra, Orquesta Sinfonica Euskadi, Orebro Chamber Orchestra; concert tours: France, Holland, Belgium, Spain, Finland, Italy, Japan, Taiwan, USA, Aust; TV and radio appearances all over Euro and the UK, ed of much 1600-1750 music, keyboard continuo with many leading Br orchs incl Acad of Ancient Music and City of London Sinfonia; *Recreations* skiing, cricket, graphic design; *Style*— Robert King, Esq; 2 Salisbury Rd, Ealing, London W13 9TX (☎ 081 579 6283, fax 081 567 8824)

KING, Robert Shirley; s of Rev William Henry King, MC, TD, of Trumpington, and Dorothy Sharpe (d 1964); *b* 12 July 1920; *Educ* Manchester GS, Univ of Cambridge (MA); *m* 1, 1947, Margaret (d 1956), da of Ernest Douglas Costain Siddall (d 1963), of Wallasey; 2 da (Janet b 1950, Rachel b 1953); m 2, 1958, Mary, da of Clifford William Rowell, CBE (d 1962), of Cambridge; 1 s (John b 1961), 2 da (Ruth b 1959, Helen b 1965); *Career* served RAF 1940-45, Corpl, Madagascar, E Africa, ME; sr dist offr Tanganyika Civil Serv 1949-62, asst sec Home Office 1962-70 and 1985-86, under sec DHSS 1971-80; govr: Chestnut Fndn 1976-83, Bell Educn Tst 1984-89; sec: Working Pty on the Rôle and Tasks of Social Workers, Nat Inst for Social Work 1980-82, Health Promotion Res Tst 1984-89; memb Cncl: SHAPE 1982-89, Br and Foreign Sch Soc 1982-89; chm Co-ordinating Ctee Save The Children Fund Cambridge Project 1984-88; *Recreations* walking, cycling, gardening, African affairs; *Style*— Robert King, Esq; 3 Nightingale Ave, Cambridge (☎ 0223 248965)

KING, Roger Douglas; MP (C) Birmingham Northfield 1983-; *b* 26 Oct 1943; *Educ* Solihull Sch; *m* 1973, Jennifer Susan (*née* Sharpe); 2 s, 1 da; *Career* engrg apprentice British Motoring Corporation 1960-66 (sales rep 1966-74), own mktg business 1974-81; Parly candidate (C) Cannock 1974; PPS to: Michael Havard, QC, MP, Min of State DOE 1987-90, Sec of State For Employment 1990-; non-exec dir National Express Holdings Ltd; vice chm All Pty Motor Indust Gp 1985-, former jt sec Commons Tourism Ctee; FIMI; *Recreations* motoring; *Style*— Roger King, Esq, MP; House of Commons, London SW1

KING, Ronald Gordon; s of Basil King, and Jacqueline, *née* Timmermans; *b* 31 Dec 1946; *Educ* Jesuit Coll Antwerp; *Career* ed: Viewpoint 1965-, Warfare 1972-, The Keys of Peter 1969-; sec: Christian Centre Pty, Napoleon Soc, Pugin Gild; *Books* Catholicism and European Unity (1980), Zionism and the Vatican (1981), Napoleon and Freemasonry (1985); *Clubs* Hon Librarian, Army and Navy; *Style*— Ronald King, Esq; 157 Vicarage Rd, London E10 5DU (☎ 081 539 3876)

KING, Hon (John) Rupert Charles; s of Baron King of Wartnaby (Life Peer); twin with Philip *qv*; *b* 1950; *Educ* Harrow; *m* 1986, Cherry M, only da of R B Jessop, OBE, of Ingoldsby, Lincs; 1 s (Philip b 1988); *Style*— The Hon Rupert King; Garden Close, Wartnaby, Melton Mowbray, Leics

KING, Dame Ruth; *née* Railton; DBE (1966); *see*: Railton, Dame Ruth

KING, Shirley Georgina (Gina); da of Dr the Hon W S Maclay, CBE (d 1964), of Millwaters, Newbury, Berkshire, and 40 Kensington Sq, London W8, and Dorothy, *née* Lennox; *b* 4 July 1933; *Educ* Westonbirt Sch Glos, St Martin's Sch of Art London; *m* 1, 25 June 1955 (m dis 1974), (Robert) David Ogden; 3 s (Robert Nicholas b 16 May 1958, Joseph Jeremy b (twin) 1958, Benjamin Patrick b 15 Nov 1966), 1 da (Emma Maclay 25 March 1961); m 2, 21 Oct 1989, Prof M S King; *Career* memb Lloyd's; memb Northants CC 1967 (chm Educn Ctee 1985-); *Recreations* painting, tennis, bridge, gardening; *Style*— Mrs Gina King; Cedar House, Hellidon, Daventry, Northamptonshire NN11 6LG (☎ 0327 61919)

KING, Stephen Harris Morley; *b* 25 Feb 1931; *Educ* Harrow, CCC Oxford (capt squash team); *Career* J Walter Thompson: joined 1957, worked on agency's maj accounts, set up UK's first account planning dept 1968, responsible for specialist units for advtg res and new product devpt, chm MRB Group 1979-86, currently non-exec dir WPP (acquired J Walter Thompson 1987); *Books* Developing New Brands (1973, 2 edn 1984); *Style*— Stephen King, Esq; WPP Group plc, 27 Farm St, London W1X 6RD (☎ 071 408 2204, fax 071 493 6819)

KING, Stephen William Pearce; s of William Raymond Pearce King, CBE (d 1980), and Edna Gertrude, *née* Swannock (d 1971); *b* 21 Jan 1947; *Educ* King Edward's Sch Birmingham; *m* 22 Sept 1973, Angela Denise, da of Dennis George Gammon, of Worcester; 2 s (Alexander b 1976, Jeremy b 1978); *Career* admitted slr 1973; princ Stephen King & Co slrs, specialists in child care, criminal and matrimonial law; *Recreations* sport, music, charity work, writing, theatre, travelling, meeting people; *Style*— Stephen W P King, Esq; Stephen King & Co, 258 High Street, Erdington, Birmingham B23 6SN (☎ 021 382 8222)

KING, Susan Dawn; da of Alfred Harold King, of Guildford, Surrey, and Anne, *née* Jones (d 1981); *b* 12 Dec 1956; *Educ* George Abbott Girls Comp Sch Guildford, Guildford Tech Coll; *m* 21 Nov 1986, Jeffrey Kenneth Houlgrave, s of Clifford Houlgrave, DFM; 1 s (James Alfred b 28 May 1990), 1 da (Jessica b 6 March 1989); *Career* TV presenter 1972-, career has included BBC children's documentaries and various appearances on both BBC and ITV nat progs, currently presenter of TV South West's evening news and magazine programme; *Books* Horses Galore (1979); *Recreations* riding, walking, reading, looking after Jessica; *Style*— Ms Susan King; TSW, Derry's Cross, Plymouth, Devon (☎ 0752 663322, fax 0752 671970, telex 45714)

KING, Sir Sydney Percy; OBE (1965); s of James Edwin King, and Florence Emily King; *b* 20 Sept 1916; *Educ* Brockley Central Sch; *m* 17 June 1944, Millicent Angela, da of Dennis Leo Prendergast; 2 da (Jennifer b 10 July 1946, Dianne b 18 March 1950, d 1 Sept 1979); *Career* dist organiser Nat Union Agric and Allied Workers 1946-80; pro chllr Univ of Leicester 1987-90 (memb Cncl 1980-); memb: N Midland Regnl Bd for Indust (vice chm 1949), Sheffield Regnl Hosp Bd 1963-73 (chm 1969-73), E Midlands Econ Planning Cncl 1965-, E Midlands Gas Bd 1970, E Midland regnl panel MAFF 1972-79 (chm 1977); chm: Kesteven Water Bd 1962-70, Trent RHA 1973-82; memb: Kesteven CC 1952-74 (Alderman 1967), Lincs Family Practitioner Ctee 1982-; JP Kesteven 1956-86; memb Labour Party; Hon LLD: Leicester 1980, Nottingham 1981; kt 1975; *Style*— Sir Sydney King, OBE; 49 Robertson Drive, Sleaford, Lincs NG34 7AL (☎ 0529 302056)

KING, Thea; OBE (1985); da of Henry Walter Mayer King, and Dorothea Louise King; *b* 26 Dec 1925; *Educ* Bedford HS, RCM; *m* Jan 1953, Frederick Thurston, who d Dec 1953; *Career* Sadler's Wells Orch 1950-52, Portia Wind Ensemble 1955-68, London Mozart Players 1956-84; current memb: English Chamber Orch, Melos Ensemble of London, Robles Ensemble; frequent soloist broadcaster and recitalist; prof: RCM 1962-87, Guildhall Sch of Music 1988-; recordings incl works by: Mozart, Brahms, Spohr, Mendelssohn, Bruch, Finzi, Stanford, Blake, Seiber, Lutoslawski; pubns: Clarinet Solos (Chester Woodwind series, 1977), arrangement of J S Bach Duets for Two Clarinets (1979), Schumann For The Clarinet (1991); FRCM, ARCM; *Recreations* cows, pillow-lace; *Style*— Ms Thea King, OBE; 16 Milverton Rd, London NW6 (☎ 081 459 3453)

KING, Rt Hon Thomas Jeremy (Tom); PC (1979), MP (C) Bridgwater March 1970-; s of John H King, JP, of Langford, Somerset; *b* 13 June 1933; *Educ* Rugby, Emmanuel Coll Cambridge; *m* 1960, (Elizabeth) Jane, 3 and yst da of Robert Tilney, CBE, DSO, TD, DL, Lord of the Manor of Sutton Bonington (maternal gs of Sir Ernest Paget, 1 Bt); 1 s, 1 da; *Career* serv Nat Serv in Somerset LI and King's African Rifles (Tanganyika and Kenya), formerly with E S & A Robinson Ltd Bristol (rising to div gen mangr), chm Sale Tilney & Co 1971-79 (dir 1965-1979); vice chm Cons Parly Indust Ctee 1974, PPS to Min Posts and Telecommunications 1970-72, min for Industl Devpt 1972-74; oppn front bench spokesman: Indust 1975-76, Energy 76-79; min of state for Local Govt and Environmental Servs DOE 1979-83; sec of state for: Enviroment Jan-June 1983, Transport June-Oct 1983, Employment Oct 1983-85, Northern Ireland 1985-July 1989, Defence July 1989-; *Style*— The Rt Hon Tom King, MP; House of Commons, London SW1

KING, Timothy John; s of Wing Cdr John Hall King, of Little Compton, Moreton-in-Marsh, Glos, and Heather Grace, *née* Baden Powell (d 1986); *b* 22 Feb 1946; *Educ* Charterhouse; *m* 28 Aug 1971, Marion Mason, wid of Christopher Parrott (d 1970), da of Herbert Ingram (d 1979); 1 da (Natasha b 1973), 1 s (Timothy b 1966), 1 da (Esther b 1969); *Career* sales dir Bass Sales Ltd 1980-84, sales admin dir Bass Mitchells & Butlers 1984-88, sales dir Belhaven Brewery Co Ltd 1988-; *Recreations* equestrianism, opera, music, scouting; *Style*— Timothy King, Esq; Easter Langlee, by Galashiels, Selkirkshire, (☎ 0896 58588); Belhaven Brewery Co Ltd, Dunbar, East Lothian, (☎ 0368 62734, car 0860 816 433)

KING, Timothy Parker; *b* 27 Nov 1954; *Educ* Westminster Sch Connecticut USA, Hobart Coll NY; *m* 3 Dec 1983, Diana Bradfield Niles; *Career* devpt dir Detroit Office Cato Johnson (subsid of Young & Rubicam) 1977-79 (md 1975-77), dir of corporate communication JP Stevens & Co NY 1979-82, exec vice pres and dir corporate identitiy Siegel & Gale NY 1982-88, dir corporate identitiy Siegel & Gale International 1988-90, md Siegel & Gale Europe 1990-; lectr at: AIGA, DMI, Bank Mktg Assoc; commentator for: BBC, Financial Times, Marketing Week, Campaign, The Economist; maj design projects: BP corporate identity 1988, Bull Worldwide Information Systems 1988, US Steel corporate identity 1989, The American Med Assoc 1989; memb: American Inst of Graphic Arts, Design Mgmnt Inst, Design Museum; *Style*— Timothy King, Esq; Siegel & Gale Ltd, 27 Fitzroy St, London W1P 5AF (☎ 071 580 0202, fax 071 436 9521)

KING, Sir Wayne Alexander; 8 Bt (UK 1815), of Charlestown, Roscommon; s of Sir Peter Alexander King, 7 Bt (d 1973); *b* 2 Feb 1962; *Style*— Sir Wayne King, Bt; 146 High St, Almonte, Ontario, Canada KOA 1AO

KING, William Lawrence; s of Ian Lawrence King (d 1974), and Maisie, *née* Cooke (d 1988); *b* 29 Dec 1947; *Educ* Oundle, Trinity Hall Cambridge (MA); *m* 24 May 1975, Jane, da of Philip George Wrixon, of Norton Canon, Hereford; 2 s (Edward b 1979, Tom b 1981); *Career* slr, Macfarlanes 1970 (ptnr 1979); memb Ct Worshipful Co of Slrs; *Recreations* beagling; *Clubs* Utd Oxford and Cambridge; *Style*— William King, Esq; Macfarlanes, 10 Norwich St, London EC4A 1BD (☎ 071 831 9222, fax 071 831 9607, telex 296381)

KING-FARLOW, Charles Roderick; s of Roderick Sydney King-Farlow, of Birmingham, and Alice Frances Joan, *née* Ashley; *b* 16 Feb 1940; *Educ* Eton, Trinity Coll Oxford (MA); *m* 1965, Tessa, da of Robert Lawrence Raikes, of Llanvethrine, nr Abergavenny; 1 s (Joshua Michael b 1971), 1 da (Alice Caroline 1968); *Career* admitted slr 1965; ptnr Pinsent & Co 1969-; dir: ISS Europe Ltd 1969-, Exec Resources Ltd 1974-, CW Cheney & Son Ltd 1980-88; memb: Bd Midlands Arts Centre 1985- (chm 1985-89); City of Birmingham Orch Cncl of Mgmnt 1972-80, Friends of Birmingham Museums and Art Gallery Ctee 1972-78 and 1983-88, Cncl Birmingham Law Soc 1976-; tstee City of Birmingham Orchestral Endowment Fndn 1971-; memb Bd City of Birmingham Touring Opera 1987-, Public Art Cmmns Agency 1990-, Taxation Ctee of Historic Houses Assoc 1980-; contrib to Taxation and International Journal of Museum Management; *Recreations* gardening, fishing, skiing; *Clubs* Oriental; *Style*— Charles King-Farlow, Esq; 8 Vicarage Rd, Edgbaston, Birmingham B15 3ES (☎ 021 455 0902); Post & Mail House, 26 Colmore Circus, Birmingham B4 6BH (☎ 021 200 1050)

KING-HALL, Hon Adrianna - Adrianna - Frances Susan; da of Baron King-Hall (Life Peer, d 1966); *b* 11 Aug 1927; *Educ* Dartington Hall, Frensham Heights, Univ Coll Exeter (BSc), Graduate Inst of Int Affairs Geneva (L ès Sciences Politiques, Int Relns), Yale Univ (Master of Public Health); *Career* asst gen sec Health Visitors Assoc 1953-56, ed International Nursing Review 1956-60, exec sec Int Union for Health Educn 1960-62, gen sec Soc for Health Educn 1962-71, dir Int Fedn of Practitioners of Natural Therapies 1978-79, project coordinator Pioneer Health Centres Ltd (founders of the Peckham Experiment); chm and advsr to nat and int voluntary orgns since 1975; *Recreations* domestic crafts, gardening; *Style*— The Hon Adrianna King-Hall; Old Barn, Northdown Rd, Woldingham, Caterham, Surrey CR3 7BD (☎ 0883 653197, fax 0883 653135)

KING-HALL, Hon Ann; da of Baron King-Hall (Life Peer, d 1966); *b* 1920; *Style*— The Hon Ann King-Hall; 11 North Side, Clapham Common, SW4 0RF

KING-HAMILTON, His Hon (Myer) Alan Barry; QC (1954); s of Alfred King-Hamilton (d 1959), of Oxshott Surrey, and Constance Clyde Druiffe (d 1962); *b* 9 Dec 1904; *Educ* Bishop's Stortford GS, Trinity Hall Cambridge (MA, pres Union Soc); *m* 1935, Rosalind Irene, da of Dr Abraham Ellis; 2 da (Mary, Jane); *Career* serv WWII Sqdn Ldr RAF; rec: Hereford 1954, Gloucester 1956, Wolverhampton 1961; dep chm Oxford County Quarter Sessions 1955, ldr Oxford Circuit 1961, cmmr of Assize 1961 and 1963, legal memb Med Practices Ctee Miny of Health 1961; additional judge Central Criminal Ct 1964, ret 1979, dep circuit judge 1980-84, legal memb ABTA Appeal Bd 1980, memb Ctee Birnbeck Housing Assoc 1982, memb Arts and Library Ctee MCC 1985-1989, Tstee Barnet Community Tst 1985-88, chm Mary Whitehouse Res and Educn Tst 1986, pres Westlon Housing Assoc 1977, pres W London Synagogue 1965-72 and 1975-83, memb Bar Cncl 1956-60, bench Middle Temple 1961; Freeman City of London 1965, Master Worshipful Co of Needlemakers 1969; *Books* And Nothing But the Truth (autobiography 1982); *Style*— His Hon Alan King-Hamilton, QC; c/o RAF Club, 128 Piccadilly, London W1

KING-HARMAN, Col Anthony Lawrence; OBE (1982), DL (Bedfordshire 1987); s of Capt Robert Douglas King-Harman, DSO, DSC, RN (d 1978), and Lily, *née* Moffatt (d 1965); *b* 28 Feb 1918; *Educ* Wellington, RMA Woolwich; *m* 21 Dec 1944, Jeanette Stella, *née* Dunkerley, step da of Frederick C Guthrie (d 1976), of Cape Province, SA; 2 s (Lt-Col (Anthony) William (RA) b 2 May 1946, Michael Charles b 10 Aug 1947); *Career* cmmnd RA 1938, served Western Desert and Burma (despatches), Staff Coll 1945, CO 39 Regt RA 1959-61, NATO Standing Gp Washington 1963-67, ret 1968; joined Int Staff NATO Brussels 1968, head Def Policy Section, ret 1982; Cmmnr St John Ambulance Beds 1983-87; OStJ 1987; *Recreations* golf, gardening; *Clubs* Army and Navy, Anglo-Belgian; *Style*— Col Anthony King-Harman, OBE, DL; Ouse Manor, Sharnbrook, Bedford MK44 1PG (☎ 0234 781439)

KING OF WARTNABY, Baron (Life Peer, UK 1983), of Wartnaby in Co of Leicestershire; John Leonard King; yr s of Albert John and Kathleen King; *m* 1, 1941, Lorna Kathleen Sykes (d 1969); 3 s (Richard, Philip, Rupert, *qqv*), 1 da (Rachel); m 2, 1970, Hon Isabel Monckton (*see* King of Wartnaby, Baroness), 3 and yst da of 8 Viscount Galway; *Career* chm: Babcock Int plc (formerly Babcock & Wilcox) 1972-, Babcock Int Inc, Br Nuclear Assocs, SKF (UK) Ltd 1976-, R J Dick Inc, Dick Corpn, NEB 1979-81, Br Airways 1981-; dir: First Union Corpn, Nat Nuclear Corpn, 1928 Investmt Tst, Tyneham Investmts Ltd, BFSS Investmts, Mill Feed Hldgs Ltd, Royal Opera House Tst, Royal Ordnance plc, Clogau Gold Mines; chm: City and Industl Liaison Cncl, Alexandra Rose Day 1980-; pres Heathrow branch Royal Aeronautical Soc; MFH: Badsworth 1949-58, Belvoir 1958-72; hon fellow Coke Oven Managers' Assoc 1983; Cdr of Royal Order of the Polar Star 1983, Freeman City of London; FBIM; kt 1979; *Clubs* White's, Pratt's, Brook (New York); *Style*— The Rt Hon the Lord King of Wartnaby; Wartnaby, Melton Mowbray, Leics LE14 3HY; Cleveland House, St James's Square, London SW1Y 4LN (☎ 071 930 9766)

KING-SMITH, Ronald Gordon (Dick); s of Capt Ronald King-Smith, DSO, MC (d 1980), of Bitton, Glos, and Gay, *née* Boucher (d 1980); *b* 27 March 1922; *Educ* Marlborough, Univ of Bristol (BEd); *m* 6 Feb 1943, Myrle, da of Gp Capt Tom Harry England, DSC, AFC (d 1975), of Malta; 1 s (Giles b 1953), 2 da (Juliet b 1945, Elizabeth (Mrs Rose) b 1948); *Career* WWII serv Lt Grenadier Gds 1941-46 (wounded Italy 1944, despatches); farmer 1947-67, teacher 1976-82, writer of children's books 1978-; *Books* incl: The Fox Busters (1978), Daggie Dogfoot (1980), The Mouse Butcher (1981), Magnus Powermouse (1982), The Queen's Nose (1983), The Sheep-Pig (1983), Harry's Mad (1984), Saddlebottom (1985), Noah's Brother (1986), Tumbleweed (1987), The Toby Man (1988), Martin's Mice (1988), George Speaks (1988), Dodos are For Ever (1989), Paddy's Pot of Gold (1990), The Water Horse (1990), Alphabeasts (1990), Jungle Jingles (1990); *Recreations* writing children's books, walking; *Style*— Dick King-Smith, Esq; Diamond's Cottage, Queen Charlton, Keynsham, Bristol BS18 2SJ (☎ 0272 864655)

KINGAN, (Thomas) John Antony; DL Co Down (1965); s of William Sinclair Kingan (d 1946), of Glenganagh, 39 Bangor Rd, Groomsport, Bangor, Co Down, and Catherine Elizabeth Margaret, OBE, JP, *née* Brett; paternal ancestry listed in Burke's Irish Family Records (1976); *b* 10 May 1923; *Educ* Stowe, Trinity Coll Oxford; *m* 11 Dec 1954, Daphne Marian, da of Rt Hon Sir Norman Stronge, 8 Bt, MC, of Tynan Abbey, Co Armagh (assas by IRA 1981); 1 s (James Anthony John b 1957); *Career* Lt IG 1943-46, serv Normandy 1944; trainee Messrs J & T Sinclair Belfast 1946-48; farmer 1948-; *Clubs* Cavalry and Guards', Ulster Reform Belfast, Royal Ulster Yacht Bangor; *Style*— Thomas Kingan, DL; Glenganagh, 39 Bangor Rd, Groomsport, Bangor, Co Down, N Ireland BT19 2JF (☎ 0247 460043)

KINGDOM, Leonard Grantley; s of Thomas Kingdom (d 1957), of Leics, and Amy Kingdom (d 1968); *b* 24 June 1919; *Educ* Wyggeston Sch Leicester, King's Coll Cambridge (MA, MB BChir), St Bartholomew's Hosp; *m* 1, 4 Dec 1943 (m dis 1969), Joyce Elizabeth Mary, da of Sqdn Ldr William Catchpole, AFC (d 1935); 1 s (Richard b 31 March 1946 d 1971), 1 da (Susan b 6 June 1948); m 2, 3 Dec 1969, Susan Elizabeth, da of William King (d 1971), of Bexley; 1 s (William b 8 Dec 1971), 1 da (Sarah b 21 Feb 1976); *Career* Capt RAMC 1943-47, graded surgical specialist BLA 1944; served: Mobile Neurosurgical Unit, Field Surgical Unit (O/C); jr hosp appts at St Bart's Hosp and Royal Free Hosp, demonstrator of anatomy Univ of Cambridge 1942, chief asst St Bart's Hosp 1948-52, conslt otologist LCC 1950-64; conslt ENT surgn: UCH 1952-78, Queen Mary's Hosp for Children 1950-64, St Lukes Hosp for the Clergy 1964-80, Hosp of St John and St Elizabeth 1978-80; now in private practice; memb of Ct City Univ 1980-85, memb Br Assoc of Otolaryngologists 1952; Freeman City of London, Liveryman Worshipful Co of Fan Makers (memb of Ct 1967-, Master 1979-80), hon sec City of London Past Masters Assoc 1980-81; FRSM 1948-, FRCS; *Recreations* travelling; *Style*— Leonard Kingdom, Esq; Stoneygate, Top Park, Gerrards Cross, Bucks SL9 7PW (☎ 0753 883615); 10/12 Bryanston Square, London W1H 8BB (☎ 071 723 1288)

KINGERLEE, Gavin John; s of Henry John Kingerlee, of Switzerland, and Constance Mary, *née* Skinner (d 1938); *b* 10 Oct 1936; *Educ* Dragon Sch Oxford, Repton; *m* 1967, Margriet Marjan; 1 s (Aidan b 1973), 2 da (Sharon b 1970, Elaine b 1971); *Career* dir: Rodenhurst Properties Ltd, Kingerlee Hldgs Ltd; chm Highcroft Investmt Tst plc; dir Aurelia Plastics Ltd; *Recreations* fishing, swimming, watching sport; *Clubs* Shark Angling of GB (pres), Kidlington and Gosford Swimming (pres), Hanborough Cricket (pres); *Style*— Gavin Kingerlee, Esq; Straits Cottage, Church Hanborough, Oxford; Aurelia Plastics Ltd, Station Approach, Kidlington, Oxford (☎ 0865 841300)

KINGHAM, His Hon Judge James Frederick; DL (Herts, 1989); s of Charles William Kingham (d 1985), and Eileen Eda, *née* Hughes (d 1986); *b* 9 Aug 1925; *Educ* Blaenau Flestionog GS, Wycliffe Coll, Queens' Coll Cambridge (BA, MA), Graz Univ Austria; *m* 1958, Vivienne Valerie Tyrrell, da of Edwin George Brown, of Barnet Herts; 2 s (Simon b 1966, Guy b 1967), 2 da (Sarah b 1960, Emma b 1962); *Career* served RN, Pacific Fleet 1943-47; called to the Bar Gray's Inn 1951; memb Gen Cncl of Bar 1954-58, Bar Cncl Sub Ctee Sentencing & Penology, dep rec Nottingham 1961-70, (rec Crown Ct 1970-73), circuit judge 1973-90, liaison judge Beds 1981-90, memb Criminal Injuries Compensation Bd 1990-, dep judge 1990-, teacher in Law Selwyn Coll Cambridge 1990-, tutor Judicial Studies Bd 1990-, lectrin Family Law 1990-; dep co cmmr Hertfordshire scouts 1971-80; venture scout ldr: Harpenden 1975-86, Kimpton 1986-; *Recreations* skiing, climbing, squash, gardening, supporting Luton Town football club; *Style*— His Hon James Kingham, DL; Stone House, High St, Kimpton, Hitchin, Herts

KINGHAM, Norman Frederick; JP (1959); s of Maj Alfred Kingham (d 1960), and Gertrude Isobel, *née* Neems (d 1971); f in law 'Billy' Williams joined the Army in 1915, and won the MM at the age of 16; he was discharged until he was old enough to rejoin as a volunteer; *b* 5 Dec 1920; *Educ* convent, Liscard HS, Univ of Liverpool (Dip Arch), Columbia Univ NY; *m* 10 March 1951, Muriel Olive, da of Chief Supt Hugh Herbert Williams (d 1974); 2 s (Paul b 1954, Timothy b 1956); *Career* TA and Nat Serv RE 1937-39, Lance Corpl Western Desert 1940 (POW 1941, excaped 1942), UK 1943, ME 1944-45; pres: Liverpool Architectural Soc 1969-71, Wallasey Boys Club 1973-; fndr memb and chm Martime Housing Assoc 1963-65, vice chm Bd of Govrs Wirral Coll of Art Design and Adult Studies 1980-82; chm: Bldg and Environment Gp Merseyside C of C 1973-76, Liverpool Ctee Br Heart Fndn 1986-, Advsy Bd Merseyside Branch of the Salvation Army 1982-, Liverpool Branch RIBA; memb: Advsy Bd Merseyside Branch Manpower Cmmn Services 1976-79; memb Cncl: RIBA 1972-74, Merseyside C of C 1973-; chm Birkenhead Ironworks and CSS Alabama Tst 1987-90 (chm Alabama Tst 1990-91); *Recreations* archaeology, ancient history; *Clubs* Royal Cwlth London, Hon Soc Knights of the Round Table, Veteran Car of GB, Fortress Study Gp; *Style*— Norman F Kingham, Esq, JP; Rock Villa, Wellington Rd, Wallasey, Merseyside L45 2NF (☎ 051 639 1731); Kingham Knight, Warrington Architects, 45-49 Berry St, Liverpool (☎ 051 708 9388, fax 051 709 5454)

KINGHORN, Dr George Robert; s of Alan Douglas Kinghorn, of Allendale, Northumberland, and Lilian Isobel, *née* Henderson; *b* 17 Aug 1949; *Educ* Royal GS Newcastle upon Tyne, Univ of Sheffield (MB ChB, MD); *m* 14 July 1973, Sheila Anne, da of Haydn Wilkinson Littlewood, of Sheffield; 1 s (Robert b 1978), 1 da (Joanne b 1982); *Career* trg in gen med Royal Hosp and Royal Infirmary Sheffield 1972-76, sr registrar in genito-urinary med Royal Infirmary Sheffield 1976-78, conslt in genito-urinary med and conslt in genito-urinary med admin charge General Infirmary Leeds 1979, hon clinical lectr i/c sub-dept of genito-urinary med Univ of Sheffield 1979; WHO conslt: Sri Lanka 1985, Tunisia 1987; EEC conslt Kenya 1988; chm Advsy Sub-Ctee on Genito-urinary Med Trent Region 1989- (memb 1978-, vice chm 1985-89), memb Trent Regnl Med Ctee, chm Special Advsy Ctee Jt Ctee on Higher Med Trg 1986-77 (memb 1981-84, sec 1984-86); hon sec: Br Co-operative Clinical Gp 1983-, Ctee on Genito-urinary Med RCP 1986- (memb 1983-86); memb UK Working Pty MRC and INSERM Concorde Study 1988-; memb: Med Soc for Study of Venereal Diseases 1976, E Midlands Soc of Physicians 1979; MRCP 1986, FRCP 1988; *Recreations* travel, home computers, sport; *Style*— Dr George Kinghorn; Dept of Genitourinary Medicine, Royal Hallamshire Hospital, Glossop Rd, Sheffield S10 2JF

KINGMAN, Sir John Frank Charles; s of Dr Frank Edwin Thomas Kingman (d 1983), and Maud Elsie, *née* Harley (d 1951); *b* 28 Aug 1939; *Educ* Christ's Coll Finchley, Pembroke Coll Cambridge (MA, ScD); *m* 16 Dec 1964, Valerie, da of Frank Cromwell, OBE, ISO (d 1978); 1 s (John b 1969), 1 da (Charlotte b 1972); *Career* mathematician; prof of maths and statistics Univ of Sussex 1966-69, prof of maths Univ of Oxford 1969-85, vice chllr Univ of Bristol 1985-; memb Brighton Co Borough Cncl 1968-71, chm Sci and Engrg Res Cncl 1981-85; vice pres Parly and Scientific Ctee 1986-89 (vice chm 1983-86), pres Royal Statistical Soc 1987-89; Freeman City of London, Liveryman Worshipful Co of Goldsmiths 1987; Hon DSc: Univ of Sussex 1983, Univ of Southampton 1985; Hon LLD Univ of Bristol 1989; FRS 1971; Officier des Palmes Académiques (France) 1989; kt 1985; *Books* Introduction to Measure and Probability (with S J Taylor, 1966), The Algebra of Queues (1966), Regenerative Phenomena (1972), Mathematics of Genetic Diversity (1980); *Clubs* Lansdowne, United Oxford and Cambridge Univ; *Style*— Sir John Kingman, FRS; Senate House, University of Bristol, Tyndall Avenue, Bristol BS8 1TH (☎ 0272 303960, fax 0272 251424)

KINGS NORTON, Baron (Life Peer UK 1965), of Wotton Underwood, Co Buckingham; Harold Roxbee Cox; s of William John Roxbee Cox (d 1931), of Birmingham, and Amelia, *née* Stern (d 1949); *b* 6 June 1902; *Educ* Kings Norton GS, Imperial Coll London (PhD, fell); *m* 1, 12 July 1927, Doris Marjorie (d 1980), da of Ernest Edward Withers (d 1939), of Northwood; 2 s (Christopher, Jeremy); m 2, 1982, Joan Ruth Pascoe, da of late W G Pack of Torquay; *Career* chm: Landspeed Ltd 1975-, Cotswold Research Ltd 1979-, Berger Jenson & Nicholson Ltd 1967-75, Metal

Box Co 1961-67; dir: Dowty Rotol 1968-75, Ricardo & Co (Engrs) 1927 Ltd 1965-77, Br Printing Corpn 1968-77, Hoechst UK 1970-75; pres: Royal Aeronautical Soc 1947-49, Royal Instn 1969-76; chm: Cncl for Scientific and Industl Res 1961-65, Cncl for Nat Academic Awards 1964-71; chllr Cranfield Inst of Technol 1969-; Medal of Freedom with Silver Palm (USA) 1947; Freeman City of London; Liveryman Guild of Air Pilots and Air Navigators; DIC, FIMechE; Hon FRAeS, Hon DSc, Hon DTech, Hon LLD; kt 1953; *Recreations* collecting aeronautical antiquities; *Clubs* Athenaeum, Turf; *Style*— The Rt Hon Lord Kings Norton; Westcote House, Chipping Campden, Glos (☎ 0386 840440)

KINGSALE, 30 Baron (I c 1340, precedence 1397); John de Courcy; Premier Baron of Ireland; s of Lt-Cdr Hon Michael de Courcy, RN (d 1940; s of 29 Baron Kingsale who was fifth in descent from the Lord Kingsale who successfully claimed from George III the hereditary privilege of keeping his hat on in front of the king; his cous and predecessor had also successfully claimed this privilege under William III, though the legend that King John granted the permission first is probably apocryphal), and Joan Reid (d 1967); *b* 27 Jan 1941; *Educ* Stowe, Sorbonne, Salzburg Univ; *Heir* 3 cous twice removed, Nevinson Russell de Courcy; *Career* 2 Lt Irish Guards 1962-65; former: bingo caller, film extra, safari park driver, barman in local pub; occasional broadcaster, plumber, builder and carpenter; chm Strand Publications 1970, Nat Assoc Serv to Realm 1979; dir: D'Olier Grantmesnil & Courcy Acquisitions 1970, Banaid Int (Brisbane) 1987, De Courcy-Daunt (Brisbane) 1987, Kinsale Devpt Corpn; pres Impex Conslts 1987, patron L'Orchestre de Monde 1987; *Recreations* shooting, palaeontology, venery; *Clubs* Cavalry and Guards'; *Style*— The Rt Hon Lord Kingsale; Crawley Farm, South Brewham, nr Bruton, Somerset

KINGSBURY, Derek John; CBE (1988); s of Maj A Kingsbury, BEM, of Virginia Water, Surrey; *b* 10 July 1926; *Educ* Strodes Secdy Sch Egham, City and Guilds Coll London (BSc); *m* 1; 1 c (and 1 c decd); m 2, 1980, Sarah; 1 c; *Career* chm and gp chief exec Fairey Group 1987 (chm of gp subsidiary cos 1982-), non-exec dir Vickers 1981-, dep chief exec Dowty Group to 1982; memb Cncl CBI 1980-86 (chm Overseas Ctee 1980-84), memb Review Bd for Govt Contracts 1986-; chm: Def Manufacturers Assoc 1987-90 (memb Cncl 1985-), Cncl for Educnl Technol Pilot Scheme Steering Ctee 1987-90; memb Engrg Cncl 1990-, pres Br Heart Fndn Horse Show 1977-; CEng, FIEE, FCGI; *Recreations* golf (capt Aircraft Golfing Soc 1982); *Clubs* MCC, RAC, Beaconsfield Golf, St Enodoc Golf; *Style*— Derek Kingsbury, Esq, CBE; Fairey Group plc, Cranford Lane, Heston, Hounslow, Middx TW5 9NQ (☎ 081 759 4811)

KINGSBURY, Lady Patricia Mary Charlemont; *née* French; da of 2 Earl of Ypres (d 1958), and his 1 w Olivia Mary, *née* John (d 1934); *b* 6 July 1919; *Educ* privately in Munich and Paris; *m* 24 Jan 1942, Henry Edmund Roland Kingsbury (d 1980), yst s of Gerald Francis Kingsbury, JP (d 1950, ggs through his mother of 1 Earl of Bradford); 2 s (Philip Charles Orlando b 1944, Gerald Richard Charlemont b 1945); *Career* civil defence 1940-41; dir: Electrolube Ltd, H K Wentworth Ltd, Automation Facilities Ltd, DCS Packaging Ltd; *Recreations* travel, theatre, racing; *Style*— The Lady Patricia Kingsbury; c/o Lloyds Bank Ltd, 6 Pall Mall, London SW1Y 5NH; Electrolube Ltd, Blakes Rd, Wargrave, Berks (☎ 0734 404031)

KINGSHOTT, (Albert) Leonard; s of Albert Leonard Kingshott, of Ingatestone, Essex, and Katherine Bridget, *née* Connelley; *b* 16 Sept 1930; *Educ* LSE (BSc); *m* 10 Aug 1957, Valerie, da of Ronald Simpson (d 1964); 2 s (Adrian b 1960, Brendan b 1962), 1 da (Nicola b 1958); *Career* RAF (FO) 1952-55; fin analyst BP Corporation 1955-59, economist British Nylon Spinners 1960-62, fin mangr Iraq Petroleum Co 1963-65; treas: Ford of Europe, Ford Motor Co, Ford of Britain 1965-70; fin dir Whitbread Group 1970-72, md fin British Steel Corporation 1972-77; dir Int Banking Div Lloyds Bank plc 1977-89 (dir Merchant Banking Div 1977); exec dir: Europe 1980, Marketing & Planning 1983 (dep chief exec 1985 and dir several assoc cos); exec dir banking The Private Bank and Tst Co Ltd 1989, appointed Crown Agent 1989; govr and assoc memb faculty Ashbridge Mgmnt Coll, memb Monopolies and Mergers Cmmn 1990; FCIS; *Books* Investment Appraisal (1967); *Recreations* reading, chess, golf; *Style*— Leonard A Kingshott, Esq; 4 Delamas, Beggars Hill, Fryerning, Ingatestone, Essex; The Private Bank & Trust Company Ltd, Lansdowne House, Berkeley Square, London W1X 5DG (☎ 071 872 3700)

KINGSLEY, Ben; s of Rahimtulla Harji Bhanji, and Anna Lyna Mary, *née* Goodman; *b* 31 Dec 1943; *Educ* Manchester GS; *Career* actor; RSC 1967-86: title roles incl Hamlet, Othello; Nat Theatre 1977-78: leading roles incl Mosca in Volpone; films incl: Gandhi, Betrayal, Turtle Diary, Harem, Silas Marner, Maurice, Slipstream, Testimony, Lenin, The Train, Pascali's Island, Without a Clue, Murderers Amongst Us, Fifth Monkey, The Children, A Necessary Love; awards incl: Oscar, BAFTA (twice), Golden Globe (twice), NY Critics, LA Critics, London Standard, Grammy, Simon Wiesenthall Humanitarian Award, Berlin Golden Camera; associate artist RSC; patron and affiliated memb of many charitable organisations; MA Salford 1984; memb: BAFTA 1983, American Acad of Motion Picture Arts and Sciences; PADMA SRI (India) 1985; *Style*— Ben Kingsley, Esq; ICM, 388-396 Oxford St, London W1N 9HE (☎ 071 629 8080)

KINGSLEY, David John; s of Walter John Kingsley, and Margery, *née* Walden; *b* 10 July 1929; *Educ* Southend HS for Boys, LSE (BSc); *m* 1, July 1965 (m dis), Enid Sophia, da of Thomas Jones, MBE (d 1985), of Llandeilo; 2 da (Nichola Sophia b 1962, Nadia b 1964); m 2, May 1968 (m dis), Gillian, da of George Leech (d 1978); 2 s (Andrew John b 1966, Paul David b 1967); m 3, Oct 1988, Gisela Irene, *née* Reichardt; *Career* dir Benton and Bowles Advertising Agency 1961-64, fndr and ptnr Kingsley Manton & Palmer Advertising Agency 1964-78, dir and chm Kimpher Group Communications Group 1969-78, ptnr and chm Kingsley & Kingsley Business Consultancy 1974-; dir: King Publications, Francis Kyle Gallery; chm: Stokecroft Arts, Inter Action Community Arts Tst, Centre for World Devpt Educn; govr LSE (memb Standing Ctee), memb Devpt Ctee RCM, hon sec The Ireland Fund (UK); Lab Parly candidate E Grinstead 1952-54; advsr to: Lab Pty and Govt on Communications 1962-70, SDP 1981-87, Pres Kaunda Zambia 1974-80, Mauritius Govt 1977-81, to SDP 1981-87; organiser and creator: The Greatest Children's Party in the World for the Int Year of the Child 1980, HM The Queen's 60th Birthday Celebration; FRS, FIPA, ASIAD; *Books* Albion in China (1979); *Recreations* music, books, creating happy public events, travel, art; *Clubs* Reform, RAC; *Style*— David J Kingsley, Esq; 99 Hemingford Rd, London N1 1BY (☎ 071 607 4866); 53 Thornhill Rd, London N1 1HX (☎ 071 609 5770, fax 071 607 8025)

KINGSLEY, Ivor; s of Harry Kaminsky (d 1959), and Bertha Kaminsky, *née* Karinski (d 1961); parents were refugees from Russia; *b* 10 Aug 1933; *Educ* Waterloo Rd Sch, Broughton M/C; *m* 4 Feb 1960, Brenda, da of James Egan, of Bury; 2 s (Mark b 1960, Paul b 1967); *Career* md Kingsley Forester plc until 1986; works in fin; semi ret; *Recreations* golf; *Clubs* Whitefield Golf; *Style*— Ivor Kingsley, Esq; 197-199 Monton Rd, Monton Green, Eccles M30 9PP (☎ 2340 607867)

KINGSLEY, Sir Patrick Graham Toler; KCVO (1962, CVO 1950); s of Gerald Kingsley; *b* 1908; *Educ* Winchester, New Coll Oxford; *m* 1947, Priscilla Rosemary, da of Capt A Lovett Cameron; 3 s, 1 da; *Career* serv WWII Queen's Royal Regt; sec and Keeper of the Records Duchy of Cornwall 1954-72 (asst sec 1930-54); *Style*— Sir Patrick Kingsley, KCVO; West Hill Farm, West Knoyle, Warminster, Wilts

KINGSLEY, Stephen Michael; s of Ernest Robert Kingsley, of Cheadle, Cheshire, and Ursula Renate, *née* Bochenek (d 1972); *b* 1 June 1952; *Educ* Cheadle Hulme Sch, Univ of Bristol (BSc); *m* 18 March 1982, Michelle, da of Oscar Solovici (d 1983), of Paris; 1 da (Natalie b 1984); *Career* Arthur Andersen & Co 1973-: mangr 1979-86, ptnr 1986-, head London Capital Markets Gp 1987-, dir euro regnl capital mkts 1988-; memb Tech Panel Securities and Investmts Bd 1985-87; FCA; *Books* Managing A Foreign Exchange Department (contrib, 1985), Currency Options (contrib, 1985); *Recreations* travel, ballet, classical music, current affairs; *Style*— Stephen Kingsley, Esq; 2 Hocroft Ave, London NW2 2EH (☎ 071 794 6542); Arthur Andersen & Co, 1 Surrey St, London WC2R 2PS (☎ 071 438 3000, 071 438 3855, fax 071 831 1133, telex 8812711)

KINGSMILL-MOORE, (John) Miles; s of Hon Mr Justice Theodore Conyngham Kingsmill-Moore (d 1979), of Hernshaw, Castle Park Rd, Rathfarnham, Dublin, and Beatrice Doreen Davidson, *née* Macnie (d 1976); *b* 20 July 1929; *Educ* St Columba's Coll Rathfarnham nr Dublin, Trinity Coll Dublin (BA, MB BCh, BAO); *m* 15 Feb 1969, Patricia Ann, da of Martin O'Brien (d 1987); 2 s (Hugh Conyngham b 4 Dec 1972, David Miles b 27 Jan 1977), 1 da (Ann Alexandra b 13 Aug 1971); *Career* conslt orthopaedic and traumatic surgn NW Thames RHA 1970, chm N Surrey Dist Mgmnt Team 1979-83, orthopaedic advsr CAA 1986-, memb NW Thames RHA Med Manpower Ctee 1989-; FRCS 1961, FRCSI 1964, FRSM 1978, fell Br Orthopaedic Soc 1979; *Style*— Miles Kingsmill-Moore, Esq; Jacaranda, Queens Hill Rise, Ascot, Berkshire SL5 7DP (☎ 0990 23100); Ashford Hospital, Ashford, Middlesex (☎ 0784 251188)

KINGSTON, 11 Earl of (I 1768); Sir Barclay Robert Edwin King-Tenison; 15 Bt (I 1682); also Baron Kingston of Rockingham (I 1764), Viscount Kingsborough (I 1766), Baron Erris (I 1800), Viscount Lorton (I 1806); s of 10 Earl of Kingston (d 1948); *b* 23 Sept 1943; *Educ* Winchester, RMA Sandhurst; *m* 1, 1965 (m dis 1974), Patricia Mary, da of E C Killip, of Beoley Lodge, Uttoxeter, Staffs; 1 s, 1 da (Lady Maria Lisette b 1970); m 2, 1974 (m dis 1979), Victoria, da of D C Edmonds, of Northwood, Middx; m 3, 9 Feb 1990, Corleen Jennifer Rathbone; *Heir* s, Robert Charles Henry, Viscount Kingsborough b 20 March 1969; *Career* late Lt Royal Scots Greys; *Style*— The Rt Hon the Earl of Kingston; c/o Midland Bank Ltd, 47 Ludgate Hill, EC4

KINGSTON, Beryl Alma; da of Herbert Edwards, and Ella, *née* Parodi; *b* 28 Jan 1931; *Educ* Streatham Secdy Sch, LCC GS, King's Coll London (BA, AKC); *m* 29 July 1950, Roy Darren Kingston; 1 s (Lawrence b 1 June 1954), 2 da (Mary b 14 July 1956, Caroline b 10 March 1959); *Career* teacher in various ILEA schs 1952-54 and 1964-75, head of English Felpham Comp 1975-85; author; memb: Nat Childbirth Tst 1956, CND 1960, Ctee of 100, Soc of Authors 1980-; *Books* Lifting the Curse (1980), Hearts and Farthings (1985), Kisses and Ha'pennies (1986), A Time to Love (1987), Tuppenny Times (1988), Fourpenny Flyer (1989), Sixpenny Stalls (1990), London Pride (1990); *Books incl:* Lifting the Curse (1980), Hearts and Farthings (1985), Kisses and Ha'pennies (1986), A Time to Love (1987), Tuppenny Times (1988), Fourpenny Flyer (1989), Sixpenny Stalls (1990), London Pride (1990); *Recreations* swimming, walking, theatre, reading, making music; *Style*— Mrs Beryl Kingston; Darley Anderson, 11 Eustace Rd, Fulham, London SW6

KINGSTON, (Thomas) David; s of Rev John Howard Kingston (d 1978), of Limavady, Co Derry, and Gertrude Elizabeth, Hare (d 1977); *b* 3 March 1943; *Educ* Portora Royal Sch Enniskillen, Wadham Coll Oxford (MA); *m* 24 June 1967, Georgina, da of William George Ashmore; 2 da (Tara Catherine b 4 June 1970, Candia Louise b 22 Sept 1971); *Career* jt asst actuary Scottish Widow's Fund Edinburgh 1967-68 (actuarial student 1964-67); Irish Life Assurance plc: sr investmt analyst and dep fund mangr 1968-73, pensions actuary 1973-74, fund mangr 1974-75, pensions mangr 1975-80, mktg ops mangr 1980-83, md 1983-; Lord Mayor's Millenium award 1988; FFA 1967, FPMI 1979, ASIA 1972; *Books* Measuring Investment Performance (1975), Pension Funds & Inflation (1978); *Recreations* tennis, windsurfing, skiing, gardening; *Style*— David Kingston, Esq; Irish Life Assurance plc, Lower Abbey St, Dublin 1, Ireland (☎ 010 704 2000, fax 010 704 1908)

KINGSTON, Jeremy Henry Spencer; s of William Henry Kingston (d 1989), of Brighton, Sussex, and Elsie, *née* Cooper (d 1980); *b* 5 Aug 1931; *Educ* Reigate GS Surrey; *m* 1967, Meg, da of James Ritchie, of Dumbarton; 2 s (Benjamin James b 1968, Rufus William b 1970); *Career* Nat Serv 2 Lt Royal Signals; casually employed Chelsea 1951-55 (coffee houses, sculpture, barr's clerk's clerk), sec to John Lehmann 1955-57; playwright: No Concern of Mine (Westminster) 1958, Signs of the Times (Vaudeville) 1973, Oedipus at the Crossroads (King's Head) 1977; theatre critic: Punch 1964-75, The Times 1985-; *Books* Love Among The Unicorns (1968), and three children's books; *Recreations* long conversations over meals; *Style*— Jeremy Kingston, Esq; 65 Romulus Court, Brentford Dock, Middx TW8 8QL (☎ 081 568 4714); The Times, Pennington St, London E1 9XN

KINGSTON, Thomas Archer; s of Leonard James Kingston (d 1982), and Patricia Elisabeth, *née* Clay; *b* 4 Feb 1952; *Educ* Lady Eden's Sch, Highgate Sch, Keble Coll Oxford (MA); *m* 19 April 1980, Margaret, da of Thomas Donnellan (d 1989); 3 da (Joanna b 1983, Philippa b 1985, Helen b 1988); *Career* fin dir Mayfair Catering Co Ltd 1978-83 (co sec 1975), conslt BTR Management Services 1980-83, sr conslt Interactive Incorp 1983-; hon treas Chipperfield Choral Soc; Freeman City of London 1974, Liveryman Worshipful Co of Vintners 1983; MBIM; *Recreations* music, children's entertainer; *Clubs* Oxford and Cambridge; *Style*— Thomas Kingston, Esq; Briarwood, Langley Rd, Chipperfield Herts WD4 9JP (☎ 0923 263 486); Interactive (UK) Ltd, 9 Marlin House, Marlins Meadow, Croxley Centre, Watford (☎ 0923 227 777)

KINGTON, Miles Beresford; s of William Beresford Nairn Kington, of Vrondeg Hall, nr Wrexham, and Jean Ann, *née* Sanders; descended from Thomas Kington (d 1857), of Charlton House, Somerset, who m Margaret, yr da and co-heiress of Laurance Oliphant, 8th Lord of Gask (sr line is Kington-Blair-Oliphant, of Ardblair Castle, Perthshire); *b* 13 May 1941; *Educ* Glenalmond, Trinity Coll Oxford (BA); *m* 1, 28 Feb 1964 (m dis), Sarah, da of Robert Paine, of Canterbury; 1 s (Thomas b 1968), 1 da (Sophie b 1966); m 2, 6 June 1987, Caroline, da of Nick Carter, of Knysna, S Africa; 1 s (Adam b 1987); *Career* freelance writer and former asst gardener in Ladbroke Square; former jazz corr The Times, double bass player with Instant Sunshine, literary ed Punch (cr Let's Parler Franglais column) 1973-80; went up Andes for BBC's Great Train Journeys of The World Series (Three Miles High) 1980; humorous columnist for: The Times (cr Moreover) 1981-87, The Independent 1987-; translator of Alphonse Allais (French humorist); *Books* incl: Miles and Miles, Moreover, Moreover Two, Nature Made Ridiculously Simple, The Franglais Lieutenant's Woman; *Recreations* bicycling, drinking, trying to remember if I have signed the Official Secrets Act; *Clubs* Garrick, Ronnie Scott's; *Style*— Miles Kington, Esq; 40 Lower Stoke, Limpley Stoke, Bath BA3 6HR (☎ 0225 722262)

KINGZETT, Jan Anthony; s of Richard Norman Kingzett, of 18 Sloane Ave, London, and Julia Mary Kingzett; *b* 25 Oct 1955; *Educ* Eton, Trinity Coll Cambridge, (MA); *Career* res staff J Henry Schroder Wagg Ltd 1977, asst dir Singapore Int Merchant Bankers Ltd 1981, dir Schroder Investmt Magmnt Ltd 1986-; *Clubs* MCC, Queen's; *Style*— Jan Kingzett, Esq; Schroder Investment Management Ltd, 36 Old Jewry,

London, EC2R 8BS (☎ 071 382 6000)

KININMONTH, James Wyatt; s of Peter Wyatt Kininmonth, of Tappington Grange, Wadhurst, Sussex, and Priscilla Margaret, *née* Sturge; *b* 26 Sept 1952; *Educ* Harrow, RMA Sandhurst; *m* 19 March 1977, Susie, da of Richard William Griffin, of Norwood, N Carolina, USA; 1 s (Charles b 1985), 2 da (Annabel b 1980, Harriet b 1983); *Career* cmmnd 5 Royal Inniskilling Dragoon Gds 1974, Capt 1977, trans to reserve 1978; dir: Kininmonth Holdings 1982-85, Kininmonth Reinsurance Brokers 1982-85; md Kininmonth Lambert North America 1987- (dir 1985-); memb Lloyds since 1983; Freeman City of London; Liveryman: Worshipful Co of Haberdashers 1982, Worshipful Co of Insurers 1985; *Recreations* shooting, skiing, tennis, golf; *Clubs* City of London; *Style—* J W Kininmonth, Esq; Lampool, Fairwarp, Sussex (☎ 082571 2447); Kininmonth Lambert North America, 53 Eastcheap, London EC3P 3HL (☎ 071 283 2000, fax 071 623 2740, telex 8814631)

KININMONTH, Peter Wyatt; s of Alec Marshall Kininmonth, MBE (d 1968); *b* 23 June 1924; *Educ* Sedbergh, Brasenose Coll Oxford; *m* 1951, Priscilla Margaret, da of Raymond Wilson Sturge, of Lords Mead, Ashmore, Dorset; 3 s, 1 da; *Career* Capt WWII; dir Lowndes Lambert Group Holdings Ltd; chm: Kininmonth Lambert Ltd, P W Kininmonth Ltd; chm Richmond Fellowship for Community Mental Health; *Recreations* golf, gardening, opera; *Clubs* Vincent's, City of London, Royal and Ancient St Andrews, Royal St George's, Swinley Forest, Rye, Portmarnock, Lahinch, Pine Valley (New Jersey), Lake Nona (Florida), Old Elm (Chicago); *Style—* Peter Kininmonth Esq; Tappington Grange, Wadhurst, Sussex (☎ 089 288 2186)

KINKEAD-WEEKES, Prof Mark; s of Lt-Col Alfred Bernard (Bill) Kinkead-Weekes, MC (d 1960), and Vida May, *née* Kinkead (d 1946); *b* 26 April 1931; *Educ* Potchefstroom Boys HS, Univ of Cape Town, Brasenose Coll Oxford; *m* March 1959, (Margaret) Joan, da of Benjamin Irvine (d 1966); 2 s (Paul b 1962, Timothy Guy b 1963); *Career* lectr Univ of Edinburgh 1958-65 (asst lectr 1956-58); Univ of Kent at Canterbury: lectr 1965-66, sr lectr 1966-74, prof of English and American lit 1974-84, pro vice chllr 1974-77, emeritus prof 1984-; govr: Christ Church Coll Canterbury, Kings Sch Rochester, London Contemporary Dance Tst; *Books* William Golding: A Critical Study (with I Gregor, 1967, 2 edn 1984), Samuel Richardson: Dramatic Novelist (1973), D H Lawrence: The Rainbow (ed, 1989); *Recreations* golf; *Style—* Prof Mark Kinkead-Weekes; 5 Albion Place, Ramsgate, Kent CT11 8HQ (☎ 0843 593168); Rutherford College, The University, Canterbury CT2 7NX (☎ 0227 764000 ext 3437)

KINLOCH, Ann, Lady; Ann Maud; da of Gp Capt Frank Leslie White, of London; *m* 2 June 1965, as his 3 w, Sir Alexander Kinloch, 12 Bt (d 1982); 1 s (James, *qv*); *Style—* Ann, Lady Kinloch; Greenacre, 87 Hepburn Gardens, St Andrews, Fife KY16 9LT

KINLOCH, Sir David; 13 Bt (NS 1686), of Gilmerton, East Lothian; s (twin with his sister Ann) of Sir Alexander Davenport Kinloch, 12 Bt (d 1982), by his 2 w, Hilda Anna, da of late Thomas Walker, of Edinburgh; *b* 5 Aug 1951; *Educ* Gordonstoun; *m* 1, 1976 (m dis 1986), Susan, da of Arthur Middlewood; 1 s (Alexander b 1978), 1 da (Alice b 1976); m 2, 1987, Maureen, da of Robert Carswell; 1 s (Christopher Robert b 1988); *Heir* s, Alexander Kinloch b 31 May 1978; *Career* civil engr; *Style—* Sir David Kinloch, Bt; Gilmerton House, Athelstaneford, North Berwick, East Lothian (☎ 062 082 207)

KINLOCH, David Oliphant; s and h of Sir John Kinloch, 4 Bt; *b* 15 Jan 1942; *Educ* Charterhouse; *m* 1, 1968 (m dis 1979), Susan Minette, da of Maj-Gen Robert Elliott Urquhart, CB, DSO; 3 da; m 2, 1983, Sabine, da of Philippe de Loës, of Geneva, Switzerland; 1 s; *Career* CA; co director; *Style—* David Kinloch, Esq; House of Aldie, Fossoway, Kinross-shire, Scotland; 29 Walpole St, London SW3 4 QS

KINLOCH, Sir John; 4 Bt (UK 1873), of Kinloch, Co Perth; s of Sir George Kinloch, 3 Bt, OBE (d 1948); *b* 1 Nov 1907; *Educ* Charterhouse, Magdalene Coll Cambridge; *m* 1934, Doris Ellaline, da of late Charles Joseph Head, of Imber Close, Esher, Surrey; 1 s, 2 da; *Heir* s, David Oliphant Kinloch; *Career* Br Miny of War Tport Iran 1942-45; employed by Butterfield & Swire in China and Hong Kong 1931-63, by John Swire & Sons Ltd London 1964-73; *Clubs* New (Edinburgh); *Style—* Sir John Kinloch, Bt; Aldie Cottage, Kinross, Kinross-shire KY13 7QH (☎ 05774 305)

KINLOSS, Lady (S Lordship 1602); Beatrice Mary Grenville; *née* Morgan-Grenville; da of Rev the Master of Kinloss (2 s of Lady Kinloss, 11 holder of title, but he suc er bro in courtesy title); suc grandmother as 12 holder of title 1944; *b* 18 Aug 1922; *Educ* Ravenscroft Sch Eastbourne; *m* 1950, Dr Greville Stewart Parker Freeman-Grenville, *qv*, s of Rev Ernest Freeman (changed name with husb to Freeman-Grenville, recognised by Lord Lyon King of Arms 1950); 1 s, 2 da; *Heir* s, Master of Kinloss; *Career* sits as Independent peer in House of Lords; memb House of Lords Ctee on European Communities (Sub Ctee C); *Clubs* Royal Cwlth Soc; *Style—* The Rt Hon Lady Kinloss; North View House, Sheriff Hutton, York YO6 1PT (☎ 03477X) 447)

KINMONT, Dr Patrick David Clifford; MBE (Mil 1945), TD (1946); s of Patrick Kinmont, JP, MD, FRCSE (d 1953), of Newark-on-Trent, and Marie Therèse Clifford (d 1942), of Ennistown, Co Meath; *b* 28 Feb 1916; *Educ* Epsom Coll, King's Coll London, King's Coll Hosp (MD); *m* 25 March 1950, Elizabeth Gladys Matilda, da of Lt Charles West, RM (d 1945), of Corfe Castle; 1 s (John b 1951), 1 da (Philippa b 1953); *Career* War Serv Maj RAMCT, serv Norway and W Desert 1940, Greece 1940-41, (despatches), sr Br offr Stalag 18A Austria 1941-45, CO Bovington Mil Hosp 1945; head of dermatology: Derby Royal Infirmary 1950-73, Univ and Gen Hosp Nottingham 1973-79; conslt dermatologist: and post grad tutor Univ of Kuwait 1979-81, (emeritus) Notts Hosps 1979; visiting lectr Univ of: (Sydney, Adelaide, Melbourne, Perth, Singapore, Dacca, Damascus, Beirut 1967), Chicago 1979, (state) Pennsylvania 1982; memb: NY Acad of Sciences 1987, E Mids Med Appeal Tbnls 1973-88, Bd of dirs The Christian Children's Fund (GB) 1983-; hon memb Dermatologists Assocs (Br, American Irish); former pres Assoc of Dermatologists: Br 1978, N of England 1969, Mids 1970; former pres: E Mids Assoc of Physicians 1966, Derby Med Soc 1972; vice pres RSM Dermatology (sec 1977); FRCP; *Books* Skin Diseases for Beginners (with R B Coles), other dermatological pubns; *Recreations* shooting, fishing; *Clubs* Kildare Street and Univ Dublin, United Services Notts, Univ Nottingham; *Style—* Dr Patrick Kinmont, MBE, TD; 11 Regent St, Nottingham (☎ 0602 475475); Carlton Ashes House, Hough on the Hill, Grantham, Lincs (☎ 0400 50189)

KINMONT, Lady Sophia; *née* Pelham; da of 7 Earl of Yarborough, JP; *b* 15 Oct 1958; *m* 1983, John Kinmont, s of Dr Patrick Kinmont, of Ermine House, Fulbeck, Lincolnshire; *Style—* The Lady Sophia Kinmont; 45 Lynette Avenue, London SW4 9HF

KINNAIRD, Lady (Germaine) Elizabeth Olive; *née* Eliot; da of 8 Earl of St Germans, KCVO, OBE (d 1960) and Helen, nee Post; *b* 1911; *m* 1, 1932 (m dis 1940) Thomas James (d 1976), s of Hon Cuthbert James, CBE, MP (s of 2 Baron Northbourne); m 2, 1950 (m dis 1963), Hon (Kenneth) George Kinnaird (d 1973), s of late 12 Lord Kinnaird; *Career* author and novelist; *Style—* The Lady Elizabeth Kinnaird; New York

KINNAIRD, 13 Lord (S 1682); Graham Charles Kinnaird; Baron Kinnaird of Rossie (UK 1860); s of 12 Lord Kinnaird, KT, KBE (d 1972); *b* 15 Sept 1912; *Educ* Eton; *m* 1, 1938 (m dis 1940), Nadia, da of Harold Augustus Fortington, OBE; m 2, 1940, Diana Margaret Elizabeth, da of late Robert Shuckburgh Copeman, of Roydon Hall, Diss, Norfolk; 1 s decd, 4 da (Hon Mrs Wigan, Hon Mrs Anna Liddell, Hon Mrs Susan Lea, Hon Mrs Mary Staib); *Heir* none; *Career* Flying Offr RAFVR, late Lt 4/5 Bn Black Watch (TA); sits as Cons in House of Lords; *Clubs* Brooks's, Boodles; *Style—* The Rt Hon the Lord Kinnaird; Rossie Priory, Inchture, Perthshire (☎ 0282 86 246)

KINNELL, Ian; QC (1987); s of Brian Kinnell (d 1960), and Grace Madeline, *née* Borer (d 1983); *b* 23 May 1943; *Educ* Sevenoaks Sch Kent; *m* 17 March 1970, Elizabeth Jane, da of David Farries Ritchie, of Hereford; 1 s (Alexander Murray b 1978), 1 da (Fiona b 1981); *Career* barr Gray's Inn 1967, SE Circuit, rec 1987-; *Style—* Ian Kinnell, Esq; 7 King's Bench Walk, Temple, London EC4Y 7DS (☎ 071 583 0404, fax 071 583 0950, telex 887491 KBLAW)

KINNIMENT, Prof David John; s of Herbert John Kinniment (d 1974), and Iris Henrietta, *née* Vivaudou (d 1987); *b* 10 July 1940; *Educ* Haberdashers' Aske's, Univ of Manchester (BSc, MSc, PhD); *m* 11 Aug 1962, Anne, da of James Lupton, of 12 St Anne's Drive, Burnley, Lancs; 2 da (Michelle Jane b 19 Aug 1964, Sarah Lynne b 15 Sept 1966); *Career* sr lectr in computer sci Univ of Manchester 1971-79 (lectr in electrical engrg 1964, lectr in computer sci 1964-71), head of Dept of Electrical and Electronic Engrg Univ of Newcastle upon Tyne 1982- (prof of electronics 1979-); SERC: memb: Sub Ctee Solid State Devices 1979-83 and Microelectronics Facilities 1982-86, Ctee Alvey Industl and Academic Liaison Ctee 1984-87 and Devices Ctee 1988-; Cncl Microelectronics Application Res Inst 1983-90; MIEE 1966, MIEEE 1970; *Books* CAD for VLSI (1985); *Recreations* travelling; *Style—* Prof David Kinniment; Electrical and Electronic Engineering Department, The University, Newcastle upon Tyne NE1 7RU (☎ 091 222 7338, fax 091 222 8180)

KINNOCK, Rt Hon Neil Gordon; PC (1983), MP (Lab) Islwyn 1983-; s of Gordon Kinnock and Mary, *née* Howells; *b* 28 March 1942; *Educ* UC Cardiff (BA, DipEd); *m* 1967, Glenys, *née* Parry; 1 s (Stephen), 1 da (Rachel); *Career* UC Cardiff: chm socialist soc 1963-66, pres SU 1965-66; tutor organiser WEA 1966-70, MP (Lab): Bedwellty 1970-83, Islmyn (new constit) 1983-, PPS to Sec State Employment 1974-75, chief oppn spokesman on educn 1979-83; memb: Nat Exec Ctee Lab Pty 1978-, Lab Shadow Cabinet 1980-; chm Lab Pty 1987-88; memb TGWU, hon fell UC Cardiff; *Books* Making Our Way - Investing in Britain's Future (1986); *Recreations* music (esp male voice choral work), rugby football, being with family; *Style—* The Rt Hon Neil Kinnock, MP; House of Commons, London SW1

KINNOULL, 15 Earl of (S 1633); Arthur William George Patrick Hay; also Viscount Dupplin and Lord Hay (S 1627, 1633, 1697), Baron Hay (GB 1711); s of 14 Earl of Kinnoull (d 1938); *b* 26 March 1935; *Educ* Eton; *m* 1961, Gay Ann, da of Sir Denys Colquhoun Flowerdew Lowson, 1 Bt (d 1975); 1 s, 3 da; *Heir* s, Viscount Dupplin; *Career* sits as Conservative in House of Lords; jr Cons whip House of Lords 1966-68; FRICS; sr ptnr Langley Taylor; memb Agricultural Valuers' Assoc; pres: National Cncl on Inland Tport 1964-76, Scottish Clans Assoc 1970; vice-pres Nat Assoc of Parish Cncls 1971; chm Property Owners' Building Soc; cncl memb Royal Nat Mission to Deep Sea Fishermen 1978-; Cons del Cncl of Europe 1983-; memb Royal Co of Archers (Queen's Body Guard for Scotland) 1965-; *Clubs* Turf, Pratt's, White's, MCC; *Style—* The Rt Hon the Earl of Kinnoull; 5 Verulam Bldgs, Grays Inn, London WC1 (☎ 071 242 5038); 15 Carlyle Square, London SW3; Pier House, Seaview, IOW

KINROSS, 5 Baron (UK 1902); Christopher Patrick Balfour; s of 4 Baron Kinross, OBE, TD, DL, and his 2 w, Helen (d 1969), da of Alan Hog and formerly w of Lt-Col Patrick Perfect; *b* 1 Oct 1949; *Educ* Eton, Univ of St Andrews, Univ of Edinburgh; *m* 1974, Susan Jane, da of Ian Robert Pitman; 2 s (Hon Alan, Hon Derek Andrew b 1981); *Heir* s, Hon Alan Ian Balfour b 4 April 1978; *Career* Writer to the Signet; *Recreations* pistol and rifle shooting, military vehicle restoration, off road Land Rover competition; *Clubs* New (Edinburgh); *Style—* The Rt Hon the Lord Kinross, WS; 11 Belford Place, Edinburgh EH4 3DH

KINROSS, John; s of James Kinross (d 1961); *b* 4 May 1922; *Educ* Co Boys' Sch Windsor; Southall Tech Coll; *m* 1, 1947, Marie (d 1969), da of Arthur Horace Lucas; 1 s, 1 da; m 2, 1972, Eileen Margaret, da of Alfred Seamarks (d 1971), 1 step da; *Career* Lancer Boss Gp: joined 1959, appointed project dir 1961, ret; received Design Cncl awards 1972 and 1976; dir Seamarks Coach & Travel Gp 1975-; CEng, MIMechE; *Recreations* creative pastimes, conservation and preservation; *Style—* John Kinross Esq; Papplewick, Oldhill Wood, Studham, Beds LU6 2NF (☎ 0582 872391)

KINROSS, Ruth, Baroness; Ruth Beverley Balfour; da of late William Henry Mill, SSC; *m* 1, Kenneth William Bruce Middleton; m 2, 1972, as his 3 w, 4 Baron Kinross, OBE, TD, DL (d 1985); *Style—* The Rt Hon Ruth, Lady Kinross; 58 India St, Edinburgh EH3 6HD

KINSMAN, Rodney; *b* 1943; *Educ* Central Sch of Art; *Career* furniture designer; md OMK Design (fndr 1966); Royal Designer to Industry 1990; visiting prof RCA 1985-86 (external examiner 1987-88); memb BA Advsy Cncl St Martins and Central Sch of Art 1989-90; work in exhibitions incl: The Way We Live Now (V & A Museum) 1979, Sit (RIBA) 1980, The Modern Chair (ICA) 1989, The Review (Design Museum London) 1989, Evolution of the Modern Chair (Business Design Centre London) 1989, BBC Design Awards (Design Centre London) 1990; also chosen to represent Britain in numerous foreign exhibitions; designs featured in: various Museum permanent collection UK and abroad incl V & Museum, numerous publications TV and radio broadcasts; awards incl: Observer Design award UK 1969, Design Council award 1984, Resources Cncl Inc 1987, Product Design award USA, Industrial Design Designers Choice USA 1988, D & AD Silver award for most outstanding Br product design for the home UK 1989, The British Design award 1991; hon FRCA 1988; fell Soc of Industl Artists and Designers (now CSD) 1983; *Clubs* Reform, Chelsea Arts, Groucho; *Style—* Rodney Kinsman, Esq; OMK Design Ltd, Stephen Building, Stephen St, London W1P 1PN (☎ 071 631 1335, fax 071 631 3227, telex 24218 OMK)

KINTORE, Delia, Countess of; Delia; o da of William Lewis Brownlow Loyd (d 1947), of Upper House, Shamley Green, Guildford, and Hon Bettine Henrietta, *née* Knatchbull-Hugessen (d 1967), 2 da of 2 Baron Brabourne; *b* 12 Sept 1915; *m* 5 March 1935, 12 Earl of Kintore (d 1989); 2 s (13 Earl, Hon Alexander David Baird, *qqv*), 1 da (Lady Diana Holman, *qv*); *Style—* The Rt Hon Delia, Countess of Kintore; 16 Garden House, Inchmarlo, Banchory, Kincardineshire AB3 1HW (☎ 03302 5025)

KINTORE, 13 Earl of (S 1677); Sir Michael Canning William John Keith; 4 Bt (UK 1897); also Lord Keith of Inverurie and Keith Hall (S 1677), Baron Stonehaven (UK 1925), and Viscount Stonehaven (UK 1938); er s of 12 Earl of Kintore (d 1989), and Delia, Countess of Kintore, *qv*; *b* 22 Feb 1939; *Educ* Eton, RMA Sandhurst; *m* 1972, Mary, o da of late Sqdn Ldr Elisha Gaddis Plum, of Rumson, New Jersey, USA; 1 s (Lord Inverurie), 1 da (Lady Iona Delia Mary Gaddis b 1978); *Heir* s, Lord Inverurie, *qv*; *Career* late Lt Coldstream Guards; *Style—* The Rt Hon the Earl of Kintore; The Stables, Keith Hall, Inverurie, Aberdeenshire (☎ 0467 20495)

KIRBY, Dr Anthony John; s of Samuel Arthur Kirby, and Gladys Rosina, *née* Welch; *b* 18 Aug 1935; *Educ* Eton, Gonville and Caius Coll Cambridge (BA, MA, PhD); *m* 1962, Sara Sophia Benjamina Nieweg; 1 s, 2 da; *Career* Nat Serv RCS 1954-55;

NATO Postdoctoral fell: Univ of Cambridge 1962-63, Brandeis Univ USA 1963-64; Univ of Cambridge: univ demonstrator 1964-68, lectr and reader in organic chemistry 1985- (lectr 1968-85), coll lectr Gonville and Caius Coll 1965- (tutor 1966-74, fell 1962-), dir of studies in natural sciences 1968-; visiting prof: Univ of Paris Orsay 1970, Université Pierre et Marie Curie Paris 1987, The Technion Haifa 1991; res fellowship Japan Soc for the Promotion of Res 1986, visiting scholar Univ of Cape Town 1987, invited lectr in numerous countries; memb: Perkin Editorial Bd RSC 1983-87, Mgmnt Ctee Organic Reaction Mechanisms Gp RSC 1983-86 (chm 1986-90), Sci and Engrg Res Cncl Organic Chemistry Sub-Ctee 1986-89, Chemistry Ctee SERC 1988-, Hooke Ctee Royal Soc 1988-, Advsy Ctee Salters Advanced Chemistry Project 1989-, Panel of Experts Univ of London 1989-; elector to 1702 Chair of Chemistry at Cambridge 1987; RSC Award in Organic Reaction Mechanisms 1983, FRS 1987; *Books* The Organic Chemistry of Phosphorus (with S G Warren, 1967), The Anomeric Effect and Related Stereoelectronic Effects at Oxygen (1983), numerous papers and review articles; *Recreations* chamber music, walking; *Style—* Dr Anthony J Kirby, FRS; University Chemical Laboratory, Cambridge CB2 1EW (☎ 0223 336370, fax 0223 336362)

KIRBY, Hon Mrs (Antonia); da of 8 Baron Rendlesham by his 2 w, Clare; *b* 17 Jan 1956; *m* 1981, Hugo Giles Stephen Astley Kirby, s of Giles Kirby, of The Manor House, South Harting, Petersfield, Hants, and Mrs Angela Kirby, of 17 Wetherby Gdns, London SW5; 1 s (Nicholas b 1983), 1 da (Natasha b 1985); *Style—* The Hon Mrs Kirby

KIRBY, Dr Brian John; s of George Kirby, of London, and Lily Ann, *née* Deighton; *b* 25 Aug 1936; *Educ* Westham GS, Univ of Leeds (MB ChB); *m* 23 July 1959, Rachel Mary, da of James Stoddart Pawson, of Halifax; *Career* house appts Leeds 1960-63, registrar Central Middx Hosp London 1963-65, res fell supported by MRC 1965-67, instr in med Med Coll Virginia 1967-68, registrar Royal Postgrad Med Sch 1968-69, lectr in med Univ of Edinburgh 1969-74, dep dir and sr lectr in Med Univ of Exeter Postgrad Med Sch 1974-, conslt physician to Royal Devon and Exeter Hosp and W of England Eye Infirmary 1974-; vice chm DHSS Review of Medicines Ctee 1987- (memb 1984); memb: DHSS Safety Efficacy and Adverse Reactions Ctee 1987-, Cncl to Exec Ctee Coronary Prevention Gp; chm SW Action on Smoking and Health Ctee; FRCP, memb RSM; *Recreations* anything hedonistic; *Style—* Dr Brian Kirby; Postgraduate Medical Schook, Barack Rd, Exeter EX25 5DW (☎ 0392 403015)

KIRBY, Hon Mrs (Cecilia Alice); *née* Clifford; da of 13 Baron Clifford of Chudleigh; *b* 15 Nov 1945; *m* 1968, Capt Nicholas Breakspear Kirby, RN, s of Ronald Ernest Kirby; 1 s, 3 da; *Style—* The Hon Mrs Kirby; Melbury Bubb House, Melbury Bubb, Evershot, nr Dorchester, Dorset

KIRBY, David Donald; s of Walter Donald Kirby (d 1958), and Margaret Irene, *née* Halstead (d 1977); *b* 12 May 1933; *Educ* Royal GS High Wycombe, Jesus Coll Oxford (MA); *m* 1955, Joan Florence, da of Frederick James Dickins; 1 s (William), 1 da (Elizabeth); *Career* BR: dir London & SE Servs 1982-85, md Sealink UK until 1981, jt md bd 1985-87, vice chm (railways) 1987-89; chm Fishguard & Rosslare Railways & Harbours until 1981; *Recreations* singing in choirs, messing about in boats; *Style—* David Kirby, Esq; Rushden, Graemesdyke Rd, Berkhamsted, Herts

KIRBY, Prof Gordon William; s of William Admiral Kirby (d 1950), of Liverpool, and Frances Teresa, *née* Townson (d 1973); *b* 20 June 1934; *Educ* Liverpool Inst HS, Liverpool Tech Coll, Gonville and Caius Coll Cambridge (MA, PhD, SCD, Schuldham Plate, 1851 Exhibition Sr studentship); *m* 4 April 1964 (m dis 1983), Audrey Jean, da of Col C E Rusbridge, of Halse, Somerset; 2 s (Giles Peter b 1968, Simon Michael b 1970); *Career* univ teacher Imperial Coll London 1960-67 (asst lectr 1960-61, lectr 1961-67), prof of organic chemistry Loughborough Univ of Technol 1967-72, regius prof of chemistry Univ of Glasgow 1972-; Corday Morgan Medal and Prize 1969, Tilden Lectureship and Medal 1974-75; memb Chemistry Ctee SERC 1971-75, chm Journals Ctee Royal Soc of Chemistry 1981-84; FRSC 1970, FRSE 1975; *Books* Progress in the Chemistry of Organic Natural Products (ed), plus many res papers in journals of the Chemical Soc; *Recreations* hill walking, amateur astronomy; *Style—* Prof Gordon Kirby, FRSE; Dept of Chemistry, Univ of Glasgow, Glasgow G12 8QQ (☎ 041 339 8855, ext 4416/4417, fax 041 330 4808, telex 777070 UNIGLA)

KIRBY, John; s of Percival Henry Kirby, of 64 Rydal Gdns, Wembley, and Dorothy Alice, *née* Southgate; *b* 31 Oct 1931; *Educ* Harrow GS, Acton Tech Coll, Chelsea Sch of Pharmacy; *m* (Phyllis) Joy, da of Charles Dodd (d 1975), of 16 Lapstone Gdns, Kenton; 4 da (Susan Elizabeth b 27 July 1956, Caroline Jane b 20 Dec 1957, Sarah Christine b 21 Dec 1958, Rebecca Charlotte b 21 Dec 1962); *Career* community pharmacist: St John's Wood 1956-61, Welwyn Gdn City 1961-; dir: Johns Kelynack Gp of Pharmacies 1962-, Stearns Pharmacies 1969-77, Scotts Pharmacies 1970-77, Focus Ltd (Gifts) 1982-88; chm: local professional assoc 1966 and 1983, Welwyn Garden Round Table 1971-72; memb Pharmaceutical Servs Negotiating Ctee 1982- (Nat Standing Pharmaceutical Advsy Ctee to HMG); former memb govrs: Applecroft Sch, Stanborough Sch; pres Welwyn Hatfield Rotary Club 1983-84, fndr memb Coll of Pharmacy Practice 1985; memb Inst of Pharmacy Mgmnt 1963, fell Royal Pharmaceutical Soc 1989 (memb 1956); *Style—* John Kirby, Esq; 2 Elmwood, Welwyn Gdn City, Herts AL8 6LE; 31 Cole Green Lane, Welwyn Gdn City, Herts AL7 3PP (☎ 0707 326043)

KIRBY, John Edward Weston; s of Lt-Col Robert Fry Kirby, DSO, MBE, of The Oak, Beaumont, Clacton-on-Sea, Essex, and Pamela Mary, *née* Weston; *b* 4 Feb 1936; *Educ* Ampleforth, CCC Oxford (MA); *m* 1, 4 Oct 1963, Teruko Frances (d 1974), da of Rear Adm Yoshio Takahashi, of Tokyo, Japan; 2 s (Patrick b 21 Nov 1966, Peter b 30 June 1974); m 2, 11 Feb 1978, Michiko, da of Junichi Wada of Tokyo Japan; 1 da (Alicia b 21 May 1981); *Career* Bank of England 1959-: fin attaché Br Embassy Tokyo 1974-76, advsr Far East and Australasia 1977-83 (W Europe 1983-85), alternate memb EC Monetary Ctee 1983-85, head Int Div (N America, W Europe and Japan) 1985-88, alternate exec dir Bank for Int Settlements 1985-88, head Int Div (developing countries and int fin insts) 1988-90, min (fin) Br Embassy Tokyo 1990-; memb UK/Japan 2000 Group; *Books* Business in Japan (contrib, 1980); *Recreations* reading, the arts, cricket; *Clubs* Vincent's; *Style—* John Kirby, Esq; Bank of England, Threadneedle St, London EC2R 8AH (☎ 071 601 4174)

KIRBY, (Phyllis) Joy; *née* Dodd; da of William Charles Dodd (d 1975), of Harrow, and Phyllis Ruby, *née* Champion-Jones; *b* 27 June 1935; *Educ* Preston Manor GS Harrow Middx, Hatfield Poly (BA); *m* John Kirby, s of Percival Henry Kirby, of Harrow; 4 da (Susan Elizabeth b 16 July 1956, Caroline Jane b 20 Dec 1957, Sarah Christine b 21 Dec 1958, Rebecca Charlotte b 21 Dec 1962); *Career* teacher 1972-82, dir Johns and Kelynack 1978-, chm Focus Gifts 1983-88; memb: Greenpeace, Friends of the Earth, CND; *Style—* Mrs Joy Kirby; Johns and Kelynack Ltd, 31 Cole Green Lane, Welwyn Garden City, Herts

KIRBY, Maj-Gen Norman George; OBE; s of George William Kirby (d 1978), and Laura Kirby (d 1980); *Educ* King Henry VIII Sch Coventry, Univ of Birmingham (MB ChB); *m* 1 Oct 1949, Cynthia Maire, da of Thomas Ian Bradley (d 1954); 1 s (Robert b 22 June 1954), 1 da (Jill b 11 Nov 1958); *Career* regtl MO 10 Parachute Regt TA 1950-51, offr i/c 5 Parachute surgical team 1956-59 (served Suez landing 1956), offr i/c surgical div BMH Rinteln 1959-60, OC and surgical specialist BMH Tripoli 1960-62, OC and conslt surgn BMH Dhekelia 1967-70, chief conslt surgn Cambridge Mil Hosp 1970-72, conslt surgn HQ BAOR 1973-78; 1978-82: dir of Army surgery, conslt surgn to the Army, hon surgn to the Queen; Hon Col: 308 Gen Hosp RAMC TA 1982-87, 144 Field Ambulance RAMC TA 1985-; Col Cmdt RAMC 1987-; surgical registrar: Plastic Surgery Unit Stoke Mandeville Hosp 1950-51, Birmingham Accident Hosp 1953-55; Postgrad Med Sch Hammersmith 1964, hon conslt surgn Westminster Hosp 1979-, dir Clinical Servs, Accidents, Emergencies and Admissions Guy's Hosp 1985- (conslt accident and emergency surgn 1982-); chm: Accidents and Emergencies Ctee SE Thames RHA 1983-88, Army Med Dept Working Pty Surgical Support for BAOR 1978-80; memb Med Ctee Defence Scientific Advsy Cncl 1979-82, examiner in anatomy RCS Edinburgh 1982-90, memb Ct of Examiners RCS 1988; pres: Br Assoc for Accident and Emergency Med 1990, Mil Surgical Assoc 1991-; vice pres Br Assoc of Trauma in Sport 1982-88; memb Cncl: Int Coll of Surgns 1980, RCS 1989; McCombe lectr RCS Edinburgh 1979, Mitchener medal RCS 1982, memb Ed Bd Br Jl Surgery and Injury 1979-82, librarian Med Soc of London 1988-; Freeman City of London 1980, Liveryman Worshipful Soc of Apothecaries of London; memb HAC; OStJ; FRCS, FICS, FRCSEd; *Books* Field Surgery Pocket Book (1981), Baillieres First Aid (1985), Pocket Reference, Accidents and Emergencies (1991); *Recreations* travel, reading, word processing, archaeology; *Clubs* surgical travellers; *Style—* Maj-Gen Norman Kirby, OBE; Guy's Hospital, London Bridge, London SE1 9RT (☎ 071 955 5000 ext 2782, fax 071 407 4823)

KIRBY, Paul Michael; s of William Raistrick Kirby (d 1968), and Laura, *née* Topham; *b* 19 Feb 1948; *Educ* Hanson GS Bradford Yorks; *m* 16 Sept 1967, Vivien, da of Jack Longstaff, of 10 Bryanstone Rd, Laisterdyke, Bradford, W Yorks; 1 s (Anthony b 1980), 2 da (Deborah b 1976, Michelle b 1978); *Career* Provident Finance Group plc: trainee programmer 1966, project mangr (customer accounting systems) 1972; systems devpt mangr ICL 1900 systems 1975, dep md HT Greenwood Ltd 1980; md: Practical Credit Services Ltd 1983, Car Care Plan (Securites Div) Ltd 1985-; *Recreations* cricket, rugby, football, squash; *Style—* Paul Kirby, Esq; 8 Glenview Close, Nab Wood, Shipley, West Yorks BD18 4AZ (☎ 0274 599877); Car Care Plan (Securities Division) Ltd, Bramley District Centre, Bramley, Leeds, West Yorks LS13 2EJ (☎ 0532 562133, fax 0532 551601, telex 557316 SAFETY G, car 0836 756150)

KIRBY, Dr Peter Linley; OBE (1976); *b* 25 June 1924; *Educ* Bedes Sch, Univ of Durham (BSc, MSc, DSc); *m* 1948, Lilian; 1 s (Paul Kelvin b 1953), 1 da (Pamela Gillian b 1956); *Career* gp dir of res Crystalate Electronics Ltd; dir: Welwyn Strain Measurement Ltd, Strainstall Ltd; visiting prof: Univ of Edinburgh, Univ of Newcastle, Univ of Durham; lectr on: intellectual property subjects for business mgmnt, microelectronics; author of over 50 pubns on electronics; vice chm Cncl Univ of Durham, chm of Govrs Durham Business Sch; *Style—* Dr Peter Kirby, OBE; 14 Woodlands, Gosforth, Newcastle upon Tyne (☎ 091 2857932)

KIRBY, Richard Charles; s of Charles Neil Vernon Kirby (d 1970), and Nora Helena, *née* Corner; *b* 18 Sept 1946; *Educ* Sevenoaks Sch, Jesus Coll Oxford (MA); *m* 1, 27 April 1974 (m dis 1985), Judith Patricia, da of Lennard Withers, of Fordcombe, Kent; m 2, 18 May 1985, Jill Christine, da of Kenneth Fernie, of Rugby, Warwicks; 2 s (Thomas b 1986, James b 1988); *Career* admitted slr 1971, managing ptnr Speechly Bircham 1989- (ptnr 1973-); cnllr Tonbridge and Malling Borough 1971-84 (ldr 1979-82), memb Ctee London Young Slrs 1973-74; memb: Exec Tonbridge and Malling Cons Assoc 1978-84 (vice chm 1979-84), Exec SE region Nat Housing and Town Planning Cncl 1980-83, Cncl Mental After Care Assoc 1982- (hon treas 1987-); slr Worshipful Co of Pewterers 1981-; *Recreations* reading, theatre, swimming; *Clubs* Carlton; *Style—* Richard Kirby, Esq; 48 Alleyn Rd, Dulwich, London SE21 8AL (☎ 081 670 2525); Bouverie House, 154 Fleet St, London EC4A 2HX (☎ 071 353 3290, fax 071 353 4825/4992, telex 22655)

KIRBY, Roger Ian Paul William; s of Vernon Kirby, of Lytham, and Audrey Georgina Kirby; *b* 3 March 1953; *Educ* Malvern, Kingston Poly (BA); *m* 1981, Kathryn Warner, da of Lewis L Warner, of USA; 1 da (Molly b 1983); *Career* md Inenco Gp; dir: Industl Energy Costs Ltd 1972-, Inenco Energy Conservation Ltd 1976-, Industl Energy Costs (telecommunications) Ltd 1978, Industl Energy Costs (systems) Ltd 1983-, Inenco Ltd 1984, Inenco Energy Performance Ltd 1985-; *Recreations* sailing, swimming; *Clubs* Ocean Cruising; *Style—* Roger Kirby, Esq; East Beach, Lytham, Lancashire; Inenco Group, Vulcan House, Orchard Road, St Annes-on-Sea, Lancs (☎ 0253 728951, telex 677155)

KIRDAR, Nemir Amin; s of Amin Jamil Kirdar (d 1958), and Nuzhet Mohammed Ali Kirdar (d 1982); *b* 28 Oct 1936; *Educ* Baghdad Coll, Univ of the Pacific California (BA), Fordham Univ (MBA), Harvard Univ; *m* 1 Feb 1967, Nada, da of Dr Adnan Shakir; 2 da (Rena b 1968, Serra b 1975); *Career* fndr and proprietor Nemir A Kirdar Business Enterprises 1963-69, trainee then asst treas rising to asst vice pres Allied Bank International NY 1969-73, vice pres Nat Bank of N America NY 1973-74, vice pres and head Gulf Div Chase Manhattan Bank NY 1974-81, fndr pres and chief exec offr INVESTCORP Bank EC Bahrain Banking Corpn Bahrain 1982-; memb: Exec Ctee Int Bd of Advsrs Inst of Social and Econ Policy ME John F Kennedy Sch of Govt Harvard Univ, N S Round Table Washington DC, Advsy Bd World Econ Forum Geneva, Inter-Religious Fndn London, Arab Bankers Assoc London, Advsy Ctee Centre for Contemporary Arab Studies Georgetown Univ Washington DC, Bd Heart Res Fndn NY, Bd Int Cncllrs Center for Strategic and Int Studies Washington DC, Visiting Ctee Fordham Univ NY; author of several articles in leading business and fin magazines; fell Sommerville Coll Oxford; author of several articles in leading business and fin magazines; *Recreations* reading, skiing, windsurfing, tennis, collecting antiques; *Clubs* Metropolitan (Washington DC); *Style—* Nemir Kirdar, Esq; Investcorp, 65 Brook St, London W1Y 1YE (☎ 071 629 6600, fax 071 499 0371, telex 28430)

KIRK, Anthony James Nigel; s of James Brian Kirk, of Balmoral House, 45 The Majestic, St Annes-on-Sea, and Lavinia Mary, *née* Kellow; *b* 3 May 1958; *Educ* Ipswich Sch, King Edward VII Sch Lytham, King's Coll London (LLB); *Career* called to the Bar Gray's Inn 1981; memb: SE circuit, Family Law Bar Assoc, Sussex Sessions Bar Mess; memb Royal Coll of Organists; *Recreations* opera, classical music; *Style—* Anthony Kirk, Esq; 4 Grassmount, Taymount Rise, Forest Hill, London SE23 3UW (☎ 081 291 7120); 1 King's Bench Walk, Temple, London EC4Y 7DB (☎ 071 583 6266, fax 071 583 2068)

KIRK, Colin; s of Edgar Thomas Kirk (d 1974), and Ethel Emma, *née* Jermy; *b* 14 March 1939; *Educ* Barton-upon-Humber GS, Univ of Edinburgh, Oxford Poly (DMS); *m* 1, 1963 (m dis 1983), Patricia Elizabeth Sparks; 2 s (James Thomas b 1964, Edmund b 1965), 1 da (Sarah b 1966); m 2, 1984, Jill Butler; *Career* trainee health serv admin Birmingham Accident Hosp 1962-64, dep admin Worcester Royal Infirmary 1964-65; admin: Bradford Royal Infirmary 1965-69 (Dip Health Serv Management 1967), Littlemore Hosp 1969-71; res offr Health Serv Evaluation Gp Oxford 1972-74, sector mangr N Oxfordshire 1974-79, planning offr Oxfordshire Health Authy 1979-84, gen mangr Mental Health Unit Hampstead Health Authy 1985-; *Recreations* literature, music, squash, France; *Style—* Colin Kirk, Esq; 1 Bridge Street, Oxford OX2 0BA; Friern Hospital, Friern Barnet Road, London N11 3BP (☎ 081 368 1288, fax 081 361 4434)

KIRK, David; s of Herbert Arthur Kirk (d 1969), of Sutton Coldfield, Warwickshire, and Constance Florence, *née* Mortimer; *b* 26 May 1943; *Educ* King Edward's Sch Birmingham, Balliol Coll Oxford, Clinical Med Sch Oxford (MA, BM BCh, DM); *m* 7 Aug 1965, Gillian Mary, da of Maj Wilson Bell Wroot, of Sutton Coldfield, Warwickshire; 1 s (Robert b 1971), 2 da (Tonya b 1969, Lucy b 1975); *Career* res med appts Radcliffe Infirmary Oxford 1968-69, univ demonstrator Univ of Oxford 1969-70; sr house offr appts 1970-72: Radcliffe Infirmary, Churchill Hosp Oxford, Bristol Royal Infirmary; surgical registrar 1973-75: Royal Infirmary Sheffield, Children's Hosp; res asst in surgery Univ of Sheffield 1975-76; sr surgical registrar 1976-78: Bristol Royal Infirmary, Royal Devon and Exeter Hosp; sr urological registrar 1978-82: Bristol Royal Infirmary, Southmead Hosp; conslt urological surgn Gtr Glasgow Health Bd 1982-, hon clinical lectr Univ of Glasgow 1982; Arris and Gale lectr RCS 1980-81; memb Cncl: Section of Urology RSM 1984-87, Br Assoc of Urological Surgns 1988-; chm Scot Urological Oncology Gp 1985-88 (sec 1983-85), memb Working Pty Sub Gp MRC, study coordinator of prostatic cancer Working Pty MRC; contrib to multiauthor books on mgmnt of urological cancer, memb Editorial Ctee Br Jl of Urology 1990-; FRCS 1973, FRSM 1981, FRCPSGlas 1989; *Recreations* skiing, hill walking, classical music, woodwork; *Style*— David Kirk, Esq; Woodend, Prospect Rd, Dullatur, Glasgow G68 0AN (☎ 0236 720778); Urology Dept, Western Infirmary, Dumbarton Rd, Glasgow (☎ 041 339 8822 ext 4388)

KIRK, Lady; Elizabeth Mary; da of Richard Brockbank Graham (d 1957), and Gertrude Anson (d 1987); *b* 9 Jan 1928; *Educ* St Leonard's Sch, Somerville Coll Oxford (MA); *m* 1950, Sir Peter Michael Kirk (d 1977; MP (C) Saffron Walden), s of Rt Rev Kenneth Escott Kirk, late Bishop of Oxford (d 1954); 3 s; *Career* memb: Countryside Cmmn 1979-87, Eastern Cncl for Sport and Recreation 1982-87; chm Peter Kirk Meml Fund, tstee Byways and Bridleways Tst; memb Regnl Advsy Ctee Forestry Cmmn 1987-; Nat Tst Regnl Ctee: East Anglia 1982-87, Yorks 1988-; DL Essex 1983-87; *Recreations* fell walking, music, riding; *Clubs* Farmers'; *Style*— Lady Kirk; Manor Farm, Newton upon Rawcliffe, Pickering, N Yorks YO18 8QA

KIRK, (Alistair) Graham; s of Alexander Charles Tansley Kirk, of Longfield, Stokeholy Cross, Norwich, Norfolk, and Dulce Marjory, *née* Ewins; *b* 10 May 1935; *Educ* Windsor GS, Berks Coll of Art and Design (NDD); *m* July 1986, Gillian Ruth, da of Mark Cresswell Bostock; 2 da (Catherine Elizabeth b 26 Oct 1987, Alexandra Claire b 30 May 1989); *Career* art dir various London advertising agencies until 1967; set up own photographic studio London 1968-, visiting lectr in photography London Coll of Printing 1969; portfolio incl: still life and food photography for advertising and editorial publications, contrib to Sunday Times and Observer magazines, photographs appear in many books on food; memb Assoc of Fashion Advertising and Editorial Photographers; FCSD 1986-; *Recreations* music and gardening; *Style*— Graham Kirk, Esq; Forge Farm House, Goudhurst, Kent TN17 2QZ; Germon 11410 Mezerville, France; Graham Kirk Photography, 122 Brad St, London SE1 8TD (☎ 071 928 7051); Oast Studio, Forge Farm House, Goudhurst, Kent TN17 2QZ (☎ 0580 211646)

KIRK, Joanna Elizabeth; da of Michael Alan Barker Kirk, of Holbrook House, The Royal Hosp Sch, Holbrook, Suffolk, and Margaret Elizabeth Kirk; *b* 19 April 1963; *Educ* Convent of Jesus and Mary, Guildford, West Surrey Coll of Art and Design Farnham (distinction for fndn course and Lena Garnade award), Goldsmith's Coll London (BA); *Career* artist; Christie's Inaugural Exhibition London 1984, Love: Sacred and Profane (Plymouth Arts Centre) 1986, Interference (Riverside Studios London) 1986, Third Eye Centre Glasgow 1987, Nicola Jacobs Gallery London 1987, Gp Show (Richard Pomeroy Gallery London) 1987, New Gallery Whitechaple Art Gallery London 1988, Vanitas Triennial Festival Norwich Sch of Art 1988, Carine Campo Gallery Antwerp 1989, Nicola Jacobs Gallery London 1989, selections from the collections of M Anwar Kamal Twentieth Century Drawing and Sculpture (Cummer Gallery of Art, Jacksonville, Florida) 1989, Subject Object (Nicola Jacobs Gallery London) 1989, Br Art Show 1990 (Macclennon Galleries Glasgow, Leeds City Art Gallery, Hayward Gallery London); winner Whitechapel Art award 1988; *Recreations* reading, going to exhibitions; *Style*— Ms Joanna Kirk; 23A Park Vista, Greenwich SE10 (☎ 081 293 5693, 701 4341); Nicola Jacobs Gallery, 9 Cork St, London W1 (☎ 071 437 3868)

KIRK, Raymond Maurice; *b* 31 Oct 1923; *Educ* County Secdy Sch W Bridgford Nottingham, Univ of London (MB BS, MS); *m* 2 Dec 1952, Margaret; 1 s (Jeremy), 2 da (Valentine, Louise); *Career* Lt RN 1942-46; conslt surgn Royal Free Hosp 1964-89 (currently hon consltg surgn); RCS: ed Annals 1985, memb Cncl 1983-, memb Ct of Examiners 1975-81, currently dir Overseas Doctors Trg Scheme; former examiner: Univ of London, Univ of Liverpool, Univ of Bristol, Univ of Khartoum, Univ of Colombo; former pres: surgical section RSM, Med Soc London; FRCS, FRSM; *Books* Gen Surgical Operations (jt ed, 2 edn 1987), Complications of Surgery of the Upper Gastrointestinal Tract (jtly, 1987), Basic Surgical Techniques (3 edn, 1988); *Recreations* squash, cycling, opera, travel; *Style*— Raymond Kirk, Esq; 10 Southwood Lane, Highgate Village, London N6 5EE (☎ 081 340 8575); Royal College of Surgeons of England, 35-43 Lincoln's Inn Fields, London WC2A 3PN (☎ 071 405 3474 ext 4040)

KIRKBY, Prof Michael John (Mike); s of John Lawrence Kirkby (d 1989), of London, and Hilda Margaret, *née* Potts (d 1974); *b* 6 May 1937; *Educ* Radley, Univ of Cambridge (BA, PhD); *m* 1, 24 July 1963 (m dis 1975), Anne Veronica Tennant, da of Philip Whyte (d 1983), of Bedford; 1 s (David b 1967), 1 da (Clare b 1970); m 2, 15 May 1976, Fiona Elizabeth, da of Donald Weston Burley; 2 s (John b 1978, Nicholas b 1982); *Career* Nat Serv 2 Lt REME 1955-57; lectr in geography Univ of Bristol 1967-72, prof of physical geography Univ of Leeds 1973-; author of numerous scientific pubns; FRGS 1963; memb: IBG 1963, BGRG 1966; *Books* Hillslope Form and Process (with MA Carson, 1972), Hillslope Hydrology (ed, 1978), Soil Erosion (ed with RPC Morgan, 1980), Computer Simulation in Physical Geography (jtly, 1987); *Recreations* hill walking, photography; *Style*— Prof Mike Kirkby; School of Geography, University of Leeds, Leeds LS2 9JT (☎ 0532 333310, fax 0532 333308)

KIRKE, Rear Adm David Walter; CB (1967), CBE (1962, OBE 1945); s of Percy St George Kirke (d 1966), and Alice Gertrude (d 1959), da of Sir James Gibson-Craig, 3 Bt; *b* 13 March 1915; *Educ* RNC Dartmouth; *m* 1, 1936 (m dis 1950), Tessa, da of Capt Patrick O'Connor; 1 s; m 2, 1956, Marion Margaret, da of late Dr James Gibb; 1 s, 1 da; *Career* chief of Naval Aviation Indian Navy New Delhi 1959-62, Flag Offr Naval Flying Trg 1965-68; *Recreations* golf; *Clubs* Army and Navy; *Style*— Rear Adm David Kirke, CB, CBE; Lismore House, Pluckley, Kent (☎ 023 384 439)

KIRKHAM, David John; s of Joseph Edward Kirkham (d 1961), of Chingford, and Doris Evelyn Kirkham; *b* 8 March 1947; *Educ* Chingford GS, Lady Lumley's GS; *m* 12 April 1971, Elizabeth Margaret, da of Edward Armstrong Hayes, of Thornton-le-Dale; 1 s (James Edward b 1981), 1 da (Charlotte Mary b 1978); *Career* ptnr Gardiners CA's Scarborough 1974-89 (mangr 1970-74, sr ptnr 1977-79), nat exec ptnr Moore Stephens E Yorks 1988-89, co sec Co Properties Gp plc 1980-88 (fin dir 1986-88); dir: Kingsley Res Ltd, Desktop Professional Systems Ltd, Glazebrook Interior Architects, Greenfield Hldgs Ltd, Marshall Gp Ltd; memb: Round Table 1972-87, Rotary 1988-, Ryedale Cons Assoc; FCA 1970; *Recreations* squash, deer stalking; *Clubs* RAC; *Style*— David Kirkham, Esq; The High Hall, Thornton-le-Dale, Pickering, N Yorks YO18 7QR (☎ 0751 74 371); Catriona, Roshven, Irine, Lochailort, Fortwilliam, Inverness-shire (☎ 0687 7271); Kingsley House, 18 Queen St, Scarborough, N Yorks (☎ 0723 500 373)

KIRKHAM, Donald Herbert; s of Herbert Kirkham (d 1987), and Hettie, *née* Trueblood; *m* 17 Sept 1960, Kathleen Mary, da of Christopher Lond; 1 s (Richard b 1963), 1 da (Sarah b 1966); *Career* Nat Serv Army 1954-56; The Woolwich Building Society: joined Lincoln Branch 1959, branch mangr Worcester 1963, gen mangr's asst 1967, business prodn mangr 1970, asst gen mangr of ops 1972, gen mangr 1976, dep chief gen mangr 1981, appointed to local bd for Scotland and NI 1979-84, memb Main Bd 1982, chief exec 1986; vice pres Chartered Bldg Socs Inst 1986 (pres 1981-82), vice pres Cncl of Inst of Chartered Secs and Admins 1991; chm Met Assoc of Bldg Socs; tstee Greenwich Festival; Freeman City of London, Liveryman Worshipful Co of Chartered Secretaries and Adminstrators; FCIS 1960, FCBSI 1965, CBIM 1986; *Recreations* boating; *Clubs* IOD; *Style*— Donald Kirkham, Esq; 2 Chaundrye Close, The Court Yard, Eltham SE9 5QB (☎ 081 298 5000, fax 0322 555 733)

KIRKHAM, John Squire; s of Wilfred Kirkham (d 1989), and Una Mary, *née* Baker; *b* 20 Sept 1936; *Educ* Gonville and Caius Coll Cambridge (MA, MB BChir, MChir), Westminster Hosp, FRCS, FRCSEd; *m* 19 Sept 1969, Charlotte, da of Paul Giersing (d 1981), of Aalborg, Denmark; 1 s (Alexander), 1 da (Sophie); *Career* ships surgn Union Castle Line MN 1962-63; house surgeon Westminster Hosp; sr house offr: Birmingham Accident Hosp, The Hosp for Sick Children Gt Ormond St, surgn registrar Aberdeen Royal Infirmary, sr surgical registrar St James's Hosp SW12, Charing Cross Hosp; conslt surgn St George's Hosp London and St James's Hosp London 1971-90, hon sr lectr St George's Hosp Med Sch, Queen Mary's Univ Hosp Roehampton 1991 (conslt in gen surgery, surgical gastroenterology and digestive endoscopy); examiner: Univ of London, Khartoum, Basra; visiting prof: Khartoum Basra, Cairo, Melbourne, Alexandria; author papers on: surgical aspects of gastroenterology, gastro-intestinal bleeding, endoscopy, various surgical topics, chapters in surgical textbooks; memb: Save Br Sci, Int Internal Dendrology Soc, Pancreatic Soc of GB and Ireland, Br Soc of Gastroenterology, Assoc of Surgns of GB and Ireland, Int Gastro-Surgical Club; FRSM; *Books* contrib to Maingot's Adbominal Operations (1984), Surgery of Obesity (1984), British Surgical Progress (1990); *Recreations* reading, dendrology, sailing, travelling, fishing; *Clubs* Athenaeum, Naval and Military; *Style*— John Kirkham, Esq; 149 Harley St, London W1N 2DH (☎ 071 935 4444)

KIRKHAM, Hon Mrs (Pamela Vivien); da and co-heiress of Baroness Berners, *qv*; *b* 30 Sept 1929; *m* 1952, Michael Joseph Sperry Kirkham; 2 s, 1 da; *Style*— The Hon Mrs Kirkham; Ashwellthorpe, 103 Charlton Lane, Cheltenham, Glos GL53 9EE

KIRKHILL, Baron (Life Peer UK 1975), in District of City of Aberdeen; John Farquharson Smith; s of Alexander Findlay Smith; *b* 7 May 1930; *Educ* Robert Gordon's Colls Aberdeen; *m* 1965, Frances Mary Walker Reid; 1 step da; *Career* lord provost of the City and Royal Burgh of Aberdeen 1971-75, min of State Scottish Office 1975-78, chm North of Scotland Hydro-Electric Bd 1979-82; memb Cncl of Europe 1987-; Hon LLD Univ of Aberdeen 1974; *Style*— The Rt Hon the Lord Kirkhill; 3 Rubislaw Den North, Aberdeen (☎ 0224 314167)

KIRKHOPE, Timothy John Robert; MP (C) Leeds NE 1987-; s of John Thomas Kirkhope, of Newcastle upon Tyne, and Dorothy Buemann, *née* Bolt (d 1973); *b* 29 April 1945; *Educ* Royal GS Newcastle upon Tyne, Coll of Law Guildford; *m* 1969, Caroline, da of Christopher Thompson Maling (d 1975), of Newcastle upon Tyne; 4 s (Justin b 1970, Rupert b 1972, Dominic b 1976, Alexander 1979); *Career* slr; ptnr with Wilkinson Maughan Newcastle upon Tyne (formerly Wilkinson Marshall Clayton & Gibson) 1977-87, conslt 1987-; cncllr Northumberland 1981-85, PPS to Min of State for the Environment and Countryside (David Trippier MP) 1989-90, asst govt whip 1990-; memb: Newcastle Airport Controlling Bd 1981-85, Cons Nat Exec Ctee, Northern Region Health Authy 1982-86; *Recreations* swimming, tennis, flying; *Clubs* Northern Counties; *Style*— Timothy Kirkhope, Esq, MP; Kirkhope, 7 Dewar Close, Collingham, Leeds LS22 5JR; 8 Castle Street, Warkworth, Northumberland NE65

KIRKMAN, William Patrick (Bill); s of Geoffrey Charles Aylward Kirkman (d 1976), of New Milton, Hampshire and Berth Winifred, *née* Hudson (d 1989); *b* 23 Oct 1932; *Educ* Churcher's Coll Petersfield Hampshire, Oriel Coll Oxford (Heath Harrison travelling scholar, MA, MA by incorporation (Cambridge)); *m* 5 March 1959, Anne Teasdale, da of Frank Fawcett (d 1975), of Minster Lovell, Oxon; 2 s (George William Fawcett b 1961, Edward Thomas Fawcett b 1964), 1 da (Eleanor Mary Fawcett b 1968); *Career* Nat Serv RASC 1950-52, Lt Intelligence Corps (TA) 1955-61; memb editorial staff Express & Star Wolverhampton 1955-57; The Times: joined editorial staff 1957, Cwlth staff corr 1960-64, Africa corr 1962-64; asst sec Oxford Univ Appts Ctee 1964-68, sec Cambridge Univ Careers Service 1968-; vice pres Wolfson Coll Cambridge (formerly Univ Coll) 1980-84 (fell 1968-), dir Press Fellowship Prog 1982-; chm: Standing Ctee Univ Appts Servs 1971-73, Cambridgeshire Cwlth Gp 1988; tstee Sir Halley Stewart Tst 1970; memb: Mgmnt Ctee Central Services Unit for Careers Servs 1972-76 and 1986-88, Univ of Cambridge Public Relations Ctee, Univ of Cambridge Bd of Extra-Mural Studies, Training Bd Econ & Social Res Cncl 1990-, South & East Regnl Advsy Cncl BBC 1990, Ely Diocesan Communications Ctee 1978-88; church warden: St Andrews Headington Oxford 1967-68, St Mary All Saints Willingham Cambridge 1977-84; FRSA 1990; *Recreations* church activities, travel; *Clubs* Commonwealth Trust (Royal Commonwealth Soc); *Style*— William Kirkman, Esq; 19 High Street, Willingham, Cambridge CB4 5ES (☎ 0954 60393); Cambridge University Careers Service, Stuart House, Mill Lane, Cambridge CB2 1XE (☎ 0223 338288, fax 0223 338281)

KIRKPATRICK, Sir Ivone Elliott; 11 Bt (NS 1685), of Closeburn, Dumfriesshire; s of Sir James Alexander Kirkpatrick, 10 Bt (d 1954); *b* 1 Oct 1942; *Educ* Wellington, St Mark's Coll Adelaide Univ; *Heir* bro, Robin Kirkpatrick; *Style*— Sir Ivone Kirkpatrick, Bt

KIRKPATRICK, Jennifer Augustine (Jenny); da of Richard Arthur Seckerson (d 1973), of Wallasey, Merseyside, and Olive Frances Maude, *née* O'Connor; *b* 7 Aug 1946; *Educ* Oldershaw GS Wallasey, Cheshire Coll of Educn, Univ of Keele Inst of Educn (BEd); *m* 4 April 1969 (m dis 1984), Jack Kirkpatrick; *Career* teacher of English Dunstable Sch Beds 1968-70, head of resources St Albans Sch Herts 1970-75 (head of English 1971-75, sr sixth form tutor 1972-75), dep head Comprehensive London Borough of Barnet 1975-79, gen sec Nat Assoc of Probation Offrs 1979-85, dir Electricity Consumers' Cncl, nat watchdog for the Electricity Supply Indust 1985-88; dir: Bursar-Marsteller 1989, The Paul Hamlyn Fndn 1988-89; writer and broadcaster; *Recreations* written and spoken word, public sector policy, anything obsessional - crosswords, bridge, puzzles, horses; *Style*— Jenny Kirkpatrick; 86 Bryanston Ct, George St, London W1 (☎ 071 831 6262)

KIRKPATRICK, Hon Mrs (Joanna Norrie); o da of 3 Viscount Daventry; *b* 8 Feb 1964; *m* 12 May 1990, Nicholas Y J Kirkpatrick, 2 s of John Kirkpatrick, of Horn Park, Beaminster, Dorset; *Style*— The Hon Mrs Kirkpatrick

KIRKPATRICK, Robin Alexander; s of Sir James Alexander Kirkpatrick, 10 Bt, and hp of bro, Sir Ivone Elliott Kirkpatrick, 11 Bt; *b* 19 March 1944; *Educ* Wellington; *Style*— Robin Kirkpatrick, Esq

KIRKPATRICK, William Brown; s of Joseph Kirkpatrick (d 1961), of Dumfriesshire, and Mary Laidlaw Kirkpatrick, *née* Brown (d 1985); *b* 27 April 1934; *Educ* George Watson's Coll Edinburgh, Strathclyde Univ (BSc Econ), Colombia Univ New York (MSc); *m* 1990, Joan Millar; *Career* Investors in Industry plc 1960-85, memb Gaming Board for GB, dir six other cos; *Recreations* Scottish paintings, porcelain pigs, current affairs; *Clubs* Caledonian; *Style*— William Kirkpatrick, Esq; 20 Abbotsbury House, Abbotsbury Rd, London W14 8EN (☎ 071 603 3087)

KIRKUP, Prof James Falconer; s of James Harold Kirkup (d 1958), and Mary Johnson (d 1973); descendant of Seymour Stocker Kirkup (DNB), Thomas Kirkup (DNB), William Falconer (DNB); *b* 23 April 1918; *Educ* S Shields Secdy Sch, King's Coll Univ of Durham (BA); *Career* lectr and prof at various univs in Br, Europe, USA and Far East, prof of comparative lit Kyoto Univ of Foreign Studies 1976-88, composer An Actor's Revenge (opera); sponsor Inst of Psychophysical Res Oxford 1970; named Ollave Order of Bards, Ovates and Druids 1974; pres Br Haiku Soc 1990-; FRSL; *Books* 20 volumes of poetry, The Sense of the Visit (1985), translator of Kawabata, Simone de Beauvoir, Kleist, Pasolini; A Poet Could Not But Be Gay (autobiography), I of All People (autobiography), Gaijin On The Ginza (novel); *Recreations* reading, music (jazz and classical), cinema, travel; *Style*— Prof James Kirkup; BM-Box 2780, Br Monomarks, London WC1N 3XX

KIRKWOOD, Andrew Tristram Hammett; QC (1989); s of Maj Tristram Guy Hammett Kirkwood, RE (ka 1944), and Margaret Elizabeth Montagu (who m 2, Rt Rev Arthur Groom Parham, MC, Bishop of Reading, and 3, Sir Neville Major Ginner Faulks, MBE, TD (d 1982)); *b* 5 June 1944; *Educ* Radley, Christ Church Oxford (MA); *m* 13 July 1968, Penelope Jane, *née* Eaton; 2 s (Tristram b 2 Jan 1972, Edward b 19 June 1977), 1 da (Sophie b 25 Oct 1969); *Career* called to the Bar Inner Temple 1966, rec Crown Ct 1987; *Recreations* the countryside; *Clubs* MCC; *Style*— Andrew Kirkwood, Esq, QC; 4 Paper Bldgs, Temple, London EC4Y 7EX (☎ 071 353 3420, fax 071 353 4979)

KIRKWOOD, (Joan) Antoinette Lindsay; da of Maj Charles Home Kingston Kirkwood (d 1966), of Chelsea, and Ivy Muriel, *née* Burlton (d 1983); *b* 26 Feb 1930; *m* 14 July 1961, Richard Owen Neil Phibbs (d 1987), s of Basil Phibbs (d 1938), of Lisheen, Sligo; 1 s (Harry b 1966), 2 da (Rebekah b 1962, Jessica b 1964); *Career* composer and publisher; works as composer: Suite for Strings, Symphony No 1, Sonata for Cello and Piano, Six Intermezzi for Piano Solo; dir Curlew Publishing; memb: Composers' Guild of GB, Performing Right Soc, ISM; *Style*— Miss Antoinette Kirkwood; 56 Sutherland St, London SW1V 4JZ (☎ 071 828 1683)

KIRKWOOD, Archibald Johnston (Archy); MP (SLD) Roxburgh and Berwickshire 1983-; s of David Kirkwood, of Glasgow, and Jessie Barclay (d 1980); *b* 22 April 1946; *Educ* Heriot-Watt Univ (BSc); *m* 1972, Rosemary Jane, da of Edward John Chester; 1 s, 1 da; *Career* slr; *Recreations* music, skiing; *Style*— Archy Kirkwood, Esq, MP; House of Commons, London SW1

KIRKWOOD, (Robert William) Cecil; OBE (1987); s of William Kirkwood (d 1988), of Lambeg, Lisburn, and Margaret, *née* Carmichael; *b* 1 May 1933; *Educ* Royal Belfast Academical Instn, Queen's Univ Belfast (BSc); *m* 25 July 1957, Isobel Margaret, da of James Henry Kerr (d 1945); 2 s (James b 12 Feb 1962, Michael b 18 Sept 1963), 1 da (Kathy b 7 Nov 1959); *Career* South Eastern Educn and Library Bd: memb 1973-85, chm 1979-81; Lisburn Borough Cncl: cncllr 1973-77, alderman 1977-81; chm Youth Ctee for NI 1981-86, memb Admin Cncl Royal Jubilee Tsts 1986-89, vice chm NI Ctee Prince's Tst 1987-; ALA 1969-; *Recreations* sports admin; *Clubs* Lisburn Rugby, Lisburn Cricket (chm 1986-88), Lisnagarvey Hockey; *Style*— Cecil Kirkwood, Esq, OBE; 4 Marnabrae, Belsize Rd, Lisburn, Co Antrim, Northern Ireland BT27 4LD (☎ 0846 664046); Queen's Univ Agric and Food Sci Centre, Newforge Lane, Belfast BT9 5PX, Northern Ireland (☎ 0232 661166)

KIRKWOOD, Colin Bennie; s of Matthew Chrystal Kirkwood, of Killearn, Stirlingshire, and Charlotte Margaret, *née* Bennie; *b* 6 Dec 1951; *Educ* Glasgow Acad, Napier Coll of Sci and Technol Edinburgh (Dip in Book and Periodical Publishing); *m* 4 April 1987, Isabel Mary, da of David Gordon Johnstone (d 1976); 1 s (Matthew b 1989), 1 da (Rosanna Mary b 1991); *Career* prodn and ed asst NFER publishing co 1972-74, gen ed Blackie & Son Ltd 1974-77; John Bartholomew & Son Ltd: editorial mangr Pictorial Div 1977-79, Book Div mangr 1979-81, publishing mangr 1981-83, assoc dir publishing 1984-86, publishing dir 1986-89; md The Aberdeen University Press Ltd 1990-; chm Scot Young Publishers Soc 1979, chm Scot Publishers Assoc 1984-86, memb Bd Edinburgh Book festival 1984-89, ed Charles Rennie Mackintosh Soc Newsletter 1976-84; *Books* The National Book League (1972); *Recreations* sailing, tennis, cooking, architecture; *Style*— Colin B Kirkwood, Esq; 37 Park Rd, Edinburgh, EH6 4LA (☎ 031 552 4398); The Aberdeen University Press Ltd (Publishers), Farmers Hall, Aberdeen AB9 2XT (☎ 0224 641672/641663, fax 0224 643286)

KIRKWOOD, 3 Baron (UK 1951); David Harvie Kirkwood; s of 2 Baron Kirkwood (d 1970, s of 1 Baron, PC, JP, MP Dumbarton Burghs 1922-50, who as David Kirkwood was deported for being the ringleader in a protest against rent increases); *b* 21 Nov 1931; *Educ* Rugby, Trinity Hall Cambridge (MA, PhD); *m* 1965, Judith, da of John Hunt, of Leeds; 3 da (Hon Ruth b 17 Sept 1966, Hon Anne b 24 April 1969, Hon Lucy b 28 July 1972); *Heir* bro, Hon James Kirkwood; *Career* warden Stephenson Hall 1974-79, sr lectr Sheffield Univ 1976-87, hon sr lectr 1987-; CEng; *Style*— The Rt Hon the Lord Kirkwood; 56 Endcliffe Hall Ave, Sheffield S10 3EL (☎ 0742 663107)

KIRKWOOD, Eileen, Baroness; Eileen Grace; da of late Thomas Henry Boalch, of Pill, Bristol; *m* 1931, 2 Baron Kirkwood (d 1970); *Style*— The Rt Hon Eileen, Lady Kirkwood

KIRKWOOD, The Hon Lord; Ian Candlish Kirkwood; QC (1970); s of John Brown Kirkwood OBE (d 1964), and Constance Kirkwood (d 1987); *b* 8 June 1932; *Educ* George Watson's Boys' Coll Edinburgh, Edinburgh Univ (MA, LLB), Univ of Michigan (LLM); *m* 1970, Jill, da of Lt-Cdr Trevor P Scott, RN (ret), of Torquay; 2 s (Jonathan b 1973, Richard b 1975); *Career* chm Medical Appeal Tribunal (until 1987); senator Coll of Justice Scotland 1987; *Recreations* tennis, golf, chess; *Style*— The Hon Lord Kirkwood; 58 Murrayfield Ave, Edinburgh, EH12 6AY (☎ 031 337 3468); Knockbrex House, nr Borgue, Kirkcudbrightshire (☎ 055 77 269)

KIRKWOOD, Hon James Stuart; s of 2 Baron Kirkwood (d 1970), and hp of bro, 3 Baron; *b* 19 June 1937; *Educ* Rugby, Trinity Hall Cambridge; FRICS; *m* 1965, Alexander Mary, da of late Alec Dyson, of Holt, Norfolk; 2 da; *Style*— The Hon James Kirkwood; The Cearne, Kent Hatch, Crockham Hill, Edenbridge, Kent

KIRKWOOD, James William; s of Robert William Cecil Kirkwood, OBE, of 4 Marnabrae, Belsize Rd, Lisburn, NI, and Isobel Margaret, *née* Kerr; *b* 12 Feb 1962; *Educ* Friends' Sch Lisburn NI; *m* Pamela Jean, *née* McMurray; *Career* hockey player; 70 Ir caps 1981-, 40 GB caps 1987-, Olympic Gold medallist Seoul 1988, 3 Ir cricket caps 1983; sales exec Forward Tst Gp 1983-; *Recreations* all sports, music; *Style*— James Kirkwood, Esq; 2 Old Mill Heights, Hillsborough NI (☎ 0846 683317); Forward Trust Ltd, 5 Donegall Sq South, Belfast, NI (☎ 0232 324 641)

KIRKWOOD, (Iona Mary) Nicole; da of 12 Baron de Fresnes (Fr), and his w, Lady Fiona, *née* Abney-Hastings, *qv*; *b* 30 June 1957; *Educ* Univ of Edinburgh (BA); *m* 1982, Timothy John Kirkwood, 2 s of Andrew and Patricia Kirkwood, of Half Acre, Corfe Castle, Dorset; 1 s (Toby John b 1989), 4 da (Harriet Mary b 1984, Matilda Alice b 1986, Jemima Jane b 1987, Phoebe Maud b 1990); *Style*— Mrs Timothy Kirkwood; Straan, Advie, Grantown-on-Spey, Moray

KIRKWOOD, Ronald Campbell; s of Maj William Campbell Kirkwood, OBE, MC (d 1965), of Glasgow, and Elizabeth Campbell, *née* Murray; *b* 23 April 1939; *Educ* Fettes, Univ of Glasgow (BSc); *m* 22 July 1963, Alice Mackay, da of Gregor MacGregor (d 1968); 3 da (Rosalind Elizabeth b 1968, Jennifer Anne (twin) b 1968, Gillian Louise b 1971); *Career* Clyde Fuel Systems 1961-62, ptnr Hulley Kirkwood 1969- (design engr 1962-69); memb: Bldg Standards Ctee Scotland, Bldg Servs Res Info Assoc Bracknell; memb Incorporation of Masons Glasgow; FCIBSE, MIMechE, MConsE; *Books* pubns: various tech papers on engrg servs and energy mgmnt; *Recreations* golf; *Clubs* Royal Scottish Automobile, Glasgow Art; *Style*— Ronald Kirkwood, Esq; Hulley and Kirkwood, Consulting Engineers, 15/16 Woodside Place, Glasgow G3 7QS (☎ 041 332 5466, fax 041 333 0091)

KIRSTEIN, Prof Peter Thomas; s of Walter Kirstein (d 1983), of London; *b* 20 June 1933; *Educ* Highgate Sch London, Gonville & Caius Coll Cambridge (BA), Stanford Univ (MSc, PhD), Univ of London (DSc); *m* 5 July 1958, Gwen Margaret Oldham; 2 da (Sarah Lynn b 1964, Claire Fiona b 1971); *Career* res assoc and lectr W W Hansen Laboratory of Physics Stanford Univ 1957-58, accelerator physicist Centre of European Nuclear Research Geneva Switzerland 1959-63, scientific rep Europe Gen Electric Company of USA 1963-67, prof of computer systems Univ of London 1970-73 (reader in information processing 1967-70); UCL: prof 1973-, head Dept of Computer Science 1980-; FBCS 1964, FIEE 1965, FInstP 1965, SMIEEE 1975, FEng 1980; *Books* Space Charge Flow (1967); *Recreations* skiing, tennis, squash; *Clubs* Alpine Ski; *Style*— Prof Peter Kirstein; 31 Bancroft Ave, London N2 0AR (☎ 071 380 7286); Department of Computer Science, University College London, Gower St, London WC1E 6BT (☎ 071 380 7286, fax 071 387 1397)

KIRWAN, Ernest O'Gorman; s of E O'G Kirwan, CIE, MD FRCSI (d 1965) and Mary D Therkelsen (d 1974); *b* 6 June 1929; *Educ* Ampleforth, Cambridge Univ (MA, MB, BChir), Middlesex Hosp; *m* 20 April 1963, Marie Christine, da of Dr J Coakley (d 1954); 3 s (Robert b 1965, Edward b 1967, Patrick b 1969), 1 da (Sarah b 1966); *Career* Capt RAMC 1954-56; civilian conslt to the RN and RAF 1962-; conslt orthopaedic surgn; Royal Nat Orthopaedic Hosp, Univ Coll Hosp 1966-; Br exec memb of Int Soc for the Study of the Lumbar Spine 1984-; exec of the Br Orthopaedic Assoc 1981-84; *Books* publications in medical journals on spinal surgery, pain and hip surgery; FRCS(E) 1960; *Recreations* sailing, skiing; *Clubs* St Albans Medical Soc; *Style*— Ernest Kirwan, Esq; 31 Newlands Avenue, Radlett, Herts; 107 Harley St, London W1

KIRWAN, Sir (Archibald) Laurence Patrick; KCMG (1972, CMG 1958), TD (1949); s of Patrick Kirwan; *b* 13 May 1907; *Educ* Wimbledon Sch, Merton Coll Oxford; *m* 1, 1933 (m dis 1945), Joan Elizabeth, da of Capt Hon Wentworth Chetwynd (bro of 8 Viscount Chetwynd, d 1914); 1 da; m 2, 1949, Stella Mary Monck, da of R Buchanan Cock; *Career* served WWII Intelligence Corps, TARO 1939-57, Hon Lt-Col; dir and sec RGS 1945-75 (hon vice pres 1981-); ed Geographical Journal 1945-78; memb: Ct of Arbitration Argentine-Chile Frontier Case 1965-68, Sec of State for Tport's Advsy Ctee on Landscape Treatment of Trunk Rds 1968-81, UN Register of fact-finding experts 1968-; memb Ct Univ of Exeter 1969-80; *Style*— Sir Laurence Kirwan, KCMG, TD; c/o Royal Geographical Society, 1 Kensington Gore, London SW7

KISHEN, Dr Roop; s of Janki Nath Sathu, of Srinagar, Kashmir, India, and Durga, *née* Raina; *b* 21 Aug 1947; *Educ* Univ of Madras (MB BS, DA, MD); *m* 4 Nov 1974, Meera, da of Col Lakshmi Narasimhan, of Chingleput, Tamilnadu, India; 1 s (Ravin b 1977), 1 da (Kavitha b 1980); *Career* conslt in intensive care med and anaesthesia 1985-; hon assoc lectr; FFARCS; *Recreations* gardening, reading; *Style*— Dr Roop Kishen; Intensive Care Unit, Hope Hospital, Eccles Old Rd, Salford M6 8H6 (☎ 061 789 7373)

KISSACK, Nigel Euan Jackson; s of Maj Henry Jackson Kissack, RE (ret), of Sydney, Aust, and formerly Isle of Man, and Ethel Valerie, *née* Kneen; *b* 8 April 1955; *Educ* King William's Coll IOM, Univ of Sheffield (LLB); *m* 11 Oct 1980, Kathryn Margaret, da of Thomas Lloyd-Jones, of Hale, Cheshire; 1 s (Richard Lloyd b 2 Aug 1984), 1 da (Annabel Laura Jayne b 4 Aug 1982); *Career* admitted slr 1979; articled clerk Foysters Manchester, currently ptnr Alsop Wilkinson; author of various professional articles; *Recreations* rugby, cricket, cycling, reading, golf, skiing; *Clubs* St James's (ctee memb), Hale Golf; *Style*— Nigel Kissack, Esq; 11 St James's Square, Manchester (☎ 061 834 7760, telex 667965, fax 061 831 7515)

KISSIN, Baron (Life Peer UK 1974), of Camden in Greater London; Harry Kissin; s of Israel Kissin, and Reusi, *née* Model; *b* 23 Aug 1912; *Educ* Basle Univ (LLD); *m* 1935, Ruth Deborah, da of Siegmund Samuel; 1 s (Hon Robert David b 1947), 1 da (Hon Evelyn Anne (Hon Mrs Singer) b 1944); *Career* chm: Lewis & Peat Ltd 1961-73, Experanza Int Servs plc 1970-83, Guinness Peat Gp plc 1973-79, Linfood Hldgs 1974-81, Lewis & Peat Hldgs 1982-87; life pres GPG plc (formerly Guinness Peat Gp plc) 1979; dir: Tycon Spa Venice 1974-, Transcontinental Servs Gp NV 1982-86; pres Lewis & Peat Hldgs Ltd 1987-; chm Cncl Inst of Contemporary Arts 1968-75, dir Royal Opera House Covent Garden 1973-84, tstee Royal Opera House Tst 1974-87 (chm 1974-80); govr: Bezadel Acad of Arts & Design 1975-87, Hebrew Univ of Jerusalem 1980-; Commandatore Ordem Nacional do Cruzeiro do Sul (Brazil) 1977, Chevalier Légion d'Honneur 1981; 1300 Years Bulgaria medal 1982; *Clubs* Reform, E India, Devonshire Sports, Public Schs; *Style*— The Rt Hon the Lord Kissin; 32 St Mary at Hill, London EC3P 3AJ (☎ 071 623 3111/9911); House of Lords, London SW1A 0AA

KISSMANN, Edna; da of Karl Kissmann (d 1983), of Jerusalem, Israel, and Frieda Mausser Kissmann, of Tel Aviv, Israel; *b* 20 Dec 1949; *Educ* Hebrew Univ HS, Hebrew Univ (BA), Univ of Baston Sch of Pub Communications (MSc); *Career* asst press sec PM's Office Govt of Israel 1975, md Ruder and Finn PR Ltd Israel 1976-77 (assoc dir 1973-75); Burson-Marsteller Inc NY: account exec 1978-79, account supervisor 1979-80, client servs mangr 1980-82, gp mangr 1982-85, vice pres then sr vice pres, exec vice pres and unit mangr i/c healthcare communications practice 1985-88; Burson-Marsteller London: EUP/unit mangr of healthcare and mktg 1988-89, jt md 1989-; winner of several internal Burson-Marsteller awards; fndr memb Israel PR Assoc 1974 (memb London 1990); *Recreations* music, theatre, travel, people, good food and wine; *Clubs* The Reform; *Style*— Miss Edna Kissmann; 15 Melton Court, Old Brompton Road, London SW7; Burson-Marsteller Ltd, 24-28 Bloomsbury Way, London WC1 2PX (☎ 071 831 6262, 071 430 1033)

KISTER, Hon Mrs (Jane Elizabeth); *née* Bridge; da of Baron Bridge of Harwich, PC; *b* 1944; *m* 1978, Prof J K Kister; *Style*— The Hon Mrs Kister

KISZELY, Hon Mrs (Arabella Jane); da of 3 Baron Herschell; *b* 1955; *m* 1984, Col John Panton Kiszley, SG, s of Dr John Kiszley, of Whitefield, Totland Bay, IOW; 3 s (Alastair b 1986, Mathew b 1987, Andrew b 1990); *Style*— Hon Mrs Kiszely

KITAJ, R B; s of Dr Walter Kitaj (d 1982), and Jeanne Brooks Kitaj; *b* 29 Oct 1932; *Educ* Royal Coll of Art; *m* 15 Dec 1983, Sandra Fisher; 2 s (Lem b 1958, Max b 1984), 1 da (Dominie b 1964); *Career* US Army 1955-57; artist; pt/t teacher: Camberwell Sch of Art 1961-63, Slade Sch 1963-67; visiting prof: Univ of California Berkeley 1968, UCLA 1970; solo exhibitions: Marlborough New London Gallery 1963 and 1970, Marlborough Gallery NY 1975 and 1974, LA Co Museum of Art 1965, Stedelijk Museum Amsterdam 1967, Museum of Art Cleveland 1967, Univ of California Berkeley 1967, Galerie Mikro Berlin 1969, Kestner Gesellschaft Hanover 1970, Boymans-van-Beuningen Museum Rotterdam 1970, Cincinnati Art Museum Ohio (with Jim Dine) 1973, Marlborough Fine Art 1977, 1980 and 1985; retrospective exhibitions: Hirshorn Museum Washington 1981, Cleveland Museum of Art Ohio 1981, Kuntshalle Düsseldorf 1982; Hon DLitt London 1982; memb US Inst of Arts and Letters NY 1982, Nat Acad of Design NY 1987; ARA 1984; *Style—* R B Kitaj, Esq; c/o Marlborough Fine Art Ltd, 6 Albemarle St, London W1

KITCHEN, Prof Kenneth Anderson; s of Leslie Dufton Kitchen, of 50 Rosefield Rd, Woolton, Liverpool, and Hannah, *née* Sheen (d 1981); *b* 8 June 1932; *Educ* Hawick HS, Kettering GS, Newark Magnus GS, Univ of Liverpool (BA, PhD); *Career* Univ of Liverpool: lectr in Egyptology 1957-74, reader in Egyptology 1974-87, prof of Egyptology (personal chair) 1987-; author numerous papers and articles; visiting prof Regent Coll Vancouver Canada 1970, visiting fell Rundle Fndn for Egyptian Archaeology Macquarie Univ Sydney Aust 1985 and 1989; TE Peet Travelling prize 1962, Sir Ernest Cassell Tst award 1970, Br Acad award 1987; *Books* Suppiluliuma and the Amarna Pharaohs (1962), Ancient Orient and Old Testament (1966), Ramesside Inscriptions, Historical and Biographical Vols I-VIII (1968-1990), The Third Intermediate Period in Egypt (1100-650 BC) (1972 and 1986), The Bible in its World (1977), Pharaoh Triumphant, Life and Times of Ramesses II, King of Egypt (1983), Catalogue of the Egyptian Collection in the National Museum Rio de Janeiro (1990); *Recreations* walking, gardening, exotic jams; *Style—* Prof Kenneth Kitchen; Oriental Studies, University of Liverpool, PO Box 147, Liverpool L69 3BX (☎ 051 794 2468)

KITCHEN, Michael; s of Arthur Kitchen, and Betty, *née* Allen; *b* 31 Oct 1948; *Educ* City of Leicester Boys GS, RADA; *m* ; 1 s (Jack b 7 Oct 1988); *Career* actor; theatre work incl: Nat Theatre 1974-84, RSC 1987 (roles incl Hogarth, Mercutio, Bolingbroke), Lenny in The Homecoming (West End); numerous TV appearances incl: Caught on a Train, Brimstone and Treacle, Home Run, Benefactors, The Brontës, Freud, No Man's Land, Savages, Justice Game, Bedroom Farce, King Lear, A Comedy of Errors, School Play, Love Song, Ball Trap at the Côte Sauvage; films incl: Out of Africa, The Russia House, Fools of Fortune, The Dive, Pied Piper, Unman Wittering and Zigo, The Bunker; writer of two screenplays and short stories; *Recreations* music, guitar, piano, composition, pilot's licence, riding, tennis, skiing, swimming; *Style—* Michael Kitchen, Esq; c/o Markham & Froggatt Ltd, Julian House, 4 Windmill St, London W1 (☎ 071 636 4412)

KITCHEN, Stanley; s of Percy Inman Kitchen, OBE (d 1963), of Solihull, and Elizabeth, *née* Green (d 1982); *b* 23 Aug 1913; *Educ* Rugby; *m* 27 Sept 1941, Jean, da of Albert Renwick Craig (d 1950), of Wellington, Salop; 2 da (Jennifer (Mrs Griffin) b 15 July 1942, Susan (Mrs White) b 31 July 1947); *Career* Nat Serv, enlisted RASC 1939, 2 Lt 1940, S/Capt WO CPO (FS) 1941, Maj 1942, DADST and ADST Br Army Staff Washington DC USA 1943-46; CA; sec and chief accountant The British Rollmakers Corpn Ltd Wolverhampton 1946-48, Birmingham ptnr Foster & Stephens 1948-65 (merged with Touche Ross & Co, ptnr 1965-81), chm Step Management Services Ltd 1978-85, dir Cobalt (UK) Ltd 1986-; memb Cncl Inst of CAs 1966-81 (pres 1976-77), memb Ctee Birmingham W Midlands Soc of CAs 1951-81 (pres 1957-58), pres Birmingham CA Students Soc 1962-63; Liveryman Worshipful Co of CAs 1977- (memb Ct 1977-85); FCA 1937, FInstD 1980; *Recreations* golf, gardening, travel; *Clubs* Lansdowne, The Birmingham, Birmingham Chamber of Commerce; *Style—* Stanley Kitchen, Esq; 1194 Warwick Rd, Knowle, Solihull, W Midlands B93 9LL (☎ 0564 772 360)

KITCHENER, Dr Henry Charles; *b* 1 July 1951; *Educ* Eastwood HS, Univ of Glasgow (MB ChB, MD); *m* 12 June 1977, Valerie Anne, da of Walter Hayes, of Glasgow; 1 da (Sophie); *Career* lectr in obstetrics and gynaecology Univ of Singapore 1983-84, William Blair-Bell memorial lectr RCOG 1985 (Florence and William Blair-Bell res fell 1980-82), sr registrar in obstetrics and gynaecology Gtr Glasgow Health Bd 1984-88, conslt obstetrician and gynaecologist specialising in gynaecological oncology Grampian Health Bd 1988-; memb Exec Ctee Br Soc for Colposcopy and Cervical Pathology 1988-; MRCOG 1980, FRCS Glasgow 1989; *Recreations* golf, hillwalking, the arts; *Clubs* Royal Aberdeen Golf, Royal Dornoch Golf; *Style—* Dr Henry Kitchener; Ewo House, Murtle Den Rd, Milltimber, Aberdeen AB1 0HS; Dept of Gynaecology, Ward 42/43, Aberdeen Royal Infirmary, Foresterhill, Aberdeen (☎ 0224 681818)

KITCHENER, Hon Mrs Charles; Ursula Hope; da of Capt C M Luck, CMG, DSO, Royal Indian Navy; *m* 1959, Hon Charles Eaton Kitchener (d 1982), yr bro of 3 Earl Kitchener of Khartoum, *qv*; 1 da (Emma Joy (Mrs Julian Fellowes, qv) b 1963); *Recreations* gardening; *Style—* The Hon Mrs Charles Kitchener; Croylands, Old Salisbury Lane, Romsey, Hants SO5l 0GD

KITCHENER OF KHARTOUM AND OF BROOME, 3 Earl (UK 1914); Henry Herbert Kitchener; TD, DL (Cheshire 1972); s of Viscount Broome (d 1928, s of 2 Earl and n of the general who won his reputation at the recapture of Khartoum); suc gf 1937; *b* 24 Feb 1919; *Educ* Winchester, Trinity Coll Cambridge; *Career* Maj RCS (TA), ret; *Clubs* Brooks's; *Style—* The Rt Hon the Earl Kitchener of Khartoum, TD, DL; Westergate Wood, Eastergate, Chichester, W Sussex PO20 6SB (☎ 0243 543061)

KITCHIN, Alan William Norman; s of Norman Tyson Kitchin, and Shirley Boyd, *née* Simpson; *b* 31 Jan 1954; *Educ* Oundle, Univ of Cambridge (BA, MA); *Career* admitted slr 1978; ptnr Ashurst Morris Crisp 1986-; *Recreations* golf, tennis; *Clubs* Walton Heath Golf; *Style—* Alan Kitchin, Esq; Ashurst Morris Crisp, 7 Eldon St, London EC2M 7HD (☎ 071 247 7666, telex 887067, fax 071 377 5659)

KITCHIN, David James Tyson; s of Norman Tyson Kitchin, and Shirley Boyd, *née* Simpson; *b* 30 April 1955; *Educ* Oundle, Fitzwilliam Coll Cambridge (MA); *Career* called to the Bar Grays Inn 1977; *Recreations* golf, fishing; *Clubs* Walton Heath, Leander, Hawks (Cambridge); *Style—* David Kitchin, Esq; 22 Perrymead St, London SW6 (☎ 071 736 2161); Francis Taylor Building, Temple, London EC4 (☎ 071 353 5657)

KITCHING, (Henry) Alan; s of Noel Kitching, JP (d 1975), and Gladys Nichols (d 1961); *b* 9 Feb 1936; *Educ* Leighton Park Reading, Peddie Inst Hightstown NJ USA; *m* 1988, Ann Margaret, *née* Britton; 2 s; *Career* serv RN Sub-Lt; stockbroker; chm Middlesbrough Warehousing Ltd; dir: Allied Provincial Securities Ltd, ST & H Nominees Ltd, Talstan Nominees Ltd; *Recreations* tennis, shooting, fishing, bridge; *Clubs* Cleveland; *Style—* Alan Kitching, Esq; Angrove House, Catton, North Yorkshire

KITCHING, Brian William; s of Thomas Kitching (d 1944), and Nora Kitching (d 1942); *b* 5 Nov 1932; *Educ* Sedbergh, Loughborough Coll, Univ of London (BSc); *m* 4 July 1959, Moira Maud, da of John Cameron, of Comrie, Perthshire; 2 s (Trevor John b 21 Sept 1961, Neil Cameron b 11 Nov 1966), 1 da (Dawn Nora b 15 July 1963); *Career* engr; M Macdonald & Partners 1956-59 and 1962-69, William Arrol & Co 1959-62, Arthur C Allen 1970-71, ptnr Allen Gordon & Co 1971-; FICE, MIStructE, MIWEM, MConsE; *Recreations* contract bridge, golf, hill walking; *Clubs* Rotary; *Style—* Brian Kitching, Esq; Allen Gordon & Co, 1 Charlotte St, Perth (☎ 0738 39881)

KITCHING WALKER, Stephen; s of Ernest Smith Walker (d 1965), and Alice Kate Walker (d 1964); *b* 22 April 1923; *Educ* Alcester GS, Gonville and Caius Coll Cambridge (MA); *m* 1, 28 July 1951, Betty Simpson; 1 s (Philip Stephen b 1956), 1 da (Catherine b 1952); m 2, 20 Feb 1971, Yvonne Teresa, da of George Albert Theakston; *Career* Sandhurst 1943, Capt 25 Dragoons, served India and Burma; admitted slr 1949; dep coroner 1954-74, clerk to Cmmrs 1954-; fndr pres Pickering and Dist Rotary Club; Paul Harris fell 1988; *Recreations* shooting, tennis, walking; *Style—* Stephen Kitching Walker, Esq; Old Maltongate Farm, Thornton-le-Dale, Pickering, N Yorks (☎ 0751 74435); 8 Market Place, Kirbymoorside, Yorks (☎ 0751 31237)

KITSON, Gen Sir Frank Edward; GBE (1985, CBE for gallantry 1972, OBE 1968, MBE 1959), KCB (1980) MC (1955, Bar 1958), DL; s of Vice Adm Sir Henry Kitson, KBE, CB, by his w Marjorie, *née* de Pass; *b* 15 Dec 1926; *Educ* Stowe; *m* 1962, Elizabeth Janet, da of Col Charles Richard Spencer, OBE, DL; 3 da; *Career* cmmnd 2 Lt Rifle Bde 1946, BAOR 1946-53, served Kenya, Malaya, Cyprus; CO 1 Bn Royal Green Jackets 1967-69, def fellow Univ Coll Oxford 1969-70, Cmd 39 Inf Bde NI 1970-72, Cmdt Sch of Infantry 1972-74, RCDS 1975, GOC 2 Div (subsequently Armoured Div) 1976-78, Cmdt Staff Coll 1978-80, Col Cmdt 2 Bn Royal Green Jackets 1979-87, dep C in C UKLF and inspr gen TA 1980-82, C in C UKLF 1982-85, Rep Col Cmdt RGJ 1982-85, Hon Col Univ of Oxford OTC (V) 1982-87, Gen 1982; ADC Gen to HM The Queen 1983-85; *Books* author of books on war incl: Gangs and Countergangs (1960), Low Intensity Operations (1971), Bunch of Five (1977), Warfare as a Whole (1987), Directing Operations (1989); *Style—* Gen Sir Frank Kitson, GBE, KCB, MC, DL; c/o Lloyds Bank, Farnham, Surrey

KITSON, Hon Mrs (Ginette Molesworth); da of 2 Baron Kindersley, CBE, MC (d 1976); *b* 1924; *m* 1, 1945 (m dis 1949), Dominick Moore Sarsfield; 2 s (Simon b 1945, Shaun b 1947); m 2, 1953, Henry James Buller Kitson; *Style—* The Hon Mrs Kitson; Nine Acres, Wallcrouch, Wadhurst, E Sussex

KITSON, Linda Frances; da of Henry James Buller Kitson, and Vivien Lorna, *née* Paget; *b* 17 Feb 1945; *Educ* Tortington Park Sussex, L'Ecole Des Beaux Arts Lyons France, St Martin's Sch of Art London (BA), RCA (MA); *Career* artist; visiting tutor (art schs) 1971-78: RCA, St Martin's, Chelsea, Camberwell, City & Guilds London; lectr RCA 1979-82, candidate Royal Acad of Art 1981, official war artist Falkland Islands Task Force (awarded S Atlantic medal with rosette) 1982, pres Army Arts and Crafts Soc 1983; one man exhibitions incl: Clare Coll Cambridge 1971, annually Illustrations Art Gallery London 1970-79; mixed exhibitions incl: annually Royal Acad 1971-, Workshop Gallery London 1979-, Imp War Museum UK Tour 1982-83, The NT 1984-85; *Books* Picnic, The Falklands War: A Visual Diary (1982), The Plague (1985), Sun Wind Sand and Stars (1989); *Recreations* dancing; *Clubs* Chelsea Arts, Dover St Arts; *Style—* Miss Linda Kitson; 1 Argyll Mansions, Kings Rd, London SW3 5ER

KITSON, Sir Timothy Peter Geoffrey; s of Geoffrey Kitson; *b* 28 Jan 1931; *Educ* Charterhouse, RAC Cirencester; *m* 1959, Diana Mary Fattorini; 1 s, 2 da; *Career* former memb Thirsk RDC & N Riding Yorks CC; formerly farmed in Australia; MP (C) Richmond (Yorks) 1959-83, PPS to Parly Sec Miny of Agriculture 1960-64, oppn whip 1967-70, PPS to Edward Heath as PM 1970-74, to same as Ldr of oppn 1974-75; chm: Provident Financial Group 1983- (dep chm 1982-83), Ryeland Holdings Ltd 1983; dir: Leeds Permanent Building Society 1983-, Alfred McAlpine plc, Bradstock Hamilton, GKR Group, Goddard Kay Rogers (Northern) Ltd; kt 1974; *Style—* Sir Timothy Kitson; Leases Hall, Leeming Bar, Northallerton, N Yorks (☎ 0677 22180)

KITSON, Hon Verona Vandeleur; OBE (1982, MBE mil 1960), TD; da of 3 Baron Airedale, DSO, MC (d 1958); *b* 28 Sept 1920; *Career* serv WWII as Jr Cdr ATS; Maj WRAC (TA); chm Riding for the Disabled Assoc 1970-82; formerly JP; Liberty of Peterborough; *Recreations* riding; *Style—* The Hon Verona Kitson, OBE, TD; Pasture House, N Luffenham, Oakham, Rutland

KITT, Stanley; s of William Edward Kitt (d 1945), of Blackpool, and Lavinia, *née* Harrington (d 1971); *b* 10 Oct 1910; *Educ* Elementary Sch; *m* 20 Sept 1937, Kathleen, da of Alfred Mitchell (d 1957), of Blackpool; 2 s (Stanley b 1951, Michael b 1960), 4 da (Lavinia b 1940, Kathleen b 1942, Ann b 1945, Susan b 1948); *Career* pres Daintee Chocolate Confectionary Co (Blackpool) Ltd; chm: Keenlift Ltd, S K Daintee (Holdings) Ltd, Daintee (Canada) Ltd, Sterling Candy Inc, Clifton Cash & Carry Ltd, James Henry Parr (Lancashire) Limited engrg and construction; *Recreations* gardening; *Clubs* Directors; *Style—* Stanley Kitt, Esq; Green Ridges, 99 Ballam Rd, Lytham St Annes, Lancs FY8 4LF (☎ 0253 735513); Daintee Chocolate Confectionary Co (Blackpool) Ltd, Clifton Road, Marton, Blackpool FY4 4QB (☎ 0253 61201, fax 0253 792006, telex 67679 DAINTE G)

KITTEL, Gerald Anthony; s of Francis William Berthold Kittel of Faraway, South View Rd, Pinner Hill, Middx, and Eileen Winifred, *née* Maybanks (d 1973); *b* 24 Feb 1947; *Educ* Merchant Taylors', Univ of Poitiers (History Dip), Ealing Poly; *m* 26 April 1975, Jean Samantha, *née* Beveridge; 2 s (Christian b 1969, Ashley b 1976), 1 da (Natalie b 1979); *Career* md Northey Bunting Kittel Advertising & Marketing and Paulsgrove Ltd; memb Int Advertising Assoc; MIPA, MInstM; *Recreations* riding, squash, tennis; *Clubs* St James, Park Place, Old Merchant Taylors' Soc; *Style—* Gerald Kittel, Esq; Valence End, Hosey Hill, French St, Westerham, Kent TN16 1PN; 20 Lime Court, Gipsy Lane, Putney, London SW15 5RJ

KITTO, Rt Hon Sir Frank Walters; AC (1983), KBE (1955), PC (1963), KC (1942); s of James Walters Kitto, OBE (d 1955), and Adi Lilian Kitto (d 1927); *b* 30 July 1903; *Educ* N Sydney HS, Sydney Univ (BA, LLB); *m* 1928, Eleanor May (d 1982), da of William Henry Howard (d 1942); 3 da (and 1 decd); *Career* Crown Slr's Office NSW 1921-27, called to the Bar NSW 1927, justice High Ct of Australia 1950-70 (ret), chm Aust Press Cncl 1976-82 (ret), chllr Univ of New England 1970-81 (ret); Hon LLD (Sydney Univ) 1982, Hon DLitt (New England Univ) 1982; *Style—* The Rt Hon Sir Frank Kitto, AC, KBE, QC; 18/243 Donnelly St, Armidale, NSW 2350, Australia

KITZINGER, Sheila Helena Elizabeth; MBE (1982); da of Alec Webster, and Clare, *née* Bond; *b* 29 March 1929; *Educ* Bishop Fox GS Taunton, Ruskin Coll Oxford, St Hugh's Coll Oxford (MLitt); *m* 1952, Uwe Kitzinger; 5 da (Celia b 1956, Nell b 1958, Tessa (twin) b 1958, Polly b 1961, Jenny b 1963); *Career* writer, lectr; Writers Fellowship Award from the Rockefeller Fndn 1988; involved with midwives' info and resource serv Nat Childbirth Tst; *Books* incl: The Experience of Childbirth (1962), Pregnancy and Childbirth (1980, revised 1989), Women's Experience of Sex (1983), Birth Over Thirty (1985, American Health Book Award), Freedom and Choice in Childbirth (1987), Being Born (1987, American Hornbook Award and Times Educnl Supplement Award), Breastfeeding Your Baby (1989), The Crying Baby (1989), Talking With Children About Things That Matter (with Celia Kitzinger, 1989), Pregnancy Day by Day (with Vickey Bailey, 1990); *Recreations* painting; *Clubs* RSM; *Style—* Ms Sheila Kitzinger, MBE; The Manor, Standlake, nr Witney, Oxford OX8 7RH (☎ 0865 300266, fax 0865 300438)

KITZINGER, Uwe; CBE (1980); *b* 12 April 1928; *Educ* Watford GS, Balliol Coll and New Coll Oxford; *m* 1952, Sheila Helena Elizabeth, *née* Webster; 5 da; *Career* with Cncl of Europe 1951-56, fell Nuffield Coll 1956-76, fndr ed Journal of Common Market Studies 1961-, prof Paris Univ 1970-73, advsr to vice pres of EEC Cmmn i/c external rels Brussels 1973-75, dean Euro Inst of Business Admin INSEAD Fontainebleau

1976-80; dir Oxford Centre for Mgmnt Studies 1980-84, pres Templeton Coll Univ of Oxford 1984-, foundr chm Major Projects Assoc 1981-86, fndr pres Int Assoc of Macro-Engr Socs 1987-; chm Oxfordshire Radio Ltd 1988; memb Cncl: RIIA 1976-85, OXFAM 1981-85, Foundation Jean Monnet 1990-; Hon LLD 1986; *Books* German Electoral Politics (1960), The Challenge of the Common Market (1961), Diplomacy and Persuasion (1973); *Recreations* sailing (ketch 'Anne of Cleves'); *Clubs* Reform, Royal Thames Yacht, Utd Oxford and Cambridge Univs; *Style—* Uwe Kitzinger, Esq, CBE; Standlake Manor, Witney, Oxon (☎ 0865 300 266); La Rivière, 11100 Bages, France (☎ 68 41 29 60)

KLARE, Hugh John; CBE (1967); s of Frederick Klare (d 1973), and Ella Helen Klare (d 1970); came to England from Austria in 1932; *b* 22 June 1916, (Berndorf, Austria); *Educ* Gymnasium Berndorf, Geneva Univ; *m* 18 Sept 1946, Eveline Alice Maria, da of Lt-Col James Dodds Rankin, MBE (d 1965); *Career* Maj (GSO II), served Middle East; dep dir Economic Organisation Div Control Cmmn for Germany; criminologist and penologist, dir Howard League for Penal Reform 1950-59 and 1961-71; seconded to Cncl of Europe Strasbourg: dep dir Div of Crime Problems 1959-61, head Div of Crime Problems 1971-72; first Sperry & Hutchinson lectr LSE 1966-, extra mural lectr in criminology Univ of London 1961-71; regular columnist Justice of the Peace 1971-85 (currently occasional contrib); memb: Parole Bd 1972-74, Glos Probation Ctee 1972-86; vice pres Glos Arthritis Tst (chm 1984-90), fndr and tstee Cheltenham & N Cotswolds Eye Therapy Trust 1980-; *Books* Anatomy of Prison (1960), Delinquency and Social Control (1966), People in Prison (1972); *Style—* Hugh Klare, Esq, CBE; 34 Herriots Ct, St George's Crescent, Droitwich Spa, Worcs (☎ 0905 776316)

KLASSNIK, Robin; s of Dr Benjamin Klassnik, and Leila Fabian, *née* Hammerschalg; *b* 28 Jan 1947; *Educ* Haverstock Comprehensive Sch, Hornsey Coll of Art, Leicester Coll of Art (BA); *m* 1 Dec 1979, Kathryn, da of Henry Halton; 1 s (Tomas b 2 Jan 1981), 1 da (Zoë b 9 Oct 1983); *Career* artist, lectr, gallery owner; gp ldr Fndn Course London Coll of Printing 1979-82, head Complementary Studies Byam Shaw Sch of Art 1982- (visiting lectr 1977-82), res asst (sculpture theory) Statens Kunstakademie Oslo Norway 1990-91; guest lectr: Poznan Acad of Fine Art, Maidstone Sch of Art, Camberwell Sch of Art, Brighton Poly, Slade Sch of Fine Art, Statens Kunstakademie Oslo, Goldsmiths Coll London, RCA London, Valands Konsthogskola Goteborg Sweden, Bath Coll of HE, Chelsea Coll of Art & Design (external examiner sculpture MA); dir New Contemporaries; solo exhibitions: Walk Through Painting (Pavilions in the Park, Croydon) 1969, Nine Till Four (Acland Burghley Sch) 1969, Postal Sculpture (Boyd Inst and James Carters Bookshop) 1970, 34' 3"x 57 x 11' 6" (New Gallery) 1970, Galeria Dois Porto Portugal 1974, Open Studio Martello St 1974, Galeria Akumulatory 2 Poznan Poland 1975, Space Open Studios 1976, Nearly a Sculpture (Galeria Akumulatory 2, Galeria Pawilon Krakow, Whitechapel Art Gallery) 1978-79, Five Pheromones The Incomplete Documentation (Matts Gallery) 1980, Three Works (Spectro Art Gallery Newcastle upon Tyne) 1981, To Be Or Not To Be Original That is The Question (Galeria Akumulatory 2, Piwna 20/26 Warsaw Poland) 1983; fndr owner and dir Matts Gallery 1979; over fifty solo exhibitions to date; publisher artists books and bookworks; *Recreations* cricket; *Clubs* Burger King; *Style—* Robin Klassnik, Esq; Matt's Gallery, 10 Martello St, London Fields, London E8 3PE (☎ 071 249 3799, 081 521 4913)

KLEANTHOUS, Christodoulos Photios; s of Photios Kleanthous (d 1971), and Zenovia Hatgipanayi (d 1977); *b* 1 March 1944, (Cyprus); *Educ* Upton House Sch Hackney E London; graduated from Sir John Cass Coll, London Univ 1967 (BSc); *m* 14 Nov 1969, Diana Margaret, da of George Smith ('Gus'-the cartoonist), of Abbotsfield, Fitzroy Rd, Fleet, Hants; 1 s (Andrea George b 1976), 1 da (Anna Zinovia b 1971); *Career* advertising; exec dir McCann-Erickson Advertising Ltd 1972- (bd memb 1979); *Recreations* swimming, hill walking; *Clubs* RAC, Pall Mall; *Style—* Christodoulos Kleanthous, Esq; McCann-Erickson Advertising Ltd, 36 Howland St, London W1A 1AT (☎ 071 580 6690)

KLEEMAN, David George; s of Jack Kleeman (d 1984), and Ruth, *née* Stephany (d 1981); *b* 20 Aug 1942; *Educ* St Paul's, Trinity Hall Cambridge (MA); *m* 1968, Manuela Rachel, da of Edouard Cori, of Ave de Wagram, Paris; 4 da (Susanna b 1970, Nicole b 1973, Julie b 1974, Jenny b 1978); *Career* dir: Bridgend Group plc, The Housing Corporation, Daman Financial Services Ltd, and other cos; slr; chm Enfield and Haringay Family Health Services Authority Co; *Recreations* fishing, reading, opera; *Clubs* MCC; *Style—* David Kleeman, Esq; 141 Hamilton Terrace, London NW8 9QS (☎ 071 624 2335); Suite 8, 44 Baker St, London W1M 1DH (☎ 071 487 4313)

KLEEMAN, Harry; CBE (1984); s of Max Kleeman (d 1947); *b* 2 March 1928; *Educ* Westminster, Trinity Coll Cambridge; *m* 1955, Avril, da of Dr Maurice Lees (d 1974); 2 s (John, Daniel), 2 da (Jacqueline, Amanda); *Career* chm Kleeman Plastics Gp 1968, pres British Plastics Fedn 1979-80 (memb Cncl 1977-85), chm CBI Small Firms Cncl 1988-90 (also memb Cncl); former chm: Mgmnt Ctee Polymer Engrg Directorate, Plastic Processing EDC of NEDO, Advsy Ctee on Telecommunications for Small Businesses 1986-88; Freeman City of London, Liveryman Worshipful Co of Horners (memb Ct and upper warden); fell Plastics & Rubber Inst (chm 1985-87, memb Cncl 1984-87); *Recreations* amateur radio, riding; *Clubs* RSA; *Style—* Harry Kleeman, Esq, CBE; 41 Frognal, London NW3 (☎ 071 794 3366), High Trees, Friday St, Dorking, Surrey (☎ 0306 730 678)

KLEIN, Bernat; CBE (1973); s of Lipot Klein (d 1964), of Senta, Yugoslavia, and Serena, *née* Weiner (d 1944); *b* 6 Nov 1922; *Educ* Bezalel Sch of Art Jerusalem, Univ of Leeds; *m* 31 March 1951, Margaret Soper; 1 s (Jonathan b 1953), 2 da (Gillian b 1957, Shelley b 1963); *Career* designer: Tootal 1948-49, Munrospun 1949-51; chm and md Colourcraft 1951-62; md: Bernat Klein Ltd 1962-66 (chm and md 1981), Bernat Klein Design Ltd 1966-81; exhibitions: E-SU 1965, Alwyn Gallery 1967, O'Hana Gallery 1969, Assoc of Arts Gallery Capetown, Goodmant Gallery Johannesburg and O'Hanna Gallery 1972; Hon FRIAS, FCSD; *Publications* Eye for Colour (1966), Design Matters (1976); *Recreations* reading, tennis; *Style—* Bernat Klein, Esq, CBE; High Sunderland, Galashiels (☎ 0750 20730)

KLEIN, David Mordechai; s of Max Israel Klein, of 26 The Square, Ilford, Essex, and Glady Doris, *née* Evans; *b* 31 Dec 1951; *Educ* Ilford Co HS, Univ of Southampton (BA), Carnegie Coll (PGCE); *m* May 1979, Jos Holt, da of Peter Bailey, of 43 Purbeck Dr, Bury, Lancs; 2 da (Esther b 9 Aug 1979, Amy b 7 July 1986); *Career* Oracle Teletext Ltd: researcher and journalist 1978, mktg mangr 1981, ed of features 1982, editorial dir 1985; *Recreations* cycling, badminton; *Style—* David Klein, Esq; Oracle Teletext Ltd, Craven House, 25-32 Marshall St, London W1V 1LL (☎ 071 434 3121, fax 071 494 0572, telex 8813039, car 0860 327832)

KLEIN, Roland; s of Fernand Klein (d 1982), and Marguerite, *née* Meyer (d 1987); *b* 3 July 1938; *Educ* CEC, BEPC and Beaux Arts Rouen France, Ecole de la Chambre Syndicale de la Haute Couture Parisienne and CAP Paris France; *Career* Nat Serv France 1959-60; asst tailor Jean Patou Paris 1958-59, asst designer Christian Dior Paris 1960-61, asst designer Jean Patou and Karl Lagerfeld 1961-63, designer Nettie Vogue London 1963-66, design dir Marcel Fenez London 1970-88 (designer 1966-70), designer Roland Klein Ltd London and Tokyo 1988-; major projects incl: conslt designer British Airways corporate image clothing 1986, Max Mara and Marina Rinaldi Italy 1988-, British Telecom corporate image clothing 1991; *Awards* Fil D'or 1987; *Style—* Roland Klein, Esq; Roland Klein Ltd, 7/9 Tryon St, London SW3 3LG (☎ 071 823 9179, 071 823 9717)

KLEIN, Prof Rudolf Ewald; s of Dr Robert Klein (d 1958), of Dumfries, and Dr Martha Klein, *née* Szidon; *b* 26 Aug 1930; *Educ* Bristol GS, Merton Coll Oxford (MA, Gibbs prize in modern history); *m* 24 May 1957, Josephine, da of Leonard Thomas Parfitt (d 1980), of Guildford; 1 da (Leonora Jane b 1963); *Career* leader writer Evening Standard London 1951-61, leader writer and leader page editor The Observer 1961-71, res assoc London Sch of Hygiene 1971-73, sr fell Centre for Studies in Social Policy 1973-78, prof of social policy Univ of Bath 1978- (dir Centre for the Analysis of Social Policy); memb: Wiltshire Area Health Authy, Bath District Health Authy, various ctees of Social Sci Res Cncl, Econ and Social Res Cncl; specialist advsr to House of Commons Social Servs Ctee; *Books* Complaints Against Doctors (1973), Inflation and Priorities (ed, 1975), The Politics of Consumer Representation (co-author Janet Lewis, 1976), The Politics of the NHS (1983), The Future of Welfare (co-ed Michael O'Higgins, 1985), Accountabilities (co-author Patricia Day, 1987); *Style—* Prof Rudolf Klein; 3 Macaulay Buildings, Widcombe Hill, Bath BA2 6AS (☎ 0225 310774); School of Social Sciences, University of Bath, Bath BA2 7AY (☎ 0225 826826)

KLEINPOPPEN, Prof Hans Johann Willi; s of Gerhard Kleinpoppen (d 1985), and Emmi, *née* Maass; *b* 30 Sept 1928; *Educ* HS Germany, Univ of Giessen Germany, Univ of Heidelberg Germany, Univ of Tübingen Germany; *Career* Privat-Dozent Univ of Tübingen 1967, visiting fell and prof Univs of Colorado and Columbia 1967-68; Univ of Stirling: prof of experimental physics 1968-, head of Physics Dept 1972-74, dir Inst of Atomic Physics 1974-81, head of Atomic and Molecular Physics Res Unit 1981-; fell Center for Theoretical Studies Univ of Miami 1973, visiting prof Univ of Bielefeld 1978-79; chm various int confs on atomic and molecular physics; co-ed Monograph Series on Physics of Atoms and Molecules, ed of eleven books on atomic and molecular physics; festschrift: Coherence in Atomic Collision Physics (1988); FInstP 1969, FAmPhysSoc 1972, FRAS 1974, FRSE 1987; *Recreations* music, fine art; *Style—* Prof Hans Kleinpoppen, FRSE; 27 Kenningknowes Rd, Stirling, Scotland; Atomic and Molecular Physics Research Unit, University of Stirling, Stirling, Scotland (☎ 0786 67800)

KLEINWORT, Joan Nightingale; *née* Crossley; MBE (1945), JP (1951), DL (W Sussex 1983); da of Dr Arthur William Crossley, CMG, CBE, FRS, LLD (d 1927, the first director of Porton Station 1916, researching poison gas), and Muriel (d 1973, having m 2, Col Sir John Wallace Pringle, CB, RE), da of Ralph Lamb, of Liverpool; *b* 3 April 1907; *Educ* St Felix Sch Southwold; *m* 29 Dec 1932, Ernest Greverus Kleinwort (d 1977), 4 s of Sir Alexander Drake Kleinwort, 1 Bt (d 1935); 1 s (Sir Kenneth Drake Kleinwort, 3 Bt, *qv*), 1 da (Gillian Mawdesley (Mrs Warren) b 1937); *Recreations* gardening; *Style—* Mrs Joan Kleinwort, MBE, JP, DL; Heaselands, Haywards Heath, W Sussex (☎ 0444 454181)

KLEINWORT, Sir Kenneth Drake; 3 Bt (UK 1909), of Bolnore, Cuckfield, Sussex; s of Ernest Greverus Kleinwort (d 1977, chm Kleinwort Benson Ltd 1961-66, 2 s of Sir Alexander Kleinwort, 1 Bt, who was ptnr of Kleinwort Sons & Co); succeeded unc, Sir Alexander Kleinwort, 2 Bt, who d 1983; *b* 28 May 1935; *Educ* Eton, Grenoble Univ; *m* 1, 1959, Lady Davina Rose Pepys (d 1973), da of 7 Earl of Cottenham (d 1968); 1 s (Richard b 1960), 1 da (Marina b 1962); m 2, 1973, Madeleine Hamilton, da of Ralph Taylor, of Buenos Aires; 2 s (Alexander b 1975, Michael b 1977), 1 da (Selina b 1981); *Heir* s, Richard Drake Kleinwort; *Career* pres Interalia Leasing LTDA Chile; dir: Heaselands Estates Ltd, Neubar SA Geneva, Trebol International Corporation USA, Kleinwort Benson Group plc, Banque Kleinwort Benson SA Geneva, Kleinwort Benson (Europe) SA Brussels; memb Cncl WWF Int Switzerland, memb Cncl and treas Wildfowl and Wetlands Tst Slimbridge, memb Environment Ctee RSA, fell World Scout Fndn Geneva; *Recreations* travel, photography, skiing, shooting, gardening; *Style—* Sir Kenneth Kleinwort, Bt; La Massellaz, 1126 Vaux-sur-Morges, Switzerland; Banque Kleinwort Benson SA, 2 Place du Rhône, 1211 Geneva 11

KLEINWORT, Richard Drake; s and h of Sir Kenneth Kleinwort, 3 Bt, by his 1 w, Lady Davina Pepys; *b* 4 Nov 1960; *Educ* Stowe, Univ of Exeter (BA); *m* 29 Nov 1989, Lucinda, da of William Shand Kydd, of London; *Career* banker Deutschebank A G Frankfurt, Biss Lancaster plc, currently Grandfield Rork Collins Financial; *Recreations* photography, travel, sports (in general); *Clubs* WWF (1001), World Scout Foundation; *Style—* Richard Kleinwort, Esq; 54 Bovingdon Rd, London SW6 2AP

KLETZ, Dr Trevor Asher; s of William Kletz (d 1974), of Manchester, and Frances, *née* Amshewitz, of London; *b* 23 Oct 1922; *Educ* King's Sch Chester, Univ of Liverpool (BSc), Loughborough Univ of Technol (DSc); *m* 28 Oct 1958, Denise Valerie (d 1980), da of Stanley Winroope; 2 s (Anthony Michael b 13 May 1961, Nigel Howard b 10 July 1963); *Career* ICI Ltd: Res Dept Billingham 1944-51, various appts in prodn rising to asst mangr Oil Works Billingham 1952-67, safety advsr Heavy Organic Chemicals (later Petrochemicals) Div 1968-82; Dept of Chemical Engrg Loughborough Univ of Technol: visiting industl prof 1978, full-time prof 1982, visiting prof 1986-; IChemE Cncl medal 1986, Loss Prevention Symposium Ctee American IChemE Bill Doyle award 1985; FIChemE 1978 (memb 1976), FRSC 1984 (assoc 1944), FEng 1984, memb American IChemE 1982; *Books* Hazop and Hazan - Notes on the Identification and Assessment of Hazards (1983, 2 edn 1986), Cheaper, Safer Plants or Wealth and Safety of Work-Notes on Inherently Safer and Simpler Plants (1984, 3 edn retitled Plant Design for Safety - A User-Friendly Approach, 1991), Myths of the Chemical Industry or 44 Things a Chemical Engineer Ought Not to Know (1984, 2 edn retitled Improving Chemical Industry Practices, A New Look at Old Myths of the Chemical Industry, 1990), What Went Wrong? - Case Histories of Process Plant Disasters (1985, 2 edn 1988), An Engineer's View of Human Error (1985, 2 edn 1991), Learning From Accidents In Industry (1988), Critical Aspects of Safety and Loss Prevention (1990); *Recreations* reading, walking, railways; *Style—* Dr Trevor Kletz; 64 Twining Brook Rd, Cheadle Hulme, Cheadle, Cheshire SK8 5RJ (☎ 061 485 3875); Senior Visiting Research Fellow, Dept of Chemical Engineering, University of Technology, Loughborough, Leics LE11 1TU

KLIMES, Michal Vladimir; s of Prof Vladimir Klimes, of Prague; *b* 9 July 1944; *Educ* Inst of Chem Technol Prague; *m* 1966, Radana Zdena, *née* Egermeyer; 2 children; *Career* gp tech dir Thomas & Green Hldgs Ltd; dir: Fourstones Paper Mills Co Ltd, Thomas Green Ltd; *Recreations* tennis; *Style—* Michal Klimes, Esq; The Cedars, Stratford Drive, Wooburn Green, Bucks (☎ 062 85 26576)

KLINE, Prof Paul; s of Maurice Victor Kline, and Ivy, *née* Simmons; *b* 8 March 1937; *Educ* Trinity Sch Croydon, Univ of Reading (BA), Univ of Aberdeen (MEd), Univ of Manchester (PhD, DSc); *m* 1, 8 Aug 1960 (m dis 1987); 1 s (Merlyn b 1963), 3 da (Anna b 1965, Naomi b 1966, Harriet b 1971); m 2, 28 Nov 1987, Penelope Mary Bennet; *Career* Univ of Exeter: lectr in educn 1966-69, lectr in psychology 1969-73, reader in psychometrics 1973-86, prof of psychometrics 1986-; *Books* Fact and Fantasy in Freudian Theory (1972), The Psychology of Vocational Guidance (1975), Psychological Testing (1976), Personality Theories and Dimensions (1976), Psychometrics and Psychology (1979), Fact and Fantasy in Freudian Theory (1981), Personality Measurement and Theory (1983), Psychology and Freudian Theory (1984), Handbook of Test Construction (1986), Psychology Exposed. The Emperor's New Clothes (1988), Psychology and Freudian Theory (1988), Intelligence; The

Psychometric View (1990); *Style—* Prof Paul Kline; Department of Psychology, University of Exeter, Exeter, Devon EX4 4QG (☎ 0392 264621)

KLOOTWIJK, Jaap; s of Jacob Leendert, of Rotterdam, and Woutrina Johanna, *née* Boer; *b* 16 Nov 1932; *Educ* Rotterdam GS, Delft Univ Holland (MSc); *Career* Lt Royal Netherlands Navy 1956-58; joined Royal Dutch Shell Group 1958; various postings in: UK, Holland, France, Sweden, Switzerland, Algeria and Kenya 1958-76; area coordinator SE Asia 1976-79, md Shell International Gas Ltd 1979-82, md Shell UK Oil and Shell UK Ltd 1983-88, chm UK Oil Pipelines Ltd 1983-88; dir The Flyfishers' Co Ltd 1985, non-exec dir Grove Holdings Ltd 1991; FRSA 1986; *Recreations* shooting, fishing, reading; *Clubs* The Flyfishers' (pres 1985-87); *Style—* Jaap Klootwijk, Esq; 26 Manor House Court, Warwick Avenue, London W9 2PZ (☎ 071 289 4276)

KLUG, Sir Aaron; s of Lazar Klug, of Durban (d 1971), and Bella Silin (d 1932); *b* 11 Aug 1926; *Educ* Durban HS, Univ of the Witwatersrand (BSc), Univ of Cape Town (MSc), Univ of Cambridge (PhD, ScD); *m* 8 July 1948, Liebe, da of Alexander Bobrow (d 1983), of Cape Town; 2 s (Adam Brian Joseph b 1954, David Rupert b 1963); *Career* Nuffield res fell Birbeck Coll London 1954-57, ldr virus res project 1958-61; Cambridge Univ: fell Peterhouse 1962- (res in molecular biology), dir of natural sci studies 1962-85, jt head structural studies 1978-86, dir of laboratory 1986-, hon prof 1989; awards: Heineken prize Royal Netherlands Acad 1974, Louisa Gross Horwitz prize Columbia Univ 1981, Nobel prize for chemistry 1982; Hon DSc: Chicago 1978, Witwatersrand 1984, Hull 1985, St Andrews 1987; hon Dr Columbia 1978, Dr hc Strassburg 1978, hon Dr Stockholm 1980, hon fell Trinity Coll Cambridge 1983, hon PhD Jerusalem 1984; Hon FRCP 1986 (Baly medal 1987), memb Biochem Soc (Harden medal 1985), FRS 1969 (Copley medal 1985); foreign assoc: Nat Acad of Sciences of USA 1984, Max-Planck-Gesellschoft FRG, Académie des Sciences .Paris 1989; kt 1988; *Recreations* reading, gardening; *Style—* Sir Aaron Klug, FRS; MRC Laboratory of Molecular Biology, Hills Rd, Cambridge CB2 2QH (☎ 0223 248011)

KLYBERG, (Charles) John; *see*: Fulham, Bishop of

KNAPMAN, Paul Anthony; s of Frederick Ethelbert Knapman, of Torquay, Devon, and Myra, *née* Smith; *b* 5 Nov 1944; *Educ* Epsom Coll, King's Coll London, St George's Hospital Medical Sch (MB BS, DMJ, MRCS, LRCP), Inns of Court Sch of Law (barrister, Gray's Inn); *m* 1970, Penelope Jane, da of Lt Cdr Michael Cox, of Torquay, Devon; 1 s, 3 da; *Career* medical practitioner and barrister; Surgn Lt RNR 1970; HM coroner Inner West London at Westminster Coroners Ct 1980-; hon lectr medical jurisprudence: St George's, United Hosps of Guy's and St Thomas's, St Mary's, Charing Cross and Westminster, Middx and Univ Coll Hosp; memb Lloyds; *Books* The Law and Practice on Coroners (jtly, 3 edn 1985), Medicine and the Law (1989), Casebook on Coroners (1989); *Recreations* squash rackets, sailing, shooting; *Clubs* Athenaeum, Royal Torbay Yacht; *Style—* Paul Knapman, Esq; c/o Westminster Coroner's Ct, Horseferry Rd, London SW1 (☎ 071 834 6515)

KNAPMAN, Roger Maurice; MP; s of Harry Arthur Blackmore Knapman of North Tawton, Devon and Joan Margo, *née* Densham (d 1970); *b* 20 Feb 1944; *Educ* St Aubyn's Sch Tiverton, All Hallows Sch Lyme Regis, RAC Circencester; *m* 25 March 1967, Carolyn Trebell, da of Sidney George Eastman of Appledore near Bideford, N Devon; 1 s (William b 1970), 1 da (Rebecca b 1971); *Career* chartered surveyor (FRICS 1967); *Recreations* fishing, snooker; *Style—* Roger Knapman, Esq, MP; 38 Tufton Court, Tufton St, London SW1; c/o Stroud Conservative Association, Carlton Gardens, London Road, Stroud, Glos

KNAPP, Edward Ronald (Ron); CBE (1979); s of Percy Charles Knapp (d 1979), and Elsie Maria, *née* Edwards (d 1978); *b* 10 May 1919; *Educ* Cardiff HS, St Catharine's Coll Cambridge (MA), Harvard Business Sch (AMP); *m* 16 April 1942, Vera Mary, da of Capt William Stephenson, of Cardiff; 2 s (Ian b 1946, William b 1951), 2 da (Vanessa b 1956, Lucille b 1959); *Career* RNVR Lt Cdr 1940-46, HMS Aurora 1941-44, US Naval Res Estab Washington DC 1944-46, Admty 1946; md: Br Timken 1969-79 (joined 1946), Timken Europe 1979-84; dir Timken Co USA 1976; rugby capt: Univ of Cambridge 1940-41, Northampton RFC 1948; played for Wales 1940; govr Nene Coll 1948-89, pres Northants RFC 1986-88; *Recreations* gardening, golf, world travel; *Clubs* East India, Northants and County, Hawks (Cambridge); *Style—* Ron Knapp, Esq, CBE; The Elms, 1 Millway, Duston, Northampton (☎ 0604 584737)

KNARESBOROUGH, Bishop of, 1986-; Rt Rev Malcolm James Menin; s of Rev James Nicholas Menin (d 1970), Vicar of Shiplake, Oxon, and Doreen, *née* Dolamore (d 1967); *b* 26 Sept 1932; *Educ* Dragon Sch, St Edward's, Univ Coll Oxford (MA), Cuddesdon Coll; *m* 11 Oct 1958, Jennifer Mary, da of Andrew Patrick Cullen (d 1966); 1 s (Andrew b 1961), 3 da (Catherine b 1959, Brigid b 1963, Sarah b 1965); *Career* deacon 1957 Portsmouth, priest 1958; asst curate Holy Spirit Southsea 1957-59, asst curate Fareham Hants 1959-62, vicar St Mary Magdalene with St James Norwich 1962-86, rural dean Norwich East 1981-86; hon canon Norwich Cathedral 1982, consecrated Bishop of Knaresborough 1986; *Recreations* carpentry, walking, gardening, photography; *Style—* The Rt Rev the Bishop of Knaresborough; 16 Shaftesbury Avenue, Leeds LS8 1DT (☎ 0532 664800)

KNATCHBULL, Hon Philip Wyndham Ashley; s of 7 Baron Brabourne and Countess Mountbatten of Burma, *qqv*; *b* 2 Dec 1961; *Educ* Gordonstoun, Univ of Kent, London Int Film Sch; *Career* film maker; *Style—* The Hon Philip Knatchbull; 41 Montpelier Walk, London SW7 1JH

KNECHT, Prof Robert Jean; s of Jean Joseph Camille Knecht (d 1970), and Odette Jeanne Eugenie Juliette, *née* Mioux (d 1983); *b* 20 Sept 1926; *Educ* Lycée Français London, Salesian Coll Farnborough, King's College Univ of London (BA, MA), Univ of Birmingham (DLitt); *m* 1, 8 Aug 1956, Sonia Mary Fitzpatrick (d 1984), da of Dr Hubert Hodge; m 2, 28 Aug 1986, Maureen Joan, *née* White; *Career* prof of French history Univ of Birmingham 1985- (asst lectr in mod history 1956-59, lectr 1959-68, sr lectr 1968-78, reader 1978-85); chm: Soc for Renaissance Studies 1989-, Bd Govrs Wroxall Abbey Sch Warwick; co fndr Soc for Study of French History; memb Société de l'Histoire de France; FRHistS; *Books* The Voyage of Sir Nicholas Carewe (1959), Francis I (1982), French Renaissance Monarchy (1984), The French Wars of Religion (1989), Richelieu (1990); *Recreations* travel, music, photography; *Clubs* New Cavendish; *Style—* Prof Robert Knecht; 79 Reddings Rd, Moseley, Birmingham B13 8LP (☎ 021 449 1916)

KNIBB, Prof Michael Anthony; s of Leslie Charles Knibb (d 1987), and Christian Vera, *née* Hoggar (d 1978); *b* 14 Dec 1938; *Educ* Wyggeston Sch Leicester, King's Coll London (BD, PhD), Union Theological Seminary NY (STM), Corpus Christi Coll Oxford; *m* 30 Dec 1972, Christine Mary, da of John Henry Thomas Burrell, of Leicester; *Career* Old Testament Studies King's Coll London: lectr 1964-82, reader 1982-86, prof 1986-; head of Theology and Religious Studies Dept King's Coll London 1989-; memb SOTS 1965, ed SOTS Book List 1980-86, hon sec Palestine Exploration Fund 1969-76, memb Studiorum Novi Testamenti Societas 1980- (joint convener of seminar on early Jewish writings and the New Testament 1986-); FBA 1989; *Books* The Ethiopic Book of Enoch (1978), Het Boek Henoch (1983), Commentary on 2 Esdras (1979), The Qumran Community (1987); *Recreations* walking; *Clubs* Athenaeum; *Style—* Prof Michael Knibb; 6 Shootersway Park, Berkhamsted, Herts HP4 3NX (☎ 0442 871459); Dept of Theology and Religious Studies, King's Coll London, Strand, London WC2R 2LS (☎ 071 873 2341, fax 071 836 1799)

KNIGHT, Andrew Stephen Bower; s of M W B Knight, and S E F Knight; *b* 1 Nov 1939; *m* 1, 1966 (m dis), Victoria Catherine Brittain; 1 s (Casimir); m 2, 1975, Begum Sabiha Rumani Malik; 2 da (Amaryllis, Agsaneh); *Career* ed The Economist 1974-86, dir Tandem Computers Inc 1984-; Daily Telegraph plc: chief exec 1986-89, ed-in-chief 1987-89; dir Reuters Holdings plc 1988-; exec chm News Int plc 1990-; memb: Bd Overseers Hoover Inst Stanford Univ 1989-, Advsy Bd Centre Econ Policy Res Stanford Univ 1981-; govr Ditchley Fndn 1981- (memb Mgmnt Cncl 1982-); *Clubs* Brooks's, Royal Automobile; *Style—* Andrew Knight, Esq; Virginia St, London E1 9XY

KNIGHT, Dr Anthony Harrington; s of Dr Bryant William Knight (d 1982), and Gladys Irene, *née* Eldridge; *b* 29 April 1940; *Educ* Univ Coll Sch, St Bartholomew's Hosp Med Sch Univ of London (MB BS); *m* 24 Aug 1963, Sheila Mary, da of Alfred Stanely Brewer (d 1989); 2 s (Jonathan Clive b 1965, Christopher Harrington b 1968); *Career* conslt physician Stoke Mandeville and Royal Bucks Hosps 1974-, fndr and physician in charge Aylesbury Diabetes Educn Treatment Centre 1978-, dist clinical tutor Univ of Oxford 1979-86, vice chm Aylesbury Vale Health Authy 1982-89; memb Br Diabetic Assoc Med Scientific and Educn Sections (sec Educn Section 1986-89), pres Aylesbury Dist Br Diabetic Assoc, chm Stoke Mandeville Hosp Post Grad Med Soc, fndr and leader Ridgeway and Vale Diabetes Club; MRCS 1963, FRCP 1980 (MRCP 1968); *Recreations* hill and mountain walking, oil painting; *Style—* Dr Anthony Knight; The Old Vicarage, 101 Aylesbury Rd, Bierton, Bucks HP22 5BT; 4 Temple Sq, Aylesbury, Bucks; The Diabetes Centre, Stoke Mandeville Hospital, Aylesbury, Bucks (☎ 0296 84111 ext 3515)

KNIGHT, Sir Arthur William; s of Arthur Frederick Knight; *b* 29 March 1917; *Educ* Tottenham Co Sch, LSE; *m* 1, 1945, Beatrice, *née* Oppenheim (d 1968); 1 s, 3 da; m 2, 1972, Sheila Whiteman; *Career* chm: Courtaulds 1975-79, Nat Enterprise Bd 1979-80; non-exec dir Dunlop Holdings 1981-84 (resigned); vice chm Cncl RIIA until 1986; kt 1975; *Style—* Sir Arthur Knight; Charlton End, Singleton, W Sussex PO18 0HX; Flat 20, Valiant House, Vicarage Crescent, London SW11 3LU (☎ 071 228 3026)

KNIGHT, Prof Bernard Henry; GSM (Malaya) 1956; s of Harold Ivor Knight (d 1984), of Cardiff, and Doris, *née* Lawes; *b* 3 May 1931; *Educ* St Illtyd's Coll Cardiff, Welsh Nat Sch of Med (MD BCh); *m* 11 June 1955, Jean Gwenllian, da of Charles Ogborne (d 1947), of Swansea; 1 s (Huw David Charles b 1964); *Career* Short Serv Cmmn Capt RAMC specialist in pathology Malaya 1956-59; called to the Bar Gray's Inn; DMJ (Path), lectr in forensic med Univ of London 1959-62, sr lectr Univ of Newcastle 1965-68, prof of forensic pathology and lectr Univ of Wales 1980- (sr lectr 1968-76, reader 1976-80), Home Office pathologist, conslt pathologist Cardiff Royal Infirmary, dir Wales Inst of Forensic Med 1989-, managing ed Forensic Sci Int; memb GMC 1979-, vice pres Int Acad of Legal Med 1982-, pres Forensic Sci Soc 1987-89, chm bd of examiners in forensic med RCPath; memb Home Office ctee on forensic pathology, memb Cncl and pres-elect Br Assoc in Forensic Med (former sec), hon memb Finnish and German Socs of Forensic Med; FRCPath, MRCP; *Books* Crime novels: The Lately Deceased (1963), The Thread of Evidence (1965), Russian Roulette (1968), Policeman's Progress (1969), Tiger at Bay (1970), Deg Y Dragwyddoldeb (1972), The Expert (1976); historical novels: Lion Rampant (1974), Madoc Prince of America (1977); biography: Autopsy - The Memoirs of Milton Helpern (1977); popular non-fiction: Murder Suicide or Accident (1971), Discovering the Human Body (1980); textbook: Legal Aspects of Medicine (5 edn, 1991), Sudden Death In Infancy (1982), Coroners Autopsy (1983), Lawyer's Guide to Forensic Medicine (1983), Forensic Medicine (1986), Essentials of Forensic Medicine (with Polson & Gee, 1985), Simpson's Forensic Medicine (10 edn, 1991), Forensic Pathology (1991); *Recreations* writing: crime and history novels, biography, radio and TV drama; *Style—* Prof Bernard Knight, GSM; 26 Millwood, Lisvane, Cardiff CF4 5TL (☎ 0222 752798); Wales Institute of Forensic Medicine, University of Wales College of Med, Royal Infirmary, Cardiff CF2 1SZ (☎ and fax 0222 484258)

KNIGHT, Brien Walter; s of Edward Alfred Knight, of Sussex, and Winifred, *née* Stolworthy (d 1976); *b* 27 June 1929; *Educ* Woodhouse GS, Sir John Cass, London Univ; *m* 1, 1955, Annette, da of Alfred Scotten (d 1964), of Barnet; 1 s (Darrell b 1963), 4 da (Carolyn b 1961, Judith b 1964, Emma b 1966, Sophie b 1966); m 2, Maria Antoinette (Rita), da of Abraham Van Der Meer (d 1958), of Holland; *Career* dir: Knight Strip Metals Ltd 1951 (chm 1970-), Sterling Springs Ltd 1952-, Knight Precision Wire Ltd 1979- (chm 1979-); Precision Metals NV (Belgium) 1973-; chm Knuway Investmts Ltd 1973-, FIOD; *Recreations* DIY, sailing; *Style—* Brien Knight, Esq; Millview, 3 Hawthorn Grove, Barnet Rd, Arkley, Herts EN5 3JZ; Knuway House, Cranborne Rd, Potters Bar, Herts EN6 3JL

KNIGHT, Capt Christopher Moreton; s of Moreton Thorpe Knight, JP (d 1982), of Cooling Castle, Cliffe, Kent, and Laura, *née* Noble (d 1964); *b* 31 May 1934; *Educ* Felsted, Sir John Cass Coll London (Master Mariner); *m* 26 Nov 1987, Janet Vivien, da of Alfred Arthur Aston (d 1984), of Sidcup, Kent; 1 s (Peter b 1989); *Career* MN; md J P Knight (offshore) Ltd 1981-, vice chm J P Knight Ltd (tugowners) 1982- (dir 1964-); chm Shaftesbury Homes Arethusa 1973-; chm Br Tugowners Assoc 1974-76, chm Ropes Cordage and Netting Standards Ctee and memb Chm's Advsy Panel BSI 1981, memb Cncl CBI 1982-83; memb Bd: Cwlth Tst 1989, Medway Housing Soc (and chm Fin Ctee) 1990-; chm Victoria League for Cwlth Friendship 1990-; Freeman City of London 1973, Liveryman Hon Co of Master Mariners 1973, Freeman Worshipful Co of Watermen and Lightemen 1985; memb Nautical Inst 1975; *Recreations* wood carving, bee-keeping; *Clubs* Naval and Military, Cwlth Tst; *Style—* Capt Christopher Knight; 47 St George's Square, London SW1V 3QN (☎ 071 821 8675); Cooling Castle, Cliffe-at-Hoo, Kent ME3 8DT; 348 High St, Rochester, Kent ME1 1DH (☎ 0634 826 633, fax 0634 829 093, telex 965016)

KNIGHT, Hon Mrs (Elizabeth Angela Veronica Rose); *née* Nall-Cain; da of 2 Baron Brocket (d 1967); *b* 3 May 1938; *m* 1, 1958 (m dis 1969), 6 Marquess of Headfort; 1 s (Christopher b 1959), 2 da (Rosanagh b 1961, Olivia b 1963); m 2, 1970 (m dis 1987), William Murless Knight; 1 s (Peregrine b 1971); *Career* Colour Cnsllr for Isle of Man; *Style—* The Hon Mrs Knight; Northfield, Kirk Andreas, Isle of Man (☎ 0624 880452)

KNIGHT, Francis William; s of Thomas Francis Knight (d 1959), and Louisa Doreen, *née* Berridge; *Educ* The Roan Sch Blackheath, St John's Coll Cambridge (MA); *m* 1 Aug 1959, Diane Beverley, *née* Knight; 1 s (Timothy Francis b 30 Oct 1973), 2 da (Susan Pernille b 26 Aug 1965, Jennifer Louise b 27 Sept 1969); *Career* Colgate-Palmolive: mktg mgmnt UK 1960-63, mktg mgmnt Denmark 1964-65, md E Africa 1966-68; mgmnt conslt Booz Allen & Hamilton International 1969-70, gp md Bristol-Myers Co 1971-77, chm and chief exec Campbells Soups 1977-81, md United Biscuits 1984-85 (dep md 1981-83), chief exec UB Foods Europe 1986-87; currently: dep gp chief exec United Biscuits (Holdings) plc, non-exec dir Ocean Group plc; *Recreations* golf, chess, opera, Dickensiana; *Style—* Francis Knight, Esq; United Biscuits (Holdings) plc, Syon Lane, Isleworth, Middlesex TW7 5NN (☎ 081 560 3131, fax 081 847 5295, telex 8954657)

KNIGHT, Geoffrey Egerton; CBE (1970); s of Arthur Egerton Knight, and Florence Gladys, *née* Clarke; *b* 25 Feb 1921; *Educ* Stubbington House, Brighton Coll Sussex; *m* 1947, Evelyn Bugle; 2 da; *Career* RM 1939-46; joined Bristol Aeroplane Co Ltd 1953; dir: Bristol Aircraft Ltd 1956, BAC Ltd 1964-77 (vice-chm 1972-76); Fenchurch

Insurance Group Ltd 1979- (chm 1980); GPA Gp Ltd 1976-, GPE plc (formerly Guiness Peat Gp) 1976- (jt dep chm 1987-89, chm 1989-), Trafalgar House plc 1980-; *Books* Concorde: the inside story (1976); *Clubs* Boodle's, White's; *Style*— Geoffrey Knight, Esq, CBE; 33 Smith Terrace, London SW3 (☎ 071 352 5391); Fenchurch Insurance Group Ltd, 136 Minories, London EC3N 1QN (☎ 071 488 2388, telex 884442)

KNIGHT, Gregory (Greg); MP (Cons) Derby North 1983-; s of Albert George Knight, of Leicester, and late Isabella, *née* Bell; *b* 4 April 1949; *Educ* Alderman Newton's GS Leicester, Coll of Law Guildford; *Career* admitted slr 1973, practising until 1983; PPS: to David Mellor then Min of Health 1988-89; Min of State at FO 1987-88, govt whip 1989, Lord Cmmr of Treasury 1990; journalist, owns a recording studio; Leicester City cnsllr 1976-79, Leicestershire co cncllr 1977-83, former chm Public Protection Ctee, former dir Leicester Theatre Tst Ltd (former chm of Fin Ctee); *Books* Westminster Words (1988), Honourable Insults (1990); *Recreations* arts especially music; *Style*— Greg Knight, Esq, MP; House of Commons, London SW1

KNIGHT, Maj (Hubert) Guy Broughton; MC (1941); s of Lt-Col F Guy Knight, MC (d 1956), of Aston Hall, Stone, Staffordshire, and Edith Rosmond, *née* Broughton-Adderley (d 1949); *b* 9 April 1919; *Educ* Eton, Sandhurst; *m* 8 July 1944, Hester, da of Arthur Thomas Loyd, OBE (Lord Lt Berks, d 1944); 2 da (Henrietta Catherine b 15 Dec 1946, Celia Elizabeth (Lady Vestey) b 11 Oct 1949); *Career* Coldstream Gds 1938-51, Western Desert Campaign 1940-43 (wounded four times), Staff Coll 1944, G2 Ops London Dist 1947-50; gen cmmr Income Tax 1950- (chm 1979-88); farmer; treas NFU 1982-89; former chm Wantage RDC, former memb Oxfordshire CC; *Recreations* shooting, fishing; *Clubs* White's, Buck's, Pratt's; *Style*— Maj Guy Knight, MC; Lockinge Manor, Wantage, Oxfordshire (☎ 0235 833 266); West Lockinge Farm, Wantage, Oxfordshire (☎ 0235 833 275, car 0860 527 044)

KNIGHT, Heather Ann; da of Jack Knight, of Diss, Norfolk, and Doris Amelia, *née* Foster; *b* 29 April 1944; *Educ* Grays Convent HS, South East Essex Tech Coll; *Career* sec to head of market res Charles Hobson & Grey 1963-65, PA to publicity offr Thames Board Mills 1965-67; PA to head PR: Benton & Bowles 1967-68, Save the Children Fund 1968-71; asst to artistic dir London Festival Ballet 1971-78, office mangr Greenhalgh & Hanson 1978-81, major examinations mangr Royal Acad of Dancing 1981, administrative dir London City Ballet 1981-84, artistic mangr London Festival Ballet 1984-85, administrative dir London City Ballet 1985-; *Recreations* all the arts particularly classical ballet, opera, classical music, travel, people; *Style*— Ms Heather Knight; 44 Mirabel Rd, London SW6 7EH (☎ 071 381 2752); London City Ballet Trust Ltd, London Studio Centre, 42-50 York Way, London N1 9AB (☎ 071 837 3133, fax 071 837 3248)

KNIGHT, Jeffrey Russell; s of Thomas Edgar Knight (d 1972), of Bristol, and Ivy Cissie, *née* Russell; *b* 1 Oct 1936; *Educ* Bristol Cathedral Sch, St Peter's Coll Oxford (MA); *m* 12 Dec 1959, Judith Marion Delver, da of Reginald Delver Podger (d 1968), of Weston-Super-Mare; 4 da (Katherine Anne b 1964, Elizabeth Jane b 1967, Emma Frances b 1968, Alison Mary b 1972); *Career* articled clerk Fuller Wise Fisher & Co 1962-66, CA 1966; The Stock Exchange: joined Quotations Dept 1967, head of dept 1973, dep chief exec 1976, chief exec 1982-89, formerly special advsr to Dept of Trade on the EEC; memb CAs Livery Co; FCA, FRSA; *Recreations* cricket, music; *Clubs* Brooks's; *Style*— Jeffrey Knight, Esq; Robin Haye, The Drive, Godalming, Surrey (☎ 0483 424399)

KNIGHT, Jeremy Plowman; s of Edwin Harry Morshead Knight, of London, and Janice Catherine, *née* Wheeler; *b* 15 July 1960; *Educ* St Paul's, Univ of Bristol (scholar, BSc Econ); *Career* Brown Shipley & Co Limited: joined 1981, vice pres NY Office 1985-87, dir Corp Fin Dept 1989-; Liveryman Worshipful Co of Founders 1990, Freeman City of London 1990; *Clubs* City Univ; *Style*— Jeremy Knight, Esq; 113 Lily Close, West Kensington, London W14; Brown Shipley & Co Ltd, Founders Court, Lothbury, London EC2R 7HE (☎ 071 606 9833)

KNIGHT, Dame (Joan Christabel) Jill; DBE (1985, MBE 1964), MP (C) Birmingham Edgbaston 1966-; da of A E Christie (d 1933); *b* 1927 July; *Educ* Fairfield Sch, King Edward GS for Girls Birmingham; *m* 1947, Montague Knight, s of Leslie Knight of Harpole Hall, Northampton; 2 s; *Career* lectr, broadcaster; memb Northampton Borough Cncl 1956-66; contested (Cons) Northampton 1959 and 1964; memb Select Ctee on Race Relations and Immigration 1969-72, chm Cons Backbench Ctee Health and Social Services 1981-, memb Cncl Europe 1977-88, chm Lords and Commons All-Pty Child Protection Gp, pres W Midlands Cons Political Centre 1980-83; memb: Exec 1922 Ctee, Select Ctee Home Affrs 1980-84; *Style*— Dame Jill Knight, DBE, MP; House of Commons, London SW1

KNIGHT, Michael James; s of Charles Knight (d 1988), of London, and Ellen, *née* Murphy; *b* 29 Aug 1939; *Educ* St Bonaventures Sch London, King's Coll London, St George's Hosp London (MB BS, MS); *m* 1981, Phyllis Mary, da of William Ansel Purcell; 1 s (William Robert Charles b 1981), 1 da (Ellen Harrison b 1983); *Career* surgical registrar: Royal Hampshire County Hosp Winchester 1965-69, St George's Hosp 1969-71 (surgical res fell 1971-72); surgical res fell Washington Univ St Louis Missouri USA 1972-73, sr surgical registrar St George's Hosp London 1973-78, Hunterian prof RCS 1975, hon sr lectr St George's Hosp Med Sch; consult surgn: St James Hosp London 1978-88, St George's Hosp London 1978-, Royal Masonic Hosp London 1979-; memb: Pancreatic Soc of GB and Ireland (pres 1987), RSM, Euro Soc of Surgical Res, Ct of Examiners RCS 1988-; examiner in surgery Univ of London; author of numerous publications on gastroentorology, hepatic, pancreatic and biliary tract diseases; FRCS 1967 (MRCS 1963), LRCP; *Recreations* music; *Clubs* Players Theatre (London), St Anthony's (Forest Gate, London); *Style*— Michael Knight, Esq; 135 Harley Street, London W1N 1DJ (☎ 071 487 3501)

KNIGHT, Sir Michael William Patrick; KCB (1983, CB 1980), AFC (1964); s of William and Dorothy Knight; *b* 23 Nov 1932; *Educ* BA; *m* 1967, Patricia Ann, *née* Davies; 1 s, 2 da; *Career* AOC No 1 Gp RAF Strike Cmd 1980-82, Air Memb for Supply and Orgn 1983-86, UK Mil Rep NATO 1986-89, Air ADC to HM The Queen 1986-89, ret as Air Chief Marshal 1989, Flag Offr RAFVR(T) 1989-; dir FR Group plc 1990-; memb: Ctee RFU 1977-, Cncl RUSI 1984-87, Cncl Taunton Sch 1987-, Cncl Air League 1989-; chm Northern Devon Healthcare Tst 1990; Hon DLitt; FRAeS; *Recreations* rugby, other sports, music, writing, lecturing; *Clubs* RAF, Colonels; *Style*— Sir Michael Knight, KCB, AFC; c/o Nat West Bank plc, 24 Derby St, Leek, Staffs ST13 5AF

KNIGHT, Dr Peter Clayton; s of Norman Knight, and Vera, *née* Jordan; *b* 8 July 1947; *Educ* Bishop Vesey GS, Univ of York (BA, DPhil); *m* 2 April 1978, Catherine Mary, da of Raymond Ward; 1 s (Andrew b 5 March 1979), 1 da (Gail b 28 Aug 1981); *Career* asst dir Plymouth Poly 1979-82, dep dir Lancashire Poly 1982-85, dir Birmingham Poly 1985-; memb: Burnham Further Educn Ctee 1976-81, Ctee on Mgmnt Public Sector Higher Educn 1977, nat advsy body for Local Authy Higher Educn 1981-84, Polys and Colls Funding Cncl 1988-; nat pres NATFHE 1978-79, chm Soc for Res into Higher Educn; FRAS, CPhys, MInstP; *Style*— Dr Peter Knight; Birmingham Polytechnic, Franchise St, Birmingham B42 2SU (☎ 021 331 5555, fax 021 331 6543)

KNIGHT, Peter John Talbot; s of John Knight, and Gillian Ann, *née* Leather; *b* 12 Oct 1961; *Educ* Malvern; *m* 21 May 1988, Deborah Ann, da of Ronald Frederick Hunter, of Reading; *Career* former gp md: Jackson Property Servs, Halifax Property Servs; md: Phoenix New Homes, P & I Properties, La Manga Property Servs; *Recreations* golf; *Clubs* Sundridge Park Golf; *Style*— Peter Knight, Esq; 2 East St, Bromley, Kent BR1 1QX (☎ 081 313 3132, fax 081 290 4562)

KNIGHT, Hon Mrs (Priscilla); *née* Dodson; da of 2 Baron Monk Bretton, CB (d 1933); *b* 1914; *m* 1935, Maj Claude Thorburn Knight; 1 s (Christopher William), 3 da (Caroline Jane, Patricia Susan, Geogiana Sarah Anne); *Style*— The Hon Mrs Knight; Idlehurst, Birch Grove, Horsted Keynes, Sussex RH17 7BT (☎ 082574 224)

KNIGHT, (Warburton) Richard; CBE (1987); s of Warburton Henry Johnston Knight (d 1987), and Alice Gweneth Knight; *b* 2 July 1932; *Educ* Trinity Coll Cambridge (MA); *m* 26 Aug 1961, Pamela, da of Leonard Charles Hearmon; 2 s (James, Matthew), 1 da (Sarah); *Career* Nat Serv 2 Lt RAEC 1950-52; teacher in Middx and Huddersfield 1956-62, asst dir for secdy schs Leicester 1967, asst educn offr for secdy schs and for special and social educn in WR 1970, dir Educn Servs Bradford Met DC 1974-; *Recreations* squash, cycling, fell walking, beekeeping; *Clubs* Royal Over-Seas League; *Style*— Richard Knight, Esq, CBE; Thorner Grange, Sandhills, Thorner, nr Leeds, W Yorks; Provincial House, Tyrrel St, Bradford, W Yorks (☎ 0274 752500)

KNIGHT, (John) Roger; s of Tom Knight (d 1966), of Pier St, Aberystwyth, and Friswyth, *née* Raymond Jones (d 1972); *b* 16 Aug 1946; *Educ* Littleover Derby; *m* 25 Oct 1980, Wendy Laurena, da of Roy Francis May, of Kynmar, Penn Rd, Chalfont-St-Peter, Gerrards Cross, Bucks; 1 s (Thomas Roger b 1983), 1 da (Lucy Jane b 1985); *Career* computer systems devpt & troubleshooting Cinema Int Corp Amsterdam 1970-72, freelance computer conslt 1972-79, dir, chm and md J Computer Logic Ltd 1980-89; memb Hereford Business Club; MBCS 1981; *Recreations* cycling, walking, food, rearing ducks and geese, restoration of ancient buildings; *Style*— Roger Knight, Esq; New Mill, Eaton Bishop, Hereford HR2 9QE (☎ 0981 251 324); Golden Valley Software Factory, New Mills, Eaton Bishop, Hereford HR2 9QE (☎ 0981 251 359)

KNIGHT, Dr Roger John Beckett; s of Lt Cdr John Beckett Knight (d 1983), of Bromley, Kent, and Alyson Yvonne Saunders, *née* Nunn; *b* 11 April 1944; *Educ* Tonbridge, Trinity Coll Dublin (MA), Univ of Sussex (PGCE), UCL (PhD); *m* 3 Aug 1968 (m dis 1980), Helen Elizabeth, da of Dr William Magowan (d 1980), of Hawkhurst, Kent; 2 s (William b 1973, Richard b 1976); *Career* National Maritime Museum: custodian Manuscripts 1977-81 (dep 1974-77) dep head Books and Manuscripts 1981-84, head Info Project Gp 1984-86, head Documentation Div 1986-88, head Collections Div and chief curator 1988-; memb: Ctee Greenwich Soc 1988-90, Cncl Soc for Nautical Res 1975-79, Cncl Navy Records Soc 1975-; FRHistS; *Books* Guide to the Manuscripts in the National Maritime Museum (1977, 1980), The Journal of Daniel Paine, 1794-1797 (with Alan Frost, 1983), Portsmouth Dockyard in the American War of Independence, 1774-1783 (1986); *Recreations* sailing, cricket, music; *Style*— Dr Roger Knight; 133 Coleraine Rd, London SE3 7NT (☎ 081 853 1912); National Maritime Museum, Greenwich, London SE10 (☎ 081 858 4422)

KNIGHT, Dr Ronald Kelvin; s of Walter Leonard Knight, and Kathleen Elizabeth, *née* Langran; *b* 12 Oct 1945; *Educ* Latymer Upper Sch, Gonville and Caius Coll Cambridge (BA, MA), St Barts Med Coll London (MB BChir, MRCP); *m* 31 March 1984, Clare Louise, da of Donald Scott, of Wrexham; 3 da (Olivia b 26 Feb 1985, Georgia b 18 Feb 1988, Imogen b 9 Sept 1989); *Career* currently conslt physician in gen and respiratory med at Frimley Park, Farnham and Royal Brompton and Nat Heart Hosps; has researched into and contributed several chapters to reference books on respiratory diseases and runs a clinic for patients with cystic fibrosis referred on a nat level; chm Dept of Med Frimley Park Hosp, med advsr Camberley and Dist Asthma Soc, memb Thoracic Assoc; *Books* contrib Chapters to a number of reference books on Respiratory Disease; *Recreations* children, running, association football; *Style*— Dr Ronald Knight; Brambley Wood, Snowdenham, Links Rd, Bramley, Guildford, GU5 0BX, (☎ 0483 894392); Frimley Park Hospital, Portsmouth Rd, Frimley, Camberley, Surrey (☎ 0276 692777); Royal and National Heart Hospitals, Fulham Rd, Chelsea, London SW3 (☎ 071 352 8121)

KNIGHT, Stephen Charles; s of Reginald Frank Knight, of 29 Blenheim Rd, Street, Somerset, and Sheila Ethel Clarice, *née* Jones; *b* 25 Nov 1954; *Educ* Colfe's Sch, Bromley Coll; *m* 30 July 1977, Lesley Joan, da of Haraold Leonard Davison, of 9 Donaldson Rd, London; 2 s (Timothy David Stephen b 1988, Joshua James Stephen b 1990); *Career* gen mangr mktg and devpt Newcross Building Society 1983-84, vice pres Citibank 1984-87, chm Private Label Mortgage Services Ltd 1987-; FCBSI 1977, MBIM 1978, MCIM 1979; *Recreations* squash, cricket, freelance writing; *Clubs* IOD; *Style*— Stephen Knight, Esq; Little Grange, Orpington Rd, Chislehurst, Kent BR7 6RA (☎ 0689 833667); Brettenham House, 14-15 Lancaster Place, London WC2E 7EB (☎ 071 379 5232, fax 071 379 4078, car 0831 380822 and 0836 243659)

KNIGHT, Wilfred Victor Robert; s of Maj Wilfred Knight (d 1972), and Edith Nell, *née* Clarkson; *b* 24 May 1940; *Educ* Watford GS, Bramshill Police Coll, Trinity Coll Cambridge (MA, MPhil); *m* 1, 1963 (m dis); m 2, Patricia Ann, *née* Liddiard; 3 s (Robert John b 4 April 1969, Gregory Iain b 6 June 1972, Alistair Grant b 7 Aug 1977); *Career* joined Met Police 1959, progressed through ranks from Detective Constable to Detective Superintendent, Special Br Protection Offr for Rt Hon Harold Wilson, PM, and Rt Hon Edward Heath, PM, and other Heads of State; staff offr to various sr police offrs, awarded Bramshill Scholarship to Trinity Coll Cambridge 1977-80 and 1982-83, served with Crime Prevention and Community Rels Branch until 1984, injured and medically ret from force 1985 following injuries received during the miners' strike (rank, Detective Superintendant); fndr Robert Gregory Assocs Ltd 1985 (security conslt, designing security systems for Architects and Developers), also acts as tech advsr to TV and Cinema (The Bill, The Sweeney, etc); coach to rowing eights for Cambridge Univ Colls; ARICS; *Recreations* squash, rowing, running; *Clubs* MPAA, CUBC; *Style*— Wilfred Knight, Esq

KNIGHT, William Arnold; CMG (1966), OBE (1954); s of William Knight (d 1953), of Llanfairfechan, and Clara, *née* Maddock (d 1987); *b* 14 June 1915; *Educ* Friars Sch Bangor, UCNW (BA); *m* 1939, Bronwen, da of Evan Parry (d 1914), of Bethesda; 1 s (William), 1 da (Gillian); *Career* Colonial Audit Dept 1938: served Kenya 1938-46, Mauritius 1946-49, Sierra Leone 1949-52, Br Guiana 1952-57, Uganda 1957-68; controller and auditor gen of Uganda 1962-68, cmmr for economy and efficiency Uganda 1969-70; *Recreations* fishing, gardening; *Clubs* East India; *Style*— William Knight, Esq, CMG, OBE; Neopardy Mills, Crediton, Devon (☎ 036 32 2513)

KNIGHT, (Christopher) William; s of Claude Thorburn Knight, of Idlehurst, Birchgrove, Horsted Keynes, Sussex, and Hon Priscilla, *née* Dodson; *b* 10 April 1943; *Educ* Eton; *m* 6 Sept 1969, Jonkvrouwe Sylvia Caroline, da of Jonkheer Emile van Lennep, of Ruychrocklaan 444, Den Haag, The Netherlands; 1 s (Christopher b 20 Oct 1973), 2 da (Alexa b 9 Nov 1971, Louisa b 15 Oct 1977); *Career* princ mangr Portuguese Branch The Bank of London and S America 1982-84; dir: Lloyds Merchant Bank 1985, Lloyds Investmt Mangrs 1987; md Lloyds Bank Fund Mgmnt 1988; *Style*— William Knight, Esq; 82 Lansdowne Rd, London W11 2LS (☎ 071 221 3911); 48 Chiswell St, London EC1Y 4GR (☎ 071 600 4500, fax 071 522 5165)

KNIGHT, William John Langford; s of William Knight, and Gertrude Alice, *née* Wallage; *b* 11 Sept 1945; *Educ* Sir Roger Manwood's Sch Sandwich Kent, Univ of

Bristol (LLB); *m* 21 April 1973, Stephanie Irina, da of Lt-Col Edward Jeffery Williams; 1 s (Sam b 1980), 1 da (Sarah b 1977); *Career* admitted slr 1969; Simmons & Simmons Slrs: joined 1967-, ptnr 1973-, i/c Hong Kong office 1979-82; memb cncl: Haydn Mozart Soc, Sickle Cell Anaemia Relief; chm Standing Ctee on Co Law for Law Soc; memb City of London Slrs Co, Law Soc; FRSA; *Books* The Acquisition of Private Companies (1975, 5 edn 1989); *Recreations* riding, piano, skiing; *Clubs* Hong Kong; *Style*— W J L Knight, Esq; 14 Dominion St, London EC2M 2RJ (☎ 071 628 2020, fax 071 588 4129, telex 888562)

KNIGHTS, Dr Brenchley William; s of Sqdn Ldr William Charles Knights, and Phyllis Dawson, *née* Rose; *b* 9 Aug 1941; *Educ* Maidstone GS, Kings Coll London; *m* 25 Aug 1984, Mairi McLean, da of John Gray Youngson, of Fleet, Hants; 3 s (Justin b 19 Sept 1968, Kingsley b 17 June 1970, Lewis b 26 March 1987), 1 da (Cembre b 19 Dec 1965); *Career* res Sask Canada 1967-70, GP Melton Mowbray 1972-76, registered psychiatrist 1976-80, conslt in child psychiatry 1980-; Nat AFT; MRCS, MRCPsych 1978, LRCP; *Recreations* sailing, skiing; *Clubs* Bedfords; *Style*— Dr Brenchley Knights; Child and Family Centre, Bethel Hospital, Norwich (☎ 0603 613411)

KNIGHTS, Baron (Life Peer UK 1987), of Edgbaston, Co West Midlands; Philip Douglas Knights; CBE (1976, OBE 1971), QPM (1964), DL (1985); s of Thomas James Knights (d 1978), of Ottershaw, Surrey, and Ethel Ginn (d 1963); *b* 3 Oct 1920; *Educ* E Grinstead Co Sch, King's Sch Grantham, Police Staff Coll; *m* 1945, Jean da of James Henry Burman (d 1972); *Career* served WWII with RAF; police cadet Lincolnshire Constabulary 1937, all ranks to Chief Supt 1957, Dep Chief Constable Birmingham City Police 1970-72 (Asst Chief Constable 1959-70); Chief Constable: Sheffield and Rotherham 1972-74, S Yorks 1974-75, West Midlands Police 1975-85; memb: Aston Univ Cncl 1985-, Ctee Warwicks CCC 1985-89; tstee Police Fndn 1979-, memb Advsy Cncl Cambridge Inst of Criminology 1986-; Kt 1980; *Recreations* sport, travel, reading; *Style*— The Rt Hon the Lord Knights, CBE, QPM, DL; House of Lords, London SW1A 0PW

KNILL, Sir John Kenelm Stuart; 4 Bt (UK 1893), of The Grove, Blackheath, Kent; s of Sir (John) Stuart Knill, 3 Bt (d 1973); *b* 8 April 1913; *Educ* Downside; *m* 1951, Violette Maud Florence Martin (d 1983), da of Leonard Martin Barnes, of Durban, S Africa; 2 s; *Heir* s, Thomas Knill; *Career* WWII Lt RNVR 1940-45; canal carrier 1948-54, farmer 1956-63, MOD 1963-77, pres Avon Tport 2000, Association of Canal Enterprises; vice pres Cotswold Canals Tst, hon life memb Inland Waterways Assoc; *Clubs* Victory Services; *Style*— Sir John Knill, Bt; Canal Cottage, Bathampton, Avon (☎ 0225 463603)

KNILL, Prof John Lawrence; s of William Cuthbert Knill (d 1983), of S Croydon, and Mary, *née* Dempsey; *b* 22 Nov 1934; *Educ* Whitgift Sch Croydon, Imperial Coll London (BSc, ARCS, PhD, DIC, DSc); *m* 16 July 1957, Diane Constance, da of John Corr Judge (d 1956), of Hagerstown, USA; 1 s (Patrick b 1966), 1 da (Fiona b 1962); *Career* geologist Sir Alexander Gibb & Ptnrs 1957; Univ of London: asst lectr 1957-59, lectr 1959-65, reader 1965-73, prof of engrg geology 1973-, head Dept of Geology 1979-88; dean Royal Sch of Mines 1980-83; chm: Natural Enviroment Res Cncl 1988-, Radioactive Waste Mgmnt Advsy Ctee; memb Nature Conservancy Cncl; hon FCGI 1988, FICE 1981, FHKIE 1982, FIGeol 1986; *Books* Industrial Geology (1978); *Recreations* viticulture; *Clubs* Athenaeum; *Style*— Prof John Knill; Highwood Farm, Shaw-cum-Donnington, Newbury, Berks RG16 9LB; Natural Environment Research Council, Polaris House, N Star Ave, Swindon, Wilts SN2 1EU (☎ 0793 411 653, fax 0793 411 501, telex 444293)

KNILL, Thomas John Pugin Bartholomew; s and h of Sir John Kenelm Stuart Knill, 4 Bt; *b* 23 Aug 1952; *m* 1977, Kathleen Muszynski; *Style*— Thomas Knill, Esq

KNIPE, Sir Leslie Francis; MBE; *b* 1913; *Educ* West Monmouth Sch Pontypool; *Career* served WWII, Maj RASC Burma; farmer; pres Cons Pty in Wales (chm 1972-77), Monmouth Cons and Unionist Assoc; *Style*— Sir Leslie Knipe, MBE; Brook Acre, Llanvihangel, Crucorney, Abergavenny, Gwent, Wales (☎ 087 382 348)

KNOCKER, Col Nigel Bedingfield; OBE (1974); s of Gp Capt John Bedingfield Knocker (d 1958), of London, and Lilian Helen *née* Gibbard (d 1975); *b* 31 Aug 1930; *Educ* Oakham Sch Rutland; *m* 1, 15 Nov 1958, Catriona Jane (d 1979), da of Gen Sir Roderick Mcleod, GBE, KCB, DL (d 1981); 1 s (Jonathan Bedingfield b 9 Sept 1961), 1 da (Fiona Camilla b 5 Nov 1963); m 2, 14 March 1981, Angela Grey, da of Maj-Gen Sir John Willoughby, KBE, CB, of Warminster, Wilts; *Career* cmmnd The Royal Sussex Regt 1950; served in: Egypt, UK, Germany, Korea, Aust, N Ireland, N Africa, Aden, Gibraltar; CO Desert Regt Sultan's Armed Forces Sultanate of Oman 1971-73; def attaché Muscat 1978-80 Cmdt Support Weapons Wing Sch of Inf 1980-82, staff of CDS MOD Oman 1982-85 (ret Army 1985); joined Wiltshire CC 1985, currently county emergency planning offr Wilts; MBIM 1972; Kt Chevalier (1 class) House of Orange (1954), DSM Oman (1973); *Recreations* skiing, tennis; *Clubs* Army and Navy; *Style*— Col Nigel Knocker, OBE; The Hatch, Seend, Melksham, Wilts SN12 6NW (☎ 0380 828609); County Hall, Trowbridge, Wilts BA14 8JE (☎ 0225 753641, fax 0225 777424, telex 44340)

KNOLLYS, 3 Viscount (UK 1911); David Francis Dudley Knollys; also Baron Knollys (UK 1902); s of 2 Viscount Knollys, GCMG, MBE, DFC (d 1966), and Margaret, da of Sir Stuart Coats, 2 Bt; *b* 12 June 1931; *Educ* Eton; *m* 1959, Hon Sheelin Virginia, da of Lt-Col the Hon Somerset Arthur Maxwell, MP (d 1942), and sis of 12 Baron Farnham; 3 s, 1 da; *Heir* s, Hon Patrick Knollys; *Career* late 2 Lt Scots Gds; *Style*— The Rt Hon the Viscount Knollys; Bramerton Grange, Norwich NR14 7HF (☎ 050 88 266)

KNOPS, Prof Robin John; s of Joseph Nicholas Jean Toussaint Knops (d 1978), of Weymouth, Dorset, and Rita Josephine, *née* Colombo; *b* 30 Dec 1932; *Educ* Thames Valley GS Twickenham, Univ of Nottingham (BSc, PhD); *m* 2 Sept 1965, Margaret Mary, da of Michael McDonald (d 1977), of Newcastle upon Tyne; 4 s (Andrew b 10 June 1966, Peter b 4 May 1968, Joseph b 12 April 1970, Robert b 22 Oct 1971), 2 da (Geraldine b 9 Aug 1974, Catherine b 9 Jan 1980); *Career* lectr in mathematics Univ of Nottingham 1959-62 (asst lectr 1956-59), reader in continuum mechanics Univ of Newcastle upon Tyne 1968-71 (lectr in applied mathematics 1962-68); Heriot-Watt Univ: prof of mathematics 1971-, head of Dept 1971-83, dean of science 1984-87, vice princ 1988; pres Edinburgh Mathematical Soc 1974-75, memb Royal Soc of Edinburgh 1975 (curator 1987-); FRSA 1989; *Books* Uniqueness Theorems in Linear Elasticity (with LE Payne, 1971); *Recreations* walking, travel, reading; *Style*— Prof R J Knops; Heriot-Watt University, Edinburgh EH14 4AS (☎ 031 451 3222, fax 031 449 5153)

KNORPEL, Henry; CB (1982), QC (1988); s of Hyman Knorpel (d 1958), of Guildford Surrey, and Dora, *née* Lukes; *b* 18 Aug 1924; *Educ* City of London Sch, Magdalen Coll Oxford (BCL, MA); *m* 1953, Brenda, da of Harry Sterling (d 1982), of Wembley, Middx; 2 da (Melanie, Helen); *Career* barr Inner Temple 1947-52 (bencher 1990); Govt Legal Serv 1952-85: MNI/MPNI 1952-65, Law Cmmn 1965-67, MSS 1967-68, asst slr DHSS 1968-71 (princ asst slr 1971-78, slr 1978-85); lectr in law 1950-, counsel to The Speaker 1985-; *Style*— Henry Knorpel, Esq, CB, QC; Conway, 32 Sunnybank, Epsom, Surrey KT18 7DX (☎ 0372 721394); House of Commons, London SW1A 0AA (☎ 071 219 3776)

KNOTT, Herbert Espenett (Herbie); s of Lt-Col Roger Birbeck Knott, OBE, MC (d 1960), of Wilmslow, Cheshire, and Eva, *née* Conroy; *b* 11 March 1949; *Educ* Rugby, Univ Coll Oxford (BA, MA); *Career* mgmnt trainee Atlas Express Ltd 1972-73; photojournalist (as Herbie Knott): London Evening Standard 1977-80, Now! magazine 1980-81, The Sunday Times 1981-86, The Independent 1986-; contrib: World Press Photo Exhibitions 1987 and 1989, Telegraph Magazine 25th Anniversary Exhibition, Br Press Photographers Assoc Exhibitions 1986-89, Witness Exhibition (NT) 1990; *Awards* Nikon Photographer of the Month June 1983 and Dec 1990, Nikon Photographer of the Election 1987; memb British Press Photographers Assoc 1986; *Books* How They Made Piece of Cake (with Robert Eagle, 1988), Black and White (1990), Glasmoth-Moscow and Back by Tiger Moth (with Jonathan Elwes, 1990); *Recreations* skiing, tennis, supporting Wimbledon FC; *Style*— Herbie Knott, Esq; The Independent, 40 City Rd, London EC1 (☎ 071 253 1222)

KNOTT, Prof John Frederick; s of Fred Knott, of Bristol, and Margaret, *née* Chesney; *b* 9 Dec 1938; *Educ* Univ of Sheffield (BMet), Univ of Cambridge (PhD); *m* 1, 16 April 1963 (m dis 1986), Christine Mary, da of William Roberts; 2 s (William Frederick b 28 April 1965, Andrew John b 10 May 1966); m 2, 15 Sept 1990, Susan Marilyn (formerly Mrs Cooke), da of William Jones; 2 step s (Paul Antony b 6 Dec 1966, James Daniel b 21 April 1981); *Career* res offr Central Electricity Res Laboratories Leatherhead 1962-66, lectr Dept of Materials Sci and Metallurgy Univ of Cambridge 1967-81, reader in mechanical metallurgy Univ of Cambridge 1981-90, prof and head of Sch of Metallurgy and Materials Univ of Birmingham 1990-, vice master Churchill Coll Cambridge 1988-90 (Goldsmith's fell 1967-91; memb: Inst of Metals Materials Engrg Ctee 1979- (chm 1990-), MOD Materials Ctee 1985-88, Co-Funding Panel SERC/CEGB 1985-90, Rolls Royce Materials and Processing Advsy Bd 1987-, UKAEA Tech Assessment Gp on Structural Integrity 1988-, Res Bd of the Welding Inst 1989-, SERC Aerospace Industs Sub Ctee 1990-; FIM 1974 (AIM 1963), CEng 1978, fell Welding Inst 1985, FRSA 1985, FEng 1988, FRS 1990; visiting fell Japan Soc for the Promotion of Sci 1980, hon fell Int Congress on Fracture 1984 (vice pres 1984-89); Sheffield Soc of Engrs and Metallurgists prize 1958, Mappin medal 1959, Nesthill medal 1959, LB Pfeil prize for Physical Metallurgy 1973, Rosenhain medal for Physical Metallurgy 1978, Leslie Holliday prize (Materials Sci Club) 1978; *Books* Fundamentals of Fracture Mechanics (1973), Worked Examples in Fracture Mechanics (with D Elliott, 1979); *Recreations* bridge, cryptic crosswords, listening to traditional jazz, playing the tenor recorder rather badly; *Style*— Prof John Knott, FRS; 6 Audley Close, St Ives, Cambridge PE17 4UJ (☎ 0480 492985); The Univ of Birmingham, Sch of Metallurgy and Materials, Edgbaston, Birmingham B15 2TT (☎ 021 414 6729, 021 414 6730, fax 021 414 5232)

KNOTT, Malcolm Stephen; s of Eric Stephen Knott, of Pequina, 39 The Mowbrays, Framlingham, Suffolk, and Grace Lilley, *née* Smith; *b* 22 Aug 1940; *Educ* Mercers' Sch Holborn; *m* 15 Sept 1962, Eileen Margaret (Meg), da of Ernest William Smith-Lane (d 1969), of 69 Barnet Rd, Potters Bar, Middx; 1 s (Mungo b 1964), 1 da (Nancy b 1967); *Career* slr 1962-67, called to the Bar 1968; head chambers Lincolns Inn 1980-85, bar Cncl 1985-89, in practice Queen's Bench and Chancery Divs London, asst rec Crown Ct; memb Adam Smith Club and Campaign for Bar; Freeman City of London 1959; *Recreations* family history, toy soldiers; *Clubs* The Players Theatre, Society of Genealogists; *Style*— Malcolm Knott, Esq; 48 Oakfield Rd, Southgate, London N14 6LX (☎ 081 882 3676)

KNOTT, Air Vice Marshal Ronald George; CB (1967), DSO (1945), DFC (1944), AFC (1956); s of Capt George Knott (d 1952), and Edith Rose, *née* Anderson (d 1981); *b* 19 Dec 1917; *Educ* Borden GS; *m* 1941, Hermione Violet, da of Col Robert Bernard Phayre (d 1964); 3 s (Terence, Nicholas (decd), Andrew), 1 da (Alexandra); *Career* RAF Dir of Op Requirements MOD 1963-67, Sr Air Staff Offr ME Air Force 1967-70, Air Offr Admin Air Support Cmd 1970-72, ret; chm Weald of Kent Preservation Soc; *Recreations* wine growing, property restoration; *Style*— Air Vice Marshal Ronald Knott, CB, DSO, DFC, AFC; Pilgrims Cottage, Charing, Ashford, Kent TN27 0DR

KNOTT, (Charlotte) Teresa; JP; da of John Stobart Keith, OBE, of 96 Barton Rd, Newnham, Cambridge, and Joan, *née* Hansell (d 1969); *b* 28 March 1940; *Educ* Prior's Field Godalming Surrey, Cordon Bleu Cookery Sch Marylebone Lane (Dip Cordon Bleu), Mon Fertile Morges Switzerland, London Coll of Secretaries; *m* 1968, William Espenett Bayly Knott, s of Lt-Col John Espenett Knott, CMG, DSO; 1 s (Richard John b 3 Feb 1971), 1 da ((Adeline) Louise b 1 Dec 1969); *Career* owner of self-created garden open to the public Glenwhan Gardens Dunragit Stranraer; Magistrate Stranraer Dist Ct, chm Nat Cncl Conservation of Plants in Gardens Dumfries and Galloway; memb: Int Dendrology Soc, Hardy Plant Soc, Scottish Rock Garden Club; Freewoman: City of London, Worshipful Co of Skinners; *Recreations* collector of early English water colour drawings, water-colour painting, swimming, gardening, fishing; *Style*— Mrs William Knott, JP; Glenwhan House, Dunragit, Stranraer DG9 8PH (☎ 05814 222)

KNOWLAND, Raymond Reginald (Ray); s of Reginald George Knowland (d 1945), and Marjorie Doris, *née* Alvis; *b* 18 Aug 1930; *Educ* Bristol GS, Sir John Cass Coll; *m* 1 Sept 1956, Valerie Mary, da of Norman Wintour Higgs (d 1969); 3 s (Paul b 1961, Peter b 1963, Jeremy b 1967); *Career* Nat Serv RAF 1955-57; BP Chemicals: works gen mangr Barry Works S Wales 1969-75 (various appts 1957-69), works gen mangr Balgan Bay Works S Wales 1975-78, md BP Chemicals Belgium Antwerp 1978-80, chief exec offr BP head office London 1983-89 (dir 1980-83); currently md BP Co plc; pres: Br Plastics Fedn 1985-86, Assoc Petrochemical Prodrs Europe 1985-88 (currently memb Steering Ctee); vice pres Chemical Industs Assoc 1988-, chm bd Chemical Indust Ecology and Toxicology Centre 1986-; Freeman: City of London, Worshipful Co of Horners; FRSC 1958, CBIM 1987 (MBIM 1958); *Recreations* sailing, photography, rugby football; *Style*— Ray Knowland, Esq; British Petroleum Company plc, Moor Lane, London EC2Y 9BU (☎ 071 920 4360, fax 071 920 4232, telex 888811, car 0836 631744)

KNOWLES, Sir Charles Francis; 7 Bt (GB 1765), of Lovell Hill, Berkshire; s of Sir Francis Gerald William, 6 Bt, FRS (d 1974); *b* 20 Dec 1951; *Educ* Marlborough, Oxford Sch of Architecture (DipArch); *m* 1979, Amanda Louise Margaret, da of Lance Bromley, of Molyneux St, London W1; 2 s ((Charles) William Frederick Lance b 1985, Edward Francis Annandale Bromley b 7 April 1989); *Heir* s, (Charles) William Frederick Lance Knowles b 27 Aug 1985; *Career* ptnr Charles Knowles Design (architects); RIBA, FRSA; *Style*— Sir Charles Knowles, Bt; Silbury Hill House, 2 Vaughan Ave, London W6 0XS

KNOWLES, Prof Christopher John; s of Frank Knowles, of Knott End, Lancashire, and Alice Clayton, *née* Sims; *b* 2 March 1943; *Educ* Univ of Leicester (BSc, PhD); *m* 14 July 1968, Denise Henriette, da of Paul Georges Fouquet (d 1976); 1 s (Peter b 1969); *Career* post-doctoral fell: Dartmouth Coll USA 1967-69, Univ of Warwick 1969-70; Univ of Kent at Canterbury: lectr 1970-77, sr lectr 1977-80, reader 1980-84, prof microbial biochemistry 1984-; sec Euro Environmental Res Orgn; CChem, FRSC 1986, FRSA 1987; *Recreations* walking, skiing, cooking; *Style*— Prof Christopher Knowles; Biological Laboratory, University of Kent, Canterbury, Kent (☎ 0227 764000)

KNOWLES, Colin George; s of George William Knowles (d 1977), and Isabelle, *née* Houghton (d 1980); *b* 11 April 1939; *Educ* King George V GS Southport, CEDEP Fontainebleau France; *m* 1981, Lesley Carolyn Angela (Carla), da of Roland Stansfield

Stamp, of Devonshire; 1 da (Marguerite Isabella (Daisy) b 1984), by earlier m, 2 da (Emma, Samantha); *Career* co sec and head of public affrs Imperial Tobacco Ltd 1960-80, chm Griffin Assoc Ltd UK 1980-83, dir TWS PR (Pty) Ltd Johannesburg 1984, chm Concept Communications (Pty) Ltd Johannesburg 1983-84, dir of devpt and public affrs Univ of Bophuthatswana 1985-, chm P R Inst of S Africa Bophutatswana region 1988-, chm St John Ambulance Fndn Bophuthatswana 1989-; dir: Assoc for Business Sponsorship of the Arts 1975-84 (chm 1975-80), The Bristol Hippodrome Tst Ltd 1977-81, The Bath Archaeological Tst Ltd 1978-81, The Palladian Tst Ltd 1979-81; memb Chllr of Duchy of Lancaster's Ctee of Honour on Business and the Arts 1980-81; Freeman City of London (1974), Liveryman Worshipful Co of Tobacco Pipe Makers and Tobacco Blenders London (1973); MInstM, MIPR, FBIM, FRSA, MPRISA, APR; CStJ; *Recreations* game watching, reading, fishing, shooting; *Clubs* Carlton, MCC; *Style—* C G Knowles, Esq; Univ of Bophuthatswana, Post Bag X2046, Mmabatho 8681, Rep of Bophuthatswana, Southern Africa (☎ 010 27 1401 21171, telex 3072 BP)

KNOWLES, Hon Mrs (Lorraine Charmian Gabrielle); *née* Carleton; da of 2 and last Baron Dorchester, and Kathleen de Blaquiere, only da of 6 Baron de Blaquiere; *b* 29 Dec 1919; *Educ* Convent of the Sacred Heart Roehampton, St Mary's Sch Calne, RCM; *m* 1947, James Metcalfe Knowles, s of Thomas Greenwood Knowles, of Halifax , Yorks; 1 s (Thomas), 1 da (Elizabeth Coleman); *Career* served WWII: VAD 1939-44 (PID 1944), SOE FANY and Force 136 India and Ceylon 1944-46; former: dist cmmr Chelsea Girl Guides, hon sec Chelsea Soc; ed FANY Gazette 1976-88, chm West Dean Parish Meeting 1979-88; *Recreations* running family vineyard, freelance writing; *Style—* The Hon Mrs Knowles; 9 St Leonard's Terrace, London SW3; Sheep Pen Cottage, Friston Forest, West Dean, nr Seaford, East Sussex

KNOWLES, Michael; MP (C) Nottingham East 1983-; s of Martin Christopher Knowles, and Anne Knowles; *b* 21 May 1942; *Educ* Clapham Coll; *m* 1965, Margaret Isabel Thorburn; 3 da; *Career* sales mangr; Parly candidate (C): Merthyr Tydfil Feb 1974, Brent East Oct 1974; memb: Surbiton Constituency Exec 1971-83, Kingston Cncl 1971-83 (ldr 1974-83), Kingston constituency exec 1974-83, London Boroughs Assoc; *Style—* Michael Knowles, Esq, MP; c/o House of Commons, London SW1A 0AA

KNOWLES, Hon Mrs (Patricia Janet); *née* Brown; yr da of Baron George-Brown, PC (Life Peer); *b* 1942; *m* 1967, Derek Knowles; *Style—* The Hon Mrs Knowles

KNOWLES, Peter Frederick; s of Frederick William Knowles (d 1984), and Lillian Mary, *née* Owen; *b* 3 Jan 1952; *Educ* Wilnecote HS Tamworth, Mathew Boulton Tech Coll Birmingham; *Career* stockbroker; Harris Allday Lea and Brookes Birmingham 1969-74, Smith Keen Cutler Birmingham 1975-85, Fyshe Horton Finney Ltd 1985- (also dir); dir Little Ted (Nominees) Ltd, Wilnecote Investments Ltd; Mayor of Tamworth 1989-90; memb London Stock Exchange, FFA; *Recreations* music, theatre, study of beers; *Style—* Peter F Knowles, Esq; 275 Hockley Rd, Hockley, Tamworth, Staffs B77 5EN (☎ 0827 283122); Charles House, 148/149 Great Charles St, Birmingham B3 3HT (☎ 021 236 3111, fax 021 236 4875)

KNOWLES, (George) Peter; s of Geoffrey Knowles, MC, RA (d 1968), of 57 Charlton Rd, Weston-super-mare, and Mabel Eveline, *née* Bowman (d 1958); *b* 30 Dec 1919; *Educ* Clifton, Queen's Coll Cambridge (MA, LLM); *m* 2 Oct 1948, (Elizabeth) Margaret (d 1991), da of John Scott, of East Lilburn, Old Bewick, Alnwick; 1 s (George b 15 Jan 1958), 2 da (Susan (Mrs Architage) b 12 March 1951, Christine (Mrs Gardner) b 29 Nov 1953); *Career* WW11 2 Indian Field Regt RA 1939-45; admitted slr 1948 (ret 1987); legal sec and registrar Archbishop of York, registrar of Convocation of York 1968-86, jt registrar of C of E Gen Synod 1970-80, chm York Rent Tbnl; memb: Rent Assesment Ctee, Mental Health Tbnl; former dep coroner for York and coroner for S dist of N Yorks; former sec York branch RSPCA, memb Merchant Adventurers of York; memb Law Soc; *Recreations* fishing, gardening; *Clubs* Yorkshire (York); *Style—* Peter Knowles, Esq; 11 Lang Rd, Bishopthorpe, York

KNOWLES, Brig Royston; CBE (1969); *b* 9 July 1919; *Educ* St John's Sch Fulham, Wandsworth Tech Coll, Regent St Poly (HND); *m* 21 Dec 1946, Christina Joyce; 1 s (Roger Ian b 1947, d 1957), 1 da (Lesley Jane b 1949); *Career* cmmnd 1941, Lt 1 AA Div 1941, Capt 18 Inf Div 1941-45 (Far East POW 1942-45), 1 AA Gp 1946-48, RMCS 1948-50, Maj Admty Estab 1950-53, HQ NORTHAG 1953-55, 3 Armd WKSP REME 1955-56, Miny of Supply 1956-58, OC 37 GW Regt WKSP 1959-60, CO radar branch 1960-63, Col ADEME MOD 1963-66, Cmdt 38 Central WRSP REME 1966-69, Brig DDEME Southern Cmd 1969-72, MOD 1972-74; memb Cncl Br Quality Assoc 1979, academician Int Acad of Quality 1980, memb Cncl Euro Orgn for Quality 1987-89, vice pres Inst of Quality Assur 1988- (sec gen 1974-88; Freeman: City of London 1984, Worshipful Co of Engrs 1984; FIEE 1947, FBIM 1959, FIQA 1974; *Books* Automatic Test Systems and Applications (1975); *Recreations* travel; *Clubs* Army and Navy; *Style—* Brig Royston Knowles, CBE; 30 Acacia Rd, Hampton, Middx TW12 3DS

KNOWLES, Timothy (Tim); s of Cyril William Knowles (d 1966), of Worcester, and Winifred Alice, *née* Hood (d 1965); *b* 17 May 1938; *Educ* Bishop Gore GS Swansea; *m* 30 Sept 1967, Gaynor, da of Edgar Ernest Hallett, of Llandaff, Cardiff; 1 da (Tracy b 1969); *Career* co sec and accountant Louis Marx & Co Ltd 1960-68, controller Modco Valentite 1968-69; md HTV Ltd: co sec 1969-78, fin dir 1975-81, asst md 1981-86, gp md HTV Gp plc 1986-88 (fin dir 1976-86), dir Welsh Water plc 1989-, fin dir Export Credits Guarantee Dept Insurance Servs 1990-; Parly candidate (Cons) Swansea E 1966; memb: S Wales Electricity Bd 1981-82, Welsh Water Authy 1982-89; FCA 1960; *Recreations* travel, walking, watching cricket; *Clubs* Cardiff and County; *Style—* Tim Knowles, Esq; Cae Ffynnon, 12 Ger-y-Llan, St Nicholas, Cardiff CF5 6SY (☎ 0446 760726)

KNOWLES, Tony; s of Kevin Knowles, of Bolton, and Bridgette (Birdie) Agnes, *née* Brogan; *b* 13 June 1955; *Educ* St Annes RC Secdy, Bolton Art Sch, Bolton Art Coll; *Career* snooker player; Nat U19 Campion 1972 and 1974; tournaments won: Pontins Autumn Open 1979, Jameson International 1982, Professional Players Tournament 1983, Winfield Aust Masters 1984; tournament runner-up: Warners Open 1978, Scottish Masters 1983, World Doubles (with Jimmy White) 1983, Tolly Cobbold Classic 1984, Jameson Int 1984, Eng Professional Championship 1985, World Team Classic (memb Eng team) 1982, World Cup (memb Eng A team) 1985; proprietor: Snooker Club Bolton, Nine Bar Bowness Winermore; *Recreations* water skiing, tennis, golf, swimming; *Style—* Tony Knowles, Esq; Trickshots Ltd, 181 Chorley New Rd, Horwich, Bolton, Lancs BL6 5QE (☎ 0204 694774)

KNOWLES, Trevor; s of Gordon Gray Knowles (d 1972), of Hull, and Leonora Mary Knowles (d 1979); *b* 23 July 1938; *m* 25 June 1966, Elaine, da of William George Day; 2 s (Philip b 8 June 1969, Stephen b 8 June 1972); *Career* gen mangr Lincolnshire Publishing Co Ltd Lincoln 1972-81, md Hull and Grimsby Newspapers Ltd Grimsby 1981-; memb Cncl Newspaper Soc, memb Cleethorpes Rotary Club; FCA 1961; *Recreations* golf; *Clubs* Cleethorpes Golf; *Style—* Trevor Knowles, Esq; 45 Cromwell Rd, Cleethorpes, Humberside DN35 0AU (☎ 0472 696703); Grimsby Evening Telegraph, 80 Cleethorpe Rd, Grimsby DN31 3EH (☎ 0472 359232, fax 0472 361093)

KNOWLSON, Prof James Rex; s of Francis Frederick Knowlson (d 1972), of Ripley, Derbyshire, and Elizabeth Mary, *née* Platt; *b* 6 Aug 1933; *Educ* Swanwick Hall GS Derbyshire, Univ of Reading (BA, DipEd, PhD); *m* Elizabeth Selby, da of Thomas Albert Coxon (d 1985); 2 s (Gregory Michael b 1960, Richard Paul b 1963), 1 da (Laura Elizabeth b 1968); *Career* asst master Ashville Coll Harrogate 1959-60, lectr in French Univ of Glasgow 1963-69 (asst lectr 1960-63), prof of French Univ of Reading 1981- (lectr 1969-75, Leverhulme res fell 1975-76, sr lectr 1975-78, reader 1978-81); memb: Soc of Authors 1987-, Soc of French Studies, Assoc of Univ Teachers; *Books* Samuel Beckett: An Exhibition (1971), Light and Darkness in The Theatre of Samuel Beckett (1972), Universal Language Schemes in England and France 1600-1800 (1975), Happy Days/Oh les beaux jours (ed, 1978), Frescoes of the Skull: The Later Prose and Drama of Samuel Beckett (with John Pilling, 1979), Samuel Beckett's Krapp's Last Tape (ed, 1980), Happy Days (ed, 1985); *Recreations* badminton, cricket, theatre; *Style—* Prof James Knowlson; Rivendell, 259 Shinfield Rd, Reading, Berks RG2 8HF (☎ 0734 866387); Dept of French, The Faculty of Letters And Social Sciences, The University of Reading, Whiteknights, Reading, Berks RG2 (☎ 0734 318776)

KNOWLTON, Richard James; CBE (1983), QFSM (1977); s of Richard John Knowlton, AM (d 1981), and Florence May, *née* Humby (d 1950); *b* 2 Jan 1928; *Educ* Bishop Wordworth's Sch Salisbury; *m* 1949, Pamela Vera, da of Charles Horne, of Salisbury; 1 s (Richard b 1950); *Career* served 42 Commando RM (Hong Kong, Malta) 1945-48; fireman Southampton FB 1949-59, station offr Worcester City & Country Fire Brigade asst div offr London Fire Brigade 1963-67, div offr London Fire Brigade 1967-69, div cdr London Fire Brigade 1969-71, firemaster: SW Scotland 1971-75, Strathclyde FB 1975-84; HM Chief Insp of Fire Services (Scot) 1984-89; chm London Branch Inst of Fire Engrs 1969, UK chm Fire Services Nat Ben Fund 1980-81, UK pres Chief & Asst Chief Fire Offrs Assoc 1980-81, Br rep Cncl Euro Assoc of Prof Fire Brigade Offrs 1979-85, pres Scot Dist Fire Serv Sports & Athletic Assoc 1985-; FBIM, FIFireE; *Style—* James Knowlton, CBE, QFSM; 5 Potters Way, Laverstock, Salisbury, Wilts SP1 1PY (☎ 0722 326487)

KNOX, Anthony Douglas (Tony); s of William Trevor Knox, of Bournemouth, and Jean, *née* Calder; *b* 23 March 1945; *Educ* St Dunstan's Coll, ChCh Oxford (MA); *m* 3 Feb 1990, Adele Josephine, *née* Knight-Harper; 1 da (Camilla Rose b 26 June 1990); *Career* dir: Broad St Group plc 1990, Financial Dynamics; *Recreations* tennis, skiing; *Clubs* Hurlingham, Oxford and Cambridge, City University; *Style—* Tony Knox, Esq; Financial Dynamics, 30 Furnival St, London EC2A 1JE (☎ 071 831 3113, fax 071 831 7961)

KNOX, Anthony James (Tony); s of Harry Cooke Knox (d 1979), of Belfast, and Lila Mary Knox; *b* 9 Oct 1949; *Educ* Royal Belfast Academical Inst, Wadham Coll Oxford (BA, MA), Queens Univ Belfast (MA); *m* 30 March 1972 (m dis), Marie-Hélène Clotilde, da of Pierre Hubert, of St Gervais, Hte Savoie, France; 2 da (Jessica b 1975, Chloe b 1980); *Career* radio prodr BBC NI 1975-82, prodr South Bank Show LWT 1982-; *Recreations* fishing; *Clubs* Kells and Conor Angling, Piscatorial Soc; *Style—* Tony Knox, Esq; LWT, London SE1 9LT (☎ 071 261 3788, fax 071 633 0842)

KNOX, Bernadette; da of Joseph Chapman Knox (d 1979), and Theresa, *née* Birney; *b* 22 Oct 1954; *Educ* Convent of the Sacred Heart GS Newcastle upon Tyne, St Anne's Coll Oxford (MA); *Career* J Walter Thompson Co Ltd: Media Dept 1976, Planning Dept 1978, dir Bd 1989, gp planning dir 1990-; accounts handled incl: Kraft, The Guardian, Findus, Elida Gibbs, Electricity Council, TSB, John Harvey & Sons, Rowntrees 1984-, Scott (Andrex) 1987-, City of Newcastle upon Tyne 1989-; *Recreations* books, cinema, listening to music, talking, worrying about getting fit; *Style—* Ms Bernadette Knox; J Walter Thompson, 40 Berkeley Square, London W1 (☎ 071 499 4040)

KNOX, Bryce Harry; CB (1986); s of Brice Henry Knox, of London, and Rose, *née* Hetty Yelland; *b* 21 Feb 1929; *Educ* Stratford GS, Univ of Nottingham (BA); *m* 1957, Norma, da of George Thomas, of London; 1 s (Daniel b 1967); *Career* dep chm Bd of Customs and Excise 1983-88, asst princ HM Customs 1953 (princ 1958), HM Treasy 1963-65, asst sec 1966, seconded to HM Dip Serv, cnsllr office of UK Perm Rep to Euro Communities 1972-74, under sec 1974, cmmr HM Customs and Excise 1975; *Recreations* reading, listening to music, tasting/discussing wine, bridge; *Clubs* Reform, MCC; *Style—* Bryce Knox, Esq, CB; 9 Manor Way, Blackheath, London SE3 9EF (☎ 081 852 9404)

KNOX, (Alexander) David; CMG (1988); s of James Knox (d 1953), and Elizabeth Maxwell, *née* Robertson (d 1961); *b* 15 Jan 1925; *Educ* The Queen's Royal Coll Trinidad W Indies, Univ of Toronto Canada (BA), LSE; *m* 15 July 1950, Beatrice Lily, da of William Benjamin Dunell (d 1963); 1 s (Andrew b 1953), 2 da (Helen b 1954, Julia b 1963); *Career* reader in economics LSE 1955-63 (joined 1949), vice pres Int Bank for Reconstruction and Devpt 1980-87 (joined 1963); *Recreations* walking, opera; *Clubs* Reform; *Style—* David Knox, Esq, CMG; Knights Barn, Manor Farm Lane, East Hagbourne, Oxfordshire OX11 9ND (☎ 0235 817792)

KNOX, David Laidlaw; MP (C) Staffs Moorlands 1983-; s of John McGlasson Knox (d 1951), of Lockerbie, and Catherine Helen Campbell, *née* Laidlaw; *b* 30 May 1933; *Educ* Lockerbie and Dumfries Acads, Univ of London; *m* 1980, Margaret E Maxwell, *née* McKenzie; *Career* economist and mgmnt consIt; contested (C): Birmingham Stechford 1964 and 1966, Nuneaton (by-election) 1967; MP (C) Leek 1970-83, jt-sec Cons Fin Ctee 1972-73, PPS to Sec State Def 1973-74; sec Cons Trade Ctee 1974, vice chm: Cons Pty 1974-75, Cons Employment Ctee 1979-80 (sec 1976-79), Cons Gp for Europe 1984-87; memb: Select Ctee Euro Legislation 1976-, Chm's Panel in the House of Commons 1983-; *Style—* David Knox, Esq, MP; House of Commons, London SW1

KNOX, Lady Elizabeth Marianne; er da of 7 Earl of Ranfurly, *qv*

KNOX, (William) Graeme; s of William Francis Knox (d 1970), of Glasgow, and Marjorie Evelyn, *née* Milroy (d 1990); *b* 18 Feb 1945; *Educ* Glasgow Acad, Christ Coll Cambridge (MA); *m* 20 June 1969, Jennifer Marion, da of Dr Thomas Russell; 1 s (Mark Tarimo b 3 Feb 1975), 1 da (Karen Ann Hazel b 31 Dec 1976); *Career* Scottish Amicable Life Assurance Society: actuarial student 1966, analyst Investmt Dept 1969, responsible for Investmt Dept and clients 1976; md Scottish Amicable Investment Managers Limited 1984-; FFA 1969; *Recreations* golf, hillwalking, singing; *Style—* Graeme Knox, Esq; Scottish Amicable Investment Managers Ltd, 150 St Vincent St, Glasgow G2 5NQ (☎ 041 248 2323, fax 041 248 3778)

KNOX, Ian Campbell; s of Eric Campbell Knox, and Mary Fyfe, *née* Beattie; *b* 18 Jan 1954; *Educ* Royal HS Edinburgh, Waid Acad Anstruther, Edinburgh Coll of Art, Br Cncl scholarship to Budapest, Nat Film Sch; *m* 19 Jan 1984, Emily Broome Green; *Career* freelance writer and director 1980-; credit incl: The Stronger 1980, The Privilege 1982, Sweet Nothings (BBC) 1983, Workhorses (BBC) 1983, Boon (Central) 1985, Shoot for The Sun (BBC) 1986, Down Where The Buffalo Go (BBC) 1987, Flying To Nowhere (Shofilm) 1988, Crossfire (Central) 1989, Proof of Death (Central) 1989, Valentine Falls (Channel 4) 1989, The Police (BBC) 1990; *awards* Scottish Radio and TV awards for Best Play (for Workhorses) 1984, BAFTA award for Best Short film (for The Privilege) 1983, Bilbao film Festival award for Best Short Fiction (The Privilege) 1983; memb Dirs' Guild 1987; *Recreations* music (bass player), motor cycling, walking; *Style—* Ian Knox, Esq; 24c Durham Terrace, London W2 5PB (☎ 071 792 0101)

KNOX, Jack; s of Alexander Knox (d 1986), of Kirkintilloch, and Jean Alexander Gray, *née* Graham (d 1988); *b* 16 Dec 1936; *Educ* Lenzie Acad, Glasgow Sch of Art D A; *m* 5 July 1960, Margaret Kyle, da of Walter Duncan Sutherland (d 1963), of Linlithgow; 1 s (Kyle Alexander b 1964), 1 da (Emily Barbara b 1967); *Career* artist; lectr Duncan of Jordanstone Coll of Art 1965-81, head Painting Studios Glasgow Sch of Art; solo exhibitions: 57 Gallery Edinburgh 1961, The Scottish Gallery Edinburgh 1966, Richard Demarco Gallery Edinburgh 1969, Serpentine Gallery London 1971, Buckingham Gallery London 1972, Civic Arts Centre Aberdeen 1972, Retrospective (Edinburgh, Fruit Market Glasgow, Third Eye and touring) 1983, The Scottish Gallery Edinburgh 1989, Kelvingrove Art Gallery and Museum Glasgow 1990; gp exhibitions incl: Scottish Art Now (Fruitmarket Gallery Edinburgh) 1982, Six Scottish Painters (Graham Gallery NY) 1983, Arte Escozia Contemporea (Nat Gallery of Brazil) 1985, Moorehead State Univ Minnesota 1987, The Compass Contribution (Tramway Glasgow) 1990, Scottish Art since 1900 (The Barbican London) 1990; pub collections incl: Scottish Nat Gallery of Modern Art, Glasgow Art Galleries, Scottish Nat Portrait Gallery, Aberdeen Art Gallery, Arts Cncl of GB, Contemporary Art Soc, Edinburgh City Arts Centre, Glasgow Univ, Hunterian Museum Glasgow, City Art Gallery Manchester, Royal Scottish Academy Collection, Scottish Arts Cncl, Scottish Television; memb: Scottish Arts Cncl 1974-79, Tstees Ctee Scottish Nat Gallery of Modern Art 1975-81, Bd of Tstees Nat Gallery of Scotland 1982-87; sec Royal Scot Academy 1990; external examiner Univ of Dundee 1990; RSA 1979, RGI 1981, RSW 1987; *Style—* Jack Knox, Esq; Glasgow School of Art, 167 Renfrew St, Glasgow (☎ 041 332 9797)

KNOX, Col James Stuart; s of Brig George Stuart Knox, CBE, of Riseley Cottage, Assheton Rd, Beaconsfield, Bucks HP9 2NP, and Heather Lindsay, *née* Eddis; *b* 14 April 1940; *Educ* Wellington, RMA Sandhurst; *m* 1 June 1985, (Elizabeth) Claire, da of Peter Jackson, of Harrogate, N Yorks; 3 s ((Benjamin) James Longley b 26 Oct 1973, Oliver James Stuart b 14 April 1986, Rupert James Stuart b 31 March 1987), 2 da ((Mary) Lucinda Claire Longley b 14 Dec 1972, Clarissa Elizabeth Heather b 5 June 1988); *Career* cmmnd 1960 15/19 King's Royal Hussars, regt duty UK and BAOR 1960-64, Capt instr RAC Gunnery Sch 1964-66, RD BAOR and UK 1966-69, instr RMAS 1969-71, Maj RD BAOR and NI 1971-72, staff Coll 1973, MA to dep C-in-C UKLF 1974-75, Maj RD (NI, UK, Cyprus, BAOR), SO2 MO2 in MOD 1978-79, Lt-Col SO1 Battle Gp Trainer BAOR 1979-80, Co 15/19 1980-83, SO1 MS5 MOD 1983-85, Div Col Staff Coll Camberley 1986-88, Defence Attaché Mexico City 1989-90; *Recreations* cricket, shooting, fishing, stalking, my family; *Clubs* MCC, IZ Free Foresters; *Style—* Col James Knox; c/o HQ United Kingdon Land Forces, Wilton, Salisbury, Wilts SP2 0AG

KNOX, Hon Mr Justice; Sir John Leonard; QC (1979); s of Leonard Needham Knox (d 1956), and Berthe Helene, *née* Knox (d 1981); *b* 6 April 1925; *Educ* Radley, Worcester Coll Oxford (MA); *m* 1953, Anne Jacqueline, da of Herbert Mackintosh; 1 s (Thomas), 3 da (Diana, Catherine, Margaret); *Career* Lt RA 1944-47; barr Lincoln's Inn 1953-85, bencher Lincoln's Inn 1977, attorney-gen Duchy of Lancaster 1984-85, justice of High Ct Chancery Div 1985, judge of Employment Appeal Tribunal 1989; kt 1985; *Style—* The Hon Mr Justice Knox; Royal Courts of Justice, Strand, London WC2

KNOX, Robert William (Bob); s of Jack Dallas Knox (d 1983), of Claygate, Surrey, and Margaret Meikle, *née* Elder; *b* 15 Dec 1943; *Educ* Cranleigh; *m* 10 Feb 1968, Susan Mary, da of Cyril Joseph O'Bryen, of Weybridge, Surrey; 2 da (Julie b 1970, Katharine b 1972); *Career* ptnr Kidsons Impey CAs 1972-, memb London (W End) Dist Trg Bd ICAEW 1980; FCA 1966; *Books* Statements of Source and Application of Funds (1977); *Recreations* occasional golf, bridge, philately; *Style—* Robert W Knox, Esq; Kidsons Impey, Russell Square House, 10-12 Russell Square, London WC1B 1AE (☎ 071 436 3636, fax 071 436 6603, telex 263901)

KNOX, Hon Sir William Edward; s of late Edward Knox (Air Cdr), and late Dr Alice, *née* Thomas; *b* 14 Dec 1927; *Educ* Melbourne HS; *m* 1956, Doris Alexia Ross; 2 s, 2 da; *Career* MLA Queensland (Lib) for Nundah 1957-89, sec Parly Lib Party 1960-64, sec Jt Govt Parties 1965, min for Transport 1965-72, chm Queensland Road Safety Cncl and memb Aust Transport Advsy Cncl 1965-72, min for Justice and attorney-gen 1971-76, dep ldr Parly Lib Party 1971-76, state treas 1976-78, dep premier and ldr Parly Lib Party 1976-78, min for Health 1978-80, min for Employment and Lab Rels 1980-83, ldr Parly Lib Pty 1983-88; chm St John's Cncl Queensland; CStJ 1990; kt 1979; *Style—* The Hon Sir William Knox; 1621 Sandgate Rd, Nundah, Queensland 4012, Australia (☎ 010 617 266 9893)

KNOX-JOHNSTON, Capt William Robert Patrick (Robin); CBE (1969), RD (1978, and Bar); s of David Robert Knox-Johnston (d 1970), and Elizabeth Mary, *née* Cree; *b* 17 March 1939; *Educ* Berkhamsted Sch; *m* 1962, Suzanne, da of Denis Ronald Singer; 1 da (Sara b 1963); *Career* yachtsman; first person to circumnavigate the world non-stop & single handed 14 June 1968-22 April 1969, holder Br Sailing Trans Atlantic Record (10 days, 14 hours, 9 mins) 1986, World Champion Class II multihulls 1985; Hon DSc Maine Maritime Acad; FRGS 1965; *Books* World of my Own (1969), Sailing (1975), Twilight of Sail (1978), Last but not Least (1978), Bunkside Companion (1982), Seamanship (1986), The BOC Challenge (1986-87), The Cape of Good Hope (1989); *Recreations* sailing; *Clubs* Royal Cruising, Royal Ocean Racing; *Style—* Capt Robin Knox-Johnston, CBE, RD; 26 Sefton St, Putney, London SW15 (☎ 081 789 0465)

KNOX-LECKY, Maj-Gen Samuel; CB (1979), OBE (1967); s of John Daniel Lecky (d 1929), of Coleraine, and Mary Thompson, *née* Knox (d 1968); *b* 10 Feb 1926; *Educ* Coleraine Acad, Queen's Univ Belfast (BSc, CEng); *m* 18 Oct 1947, Sheila Constance, da of Hugh Jones (d 1952) of Liverpool; 1 s (Paul b 1955), 2 da (Karla b 1949, Jennifer b 1952); *Career* Army 1946-79, cmmnd REME 1946, DEME BAOR and Cmdt SEME as Brig; DMAO (MOD) and Min (DS) Br Embassy Tehran as Maj-Gen, Hon Col QUB OTC 1978-83, Col Cmdt REME 1980-86; dir-gen Agric Engrs Assoc 1980-88; FIMechE; *Recreations* fishing, sailing; *Style—* Maj-Gen Samuel Knox-Lecky, CB, OBE

KNOX-PEEBLES, Brian Philip; s of Lt-Col George Edward Knox-Peebles, RTR, DSO (d 1969), and Patricia, *née* Curtis-Raleigh; *b* 19 June 1936; *Educ* Wellington, Göttingen Univ W Germany, BNC Oxford (MA); *m* 20 Aug 1960, Rose Mary, da of Capt Cyril Telford Latch; 1 s (Brendan b 21 Sept 1965), 3 da (Nina b 16 Nov 1962, Fleur b 3 Feb 1964, Bryonie b 16 Nov 1967); *Career* Daily Mail 1963-64, Evening Standard 1964-65, The Times 1965-67, United Newspapers plc 1967-89; dir: Bradbury Agnew Ltd 1979-82, United Prov Newspapers 1981-89, gp mktg dir United Newspapers plc 1974-89; guest lectr: Stanford Univ Calif, Univ of Texas, Univ of Alabama, Univ of Mo, Univ of Louisiana, Univ of N Carolina, Univ of Conn, Univ of Columbia, Columbia Univ NY; dir Webster & Horsfall 1987-, chm Oceanwide Publishing Enterprises Ltd 1990-; fndr and chm Consultants in Media Ltd; fndr memb and first pres Int Newspaper Mktg Assoc (Europe); Euro dir Int Circulation Manager Assoc; memb: Mktg Soc, Int Advertising Assoc, Newspaper Res Cncl (USA), Mkt Res Soc; FInstD; *Books* The Fleet Street Revolution; *Recreations* cinema, walking, swimming, reading, writing; *Clubs* Hurlingham; *Style—* Brian Knox-Peebles, Esq; Webster & Horsfall Ltd, Hay Mills, Birmingham B25 8DW (☎ 021 772 2555); Consultants in Media Ltd, CGA, Central House, Medwin Walk, Horsham, Surrey RH12 1AG; 2 Campden House Terrace, Kensington Church St, London W8 4BQ (☎ 071 727 9595)

KNUTSFORD, 6 Viscount (UK 1895); Michael Holland-Hibbert; DL (1977 Devon); also Baron Knutsford, of Knutsford, Co Chester (UK 1888), and 7 Bt (UK 1853); o s of Hon Wilfrid Holland-Hibbert (d 1961; 2 s of 3 Viscount), and Isabel Audrey, *née* Fenwick; s cousin 5 Viscount 1986; *b* 27 Dec 1926; *Educ* Eton, Trinity Coll Cambridge (BA); *m* 8 May 1951, Hon Sheila Constance Portman, er da of 5 Viscount Portman (d 1942); 2 s (Hon Henry Thurstan, Hon James Edward b 19 May 1967), 1 da (Hon Lucy Katherine b 27 June 1956); *Heir* s, Hon Henry Thurstan Holland-Hibbert b 6 April 1959; *Career* SW regnl dir Barclays Bank 1956-86; memb various ctees Nat Tst 1965-86 (memb Finance Ctee 1986); High Sheriff of Devon 1977-78; *Clubs* Brooks's; *Style—* The Rt Hon the Viscount Knutsford, DL; Broadclyst House, Exeter, Devon EX5 3EW (☎ 0392 61244)

KNUTSFORD, Viscountess; Sheila Constance; *née* Portman; er da of 5 Viscount Portman (d 1942); *b* 25 June 1927; *m* 8 May 1951, 6 Viscount Knutsford, *qv*; 2 s, 1 da; *Style—* The Rt Hon the Viscountess Knutsford; Broadclyst House, Exeter EX5 3EW (☎ 0392 61244)

KOCH, Frederick Robinson; s of Fred Chase Koch (d 1967), of Wichita, Kansas, USA, and Mary Clementine, *née* Robinson (d 1990); *b* 26 Aug 1933; *Educ* Hackley Sch Tarrytown NY, Harvard Coll Cambridge Mass (BA), Harvard Law Sch, Yale Drama Sch (MFA); *Career* US Naval Res 1956-58; dir: Agnes de Mille Dance Theatre, The Asia Soc, Caramoor Center for Music and the Arts, 825 Fifth Ave Corp, New York City Opera; sec The Lincoln Center Theatre Co, vice pres Spoleto Festival, memb American Friends of Glyndebourne Opera, govr City Center of Music and Drama, vice chm Cncl of Fells The Pierpont Morgan Library; memb: Standing Ctee Harvard Univ Library, Visiting Ctee to Dept of Euro Paintings The Met Museum of Art, Friends of the Theatre Collection Museum of the City of NY, Nat Cncl Santa Fe Opera; currently: dir Film Soc of Lincoln Center, advsy dir Met Opera Assoc, pres Sutton Place Fndn, pres Frederick R Koch Fndn, govr Royal Shakespeare Co, memb Ctee Harvard Theatre Collection, hon curator of theatre arts Harvard Coll Library; *Recreations* attending theatre, concerts and opera; *Clubs* Brooks's, Turf, Mark's, Harry's Bar, Doubles (NY), Grolier (NY), Harvard (NY), Century (NY), Met Opera (NY), NY Athletic; *Style—* Frederick R Koch, Esq; 825 Fifth Ave, New York, New York 10021 USA; Sutton Place, nr Guildford, Surrey GU4 7QV; Schloss Bluehnbach, A-5451 Tenneck, Land Salzburg, Austria; Villa Torre Clémentina, Rue Impératrice Eugènie, 06190 Roquebrune Cap-Martin, France

KOECHLIN-BERESFORD, Hon Mrs (Clare Antoinette Gabrielle de la Poer); *née* Beresford; 2 da of 6 Baron Decies (by 2 w); *b* 31 Dec 1956; *m* Jorge J Koechlin; 1 s (Michael Joseph Tristam b 1986); *Style—* The Hon Mrs Koechlin; c/o Coutts and Co, 1 Old Park Lane, London W1Y 4BS

KOECHLIN-SMYTHE, Patricia Rosemary; OBE (1956); da of Capt Eric Hamilton Smythe, MC (d 1945), and Frances Monica Curtoys (d 1952); *b* 22 Nov 1928; *Educ* Pates GS Cheltenham, St Michael's Cirencester, Talbot Heath Bournemouth; *m* 1963, Samuel Koechlin (d 1985), s of Hartmann Koechlin (d 1961), of Basel, Switzerland; 2 da (Monica b 1966, Lucy b 1968); *Career* equestrian; memb Br Show Jumping Team 1947-64, has won numerous prizes incl: Leading Show Jumper of the Year 1949, 1958 and 1962, set Ladies' record for high jump Brussels 1954 (2m 20cm); with Br Equestrian Olympic Team: Stockholm (1956, won Show Jumping Team Bronze Medal, tenth individual), Rome (1960, tenth Individual); British Show Jumping Association: memb Br Affrs Ctee, memb Selection Ctee; memb: World Wide Fund For Nature Int Cncl and UK Cncl, Achievement Bd Int Cncl for Bird Preservation 1990, Bd Earthwatch Europe 1990; pres Br Show Jumping Assoc 1982-86; writer; landowner; Freeman: Worshipful Co of Farriers 1955, City of London 1956, Worshipful Co of Loriners 1961, Worshipful Co of Saddlers 1963; *Books* (as Pat Smythe) Jump for Joy: Pat Smythe's Story (1954), Pat Smythe's Book of Horses (1955), One Jump Ahead (1956), Jacqueline Rides for a Fall (1957), Three Jays Against the Clock (1957), Three Jays on Holiday (1958), Three Jays Go to Town (1959), Three Jays Over the Border (1960), Three Jays Go to Rome (1960), Three Jays Lend a Hand (1961), Horses and Places (1959), Jumping Round the World (1962), Florian's Farmyard (1962), Flanagan My Friend (1963), Bred to Jump (1965), Show Jumping (1967), A Pony for Pleasure (with Fiona Hughes, 1969), A Swiss Adventure (1970), Pony Problems (with Fiona Hughes, 1971), A Spanish Adventure (1971), Cotswold Adventure (1972); *Recreations* sport, music; *Style—* Mrs Patricia Koechlin-Smythe, OBE; Sudgrove House, Miserden, nr Stroud, Glos GL6 7JD (☎ 028582 360)

KOELLE, Lady; Elizabeth Anne; da of Sir Philip Henry Devitt, 1 Bt (d 1947, when Btcy became extinct); *b* 1921; *m* 1948, as his 2 w, Vice-Adm Sir Harry Philpot Koelle, KCB (d 1980); 2 da; *Style—* Lady Koelle; Pippins, Longburton, Sherborne, Dorset

KOENIGSBERGER, Prof Otto Heinrich Gustav; s of Georg F Koenigsberger (d 1932), of Oberbaurat, Berlin, and Katharine Mathilde, *née* Born (d 1953); *b* 13 Oct 1908; *Educ* Tech Univ Berlin (Dr-Ing); *m* 20 Dec 1957, Dr Renate Ursula Born, da of Dr Wolfgang Born (d 1949), of Vienna; *Career* memb Swiss Inst for the History of Ancient Egyptian Architecture 1933-35, chief architect and planner Mysore State India 1939-48, dir of housing, Miny of Health Govt of India and planning advsr Basildon New Town Essex 1948-51; UN planning and housing, advsr 1956-63 to Govts of: Ghana, Nigeria, Pakistan, Phillippines, Ceylon and Singapore; planning conslt 1956-63 to Govts of: Zambia, Brazil and Costa Rica; housing advsr to UN Econ Cmmn for Africa 1966-70, Mellon prof of planning Columbia Univ NY 1968, head Dept of Devpt and Tropical Studies Architectural Assoc London 1957-72; UCL: prof of devpt planning and head Devpt Planning Unit 1973-78, emeritus prof and hon res fell 1979-; ed Habitat Int 1976-; UN Centre for Human Settlements Award Habitat Scroll of Honour 1989; Hon Dr-Ing Univ of Stuttgart 1979; fndr memb Inst of Town Planners (India) 1948-, memb A E V Berlin 1932, MRTPI 1952, ARIBA 1968; author of numerous pubns 1932- on: architectural and applied climatology, planning and housing: practice and consultancy reports, planning and housing: theory and education; *Recreations* sailing; *Clubs* Architectural Assoc; *Style—* Prof Otto Koenigsberger; 300 West End Lane, (Ground Floor), London NW6 1LN (☎ 071 794 3475); Development Planning Unit, University College London, 9-11 Endsleigh Gardens, London WC1H 0ED (☎ 071 388 7581)

KOFFMANN, Pierre; *b* 21 Aug 1948; *Educ* Ecole Jean Jacques Rousseau Tarbes France, Cap de Cuisine et de Salle Tarbes; *m* 16 Sept 1972, Annie; 1 da (Camille b 26 Oct 1983); *Career* Military Service 1967-69; commis Restaurant L'Aubette Strasbourg 1966, commis Grand Hôtel Palais Juan Les Pins 1967, Restaurant Le Provencal La Ciotat 1969-70, Restaurent La Voile d'Or Lausanne 1970, Gavroche Restaurant 1970-71, chef Brasserie Benoist 1971, Waterside Inn Restaurant Bray on Thames Berks 1971-77, chef and proprietor La Tante Claire Restaurant 1977-; 2 Michelin stars, Restaurant Assoc Best Restaurant of the Year, The Caterer Best Chef of the Year, Egon Ronay Restaurant of the Year; Top Mark: AA Guide, Egon Ronay, Gault et Millau; memb Relais et Chateaux et Academie Culinaire de France; *Books* Memories of Gascony (1990); *Style—* Pierre Koffmann, Esq; Tante Claire Restaurant Ltd, 68 Royal Hospital Rd, Chelsea, London SW3 (☎ 071 352 6045, 071 351 0227, fax 071 352 3257)

KOHNER, Prof Eva Maria; da of Baron George Nicholas Kohner, of Szaszberek (d 1944), of Hungary, and Andrea Kathleen, *née* Boszormenyi (d 1985); *b* 23 Feb 1929; *Educ* Baar-Madas Presbyterian Boarding Sch for Girls, Royal Free Hosp Sch of Med London Univ (BSc, MB BS, MD); *m* 26 April 1961 (m dis 1979), Steven Ivan

Warman; *Career* med registrar med ophthalmogy Lambeth Hosp 1963-64, res fell Royal Postgraduate Med Sch Hammersmith Hosp London 1965-68, MRC Alexander Wernher Piggott Meml fell NY 1968-69; Moorfields Eye Hosp and Hammersmith Hosp: sr registrar and lectr 1970-77, conslt med ophthalmologist 1977-88, prof med ophthalmology (first full-time prof in Britain) 1988-; worked in field of treatment of diabetic eye disease by laser (in part instrumental in this treatment now being available to all patients in Britain) and pathogenic mechanisms in diabetic eye disease; MRCP 1963, FRCP 1977; *Books* over three hundred publications in field of retinal vascular disease; *Recreations* art, travel; *Style—* Prof Eva Kohner; 32 Monckton Ct, Strangways Terrace, London W14 8NF

KOLBERT, His Hon Judge Colin Francis; s of Arthur Richard Alexander Kolbert, of Barnet and Barnstaple, and Dorothy Elizabeth, *née* Fletcher; *b* 3 June 1936; *Educ* Queen Elizabeth's Barnet, St Catharine's Coll Cambridge (MA, PhD), St Peter's Coll Oxford (MA, DPhil); *m* 12 Sept 1959, Jean Fairgrieve, da of Stanley Hutton Abson (d 1964), of Friern Barnet; 2 da (Julia Catharine b 1963, Jennifer Sally b 1965); *Career* RA 1954-56, Cambridge Univ OTC (TAVR) 1969-74; called to the Bar Lincoln's Inn 1961; fell and tutor in jurisprudence St Peter's Coll Oxford 1964-68, fell Magdalene Coll Cambridge 1968- (tutor 1969-88), lectr in law Dept of Land Economy Cambridge 1968-88; rec SE Circuit 1985-88, circuit judge 1988-; *Clubs* Hawks' (Cambridge), MCC, Farmers', Cambridge Univ Rugby; *Style—* His Hon Judge Colin Kolbert; Magdalene Coll, Cambridge CB3 0AG (☎ 0223 332150); Lamb Building, Temple, London EC4Y 7AS (☎ 071 353 6381, fax 071 583 178)

KOLTAI, Ralph; CBE (1983); s of Dr Alfred Koltai, of Budapest, Vienna, Berlin, Brussels, Havana and London (d 1970), and Charlotte, *née* Weinstein (d 1987); *b* 31 July 1924; *Educ* Berlin, Central Sch of Arts and Crafts London (Dip Art/Design); *m* 29 Dec 1954 (m dis 1976), Mary Annena, da of late George Stubbs, of Liverpool; *Career* RASC attached Intelligence Corps served Nuremburg War Crimes Trial and London Interrogation Unit 1944-47; freelance stage designer for drama opera and dance; assoc designer RSC 1963-66 and 1976-; first prodn Angelique for London Opera Club 1950; designs for: Royal Opera House, Sadlers Wells, Scottish Opera, Nat Welsh Opera, Ballet Rambert; RSC prodns incl: The Caucasian Chalk Circle 1962, The Representative 1963, The Birthday Party 1964, The Jew of Malta 1964, Timon of Athens 1965, Little Murders 1967, Major Barbara 1970, Old World 1976, Wild Oats 1977, The Tempest 1978, Hamlet 1980, Molière 1982, Much Ado About Nothing 1982, Cyrano de Bergerac (SWET award) 1984; for Nat Theatre: As You Like It 1967, Back To Methuselah 1969, State of Revolution 1977, Brand (SWET award) 1978, Richard III 1979, Man and Superman 1981; has worked throughout Europe and in Argentine, USA, Canada, Australia; other prodns incl: Wagners complete Ring Circle (ENO) 1973, Tannhauser (Sydney) 1973 and Geneva 1986, Fidelio (Munich) 1974, Bugsy Malone 1983, Pack of Lies 1983, Metropolis 1989, dir and designer of The Flying Dutchman 1987 and La Traviata 1990, The Planets Royal Ballet 1990, Hong Kong Arts Festival; elected RDI RSA 1984, vice chm Assoc Br Theatre Designers; BSA; co winner Individual Gold Medal Prague Quadrienal 1975, Golden Troika 1979, Individual Silver Medal 1987; *Recreations* wildlife photography; *Style—* Ralph Koltai, Esq, CBE; c/o MLR 2000, Fulham Rd, London SW10

KOLVIN, Prof Israel; s of Philip Kolvin (d 1936), of Johannesburg; *b* 5 May 1929; *Educ* Univ of S Africa (BA), Univ of Witwatersrand (MB BCh, MD), Univ of Edinburgh (DPsych); *m* 27 June 1954, Rona, da of Joseph Samuel Idelson (d 1975), of Johannesburg; 1 s (Philip Alan b 4 Aug 1961), 1 da (Jennifer Lee (Mrs Jacobs) b 2 Nov 1957); *Career* registrar Royal Hosp for Sick Children Edinburgh , sr registrar Warneford and Park Hosp Oxford 1961-63, conslt Dept of Psychiatry Univ of Newcastle 1964-90, prof of child psychiatry Univ of Newcastle 1977-90 (former reader, dir of Human Devpt Unit 1974-90); memb Ctee of Advsrs to Chief Scientist Mental Health Res Fndn 1986-, chm Exec Ctee Child and Adolescent Section RCPsych 1985-89; memb: Educn Ctee Manpower, Res Cncl Court of Electors RCPsych; pres Psychiatric Section RSM 1982-83; res into low birth weight, deaf children, infantile autism, evaluation of psychotherapy, depression in childhood; FRCPsych 1972; memb: Paediatric Assoc, RSM; *Books* Bladder Control and Enuresis (jtly, 1973), Born Too Soon, Born Too Small (jtly, 1976), Speech Retarded & Deaf Children (jtly, 1979), Help Starts Here (jtly, 1981), Cycle of Deprivation (jtly, 1990); *Recreations* travel, theatre, bridge badly, golf poorly; *Style—* Prof Israel Kolvin; The Tavistock Centre, 120 Belsize Lane, London NW3 5BA (☎ 071 435 7111); The Royal Free Hospital, School of Medicine, Pond St, Hampstead, London NW3 2QG (☎ 071 794 0500)

KOMIEROWSKA, Hon Mrs (Katharine Mary); *née* Godley; da of 2 Baron Kilbracken, CB, KC (d 1950); *b* 1923; *Educ* (BSc); *m* 1944, Capt Peter Komierowski; 1 s, 1 da; *Style—* The Hon Mrs Komierowska; 4 Stanley Mansions, Park Walk, SW10

KONDRACKI, Henry Andrew; s of Pawel Kondracki (d 1986), of 12 Union St, Edinburgh, and Boyce Matilda, *née* Hills (d 1988); *b* 13 Feb 1953; *Educ* Bellevue Secdy Sch Edinburgh, Byam Shaw Sch of Art London, Slade Sch UCL (BA, Sir William Coldstream prize for best figurative work, Slade prize for Fine Art); *m* 2 Oct 1985, Sara, da of Dr Mohamed Gawad Elsarrag; 1 s (Patrick Samuel); *Career* artist; one man shows: Traverse Theatre Club Edinburgh 1979, The Artist's Collective Gallery Edinburgh 1984, Vanessa Devereux Gallery London 1987 and 1989, Michael Wardell Gallery Melbourne Aust 1988; gp exhibitions: Off the Wall 1988, Contemporary Drawings (Vanessa Devereux Gallery London) 1989, Royal Acad Summer Sch 1989; collections: Granada Fndn Manchester 1983, Br Arts Cncl 1986 and 1989, UCL 1986; awards: materials and cost award Scot Art Cncl 1978 (minor bursary 1979), South Bank Bd prize 1987; selected to participate in The Peter Moores Exhibition (Walker Gallery Liverpool) 1986; memb Cncl Edinburgh Printmakers Workshop; *Style—* Henry Kondracki, Esq; 4 Albion Terrace, Edinburgh (☎ 031 661 9894); William Jackson Gallery, 28 Cork St, London W1 (☎ 071 287 2121)

KONIG, Martyn; s of Peter Hans Konig, of Guildford, Surrey, and Dorothy, *née* Vernon; *b* 21 Sept 1957; *Educ* Godalming GS, Univ of Liverpool (LLB); *Career* barr; called to the Bar Gray's Inn 1979; N M Rothschilds: bullion dealing in Treasy Dept 1980-87, asst dir Bullion Trading (USA, Africa, Asia, Aust) 1987-90, dir trading Treasy Div 1990-; memb: Gray's Inn, Chartered Inst of Bankers; *Recreations* motor racing, classic cars, boating; *Style—* Martyn Konig, Esq; N M Rothschild & Sons Ltd, PO Box 185, New Court, St Swithin's Lane, London EC4P 4DU (☎ 071 280 5000)

KONYN, Gerald; s of Hartog Konyn (d 1956), and Katherine, *née* Binderman (d 1965); *b* 18 July 1916; *Educ* Northern Poly (BSc); *m* 1, 1942, Ida (d 1956), da of Howard Levene (d 1957), of Hendon; 1 s (Hartog b 1950), 1 da (Ruth b 1946); m 2, 10 Aug 1967, Marie Claire Aimee, *née* Gouges; 2 da (Geraldine b 1968, Pascale b 1970); *Career* bookseller: Handel Smithy Bookshop, J & E Bumpus (booksellers to HM The Queen); chm: The Book Guild, Guild Large Print Books; *Books* The Story of Philosophy (1967); *Recreations* reading, writing 500 words a day, swimming; *Clubs* RAC; *Style—* Gerald Konyn, Esq; Beresford Manor Farm, Plumpton Green, Sussex BN8 4EN (☎ 0273 890171); Temple House, 25/26 High St, Lewes, Sussex BN7 2LU (☎ 0273 472534, fax 0273 476472)

KOOPS, Eric Jan Leendert; s of Leendert Koops (d 1990), of Hellingly, Sussex, and Daphne Vera, *née* Myhill; *b* 16 March 1945; *Educ* Eastbourne Coll, Univ of Lancaster (BA); *m* 1, 1968 (m dis 1985), Glenys Marie Baker; 1 s (Mark Alexander b 20 Feb 1975), 1 da (Amanda Charlotte b 25 Sept 1972); m 2, 11 Sept 1987, Hon Mary Claire Hogg, QC, da of Baron Hailsham of St Marylebone, KG, CH, *qv*; 1 da (Katharine Mary b 17 March 1989); *Career* TA 2 Lt 4/5 KORR 1964-67; investmt banker and dir of several public and private cos in UK and the Benelux; hon dir The Duke of Edinburgh's Award World Fellowship; tstee: Inst for Policy Res, Winnicott Clinic of Psychotherapy Charitable Tst; Parly candidate (Cons) Wakefield 1974; chm Political Ctee Carlton Club 1984-88; FCA 1971; *Publications* Money for our Masters (1970), Airports for the Eighties (1980); *Recreations* travel, cricket, biographies; *Clubs* Buck's, Carlton, MCC; *Style—* Eric Koops, Esq; 16 Moreton Place, London SW1V 2NP (☎ 071 834 5615)

KOOPS, Hon Mrs (Mary Claire); *née* Hogg; QC (1989); er da of Baron Hailsham of St Marylebone, KG, CH, FRS, PC, and his 2 w, Mary Evelyn, *née* Martin (d 1978); *b* 15 Jan 1947; *Educ* St Paul's Girls' Sch; *m* 11 Sept 1987, Eric Jan Leendert Koops, *qv*, s of Leendart Koops (d 1990), of Hellingly, Sussex; 1 da (Katharine Mary b 17 March 1989); *Career* barr Lincoln's Inn 1968, asst rec 1986-90, rec 1990-; govr Poly of Central London 1983-; tstee Harrison Homes 1986-; memb Nat Cncl Church of England Children's Soc 1990-; Freeman City of London 1981; *Style—* The Hon Mrs Koops, QC; 1 Mitre Court Buildings, Temple, London EC4

KOPELOWITZ, Dr Lionel; JP (Northumberland 1964); s of Dr Maurice Kopelowitz (d 1971), and Mabel, *née* Garston (d 1949); *b* 9 Dec 1926; *Educ* Clifton, Trinity Coll Cambridge (BA), Univ Coll Hosp London (MA); *m* 29 July 1980, Mrs Sylvia Waksman, *née* Galter; *Career* Flt Lt RAF Med Branch 1952-53; princ in gen practice in Newcastle upon Tyne 1953-87; chm: BMA Newcastle Div 1969-70, Newcastle Family Practitioner Ctee 1979-85, Newcastle Local Med Ctee 1980-86; pres: Soc of Family Practitioner Ctees 1978-79, BMA Northern Regnl Cncl 1984-88, Bd of Deps of Br Jews 1985-, Nat Cncl for Soviet Jewry 1985-, Euro Jewish Congress 1988-; memb: Gen Optical Cncl 1979-, BMA Cncl 1982-, GMC 1984-; hon sec BMA Northern Regnl Cncl 1975-84; Liveryman Worshipful Soc of Apothecaries 1966; memb Assur Med Soc 1987; life vice pres Tyneside Cncl of Christians and Jews; vice pres: Trades Advsy Cncl, Br Cncl of Sha'are Zedek Med Centre Jerusalem; former memb Bd Govrs Haifa Technion 1977-89; *Books* Medical Annual (contrib 1985); *Recreations* contract bridge, continental travel; *Clubs* Athenaeum, Cambridge Union Soc; *Style—* Dr Lionel Kopelowitz, JP; 10 Cumberland House, Clifton Gardens, London W9 1DX (☎ 071 289 6375); Woburn House, Tavistock Square, London WC1 (☎ 071 387 3952, fax 071 383 5848)

KOPPEL, Jessica Esther (Jess); da of Heinz Koppel (d 1980), of Cwmerfyn, Aberystwyth, and Renate Hanni, *née* Fischl; *b* 4 April 1963; *Educ* Penglais Aberystwyth, Cardiff Coll of Art (Higher Nat Dip Photography); partner Ceri Huw James; *Career* photographer; asst to Bryce Attwell 1984-85, freelance photographer 1985- (specialising in food and still life); numerous exhibitions incl: Stages Photographers Gallery 1988, Assoc of Photographers Gallery, F45 Womens Exhibition every year; winner: Silver award Assoc of Photographers, Clio Gold award Int Food Packaging 1988, award of Excellence Mead Show 1989; memb Assoc of Photographers 1985; *Books* Sophie Grigson's Ingredients Book (contrib, 1991), 10 Minute Cuisine (contrib, 1991); *Style—* Ms Jess Koppel; Jess Koppel Photography, 65/69 Leonard Street, London EC2A 4QS (☎ 071 739 6642)

KOPPEL, Hon Mrs (Jessica Gwendolen); *née* St Aubyn; da of 3 Baron St Levan (d 1978), and Hon Clementina Gwendolen Catherine Nicolson, o da of 1 Baron Carnock; sis of Giles St Aubyn, the writer; niece of late Sir Harold Nicolson; *b* 8 Feb 1918; *m* 1939, John Patrick Koppel, late Maj Welsh Gds and former dep chm Courtaulds, s of Percy Alexander Koppel, CMG, CBE (d 1932); 1 s, 2 da; *Career* assoc memb Save the Children Fund, memb Cons Assoc NW Hants; *Recreations* gardening; *Clubs* Army & Navy; *Style—* The Hon Mrs Koppel; Goodworth House, Goodworth Clatford, Andover, Hants (☎ 0264 66539)

KORALEK, Paul George; CBE (1984); s of Mr Ernest Koralek (d 1983), and Alice, *née* Muller (d 1989); *b* 7 April 1933; *Educ* Aldenham, Architectural Assoc Sch of Arch (AA Dip); *m* 13 Dec 1958, (Audrey) Jennifer, da of Capt Arthur Vivian Chadwick (d 1980); 1 s (Benjamin b 14 July 1967), 2 da (Catherine b 16 March 1961, Lucy b 19 Dec 1962); *Career* ptnr and dir Ahrends Burton & Koralek Architects 1961-; princ works incl: Trinity Coll Dublin (Berkeley Library 1972, Arts Faculty bldg 1979), residential bldg Keble Coll Oxford 1976, Templeton Coll Oxford 1969-88, Nebenzahl House Jerusalem 1972, warehouse and showroom for Habitat Wallingford, factory for Cummins Engines Shotts, J Sainsbury Supermarket Canterbury 1984, retail HQ WH Smith Swindon 1985, Kingston dept store John Lewis, St Marys Hosp Newport IOW, Heritage Centre Dover, stations for extention Docklands Railway, new Br Embassy Moscow; RIBA 1957, ARA 1986; *Style—* Paul Koralek, Esq, CBE; 3 Rochester Rd, London NW1 9JH (☎ 071 485 9143); Ahrends Burton & Koralek, Unit 1, 7 Chaleot Rd, London NW1 8LH (☎ 071 586 3311)

KORN, Jacqueline; da of Harry Korn (d 1989), of London, and Essie, *née* Simmons; *b* 15 April 1938; *Educ* Harrow Weald Co GS; *m* 14 March 1965, Ralph Glasser; 1 s (Roland b 5 Feb 1973), 1 da (Miranda b 29 Sept 1975); *Career* authors' agent; became jt owner David Higham Associates 1972 (joined 1958); *Recreations* music, theatre, reading, walking; *Clubs* Groucho, RAC; *Style—* Miss Jacqueline Korn; David Higham Assocs Ltd, 5-8 Lower John St, Golden Square, London W1R 4HA (☎ 071 437 7888, fax 071 437 1072)

KORNBERG, Prof Sir Hans (Leo); s of Max Kornberg; *b* 14 Jan 1928; *Educ* Queen Elizabeth GS Wakefield, Univ of Sheffield; *m* 1956, Monica King (d 1989); 2 s (Jonathan, (twin) Simon), 2 da (Julia, Rachel); *Career* prof biochemistry Univ of Leicester 1960-75, Sir William Dunn prof biochemistry Univ of Cambridge, fell Christ's Coll Cambridge 1975- (master of Christ's 1982-); a managing tstee Nuffield Fndn 1973-, chm Royal Cmmn Environmental Pollution 1976-81, chm Sci Advsy Ctee and chm Kuratorium Max-Planck Inst Dortmund 1979-89, memb AFRC 1981-85, memb Advsy Cncl for Applied Res & Devpt 1982-85, chm Advsy Ctee for Genetic Modification 1986-, memb Priorities Bd for Res in Agric and Food 1985-90, tstee Wellcome Tst 1990-; pres: Biochemistry Soc 1990-, Int Union Biochemistry 1991-, Assoc Sci Educn 1991-; Hon DSc: Cincinnati, Warwick, Leicester, Sheffield, Bath, Strathclyde; Hon DUniv Essex, Hon MD Leipzig, also memb various int acads; pres Br Assoc 1984-85 FIBiol, FRSA, Hon FRCP 1989, FRS 1965; *Clubs* United Oxford and Cambridge Univ; *Style—* Prof Sir Hans Kornberg, FRS; The Master's Lodge, Christ's Coll, Cambridge CB2 3BU

KORNBERG, Justin Anthony; s of late Isaac Eugene Kornberg, and Bessie, *née* Nathan; *b* 16 Aug 1928; *Educ* Bronx HS of Sci (USA), Clifton, Trinity Coll Cambridge, Bradford Tech, LSE; *m* 1961, Elizabeth Ann, *née* Oppenheim; 1 s, 2 da; *Career* chm Lister & Co Ltd; memb: Cncl Anglo-Israel C of C, Aims the Free Enterprise Orgn, Freedom Assoc Ltd; fndr and chm Transpennine Gp; *Recreations* reading, fishing, golf; *Clubs* Athenaeum; *Style—* Justin Kornberg, Esq; 15 Portland Place, London W1N 3AA

KORNICKA, Lady Lepel (Sophia); *née* Phipps; da of 4 Marquess of Normanby, CBE; *b* 1952; *m* 1975, Richard Kornicki; 2 s, 1 da; *Style—* The Lady Lepel Kornicka; 15 Castello Ave, London SW15

KOSSOFF, David; s of Louis Kossoff (d 1941), and Anne Kossoff, *née* Shaklovitz (d 1966); *b* 24 Nov 1919; *Educ* Northern Poly (Sch of Architecture and Design); *m* 1947, Jennie, da of Frank Jenkins; 2 s (Simon, Paul (decd)); *Career* commercial artist 1937, draughtsman 1937-38, furniture designer 1938-39, tech illustrator 1939-45, began acting 1943, worked as actor and illustrator 1945-52, as actor and designer 1952-; BBC Repertory Co 1945-51; actg parts incl: Col Alexander Ikonenko in the Love of Four Colonels 1952, Sam Tager in The Shrike 1953, Morry in The Bespoke Overcoat, Tobit in Tobias and the Angel 1953, Prof Lodegger in No Sign of the Dove 1953, Nathan in The Boychik 1954, Mendele in The World of Sholom Aleichen 1955 (Johannesburg 1957), one-man show One Eyebrow Up 1957, Man on Trial 1959, Stars in Your Eyes 1960, The Tenth Man 1961, Come Blow Your Horn 1962, one-man show Kossoff at the Prince Charles 1963 (later called A Funny Kind of Evening), Enter Solly Gold 1970, Cinderella 1971, Bunny 1972; own bible storytelling programmes on radio and TV as writer and teller 1964-69; solo performance (stage) As According to Kossoff 1970-, Late Great Paul (anti-drugs performance in schools) 1981-; has appeared in many films, won Br Acad award 1956; FRSA; Hon D Litt; *Books* Bible Stories retold by David Kossoff (1968), The Book of Witnesses (1971), The Three Donkeys (1972), The Voices of Masada (1973), The Little Book of Sylvanus (1975), You Have a Minute, Lord? (1977), A Small Town is a World (1979), Sweet Nutcracker (1985); *play* Big Night for Shylock (1968); *Recreations* reading, conversation; *Style—* David Kossoff Esq; 45 Roe Green Close, Hatfield, Herts AL10 9PD (☎ 0707 263475)

KOSTICK, Marjorie Phyllis; da of Roy Tudball (d 1984), and Annie Elizabeth Webber; *b* 6 Oct 1938; *Educ* Univ of London, Univ of Exeter (BA); *m* 26 Dec 1961, Gerald, s of Nathan Kostick (d 1950); 2 s (Conor Patrick b 1964, Gavin Michael b 1966); *Career* CA; ptnr M Kostick & Co Chester; dir: Hunter Street Financial Services Ltd, Clwyd Refractory Fibres Ltd; FCA, ATII, MBIM; *Style—* Mrs Marjorie Kostick; 14 Walpole St, Chester CH1 4HG (☎ 0244 375789); 8 St John St, Chester CH1 1DA (☎ 0244 341220, fax 0244 341263)

KOVAR, Dr Ilya Zdenek; s of Victor Kovar (d 1971), and Nina, *née* Klein; *b* 17 March 1947; *Educ* Sydney Boys HS Aust, Univ of Sydney (MB BS); *m* 29 Dec 1974, Cynthia Rose, da of Norbert Sencier; 3 s (Simon b 10 Oct 1976, Benjamin b 23 March 1979, David b 31 May 1984), 1 da (Sarah b 31 May 1984); *Career* currently sr lectr in child health at Charing Cross and Westminster Schs and conslt paediatrician Charing Cross Hosp London; author of med, scientific, clinical articles and med texts; memb: BPA, AAP, FRCP, FRCPC, FAAP, DRCOG; *Books* Textbook for DCH (1984), Make it Better (1982); *Recreations* riding, reading, music; *Style—* Dr Ilya Kovar; Dept Child Health, Charing Cross Hospital, London W6 8RF (☎ 081 8467195)

KRAEMER, (Thomas Wilhelm) Nicholas; s of Dr William Paul Kraemer (d 1982), of London, and Helen, *née* Bartrum; *b* 7 March 1945; *Educ* Lancing, Dartington Coll of Arts, Univ of Nottingham (BMus, ARCM), Guildhall Sch of Music; *m* 22 April 1984, Elizabeth Mary, da of John Anderson; 1 s (Dominic b 1988), 1 da (Emma b 1986); *Career* harpsichordist: Monteverdi Orchestra and English Baroque Soloists 1970-80, Acad of St Martin in the Fields 1972-80; musical dir: Unicorn Opera Abingdon 1971-75, West Eleven Childrens Opera 1971-88; fndr and dir Raglan Baroque Players 1978-, musical dir Opera 80 1980-83, princ conductor Divertimenti 1980-, assoc conductor BBC Scottish Symphony Orchestra 1983-85, artistic dir London Bach Orchestra 1985-, Irish Chamber Orch 1985-90; memb Royal Soc Musicians; *Recreations* tennis, active fatherhood; *Clubs* Hornsey; *Style—* Nicholas Kraemer, Esq; 35 Glassyln Rd, London N8 8RJ (☎ 081 340 6941)

KRAIS, Maurice; *Educ* Stationers' Company's Sch, Regent St Poly; *Career* RAF; ed asst Reuters, chief reporter Walthamstow Post; ed 1951-80: Marylebone Mercury, Paddington Mercury, Queen's Park Advertiser; former gp ed West London Newspaper Group; former ed and fndr: Mayfair News, Holborn Guardian; assoc news ed The People 1980-; *Recreations* overseas travel, theatre, walking, sport; *Style—* Maurice Krais, Esq; Mirror Group Newspapers, Holborn Circus, London EC1P 1DQ

KRAPEZ, Dr John Robert; s of Ivan Krapez (d 1988), of Dudley, Worcs, and Anne Krapez; *b* 8 July 1948; *Educ* Tividale Sch, Westminster Med Sch (MB BS); *m* 28 Nov 1975, Marilyn Eva Harding, da of Maj Leslie Harding Barnes, MBE (d 1987), of Greatstone, New Romney, Kent; 1 s (Timothy b 17 Sept 1977), 1 da (Nicola 3 July 1981); *Career* St Bartholomew's Hosp: lectr depts of clinical pharmacology and anaesthesia 1976-78, conslt anaesthetist and hon sr lectr Dept of Anaesthesia and Med Coll 1978-; tutor Coll of Anaesthetists; FC Anaesthetists 1975; *Recreations* skiing, model railways and aircraft, carpentry; *Style—* Dr John Krapez; 73 Harley St, London W1 (☎ 071 486 0725)

KRAUSHAR, Christopher Arthur Anthony; s of Casimir Kraushar (d 1948); *b* 8 Feb 1940; *Educ* St Paul's, Christ's Coll Cambridge (MA); *m* 1963, Alison Margaret, da of Alexander Graham, of Peterborough; 1 s (Robert b 1967), 1 da (Alison b 1964); *Career* md: Gaskell & Chambers Ltd 1980-83, Dreamland Electrical Gp 1983-85, Autonumis Ltd 1985-87, Fordham Bathrooms & Kitchens Ltd 1987-; dir: Perkins Engines Gp 1978-80, MKR Hldgs 1980-83, Hepworth Plastics Ltd 1987-; CEng, FBIM, FID; *Recreations* badminton, squash, windsurfing; *Style—* Christopher Kraushar, Esq; Highfields, 26 Tinacre Hill, Wightwick, nr Wolverhampton, Staffs WV6 8DA (☎ 0902 761053)

KRAUSHAR, Peter Maximilian; s of Casimir Kraushar (d 1948) and Maria Dauksza (d 1960); Polish by origin; *b* 30 Aug 1934; *Educ* St Paul's Sch, Univ of Cambridge (MA); *m* 4 April 1959, Rosalind, da of Dr Harold Pereira (d 1976); 3 s (Mark b 1960, Gregory b 1964, Justin b 1966), 1 da (Joanna b 1962); *Career* chm: KAE Group Ltd 1969, Mintel 1985, IIS Ltd 1984, Partime Careers Ltd 1980; pres KAE Development 1990, (chm 1969-90); chm: Mktg Soc 1973-74 and 1974-75; *Books* New Products and Diversification (1977), Practical Business Development - What Succeeds What Does Not (1985); *Recreations* bridge, tennis, travel, reading, writing; *Style—* Peter Kraushar, Esq; 2 Lauradale Road, London N2 9LU (☎ 081 883 4736)

KREBS, Prof John Richard; s of Sir Hans Krebs (d 1981), of Oxford, and Margaret Cicely, *née* Fieldhouse; *b* 11 April 1945; *Educ* City of Oxford HS, Pembroke Coll Oxford (MA, DPhil); *m* 3 Aug 1968, Katharine Anne, da of John Fullerton (d 1973), of Newport, Gwent; 2 da (Emma Helen b 1977, Georgina Clare b 1980); *Career* asst prof Inst of Animal Resource Ecology Univ of BC 1970-73, lectr in zoology Univ Coll N Wales Bangor 1973-75, fell Wolfson Coll Oxford 1975-81, lectr in zoology Edward Grey Inst Oxford 1975-88 (demonstrator in Ornithology 1970), Royal Soc res prof and fell Pembroke Coll 1988- (EP Abraham fell 1981-88); memb: AFRC 1988-; Max Planck Soc 1985-; FRS 1984; *Books* Behavioural Ecology (with N B Davies, 1978, 1984 and 1991), Introduction to Behavioural Ecology (with N B Davies, 1981 and 1987), Foraging Theory (with D W Stephens, 1986); *Style—* Prof John R Krebs; 11 Brookside, Oxford OX3 7PJ (☎ 0865 63211); Dept of Zoology, South Parks Rd, Oxford OX1 3PS (☎ 0865 271166, 0865 310447)

KREBS, Lady; Margaret Cicely; da of J L Fieldhouse, of Wickersley, Yorks; *b* 30 Oct 1913; *Educ* Manchester Univ; *m* 1938, Sir Hans Krebs, FRS, FRCP, Nobel Laureate & sometime prof of Biochemistry at Sheffield & Oxford Univs; 2 s, 1 da; *Career* teaching; *Style—* Lady Krebs; 25 Abberbury Rd, Iffley, Oxford OX4 4ET (☎ 0865 777534)

KREMER, Lady Alison Emily; *née* Balfour; yr da of 3 Earl of Balfour (d 1968); *b* 16 Nov 1934; *m* 8 May 1963, Thomas Kremer, s of Bernard Kremer, of Kolozsvar, Transylvania; 1 s, 2 da; *Style—* The Lady Alison Kremer

KRETSCHMER, John Martin; s of Dr Eric Kretschmer (d 1954); *b* 1 April 1916; *Educ* Ottershaw Coll, King's Coll London (BSc); *m* 1943, Noel Mary, da of George Herbert Tapsfield; 2 s (Robin James, Richard Andrew), 1 da (Katharine Anne Dures); *Career* Maj RE; chm: Reed & Mallik Ltd, Reed & Stuart (Pty) Ltd; dir Rush & Tompkins Gp Ltd 1978, ret 1982; memb Cncl: Inst CEng 1979, Fedn of CE Contractors; elected memb Engrg Assembly 1985; treas: Mt Everest Fndn, Salisbury, S Wilts Museum Tst; CEng, FICE, FIStructE, FRGS; *Recreations* mountaineering, natural history; *Clubs* Alpine; *Style—* John Kretschmer, Esq; Tower House, Redlynch, Salisbury, Wilts (☎ 0725 20401)

KRIKLER, Dennis Michael; s of Barnet Krikler, and Eva Krikler (d 1986); *b* 10 Dec 1928; *Educ* Muizenberg HS, Univ of Cape Town SA (MB ChB); *m* 3 July 1955, Anne, da of August Winterstein (d 1974), of Bad Krozingen, Germany; 1 s (Paul Alan b 1961), 1 da (Shirley Jean b 1957); *Career* fell Lahey Clinic Boston 1956, C J Adams Meml Travelling Fell 1956, sr registrar Groote Schuur Hosp 1957-58 (house physician and registrar 1952-55); conslt physician: Salisbury Central Hosp Rhodesia 1958-66, Prince of Wales Hosp London 1966-73; conslt cardiologist Hammersmith and Ealing Hosps 1973-, sr lectr in cardiology Royal Postgrad Med Sch 1973-, ed expert clinicien en cardiologie Ministére des Affaires Sociales Santé France 1983, int lectr American Heart Assoc 1984 (Paul Dudley White Citation for int achievement); visiting prof 1985: Baylor Univ, Indiana Univ, Univ of Birmingham; visiting prof Boston, Kentucky, and UCLA 1988; Joseph Welker lectr Univ of Kansas, George Burch lectr Association of Univ Cardiologists USA 1989, Henri Denolin lectr Euro Soc of Cardiology, Hideo Meda lectr Japan Soc of Electrocardiology 1990; papers on cardiology in nat and int jls; ed British Heart Journal 1981-; memb Ed Ctee: Cardiovascular Res 1975-, Archives des Maladies du Coeur et des Vaisseaux 1980-; hon memb: Soc di Cultura Medica Vercellese Italy, Soc de Cardiologia de Levante Spain, Soc Francaise de Cardiologie 1981-; memb Scientific Cncl Revista Portuguese de Cardiologia 1982-, hon fell Cncl on Clinical Cardiology American Heart Assoc 1984; McCullough prize 1949, Sir William Osler Award Miami Univ 1981, medal of Honour Euro Soc of Cardiology; Freeman: Worshipful Soc of Apothecaries 1989, City of London 1990; memb Br Cardiac Soc 1971, FACC 1971, MD 1973, FRCPE 1970, FRCP 1973; *Books* Cardiac Arrhythmias (with J F Goodwin, 1975), Calcium Antagonism in Cardiovascular Therapy (with A Zanchetti, 1981), Amiodarone and Arrhythmias (with D A Chamberlain and W J McKenna, 1983), Workshop on Calcium Antagonists (with P G Hugenholtz, 1984); *Recreations* photography, history; *Style—* Dennis Krikler, Esq; 55 Wimpole St, London W1M 7DF

KRIKLER, His Hon Judge Leonard Gideon; s of Maj J H Krikler, OBE, ED (d 1971), of St Brelade Jersey CI, and Tilly Krikler (d 1974); *b* 23 May 1929; *Educ* Milton Sch Bulawayo S Rhodesia; *m* 1955, Thilla (d 1973); m 2, 1975, Lily; 6 s, 2 da; *Career* recorder of Crown Cts 1980-84; *Recreations* drawing, painting; *Style—* His Hon Judge Leonard Krikler; Lambs Bldgs, Temple, London EC4Y 7AS (☎ 071 435 3348)

KRIWACZEK, Paul; Oscar Kriwaczek (d 1960), and Alice Lunzer; *b* 30 Nov 1937; *Educ* Kilburn GS, London Hospital Med Coll (BDS, LDS); *m* 29 Jan 1966, Jeannette Ann, da of Leslie Donald Parsons, of Timbarra, Neals Lane, Chetnole, Dorset; 2 s (Rohan b 1968, Tamor b 1972), 1 da (Nandi b 1974); *Career* prodr/dir BBC TV: Ancestral Voices (David Munrow) 1975, BBC Computer Literacy Project (RTS prize) 1980, Bellamy's Backyard Safari (BAAS prize) 1982, Orchestra with Jane Glover 1984, Mozart with Jane Glover 1986; writer/prodr: Parosi (BBC TV) 1978, The Well 1989; exec prodr BBC TV 1987-; memb RCS; AIEE 1988; *Style—* Paul Kriwaczek, Esq; BBC Television, Continuing Education, The Broadway, Ealing, London W5 2PA (☎ 081 991 8001, fax 081 567 9356)

KROCH, Henry Justus; CBE (1983, OBE 1968); s of Dr Curt Kroch (d 1960), of Leipzig, and Lilly, *née* Rummelsburg (d 1971); Kroch jr family bank 1870-1940 Leipzig Germany; *b* 28 Oct 1920; *Educ* St Gall & Winterthur Switzerland; *m* 8 March 1956, Margot Emma Natalie, da of late Adolf Kohlstadt; 2 s (Anthony, Ian), 1 da (Margaret (Mrs Cottam)); *Career* AB Electronic Prods Gp plc: joined 1951, dir 1957, md 1964, chm and chief exec 1978, currently pres and non-exec dir; former: pres (currently hon pres) Euro Electronic Component Manufacturers Assoc Brussels, chm Electronic Components Bd, Cncl memb (currently tstee) Electronic Components Industry Fedn; memb: Cncl CBI Wales 1966-77, Welsh Cncl 1968-79; pres Engrg Employers Assoc of S Wales 1969-70, dir Devpt Corp for Wales 1971-82, chm Inst of Welsh Affairs 1987-; Master Worshipful Co of Scientific Instrument Makers 1987-88, Hon Freeman Borough of Cynon Valley 1987; hon fell and life govr Univ Coll Cardiff, hon fell Poly of Wales; CIEE, FBIM; Golden Order of Merit State of Salzburg Austria 1986; *Recreations* music, mountains, swimming; *Clubs* East India, Cardiff & County, City Livery, United Wards of City of London; *Style—* Henry Kroch, Esq, CBE; AB Electronic Products Gp plc, Abercynon, Mid Glamorgan CF45 4SF (☎ 0443 740331, telex 498606 ABEC G)

KROLL, Natasha; da of Dr Hermann Kroll, and Sophie, *née* Rabinovich; b 20 May 1914; *b* 20 May 1914, (Moscow); *Educ* Berlin HS; *Career* TV and film designer; teacher of window display Reimann Sch of Art London 1936-40; display mangr: Rowntrees Yorks 1940-42, Simpson Piccadilly 1942-55; sr designer BBC TV 1955-66, freelance 1966-; RDI, FSIAD; *Recreations* painting, entertaining; *Style—* Ms Natasha Kroll; 5 Ruvigny Gardens, London SW15 (☎ 081 788 9867)

KROLL, Dr Una Margaret Patricia (Novice Una SSC); da of Brig George Arthur Hill, CB, DSO, MC (d 1970), and Hilda Evelyn Hill, *née* Pediani (d 1965); *b* 15 Dec 1925; *Educ* Malvern Girls' Coll, Cambridge Univ (MA, MB BChir); *m* 1957, Leopold Kroll, s of Bishop Leopold Kroll (d 1949), of New York; 1 s (Leopold), 3 da (Florence, Elisabeth, Una); *Career* medical practitioner Missionary Serv in Liberia and Namibia 1953-61, GP (England) 1961-81, community health doctor 1981-; deaconess (C of E) 1970-; memb: Christian Medical Cmmn 1978-85, CRAC (Churches Religious Advsy Cncl to BBC) 1980-85, Gen Synod of C of E (diocese of Chichester) 1980-87; deacon Church in Wales Dec 1988; *Books* A Signpost to the World (1975), Flesh of my Flesh (1976), Lament for a Lost Enemy (1978), Sexual Counselling (1980), A Spiritual Exercise Book (1985), Growing Older (1988); *Style—* Novice Una SSC; Society of Sacred Cross, Tymawr Convent, Lydart, Monmouth, Gwent NP5 4RW

KROMBERG, Peter Heinz; s of Heinz Kromberg (d 1941), and Hilde, *née* Fuerst; *b* 29 Dec 1940; *m* 25 March 1972, Nicole, da of Simone Baldini; 2 s (Olivier, Jean-Pierre); *Career* chef's apprenticeship Hotel Duisburger Hof Germany 1955-58, seasonal jobs in leading hotels in Switzerland and Bavaria 1958-63, chef de partie gardemanger Athens Hilton 1963-66; exec chief: Siam Inter-Continental Hotel Bangkok 1966-70, Portman Inter-Continental London 1971-75, Hotel Inter-Continental London 1975-; apprentice of the year 1958, Gold medal winner with distinction Cookery Olympics Germany 1972 and 1976, winner of CATEY award 1987, selected as guest chef on tv series Take Six Chefs; memb: Académie Culinaire of GB, Assoc Internationale Des Mâitres Conseils on Gastronome Francaise, Guild Des Fromagers; hon memb Restaurateurs Assoc of GB, hon int pres Toques Blanches; *Recreations* gardening, skiing, cycling, swimming and squash; *Clubs* Club 9; *Style—* Peter Kromberg, Esq; Hotel Inter-Continental London, One Hamilton Place, London W1V 0DY (☎ 071 409 3131 ext 79256 or 071 493 9502, fax 071 493 3476)

KRUSIN, Sir Stanley Marks; CB (1963); *b* 8 June 1908; *Educ* St Paul's Sch, Balliol Coll Oxford; *m* 1, 1937 (w d 1972); 1 s, 1 da; m 2, 1976 (w d 1988); *Career* served WWII RAFVR; called to the Bar Middle Temple 1932, Parly counsel 1953-69, second

Parly counsel 1970-73; kt 1973; *Style*— Sir Stanley Krusin, CB; 5 Coleridge Walk, London NW11 (☎ 081 458 1340)

KUDIAN, Mischa; *Career* writer, ed, poet, lectr, painter, specialist trans of Armenian literature, and children's fiction writer; *publications* trans: Scenes from an American Childhood by Vahan Totovents (1962, 2 ed 1980), Selected Works by Avetik Issahakian (1976), Komitas, the Shepherd Songs by Levon Miridjanian (1983) The Tailor's Visitors by Shahan Shahnour (1984), Jesus the Son by Nerses Shnorhali (1986); ed and trans: The Bard of Loree by Hovannes Toumanian (1970), Tell Me, Bella by Vahan Totovents (1972), Soviet American Poetry (1974), The Muse of Sheerak by Avetik Issahakian (1975), Lamentations of Narek by Grigor Narekatsi (1977), Honourable Baggars by Hagop Baronian (1978), Retreat Without Song by Shahan Shahnour (1982), Jonathan Son of Jeremiah by Vahan Totovents (1985); ed and reteller The Saga of Sassoun by Mischa Kudian (1970); poetry: Candy Floss (1980), Flutterby (1984), This Day and Age (1984), Tenpence a Laugh (1984), Witricks Galore! (1984); books: Three Apples Fell from Heaven (1969), More Apples Fell from Heaven (1982); *Style*— Mischa Kudian, Esq

KUDLICK, Martin; s of Joseph Kudlick and Raie Kudlick; *b* 27 Dec 1933; *Educ* Westcliff High; *m* 16 Sept 1962, Margaret Helen, da of David Fisher; 1 s (Jonathan b 1970), 2 da (Suzanne b 1968, Nicola b 1973); *Career* CA; sr ptnr H W Fisher & Co; *Recreations* walking, jogging, reading, music; *Clubs* Reform; *Style*— Martin Kudlick, Esq; 36 Paines Lane, Pinner, Middx (☎ 081 868 4055); 69/76 Long Acre, London WC2 E9JW (☎ 071 379 3461, fax 071 831 1290)

KUENSSBERG, Nicholas; s of Dr Ekkehard Von Kuenssberg, CBE, of Little Letham, Haddington, E Lothian, and Constance, *née* Hardy; *b* 28 Oct 1942; *Educ* Edinburgh Acad, Wadham Coll Oxford (BA); *m* 27 Nov 1965, Sally, da of Hon Lord Robertson (Lord of Session), of 13 Moray Place, Edinburgh; 1 s (David b 1971), 2 da (Joanna b 1973, Laura b 1976); *Career* chm Dynacast International Ltd 1978-; dir: J & P Coats Ltd 1978-, West of Scotland Bd Bank of Scotland 1984-88, South of Scotland Electricity Bd (now Scottish Power plc) 1984-, Coats Patons plc 1985-, Coats Viyella plc 1986-, Standard Life Assurance Co 1988-; visiting prof Strathclyde Business Sch 1988- (visiting fell 1986-87), govr Queen's Coll Glasgow 1989-; FCIS 1977, CBIM 1989; *Recreations* travel, languages, opera, sport; *Style*— Nicholas Kuenssberg, Esq; 6 Cleveden Drive, Glasgow G12 OSE; Coats Viyella plc, 155 St Vincent St, Glasgow G2 5PA (☎ 041 221 8711, fax 041 248 2512)

KUHRT, Ven Gordon Wilfred; s of Wilfred Nicholas Henry Kuhrt, and Doris Adeline, *née* Goddard; *b* 15 Feb 1941; *Educ* Colfe's GS, Univ of London (BD), Oakhill Theol Coll; *m* 31 Aug 1963, Olive Margaret, da of Raymond Frank Alexander Powell; 3 s (Martin b 1966, Stephen b 1969, Jonathan b 1972); *Career* religious educn teacher 1963-65, vicar Shenstone Dio of Lichfield 1973-79, vicar Emmanuel Croydon Dio of Southwark 1979-89, rural dean Croydon Central 1981-86, hon canon Southwark Cathedral 1987-89, biblical studies lectr Univ of London 1984-89, memb Gen Synod C of E 1986-, archdeacon Lewisham Dio of Southwark 1989-; *Books* Handbook for Council and Committee Members (1985), Believing in Baptism (1987); *Style*— The Ven the Archdeacon of Lewisham; 3A Court Farm Rd, Mottingham, London SE9 4JH (☎ 081 857 7982)

KUIPERS, Dr John Dennis; s of Joannes Kuipers (d 1961), of Holland, and Marion, *née* Sewell (d 1973), of UK; *b* 9 July 1918; *Educ* St John's Coll Cambridge (MA), Univ of London (MSc), Univ of Amsterdam (DSc), Univ of Strathclyde (LLD); *m* 17 Feb 1940, Johanna Adriana, da of Machiel Pieter De Roon (d 1968), of Holland; 3 s (Francis b 1941, Adrian b 1944, Richard b 1946); *Career* SOE 2 Lt and Capt 1941-44, Royal Netherlands Army Gen Serv Capt and Maj 1944-45; chm Royal De Betue Co Ltd Holland 1945-65 (dir), memb EEC Indust Fedn 1964-74, pres ESC of EEC 1970-72 (memb 1962-74), vice pres Fedn of Netherlands Industs 1970-75, chm Foreign Affrs Ctee Cncl of Netherlands Indust Fedns 1970-75, visiting prof Strathclyde Business Sch 1973-78; Kt Order Netherlands Lion (1974), Offr Orange Nassau (1969), Cdr Italian Order of Merit (1972), Cdr Order of Leopold II Belgium (1972), Offr Order of George I Greece (1964); *Books* Resale Price Maintenance in GP (1950); *Recreations* study of art and history, music; *Style*— Dr Dennis Kuipers; Los Algarrobos, PU 106, 03730 Javea, Alicante, Spain (☎ 6 579 1334); 7 Avenue Paul Hymans, (Bte 5) Brussels 1200 (☎ 2 762 7173)

KULUKUNDIS, Elias George (Eddie); OBE; s of George Elias Kulukundis (d 1978), and Eugenia, *née* Diacakis; 5 generation shipping family; *b* 20 April 1932; *Educ* Collegiate Sch NYC NY, Salisbury Sch Salisbury Connecticut, Yale Univ; *m* 4 April 1981, Susan Hampshire (actress), *qv*, da of George Kenneth Hampshire (d 1964); *Career* dir: Rethymnis & Kulukundis Ltd, 1964-, London & Overseas Freighters plc 1980-86 and 1989-; chm: Knightsbridge Theatrical Productions Ltd 1970-, Theatres Trust, Theatre Museum Assoc, Sports Aid Foundation Ltd 1988-; vice chm: Royal Shakespeare Theatre Trust 1983- (memb Cncl of Management), Hampstead Theatre Ltd; vice pres: Greenwich Theatre Ltd, Traverse Theatre Club; govr Royal Shakespeare Theatre; tstee: The Raymond Mander and Joe Mitchenson Theatre Collection Ltd, Hampstead Theatre Trust; memb: Baltic Exchange 1959-, Lloyd's 1964- (memb Cncl 1983-89), Exec Cncl SWET; tstee Salisbury Sch Conn; theatrical prodr; London prodns incl (some jtly): Enemy, The Happy Apple, Poor Horace, The Friends, How the Other Half Loves, Tea Party and The Basement (double bill), The Wild Duck, After Haggerty, Hamlet, Charley's Aunt, Straight Up, London Assurance, Journey's End, Small Craft Warnings, A Private Matter, Dandy Dick, The Waltz of the Toreadors, Life Class, Pygmalion, Play Mas, The Gentle Hook, A Litle Night Music, Entertaining Mr Sloane, The Gay Lord Quex, What the Butler Saw, Travesties, Lies, The Sea Gull, A Month in the Country, A Room With a View, Too True to Be Good, The Bed Before Yesterday, Dimetos, Banana Ridge, Wild Oats, Candida, Man and Superman, Once a Catholic, Privates on Parade, Gloo Joo, Bent, Outside Edge, Last of the Red Hot Lovers, Beecham, Born in the Gardens, Tonight at 8.30, Steaming, Arms and the Man, Steafel's Variations, Messiah, Pack of Lies, Of Mice and Men, The Secret Diary of Adrian Mole Aged 13 and 3/4, Camille, The Cocktail Party, Curtains, Separation, South Pacific, Over My Dead Body, Never the Sinner, King and I; NY prodns (jtly): How The Other Half Loves, Sherlock Holmes, London Assurance, Travesties, The Merchant, Players, Once a Catholic; FRSA; *Recreations* theatre; *Clubs* Garrick; *Style*— Eddie Kulukundis, Esq, OBE; Winchmore House, 15 Fetter Lane, London EC4A 1JJ (☎ 071 583 2266, fax 071 583 0046, telex 8811736 RANDK G)

KUMAR, Prof (Jagdish) Krishan; *b* 11 Aug 1942; *Educ* William Ellis Sch London, St John's Coll Cambridge (BA, MA), LSE (MSc); *Career* prodr Talks Dept BBC 1972-74, prof of social thought Univ of Kent 1987- (lectr in sociology 1967-77, reader in sociology 1977-87); tstee Action Soc Tst; *Books* Prophecy and Progress (1978), Utopia and Anti-Utopia in Modern Times (1987), Rise of Modern Society (1988), Utopianism (1991); *Style*— Prof Krishan Kumar; Keynes College, University of Kent, Canterbury CT2 7NP (☎ 0227 764000)

KUMI, Ishmael Job Ayeh; s of Dr Emmanuel Ayeh Kumi (d 1989), of Ghana, and Sabina, *née* Cromwell; *b* 15 Sept 1939; *Educ* Adisadel Coll Cape Coast Ghana, Oxford (MA), Sorbonne (Maîtrise); *Career* lectr in classics Cape Coast Univ Ghana; called to the Bar Gray's Inn 1977; gen sec Ghana Red Cross; *Recreations* tennis (lawn); *Style*— Ishmael Kumi, Esq; Warrington Mansions, 212 Kilburn High Rd, London NW6 4JH (☎ 071 372 2023, fax 071 372 2023)

KUNKLER, Dr Ian Hubert; s of Dr Peter Bertrand Kunkler, of Las Fuentes, Spain, and Pamela, *née* Hailey (d 1988); *b* 22 July 1951; *Educ* Clifton, Univ of Cambridge (BA, MA), Barts (MB BChir, MRCP); *m* 18 July 1981, Dr (Alison) Jane Kunkler, da of late Ronald George Pearson, of Kenya; *Career* house offr Univ of Leicester Med Sch 1978-79, sr house offr in gen med Nottingham City Hosp 1979-81, sr registrar Western Gen Hosp Edinburgh 1984-88 (registrar 1981-83), EEC and French Govt clinical res fell Inst Gustave Roussy Paris 1986-87; author papers on: bone scanning in breast cancer, radiotherapy in breast and laryngeal cancer, the value of clinic follow-up in cervical cancer; pres London Med Gp 1977, convener annual conference Pain-A Necessity? Charing Cross Med Sch; memb BMA 1978, DMRTEd 1983, FRCR 1985, FRSM 1989; *Books* Cambridge University Medical Journal (ed 1974); *Recreations* fly fishing; *Style*— Dr Ian Kunkler; Weston Park Hospital, Whitham Rd, Sheffield S10 2SJ (☎ 0742 670222, fax 0742 684193)

KUNZ, Gerald Charles (Gerry); OBE (1985); s of Charles Kunz (d 1958), and Eva Dorothy, *née* Lloyd (d 1940); *b* 24 March 1927; *Educ* privately; *m* 22 March 1958, (Elizabeth) Anne, da of Horace Charles Pitt (d 1962); 2 s (Simon Charles b 15 Oct 1962, Jeremy Lloyd b 21 Feb 1965); *Career* Fleet Air Arm Royal Sussex Regt, RHG 1944-48; asst exhibition mangr 1958, exhibition mangr 1969, gen mangr exhibitions 1980; cncl memb Assoc of Exhibition Organisers; Castrol Gold Medal Award 1984; Freedom of the City of London 1976; Liveryman Worshipful Co of Coachmakers and Coach Harness Makers 1976; *Recreations* golf, reading, cards, music; *Clubs* Royal Mid-Surrey Golf; *Style*— Gerry Kunz, Esq, OBE; Society of Motor Manufacturers & Traders Ltd, Forbes House, Halkin St, London SW1X 7DS (☎ 071 235 7000, fax 071 235 7112, telex 21628)

KUNZELMANN, C Dixon; s of Fabian W Kunzelmann, of Old Bennington, Vermont, USA, and Helen Dixon; *b* 19 Dec 1941; *Educ* St Paul's Sch Concord NH USA, Univ of Freiburg W Germany, Hobart Coll Geneva NY USA, Amos Tuck NH USA; *m* 3 Feb 1968, Joan, da of Rawson Atwood, of Rumson, NJ, USA; 1 s (Christopher Ely b 1970), 1 da (Laura Rawson b 1973); *Career* JP Morgan: joined 1965, personnel SVP London 1982-89, Securities Gp SVP NYC 1989-90, corp staffing SVP NYC 1990-; tstee Hobart Coll 1990-, vice pres American Friends of Georgian Gp 1989; *Recreations* shooting, fishing, driving; *Clubs* Flyfishers, Annabels, Queens, Pilgrims, Guards Polo, Links (NY), Union (NY), Hay Harbor (NYC), Adirondarck League (NYC); *Style*— C Dixon Kunzelmann, Esq; 1220 Park Ave, New York City, NY 10128, USA (☎ 212 722 8409); PO Box 68, Boonton, NJ 07005, USA (☎ 201 334 0594); J P Morgan & Co, 60 Wall St, NYC, NY 10260 (☎ 212 648 6622)

KUPER, Prof Adam Jonathan; s of Simon Meyer (d 1963), of Johannesburg, and Gertrude, *née* Hesselson (d 1987); *b* 29 Dec 1941; *Educ* Parktown Boys HS Johannesburg, Univ of the Witwatersrand Johannesburg (BA), King's Coll Cambridge (PhD); *m* 16 Dec 1966, Jessica Sue, da of Sidney Cohen (d 1986), of Johannesburg; 2 s (Simon b 1969, Jeremy b 1971), 1 da (Hannah b 1974); *Career* lectr in social anthropology Makerere Univ of Kampala Uganda 1967-70, lectr in anthropology UCL 1970-76, prof of African anthropology and sociology Univ of Leiden 1976-85, prof of social anthropology and head of Dept of Human Sciences Brunel Univ 1985-; visiting appts: asst prof Univ of California 1969, planner Nat Planning Agency Office of PM Jamaica 1972, prof Univ of Gothenburg Sweden 1975; fell Centre for Advanced Study in the Behavioural Sci California 1980-81; chm of Euro Assoc of Social Anthropologists 1989-90; hon doctorate Univ of Gothenburg 1978; *Books* Kalahari Village Politics (1970), Wives for Cattle: Bridewealth and Marriage in Southern Africa (1982), Anthropology and Anthropologists: The Modern British School (1983), South Africa and the Anthropologist (1987), The Invention of Primitive Society: Transformations of an Illusion (1988); Councils in Action (ed, 1971), The Social Anthropology of Radcliffe-Brown (ed, 1977), The Social Science Encyclopaedia (ed, 1985); *Recreations* cricket; *Style*— Prof Adam Kuper; 16 Muswell Rd, Muswell Hill, London N10 2BG (☎ 081 883 0400); Brunel University, Dept of Human Sciences, Uxbridge, Middx UB8 3PH (☎ 0895 56461, fax 0895 32806, telex 261173 Brunel G)

KUPFERMANN, Jeannette Anne; s of Nathaniel Weitz (d 1988), and Era Tarnofsky; *b* 28 March 1941; *Educ* Hendon Co GS, LSE (BA), Univ Coll London (MPhil); *m* 21 June 1964, Jacques H Kupfermann (d 1988), s of Elias Kupfermann (k ca 1940); 1 s (Elias Jonathan b 16 April 1965), 1 da (Mina Alexandra b 10 May 1967); *Career* anthroplogy; res librarian Wenner-Gren Fndn Anthropological Res NY 1963-65, actress Woodstock Playhouse NY 1964-67, res asst Univ of London 1976-77; bdcasting 1972-; writer: Man and Myth (Radio 3, award for best radio documentary series 1976), An Introduction to Social Anthropology (1980); presenter and contrib LWT and Thames TV 1970-, panelist on Tomorrow's Child; tech advsr to film dirs: Fred Zinnemann (The Dybbuk) 1972, Barbara Streisand (Yentl) 1982; journalist: Woodstock Times 1965-67, Sunday Times 1984-88, Daily Telegraph 1987; TV critic and feature writer: Daily Mail 1984-, Sunday Times Magazine, You, She, New Woman; memb Br Bdcasting Press Guild 1988; *Books* The Mistaken Body (1978); *Recreations* dancing (jazz ballet, tap), gardening, walking, painting (water colours), studying cosmology; *Clubs* Chelsea Arts; *Style*— Ms Jeanette Kupfermann; Television Dept, Daily Mail, Northcliffe House, 2 Derry Street, London W8 5EE (☎ 071 583 8000)

KURLAND, Dr Philip; s of Peter Kurland (d 1975), and Esther Kurland (d 1983); *b* 6 May 1935; *Educ* Strodes Fndn, Univ of London, Guy's Hospital; *m* Michelle, da of William Dillon; 5 c (Nicola b 1973, Paul b 1975, Matthew b 1986, Edward b 1988, Thomas b 1988); *Career* dental surgn; private practice 1959-, contribs to learned jls; memb: Br Standards Inst, LDS Club; GDPA 1959, EUD 1970, LDS, FRCS, FInstD; *Books* Intravenous Techniques in Dentistry (1967); *Recreations* tennis; *Style*— Dr Philip Kurland; 22 Harley St, London W1N 1AA (☎ 071 637 0491)

KURLANSKY, Mervyn Henry; s of Joseph Kurlansky, of Johannesburg, SA, and Jean, *née* Isaacs; *b* 3 March 1936; *Educ* Highlands North HS Johannesburg, Central Sch of Arts London; *m* (m dis), 2 da (Karen b 6 April 1962, Dana b 2 July 1965); *Career* graphic designer; freelance practice 1961-62, Planning Unit Knoll International 1962-67, freelance practice 1967-69, Crosby Fletcher Forbes 1969-72, fndr ptnr Pentagram Design Limited 1972-; clients incl: Penguin Books 1967-80, Renters 1972-90, Rank Xerox 1972, British Telecom (Prestel) 1977, Shiseido 1977 and 1988, Johnnie Walker 1980, ICI 1982, Barclaycard 1983, Faber & Faber 1983, Eureka! The Children's Museum 1987-, Museum of Modern Art Oxford 1988-, British Library 1988-, Edinburgh Park 1991; various int exhibitions; books: Pentagram (1972), Watching My Name Go By (1974), Living By Design (1978), Ideas On Design (1968); *awards*: Design & Art Direction silver 1972 and 1973, Brno bronze 1978, New York Art Directors Club silver 1988, Japanese Package Design Cncl gold 1988; memb: Designers & Art Directors Assoc, Alliance Graphique Internationale; FCSD, FSTD; *Recreations* horseriding, running, swimming, skiing, windsurfing, music; *Clubs* RAC; *Style*— Mervyn Kurlansky, Esq; Pentagram Design Limited, 11 Needham Rd, London W11 2RP (☎ 071 229 3477, fax 071 727 9932)

KUT, David; s of Jakob Kut (d 1962), of London, and Frieda Sachs (d 1979); *b* 5 May 1922; *Educ* Adass Real Gymnasium of Berlin Germany, ORT Tech Sch Berlin, Northampton Poly London, Univ of London (BSc); *m* 2 Nov 1952, Seena, da of Itzak

Assuschkewitz (d 1950), of London; 1 s (Steven Humphrey b 1959), 1 da (Deborah Helen b 1962); *Career* WWII Aux War Serv; draughtsman Benham and Sons (Engrs) Ltd 1943-46, jr engr Oscar Faber & Ptnrs Consulting Engrs 1946-49, sr engr Powell Duffryn Tech Servs Ltd 1949-54; David Kut and Ptnrs: fndr 1954, sr ptnr 1954-87, conslt 1988-; chm Professional Affairs Sub Ctee Engrg Cncl Regnl Orgn Ctee London Central, former memb Guide Ctee Inst of Heating and Ventilating Engrs; CEng, MInstE, MConsE, FIMechE, FCIBS, FCIArb: Eur Ing; *Books* Heating and Hot Water Services in Buildings (1968), Warm Air Heating (1970), Applied Waste Recycling for Energy Conservation (with G Hare, 1981), District Heating and Cooling for Energy Conservation (with R E Diamant, 1981), Dictionary of Applied Energy Conservation (1982), Applied Solar Energy (with G Hare, 1983), Efficient Waste Management (with G Hare, 1989), Illustrated Dictionary of Engineering Services (1991); *Recreations* graphology, chess, yoga, tropical fish, swimming; *Style—* Eur Ing David Kut; 5 Thornton Way, London NW11 6RY (☎ 081 455 7018); David Kut & Ptnrs, Rosebery House, Tottenham Lane, London N8 9BY (☎ 081 348 5171/6, fax 081 340 8926, telex 291347)

KUYPERS, (Andreas) Neville; s of Andreas Kuypers (d 1982), of Liverpool, and Ellen Margaret, *née* Rodgers (d 1987); *b* 18 April 1934; *Educ* Quarry Bank GS Liverpool; *m* Isobel Jean, da of John Clark; 2 s (Timothy John b 3 Nov 1967, Matthew Yacine b 10 March 1971), 2 da (Andrea Jane b 10 March 1964, Nina Sophia b 3 Nov 1972); *Career* Nat Serv jr technician photographer RAF 1954-56; photographer; Elsam Mann and Cooper Ltd 1949-73 (apprentice rising to studio mangr and co dir), formed partnership C J Studios 1973-86, chm Neville Kuyper Photography Ltd 1990- (estab co 1986); memb BIPP 1951- (memb Admissions and Qualifications Bd 1990-); awards from BIPP (NW region) incl: Industl award, Commercial award, Scientific award, numerous Merit awards; non-stipendar minister The United Reformed Church; *Clubs* Non-Stipendary Minister of The United Reformed Church; *Style—* Neville Kuypers, Esq; Neville Kuypers Photography Ltd, 93 New Chester Rd, New Ferry, Wirral, Merseyside L62 1AB (☎ 051 645 0544, fax 051 645 8531)

KVERNDAL, Simon Richard; s of Ole Sigvard Kverndal, of Colgates, Halstead, Kent, and Brenda, *née* Skinner; *b* 22 April 1958; *Educ* Haileybury, Sidney Sussex Coll Cambridge (MA); *Career* called to the Bar Middle Temple 1982, practising barr in commercial and maritime law 1983-; memb London Diocesan Fin Ctee; Liveryman Worshipful Co of Shipwrights 1983; *Recreations* real tennis, rackets, squash, wine tasting, opera, the Church of England; *Clubs* Hawks, Queen's, MCC; *Style—* Simon Kverndal, Esq; 48 Ebury St, London SW1W 0LU (☎ 071 730 4274); 2 Essex Court, Temple, London EC4Y 9AP (☎ 071 583 8381, fax 071 353 0998, telex 8812528)

KWIATKOWSKI, Lady Barbara; *née* Legge; da of late 7 Earl of Dartmouth; *b* 1916; *m* 1945, Adam Kwiatowski, Lt Polish Army; 4 s; *Career* formerly in First Aid Nursing Yeo; *Style—* The Lady Barbara Kwiatkowski; The Bothy, Patshull Park, Wolverhampton, W Midlands

KYLE, Andy; *Career* picture editor Daily Mail; *Style—* Andy Kyle, Esq; Daily Mail, Northcliffe House, 2 Derry St, London W8 5TT (☎ 071 938 6373, fax 071 937 5560)

KYLE, James; CBE (1989); s of John Kyle (d 1978), of Brocklamont, Ballymena, N Ireland, and Dorothy Frances, *née* Skillen (d 1967); *b* 26 March 1925; *Educ* Ballymena Acad, Queen's Univ Belfast (MB BCh, MCh, DSc); *m* 31 July 1950, Dorothy Elizabeth, da of Alexander Galbraith (d 1945); 2 da (Frances b 1952, Maureen b 1956); *Career* lectr in surgery Univ of Liverpool 1957, sr lectr Univ of Aberdeen 1959, sr surgn Aberdeen Royal Infirmary, chm Grampian Health Bd; former chm: BMA Rep Body 1984-87, Scot Ctee for Hosp Med Servs 1977-81, Scot Jt Conslts Ctee, 1984-89; memb Gen Med Cncl 1979-; FRCS 1954, FRCSI 1954, FRCSEd 1964; *Books* Pye's Surgical Handicraft (1962), Peptic Ulceration (1960), Crohn's Disease (1972), Scientific Foundations of Surgery (1967); *Recreations* skiing, amateur radio GM4CHX, philately; *Clubs* Royal Northern, University; *Style—* James Kyle, Esq, CBE; Grianan, 74 Rubislaw, Den North, Aberdeen AB2 4AN (☎ 0224 317 966); Aberdeen Royal Infirmary, AB9 2ZB (☎ 0224 681 818); Grampian Health Board, 1 Albyn Place, Aberdeen (☎ 0224 589 901)

KYLE, Kenneth Francis; s of Capt Samuel Kyle (d 1977), of Bangor, N Ireland, and Jean, *née* McClintock; *b* 19 Aug 1934; *Educ* Coleraine Acad, Queens Univ Belfast (MB ChB, BAO, MCh, MD); *m* 11 July 1958, Barbara Margaret, da of George Wilson (d 1987), of Belfast; 1 s (Mark Christopher b 20 May 1959), 1 da (Stephanie b 6 Aug 1961); *Career* Lt-Col TA 1952-65; conslt urologist i/c Dept of Urology Western Infirmary Glasgow, hon lectr urology Univ of Glasgow; pres Scottish Urological Assoc 1990-; contrib Robb and Smith Operative Surgery 1970, pubns on ultrasound and renal transplantation in nat jls; FRCS 1963; memb: Br Assoc Urological Surgns, BMA; *Recreations* golf, walking; *Style—* Kenneth Kyle, Esq; 13 Campsie View Dr, Strathblane, Stirlingshire G63 9JE (☎ 0360 70522); Department of Urology, Western Infirmary, Glasgow (☎ 041 339 8822)

KYLE, Dr Peter McLeod; s of Andrew Brown Kyle, of Ravens Court, Thorntonhall, and late Janet, *née* McLeod; *b* 19 Aug 1951; *Educ* Glasgow HS, Univ of Glasgow (MB ChB); *m* 25 March 1982, Valerie Anne, da of James Steele, of Mairi Lodge, Hamilton; 1 s (Alasdair b 23 Jan 1983), 2 da (Catriona Jane b 20 Dec 1984, Gillian Fiona b 16 Feb 1989); *Career* conslt ophthamologist Great Glasgow Health Bd 1982, memb Med Appeal Tbnl 1985-, hon clinical lectr Univ of Glasgow 1985 (lectr in ophthalmology 1980-84), ophthalmic advsr Queens Coll Glasgow 1985-; FRCS (Glasgow and Edinburgh), FCOphth; *Clubs* Glasgow Art, Golf House (Elie); *Style—* Dr Peter Kyle

KYLE, Peter William (*né* Buchan-Kyle); s of Robert Buchan-Kyle (d 1960), and Evelyn, *née* Palliser-Bosomworth; *b* 21 Nov 1948; *Educ* Rambert Sch of Ballet London, Institut For Bühnentanz Köln Germany; *m* Kathryn Anna, *née* Grundy; 2 da (Abigail b 1 Nov 1971, Charlotte b 22 Dec 1975); *Career* solo dancer and choreographer: Northern Dance Theatre Manchester 1970-74, NZ Ballet 1974-75; dance advsr Leicestershire Educn Authy 1975-81, dance offr Arts Cncl of GB 1981-83, artistic dir Queens Hall Arts Centre Hexham Northumberland 1983-88, chief exec The Scottish Ballet 1988-; fndr: Leicestershire Co Sch of Dance, Nat Festival of Youth Dance, Nat Youth Dance Co; FRSA; *Recreations* education, cinema, music, drama, visual arts; *Style—* Peter Kyle, Esq; The Scottish Ballet, 261 West Princes St, Glasgow, Scotland G4 9EE (☎ 041 331 2931, fax 041 331 2629)

KYLE, (James) Terence; s of James Kyle (d 1976), of Belfast, and Elizabeth, *née* Cinnamond; *b* 9 May 1946; *Educ* The Royal Belfast Acad Inst, Christ's Coll Cambridge (MA); *m* 17 May 1975, Diana, da of Duncan Sager Jackson, of Buxton; 1 s (Robin b 1984), 2 da (Susan b 1979, Alison b 1981); *Career* ptnr Linklaters & Paines 1979- (asst slr 1972-79); memb City of London Slrs Co 1979; memb Law Soc 1972; *Recreations* cricket, squash; *Style—* Terence Kyle, Esq; Linklaters & Paines, Barrington House, 59-67 Gresham St, London EC2Y 7JA (☎ 071 606 7080, fax 071 606 5113, telex 884349)

KYNGE, Maj (John) Julian; s of Lt Col Sydney John Kynge, MC and bar (d 1950), and Marian Hinchcliffe, *née* Lancaster (d 1977); *b* 15 Jan 1932; *Educ* Canford, RMA Sandhurst, RMC of S Schrivenham; *m* 18 Nov 1961, Augusta Pauline Foster, da of Rev Clifford Hubert Davies (d 1980), Canon of York; 1 s (James b 1963), 2 da (Marian b 1962, Madelaine b 1969); *Career* Regular Army Offr, Maj; served: Korea, Japan, Malaya, Hong Kong, Cyprus, Aden, Malaysia; farmer and landowner; *Recreations* game shooting, fishing, cricket; *Clubs* Army and Navy, Farmers; *Style—* Maj Julian Kynge; Potto Grange, Northallerton, N Yorks, (☎ 0642 700212)

KYRLE POPE, Vice Adm Sir Ernle John; KCB (1976); s of Cdr Rowland Cecil Kyrle Pope (d 1976), and late Agnes Jessie MacDonald; *b* 22 May 1921; *Educ* RNC Dartmouth; *m* 21 Dec 1968, Phyllis Mary Webber; 5 s (Christopher, Andrew, Nicholas, Martin, Jonathan); *Career* served WWII HMS Decoy 1962-64, dir Naval Equipment 1964-66, CO HMS Eagle 1966-68, Flag Offr Western Fleet Flotillas 1969-71, COS to C in C Western Fleet 1971-74, Cdr Allied Naval Forces S Europe 1974-76, Rear Adm 1969, Vice Adm 1972; pres RN Assoc; *Clubs* Army and Navy; *Style—* Sir Ernie J Kyrle Pope, KCB; Homme House, Much Marcle, Ledbury, Hereford

KYRLE POPE, Rear Adm Michael Donald; CB (1969), MBE (1945), DL (Hertfordshire 1983); s of Cdr Rowland Kyrle Cecil Pope, DSO, OBE, DL, RN (d 1976), of Ledbury, Herefordshire, and Agnes Jessie, *née* Macdonald (d 1968); *b* 1 Oct 1916; *Educ* Wellington; *m* Angela Suzanne, da of Adm Sir Geoffrey Layton, GBE, KCMG, DSO (d 1964), of Rowland's Castle, Hants; 1 s (James), 1 da (Emma); *Career* joined RN 1934-70, Submarine Serv, HMS Vanguard 1946-47, Sr Naval Offr Persian Gulf 1962-64, Cdre Intelligence Def Intelligence Staff MOD 1965-67, Rear Adm COS to C-in-C Far East Singapore 1967-69; gen mangr Middle East Navigation Aids Serv (Bahrain) 1971-77, dir Jerusalem and East Mission Tst 1978-; dean's administrator St Albans Cathedral 1977-80; *Recreations* country interests, sailing; *Clubs* Army & Navy; *Style—* Rear Adm Michael Kyrle Pope, CB, MBE, DL; Hopfields, Westmill, Buntingford, Herts

KYTE, Thomas; *b* 4 June 1947; *m* 1970, Lynn Dora Harding; 2 da, 1 s; *Career* H M Inland Revenue 1963-65, investment commentator Financial Times 1970-77 (statistician 1966-70), writer Questor column Daily Telegraph 1977-86, city ed The Independent 1987-88 (dep city ed 1986-87), dir Brunswick Public Relations 1988-; *Recreations* sports, literature, cooking; *Style—* Thomas Kyte, Esq; Brunswick Public Relations, 15 Lincolns Inn Fields, London WC2A 3ED (☎ 071 404 5959, fax 071 831 2823)

L

L'ETANG, Dr Hugh Joseph Charles James; s of Dr Joseph Georges L'Etang (d 1966), of London, and Frances Helène Maas (d 1961); *b* 23 Nov 1917; *Educ* Haileybury, St John's Coll Oxford (BA), Bart's (BM BCh), Harvard Sch of Public Health; *m* 1951, Cecily Margaret, da of Frank Stanley Tinker (d 1923), of Barrowmore Hall, Cheshire; 1 s (Guy), 1 da (Jacqueline); *Career* RAMC 1943-46, RMO 5 Bn Royal Berks Regt, served Normandy and NW Europe 1944-46 (despatches), RAMC (TA) 1947-55, Lt-Col RAMC 1953-56, OC 167 Field Ambulance (TA); med advsr: Sun Life Assurance Society 1947-5, N Thames Gas Board 1948-56, British European Airways 1956-58; head of Med Dept John Wyeth & Bros Ltd 1964-69 (med advsr 1958-64); ed: The Practitioner 1973-82 (dep ed 1969-72), Travel Medical International 1982-; ed in chief RSM Round Table Series, conslt ed The Physician; memb Royal Utd Servs Inst, Int Inst Strategic Studies, Mil Commentators Circle; hon fell Coll of Physicians of Philadelphia 1985; *Books* The Pathology of Leadership (1969), Fit to Lead? (1980); *Recreations* reading, study of medical aspects of military and foreign affrs; *Clubs* United Oxford & Cambridge Univ; *Style—* Dr Hugh L'Etang; 27 Sispara Gardens, West Hill Rd, London SW18 1LG (☎ 081 870 3836)

LA ROCHE, Anthony Philip; TD (1978); s of Philip La Roche (d 1988), and Ruby, *née* Peach; *b* 10 July 1944; *Educ* St George's Coll Weybridge Surrey; *m* 18 Sept 1965, Jane Elizabeth, da of Herbert Custerson; 2 da (Amy Jane b 1972, Sophie Elizabeth b 1979); *Career* TA 1962-82; md: Allen Harvey Ross Ltd 1976-81, Cater Allen Futures Ltd 1981-; dir: Cater Allen Hldgs plc 1982-, London Int Fin Futures Exchange 1984-; *Recreations* swimming, cycling, field sports; *Clubs* City of London; *Style—* Anthony La Roche, Esq, TD; Cater Allen Futures Ltd, 20 Birchin Lane, London, EC3V 9DJ (☎ 071 283 7432, fax 071 283 7001)

LA TROBE-BATEMAN, Richard George Saumarez; s of John Saumarez La Trobe-Bateman, of Sark, CI, and Margaret Jane, *née* Schmid; *b* 17 Oct 1938; *Educ* Westminster, St Martin's Sch of Art, RCA (MDesRCA); *m* 26 April 1969, Mary Elizabeth, da of Arthur Jolly, JP (d 1984), of Hove; 1 s (Will b 1973), 2 da (Emily b 1971, Alice b 1976); *Career* studied sculpture under Anthony Caro at St Martin's Sch of Art 1958-61, studied furniture under David Pye at RCA 1965-68; exhibited: UK Design Centre, Crafts Cncl, V & A, Br Craft Centre, Contemporary Applied Art; exhibited in: Belgium, Holland, Denmark, Austria, France, USA, Japan; works in pub collections incl: V & A, Crafts Cncl, Leeds City Art Collection, Tyne and Wear Art Collection, Shipley Gallery, Portsmouth Gallery, Craft Study Centre (Bath); memb Crafts Cncl 1982-86 (work presented to HRH Prince of Wales by Craft Cncl 1984); prof of furniture San Diego State Univ USA 1986-87; *Clubs* Contemporary Applied Arts; *Style—* Richard La Trobe-Bateman, Esq; Elm House, Batcombe, Shepton Mallet, Somerset BA4 6AB (☎ 074 985 442)

LABAND, Paul Alexander Kenneth; s of Oliver Ernest Kenneth Laband, MBE, of Glenyra, Earlsferry, Elie, Fife, and Margaret Ann, *née* MacCallum; *b* 15 Aug 1948; *Educ* Strathallan Sch Forgandenny Perth, Downing Coll Cambridge (BA); *m* 22 Aug 1970, Sheila, da of Albert Russell, of Poole, Dorset; 2 da (Kathryn b 14 June 1974, Caroline b 15 Feb 1977); *Career* stockbroker Simon & Coates 1970-73, asst exec dir Abbey Life 1984-86 (portfolio mangr 1973-84), dep md Abbey Life Investment Services Ltd 1989 (dir 1986-88); ASIA; *Recreations* athletics, sailing, singing; *Style—* Paul Laband, Esq; Compton Cottage, 5 Canford Crescent, Canford Cliffs, Poole, Dorset BH13 7NB (☎ 0202 700460); Abbey Life Assurance Co Ltd, 80 Holdenhurst Rd, Bournemouth BH8 8AL (☎ 0202 292373, fax 0202 296816, telex 41310)

LABOUCHERE, Sir George Peter; GBE (1965), KCMG (1951); s of Lt-Col Frank Anthony Labouchere (d 1948), of 15 Draycott Ave, London; *b* 2 Dec 1905; *Educ* Charterhouse, La Sorbonne; *m* 1943, Rachel Katharine, da of Hon Eustace Hamilton-Russell (d 1962, 6 s of 8 Viscount Boyne); *Career* FO 1929, cnsllr Nanking 1946, Buenos Aires 1948; min: Vienna 1950-53, Hungary 1953-55; ambass to: Belgium 1955-60, Spain 1960-66 (ret); pres Shropshire branch of CPRE; FRSA; *Recreations* shooting, fishing, oriental ceramics, modern art; *Clubs* White's, Brooks's, Beefsteak, Pratt's, Dilettante Soc; *Style—* Sir George Labouchere, GBE, KCMG; Dudmaston, Bridgnorth, Shropshire (☎ 0746 780 351)

LABOVITCH, Carey Elizabeth (Mrs S Tesler); da of Neville Labovitch, MBE, and Sonia Deborah, *née* Barney; *b* 20 April 1960; *Educ* Lyçée Français De Londres, St Paul's Girls' Sch London, St Hilda's Coll Oxford (MA); *m* 1990, S Tesler; *Career* magazine publisher 1980-; md The Cadogan Press Group Ltd, fndr publisher of Blitz Magazine 1980 and The MDB Magazine Directory Book 1984, The HMV Christmas Magazine, The Guardian Impact Magazine; awards for publishing: Guardian Best Graphics award 1981, Magazine Publishing Entrepreneur of the Year award (highly commended) 1984, BBC Enterprise award for Small Businesses 1985, Businesswoman of the Year award 1986, Blitz Best feature in a Consumer Magazine 1989, Impact Colour Supplement of the Year Award 1990; yst ever finalist in Veuve Clicquot/ IOD, judge for Guardian/NUS Student Media Awards 1987, 1988 1989 and BBC Enterprise Awards 1987; patron of the Virgin Charitable Fndn; *Recreations* cartooning, cinema, photography, reading; *Style—* Ms Carey Labovitch; 40-44 Newman Street, London W1P 5PA (☎ 071 436 5211, fax 071 436 5290)

LACAMP, Philippe Frederick; s of Philippe Albert Lacamp (d 1982), of Milton Regis, Kent, and Dorothea Jeanette, *née* Barker; *b* 12 March 1940; *Educ* City of London Sch; *m* 31 July 1965, Marie-Louise, da of Capt Peter Stephens Impey, of High Barn, Finstall, Worcs; 1 s (Philippe Paul b 5 Feb 1969), 2 da (Melissa b 26 April 1971, Camilla b 18 Dec 1972); *Career* dir Allders Ltd 1973-82, independent conslt 1982-; mangr C of E primary sch, tstee Contacts Charity for Handicapped Children, chm St Mary's Norton Restoration Ctee; Freeman: City of London 1961, Worshipful Co of Blacksmiths 1966; MBCS 1963; *Books* Microcomputers in Retail (1984); *Recreations* singing, piano, tennis, golf; *Clubs* Kent and Canterbury; *Style—* Philippe Lacamp, Esq; Prospect House, High St, Westerham, Kent TN16 1RG (☎ 0959 644 22, fax 0959 644 22)

LACE, John Herbert; s of William Stanley Lace (d 1958), and Helen (d 1985); *b* 12 Sept 1934; *Educ* King William's Coll; *m* 2 Sept 1961, Ann Morwen; 1 s (Jonathan b 1967), 1 da (Victoria b 1970); *Career* REME 1953-55; currently Lt-Col Engr and Staff Corps RE; md: Babcock Energy Ltd 1987- (projects dir 1984-87, construction dir 1977-84); exec dir Babcock International Group 1989; *Recreations* cycling, golf, aviation; *Clubs* Royal Troon Golf; *Style—* John Lace, Esq; Brackenhurst, 13 Symington Road, North Symington, Ayrshire KA1 5PZ; Babcock Energy Ltd, Porterfield Rd, Renfrew PA4 8DJ (☎ 041 885 3340, fax 041 885 3346)

LACEY, Dr (John) Hubert; s of Percy Hubert Lacey, of Leics, and Sheila Margaret, *née* Neal; *b* 4 Nov 1944; *Educ* Loughborough GS, Univ of St Andrews (MB ChB), Univ of London (MPhil), Univ of Dundee (MD), RCOG (DipObst); *m* 7 Feb 1976, Susan Millicent, da of Richard England Liddiard, CBE, *qv*, of Oxford Lodge, Wimbledon SW19; 2 s (Ben William Hubert b 1979, Jonathan Rupert Neal b 1982), 1 da (Emma Louise Susan b 1978); *Career* jr hosp appts Dundee, St Thomas's and St George's Hosps 1969-78; hon conslt psychiatrist: Middx Hosp 1978-80, St George's Hosp 1980-; conslt i/c Bulimia Clinic 1980-, reader Univ of London 1987- (sr lectr 1978-86), head of adult psychiatry St Georges Hosp Med Sch 1987-; author of several res papers on anorexia, bulimia, psychosomatic med and psychopharmacology; patron Eating Disorders Assoc; sec: gen psychiatry RCPsych, Psychiatry Ctee Univ of London, Div of Psychiatry Wandsworth and Merton Health Authy; memb Int Coll of Psychosomatic Med; Freeman: City of London 1986, Worshipful Co of Plasterers 1986; memb RSM, MRCPsych 1974, FRCPsych 1985; *Books* Psychological Management of the Physically Ill (1989); *Recreations* reading, interior decoration, hill walking; *Clubs* Athenaeum; *Style—* Dr Hubert Lacey; 5 Atherton Drive, Wimbledon, London SW19 5LB (☎ 081 947 5976); Rock Cottage, Church St, Amberley, W Sussex (☎ 0798 831209); Reader & Head, Adult Psychiatry Section, Academic Dept of Psychiatry, Jenner Wing, St George's Hosp Med Sch, Tooting, London SW17 0RE (☎ 081 372 9944 ext 55528, fax 081 767 4696, telex 845291)

LACEY, Nicholas Stephen; s of John Stephen Lacey, of Highgate, London, and Norma, *née* Hayward; *b* 20 Dec 1943; *Educ* Univ Coll Sch, Emmanuel Coll Cambridge (MA), Architectural Assoc London (AADip); *m* 1, 1965 (m dis 1976), Nicola, da of Dr F A Mann; 2 s (Joshua b 1968, William b 1973), 1 da (Olivia b 1970); *m* 2, 1981, Juliet, da of Dr Wallace Aykroyd, CBE (d 1979); 2 da (Laetitia b 1978, Theodora b 1980); *Career* ptnr: Nicholas Lacey & Assoc Architects 1971-83, Nicholas Lacey Jobst & Ptnrs Architects 1983-; winner: Wallingford Competition 1972, Crown Reach 1977; jt winner Arunbridge 1977, prize winner Paris Opera House Competition 1983; *Recreations* music, theatre, sailing; *Style—* Nicholas Lacey, Esq; Nicholas Lacey, Jobst & Partners, Reeds Wharf, Mill St, London SE1 (☎ 071 231 5154, home: 071 237 6281)

LACEY, Peter William; s of Maj Eric Oliver Lacey (d 1947), of Moseley, Birmingham, and Edna Joyce Annie (Joy), *née* Bennett (d 1986); *b* 13 Nov 1945; *Educ* The Old Hall Wellington Salop Solihull Warwickshire; *m* 22 Nov 1969, Pamela Muriel, da of Neville Nicholl (d 1981), of Musbury, Devon; 3 s (David b 1972, Guy b 1975, Benjamin b 1980); *Career* CA; articled clerk Chas Richards & Co Birmingham 1964-68, Goodland Bull & Co Taunton, Robson Rhodes Taunton, Apsleys Wellington 1969-90; dir Community Cncl for Somerset 1990-, co sec Somerset Assoc of Local Cncls 1990-; chm of govrs: Court Fields Sch Wellington, W Buckland Co Primary Sch; formerly chm W Buckland Parish Cncl, former memb Somerset Co Jt Ctee COSIRA, former memb Ctee Community Cncl for Somerset, former chm Somerset Customer Consultative Ctee Wessex Water, chm Somerset Assoc of Local Cncls 1986-89, memb Regnl Bd Wessex and chm Regnl Rivers Advsy Ctee NRA 1989-; ACA 1969, FCA 1979; *Recreations* gardening; *Clubs* Old Silhillians; *Style—* Peter Lacey, Esq; The Old Forge, West Buckland, Wellington, Somerset TA21 9JS (☎ 0823 662376); Community Council for Somerset, St Margarets, Hamilton Rd, Taunton, Somerset (☎ 0823 331222)

LACEY, Prof Richard Westgarth; s of Jack Lacey, and Sybil Lacey; *b* 11 Oct 1940; *Educ* Felsted, Jesus Coll cambridge (BA, MB BChir, MD), The London Hosp (DCH); *m* Fionna; 2 da (Miranda, Gemma); *Career* The London Hosp 1964-66, Bristol Royal Infirmary 1966-68, reader Univ of Bristol 1973-74 (lectr 1968-73), conslt in infectious diseases King's Lynn E Anglia RHA 1974-83, conslt in chemical pathology King's Lynn Queen Elizabeth Hosp 1975-83, prof of clinical microbiology Univ of Leeds 1983-; numerous pubns in jls; memb: Pathological Soc of GB, Br Soc for AntiMicrobial Chemotherapy, conslt to WHO; FRCPath; *Books* Safe Shopping, Safe Cooking, Safe Eating (1989); *Recreations* gardening, antique restoration (intermittently); *Style—* Prof Richard Lacey; Department of Microbiology, University of Leeds, Leeds LS2 9JT (☎ 0532 335596, fax 0532 335596)

LACEY, Timothy John Twyford; s of William Joseph Lacey, of Sunbury on Thames, and Phyllis Edith, *née* Thomas; *b* 17 May 1935; *Educ* Downside; *m* 24 March 1962, Anne Patricia, da of Maj Reginald William Henly-Stuart (d 1987), of Hereford; 2 s (Michael b 1963, Christopher b 1965); *Career* chief exec William Lacey Group plc and of all subsid cos; *Recreations* golf, farming; *Style—* Timothy Lacey, Esq; Little Wildwood Farm, Wildwood Lane, Cranleigh, Surrey GU6 8JR; Elmbridge House, Elmbridge Lane, Woking, Surrey GU22 9AF (☎ 0483 740700, fax 0483 740675, car 0836 713060)

LACHELIN, Dr Gillian Claire Liborel; da of Pierre Joseph Augustin Lachelin (d 1977), and Joan Kathleen Moncaster, *née* Hilbery (d 1963); *b* 5 Feb 1940; *Educ* Princess Helena Coll Sch for Girls, Girton Coll Cambridge (MA, MB BChir), Univ of London (MD); *Career* registrar in obstetrics and gynaecology UCH London 1969-72, lectr and hon sr registrar Univ Coll Med Sch and UCH 1972-77, reader and hon conslt in obstetrics and gynaecology UCL and Middx Sch of Med 1977-; memb: Blair Bell Res Soc 1975, Soc for Endocrinology 1979, Br Fertility Soc 1981, Soc for Gynaecologic Investigation USA 1982; FRCOG 1982 (MRCOG 1969); *Books* Miscarriage The Facts (1985), Practical Gynaecology (with D L Y Liu, 1989), Clinical Reproductive Endocrinology (1991); *Recreations* travel, photography, gardening; *Style—* Dr Gillian Lachelin; Obstetric Unit, 88-96 Chenies Mews, Huntley St, London WC1 (☎ 387 9300 ext 5410)

LACHS, His Hon Judge Henry Lazarus; s of Samuel Lachs (d 1960); *b* 31 Dec 1927; *Educ* Liverpool Inst HS, Pembroke Coll Cambridge; *m* 1959, Dr Edith Lachs, JP, da of Ludwig Bergel; 4 da; *Career* rec of the Crown Ct 1972-79, circuit judge 1979-; regnl chm Mental Health Review Tbnl 1968-79; *Style—* His Hon Judge Lachs; 41 Menlove Gdns West, Liverpool L18 (☎ 051 722 5936)

LACK, Alastair Iliffe; s of Gordon Iliffe Lack (d 1985), and Joan Hardwick, *née* Riddell; *b* 25 Dec 1944; *Educ* Whitgift Sch, Univ Coll Oxford (BA); *m* 9 Jan 1971,

Catherine Noel, da of John Conran Smerdon (d 1984); 1 da (Sarah Charlotte b 10 Dec 1975); *Career* prodn asst further educn BBC TV 1975, prodr evening sequences BBC radio 1977; World Service: talks writer 1971, prodr 1971-77, sr prodr 1977-84, exec prodr 1984-87, asst head current affrs 1987-88, dep head 1988-90, head of prodns in English 1990; *Recreations* travel, sport, literature; *Clubs* MCC; *Style*— Alastair Lack, Esq; 77 Whitmore Rd, Harrow, Middlesex HA1 4AE (☎ 081 423 2755); BBC World Service, Bush House, Aldwych, London WC2 (☎ 071 257 2782)

LACK, Dr (John) Alastair; s of Prof C H Lack, of Meads Cottage, Coombe Bissett, Salisbury, Wilts, and Janet Doreen, *née* Steele; *b* 1 Sept 1942; *Educ* Westminster, UCH (MB BS), Imperial Coll London (DIC); *m* 2 July 1966, (Patricia) Margaret, da of Alec Reynolds; 1 s (Christopher b 7 Jan 1975), 2 da (Juliette b 14 March 1970, Katherine b 18 May 1973); *Career* asst prof anaesthesia Stanford Hosp San Francisco USA 1971-73, conslt anaesthetist Salisbury Hospitals 1974-, regn mgmnt Salisbury Health Authy; chm Computing Anaesthesia Soc GB and NI; FFARCS 1968; *Books* On Computing and Technology in Anaesthesia and Intensive Care; *Recreations* music, wine, swimming, gardening; *Style*— Dr Alastair Lack; The River House, Coombe Bissett, Salisbury, Wilts SP5 4LX (☎ 0722 77303); Anaesthetic Department, Odstock Hospital, Salisbury, Wilts SP2 8BJ (☎ 0722 336262)

LACON, Edmund Richard Vere; s and h of Sir Edmund Vere Lacon, 8 Bt; *b* 2 Oct 1967; *Style*— Edmund Lacon, Esq

LACON, Sir Edmund Vere; 8 Bt (UK 1818); s of Sir George Vere Francis Lacon, 7 Bt (d 1980), by his 1 w Hilary; *b* 3 May 1936; *Educ* Woodbridge Sch Suffolk; *m* 1963, Gillian, da of Jack Henry Middleditch, of Wrentham, Suffolk; 1 s, 1 da; *Heir* s, Edmund Richard Vere b 2 Oct 1967; *Career* gen mangr; *Style*— Sir Edmund Lacon, Bt

LACY, Ernest Joseph Henry; JP; s of James Herbert Lacy (d 1959), and Amelia Mary, *née* Gilbert (d 1969); *b* 6 Oct 1912; *Educ* Willesden Tech Coll; *m* 24 March 1940, Irene Sara Lynforth, da of John Alfred Pike (d 1934); 2 da (Diane Lynforth (Mrs Bell) b 1941, Jennifer Mary (Mrs Picklance) b 1947); *Career* bldg and public works contractor; chm and md of own business; chm Arun DC 1984 (chm Planning and Devpt Ctee), fin and admin memb Littlehampton Harbour Bd; tstee Arundel Castle; Freeman: City of London, Worshipful Co of Paviors; FCIOB; *Recreations* local affairs, deep sea fishing, wood carving; *Clubs* City Livery; *Style*— Ernest Lacy, Esq, JP; Seafurl, Second Ave, Felpham, West Sussex PO22 7LJ (☎ 0243 582 157)

LACY, John Trend; CBE (1982); s of Rev Hubert Lacy (d 1982), and Gertrude Markham (d 1983); *b* 15 March 1928; *Educ* Kings Sch Ely Cambs; 16 June 1956, Pamela, da of John Guerin; 1 s (Nicholas b 23 Dec 1957); *Career* RN 1945-48; Cons Pty agent London and Bucks 1950-60, CCO agent W Mids N and SE 1960-85, gen dir Cons Pty Campaigning 1989- (dir 1985-89); memb Nat Soc Cons and Unionist Agents; *Recreations* politics, family; *Clubs* St Stephen's, Carlton; *Style*— John Lacy, Esq, CBE; Conservative Central Office, 32 Smith Square, London SW1P 3HH (☎ 071 222 9000, fax 071 222 1135)

LACY, Patrick Bryan Finucane; s of Sir Maurice John Pierce Lacy, 2 Bt (d 1965); and hp to Btcy of bro, Sir Hugh Maurice Pierce Lacy, 3 Bt; *b* 18 April 1948; *Educ* Downside; *m* 1971, Phyllis Victoria, da of Edgar P H James; 1 s, 1 da; *Style*— Patrick Lacy, Esq; 11 Tudor Gdns, Barnes, SW13

LADD, Capt Martin Leonard; OBE (1982); s of Leonard Stanley Ladd (d 1968), of London and Yorks, and Mary, *née* Whitelock; *b* 1 June 1944; *Educ* Marist Coll Hull, Britannia Royal Naval Coll Dartmouth; *Career* joined RN as Aircraft Artificier 1960, commissioned as Upper Yardman 1963, BRNC Dartmouth 1963-64 and 1965-66, HMS Aurora 1964-65, HMS Tenby 1967-68, Exec Offr HMS Lewiston 1968-70, Navigating Offr HMS NAIAD 1971-72, Ops Offr HMS Arethusa and Achilles 1972-74, Staff Offr BRNC Dartmouth 1975-77, Exec Offr HMS Avenger 1977-79, staff of Flag Sea Trg 1979-80, Cdr MOD in DNW and C-in-C fleet Staff 1980-84; CO Type 42 Destroyers: HMS Birmingham 1984, HMS Edinburgh 1986; Mil Asst to Vice-Chief Def Staff 1987-88, Capt 1987, Asst Dir Requirements (Ships) MOD and pres Admiralty Interview Bd 1988-90; left RN 1990; dir: Brighter Prospects Ltd 1990-; Future Training Services (Winchester) 1990-, FBIM 1991; *Recreations* youth training, golf; *Clubs* Winchester C of C, RN, Andover Golf; *Style*— Capt Martin Ladd, OBE; c/o Midland Bank, High St, Winchester, Hampshire

LADENBURG, Michael John Carlisle; s of John Arthur George Ladenburg (d 1990), of W Sussex, and Yvonne Rachel Bankier, *née* Carlisle (d 1968); *b* 2 Feb 1945; *Educ* Charterhouse, Christ Church Oxford (MA); *m* 1971, Susan Elizabeth, da of Dr George Denys Laing, of Surrey; 1 s (William b 1980), 2 da (Harriet b 1975, Olivia b 1978); *Career* merchant banker; dir: J Henry Schroder Wagg & Co Ltd 1979-88, Robert Fleming & Co Ltd 1988-; *Recreations* music, sailing, golf, skiing, reading, tennis; *Clubs* Hurlingham, Tandridge Golf; *Style*— Michael Ladenburg, Esq; 62 Cloncurry St, London SW6 6DU (☎ 071 736 5605); Robert Fleming & Co Ltd, 25 Copthall Ave, London EC2R 7DR (☎ 071 638 5858)

LADENIS, Nicholas Peter (Nico); s of Peter Ladenis (d 1960), of Kenya, and Constance, *née* Antoniadis (d 1976); *b* 22 April 1934; *Educ* Prince of Wales Sch Nairobi, Regent St Poly, LSE, Univ of Hull (BSc Econ); *m* 29 June 1963, Dinah-Jane, da of Theodore Zissu (d 1942); 2 da (Natasha Nicole b 29 April 1964, Isabella Therese b 28 June 1966); *Career* restaurateur; various appointments incl: Caltex Kenya 1962, Ford Motor Company, Sunday Times; opened first restaurant in 1971, fndr chef and patron Chez Nico 1973- (with wife Dinah-Jane as ptnr); first distinction Good Food Guide 1976, second Michelin 1984 (first 1981), Chef of the Year 1988; *Books* My Gastronomy (1987); *Recreations* food, travelling, family; *Style*— Nico Ladenis, Esq; Chez Nico Ltd, 35 Great Portland Place, London W1N 5DD (☎ 071 436 8846, fax 071 436 0134)

LADER, Prof Malcolm Harold; s of Abe Lader (d 1979), of Liverpool, and Minnie, *née* Sholl; *b* 27 Feb 1936; *Educ* Liverpool Inst HS, Univ of Liverpool (BSc, MB ChB, MD), London Univ (PhD, DPM, DSc); *m* 16 April 1961, Susan Ruth, da of Louis Packer (d 1990), of Hendon, Middx; 3 da (Deborah b 1966, Vicki b 1969, Charlotte b 1972); *Career* memb external scientific staff MRC 1966-, conslt Bethlem Royal and Maudsley Hosp 1970-, prof of clinical psychopharmacology Univ of London 1978-; tstee Mental Health Fndn; memb Advsy Cncl Misuse of Drugs; FRCPsych 1971; *Books* Psychiatry on Trial (1977), Dependence on Tranquillizers (1984), Biological Treatments in Psychiatry (1990); *Recreations* antiques, English watercolours; *Clubs* RSM; *Style*— Prof Malcolm Lader; 11 Kelsey Way, Beckenham, Kent BR3 3LP (☎ 081 650 0366); 10 Dedham Mill, Dedham, Essex CO7 6DH; Inst of Psychiatry, Decrespigny Park, London SE5 8AF (☎ 071 703 0770, fax 071 703 5796)

LAFLIN, Reginald Ernest; s of Sydney Ernest Laflin (d 1975), of The Crescent, Rustington, West Sussex, and Rosie, *née* Nichols (d 1988); *b* 21 March 1926; *Educ* Sir Walter St John's Public Sch, Battersea Poly (HNC), Borough Poly (HNC); *m* 28 Sept 1952, (Ruby) Elsie, da of George Francis Brown; 1 s (Michael John), 1 da (Susan); *Career* WWII pilot/navigator in trg RAFVR 1943-45; md APV Paralec Ltd (chief engr APV Paramount Ltd) 1952-75, assoc ptnr Revell Hayward & Ptnrs 1975-78, ptnr EG Phillips Son & Ptnrs 1978-88, ptnr Nordale Assocs 1988-; CEng, FIEE, FIMechE, FICBSE, FIMechIE, MIM, FID; *Clubs* Directors; *Style*— Reginald Laflin, Esq; 9 Gorham Ave, Rottingdean, Brighton, E Sussex (☎ 0273 300 106); Noredale Assocs, 51-53 Burney Rd, Greenwich, London SE10 8EX (☎ 081 858 4482, fax 081 858 5876, telex 8951039)

LAGDEN, Ronald Gordon; s of Reginald Bousfield Lagden, OBE, MC (d 1944), and late Christine, *née* Haig; *b* 4 Sept 1927; *Educ* Marlborough, RMC Sandhurst (Sword of Honour), Harvard, AMP Univ; *m* 1951, Elizabeth Veronica, da of John Kenneth Mathews (d 1972); 2 s, 1 da; *Career* Lt Queen's Own Cameron Highlanders serv Italy; Maconochie Foods 1947-53, Bowater Scott Corporation 1953-63, md Findus Ltd 1963-68, chm and md Quaker Oats Ltd 1968-71 (chm and pres (Europe) Quaker Oats Co 1971-85, non-exec dir 1985-); non-exec dir: WA Baxter & Sons Ltd, Eldridge Pope; dir Pagepine Ltd, chm Golf Development International (Brussels); *Books* Principles and Practices of Management (jtly); *Recreations* golf, gardening, reading, bridge, family; *Clubs* Royal and Ancient Golf, Sunningdale Golf, Royal Golf de Belique, Pulborough/Anglo Belge (Knightsbridge); *Style*— Ronald Lagden, Esq; Spear Hill Cottage, Ashington, Sussex

LAGESEN, Air Marshal Sir Philip Jacobus; KCB (1979, CB 1974); *Career* Air Cdre RAF 1970, SASO Strike Cmd 1972, Air Vice-Marshal 1972, dep cdr RAF Germany 1973-75, AOC No 1 Gp RAF Strike Cmd 1975-78; AOC 18 Gp Northwood 1978-; *Style*— Air Marshal Sir Philip Lagesen, KCB; c/o Lloyds Bank, 6 Pall Mall, London SW1

LAIDLAW, Charles David Gray; s of George Gray Laidlaw, and Margaret Orr, *née* Crombie; *b* 23 Jan 1954; *Educ* Strathallan Sch, Univ of Edinburgh (LLB); *m* 27 June 1986, Lucy Elizabeth, *née* Brooks; 1 s (Robert Gray b 27 June 1989); *Career* political writer D C Thompson Group 1977-79 (reporter 1975-77), reporter Sunday Express 1980, def intelligence analyst MOD 1980-83, exec Good Relations 1983-85, mangr PA Consulting Group 1985-87, gp mangr Reginald Watts Associates 1987-88; dir: Burson-Marsteller and Burson-Marsteller Financial 1988-90, TMA Group 1990-; Freeman City of Glasgow (hereditary); MIPR 1986, memb Grand Antiquary Soc; *Recreations* rugby, running, writing; *Clubs* London Scottish; *Style*— Charles Laidlaw, Esq; TMA Communications, 6 Victoria Crescent Rd, Glasgow G12 9DB (☎ 041 339 9305, car 0836 702038)

LAIDLAW, Sir Christophor Charles Fraser; s of late Hugh Alexander Lyon Laidlaw; *b* 9 Aug 1922; *Educ* Rugby, St John's Coll Cambridge; *m* 1952, Nina Mary Prichard; 1 s, 3 da; *Career* BP Co Ltd: dir of ops 1971-72, md 1972, dep chm 1980-81; chm BP Oil 1977-81; exec chm ICL plc 1981-84; dir: Commercial Union Assurance 1978-83, Barclays Bank Int 1980-87, Barclays Bank plc 1981-88, Amerada Hess Corporation 1983-, Dalgety plc 1984-, Redland plc 1984-, Mercedes Benz (UK) 1985-; chm Bridon plc 1985-90; pres Chamber of Indust and Commerce in UK 1983-84, dir INSEAD and chm UK Advsy Bd 1987-; Master Worshipful Co of Tallow Chandlers 1988-89; kt 1982; *Style*— Sir Christophor Laidlaw; 22 Hill St, Mayfair, London W1X 7FU

LAIDLAW, (Henry) Renton; s of Henry Renton Laidlaw (d 1989), of Broughty Ferry, Dundee, and Margaret McBeath, *née* Raiker; *b* 6 July 1939; *Educ* James Gillespie's Edinburgh, Daniel Stewart's Coll Edinburgh; *Career* golf corr Evening News Edinburgh 1957-68, news presenter Grampian TV Aberdeen 1968-70, news presenter and reporter BBC Scotland Edinburgh 1970-73, golf corr The London Evening Standard 1973-; ITV, TWI Eurosport, BSB; golf presenter 1973-: presenter BBC Sport on 2 1985-88; *Books* Play Golf (with Peter Alliss), Tony Jacklin: The First 40 Years (with Tony Jacklin), Play Better Golf, Golfing Heroes, Ryder Cup; *Recreations* theatre-going, playing golf, travelling; *Clubs* Caledonian, Sunningdale Golf, Wentworth Golf, Royal Burgess Golf; *Style*— Renton Laidlaw, Esq; Evening Standard, Derry St, London W8 1EE

LAIDLAW, Robin David; s of Alexander Banatyne Stewart Laidlaw (d 1968), and Margaret Alicia, *née* Hutt (d 1981); *b* 8 Oct 1928; *Educ* George Watson's Coll, Heriot Watt Univ; *m* 29 Nov 1951, Noreen Frances, da of Reginald Wilson (d 1979); 1 s (David b 1956), 1 da (Deborah b 1953); *Career* combustion engr; dir: Laidlaw Drew & Co Ltd 1965-, St Serf's Sch Tst 1975- (chm 1967-75); sec Scottish Sailing Assoc 1977-81; CEng, MIMechE; *Recreations* flying (light aircraft, previously Rang gliders and microlights), photography, sailing; *Clubs* Edinburgh Flying, Edinburgh Photographic Society; *Style*— Robin Laidlaw, Esq; The Smiddy, Dalmeny, W Lothian, EH30 9TU; Laidlaw Drew & Co Ltd, Sighthill, Edinburgh EH11 4HG (☎ 031 453 5445, telex 72609, fax 031 453 4793)

LAIDLAW THOMSON, Hilary Dulcie; da of Dr Edward Laidlaw Thomson, Surgn Capt RNVR, and Dulcie Elspeth Mary, *née* Redfearn; *b* 9 July 1939; *Educ* internationally; *m* 26 Oct 1962, Antony Meysey Wigley Severne, s of Charles Edward Severne; 1 s (Charles Edward); *Career* chief exec Media Relations Ltd; *Recreations* gardening, writing, skiing; *Style*— Ms Hilary Laidlaw Thomson; Media Relations, 125 Old Brompton Rd, London SW7 3RN (☎ 071 835 1000)

LAIDLOW, Dr John Michael; s of Dr E V Laidlow, of Rectory Cottage, Rectory Rd, Retford, Notts, and Doreen Waugh, *née* Simpson; *b* 6 June 1948; *Educ* Stonyhurst, Bart's and Univ of London (MB BS); *m* 25 Sept 1977, Heather; 3 da (Charlotte b 5 Sept 1978, Annalise b 8 Jan 1981, Alexa b 20 Oct 1982); *Career* conslt radiologist Royal Hants Co Hosp, med registrar St Mark's Hosp London, house med physician St Bartholomew's Hosp London (former sr registrar radiology); sec Winchester Div BMA; memb BMA, MRCP 1976, FRCR 1983; *Recreations* sports, squash, golf, tennis, skiing; *Style*— Dr John Laidlow; Royal Hampshire County Hospital, Romsey Rd, Winchester, Hants S022 5DG (☎ 0962 863535)

LAIGHT, Barry Pemberton; OBE (1970); s of Donald Norman Laight (d 1935), of Astwood Bank, and Norah, *née* Pemberton (d 1946); *Educ* Johnston Sch Durham, Birmingham Central Tech Coll, Merchant Venturers Tech Coll Bristol, Univ of Bristol (MSc); *m* 17 Feb 1951, Ruth da of Alfred Sutro Murton, DCM, MM (d 1975), of Warsash, Hants; 1 s (Timothy b 1952), 1 da (Deborah b 1954); *Career* chief aerodynamicist Bristol Aeroplane Co 1947-52, tech dir Blackburn and General Aircraft 1952-61, dir mil projects Hawker Siddeley Aviation 1961-77, engrg dir Short Bros 1977-82, sec RAeS 1982-85 (pres 1974-76), conslt DTI, Vertical Axis Wind Turbines 1985-; memb: NATO Advsy Gp on Aerospace R & D, Aircraft Res Assoc, Int Cncl Aeronautical Scis, AERO, Mensa; govr Kingston Poly; FRAes 1955, FInstD 1975, MAIAA 1982, FEng 1981, FIMechE 1983, Eur Ing 1989; *Recreations* music, mathematics, walking; *Clubs* Athenaeum; *Style*— Eur Ing Barry Laight, OBE; Dunelm, 5 Littlemead, Esher, Surrey, KT10 9PE (☎ 0372 63216)

LAINE, Cleo - Clementine Dinah (Mrs John Dankworth); OBE (1979); da of Alexander Campbell, and Minnie, *née* Bullock; *b* 28 Oct 1927; *m* 1, 1947 (m dis 1958), George Langridge; 1 s; m 2, 1958, John Philip William Dankworth; 1 s, 1 da; *Career* vocalist; with The Dankworth Orchestra 1953-58; lead roles in: Seven Deadly Sins Edinburgh Festival and Sadler's Wells 1961, Showboat 1972; acting roles in: A Time to Laugh, Hedda Gabler, The Women of Troy, Edinburgh Festival 1966 and 1967, Collette 1980, The Mystery of Edwin Drood 1986 (winner of Theatre World award, nominated for a Tony award and a Drama Desk award), Into The Woods 1989 (US Nat Tour); record albums incl: That Old Feeling 1985, Cleo Sings Sondheim 1988, Woman to Woman 1989; Gold records incl: Feel the Warm, I'm a Song, Live in Melbourne; Platinum records incl: Best Friends, Sometimes When We Touch; awards incl: Golden Feather award LA Times 1973, Edison award 1974, Variety Club 1977, Singer of the Year (TV Times) 1978, Grammy award (best female jazz vocalist) 1985, Theatre

World award 1986; has appeared on television numerous times and made guest appearances with symphony orchestras in England and abroad; Hon MA Open Univ 1975, Hon DMus Berklee Coll of Music; *Style*— Miss Cleo Laine, OBE; International Artistes Ltd, Regent House, 235 Regent St, London W1 (☎ 071 439 8401)

LAINE, John Bunch; s of John Laine (d 1977), of Springfield, Marford, Wrexham, N Wales, and Marjorie, *née* Bunch (d 1988); *b* 14 Nov 1930; *Educ* Worksop Coll, Univ of Liverpool (MB ChB); *m* 21 Sept 1985, Christine Helen, da of Harry Stephenson (d 1965); 1 da (Charlotte Claire Louise b 18 May 1986); *Career* RNVR 1955-57; conslt surgn: Bolton Royal Infirmary, Maelor Gen Hosp Wrexham; sr examiner and regnl advsr RCSEd, former tutor RCS; fell Assoc of Surgns GB and Ireland, FRCS, FRCSEd; *Recreations* music, flying; *Clubs* Ravenair; *Style*— John Laine, Esq; Maelor Gen Hospital, Wrexham (☎ 0978 291 100)

LAING, Alastair Stuart; CBE (1980), MVO (1959); s of Capt Arthur Henry Laing (d 1943), and Clare May, *née* Ashworth (d 1959); *b* 17 June 1920; *Educ* Sedbergh; *m* 17 July 1946, Audrey Stella, da of Dr Frederick William Hobbs (d 1924); 1 s (Stuart b 1956, d 1961); *Career* WWII: Capt 10 Gurkha Rifles IA 1940-46, 3/10 Gurkha Rifles 1941-42, 10 Gurkha Rifles Regtl Centre 1943-44, seconded to civil admin in Bengal 1944-46; dep dir gen Cwlth War Graves Cmmn 1975-83 (various appts 1947-75); chm Vale of Aylesbury Hunt 1981-87 (jt sec 1970-81); *Recreations* gardening, racing, hunting, history; *Style*— Alastair Laing, Esq, CBE, MVO; Wagtails, Lower Wood End, nr Marlow, Bucks SL7 2HN (☎ 062 844 481)

LAING, Dr Gordon James; ISO (1985); s of James William Laing (d 1941), of Oldham, Lancs, and Mary, *née* Shaw (d 1978); *b* 12 Jan 1923; *Educ* Eltham Coll London, Oldham Hulme GS, Oldham Tech Coll, UMIST, Univ of Sussex (MSc), Univ of London (PhD); *m* 8 Feb 1975, Frances, da of John Wilson (d 1958); 1 s (Fraser James b 9 Nov 1976); *Career* res engr Nat Gas and Oil Engine Co Ltd until 1949; Miny of Supply: scientific offr 1949, sr scientific offr i/c of an RARDE outstation 1951, princ scientific offr 1955, trials dir overseas ops, sr princ scientific offr 1983, left DOAE 1985; qualified NHBC builder; formed Surrey Residential Devpts Ltd; currently exec dir and mgmnt conslt for socs dealing with the homeless or the incurably sick; Freeman: City of London 1973, Worshipful Co of Bakers 1973; CEng, MIMechE, MIEE 1947, MORS 1970; *Books* Building Scientific Models (1986); *Recreations* tennis, painting; *Style*— Dr Gordon Laing, ISO; 23 Woodend Park, Cobham, Surrey KT11 3BX

LAING, Maj Hugh Charles Desmond; s of Capt Hugh Desmond Bertram Laing (d 1953), and Dorothy Linton, *née* Harvey (d 1986); *b* 24 Dec 1931; *Educ* King's Coll Sch Canada, Millfield, RMA Sandhurst; *m* 2 May 1959, Hon Rosemary Cornwall-Legh, da of 5 Baron Grey of Codnor, CBE, AE, DL, *qv*; 1 adopted da (Camilla Catherine Harvey b 29 June 1964); *Career* cmmnd 2 Lt Scots Gds 1952, Adj Gds Trg Bn Pirbright, GSO3 16 Ind Parachute Bde, Staff Coll Camberley, GSO2 Int Coord Jt Int Staff Hong Kong, Co Cmd Scots Gds, Sqdn Ldr 22 SAS Regt, GSO2 Br Def Liaison Staff Washington, ret 1973; Sqdn Ldr Duke of Lancaster's Own Yeo 1984-88; called to the Bar Inner Temple 1976, practising Northern Circuit Manchester 1976-91; pres Scots Gds Assoc Manchester Branch; *Recreations* golf, walking, shooting, photography; *Clubs* Special Forces; *Style*— Maj Hugh Laing; Cherry Hall, Cherry Lane, Lymm, Cheshire (☎ 0925 75 5954)

LAING, Dr Ian Geoffrey; s of George Edward Laing, and Frances May, *née* Hutton; *b* 15 May 1933; *Educ* Leeds GS, Univ of Leeds (BSc, PhD); *m* 5 April 1958, Una, da of Albert Hannam (d 1982); 2 s (Andrew Nicholas b 1962, Jonathan Richard b 1964), 2 da (Deborah Claire b 1960, Rebecca Sarah b 1967); *Career* tech dir Clayton Aniline Co Ltd 1978-85 (prodn dir 1971-77, prodn mangr 1966-71, memb Bd 1971-), dir of health safety and environment protection Ciba-Geigy plc 1986-; memb Health and Safety Cmmn's Advsy Ctee on Toxic Substances 1978-85; CIA: memb Cncl for Industl Safety Health and Environmental Control 1985-, Carcinogenic Substances Ctee 1963, chm 1974-86; chm Task Force for Carcinogens Mutagens and Teratagens 1985-, memb Cncl Br Industl Biological Res Assoc 1989-; FRSC, FSDC, FBIM; *Recreations* photography, oil and water colour painting, skiing, walking, cycling; *Style*— Dr Ian Laing; Shieldaig, Calrofold Lane, Rainow, nr Macclesfield, Cheshire SK11 0AA (☎ 0625 420552); Ciba-Geigy plc, Hulley Rd, Macclesfield, Cheshire SK10 2NX (☎ 0625 421933, fax 0625 619637)

LAING, Sir John Maurice; s of Sir John William Laing, CBE (d 1978), of Mill Hill, London NW7, and Beatrice, *née* Harland (d 1972); *b* 1 Feb 1918; *Educ* St Lawrence Coll Ramsgate; *m* 20 March 1940, Hilda Violet, da of William Tom Steeper Richards (d 1946), of Ramsgate; 1 s (John Hedley b 1959); *Career* WWII RAFVR 1941-45 (seconded Glider Pilot Regt for Rhine crossing 1945); dir: John Laing plc 1939-87 (jt md 1947-54, md 1954-76, dep chm 1966, chm 1976-82), Bank of England 1963-80; pres: Br Employers' Confedn 1964-65, CBI 1965-66, Export Gp for the Constructional Industs 1976-80, Fedn of Civil Engrg Contractors 1977, RYA 1983-87; memb: Export Guarantees Advsy Cncl 1959-63, Econ Planning Bd 1961, NEDC 1962-66, NIESR 1964-82, Admin Staff Coll 1965-70; Insignia Award CGLI 1978; Hon LLD Strathclyde 1967; Freeman Municipality of Surrey BC Canada 1978; MCIOB 1981; *Recreations* sailing, swimming; *Clubs* Royal Yacht Sqdn, Royal Ocean Racing, Arts; *Style*— Sir Maurice Laing; John Laing plc, Page St, Mill Hill, London NW7 2ER

LAING, John Stuart; s of Dr Denys Laing, of Limpsfield, Surrey, and Dr J Dods; *b* 22 July 1948; *Educ* Rugby, Corpus Christi Coll, Cambridge; *m* 12 Aug 1972, Sibella, da of Sir Maurice Dorman, GCMG, GCVO, of West Overton, Wiltshire; 1 s (James b 1974), 2 da (Catriona b 1979, Hannah b 1985); *Career* Dip Serv 1971-: FCO 1971-72, Mecas Lebanon 1972-73, HM Embassy Jeddah 1973-75, UK perm rep to EC 1975-78, FCO 1978-83, HM Embassy Cairo 1983-87, FCO 1987-89, HM Embassy Prague 1989-; *Recreations* music, hill walking; *Style*— Stuart Laing, Esq; c/o British Embassy, Prague; c/o FCO, King Charles St, London SW1A 2AH (☎ 422 53 33 47)

LAING, Sir (William) Kirby; JP (Middx 1965), DL (1978); s of Sir John Laing, CBE (d 1978), and Beatrice, *née* Harland (d 1972); *b* 21 July 1916; *Educ* St Lawrence Coll Ramsgate, Emmanuel Coll Cambridge (MA); *m* 1, 1939, Joan Dorothy (d 1981), da of Capt E C Bratt (d 1965); 3 s; m 2, 1986, Isobel Lewis, da of late Edward Wray; *Career* chm Laing Properties plc 1978-87, dir John Laing plc 1939-80; pres: Nat Fedn of Bldg Trades' Employers 1965 and 1967, Inst of Civil Engrs 1974, Royal Albert Hall 1979-; hon fell Emmanuel Coll Cambridge 1983; kt 1968; *Clubs* Naval & Military, Royal Fowey Yacht; *Style*— Sir Kirby Laing, JP, DL; 133 Page St, London NW7 2ER

LAING, Hon Mrs (Lucy Ann Anthea); *née* Low; da of 1 Baron Aldington, KCMG, CBE, DSO, TD, PC; *b* 1956; *Educ* Cranborne Chase Sch; *m* 1979, Alasdair North Grant Laing; 1 da (Emma Mary b 1980), 2 s (Alexander William b 1982, Frederick Charles b 1985); *Style*— The Hon Mrs Laing; Relugas, Forres, Moray, Scotland

LAING, Peter Anthony Neville Pennethorne; s of Lt-Col Neville Ogilvie Laing, DSO (d 1950); *b* 12 March 1922; *Educ* Eton, Paris Univ; *m* 1958, Penelope Lucinda, da of Sir William Pennington-Ramsden, 7 Bt, of Muncaster Castle, Cumberland; 2 da; *Career* attaché Br Embassy, Madrid 1944-46; int mktg conslt in: Western Europe, US, Caribbean, Latin America; dir ITC Project for UN 1975-; *Style*— Peter Laing, Esq; Sotogrande, Guardiaro, Cadiz, Spain

LAING, Ronald David; s of D P M Laing, and Amelia Laing; *b* 7 Oct 1927; *Educ* Glasgow Univ (MB CHB, DPM); *Career* West of Scotland Neurosurgical Unit 1951, Central Army Psychiatric Unit Netley 1951-52, Dept of Psychological Med Glasgow Univ 1953-56, Tavistock Clinic 1956-60, Tavistock Inst of Human Relations 1960-, fell Fndns Fund for Res in Psychiatry 1960-67, dir Langham Clinic for Psychotherapy 1962-65, fell Tavistock Inst of Med Psychology 1963-64, princ investigator Schizophrenia and Family Research Unit Tavistock Inst 1964-67, chm Philadelphia Assoc 1964-82; *Books incl:* The Divided Self (1960), The Self and Others (1961), The Politics of Experience and the Bird of Paradise (1967), Knots (1970), The Politics of the Family (1971), The Facts of Life (1976), Do You Love Me (1977), Conversations with Children (1978), Sonnets (1979), The Voice of Experience (1982); *Style*— Ronald Laing, Esq

LAING, Hon Mrs (Rosemary); *née* Cornwall-Legh; er da of 5 Baron Grey of Codnor, CBE, AE, DL, *qv*; *b* 11 March 1932; *m* 2 May 1959, Maj Hugh Charles Desmond Laing, *qv*; 1 adopted da (Camilla Catherine Harvey b 29 June 1964); *Style*— The Hon Mrs Laing; Cherry Hall, Cherry Lane, Lymm, Cheshire (☎ 0925 755954)

LAING OF DUNPHAIL, Baron (Life Peer UK 1991), of Dunphail in the District of Moray; Sir Hector Laing; s of Hector Laing; *b* 12 May 1923; *Educ* Loretto, Jesus Coll Cambridge; *m* 1950, Marian Clare, da of Maj-Gen Sir John Emilius Laurie, 6 Bt, CBE, DSO (d 1983); 3 s (Hon Mark Hector b 1951, Hon Robert John b 1953, Hon Anthony Rupert b 1955); *Career* WWII served Scots Gds 1942-47 (despatches 1944), demob bed Capt; joined McVitie & Price 1947 (chm 1963), dir United Biscuits 1953 (md 1964, chm United Biscuit's Hldgs 1972); chm: Food and Drink Industs Cncl 1977-79, Scottish Business in the Community 1982, City and Industl Liaison Cncl 1985, Business in the Community 1987; dir: Bank of England 1973, Exxon Corp Inc 1984; pres: Goodwill 1983, The Weston Spirit 1989; govr Nat Inst of Econ and Social Res 1985, memb Cncl for Indust and Higher Educn 1985, jt treas Cons Pty 1988, jt chm The Per Cent Club 1986, chm the tstees The Lambeth Fund 1983, govr Wycombe Abbey Sch 1981; Hon DUniv: Univ of Stirling, Heriot-Watt Univ; kt 1978; *Recreations* gardening, walking, flying; *Style*— The Rt Hon Lord Laing of Dunphail; United Biscuits, Grant House, Syon Lane, Isleworth, Middx TW7 5NN

LAIRD, Endell Johnston; *b* 6 Oct 1933; *Educ* Forfar Academy; *m* 5 Sept 1958, June; 1 s (David b 1965), 2 da (Susan b 1960, Jackie b 1963); *Career* ed-in-chief and dir: Scottish Daily Record, Sunday Mail; former chm Scottish Editors Ctee; memb D-Notice Ctee 1986-, hon pres Newspaper Press Fund; *Recreations* walking, golf, bridge; *Clubs* Bishopbriggs Golf, Bishopbriggs Bridge; *Style*— Endell J Laird, Esq; 10 Glenburn Gdns, Bishopbriggs, Glasgow; Scottish Daily Record and Sunday Mail, Anderston Quay, Glasgow G3 8DA (☎ 041 242 3353, fax 041 204 0770, telex 778277)

LAIRD, Gavin Harry; CBE (1988); s of James Laird, and Frances Luxton Laird; *b* 14 March 1933; *Educ* Clydebank HS; *m* 4 Oct 1956, Catherine Gillies (Reena), *née* Campbell; 1 da (Fiona Campbell b 14 April 1961); *Career* AEU: elected regnl offr Scotland 1972, memb Exec Cncl 1975-82, gen sec 1982-; non-exec dir: Highlands and Islands Development Board 1973-75, Scottish TV 1986-, Court of The Bank of England 1986-, FS Assurance 1988- (became Britannia Life 1990); pt/t memb: British National Oil Corporation 1976-86, Scottish Development Agency 1986-, GSL Scotland; memb: Gen Cncl of Scottish TUC 1972-75, Arts Cncl of GB 1983-86, Ed Bd European Business Journal; govr: London Business Sch 1988-, Atlantic Coll 1988-, Napier Technical Coll 1989-; hon fell Paisley Tech Coll; *Recreations* hill walking, music, reading, avoiding work; *Clubs* Royal Scottish Automobile, North Kent Ramblers' Assoc; *Style*— Gavin H Laird, Esq, CBE; 35 Southlands Grove, Bromley, Kent BR1 2DA; Amalgamated Engineering Union, 110 Peckham Road, London SE15 5EL (☎ 071 703 4231, fax 071 701 7862)

LAIRD, John; s of John Laird (d 1962), and Mary, *née* McGalliard; *b* 16 March 1936; *Educ* Oatlands Sch, Royal Coll of Sci and Technol (MSc); *m* 1957, Joan Norma, da of late John Shrigley (d 1981); 1 s (Andrew b 1958), 1 da (Joanna b 1964); *Career* dir Lahoud Engrg Co (UK) Ltd; CEng, FIMarE; *Recreations* music, reading; *Clubs* Naval; *Style*— John Laird, Esq; 1 Hill St, Berkeley Sq, London W1X 7FA (☎ 071 493 1293)

LAIRD, Margaret Heather; da of William Henry Polmear (d 1966), and Edith, *née* Tippett; *b* 29 Jan 1933; *Educ* The HS Truro, Westfield Coll Univ of London (BA), King's Coll (Cert in Religious Knowledge); *m* 14 Jan 1961, The Rev Canon John Charles Laird; 2 s (Andrew John William b 1963, Stephen Charles Edward b 1966); *Career* divinity mistress: Grey Coat Hosp 1955-59, St Albans HS 1960-62; head of Religious Studies Dept The Dame Alice Harpur Sch 1970-88, cmmr Third Church Estates 1988-; memb Gen Synod 1980-; *Recreations* medieval art, architecture, pilgrims' routes; *Clubs* Utd Oxford and Cambridge; *Style*— Mrs Margaret Laird; Church Commissioners, 1 Millbank, London SW1P 3JZ (☎ 071 222 7010)

LAIRD, Michael Donald; OBE (1983); s of George Donald Struthers Laird (d 1980), and Catherine Brown Dibley, *née* Tennent; *b* 22 March 1928; *Educ* Loretto, Edinburgh Coll of Art (Dip Arch); *m* 23 March 1957, Hon Kirsty Noel-Paton, da of Baron Ferrier (Life Peer), *qv*; 2 s (Simon b 1958, Magnus b 1962), 1 da (Nicola b 1958); *Career* lectr Dept of Architecture Edinburgh Univ and Coll of Art 1954-57, architect and industl designer Michael Laird & Ptnrs 1954-, MacLaren Fellowship 1956-58; works incl: Edinburgh Univ Central Facilities Bldg, head office Standard Life Assur Co, computer HQ Royal Bank of Scotland; sundry awards: Saltire Soc, Br Steel, Civic Tst, Royal Scottish Acad (gold medallist 1968); FRSA, FSIA, FRIAS, ARIBA; *Recreations* sailing, skiing, hill walking; *Clubs* New (Edinburgh); *Style*— Michael Laird, Esq, OBE; 22 Moray Place, Edinburgh EH3 6DB (☎ 031 225 5859); The Michael Laird Partnership, 5 Forres St, Edinburgh EH3 6DE (☎ 031 226 6991, fax 031 226 2771)

LAIRD, Robert Edward; s of Robert Laird (d 1975), of Seaford, Sussex, and Esther Margaret, *née* Stoney (d 1976); *b* 25 Dec 1940; *Educ* Aldenham, Harvard Univ; *m* 8 Aug 1964, Mary Theresa, da of Martin Cooke (d 1969), of Galway, Ireland; 2 s (Robert Richard Martin b 1964, Julian Alexander b 1968) 1 da (Caroline b 1971); *Career* various appts Unilever Ltd 1959-76, dir Carnation Foods 1977-80, md Vandemoortele 1980-86, chm Polar Entertainment Group 1986-88, dir Keith Butters Ltd 1988-89, head of mktg Tate & Lyle Sugars 1989; memb cncl Coronary Prevention Gp; Freeman: City of London 1984, Worshipful Co of Upholders 1984; MInsTM 1978, FBIM 1980, MIOD 1982; *Recreations* golf, squash, jogging, reading, genealogy; *Clubs* Old Aldenhamians, Harvard Business Sch Club of London, The Sportsman; *Style*— R E Laird, Esq; 42 Elsham Rd, Kensington, London W14 8HB (☎ 071 602 2843); Tate & Lyle Sugars, Enterprise House, 45 Homesdale Rd, Bromley, Kent BR2 9TE (☎ 081 464 6556, fax 081 290 0721, telex 917184)

LAIRD CRAIG, Hon Mrs (Roxane); *née* Balfour; o da of 2 Baron Balfour of Inchrye, *qv*; *b* 8 Sept 1955; *m* 1978, Adrian Laird Craig; 1 s (Robert Joseph b 1982), 2 da (Mary Ann Josephine b 1984, Alethea Katharine b 1986); *Style*— The Hon Mrs Laird Craig; The Rowantrees, Biggar, Lanarkshire

LAISTER, Peter; s of late Horace Laister; *b* 24 Jan 1929; *Educ* King Edward's Sch Birmingham, Manchester Univ Coll of Technol; *m* 1, 1951, Barbara Cooke; 1 s, 1 da; m 2, 1958, Eileen Alice Goodchild, *née* Town; 1 da; *Career* RAF 1949-51; Esso Petroleum Co 1951-66, gp md Br Oxygen Co Ltd (BOC Int Ltd) 1969-79, Ellerman Lines Ltd 1976-79, chief exec Thorn EMI 1983- (chm 1984-); chm: BOC Fin Corpn (USA) 1974-75, Tollemache & Cobbold Breweries 1978-79, London & Hull Insur Co 1976-79, BMCL 1984- (dir 1976-), Park Hotels plc 1985-, Tower Gp 1985-, Contec plc, Inchcape plc 1982-, Fluor Daniel 1985-, Maxwell Communication Corp 1985, Nimbus records Ltd 1987-; dir Mirror Gp Newspapers Ltd 1985-; memb Industl Devpt Advsy Bd 1981-; cncl memb: Industl Soc 1971, UCL 1978 chm Br Fndn for Age Res 1982-; *Recreations* private flying, boating, angling, gardening, photography; *Clubs* Athenaeum; *Style—* Peter Laister, Esq; Thatches, 92 Staines Rd, Wraysbury, Bucks

LAITHWAITE, Prof Eric Roberts; s of Herbert Laithwaite (d 1954), of Kirkham, Lancs, and Florence, *née* Roberts (d 1966); *b* 14 June 1921; *Educ* Kirkham GS, Manchester Univ (BSc, MSc, PhD, DSc); *m* 8 Sept 1951, Sheila Margaret, da of Arthur Haighton Gooddie (d 1981), of Hawkinge, Kent; 2 s (Martin b 1954, Dennis b 1965), 2 da (Helen (Mrs Boam) b 1956, Louise b 1962); *Career* WWII RAF 1941-46 (RAF Farnborough 1943-46); lectr Manchester Univ 1951-64, prof of heavy electrical engrg Imperial Coll London 1964-86 (emeritus prof 1986-); pres Assoc for Sci Educn 1970; dir: Linear Motors Ltd 1971-86, Landspeed Ltd 1975-86, Cotswold Res Ltd; conslt Brian Colquhoun & Ptnrs 1975-; former conslt: Br Rail, Tracked Hovercraft Ltd, GEC, Pilkington Bros; RS SG Brown Award and Medal 1966, fell Univ of Hong Kong 1986; Nikola Telsa Award; fell Imperial Coll 1990; TV and radio progs incl: Tomorrow's World, Horizon, The World Around Us, Science Now, Dial a Scientist; CEng, FIEEE, FIEE, FRCA; *Books incl:* Induction Machines for Special Purposes (1966), Propulsion Without Wheels (1966), The Engineer in Wonderland (1967), How to Invent (1970), Engineer Through the Looking Glass (1974), Dictionary of Butterflies and Moths (1981), Invitation to Engineering (1984), Shape is Important (1986), History of Linear Electric Motors (1988); *Recreations* entomology, gardening; *Clubs* Athenaeum; *Style—* Prof Eric Laithwaite; Department of Electrical Engineering, Imperial College, London SW7 (☎ 071 589 5111, ext 5112)

LAJTHA, Prof Laszlo George; CBE (1983); s of Laszlo John Lajtha (d 1963), of Budapest, and Rose Stephanie Emily, *née* Hollos; *b* 25 May 1920; *Educ* Presbyterian HS Budapest, Univ Med Sch Budapest (MD), Exeter Coll Oxford (DPhil); *m* 28 Aug 1954, Gillian MacPherson, da of Dr Alastair Wingate Henderson (d 1985); 2 s (Christopher b 1955, Adrian b 1957); *Career* asst prof of physiology Univ of Budapest 1944-46, res assoc in haematology Radcliffe Infirmary Oxford 1947-50, head Radiobiology Laboratory Churchill Hosp Oxford 1951-62, res fell in pharmacology Univ of Yale USA 1954-55, dir Paterson Inst of Cancer Res Christie Hosp Manchester 1962-83, prof experimental oncology Univ of Manchester 1970-83 (emeritus 1983), ed British Journal of Cancer 1972-82; pres: Br Soc of Cell Biology 1977-80, Euro Orgn for Res and Treatment of Cancer 1979-81; memb: Bd Govrs Pownall Hall Prep Sch Wilmslow 1972-83, Cncl All Saints Sch Bloxham 1986-; Hon Citizen Texas 1964, hon memb Hungarian Acad of Scis 1983; Hon MD Univ of Szeged Hungary 1980; FRCPath 1973, FRCPE 1980; *Books* Use of Isotopes in Haematology (1961); *Recreations* archaeology, medieval history, baroque music, alpine gardening, bonsai; *Clubs* Athenaum, RN Med; *Style—* Prof Laszlo Lajtha, CBE; Brook Cottage, Little Bridge Rd, Bloxham, Oxfordshire OX15 4PU (☎ 0295 720 311)

LAKE, Sir (Atwell) Graham; 10 Bt (GB 1711), of Edmonton, Middx; s of Capt Sir Atwell Henry Lake, 9 Bt, CB, OBE, RN (d 1972); *b* 6 Oct 1923; *Educ* Eton; *m* 1983, Mrs Katharine Margaret Lister, da of D W Last; *Heir* bro, Edward Geoffrey Lake; *Career* serv in Gilbert & Ellice Mil Forces 1944-45, Col Admin Serv 1945-55, sec to Govt of Tonga 1950-53, Br High Cmmn New Delhi 1966-68, FCO 1969-72; sr tech advsr MOD to 1983, ret; *Recreations* bridge, chess, tennis, skiing; *Clubs* Lansdowne; *Style—* Sir Graham Lake, Bt; Magdalen Laver Hall, Chipping Ongar, Essex

LAKE, John Walter; s of Norman Lake (d 1952), of Derby, and Ella, *née* Mills (d 1984); *b* 7 May 1930; *Educ* Repton; *m* 4 Sept 1959, Anne Patricia, da of Thomas Ash (d 1982), of Derby; 1 s (John Emmerson b 1965); *Career* builders' merchant; chm and md: E & J W Lake (Holdings) Ltd 1979-, J H Thornhill (Coal and Haulage) Ltd 1964-, E & J W Lake Ltd 1964-; chm: Gt Central Merchants Ltd 1961-, Brookhouse Johnson Ltd 1975-, Magiglide Leisure Ltd 1975-, N Midland Building Supplies 1969-, Belper Building Supplies 1980-; Freeman City of London 1982, Liveryman Worshipful Co of Builders' Merchants 1982; FIBM 1969, FInstD 1965, FBIM 1982; *Recreations* squash, tennis, hockey; *Clubs* The Carrington, Derby Hockey; *Style—* John W Lake, Esq; Flower Lillies, Windley, Derbyshire DE5 2LQ (☎ 077 389 455); Lake House, Parcel Terrace, Derby DE1 1LQ (☎ 0332 49083, telex 37131)

LAKE, Richard Lawrence Geoffrey; s of Albert Lake (d 1968), and Elsie; *b* 11 Nov 1939; *m* 17 Oct 1964, Sheila June, da of Charles Douglas Marsh; 2 da (Amanda b 18 April 1967, Katharina b 1 May 1980); *Career* chartist Laurie Milbank 1969-72; equity ptnr: Zorn and Leigh-Hunt 1972-76, Grieveson Grant 1976-84, Raphael Zorn 1984-86; dir Swiss Bank Corp 1986-89, chm World Stockmarket Analysis 1989-90, dir Hoare Govett Securities 1991-; memb Soc of Investment Analysts, fell Soc of Technical Analysts; memb Duke St Baptist Church Richmond; *Recreations* cycling, walking; *Style—* Richard Lake, Esq; 285 Petersham Rd, Petersham, Richmond, Surrey (☎ 081 940 3795); Hoare Govett Investment Research Limited, 4 Broadgate, London EC2M 7LE (☎ 071 601 0101, fax 071 374 7353, telex 297801 HORGOV-G)

LAKE, Terence Edward; s of Walter Joseph Lake (d 1978), and Maud, *née* Ford (d 1951); *b* 26 July 1933; *Educ* East Ham GS for Boys, Leicester Univ (BSc); *m* 11 June 1955, Margaret, da of Gerald Steechman: 2 da (Hazel (Mrs Anwell) b 2 June 1957, Helen (Mrs Kitchingham) b 24 Jan 1959); *Career* Nat Serv 1954-56, Sch of Ammunition Bromley (Sgt ammunition examiner); gp fin controller Elliott Automation 1960-68, commercial dir and md Instrument Maintenance and Erection Co 1968-75, dir Roxby Engrg Ltd 1981-; Liveryman Worshipful Co of Scientific Instrument Makers; *Recreations* reading, gardening, travel, wine; *Style—* Terence Lake, Esq; 7 Lawpings, New Barn, Longfield, Kent DA3 7NH (☎ 04 747 4190); Roxby House, Station Rd, Sidcup DA15 7EJ (☎ 081 300 3393, fax 081 300 4400, telex 896172 ROXBY G)

LAKER, Sir Frederick Alfred (Freddie); *b* 6 Aug 1922; *Educ* Simon Langton Sch Canterbury; *m* 1, 1942 (m dis 1968), Joan; 1 s (decd), 1 da (Elaine); m 2, 1968 (m dis 1975), Rosemary Black; m 3, 1975 (m dis 1982), Patricia Gates, of Oklahoma; 1 s (Freddie Jr b 1978); m 4, 1985, Jacqueline Ann Harvey; *Career* with Short Bros Rochester 1938-40, Gen Aircraft 1940-41, ATA 1941-46, md Aviation Traders Gp 1946-65, md Br Utd Airways 1960-65, chm and md Laker Airways (Int) Ltd 1966-82, established Skytrain Holidays 1983; memb Airworthiness Requirements Bd until 1982, aviation and travel conslt 1982-; Lloyd's underwriter 1954-; chm benevolent fund Guild of Air Pilots and Air Navigators; hon fell UMIST; Hon DSc City Univ, Hon DSc Cranfield Inst of Technol, Hon LLD Manchester; kt 1978; *Clubs* Jockey, Eccentric, Little Ship; *Style—* Sir Freddie Laker; Furzegrove Farm, Chailey, E Sussex (☎ 082 572 2648)

LAKER, Dr Michael Francis; s of Sqdn Ldr Walter John Laker, of Ledbury, and Joyce, *née* Ashill; *b* 9 June 1945; *Educ* Newport HS, Univ of London (MD, BS, Dip BioChem); *m* 13 Dec 1969, Alison Jean, da of Thomas Borland (d 1986), of Tunbridge Wells; 2 s (Christopher b 1981, Jonathan b 1983), 2 da (Hannah b 1974, Bethan b 1977); *Career* lectr in chemical pathology and metabolic disorders St Thomas Hosp Med Sch 1973-80, res fell Dept of Med Univ of California San Diego 1979-80, sr lectr in clinical biochemistry and metabolic med Univ of Newcastle and conslt chemical pathologist Newcastle Health Authy 1980-89, reader in clinical biochemistry and metabolic med Univ of Newcastle upon Tyne 1989-; memb Ctee Br Hyperlipidaemia Assoc; FRCPath 1988; *Books* Short Cases in Clinical Biochemistry (1984); *Recreations* music, computing, gardening; *Style—* Dr Michael Laker; 9 Campus Martius, Heddon On The Wall, Northumberland NE15 0BP (☎ 0661 853 798); Dept of Clinical Biochemistry and Metabolic Medicine, Univ of Newcastle upon Tyne, Medical School, Framlington Plc, Newcastle upon Tyne NE2 4HH (☎ 091 2325131 ext 24566)

LAKES, Gordon Harry; CB (1987), MC (1951); s of Harry Lakes (d 1980), and Annie, *née* Butcher (d 1970); *b* 27 Aug 1928; *Educ* Army Tech Sch Arborfield, RMA Sandhurst; *m* 2 Oct 1950, Nancy, da of Joseph Watters Smith (d 1952); 1 da (Alison b 1953); *Career* cmmnd RA 1948, 39 Medium Regt 1949-50, Lt 1950, 170 Ind Mortar Batty 1950-52, pilot 657 Air Op Sqdn RAF 1952-54, Capt 1953, Adj 383 Light Regt RA (DCRH) TA 1954-56, 2 Ind Field Batty RA 1956-58, promoted Maj to cmd Ghana Recce Sqdn Ghana Army 1958-60, ret 1960; called to the Bar Middle Temple 1960; asst govr HM Prison Serv 1961, HM Borstal Feltham 1962-65, asst princ Offrs Trg Sch Leyhill 1965-68, govr HM Remand Centre Thorp Arch 1968-70, Prison Serv HQ 1970, govr class 3 1971, HM Prison Pentonville 1974, govr class 2 1975, HM Prison Gartree 1975, Prison Serv HQ 1977, govr class 1 1979, asst controller and HM dep chief inspr of prisons 1982, AUSS and dep dir gen of Prison Serv 1985, memb Cncl of Europe Ctee for Cooperation in Prison Affrs 1986, ret 1988; memb Parole Bd 1989-, assessor to Lord Justice Woolf's Inquiry into Prison Disturbances 1990-, commissioner Mental Health Act 1991-; *Recreations* golf, photography; *Style—* Gordon Lakes, Esq, CB, MC; Havelock House, New St, Charfield, Wotton-Under-Edge, Glos GL12 8ES (☎ 0453 842 705)

LAKEY, Prof John Richard Angwin; s of late William Richard Lakey, and late Edith; *b* 28 June 1929; *Educ* Morley GS, Univ of Sheffield (BSc, PhD); *m* 22 Dec 1955, Dr Pamela Janet Lakey, JP, da of late Eric Clifford Lancey; 3 da (Joanna Margaret, Philippa Mary (Mrs Lewry), Nicola Janet (Dr King)); *Career* res posts Simon Carves Ltd, secondment to AERE Harwell and GEC 1953-60; RNC Greenwich: asst prof 1960-80, prof 1980-89, dean 1984-86 and 1988-89; reactor shielding conslt DG Ships 1967-89, radiation conslt WHO 1973-74, visiting prof Univ of Surrey 1988, fndr John Lakey Assocs 1989, memb CNAA Physics Bd 1973-82, pubns dir Int Radiation Protection Assoc 1979-88, external examiner Univ of Surrey 1980-86, visiting lectr Harvard Univ 1984-, memb Ed Bd Physics in Med and Biology 1980-83, news ed Health Physics 1980-88; regnl scientific advsr No5 Region 1984-, chm UK Liaison Ctee for Scis Allied to Med and Biology 1984-87, pres Inst Nuclear Engrs 1988-90 (vice pres 1983-87), vice pres London Int Youth Sci Fortnight 1988-, pres Int Radiation Protection Assoc 1988-; vice pres Euro Nuclear Soc 1989-, memb Medway Health Authy 1987-90; Freeman City of London 1988, Liveryman Worshipful Co of Engineers 1988; Eur Ing, CEng, FINucE, FInstE, CPhys; memb: Soc for Radiological Protection, American Nuclear Soc, FRSP; *Books* Protection Against Radiation (1961), Radiation Protection Measurement: philosophy and implementation (1975), ALARA principles and practices (1987), IRPA Guidelines on Protection Against Non-Ionizing Radiation (1991), papers on nuclear safety, radiological protection and management of emergencies; *Recreations* yachting, photography, conversation; *Clubs* Athenaeum, Medway Yacht, RNSA; *Style—* Prof John Lakey; John Lakey Associates, 5 Pine Rise, Meopham, Gravesend, Kent (☎ 0474 812551)

LAKIN, Hon Mrs (Helena Daphne); *née* Pearson; da of 2 Viscount Cowdray, JP, DL (d 1933); *m* 1939, Lt-Col John Lakin, TD, JP, DL (d 1989), s of Henry Gilbert Lakin (d 1964), of Pipers Hill, Warwicks; 1 s (Michael, b 1955); *Style—* The Hon Mrs Lakin; Hammerwood House, Iping, nr Midhurst, W Sussex GU29 0PF (☎ 0730 813635)

LAKIN, Sir Michael; 4 Bt (UK 1909); s of Sir Henry Lakin, 3 Bt (d 1979); *b* 28 Oct 1934; *Educ* Stowe; *m* 1, 1956 (m dis 1963), Margaret, da of Robert Wallace, of Mount Norris, Co Armagh; m 2, 1965, Felicity, da of Anthony Denis Murphy, of Londiani, Kenya; 1 s, 1 da; *Heir* s, Richard Anthony Lakin b 26 Nov 1968; *Style—* Sir Michael Lakin, Bt; Torwood, Post Office, Rosetta, Natal, S Africa

LAKIN, Noel Oscar Ernest; s of Oscar Dennis Lakin (d 1953), and Beryl Ann, *née* Danert (d 1968); *b* 19 Oct 1924; *Educ* Irish Christian Bros Schs in India; *m* 1958, Aurela Avadney Barbara, da of Thomas William Tristram (d 1968); 3 s (Peter b 1959, Andrew b 1966, Russell b 1968), 3 da (Paula b 1960, Noeline b 1962, Ursula b 1964); *Career* md Taymel 1982 (dep chm Taymel 1985), dir Taylor Woodrow Cons Ltd; *Recreations* tennis; *Style—* Noel Lakin, Esq; Alpha House, Westmount Centre, Delamere Road, Hayes Middx UB4 0HD

LAKIN, Peter Maurice; s of Ronald Maurice Lakin (d 1985), of Coventry, and Dorothy Kathleen, *née* Cowlishaw; *b* 21 Oct 1949; *Educ* King Henry VIII GS Coventry, Univ of Manchester (LLB); *m* 11 Dec 1971, Jacqueline, da of John Alexander Jubb; 1 s (Michael John b 25 May 1975), 1 da (Emma Jane b 14 May 1977); *Career* asst slr Conn Goldberg Solicitors 1974-76 (articled clerk 1971-74), ptnr (i/c Forensic Litigation Criminal and Motoring Law) Pannone Blackburn Solicitors 1976-; asst rec Crown Court 1989, hon sec Manchester and Dist Medico Legal Soc; memb Law Soc 1974; *Recreations* fell walking, gardening, opera; *Style—* Peter Lakin, Esq; Pannone Blackburn Solicitors, 123 Deansgate, Manchester (☎ 061 832 3000, fax 061 834 2067)

LAL, Prof Deepak Kumar; s of Nand Lal (d 1984), of New Delhi, and Shanti, *née* Devi; *b* 3 Jan 1940; *Educ* Doon Sch Dehra Dun, Stephen's Coll Delhi (BA), Jesus Coll Oxford (MA, BPhil); *m* 11 Dec 1971, Barbara, da of Jack Ballis (d 1987), of New York; 1 s (Akshay b 18 Aug 1981), 1 da (Deepika b 17 March 1980); *Career* Indian Foreign Serv 1963-65, lectr Christchurch Coll Oxford 1966-68, res fell Nuffield Coll Oxford 1968-70, reader political econ UCL 1979-84 (lectr 1970-79), prof political econ Univ of London 1984-, James S Colman prof of devpt studies Univ of Calif at Los Angeles (UCLA) 1990-; conslt Indian Planning Cmmn 1973-74, res admin World Bank Washington DC 1983-87; conslt 1970-: ILO, UNCTAD, OECD, UNIDO, World Bank, Miny of Planning S Korea and Sri Lanka; *Books* Wells and Welfare (1972), Methods of Project Analysis (1974), Appraising Foreign Investment in Developing Countries (1975), Unemployment and Wage Inflation in Industrial Economies (1977), Men or Machines (1978), Prices for Planning (1980), The Poverty of Development Economics (1983), Labour and Poverty in Kenya (with P Collier, 1986), Stagflation, Savings and the State (ed with M Wolf, 1986), The Hindu Equilibrium (1988 and 1989), Public Policy and Economic Development (ed with M Scott, 1990); *Recreations* opera, theatre, tennis; *Style—* Prof Deepak Lal; 2 Erskine Hill, London NW11 6HB (☎ 081 458 3713); A 30 Nizamuddin West, New Delhi 110013, India (☎ 010 9111 698225); Department of Economics, University College London, Gower St, London WC1E 6BT (☎ 071 387 7050 ext 2300, fax 071 383 7127)

LALANDI-EMERY, Lina Madeleine; OBE (1975); da of late Nikolas Kaloyeropoulos, and the late Toula, *née* Gelekis; *Educ* Athens Conservatoire, privately in England; *m* Ralph Emery; *Career* first appeared as harpsichord soloist Royal Festival Hall 1954, int career in concert radio and TV, dir Eng Bach Festival Trust 1963- (fndr 1962) (specialises baroque opera and dance); appearances incl: Covent Gdn, Versailles and numerous festivals of music (Granada, Athens, Monte Carlo, Madrid); Offr Dans L'Ordre des Arts et Des Lettres France 1978; *Recreations* cats, cooking, reading, knitting; *Style—* Mrs Lina Lalandi-Emery, OBE; 15 South Eaton Place, London SW1W 9ER (☎ 071 730 5925); English Bach Festival Trust, 15 South Eaton Place, London SW1W 9ER (☎ 071 730 5295, fax 071 730 1456)

LAM, Martin Philip; *b* 10 March 1920; *Educ* Univ Coll Sch Hampstead, Gonville and

Caius Coll Cambridge; *m* 1953, Lisa, *née* Lorenz; 1 s (Stephen), 1 da (Jenny); *Career* WWII 1940-45: Air Formation Signals, Special Forces, Capt Mil Govt Italy; assoc conslt: BIS Mackintosh 1979-, Gen Technol Systems, ScanEurope; on loan to Euro Cmmn DG XIII 1986-88; Bd of Trade Miny of Materials 1947-78, Nuffield fell on aspects of econ devpt in Latin America 1952, memb UK Delgn to OECD 1963-65, official ldr of Delgn to UNCTAD 1972, under sec Computer Systems and Electronics DTI; *Style—* Martin Lam, Esq; 22 The Avenue, Wembley, Middx, HA9 9QJ (☎ 081 904 2584)

LAMARQUE, Lady Emma Elizabeth Anne; da of 7 Earl of Rosebery, DL; *b* 12 Sept 1962; *m* 1984, William Lamarque, s of late W G Lamarque, of Coxwold, York; 1 s (Victor George b 1986), 1 da (Francesca b 1988); *Style—* The Lady Emma Lamarque

LAMB, Adrian Frank; s of Frank Lamb (d 1981), and Mary Elizabeth Graham, *née* Chambers (d 1977); *Educ* Gateshead GS; *m* 4 May 1974, Jane, da of William Moore, of Spital Farm, Blyth, Notts; 1 s (Richard b 1982), 3 da (Katharine b 1976, Amy b 1978, Jennifer b 1982); *Career* CA; Richard Ormond Son & Dunn 1960-65, ptnr Coopers & Lybrand 1975-, seconded to Civil Serv Dept 1970; hon treas Int Fedn of Multiple Sclerosis Socs; FCA 1966; *Books* Analysed Reporting (1977), Internal Audit in the Civil Service (jtly, 1971); *Recreations* tennis, bridge, music, gardening; *Style—* Adrian Lamb, Esq; Lynbury House, Burtons Way, Chalfont St Giles, Bucks HP8 4BP (☎ 0494 764810); Coopers & Lybrand Deloitte, Plumtree Court, London EC4A 4HT (☎ 071 583 5000, fax 071 822 4652, telex 887470)

LAMB, Sir Albert Thomas (Archie); KBE (1979, MBE 1953), CMG (1974), DFC (1945); s of Reginald Selwyn Lamb (d 1970), and Violet, *née* Haynes (d 1980); *b* 23 Oct 1921; *Educ* Swansea GS; *m* 8 April 1944, Christina Betty, da of Albert Henry Wilkinson (d 1960) ; 1 s (Robin b 1948), 2 da (Elizabeth b 1945, Kathryn b 1959); *Career* RAF 1941-46; FO 1938-41, Rome Embassy 1947-50, Genoa Consulate 1950, Bucharest Legation 1950-53, FO 1953-55, MECAS 1955-57, Bahrain (political residency) 1957-61, FO oil desk 1961-65, Kuwait Embassy 1965, political agent Abu Dhabi 1965-68, chief inspr Dip Serv 1968-74; ambass: Kuwait 1974-77, Norway 1978-80; memb Bd BNOC 1981-82, dir Britoil plc 1982-88, memb Bd Samuel Montagu & Co Ltd 1981-85 (advsr 1985-88), sr assoc Conant & Assocsiate Ltd Washington DC 1985-; *Recreations* gardening; *Clubs* RAF; *Style—* Sir Archie Lamb, KBE, CMG, DFC

LAMB, Andrew Martin; s of Harry Lamb, of Abergele, Clwyd, and Winifred, *née* Emmott; *b* 23 Sept 1942; *Educ* Werneth Sch Oldham, Manchester GS, CCC Oxford (MA); *m* 1 April 1970, Wendy Ann, da of Frank Edward Davies, of Shirley, Solihull, Warwicks; 1 s (Richard Andrew b 1976), 2 da (Helen Margaret b 1972, Susan Elizabeth b 1973); *Career* investmt mangr then asst gen mangr MGM Assur 1985-88, chief investmt mangr Friends Provident Life Office 1988-; musicologist; FIA 1972, AMSIA; *Books* Jerome Kern in Edwardian London (1985), Gänzl's Book of the Musical Theatre (with Kurt Gänzl, 1988); contrib to: Gramophone, The Musical Times, The New Grove Dictionary of Music & Musicians; *Recreations* cricket, music, family; *Clubs* Lancashire CCC; *Style—* Andrew Lamb, Esq; 12 Fullers Wood, Croydon, CR0 8HZ; Friends Provident Life Office, 15 Old Bailey, London EC4M 7AP (☎ 071 329 4454)

LAMB, Colin Anthony; s of Wilfred Samuel Lamb (d 1978), of London, and Evelyn Mabel, *née* Straker (d 1982); *b* 17 Nov 1928; *Educ* Dulwich; *m* 7 May 1960, José Dorothy, da of Harold Punt (d 1973), of Hartoft, N Yorkshire; 1 s (Rupert b 22 Oct 1967), 2 da (Henrietta b 26 March 1962, Isabella b 11 Sept 1963); *Career* Nat Serv 2 Lt RASC 1947-49, Capt Middx Regt TA 1954; insurance broker Lloyds 1950-56, dist police special branch and game dept Tanganyika HM Overseas Civil Serv 1956-64; called to the Bar Middle Temple 1966, examiner under Ecclesiastical Jurisdiction Measure 1978-, rec Crown Ct 1989-; *Recreations* cricket, music; *Clubs* The Norfolk; *Style—* Colin Lamb, Esq; Bure Hse, Millgate, Aylsham, Norfolk (☎ 0263 732555)

LAMB, Hon David Charles; s and h of 2 Baron Rochester, *qv*; *b* 8 Sept 1944; *Educ* Shrewsbury Sch, Univ of Sussex; *m* 9 April 1969, Jacqueline Agnes, yr da of John Alfred Stamp, of Torquay, Devon; 2 s (Daniel b 1971, Joe b 1972); *Career* journalist; *Style—* The Hon D C Lamb; 14 Stamford Rd, Bowdon, Cheshire WA14 2JU (☎ 061 928 9030)

LAMB, Eric Alan; s of Eric Lamb, of the Wirral, and Edna Marjorie, *née* Wright; *b* 3 March 1953; *Educ* Park HS Birkenhead, Univ of Liverpool (LLB); *m* 5 April 1980, Elizabeth Ann, da of Douglas Gill, of the Wirral; *Career* called to the Bar Lincoln's Inn 1975; *Recreations* boating, tennis; *Clubs* Athenaeum, Liverpool Racquet; *Style—* Eric Lamb, Esq; 1 Exchange Flags, Liverpool (☎ 051 236 7747)

LAMB, Air Vice-Marshal George Colin; CB (1977), CBE (1966), AFC (1947); s of George Lamb, of Wryville, Hornby, Lancs (d 1953), and Bessie Lamb; *b* 23 July 1923; *Educ* Lancaster Royal GS; *m* 1, 1945, Nancy Mary, da of Ronald Godsmark, of Norwich; 2 s; m 2, 1981, Mrs Maureen Margaret Mepham, da of Thomas Bamford (d 1967), of Hounslow, Middx; *Career* asst cmdt RAF Coll Cranwell 1964-65, dep cdr Air Forces Borneo 1965-66, Air Cdre 1968, OC RAF Lyneham 1969-71, RCDS 1971-72, dir of control (ops) Nat Air Traffic Serv 1972-74, Cdre Southern Maritime Air Region 1974-75, COS No 18 Gp 1975-78, RAF vice pres Combined Cadet Forces Assoc 1978-; md Yonex UK Ltd 1990- int rugby football referee 1967-72, chief exec Badminton Assoc of England 1978-89, memb Sports Cncl 1983; chm: Lilleshall Nat Sports Centre 1983, Sports Ctee Princes Tst 1985; privilege memb RFU 1985 (memb Ctee 1973-85), gen sec London Sports Med Inst 1989-90, Br Int Sports Ctee 1989-, memb Sports Cncl Drug Abuse Advsy Gp 1984-; FBIM; *Recreations* rugby union football, cycling, gardening; *Clubs* RAF; *Style—* Air Vice-Marshal George Lamb, CB, CBE, AFC; Hambledon, 17 Meadway, Berkhamsted, Herts HP4 2PN (☎ 044 27 2583; office: 071 251 0583)

LAMB, Maj Gilbert Wrightson; s of His Hon Percy Charles Lamb, QC (d 1973), of Chislehurst, Kent, and Constance, *née* White (d 1981); *b* 29 April 1924; *Educ* Clifton; *m* 1 Aug 1957, Sarah Geraldine Ruth, da of Ralph Tennyson-d'Eyncourt, MBE, of Bayons Manor, Lincs; 1 s (Matthew Gilbert Peregrine b 1966), 2 da (Joanna Elizabeth b 1958, Emma Harriet b 1961); *Career* WWII enlisted 1943, cmmnd Grenadier Gds, served Italy (wounded 1944, despatches 1945); Army Staff Coll Camberley 1954, DAA & QMG 1 Gds Bde 1956-58, DAMS London Dist 1960-62, ret 1962; called to the Bar Grays Inn 1962; Formica Ltd 1962-70: gen mangr (Switzerland) 1964-65, gen mangr (India) 1965-68, md 1968-70; dir: Inc Soc of Br Advertisers 1971-79, public affrs TI Gp plc 1979-85; chm Taunton Conservative Assoc 1986-89; memb Somerset Co Cncl; *Recreations* hunting, gardening; *Clubs* Cavalry and Guards; *Style—* Maj Gilbert Lamb

LAMB, Prof Hubert Horace; s of Prof Ernest Horace Lamb (d 1946), of London, and Lilian, *née* Brierley (d 1969); *b* 22 Sept 1913; *Educ* Oundle, Trinity Coll Cambridge (BA, MA, ScD); *m* 7 Feb 1948, (Beatrice) Moira Milligan, da of Rev Oswald Milligan, DD (d 1940), of Corstorphine, Edinburgh; 1 s (Norman Peter b 1957), 2 da (Catherine Ann (Mrs Gilbride) b 1948, Kirsten Mary (Mrs Reilly) b 1954); *Career* entered Meteorological Office 1936, seconded Irish Meteorological Serv 1939 (later transfd), head forecaster transatlantic civil passenger route 1941-44, researcher UK Meteorological Office 1945-71, forecaster whaling in Antarctic 1946-47, fndr and first dir Climatic Res Unit UEA 1972-78; memb Nat Antarctic Res Ctee 1960-78, former vice pres RMS (Symons Medallist 1987), vice chm N Norfolk Lib Democrats; author of entries in Encyclopaedia Britannic and Oxford Dictionary of Natural History etc; Hon DSc UEA 1981, Hon LLD Univ of Dundee 1981; Vega medal Royal Swedish Geographical Soc 1984; hon corresponding memb: Danish Natural History Soc 1978-, Royal Acad of Arts and Sciences Barcelona 1985-; FRMetS 1938, FRGS 1947; *Books* Climate: Present, Past and Future (vol 1 1972, vol 2 1977), Climate, History and the Modern World (1982), Weather, Climate and Human Affairs (1988); *Recreations* travel, hill walking; *Style—* Prof Hubert Lamb; Climatic Res Unit, Univ of East Anglia, Norwich NR4 7TJ (☎ 0603 56161)

LAMB, Prof John; CBE (1986); s of Walter Lamb (d 1981), and Fanny, *née* Atkinson (d 1961); *b* 26 Sept 1922; *Educ* Accrington GS, Univ of Manchester (BSc, Fairbairn Prizeman, MSc, PhD, DSc); *m* 1947, Margaret May, da of John Livesey; 1 da (Alison Margaret b 1950), 2 s (John Garth b 1951, Nigel Thomas b 3 Sept 1954); *Career* extra mural res (Univ of Manchester) Miny of Supply 1943-46; Imperial Coll London: asst lectr 1946-47, lectr 1947-56, reader 1956-61, asst dir Dept of Electrical 1958-61; James Watt prof of electrical engrg Univ of Glasgow 1961-; memb Nat Electronics Cncl 1963-78, fndr memb CNAA 1964-70, pres Br Soc of Rheology 1970-72, chm Scottish Indust-Univ Ctee in Engrg 1969-71, memb Cncl RSE 1980-83 and 1986- (vice pres 1989-), vice princ Univ of Glasgow 1977-80, scientific advsr Scottish Office Indust Dept 1987-; Gledden fell Univ of W Aust 1983; fell Acoustical Soc of America 1960, FInstP 1960, hon fell Inst of Acoustics 1980, FEng 1984, FIEE 1984, FRSE 1968; *Books* Proceedings Fourth European Conferance on Integrated Optics (jt ed 1987), Integrated Optics (contrib 1983, ed S Martellucci and RN Chester), Acoustics And Spectroscopy (contrib 1979), Molecular Basis of Transitions and Relaxations (contrib 1978, D J Meier), Molecular Motions in Liquids (contrib 1974), Interdisciplinary Approach to Liquid Lubricant Technology (contrib 1973); *Recreations* classical music, hill walking; *Style—* Prof John Lamb, CBE; 5 Cleveden Crescent, Glasgow G12 OPD (☎ 041 339 2101); Department of Electronics and Electrical Engineering, The University, Glasgow G12 8QQ (☎ 041 330 4799, fax 041 330 4907)

LAMB, Prof Joseph Fairweather; s of Joseph Lamb (d 1972), of Balnacake, Brechin, Angus, and late Agnes May, *née* Fairweather; *b* 18 July 1928; *Educ* Auldbar Public Sch, Brechin HS, Univ of Edinburgh (MB ChB, BSc, PhD); *m* 1, 10 Sept 1955 (m dis 1989), Olivia Jane, da of Robert Horne (d 1960), of Uganda; 5 s (Joseph William b 1958, John Robert b 1962, Andrew Noel b 1964, James Gerald b 1985, William Finlay b 1987), 1 da (Angela Gail b 1956); m 2, 21 April 1989, Bridget Cecilia, da of John Kingsley Cook, of London; *Career* Nat Serv RAF 1947-49, house offr appts 1955-56, lectr Royal (Dick) Vet Coll Univ of Edinburgh 1958-61, lectr then sr lectr physiology Univ of Glasgow 1961-69, Chandos prof physiology Univ of St Andrews 1969-; sec Physiological Soc 1982-85, chm and fndr memb Save Br Sci 1986-; memb RSM, FRCPE 1984, FRSE 1986, FRSA 1987; *Books* Essentials of Physiology (1980); *Recreations* sailing; *Clubs* Sceptre Sailing, RSM, Sloane; *Style—* Prof Joesph Lamb, FRSE; Kenbrae, Millbank, Cupar, Fife KY15 5DP (☎ 0334 52791); Dept of Biology & Pre-Clinical Med, Bute Medical Buildings, Univ of St Andrews, Fife KY16 9TS (☎ 0334 76161/7233, fax 0334 52791)

LAMB, Katherine Margaret; da of Charles Gordon Wallace, of 31 Charteris Rd, Longnidory, East Lothian, and Emelia Campbell, *née* Stewart; *b* 9 Oct 1952; *Educ* St George's Sch For Girls Edinburgh, Univ of Aberdeen (BSC); *m* 27 Dec 1980, John Crawford Lamb, s of William Lamb (d 1980); 1 s (Gordon), 1 da (Rosie); *Career* personnel mangr William Thyne 1974-86, dir William Sommerville & Son Ltd 1986-; *Recreations* golf, skiing, swimming, hill walking; *Clubs* Dundas GC; *Style—* Mrs Katherine Lamb

LAMB, Hon Kenneth Henry Lowry; CBE (1985); s of 1 Baron Rochester, CMG (d 1955); *b* 23 Dec 1923; *Educ* Harrow, Trinity Coll Oxford (MA); *m* 1952, Elizabeth Anne, da of Douglas Arthur Saul (d 1981); 1 s, 2 da; *Career* WWII instr Lt RN 1944-46; pres Oxford Union 1944; sr lectr history and English RN Coll Greenwich 1946-53; BBC 1955-80: head of religious broadcasting 1963-66, sec 1967-68, dir public affrs 1969-77, special advsr broadcasting res 1977-80; sec to Church Cmmrs 1980-85; chm Charities Effectiveness Review Tst 1987-; FRSA; *Recreations* golf, cricket, music; *Clubs* MCC, Nat Lib, Royal Fowey Yacht, Highgate Golf; *Style—* The Hon Kenneth Lamb, CBE; 25 South Terr, London SW7 2TB (☎ 01 584 7904)

LAMB, Sir Larry; *b* 15 July 1929; *Educ* Rastrick GS; *m* Joan Mary Denise, *née* Grogan; 2 s, 1 da; *Career* ed: Daily Mail (Manchester) 1968-69, The Sun 1969-72 and 1975-81 (ed dir 1971-81, dep chm News Gp 1979-81), dep chm and ed-in-chief Western Mail Ltd W Aust 1981-82; ed: The Australian 1982, Daily Express 1983-86; chm Larry Lamb Assocs 1986-; kt 1980; *Recreations* cricket, fell-walking, fishing; *Style—* Sir Larry Lamb; Bracken Cottage, Bratton Fleming, N Devon EX31 4TG

LAMB, Lady (Margaret) Pansy Felicia; da of 5 Earl of Longford, KP, MVO (ka 1915); *b* 1904; *m* 1928, Henry Lamb, RA, MC (d 1960); 1 s, 2 da; *Style—* The Lady Pansy Lamb; 22 Via di San Stefano del Cacco, Rome, Italy

LAMB, Peter John; s of Henry Robert Lamb, of St Ives, Cambs, and Lilly Greensitt (d 1954); *b* 4 July 1944; *Educ* Ramsey Abbey Sch, Coll Mid-Essex Chelmsford (HNC); *m* 1987, Suzanne Beverley, da of Paul Ryder, of Swansea, Wales; 2 s (Jonathan b 1983, Tobias b 1985), 2 da (Nicola b 1966, Alison b 1968); *Career* dir Gyproc Insulation Ltd 1985-, md Insulation Techniques and Materials Ltd 1983-85, md West Anglia Insulation Ltd 1985-; *Recreations* sailing, teaching meditation; *Clubs* Haven Ports Yacht, Br Meditation Soc; *Style—* Peter Lamb, Esq; Gyprol Insulation, 10 Leather Lane, Braintree, Essex CM7 7UZ (☎ 0376 22713, telex 987804)

LAMB, Richard Anthony; s of Maj Stephen Eaton Lamb, of 30 Redcliffe Square, London, and Leila Mary, *née* Whyte; *b* 11 May 1911; *Educ* Downside, Merton Coll Oxford (MA); *m* 18 Feb 1948, Daphne, da of Sir Paul Butler, KCMG; 2 s (Richard Michael b 1952, Peter Stephen b 1954), 2 da (Rosemary Anita b 1951, Penelope Mary b 1956); *Career* 12A (TA) 1939, Capt AFHQ 1943 (Algiers), Maj GSO2 RA with Friuli Italian Div 1943-45; dir Hartley Main Collieries 1939-49; ed: City Press 1966-76, Military History Monthly (formerly War Monthly) 1979-82; memb Cumberland CC 1946-52, Parly candidate: (Lib) Lichfield Gen Election 1945, (C) Stockton on Tees 1950, (Lib) N Dorset 1964-66; *Books* Montgomery in Europe (1983), Ghosts of Peace (1987), Failure of Eden Government (1987), Drift to War 1922-39 (1989); *Recreations* lawn tennis, travelling; *Clubs* Hurlingham, Utd Oxford and Cambridge, Nat Lib; *Style—* Richard Anthony Lamb, Esq; Knighton Manor, Broad Chalk, Salisbury, (☎ 0722 780 206)

LAMB, Rev Hon Roland Hurst Lowry; s of 1 Baron Rochester, CMG (d 1955); *b* 1917; *Educ* Mill Hill, Jesus Coll Cambridge; *m* 1943, Vera Alicia, da of Arthur Morse (d 1974), of Edgware, Middx; 1 s, 3 da; *Career* chaplain RAF 1942, Middle E 1944, supt Aberystwyth Eng Methodist circuit 1955-61, Callington 1961, resigned Methodist Miny 1967; gen sec Br Evangelical Cncl 1967-82; *Style—* The Rev the Hon Roland Lamb, MA; Meadowside, 13 Eversleigh Rise, South Darley, Matlock, Derbys DE4 2JW (☎ 0629 732645)

LAMB, Stuart Howard; s of William Lamb (d 1966), of Fairways, Walton Lane, Wakefield, and Ruth Evelyn, *née* Mellor; *b* 21 April 1948; *Educ* Queen Elizabeth GS Wakefield, Leicester Poly; *m* 1, 10 Sept 1969 (m dis 1974), Gillian Margaret, da of Robert Stuart Hadfield of Scarborough; 1 s (William Robert Stuart b 8 April 1970), 1 da (Deborah Jayne b 14 July 1972); m 2, 14 April 1979, Jean Lesley, da of Charles Willy Wagstaff, of Chevet Grange, Sandal; 2 da (Ruth Caroline b 11 March 1981, Charlotte Jane b 16 July 1983); *Career* chm William Lamb & Co (Footwear) Ltd 1967

1982 (dir 1967, jt md 1969), gp chm Gola Gp of Cos 1987; ABSI 1968; *Recreations* motor sailing, golf; *Clubs* Woodthorpe Golf; *Style*— Stuart Lamb, Esq; Walton Common Farm, Common Lane, Walton, Wakefield, W Yorkshire (☎ 0924 255376); 13B Bahia d'Or, Porto Petre, Mallorca, Balearics, Spain; Gola Gp of Cos, Stanley, Wakefield, W Yorkshire (☎ 0924 823541, fax 0924 820297, car 0860 618490)

LAMB, Hon Timothy Michael (Tim); s of 2 Baron Rochester; *b* 24 March 1953; *Educ* Shrewsbury, The Queen's Coll Oxford (MA); *m* 23 Sept 1978, Denise Ann, da of John Buckley, of Witham, Essex; 1 s (Nicholas b 9 Nov 1985), 1 da (Sophie b 15 Sept 1983); *Career* professional cricketer with Middlesex CCC 1974-77, Northants County Cricket Club 1978-83; sec/gen mangr Middlesex CCC 1984-88; cricket sec Test and County Cricket Bd 1988-; *Recreations* cricket, golf, travel; *Clubs* MCC, Lord's Taverners; *Style*— The Hon Tim Lamb; c/o Test and County Cricket Board, Lord's Ground, London NW8 8QZ (☎ 071 286 4405, fax 071 289 5619, telex 24462 TCCB G)

LAMB, Dr Trevor Arthur John; s of Arthur Bradshaw Lamb, and Ruth Ellen, *née* Eales; *b* 7 Dec 1929; *Educ* Wanstead GS Essex, QMC Univ of London (BSc, PhD); *m* 1952, Shirley Isabel, da of Sidney Charles Hubbard (d 1971); 2 s (John b 1957, Martin b 1960), 2 da (Susan b 1960, Karen b 1964); *Career* pt/t lectr Univ of London 1950-52, section ldr Bristol Aeroplane Co Engine Div 1952-56 (tech offr), section head Imperial Chemical Industs 1956-58 (mangr machine and press shops), gen mangr Leeds Plant Marston Excelsior Ltd (subsid of ICI Metals Div, became Imperial Metal Industs Ltd, styled IMI Ltd) 1958-62 (factory mangr); IMI Ltd: md Radiator Gp 1966, md Marston Radiators, Marston Radiator Servs Ltd, Paxman Coolers Ltd, Marston Refrigeration Ltd; dir Overseas and Mktg Main Bd 1974-87, dir Australasian Refinery and Fabrication Gps main bd 1974-77, responsible for Value Gp 1977-89 and Fluid Power Gp 1981-; non-exec dir bd W Canning Ltd 1980-, dir IMI plc, dir IMI Gp Inc USA, govr The City Technol Coll Kingshurst; chm: IMI Int Ltd, IMI Fluid Power Int Ltd, Norgren Co USA, Watson Smith Ltd, Norgren Martonair Ltd, Webber Electro Components Ltd; chm Norgren Martonair: Pacific Pty Ltd Aust, Europa GmbH Germany, SpA Italy, SA Spain, Pty Ltd Aust, (NZ) Ltd; *Recreations* tennis, swimming; *Style*— Dr Trevor Lamb; Mead End, Bushwood Drive, Dorridge, Solihull, W Mids B93 8JL (☎ 0564 773877); IMI plc, PO Box 216, Witton, Birmingham B6 7BA (☎ 021 356 4848, fax 021 344 3249, telex 336771)

LAMBART, Lady Katherine Lucy; *née* Lambart; da of 12 Earl of Cavan, TD, DL; *b* 2 March 1955; *Educ* St Mary's Sch Wantage, L'Institut Alpin Videmanette (Alliance Française) Vaud Switzerland; *m* 1978 (m dis 1986), Lorenzo Ruiz Barrero, s of Don Lorenzo Ruiz Jimenez, of Madrid; 1 s (Lorenzo b 1980), 1 da (Natasha b 1982); *Style*— The Lady Katherine Lambart; 174 Broomwood Rd, London SW11

LAMBE, Lady; Petra Rachel; changed first name from Lesbia 1966; only da of Sir Walter Orlando Corbet, 4 Bt, JP, DL (d 1910); *b* 27 Jan 1905; *Educ* Downe House Sch; *m* 1, 1927 (m dis 1940), Cdr Victor Ivor Henry Mylius, formerly RN, only s of Henry Mulius, of Villa Olivetta, Lago di Como; 1 s (Andrew); m 2, 1940, Adm of the Fleet Sir Charles Edward Lambe, GCB, CVO (d 1960); 1 s (James, *see* Fairfax-Lucy, Hon Lady), 1 da (Louisa); *Career* vice-chm Women's Cncl; *Recreations* music, gardening, reading, translating; *Style*— Lady Lambe; Knockhill House, St Fort, Newport on Tay, Fife (☎ 0382 542152); 21 Stafford Place, London SW1 (☎ 071 828 3953)

LAMBERT *see also*: Drummond Lambert

LAMBERT, Dr Andrew David; s of David George Lambert, of Toad Hall, Beetley, Norfolk, and Nola, *née* Burton; *b* 31 Dec 1956; *Educ* Hamond's Sch Swaffham, City of London Poly (BA), King's Coll London (MA, PhD); *m* 27 Nov 1987, Zohra, da of Mokhtar Bouznat, of Casablanca, Morocco; *Career* lectr modern int history Bristol Poly 1983-87, conslt Dept of History and Int Affrs RNC Greenwich 1987-89, sr lectr in war studies RMA Sandhusrt; dir SS Great Britain Project 1989-, cncllr Soc Navy Records 1985; *Books* Battleships in Transition: The Creation of the Steam Battlefleet 1815-1960 (1984 and 1985), Warrior: Restoring The World's First Ironclad (1987), The Crimean War: British Grand Strategy Against Russia 1853-56 (1990); *Recreations* running, motorcycling; *Clubs* Vintage Motorcycle; *Style*— Dr Andrew Lambert; 47 Fane House, Waterloo Gdns, London E2 9HY

LAMBERT, Angela Maria; da of John Donald Helps, of Sherborne, Dorset, and Ditha Helps, *née* Schroeder; *b* 14 April 1940; *Educ* Wispers Sch, St Hilda's Coll Oxford (BA); *m* 1962, (m dis 1967), Martin John Lambert; 1 s (Jonathan Martin Andrew), 2 da (Carolyn Ruth (Mrs Butler), Marianne Jane Colette); *Career* private sec to Earl of Longford, PC 1964-67, freelance writer and journalist 1967-71; reporter: ITN (News At Ten) 1972-76, LWT 1976-77, Thames TV 1978-88; columnist and feature writer The Independent 1988-; memb: RSA, PEN; *Books* Unquiet Souls (1984), 1939: The Last Season of Peace (1989), Love Among The Single Classes (1989), No Talking After Lights (1990); *Recreations* France, family, cats, books, wine, foreign films in black and white with subtitles; *Clubs* Fred's; *Style*— Mrs Angela Lambert; Flat 4, 15 Collingham Rd, London SW5 ONU (☎ 071 244 9762, fax 071 244 8297); The Independent, Newspaper Publishing plc, 40 City Rd, London EC1Y 2DB (☎ 071 956 1879)

LAMBERT, Sir Anthony Edward; KCMG (1964, CMG 1955); s of Reginald Everitt Lambert (d 1968), of Pensbury House, Shaftesbury, Dorset, and Evelyn Lambert (d 1968); *b* 7 March 1911; *Educ* Harrow, Balliol Coll Oxford; *m* 28 April 1948, Ruth Mary, da of Sir Arthur Percy Morris Fleming, CBE (d 1960); 3 da (Jane b 1949, Katherine b 1950, Julia b 1953 d 1958); *Career* entered Foreign Serv 1934; cnsllr: Stockholm 1949 and Athens 1951; min to Bulgaria 1958; ambass: Tunisia 1960, Finland 1963, Portugal 1966-70; *Clubs* Brooks's; *Style*— Sir Anthony Lambert, KCMG; 16 Kent Hse, 34 Kensington Ct, London W8 5BE (☎ 071 937 7453)

LAMBERT, Barry Unwin; s of Henry Benjamin Lambert (d 1981), and Elsie, *née* Organ (d 1977); *b* 28 Jan 1934; *Educ* The John Lyon Sch, Harrow GS, Br Sch of Osteopathy (DO, MRO); *m* 3 Oct 1959, Penelope Frances, da of Harold David Frearson (d 1982); 3 s (Simon b 1960, Jonathan b 1962, Christopher b 1967); *Career* registered osteopath; chm of the Gen Cncl & Register of Osteopaths 1971-76 and 1983-, memb Osteopathic Educn Fndn Cncl of Mgmnt 1968-; memb Nat Tst and RSPB; *Recreations* fly fishing, field sports, sailing, wood engraving, wood carving, etching; *Clubs* RSM, Rotary; *Style*— Barry U Lambert, Esq; Fairlead, Chart Lane, Reigate, Surrey (☎ 0737 245500, 0737 245041)

LAMBERT, Colin Joseph; s of Virgil Joseph (d 1978), of Mangus-Colorado, and Elynor Marie, *née* Keefe; *b* 17 Jan 1948; *Educ* Chouinard Art Inst Los Angeles California; *m* 25 Sept 1983, Catherine Mary, da of Joseph Finn, of 71 Kenilworth Park, Dublin 6, Ireland; *Career* sculptor; works incl: Within Reach six 9 foot bronze figures Stamford Forum Stamford Connecticut USA 1987, Equilibrium two 6 foot figures in bronze London United Bldg London 1988, The Harvest Was Great Renaissance Vineyard California 1989, winner competition for public sculpture for shopping dist Warminster Wilts; memb Free Painters and Sculptors; *Recreations* working; *Style*— Colin Lambert, Esq; Flint Barn Studio, West End, nr Essendon, Hatfield, Herts AL9 5RQ

LAMBERT, David John; s of Edward Lambert (d 1959), of London, and Gladys Julia, *née* Coleman (1966); *b* 16 July 1938; *Educ* St Pauls Way Secdy Sch Bow London; *m* 26 Sept 1959, Vera Margaret, da of John Hatcher, BEM (d 1976), of Wilton, Wilts; 1 s (Simon David b 1967), 1 da (Jacqueline Anne (Mrs Fuller) b 1963); *Career* RAPC; trainee estimator then dir of estimating and survey Nat Painting Contractors, chm and md John Ruskin Co Ltd; former pres: Horley Lions Club, Friends of Farmfield Hosp; pres: Mid Surrey Construction Trg Gp, E Surrey Assoc of Bldg Employers Confedn; former nat pres Nat Fedn of Painting and Decorating Contractors; FICM 1981, FBIM 1982, FFB 1985; *Recreations* rambling, swimming, gardening, reading; *Style*— David Lambert, Esq; Long Melford, 76 Oakwood Rd, Horley, Surrey RH6 7BX (☎ 0293 773 262); John Ruskin Co Ltd, Old Carters Yard, 65B Lumley Rd, Horley, Surrey RH6 7RF (☎ 0293 774521)

LAMBERT, Sir Edward Thomas; KBE (1958), CVO (1957); s of Brig-Gen Thomas Stanton Lambert, CB, CMG (d 1921); *b* 19 June 1901; *Educ* Charterhouse, Trinity Coll Cambridge; *m* 1936, Rhona Patricia Gilmore, da of Harold St George Gilmore (decd), and of Mrs J H Molyneux (decd); 1 s, 1 da; *Career* entered HM Foreign Serv 1926; served: at Bangkok, Batavia, Medan, Curacao; FO: consul-gen Geneva 1949-53, Paris 1953-59; *Style*— Sir Edward Lambert, KBE, CVO; Crag House, Aldeburgh, Suffolk

LAMBERT, Hon Grace Mary; da of 1 Viscount Lambert, PC (d 1958); *Style*— The Hon Grace Lambert; 1 St Germans, Exeter, Devon (☎ 0392 74219)

LAMBERT, Sir Greville Foley; 9 Bt (GB 1711); s of Lionel Foley Lambert (d 1934, 4 s of 6 Bt); suc cousin, Sir John Foley Grey, 8 Bt, 1938; *b* 17 Aug 1900; *Educ* Rugby; *m* 1932, Edith Roma, da of Richard Batson; 3 da; *Heir* kinsman, Peter John Biddulph Lambert; *Style*— Sir Greville Lambert, Bt; Flat 5, Henleydale, Stratford Rd, Shirley, Solihull, W Midlands

LAMBERT, Harry Paul; s of James Lambert (d 1979), of Kent, and Irene, *née* Kennedy; *b* 20 Feb 1944; *Educ* Chorlton Tech High, Stockport Coll; *m* 1974, Shan Elizabeth Rose, da of Trevor Watkins, of Kent; 1 s (Mark James Trevor b 1981), 1 da (Katie Elizabeth b 1982); *Career* chm and chief exec The Adscene Gp plc (dir 1974-); dir Assoc of Free Newspapers 1983-; *Style*— Harry Lambert, Esq; Newspaper House, Wincheap, Canterbury, Kent CT1 3YR

LAMBERT, Henry Uvedale Antrobus; s of Roger Uvedale Lambert, MBE (d 1985), of Cuckseys Farm, Blechingley, Surrey, and Muriel Froude (d 1982), da of Sir Reginald Antrobus, KCMG, CB; *b* 9 Oct 1925; *Educ* Winchester, New Coll Oxford (MA); *m* 19 Jan 1951, Diana Elsworth, da of Capt Henry Eric Dumbell, Royal Fus (d 1957), of Bridge Vere, Farnham, Surrey; 2 s (Michael Uvedale b 1952, Roger Mark Uvedale b 1959), 1 da (Jennifer b 1955); *Career* RN 1939-45, Sub Lt RNVR, later RNR Lt Cmdr (ret); chm Barclays Bank Int Ltd 1979-83 (joined Barclays 1948, dir 1966, vice chm 1973, dep chm Barclays Bank plc 1979-85); chm: Barclays Bank UK Ltd 1983-85, Sun Alliance & London Insur Gp 1985 (vice chm 1978-83, dep chm 1983-85), Agric Mortgage Corpn plc 1985 (dep chm 1977-85); dir BA 1985-89; fell Winchester Coll 1979; FCIB 1967; *Recreations* fishing, gardening, naval history; *Clubs* Brooks's, MCC; *Style*— Henry Lambert, Esq; c/o Agricultural Mortgage Corporation plc, Royal Bank of Canada Centre, 71 Queen Victoria Street, London EC4V 4DE

LAMBERT, Sir John Henry; KCVO (1980), CMG (1975); s of Col R S Lambert, MC (d 1976), and Mrs H J F Mills; *b* 8 Jan 1921; *Educ* Eton, Sorbonne, Trinity Coll Cambridge; *m* 1950, Jennifer Ann, da of Sir Robert Urquhart, KBE, CMG; 1 s, 2 da; *Career* served Grenadier Gds 1940-45; entered Foreign Serv 1945: cnsllr Stockholm 1964, commercial cnsllr and consul-gen Vienna 1971-74, min and dep cmdt Br Mil Govt Berlin 1974-77, ambass to Tunisia 1977-81; dir Heritage of London Tst 1981-; chm Channel Tunnel Investmts plc 1986-; Grand Offr Order of Tunisian Republic 1980; *Clubs* Hurlingham, MCC, Royal St Georges Golf, Sandwich; *Style*— Sir John Lambert, KCVO, CMG; 103 Rivermead Court, London SW6 3SB (☎ 071 731 5007; office: 071 973 3809)

LAMBERT, Hon Margaret Barbara; CMG (1965); da of 1 Viscount Lambert, PC (d 1958); *b* 1906; *Educ* Lady Margaret Hall Oxford, LSE; *Career* serv WWII in Euro Service of BBC; asst ed Br Documents of Foreign Policy 1946-50, lectr in modern history Univ Coll of South West 1950-51, ed-in-chief of German Diplomatic Archives FO 1951-, lectr in modern history St Andrew's Univ 1956-60; *Style*— The Hon Margaret Lambert, CMG; 39 Thornhill Rd, London N1 (☎ 01 607 2286)

LAMBERT, 3 Viscount (UK 1945); Michael John Lambert; yr s of 1 Viscount Lambert, PC (d 1958); suc bro, 2 Viscount 1989; *b* 29 Sept 1912; *Educ* Harrow, New Coll Oxford; *m* 5 Sept 1939, Florence Dolores, da of Nicholas Lechmere Cunningham Macaskie, QC; 3 da (Hon Sophia Jane b 1943, Hon Caelia Anne Georgiana (Hon Mrs Pereira) b 1946, Hon Flavia Mary b 1949); *Heir* none; *Style*— The Rt Hon the Viscount Lambert; Casanuova di Barontoli, 53010 Rocco a Pilli, Siena, Italy

LAMBERT, Maj Olaf Francis; CBE (1984), DL (1989); s of Walter Lambert (d 1965), of London, and Edith Jemima, *née* Gladstone (d 1963); *b* 13 Jan 1925; *Educ* Caterham Sch, RMA Sandhurst (wartime); *m* 1950, Lucy, da of John Adshead (d 1943), of Macclesfield; 2 s (Simon, Charles), 2 da (Sarah, Harriet); *Career* cmmnd RTR, served NW Europe 7th Armoured Div, and BAOR, ret as Maj 1959, Hon Col Royal Mil Police (TA) 1984; landowner; AA: joined 1959, md 1973-77, dir gen 1977-87, vice pres 1987-, dir of all associated AA cos up to 1987; dir Mercantile Credit Ltd 1980-85; memb: Int Advanced Motorist Cncl 1965-89, Jt Standing Ctee RAC, AA, RSAC 1968-87; world pres Int Touring Alliance 1983-86 (memb 1973-87); chm: Friendly Soc 1986-, Br Road Fedn 1987-; memb Driving and Vehicle Licensing Agency Advsy Bd 1990-, memb: Hants Ctee Army Benevolent Fund, Winchester Cathedral Tst Cncl; Freeman City of London, Liveryman Worshipful Co of Coachmakers and Coach Harness Makers; FRSA, CBIM, FIMI; *Recreations* hunting, skiing, walking, music; *Clubs* Army & Navy; *Style*— Maj O F Lambert, CBE, DL; Elm Farm, Baybridge, Owslebury, Hampshire

LAMBERT, Patricia (Pat); OBE (1980); da of Frederick Burrows (d 1961), and Elsie, *née* Mummery (d 1971); *b* 16 March 1926; *Educ* Malet Lambert HS Hull, West Bridgford GS Nottingham; *m* 1949, (m dis 1982), George Richard, s of Richard Palin Lambert (d 1982); 1 s (Warwick b 1954), 1 da (Margaret b 1952); *Career* memb Nat Consumer Cncl 1978-82; Br Standards Inst 1972-, chm Consumer Standards Advsy Ctee (now Consumer Policy Ctee) 1972-, memb Bd 1980-86, chm Consumer Standards Advsy Cncl 1980-86, memb Quality Assur Bd 1986 (govr 1986-), memb various other BSI ctees; memb: Unit Tst Assoc Consumer Affrs Panel (now Consumer Standards Ctee) 1981, Advsy Ctee on Safety of Electrical Appliances Br Tech Approval Bd 1980-86, Direct Mail Servs Standards Bd 1983- (dir 1986-); dir and vice chm Think Br Campaign 1983 (now Invest in Britain); memb: Advsy Panel UTA 1981, Nat House Building Cncl 1980; public interest dir Life Assur & Unit Tst Regulatory Orgn 1986, memb Gas Consumers Cncl (E Mids Panel) 1988; *Style*— Pat Lambert, OBE; 42 Tollerton Lane, Tollerton, Nottingham (☎ 06077 2412)

LAMBERT, Sir Peter John Biddulph; 10 Bt (GB 1711), of London, but does not yet appear on the Official Roll of the Baronetage; o s of John Hugh Lambert (d 1977), and Edith, *née* Bance (d 1988); suc kinsman Sir Greville Foley Lambert, 9 Bt (d 1988); *b* 5 April 1952; *Educ* Upper Canada Coll, Trent Univ Peterborough (BSc), Univ of Manitoba Winnipeg (MA); *m* 1989, Leslie Anne, da of Richard Welkos Lyne; *Heir* uncle, Robert William Lambert b 6 June 1911; *Style*— Sir Peter Lambert, Bt; c/o 483 Spadina Rd, Toronto, Ontario, Canada M5P 2W6

LAMBERT, Lady; (Edith) Roma; *née* Batson; da of Richard Batson; *m* 15 July 1932, Sir Greville Foley Lambert, 9 Bt (d 1988); 3 da; *Style*— Lady Lambert; 12 Newborough Rd, Shirley, Solihull, Warwicks

LAMBERT, Stephen; s of Roger Lambert, of London, and Monika, *née* Wagner; *b* 22 March 1959; *Educ* Thames Valley GS, UEA, Univ of Oxford; *m* 8 April 1988, Jenni, da of Martin Russell, of SA; 1 da (Jessica b 1988); *Career* BBC TV 1983-: documentary features; prodr and dir: 40 Minutes 1987-, Inside Story 1987-, East Side Story 1987, Dolebusters 1988, Greenfinches 1988, Who'll Win Jeanette? 1989, Crack Doctors 1989, Hilary's In Hiding 1990, Malika's Hotel 1990, Children of God 1991; memb BAFTA; *Books* Channel Four (1982); *Recreations* sailing; *Style*— Stephen Lambert, Esq; BBC TV, Kensington House, Richmond Way, London W14 (☎ 081 895 6257/8)

LAMBERT, Prof Thomas Howard; s of Henry Thomas Lambert, and Kate Lambert; *b* 28 Feb 1926; *Educ* Univ of London (BSc, PhD); *Career* UCL: lectr 1951-63, sr lectr 1963-65, reader 1965-67, Kennedy prof of mechanical engrg 1967; hon memb RCNC, FRINA, FIMechE; *Recreations* gardening; *Style*— Prof Thomas Lambert; Department of Mechanical Engineering, University College London, Gower St, London WC1 7JE (☎ 071 387 7050, tlx 296273)

LAMBERT, Thomas Peter; s of Thomas Lambert (d 1938); *b* 7 Oct 1927; *Educ* Stowe, RMA Sandhurst; *m* 1956, Davinia Margaret, *née* Walford; 4 children; *Career* Capt Inniskilling Dragoon Gds; pres Bradford C of C 1975-77, regnl dir Nat West Bank Ltd 1977, jt md John Foster & Son Ltd 1980, chm Wool Industry Res Assoc 1981; *Recreations* shooting, tennis, gardening; *Style*— Thomas Lambert, Esq; The Old Vicarage, S Stainley, Harrogate, N Yorks (☎ 0423 770169)

LAMBERT, Verity Ann; da of Stanley Joseph Lambert, and Ella Corona Goldburg; *b* 27 Nov 1935; *Educ* Roedean, Sorbonne; *Career* prodr BBC TV 1963-74, controller Drama Dept Thames TV 1974-76, chief exec Euston Films 1976-82, dir of prodn and exec prodr Thorn EMI Screen Entertainment 1982-85, ind film prodr 1985- (co name Cinema Verity Ltd), prodr A Cry in the Dark, exec prodr May to December BBC TV; series incl: Sleepers (BBC), GBH (C4), Boys from the Bush (BBC), Coasting (Granada TV); *Recreations* good books, good food; *Style*— Ms Verity Lambert; Cinema Verity Ltd, The Mill House, Millers Way, 1A Shepherds Bush Rd, London W6 7NA (☎ 081 749 8485)

LAMBIE, Alexander Ogilvie; s of J M S Lambie (decd); *b* 24 Oct 1938; *Educ* Mill Hill Sch, Univ of Durham; *m* 1969, Diana Margaret, *née* Owen; 1 da; *Career* md Cammell Laird Shipbuilders Ltd 1979-84, chm Cammell Laird (Training) Ltd 1976-84, dep md British Shipbuilders 1984-85; dir: A+P Appledore Ltd 1985-; A&P Appledore International Ltd 1989-; md A&P Appledore Aberdeen Ltd 1989-, dir A+P Appledore Holdings Ltd 1990; FRSA 1984: Liveryman Worshipful Co of Shipwrights 1987; *Style*— Alastair Lambie, Esq; St Nicholas House, Burton, South Wirral, Cheshire L64554

LAMBIE, David; MP (Lab) Cunninghame S 1983-; s of late Robert Lambie, JP (d 1985); *b* 13 July 1925; *Educ* Ardrossan Acad, Univ of Glasgow (BSc, DipEd), Univ of Geneva; *m* 1954, Netta May, da of Alexander Merrie (d 1985), of Barnett Court, Saltcoats, Ayr; 1 s, 4 da; *Career* teacher; chm Scottish Lab Pty 1965-66, MP (Lab) Central Ayrshire 1970-1983, memb Select Ctee on Parly Cmmr for Admin 1974-83, chm Select Ctee Scottish Affrs 1982-87 (memb 1979-87), sec All Pty Parly Energy Gp; memb Cncl of Europe and Western Euro Union (alternate memb 1987-), USDAW Sponsored, FEIS; *Recreations* watching football; *Clubs* Cunninghame North Labour (Saltcoats); *Style*— David Lambie, Esq, MP; 11 Ivanhoe Drive, Saltcoats, Ayrshire (☎ 0294 64843; office 76844); House of Commons, London SW1 (☎ 071 219 5140)

LAMBLE, Lloyd Nelson; s of William Henry Sylvester Lamble (d 1956), of Melbourne, Australia, and (Francis) Alma Spencer, *née* Potter (d 1971); *b* 8 Feb 1914; *Educ* Wesley Coll Melbourne, Melbourne Univ Conservatorium of Music; *m* m 1, Marjorie Ellerton, *née* Barrett; m2, (Doris) Barbara, da of Dr S A Smith; 1 s (Lloyd William Addison (Tim) b 5 Sept 1941), 1 da (Elizabeth (Mrs Danny Gillespie) b 22 Sept 1944); m 3, (Joyce) Lesley Wallis, *née* Jackson; 1 adopted s (Lloyd Wallis Addison b 21 Dec 1962), 1 adopted da (Helene Caroline (b 28 March 1963); *Career* aommenced piano studies at age 4, joined travelling circus, became world's youngest radio announcer at age of 17, freelance radio acting, first theatre appearance in Novello's Fresh Fields (comedy Theatre Melbourne), first starring role as Danny in Night Must Fall (comedy Theatre Melbourne) 1936, lead in first musical comedy Wild Violets (His Majesty's Melbourne) 1937, founded own drama sch Radio Theatre Guild 1938, formed own company to tour NSW and Queensland 1945, 1 year on fair grounds 1946, first London play The Martin's Nest (Westminster Theatre) 1952, first tv appearance The Passing Parade (BBC) 1952; films incl: Where no Vultures Fly 1952, The Story of Gilbert and Sullivan 1953, The Straw Man 1954, The Dambusters 1954, The Bells of St Trinians (as Inspr Sammie Kemp-Bird) 1954, The Man Who Knew Too Much 1956, The Good Companions, Quatermass 2 1957, Blue Murder at St Trinians 1957, Our Man in Havana 1959, The Pure Hell of St Trinians 1960, No Sex Please We're British 1973, Eskimo Nell 1974; tv incl: Corridors of Power, Z Cars, Softly Softly, Armchair Theatre, Lady Killers, The Naked Civil Servant, Howard's Way; recent theatre incl: The Picture of Dorian Gray (Greenwich), Having a Ball (Liverpool, Salisbury, Hornchurch), On Golden Pond (Dundee), Habeas Corpus, School for Scandal (Pitlochry), Gigi (Cardiff); currently Charles in Me and My Girl (Adelphi Theatre); 60 years in showbusiness June 1991; *Recreations* classical music, swimming, tennis, golf, writing, philosophy, house building; *Style*— Lloyd Lamble, Esq; 55 Greencroft Gardens, London NW6 3LL (☎ 071 624 4320); Janet Mills Associates, Bycopse Cottage, 2 Old Derry Hill, Calne, Wilts SN11 9PJ (☎ 0249 658189)

LAMBTON, Viscount; (*see*: Durham, Baron)

LAMBTON, Antony Claud Frederick; (Viscount Lambton, by which courtesy title he was known in House of Commons); s of 5 Earl of Durham (d 1970); disclaimed peerages (Earldom of Durham, Barony of Durham and Viscountcy of Lambton) for life 1970; *b* 10 July 1922; *m* 1942, Belinda, da of Maj Douglas Holden Blew-Jones, of Westward Ho, N Devon; 1 s, 5 da; *Heir* to renounced Earldom of Durham, s, Lord (courtesy title of Baron) Durham; *Career* MP (C) Northumberland (Berwick-on-Tweed) 1951-73; PPS to Min of Supply 1954, parly under-sec of state for Def (RAF) 1970-73; *Books* Snow and Other Stories (1983); *Style*— Antony Lambton, Esq; Biddick Hall, Lambton Park, Chester-le-Street, Durham; Lambton Castle, Fence Houses, Durham (☎ Fence Houses 36)

LAMBTON, Lady Elizabeth Mary; *née* Petty-FitzMaurice; yr da of 6 Marquess of Lansdowne, DSO, MVO (d 1936); *b* 1927; *m* 1950, Maj Charles William Lambton (s of Brig-Gen Hon Charles Lambton, DSO, himself 4 s of 2 Earl of Durham); 3 s, 1 da; *Style*— The Lady Elizabeth Lambton; The Old Rectory, Calstone, Calne, Wilts SN11 8PZ (☎ 0249 812149)

LAMBTON, Hon John George; s of 5 Earl of Durham (d 1970), and his 2 w, Hermione, *née* Bullough (d 1990); *b* 1932; *Style*— The Hon John Lambton; 39 Hill Street, London W1

LAMBTON, Lucinda; *née* Lambton; eldest da of Antony Lambton (6 Earl of Durham who disclaimed peerage 1970); *b* 10 May 1943; *m* 1, 16 Jan 1965, Henry Mark Harrod, s of Sir (Henry) Roy Forbes Harrod; 2 s (Barnaby, Huckleberry); m 2, 11 Jan 1986 (m dis), Sir Edmund Fairfax-Lucy, 6 Bt, of Charlecote Park, Warwick; *Career* photographer, writer; presenter producer and dir of television programmes: On The Throne, Animal Crackers, Cabinet of Curiosities, The Great North Road, Desirable Dwellings; six pt series: Hurray for Today on modern architecture, Hurray for Today USA; 18 pt series The A-Z of Britain; *Books* Vanishing Victoriana, Temples of Convenience, Chambers of Delight, Beastly Buildings, Album of Curious Houses; *Style*— Lucinda Lambton; The Old Rectory, Hedgerley, Buckinghamshire SL2 3UY

LAMBTON, Hon Mrs (Monica Dorothy); *née* Brand; da of 3 Viscount Hampden, GCVO, KCB, CMG (d 1958); *b* 3 March 1914; *m* 1933, D'Arcy Lambton (d 1938), s of Hon Claud Lambton (decd); 2 children; *Style*— The Hon Mrs Lambton; Saxon House, Shottisham, Woodbridge, Suffolk IP12 3HG (☎ 0394 411322)

LAMDIN, Ian David; s of David Robert Lamdin, and Zara Patricia, *née* Berry; *b* 5 April 1960; *Educ* Pinewood Sch, Radley, Pembroke Coll Oxford (BSc); *Career* jt venture auditor Petrofina UK Ltd 1988; Freeman Worshipful Co of Distillers 1983; ACA; *Style*— Ian Lamdin, Esq; Petrofina (UK) Ltd, Petrofina House, 1 Ashley Ave, Epsom, Surrey KT18 5AD (☎ 03727 44712)

LAMMIMAN, Surgn Rear Adm David Askey; LVO (1978); s of Herbert Askey Lammiman (d 1943), and Lilian Elsie, *née* Park (d 1981); *b* 30 June 1932; *Educ* Wyggeston Sch Leicester, St Bartholomew's Hosp (MB BS, DA, DObstRCOG); *m* 1, 7 Sept (m dis 1984), Sheila Mary, da of Frederick Graham (d 1963); 3 s (Christopher b June 1958, Robert b April 1960, Michael b March 1969), 1 da (Susie b Feb 1967); m 2, 30 Oct 1984, Caroline Dale, da of Francis John Brooks (Lt Cdr RN, ret); *Career* res house offr Redhill County Hosp and St Bartholomew's Hosp 1957-58; joined RN 1959; clinical asst 1966-69: Southampton Gp of Hosps, Alder Hey Children's Hosp, Liverpool/Radcliffe Infirmary Oxford; conslt anaesthetist RN Hosp Malta 1969-71, RN Hosp 1971-73 and 1978-82, RN Hosp Gibraltar 1973-75, RN Hosp Plymouth 1975-76; serv in ships: HMS Chaplet 1959, HMS Eagle 1967-68, HMY Britannia 1976-78; dir of med personnel MOD 1982-84; med offr i/c: RN Hosp Plymouth 1984-86, RN Hosp Haslar 1986-88; Surgn Rear Adm (Support Med Servs) 1989-90, Med Dir Gen (Naval) Oct 1990-; QHS 1987; memb Assoc of Anaesthetists 1962, FFARCS 1969; *Recreations* fly fishing, golf, tennis; *Clubs* Navy and Military, RN Sailing Assoc (Portsmouth); *Style*— Surgn Rear Admiral David Lammiman, LVO; Defence Medical Services Directorate, Ministry of Defence, Room 624, First Avenue House, 40-48 High Holborn, London WC1V 6HE (☎ 071 430 5890, fax 071 430 5095)

LAMOND, James Alexander; JP (Aberdeen), MP (Lab) Oldham Central and Royton 1983-; s of Alexander Lamond (d 1965), of Burrelton, Perthshire; *b* 29 Nov 1928; *Educ* Burrelton Sch, Coupar Angus; *m* 1954, June Rose, da of Joseph Wellburn, of Aberdeen; 3 da; *Career* draughtsman; MP (Lab) Oldham E 1970-83, Lord Provost and Lord-Lt of Aberdeen 1970-71; vice-pres World Peace Cncl; memb Chms Panel North Atlantic Assembly 1979; *Style*— James Lamond, Esq, JP, MP; 15 Belvidere St, Aberdeen (☎ 0224 638074); Flat 7, 26 Medway St, London SW1 (☎ 071 222 1874); House of Commons, London SW1A 0AA (☎ 071 219 4154); Bartlam Place, Oldham (☎ 061 620 0118)

LAMOND, William; s of Robert Lamond (d 1973); *b* 26 April 1925; *Educ* Shawlands Acad; *m* 1950, Kathleen Mary; 2 s, 1 da; *Career* CA; dir James Finlay plc; *Recreations* golf, bridge; *Clubs* Oriental, Western (Glasgow); *Style*— William Lamond, Esq; Windward, Ferniegair Ave, Helensburgh, Scotland (☎ 0436 75014)

LAMONT, Norman Stewart Hughson; PC (1986), MP (C) Kingston upon Thames 1972-; s of Daniel Lamont; *b* 8 May 1942; *Educ* Loretto, Fitzwilliam Coll Cambridge; *m* 1971, Alice Rosemary, da of Lt-Col Peter White; 1 s, 1 da; *Career* PA to Duncan Sandys 1965, CRD 1966-68, N M Rothschild & Sons 1968-79, contested (C) Hull E 1970; chm: Coningsby Club 1970-71, Bow Gp 1971-72; PPS to Arts Min 1974; oppn spokesman: Consumer Affairs 1975-76, Industry 1976-79; under-sec of state Dept of Energy 1979-81; min of state: DTI 1981-85, Defence Procurement 1985-86; financial sec to Treasy May 1986-July 1989, chief sec to the Treasy July 1989-Nov 1990; Chancellor of the Exchequer Nov 1990-; *Style*— The Rt Hon Norman Lamont, MP; 11 Downing Street, London SW1

LAMONT, Prof William Montgomerie; s of Hector Lamont (d 1985), of Harrow, London, and Hughina Carmichael, *née* MacFadyen (d 1982); *b* 2 Feb 1934; *Educ* Harrow Weald County GS, Univ of London (BA, PGCE, PhD); *m* 5 April 1961, Linda Mary, da of Lionel Stanley Cuthbert Murphy; 3 da (Catriona b 1 Jan 1962, Ailsa b 10 May 1963, Tara b 26 June 1965); *Career* schoolmaster Hackney Downs Secdy Sch 1959-63, lectr Aberdeen Coll of Educn 1963-66, prof of history Univ of Sussex 1966- (lectr 1966, reader 1970), dean Sch of Cultural and Community Studies Univ of Sussex 1981-86, dir Centre for the History of Br Political Thought Folger Library Washington; FRHistS 1969; *Books* Marginal Prynne (1963), Godly Rule (1969), The Realities of Teaching History (ed, 1972), Politics Religion and Literature in the 17th century (jtly, 1975), Richard Baxter and the Millennium (1979), The World of the Muggletonians (jtly, 1983); *Recreations* watching Arsenal; *Style*— Prof William Lamont; Arts Building, University of Sussex, Falmer, Brighton SU1 1CX (☎ 0273 606755)

LAMONT OF THAT ILK, Peter; Chief of Clan Lamont; s of Noel Brian Lamont of that Ilk (decd); *b* 1955; *Career* student St Patrick's Coll Manly, NSW, Australia; *Style*— Peter Lamont of that Ilk; St Patrick's College, Darley Rd, Manly, NSW 2025, Australia

LAMPARD, Martin Robert; s of Austin Hugo Lampard (d 1964); *b* 21 Feb 1926; *Educ* Radley, Christ Church Oxford; *m* 1957, Felice, da of John MacLean (d 1944); 3 da; *Career* Sub Lt RNVR North Atlantic; slr 1952, Ashurst Morris Crisp & Co ptnr 1957, sr ptnr 1974; dir: Allied Breweries 1981-, Laird Gp, Canadian Overseas Packaging Industs Ltd, Hambros 1983-; *Recreations* farming in E Anglia, sailing, shooting; *Clubs* Royal Yacht Squadron, Royal Ocean Racing; *Style*— Martin Lampard, Esq; c/o Ashurst Morris Crisp, 7 Eldon Drive, London EC2 (☎ 071 247 7666); 507 Willoughby House, Barbican, London EC2Y 8BN (071 588 4048); Theberton House, Theberton, nr Leiston, Suffolk (☎ 0728 830510)

LAMPERT, Catherine Emily; da of Lt Cdr Chester Graham Lampert (d 1981), of Washington DC, USA, and Emily Schubach Lampert; *b* 15 Oct 1946; *Educ* Brown Univ (BA), Temple Univ (MA); *m* 22 Dec 1971, Robert Keith, s of Harry Mason (d 1960); *Career* sr exhibition organiser Arts Cncl of GB 1973-88, dir Whitechapel Art Gallery 1988-; organiser of several exhibitions incl retrospectives of: Frank Averbach, Lucian Freud, Michael Andrews, Anthony Caro, Henri Matisse, Drawings and Sculputure, Auguste Rodin, In the Image of Man, Arshile Gorky, Euan Uglow; memb Slade Ctee Univ of London; memb ICOM, CIMAM; *Books* The Drawings and Sculpture of Auguste Rodin (1977); *Style*— Mrs Catherine Lampert; Whitechapel Art Gallery, 80-82 Whitechapel High St, London E1 (☎ 071 377 5015, fax 071 377 1685)

LAMPERT, Hon Mrs (Jill Mary Joan); 3 da of 3 Baron Acton, CMG, MBE, TD (d 1989); *b* 15 June 1947; *m* 1969, Nicholas Lampert; 2 da; *Style*— The Hon Mrs Lampert; 46 Clarence Road, Moseley, Birmingham B13 9UH

LAMPITT, Stuart Richard; s of Joseph Charles Lampitt, of 38 Bridgnorth Rd, Wombourne, nr Wolverhampton, and Muriel Ann Lampitt; *b* 29 July 1966; *Educ* Kingswood Sch, Dudley Coll of Technol; *Career* professional cricketer; Worcestershire CCC 1985- (awarded county cap 1989); jr Himley 1976-80, Dudley 1980-85, Stourbridge 1985-90, represented Worcs Cricket Assoc under 16 and under 19 (capt), S England under 19 int youth cricket tournament Bermuda 1985, under 25 v India

Edgbaston 1990, player and coach Mangere NZ 1986-87 and 1987-88; record for number of runs in a season Worcs Schs Cricket Assoc under 19; hon with Worcestershire: Co Championship 1988 and 1989, Refuge Assurance League 1988; footballer: Brierly Hill & Dudley Schs, West Midlands Co Schs, Kingwinford Wanderers, Handrahans Timbers, Sandwell Borough, Oldbury, training sessions with various Football Leaugue clubs; *Recreations* golf, any other ball sports; *Style*— Stuart Lampitt, Esq; Worcestershire CCC, New Road, Worcester (☎ 0905 422694)

LAMPL, Sir Frank William; s of Dr Otto Lampl (d 1934), and Olga, *née* Jellinek (d Auschwitz 1944); *b* 6 April 1926; *Educ* Faculty of Architecture and Engrg Tech Univ Brno Czechoslovakia; *m* 1948, Blanka, da of Jaroslav Kratochvil (d 1981); 1 s (Thomas b 1950); *Career* emigrated from Czechoslovakia to the UK 1968, exec dir Bovis Construction 1974, md Bovis Int 1978, dir Bovis Ltd 1979, chm Bovis Construction and Bovis Int 1985, exec dir Peninsular and Oriental Steam Navigation Co (P&O) 1985, dir Lehrer McGovern Bovis Inc New York 1986, chm Bovis (Far E) Ltd 1987; CBIM, FCIOB; kt 1990; *Clubs* RAC; *Style*— Sir Frank Lampl; Liscartan House, 127 Sloane St, London SW1X 9BA (☎ 081 422 3488, fax 071 730 4722, telex 919435)

LAMPLUGH, Diana Elizabeth; da of David Gwynydd Howell (d 1971), of Cheltenham, and Eileen Mary, *née* Weddell; *b* 30 July 1936; *Educ* Seven Springs Cheltenham, Westonbirt Sch Tetbury, West London Inst of Higher Education (Dip Ed, Swimming Teachers Dip); *m* 18 Oct 1958, Paul Crosby Lamplugh, s of Eric Crosby Lamplugh; 1 s (Richard b 21 Jan 1960), 3 da (Susannah Jane (Suzy) b 3 May 1961, disappeared 28 July 1986, presumed murdered, Tamsin Rose b 13 July 1962, Elizabeth Madge b 16 June 1970); *Career* sec to: headmaster Wycliffe Coll 1955-57, dir Carl Rosa Opera Co 1957-58, controller of programmes BBC TV 1958-60; teacher of swimming Richmond Adult and Further Educn (specialist in elderly and disabled) 1968-, fndr and dir BR Slimnastics Assoc 1973-89, teacher of slimnastics relaxation and tension control Richmond Adult and Community Coll 1974-88, tutor and assessor of slimnastics teachers 1973-89 (created concept of Whole Person Approach to Fitness), res project Disabled Living Fndn 1985 (Sports and Exercise for the Visually Handicapped, published 1989), fndr memb Exec Ctee of Int Stress & Tension Control Soc UK, memb Ctee on Violence Health & Safety Exec, fndr and dir The Suzy Lamplugh Trust 1986- (campaigner for action on personal safety for people at work and about their daily lives, care and help for seekers of missing persons and changes in sentencing and treatment of sex offenders); tstee The Gracewell Inst; *Books* Slimnastics (1970), Stress and Overstress (1974), A Guide to Good Living (1980), The Whole Person Approach to Fitness (1984, all with Pamela Nottidge), Beating Aggression (1988), Survive the 9-5 (1989), Physical Activities for Visually Handicapped People (1989); ed and writer Br Slimnastics Assoc booklets; author of numerous articles and manuals; *Recreations* opera, boats, riding, swimming, teaching, speaking, enjoying my children, being alone with my husband; *Clubs* soroptimists UK Int, IOD; *Style*— Mrs Diana Lamplugh; 14 East Sheen Ave, London SW14 8AS (☎ home 081 876 1838; business 081 392 1839, fax 081 392 1830)

LAMPRELL-JARRETT, Peter Neville; s of Reginald Arthur Lamprell-Jarrett (d 1966); *b* 23 June 1919; *Educ* Cliftonville Coll; *m* 1944, Kathleen, da of Percival Francis Furner (d 1973); 2 children; *Career* architect and surveyor 1954-; pres Incorporated Assoc of Architects and Surveyors 1967-68; life vice pres London Caledonian Catholic Assoc; Freeman City of London 1978, Liveryman Worshipful Co of Wheelwrights; FFB, FRSA, FSAScot; KCSG 1975, KCHS 1974, Cdr Cross Polonia Restituta (Poland) 1982; *Recreations* painting, fishing, walking, classical music; *Clubs* Royal Cwlth Soc, Lighthouse; *Style*— Peter Lamprell-Jarrett, Esq; Hramsa, Reeds Lane, Sayers Common, Hassocks, W Sussex; Carrick House, Carrick Castle, by Lochgoil, Argyll (☎ 030 13 394); 42 Mall Chambers, Kensington Mall, London W8 4DZ (☎ 071 229 8247)

LAMPSON, Hon Victor Miles George Aldous; s of 1 Baron Killearn, GCMG, CB, MVO, PC (d 1964), by his 2 w Jacqueline (herself da of Marchese Senator Aldo Castellani, KCMG); hp of half-bro, 2 Baron; *b* 9 Sept 1941; *Educ* Eton; *m* 1971, Melita Amaryllis Pamela Astrid, da of Rear Adm Sir Morgan Charles Morgan Giles, DSO, OBE, lately MP Winchester; 2 s, 2 da; *Career* late Capt Scots Gds; *Style*— The Hon Victor Lampson; Franchise Manor, Burwash, Sussex

LAN, Henry Hing-Kam; s of Kim Fa Lan (d 1971), and Sun Yin Lan *née* Chan (d 1987); *b* 9 Nov 1948; *Educ* St Joseph Coll Mauritius; *m* 5 Jan 1977, Christiane, da of Felix Li-Kwet-Liit (Mauritius); 2 s (Oliver b 20 Sept 1979, Nigel b 1 Aug 1983); *Career* CA, ptnr David Rubin & Co; *Recreations* tennis, squash; *Style*— Henry Lan, Esq; 14 Parkfield Gardens, N Harrow, Middx HA2 6JR; David Rubin & Co, Pearl Assurance House, 319 Ballards Lane, N Finchley, London N12 8LY (☎ fax 01 446 2994)

LANCASTER, Christopher; s of George Lancaster (d 1959), of Headingley, Leeds, and Grace Evelyn, *née* Foster (d 1974); *b* 10 Aug 1932; *Educ* Queen Elizabeth GS Wakefield, Trinity Hall Cambridge (MA, LLM); *m* 12 Sep 1959, Aase,da of Kristoffer Böe (d 1965), of Bergen, Norway; 2 s (Stephen b 1960, Richard b 1962), 1 da (Anne-Lise b 1964); *Career* articled clerk Booth and Co 1956-59, asst slr William Henry and Co 1959-60 (ptnr 1960-72), ptnr Willey Hargrave 1972-88 (conslt 1988-), pres Leeds Law Soc 1979-80 (press offr 1972-79); memb: Headingley Rotary 1974-84, Leeds Skyrack Lions Club 1965-69, tstee Grassington Angling Club 1972-85, Law Soc 1959; *Recreations* fly-fishing, English history, jazz piano; *Style*— Christopher Lancaster Esq; Park Lane House, Westgate, Leeds, LS1 2RD (☎ 0532 441 151, fax 0532 436 050, telex 265871)

LANCASTER, Graham; s of Eric Lancaster, of Salford, Gtr Manchester, and Edna, *née* Butterworth; *b* 24 Feb 1948; *Educ* Salford GS, Mid Cheshire Coll (HND); *m* 10 Oct 1971, Lorna Mary, da of William Thomas White (d 1979); *Career* Hawker Siddeley Aviation 1968-69, asst to dir of info and educn The Textile Cncl 1969-70, trg devpt offr Corah Ltd 1971, policy coordinator to pres CBI 1972-77, head of public affrs ABTA 1977, chm Biss Lancaster plc 1978-; MInstM, MIPR, FRSA; *Books* The Nuclear Letters (1979), Seward's Folly (1980), The 20 Percent Factor (1987); *Recreations* writing; *Clubs* Groucho's; *Style*— Graham Lancaster, Esq; Biss Lancaster plc, 69 Monmouth Street, London WC2H 9DG (☎ 071 497 3001, fax 071 497 8915, telex 894767 BISSPR G)

LANCASTER, Dame Jean; DBE (1963); da of Richard C Davies, of Blundellsands, Lancs; *b* 11 Aug 1909; *Educ* Merchant Taylors' Crosby Lancs; *m* 1967, Roy Cavander Lancaster; *Career* dir WRNS 1961-64; *Style*— Dame Jean Lancaster; Greathed Manor, Dormansland, Lingfield, Surrey

LANCASTER, Bishop of (RC) 1985-; Rt Rev John Brewer; s of Eric Winston Brewer (d 1977), of Derbyshire, and Laura Helena Webster (d 1987); *b* 24 Nov 1929; *Educ* Ushaw Coll Durham, Venerable English Coll Rome, Gregorian Univ Rome (STL, JCL, PhL); *Career* vice-rector Ven English Coll Rome 1964-71, auxiliary bishop of Shrewsbury 1971-83, co-adjutor to Bishop of Lancaster 1983-85, Bishop of Lancaster 1985-; *Style*— The Rt Rev the Bishop of Lancaster; Bishop's House, Cannon Hill, Lancaster LA1 5NG (☎ 0524 32231)

LANCASTER, John Meredith; s of Dr Zikmund F Foltin, and Alica Foltinova, *née* Polakova; *b* 23 Aug 1919; *Educ* Komenius Univ Bratislava, Coll of Aeronautical Engrg London, LSE; *m* 12 June 1943, Jean Gertrude, da of Lt-Col George William Thomas Coles, TD; 2 s (Michael John b 1944, David John b 1967), 3 da (Jane Deirdre (Mrs Brentnall) b 1949, Sally Jean (Mrs de Elye Cole) b 1951, Judith Elisabeth b 1953); *Career* RAOC Workshop Unit 6 AA Div 1940-42, cmmnd E Surrey Regt 1942, Intelligence Corps, Interservice Topographical Dept 1943-46, Maj GSO2; head of mkt res Rio Tinto Co Ltd 1947-51, mktg exec Metallo-Chemical Refining Co 1952; The British Sulphur Corporation Ltd: joined 1953, md 1954-85, chm 1970-89, non-exec dir 1989-; dir CRU Holdings Co Ltd 1986-; chm and md: L & B Consultants Ltd 1985-, Seven Rocks Mining Ltd 1989-; chm: Orlestone Parish Cncl 1961-, Hamstreet Victory Hall 1966-, Hamstreet and Warchorme Branch Ashford Cons Assoc 1963- (memb Exec Ctee); memb: CPRE, Romney Marsh Level, Fertiliser Soc; Francis New Meml Medal; Lord of the Manor of Orlestone 1969-; Freeman City of London 1978, Liveryman Worshipful Co of Stationers and Newspaper Makers 1978; *Books* World Survey of Sulphur Resources (1966); *Recreations* swimming, skiing, gardening; *Clubs* Carlton; *Style*— John Lancaster, Esq; Court Lodge, Orlestone, Ashford, Kent (☎ 0233 732 339); 4 Eccleston Square, London SW1; 31 Mount Pleasant, London WC1X 0AD (☎ 071 837 5600, fax 071 837 0292, telex 918918 LONDON SULFEX G)

LANCASTER, Vice Adm Sir John Strike; KBE (1961), CB (1958); s of George Henry Lancaster (d 1955), of Plymouth; *b* 26 June 1903; *Educ* King Edward VI Sch Southampton; *m* 1927, Edith Laurie (d 1980), da of late Ernest Robert Jacobs; 2 da; *Career* Rear Adm Personnel Home Air Cmd 1956-59, Vice Adm 1959, dir-gen Manpower Admty and Chief Naval Supply and Secretariat Offr 1959-62, ret 1962; *Recreations* gardening; *Style*— Vice Adm Sir John Lancaster, KBE, CB; Moorings, 59 Western Way, Alverstoke, Gosport, Hants PO12 2NF (☎ 0705 584172)

LANCASTER, (Christopher Ronald) Mark; s of Charles Ronald Lancaster (d 1978), and Muriel, *née* Roebuck (d 1977); *b* 14 May 1938; *Educ* Bootham Sch York, Univ of Newcastle upon Tyne (BA); *Career* artist; exhibited London and NY 1965-, artist in res Kings Coll Cambridge 1968-70, designer Merce Cunningham Dance Company NY 1974-, works in pub collections include Tate Gallery, V & A, Arts Cncl, Br Cncl, Fitzwilliam Museum Cambridge, Museum of Modern Art NY; NY dance and performance award 1989 (Bessie); *Style*— Mark Lancaster, Esq; Dunselma Castle, Strone, Argyll, Scotland PA23 8RU; Mayor Rowan Gallery London, 31a Burton Place, London W1 (☎ 071 499 3011, fax 071 355 3486)

LANCASTER, Noel Brownrigg; s of Thomas William Carruthers Lancaster (d 1938), and Margaret Mary, *née* Callander (d 1964); *b* 25 Dec 1925; *Educ* Nelson Sch Wigton, Queen Elizabeth GS Penrith; *m* 6 Jan 1955, Elizabeth Susan, da of James Lamb Chalmers (d 1961); 2 s (Ian Callander, David Forbes d 1958), 1 da (Hilary Elizabeth Margaret); *Career* ptnr NB Lancaster & Co CAs; former sec, Cumberland Agric Soc 1961-68; farmer W Mains, Penton, Carlisle; Lord of the Manor of Docker; FCA; *Recreations* golf, fishing, shooting; *Clubs* Powfoot Golf, Brampton Golf, Carlisle Golf; *Style*— Noel B Lancaster, Esq; Little Drawdykes, Whiteclosegate, Carlisle, Cumbria; N B Lancaster & Co, Chartered Accountants, St Cecil Street, Carlisle, Cumbria (☎ 0228 25788)

LANCASTER, Patricia Margaret; da of Vice Adm Sir John Lancaster, CBE, CB, qv, of Moorings, 59 Western Way, Alverstoke, nr Gosport, Hants, and Edith Laurie, *née* Jacobs (d 1980); *b* 22 Feb 1929; *Educ* Univ of London (BA), Univ of Southampton (PGCE); *Career* teacher St Mary's Sch Calne Wilts 1951-58, housemistress and teacher of English St Swithun's Winchester 1958-62; headmistress: St Michaels Petworth 1962-73, Wycombe Abbey Sch Bucks 1974-88; pres GSA 1980-81; church cmmr 1989; govr: Berkhamsted Sch, Marlborough Coll, St Mary's Calne, St Swithun's Winchester, Repton Sch; *Recreations* theatre, art galleries; *Style*— Miss Patricia Lancaster; 8 Vectis Rd, Alverstoke, nr Gosport, Hants (☎ 0705 583 189)

LANCASTER, Reg; s of Tim Lancaster, of Leasingham, Lincs, and Elizabeth, *née* McLean; *b* 6 April 1935; *Educ* Bearsden Acad Dumbartonshire, Ballyclare HS Co Antrim; *m* 25 March 1957, Annabelle McLaren, da of John M Allan; 1 s (Raymond b 7 July 1958), 1 da (Heather b 16 June 1960); *Career* photographer; joined Daily Express Scotland 1951-62, Daily Express London 1962- (seconded to Paris office 1965-73); Sports Picture of 1960 Encyclopedia Britannica award, News Picture of 1978 and 1987, Br Press Awards, Royal Picture 1987 Kodak awards, winner of many awards at regnl nat and int film-making competitions; fell Inst of Amateur Cinematographers; *Recreations* film-making; *Style*— Reg Lancaster, Esq; Daily Express, Ludgate House, 245 Blackfriars Rd, London EC1P 1DQ (☎ 071 928 8000)

LANCASTER, Dr Richard; s of Norman Gerald Lancaster (d 1981), and Elizabeth Lynda, *née* Theobald; *b* 25 March 1938; *Educ* Rugby, Sidney Sussex Coll Cambridge (MA), Middx Hosp (MB BChir, PhD); *m* Helen Elizabeth, da of Rev John York Barber; 2 s (Adam Henry b 6 March 1971, Harry John b 16 Jan 1975), 1 da (Amelia Clare b 15 Jan 1970); *Career* house physician and house surgn Middx Hosp 1964-65 (med registrar 1966-67, lectr in clinical pharmacology 1967-73); conslt physician St Mary's and St Charles Hosps 1973-; FRCP 1979, MRCP 1966; memb RSM 1968; *Books* Pharmacology in Clinical Practice (1980); *Recreations* sports, cycling, chess; *Clubs* RSM; *Style*— Dr Richard Lancaster; 3 Alexander St, London W2 (☎ 071 727 7936); 54 Wimpole St, London W1 (☎ 071 487 3504, fax 071 486 7797)

LANCASTER SMITH, Dr Michael John; s of Ronald Lancaster Smith, of Hastings, Sussex, and Marie, *née* Wright; *b* 4 Sept 1941; *Educ* Hastings GS, London Hosp Med Sch Univ of London (BSc, MB BS, MD); *m* 11 April 1964, Susan Frances Bayes, da of Lt Arthur Bannister (d 1946); 1 s (Daniel b 1969), 2 da (Catherine b 1966, Naomi b 1971); *Career* registrar and sr registrar The London Hosp 1969-73 (house physician and surgn 1966-68), sr lectr St Bartholomews Hosp 1973-74, conslt physician Queen Marys Hosp Sidcup Kent 1974-; memb Br Soc of Gastroenterology, vice chm Bexley Health Authy 1986-89; memb BMA; FRCP; *Books* Problems in Practice - Gastroenterology (1982), Problems in Management - Gastroenterology (1985), Ulcer and Non Ulcer Dyspepsia (1987); *Recreations* cricket, music, theatre; *Style*— Dr Michael Lancaster Smith; Stableside House, 36 Southborough Rd, Bickley, Bromley, Kent BR1 2EB (☎ 081 464 4184); Queen Marys Hospital, Sidcup, Kent (☎ 081 302 2678 ext 4231); Blackheath Hospital, London SE3; The Sloane Hospital, Beckenham, Kent

LANCE, Prof (Edward) Christopher; s of F Nevill Lance (d 1987), and Elizabeth, *née* Bagnall (d 1989); *b* 17 Jan 1941; *Educ* Dulwich, Trinity Coll Cambridge (MA, PhD); *m* 9 April 1966, Mary Margaret *née* Hall; 1 s (Stephen b 1969), 1 da (Elizabeth b 1971); *Career* lectr in pure maths Univ of Newcastle 1965-73, reader Univ of Manchester 1973-78, visiting prof Univ of Pa USA 1978-80 (1971-72), prof Univ of Leeds 1980-; vice-pres London Mathematical Soc 1989-; *Recreations* hill walking, music; *Style*— Prof Christopher Lance; School of Mathematics, The University of Leeds, Leeds, W Yorks LS2 9JT (☎ 0532 335142, 556473, fax 0532 429925, telex 0532 429925)

LANCELEY, Ian Kenneth; s of Thomas Peter Kenneth Lanceley, of Paignton, Devon, and Barbara Doreen, *née* Allen; *b* 12 Feb 1946; *Educ* Blundell's, Coll of Law; *m* 12 Dec 1980, Valerie, da of Frederick William Kay (d 1987), of Kirby Hill, Richmond, North Yorks; 2 s (Adam b 1981, Charles b 1983); *Career* admitted slr 1971; ptnr Freeborough Slack & Co 1977-85, jt sr ptnr Freeboroughs 1985-; *Recreations* squash, golf; *Clubs* Roehampton; *Style*— Ian K Lanceley, Esq; 14/15 Vernon St, West Kensington, London W14 (☎ 071 602 3474, fax 071 603 7004, car 0836 256 167)

LANCELOT, James Bennett; s of Rev Roland Lancelot (d 1983), and Margaret, *née* Tye; *b* 2 Dec 1952; *Educ* St Paul's Cathedral Choir Sch, Ardingly, RCM, King's Coll Cambridge (MA, MusB); *m* 31 July 1982, Sylvia Jane, da of Raymond Hoare, of Cheltenham; 2 da (Rebecca b 1987, Eleanor b 1989); *Career* asst organist Hampstead Parish Church and St Clement Danes Church 1974-75, sub-organist Winchester Cathedral 1975-85, master of the choristers and organist Durham Cathedral 1985-, conductor Univ of Durham Choral Soc 1987, numerous recordings; memb Cncl RCO; FRCO (chm 1969), ARCM 1970; *Recreations* railways; *Style—* James Lancelot, Esq; 6 The College, Durham DH1 3EQ (☎ 091 386 4766)

LANCHBERY, John; OBE (1990); *Educ* RAM (Henry Smart scholar); *Career* served WWII RAC 1942-45; conductor; musical dir Metropolitan Ballet 1947-49, freelance 1949-51, conductor Sadler's Wells Theatre Ballet 1951-60, princ conductor Royal Ballet (arranged ballet scores La Fille Mal Gardee, The House of Birds, The Dream) 1960-72, musical dir Australian Ballet (arranged ballet scores incl Don Quixote, Mayerling, The Merry Widow) 1972-76, guest conductor The Royal Ballet 1976-, music dir American Ballet Theatre 1978-80, guest ballet conductor world's leading opera houses; composer music for film and tv incl: The Tales of Beatrix Potter, The Turning Point, The Evil under the Sun, Nijinsky; awards: Bolshoi medal, Queen Elizabeth II Coronation award (From Royal Acad of Dance), Carina Ari medal; *Style—* John Lanchbery, Esq, OBE; c/o Roger Stone, Concert /Artist Management, West Grove, Hammers Lane, Mill Hill, London NW7 4DY (☎ 071 855 0222, telex 896061 AscogG)

LANCHIN, Gerald; s of Samuel Lanchin (d 1969), of London, and Sara, *née* Bernstein (d 1967); *b* 17 Oct 1922; *Educ* St Marylebone GS, LSE (BCom); *m* 1951, Valerie Sonia, da of Charles Lyons (d 1970), of London; 1 s (Michael), 2 da (Wendy, Judith); *Career* HM Forces 1942-46; under sec Dept of Trade 1971-82; chm Direct Mail Servs Standards Bd 1983-89, consIt trade practices; memb: Cncl Consumers' Assoc 1983-88, Data Protection Tbnl 1985-; vice pres Nat Fedn of Consumer Gps 1984-; *Books* Government and the Consumer (1985); *Recreations* photography, music, walking; *Clubs* Reform; *Style—* Gerald Lanchin, Esq; 28 Priory Gardens, Berkhamsted, Herts HP4 2DS (☎ 0442 875283)

LAND, (Harold) Brook; s of David Land, of London, and Zara, *née* Levinson; *b* 12 March 1949; *Educ* St Paul's; *m* 7 Dec 1975, Anita Penny, da of Leslie Grade; 1 s (Daniel Edward b 30 April 1983), 1 da (Lesley Olivia b 19 Jan 1981); *Career* Nabarro Nathanson Solicitors: articled clerk 1967-72, asst slr 1972-74, ptnr 1974-; memb Law Soc 1972; *Recreations* reading, TV, poker; *Clubs* Annabel's; *Style—* Brook Land, Esq; Nabarro Nathanson, 50 Stratton St, London W1X 5FL (☎ 071 493 9933, fax 071 629 7900)

LAND, David; s of Solomon Land (d 1952), and Sarah Land; *b* 22 May 1918; *Educ* Davenant Fndn GS London; *m* 1945, Alexandra Zara, da of Capt A V Levinson, RFC; 2 children; *Career* serv WWII with RASC; impresario and prodr; fndr David Land (Agency) Ltd which introduced Harlem Globetrotters to Europe, personal mangr to Tim Rice and Andrew Lloyd Webber 1969, dep chm Robert Stigwood Gp Ltd 1979; co-productions: Jesus Christ Superstar (NY 1971, London 1972), Joseph and the Amazing Technicolor Dreamcoat (London 1973), Jeeves (London 1975), Evita (with Robert Stigwood, London 1978, Olivier Award and NY 1979, Tony and Drama Desk Awards), Swan Esther (1983); admin Dagenham Girl Pipers 1948-, chm and exec dir Theatre Royal Brighton, chm Young Vic Theatre London; *Recreations* theatre and youth organisations, poker, cricket; *Style—* David Land, Esq; Nevill House, Nevill Rd, Rottingdean, Sussex; Robert Stigwood Group Ltd, 118-120 Wardour St, London W1V 4BT (☎ 071 437 3224)

LAND, James Gordon Murray; OBE (1979); s of Gordon William Land (d 1964), Marion Lina, *née* King (d 1978); *b* 10 Sept 1932; *Educ* Marlborough; *m* 18 Aug 1956, Betty Winifred; 1 s (Tristram b 1957), 1 da (Teresa b 1959); *Career* ptnr ;Price Waterhouse 1968-(joined 1955, served Spain Italy and Libya); pres Br C of C Spain 1977-79, vice pres cncl Br C of C Continental Europe; memb ICAEW (cncl memb rep EEC); *Recreations* cooking, painting, photography; *Style—* James Land, Esq, OBE; Price Waterhouse, Paseo Du La Castellana 43, 28046 Madrid, Spain (☎ 010 34 1 308 35 00, fax 010 341 308 35 66, telex 42164 PWCOE)

LAND, Prof Michael Francis; s of Prof Frank William Land (d 1990), and Nora Beatrice, *née* Channon (d 1985); *b* 12 April 1942; *Educ* Birkenhead Sch Cheshire, Jesus Coll Cambridge (BA, Frank Smart prize in Zoology), UCL (PhD); *m* 1, (m dis 1980), Judith Drinkwater; 1 s (Adam Michael b 1969); m 2, 10 Dec 1980, Rosemary, da of James Clarke; 2 da (Katherine Rosemary b 1981, Penelope Frances b 1983); *Career* asst prof Univ of Calif Berkeley 1969-71 (miller fell 1967-69); Biological Sciences Univ of Sussex: lectr 1972-78, reader 1978-84, prof 1984-; sr visiting fell Aust Nat Univ Canberra 1982-84; memb Cncl of the Marine Biological Assoc 1987-91; memb Editorial Bd: Proceedings of Royal Soc, Jl of Experimental Biology, Jl of Comparative Physiology; FRS 1982; *publications:* 70 publications on aspects of animal vision in learned jls and popular sci jls; *Recreations* gardening, music; *Style—* Prof Michael Land, FRS; White House, Cuilfail, Lewes, East Sussex BN7 2BE (☎ 0273 476780); Sch of Biological Sciences, Univ of Sussex, Brighton BN1 9QG (☎ 0273 606755)

LAND, Peter Anthony; s of Anthony Land (d 1973), and Barbara Williamson, *née* Markland (d 1980); *b* 14 April 1927; *Educ* Bemrose Sch Derby; *m* 15 April 1952, Dorothy Jessica, da of Samuel Robert Pritchard (d 1989); 1 s (Patrick b 1956), 2 da (Jane b 1955, Sally b 1961); *Career* cmmnd Sherwood Foresters 1945-48; md Br Tport Hotels 1978-83, md Nat Carriers 1967-77; chief accountant: BTR Industries 1958-63, BR Western Region 1963-67; chm: J N Dobbin (Hldgs) Ltd 1980-85, Bisham Abbey Nat Sport Centre 1980-84, Wycombe Health Authy 1986-; tstee HRH Princess Christian's Hosp 1984-; Freeman: City of London, Worshipful Co of Cooks; FCA 1950, CBIM 1975; *Recreations* golf, travel, formerly cricket, hockey (former Capt Derbys); *Clubs* MCC; *Style—* Peter Land, Esq; South Riding, Bisham Rd, Marlow, Bucks (☎ 06284 2898); 3 Vicarage St, Colyton, Devon EX13 6JR (☎ 0297 52092)

LANDA, Clive Hugh Alexander; MBE (1980); s of Basil Walter Landa, of London, and Alice Applebaum (d 1956); *b* 11 July 1945; *Educ* William Ellis School, Queen's Coll Oxford (MA), London Graduate School of Business Studies (MSc); *m* 1981, Lynda, da of Sidney Henry James Bates (d 1986); *Career* md: Pearl & Dean Gp Ltd, Shepperton Studios Ltd, Air Call Teletext Ltd, Allen Computers Int Ltd; *Recreations* tennis, bridge; *Clubs* Carlton; *Style—* Clive Landa, Esq, MBE; Allen House, Station Rd, Egham, Surrey (☎ 0784 37411, car 0836 503165)

LANDALE, David William Neil; s of David Fortune Landale (d 1970), and Louisa D M C, *née* Forbes, (d 1956), yst da of Charles Forbes of Callander House, Falkirk, Stirlingshire; *b* 27 May 1934; *Educ* Eton, Balliol Coll Oxford (MA); *m* 1961, Norah Melanie, da of Sir Harold Roper, MC, MP (C) for N Cornwall 1949-59 (d 1969); 3 s (Peter b 1963, William b 1965, Jamie b 1969); *Career* Black Watch Royal Highland Regt 1952-54; Jardine Matheson & Co Ltd 1958-75: Hong Kong, Thailand, Taiwan, Japan (dir 1967-75); dir: Matheson & Co Ltd 1975-, Pinneys Hldgs Ltd 1982-87; chm: T C Farries & Co Ltd 1982-, Timber Growers UK Ltd 1985-87; appointed sec and keeper of Records of The Duchy of Cornwall 1987, dep Lord Lieut Nithsdale and Annandale (Dumfriesshire); *Recreations* all countryside pursuits, theatre, reading (history); *Clubs* Boodle's, Pratt's, New (Edinburgh); *Style—* David W N Landale, Esq; Duchy of Cornwall, 10 Buckingham Gate, London SW1E 6LA (☎ 071 834 7346; fax 071 931 9541)

LANDAU, Sir Dennis Marcus; s of late Michael Landau, metallurgist; *b* 18 June 1927; *Educ* Haberdashers' Aske's; *Career* chief exec Co-op Wholesale Soc, dep chm Co-op Bank plc; kt 1987; *Style—* Sir Dennis Landau; Co-operative Wholesale Society Ltd, PO Box 53, New Century House, Manchester M60 4ES (☎ 061 834 1212, telex 667046)

LANDAU, Hon Mrs (Jane Malca); *née* Mishcon; da of Baron Mishcon (Life Baron); *b* 1950; *m* m 1, 1971 (m dis), Anthony Jay; 1 s (Adam), 1 da (Lucy); m 2, 30 Oct 1990, Edward Landau; *Career* barr (under maiden name); *Style—* The Hon Mrs Landau

LANDAU, Steven Martin; s of Capt John Joseph Landau, of 11 Gay Close, London NW2, and Gloria Violet Landau, *née* Harvey; *b* 5 Dec 1949; *Educ* Warwick University (MSc); *m* 1977, Kay, da of Detective Inspector Roy Woolley, of 25 Denbigh Place, Lutterworth, Leics; 2 da (Kelly Elizabeth b 1980, Laura Jane b 1982); *Career* fin controller Levi Strauss N Europe 1978-80, md Herondrive 1985-88 (fin dir 1980-85); md Norfolk Fin 1988-; *Recreations* sport; *Style—* Steven Landau, Esq; Ashburton Hse, Lashbrook Rd, Lower Shiplake, Henley-on-Thames, Oxen RG9 3NX (☎ 073522 2203, car 0860 748632)

LANDER, John Hugh Russell; s of Hugh Russell Lander, of IOW, and Maude Louise, *née* Ellis; *b* 25 Feb 1944; *Educ* Sandown GS, Univ of Sheffield (BSc), Imperial Coll London (MSC, DIC); *m* 1972, Veronica Elvira, da of Peter Mathew Van Eijk, of Holland; 2 s (Robert b 1976, Edward b 1983), 2 da (Melody b 1975, Annabel b 1982); *Career* exploration dir RTZ Oil & Gas Ltd 1983-89, vice pres Exploration Platt Energy Corp 1983-86, md PICT Petroleum plc 1989-; *Recreations* sailing, squash; *Clubs* RAC, Lagos Yacht; *Style—* John Lander, Esq; 45 Burgh Heath Rd, Epsom, Surrey; Pict Petroleum plc, 33-37 Lower Regent Street, London SW1 (☎ 071 287 4393, telex 8811305)

LANDER, Maxwell; s of Gustave Lander (d 1948); *b* 10 May 1914; *Educ* King Edward's Sch Birmingham; *m* 1939, Helena Margaret, da of Wolf Halon; 1 da (Pamela Marjorie (Mrs Lander Brinkley)); *Career* former Col GHQ India Cmd; conslt actuary, jt sr ptnr Duncan C Fraser & Co 1950-84 (ptnr 1984-86), conslt William M Mercer Fraser Ltd 1986-, asst sec Admty 1947-50; pres Nat Assoc of Pension Funds 1981-85; Master Worshipful Co of Actuaries 1986-87; holder of Queen's Silver Jubilee medal; *Recreations* fast cars, reading, theatre, music, food and wine; *Clubs* RAC; *Style—* Maxwell Lander, Esq; 1st Floor, 189 Pall Mall House, Tithebarn St, Liverpool L2 2QU (☎ 051 236 9771); Flat 124, 25 Porchester Place, London W2 2PF (☎ 071 262 4119); 83 Waterloo Rd, Hillside, Southport, Merseyside PR8 2NW (☎ 0704 67408)

LANDERS, Brian Whitfield; s of William Reginald Harry Whitfield Landers (d 1964), of Beckenham, and Gladys Winifred, *née* Widgery (d 1979); *b* 22 March 1921; *Educ* City of London Sch; *m* 7 Sept 1943, Elizabeth Joan Marguerite, da of John Pearce, of Wooburn Green, Bucks (d 1950); 2 da (Valerie Elizabeth b 1947, Rosalind Mary b 1954); *Career* Pilot RAF 1941-46, Flt Lt, Flying Boat Capt with coastal cmd; slr; sr ptnr Waterhouse and Co London 1982-86; chm Castle Baynard Ward Club 1973-74; pres: City of Westminster Law Soc 1977-78, John Carpenter Club 1981-82; Liveryman Worshipful Co of Basketmakers 1956-; *Recreations* photography, cricket; *Clubs* MCC, Forty, City Livery, John Carpenter (Old Citizens' Assoc); *Style—* Brian W Landers, Esq; Cobbleston, The Glen, Farnborough Park, Kent BR6 8LR (☎ 0689 856209)

LANDES, Emil; s of Wilhelm Landes (d 1983), of London, and Toni, *née* Held; *b* 13 July 1932; *Educ* Parmiter's Sch, King's Coll Hosp London (BDS); *m* 7 Feb 1960, Suzanne Dorrit, da of Paul Fraenkel, of Stockholm, Sweden; 2 s (Anthony b 1963, Jeremy b 1966), 1 da (Viveca b 1961); *Career* Flt Lt dental branch RAF 1958-59 (Flying Offr 1957-58); dental surgn St Thomas' Hosp, St Mary's Hosp, currently in private practice Harley St; int tstee Alpha Omega Dental Fraternity; Freeman City of London 1971; GDC 1956, BDA 1956, SAAD 1971, RSM 1974, EDS 1983; *Recreations* golf, tennis, skiing, chess, reading, biographies; *Clubs* RAC, RAF; *Style—* Emil Landes, Esq; Penthouse West, Thornbury Sq, London N6 5YW (☎ 071 281 1843); 22 Harley St, London W1 (☎ 071 637 0491, car 0836 248529)

LANDINI, Mark Robert; s of Fernado Landini (d 1978), and Girleen Merrilees Hopgood; *b* 12 May 1958; *Educ* Downside, Kingston Art Sch, Middlesex Art Sch (BA); *m* 9 Aug 1986, Erica Jane, da of Eric Houghton; 1 s (Tom Dino b 15 Nov 1986), 1 da (Lucy Ieshia b 26 Feb 1990); *Career* Architetto Costantini Rome 1978-79, interior designer Design Research Unit London 1979-80, office designer Norah Tew London Ltd 1980-81, office and restaurant designer GMW Arch's London 1981-82; retail and leisure design Fitch & Co London 1982-89: joined as jr designer, assoc dir 1984, creative dir Retail Div and memb Bd 1987-90; creative and jt managing dir RSCG Conran Design London 1990-; D & AD Silver award for Most Complete Retail Design Programme (for Midland Bank work) 1987, World Store award for lighting design (for Esprit du Vin work)1989; memb: CSD 1978, D & AD 1987; *Recreations* squash, theatre, jazz, 20th century lit; *Clubs* Fred's (Soho), YMCA; *Style—* Mark Landini, Esq; RSCG Conran Design Ltd, The Clove Building, 4 Maguire St, London SE1 2NQ (☎ 071 522 2225, fax 071 522 2226)

LANDON, Prof (Howard Chandler) Robbins; s of William Grinell Landon (d 1979), and Dorothea, *née* Le B Robbins (d 1982); *b* 6 March 1926; *Educ* Asheville Sch, Lenox Sch, Swarthmore Coll, Boston Univ (MBus); *m* 1, (m dis 1957), Christa; m 2, Else Radant, da of Fritz Schmidt (d 1975); *Career* guest Queens Coll NY 1969, visiting prof Univ Coll Cardiff 1978- (visiting professional fell 1971-77, chm John Bird Prof of music history), guest prof Univ of California 1979 (1970 and 1975); Hon DMus: Boston Univ 1969 Queens Coll Belfast 1971, Univ of Bristol 1975, New England Conservatory of Music 1988; Verdientskreuz fur Kunst und Wissenschaft Austria first class (second class 1975), Golden Cross City of Vienna (1986); *Books* Haydn-Chronicle and Works (5 vols 1978-80), 1791 Mozarts Last Year (1988), Mozart-The Golden Years 1781-91 (1989), the Mozart Compendium (ed, 1990); *Recreations* swimming, walking, cooking; *Style—* Prof Robbins Landon; Château de Foncoussières, 81800 Rabastens, (Tarn) France (☎ 01033 63 40 61 45); Anton Frankgasse 3, Vienna 1180, Austria Music Dept, PO Box 78, Univ of Wales, Cardiff CF1 1XL (☎ 0222 874000, fax 010 33 63 33 76 36)

LANDON, Theodore Luke Giffard; s of Rev Sylvanus Luke Landon (d 1979; his m was Jane Mary Giffard, *see* Halsbury, 3 Earl of), formerly vicar of Marldon, Devon, and Florence Faith Loetitia Trelawny, *née* Lowe (d 1972; her m was Eleanor Salusbury-Trelawny, *see* Sir John Salusbury Trelawny 13 Bt), Mr Landon is the head of the French Huguenot family of Landon, founded in England by Samuel Landon in 1683; *b* 10 Oct 1926; *Educ* Blundell's, Univ of London; *m* 1956, Joan, da of Frederic Archibald Parker (d 1977), of Alresford, Hants (s of Rev Hon Archibald Parker, sometime rural dean of Wem, Salop, and Hon Maud Bateman-Hanbury, da of 2 Baron Bateman; the dean was 9 s of 6 Earl of Macclesfield); 3 s (Mark b 1958, Philip b 1962, Benjamin b 1967), 2 da (Felicity b 1960, Rohais b 1964); *Career* dep chm and md Terra Nova Insur Co Ltd 1970-79, dep chm C T Bowring Underwriting Hldgs Ltd 1979-83; dir: English and American Insur Co Ltd 1982-89, English and American Pension Tst 1984-; memb Lloyd's 1961-; govr Kelly Coll Tavistock 1969-; tstee Huguenot Soc 1973- (pres 1989-); *Recreations* history, music, genealogical research; *Clubs* East India, Gresham; *Style—* Theodore Landon, Esq; Three Quays, Tower Hill,

London EC3R 6DSD (☎ 071 283 7575); Great Bromley House, Great Bromley, Colchester, Essex CO7 7TP (☎ 0206 230 385)

LANE, Anthony John; s of Eric Marshal Lane, and Phyllis Mary, *née* Hardwick; *b* 30 May 1939; *Educ* Caterham Sch, Balliol Coll Oxford; *m* 1967, Judith Sheila, da of William Herbert Dodson (d 1968); 2 s (Barnaby b 1969, Robin b 1972), 1 da (Lucinda b 1976); *Career* dep sec DTI; *Recreations* music; *Style—* Anthony Lane, Esq; Department of Trade & Industry, 151 Buckingham Palace Road, London SW1

LANE, Dr Anthony Milner; s of Herbert William Lane (d 1977), and Doris Ruby, *née* Milner (d 1965); *b* 27 July 1928; *Educ* Trowbridge Boys' GS, Univ of Cambridge (BA, PhD); *m* 28 Aug 1952, Anne Sophie (d 1980), da of Isaac Zissman (d 1964); 2 s (Michael b 1964, Mark b 1970), 1 da (Galina b 1961); m 2, 26 Oct 1983, Jill Valerie, *née* Lander; *Career* chief scientist UKAEA Harwell 1977-89 (scientist 1953-); FRS 1974; *Recreations* walking; *Style—* Dr Anthony Lane, FRS; 6 Walton St, Oxford, OX1 2HG (☎ 0865 56565)

LANE, Maj-Gen Barry Michael; CB (1984), OBE (1974, MBE 1965); *b* 10 Aug 1932; *Educ* Dover Coll; *m* 1, 1956, Eveline Jean (d 1986), da of Vice Adm Sir Harry Koelle, KCB; 1 s (Anthony b 1962), 1 da (Juliet b 1959); m 2, 1987, Shirley Ann, da of E V Hawtin; *Career* cmmnd LI 1954; cmd: 1 LI 1972-75, II Armd Bde 1977-78; RCDS 1979, DAQ 1981-82, vice QMG 1982-83, GOC S W Dist 1984-87, Col LI 1982-87; chief exec Cardiff Bay Devpt Corp 1987-90; *Recreations* cricket, travel, wines; *Clubs* Army and Navy; *Style—* Maj-Gen Barry Lane, CB, OBE; c/o National Westminster Bank, Tadworth, Surrey KT20 5AF

LANE, David Goodwin; s of James Cooper Lane (d 1981), of Gloucester, and Joyce Lilian, *née* Goodwin; *b* 8 Oct 1945; *Educ* Crypt Sch Gloucester, King's Coll London (LLB, AKC); *Career* called to the Bar Gray's Inn 1968, rec Crown Ct; memb Royal Soc of St George; Freeman City of London; *Style—* David Lane, Esq; 2 All Saints' Court, Bristol BS1 1JN

LANE, David Neil; CMG (1983); s of A C Lane (d 1974), of Bath, and H M Lane, *née* Tonner (d 1980); *b* 16 April 1928; *Educ* Abbotsholme Sch, Merton Coll Oxford (MA); *m* 1968, Sara, da of C J Nurcombe, MC (d 1988), of Timberscombe, Somerset; 2 da (Harriet b 1969, Victoria b 1973); *Career* HM Foreign (later Diplomatic) Serv 1951-88, Br high cmmr Trinidad and Tobago 1980-85, ambass to the Holy See 1985-88; *Recreations* music; *Clubs* Travellers'; *Style—* David Lane, Esq, CMG; 6 Montagu Sq, London W1H 1RA (☎ 071 486 1673)

LANE, Sir David William Stennis Stuart; s of Hubert Samuel Lane, MC; *b* 24 Sept 1922; *Educ* Eton, Trinity Coll Cambridge, Yale; *m* 1955, Lesley Anne Mary, da of Sir Gerard Clauson, KCMG, OBE (d 1974); 2 s; *Career* serv WWII RNVR; called to the Bar Middle Temple 1955, Br Iron and Steel Fedn 1948-59 (sec 1956), with Shell International 1959-67; MP (C) Cambridge 1967-76 (had contested Lambeth (Vauxhall) 1964, Cambridge 1966), PPS to Employment Sec 1970-72, Parly under sec Home Office 1972-74; chm: N Kensington Cons Assoc 1961-62, Cmmn for Racial Equality 1977-82, Nat Assoc of Youth Clubs 1982-87; kt 1983; *Recreations* travel, walking, golf; *Clubs* MCC; *Style—* Sir David Lane; 5 Spinney Drive, Great Shelford, Cambridge CB2 5LY (☎ 0223 843437)

LANE, (Sara) Elizabeth; da of Rt Hon Sir Lionel Heald, QC, MP (d 1981), of Chilworth Manor, Surrey, and Daphne Constance Heald, CBE; *b* 30 April 1938; *Educ* Heathfield and Paris; *m* 15 May 1963, George Henry Lane, MC, s of Ernest Lanyi, of Budapest, Hungary; *Career* dir Seek & Find Ltd 1963-68, advsr on works of art and assoc Baron Martin von Koblitz 1968-78, dir Christie Manson & Woods Ltd 1978-; *Recreations* country pursuits; *Style—* Mrs George Lane; 12 Petersham Place, London, SWY 5PX (☎ 071 584 7840); Christie Mansion Woods Ltd, 8 King St, St James, London SW1 (☎ 071 839 9060)

LANE, Baron (Life Peer UK 1979), of St Ippollitts, Co Hertfordshire; Geoffrey Dawson Lane; AFC (1943), PC (1974); s of late Percy Albert Lane, of Lincoln; *b* 17 July 1918; *Educ* Shrewsbury, Trinity Coll Cambridge; *m* 1944, Jan, da of Donald Macdonald; 1 s (Hon Richard b 1948); *Career* served RAF 1939-45, Sqdn Ldr 1942; barr 1946, QC 1962, bencher 1966, dep chm Beds QS 1960-66, rec Bedford 1963-66, judge High Ct of Justice (Queen's Bench) 1966-74, Lord Justice of Appeal 1974-79, Lord of Appeal-in-Ordinary 1979-80, Lord Chief Justice 1980-, hon master of the bench Inner Temple 1980-; Hon DCL Cambridge 1984; kt 1966; *Style—* The Rt Hon the Lord Lane, AFC; Royal Courts of Justice, Strand, London WC2; House of Lords, London SW1

LANE, (formerly Lanyi) George Henry; MC; s of Ernest Lanyi (d 1945), of Budapest, and Theresa, *née* Schweitzer (d 1938); *b* 18 Jan 1915; *Educ* Eotvos Jozsef Foreal Budapest, Univ of London; *m* 1, 1943 (m dis 1956), Hon Miriam Rothschild; 1 s, 3 da; m 2, 15 May 1963, (Sara) Elizabeth, da of Rt Hon Sir Lionel Heald, QC, MP; *Career* cmmnd Buffs served 10 Commando, carried out special ops (small scale raids), captured 1944 (POW); farmer Ashton Wold Peterborough 1946-56; treas De Pontet & Co NY Stock Exchange 1956-61, exec vice pres Euro Econ News Agency 1961-86; pres Br Legion Oundle Northants, area chm Cons Pty Soke Peterborough, chm Oundle branch NFU, memb American C of C; MInstM; *Recreations* shooting, skiing; *Style—* George Lane, Esq, MC; 12 Petersham Place, London SW7 5PX, (☎ 071 584 7840)

LANE, (John) Godfrey; s of Vivian Charles Thomas Lane (Wing Cdr 1945, d 1982), of Hale, Cheshire, and Myra Victoria Lane; *b* 5 Jan 1932; *m* 1958, Winifred Lily, da of John Henry Brooks (d 1972); 3 s (Paul Bruce, Gordon Stuart, Michael John); *Career* CA 1954; 2 yr Nat Serv; employed on Internal Audit with Esso 1957-58, fin/distribution dir Abbots Packaging Ltd 1958 (md 1981-86); dir: MacFarlane gp (Clansman) plc, Abbott's Packaging Ltd; FCA; *Recreations* yachting, golf, swimming, ballet; *Clubs* Poole Harbour Yacht, South Heats Golf, Porsche; *Style—* Godfrey Lane, Esq; Abbott's Packaging Ltd, Gordon House, Oakleigh Rd South, New Southgate, London N11 1HL (☎ 081 368 1266)

LANE, John; CB (1981); s of Roger James Iddison Lane (d 1972), and Mary Elizabeth Lily, *née* Roberts (d 1982); *b* 23 Oct 1924; *Educ* John Lyon Sch, Harrow, Univ Coll Hull, LSE (BSc); *m* 1954, Ruth Ann, da of Thomas Victor Crocker (d 1941); 1 s (Robert); *Career* civil servant; under sec Depts of the Environment and Tport 1972-78, dep dir Central Statistical Office 1978-81, dep sec, ret; *Recreations* theatre, music, golf; *Clubs* Civil Service; *Style—* John Lane, Esq, CB; Fern Hill, 67 Mount Ephraim, Tunbridge Wells, Kent

LANE, John Anthony; s of Walter William Lane, of Harrow, Middx, and Phyllis Gwendoline, *née* Jones; *b* 30 June 1946; *Educ* Harrow Co GS; *m* 8 Aug 1970, Joan Elizabeth, da of Harold Burgess, of Harrow, Middx; 2 s (Andrew Michael b 1977, Stuart Christopher b 1981); *Career* CA; sr ptnr Lane & Co; former ptnr: Josolyne Layton-Bennett & Co, Arthur Young McClelland Moores & Co, Everett Collins & Loosley; *Clubs* Tring Lions; *Style—* John Lane, Esq; Far Hills, Grove Rd, Tring, Herts HP23 5PA (☎ 044 282 2766); Exchange House, Lake Street, Leighton Buzzard, Beds LU7 8RS (☎ 0525 373 767)

LANE, John Armstrong; s of Dr Sidney William Lane (d 1952), of Leicester, and Freda Lydia, *née* Robinson (d 1980); *b* 7 April 1935; *Educ* Ashby-de-la-Zouch GS, Leicester Sch of Architecture (Dip Arch); *m* 23 June 1983, Patricia Anne, da of Rowland Fletcher, of Derby; 2 da (Dawn b 9 July 1967, Sonia b 2 Nov 1971); *Career* Nat Serv RAF; fndr Lane, Bremner & Garnett Architects 1961: former govr Glasgow Sch of Art, former pres RIAS; FRIBA; *Recreations* family, country house, travel, competitions; *Clubs* Art (Glasgow); *Style—* John Lane, Esq; 18 Whittingehame Drive, Glasgow G12 0XX (☎ 041 339 7101); Planetree, Planetree Park, Gatehouse of Fleet, Castle Douglas, Kirkcudbrightshire; Lane, Bremner and Garnett, Chartered Architects, 69 Berkeley St, Glasgow G63 7DX (☎ 041 221 8148, fax 041 221 6057)

LANE, (Henry) John Noxon; s of Henry Audley Lane (d 1965), and Annie Elizabeth, *née* Larking; *b* 15 Oct 1928; *m* 25 April 1959, Maureen Edith, da of Reginald Morris (d 1979); 1 s (Jon b 1967), 3 da (Susan b 1960, Philippa b 1964, Jacky (twin) b 1964); *Career* Nat Serv RM 1947-49; dir: Stylus Supplies (Mountings) Ltd 1970-, TEE (Heat Treatment) Ltd 1975-; sr ptnr George Hay and Co 1975- (accountant, ptnr 1956-); fndr memb: Biggleswade Round Table 1954, Rotary Club 1966; FCA 1953; *Recreations* work and walking; *Style—* John Lane, Esq; Parkside, The Avenue, Sandy, Bedfordshire (☎ 0767 680550), Brigham House, 93 High St, Biggleswade, Bedfordshire (☎ 0767 315010, fax 0767 318388)

LANE, Josiah Bowen; s of Josiah Bowen Lane (d 1947), of Sandhills House, Walsall Wood, Staffordshire, and late Harriot Anne, *née* Kircham; *b* 2 Oct 1924; *Educ* Rossall Sch, Clare Coll Cambridge; *m* 30 April 1955, Anita Joy, da of Harold Andrews (d 1974), of 62 Wake Green Rd, Moseley, Birmingham; 2 da (Claire b 1956, Fleur b 1959); *Career* WWII RE 1943, cmmnd RE 1945, serv 1945-47, Bombay Sappers and Miners, 401 Field Sqdn 3 Indian Armd Bde (Burma and NW Frontier India); Lane Bros Tar Distillers Ltd 1947- (Lancs Tar Distillers Ltd): dir 1948 (later jt md), chm 1973-; Freeman: City of London, Worshipful Co of Paviors; *Recreations* skiing, watching cricket, shooting; *Clubs* Livery, MCC; *Style—* Josiah Lane, Esq; 24 Bowgreen Rd, Bowdon, Altrincham, Cheshire WA14 3LX; Lancashire Tar Distillers Ltd, Liverpool Rd, Cadishead, Manchester (☎ 061 775 2644, fax 061 776 1077, telex 668620)

LANE, Kenneth Alexander; OBE; s of Lt Alexander William Lane, MBE, RN (d 1970); *b* 20 March 1924; *Educ* Winchester, Christ's Coll Cambridge (MA); *m* 1, 1945, Peggy (d 1973), da of Patrick Murphy (d 1942); 3 s, 3 da; m 2, 1975, Delma, da of Walter Garrod, of Kings Lynn; *Career* Admty Scientific Serv 1943-45; Avon Rubber Co 1946-53, Eng Electric Co 1953 (dir various subsid cos until 1969), dep md Bowthorpe Hellermann Ltd 1970-72, md Porvair Ltd 1973-75, exec chm Kearney and Trecker Marwin Ltd 1976-81, dir gen The Machine Tool Trades Assoc 1981-85; chm: Kemptown Cons Assoc 1979-81, Brighton Cons Assoc 1986-88, treas Hove Cons Assoc 1987-90; rear cdre Brighton Marina Yacht Club 1988-90; FCA, FInstD; *Clubs* St Stephen's, IOD; *Style—* Kenneth Lane, Esq, OBE; 83 Kingsway Court, Hove, E Sussex BN3 2LR

LANE, Margaret; *see*: Huntingdon, Countess of

LANE, Hon Mrs (Miriam Louisa); *née* Rothschild; CBE (1982); eld da of Hon Nathaniel Charles Rothschild (d 1923); sis of 3 Baron Rothschild; granted the rank and precedence of a Baron's da 1938; *b* 5 Aug 1908; *Educ* privately; *m* 14 Aug 1943 (m dis 1957), Capt George Henry Lane, MC; 1 s, 3 da (1 s and 1 da decd); *Career* serv WWII FO (Def Medal); farmer & biologist (300 Scientific publns); tstee Br Museum 1967-75; visiting prof Biology Royal Free Hosp 1970-74, Romanes lectr 1985; memb: Zoological and Entomological Res Cncl, Marine Biological Assoc, Royal Entomological Soc, Systematics Assoc, Soc for Promotion of Nature Reserves, Pubns Ctee ZS; Wrigglesworth medal Royal Entomological Soc, Victoria medal RHS 1991; hon fell St Hugh's Oxford; Hon DSC: Oxford, Gotenberg, Hull, North Western (Chicago), Leicester, Open Univ; FRS; *Books* Fleas Flukes and Cuckoos (5 edn), Dear Lord Rothschild (1983), Catalogue of the Rothschild Collection of Fleas (6 vols) (1953-82), The Butterfly Gardener (1983), Atlas of Insect Tissue (1985), Animals and Man (1986), Butterfly Cooing Like a Dove (1991); *Recreations* natural history, conservation; *Clubs* Queens; *Style—* The Hon Mrs Miriam Lane, CBE, FRS; Ashton Wold, Peterborough PE8 5LZ

LANE, Dr Peter Edward; OBE (1985); s of Harry Edward Lane (d 1961), and Louisa Carrie, *née* Jones (d 1979); *b* 8 Sept 1925; *Educ* Sutton GS, Univ of Durham (BSc, PhD); *m* 1960, Freda Dorothy, da of Roland Towers Irving, of Cumbria (d 1985); 1 s (Nigel b 1966); 1 da (Nicola b 1964); *Career* RAF Aircrew War 1983-85; dir BP Shipping Ltd 1983-85, chief exec dir BP Exploration Co Ltd 1982-85 (ret), chm Oceaneering International Services Ltd 1985-88, dir Trafalgar House Offshore and Structural Ltd 1985-; CEng, CPhys, FInstPet, MIEE, MInstP; *Recreations* motor cruising, music, reading; *Clubs* Phyllis Court, Henley; *Style—* Dr Peter Lane, OBE; Pine Lodge, River Rd, Taplow, Bucks SL6 0BG (☎ 0628 30364)

LANE, Terence Maurice; s of Alexander Uriah Lane (d 1927), of Fleet, Hants, and Hilda Rachel, *née* Smith (d 1976); *b* 5 Oct 1918; *Educ* London Univ (BA), Indiana Univ (AB), Coll of Law; *m* 15 Aug 1944, (Bruce) Jacqueline, da of Bruce Alexander Johnston Dunlop, MC; 3 s (Jeremy, Piers, Crispin), 4 da (Litan, Rafael (Mrs Hall), Halcyon (Mrs Day), Meredith (Mrs Sanders)); *Career* RA 1940, cmmnd 2 Lt 1941, seconded 2 Indian Anti-Tank Regt and 28 Mountain Regt RIA 1941, Capt 1944, Maj 1944 (mentioned in despatches); Colonial Admin Serv Tanganyika Territory (now Tanzania) 1946, dist cmmr Chunya Dist 1948, invalided from serv 1949; slr 1953, fndr ptnr Baker & McKenzie 1961, sr ptnr Lane & Ptnrs 1974, ptnr Marks Murase & White NYC 1974; Freeman City of London 1987, Liveryman Worshipful Co of Arbitrators 1987; memb Law Soc 1954, FCIArb 1977; *Books* International Licensing Agreements (1973); *Recreations* riding, hunting, racing; *Clubs* Savage, Hampshire Hunt; *Style—* Terence Lane, Esq; Peregrine House, Rake, Liss, Hants (☎ 073089 3138); 46-47 Bloomsbury Square, London WC1A 2RU (☎ 071 242 2626 , fax 071 242 0387, telex 8812495)

LANE FOX, Hon Mrs (Janet); o da of 3 Baron Hamilton of Dalzell, GCVO, MC (d 1990), and Rosemary Olive, *née* Coke; *b* 8 Sept 1936; *m* 11 June 1960, Richard Sackville Lane Fox, s of Col Francis Gordon Ward Lane Fox (d 1989), of The Little House, Bramham Park, Wetherby, York; 1 s, 1 da; *Style—* The Hon Mrs Lane Fox; 17 Princedale Rd, London W11 4NW (☎ 071 727 4330); Kingsley Mill, Black Torrington, Beaworthy, Devon (☎ 040 923 209)

LANE FOX, Robin James; s of James Henry Lane Fox, of Middleton Cheney, Oxon, and Anne, *née* Loyd; *b* 5 Oct 1946; *Educ* Eton, Magdalen Coll Oxford (MA); *m* 26 June 1970, Louisa Caroline Mary, da of Maj Charles Farrell, MC, of Cutmill House, Watlington, Oxon; 1 s (Henry b 19 Oct 1974), 1 da (Martha b 10 Feb 1973); *Career* fell Magdalen Coll Oxford 1970-73, lectr in classics Worcester Coll Oxford 1974-76, res fell classical and Islamic history Worcester Coll 1976-77, fell and tutor New Coll Oxford 1977-, univ reader in ancient history 1989-; gardening columnist Finanical Times 1970-, Br Press Award Leisure Journalist of Year 1988; garden master New Coll 1979-; FRSL 1974; *Books* Alexander The Great (1973), Variations On A Garden (1974), Search for Alexander (1980), Better Gardening (1982), Pagan and Christians (1986); *Recreations* gardening, hunting, travelling; *Clubs* Beefsteak; *Style—* Robin Lane Fox, Esq; c/o New College, Oxford (☎ 0865 279 555)

LANE OF HORSELL, Baron (Life Peer UK 1990), of Woking in the County of Surrey; Sir Peter Stewart Lane; JP (Surrey 1976); s of Leonard George Lane (d 1950); *b* 29 Jan 1925; *Educ* Sherborne; *m* Doris Florence (d 1969), da of Robert Simpson Botsford (d 1955); 2 da (of whom Rosalie m 2 Baron Trefgarne, *qv*); *Career* serv Sub Lt RNVR 1943-46; sr ptnr BDO Binder Hamlyn CA 1979-, ptnr int firm BDO

Binder, chm Brent Chemicals Int plc, dep chm More O'Ferrall plc; dep chm Nuffield Nursing Homes Tst, chm Air Travel Tst Ctee; Nat Union of Cons and Unionists Assocs: vice chm 1981-83, chm 1983, chm exec ctee 1986-, hon vice pres 1984-; kt 1984; *Clubs* Boodle's, MCC; *Style*— The Rt Hon Lord Lane of Horsell, JP; c/o House of Lords, London SW1; BDO Binder Hamlyn, 20 Old Bailey, London EC4M 7BH (☎ 071 489 9000)

LANE-SMITH, Roger; s of Harry Lane-Smith (d 1979), of Cheshire, and Dorothy, *née* Shuttleworth; *b* 19 Oct 1945; *Educ* Stockport GS, Guildford Coll of Law (Robert Ellis Memorial prizeman); *m* 1969, Pamela Mary, da of Leonard Leigh; 1 s (Jonathan Roger b 10 Nov 1973), 1 da (Zoe Victoria b 21 June 1971); *Career* admitted slr 1969; ptnr David Blank & Co Manchester 1973-77; Alsop Wilkinson: ptnr 1977-; managing ptnr: Manchester Office 1977-88, London Office 1988-; winner Robert Ellis Meml prize; memb Law Soc; *Recreations* golf, tennis, shooting, deep sea fishing; *Clubs* Mark's, St James'; *Style*— Roger Lane-Smith, Esq; Alsop Wilkinson, 6 Dowgate Hill, London EC4R 2SS (☎ 071 248 4141, fax 071 623 8286, car 0860 525986)

LANESBOROUGH, 9 Earl of (1756); Denis Anthony Brian Butler; TD, JP (Leics 1967), DL (1962); also Baron of Newtown-Butler (I 1715, but eldest s & h usually styled Lord Newtown-Butler), and Viscount Lanesborough (I 1728); s of 8 Earl of Lanesborough (d 1950), by his 2 w Grace, da of Sir Anthony Abdy, 3 Bt; *b* 28 Oct 1918; *Educ* Stowe; *m* 1939 (m dis 1950), Bettyne Ione (d 1989), da of Sir Lindsay Everard, JP, DL, MP (d 1949); 2 da (1 decd); *Heir* Major Henry Butler; *Career* Lt Leics Yeo 1939, Maj RA (TA) 1945; memb Nat Gas Consumers' Cncl 1973-78, Trent RHA 1974-85; chm Loughborough & Dist Housing Assoc 1978-; *Style*— The Rt Hon Earl of Lanesborough, TD, JP, DL; Alton Lodge, Kegworth, Derby (☎ 0509 672243)

LANG, Prof Andrew Richard; s of late Ernest Lang; *b* 9 Sept 1924; *Career* asst prof Harvard Univ 1954-59; Univ of Bristol: physics lectr 1960-66, reader 1966-79, prof of physics 1979-87, prof emeritus 1987-; FRS 1975; *Style*— Prof Andrew Lang, FRS; 1B Elton Rd, Bristol BS8 1SJ

LANG, Belinda Lucy; da of Jeremy Hawk, of London, and Joan, *née* Heal; *b* 23 Dec 1953; *Educ* Lycee Français de Londres, Central Sch of Speech and Drama; *m* 15 Oct 1988, Hugh Munro, s of John Hugh Munro Fraser (d 1987); *Career* actress; tv credits incl: To Serve Them All My Days (BBC 1980), Dear John (BBC 1985), The Bretts (Central TV 1986), Bust (LWT 1988) Alteyn Mysteries (BBC 1990), Second Thoughts (LWT 1991); stage credits incl: Present Laughter (Vaudeville Theatre 1981), Hobsons Choice (Haymarket 1982), Antigone and Tales from Hollywood (Nat Theatre 1983-84), Clandestine Marriage (Albery 1984), Mrs Klein (Apollo 1989), Thark (Lyric Hammersmith 1989); *Recreations* walking, cycling, reading; *Style*— Miss Belinda Lang; c/o Ken McReddie, 91 Regent St, London W1 (☎ 071 439 1456)

LANG, Hon Mrs (Cecilia Alexandra Rose); *née* Alport; JP (Inner London); er da of Baron Alport, PC, TD (Life Peer), *qv*; *b* 3 Sept 1946; *Educ* County High Sch Colchester, Arundel Sch Harare Zimbabwe, Queensgate Sch; *m* 1969, Rev Geoffrey Wilfrid Francis Lang, MA, s of Frederick Lang of Croxley Green, Herts; 1 s (Oliver James Alport b 1971), 1 da (Imogen Eileen Cecilia b 1973); *Style*— The Hon Mrs Lang, JP; 17 Ravenscourt Road, London W6 0UH

LANG, David Louis; s of Howard J Lang, and Helen, *née* Grant; *b* 6 Oct 1939; *Educ* Univ of Western Ontario (BA); *m* 1963, Elizabeth Anne Holton; 2 s (Alen b 1969, Douglas b 1970), 2 da (Cynthia Anne b 1964, Catherine Elaine b 1966); *Career* dir: Coopers and Lybrand 1962-66, Bank of Montreal 1966-69, Cochran Murray and Wisener 1969-75, Crang and Ostiguy (Investmt Dealers) 1975-77, Citicorp International Gp 1977-80, Lloyds Bank International Ltd 1980-83; vice-pres treasy ops Canadian Imp Bank Gp 1983-88, dir and risk mangr Girozentrale Gilbert Eliott; former memb Bd of Govrs Montreal Childrens Hosp; *Recreations* hunting, fishing, squash; *Clubs* Toronto, Hurlingham; *Style*— David Lang, Esq; Broom Close, Esher, Surrey KT10 9ET

LANG, Lt-Gen Sir Derek Boileau; KCB (1967, CB 1964), DSO (1944), MC (1941), DL (Edinburgh 1978); s of Lt-Col C F G Lang (d 1961), of Whytegates, Church Crookham, Hants; *b* 7 Oct 1913; *Educ* Wellington, RMC Sandhurst; *m* 1, 1942, Morna Helena Casey (d 1953), da of Charles Massy-Dawson, of Sussex; 1 s, 1 da; m 2, 1953 (m dis 1969), Anita Lewis Shields; m 3, 1969, Elizabeth H Balfour (d 1982); m 4, 1983, Maartje McQueen, wid of Charles N McQueen; *Career* 2 Lt Cameron Highlanders 1933, Brig 1958, COS Scot Cmd 1960-61, GOC 51 Highland Div 1962-64, dir Army Trg MOD 1964-66, GOC-in-C Scot Cmd and govr of Edinburgh Castle 1966-69, Lt-Gen 1966, ret 1969; sec Univ of Stirling 1970-74, assoc conslt PA Mgmnt Conslts Ltd 1975-83; OStJ; *Recreations* golf, shooting, fishing, music; *Clubs* Hon Co of Edinburgh Golfers, New (Edinburgh), Muthaiga (Kenya), Sr Golfers; *Style*— Lt-Gen Sir Derek Lang, KCB, DSO, MC, DL; Templeland, Kirknewton, Midlothian EH27 8DJ (☎ 0506 883211)

LANG, Rear Adm (William) Duncan; CB (1981); s of James Hardie Lang (d 1936), of Edinburgh, and Elizabeth Foggo Paterson, *née* Storie (d 1965); *b* 1 April 1925; *Educ* Edinburgh Acad; *m* 1947, Joyce Rose, da of Alfred Henry Weeks (d 1936), of Catford; 1 s (James), 1 da (Celia); *Career* serv WWII RN 1943; pilot in 800, 816 and 825 Sqdns, flying instr and test pilot, CO 802 Sqdn 1958-59, CO RNAS Lossiemouth 1970-72, COS to Flag Offr Naval Air Cmd 1975-76, Naval ADC to HM The Queen 1978, Mil Dep to Head of Def Sales 1978-81; dir Naval Security 1981-86; *Recreations* golf (pres RNGS 1979-85); *Clubs* Army & Navy; *Style*— Rear Adm Duncan Lang, CB; c/o Midland Bank, 19 High Street, Haslemere, Surrey GU27 2HQ

LANG, Hugh; ERD (1967); s of Hugh Lang (d 1981), of Holmwood, Surrey, and Lilian Maydee, *née* Mackay; *b* 22 Dec 1934; *Educ* St Edmunds Sch Hindhead, Harrow; *m* 11 March 1961, Rosanne Auber, da of Col Richard Quentin Charles Mainwaring (d 1983), of Cortown, Kells, Co Meath Ireland; 2 s (Alistair Hugh b 15 July 1963, James Richard b 13 March 1966); *Career* 2 Lt 5 Royal Inniskilling Dragoon Gds cmmnd 1954, RARO (AER) 1956-67, Maj 1964; ptnr John Prust & Co 1963-70, Laurence Prust & Co 1970-80, non-exec dir Wallace Smith Trust Co Ltd 1985; memb Stock Exchange 1962-, chief exec and sec The Stock Exchange Benevolent Fund 1980; govr Crossways Trust Ltd, tstee Poyle Charity, memb Exec and Fin Ctee Offrs Assoc; hon fin advsr Royal National Coll for the Blind; Freeman City of London 1956, Liveryman Worshipful Co of Skinners 1956; *Recreations* shooting, skiing, gardening, wine; *Clubs* The Cavalry & Guards', The City of London, MCC; *Style*— Hugh Lang, Esq, ERDL; Durfold Hatch Cottage, Fisher Lane, Chiddingfold, Surrey GU8 4TF (☎ 0428 684286); Stock Exchange, London EC2N 1HP (☎ 071 588 2355)

LANG, Hugh Montgomerie; CBE (1978); s of John Montgomerie Lang; *b* 7 Nov 1932; *Educ* Univ of Glasgow (BSc); *m* 1, 1959 (m dis 1981), Marjorie Armour; 1 s, 1 da; m 2, 1981, Susan Lynn Hartley; *Career* REME 1953-55; chm: P-E International 1980- (dir 1972-, chief exec 1977-), Redman Heenan Int 1982-86 (dir 1981-86); Brammer 1990- (dir 1990-), Technol Transfer Servs Advsy Ctee 1982-85 (memb 1978-85); dir: Fairey Holdings 1978-82, UKO International 1985-6; non-exec dir: B Elliott plc 1986-88, Renaissance Holdings plc 1987-, Siebe plc 1987-, Strong & Fisher (Holdings) plc 1988-90, Co-ordinated Land and Estates plc 1988-; memb: Business Educn Cncl 1980-81, CBI Industl Policy Ctee 1980-83, Design Cncl 1983-90 (dep chm 1987-90), Engrg Cncl 1984-86; CEng, FIProdE, FIMC, CBIM, FRSA; *Recreations* fishing, gardening, golf, reading; *Clubs* Denham Golf, Army and Navy; *Style*— Hugh Lang, Esq, CBE; Mount Hill Farm, Gerrards Cross, Bucks SL9 8SU (☎ 0753 662406)

LANG, Rt Hon Ian Bruce; PC (1990), MP (C) Galloway and Upper Nithsdale 1983-; s of James Fulton Lang, DSC; *b* 27 June 1940; *Educ* Lathallan Sch Kincardineshire, Rugby, Sidney Sussex Coll Cambridge (BA); *m* 1971, Sandra Caroline, da of John Alastair Montgomerie, DSC; 2 da; *Career* contested (C): Central Ayrshire 1970, Glasgow Pollok 1974; MP (C) Galloway 1979-83, asst govt whip 1981-83, lord cmmr Treasy 1983-86; Parly Under Sec of State: Dept of Employment 1986, Scottish Office 1986-87; min of State Scottish Office 1987-90; sec of state for Scotland 1990-, vice-chm Scottish Cons Pty 1983-86; memb Lloyd's; tstee W of Scotland Tstee Savings Bank 1974-81; dir: Hutchison and Craft Ltd 1975-81, Hutchison and Craft (Underwriting Agents) Ltd 1976-81; dir Glasgow C of C 1978-81; memb Royal Co of Archers (Queen's Body Guard for Scotland) 1974; OStJ 1974; *Clubs* Western (Glasgow), Prestwick Golf, Pratt's; *Style*— Rt Hon Ian Lang, MP; House of Commons, London SW1A 0AA

LANG, The Very Rev John Harley; s of Frederick Henry Lang (d 1973), of Rickmansworth, Herts, and Eileen Annie Harley (d 1966); *b* 27 Oct 1927; *Educ* Merchant Taylors', King's Coll London, Emmanuel Coll Cambridge (MA, BD); *m* 1972, Frances Rosemary, da of Reginald Widdowson, of Budleigh, Salterton, Devon; 3 da (Henrietta b 1973, Victoria b 1975, Charlotte b 1977); *Career* curate St Mary's Portsea 1952-54, priest vicar Southwark Cathedral 1957-60, chaplain Emmanuel Coll Cambridge 1960-64, head of religious broadcasting BBC 1971-80 (asst head 1964-71), chaplain to HM The Queen 1976-80, dean of Lichfield 1980-; Hon DLitt Univ of Keele 1988; *Recreations* music; *Clubs* Cavalry and Guards; *Style*— The Very Rev the Dean of Lichfield; The Deanery, Lichfield, Staffs WS13 7LD

LANG, Hon Mrs (Victoria Mary); *née* Sackville-West; da (by 1 m) of 6 Baron Sackville; *b* 26 April 1959; *m* 16 Dec 1989, Jonathan G F Lang, yr s of John Lang, of Nairobi, Kenya; *Style*— The Hon Mrs Lang; 107 Ashley Gdns, Thirleby Rd, London SW1P 1HJ

LANGDALE, Simon John Bartholomew; s of Geoffrey Ronald Langdale (d 1977), of Tunbridge Wells, and Hilda Joan, *née* Bartholomew; *b* 26 Jan 1937; *Educ* Tonbridge, St Catharine's Coll Cambridge (MA); *m* 30 July 1962, Diana Marjory, da of Roger Wilby Hall, MVO, JP (d 1973), of Glebe House, West Grinstead, Sussex; 2 s (Andrew Rupert b 1964, Mark Simon b 1970), 1 da (Philippa Kate b 1967); *Career* housemaster Radley Coll 1968-73 (master 1959-73); headmaster: Eastbourne Coll 1973-80, Shrewsbury 1981-88; dir educational and gen grants The Rank Fndn 1988-; *Recreations* books, gardening, golf; *Clubs* East India, Hawks; *Style*— Simon Langdale, Esq; Park House, Culworth, Banbury, Oxon OX17 2AP (☎ 0295 76 222); 12 Warwick Square, London SW1V 2AA (☎ 071 834 7731)

LANGDON, David; OBE; s of Bennett Langdon, and Bess Langdon; *b* 24 Feb 1914; *Educ* Davenant GS; *m* 1955, April Yvonne Margaret, *née* Sadler-Phillips; 2 s (Ben, Miles), 1 da (Beth); *Career* Sqdn Ldr RAFVR 1945; cartoonist & illustrator; memb of Punch Table, contrib Punch, New Yorker, and others; official artist to: Centre Internationale Audio-Visuel, D'Etudes et de Recherches; *Books* various cartoon collections; *Recreations* golf; *Clubs* RAF; *Style*— David Langdon, Esq, OBE; Greenlands, Honor End Lane, Prestwood, Great Missenden, Bucks HP16 9QY (☎ 02406 2475)

LANGDON, (Augustus) John; s of late Rev Cecil Langdon, and Elizabeth Mercer Langdon, MBE; *b* 20 April 1913; *Educ* Berkhamsted Sch, St John's Coll Cambridge (MA); *m* 1; 2 da; m 2, 1949, Doris Edna, *née* Clinkard; 1 s; *Career* chartered surveyor and land agent; supt land offr Admty 1937-45, ptnr to J Carter Jonas & Sons Oxford 1945-48 (ptnr 1936-37), regnl land cmmr Miny of Agric 1948-65, dep dir of agric Land Serv Miny of Agric 1965-71, chief surveyor Agric Devpt and Advsy Serv MAFF 1971-74, Nat Tst London 1974-76; chm Statutory Ctee on Agric Valuation; memb: Gen Cncl RICS, Land Agency and Agric Divnl Cncl 1971-75; FRICS, FRSA; *Books* Rural Estate Management (contrib), Fream's Elements of Agriculture (contrib); *Recreations* gardening, walking, collecting; *Clubs* United Oxford and Cambridge; *Style*— John Langdon, Esq; Thorn Bank, Long Street, Sherborne, Dorset DT9 3BS

LANGDON, Capt Jonathan Bertram Robert Louis; s of Capt John Edward Langdon, RN, of Hayling Is, and Nancy Langdon; *b* 1 Nov 1939; *Educ* Hurstpierpoint Coll, RNC Dartmouth; *m* 31 March 1962, Hilary Jean, da of John William Fox Taylor, OBE (d 1988), of Spain; 2 s (Andrew William b 1964, Stephen John (twin) b 1964), 1 da (Claire Fiona b 1967); *Career* RNC Dartmouth 1958, HM Ships Bermuda, Lincoln, Daring 1960-68; called to the Bar Gray's Inn 1970; Far East legal advsr Hong Kong 1973-75, RN Supply Sch 1975-77, Cdr 1977, HMS Norfolk 1977-79, MOD 1979-81, staff of C-in-C Naval Home Cmd 1981-83, asst rec SE Circuit 1983, sec to Naval Sec MOD 1983-86, Capt 1986, postgrad trg int law 1987-88, Chief Naval Judge Advocate 1988-90, rec SE Circuit 1989, sec to C-in-C Naval Home Cmd 1990-; *Recreations* sailing, gardening, history; *Style*— Capt Jonathan Langdon, RN; c/o Lloyds Bank, High Street, Sittingbourne, Kent

LANGDON, Michael; CBE (1973); s of Henry Birtles (d 1931), of Wolverhampton, and Violet Mary Price (d 1966); *b* 12 Nov 1920; *Educ* Bushbury Hill Sr Boys Sch; *m* 1947, Vera Laura, da of Robert Duffield (d 1958), of Norfolk; 2 da (Christine b 1948, Diana b 1950); *Career* opera singer Royal Opera House 1950-80; sang internationally at Metropolitan Opera: San Francisco, Chicago, Seattle, Los Angeles, Miami, San Diego, Houston, Bueonos Aires, Paris, Aix En Provence, Marselliese, Monte Carlo, Lisbon, Brussels, Zurich, Lausanne, Geneva, Berlin, Stuttgart, Munich, Cologne, Copenhagen, Budapest and Rhodesia; also with Scot Opera, WNO, Opera N, and Glyndebourne; many performances on BBC Radio & TV, also on BBC in full length operas and lieder recitals, dir Nat Opera Studio 1978-87; *Books* Notes From a Low Singer (1982); *Recreations* assoc football, cricket, baseball, reading sci fiction; *Style*— Michael Langdon, Esq, CBE; 34 Warnham Court, Grand Avenue, Hove, Sussex BN3 2NJ (☎ 0273 733120)

LANGDON, Richard Norman Darbey; s of Norman Langdon (d 1959), of Shrewsbury, and Dorothy Hewitt, *née* Darbey; *b* 19 June 1919; *Educ* Shrewsbury; *m* 1 Nov 1944, June Phyllis, da of Alexander Ernest Dixon (d 1954), of Kingston, Surrey; 2 s (John Richard Darbey b 1946, Michael Robert Finch b 1948); *Career* offr RA 1939-46; ptnr Spicer and Pegler 1951-84 (managing ptnr 1971-84, sr ptnr 1978-84); chm: Finlay Packaging plc 1984-, First Nat Fin Corp 1984-, Time Prods plc 1984-; dep chm Chemring Gp 1984-, dir Rockware Gp plc 1985-; chm Beeson Gregory Ltd 1989-; *Recreations* sailing, gardening, bricklaying; *Clubs* City of London, Old Salopian; *Style*— Richard Langdon, Esq; Rough Hill House, Munstead, nr Godalming, Surrey GU8 4AR (☎ 04868 21507); First National Finance Corporation plc, P O Box 505, St Alphage House, Fore Street, London EC2P 2HJ (☎ 071 638 2855, fax 071 628 9963, car 0680 380849)

LANGDON-DAVIES, Peter Guy; s of John Eric Langdon-Davies (d 1972), and Constance Rina, *née* Scott (d 1955); *b* 23 June 1919; *Educ* Leighton Park Sch, Trinity Coll Cambridge (MA); *m* 14 Feb 1952, Cynthia Marguerite, da of William Richard Wall, OBE (d 1972); 1 s (Thomas b 1952), 1 da (Jane b 1955); *Career* WWII serv 1939-46; Capt RA: France 1940, Iceland 1940-41, ME and N Africa 1942-43, Italy 1943-44, Allied Control Cmmn for Austria political div 1946; called to the Bar Inner Temple 1951 (master of the bench 1982); standing counsel: MAFF and Forestry Cmmn 1964-

85, Miny of Land and Natural Resources 1966-68, Intervention Bd for Agric Produce 1972-85; commons cmmr 1985, chief commons cmmr 1986-; pres Agric Law Assoc 1984- (chm 1975-80, vice pres 1981-84), pres Comité Européen de Droit Rural 1987-89 (vice pres 1975-87); *Style*— Peter Langdon-Davies, Esq; 5 Kings Bench Walk, Temple, London EC4Y 7DN (☎ 071 353 3941); Ty'r Ywen, Partrishow, Abergavenny, Gwent (☎ 0873 890 308); Commons Commissioners, Golden Cross House, Duncannon Street, London WC2N 4JF (☎ 071 210 4584)

LANGDON-DAVIES, Robin Harry; DFC (1944); s of John Eric Landgon-Davies, MBE (d 1971), of Sevenoaks, and Constance Rina, *née* Scott (d 1954); *b* 9 Sept 1920; *Educ* Laighton Park Sch; *m* 11 Feb 1942, Cicely Frances, da of Frank Dyer (d 1978); 1 s (Michael Anthony b 1953), 1 da (Anna Francesca b 1949); *Career* RAF, enlisted 1940, cmmnd 1941, cmd 6 Sqdn Balkan Air Force; CA; Thornton & Thornton; articled (Oxford) 1940, qualified (Banbury) 1950, ptnr (Banbury) 1951, ptnr (Oxford) 1953; ptnr: Grace Darbyshire & Todd (Bristol) 1962, Harmood Banner Cash Stone & Mounsey (Bristol) 1965, Dearden Lord Annan Morrish (Bristol) 1975, ret 1985; hon treas Oxfam 1960-73, chm Oxford CA Gp 1960, chm Bristol Area Soc CA 1973, pres W Eng Soc CA 1980; FCA (1961, ACA 1950); *Recreations* ornithology; *Style*— Robin Langdon-Davies, Esq, DFC

LANGE, Leo Stanley; s of Jacob Lange (d 1966), and Gertrude, *née* Wolfowitz (d 1969); *b* 25 July 1931; *Educ* Worcester HS for Boys, Univ of Cape Town (MB ChB, MD); *m* 7 Jan 1962, Natasha, da of Dr Maurice Rose (d 1982); 3 da (Claire b 1963, Annushka b 1967, Tamara b 1968); *Career* conslt neurologist Charing Cross Hosp; contrib various pubns and scientific jls; FRCP; *Books* author of various pubns in scientific jls; *Recreations* music, sailing; *Clubs* Athenaeum; *Style*— Dr Leo Lange; 17 Harley St, London W1N 1DA (☎ 071 631 0770)

LANGER, Air Cdre John Francis; CBE (1973), AFC, (1958) DL (Gtr London 1983); s of Cecil Edward Langer (d 1966), and Emma Elizabeth Maud, *née* Tucker (d 1988); *b* 24 June 1925; *Educ* Wimbledon Coll; *m* 1951, Doreen (stage name Jane), da of Wilfrid Newland-Hodges; 2 s, 1 da; *Career* RAF Serv WWII in SE Asia Cmd, Flt Cdr No 33 Sqdn 1948-50, QFI Cambridge Univ Air Sqdn 1951-53, Cdr Singapore Sqdn MAAF 1953-56, Sqdn Cdr No 43 (Fighting Cocks) Sqdn 1957-59, chief instr Central Flying Sch 1962-64, Station Cdr RAF Valley 1970-71, dep dir Air Plans MOD 1972, Cdr Singapore Air Force 1973-75, dir Flying Trg MOD 1975-79, ret; UK govt advsr on aviation security 1979-1987; vice chm (Air) TAVR Assoc for Gtr London 1980-1988; aviation security conslt 1987-; rep DL for Hillingdon 1987-; *Recreations* cat watching; *Clubs* RAF; *Style*— Air Cdre John Langer, CBE, AFC, DL; 29 Beechwood Ave, Kew, Surrey TW9 4DD (☎ 081 878 3932)

LANGFORD, Bonita (Bonnie); *b* 22 July 1964; *Educ* Arts Educational Sch London, Italia Conti Stage Sch; *Career* actress; theatre work incl: West End debut (aged seven) Bonnie Butler in Gone With The Wind (Theatre Royal Drury Lane), Baby June in Gypsy (Piccadilly Theatre), Kate in Pirates of Penzance (Theatre Royal Drury Lane), Rumpleteazer in Cats (New London Theatre), title role Peter Pan - The Musical (Aldwych Theatre), Gypsy (Winter Gardens Theatre Broadway NY and touring), Charlie Girl (Opera House Manchester and Hippodrome Birmingham) 1987, Sally Smith in Me And My Girl 1988, Dames At Sea (Haymarket Theatre) 1989, title role in Mabel 1990; pantomine incl: debut title role Cinderella (Guildford) 1978, the princess in Jack And The Beanstalk (Lewisham Concert Hall) 1983 and 1984, title role Cinderella (Wimbledon Theatre) 1984-85 and 1990; tv work incl: debut singing On The Good Ship Lollipop on Opportunity Knocks (aged six), co-host Junior Showtime (Yorkshire TV), Violet Elizabeth in Just William 1976, Lena and Bonnie (Thames TV) 1978, The Hot Shoe Show 1983, Rub-a-dub-tub (TV-am), co-host The Saturday Starship (Central TV) 1984, Melanie in Doctor Who (BBC TV) 1986, This is Your Life 1986, A Royal Birthday Gala (for the Queen Mother's 90th birthday) 1989, numerous guest appearances; film work incl: Bugsy Malone, Wombling Free 1980; debut single (on Tembo Records) Just One Kiss 1984; *Style*— Miss Bonnie Langford; Mark Hudson Ltd, 3rd Floor, 146 Strand, London WC2R 1JH (☎ 071 240 8851, fax 071 397 0089)

LANGFORD, 9 Baron (I 1800); Col Geoffrey Alexander Rowley-Conwy; OBE (mil 1943), DL (Clwyd 1977); s of Maj Geoffrey Seymour Rowley-Conwy (ka 1915, himself ggs of 1 Baron, who in his turn was 4 s of 1 Earl of Bective, the Earldom of the same now forming one of the subsidiary dignities of the Marquesses of Headfort), of Bodrhyddan, Rhuddlan, Flintshire; suc 2 cous once removed, 8 Baron Langford, 1953; *b* 8 March 1912; *Educ* Marlborough, RMA Woolwich, Staff Coll Quetta; *m* 1, 1939 (m dis 1956), Ruth St John, da of late Albert St John Murphy; m 2, 1957, Grete (d 1973), da of late Col E T von Freiesleben, Danish Army; 3 s; m 3, 1975, Susan, da of C Denham; 1 s (Hon Christopher b 1978), 1 da (Hon Charlotte b 1980); *Heir* s, Hon Owain Grenville Rowley-Conwy b 1958; *Career* cmmnd RA 1932, Lt 1935, Capt 1939, Maj 1941, Lt-Col 1945, serv 1939-45, with RA in Singapore (POW escaped), with Indian Mountain Artillery in Burma, DAQMG Berlin Airlift, FASSBERG 1948-49, GSO1 42 Inf Div TA 1949-52, ret 1957, Hon Col 1967; constable of Rhuddlan Castle, lord of the manor of Rhuddlan; Freeman City of London; *Clubs* Army and Navy; *Style*— Col The Rt Hon the Lord Langford, OBE, DL; Bodrhyddan, Rhuddlan, Clwyd LL18 5SB (☎ 0745 590414)

LANGFORD, Gerald Percival; s of Percival Claude Smith Langford (d 1968), and Margaret Winifred, *née* Hamill (d 1990); *b* 27 July 1943; *Educ* Gresham House Sch Motherwell Scotland; *m* Anne, da of John Rochford (d 1984); 2 s (Robert Gerald b 19 May 1979, Andrew John b 30 May 1982), 1 da (Valerie Anne b 1 Feb 1977); *Career* Scottish Union and Nat Insur Co Edinburgh 1959-67, Associated Life & Pensions Ltd Dublin 1967-70, pensions mangr Royal Trust Co (Ireland) Ltd Dublin 1970-76; md Smurfit Group Pension Trustees Ltd Dublin and Smurfit UK Pensions Trustees Ltd Manchester 1976-87, md Beech Hill Pension Trustees Ltd Dublin 1982-87, jt md L & P Finan Trustees of Ireland Ltd 1987-, dir L & P Financial Trustees Ltd Manchester 1987-, Irish Assoc of Pension Funds: fndr sec, memb Cncl 1971-83, pres 1982-83; FPMI 1980, fell Irish Inst of Pension Mangrs 1990; *Recreations* golf, tennis, music; *Clubs* Howth/Sutton Lions, Howth Golf, Sutton Lawn Tennis; *Style*— Gerald Langford, Esq; 38 Offington Lawn, Sutton, Dublin 13, Ireland (☎ 0001 390274); 62 Northumberland Rd, Ballsbridge, Dublin 4, Ireland (☎ 0001 682899, fax 0001 687566)

LANGFORD, Martin Peter Neil; s of Charles William Langford (d 1972), and Barbara Mary Langford (d 1990); *Educ* Dulwich Coll; *m* 1 Sept 1979, Kathleen Langford, da of Hugh Peter Lim; 2 da (Kirstyn Jane b 25 Feb 1985, Katherine Mary b 23 Nov 1986); *Career* PR conslt; Peter West & Associates 1969-70, Russell Greer & Associates 1970-71; Burson-Marstellar: London 1971-73, Hong Kong 1973-79, mangr Creative Servs London 1979-86, md 1986-88, dep chm 1988-89, md 1989-; PR Professional of the Year award (PR Week Indust) 1987; vice chm PR Conslts Assoc; MIPR 1984; *Recreations* game fishing; *Clubs* Mosimann's; *Style*— Martin Langford, Esq; 55 Oakley Rd, Warlingham, Surrey CR3 9BE (☎ 0883 624719); Burson-Marsteller Ltd, 24-28 Bloomsbury Way, London WC1A 2PX (☎ 071 831 6262, fax 071 404 1146, car 0836 233528)

LANGFORD, Philip Baber; s of Percy Norman Langford (d 1968), and Elizabeth Ellen, *née* Jones (d 1987); *b* 23 March 1934; *Educ* Bromsgrove, BNC Oxford (MA), Univ of London (LLB); *m* 10 March 1987, Catherine Judith, da of William Arthur Gibbon, of 132 The Close, Salisbury, Wiltshire; 2 step s (Edward b 1977, Richard b 1979); *Career* Nat Serv 2 Lt RAEC attached to 2 bn Coldstream Guards 1959-61; admitted slr 1959; asst slr Kent CC 1961-63, ptnr Thomson Snell & Passmore 1965- (joined 1963); former chm SE Area Legal Aid Ctee, former pres Tunbridge Wells Tonbridge and Dist Law Soc; memb Law Soc; *Recreations* tennis, reading, travel; *Style*— Philip Langford, Esq; Baber House, Ticehurst, Wadhurst, East Sussex TN5 7HT (☎ 0580 200978); Thomson Snell & Passmore, 3 Lonsdale Gardens, Tunbridge Wells, Kent TN1 1NX (☎ 0892 510000, telex 95194 TSANDP G, fax 0892 549884)

LANGFORD, Ruth, Lady; Ruth St John; da of Albert St John Murphy, of The Island House, Little Island, Co Cork; *m* 1939 (m dis 1956), 9 Baron Langford; *Style*— Ruth, Lady Langford; Somerdale, Midleton, Co Cork, Eire

LANGFORD-HOLT, Lt Cdr Sir John Anthony; s of late Ernest Langford-Holt; *b* 30 June 1916; *Educ* Shrewsbury; *m* 2, 1953 (m dis 1969), Flora Evelyn Innes, da of late Ian St Clair Stuart; 1 s, 1 da; m 3, 1983, Irene; *Career* joined air branch RN 1939, Lt Cdr 1944; MP (C) Shrewsbury 1945-83, sec Cons Parly Labour Ctee 1945-50, jt sec House of Commons Branch Br Legion 1945-50; memb: Parly and Scientific Ctee, Cwlth Parly Assoc; chm: Anglo-Austrian Soc 1960-63 and 1971-83, Select Ctee Defence 1980-83; Freeman and Liveryman City of London, memb Ct Worshipful Co of Horners 1967; chllr Primrose League 1989; Austrian Grand Decoration of Honour in Silver with Star, Order of Civic Merit (France); kt 1962; *Clubs* White's; *Style*— Lt Cdr Sir John Langford-Holt; Studdale House, 20 Brook Ave, New Milton, Hants BH25 5HD

LANGHAM, Sir James Michael; 15 Bt (E 1660), TD; s of Sir John Charles Patrick Langham, 14 Bt (d 1972); *b* 24 May 1932; *Educ* Rossall; *m* 1959, Marion Audrey Eleanor, da of Oswald Barratt; 2 s, 1 da; *Heir* s, John Stephen Langham; *Style*— Sir James Langham, Bt, TD; Claranagh, Tempo, Enniskillen, Co Fermanagh, N Ireland

LANGHAM, John Michael; CBE (1976); s of George Langham (d 1951); *b* 12 Jan 1924; *Educ* Bedford Sch, Queen's Coll Cambridge (MA), Admin Staff Coll; *m* 1949, Irene Elizabeth, *née* Morley; 2 s, 1 da; *Career* served RN 1944-46; exec chm Stone Manganese Marine Ltd 1967-, divnl chm Stone-Platt Industs Ltd 1967-81, chm Vacu-Lug Traction Tyres Ltd 1973-, dir BPB Industs Ltd 1976-, chm and md Langham Industs Ltd 1981-; chm: Langham Overseas Ltd 1981-, Weardale Steel (Walsingham) Ltd 1983-, Appledore Shipbuilders Ltd 1989-; exec bd memb BSI 1969-76 (dep chm Quality Assur Cncl 1971-79); memb: CBI Cncl 1967-79 (chm CBI Prodn Ctee 1970-79), Gen Cncl Engrg Employers Fedn 1974-82 (memb Mgmnt Bd 1979-82); Br Foundry Medal and Prize 1954, Award of the American Foundrymens Soc 1962; *Recreations* skiing, sailing, farming; *Style*— John Langham, Esq, CBE; Bingham's Melcombe, Dorchester, Dorset (☎ 0258 880808)

LANGHAM, John Stephen; s and h of Sir James Michael Langham, 15 Bt; *b* 14 Dec 1960; *Style*— John Langham, Esq; Claranagh, Tempo, Enniskillen, Co Fermanagh

LANGHAM, Rosamond, Lady; Rosamond Christabel; MBE (1969); da of Arthur Rashleigh (d 1952), of Killiney, Dublin; *b* 3 July 1903; *Educ* in England with governess at home and music, riding & dancing masters; *m* 1930, Sir John Charles Patrick Langham, 14 Bt (d 1972), s of Sir Herbert Langham, 13 Bt (d 1951); 1 s (15 Bt) Sir James Langham-present Bart; *Career* patron NIGFAS for N Ireland and life long interest in Girl Guides: County Commission for Carlow, Eire, for 21 yrs & for Co Fernanagh N Ireland for 12 yrs; memb of Br Red Cross; medal of Merit from World Chief Guide (Lady BP) in 1959; *Books* All Things Bright and Beautiful (book of poems 1982); *Recreations* gardening, flower arranging, ballroom and folk dancing; *Style*— Rosamond, Lady Langham, MBE; Tempo Manor, Tempo, Enniskillen, Co Fermanagh, N Ireland (☎ 036 554 202)

LANGHORNE, Richard Tristan Bailey; s of Eadward John Bailey Langhorne, MBE, of Chichester, and Rosemary, *née* Scott-Foster; *b* 6 May 1940; *Educ* St Edward's Sch Oxford, St John's Coll Cambridge (BA, MA); *m* 18 Sept 1971, Helen Logue, da of William Donaldson, CB (d 1988); 1 s (Daniel b 22 Nov 1972), 1 da (Isabella b 29 Aug 1975); *Career* lectr in history Univ of Kent 1966-75 (master Rutherford Coll 1971-74), fell St John's Coll Cambridge 1975- (steward 1975-79, bursar 1975-87), dir Centre of Int Studies Univ of Cambridge 1987-, visiting prof Sch of Int Rels Univ of S California 1986; chm Br Int History Assoc 1988; FRHistS 1985; *Books* The Collapse of the Concert of Europe 1890-1914 (1982), Diplomacy and Intelligence during the Second World War (ed, 1985); *Recreations* cooking, music, railways; *Clubs* Athenaeum; *Style*— Richard Langhorne, Esq; 15 Madingley Road, Cambridge CB3 0EG (☎ 0223 635 41); Centre of Int Studies, West Rd, Cambridge and St John's Coll, Cambridge CB2 1TP (☎ 0223 335 333/338 641)

LANGLAIS, Hon Mrs (Joanna Harriet Nevill); da of 7 Baron Latymer, *qv*; *b* 1928; *m* 1951, Pierre Langlais; 1 s, 4 da; *Style*— The Hon Mrs Langlais; PO Box 113, North Hartland, Vermont 05052, USA

LANGLANDS, Alastair Francis; s of Alexander Langlands (d 1969), and Elizabeth Langlands; *b* 20 Sept 1932; *Educ* Shawlands Acad, Agric Coll Univ of Glasgow, Univ of York, Univ of Toronto; *m* 1 Nov 1969, Fiona Cameron, *née* Mckenzie; *Career* brand mangr General Foods Corp 1961-67, conslt PA International Ltd 1967-72, md Superlamp Metallic 1972-76, md Bestobell Engineering Products 1976-81, chief exec Hawthorn Leslie Group plc 1981-, Bishop Industrial Controls Ltd, Briticent International Ltd, British Central Electrical Ltd, J Dyson & Co Ltd, Electrical Trades Supply Ltd, Shakeshaft Electrical Wholesale Ltd; *Recreations* tennis, athletics, football; *Clubs* Caledonian; *Style*— Alastair Langlands, Esq; Hawthorn Leslie Group plc, Lancashire House, 39-43 Monument Hill, Weybridge, Surrey KT13 8RN (☎ 0932 858322, fax 0932 849517, car 0836 210695)

LANGLANDS, Dr Ross William Duff; s of Ronald Ross Langlands (d 1959), of Dundee, and Mary Duff, *née* Jolly; *b* 1 Nov 1948; *Educ* Kirkton HS Dundee, Univ of Edinburgh (BSc, MB ChB), East of Scotland Coll of Agric (Dip); *m* 30 June 1973, Diana Elizabeth, da of Ronald Nelson Holton, of Newhall Port, Gifford; 2 s (Alasdair b 1982, Niall b 1983); *Career* gen medical practitioner 1977-; trainer in gen practice 1986; RCGP scholarship to E Germany 1988; MRCGP; *Recreations* shooting, reading, gardening, good food and wine, opera, German language; *Style*— Dr Ross W D Langlands; Ardlea, Gifford, E Lothian EH41 4JD (☎ 062 081 564); Newton Port Surgery, Haddington, E Lothian EH41 3NF (☎ 062 082 5051)

LANGLEY, Maj-Gen Sir (Henry) Desmond Allen; KCVO (1983), MBE (1967); s of Col Henry Langley, OBE; *b* 16 May 1930; *Educ* Eton, RMA Sandhurst; *m* 1950, Felicity, da of Lt-Col K J P Oliphant, MC; 1 s, 1 da; *Career* cmmnd Life Gds 1949, cmd Life Gds 1969-71, Lt-Col cmdg Household Cavalry and Silver Stick-in-Waiting 1972-75, Cdr 4 Gds Armd Bde 1976-77, RCDS 1978, Brig Gen Staff HQ UK Land Forces 1979, GOC London Dist and Maj-Gen cmdg Household Div 1979-83, Cdr British Forces Cyprus and Admin Sovereign Base Areas 1983-85, govr and C in C Bermuda 1988-; govr Church Lads' and Church Girls' Bde 1986-; *Style*— Maj-Gen Sir Desmond Langley, KCVO, MBE; Government House, Bermuda

LANGLEY, Edward Noel; s of Edward George Langley (d 1975), of Kings Lynn, and Katie ELizabeth, *née* Wright (d 1981); *b* 28 Dec 1926; *Educ* Gt Yarmouth GS; *m* 9 June 1951, Audrey Alicia Betty, da of Leslie Edward Dugmore (d 1966), of Birmingham; *Career* Sgt RCS Germany 1947-48; sales engr Coventry Climax Engines 1950-52, md Isaac Bentley & Co Ltd 1970-85 (sales dir 1962-70), gp md Marston Bentley Group 1985-, main bd dir W Canning plc 1984, chm Marston Bentley Group

1989-; memb: Diecasting Soc, IOD; *Recreations* hiking, sport in general; *Style*— Edward Langley, Esq; Hylo House, Cale Lane, New Springs, Wigan WN2 1JR (☎ 0942 824 242, fax 0942 826 653, car 0831 315332, telex 67230)

LANGLEY, (Julian Hugh) Gordon; QC (1983); s of Gordon Thompson Langley (d 1943), and Marjorie, *née* Burgoyne; *b* 11 May 1943; *Educ* Westminster, Balliol Coll Oxford (BA, BCL); *m* 20 Sept 1968, Beatrice Jayanthi, da of Simon Tennakoon (d 1986), of Colombo, Sri Lanka; 2 da (Ramani Elizabeth b 1969, Sharmani Louise b 1972); *Career* called to the Bar Inner Temple 1966, rec 1986; *Recreations* music, sport; *Clubs* Travellers; *Style*— Gordon Langley, Esq, QC; Fountain Court, Temple, London EC4Y 9DH (☎ 071 583 3335, fax 071 353 0329, telex 881 3408 FONLEG G)

LANGLEY, (Michael) John; s of Charles Walter Langley, of Bristol, and Ruth Cullis, *née* Blythe; *b* 11 May 1951; *Educ* Bristol GS, Gonville and Caius coll Cambridge (BA), Coll of William and Mary Virginia USA (MA); *Career* theatre mangr Nat Theatre 1987-; *Recreations* reading, cricket; *Clubs* Groucho; *Style*— John Langley, Esq; 7 North Street, Clapham, London SW4 0HQ (☎ 071 622 9433); National Theatre, South Bank, London SE1 9PX (☎ 071 928 2033, fax 071 620 1197)

LANGLEY, John William Frederick; s of Reginald John William Langley (d 1973), of Torquay, Devon, and Veronica Mary, *née* King; *b* 17 Feb 1932; *Educ* Hornchurch GS; *m* 23 Sept 1961, Margaret Tait, da of Thomas Ormiston Gow; 1 s (Michael John b 25 Nov 1965), 1 da (Clare Caroline b 28 Nov 1963); *Career* journalist; contrib to local weekly newspapers whilst at sch, reporter The Romford Times 1949-, industl corr Western Morning News and Evening Herald Plymouth, joined News Chronicle (Manchester office) 1954, motoring corr Daily Sketch 1956-57, re-joined News Chronicle, gen reporter and motoring writer Daily Telegraph 1961- (motoring corr 1965-); fndr memb and first chm Fleet St Motoring Gp; hon ed Waterfowl (magazine of Br Waterfowl Assoc) 1975-85; *Awards* Motoring Writer of the Year award (twice); memb: Guild of Motoring Writers, Wildfowl Tst, Br Waterfowl Assoc, Kent Tst for Nature Conservation; *Recreations* breeding and watching wildfowl, secondhand books, looking at trees, wildlife, music, real ale, motoring, fishing; *Style*— John Langley, Esq; Hunters End, Chiddingstone Hoath, Edenbridge, Kent (☎ 0892 870291); The Daily Telegraph, Peterborough Court, South Quay Plaza, 181 Marsh Wall, Isle of Dogs, London E14 9SR (☎ 071 538 5000, fax 071 538 7842)

LANGLEY, Kenneth William; s of William Thomas Charles Langley (d 1984), of Osmont House, Grove Park, Wanstead, London, and Ada Winifred, *née* Looke (d 1979); *b* 13 Jan 1932; *Educ* East Ham Tech HS, East Ham Tech Coll; *m* 16 March 1957, Daisy Rosina, da of Frederick Charles Parsons (d 1956), of Essex; 3 da (Gillian b 1959, Susan b 1961, Elizabeth b 1964); *Career* Nat Serv Sgt RE Egypt and Jordan; memb: Greenwich Chamber of Trade, Kent Branch Jt Consultative Ctee for Bldg Indust, CBI, Divnl Cncl RICS; memb Rotary Club Gravesend; Freeman City of London 1972, Liveryman Worshipful Co of Basketmakers 1977; FCIOB 1957, FRICS 1960, ACIArb 1966; *Recreations* music, reading, golf; *Clubs* City Livery; *Style*— Kenneth Langley, Esq; Wm Bryen Langley & Co, 58 Footscray Rd, London SE9 2SU (☎ 081 850 7775, fax 081 850 6772)

LANGMAN, Lady; Iris Pamela Gaskell; *née* Kennard; o da of Capt (Alan) Spencer Gaskell Kennard (d 1951), formerly of Purslow Hall, Craven Arms, Shropshire, and Agatha Frances, *née* Colfox; *b* 1 May 1912; *m* 18 July 1936, Sir John Lyell Langman, 3 and last Bt (d 1985); 3 da (1 decd); *Style*— Lady Langman; The Goslings, Gooseacre Lane, Cirencester, Glos GL7 2DS

LANGMAN, Prof Michael John Stratton; *b* 30 Jan 1935; *Educ* St Pauls, Guys Hosp Med Sch (BSc, MB, MD); *m* Rosemary Ann Langman, JP; 2 s (Nicholas, Benjamin), 2 da (Suzannah, Victoria); *Career* conslt physician, sr lectr, then reader in med Nottingham Teaching Hosps 1968-73, Boots prof of therapeutic med Univ of Nottingham Med Sch 1974-87, William Withering prof of med Univ of Birmingham Med Sch 1987-; memb: Ctee on Review of Medicines 1980-86, Ctee on Safety of Medicines 1987, Br Soc of Gastroenterology; MRCP 1960, FRCP 1974; *Recreations* squash, cricket, opera-going; *Clubs* MCC; *Style*— Prof Michael Langman; Queen Elizabeth Hosp, Birmingham B15 2TH (☎ 021 472 1311)

LANGRIDGE, Edward James; s of Edward Victor Langridge (d 1977), of Eastbourne, Sussex, and Edith Mabel, *née* Blair; *b* 7 Aug 1946; *Educ* Eastbourne GS; *m* 1, 1967 (m dis 1983), Margaret Dally, *née* Scott; 1 s (Stuart Edward b 12 Oct 1973), 1 da (Nicola Ann b 7 March 1972); m 2, 1982, Judith Anne, da of Stanley Frederick Hammersley; 1 s (Alexander James b 2 July 1988), 1 da (Sophie Clare Henrietta b 9 Feb 1990); *Career* prodn mangr Gordon Scott & Barton Ltd 1966-72 (prodn trainee 1963-66); Smedley McAlpine Ltd: prodn mangr 1972, assoc dir 1975, dir 1980, dep md 1983, md 1987-; FBIM, MInstM; *Recreations* classic cars, golf; *Clubs* Jaguar Drivers, Poult Wood Golf; *Style*— Edward Langridge, Esq; Byeways, Gipps Cross Lane, Langton Green, Tunbridge Wells, Kent TN3 0DH (☎ 089 286 2006); Smedley McAlpine Ltd, 140 Camden Street, London NW1 9PB (☎ 071 267 7070, fax 071 267 2707, car 0860 657985)

LANGRIDGE, Philip Gordon; s of Arthur Gordon, and Elsie Kate, *née* Underhill; *b* 16 Dec 1939; *Educ* Maidstone GS, Royal Acad of Music; *m* 1, 2 Aug 1962, (Margaret) Hilary, da of Rev George Davidson; 1 s (Stephen Maitland b 28 May 1962), 2 da (Anita James b 11 June 1966, Jennifer Mary b 19 Dec 1970); m 2, 6 June 1981, Ann, da of Joseph Eugene Murray, of Dublin; 1 s (Jonathan Philip b 20 Oct 1986); *Career* concert and opera singer (tenor); debut Glyndebourne Festival 1964 and BBC Promenade Concerts 1970; first appearance: in Indomeneo at Angers 1975, at La Scala in Boris Godunov with Abbado 1979; performances incl: Indomeneo at Glyndebourne 1983, Boris Godunov and Royal Opera Covent Garden, Cosi Fan Tutte at The Met New York 1985, world premier of Mask of Orphens (Birtwistle) ENO 1986, new prodn of Billy Budd (Britten) ENO 1988; sang Aron at Salzburg Fest 1987 and 1988; Grammy Award for Moses und Aron (Schonberg) under Solti 1986, Olivier Award for O Sud (Janacek) 1984, winner of RPS Charles Heidsieck Singer of the Year 1988-89; served on Music Panel for Arts Cncl of GB; over 50 recordings of early, baroque, classical, romantic and modern music; LRAM, GRSM, FRAM, ARAM; *Recreations* collecting watercolours; *Style*— Philip Langridge, Esq; c/o Allied Artists, 42 Montpelier Sq, London SW7 1JZ (☎ 071 589 6243)

LANGRISHE, Hon Lady (Grania Sybil Enid); *née* Wingfield; da of 9 Viscount Powerscourt (d 1973), and Sheila, Viscountess Powerscourt *qv*; sis of 10 Viscount; *b* 25 April 1934; *m* 1955, Sir Hercules Ralph Hume Langrishe, 7 Bt; 1 s, 3 da; *Style*— The Hon Lady Langrishe; Ringlestown House, Kilmessan, Co Meath, Ireland (☎ 010 353 46 25243)

LANGRISHE, Sir Hercules Ralph Hume; 7 Bt (I 1777), of Knocktopher Abbey, Kilkenny; s of Capt Sir Terence Hume Langrishe, 6 Bt (d 1973), of Knocktopher Abbey, Co Kilkenny; *b* 17 May 1927; *Educ* Summer Fields (St Leonards), Eton; *m* 1955, Hon Grania Sybil Enid, *qv*, da of 9 Viscount Powerscourt; 1 s, 3 da (Miranda, Georgina, Atalanta); *Heir* s, James Hercules Langrishe; *Career* 2 Lt 9 Lancers 1947, Lt 1948, ret 1953; *Clubs* Kildare Street and Univ (Dublin); *Style*— Sir Hercules Langrishe, Bt; Ringlestown House, Kilmessan, Co Meath, Ireland (☎ 010 353 46 25243)

LANGRISHE, James Hercules; s and h of Sir Hercules Ralph Hume Langrishe, 7 Bt; *b* 3 March 1957; *m* 1985, Gemma, da of Patrick O'Daly, and Rita, *née* Hickey, of Kiltale, Co Meath; 1 s (b 8 April 1988), 1 da (b 1986); *Style*— James Langrishe, Esq; Ringlestown House, Kilmessan, Co Meath (☎ 010 353 46 25243)

LANGSTAFF, Brian Frederick James; s of Frederick Sydney Langstaff, of 2 Parsonage Farm, Church St, Boxted, Essex, and Muriel Amy Maude, *née* Griffin; *b* 30 April 1948; *Educ* George Heriot's Sch Edinburgh, St Catharine's Coll Cambridge (BA); *m* 19 July 1975, Deborah Elizabeth, da of Samuel James Weatherup (d 1953), of NI; 1 s (Nicholas b 1980), 1 da (Kerry b 1978); *Career* called to the Bar Middle Temple 1971, sr lectr in law (former lectr) Chelmer Coll 1971-75, Harmsworth Scholar 1975, in practice 1975-; chm of govrs Stoke-by-Nayland VCP Sch, parochial church cncllr Stoke-by-Nayland; *Books* Concise College Casenotes Series: Equity & Trusts (1975); *Recreations* tennis, swimming, walking, travel, watching TV, mowing the lawn; *Style*— Brian Langstaff, Esq; The Pyghtle, Scotland St, Stoke-by-Nayland, Suffolk (☎ 0206 262257); Cloisters, 1 Pump Ct, Temple, London EC4 (☎ 071 583 0303, fax 071 583 2254)

LANGTON, Bryan David; CBE (1988); s of Thomas Langton (d 1974), and Doris, *née* Brown (d 1987); *b* 6 Dec 1936; *Educ* Accrington GS, Westminster Tech Coll (Dip Hotel Operation), Ecole Hotelière de la SSA Lausanne (Operations Dip); *m* 23 Sept 1960, Sylva, da of Herman Heinrich Leo Degenhardt, of Richterstrasse 11, Braunschweig, W Germany; 2 da (Suzanne (Mrs Boyette) b 1962, Michele (Mrs Wijegoonaratna) b 1964); *Career* dir Bass plc 1985-; chm Crest Hotels Ltd 1985- (md 1982-88), Bass Horizon Hotels 1985-89, Holiday Inns Int 1988-, Toby Restaurants Ltd 1988-; memb: Grand Cncl of Hotel and Catering Benevolent Assoc, exec ctee of Int Hotel Assoc, bd of mgmnt British Hotels, Restaurants and Caterers Assoc; hon fell Manchester Poly 1986; FHCIMA; *Recreations* golf, reading, cricket, theatre; *Style*— Bryan D Langton, Esq, CBE; Westward Lodge, Shilton Road, Burford, Oxon OX8 4PA (☎ 099 382 2599); Bass Hotels and Restaurants Division, 24-26 Bridge St, Banbury, Oxon OX16 8RQ (☎ 0295 252555, fax 0295 267339, telex 837294, car 0836 601588)

LANGTON, Edward Langton; s of Lewis Langton, and Louisa Kate, *née* Levy; *b* 30 Oct 1921; *Educ* City of London Sch; *m* 1 Sept 1949, Joye Amelia, da of Jack Isaacs (d 1962); 1 s (Timothy John b 25 July 1953), 1 da (Louise (Mrs Rawlins) b 26 June 1950); *Career* WWII serv: Flt Lt and Sqdn Navigation Offr RAF 1941-46; CA; sr ptnr Stoy Hayward 1968-85 (ptnr 1951-86); memb Exec Cncl Horwath and Horwath International 1975-86 (currently Euro regnl dir); chm: Oak Hotels plc, Sinclair Goldsmith Holdings plc; dir Court Holdings Ltd; pres John Carpenter Club, memb Exec Bd Variety Club of GB, chm Jewish Home and Hosp Tottenham; Liveryman Worshipful Co of Chartered Accountants; FCA; *Recreations* golf, cricket; *Clubs* Hurlingham, RAC, MCC; *Style*— Edward Langton Langton, Esq; Flat 8, 40 Chester Square, London SW1W 9HT (☎ 071 730 1847); 8 Baker St, London W1M 1DA (☎ 071 486 5888)

LANGTON, Lord; James Grenville Temple-Gore-Langton; s and h of 8 Earl Temple of Stowe, *qv*; *b* 11 Sept 1955; *Educ* Winchester; *Style*— Lord Langton; c/o The Rt Hon Earl Temple of Stowe, Garth, Outertown, Stromness, Orkney

LANGTON, John Leslie; s of Arthur Laurence Langton (d 1976), and Sarah Jane, *née* Baker; *b* 23 Nov 1948; *Educ* Roan GS Greenwich; *m* 10 Aug 1979, Raymonde, da of Raymond Glinne, of Gembloux, Belgium 5030; 1 da (Jennifer Marie-Anne b 8 Dec 1983); *Career* Strauss Turnbull & Co 1965-69, Scandinavian Bank Ltd 1969-73, Williams & Glyns Bank 1973-74, Bondtrade in Brussels 1974-77, Morgan Stanley International 1977-78, dir Amex Bank Ltd 1979-80, sr exec dir Orion Royal Bank Ltd 1980-85, exec dir Security Pacific Hoare Govett Ltd 1986-87, md Gintel & Co Ltd 1987-89, chm AIBD (Systems & Information) Ltd 1990-, (memb Bd AIBD Zurich 1981-); chief exec and sec gen The Assoc of Int Bond Dealers; *Recreations* wine, food, books, backgammon, travel; *Style*— John L Langton, Esq; 8 Beckenham Rd, West Wickham, Kent BR4 0QT (☎ 081 777 1202); Schwanengasse 2, 8001 Zurich, Switzerland; The Association of International Bond Dealers, Rigistrasse 60, CH-8033, Zurich, Switzerland (☎ 010 411 363 4222, fax 010 411 363 7772, telex 815812); AIBD (Systems & Information) Ltd, 7 Limeharbour, Docklands, London E14 9NQ (☎ 071 538 5656, fax 071 538 4902, telex 8813069)

LANGTON, John Raymond; *b* 28 May 1929; *Educ* Stationers' Co Sch; *m* 4 April 1953, Brenda Olive; 1 s (Toby b 1970), 2 da (Fiona b 1962, Charlotte b 1966); *Career* fndr and md Sun Life Unit Services Ltd 1980-89, chm Valens Associates Ltd 1989-; ACII 1953; *Style*— John Langton, Esq; 25 Brandon Mews, Barbican, London EC2Y 8BE (☎ 071 588 6108)

LANGTON, Col Roland Stephen; LVO (1953), MC (1945); s of Leslie Langton (d 1952), memb Lloyd's; *b* 1921; *Educ* Radley, Jesus Coll Cambridge; *m* 1948, Pamela Elvira, da of Kenneth Headington, MC (decd), of Paley St, Berks; 3 s, 1 da; *Career* served 1939-45 with Irish Gds, NW Europe 1940-45 (despatches), Palestine (despatches), Egypt, Cyprus, BAOR; psc, jssc; cmd 1 Bn Irish Gds 1961-64, AAG MOD (PS12 Army) 1964-66, sr Army rep Defence Operational Analysis Estab 1966-69; underwriting memb of Lloyd's; dir: Langton Underwriting Agents Ltd, Milestone Underwriting Mgmnt Ltd; memb Ct of Assistants Worshipful Co of Merchant Taylors 1971 (Master 1978), memb Ct of Corpn of Sons of the Clergy; FRSA, FBIM; *Recreations* enjoying retirement; *Clubs* City of London, Leander, London Rowing; *Style*— Col Roland Langton, LVO, MC; Keeper's Cottage, Crowsley Park, Harpsden, Henley-on-Thames, Oxon RG9 4JB (☎ Henley 573698)

LANGTRY, (James) Ian; s of Rev Herbert James Langtry (d 1942), and Irene Margaret, *née* Eagleson; *b* 2 Jan 1939; *Educ* Coleraine Academical Instn, Queen's Univ Belfast (BSc); *m* 1959, (Eileen Roberta) Beatrice, da of James Burnside Nesbitt (d 1957); 1 s (James Paul Eagleson b 1960), 1 da (Anna Beatrice b 1965); *Career* asst master Bangor GS 1960-61, lectr Belfast Coll of Technol 1961-66, asst dir Civil Serv Cmmn 1966-70; Dept of Educn and Sci: princ 1970-76, asst sec 1976-82, under sec 1982-87; under sec Dept of Health and Social Security 1987-88; educn offr Assoc of CCs 1988-; *Recreations* golf, sailing; *Clubs* Royal Portrush Golf, West Kent Golf; *Style*— Ian Langtry, Esq; Association of County Councils, Eaton House, 66a Eaton Square, London SW1W 9BH (☎ 071 235 1200)

LANIGAN, Denis George; s of George Lanigan (d 1961), and Ada Lanigan (d 1988); *b* 26 Jan 1926; *Educ* Drayton Manor Sch, Kings Coll Cambridge (MA); *m* 5 Oct 1959, Jean, *née* Sanderson; 1 s (Mark b 1960), 1 da (Kate b 1962); *Career* J Walter Thompson Company: chief exec JWT Germany 1959-64, md UK 1966-74, chm UK 1974-76, pres JWT Europe 1976-80, vice chm Worldwide 1980-82, chief operating offr Worldwide 1982-86; currently: dir Marks and Spencer plc, non-exec dir TSB Bank 1987-90, chm MM and K Ltd 1988-; memb: Cambridge Univ Appt Bd 1974-78, East Sussex Area Health Authy 1972-74, Overseas Trade Bd N Americn Advsy Ctee 1986-91 (chm 1991); dir Money Mgmnt Cncl 1986-; *Recreations* music, theatre, gardening; *Clubs* Arts, University (NY); *Style*— Denis Lanigan, Esq; 21 Queens Gate Gardens, London SW7 5LZ (☎ 071 268 7410); Annes, Hadlow Down, East Sussex TN22 4HU; Marks and Spencer plc, Michael House, 35/67 Baker St, London W1A 1DN (☎ 071 268 7410)

LANKESTER, Richard Shermer; s of Richard Ward Lankester (d 1969), and Elsie Marion, *née* Shermer; *b* 8 Feb 1922; *Educ* Haberdashers' Aske's, Hampstead Sch, Jesus Coll Oxford (MA); *m* 30 May 1950, Dorothy, da of Raymond Jackson (d 1966), of Worsley, Lancs; 3 s (Simon b 1951, d 1989, Toby b 1960, Thomas b 1964), 1 da

(Ruth b 1955); *Career* serv Hants RHA Regt Italy 1943-45, RA 1942-45, Lt; Clerks Dept House of Commons 1947, co ed The Table 1962-67, clerk of Standing Ctees 1973-75, clerk to Expenditure Ctee 1975-79, registrar of Members' Interests 1976-87, clerk of Select Ctees House of Commons 1979-87; *Style*— Richard Lankester, Esq; The Old Farmhouse, The Green, Boughton Monchelsea, Kent (☎ 0622 743749)

LANSDOWNE, 8 Marquess of (GB 1784); Maj George John Charles Mercer Nairne Petty-Fitzmaurice; PC (1964), JP (Perthshire 1950); also Baron Kerry and Lixnaw (I 1295), Earl of Kerry, Viscount Clanmaurice (both I 1723), Viscount FitzMaurice, Baron Dunkeron (both I 1751), Earl of Shelburne (I 1753), Lord Wycombe, Baron of Chipping Wycombe (GB 1760), Earl Wycombe, and Viscount Calne and Calston (both GB 1784); assumption of additional surnames of Petty-Fitzmaurice recognised by decree of Lord Lyon 1947; s of Maj Lord Charles Mercer-Nairne, MVO (ka 1914, himself 2 s of 5 Marquess, sometime Viceroy of India and Foreign Sec), and Lady Violet Mary Elliot Murray-Kynynmound, da of 4 Earl of Minto; suc 7 Marquess (first cousin, who was ka 1944); *b* 27 Nov 1912; *Educ* Eton, Ch Ch Oxford; *m* 1, 1938, Barbara (d 1965), da of Harold Stuart Chase, of Santa Barbara, California; 2 s, 1 da (and 1 decd); m 2, 1969 (m dis 1978), Hon Selina Polly Dawson, da of 1 Viscount Eccles, KCVO, PC; m 3, 1978, Gillian Ann (d 1982), da of Alured Morgan; *Heir* s, Earl of Shelburne; *Career* served WWII Capt Scots Greys & Maj Free French; private sec to Duff Cooper (1 Visc Norwich) when ambass in Paris 1944; 2 Lt Scottish Horse (TA), a lord in waiting to HM The Queen 1957-58, jt parly under-sec state FO 1958-62, min of state Colonial Affairs 1962-64, DL Wilts 1952-73, sec Junior Unionist League for E Scotland 1939; memb Royal Company of Archers (Queen's Body Guard for Scotland); chm Franco-British Soc 1972- (and pres); patron of two livings; *Clubs* Turf, New (Edinburgh); *Style*— The Most Hon the Marquess of Lansdowne; Meikleour House, Perthshire (☎ 025 083 210)

LANSDOWNE, Peter William; s of William Marks Lansdowne (d 1972), and Bessie Maria, *née* Eales; *b* 1 Feb 1938; *Educ* Boys GS Gowerton, Univ Coll Swansea (BSc); *m* 1, 12 July 1963 (m dis), Anna Deborah, da of Howell Vernon David (d 1966); 3 s (Simon b 1966, Nicholas b 1968, Anthony b 1971), 1 da (Amanda b 1964); m 2, 3 Aug 1990, Beverley Anne, da of Griffith John Philips; *Career* divnl dir Binnie and Ptnrs 1989-; vicars warden All Saints Oystermouth; memb Assoc of Consulting Engrs, FIChemE 1979 (former memb Cncl and chm S Wales Branch), MIWE 1979; *Recreations* cycling; *Clubs* Bristol, Channel Yacht, Rotary; *Style*— Peter W Lansdowne, Esq; 4 Caswell Bay Road, Bishopston, Swansea, SA3 3DD (☎ 044 128 2442); Binnie and Partners, Pembroke Hse, Charter Crt, Phoenix Way, Swansea SA7 9EH (☎ 0792 781 935, fax 0792x 781 947)

LANSDOWNE, Polly, Marchioness of; (Selina) Polly Dawson; da of 1 Viscount Eccles, KCVO, PC, *qv*; *b* 1937; *Educ* Sherborne Sch for Girls, London Univ; *m* 1, 1962 (m dis 1968), Robin Andrew Duthac Carnegie, late Capt Queen's Dragoon Gds; 1 s; m 2, 1969 (m dis 1978), 8 Marquess of Lansdowne; *Style*— Polly, Marchioness of Lansdowne; 29 St Dionis Rd, London SW6 4UQ

LANTOS, Prof Peter Laszlo; s of Sandor Leipniker (d 1945), and Ilona, *née* Somlo (d 1968); *b* 22 Oct 1939; *Educ* Med Sch Szeged Univ Hungary (MD), Univ of London (PhD); *Career* Wellcome res fell 1968-69, sr lectr and hon conslt in neuropathology Middx Sch of Med 1976-79 (res asst 1969-73, lectr in neuropathology 1974-75), prof of neuropathology Inst of Psychiatry 1979-; hon conslt in neuropathology: Bethlem Royal and Maudsley Hosps 1979-, KCH 1985-; chm: Scientific Advsy Panel Brain Res Tst 1985-, Neuropathology Sub Ctee RCPath 1986-89 (chm Panel of Examiners in Neuropathology 1983-89), Academic Bd Inst of Psychiatry 1988-; memb: Pathologic Soc GB and I 1971-, Br Neuropathological Soc 1972-; MRCPath 1975; *Books* contrib: Brain Tumours: Scientific Basis, Clinical Investigation and Current Therapy (1980), Histochemistry in Pathology (1983), Scientific Basis of Clinical Neurology (1985), Schizophrenia: The Major Issues (1988); *Recreations* travel, theatre, fine arts; *Clubs* Athenaeum; *Style*— Prof Peter Lantos; Institute of Psychiatry, London SE5 8AF (☎ 071 703 5411)

LANYON, Prof Lance Edward; s of Harry Lanyon (d 1947), of London, and Heather Gordon, *née* Tyrell; *b* 4 Jan 1944; *Educ* Christ's Hosp, Univ of Bristol (BVSc, PhD, MRCVS); *m* 15 April 1972, Mary, da of Harold Kear (d 1966), of Sevenoaks, Kent; 1 s (Richard b 1975), 1 da (Alice b 1977); *Career* reader vet anatomy Univ of Bristol 1967-79 (lectr 1967-79), prof Tufts Sch of Vet Med Boston Mass USA 1983-84 (assoc prof 1980-83); The Royal Vet Coll London: prof vet anatomy 1984-89, head Dept of Vet Basic Sci 1987-88, princ 1989-; FBOA; memb: Euro Soc for Biomechanics, Orthopaedic Res Soc (US), Anatomical Soc, Bone and Tooth Soc, American Soc for Bone and Mineral Res; MRCVS 1966; *Books* numerous chapters in books on Orthopaedics, Osteoporosis and Athletic Training, and various scientific articles in orthopaedic and bone related jls; *Recreations* building, home improvements, sailing; *Clubs* Christ's Hosp; *Style*— Prof Lance Lanyon; The Royal Veterinary College, Royal College St, London NW1 0TU (☎ 071 387 2898, fax 071 387 7386)

LAPOTAIRE, Jane Elizabeth Marie; da of Louise Elise Burgess Lapotaire; *b* 26 Dec 1944; *Educ* Northgate GS Ipswich, Bristol Old Vic Theatre Sch; *m* 1, 1965, Oliver Wood (m dis 1967); 1 s (Rowan b 1973); m 2, 1974, Roland Joffé (m dis 1982); *Career* actress; Bristol Old Vic Co 1965-67; NT Co 1967-71: Measure for Measure, Flea in Her Ear, Dance of Death, Way of the World, Merchant of Venice, Oedipus, The Taming of the Shrew; freelance in films (Paramount, MGM, United Artists) and TV 1971-74 and 1976-78; RSC 1974-75: Viola in Twelfth Night, Sonya in Uncle Vanya; Prospect Theatre Co West End 1975-76: Vera in A Month in the Country, Lucy in Honeychurch in As Room with a View; Rosalind in As You Like It Edinburgh Festival 1977; RSC 1978-81: Rosaline in Love's Labours Lost 1978-79; title role in Piaf: The Other Place 1978, Aldwych 1979, Wyndhams 1980, Broadway 1981; NT: Eileen in Kick for Touch 1983, Belvidera in Venice Preserv'd, Antigone 1984; St Joan (title role) Compass Co 1985, Double Double Fortune Theatre 1986, RSC 1986-87 (Misalliance 1986, Archbishop's Ceiling 1986), Greenland Royal Court Theatre 1988, Joy Davidman in Shadowlands Queen's Theatre Shaftesbury Ave 1990; TV: Marie Curie 1977, Anthony and Cleopatra 1981, Macbeth 1983, Seal Morning 1985, Napoleon and Josephine 1987, Blind Justice 1988, The Dark Angel 1989; films: Eureka 1983, Lady Jane 1986; Emmy and BAFTA nominations 1976; awards for performance in Piaf: SWET Award 1979, London Critics Award 1980, Variety Club Award 1980, Broadway Tony Award 1981; for Blind Justice Br Press Guild Best Actress Award 1988, Variety Club Award 1989; pres Bristol Old Vic Theatre Club 1985-, memb Marie Curie Meml Fndn Appeals Ctee 1986-88, hon pres Friends of Southwark Globe 1986-, visiting fell Univ of Sussex 1986-; *Books* Grace and Favour (autobiog, 1989); *Recreations* walking, water colours; *Style*— Ms Jane Lapotaire; c/o International Creative Management, 388 Oxford St, London W1 (☎ 071 629 8080)

LAPPERT, Prof Michael Franz; s of the late Julius Lappert, of Brno, Czechoslovakia, and the late Kornelie, *née* Beran; *b* 31 Dec 1928; *Educ* Wilson's GS London, Northern Poly London (BSc, PhD, DSc); *m* 14 Feb 1980, Lorna, da of David McKenzie (d 1974), of Seaton, Workington; *Career* sr lectr N Poly London 1955-59 (asst lectr 1952-53, lectr 1953-55), sr lectr Univ of Manchester Inst Sci and Technol 1961-64 (lectr 1959-61), prof Univ of Sussex 1969- (reader 1964-69); sr fell Univ of Sussex SERC 1980-85; author of c 500 papers on organometallic and inorganic chemistry; pres Dalton Div RSC 1989-91; Hon Dr Rer Nat Munchen 1989; FRS, FRCS, MACS; *Books* Metal and Metalloid Amides: Syntheses, Structures and Physical and Chemical Properties (with P P Power, A R Sanger, R C Srivastava, 1980), Chemistry of Organo-Zirconium and Hafnium Compounds (with D J Cardin, C L Raston, 1986); *Recreations* theatre, opera, art, tennis, walking; *Style*— Prof Michael Lappert; 4 Varndean Gardens, Brighton BN1 6WL (☎ 0273 503 661); School of Chemistry and Molecular Sciences, Univ of Sussex, Brighton BN1 9QJ (☎ 0273 678 316)

LAPPING, Peter Herbert; s of Dr Douglas James Lapping, MBE (d 1989), of Swaziland, and Dorothy, *née* Horrocks (d 1971); *b* 8 Aug 1941; *Educ* St John's Coll Johannesburg, Univ of Natal (BA), Lincoln Coll Oxford (MA, played cricket for OU Authentics); *m* 1 April 1967, Diana Dillworth, da of Lt Col Eric S G Howard, MC (d 1977), of Stroud, Glous; 1 s (Mark Edward b 1969), 1 da (Joanna Venka b 1970); *Career* asst master Reed's Sch 1966-67, head of hist Lomretto Sch 1967-79 (house master Pinkie House 1972-79); headmaster: Shiplake Coll 1979-88, Sherborne 1988-; memb: HMC, SHA; *Recreations* walking, gardening, travel; *Clubs* Vincents (Oxford), MCC, East India, Devonshire Sports and Public Schools; *Style*— Peter Lapping, Esq; Sherborne School, Dorset DT9 3AP (☎ 0955 812646, fax 0935 816628)

LAPSLEY, (Alastair Gourlay) Howard; s of Rev Claude William Lapsley (d 1976), and Florence Lapsley; *b* 20 May 1940; *Educ* Dulwich, Coll of Law; *m* 5 June 1965, Susan Elizabeth, da of Charles Henry Bassingthwaighte (d 1988), of Diss, Norfolk; 1 s (Angus b 1970), 1 da (Catriona b 1972); *Career* admitted slr 1964; dir: JA Gadd Ltd 1975-, Hubdean Ltd 1981-; RAC Motor Sports Assoc Ltd 1986-, Bugatti Owners Club Ltd 1986-; memb Br Motor Sports Cncl 1984-; Br Rally Champion (1300 cc) 1983; memb Law Soc; *Recreations* motor sport, music, travel; *Clubs* RAC; *Style*— Howard Lapsley, Esq; 8 Horsefair, Chipping Norton, Oxon (☎ 0608 642063, fax 0608 644429)

LAPSLEY, Air Marshal Sir John Hugh; KBE (1969), CB (1966), DFC (1940), AFC (1950); s of Edward John Lapsley (d 1918), and Norah Gladys, *née* Kelly (d 1972); *b* 24 Sept 1916; *Educ* Wolverhampton Sch, RAF Coll Cranwell; *m* 1, 1942, Jean Margaret (d 1979), da of Douglas Tait MacIvor (d 1958), of Gravesend; 1 s, 1 da; m 2, 1980, Mrs Millicent Rees, da of Charles Hubert Beadnell (d 1936), and wid of T A Rees; *Career* RAF 1933, Lord Wakefield scholarship to RAF Coll Cranwell 1936, WWII (Egypt, UK, France and Germany), Gp Capt 1956, Air Cdre 1961, Dep COS (Air) 2 TAF 1961-62, Air Vice-Marshal 1965, sec to Chiefs of Staff Ctee, MOD 1964-66, Air Marshal 1968, AOC-in-C Coastal Cmd RAF 1968-69, head of Br Def Staff, Washington 1970, ret 1973; dir gen Save the Children Fund 1974-75, dir Falkland Is R & D Assoc Ltd 1978-83, vice pres The UK Falklands Is Ctee 1986; cncllr Suffolk Coastal DC 1979-87 (vice chm 1982-83, chm 1983-84); *Recreations* golf, fishing, ornithology; *Clubs* RAF, Aldeburgh Golf, Suffolk Fly Fishers'; *Style*— Air Marshal Sir John Lapsley, KBE, CB, DFC, AFC; 149 Saxmundham Rd, Aldeburgh, Suffolk IP15 5PB (☎ 0728 453957)

LARCOM, Sir (Charles) Christopher (Royde); 5 Bt (UK 1868); s of Sir Philip Larcom, 4 Bt (d 1967); *b* 11 Sept 1926; *Educ* Radley, Clare Coll Cambridge; *m* 1956, Barbara Elizabeth, da of Balfour Bowen; 4 da; *Career* memb The Stock Exchange London 1959-1987 (memb Cncl 1970-1980), ptnr Grieveson Grant and Co stockbrokers 1960-1986, fin dir Kleinwort Grieveson 1986; *Recreations* sailing, music; *Clubs* Naval and Military, Cruising Assoc, Ocean Cruising, Itchener Sailing, Island Sailing, Blackwater Sailing; *Style*— Sir Christopher Larcom, Bt; 8 The Postern, Barbican, Wood Street, London EC2Y 8BJ; and 4 Marinacay, PO Box 145, Road Town, Tortola, British Virgin Islands

LARDNER, Bernard John; s of Oswald Henry Lardner, of Gillingham, Kent, and Elizabeth Kathleen Lardner; *b* 12 Jan 1944; *Educ* Finchley GS; *m* 1, Vanessa Joy, *née* Davidson (d 1974); 1 da (Claire Louise b 17 March 1972); m 2, 1 Aug 1975, Betty Ann, *née* Carrott; 1 s (Mark b 30 July 1976), 1 da (Zoe Jayne b 1 May 1978); *Career* res and exec dir Laing and Cruickshank (Stockbrokers) 1980 (dir 1975); Alexanders Laing & Cruickshank Holdings Ltd: main bd dir 1984, main bd dir CL ALCH 1987, dir corporate fin 1987; dir Harvey & Thompson plc 1989; Freeman City of London 1987; AMSIA; *Recreations* golf, fishing, skiing; *Clubs* St George's Hill Golf; *Style*— Bernard Lardner, Esq; 43 Dover St, London W1X 3RE (☎ 071 495 6702, fax 071 495 2746, telex 883757 HARVEY G)

LARDNER-BURKE, Thomas David; s of Desmond William Lardner-Burke (d 1984), of Zimbabwe, and Alice May, *née* Fraser; f was Min of Justice and Min of Commerce and Indust in Mr Ian Smith's Rhodesian Govt; *b* 9 Dec 1937; *Educ* St Andrew's Coll Grahamstown SA, Brixton Sch of Building; *m* 1966, Virginia Alicia, *née* Allison; 3 da (Claire Olivia b 1968, Amanda May b 1969, Katherine Anna b 1975); *Career* chm: Building Brokers Ltd 1964, Trac Office Contracts Ltd 1968, Home Secretaries Ltd 1989; dir Trac Telecom Ltd 1982; chm Anglo Rhodesian Soc 1969-80; *Recreations* tennis, golf, travel; *Clubs* Harare, IOD; *Style*— T D Lardner-Burke, Esq; Thornton House, Thornton Road, London SW19 4NG (☎ 081 944 6888, car 0836 233355)

LAREDO, Jaime; *b* 1940; *Career* musician; pupil of: Antonio de Grassi, Frank Houser, Josef Gingold, Ioan Galamian; debut recital 1948, orchestral debut 1951, youngest winner ever Queen Elizabeth competition Brussels 1959, festival appearances with major orchestras worldwide incl: Spoleto, Tanglewood, Hollywood Bowl, Mostly Mozart, Ravinia, Blossom, Marlboro, Edinburgh, The Proms; dir Chamber Music at the 92nd Street Y series NY, memb Kalichstein/Laredo/Robinson Trio, teacher Artist Faculty Curtis Inst, chamber musician, dir and soloist with int chamber orchestras incl St Paul and the Scottish Chamber, numerous tours worldwide; awarded Handel medallion NY; *Style*— Jaime Laredo; Harold Holt Ltd, 31 Sinclair Road, London W14 0NS (☎ 071 603 4300, fax 071 603 0019, telex 22339 HUNTER)

LARGE, Andrew Mcleod Brooks; s of Maj-Gen Stanley Eyre Large, MBE, of Drumcrannog, Dalbeattie, Kirkcudbrightshire, and Janet Mary, *née* Brooks; *b* 7 Aug 1942; *Educ* Winchester, Univ of Cambridge (BA), Insead Fontainebleau (MBA); *m* 17 June 1967, Susan Mary, da of Sir Ronald Melville, KCB, *qv*; 2 s (Alexander b 1970, James b 1972), 1 da (Georgina b 1976); *Career* British Petroleum Ltd 1964-71, md Orion Bank Ltd 1971-79, chief exec and dep chm Swiss Bank Corp International 1983 (md 1980), gp chief exec and dep chm Swiss Bank Corp International 1987, memb Exec Bd Swiss Bank Corp 1988-89; non-exec dir: Nuclear Electric PLC 1990-, Ranks Hovis McDougall PLC 1990-, Phoenix Securities Ltd 1990-; non-exec chm Luthy Baillie Dowsett Pethick & Co Limited 1990-, chm Large Smith Walter Limited 1990-; dep chm International Securities Regulation Organisation 1985-86, chm The Securities Assoc 1986-87, memb Cncl International Stock Exchange 1986-87; *Recreations* skiing, walking, photography, music, weather, sailing, gardening; *Clubs* Brooks's; *Style*— Andrew Large, Esq; Stokes House, Ham St, Richmond, Surrey (☎ 081 940 2403)

LARGE, Hon Mrs (Elisabeth); da of Baron Edmund-Davies, PC (Life Peer); *b* 1939; *m* 1, 1965 (m dis 1975), Richard Owen Roberts; m 2, 1988, Alan Large; *Style*— The Hon Mrs Large; 7 Swaledale Avenue, Reedley, Burnley, Lancs BB10 2LJ

LARGE, Prof John Barry; s of Tom Large (d 1975), and Ada Large; *b* 10 Oct 1930; *Educ* QMC, Purdue Univ Indiana USA, Cornell Univ NY USA, Harvard Univ Mass USA; *m* 18 Oct 1958, Barbara Alicia, da of William A Nelson (d 1965), of New Westminster, BC, Canada; 2 s (Jonathan William b 13 March 1968, Jeremy Thomas (twin)); *Career* chief acoustics The Boeing Co Seattle USA 1958-70, prof applied acoustics Univ of Southampton 1970: dir Inst of Sound and Vibration Res, dean Faculty of Engrg, chief exec Univ of Southampton Hldgs Ltd, dir industl affrs; conslt: US Dept of Transportation, UK Civil Aviation Authy, BAA plc (formerly Br Airports Authy), BR Bd, Euro Community Environmental Serv; non-exec dir Sarasota Automation Ltd; dir Southampton C of C, exec memb Hants Devpt Assoc; fell Royal Acoustical Soc; memb Acoustical Soc of America, MSAE (USA), corresponding memb Inst of Noise Control Engrg USA; *Recreations* flying, skiing; *Style*— Prof John Large; Chinook, Southdown Rd, Shawford, Hants SO21 2BY (☎ 0962 712307); Univ of Southampton, Southampton, Hants SO9 5NH (☎ 0703 592296 fax 0703 559308 telex 47661)

LARGE, Peter; MBE (1974), CBE (1987); s of Rossyln Victor Large (d 1955), and Ethel May, *née* Walters (d 1981); *b* 16 Oct 1931; *Educ* Enfield GS, UCL (BSc); *m* 27 April 1962, Susy (d 1982), da of Dr Bernard Fisher (d 1960); 1 s (George b 1957), 2 da (Julia b 1947, Anne b 1953); *Career* Nat Serv Sub Lt (E) HM Submarines 1953-55; Shell Int: joined 1956, Nigeria 1957, Ghana 1957-60, SE Arabia 1960-61, Indonesia 1961-62; paralysed by Poliomyelitis; Civil Serv 1966-; chm: Jt Ctee on Mobility for Disabled People 1971-, Assoc Disabled Professionals 1971-; memb: Exec Ctee Royal Assoc for Disability and Rehabilitation 1977-, Access Ctee for England 1984-, Nat Advsy Cncl on Employment of Disabled People 1987-; govr Motability 1978-, vice chm Disablement Income Gp 1985- (Parly advsr 1973-), dep chm Disabled Persons Tport Advsy Ctee 1986-; *Recreations* living with siamese cats; *Style*— Peter Large, Esq, CBE; 14 Birch Way, Warlingham, Surrey, CR6 9DA (☎ 0883 623801)

LARK, Robert John (Bob); s of John Frederick Lark, Lowestoft, Suffolk, and Elizabeth Mary, *née* Hunt; *b* 7 Jan 1946; *Educ* Roman Hill Secdy Sch Lowestoft; *m* 1, 18 Sept 1965, Valerie Ann, da of James Malcolm; 2 s (David Robert b 23 Feb 1967, Jonathan Paul b 8 Feb 1971); m 2, 3 Nov 1984, Ann Elizabeth, da of Bernard Mozley; 1 s (Nicholas William b 1 Jan 1989); *Career* apprentice Royal Corps of Signals 1960-63; fault finder Pye Television Ltd 1964-68, Hughes (Lowestoft) Ltd 1968-80 (engr, retail supervisor, buyer), sales dir Baskills Ltd 1980-89, chief exec Derbyshire CCC 1989-; *Recreations* cricket, golf, snooker, travelling; *Style*— Bob Lark, Esq; 31 Strettea Lane, Higham, Derbyshire DE5 6EJ (☎ 0773 835042); Derbyshire County Cricket Club, County Ground, Nottingham Rd, Derby DE2 6DA (☎ 0332 383211, fax 0332 290251)

LARKEN, Cmdt Anthea; CBE (1990); da of Frederick William Savill, of Winchester, and Nance, *née* Williams; *b* 23 Aug 1938; *Educ* Stafford Girls' HS; *m* 19 Dec 1987, Rear Adm (Edmund Shackleton) Jeremy Larken, DSO, s of Rear Adm Edmund Thomas Larken, CB, OBE (d 1965), of Yarmouth, IOW; *Career* range assessor WRNS 1956, cmmnd 1960, qualified photographic interpreter 1961, qualified WRNS Sec Offr 1967, i/c WRNS offrs trg BRNC Dartmouth 1977-79, RN Staff Coll 1978-79, NATO Mil Agency for Standardisation Brussels 1981-84, Chief Staff Offr (admin) to Flag Offr Plymouth 1985-86, Royal Coll of Def Studies 1987, Dir WRNS ADC to HM The Queen 1988-90; *Recreations* theatre, music, reading, home, family and friends; *Clubs* Royal Cwlth Soc; *Style*— Cmdt Anthea Larken, CBE, ADC, WRNS; c/o The Naval Secretary, MOD, Old Admiralty Building, Spring Gardens, London SW1A 2BE

LARKEN, Jasper Wyatt Royds; s of Capt Francis Wyatt Rawson Larken (d 1985), of Rushall Manor, Pewsey, Wilts, and Florence Meriel, *née* Royds, (see Burke's Landed Gentry, 18th Edn Vol 1 1965); *b* 12 Sept 1939; *Educ* Winchester; *m* 20 April 1968, Caroline Lucia Marie, da of Stuart West Little, of Fenwick, Old Saybrook, Connecticut, USA; 1 s (Jonathan b 1973), 1 da (Melissa b 1970); *Career* Grenadier Gds 1958-61; md Financial Intelligence UK Ltd 1978-; *Recreations* bridge, hunting, tennis, golf; *Clubs* Boodle's, MCC, Berkshire; *Style*— Jasper Larken, Esq; 24 Astell St, London SW3 3RU; The Green, Fifield, Milton-under-Wychwood, Oxon (☎ 071 352 1796); 10 St James Place, London SW1A 1NP (☎ 071 491 8147, fax 071 499 6755)

LARKEN, Rear Adm (Edmund Shackleton) Jeremy; DSO (1982); s of Rear Adm Edmund Thomas Larken, CB, OBE (d 1965), and Eileen Margaret, *née* Shackleton; *b* 14 Jan 1939; *Educ* Bryanston, Britannia RNC Dartmouth; *m* 1, 1963 (m dis 1987), Wendy Nigella, *née* Hallett; 2 da (Juliet b 1963, Henrietta b 1968); m 2 , 1987, Cmdt Anthea Larken, WRNS, da of Frederick William Savill, of Winchester; *Career* joined RN 1957; submarines 1961 served: HMS Finwhale, Tudor, Ambush and Narwhal; Navigation Offr HMS Valiant 1963, 1 Lt HMS Otus 1967, exchange with USN Submarine Force 1971-73; cmd: HMS Osiris 1969-70, Glamorgan 1975, Valiant 1976-77, Neptune (SM3) 1979-81, HMS Fearless 1981-83 (incl Falklands Campaign); Naval Plans 1983-84, Dir Naval Staff Duties 1985, Cdre Amphibious Warfare and Cmd UK/NL Amphib Force 1985-87, Asst Chief of Def Staff (Overseas) 1988-90, Rear Adm 1988; govr Bryanston Sch 1988; *Recreations* maritime and aviation interests, history and strategy, theatre, reading, home, family and friends; *Clubs* Royal Cwlth Soc; *Style*— Rear Adm Jeremy Larken, DSO; c/o The Naval Secretary, Ministry of Defence, Old Admiralty Building, Whitehall, London SW1

LARKIN, Judith Mary; da of Patrick John Larkin, and Sylvia May, *née* Silverthorne; *b* 22 May 1952; *Educ* The North London Coll Sch, City of London Poly; *Career* trainee Unilever plc 1971, corporate PR specialist IT/ Telecommunications and Electronics Industries, head of corporate PR Logica plc 1979-84, dir: Traverse-Healy & Regester 1984-87, Charles Barker 1987; md Fleishman-Hillard UK Ltd 1990; MIPR 1985, chm Br Gp Int PR Assoc; *Style*— Ms Judith Larkin; 101 Shakespeare Tower, Barbican, London EC2Y 8DR (☎ 071 628 3372); Fleishman-Hillard UK Ltd, 25 Wellington St, Covent Garden, London WC2E 7DA (☎ 071 306 9000, fax 071 497 0096)

LARKIN, Prof Maurice John Milner; s of Terence John Larkin (d 1964), of Birmingham, and Winifred, *née* Richards; *b* 12 Aug 1932; *Educ* St Philip's GS Birmingham, Trinity Coll Cambridge (BA, MA, PhD); *m* 17 Dec 1958, Enid Thelma, da of Clifford Enoch Lowe (d 1988), of Haddington; 1 s (John b 1962), 1 da (Katie b 1965); *Career* Nat Serv 2Lt RAEC 1950-51, TA Serv Lt RA 1951-55; lectr in history Univ of Glasgow 1961-65 (asst lectr 1958-61), reader in history Univ of Kent 1976 (lectr 1965-68, sr lectr 1968-76), Richard Pares prof of history Univ of Edinburgh 1976-; fell Royal Historical Soc 1986; *Books* Gathering Pace: Continental Europe 1870-1945 (1969), Church and State after the Dreyfus Affair (1974), Man and Society in Nineteenth Century Realism: Determinism and Literature (1977), France Since the Popular Front: Government and People 1936-86 (1988); *Recreations* bird-watching, music, cinema; *Style*— Prof Maurice Larkin; 5 St Baldred's Cres, N Berwick, E Lothian, Scotland EH39 4PZ (☎ 0620 2777); Dept of History, University of Edinburgh, William Robertson Building, George Sq, Edinburgh EH8 9JY (☎ 031 667 1011, fax 44 31 6677938, telex 727442 UNIVED G)

LARKINS, Derrick Alfred; CBE (1987); s of Walter Arthur Larkins (d 1950), and Ada Aelia Larkins (d 1966); *b* 5 July 1926; *Educ* Royal Liberty Sch Romford; *m* 1960, Noël Sarah, da of William White, of Co Meath, Ireland; 1 s (Barry b 1966), 1 da (Trudi b 1968); *Career* WWII served RN Patrol Serv 1943-46; Apex Oilfields Trinidad 1951-54, Ford Motor-Co & Chrysler Motors 1954-61, dep chm (formerly chief accountant and jt md) Lansing Bagnall 1961-89; FCMA; *Recreations* gardening, watching sport, music, reading; *Clubs* MCC; *Style*— Derrick Larkins, Esq, CBE; Kneledore, Barn Close, Church Rd, Tadley, Hants RG26 6AU (☎ 0734 814730)

LARKINS, Hon Mrs (Miranda); da of Sir Richard Sharples (d 1972), of Government House, Bermuda, and Baroness Sharples, *née* Newall; *b* 26 Nov 1951; *m* 1981, Nicholas John Larkins, s of Dr Nicholas Larkins, of Sydney, Australia; 1 s (Harry b 1985), 1 da (Amelia b 1989); *Style*— The Hon Mrs Larkins; The Old Rectory, Stoke Wake, Blandford, Dorset

LARLHAM, Christopher; s of Maj Percival Edward Larlham (d 1968), of London, and Cecelia Louise, *née* Farrell; *b* 8 Nov 1949; *Educ* Dulwich; *m* 3 May 1973 (m dis 1984), Caroline Jane, da of Stanley Godfrey, of Ruislip; 3 s (Edward b 1976, Guy b 1978, George b 1980); *Career* admitted slr 1975; articled clerk Allibones 1969-75 (merged with Cameron Kemm Nordon 1973), ptnr Cameron Kemm Nordon 1976-80 (merged with Markbys 1980), ptnr Cameron Markby 1980-89 (merged with Hewitt Woollacott & Chown and with Brafman Morris 1989), ptnr Cameron Markby Hewitt 1989- (Managing ptnr 1990-); hon fixture sec Incogniti CC, capt Saffron Walden Bridge Club; Liveryman Worshipful Co Slrs; memb Law Soc; *Recreations* cricket, bridge, wine; *Clubs* MCC; *Style*— Christopher Larlham, Esq; Sceptre Court, 40 Tower Hill, London EC3N 4BB (☎ 071 702 2345, fax 071 702 2303, telex 925779 CAMLAW G)

LARMINIE, (Ferdinand) Geoffrey; OBE (1971); s of Ferdinand Samuel Larminie (d 1963), of Dublin, Ireland, and Mary, *née* Willis; *b* 23 June 1929; *Educ* St Andrew's Coll Dublin, Trinity Coll Dublin (BA, MA); *m* 3 April 1956, Helena Elizabeth Woodside, da of late Ralph Coburn Carson, of Inch House, Kilkenny, Ireland; 1 s (Christopher b 8 June 1969), 1 da (Susan b 23 Dec 1963); *Career* asst lectr in geology Univ of Glasgow 1954-56, lectr in geology Univ of Sydney 1956-60; British Petroleum plc: joined 1960, Exploration Dept in Sudan, Greece, Canada, Libya, Kuwait, California, NY, Alaska and Thailand, scientific advsr Info Dept London 1974-75, gen mangr Public Affrs and Info Dept 1975-76, gen mangr Environmental Control Centre London 1976-84, external affrs co-ordinator health safety and environmental servs 1984-87, ret 1987-89; dir Br Geological Survey 1987-90; pres: Alaska Geological Soc 1969, Soc for Underwater Technol 1987-; govr Bangkok Patana Sch Thailand 1972-74; memb: Royal Cmmn on Environmental Pollution 1979-83, Gen Advsy Cncl IBA 1980-85, Bd of Mgmnt Inst of Offshore Engrg Heriot-Watt Univ 1981-90, Natural Environment Res Cncl 1983-87, Polar Res Bd Nat Res Cncl Washington DC 1984-88, Cncl RGS 1984-90 (vice pres 1987-90); scientific tstee Bermuda Biological Station for Res; hon fell Trinity Coll Dublin 1989; Freeman City of Fairbanks Alaska; Gold Pan Award; FGS, FRSA, FRGS; *Recreations* archaeology, natural history, reading, shooting; *Style*— Geoffrey Larminie, Esq, OBE; Lane End, Lane's End, nr Tring, Herts HP23 6LF

LARMINIE, Maj John Charles; s of John Peel Alexander Larminie (d 1958), of Monk Sherborne, Hants, and Alison Yorke, *née* Lyle (d 1978); *b* 12 July 1926; *Educ* Winchester, RMCS; *m* 30 Dec 1950, Carola Anne, da of Brig Thomas Farquaharson Ker Howard (d 1963); 2 s (James b 1952, Oliver b 1953), 2 da (Annabelle b 1958, Penelope b 1961); *Career* Br Army 1944-72, Maj 1 Queen's Dragoon Gds; consulting mechanical engr 1972-; author of several technical and historical books; *Recreations* sailing; *Clubs* Army and Navy, Poole Yacht; *Style*— Maj John Larminie; Tithe Barn, Lytchett Matravers, Poole, Dorset BH16 6BJ (☎ 092 945 201)

LARMOUR, Sir Edward Noel; KCMG (1977, CMG 1966); s of Edward Larmour; *b* 25 Dec 1916; *Educ* Royal Belfast Academical Inst, Trinity Coll Dublin, Univ of Sydney; *m* Agnes Margaret, da of Thomas Bill; 1 s, 2 da; *Career* served Royal Inniskilling Fus and 15 Indian Corps in Burma 1940-46, joined CRO 1948, Br high cmmr in Jamaica and ambassador (non res) to Haiti 1970-73, Br high cmmr for New Hebrides (res in London) 1973, dep under sec of state FCO 1975-76; *Style*— Sir Edward Larmour, KCMG; 68 Wood Vale, London N10 (☎ 081 444 9744)

LARMOUTH, Prof John; TD (1974); s of Herbert Larmouth (d 1963), of 12 Northumberland Rd, Thornaby, Teesside, Cleveland, and Elsie, *née* Grimwood (d 1989); *b* 17 Sept 1941; *Educ* The GS Yarm, Emmanuel Coll Cambridge; *m* 14 April 1973, Carol Anne, da of Albert George Grover (d 1987), of 11 Ascham Rd, Cambridge; 1 s (James b 1984), 1 da (Sarah-Jayne b 1984); *Career* cmmnd TA 1964, transferred RARO Maj 1983; computing laboratory Univ of Cambridge 1967-76; Univ of Salford dir of: computing serv 1976-82, computing systems res and devpt 1982-86, Info Technol Inst 1986-; FBCS 1974, CEng 1988; *Books* Standards for Open Systems Interconnection (1987); *Style*— Prof John Larmouth; 1 Blueberry Rd, Bowdon, Altrincham, Cheshire WA14 3LS (☎ 061 928 1605); Information Technology Institute, University of Salford, Salford M5 4WT (☎ 061 745 5657, fax 061 745 8169, tlx 668680 SULIB)

LARNER, Gerald; s of Clifford Larner (d 1968), of Leeds, and Minnie, *née* Barraclough (d 1985), of Leeds; *b* 9 March 1936; *Educ* Leeds Modern Sch, New Coll Oxford (sr scholarship, BA); *m* 1, 1959 (m dis 1988), Celia Ruth Mary, da of late Harry Gordon Norman White; 2 da (Alice Elizabeth b 1960, Melissa Ruth b 1962); m2, 1989, Lynne Catherine Telfer, da of late Stuart George Cameron Walker; *Career* asst lectr German Dept Univ of Manchester 1960-62; The Guardian: freelance music critic 1960-62, features sub ed 1962-64, dep features ed 1964-65, regnl music and opera staff critic 1965-; frequent contrib to musical and other jls incl: Musical Times and Opera; specialist writer of prog and sleeve/liner notes, occasional lectr on music and opera; tv and radio broadcaster; memb: NW Arts Music Panel 1975-80, Hallé Orch Advsy Ctee 1990-; artistic dir Bowden Festival 1980-84; memb The Critics Circle 1966; *Books* translated librettist Wolf's Der Corregidor (1966), librettist McCabe's The Lion The Witch and the Wardrobe (1971), The Glasgow Style (1979), contrib The New Grove (1980); *Recreations* visual arts incl decorative arts and design, theatre literature, travel, country walking, writing about food and wine, watching and playing tennis; *Style*— Gerald Larner, Esq; 38 Heyes Lane, Alderley Edge, Cheshire SK9 7JY (☎ 0625 585378); The Guardian, 119 Farringdon Rd, London EC1R 3ER (☎ 071 278 2332)

LARRAIN, Prof Jorge; s of Alberto Larrain, of Santiago, Chile, and Rosa, *née* Ibañez; *b* 7 May 1942; *Educ* Catholic Univ of Chile (BTheol, Licenciate of Sociology), Univ of Sussex (MA DPhil); *m* 26 Dec 1969, Mercedes, da of Alberto Pulido, of Santiago, Chile; 1 da (Caroline); *Career* Univ of Birmingham: lectr in sociology 1977, sr lectr 1984, reader 1987, hd Dept of Cultural Studies 1988-, prof of social theory 1990; *Books* The Concept of Ideology (1979), Marxism Ideology (1983), A Reconstruction of Historical Materialism (1986), Theories of Development (1989); *Recreations* tennis; *Style*— Prof Jorge Larrain; University of Birmingham, Department of Cultural Studies, PO Box 363, Birmingham B15 2TT (☎ 021 414 6216)

LARRECHE, Prof Jean-Claude; s of Pierre Albert Alexis Larreche, of Pau, France, and Odette Jeanne Madeleine, *née* Hau-Sans; *b* 3 July 1947; *Educ* Lyon France (INSA), Univ of London (MSc), Fontainebleau France (MBA), Stanford Univ USA (PhD); *m* 10 Sept 1971, Denyse Michèle Joséphine, da of Michel Francis Henri Gros, of Besancon, France; 1 s (Philippe b 1978), 1 da (Sylvie b 1975); *Career* prof of mktg INSEAD 1974-, non-exec dir Reckitt and Colman plc London 1983-, dir Euro Strategic Mktg Inst INSEAD 1985-89, chm Strat X Veneux France 1985-, memb Bd The Mac Group Boston 1986-89; memb: America Mktg Assoc 1973, Inst of Mgmnt Sci 1975, FInstD; *Recreations* tennis; *Style*— Prof Jean-Claude Larreche; 85 Rue Murger, 77780, Bourron Marlotte, France (☎ 1 64456200, fax 1 64459876); INSEAD, 77305, Fontainebleau, France (☎ 1 60724000, fax 1 60724242, telex 690389 F)

LARSEN, Gerd Elly (Mrs Turner); da of Leonard Larsen (d 1948), of Oslo Norway, and Elly, *née* Jensen (d 1958); *b* 19 Feb 1920; *Educ* Norwegian Girls Sch, Margaret Graske Dance Sch London; *m* 1, George Konried; m2 19 March 1944, Harold Turner, s of Harold Turner, of Manchester; 1 da (Solveig Anne); *Career* Mil Serv ENSA (with Royal Ballet, Sadlers Wells); memb Royal Ballet 1944-; *Style*— Ms Gerd Larsen; The Royal Ballet, Royal Opera House, 8 Covent Garden, London WC2

LASCELLES, Angela Marion; da of James Anthony Greig (d 1967), of Mersham, Kent, and Juliet Felicia, *née* Colville; *b* 25 Aug 1947; *Educ* Ashford Sch Kent, Univ of London (BA); *m* 8 June 1974, Richard Anthony Finlayson Lascelles, s of Dr William Finlayson Lascelles; 2 s (Edward b 3 Oct 1975, Simon b 31 Dec 1978), 1 da (Rosalind b 24 July 1981); *Career* graduate trainee private clients Phillips & Drew Stockbrokers 1968-70, investmt analyst Spencer Thornton Stockbrokers 1970-72, investmt mangr Dawnay Day (Merchant Bank) 1972-74; asst investmt mangr: Associated British Foods Pension Fund 1975-79, Courtaulds Pension Fund 1979-86; exec dir OLIM Ltd 1986-; jt investmt dir: OLIM Convertible Trust plc 1989, Value & Income Trust plc 1986-; govr The London Inst; ASIA; *Recreations* tennis, music; *Style—* Mrs Angela Lascelles; OLIM Ltd, Pollen House, 10-12 Cork St, London W1X 1PD (☎ 071 439 4400, fax 071 734 1445)

LASCELLES, Maj-Gen (Henry) Anthony; CB (1967), CBE (1962), DSO (1944); s of Edward Charles Ponsonby Lascelles, OBE (d 1951), of Woolbeding, Midhurst, Sussex, and Leila Winifred Leonora, *née* Kennett-Barrington (d 1979); *b* 10 Jan 1912; *Educ* Winchester, Oriel Coll Oxford (MA); *m* 5 March 1941, Ethne Hyde Ussher, *née* Charles; *Career* WWII served Egypt, N Africa, Sicily, Italy; instr Nato Defence Coll 1955-56, Brig RAC 1956-57, NDC Canada 1958, BGS Mo War Office 1959-62, COS NI 1962-63, MGGS far east 1963-66; tstee Winston Churchill Meml Tst 1980- (dir gen 1966-80), pres Br Water Ski Fedn 1979-; *Recreations* squash, tennis, music; *Clubs* Naval and Military; *Style—* Maj-Gen Anthony Lascelles, CB, CBE, DSO; Manor Farm Cottage, Hedgerley Green, Bucks SL2 3XG (☎ 0753 883582)

LASCELLES, Viscount; David Henry George Lascelles; s of 7 Earl of Harewood; *b* 21 Oct 1950; *Educ* The Hall Sch, Westminster; *m* 12 Feb 1979, Margaret Rosalind, da of Edgar Frank Messenger; 3 s (Hon Benjamin b 9 Sept 1978, Hon Alexander, Hon Edward b 19 Nov 1982), 1 da (Hon Emily b 23 Nov 1975); *Heir* 2 s (but 1 b in wedlock), Hon Alexander Edgar Lascelles b 13 May 1980; *Style—* Viscount Lascelles; 2 Orme Sq, London W2

LASCELLES, Hon Gerald David; yr s of 6 Earl of Harewood, KG, GCVO, DSO, TD (d 1947), and HRH The Princess Royal (d 1965, da of George V); *b* 21 Aug 1924; *Educ* Eton; *m* 1, 1952 (m dis 1978), Angela, da of Charles Stanley Dowding (d 1972); 1 s (Henry Ulick b 1953, m 1979 Alexandra Clare Ruth, da of Peter Morton); m 2, 1978, Elizabeth Evelyn, da of Brig Sydney Collingwood, CMG, CBE, MC; 1 s (Martin David b 1962); *Career* pres Br Racing Drivers Club 1964-, dir Silverstone Circuits Ltd and subsidiaries, pres Inst of the Motor Indust 1969-73 and 1975-77; *Recreations* shooting, gardening; *Clubs* RAC; *Style—* The Hon Gerald Lascelles; Cliffordine House, Rendcomb, Cirencester GL7 7ER (☎ 028 583 321)

LASCELLES, Hon James Edward; s of 7th Earl of Harewood, *qv*; *b* 5 Oct 1953; *Educ* Westminster; *m* 1, 4 April 1973 (m dis 1985), Fredericka Ann, da of Prof Alfred Duhrsson, of Majorca; 1 s, 1 da; m 2, 4 May 1985, Lori (Shadow), da of J R Lee of Arizona, USA; 1 s, 1 da; *Career* leader of rock groups Breakfast Band, Cuckoo; session work and composer; dir Tribal Music Int (tape co, releasing American Indian music); part-time disc jockey at Albuquerque Univ Station; *Style—* The Hon James Lascelles; 1 Orme Lane, London W2 (☎ 071 727 1163)

LASCELLES, Hon Mark Hubert; s of 7 Earl of Harewood, *qv*; *b* 5 July 1964; *Style—* The Hon Mark Lascelles

LASCELLES-HADWEN, Francis Edward; s of Edward Hubert Lascelles Hadwen (d 1947), and Margaret, *née* Fernie Turnball; *b* 13 Dec 1926; *Educ* The Hall, St Paul's, Magdalen Coll Oxford (MA), Univ of Aston (DPM); *m* 1 (m dis), Lady Julia Blunt-Mackenzie, da of 4 Earl of Cromartie MC, JP, DL; 1 s, 1 da; m 2 (m dis), Clare, da of HG Liversidge, of Nairobi; 2 s; *Career* Nat Serv RN 1945-47, sec to Capt HMS Woodbridge Haven, asst to Cdre HMS Pembroke; Army SSC 1963-66, instr Sandhurst candidates ASE Beaconsfield; educn and trg offr: Tournai and Oudenarde Barracks, Aldershot, attached Welch Regt, Sch of Infantry Warminster; various commercial positions City of London; visiting lectr in econs Brighton Tech Coll and Poly 1967-70; exec dir Partington's advertising and PR; broker Lloyd's of London, Stock Exchange with Coates Son & Co; dir Finchcastle Ltd fin conslts; memb: LCC for Clapham Div of Wandsworth 1955-58, Housing, Town Planning and Rivers Ctees, TA Forces Assoc Co of London; govr Larkhall and Heathbrook Schs London, hon sec personal staff Rt Hon Sir W Churchill prior to second admin joined Lab Pty after Suez, former chm E Sussex Fabian Soc; memb: Ladywood Police Consultative Ctee 1987-89, Harborne and Quinton Police Liaison Ctee 1987, Birmingham City Centre Crime Prevention Panel 1987- (chm 1989-90), Birmingham and Sutton Coldfield Crime Prevention Panel 1987-89 (Memb 1989-), Quinborne Community Assoc Cncl 1987-89; convenor local Neighbourhood Watch Scheme; sch govr: Duddeston Manor (vice chm 1989-90), St Georges C of E Jl (vice chm 1989-); chm Fin Ctee (support) SSAFA and FHS W Mids Central 1989-90, vice chm Birmingham Lib Democratic Pty 1989-90, memb Regnl Cncl SLD; memb SLD: Coordinating Ctee Birmingham Area Pty, Candidates Selection Panel, Election Sub Ctee; chm Edgbaston Lib Democratic Pty 1990 (memb Exec Ctee Selly Oak and Northfields SLD 1990); del: Ladworth project Inter-Agency Conference 1988, delegate Birmingham Heartlands Inter-Agency Conference 1988-89; police lay visitor 1988-, memb: Harborne and Quinton Police Consultative Ctee 1989-, memb Birmingham Vol Serv Cncl 1989-, invited to give evidence to Ctee on Press Privacy and Related Matters 1989, memb sub ctee to report on police leadership and composition to the PM and Home Sec 1990); del: for Birmingham Crime Concern Tst Conf Westminster 1989, Lay Visitors Conf Univ of London 1990; memb Rann Project Steering Ctee 1989-90, currently engaged in academic res into means of mitigating nuclear arms race and termination of cold war politics; FRSA; *Recreations* the South of France, Monte Carlo, 18 Century Dukes, owning Pekingese dogs, the second chamber and the constitution; *Clubs* Oxford Union, The Barons (Birmingham); *Style—* Francis Lascelles-Hadwen, Esq; 22 Rodbourne Rd, Harborne, Birmingham B17 0PN

LASDUN, Sir Denys Louis; CBE (1965); s of Norman Lasdun; *b* 8 Sept 1914; *Educ* Rugby, Architectural Assoc; *m* 1954, Susan Bendit; 2 s, 1 da; *Career* served WWII RE; architect; in practice with Peter Softley 1960-; works incl: Royal Coll of Physicians London, Flats 26 St James's Place, Univ of London (SOAS, Inst of Educn, Law Inst, project for Courtauld Inst), Nat Theatre and IBM Central Marketing Centre, South Bank London, office bldgs Fenchurch St EC4 and Milton Gate EC2, EEC HQ for Euro Investmt Bank, Luxembourg, Univ of East Anglia, Christ's Coll extensions Cambridge, Cannock Community Hosp, design for new Hurva Synagogue Old City Jerusalem, Genoa Opera House competition; tstee British Museum 1975-85; memb: Academie d'Architecture 1984, Slade Ctee Int Acad of Architecture Bulgaria 1986; Hon Fell American Inst of Architects 1966; Hon DLitt: E Anglia 1974, Sheffield 1978; Accademia Nazionale di San Luca 1984; RIBA Gold medal 1977; FRIBA; kt 1976; *Books* Architects' Approach to Architecture (1965), A Language and a Theme (1976), Architecture in the Age of Scepticism (1984); *Style—* Sir Denys Lasdun, CBE; 146 Grosvenor Rd, London SW1V 3JY (☎ 071 630 8211, fax 071 821 6191)

LASHMORE, Cdr Martin Ernest (Tony); DSO (1943), OBE (1961), DSC (1942); s of Rear Adm Harry Lashmore, CB, DSO (d 1945), and Beatrice, *née* Evans (d 1960); *b* 9 Nov 1911; *Educ* RNC Dartmouth and Greenwich, HMS Bacchante; *m* 11 Feb 1939, Iona Stuart (Bunty), da of Ian Mackay (d 1933); 1 s (Richard Anthony b 1956), 3 da (Diana b 1940, Susan b 1946, Elisabeth b 1950); *Career* RN career; HMS Queen Elizabeth 1929, HMS Emerald 1930, HMS Enterprise 1930-31, RNC Greenwich 1931, HMS Sussex 1932-33, HMS Orion 1933-35, HMS Dragon 1936-37, HMS Douglas 1937-38, observer's course 1938-39, HMS Ark Royal 1939-40, various flying appts 1940-42, SO Naval Air Sqdn Halfar Malta 1942, admiralty Naval Air Organisation Div, Naval Staff course 1944, planned invasion Rangoon and Malaya 1945, dep asst cmdt Sch of Land-Air Warfare Old Sarum 1946-47, staff officer Intelligence Hong Kong 1949-52, and HMS Whitesand Bay 1952-53, SO's war course Greenwich 1953, admiralty Naval Intelligence Div 1954-56, asst dir Naval Intelligence 1956-63, ret from Navy 1963, dip serv 1963-67, administered Sch of Architecture Portsmouth 1969-76; *Style—* Cdr Tony Lashmore, DSO, OBE, DSC, RN; 7 South Normandy, Warblington Street, Old Portsmouth, Hampshire PO1 2ES (☎ 0705 828981)

LASK, Dr Bryan; s of Dr Aaron Lask, and Rita, *née* Flax (d 1989); *b* 18 Feb 1941; *m* 15 Sept 1973, Judith, da of Norman Stubbs (d 1981); 2 s (Gideon, Adam); *Career* conslt psychiatrist Hosp for Sick Children Gt Ormond St London, sr lectr Inst of Child Health London, former ed Jl of Family Therapy; memb BMA; FRCPsych; *Books* Child Psychiatry & Social Work (1981), Childrens Problems (1985), Childhood Illness - The Psychosomatic Approach (1989); *Recreations* sports, theatre, music; *Style—* Dr Bryan Lask; Hospital for Sick Children, Gt Ormond St, London WC1 (☎ 071 405 9200, 071 829 8657)

LASOK, Prof Dominik; QC (1982); s of Alojzy Lasok of Turza (Poland) (d 1956); *b* 4 Jan 1921; *Educ* elementary educn in Poland and Switzerland, Univ of Fribourg (Licence en Droit), Univ of Durham (LLM), Univ of London (PhD, LLD), Polish Univ Abroad (Dr Juris); *m* 7 Aug 1952, Sheila May, da of James Corrigan; 2 s (Paul b 1953, Marc b 1960), 3 da (Pia b 1962, Teresa b 1962, Carmen b 1965); *Career* WWII in Polish Army (cmmnd 1944), served Poland, France and Italy 1939-46 (holds Polish, French and British decorations); employed in indust 1948-51; called to the Bar 1954; legal advsr 1954-58, prof of Euro law Univ of Exeter 1968-86, emeritus prof; visiting prof: Williamsburg (1966-67 and 1977), McGill Univ 1976-77, Rennes Univ 1980-81 and 1986, College d'Europe Bruges 1984-86, Aix-Marseille Univ 1986 and 89, Marmara Univ Istanbul 1987-91; Hon LLD Aix-Marseille 1987; Officier dans L'Ordre des Palmes Academiques France 1983; *Books* Polish Family Law (1968), Law and Institutions of the European Communities (1972, 5 edn 1991), Polish Civil Law (1975), The Law of the Economy of the European Communities (1980), The Customs Law of the European Community (1983, 2 edn 1991), Professions and Services in the EEC (1986), Conflict of Laws in the European Community (1987); *Style—* Prof Dominik Lasok, QC; Reed, Barley Lane, Exeter (☎ 0392 72582); Ground Floor, Lamb Building, Temple, London 4Y 7AS

LASOK, Dr (Karol) Paul Edward; s of Dominik Lasok, QC, of Reed Cottage, Barley Lane, St Thomas, Exeter, Devon, and Sheila May, *née* Corrigan; *b* 16 July 1953; *Educ* Jesus Coll Cambridge (MA), Univ of Exeter (LLM, PhD); *Career* called to the Bar Middle Temple 1977, legal sec Ct of Justice of Euro Communities 1980-84 (locum tenens March-May 1985); private practice: Brussels 1985-87, London 1987-; memb Cons Pty; memb Editorial Bd: European Competition Law Review, Law and Justice; *Books* The European Court of Justice Practice and Procedure (1984); contrib to: Halsbury's Laws of England 4 edn vols 51 and 52 (1986), Stair Memorial Encyclopaedia of the Laws of Scotland; *Recreations* walking, music; *Style—* Dr Paul Lasok; 75 Brokesley St, Bow, London E3 4QJ (☎ 081 980 2948); 4 Raymond Buildings, Grays Inn, London WC1R 5BP (☎ 071 405 7211, fax 071 405 2084)

LASS, Jonathan Daniel; s of Jacob Lass, of 57 Southway, London NW11, and Regina, *née* Weinfeld; *b* 22 Feb 1946; *Educ* Univ Coll Sch, Downing Coll Cambridge (MA); *m* 24 March 1985, Andria Mina, da of Mervyn Thal; 2 s (Saul Alexander Yentis, Gregory Michael); *Career* Herbert Oppenheimer Nathan & Vandyk 1970-75; admitted slr 1972, slr Crawley & De Reya 1975-77, vice pres and legal advsr Citibank NA 1977-86, ptnr Lovell White Durrant (formerly Lovell White & King) 1986-89, ptnr Lass Salt Garvin Slrs 1990-; memb: Law Soc, Int Bar Assoc; *Recreations* history, opera, theatre, art, antiques, swimming, tennis; *Clubs* RAC, Annabels; *Style—* Jonathan Lass, Esq; 4 North Square, London NW11 (☎ 081 458 0333); 16 Bell Yard, London WC2A 2JR (☎ 071 831 4344)

LASSEN-DIESEN, David Peter; s of Sigurd Lassen-Diesen (d 1986), and Mary Margaret, *née* Wright; *b* 30 Jan 1938; *m* 7 Sept 1968, Valerie Jane, da of Joseph John Ive (d 1964); 2 s (David b 1974, Piers b 1977), 1 da (Karen b 1971); *Career* fndr Finance Centre, first money shop business in UK 1967, fndr ptnr Diesen Property Co 1967; dir: Frost Holdings 1972-74, Konrad Roberts Ltd 1978, Konrad Roberts plc 1985-; *Recreations* golf; *Style—* David P Lassen-Diesen, Esq; Roundwood Hall, Norwood Hill, Horley, Surrey RH6 0HS (☎ 0293 862798, fax 0293 862846, car 0836 289209)

LASSETER, Ronald Sydney Gaston; s of Ronald Edwin Lasseter, of 3 Highfield Place, Coneyhill Rd, Gloucester, and Marcelle, *née* Gondry; *b* 26 May 1947; *Educ* Prince Rupert Sch Wilhelmshaven W Germany, Univ of Exeter (BSc); *m* 1971, Diane, da of Arthur Ronald Ellis, of 5 Whitestones, Cranford Ave, Exmouth, Devon; 1 s (Michael b 1975), 1 da (Emma b 1978); *Career* currently md of Pilkington's Tiles Hldgs Ltd and chm of its subsidiaries; FCA; *Recreations* tennis, squash; *Style—* R S G Lasseter, Esq; PO Box 4, Clifton Junction, Manchester M27 2LP (☎ 061 794 2024, telex 667663, fax 061 794 5455)

LAST, Maj-Gen Christopher Neville; CB (1990), OBE (1976); s of Jack Neville Last, and Lorna Kathleen Mary, *née* Goodman; *b* 2 Sept 1935; *Educ* Culford Sch, Brighton Tech Coll; *m* 11 Feb 1961, Pauline Mary, da of Henry Percy Lawton (d 1981); 2 da (Caroline Victoria Neville (Mrs Ludwig) b 3 Aug 1964, Alexandra Louise Neville b 10 June 1969); *Career* Regular Army, Royal Signals Troop Cdr 1956-67: served Germany, UK 16 Para Bde, 44 Para Bde, Far East Borneo Campaign 1967, Maj and Cdr 216 Para Signal Sqdn in UK, GS01 Signals HQ BAOR 1973, Cdr Royal Signals NI 1974-76, GS01 Directorate of Combat Devpt MOD 1976, GS01 Directorate of Mil Ops MOD 1977, Col asst dir Long Range Surveillance and Cmd and Control Projects (Army) 1977, Cdr 8 Signal Regt 1980, Brig and Cdr 1 Signal Bde HQ 1 (Br) Corps Germany 1981-83; dir of Mil Cmd and Control Projects (Army) UK 1984, dir of Procurement Policy (special studies) for Chief of Def Procurement 1985, Maj-Gen and Vice Master Gen of the Ordnance 1986, mil dep to Head of Def Export Servs 1988, Col Cmdt RCS 1990; Chief Exec Clwyd FHSA 1990; memb: CLA, Br Field Sports Soc, Nat Tst; hockey rep Corps Army and Combined Servs; Freeman: Worshipful Co of Info Technologists 1988, City of London 1988; *Recreations* shooting, sailing, skiing, ballet; *Clubs* Special Forces; *Style—* Maj Gen Christopher Last, CB, OBE; c/o Nat West Bank plc, 34 North Rd, Lancing, Sussex BN15 9AB

LAST, Prof Joan Mary; OBE (1988); da of Dr Cecil Edward Last (d 1971), of Bletsoe, Littlehampton, Sussex, and Grace Bevington, *née* Jarvis (d 1913); *b* 12 Jan 1908; *Educ* Godolphin Sch Salisbury, piano student Mathilde Verne; *Career* brief career as pianist ended with injury to hand; prof of piano RAM 1959-83; teaching seminars and master classes in USA, Canada, Aust, NZ, Africa, Bermuda, Hong Kong, Scandinavia: compiled over 100 albums of educnl music and 3 textbooks for Piano Teachers; voluntary work as music presenter Voice of Progress cassette magazine for the blind; memb: Inc Soc of Musicians 1940, EPTA, Composers Guild, Performing Rights Soc; Hon ARAM 1965, Hon RAM 1975; *Recreations* photography; *Clubs* RAM, RAM Guild;

Style— Prof Joan Last, OBE; Surya, 11 St Mary's Close, Littlehampton, Sussex BN17 5PZ (☎ 0903 713522)

LAST, John William; CBE (1989); s of late Jack Last (d 1986), and Freda Edith, *née* Evans (d 1976); *b* 22 Jan 1940; *Educ* Sutton GS Surrey, Trinity Coll Oxford (MA); *m* 1967, Susan Josephine, da of John Holloway Farmer, of Knaresborough; 3 s (Andrew John b 2 Jan 1969, Philip James b 12 June 1971, Peter Charles b 7 June 1973); *Career* head of corp affrs Littlewoods Orgn (joined 1969), fndr Merseyside Maritime Museum; chm: Walker Art Gallery Liverpool 1977-81, Royal Liverpool Philharmonic Orch 1977-; memb: Arts Cncl 1980-84, Press Cncl 1980-86, Museums Cmmn 1983-; tstee: Theatre Museum 1983-86, V&A 1983-6 (memb Advsy Cncl); vice pres Museums Assoc 1983-84; visiting prof in arts admin City Univ 1985-, hon fell Liverpool Poly 1989, Christie lectr 1990, vice chm Northern Ballet Theatre, chm Museums Trg Inst 1990; Freeman City of London 1985, Liveryman Worshipful Co of Barber Surgns 1986; *Recreations* Victoriana, music, swimming; *Clubs* RAC, Racquet (Liverpool); *Style*— John Last, Esq, CBE; 25 Abbey Rd, West Kirby, Wirral, Merseyside L48 7EN; 100 Old Hall St, Liverpool L70 1AN (☎ 051 235 2222, fax 051 235 4900)

LAST, Richard Patrick; s of Cyril Clarence Last (d 1960), of Virgina Water, Surrey, and Winifred Kathleen, *née* Clarke (d 1977); *b* 19 July 1927; *Educ* St George's Coll Weybridge; *m* 1964, Pauline Agnes, da of Joseph Robert Newton (d 1986); 5 da (Penelope Jane b 27 Feb 1965, Elizabeth Clare b 23 July 1966, Amanda Mary b 11 Nov 1968, Charlotte Alexandra b 9 Dec 1969, Victoria Christine b 30 June 1972); *Career* reporter Gloucestershire Echo Cheltenham 1949-54, baritone Carl Rosa Opera Co 1954-55, music and theatre critic Nottingham Evening Post 1956-58, music critic and feature writer Daily Herald London 1959-64, feature writer and dep TV critic The Sun 1964-69; Daily Telegraph: dep broadcasting corr and TV critic 1970-86, chief TV critic 1986-; winner Rose Bowl (supreme vocal trophy) Cheltenham Competitive Festival 1956; chm: Press Jury Montreux Golden Rose 1975, Broadcasting Press Guild 1984-85; memb: BAFTA 1973, RTS 1979; *Books* Annual Register of Events (contrib 1976-83); *Recreations* music, reading, travel; *Clubs* BAFTA Piccadilly; *Style*— Richard Last, Esq; Tiverton, The Ridge, Woking, Surrey; Daily Telegraph, 181 Marsh Wall, London E14 9SR (☎ 0483 764 895)

LASZLO; *see*: de Laszlo

LATCHMORE, Andrew Windsor; s of Arthur John Craig Latchmore, MBE, of Windrush Coll Farm Lane, Linton, Nr Wetherby, W Yorks, and Joyce Mary, JP, *née* Raper; *b* 9 Feb 1950; *Educ* Oundle, Univ of Leeds (LLB); *m* 1, 20 June 1976 (m dis 1989), Jillian Amanda, da of Victor Hugo Watson, of Moatfield, E Keswick, Nr Leeds; 1 s (Jolyon Guy 1981), 1 da (Lucy Emma 1979); m 2, Clarissa Mary, da of Maj Peter J Orde; *Career* admitted slr 1975; ptnr Hepworth and Chadwick 1978; sec to govrs Gateways Sch 1977, hon sec Leeds Law Soc 1982; memb The Law Soc; *Recreations* music, opera, golf, tennis, skiing, walking, travel; *Clubs* Alwoodley Golf, The Terrace Tennis (Boston Spa), Collingham Squash; *Style*— Andrew Latchmore, Esq; Hepworth and Chadwick, Cloth Hall Court, Infirmary Street, Leeds LS1 2JB (☎ 0532 430391, fax 0532 456188, telex 557917)

LATEY, Rt Hon Sir John Brinsmead; MBE (1943), PC (1986); s of William Latey, CBE, QC (d 1976), and Annie (d 1983); *b* 7 March 1914; *Educ* Westminster Sch, Ch Ch Oxford; *m* 1938, Betty Margaret, da of Dr Edwyn Henry Beresford of London; 1 s, 1 da; *Career* served WWII MEF and WO (Lt-Col); called to the Bar Middle Temple 1936, QC 1957; bencher Middle Temple 1964-; a judge of High Court of Justice (Probate, Divorce and Admty Div, now Family Div) 1965-89; chm Lord Chllr's Ctee on Age of Majority 1965-67, dep chm Oxfordshire quarter sessions 1966; kt 1965; *Recreations* golf, fishing, chess, bridge; *Clubs* United Oxford and Cambridge Univs; *Style*— The Rt Hon Sir John Latey, MBE; 16 Daylesford Ave, Roehampton, London SW15 5QR (☎ 081 876 6436)

LATHAM, Cecil Thomas; OBE (1976); s of Cecil Frederick James Latham (d 1942), and Elsie Winifred, *née* Lewis (d 1959); *b* 11 March 1924; *Educ* Rochester Cathedral Choir Sch, King's Sch Rochester; *m* 8 Aug 1945, Ivy Frances, da of Thomas William Fowle (d 1935); 1 s (Martin John b 1954), 1 da (Helen Susan b 1952); *Career* war serv 1942-45; asst clerk Magistrate's Courts: Chatham 1939-42, Maidstone 1945, Leicester 1948-54, Bromley 1954-63; dep clerk to the Justices: Liverpool 1963-65, Manchester 1965-76 (clerk); stipendiary magistrate Greater Manchester (Salford) 1976-; memb: Royal Cmmn on Criminal Procedure 1978-81, Criminal Law Revision Ctee 1981-; Hon MA Univ of Manchester 1984; *Books* Stone's Justices' Manual (editions 101-109); fndr ed: Family Law Reports 1980-86, Family Court Reporter 1987-; specialist ed J P Reports 1986-; *Style*— Cecil Latham, Esq, OBE; 19 Southdown Crescent, Cheadle Hulme, Cheshire SK8 6EQ (☎ 061 485 1185); Magistrates' Court, Bexley Square, Salford M3 6DJ

LATHAM, Christopher George Arnot; s of Edward Bryan Latham, CBE (d 1980), and Anne Arnot, *née* Duncan (d 1989); *Educ* Stowe, Clare Coll Cambridge (MA); *m* 1 June 1963, Jacqueline Yvette Renée, da of Captaine Gaston Cabourdin (d 1970); 3 s (Patrick b 1964, Charles b 1965, Paul b 1969); *Career* articled CA Fitzpatrick Graham 1951-54; chm: Timber Research and Development Association 1972-74, Commonwealth Forestry Association 1972-74; forestry cmmr 1973-78, exec chm James Latham plc 1987- (joined 1955, dir 1959-87), dir Cilntec; chm Psychiatric Rehabilitation Assoc, tstee Timber Trade Benevolent Soc; Freeman Worshipful Co of Builders Merchants 1985; FCA, FIWSc; *Recreations* forestry, beagling; *Style*— Christopher Latham, Esq; 5 Canonbury Square, London N1 2AN; James Latham PLC, Lesside Wharf, Clapton, London E5 9NG (☎ 081 806 3333, fax 081 806 7249, telex 265670)

LATHAM, David Nicholas Ramsay; QC (1985); s of Robert Clifford Latham, CBE, of Cambridge, and Eileen Frances, *née* Ramsay (d 1969); *b* 18 Sept 1942; *Educ* Bryanston, Queens' Coll Cambridge (MA); *m* 6 May 1967, Margaret Elizabeth, *née* Forrest; 3 da (Clare Frances b 2 Aug 1969, Angela Josephine b 23 Jan 1972, (Rosemary) Harriet b 10 Dec 1974); *Career* called to the Bar Middle Temple 1964; jr counsel to the Crown Common Law 1979-85, jr counsel to Dept of Trade in export credit guarantee matters 1982-85; memb: Gen Cncl of the Bar 1986-, Judicial Studies Bd 1988-, Cncl Legal Education 1988-; bencher Middle Temple 1989; *Recreations* reading, music, food, drink; *Clubs* Leander; *Style*— David Latham, Esq, QC; The Firs, Church Rd, Sunningdale, Ascot, Berks (☎ 0990 22686); 1 Crown Office Row, London EC4 (☎ 071 353 1801, fax 071 583 1700)

LATHAM, David Russell; s of Russell Latham CBE, MC, JP (d 1964), and Elsa Mary, *née* Andrews (d 1980); *b* 9 Nov 1937; *Educ* Rugby; *m* 1963, Susan Elisabeth, da of Charles Alfred Bryant (d 1984); 2 s (Jonathan b 1966, Nicholas b 1968), 1 da (Katherine b 1970); *Career* md James Latham plc; *Recreations* tennis, golf, skiing; *Style*— D R Latham; James Latham plc, Leeside Wharf, Clapton E5 9NG (☎ 081 806 3333)

LATHAM, Derek James; s of James Horace Latham, DFC, of Newark-on-Trent, and Mary Pauline, *née* Turner (d 1974); *b* 12 July 1946; *Educ* King Edward VI GS Retford, Leicester Sch of Architecture, Trent Poly Nottingham (Dip Arch, Dip TP, Dip LD, ALI); *m* 14 Sept 1968, Pauline Elizabeth, da of Philip George Tuxworth, of Lincs; 2 s (Benjamin James b 1974, Oliver James b 1981), 1 da (Sarah Jane b 1972); *Career* Clifford Wearden & Assocs (architects and planners) London 1968-70, housing architect and planner Derby CC 1970-73, design and conservation offr Derbyshire CC 1974-78, tech advsr Derbyshire Historic Bldgs Tst 1978, princ Derek Latham and Assocs 1980-, external examiner Leicester Sch of Architectural Conservation Studies 1983-86, md Michael Saint Developments Ltd 1984, architectural advsr Peak Park Tst 1986, concept co-ordinator Sheffield Devpt Corp 1987-, external examiner Leicester Sch of Architecture 1988-; memb Exec Ctee Cncl for Care of Churches 1985-, govr Nottingham Sch of Interior Design 1986-; *Recreations* squash; *Clubs* Duffield Squash and Lawn Tennis; *Style*— Derek J Latham, Esq; Hieron's Wood, Vicarage Lane, Little Eaton, Derby DE3 5EA (☎ 0332 832371); Derek Latham and Company, St Michaels, Derby DE1 3SU (☎ 0332 365777)

LATHAM, 2 Baron (UK 1942); Dominic Charles Latham; er (twin) s of Hon Francis Charles Allman Latham (d 1959), and his 3 w Gabrielle Monica, *née* O'Riordan (d 1987), and gs of 1 Baron Latham (d 1970); *b* 20 Sept 1954; *Educ* NSW Univ (BEng 1977, MEngSc 1981); *Heir* bro, Anthony Latham; *Career* civil engr with Electricity Cmmn of New South Wales 1979-88; structural engr with Rankine & Hill consulting engrs 1988-; *Recreations* tennis, squash, snooker, electronics, sailboarding; *Style*— The Rt Hon the Lord Latham; PO Box 355, Kensington, NSW 2033, Australia

LATHAM, Hon Mrs Francis; Gabrielle; da of Dr S M O'Riordan; *m* 1951, as his 3 w, the Hon Francis Charles Allman Latham (d 1959, s of 1 Baron Latham); *Style*— The Hon Mrs Francis Latham; 6/226 Rainbow St, S Coogee 2034, Sydney, NSW, Australia

LATHAM, Lady Gwendoline Lucy Constance Rushworth; da of Adm of the Fleet 1 Earl Jellicoe, GCB, OM, GCVO (d 1935); *b* 14 April 1903; *m* 1935, Lt-Col Edward Latham, MC (d 1957); 2 s, 1 da; *Style*— The Lady Gwendoline Latham; Oak Knoll, Sunningdale, Berks (☎ 0990 22842)

LATHAM, James Miles; s of Maj James Francis Latham, TD, JP (d 1966); *b* 24 Jan 1940; *Educ* Haileybury; *m* 1968, Margaret Eleanor, *née* Gray; 2 s; *Career* wood merchant, dir James Latham plc; memb Cncl: Timber Trade Fedn of UK 1974-, Timber Res and Devpt Assoc 1975-, Assoc of Br Plywood and Veneer Mfrs; *Recreations* golf, gardening, field sports; *Clubs* Royal Worlington, Newmarket Golf; *Style*— James Latham, Esq; Gills Farm, Epping Upland, Essex CM16 6PL; James Latham plc, Leeside Wharf, Clapton, London E5 9NG (☎ 081 806 3333, fax 081 806 7249, telex 265670)

LATHAM, John Aubrey Clarendon; s of Geoffrey Chitty Latham (d 1980), of Farnham, Surrey, and Kathleen Anne Clavedon, *née* Godfrey (d 1970); *b* 23 Feb 1929; *Educ* Winchester, various art colls; *m* 1951, Barbara Mary Leslie, da of Leo Steveni; 2 s (Peter Noa b 1952, John-Paul b 1954), 1 da (Xenia b 1963); *Career* CO RN 1944; artist; fndr Inst for Studies of Mental Images 1954, co-fndr Artist Placement Gp 1965, teacher St Martin's Sch of Art 1965-67; works in pub collections: Museum of Modern Art NY (Shem, Art and Culture), Tate Gallery, Newark Museum New Jersey, Modern Art Museum Caracas, Belfast National Gallery of Modern Art, Washington Gallery of Modern Art, Musee de Calais France, Washington Art Centre Minneapolis USA; one man exhibitions incl: Kingly Gallery London 1948, Bear Lane Gallery Oxford 1963, Kasmin Gallery London 1963, Alan Gallery NY 1964, Lisson Gallery London 1970 1987 and 1989, Gallery House London 1972-73, Stedelijk Van Abbemuseum Eindhoven 1983, Josh Baer Gallery NY 1987 and 1989, Art after Physics (Staatsgalerie Stuttgart) 1991; several films, videos, tapes; many articles, happenings, performances and demonstrations; pubns incl: Report and Offer For Sale (1971), Concept of Order from a Time Based Viewpoint (1978), Event-Structure, Approach to a Basic Contradiction (1981), Sub Quantum (with Andrew Dipper, 1983), Report of a Surveyor (1984), Dimension: framework of "event" discovered via art (with Munro, 1989); *Style*— John Latham; 210 Bellenden Rd, London SE15 4BW (☎ 071 639 3597)

LATHAM, (John) Martin; s of William John Lawrence Latham, of Leatherhead, Surrey, and Kathleen Louise, *née* Ward; *b* 28 July 1942; *Educ* Bradfield Coll Berks, Fitzwilliam Coll Cambridge (MA); *Career* articled clerk and asst mangr Peat Marwick Mitchell & Co London 1965-74; James Capel & Co: corp fin exec 1974-76, co sec 1976-87, head of secretariat 1987-; memb The Stock Exchange 1978, FCA 1979; *Recreations* tennis, golf, yachting; *Clubs* MCC, Roehampton; *Style*— Martin Latham, Esq; 6 Cranleigh, 139 Ladbroke Rd, Holland Park, London W11 3PX (☎ 071 727 6226); James Capel & Co, James Capel House, 6 Bevis Marks, London EC3A 7JQ (☎ 071 621 0011, fax 071 621 0844, telex 888866)

LATHAM, Michael Anthony; MP (C) Rutland and Melton 1983-; *b* 20 Nov 1942; *Educ* Marlborough, King's Coll Cambridge, Dept of Educn Univ of Oxford; *m* 1969, Caroline Susan, da of Maj T A Terry, RE (d 1971); 2 s; *Career* CRD 1965-67, co-opted memb GLC Housing Ctee 1967-73, memb Westminster City Cncl 1968-71, dir and chief exec House Builders Fedn 1971-73, former memb Mgmnt Bd Shelter; MP (C) Melton 1974-83, vice chm Cons Parly Environment Ctee 1979-83, hon sec Cons Parly Countryside Sub-Ctee 1979-83; memb: Select Ctee Energy 1979-82, Public Accounts Ctee 1983-, Advsy Cncl on Public Records 1985-; vice pres Bldg Socs Assoc; *Recreations* cricket, fencing, gardening, listening to classical music; *Clubs* Carlton; *Style*— Michael Latham, Esq, MP; House of Commons, London SW1

LATHAM, (Edward) Michael Locks; s of Edward Bryan Latham, CBE (d 1980); *b* 7 Jan 1930; *Educ* Stowe, Clare Coll Cambridge; *m* 1955, Joan Doris, da of Charles Ellis Merriam Coubrough (d 1967); 1 s, 2 da; *Career* chm: Trebartha Estates Ltd, G A Day Timber Centres Ltd, Malcolm Turner Bldgs Supplies Ltd, The Lanlivery Tst 1989-; dir James Latham plc 1987- (chm 1973-87); pres: Sandringham Assoc of Royal Warrant Holders 1982-83, Fedn of Tropical Timber Trade in EEC 1980-82, Timber Trade Fedn 1984-85; memb Exec Ctee Nat Cncl of Bldg Material Prodrs 1985; pres Int Tech Assoc of Tropical Timber, govr St Dunstan's Abbey Sch 1988-; *Recreations* tennis, the countryside, classic cars, books; *Clubs* Launceston Golf; *Style*— E Michael Latham, Esq; Trebartha Lodge, Launceston PL15 7PD; James Latham plc, Yate, Bristol BS17 5JX (☎ 0454 315 421, telex 449418)

LATHAM, Air Vice-Marshal Peter Anthony; CB (1980), AFC (1960); s of Oscar Frederick Latham (d 1945), of Birmingham, and Rhoda, *née* Archer; *b* 18 June 1925; *Educ* St Phillip's GS Birmingham, St Catharine's Coll Cambridge; *m* 19 Sept 1953, Barbara Mary, da of Reginald des Landes Caswell (d 1984), of Birmingham; 2 s (Mark b 1958, Phillip b 1960), 6 da (Jane (Mrs Foskett) b 1954, Sarah (Mrs Street) b 1955, Anne (Mrs Lewis) b 1956, Katharine (Mrs Hampden-Smith) b 1959, Margaret (Mrs Lindsell) b 1962, Josephine b 1965); *Career* joined RAF 1944, served in 26, 263, 614, 247 sqdns 1946-54, cmd III Sqdn (ldr Black Arrows Aerobatic Team) 1958-60, MOD jt planning staff 1962-64, cmd NEAF strike and PR wing 1964-66, Gp Capt Ops 38 Gp 1967-69, cmd RAF Tengah, Singapore 1969-71, MOD central staff 1971-73, AOC Offr and Aircrew Selection Centre Biggin Hill 1973-74, SASO 38 Gp 1974-76, dir def ops MOD 1976-77, AOC II Gp 1977-78, Cdre RAF Sailing Assoc 1974-80, pres Assoc of Service Yacht Clubs 1978-81, ret RAF 1981; princ Oxford Air Trg Sch and dir CSE Aviation 1981-85, sr air advsr Short Bros plc 1985-90, ptnr Peter Latham Clocks; memb ctee East Wessex TAVR; Freeman City of London 1988, memb of Ct of Assistants Worshipful Co of Clockmakers 1990-; *Recreations* sailing, horology; *Clubs* RAF; *Style*— Air Vice-Marshal P A Latham, CB, AFC; Lloyd's Bank, 193 High St, Deritend, Birmingham B12 OLJX

LATHAM, Peter Douglas Langdon; s of Lt-Col James Douglas Latham TD (d 1985), of Stondon Massey House, nr Brentwood, Essex, and Rosemary Langdon Buckley; *b* 6 Feb 1951; *Educ* Repton, Univ of Exeter (BA); *m* 1977, Barbara Frances, da of Frank John Neve, OBE; 2 s (Simon b 1980, Martin b 1982); *Career* dir: James Latham plc 1985-, Richard Graefe Ltd 1977-90; chm Latham Timber Centres (Holdings) Ltd 1983-; pres: Wood Forum 1981-84, High Wycombe Furniture Mfrs Soc 1984-86; *Recreations* squash, beekeeping, mountaineering; *Style—* Peter Latham, Esq; Latham Timber & Building Supplies, Simpson Rd, Bletchley, Milton Keynes MK1 1BB (☎ 0908 644222, car 0836 210 154)

LATHAM, Sir Richard Thomas Paul; 3 Bt (UK 1919); s of 2 Bt (d 1955); *b* 1934; *Educ* Eton, Trinity Coll Cambridge; 1958, Marie-Louise Patricia, da of Frederick H Russell, of Vancouver, BC, Canada; 2 da; *Style—* Sir Richard Latham, Bt; 2125 Birnam Wood Drive, Santa Barbara, Calif 93108, USA

LATHAM, Robert Sidney; s of Ronald Geoffrey Latham (d 1951), of Ridge Park, Bramhall, Ches, and Doris, *née* Greenhalgh (d 1940); *b* 4 Feb 1929; *Educ* Repton, Trinity Coll Oxford (MA); *m* 1 June 1963, Suzannah, da of Ralph Herbert Lane, of Leigh Place, Reigate, Surrey; 3 s (Simon b 1964, Harry b 1964, William b 1967), 1 da (Sophie b 1970); *Career* Nat Serv Ches Regt 1947-49; asst slr Farrer & Co 1956-58, dep slr Nat Tst 1959-64 (slr 1964-89); govr and tstee St Mary's Prep and Choir Sch Reigate 1984-, church warden St Philip's Reigate 1984-; memb Law Soc 1956-; *Recreations* allotment, environment; *Style—* Robert Latham, Esq; The Old Granary, Park Lane, Reigate, Surrey RH2 8JX (☎ 0737 242203)

LATHAM, Simon John; s of Peter George Latham, and Audrey, *née* Turner; *b* 20 May 1957; *Educ* Univ of Exeter (LLB); *Career* admitted slr 1981, asst slr Ince and Co 1981, ptnr 1987; memb Law Soc; *Recreations* yachting; *Style—* Simon Latham, Esq; Ince & Company, Knollys House, 11 Byward St, London EC3R 5EN (☎ 071 623 2011, telex 8955043, fax 071 623 3225)

LATHBURY, Lady; Mairi Zoë; da of late Arthur MacMillan; *m* 1, Patrick Somerset Gibbs (decd); m 2, 1972, Gen Sir Gerald William Lathbury, GCB, DSO, MBE, DSC (d 1978); *Style—* Lady Lathbury; Casa San Pedro, Gata de Gorgos, Prov Alicante, Spain

LATIEF, Hon Mrs (Annette Yvonne); *née* Curzon; da (by 1 m) of 3 Viscount Scarsdale; *b* 28 Oct 1953; *m* 1979, Capt Hani Talaat Latief, of Cairo; 2 s (Sagi b 1982, Shadi b 1989); *Style—* The Hon Mrs Latief; 7 Dr Ismaiel Ghanem St, Nozha Geddida, Heliopolis, Cairo, Egypt

LATIMER, Dr Raymond Douglas (Ray); s of Kenneth Eric Latimer, MBE (d 1975), of London, and Doris Evelyn, *née* Friend; *b* 15 Aug 1941; *Educ* City of London Sch, Univ of Cambridge (MA), Middlesex Hosp Med Sch (LRCP, MRCS, MB BS); *m* 15 May 1965, Patricia Mary, da of Frank Theodore Page; 3 s (Paul b 1968, Mark b 1970, Andrew b 1978), 1 da (Sarah b 1971); *Career* cardiothoracic anaesthetist Papworth Hosp, assoc lectr Univ of Cambridge, ed Jl of Cardiothoracic Anaesthesia; guest lectr: China 1987, Iran 1989; fndr Assoc of Cardiothoracic Anaesthetists of GB and I, sec and treas Euro Assoc of Cardiothoracic Anesthesiologists; FFARCS; *Books* author of chapters in pubns on anaesthesia for heart and lung transplantation and selective phosphodieterase inhibitors in treatment of heart failure; *Recreations* sailing, Christian Youth Leader (Pathfinders); *Clubs* Christian Med Fellowship; *Style—* Dr Ray Latimer; Oaksway, 15 Braggs Lane, Hemingford Grey, Huntingdon, Cambs PE18 9BW (☎ 0480 63582); Papworth Hospital, Papworth Everard, Cambridge CB3 8RE (☎ 0480 830 541, fax 0480 831146)

LATIMER, Sir (Courtenay) Robert; CBE (1958, OBE 1948); s of Sir Courtenay Latimer, KCIE, CSI (d 1944), and Isabel Primrose, *née* Aikman (d 1981); *b* 13 July 1911; *Educ* Rugby, Ch Ch Oxford (MA); *m* 1, 3 Oct 1944, Elizabeth Jane Gordon (d 1989), da of William Mitchell Smail (d 1971); 1 s (Colin b 1947), 1 da (Penelope b 1953); m 2, 4 Jan 1990, Frederieka Jacoba Blankert, da of Hermanus Witteveen (d 1959); *Career* ICS and IPS 1935-47, HM Overseas Serv 1948-64 (dep high cmmr for Basutoland, Bechuanaland Protectorate and Swaziland 1960-64), min (Territories) in Br Embassy Pretoria 1964-66; registrar Kingston Poly 1967-76; *Recreations* golf; *Style—* Sir Robert Latimer, CBE; Benedicts, Old Avenue, Weybridge, Surrey KT13 0PS (☎ 0932 842381)

LATNER, Prof Albert Louis; s of Harry Latner (d 1971), of Finchley, London, and Miriam, *née* Gordon (d 1978); *b* 5 Dec 1912; *Educ* Imperial Coll London (BSc, MSc, ARCS, DIC), Univ of Liverpool (MD, DSc); *m* 3 Sept 1936, Gertrude (d 1986), da of Rev Sabita Franklin (d 1920), of Newcastle upon Tyne; *Career* RAMC 1941-46; lectr Dept Physiology Univ of Liverpool 1939-41 (asst lectr 1933-36), sr registrar Br Postgraduate Med Sch 1946-47; Univ of Durham: lectr in chem pathology 1947-55, reader in med biochem 1955-61; Univ of Newcastle upon Tyne: prof of clinical biochem 1961-78, dir Cancer Res Unit 1967-78; conslt Royal Victoria Infirmary Newcastle upon Tyne 1947-78; pres Assoc of Clinical Biochem 1961 and 1962, memb Cncl Assoc Clinical Pathologists 1967-70; memb: Ctee Standards Int Fedn Clinical Chem 1967-70, Br Nat Ctee for Biochem 1967-77; titular memb Int Union Pure & Applied Chem 1967-73; FRIC 1953, FRCPath 1963, FRCP 1964, Hon FNACB USA 1977; *Books* Isoenzymes in Biology and Medicine (with A W Skillen, 1968), Clinical Biochemistry (Cantarow and Trumper 1975); *Recreations* photography, gardening; *Clubs* Athenaeum; *Style—* Prof Albert L Latner; Ravenstones, 50 Rectory Rd, Newcastle upon Tyne NE3 1XP (☎ 091 285 8020)

LATOUR-ADRIEN, Hon Sir (Jean Francois) Maurice; s of Louis Constant Emile Adrien (decd); *b* 4 March 1915; *Educ* Royal Coll Mauritius, UCL; *Career* chief justice of Mauritius 1970-77; kt 1971; *Style—* The Hon Sir Maurice Latour-Adrien; Vacoas, Mauritius

LATTANAN, Pornlert; s of Gp-Capt Lek Lattanan, and Praphit Lattanan; *b* 13 Nov 1953; *Educ* Assumption Coll Bangkok, Chulalongkorn Univ Bangkok (BSc), Columbia Univ NYC (MBA); *m* 14 Nov 1980, Rinthan, da of Virat Sivakoses; 2 s (Prom b 29 March 1984, Pat b 23 Feb 1986); *Career* Geschaeftsleter Thai Farmers Bank, Hamburg Branch 1983, vice pres and branch mangr Thai Farmers Bank London Branch 1987; *Recreations* tennis, golf; *Clubs* Overseas Bankers; *Style—* Pornlert Lattanan, Esq; 80 Cannon St, London EC4N 6HH (☎ 071 623 4975, fax 2837437, telex 8811173)

LATTER, (Henry) James Edward; s of Henry Edward Latter, of Horley, Surrey, and Hilda Bessie, *née* Gyford; *b* 19 April 1950; *Educ* Reigate GS, Trinity Hall Cambridge (BA, MA); *m* 27 May 1978, Penelope Jane, da of Douglas Arthur Morris, of Pto del Duquesa, Spain; 1 s (Christopher b 1983), 1 da (Sarah b 1985); *Career* called to the Bar Middle Temple 1972; chm Disciplinary Ctee Potato Mktg Bd 1988; churchwarden Parish of Horley 1982-86, reader C of E 1990; *Recreations* gardening, reading; *Style—* James Latter, Esq; 1 Harcourt Buildings, Temple, London EC4Y 9DA (☎ 071 353 9421, fax 071 353 4170, telex 8956718 CRIPPSG)

LATTO, Dr Douglas; s of David Latto (d 1946), of Dundee, and Christina, *née* Gordon (d 1960); *b* 13 Dec 1913; *Educ* St Andrews Univ (MB ChB, DObst); *m* 11 Oct 1945, Dr Edith Monica Lotto, da of Capt Arthur Edward Druitt; 1 s (Conrad b 1948), 3 da (Christina b 1947, Elizabeth b 1952, Veronica b 1957); *Career* house surgn Dundee Royal Infirmary 1939, house physician Cornelia and E Dorset Hosp Poole 1940, res obstetrician and gynaecologist Derbys Hosp for Women Derby 1940, res surgical offr Birmingham Accident Hosp 1944, casualty offr Paddington Gen Hosp London 1944, asst obstetrics and gynaecology Mayday Hosp Croydon 1945, res obstectrics and gynaecologist Southlands Hosp Shoreham-by-Sea Sussex 1946-49, Nuffield Dept of Obstetrics and Gynaecology Radcliffe Infirmary Oxford 1949-51; chm Br Safety Cncl 1971- (Sword of Honour 1985); Freeman City of London 1988, Liveryman Worshipful Soc of Apothecaries 1988; memb BMA, FRPSL 1975, FRCOG 1989; *Recreations* squash, travelling, gardening, philately; *Clubs* RAC, Rolls-Royce Enthusiasts; *Style—* Dr Douglas Latto; Lethnot Lodge, 4 Derby Road, Caversham, Reading, Berks RG4 0EZ (☎ 0734 472282); 59 Harley St, London W1N 1DD (☎ 071 580 1070)

LATYMER, 8 Baron (E 1431-32); Hugo Nevill Money-Coutts; s of 7 Baron Latymer (d 1987); *b* 1 March 1926; *Educ* Eton; *m* 1, 1951 (m dis 1965), Hon (Penelope) Ann Clare, da of Thomas Addis Emmet (d 1934), and Lady Emmet of Amberley (Life Peeress); 2 s (Crispin b 1955, Giles b 1957), 1 da (Clare b 1952); m 2, 1965, Jinty, da of Peter Calvert (d 1970); 1 s (Henry b 1967), 2 da (Vera b 1972, Fanny b 1973); *Heir* s, Hon Crispin; *Career* gardener; *Style—* The Rt Hon the Lord Latymer; Vivero Hortus, Santa Maria, Mallorca

LAUD, Derek George Henry; s of Alexander Laud; *Career* professional speech writer and special advsr to Cons MP and Govt Mins, campaign mangr gen election 1987, asst Campaign Team for Rt Hon John Major, MP 1990, parly conslt to Strategy Network Int, dir First Market Intelligence Publishing Co, occasional journalist and broadcaster; local govt candidate 1986 and 1990, memb Cons Pty: Westminster Assoc, Battersea Assoc, Norwood Assoc; *Recreations* reading poetry, fox hunting, music, staying with the Welbys; *Style—* Derek Laud, Esq; House of Commons, London SW1A 0AA (☎ 071 222 4140); Clutha House, 10 Storeys Gate, London SW1

LAUDERDALE, Irene, Countess of Lauderdale; Irene Alice May Maitland; *née* Shipton; da of Rev C P Shipton (d 1933), of Halsham, Yorks, by his w Lory (Florence Leslie, d 1962); *b* 1 May 1900; *Educ* Maynard Sch Exeter, St Hilda's Sch Whitby, Battersea Poly; *m* 1940, as his 2 w, 16 Earl of Lauderdale (d 1968); *Books* Of Shoes and Ships and Sealing Wax, Of Cabbages and Kings (poems); *Recreations* travel, reading, writing verse, naval history; *Style—* The Rt Hon Irene, Countess of Lauderdale; Flat 11, West Preston Manor, Station Rd, Rustington, W Sussex BN16 3AX (☎ 0903 782720)

LAUDERDALE, 17 Earl of (S 1624); Sir Patrick Francis Maitland; 13 Bt (NS 1680); also Lord Maitland of Thirlestane (S 1590), Viscount of Lauderdale (S 1616), Viscount Maitland, and Lord Thirlestane and Boltoun (both S 1624); s of Rev Hon Sydney George William Maitland (d 1946; 2 s of 13 Earl), and gggggg nephew of 2 Earl and 1 Duke of Lauderdale (the 'L' of Charles II's acronymic CABAL); suc bro, 16 Earl, 1968; f of Lady Olga Maitland (*see* Hay, Lady Olga); *b* 17 March 1911; *Educ* Lancing, Brasenose Coll Oxford; *m* 1936, Stanka, da of Prof Milivoje Lozanitch, of Belgrade Univ; 2 s, 2 da; *Heir* s, Master of Lauderdale, Viscount Maitland; *Career* sits as Cons in House of Lords; journalist 1933-59, fndr and sometime ed Fleet Street Letter Service, sometime ed The Whitehall Letter; war corr: The Times (Central Europe) 1939-41, News Chronicle (Pacific) 1941-43; MP (C) Lanarkshire (Lanark Div) 1951-59 (resigned whip 1956-58 in protest at withdrawal from Suez); fndr and chm Expanding Cwlth Gp at House of Commons 1955-59 (re-elected chm 1959), chm House of Lords Sub-ctee on Energy Tport and Res 1974-79; dir Elf Aquitaine UK Holdings 1980-; pres The Church Union 1956-61, memb (emeritus) Coll of Guardians Nat Shrine of Our Lady of Walsingham 1955-; FRGS; *Clubs* New (Edinburgh), RSAC (Glasgow); *Style—* The Rt Hon the Earl of Lauderdale; 12 St Vincent St, Edinburgh (☎ 031 556 5692); 10 Ovington Square, London SW3 1LH (☎ 071 589 7451)

LAUGHLAND, (Graham Franklyn) Bruce; QC (1977); s of Andrew Percy Laughland, of Birmingham (d 1962); *b* 18 Aug 1931; *Educ* King Edward's Sch Birmingham, Ch Ch Oxford; *m* 1969, Victoria Nicola Christina, da of A S Jarman, of Brighton; 1 s; *Career* called to the Bar Inner Temple 1958, standing counsel to the Queen's Proctor 1968-; prosecuting counsel to Inland Revenue (Midland & Oxford circuit) 1973-77; a recorder of Crown Ct 1972-; bencher of the Inner Temple 1985; *Style—* Bruce Laughland, Esq, QC; 4 King's Bench Walk, Temple, EC4 (☎ 071 353 3581); 30 Monmouth Rd, London W2 (☎ 071 229 5045)

LAUGHLAND, Hugh William; s of William Laughland (d 1949), and Eleanor Anne Gordon, *née* Wilson; *b* 20 Dec 1931; *Educ* Ayr Acad, Merchiston Castle Sch; *m* 24 Aug 1961, Louise Osborne; 1 s (Brian b 1963), 1 da (Tracy b 1966); *Career* Fleet Air Arm 1954-56; dir Scottish Aviation Ltd 1970-75 (joined 1957), chief exec Scottish Universal Investment 1976-79; dir: Thomas Tilling plc 1981-83 (joined 1980), BTR plc 1983-, Lowandbonar plc, Bryant Group plc, Wace GP plc; jt chief exec Euro Reg (1984-88); chm: Stoddard Sekers International plc; Ibex Holdings plc; jt exec chm Euro Reg (1984-88); CA, ATII; *Recreations* golf, gardening; *Clubs* Caledonian; *Style—* Hugh Laughland, Esq; Staple, Higher Stratton, Stratton Chase Drive, Chalfont St Giles, Bucks HP8 4NS

LAUGHLAND, Iain Hugh Page; s of Hugh Norman Wilson Laughland (d 1984), and Morag Laughland; *b* 29 Oct 1935; *Educ* Merchiston Castle Sch; *m* 1972, Ann Stewart, da of Andrew Blackwood Stewart Young, of Belhaven, Troon, Ayrshire, Scot; 1 s (Andrew Iain Stewart b 1965), 1 da (Rosemary Ann b 1963); *Career* 2 Lt 1 Bn Seaforth Highlanders, serv Egypt, Aden, Gibraltar 1955-56; dir press: Coomberlands 1964-68, Benn Pubns Ltd 1977-87, Farm Holiday Guides Ltd 1981-84; 31 Caps Scotland Rugby XV 1959-66, capt 1965, record 5 wins Middx Sevens; *Recreations* golf; *Clubs* Rye, Caledonian, London Scottish Football; *Style—* Iain Laughland, Esq; School House Farm, School House Lane, Horsmonden, Tonbridge, Kent TN12 8BN

LAUGHTON, Prof Michael Arthur; s of William Arthur Laughton (d 1986), of Barrie, Ontario, Canada, and Laura, *née* Heap (d 1987); *b* 18 Dec 1934; *Educ* King Edward Five Ways Birmingham, Etobicoke Collegiate Inst Toronto Canada, Univ of Toronto (BASc), Univ of London (PhD, DSc(Eng)); *m* 1960, Margaret Mary, yr da of Brig George Vincent Leigh Coleman, OBE (QVOCG Indian Army, d 1970); 2 s (Mark Michael b 30 July 1968, Thomas George b 16 May 1971), 2 da (Joanna Margaret (Mrs Brogan-Higgins) b 28 June 1963, Katherine Alice b 22 Nov 1965); *Career* graduate apprentice GEC Witton Birmingham 1957-59, project engr GEC Engineering Computer Services 1959-61; Queen Mary Coll (now Queen Mary and Westfield Coll) Univ of London: DSIR res student 1961-64, lectr Dept of Electrical Engrg 1964-72, reader in electrical engrg 1972-77 (prof 1977-), dean Faculty of Engrg 1983-85, pro-princ QMC 1985-89; dean of engrg Univ of London 1990-; visiting prof: Univ of Purdue USA 1966, Univ of Tokyo Japan 1977; external examiner numerous univs UK and abroad 1970-; co-ed and fndr Int Journal of Electrical Power and Energy Systems 1978-; chm: Tower Shakespeare Company Ltd 1985-, Queen Mary College Industrial Research Ltd 1988- (dir 1979); organising sec Power Systems Computation Confs 1963-81 (chm Organising Ctee 1981-); chm: IEE Working Gp on Applications of New Electronic Techniques in Publishing 1983-87, Working Gp on Renewable Energy 1986-90 (Watt Ctee Exec 1986-); memb: Info Ctee Royal Society 1988-, House of Lords Select Ctee on the Euro Communities 1988- (specialist advsr to Sub Ctee B (Energy, Tport and Technol) on Inquiries into Renewable Resources 1988 and Efficiency of Electricity Use 1989), Cncl IEE 1990; memb of Ct of Cranfield Inst of Technol 1991-; Freeman: City of London 1990, Worshipful Co of Barbers 1990; MRI 1973, FIEE 1977 (MIEE 1968), FEng 1989; *Publications* Electrical Engineers Reference Book (with M G Say, 1985), Expert System Applications in Power Systems (ed with T S Dillon, 1990), Renewable

Energy Sources (ed 1990); author of numerous papers on electrical power and energy systems, control and computation; *Recreations* following rugby and cricket; *Clubs* Athenaeum; *Style*— Prof M A Laughton; 209 East Dulwich Grove, London SE22 8SY (☎ 081 693 3555); Department of Electonic Engineering, Queen Mary & Westfield College, University of London, Mile End Rd, London E1 4NS (☎ 071 975 5331, fax 081 981 0259)

LAUGHTON-SCOTT, Rachel Annabel; da of Martin Alfred Butts Bolton, JP, DL, and Margaret Hazel, *née* Kennaway; *b* 24 Aug 1957; *Educ* Moreton Hall Sch, Univ of Exeter (BA); *m* 5 Sept 1981, Charles Gilbert Foster Laughton-Scott, s of His Hon Judge (Edward Hey) Laughton-Scott, QC (d 1978); 2 s (Rory Edward b 6 Dec 1986, Sam Alexander b 15 May 1989); *Career* publishing dir Reed Publishing Servs 1985-; *Style*— Mrs Rachel Laughton-Scott; Reed Publishing Services, 7-11 St John's Hill, London SW11 (☎ 071 228 3344)

LAUNDER, Victor Charles; s of Charles Walter Launder (d 1974), of Carisbrooke, IOW, and Millicent Alice, *née* Missen (d 1986); *b* 13 July 1916; *Educ* Newport IOW Co Secdy Sch, Southern Coll of Art Portsmouth, Univ of Bristol; *m* 23 July 1955, Audrey Ann, da of Thomas Maynard Vowleş (d 1973), of Backwell, nr Bristol; 2 da (Susan b 1956, Robina b 1960); *Career* war serv; aircraft prodn engr Saunders-Roe Ltd 1939-45; architect; lectr Southern Coll of Art Portsmouth 1947-59; vice princ Royal West of Eng Acad Sch of Architecture 1960-64; sr lectr Sch of Architecture Univ of Bristol 1964-81; author numerous book reviews; ARIBA; *Books* Foundations (1972); *Recreations* walking, cycling, archaeology, photography; *Style*— Victor Launder, Esq; 9 Lower Gurnick Road, Newlyn, Penzance TR18 5QN (☎ 0736 64655); Casa Marina, Pla del Mar 157, Moraira (Alicante Prov), Spain

LAUNER, Dr Michael Andrew; s of Ellis Launer (d 1978), of Manchester, and Sylvia Launer, *née* Cohen (d 1985); *b* 29 May 1947; *Educ* Manchester GS, Univ of Leeds (DPM), Open Univ (BA); *m* Nov 1972, Hilary Elizabeth, da of Herbert Frederick Coates (d 1955), of Milford Haven, Wales; 1 s (Jack Simon b 1974); *Career* conslt psychiatrist Burnley Pendle and Rossendale 1977-, fndr Psychonutritional Unit for the Treatment of Eating Disorders Burnley 1984; freelance contrib: World Medicine, Hospital Doctors, local radio and newspapers; hon conslt: Samaritans, Relate; hon lectr Cruse, listed by Anorexic Aid, second opinion doctor Mental Health Cmmn, Law Society approved expert witness, advsr Nat Ctee for Sick Doctor, vice chm Special Prof Panel for Sick Doctors, LRCP, MRCS 1970, MRCPsych 1975, memb BMA; *Recreations* writing, sport as a spectator; *Style*— Dr Michael Launer; Lamont Clinic, Burnley General Hosp, Casterton Ave, Burnley, Lancs BB10 2PQ (☎ 0282 25071 ext 4736)

LAURENCE, Dan H; *b* 28 March 1920; *Educ* Hofstra Univ (AB), New York Univ (AM); *Career* WWII radar specialist Fifth AF (USA) 1942-45; served: Aust, New Guinea, Philippines; prof of English NY Univ 1967-70 (assoc prof 1962-67); visiting prof: Indiana Univ 1969, Univ of Texas at Austin 1974-75, Tulane Univ (Andrew Mellon prof in humanities) 1981, Univ of BC 1984; John Guggenheim Meml fell 1960, 1961, 1972, visiting fell Inst for Arts and Humanistic Studies Pennsylvania State Univ 1976, Montgomery fell Dartmouth Coll 1982, adjunct prof of drama Univ of Guelph 1986-91 (visiting prof 1983); literary and dramatic advsr Estate of George Bernard Shaw 1973-90, assoc memb RADA 1979, assoc dir Shaw Festival Ontario 1988-91 (literary advsr 1982-91); Hon Phil Beta Kappa 1967; *Books* Henry James: A Bibliography (with Leon Edel, 1957, 3 edn, 1981), Bernard Shaw: A Bibliography (1983), A Portrait of The Author as a Bibliography (1983), Collected Letters of Bernard Shaw (ed vols 1965, 1972, 1985, 1988), Bernard Shaw Collected Plays with their Prefaces (ed 7 vols 1970-74), Shaw's Music (ed, 3 vols 1981-89), Shaw on Dickens (with Martin Quinn, 1985); *Style*— Dan H Laurence, Esq; 102 Rampart Drive, San Antonio, 78215 Texas, USA (☎ 512 344 9666)

LAURENCE, John Kellock; TD (1946); s of Robert Peter Gow Laurence (d 1956), and Janetta Maclean, *née* Kellock (d 1939); *b* 8 Oct 1913; *Educ* George Watson's Coll, Univ of Edinburgh (BL); *m* 11 Dec 1940, Mary, da of Bartholomew Davison (d 1960); 3 da (Katherine Patricia Ivens, Veronica Gail Trenchard, Pamela Rosamund Morgan); *Career* Capt RA; served: Western Desert, Sicily, Europe; CA 1938; sr ptnr Hays Allan 1976-83; chm: Dencora plc 1981-, KLP plc 1983-; *Recreations* walking, gardening; *Clubs* Caledonian, London Scottish Rugby Football; *Style*— John Laurence, Esq, TD; Cardross House, Church Rd, Ham Common, Richmond TW10 5HG (☎ 081 940 8708)

LAURENCE, Michael; s of Jack Laurence, MBE (d 1960), of 31 Deansway, London N2, and Eveleen, *née* Lewis (d 1988); *b* 18 June 1930; *Educ* Stonyhurst, St Mary's Hosp Med Sch, Univ of London (MB BS); *m* 12 Sept 1967, Parvin, da of Jamshid Faruhar (d 1969), of Iran; 1 s (Arian b 1968), 2 da (Nicola b 1970, Hotessa b 1973); *Career* RAMC Capt specialist anaesthetics MELF 1955-57; orthopaedic surgn and consltt: Guy's Hosp 1970- (St Olave's Hosp, New Cross Hosp, Lewisham Hosp), Hosp of St John and St Elizabeth; conslt orthopaedic surgn: Hammersmith Hosp 1968-70, Royal Nat Orthop Hosp Stanmore 1968-70; sr lectr inst of orthopaedics London Univ 1968-70, lectr Dept of Surgery Royal Post Graduate Med Sch 1968-70, chm med staff ctee Hosp of St John & St Elizabeth 1982-88; author of many articles papers and chapters in books on the subject of Reconstuctive Joint Surgery in Chronic Arthritis; pres Rheumatical Arthritis Surgical Soc 1978-79 and 1988-89; FRCS; *Recreations* sailing, golf; *Clubs* Island Sailing (Cowes); *Style*— Michael Laurence, Esq; 2 Lyndhurst Terrace, Hampstead NW3 5QA; Billingham Manor, nr Newport IOW PO30 3HE; 106 Harley St, W1N 1AF (☎ 01 486 3131)

LAURENCE, Prof (Kurt) Michael; s of Gustav Leobenstein (d 1924), of Berlin, and Grete, *née* Heymann (d 1990); *b* 7 Aug 1924; *Educ* Newcastle under Lyme HS, Trinity Hall Cambridge (BA, MA), Univ of Liverpool (MB BCh), Univ of Wales (DSc); *m* 9 July 1949 (Ethel) Rose, da of Thomas James Settle (d 1976), of Coventry; 1 s (Anthony Stephen b 1950), 2 da (Amanda Rose b 1959, Elizabeth Clare b 1961); *Career* registrar in pathology Portsmouth 1953-55, res fell in hydrocephalus and spina bifida Hosp for Sick Children Gt Ormond St London 1955-58, reader in applied genetics Welsh Nat Sch for Med 1969-76 (sr lectr paediatric pathology 1959-69), prof of paediatric res Univ of Wales Coll of Med 1976-89, hon conslt clinical geneticist S Glam Health Authy 1976-89, co-dir Inst of Med Genetics 1976-89, emeritus prof Univ of Wales 1989-; over 300 sci papers on congenital malformations, clinical genetics, paediatric congenital malformations, paediatric pathology, hydrocephalus and spina bifida, parental diagnosis, prevention of malformations; FRCPE, FRCPath; memb: Clinical Genetics Soc (past pres), Br Paediatric Assoc, Soc for Res into Hydrocephalus and Spina Bifida (past pres), Paediatric Pathology Soc; *Books* Fetoscopy (jtly, 1981), Fetal and Neonatal Pathology (contrib, 1987), Principles and Practice of Med Genetics (contrib, 1990); *Recreations* music, painting, current affairs, skiing, walking; *Clubs* Athenaeum; *Style*— Prof Michael Laurence; Springside, Pen-y-Turnpike, Dinas Powys, South Glamorgan CF6 4HG (☎ 0222 513248); Department of Child Health, University of Wales College of Medicine, Heath Park, Cardiff CF4 4XN (☎ 0222 747747, fax 0222 747603)

LAURENCE, Sir Peter Harold; KCMG (1981, CMG 1976), MC (1944), DL (Devon 1989); s of Ven George Laurence (d 1953); *b* 18 Feb 1923; *Educ* Radley, Ch Ch Oxford; *m* 1948, Elizabeth Aïda, da of H C B Way; 2 s, 1 da; *Career* diplomat; political advsr Berlin 1967-69, visiting fell All Souls Coll Oxford 1969-70, cnsllr (commercial) Paris 1970-74, chief inspr Dip Serv 1974-78, ambass Ankara 1980-83, ret; chm: Br Inst of Archaeology at Ankara 1984-, Community Cncl of Devon 1986-; fell Woodard Corp, chm of govrs Grenville Coll Bideford 1988-, memb Cncl Univ of Exeter 1989-; *Clubs* Army and Navy; *Style*— Sir Peter Laurence, KCMG, MC, DL; Trevilla, Beaford, Winkleigh, N Devon EX19 8NS

LAURENSON, James Tait; s of James Tait Laurenson (d 1986), of Seal, Kent, and Vera Dorothy, *née* Kidd (d 1968); *b* 15 March 1941; *Educ* Eton, Magdalene Coll Cambridge (MA); *m* 13 Sept 1969, Hilary Josephine, da of Alfred Howard Thompson, DFC, of Eweside House, Cockburnspath, Berwickshire; 1 s (Fergus b 1976), 3 da (Emily b 1972, Marianne b 1974, Camilla b 1978); *Career* banker; Adam & Co Group plc (formerly Ivory & Sime Investment Managers): joined 1968, ptnr 1970, dir 1975, dep chm and md 1983; dir: United Scientific Holdings plc 1971, First Charlotte Assets Trust plc 1983; chm Nippon Assets Investments SA 1984; Freeman City of Edinburgh, memb Ct Worshipful Co of Merchants of City of Edinburgh; FCA 1968; *Recreations* tennis, gardening, skiing, shooting, stalking; *Clubs* New (Edinburgh); *Style*— James Laurenson, Esq; Hill House, Kirknewton, Midlothian EH27 8DR (☎ 0506 881990); 22 Charlotte Square, Edinburgh EH2 4DF (☎ 031 225 8484, fax 031 225 5136)

LAURENT, Hon Mrs (Isabelle); da of Baron Lever of Manchester, PC and his 2 w Diane, *née* Bashi; *m* 17 Sept 1988, Dr Antony Laurent (as Antoine Laurent author of Cuisine Novella), er s of the late Jacques Condou and Mme Jacques Bertheau; *Style*— The Hon Mrs Laurent; c/o The Rt Hon Lord Lever of Manchester, House of Lords, London SW1

LAURIE, Sir (Robert) Bayley Emilius; 7 Bt (UK 1834), of Bedford Sq, Middlesex; s of Maj-Gen Sir John Emilius Laurie, 6 Bt, CBE, DSO (d 1983), and Evelyn, *née* Richardson-Gardener (d 1987); *b* 8 March 1931; *Educ* Eton; *m* 1968, Laurelie Meriol Winifreda, da of Sir Reginald Lawrence William Williams, 7 Bt, MBE, ED (d 1971); 2 da (Clare b 1974, Serena b 1976); *Heir* kinsman, Andrew Ronald Emilius Laurie b 1944; *Career* Capt 11 Bn Seaforth Highlanders (TA) 1951-67; Samson Menzies Ltd 1951-58, CT Bowring & Co Ltd 1958-88, dir CT Bowring (Underwriting Agencies) Ltd 1967-83, chm Bowring Membs Agency Ltd 1983-88, dir Murray Lawrence Membs Agency Ltd 1988-; elected memb Lloyd's 1955; *Style*— Sir Bayley Laurie, Bt; The Old Rectory, Little Tey, Colchester, Essex (☎ 0206 210410)

LAURIE, Richard Thomas; s of Thomas Werner Laurie (d 1944), of 9 Lytton Grove, Putney, London SW15, and Elizabeth Mary Beatrice, *née* Blackshaw (d 1967); *b* 4 Oct 1935; *Educ* Bradfield Coll; *m* 29 June 1959 (m dis), Susan, da of John Dring, OBE, of Fakenham, Norfolk; 2 s (Daniel b 1959, Thomas b 1963), 1 da (Sophie b 1961); *Career* Nat Serv RASC 1954-56, 2 Lt; creative dir Brockie Haslam Advertising 1970-81; freelance journalist and copywriter; professional jazz musician; memb: of exec ctee Soho Soc 1977-, ed Soho Clarion 1977-; MIPA; *Recreations* book collecting, magazine editing; *Style*— Richard T Laurie, Esq; 27 Clarendon Drive, Putney, London, SW15 1AW (☎ 01 780 1939, fax 071 780 2137)

LAURIE, Capt Robert Peter; JP (1974), DL (1979); s of Col Vernon Stewart Laurie, CBE, TD, DL (d 1981), of The Old Vicarage, S Weald, Brentwood, Essex (*see* Burke's Landed Gentry 18th Edn, vol iii), and Mary (d 1989), 2 da of late Selwyn Robert Pryor, of Plaw Hatch, Bishop's Stortford, Essex; *b* 20 Aug 1925; *Educ* Eton; *m* 26 Nov 1952, Oonagh Margaret Faber, 3 da of late William Preston Wild, of Warcop Hall, Westmorland; 3 s (Ranald Martin b 1956, Benjamin William b 1959, Andrew Robert b 1963), 1 da (Marian Doone b 1955); *Career* Coldstream Gds 1943-47 (hon Capt); farmer (ret); memb Stock Exchange 1953-87; ptnr Heseltine Powell & Co (then Heseltine Moss & Co) 1953-80 (conslt 1980-85), dir Br Empire Securities & Gen Tst plc 1954- (chm 1973-84); memb Ct Essex Univ 1979-; govr: Brentwood Sch 1974-, Alleyn's Sch 1984-; chm Essex Assoc of Boys Clubs 1977-86 (pres 1986-), a vice-pres Nat Assoc of Boys Clubs 1986-; pres: Essex Agric Soc 1986-87, Essex Home Workers 1986-, Essex Shire Horse Assoc 1987-, Chelmsford and Mid Essex Samaritans 1986-, The Essex Club 1984; High Sheriff of Essex 1978-79 (Vice-Lord Lieut 1985-); chm Essex Co Ctee TAVRA 1987-91, memb Cncl CGLI 1984-; Master Worshipful Co of Saddlers 1981-82; *Recreations* foxhunting, gardening, reading, attempting to behave, agriculture; *Clubs* City Livery; *Style*— Capt Robert P Laurie, JP, DL; Heatley's, Ingrave, Brentwood, Essex (☎ 0277 810224)

LAURISTON, His Hon Judge Alexander Clifford; QC (1972); s of Alexander Lauriston, MBE (d 1960); *b* 2 Oct 1927; *Educ* Coatham Sch Redcar, Trinity Coll Cambridge; *m* 1954, Inga Louise, da of E Gregor (d 1987), of Tunbridge Wells; 2 da; *Career* called to the Bar Inner Temple 1952, rec Crown Ct 1972-76, circuit judge 1976-; Freeman: City of London 1969, Worshipful Co of Loriners 1969; *Clubs* Berkshire Golf, Utd Oxford and Cambridge; *Style*— His Hon Judge Lauriston, QC; 2 Harcourt Buildings, Temple, London EC4

LAURITZEN, Lady Rose Deirdre Margaret; *née* Keppel; raised to rank of an Earl's da 1980; da of Viscount Bury (d 1968), and gda of 9 Earl of Albemarle, MC (d 1979); *b* 11 Dec 1943; *Educ* Heathfield; *m* 1975, Peter Lathrop Lauritzen, s of George Lauritzen, of Chicago; 1 s (Frederick Alexander Mark b 1977); *Style*— The Lady Rose Lauritzen; Palazzo da Silva, Cannaregio 1468, Venice, Italy (☎ 715006)

LAUTERPACHT, Elihu; CBE (1989), QC (1970); s of Sir Hersch Lauterpacht, QC (d 1960), and Rachel, *née* Steinberg (d 1989); *b* 13 July 1928; *Educ* Harrow, Trinity Coll Cambridge (MA, LLM); *m* 1, 1955, Judith Maria (d 1970), er da of Harold Hettinger; 1 s (Michael), 2 da (Deborah, Gabriel); m 2, 1973, Catherine Josephine, da of Francis Daly (d 1960); 1 s (Conan b 1980); *Career* int lawyer; called to the Bar Gray's Inn 1983; reader in int law & dir Res Centre for Int Law Univ of Cambridge, judge World Bank Admin Tbnl; *Clubs* Athenaeum; *Style*— Elihu Lauterpacht, Esq, CBE, QC; Res Centre for Int Law, 5 Cranmer Rd, Cambridge CB3 5BL (☎ 0223 335358)

LAVAN, Hon Mr Justice; Hon Sir John Martin; s of M G Lavan, KC (d 1925), and Amy Alice Lavan (d 1925); *b* 5 Sept 1911; *Educ* Aquinas Coll Perth, Xavier Coll Melbourne; *m* 1939, Leith, da of W E Harford; 1 s, 3 da; *Career* private law practice 1934-69, memb Barr's Bd WA 1960-69, justice of Supreme Ct of W Aust 1969-, pres Law Soc WA 1964-66, chm Parole Bd WA 1969-76; KStJ, kt 1981; *Style*— The Hon Mr Justice Lavan; 165 Victoria Ave, Dalkeith, WA 6009, Australia

LAVELLE, Roger Garnett; s of Dr Henry Allman Lavelle (d 1955), and Dr Evelyn Alice Garnett (d 1986); *b* 23 Aug 1932; *Educ* Leighton Park Reading, Trinity Hall Cambridge (BA, LLB); *m* 7 Dec 1956, Gunilla Elsa, da of Prof Hugo Odeberg (d 1973); 3 s (Barnaby b 22 March 1962, Richard b 10 March 1967, Edward b 4 May 1972); 1 da (Katharine b 18 July 1959); *Career* special asst (Common Market) Lord Privy Seal 1961-63, private sec to Chllr of Exchequer 1965-68; HM Treasy: under sec 1975, dep sec 1985-87; head Euro Secretariat Cabinet Office 1987-89, vice pres Euro Investment Bank 1989-; *Recreations* music, gardening; *Style*— Roger Lavelle, Esq; c/o European Investment Bank, 100 Boulevard Conrad, Adenauer, L2950 Luxembourg

LAVENDER, Gp Capt Brian William; OBE (1975), AFC (1965); s of John Ernest Lavender, MBE (d 1973), and Margaret Vessey Lavender (d 1981); *b* 25 April 1935; *Educ* Exeter Sch, Indian Def Servs Staff Coll, USAF Staff Coll; *m* 27 March 1965, Caroline, da of Arthur Richard King, of 171 New Bedford Rd, Luton, Beds; 2 s (Guy b 8 July 1967, Mark b 15 Sept 1972); *Career* pilot training 1953-54, sqdn pilot Germany 1955-59, flying instr 1960-61, air advsr Khartoum Sudan 1962-64, sqdn cdr 1965-67, staff HQ 1968-69, CO 6 and 29 Sqdns 1972-75, skyflash trials California 1976-77, Station Cdr Wildenrath Germany 1979-81, Air Cdr Falkland Islands 1983-84, ACOS HQ Afnorth Oslo 1985-87, MOD 1988-89 (1970-72, 1978, 1982), Regnl Cmdt air cadets HQ London and SE 1989-; memb RUSI 1979, FBIM 1987; *Recreations* skiing, sailing, jogging, video photography; *Clubs* RAF; *Style—* Gp Capt Brian Lavender, OBE, AFC; Regional Commandant, Headquarters Air Cadets (London & South East), Royal Air Force Northolt, Ruislip, Middx HA4 6NG (☎ 01 845 2300 ext 352, fax 01 845 2300 ext 391)

LAVENDER, (Christopher) Justin; s of Alexander Desmond Lavender, of 12 St Catherine's Way, Christchurch, Dorset, and Hilary May, *née* Coleman; *b* 4 June 1951; *Educ* Bedford Modern Sch, QMC London, Guildhall Sch of Music and Drama; *m* 1; 1 s (William b 4 May 1982), 1 da (Catherine b 21 Jan 1984); m 2; Louise, da of Derek William Crane; *Career* opera singer; debut with Victoria State Opera (Nadir in Pearl Fishers) Sydney Opera House 1980, Male Chorus (Rape of Lucretia) and Belmont (Entführung) Palermo 1983, video recording Le Berger (Oedipus Rex) with Haitink and Amsterdam Concertgebouw Orch 1983, created leading tenor role of Lorenzi in Arrigo's Il Ritorno di Casonova Geneva 1984 (revived Paris 1985), Don Ottavio (Don Giovanni) Rome 1985, The Painter (Lulu) Scottish Opera 1987, Pilade (Rossini's Ermione) Madrid 1988, Schubert's Mass in E flat with Giulini and Berlin Philharmonic 1988, Bartók's Cantata Profana with Solti and London Philharmonic 1989, title role in Gounod's Faust at Brighton Festival 1989, created role of Montezuma (Prodromidés' La Noche Triste) in Nancy and Paris 1989, recording of La Noche Triste released on MFA label 1991, Arnold (Rossini's Guillaume Tell) Royal Opera House Covent Garden 1990, Almaviva (Barbiere) Royal Opera House 1990, Tamino (Die Zauberflöte) Summer Festival at Vienna State Opera 1990, Rossini's Stabat Mater with Accardo and the Academia di Santa Cecilia Rome 1990, Don Ottavio (Don Giovanni) Prague Spring Festival 1990, debut at Teatro alla Scala Milan in title role of Rossini's Le Comte Ory 1991; performances with all major Br orchs (particulary known for Verdi's Requiem, Elgar's The Dream of Gerontius, Handel's Messiah); *Recreations* walking, cycling, good food, reading, carpentry, railway modelling; *Style—* Justin Lavender, Esq; Milestone, Castle St, Mere, Wiltshire BA12 6JQ; Kaye Artists Management, 250 King's Rd, London SW3 5UE (☎ 071 376 3456, fax 071 376 5171)

LAVER, Prof John David Michael Henry; s of Harry Frank Laver (d 1985), and Mary, *née* Brearley; *b* 20 Jan 1938; *Educ* Churcher's Coll, Univ of Edinburgh (MA, Dip Phon, PhD); *m* 1, 29 July 1962 (m dis 1974), Avril Morna Anel Macqueen, *née* Gibson; 2 s (Nicholas b 1963, Michael b 1965), 1 da (Claire b 1968); m 2, 1 Aug 1974, Sandra, da of Alexander Traill, of Bonnyrigg, Midlothian; 1 s (Matthew b 1972); *Career* Univ of Ibadan: asst lectr phonetics 1963-64, lectr phonetics 1964-66; Univ of Edinburgh: lectr phonetics 1966-76, sr lectr 1976-80, reader 1980-85, personal chair in phonetics 1985-, chm Centre for Speech Tech Res 1989- (dir 1984-89); memb: Cncl of Int Phonetics Assoc, Bd of the Euro Speech Communication Assoc; FIOA 1988-, FBA 1990; *Books* The Phonetic Description of Voice Quality (1980); *Recreations* travel; *Style—* Prof John Laver; Centre for Speech Technology Research, University of Edinburgh, 80 South Bridge, Edinburgh EH1 1HN (☎ 031 225 8883, fax 031 226 2730, telex UNIVEDG 727 442)

LAVERACK, Prof Michael Stuart; s of Clifford Laverack (d 1952), and late Rachel Frances, *née* Melvin; *b* 19 March 1931; *Educ* Selhurst GS Croydon, Univ of Southampton (BSc, PhD); *m* 25 March 1961, Maureen Ann, da of Richard Cole (d 1984), of Tower Wood Cottage, Tower Wood, Windermere; 2 s (Giles Kevin b 1964, Neville Murray b 1968), 1 da (Julia Kirsten b 1962); *Career* sci offr Nature Conservancy 1958-60; Univ of St Andrews: lectr zoology 1960-67, sr lectr in zoology 1967-69, prof of marine biology 1969-; dir Gatty Marine Lab St Andrews 1969-85; memb: Soc of Experimental Biology, Marine Biological Assoc; FRSE, CBiol, FIBiol 1970; *Books* Physiology of Earthworms (1963), Fauna and Flora of St Andrews Bay (with Dr M Blackler, 1974), Lecture Notes in Invertebrate Zoology (with J Dando, 3 edn 1987), Coastal Marine Zooplankton (with C D Todd, 1991); *Recreations* walking, photography, reading, gardening; *Clubs* Rotary (St Andrews); *Style—* Prof Michael Laverack, FRSE; Branxton, Boarhills, St Andrews, Fife KY16 8PR (☎ 0334 88241); Gatty Marine Laboratory, St Andrews, Fife KY16 8LB (☎ 0334 76161 ext 7101, fax 0334 78299)

LAVERICK, Peter Michael; s of Cdr Roy Carpenter, and Joyce Margaret Carpenter; *b* 7 June 1942; *Educ* Canford Sch, Sch of Law; *m* 26 Feb 1972, Elaine Ruth, da of Leopold Steckler; 2 da (Helen Tanya b 1973, Elise Mary b 1975); *Career* Capt GS (attached Coldstream Guards) 1968-71; slr 1966, Notary public 1985, ptnr Bellamy Knights & Griffin Worthing; *Recreations* sailing & skiing, former tideway oarsman; *Clubs* RORC, Island Sailing, Ski Club of GB, Martlake Angliaux Boat; *Style—* Peter M Laverick, Esq; North Barn, Poling, W Sussex (☎ (0903) 883205); 23 Warwick Street, Worthing, W Sussex (☎ 0903 210781, fax 0903 37625)

LAVIN, Deborah Margaret; da of George E Lavin (d 1987), of Johannesburg, SA, and Laura Kathleen Lavin (d 1987); *b* 22 Sept 1939; *Educ* Roedean Sch Johannesburg SA, Rhodes Univ Grahamstown SA, Lady Margaret Hall Oxford (BA, DipEd, MA); *Career* lectr Dept of History Univ of Witwatersrand SA 1962-64, lectr then sr lectr Dept of History Queen's Univ Belfast 1965-80; Univ of Durham: princ Trevelyan Coll 1980-, dep dean of colleges 1990-; *Style—* Miss Deborah Lavin; Hickmans Cottages, Cat St, East Hendred, Wantage, Oxon OX12 8JT; Trevelyan College, University of Durham, Elvet Hill Road, Durham DH1 3LN (☎ 091 374 3761)

LAVINGTON, Dr Michael Richard; s of Richard Lavington; *b* 21 Feb 1943; *Educ* Whitgift, Cambridge, Columbia Univ New York, Univ of Lancaster (BA, MA, PhD); *m* 1966, Claire June, da of James Watford; 2 da (Susan b 1969, Victoria b 1970); *Career* pres Black Starr & Frost (New York), Kay Jewellers (Alexandria Va); dir: Ralli Australia 1970-71; Bodwater-Ralli America 1971-74; *Recreations* theatre, chess, bridge, travel; *Style—* Dr Michael R Lavington; 6615 Georgetown Pike, Mclean, VA 22101 USA (☎ business 703 683 683 3800)

LAVINGTON, Prof Simon Hugh; s of Edgar Lavington (d 1982), of Wembley Park, London, and Jane, *née* Nicklen; *b* 1 Dec 1939; *Educ* Haileybury & ISC, Univ of Manchester (MSc, PhD); *m* 6 Aug 1966, Rosalind Margaret, da of Rev George Charles William Twyman, ISO, of Herstmonceux, Sussex; 2 s (Damian b 25 Aug 1968, Dominic b 9 April 1970), 2 da (Hannah b 7 Sept 1971, Tamsin b 19 May 1973); *Career* sr lectr Univ of Manchester 1974-86 (lectr 1965-74); prof: Univ of Ife Nigeria 1976-77, Univ of Essex 1986-; memb: various BCS and IEE ctees; DTI and SERC PNA Ctee; UN tech expert 1975: C Eng, FBCS 1978, FIEE 1985, FRSA 1988; *Books* Logical Design of Computers (1969), History of Manchester Computers (1975), Processor Architecture (1976), Early British Computers (1980), Information Processing 80 (1980); *Recreations* sailing, walking; *Clubs* Thames Barge Sailing; *Style—* Prof Simon Lavington; Lemon Tree Cottage, 46 High St, Sproughton, Suffolk IP8 3AH (☎ 0473 748478); Department of Computer Science, University of Essex, Colchester CO4 3SQ (☎ 0206 872677, fax 0206 873598, telex 98440 unilib g)

LAW, Hon Andrew Bonar; s of 1 Baron Coleraine, PC (d 1980); *b* 27 July 1933; *Educ* Rugby, Trinity Coll, Dublin; *m* 11 March 1961, Joanna Margarette, da of Raymond Neill, of Fairview, Delgany, Co Wicklow, Ireland; 1 s (Richard Pitcairn Bonar b 1963), 1 da (Charlotte Mary de Montmorency Bonar b 1964); *Books* various books on Irish Cartography; *Style—* The Hon Andrew Bonar Law; Shankill Castle, Shankill, Co Dublin, Ireland

LAW, Anthony John; s of Victor Frank Law, of London, and Hilda Ellen, *née* Whitaker; *b* 19 April 1940; *Educ* Christ's Coll Blackheath; *m* 18 July 1970, Pamela Ann, da of late Nelson Stuart Middleton; 2 da (Alexandra Michelle Jane b 7 Feb 1978, Nicola Anne-Marie b 28 May 1980); *Career* publisher Apollo Magazine, The International Magazine of Art and Antiques; chm Bd of Govrs Christ's Coll Blackheath; memb Inst of Journalists; *Clubs* Rugby; *Style—* Anthony Law, Esq; 10 Strathmore Close, Caterham, Surrey CR3 5EQ (☎ 0883 348082); Apollo Magazine Ltd, 3 St James's Palace, London SW1A 1NP (☎ 071 629 3061, fax 071 491 1676)

LAW, Hon Cecil Towry Henry; s of 7 Baron Ellenborough, MC (d 1945); *b* 17 Oct 1931; *Educ* Eton; *m* 22 Feb 1957, (Daphne Mary) Jean, da of Hon Laurence Paul Methuen (d 1970); 1 s, 3 da; *Career* Lt 1 King's Dragoon Gds 1950-52; Lloyd's insur broker 1952; chm Towry Law (Hldgs) Ltd 1958-, and all assoc cos in Towry Law Gp; *Style—* The Hon Cecil Law; 6 Sussex Square, London W2 2SJ; Towry Law (Holdings) Ltd, Towry Law House, High St, Windsor, Berks SL4 1LX

LAW, Charles Ewan; s of Robert Charles Ewan Law, DSO, DFC (ret Gp Capt), of Constantine Bay, Cornwall, and Norah, *née* Eaden; *b* 12 Aug 1946; *Educ* Wrekin Coll, Univ of Nottingham (BSc), Manchester Business Sch (MBA); *m* 5 Sept 1970, Clodagh Susan Margaret, da of Lt-Col Eric Steele-Baume, MBE (d 1968); 2 s(Huw b 1974, Henry b 1980), 1 da (Angharad b 1972); *Career* metallurgist BSC 1969-71, mangr Utd Int Bank 1973-79, vice pres Merrill Lynch Int Bank 1979-81, exec dir First Interstate Ltd 1984-87, non-exec dir Continental Illinois Ltd 1987- (exec dir 1981-84), md Continental Bank 1988-; *Recreations* sailing, theatre; *Clubs* RAC; *Style—* Charles Law, Esq; 162 Queen Victoria St, London EC4V 4BS (☎ 071 860 5153, fax 071 236 3099, telex 946246)

LAW, David Charles; s of Charles Law, of 50 Savage Lane, Sheffield (d 1975), and Florence Gladys Wainwright; *b* 9 Sept 1930; *Educ* King Edward VII Sheffield, BNC Oxford (MA); *m* 25 Jan 1956, Mary, da of Joseph William Senior, of Sheffield (d 1967); 1 s (Richard b 1962), 1 da (Sally b 1956); *Career* slr; sr ptnr David Law & Co Sheffield, dir Gilleyfield Investments Ltd 1960-, exec chm Hallamshire Electric Co Ltd 1972-78; dir: The Chris Fund Ltd 1980-, Wigfalls plc 1983-85, Sheffield Boy Scouts (Holdings) Ltd 1970-; hon consul for Belgium in Sheffield; sporting records: Oxford full blues track & cross county, Univ 3 Mile and cross country record, UAU 1 mile champion 1952, world student 1500 m 1953, world record 4 x 1500 m relay champion 1953, Br Cwlth record 4 x 1 mile relay, 1 mile finalist Br Empire games 1954; *Recreations* golf, skiing, game shooting; *Clubs* Sheffield, Abbeydale Golf, Abersoch Golf, S Caernarvon Yacht; *Style—* David Law, Esq; Dore Lodge, 79 Dore Rd, Sheffield S17 3ND; David Law & Co Telegraph House, High St, Sheffield S1 1PT (☎ 0742 700 999, fax 0742 739 292, car 0836 250 893)

LAW, David Thomas; s of David Philip Law (d 1971), and Florence Isabella, *née* Hyslop; *b* 17 Nov 1939; *Educ* Swanwick Hall GS Derby, Derby Tech Coll; *m* 5 Oct 1963, Jeane Beryl, da of Albert Edward Parsons; 1 s (Graham Cameron b 1971), 1 da (Deborah Jane b 1969); *Career* apprentice Rolls-Royce Aero Engines Ltd 1955-61; engr: Schlumberger Gp 1961-63, Elliott Bros Ltd 1963-69; res mangr Plessey Telecommunications Research Ltd 1969-73, conslt Software Sciences Ltd 1973-79, fndr and md Transaction Security Ltd 1979-83; fndr and chm: Crypto Systems Ltd 1984-, Strategic Research Europe Ltd 1989-; memb Co of Information Technologists 1989-, fndr and tstee Quality in the Community 1991; CEng, MIEE; *Recreations* reading, country walking, travel, gardening; *Style—* David Law, Esq; Talgarth, 181 Upper Chobham Rd, Camberley, Surrey GU15 1EH (☎ 0276 26303, fax 0276 24475)

LAW, Hon Edmund Ivor Cecil; 2 s of 8 Baron Ellenborough; *b* 21 Dec 1956; *Educ* Peterhouse Cambridge (MA); *m* 1982, Susan, er da of Derek Baker, of 5 Jermyn Close, Cambridge; 2 s (David Christopher b 8 March 1984, John Christian b 6 Feb 1986); *Style—* The Hon Edmund Law; 213 Waterhouse Moor, Harlow, Essex CM18 6BW

LAW, George Llewellyn; s of George Edward Law, MC (d 1974), of Maplehurst, Sussex, and Margaret Dorothy, *née* Evans, OBE (d 1980); *b* 8 July 1929; *Educ* Westminster, Clare Coll Cambridge (BA); *m* 26 March 1960, Anne Stewart, da of Arthur Adolphus Wilkinson (d 1974), of Chelsea, London; 1 da (Jane b 1962); *Career* Nat Serv RCS 1948-49; ptnr Slaughter and May slrs 1961-67 (joined 1952); dir: Morgan Grenfell & Co Ltd 1968- (exec 1968-88), Morgan Grenfell Group plc 1971-89 (vice chm 1987-88, sr advsr 1988-); memb: City of London Slrs Co, The Law Soc; FRSA; *Recreations* opera, ballet, classical music, theatre, art, art history; *Clubs* Brooks's, MCC; *Style—* George Law, Esq; 6 Phillimore Gardens Close, London W8 7QA (☎ 071 937 3061); Gainsborough Cottage, Cley-next-the-Sea, Holt, Norfolk; 23 Great Winchester St, London EC2P 2AX (☎ 071 588 4545, fax 071 588 5598, telex 8953511 MGLDN G)

LAW, Gordon Malcolm; s of Robert Law (d 1989), of Sheffield, and Elizabeth Black, *née* Cassells; *b* 7 Nov 1932; *Educ* King Edward VII GS Sheffield, Univ of Sheffield (BA); *m* 31 Aug 1957, Elaine, da of Thomas Whittingham (d 1942); 3 da (Helen b 15 Nov 1959, Mary b 4 Feb 1961, Charlotte b 12 Oct 1965); *Career* Nat Serv 12th Royal Lancers (POW) 1955-57; staff offr Jessop-Saville Ltd Sheffield 1960-62 (graduate trainee 1957-60), gp estab offr Shepherd Building Group Ltd York 1965-70 (personnel offr 1962-65); Woolwich Building Society: personnel mangr 1970-72, asst gen mangr personnel 1972-76, gen mangr personnel and trg 1976-90, ret 1990; memb cncl: Nat Interactive Video Centre, Nat Cncl for Educnl Technol, Chartered Bldg Socs Inst (CBSI); memb: York Tourist Advsy Bd 1968-70, York Crime Prevention Ctee 1967-70; govr Thames Poly (chm Ct of Govrs 1985-88), past pres York Jr C of C; Freeman City of London, Liveryman Worshipful Co of Distillers; hon FCBSI 1977, hon FBIM 1975, FIPM 1960; *Books* Personnel Policy and Line Management (1974, revised 1983); *Recreations* golf, philately; *Clubs* City Livery, W Kent GC; *Style—* Gordon Law, Esq; 6 Hawthorne Close, Bickley, Bromley, Kent BR1 2HJ

LAW, Adm Sir Horace Rochfort; GCB (1972, KCB 1967, CB 1963), OBE (1951), DSC (1941); s of Dr Samuel Horace Law, MD (d 1940), of Dublin, and Sybil Mary, *née* Clay; *b* 23 June 1911; *Educ* Sherborne; *m* 13 Dec 1941, Heather Valerie, da of Rev Henry Haworth Coryton (d 1956); 2 s (Robert b 1946, Edward b 1952), 2 da (Philippa b 1942, Deborah b 1948); *Career* joined RN 1929; CO: HMS Duchess 1952, HMS Centaur 1958; Capt Britannia RNC Dartmouth 1960; Rear Adm, Flag Offr Sea Trg 1962, Submarines 1963; Vice Adm Controller of the Navy 1965-70; Adm, C-in-C Naval Home Cmd and First and Princ Naval ADC to HM The Queen 1970-72; ret 1972; chm Hawthorn Leslie 1973-81; pres RINA 1979-81; chm Church Army Bd 1979-86; pres offr Christian Union 1970-86; chm Agnes Weston's Royal Sailors Rest 1958-85; Order of William of Orange 1 Class (Netherlands) 1972; *Style—* Adm Sir Horace Law, GCB, OBE, DSC; Cowpers, West Harting, Petersfield, Hants (☎ 073 825 511)

LAW, James; QC (Scotland 1970); s of George Law (d 1961), and Isabella Rebecca, *née* Lamb (d 1985); *b* 7 June 1926; *Educ* Kilmarnock Acad, Girvan HS, Univ of Glasgow (MA, LLB); *m* 1956, Kathleen Margaret, da of Alexander Gibson (d 1984); 2 s (George, Bruce), 1 da (Catriona); *Career* advocate dep 1957-64, memb Criminal Injuries Compensation Bd 1970-; chm Temp Sheriffs' Assoc 1975-; *Clubs* New

(Edinburgh), Caledonian (Edinburgh); *Style—* James Law, Esq, QC; 7 Gloucester Place, Edinburgh EH3 6EE (☎ 031 225 2974); Advocates Library, Edinburgh EH1 1RF (☎ 031 226 5071)

LAW, Laurence Arthur; s of Frederick Charles Law, of 29 Jedburgh Gardens, Newcastle upon Tyne, and Lilian Boland; *b* 2 June 1937; *Educ* Rutherford GS Newcastle, Open Univ (BA); *m* 1963, Orray; 2 s (Keith b 1965, Anthony b 1968), 2 da (Julie b 1964, Helen b 1970); *Career* div dir Alexander Stenhouse UK Ltd (dir 1974-), pres Newcastle upon Tyne Chartered Insur Inst 1980-81, chm Br Insur Brokers Assoc Northern Reg 1981-82; *Recreations* choral singing, music, badminton; *Style—* L A Law, Esq; Alexander Stenhouse UK Ltd, 230 High St, Potters Bar, Herts EN6 5BU (☎ 0707 51222, telex 2987785, fax 0707 46092)

LAW, Richard William Evan; s of George Edward Law (d 1974), of Court-up-Hill, Maplehurst, Sussex, and Margaret Dorothy, *née* Evans, OBE (d 1979); *b* 17 May 1926; *Educ* Westminster, ChCh Oxford (BA, MA); *m* 11 Feb 1955, Joy Patricia, da of Dr Jean-Jacques Spira (d 1972), of London; 1 s (Nicholas b 1957), 2 da (Jennifer b 1957, Katie b 1959); *Career* mgmnt trainee Seligman Brothers 1951-53, Gillett Bros Discount Co 1953-83 (md 1968), chm Int CD Market Assoc 1972-73, dir Kirkland Whittaker Ltd 1974-81, chm Kirkland Whittaker (Italia) Spa Milan 1974-78, cmmr Public Works Loans Bd 1977-89, London advsr to Banca Commerciale Italian Milan 1983-86, dept chm BCI Ltd 1983-86, chm Euromed Investmts plc 1986-; numerous pubns in jls; annual lectr on banking and money markets to Br Cncl 1968-84, chm Council for Music in Hospitals 1982-, govr Br Inst of Florence 1984-, memb Cncl of St John's Smith Square 1983-; *Books* Banking (as Evan Hughes, 1974); *Recreations* music, travel, cooking; *Clubs* Brooks's, Garrick; *Style—* Richard Law, Esq; Euromed Investments PLC, 7 Bury Place, London WC1A 2LA (☎ 071 831 7430, fax 071 430 1637)

LAW, Maj the Hon Rupert Edward Henry; s and h of 8 Baron Ellenborough; *b* 28 March 1955; *Educ* Eton; *m* 1981, Hon Grania Boardman, only da of Baron Boardman (Life Peer); 2 s (James Rupert Thomas b 8 March 1983, Frederick George Towry Gray b 9 Sept 1990), 1 da (Georgina b 16 Dec 1984); *Career* Coldstream Gds until 1988; Coutts and Co 1988-; *Style—* Maj the Hon Rupert Law; Bridge House, Clipston, Market Harborough, Leicestershire LE16 9RX (☎ 085 886 380)

LAWDEN, James Anthony Henry; s of Maj Henry Tipping Lawden, MC (d 1981), of Roehampton SW15, and Claire Phyllis, *née* Berthoud (d 1962); *b* 10 Aug 1955; *Educ* Winchester, New Coll Oxford; *Career* admitted slr 1981; Freshfields: joined 1979, ptnr 1988 (seconded with Aoki, Christensen & Nomoto Tokyo 1985); memb Law Soc; *Recreations* tennis, squash, travelling; *Clubs* Naval and Military, Roehampton; *Style—* James Lawden, Esq; Freshfields, Whitefriars, 65 Fleet St, London EC4Y 1HS (☎ 071 936 4000, fax 071 248 3487/8/9, telex 889292)

LAWDER, Simon David Patrick; s of Lt Col Frederick Herbert Lawder, MC, TD (d 1986), and Pauline Winifred, *née* Thompson; *b* 27 July 1944; *Educ* Denstone Coll; *m* 23 May 1970, Bridget Ann, da of Ernest Nelson Staker (d 1973); 1 s (James b 1973), 1 da (Anna b 1978); *Career* mangr: Barclays Bank DCO Sierra Leone and Malawi 1965-67, Kleinwort Benson Ltd 1968-69; account dir: Winship Webber & Co 1969-74, Allen Brady & Marsh 1974-75; dir Harrison Cowley Bristol 1975-86, md RS Alliance International 1986-90 (chm 1990-); head of Lions Int Aid Prog UK and I 1984-86, dir The Bristol Initiative, tstee Westmorland Devpt; MIPA 1986-; *Recreations* golf, France, family, Lions Club; *Style—* Simon Lawder, Esq; 47 North Road, Wells, Somerset BA5 2TL (☎ 0749 73941); Europa House, Queens Rd, Clifton, Bristol BS8 1EE (☎ 0272 731181, fax 0272 744196)

LAWLER, Geoffrey John; s of Maj Ernest Lawler, and Enid Florence Lawler, of Richmond, N Yorks; *b* 30 Oct 1954; *Educ* Colchester Royal GS, Richmond Sch, Univ of Hull (BSc); *m* 1989, Christine Roth, da of Mr C Roth, of Wyoming USA; *Career* Cons Res Dept 1980-82, PR exec 1982-83, md Lawler Assocs 1987-, vice pres Int Access Inc 1987-; MP (C) Bradford North 1983-87; pres: Univ of Hull Students' Union 1976-77, pres Br Youth Cncl 1984-87; memb cncl UKIAS 1987-; Freeman City of London; *Recreations* cricket, travel; *Style—* Geoffrey Lawler, Esq; Lawler Assocs, Westfield Rd, Leeds LS3 1DG

LAWLER, Ivan; s of Roland James Lawler, and Diana Mary, *née* Rabjohns; *b* 19 Nov 1966; *Educ* Hampton Sch; *Career* canoeist: nat marathon champion 1986, 1987, 1988, Olympic team 1988, world marathon champion 1989 (runner up 1988 and 1990), winner 10,000 World Spring Championships, mens double kayaks 1990 (runner up 1989); ptnr Grayson Bourne; holder of 4 nat sprint titles 1989, ranked no 1 nationally in marathon and sprint; *Style—* Ivan Lawler, Esq

LAWLEY, Susan (Sue); da of Thomas Clifford Lawley (d 1972), and Margaret Jane Lawley; *b* 14 July 1946; *Educ* Dudley Girls' HS, Univ of Bristol (BA); *m* 1, David Arnold Ashby; 1 s (Thomas David Harvey b 1976), 1 da (Harriet Jane b 1980); m 2, Roger Hugh Williams; *Career* trainee reporter and sub ed Western Mail and South Wales Echo 1967-70, BBC Plymouth 1970-72 (freelance reporter, sub ed, TV presenter); TV presenter BBC: Nationwide 1972-75 and 1977-81, Tonight 1976, Budget and gen election progs Nine O'Clock News 1981-82, Six O'Clock News 1982-86, Saturday Matters 1986-90, guest presenter Wogan and Question Time, documentaries and other special progs; presenter Desert Island Discs BBC Radio Four 1986-, presenter Granada TV Ltd 1991-; Hon LLD Univ of Bristol 1989, Hon MA Univ of Birmingham 1989; govr Nat Film and TV Sch 1990-; *Recreations* family life, eating, other people's biographies, guarding my own privacy; *Style—* Ms Sue Lawley

LAWLOR, Prof John James; s of Albert John Lawlor (d 1938), and Teresa Anne Clare, *née* Knight (d 1954); *b* 5 Jan 1918; *Educ* Ryders Sch, Magdalen Coll Oxford (BA, MA, DLitt); *m* 1, 26 April 1941 (m dis 1979), Thelma Joan, da of Charles Edward Parkes Weeks (d 1964); 1 s (John b 1954), 3 da (Teresa Anne (Mrs Rigby) b 1945, Judith Mary (Mrs Griffiths) b 1947, Penelope Jane (Mrs Jeffrey) b 1949); m 2, 7 Nov 1984, Prof Kimie Imura, *née* Fukuda; *Career* WWII Devonshire Regt 1940-45, cmmnd 1941, Capt 1942-45; asst chief instr Artists' Rifles OCTU 1943-44, serv in Italy with Royal West Kent and Hamps Regts 1944-45, mil govt Austria 1945; lectr in English BNC and Trinity Coll Oxford 1947-50, univ lectr in English lit 1949-50, prof of English language and lit Univ of Keele 1950-80, fell Folger Shakespeare Library Washington DC 1962, Ziskind visiting prof Brandeis Univ USA 1966, visiting prof Univ of Hawaii 1972; pres N Staffs Drama Assoc 1955-72, jt sec Advsy Ctee for Adult Educn N Staffs 1957-60; sec gen and tres Int Assoc of Univ Profs of English 1971-; FSA 1966; *Books incl* The Tragic Sense in Shakespeare (1960), Piers Plowman: An Essay in Criticism (1962), Patterns of Love and Courtesy (1966), To Nevill Coghill From Friends (with W H Auden, 1966); *Recreations* any sort of seafaring; *Clubs* Athenaeum; *Style—* Prof John Lawlor, FSA; Penwithian, Higher Fore St, Marazion, Cornwall (☎ 0736 711 180); 967-24 Misawa, Hinohi, Toyko 191 (☎ 0425 94 4177)

LAWLOR, Thomas Francis Christopher; s of Thomas Francis Lawlor (d 1976), of Dublin, Repub of Ireland, and Elizebeth Hendrick Lawlor; *b* 17 June 1938; *Educ* Christian Brothers' Sch Dublin, Univ Coll Dublin (BA); *m* 1, 21 Sept 1963, Marcia (d 1969), da of late William Carew, of Dublin; m 2, 2 Aug 1971 (m dis 1981), Pauline, da of late Francis Wales, of Stockton on Tees; 1 da (Frances b 19 Jan 1971); m 3, 21 June 1982, Ghislaine Ruby Solange, da of Joseph Raymond Labour, of Beau Basin, Mauritius; *Career* bass-baritone opera singer; has sung over 60 operatic roles 1963-71, princ baritone D'Oyly Carte Opera Co touring USA and Canada 1964, 1966 and 1968, performed with New Sadlers Wells Opera House Central City Opera Festival USA 1968, Prom Concerts 1968-1988; debut: Glyndebourne 1971, Kent Opera and Royal Opera House 1972, ENO 1975, Opera North 1979; Carnegie Hall NY 1976-86, Singapore Festival of the Arts 1988, Valencia Festival 1988, Wexford Festival 1989 and 1990, Opera NI 1990, Dublin Grand Opera; adjudicator memb Br Fedn of Music Festivals, memb Faculty Bay View Summer Conservatory of Music Michigan USA; Hon Citizen Central City Colorado USA 1968; *Clubs* Nat Univ of Ireland (London); *Style—* Thomas Lawlor, Esq; 31 Bridge Lane, Ilkley, W Yorks (☎ 0943 608 913)

LAWRANCE, (June) Cynthia; da of Albert Isherwood Emmett (d 1985), and Ida Emmett; *b* 3 June 1933; *Educ* 9 Schs (wartime), St Anne's Coll Oxford (BA, MA); *m* 27 Jun 1957, Rev David Lawrance, s of David Lawrance; 3 da (Elizabeth b 1958, Mary b 1960, Ruth b 1963); *Career* teacher: Inst Britannique Univ de Paris 1954-57, Br Cncl Cyprus 1957-58, Ahlyyah Sch Amman Jordan 1958-61, Counthill GS Oldham 1962-64; dep headmistress Chadderton GS for Girls 1965-70; headmistress: Broughton HS 1970-74, Harrogate Ladies' Coll 1974-; memb: SHA, NAHT, GSA; *Recreations* music, chess, French literature; *Style—* Mrs Cynthia Lawrance; 21 Clarence Drive, Harrogate HG1 2QE (☎ 0423 504050); 5 Cavendish Mansions, Mill Lane, Hampstead, London NW6 1TE; Harrogate Ladies' College, Clarence Drive, Harrogate, North Yorkshire HG1 2QG (☎ 0423 504543)

LAWRENCE, Hon Mrs ((Christine) Alexandra Canning); da of 5 Baron Garvagh; *b* 20 Sept 1949; *Educ* RNS Haslemere, Guildford Tech Coll; *m* 1971 (m dis 1987), Louis David Lawrence; 2 s (Stafford, Lucas); *Career* arts admin; *Style—* The Hon Mrs Lawrence; 4 Artesian Rd, London W2 4AP

LAWRENCE, Christopher Nigel; s of Rev William Wallace Lawrence (d 1979), and Millicent, *née* Atkinson (d 1983); *b* 23 Dec 1936; *Educ* Westborough HS Westcliff on Sea, Central Sch of Arts and Crafts London (NDD); *m* 1958, Valerie Betty; 2 s (Adrian, Robin), 2 da (Fay, Verity); *Career* goldsmith, silversmith and industl designer 1968-; one-man exhibitions: Galerie Jean Renet London 1970-71, Hamburg 1972, Goldsmiths' Hall 1973, Ghent 1975, Hasselt 1977; maj cmmns: Br Govt, city livery cos, banks, mfrg cos; judge and external assessor for art colls, specialist in symbolic presentation pieces and limited edns of decorative pieces, industl designer to leading mfrs of cutlery and hollow ware; TV and radio bdcaster; chm Goldsmiths' Craft Cncl 1976-77; Jacques Cartier Meml Award for Craftsman of the Year 1960 1963 and 1967 (unique achievement); Liveryman Worshipful Co of Goldsmiths 1978-; FTC, FIPG; *Recreations* cruising on family's narrow boat, badminton, carpentry; *Style—* Christopher Lawrence, Esq; 20 St Vincent's Rd, Westcliff-on-Sea, Essex SS0 7PR (☎ 0702 338443); 172 London Road, Southend-on-Sea, Essex SS1 1PH (☎ 0702 344897)

LAWRENCE, Dr Clifford Maitland; s of Ronald Douglas Lawrence, and Irene Rose Emma, *née* Abell; *b* 29 Nov 1950; *Educ* East Ham GS, Univ of Sheffield Med Sch (MB ChB, MD); *m* 2 April 1977, (Patricia) Anne; 2 s (Thomas b 12 Sept 1981, Christopher b 22 June 1986), 1 da (Joanna b 23 Feb 1984); *Career* dermatologist N Staffs Hosp Centre and Royal Victoria Infirmary Newcastle; author of papers on: skin surgery, psoriasis, dithranol inflammation; MRCP 1978; *Recreations* gardening; *Style—* Dr Clifford Lawrence; Dept of Dermatology, Royal Victoria Infirmary, Newcastle NE1 4LP (☎ 091 232 5131)

LAWRENCE, Clive Wyndham; s of Lt-Col Sir (Percy) Roland Bradford Lawrence, MC, and hp to Btcy of bro, Sir David (Roland Walter) Lawrence; *b* 6 Oct 1939; *Educ* Gordonstoun; *m* 1966, Sophia Annabel Stuart, da of Ian Hervey Stuart Black; 3 s; *Career* late Lt Coldstream Gds; *Style—* Clive Lawrence, Esq; Woodside, Frant, nr Tunbridge Wells, Kent TN3 9HW

LAWRENCE, 5 Baron (UK 1869); Sir David John Downer Lawrence; 5 Bt (UK 1858); s of 4 Baron (d 1968) by his 1 w, Margaret; *b* 4 Sept 1937; *Educ* Bradfield; *Style—* The Rt Hon the Lord Lawrence; c/o Bird & Bird, 2 Gray's Inn Sq, London WC1

LAWRENCE, Sir David Roland Walter; 3 Bt (UK 1906); s of Lt-Col Sir (Percy) Roland Bradford Lawrence, 3 Bt, MC (d 1950); *b* 8 May 1929; *Educ* Radley, RMC; *m* 1955, Audrey (formerly w of 11 Duke of Leeds), da of Brig Desmond Young, CIE, OBE, MC; *Heir* bro, Clive Wyndham Lawrence; *Career* late Capt Coldstream Gds; *Clubs* Cavalry & Guards; *Style—* Sir David Lawrence, Bt; 28 High Town Rd, Maidenhead, Berks

LAWRENCE, Edward George; s of Capt Edward Sear Lawrence (d 1964), of Southgate, London, and Ethel May, *née* Lambert; *b* 26 Feb 1927; *Educ* Edmonton Co GS; *Career* dir Lawrence Bros (Transport) Ltd 1949-77, ret; memb Heraldry Soc 1952-, life govr Royal Soc of St George 1953 (memb Exec Cncl for eight years), silver staff usher Jubilee HM Queen Elizabeth II 1977, wandsman St Paul's Cathedral London 1977-88, usher at wedding of TRH The Prince and Princess of Wales 1981; memb Ctee Middx Fedn of Old Grammarian Socs 1955-64, asst dir of ceremonies of Most Venerable Order of St John 1980; CStJ 1979, KStJ 1989; Freeman City of London 1959; Liveryman: Worshipful Co of Carmen 1960, Worshipful Co of Scriveners 1983; AMInstTA 1947, FFCS 1954, FInstD 1955, FRSA 1963; *Recreations* heraldry, deipnosophism, ceremonial, official and academic dress; *Clubs* City Livery, Wig and Pen, IOD; *Style—* Edward Lawrence, Esq; 77 Prince George Ave, Southgate, London N14

LAWRENCE, Felicity Jane Patricia; da of Prof Clifford Hugh Lawrence, and Helen Maud, *née* Curran; *b* 15 Aug 1958; *Educ* Ursuline Convent Wimbledon, St Anne's Coll Oxford (BA); *Career* ed New Health Magazine 1984-86; Daily Telegraph plc: ed Sunday Magazine 1986-88, ed Weekend Magazine 1988-, head of devpt magazines 1988-; *Publications* Additives: Your Complete Survival Guide (ed); *Style—* Ms Felicity Lawrence; Daily Telegraph plc, Peterborough Court, at South Quay, 181 Marsh Wall E14 9SR (☎ 01 538 5000)

LAWRENCE, Francine; *Educ* Twickenham Art Sch; *Career* won Thames TV Design bursary and travelled Caribbean, holding exhibition of photographs on her return; New English Library, worked with several design gps; asst art dir: Fontana and freelanced for Virago Books, Woman's Journal, art dir and assoc ed Living, ed Country Living 1989- (art dir 1985); Designer of The Year award Periodical Pubns Assoc 1988, Mark Boxer award for Art Editors 1989; chair Br Soc Magazine Eds 1991; *Recreations* photography, cats, gardening, watching The Archers; *Style—* Ms Francine Lawrence; c/o Julie Turner, The National Magazine Co Ltd, 72 Broadwick St, London W1V 2BP (☎ 071 439 5000, fax 071 439 5177, telex 263879)

LAWRENCE, George Alexander Waldemar; s of Sir Alexander Waldemar Lawrence, 4 Bt and hp of bro, Sir John Waldemar Lawrence, 6 Bt, OBE; *b* 22 Sept 1910; *Educ* Eton, Trinity Cambridge; *m* 1949, Olga, da of Peter Schilovsky; 1 s, 2 da; *Style—* George Lawrence, Esq; Brockham End, Bath, Avon

LAWRENCE, Gordon Charles; s of Alfred Charles Lawrence, and Gertrude Emily, *née* Frost; *b* 2 March 1931; *Educ* Isleworth GS; *m* 17 July 1954, Barbara Mary Rees, da of Francis Charles Rees Deacon, MBE (d 1983); 2 s (Simon b 1957, Jonathan b 1963), 1 da (Catriona b 1959); *Career* fin conslt; dir: Schreiber Industs Ltd 1967-70, Helena Rubinstein Ltd 1970-74; National Trust: dir of fin 1977-88, memb Wessex Regnl Ctee 1988-; FCA, FCMA, JDip MA; *Recreations* music, sailing; *Style—* Gordon Lawrence, Esq; The Chantry, Bromham, Wilts (☎ 0380 850294)

LAWRENCE, Sir Guy Kempton; DSO (1943), OBE (1945), DFC (1941); s of Albert Edward Lawrence (d 1951); *b* 5 Nov 1914; *Educ* Marlborough; *m* 1947, Marcia Virginia, da of Prof Harold Clark Powell; 2 s, 1 da; *Career* memb Stock Exchange London 1937-45, chm Findus (UK) Ltd 1967-75; dep chm: Spillers French Hldgs Ltd 1972-75, J Lyons & Co Ltd 1950-75; chm Food and Drink Industs Cncl 1973-77, dir Eagle Aircraft Servs Ltd 1977, chm Eggs Authy 1978-81; kt 1976; *Recreations* Br ski team 1937-38, farming, squash, carpentry; *Clubs* RAF; *Style—* Sir Guy Lawrence, DSO, OBE, DFC; Courtlands, Kier Park, Ascot, Berks (☎ 0990 21074)

LAWRENCE, Prof (Clifford) Hugh; s of Ernest William Lawrence, (d 1956), of London, and Dorothy Estelle, *née* Mundy; *b* 28 Dec 1921; *Educ* Stationers' Co Sch, Lincoln Coll Oxford (BA, MA, D Phil); *m* 11 July 1953, Helen Maud, da of Felix Curran, of Dublin and Yorks; 1 s (Peter), 5 da (Clare, Margaret, Felicity, Katherine, Julia); *Career* 2 Lt RA 1943, Lt 1944, Capt Beds and Herts 1945, Maj 1945-46; Bedford Coll Univ of London: lectr in history 1951-62, dean Faculty of Arts 1975-77, head Dept of History 1980-85; prof of medieval history Univ of London 1970-87 (reader 1962-70); author: St Edmund of Abingdon, a study in Hagiography and History (1960), The English Church and the Papacy in the Middle Ages (1965), Medieval Monasticism, Forms of Religious Life in Western Europe in the Middle Ages (1984), 'The University in Church and State' in History of University of Oxford (vol 1, ed J Catto); memb: Press Cncl 1976-80, governing body Westfield Coll 1982-86; vice chm of govrs Heythrop Coll 1988- (memb governing body 1980-); FRHistS 1960, FSA 1985; *Recreations* reading, painting, sightseeing; *Style—* Prof Hugh Lawrence, FSA; 11 Durham Road, London, SW20 OQH (☎ 081 946 3820)

LAWRENCE, Ivan John; QC (1981), MP (C) Burton 1974-; s of Leslie Lawrence; *b* 24 Dec 1936; *Educ* Brighton Hove and Sussex GS, Ch Ch Oxford (MA); *m* 1966, Gloria Helene; 1 da; *Career* called to the Bar Inner Temple 1962; SE Circuit, rec of the Crown Cts 1987, bencher Inner Temple 1990-; chm: Cons Parly Legal Ctee, Cons Parly Home Affrs Ctee, All-Pty Jt Parly Barristers Gp; memb: Foreign Select Ctee, Cncl of Justice, vice chm Cwlth Parly Assoc (Br branch); *Style—* Ivan Lawrence, Esq, QC, MP; Dunally Cottage, Lower Halliford Green, Shepperton, Middx (☎ 0932 224692); Grove Farm, Drakelow, Burton upon Trent, Staffs (☎ 44360)

LAWRENCE, Jeffrey; s of Alfred Silver (d 1957), and Sylvia, *née* Fishgold; *b* 28 March 1946; *Educ* Carmel Coll, London Business Sch; *m* 8 April 1971, Vivienne Lesley, da of Clifford Arch (d 1987); 2 da (Faith b 1973, Sarah b 1975); *Career* Merrill Lynch: office mangr 1980-84, md corporate fin servs 1984-87, regnl mangr Scandanavia and Netherlands 1987-89; currently md Merrill Lynch Global Asset Mgmnt; memb ctee and Old Age Home; FInstD; *Recreations* golf, race horse owner; *Clubs* RAC; *Style—* Jeffrey Lawrence, Esq; Moor Land House, Moor Lane, Sarratt, Herts; 99 Park St, London W1 (☎ 01 499 7812)

LAWRENCE, John; OBE (1974); s of William Lawrence (d 1988), and Nellie Rhoda, *née* Smith (d 1975); *b* 22 April 1933; *Educ* Wellington GS, Luton GS, Queens' Coll Cambridge (BA, CertEd), Univ of Indiana (MA); *m* 1, (m dis); m 2, 1 Oct 1988, Khaw Yew-Mei, da of Khaw Kai Boh (d 1974); *Career* Nat Serv RAF 1951-53; Br Cncl 1961-: HQ appts 1961-65, regnl rep Sabah 1965-68, rep Zambia 1968-73, rep Sudan 1974-76, rep Malaysia 1976-80, dir South Asia Dept 1980-82, controller Americas Pacific and South Asia Div 1982-86, rep Brazil 1987-90, controller Africa and Middle East Div 1990-; *Recreations* walking; *Style—* John Lawrence, Esq, OBE; British Council, 10 Spring Gardens, London SW1A 2BN (☎ 071 389 4784, fax 071 839 6347, telex 8952201)

LAWRENCE, John Eugene; JP (Essex) 1966; s of Ernest Eugene Oliver Lawrence (d 1970), of Welbeck, Long Rd, Canvey Is, Essex, and Irene Muriel, *née* Kynoch; *b* 29 April 1927; *Educ* Brentwood Sch; *m* 15 Sept 1955, Vera Edna, da of George Henry Bigsby (d 1976), of Wall Rd, Canvey Is, Essex; *Career* cmmnd RASC (T/Capt) 1945-48; chm Canvey Supply Co Ltd 1970-, md Canvey Wharf Co Ltd 1970-; Freeman City of London, Liveryman Worshipful Co of Builders Merchants 1979; FInstB; *Recreations* boating, skiing; *Style—* John Lawrence, Esq, JP; 40 Chapman Rd, Canvey Island, Essex SS8 7QS (☎ 0268 682204, fax 0268 696 724)

LAWRENCE, Air Vice-Marshal John Thornett; CB (1975), CBE (1967, OBE 1961), AFC (1945), AE; s of Tom Lewis Lawrence, JP (d 1970), and Beatrice Mary Sollars (d 1977); *b* 16 April 1920; *Educ* Crypt Sch Gloucester; *m* 2 June 1951, Hilary Jean, da of Lewis Davis Owen (d 1968); 3 s (Patrick b 1952, Christopher b 1955, Andrew b 1959), 1 da (Tessa b 1964); *Career* RAFVR 1938-, WWII Coastal Cmd 235, 202 and 86 Sqdns, dir staff RAF Flying Coll 1949-53, Co No 14 Sqdn 1953-55, so 2ATAF Turkey 1956-58, OC Flying RRFU 1958-61, Gp Capt Ops AFME Aden 1962-64, Co RAF Wittering 1964-66, AOC No 3 Gp Bomber Cmd 1967, Student IDC 1968, dir Orgn and Admin Plans RAF 1969-71, dir Gen Personnel Mgmnt RAF 1971-73, Air Offr Scot and NI 1973-75, ret April 1975; Rolls Royce Ltd 1975-81; vice pres SSAFA Glos 1990-; Order of Leopold II Belgium 1945, Croix De Guerre Belgium 1945; *Recreations* golf, bridge; *Clubs* RAF; *Style—* Air Vice-Marshal John Lawrence, CB, CBE, AFC, AE

LAWRENCE, Sir John Waldemar; 6 Bt (UK 1858), OBE (1945); s of Sir Alexander Waldemar Lawrence, 4 Bt (d 1939), and Anne Elizabeth Le Poer, *née* Wynne (d 1948); suc bro, Sir Henry Eustace Waldemar Lawrence, 5 Bt (d 1967); *b* 27 May 1907; *Educ* Eton, New Coll Oxford (MA); *m* 1, 1947, Jacynth Mary (d 1987), da of Rev F G Ellerton; m 2, 1988, Audrey Viola Woodiwiss, w of late John Woodiwiss; *Heir* s, George Alexander Waldemar Lawrence; *Career* with BBC 1940-42 (Euro intelligence offr and subsequently Euro services organiser), press attaché Moscow 1942-45, chm Centre for Study of Religion and Communism (now Keston Coll) 1969-83, pres Keston Coll 1983-; chm GB-USSR Assoc 1970-85; ed Frontier 1958-75; *Books* A History of Russia (1960), Russians Observed (1969), The Journals of Honoria Lawrence (with Audrey Woodiwiss, 1980), The Hammer & The Cross (1986), Lawrence of Lucknow (1990); *Recreations* walking, argument and reading in ten languages; *Clubs* Athenaeum; *Style—* Sir John Lawrence, Bt, OBE; 24 St Leonards Terrace, London SW3 4QG (☎ 071 730 8033); 1 Naishe's Cottage, Northstoke, Bath BA1 9AT (☎ 0272 326076)

LAWRENCE, John Wilfred; s of Wilfred James Lawrence, and Audrey Constance, *née* Thomas; *b* 15 Sept 1933; *Educ* Salesian Coll Cowley Oxford, Hastings Sch of Art, The Central Sch of Art and Design; *m* 14 Dec 1957, Myra Gillian, da of Dr George Douglas Hutton Bell, CBE; 2 da (Emma b 26 July 1958, Kate b 6 Feb 1960); *Career* book illustrator and lectr illustration: Brighton Poly 1960-68, Camberwell Sch of Art 1960-; external assessor illustration: Bristol Poly 1978-82, Brighton Poly 1982-85, Exeter Coll of Art 1986-89, Duncan of Jordanstone Coll of Art 1986-89, Kingston Poly 1990-, Edinburgh Coll of Art 1991-; work represented in: Ashmolean Museum, V & A, Nat Museum of Wales, collections abroad; memb Art Workers Guild 1972 (master 1990), RE 1987, Soc of Wood Engravers; *Books* The Giant of Grabbist (1968), Pope Leo's Elephant (1969), Rabbit and Pork Rhyming Talk (1975), Tongue Twisters (1976), George His Elephant and Castle (1983), Good Babies Bad Babies (1987); illustrator of more than 90 books; *Clubs* Double Crown; *Style—* John Lawrence, Esq; 22A Castlewood Rd, London N16 6DW (☎ 081 809 3482)

LAWRENCE, Hon Mrs (Louise Eleanor Alice); *née* Canning; yr da of 5 Baron Garvagh; *b* 14 April 1951; *m* 1975, Mark Lawrence; 2 s (Jack Canning b 1982, Rufus Powell b 1986); *Style—* The Hon Mrs Lawrence; Croft House, All Cannings, Devizes, Wiltshire (☎ 038 086 339)

LAWRENCE, Lady; Marjorie Avice; da of Charles Angelo Jones (decd), of Bodney Hall, Norfolk; *m* 1941, Hon Mr Justice (Sir Frederick) Geoffrey Lawrence (d 1967); *Style—* Lady Lawrence; Bridge Farm, Burgess Hill, Sussex

LAWRENCE, (Walter Nicholas) Murray; s of Henry Walter Neville Lawrence (d 1959), and Sarah Schuyler (d 1947), da of Nicholas Murray Butler who was pres of Columbia Univ in NY and USA Republican vice pres candidate 1912 (under Taft); *b* 8 Feb 1935; *Educ* Winchester, Trinity Coll Oxford (BA, MA); *m* 29 April 1961, Sally Louise, da of Col Alleyn Becher O'Dwyer (d 1973); 2 da (Sarah Louise, Catherine Jane); *Career* Treaty Dept C T Bowring & Co Ltd 1957-62, underwriter Harvey Bowring & others 1970-84 (asst underwriter 1962-70); dir: C T Bowring & Co Ltd 1976-84, C T Bowring (Underwriting Agencies Ltd 1973-84); chm: Murray Lawrence Holdings Ltd 1988-, Murray Lawrence Members Agency Ltd 1988-, Murray Lawrence & Partners Ltd 1989- (sr ptnr 1985-89), chm Lloyds 1988, 1989 and 1990 (memb Ctee 1979-82 and 1991, dep chm 1982 and 1984-87); Liveryman Worshipful Co of Insurers; FCII 1979; *Recreations* golf, opera, travelling; *Clubs* Boodle's, MCC, Royal and Ancient GS (St Andrews), Woking Golf, Swinley GS, Royal St George's GS, Rye Golf; *Style—* Murray Lawrence, Esq; Murray Lawrence & Partners, 32 Threadneedle St, London EC2R 8AY (☎ 071 588 7447)

LAWRENCE, Sir (John) Patrick Grosvenor; CBE (1983); s of Ernest Victor Lawrence, and Norah Grosvenor, *née* Hill; *b* 29 March 1928; *Educ* Denstone Coll Staffs; *m* 1954, Anne Patricia, da of Dr Charles Auld; 1 s, 1 da; *Career* RNVR 1945-48; admitted slr 1954; sr ptnr Wragge & Co Birmingham 1982- (ptnr 1959-82); chm: Nat Union of Cons and Unionist Assoc 1986-87, W Midlands Cons Cncl 1979-82 (pres 1988-89), chm Birmingham Cathedral in Need Appeal 1990; memb: Bromsgrove RDC 1967-74 (chm Rent Assessments Panel 1971-), Cncl Shooting Sports Tst Ltd (also slr); vice chm Br Shooting Sports Cncl 1985-; memb Cncl: Denstone Coll 1989-, Univ of Aston 1990-; kt 1988; *Clubs* Carlton, Law Soc's Yacht, Bean (Birmingham); *Style—* Sir Patrick Lawrence, CBE; Bank House, 8 Cherry St, Birmingham B2 5JY (☎ 021 632 4131)

LAWRENCE, Hon Patrick John Tristram; s and h of 4 Baron Trevethin and 2 Baron Oaksey; *b* 29 June 1960; *m* 20 May 1987, Lucinda H, eldest da of Demetri Marchessini, of Wilton Crescent, SW1; 1 s (b 17 May 1990), 1 da (b 1987); *Clubs* New World; *Style—* The Hon Patrick Lawrence; 21 Dewhurst Rd, London W14 (☎ 071 603 2303)

LAWRENCE, Dr Peter Anthony; s of Instr Lt Ivor Douglas Lawrence (RN ret), of Swanage, Dorset, and Joy Frances, *née* Liebert; *b* 23 June 1941; *Educ* Wennington Sch Wetherby Yorks, Univ of Cambridge (MA, PhD); *m* 9 July 1971, (Ruth) Birgitta, da of Prof Ake Haraldson (d 1985), of Uppsala, Sweden; *Career* Cwlth (Harkness) fell 1965-67, Genetics Dept Univ of Cambridge 1967-69, MRC Lab of Molecular Biology Cambridge 1969-; parish cnllr; FRS 1983; *Books* Insect Development (ed, 1976); *Recreations* fungi, gardening, golf, theatre, trees; *Style—* Dr Peter Lawrence, FRS; 9 Temple End, Gt Wilbraham, Cambridge CB1 5JF (☎ 0223 880505); MRC Laboratory Molecular Biology, Hills Rd, Cambridge CB2 2QH (☎ 0223 248011, fax 0223 213556, telex 81532)

LAWRENCE, Professor Raymond John; s of Herbert Lawrence (d 1959), of Ruislip, and Nellie Grace, *née* Martin (d 1982); *b* 3 July 1925; *Educ* St Paul's Sch, Pembroke Coll Cambridge (BA, MA), Univ of Berkeley Calif; *m* 27 Dec 1952, Antonia Victorine, da of Coenraad Jan Graadt Van Roggen (d 1934), of Rotterdam, Holland; 1 da (Caroline Mary b 1959), 1 adopted s (Steven Martin b 1963); *Career* WWII Lt Intelligence Corps, served: Philippines, India, Malaya, Singapore, W Germany; mgmnt trainee Unilever Ltd 1950-52, product mangr (Summer County Margarine) Van der Berghs Ltd London 1953-56, PA to md Savonneries Lever Paris 1956-59, advertising mangr Unilever Aust Pty Ltd 1959-62; prof of mktg (first Univ chair in mktg) Univ of Lancaster 1965-88, prof emeritus 1988; FInstM 1988; *Books* Modern Marketing Management (1971); *Recreations* tennis, golf, chess, bridge; *Style—* Prof Raymond Lawrence; Toll Bar Cottage, 41 Toll Bar Crescent, Lancaster LA1 4NR (☎ 0524 65059); Department of Marketing, University of Lancaster, Bailrigg, Lancaster LA1 4YX (☎ 0524 65201)

LAWRENCE, Ruth Isabel; da of Frederick Lawrence, of London, and Clare, *née* Rosenblatt; *b* 13 May 1957; *Educ* E Barnet GS, Clare Coll Cambridge Univ (MA); *Career* managing ed Sweet and Maxwell Ltd 1980-85, head of publishing Law Soc of Eng and Wales 1986- (press offr 1985-86); memb: N Barnes Residents Assoc, Hon Soc of Middle Temple; Hon MA Univ of Cambridge; *Recreations* flying light aircraft, classical guitar, walking; *Style—* Ms Ruth Lawrence; Barnes, London SW13; The Law Society, 113 Chancery Lane, London W12A 1PL (☎ 071 242 1222)

LAWRENCE, Sandra Elizabeth; da of Brig Roderick Lawrence, OBE (d 1976), and Gillian Winifred, *née* Bishop; *b* 2 Jan 1945; *Educ* St Mary's Sch Wantage, St Martin's Sch of Art London; *Career* painter; exhibited Royal Acad, Francis Kyle, Fischer Fine Art, Pastel Soc, Royal Inst of Oil Painters, Inst of Fine Arts Glasgow, New York, Caracas, Palm Beach; designed Overlord Embroidery D-Day Museum Portsmouth 1968-72; ROI 1980; *Recreations* travel, music, reading; *Clubs* Chelsea Arts; *Style—* Ms Sandra Lawrence; 2B Avenue Studios, Sydney Close, London SW3 6HW (☎ 071 589 8460)

LAWRENCE, Stephen Richard; s of Richard Lawrence, of Thrussington, Leicestershire, and Joyce, *née* Howarth; *b* 6 Sept 1951; *Educ* Longslade Coll Leics; *m* 9 April 1983, Linda Corina, *née* Hillier; *Career* pilot offr cadet RAF 1971; Civil Service 1969-71, advtg mangr Loughborough Monitor 1971-72, reporter and features writer Leicester Mercury 1972-76, ed Leicester Shopwindow 1976-78, chief sub ed Gulf Mirror Bahrain 1978-79, sr ed Daily Nation Nairobi Kenya 1979-82, fndr Media Management Kenya 1983-86 and London 1986-87, ptnr Raitt Orr & Associates Public Relations 1988-90, external relations advsr BP Chemicals 1990-; MIPR 1986; *Books* The Complete Guide To Amboseli National Park (1983), The Total Guide To Nairobi National Park (1986), The Total Guide To Amboseli National Park (1986); *Recreations* ocean sailing, sub aqua, natural history; *Clubs* Royal Yachting Assoc (qualified skipper), BP Yacht, Pemba Channel Fishing (Kenya), British Sub Aqua, Kenya Soc; *Style—* Stephen Lawrence, Esq; BP Chemicals, 76 Buckingham Palace Road, London SW1W 0SU (☎ 071 581 6804, fax 071 581 6475)

LAWRENCE, His Hon Judge Timothy; s of Alfred Whiteman Lawrence, MBE, and Phyllis Gertrude, *née* Lloyd-Jones; *b* 29 April 1942; *Educ* Bedford Sch; *Career* Slrs Dept New Scotland Yard 1967-70, ptnr Claude Hornby and Cox 1970-86 (sr ptnr 1976), rec 1983, circuit judge 1986-; memb: criminal law ctee Law Soc 1978-86, No 13 Area Legal Aid Ctee 1983-86, Judicial Studies Bd 1984-87 (criminal ctee until 1988); chm No 14 Area Duty Slr Ctee 1984-86; pres: London Criminal Cts Slrs Assoc 1984-86 (sec 1974-84), Industrial Tribunals for England and Wales 1991-; *Clubs* Hurlingham; *Style—* His Honour Judge Lawrence; 8 Slaidburn Street, London SW10 0JP

LAWRENCE, Timothy Gordon Roland (Tim); s of Lionel Arthur Lawrence (d 1975), and Patricia Mary Young; *b* 22 Aug 1936; *Educ* Wimbledon Coll, St George's Coll Weybridge; *m* 19 Sept 1964, (Mabyn) Ann, da of Robert Hugh Shuttleworth Petherbridge; 1 s (Stephen Robert Anthony b 3 April 1966), 2 da (Katherine Ann b 15

July 1977, Joanna Frances b 22 Feb 1977); *Career* Nat Serv 1958-60 (cmmnd Royal Irish Fusiliers); articled clerk Wilson De Zouche & Mackenzie (later Wilson Davis & Co) 1953-58, CA 1958 (won Gold medal of ICAEW for first place in final examination); Cooper Brothers & Co (now Coopers & Lybrand Deloitte): joined 1960-, ptnr 1967-, memb Governing Bd 1975-90, vice chm 1988-90; chm London Soc of Chartered Accountants 1984-85; FCA; *Recreations* bridge, golf; *Clubs* MCC, Stoke Poges Golf, Austenwood Bridge; *Style*— Tim Lawrence, Esq; Whitethorn, Collinswood Rd, Farnham Common, Slough, Berkshire SL2 3LH (☎ 0753 645377); Coopers & Lybrand Deloitte, Plumtree Court, London EC4A 4HT (☎ 071 583 5000, fax 071 822 4863)

LAWRENCE, Vernon John; s of Arthur Douglas Lawrence, of Berlin, W Germany, and Lilian Cecily, *née* Collings (d 1956); *b* 30 April 1940; *Educ* Ingleside Coll, Dulwich Coll, Kelham Coll; *m* 10 Sept 1960, Jennifer Mary, da of Maj Michael Henry Cecil Drewe, MBE, JP (d 1986), of Sidmouth, Devon; 2 s (James William b 1964, Jeremy Robert b 1966), 1 da (Sarah Katherine b 1961); *Career* prodr BBC Radio 1963 (studio mangr 1958), prodr BBC TV 1967 (dir 1964); programmes incl: Top of the Pops, Lulu, Omnibus, Full House, Cilla; controller entertainment Yorks TV 1985 (asst head 1974); progs incl: The Darling Buds of May, Let's Face the Music, Rising Damp, Song by Song, Only When I Laugh, Duty Free, The New Statesman, Bit of a Do, Home to Roost, Haggard, Beecham, James Galway, Stay Lucky; memb: BAFTA 1985, RTS; *Recreations* walking, fishing, gardening, art; *Style*— Vernon Lawrence, Esq; Yorkshire Television, Television Centre, Leeds LS3 1JS (☎ 0532 438283/071 242 1666, fax 4058062)

LAWRENCE, Sir William Fettiplace; 5 Bt (UK 1867), of Ealing Park, Middx; s of Sir William Lawrence, 4 Bt (d 1986); *b* 23 Aug 1954; *Educ* King Edward VI Sch Stratford-upon-Avon; *Heir* cousin, Peter Stafford Hayden Lawrence; *Career* asst fin accountant: W B Bumpers Ltd, Rockwell Int 1980-81; gen mangr Newdawn & Sun Ltd 1981-, proprietor William Lawrence Wines; chm Stratford-on-Avon Dist Cncl 190-91 (memb 1982-90); memb: S Warwickshire Health Authy 1984-, W Midlands Arts 1984-; pres Stratford and Dist MENCAP 1990, dir English Tourist Bd 1990, tstee Action Unlimited Tst; *Recreations* horse racing, wine; *Style*— Sir William Lawrence, Bt; The Knoll, Walcote, nr Alcester, Warks B49 6LZ (☎ 0789 488303)

LAWRENCE-JONES, Sir Christopher; 6 Bt (UK 1831); s of Cdr Bertram Edward Jones, RN (d 1958); suc Sir Lawrence Evelyn Jones, 5 Bt, MC, TD (d 1969); *b* 19 Jan 1940; *Educ* Sherborne, Gonville and Caius Coll Cambridge, St Thomas's Hosp (MA, MB BChir, DIH, FFOM); *m* 1967, Gail, da of C A Pittar; 2 s; *Heir* s, Mark Christopher Lawrence-Jones b 28 Dec 1968; *Career* med advsr to various organisations 1967-; ICI Dyestuffs Div 1967-70, BP Co Ltd 1970-73, Health and Safety Exec 1973-75, ICI Paints Div 1975-79, centl med advsr ICI 1979-85, chief med offr ICI Gp HQ Millbank SW1 1985-, chm Medichem 1986-; memb bd Faculty of Occupational Med RCP 1988-, pres Section of Occupational Med Royal Soc of Med 1990; *Recreations* cruising under sail (Yacht 'Seago'); *Clubs* Royal Cruising; *Style*— Sir Christopher Lawrence-Jones, Bt; c/o Coutts & Co, 440 Strand, London, WC24 0QS

LAWRENCE-MILLS, Rowena Margaret; da of Edward Charles Leader (d 1982), and Blanche Linda, *née* Calcott (d 1979); *b* 14 July 1931; *Educ* North London Collegiate Sch for Girls, UCL (BSc); *m* 3 Sept 1955, John, s of Herbert Harold (d 1964); 1 s (Charles Sebastian b 1966), 1 da (Alexandra Louise b 1968); *Career* chm and chief exec Rowena Mills Assocs Ltd, former economist Metal Box Co Ltd, chm packaging working pty NEDO 1988-90, memb: Ctee of Investigation MAFF 1988-, financial Reporting Cncl 1990-; cncllr CBI London Region 1985-88; Freeman City of London, Liveryman Worshipful Co of Plumbers, Fellow Inst of Packaging; *Recreations* work, riding, music, theatre, reading, writing; *Clubs* Naval and Military; *Style*— Mrs Rowena Lawrence-Mills; Peart Hall, Spaxton, Bridgwater, Somerset TA5 1DA (☎ 027 867 343, fax 027 867 209); 50 Pembroke Rd, Kensington, London W8 6NX; Rowena Mills Associates Ltd, PO Box 594, London W8 7DE (☎ 071 937 4035, fax 071 603 7461)

LAWRENSON, Prof Peter John; s of John Lawrenson (d 1949), of Prescot, and Emily, *née* Houghton (d 1979); *b* 12 March 1933; *Educ* Prescot GS, Univ of Manchester (BSc, MSc, DSc); *m* 5 April 1958, Shirley Hannah, da of Albert Edward Foster, of Macclesfield; 1 s (Mark b 1958), 3 da (Ruth b 1960, Rachel b 1963, Isobel b 1965); *Career* res engr GEC 1956-61; Univ of Leeds: lectr 1961, reader 1965, prof 1966, head Dept of Electrical and Electronic Engrg 1974-84, chm Faculty of Sci and Applied Sci 1978-80, chm Faculty of Engrg 1980-81; chm and chief exec Switched Reluctance Drives Ltd 1980-; dir: Dale Electric International plc 1988-, Allenwest Ltd 1988-; author of over 120 papers for various sci jls; awards: Inst Premium IEE 1981, Alfred Ewing Gold Medal Royal Soc and Inst of Civil Engrs 1983, Esso Energy Gold Medal Royal Soc 1985, Faraday Medal IEE 1990; dep pres IEE 1990-; memb Cncl Univ of Buckingham; FIEE 1974, FIEEE 1975, FEng 1980, FRS 1982; *Books* Analysis and Computation of Electric & Magnetic Fields (with K J Binns, 1963 and 1973), Per Unit Systems (with M R Harris & J M Stephenson, 1970); *Recreations* chess, bridge, squash, walking; *Style*— Prof Peter Lawrenson, FRS; Switched Reluctance Drives Ltd, Springfield House, Hyde Terrace, Leeds LS2 9LN; University of Leeds, Leeds LS2 9JT (☎ 0532 332014, 0532 443844, fax 0532 423179, telex 0532 556578)

LAWREY, Keith; JP (Inner London); s of Capt George William Bishop Lawrey, of Bognor Regis, W Sussex, and Edna Muriel, *née* Gass; *b* 21 Aug 1940; *Educ* Colfe's Sch, Birkbeck Coll London (LLB, MScEcon); *m* 20 Dec 1969, (Helen) Jane, da of James Edward Marriott, MBE, and Betty Evelyn, *née* Church; 2 s (David Keith b 1972, Andrew Charles Keith b 1976), 2 da (Sarah Jane b 1970, Katherine Jane b 1979); *Career* called to the Bar Gray's Inn 1972; educn offr Plastics and Rubber Inst 1960-68, lectr and sr lectr Bucks Coll of Higher Educn 1968-74, head Dept Business Studies Mid-Kent Coll of Higher and Further Educn 1974-78, sec gen The Library Assoc 1978-84, dean of Faculty of Business and Mgmnt Harrow Coll of Higher Educn 1984-90, sec and registrar RCVS 1990-; hon treas Coll of Preceptors 1987- (also examiner), lay preacher Methodist church; Freeman City of London, Liveryman Worshipful Co of Chartered Secretaries and Administrators; FCIS 1967, FCollP 1980; *Recreations* preaching, sailing, swimming, theatre, gardening; *Clubs* Dell Quay Sailing, Old Colfeians' Assoc; *Style*— Keith Lawrey, Esq, JP; Royal College of Vetinary Surgeons, 32 Belgrave Square, London SW1X 8QP (☎ 071 235 4971)

LAWS, Brian; s of John Robert Laws, of Washington, Tyne & Wear, and Ellen, *née* McCormick (d 1988); *b* 14 Oct 1961; *Educ* 29 May 1982, Margaret Sinclair, da of George Albert Evans; 1 s (Jamie b 11 June 1984), 1 da (Danielle Sinclair b 1 March 1983); *Career* professional footballer; Burnley 1976-83 (debut 1979 v Watford), Huddersfield Town 1983-85, Middlesbrough 1985-88, Nottingham Forest 1988-; in England B squad v Algeria 1990, represented Barclays League England v Ireland 1990; winner's medals: Littlewoods Cup 1989 and 1990, Simod Cup 1989: qualified football coach 1989; proprietor Show-Offs Marketing Ltd; *Recreations* golf; *Style*— Brian Laws, Esq; Nottingham Forest FC, City Ground, Nottingham (☎ 0602 405111, fax 0602 405101)

LAWS, Courtney Alexander Henriques; OBE (1987); s of Ezekiel Laws (d 1986), and Agatha, *née* Williams (d 1983); *b* 16 June 1934; *Educ* Lincoln Coll, Nat Coll Youth Workers Leicester, Cranfield Coll Bedford; *m* 7 Sept 1955, Wilhel (Rubie), da of Nikana Brown (d 1962); 1 s (Clive Anthony b 3 Jan 1959), 2 da (Carole Alexandra b 14 March 1964, Claudette Joanna b 13 Oct 1967); *Career* dir Brixton Neighbourhood Community Assoc Ltd 1971-; memb: St John's Inter Racial Club 1958, W Indian Standing Conf 1959, NCII 1960; involved with Campaign Against Racial Discrimination 1960, memb Works Ctee Peak Freans Biscuit Co 1960-69, shop steward TAWU 1960-70; memb: Central Ctee Br Caribbean Assoc 1960, Assoc Jamaicans 1965, West Indians' Sr Citizens Assoc 1973, Consultative Ctee ILEA 1975, Cmmn Racial Equality 1977-80, Consortium Ethnic Minorities 1978, S Eastern Gas Consumer Cncl 1980; non-exec dir Voice Communications Group Ltd; memb: Lambeth Cncl for Community Rels 1964, Geneva and Somerleyton Community Assoc 1966; govr Brixton Coll, memb Consultative Cncl City and East London Coll 1975; Order of Distinction Jamaica 1978, Prime Minister of Jamaica medal of Appreciation 1987; *Recreations* reading, music; *Clubs* Brixton United Cricket, Oasis Sports and Social, Brixton Domino; *Style*— Courtney A Laws, Esq, OBE; 164 Croxted Rd, W Dulwich, London SE21 8NW; 71 Atlantic Rd, London SW9 8PU (☎ 01 274 0011)

LAWS, Frederick Geoffrey; s of Frederick Roberts Laws (d 1987), and Annette Kirby (d 1975); *b* 1 Aug 1928; *Educ* Arnold Sch Blackpool, London Univ (LLB); *m* 8 June 1955, Beryl Holt; 2 da (Amanda (Mrs Leslie) b 16 Nov 1957, Diana (Mrs Howers) b 30 Sept 1961); *Career* Nat Serv RA 1947-49; admitted slr 1952; asst slr: Blackpool Corpn 1952-54, Bournemouth Corpn 1955-59, Southend on Sea Corpn 1959-71, Town Clerk Southend on Sea 1971-84; local ombudsman; capt Thorpe Hall Golf Club 1983 (chm 1984-90); Freedom Borough of Southend on Sea 1985; memb Law Soc; *Recreations* golf; *Clubs* Thorpe Hall Golf, Anthenaeum; *Style*— Frederick Laws, Esq; 270 Maplin Way North, Southend-on-Sea, Essex (☎ 0702 587 459), Commission for Local Administration in England, The Oaks, Westwood Business Park, Westwood Way, Coventry CV4 8JB (☎ 0203 695 999)

LAWS, Iain McOlvin; TD (1981); s of Capt Edmund Francis Laws (d 1976), of Banchory, Scotland, and Marion, *née* Cruickshank; *b* 23 Feb 1938; *Educ* Robert Gordon's Coll Aberdeen, Univ of St Andrews (BDS), Univ of Aberdeen (MB ChB); *m* 21 Sept 1963, (Mary) Bridget, da of Thomas Hugh Maguire (d 1952), of Manor Hamilton, Eire; 2 s (Stephen b 3 April 1969, Gavin b 16 May 1973), 2 da (Siobhan b 3 Aug 1964, Diane b 14 Feb 1967); *Career* TA 1969-; sr house offr Nottingham Gen Hosp 1962-63, registrar Mount Vernon Hosp 1963-65, lectr and sr registrar Kings Coll Hosp 1970-73; conslt in oral and maxillo-facial surgery: Whittington and Royal Free Hosps 1973-86, Hampstead Health Authy 1986-; FDS, FRCS(Eng); *Recreations* fishing; *Style*— Iain Laws, Esq, TD; 53 Wimpole St, London W1M 7DF (☎ 071 935 6809)

LAWS, Dr Richard Maitland; CBE (1983); s of Percy Malcom Laws (d 1962), and Florence May Laws, MBE, *née* Heslop (d 1983); *b* 23 April 1926; *Educ* Dame Allan's Sch Newcastle upon Tyne, St Catharine's Coll Cambridge (open scholarship, res scholarship, MA, PhD); *m* Maureen Isobel Winifred, da of Late George Leonard Holmes; 3 s (Richard Anthony, Christopher Peter, Andrew David); *Career* biologist Falkland Is Dependencies Survey 1947-53, biologist and whaling inspr on factory ship Balaena in Antarctic 1953-54, PSO Nat Inst of Oceanography 1954-61; dir: Nuffield Unit of Tropical Animal Ecology Uganda and Univ of Cambridge 1961-67, Tsavo Res Project Kenya 1967-68; Smuts Meml fellowship Univ of Cambridge 1968-69, Leverhulme fellowship 1969, head Life Sciences Div Br Antarctic Survey 1969-73; dir: Br Antarctic Survey 1973-87, NERC Sea Mammal Res Unit 1977-87, master St Edmund's Coll Cambridge 1985-; author of numerous res pubns in scientific journals, books and reviews; Bruce Meml medal for Antarctic work RSE 1954, scientific medal Zoological Soc of London 1966, polar medal 1976, hon fellowship St Catharine's Coll Cambridge 1982; SCAR: UK memb working Gp on Biology 1972-, memb Gp of Specialists on Seals 1972- (convenor 1972-88), chm Working Gp on Biology 1980-86, pres BIOMASS Exec 1990- (memb 1976-); FZS 1960 memb Cnl 1982-84, vice pres 1983, sec 1984-87; FIBiol 1973 (vice pres 1983), FRS 1980 (chm Interdisiciplinary Scientific Ctee on Antarctic Res 1988); *Books* Elephants and their Habitats (with I S C Parker and R C B Johnstone, 1975), Research in the Antarctic (jt ed with V E Fuchs, 1977), Antarctic Ecology (ed 1984), Antarctic Nutrient Cycles and Food Webs (jt ed with W R Siegfried and P R Condy, 1985), Antarctica: the Last Frontier (1989), Life at Low Temperatures (jt ed with Franks, 1990); *Style*— Dr Richard Laws, CBE, FRS; 3 The Footpath, Coton, Cambridge CB3 7PX (☎ 0954 210567); The Master, St Edmund's College, Cambridge CB3 0BN (☎ 0223 350398)

LAWSON, Anthony Raymond; s of Alexander Lawson (d 1965), of Redcroft, Whitefield, Manchester, and Jeanne Alexandra Lawson (d 1968); *b* 26 Aug 1931; *Educ* Repton; *m* 1, 1955, Anne, da of Dr Walter Martin, MC, of Bury, Lancs; 1 s, 1 da; m 2, 1980, Patricia Jane, da of Dr F Lascelles, MC, of Formby, Lancs; *Career* chm and chief exec Hollas Gp plc; memb: Lloyd's, IOD; FBIM; *Recreations* tennis; *Style*— Anthony Lawson, Esq; Balgownie, Chelford Rd, Knutsford, Cheshire WA16 8QP (☎ 0565 3075); Hollas Group plc, 1 Adams Court, Adams Hill, Knutsford, Cheshire WA16 6BA (☎ 0565 50305, fax 0565 55687)

LAWSON, Hon Mrs (Carole); *née* Samuel; da of Baron Samuel of Wych Cross (Life Peer) *qv*; *b* 1942; *m* 1963, Geoffrey Clive Henry Lawson (a slr of Supreme Ct 1963-); 2 s; *Style*— The Hon Mrs Lawson; Stilemans, Brighton Rd, Munstead, Godalming, Surrey (☎ 048 68 28782)

LAWSON, Lady Caroline; *née* Lowther; da of 7 Earl of Lonsdale; *b* 11 March 1959; *m* 1, 1978 (m dis), Guy Forrester; m 2 (m dis), Steven Hunt; 1 s (George b 1982); m 3, 18 Sept 1987, Charles John Patrick Lawson, s of Sir John Charles Arthur Digby Lawson, 3 Bt, DSO, MC; 1 da (Tess b 1988); *Style*— The Lady Caroline Lawson; Heckwood, Sampford Spiney, Yelverton, Devon PL20 6L9

LAWSON, Charles John Patrick; s and h of Sir John Charles Arthur Digby Lawson, 3 Bt, DSO, MC; *b* 19 May 1959; *Educ* Harrow, Univ of Leeds, RAC, Cirencester; *m* 18 Sept 1987, Lady Caroline Lowther, da of 7 Earl of Lonsdale; 1 da (Tessa b 30 Oct 1988); *Style*— Charles Lawson, Esq; 46 High Street, Helmsley, North Yorkshire

LAWSON, Sir Christopher Donald; *b* 1922; *Educ* Magdalen Coll Sch Oxford; *m* 1945, Marjorie Patricia, *née* Bristow; 2 s, 1 da; *Career* serv RAF 1941-50 Sqdn Ldr; joined Thomas Hedley Ltd (sales mangr, mktg, personnel), retail sales mangr Cooper McDougal & Co, md Mars Foods, dir Mars Ltd, pres Mars Snack Master; chm: Spearhead Ltd, Goodblue Ltd; dir Cons Central Office 1981-; dir: Grant Maintained Schools Ltd, Choice in Educations Ltd; *Clubs* RAF, MCC, Gloucester RFC, Lillybrook, Doublegate (USA), Thurlstone Golf; *Style*— Sir Christopher Lawson; Church Cottage, Great Witcombe, Glos GL3 4TT (☎ 0452 862591); Luggers, S Milton, Devon

LAWSON, Prof David Hamilton; s of David Lawson (d 1956), of East Kilbride, and Margaret Harvey, *née* White (d 1982); *b* 27 May 1939; *Educ* HS of Glasgow, Univ of Glasgow (MB ChB, MD); *m* 7 Sept 1963, Alison, da of William Diamond (d 1974), of Sale; 3 s (Derek b 1965, Iain b 1967, Keith b 1970); *Career* visiting conslt Univ Med Center Boston Mass 1972-; conslt physician: Royal Infirmary Glasgow 1973-, Dental Hosp Glasgow 1984-; visiting prof Sch of Pharmacy Univ of Strathclyde 1976-; advsr on adverse drug reactions WHO Geneva 1984-, external assessor Scientific Branch Civil Serv Cmmn 1986-; Dept of Health London: chm Ctee on Review of Med 1987- (memb 1979-), memb Ctee on Safety of Med 1987-; memb: Br Pharmacological Soc 1976, Assoc Physicians GB & Ireland 1979, Scottish Soc Physicians 1975; FRCPE, FRCP Glas, FFPM, fell American Coll of Clinical Pharmacology; *Books* Clinical

Pharmacy & Hospital Drug Management (with R M E Richards, 1982), Current Medicine-2 (1990); *Recreations* hill-walking, photography, bird-watching; *Clubs* Royal Commonwealth Soc, London; *Style—* Prof David Lawson; 43 Drumlin Drive, Milngavie, Glasgow G62 6NF (☎ 041 956 2962); Wards 4 and 5, Royal Infirmary, Glasgow G4 0SF (☎ 041 552 2335 ext 4291, fax 041 552 8933)

LAWSON, Denis Stamper; s of Lawrence Lawson (d 1981), of Crieff Perthshire Scotland and Phyllis Lawson; *b* 27 Sept 1947; *Educ* Crieff Secdy Sch, Morrisons Acad Crieff, RSAMD; *m* 1 s (Jamie Fletcher b 3 June 1979); *Career* actor; theatre roles incl: Pal Joey at Albery Theatre 1980-81, Mr Cinders at Fortune Theatre 1983, Lend Me A Tenor at Globe Theatre 1987, Mosca in Volpone at Almeida Theatre 1990; tv work incl: Dead Head (by Howard Brenton) BBC, That Uncertain Feeling (by Kingsley Amis) BBC, Love After Lunch Screen 2 BBC, One Way Out Screen 1 BBC; films incl: Providence 1977, Local Hero 1983; awards: Drama magazine award for Most Promising Actor (for Pal Joey) 1981, SWET award for Best Actor in a Musical (Mr Cinders) 1983; *Recreations* Sheila Gish, music; *Style—* Denis Lawson, Esq; James Sharkey Assoc, 15 Golden Square, London W1R 3AG (☎ 071 434 3801)

LAWSON, Dominic Ralph Campden; s of Rt Hon Nigel Lawson, MP, *qv*, and Vanessa Mary Addison, *née* Salmon (d 1985); *b* 17 Dec 1956; *Educ* Westminster, ChCh Oxford; *m* 11 Sept 1982, Jane Fiona, da of David Christopher Wastell Whytehead, of The Cottage, Brightlands, Gallery Rd, W Dulwich, London SE21 7AB; *Career* res The World Tonight Radio 4 1979-81; The Financial Times: joined staff 1981, energy corr 1983-86, Lex 1986-87; ed The Spectator 1990- (dep ed 1987-90), columnist for The Sunday Correspondent 1990; *Books* Korchnoi - Kasparov: The London Contest (with Raymond Keene, 1983), Britain in the Eighties (contrib, 1989); *Recreations* chess, cricket; *Clubs* Academy, MCC; *Style—* Dominic Lawson, Esq; 16 Bisham Gardens, Highgate Village, London N6 6DD; The Spectator, 56 Doughty St, London WC1 (☎ 071 405 1706, fax 071 242 0603, telex 27124)

LAWSON, Eileen Day; da of Maurice Day (d 1952), of 71 Harley House, London NW1, and Henrietta, *née* Goldstein (d 1975); *b* 12 Dec 1919; *Educ* South Hampstead HS, Lycee de Versailles France, Sorbonne Paris; *m* 21 June 1949, Ernest Lawson, s of Jack Lawson; 1 s (Maurice Day b 26 March 1952), 2 da (Neroli Louise Day b 8 May 1960, Virginia Ann Day (twin)); *Career* chm Fuerst Day Lawson Gp 1956-86; *Style—* Mrs Ernest Lawson; 1 Eaton Mansions, Cliveden Place, London SW1 (☎ 071 730 5788, fax 071 488 9927, telex 887871)

LAWSON, Elizabeth Ann; QC (1989); da of Alexander Edward Lawson, of Croydon, Surrey, and Helen Jane, *née* Currie (d 1989); *b* 29 April 1947; *Educ* Croydon HS for Girls, Univ of Nottingham (LLB); *Career* called to The Bar 1969; chaired: inquiries into child abuse London Borough of Lewisham 1985, Islington Area Child Protection Ctee 1989; sec St Paul's Bayswater United Reformed Church; *Recreations* knitting, cake decoration; *Style—* Miss Elizabeth Lawson, QC; Cloisters, Temple, London EC4 (☎ 071 583 0303, fax 071 583 2254)

LAWSON, Hon Hugh John Frederick; s of 4 Baron Burnham, CB, DSO, MC (d 1963), and hp of bro, 5 Baron Burnham; *b* 1931; *Educ* Eton, Balliol Coll Oxford; *m* 1955, Hilary, da of Alan Hunter, of Huntingtowerfield House, Almondbank, Perthshire; 1 s, 2 da; *Career* Lt Scots Gds (SR) 1952; *Style—* The Hon Hugh Lawson; Woodlands Farm, Beaconsfield, Bucks

LAWSON, Hon Mrs (Irene); da of 1 Baron Lawson (d 1965); *b* 1909; *m* 1935, Charles Frederick Campbell Lawson (d 1985); 3 da; *Style—* The Hon Mrs Lawson; Dourene, Park Rd North, Chester-le-Street, Co Durham

LAWSON, John Arthur; DFC; s of Charles Lawson (d 1975), of Bognor Regis, Sussex, and May, *née* Holland (d 1978); *b* 19 Oct 1920; *Educ* Dunstable GS; *m* 3 May 1947, Olive Mary, da of Charles Albert Hulford (d 1977); *Career* Flt Lt RAF (bomber cmd) 1941-46; accountant Electricity Supply 1946-52, accountant (reorganisation) United Yeast Co 1952-55, supervising consultant (mgmnt) Associated Industrial Consultants (INBUCON) 1955-66; dir: Carrington & Dewhurst plc 1966-70, Reed International Ltd 1970-79, Tavener Rutledge plc 1979-86, Butler & Tanner Ltd 1981-90; exec chm Lawrence-Allen Ltd 1986-90, non-exec dir Rubery Owen (Hldgs) Ltd 1984-91; now ret; Assoc Inst Mgmnt Accountants, FID; *Recreations* golf, swimming; *Style—* John A Lawson, Esq, DFC; Manor Stables Cottage, Great Somerford, Chippenham, Wilts SN15 5EH

LAWSON, Col Sir John Charles Arthur Digby; 3 Bt (UK 1900), of Weetwood Grange, Headingley-cum-Burley, W Yorks, DSO (1943), MC (1940); s of Maj Sir Digby Lawson, 2 Bt, TD, JP (d 1959), and Iris Mary Fitzgerald (d 1941); *b* 24 Oct 1912; *Educ* Stowe, RMC, Staff Coll Camberley; *m* 1, 17 March 1945 (m dis 1950), Rose (d 1972), da of David Cecil Bingham (d 1914); m 2, 22 Dec 1954, Tresilla Anne Eleanor (d 1985), da of late Maj Eric Buller Leyborne Popham, MC, of Downes, Crediton; 1 s; *Heir* s Charles John Patrick Lawson, *qv*; *Career* 2 Lt 11 Hussars (PAO) 1933, served Palestine 1936 (despatches), seconded Trans/Jordan Frontier Force 1939-40, Western Desert 1940-43 (wounded despatches 3), Temp Lt-Col 1943 as Gen Montgomery apptd advsr on armoured reconaissance to Gen Patton N Africa 1943 (wounded), US Marine Staff Course Quantico Virginia 1944-, Personal Liaison Offr to Gen Montgomery at 21 Army GP N France 1944-, cmdg Inns of Court regt 1944-46, ret 1947, Col 11 Hussars (PAO) 1965-69, Col R Hussars 1969-72; chm Fairbairn Lawson Ltd and subsidiary cos 1968-79, memb Cncl Univ of Leeds 1972-79; US Legion of Merit 1943; *Recreations* golf, gardening, country pursuits; *Clubs* Cavalry and Guards', MCC; *Style—* Col Sir John Lawson, Bt, DSO, MC; Hillmore Cottage, Bishops Hull Rd, Taunton, Somerset TA1 5ER (☎ 0823 321456)

LAWSON, Mark Gerard; s of Francis Lawson, of Harpenden, Herts, and Teresa, *née* Kane; *b* 11 April 1962; *Educ* St Columba's Coll St Albans Herts, UCL (BA); *m* 1990, Sarah Gillian Jane, da of Alan John Gilbert Bull; *Career* journalist; jr reporter and TV critic The Universe 1984-85, TV previewer The Sunday Times 1985-86, asst arts ed and TV critic The Independent 1986-89 (Parly sketchwriter 1987-88) chief feature writer The Independent Magazine 1988, TV critic The Independent on Sunday 1990; freelance contrib to numerous pubns 1984- incl: The Times, Time Out, The Listener, Mirabella; writer and presenter TV documentary Byline: Vote For Ron (BBC) 1990; *Awards* British Press award 1987, British Press Arts Journalism awards 1989 and 1990, TV-AM Critic of the Year 1989, TV-AM Broadcast Journalist of the Year 1990; *Books* contrib: House of Cards: A Selection of Modern Political Humour (1988), Fine Glances: an anthology of cricket writing (1990); *Recreations* theatre, watching cricket, red wine, reading; *Style—* Mark Lawson, Esq; The Independent/The Independent on Sunday, Newspaper Publishing plc, 40 City Rd, London EC1 1OA (☎ 071 756 1551, fax 071 962 0016)

LAWSON, Maurice Day; s of Ernest Lawson, of Eaton Mansions, St John's Wood, and Eileen, *née* Day; *b* 26 March 1952; *Educ* Harrow, Exeter Coll Oxford (MA), Harvard Business Sch; *m* 14 Sept 1985, Charlotte Mary Clare, da of Sir William Godfrey Agnew, KCVO, of Pinehurst, South Ascot, Berks; 2 da (Eloise Ruth b 1987, Alicia Dorothie Day b 1989); *Career* commodity trader; dir and chief exec: Fuerst Day Lawson Ltd, Fuerst Day Lawson Holdings Ltd, Union Merchants Overseas Ltd, Fuerst Day Lawson Citrus Ltd, Fuerst Schneider Chemicals Ltd, R Verney & Co Ltd; *Recreations* tennis, squash, sailing; *Clubs* RAC, Royal Motor Yacht, Sandbanks; *Style—* Maurice Lawson, Esq; 42 Holland Park Avenue, London W11 3QY (☎ 071 229 1346, telex 887871, fax 071 488 9927); Fuerst Day Lawson Holdings Ltd, St Clare House, 30-33 Minories, London EC3N 1LN

LAWSON, Hon Mrs (Miranda Jane); *née* Newall; da of 2 Baron Newall; *b* 25 Feb 1959; *m* 31 May 1986, Timothy Guy Lawson, son of Derek C Lawson, of Sherbourne, Warwick; 1 s (George Thomas Guy b 1987); *Style—* The Hon Mrs Lawson; The Pointed House, Meeting House Lane, Brant Broughton, Lincoln LN5 0SH

LAWSON, (Hon) Sir Neil; QC (1955); s of Robb Lawson (decd); *b* 1908; *Educ* Hendon County Sch, London Univ; *m* 1933, Gweneth Clare, da of late Sidney Wilby, FCA (decd), of Leicester; 1 s, 1 da; *Career* served with RAFVR 1940-45; barrister Inner Temple 1929, bencher 1961, law commissioner 1965-71, a judge of High Court (Queen's Bench Div) 1971-83, ret; kt 1971; *Style—* Sir Neil Lawson, QC; 30a Heath Drive, Hampstead, London NW3 (☎ 071 794 2585)

LAWSON, Rt Hon Nigel; PC (1981), MP (C) Blaby 1974-; s of Ralph Lawson, and Joan Elisabeth, *née* Davis; *b* 11 March 1932; *Educ* Westminster, ChCh Oxford; *m* 1, 1955 (m dis 1980), Vanessa Mary Addison, *née* Salmon; 1 s (Dominic Ralph Campden b 1956, *qv*), 3 da; m 2, 1980, Thérèse Mary Maclear; 1 s, 1 da; *Career* Sub-Lt RNVR 1954-56; memb editorial staff Financial Times 1956-60, city ed Sunday Telegraph 1961-63, ed The Spectator 1966-70; Parly candidate (C) Eton and Slough 1970, oppn whip 1976-77, oppn spokesman on Treasy and Economic Affrs 1977-79, fin sec to the Treasy 1979-81, Energy sec 1981-83, Chancellor of the Exchequer 1983-Oct 1989 (resigned); dir and pt/t conslt Barclays Bank 1990-, dir Guinness Peat Aviation 1990-, chm Central Europe Trust 1990; special advsr Cons HQ 1973-74, vice chm Cons Political Centre Nat Advsy Ctee 1972-75; *Style—* The Rt Hon Nigel Lawson, MP; House of Commons, London SW1

LAWSON, Gen Sir Richard George; KCB (1980), DSO (1962), OBE (1968); s of John Lawson, and Florence Rebecca Lawson; *b* 24 Nov 1927; *Educ* St Alban's Sch, Univ of Birmingham; *m* 1956, Ingrid, da of Dr Sture Nikolaus Montelin, of Sweden (d 1979); 1 s; *Career* served with UN peacekeeping force Zaire 1962 when he rescued Belgian priest from 800 rebels armed only with a swagger-stick (DSO); CO Ind Sqdn Royal Tank Regt Berlin 1963-64, GSO 2 MOD 1965-66, COS S Arabian Army 1967, CO 5 Royal Tank Regt 1968-69, Cdr 20 Armoured Bde 1972-73, Asst Mil Dep to Head of Def Sales 1975-77, GOC 1 Armd Div 1977-79, GOC NI 1979-82, Gen 1982, C-in-C Allied Forces N Europe 1982-84; Col Cmdt Royal Tank Regt 1980-82; Order of Leopold (Belgium) 1962, Kt Cdr Order of St Sylvester (Vatican) 1962; kt 1979; *Books* Strange Soldiering (1963), All The Queen's Men (1967), Strictly Personal (1972); *Recreations* sailing, writing; *Clubs* Army and Navy; *Style—* Gen Sir Richard Lawson, KCB, DSO, OBE

LAWSON, Richard Henry; s of Sir Henry Brailsford Lawson, MC (d 1980), of Churchmead, Pirbright, Surrey, and Mona, *née* Thorne (d 1990); *b* 16 Feb 1932; *Educ* Lancing; *m* 1958, Janet Elizabeth, da of Hugh Govier, of Shere, nr Guildford, Surrey; 3 s (Anthony b 1966, Charles b 1969, Philip b 1972), 1 da (Sally d 1975); *Career* jt sr ptnr W Greenwell & Co 1980-86; memb: Stock Exchange 1959, Cncl of Stock Exchange (dep chm 1985-86); dep chm Security Assocs 1986, chm Greenwell Montagu Stockbrokers Ltd 1987, dir The Investors Compensation Scheme 1987; *Recreations* golf, tennis, walking, birdwatching, skiing; *Clubs* Naval and Military; *Style—* Richard Lawson, Esq; Cherry Hill, Burrows Lane, Gomshall, Surrey GU5 9QE; Greenwell Montagu Stockbrokers, 114 Old Broad St, London EC2P 2HY (☎ 071 588 8817, telex 925363, fax 071 588 1673)

LAWSON, Robert Alexander Murdoch; s of Robert McKenzie Lawson (d 1944), and Margaret Perrins Murdoch (d 1985); *b* 11 Feb 1938; *Educ* George Watsons Boys Coll Edinburgh, Univ of Edinburgh (MB ChB); *m* 13 Nov 1965, Elizabeth Ettie, da of Tom Clark (d 1971); 1 s (Tom b 1973), 4 da (Rebecca b 1966, Catherine b 1969, Elizabeth b 1970, Hannah b 1981); *Career* registrar in surgery Bangour Gen Hosp W Lothian 1966-69, registrar then sr registrar Shotley Bridge cardio-Thoracic Unit Co Durham 1969-72, res fell St Vincents Hosp Univ of Oregon Med Sch USA 1973-75, sr registrar Nat Heart and London Chest Hosp Brompton 1975-77, currently conslt cardio-thoracic surgn Wythenshawe Hosp Manchester; memb: Br Cardiac Soc, Soc of Thoracic and Cardiovascular Surgns of UK and Ireland; FRCS Ed 1966, FRCS 1971; *Recreations* walking; *Style—* Robert Lawson, Esq; The Hollies, 8 Harboro Road, Sale, Cheshire M33 5AB (☎ 061 973 3295); Cardio-Thoracic Unit, Wythenshawe Hospital, South Manchester (☎ 061 998 7070)

LAWSON, Roger Hardman; *b* 3 Sept 1945; *m* Jeni; 3 da (Sarajane, Annabel, Louise); *Career* head Int Dept 3i plc; dir: 3i Australia Ltd, 3i Guernsey Ltd, 3i Jersey Ltd, 3i Corporation (US); memb Ct City Univ, chm Bd for Chartered Accountants in Business; FCA (memb Cncl and Mgmnt Ctee); *Recreations* golf; *Clubs* Royal Wimbledon Golf; *Style—* Roger Lawson, Esq; 3i plc, 91 Waterloo Rd, London SE1 8XP (☎ 071 928 3131, fax 071 928 0058)

LAWSON, Sonia; da of Frederick Lawson (d 1968), of Castle Bolton, North Yorks, and Muriel Mary, *née* Metcalfe; *b* 2 June 1934; *Educ* RCA (postgrad travelling scholarship); *m* 14 Jan 1969, Charles William Congo; 1 da (b 27 May 1970); *Career* artist; currently tutor Royal Acad Schs and visiting tutor RCA, Lorne award 1987; solo exhibitions incl: Zwemmer Gallery London 1960, New Arts Centre London 1963, Queens Square Gallery Leeds 1964, Trafford Gallery London 1967, Billingham/Middlesbrough 1973, Harrogate Art Gallery 1979, Central Art Gallery Milton Keynes 1982, Mappin Gallery Sheffield 1982, Cartwright Gallery Bradford 1982, Leicester Kimberlin and Hull Ferens 1983, City Arts Gallery Manchester 1987, Wakefield City Arts Gallery 1988, Boundry Gallery London 1989, Bradford Cartwright 1989; public and private collections: Imperial War Museum London, Arts Cncl GB, Sheffield Graves, Belfast Art Gallery, Leeds Univ, Middlesbrough Art Gallery, Miny Works, RCA Collection, Wakefield, Carlisle and Rochdale Galleries, various educn authys, Vatican Rome, Chatsworth House collection; private collections: Europe, USA, Canada, Aust; gp exhibitions incl: London Gp, Royal Acad, RWS, 25 Years of British Art (Royal Acad Jubilee) 1977, Moira Kelly Fine Art (London 1982 and NY 1983), Tully Cobbold Tour 1982-83 and 1985-86, Leeds Poly 'New Art' 1987, Manchester City Art Gallery 1988, London RCA Centinary 1988, Olympia Festival 1989, Bath Festival 1989, China Br Touring Exhib 1989-90, Royal Inst of Fine Art Glasgow 1990, The Infernal Method etchings, Royal Acad of Arts 1990; Eastern Arts drawing prize (first prize 1984 and 1986); ARCA 1959, RWS 1987 (Assoc 1984), RA 1991 (ARA 1982); *Recreations* Denizen watching; *Clubs* Arts; *Style—* Ms Sonia Lawson, RA; Royal Academy of Arts, Burlington House, Piccadilly, London W1 (☎ 071 439 7438, fax 071 434 0837, 21812)

LAWSON, Thomas Vincent; s of John Boyd Lawson, MBE (d 1952), and Mary Alexandra, *née* Chambers (d 1945); *b* 22 Jan 1925; *Educ* Denstone Coll, Univ of Leeds (BSc), Imperial Coll London (DIC); *m* 6 Aug 1948, Pauline Elizabeth, da of William Arthur Gaunt (d 1924); 2 s (Theodore Thomas b 23 Oct 1953, Oscar Charles b 18 May 1958), 4 da (Alexandra Barbara b 14 Oct 1952, Charity Jenny b 5 Sept 1956, Pandora Pauline b 20 July 1964, Darcie Tabitha b 11 Jan 1966); *Career* Univ of Bristol: lectr in aeronautical engrg 1949-62, sr lectr in aeronautical engrg 1962-72, reader in industrial aerodynamics 1972-83, hon sr res fell in aerospace engrg 1983-; conslt in industl aerodynamics and wind engrg 1983-; chm ESDU Wind Engrg Ctee; memb: ESDU Structural Vibration Ctee, BSI BS 6399 Wind Loading Ctee; memb Editorial Bd: Journal of Atmospheric Environment, Journal of Wind Engineering and Industrial

Aerodynamics; *Books* Wind Effects on Buildings (2 vols, Design Applications, Statistics and Meteorology, 1980); *Recreations* gardening, drawing; *Style—* Thomas Lawson, Esq; Hamel Green House, Ham Green, Pill, Bristol, Avon BS20 0HF (☎ 0275 372263); Dept of Aerospace Engineering, University of Bristol, Bristol, Avon BS8 1TR (☎ 0272 303266, fax 0272 251154)

LAWSON, Lady Grant; Virginia; da of Sidney Butler Dean (decd), of St Paul, Minnesota, USA; *m* 1940, Col Sir Peter Grant Lawson, 2 Bt (d 1973); *Style—* Lady Grant Lawson; Dorridge Farm, Fordingbridge, Hants

LAWSON JOHNSTON, Hon (George) Andrew; s of 2 Baron Luke, KCVO, TD; *b* 1944; *Educ* Eton; *m* 1968, Sylvia Josephine Ruth, da of Michael Richard Lloyd Hayes; 3 s, 1 da; *Career* artist and engraver of glass; *Style—* The Hon Andrew Lawson Johnston

LAWSON JOHNSTON, Hon Arthur Charles St John; DL (Beds 1989); s and h of 2 Baron Luke, KCVO, TD, by his w Barbara, da of Sir FitzRoy Hamilton Anstruther-Gough-Calthorpe, 1 Bt; *b* 13 Jan 1933; *Educ* Eton, Trinity Coll Cambridge (BA); *m* 1, 6 Aug 1959 (m dis 1971), Silvia Maria, da of Don Honorio Roigt, former Argentine Ambass at The Hague; 1 s, 2 da; m 2, 1971, Sarah Louise, da of Richard Hearne, OBE; 1 s; *Career* art dealer, farmer; councillor Beds 1966-70 (chm of Staffing Ctee 1967-70), High Sheriff Beds 1969-70, pres Nat Assoc of Warehouse-Keepers 1960-78; cmmr St John Ambulance Bde in Beds 1972-85; cdr St John Ambulance Beds 1985-90; KStJ; *Recreations* shooting, fishing; *Style—* The Hon Arthur Lawson Johnston, DL; Odell Manor, Beds MK43 7BB (☎ 0234 720416)

LAWSON JOHNSTON, Hon Hugh de Beauchamp; TD (1951), DL (Beds 1964); s of 1 Baron Luke, KBE (d 1943), by his w Hon Edith Laura St John (d 1941), da of 16 Baron St John of Bletso; *b* 7 April 1914; *Educ* Eton, Chillon Coll, Corpus Christi Cambridge (BA, MA); *m* 1946, Audrey Warren, da of Col Frederick Warren Pearl (decd); 3 da; *Career* Capt 5 Bn Bedfordshire Regt (TA Reserve); with Bovril Ltd 1935-71 (latterly chm), chm Tribune Investmt Tst Ltd 1950-86, Pitman Ltd (chm to 1981); chm of Ctees United Soc for Christian Literature 1949-82; High Sheriff Beds 1961-62; *Style—* The Hon Hugh Lawson Johnston, TD, DL; Flat 1, 28 Lennox Gdns, SW1 (☎ 071 584 1446); Woodleys Farmhouse, Melchbourne, Bedfordshire (☎ 0234 708282)

LAWSON JOHNSTON, Hon Ian Henry Calthorpe (Harry); s of 2 Baron Luke, KCVO, TD; *b* 1938; *Educ* Harrow; *m* 1970, Lady (Pamela) Lemina Gordon, da of 12 Marquess of Huntly; 1 s, 1 da; *Clubs* Boodle's; *Style—* The Hon Harry Lawson Johnston; Coombe Slade Farm, Brailes, Banbury, Oxon OX15 5AF

LAWSON JOHNSTON, Lady (Pamela) Lemina; *née* Gordon; da of 12 Marquess of Huntly; *b* 1942; *m* 1970, Hon Ian Henry Calthorpe Lawson Johnston; 1 s, 1 da; *Style—* The Lady Lemina Lawson Johnston; Coombe Slade Farm, Brailes, Banbury, Oxon OX15 5AF

LAWSON JOHNSTON, Hon Olive Elizabeth Helen; *née* Lawson-Johnston; eldest da of 1 Baron Luke, KBE (d 1943), and Hon Edith Laura (d 1941), 5 da of 16 Baron St John of Bletso; *b* 22 Jan 1904; *m* 18 Dec 1934 (m dis 1936), Frederick Lothair Lawson Johnston (d 1963), s of W E Lawson Johnston, of 29 Wilton Crescent, London SW1; *Career* Sr Cmdt ATS 1938-40, 2 Officer WRNS 1941-45; *Style—* The Hon Olive Lawson Johnston; Muir Lan Morrach, Rue Road, Arisaig, Inverness-shire PH39 4NU (☎ 06875 264)

LAWSON JOHNSTON, Hon (Laura) Pearl; OBE (1946), JP (Beds 1941-84), DL (1976); da of 1 Baron Luke, KBE (d 1943); *b* 18 Aug 1916; *Career* county pres St John Ambulance Brigade 1971-; CStJ 1981-90; High Sheriff of Bedfordshire 1985-86; *Recreations* racehorse breeder; *Style—* The Hon Pearl Lawson Johnston, OBE, JP, DL; Woodleys Stud House, Melchbourne, Beds MK44 1AG (☎ 0234 708 266)

LAWSON JOHNSTON, Hon Philip Richard; 4 and yst s of 2 Baron Luke, KCVO, TD; *b* 20 Nov 1950; *Educ* Eton; *m* 1977, (Saskia) Moyne, da of Terence George Andrews, MBE; 3 s (incl twins), 1 da; *Career* glass engraver and song writer; *Style—* The Hon Philip Lawson Johnston; 307 Woodstock Rd, Oxford OX2 7NY

LAWSON ROGERS, (George) Stuart; s of George Henry Roland Rogers, CBE (d 1983), of Bournemouth, and Mary Lawson (d 1983); *b* 23 March 1946; *Educ* Buckingham Coll Harrow Middx, LSE (LLB); *m* 19 July 1969, Rosalind Denise, da of Lt Dennis Ivor Leach, of Bournemouth; 1 s (Dominic b 1971), 1 da (Lucy b 1972); *Career* called to the Bar Gray's Inn 1969; asst boundary cmmr Boundary Cmmn (Parly) for England and Wales 1981, ad hoc appt asst boundary cmmr Local Govt Boundary Cmmn for England and Wales 1983, appt to Panel of Chairmen of Structure Plan Examinations in Public Dept of Environment 1984, asst rec 1986, appt to Panels of Legal Assessors to GMC and Gen Dental Cncl 1988, inspector Dept of Transport (Merchant Shipping Act 1988 investigations) 1989, inspector DTI (insider dealing investigation) 1989,Standing Counsel to H M Customs and Excise (Criminal S E Circuit) 1989, Crown Ct 1990; dir Watford AFC 1990, memb local Horticultural Soc, memb Hon Soc Gray's Inn, memb RCA; *Recreations* gardening, reading; *Style—* Stuart Lawson Rogers, Esq; 36 Essex St, London WC2 3AS (☎ 071 413 0353, 071 353 3533, fax 071 413 0374 DX LDE 148)

LAWSON-TANCRED, Andrew Peter; s and h of Sir Henry Lawson-Tancred, 10 Bt, of Boroughbridge, Yorkshire and Jean Veronica, *née* Foster (d 1970); *b* 18 Feb 1952; *Educ* Eton, Univ of Leeds; *Career* barr at Law, Hon Soc of the Middle Temple; *Recreations* flying; *Style—* Andrew Lawson-Tancred, Esq; 1 Cristowe Rd, London SW6 3QF; W H Smith Television, The Quadrangle, 180 Wardour St, London W1V 4AE (☎ 071 439 1177, fax 071 439 1177)

LAWSON-TANCRED, Sir Henry; 10 Bt (E 1662), JP (WR Yorks 1967); s of Maj Sir Thomas Selby Lawson-Tancred, 9 Bt (d 1945); *b* 1924; *Educ* Stowe, Jesus Coll Cambridge; *m* 1, 1950, Jean Veronica (d 1970), da of Gerald Robert Foster (d 1962); 5 s, 1 da; m 2, 1978, Susan Dorothy Marie-Gabrielle, da of late Sir Kenelm Cayley, 10 Bt, and formerly w of Maldwin Drummond; *Heir* s, Andrew Peter Lawson-Tancred; *Career* served with RAFVR 1942-46; *Style—* Sir Henry Lawson-Tancred, Bt, JP; Aldborough Manor, Boroughbridge, Yorks (☎ 0423 322716)

LAWSON-TURNER, Wilberforce; s of Arthur Lawson-Turner (d 1959), of Maitlands, Chapel-en-le-Frith, Derbys, and Alice Ewart, *née* Pearson (d 1974); *b* 21 April 1918; *Educ* Buxton Coll; *m* 1951, Felicity Marion, da of William Reader; 2 s (Simon b 31 Aug 1956, Guy b 17 May 1953); *Career* RNR Naval Communications Offr 1940-46; dir Surbiton Aircraft Weybridge Surrey 1949-; Liveryman Worshipful Co of Playing Card Makers 1962; *Recreations* flat racing, bridge; *Style—* Wilberforce Lawson-Turner, Esq; Wild Acre, Broad Lane, Hale, Ches WA15 ODG

LAWTON, Capt Alan Frederick; s of Frederick Lawton (d 1974), of Berkhamsted, and Ivy, *née* Parker (d 1989); *b* 14 Feb 1939; *Educ* Berkhamsted Sch, Britannia RNC Dartmouth, Royal Naval Engrg Coll, Univ of London (BSc), RCDS; *m* 21 Jan 1967, Susan Russell, da of John Torrie Johnston (d 1978), of Glasgow; 2 da (Tina b 1967, Jennifer b 1970); *Career* RNC Dartmouth 1957, Cdr 1975, Trg Cdr HMS Caledonia 1976-78, Dir marine engrg RNZN 1978-79, Chief Tech Servs RNZN 1979-80, Marine Engr Offr HMS Bristol 1980-82, Offr i/c Machinery Trials units 1982-83, Capt 1984, Offr i/c fleet maintenance Falklands Is 1984, Asst Dir Naval Plans and Progs 1985-87, memb Royal Coll of Def Studies 1988, Dir naval logistic planning 1989-; MIMechE 1969; *Recreations* golf, tennis, watching cricket and rugby; *Style—* Capt Alan Lawton, RN; Director of Naval Logistic Planning, Room 9326, Main Building, Ministry of Defence, Whitehall, London SW1A 2HB (☎ 01 218 3287)

LAWTON, Charles Henry Huntly; s of Philip Charles Fenner Lawton CBE, DFC, and Emma Letitia Gertrude Lawton, *née* Stephenson; *b* 17 April 1946; *Educ* Westminster Sch; *m* 21 April 1979, Sarah Margaret, da of Rev Christopher Lambert; 1 s (Timothy b 1982), 1 da (Hermione b 1984); *Career* admitted slr 1970; legal advsr and head legal dept RTZ Corp plc 1985-; *Recreations* walking, reading, fishing; *Clubs* White's; *Style—* Charles Lawton, Esq; 26 Abingdon Villas, London W8 (☎ 01 937 9148); 6 St James's Square, London SW1 (☎ 01 930 2399)

LAWTON, Rt Hon Sir Frederick Horace; PC (1972), QC (1957); s of William John Lawton, OBE; *b* 21 Dec 1911; *Educ* Battersea GS, CCC Cambridge; *m* 1937, Doreen, da of Richard John Maker Wilton (d 1979), of Bodmin, Cornwall; 2 s; *Career* WWII London Irish Rifles 1939-41; judge of the High Ct 1961-72, lord justice of appeal 1972-86; chm: Standing Ctee for Criminal Law Revision 1977-86, Advsy Ctee on Legal Educn 1976-86, pres British Acad of Forensic Scis 1964; kt 1961; *Style—* The Rt Hon Sir Frederick Lawton; 1 The Village, Skelton, York YO3 6XX (☎ 0904 470441); Mordryg, Stoptide, Rock, nr Wadebridge, Cornwall (☎ 0208 863375)

LAWTON, Prof John Hartley; s of Frank Hartley Lawton (d 1982), of Leyland, Lancashire, and Mary, *née* Cuerden; *b* 24 Sept 1943; *Educ* Balshaw's GS Leyland, Univ Coll Durham (BSc, PhD); *m* 22 Oct 1966, Dorothy, da of Harold Grimshaw (d 1960), of Leyland Lancs; 1 s (Graham John b 1969), 1 da (Anna Louise Lawton b 1968); *Career* Univ of Oxford: departmental demonstrator in zoology 1968-71, lectr in zoology Lincoln Coll 1970-71, lectr in zoology St Annes Coll 1970-71; Dept of Biology Univ of York: lectr 1971-78, sr lectr 1978-82, reader 1982-85, prof 1985-89; Imperial Coll of Sci Technol and Med Univ of London (prof of community ecology and dir Res Centre for Population Biology 1989-); memb: Royal Cmmn on Environmental Pollution, Cncl for Royal Soc for the Protection of Birds, American Soc of Naturalists, Br Ecological Soc; fell: Royal Entomological Soc, Br Tst for Ornithology, Royal Soc of London; former Cncl memb Freshwater Biological Assoc; *Books* Insects on Plants: Community Patterns and Mechanisms (1984), Blackwell Scientific Oxford (with T R E Southwood and D R Strong); *Recreations* bird watching, gardening, photography, running, hill walking, travel; *Style—* Prof John Lawton; 17 Course Rd, Ascot SL5 7HQ (☎ 0344 26819); 21 Lime Ave, York YO3 0BT (☎ 0904 424873); Centre for Population Biology, Imperial College, Silwood Park, Ascot SL5 7PY (☎ 0344 294354, fax 0344 873173)

LAX, Peter Andrew; s of Carl Werner Lax, BEM, and Lilly Lax; *b* 27 March 1958; *Educ* Barnard Castle Sch, Hatfield Coll Univ of Durham (BA); *m* 27 July 1985, Angela Clare, da of Kenneth Sidney Ansell Davis, of Gayton, Wirral; *Career* admitted slr 1982; articled clerk John Buckingham Duggan Lea & Co 1980-82, ptnr Pinsent & Co Slrs 1988; memb Birmingham Canal Navigation Soc, organiser legal advice session Birmingham CAB; memb Law Soc 1982; *Recreations* rabbit watching; *Style—* Peter Lax, Esq; The Warren, 18 Joy Berry Drive, Old Swinford, Stourbridge, West Midlands DY8 2EF (☎ 0384 377748); Pinsent & Co, Post & Mail House, 26 Colmore Circus, Birmingham B4 6BH (☎ 021 200 1050, fax 021 200 1040, car 0836 648715)

LAY, David John; s of Walter Charles Frederick Lay (d 1984), and June Barbara, *née* Cadman; *b* 15 Aug 1948; *Educ* Magdalen Coll Sch Oxford, CCC Oxford (MA); *m* 1 Sept 1973, Tamara Said, da of Said Pasha Mufti (d 1989), former PM of Jordan; 1 s (Taimour b 1982), 3 da (Sima b 1977, Maya b 1980, Lana b 1982); *Career* BBC radio news reporter 1974-79, presenter Twenty-four Hours BBC World Serv 1979-, managing ed Oxford Analytica 1988-; *Recreations* tennis, foreign travel, ME politics; *Clubs* David Lloyd Slazenger; *Style—* David Lay, Esq; 215 Ashburnham Rd, Ham, Richmond, Surrey TW10 7SE (☎ 081 948 2370)

LAY, Patrick William; s of William Henry Lay (d 1984), of Cockfosters, Enfield, and Ellen Louise, *née* Cole (d 1972); *b* 24 July 1930; *Educ* Edmonton Co GS; *m* 24 Dec 1955, Lois, da of Robert Henry Thornton-Berry (d 1987), of Bristol; 1 da (Karen b 1956); *Career* Nat Serv RN; fin jounalist: Lloyds List Shipping Gazette 1954-56, Reuters 1956-59, The Times 1959-61, Evening News; dep fin ed Daily Mirror, dir fin PR co Shareholder Relations (An PR) 1970-74, fin journalist Daily Mail 1974-76, fin ed Daily Express 1983-86 (dep fin ed 1976-83), city ed Sunday Express 1986-89; conslt on media affrs to: Dewe Rogerson fin PR, City Univ Business Sch; *Recreations* cricket, walking, Weimaraner dogs; *Clubs* MCC; *Style—* Patrick Lay, Esq; Didgemere Lodge, Epping Rd, Roydon, Essex, CM19 5DB (☎ 027979 2258)

LAY, Richard Neville; s of Edward John Lay, of Banstead, Surrey, and Nellie, *née* Gould (d 1987); *b* 18 Oct 1938; *Educ* Whitgift Sch; *m* 12 Sept 1964, 1 s (Martin Richard Forbes b 1969), 1 da (Melaine St Clair b 1965); *Career* chartered surveyor; ptnr Debenham Tewson & Chinnocks 1965-87, chm Debenham Tewson & Chinnocks Holdings plc and subsid cos 1987-; surveyor to the Worshipful Co of Armourers & Brasiers 1983-; memb West End Bd Sun Alliance and London Insurance Group, tstee Tate Gallery Fndn; FRICS; *Recreations* gardening; *Clubs* RAC; *Style—* Richard Lay, Esq; 15 Clareville Grove, London SW7 5AU; 44 Brook St, London W1 (☎ 071 408 1161, fax 071 491 4593, TELEX 22105)

LAYARD, Rear Adm Michael Henry Gordon; CBE (1983); s of Edwin Henry Frederick Layard (d 1972), of Colombo, Sri Lanka, and Doris Christian Gordon, *née* Spence (d 1965); *b* 3 Jan 1936; *Educ* Pangbourne Coll, BRNC Dartmouth; *m* 17 Dec 1966 Elspeth Horsley Fisher, da of late Rev L C Fisher; 2 s (James Henry Gordon b 1967, Andrew Charles Gordon b 1969); *Career* RN: Seaman Offr 1954-58, trainee fighter pilot 1958-60, fighter pilot 1962-70, air warfare instr 1964; Cmd: 899 Naval Air Sqdn (Sea Vixens) 1970-71, HMS Lincoln 1971-72; NDC 1974, Directorate Naval Air Warfare MOD 1975-77, Cdr (Air) HMS Ark Royal 1977-78, CSO (Air) to flag offr Naval Air Cmd 1979-82, SNO SS Atlantic Conveyor Falklands conflict 1982; cmd: RNAS Culdrose 1982-84, HMS Cardiff 1984-85 (leader Task Force to Persian Gulf); dir Naval Warfare (Air) MOD 1985-88, flag offr Naval Air Command 1988-90, dir Gen Naval Manpower Trg 1990-; chm Tstees of the Fleet Air Arm Museum 1988-90, pres RN Golfing Soc, tstee Tout Quarry Portland Sculpture Park; memb: RN Sailing Assoc, Fleet Air Arm Offrs Assoc; Ordre de Chevalier Bretvin; *Recreations* music, history, painting, golf, sailing; *Clubs* Commonwealth, Royal Navy Club of 1765 & 1785; *Style—* Rear Adm Michael Layard, CBE; c/o Lloyds Bank plc, Cheapside, Langpore, Somerset

LAYARD, Prof (Peter) Richard Grenville; s of John Willoughby Layard (d 1974), and Doris, *née* Dunn (d 1973); *b* 15 March 1934; *Educ* Eton, Univ of Cambridge (BA), LSE (MSc); *Career* 2 Lt 4 RHA 1953-54, RA 1952-54; sch teacher LCC 1959-61, sr res offr Robbins Ctee of Higher Educn 1961-64; LSE: dep dir Higher Educn Res Unit 1964-74, lectr 1968-75, head Centre of Lab Econs 1974-, reader 1975-80, prof of econs 1980-, dir Centre of Econ performance 1990-; memb Univ Grants Ctee 1985-89, chm Exec Ctee Employment Inst until 1986 and chm 1987-; fell Econometric Soc; *Books* More Jobs, Less Inflation (1982), How to Beat Unemployment (1986), Restoring Europe's Prosperity (with O Blanchard and R Dornbusch, 1986), Microeconomic Theory (with A Walters, 1978, reissued 1987), The Performance of the British Economy (with R Dornbusch, 1987); *Recreations* walking; *Style—* Prof Richard Layard; 18 Provost Rd, London NW3 4ST (☎ 071 722 6347); Centre for Economic Performance LSE, Houghton St, London WC2A 2AE (☎ 071 995 7281, fax 01 955 7595)

LAYCOCK, Lady; Angela Clare Louise; yr da of Rt Hon William Dudley Ward, PC (d 1946, gn of 1 Earl of Dudley), and Winifred May, *née* Birkin, later Marquesa de Casa Maury (d 1982); *b* 1916; *m* 24 Jan 1935, Maj-Gen Sir Robert Edward Laycock, KCMG, CB, DSO, Royal Horse Guards (d 1968), s of Brig-Gen Sir Joseph Laycock, KCMG, DSO, TD, JP, DL, by Katherine, formerly w of 6 Marquess of Downshire and da of Hon Hugh Hare, 4 s of 2 Earl of Listowel, KP; 2 s (Joseph William (decd), Benjamin Richard), 3 da (Tilly Jane m Sidney Davis, Emma Rose m Richard Temple, Katherine Martha m David Mlinaric, *qv*); *Career* former CC and JP Notts; DStJ; *Style—* Lady Laycock, JP; La Canada Real, Sotogrande, (PA) Cadiz, Spain

LAYCOCK, Lady; Hilda Florence; da of Christopher Ralph Carr, of Harrogate, and Florence Margaret, *née* Taylor; *b* 22 Jan 1908; *Educ* Birklands Sch Harrogate, St Cuthbert's Sch Bournemouth; *m* 18 April 1931, Sir Leslie Ernest Laycock, CBE, JP (d 1981), s of Ernest Bright Laycock, OBE, of Harrogate and Leeds; 2 s (Michael Peter Latham b 1938, (John) Patrick Latham b 1944); *Career* dir: Peter Laycock Ltd, Buslingthorpe Estates Ltd, Latham Investments Ltd, LEL Estates Ltd, Blacktoft Estates Ltd, Latham Wool Co Ltd, Marville Properties Ltd; past chm WRVS Harrogate Area (Housing); *Recreations* bridge, tennis, badminton; *Style—* Lady Laycock; The Gables, Rayleigh Rd, Harrogate, N Yorks HG2 8QR (☎ 0423 566219); 32 Acfold Road, London SW6 2AL (☎ 071 736 1536)

LAYCOCK, Mrs Peter; Patricia; da of Kenneth Richards, of NSW; *b* 20 Jan 1914; *m* 1, 1932 (m dis 1937), as his 1 w, 9 Earl of Jersey; 1 da (Lady Caroline Ogilvy); m 2, 1937, Maj Robin Filmer-Wilson (k 1944); 1 s, 1 da; m 3, 1953, Lt-Col Peter Laycock (d 1978); *Style—* Mrs Peter Laycock; 80 Eaton Sq, London SW1

LAYDEN, Sir John; JP (1965); s of Thomas Henry Layden (d 1961), of 7 Millicent Square, Maltby, Rotherham, South York, and Annie, *née* Peach (d 1959); *b* 16 Jan 1926; *Educ* Maltby Hall Sch, Univ of Sheffield; *m* 26 March 1949, (Dorothy) Brenda, da of James McLean (d 1949), of Manor House, Maltby, Rotherham, South York; 2 s (John b 13 March 1956, Keith b 18 Oct 1959); *Career* chm Assoc Met Authys, ldr Rotherham Met BC, vice-pres Br Section Int Univ Local Authys; Freeman City of London 1988, kt 1988; *Recreations* watching football, reading; *Style—* Sir John Layden, JP; Rotherham Met Borough Cncl, The Civic Suite, Elliott House, Frederick Street, Rotherham S60 1QW (☎ 0709 823 580, fax 0709 371 597, car 0836 508 292)

LAYFIELD, Sir Frank Henry Burland Willoughby; QC (1967); s of Henry Layfield (d 1960); *b* 9 Aug 1921; *Educ* Sevenoaks; *m* 1965, Irene Partricia, da of Capt J D Harvey, RN; 1 s, 1 da; *Career* called to the Bar 1954; chm: Inquiry into Greater London Plan 1970-72, Ctee of Inquiry into Local Govt Fin 1974-76, NEDO Working Pty on Constructional Steel Work 1977-82; Counsel to Univ of Oxford 1972, bencher Gray's Inn 1974, memb Sec of State's Housing Fin Policy Review 1975-77, general cmmr of taxes 1977-, rec of the Crown Ct 1979-, govt inspr on inquiry into Sizewell B Nuclear Power Station; pres Assoc of CCs, chm Tribunal for the Protection of St Paul's Cathedral 1971-; hon fell: Coll of Estate Mgmnt 1981, Inst of Landscape Architects 1989, Inc Soc of Valuers and Auctioneers; memb Ct of Assts Worshipful Co of Pewterers 1982-; Lincoln Land Inst Gold Medal 1983; ARICS; kt 1976; *Style—* Sir Frank Layfield, QC; 2 Mitre Court Bldgs, Temple, London EC4 (☎ 01 583 355); Grove House, Beckley, Oxford

LAYLAND, Hon Mrs (Sheila Hamnett); da of Baron Hamnett (Life Peer); *b* 24 July 1933; *Educ* Levenshulme HS, City of Portsmouth Training Coll; *m* 1962, Eric Layland; 1 s, 1 da; *Style—* The Hon Mrs Layland; 31 Sevenoaks Ave, Heaton Moor, Stockport, Cheshire (☎ 061 432 8083)

LAYMAN, Rear Adm Christopher Hope; CB (1990), DSO (1982), LVO (1977); s of Capt Herbert F H Layman, DSO, RN (d 1989), and Elizabeth, *née* Hughes (d 1990); *b* 9 March 1938; *Educ* Winchester; *m* 15 Aug 1964, Katharine Romer, da of Capt Stephen Romer Ascherson, RN (d 1955); 1 s (James b 1965), 1 da (Alexandra b 1969); *Career* joined RN 1956, specialised communications and electronic warfare 1966; cmd: HMS Hubberston 1968-70, HMS Lynx 1972-74; exec offr HM Yacht Britannia 1976-78, Capt 7 Frigate Sqdn 1981-83; cmd: HMS Argonaut 1981-82, HMS Cleopatra 1982-83, HMS Invincible 1984-86; Cdr Br Forces Falkland Islands 1986-87, asst dir (CIS) Int Mil Staff NATO HQ 1988-; *Publications* Man of Letters (1990); *Recreations* fishing, archaeology; *Clubs* New (Edinburgh); *Style—* Rear Adm C H Layman, CB, DSO, LVO; c/o Drummonds, 49 Charing Cross, London, SW1A 2DX

LAYTE, James Douglas; s of George Douglas Layte (d 1978), and Phyllis Joan, *née* Bullock; *b* 29 July 1951; *Educ* Monkton Combe Sch Bath, Tabor Acad Marion Mass USA, Univ of East Anglia (BA); *m* 20 June 1974, Caroline Clare Gage, da of late Peter Bruce Gage Miller, of Norwich; 2 s (Samuel b 1974, Henry b 1977); *Career* antique and fine art dealer; memb Vetting Ctee Fine Art and Antiques Fair Olympia 1980-; *Recreations* gardening, travel; *Style—* James D Layte, Esq; Waterfall Cottage, Mill St, Swanton Morley, Norfolk; 3 Fish Hill, Holt, Norfolk

LAYTON, Hon Christopher Walter; s of 1 Baron Layton, CH, CBE (d 1966); *b* 31 Dec 1929; *Educ* Oundle, King's Coll Cambridge; *m* 1, 1952 (m dis 1957), Anneliese Margarethe, da of Joachim von Thadden, of Hanover; 1 s, 1 da; m 2, 1961, Margaret Ann, da of Leslie Moon; 3 da; *Career* dir Computer Electronics, Telecommunications and Air Transport Equipment Manufacturing, Directorate-General of Internal Market and Industrial Affairs Commission of the European Communities 1973-; *Style—* The Hon Christopher Layton; Directorate-General of Internal Market & Industrial Affairs, Commission of the European Communities, 200 rue de la Loi, 1049 Brussels, Belgium; Ave Albert Lancaster, 95B, 1080 Brussels, Belgium

LAYTON, Dr Clive Allan; s of Peter Eric Layton (d 1979), and Joan, *née* Sims; *b* 17 April 1944; *Educ* City of London Sch, King's Coll London, St George's Hosp Med Sch London (MB, BS); *m* 2 April 1971, Helen MacLean, da of William Paxton (d 1953); 2 da (Charlotte b 1972, Sarah b 1974); *Career* sr registrar in cardiology The London Hosp 1972-77; conslt cardiologist: Nat Heart and Chest Hosps The London Chest Hosp 1977-, NE Thames Regnl Health Authy 1977-; non exec dir Medihome Ltd; contrib to pubns on cardiology and intensive care; serving memb Ctee of Essex Hunt Branch of Pony Club; former memb English Fencing Team (Br Schs, Public Schs and Br Junior Fencing Champion); MRCP 1969; *Recreations* equestrian activities; *Style—* Dr Clive Layton; 22 Upper Wimpole St, London W1M 7TR (☎ 071 486 8961, fax 071 486 7918, car 0836 289 087, telex 23621 CARDIO G)

LAYTON, Lt-Col Hon David; MBE (1946); s of 1 Baron Layton, CH, CBE (d 1966), and Eleanor Dorothea (d 1959), da of Francis Beresford Plumptre Osmaston; uncle and hp of 3 Baron Layton, *qv*; *b* 5 July 1914; *Educ* Gresham's Sch Holt, Trinity Coll Cambridge; *m* 1, 1939, Elizabeth, da of Rev Robert Millar Gray, of Hampstead; 2 s, 1 da; m 2, 1972, Joy Parkinson; *Career* 2 Lt RE 1939; md Incomes Data Services; *Style—* Lt-Col the Hon David Layton, MBE; 18 Grove Terrace, Highgate Rd, London NW5

LAYTON, Dr Denis Noel; s of Reginald Frank Layton (d 1966), of Banstead, Surrey, and Ida Mary, *née* Pinker (d 1976); *b* 29 Dec 1925; *Educ* City of London Freemen's Sch, Imperial Coll London (PhD, MSc); *m* 12 July 1958, Margaret Alison, da of Richard Kestell Floyer (d 1975), of Mayfield; 2 da (Frances b 1961, Hilary b 1963); *Career* Capt REME 1946-48; various appts GKN Group 1952-62; dir: Mountford (GKN Group) 1962-76 (md 1967-76), Hoskins & Horton plc 1978-82; chm CSM Plating Ltd 1979-89; chm DTI Ctee on Corrosion 1975-78, memb DTI Ctee for Industl Technols, pres Inst of Metal Finishing 1988-90; FBIM, FIMF, MInstP; *Recreations* campanology, music; *Style—* Dr Denis Layton; The Gardens, Clows Top, Kidderminster, Worcs DY14 9HW

LAYTON, Dorothy, Baroness; Dorothy Rose Layton; *née* Cross; da of Albert Luther Cross, of Rugby; *m* 1938, 2 Baron Layton (d 1989); 1 s (3 Baron, *qv*), 1 da (Hon Dr Jennings, *qv*); *Career* proprietor Layton Antiques Richmond 1965-; JP Middx 1954-67; *Style—* The Rt Hon Dorothy, Lady Layton; 6 Old Palace Terrace, Richmond Green, Richmond, Surrey TW6 1NB (☎ 081 940 0834)

LAYTON, 3 Baron (UK 1947); Geoffrey Michael Layton; o s of 2 Baron Layton (d 1989); *b* 18 July 1947; *Educ* St Paul's, Stanford Univ Calif, Univ of Southern Calif; *m* 1, 1969 (m dis 1971), Viviane, da of François P Cracco, of Louvain, Belgium; m 2, 1989, Caroline Jane, da of William Thomas Mason, of Fairford, Glos, and formerly w of Adm Spyros Soulis, of Athens; *Heir* uncle, Hon David Layton, MBE, *qv*; *Style—* The Rt Hon the Lord Layton; c/o House of Lords, London SW1

LAZARUS, Sir Peter Esmond; KCB (1985, CB 1975); s of Kenneth Michaelis Lazarus (d 1961), of London, and Mary Rebecca, *née* Halsted (d 1982); *b* 2 April 1926; *Educ* Westminster, Wadham Coll Oxford; *m* 1950, Elizabeth Anne Marjorie, da of Leslie H Atwell, OBE (d 1971), of London; 3 s (Richard, Stephen, James); *Career* perm under sec Dept of Tport 1982-85, memb Bd CAA 1986-, dir Manchester Ship Canal Co 1986-, chm Ctee for Monitoring Agreements on Tobacco Advertising and Sponsorship 1986-90; Bde Cmdt Jewish Lads and Girls Bde, vice pres Anglo Jewish Assoc, chm Lib Jewish Synagogue; *Recreations* music, reading; *Clubs* Athenaeum; *Style—* Sir Peter Lazarus, KCB; 28 Woodside Ave, London N6 4SS (☎ 071 883 3186)

LAZENBY, David William; s of George William Lazenby, of Walton-on-Thames, Surrey, and Jane, *née* Foster; *b* 13 Oct 1937; *Educ* Canford, Battersea Coll of Technol, Imperial Coll London (DIC), City Univ London (Dip, CU); *m* 2 Sept 1961, Valerie Ann, da of Lewis Edward Kent, OBE (d 1972); 1 s (Jonathan b 22 Jan 1965), 1 da (Andrea b 23 Feb 1968); *Career* chm Andrews Kent & Stone consulting engrs 1983- (joined 1962, ptnr 1972); civil and structural engrg work includes: Nat Library of Wales, Merchant Navy Coll, E Sussex County Hall; Pres IStructE, chm Br Standards Inst Construction Codes Ctee, visitor to Building Res Estab; Eur Ing, FICE, FIStructE, MAssocCE; *Books* 1936/85 Structural Steelwork for Students (jtly, 1985), Structural Mechanics for Students (1984), Cutting for Construction (1978); *Recreations* travel, tennis, opera, good food and wine; *Style—* David W Lazenby, Esq; Paddock Hse, Bennett Way, West Clandon, Guildford, Surrey (☎ 0483 223 104); Andrews Kent & Stone, 1 Argyll St, London W1V 2DH (☎ 071 437 6136, fax 071 437 1035, telex 291585)

LE BAILLY, Vice Adm Sir Louis Edward Stewart Holland; KBE (1972, OBE 1952), CB (1969), DL (Cornwall 1982); s of Robert Francis Le Bailly; *b* 18 July 1915; *Educ* RNC Dartmouth, RN Engrg Coll Devonport; *m* 1946, Pamela Ruth, da of Rear Adm Charles Pierre Berthon; 3 da; *Career* joined RN 1929, served WWII, Cdr British Navy Staff and naval attaché Washington DC 1967-69, dir Serv Intelligence MOD 1970, ret 1972; DG of Intelligence MOD 1972-75; memb Cncl The Pilgrims; CEng, FIMechE, MIMarE, FInstPet; *Clubs* Naval and Military; *Style—* Vice Adm Sir Louis Le Bailly, KBE, CB, DL; Garlands House, St Tudy, Bodmin, Cornwall

LE BAS, Caroline; da of Rt Hon Dr John Gilbert, MP, and Josephine, *née* Kealworthy (d 1988); *b* 29 Oct 1950; *Educ* Millfield Sch; *Career* business devpt dir (Europe) Young and Rubicam; memb IAA; *Recreations* sailing and skiing; *Clubs* Royal Solent Yacht; *Style—* Ms Caroline Le Bas; 36 Redfield Lane, London SW5 (☎ 071 373 7089); Young and Rubicam Europe, Greater London House, Hampstead Rd, London NW1 (☎ 071 387 9366, fax 071 380 6570)

LE BRUN, Lady Carina Doune; *née* Brudenell-Bruce; 2 da (yr da by 1 m) of 8 Marquess of Ailesbury and his 1 w, Edwina Sylvia de Winton, da of Lt-Col Sir Edward Wills, 4 Bt; *b* 13 Jan 1956; *Educ* Lawnside; *m* 1982 (m dis 1988), Anthony Le Brun, only s of Basil Le Brun, of Beauchamp, St John, Jersey, and Mrs Elaine Le Brun, of Le Douet, St John, Jersey; *Career* pottery decorator; *Style—* The Lady Carina Le Brun; Beauchamp, St John, Jersey, Channel Islands; Jersey Pottery, Goray, Jersey

LE BRUN, Christopher Mark; s of John Le Brun, BEM, QSM, RM (d 1970), of Portsmouth, and Eileen Betty, *née* Miles; *b* 20 Dec 1951; *Educ* Southern GS Portsmouth, Slade Sch of Fine Art (DFA), Chelsea Sch of Art (MA); *m* 31 March 1979, Charlotte Eleanor, da of Gp Capt Hugh Beresford Verity, DSO, DFC, of Richmond, Surrey; 2 s (Luke b 1984, Edmund b 1990), 1 da (Lily b 1986); *Career* artist; one man exhibitions incl: Nigel Greenwood Gallery London (1980 1982 1985 and 1989), Gillespie-Laage-Salomon Paris 1981, Sperone Westwater NY (1983 1986 and 1988), Fruitmarket Gallery Edinburgh 1985, Arnolfini Gallery Bristol 1985, Kunsthalle Basel 1986, DAAD Galerie Berlin 1988, Galerie Rudolf Zwirner Cologne 1988; gp exhibitions incl: Nuova Imagine Milan Triennale 1980, Sydney Biennale 1982, New Art (Tate Gallery London) 1983, An Int Survey of Recent Painting and Sculpture (Museum of Mod Art NY) 1984, The Br Show (toured Australia and NZ) 1985, Paris Biennale 1985, San Francisco Biennale 1986, Venice Biennale 1982 and 1984, Falls the Shadow (Recent Br and Euro Art Hayward Gallery London) 1986, British Art of the 1980's (Museum of Modern Art: Oxford, Budapest, Warsaw, Prague) 1987; Avant Garde in the Eighties (LA County Museum LA) 1987, Br Art of the 1980's (Liljevalchs Museum Stockholm) 1987, The Br Picture (LA Louver Gallery LA) 1988, New Br Painting (Cincinnati Museum and American tour) 1988-89, Br Art Now (Setagaya Art Museum and Japanese tour) 1990-91; awards and cmmns: prizewinner John Moores Liverpool Exhibitions 1978 and 1980, Calouste Gulbenkian Fndn Printmakers Commission Award 1983, designer Ballet Imperial Royal Opera House Covent Garden 1985; DAAD Fellowship Berlin 1987-88; tstee Tate Gallery 1990; *Style—* Christopher Le Brun, Esq; c/o Nigel Greenwood Gallery, 4 New Burlington St, London W1X 1FE (☎ 071 434 3795)

LE CARPENTIER, Francis Stewart; s of Frank Henry Le Carpentier, of Worthing, W Sussex, and Elizabeth, *née* Stafford (d 1961); *b* 26 Feb 1949; *Educ* Royal Wolverhampton Sch; *m* 2 July 1976, Nicole Madeleine Fischer Corderior, da of Willey Fischer, of Brussels; 1 s (Philipe Alexandre), 1 da (Mercedes Elizabeth); *Career* offr US Armed Forces 1969-71 served Europe and Far East; until 1969 retail mangr, gp sales dir Int Property Developers 1971-74, chm and chief exec Paramount Gp 1974-; MInstD 1988; *Recreations* skiing, shooting (not animals), motorsports and powercraft racing; *Clubs* Annabeles (London), various in rest of world; *Style—* Francis Le Carpentier, Esq; Paramount Group, 241 Kings Road, London SW3 (☎ 071 351 3135)

LE CARRÉ, John - David John Moore Cornwell; s of Ronald Thomas Archibald Cornwell and Olive, *née* Glassy; *b* 19 Oct 1931; *Educ* Sherborne, Univ of Berne, Lincoln Coll Oxford (BA); *m* 1, 1954 (m dis 1971), Alison Ann Veronica Sharp; 3 s; m 2, 1972, Valerie Jane Eustace; 1 s; *Career* schoolmaster Eton 1956-58; British Foreign Serv 1960-64; novelist; hon fell Lincoln Coll Oxford 1984, Hon Dr Exeter Univ 1990; *Books* Call for the Dead (1961), A Murder of Quality (1962), The Spy Who Came in from the Cold (1963), The Looking-Glass War (1965), A Small Town in Germany (1968), The Naïve and Sentimental Lover (1971), Tinker, Tailor, Soldier, Spy (1974), The Honourable Schoolboy (1977), Smiley's People (1980), The Little Drummer Girl (1983), A Perfect Spy (1986), The Russia House (1989), The Secret Pilgrim ((1991); *books include* The Spy Who Came In From The Cold (1963, also feature film), Tinker,

Tailor, Soldier, Spy (1974, also TV series), Smiley's People (1980, also TV series), The Little Drummer Girl (1983, also feature film), A Perfect Spy (1986, also TV series), The Russia House (1989, also feature film); *Style—* David Cornwell, Esq; David Higham Associates, 5-8 Lower John Street, London W1R 4HA

LE CHEMINANT, Air Chief Marshal Sir Peter de Lacey; GBE (1978), KCB (1972, CB 1968), DFC (1943, and bar 1951); s of Col Keith Le Cheminant, TD, of Guernsey, CI, and Blanche Etheldred Wake Clark; *b* 17 June 1920; *Educ* Elizabeth Coll Guernsey, RAF Coll Cranwell; *m* 1940, Sylvia, da of J van Bodegom (d 1963); 1 s, 2 da; *Career* joined RAF 1939, Cmdt Joint Warfare Establishment 1968-70, asst chief of Air Staff (Policy) 1972, memb Permanent Mil Deputies Gp Cen Treaty Orgn 1972-74, vice chief of Defence Staff 1974-76, dep C-in-C Allied Forces Central Europe 1976-79, Lt-govr and C-in-C Guernsey 1980-85; *Recreations* golf, sailing; *Clubs* RAF; *Style—* Air Chief Marshal Sir Peter Le Cheminant, GBE, KCB, DFC; La Madeleine de Bas, Ruette de La Madeleine, St Pierre du Bois, Guernsey, Channel Islands

LE CONTE, Frederick James; s of William Le Conte (d 1980), of Islington, and Dorothy Emily, *née* Kingsley (d 1980); *b* 27 Nov 1941; *Educ* Islington Green Sch; *m* 22 Sept 1962, Lola Louise, da of Frank John Downer; 2 s (William b 18 May 1966, Dean b 9 June 1970); *Career* scenic artist ENO 1977-85, Royal Opera House Covent Garden 1985- (1963-77); *Style—* Frederick Le Conte, Esq; Royal Opera House, Covent Garden, London WC2; Scenic Studio HOD (☎ 071 240 1200)

LE FANU, Hon Mrs (Juliet Louise); *née* Annan; yr da of Baron Annan, OBE (Life Peer), *qv*; *b* 7 Jan 1955; *Educ* Francis Holland Sch, King's Coll Cambridge (MA); *m* 4 April 1987, Dr James Richard Le Fanu, 2 s of Richard Le Fanu, of 8 Malvern Terrace, London N1; 1 s (Frederick James b 23 May 1989); *Career* publisher with William Collins Publishers London; *Style—* The Hon Mrs Le Fanu; 24 Grafton Square, London SW4 0DB

LE FANU, Mark; s of Adm of the Fleet Sir Michael Le Fanu (d 1970), and Prudence, *née* Morgan (d 1980); *b* 14 Nov 1946; *Educ* Winchester, Univ of Sussex (BA), Coll of Law; *m* 1976, Lucy Rhoda, da of John Cowen (d 1982), of Bisley, Stroud, Glos; 3 s (Thomas b 1980, Matthew b 1982, Caspar b 1986), 1 da (Celia b 1985); *Career* Lt RN 1964-73; slr McKenna & Co 1973-78; memb Soc of Authors 1979- (gen sec 1982-); *Recreations* canals, sailing, rough travelling; *Style—* Mark Le Fanu, Esq; 25 St James's Gardens, London W11 4RE (☎ 071 603 4119); Soc of Authors, 84 Drayton Gardens, London SW10 9SB (☎ 071 373 6642)

LE FLEMING, Morris John; s of Maj Morris Ralph Le Fleming (d 1969), of Durham, and Mabel, *née* Darling (d 1980); *b* 19 Aug 1932; *Educ* Tonbridge Sch, Magdalene Coll Cambridge (BA); *m* 27 Aug 1960, Jenny Rose, da of Reginald McColvin Weeks, of Bristol; 1 s (Daniel b 1963), 3 da (Emma b 1961, Bridget b 1965, Alice b 1969); *Career* Nat Serv 2 Lt RA 1951-52, Capt TA 1952-61; admitted slr 1958; asst slr: Worcestershire CC 1958-59, Middx CC 1959, Nottinghamshire CC 1959-63; asst clerk Lincolnshire CC 1963-69; Hertfordshire CC: dep clerk 1969-73, county sec 1973-79, chief exec 1979-90, clerk to the Lieutenancy 1979-90, clerk to Magistrates Cts Ctee 1979-90, sec to Probation Ctee 1979-90; Prince's Youth Business Tst Reg Bd 1987-90, dir Herts TEC 1989-90; CBIM; *Recreations* theatre, family history, gardening, architecture; *Style—* Morris le Fleming, Esq; Swangleys Lane, Knebworth, Herts SG3 6AA (☎ 0438 813 152); County Hall, Hertford (☎ 0992 555 600, telex 81272 HERBKS)

LE FLEMING, Noveen, Lady; Noveen Avis; da of the late C C Sharpe, of Rukuhia, Hamilton, New Zealand; *m* 28 April 1948, Sir William Kelland Le Fleming, 11 Bt (d 1988); 3 s, 4 da; *Style—* Noveen, Lady Le Fleming; Green Road, 6 Kopane Rural Delivery, Palmerston North, New Zealand

LE FLEMING, Sir Quentin John; 12 Bt (E 1705), of Rydal, Westmorland; s of Sir William Kelland Le Fleming, 11 Bt (d 1988); *b* 27 June 1949; *m* 26 June 1971, Judith Ann, da of C J Peck, JP, of Ashhurst, Manawatu, NZ; 2 s (David Kelland, Andrew John b 4 Oct 1979), 1 da (Josephine Kay b 31 July 1973); *Heir* s, David Kelland Le Fleming b 12 Jan 1976; *Style—* Sir Quentin Le Fleming, Bt; 147 Stanford St, Ashhurst, Manawatu, New Zealand

LE GOY, Raymond Edgar Michel; s of Jean Andre Stanhope Nemorin Michel Le Goy (d 1966), of Mauritius, and May, *née* Callan (d 1976); *b* 20 April 1919; *Educ* William Ellis Sch, Caius Coll Cambridge (MA); *m* 27 Aug 1960, (Silvia) Ernestine, da of Philip Luther Burnett (d 1947), of Trelawny, Jamaica; 2 s (Keith b 1962, Mark b 1964); *Career* Br Army: joined 1940, cmmnd 1941, Staff Capt HQ E Africa 1943-45, Maj 1945; London Passenger Transport Bd 1947, UK civil servant 1947-, princ 1948, asst sec 1958, under sec 1968; EC: DG for Transport 1973-81, a DG 1982-; chm Union of Univ Liberal Soc 1939-40, sec Cambridge 1939; FCIT; *Books* The Victorian Burletta (1953); *Recreations* theatre, music, race relations; *Clubs* United Oxford and Cambridge University, National Liberal; *Style—* Raymond Le Goy, Esq; Societe Generale De Banque, Agence Europbenne, Rond Point Schuman, Brussels B 1040, Belgium

Le GRAND, Julian Ernest Michael; s of Roland John Le Grand (d 1976), of Taunton, Somerset, and Eileen Joan, *née* Baker; *b* 29 May 1945; *Educ* Eton, Univ of Sussex (BA), Univ of Pennsylvania (PhD); *m* 19 June 1971, Damaris May, da of Rev Nigel Robertson-Glasgow, of Fakenham, Norfolk; 2 da (Polly b 1978, Zoe b 1981); *Career* lectr in economics: Univ of Sussex 1971-78, LSE 1978-85; sr res fell Suntory-Toyota Int Centre for Econs and Related Disciplines LSE 1985-87, prof of public policy Sch for Advanced Urban Studies Univ of Bristol 1987-; conslt: OECD, Euro Cmmn, Open Univ, French Govt; ESRC: memb Social Affrs Ctee 1982-86, memb Res Grants Bd 1988-; co-fndr Socialist Philosophy Gp, memb Ctee Fabian Soc; *Books* The Economics of Social Problems (with R Robinson, 1 edn 1976, 2 edn 1984), The Strategy of Equality (1982), Privatisation and the Welfare State (ed with R Robinson, 1984), Not Only the Poor (with R Goodin, 1987), Market Socialism (ed with S Estrin, 1989), Equity and Choice (1991); *Recreations* drawing, juggling; *Style—* Julian Le Grand, Esq; 31 Sydenham Hill, Cotham, Bristol BS6 5SL (☎ 0272 425253); School for Advanced Urban Studies, University of Bristol, Rodney Lodge, Grange Rd, Bristol BS8 4EA (☎ 0272 741117, fax 0272 737308)

LE GRICE, (Andrew) Valentine; s of Charles Le Grice (d 1982), of Penzance, and Wilmay, *née* Ward; *b* 26 June 1953; *Educ* Shrewsbury, Collingwood Coll Univ of Durham (BA); *m* 17 dec 1977, Anne Elizabeth, da of Philip Moss, of Gt Bookham; 2 s (Charles b 8 Oct 1984, Philip b 16 Aug 1986), 1 da (Alexandra b 24 Nov 1989); *Career* called to the Bar Middle Temple 1977; *Clubs* Travellers', Royal Yacht Sqdn; *Style—* Valentine Le Grice, Esq; 1 Mitre Court Bldgs, Temple, London EC4Y 7BS

Le MARCHAND, Capt Thomas Maitland; s of Col L P Le Marchand, OBE (d 1977), and Sibyl, *née* Rouse; *b* 14 May 1941; *Educ* Tonbridge Sch, Britannia RNC Dartmouth; *m* 29 June 1963, Valerie, da of L Reynolds (d 1963); 1 s (Philip b 4 July 1973), 3 da (Zoë b 15 April 1964, Helen b 26 Sept 1966, Anna b 19 Dec 1968); *Career* joined RN 1959, cmmnd 1962, submarine serv 1963; cmd: HMS Narwhal 1972-74, HMS Valiant 1977 and 1981-83 (Falklands War (despatches 1982)), HMS Cleopatra and 7 Frigate Sqdn 1987-89, 3 Submarine Sqdn 1989-; *Recreations* squash (Suffolk county veterans 1988); *Clubs* Royal Navy Club of 1765 and 1785; *Style—* Capt Thomas Le Marchand; c/o Naval Secretary, MOD, Old Admiralty Building, Whitehall, London SW1 (☎ 071 218 3171)

LE MARCHANT, Sir Francis Arthur; 6 Bt (UK 1841); s of Sir Denis Le Marchant, 5 Bt (d 1987), and Elizabeth Rowena Worth; *b* 6 Oct 1939; *Educ* Gordonstoun, Royal Acad Schs; *Heir* kinsman, Michael Le Marchant b 1937; *Career* painter; *Style—* Sir Francis Le Marchant, Bt; c/o Midland Bank, 88 Westgate, Grantham, Lincs

LE MARCHANT, Lady; Lucinda Gaye; *née* Leveson Gower; o da of Brig Hugh Nugent Leveson Gower (ggggs of Adm Hon John Leveson-Gower, yr s of 1 Earl Gower), of Tilford, and his 1 w, Avril Joy, *née* Mullens; *b* 12 Nov 1935; *m* 5 May 1955, Sir Spencer Le Marchant (d 1986); 2 da; *Style—* Lady Le Marchant; 29 Rivermill, Grosvenor Rd, London SW1 (☎ 071 821 9191); The Saltings, Yarmouth, Isle of Wight (☎ 0983 760223)

LE MARECHAL, Robert Norford; s of Reginald Le Marechal (d 1976), of Southampton, and Margaret, *née* Cokely; *b* 29 May 1939; *Educ* Taunton's Sch Southampton; *m* 21 Dec 1963, Linda Mary, da of Noel Stanley Williams (d 1983), of Ludlow; 2 da (Kate b 1969, Rebecca b 1971); *Career* Sgt RAEC 1958-60; sr auditor MOD 1971-76 (joined Exchequer and Audit Dept 1957), chief auditor DOE 1976-80, dep dir of audit 1980-83, dir of policy and planning NAO 1984-86, asst auditor gen 1986-89, dep comptroller and auditor gen 1989-; *Recreations* reading, gardening; *Style—* Robert Le Marechal, Esq; 62 Woodcote Hurst, Epsom, Surrey (☎ 03727 21291); National Audit Office, Buckingham Palace Road, Victoria, London (☎ 071 798 7381)

LE MASURIER, Sir Robert Hugh; DSC (1942); s of William Smythe Le Masurier (d 1955); *b* 29 Dec 1913; *Educ* Victoria Coll Jersey, Pembroke Coll Oxford; *m* 1941, Helen Sophia Sheringham; 1 s, 2 da; *Career* serv in 1939-45 war; slr gen Jersey 1955-58 (attorney gen 1958-62), bailiff Jersey 1962-74, a judge of Guernsey Ct of Appeal 1964-; kt 1966; *Style—* Sir Robert Le Masurier, DSC; 4 La Fantasie, Rue Du Huquet, St Martin, Jersey, CI

LE MOIGNAN, Martine; MBE (1990); da of Alan George le Moignan, and Hazel May, *née* Toudic; *b* 28 Oct 1962; *Educ* Cordier Hull, Blancheland Coll; *Career* professional squash player; former county player Hants and Notts, currently Essex; 71 full caps England; honours incl: memb England team World Team Championship winners 4 times (Ireland, NZ, Holland, Aust), world champion Holland 1989 (runner up Aust 1990); record for most England caps; *Recreations* all sport, travelling, reading, yoga, aerobics, jazz music; *Style—* Miss Martine le Moignan, MBE; c/o Steven Ivell, 19 Gainsborough Drive, Lawford Dale, Manningtree, Essex (☎ 0206 391282)

LE PARD, Geoffrey; s of Desmond Allen Le Pard, Silver Crest, Silver St, Sway, Lymington, and Barbara Grace, *née* Francis; *b* 30 Nov 1956; *Educ* Purley GS, Brockenhurst GS, Univ of Bristol (LLB); *m* 19 May 1984, Linda Ellen, da of Leslie Jones, of 42 Ruskin Rd, Costessey, Norwich; 1 s (Samuel William b 23 April 1990); *Career* articled clerk Corbould Rigby & Co 1979-81, ptnr Freshfields 1987- (asst slr 1981-87); memb City of London Slrs Co; *Recreations* cricket, rugby, squash, theatre, good food; *Clubs* Law Soc RFC, Dulwich CC; *Style—* Geoffrey Le Pard, Esq; Whitefriars, 65 Fleet St, London EC4 (☎ 071 936 4000)

LE POER TRENCH, Brinsley; *see*: Clancarty, Earl of

LE QUESNE, Sir (John) Godfray; QC (1962); 3 s of Charles Thomas Le Quesne, QC (d 1954), of London and Jersey, and Florence Elizabeth Eileen, *née* Pearce Gould (d 1977); bro of Sir Martin and Prof Leslie, *qv*; *b* 18 Jan 1924; *Educ* Shrewsbury, Exeter Coll Oxford (MA); *m* 6 April 1963, Susan Mary, da of Rev Thomas Woodman Gill; 2 s, 1 da; *Career* called to the Bar Inner Temple 1947, admitted to Bar of St Helena 1959; dep chm Kesteven Lincs QS 1963-71, judge Cts of Appeal of Jersey and Guernsey 1964-, rec of Crown Ct 1972- (resumed practice 1988); chm: Cncl Regent's Park Coll Oxford 1958-87, Monopolies and Mergers Cmmn 1975-87; Dato Order of the Crown of Brunei 1978; kt 1980; *Recreations* music, railways, walking; *Style—* Sir Godfray Le Quesne, QC; 1 Crown Office Row, Temple, London EC4 7HH (☎ 071 583 9292, telex 8953152)

LE QUESNE, Prof Leslie Philip; CBE (1984); 2 s of Charles Thomas Le Quesne, QC (d 1954), and (Florence Elizabeth) Eileen (d 1977), 3 da of Sir Alfred Pearce Gould, KCVO, FRCS; bro of Sir Martin and Sir Godfray, *qqv*; *b* 24 Aug 1919; *Educ* Rugby, Exeter Coll Oxford (DM, MCh); *m* 1969, Pamela Margaret, da of Dr Archibald Fullerton, MC (d 1972), of Batley, Yorks; 2 s (Thomas b 1973, William b 1975); *Career* prof of surgery Middx Hosp and dir Surgical Studies Dept 1963-84, dep vice chllr and dean Faculty of Med Univ of London 1980-84; medical awards administrator Commonwealth Scholarship Cmmn 1984-91; FRCS; *Recreations* fishing, sailing; *Clubs* Reform; *Style—* Prof Leslie Le Quesne, CBE; 8 Eton Villas, London NW3 4SX (☎ 071 722 0778)

LE QUESNE, Sir (Charles) Martin; KCMG (1974); s of Charles Thomas Le Quesne, QC (d 1954); bro of Prof Leslie and Sir Godfray, *qqv*; *b* 10 June 1917; *Educ* Shrewsbury, Exeter Coll Oxford; *m* 1948, Deidre Noel Fisher; 3 s; *Career* entered Foreign Office 1946; ambass to: Republic of Mali 1961-64, Algeria 1968-71; dep under sec FCO 1971-74, high cmmr Nigeria 1974-76; memb of the States of Jersey 1978-90; hon fell Univ of Oxford 1990; *Style—* Sir Martin Le Quesne, KCMG; Beau Desert, St Saviour, Jersey, CI (☎ 0534 22076)

LE SAUX, Graeme Pierre; s of Pierre Le Saux, of Jersey, CI, and late Daphne, *née* Brown; *b* 17 Oct 1968; *Educ* D'Hautree Sch Jersey, Hautlieu, Kingston Poly; *Career* professional footballer; debut Chelsea v Portsmouth 1989; 4 England under 21 caps; *Recreations* tennis, jazz music, antiques, art, literature, media; *Style—* Graeme Le Saux, Esq; Chelsea FC, Stamford Bridge, Fulham Rd, London SW6 1HE (☎ 071 385 5545)

LE TISSIER, Matthew Paul; s of Marcus Le Tissier, of Guernsey, and Ruth Elizabeth, *née* Blundel; *b* 14 Oct 1968; *Educ* La Mare De Carteret Secdy Sch CI; *m* 23 June 1990, Catherine Claire, *née* Loveridge; *Career* professional footballer; Southampton 1986-: apprentice then professional, debut 1986, over 160 appearances; 2 England B caps v Republic of Ireland and Czechoslovakia 1990; Young Player of the Year Professional Footballers' Assoc 1990, Barclays Young Eagle of the Year 1990; *Recreations* snooker, golf, tv; *Style—* Matthew Le Tissier, Esq; Jerome Anderson Management Ltd, 248 Statron Rd, Edgware, Middlesex HA8 7AU (☎ 081 958 7799, fax 081 958 2000)

LEA, His Hon Christopher Gerald; MC; yst s of late George Percy Lea, and Jocelyn Clare, *née* Lea, of Franche, Kidderminster, Worcs; *b* 27 Nov 1917; *Educ* Charterhouse, RMC Sandhurst; *m* 1952, Susan Elizabeth, da of Maj Edward Pendarves Dorrien Smith; 2 s, 2 da (1 decd); *Career* called to the Bar Inner Temple 1948; memb: Assistance Bd Appeal Tribunal Oxford Area 1961-63, Mental Health Review Tbnl 1962-68 and 1983-, met magistrate 1968-72, dep chm Berks QS 1968-71, circuit judge 1972-90; *Style—* His Hon Christopher Lea, MC; Simms Farm House, Mortimer, Reading, Berks (☎ 0734 332 360)

LEA, Diana, Lady; Diana Silva; *née* Thompson; only da of James Howard Thompson, MIME, of Coton Hall, Bridgnorth, Shropshire, and Gladys, *née* Yates; *m* 1, 1945 (m dis 1947), Capt Guy William Bannar-Martin, IA; m 2, 1950, as his 2 wife, Sir Thomas Claude Harris Lea, 3 Bt (d 1985); *Style—* Diana, Lady Lea

LEA, Harold Rodney; DFC (1945); s of Albert Lea (d 1967), of Fordingbridge, Hants, and Elsie, *née* Tattersall (d 1934); *b* 31 March 1922; *Educ* King's Norton GS Birmingham; *m* 1, 16 March 1946, Pamela Alice, da of late John Leicester, of Ashtead, Surrey; m 2, 2 June 1951, Ruby, da of Rueben Tallon, of Storth, Milnthorpe, Cumbria;

1 s (Timothy John b 1959), 1 da (Suzanne Elizabeth b 1954); *Career* WWII joined RAFVR 1940; Fighter Cmd Flt Lt served: N Africa, Malta, Sicily, Italy, Holland, Belgium; instr: Central Gunnery Sch RAF 1944, Fighter Ldrs Sch RAF 1945-46; served RAF Korean War; joined Br Euro Airways (attaining cmd) 1964; hi-jacked 1975 on a flight Manchester to London; ret 1976; flew photographic aircraft for Arthur Gibson specialising in air to air photography; chm and pres West Berks Cons Assoc 1979-85; Queen's Commendation for Valuable Serv in the Air 1976; *Recreations* gardening, golf, reading; *Clubs* Penina GC (Algarve, Portugal); *Style*— Harold Lea, Esq, DFC; Casa Dos Bunkers, Falfeira, Portelas, 8600 Lagos, Algarve, Portugal (☎ Lagos 082 63937)

LEA, Vice Adm Sir John Stuart Crosbie; KBE (1979); s of Lt-Col Edward Heath Lea (d 1947), and Aileen Beatrice, *née* Hawthorne (d 1973); *b* 4 June 1923; *Educ* Boxgrove Sch, Shrewsbury, RNEC Keyham; *m* 1947, Patricia Anne, da of William Martin Thoseby (d 1955); 1 s, 2 da; *Career* joined RN 1941, Capt 1966, dir of Naval Admin Planning 1970-71, Cdre HMS Nelson 1972-75, Rear Adm 1975, asst chief of Fleet Support 1976-77, dir gen Naval Manpower and Trg 1977-80, Vice Adm 1978, ret; chm GEC Marine and Industl Gears Ltd 1980-87; chm: Portsmouth Naval Heritage Tst 1983-87, chm Hayling Island Horticultural Soc 1980, chm Regular Forces Employment Assoc 1987-89, Vice Pres RFEA 1990; pres Hampshire Autistic Assoc 1988; Master Worshipful Co of Plumbers 1988-89; *Recreations* walking, woodwork, gardening; *Style*— Vice Adm Sir John Lea, KBE; Springfield, 27 Bright Lane, Hayling Island, Hants (☎ 070 5 463801)

LEA, (Francis) Peter; s of Francis William Lea (d 1977), and Margaret Anne, *née* Washer (d 1981); *b* 8 Aug 1935; *Educ* St Joseph's Acad Blackheath London; *m* 3 Aug 1959, Virginia Daisy, da of Harold Edward Munday (d 1977); 2 s (David b 1960, Michael b 1971), 4 da (Alison b 1961, Ruth b 1963, Joanne b 1965, Catherine b and d 1970); *Career* Nat Serv RA 1954-56; chief sports sub ed Daily Sketch 1966 (joined 1960, dep chief sports sub ed 1964), sports ed Daily Mail 1988 (joined 1971, asst sports ed 1974, dep sports ed 1982), ret 1990; *Recreations* swimming, golf, music, reading; *Clubs* Scribes West Int; *Style*— Peter Lea, Esq

LEA, Prof Peter John; s of Dr Alan Joseph Lea (d 1983), of Tamworth, and Jessie, *née* Farrall; *b* 1 Dec 1944; *Educ* Arnold Sch Blackpool, Univ of Liverpool (BSc, PhD, DSc); *m* 30 July 1965, Christine, *née* Shaw; 1 da (Julia b 5 Dec 1966); *Career* res fell Royal Soc 1972-75, princ scientific offr Rothamsted Experimental Station Harpenden Herts 1978-84 (sr scientific offr 1975-78), head Div Biological Scis Univ of Lancaster 1988- (prof biology 1985-); chm Phytochemical Soc Europe (sec 1982-87); FIBiol; *Books* incl: The Genetic Manipulation of Plants and its Application to Agriculture (with G R Stewart, 1984), The Biochemistry of Plant Phenolics (with C F van Sumere, 1986), Biologically Active Natural Products (with K Hostettmann, 1987), Methods in Plant Biochemistry (1989), The Biochemistry of plants (with B J Miflin, 1990); *Recreations* cricket, collecting wedgwood pottery; *Style*— Prof Peter Lea; The Old Sch, Chapel Lane, Ellel, Lancaster LA2 0PW (☎ 0524 751156); Univ of Lancaster, Div of Biological Sciences, Bailrigg, Lancaster LA1 4YQ (☎ 0524 65201 ext 3510, fax 0524 382212)

LEA, Philip; s of Herbert James Lea (d 1932), and Elizabeth, *née* Maskery; *b* 28 July 1915; *Educ* Sandbach Sch Cheshire; *m* Oct 1940, Vera Nadine (d 1986), da of Albert Cope (d 1969); 1 s (John Edward), 1 da (Anne Arden (Mrs Borrowdale)); *Career* chm and md Morning Foods Ltd North Western Mills 1942-; dir: H J Lea & Sons, P J Lea Consulting Services Ltd, Mornflake Oats Ltd, Wheelock Estates Ltd, Trustlea Ltd, Walter Brown & Sons Ltd, Assoc of Cereal Food Manufacturers; engrg conslt UK Agric Supply Trade Assoc; life govr The Royal Agric Soc of Eng, fell Nat Inst of Agric Botany Cambridge; Freeman City of London, memb Worshipful Co of Farmers; *Recreations* shooting, golf, boar hunting; *Clubs* Farmers', City Livery, RAC; *Style*— Philip Lea, Esq; Calveley Court, Tarporley, Cheshire (☎ 027 073 222); St Petrock's, Marine Drive, Llandudno (☎ 0492 77367); Morning Foods Ltd, North Western Mills, Crewe, Cheshire CW2 6HP (☎ 0270 213261, fax 0270 500291, telex 36548)

LEA, Robert Francis Gore; OBE (1942); s of Sir (Thomas) Sydney Lea, 2 Bt (d 1946), of Dunley Hall, nr Stourport, Worcs, and Mary Ophelia, *née* Woodward; *b* 22 Jan 1906; *Educ* Lancing, Clare Coll Cambridge (BA, MA); *m* 1, 5 March 1936, Valerie Josephine (d 1948), da of Lt Sir James Henry Domville 5 Bt; 1 da (Annabel Clare Ophelia b 1945); m 2, 3 May 1956, Susan, da of John Greenwood, of Dorset; 1 s ((Francis) Rupert Chad Lea b 1957); *Career* Aux Airforce 600 City of London F Sqdn 1930, enlisted 1939, served at Hornchurch Battle of Br, Siege of Malta 1941-42, Wing-Cdr 1943 (despatches); Lloyds of London 1928-36, commercial dir Aero-Res Ltd Duxford 1955-60 (joined 1937), md CIBA Duxford 1960 (jt md and dep chm 1963), chm TECHNE Ltd 1975-88; amateur breeder of roses, created the gardens at Duxford Mill opens for charity six times a year; fell Woodland Corpn 1939-56; *Recreations* gardening, shooting, fishing; *Style*— Robert Lea, Esq, OBE

LEA, Hon Mrs (Susan); da of 13 Lord Kinnaird; *b* 31 Dec 1956; *m* 1987, Francis Rupert Chad Lea, s of Robert Francis Gore Lea, OBE, of Duxford Mill, Cambridge (2 s of Sir Thomas Sydney Lea, 2 Bt); *Style*— The Hon Mrs Lea

LEA, Sir Thomas William; 5 Bt (UK 1892), of The Larches, Kidderminster, Worcestershire, and Sea Grove, Dawlish, Devon; eldest s of Sir (Thomas) Julian Lea, 4 Bt (d 1990), and Gerry Valerie, o da of late Capt Gibson Clarence Fahnestock, USAF; *b* 6 Sept 1973; *Heir* bro, Alexander Julian Lea b 1978; *Style*— Sir Thomas Lea, Bt; Bachelors Hall, Hundon, Sudbury, Suffolk CO10 8DY

LEACH, Allan William; s of Frank Leach (d 1938), of Rotherwick Hants, and Margaret Ann, *née* Bennett (d 1973); *b* 9 May 1931; *Educ* Watford GS, Loughborough Coll, Open Univ (BA, DPA); *m* 1962, Betty, da of William George Gadsby, of Bramcote, Notts; 1 s (William b 1967), 1 da (Sarah b 1969); *Career* county librarian Bute 1965-71, burgh librarian Ayr 1971-74; dir of Library Servs Kyle and Carrick 1974-82, dir gen and librarian Nat Library for the Blind 1982-; memb Standing Ctee IFLA Section of Libraries for the Blind 1983- (chm 1985-87); *Recreations* people, music, the countryside; *Style*— Allan Leach, Esq; 4 Windsor Rd, Hazel Grove, Stockport, Cheshire SK7 4SW (☎ 061 483 6418); Nat Library for the Blind, Cromwell Rd, Bredbury, Stockport, Cheshire SK6 2SG (☎ 061 494 0217)

LEACH, Clive William; s of Stanely Aubrey Leach, of Kessingland, Suffolk, and Laura Anne, *née* Robinson; *b* 4 Dec 1934; *Educ* Sir John Leman Sch Beccles Suffolk, Univ of Birmingham; *m* 1, 25 Oct 1958; 3 s (Christopher b 1959, Stuart b 1961, Adrian b 1964); m 2, 25 Sept 1980, Stephanie Miriam, da of Patrick McGinn, of Newlands Rd, Sidmouth, Devon; 1 s (Damian b 1981); *Career* md Yorks TV Ltd, chm Yorks TV Enterprises Ltd; played first class cricket for Warwicks 1955-57, also for Durham and Bucks counties; *Recreations* golf, travel, entertaining; *Clubs* Harewood Downs Golf, Warwickshire County Cricket, Bucks County Cricket, Clermont, MCC; *Style*— C W Leach, Esq; Yorkshire Television Ltd, 32 Bedford Row, London WC1

LEACH, David Andrew; OBE (1987); s of Bernard Howell Leach, CH, CBE (d 1979), of Cornwall, and Edith Muriel, *née* Hoyle (d 1955); *b* 7 May 1911; *Educ* Dauntsey's Sch; *m* 23 April 1938, (Mary) Elizabeth, da of Surgn Cdr Samuel Henry Facey (d 1942), of The Firs, Nyewood, Petersfield, Hants; 3 s (John Henry b 1939, (Paul) Jeremy David b 1941, Simon Andrew b 1956); *Career* WWII DCLI 1941-45; potter: student to Bernard Leach (father), in practise 1930-; former chm Craftsman Potters Assoc GB, chm Devon Guild Craftsmen 1985-88; gold medalist Int Acad Ceramists; memb: Craftsmen Potters Assoc, Crafts Cncl, Devon Guild of Craftsmen; *Recreations* hockey and tennis; *Style*— David Leach, Esq, OBE; Lowerdown Cross, Bovey Tracey, Devon TQ13 9LE (☎ 0626 833408); Lowerdown Pottery, Lowerdown Cross, Bovey Tracey, Devon TQ13 9LE (☎ 0626 833408)

LEACH, Frank; s of George Manley Leach (d 1954), and Ethel Leach (d 1968); *b* 1 May 1935; *Educ* Wirral GS, Univ of London (BA); *m* 1959, Marion, da of Reginald Edwards (d 1975); 2 s; *Career* chartered sec; gp sec The Cunard S/S Co Ltd 1968-74; dir: Br Lion Films Ltd 1974-76, Thorn EMI Screen Entertainment 1977-86, Weintraub Entertainment 1987-; *Recreations* painting, gardening; *Style*— Frank Leach, Esq; 11 Upton Quarry, Langton Green, Tunbridge Wells, Kent (☎ 089 286 2733); Weintraub Entertainment, 167/9 Wardour St, London W1 (☎ 071 439 1790)

LEACH, Graham John; s of Vernon Richard Henry Leach, of Surrey, and Doris Elsie Margaret, *née* Richardson; *b* 1 Oct 1948; *Educ* Battersea GS London, Univ of Liverpool (BA); *m* 14 Dec 1974, Ruth, da of Noel Barsby, of Woburn; 3 s (Thomas b 1980, William b 1983, Oliver b 1985); *Career* BBC journalist; news trainee 1971-2, regnl news corr Belfast 1972-74, radio reporter London 1974-77, Bonn corr 1977-81, ME corr 1981-83, SA radio corr 1983-89, Europe corr 1989-; Sony Radio Reporter of the Year 1987; *Books* South Africa No Easy Path to Peace (1985), The Afrikaners Their Last Great Trek (1989); *Recreations* theatre, cycling; *Style*— Graham Leach, Esq; British Broadcasting Corporation, International Press Centre, BP 5O, 1 Boulevard Charlemagne, 1040 Brussels, Belgium (☎ 010 32 2302120, fax 010 32 2302688, telex 25912, car 017 415160)

LEACH, Adm of the Fleet Sir Henry Conyers; GCB (1978, KCB 1977); s of Capt John Caterall Leach, MVO, DSO, RN (ka 1941), and Evelyn Burrell, *née* Lee (d 1969); *b* 18 Nov 1923; *Educ* RNC Dartmouth and Greenwich; *m* 15 Feb 1958, Mary Jean, da of Adm Sir Henry William Urquhart McCall, KCVO, KBE, CB, DSO (d 1980); 2 da (Henrietta b 1959, Philippa b 1964); *Career* joined RN 1937, Capt 1961, dir Naval Plans 1968-70, Rear Adm 1971, asst chief Naval Staff (Policy) 1971-73, Vice Adm 1974, Flag Offr First Flotilla 1974-75, Vice Chief of Def Staff 1976-77, Adm 1977, C-in-C Fleet and Allied C-in-C Channel and Eastern Atlantic 1977-79, chief of Naval Staff and First Sea Lord 1979-82, Adm of the Fleet 1982, first and princ Naval ADC to the Queen 1979; chm St Dunstan's 1983-; pres: Regal Naval Benevolent Soc 1983-, Sea Cadet Assoc 1984-; vice pres SSAFA 1984-, sr pres Offrs Assoc 1991-, chm Cncl King Edward VII Hospital 1987-; Freeman: City of London 1982, Worshipful Co of Shipwrights', Merchant Taylors' Co; *Recreations* fishing, shooting, gardening, repairing antique furniture; *Clubs* Farmers'; *Style*— Adm of the Fleet Sir Henry Leach, GCB; Wonston Lodge, Wonston, Winchester, Hants (☎ 0962 760327)

LEACH, Peter Timothy Lionel; s of Lt-Col Lionel Robert Henry Gerald Leach, MC, JP, DL, of Benington Park, Stevenage, Herts, and Joan Mary, *née* Rochford; *b* 2 Oct 1945; *Educ* Ampleforth; *m* 1972, Stephanie, da of Geoffrey Haig Pike (d 1981), 2 s (Robert b 1974, Mark b 1980); 2 da (Emma b 1973, Sarah b 1977); *Career* CA; dir Joseph Rochford Gp 1983; *Recreations* field sports; *Style*— P T L Leach, Esq; Wormley House, 82 High Rd, Wormley, Broxbourne, Herts (☎ 0992 466324)

LEACH, Maj Robert Francis (Robin); s of late Maj Robert Wild Leach, and Jocelyn Mary, *née* Hudson (d 1979); *b* 25 May 1926; *Educ* Marlborough, RMA Sandhurst; *m* 13 Feb 1954, Christine Rosemary, da of Robert Christopher Giles, of Terwick Hill, Rogate, Sussex; 2 s (Robert Charles b 1957, Andrew Christopher b 1963), 1 da (Frances Columbel (Mrs Andrew Kerr) b 1955); *Career* WWII cmmnd 3 Kings Own Hussars served: Palestine, UK, Germany; Capt: GSO3 11 Armd Div HQ, staff 23 Armd Bde TA; instr RMA Sandhurst; Maj: Staff Mil Ops Branch MOD, HQ Aldershot Dist; cmd sqdn 4/7 Royal Dragoon Gds Catterick, ret Maj 1963; memb mgmnt consumer div Kimberley Clarke 1963-65; Time-Life Int: Life Magazine 1965-70, Advertising Dept Time Magazine London 1970-76, mangr Time M East (also Scotland and Ireland) 1977-83; dir C W Assocs Ltd Int Media Reps 1983-91; memb Int Advertising Assoc 1965-83, pres Pirbright Br Legion, cncllr (also church warden and vice chm) Pirbright PCC; Past Master Sandhurst Beagles; *Recreations* golf, tennis, travel, field sports; *Clubs* Cavalry Guards, Worplesdon Golf; *Style*— Maj Robin Leach; Greengates, The Green, Pirbright, nr Woking, Surrey (☎ 04867 2215); C W & Associates Ltd, 185-187 Brompton Rd, London SW3 1NE (☎ 071 584 8588)

LEACH, Robin Anthony Langley; s of Col Anthony Pearce Leach, TD, DL (d 1984), of Clifford, Wetherby, Yorks, and Jeanette Helen Leach; *b* 20 March 1955; *Educ* Sherborne, Univ of St Andrews (MA); *m* 19 Sept 1987, Fiona Susan, da of Hamish Tait Easdale, of Polkerris, Camp Rd, Gerrards Cross, Bucks; *Career* called to the Bar Lincolns Inn 1979; *Recreations* golf, cricket, squash, fishing, shooting, horseracing, photography, travel; *Clubs* MCC, RAC; *Style*— Robin Leach, Esq; 2 Harcourt Buildings, Temple, London EC4 (☎ 071 353 2112)

LEACH, Robin Dudley; s of Ronald Frederick Leach, and Mabel Ellen, *née* Pretty; *b* 7 May 1947; *Educ* Ealing GS, St Thomas Hosp London (MB BS, MS); *m* 15 Feb 1975, Susan Mary, da of Dafydd W Jones-Williams; 1 adopted s (Simon Charles b 7 Sept 1977); *Career* conslt surgn Kingston Hosp 1984-; pres clinical section RSM 1989, clinical tutor Kingston Hosp Univ of London 1989; memb RSM 1989, FRCS 1975; *Books* The Longest Race (Chapter on Medical Aspects, 1975), Sailing (Chapter on Medical Aspects, 1981); *Recreations* First English doctor to race around world (1973-4) Whitbread Round the World Yacht Race; *Style*— Robin Leach, Esq; Oak Cottage, Common Lane, Claygate, Surrey KT10 0HY; Kingston Hosp, Kingston upon Thames, Surrey (☎ 081 546 7711); New Victoria Hosp, 184 Coombe Lane West, Kingston, Surrey (☎ 081 949 1661)

LEACH, Dr Rodney; s of Edward Leach (d 1951), of Thornton Cleveleys, Lancs, and Alice Matthews, *née* Marcroft; descendant of one of the Rochdale Pioneers who founded the Worldwide Co-operative movement; *b* 3 March 1932; *Educ* Baines GS, Poulton le Fylde Lancs, Univ of Birmingham (BSc, PhD); *m* 1958, Eira Mary, da of David Arthur Tuck (d 1975), of Caterham, Surrey; 3 s (Michael, Stephen, Alan), 1 da (Alison); *Career* ptnr McKinsey & Co Inc 1970-74, exec dir P & O Steam Navigation Co 1974-85; chm: P & O Euro Tport Servs Ltd 1974-85, P & O Cruises Ltd 1980-85; chief exec and md VSEL Consortium plc 1985-88, chm and chief exec Vickers Shipbuilding and Engineering Ltd 1986-88; dir: NW Water Group plc 1989-, Jasmin plc 1989-, Rennaissance Arts Theatre Tst Ltd 1989-; memb NW Water Authy 1989, conseiller Spécial Chambre de Commerce et d'Industrie de Boulogne sur Mer 1989-, memb Gen Cncl Cumbria Tourist Bd 1987-; Freeman City of London, Liveryman Worshipful Co of Shipwrights; CEng, FRINA, FCIM, FIIM; *Recreations* sailing, reading, gardening, fell walking; *Clubs* RAC, Royal Yachting Assoc; *Style*— Dr Rodney Leach; Cleeve Howe, Windermere, Cumbria LA23 1AS

LEACH, Sir Ronald George; GBE (1976); s of William T Leach; *b* 1907; *Educ* Alleyns; *m* Margaret Alice, da of Henry Binns; *Career* dep fin sec Miny of Food 1939-46; memb: Departmental Ctee on Flooding 1953, Ctee of Inquiry into Shipping 1967; chm: Standard Chartered Bank (CI) Ltd, Standard Chartered Trust Co (CI) Ltd; Consumers Ctee for GB 1957-66, sr ptnr Peat Marwick Mitchell & Co Chartered Accountants 1966-77; dir: Samuel Montagu & Co 1977-80, Banque Nationale de Paris Ltd 1977-80, Samuel Montagu & Co (Jersey) Ltd 1980-87, International Investment Trust of Jersey Ltd, Ann St Brewery; pres Inst of CAs 1969-70; Govett America

Endeavour; kt 1970; *Style*— Sir Ronald Leach, GBE; La Rosière, Mont de la Rosière, St Saviour, Jersey (☎ 0534 77039); Limeuil, Dordoyne, France

LEACH, Stephen Michael Joseph; s of Lt-Col Lionel Robert Henry Gerald Leach MC, JP, DL, of Benington Park, Stevenage, Herts, and Joan Mary, *née* Rochford, MD; *b* 5 Nov 1947; *Educ* Ampleforth; *m* 24 July 1976, Sarah Margaret Young, da of Maj Edward Young Dobson (d 1972); 1 s (Timothy b 1979), 2 da (Rebecca b 1978, Katie b 1982); *Career* admitted slr 1973; sec Woodbridge Rotary Club, clerk Ufford Tstees; memb: Law Soc 1973; prov Notaries Soc; *Recreations* fishing, shooting; *Style*— Stephen Leach, Esq; 28 Church Street, Woodbridge, (☎ 0394 385161 fax 0394 380134)

LEACH, (Ernest) Terrance; s of Ernest Terrance Leach (d 1982), of St Anton, Pear Tree Lane, Whitchurch, Shropshire, and Alice Maud, *née* Hollyhead; *b* 21 Jan 1933; *Educ* Whitchurch GS, Univ of Nottingham (LLB); *m* 21 March 1959, Patricia, da of Ralph Cook (d 1987), of The Cottage, Edgeley Hall, Whitchurch, Shropshire; 2 da (Stephany b 9 April 1962, Stella b 11 May 1965); *Career* called to the Bar Grays Inn 1960; ptnr: quantity surveyors The Leach Partnership (former E T Leach and Ptnrs) 1963-83, Leach International SA 1970-83, ptnr quantity surveying and construction claims consultancy E T Leach and Assoc (UK) 1983-; former govr Sir John Talbots Sch; former chm Whitchurch Shropshire branch RNLI, Save the Children Fund; Freeman City of London 1985, Liveryman Worshipful Co of Arbitrators; FCIArb 1965, hon fell Inst of Quantity Surveyors 1975, FInstCES 1980, FRICS 1985, BACFI 1985; *Recreations* yachting, model making and painting; *Style*— Terrance Leach, Esq; Trem-y-Garn, Barmouth, Gwynedd LL42 1PH (☎ 0341 281364)

LEACHMAN, Jack Ramsay; s of William Thomas Leachman (d 1985), of Colwyn Bay, and Grace, *née* Stamper (d 1979); *b* 14 Jan 1924; *Educ* Northampton Town and County Sch; *m* 26 Sept 1949, (Isobel) Patricia, da of Henry McIntyre Whent (d 1949); 1 s (Robert b 1952), 2 da (Sara b 1955, Emma b 1964); *Career* WWII Flt Lt RAF Saudi Arabia 1943-47; dir Bass plc 1975-86 (brewer 1951-86), chm Bass Brewing Ltd 1978-86, dir Grinkle Park Estate 1984-; memb Sail Trg Assoc, Royal Warrant Holder 1978-84, tstee Game Conservancy Assoc 1990; City of London 1981; FIBrew 1989; *Recreations* shooting, fishing, cricket; *Clubs* MCC, Boodle's; *Style*— Jack Leachman, Esq; Pear Trees, Egton Bridge, Whitby, N Yorks YO21 1UZ (☎ 0947 85219); Grinkle Park Estate, Loftus, Saltburn, Cleveland TS13 4UB (☎ 0287 640468, fax 0287 641278)

LEADBETTER, Prof Alan James; s of Robert Pichavant Leadbetter (d 1989), and Edna, *née* Garlick; *b* 28 March 1934; *Educ* Univ of Liverpool (BSc, PhD), Univ of Bristol (DSc); *m* 23 Oct 1957, (Jean) Brenda, da of Percy Williams (d 1966); 1 s (Andrew Robert b 1 Aug 1964), 1 da (Jane b 22 Dec 1966); *Career* postdoctoral res fell Nat Res Cncl Canada Ottawa 1957-59; Univ of Bristol Sch of Chemistry: res asst 1959-62, lectr 1962-72, reader in physical chemistry 1972-74; prof of physical chemistry Univ of Exeter 1975-82; SERC: assoc dir Sci Bd and head Neutron Div 1982-87, assoc dir and head Science Dept (Rutherford Appleton Laboratory) 1987-88, dir Daresbury Laboratory 1988-; FRSC, FInstP; *Publications* author of numerous articles in scientific jls; *Recreations* cooking, walking; *Style*— Prof Alan Leadbetter; SERC, Daresbury Laboratory, Warrington WA4 4AD (☎ 0925 603119, fax 0925 603100, telex 629609)

LEADBETTER, Martin John; s of Albert Walter Leadbetter (d 1988), and Mildred Joan Leadbetter; *b* 6 April 1945; *Educ* Sir Christopher Wren Sch London, Trinity Coll of Music London; *m* 7 June 1969, Ivy Georgina, da of George William Goody, of Hayes, Middx; 2 s (Simon John b 13 Sept 1973, Mark Edward b 22 Nov 1974); *Career* fingerprint expert Herts Police, currently on Home Office attachment; conductor; dir of music Herts Police, conductor of Police Choir; composer; compositions incl: An English Requiem, Te Deum, The Chequered Band, Fanfare in Praise of Children, A Royal Birthday Greeting; Fell and Sec The Fingerprint Soc, regnl vice pres Int Assoc for Identification, asst ed Fingerprint Whorld, memb Composers Guild of GB; *Recreations* general knowledge quizzes (past contender Mastermind), philately, foreign travel, natural sciences, drama and reading, cookery and wine making; *Style*— Martin Leadbetter, Esq; Hertfordshire Police HQ, Welwyn Garden City, Herts AL8 6XF (☎ 0707 331177)

LEADBITTER, Edward; MP (Lab) Hartlepool 1964-; s of Edward Leadbitter, of Easington, Co Durham; *b* 18 June 1919; *Educ* State Sch, Teachers' Training Coll; *m* 1940, Phyllis Irene Mellin; 1 s, 1 da; *Career* cmmnd Royal Artillery 1941, served WWII; teacher; memb W Hartlepool Borough Cncl; organizer of Exhibition on History of Lab Movement 1956; chm: PLP Transport Gp 1978-87, PLP Ports Gp 1978-87, Anglo-Tunisian Parly Gp 1977-; memb House of Commons Chairmen's Panel 1980-; sponsored Registration of Children's Homes Bill 1981 successfully; hon Freeman Borough of Hartlepool 1981, Freeman City of London 1986; *Style*— Edward Leadbitter, Esq, MP; 8 Warkworth Drive, Hartlepool, Cleveland

LEAF, Ian Andrew; s of Walter Murray Leaf, and Norma, *née* Asquith; *b* 29 Nov 1953; *Educ* Univ College Sch London, Business Sch London (BA); *m* 1, 12 Sept 1976, Sandra Gillian, da of John Davis; 1 s (Jarrod b 1980), 1 da (Marisa b 1978); m 2, 16 Dec 1984, Caroline Lesley, da of Michael Nayor Bruck (d 1973); 2 s (Harrison b 1986, Robert b 1987); *Career* mgmnt trainee Br Petroleum Co Ltd, chm Rapport International gp 1975-82, Gp chm Symbol International plc 1980-86 (ret 1986); Liveryman Worshipful Co of Coachmakers and Coach Harness Makers 1981; memb Lloyds 1981; *Recreations* flying, sailing, hunting, piano, tennis, squash, skiing; *Clubs* Royal Naval, Mensa; *Style*— Ian Leaf, Esq

LEAF, Robert Stephen; s of Nathan Leaf, and Anne, *née* Feinman; *b* 9 Aug 1931; *Educ* Univ of Missouri (Bachelor of Journalism, MA); *m* 8 June 1958, Adele Renee; 1 s (Stuart b 4 June 1961); *Career* Burson-Marsteller International: joined 1957, vice pres 1961, exec vice pres 1965, pres 1968, chm 1985; writer in various trade and business pubns for USA, Europe and Asia; speaker on PR marketing and communications in W and E Europe (incl Russia), Asia (incl China), Australia, N and S America; memb: PR consltg (former bd memb), Int Advertising, Foreign Press, PR Soc of America; MIPR; *Recreations* tennis, travel, theatre; *Clubs* Hurlingham; *Style*— Robert Leaf, Esq; 3 Fursecroft, George St, London W1H 5LF (☎ 071 262 4846); office 24-28 Bloomsbury Way, London WC1A 2PX (☎ 071 831 6262, fax 071 430 1033, telex 267531)

LEAHY, Sir John Henry Gladstone; KCMG (1981), CMG (1973); s of William Henry Gladstone Leahy (d 1941), and Ethel, *née* Sudlow (d 1967); *b* 7 Feb 1928; *Educ* Tonbridge, Clare Coll Cambridge (BA), Yale (MA); *m* 1954, Elizabeth Anne, da of John Hereward Pitchford, CBE, *qv*; 2 s, 2 da; *Career* serv RAF 1950-52; entered FO 1952, head of chancery Tehran 1965-68, FCO 1968, head personnel servs FCO 1969, head News Dept FCO 1971-73, cnsllr and head of chancery Paris 1973-75, asst under sec state on loan to NI Office 1975-77, asst under sec state FCO 1977-79, ambass SA 1979-82, dep under sec state (Africa and ME) FCO 1982-84, high cmmr Aust 1984-88; chm Franco-Br Cncl; dir: The Observer, Urban Fndn; govr: ESU, Skinners' Girl's Sch Hackney; pro chllr City Univ, vice chm Maritime Tst, warden Worshipful Co of Skinners; *Recreations* tennis, golf; *Clubs* Oxford & Cambridge, Lords Taverners; *Style*— Sir John Leahy, KCMG; Manor Stables, Bishopstone, Seaford, E Sussex BN25 2UD (☎ 0323 898898)

LEAKE, Prof Bernard Elgey; s of Norman Sidney Leake (d 1963), and Clare Evelyn, *née* Walgate (d 1970); *b* 29 July 1932; *Educ* Wirral GS Bebington, Univ of Liverpool (BSc, PhD), Univ of Bristol (DSc); *m* 23 Aug 1956, Gillian Dorothy, da of Prof Charles Henry Dubinson, CMG, 5 s (Christopher b 1958, Roger b 1959, Alastair b 1961, Jonathan b 1964, Nicholas b 1966); *Career* Leverhulme res fell Univ of Liverpool 1955-57, res assoc Berkeley California 1966, reader in geology Univ of Bristol 1968-74 (lectr 1957-68); Univ of Glasgow 1974-: prof and head Dept of Geology and Applied Geology, hon keeper of geological collections Hunterian Museum; author of over 100 res papers and maps, especially of Connemara Western Ireland; treas Geological Soc London 1980-85 and 1989- (pres 1986-88); FGS 1956, FRSE 1976; *Books* Catalogue of Analysed Calciferous Amphiboles (1968); *Clubs* Geological Soc; *Style*— Prof Bernard Leake, FRSE; Dept Geology & Applied Geology, University of Glasgow, Glasgow G12 8QQ

LEAKE, Christopher Jonathan Piers; s of Kenneth Piers Leake (d 1988), of Frodsham, Cheshire, and Sheila Mary, *née* Salt; *b* 17 May 1951; *Educ* St Olave's Sch York, St Peter's Sch York; *m* 1976, Carol Joan, da of Lawrence Miveld, of Hartford, Cheshire; 1 s (Gerard William b 13 Dec 1982), 1 da (Claire Louise b 21 Oct 1978); *Career* journalist; reporter W Cheshire Newspapers 1970-74, Express and Star Wolverhampton 1974-79 (reporter, industl corr), The Daily Telegraph 1979-82 (Scottish corr, memb industl staff), industl and consumer affrs ed The Mail on Sunday 1982-; *Recreations* squash, running, people, films; *Style*— Christopher Leake, Esq; The Mail on Sunday, Associated Newspapers plc, Northcliffe House, 2 Derry St, Kensington, London W8 5TS (☎ 071 938 7034, fax 071 937 3829)

LEAKER, Dudley Roberts; s of Charles Henry Leaker (d 1941), and Mabel Gwendoline Leaker (d 1967); *b* 22 Dec 1920; *Educ* Dynevor Sch Swansea, Welsh and RWA Schs of Architecture UCL, Strathclyde Univ; *m* 12 June 1945, Mary Venn (Molly), da of Sydney James (d 1958); 1 s (David Charles b 1949), 3 da (Margaret (Mrs Halstead) b 1947, Jane (Mrs Smith) b 1953, Patricia (Mrs Eynon) b 1956); *Career* Civil Def; architect on bomb-damaged cities: Bristol, Plymouth, Coventry 1945-52; sr architect Stevenage New Town 1952-56; chief architect and planner: Cumbernauld New Town 1962-70, Warrington New Town 1970-75; architectural advsr and exec dir Milton Keynes New City 1975-78, hon res fell Open Univ 1979-84, exchange prof of architecture Pennsylvania State Univ 1981-82; chm Int Study Gp invited to Tokyo by Japanese govt 1985, sr ind inspr at major public inquiries 1978-, head of team winning Reynolds Award for Community Architecture, and various other architectural awards; chm: Int Working Party on New Towns 1976-87, Bd of Tstees Inter Action (Milton Keynes) 1976-78; external examiner Strathclyde and Sheffield Univs; memb Bd: Oxford Citizen's HSG Assoc 1978-85, S Shrops Rural HSG Assoc 1988-; hon life memb Int Fedn of HSG & Planning, fndr memb Cottage Theatre Cumbernauld; JP Dunbartonshire 1968-75; FRIBA 1952, FRIAS 1958, memb ISOCARP 1962; *Books* New Towns in National Development (1980), New Towns Worldwide (1985); *Recreations* painting, music, travel; *Style*— Dudley Leaker, Esq; Anchorsholme, Heighway Lane, All Stretton, Shrops SY6 6HN (☎ 0694 722095)

LEAKEY, Dr David Martin; s of Reginald Edward Leakey (d 1969), of Redhill, Surrey, and Edith Doris, *née* Gaze (d 1974); *b* 23 July 1932; *Educ* Imperial Coll London (BSc, PhD, DIC); *m* 31 Aug 1957, Shirely May, da of George Clifford Webster (d 1968), of Bridlington, Yorks; 1 s (Graham Peter b 1967), 1 da (Pamela Susan b 1961); *Career* tech dir GEC Telecoms Ltd 1969-84; dir: Fulcrum Telecommunications Ltd 1985-, Mitel Inc Canada 1986-; chief scientist BT 1986- (dep engr-in-chief 1984-86); Liveryman Worshipful Co of Engrs, Freeman City of London; FEng, FIEE, FCGI; *Recreations* horticulture; *Style*— Dr David Leakey; British Telecom Centre, 81 Newgate St, London EC1A 7AJ (☎ 071 356 5315, telex 883051)

LEAKEY, Dr Mary Douglas; *née* Nicol; da of Erskine Edward Nicol (d 1926), and Cecilia Marion Elizabeth, *née* Frere; *b* 6 Feb 1913; *Educ* privately; *m* 1936, Dr Louis Seymour Bazett Leakey FBA (d 1972), s of Canon Henry Leakey (d 1940); 3 s; *Career* archaeologist; former dir of res Olduvai Gorge Excavations; Hon DSc Witwatersrand 1965, Hon DSocSc Yale 1976, Hon DSc Chicago 1981, Hon DLitt Oxford 1982, Hon DSc Cambridge 1987, Hon DSc Emory Univ 1989, Hon DSc Univ of Mass 1989, Hon DSc Brown Univ 1990; FBA, FSA, FRAI, memb US Nat Acad Sc; *Recreations* reading, game watching; *Clubs* Women's Univ Club; *Style*— Dr Mary Leakey; c/o National Museum, Box 30239, Nairobi, Kenya

LEAMON, Sandra Roslyn; da of Arthur Leamon, of Cheadle Hulme, Cheshire, and Irene, *née* Sutton; *b* 22 June 1943; *Educ* Cheadle County GS for Girls, Manchester Coll of Commerce (Dip Business Studies); *Career* trainee copywriter Pritchard Wood 1967, copywriter Waseys' 1969, jt creative dir McCormick Richards (now Publicis) 1970-76; J Walter Thompson: joined as copywriter 1976, gp head 1987, bd dir 1988, currently creative gp head; winner various awards incl: D & AD, Br Television Advtg, Creative Circle, Cannes Film Festival Clios, Pegasus, Irish Film Festival, Euro Grand Prix 1990; memb D & AD 1974-; *Recreations* fair weather skiing, learning to speak French, Times crossword; *Clubs* Groucho; *Style*— Ms Sandra Leamon; J Walter Thompson, 40 Berkeley Square, London W1 (☎ 071 499 4040)

LEAMY, Stuart Nigel; s of Charles Kitchener Leamy, of 13 Buckingham Gdns, E Molesey, Surrey, and Constance Patricia, *née* Buckingham; *b* 9 July 1946; *Educ* Christ's Hosp Pembroke Coll Oxford (BA, MA); *m* 31 July 1971, Carol Juliet, da of Donald Thomson (d 1949); 2 s ((Charles) Edmund b 1975, Selwyn b 1977); *Career* CA; fin dir: Progressive Publicity Gp 1989, Hampton Pool Ltd 1984; FCA; *Recreations* swimming, watching cricket, medieval history; *Clubs* St Stephen's Constitutional; *Style*— Stuart Leamy, Esq; Shaftesbury House, 2 Shaftesbury Rd, London N18 1SQ (☎ 081 884 3304, fax 081 884 2612)

LEAN, (George) Alastair; OBE (1971); s of Daniel Lean (d 1960), of Glasgow, and Edith Janet, *née* Maclellan (d 1966); *b* 19 June 1921; *Educ* Loretto, Musselburgh, Royal Technical Coll Glasgow (now Univ of Strathclyde); *m* 1, June 1946 (m dis 1966), Iona Edith Hope, da of Charles Hope Murray (d 1938), of Beith; 1 s ((Daniel) Graham), 2 da (Ferelith Iona, Bryony Edith); m 2, (Margaret) Anne Little, da of Sir Rennie Izat, CIE (d 1966), of Balliliesk, Muckhart; *Career* RAF Coastal Cmd, Sqdn Ldr 1940-46 (despatches); studied med 1938-40, entered textile indust 1946, dir of various textile mfrg cos 1950-66; md: Carse of Allan Ltd 1966-81, Pauline Hyde & Associates Ltd (outplacement conslts) Scotland 1982, ret 1988; freelance contrib to radio and jls; memb Glasgow Valuation Appeals Ct 1955-67, chm Savings Bank of Glasgow 1964-66 (tstee 1955-83), vice chm Scot Woollen Mfrs Assoc 1965, gen cmmr of Income Tax 1970-, consul for Finland Glasgow 1973-, chm Personnel Gp Tstee Savings Bank Central Bd 1977-82 (Employers Cncl 1966-76), dir Merchants House of Glasgow 1985-; dean Glasgow Consular Corps 1987-89; Freeman City of Glasgow 1985, memb Incorp of Weavers Glasgow 1985; FInstD 1960-; Kt (Class 1) Order of the White Rose (Finland) 1985; *Recreations* shooting, countryside, Finnish matters; *Clubs* Western (Glasgow), Clyde Corinthian Yacht (Rhu); *Style*— G Alastair Lean, Esq, OBE; Birkhill, Muckhart, By Dollar, Scotland FK14 7JW

LEAN, Sir David; CBE (1953); s of late Francis William le Blount Lean and Helena Annie Tangye; *b* 25 March 1908; *Educ* Leighton Park Sch Reading; *m* 1, 28 June 1930, Isabel Margo, da of Edmund Wylde Lean; 1 s (Peter David Tangye b 2 Oct 1930); m 2, Nov 1940 (m dis 1949), Kay Walsh; m 3, 21 May 1949 (m dis 1957), Ann

Todd (actress); m 4, 4 July 1960 (m dis 1978), Mrs Leila Devi Matkar (d 1988); m 5, 1981 (m dis 1985), Sandra Hotz; *Career* film dir: In Which We Serve (co-director with Noël Coward), This Happy Breed, Blithe Spirit, Brief Encounter, Great Expectations, Oliver Twist, The Passionate Friends, Madeleine, The Sound Barrier, Hobson's Choice, Summer Madness, The Bridge on the River Kwai (US Academy Award 1957), Lawrence of Arabia (US Academy Award 1963), Dr Zhivago, Ryan's Daughter, Passage to India (1984); kt 1984; *Style*— Sir David Lean, CBE

LEAPER, David John; s of David Thomas Leaper, of Leeds, and Gwendoline, *née* Robertson; *b* 23 July 1947; *Educ* Leeds Modern GS, Univ of Leeds (MB ChB, MD, ChM); *m* 1 s (Charles David Edward), 1 da (Alice Jane Sophia); *Career* Univ of Leeds: house offr 1970-71, MRC res fell 1971-73, registrar surgery 1973-76; Univ of London: CRC res fell, sr registrar in surgery 1976-81; conslt sr lectr in surgery Univ of Bristol 1981-, Hunterian prof of surgery RCS 1981-82, prof of surgery Hong Kong Univ 1988-90; memb Cncl and vice pres RSM (surgery) 1982-88, fndr memb Surgical Infection Soc of Europe, memb Ctee Surgical Res Soc (UK) 1987-88; FRCS(Eng) 1975, FRCSEd 1974, FICA 1984; *Clubs* RSM London; *Style*— David Leaper, Esq; University Department of Surgery, Medical School Unit, Southmead Hospital, Bristol BS10 5NB (☎ 0272 505050 ext 3836, fax 0272 590145)

LEAPMAN, Hon Mrs (Anne Cynthia Veronica Tempest); da of 2 and last Viscount Plumer (d 1944); *b* 22 April 1921; *m* 19 July 1952, John Frederick Martyn Leapman, s of Lt-Col H M Leapman, of Hove, Sussex; 3 da (Joanna b 1953, Emma b 1956, Sarah b 1961); *Style*— The Hon Mrs Leapman; 4 Upper King's Cliff, St Helier, Jersey

LEAPMAN, Edwina; da of Charles Morris Leapman (d 1962), of London, and Hannah, *née* Schonfield (d 1988); *b* 21 Oct 1931; *Educ* Farnham Sch of Art, Slade Sch of Fine Art, The Central Sch of Art; *m* Dec 1957 (m dis 1969), John Saul Weiss; *Career* artist; solo exhibitions: The New Art Centre London 1974, Annely Juda Fine Art London 1976 and 1980, Gallery Noyse Oppenheim Nyon Switzerland 1979, Gallery Artline The Hague Holland 1979, Juda Rowan Gallery London 1987, Galerie Konstrucktiv Tendens Stockholm Sweden 1990, The Serpentine Gallery London 1991; gp exhibitions incl: Signals Gallery London 1956, Four Abstract Painters (ICA, London) 1967, Survey '67 (Camden Art Centre, London) 1967, Silence (Camden Art Centre) 1971, John Moores Exhibition Liverpool 1972, 1974 and 1976, Post Minimal Painting (Scottish Arts Cncl, Edinburgh) 1974, Pini Dippel: A Selection of Six Painters (Air Gallery, London) 1976, Gallerie Noyce Oppenheim Nyon Switzerland 1977, Hayward Annual '78 (Hayward Gallery, London) 1978, A Free Hand (Arts Cncl Touring Exhibition) 1978, The Arts Cncl Collection (Hayward Gallery) 1980, Masters of the Avant-Garde & Three Decades of Contemporary Art (Annely Juda/Juda Rowan) 1986, A Disquieting suggestion (John Hansard Gallery Southampton) 1988, The Presence of Painting: Aspects of British Abstraction (South Bank Touring Exhibition) 1989, The Experience of Painting: Eight Modern Artists (Laing Art Gallery Newcastle, S Bank Touring Exhibition) 1989, From Picasso to Abstraction (Annely Juda Fine Art) 1989; *Style*— Ms Edwina Leapman; Annely Juda Fine Art, 23 Dering St, London W1R 9AA (☎ 071 722 5311)

LEARMOND, Hon Mrs (Virginia Mary); yr da of Baron Marshall of Leeds (Life Peer, d 1990); *b* 1949; *Educ* Queen Margaret's Sch York, Cygnets House London; *m* 1972, Nigel James Alexander Learmond; 1 s (Alexander Marshall b 1978), 1 da (Marissa Virginia Stuart b 1973); *Career* teacher; FRSA; *Recreations* music, theatre; *Style*— The Hon Mrs Learmond; 52 Marryat Rd, Wimbledon SW19

LEARMONT, Lt-Gen Sir John (Hartley); KCB (1989), CBE (1980, OBE 1975); s of Capt Percy Hewitt Learmont, CIE (d 1983), of Curry Rivel, Somerset, and Doris Orynthia, *née* Hartley (d 1982); *b* 10 March 1934; *Educ* Fettes, RMA Sandhurst; *m* 2 March 1957, Susan, da of Thomas Jefferson Thornborrow, (d 1971), of Penrith; 3 s (Mark b 7 Jan 1958, Richard John b 8 June 1960, James Jefferson b 9 Feb 1967); *Career* cmmnd RA 1954, Instr RMA 1960-63, student Staff Coll 1964, served 14 Fld Regt, Staff Coll and 3 RHA 1965-70, MA to C-in-C BAOR 1971-73, CO 1 RHA 1974-75 (despatches 1974), HQ BAOR 1976-78, Cdr 8 Fld Force 1979-81, Dep Cdr Cwlth Monitoring Force Rhodesia 1979-80, student RCDS 1981, Chief of Mission Br C-in-C Mission to Soviet Forces in Germany 1982-84, Cdr Artillery 1 (Br) Corps 1985-87, Chief of Staff UKLF 1987-88, Cmdt Staff Coll Camberley 1988-89, Col Cmdt Army Air Corps 1988-, Col Cmdt RA 1989-, Col Cmdt RHA 1990-, Hon Col 2 Bn The Wessex Regt 1990-, pres Army Athletic Assoc 1988-, Mil Sec MOD 1989-; FBIM; *Recreations* fell walking, all sport, theatre; *Clubs* Naval and Military; *Style*— Lt-Gen Sir John Learmont, KCB, CBE

LEAROYD, Lady (Mary) Sarah-Jane Hope; da of 3 Marquess of Linlithgow, MC; *b* 25 May 1940; *Educ* Heathfield Ascot, Paris; *m* 1967 (m dis 1978), Michael Gordon Learoyd; 1 s (Jeremy b 1971); *Style*— The Lady Sarah-Jane Learoyd

LEARY, Brian; QC; s of late A T Leary, and late M C Leary, *née* Bond; *b* 1 Jan 1929; *Educ* Kings Sch Canterbury, Wadham Coll Oxford (MA); *m* 14 April 1965, Myriam Ann, da of late Kenneth Bannister, CBE, of Mexico City; *Career* called to the Bar Middle Temple 1953; sr prosecuting counsel to Crown 1971-78 (jr 1964-71), master of the bench 1986; chm Br Mexican Soc; *Recreations* travel, sailing, growing herbs; *Style*— Brian Leary, Esq, QC; East Farleigh House, East Farleigh, Kent (☎ 0622 726295); 5 Paper Buildings, Temple EC4 (☎ 071 583 6117)

LEASK, Annie Carol; da of Kenneth Roy Leask, of Hatfield, South Yorkshire, and Marion Gladys, *née* Dixey; *b* 23 July 1965; *Educ* Thorne GS, Univ of Kent Canterbury (BA), Nat Cncl for Training Journalists proficiency cert; *Career* trainee Croydon Advertiser Newspaper Group 1986-89, presenter and reseacher daily news bulletins Croydon Cable TV 1987-88, freelance journalist 1989 (Thames TV, Sunday Mirror, Evening Standard), showbusiness reporter and music critic Daily Express 1989-; memb NUJ 1986; *Recreations* horse riding, squash, skiing, reading; *Style*— Ms Annie Leask; Daily Express, Ludgate House, 245 Blackfriars Rd, London SE1 9UX (☎ 071 922 7051, fax 071 922 7970/7974, car 0831 237092)

LEASK, Lt-Gen Sir Henry Lowther Ewart Clark; KCB (1970, CB 1967), DSO (1945), OBE (1957, MBE 1945); s of Rev James Leask, rector of Scruton Yorks, and Margaret Ewart Leask; *b* 30 June 1913; *m* 1940, Zoë de Camborne, da of Col William Patterson Paynter, DSO (d 1958), of Dogmersfield Lodge, Odiham, Hants; 1 s, 2 da; *Career* 2 Lt Royal Scots Fus 1936, served WWII (India, Med and Italy), GSO 1942, Bde Maj Inf Bde 1943, 2 i/c (later CO) 8 Bn Argyll and Sutherland Highlanders 1944-45, CO 1 Bn London Scottish 1946-47, Gen Staff Mil Ops WO 1947-49, Instr Staff Coll 1949-51, CO 1 Bn Parachute Regt 1952-54, asst mil sec to Sec of State for War 1953-57, Cmdt Tactical Wing Sch of Inf 1957-58, cmd Inf Bde 1958-61, Brig 1961, idc 1961, dep mil sec to Sec of State for War 1962-64, Col Royal Highland Fus 1964-69, Col Cmdt Scottish Inf 1968, GOC 52 Lowland Div 1964-66, Maj-Gen 1964, Dir Army Trg MOD 1966-69, Lt-Gen 1969, GOC Scotland 1969-72; ret; govr of Edinburgh Castle 1969-72; *Recreations* shooting, fishing; *Clubs* New (Edinburgh), Hurlingham, Carlton; *Style*— Lt-Gen Sir Henry Leask, KCB, DSO, OBE; 9 Glenalmond House, Manor Fields, London SW15 (☎ 081 788 6949)

LEASK OF LEASK, Madam Anne Meredith Gordon Fleming; 22 Chief of Clan Leask; da of Alexander Leask Curr, univ lectr; suc Alexander Graham Leask of that Ilk 1968; *b* 1915; *Educ* Lonsdale Sch for Girls Norwich, Univ of London (BA), Sorbonne (Diplôme), Univ of Colorado (MA, PhD); *Career* instr Univ of Colorado, asst and assoc prof Univ of Toledo (Ohio) and Kalamazoo Coll (Michigan), prof Cedar Cres Coll (Pa), lectr Inst of Adult Educn Norwich; personally involved with Clan Leask Soc and membs worldwide and with charitable orgns; Chev de l'Ordre des Palmes Académiques; *Books* La Littérature Française Contemporaire (1970), French Grammar, Spanish Grammar, The Leasks (1980); *Recreations* theatre, music, swimming; *Clubs* Royal Overseas League; *Style*— Madam Leask of Leask; 1 Vincent Rd, Sheringham, Norfolk; Leask, Aberdeenshire

LEASOR, (Thomas) James; s of Richard Leasor, (d 1959), of Erith, Kent, and Christine, *née* Hall (d 1949); *b* 20 Dec 1923; *Educ* City of London Sch, Oriel Coll Oxford (BA, MA); *m* 1 Dec 1951, Joan Margaret, da of Capt Roland S Bevan (d 1968), of Crowcombe, Somerset; 3 s (Jeremy b 1953, Andrew b 1956, Stuart b 1958); *Career* WWII vol Royal E Kent Regt 1942, cmmnd 2 Lt Royal Berks Regt 1944; serv 1 Lincolns: Burma, India, Malaya, ret Capt 1946; ed staff London Daily Express 1948-55, magazine conslt Geo Newnes Ltd (later IPC) 1955-59, co fndr and dir Elm Tree Books; underwriting memb Lloyds; FRSA; OStJ; *Books* author of 30 books incl: the Dr Jason Love series of suspense books, The Red Fort (1954), War at the Top (1959), Hess, The Uninvited Envoy (1962), Singapore, The Battle that Changed the World (1968), Green Beach (1975), Open Secret (1983), Ship of Gold (1984), Tank of Serpents (1986); *Recreations* walking dogs, swimming, vintage sports cars; *Clubs* Garrick; *Style*— James Leasor, Esq; Swallowcliffe Manor, Salisbury, Wilts SP3 5PB; Casa Do Zimbro, Praia da Luz, Lagos, Algarve, Portugal

LEATES, Margaret; da of Henry Arthur Sargent Rayner, and Alice, *née* Baker; *b* 30 March 1951; *Educ* Lilley and Stone Girls' HS Newark, King's Coll London (LLB, LLM, AKC); *m* 26 May 1973, Timothy Philip Leates; 1 s (Benjamin b 15 April 1982), 1 da (Lydia b 14 July 1983); *Career* admitted slr; dep parly counsel 1986-; memb Law Soc; *Recreations* junk, gardening; *Clubs* Whitstable Yacht; *Style*— Mrs Margaret Leates; Crofton Farm, 161 Crofton Lane, Orpington, Kent BR6 0BP (☎ 0689 820192)

LEATHAM, Philip William; s of Maj Patrick Magor Leatham (d 1950), and Hon Cecily, *née* Berry (d 1976), da of 1 Baron Buckland (d 1928 when title extinct); bro Simon Leatham, *qv*; *b* 30 Aug 1946; *Educ* Eton, Magdalene Coll Cambridge; *m* 1971, Hon Rowena Margaret, *née* Hawke, *qv* da 9 Baron Hawke; 2 s (Patrick b 1974, Frederick b 1981), 1 da (Arabella b 1976); *Career* chartered accountant; *Recreations* riding, shooting; *Clubs* Boodle's; *Style*— Philip Leatham, Esq; Glebe House, Sapperton, Glos

LEATHAM, Simon Patrick; eldest s of Maj Patrick Magor Leatham (d 1951), and Hon Cecily Eveline, *née* Berry (d 1976), da of 1 and last Baron Buckland (d 1928); bro of Philip Leatham, *qv*; *b* 9 Nov 1944; *Educ* Eton, Trinity Coll Cambridge; *m* 25 April 1967, Lady Victoria Diana, *née* Cecil, da of 6 Marquess of Exeter (d 1982); 1 s (Richard b 1971), 1 da (Miranda b 1969); *Career* chartered accountant; chief exec Oceanic Finance Corp Ltd 1982-; *Clubs* Boodles; *Style*— Simon P Leatham, Esq; Burghley Ho, Stamford, Lincolnshire PE9 3JY (☎ 0780 63 131); Flat 18, Chelsea Ho, St Lowndes St, London SW1X 9JE (☎ 071 245 6366); Albemarle House, 1 Albemarle St, London (☎ 071 491 4294, telex 8812315 OCFIN G)

LEATHAM, Lady Victoria Diana; *née* Cecil; da of 6 Marquess of Exeter, KCMG, and 2 w, Diana, da of Hon Arnold Henderson, OBE (d 1933, 5 s of 1 Baron Faringdon, CH); *b* 1947; *m* 1967, Simon Patrick Leatham, *qv*; 1 s, 1 da; *Career* dir: Preservation Tst, Burghley House; Sotheby's; presenter of tv progs on stately homes; lectr on antiques UK and overseas; memb Finance and Planning Ctee HHA; tstee Samuel Courtauld Tst; *Style*— The Lady Victoria Leatham; Burghley House, Stamford, Lincs (☎ 0780 63131); Flat 18, 24 Lowndes St, London SW1 (☎ 071 245 6366)

LEATHER, Sir Edwin Hartley Cameron; KCMG (1974), KCVO (1975); s of Harold H Leather, MBE; *b* 1919; *Educ* Trinity Coll Sch Ontario, RMC Kingston Ontario; *m* 1940, Sheila Alexie, da of A H Greenlees; 2 da; *Career* dir Hogg Robinson and Capel-Cure Ltd and subsid cos 1946-64; MP (C) Somerset N 1950-64; pres Inst of Mktg 1963-67, dir William Baird and Co Ltd 1966-73, chm Nat Union of Cons Assocs 1969-70, govr and C-in-C Bermuda 1973-77, dir N M Rothschild (Bermuda) 1978-, and others; broadcaster and author; nat govr The Shaw Festival Canada, memb Hon Ctee of the Canadian Meml Fndn; Hon LLD Univ of Bath 1975; hon FRSA, hon citizen Kansas City, medal of merit Royal Canadian Legion, Gold medal Nat Inst of Social Sciences NY; KStJ 1973; kt 1962; *Books* The Vienna Elephant, The Mozart Score, The Duveen Letter; *Recreations* travel, reading, music; *Clubs* Royal Bermuda Yacht, York (Toronto), Hamilton (Ontario); *Style*— Sir Edwin Leather, KCMG, KCVO; Chelsea, Inwood Close, Paget, Bermuda (☎ 809 236 0240); 130 St Joseph's Drive, Hamilton, Canada L8N 2E8 (☎ 416 527 1917)

LEATHER, Dr Hugh Moffat; s of Douglas John Leather (d 1976), of Birmingham, and Edith, *née* Walker (d 1981); *b* 30 Aug 1925; *Educ* King Henry VIII Sch Coventry, Ellesmere Coll, Univ of Birmingham (MB ChB), Univ of Bristol (MD); *m* 25 June 1955, Catherine Margaret, da of Robert John Stephen (d 1969), of Bristol; 1 s (Andrew b 1960), 2 da (Susan b 1956, Hilary b 1958); *Career* Capt RAMC 1948-50; conslt physician Plymouth Health Dist 1962-90, vice chm Plymouth Health Authy 1984-90, cncllr RCP 1980-85 (examiner 1989-); FRCP 1968; *Books* Synopsis of Renal Disease and Urology (jt author, 1966); *Recreations* music, golf, gardening; *Clubs* Athenaeum; *Style*— Dr Hugh Leather; Leatside, Yelverton, South Devon PL20 6HY (☎ 0822 85 2898)

LEATHERDALE, Dr Brian Anthony; s of Dennis Hector Leatherdale, and Mary Ann, *née* Sheilds (d 1984); *b* 30 Nov 1942; *Educ* St Josephs Coll Birkfield, London Hosp Med Coll (BSc, MD, DiplObst); *m* 27 April 1968, Salliebelle, da of Joseph Gilley Dathan (d 1987); 2 s (Anthony Stephen b 15 May 1971, Daniel Brian b 23 March 1973); *Career* sr med registrar King's Coll Hosp 1972-75, conslt physician Dudley Rd Hosp Birmingham 1975-81, conslt physician Royal S Hants Hosp Southampton 1981-(post grad tutor 1983-88); dep regnl advsr Wessex RCP 1988-; memb BMA, memb RSM, FRCP 1985; *Recreations* cricket, golf, assoc football; *Clubs* Brockenhurst Manor Golf; *Style*— Dr Brian Leatherdale; Hewers Orchard, Newtown, Minstead, nr Lyndhurst, Hants (☎ 0703 812789); Royal South Hants Hospital, Graham Rd, Southampton SO9 4XY (☎ 0703 634288)

LEATHERLAND, Baron (Life Peer UK 1964), of Dunton, Co Essex; Charles Edward Leatherland; OBE (1951), MSM, JP (Essex 1944), DL (Essex 1963); s of John Edward Leatherland (d 1945), of Churchover, Warwicks; *b* 18 April 1898; *Educ* Harborne Sch Birmingham; *m* 1922, Mary Elizabeth (d 1987), da of Joseph Henry Morgan, of Shareshill, Staffs; 1 s (Hon John Charles b 1929), 1 da (Hon Irene Mary (Hon Mrs Richards) b 1923); *Career* sits as Labour peer in House of Lords; served WWI Co Sgt-Maj Royal Warwicks Regt, Somme and Ypres (MSM and despatches), army of occupation Bonn; vice-chm Essex CC 1952-55 and 1958-60 (chm 1960-61, chm Finance Ctee 1952-55 and 1958-60); tres and memb Essex Univ Cncl 1961-73; memb: Basildon Dvpt Corpn 1967-71, Monopolies Cmmn to consider newspaper mergers 1969; hon Doctor of the Univ (DU) Essex; won both Prince of Wales's Gold Medals for essays on economic subjects 1923 and 1924; *Books* Book of the Labour Party (part author); *Recreations* formerly fox hunting, now walking; *Style*— The Rt Hon the Lord Leatherland, OBE, MSM, JP, DL; 19 Starling Close, Buckhurst Hill, Essex (☎ 081 504 3164)

LEATHERLAND, Hon John Charles; s of Baron Leatherland, OBE (Life Peer) *qv*; *b*

2 July 1929; *Educ* Brentwood; *m* 1954, Esther, da of Mrs Dora Steckman, of London; 2 da; *Style—* The Hon John Leatherland; 4 Manor Way, Chingford Hatch, London E4 6NW (☎ 081 529 0347)

LEATHERS, Hon Christopher Graeme; s and h of 2 Viscount Leathers, *qv*; *b* 31 Aug 1941; *Educ* Rugby; *m* 1964, Maria Philomena, da of Michael Merriman, of Charlestown, Co Mayo; 1 s (James Frederick b 1969), 1 da (Melissa Maria b 1966); *Career* civil servant; Dept of Tport; memb Inst of Chartered Shipbuilders, MBIM; Liveryman Worshipful Co of Shipwrights; *Style—* The Hon Christopher Leathers; Sunhill, Mold Rd, Bodfari, Denbigh, Clwyd LL16 4DP

LEATHERS, 2 Viscount (UK 1954); Frederick Alan Leathers; also Baron Leathers (UK 1941); s of 1 Viscount Leathers, CH, PC (d 1965); *b* 4 April 1908; *Educ* Brighton Coll, Emmanuel Coll Cambridge; *m* 1, 1940 (m dis 1983), Elspeth Graeme, da of Sir Thomas Alexander Stewart, KCSI, KCIE (d 1964); 2 s (Hon Christopher, Hon Jeremy *qqv*), 2 da (Hon Mrs Arthur Centner b 1944, Hon Mrs Richard Pitt b 1974); m 2, 1983, Mrs Lorna Barnett, widow of A A C Barnett; *Heir* s, Hon Christopher Graeme Leathers; *Career* chm Missions to Seamen; memb Baltic Exchange; former chm of various shipping and cement cos; former dir Nat Westminster Bank (outer London regn); memb: Worshipful Co of Shipwrights, Worshipful Co of Watermen and Lightermen; FRPSL, FRSA, MInstPet; *Clubs* RAC; *Style—* The Rt Hon the Viscount Leathers; Park House, Chiddingfold, Surrey GU8 4TS (☎ 042 879 3222)

LEATHERS, Hon Jeremy Baxter; s of 2 Viscount Leathers, *qv*; *b* 11 April 1946; *Educ* Rugby, Trinity Coll Dublin (BBS); *m* 1969, Fiona Lesley, eldest da of late George Stanhope Pitt, of Rowbarns Manor, Horsley, Surrey; 1 s (Luke Alexander b 1974), 2 da (Tara Charlotte b 1972, Fern Griselda b 1979); *Career* md Stocksigns 1988-; dir: Applied Environmental Research Co (AERC) 1988-, British & Foreign Wharf 1977-; *Recreations* sailing, tennis, reading ski brochures; *Style—* The Hon Jeremy Leathers; Stocksigns Ltd, Ormside Way, Redhill, Surrey RH1 2LG (☎ 0737 764764, fax 0737 763763)

LEATHERS, Hon Leslie John; s of 1 Viscount Leathers, CH, PC (d 1965); *b* 25 Nov 1911; *Educ* Brighton Coll; *m* 1937, Elizabeth Stella, da of Thomas Stanley Nash (d 1964); 2 s (Michael b 1938, David b 1942), 1 da (Mrs Winfried Bischoff, *qv*); *Career* Lt-Col (AQMG); Staff Coll 1943; slr 1934; memb Cncl London C of C 1955-65; gen cmmr of Income Tax 1958-75; memb Worshipful Co of Coachmakers and Coach Harness Makers; *Clubs* Brooks's, Hurlingham, Rand (Johannesburg); *Style—* The Hon L J Leathers; Middleton Park, Middleton Stoney, nr Bicester, Oxfordshire OX6 8SQ

LEAVER, Sir Christopher; GBE (1981), JP (Inner London); s of Dr Robert Leaver, and Audrey, *née* Kerpen; *b* 3 Nov 1937; *Educ* Eastbourne Coll; *m* 1975, Helen Mireille Molyneux Benton; 1 s (Benedict), 2 da (Tara, Anna); *Career* cmmnd RAOC 1956-58, Hon Col 151 (Gtr London) Tport Regt RCT (V) 1983-88, Hon Col Cmdt RCT 1988-; dep chm Thames Water plc 1983-; dir: Bath & Portland Gp plc 1983-85, Thermal Scientific plc 1985-88; chm: Russell & McIver Gp (wine merchants), Thames Line plc 1987-89; memb: Cncl RBKC 1970-73, Bd Brixton Prison 1975-78, Cmmn of Lt for City of London 1982, fin ctee London Diocesan Fund 1983-86; Alderman Ward of Dowgate City of London 1974- (memb Ct of Common Cncl 1973), church warden St Olave's Hart St 1975-89; govr: Christs' Hosp Sch 1975-, City of London Girls Sch 1975-78, City of London Freemen's Sch 1980-81, Music Therapy Tst 1981-89; Sheriff City of London 1979-80; chm: Young Musicians Symphony Orchestra Tst 1979-81, London Tourist Bd 1983-89, Eastbourne Coll 1988-; Lord Mayor London 1981-82, Chllr City Univ 1981-82 (govr 1978-), church cmmr 1982-; tstee: London Symphony Orchestra 1983-90, Chichester Festival Theatre; vice pres: Cncl Mission to Seamen 1983-, Nat Playing Fields Assoc 1983-, Bridewell Royal Hosp 1983-89; hon memb GSM 1982-; Hon DMus City Univ 1982; Freeman Worshipful Co of Watermen and Lightermen; Hon Liveryman: Worshipful Co of Farmers, Worshipful Co of Environmental Cleaners 1982-; Master Worshipful Co of Carmen 1987-88; KStJ 1982; FRSA, FCIT; *Style—* Sir Christopher Leaver, GBE, JP; The Rectory, St Mary-at-Hill, London EC3R 8EE (☎ 071 283 3575)

LEAVER, Prof Christopher John; s of Douglas Percival Leaver (d 1978), and Elizabeth Constance, *née* Hancock; *b* 31 May 1942; *Educ* Lyme Regis GS, Imperial Coll London (BSc, ARCS, DIC, PhD), Oxford Univ (MA); *m* 8 Oct 1971, Anne, da of Prof Hastings Dudley Huggins (d 1970); 1 s (Tristan), 1 da (Anya); *Career* Fulbright scholar Purdue Univ USA 1966-68, sci offr ARC Plant Physiology Unit Imperial Coll 1968-69, prof of plant molecular biology Univ of Edinburgh 1986-89 (SERC sr res fell 1985-89, reader 1980-86, lectr 1969-80), Sibthorpian prof of plant sci Oxford 1990-; fell St Johns Coll Oxford; tstee John Innes Inst 1987-; memb: Cncl AFRC, priorities Bd MAFF; T H Huxley Gold medal Imperial Coll 1970, Tate and Lyle Award Phytochem Soc of Europe 1984, Acadamea Europea 1988; EMBO 1982, FRS 1986, FRSE 1987; *Recreations* walking and talking in Upper Coquetdale; *Style—* Prof Christopher Leaver, FRS, FRSE; Dept of Plant Science, South Parks Rd, Oxford OX1 3RA (☎ 0865 275143, fax 0865 275144)

LEAVER, Colin Edward; s of Edward Roy Leaver, of West Wittering, West Sussex, and Freda Eleanor, *née* Toogood; *b* 25 May 1958; *Educ* Haywards Heath GS, Lincoln Coll Oxford (MA); *m* 10 May 1986, Maria Victoria, da of John Hutton Simpkins, of Alicante, Spain; 1 da (Chirstina b 1987); *Career* Simmons & Simmons: articled clerk 1980-82, asst slr 1982-86, ptnr 1986-; *Recreations* hockey, philately, aviation; *Style—* Colin Leaver, Esq; The Coppice, Birtley Rise, Bramley, Nr Guilford, Surrey; 14 Dominion St, London EC2M 2RJ (☎ 071 628 2020, fax 071 588 4129, telex 888 526 SIMMON G)

LEAVER, Hon Mrs (Margaret); *née* Cavendish; da of 6 Baron Waterpark (d 1949); *b* 1907; *m* 1934, Wallace Thomas Leaver (d 1972); 2 da (Diana (Mrs Peter Wiggins) b 1938, Elizabeth b 1942); *Style—* The Hon Mrs Leaver; St Benets, Beech Hill, Bridge, Canterbury, Kent

LEAVER, Peter Lawrence Oppenheim; QC (1987); s of Marcus Isaac Leaver (d 1966), of London, and Lena, *née* Oppenheim (d 1984); *b* 28 Nov 1944; *Educ* Aldenham Sch, Univ of Dublin; *m* 2 June 1969, Jane Rachel, o da of Leonard Pearl (d 1983), of London; 3 s (Marcus, James, Benjamin) 1 da (Rebecca); *Career* called to the Bar Lincoln's Inn 1967; memb Gen Cncl Bar 1987-90; chm: Bar Ctee 1989 (vice chm 1988-89), Int Practice Ctee 1990; memb: Ctee on Future of Legal Profession 1986-88, Cncl Legal Educn 1986-; *Recreations* refereeing football matches, sport, wine, theatre, opera; *Clubs* Athenaeum, MCC; *Style—* Peter Leaver, Esq, QC; 5 Hamilton Terrace, London NW8 9RE (☎ 071 286 0208); 1 Essex Ct, Temple, London EC4Y 9AR (☎ 071 583 2000, fax 071 583 0118, telex 889109 ESSEX G)

LEAVETT-SHENLEY, John; s of Ernest Leavett-Shenley (d 1974); *b* 21 May 1930; *m* 1961, Alison Yvonne (d 1990), da of Cdr The Hon Henry Cecil, OBE (d 1962, 4 s of Baroness Amherst of Hackney, OBE, by her husb Col Lord William Cecil, CVO, who in his turn was 3 s of 3 Marquess of Exeter); 2 s, 1 da; *Career* Welsh Gds 1948-53; farmer and forester; pres Devon Cattle Breeders Soc 1978, High Sheriff of Hants 1985-86; *Recreations* racing, shooting, fishing; *Clubs* Cavalry and Guards', Welsh Guards; *Style—* John Leavett-Shenley, Esq; The Holt, Upham, nr Southampton, Hants SO3 1HR (☎ 0489 893452)

LEBERL, Geoffrey Albert; s of Francis Albert Leberl, and Nancy Reay, *née* Harrison; *b* 23 Aug 1943; *Educ* Archbishop Tenisons GS; *m* 18 June 1966, Pauline, da of Redvers Buller Percy Mee; 1 s (Martin b 1970), 1 da (Samantha b 1967); *Career* dir Leberl Advertising Ltd 1965-; MIPA; *Recreations* half marathon running, badminton, swimming, gardening, music, theatre; *Clubs* Honor Oak Sports; *Style—* Geoffrey A Leberl, Esq; c/o 7 Brooks Court, Kirtling Street, Battersea, London SW8 5BX (☎ 071 720 1966, fax 071 622 0034)

LEBUS, Hon Mrs (Christina); da of 2 Baron Strathalmond, CMG, OBE, TD (d 1976); *b* 1954; *m* 1974, Timothy Andrew Lebus; 1 s (David b 1983); *Style—* The Hon Mrs Lebus; 70 Ellerby St, London SW6 6EZ

LEBUS, John Edward Louis; s of Louis Solomon Lebus (d 1983), and Edith Anne, *née* Mannheim (d 1978); *b* 28 May 1932; *Educ* Montezuma Mountain Sch Calif USA, Canford, Pembroke Coll Cambridge (MA); *m* 15 Dec 1956, Jane Penelope, da of Lionel Livingstone, OBE (d 1962); 3 s (Simon b 1957, Matthew b 1959, Andrew b 1961), 1 da (Amanda Suzanne b 1964); *Career* md: Kitchen Range Foods Ltd, Common Mktg Ltd; dir Hernitage Projects Ltd, vice pres Br Frozen Food Food Fedn; vice chm Cambridge Symphony Orch; *Clubs* HAC; *Style—* John Lebus, Esq; Farriers, Newton Rd, Whittlesford, Cambridge CB2 4PF; Kitchen Range Foods Ltd, Bar Hill, Cambridge CB3 8EX (☎ 0954 780078, fax 0954 789813)

LECHLER, Robert Ian; s of Dr Ian Sewell Lechler (d 1972), and Audrey Florence, *née* Wilson (d 1979); *b* 24 Dec 1951; *Educ* Monkton Combe Sch, Univ of Manchester (MB ChB), Univ of London (PhD); *m* Valerie Susan Lechler, da of Harold Ord Johnston (d 1988); 2 s (Alastair Robert b 4 Feb 1980, Toby Ian b 23 Dec 1982), 1 da (Suzannah Jane b 24 Feb 1988); *Career* sr renal registrar Professorial Med Unit Hammersmith Hosp 1983-84 (renal registrar 1982-83), Wellcome Tst Travelling Fellowship Laboratory of Immunology Bethesda Maryland USA 1984-86, reader in immunology and hon conslt in med Royal Postgrad Med Sch 1989 (sr lectr in immunology 1986-89); memb: Cncl Nat Kidney Res Fund, Ctee Med Res Soc, Editorial Bd Transplantation Jl; chm Leadership Ctee Local Anglican Church; memb: RCP 1978, Renal Assoc 1980, Int Transplantation Soc 1987, Med Res Club 1987, Assoc of Physicians 1988; FRCP; *Recreations* classical music, theatre, family; *Style—* Robert Lechler, Esq; Department of Immunology, Royal Postgraduate Medical School, Hammersmith Hospital, Du Cane Rd, London W12 0NN

LECHMERE, Sir Berwick Hungerford; 6 Bt (UK 1818), JP (Worcs 1966); s of Capt Sir Ronald Berwick Hungerford Lechmere, 5 Bt (d 1965), and Constance, *née* Long; the estate of Severn End at Hanley Castle, formerly known as Lechmere's Place has been in the family since 11th century; Nicholas Lechmere, chancellor of Duchy of Lancaster for Life 1717 cr. Baron Lechmere 1721, *dsp* 1727; *b* 21 Sept 1917; *Educ* Charterhouse, Magdalene Coll Cambridge; *m* 1, 24 May 1952 (m annulled 1954), Susan Adele Mary, o child of late Cdr George Henry Maunsell-Smyth, RN; m 2, 17 Nov 1954, Norah Garrett, eldest da of late Lt-Col Christopher Garrett Elkington, DSO, DL, of The Moat House, Cutnall Green, Worcs; *Heir* kinsman, Reginald Anthony Hungerford Lechmere; *Career* High Sheriff Worcs 1962, vice Lord-Lt Hereford and Worcester 1977- (DL 1972); FICS; CStJ (1980); *Style—* Sir Berwick Lechmere, Bt, JP; Church End House, Hanley Castle, Worcester (☎ 068 46 2130)

LECHMERE, Reginald Anthony Hungerford; s of Anthony Hungerford Lechmere (d 1954, 3 s of 3 Bt); hp of kinsman, Sir Berwick Hungerford Lechmere, 6 Bt; *b* 24 Dec 1920; *Educ* Charterhouse, Trinity Hall Cambridge; *m* 1956, Anne Jennifer, da of late A C Dind, of Orbe, Switzerland; 3 s (Nicholas b 1960, Adam b 1962, Mark b 1966), 1 da (Jennifer b 1959); *Career* formerly Capt 5 Royal Inniskilling Dragoon Gds; antiquarian bookseller; *Style—* Reginald Lechmere, Esq; Primeswell, Evendine Lane, Colwall, nr Malvern, Worcs (☎ 0684 40 340)

LECK, Prof Ian Maxwell; s of Rev Arthur Simpson Leck (d 1952), and Margaret Mortimer, *née* Jagger (d 1983); *b* 14 Feb 1931; *Educ* Kingswood Sch Bath, Univ of Birmingham (MB ChB, PhD, DSc); *m* 25 July 1959, Ann Patricia, da of Arnold Wilfred Sarson (d 1973); 2 s (Christopher b 1962, Jonathan b 1967), 2 da (Susan b 1960, Patricia b 1965); *Career* Lt 1955-56 and Capt 1956-57 RAMC; house offr Walsall Gen Hosp 1954-55, lectr in social med Univ of Birmingham 1959-66 (res fell 1957-59), sr lectr in community med Univ Coll Hosp Med Sch London 1966-71, prof of community med then prof of epidemiology Univ of Manchester 1979- (reader in social and preventive med later community med 1971-78), hon specialist in community med then pub health med Manchester Area (later Central Manchester Dist) Health Authy 1979-; author of papers and chapters on epidemiology of malformations and cancer; assoc ed Teratology: the Journal of Abnormal Development 1972-80; memb: Ctee Soc for Social Med 1974-77, Ed Bd Journal of Epidemiology and Community Health 1978-; associateship of Faculty of Occupational Med 1982-, hon sec and treas Heads of Academic Depts Gp (social and community med) 1985-87, examiner for and for membership of Faculty of Community Med 1986- (now faculty if Public Health Med); MSc (ex officio) Manchester 1982; FFCM 1972, FRCP 1985; *Books* Childhood Cancer in Britain: Incidence, Survival and Mortality (with G J Draper, 1982), God of Science, God of Faith (with D Bridge, 1988); *Recreations* cycling, walking; *Style—* Prof Ian Leck; Pembury, 54 Alan Road, Heaton Moor, Stockport, Cheshire SK4 4LE (☎ 061 442 0033); Department of Public Health and Epidemiology, University of Manchester, Stopford Building, Oxford Rd, Manchester M13 9PT (☎ 061 275 5195)

LECKY, Ian Cecil Hamilton Browne; s of Capt Halton Stirling Lecky, CB, AM, RN (d 1940), and Agnes, *née* Close (d 1976); *b* 16 Dec 1924; *Educ* RNC Dartmouth; *Career* WWII 1942-44 Midshipman (later Sub Lt) RN served Med ops Pedestal, Torch Husky and Avalanche: admitted slr 1949, airline pilot Br United Airways 1955-66, slr private practice 1967-, conslt Batchelors; memb Law Soc 1949; *Recreations* flying (flying instr), sub aqua diving, under water photography; *Style—* Ian Lecky, Esq; 22 Andsell Terrace, Kensington, London W8 5BY; Batchelors, The Outer Temple, 222-225 Strand, London WC2R 1BG (☎ 071 353 5134, fax 071 353 2766, telex 262 363)

LECOMBER, Brian Kenneth; *b* 12 July 1945; *Educ* Dr Challoner's GS Amersham Bucks; *m* 15 Dec 1978, Barbara Joyce, da of Frank Moore; 1 da (Amy b 1987); *Career* journalist 1962-70, wing walker Roaring 20s Flying Circus 1970, chief flying instr Antigua Aero Club WI 1971-73, novelist 1973-78, display aerobatic pilot 1978; memb Rothmans Aerobatic Team touring: UK, Europe, Middle and Far E 1979-80; fndr Firebird Aerobatics 1981-, flown a record breaking 1350 pub aerobatic displays, Br freestyle aerobatic champion 1984 and 1988; flown at: Farnborough, Paris, Royal Show, Grand Nat; memb: Historic Aircraft Assoc, Br Aerobatic Assoc, Aircraft Operators and Pilots Assoc; display evaluator CAA; memb Worshipful Co of Air Pilots and Air Navigators; *Books* Turn Killer (1974), Dead Weight (1976), Talk Down (1978); *Recreations* gardening; *Style—* Brian Lecomber, Esq; Elmers, 94 Ellesborough Road, Wendover, Bucks HP22 6EW (☎ 029996 625770); Firebird Aerobatics Ltd, 11 High St, Wendover, Bucks HP22 6DU (☎ 0296 622739, fax 0296 625883)

LEDEN, Judy (Mrs Trevor Gardner); MBE (1989); da of Thomas Leden, of Wraysbury, Berks, and Nina Mary, *née* Nowell; *b* 23 Dec 1959; *Educ* St Bernard's Convent Slough, Welsh Nat Sch of Med; *m* 24 Nov 1990, Dr Trevor Gardner, s of D Gardner, of Sydney, Australia; *Career* hang gliding champion; holder of womens world open distance record 1983, Br Womens Open Champion 1983, Euro Womens Champion 1986, World Womens Champion 1987, holder of two womens world records

1990, first female capt Br mixed team 1990; memb: competitions ctee Br Hang Gliding Assoc, Br Womens Pilots Assoc, Womens Sports Fndn; Diplome de Performance French Aeroclub 1988; *Recreations* microlight flying, paragliding, swimming, reading, travel, theatre; *Style*— Miss Judy Leden, MBE; 8 Burnham Manor, Gibbet Lane, Camberley, Surrey GU15 3UP (☎ 0276 28649)

LEDERER, Peter J; *Career* Four Seasons Hotels Canada 1972-79, vice pres Wood Wilkings Ltd Toronto Canada 1979-81; gen mangr: Plaza Group of Hotels Toronto Canada 1981-83, The Gleneagles Hotel 1983-87; ops dir Guinness Enterprises 1987-, md Gleneagles Hotels plc (The Champney Group) 1987-; govr: Ardvreck Sch Crieff, Duncan of Jordanston Coll of Art Dundee; external advsr Bd of Studies Univ of Dundee, memb Editorial Panel Inside Hotels, dir Scottish Enterprises Tayside Ltd; Master Innholder Worshipful Co of Innholders, Freeman City of London; memb: Canadian Hospitality Inst, IOD; MBIM; FHCIMA; *Style*— Peter J Lederer, Esq

LEDERMAN, Colin Stuart; s of Morris Lederman, of London, and Rachel, *née* Baroness Iglitski (d 1988); *b* 4 March 1937; *Educ* City of London Sch; *m* 15 May 1960, Jill, da of Capt Maxwell Lincoln (d 1985), of London; 1 s (Martin David b 1962), 1 da (Meryl Ruth b 1965); *Career* CA; ptnr: Frank Dymond & Co London 1965-69, Backhouse Young Partnership (formerly B & E Backhouse) 1970-88; dir: Loggia Ltd Film distributors 1987-, Atlantis Devpt Corpn Ltd 1988-; former del Bd of Deps for Br Jews; Lord of the Manor of Ashton, ACA 1962, FCA 1969, MBIM 1987; *Recreations* golf, badminton; *Style*— Colin Lederman, Esq; PO Box 1433, London NW4 1TZ (☎ 081 203 6727, fax 081 203 7502, car 0836 739 697)

LEDERMAN, Geoffrey Lewis Harry; s of David Lederman (d 1945), and Sylvia Doris, *née* Langbart; *b* 9 July 1929; *Educ* Whittinghame Coll; *m* 29 April 1963, Olivia, da of Frederick Russell (d 1978); 2 da (Amanda (Mrs Pinder) b 1965, Caroline b 1968); *Career* ptnr Smith Bros 1960-73 (joined 1951), jt chief exec Smith New Court plc 1987-89 (dir 1973-87); memb Stock Exchange; *Recreations* cricket, squash, tennis, golf; *Clubs* MCC, RAC, Incogniti, Annabels; *Style*— Geoffrey Lederman, Esq; 145 Hamilton Terrace, London NW8 (☎ 071 624 4986); Smith New Court plc, Chetwynd House, 24 St Swithins Lane, EC4 8AE (☎ 071 626 1544, car 0836 286339)

LEDERMAN, Paul; s of François Lederman (Belgian Médaille Commémorative de la Guerre with 2 crossed swords), of 99 Penshurst Gdns, Edgware, Middx, and Elena, *née* Attias; *b* 2 Aug 1942; *Educ* Lycée Français, London, Finchley Co Gs, Univ of London, and Birklands Mgmnt Centre; *m* 1, 16 Dec 1973 (m dis 1983), Nicole Marie, da of Henri Deparmentier (d 1972); 2 s (Henry b 1976, David b 1979); m 2, 20 Oct 1985, Barbara, da of Simon Dove (d 1989); *Career* CA (1968), sole practitioner 1977-; prop P L Advertising 1976-, mgmnt conslt 1976-80; dir: Skyparks 1982-, Elena Chocolates Ltd (founded by mother) 1984-86, md Skylinks Ltd, exec Airline 1985-89; Freeman: Worshipful Co of Air Pilots and Air Navigators 1965-, City of London 1967-; lectr in accountancy: Cambridge Graduate Centre, Hatfield & Middx Polys 1978-81; memb Economic Res Cncl 1981-; patented: aero engine 1982, Dynafloat 1990; DMS, FCA, FBIM, MInstPI; *Recreations* music, countryside, former private pilot; *Clubs* The Roof Gardens Kensington; *Style*— Paul Lederman, Esq; 18 Wheatley Close, Hendon, London NW4 4LG (☎ 081 203 5513)

LEDERMANN, Dr Erich Kurt; s of William Ledermann (d 1949), of London, and Charlotte, *née* Apt (d 1980); *b* 16 May 1908; *Educ* Univ of Berlin (MD), Univ of Heidelberg, Univ of Freiburg, Royal Coll Edinburgh and Glasgow (LRCPSE, LRFPS); *m* 21 June 1941, Marjorie Alice, da of Herbert Francis Smith (d 1938), of Harpenden, Herts; 1 s (David b Feb 1942), 1 da (Elizabeth b July 1944); *Career* natural therapy physician Nature Clinic London, conslt physician Royal London Homoeopathic Hosp 1965 (sr hosp med offr 1956), conslt psychiatrist Marlborough Day Hosp 1973 (sr hosp med offr 1956); FFHom, FRCPsych; memb BMA 1936; *Books* Natural Therapy (1953), Philosophy and Medicine (1970, revised edn 1986), Existential Neurosis (1972), Good Health Through Natural Therapy (1976), Mental Health and Human Conscience, The True and the False Self (1984), Your Health In Your Hands, A Case for Natural Medicine (1989); *Recreations* writing, walking; *Style*— Dr Erich Ledermann; 13 Ardwick Rd, London NW2 2BX (☎ 071 435 5133); 121 Harley St, London W1 (☎ 071 935 8774)

LEDGER, Christopher John Walton; s of Peter Walton Ledger, of Truro, Cornwall, and Barbara Nancy, *née* Eve; *b* 5 Feb 1943; *Educ* The Nautical Coll Pangbourne; *m* 1, 21 April 1971 (m dis 1973); m 2, 17 Sept 1977, Gillian Penelope, da of Col Paul Heberden Rogers (d 1972); 1 s (James Walton Herberden b 17 July 1981), 1 da (Nicola Kate b 10 Aug 1978); *Career* cmmnd 2 Lt RM 1962, offr 43 Commando 1964, OC Recce Tp 45 Commando 1965-66, ATURM Poole 1966-67, OC HMS Bulwark 1967-69, Adj RM Pool 1969-72, ATT HQ CO Forces 1972-74; Shell UK Ltd: joined 1974, PA mangr Expro 1976-77, mangr Small Business Initiative Films and Educnl Serv 1978-81, dir of PA 1981-84, chief exec World Energy Business 1984-86, chief exec The Phoenix Initiative 1986-; dir: Manchester Phoenix, Salford Phoenix, Lewisham Development Corporation; tstee Prospect Tst; Liveryman Worshipful Co of Grocers' 1972; FRSA, FInstPet; *Recreations* sailing, shooting; *Clubs* Royal Cornwall Yacht, Reform, Special Forces, Tamesis; *Style*— Christopher Ledger, Esq; The Willows, 29 Broom Water, Teddington, Middx TW11 9QJ (☎ 081 977 3451); The Phoenix Initiative, 26 Store St, London WC1E 7BT (☎ 071 436 1561)

LEDGER, Frank; OBE (1985); s of Harry and Doris Ledger; *b* 16 June 1929; *Educ* Univ of London (BSc); *m* 1953, Alma, *née* Moverley; 2 s; *Career* student apprentice Leeds Corp Electricity Dept 1947, station mangr Cottam 1965, gp mangr Midlands Region 1968, dir computing CEGB 1980, dir operations CEGB 1981, memb Bd for Prodn CEGB 1986-89, dep chm Nuclear Electric 1989; FEng 1990; *Style*— Frank Ledger, Esq, OBE; CEGB, 15 Newgate Street, London EC1 (☎ 071 634 6673)

LEDGER, Dr Philip Stevens; CBE (1985); s of Walter Stephen Ledger (d 1986), of Bexhill-on-Sea, and Winifred Kathleen, *née* Stevens; *b* 12 Dec 1937; *Educ* Bexhill GS, King's Coll Cambridge (MA, MusB); *m* 15 Apr 1963, Mary Erryl, *née* Wells; 1 s (Timothy b 1964), 1 da (Katharine b 1966); *Career* master of music Chelmsford Cathedral 1962-65, dir of music UEA 1965-73 (dean Sch of Fine Arts and Music 1968-71), conductor Univ of Cambridge Musical Soc 1973-82, dir of music and organist Kings Coll Cambridge 1974-82, RSAMD 1982-; Hon LLD Univ of Strathclyde 1987; FRCM 1983, HonRAM 1984, FRNCM 1989, HonGSM 1989, FRSE 1990, FRCO; *Recreations* swimming, theatre-going; *Clubs* Athenaeum; *Style*— Dr Philip Ledger, CBE, FRSE; Royal Scottish Academy of Music and Drama, 100 Renfrew St, Glasgow G2 3DB (☎ 041 332 4101, fax 041 332 8901)

LEDINGHAM, Prof John Gerard Garvin; s of Dr John Ledingham (d 1970), of 47 Ladbroke Square, London, and Dr Una Christina, *née* Garvin (d 1965); *b* 19 Oct 1929; *Educ* Rugby, New Coll Oxford (MA, DM), Middx Hosp Med Sch Univ of London (BM BCh); *m* 3 March 1962, Elaine Mary, da of Richard Glyn Maliphant (d 1977), of 49 Cathedral Rd, Cardiff; 4 da (Joanna b 23 March 1963, Catherine b 21 May 1964, Clare b 10 Oct 1968, Sarah b 20 Nov 1971); *Career* Nat Serv 2 Lt RA 1949-50; registrar in med Middx Hosp London 1960-62 (house offr 1957-58), sr registrar Westminster Hosp London 1963-65, visiting fell Univ of Columbia NY 1965-66, conslt physician United Oxford Hosps 1966-74, May reader in Med Univ of Oxford 1974- (prof 1989); contrib various med and science jls; tstee: Nuffield Prov Hosps Tst, Beit Tst, Oxford Hosp Devpt and Improvement Fund, Oxford Hosps Servs and Devpt Tst, memb Animal Procedures Ctee of Home Sec; chm MRS; examiner in med Univs of: Cambridge, Glasgow, Oxford, London, Southampton, Sheffield; examiner RCP; former hon sec and hon treas Assoc of Physicians of GB and Ireland, former pres Hypertension Soc, censor RCP, memb Supra Regnl Servs Ctee Dept of Health; fell New Coll Oxford 1974; FRCP 1971; *Books* Oxford Textbook of Medicine (ed with D J Weatherall and D A Warrell, 1983); *Recreations* music, golf; *Clubs* Vincent's (Oxford); *Style*— Prof John Ledingham; 22 Hid's Copse Rd, Cumnor Hill, Oxford OX2 9JJ (☎ 0865 862023); Nuffield Department of Clinical Medicine, John Radcliffe Hospital, Oxford OX3 9DU (☎ 0865 221329, fax 0865 750506)

LEDLIE, John Kenneth; OBE (1977); s of Reginald Cyril Bell Ledlie (d 1966), and Elspeth Mary, *née* Kaye (d 1982); *b* 19 March 1942; *Educ* Westminster, Brasenose Coll Oxford (MA); *m* 27 Nov 1965, Rosemary Julia Allan, da of Francis Glen Allan (d 1974); 3 da (Rebecca b 1969, Kate b 1971, Joanna b 1973); *Career* UK delgn to NATO Brussels 1973-76, head Def Section 19 MOD 1983, chief PR MOD 1985-87, under sec MOD 1987, dep sec NI Office 1990, fell Centre for Int Affrs Harvard Univ 1987-88; *Recreations* cricket, tennis, squash, ornithology, hill-walking, opera; *Clubs* Oxford and Cambridge; *Style*— John Ledlie, Esq, OBE; c/o Northern Ireland Office, Old Admiralty Building, Whitehall, London SW1

LEDWARD, Lady Jane Annabelle; *née* Howard; da of 12 Earl of Carlisle; *b* 1947; *m* 1, 1968 (m dis 1977), John David Vaughan Seth-Smith, only s of Lt-Cdr David Keith Seth-Smith, RN; 1 da (Gemma b 1972); m 2, 1983, Rodney S Ledward, s of late Arthur Ledward; *Style*— The Lady Jane Ledward

LEDWARD, Rodney Spencer; s of Arthur Ledward (d 1984), of Stone, Staffs, and Beatrice Maud, *née* Pritchard (d 1986); *b* 30 June 1938; *Educ* Alleynes GS, Univ of Manchester (BSc, MPS), Univ of Liverpool (MB ChB), Univ of Virginia Charlottesville, Brown Univ RI, Univ of Nottingham (DM); *m* 26 Aug 1983, Lady Jane Annabelle Howard; 1 s (Bertie Arthur Ruthven b 7 Nov 1985); *Career* conslt in obstetrics and gynaecology SE Kent Health Dist 1980-; private gynaecological practice: St Saviour's Hosp Hythe Kent, Chaucer Hosp Canterbury, London Med Centre, London Bridge Hosp; md Tutorial Systems International; hon sr teaching fell Dept Obstetrics and Gynaecology The Royal London Hosp, dean Ross Univ Med Sch Ross Univ NY; FRCS 1974, FRSM 1974, FRCOG 1986; *Books* Drug Treatment in Obstetrics (1982, 2 edn 1990), Drug Treatment in Gynaecology (1984), Handbook of Obstetrics and Gynaecology (1986); *Recreations* swimming, riding; *Clubs* RSM; *Style*— Rodney Ledward, Esq; Beaulieu, The Riviera, Sandgate CT20 3AB (☎ 0303 40104); Consulting Rooms, St Saviours Hospital, Hythe (☎ 0303 265 581); Chaucer Hospital, Canterbury (☎ 0227 455 466); 144 Harley St, London (☎ 071 935 0023); London Bridge Hospital (☎ 071 403 488)

LEDWIDGE, Sir (William) Bernard John; KCMG (1974, CMG 1964); s of Charles Bernard Arthur Ledwidge (d 1945); *b* 9 Nov 1915; *Educ* Cardinal Vaughan Sch, King's Coll Cambridge, Princeton Univ USA; *m* 1, 1948 (m dis 1970), Anne, da of George Henry Kingsley (d 1959); 1 s, 1 da; m 2, Flora, da of André Groult (d 1967); *Career* entered India Office 1939, Indian Army 1941-46, NW Frontier; FO 1948, first sec Kabul 1952-56, political advsr Br Mil Govt Berlin 1956-61, cnsllr FO 1961, head of Western Dept FO 1963-65, min Paris 1965-69; ambass: Finland 1969-72, Israel 1972-75; chm UK Ctee for UNICEF 1976-89, memb Police Complaints Bd 1977-82; *Books* Frontiers (1980), Des Nouvelles de la Famille (1981), De Gaulle (1982), De Gaulle et les Americains (1984), Sappho la Premiere Voix de Femme (1987); *Clubs* Travellers (London and Paris), MCC; *Style*— Sir Bernard Ledwidge, KCMG; 54 Rue de Bourgogne, 75007 Paris France (☎ 705 8026); 19 Queen's Gate Terrace, SW7 5PR (☎ 071 584 4132)

LEE, (Edward) Adam Michael; s of His Hon Judge Michael Lee, DSC, DL (d 1983), of The Manor Farm House, Easton, Winchester, Hampshire, and Valerie Burnett Georges, *née* Drake-Brockman; *b* 29 June 1942; *Educ* Winchester, ChCh Oxford (MA); *m* 5 July 1975, Carola Jean, da of Capt Frederick Le Hunte Anderson (d 1989), of Standen Manor Farm, Hungerford, Berks; 2 s ((Frederick) Edward Maconchy b 1977, (James) Michael Maconchy b 1981); *Career* called to the Bar Middle Temple 1964; cadet Glyn Mills & Co 1964; William & Glyn's Bank: sr planner 1969, dep dir City Div 1974; local dir: Child & Co 1977-87, Holts Branches 1978-87; asst gen mangr Royal Bank of Scotland 1985-87, conslt Adam & Co 1988-90 (gp devpts dir 1988-90), dir Duncan Lawrie Tst Corp 1990-, sec and treas Inveforth Charitable Tst; tstee: Chelsea Opera Gp, Southern Pro Arte Orchestra; published articles in: Three Banks Review, Royal Bank of Scotland Review, Humberts Commentary; Freeman City of London, Liveryman Worshipful Co of Dyers 1984; FCIB 1981; *Recreations* opera, fly fishing, food, travel; *Clubs* Travellers', Rye Golf, Chatham Dining (memb ctee); *Style*— Adam Lee, Esq; The Farm, Northington, Alresford, Hants SO24 9TH (☎ 0962 732 205)

LEE, Barry Thomas; s of Thomas John Lee (d 1960), of London, and Lilian Violet, *née* Felstead; *b* 2 June 1946; *Educ* Latymer Upper Sch, Queen's Coll Oxford (MA); *m* 1 March 1976, Rosemarie Ann, da of Gerald Plumridge, of Haverhill, Suffolk; 1 s (Thomas b 1980), 1 da (Caroline b 1977); *Career* res exec Br Market Res Bureau 1968-71, divnl head Louis Harris Int 1972-73, dir Public Attitude Surveys Ltd 1974-86, md Public Attitude Surveys Ltd 1987-; memb: MRS 1970, Euro Soc For Opinion and Mktg Res 1989; *Clubs* Oxford Union; *Style*— Barry Lee, Esq; Public Attitude Surveys Ltd, Rye Park House, London Road, High Wycombe, Bucks HP11 1EF (☎ 0494 32771, fax 0494 21404)

LEE, Charles Barnaby; s of Capt RA Lee, DFC, of The Manor House, Byfleet, Surrey, and BJ Lee; *b* 22 Oct 1943; *Educ* Tonbridge; *m* 1 Oct 1970, Meryan Patricia Louise, da of Maj PTV Leith (d 1967); 3 da (Melissa b 23 Aug 1974, Catriona b 26 June 1976, Alice b 30 Oct 1982); *Career* ptnr (later dir) RA Lee Fine Arts Ltd, md Ronald A Lee plc; chm Grosvenor House Antiques Fair 1983, First Int Art Fair Johannesburg SA 1984, pres BADA 1981-83, memb Ctee Burlington House Fair, co-prodr and res Br Clocks 1600-1850 (film), chm Art Trade Liasion Ctee 1990-, memb Horological Industry Ctee; Freeman City of London, Liveryman Worshipful Co of Clockmakers 1973 (steward 1980); *Clubs* Garrick, Bucks, Bembridge SC; *Style*— Charles Lee, Esq; 80 Thurleigh Rd, London SW12 8UD; 1-9 Bruton Place, Mayfair, London W1X 7AD (☎ 071 499 6266, 071 629 5600, fax 071 629 2642)

LEE, Christopher Frank Carandini; s of Lt-Col Geoffrey Trollope Lee (d 1941), and Contessa Estelle Marie Carandini (d 1981); m descends from one of the six oldest Italian families, created Count 1184 and granted Arms Emperor Charlemagne by Emperor Frederick Barbarossa; *b* 27 May 1922; *Educ* Eton, Wellington Coll; *m* 1961, Birgit, da of Richard Emil Kroencke (d 1982); 1 da (Christina b 1963); *Career* served WWII RAF 1941-46, Flt Lt, Intelligence and Special Forces, W Desert, Malta, Sicily, Italy and Central Europe (despatches 1944); actor (entered film indust 1947), author, singer; appeared in over 200 feature films worldwide incl: Moulin Rouge, Tale of Two Cities, Dracula, Rasputin, The Devil Rides Out, Private Life of Sherlock Homes, The Wicker Man, The Three Musketeers, The Four Musketeers, Man with a Golden Gun, To the Devil a Daughter, Airport 77, The Far Pavilions, 1941, The Return of Captain Invincible, The Disputation (TV), Round the World in 80 Days (TV), The Return of Musketeers, Gremlins II, The French Revolution (TV); also theatre, opera and TV; Offr Arts Sciences et Lettres France 1974, OStJ 1986; *Books* Christopher Lee's X

Certificate (1975), Archives of Evil (1975), Tall, Dark and Gruesome (1977); *Recreations* golf, travel, languages, opera; *Clubs* Buck's, MCC, Hon Co of Edinburgh Golfers, Travellers (Paris); *Style*— Christopher Lee, Esq; c/o James Sharkey, 15 Golden Square, London W1 (☎ 071 434 3801)

LEE, Capt (John) Colin Leonard Thornton; JP (1980); s of John Lee (d 1946), of Birkenhead, and Ann Rebecca, *née* Thornton (d 1979); *b* 14 Jan 1933; *Educ* Birkenhead Sch, Liverpool Poly, RNC Greenwich, Univ of Wales Cardiff; *m* 7 Oct 1961, Jean Pauline, da of Norman Drummond Wilson (d 1977); 1 s (Mark b 8 Feb 1967), 2 da (Alison b 3 March 1963, Catherine b 31 July 1964); *Career* cadet Ellerman Hall Line 1950-54; Ellerman and Bucknall Line: 4 Offr 1955, 3 Offr 1956, 2 Offr 1958, Chief Offr 1962, Master 1966; assoc dir AE Smith Coggins Stevedores and Master Porters Liverpool 1967-72, sr commercial mangr Mersey Docks and Harbour Co 1979-82 (operations mangr 1972-75, customer servs mangr 1975-78), md Delphic Ltd 1982-85, int mgmnt and mkting conslt Alan Marshall Partnership 1985-; Knight Remembrancer Hon Soc of Knights of the Round Table, memb St John Cncl for Merseyside, fndr memb and past pres Rotary Club of Liverpool Exchange, N W area rep chm Sea Cadet Corps, life vice pres Bebington Unit Sea Cadet Corps, dir Centre for Brain Injury Rehabilitation and Devpt Chester; memb: Environment and Public Affrs Ctee Merseyside C of C, Merseyside Advsy Bd Salvation Army, Seven Seas Club, Tower Ward Club; Freeman City of London 1985, memb of Ct of Assts Hon Co of Master Mariners 1989 (memb 1984, chm and sec NW Area 1987); FBIM 1983; *Recreations* travel, gardening, naval and maritime history; *Clubs* Athenaeum (Liverpool), Royal Over-seas League, Wig and Pen; *Style*— Capt Colin Lee; Three Oaks, Grove Rd, Mollington, Chester CH1 6LG (☎ 0244 851 253); Alan Marshall Partnership, 11/13 Victoria St, Liverpool L2 5QQ (☎ 051 227 2892, fax 051 227 4943)

LEE, Prof David John; CBE (1989); s of Douglas Lee (d 1987), and Mildred Amy, *née* Checkley (d 1955); *b* 28 Aug 1930; *Educ* Chislehurst & Sidcup Co GS, Univ of Manchester (BSc), Imperial Coll London (DIC); *m* 6 Dec 1957, Helga; 1 s (Graham b 1961), 1 da (Caroline b 1960); *Career* Nat Serv RE 1950-52, Col Engr and Tport Staff Corps RE (TA) 1990 (Maj 1978, Lt-Col 1982); chm G Maunsell & Partners 1984- (joined 1955, ptnr 1966, managing ptnr 1978-84), dir Maunsell International Group; visiting prof: Imperial Coll London, Univ of Newcastle upon Tyne; author of many papers published in learned jnls; Freeman City of London, Liveryman Worshipful Co of Engrs; FICE 1966, FIStructE 1968 (pres 1985-86), FEng 1980; *Books* Theory and Practice of Bearings and Expansion Joints for Bridges (1971), Civil Engineering Reference Book (contrib); *Clubs* East India; *Style*— Prof David Lee, CBE; G Maunsell & Partners, Yeoman House, 63 Croydon Rd, Penge, London SE20 7TP (☎ 081 778 6060, fax 081 659 5568, telex 946171)

LEE, Air Chief Marshal Sir David John Pryer; GBE (1969, KBE 1965, CBE 1947, OBE 1943), CB (1953); s of John Lee (d 1955), and Gertrude Ethel Lee (d 1964), of Bedford; *b* 4 Sept 1912; *Educ* Bedford Sch, RAF Coll Cranwell; *m* 1938, Denise, da of Louis Hartoch (d 1934), of Bedford; 1 s, 1 da; *Career* joined RAF 1930, serv WWII, Cmdt RAF Staff Coll Bracknell 1962-64, air memb for Personnel 1965-68, UK Mil Rep NATO 1968-71, ret 1972; chm Grants Ctee RAF Benevolent Fund 1971-88, dir United Services (tstee 1972-88), chm Exec Ctee Nuffield Tst for the Forces of the Crown 1975-, pres Corps of Commissionaires 1984-88; *Books* Flight From the Middle East (1980), Eastward (1983), Never Stop the Engine When Its Hot (1983), Wings in the Sun (1989); *Recreations* golf; *Clubs* RAF; *Style*— Air Chief Marshal Sir David Lee, GBE, CB; Danemore Cottage, Danemore Lane, South Godstone, Surrey (☎ 0342 893162)

LEE, David Stanley Wilton; DL (1984); s of Col Kenneth C Lee, TD (d 1964); *b* 17 Sept 1933; *Educ* Uppingham, Queens' Coll Cambridge; *m* June 1957, Jennifer Ann, da of Col John P Hunt, TD (d 1971); 3 s, 2 da; *Career* dir Arthur Lee & Sons 1965-; non exec dir: Halifax Building Soc 1977-, Iron Trades Insurance 1978-; chm SSAFA Sheffield; *Recreations* golf, shooting, fishing, farming; *Clubs* The Club (Sheffield), Farmers'; *Style*— David Lee, Esq, DL; Arthur Lee & Sons plc, PO Box 54, Meadow Hall, Sheffield S9 1HU (☎ 0742 437272, fax 0742 439782, telex 54165 CROWN G)

LEE, Sir (Henry) Desmond (Pritchard); s of Rev Canon Henry Burgass Lee (d 1951), and Ida Marian, *née* Pritchard (d 1963); *b* 30 Aug 1908; *Educ* Repton, CCC Cambridge (MA); *m* 1935, Elizabeth, da of Col Arthur Crookenden (d 1962); 1 s, 2 da; *Career* lectr in Classics Cambridge 1937-48; Miny of Home Security 1940-44; headmaster: Clifton 1948-54, Winchester 1954-68; chm Headmaster's Conference 1959-60 and 1967; memb Secdy Schs Examination Cncl and Schools Cncl 1952-68; pres Hughes Hall Cambridge 1974-78; Hon LittD Nottingham, life fell CCC Cambridge; kt 1961; *Recreations* philosophy, carpentry; *Clubs* East India, Devonshire Sports, Public Schools; *Style*— Sir Desmond Lee; 8 Barton Close, Cambridge CB3 9LQ (☎ 0223 356553)

LEE, Hon Mrs (Doris); da of Baron Williams of Barnburgh, Life Peer (d 1967); *b* 1916; *m* 1939, Robert Kesteven Lee (d 1967); *Style*— The Hon Mrs Lee; 346 Thorne Rd, Doncaster

LEE, Edward David; s of Walter George Lee (d 1974), and Annie Rosina, *née* Wriggle; *b* 23 Dec 1947; *Educ* Southend HS for Boys, Coll of Law; *m* 9 May 1971 (m dis 1986), Janet Laurie, da of Jack Cyril Mitchell, of Southend-on-sea, Essex; 1 s (Matthew Mitchell b 13 May 1978), 1 da (Michelle Alexandria b 10 June 1976); *Career* slr; Rochford DC: princ legal asst 1980-84, slr to cncl 1984-85, asst slr 1990-91; ptnr: Wiseman Lee Marshall Essex 1985-89, Kloosmans 1991-; treas Southend on Sea Playbus Ctee, sec Abbeyfield Rochford and Dist Soc Ltd, govr Grove Co Infants and Jr Schs; memb Law Soc 1977; Dip Local Govt; FInstLEx 1967; *Recreations* musician; *Style*— Edward Lee, Esq; 4 Newhall, Ashingdon, Essex (☎ 0702 548821)

LEE, Geoffrey; OBE (1980); s of Clifford Lee, of Bolton, Lancs, and Florence Lee (d 1988); *b* 7 Jan 1931; *Educ* Sunning Hill Sch, Lords Commercial Coll Bolton; *m* 1955 (m dis 1986), Shirley, *née* Massey; 2 da (Janet b 1958 d 1981, Caroline b 1956); *Career* insur and investmt broker; dep regnl chm CE Heath (UK) Ltd Insurance Brokers, underwriting memb Lloyds; memb Appeals Tbnl for Miny of Pensions and Nat Insur 1961-64, pres Altrincham and Dist C of C and Trade 1965 (treas 1963, chm 1964, memb Exec Ctee 1960-81, chm Past Pres Ctee 1982-); chm Assoc of Insur Brokers NW Area 1968-70 (memb Nat Exec Ctee), vice chm NW Industl Cncl 1973-87 (memb Ctee 1968-); Altrincham & Sale Cons Assoc: treas 1969-75, vice pres 1975-83; memb Exec Ctee Knutsford Constituency Cons Assoc 1975-77; memb: Northern Exec Ctee French C of C 1982-87, Cons Manchester Action Ctee 1988-; ABIBA, FIMBRA, IBRC; *Recreations* weight training, keeping fit; *Clubs* Mere Golf and Country (Knutsford); *Style*— Geoffrey Lee, Esq, OBE; Mode Cottage, Church Lane, Mobberley, Cheshire WA16 7RA (☎ 0565 873485); B E Heath (UK) Ltd, Station House, Stamford, New Rd, Altrincham, Cheshire WA14 1EP (☎ 061 928 3483)

LEE, Brig Sir (Leonard) Henry; CBE (1964, OBE 1960); s of Henry Robert Lee (d 1969), of Southsea, Hants, and Nellie, *née* Randall; *b* 21 April 1914; *Educ* Portsmouth GS, Univ of Southampton; *m* 1949, Peggy Metham; *Career* serv WWII BEF, Maj Royal Scots Greys (despatches 1945), Lt-Col 1954, Chief of Intelligence to Dir of Ops of Malaya 1957-60, Col naval and mil attaché Saigon 1961-64, Chief of personnel and admin Allied Land Forces Central Europe (France) 1964-66, Brig Chief of Intelligence Allied Forces Central Europe (Netherlands) 1966-69, ret 1969; dep dir Cons Party Bd of Fin 1970-; kt 1983; *Recreations* gardening, golf; *Clubs* Kingswood Golf; *Style*— Brig Sir Henry Lee, CBE; Fairways, Sandy Lane, Kingswood, Surrey (☎ 0737 832577); Conservative Party Central Office, 32 Smith Sq, London SW1 (☎ 071 222 9000)

LEE, Hermione; da of Dr Benjamin Lee, and Josephine Lee; *b* 29 Feb 1948; *Educ* Lycée de Londres, City of London Sch, Queen's Coll and St Hilda's Coll Oxford (BA, BPhil); ptnr 1975- John M Barnard; *Career* instr William and Mary Coll Williamsburg USA 1970-71, lectr Univ of Liverpool 1971-77, reader in English Univ of York 1990- (lectr 1977-88, sr lectr 1988-90); judge: Faber Prize 1981, Booker Prize 1981, W H Smith Prize 1987-, Cheltenham Prize 1987; presenter: Book Four (C4) 1982-86, Booker Prize (LWT) 1984-86; memb: Mgmnt Ctee Lumb Bank Arvon Fndn, Advsy Ctee Centre for the Book Br Library; *Books* The Novels of Virginia Woolf (1977), Elizabeth Bowen (1981), Philip Roth (1982), Willa Cather: A Life Saved Up (1989), editions and anthologies of: Kipling, Trollope, Woolf, Bowen, Cather; The Secret Self (short stories by women writers); *Clubs* Academy; *Style*— Ms Hermione Lee; Dept of English, University of York, Heslington, York YO1 5DD (☎ 0904 433361)

LEE, James Giles; s of John Lee, CBE, and Muriel, *née* Giles; *b* 23 Dec 1942; *Educ* Trinity Coll Glenalmond, Univ of Glasgow, Harvard Univ; *m* 1966, Linn, *née* MacDonald; 1 s (John b 1974), 2 da (Maggie b 1968, Katie b 1971); *Career* conslt McKinsey & Co 1969-80, dep chm and chief exec Pearson, conslt McKinsey & Co 1969-80, dep chm and chief exec Pearson Longman 1980-83; chm: Penguin Publishing Co 1980-84, Longman Gp 1980-84; dir S Pearson & Son 1981-84, dep chm Yorkshire TV 1982-88, chief exec Goldcrest Films and TV 1983-85 (chm 1981-85), chm Direct Bdcasting by Satellite Consortium 1986-87, dir Boston Consulting Group Ltd 1987-; *Books* Planning for the Social Services (1978), The Investment Challenge (1979); *Recreations* photography, travelling, sailing; *Clubs* Reform, Harvard (NY); *Style*— J G Lee, Esq; Meadow Wood, Penshurst, Kent (☎ 0892 870309); Devonshire House, Mayfair Place, London W1X 5FH (☎ 071 493 3222, telex 28975, fax 071 499 3660)

LEE, Jennifer Elizabeth; da of Ernest J M B Lee, and Mary, *née* Fowlie; *b* 21 Aug 1956; *Educ* St Margaret's Sch for Girls Aberdeen, Edinburgh Coll of Art (Dip AD), RCA (MA); *m* 29 March 1990, Jake Tilson, s of Joe Tilson; *Career* potter; one woman exhibitions: The Scottish Gallery Edinburgh 1981, Anatol Orient London 1984, Crafts Cncl Sideshow ICA London 1985, Rosenthal Studio-Haus London 1985, Craft Centre Royal Exchange Theatre Manchester 1986, Crafts Cncl Shop V & A 1987, Craft Centre and Design Gallery City Art Gallery Leeds 1987, Galerie Besson London 1990, Graham Gallery NY 1991; selected gp exhibitions incl: Three Generations British Ceramics (Maya Behn Zurich) 1984, Jugend Gestaltet (Exempla Munich) 1985, Jugend Formt Keramik (Mathildenhöhe Darmstadt Germany) 1985, British Ceramic Art (Transform NY) 1985, Zeitgenössiche Keramik Aus Grossbritannien (Keramik Studio Vienna) 1986, New British Design (Osaka and Tokyo) 1987, On a Plate (The Serpentine Galley) 1987, British Ceramics (Marianne Heller Galerie Sandhausen Germany) 1987, The New Spirit (Crafts Cncl Gallery London and tour) 1987, Craft and Folk Museum (Los Angeles) 1988, Ton in Ton (Landesmuseum Germany) 1988, Christmas Exhibition (Galerie Besson London) 1988, Sotheby's Decorative Award Exhibition (Yorakucho Seibu Japan) 1988, Galleri Lejonet (Stockholm) 1989, L'Europe des Ceramistes (Auxerre France touring Spain, Austria, Hungary) 1989, The Royal Scottish Museum (Edinburgh) 1989, Lucie Rie Hans Coper and their Pupils (Sainsbury Centre Norwich) 1990, Int Art Fair (Chicago) 1990, The Fitzwilliam Museum (Cambridge) 1991, British Ceramics (Int Art Fair Bologna Italy) 1991; pub collections incl: V & A London, Royal Scottish Museum, Glasgow Museums and Art Galleries, The Scottish Collection SDA Edinburgh, Los Angeles Co Museum of Art, Leeds City Art Gallery, Contemporary Art Society, Crafts Cncl Collection, The Sainsbury Centre (Norwich), Hawkes Bay Art Gallery New Zealand; David Gordon meml tst prize 1979, Andrew Grant travelling scholarship 1979, Allen Lane Penguin book award 1983, Mathildenhöhe award Rosenthal Germany 1984, Jugend Gestaltet prize Munich 1985, Crafts Cncl Grant 1987, Br Cncl Exhibitions Grant 1991; *Style*— Ms Jennifer Lee; c/o Galerie Besson, 15 Royal Arcade, 28 Old Bond St, London W1X 3HD (☎ 071 491 1706)

LEE, Jeremy Charles Roger Barnett; s of Lt Cdr Charles Alexander Barnett Lee, RNR (d 1982), of Phyllis Kathleen Mary, *née* Gunnell (d 1986); *b* 10 July 1944; *Educ* Bristol Cathedral Sch; *m* 4 April 1972 (m dis 1983), Patricia Margaret, *née* Coleridge; 3 da (Veryan Georgina Coleridge b 1974, Isobel Mary b 1977, Caroline Sybella b 1978); *Career* RM: 2 Lt 1962, Troop Cdr 40 Commando serving in Malaya and Sabah 1964-65, Lt 1965, Coy Cdr Sultan's Armed Forces Muscat and Oman 1967-69, Adj (later Co Cdr) 40 Commando serving in NI, Cyprus during Turkish invasion 1972-74, Capt 1973, invalided 1976; admitted slr 1978; sr ptnr Symes Robinson & Lee (Exeter, Crediton, Budleigh Salterton) 1983-; area treas Crediton Cons Assoc 1980-, chm Coldridge Brushford and Nymet Rowland Cons Assoc 1981-; rugby: Capt RM 1971, RN 1971, Exeter FC 1965-67 and 1969-72; memb: Anglo Omani Soc, Law Soc; ASBAH's Conversationalist of the Year 1990; Sultan's Bravery Medal 1968; *Recreations* tennis, fox-hunting, walking, gardening, cycling; *Clubs* Army and Navy; *Style*— Jeremy Lee, Esq; Frogbury, Coldrige, nr Crediton, Devon EX17 (☎ 0363 83484); Symes Robinson and Lee, Manor Office, North St, Crediton, Devon (☎ 03632 5566)

LEE, Prof John Anthony; s of Cecil John Lee (d 1977), of Southsea, Hants, and Phyllis Gwendoline, *née* Fry; *b* 18 March 1942; *Educ* The Portsmouth GS, Univ of Sheffield (BSc, PhD); *m* 17 April 1965, Barbara Lee, da of Thomas Harold Wright, of Burton-in-Kendal, Cumbria; 2 s (Richard b 1968, Peter b 1971); *Career* Univ of Manchester: asst lectr in botany 1967, lectr 1970, sr lectr 1979, head of dept and prof of environmental biology 1988-; ed The Journal of Ecology 1983-90, author of several scientific papers; memb Cncl The Br Ecological Soc 1983-90, vice pres Int Ecology Soc 1989-; memb: Soc for Experimental Biology, Br Ecological Soc; *Recreations* theatre, cricket and hill walking; *Style*— Prof John Lee; Dept of Environmental Biology, University of Manchester, Manchester M13 9PL (☎ 061 275 3888)

LEE, John Desmond (Des); s of Ernest Wilson Lee (d 1988), of Doncaster, and Sarah, *née* Murphy (d 1958); *b* 18 Jan 1942; *Educ* Belmont Abbey Hereford, Doncaster Tech Coll; *m* 30 April 1964, Susan, da of Eric Bott (d 1974), of Doncaster; 1 s (Ryan b 18 March 1970), 1 da (Tracy b 25 April 1967); *Career* computer supervisor NCB 1960-65, computer servs mangr Centre File 1965-67, sr mangr GMS Rowntree Ltd 1967-81, mgmnt servs controller Brooke Bond Oxo Ltd 1981-86, gp head of systems and communications Lloyds of London 1986-90, info technol dir B&Q PLC (part of Kingfisher Group) 1990-; fndr London Insur Mkt Network (LIMNET), chm IBM Computer Users Assoc 1979-81 (hon life pres), int conf speaker on info technol; former memb York 65 Round Table; Freeman: Worshipful Co of Info Technologists 1987, City of London 1987; FBCS 1981, FIDPM 1978; *Recreations* tennis, motor racing; *Style*— Des Lee, Esq; B&Q PLC, Portswood House, 1 Hampshire Corporate Park, Chandlers Ford, Hampshire SO5 3YX (☎ 0703 256256 ext 6002, fax 0703 256095, telex 47233)

LEE, John Michael Hubert; s of Victor Lee (d 1978), of Wentworth, Surrey, and Reneé Annette, *née* Harburn (d 1960); *b* 13 Aug 1927; *Educ* Reading Sch, Christ Coll Cambridge (MA), SOAS Univ of London; *m* 16 July 1960, Margaret Ann, da of James McConnell Russell, ICS; 1 s (Julian b 1968), 1 da (Joanna b 1963); *Career* HM Colonial

Serv Gold Coast (Ghana) 1951-58; cadet dist cmmr Transvolta Togoland 1951-52, asst sec Accra 1952-53, asst govt agent (dist cmmr) Koforidua 1953, sec to Regnl Office (Prov Cmmr) 1953-54, asst govt agent Kibi 1954-55, govt agent Koforidua and Akuse 1955-58, princ asst sec Accra 1958; on staff BBC 1959-65; called to the Bar Middle Temple 1960, in practice Midland circuit 1965-; MP (Lab): Reading 1966-70, Handsworth 1974-79; Parly candidate (Lab) Reading 1964, chm W Midland Gp of Lab MPs 1974-75, memb Parly Ctee on Obsolete Legislation; *Recreations* gardening, watching cricket and tennis, reading, listening to classical music; *Clubs* Royal Over-Seas League; *Style*— J M H Lee, Esq; 2 Dr Johnson's Building, Temple, London EC4Y 7YR (☎ 071 353 5371)

LEE, John Preston; TD (1969); s of George Thomas Lee (d 1982), and Margaret Preston (d 1989); maternal gf Hubert Preston, former ed of Wisden; *b* 4 Oct 1934; *Educ* Emmanuel Sch; *m* 16 Sept 1961, Jeanette Mary, da of John William Arthur Knapman (d 1975), of Salters Heath, Sevenoaks, Kent; 1 da (Vivienne b 1966); *Career* Capt RA 1952-54, TA 1954-71; area mangr Midland Bank plc Guernsey CI; dir: Midland Bank Tst Corp Guernsey Ltd 1981-, Thomas Cook Guernsey Ltd 1981-, Midland Bank Nominees Guernsey Ltd 1981-, Griffin Insur Ltd 1987-, Thai Investmt Fund Ltd 1988, Automotive Fin Insur Ltd 1988, Maxfort Insurance Ltd, JCB Insurance Ltd; FCIB 1985; *Recreations* yachting; *Clubs* United (Guernsey), Royal Channel Island Yacht, Guernsey Yacht; *Style*— John Lee, Esq, TD; La Girouette, Rue de la Mare, St Andrews, Guernsey, CI; Midland Bank plc, Box 31, St Peter Port, Guernsey, CI (☎ 0481 24201)

LEE, John Robert Louis; MP (C) Pendle 1983-; s of Basil Lee (d 1983), and Miriam Lee (d 1982); *b* 21 June 1942; *Educ* William Hulme's GS Manchester; *m* 1975, Anne Monique, *née* Bakirgian; 2 da; *Career* accountancy articles 1959-64, Henry Cooke Lumsden & Co Manchester stockbrokers 1964-66, founding dir Chancery Consolidated Ltd investmt bankers, dir Paterson Zochonia (UK) Ltd 1975-76; vice chm NW Conciliation Ctee Race Relations Bd 1976-77, political sec to Rt Hon Robert Carr (now Lord Carr of Hadley) 1974, contested (C) Manchester Moss Side Oct 1974, MP (C) Nelson and Colne 1979-83; chm cncl Nat Youth Bureau 1980-83, jt sec Cons Back Bench Indust Ctee 1979-80, pps to Min of State for Indust 1981-83, pps to Sec of State for Trade and Indust 1983; parly under sec of state: MOD 1983-86, Dept of Employment 1986-86; min for tourism 1987-89; non exec chm Country Holidays Ltd 1989-; conslt: Trust House Forte plc 1989-, PS Turner (Hldgs) Ltd 1989-; non exec dir Paterson Zochonis 1990-; FCA; *Recreations* fly fishing, collecting; *Style*— John Lee, Esq, MP; House of Commons, London SW1A 0AH (☎ 071 219 4002)

LEE, His Honour Judge; John Thomas Cyril Lee; s of Cyril Lee (d 1974), and Dorothy Lee (d 1985), of Leadon Bank, Ledbury; *b* 14 Jan 1927; *Educ* Holly Lodge GS, Emmanuel Coll Cambridge (MA, LLB); *m* 1956, Beryl, da of John T Haden (d 1959); 1 s, 3 da; *Career* served HM Forces 1945-48, Royal W African Frontier Force; called to the Bar Gray's Inn 1952; chm various tbnls, circuit judge Midland and Oxford 1972-; *Recreations* golf; *Clubs* Union & County, Worcester Golf & Country; *Style*— His Hon Judge John Lee; The Red House, Upper Colwall, Malvern, Worcs

LEE, Julian Francis Kaines; s of Dr Terence Joseph Lee, and Dr Gwen Elizabeth, *née* Kaines (d 1974); *b* 17 July 1945; *Educ* Worth Abbey; *m* 6 Sept 1975, Lesley Jane Menzies, da of George William Rumford; 2 s (Simon b 1978, Marcus b 1986), 3 da (Charlotte b 1979, Georgina b 1981, Arabella b 1983); *Career* ptnr: Tansley Witt & Co 1975-78, Arthur Andersen & Co 1978-82; dir and chief operating offr Phibro Solomon Ltd 1984-86, jt md British and Commonwealth Holdings plc 1987-88 (dir 1986-88), chief exec The Bricom Group Ltd 1988-90; FCA 1975 (ACA 1969); *Recreations* family, farming, reading; *Clubs* Brooks's; *Style*— Julian Lee, Esq; Fen Place Mill, Tutners Hill, Sussex

LEE, (Harry) Lincoln; s of Harry Lee (d 1965), of Cheshire, and Florence Catherine, *née* Harrison (d 1980); *b* 7 Jan 1922; *Educ* Stockport GS; *m* 6 July 1945, Helen Hunter, da of Charles Hunter McCallum (d 1958), of W Dulwich; 3 s (Neil b 1948, Nicholas b 1950, Dougal b 1959); *Career* RAF pilot 1940, cmmd 1941 (demob 1946); capt BSAA 1947 (then BOAC, pilot 1946), master air pilot 1965, regnl tech dir Int Air Tport Assoc N Atlantic and N America 1968 (joined 1965), aviation conslt and author 1988-; served on numerous aviation ctees and panels both Br and Int; Freeman City of London 1966, Upper Freeman Guild of Air Pilots and Air Navigators; FRIN 1974; *Books* Three-Dimensioned Darkness (1962), Torwolf the Saxon (1988); *Clubs* RAF; *Style*— Lincoln Lee, Esq; 7 Saxon Gdns, Taplow, Berks SL6 0DD (☎ 0628 20826, 0628 24005)

LEE, Malcolm Kenneth; QC (1983); s of Thomas Marston Lee (d 1972), of Birmingham, and Fiona Margaret, *née* Mackenzie; *b* 2 Jan 1943; *Educ* King Edward's Sch Birmingham, Worcester Coll Oxford (MA); *m* 16 May 1970, (Phyllis) Anne Brunton, da of Andrew Watson Speed, of Bromsgrove, Worcs; 3 s (Oliver b 1973, Dominic b 1974, Adrian b 1977), 4 da (Phyllis b and d 1972, Lydia b 1976, Flora b 1979, Georgina b 1981); *Career* Lt 268 Regt (RA) TA 1965-69; called to the Bar Inner Temple 1967; practised Midland Circuit 1967-71, Midland and Oxford Circuit 1972-; jr counsel to DHSS 1979-83; dep chm Agric Land Tribunal E Midland area and Midland area 1978-; rec Crown Ct 1980-; *Recreations* squash, tennis, walking, reading; *Clubs* Edgbaston Priory; *Style*— Malcolm Lee, Esq, QC; 24 Estria Rd, Edgbaston, Birmingham B15 2LQ (☎ 021 440 4481); 4 Fountain Ct, Steelhouse Lane, Birmingham B4 6DR (☎ 021 236 3476)

LEE, Prof Mark Howard; s of Clifford Howard Lee, of Derby, and Peggy Alice, *née* Osborne; *b* 9 April 1944; *Educ* Univ of Wales (BSc, MSc), Univ of Nottingham (PhD); *m* 24 July 1971, Elizabeth Anne, da of Rev Frank Andrew Willmot (d 1976), of London, 2 s (Matthew Peter Howard b 13 Oct 1976, Joseph Jonathan b 28 March 1979), 1 da (Bethan Louisa b 3 Jan 1984); *Career* lectr City of Leicester Poly 1969-74, prof Univ of Wales Averystwyth 1987- (lectr 1974-85, sr lectr 1985-87), visiting prof Univ of Aukland NZ 1988; FRSA, MIEE, CEng; *Books* Intelligent Robotics (1989); *Recreations* mountaineering; *Style*— Prof Mark Lee; Department of Computer Science, University College of Wales, Penglais, Aberystwyth, Dyfed SY23 3BZ (☎ 0970 622421, telex 35181, fax 0970 627172)

LEE, Michael James Arthur; s of Brian Arthur Frederick Lee (d 1983), of Newton Abbot, Devon, and Rachel Dorothy Strange, *née* Wickham; *b* 22 June 1942; *Educ* Blundell's Sch, Univ of Durham (LLB); *m* 4 March 1974 (m dis 1984), Judith Mary, da of Humphrey David Oliver of Alresford Hants; 1 da (Henrietta Victoria b 4 Oct 1976), 1 step s (Rory Charles McGregor Aird b 28 Jan 1968), 1 step da (Imogen Holly Aird b 25 May 1969); *Career* admitted slr 1966; articled clerk Lovell White and King 1963-66 (asst slr 1966-67); legal asst New Scotland Yard 1967-69; Norton Rose: asst slr 1970-73, ptnr 1973-; memb Worshipful Co of City of London Slrs; memb Law Soc, ACIArb; *Recreations* sailing, skiing; *Clubs* RAC, Lttle Ship; *Style*— Michael Lee, Esq; Norton Rose, Kempson House, Camomile St, London EC3A 7AN (☎ 071 283 2434, telex 883652, fax 071 588 1181, car 0836 231979)

LEE, Prof (John) Michael; s of John Ewart Lee (d 1975), of Castle Donington, and May, *née* Humber; *b* 29 March 1932; *Educ* Henry Mellish GS Nottingham, ChCh Oxford (MA, BLitt); *m* 23 June 1962, Mary Joy, da of James Philip Sorby Bowman (d 1962), of Barnack; 1 s (Matthew b 1964), 1 da (Helen b 1966); *Career* lectr and sr lectr in govt Univ of Manchester 1958-67, princ (academic secondment) HM Treasy 1967-69, sr lectr Inst of Cwlth Studies 1969-72, reader in politics Birkbeck Coll 1972-81, dean of Faculty of Social Sciences Univ of Bristol 1987- (prof of politics 1981-); jt ed Jl of RIPA; FRHistS 1971; *Books* Social Leaders and Public Persons (1963), Colonial Development and Good Government (1967), African Armies and Civil Order (1969), The Churchill Coalition (1980); *Style*— Prof Michael Lee; 29 Castlebar Rd, Ealing, London W5 2DL (☎ 081 997 9006); 212 High Kingdown, Bristol BS2 8DG (☎ 0272 290249); University of Bristol, Senate House, Tyndall Avenue, Bristol BS8 1TH (☎ 0272 303030)

LEE, Prof Michael Radcliffe; s of Harry Lee (d 1982), of Manchester, and Jean Adelaide, *née* Radcliffe (d 1976); *b* 21 Nov 1934; *Educ* Manchester GS, Univ of Oxford (MA, DM, DPhil); *m* 27 Aug 1960, Judith Ann, da of Reginald Horrocks, of Leyland Lancashire; 1 s (Stephen Michael b 21 Dec 1962), 1 da (Karen Elizabeth b 11 March 1965); *Career* lectr in med: Univ of Oxford 1965-69, St Thomas' Hosp 1969-71; med dir then md Weddell Pharmaceuticals 1971-73, sr lectr in clinical pharmacology Univ of Leeds 1973-84, prof Univ of Edinburgh 1984-; memb: Assoc of Physicians of GB and I, Br Hypertension Soc; FRCP 1976, FRCPE 1985, FRSE 1990; *Books* Renin and Hypertension (1969), Clinical Toxicology (jtly, 1982); *Recreations* gardening, collecting cricket and naval books; *Style*— Prof Michael Lee, FRSE; 112 Polwarth Terrace, Edinburgh EH11 1NN (☎ 031 337 7386); Clinical Pharmacology Unit, University of Edinburgh Medical School, Royal Infirmary, Edinburgh EH3 9YW (☎ 031 229 2477, telex 727442 UNICED S)

LEE, Michael Richard; OBE (1974); s of Maj Thomas Lee (ka 1941), and Laura Myfanwy, *née* Bushman (d 1987); *b* 1 Nov 1934; *Educ* Eton, RMA Sandhurst; *m* 5 July 1969, Jane Patricia, da of Sidney George Harris; 1 s (William b 1970), 1 adopted da (Prue b 1966); *Career* cmmnd Welsh Gds 1955, DAA and QMG HQ 99 Gurkha Inf Bde 1966, Bde Maj 4 Gds Armd Bde 1969, CO 1 Bn Welsh Gds 1972, Regtl Lt-Col Welsh Gds 1976; Col gen staff: SHAPE 1978, HQ BAOR 1981, HQ UKLF 1983; Cdr 2 Inf Bde and Dep Constable Dover Castle 1984, pres RCB 1988 dep dir Army Security 1990; *Recreations* game shooting, bird watching, military history; *Clubs* Pratt's; *Style*— Brigadier Michael Lee, OBE

LEE, Nicholas John (Nick); s of Percy Horatio Lee, and Vera Maud, *née* West; *b* 14 Aug 1942; *Educ* Colchester Royal GS; *m* 17 Sept 1966, Wendy Elizabeth, da of Norman Frederick White (d 1968); 1 s (Simon John b 19 Feb 1969), 1 da (Sarah Jayne b 15 Nov 1967); *Career* Arthur Goddard and Co 1959-68 (qualified as CA 1964); Jardine Insurance Brokers (formerly Pickford Dawson and Holland Ltd) 1968-: joined as accountant and progressed to co sec and fin dir; memb St Osyth PCC; FCA 1969; *Recreations* golf, tennis, skiing; *Clubs* Royal Oversea's League; *Style*— Nick Lee, Esq; 31 St Clairs Rd, St Osyth, Clacton-on-Sea, Essex (☎ 0255 821163); Jardine Insurance Brokers Ltd, PO Box 861, 91-99 New London Rd, Chelmsford, Essex CM2 OPL (☎ 0245 490949, fax 0245 491664)

LEE, Maj-Gen Patrick Herbert; CB (1982), MBE (1964); s of Percy Herbert Lee, and Mary Dorothea Lee; *b* 15 March 1929; *Educ* King's Sch Canterbury, Univ of London (BSc); *m* 1952, Peggy Eveline, *née* Chapman; 1 s, 1 da; *Career* cmmnd RMA Sandhurst 1948, Staff Coll 1960, WO Staff duties 1961-63, CO Parachute Workshop 1964-65, JSSC 1966, mil asst to Master of Gen Ordnance 1966-67, directing staff Staff Coll 1968-69, Cdr REME 2 Div 1970-71, Col AQ Br Corps 1972-75, Dep Cmdt Sch of Electrical Mech Engrg (Army) 1976-77, Cmdt REME Trg Centre 1978-79, DG REME 1980-83, Col Cmdt REME 1983-89; dir Wincanton Distribution Services Ltd 1983-; memb Wessex Water Authy 1983-88, dir Road Haulage Assoc 1988-, vice chm RHA 1990-; CEng, FIMechE, FBIM, FInstD; *Recreations* gardening, railways, Roman history, industrial archeology; *Clubs* Army and Navy; *Style*— Maj-Gen Patrick Lee, CB, MBE

LEE, Paul Anthony; s of Wilfred Lee (d 1970), of Manchester, and Anne, *née* Molyneux; *b* 26 Jan 1946; *Educ* Central GS Manchester, Clare Coll Cambridge (MA, LLB); *m* 16 Sept 1977, Elisabeth Lindsay, da of Maj Geoffrey Robert Taylor, of Manchester; 2 s (Jonathan b 1980, William b 1985), 1 da (Antonia b 1983); *Career* admitted slr 1970; ptnr Addleshaw Sons & Latham Manchester; dir: Robert H Lowe plc 1985- (dep chm 1990), Davies & Metcalfe plc 1986, Pugh Davies & Co Ltd 1976-, Royal Exchange Theatre Co 1986-, Leaf Properties Ltd (chm) 1986-, Classic Car Conslts Ltd 1988-; chm Patron and Assocs Manchester City Art Gallery, Ffeoffee Chethams Hosp and Library, govr Chethams Sch of Music; *Recreations* the arts, travel, tennis, wine; *Clubs* Oxford and Cambridge, St James's Manchester, Real Tennis and Racquets Manchester; *Style*— Paul A Lee, Esq; Riverbank Cottage, Stanton Avenue, W Didsbury, Manchester M20; Dennis House, Marsden Street, Manchester M2 1JD (☎ 061 832 5994)

LEE, Peter Gavin; s of Lt Cdr John Gavin Lee, RNVR, of Burygate, Felsted, Essex, and late Helena Frances, *née* Whitehead; *b* 4 July 1934; *Educ* Midhurst GS, Wye Coll; *m* 27 April 1963, Caroline Mary, da of Cdr EN Green, RN (d 1976); 2 s (William Gavin b 1964, Jonathan Campbell b 1966), 1 da (Olivia Alice b 1969); *Career* RA Nat Serv 1953-55; chartered surveyor Strutt & Parker 1957- (sr ptnr 1979-), chm Anglo American Liaison Ctee Wethersfield USAF; High Sheriff of Essex 1990-91; govr Felsted Sch; Freeman City of London 1977, Liveryman Worshipful Co of Chartered Surveyors 1977; FRICS; *Recreations* piloting, country pursuits, vintage cars and aircraft; *Clubs* Boodles; *Style*— Peter Lee, Esq; Fanners, Great Gt Waltham, Essex CM3 1EA (☎ 0245 360 470); 13 Hill St, London W1 (☎ 071 629 7282, fax 071 495 3176)

LEE, Robin John; s of John Johnson Lee, of Dublin, and Adelaide Elizabeth, *née* Hayes; *b* 23 Oct 1952; *Educ* Wesley Coll Dublin, Trinity Coll Dublin (BA, MB BCh, MA, MD); *m* 23 Sept 1981, (Sylvia) Jane Lucette, da of Ernest Herbert Bodell, of Dublin; 2 s (Charles b 25 Dec 1982, Christopher (twin) b 25 Dec 1982), 1 da (Sarah b 31 Jan 1981); *Career* sr registrar in otolaryngology: Royal Victoria Eye and Ear Hosp Dublin 1985, Federated Dublin Vol Hops 1986, Beaumont Hosp Dublin 1988; res fell Dept of Otolaryngology Head and Neck Surgery Univ of Iowa 1987, conslt ENT surgn Kettering Gen Hosp 1988-; memb Ctee Young Consultants in Otolaryngology Head and Neck Survery 1989-; memb: BMA 1988, RSM 1988, Br Assoc of Otolaryngologists 1988, Irish Otolaryngological Soc 1983; FRCSI 1984; *Style*— Robin Lee, Esq; Kettering General Hospital, Rothwell Rd, Kettering, Northants NN16 8UZ (☎ 0536 410666 ext 272)

LEE, Rosa; da of William W Y Lee, and Joyce Ying Lee (d 1987); *b* 1 Feb 1957; *Educ* Univ of Sussex (BA), Brighton Poly Faculty of Art and Design, St Martin's Sch of Art (BA), RCA (MA); *Career* artist; solo exhibitions: Artist of the Day (Flowers East Gallery) 1989, Ellipsis (The Winchester Gallery) 1989 (touring 1990), Interface (Todd Gallery London) 1990; gp exhibitions incl: Universiad Exhibition (Kobe Japan) 1985, The Class of '86 (ILEA London Inst Show Royal Festival Hall) 1986, The Marlow Art Collection (Rank Xerox '86, The Nat Theatre) 1986, Harrogate Colour Festival 1986, The Three Year Itch (Recent Graduates Work from St Martin's Sch of Art, Smiths Gallery Covent Garden) 1986, London Art Schools in Brussels (Ecoles en Galerie Brussels) 1988, Whitechapel Open (Whitechapel Gallery) 1989, John Moores 16 (Walker Art Gallery Liverpool) 1989-90, Opening Gp Exhibition (Todd Soho Gallery) 1989, 3 Ways (RCA/Br Cncl touring exhibition) 1990, Works on Paper (Todd Gallery London) 1990, Broadgate Art Week 1990, Group Show (Todd Gallery London) 1991;

work in three public collections; pt/t fine art lectr; *Awards* ABTA Award 1986, Cwlth Festival prizewinner 1986, Mario Dubsky travel award 1988, visiting fell in painting Winchester Sch of Art 1988-89, John Moores 16 prizewinner 1989, Gtr London Arts award 1989; *Style*— Ms Rosa Lee; 1-5 Needham Rd, London W2 (☎ 081 960 6209)

LEE, Samuel George; s of George Alles Lee (d 1966), and Nancy, *née* Moore; *b* 16 Oct 1939; *Educ* Rossall; *m* 12 May 1965, Jennifer Anne Nye, da of Rev J A K Nye, of Lytham St Annes; 2 s (Matthew Everett b 1968, Joseph James b 1970); *Career* admitted slr 1963; coroner Blackpool and Fylde Dist 1989; chm: Fylde Arts Assoc 1977-81, Blackpool District CC 1986: vice chm Blackpool Grand Theatre Tst 1980; govr: Rossall Sch 1981, Blackpool Fylde Coll 1990; *Recreations* squash, reading, watching rugby; *Style*— Samuel G Lee, Esq; The Croft, 7 St Clements Ave, Blackpool FY3 8LT (☎ 0253 391990); John Budd & Co, 283 Church St, Blackpool FY1 3PG (☎ 0253 26557)

LEE, Maj-Gen (James) Stuart; MBE (1970), CB (1990); s of George Lee (d 1974), and Elizabeth, *née* Hawkins (d 1952); *b* 26 Dec 1934; *Educ* Normanton GS, Univ of Leeds (BA), King's Coll London (MA); *m* 21 March 1960, Lorna Alice, da of James Leonard Powell (d 1983); 1 s (James Alastair Spencer b 29 Dec 1964); *Career* educn offr UK Trg Units 1959-64, mil trg offr Beaconsfield 1964, RMCS and Staff Coll 1964-65; DAQMG HQ: Cyprus Dist 1966, NEARELF 1967; SO2 MOD 1968-70, DAA & QMG HQ NEARELF 1970, GSO2 HQ FARELF 1970-71, OC offr trg wing Beaconsfield 1971-74, gp educn offr Rheindahlen 1974-75, chief educn offr NE Dist 1976-78, head offr Educn Branch 1978-79, SO1 trg HQ UKLF 1979, Col Chief Inspr Res 1980-82, Cdr educn HQ BAOR 1983-87, dir army educn 1987-90, non-exec dir Exhibition Consultants Ltd 1990; pres Leeds Univ Union 1958-59, res assoc Int Inst of Strategic Studies 1982-83, dep co cmmr Br Scouts Western Europe 1983-87, tstee and sec Gallipoli Meml Lecture 1987-90, pres Army Canoe Union 1987-90, pres Army Chess 1987-90; memb: Bd of Mgmnt Nat Fndn for Educnl Res 1987-, Nat Advsy Ctee Duke of Edinburgh's award 1987-90, Cncl Scout Assoc 1988-, Cncl and chm Sr Awards Ctee City and Guilds of London Inst 1990-; FRSA 1987; *Recreations* theatre, boats; *Style*— Maj-Gen Stuart Lee, MBE; c/o Royal Bank of Scotland, Holt's Branch, Kirkland House, Whitehall, London SW1A 2EB

LEE, Rev Terence; s of (John) Denis Lee (d 1967), of Newcastle upon Tyne, and Kathleen, *née* Meakin; *b* 5 Dec 1946; *Educ* Barnard Castle Sch Co Durham, Oxford NSM Course; *m* 1 Jan 1972 (m dis 1989), Susan Anne, da of Kenneth Spence, of Leyburn, N Yorks; 1 s (James Denis b 1975), 1 da (Victoria Ann b 1973); *Career* practised as a CA: Newcastle upon Tyne 1971-73, Gallon Lee and Co 1971-76, Haines Watts 1978-84; ptnr Feltons Chartered Accountants (Welbeck Street and Windsor) 1984-; trained under the Oxford Non Stipendiary Ministry Ct 1980-83, ordained deacon 1983 and priest 1984; asst priest: Calcot Reading 1983-86, Burghfield Saint Mary the Virgin Oxon 1986-88; chm Thames Valley Soc of CAs 1985-; ACA 1971, FCA 1976; *Recreations* singing solo tenor, shooting, fishing, riding, squash, eating, cooking; *Clubs* Athenaeum; *Style*— The Rev Terence Lee; 45 Christchurch Rd, Reading, Berks RG2 7AN; 12 Sheet St, Windsor, Berks SL4 1BG (☎ 0753 840111, fax 0753 850028); 55 Welbeck St, London W1

LEE, Thomas Albert; s of Thomas Ernest Lee (d 1978), of Kensington, and Harriet Elizabeth, *née* Halesworth; *b* 2 Feb 1901; *Educ* Surrey Co GS, RAF Coll Cranfield, Kenya Univ Nairobi; *m* 27 July 1958, Nancy Marie Terese, da of John Augustus Hope (d 1957), of Ireland; 2 s (Gerald b 1962, Nathan (twin, still born)); *Career* RAF 1950-56; md: Rocke International Ltd 1968-71, Lee Engineering Ltd 1971-; memb Cons Pty; memb Royal Aeronautical Soc; *Recreations* motor racing; *Clubs* RAC; *Style*— Thomas Lee, Esq; Rebels Beech, Portnall Rise, Wentworth, Surrey GU25 4JZ (☎ 0344 843256); Lee Engineering Ltd, Sky Business Park, Thorpe, Surrey TW20 8RF, (☎ 0784 471166, fax 0784 471160)

LEE, Prof Thomas Alexander; s of Thomas Henderson Lee (d 1970), of Edinburgh, and Dorothy Jane Paton, *née* Norman (d 1990); *b* 18 May 1941; *Educ* Melville Coll Edinburgh, ICAS, Univ of Edinburgh, Inst of Taxation, Univ of Strathclyde (MSc, D Litt); *m* 14 Sept 1963, Ann Margaret, da of John Brown (d 1971), of Edinburgh; 1 s (Richard Thomas b 19 July 1968), 1 da (Sarah Ann (Mrs Birchall) b 17 August 1965); *Career* auditor J Douglas Henderson & Co and Peat Marwick Mitchell 1959-64, lectr Univ of Strathclyde 1966-69; prof: Univ of Liverpool 1973-76, Univ of Edinburgh 1976-90 (lectr 1969-73), Culverhouse prof of accounting Univ of Alabama 1991-; dir accounting and auditing res ICAS 1983-84, memb Exec Ctee AUTA (BAA) 1971-84, ed AUTA News Review 1971-75; ICAS: memb and convener Scottish Accounting History Ctee 1971-, memb Educn Ctee 1982-88, memb Advsy Ctee on Accounting Educn 1985-87, memb Company Law Strategy Unit 1986-88, memb Res Ctee 1988-90, memb cncl 1989-90; memb Cncl Br Fin and Accounting Assoc 1973-77; memb ed bd: Journal of Business Fin and Accounting 1976-82, Accounting Review 1977-80, Accounting and Business Res 1981-; elder church of Scotland 1984-, memb academic advsy ctee ASC 1987-90; memb: ICAS 1964, IT 1966, AAA 1969, AAH 1974, EAA 1978; FRSA 1983; *Books* Books incl: Company Auditing (1972), Income and Value (1974), Company Financial Reporting (1976), Cash Flow Accounting (1984), Towards a Theory and Practice of Cash Flow Accounting (1986), The Closure of the Accounting Profession (1989); *Recreations* road running, cricket, history; *Style*— Prof Thomas Lee; 2013 Foxridge Road, Tuscaloosa, Alabama 35406, USA; Culverhouse School of Accountancy, Univesity of Alabama, 375 Bidgood Hall, Box 870220, Tuscaloosa, Alabama, AL 35487-0220, USA (☎ 0101 205 348 7915)

LEE, Vernon Harry; s of Robert Lee (d 1970), and Elsie, *née* Ward (d 1982); *b* 11 April 1924; *Educ* Nunthorpe GS York, Univ of Liverpool Sch of Architecture (B Arch, Dip CD); *m* 1; 5s (Matthew b 30 May 1953, Marcus b 24 Oct 1955, Timothy b 5 March 1959, Jeremy b 28 May 1960, David b 17 May 1964), 1 da (Helen b 15 July 1951); m 2, 20 Dec 1983, Anne Downing Ghinn; *Career* Nat Serv Univ Air Sqdn RAF 1942, invalided out of fighter pilot training 1943; sr architect Farmer & Dark London 1955-57, sr architect gp ldr Schs Div Herts CC 1951-55 and 1957-60, res architect Miny of Health 1960, dep regnl architect NW Regnl Met Bd 1960-63; Robert Matthew Johnson Marshall and Ptnrs Scot: gp ldr, ptnr 1963, chm; planning advsr to Urban Planning Office Shenzhen Econ Free Zone; chm Cncl Br Conslts Bureau 1980-82 (memb Cncl 1972-83); MRTPI, FRIBA, ARIAS, FRSA; *Recreations* swimming, walking, touring, music, travel, golf, fishing, books; *Clubs* New (Edinburgh), Royal Overseas League; *Style*— Vernon Lee, Esq; RMJM Scotland Ltd, 10 Bells Brae, Edinburgh EH4 3BJ (☎ 031 225 2532, fax 031 226 5117, telex 727411 RUMJUM EDIN)

LEE, Col Sir William Allison; OBE (1945), TD (1948), DL (1965 Co Durham); s of Samuel Percy Lee (d 1939), of Darlington, and Florence Ada, *née* Short (d 1944); *b* 31 May 1907; *Educ* Queen Elizabeth GS Darlington; *m* 1, 1933, Elsa Norah (d 1966), da of Thomas Hanning (d 1943); m 2, 1967, Mollie Clifford (d 1989), da of Sir Cuthbert Whiteside (d 1968); *Career* served in Royal Signals 1935-53, TA Col 150 and 151 Inf Bdes 1953-58; chm: Newcastle Regnl Hosp Bd 1970-73, Northern RHA 1973-78; ret branch mangr Guardian Royal Exchange Assurance Group; High Sheriff 1978, pres Darlington SSAFA, memb St John Cncl Co Durham; OStJ 1980; kt 1975; *Recreations* gardening; *Style*— Col Sir William Lee, OBE, TD, DL; Whiteside, 23 Low Green, Gainford, Co Durham (☎ 0325 730564)

LEE-BROWNE, Col Martin Shaun Lee; CBE (1989, OBE, 1974), TD, DL (Glos); s of Denis William Lee-Browne (d 1960), of Cirencester, and Freda Rosamund Austin (d 1974); *b* 17 Oct 1931; *Educ* Leighton Park Sch Reading, Emmanuel Coll Cambridge; *m* 14 Sept 1957, Diana Frances, da of Dr Geoffrey Richard Ford of Dartford, Kent; 3 s (Jeremy b 1960, Patrick b 1964, Rupert b 1966), 1 da (Alison b 1962); *Career* Col TA (ret 1981), Dep Col The Glos Regt; Hon Col: 1 Bn The Wessex Regt, 1 (Cadet) Bn The Glos Regt ACF; slr; sr ptnr Wilmot & Co; dir: Clements (Watford) Ltd, Coln Gravel Co Ltd; chm Western Wessex TAVR Assoc 1982-90, vice chm Cncl of TAVR Assocs 1987-90; *Recreations* music, sailing; *Clubs* Army and Navy; *Style*— Col M S Lee-Browne, CBE, TD, DL; Park Farm House, Fairford, Glos GL7 4JL (☎ 0285 712102)

LEE OF NEWTON, Baroness; Amelia; *née* Shay; da of William Shay; *m* 1938, Baron Lee of Newton, PC (Life Peer) (d 1984); 1 da (Hon Mrs Flint, *qv*); *Style*— The Rt Hon Lady Lee of Newton; 52 Ashton Road, Newton-le-Willows, Merseyside, EA12 0AE

LEE-POTTER, Dr Jeremy Patrick; s of Air Marshal Sir Patrick Lee Potter, KBE, (d 1983), of Wittersham, Kent, and Audrey Mary, *née* Pollock; *b* 30 Aug 1934; *Educ* Epsom Coll, Guy's Hosp Univ of London (MB BS); *m* 26 Oct 1957, Lynda, da of Norman Higginson, of Culcheth, Lancs; 1 s (Adam b 1968), 2 da (Emma b 1958, Charlotte b 1960); *Career* Sqdn Ldr Med Branch RAF 1960-68, sr specialist in pathology RAF Inst of Pathology and Tropical Med; lectr in haematology St Georges Hosp Med Sch Univ of London 1968-69, conslt haematologist E Dorset Health Authy 1969-; BMA: dep chm Central Conslts and Specialists Ctee 1988-, memb Standing Med Advsy Ctee 1990-, chm Cncl 1990-; FRCPath 1979; *Recreations* printing, print-making, visual arts; *Style*— Dr Jeremy Lee-Potter; Icen House, Stoborough, Wareham, Dorset BH20 5AN ; 8 Strathmore Gardens, London W8 4RZ Dept of Haematology, Poole Gen Hosp, Longfleet Rd, Poole, Dorset (☎ 0202 675100); British Medical Association, Tavistock Square, London WC1H 9JP (☎ 071 383 6000)

LEE-STEERE, Gordon Ernest; s of Charles A Lee-Steere (ka 1940), of Jayes Park, Ockley, Surrey, and Patience Hargreaves, *née* Pigott-Brown; *b* 26 Dec 1939; *Educ* Eton, Trinity Coll Cambridge (MA); *m* 14 July 1966, Mary Katharine, da of Lt-Col Innes Stuart of Ethie Mains, of Inverkeilor, Angus; 1 s (James b 1976), 3 da (Henrietta b 1969, Lucinda b 1971, Marina b 1973); *Career* mgmnt conslt Deloitte Robson Morrow 1968-74, pres Country Landowners Assoc 1987-89; chm Surrey Branch CPRE 1982-, dist cncllr Mole Valley 1983-, parish cncllr Ockley 1976-, chm of govrs Sondes Place Sch Dorking; MIMC, MBCS; *Recreations* country; *Clubs* Boodle's, Farmer's; *Style*— Gordon Lee-Steere, Esq; Jayes Park, Ockley Surrey, RH3 5RA (☎ 030 670 223)

LEECE, Geoffrey Robert; s of Robert Sydney Leece (d 1984), and Edith, *née* Stevenson; *b* 1 Dec 1931; *Educ* Alsop HS, Prescot GS; *m* 16 May 1973, Janet Kate, da of Colin McCaig (d 1979); 2 s (Stuart b 1975, Alastair b 1977); *Career* CA; sr ptnr Pannell Kerr Forster CA Liverpool 1970-; FCA 1954; *Recreations* golf, watching Everton FC; *Clubs* Athenaeum (Liverpool), Huyton and Prescot Golf, Heswall Golf, Soc of Liverpool Golf Captains (Capt 1987/88); *Style*— Geoffrey Leece, Esq; Thornhill, Briardale Rd, Willaston, S Wirral, L64 1TD; 52 Mount Pleasant, Liverpool L3 5UN (☎ 051 708 8232)

LEECH, Prof Geoffrey Neil; s of Charles Richard Leech (d 1973), of Overstone, Bredon, Worcs, and Dorothy Eileen Leech (d 1967); *b* 16 Jan 1936; *Educ* Tewkesbury GS, UCL (BA, MA, PhD); *m* 29 July 1961, Frances Anne, da of George Berman, MBE (d 1985), of 60 Greaves Rd, Lancaster; 1s (Thomas b 1964), 1 da (Camilla b 1967); *Career* Nat Serv SAC RAF 1954-56; Harkness fell Mass Inst of Technol 1964-65, lectr English UCL 1965-69 (asst lectr 1962-64), visiting prof Brown Univ USA 1972, prof of linguistics and modern Eng language Univ of Lancaster 1974- (reader in Eng language 1969-74); memb: Cncl The Philological Soc 1979-83, Eng Teaching Advsy Ctee The Br Cncl 1983-, Academia Europaea 1990-; Fil Dr Lund Univ Sweden 1987; FBA 1987; *Books* English in Advertising (1966), A Linguistic Guide to English Poetry (1969), A Grammar of Contemporary English (with Randolph Quirk Sidney Greenbaum and Jan Svartvik, 1972), Semantics (1974), Studies in English Linguistics: For Randolph Quirk (ed with Sidney Greenbaum and Jan Svartvik, 1980), Style in Fiction: A Linguistic Introduction to English Fictional Prose (with Michael H Short, 1981), A Comprehensive Grammar of the English Language (with Randolph Quirk Sidney Greenbaum and Jan Svartvik, 1985), An A-Z of English Grammar and Usage (1989); *Recreations* chamber music, playing the piano; *Style*— Prof Geoffrey Leech; Department of Linguistics and Modern English Language, University of Lancaster, Bailrigg, Lancaster LA1 4YT (☎ 0524 65201, fax 0524 63806, telex 65111 LANCUL G)

LEECH, Maj John Cooper; s of Raymond Alan Leech (d 1979), of Ipswich, Suffolk, and May Daisy Gertrude, *née* Pledger (d 1971); *b* 25 Feb 1928; *Educ* Northage GS Ipswich, Inst of Educn Univ of London; *m* 25 April 1964, Pauline Mary, da of Russell James Forth (d 1963), of Cheltenham, Gloucestershire; *Career* cmmnd RASC 1947, RAEC 1953 (served Aust, Malaya, Borneo, Malta, N Africa, BAOR), ret 1978; Chamberlain Lincoln Cathedral 1978-79, State Invitations Asst Lord Chamberlain's Office Buckingham Palace 1979-; voluntary steward of St George's Chapel Windsor; Chevalier du Wissam Alouite (Morocco) 1987, Cavaliere Ordine Al Merito della Repubblica Italiana 1990; *Recreations* Ciné photography, restoration of old furniture, history, swimming; *Clubs* Army and Navy; *Style*— Major John Leech; 10 Cumberland Lodge Mews, The Great Park, Windsor, Berkshire SL4 2JD (☎ 0784 431611), Lord Chamberlain's Office, Buckingham Palace, London SW1A 1AA (☎ 071 9304832)

LEECH, Rev Kenneth; s of John Leech, and Annie Leech; *b* 15 June 1939; *Educ* Hyde GS Tameside, King's Coll London (Sambrooke scholar, BA, Barry prize in divinity, AKC), Trinity Coll Oxford (BA), St Stephen's House Oxford; *m* 1970, Rheta; *Career* ordained: deacon 1964, priest 1965; asst priest: Holy Trinity Hoxton London 1964-67, St Annes Soho 1967-71; fndr and dir: Soho Drugs Gp 1967-71, Centrepoint Soho Emergency Night Shelter 1969-71; chaplain and tutor St Augustine's Coll Cambridge 1971-74, relief chapain HM Prison Canterbury 1971-74, rector St Matthew's Bethnal Green 1974-80, i/c post-ordination training Stepney Episcopal Area 1975-80, advsr on exorcism and the occult to the London Bishops 1976-79; visiting theologian: St Stephen's House Chicago 1978-89, Bishop Brent House Chicago 1990-; race rels field offr General Synod Board Social Responsibility 1980-87, hon asst priest St Clements Notting Dale 1982-88, dir Runnymede Trust 1987-90, chm Maze Drug Prevention Project 1989-, memb Drug Policy Review Gp 1988-, Christendom fell St Botolph's Church Aldgate 1991; former memb Ctee: Soho Project, Avenues Unlimited Youth Project, Br and Foreign Schs Soc, Inst for Study of Drug Dependence; giver of numerous lectures at Univs and Colls Britain and America; *Books* Drugs for Young People: their use and misuse (with Brenda Jordan, 1967), Keep the Faith Baby (1973), Brick Lane 1978: the Events and their Significance (1980), The Social God (1981), Care and Conflict: leaves from a pastoral notebook (1990), contrib to numerous learned jls; *Recreations* cartoon drawing, Lancashire dialect poetry, pubs; *Style*— Rev Kenneth Leech; St Botolph's Crypt, Aldgate, London EC3N 1AB (☎ 071 283 6810)

LEECH, His Honour Robert Radcliffe; s of Edwin Radcliffe Leech (d 1947); *b* 5 Dec 1919; *Educ* Monmouth Sch, Worcester Coll Oxford; *m* 1951, Vivienne Ruth, da of A J

Rickerby; 2 da; *Career* served Border Regt (despatches twice) 1940-44; called to the Bar Middle Temple 1949, dep chm Cumberland QS 1966, co ct judge 1970, circuit judge 1971-86, hon rec City of Carlisle 1985-86; *Recreations* sailing, golf; *Clubs* Oriental, Border and Co (Carlisle); *Style—* His Hon Robert Leech; Scaur House, Cavendish Terrace, Stanwix, Carlisle CA3 9ND (☎ 0228 21946)

LEEDALE, Prof Gordon Frank; s of William Henry Leedale, and Ivy Victoria Alexandra, *née* Hampton; *b* 10 Oct 1932; *Educ* E Ham GS, QMC (BSc, PhD, DSc); *m* 24 July 1954 (m dis 1981), Hazel Doris, da of Harry Dudley Leeson (d 1984); 1 s (Jonathan Paul b 7 Dec 1967), 2 da (Wanda Siriol Jane b 8 Feb 1960, Siân Vanessa b 13 March 1964); *Career* res fell in pure sci Univ of Durham 1957-59, res fell Devpt Cmmn 1959-60; Univ of Leeds: lectr in botany 1960-65, reader in botany Dept of Plant Sciences 1965-79, prof of botany 1980-, head Dept of Plant Sciences 1986-87, head Dept of Pure and Applied Biology 1987-90; Darwin lectr Br Assoc 1965, sec Br Phycological Soc 1965-67, hon ed British Phycological Journal 1967-75, pres Soc of Evolutionary Protistology 1977-79; FIBiol 1981, FLS 1981; *Books* Euglenoid Flagellates (1967); *Recreations* classical music, biological photography; *Style—* Prof Gordon Leedale; The Cottage, Rigton Hill, N Rigton, Leeds LS17 0DJ (☎ 0423 734348); Dept of Pure and Applied Biology, University of Leeds, Leeds LS2 9JT (☎ 0532 332870, fax 0532 332882)

LEEDHAM, Dr Peter William; s of William Marshall Leedham, and Winifred, *née* Doswell; *b* 17 March 1941; *Educ* Collyer's Sch Horsham Sussex, King's Coll Hosp Med Sch London (MB BS); *m* 12 June 1965, (Dorothy) Elaine, da of Walter John Witcombe, of Magor, Newport, Gwent; 2 s (Richard b 1966, David b 1971), 1 da (Ruth b 1968); *Career* lectr in morbid anatomy Kings Coll Hosp Med Sch 1967 (demonstrator in pathology 1966), lectr in morbid anatomy The London Hosp Med Coll 1969, conslt histopathologist Shropshire Health Dist 1972-; memb Shropshire local Med Ctee, past memb Shropshire Health Authy 1979-87, past memb regnl scientific ctee and past chm combined laboratory servs ctee W Midlands RHA, memb Shrewsbury Rotary Club; memb: ACP, BMA, Pathological Soc of GB and Ireland, Int Acad Pathology (former cncl memb); LRCP, MRCS, FRCPath; *Recreations* golf, gardening; *Style—* Dr Peter Leedham

LEEDS, Archdeacon of; *see*: Comber, Ven Anthony James

LEEDS, Aubrey; s of William Henry Leeds (d 1947, gs of 2 Bt), and Mary (d 1956), eld da of James Fyfe-Jamieson, of Renfrews; hp of cous Sir Christopher Leeds, 8 Bt, *qv*; *b* 4 Aug 1903; *m* 1933, Barbara, only child of J Travis, of Lightcliffe, Yorks; 1 s (Antony b 1937), 2 da (Mrs John Nation b 1936, Sharman b 1953); *Career* rubber planter; *Recreations* angling; *Clubs* 22; *Style—* Aubrey Leeds, Esq; 17 Atwood Avenue, Kew Gardens, Surrey (☎ 081 876 2038)

LEEDS, Sir Christopher Anthony; 8 Bt (UK 1812); s of Maj Geoffrey Hugh Anthony Leeds (d 1962, yr bro of 6 Bt) by his w Yolande Therese Barre, *née* Mitchell (d 1944); suc cous, Sir Graham Mortimer Leeds, 7 Bt, in 1983; *b* 31 Aug 1935; *Educ* King's Sch Bruton, LSE (BSc), Univ of S California (MA); *m* 1974 (m dis 1980), Elaine Joyce, da of late Sqdn Ldr Cornelius Harold Albert Mullins; *Heir* cous, Aubrey Leeds, *qv*; *Career* asst master: Merchant Taylors' Sch 1966-68, Christ's Hosp 1972-75, Stowe 1978-81; sr lectr Univ of Nancy II; visiting lectr Univ of Strasbourg I 1983-87; author, memb Conflict Res Soc; *Books* incl: Political Studies (1968, third edn 1981), European History 1789-1914 (1971, second edn 1980), Italy under Mussolini (1972), Management and Business Studies (with R S Stainton and C Jones, 1974, third edn 1983) World History-1900 to the present day (1987), Peace and War (1987), English Humour (1989); *Recreations* tennis, modern art, travel; *Clubs* Lansdowne; *Style—* Sir Christopher Leeds, Bt; 6 Hurlingham, 14 Manor Way, Eastcliffe, Bournemouth, Dorset; 7 Rue de Turique, 54000 Nancy, France (☎ 010 33 83 96 43 838)

LEEDS, Bishop of (RC) 1985-; Rt Rev David Every Konstant; s of Antoine Konstant (d 1985), and Dulcie Marion Beresford Leggatt (d 1930); *b* 16 June 1930; *Educ* St Edmund's Coll Ware, Christ's Coll Cambridge (MA), Univ of London Inst of Education (PGCE); *Career* priest Diocese of Westminster 1954, Cardinal Vaughan Sch Kensington 1959, diocesan advsr on religious educn 1966, St Michael's Sch Stevenage 1968, dir Westminster Religious Educn Centre 1970, auxiliary bishop of Westminster (bishop in Central London) 1977-85; chm Nat Bd of Religious Inspectors and Advisers 1970-75; episcopal advsr: Catholic Teachers' Fedn 1980-88, Catholic Inst for Int Relations 1982-; chm: Oxford and Cambridge Catholic Education Bd 1984-, Dept of Catechetics Bishops Conf 1978-84, Dept of Catholic Educn 1984-, W Yorks Ecumenical Cncl 1986-87; Freeman City of London 1984; author of various books on religious educn and liturgy; *Recreations* music, sport of most kinds; *Style—* The Rt Rev the Bishop of Leeds; Bishop's House, 13 North Grange Road, Headingley, Leeds LS6 2BR (☎ 0532 304533, fax 0532 789890)

LEEK, Anthony Thomas (Tony); s of Thomas Henry Howard Leek (d 1988), and Mary, *née* Curtis; *b* 15 Feb 1947; *Educ* Forest Sch Snaresbrook, Univ of Southampton (LLB); *Career* admitted slr 1975; ptnr: Austin Ryder & Co 1977-86, Alsop Wilkinson 1987-; memb Law Soc; *Recreations* cricket, theatre, music; *Style—* Tony Leek, Esq; 6 Dowgate Hill, London EC4 R 2SS (☎ 071 248 4141, fax 071 623 8286, telex 995593)

LEEMING, Charles Gerard James; s of Gerard Paschal de Pfyffer Leeming, of Field Dalling Hall, Holt, Norfolk, and Joan Helen Mary (d 1954), da of Edmund Trappes-Lomax (d 1927, *see* Burke's Landed Gentry 1952); *b* 4 May 1936; *Educ* Ampleforth; *Career* admitted slr 1959, sr ptnr Wilde Sapte London 1987, (ptnr 1963-); chm Banking Sub-ctee London Law Soc, memb Lloyds; memb Worshipful Co of Watermen and Lightermen of the River Thames, Freeman Worshipful Co of Slrs; *Recreations* sailing, music, art, books, bee-keeping, collecting electronic gadgets; *Clubs* Little Ship, Cruising Assoc; *Style—* Charles Leeming, Esq; Picton House, 45 Strand-on-the-Green, Chiswick, London W4 3PB (☎ 081 994 0450); Wilde Sapte, Queensbridge House, 60 Upper Thames St, London EC4V 3BD (☎ 071 236 3050, fax 071 236 9624, telex 887793)

LEEMING, David Roger; s of Stanley James Robert Leeming and Ada; *b* 29 Aug 1947; *Educ* Felsted Sch, Clare Coll Cambridge (MA); *m* 18 May 1974, Geraldine Margaret, da of Antony Duke Coleridge; 2 s (Robert b 1978, Toby b 1981); *Career* chm: Platignum plc (managing) 1985, all subsidiary and assoc cos; *Style—* David Leeming, Esq; PO Box 1, Royston, Herts (☎ 0763 44133)

LEEMING, Lady Elizabeth Mary Cecilia; *née* Bowes Lyon; da of 17 Earl of Strathmore and Kinghorne (d 1987); *b* 23 Dec 1959; *Educ* St Hilda's Coll Oxford (BA); *m* 1 Sept 1990, Antony Richard Leeming, eldest s of late Richard Leeming, of Skirsgill Park, Penrith, Cumbria; *Style—* The Lady Elizabeth Leeming

LEEMING, Ian; QC (1988); s of FLt Lt Thomas Leeming (d 1981), of Preston, Lancs, and Lilian, *née* Male; *b* 10 April 1948; *Educ* Catholic Coll Preston, Univ of Manchester (LLB); *m* 26 May 1973, Linda Barbara, da of Harold Cook, of Walton-le-Dale, Preston, Lancs; 1 s (Charles b 1985), 2 da (Lucinda b 1976, Angela b 1981); *Career* called to the Bar Gray's Inn 1970, Lincoln's Inn (Ad Eundem); Northern Circuit 1971, in practice at the Chancery and Commercial Bars 1971-, fndr memb Northern Soc of Cons Lawyers (vice chm 1985-89), asst rec 1986, rec 1989, chm of Heaton Cons 1986-88, former pt/t lectr in law Univ of Manchester; *Recreations* squash, real tennis, occasional racquets; *Clubs* Athenaeum, Carlton, Manchester Tennis and Racquets; *Style—* Ian Leeming, Esq, QC; 11 Stone Bldgs, Lincoln's Inn, London (☎ 071 404 5055); Crown Square Chambers, Deans Ct, Crown Square, Manchester (☎ 061 833 9801)

LEEMING, James Thompson; *b* 13 Sept 1927; *Career* conslt physician in med for the elderly: Bolton 1963-67, Univ Hosp of S Manchester 1967-77, Manchester Royal Infirmary and Barnes Hosp 1979-; full time memb course team working on An Ageing Population (covering all aspects of elderly population 1977-79), sec Br Geriatrics Soc 1975-78; FRCP 1974; *Style—* James Leeming, Esq; Barnes Hospital, Cheadle, Cheshire SK8 2NY

LEEMING, Jan (Mrs Steenson); da of Ivan Terrence Atkins, MBE, of Nailsworth, Glos, and Hazel Louise Wyatt, *née* Haysey; *b* 5 Jan 1942; *Educ* St Joseph's Convent GS, Abbey Wood Kent; *m* 1, 10 April 1980 (m dis July 1986), Patrick Geoffrey Lunt, s of Rev Canon Ronald Lunt, of Ledbury, Herefordshire; 1 s (Jonathan Patrick Geoffrey b 18 May 1981); m 2, 8 Aug 1988, John Eric Steenson; *Career* TV newsreader and presenter; TV announcer NZ 1962, first woman TV newsreader Sydney Aust 1963, theatre actress 1963-66; presenter: Women Only and Report West HTV West 1970-76, Pebble Mill at One and various outside broadcast specials 1976-80; announcer Radio 2, newsreader BBC 1980-87; presenter: The Garden Party (BBC TV) 1989, Makers (ITV This Morning) 1989, 1990, 1991; compere Eurovision Song Contest 1982, contrib holiday articles to Travelling Magazine; winner: newsreader of the Year 1981 and 1982, TV Personality of the Year 1982; charities: Fight for Sight, Stars Orgn for Spastics; involved in corporate videos, presentations and conferences; memb Guild of Freemen City of London 1988; *Books* Working in Television (1980), Simply Looking Good (1984); *Style—* Miss Jan Leeming; c/o Anne Sweetbaum, Arlington Enterprises, 1-3 Charlotte Street, London W1P 1HD (☎ 071 580 0702, fax 071 580 4994)

LEEMING, John Coates (Jack); s of late James Arthur Leeming, and Harriet Leeming (d 1950); *b* 3 May 1927; *Educ* Chadderton GS Lancs, St John's Coll Cambridge (MA); *m* 1, 14 April 1949, Dorothy, da of late Joseph Carter; 2 s (Barry b 1950, Peter b 1959); m 2, 7 Dec 1985, Cheryl Elise Kendall, da of Adam Mitchell Gillan (d 1979); *Career* teacher 1948-50, HM Customs and Excise 1950-56, HM Treasy 1958-67, World Bank Washington DC 1967-70, Civil Serv Dept 1970-75, cmmr of Customs and Excise 1975-78, DTI 1978-86, dir gen Br Nat Space Centre 1987-88, space conslt 1988-, golf capt RAC Woodcote Park 1988; *Recreations* golf; *Clubs* RAC; *Style—* Jack Leeming, Esq; 9 Walnut Close, Epsom, Surrey KT18 5JL (☎ 03727 25397); 4 Astral House, Maunsel St, London SW1P 2EA (☎ 071 630 9243)

LEEPER, (Thomas William) Brian; s of Richard Leeper, of W Byfleet; bro of Desmond Leeper, *qv*; *b* 16 June 1927; *Educ* Downside, Magdalene Coll Cambridge; *m* 1951, Edreen Diana, da of Capt Edric Lyte; 4 s (Patrick b 1953, Michael b 1955, James b 1957, Timothy b 1965), 2 da (Mrs Andrew Bruce b 1952, Mrs Johnathon Gidley b 1959); *Career* Mil Serv Irish Gurds 1945-48; dir LEP Gp Ltd 1970-86; homoeopath 1989; *Recreations* aviculture, horticulture, herbalism, photography; *Clubs* Cavalry & Guards; *Style—* Brian Leeper, Esq; Bonners, Hambledon, Godalming, Surrey

LEEPER, (Richard John) Desmond; s of Richard Leeper, of W Byfleet; bro Brian Leeper, *qv*; *Career* chm and md LEP Gp Ltd; *Style—* Desmond Leeper, Esq; LEP Gp Ltd, Sunlight Wharf, Upper Thames St, London EC4

LEES, Dr Andrew John; s of Lewis Lees, of Villa Chant D'Oiseaux, Chemin de la Croix, Plascassier, France, and Muriel, *née* Wadsworth; *b* 27 Sept 1947; *Educ* Roundhay Sch, London Hosp Med Coll (MD); *m* 21 July 1973, Juana Luisa Pulin Perez-Lopez, da of Juan Luis Pulin, of Geneva; 1 s (George Luis b 9 April 1975), 1 da (Nathalie Jasmine b 23 June 1976); *Career* conslt neurologist to the Nat Hosp for Neurology and Neurosurgery UCL and Middx Hosps; med advsr Parkinsons Disease Soc, chm Med Advsy Panel Gilles de la Tourette Assoc UK; FRSM, FRCP; *Books* Parkinsons Disease - The Facts (1982), Tics and Related Disorders (1985); *Recreations* Hispanic and Latin American studies, memb Saracens RFC AND Liverpool FC; *Clubs* Taurino De Londres; *Style—* Dr Andrew Lees; The National Hospital for Neurology and Neurosurgery, Queen Square, London WC1 (☎ 071 837 3611)

LEES, Sir (William) Antony Clare; 3 Bt (UK 1937); s of Sir William Hereward Clare Lees, 2 Bt (d 1976); *b* 14 June 1935; *Educ* Eton, Magdalene Coll Cambridge (MA); *m* 1986, Joanna Olive Crane; *Style—* Sir Antony Lees, Bt

LEES, Col Brian Musson; LVO (1979), OBE (1978); s of John Lees (d 1978), and Margaret *née* Musson (d 1942), of Tamworth; *b* 9 Oct 1931; *Educ* Queen Elizabeth GS Tamworth, Univ of Leeds (BA); *m* 1963, Diana Caroline, da of John Harold Everall; 2 da (Diana b 1964, Alexia b 1966); *Career* Cmmnd KOYLI 1954; served: Kenya (Mau Mau campaign), Cyprus (EOKA campaign), Arabian Peninsula (S Yemen emergency); CO 5 Bn LI 1971-73, Def Attaché Jedda 1975-79, Def Intelligence Staff MOD 1979-82, Head Br Def Intelligence Liaison Staff Washington 1982-84, Def Attaché Muscat 1984-1986, ret 1987; ME conslt; FRGS (1989); *Books* The Al Sa'ud, Ruling Family of Saudi Arabia (1980); *Recreations* music, gardening, reading; *Clubs* Army & Navy, MCC, Royal Soc for Asian Affrs; *Style—* Col B M Lees, LVO, OBE; The Old Rectory, Kenley, Shropshire SY5 6NH (☎ 069 44 281); 74 Leith Mansions, Grantully Rd, London W9 1LJ (☎ 071 289 7559)

LEES, His Honour Judge; Charles Norman; s of Charles Lees; b 4 Oct 1929; *b* 4 Oct 1929; *Educ* Stockport Sch, Univ of Leeds; *m* 1961, Stella (d 1987), da of Hubert Swann; 1 da (Rosemary); *Career* called to the Bar Lincoln's Inn 1951, a dep chm Cumberland QS 1969-72, rec of Crown Ct 1972-80, circuit judge 1980-; legal chm Disciplinary Ctee of the Potato Mktg Bd 1965-80, memb Mental Health Review Tbnl Manchester Reg 1971-80, (chm 1977-80)G; *Style—* His Hon Judge Lees; 1 Deans Court, Crown Sq, Manchester 3

LEES, Christopher James; s and h of Sir Thomas Edward Lees, 4 Bt; *b* 4 Nov 1952; *Educ* Eton, Edinburgh Univ; *m* 1, 1977 (m dis 1988), Jennifer, da of John Wyllie, of Newton Stewart, Wigtownshire; m 2, 1989, Clare, da of Austen Young, of Sheffield; *Career* farmer; county cncllr; *Style—* Christopher Lees Esq; Cuzenage, Foxhills Road, Lytchett Matravers, Poole, Dorset

LEES, Col Colin Anthony; s of Wallace Hall Lees, of Blackpool, Lancs, and Olga Irene, *née* Livingstone; *b* 18 July 1937; *Educ* Arnold Sch, RMA Sandhurst, Univ of London (LLB); *m* 19 Dec 1964, (Mary) Christine da of Neil Walmsley (d 1986); 2 s (Christopher b 4 June 1967, Jeremy b 17 Dec 1973), 1 da (Vanya b 8 Feb 1971); *Career* cmmnd E Lancs Regt 1958, serv with Lancs Regt in Hong Kong Germany Swaziland UK 1959-68, transferred 7 Gurkha Rifles 1968, GS03 6 ARMD Bde Germany 1971-73, SO2 HQ BAOR Germany 1975-77, 831 CO 10 Gurkha Rifles Brunei and Hong Kong 1980 (second in cmd 1977-79), def attaché Kathmandu 1986-87, def attaché Peking 1988-; Gurkha Dakshin Bahu Nepal 1987; *Recreations* travel, golf, hill walking; *Clubs* Royal Overseas League, Royal Hong Kong Golf; *Style—* Col Colin Lees; British Embassy Peking, FLO Outward Bag, King Charles St, London SW1A 2AH (☎ 010 86 1 532 1961, telex 22191 PRDRM CN)

LEES, David Bryan; s of Rear Adm Dennis Marescaux Lees, CB, DSO (d 1973), and Daphne May, *née* Burnett; *b* 23 Nov 1936; *Educ* Charterhouse; *m* 1961, Edith Mary, da of Brig Ronald Playfair St Vincent Bernard, MC, DSO (d 1943); 2 s, 1 da; *Career* served Nat Serv 2 Lt RA 1955-57; articled clerk with Binder Hamlyn & Co (chartered accountants) 1957-62, sr audit clerk 1962-63, chief accountant Handley Page Ltd

1964-68, fin dir Handley Page Aircraft Ltd 1969; GKN Sankey Ltd (now GKN plc): chief accountant 1970-72, dep controller 1972-73, dir sec and controller 1973-76, gp fin exec 1976-77, gen mangr (fin) 1977-82, fin dir 1987, gp md 1987-88, chm and chief exec 1988; pres GKN N America Inc 1986-; dir: GKN (UK) plc 1982, United Engrg Steels Ltd 1986-; cmmr Audit Cmmn 1983-90; EEF: memb commercial and economic ctee 1985-87, ex-officio memb mgmnt bd and gen cncl 1987-, policy ctee 1988-, vice pres 1988, sr dep pres 1989, pres 1990; memb SMMT exec ctee and cncl 1987-89; CBI: memb cncl 1988, memb econ and financial policy ctee 1988 (chm Nov 1988), memb pres's ctee 1988-; memb: Midlands Industl Cncl 1988-, DTI engrg mkts advsy ctee 1989-; CBIM 1983, fell Royal Soc for the Encouragement of the Arts, Manufacturers and Commerce 1988-; *Recreations* golf, music; *Clubs* MCC; *Style*— David Lees, Esq; GKN plc, P O Box 55, Ipsley House, Ipsley Church Lane, Redditch, Worcs B98 OTL (☎ 0527 517715, fax 0527 517715, telex 336321)

LEES, Dorothy, Lady; Dorothy Gertrude; da of Francis Alexander Lauder; *m* 1930, Sir William Hereward Clare Lees, 2 Bt (d 1976); 1 s (Sir (William) Antony Clare Lees, 3 Bt, *qv*), 1 da (Jennifer Dorothy Clare (Mrs Wallinger) b 1932); *Style*— Dorothy, Lady Lees

LEES, George Robert; s of Lt-Col Lawrence Werner Wyld Lees (d 1976), of Tunstall Hall, Market Drayton, Salop, and Gwendolen Bessie St Clare, *née* Daniel (d 1976); *b* 10 Aug 1924; *Educ* Stowe, Trinity Coll Cambridge (MA); *m* 13 Dec 1958, Lois Marian, da of Capt Stuart Scimgeour, MC (d 1956), of 16 Launcheston Place, S Kensington, London; 2 da (Maryanne b 1961, Henrietta b 1963); *Career* service Normandy 1943-47, Palestine 1944, AER 1 King's Dragoon Guards 1951-61 (Lt 1945-47), Maj Queens Dragoon Guards 1959; articled clerk CA 1950-53, asst to investment firm Philip Hill Investment Tst Ltd 1956-63, mangr Pension Fund and Charities Investmt Dept Philip Higginson Erlangers and later Hill Samuel Ltd 1963-68, assoc dir Leopold Joseph and Sons Ltd 1968-76, portfolio mangr 1976-84 TSB Pension Fund Equity, chm GR Lees and Ptnrs Ltd 1984-; FCA; *Books* Stabilized Accounting (1951); *Recreations* riding, shooting; *Clubs* Cavalry & Guards; *Style*— George Lees, Esq; Taylor Young Investment Management Ltd, 45 Curlew St, London SE1 2ND (☎ 071 407 3452, 071 4073533)

LEES, Helen, Lady; Helen Agnes Marion; da of Charles C Chittick (decd), and widow of Thomas Orr Gibb; *m* 1927, Sir Arthur Henry James Lees, 5 Bt (d 1949); *Style*— Helen, Lady Lees; 3 Valsayn Ave, Valsayn Park, Curepe, Trinidad

LEES, John Cathcart; s of John Rutherford D'Olier-Lees (decd); descends from Sir John Lees 1 Bt successively Usher of Black Rod, Sec of State for War and sec to PO in Ireland d 1811, hp of kinsman, Sir Thomas Harcourt Ivor Lees, 8 Bt, *qv*; *b* 12 Nov 1927; *m* 1957, Wendy Garrold, da of Brian Garrold Groom (decd), of Edinburgh; 2 s (John b 1961, James b 1963); *Career* formerly Lt 12 Bn Border Regiment and SAS Regiment (Artists Rifles) TA; *Style*— John Lees, Esq; 5 Pound Close, Ringwood, Hants

LEES, Dr Kenneth; s of Noel Darwin Lees (d 1974), and Doris Lees (d 1947); *b* 19 March 1925; *Educ* Audenshaw GS, Univ of London (BSc, PhD); *m* 1 Sept 1951, Mary Eastwood, da of Arthur Horrabin (d 1943); 2 s (Roderic b 1956, Nicholas b 1960), 2 da (Amanda b 1958, Rebecca b 1965); *Career* mangr Wool Industs Res Assoc 1960-69 (chemist 1946-60); tech dir: London Textile Testing House Ltd 1969-86, Wool Testing Services International Ltd 1973-77; dir Wool Testing Services NZ 1977-85; md Quality Control International Ltd 1980-89 (tech dir 1977-80), dir ICCH Pension Fund 1983-85, ret; conslt to SGS Testing Div (parent co of QCI Ltd); *Recreations* tennis, badminton, squash, gardening, mountain walking; *Style*— Dr Kenneth Lees; Game Cottage, Pollards Park, Nightingales Lane, Chalfont St Giles, Bucks HP8 4SN; Gaw House, Alperton Lane, Wembley, Middlesex HA0 1WU fax 081 997 9723, telex 25658)

LEES, Michael Edward; s of Robert Edward (d 1940), of The Vicarage, Thornton-Le-Fylde, Lancs, and Gladys Mary, *née* Prescott (d 1985); *b* 28 Oct 1937; *Educ* St Edmund's Sch Canterbury, Gonville and Caius Coll Cambridge (BA, MA); *m* 15 Jan 1966, Jill Virginia, da of Raymond Cawthorne, of The Chalet, Croft Meadow, Sampford Brett, Somerset; 2 s (Andrew b 1970, Richard b 1973); *Career* Royal Army Educnl Corps 1958-76, Maj Scotland 1959-64, Aden 1964-67, London 1967-71, ANZUK Force Singapore 1971-74, Winchester 1974-76; corp security exec The Plessey Co plc 1979-; *Recreations* offshore sailing, travel, walking, gardening; *Clubs* Royal Lymington Yacht; *Style*— Michael Lees, Esq; Knowle Lodge, Brighton Rd, Sway, Lymington, Hants (☎ 0590 683408); Siemens Plessey Eletronic Systems, Grange Rd, Christchurch, Dorset (☎ 0202 404905, telex 404499)

LEES, Air Vice-Marshal Robin Lowther; CB (1985), MBE (1962); s of Air Marshal Sir Alan Lees, KCB, CBE, DSO, AFC (d 1973), of Newbury, Berks, and Norah Elizabeth, *née* Thompson (d 1974); *b* 27 Feb 1931; *Educ* Wellington, RAF Cranwell; *m* 1966, Alison, da of Lt-Col Cuthbert Benson Carrick, MC, TD, JP (d 1966), of Newcastle upon Tyne; 3 s (Timothy, Anthony, Edward); *Career* RAF 1949-86, Air Offr Admin RAF Support Cmd and Head of RAF Admin Branch 1982-86 (AVM); chief exec Br Hotels Restaurants and Caterers Assoc 1986-; memb Cncl CBI 1990-, govr Wellington Coll 1990-; rep: Hants Combined Servs and RAF at squash, RAF at tennis and Cambs at hockey; *Recreations* lawn tennis, real tennis, squash, rackets, golf; *Clubs* All England Lawn Tennis, Jesters, RAF; *Style*— Air Vice-Marshal Robin Lees, CB, MBE; c/o Barclays Bank Ltd, 6 Market Place, Newbury, Berks; 40 Duke St, London W1M 6HR (☎ 071 499 6641)

LEES, Ronald; s of Arthur Lees (d 1946), of Stockport, Cheshire, and Eva, *née* Smith (d 1983); *b* 28 Sept 1933; *Educ* Stockport Coll; *m* 1 June 1957, Airline Margot, da of Albert Williamson (d 1978), of Stockport, Cheshire; *Career* works chemist CWS Ltd until 1959, res chemist Food Industs Res Assoc 1960-65, Info Servs for Industl Miny of Technol 1965, princ Small Firms Info Serv Dept of Indust 1971, Supt Laboratory of the Govt Chemist 1978; author of over 260 articles on food topics; former pres: Kingston Philatelic Soc, Weybridge Philatelic Soc; FRSC, FRSH, MIFST, CChem; *Books* Sugar Confectionary and Chocolate Manufacture (1973), Food Analysis (1975), Faults, Causes and Remedies in the Sweet and Chocolate Industry (1981), Chemical Nomenclature Usage (ed, 1983) Design Construction and Refurbishment of Laboratories (ed, 1984), A Hisory of Sweet and Chocolate Making (1988); *Recreations* walking, postal history; *Style*— Ronald Lees, Esq; Laboratory of the Government Chemist, Queens Road, Teddington, Middlesex TW11 OLY (☎ 081 943 7320, fax 081 943 2767, telex 9312132476)

LEES, Dr (David Arthur) Russell; s of Dr David Lees, CBE (d 1986), of Larch Rd, Glasgow, and Olive Willington; *b* 16 Jan 1948; *Educ* Hamilton Acad, Univ of Glasgow; *m* 21 June 1971, Marie; 4 s (Russell b 1972, Andrew b 1975, Alister b 1982, Peter b 1984); *Career* registrar Dept of Obstetrics and Gynaecology: Robroyston Hosp Glasgow 1974-76, Stobhill Hosp Glasgow 1978-80; sr registrar Queen Mother's Hosp Glasgow 1980-81, conslt obstetrician and gynaecologist Raigmore Hosp Inverness 1981-; area advsr for the handicapped Inverness, Medal of Merit for servs to Scout Assoc; memb Highland Med Soc; FRCOG; *Style*— Dr Russell Lees; Crofthill, Daviot (west), Inverness IVI 2XQ (☎ 0463 85230); Dept of Obstetrics, Raigmore Hospital, Inverness IV2 3UJ (☎ 0463 234151)

LEES, Sir Thomas Edward; 4 Bt (UK 1897), JP (1951) Dorset; s of Col Sir John Victor Elliott Lees, 3 Bt, DSO, MC (d 1955); *b* 1925; *Educ* Eton, Magdalene Coll Cambridge; *m* 1949, Faith Justin, JP (1963), da of Gaston Jessiman; 1 s, 3 da (Sarah (Mrs Omond) b 1951, Bridget (Mrs Green) b 1954, Elizabeth b 1957); *Heir* s, Christopher James Lees; *Career* serv RAF 1943-45; High Sheriff of Dorset 1960; memb: Dorset CC 1951-72, General Synod 1970-90; *Recreations* sailing; *Clubs* Royal Cruising; *Style*— Sir Thomas Lees, Bt, JP; Post Green, Lytchett Minster, Dorset (☎ 0202 622048)

LEES, Sir Thomas Harcourt Ivor; 8 Bt (UK 1804), of Blackrock, Dublin; s of Sir Charles Archibald Edward Ivor Lees, 7 Bt (d 1963); *b* 6 Nov 1941; *Heir* kinsman, John Cathcart D'Olier Lees, *qv*; *Style*— Sir Thomas Lees, Bt

LEES, William; CBE (1971), TD (1962 bar 1968); s of Maj William Lees (d 1986), and Elizabeth, *née* Massey (d 1962); *b* 18 May 1924; *Educ* Queen Elizabeth Sch Blackburn, Victorian Univ Manchester (MB ChB, DPH); *m* 4 Oct 1947, (Winifred) Elizabeth, da of Robert Archibald Hanford (d 1964), of Cheshire; 3 s (William b 1948, John b 1953, Christopher b 1959); *Career* RAMC 1948-50; TA 1950-71: Col Cmdg 257 Gen Hosp TA 1966-71, Col Cmdt NW sector ACF 1971-77; lectr and gynaecologist St Mary Hosp Manchester 1950-59, sr princ med offr Miny of Health DHSS 1959-81 (under sec 1977-81), conslt advsr on med manpower and post graduate educn SW Thames RHA 1981-87; chm Dacorum Cancer Relief and McMillan Fund; Hon Physician HM The Queen 1970-72; Liveryman Worshipful Co of Apothecaries; OStJ 1968; FROCG 1964, MFCM 1973; *Recreations* golf, music, travel; *Clubs* Athenaeum, St Johns; *Style*— Dr William Lees, CBE, TD; 13 Hill Park Hill, Berkhamsted, Herts HP4 2NH (☎ 0442 863010)

LEES-MILNE, James; s of George Crompton Lees-Milne (d 1949), of Crompton Hall, Lancashire, and Wickhamford Manor, Evesham, Worcs, and Helen Christina (d 1962), da of Henry Bailey, DL, and gda of Sir Joseph Bailey, 1 Bt, of Glanusk Park, Crickhowell, Powys; *b* 6 Aug 1908; *Educ* Eton, Magdalen Coll Oxford, Grenoble Univ; *m* 19 Nov 1951, Alvilde, da of late Lt-Gen Sir Tom Molesworth Bridges, KCB, KCMG, DSO, former wife of 3 Viscount Chaplin; *Career* 2 Lt Irish Gds 1940-41 (invalided); private sec to 1 Baron Lloyd 1931-34, staff at Reuters 1935-36, on staff Nat Tst 1936-66, advsr on historic bldgs Nat Tst 1951-66; FRSL 1957, FSA 1974; *Books* The National Trust (ed, 1945), The Age of Adam (1947), National Trust Guide: Buildings (1948), Tudor Renaissance (1951), The Age of Inigo Jones (1953), Roman Mornings (Heinemann Award, 1956), Baroque in Italy (1959), Baroque in Spain and Portugal (1960), Earls of Creation (1962), Worcestershire: A Shell Guide (1964), St Peter's (1967), English Country Houses: Baroque 1685-1714 (1970), Another Self (1970), Heretics in love (1973), Ancestral Voices (1975), William Beckford (1976), Prophesying Peace (1977), Round the Clock (1978), Harold Nicolson (vol 1 1980, vol II 1981, Heineman Award 1982), Images of Bath (with David Ford, 1982), The Country House (1982), Caves of Ice (1983), The Last Stuarts (1983), Midway on the Waves (1985), The Enigmatic Edwardian (1986), Some Cotswold Country Houses (1987), Venetian Evenings (1988), The Fool of Love (1990); *Recreations* walking; *Clubs* Brooks's; *Style*— James Lees-Milne, Esq, FSA; Essex House, Badminton GL9 1DD (☎ 045 421 288)

LEES-SPALDING, Rear Adm Ian Jaffery; CB (1973); s of Frank Souter Lees-Spalding (d 1970); *b* 16 June 1920; *Educ* Blundells; *m* 1946, June Sandys Lyster, da of Maj Warren Lyster Sparkes, of Devon; 2 da; *Career* joined RN 1938, awarded commendation 1940, joined submarines 1945, CSO (tech) to C-in-C Fleet and inspr gen Fleet Maintenance 1971, ret 1974, ADC 1971; admin London Int Film Sch 1975-79; *Books* Macmillan and Silk Cut Nautical Almanac (ed), Macmillan and Silk Cut Yachtsman's Handbook (ed); *Recreations* sailing, travel, gardening; *Clubs* Army and Navy; *Style*— Rear Adm Ian Lees-Spalding, CB; St Olaf's, Wonston, Winchester, Hants SO21 3LP (☎ 0962 760249)

LEESE, Arthur; s of Henry Leese (d 1969), and Edith Mabel, *née* Baker (d 1952); *b* 4 May 1931; *Educ* Battersea GS; *m* 18 July 1959, Marian, da of Walter Thomas Bryant (d 1989); 1 s (Simon b 1967), 1 da (Sarah b 1971); *Career* dir: Columbia Pictures Corporation Ltd 1980-, Columbia Pictures Video Ltd 1982-, Colgems Productions Ltd 1983-, Columbia Video Europe Ltd 1990, Seven Seas Films Ltd 1990-, Darby Films Ltd 1990-; *Recreations* reading, walking, fishing; *Style*— Arthur Leese, Esq; 53 Chieveley Drive, Tunbridge Wells, Kent TN2 5HQ (☎ 0892 30706); 19/23 Wells St, London W1P 3FP (☎ 071 580 2090, telex 263392, fax 071 528 8980)

LEESE, Sir John Henry Vernon; 5 Bt (UK 1908); s of Vernon Francis Leese, OBE (d 1927), 2 s of 1 Bt; suc kinsman, Sir Alexander William Leese, 4 Bt, 1979; *b* 7 Aug 1901; *Style*— Sir John Leese, Bt

LEESON, Ian Arthur; s of Alister Curtis Leeson, of Heathfield, Chilworth, nr Southampton, Hants, and Nancy Avis Louise, *née* Cayzer; *b* 13 March 1937; *Educ* Rugby, Univ Coll Oxford (MA); *m* 7 Aug 1965, (Eileen) Margaret, da of Col Anderson Kirkwood Tennent, OBE (d 1971); 2 da (Sally b 1968, Patricia b 1971); *Career* CA, ptnr Ernst & Young 1970-; FCA 1964; *Recreations* golf, tennis; *Clubs* Woking Golf, St Georges Hill Lawn Tennis; *Style*— Ian Leeson, Esq; Talana, Esher Close, Esher, Surrey (☎ 0372 466683); c/o Ernst & Young, Becket House, 1 Lambeth Palace Road, London SE1 7EU (☎ 071 928 2000, fax 071 928 1345)

LEFANU, Nicola Frances; da of William Richard LeFanu, and Elizabeth Violet Maconchy, DBE; *b* 28 April 1947; *Educ* St Mary's Sch Calne Wilts, St Hilda's Coll Oxford (BA, MA); Harkness fellowship; Univ of London (DMus); *m* 16 March 1979, David Newton Lumsdaine; 1 s (Peter LeFanu b 13 Nov 1982); *Career* composer; memb: Music Panel ACGB, Cncl SPNM, fndr WIM; *Books* author of forty musical compositions; *Recreations* conservation, natural history, feminism; *Style*— Dr Nicola LeFanu; 9 Kempe Rd, London NW6 6SP (☎ 081 960 0614)

LEFEVER, Andrew Maitland; s of Henry Charles Lefever, of Canterbury, Kent, and Evelyn, *née* Stewart; *b* 28 June 1941; *m* 14 Aug 1965, Elizabeth Jill, da of George Monkhouse; 1 s (Michael James b 1 Oct 1969), 2 da (Clare Jane b 9 March 1969, Ann Margaret b 13 April 1971); *Career* slr; Pinsent & Co: joined 1961, qualified 1966, ptnr 1969-, opened London Office 1987; winner Law Soc's Honours prize (Birmingham); Freeman City of London 1989, memb Worshipful Co of Needlemakers' 1989; memb Law Soc 1966; *Recreations* renovation of old properties, sport, theatre, classical music; *Clubs* The Thunders'; *Style*— Andrew Lefever, Esq; Flat 3, 148 Wapping High St, London E1 9XG (☎ 071 702 9511); Pinsent & Co, Dashwood House, Box 736, 60 Old Broad St, London EC2M 1NR (☎ 071 638 3899, fax 071 638 3911)

LEFEVER, Col Paul Stuart Hale; s of Stuart Edwin Hale Lefever (d 1968), of Marlborough, Wilts, and Edna Maud Muriel, *née* Jacob; *b* 1 Oct 1937; *Educ* Wrekin Coll Shropshire; *m* 31 Aug 1963, Judith Ann, da of Edmund Esward Webster (d 1981), of Marlborough, Wilts; 2 s (Andrew b 1965, James b 1967), 1 da (Helen b 1972); *Career* cmmnd RA 1959, various staff and regimental appts 1959-79, Nat Defence Coll 1980, UK delegation to NATO 1981-84, defence attaché Sofia Bulgaria 1985-88, defence advsr Caribbean 1988-; *Recreations* music, reading, travel, things mechanical; *Style*— Col Paul Lefever; 21 Millsborough Ave, Kingston, Jamaica (☎ 010 1809 92 76198); British High Commission, Kingston, Jamaica (☎ 010 1809 92 69050)

LEFEVRE, Frank Hartley; s of Charles Wilson Lefevre of 3 Harlaw Terrace, Aberdeen, and Ethil Edith, *née* Hartley (d 1956); *b* 4 Dec 1934; *Educ* Robert Gordon's Coll Aberdeen, Aberdeen Univ (MA, LLB); *m* 20 Aug 1960, Hazel, da of Magnus

Harper Gray (d 1981), of 30 Albert Terrace, Aberdeen; 1 s (Paul b 1964), 2 da (Tracey b 1961, Julie b 1966); *Career* slr & advocate in Aberdeen; firm of Lefevre & Co; dir: Quantum Claims Compensation Specialists Ltd, conslt in law Albervic Ltd 1968-; Notary Public; former pres Grampian Squash Racquets Assoc; *Recreations* golf, squash racquets, musical appreciation; *Clubs* Royal Northern & Univ, Royal Aberdeen Golf, Aberdeen Sportsmans, Aberdeen Squash Racquets, Sloan; *Style*— Frank Lefevre, Esq; Braco Lodge, 11 Rubislaw Den North, Aberdeen; 1 Queens Cross, Albyn Place, Aberdeen AB1 6XW (☎ 0224 208208, fax 0224 311998)

LEFEVRE, Garry Ernest Grant; s of Maj Jack Ernest Lefevre, of Zimbabwe, and Irene Kathleen, *née* Osborne; *b* 6 May 1938; *Educ* Clifton Sch SA, Kingston Coll; *m* 4 April 1977, Inge, da of Hans Rosted (d 1985), of Copenhagen, Denmark; 1 da (Tanya b 1 March 1980); *Career* RAF 1958-60; audit mangr Price Waterhouse 1965-70, controller Morgan Guarantee Tst 1970-73, fin dir Interdan 1973-77, mangr TSB Gp 1977-81, Nationwide Building Soc 1982-86; dir 1986-: Meteor Holdings, Meteor Mercantile, Confederation Bank, Intermega Giltra (Denmark); FCCA 1965; *Recreations* golf, bridge; *Clubs* Wentworth Golf; *Style*— Garry Lefevre, Esq; Hillside, Gorse Hill Lane, Wentworth, Surrey (☎ 0344 842 440)

LEFÈVRE, Robin Charles; s of Jack Lefèvre, and Jean, *née* Syme; *b* 5 May 1947; *Educ* Irvine Royal Acad, The Royal Scottish Acad of Music and Dramatic Art; *m* 2 Oct 1970, Maureen, da of George Webster; 1 da (Laura b 15 Aug 1971); *Career* assoc dir Hamstead Theatre; prodns at Hamstead incl: Then and Now, Threads, Writer's Cramp, On the Edge, Fall, Bodies (transfd Ambassador's Theatre), Aristocrats (Evening Standard Best Play award 1988, NY Drama Critics Best Foreign Play award) Valued Friends (Evening Standard award, at Long Wharf Connecticut); dir: Outside Edge (Queens Theatre), Rocket to the Moon (Apollo), Are You Lonesome Tonight? (Evening Standard Best Musical award), Rowan Atkinson's New Review (Shaftesbury), The Entertainer (Shaftesbury), The Country Girls (Apollo), When We Are Married (NT), Poor Beast in the Rain (Bush), Rocky Horror Show (Piccadilly); *Style*— Robin Lefèvre, Esq

LEFF, Prof Julian Paul; s of Dr Samuel Leff (d 1962), of London, and Vera Miriam, *née* Levy (d 1980); *b* 4 July 1938; *Educ* Haberdashers' Askes', UCL (BSc, MD); *m* 31 Jan 1975, Joan Lillian, da of Jacob Raphael (d 1970), of Tel Aviv, Israel; 3 s (Alex b 1967, Jonty b 1976, Adriel b 1980), 1 da (Jessica b 1975); *Career* career scientist MRC 1972, hon conslt physician Maudsley Hosp 1973, hon sr lectr London Sch of Hygeine 1974-89, asst dir MRC Social Psychiatry Unit 1974-89, clinical sub-dean Inst of Psychiatry 1974-79, dir Team For Assessment of Psychiatric Servs 1985, dir MRC Social and Community Psychiatric Unit 1989 (prof of Social and cultural Psychiatry 1987); memb: prof advsy ctee Nat Schizophrenia Fellowship, cncl Richmond Fellowship; FRCPsych, MRCP; *Books* Psychiatric Examination in Clinical Practice (1978), Expressed Emotion in Families (1985), Psychiatry Around the Globe (1988); *Recreations* squash, swimming, croquet, chess, piano; *Clubs* The 52; *Style*— Prof Julian Leff; Inst of Psychiatry, De Crespigny Park, London SE5 8AF (☎ 071 703 5411, fax 071 703 0458)

LEGARD, Christopher John Charles; s and h of Sir Charles Thomas Legard, 15 Bt, *qv*, and Elizabeth (who m 2, 1988, Patrick M L Hibbert-Foy), da of John M Guthrie; *b* 19 April 1964; *Educ* Eton Coll; *m* 1986, Miranda, da of Maj Fane Travers Gaffney, of Crossbank Hill, Hurworth, Co Durham; *Career* chartered accountant; *Recreations* skiing, shooting, photography; *Style*— Christopher Legard, Esq; 177 Boundaries Rd, Balham, London SW12 8HE (☎ 081 672 7176)

LEGG, Barry Charles; s of Henry Wellman Legg, of Hucclecote, Glos, and Elfreda, *née* Thorp; *b* 30 May 1949; *Educ* Sir Thomas Rich's GS Gloucester, Manchester Univ; *m* 16 March 1974, Margaret Rose, da of Roy Stewartson, of Roath Park, Cardiff; 1 s (George Alexander b 27 Nov 1987), 2 da (Victoria Rose b 21 Jan 1981, Elizabeth Fiona b 12 Sept 1984); *Career* CA, Courtaulds Ltd 1971-76, Coopers & Lybrand 1976-78, exec dir Hillsdown Hldgs plc 1978-; memb Westminster City Cncl 1978 (chm fin ctee 1986, chief whip Cons gp 1983); parly candidate (Cons) Bishop Auckland 1983; FCA 1975, ATII 1976; *Recreations* cricket; *Clubs* Glos Co Cricket, Glos Exiles; *Style*— Barry Legg, Esq; 22 Chapel St, London SW1 7BY (☎ 071 235 4944); Hillsdown Holdings plc, Hilldown House, 32 Hampstead High St, London NW3 1QD (☎ 071 794 0677)

LEGG, (Cyrus) Julian Edmund; s of Cyrus Daniel Jasper Edmund Legg, of Pevensey Bay, E Sussex, and Eileen Doris, *née* Hopkins; *b* 5 Sept 1946; *Educ* Tiffin Sch Kingston-on-Thames; *m* 21 Jan 1967, Maureen Jean, da of James Grahame Lodge (d 1966); 2 s (Cyrus James Grahame b 1968, Julian Clive Edmund b 1969); *Career* Civil Serv Dept 1970-74, ARC 1974-83 (and 1966-70), HM Treasy 1983-87, museum sec The Natural History Museum 1987; *Recreations* sailing, gardening; *Style*— Julian Legg, Esq; The Natural History Museum, Cromwell Rd, London SW7 5BD (☎ 071 938 8733, fax 071 938 8799)

LEGG, Dr Nigel John; s of John Burrow Legg, MBE (d 1957), of Harrow, and Constance Violet, *née* Boatwright (d 1984); *b* 5 Feb 1936; *Educ* Univ Coll Sch, St Mary's Med Sch Univ of London (MB BS); *m* 10 Sept 1960, Margaret Lilian, da of Frank Donald Charles (d 1958), of Harrow; 1 s (Benedick b 1967), 2 da (Kina b 1964, Fiona b 1962); *Career* sr conslt neurologist Hammersmith Hosp, sr lectr in neurology Royal Postgrad Med Sch and Inst of Neurology 1975-; pubns on: Parkinsons disease, multiple sclerosis, other neurological diseases; specialises in migraine; pres Soc for the Relief of Widows and Orphans of Med Men; memb: Assoc Br Neurologists, Brain Res Assoc; Liveryman Worshipful Soc of Apothecaries, Freeman City of London 1981; *Books* Neurotransmitter Systems and their Clinical Disorders (ed, 1978); *Recreations* Dr Johnson, chamber music; *Clubs* Athenaeum, RSM; *Style*— Dr Nigel Legg; 12 Rosemont Rd, London NW3 6NE (☎ 071 794 2630); 152 Harley St, London W1N 1HH (☎ 071 935 8868)

LEGG, Thomas Stuart; CB (1985), QC (1990); s of Francis Stuart Legg (d 1988), and Margaret Bonté Sheldon, *née* Amos; *b* 13 Aug 1935; *Educ* Horace-Mann Lincoln Sch NY, Frensham Heights Sch Surrey, St John's Coll Cambridge (MA, LLM); *m* 1, Aug 1961 (m dis 1983), Patricia Irene, da of David Lincoln Dowie; 2 da (Lucy b 1969, Isobel b 1972); m 2, 1983, Marie-Louise Clarke, da of late Humphrey Jennings; *Career* RM 1953-55; called to the Bar Inner Temple 1960; Lord Chllr's Dept: joined 1962, private sec to Lord Chllr 1965-68, asst slr 1975, under sec 1977-82, SE circuit admin 1980-82, dep sec 1982-89, dep clerk of crown 1986, sec cmmns 1988, perm sec to Lord Chllr and clerk of crown in Chancery 1989; Master of Bench 1984; *Clubs* Garrick; *Style*— Thomas Legg, Esq, CB, QC; Lord Chancellor's Dept, House of Lords, London SW1 (☎ 071 219 3246)

LEGGATT, Rt Hon Lord Justice; Rt Hon Sir Andrew Peter; PC (1990); s of Capt W R C (Peter) Leggatt, DSO, RN (d 1983), of Odiham, Hants, and (Dorothea Joy), *née* Dreyer; *b* 8 Nov 1930; *Educ* Eton, King's Coll Cambridge (MA); *m* 17 July 1953, Gillian Barbara (Jill), da of Cdr C P Newton, RN (d 1970), of Petersfield, Hants; 1 s (George b 1957), 1 da (Alice b 1960); *Career* served Rifle Bde 1949-50 and TA 1950-59; called to the Bar Inner Temple 1954, QC 1972, rec of Crown Ct 1974-82, bencher 1976, High Ct judge 1982-90; Lord Justice of Appeal 1990-; memb: Bar Cncl 1971-82 (chm 1981-82), Top Salaries Review Body 1979-82; kt 1982; *Recreations* listening to music, personal computers; *Clubs* MCC; *Style*— The Rt Hon Lord Justice Leggatt; Royal Cts of Justice, Strand, London WC2A 2LL (☎ 071 936 6635)

LEGGATT, Sir Hugh Frank John; s of Henry Alan Leggatt (d 1951), of London, and Beatrice Grace, *née* Burton (d 1934); *b* 27 Feb 1925; *Educ* Eton, New College Oxford; *m* 1, 1953 (m dis 1990), Jennifer Mary, da of Paul Hepworth (d 1964); 2 s (Charles b 1954, Martin b 1955); m 2, 2 Jan 1991, (Caroline) Gaynor, yr da of William Leonard Tregoning, CBE, of Landue, Cornwall; *Career* joined Leggatt Bros 1946 (ptnr 1952, sr ptnr 1962); pres Fine Art Provident Inst 1960-63, chm Soc of London Art Dealers 1966-70, memb Museums & Galleries Cmmn 1983-; hon sec Heritage in Danger 1974; kt 1988; *Recreations* the arts; *Clubs* Whites; *Style*— Sir Hugh Leggatt; Flat 1, 10 Bury St, St James', London SW1Y 6AA (☎ 071 839 4698); 17 Duke St, St James', London SW1Y 6DB (☎ 071 930 3772)

LEGGE, (John) Michael; s of Dr Alfred John Legge, of Guildford, Surrey, and Marion Frances, *née* James; *b* 14 March 1944; *Educ* Royal GS Guildford, ChCh Oxford (BA, MA); *m* 24 July 1971, Linda, da of John Wallace Bagley, of Haywards Heath, Sussex; 2 s (Christopher b 18 March 1975, Richard b 12 Nov 1978); *Career* MOD 1966-: asst private sec to def sec 1970, princ 1971, first sec UK delgn to NATO 1974-77, asst sec 1978; Rand Corp Santa Monica California 1982, asst under sec of state for policy 1987, asst sec-gen for def planning and policy NATO 1988; *Books* Theatre Nuclear Weapons and the Nato Strategy of Flexible Response (1983); *Recreations* golf, gardening; *Clubs* Puttenham Golf, Duisberg Golf; *Style*— Michael Legge, Esq; Assistant Secretary General DPP, NATO Headquarters, 1110 Brussels, Belgium (☎ 010 322 728 40 58)

LEGGE, Hon Rupert; s of 9 Earl of Dartmouth, and Countess Spencer, *qv*; *b* 1 Jan 1951; *Educ* Eton, ChCh Oxford (MA); *m* 1984, Victoria, da of Lionel Edward Bruce Ottley, of Tichborne Park Cottage, Alresford, Hants; 1 s (Edward Peregrine b 1986), 1 da (Claudia Rose b 1989); *Career* called to the Bar Inner Temple 1975; *Books* The Children of Light (1986), Fashionable Circles (1991); *Style*— The Hon Rupert Legge; Hamswell House, nr Bath BA1 9DG

LEGGE-BOURKE, Hon Mrs (Elizabeth Shân Josephine); *née* Bailey; LVO; o child of 3 Baron Glanusk, DSO (d 1948), and Margaret (who later m 1 Viscount De L'Isle, *qv*); *b* 10 Sept 1943; *m* 2 June 1964, Capt William Nigel Henry Legge-Bourke, er s of Sir Harry Legge-Bourke, KBE, DL, and Lady Legge-Bourke; 1 s, 2 da; *Career* lady-in-waiting to HRH The Princess Royal 1978-; pres Welsh Cncl of Save the Children Fund; chief pres for Wales St John's Ambulance Bde; memb Brecon Beacons Nat Park Authority 1989-; High Sheriff of Powys 1991; *Style*— The Hon Mrs Legge-Bourke, LVO; Penmyarth, Glanusk Park, Crickhowell, Powys NP8 1LP (☎ 0873 810230)

LEGGE-BOURKE, Lady; (Catherine) Jean; da of Col Sir Arthur Grant of Monymusk, 10 Bt, CBE, DSO (d 1931); *b* 18 Aug 1917; *m* 1938, Maj Sir Harry Legge-Bourke, KBE, MP, DL (d 1973, *see* Peerage Earl of Dartmouth); 2 s (William m Hon Elizabeth, *née* Bailey, *qv*; Heneage b 1948 m Maria Clara *née* de Sá-Carneiro: 1 s, 1 da), 1 da (Victoria, *qv*); *Style*— Lady Legge-Bourke; Flat 2, 121 Dovehouse St, London SW3 6JZ (☎ 071 352 5911)

LEGGE-BOURKE, Victoria Lindsay; LVO (1986); da of Maj Sir Harry Legge-Bourke, KBE, DL, MP (d 1973), and Lady Legge-Bourke, *qv*; *b* 12 Feb 1950; *Educ* Benenden, St Hilda's Coll Oxford; *Career* dir Junior Tourism Ltd 1974-81; lady-in-waiting to HRH The Princess Royal 1974-86, extra lady-in-waiting to HRH The Princess Royal 1986-; special asst American Embassy London 1983-89 Price Investments Kansas City Mo USa 1989-; *Style*— Miss Victoria Legge-Bourke, LVO; 21 Eccleston Square, London SW1V 1NS (☎ 071 834 0978); Apartment 1105, 4550 Warwick Boulevard, Kansas City, Missouri 64111, USA (☎ 861 561 3038)

LEGGE-BOURKE, William Nigel Henry; er s of Sir Harry Legge-Bourke, KBE, DL, MP (d 1973), and (Catherine) Jean, *née* Grant of Monymusk (*see* Lady Legge-Bourke); *b* 12 July 1939; *Educ* Eton, Magdalene Coll Cambridge (MA); *m* 2 June 1964, Hon (Elizabeth) Shân Josephine Bailey, LVO, da of 3 Baron Glanusk, DSO (d 1948) (*see* Hon Mrs Legge-Bourke); 1 s (Harry Russell b 1972), 2 da (Alexandra Shân b 1965, Zara Victoria b 1966, m 1985, Capt R Plunkett-Ernle-Erle-Drax); *Career* cmmnd Royal Horse Guards (The Blues) 1958, Capt and Adj, ret 1968; memb Int Stock Exchange; ptnr Grieveson Grant & Co 1974-86, dir Kleinwort Benson Securities Ltd 1986-; memb: Cncl ISE 1988-, Representative Body of the Church in Wales; chm Fin Ctee The Scout Assoc; *Recreations* country sports; *Clubs* White's; *Style*— William Legge-Bourke, Esq; Penmyarth, Glanusk Park, Crickhowell, Powys NP8 1LP (☎ 0873 810230); 8 Kensington Mansions, Trebovir Road, London SW5 9TF; Kleinwort Benson Securities Ltd, 20 Fenchurch Street, London EC3P 2DB (☎ 071 623 8000)

LEGGETT, Dr Jeremy Kendal; s of Dennis Leslie Kendal Leggett, and Audrey Pamela, *née* Holton; *b* 16 March 1954; *Educ* Hastings GS, Univ of Wales Aberystwyth (BSc), Univ of Oxford (DPhil); *m* 1971 (m dis 1976); 1 da (Jessie b 26 April 1972); m 2, 1990, Abigail Charlot Rebecca Munson; *Career* reader in stratigraphy Imp Coll of Sci and Techol 1987-89 (lectr in geology Royal Sch of Mines 1978-87), dir of sci Greenpeace UK 1989-; represented UK on Thematic Advsy Panel to Int Ocean Drilling Prog; author of over 50 research papers and numerous articles on environmental issues and policy: The Guardian, The Independent, The Times, The Sunday Times, The Observer, New Scientist, New Statesman; winner of: Presidents Prize of Geological Soc 1980, Lyell Fund of Geological Soc 1987; treas Save British Sci Soc 1985-86, dir Verification Technol Info Centre 1986-89; FGS 1975; *Books* Trench Fore-arc Geology (1982), Marine Clastic Sedimentology: Models and Case Histories (with G G Zuffa, 1988), Global Warming: the Greenpeace Report (1990), Operation Earth (1991); *Recreations* non-violent direct actions in defence of the natural environment; *Clubs* Oxford and Cambridge Golfing Soc; *Style*— Dr Jeremy Leggett; Greenpeace, 30-31 Islington Green, London N1 8XE (☎ 071 354 5100, fax 071 359 4062, telex 25245)

LEGGETT, Keith Arnold; s of Jack Eric Leggett, of 22 Danes Close, Kirkham, Preston, Lancashire, and Marian Lois, *née* Perkins; *b* 18 March 1940; *Educ* Monkton Combe Sch, Cloverley Hall Whitchurch Salop; *m* 4 Sept 1964, Sonja Ruth, da of Marco Fortune Gareh, of 14 Linden Aven, Thornton Cleveleys, Fylde; 3 s (Stephen b 1966, Oliver b 1968, Robert b 1972); *Career* estate agent, valuer, surveyor and auctioneer; princ N Routledge & Co Sale Cheshire 1964-87; residential sales dir Nationwide Anglia Beresfords Estate Agents 1987-89, dir of recruitment Keith Leggett Consultancy 1989-; former chm: Sale and Dist Round Table, Manchester Branch of Inc Soc of Valuers and Auctioneers, North Cheshire and Sale 41 Club, Sale Festival of Sport and Drama; FSVA, FCIArb, IRRV; *Recreations* golf, gardening; *Clubs* Hale Golf, N Cheshire 41; *Style*— Keith Leggett, Esq; The Ridge, York Drive, Bowdon, Altrincham, Cheshire WA14 3HF (☎ 061 941 2997); The Ridge, York Drive, Bowdon, Altrincham, Cheshire WA14 3HF (☎ 061 941 2997, fax : 061 928 7683)

LEGGOTT, (James Peter) Bruce; s of Walter Leggott (d 1980), and Miriam Moss, *née* Weston (d 1966); *b* 1 Nov 1950; *Educ* Monkton Combe Sch, Shuttleworth Agric Coll; *m* 28 Dec 1974, Elizabeth Maltby, da of Cncllr Ronald Hubert Fielding, of Courcelle, 35 Windmore Ave, Potters Bar, Herts; 1 s (Thomas b 1980), 1 da (Claire b 1981); *Career* farmer; agric instr Kenya VSO 1971-73, ptnr in W Leggott & Son (family business) 1974-; chm Lincs and S Humberside Farming and Wildlife Advsy Gp 1984-; *Recreations* sailing, skiing, photography; *Clubs* SCGB; *Style*— Bruce Leggott, Esq; Manor Farm, Burtoft, Boston, Lincs PE20 2PD (☎ 0205 460283)

LEGH, Charles Francis; s of Cdr Ralph Armitage Broughton, RN (d 1975), and

Cynthia Combermere Broughton Legh, OBE (d 1983), of Adlington Hall; assumed surname of Legh in lieu of patronymic 1940; Legh family have lived at Adlington Hall since 1315 (*see* Burke's Landed Gentry 1952; cadet line cr Bt 1611 and Baron 1643, extinct 1786, 2 cr 1839, *see* Peerage, Alice Leigh cr Duchess of Dudley for Life 1644 *dsp* 1669); *b* 2 Feb 1922; *Educ* Stowe, Trinity Coll Cambridge; *m* 1, 24 Sept 1954 (m dis 1974), Jane Mary Chaworth, da of Fergus Munro Innes, CIE, CBE, of Woking, Surrey; 1 s (Robert b 1955, d 1962), 1 da (Camilla b 1960, m 16 Sept 1989, Andrew Shuttleworth Barnett, who has assumed the name of Barnett Legh); 2, 28 May 1989, Sarah Hanby, widow of Charles John Hines, of Casey Key, Florida, USA; *Career* served 2 KE VII own Gurkha Rifles 1942-46; served in India and Burma; broker Lloyds 1954-67, underwriting memb Lloyds 1956-; historic house and landowner; *Recreations* gardening, historical research; *Clubs* Arts; *Style—* Charles F Legh, Esq; Adlington Hall, Macclesfield, Cheshire SK10 4LF (☎ 0625 829508)

LEGH, Hon David Piers Carlis; s of 4 Baron Newton; *b* 21 Nov 1951; *Educ* Eton, RAC Cirencester; *m* 1974, Jane Mary, da of John Roy Wynter Bee, of Heather Hills, West End, Woking, Surrey; 2 s (Hugo b 1979, Thomas b 1984), 1 da (Charlotte Mary b 1976); *Career* chartered surveyor; ptnr John German chartered surveyors; FRICS, MRAC; *Clubs* Farmers; *Style—* The Hon David Legh; Cubley Lodge, Ashbourne, Derbys (☎ 0335 330297); The Rotunda, High St, Burton-on-Trent (☎ 0283 42051)

LEGH, Hon Richard Thomas; s and h of 4 Baron Newton; *b* 11 Jan 1950; *Educ* Eton, Ch Ch Oxford; *m* 1978, Rosemary Whitfoot, da of Herbert Clarke, of Eastbourne; 1 s; *Style—* The Hon Richard Legh; 101 Eton Rise, Eton College Rd, London NW3

LEGON, Prof Anthony Charles; s of George Charles Legon, and Emily Louisa Florence, *née* Conner; *b* 28 Sept 1941; *Educ* Coopers' Company Sch, UCL (BSc, PhD, DSc); *m* 20 July 1963, Deirdre Anne, da of Edgar Albert Rivers (d 1944); 2 s (Anthony Daniel Charles b 14 Nov 1979, Edward James b 14 July 1989), 1 da (Victoria May b 11 March 1977); *Career* Turner and Newall fell Univ of London 1968-70, lectr in Chemistry UCL 1970-83 (reader 1983-84), prof physical chemistry Univ of Exeter 1984-89, Thomas Graham prof of chemistry UCL 1989-90, prof physical chemistry, Univ of Exeter 1990-, Tilden lectr and medallist Royal Soc of Chemistry 1989-90; 160 sci papers published; memb Physical Chemistry Subctee Chemistry Ctee of SERC 1984-87; FRSC 1977; *Recreations* cricket; *Style—* Prof Anthony Legon; Dept of Chemistry, University of Exeter, Stocker Rd, Exeter EX4 4QD (☎ 0392 263 488, fax 0392 263 434, telex 42894 EXUNIV G)

LEGRAIN, Gérard Marie Francois; s of Jean Legrain (d 1985), and Marie Hélène, *née* Merica (d 1962); *b* 16 April 1937; *Educ* Ecole St Louis de Gonzague, Sorbonne, Faculté de Droit, Inst d' Etudes Politiques, Ecole Nationale d'Aministration Paris; *m* 1969, Katrin Ines, da of Harald Tombach, of Altadena, California, USA; 2 s (Philippe b 1973, Pierre b 1980), 1 da (Milli b 1976); *Career* Sub Lt 27 and 15 Bataillons de Chasseurs Alpins 1962; Citibank: Paris 1965, NY 1967, Mexico City 1969; vice pres Citicorp International Bank Ltd London 1972; md Int Mexican Bank Ltd London 1974; *Recreations* skiing, swimming, tennis; *Clubs* Hurlingham; *Style—* Gérard Legrain, Esq; Intermex, 29 Gresham Street, London EC2V 7ES (☎ 071 600 0880, fax 071 6009891, telex 881 017)

LEGUM, Colin; s of Louis Samuel Legum (d 1933), of Kestell, SA, and Jane, *née* Horvich (d 1979); *b* 3 Jan 1919; *Educ* Piet Retief HS Kestell Orange Free State SA; *m* 1, 5 June 1941, Eugenie Maud (d 1957), da of L O Leon (d 1959), of Evenrond, Tzaneen, SA; 1 s (David b 20 Jan 1943); m 2, 15 May 1961, Margaret Jean, *née* Roberts; 3 da (Kate b 7 Dec 1964, Elizabeth b 27 Jan 1966, Josephine b 17 Sept 1968); *Career* political corr Sunday Express Johannesburg 1937; ed: Forward Johannesburg 1939-41, Labour Bulletin 1942-48; assoc ed The Observer London 1949-81; ed: Africa Contemporary Record 1968-89, Third World Reports 1981-; memb Johannesburg City Cncl 1941-48, gen sec SA Lab Pty 1946-49; memb: Africa Bureau, Africa Pubns Tst, Africa Educn Tst London; UKSA 1949, NUJ 1951, RIAA 1952, IISS 1952, ASA (US) 1956, ASA (Canada) 1963, CWDA 1965, IHR 1972; Award of Anciens Nato Def Coll Rome 1978 and 1987, medal of Instituto da Defensa Nacionale Portugal 1987 and 1989; *Books* incl: Attitude to Africa (jtly, 1951), Congo Disaster (1960), Ethiopia - The Fall of Haile Selassie's Empire (1975), The Year of the Whirlwind (1977), The Western Crisis over Southern Africa (1979), Communism in Africa (jtly, 1979), The Battle Fronts of Southern Africa (1988); *Recreations* fishing, gardening, photography; *Style—* Colin Legum, Esq; Wild Acre, Plaw Hatch, Sharpthorne, West Sussex RH19 4JL (☎ 0342 810875); 28 Augustus Close, Brentford Dock, Brentford, Middx TW8 8QE (☎ 081 568 5903)

LEHANE, Maureen Theresa (Mrs Peter Wishart); da of Christopher Lehane (d 1970), of London, and Honor, *née* Millar; *Educ* Queen Elizabeth's Girls' GS Barnet, Guildhall Sch Music and Drama; *m* 26 May 1966, Peter Wishart (d 1984); *Career* concert and opera singer; studied under: Hermann Weissenborn, John and Aida Dickens; debut Glyndebourne 1967; speciality Handel, numerous leading roles with Handel opera socs in: England, America, Poland, Sweden, Germany; numerous master classes on the interpretation of Handel's vocal music; title roles in: Handel's Ariodante Sadlers Wells 1974, Peter Wishart's Clytemnestra London 1974, Purcell's Dido and Aeneas Netherlands Opera 1976, castrato lead JC Bach's Adriano London 1982; female lead Hugo Cole's The Falcon Somerset 1983, Peter Wishart's The Lady of the Inn Reading Univ 1983; festival appearances incl: Stravinsky Festival Cologne, City of London, Aldeburgh, Cheltenham, Three Choirs, Bath, Oxford Bach, Göttingen Handel Festival; tours incl: N America, Australia, Far East, Middle East; visits incl: Holland, Belgium, Berlin, Lisbon, Poland, Rome, Warsaw; recordings incl: Bach, Haydn, Mozart, Handel (Cyrus in first complete recording Belshazzar); tv appearances incl: BBC, ABC Australia, Belgian TV; regular appearances promenade concerts; memb Jury Int Singing Comp Hertogenbosch Festival Holland 1982-, fndr Great Elm Music Festival; *Books* Songs of Purcell (co ed Peter Wishart); *Recreations* cooking, gardening, reading; *Style—* Miss Maureen Lehane; Bridge House, Great Elm, Frome, Somerset BA11 3NY

LEHMAN, Hon Mrs (Karen Jean); da of 9 Viscount Doneraille (d 1983), and Melva, Viscountess Doneraile, *qv*; *b* 1955; *m* 1977, R Lehman; *Style—* The Hon Mrs Lehman

LEHMAN, Prof Meir M; s of Benno Lehman (d 1935), and Theresa, *née* Wallerstein (d 1988); *b* 24 Jan 1925; *Educ* Letchworth GS, Imperial Coll (BSc, ARCS, PhD, DIC, DSc); *m* 26 Aug 1953, Chava, da of Moses Robinson (d 1948); 3 s (Benjamin Moses, Jonathan David, Raphael Dan), 2 da (Machla Lea, Esher Dvora); *Career* apprentice Murphy Radio Ltd 1942-50, jr logic designer Ferranti Ltd 1956-57, head digital computers Sci Dept Israel Miny of Defense 1957-64, res staff memb mangr project IMP IBM res div 1964-72; Imp Coll of Sci and Technol: prof of computing sci 1972-84, head Dept of computing dept 1979-84) (head section 1972-79), emeritus prof Dept of Computing 1984-, sr res fell 1989; fundr and dir IST Ltd 1982-88 (chm 1982-84), fndr and md Lehman Software Technol Assocs Ltd 1984-; author of and numerous papers; FEng, FIEE, FBCS, FIEEE, MACM; *Books* Program Evolution - Processes of Software Change (1985); *Recreations* Talmudic studies, DIY, fund raising for charity; *Style—* Prof Meir Lehman; Department of Computing, Imperial College of Science, Technology & Medicine, 180 Queen's Gate, London SW7 2BZ (☎ 071 589 ext 5009, fax 071 581 8024)

LEHMANN, Dr Geoffrey Donald; MBE (1974); s of Paul Samuel Lehmann (d 1950), of Woodland House, Woodford Wells, Essex, and Lilian Ruth, *née* Harris (d 1954); *b* 5 Jan 1904; *Educ* Highgate Sch, Queen Mary's Coll London, Univ Coll Oxford (BSc, DPhil), UCH London (MRCS, LRCP), Univ of Liverpool (DTM, DOMS); *m* 16 Sept 1933, Monica Elizabeth, da of Henry Deacon Allen (d 1919), of The Retreat, Cawnpur, India; 1 s (Donald John b 21 May 1940), 3 da (Prilla (Mrs Coole) b 25 Jan 1935, Petronella (Mrs Young) b 25 March 1938, Su (Mrs East) b 15 Dec 1946); *Career* Vol IMS India 1942-46, Staff Maj DADP, Central Cmd Meerat India; specialist in eye surgery, pioneered certain new surgery techniques India, jt fndr with Mrs Monica Lehmann Herbertpur Christian Hosp Himalayan Doon Valley 1936 (sole permanent dir until 1973), chm Wyberg Allen Sch Mussouria India 1973-84; engr; dir: Lehmann Archer Lane (later Tap and Dies Ltd), Dunsterville Allen plc (Property Co); fndr of Charitable Tst; fndr: Herbertpur Tst UK 1935, NEED Non-profit Corp USA 1956, Herbertpur Tst Assoc India 1976; fndr dir Int Films Ltd; chm: Sunda Ltd, Calamus Ltd; Name at Lloyds 1954; fell Soc of Tropical Medicine and Hygiene; *Books* incl: Lyrics (1980), On the Trial of a Spy (1981), The Red Gang (with B Norman, 1983), Danger on The Sonita (1985), Saved by Fire (1990); *Recreations* tennis, golf; *Style—* Dr Geoffrey Lehmann, MBE

LEHNHOFF, Dr Nikolaus; *b* 20 May 1939; *Educ* Univ of Munich, Univ of Vienna (PhD); *Career* asst stage dir: Berlin Opera 1962-66, Bayreuth Festival 1963-66, Metropolitan Opera NY 1966-71, Die Frau Ohne Schatten (Paris 1972, Stockholm 1975), Tristan Und Isolde (Orange Festival 1973, Frankfurt 1977), Fidelio (Bremen 1974, Bonn 1983), Electra (Chicago 1975), L'Enfant et Les Sortileges (Berlin 1979), Cosi Fan Tutte (Bonn 1981), Der Ring (San Francisco 1983-85, Munich 1987), Katia Kabanova (Glyndebourne 1988), Hollander (Santa Fe 1988), Salome (Metropolitan Opera NY 1989), Jenufa (Glyndebourne 1989), Die Meistersinger (Milano, Scala 1990), Idomeneo (Salzburg Festival 1990); *Books* Es war Einmal....The Munich Ring (1987); *Style—* Dr Nikolaos Lehnhoff; 4000 Duesseldorf 12, Gut Holt, Holterweg 72, W Germany (☎ 211 298171, fax 211 294488)

LEICESTER, 6 Earl of (UK 1837); Anthony Lovel Coke; also Viscount Coke (UK 1837); s of Lt the Hon Arthur Coke (2 s of 3 Earl); suc first cous 1976; *b* 11 Sept 1909; *Educ* Gresham's Sch Holt; *m* 1, 1934 (m dis 1947), Moyra (d 1987), da of Douglas Crossley; 2 s, 1 da; m 2, 1947, Vera (d 1984), da of Herbert Haigh, of Salisbury, Rhodesia (now Zimbabwe); m 3, 1985, Elizabeth Hope, da of Clifford Arthur Johnstone, of Kiswani, Addo, CP, S Africa; *Heir* s, Viscount Coke; *Career* served WWII RAF; rancher, farmer retired; *Style—* The Rt Hon the Earl of Leicester; Hillhead, Pendeen Crescent, Plettenberg Bay, Cape Province 6600, S Africa; PO Box 544, Piettenberg Bay 6600, RSA (☎ 04457 32255)

LEICESTER, Lady; Marthe; da of Louis de Miéville de Rossens; *m* 1930, as his 2 w, Sir Peter Fleming Frederic Leicester, 8 Bt (d 1945); *Style—* Lady Leicester; Shearwater, Downderry, Cornwall

LEIFLAND, HE Leif; GCVO; The Swedish Ambassador; s of Sigfrid Leifland (d 1970), and Elna Jonson (d 1985); *b* 30 Dec 1925; *Educ* Univ of Lund (LLB); *m* 1954, Karin Kristina, da of Gustaf Abard (d 1982); 1 s (Karl), 2 da (Christina, Eva); *Career* joined Swedish Miny of Foreign Affrs 1952; served: Athens 1953, Bonn 1955, Stockholm 1958, Washington 1961, Stockholm 1964, Washington 1970, Stockholm 1975; perm under sec of state 1977-82, ambass London 1982; Grand Cross of: Austria, Finland, Fed Rep of Germany, Iceland, Rep of Korea, Mexico, Spain, Yugoslavia; *Books* The Blacklisting of Atel Wenner-Gwen (1989); *Style—* HE the Ambassador of Sweden; 27 Portland Place, W1; 11 Montagu Place, W1H 2AL (☎ 071 724 2101)

LEIGH, Hon Benjamin Chandos; s of 4 Baron Leigh, TD (d 1979), and Anne Hicks Beach (d 1977); *b* 24 Oct 1942; *Educ* Eton, Mons OCS; *m* 1979, Jennifer Vivian, da of late Capt Peter Winser, and formerly w of Hon Richard Henry Strutt, el s 4 Baron Belper; 1 da (Samantha Jane Hazel b 1980), 2 step-children (*see* Lord Belper); *Career* Lt 11 Hussars (PAO) 1960-65; *Recreations* racing, shooting; *Clubs* Turf; *Style—* The Hon Benjamin Leigh; Little Rissington House, Little Rissington, Cheltenham, Glos GL54 2NB

LEIGH, Bernard Malcolm; s of Lionel Leigh, of London, and Cecilia, *née* Ruderman; *b* 7 Feb 1950; *Educ* William Ellis GS, London Hosp Dental Inst Univ of London (BDS), Eastman Hosp Inst of Dental Surgery; *m* 25 Nov 1973, Yvonne Pamela, da of Leslie Wolfe; 4 s (Daniel b 6 Nov 1976, Jeremy b 24 March 1979, Joshua b 25 July 1984, Avram b 27 July 1989), 2 da (Sara b 20 Nov 1974, Talia b 18 Oct 1980); *Career* house offr London Hosp 1973; practiced: City of London 1974-75, Hemel Hempstead 1976-82, London NW11 1976-84, Harley St 1982-; hon clinical asst Dept of Cons Dentistry Inst of Dental Surgery Eastman Dental Hosp 1979-; memb: Alpha Omega (Ctee 1984-88), Br Endodontic Soc (Ctee 1981-82), Gen Dental Practitioners Assoc; *Recreations* music, computers, photography; *Style—* Bernard Leigh, Esq; 137 Harley St, London W1N 1DJ (☎ 071 935 3394, 071 487 4369)

LEIGH, Hon Christopher Dudley Piers; er s (but only one by 1 w) and h of 5 Baron Leigh; *b* 20 Oct 1960; *Educ* Eton, RAC Cirencester; *m* 15 Aug 1990, Sophy-Ann, da of Richard Burrows, of The Old Hall, Groby, Leics; *Career* memb: British Field Sports Soc, Royal Agric Soc of England; *Recreations* racing, tennis; *Clubs* Turf; *Style—* The Hon Christopher Leigh; Fern Farm, Adlestrop, Moreton-in-the-Marsh, Gloucs GL56 OYL (☎ 0608 658203)

LEIGH, Christopher Humphrey de Verd; QC (1989); s of Wing Cdr Humphrey de Verd Leigh, OBE, DFC, AFC (d 1981), and Johanna Emily, *née* Whitfield Hayes; *b* 12 July 1943; *Educ* Harrow; *m* 18 July 1970, Frances Raymonde, da of Col Raymond Henry Albert Powell, OBE, MC; *Career* called to the Bar Lincoln's Inn 1967, rec Crown Ct 1985; *Recreations* travel; *Style—* Christopher Leigh, Esq, QC; Dennetts, Broughton, Stockbridge, Hants SO20 8AD (☎ 0794 3071 387); 1 Paper Buildings, Temple, London EC4Y 7EP (☎ 071 353 3728)

LEIGH, David Irvine; s of Frederick Leigh (d 1980), of Glasgow, Scotland, and Mary, *née* David; *b* 16 April 1944; *Educ* Glasgow Sch of Art, Edinburgh Coll of Art Heriot Watt Univ (DA); *m* 30 Aug 1975, Lynda, da of Frank Thomas Taylor (d 1970), of Hawkhurst, Kent; 1 s (Elliot b 1983), 1 da (Claire Francesca b 1971); *Career* architect; ptnr R J Wood Chapman and Hanson 1974, chm and md Chapman and Hanson 1989- (dir 1981); designed HQ bldgs: Charrington & Co London 1978, R S Components Corby 1984, Electrocomponents Knightsbridge 1987, W M Lighting Northampton 1989; chm Fairlight Tennis Club; MRIBA 1969; *Recreations* tennis, swimming, cycling, computing; *Clubs* St Stephens, Inigo Jones; *Style—* David Leigh, Esq; Chapman & Hanson, Chartered Architects and Interior Designers, 29 Widmore Rd, Bromley, Kent BR1 1RT (☎ 081 460 8834, fax 081 460 8838)

LEIGH, Edward Julian Egerton; MP (C) Gainsborough and Horncastle 1983-; s of Sir Neville Leigh, KCVO, *qv*, and Denise Yvonne, *née* Branch; *b* 20 July 1950; *Educ* The Oratory, Lycée Francais de Londres, Univ of Durham; *m* 25 Sept 1984, Mary, eldest da of Philip Henry Russell Goodman, of 21 Upper Phillimore Gardens, London, and Sophie (Sonia), o da of late Count Vladimir Petrovitch Kleinmichel, CVO; 1 s, 3 da; *Career* barr; former: pres Durham Union Soc, chm Durham Univ Cons Assoc; Parly candidate Middlesborough 1979, dir Coalition for Peace through Security, chm Nat Cncl for Civil Defence 1980-83, memb House of Commons Select Ctee for Defence 1983-87, vice chm and sec for Backbench Ctees on Agric Employment and Defence 1983-90, Parly private sec and min of state Home Office 1990-; memb:

Richmond Borough Cncl 1977-81, GLC 1977-81; Parly under sec of state Dept of Trade and Industry 1990-; *Publications* Right Thinking (1976); *Style—* Edward Leigh, Esq, MP; House of Commons, London SW1

LEIGH, Sir Geoffrey Norman; s of Morris Leigh, and Rose Leigh; *b* 23 March 1933; *Educ* Haberdashers' Aske's, Univ of Michigan; *m* 1976, Sylvia, *née* King; 5 c; *Career* industrialist; chm: Allied London Properties plc, Sterling Homes Hldgs Ltd; memb: Int Advsy Bd The American Univ 1983-, Advsy Cncl Prince's Youth Business Tst 1985-; sponsor Leigh City Technol Coll 1988-, govr City Literary Inst; memb Cncl: London Historic Home Museums Tst (until 1987), Friends of Br Library 1987-; Freeman City of London; FRSA; kt 1990; *Clubs* Carlton, Royal Automobile, Savile, Hurlingham; *Style—* Sir Geoffrey Leigh; 26 Manchester Square, London W1A 2HU (☎ 071 486 6080)

LEIGH, Guy Ian Frederick; s of Arthur Benjamin Leigh, and Amelia, *née* Berger; b 22 Nov 1944; *Educ* Univ of Pennsylvania (BA), Law Sch Univ of Penn Sylvania (JD), Trinity Hall Cambridge (DipIntLaw); *m* 9 Aug 1968, Mary Eleanor, da of Maj Ralph Siggins Merkle, of Emporium, Pennsylvania; 1 s (Alexander b 2 May 1976), 1 da (Sarah b 5 May 1980); *Career* admitted slr 1974; articled to Clifford Turner 1972-74; Theodore Goddard: joined 1974, ptnr 1978-, memb responsible for competition/anti-trust practice Mgmnt Ctee 1988-90; memb: Ctee Competition Law Assoc, Law Soc of Eng and Wales, Jt Competition Working Pty of the Bars and Law Socs of UK; dep gen rapporteur Int League of Competition Law; *Books* The EEC and Intellectual Property (with Diana Guy, 1981), various articles on EEC competition law; *Recreations* languages (German, Italian, Spanish and French), travel, photography; *Style—* Guy I F Leigh, Esq; Theodore Goddard, 150 Aldersgate St, London EC1A 4EJ (☎ 071 606 8855, fax 071 606 4390, telex 884678)

LEIGH, Dr Irene May; da of Archibald Allen, of Liverpool, and May Lilian, *née* Whalley; *b* 25 April 1947; *Educ* Merchant Taylors', London Hosp Med Coll (BSc, MB BS); *m* 21 June 1969, Prof (Peter) Nigel Leigh, s of Dr (Archibald) Denis Leigh, of Otford, Kent; 1 s (Piers Daniel b 24 June 1973), 3 da (Andrea Yseult b 11 Oct 1975, Miranda Chloe b 17 June 1982, Rosalino Clio b 12 Jan 1988); *Career* conslt dermatologist London Hosp 1983, hon dir ICRF Skin Tumour Unit 1986, sr lectr dermatology London Hosp Med Coll 1987-; FRCP 1989; *Books* Coping with Skin Diseases (1984); *Style—* Dr Irene Leigh; Dept of Dermatology, London Hospital Medical College, London E1 1BB (☎ 071 377 7000, fax 071 377 7677)

LEIGH, 5 Baron (UK 1839); John Piers Leigh; s of 4 Baron Leigh (d 1979), and Anne, da of Ellis Hicks Beach (nephew of 1 Earl St Aldwyn); *b* 11 Sept 1935; *Educ* Eton, Oriel Coll Oxford, London Univ; *m* 1, 1957 (m dis 1974), Cecilia Poppy, da of late Robert Cecil Jackson; 1 s (Hon Christopher, *qv* b 1960), 1 da (Hon Camilla, *qv*, b 1962) (and 1 da decd); m 2, 1976 (m dis 1982), Susan, da of John Cleave, of Whitnash, Leamington Spa; 1 s (Hon Piers b 1979); m 3, 1982, Lea, o da of Col Harry Noel Havelock Wild, and Violet, yst da of Henry Selby-Lowndes, formerly w of Lt Col Brian Gustavus Hamilton-Russell (*see* Peerage, Viscount Boyne, by whom she had 1 s (Henry b 1969) and 1 da (b 1976)); *Heir* s, Hon Christopher Dudley Piers Leigh; *Style—* The Rt Hon the Lord Leigh; Stoneleigh Abbey, Kenilworth, Warwickshire (☎ 0926 52116/57766); Unicorn Lodge, 12 Briar Walk, Putney, London SW15

LEIGH, John Roland; s of Adam Dale Leigh (d 1978); *b* 11 March 1933; *Educ* Winchester, King's Coll Cambridge; *m* 1957, Rosemary Renée, da of late Capt Gordon Furze, MC; 1 s, 3 da; *Career* merchant banker; ptnr Rathbone Bros & Co 1963-88; dir: Greenbank Trust Ltd 1969-81, Albany Investment Trust plc 1979-, Rathbone Brothers plc 1988-; chm Blackburn Diocesan Bd of Fin Ltd 1976-; *Clubs* Flyfishers', Athenaeum (Liverpool); *Style—* John Leigh, Esq; Robin Hood Cottage, Blue Stone Lane, Mawdesley, Ormskirk, Lancs (☎ 0704 822641)

LEIGH, Prof Leonard Herschel; s of Leonard William Leigh (d 1976), of Edmonton, Canada, and Lillian Mavis, *née* Hayman (d 1965); *b* 19 Sept 1935; *Educ* Strathcona HS Edmonton Canada, Univ of Alberta (BA, LLB), Univ of London (PhD); *m* 17 Dec 1960, Jill Diane, da of George Gale (d 1986); 1 s (Matthew b 1967), 1 da (Alison Jane b 1965); *Career* cmmnd Royal Canadian Artillery 1955, transferred Kings Own Calgary Regt 1959-62; called to the Bar NW Territories 1960 (Alberta 1958); private practice Alberta 1958-60, advsy counsel Dept of Justice Canada 1960-62; LSE: asst lectr 1964-65, lectr in law 1965-71, reader 1971-82, prof of criminal law 1982-, convenor Law Dept 1987-; visiting prof Queens Univ Kingston Ontario 1973-74; UK corr: La Revue de Science Criminelle (Paris), La Revue de Droit Penal et de Criminologie (Belgium), La Revue de Droit Africaine (Cameron), La Revue Trimestrielle des Droits de l'Homme (Belgium); UK chm: Int Assoc of Penal Law 1986-, Université de l'Europe 1986-90; pt/t consIt to govts of: Canada, Quebec, Alberta; *Books* The Criminal Liability of Corporations in English Law (1969), Northey & Leigh, Introduction to Company Law (4 edn 1987), Police Powers in England and Wales (2 edn 1985), Strict and Vicarious Liability (1982), Leigh and Edey, Companies Act 1981 (1982), A Guide to the Financial Services Act 1986 (jtly 1986); *Recreations* music, walking; *Style—* Prof Leonard Leigh; Rowan Cottage, 20 Woodside Ave, Beaconsfield, Bucks HP9 1JJ (☎ 0494 672 787); Law Dept, London Sch of Economics and Political Science, Houghton St, Aldwych WC2 2AE (☎ 071 955 7254)

LEIGH, Hon Michael James; s of 4 Baron Leigh, TD (d 1979); *b* 1945; *Educ* Eton, Keble Coll Oxford; *m* 1972 (m dis 1980), Cherry Rosalind, da of late David Long-Price; *Style—* The Hon Michael Leigh

LEIGH, Mike; s of Alfred Abraham Leigh (d 1985), and Phyllis Pauline, *née* Cousin; *b* 20 Feb 1943; *Educ* Salford GS, RADA, Camberwell Sch of Arts and Crafts, Central Sch of Art and Design (Theatre Design Dept), London Film Sch; *m* 15 Aug 1973, Alison, da of George Percival Steadman; 2 s (Toby b 1978, Leo b 1981); *Career* dramatist; theatre, tv and film dir; assoc dir Midlands Arts Centre for Young People 1965-66, asst dir RSC 1967-68, lectr in drama Sedgley Park and De La Salle Colls Manchester 1968-69, lectr London Film Sch 1970-73; memb: Drama Panel Arts Cncl GB 1975-77, Dir's Working Pty and Specialist Allocations Bd 1976-84, Accreditation Panel Nat Cncl for Drama Trg 1978-, Gen Advsy Cncl IBA 1980-82; writer-dir: Nat Film Theatre Retrospective 1979, BBC TV Retrospective (incl Arena: Mike Leigh Making Plays) 1982; writer- dir stage plays incl: The Box Play 1965, My Parents Have Gone To Carlisle, The Last Crusade of the Five Little Nuns (Midlands Arts Centre), Nenaa (RSC Studio Stratford-upon-Avon) 1967, Individual Fruit Pies (E15 Acting Sch) 1968, Down Here And Up There (Royal Ct Theatre Upstairs) 1968, Big Basil 1968, Glum Victoria And The Lad With Specs (Manchester Youth Theatre) 1969, Epilogue (Manchester) 1969, Bleak Moments (Open Space) 1970, A Rancid Pong (Basement) 1971, Wholesome Glory, Dick Whittington and his Cat (Royal Ct Theatre Upstairs) 1973, The Jaws of Death (Traverse, Edinburgh Festival) 1973, Babies Grow Old (Other Place) 1974 ICA 1975, The Silent Majority (Bush) 1974, Abigail's Party (Hampstead) 1977, Ecstasy (Hampstead) 1979, Goose-Pimples (Hampstead, Garrick) 1981 (Standard Best Comedy award), A Smelling a Rat (Hampstead) 1988, Greek Tragedy (Belvoir St Theatre Sydney 1989, Edinburgh Festival and Theatre Royal Stratford East) 1990; writer- dir BBC Radio play Too Much of A Good Thing (banned) 1979; dir BBC TV plays and films: A Mug's Game 1972, Hard Labour 1973, The Permissive Society, Afternoon, A Light Snack, Probation, Old Chums, The Birth Of The 2001 FA Cup Final Goalie 1975, Nuts in May, Knock For Knock 1976, The Kiss of Death, Abigail's Party 1977, Who's Who 1978, Grown-Ups 198, Home Sweet Home 1982, Four Days In July 1984; writer- dir Channel Four films: Meantime 1983, The Short And Curlies 1987; writer- dir feature films incl: Bleak Moments 1971 (Golden Hugo, Chicago Film Festival 1972, Golden Leopard Locarno Film Festival 1972), High Hopes 1989 (Critics' Prize Venice Film Festival 1988), Life Is Sweet (1990); *Style—* Mike Leigh, Esq; c/o Peters Fraser & Dunlop, The Chambers, Chelsea Harbour, Lots Rd, London SW10 OXF (☎ 071 376 7676)

LEIGH, Sir Neville Egerton; KCVO (1980, CVO 1967); s of Capt Cecil Egerton Leigh (d 1930); *b* 4 June 1922; *Educ* Charterhouse and abroad; *m* 1944, Denise, da of C D Branch, MC (d 1977), of Paris, France; 2 s (Edward J E Leigh, MP, *qv*), 1 da; *Career* served in RAFVR 1942-47; called to the Bar Inner Temple 1948; legal asst Treasy Slrs Dept 1949-51, sr clerk Privy Cncl Office 1951-65, clerk of the Privy Cncl 1974-84 (dep clerk 1965-74), conslt Royal Coll of Nursing 1985-88, a chm Central London Valuation and Community Charge Tbnl; pres Br Orthoptic Soc 1984-; tstee: Dept Tst for Young Disabled, Royal Home and Hosp Putney 1985-90; govr Sutton's Hosp in Charterhouse 1986-; public memb Press Council 1986-88; *Style—* Sir Neville Leigh, KCVO; 11 The Crescent, Barnes, London SW13 0NN (☎ 081 876 4271)

LEIGH, Peter William John; s of John Charles Leigh, JP (d 1961), of Harrow, and Dorothy Grace Jepps Leigh (d 1962); *b* 29 June 1929; *Educ* Harrow Weald Co GS, Coll of Estate Mgmnt; *m* 9 June 1956, Mary Frances, *née* Smith; 2 s (Simon b 1960, Howard b 1965), 1 da (Alison b 1961); *Career* Nat Serv RCS 1947-49; in private surveying practice 1949-53, valuation asst Middx CC 1953-60, commercial estates offr Bracknell Development Corporation 1960-66; dir: valuation and estates GLC 1981-84 (sr appts 1966-81), property servs Royal Co of Berks, 1984-88; surveying and property conslt 1988-; memb: Exec Local Authy Valuers Assoc 1981-88, Gen Cncl RICS 1984-86, Govt Property Advsy Gp 1984-88; vice chm Mid-Berks Housing Assoc 1988-; FRICS 1954; *Recreations* drawing and painting, exploring Cornwall, gardening; *Style—* Peter Leigh, Esq; 41 Sandy Lane, Wokingham, Berks RG11 4SS (☎ 0734 782732); Quinley, Bodinnick-by-Fowey, Cornwall PL23 1LX

LEIGH, Richard Henry; s of Eric Leigh (d 1982), and his 1 w, Joan Fitzgerald Lane (d 1973), eldest da of M C L Freer; hp to unc Sir John Leigh, 2 Bt; *b* 11 Nov 1936; *Educ* England and Switzerland; *m* 1, 1962 (m dis 1977), Barbro Anna Elizabeth, eldest da of late Stig Carl Sebastian Tham, of Sweden; m 2, 1977, Chérie Rosalind, eldest da of D D Dale, of La Blanchie, Cherval, France, and widow of A Reece, RMS; *Style—* Richard Leigh, Esq; Trythall Vean, Madron, nr Penzance, Cornwall

LEIGH FERMOR, Hon Mrs (Joan Elizabeth); *née* Eyres Monsell; da of 1 Viscount Monsell, GBE (d 1969); *b* 5 Feb 1912; *m* 1, 1939 (m dis 1947), William John Rayner, CBE; m 2, 1968, Patrick Michael Leigh Fermor, DSO, OBE, *qv*; *Style—* The Hon Mrs Leigh Fermor; c/o Messrs John Murray, 50 Albemarle St, London W1

LEIGH FERMOR, Patrick Michael; DSO (1944), OBE (1943); s of Sir Lewis Leigh Fermor, OBE, FRS, DSc, and Muriel Eileen, *née* Ambler; *b* 11 Feb 1915; *Educ* King's Sch Canterbury; *m* 1968, Hon Joan Elizabeth, *née* Eyres-Monsell, *qv*; *Career* served WWII Irish Gds, Intelligence Corps, in Greece and Germany, Maj 1943; dep dir Br Inst Athens 1936; author; corresponding memb Athens Acad; hon citizen: Herakleion (Crete), Gythion (Laconia), and Kardamyli (Messenia) all in Greece; awarded Gold medal of Honour of Municipality of Athens 1988; *Books* The Travellers Tree (1950), A Time to Keep Silence (1953), The Violins of St Jacques (1953), Mani (1958), Roumeli (1966), A Time of Gifts (1967), Between the Woods and the Water (1986); *Recreations* walking, swimming, travel, reading, music; *Clubs* Travellers', White's, Pratt's, Beefsteak, Puffins (Edinburgh), Special Forces; *Style—* Patrick Leigh Fermor, Esq, DSO, OBE; c/o John Murray Ltd, 50 Albemarle St, London W1

LEIGH PEMBERTON, Jeremy; s of late Robert Douglas Leigh Pemberton, MBE, MC, JP, and late Helen Isabel, *née* Payne-Gallwey; bro of Rt Hon Robin Leigh Pemberton, qv; *b* 25 Nov 1933; *Educ* Eton, Magdalen Coll Oxford (MA), INSEAD Fontainebleau (MBA); *m* 1, 30 May 1968 (m dis 1980), Mary, da of John Ames, of Boston, Mass; 1 s (Richard b 13 Dec 1971); m 2, 3 June 1982, Virginia Marion, da of Sir John Curle, KCVO, CMG, qv; *Career* Nat Serv Grenadier Gds 1952-54, cmmnd 2 Lt 1953; Brooke Bond Liebig 1957-69 (rising to gp mktg controller), md W & R Balston Group 1973-74 (gp mktg controller and corporate planner 1970-73), dep chm Whatman plc (formerly Whatman Reeve Angel plc) 1990- (md 1974-89); chm: Mid Kent Holdings plc, Kent Co Crematorium plc; dir: London & Manchester Group plc, Fleming Fledgeling Investment Trust plc, Kent Economic Development Board, Bailey Products Ltd, Kent TEC Ltd, Genzyme (UK) Ltd, Southern Advsy Bd National Westminster Bank plc; CBI: former memb Nat Cncl, former memb Econ and Fin Policy Ctee, former memb Fin and Gen Purposes Ctee, fndr chm Kent Area Ctee (later chm SE Regnl Cncl); visiting prof in mktg at INSEAD 1965-70; pres: INSEAD Int Alumni Assoc 1962-66, Kent branch Chartered Inst of Mktg 1988-91; chm Fin Ctee Kent Branch Red Cross, SE memb Nat Employers' Liaison Ctee, memb Rates Consultative Ctee Kent CC; tstee: Understanding Indust Tst (chm Mgmnt Bd), Lord Cornwallis Meml Fund; FCIM, FInstD, FRSA; *Recreations* opera, fishing; *Style—* Jeremy Leigh Pemberton, Esq; Hill House, Wormshill, Sittingbourne, Kent ME9 OTS; Whatman plc, Whatman House, 20/20 Maidstone, Kent, ME16 OLS (☎ 0622 676 670, fax 0622 687408)

LEIGH-PEMBERTON, Rt Hon Robin (Robert); PC (1987); s of Capt Robert Leigh-Pemberton, MBE, MC (d 1964), of Torry Hill, Sittingbourne, Kent, and Helen Isabel, *née* Payne-Gallwey (d 1985); *b* 5 Jan 1927; *Educ* Eton, Trinity Coll Oxford; *m* 8 July 1953, Rosemary Davina, da of Lt-Col David Walter Arthur William Forbes, MC (ka 1943), of Callander, Falkirk, and Diana (d 1982; who m 2, 1946, 6 Marquess of Exeter who d 1981), gda of 1 Baron Faringdon; 5 s (John b 16 March 1955, James b 10 Dec 1956, Edward b 10 Jan 1959, Thomas b 22 Sept 1961, William b 20 march 1964); *Career* Lt Grenadier Gds, served Palestine 1946-48; Hon Col: Kent and Sharpshooters Yeo Sqdn, 265 (KCLY) Signal Sqdn (V), 5 (Vol) Bn The Queen's Regt; pres: SE TA & VR Assoc, Kent SSAFA; hon pres: Kent Wing Air Trg Corps; called to the Bar Inner Temple 1954, practised London and SE Circuit 1954-60, hon bencher 1983; dir: Birmid Qualcast 1966-83 (dep chm 1970, chm 1975-77), University Life Assurance Society 1967-78, Redland Ltd 1972-83, Equitable Life Assurance Society 1979-83 (vice pres 1982-83); chm: National Westminster Bank 1977-83 (dir 1972-83, dep chm 1974), Ctee of London Clearing Bankers 1982-83; govr Bank of England 1983-; Lord-Lieut of Kent 1982- (DL 1970, vice Lord-Lieut 1972-82), JP 1961-75, co cncllr Kent 1961-77 (chm Cncl 1972-75); memb NEDC 1982-; tstee: Royal Acad of Arts Tst 1982-87 (now tstee emeritus), Kent CCC, Kent Co Playing Fields Assoc, Kent Co Agric Soc, Rochester Cathedral Tst, The Kent Fndn; chm Canterbury Cathedral Appeal Tst Fund; pres: Kent Co Agric Soc 1984-85, Royal Agric Soc of England 1989-90, Kent Rural Community Cncl, Kent Assoc of Youth Clubs, St John Cncl for Kent; hon fell Trinity Coll Oxford 1984, pro chllr Univ of Kent 1977-83, seneschal of Canterbury Cathedral 1983-; Hon DCL Univ of Kent 1983, Hon DLitt: City of London 1988, Loughborough 1989, City Poly 1990; memb RSA, FCIB, KStJ 1983; *Recreations* country pursuits, the arts; *Clubs* Brooks's, Cavalry & Guards', Kent CCC; *Style—* The Rt Hon Robin Leigh-Pemberton; Torry Hill, Sittingbourne, Kent ME9 0SP (☎ 0795 83258); Bank of England, Threadneedle Street, London EC2R 8AH (☎ 071 601 4444)

LEIGH-SMITH, (Alfred) Nicholas Hardstaff; s of Lt-Col Alfred Leigh Hardstaff

Leigh-Smith, TD, DL (d 1978), of Stanwell Moor, Middx, and Marguerite Calvert, *née* Calvert-Harrison (d 1983); *b* 21 Dec 1953; *Educ* Epsom Coll, Univ of Leeds (LLB); *Career* called to the Bar Lincoln's Inn 1976; dep clerk: Bromley Justices 1985, Brent Justices 1989; *Recreations* rugby union football, clay pigeon shooting, reading, walking; *Style*— Nicholas Leigh-Smith, Esq; 163 Elborough St, London SW18 (☎ 081 874 1217); 3-4 John St, Penmachno, North Wales; The Magistrates Courts, Brent, 448 High Rd, London NW10 2DZ (☎ 081 451 2425, fax 081 451 6227)

LEIGHTON, (Henry) Gerard Mather; s of Wilfrid Leighton (d 1967), of Burnett, Somerset, and Margaret, *née* Mather; *b* 15 Aug 1932; *Educ* Winchester, Corpus Christi Coll Oxford (MA); *m* 5 June 1982, Amanda Juliet, da of Brig Cedric George Buttenshaw, CBE, DSO, of Worton, nr Devizes, Wiltshire; 1 s (Henry b 1984), 1 da (Alice b 1985); *Career* CA; ptnr Grace Darbyshire & Todd Bristol 1959-68; dir: Tyndall Group Ltd and subsids 1962-86, Gateway Securities Ltd 1965-77; chm Jordan Group Ltd 1985- (dir 1968-), dep chm W of England Tst Ltd 1982- (dir 1972); hon treas Bristol and Glocs Archaeological Soc 1971-; chm: Bristol Diocesan Advsy Ctee for Care of Churches 1974-, Somerset Record Soc 1977-; dep chm: Wells Cathedral Fabric Ctee 1987-, Bristol Cathedral Fabric Ctee 1989-; FSA; *Recreations* gardening, hunting, archaeology; *Clubs* Travellers; *Style*— Gerard Leighton, Esq; Hassage Manor, Faulkland, nr Bath, Somerset (☎ 0373 834449); 21 St Thomas St, Bristol (☎ 0272 299292)

LEIGHTON, Ian; s of James Horsburgh Leighton, and Kathleen, *née* Paton; *b* 2 Sept 1954; *Educ* Madras Coll St Andrew, Kirkcaldy Tech Coll Univ of Liverpool (BA, BArch); *m* 20 Aug 1977, Joan, da of Robert Porter; 1 s (David b 1982), 1 da (Christine b 1980); *Career* chartered architect; ptnr in own practice specialising in technol consultancy and defects investigation; previous appointments have incl res asst Liverpool Univ Sch of Architecture 1975; memb: RIBA Merseyside Branch Ctee 1985-87, Liverpool Architectural Soc Cncl 1987-88, Liverpool Regnl Jt Consultative Ctee for Bldg 1988-; RIBA 1981-; *Recreations* badminton; *Style*— Ian Leighton, Esq; 15 Ennis Rd, Liverpool L12 9JD (☎ 051 228 2180)

LEIGHTON, Kathleen, Lady; Kathleen Irene Linda; da of Maj Albert Ernest Lees, of Rowton Castle, Shrewsbury; *m* 1932, Col Sir Richard Tihel Leighton, 10 Bt, TD (d 1957); 1 s (Sir Michael, 11 Bt, *qv*), 3 da (Mrs Edward Bonner-Maurice b 1932, Judy b 1937, Mrs Vyvian Clover b 1938); *Style*— Kathleen, Lady Leighton; The Spawns, Shrewsbury

LEIGHTON, Sir Michael John Bryan; 11 Bt (E 1693); s of Col Sir Richard Tihel Leighton, 10 Bt, TD (d 1957); *b* 8 March 1935; *Educ* Stowe, RAC, Cirencester, Tabley House Agric Sch; *m* 1974 (m dis 1980), Amber Mary Ritchie; *Career* photographer of wild life; ornithologist; *Recreations* panel 'A' gun dog judge, cricket, tennis, golf, writing poetry, cooking; *Clubs* MCC; *Style*— Sir Michael Leighton, Bt; Loton Park, nr Shrewsbury, Shropshire (☎ 074 378 232)

LEIGHTON, Ronald; MP (Lab) Newham North East 1979-; s of Charles Leighton; *b* 24 Jan 1930; *Educ* Monteagle and Bifrons Sch Barking; *m* 1951, Erika Wehkin; 2 s; *Career* chm: Labour Common Market Safeguards Ctee, House of Commons Select Ctee on Employment; *Style*— Ronald Leighton, Esq, MP; House of Commons, London SW1

LEIGHTON, Tom James; s of Thomas James Leighton (d 1974), and Winifred Barclay, *née* Mearns; *b* 2 Oct 1944; *Educ* Cardinal Newman Coll Buenos Aires Argentina, Austin Friars Sch Carlisle, Derby Coll of Art (Dip Photography); *m* 1, 1964 (m dis 1969), Margaret Louise Lockhart Mure; 1 s (Lee Lockhart-Mure b 20 April 1967); m 2, 1970, Susan Gillian, da of Albert George Hollingsworth; *Career* photographer; asst with several photographers incl: Christa Peters, David Anthony, Graham Hughes 1972-75; fashion photographer for many magazines advertising agencies and catalogues 1975-81, interiors photographer 1981-; assignments incl: America Vogue, World of Interiors, Sunday Times Magazine, Telegraph Magazine, Casa Vogue (Spain), La Casa de Marie Claire (Spain), Domino (Canada), Country Living, Homes and Gardens, Elle Decoration; Merit award from Art Dirs Club of Toronto 1989 for work published in Domino magazine; *Photography Books*: Grand Illusions (1988), The Painted House (1988); *Clubs* Sutton Lane Gym; *Style*— Tom Leighton, Esq; 17 Cedar Court, Sheen Lane, London SW14 8LY (☎ 081 876 8497)

LEIGHTON OF ST MELLONS, 2 Baron (UK 1962); Sir John Leighton Seager; 2 Bt (UK 1952); s of 1 Baron, CBE (d 1963), and Marjorie, Lady Leighton of St Mellons *qv*; *b* 11 Jan 1922; *Educ* Caldicott Sch, Leys Sch Cambridge; *m* 1, 31 Oct 1953, Elizabeth Rosita (d 1979), o da of late Henry Hopgood, of Cardiff; 2 s (Hon Robert b 1955, Hon Simon b 1957), 1 da (Hon Carole b 1958) and 1 da decd; m 2, 1982, Ruth Elizabeth, wid of John Hopwood; *Heir* s, Hon Robert William Henry Leighton Seager; *Career* dir Watkin Williams & Co, conslt Principality Building Soc, former chm Cardiff & Bristol Channel Shipowners Assoc, former dir W H Seager & Co Ltd; *Recreations* gardening, photography, being educated by my grandchildren; *Style*— The Rt Hon the Lord Leighton of St Mellons; 346 Caerphilly Road, Cardiff

LEIMAN, Russell Michael; s of Dr Norman Cecil Leiman (d 1983), and Edith Helen, *née* Rosenberg; *b* 26 Oct 1947; *Educ* King Edward VII Sch Johannesburg S Africa; *m* 15 April 1973, Ashley Elizabeth Chesler, *née* Beer; 2 step da (Samantha Jane b 13 March 1969, Vanessa Claire b 13 April 1971); *Career* clerk I Jacobs (memb Johannesburg Stock Exchange 1968-71); Vickers Da Costa: arbitrage trader London 1971-74, Hong Kong 1974-77, assoc gen mangr Tokyo Branch 1977-85, pres Vickers Da Costa Securities Inc (NY) 1985-88; chief exec Citicorp Scrimgeour Vickers International Ltd (London) 1988-89 (formerly Vickers Da Costa Ltd), chief exec Credit Lyonnais Securities and Laing & Cruickshank Institutional Equities Ops UK 1989-90, dir Int Equity Div Credit Lyonnais 1990; memb: Int Stock Exchange, Int Ctee NASD Washington 1988; *Recreations* theatre, music, photography; *Style*— Russell Leiman, Esq; 7 Kent Terrace, London NW1 4RP (☎ 071 724 2234); Credit Lyonnais Capital Markets, Broadwalk House, 5 Appold St, London EC2A 2DA (☎ 071 588 4000, fax 071 588 0301); 19 Boulevard Des Italiens, 75002, Paris (☎ 4295 7000)

LEINSTER, 8 Duke of (I 1766); Gerald FitzGerald; Premier Duke, Marquess and Earl in the Peerage of Ireland, also Baron of Offaly (I *ante* 1203 restored 1554), Earl of Kildare (I 1316), Viscount Leinster of Taplow (GB 1747), Marquess of Kildare, Earl of Offaly (both I 1761), and Baron Kildare (UK 1870); s of 7 Duke of Leinster (d 1976, descended from common ancestors of (1) The Earls of Plymouth, (2) Giraldus Cambrensis the medieval historian, (3) the Earls of Desmond (now extinct), (4) the hereditary Knights of Glin and Kerry and the (extinct) White Knight, (5) the Marquesses of Lansdowne), and his 1 w May, *née* Etheridge (d 1935); *b* 27 May 1914; *Educ* Eton, Sandhurst; *m* 1, 17 Oct 1936 (m dis 1946), Joane, eldest da of late Maj Arthur McMorrough Kavanagh, MC; 2 da (Lady Rosemary Wait b 1939, Lady Nesta Tirard b 1942), and 1 decd; m 2, 12 June 1946, Anne, yr da of Lt-Col Philip Eustace Smith, MC, TD; 2 s (Marquess of Kildare, *qv*, Lord John b 1952); *Heir* s, Marquess of Kildare, *qv*; *Career* served WWII with 5 Royal Inniskilling Dragoon Gds (wounded in Normandy); master: N Kilkenny foxhounds 1937-40, W Percy foxhounds 1945-46, Portman foxhounds 1946-47; *Recreations* shooting, fishing; *Style*— His Grace the Duke of Leinster; Kilkea House, Wilcote Lane, Ramsden, Oxon OX7 3BA

LEINSTER, Samuel John; s of Victor Leinster, of Birmingham, and Jemina Eileen Eva, *née* McGeown; *b* 29 Oct 1946; *Educ* Boroughmuir Sr Secdy Sch Edinburgh, Univ of Edinburgh (BSc, MB ChB), Royal Coll of Surgns Edinburgh (FRCS), Univ of Liverpool (MD); *m* 17 July 1971, Jennifer, da of James Woodward, of Wirral; 3 s (Alistair b 1975, David b 1979, Benjamin b 1988), 1 da (Angela b 1972); *Career* RAF Med Branch: PO 1969, Flying Offr 1971, Flt Lt 1972, MO 1972-77, Sqdn Ldr 1977, surgical specialist, ret 1977; lectr in surgery Welsh Nat Sch of Med 1978-81, sr lectr in surgery Univ of Liverpool and hon conslt surgn Liverpool Health Authy 1982-90, reader in surgery Univ of Liverpool 1990-; memb: BMA, Surgical Res Soc, Assoc of Surgns of GB and I, Assoc for the Study of Med Educn, Br Assoc of Surgical Oncology, Christian Med Fellowship, Gideons Int; *Books* Systemic Diseases for Dental Students (with T J Bailey, 1983); *Recreations* local preacher, DIY enthusiast, reading, swimming; *Style*— Samuel Leinster, Esq; 7 Roman Rd, Meols, Wirral, Merseyside L47 6AG (☎ 051 632 4468); Dept of Surgery, University of Liverpool, PO Box 147, Liverpool (☎ 051 709 0141)

LEINSTER, Dowager Duchess of; Vivien Irene; da of Thomas Albert Felton (d 1957), and his w Lilian Adshead; *b* 19 Feb 1920; *m* 1, 1937 (m dis 1965), George William Conner; 1 s; m 2, 1965, as his 4 w, 7 Duke of Leinster, Premier Duke, Marquess and Earl of Ireland (d 1976); *Career* medical sec Royal Marsden Hosp 1977-81; gift shop admin Help the Aged 1976; *Style*— Her Grace the Dowager Duchess of Leinster; 26 The Albemarle, Marine Parade, Brighton, East Sussex BN2 1TX (☎ 0273 680827)

LEISHMAN, James; s of Mitchell Ramsay Leishman, of 165 Lumphinnans Rd, LochGelly, and Mary, *née* McAneeny; *b* 15 Nov 1953; *Educ* Cowdenbeath Sr High Sch; *m* 24 Feb 1978, Mary Haldane, da of John Smith, of Burnside House Kelty Bridge, Kelty; 1 s (Jamie b 1988), 1 da (Kate b 1981); *Career* professional footballer 1970-76, Cowdenbeath Job Centre 1977-85, pt/t football mangr 1983-85, full-time football mangr Dunfermline Athletic 1985-; Scot second div championship 1985-86, runners-up Scot first div 1986-89, Scot first div championship 1988-89; twice mangr of the month, St Andrews Boxing Club personality of the Year; scout leader; *Recreations* sport, amateur musicals, poetry; *Style*— James Leishman, Esq; Burnside House, Kelty Bridge, Blairadam, Kelty, Fife (☎ 0383 831 834); Dunfermline Athletic Football Club, East End Park, Halbeath Rd, Dunfermline, Fife (☎ 0383 724295, fax 0383 723468)

LEISHMAN, Hon Mrs (Marista Muriel); da of 1 Baron Reith, KT, GCVO, GBE, CB, TD (d 1971); *b* 10 April 1932; *Educ* St George's Ascot, Univ of St Andrews (MA); *m* 1960, Murray Leishman (psychotherapist); 1 s (Mark b 1962), 3 da (Iona b 1963, Martha b 1965, Kirsty b 1969); *Career* head of education Nat Tst for Scotland 1978-86, dir The Insite Tst, management and trg conslt in Heritage Presentation 1987-; Nat Trg award winner 1989; FRSA 1988; *Recreations* music, writing, painting, walking; *Style*— The Hon Mrs Leishman; Hunter's House, 508 Lanark Rd, Edinburgh EH14 5DH (☎ 031 453 4716)

LEITCH, Alexander Park (Sandy); s of Donald Leitch (d 1949), of Blairhall, Fife, and Agnes Smith, *née* Park; *b* 20 Oct 1947; *Educ* Dunfermline HS; *m* 22 March 1970, Valerie Beryl, da of Douglas Hodson; 3 da (Fiona b 1971, Joanne b 1973, Jacqueline b 1975); *Career* chief systems designer National Mutual Life 1969, Hambro Life 1971 (bd dir 1981), dep chm Allied Dunbar 1990 (md 1988); govr Stonar Sch; MBCS 1966; *Recreations* tennis, books; *Style*— Sandy Leitch, Esq; York Place, Richmond Rd, Lansdown, Bath (☎ 0225 311011) Allied Dunbar, Swindon SN1 1EL (☎ 0793 514 514, car 0836 212 494)

LEITCH, Sir George; KCB (1975, CB 1963), OBE (1945); s of late James Simpson Leitch, and Margaret Leitch; *b* 5 June 1915; *Educ* Wallsend GS, King's Coll Durham Univ; *m* 1942, Edith Marjorie, da of late Thomas Dawson Maughan; 1 da; *Career* served WWII (despatches), Brig 1946; entered Civil Service 1947, dep under sec of state MOD 1965-72, sec (procurement exec) 1972-74, chief exec (perm sec) 1974-75, ret; chm: Short Brothers 1976-83, Standing Advsy Ctee on Trunk Rd Assessment 1977-80; *Style*— Sir George Leitch, KCB, OBE; 10 Elmfield Rd, Gosforth, Newcastle-upon-Tyne (☎ 091 284 6559); Black Brae, Port Charlotte, Islay, Argyll (☎ 049 685 430)

LEITCH, Dr (Andrew) Gordon; s of Andrew Leitch, and Elizabeth, *née* Ramsay; *b* 12 Dec 1945; *Educ* Royal High Sch Edinburgh, Univ of Edinburgh (BSc, MB ChB, PhD); *m* 9 July 1976, Jean Elizabeth Brawn, da of Henry James Brawn Miller; 2 s (Andrew b 1979, Henry b 1985), 1 da (Elizabeth b 1982); *Career* conslt physician; memb Br Thoracic Soc, FRCPE, FCCP; *Books* Respiratory Diseases (1989); *Recreations* fishing, golfing; *Clubs* Luffness; *Style*— Dr Gordon Leitch; 16 Wilton Rd, Edinburgh EG16 5NX (☎ 031 667 5812); 14 Moray Plc, Edinburgh EH3 6DT (☎ 031 225 5320)

LEITCH, Jonathan Andrew; OBE (1988); s of Andrew Macintosh Leitch (d 1953), of Buenos Aires, Argentina, and Beryl Roscoe, *née* Allen (d 1951); *b* 31 March 1932; *Educ* Charterhouse, Cranfield (MSc); *m* 27 Feb 1954, Barbara, da of late William Louis Lovell; 1 s (Jamie b 1958), 2 da (Lesley b 1956, Joanna b 1963); *Career* apprentice engr: Rolls Royce Ltd 1950-55, Bristol Aircraft Ltd 1957; mfrg mangr Bristol Guided Weapons Div 1965, works mangr Opperman Gears Ltd 1966, dir BAC Guided Weapons Div 1978, dep md BAC Weapons Div 1980, ops dir BAC Dynamics Div 1988, ret; various offices Local Cons Assocs; *Recreations* historic vehicles, aeromodelling, travel; *Clubs* VCC, VMCC, BMFA, and others; *Style*— Jonathan Leitch, Esq, OBE; The Coach House, 16B High St, Brampton, Cambs PE18 8TG (☎ 0480 51622)

LEITCH, Maurice Henry; s of Andrew Leitch (d 1983), of Templepatrick, Co Antrim, NI, and Jean, *née* Coid (d 1973); *b* 5 July 1933; *Educ* Methodist Coll Belfast, Stranmills Trg Coll Belfast (teaching dip); *m* 1, 23 July 1956, Isobel, da of James Scott; 1 s (Paul b 17 Feb 1967), 1 da (Bronagh b 17 Sept 1965); m 2, 18 Nov 1972, Sandra, da of Alfred Hill; 1 s (Daniel b 29 April 1974); *Career* teacher Antrim NI 1954-60; BBC Radio: features prodr Belfast 1960-70, drama prodr London 1970-77, prodr Book at Bedtime 1977-89; author of several tv screenplays, radio dramas, features and short stories; Guardian Fiction Prize 1969, Whitbread Fiction Prize 1981, Pye award most promising writer new to tv 1980-1981, memb Soc of Authors 1989; *Style*— Maurice Leitch, Esq; Deborah Rogers, 20 Powis Mews, London W2 (☎ 071 221 3717)

LEITH, Hon (John) Barnabas; s of 6 Baron Burgh (d 1959); *b* 27 Dec 1947; *Educ* Wellington, Univ of Exeter (BA), Univ of Birmingham (PGCE), Univ of Kent at Canterbury (BA); *m* 1970, Erica Jane, da of David M Lewis, of Winchester; 2 s (Alexander David Kalimat b 1973, Thomas Magnus b 1976), 1 da (Angharad Jane b 1977); *Career* teacher: King Charles I Sch Kidderminster 1972-74, Scalloway Jr HS Shetland 1975-79, Anderson HS Lerwick Shetland 1979-81; dir Alcoholism Counselling Centre Lerwick 1981-84; mangr George Ronald Publisher Ltd 1987-88; asst to Sec-Gen Nat Assembly of Bahá'ís of the UK 1989-91; memb Auxiliary Bd for protection of the Bahá'í Faith; *Recreations* writing, photography, computing, study of religion, science and philosophy, public speaking; *Style*— The Hon Barnabas Leith; 24 Gardiner Close, Abingdon, Oxon OX14 3YA (☎ 0235 35224)

LEITH, Hon (Alexander) Gregory Disney; s and h of 7 Baron Burgh; *b* 16 March 1958; *m* 1984, Catharine Mary, da of David Parkes; 2 s (Alexander James Strachan b 1986, Benjamin David Willoughby b 1988); *Style*— The Hon Gregory Leith; 28 High Street, Nettlebed, Henley-on-Thames, Oxon

LEITH, Prudence Margaret; OBE (1989); da of Stewart Leith (d 1961), of Johannesburg, SA, and Margaret, *née* Inglis; *b* 18 Feb 1940; *Educ* St Mary's Sch

Johannesburg, Univ of Cape Town, Sorbonne Paris (Cours de la Civilisation Francaise); *m* 1974, (Charles) Rayne Kruger (author); 1 s (Daniel b 1974), 1 da (Li-Da b 1974); *Career* restaurateur, caterer, author, journalist; fndr: Leith's Good Food 1961, Leith's Restaurant 1969, Prudence Leith Ltd 1972, Leith's Sch of Food and Wine 1975, Leith's Farm 1976; dir: Br Transport Hotels Ltd 1977-83, Travellers-Fare 1977-85, BR Bd 1980-85 (pt/t memb), Prudence Leith Ltd 1972- (md), Leith's Good Food Ltd 1961-, Leith's Restaurant Ltd 1969-, Leith's Promotions Ltd 1975-, Leith's Farm Ltd 1976-, Location (Kensington) Ltd, Ettington Park Hotel plc 1984-87, Argyll Group plc; non-exec dir Safeway plc; memb Cncl: Food From Britain 1983-87, Museum of Modern Art 1984; appeared in: 26-part TV cookery series on Tyne-Tees TV, Best of Br BBC TV, The Good Food Show, Take 6 Cooks; memb: Econ Devpt Ctee for the Leisure & Tourism Industs 1986-90, Nat Trg Task Force, Dept of Employment 1989; *Books* written 11 cookery books between 1972 and 1987; *Recreations* riding, tennis, old cookbooks; *Style—* Miss Prudence Leith, OBE; 94 Kensington Park Rd, London W11 2PN (☎ 071 221 5282)

LEITH, Hon Rebecca Moraigh Eveleigh; da of 7 Baron Burgh; *b* 17 Dec 1959; *Educ* St Margaret's Exeter; *m* 1978 (m dis 1983), David K O Brandler; resumed her maiden name; *Style—* The Hon Rebecca Leith; 66 Cumberland Road, Spike Island, Bristol BS1 6UF

LEITH, William; s of George Manderson Leith, of 7 Lockitt Way, Kingston, Lewes, Sussex, and Mavis, *née* Moffat; *b* 30 April 1960; *Educ* Brighton Coll, Univ of Warwick (BA), Corpus Christi Coll Cambridge; partner, Miriam Darlington; *Career* freelance journalist (Guardian, NME) 1985-87; contrib ed: Tatler Magazine (freelance Sunday Telegraph, The Face, Arena) 1987-89, Sunday Correspondent Magazine (freelance GQ, Daily Telegraph, Sunday Telegraph, tv critic The Times) 1989-90; feature writer The Independent on Sunday 1990-; *Style—* William Leith, Esq; 10 Grange Road, Lewes, E Sussex (☎ 0273 473620); 51 Durlston Road, London E5; The Independent on Sunday, 40 City Road, London EC1 (☎ 071 415 1367)

LEITH-BUCHANAN, Barbara, Lady; Barbara Deane; da of Willard Phelps Leshure, of Springfield, Mass; *b* 28 Feb 1904; *Educ* Emme Willard Sch Troy NY, New England Conservatory of Music Boston; *m* 16 Sept 1933, Sir George Hector Macdonald Leith-Buchanan, 6 Bt (d 1973); *Recreations* music, gardening, youth welfare; *Style—* Barbara, Lady Leith-Buchanan; Drummakill, Alexandria, Dunbartonshire (☎ 038 983 232)

LEITH-BUCHANAN, Sir Charles Alexander James; 7 Bt (1775); s of John Wellesley MacDonald Leith-Buchanan (d 1956); suc kinsman Sir George Hector MacDonald Leith-Buchanan, 6 Bt (d 1973); *b* 1 Sept 1939; *m* 1962 (m dis 1987), Marianne, da of Col Earle Wellington Kelly; 1 s, 1 da; *Heir* s, Gordon Kelly McNicol Leith-Buchanan b 18 Oct 1974; *Career* pres United Business Machines Inc 1978; *Style—* Sir Charles Leith-Buchanan, Bt; 7510 Clifton Road, Clifton, Virginia 22024, USA

LEIVERS, Roger William; s of William Harold Leivers, of 23 Mews Lane, Calverton, Notts, and Joan Margaret, *née* Smith; *b* 8 Feb 1949; *Educ* Minster GS Southwell Notts; *m* 1973, Kathrine Anne, da of Michal Czarnopolski; *Career* CA; former articled clerk then PA to sr Ptnr Pannell Kerr Forster Nottingham; Cooper Parry Watson Sowter: mangr 1976-78, ptnr i/c Dept of Business Recovery and Insolvency 1978-; memb: Post Qualification Educn Ctee Inst of CA's 1990 (memb Insolvency Practitioners Ctee 1989), Fin and Gen Purposes Ctee and Cncl Soc of Practitioners in Insolvency 1990; FCA 1979 (ACA 1972); *Recreations* gardening, travel, politics; *Style—* Roger Leivers, Esq; Brook Lea, Clifton, Ashbourne, Derbyshire DE6 2GL (☎ 0335 42794); Cooper-Parry Watson Sowter, Chartered Accountants, 102 Friar Gate, Derby DE1 1FH (☎ 0332 295544, fax 0332 295600)

LELLO, Walter Barrington (Barry); s of Walter Joseph Lello (d 1978), of Anfield, Liverpool, and Louisa McGarrigle (d 1974); *b* 29 Sept 1931; *Educ* Liverpool Inst HS; *m* 30 July 1959, Margaret, da of Alexander McGregor (d 1979), of Aintree, Liverpool; *Career* Nat Serv coder (educnl) RN 1950-52; Civil Serv 1949-; shipping and air transport 1952-54, Ministry of Aviation 1954-64, seconded to FCO, asst civil aviation rep Far East Hong Kong 1964-67, promoted to admin class (princ) Bd of Trade 1968, Middle East civil air attachè in Beirut 1971-76, asst sec Dept of Trade London 1976, dir gen Saudi-British Econ Co-op Office Riyadh 1978-81, seconded to industry 1981-83, seconded to FCO counsellor commercial econ and aid, British Embassy Cairo 1984-88, dep regnl dir NW region DTI 1988-; *Recreations* mountaineering, sailing, reading, theatre; *Style—* Barry Lello, Esq; Deputy Regional Director, Dept of Trade and Industry, Graeme House, Derby Square, Liverpool L2 7UP (☎ 051 224 6333, telex 627647 DTILPLG)

LEMAITRE, Jean-Conrad; s of Bernard Lemaitre, of 69 Ave Georges Mandel, 75016 Paris, France, and Marie Rose, *née* De Witt; *b* 5 June 1943; *Educ* Ecole Superieure de Commerce Paris, INSEAD (MBA); *m* 1 Oct 1970, Isabelle, da of Baron Hubert de Turckheim, of Rue Chalgrin, Paris 75016; 1 s (Amaury b 18 June 1978), 1 da (Geraldine b 4 April 1974); *Career* Res Lt French Navy 1968-70; account offr Banque NSM 1970-73, corporate head Paris Branch Chemical Bank 1973-77, corporate head Northern and Southern Europe (Chemical Bank NY) 1977-80, head Nordic Div Chemical Bank London 1980-82, dep gen mangr Spain Chemical Bank Madrid 1982-86, head int private banking (Europe, N America) Chemical Bank London 1986-89, head private banking Bank Brussels Lambert; Knight of St Johanni's Von Spital Zu Jerusalem Order Germany 1977; *Clubs* Automobile de France, RAC; *Style—* Jean-Conrad Lemaitre, Esq; 9 Rue Alfred Giron, Brussels, Belgium; Chemical Bank House, 180 Strand, London WC2R 1EX, (☎ 071 380 5452)

LEMAN, Richard Alexander; s of Dennis Alexander George Leman, and Joyce Mabyn, *née* Pickering; *b* 13 July 1959; *Educ* Gresham's Sch Holt; *Career* hockey player; Bronze Medal Olympic Games (LA) 1984; Silver Medal: World Cup (London) 1986, European Cup (Moscow) 1987; Gold Medal Olympic Games (Seoul) 1988; *Recreations* golf; *Clubs* E Grinstead Hockey; *Style—* Richard Leman, Esq; Dartel House, 2 Lumley Road, Horley, Surrey (☎ 0293 785633, fax 0293 772053)

LEMKIN, James Anthony; CBE (1986); s of William Lemkin, CBE, of Wherwell, Hants, and Rachel Irene, *née* Faith (d 1958); *b* 21 Dec 1926; *Educ* Charterhouse, Merton Coll Oxford (MA); *m* 23 Nov 1960, Joan Dorothy Anne, da of Thomas Casserley (d 1945), of Wellington, NZ; 2 s (Robert b 1961, David b 1968), 2 da (Judith b 1966, Alix b 1968); *Career* served RN 1945-48; admitted slr 1953; ptnr Field Fisher Waterhouse (and predecessors) 1959-90, ret; memb GLC 1973-86: chm Legal and Parly Ctee 1977-78, chm Scrutiny Ctee 1978-81, Cons spokesman on police 1981-82, oppn chief whip 1982-86; chm Bow Gp 1952, 1956 and 1957-; vice chm Soc of Cons Lawyers 1990-; govr: Westfield Coll London 1970-83, Royal Marsden Hosp 1984-90; memb Cwlth Inst 1985-; Parly candidate: (Cons and NL) Chesterfield 1959, (L) Cheltenham 1964; memb Law Soc; *Books* Race and Power (ed, 1956); *Recreations* cricket umpiring, fishing; *Clubs* Athenaeum, Carlton; *Style—* James A Lemkin, Esq, CBE; c/o Field Fisher Waterhouse, 41 Vine St, London EC3 (☎ 071 481 4841)

LEMMON, Mark Benjamin; s of Edmund Lemmon (d 1984), of 27 Childs Hall Rd, Gt Bookham, and Mary Patricia, *née* Bryan; *b* 15 April 1952; *Educ* Wimbledon Coll, Univ Coll London (BA), LSE (MSc); *m* 8 Aug 1980, Anna, da of Prof Tamas Szekely, of Budapest; 3 da (Esther b 1981, Patricia b 1985, Bernadette b 1990); *Career* Touche Ross, Grindlays Bank, Guinness Mahon, sr corporate mangr Hong Kong and Shanghai Banking Corp; Freeman City of London, memb Billingsgate Ward Club; FCA 1978, ATII 1979, ACIB 1982; *Recreations* squash, skiing, opera; *Clubs* Wimbledon Squash and Badminton; *Style—* Mark Lemmon, Esq; The Hong Kong & Shanghai Banking Corp Ltd, 99 Bishopsgate, London EC2P 2LA

LEMON, Sir (Richard) Dawnay; CBE (1958), QPM; s of Lt-Col Frederick Joseph Lemon, CBE, DSO (d 1952); *b* 1912; *Educ* Uppingham, RMC; *m* 1939, Sylvia Marie, da of Lt-Col L W Kentish, of Burnham, Bucks; 1 s, 2 da (1 decd); *Career* joined W Yorks Regt 1932; Met Police 1934-37, Leics Constabulary 1937-39; chief constable: E Riding Yorks 1939-42, Hampshire and IOW 1942-62, Kent 1962-74; memb Cncl Friends of Canterbury Cathedral; kt 1970; *Recreations* golf; *Clubs* Band of Brothers Cricket, Free Foresters Cricket, Naval and Military, Royal St George's Golf; *Style—* Sir Dawnay Lemon, CBE, QPM; Rosecroft, Ringwould, nr Deal, Kent (☎ 030 45 67 554)

LEMON, Roy; s of Leslie George Lemon, of Poole, Dorset, and Aubrey May, *née* Weller; *b* 31 March 1946; *Educ* Royal GS Guildford (LLB); *m* 22 March 1969, Barbara Denise, da of Herbert David Jackson, of Leeds, W Yorks; 2 s (Benedict Mathew b 31 May 1975, Luke Kitson b 10 Feb 1987), 1 da (Rebecca Kate b 16 July 1977); *Career* called to the Bar Gray's Inn 1970; *Recreations* sailing and other displacement activities; *Style—* Roy Lemon, Esq; Devereux Chambers, Devereux Ct, Temple, London, WC2R 3JJ (☎ 071 353 7534, fax 071 353 1724)

LEMOS, Costas George; s of George Constantine Lemos (d 1985), of London, and Chrysanthi Lemos (d 1979); *b* 2 Jan 1937; *Educ* St Paul's, Pembroke Coll Cambridge (BA); *m* 3 April 1985, Catherine (Kitty), da of Alexander N Vernicos, of Athens; 2 step s (John b 8 Oct 1970, Alexander b 11 Oct 1975), 1 step da (Marina b 12 June 1972); *Career* co fndr and ptnr Poseidon Shipping Agencies 1964 (partnership dis 1970), fndr Lemos Maritime Co Ltd 1970-; *Recreations* travelling and reading, antiquarian book collection; *Clubs* Annabel's; *Style—* Costas Lemos, Esq; Lemos Maritime Co Ltd, 107 Fleet St, London EC4 (☎ 071 583 8441)

LEMOS, Capt Marcos Dimitris; s of Dimitris Marcos Lemos (d 1956), of Greece, and Kalliopy, *née* Lyras (d 1943); *b* 7 Oct 1927; *Educ* Gymnasium Athens; *m* 1, 1952 (m dis 1981), Chrysanthi; 1 s (Dimitris b 1956), 2 da (Kalliopy b 1958, Elly b 1959); m 2, 1981, Penelope Anne; 1 s (Antonis b 1984), 1 da (Loukia b 1987); *Career* Greek Mercantile Marine 1947-52; racehorse owner and breeder 1960-, first horse owned Marathon Runner; former owner: Warren Hill Stud, Ashley Heath Stud, Fitzroy Stables Newmarket; best horses owned: Petingo (1000 Guineas 1984), Averof, Cavo Doro, Julio Mariner (St Leger 1978), Pebbles; best horses bred: Averof, Pebbles (1000 Guineas, Champion Stakes, Eclipse, Breeders Cup); md: Lemos & Pateras Ltd 1956-87, Eurodynamic Construction SA Greece 1987-; hon memb Jockey Club; *Recreations* horse racing, sailing, reading, swimming; *Style—* Capt Marcos Lemos; (☎ 301 8944120, fax 301 894976)

LEMPRIERE-ROBIN, Brig Raoul Charles; OBE (1956); s of Capt Charles Harold Robin (ka 1917), and Yvonne, da and heiress of Jurat Reginald Raoul Lempriere, CBE, of Rosel Manor, Jersey (she m 2, 1931, Lt-Col Christopher J M Riley, MC, and d 1948) (*see* Burke's Landed Gentry, 18 edn, vol iii); *b* 6 Sept 1914; *Educ* Eton, Univ Coll Oxford (MA); *m* 6 Jan 1955, Sheelagh, da of Lt-Col Charles Edgar Maturin-Baird, of Langham, Colchester; 1 da (Emma b 1965); *Career* cmmnd Coldstream Gds 1935, served in BEF 1939, Madagascar, India, Italy, Malaya, M East and Jordan (ret as Brig 1966); memb States of Jersey 1969-78; Seigneur de Rosel, Jersey; Hereditary Butler to HM The Queen in Jersey; *Recreations* gardening, sailing; *Clubs* White's; *Style—* Brig Raoul Lempriere-Robin, OBE; Rosel Manor, Jersey (☎ 0534 52611)

LENG, Gen Sir Peter John Hall; KCB (1978, CB 1975), MBE (1962), MC (1945); s of J Leng; *b* 9 May 1925; *Educ* Bradfield; *m* 1 (m dis), Virginia Rosemary Pearson; 3 s, 2 da; m 2, 1981, Mrs Flavia Tower, da of Lt-Gen Sir Frederick Browning, KCVO, DSO (d 1965), and Dame Daphne du Maurier, DBE (d 1989); *Career* cmmnd 1944, served WWII, Cdr Land Forces NI 1973-75, Dir Mil Operations MOD 1975-78, Cdr 1 (Br) Corps 1978-80, Master-Gen of the Ordnance 1981-83, ret; Col Cmdt: RAVC 1976, RMP 1976; *Style—* Gen Sir Peter Leng, KCB, MBE, MC; 409 Hawkins House, Dolphin Sq, London SW1V 3LX

LENG, Virginia Helen Antoinette; MBE (1986); da of Col Ronald Morris Holgate (d 1980), and Heather Alice Mary, *née* Rice; *b* 1 Feb 1955; *Educ* abroad, Bedgebury Park Goudhurst Kent; *m* 7 Dec 1985 (m dis 1989), Hamish Peter Leng, s of Gen Sir Peter Leng, KCB, MBE, MC, *qv*; *Career* equestrian; Three Day Event wins incl: Jr Euro Champion 1974, Mini Olympics 1975, Euro Championships (team Gold) 1981, World Championships (team Gold) 1982, Euro Championships (team Silver) 1983, Olympic Games (team Silver) 1984, Euro Championships (team Gold) 1985, World Championships (team Gold) 1986, Olympic Games (team Silver) 1988; winner Burghley 1983, 1984, 1985, 1986, 1989 (Euro Championship, horse Master Craftsman); winner Badminton 1985, 1989 (horse Master Craftsman); individual Euro champion 1985, 1987 and 1989; World champion 1986; Olympics (individual Bronze 1984,1988); dir P and N Co; involved in Riding for the Disabled; Hon Freeman (Loriners) Worshipful Co of Saddlers 1990; *Recreations* skiing, sunning, sightseeing; *Style—* Mrs Virginia H A Leng, MBE; Ivyleaze, Acton Turville, Badminton, Avon (☎ 045421 681)

LENHAM, Neil John; s of Leslie John Lenham, and Valerie Ann, *née* Corney; *b* 17 Dec 1965; *Educ* Brighton Coll; *Career* professional cricketer; debut Sussex CCC 1984, awarded county cap 1990; capt Young England tour W Indies 1984; public schs record for runs scored in a season (1534 in 1984); Sussex player of the year 1990; *Recreations* music, golf, squash; *Style—* Neil Lenham, Esq; Sussex CCC, County Cricket Ground, Hove, Sussex (0273 732161)

LENNARD, Thomas William Jay; s of Thomas Jay Lennard, MBE, of 36 Heugh St, Falkirk, Stirlingshire, Scotland, and Elizabeth Jemima Mary Patricia, *née* Poole; *b* 25 Oct 1953; *Educ* Clifton, Univ of Newcastle Upon Tyne (MB BS, MD); *m* 8 July 1978, Anne Lesley, da of Cyril Barber, of 29 Athold St, Queens Drive, Ossett, W Yorks; 2 s (James Matthew Thomas b 1984, Jonathan Alexander Thomas b 1987); *Career* lectr in surgery Univ of Newcastle Upon Tyne 1982-88, sr lectr and conslt surgn Univ of Newcastle Upon Tyne and Royal Victoria Infirmary Newcastle 1988-; memb N of England Surgical Soc; FRCS 1980; *Books* Going into Hospital (1988); *Recreations* fly fishing, gardening; *Style—* Thomas Lennard, Esq; Ward 1, Royal Victoria Infirmary, Queen Victoria Rd, Newcastle Upon Tyne NE1 4LP (☎ 091 2325131)

LENNARD-JONES, Prof John Edward; s of Sir John Lennard-Jones, KBE (d 1954), of The Clock House, Keele, Staffs, and Kathleen Mary, *née* Lennard; *b* 29 Jan 1927; *Educ* King's Coll Choir Sch Cambridge, Gresham's, CCC Cambridge (MA, MD), UCH Med Sch London; *m* 19 Feb 1955, Verna Margaret, da of Ebenezer Albert Down (d 1960); 4 s (David b 1956, Peter b 1958, Andrew b 1960, Timothy b 1964); *Career* memb MRC Gastroenterology Res Unit Central Middx Hosp 1963-65, conslt gastroenterologist St Marks Hosp London 1965- (emeritus prof), conslt physician UCH 1965-74, prof of gastroentology London Hosp Med Coll 1974-87; author scientific papers on: gen med, gastroenterology, nutrition; Sir Arthur Hurst Lecture Br Soc of Gastroenterology 1973, Humphrey Davy Rolleston Lecture RCP 1977, Schorstein Lecture London Hosp Med Coll 1987; chm Med Ctee St Mark's Hosp 1985-90; Br Soc of Gastrenterology: hon sec 1965-70, memb Cncl 1965-90, pres 1983; memb Cncl

RCP 1986-89 (chm Gastroenterology Ctee 1985-89), vice chm Nat Assoc for Colitis and Crohn's Disease 1987-89 (chm Med Advsy Ctee 1979-90), hon memb Swedish Soc of Gastroenterology; membre d'honneur: Swiss Soc of Gastroenterology, French Soc of Gastroenterology; circuit steward Wembley and Golders Green Methodist Circuit; FRCP 1968; *Books* Clinical Gastroentology (jtly, 1968); *Recreations* ornithology, golf, gardening; *Style—* Prof John Lennard-Jones; 55 The Pryors, East Heath Rd, London NW3 1BP (☎ 071 435 6990); St Mark's Hospital, City Rd, London EC1V 2PS (☎ 071 601 7910)

LENNON, Dennis; CBE (1968), MC (1942); s of John Joseph Lennon (d 1978), and Eleanor, *née* Farrell (d 1974); *b* 23 June 1918; *Educ* Merchant Taylors', UCL; *m* 3 Sept 1947, Else Bull, da of Bjarna Bull Anderssen, of Bergen, Norway; 3 s (Christopher b 1950, Nicolas b 1952, Peter b 1956); *Career* WWII Maj Royal Engr (despatches 1940), 1 Armed Div France 1940, 7 Armed Div N Africa Alamein to Tunis, Italy, South to North 6 Armed Div, taken prisoner in St Valery and escaped through France and Spain to Gibraltar; architect private practice; Main Chalcot Estate Camden, Ridgeway Hotel Lusaka, RST HQ Building Lusaka, Royal Opera House (conslt for 10 years incl 6 State Galas), hotels and restaurants for J Lyons, Jaeger thirty shops, Harrow Sch, Shepherd Churchill Hall; co-ordinator and principle designer of: the interior design of Queen Elizabeth 2, Glyndeborne set for Richard Strauss Capriccio, Leeds Castle, Ritz Hotel, Stafford Hotel, Docklands Ind Estate, Commercial Union Main Executive Floors, Sainsburys HQ, Rothschild HQ, The Arts Club Dover St, planning permission for Criterion site Piccadilly; FRIBA, FSIA, FRSA; *Recreations* the arts; *Clubs* Savile, Royal Thames Yacht; *Style—* Dennis Lennon, Esq, CBE, MC; Hamper Mill, Watford, Herts (☎ 0923 34445); 3 Fitzhardinge St, London W1 (☎ 071 935 1181)

LENNOX; *see*: Gordon Lennox

LENNOX, Annie; da of Thomas A Lennox (d 1986), and Dorothy, *née* Ferguson; *b* 25 Dec 1954; *Educ* Aberdeen HS for Girls, RAM (ARAM); *m* Uri Fruchtmann, s of Benjamin Fruchtmann; 1 da (Lola Lennox Fruchtmann b 10 Dec 1990); *Career* singer/songwriter; band memb: The Tourists (formed 1978, split 1980), The Eurythmics (formed with Dave Stewart 1982); Eurythmics tours: Folie a Deux (UK Feb-March 1983, Europe March 1983), Kiss Me Quick (UK June 1983, USA (first tour) Aug-Sept 1983), Only Fools and Horses (UK Oct-Dec 1983), Touch (Europe Feb-May 1984, USA May and Aug-Oct 1984), Revenge (World tour Aug 1986-March 1987), Revival (World tour Sept 1989-Jan 1990); Singles awards: Sweet Dreams (Silver UK, Gold Canada), Who's That Girl (Silver UK), Here Comes The Rain Again (Gold Canada); Album awards: Sweet Dreams (Platinum UK and Canada), Touch (Double Platinum Canada, Platinum RIAA and UK), Sweet Dreams (Double Platinum Canada), Be Yourself Tonight (Triple Platinum Aust, Double Platinum Canada), Revenge (Triple Platinum Aust, Platinum UK), We Two Are One (Platinum UK and Canada), Savage (Gold Sweden); other awards incl: best UK video (for Love Is A Stranger) 1982, best video album (for Sweet Dreams) Grammy Awards, best female performance (for Sweet Dreams), Ivor Novello award for best pop song (Sweet Dreams) Br Acad of Songwriters, winner American Soc of Composers award, BPI award for best female vocalist 1982/83, 1987/88 and 1989/90; other Album awards: Replity Effect (with The Tourists, Silver UK, winner Silver UK for single I Only Wanna Be With You), Who's Zoomin Who! (Aretha Franklin, Silver UK); *Style—* Ms Annie Lennox; c/o 19 Management, Unit 32, Ransomes Dock, 35-37 Parkgate Rd, London SW11 4NP (☎ 071 228 4000, fax 071 924 1608)

LENNOX, Michael James Madill; s of Rev James Lennox, of 30 Hazel Beck, Bingley, Yorks, and May Ester, *née* Rosenthal; *b* 11 Sept 1943; *Educ* St John's Sch Leatherhead; *m* 4 May 1968, Ingrid Susan Elizabeth, da of Ronald Ewart Binns; 1 s (Timothy b 6 Dec 1974), 1 da (Rebecca b 6 Oct 1972); *Career* CA; Armitage & Norton Bradford 1961-68, Price Waterhouse (Montreal) 1968-70, asst controller Honeywell Ltd Toronto 1970-73, euro business planning controller Honeywell Europe Brussels 1973-78, fin dir Cutler Hammer Europa Ltd (Bedford) 1978-85; gp fin dir: C P Roberts & Co Ltd 1985-88, Central Trailer Rentco Ltd 1988-90; fin dir Charterhouse Development Capital Ltd 1990 FCA; *Recreations* tennis, squash, skiing; *Style—* Michael Lennox, Esq; Old Cottage Farm, Top End, Renhold, Bedford MK41 OLS (☎ 0234 870370)

LENNOX-BOYD, Hon Benjamin Alan; s and h of 2 Viscount Boyd of Merton; *b* 21 Oct 1964; *Educ* Millfield; *Style—* The Hon Benjamin Lennox-Boyd; Wiveliscombe, Saltash, Cornwall

LENNOX-BOYD, Hon Charlotte Mary; da of 2 Viscount Boyd of Merton; *b* 16 April 1963; *Educ* Cheltenham Ladies' Coll, UCL; *Style—* The Hon Charlotte Lennox-Boyd; 9 Eland Rd, London SW11

LENNOX-BOYD, Hon Christopher Alan; s of 1 Viscount Boyd of Merton, CH, PC, DL (d 1983), and Patricia, Viscountess Boyd of Merton, *qv*; bro of 2 Viscount Boyd of Merton, *qv*, and Hon Mark Lennox-Boyd, MP, *qv*; *b* 22 July 1941; *Educ* Eton, ChCh Oxford; *Books* Axel Herman Haig, The Victoria Vision of the Middle Ages (co-author), George Stubbs, The Complete Graphic Works (co-author); *Clubs* Carlton, Brooks's; *Style—* The Hon Christopher Lennox-Boyd

LENNOX-BOYD, Hon Mark Alexander; MP (C) Morecambe and Lunesdale (formerly Lonsdale) 1983-; s of 1 Viscount Boyd of Merton, CH, PC, DL (d 1983), and Patricia, Viscountess Boyd of Merton, *qv*; bro of 2 Viscount Boyd of Merton and Hon Christopher Lennox-Boyd, *qqv*; *b* 4 May 1943; *Educ* Eton, Ch Ch Oxford; *m* 1974, Mrs Arabella Lacloche, o da of Piero Parisi, of Rome; 1 da (Patricia Irene b 1980); *Career* called to the Bar Inner Temple 1968; MP (C) Morecambe and Lonsdale 1979-83; PPS to Chllr of Exchequer (Rt Hon Nigel Lawson) 1983-84; govt whip 1984-88, PPS to the Prime Minister 1988-90, Parly Under-Sec of State FCO 1990-; *Style—* The Hon Mark Lennox-Boyd, MP; House of Commons, London SW1

LENON, Andrew Ralph Fitzmaurice; s of Philip John Fitzmaurice, of Dinton, Wilts, and Jane Alethia, *née* Brooke; *b* 7 April 1957; *Educ* St Johns Sch Leatherhead, Lincoln Coll Oxford (BA); *m* 5 Sept 1987, Sheila, da of Donald Cook (d 1977); 1 s (George b 1989); *Career* called to the Bar Lincoln's Inn 1982; *Style—* Andrew Lenon, Esq; 1 Essex Court, Temple, London EC4Y 9AR (☎ 071 583 2000)

LENOX-CONYNGHAM, Charles Denis; s of Capt Alwyn Douglas Lenox-Conyngham, RN, of Benenden, Kent, and Margaret Cecilia, *née* Clear; *b* 24 Jan 1935; *Educ* Winchester, Magdalen Coll Oxford (MA), Wharton Sch of Business Admin, Univ of Pennsylvania; *m* 15 April 1972, Helga Gerrit, da of Lt-Gen Hans von Liebach (d 1966), of Berlin; 1 s (Patrick b 1972), 1 da (Laura b 1974); *Career* cmmnd 2 Lt Royal Hussars, served Germany 1954-56; md: Blue Funnel Line 1970, Price and Pierce 1985; exec dir Ocean Transport & Trading 1972-85, chm and chief exec Sealink (UK) Ltd 1985-90; *Recreations* family, gardening, tennis, squash, skiing; *Clubs* RAC; *Style—* Charles Lenox-Conyngham, Esq; Yew Tree House, Benenden, Kent TN17 3EJ (☎ 0580 240 630); Sealink Stena Line, Charter House, Park Street, Ashford, Kent TN24 8EX

LENSKA, RULA (aka Rozamaria Luara Lubienska); da of Count Ludwig Lubienski, and Elizabeth Carroll, *née* Tyszkiewicz; *b* 30 Sept 1947; *Educ* Jesus & Mary Covent Willesden Green, Ursuline Convent Westgate-on-Sea, Pitmans Secretarial Coll Holborn, Weber Douglas Acad of Dramatic Art; *m* 1 (m dis), Brian Deacon; 1 da (Lara b 17 Aug 1979); m 2, Dennis Waterman; *Career* actress; theatre: Suddenly At Home (Durbridge, Windsor, Fortune Theatre) 1970-72, Secretary Bird, Lady Capulet in Romeo and Juliet, Titania in Midsummer Night's Dream (Regents Park Open Air Theatre), Regina in Ghosts (Swan Theatre), Doris in Suddenly At Home (Old Vic, Aust, NZ), Double Double, The Real Thing (Guildford, Aust), Elvira in Blithe Spirit (Lyric Hammersmith), Temptation (Palace Theatre London), The Physicists; TV appearances incl: Dixon of Dock Green, Rock Follies, Amazing Stories, Take a Letter Mr Jones, Robin of Sherwood, Return of the Native, Design for Living, Conversations with a Stranger, Aubrey Beardsley, Jackanory, The Saint, The Godmother, Cluedo; many appearances on panel games; co-presenter woman's prog (Sky TV); fluent in Polish, French, Italian, German; hot air balloon pilot; fndr memb Elefriends, hon vice pres Operation Raleigh, tstee Angels International; *Recreations* music, reading, snooker, photography, conservation, travel, embroidery, making jewellery, alternative medicine and healing; *Clubs* Tramp, Stringfellows, Polish Hearth; *Style—* Ms Rula Lenska; Vernon Conway, 5 Spring St, Paddington, London W2 (☎ 071 262 5506/7)

LENT, Martin Victor; s of Eric Lent, of Pinner, Middx, and Tina, *née* Koten (d 1990); *b* 18 June 1954; *Educ* John Lyon Sch Harrow-on-the-Hill; *m* 16 Sept 1979 (m dis 1990), Melanie Ruth, *qv*, da of Cyril Searle, of London; *Career* Malvern & Co 1973-77, Emile Woolf and Assocs 1977-79, Premier Clay Litho Ltd 1979-80, Crocodile 1980-81; chm: Pamplemousse 1982-, Br Fashion Cncl Exec, Br Fashion Cncl Exhibitors Ctee; ACA, FCA 1981; *Recreations* tennis, skiing, theatre, gourmet, travel, reading; *Clubs* Vanderbilt, Stocks, Ragdale; *Style—* Martin Lent, Esq; The Tower, Well Rd, Hampstead, London NW3; Pamplemousse, 8-14 St Pancras Way, Camden Town, London NW1 OQJ (☎ 071 387 8797, fax 071 383 3602)

LENT, Melanie Ruth; da of Cyril Searle, of Woodford, Essex, and Ita, *née* Bursztyn; *b* 31 Aug 1958; *Educ* Caterham Co Sch Essex, London Sch of Fashion, Ravensbourne Coll of Art (BA); *Career* designer: Polly Peck plc 1979-80, Fitrite 1980-81; design dir Pamplemousse 1982-; *Recreations* skiing, linguistics, aerobics, travel; *Clubs* Champneys Heath; *Style—* Mrs Melanie Lent; Pamplemousse, 8-14 St Pancras Way, Camden Town, London NW1 OQS (☎ 071 387 8797, fax 071 387 0320, telex 295383 PAMPLE G)

LENTON, (Aylmer) Ingram; s of Albert Lenton (d 1981), and Olive Lenton; *b* 19 May 1927; *Educ* Leeds GS, Magdalen Coll Oxford, Univ of Leeds; *m* 1951, Ursula Kathleen, da of Cyril Henry Brownlow King (d 1964); 1 s, 2 da; *Career* md South African Nylon Spinners 1964-66, dir ICI Fibres 1966-67, md John Heathcoat & Co 1967-75; chm: Bowater UK Paper Co 1976-78, Bowater UK Ltd 1979-81, John Heathcoat & Co (Hldgs) Ltd 1984; md Bowater Corp 1981-84 (dir 1979-), chm and md Bowater Industs plc 1984-87, dep chm Watts Blake Bearne & Co plc 1989 (dir 1987-); chm: Atkins Holdings Ltd 1989 (dir 1987-), Crown Agents 1987, Chapman Industries plc 1988-89, Scapa Group plc 1988, Compass Group plc 1987; memb Ct of Assts Worshipful Co of Stationers and Newspaper Makers; hon fell Br Orthopaedic Assoc 1990; *Recreations* golf, fencing, walking, fishing; *Clubs* IOD; *Style—* Dr A I Lenton

LENTON, John Robert; s of Rev Robert Vincent Lenton, vicar of Lacock, Wilts (ret); *b* 13 May 1946; *Educ* Prince of Wales Sch Nairobi, Exeter Coll Oxford, Harvard Business Sch; *m* 1967, Ann Cathrine; 1 s, 1 da; *Career* specialist in fin mktg; International Factors Ltd: dir sales and mktg 1976, dir operations 1977, dir sales and mktg 1979; sr vice pres Euro operating centre and customer servs American Express 1988- (vice pres fin and planning 1982-86, vice pres and gen mangr N Europe 1986-88); *Recreations* skiing, choral singing, treble recorder; *Style—* John Lenton, Esq; 11 Wilbury Gdns, Hove, Sussex (☎ office 0273 693555)

LENYGON, Bryan Norman; s of the late Maj Frank Norman Lenygon, of Highfield, Bells Yew Green, E Sussex, and Marjorie Winifred, *née* Healey; *b* 6 May 1932; *Educ* Univ of London (MA, LLB); *m* 27 Oct 1967, Diana Jane, da of Betty Patricia Baxter, of Hingham, Norfolk; 2 da (Fiona b 1957, Sally b 1961); *Career* called to the Bar Gray's Inn 1976; dir: English-Caledonian Investment plc, The HMG Group plc, North American Gas Investment Trust plc, The Turkey Trust plc; gen cmmr City of London; Freeman City of London; FCA, FCIS, ATII; *Recreations* tennis; *Clubs* City of London, City Livery; *Style—* Bryan Lenygon, Esq; Highfield, Bells Yew Green, E Sussex TN3 9AP (☎ 0892 75 343)

LEON, Alexander John; s and h of Sir John Ronald Leon, 4 Bt; *b* 3 May 1965; *Educ* Bryanston; *Career* music prodn asst; *Recreations* skiing, watersports, tennis, cricket; *Style—* Alexander Leon, Esq; 8 Markham St, London SW3 (☎ 071 589 2230)

LEON, Dowager Lady; Alice Mary; da of late Dr Thomas Holt; *b* 10 Sept 1919; *Educ* Queen Ethelburga's Sch Harrogate; *m* 1947, as his 3 w, Sir Ronald George Leon, 3 Bt (d 1964); *Career* served FANY 1941-46; *Style—* Dowager Lady Leon; 83 Lexham Gdns, London W8

LEON, Sir John Ronald; 4 Bt (UK 1911); s of Sir Ronald George Leon, 3 Bt (d 1964), and his 1 w, Dorothy Katharine (the actress Kay Hammond; d 1980), da of Cdr Sir Guy Standing, KBE (d 1937), and who m 2, Sir John Clements, CBE, *qv*; *b* 16 Aug 1934; *Educ* Eton, Millfield, Byam Shaw Sch of Art; *m* 1, 1961 (m dis 1972), Jill, da of Jack Melford, actor; 1 s (Alexander); m 2, 7 April 1984, Sarah Kate, da of Bryan John Forbes, film dir; 1 s (Archie b 28 July 1986), 2 da (India b 25 June 1985, Octavia b 3 Nov 1989); *Heir* s, Alexander John Leon, *qv*; *Career* 2 Lt KRRC 1953-55; actor (as John Standing); stage plays include: The Importance of Being Earnest (1968), Ring Round the Moon (1969), Arms and the Man (1970), Sense of Detachment (1972), Private Lives (1973), St Joan (1973), Jingo (1976), The Philanderer (1978), Plunder (1978), Close of Play (1979), Tonight at 8.30 (1981), Biko Inquest (1984), Rough Crossing (1985); films include: King Rat (1965), Walk Don't Run (1965), The Eagle Has Landed (1976), Rogue Male (1976), The Legacy (1977); television performances: The First Churchills, Charley's Aunt, Tinker, Tailor, Soldier, Spy; American television: Lime Street (1985), Murder She Wrote (1989), LA Law (1990); artist (watercolours); memb Green Peace; *Recreations* painting, fishing; *Style—* Sir John Leon, Bt; c/o William Morris, 31-32 Soho Square, London W1V 5DG

LEON, Ronald; s of Capt Alec Leon (D 1973), and Capt Perla Glucksmann (d 1970); *b* 11 Dec 1931; *Educ* Arnold Sch Blackpool, Royal Tech Coll Salford; *m* 19 Nov 1971, Susana, da of Alberto Mamrud, of Buenos Aires, Argentina; 2 s (Nick b 1972, Andrew b 1974); *Career* Army Cadet Force 1943-50; regnl mangr Latin America Werner Managment Consultants NY 1960-73; dir: International Business Development 1973-76, Visa International Inc San Francisco California 1973-76; md Occidental Petroleum's subsids Mexico and Venezuela 1976-80; chm: Oxy Metal Industries GB Ltd 1980-84, EFCO Ltd 1984-; chm Br Industl Furnace Constructors Assoc, pres Euro Furnace Manufacturers Assoc; ATI, ARTCS; *Recreations* hiking; *Style—* Ronald Leon, Esq; Sefton, The Hockering, Woking, Surrey (☎ 04837 60292); Efco Ltd, Forsyth Rd, Sheerwater, Woking, Surrey GU21 5RZ (☎ 04837 26433, fax 04837 73818, telex 859465)

LEONARD, Baroness; Glenys Evelyn; da of Ernest Kenny; *m* 1945, Baron Leonard, OBE (Life Peer, d 1983); 1 s, 1 da; *Style—* The Rt Hon the Lady Leonard; 19 Queen Anne, Cardiff

LEONARD, Rt Rev and Rt Hon Graham Douglas; *see*: London, Bishop of

LEONARD, His Hon James Charles Beresford Whyte; s of late Hon James Weston Leonard, KC, of Johannesburg; *b* 1905; *Educ* Clifton, ChCh Oxford; *m* 1939,

Barbara Helen (d 1989), da of Capt William Incledon-Webber (d 1938), of Buckland House, Braunton, N Devon; 2 s, 1 da; *Career* barr Inner Temple 1928, rec of Walsall 1951-64, bencher 1961; dep chm: Oxfordshire QS 1962-71, County and Inner London QS and Middx QS 1965-72; circuit judge 1972-79, judge of Mayor's and City of London Ct 1973-79; junior counsel min: Agriculture Fisheries and Food, Forestry Cmmn; Statutory Ctee Pharmaceutical Soc of GB 1962-65; *Style—* His Hon James Leonard; Cross Trees, Sutton Courtenay, Oxon (☎ 0235 848230)

LEONARD, Dr John Cyril; s of Cyril Leonard (d 1985), of Pinner, and Kate, *née* Whyte (d 1955); *b* 19 June 1927; *Educ* Ealing GS, Westminster Hosp Med Sch Univ of London (MD, MRCP, FRCP); *m* 20 July 1963, Edith Marjorie, da of Arthur Creighton, of Rotherham; 2 s (Richard b 1964, Andrew b 1967); *Career* unit conslt physician Withington Hosp Manchester 1963-89 (Unit gen mangr 1985-89); *Books* A Guide to Cardiology (1961); *Recreations* visiting ancient churches; *Style—* Dr John Leonard; 87 Palatine Road, Manchester

LEONARD, Hon Mr Justice; Hon Sir (Hamilton) John Leonard; s of Arthur Leonard; *b* 28 April 1926; *Educ* Dean Close Sch Cheltenham, BNC Oxford; *m* 1948, Doreen, yr da of late Lt-Col Sidney Parker, OBE; 1 s, 1 da; *Career* served Coldstream Gds (Capt) 1944-47; called to the Bar Inner Temple 1951, cmmr Central Criminal Ct 1969-71, dep chm Surrey QS 1969-71, QC 1969, rec Crown Court 1972-78, circuit judge 1978-81, high court judge Queen's Bench 1981-, presiding judge Wales and Chester Circuit 1982-86; Common Serjeant City of London 1979-81; memb: Gen Cncl of Bar 1970-74, Judicial Studies Bd 1979-82, Cncl Hurstpierpoint Coll 1975-82; govr Dean Close Sch 1986-, former chm Criminal Bar Assoc; Liveryman Worshipful Co of Plaisterers; HM Lt City London 1980-81; kt 1981; *Style—* The Hon Mr Justice Leonard; Royal Courts of Justice, Strand, London WC2A 2LL

LEONARD, John Patrick; s of Rt Rev MPG Leonard, DSO (d 1963), and Kathleen Mary, *née* Knights-Smith; *b* 3 Sept 1935; *Educ* Glasgow Acad, Trinity Coll Glenalmond, Selwyn Coll Cambridge (BA), Sch of Mil Survey Hermitage (Dip land surveying), Univ Coll Cambridge (Dip Devpt Studies); *m* 6 Aug 1960, Christine Joan, da of Eric Mayer; 1 s (Adam Patrick b 1965 d 1984), 2 da (Catherine b 1963 d 1965, Rachel Ann b 1967); *Career* Midshipman and Sub Lt RN 1954-56; maths teacher Town Close Prep Sch 1957; Directorate of Overseas Surveys (i/c Survey Parties Jamaica, Br Honduras, Nigera, Sierra Leone, Mauritius and Sarawak) 1961-71; Ordnance Survey: regnl mangr W Midlands 1972-78, asst dir surveys 1978-82, head of prodn 1982-84, dir mktg planning and devpt 1984-; pres Land Surveyors Div RICS 1990-91; FRICS 1985 (ARICS 1964); *Recreations* mountaineering, golf, photography; *Style—* John Leonard, Esq; Dellbrook, Hubert Road, St Cross, Winchester, Hants S023 9RG (☎ 0962 865093); Ordnance Survey, Romsey Rd, Maybush, Southampton, Hants S09 4DH (☎ 0703 792558, fax 0703 792888)

LEONARD, John Thirlestane; CBE (1984); o s of John Gifford Leonard, of Oxhey Cottage, Oxhey Woods, Northwood, Middx; *b* 10 July 1922; *Educ* Rugby; *m* 1946, Gabrielle Mary Leonard, MBE, da of Felix Feeny, of 89 Bromley Rd, Beckenham, Kent; 3 s, 2 da; *Career* RN 1941-46, Lt RNVR; chm and chief exec Carless Capel and Leonard plc 1977-89 (chief exec 1964-77), chm British International Oil Exploration Cos (BRINDEX) 1983; chm London C of C and Indust 1984-86, vice pres Inst of Petroleum 1985-88, memb Cncl Univ of Southampton 1989-; FCA, CBIM, FInstPet; *Recreations* yachting, gardening, reading; *Clubs* Naval, Royal Solent Yacht (tstee), Little Ship; *Style—* John Leonard, Esq, CBE; Solent View Cottage, Long's Wharf, Yarmouth, Isle of Wight PO41 0PW (☎ 0983 760390, fax 0983 761105)

LEONARD, (James) Nigel Robert; s of Norman Arthur Leonard, of Limpsfield Chart, Surrey, and Patricia Jessie, *née* Barrett; *b* 23 March 1952; *Educ* Forest Sch, RCM; *Career* operatic bass; work at ENO incl: Aida and Damnation of Faust 1980, Fidelio and Tosca 1981, The Flying Dutchman and Boris Godunov 1982, Don Carlos and The Magic Flute 1983, Rigoletto and Mazeppa 1984, Faust and the Mastersingers 1985, Don Giovanni and Parsifal 1986, Akhnaten and Queen of Spades 1987, La Bohème and King Lear 1988-89; Simone Boccanegra Royal Opera House 1980; notable roles incl: Sarastro in The Magic Flute, Zaccariah in Nabucco, King Philip in Don Carlos, Fiesco in Simone Boccanegra; TV appearances incl: Rigoletto, Lady Macbeth, Akhnaten, Mary Stuart; ARCM; *Recreations* sailing, collecting fountain pens, bridge; *Clubs* Players Theatre; *Style—* Nigel Leonard, Esq; 2 Lower Chart Cottages, Chart Lane, Brasted Chart, nr Westerham, Kent TN16 1LN (☎ 0959 62847); c/o English National Opera, St Martins Lane, London WC2; Flat 2, 24 Sutherland St, London SW1

LEONARD, Paul Michael; *b* 14 Jan 1942; *Educ* Finchley GS, Univ of Sheffield (LLB); *m* 1970, Diana Clare, *née* Bryce-Curtis; 2 s (Nick, Guy), 1 da (Emily); *Career* admitted slr 1966; Freshfields: articled clerk 1964-66, asst slr 1966-72, litigation ptnr 1972-, managing ptnr Litigation Dept 1988-90, jtly responsible for recruitment of trainee slrs; memb DTI panel for appeals under Consumer Credit and Estate Agents Acts; memb Cncl Trinity Hospice (chm House Ctee); *Recreations* cricket, skiing, Aston Martins, paintings of Paul Marny; *Clubs* MCC; *Style—* Paul Leonard, Esq; Freshfields, Whitefriars, 65 Fleet St, London EC4Y 1HS (☎ 071 936 4000, fax 071 832 7246)

LEONARD, Peter Ernest; s of Derrick Edward Leonard, and Peggy May, *née* Hobbs; *b* 14 Feb 1954; *Educ* Soham GS, Kingston Poly (BA), Northwestern Univ (MA); *Career* Frederick Gibberd and Partners 1978-79, Conran Associates 1979-81, chm Peter Leonard Associated 1981-; *Style—* Peter Leonard, Esq; 535 Kings Rd, London SW10 (☎ 071 352 1717, fax 071 351 4307)

LEONARD, Dr Robert Charles Frederick; s of André Lucien Maxime Leonard (d 1977), of Merthyr Tydfil, Wales, and Rosa Mary, *née* Taylor; *b* 11 May 1947; *Educ* Merthyr Tydfil Co GS, Charing Cross Hosp Med Sch (BSc, MB BS, MD); *m* 2 June 1973, Tania, da of Roland Charles Smith, of Louth, Lincs; 3 da (Victoria b 26 Sept 1974, Louisa b 26 Feb 1978, Emily b 18 Sept 1980); *Career* sr house offr: Charing Cross Hosp 1972, Hammersmith Hosp 1973; registrar Oxford Hosps 1974-76, fell Leukaemia Res Fund 1976-79, lectr and sr registrar Newcastle Hosps 1979-82, fell Cancer Res Campaign 1981-82, res fell Dana Farmer Cancer Inst Harvard Med Sch Boston 1982-82, hon conslt physician and sr lectr Clinical Oncology Edinburgh 1983-; chm: Lothian Health Bd Ethical Ctee on Med and Oncology, Educnl Ctee Assoc of Cancer Physicians; memb Ed Bd British Journal of Cancer; FRCPE 1984, American Soc of Clinincal Oncology; *Books* Understanding Cancer (1985); *Recreations* music, piano, soccer; *Style—* Dr Robert Leonard; 19 Craigcrook Rd, Edinburgh (☎ 031 332 2033); Department Clinical Oncology, Western General Hospital, Edinburgh (☎ 031 332 2525)

LEPLEY, Stephen Keith (Steve); s of Ernest Joseph Lepley (d 1989), and Joyce Elsie, *née* Walker; *b* 20 Aug 1954; *Educ* Stratford GS; *m* 11 Dec 1982, Tracey Ann, da of Terry Richardson; 1 s (Samuel b 17 July 1985), 2 da (Ann-Marie b 24 Sept 1979, Lauren b 28 July 1983); *Career* Cartwright Brice Ltd 1970-75 (trainee accountant, asst co accountant), co accountant Owlcliff Ltd 1975-78, asst gp accountant Victoria Sporting Group of Companies (take over by Playboy 1980) 1978-81, chief accountant McCormick Publicis Ltd 1983-84 (regnl accountant 1981-83), fin controller (assoc dir) Gold Greenless Trott Advertising 1986-88 (accountant 1984-86), fin dir Simons Palmer Denton Clemmow & Johnson Ltd 1988-; *Recreations* most sports particularly rugby and soccer; *Style—* Steve Lepley, Esq; 56 Inchbonnie Rd, 5 Woodham Ferrers, Chelmsford, Essex CM3 5GE (☎ 0245 323057); Simons Palmer Denton Clemmow & Johnson Ltd, 19-20 Noel St, London W1V 3PD (☎ 071 287 4455, fax 071 287 2672)

LEPPARD, Raymond John; CBE (1983); s of Albert Victor Leppard, and Bertha May, *née* Beck; *b* 11 Aug 1927; *Educ* Trinity Coll Cambridge; *Career* fell and lectr in music Trinity Coll Cambridge 1958-68, princ conductor BBC Northern Symphony Orch 1972-80, princ guest conductor St Louis Symphony Orch 1984-90, music dir Indianapolis Symphony Orch 1987-; Hon D Univ Bath 1972; hon memb: RAM 1972, GSM 1984; Hon FRCM 1984; Commendatore al Merito Della Republica Italiana 1974; *Books* Monteverda: IL Ballo Della Ingrate (1958), L'incoronazione Di Poppea (1962), L'Orfeo (1965), Cavalli: Messa Concertata (1966), L'Ormindo (1967), La Calisto (1969), IL Ritorno D'Ulisse (1972), L'Eqisto (1974), L'Orione (1983), Authenticity in Music Realisations (1988); *Recreations* theatre, books, friends, music; *Style—* Raymond Leppard, Esq, CBE; Colbert Artists Management, 11 West 57th Street, New York, NY 10019, USA (☎ 212 757 0782, fax 212 541 5179)

LEPSCHY, Giulio; s of Emilio Lepschy, and Sara, *née* Castelfranchi (d 1984); *b* 14 Jan 1935; *Educ* Liceo Marco Polo Venice, Univ of Pisa (Dott Lett), Scuola Normale Superiore (Dip & Perf Sc Norm Sup); *m* 20 Dec 1962 (Anna) Laura, da of Arnaldo Momigliano, Hon KBE (d 1987); *Career* Univ of Reading; lectr 1964-, reader 1967-, prof 1975-; FBA 1987-; *Publications* Saggi di Linguistica Italiana (1978), Intorno a Saussure A Survey of Structural Linguistics (1970), The Italian Language Today (with A L Lepschy, 1977), (1979), Mutamenti di Prospettiva nella Linguistica (1981), Nuovi Saggi di Linguistica Italiana (1989), Sulla Linguistica Moderna (1989), Storia della Linguistica (1990); *Style—* Prof Giulio Lepschy; Department of Italian Studies, The University, Whiteknights, Reading RG6 2AA (☎ 0734 875123 ext 7401)

LEPSCHY, Prof (Anna) Laura; da of Arnaldo Dante Momigliano, KBE (d 1987), of London, and Gemma Celestina, *née* Segre; *b* 30 Nov 1933; *Educ* Headington Sch Oxford, Somerville Coll Oxford; *m* 20 Dec 1962, Giulio Ciro Lepschy, s of Emilio Lepschy, of Venice; *Career* jr fell Univ of Bristol 1957-59, lectr in Italian Univ of Reading 1962-68 (asst lectr 1959-62), UCL: lectr in Italian 1968-79, sr lectr 1979-84, reader 1984-87, prof 1987-; memb: Soc for Italian Studies, Assoc for Study of Modern Italy, Pirandello Soc, Comparative Lit Assoc, Modern Humanities Res Assoc, Associazione Internazionale Studi Lingua and Letteratura Italiana; *Books* Santo Brasca, Viaggio in Terrasanta 1480 (ed, 1967), Tintoretto Observed (1983), Narrativa e Teatro fra Due Secoli (1984); *Recreations* swimming; *Style—* Prof Laura Lepschy; Department of Italian, University College, Gower St, London WC1 (☎ 071 387 7050, fax 071 387 8057)

LEROY-LEWIS, David Henry; s of Stuyvesant Henry LeRoy-Lewis (d 1956); *b* 14 June 1918; *Educ* Eton; *m* 1953, Cynthia Madeleine, da of Cdr John Christian Boldero, DSC, RN (d 1984), of Bridport, Dorset; 3 da (Jennifer (Mrs Herford), Zara (Mrs Webb), Victoria (Mrs Meakin)); *Career* former chm Akroyd & Smithers Ltd 1976-81, dep chm The Stock Exchange London 1973-76 (cncl memb 1961-81), chm TR North America Investmt Trust plc 1974-88, dep chm Touche Remnant & Co 1981-88 (dir 1974-88); non exec chm: R P Martin plc 1981-85, Henry Ansbacher Holdings plc 1982-88, Hill Martin plc 1989-; dir: TR Industrial & General Trust 1967-88, TR Trustees Corporation plc 1973-88, TR Energy plc 1980-89; memb IOD; FCA; *Clubs* MCC, Naval and Military; *Style—* David LeRoy-Lewis, Esq; Stoke House, Stoke, Andover, Hants SP11 0NP (☎ 0264 738 548)

LERWILL, Robert Earl; s of Colin Roy F Lerwill, and Patricia (Luck) Lerwill; *b* 21 Jan 1952; *Educ* Barnstaple GS, Gosport GS, Univ of Nottingham (BA); *m* Dec 1980, Carol H G Ruddock 1 s (Henry Robert b June 1985); *Career* Arthur Anderseon & Co: joined as articled clerk 1973, mangr 1978, sr mangr 1981-86; gp fin dir WPP Group plc 1986-; FCA (ACA 1977), MInstD 1987; *Recreations* travel; *Style—* Robert Lerwill, Esq; WPP Group plc, 27 Farm St, London W1X 6RD (☎ 071 408 2204, fax 071 493 6819)

LESEBERG, Michael; s of Lt Walter Leseberg (ka 1944), of Hamburg, and Karla, *née* Menge (d 1977); *b* 16 Feb 1940; *Educ* Germany Business Studies; *m* 27 Sept 1962, Traute, da of Johannes Plueschau, of Hamburg; 3 da (Birte b 1964, Petra b 1966, Katja b 1968); *Career* dir: Orimex Handelsgesellschaft MBH Hamburg 1969, Gilbert J McCaul (overseas) Ltd 1977, London Potato Futures Assoc 1983 (formerly chm), London Commodity Exchange Ltd 1984-87, Baltic Int Freight Futures Exchange 1985; md Gilbert J McCaul Ltd 1987 (overseas 1988); memb Cncl AFBD 1984-86; Stour Valley Music Soc; memb Baltic Exchange; *Recreations* music, tennis; *Style—* Michael Leseberg, Esq; Bridge House, 4 Borough High St, London, SE1 9QZ, (☎ 071 378 1415, fax 071 378 1126)

LESLIE, Sir (Colin) Alan Bettridge; s of Rupert Colin Leslie, and Gladys Hannah, *née* Bettridge; *b* 10 April 1922; *Educ* King Edward VII Sch Lytham, Merton Coll Oxford (MA); *m* 1, 1963, Anne Barbara, *née* Coates (d 1982); 2 da; m 2, 1983, Jean Margaret (Sally), wid of Dr Alan Cheatle; *Career* cmmnd RSF 1941-46; slr Stafford Clark & Co 1948-60, head of Legal Dept and co sec BOC Group (formerly BOC International, (British Oxygen Co)) 1960-83; Foreign Compensation Cmmn 1986-90, adjudicator Immigration Appeals 1990; pres Law Soc 1985-86 (vice pres 1984-86); kt 1986; *Recreations* fishing; *Clubs* United Oxford and Cambridge Univ; *Style—* Sir Alan Leslie; Tile Barn Cottage, Alfriston, East Sussex (☎ 0323 870 388); 36 Abingdon Rd, London W8 (☎ 071 937 2874)

LESLIE, Capt Alastair Pinckard; TD; s of Hon John Wayland Leslie (s of 19 Earl of Rothes); *b* 29 Dec 1934; *Educ* Eton; *m* 1963, Rosemary, da of Cdr Hubert Wyndham Barry, RN; 1 s (David b 1967, d 1989), 2 da (Fiona b 1965, Ann b 1973); *Career* Capt Royal Scots Fusiliers (TA); md Willis Faber & Dumas (Agencies) Ltd 1976-85, dir A P Leslie Underwriting Agency Ltd and other Lloyds underwriting agencies, dir Utd Goldfields NL until 1988; memb Queen's Body Guard for Scotland (The Royal Co of Archers); Liveryman Worshipful Co of Clothworkers; *Recreations* fishing, stalking, shooting; *Clubs* Boodle's, Pratt's; *Style—* Capt Alastair Leslie, TD; Seasyde House, Errol, Perthshire (☎ 082 12 500); 7 Wallgrave Rd, London SW5 0RL (☎ 071 370 7017); Office: Marlon House, 71 Mauk Lane, EC3 (☎ 071 702 3891)

LESLIE, Hon Alexander John; s of 21 Earl of Rothes; *b* 1962; *Educ* Eton; *m* 24 Feb 1990, Tina L, da of Dr T E Gordon, of Westmoreland Drive, Orlando, Florida, USA; *Career* wine trade, insurance broking, conference organisation; *Style—* The Hon Alexander Leslie; Flat B, 25 Bolton Gardens, London SW5

LESLIE, David Carnegie; Baron of Leslie; o s of David Brown Leslie (d 1985), of Aberdeen, and Ethel Watson, *née* Kenn; *b* 1 Feb 1943; *Educ* Aberdeen GS, Scott Sutherland Sch of Architecture (Dip Arch); *m* 7 June 1967, Leslie Margaret, da of Roderick Allen Stuart (d 1970), of Aberdeen; 2 da (Angela Elizabeth b 1970, Yvonne Margaret b 1972); *Career* chartered architect; ptnr Leslie Castle by Insch; restorer of ruined Leslie Castle, ancestral home of the Leslies; Freeman of City of London 1987, Burgess of Trade Aberdeen 1979, Burgess of Guild Aberdeen 1984; RIBA 1974, ARIAS 1979, FSA (Scot) 1981; KSG 1984; *Recreations* skiing, shooting, gardening, genealogy; *Clubs* Conservative; *Style—* The Much Honoured Baron of Leslie; Leslie Castle, Leslie, by Insch, Aberdeenshire (☎ 0464 20869)

LESLIE, Desmond Arthur Peter; s of Sir (John Randolph) Shane Leslie, 3 Bt (d 1971), and hp of bro Sir John Norman Ide Leslie, 4 Bt; *b* 29 June 1921; *Educ* Ampleforth, Trinity Coll Dublin; *m* 1, 1945, Agnes, o da of Rudolph Bernauer, of Budapest, Hungary; 2 s, 1 da; m 2, 1970, Helen Jennifer, da of late Lt-Col E I E

Strong, of Wiveliscombe, Som; 2 da; *Career* WWII Flt Sgt Pilot 313 and 131 Squadrons 1942-44; composer, author, film producer, discologist; musical compositions: The Living Shakespeare (an album of 12 LPs of electronic music for Old Vic Cast, Macbeth, Hamlet, Othello, Midsummer Night's Dream, The Tempest, Julius Caesar, Antony and Cleopatra, Measure for Measure, King Lear, Richard III, Henry V); film music: The Day the Sky Fell In, Dr Strangelove, Yellow Submarine, Death of Satan, also numerous library music pieces for Joseph Weinberger; produced and dir films: The Missing Princess, Stranger at My Door; author of: Careless Lives, Pardon My Return, Angels Weep, Hold Back the Night, The Amazing Mr Lutterworth, The Jesus File, The Daughters of Pan; humour: How Britain Won the Space Race, Susie Saucer and Ronnie Rocket; *Books* Flying Saucers Have Landed (1,000,000 copies sold; 21 translations to other languages); *Recreations* building cross country courses, falling off horses, teasing evil minded officials, investigating spiritualist and psychic phenomena; *Style*— Desmond Leslie, Esq; Castle Leslie, Gaslough, co Monaghan, Ireland

LESLIE, Prof Frank Matthews; JP (1984); s of William Ogilvy Leslie (d 1946), of Dundee, and Catherine Pitkethly, *née* Matthews (d 1969); *b* 8 March 1935; *Educ* Harris Acad Dundee, Queen's Coll Dundee, Univ of St Andrews (BSc), Univ of Manchester (PhD); *m* 19 Aug 1965, Ellen Leitch, da of William Reoch (d 1945), of Lochee, Dundee; 1 s (Calum William b 6 June 1974), 1 da (Sheena Reoch b 13 June 1969); *Career* asst lectr in mathematics Univ of Manchester 1959-61, res assoc in mathematics MIT USA 1961-62, lectr in mathematics Univ of Newcastle upon Tyne 1962-68, visiting asst prof in mechanics John Hopkins Univ USA 1966-67, visiting prof in engrg Tulane Univ USA 1978, professor of mathematics Univ of Strathclyde 1982- (sr lectr 1968-71, reader 1971-79, personal prof 1979-82), visiting prof in engrg Hokkaido Univ Japan 1985; memb ed bd: J Non-Newtonian Fluid Mechanics 1980-, Liquid Crystals 1985-, Continuum Mechanics and Thermodynamics 1988-; chm Br Liquid Crystal Soc 1987-; FIMA 1969, FInst Phys 1978, FRSE 1980; *Recreations* golf, hill-walking, gardening; *Style*— Prof Frank Leslie, JP; Mathematics Department, University of Strathclyde, Livingstone Tower, Richmond St, Glasgow G1 1XH (☎ 041 552 4400 ext 3655, fax 041 552 0775, telex 77 472 (UNSLIB G)

LESLIE, Ian James; s of James Beattie Leslie (d 1973), of Brisbane, Aust, and Margaret Jean, *née* Ryan; *b* 23 Jan 1945; *Educ* Brisbane Boys Coll, Univ of Queensland (MB BS), Univ of Liverpool (MCh Orth); *m* 1 Sept 1975, Jane Ann, da of Col (Allan) Rex Waller, MBE, MC (d 1985), of Waddesdon, Bucks; 1 s (James Henry Rex b 1982), 1 da (Charlotte Ann b 1978); *Career* RAAF 1968-72 (flying offr 1968, Flt Lt 1969, Sqdn Ldr 1971); res MO Royal Brisbane Hosp Aust 1969, MO RAAF 1970-72 (sr MO Vietnam 1971), teaching surgical registrar Princess Alexandra Hosp Brisbane 1973, sr registrar Nuffield Orthopaedic Centre Oxford 1974-77, sr lectr Univ of Liverpool 1978-81, conslt orthopaedic surgn Bristol Royal Infirmary and clinical lectr Univ of Bristol 1982-; treas Br Orthopaedic Res Soc, past memb Cncl Br Soc Hand Surgery, ed Sec Br Orthopaedic Assoc; memb Ed Bd: Journal of Bone and Joint Surgery, British Journal of Hand Surgery, Current Orthopaedics; FRCSEd 1974; *Books* Watson-Jones Fractures (contrib), Arthroscopy in Operative Orthopaedics (1979), Operative Treatment of Fractures In Children And Surgery of Wrist in Operative Othopaedics (1989); *Style*— Ian Leslie, Esq; Collingwood, Easter Compton, Bristol BS12 3RE (☎ 04545 2255); Bristol Royal Infirmary, Marlborough St, Bristol BS2 8HW (☎ 0272 230000); 2 Clifton Park, Clifton Bristol BS8 3BS (☎ 0272 737113)

LESLIE, James Francis; TD (1974), JP (Co Antrim 1967), DL (Co Antrim 1973); s of Seymour Argent Sandford Leslie, CMG, DL (d 1953), and Eleanor Mary, *née* Stuart (d 1990); *b* 19 March 1933; *Educ* Eton, Queens' Coll Cambridge (MA); *m* 16 June 1956, (Patricia) Elizabeth Jane, da of Col William Anderson Swales, OBE, MC, TD (d 1955); 2 s (James b 1958, John b 1960), 1 da (Rosejane b 1964); *Career* cmmnd N Irish Horse (TA) 1963, Maj Royal Yeo (V) 1968; colonial serv (dist offr) Tanganyika 1956-59; farmer 1960-; pres Local Branch Royal Br Legion, chm TA & VRA (NI) 1986-; High Sheriff of Co Antrim 1967, Vice Lt 1983; *Recreations* shooting, fishing; *Style*— James Leslie, Esq, TD, JP, DL; Leslie Hill, Ballymoney, Co Antrim BT53 6QL

LESLIE, Lord; James Malcolm David Leslie; s and h of 21 Earl of Rothes; *b* 4 June 1958; *Educ* Eton; *Style*— Lord Leslie; 8 Kinnoul Rd, London SW6

LESLIE, Capt Sir John Norman Ide; 4 Bt (UK 1876); s of Sir (John Randolph) Shane Leslie, 3 Bt (d 1971), and Marjory Mary Ide (d 1951); branch of Earls of Rothes; *b* 6 Dec 1916; *Educ* Downside, Magdalene Coll Cambridge (BA); *Heir* bro, Desmond Arthur Peter Leslie, of Castle Leslie, Glaslough, Co Monaghan; *Career* served WWII Irish Gds (POW 1940-45); artist, ecologist, restorer of old buildings; Knight of Honour and Devotion SMO Malta, Knight Cdr Order of St Gregory the Great; landowner (900 acres), previous to Irish Land Act 1910 fortynine thousand acres; *Recreations* ornithology, forestry; *Clubs* Travellers', Circolo della Caccia (Rome); *Style*— Capt Sir John Leslie, Bt; 19 Piazza in Piscinula, Rome 00153, Italy

LESLIE, Hon John Wayland; s of 19 Earl of Rothes (d 1927); *b* 16 Dec 1909; *Educ* Stowe, CCC Cambridge; *m* 1932, Coral Angela, da of George Henry Pinckard, JP (d 1950), of Combe Court, Chiddingfold, Surrey, and of 9 Chesterfield St, Mayfair; 1 s, 1 da; *Career* served WWII RAFVR Flt Lt (invalided 1943); memb Royal Co of Archers (Queen's Body Guard for Scotland); Liveryman Worshipful Co of Clothworkers; *Recreations* fishing, shooting; *Clubs* Boodle's; *Style*— The Hon John Leslie; Guildford House, Castle Hill, Farnham, Surrey GU9 7JG (☎ 0252 716975)

LESLIE, Peter Evelyn; s of Patrick Holt Leslie (d 1972), of Oxford, and Evelyn de Berry; *b* 27 March 1931; *Educ* Dragon Sch Oxford, Stowe, New Coll Oxford; *m* 1975, Charlotte, da of Sir Edwin Arthur Chapman-Andrews, KCMG, OBE (d 1979); 2 step s (Francis, Mathew), 2 step da (Alice, Jessica); *Career* cmmnd Argyll and Sutherland Highlanders 1951, served 7 Bn (TA) 1952-56; dep chm Barclays Bank 1987- (gen mangr 1973-76, dir 1980, chief gen mangr and md 1985-88); chm Exec Ctee Br Bankers Assoc 1978-79; govr: Nat Inst of Social Work 1973-83, Stowe Sch 1983-; chm: Exports Guarantee Advsy Cncl 1987- (memb 1978-81, dep chm 1986-87), Overseas Devpt Inst 1988-, Queen's Coll 1989; Cwlth Devpt Corp 1989-; *Recreations* natural history, historical research; *Style*— Peter Leslie, Esq; 54 Lombard St, London EC3

LESLIE, Richard Andrew; s of Cyril Leslie, of Middx, and Rozella, *née* Keen; *b* 24 April 1954; *Educ* Kingbury HS, Morehead State Univ Kentucky USA (MBA); *m* 7 Aug 1982, Margaret Elizabeth, da of Colston Henry Harrison, of Bristol, Avon; *Career* CA; proprietor of R A Leslie & Co; Middx Co: tennis player 1970-87, squash player 1976-78; twice capt England Sr Tennis Team, formerly Br under 18 and 21 Doubles champion; *Recreations* tennis, squash, snooker; *Clubs* Lansdown, formerly All England Wimbledon; *Style*— Richard A Leslie, Esq; The Old School House, Tormarton, nr Badminton GL9 1HZ (☎ 045 421 370, car phone 0860 821296)

LESLIE, Robin; s of Lt-Col John Leslie (d 1965), of Brancaster, Norfolk; *b* 6 Nov 1924; *Educ* Eton; *m* 1, 1949, Susan Mary, yr da of Maj-Gen James Francis Harter, DSO, MC (d 1960); 2 da (Sarah Jane b 1950, Belinda b 1952); m 2, 1983, June Rose, da of Lt-Gen Frederick George Beaumont Nesbitt, CVO, CBE, MC (d 1972); *Career* served WWII Capt 12 Royal Lancers; fruit farmer; dir: Home Grown Fruits Ltd 1969-73, Colchester Oyster Fishery Ltd 1965-89 f; *Recreations* golf, gardening; *Clubs* White's (chm 1987-90); *Style*— Robin Leslie, Esq; Orchard House, Malting Farm, Langham, Colchester, Essex CO4 5HX (☎ 0206 271087)

LESLIE, (Percy) Theodore; heir to btcy of Leslie of Wardis and Findrassie (NS 1625); succession, as 10 Bt, pending at time of going to press; s of (Frank Harvey) Leslie (d 1965); ggs of Sir John Leslie, 4 Bt, who assumed the title in 1800, after a period of dormancy), and Amelia Caroline (d 1918), da of Alexander Russon; *b* 19 Nov 1915; *Educ* London, privately; *Career* engineer British Aerospace, ret 1980; Freeman City of London 1978; FSA (Scot); KASG; *Recreations* chess, gardening, visiting places of historic interest; *Style*— Theodore Leslie, Esq; c/o National Westminster Bank, 5 Market Place, Kingston-upon-Thames, Surrey

LESLIE, Thomas Gerard; s of Thomas Leslie, JP (d 1985), of Manuel, Muiravonside, and Ellen Slaven (d 1976), da of Hugh Francis McAllister; *b* 1 Aug 1938; *Educ* St Joseph's Coll Dumfries, Mons Offr Cadet Sch Aldershot; *m* 12 June 1982, Sonya Anne, da of Leslie John Silburn (d 1980); 1 s (Thomas b 1985); *Career* Nat Serv Scots Gds 1958, cmmnd Argyll and Sutherland Highlanders 1959, Lt HAC RARO; various exec posts: Canada Dry (UK) Ltd, Booker McConnell Ltd, Thos de la Rue; The Corps of Commissionaires; memb The Company of Pikemen and Musketeers HAC; Freeman City of London 1974; FSA (Scot) 1980; chm London Caledonian Catholic Assoc 1983-87; *Recreations* shooting, heraldry, genealogy; *Clubs* British American Forces Dining; *Style*— Thomas Leslie, Esq, FSA; 3 Crane Court, Fleet St, London EC4A 2EJ (☎ 071 353 1125)

LESLIE MELVILLE, Hon Alan Duncan; s of 13 Earl of Leven and 12 of Melville, KT (d 1947); *b* 1928; *Educ* Eton; *Career* Capt Rifle Bde 1954, ret 1956; *Style*— The Hon Alan Leslie Melville; Fingask, Kirkhill, Inverness

LESLIE MELVILLE, Hon Archibald Ronald; yr s of 14 Earl of Leven and (13 of) Melville; hp to er bro, Lord Balgonie; *b* 15 Sept 1957; *Educ* Gordonstoun; *m* 4 April 1987, Julia Mary Greville, yr da of Basil Fox, of 32 Pembroke Gardens, London W8; 1 da (Alice Catherine b 12 Nov 1990); *Career* 2 Lt Queen's Own Highlanders to 1981, Lt 1981, Lt RARO 1982; *Style*— The Hon Archibald Leslie Melville; Glenferness House, Nairn, Scotland IV12 5UP

LESLIE MELVILLE, Lady Elizabeth (Eliza); *née* Compton; DL (Ross and Cromarty, Sleye and Lochalsh); da of 6 Marquess of Northampton, DSO (d 1978), and Virginia Lucie Hussey, *née* Heaton; *b* 7 Dec 1944; *m* 1968 (Ian) Hamish Leslie Melville, s of Maj Michael Ian Leslie Melville, of Bridgelands, Selkirk; 2 s (James Ian b 1969, Henry Bingham b 1975); *Clubs* Turf; *Style*— The Lady Eliza Leslie Melville, DL; Lochluichart Lodge, by Garve, Ross-shire

LESLIE MELVILLE, Hon George David; s of 13 Earl of Leven and 12 of Melville, KT (d 1947); *b* 13 May 1924; *Educ* Eton, Trinity Coll Cambridge; *m* 1955, Diana Mary, da of Brig Sir Henry Houldsworth, KBE, DSO, MC (d 1963); 1 s, 1 da; *Career* late Rifle Bde, served 1942-45 (wounded 1945), Maj Black Watch TA, chartered land agent; FRICS; *Recreations* shooting, skiing; *Clubs* Naval and Military; *Style*— The Hon George Leslie Melville, JP; Inneshewen, Aboyne, Aberdeenshire AB3 5BH

LESLIE MELVILLE, (Ian) Hamish; o s of Maj Michael Leslie Melville, TD, DL, s of Lt-Col Hon Ian Leslie Melville (4 s of 11 Earl of Leven and 10 Earl of Melville), and Cynthia, da of Sir Charles Hambro, KBE, MC; *b* 22 Aug 1944; *Educ* Eton, Ch Ch Oxford (BA, MA); *m* 1968, Lady Elizabeth Compton, yr da of 6 Marquess of Northampton; 2 s (James b 1969, Henry b 1975); *Style*— Hamish Leslie Melville, Esq; Lochluichart Lodge, by Garve, Ross-shire (☎ 09974 242)

LESNIAK, Alicja Barbara; s of Jozef Lesniak, and Maria, *née* Stachy; *b* 4 Dec 1951; *Educ* Imperial Coll London (BSc), ARCS; *Career* tax sr Arthur Andersen & Co 1974-76 (audit asst 1973-74), project accountant WEA Records Ltd 1976-77, chief accountant Crest 1977-79, mangr Mgmnt Info Systems Lummus & Co 1979-80; Arthur Andersen & Co: asst controller 1980-82, fin controller 1982-86, UK dir of fin 1986-87; Euro gp controller WPP Group plc 1987-89, UK gp fin dir J Walter Thompson Co Limited 1989-; *Style*— Ms Alicja Lesniak; J Walter Thomspon Compnay Limited, 40 Berkeley Square, London W1 (☎ 071 499 4949, fax 071 493 8432)

LESSELS, Norman; s of John Clark Lessels (d 1981), of Edinburgh, and Gertrude Margaret Ellen, *née* Jack; *b* 2 Sept 1938; *Educ* Melville Coll, Edinburgh Acad; *m* 1, 31 Dec 1960, Gillian Durward, *née* Clark (d 1979); 2 s (Alasdair b 1963, James b 1967, d 1979), 1 da (Sarah b 1965, d 1979); m 2, 27 Jan 1981, Christine, da of George Stevenson Hitchman (d 1971), of Gullane, E Lothian; *Career* admitted CA 1961; ptnr: Ernst Whinney (and predecessor firms) 1962-80, Chiene and Tait CA 1980-; non-exec dir: Scottish Eastern Investment Trust plc 1980-, Bank of Scotland 1988-, Scottish Homes 1988-, Havelock Europa plc 1989-, Securities and Investments Bd 1989-; dep chm and non-exec dir Cairn Energy plc 1988-, non-exec govr British United Provident Assoc Ltd; *Recreations* golf, music, bridge; *Clubs* New Edinburgh, Hon Co of (Edinburgh) Golfers, R & A, Bruntsfield Links Golfing Soc; *Style*— Norman Lessels, Esq; 11 Forres St, Edinburgh EH3 6BJ (☎ 031 225 5596); 3 Albyn Place, Edinburgh EH2 4NQ (☎ 031 225 7515, fax 031 220 1083)

LESSER, Anton; s of David Lesser (d 1985), of Birmingham, and Amelia Mavis, *née* Cohen (d 1984); *b* 14 Feb 1952; *Educ* Mosely GS Birmingham, Univ of Liverpool (BA), RADA (Bancroft gold medal); Partner, Madeleine Adams; *Career* actor; theatre: Richard in Henry VI (RSC), Dance of Death (RSC), Michael in Sons of Light (RSC), Anthony in Julius Caesar (Tyne and Wear), Betty/Edward in Cloud Nine (Liverpool Everyman), Romeo in Romeo and Juliet (RSC), Darkie in The Fool (RSC), Constantin in The Seagull (Royal Ct), Hamlet in Hamlet (Warehouse), Kissing God (Hampstead Theatre Club), Troilus in Troilus and Cressida (RSC Stratford), Carlos Montezuma in Melons (RSC The Pit), Bill Howell in Principia Scriptoriae (RSC The Pit), Family Voices (Lyric Hammersmith), Feste in Twelth Night (Riverside Studios), Gloucester in Henry VI (RSC Stratford, The Barbican), Richard III in Richard III (RSC Stratford, The Barbican), Joe in Some Americans Abroad (RSC The Barbican), Bolingbroke in Richard II (RSC Stratford) Forest in Two Shakespearian Actors (RSC Stratford); television: Orestes in The Oresteia (BBC), Philip in The Mill on the Floss (BBC), Ken in The Daughters of Albion (YTV), Abesey Ivanovitch in The Gambler (BBC), Troilus in Troilus and Cressida (BBC), Trofimov in The Cherry Orchard (BBC), Crown Court (Granada TV), Edgar in King Lear (BBC), Wilheim Fliess in Freud (BBC), Cox in Good and Bad At Games (C4), Valerie Chaldize in Sakharov (C4), Willy Price in Anna of The Five Towns (BBC), Stanley in Stanley Spencer (BBC), Vincenzo Rocca in Airbase (BBC), London Embassy (Thames TV), Feste in Twelth Night (BBC), Wiesenthal (TVS/HBO), The Strauss Dynasty (mini-series) film: The Missionary, Monseigneur Quixote; assoc artist RSC, vice pres Friends of Br Theatre; *Style*— Anton Lesser, Esq; c/o Jeremy Conway Ltd, 18-21 Jermyn St, London SW17 6HP (☎ 071 287 0077, fax 071 287 1940)

LESSER, Dr Jeffrey; s of Louis Lesser (d 1952), of Hampstead, and Gaby, *née* Katz (d 1974); *b* 18 Feb 1927; *Educ* City of London (Corpn Scholar), Univ of London (MB BS, BDS, LDS, RCS Eng), Dip in Archaeology 1990; *m* 13 Nov 1955, Sheila, da of Mark Goldstein (d 1980), of Horsmonden, Kent; 2 s (Adam b 1958, Jeremy b 1962); *Career* Capt RAMC; physician, dental surgeon; past chm: Univ of London J Students Union, Univ of London J Graduates, Alpha Omega Int; *Recreations* squash; *Style*— Dr Jeffrey Lesser; The Maverns, 4 Hill Crescent, Totteridge (☎ 081 445 8280); 82 Harley Street, London W1 (☎ 071 636 7170)

LESSER, Leslie Hugh; s of Isaac Lesser (d 1960); *b* 7 Jan 1934; *Educ* Westcliff HS;

m 1956, Joyce; 1 s (Guy Fenton), 1 da (Vivien Adele); *Career* dir: Blacks Leisure Group plc, Greenfield Milletts International Ltd Hong Kong, Rheilffordd Llyn Padarn Cyfyngedig, City Tenancies plc, Home Tenancies plc, vice chm Southend United Football Club Ltd; FCA; *Recreations* golf, fishing, Shakespearean theatre; *Style*— Leslie Lesser, Esq; 130 Rivermill, SW1; 17 Burlescoombe Rd, Thorpe Bay, Essex

LESSER, Sidney Lewis; s of Joseph Lesser (d 1944), and Rachel, *née* Arram (d 1969); *b* 23 March 1912; *Educ* Raine's GS; *m* 10 July 1938, Nina, da of Robert Lowenthal (d 1971); 2 da (Susan Raymonde b 27 Sept 1942, Janis Erica b 17 June 1947); *Career* slr; vice-pres of the RAC (former exec chm); memb Law Soc; *Recreations* foreign travel, golf; *Clubs* RAC, The Propeller Club of USA; *Style*— Sidney L Lesser, Esq; 37 Fairfax Place, Hampstead, London NW6 4EJ (☎ 071 328 2607)

LESSING, Charlotte; da of George Fainstone, and Helene Peretz; *b* 14 May 1924; *Educ* Henrietta Barnet Sch, Univ of London (Extension Course Dip Eng Lit); *m* 25 May 1948, Walter Lessing; 3 da (Diana b 1953, Judith b 1954, Nicola b 1957); *Career* writer of short stories, travel articles, features and occasional broadcaster; ed-in-chief: Good Housekeeping 1987- (ed 1973-87, dep ed 1964-73), Country Living 1985-86; ed conslt 1988-; Ed of the Year Award Periodical Publisher Assoc 1983; *Recreations* travel, wine; *Clubs* Groucho; *Style*— Mrs Charlotte Lessing; 2 Roseneath Rd, London SW11 6AH (☎ 071 228 0708)

LESSING, Doris May; da of Alfred Cook, and Emily Maude, *née* McVeagh; *b* 22 Oct 1919; *m* 1, 1939 (m dis 1943), Frank Charles Wisdom; 1 s (John), 1 da (Jean); m 2, 1945 (m dis 1949), Gottfried Anton Nicholas Lessing; 1 s (Peter); *Career* author; Mondello Prize (Italy) 1946, Somerset Maugham Award 1954, Prix Medici 1976, Austrian State Prize for Euro Lit 1981, Shakespeare Prize Hamburg 1982, WH Smith Lit Award 1986, Grinzane Cavour (Italy-Foreign Fiction) 1989; memb: Nat Inst Arts and Letters, Inst Cultural Res; *Books* The Grass is Singing (1950), Children of Violence (five vols, 1951-69), The Golden Notebook (1962), Briefing for a Descent into Hell (1971), The Summer Before the Dark (1973), The Memoirs of a Survivor (1975), Canopus in Argos, Archives (5 vols 1979-83), The diaries of Jane Somers: Diary of a Good Neighbour (1983) and If the Old Could..(1984) published under pseudonym Jane Somers, The Good Terrorist (1985), The Fifth Child (1988); short stories incl: African Stories (two vols), This was the Old Chief's Country, The Sun Between Their Feet, Collected Stories (two vols), To Room 19, The Temptation of Jack Orkney; non-fiction incl: The Wind Blows Away our Words, Documents Relating to the Afghan Resistance (1974), Prisons We Choose to Live Inside (1986); essays incl A Small Personal Voice (1974), poetry incl Fourteen Poems (1959), Play With A Tiger (play, 1962); *Style*— Mrs Doris Lessing; c/o Jonathan Clowes Ltd, 10 Iron Bridge House, Bridge Approach, London NW1 8BD

LESSORE, John Viviand; s of Frederick Lessore (d 1951), of London, and Helen Lessore, OBE, *née* Brook; *b* 16 June 1939; *Educ* Merchant Taylors', Slade Sch of Fine Art; *m* 1962, Paule Marie, da of Jean Achille Reveille (Officier de la légion d'honneur, d 1967), of Paris; 4 s (Remi b 1962, Vincent b 1967, Timothy b 1973, Samuel b 1977); *Career* artist; princ exhibitions incl: Beaux Arts Gallery 1965, New Art Centre 1971, Theo Waddington 1981, Stoppenbach & Delestre 1983 and 1985, Nigel Greenwood 1990; works in public collections incl: Leicester Educn Ctee, Arts Cncl Collection, Royal Acad of Arts, Westminster Hosp, Tate Gallery, Swindon Museum and Art Gallery, CAS, Norwich Castle Museum, Br Cncl; *Style*— John Lessore, Esq

LESTER, Anthony John; s of Donald James Lester, of Wallingford, Oxon, and Edith Helen Hemmings (d 1982); *b* 15 Sept 1945; *Educ* Gaveston Hall Nuthurst Sussex, St John's Coll Co Tipperary Eire; *Career* ind fine art conslt, valuer, art critic, book reviewer and lectr; contribs to numerous magazines incl: Woman, Antique Collecting, Artist's and Illustrator's Magazine, Antique Dealer and Collectors Guide, Limited Edition, The World of Antiques, The Speculator; featured in Farmer's Weekly, Radio Times, Sunday Express Magazine, British Midland Voyager Magazine; regular broadcaster TV Antiques Roadshow 1986-89; *Books* The Exhibited Works of Helen Allingham (1979), The Stannards of Bedfordshire (1984), BBC Antiques Roadshow-Experts on Objects (contrib, 1987); memb Int Assoc of Art Critics (AICA); *Recreations* travel, entertaining friends, charity work; *Style*— Anthony J Lester, Esq; The Dower House, Hithercroft, Wallingford, Oxfordshire OX10 9ES (☎ 0491 36683); Old Hithercroft House, Hithercroft, Wallingford, Oxfordshire OX10 9ES (☎ 0491 37552)

LESTER, Anthony Paul; QC (1975); s of Harry Lester (d 1984), of London, and Kate, *née* Cooper-Smith; *b* 3 July 1936; *Educ* City of London Sch, Trinity Coll Cambridge (BA), Harvard Law Sch (LLM); *m* 29 July 1971, Catherine Elizabeth Debora, da of Michael Morris Wassey (d 1969), of London; 1 s (Gideon b 1972), 1 da (Maya b 1974); *Career* 2 Lt RA 1956; called to the Bar Lincolns Inn 1963 (bencher 1985), memb Northern Ireland Bar and Irish Bar; rec S Eastern circuit 1987; special advsr to: Home Sec 1974-76, Standing Cmmn on Human Rights in NI 1975-77; chm: Bd of Govrs James Allens Girls Sch, Interights (Int Centre for Legal Protection of Human Rights); chm Runnymede Tst, govr LSE Science; hon visiting prof of law UCL; CIArb; *Books* Justice in the American South (1964), Shawcross and Beaumont on Air Law (ed jtly, 3 edn 1964), Race and Law (jtly 1972); contrib: British Nationality, Immigration and Race Relations in Halsbury's Laws of England (4 edn, 1973), The Changing Constitution (ed Powell and Oliver, 1985); *Recreations* walking, sailing, golf, water colours; *Clubs* Garrick, RAC; *Style*— Anthony Lester, Esq, QC; 2 Hare Court, Temple, London EC4Y 7BH (☎ 071 583 1770, fax 071 583 9269, telex 27139 LINLAW)

LESTER, James Theodore; MP (C) Broxtowe 1983-; s of Arthur Ernest and Marjorie Lester; *b* 23 May 1932; *Educ* Nottingham HS; *m* 1, 1953 (m dis 1989), Iris; 2 s; m 2, Jan 1989, Merry Lee's; *Career* MP (C) Beeston Feb 1974-83, oppn whip 1975-79, parly under sec state Employment 1979-81, fndr memb CARE (Cons Action to Revive Employment), dep chm all party gp on Overseas Devpt; *Style*— James Lester, Esq, MP; 4 Trevose House, Orsett Street, London SE11

LESTER, Nigel Martin; s of Geoffrey Charles Lester, of Littlehampton, Sussex, and Pamela Anne, *née* Goddard (d 1981); *b* 26 March 1953; *Educ* Banbury GS, Univ of Sussex (BSc); *m* 1982, Rosemarie Anne, da of Eric George Skoll; 1 s (Jonathan Robert Anthony b 1987), 1 da (Charlotte Nicole Pamela b 1984); *Career* int equity fund mangr Legal and General Assurance Society Ltd London 1974-81, asst dir and sr mangr Schroders and Chartered Hong Kong 1981-84, md Aetna Investment Management (FE) Hong Kong 1984-88, County Nat West Investment Management 1990- (vice pres, chief investmt offr and sr vice pres International); FIA 1980; *Recreations* real tennis, squash, theatre; *Clubs* MCC, Hong Kong; *Style*— Nigel Lester, Esq; 3 Cornwall Mansions, 33 Kensington Court, London W8 5BG (☎ 071 937 7735); County Natwest Investment Management Ltd, 43-44 Crutched Friars, London EC3N 2NX (☎ 071 374 3000, fax 071 374 3248)

LESTER, Richard; s of Elliott Lester (d 1951), of Pennsylvania, USA, and Ella Young Lester (d 1969); *b* 19 Jan 1932; *Educ* William Penn Charter Sch, Univ of Pennsylvania (BA); *m* 1956, Deirdre Vivian, da of Sqdn Ldr Frederick James Smith (d 1970); 1 s (Dominic), 1 da (Claudia); *Career* TV dir: CBS USA 1951-54, AR (dir TV Goon shows 1956); directed The Running, Jumping and Standing Still Film (Academy award nomination, 1st prize San Francisco Festival 1960); feature films directed incl: It's Trad, Dad (1962), Mouse on the Moon (1963), A Hard Day's Night (1964), The Knack (1964, Grand Prix Cannes Film Festival), Help (1965, Best Film Award and Best Dir Award Rio de Janeiro Festival), A Funny Thing Happened on the Way to the Forum (1966), How I won the War (1967), Petulia (1968), The Bed Sitting Room (1969, Gandhi Peace Prize Berlin Film Festival), The Three Musketeers (1973), Juggernaut (1974, Best Dir Award Teheran Film Festival), The Four Musketeers (1974), Royal Flash (1975), Robin and Marian (1976), The Ritz (1976), Butch and Sundance: The Early Days (1979), Cuba (1979), Superman II (1981), Superman III (1983), Finders Keepers (1984), Return of the Musketeers (1989), Get Back (1990); awarded Grand Prize Avoriaz Festival 1977; Order of Academy of Arts and Letters (France) 1973; *Style*— Richard Lester, Esq; Courtyards, River Lane, Petersham, Surrey; Courtyard Films Ltd, Twickenham Studios, St Margarets, Middlesex TW1 2AW (☎ 081 892 4477)

LESTOR, Joan; MP (Lab) Eccles 1983-; *b* 1931,Vancouver; *Educ* Blaenavon Secdy Sch (Monmouth), William Morris Secdy Sch Walthamstow, London Univ; *m* ; 1 s, 1 da (both adopted); *Career* nursery sch teacher 1959-66, memb LCC 1962-64; MP (Lab) Eton and Slough 1966-83; Parly under-sec of state Dept of Education and Science 1969-70 & 1975-76, memb Labour Party NEC 1967-82 (chm 1977-78), Parly under-sec of state FCO 1974-75, co-chm Jt Ctee Against Racism 1978-, chm Int Ctee Labour Party 1978-; oppn front bench spokesman Women's Rights & Welfare 1981-; Lab spokesperson: aid and devpt 1987-98, children juvenile offenders and race 1989-; *Style*— Miss Joan Lestor, MP; House of Commons, SW1

LETANKA, Lady Christina; *née* Gathorne-Hardy; da of 4 Earl of Cranbrook, CBE; *b* 1 May 1940; *m* 1967, Stanley Edward Letanka; 1 s (Peter Edward b 1974), 2 da (Stella Dorothy b 1968, Florence Ruth b 1969); *Style*— The Lady Christina Letanka; Pepsal End, Pepperstock, nr Luton, Beds LU1 4LH (☎ 0582 23861)

LETCHER, (Robert) Peter; s of (Henry) Percival Letcher (d 1990), of St Ives House, Ringwood, Hants, and Catherine Jessie, *née* Harris (d 1980); *b* 12 Aug 1924; *Educ* Radley; *m* 1, 22 Aug 1947 (m dis 1955), Patricia Enid, da of Eugene Baerselman; m 2, 27 July 1957, Virginia Rose Lou, da of Gurth Kemp Fenn-Smith; 2 s (Piers b 15 Aug 1960, Peregrine b 20 Nov 1961); *Career* Lt Grenadier Guards 1944, King's Co N W Europe (wounded, despatches), Capt Control Cmmn 1945, ADC to Regnl Cmmr N Rhine and Westphalia 1946-47; admitted slr 1948; ptnr Letcher & Son 1949-90, conslt 1990-; NP; chm Industl Tbnls 1976-79; *Recreations* skiing, shooting, racing, photography; *Clubs* Army and Navy; *Style*— Peter Letcher, Esq; Honeypound, Martin, Fordingbridge, Hants SP6 3LR (☎ 072 589 389); Letcher & Son, 24 Market Place, Ringwood, Hants BH24 1BS (☎ 0425 471 424, fax 0425 470 917)

LETHBRIDGE, John Francis Buckler Noel; s and h of Sir Thomas Periam Hector Noel Lethbridge, 7 Bt; *b* 10 March 1977; *Educ* Ravenswood Devon, Wilken Park Bucks; *Recreations* running, swimming; *Style*— John Lethbridge, Esq; Lloyds House, Honeymead, Simonsbath, Minehead, Somerset

LETHBRIDGE, Sir Thomas Periam Hector Noel; 7 Bt (UK 1804); s of Sir Hector Wroth Lethbridge, 6 Bt (d 1978), and Diana Evelyn Noel; *b* 17 July 1950; *Educ* Milton Abbey, RAC Cirencester; *m* 1976, Susan (Suzie) Elizabeth, da of Lyle Rocke, of Maryland; 4 s (John b 1977, Edward b 1978, Alexander b 1982, Henry b 1984), 2 da (Georgina b 1980, Rachel b 1986); *Heir* s, John Francis Buckler Noel Lethbridge; *Career* art dealer in sporting subjects of 1700 to date, int agent for distinguished retail names; *Clubs* Farmers', Naval and Military; *Style*— Sir Thomas Lethbridge, Bt; Lloyds House, Honeymead, Simonsbath, Minehead, Somerset TA24 7JX

LETLEY, Peter Anthony; s of Sidney Charles Letley (d 1978), of Woodbridge, Suffolk, and Ruby, *née* Berry; *b* 11 Nov 1945; *Educ* Woodbridge Sch Suffolk, St John's Coll Oxford (BA); *m* 21 March 1970, (Alice) Emma Campbell, da of Lt-Col Campbell K Finlay, of W Ardhu, Isle of Mull, Argyll; 1 s (Alfred Thomas b 4 Sept 1988); *Career* joined Hong Kong Bank Group 1974; Wardley Ltd: head of Lending Dept 1974-78, dir overseas ops and dir 1978-82, jt md Aust 1982-83, chief exec Hong Kong International Trade Finance Ltd (London) 1983-86; fin dir: James Capel Bankers Ltd 1986-87 (md 1987-88), James Capel & Co 1988-; *Recreations* theatre, opera, reading; *Clubs* Hong Kong Jockey; *Style*— Peter Letley, Esq; 24 Princedale Rd, London W11 4NJ (☎ 071 229 1398); James Capel and Co, James Capel House, 6 Bevis Marks, London EC3A 7JQ (☎ 071 621 0011, telex 888866)

LETTS, Anthony Ashworth; s of Leslie Charles Letts, of Old Swaylands, Penshurst, Kent (d 1984), and Elizabeth Mary, *née* Gibson (d 1971); John Letts (gggf) founded Diary Publishing Business in 1796 as stationer, first Diary 1812, co still family controlled; *b* 3 July 1935; *Educ* Marlborough, Magdalene Coll Cambridge (MA); *m* 15 Sept 1962, Rosa Maria, da of Avvocato Aminta Ciarrapico, of Rome, Italy (d 1985); 1 s (Philip Leslie b 1966), 1 da (Adalgisa b 1965); *Career* Nat Serv 1954-56 Lt; md Charles Letts & Co Ltd 1965, chm Charles Letts (Hldgs) Ltd 1977; dir: Charles Letts & Co Ltd 1963, Charles Letts Scotland Ltd 1978, Charles Letts Gp Servs 1978, Letts of London (USA) 1978, Letts of London Pty (Australia) 1986, Mascot Developments 1984; *Recreations* tennis, sailing, hill walking, theatre; *Clubs* Hurlingham; *Style*— A A Letts, Esq; Fairlight, Kingston Hill, Kingston-upon-Thames, Surrey KT2 7LX (☎ 081 546 5757); Charles Letts (Hldgs) Ltd, 77 Borough Rd, London SE1 1DW (☎ 071 407 8891, telex 884498 LETTS G, fax 071 403 6729)

LETTS, John Campbell Bonner; OBE (1980); s of (Christian) Francis Campbell Letts, of Oakley Hall, Cirencester, Glos (d 1963), and Eveleen Frances Calthrop, *née* Bonner (d 1969); *b* 18 Nov 1929; *Educ* Haileybury, Jesus Coll Cambridge (BA); *m* 21 Sep 1957, Sarah Helen, da of E Brian O Rorke, RA; 3 s (Robert b 1959, Matthew b 1961, Daniel b 1963) 1 da (Vanessa b 1966); *Career* Penguin Books 1959, J Walter Thompson 1960-63, Sunday Times Publications 1964-66, gen mangr Book Club Assoc 1966-69, mktg dir Hutchinson 1969, jt chm (ed and mktg dir) Folio Soc 1971-87; fndr and chm Nat Heritage 1972, tstee and memb ctee Euro Museums Tst, tstee Museum of Empire and Cwlth Tst, fndr and chm The Trollope Soc 1987-; FRSA; *Poetry* A Little Treasury of Limericks (1973); *Recreations* walking in Scotland, reading visiting museums, gardening; *Clubs* Reform; *Style*— John Letts, Esq, OBE; 83 West Side, Clapham Common, London SW4 (☎ 071 228 9448); The Trollope Society, 9a North St, London SW4 0HN (☎ 071 720 6789/ 071 924 1146)

LETTS, (John) Martin; s of Leslie Charles Letts (d 1985 direct descendent of John Letts first diary publisher), and Elizabeth Mary, *née* Gibson (d 1972); *b* 15 Feb 1934; *Educ* Marlborough; *m* 6 March 1964, Eildon Patricia, da of Brig D W McConnel, of Hawick, Roxburghshire; 2 s (Charles b 1965, Anthony b 1966, d 1976), 1 da (Diana b 1971); *Career* currently dir of companies incl: Charles Letts (Holdings) Ltd, College Valley Estates, Charles Letts (Scot) Ltd (chm); huntsman Bolebroke Beagles 1956-63; master and huntsman: Eastern Counties Otterhounds 1958-63, College Valley Foxhounds 1964-82, College Valley Foxhounds (N Northumberland) 1982-; *Recreations* foxhunting, fishing, gardening; *Style*— Martin Letts, Esq; Hethpool, Wooler, Northumberland; Thornybank Estate, Dalkeith, Lothian, Scotland

LETTS, Quentin Richard Stephen; s of R F B Letts, of Cirencester, Glos, and Jocelyn, *née* Adami; *b* 6 Feb 1963; *Educ* Haileybury, Bellarmine Coll Kentucky, Trinity Coll Dublin, Jesus Coll Cambridge; *Career* dustman and waiter 1981-84; ed: Oxon Magazine Oxford 1984-85, Mayday Magazine Dublin 1985-86, Filibuster

Magazine Dublin 1986-87; journalist The Daily Telegraph 1988-; *Recreations* restaurants, gossip; *Clubs* Frogs Cricket, Pre-Prandial Soc; *Style—* Quentin Letts, Esq; 16 Chilworth St, London W2 (☎ 071 706 4874); The Daily Telegraph, 181 Marsh Wall, London E14 (☎ 071 538 5000)

LEUCH, Werner; s of Ulrich Leuch, of Appenzell, Switzerland and Aline, *née* Baenziger (d 1984); *b* 8 Dec 1937; *Educ* ATZ Zurich (BSc); *m* 1963, Barbara Helen Elise, da of Alfred Mottet of Gossau, Switzerland; *Career* Maj Swiss Air Force 1981; md BMARC 1977-88; vice chm Swiss Economical Cncl; former govr The Kings Sch Grantham; *Recreations* skiing, swimming, fishing, shooting; *Style—* Werner Leuch, Esq; zur Weid 699, CH 8493 Saland, Switzerland

LEUCHARS, Hon Mrs (Gillian Wightman); *née* Nivison; da of 2 Baron Glendyne (d 1967); *b* 1931; *m* 1953, Maj-Gen Peter Raymond Leuchars, CBE (*qv*); 1 s; *Style—* The Hon Mrs Leuchars; 5 Chelsea Sq, London SW3

LEUCHARS, Maj-Gen Peter Raymond; CBE (1966); s of Raymond Leuchars (d 1927), and Helen Inez, *née* Copland-Griffiths (d 1979); *b* 29 Oct 1921; *Educ* Bradfield; *m* 1953, Hon Gillian Wightman Nivison, da of 2 Baron Glendyne (d 1967), of E Grinstead, Sussex; 1 s (Christopher); *Career* cmmnd in Welsh Guards 1941, served NW Europe and Italy 1944-45, Adj 1 Bn Welsh Guards Palestine 1945-48, Bde Maj 4 Bde Germany 1952-54, GSO 1 (Instr) Staff Coll Camberley 1956-59, GSO1 HQ 4 Div BAOR 1960-63, cmd 1 Bn Welsh Guards 1963-65, Princ SO to Dir of Ops Borneo 1965-66, cmd 11 Armd Bde BAOR 1966-68, cmd Jt Operational Computer Projects Team 1969-71, Dep Cmdt Staff Coll Camberley 1972-73, GOC Wales 1973-76, Col The Roy Welch Fus 1974-84; pres Gds Golfing Soc 1977-; St John Ambulance: cmmr-in-chief 1978-80 and 1985-86, chief cdr 1981-89; chm St John Fellowship 1989-; Order of Istiqlal (Jordan) 1946; KStJ 1978, GCStJ 1989; *Recreations* golf, shooting, travel, photography; *Clubs* Royal and Ancient Golf, Sunningdale Golf (capt 1975); *Style—* Maj-Gen Peter Leuchars, CBE; 5 Chelsea Sq, London SW3 6LF (☎ 071 352 6187)

LEUNG, Prof Clement; s of Hon Ming Leung, MBE, of Melbourne, and Suk Wan Leung (d 1954); *b* 10 May 1949; *Educ* McGill Univ Canada (BSc), Univ of Oxford (MSc), UCL (PhD); *m* 24 March 1979, Qui Hoon, da of Suat Eng Choo, of Singapore; 2 s (Timothy b 1986, Philip b 1990); *Career* conslt in mgmnt scis British Oxygen Ltd 1978; lectr in computer sci: Univ of Reading 1979-82, UCL 1982-86; prof of computer sci Birkbeck Coll 1986-; memb Br Computer Soc; CEng; *Books* Quantitative Analysis of Computer Systems (1988); *Recreations* jazz piano, philosophy of religion; *Style—* Prof Clement Leung; Birkbeck College, University of London, Malet St, London WC1E 7HX (☎ 071 580 6622, fax 071 636 4971)

LEUTHOLD, Rudolph; s of Eugen Albert Leuthold (d 1981), of Zurich, and Anna, *née* Wild; *b* 10 May 1949; *Educ* Gymnasium Zurich, Univ of Geneva (Lic Sc Eco), McGill Univ Montreal (MBA); *Career* vice pres Morgan Guaranty Tst NY 1981-, md JP Morgan Investmt Inc 1984-; memb Soc of Investmt Analysts 1978; *Recreations* music, theatre, literature, skiing; *Clubs* Royal Automobile; *Style—* Rudolph Leuthold, Esq; J P Morgan Investment Management Inc, 83 Pall Mall, London SW1 5ES (☎ 071 839 4145, fax 071 839 3115/3117, telex 8954543)

LEVEN AND MELVILLE, 14 Earl of Leven and 13 of Melville (S 1641); Alexander Robert Leslie Melville; also Lord Melville of Monymaill (S 1616), Lord Balgonie (S 1641), Viscount Kirkaldie, and Lord Raith, Monymaill and Balwearie (both S 1690); DL (Co of Nairn 1961); s of 13 Earl of Leven and (12 of) Melville, KT (d 1947), and Lady Rosamond Foljambe (da of 1 Earl of Liverpool); *b* 13 May 1924; *Educ* Eton; *m* 1953, Susan, da of late Lt-Col Ronald Steuart-Menzies of Culdares; 2 s, 1 da; *Heir* s, Lord Balgonie; *Career* vice pres Highland Dist TA, 2 Lt Coldstream Gds 1943, Capt 1947; chm Cairngorm Chairlift Co; late ADC to Govr-Gen NZ; pres Br Ski Fedn 1981-85; convener Nairn Co Cncl 1970-74, chm Bd of Govs Gordonstoun Sch 1971-89; *Recreations* shooting, skiing, fishing; *Clubs* New (Edinburgh); *Style—* The Rt Hon the Earl of Leven and Melville, DL; Glenferness House, Nairn, Scotland (☎ 030 95 202)

LEVENE, Ben; s of Mark Levene (d 1987), of London, and Charlotte, *née* Leapman (d 1987); *b* 23 Dec 1938; *Educ* St Clement Danes GS, Slade Sch of Fine Art (DFA); *m* 1; 2 da (Rachel Clare b 19 April 1959, Sophie Rebecca b 22 Sept 1962); m 2, 14 Feb 1978, Susan Margaret; 1 s (Jacob Daniel b 23 April 1979); *Career* artist; pt/t lectr: Camberwell Sch of Art 1963-90, RA Schs 1980-; solo exhibitons: Thackeray Gallery London 1973, 1975, 1978 and 1981, Browse and Darby London 1988 (gallery artist); exhibited in various gp exhibitions, regular exhibitor at RA Summer Show, works shown in Jasper Galleries (Houston and NY); works in various private collections in Eng and America; RA 1986 (ARA 1975); *Recreations* gardening under the supervision of my wife; *Style—* Ben Levene, Esq; c/o Royal Academy of Arts, Piccadilly, London W1V 0DS (☎ 071 439 7438)

LEVENE, Sir Peter Keith; KBE (1989), JP (City of London) 1984-; s of Maurice Pierre Levene (d 1970), and Rose Levene; *b* 8 Dec 1941; *Educ* City of London Sch, Univ of Manchester (BEcon); *m* 1966, Wendy Ann, da of Frederick Fraiman; 2 s, 1 da; *Career* chm: Utd Sci Hldgs plc 1982-85 (dir 1968-85), Def Mfrs Assoc 1984-85; chief of def procurement MOD 1985-, dir UK Nat Armaments 1988-, chm IEPG (Euro) Nat Armaments Dirs 1989-90; personal advsr to sec state for def 1984-, dep chm Wasserstein Perella & Co 1991-; govr: City of London Sch for Girls 1984-85, City of London Sch 1985-, Sir John Cass Primary Sch 1985- (dep chm); vice pres City of London Red Cross, memb Ct HAC, chm London Homes for the Elderly; common cncllr Ward of Candlewick 1983-84, Alderman Ward of Portsoken 1984-; *Recreations* skiing, swimming, watching association football, travel; *Clubs* Guildhall, City Livery; *Style—* Sir Peter Levene, KBE, JP; 10-11 Park Place, London SW1A 1LB (☎ 071 499 4664)

LEVENE, Victor; s of George Levene, and Rose, *née* Tencer; *b* 20 Feb 1939; *Educ* Latymer Upper Sch, UCL (LLB); *m* 1 (m dis); 2s (Adam b 1971, Gideon b 1972), 1 da (Nadia b 1968); m 2, 1980, Jacqueline Anne, da of Clarence Perry; 1 s (Nicolas b 1981); *Career* called to the Bar Middle Temple 1961; in practice both civil and criminal spheres 1961-; *Recreations* cinema, philately, numismatics; *Clubs* BFI; *Style—* Victor Levene, Esq; Lamb Buildings, Temple, London EC4Y 7AS (☎ 071 353 0774, fax 071 353 0535)

LEVENTHAL, Colin David; *b* 2 Nov 1946; *Educ* Univ of London (BA); *Career* slr 1971; head of copyright BBC to 1981; head of programme acquisition Channel Four TV 1981-86, dir of programme acquisition and sales Channel Four TV 1987-; *Recreations* film, television, theatre; *Style—* Colin Leventhal, Esq; Channel Four TV Co Ltd, 60 Charlotte St, London W1 (☎ 071 631 4444)

LEVENTHORPE, Richard Christopher; s of Col Graham Sidney Leventhorpe, DSO (d 1963), and Dorothy, *née* Leyland (d 1965); *b* 19 June 1927; *Educ* Eton, King's Coll Cambridge (BA); *m* 14 Jan 1959, Penelope, da of Cdr Ross Leonard William Moss (d 1960); 3 s (John b 1961, Adrian b 1963, Thomas b 1965), 1 da (Susan b 1959); *Career* Lt Coldstream Gds served Palestine (despatches); dir: Four Leaf Farm Supplies Ltd 1976-79, Devon Gp Feeds 1976-82; memb House of Keys 1986; *Recreations* shooting, gardening; *Style—* Richard Leventhorpe, Esq; Hillberry Manor, Little Mill, Onchan, IOM (☎ 0624 661660); Govt Buildings, Bucks Rd, Douglas (☎ 0624 26262)

LEVER, Hon Bernard Lewis; s of Baron Lever (Life Peer, d 1977), by his w Ray, *see* Baroness Lever; n of Baron Lever of Manchester (Life Peer); *b* 1 Feb 1951; *Educ* Clifton, Queen's Coll Oxford (MA); *m* 1985, Anne Helen, da of Patrick Chandler Gordon Ballingall, MBE, of Seaford, E Sussex; 2 da (Helen b 19.., Isabel Elizabeth Rose b 2 March 1991); *Career* called to the Bar Middle Temple 1975, co-fndr of SDP in NW 1981, Parly candidate contested (SDP) Manchester Withington 1983; *Recreations* walking, music, skiing; *Clubs* Vincent's; *Style—* The Hon Bernard Lever; 2 Old Bank St, Manchester M2 7PF (☎ 061 832 3791)

LEVER, Sir (Tresham) Christopher Arthur Lindsay; 3 Bt (UK 1911); s of Sir Tresham Joseph Philip Lever, 2 Bt, FRSL (d 1975), stepson of Pamela Lady Lever, da of late Lt Col Hon Malcolm Bowes Lyon; *b* 9 Jan 1932; *Educ* Eton, Trinity Coll Cambridge (MA); *m* 1, 1970 (m dis 1974), Susan Mary, da of late John A Nicholson, of Crossmolina, Co Mayo; m 2, 1975, Linda Weightman McDowell, da of late James Jepson Goulden, of Tennessee, USA; *Heir* none; *Career* Lt 17/21 Lancers 1950; Peat, Marwick, Mitchell & Co 1954-55, Kitcat & Aitken 1955-56, dir: John Barran & Sons Ltd (plc) 1956-64; author; patron: Rhino Rescue Tst 1985- (tstee 1986-91), Tusk Tst 1990- (chm 1990-) Cncl Soc for the Protection of Animals in N Africa 1986-88, conslt Zoo Check Tst 1984-; tstee: Int Tst for Nature Conservation 1980- (vice pres 1986-), Migraine Tst 1983-89, Nat Eczema Soc 1989-; chm: African Fund for Endangered Wildlife (UK) 1987-90, Br Tst for Ornithology Nat Centre Appeal 1987-91; memb: Cncl Br Tst for Ornithology 1988-91, Ruaha Tst 1990-, Int Union for Conservation of Nature and Natural Resources Species Survival Cmmn 1988-; hon life memb Brontë Soc 1988; MBOU, FLS; *Books* Goldsmiths and Silversmiths of England (1975), The Naturalized Animals of the British Isles (1977, paperback edition 1979), Wildlife 80: the World Conservation Yearbook (contrib 1980), Evolution of Domesticated Animals (contrib 1984), Naturalized Mammals of the World (1985), Beyond the Bars: The Zoo Dilemma (contrib 1987), Naturalized Birds of the World (1987), For the Love of Animals (contrib 1989), The Mandarin Duck (1990); *Recreations* watching and photographing wildlife, fishing, golf; *Clubs* Buck's; *Style—* Sir Christopher Lever, Bt; Newell House, Winkfield, Windsor, Berks SL4 4SE (☎ 0344 882604)

LEVER, Colin David; s of Michael Lever, of London, and Susan, *née* Cohen (d 1987); *b* 4 Sept 1938; *Educ* Hendon GS, Balliol Coll Oxford (MA); *m* 2 Sept 1962, Ruth, da of Rev Harry Bornstein (d 1943); 1 s (Alexander b 1968), 3 da (Claire b 1966, Joy b 1970, Naomi b 1973); *Career* sr ptnr Bacon & Woodrow 1982- (actuarial trainee 1960, ptnr 1966); chm Nat Assoc Pension Funds 1985-87 (memb Cncl 1981-83, vice-chm 1983-85); FIA 1965; *Books* Pension Fund Investment (with D P Hager, 1989); *Recreations* gardening, narrow boating; *Style—* Colin Lever, Esq; 38 Oakleigh Park South, London N20 9JN (☎ 081 445 7880); Bacon & Woodrow, St Olaf House, London Bridge City, London SE1 2PE (☎ 071 357 7171, fax 071 378 8428/8470, telex 895 3206 BWLON G)

LEVER, Dr Eric G; s of Sam Lever (d 1978), and Freda, *née* Mann; *b* 5 April 1947; *Educ* Quintin Sch, Trinity Coll Cambridge (MA, MB BChir), Univ Coll Med Sch, Univ of Chicago (Endocrinology Diabetes fell), MRCP 1978; *m* 26 Aug 1985, Nicola, da of Bernard Langdon; 2 s (Elliott b 21 Jan 1988, Michael b 2 May 1989); *Career* jr hosp dr appts 1975-88: Univ Coll Hosp, Edgware Gen Hosp, Univ Hosp Nottingham, Royal Marsden Hosp, Hammersmith Hosp, King's Coll Hosp London, Billings Hosp Chicago; full-time private conslt in endocrinology diabetes and gen med 1988-: London Clinic, Humana Hosp Wellington, Lister Hosp; FRSM 1988; author of many papers on endocrinology and diabetes; *Recreations* art, music and the philosophy of ideas; *Style—* Dr Eric G Lever; 130 Harley St, London W1 (☎ 071 935 6558, 071 935 2190)

LEVER, Prof Jeffrey Darcy; s of John Roger Lever (d 1948), of Manchester, and Dorothy May, *née* Letts (d 1982); *b* 29 March 1923; *Educ* Westminster, Trinity Coll Cambridge (MB BChir, MA, MD, ScD), St Thomas' Hosp London; *m* 21 Dec 1950, Margaret Emily, da of Shepherd Eastwood (d 1973), of Aughton, Lancs; 2 s (John b 1952, James b 1954); *Career* Nat Serv Lt surgn RNVR 1947; Univ of Cambridge: demonstrator in anatomy 1950, lectr 1955-61, dir of med studies Trinity Coll, fell Trinity Coll; visiting fell Dept of Anatomy Washington Univ St Louis Mo USA 1954, prof and chm Dept of Anatomy Univ of Wales 1961-90, dep princ UC Cardiff 1984-86; author of numerous res pubns and contrib to med books; pres Anatomical Soc of GB and Ireland 1986-88; *Books* Introducing Anatomy (1980); *Recreations* rowing, yachting, downhill skiing; *Clubs* Leander (Henley on Thames), East India, London Rowing, Llandaff Rowing; *Style—* Prof Jeffrey Lever; Troedyrhiw Farm, Ystrad Mynach, Hengoed, Mid Glamorgan (☎ 0443 812175)

LEVER, Jeremy Frederick; QC (1972); s of Arnold Lever (d 1980), and Elizabeth Cramer, *née* Nathan; *b* 23 June 1933; *Educ* Bradfield, Univ Coll Oxford, Nuffield Coll Oxford, All Souls Coll Oxford (MA); *Career* 2 Lt RA (E African Artillery) 1952-53; called to the Bar Gray's Inn 1957, bencher 1985; pres Oxford Union Soc 1957 (tstee 1972-77 and 1988-); dir (non exec): Dunlop Holdings Ltd 1973-80, Wellcome Fndn Ltd 1983-; govr Berkhamsted Schs 1985-; sr dean All Souls Coll Oxford 1988- (fell 1957-, sub warden 1982-84); memb: Arbitral Tbnl US/UK Arbitration concerning Heathrow Airport User Changes 1988-, Cncl and Ctee of Mgmnt Br Inst of Int and Comparative Law; *Books* The Law of Restrictive Trading Agreements (1964), Chitty on Contracts (ed 1961, 1968, 1972, 1977); *Recreations* mountain walking, music; *Clubs* Garrick; *Style—* Jeremy Lever, Esq, QC; 59 Doughty St, London WC1N 2LS (☎ 071 831 0351, fax 071 405 1675); All Souls College, Oxford OX1 4AL (☎ 0865 279379, fax 0865 279 299); Gray's Inn Chambers, Gray's Inn, London WC1R 5JA (☎ 071 405 7211, fax 071 405 2084)

LEVER, John Kenneth; , MBE; s of Kenneth Lever, and Doris Lever; *b* 24 Feb 1949; *Educ* Dane Secdy Sch Ilford; *m* 1983, Christine Ann, da of John Wilkinson; 1 da; *Career* cricketer; has played for England in 21 test matches; *Clubs* Eccentric, Wanstead Golf; *Style—* John Lever, Esq, MBE; c/o Bancroft's School, High Road, Woodford Green, Essex

LEVER, (Justin) Lawrence; *b* 22 July 1957; *Educ* Manchester GS, The Sorbonne Paris, BNC Oxford; *Career* journalist; slr Withers & Co 1983, freelance journalist contributing to Times Financial Times Telegraph Gaurdian 1983-85, asst city editor The Times 1988-89 (city reporter 1985-88), fin editor The Mail on Sunday 1989-; *Style—* Lawrence Lever, Esq; The Mail on Sunday, Temple House, Temple Avenue, London EC4 (☎ 071 938 6000)

LEVER, Pamela, Lady; (Clodagh) Pamela; da of Lt-Col the Hon Malcolm Bowes-Lyon, CBE (d 1957), and former w of Lord Malcolm Avondale Douglas-Hamilton, OBE, DFC (d 1964); *b* 15 July 1908; *m* 1962, as his 2 w, Sir Tresham Joseph Philip Lever, 2 Bt (d 1975); *Style—* Pamela, Lady Lever; Lessudden, St Boswells, Melrose, Roxburghshire

LEVER, Paul Ronald Scott; s of Thomas Denis Lever, of Conningsby House, Sandygate, Sheffield, and Mary Barclay, *née* Scott; *b* 9 Dec 1940; *m* 23 Sept 1964, Elisabeth Barbra, da of Sir Richard Hughes, Bt (d 1970), of Rivelin Cottage, Hollow Meadows, Sheffield; 1 s (Christopher Mark b 17 July 1965), 2 da (Alison Clare b 25 Feb 1967, Catherine Elisabeth b 17 June 1969); *Career* md Tower Housewares (subsidiaries of TI Gp) 1979-83, chm Darius Industl Investmts 1983-86, md Crown Paints Div (subsidiary of Reed Int) 1986-88, md Crown Berger Europe Ltd 1988-89 (chm Ireland 1988-89); chm: Curpinol Ltd 1988-89, Williams Euro Consumer Prodns Div (subsidiaries of Williams Hldgs plc) 1989; exec chm Lionheart plc 1989-; chm Alexander Drew & Sons Ltd 1990-; Int Mgmnt Centre Europe: industl fell mktg and business policy 1984, industl prof strategic mgmnt 1986, elected master teacher 1987, elected cncl memb 1988; memb Ed Bd Management Digest 1987; *Recreations* listening to classical music, watching cricket, fishing, shooting; *Clubs* Reform; *Style—* Paul Lever, Esq; Lionheart plc, 3 Adams Court, Adams Hill, Knutsford, Cheshire WA16 6BA (☎ 0565 650003, fax 0565 650004)

LEVER, Baroness; Ray Rosalia; JP (Manchester); da of Dr Leonard Levene (d 1971), of Leicester, by his w Yetta (d 1965); *b* 23 Sept 1916; *Educ* Cheltenham Ladies' Coll; *m* 1939, Baron Lever (Life Peer, d 1977), s of Bernard Lever (d 1942); 1 s, 1 da; *Style—* The Rt Hon the Lady Lever, JP; 9 Plowley Close, Didsbury, Manchester M20 8DB (☎ 061 445 3456)

LEVER OF MANCHESTER, Baron (Life Peer UK 1979), of Cheetham, City of Manchester; (Norman) Harold Lever; PC (1969); s of late (Hyman) Bernard Lever, and Bertha Lever, of Manchester; *b* 15 Jan 1914; *Educ* Manchester GS, Manchester Univ (LLB); *m* 1, 1939 (m dis), Ethel, da of Mendel Samuel, and former w of Harris Sebrinski (otherwise Samuels); m 2, 1 March 1945, Betty (Billie) (d 1948), da of Myer Woolfe, and formerly w of Monty Featherman; 1 da (Hon Judith b 1947); m 3, 1962, Mrs Diane Zilkha, da of late Saleh Bashi, of Geneva; 3 da (Hon Annabelle b 1962, Hon Isabelle (Hon Mrs Laurent) b 1964, Hon Donatella Arabelle Yasmine b 1966); *Career* sits as Lab Peer in House of Lords; called to the Bar Middle Temple; MP (L) Manchester Exchange 1945-50, Manchester Cheetham 1950-74, Manchester Central 1974-79; jt parly under-sec of state Dept of Economic Affairs 1967, fin sec to the Treasy 1967-69, paymaster gen 1969-70, chm Public Accounts Ctee 1970-73; treas Socialist Int 1971-73, chllr Duchy of Lancaster 1974-79; dir: Guardian and Manchester Evening News 1979-, Singer & Friedlander 1984-, Britannia Arrow Hldgs plc; chm London Interstate Bank Ltd, dir memb of the Int Advsy Bd of the Creditanstaldt Bankverein; chm Jt Ctee on Art and Antiques Trade and Auction Houses 1982-85, memb Franks Ctee on Falklands 1982; govr: LSE, Manchester Univ; chm: English-Speaking Union, Tstees of Royal Acad Tst, 1981-87; tstee Royal Opera House 1974-82, memb House of Lords Bridge Team in match against Commons; *Style—* The Rt Hon the Lord Lever of Manchester, PC; House of Lords, SW1

LEVERHULME, 3 Viscount (UK 1922); Sir Philip William Bryce Lever; 3 Bt (1911), KG (1988), TD, JP; also Baron Leverhulme (UK 1917); s of 2 Viscount (d 1949), by his 1 w, Marion; *b* 1 July 1915; *Educ* Eton, Trinity Coll Cambridge; *m* 1937, Margaret Ann (d 1973), da of John Moon, of Tiverton, Devon; 3 da (Hon Mrs Susan Pakenham, Hon Mrs Peter Tower, Hon Mrs Heber-Percy); *Heir* none; *Career* advsy dir Unilever Ltd; Lord-Lt for City and County of Chester 1949-90; Hon Col: Queen's Own Yeo 1979-, RAC TAVR 1972-; memb Nat Hunt Ctee 1961 (steward 1965-68), dep sr steward Jockey Club 1970-73 (sr steward 1973-76); chllr Liverpool Univ 1980-; pres NW Tourist Bd 1982-; FRCS; KStJ; *Clubs* Boodle's, Jockey; *Style—* The Rt Hon the Viscount Leverhulme, KG, TD, JP; Thornton Manor, Thornton Hough, Wirral, Merseyside (☎ 051 336 4834); Flat 6, Kingston House East, Princes Gate, Kensington, London SW7 1LJ (☎ 071 589 9322); Badanloch, Kinbrace, Sutherland

LEVESON, Brian Henry; QC 1986; s of Dr Ivan Leveson (d 1980), of Liverpool, and Elaine, *née* Rivlin (d 1983); *b* 22 June 1949; *Educ* Liverpool Coll, Merton Coll Oxford (MA); *m* 20 Dec 1981, Lynne Rose, da of Aubrey Fishel (d 1987), of Wallasey; 2 s (Andrew b 1983, James b 1989), 1 da (Claire b 1984); *Career* called to the Bar Middle Temple 1970; lectr in Law Univ of Liverpool 1971-81, rec of the Crown Ct 1988; memb Cncl Univ of Liverpool 1983; *Clubs* Athenaeum, Liverpool; *Style—* Brian Leveson, Esq, QC; 5 Essex Ct, Temple, London EC4Y 9AH (☎ 071 353 4363, fax 071 583 1491); 25 Byrom St, Manchester M3 4PF (☎ 061 834 5238, fax 061 834 0394)

LEVESON, Lord; Granville George Fergus Leveson Gower; s and h of 5 Earl Granville, MC; *b* 10 Sept 1959; *Career* a page of honour to HM Queen Elizabeth, the Queen Mother 1973-; *Style—* Lord Leveson

LEVEY, Lady Melissa Geraldine Florence; *née* Bligh; da (by 3 w) of 9 Earl of Darnley (d 1955); *b* 1945; *m* 1965, Don Manuel Torrado y de Fontcuberta (d 1980); 1 s (Manuel Ivo b 1966), 2 da (Maria Melissa b 1968, Victoria Irene b 1973); m 2, 1985, Rev Colin Russell Levey; *Style—* The Lady Melissa Levey; The Rectory, Elmley Lovett, Droitwich, Worcs WR9 0PU (☎ 0299 250255)

LEVEY, Sir Michael Vincent; LVO (1965); s of O L H Levey and Gladys Mary Milestone; *b* 8 June 1927; *Educ* Oratory Sch, Exeter Coll Oxford; *m* 1954, Brigid Brophy, *qv*; 1 da; *Career* served Army 1945-48; Slade prof of fine art Cambridge 1963-64, dir Nat Gallery 1973-86 (asst keeper 1951-66); hon fellow Exeter Coll Oxford 1973; Hon DLitt Univ of Manchester; FBA, FRSL; kt 1980; *Books* 14 vols non fiction, 3 vols fiction; *Style—* Sir Michael Levey; Flat 3, 185 Old Brompton Rd, London SW5 0AN (☎ 071 373 9335)

LEVEY, Hon Mrs (Moyra Christine); *née* Wilson; da of Baron Wilson of Radcliffe (d 1983); *b* 5 Feb 1943; *Educ* Stand GS Whitefield, Birmingham Univ; *m* 1964, Dr Arthur Crowther (d 1979); 2 da (Katherine, Caroline); m 2, 1983, Joseph Levey (d 1985); *Recreations* badminton, golf, bridge; *Style—* The Hon Mrs Levey; 8 Delfur Road, Bramhall, Cheshire

LEVI, Prof Peter (Chad Tigar); s of Herbert Simon Levi (d 1956), of Ruislip, Middlx, and Edith Mary Tigar (d 1973); *b* 16 May 1931; *Educ* Beaumont Oxford (MA); *m* 31 March 1977, Deirdre, da of Hon Dennis Craig, MBE (d 1971), of Bath; *Career* Jesuit priest; tutor and lectr Campion Hall Oxford 1965-76, lectr in classics Christ Church Oxford 1979-82, prof of poetry Univ of Oxford 1984-89; fell St Catherine's Coll 1977-; author numerous volumes of poetry and some prose; poetry: The Gravel Ponds (1960), Water Rock and Sand (1962), The Shearwaters (1985), Fresh Water Sea Water (1966), Ruined Abbeys (1968), Life is a Platform (1971), Death is a Pulpit (1971), Collected Poems (1976), Five Ages (1978), Private Ground (1981), The Echoing Green (1983), Shakespeare Birthday (1985), Shadow and Bone (1989), Goodbye to the Art of Poetry (1989); prose: Beaumont (1961), The Lightgarden of the Angel King (1973), In Memory of David Jones (1975), The Noise Made By Poems (1976), The Hill of Kronos (1980), The Flutes of Autumn (1983), A History of Greek Literature (1985), The Frontiers of Paradise (1987), To The Goat (1988), Life and Times of William Shakespeare (1988), Boris Pasternak (1989); thrillers: The Head in the Soup (1979), Grave Witness (1985), Knit One Drop One (1987); translations: Yevtushenko (1963), The Psalms (1976), Marko the Prince (1983), The Holy Gospel of St John (1985); FSA, FRSL; *Recreations* a little quiet touring, visiting small museums; *Clubs* Beefsteak; *Style—* Prof Peter Levi; St Catherines Coll, Oxford

LEVI, Renato (Sonny); s of Mario Levi (d 1972), and Eleonora, *née* Ciravegna; *b* 3 Sept 1926; *Educ* College de Cannes France, St Paul's Darjeeling, Bishop Cotton Simla India, Coll Aeronautical Engineering London; *m* 12 June 1954, Ann Joan, da of John Douglas Watson (d 1969); 2 s (Martin b 1958, Christopher b 1962), 1 da (Gina b 1955); *Career* RAF: joined 1945, cmmnd 1946, demob 1948; designer highspeed watercraft AFCO Bombay India 1951-60, chief designer Navaltecnica Anzio Italy 1960-65, freelance designer 1965-; work incl: Cowes-Torquay powerboat race winners, A Speranziella 1963, Surfury 1967, (Blue Riband holder) Virgin Atlantic Challenger II; originator of Delta hulls and Levi Drive Surface Propulsion; RDI 1987, FCSD 1989; *Books* Dhows to Deltas (1971); *Recreations* power boating and travelling; *Clubs* Royal London Yacht; *Style—* Sonny Levi, Esq; Sandhills Farmhouse, Porchfield, nr Newport, IOW (☎ 0983 524713, fax 0983 527238)

LEVIN, (Henry) Bernard; s of late Phillip Levin, and Rose, *née* Racklin; *b* 19 Aug 1928; *Educ* Christ's Hosp, LSE (BSc); *Career* journalist, author; *Style—* Bernard Levin, Esq; c/o Curtis Brown Ltd, 162-168 Regent St, London W1

LEVIN, Enny; s of Moses Levin, of London, and Sarah, *née* Greenberg (d 1983); *b* 20 March 1932; *Educ* Benoni HS, SA, Univ of Pretoria (BChD); *m* Osnuth, *née* Bregman; 2 s (Daniel, Phillip); *Career* dentist; gen practice 1955-56; teacher Hadassa Dental Hosp Jerusalem 1956, Health Serv 1957-65, Harley St practice 1965-, pt/t teacher London Dental Hosp 1965-69; author of papers and int lectr; memb: BDA, RSM, Alpha Omega, Myoforctional Inst USA; FDS; *Recreations* sailing, walking, gardening, study of religion, mysticism, psychology; *Style—* Enny Levin, Esq; 42 Harley St, London W1N 1AB (☎ 071 935 6202)

LEVIN, Gerald; s of Solomon Levin (d 1940), of Bulawayo (Rhodesia) Zimbabwe, and Anna, *née* Kosina; *b* 8 Feb 1934; *Educ* Milton Sr Sch Bulawayo, Univ of Cape Town SA (BArch), Regent St Poly (MRTPI); *Career* architect; Basil Spence & Ptnrs 1957, ptnr Renton Howard Wood Levin Partnership 1970- (joined 1962); projects incl: schemes for the London Surrey Docks, redevelopment of Nelson Harbour Antigua, Tolmers Square Euston Rd London, St Katharine Docks London, new HQ Bp Oil (UK) Ltd Hemel Hempstead, Trinity Square Chapel Lane Hounslow, Albany St London, Red Lion Square London, Exeter Skypark Exeter, Sci Res Park Emersons Green Bristol, Thomas Neal's Covent Garden, Edgware Rd Underground Station Redevelopment; studies incl: Travallator Transport study for DOE, Effect of Motor Car on Environment Ventris study 1962, Effect of Movement Systems on New Town Design (RTPI thesis) 1964, River Clyde study 1974; memb RTPI Planning Gain Working Pty (reported to DOE 1985), organiser (on behalf of Renton Howard Wood Levin Partnership) 150 Anniversary function at Hampton Ct 1984; pres Arch Assoc 1985-86, tstee and dir Pub Art Devpt Tst 1985, tstee Camden Festival 1985, chm Patrons of New Art 1990, memb Cncl and dir Friends to the Tate Gallery; *Awards* jt winner Int Ideas Competition, second place Sydney Worldwide Competition, winner AA Michael Ventris award 1962; memb Arch Assoc 1958- MRIBA 1960, MRTPI 1970; *Recreations* playing the cello; *Clubs* Reform, Groucho's, Mosimann's; *Style—* Gerald Levin, Esq; 6 Market House, 12-16 Parker St, London WC2B 5PH (☎ 071 831 9582); Renton Howard Wood Levin Partnership, 77 Endell St, London WC2H 9AJ (☎ 071 379 7900, fax 071 836 4881)

LEVIN, Richard; Sandells House, West Amesbury, Wilts SP4 7BH

LEVINE, Sir Montague Bernard; s of late Philip Levine; *b* 15 May 1922; *Educ* RCS in Ireland, RCP in Ireland; *m* 1959, Dr Rose Gold; 1 s, 1 da; *Career* gen practitioner; dep coroner Inner S London, clinical tutor in gen practice St Thomas' Hosp 1972-; author; kt 1979; *Books* Interparental Violence and its Effect on Children; *Style—* Sir Montague Levine; Gainsborough House, 120 Ferndene Rd, Herne Hill, SE24 (☎ 071 274 5554)

LEVINE, Sydney; s of Rev Isaac Levine (d 1957), of Bradford, and Miriam, *née* Altman (d 1967); *b* 4 Sept 1923; *Educ* Bradford GS, Univ of Leeds (LLB); *m* 29 March 1959, Cécile Rona, da of Joseph Rubinstein (d 1987), of Dublin; 3 s (Iain David b 1960, Simon Mark b 1962, Colin Philip b 1964), 1 da (Emma Rachel b 1969); *Career* called to the Bar Inner Temple 1952, rec of the Crown Ct 1975; *Recreations* acting and directing in amateur theatre, gardening, marathon running; *Style—* Sydney Levine, Esq; 2A Primley Park Road, Alwoodley, Leeds 17 (☎ 0532 683769); Broadway House, 9 Bank St, Bradford 1 (☎ 0274 722560, fax 0274 370708)

LEVINGE, Jane, Lady; Jane Rosemary; *née* Stacey; *m* 1976, as his 2 w, Maj Sir Richard Vere Henry Levinge, 11 Bt, MBE (d 1984); *Clubs* Naval; *Style—* Jane, Lady Levinge; Abbey Lodge, Rectory Lane, Itchen Abbas, Hants

LEVINGE, Sir Richard George Robin; 12 Bt (I 1704), of High Park, Westmeath; s of Sir Richard Vere Henry Levinge, 11 Bt, MBE (d 1984), and his 1 w, Barbara, da of George Jardine Kidston, CMG; *b* 18 Dec 1946; *m* 1, 1969 (m dis 1978), Hilary Jane, da of Dr Derek Mark, of Wingfield, Bray, Co Wicklow; 1 s (Richard Mark b 1970); m 2, 1978, Donna Maria Isabella d'Ardia Caracciolo, yr da of Don Ferdinando d'Ardia Caracciolo dei Principi di Cursi, of Haddington Road, Dublin 4; 1 s (Robin Edward b 1978), 1 da (Melissa Louise b 1980); *Heir* s, Richard Mark Levinge b 1970; *Style—* Sir Richard Levinge, Bt; Clohamon House, Bunclody, Co Wexford

LEVISON, Nicholas Timothy; s of Isaac Harry Levison, of London, and Ann, *née* Harris; *b* 1 Aug 1935; *Educ* Malvern; *m* 2 June 1971, Fosca, da of Aldo Foschi, of Forli, Italy; 1 s (James b 24 Feb 1977); *Career* slr, sr ptnr Lawrance Messer & Co 1985-89, ptnr Turner Kenneth Brown 1989-; memb: Law Soc 1958, Int Bar Assoc; *Recreations* golf, reading, theatre, skiing; *Clubs* City of London; *Style—* Nicholas Levison, Esq; Turner Kenneth Brown, 100 Fetter Lane, London EC4A 1DD (☎ 071 242 6005, fax 071 242 3003, telex 297696 TKBLAW G)

LEVISON, Victor Bernard; *Educ* Univ of London (MB BS); *Career* house surgn Radiotherapy Dept Westminster Hosp, sr registrar Radiotherapy Centre Addenbrooke's Hosp Cambridge, conslt radiotherapist Dudley Road Hosp Birmingham and Coventry; currently conslt radiotherapist: N Middx Hosp & Annexes, St Margaret's Hosp Epping, Highlands Hosp London; memb Medico-Legal Soc; MRCS, LRCP 1945, DMRT 1949, FFR 1954, FRCR 1975; *Publications* Pre-operation Radiotherapy and Surgery in the Treatment of Oat Cell Carcinoma of the Bronchus (Clinical Radiology, 1980), What is the Best Treatment of Early Operable Small Cell Carcinoma of the Bronchus? (Thorax, 1980), Effect on Fertility, Libido, Sexual Function of Post-operative Radiotherapy and Chemotherapy for Cancer of Testicle (Clinic Radiology, 1986); *Style—* Victor Levison, Esq; 20 Priory Close, Totteridge, London N20 8BB (☎ 081 445 1481); North London Nuffield Hospital, Cavell Drive, Uplands Park Ed, Enfield, Middx EN2 7PR (☎ 081 366 2122)

LEVITT, Roger Joseph; s of Maj Ben Levitt, of Finchley, London, and Esther, *née* Schofield; *b* 2 May 1949; *Educ* Wellingborough Sch; *m* 30 July 1972, Diana Marilyn, da of Lt Cdr Alfred Anthony Steyne (d 1979), of Hampstead, London; 2 s (James b 15 Nov 1974, Matthew b 7 Sept 1977), 2 da (Annabel b 28 March 1980, Georgina b 1 Sept 1983); *Career* Imperial Life of Canada 1970-72, Crown Life 1972-76, R J Levitt Insurance Brokers 1976-80, R J Levitt Pension Conslts 1980-83, R J Levitt Group of Companies 1983-85, chm The Levitt Gp plc 1985-; hon fell Oriel Coll Oxford 1989; FIMBRA, LIA; *Style—* Roger Levitt, Esq; The Levitt Group (Holdings) plc, Devonshire House, 1 Devonshire St, London W1N 1FX (☎ 071 636 5992, fax 071 637 5088)

LEVY, Allan Edward; QC (1989); s of Sidney Levy, and Mabel, *née* Lewis; *b* 17 Aug 1942; *Educ* Bury GS, Univ of Hull (LLB), Inns of Ct Law; *Career* called to the Bar Inner Temple 1969, asst rec South Eastern Circuit 1990; memb Cncl of Justice; hon legal advsr Nat Children's Bureau 1990-, Memb Cncl of the Medico-Legal Soc, speaker at Seventh Int Congress on Child Abuse in Rio de Janeiro 1988, chm Staffordshire Child Care Inquiry 1990; *Books* Wardship Proceedings (1982, 2 edn 1987), Custody and Access (1983), Adoption of Children (with J F Josling, 10 edn 1985), Focus on Child Abuse (ed and contrib 1989); *Recreations* travel, reading; *Clubs* Reform; *Style—* Allan Levy, Esq, QC; 1 Temple Gardens, Temple, London, EC4Y 9BB (☎ 071 353 3737, fax 071 583 0018)

LEVY, Sir Ewart Joseph Maurice; 2 Bt (UK 1913), JP (Leics 1934); s of Sir Maurice Levy, 1 Bt, DL, JP (d 1933); *b* 10 May 1897; *Educ* Harrow; *m* 1932, Hylda Muriel (d

1970), da of Sir Albert Levy (d 1937); 1 da; *Career* Royal Pioneer Corps 1940-45 (despatches), Lt-Col 1944; High Sheriff Leics 1937; *Clubs* Reform; *Style*— Sir Ewart Levy, Bt, JP; Welland House, Weston-by-Welland, Market Harborough, Leics

LEVY, George Joseph; s of Percy Levy (d 1967); *b* 21 May 1927; *Educ* Oundle; *m* 1952, Wendy Yetta, da of Philip Blairman (d 1972); 1 s, 3 da; *Career* chm H Blairman & Sons Ltd 1965- (dir 1955), pres Br Antique Dealers Assoc 1974-76; chm: Grosvenor House Antiques Fair 1978-79, Somerset House Art Treasures Exhibition 1979, Friends of Kenwood 1979-, Burlington Fine Art and Antique Dealers Fair 1980-82, London Historic House Museums Liaison Gp English Heritage 1985; memb Cncl Jewish Museum 1978; *Recreations* photography, theatre, tennis; *Style*— George Levy, Esq; Flat 4, 6 Aldford St, London W1 (☎ 071 495 1730)

LEVY, Prof John Court (Jack); OBE (1984); s of Alfred Levy (d 1978), and Lily, *née* Court (d 1976); *b* 16 Feb 1926; *Educ* Owens Sch, Univ of London, Univ of Illinois; *m* 6 April 1952, Sheila Frances, da of Noah Krisman; 2 s (Richard b 1960, Robert b 1967), 1 da (Ruth b 1957); *Career* The City Univ London: head Dept of Mech Engrg 1966-83, pro vice chllr 1976-82; dir engrg profession The Engrg Cncl London 1983-90, project dir IEE/IMechE proposed amalgamation 1990-; FEng, FIMechE, FRAes, FCGI; *Recreations* theatre, chess; *Clubs* Island Sailing (IOW); *Style*— Prof Jack Levy, OBE; 18 Woodberry Way, Finchley, London N12 0HG (☎ 081 445 5227); 137 Gurnard Pines, Cockleton Lane, Gurnard, IOW

LEVY, Prof John Francis; s of Donald Myer Levy (d 1967), and Hilda Rose, *née* Stephens (d 1977); *b* 30 June 1921; *Educ* Ewell Castle Sch Ewell Surrey, Imperial Coll of Sci Technol and Med (BSc, DSc); *m* 3 April 1954, Hazel, da of Bernard Shilton (d 1975); 2 s (Martin John, Timothy James), 2 da (Jain Heather (Mrs Morrissey), Wendy Susan (Mrs Tough)); *Career* Imperial Coll of Sci Technol and Med Univ of London: joined teaching staff Dept of Botany and Plant Technol 1945, lectr 1949, sr lectr in timber technol Dept of Botany 1963, asst dir Dept of Botany 1967-74, reader in wood sci 1974, prof of wood sci 1981, head of plant technol section Dept of Pure and Applied Biology 1983, emeritus prof of wood sci 1986, sr res fell 1986; visiting prof Dept of Botany Kuwait Univ 1970, guest res worker CSIRO Div of Bldg Res Highett Victoria Aust 1977; warden Weeks Hall Imperial Coll 1959-69; hon fell: Portsmouth Poly, Imperial Coll; Inst of Wood Scis: cncl memb 1957-90, pres 1971-73; Br Wood Preserving Assoc: cncl memb 1957-, hon treas 1960-69, vice pres 1968-76, dep pres 1976-78, pres 1978-80; BSI: memb Chemical Div Cncl 1982-90, chm Wood Preservation Standards Policy Ctee 1982-90; memb: Euro Homologation Ctee 1965-73, Wood Protection Sub Gp Int Union of Forestry Res Orgns 1966-, Advsy Ctee for Forest Res Forestry Cmmn 1968-80, Int Res Gp on Wood Preservation 1968-, Cncl Timber Res and Devpt Assoc 1980-90, Hull Advsy Panel Mary Rose Tst 1982-, Panel for Evaluation of Efficacy of Wood Preservative Food and Environment Protection Act 1987-; chm Review Gp on Wood Sci and Processing Forestry Res Co-ordinating Ctee 1983, dir Guarantee Protection Tst 1985-; memb governing body: Ewell Castle Sch Surrey, Old Palace Sch Surrey; hon memb Royal Sch of Mines Assoc 1989, ARCS, FLS, fell Int Acad of Wood Scis, CBiol, FIBiol, FIWSc; *Recreations* rowing, cricket watching, reading, music; *Clubs* Athenaeum, Leander, Surrey CCC, Thames Rowing (vice pres), Imperial Coll Boat (pres); *Style*— Prof John Levy; 5 Washington Rd, Barnes, London SW13 9BG (☎ 081 748 0020); Department of Biology, Imperial College of Science, Technology and Medicine, London SW7 2AZ (☎ 071 589 5111 ext 7436)

LEVY, Paul; s of Hyman Solomon Levy (d 1980), of Kentucky USA, and Mrs Shirley Singer Meyers; *b* 26 Feb 1941; *Educ* Univ of Chicago (BA, MA), Univ Coll London, Harvard Univ (PhD), Nuffield Coll Oxford; *m* 1977, Penelope, da of Clifford Marcus (d 1952); 2 da (Tatyana b 1981, Georgia b 1983); *Career* journalist and lapsed don; food and wine ed The Observer 1980-, frequent broadcaster on radio and TV; national press specialist Writers Commendations 1985 and 1987; tstee: Strachey Tst, Jane Grigson Tst; FRSL; *Books* G E Moore and the Cambridge Apostles (1977, 2 edn 1989), The Shorter Strachey (ed with Michael Holroyd, 1980, 2 edn 1989), The Official Foodie Handbook (with Ann Barr, 1984), Out to Lunch (1986), Finger-lickin' Good (1990); *Recreations* being cooked for, drinking better wine; *Clubs* Groucho, Wednesday; *Style*— Paul Levy, Esq; c/o The Observer, Chelsea Bridge House, Queenstown Rd, London SW8 4NN (☎ 071 350 3466)

LEVY, Peter Lawrence; s of Joseph Levy, CBE, BEM (d 1990), of 12 Avenue Rd, London, and (Frances) Ninot, *née* Henwood; *b* 10 Nov 1939; *Educ* Charterhouse, Univ of London (BSc); *m* 29 June 1961, Colette, da of Harry Lynford, of 20 Fairacres, Roehampton Lane, London SW15; 1 s (Jonathan David b 8 Aug 1967), 2 da (Claudia Simone b 15 Nov 1962, Melanie Tamsin b 29 June 1965); *Career* ptnr DE & J Levy (surveyors) 1966-87, dir Stock Conversion plc 1985-86, chm Shaftesbury plc 1986-; chm Cystic Fibrosis Res Tst, Freeman City of London; FRICS; *Recreations* tennis, golf, cricket, walking; *Clubs* RAC, Reform; *Style*— Peter Levy, Esq; Shaftesbury plc, 11 Waterloo Place, London SW1Y 4AU (☎ 071 839 4024, fax 071 839 1933)

LEVY, Philip Grenville; s of Sydney George Levy, of London, and Ella-Mary, *née* Jacob (d 1952); *b* 11 Sept 1946; *Educ* Clifton, Univ of Manchester (LLB); *m* 16 July 1972, Sheila Michelle, da of Ian Baxter, of London; 1 s (James b 1980), 1 da (Tania b 1977); *Career* called to the Bar Inner Temple Gray's Inn; chm Harrow SDP 1986-87; elected memb Harrow Police and Community Consultative Ctee 1987-90; writer of programme notes for public chamber concerts; *Recreations* bridge, music; *Style*— Philip Levy, Esq; 11 South Square, Grays Inn, London WC1 (☎ 071 831 6974)

LEVY, Prof Philip Marcus; s of Rupert Hyam Levy (d 1951), and Sarah Beatrice, *née* Naylor; *b* 4 Feb 1934; *Educ* Leeds Mode Sch, Univ of Leeds (BA), Univ of Birmingham (PhD); *m* 8 March 1958, Gillian Mary Levy, da of Ronald Edward Harker, of Grassington, Yorks; 2 da (Lucy b 11 Aug 1965, Mary b 3 Sept 1967); *Career* Nat Serv RAF Flying Offr and psychologist 1959-62; sr res fell then lectr in psychology Inst of Educn Univ of Birmingham 1962-65 (res fell 1956-59), sr lectr in psychology Univ of Birmingham 1969-72 (lectr Dept of Psychology 1965-69), prof of psychology Univ of Lancaster 1972-; ed The British Journal of Mathematical and Statistical Psychology 1975-80; pres Br Psychological Soc 1978-79 (involved since 1960); ESRC: memb Psychology Ctee 1976-79, chm Psychology Ctee 1979-82, chm Educn and Human Devpt Ctee 1982-87, memb Cncl ESRC 1983-86 and 1987-89, chm Human Behaviour and Devpt Res Gp 1987-89; FBPsS 1970 (memb 1960); *Books* Tests in Education (with H Goldstein, 1984), Cognition in Action (with M Smyth, 1987); *Style*— Prof Philip Levy; Dept of Psychology, University of Lancaster, Lancaster LA1 4YF (☎ 0524 65201, fax 0524 843087, telex 65111 Lancul G)

LEVY, Victor Raphael; s of Moise Edward Joseph Levy, and Thelma, *née* Goide; *b* 14 April 1951; *Educ* UCS, Univ of Manchester (BSc); *Career* tax ptnr Arthur Andersen and Co; FCA, FTII; *Style*— Victor Levy, Esq; Arthur Anderson & Co, 1 Surrey St, London WC2R 2PS (☎ 071 438 3473, fax 071 831 1133, telex 8812711)

LEW, Dr Julian David Mathew; s of Rabbi Maurice Abram Lew (d 1989), of London, and Rachel Lew, JP, *née* Segalov; *b* 3 Feb 1948; *Educ* Univ of London (LLB), Catholic Univ of Louvain (Doctorate Int Law); *m* 11 July 1978, Margot Gillian, da of Dr David Isaac Perk, of Johannesberg, SA; 2 da (Ariella b 1981, Lauren b 1983); *Career* called to the Bar Middle Temple 1970, assoc prof Univ of Namur Belgium 1976-79, assoc lawyer Dilley & Custer Brussels 1977-79, UK res counsel Briger & Assocs NY London 1979-86, admitted slr 1981, attorney at law state of NY 1985, head Sch of Int Arbitration Queen Mary and Westfield Coll Univ of London 1985-, S J Berwin & Co 1986-; dir London Ct of Int Arbitration (vice chm Cncl of Mgmnt London); Freeman: City of London 1985, Worshipful Co of Arbitrators 1985; FCIArb 1976; *Books* Selected Bibliography on East West Trade Law (1976), Applicable in International Commercial Arbitration (1978), Selected Bibliography on International Commercial Arbitration (1979), Contemporary Problems in International Commercial Arbitration (ed, 1986), International Trade: Law and Practice (ed jtly, 1985, 2 edn 1990), The Immunity of Arbitrators (1990); *Recreations* tennis, reading, religion; *Style*— Dr Julian Lew; S J Berwin & Co, 236 Grays Inn Road, London WC1X 8HB (☎ 071 278 0444, fax 071 833 2860, telex 8814928 Winlaw)

LEWANDO, Sir Jan Alfred; CBE (1968); s of Maurice Lewando, of Manchester, and Eugenie, *née* Goldsmid; *b* 31 May 1909; *Educ* Manchester GS, Univ of Manchester; *m* 1948, Nora, da of William Slavouski; 3 da; *Career* served Br Army WWII in Europe, ME and Far East 1939-45, Br Army Staff Washington DC and Br Miny of Supply Mission 1941-45, Lt-Col 1943; joined Marks & Spencer Ltd 1929 (dir 1954-70), chm Carrington Viyella Ltd 1970-75; pres Br Textile Confedn 1972-73; dir: Heal and Son Holdings Ltd 1975-82, Bunzl Group 1976-86, W A Baxter & Sons Ltd 1975-, Johnston Industs Inc (USA) 1976-84, Royal Worcester Spode Ltd 1978-79, Edgars Stores Ltd SA 1876-82; memb: Br Overseas Trade Bd 1972-77, European Trade Ctee 1973-83, Br Nat Export Cncl 1969-71; chm Appeal Ctee Br Inst Radiology 1979-84, vice pres Tport Tst 1973-89 (PRS 1989-), vice chm Clothing Export Cncl 1966-70; CBIM, FRSA; Companion Textile Inst 1972, Legion of Merit (USA) 1946; kt 1974; *Style*— Sir Jan Lewando, CBE; Davidge House, Knotty Green, Beaconsfield, Bucks (☎ 0494 674987)

LEWER, Michael Edward; QC (1983); s of Lt-Col Stanley Gordon Lewer (d 1985), of Ashtead, Surrey, and Jeanie Mary, *née* Hay (d 1980); *b* 1 Dec 1933; *Educ* Tonbridge, Oriel Coll Oxford (MA); *m* 1965, Bridget Mary, da of Harry Anderson Clifford Gill (d 1980), of Buckland, Surrey; 2 s (William b 1966, Simon b 1969), 2 da (Natasha b 1967, Louise b 1977); *Career* called to the Bar Gray's Inn 1958; rec 1983; memb Criminal Injuries Compensation Bd 1986; *Clubs* Western (Glasgow); *Style*— Michael Lewer, Esq, QC; 99 Queens Drive, London N4; Whitehouse Cottage, Horham, Suffolk; Farrars Building, Temple, London EC4

LEWERS, Very Rev Benjamin Hugh; s of Dr H B Lewers, DSO, OBE (d 1950), of Ilfracombe, Devon, and Coral Helen Lewers; *b* 25 March 1932; *Educ* Sherborne, Selwyn Coll Cambridge (MA); *m* 1957, Sara, da of Cyprian Claud Blagden; 3 s (Timothy, Michael, Thomas); *Career* Nat Serv 2 Lt The Devon Regt; ordained: deacon 1962, priest 1963; curate St Mary Northampton 1962-65, priest i/c Church of The Good Shepherd Hounslow 1965-68, industl chaplain Heathrow Airport 1968-75, vicar Newark 1975-80, rector 1980-81, provost Derby 1981-, church cmmr; *Recreations* cricket, gardening, music, wine, rug-making; *Style*— The Very Rev the Provost of Derby; The Provost's House, 9 Highfield Rd, Derby DE3 1GX (☎ 0332 42971); Cathedral Office, St Michael's House, Queen St, Derby DE1 3DT (☎ 0332 41201)

LEWES, Bishop of 1977-; Rt Rev Peter John Ball; s of Thomas James Ball (Capt WWI, d 1966), of Eastbourne, and Kathleen Obena, *née* Bradley-Morris (d 1980); *b* 14 Feb 1932; *Educ* Lancing, Queens' Coll Cambridge (MA, Squash blue), Wells Theol Coll; *Career* ordained: deacon 1956, priest 1957; curate Rottingdean Chichester 1956-58, novice Society of the Sacred Mission 1958-60, prior Community of the Glorious Ascension 1960-77, licence to officiate Birmingham 1965-66, priest i/c Hoar Cross Lichfield 1966-69, licence to officiate Bath and Wells 1969-77, canon and prebendary Chichester 1977-; fell Woodard Corp 1961-88; memb Advsy Cncl for Religious Ctees 1980-; govr: Wellington Coll 1986-, Radley Coll 1987-, Eastbourne Coll 1978- Lancing Coll 1965-90; select preacher Univ of Oxford 1988; *Recreations* squash, music; *Style*— The Rt Rev the Bishop of Lewes; Beacon House, Berwick, Polegate, East Sussex BH26 6ST (☎ 0323 870387)

LEWIN, Christopher George; s of George Farley Lewin, of Ascot, Berks, and Hilda Mary Emily, *née* Reynolds; *b* 15 Dec 1940; *Educ* Coopers' Cos Sch Bow London; *m* 1 Nov 1985, Robin Lynn, da of Robert Harry Stringham; 2 s (Andrew Christopher Philip b 3 July 1987, Peter Edward James b 19 Oct 1990); *Career* actuarial asst: Equity & Law Life Assurance Society 1956-63, London Transport Bd 1963-67; Br Railways Bd: actuarial asst 1967-70, controller corp pensions 1970-80, seconded memb Fin Insts Gp DOE 1981-82, co-ordinator private capital 1980-88; pensions dir Associated Newspapers Holdings Ltd 1989-; winner: Joseph Burn prize Inst of Actuaries 1962, Messenger and Brown prize Inst of Actuaries 1968; chm Nat Fedn of Consumer Gps 1984-86; FIA 1964, FSS, FPMI; author of numerous articles in various actuarial jls 1970-; *Recreations* family life, old books and manuscripts relating to English social history, old board games; *Clubs* Argonauts, Gallio; *Style*— Christopher Lewin, Esq; Associated Newspapers Ltd, Temple House, Temple Avenue, London EC4Y 0JA (☎ 071 938 6933)

LEWIN, John; s of Bernard Sidney Lewin (d 1987), of Newport, Dyfed, and Ruth French, *née* Smith (d 1972); *b* 7 May 1940; *Educ* King Edward's Sch Bath, Univ of Southampton (BA, PhD); *m* 9 July 1966, Jane Elizabeth Sarah, da of Capt Cecil Joy (d 1979), of Newport, Dyfed; 2 da (Jenny b 1967, Marianna b 1971); *Career* asst lectr Univ of Hull 1965-68, dean Faculty of Sci Univ Coll of Wales Aberystwyth 1989- (former lectr, sr lectr, reader, prof 1968-); FRGS 1963; *Books* Timescales in Geomorphology (ed, 1980), British Rivers (ed, 1981), Modern and Ancient Fluvial Systems (ed, 1983), Palaeohydrology in Practice (ed, 1987); *Recreations* walking, reading; *Style*— Prof John Lewin; Institute of Earth Studies, University College of Wales, Aberystwyth, Dyfed SY23 3DB (☎ 0970 623111)

LEWIN, Hon Jonathan James; yr s of Adm of the Fleet Baron Lewin, KG, GCB, LVO, DSC; *b* 20 May 1959; *Educ* Merchant Taylors', Trinity Coll Cambridge (BA); *Career* journalist, asst ed Making Music magazine; *Recreations* music, writing; *Style*— The Hon Jonathan Lewin

LEWIN, Lucille; da of Michael Witz (d 1969), of SA, and Elaine, *née* Hoffenberg (now Mrs Samuelson); *b* 27 July 1948; *Educ* Redhill Sch for Girls, Univ of Witwatersrand; *m* 1969, Richard Lewin; 2 s (Joseph Michel b 1983, Jonathan Toby b 1988); *Career* fashion designer; design res Boston USA 1969-71, buyer Harvey Nichols 1973-76, fndr Whistles 1976-; *Style*— Ms Lucille Lewin; Whistles, 12 St Christophers Place, London W1 (☎ 071 487 4484)

LEWIN, Adm of the Fleet Baron (Life Peer UK 1982), of Greenwich, in Greater London; Terence Thornton Lewin; KG (1983), GCB (1976, KCB 1973), LVO (1959), DSC (1942); s of E H Lewin (d 1963); *b* 19 Nov 1920; *Educ* Judd Sch Tonbridge; *m* 1944, Jane, da of Rev Charles James Branch Evans (d 1956); 2 s (Hon Timothy Charles Thornton b 1947, Hon Jonathan James b 1959), 1 da (Hon Susan (Hon Mrs Roe) b 1949); *Career* RN 1939, served WWII Home and Med Fleets (despatches), cmd HMS Corunna 1955-56, HMY Britannia 1957-58, Capt 1958, cmd HMS Urchin 1962, HMS Tenby 1963, Dartmouth Trg Sqdn 1962-63, HMS Hermes 1966-67, Rear Adm 1968, asst chief of Naval Staff (Policy) MOD 1968-69, Flag Offr second in cmd Far E Fleet 1969-70, Vice Adm 1970, vice chief of Naval Staff 1971-73, Adm 1973, C-in-C Fleet, Allied C-in-C Channel and C-in-C Eastern Atlantic Area 1973-75, C-in-C Naval Home Cmd 1975-77, chief of Naval Staff and First Sea Lord

1977-79, Adm of the Fleet 1979, chief of Def Staff 1979-82; Naval ADC to HM The Queen 1967-68, Flag ADC to HM The Queen 1975-77 (first and princ ADC 1977-79); chm of tstee Nat Maritime Museum 1981-87, elder brother Trinity House 1975; pres: Br Schs Exploring Soc, Shipwrecked Mariners Soc; Hon Freeman Skinners' Co and Shipwrights' Co; Hon DSc City Univ; *Style—* Adm of the Fleet the Rt Hon the Lord Lewin, KG, GCB, LVO,DSC; House of Lords, London SW1

LEWIN, Hon Timothy Charles Thornton; er s of Adm of the Fleet Baron Lewin, KG, GCB, LVO, DSC (Life Peer), *qv*; *b* 1947; *m* 1973, Carolyn Thain; *Style—* The Hon Timothy Lewin; c/o Adm of the Fleet the Rt Hon the Lord Lewin, KG, GCB, LVO, DSC, House of Lords, London SW1

LEWINSOHN, Max Robert; *b* 12 Oct 1946; *m* Joan Krystyna, 3 children; *Career* chm Industrial Trade and Finance Ltd, sr ptnr Maxwell Allen; former chm: Dominion International Group plc, Southwest Resources plc; FCA, ATII; *Recreations* tennis, skiing, windsurfing; *Style—* Max Lewinsohn, Esq; 3 Church Rd, Croydon CR0 1SG (☎ 0342 811031, fax 0342 810797)

LEWINTON, Christopher; s of Joseph Lewinton, and Elizabeth Lewinton; *b* 6 Jan 1932; *Educ* Acton Tech Coll, Univ of London; *Career* Lt REME; pres Wilkinson Sword USA 1960-70, chief exec Wilkinson Sword Gp (acquired by Allegheny International 1978) 1970-85, chm: Int Ops Allegheny International 1976-85, TI Group plc 1989- (chief exec 1986-), non-exec dir Reed International; *Recreations* golf, tennis, boating; *Clubs* Buck's Sunningdale Golf, Metropolitan (NY), Key Biscayne Yacht (Florida); *Style—* Christopher Lewinton, Esq; TI Group plc, 50 Curzon St, London W1Y 7PN (☎ 071 499 9131, fax 071 493 6533, telex 263740 TIGRUP G)

LEWIS, Alan; s of Albert Harold Lewis (d 1982), of Rochdale, and Annie, *née* Quinn; *b* 11 Sept 1940; *Educ* Salford GS; *m* 5 Feb 1966, Jean da of Roy Maclarty (d 1958), of Carshalton Beeches, Surrey; 1 s (Matthew b 1976), 1 da (Clare b 1973); *Career* copy gp head Dorland Advertising London 1967-69, creative dir J Walter Thompson Co Cape Town S Africa 1971-76 (copy chief Johannesburg 1969-71), creative dir Campbell-Ewald Pty Ltd Cape Town S Africa 1976-78, dep creative dir Lovell and Rupert Curtis Ltd London 1978-82, exec creative dir Ogilvy & Mather Scotland 1982-89, gp creative dir Robertson Marketing Servs Gp Edinburgh 1989-; MIPA 1986; *Recreations* good food, good drink and good jazz; *Style—* Alan Lewis, Esq; Ardrhu, 22 Milling St, Helensburgh, Dunbartonshire G84 9PN (☎ 0436 74722); Robertson Marketing Services Group Ltd, 90 Haymarket, Edinburgh (☎ 031 346 1777)

LEWIS, HE Sir Allen Montgomery; GCMG (1979), GCVO (1985), GCSL (1986); s of late George Ferdinand Montgomery Lewis, and Ida Louisa, *née* Barton; *b* 26 Oct 1909; *Educ* St Mary's Coll St Lucia, Univ of London (LLB, external); *m* 1936, Edna Leofrida, da of late Thomas Alexander Theobalds; 3 s, 2 da; *Career* called to Bar: St Lucia 1931, Middle Temple 1946; MLC St Lucia 1943-51; actg puisne judge Windward and Leewards Islands 1955-56, QC 1956, cmmr for reform and revison of laws St Lucia 1954-58; judge: Fed Supreme Ct 1959-62, Br Caribbean Ct of Appeal 1962, Ct of Appeal Jamaica 1962-67 (actg pres Ct of Appeal 1966, actg chief justice Jamaica 1966), chief Justice WI Assoc States Supreme Ct 1967-72, chm National Development Corporation St Lucia 1972-74; govr of St Lucia 1974-79, govr-gen of St Lucia 1979-80 and 1982-87; chllr Univ of the WI 1975-89; Hon LLD UWI 1974; KStJ 1975; kt 1968; *Publications* Revised Edition of Laws of St Lucia (1957); *Recreations* gardening, swimming; *Clubs* St Lucia Yacht, St Lucia Golf; *Style—* HE Sir Allen Lewis, GCSL, GCMG, GCVO, QC; Beaver Lodge, The Morne, PO Box 1076, Castries, St Lucia (☎ 27285)

LEWIS, Adm Sir Andrew Mackenzie; KCB (1971); s of late Rev Cyril F Lewis, of Gilston, Herts, and Effie, *née* Mackenzie; *b* 24 Jan 1918; *Educ* Haileybury; *m* 1, 1943, Rachel Elizabeth (d 1983), da of Vice Adm Eustace La Trobe Leatham, CB (d 1935); 2 s (Christopher, David); m 2, 1989, Primrose Christina, da of J D R Sadler-Phillips; *Career* Second Sea Lord 1970-71, C-in-C Naval Home Cmd 1972-74, DL Essex 1975, Lord Lt Essex 1978-; *Clubs* Brooks's; *Style—* Adm Sir Andrew Lewis, KCB; Coleman's Farm, Finchingfield, Essex CM7 4PE

LEWIS, Annette Sylvia (Nettie); da of Alan Lewis, and Shirley, *née* Vasner; *b* 7 Oct 1964; *Educ* West Hatch GS; *m* 12 Aug 1989, James Patrick Dudwell Miller, s of Patrick Reginald Miller, of Hong Kong; *Career* horsewoman and competitive showjumper; sr memb Br Young Riders Showjumping Team, nat young riders champion, Vauxhall showjumper of the future 1985-86, nat ladies champion 1988, abroad winner Royal Windsor Grand Prix 1989; wins also at: Horse of the Year Show, Wembley, Olympia, RTHS; memb Br Showjumping Assoc, memb Federation Equestrian Internationale; *Recreations* cooking, sports; *Style—* Ms Annette Lewis; The Paddock Grove Lane, Chigwell Row, Essex (☎ 081 500 5040)

LEWIS, Anthony (Tony); s of Wilfrid Llewellyn (d 1981), of Swansea, and Florence Majorie, *née* Flower; *b* 6 July 1938; *Educ* Neath GS, Christ's Coll Cambridge (MA); *m* 22 Aug 1962, Joan, da of Owen Pritchard, of Neath; 2 da (Joanna Clare b 29 Nov 1967, Anabel Sophia b 28 July 1969); *Career* cricketer; Glamorgan 1955-74, Glamorgan capt 1967-72, Eng capt tour to India, Ceylon and Pakistan 1972-73; sports presenter and commentator: HTV Wales 1971-82, BCC Radio and TV cricket progs 1974-, Sport on Four Radio Four 1977-84; cricket corr The Sunday Telegraph 1974-; memb Sports Cncl for Wales 1972-75; chm: Glamorgan CCC 1987-; Wales chm ABSA (Assoc of Business Sponsership of the Arts) 1988-; Univ of Cambridge: Rugby blue 1959, Cricket blue 1960-62 (capt 1962); *Books* Summer of Cricket (1975), Playing Days (1985), Double Century (1987); Summer of Cricket (1975), Playing Days (1985), Double Century (1987); *Recreations* golf, classical music; *Clubs* MCC, E India, Cardiff and Co, Royal Porthcawl Golf, Royal Worlington and Newmarket Golf; *Style—* Tony Lewis, Esq; Ewenny Isaf, Ewenny, Mid Glamorgan (☎ 0656 663849)

LEWIS, Anthony Meredith; s of Lt-Col G V L Lewis (d 1985), and G Lewis, *née* Fraser; *b* 15 Nov 1940; *Educ* Rugby, St Edmund Hall Oxford (MA); *m* 26 July 1970, Ewa Maria Anna, da of Stanislaw Strawinski (d 1980); 1 s (Alexander Edward Meredith (Beetle) b 1 Oct 1976), 1 da (Antonina Kathryn (Nina) b 18 Sept 1981); *Career* articled clerk Freshfields 1964-70; admitted slr 1965; sr ptnr Joynson-Hicks 1986-89 (ptnr 1971-86), jt sr ptnr Taylor Joynson Garret 1989-; memb Law Soc; *Recreations* shooting, skiing, tennis, opera, cricket; *Style—* Anthony Lewis, Esq; 10 Maltravers St, London WC2R 3BS (☎ 071 836 8456, fax 071 379 7196, telex 268014 JHICKS G)

LEWIS, Hon Antony Thomas; JP (1979); s of 3 Baron Merthyr, KBE, PC (d 1977), and Violet, *née* Meyrick; *b* 4 June 1947; *Educ* Eton, Univ of Wales (LLM); *m* 1974, Mary Carola Melton, da of Rev Humphrey John Paine; *Career* called to the Bar Inner Temple 1971; lectr in law Univ Coll Cardiff 1976-89, chm Powys Family Health Servs Authy 1990-; *Style—* The Hon Antony Lewis, JP; The Skreen, Erwood, Builth Wells, Powys

LEWIS, Arthur James Winterbotham (Jimmie); s of Arthur Blount Lewis (d 1925), of The Park, Nottingham, and Elsie, *née* Snell (d 1978); *b* 18 June 1929; *Educ* Eton; *m* 29 July 1952, (Audrey) Celia, da of Jack Dobson; 2 s (James Blount b 22 Aug 1954, William Winterbotham b 21 Nov 1958), 1 da (Lucy Mary Maud b 27 May 1953); *Career* apprenticed J B Lewis & Sons 1947 (became Meridian Ltd), dir Meridian Ltd 1957 (sold to Courtaulds Ltd 1964); Courtaulds Ltd: dir Mktg Div 1970, dir Consumer Products Gp 1984, dir Mktg Servs Courtaulds Textiles Gp 1988, ret 1989; conslt: Courtaulds Textiles plc 1989-, Yamata International Inc Tokyo 1989-; memb Euro Trade Ctee BOTB, chm Euro Clothing Mfrs Assoc, Br Knitting and Clothing Export Cncl, pres Knitting Indust Fedn; vice pres: Br Knitting and Clothing Cncl, Br Clothing Indust Assoc; *Recreations* sailing, shooting, tennis; *Clubs* coodles', Hurlingham, Aldeburgh Yacht (former cdre); *Style—* Jimmie Lewis, Esq; 11 Amner Rd, London SW11 6AA (☎ 071 223 2382); Courtaulds Textiles, 13-14 Margaret St, London W1A 3DS (☎ 071 436 5080, fax 071 323 6523)

LEWIS, Sir (William) Arthur; s of George Ferdinand Lewis, of Castries, St Lucia, W Indies, by his w Ida Louisa, *née* Barton; bro of Sir Allen Lewis (*qv*); *b* 23 Jan 1915; *Educ* St Mary's Coll Castries, LSE (BCom, PhD); *m* 1947, Gladys Isabel, da of William Jacobs, of Grenada; 2 da; *Career* lectr LSE 1938-48, Stanley Jevons prof of political economy at Univ of Manchester 1948-1959, vice-chllr Univ of West Indies 1959-63; Princeton Univ: prof of econs and int affrs 1963-68, James Madison prof of political econ 1963-82, James S McDonnell Distinguished Univ prof of econs and int affrs 1981-83 (emeritus 1983-); princ BOT then Colonial Office 1943-44, memb Econ Advsy Cncl 1945-49, dir Colonial Devpt Corp 1950-52, memb Departmental Ctee on Fuel and Power 1951-52, econ advsr to the PM of Ghana 1957-58, dep md UN Special Fund 1959-60, special advsr to the PM of the WI 1961-62; dir: Industl Devpt Corp Jamaica 1961-63, Central Bank of Jamaica 1961-62; pres Caribbean Devpt Bank 1970-73, chllr Univ of Guyana 1970-73; memb Cncl Royal Econ Soc 1949-58, pres Manchester Statistical Soc 1956, memb American Philosophical Soc 1966-, corresponding fell Br Acad 1977-, pres American Econ Assoc 1983; author of numerous articles official papers and monographs; hon fell: LSE 1959, Weizman Inst 1961, American Geographical Soc 1987; hon foreign memb American Acad of Arts and Scis 1962; over 30 hon degrees; Nobel Laureate 1979; kt 1963; *Style—* Sir Arthur Lewis; Woodrow Wilson School, Princeton University, Princeton, New Jersey, USA

LEWIS, Dr Barry Winston; s of Alfred Lewis (d 1967), of Essex, and Winifred Alice, *née* Doggett (d 1984); *b* 31 March 1941; *Educ* Hornchurch GS, UCH Med Sch (MB BS, DCH); *m* 1, 17 April 1962 (m dis 1982), Rosemary Agnes, da of James Bryant Petter (d 1988); 1 s (Timothy John Barry b 1962), 1 da (Catherine Rosemary b 1964); m 2, 24 June 1982, Josephine Caroline, da of Robert William Cunningham (d 1987), of Swansea; 2 s (Hugo Frederick b 1987, d 1988, Edgar William b 1989); *Career* conslt paediatrician London 1973-, chm London Children's and Women's Hosp 1987- (dir 1981-); fell Hunterian Soc (1983); memb: BPA 1973 (memb Cncl 1979-82), BMA; FRSM, FRCP; *Recreations* shooting, horses (racing and breeding), cricket; *Clubs* RSM; *Style—* Dr Barry Lewis; Bungeons Farm, Barking, Suffolk IP6 8HN (☎ 0449 721 992); 17 Wimpole St, London W1M 7AD (☎ 071 486 0044, car 0836 271 020)

LEWIS, His Hon Bernard; s of late Solomon Lewis, and Jeannette Lewis; *b* 1 Feb 1905; *Educ* Trinity Hall Cambridge (MA); *m* 1934, Harriette, da of late I A Waine, of Dublin, London and Nice; 1 s (Bryan Timothy Brendan); *Career* called to the Bar Lincoln's Inn 1929; co ct judge 1966, circuit judge 1972-80; *Recreations* revolver shooting, bricklaying; *Clubs* Reform, Ham & Petersham Rifle & Pistol, Aula, Cambridge Soc; *Style—* His Hon Bernard Lewis; Trevelyan House, Arlington Rd, St Margarets, Twickenham, Middx (☎ 081 892 1841)

LEWIS, Bernard Walter; CBE (1973), JP (Essex 1970); s of Walter Watson Lewis (d 1949), of Lincoln, and Florence Teresa, *née* Greenbury (d 1979); *b* 24 July 1917; *Educ* Lincoln Sch, Univ of Manchester; *m* 12 May 1943, Joyce Ilston, da of James Issac Storey (d 1932), of Rothbury, Northumberland; 1 s (John Michael b 6 Aug 1947), 1 da (Susan Joan Ilston b 29 June 1945); *Career* joined King's Own Regt 1940, RASC 1941, Capt 1942, Maj 1943, served Middle E 1940-46; chm and md Green's Flour Mills Ltd 1955-90; chm Edward Baker Holdings Ltd 1983-89, chm Flour Advsy Bureau 1979-88; pres Nat Assoc of Br and Irish Millers 1985-86; chm: Dengie and Maldon Essex bench 1970-88, Maldon Harbour Cmmrs 1978-; Gen Tax Cmmr 1957-; memb and chm Fin Bd Cons Pty 1966-75, chm Bd of Govrs Plume Sch 1968-83; Liveryman Worshipful Co of Bakers 1973; *Recreations* travel, gardening; *Clubs* RAC, United and Cecil, Essex; *Style—* Bernard Lewis, Esq, CBE, JP; Roughlees, 68 Highlands Drive, Maldon, Essex (☎ 0621 852981)

LEWIS, Brian Geoffrey Marshall; s of Col Geoffrey Archibald Ernest Lewis (d 1977), of Tunbridge Wells, and Joan Isabel, *née* Stratford; *b* 1 Dec 1943; *Educ* Bethany Sch Goudhurst; *m* 29 June 1974, Elizabeth Jane, da of John Alexander Miller, of Heathfield, Sussex; 3 da (Sarah Isabel b 2 Aug 1976, Anna Charlotte b 10 April 1979, Claire Victoria (twin) b 10 April 1979); *Career* exec positions H J Heinz Ltd and Canada Dry (UK) Ltd; md Heron Cruisers Ltd Kent, dir Stanton Asset Management Kent; *Recreations* motor sports, point-to-point, eventing; *Style—* Brian Lewis, Esq; Stanton Asset Management Ltd, Stanton House, Romford Rd, Pembury, Kent TN2 4AY (☎ 089 282 5454, fax 089 282 2482, telex 94013002 LEAS G)

LEWIS, Charles William; s of Judge Peter Edwin Lewis (d 1976), of Seaford, and Mary Ruth, *née* Massey; *b* 25 June 1954; *Educ* Eastbourne Coll, Univ Coll Oxford (MA); *m* 20 Sept 1986, Grace Julia Patricia, da of Alphonsus McKenna, of Dublin; *Career* called to the Bar Inner Temple 1977; *Recreations* skiing, bridge, shooting; *Clubs* East India, Northampton County; *Style—* Charles Lewis, Esq; The Dower House, Church Walk, Gt Billing, Northampton NN3 4ED (☎ 0604 407189); 1 King's Bench Walk, Temple, London EC4Y 7DB (☎ 071 353 8436)

LEWIS, Prof Clifford Thomas; s of Arthur Charles Lewis, of Newport, Gwent (d 1975), and Florence Lewis, *née* Golding (d 1973); *b* 29 Aug 1923; *Educ* Newport HS, Queens' Coll Cambridge (MA), Imperial Coll London (PhD); *m* 19 July 1949, (Ada) Joan Lewis, da of George Augustine Willey (d 1964), of Newport, Gwent; 1 s (Julian b 12 Feb 1956), 1 da (Rosalind b 1958); *Career* Imperial Coll London: lectr insect physiology 1955-65, sr lectr 1965-74, reader 1974-78; Royal Holloway Coll (later Royal Holloway and Bedford New Coll): prof of zoology 1978-88, vice princ 1981-85, emeritus prof 1988-; visiting prof: UCLA Calfornia 1975, Ghana 1976, La Trobe Australia 1986; *Recreations* painting, sculpture, fell-walking; *Clubs* Athenaeum; *Style—* Prof Clifford Lewis; 9 Silwood Close, Ascot, Berks

LEWIS, Clive Hewitt; s of Sqdn Ldr Thomas Jonathen Lewis, OBE, AE (d 1990), of Sway Wood Paddock, Mead End Rd, Sway, Hants, and Marguerita Eileen, *née* De Bfule (d 1987); *b* 29 March 1936; *Educ* St Peter's Sch York; *m* 7 July 1961, Jane Penelope (Penny), da of Rowland Bolland White (d 1970), of Carr Lane, Sandal, Wakefield, Yorks; 2 s (Simon Nicholas Hewitt b 1962, Mark Hewitt b 1966), 1 da (Victoria Jane b 1968); *Career* Pilot Officer RAF 1956-58, Lt 40/41 Royal Tank Regt (TA) 1958-62; sr ptnr Clive Lewis and Ptnrs 1963-, dir St Modwen Properties plc 1985-, chm RICS Journals Ltd 1987-, dir Surveyors Hldgs Ltd 1987-, pres gp div RICS 1989-90, dep chm Mersyside Devpt Corp 1989- (bd memb 1986), Northern Co's Sprint Champion 1957, Cheshire Co athlete; pres: Land Aid Charitable Tst, Worldwide FIABCI 1983-84; Freeman: City of London 1983, Worshipful Co of Chartered Surveyors; FRICS 1961, FSVA 1980; *Recreations* cricket, tennis; *Clubs* Totteridge CC, MCC, Forty Club; *Style—* Clive Lewis, Esq; Oakhurst, 7 Totteridge Common, London N20 8AP (☎ 081 445 5109); 8/9 Stratton St, London W1X 5FD (☎ 071 499 1001, car 0860 327 127)

LEWIS, (Peter) Daniel Nicolas David; s of Maj R C Lewis, TD, of Shere, Surrey, and Miriam Lorraine, *née* Birnage; *b* 14 Oct 1957; *Educ* Westminster; *Career* day centre dep warden Age Concern Westminster 1976-79, mangr London Business Sch

Bookshop 1979-82, ptnr London Town Staff Bureau 1982-88 (taken over by Burns Anderson Recruitment plc 1988), then divnl md Burns Anderson Recruitment plc London Town Div; govr IEC 1989; memb Inst Employment Consits 1984 (vice pres 1990-); *Recreations* driving, Africa, flying, bridge; *Style*— Daniel Lewis, Esq; 2 Dealtry Rd, London SW15 6NL (☎ 081 780 1699); 19 Broad Ct, London WC2B 5QN (☎ 071 836 0627, fax 071 836 1997)

LEWIS, David; s of Leonard Lewis (d 1945), of London, and Clara, *née* Tauber (d 1974); *b* 2 June 1924; *m* 24 June 1951, Esther Elizabeth Ruth, da of Joseph Benjamin, of London; 3 s (Julian, Simon, Ben (twin)), 2 da (Debbie, Rachel (twin)); *Career* WWII navigator RAF Bomber Cmd 1943-47; CA; chm Lewis Trust Group Ltd 1956-; FCA 1950-; *Recreations* flying, skiing, sailing; *Style*— David Lewis, Esq; Chelsea House, West Gate, Ealing, London W5 (☎ 081 998 8822)

LEWIS, David Gwyn; s of Rev Gwyn Lewis, (d 1984), of Bridport, Dorset, and Annie Millicent (Nancy), *née* Thomas; *b* 5 Aug 1941; *Educ* Ellesmere Coll Salop, Coll of Law London; *m* 8 April 1972, Veronica Mary Viola, da of Alban Edward Courtney Wylde, of RAX House, Birdport, Dorset; 1 da (Angharad b 1976); *Career* 2 Lt 5 Bn The Welch Regt (TA) 1960-63; admitted slr 1966; prosecuting slr: Merthyr CBC 1966-68, Dorset and Bournemouth Police Authy 1968-70, Birmingham City 1970-71; dep chief prosecuting slr Sussex Police Authy 1976-84 (prosecuting sr princ slr 1971-76); chief prosecuting slr: Warwicks 1984-86, Lincs 1986; chief crown prosecutor Cambs and Lincs 1986-; memb local branch Br Legion; Freeman City of London 1986; memb: Law Soc, Cambridge and Dist Law Soc, Peterborough and Dist Law Soc, Lincs Law Soc; *Recreations* cricket, tennis, horse racing (spectator), motoring; *Clubs* MCC, Cambridge Univ CC, Glamorgan CCC; *Style*— David Lewis, Esq; Crown Prosecution Service, Justinian House, Spitfire Close, Ermine Business Park, Huntingdon, Cambs PE18 6XY (☎ 0480 432333, fax 0480 432313)

LEWIS, David Gwynder; s of Gwynder Eudaf Lewis (d 1963), of Bryn-y-Groes, Sketty, Swansea, and Gwyneth, *née* Jones (d 1979); *b* 31 Aug 1942; *Educ* Rugby; *m* 2 July 1966, Susan Joyce, da of Andrew Agnew, of Crowborough; 1 s (George b 1972), 1 da (Alexandra b 1969); *Career* Warrant Offr TA C Battery Hon Artillery Co; banker Hambros Bank Ltd 1961- (dir 1979), md Hambro Pacific Hong Kong 1974-82, pres Hambro America New York 1982-85, dir Hambro Countrywide plc and other Hambro Gp Cos; ACIOB 1967; *Recreations* fishing, music, shooting; *Clubs* Turf, RAC, Madison Square Garden (NY); *Style*— D G Lewis, Esq; 57 Victoria Rd, London W8 5RH (☎ 071 937 2277); Hambros Bank Ltd, 41 Tower Hill, London EC3N 4HA (☎ 071 480 5000, fax 071 702 9827, car 0836 290027, telex 883851)

LEWIS, David John; *b* 17 May 1939; *Educ* Grocers' Sch, Univ of London (BSc); *m* 1961; 4 c; *Career* chartered surveyor; Town & City Properties 1959-62, David Lewis & Partners 1964-, Cavendish Land Co 1972-73, Hampton Trust 1984-87, chm Molyneux Estates 1989-; chm: Jewish Blind Soc 1979-89, Jewish Care 1991;FRICS 1969 (ARICS 1961); *Recreations* art, music; *Style*— David Lewis, Esq; Marylebone Property Corporation, 76 Gloucester Place, London W1 (☎ 071 487 3401)

LEWIS, David John; s of Eric John Lewis, of Nuneaton, Warks, and Vera May, *née* Heath (d 1981); *b* 18 Oct 1942; *Educ* King Edward VI GS Nuneaton; *m* 5 Aug 1967, Vyvian Christine Dawn, da of Eric Hutton Stewart (d 1981), of Coventry; 2 da (Sophie b 1972, Anna b 1975); *Career* qualified CA 1966; Pannell Kerr Forster: Belize 1967-70, Barbados 1970-75 (ptnr 1972), Leeds 1975 (ptnr 1976, sr ptnr and chm 1986); memb: Leeds Jr C of C 1978-83, Ctee W Yorks Soc of CAs 1982 - (treas 1982-85, sec 1985-89, vice pres 1989-90, dep pres 1990-91); pres CAs Student Soc of Leeds 1984-85; govr Prince Henry's GS Otley 1988-; memb: Leds Family Health Serv Authy 1990-, Otley Round Table 1980-83 (pres 1988), Rotary Club of Otley Chevin 1989- (fndr pres 1989-90); FICA 1966; *Clubs* Leeds, Leeds Taverners; *Style*— David J Lewis, Esq; 1 Craven Park, Menston, Ilkley, W Yorks LS29 6EQ; Pannell Kerr Forster, Pannell House, 6 Queen St, Leeds LS1 2TW (☎ 0532 443 541, fax 0532 445 560)

LEWIS, Prof David Malcolm; s of Kenneth Stanley Lewis, and Kathleen Elsie, *née* Mann; *b* 25 May 1941; *Educ* Marling Sch Stroud Glos, Univ of Leeds (BSc, PhD); *m* 14 Aug 1965, Barbara, da of Alfred Taylor (d 1965); 2 s (Stephen b 7 March 1967, Matthew b 15 April 1971), 1 da (Catherine b 5 May 1969); *Career* princ devpt offr Int Wool Secretariat 1965-78, sr res scientist CSIRO Geelong Aust 1978-79, princ devpt scientist IWS 1979-87, prof and head of dept Univ of Leeds 1987-; hon visiting prof Xian Textile Inst, Xian Peoples Repub of China 1988; memb Br Nat Ctee for Chemistry, memb and former chm WR Region Soc of Dyers and Colourists; fell Royal Soc of Chemistry 1984, FRSA 1989; *Recreations* tennis, badminton, golf, walking; *Style*— Prof David Lewis; Dept of Colour Chemistry and Dyeing, Univ of Leeds, Leeds LS2 9JT (☎ 0532 332931, fax 0532 332947, telex 556473 UNILDS G)

LEWIS, David Thomas Rowell; s of Thomas Price Merfyn Lewis (d 1989); *b* 1 Nov 1947; *Educ* St Edward's Sch, Jesus coll Oxford (BA, MA); *m* 25 July 1970, Theresa Susan, *née* Poole; 1 s (Tom b 1976), 1 da (Suzannah b 1974); *Career* admitted slr 1972 (Hong Kong 1977); currently corp fin ptnr Norton Rose (articles 1969, Hong Kong Office 1979-82); memb Co Law Ctee City Law Soc, govr Dragon Sch Oxford; memb Law Soc; *Recreations* keeping fit, collecting maps, travel; *Clubs* Hong Kong; *Style*— David Lewis, Esq; Norton Rose, Kempson House, Camomile St, London EC3A 7AN (☎ 071 283 2434, fax 071 588 1181, tlx 883652)

LEWIS, David Wyn; s of Albert Brinley Lewis, of Newcastle-under-Lyme, Staffs, and Eiluned Gwynedd, *née* Hughes; *b* 1 Nov 1944; *Educ* High Storrs GS, Univ of Sheffield (BArch); *m* 10 July 1971, Meirlys; 1 s (Steffan Gwynedd b 1972), 1 da (Bethan Rhiannon b 1975); *Career* architect and interior designer; sr ptnr David Lewis Assoc 1978- (specialising in large industl buildings, commercial devpt, housing devpt, public houses and listed buildings); pres Sheffield and S Yorks Soc of Architecture 1982-84; ARIBA 1971; *Recreations* gardening; *Style*— David Lewis, Esq; Delf View House, Eyam, Sheffield S30 1QW

LEWIS, Denice D; da of Richard Clifton Lewis, of Houston, Texas, and Wanda Joy, *née* Watson; *b* 28 Nov 1960; *Educ* Northshore HS, San Jacinto Jr Coll Houston Texas; *Career* fashion model 1983-; *Style*— Ms Denice Lewis; Models I, Omega House, 471-473 Kings Rd, London SW10 (☎ 071 351 1195)

LEWIS, Dr Dennis Aubrey; s of Joseph Lewis and Minnie *née* Coderofsky; *b* 1 Oct 1928; *Educ* Latymer Upper Sch Hammersmith, Chelsea Coll Univ of London (BSc, PhD); *m* 10 Nov 1956, Gillian Mary da of George Arthur Bratby; 2 s (Ian Andrew); *Career* serv RAF 1947-49; res chemist ICI Plastics Div 1956-68 (intelligence mangr 1968-81), dir ASLIB (The Assoc for Information Mgmnt) 1981-89; CBI rep Br Library Advsy Cncl 1976-80, memb Br Cncl Library Advsy Ctee 1981-; cncllr Welwyn Garden Urban Dist 1968-74, Welwyn Hatfield Dist 1974- (chm Cncl 1976-77); fndr Welwyn Hatfield Cncl of Voluntary Serv 1968-, pres Welwyn Hatfield Mencap Soc 1981-, fndr pres Welwyn Garden City Chamber of Trade and Commerce 1984-86; FIInfSc 1982; *Recreations* walking, trying to avoid gardening, admiring old churches; *Style*— Dr Dennis Lewis; 11 The Links, Welwyn Garden City, Herts

LEWIS, Derek Compton; s of Kenneth Compton Lewis (d 1982), of Zeal Monachorum, Devon, and Marjorie, *née* Buick; *b* 9 July 1946; *Educ* Wrekin Coll, Queens' Coll Cambridge (MA), London Business Sch (MSc); *m* 26 April 1969, Louise, da of Dr D O Wharton (d 1986), of Colwyn Bay, North Wales; 2 da (Annabel b 1983, Julia b 1984); *Career* chief exec Granada Gp plc; *Clubs* Caledonian; *Style*— Derek Lewis, Esq; 36 Golden Square, London W1R 4AH

LEWIS, Derek William; s of Arthur George Lewis, of Manor Barn, Snowshill, nr Broadway, Worcs, and Hilda, *née* Rushton; *b* 23 Oct 1944; *Educ* Dean Close Sch Cheltenham; *m* 21 Oct 1972, Bridget Jennifer, da of Maj Bowes Bindon Stoney, of Frant, Sussex; 2 s (Christopher b 4 Feb 1977, James b 14 Feb 1980), 1 da (Sarah-Jane b 30 May 1974); *Career* admitted slr 1967; Theodore Goddard 1970; memb: City of London Slrs Co, Law Soc, Int Bar Assoc; *Recreations* horse racing, golf, tennis; *Clubs* Royal Wimbledon Golf, Roehampton; *Style*— Derek Lewis, Esq; 25 Denbigh Gardens, Richmond, Surrey TW10 6EL (☎ 081 940 4801); 150 Aldersgate St, London EC1A 4EJ (☎ 071 606 8855, fax 071 606 4390, telex 884678)

LEWIS, Derek William Richard; s of Percy William Lewis, of Worcs, and Edith, *née* Wisdom (d 1941); *b* 6 July 1936; *Educ* King's Sch Worcester; *m* 16 April 1963, Hedwig Albertine, da of Karl Kamps, of St Arnold, Rheine, W Germany; 2 s (Thomas b 1964, Ron b 1968), 1 da (Stephanie b 1967); *Career* RAEC 1957-59; The Hereford Times 1953-61, The Press Assoc 1961-62; BBC: joined seconded head of news Radio Zambia Lusaka 1966-68, TV news 1968, dep ed 1970-74 (The World at One, PM, The World This Weekend) ed 1974-76 (The World Tonight, Newsdesk, The Financial World Tonight) ed 1976-88 (The World at One (Radio Programme of the year 1976 and 1979), PM, The World this Weekend (Best Current Affrs Programme 1983); media relations conslt Royal Botanic Gardens and Cwlth Devpt Corp, dir Skan Film Productions International Ltd, md Diplomatic News Services 1988-; chm of planning London Borough of Ealing 1990- (cnsllr 1989), Cncl memb The Royal Albert Hall; assoc memb Press Assoc in London; *Recreations* music, assoc football, exploring US Nat Parks; *Clubs* Norwegian, Castaways, Ritz; *Style*— Derek Lewis, Esq; 4 Campbell Rd, London W7 3EA (☎ 081 567 2478)

LEWIS, Edward Trevor Gwyn; s of Rev Gwyn Lewis (d 1984), and Annie Millicent, *née* Thomas; *b* 16 March 1948; *Educ* Ellesmere Coll, King's Coll London; *m* 6 April 1974, (Pamela) Gay, da of Lt-Col Jimmy Wilson, DL, of Manor Farm, Wraxall, Dorchester, Dorset; 3 da (Leone b 28 Feb 1975, Kim b 23 Jan 1979, Tamsin (twin) b 23 Jan 1979); *Career* called to the Bar Grays Inn 1972, dep legal mangr Mirror Group Newspapers 1980-83, JP S Westminster Div 1981-84, prosecuting counsel Western Circuit DHSS 1985-, actg stipendiary magistrate 1988-; *Recreations* riding, opera, jogging, skiing, family, motor cars; *Clubs* Garrick; *Style*— Edward Lewis, Esq; 77 Lexham Gdns, London W8 (☎ 071 370 3045); Francis Taylor Bldg, Temple, London EC4 (☎ 071 353 7768)

LEWIS, His Hon Judge Esyr Gwilym; QC (1971); s of Rev Thomas William Lewis (d 1946), of Stamford Hill, London, and Mary Jane May, *née* Selway (d 1974); *b* 11 Jan 1926; *Educ* Mill Hill, Trinity Hall Cambridge (MA, LLB); *m* 1957, Elizabeth Anne Vidler, da of William Origen Hoffmann, of Bassett, Southampton; 4 da (Emma, Clare, Alice, Charlotte); *Career* Intelligence Corps 1944-47; circuit judge (official referee) 1984; memb Criminal Injuries Compensation Bd 1977-84, bencher Gray's Inn 1978, ldr Wales & Chester Circuit 1978-80; *Recreations* watching rugby football; *Clubs* Garrick; *Style*— His Hon Judge Esyr Lewis, QC; 2 South Sq, Gray's Inn, London WC1R 5HP (☎ 01 405 5918); Official Referee's Cts, St Dunstan's House, 133-137 Fetter Lane, London EC4A 1HO

LEWIS, Prof Geoffrey; s of Ashley Lewis (d 1971), of London, and Jeanne Muriel, *née* Sintrop (d 1960); *b* 19 June 1920; *Educ* Univ Coll Sch Hampstead, St John's Coll Oxford (BA, MA, D Phil); *m* 26 July 1941, Raphaela Rhoda, da of Reuben Bale Seideman; 1 s (Jonathan b 1949), 1 da (Lalage b 1947, d 1976); *Career* WWII RAF pilot 1940-41, radar 1941-45; Univ of Oxford: lectr in Turkish 1950-54, sr lectr in Islamic studies 1954-64, sr lectr in Turkish 1964-86, prof of Turkish 1986-87, emeritus prof 1987-; visiting prof: Robert Coll Istanbul 1959-68, Princeton Univ 1970-71 and 1974, UCLA 1975, Br Acad Leverhulme Turkey 1984; St Antony's Coll Oxford: fell 1961-87, sub warden 1984-85, sr tutor 1985-87, emeritus fell 1987-; memb Br Turkish Mixed Cmmn 1975-; Dr (Honoris Causa) Univ of the Bosphorus Istanbul 1986; corresponding memb Turkish Language Soc 1953, FBA 1979; Turkish Govt Cert of Merit 1973; *Books* Plotiniana Arabica (1959), Albucasis on Surgery and Instruments (1973), The Book of Dede Korkut (1974), Turkish Grammar (1988), Thickhead and other Turkish Stories (1988); *Recreations* bodging, etymology; *Style*— Prof Geoffrey Lewis; 25 Warnborough Rd, Oxford; Le Baousset, 06500 Menton, France

LEWIS, Geoffrey David; s of David Lewis (d 1973), of Brighton, E Sussex, and Esther Grace, *née* Chatfield (d 1978); *b* 13 April 1933; *Educ* Varndean Sch Brighton, Univ of Liverpool (MA); *m* 7 July 1956, Frances May, da of Frederick John Wilderspin (d 1959), of Hove, E Sussex; 3 da (Jennifer b 1958, Heather b 1959, Esther b 1971); *Career* asst curator Worthing Museum and Art Gallery 1950-60, dep dir and keeper of antiquities Sheffield City Museum 1960-65; dir: Sheffield City Museums 1966-72, Liverpool City Museums 1972-74, Merseyside County Museums 1974-77, museum studies Univ of Leicester 1977-89; assoc teacher 1989-; memb Bd of Tstees of the Royal Armouries 1990-; pres: Yorks and Humberside Fedn of Museums and Art Galleries 1969-70, NW Fedn of Museums and Art Galleries 1976-77, Museums Assoc 1980-81, Int Cncl of Museums 1983-89; advsr at various times to: UNESCO, Egyptian Antiquities Orgn, Assoc of Met Authorities, Audit Cmmn for Local Authorities in England and Wales; FMA 1966, FSA 1969, Hon FMA 1989; *Books* Manual of Curatorship (co-ed with J M A Thompson et al, 1984, second edn 1991), For Instruction and Recreation: a Centenary History of the Museums Association (1989); *Recreations* reading, writing, walking, computing; *Style*— Geoffrey Lewis, Esq, FSA; 4 Orchard Close, Wolvey, Hinckley, Leics LE10 3LR (☎ 0455 220708)

LEWIS, Geoffrey Maurice; s of Sidney Lewis (d 1977), of Edghill, Vicarage Rd, Minehead, Somerset, and Helen, *née* Redwood (d 1988); *b* 11 July 1929; *Educ* Taunton Sch, Trinity Hall Cambridge (MA); *m* 27 Aug 1960, Christine Edith, da of Lt-Col A D May, of The Barn, Wenden Hall, Wendens Ambo, Essex; 1 s (Gregory b 1969), 3 da (Joanna b 1961, Sophie b 1964, Penelope b 1965); *Career* Nat Serv 2 Lt RA 1948-9; admitted slr 1955, sr ptnr Hong Kong Office Herbert Smith 1983-86 (ptnr Herbert Smith 1960), seconded advsr securities legislation Hong Kong Govt 1988; memb Int Bar Assoc 1975; *Books* Lord Atkin (1983); *Recreations* music, walking, watching football; *Clubs* Garrick; *Style*— Geoffrey Lewis, Esq; Wenden Hall, Wendens Ambo, Saffron Walden, Essex CB11 4JZ (☎ 0799 40 744); Exchange House, Primrose St, London EC2A 2HS (☎ 071 374 8000, fax 071 496 0043, telex 886633)

LEWIS, Henry Nathan; *b* 20 Jan 1926; *Educ* Univ of Manchester (BCom), LSE; *m* 18 Oct 1953, Jenny; 1 s (Jonathan Morris b 1956), 2 da (Deborah Freda (Mrs Goulden) b 1958, Julia Rose b 1968); *Career* Flt-Lt RAF 1948; formerly jt md Marks & Spencer plc, chm J & J Fashions, dep chm Berisford Int plc; dir: Dixons Gp plc, Hunter Saphir plc, Porter Chadburn plc, Delta Galil; *Style*— Henry Lewis, Esq; 62 Frognal, London NW3 6XG

LEWIS, Hon Mrs (Hilary Zaraz); *née* Morris; da of 1 Baron Morris of Kenwood (d 1954); *b* 1932; *m* 1964, Ronald Graham Lewis (b 5 June 1919); *Recreations* bridge; *Style*— The Hon Mrs Lewis; Zaraz, Littlewick Green, Maidenhead, Berks (☎ 062 882 3183)

LEWIS, Hugh Wilson; s of Cdr Hubert Thomas Lewis, OBE, RN (d 1989), of Midford Rd, Combe Down, Bath, Avon, and Gwyneth, *née* Ridgway; *b* 21 Dec 1946; *Educ*

Clifton, Univ of Birmingham (LLB); *m* 2 Dec 1972, Philippa Jane, da of Lt-Col John Rose Terry (d 1988), of Ensworthy, Gidleigh, Chagford, Devon; 3 s (Edward b 1973, Thomas b 1975, Christopher b 1984), 1 da (Katharine b 1979); *Career* called to the Bar Middle Temple 1970; memb: Western Circuit, Family Law Bar Assoc; *Recreations* walking Dartmoor, fly-fishing, skiing, surfing; *Clubs* Naval & Military, Devon and Exeter Inst; *Style—* Hugh Lewis, Esq; 25 Southernhay East, Exeter (☎ 55777 431005, fax 412007); Creaber Cottage, Gidleigh, Chagford, Devon

LEWIS, Ian Talbot; s of Cyril Frederick Lewis, CBE, and Marjorie, *née* Talbot; *b* 7 July 1929; *Educ* Marlborough; *m* 1, 1962, Patricia Anne, da of Rev William Dalrymple Hardy (d 1982); 2 s (James b 1964, Charles b 1966); m 2, 1986, Susan Lydia, da of Henry Alfred Sargant, of Putney, London; *Career* Nat Serv KOH and QOH followed by AER Serv (Capt) 1952-61; under sec (legal) Treasy Slrs Office 1982-90, memb Law Cmmn Working Gp on Commonhold 1986-87; pres Fordcombe Village Hall 1989-, chm Fordcombe Soc 1990-, govr Fordcombe C of E (Aided) Primary Sch 1990-; memb Ctee Marlburian Club 1984-87, pres Blackheath FC (RU) 1985-88, hon vice pres Blackheath CC; Liveryman Worshipful Co of Merchant Taylors; *Recreations* sport, countryside, theatre, reading, films; *Clubs* Cavalry and Guards', MCC, Blackheath FC (RU), Piltdown Golf; *Style—* Ian Lewis, Esq; South Cottage, Fordcombe, Tunbridge Wells, Kent TN3 0RY (☎ 0892 740413)

LEWIS, Ven John Arthur; s of Lt-Col Harry Arthur Lewis (d 1963), and Evaline Helen Ross, *née* Davidson (d 1976); *b* 4 Oct 1934; *Educ* Parkend, Bell's GS Coleford, Univ of Oxford (MA); *m* 6 June 1959, Hazel Helen Jane, da of Albert Morris (d 1942); 1 s (b 1964), 1 da (b 1962); *Career* Nat Serv 1956-58; asst curate: Prestbury Glos 1960-63, Wimborne Minster 1963-66; rector Eastington and Frocester 1966-70; vicar of: Nailsworth 1970-78, Cirencester 1978-88; chaplain Memorial Hosp and Querns Hosp Cirencester 1978-88, archdeacon of Cheltenham 1988-; hon chm Gloucestershire Constabulary; *Recreations* gardening, travel, walking, music; *Style—* The Ven the Archdeacon of Cheltenham; Westbourne, 283 Gloucester Rd, Cheltenham, Glos GL51 7AD (☎ 0242 522923); Church House, College Green, Gloucester GL1 2LY (☎ 0452 410022, fax 0452 308324)

LEWIS, (Clifford) John; *b* 16 March 1940; *Educ* Caterham Sch Surrey; *m* m; 2 s, 1 da; *Career* actuarial student Royal Exchange Assurance 1958; Phillips & Drew: res analyst 1964, gilt edged mkt specialist 1967, ptnr 1970, dir 1985; vice chm UBS Phillips & Drew 1988-; currently: dir UBS Phillips & Drew Securities Ltd, chm UBS Phillips & Drew Gilts Ltd, chm UBS Phillips & Drew Futures Ltd FIA, FSS, memb ORS, ASIA; *Clubs* London Welsh; *Style—* John Lewis, Esq; UBS Phillips & Drew, 100 Liverpool St, London EC2M 2RH (☎ 071 901 1947, fax 071 901 4908)

LEWIS, Hon John Frederick; s of 3 Baron Merthyr, KBE, PC (d 1977); *b* 30 Dec 1938; *Educ* Eton, St John's Coll Cambridge; *m* 1966, Gretl, twin da of Lt-Col J W Lewis-Bowen; 1 s, 2 da; *Career* organiser Citizens' Advice Bureau; *Recreations* DIY; *Clubs* Island Sailing; *Style—* John Lewis; 1 Cedar Hill, Carisbrooke, Newport, IOW (☎ 0983 522014)

LEWIS, John Henry James; s of Leonard Lewis, QC, of East Park House, Newchapel, nr Lingfield, Surrey, and Rita Jeanette, *née* Stone; *b* 12 July 1940; *Educ* Shrewsbury, UCL (LLB); *m* 30 Nov 1984, Susan Mary Frances, da of Maj Robert Ralph Merton, of The Old Rectory, Burghfield, Berks; 1 s (Barnaby Ralph James b 29 June 1989), 2 da (Daisy Leonora Frances b 1 Jan 1985, Lily Charlotte Frances b 23 Feb 1986); *Career* admitted slr 1966; ptnr Lewis Lewis & Co 1966-82, conslt Jaques & Lewis 1982-; chm: Blakeney Holdings Ltd, Cliveden Group Ltd; vice chm John D Wood & Co plc; dir: The Brent Walker Group plc, GR (Holdings) plc; BTA: memb, chm Heritage Ctee; chm The Attingham Tst; Freeman City of London, memb Worshipful Co of Gunmakers; memb Law Soc; *Recreations* sculpture, architecture, tennis, shooting; *Clubs* Brooks's, Garrick; *Style—* John Lewis, Esq; 5 West Eaton Place, London SW1X 8LU (☎ 071 285 1052); 243-247 Pavilion Rd, London SW1X 7BP (☎ 071 730 5420, fax 071 730 6608)

LEWIS, Maj John Henry Peter Sebastian Beale; s of Maj Peter Beale Lewis, MC (d 1961), and Mary Evelyn Louise Piers, *née* Dumas (d 1970); *b* 7 July 1936; *Educ* Eton; *m* 21 Dec 1971, Mary Virginia, da of Charles Barstow Hutchinson (d 1978); 2 s (Rupert Henry Alexander b 1974, Antony Rhydian b 1977); *Career* Maj 11 Hussars (PAO) 1955-69; dir: Br Bloodstock Agency plc 1976-, Lower Burytown Farm 1983-, Nawara Stud Co 1985-; rode over 25 winners under Jockey club rules; represented GB in Bobsleigh; *Clubs* Calvalry and Gds, MCC; *Style—* Maj J Lewis; Queensberry House, Newmarket, Suffolk (☎ 0638 665021, fax 0638 660283, telex 817157)

LEWIS, Jonathan Malcolm; s of Harold Lewis, of London, and Rene, *née* Goldser; *b* 27 March 1946; *Educ* Harrow, Downing Coll Cambridge (BA, MA); *m* 4 July 1971, Rosemary, da of Lewis Mays (d 1971); 2 s; *Career* admitted slr 1971, ptnr and jt head of Co/Commercial Dept D J Freeman & Co 1974- (asst slr 1971-74), columnist (City Comment) Law Soc Gazette 1983-90, insolvency practitioner 1986-; lectr and author on various legal topics; involved in the Scout movement; memb: Law Soc 1971, Int Bar Assoc 1981; Freeman Worshipful Co of Solicitors; *Recreations* walking, theatre, family; *Style—* Jonathan M Lewis, Esq; D J Freeman & Co, 43 Fetter Lane, London EC4A 1NA (☎ 071 583 4055, fax 071 353 7377, telex 894579)

LEWIS, Joseph Henry; s of Charles William Lewis (d 1934), of Stepney, London, and Louisa, *née* Price (d 1945); *b* 13 Feb 1924; *Educ* Cayley Street Secdy Sch, Trafalgar Square Secdy Sch; *m* 1973, Eva May; *Career* boxing administrator; hon sec Amateur Boxing Assoc 1986-; former amateur boxer: joined Broad Street Club Stepney 1936 (32 contests), 24 contests Army 1943-46, Western Command bantamweight champion 1943; other sports: cricket and football Army 1943-46, cricket Warnes Rubber Manufacturers 1947-48; accounts clerk WC Marks 1940-42, sr forman Port of London Authority 1948-74, Inchcape Management Services 1975-84; Freeman City of London; *Recreations* classical music, opera, reading; *Style—* Joseph Lewis, Esq; 53 Shellbeach Rd, Canvey Island, Essex SS8 7NT (☎ 0268 685007); Amateur Boxing Association of England, Franics House, Francis Street, London SW1P 1DE (☎ 071 976 5361, fax 071 828 8571)

LEWIS, Keith Allan; s of John William Lewis (d 1979), of London, and Violet, *née* Hill; *b* 17 March 1946; *Educ* Henry Thornton GS; *m* 30 March 1968, Sandra Elaine, da of William Slade; 4 s (Clive Matthew b 20 March 1970, David Spencer b 29 Feb 1972, Andrew Christian b 29 June 1973, Jonathan Stuart b 10 June 1976); *Career* Financial Times 1962-78 (Journalist, stock market reporter, co commentator, Lex contributor, head City Desk), dir fin pub rels Universal McCann 1978-81; dir: City & Commercial Communications 1981-82, Grandfield Rork Collins Financial 1982-85, Financial Strategy 1985 (merged with Streets); former md Streets Financial Marketing, chief exec Streets Communications 1987-, chm Streets Direct Marketing, non-exec dir BdO Group Guernsey; *Recreations* walking, photography, films; *Clubs* Wig and Pen; *Style—* Keith Lewis, Esq; Streets Communications Ltd, 18 Red Lion Court, Fleet St, London EC4A 3HT (☎ 071 353 1090, fax 071 583 0661)

LEWIS, Sir Kenneth; DL (Rutland 1973); s of William Lewis (d 1977), and Agnes, *née* Bradley (d 1980); *b* 1 July 1916; *Educ* Jarrow Central Sch, Univ of Edinburgh; *m* 1948, Jane, da of Samuel Pearson; 1 s, 1 da; *Career* serv WWII; memb Lloyd's; contested (C): Newton 1945 and 1950, Ashton-under-Lyne 1951, MP (C) Rutland and Stamford 1959-83 and Stamford and Spalding 1983-87; chm Cons Back Bench Labour Ctee 1963-64; chm and chief exec Business and Holiday Travel Ltd; *Clubs* Carlton, RAF, Pathfinders; *Style—* Sir Kenneth Lewis, DL; 96 Green Lane, Northwood, Middx (☎ 09274 23354); Redlands, Preston, Uppingham, Rutland (☎ 057 285 320); Business and Holiday Travel Ltd, 49 Lambs Conduit St, London WC1 (☎ 071 831 8691)

LEWIS, Lady; Lesley Lisle; *née* Smith; da of Frank Lisle Smith (d 1974), and Dorothy Sutcliffe (d 1973); *b* 4 July 1924; *Educ* St Hildas Collegiate Sch Dunedin NZ, Sch of Physiotherapy Dunedin NZ; *m* 1959, Prof Sir Anthony Carey Lewis, CBE (d 1983, princ Royal Acad of Music 1968-82); *Recreations* golf, gardening; *Style—* Lady Lewis; High Rising, Holdfast Lane, Haslemere, Surrey (☎ 0428 643920)

LEWIS, Hon Mrs (Lucia Anne); *née* FitzRoy; er da of Cdr Hon John Maurice FitzRoy Newdegate, RN (d 1976), and sis of 3 Viscount Daventry, *qv*; raised to the rank of a Viscount's da 1988; *b* 28 March 1920; *m* 4 July 1942, Maj Timothy Stuart Lewis, *qv*; 1 s (decd), 1 da (Caroline Anne, m Sir Frederick Douglas David Thomson, 3 Bt, *qv*); *Style—* The Hon Mrs Lewis; Inchdura House, North Berwick, Scotland

LEWIS, Lynn Alexander Mackay; s of Victor Lewis (d 1982), of London , latterly of Malta, and Maysie, *née* Mackay; *b* 23 Aug 1937; *Educ* Elizabeth Coll Guernsey, Trinity Kandy Sri Lanka; *m* 23 May 1959, Valerie Elaine, da of Harry Procter, of London; 1 s (Lindon b 1961), 1 da (Carol b 1959); *Career* fndr Corby News 1961, Rome bureau chief Sunday Mirror 1966-68, reporter and presenter Nationwide (BBC TV) 1969-74, fndr and md Nauticalia Ltd 1974 (chm 1988-); chm Marine Trades Assoc 1986-89, memb Cncl Br Marine Indust Fedn 1986-, dir Nat Boat Shows Ltd 1988-; *Recreations* cricket, bridge; *Style—* Lynn Lewis, Esq; Riverdell, Thames Meadow, Shepperton-on-Thames, Middx (☎ 0932 220 794); Nauticalia Ltd, Ferry Works, Shepperton-on-Thames, Middx (☎ 0932 244 396, fax 0932 241 679, mobile (☎ 0831 113 501)

LEWIS, Mark Robin Llewelyn; s of Gp Capt Howard Llewelyn Lewis, and Joan Blodwen, *née* Williams; *b* 6 Nov 1953; *Educ* Millfield, Exeter Coll Oxford (BA); *m* 29 June 1974, Fay Catherine, da of Patrick Alfred Tester; *Career* Allen & Overy: articles 1976-78, admitted slr 1978, asst slr 1978-81 and 1982-85, ptnr 1985-90; asst slr Cunningham John & Co 1981-82, ptnr Bevan Ashford 1990-; memb Law Soc; *Recreations* golf, cycling, walking, reading; *Style—* Mark Lewis, Esq; Bevan Ashford, Curzon House, Southernhay Crest, Exeter, Devon EX4 3LY (☎ 0392 411111, fax 0392 50764)

LEWIS, Martyn John Dudley; s of Thomas John Dudley Lewis (d 1979), of Coleraine, NI, and Doris *née* Jones; *b* 7 April 1945; *Educ* Dalriada GS Ballymoney NI, Trinity Coll Dublin (BA); *m* 20 May 1970, Elizabeth Anne, da of Duncan Carse, of Fittleworth, Sussex; 2 da (Sylvie b 11 May 1975, Kate b 24 July 1978); *Career* TV journalist, presenter and newsreader: presenter BBC Belfast 1967-68, journalist and broadcaster HTV Wales 1968-70, joined ITN 1970, set up and ran ITN's Northern Bureau Manchester 1971-78; newsreader and foreign corr ITN: News at Ten, News at 5.45 1978-86; ITN reports 1970-86 incl: Cyprus War, Seychelles Independence, Fall of Shah of Iran, Soviet Invasion of Afghanistan, Vietnamese Boat People; co-presenter: ITV gen election programmes 1979 and 1983, ITV Budget programmes 1981-84, wrote and produced Battle for the Falklands video, wrote and presented The Secret Hunters documentary (TVS), joined BBC as presenter One O'Clock News 1986, presenter Nine O'Clock News 1987-; BBC documentaries: MacGregor's Verdict, Royal Tournament, Royal Mission Great Ormond Street - A Fighting Chance, Princess Anne - Save The Children, Help is There, Indian Summer, Fight Cancer, Living with Dying; The Giving Business, Health UK; chm Drive for Youth, pres United Response; vice pres: Help the Hospices, Marie Curie Cancer Care, and dir Cancer Relief Macmillan Fund; dir: Hospice Arts, CLIC UK, Cities in Schools, Adopt-A-Student; patron: Cambridge Children's Hospice, London Lighthouse; memb Tidy Britain Gp Policy Advsy Ctee; Freeman City of London 1989; *Books* And Finally (1984), Tears and Smiles - The Hospice Handbook (1989); FRSA 1990; *Recreations* photography, tennis, good food; *Style—* Martyn Lewis, Esq; BBC TV News, BBC TV Centre, London W12 7RJ (☎ 081 576 7779, fax 081 749 7534)

LEWIS, (Patricia) Mary; da of late Donald Leslie Cornes, of Lythwood Farm, Bayston Hill, nr Shrewsbury, and Eleanor Lillian, *née* Roberts; *Educ* Stonehurst Sch Shrewsbury, St Margaret's Yeaton Peverey Shropshire, Shrewsbury Sch of Art, Camberwell Sch of Arts and Crafts (BA), Central Sch of Art Middx Poly; *m* 17 Aug 1974 (m dis), Garth David Lewis, s of David Lewis; *Career* graphic designer; creative dir and founding ptnr Lewis Moberly Design Conslts (specialists in packaging design) 1984-; memb 1989 Design and Art Direction Exec Ctee; design awards incl: 17 Clio Gold awards for Int Packaging Design, Design and Art Direction Gold award for Outstanding Design 1988, Design and Art Direction Siver award for the Most Outstanding Packaging Range 1988, 1990; juror: BBC Design Awards 1987, Design and Art Direction Awards, Assoc of Illustrators Awards; work exhibited: London, Los Angeles, Japan, NYC; MCSD; *Recreations* design; *Style—* Ms Mary Lewis; 33 Gresse St, London WIP 1PN (☎ 071 580 9252, fax 071 255 1671)

LEWIS, Prof Mervyn Keith; s of Norman Malcolm Lewis (d 1982), of Adelaide, and Gladys May Valerie, *née* Way; *b* 20 June 1941; *Educ* Unley HS, Univ of Adelaide (BSc, PhD); *m* 24 Nov 1962, Kay Judith, da of Lt Royce Melvin Wiesner (d 1977), of Adelaide; 4 da (Stephanie b 1966, Miranda b 1967, Alexandra b 1969, Antonia b 1972); *Career* Elder Smith & Co Ltd 1957-58, Cwlth Bank of Aust 1959-64, assoc dean Univ of Adelaide 1981-83 (tutor and lectr 1965-84, sr lectr 1973-79, reader 1979-84), visiting scholar Bank of England 1979-80, conslt Aust fin System Inquiry 1980-81, Midland Bank prof of money and banking Univ of Nottingham 1984-, visiting prof of econs Flinders Univ of S Aust 1987-; pres of Cncl Kingston Coll of Advanced Ed 1978-79; elected fell of the Acad of the Social Sciences in Aust 1986; *Books* Monetary Policy in Australia (1980), Australian Monetary Economics (1981), Monetary Control in the United Kingdom (1981), Australia's Financial Institutions and Markets (1985), Personal Financial Markets (1986), Domestic and International Banking (1987); *Recreations* rambling, tennis, music; *Clubs* East India; *Style—* Prof Mervyn Lewis; 4 Wortley Hall Close, University Park, Nottingham NG7 2QB (☎ 0602 787495); The University of Nottingham, Dept of Econs, University Park, Nottingham NG7 2RD (☎ 0602 484848, fax 0602 420825, telex 37346 UNINOT G)

LEWIS, Michael ap Gwilym; QC (1975); s of Rev Thomas William Lewis (d 1946), of London, and Mary Jane May, *née* Selway (d 1975); *Educ* Mill Hill, Jesus Coll Oxford (MA); *m* 3 s (Meyric b 1962, Gareth b 1964, Evan b 1966), 1 da (Bronwen b 1960); *Career* cmmnd RTR 1952-53; called to the Bar Gray's Inn 1956, memb of Senate 1976-9, bencher Gray's Inn 1986-; churchwarden Wootton Kent; *Style—* Michael Lewis, Esq, QC; 3 Hare Ct, Temple, London EC4

LEWIS, Michael Samuel; s of late Nicholas Samuel Japolsky, and late Annie Catherine Lewis; *b* 18 Oct 1937; *Educ* St Paul's Balliol Coll Oxford (BA), King's Coll London (PhD); *m* 1962, Susan Mary Knowles; 1 s, 1 da; *Career* Nat Serv RN 1956-58; graduate apprentice United Steel Cos 1961-62, asst lectr in geology Univ of Glasgow 1965-68; The Br Cncl 1968-75: gen serv offr London 1968-69, asst rep Calcutta India 1969-73, sci offr Benelux 1973-75; asst sec South Bank Poly London 1975-78, asst registrar for Res Degrees CNAA 1978-80, registrar (chief admin offr) and clerk to Governing Body Oxford Poly 1980-83, sec to Ctee of Dirs of Polys London 1983-91; memb: Geologists' Assoc, Assoc of Poly Admins, Soc for Res into Higher Educn;

FGS; *Pubns* author various articles in learned jls; *Recreations* geology, music, shaping gardens; *Style—* Dr Michael Lewis, Esq; 50 Denton Rd, Twickenham, Middx TW1 2HQ

LEWIS, Dr Mitchell; s of Coleman James Lewis (d 1966), and Fanny, *née* Zweiback (d 1959); *b* 3 April 1924; *Educ* Christian Brothers Coll Kimberley SA, Univ of Capetown (BSc, MB ChB, MD); *m* 23 Oct 1959, Ethel Norma, da of Rachmiel Nochumowitz (d 1958); 1 s (Raymond b 1962); *Career* conslt haematologist Hammersmith Hosp 1961-, sr res fell Royal Postgrad Med Sch 1989-, emeritus reader Univ of London 1989- (reader in haematology 1970-89); chm Int Cncl for Standardization in Haematology, cnsllr-at-large Int Soc of Haematology, past pres Br Soc for Haematology; FRCPath; *Books* Modern Concepts in Haematology (1972), Dyserythropoiesis (1977), The Spleen (1983), Thomboplastia Calibration (1984), Myelofibrosis (1985), Biopsy Pathology and Bone and Marrow (1985), Quality Assurance in Haematology (1988), Postgraduate Haematology (1989), Practical Haematology (1991); *Recreations* photography, reading, music; *Style—* Dr Mitchell Lewis; 6 Salisbury House, Somerset Rd, Wimbledon, London SW19 5HY (☎ 081 946 2727); Royal Postgraduate Medical School, London W12 0NN (☎ 081 746 1418, fax 081 746 1162)

LEWIS, Neville Julian Spencer; s of Raymond Malcom Lewis (d 1980), of Llanishen, Cardiff, and Constance Margaret, *née* Jones; *b* 17 March 1945; *Educ* Radley, Pembroke Coll Oxford (MA); *m* 14 July 1967, Caroline Joy, da of Robin Homes (d 1987), of Oare, Wiltshire; 1 s (David b 1978), 1 da (Miranda b 1974); *Career* barr; Parly candidate (Lib) Paddington Feb and Oct 1974; *Books* Guide to Greece (1977), Delphi and the Sacred Way (1987); *Clubs* Nat Lib; *Style—* Neville Spencer Lewis, Esq; 20 South Hill Park Gardens, London NW3; 12 Kings Bench Walk, Temple, London EC4 (☎ 071 353 5892)

LEWIS, Nigel Wickham; s of Henry Wickham Lewis, and Marjorie, *née* Greene; *b* 3 Jan 1936; *Educ* Gayhurst Sch Gerrards Cross Bucks, Greshams' Sch Holt Norfolk, Clare Coll Cambridge (MA); *m* 21 Oct 1961, Chloe Elizabeth, da of John Hershell Skinner; 1 s (Tristram b 1967), 2 da (Derryn b 1964, Venetia b 1969); *Career* graduate apprentice and design engr Vickers-Armstrongs (Aircraft) Ltd 1958-62, sr engr Glacier Metal Co Ltd 1962-68, mgmnt conslt McKinsey & Co Inc 1968-72, md Security Control Engineering Ltd 1972-76, dir and chief industl advsr 3i plc 1977-; Liveryman Worshipful Co of Cordwainers; CEng, MIMechE, MBCS; *Recreations* lawn tennis, real tennis, garden supression, music; *Style—* Nigel Lewis, Esq; Cadsden House, Princes Risborough, Aylesbury, Bucks HP17 0NB (☎ 08444 3020); 3i plc, 91 Waterloo Rd, London SE1 8XP (☎ 071 928 3131, fax 072 928 0058)

LEWIS, Lt-Col Hon Peter Herbert; JP (1990); 2 s of 3 Baron Merthyr, KBE, PC (d 1977); *b* 25 March 1937; *Educ* Eton; *m* 1974, Caroline Monica, da of Erik Cadogan, JP, of Wasperton Hill, Barford, Warwicks (gs of Capt Hon Charles Cadogan, 4 s of 4 Earl Cadogan) by his w Caroline, da of Count Hans Wachtmeister (there are two creations of Count for this family, which was ennobled in 1578; one by Charles XI of Sweden 1687; the other by Frederick William III of Prussia in 1816), of Malmö, Sweden; 1 da (Amanda Caroline b 1977); *Career* formerly Maj 15/19 Hussars, Lt-Col cmdg 9/12 Royal Lancers (Prince of Wales's) to 1982; memb Hon Corps of Gentlemen at Arms 1988; *Style—* Lt-Col the Hon Peter Lewis, JP; The Old Rectory, Chilfrome, Dorchester, Dorset

LEWIS, Peter Tyndale; s of Oswald Lewis (d 1966), of Beechwood, Highgate, MP for Colchester 1929-45, and Frances Merriman Cooper; gf founded John Lewis, Oxford St in 1864, uncle John Spedan Lewis founded John Lewis Partnership 1929; *b* 26 Sept 1929; *Educ* Eton, ChCh Oxford (MA); *m* 22 July 1961, Deborah Anne, da of Sir William Collins, CBE (d 1976), of St James's Place, London SW1; 1 s (Patrick b 1965), 1 da (Katharine b 1962); *Career* Nat Serv Coldstream Gds 1948-49; called to the Bar Middle Temple 1956; joined John Lewis Partnership 1959; chm: John Lewis Partnership 1972-, Retail Distributors Assoc 1972; memb: Cncl Industl Soc 1968-79, Design Cncl 1971-74; govr: Windlesham House Sch 1979-, NIESR 1983-; tstee: Jt Educnl Tst 1985-87, Bell Educnl Tst 1987-; CBIM, FRSA; *Recreations* golf; *Clubs* MCC; *Style—* Peter Lewis, Esq; John Lewis Partnership plc, 171 Victoria St, London SW1E 5NN (☎ 071 828 1000)

LEWIS, Philip Stuart; s of Harold Charles Lewis, of Buckhurst Hill, Essex, and Olwyn, *née* Witcombe; *b* 20 March 1947; *Educ* Buckhurst Hill County HS Chigwell Essex, St Thomas's Hosp Med Sch (BSc, MB BS); *m* 4 April 1970, (Eunice) Brenda, da of Kenneth Herbert Harold Johnson, of E Wittering, W Sussex; 2 s (John b 1985, Charles b 1987), 6 da (Sophia b 1972, Stephanie b 1974, Justine b 1975, Timothea b 1977, Davita b 1978, Octavia b 1990); *Career* house physician St Thomas's Hosp 1972, med registrar W Middx Hosp 1974-76, res fell Dept of Clinical Pharmacology St Mary's Hosp London 1976-78, sr med registrar St Mary's Hospital and Edgware 1978-83, lectr in med Central Middx Hosp 1983-84, conslt cardiovascular physician Stepping Hill Hosp Stockport and Alexandra Hosp Cheadle 1984-; memb Lipid Cncl MEDAC UK; memb: Br Hypertension Soc, Vineyard Christian Fellowship, Manchester; MRCP 1984; *Recreations* walking, painting; *Style—* Dr Philip Lewis; Stepping Hill Hospital, Poplar Grove, Stockport, Cheshire SK2 7JE (☎ 061 419 5478, Fax 061 483 1470)

LEWIS, (Arthur) Raymond; s of Harold Arthur Lewis (d 1981), of 8 Moorlands, Wilderness Rd, Chislehurst, Kent, and Gladys Nellie, *née* Thompson; *b* 13 Oct 1933; *Educ* Tonbridge; *m* 13 Sept 1957, Anne Margaret Elizabeth, da of John Christie Wishart, MBE (d 1977), of 86 Widmore Rd, Bromley, Kent; 1 s (Andrew b 1961), da (Katharine b 1962); *Career* PO RAF 1952-54; CA; dir Salamander Property Gp Ltd and subsidiaries; *Recreations* swimming, music, gardening, reading, gourmet eating; *Style—* Raymond Lewis, Esq; Hilltop, Ruxley Crescent, Claygate, Esher, Surrey KT10 0TX (☎ 0372 462543); Salamander Property Group Limited, 29 Catherine Place, London SW1E 6DY (☎ 071 821 1775, fax 071 834 4367)

LEWIS, Dr Richard Alexander; s of Harold Charles Lewis, of Buckhurst Hill, Essex, St Thomas' Hosp Med Sch, Univ of London (DM, BSc, MB BS, MRCP); *b* 4 Nov 1949; *m* 26 May 1973, Dr Anne Margaret Lewis, da of Cdr Donald Maclennan, of Tong, Stornoway, Isle of Lewis; 2 s (Christopher b 1977, Peter b 1986), 1 da (Elizabeth b 1982); *Career* house physician St Thomas Hosp London 1975, rotational sr house offr in med Southampton Gen Hosp and Dist Hosp 1976-77, rotational registrar in gen med St Richards Hosp Chichester and St Thomas' Hosp London 1977-79, res fell Dept of Respiratory med unit one Univ of Southampton 1979-82, sr registrar in gen and thoracic med Southampton and Portsmouth Dist Hosp 1982-86, conslt physician specialising in diseases of the chest to Worcester and Dist Health Authy Worcester Royal Infirmary 1986-; memb: Br Thoracic Soc, Med Res Soc, Christian Med Fellowship; govr St Richards Hospice Worcester, pres Vale of Evesham Asthma Soc; MRCS, LRCP; *Books* contrib: Pharmacology of Asthma (1983), Drugs and the Lung (1984), Current Treatment of Ambulatory Asthma (1986); *Recreations* running, cycling, mountain walking, gardening, music; *Style—* Dr Richard Lewis; Crews Court, Suckley, Worcester WR6 5DW (☎ 0886 884552), Worcester Royal Infirmary, Castle St Branch, Worcester WR1 3AS (☎ 0905 763333)

LEWIS, (John Hubert) Richard; s of The Ven John Wilfred Lewis (d 1984), and Winifred Mary, *née* Griffin; *b* 10 Dec 1943; *Educ* Radley, King's Coll London (AKC); *m* 17 April 1968, Sara Patricia, da of Rev Gerald Murray Percival (Peter) Hamilton; 3 s (Peter John b 1970, Michael James b 1972, Nicholas Richard b 1975); *Career* curate of Hexham 1967-70, industl chaplain Diocese of Newcastle 1970-77, communications offr Diocese of Durham 1977-82, agric chaplain Diocese of Hereford 1982-87, archdeacon of Ludlow 1987-; nat chm Small Farmers Assoc 1984-88; *Books* The People, The Land and The Church (jt ed, 1987); *Recreations* walking, bricklaying; *Style—* The Ven the Archdeacon of Ludlow; Glendale House, 51 Gravel Hill, Ludlow, Shropshire SY8 1QS (☎ 0584 872862)

LEWIS, Richard Simon Kirk; s of K J Lewis, of Norfolk, and Josephine, *née* Breadmore; *Educ* Lancing, Andrew Cairns GS Sussex; *m* (m dis); 2 s (Joshua b 17 Sept 1973, Joel b 31 July 1978); partner, Alison Brand; *Career* advertising exec; account exec: Lonsdale Hands Advertising (Lonsdale Crowther) London 1967-68 (trainee 1965-67), Alexander Butterfield and Ayer 1968-71; account mangr Rupert Chetwynd & Partners (Chetwynd Haddons) London 1971-75 (accounts handled incl: Lloyds Bank, Carlsberg Lager, Eggs Authority), md Chetwynd Streets Midlands Ltd Leicester 1976-82 (account dir and Bd dir 1975-76), dir Chetwynd Streets (Holdings) Ltd London 1978-82, md Wells O'Brien London and Regions 1982-83, md and fndr ptnr Singer Lewis & Associates 1983-85 (accounts handled incl: Valor Heating, Valor Home Products, Courtaulds Hosiery Acamas Toys, Greenhall Whitley, Robinsons of Chesterfield, TVR Cars), business devpt dir Graham Poulter Partnership PLC Leeds 1985-, MIPA, memb Mktg Soc; *Style—* Richard Lewis, Esq; Graham Poulter Partnership plc, 2 Burley Road, Leeds, West Yorkshire LS3 1N3 (☎ 0532 469611, fax 0532 448796)

LEWIS, Rev Canon Robert Hugh Cecil; s of Herbert Cecil Lewis, OBE (Capt Welsh Regt, d 1967), and Olive Francis, *née* Marsden (d 1980); *b* 23 Feb 1925; *Educ* Swansea GS, Manchester GS, New Coll Oxford (BA, MA), Westcolt House; *m* 15 July 1948, Joan Dorothy, da of Ernest Gordon Hickman (Maj Cheshire Regt, d 1970); 1 s (David b 15 June 1949), 1 da (Ruth b 17 Nov 1952); *Career* aat Serv 1942-47, PO RAFVR 1945, Flying Offr 1946, Flt Lt 1947; ordained: deacon 1952, priest 1953; curate: St Mary Crumpsall 1952-54, St James New Bury 1954-56; incumbent: St Peter Bury 1956-63, St George Poynton 1963-; rural dean: Stockport 1972-84, Cheadle 1984-86; hon canon Chester Cathedral 1973-, chaplain to HM the Queen 1987; county ecumenical offr for Cheshire 1986-; *Style—* The Rev Canon Robert Lewis; The Vicarage, Poynton, Stockport, Cheshire SK12 1AF

LEWIS, Hon Robin William; OBE (1988); 4 s of 3 Baron Merthyr, KBE, PC (d 1977), and Violet, *née* Meyrick; *b* 7 Feb 1941; *Educ* Eton, Magdalen Coll Oxford (BA, MA); *m* 28 April 1967, Judith Ann, o da of (Vincent Charles) Arthur Giardelli, MBE, of The Golden Plover, Warren, Pembroke, Dyfed; 1 s (Christopher b 1970), 1 da (Katharine b 1972); *Career* Cwlth Devpt Corp 1964-66, Alcan Aluminium Corporation 1967-68, Westminster Bank Ltd 1968-72, Devpt Corp for Wales 1972-82, md Novametrix Medical Systems Ltd 1982-90 (chm 1989-90), chm and md Magstim Co Ltd 1990-; High Sheriff of Dyfed 1987-88; chm Gen Advsy Cncl of Ind Bdcasting Authy 1989-90 (memb 1985-90); *Recreations* sailing; *Clubs* Leander; *Style—* The Hon Robin Lewis, OBE; Orchard House, Llanstephan, Carmarthen, Dyfed SA33 5HA (☎ 026783 254); The Magstim Co Ltd, Whitland, Dyfed SA34 0HR (☎ 0994 240798, fax 0994 240061, telex 48523)

LEWIS, Roger Charles; s of Griffith Charles John Lewis, and Dorothy, *née* Russ; *b* 24 Aug 1934; *Educ* Cynffig Sch, Univ of Nottingham (BMus); *m* 5 July 1980, Dr Christine Lewis, da of Leslie Trollope; 2 s (Owen Rhys b 29 March 1985, Thomas Griffith b 16 Feb 1988); *Career* freelance musician 1976-80, music offr Darlington Arts Centre 1980-82, presenter Radio Tees 1982-84, prodr Capital Radio 1984-85, head music Radio 1 BBC 1987-90 (prodr 1985-87), dir Classical Div EMI Records 1990-; awards incl: Sony Award 1987, 88, 89, NY Grand Award Winner and gold medal 1987 (finalist 1989); Monaco Radio Festival Finalist 1989; chm Music Conf of the Radio Acad 1990; *Style—* Roger Lewis, Esq

LEWIS, Roger St John Hulton; s of Dr John Edward Lewis, of Beaupre, Jersey, Channel Islands, and Ann, *née* Hulton; *b* 26 June 1947; *Educ* Eton; *m* 1973, Vanessa Anne, da of late Michael A England, and Mrs J A Lawrence, of Scotland Hall, Stoke-by-Nayland; 3 s (Harry b 1975, Alexander b 1977, James b 1981); *Career* CA with Peat Marwick Mitchell & Co in London and Spain 1970; joined Crest Homes plc as gp accountant 1972; dir Crest Homes 1973 (md 1975); dir Crest Nicholson Gp 1979 (gp chief exec 1983); *Style—* Roger Lewis, Esq; Ashford Farm House, Stoke D'Abernon, Surrey KT11 3HS (☎ 0932 862025); Crest Nicholson plc, Crest House, Station Rd, Egham, Surrey (☎ 0784 38771)

LEWIS, Roland Peter; s of Peter Oliver Lewis, and Lily May, *née* Rice; *b* 11 March 1951; *Career* CA; dir Resort Hotels plc; *Recreations* skiing, windsurfing, flying; *Style—* Roland P Lewis, Esq; Driftstone Manor, Kingston Gorse, Sussex BN16 1SB; Lewis & Co, 20 Springfield Rd, Crawley, Sussex (☎ 0293 542244, fax 510566, car tel 0860 614767)

LEWIS, Prof Roland Wynne; s of David Lewis (d 1958), of 10 Maesyberllan, Betws, Ammanford, Carms, and Mary Gladys, *née* Davies (d 1981); *b* 20 Jan 1940; *Educ* Amman Valley GS, Univ College Swansea (BSc, PhD, DSc); *m* 17 April 1965, Celia Elizabeth, da of Haydn Elgar Morris, of 19 High St, Ammanford, Carms; 1 s ((David) Andrew b 4 March 1971), 2 da (Caroline b 16 June 1969, Angharad b 11 Feb 1973); *Career* res engr ESSO Canada 1965-69, prof Univ Coll Swansea 1984- (lectr 1969-79, sr lectr 1979-82, reader 1982-84); chm Thermofluids Gp Nat Agency for Finite Element Methods and Standards; MICE 1973; *Books* Civil Engineering Systems-Analysis and Design, Finite Elements in the Flow and Deformation of Porous Media; *Recreations* golf, photography, gardening; *Clubs* La Quinta, Spain, Clyne Golf, Swansea; *Style—* Prof Roland Lewis; Oakridge, 331 Gower Road, Killay, Swansea SA2 7AE (☎ 0792 203166), Civil Engineering Dept, University College of Swansea, Swansea SA2 8PP (☎ 0792 295253, fax 0792 295705)

LEWIS, Stephen; *b* 11 Jan 1959; *Educ* Deyes HS Maghull Merseyside, Southport Coll of Art, Manchester Poly (BA), Jan Van Eyck Academie Maastricht Netherlands; *Career* artist; visiting artist: Cyprus Sch of Art, Voss Sch Norway, Triangle Artists Workshop NY, Emma Lake Workshop Canada, Hardingham Sculpture Workshop UK; lectr at various art colls and polys; solo exhibitions: Francis Graham-Dixon Gallery 1988 and 1990, Holden Gallery Manchester 1990; gp exhibitions: New Contemporaries (ICA), Northern Young Contemporaries (Whitworth Gallery Manchester), The First Picture Show (Norwich), Art in Europe 1991 (Freiberg Germany); work in various int collections; *Style—* Stephen Lewis, Esq; Francis Graham-Dixon Gallery, 17-18 Great Sutton St, London EC1V 0DN (☎ 071 250 1962, fax 071 490 1069)

LEWIS, Stephen John; s of Douglas John Lewis, of Codsall, Staffs, and Dorothy Pauline, *née* Shaw; *b* 8 March 1948; *Educ* Wolverhampton GS, Balliol Coll Oxford (BA); *Career* Phillips & Drew: ptnr 1980-85, dir Securities Ltd 1985-88, md Fifth Horseman Pubns Ltd 1988-; *Recreations* antiquities; *Clubs* Reform; *Style—* Stephen Lewis, Esq; 17 Solar Court, Etchingham Park Rd, London N3 2DZ (☎ 081 349 1439)

LEWIS, Stephen Michael; s of Harry Lewis, of Stanmore, Middlesex, and Celia, *née* Softness; *b* 23 Aug 1949; *Educ* Orange Hill Co GS for Boys, St Catherine's Coll Oxford (open exhibition, BA), Univ of London (LLB); *m* 3 March 1974, Erica, da of Jacob Pesate; 1 s (Adrian William b 9 April 1979), 2 da (Ann Marie b 25 April 1976,

Francesca Rose b 2 Sept 1986); *Career* mgmnt trainee Reed International 1970-71, articled clerk Clintons (solicitors) 1971-74, legal asst Law Cmmn 1975-80, ptnr Clifford Turner (became Clifford Chance) 1985-90 (asst slr 1980-85); memb: Law Soc, Sub Ctee on Insurance Law City of London Law Soc; *Recreations* music, reading, swimming, politics; *Style—* Stephen Lewis, Esq; Clifford Chance, Blackfriars House, 19 New Bridge St, London EC4V 6BY (☎ 071 353 0211, fax 071 489 0046)

LEWIS, (John) Stuart; s of John Charles Lewis, OBE, JP, of 34 Moss Close, Pinner, Middx, and Kathleen Gertrude Clara, *née* Pennick (d 1973); *b* 9 March 1944; *Educ* Downer GS; *m* 19 July 1969, Bridget Margaret, da of Eric Billingham Nash (d 1987); 2 s (James b 1971, Edward b 1983), 1 da (Anna b 1973); *Career* ptnr Fielding Newson-Smith & Co 1975, first vice pres Drexel Burnam Lambert Inc 1986 (vice pres 1980), md Private Fund Managers Ltd 1988, chm Musicale plc; dir: WIB (Publications) Ltd, Trio Investment Trust plc; fell Royal Soc for Encouragement of Arts Manufacturers and Commerce; govr Beechwood Park Sch Markyate; Freeman City of London; FCIS 1974; *Recreations* shooting, tennis, opera, reading, travel; *Clubs* City of London; *Style—* J Stuart Lewis, Esq; Greenaway House, Rose Lane, Wheathampstead, Herts AL4 8RA (☎ 05 8283 2132)

LEWIS, Terence (Terry); MP (Lab) Worsley 1983-; s of Andrew Lewis; *b* 29 Dec 1935; *m* 1958, Audrey, da of William Clarke; *Style—* Terry Lewis, Esq, MP; House of Commons, London SW1

LEWIS, Thomas Loftus Townshend; CBE (1975); s of A Neville Lewis, RP (d 1972), of Stellenbosch, Cape, SA, and Theodosia, *née* Townshend (d 1978); *b* 27 May 1918; *Educ* Diocesan Coll Rondesbosch S Africa, St Paul's, Univ of Cambridge (BA), Guy's Hosp (MB BChir); *m* 27 Nov 1946, (Kathleen) Alexandra Ponsonby Lewis, da of late Wentworth W T Moore; 5 s (John, Anthony, Robert, Charles, Richard); *Career* WWII, Capt RAMC serv Italy and Greece 1944-45; obstetric and gynaecological surgn: Guy's Hosp 1948-83, Chelsea Hosp for Women 1950-83, Queen Charlottes Maternity Hosp 1952-83; hon conslt Br Army 1973 (now emeritus), pres Obstetric Section RSM 1980-81, memb Bd of Dirs Private Patients Plan Ltd (ret); played rugby for Guy's Hosp, Middx Co, London Counties 1945-48, travelling res for England (full back) 1948-49; Freeman City of London, Liveryman Apothecaries Soc; FRCS Eng, FRCOG (vice pres 1975-78); *Books* Progress in Clinical Obstetrics and Gynaecology (1964), French's Index of Differential Diagnosis (12 edn, 1985), Ten Teachers Obstetrics (15 edn, 1990), Ten Teachers Gynaecology (15 edn, 1990); *Recreations* golf, windsurfing, skiing, dinghy sailing, collecting wine; *Clubs* Royal Wimbledon Golf; *Style—* Thomas Lewis, Esq, CBE; 13 Copse Hill, Wimbledon, London SW20 0NB (☎ 081 946 5089); Parkside Hospital, Wimbledon, London SW19 (☎ 081 946 4202)

LEWIS, Major Timothy Stuart; s of Col William Herbert Lewis, DSO, MC (d 1966), and Kathleen Campbell Naylor (d 1982); *b* 26 Nov 1921; *Educ* Cheltenham, RMA Sandhurst; *m* 4 July 1942, Hon Lucia Anne, da of Cdr the Hon John Maurice FitzRoy Newdegate (d 1976), of Arbury Hall, Nuneaton; 1 s (Michael b 1943 d 1963), 1 da (Caroline b 1946, m Sir David Thomson, 3 Bt); *Career* Coldstream Gds 1941-47 (NW Europe 1944-45), Royal Scots Greys 1947-52; Scot and Newcastle Breweries 1964-78, Securities Tst of Scot 1975-89 (chm 1985-89); *Recreations* shooting, fishing, golf; *Clubs* Hon Company of Edinburgh Golfers (capt 1978-80); *Style—* Major Timothy Lewis; Inchdura House, North Berwick, Scotland

LEWIS, Prof Trevor; s of Harold Lewis (d 1982), and Maggie, *née* Bakewell; *b* 8 July 1933; *Educ* Imperial Coll London (PhD, DIC), Univ of Cambridge (MA), Univ of Nottingham (BSc, DSc); *m* 21 March 1959, Margaret Edith, da of Frederick George Wells (d 1977); 1 s (Roger b 1 Oct 1963), 1 da (Heather b 15 April 1961); *Career* univ demonstrator in agric zoology Sch of Agric Cambridge 1958-61; Rothamsted Experimental Station 1961-; head Entomology Dept 1976-83, head Crop Protection Div and dep dir 1983-87, head Crop and Environment Protection Div 1987-89, head and actg dir Inst Arable Crops Res 1989-; seconded ODA 1970, sr res fell Univ of West Indies 1970-73, visiting prof invertebrate zoology Univ of Nottingham 1977- (special lectr 1968-69 and 73-75); AFRC assessor, memb MAFF Advsy Ctee on Pesticides 1984-89; memb: Cncl Br Crop Protection Cncl 1985-, R & D Ctee Potato Mktg Bd 1985-89; pres Royal Entomological Soc London 1985-87 (memb 1956-); memb: Br Ecological Soc, Assoc Applied Biologists; FIBiol, FRSA; *Books* Introduction to Experimental Ecology (with L R Taylor, 1967), Thrips-their Biology, Ecology and Economic Importance (1973), Insect Communication (ed 1984), contrib to sci jls on topics in entomology and agriculture; *Recreations* gardening, music; *Style—* Prof Trevor Lewis; Institute of Arable Crops Research, Rothamsted Experimental Station, West Common, Harpenden, Hertfordshire AL5 2JQ (☎ 0582 763133, fax 0582 461366, telex 825726)

LEWIS, Trevor Oswin; CBE (1983), JP (Dyfed 1969); suc as 4 Baron Merthyr (UK 1911) in 1977, but disclaimed Peerage for life, and does not use his title of Bt (UK 1896); s of 3 Baron Merthyr, KBE, TD, PC (d 1977); *b* 29 Nov 1935; *Educ* Eton, Magdalen Coll Oxford; *m* 18 April 1964, Susan Jane, da of A J Birt-Llewellin; 1 s, 3 da (Lucy b 1967, Anne b 1970, Jessamy b 1972); *Heir* to Btcy and disclaimed Barony, s, David Trevor Lewis b 21 Feb 1977; *Career* memb: Dept of Transport Landscape Advsy Ctee 1968, Countryside Cmmn 1973-83; *Style—* Trevor Lewis, Esq, CBE, JP; Hean Castle, Saundersfoot, Dyfed (☎ 0834 812222)

LEWIS-BOWEN, His Hon Judge; Thomas Edward Ifor; s of Lt-Col J W Lewis-Bowen (d 1990), and Kathleen, *née* Rice (d 1981); *b* 20 June 1933; *Educ* Ampleforth, St Edmund Hall Oxford; *m* 1965, Gillian, da of the late Reginald Brett, of Puckington, Somerset; 1 s, 2 da; *Career* barr Middle Temple 1958, rec of Crown Ct 1974-80, circuit judge (Wales and Chester) 1980-; *Style—* His Hon Judge Lewis-Bowen; Clynfyw, Boncath, Dyfed (☎ 023 9841 236); 4 Asquith Court, Swansea, W Glamorgan SA1 4QL (☎ 0792 473736)

LEWIS-JONES, Dr (Margaret) Susan; da of Ian Robert Munro Campbell, of 25 Reform St, Tayport, Fife, Scotland, and Jean Douglas, *née* Ramsay; *b* 12 April 1948; *Educ* Tudor Grange Girls GS Solihull, Univ of Liverpool Med Sch (MB ChB); *m* 7 Aug 1971, David Iwan Lewis-Jones, s of Capt Robert Gwilym Lewis-Jones, RN, CBE, of Man Siriol, Cae Deintur, Dolgellau, Gwynedd, N Wales; 1 s (Sion b 20 Jan 1976), 1 da (Alŷs b 19 May 1978); *Career* medical and surgical house offr 1972-73, demonstrator in anatomy Univ of Liverpool 1973-74, GP 1974-77, medical registrar 1982, conslt dermatologist 1987- (registrar 1982-85, sr registrar 1985-87), currently hon lectr in dermatology Univ of Liverpool; memb: BMA, Br Assoc of Dermatologists, American Acad of Dermatology, North of England Dermatological Soc, Liverpool Med Inst; MRCP 1982; *Recreations* golf, skiing, music; *Clubs* Upon-by-Chester Golf, Dolgellau Golf; *Style—* Dr Susan Lewis-Jones; Maelor General Hospital, Croes/Newydd Rd, Wrexham, Clywd, N Wales LL13 7TD (☎ 0978 291100, fax 0244 680444); Grosvenor Nuffield Hospital, Wrexham Rd, Chester, Cheshire (☎ 0244 680444)

LEWIS OF NEWNHAM, Baron (Life Peer UK 1989), of Newnham in the Co of Cambridgeshire; Sir Jack Lewis; *b* 13 Feb 1928; *Educ* Barrow GS, Univ of London (BSc, DSc), Univ of Nottingham (PhD), Univ of Manchester (MSc), Univ of Cambridge (MA, ScD); *m* 1951, Elfreida Mabel, *née* Lamb; 1 s, 1 da; *Career* sits as an Independent in the House of Lords; lectr: Univ of Sheffield 1954-56, Imperial Coll London 1956-57, lectr/reader Univ Coll London 1957-61; prof of chemistry: Univ of Manchester 1961-67, Univ Coll London 1967-70, Univ of Cambridge 1970-; warden Robinson Coll Cambridge 1975-; Firth Visiting Prof Sheffield Univ 1967; memb: SRC Poly Ctee 1973-79, SRC Sci Ctee 1975-80, SRC Sci Bd 1975-79, Univ Grants Ctee for Physical Scis 1975-80, Jt Ctee SERC/SSRC 1979-81, SERC Cncl 1980-86, Cncl Royal Soc 1982-84, Nato Sci Ctee; chm: Royal Cmmn on Environmental Pollution 1985-, DES visiting Ctee to Cranfield Inst 1984-; pres Royal Soc of Chemistry 1986-88; Hon DUniv: Open Univ 1982, Rennes Univ 1980; Hon DSc: UEA 1983, Univ of Nottingham 1983; FRS, FRIC, FRSA; kt 1982; *Style—* The Rt Hon Lord Lewis of Newnham, FRS; Warden's Lodge, 4 Sylvester Rd, Cambridge (☎ 0223 60222); University Chemical Laboratory, Lensfield Rd, Cambridge (☎ 0223 336300)

LEWISHAM, Viscount; William Legge; s and h of 9 Earl of Dartmouth by Raine, now Countess Spencer; *b* 23 Sept 1949; *Educ* Eton, Christ Church Oxford, Harvard Business Sch; *Career* contested (C): Leigh Lancs 1974, Stockport South 1974; FCA; chm and fndr Kirklees Cable; *Style—* Viscount Lewisham; Slaithwaite, nr Huddersfield, W Yorks

LEWISOHN, His Hon Judge; Anthony Clive Leopold Lewisohn; s of John Lewisohn (d 1939); *b* 1 Aug 1925; *Educ* Stowe, Trinity Coll Oxford; *m* 1957, Lone Ruthwen Jurgensen; 2 s; *Career* serv Oxfordshire & Bucks LI 1946-47, Lt; called to the Bar Middle Temple 1951, circuit judge 1974-; *Style—* His Hon Judge Lewisohn; Brackenhurst, Fairoak Lane, Oxshott, Leatherhead, Surrey

LEWISOHN, Oscar Max; s of Max Lewisohn (d 1973), of Copenhagen, Denmark, and Jenny Lewisohn (d 1984); *b* 6 May 1938; *Educ* Sortedam Gymnasium Copenhagen Denmark; *m* 1, 4 Aug 1962, Louisa Madeleine (d 1985), da of Henry Grunfeld, of London; 3 s (Mark b 1963, Richard b 1965, James b 1970), 1 da (Anita b 1967); m 2, 24 Oct 1987, Margaret Ann, da of Don Paterson, of Wellington, NZ; 2 da (Jenny b 1989, Sophie b 1990); *Career* SG Warburg and Co Ltd 1962-: exec dir 1969, dep chm 1987; dir SG Warburg plc 1985; life govr Imperial Cancer Res Fund; kt order of the Dannebrog (Denmark); *Recreations* music; *Style—* Oscar Lewisohn, Esq; 1 Finsbury Ave, London EC2M 2PK (☎ 071 606 1066)

LEWITH, Dr George Thomas; s of Frank Lewith (d 1965), and Alice, *née* Schallinger; *b* 12 Jan 1950; *Educ* Queen's Coll Taunton, Trinity Coll Cambridge (MA), Westminster Hosp London (MB BChir); *m* 7 May 1977, Nicola Rosemary, da of Lt Bonham Ley Bazeley, DSC, of Gatehouse Standish, Stonehouse, Gloucestershire; 2 s (Thomas b 1981, Henry b 1986), 1 da (Emily b 1983); *Career* paediatric intern McMaster Univ Ontario 1974, jr positions Westminster Hosp and UCH 1974-78, GP Queensland Australia 1978, WHO studentship in acupuncture Nanjing Coll of Traditional Chinese Med 1978, lectr in general practice (initially trainee) Dept of Gen Practice Univ of Southampton 1979-82, co-dir Centre for the Study of Complementary Med 1982-; author of numerous learned books and articles, ed Complementary Medical Res; memb: Cncl Res Cncl for Complementary Med, RSM; formerly: vice chm Br Med Acupuncture Soc, chm Koestler Fndn; memb numerous med orgns and ctees; MRCP 1977, MRCGP 1980; *Recreations* swimming, skiing, sailing, antique collecting, bee keeping, theatre; *Clubs* Royal Lymington Yacht, RSM; *Style—* Dr George Lewith; Swaywood House, Mead End Road, Sway, Lymington, Hampshire SO41 6EE (☎ 0590 682129); Centre for the Study of Complementary Medicine, 51 Bedford Place, Southampton, Hampshire SO1 2DG (☎ 0703 334752, fax 0703 702459)

LEWTHWAITE, Brig Rainald Gilfrid; CVO (1975), OBE (1974), MC (1943); s of Sir William Lewthwaite, 2 Bt, JP (d 1933), and hp of bro, Sir William Anthony Lewthwaite, 3 Bt; *b* 21 July 1913; *Educ* Rugby, Trinity Coll Cambridge; *m* 1936, Margaret Elizabeth, MBE (d 1990), da of Harry Edmonds (d 1982), of NY, USA; 1 s (1 s decd), 1 da (1 da decd); *Career* cmmnd Scot Gds 1934, 1939-45 served ME and NW Europe, Brig Scots Gds; mil attaché 1964 and def attaché Br Embassy Paris 1964-68, Cabinet Office 1952-55, NATO HQ Paris 1961-64, ret 1968; dir Protocol Hong Kong 1969-76; *Recreations* country life; *Style—* Brig Rainald Lewthwaite, CVO, OBE, MC; Broadgate, Millom, Cumbria LA18 5JY

LEWTHWAITE, Sir William Anthony; 3 Bt (UK 1927); s of Sir William Lewthwaite, 2 Bt, JP (d 1933), and Beryl Mary Stopford (d 1970), *née* Hickman; *b* 26 Feb 1912; *Educ* Rugby, Trinity Coll Cambridge (BA); *m* 1936, Lois Mairi, da of Capt Struan Robertson Kerr-Clark (ka 1915; bro of 1 Baron Inverchapel, GCMG, PC), and Lady Beatrice Minnie Ponsonby Moore (d 1966, having m 2, 1941, 1 Lord Rankeillour, PC; she was da of 9 Earl of Drogheda); 1 da (Catherine Jane b 1954, m 1986 William Tobias Hall), and 1 da decd; *Heir* bro, Brig Rainald Gilfrid Lewthwaite, CVO, OBE, MC; *Career* served Grenadier Gds 1943-46; slr 1937; memb: Cncl Country Landowners Assoc 1948-64, Ctee Westminster Law Soc 1964-73; *Recreations* forestry; *Style—* Sir William Lewthwaite, Bt; 114 Cranmer Court, London SW3 3HE (☎ 071 584 2088/7)

LEY, Sir Francis Douglas; 4 Bt (UK 1905), MBE (1961), TD, JP (Derbys 1939), DL (1957); s of Maj Sir Henry Gordon Ley, 2 Bt (d 1944); *b* 1907; *Educ* Eton, Cambridge; *m* 1931, Violet Geraldine (d 1991), da of Maj Gerald Johnson, of Foston, Derbys; 1 s, 1 da; *Heir* s, Ian Francis Ley; *Career* chm: Ley's Malleable Castings Co Ltd, Ewart Chainbelt Co Ltd, Ley's Foundries & Engineering Ltd; High Sheriff of Derbys 1956; *Style—* Sir Francis Ley, Bt, MBE, TD, JP, DL; Pond House, Shirley, Derby (☎ 0335 60327)

LEY, Ian Francis; s and h of Sir Francis Douglas Ley, 4 Bt, MBE, TD; *b* 12 June 1934; *Educ* Eton; *m* 1957, Caroline Margaret, da of late Maj George H Errington, MC, of Zimbabwe; 1 s, 1 da; *Career* formerly chm: Ley's Foundries & Engineering, Ley's Malleable Castings, Ewart Chainbelt Co, Beeston Boiler Co (Successors) Ltd, W Shaw & Co (ret 1982 on takeover of the gp); chm S Russell & Son Ltd 1983-; *Recreations* tennis, shooting; *Clubs* White's; *Style—* Ian Ley, Esq; 23 Bywater St, London SW3 (☎ 071 584 4125); Fauld Hall, Tutbury, Staffs DE13 9HR (☎ 0283 812266)

LEYLAND, (John) Roger Nowell; s of Sidney Leyland (d 1976), and Evelyn, *née* Place (d 1979); *b* 10 Jan 1953; *Educ* Friend's Sch Saffron Walden Essex, RAM; *Career* admitted slr 1980; ptnr Herbert Smith 1987- (joined 1985); LRAM 1971; memb Law Soc 1980-; *Recreations* music, tennis, bridge, travel, languages; *Style—* Roger Leyland, Esq; Herbert Smith, Exchange House, Primrose St, London EC2A 4HS (☎ 071 374 8000, telex 886633, fax 071 496 0043)

LEYSHON, Robert Lloyd; s of Sqdn Ldr Mervyn Leyshon, of Pencoed, Bridgend, Mid Glamorgan, and Joan Hilton, *née* Lloyd (d 1950); *b* 12 Feb 1948; *Educ* Ogmore Vale GS, St Mary's Hosp (BSc, MB BS); *m* 16 July 1977, Catherine (Kay), da of Luther Edwards (d 1984); 1 s (Aled Lloyd b 18 Nov 1978), 1 da ((Catherine) Nia b 23 Feb 1980); *Career* house surgn and casualty offr St Mary's Hosp 1972-74, rotating surgical registrar Cardiff Hosp 1974-77, sr orthopaedic registrar Cardiff and Swansea Hosp 1979-83, sr lectr in orthopaedic surgery Welsh Sch of Med 1983-84, conslt orthopaedic surgn Morriston Hosp Swansea 1984-; author of papers: use of carbon fibre as ligament replacement, research into post menopausal osteoporosis, review of hip prostheses in fractures of femoral neck; hon orthopaedic surgn Llanelli RFC and Welsh U21 rugby squad; FRCS 1977, fell Br Orthopaedic Assoc 1983; *Recreations* cricket, tennis, golf; *Clubs* Clyne Golf; *Style—* Robert Leyshon, Esq; 19 Westport Ave, Mayals, Swansea SA3 5EA (☎ 0792 403003); St Davids House, 1 Uplands Terr, Swansea SA2 0GU (☎ 0792 472922); Orthopaedic Dept, Morriston Hospital, Swansea SA6 6NL (☎ 0792 703450)

LIARDET, Maj-Gen Henry Maughan; CB (1960), CBE (1945, OBE 1942), DSO (1945), DL (Sussex, later W Sussex 1965); s of Maj-Gen Sir Claude Liardet, KBE, CB, DSO, TD, DL (d 1966), of Ballsdown, Chiddingfold, Surrey, and Dorothy, *née* Hopper (d 1968); *b* 27 Oct 1906; *Educ* Bedford Sch; *m* 25 Feb 1933, Joan Sefton, da of Maj Guy Sefton Constable, MC, JP (d 1935), of Warningcamp House, Arundel, W Sussex; 3 s (Guy Francis b 1934, Timothy William b 1936, Andrew John b 1939); *Career* cmmnd 106 (Lancs Hussars) Bde RHA (TA) 1924; regular cmmn RTC 1927 serv: UK, India, Egypt; Staff Coll 1939, WO, GHQ ME, Cdr Tank Regt 7 Armd Div Western Desert, GSO1 10 Armd Div Alamein 1942, served Palestine, Iraq and Italy 1943-45, 2 i/c 25 Tank Bde 1944-45, cmd 25 Armd Engr Bde April-Aug 1945, Col i/c admin Kent Dist UK 1946, 2 i/c 6 Armd Bde Italy and Palestine 1946-48, Brig RAC ME 1948-50, Co 8 RTR 1950, various staff appts WO, Co 23 Armd Bde 1954-55, Imperial Def Coll 1955, COS Army Staff Br Jt Servs Mission Washington DC 1956-58, dir gen fighting vehicles WO 1958-61, dep master gen of the ordnance WO 1961-64, ret 1964; ADC to HM The Queen 1956-58, Col Cmdt RTR 1961-67; W Sussex CC: memb for Arundel 1965-70, Alderman 1970-74; pres Royal Br Legion Sussex Cncl 1965-78, chm W Sussex SSAFA 1965-85; *Recreations* shooting, gardening; *Clubs* Army and Navy, Sussex; *Style*— Maj-Gen Henry Liardet, CB, CBE, DSO, DL; Warningcamp House, nr Arundel, W Sussex BN18 9QY (☎ 0903 882533)

LIBBY, Dr Donald Gerald; s of Herbert Lionel Libby (d 1958), and Minnie, *née* Green (d 1986); *b* 2 July 1934; *Educ* RMA Sandhurst, Univ of London (BSc, PhD); *m* 1, 13 May 1961, Margaret Elizabeth Dunlop (d 1979), da of John Kennedy Dunlop McLatchie; 1 da (Fiona b 1966); m 2, 26 March 1982, June, da of Collin George Belcher, of Newmarket, Suffolk; *Career* Dept of Educn and Science: princ scientific offr 1967-72, princ 1972-74, asst sec 1974-80, asst under-sec of state planning and int rels branch 1980-82, architects bldg and schs branch 1982-86, further and higher educn branch 1986-; CEng, MIEE; *Recreations* music, rowing, tennis; *Style*— Dr Donald Libby; Lygon Cottage, 26 Wayneflete Tower Ave, Esher, Surrey KT10 8QG; Dept of Education and Science, Elizabeth House, York Rd, London SE1 7PH (☎ 071 934 9927)

LIBRACH, Dr Israel Mayer; s of Maurice Librach (d 1952), of 9 Brookvale Drive, Belfast, and Annie, *née* Bogen (d 1940); *b* 23 Nov 1914; *Educ* Royal Belfast Academical Inst, Queen's Univ Belfast (MB BCH, BAO, DPH), Univ of London (DCH England); *m* 11 April 1945, Enid Mina, da of Arthur Lewis (d 1967), of 23 The Chase, London SW4; *Career* med supt City Isolation Hosp Nottingham 1945-47, lectr in hygiene Univ Coll Nottingham 1945-47, asst MOH Nottingham 1945-47, physician Chadwell Heath Hosp Ilford 1948-83, conslt for smallpox DHSS 1960-; chm Ilford Med Soc, ctee memb Barking and Havering branch BMA, lectr and examiner St John's Ambulance and Br Red Cross, memb Ilford and Barking Med Advsy Ctee; Freeman City of London 1966, Liveryman Worshipful Soc of Apothecaries 1968; Hon MRCGP 1986, Hon MFCH 1989; memb BMA 1938, FRSM 1942, fell Med Soc of London 1952; *Recreations* antiquarian, gardening, book collecting; *Style*— Dr Israel Librach; 2 Fauna Close, Chadwell Heath, Romford, Essex RM6 6AS (☎ 081 590 9727)

LICHFIELD, Archdeacon of; *see*: Ninis, Ven Richard Betts

LICHFIELD, Dean of; *see*: Lang, Very Rev John Harley

LICHFIELD, 97 Bishop of, 1984-; Rt Rev Keith Norman Sutton; the see of Lichfield was founded by Oswy, King of Mercia in 656; in 1075 it was removed to Chester, in 1102 to Coventry, and finally to its original foundation at Lichfield; patron of one hundred and thirty-four livings, the canonries and prebends in his cathedral and the archdeaconries of Stafford, Salop and Stoke-upon-Trent; s of Norman and Irene Sutton; *b* 23 June 1934; *m* 1963, Edith Mary Jean Geldard; 3 s, 1 da; *Career* curate St Andrew's Plymouth 1959-62, chaplain St John's Coll Cambridge 1962-67, tutor and chaplain Bishop Tucker Coll Mukono Uganda 1968-73, princ Ridley Hall Cambridge 1973-78, bishop of Kingston-upon-Thames 1978-83, select preacher Univ of Cambridge 1987; admitted House of Lords 1989; chm: bd of govrs Queen's Coll Birmingham 1987-, bd of mission and unity of the Gen Synod 1989-; memb: Gen Synod Standing Ctee, governing body Cranmer Hall Durham, admin cncl Royal Jubilee Tst, African RC Conf; *Books* The People of God (1982); *Recreations* russian literature, baroque music, walking, travel in France and Africa; *Style*— The Rt Rev the Bishop of Lichfield; Bishop's House, The Close, Lichfield, Staffs WS13 7LG

LICHFIELD, 5 Earl of (UK 1831); (Thomas) Patrick John Anson; also Viscount Anson and Baron Soberton (both UK 1806); s of Lt-Col Viscount Anson (d 1958, s and h of 4 Earl, who he predeceased) by his 1 w Anne Ferelith Fenella (d 1980, having m 1950 HH Prince George of Denmark, CVO, who d 1986), da of Hon John Bowes-Lyon (s of 14 Earl of Strathmore and bro of HM Queen Elizabeth The Queen Mother); suc gf 1960; *b* 25 April 1939; *Educ* Harrow, RMA Sandhurst; *m* 1975 (m dis 1986), Lady Leonora Mary Grosvenor, da of 5 Duke of Westminster, TD, and sis of Duchess of Roxburghe; 1 s, 2 da (Lady Rose Meriel Margaret b 1976, Lady Eloise Anne Elizabeth b 1981); *Heir* s, Viscount Anson; *Career* served in Grenadier Gds 1959-62 (Lt); photographer; fell: Royal Photographic Soc, The Br Inst of Professional Photographers; *Books* The Most Beautiful Women (1981), Lichfield on Photography (1981), A Royal Album (1986), Lichfield on Travel Photography (1986), Not The Whole Truth (autobiography 1986), Unipart Calendar Books (1985), Creating the Unipart Calendar (1983), Hotfoot to Zabriskie Point (1985), Lichfield in Retrospect (1988), Courvoisier Book of the Best (ed); *Recreations* arboriculture; *Clubs* White's; *Style*— The Rt Hon the Earl of Lichfield; Shugborough Hall, Stafford (☎ 0889 881454); studio: 133 Oxford Gdns, London W10 6NE (☎ 081 969 6161, fax 081 960 6494)

LICHT, Leonard Samuel; s of Bernhard Licht (d 1982), and Hilde Licht; *b* 15 March 1945; *Educ* Christ's Coll Finchley; *m* 1973, Judith, da of Albert Grossman (d 1980); 1 s, 1 da; *Career* investmt banker; vice chm and dir Mercury Asset Mgmnt Gp plc 1985, chm Channel Islands and Int Investmt Tst Ltd 1988; dir: Keystone Investmt Tst plc 1988, Beneficial Arts Ltd 1989, Royal Free NHS Tst (non-exec); *Recreations* philately, tennis, eighteenth century pottery, wine and food; *Clubs* Brooks's; *Style*— Leonard Licht, Esq; 33 King William St, London EC4R 9AS

LICKLEY, Sir Robert Lang; CBE (1973); *b* 19 Jan 1912; *Educ* Dundee HS, Univ of Edinburgh, Imperial Coll (fell 1973); *Career* chief project engr Hawker Aircraft Design Office 1940-46 (joined 1933), prof of aircraft design Coll of Aeronautics Cranfield 1946-51, md Fairey Aviation Ltd 1959-60, dir Hawker Siddeley Aviation Ltd 1960-76 (asst md 1965-76), head of Rolls Royce support staff NEB 1976-79, non-exec dir Fairey Co 1979-85; Hon: MSME, FIMechE; pres: IMechE 1971, IProdE 1987; Hon DSc: Univ of Edinburgh 1973, Univ of Strathclyde 1976; FRSE, FEng, FRAeS, FIProdE; kt 1984; *Style*— Sir Robert Lickley, CBE; Foxwood, Silverdale Ave, Walton-on-Thames, Surrey KT12 1EQ (☎ 0932 225 058)

LICKORISH, Adrian Derick; s of Leonard John Lickorish, CBE, *qv*, of 46 Hillway, Highgate, London N6, and Maris, *née* Wright; *b* 29 Oct 1948; *Educ* Highgate Sch, Univ of London (LLB, LLM); *m* 16 May 1987, Vivien Mary, da of John Bernard Gould, of Wirswall Hall, Whitchurch, Shrops; *Career* slr 1974; ptnr: Durrant Piesse 1981, Lovell White Durrant 1988; memb Law Soc; *Recreations* farming, shooting, fishing, mil history; *Clubs* Royal Over-Seas League; *Style*— Adrian Lickorish, Esq; Woodhouse Farm, Avening, Gloucestershire GL8 8NH; 65 Holborn Viaduct, London (☎ 071 236 0066)

LICKORISH, Leonard John; CBE (1975); s of Adrian Joseph Lickorish (d 1957), and Josephine, *née* Rose (d 1953); *b* 10 Aug 1921; *Educ* St Georges Coll Weybridge, UCL (BA); *m* 1945, Eileen Maris (d 1983); 1 s (Adrian Lickorish, *qv*); *Career* serv WWII RAF Flt Lt 1941-46; gen mangr Br Travel Assoc 1963-69, dir gen Br Tourist Authy 1970-86; chm Euro Travel Cmmn 1984-86, hon vice chm Euro Travel Cmmn and sec Euro Tourism Action Gp 1987, dir of studies (tourism) Royal Inst of Public Admin 1987, visiting prof Univ of Strathclyde 1989, vice pres Exhibitions Indust Fedn Ctee 1989; Order of the Crown of Belgium 1967; *Books* The Travel Trade (1958), Reviews of UK Statistical Sources Tourism (1975), Marketing Tourism (1989); numerous int pubns; *Recreations* gardening, sailing, walking; *Clubs* Royal Overseas League; *Style*— Leonard Lickorish, Esq, CBE; 46 Hillway, London N6 6EP (☎ 081 340 8920)

LIDBURY, Sir John (Towersey); s of John Lidbury (d 1950); *b* 25 Nov 1912; *Educ* Owen's Sch; *m* 1939, Audrey Joyce, da of Harold Wigzell; 1 s, 2 da; *Career* joined Hawker Aircraft Ltd 1940 (dir 1951, md 1959, chm 1961-77), dep chm and chief exec Hawker Siddeley Aviation Ltd 1959-77; chm: Hawker Siddeley Dynamics Ltd 1971-77, High Duty Alloys Ltd 1978-79 (dep chm 1970-78), Carlton Industs plc 1981-83 (dir 1978-81); vice chm Hawker Siddeley Gp plc 1970-83 (dir 1960-83, dep md 1970-81); dir: Hawker Siddeley Int Ltd 1963-83, Invergordon Distillers (Hldgs) plc 1978-83, Smiths Industs plc 1978-85; JP Kingston-upon-Thames 1952-62, pres Soc of Br Aerospace Cos Ltd 1969-70; FRAeS, CBIM; kt 1971; *Style*— Sir John Lidbury; c/o Hawker Siddeley Group plc, 18 St James's Sq, London SW1Y 4LB (☎ 071 930 6177)

LIDDELL, Alasdair Donald MacDuff; s of Ian Donald Macduff Liddell (d 1976), and Barbara Macduff, *née* Dixon; *b* 15 Jan 1949; *Educ* Fettes Coll Edinburgh, Balliol Coll Oxford (BA), Thames Poly (DMS); *m* 20 Feb 1976, Jennifer Gita, da of Prof Chimen Abramsky, of London; 1 s (Rob b 22 Feb 1977), 1 da (Maia b 11 Dec 1979); *Career* admin (Planning and Policies) Tower Hamlets Dist 1977-79, area gen admin Kensington Chelsea and Westminister AHA 1979-82, dist admin Hammersmith and Fulham Health Authy 1984-85, dist gen mangr Bloomsbury Health Authy 1985-88, regnl gen mangr E Anglian RHA 1988-; chm of tstees Public Mgmnt Fndn; *Recreations* skiing, personal computers, buying wine; *Clubs* Royal Soci of Medicine; *Style*— Alasdair Liddell, Esq; East Anglian Regional Health Authority, Union Lane, Chesterton, Cambridge CB4 1RF (☎ 0223 375266, fax 0223 312594)

LIDDELL, Hon Mrs (Anna); *née* Kinnaird; 2 da of 13 Lord Kinnaird, *qv*; *b* 18 Dec 1952; *m* 3 Sept 1988, Edward Henry (Harry) Liddell, eld s of Thomas Liddell, of Dormans Corner, Lingfield, Surrey; *Style*— The Hon Mrs Liddell; 97 Narbonne Avenue, London SW4

LIDDELL, (Andrew) Colin MacDuff; WS (1980); s of Ian Donald MacDuff Liddell, WS (d 1976), and Barbara, *née* Dixon; descendent of MacDuffs of Strathbraan, Perthshire; *b* 21 June 1954; *Educ* Cargilfield Sch Edinburgh, Fettes, Balliol Coll Oxford (BA), Univ of Edinburgh (LLB); *m* 11 Aug 1979, Katrina Louise, da of Dr Kenneth Terence Gruer, MC, of Edinburgh; 2 da (Iona Michelle b 1983, Bryony Marsali b 1985); *Career* slr, ptnr Messrs J & H Mitchell, Pitlochry and Aberfeldy 1981; sr pres Speculative Soc of Edinburgh 1983-84, sec Highland Perthshire Development Co Ltd 1985-; govr Cargilfield Sch Edinburgh 1985- (vice chm 1987-); *Recreations* skiing, windsurfing, hill walking, curling; *Style*— Colin Liddell, Esq, WS; Messrs J & H Mitchell WS, 51 Atholl Rd, Pitlochry PH16 5BU (☎ 0796 2606, fax 0796 3198)

LIDDELL, Douglas Gerard; s of Gen Sir Clive Liddell, KCB, CMG, CBE, DSO (d 1956), and Hilda Jessie Bissett, *née* Kennedy; *b* 2 Sept 1919; *Educ* Wellington, Peterhouse Cambridge; *m* 1 March 1940, Doreen Joyce, *née* Ducker; 3 da (Anita, Serena, Simone); *Career* serv WWII, Maj; ret; conslt Spink & Sons Ltd; *Recreations* reading, theatre, music, cricket; *Clubs* Oxford & Cambridge Univ; *Style*— Douglas Liddell, Esq, WS; Terrys Cross Cottage, Bramlands Lane, Woodmancote, Henfield, W Sussex BN5 9TR (☎ 0273 49 3596); Spink & Son Ltd, 5-7 King St, St James's, London SW1 6QS (☎ 071 930 7888, telex 916711)

LIDDELL, Hamish George Macduff; WS (1949); s of Buckham William Liddell (d 1950), and Katharine, *née* MacDuff (d 1957); *b* 20 Feb 1924; *Educ* Cargilfield Sch Edinburgh, Fettes, Balliol Coll Oxford (BA), Univ of Edinburgh (LLB); *m* 9 July 1965, Mary Elizabeth, da of Leslie George Milliken (d 1981); 1 s (Duncan b 1969), 1 da (Diana b 1971); *Career* WWII Lt Black Watch & KAR served E Africa, India, Burma 1943-46; practising slr 1949-; memb Scottish Sports Cncl 1972-76, pres Scottish Nat Ski Cncl 1973-78 (chm 1963-73), hon life memb Br Ski Fedn, invitation life memb SCGB; awarded Queen's Jubilee Medal 1977; *Recreations* field sports, skiing, sailing; *Style*— Hamish Liddell, Esq; 51 Atholl Rd, Pitlochry (☎ 0796 2606)

LIDDELL, Helen Lawrie; da of Hugh Reilly, of Falkirk, Stirlingshire, and Bridget, *née* Lawrie (decd); *b* 6 Dec 1950; *Educ* Univ of Strathclyde (BA); *m* 22 July 1972, Dr Alistair Henderson, s of Robert Liddell, of Coatbridge, Lanarks; 1 s (Paul b 1979), 1 da (Clare b 1985); *Career* head Econ Dept Scot TUC 1971-75 (asst sec 1975-76), econ corr BBC Scotland 1976-77, Scottish sec Lab Pty 1977-88, dir personnel and pub affrs Scottish Daily Record and Sunday Mail (1986) Ltd 1988-; parly candidate (L) E Fife 1974, cabinet rep Int Women's Year Ctee 1975, memb Nat Jt Cncl for Academic Salaries and Awards 1974-76; *Recreations* writing, walking; *Style*— Mrs Helen Liddell; Glenisla, Main Rd, Langbank, Port Glasgow, Renfrewshire, PA14 6XP (☎ 047 554 344); Largiemore, Argyll; Scottish Daily Record and Sunday Mail (1986) Ltd, Anderston Quay, Glasgow G3 8DA (☎ 041 242 3331, fax 041 204 0703, telex 778277)

LIDDELL, Mark Charles; s of Peter John Liddell, DSC (d 1979), of Moorhouse Hall, Carlisle, Cumbria, and Priscilla, *née* Downes; *b* 19 Sept 1954; *Educ* Ampleforth; *m* 21 July 1979, Hon Lucy Katherine, da of 6 Viscount Knutsford, *qv*; 1 s (James b 23 Jan 1987), 2 da (Katherine b 4 June 1983, Sophie b 24 June 1990); *Career* Lloyds broker 1974-81; dir: Lycetts (Cumbria) Ltd 1981-87, Lycetts (Insurance Brokers) Ltd 1987-, Lycetts (Financial Services) Ltd 1987-; memb of Lloyds 1981; *Recreations* shooting, cricket, snooker; *Clubs* Northern Counties; *Style*— Mark Liddell, Esq; Cumrew House, Cumrew, Carlisle, Cumbria CA4 9DD; Lycetts, Milburn House, Dean St, Newcastle upon Tyne NE1 1PP (☎ 091 232 1151, fax 091 232 1873)

LIDDELL, Hon Thomas Arthur Hamish; s and h of 8 Baron Ravensworth; *b* 27 Oct 1954; *m* 8 June 1983, Linda, da of Henry Thompson (d 1986), of Hawthorn Farm, Gosforth, Newcastle-upon-Tyne; 1 s (Henry b 27 Nov 1987), 1 da (Alice b 24 April 1986); *Career* branch chm local NFU and other ctees Northumberland NFU 1989-90; memb ctee Northumberland CLA 1990-; *Recreations* shooting; *Style*— The Hon Thomas Liddell; c/o Eslington Park, Whittingham, Alnwick, Northumberland NE66 4UR (☎ 0665 74239, car 0836 359861)

LIDDELL-GRAINGER, David Ian; Baron of Ayton (territorial); s of Capt Henry H Liddell-Grainger, JP, DL (d 1935), of Ayton Castle, Berwicks, and Lady Muriel Felicia Vere, *née* Bertie (d 1981), da of 12 Earl of Lindsey and Abingdon; *b* 26 Jan 1930; *Educ* St Peter's Coll Adelaide SA, Eton, Univ of London; *m* 14 Dec 1957 (m dis 1982), Anne Mary, da of Col Sir Henry Abel Smith, KCMG, KCVO, DSO, DL, of Barton Lodge, Windsor, Berks, and Lady May Cambridge, da of 1 Earl of Athlone and HRH Princess Alice, gda of Queen Victoria through the Queen's 4 s, the Duke of Albany; 4 s (Ian Richard Peregrine b 1959, Charles Montague b 1960, Simon Rupert b 1962, Malcolm Henry b 1967), 1 da (Alice Mary b 1964); issue by Christine, Lady de la Rue; 2 s (David Henry b 1983, Maximilian b 1985); *Career* Scots Gds 1948-50;

property developer and farmer; cncllr 1958-73, has served on Scottish Gas Cncl and cncls of: RNLI, Scot Scout Assoc, Nat Tst for Scot, Royal Agric Soc of England, Scot Landowners Fedn; dep chm Timber Growers UK 1985-88, memb Regnl Advsy Ctee Forestry Cmmn, area cmmr for Scouts in Borders; DL (1962-85); hospitaller Order of St John (Scot) 1977-82, KStJ 1974; Grand Master Mason of Scot 1969-74, memb Queen's Bodyguard for Scotland (Royal Co of Archers) 1955-83; FSA (Scot); *Recreations* flying, model engineering, history; *Clubs* New (Edinburgh), MCC; *Style—* David Liddell-Grainger, Esq; Ayton Castle, Berwickshire TD14 5RD (☎ 08907 81212)

LIDDERDALE, Sir David William Shuckburgh; KCB (1975, CB 1963), TD; s of late Edward Wadsworth Lidderdale; *b* 30 Sept 1910; *Educ* Winchester, King's Coll Cambridge; *m* 1943, Lola, da of late Rev Thomas Alexander Beckett; 1 s; *Career* served WWII The Rifle Bde (TA), active serv N Africa, Italy; asst clerk House of Commons 1934, clerk of the House 1974-76; hon vice pres Assoc of Secs-Gen of Parl (Inter-Parly Union); *Publications* The Parliament of France (1951); *Clubs* Travellers', MCC, Pilgrim Soc; *Style—* Sir David Lidderdale, KCB, TD; 46 Cheyne Walk, London SW3 5LP

LIDDIARD, Michael Richard; s of Richard England Liddiard, CBE, of Oxford Lodge, Wimbledon, and Constance Lily, *née* Rook; *b* 15 Nov 1946; *Educ* Oundle, Univ of Exeter (BA), London Business Sch; *m* 14 March 1970, Judith Elizabeth Best, da of Wing Cdr Frederick John Edward Ison, DFC, RAF (d 1978); 1 s (James Stratton b 1973), 1 da (Amanda Brooke b 1975); *Career* C Czarnikow Ltd 1969-: dir 1981, vice chm 1983, dir Czarnikow Hldgs 1984-; dir Lion Mark Hldgs 1983-; memb: Cncl Assoc of Futures Brokers and Dealers 1986-90, London Clearing House Bd 1987-; Freeman City of London 1970, ct asst Worshipful Co Haberdashers 1987 (Liveryman 1971); *Recreations* tennis, shooting; *Clubs* Carlton, Hurlingham, RAC; *Style—* Michael Liddiard, Esq; 5 Edwardes Place, Kensington, London W8 6LR (☎ 071 603 0199); C Czarnikow Ltd, 66 Mark Lane, London EC3P 3EA (☎ 071 480 9322, fax 071 480 9500)

LIDDIARD, Richard England; CBE (1977); s of Edgar Stratton Liddiard, MBE (d 1963), and Mabel Audrey, *née* Brooke (d 1968); *b* 21 Sept 1917; *Educ* Oundle, Worcester Coll Oxford (MA); *m* 16 Oct 1943, Constance Lily, da of Sir William Rook (d 1958); 1 s (Michael Richard b 1946); 3 da (Susan Millicent b 1949, Diana Brooke b 1951, Penelope Jane b 1954); *Career* WWII RCS 1939-46 (despatches 1944), Temp Lt-Col 1945 head of Ceylon Signal Corps; C Czarnikow Ltd 1946 (dir 1948, chm 1958-74); chm: Sugar Assoc of London 1960-78, Br Fedn of Commodity Assocs 1963-71 (vice chm 1971-77), London Commodity Exchange 1972-75, Czarnikow Gp 1974-84, Lion Mark Hldgs 1983-88 (dep chm 1988-); memb ctee of Invisible Exports 1964-67; chm: Bargs Res Devpt Tst 1988-, Bd of Govrs Haberdashers' Aske's, Elstree Schs 1981-87; Silver Jubilee Medal 1977; Master Worshipful Co of Haberdashers' 1977-78; Polish MC 1942; *Recreations* walking, reading; *Clubs* RAC; *Style—* Richard Liddiard, Esq, CBE

LIDDIARD, Ronald; s of Tom Liddiard (d 1954), and Gladys Marion, *née* Smith (d 1970); *b* 26 July 1932; *Educ* Canton HS Cardiff, Coll of Advanced Technol and Commerce Cardiff, Inlogov Univ of Birmingham; *m* 7 Sept 1957, June Alexandra, da of James George Ford; 2 da (Angela J b 1959, Clare A b 1961); *Career* social worker: Cardiff 1960-61, Bournemouth 1961-64; chief admin offr Welfare Servs Co Borough of Bournemouth 1964-70; dir of social servs: City of Bath 1971-74, Birmingham 1974-85; mgmnt and soc admin conslt pilot (air tport); dir Prospect Hall Coll for Disabled, govr Bluecoat Sch Birmingham; memb Assoc Dir of Soc Servs 1971; *Books* How to Become an Airline Pilot (1989); chapters in: Innovations in the Care of the Elderly (1984), Self Care and Health in Old Age (1986); *Recreations* flying instruction, travel, wines, writing; *Style—* Ronald Liddiard, Esq; Whitefriars, Portway, Alvechurch, Worcs B48 74P (☎ 0564 826235)

LIDSTER, Felicity; da of Harold Roberts (d 1981), of Monk Bretton, Barnsley, and Winifred, *née* Beaumont; *b* 7 May 1952; *Educ* Broadway GS, Huddersfield Poly (BSc); *m* 9 Feb 1970, Eric James Lidster, s of James Henry Lidster, of Stocksbridge, Sheffield; 2 s (Harvey James b 1970, Anthony John b 1972), 1 da (Charlotte Marie b 1982); *Career* dir: E J Lidster & Sons Ltd 1983, E J Lidster (Construction) Ltd 1984, Barnsley Mini-Skips Ltd 1983, Fellmoor Ltd 1985, Levelmanor Ltd 1989; *Recreations* hockey, squash; *Style—* Mrs Eric Lidster; Arunden House, Lund Lane, Burton Grange, Barnsley, S Yorks (☎ 0226 289859/298484, car 0860 614952)

LIDSTONE, John Barrie Joseph; s of Arthur Richard Francis Lidstone (d 1930), and Lillian May, *née* Teppett (d 1973); *b* 21 July 1929; *Educ* Presentation Coll Reading, Univ of Manchester, RAF Educn Officers' Course; *m* 1957, Primrose Vivien, da of Vincent Russell (d 1947), of Derby; 1 da (b 1960); *Career* Nat Serv RAF 1947-48; English master Repton 1949-52; Shell-Mex and BP Group and assoc cos 1952-62, dep md Vicon Agricultural Machinery Ltd 1962-63, dir and gen mangr Marketing Selections Ltd 1969-72; Marketing Improvements Group: joined 1965, dir 1968-, dir and gen mangr 1972-74, dep md 1974-88, dep chm 1988-89; non exec dir 1989-; non exec dir: Kalamazoo plc, North Hampshire Trust Co Ltd, St Nicholas School Fleet Educational Trust Ltd 1982-90; UK Mgmnt Consultancies Assoc 1978-88: vice chm 1985-86, chm 1986-87; articles contrib to: The Times, Daily Telegraph, Financial Times, Observer, Sunday Times, Sunday Telegraph, Long Range Planning, International Management, Marketing, Marketing Week, Management Today; ed Lidstorian 1985-88; voted top speaker on mktg in Europe 1974, Dartnell lecture tours USA 1978-82; memb Nat Exec Ctee Chartered Inst of Mktg 1985-90; Freeman City of London, Liveryman Worshipful Co of Marketors; memb BAFTA, FIMC, FBIM, FIOD, FCIM; *Films and Video*: technician, advsr and script writer: The Persuaders (1975), Negotiating Profitable Sales (1979), Training Salesmen on the Job (1981, won highest award for creative excellence at US Industl Film Festival 1982), Marketing for Managers (1985), Marketing To-Day (1985), Reaching Agreement and Interviewing (1987, 1988); *Books* Training Salesmen on the Job (1975, 2 edn 1986), Recruiting and Selecting Successful Salesmen (1976, 2 edn 1983), Negotiating Profitable Sales (1977, made into two part film by Video Arts 1979), Motivating your Sales Force (1978), Making Effective Presentations (1985), The Sales Presentation (jtly, 1985), Profitable Selling (1986), Marketing Planning for the Pharmaceutical Industry (1987), Manual of Sales Negotiation (1991), Beyond the Pay Packet (1991); *Recreations* writing, cricket, golf; *Clubs* Naval, N Hants Golf, BAFTA; *Style—* John B J Lidstone, Esq; Marketing Improvements Group plc, Ulster House, 17 Ulster Terrace, Regent's Park, London NW1 4PJ (☎ 071 487 5811, fax 071 935 4839, telex 299723 MARIMP G)

LIEBER, Ian Steven; s of Alfred Abraham Lieber (d 1952), and Eva Rosa *née* Yakar (d 1982); *b* 14 July 1941; *Educ* Cottesmore Secdy Sch Nottingham; *Career* interior designer; estab own practice 1969, designer numerous homes and commercial projects worldwide; work features in many interior magazines, lectr on interior design; *Style—* Ian Lieber, Esq; The Shop, 29 Craven Terrace, Lancaster Gate, London W2 3EL (☎ 071 262 5505)

LIEBERMAN, Prof (Alexander) Robert; *b* 7 July 1942; *Educ* Univ of London (BSc, PhD, DSc); *m* 1, (m dis 1975); 2 s (Gerald b 1963, Nicholas b 1967); m 2, 7 July 1976, Dr Margaret Mary Bird; 2 da (Elizabeth b 1977, Georgina b 1979); *Career* UCL: asst lectr Dept of Anatomy 1965-68, lectr 1968-74, sr lectr 1974-76, reader 1976-87, prof of anatomy Univ of London 1987-, dean faculty life Med sciences (biological and medical) 1990-, vice dean University College and Middlesex School of Medicine 1990-; prof of anatomy (neurobiology) Univ of Aarhus Denmark 1983-85; ed-in-chief Jl of Neurocytology 1972-; memb: BRA, IBRO, ENA, RDA, Phys Soc, Anat Soc; *Books* contrib: International Review of Neurobiology (1971), Essays On The Nervous System (1974), The Peripheral Nerve (1976), Neuron Concept Today (1976), Local Circuit Neurons (1976); *Recreations* cards, chess, backgammon; *Style—* Prof Robert Lieberman; Dept of Anatomy and Developmental Biology, University College London, Gower St, London WC1E 6BT (☎ 071 387 7050 ext 3357, fax 071 380 7349)

LIEBERMAN, Dr Stuart; s of Jerome Leon Lieberman, of 69 NW 40 Court Miami, Florida, USA, and Libby, *née* Mizus; *b* 4 Oct 1942; *m* 1, 1965 (m dis 1981), Susan Joan Lieberman; 3 s (Samuel, Steven, Simon); m 2, 30 Oct 1986, Sybil Margaret Battersby, da of Joseph Heath, of Wallheath Wolverhampton; 3 da (Abigail, Gemma, Mel); *Career* Capt USAF 1965-70; sr lectr and conslt psychiatrist St George's Hosp Med Sch 1975-; fndr memb and treas Inst of Family Therapy London 1976-79, fndr memb and sec Assoc of Family Therapy 1975-8, chm Hooley Community Assoc 1978-80; FRCPsych 1983; *Books* Transgenerational Family Therapy (1 edn 1979, 2 edn 1980); *Recreations* golf, swimming; *Style—* Dr Stuart Lieberman; St George's Hospital Medical School, Cranmer Terrace, London SW17 0RE (☎ 081 672 9944 ext 55542, fax 081 767 4696)

LIEBMANN, Dr Stephen James; s of Dr Gehard Liebmann (d 1955), of Aldermaston, and Dora, *née* Badt (d 1989); *b* 4 Sept 1945; *Educ* Reading Sch, Univ of Sheffield (BEng, PhD); *m* 1972, Felicity Anne, da of Geoffrey A E Hodgkinson; 1 s (Nicholas b 11 Jan 1975), 1 da (Charlotte b 22 July 1978); *Career* BBC Radio Sheffield 1966-69 (Freelance radio news and feature reporter, prog prodr and editor), journalist Electronics Weekly IPC Business Press 1969-72, Investors Chronicle Throgmorton Pubns 1972-77 (fin journalist, sr memb Editorial and Prodn Team); investmt researcher: J M Finn & Co (stockbrokers) 1977-81, Seymour Pierce & Co (stockbrokers) 1981-83; ptnr i/c private catering business 1983-86, fin conslt 1983-86, gp chief press offr TSB Group plc 1986-1987, dir Binns Cornwall Limited (now renamed Buchanan Communications Ltd) 1987-; *Recreations* sailing; *Style—* Dr Stephen Liebmann; Buchanan Communications Ltd, 36 St Andrews Hill, London EC4V 5DE (☎ 071 489 1441, fax 071 489 1437)

LIESNER, Hans Hubertus; CB (1980); s of Curt Liesner, and Edith, *née* Neumann; *b* 30 March 1929; *Educ* German Schs, Univ of Bristol (BA), Nuffield Coll Oxford; *m* 1968, Thelma; 1 s (Jeremy), 1 da (Raina); *Career* teaching appts 1955-70: LSE, Emmanuel Coll, Univ of Cambridge; under sec HM Treasy 1970-76, chief econ advsr and dep sec DTI 1976-; *Recreations* gardening, walking, skiing, cine photography; *Style—* Hans Liesner, Esq, CB; Dept of Trade and Industry, 1 Victoria St, London SW1H 0ET (☎ 07F 215 4258)

LIFFORD, 9 Viscount (I 1781); (Edward) James Wingfield; also Baron Lifford (I 1768); s and h of 8 Viscount Lifford (d 1987), and Alison Mary Partricia, *née* Ashton; *b* 27 Jan 1949; *Educ* Aiglon Coll Switzerland; *m* 1976, Alison, da of Robert Law, of Turnpike House, Withersfield, Suffolk; 1 s (James Thomas Wingfield b 1979), 2 da (Annabel Louise b 1978, Alice Mary b 1990); *Heir* s, James Thomas b 26 Sept 1979; *Career* stockbroker; dir: Cobbold Roach Ltd, Hampshire Building Soc, City of Winchester Assured Tenancies plc; *Recreations* country sports; *Clubs* Boodle's, Pratt's; *Style—* The Rt Hon Viscount Lifford; Field House, Hursley, nr Winchester, Hants SO21 2LE

LIFFORD, Mary, Viscountess; (Alison) Mary Patricia; *née* Ashton; 2 da of Thomas Wingrave Ashton, of The Cottage, Hursley, nr Winchester; *b* 17 Feb 1910; *Educ* private; *m* 16 Jan 1935, Alan William Wingfield Hewitt, 8 Viscount Lifford (d 1987); 1 s (9 Viscount b 1949), 3 da (Hon Mrs Swann, Hon Mrs Warburton, Hon Mrs Henderson); *Style—* Mary, Viscountess Lifford; The Barn, Hursley, Winchester, Hants (☎ 0962 75515)

LIGENZA-MILDENHALL, Gabriela Maria; da of Tadeusz Ligenza, of Gdynia, Poland, and Gertruda, *née* Szydlowska; *b* 14 May 1959; *Educ* Acad of Fine Arts in Warsaw (MA, UNESCO award); *m* 1 (m dis), 1978, Count Andrzej Borkowski; 1 da (Alicja b 13 Oct 1980); m 2, 1988, Richard Mildenhall; 1 s (Oscar b 8 Nov 1988); *Career* collaboration with Akademia Ruchu visual avangarde theatre in Warsaw and participation in many euro theatre festivals 1976-83; fndr Gabriela Ligenza (high fashion hats design) 1985-; designed own collections and collaborated with others (incl: Missoni, Alistair Blair, Caroline Charles, Jasper Conran, Paul Smith, Roland Klein, Laura Ashley, Myrene de Premonville); *Clubs* Chelsea Arts; *Style—* Mrs Gabriela Ligenza-Mildenhall; Gabriela Ligenza, 1 Mere Close, London SW15 3HX (☎ 081 788 4499, fax 081 877 1173)

LIGGINS, Sir Edmund Naylor; TD; s of Arthur William Liggins; *b* 21 July 1909; *Educ* King Henry VIII Sch Coventry, Rydal Sch; *m* 1952, Celia Jean, CBE (1991), da of William Henry Lawrence; 3 s, 1 da; *Career* admitted slr 1931; Liggins & Co Slrs; Hon LLD Univ of Warwick 1988; pres Law Soc 1975-76; kt 1976; *Recreations* travel, cricket, rugby, football, squash, rackets; *Clubs* MCC, Army and Navy; *Style—* Sir Edmund Liggins, TD; Hareway Cottage, Hareway Lane, Barford, Warwicks CV35 8DB (☎ 0926 624246); Liggins & Company, 150 Station Rd, Balsall Common, W Midlands CV7 7FF

LIGHT, Laurie; s of Laurie Light, and Edna Mary Light (d 1987); *b* 16 April 1949; *Educ* Wolverhampton GS, Wolverhampton Coll of Art (BA); *m* 10 March 1973, Rowena Glennis, da of Joseph Tunnicliffe; 1 s (Alexander Matthew b 19 July 1977), 1 da (Helen Victoria b 10 March 1980); *Career* Cassons Advertising 1971-75, Paul Hollands Associates 1975-81, fndr and md Light and Coley 1982-; *Recreations* flyfishing; *Clubs* Water Rats, Flyfishing; *Style—* Laurie Light, Esq; Griffin House, Green Lane Close, Chertsey, Surrey KT13 9QW (☎ 0932 564035); Light and Coley, 20 Fulham Broadway, London SW6 1AH (☎ 071 381 6644, fax 071 381 2833)

LIGHTBOWN, David Lincoln; MP (C) Staffs S E 1983-; *b* 30 Nov 1932; *Career* former md W Midlands Engrg Gp of Cos until entry into Parly, appt govt asst whip 1986, Lord Cmmr HM Treasy 1987, Comptroller HM's Household and govt chief whip 1990-; memb: Staff CC 1976-84, Lichfield Dist Cncl 1974-87; *Style—* David Lightbown Esq, MP; House of Commons, London SW1

LIGHTERNESS, (Thomas John) Tony; s of Thomas Charles Lighterness (d 1980), of Wimborne, Dorset, and Eleanor Mary Jones (d 1986); *b* 20 Jan 1932; *Educ* Royal Liberty Sch Gidea Park Essex; *m* 21 Feb 1959, Margaret; 1 s (David b 1961), 3 da (Elizabeth b 1959, Catherine (twin) b 1959, Janine b 1963); *Career* The RTZ Corp plc; FCIS, FCT; *Recreations* skiing, cycling, photography; *Clubs* RAC, St James'; *Style—* Tony Lighterness, Esq; 6 St James Sq London SW1Y 4LD (☎ 071 930 2399, telex 24639)

LIGHTFOOT, Elizabeth (Liz); da of John Richard Lightfoot, of Healing, nr Grimsby, S Humberside, and Ethne, *née* Stanton; *b* 27 Sept 1950; *Educ* Cleethorpes Girls GS, Univ of Newcastle (BA), Univ of Durham (MA); *Career* journalist; Hendon Times 1978-81, freelance 1981-83, Parly corr Press Association 1984-86, educn corr Mail on Sunday 1986-; *Style—* Ms Liz Lightfoot; Mail On Sunday, Associated Newspapers Ltd, Northcliffe House, London W8 5TT (☎ 071 938 7032)

LIGHTFOOT, James Cecil Emerson; s of George Cecil Lightfoot, of Woodbridge, Suffolk, and Ghetal Angelita, *née* Herschell; *b* 16 Nov 1949; *Educ* Charterhouse Univ of Oxford; *m* 7 Jan 1977, Hilary Pleydell, da of Robert Cecil Crowhurst, of Newmarket, Suffolk; 2 s (George William b 1980, Harry Robert b 1988), 1 da (Rosalie Pleydell b 1983); *Career* admitted slr, started own practice 1973, currently sr ptnr Lightfoot and O'Brien Marshall; *Recreations* sports; *Style*— James Lightfoot, Esq; Spaldings Barn, Hall Lane, Framsden, Stowmarket, Suffolk IP14 6HU; Lightfoot and O'Brien Marshall, 69 The Thoroughfare, Woodbridge, Suffolk IP12 1AH (☎ 03943 6336, fax 0394 380098, telex 987116 LITLAW)

LIGHTFOOT, His Hon Judge (George) Michael; s of Charles Herbert Lightfoot (d 1941), of Leeds, and Mary, *née* Potter (d 1974); *b* 9 March 1936; *Educ* St Michael's RC Coll Leeds, Exeter Coll Oxford (MA); *m* 20 July 1963, Dorothy, da of Thomas Miller (d 1977), of Rosecroft Farm, Loftus, Cleveland; 2 s (John b 1970, David b 1977), 2 da (Catherine b 1968, Anne b 1973); *Career* Nat Serv 1955-57, York and Lancaster Regt, Intelligence Corps; schoolmaster 1962-66; called to Bar Inner Temple 1966, practised NE circuit 1967-86, rec of Crown Ct 1985-86, appointed a circuit judge NE circuit 1986-; pres: MENCAP Leeds, Leeds Friends of the Home Farm Tst; *Recreations* cricket and sport in general, reading; *Clubs* Lansdowne, Catenian Assoc, City of Leeds Circle; *Style*— His Hon Judge Lightfoot; 4 Shadwell Park Close, Leeds LS17 8TN (☎ 0532 665673)

LIGHTHILL, Sir (Michael) James; s of Ernest Balzar Lighthill; *b* 23 Jan 1924; *Educ* Winchester, Trinity Coll Cambridge; *m* 1945, Nancy Alice Dumaresq; 1 s, 4 da; *Career* Lucasian prof of mathematics Univ of Cambridge 1969-79, provost of UCL 1979-89 (hon fell 1982); awarded Gold medal by Inst of Mathematics and Its Applications 1982; kt 1971; *Style*— Sir James Lighthill; University College London, Gower St, London WC1

LIGHTMAN, Lionel; s of Abner Lightman (d 1937), of London, and Gitli Szmul (d 1972); *b* 26 July 1928; *Educ* City of London School (LCC Scholar) Wadham College Oxford (Open Scholarship, MA); *m* 11 Nov 1952, (Molly) Helen Lightman, da of Rev Abraham Shechter (d 1958), of London; 2 da (Marion Esther (Mrs Kinshuck) b 1958, Amanda Judith (Mrs Goodman) b 1961); *Career* Nat Serv RAEC temp Capt HQ Army of the Rhine 1951-53; Bd of Trade: asst princ and private sec to Perm Sec 1953-58, princ 1958-67, trade cmmr Ottawa 1960-64, asst sec 1967-74; Office of Fair Trading: asst dir 1973-74, under sec 1974-84, dir of competition 1981-84; lay observer attached Lord Chllr's Dept 1986-90; *Style*— Lionel Lightman, Esq; 73 Greenhill, London NW3 5TZ (☎ 071 435 3427)

LIGHTMAN, Prof Stafford Louis; s of Harold Lightman, QC, of 4 Stone Buildings, Lincoln's Inn, London, and Gwendoline Joan, *née* Ostrer; *b* 7 Sept 1948; *m* 1 May 1977, Susan Louise, da of John Stubbs, of 31 York Ave, London; 3 s (Sarne Louis b 1978, Joel David b 1979, Leon Alexander b 1982), 1 da (Elewys Gemma b 1987); *Career* prof of clinical neuroendocrinology 1988-, ed journal of Neuroendocrinology 1988-; FRCP; *Books* Neuroendocrinology (with B J Everitt); *Style*— Prof Stafford Lightman; Neuroendocrinology Unit, Charing Cross Hospital, Fulham Palace Rd, London W6 8RP (☎ 081 846 7500, fax 081 846 7511)

LIGHTON, Lt-Col Sir Christopher Robert; 8 Bt (I 1791), of Merville, Dublin, MBE (1945), JP (Somerset); s of Sir Christopher Lighton, 7 Bt, JP, DL (d 1929); *b* 1897; *Educ* Eton, RMC; *m* 1, 1926 (m dis 1953), Rachel Gwendoline, da of Rear Adm Walter S Goodridge, CIE (d 1929); 2 da; m 2, 1953, Horatia Edith (d 1981), da of A T Powlett; 1 s, 2 da; m 3, 1985, Eve, da of late Rear Adm Alexander Mark-Wardlaw, and wid of Maj Stopford Ram; *Heir* s, Thomas Lighton b 1954; *Career* served in WW1 1914-18 with KRRC, re-employed 1939-45 on staff; *Style*— Lt-Col Sir Christopher Lighton, Bt, MBE, JP; Fairview, Dirleton, E Lothian

LILEY, John Garin; s of Warren Stuart Liley, of 6 St Johns Avenue, Wakefield, and Barbara Mary, *née* Gloyne; *b* 21 Aug 1967; *Educ* Eastmoor HS, Wakefield Dist Coll; *Career* Rugby Union full back Leicester FC and England; clubs: Sandal RUFC 1985-87, Wakefield RFC 1987-88, Leicester FC 1988- (59 appearances); rep: Yorks Colts 1985-86, Yorks U21 1986-88, North of Eng U21 1988, England B (debut v Namibia 1990); England: debut v Banco Nacion 1990, toured Argentina (replacement in 2 tests) 1990; holder record no of points (439) for Leicester in a season 1989/90; sports attendant 1985-89, trainee accountant 1990-91; *Recreations* outdoor activities (sports), photography, travelling; *Style*— John Liley, Esq; 25 Dorset Avenue, Glenfield, Leicester LE3 8BD (☎ 0533 313998, 0533 709228); Leicester FC, Welford Rd, Aylestone Rd, Leicester LE2 7LF (☎ 0533 541607)

LILFORD, 7 Baron (GB 1797); George Vernon Powys; s of Robert Horace Powys (d 1940, gggs of 2 Baron Lilford), by his w Vera Grace (d 1989); suc 6 Baron (2 cous twice removed) 1949; *b* 8 Jan 1931; *Educ* St Aidan's Coll Grahamstown SA, Stonyhurst; *m* 1, 1954 (m dis), Mrs Eveline Bird; m 2, 1957 (m dis 1958), Anuta, da of L F Merritt, of Johannesburg; m 3, 1958 (m dis 1961), Norma Yvonne, da of V Shell, of Johannesburg; m 4, 1961 (m dis 1969), Muriel, *née* Cooke; 2 da; m 5, 1969, Margaret, da of Archibald Penman (d 1983), of Roslin, Midlothian; 1 s, 2 da (Hon Sarah b 1971, Hon Hannah b 1974); *Heir* s, Hon Mark Vernon Powys b 16 Nov 1975; *Recreations* golf, cricket; *Style*— The Rt Hon the Lord Lilford; Le Grand Câtelet, St John, Jersey JE3 4EA, CI (☎ 0534 63871, fax 0534 64530)

LILFORD, Prof Richard James; s of Maj Victor Lilford, and Eileen, *née* Gifford; *b* 22 April 1950; *Educ* St John's Coll Johannesburg; *m* 23 May 1981, Victoria Alice Lilford; 1 s (Peter), 2 da (Nicola, Philippa); *Career* conslt obstetrician and gynaecologist Queen Charlottes Hosp London, prof of obstetrics and gynaecology Univ of Leeds; memb: Cncl RCOG, Leeds E Health Authy; PhD, MRCOG, MRCP; *Books* Basic Science for Obstetrics and Gynaecology (1984, 3 edn 1989), Prenatal Diagnosis and Prognosis (1990); *Recreations* flying; *Style*— Prof Richard Lilford; 29 Shire Oak Rd, Leeds (☎ 0532 787239); St James's University Hospital, Leeds (☎ 0532 433144, car 0860 629752)

LILL, John Richard; OBE (1978); s of G R Lill; *b* 17 March 1944; *Educ* Leyton County HS, Royal Coll Music; *Career* concert pianist, soloist with leading orchestras, worldwide TV and radio appearances, prof Royal Coll Music, winner of Int Tchaikowsky competition Moscow 1970; *Recreations* amateur radio, chess, computing; *Style*— John Lill Esq, OBE; c/o Harold Holt Ltd, 31 Sinclair Road, London W14 (☎ 071 603 4600)

LILLEY, Prof Geoffrey Michael; OBE (1981); s of Morland Michol Dessau (d 1946), of Ealing, and Emily Lilley (d 1977); *b* 16 Nov 1919; *Educ* Isleworth GS, Imperial Coll London; *m* 18 Dec 1948, Leslie Marion, da of Leonard Frank Wheeler (d 1955), of Cranfield, Beds; 1 s (Michael Moreland b 1957), 2 da (Grete Dorothea b 1950, Elisabeth Meta b 1953); *Career* served RAF 1935-36; engrg apprentice 1936-40, asst to chief engr Kodak Ltd 1939-40, Drawing Office, Design, Wind Tunnel and Aerodynamics Dept Vickers Armstrongs Weybridge and Vickers Armstrongs Supermarine Hursley Park 1940-46; lectr then prof of experimental fluid mechanics Coll of Aeronautics 1946-63; prof of aeronautics and astronautics Univ of Southampton 1963-83 (prof emeritus 1983-); memb: Aeronautical Res Cncl 1957-81, Noise Advsy Cncl (chm Noise from Air Traffic) 1969-81; dir Hampshire Technol Centre 1987-; MIMechE, FRAeSoc, FIMA; *Books* Complex Turbulent Flows (jtly with S J Kline and B J Cantwell, 1982); *Recreations* hiking, chess, opera; *Clubs* Athenaeum; *Style*— Prof Geoffrey Lilley, OBE; Highbury, Pine Walk, Chilworth, Southampton SO1 7HQ (☎ 0703 769109); Dept of Aeronautics and Astronautics, University of Southampton, Southampton SO9 5NH (☎ 0703 595000, ext 2325)

LILLEY, Rt Hon Peter Bruce; PC (1990), MP (C) St Albans 1983-; s of Arnold Francis Lilley, and Lillian, *née* Elliott; *b* 23 Aug 1943; *Educ* Dulwich, Clare Coll Cambridge; *m* 1979, Gail Ansell; *Career* energy industs investmt advsr; Parly candidate (C) Haringey Tottenham Oct 1974, former chm Bow Group; sec Cons Backbench Energy Ctee 1983-84, memb Treasy Select Ctee 1983-84, PPS to Min of State for Local Govt 1984, PPS to Chllr of Exchequer 1985-87, Treasy: econ sec 1987- 89, fin sec 1989-90; sec of state for Trade and Industry July 1990-; FInstPet 1978; *Books* Delusions of Incomes Policy (with Samuel Brittan); *Style*— The Rt Hon Peter Lilley, MP; House of Commons, London SW1

LILLICRAP, Dr David Anthony; s of Albert Ernest Lillicrap (d 1984), and Margaret, *née* Baldwin (d 1958); *b* 26 Oct 1930; *Educ* St Edward's Sch Oxford, St Edmund Hall Oxford, Guy's Hosp London (BM BCh, MA); *m* 15 June 1957, Gwyneth Frances, da of Philip Lister Roberts (d 1987); 3 s (Stephen b 1958, Richard b 1964, Peter b 1965), 1 da (Susan b 1960); *Career* sr registrar in med Guy's Hosp 1962-66, res fell John Hopkins Hosp Baltimore 1964-65, conslt physician Thanet Dist Hosp 1966-90, conslt endocrinolist Canterbury Hosp Kent 1966-90; memb: Margate Rotary Club, Dist Health Authy Canterbury Thanet until 1990; FRCP 1974; *Recreations* squash, dinghy sailing, bridge; *Style*— Dr David Lillicrap; 29 Princes Gardens, Cliftonville, Margate, Kent CT9 3AR (☎ 0843 292 335); Thanet Dist Gen Hosp, Margate, Kent (☎ 0843 225 544)

LILLINGSTON, Lady Vivienne Margaret Nevill; da of 5 Marquess of Abergavenny, KG, OBE; *b* 15 Feb 1941; *m* 1962, Alan Lillingston, s of Capt Luke Theodore Lillingston (ka Normandy Invasion Aug 1944); 2 s (Luke b 1963, Andrew b 1972), 2 da (Georgina (Mrs Michael Bell) b 1965, Sophie b 1968); *Style*— The Lady Vivienne Lillingston; Mount Coote, Kilmallock, Co Limerick, Ireland (☎ 063 98111)

LILLY, Prof Malcolm Douglas; s of Charles Victor Lilly (d 1977), and Amy, *née* Gardner; *b* 9 Aug 1936; *Educ* St Olave's GS, UCL (BSc, PhD), Univ of London (DSc); *m* 19 Sept 1959, Sheila Elizabeth, da of George Frederick Andrew Stuart (d 1973); 2 s (Andrew Stuart b 14 Nov 1966, Duncan Stuart b 12 May 1968); *Career* RNVR 1953-54, Nat Serv RN 1954-56; prof biochem engrg UCL 1979- (lectr 1963-72, reader 1972-79), dir Whatman Biochemicals 1968-71, visiting prof Univ of Pennsylvania USA 1969, chm Int Orgn for Biotechnol and Bioengrg 1972-80, memb Cncl Soc of Gen Microbiology 1979-83, memb Br Gas Res Ctee 1982-, dir Inst Biotechnol Studies 1983-89, visiting res fell Merck Sharp and Dohme USA 1987, Bd memb Public Health Lab Serv 1988-, fell UCL 1988-, dir Int Inst of Biotechnol 1989-; vice chm Govrs St Olaves GS Orpington, observer SE Gp Inst of Advanced Motorists; FIChemE 1980, FEng 1982; *Books* Fermentation and Enzyme Technology (jtly, 1979); *Recreations* advanced motoring, sailing, swimming; *Style*— Prof Malcolm Lilly; Collingwood, 8 Tower Rd, Orpington, Kent BR6 0SQ (☎ 0689 821762); Dept of Chemical and Biochemical Engineering, University College London, Torrington Place, London WC1E 7JE (☎ 071 380 7368, fax 071 388 0808)

LILLY, Michael Hugh; s of Archibald Hugh Rendall Lilly, of Mount Agar, Carnon Downs, Truro, Cornwall, and Beryl Calenda, *née* Pryor (d 1986); *b* 11 March 1951; *Educ* Hardyes Sch Dorset, Oxford Sch of Architecture (Dip Arch); *m* 20 Sept 1980, Penelope Sarah Jane, da of Ronald Horace Cranton, of Steeple Leaze Farm, Steeple, Dorset; 2 s (James b 1983, Alexander b 1985); *Career* scholarship awarded by Worshipful Co of Carpenters to study in Philadelphia USA 1978, design tutor (pt/t) Plymouth Sch of Architecture 1980-83, ptnr John Crowther & Assocs Truro 1983-; chm Cornwall Branch Assoc of Conslt Architects; memb: exec ctee Truro Civic Soc, educn ctee Carpenters Co; Freeman City of London, Liveryman Worshipful Co of Carpenters 1982; RIBA 1978; *Recreations* travel, windsurfing, walking, art; *Style*— Michael Lilly, Esq; Clifden, Carnon Downs, Truro, Cornwall TR3 6LE (☎ 0872 863 942); c/o John Crowther & Assoc, 26-28 Charles St, Truro, Cornwall TR1 2PH (☎ 0872 755 44, fax 0872 401 54)

LIM, Eileen Yee Ling; da of Hugh Peter Lim (d 1968), of Hong Kong, and Amy Yuk Mui, *née* Wong; *b* 19 Oct 1954; *Educ* Maryknoll Sisters Sch, Univ of Hawaii (BA); *Career* asst ed Femina Magazine (Hong Kong) 1977-78; Burson-Marsteller: account exec Hong Kong 1978-80, account exec New York 1980-81, gp mangr Hong Kong 1981-84; account supervisor Edelman New York 1984-86, dir Burson-Marsteller London 1987-; MIPR 1988; *Clubs* Foreign Correspondents (Hong Kong); *Style*— Ms Eileen Lim; Burson-Marsteller, 24-28 Bloomsbury Way, London WC1A 2PX (☎ 071 831 6262, fax 071 430 1033)

LIM, Dr Frederick Thomas Keng Sim; s of late Khye Seng Lim, OBE, of Penang, Malaysia, and late Lian Hioh, *née* Goh; *b* 19 April 1947; *Educ* Radley, Middx Hosp London (MB BS); *m* July 1971, Catherine Mary; *Career* Middx Hosp: house surgn 1971, registrar 1974, sr registrar 1977-78; house physician QEII Hosp Welwyn Garden City 1972, sr house offr Lister Hosp 1973, sr registrar Charing Cross Hosp 1975; conslt physician in: genito-urinary med Kings Coll Hosp 1979-86, private practice 1986-; fell Huntarian Soc; memb: Hampstead Med Soc, MSSVD; MRCP 1974; *Books* Textbook of Genito-Urinary Surgery (jtly, 1985); *Recreations* tennis, music, antiques, travel; *Style*— Dr Frederick Lim; 26 Devonshire Place, London W1N 1PD (☎ 071 487 3529, fax 071 224 1784)

LIM, Kim; *b* 16 Feb 1936; *Educ* St Martins Sch of Art, Slade Sch of Art, Univ Coll London (Dip Fine Art); *m* William Turnbull; 2 s (Alexander b 26 July 1962, Jonathan 29 July 1963); *Career* artist; solo exhibitions: Axiom Gallery 1966 1968, Waddington Galleries 1973 1990, Alpha Gallery Singapore 1974, Museum of Modern Art Oxford 1975, Experimental Series (Felicity Samuel Gallery) 1975, Temporary Print Exhibition (Tate) 1977, Roundhouse Gallery 1979, Southampton Museum & Art Gallery 1981, Nicola Jacobs Gallery 1982, Arcade Gallery Harrogate 1983, Prints & Drawings 1972-80 (Nicola Jacobs Gallery) London 1984, Nat Museum of Art Singapore 1984, Nicola Jacobs Gallery 1985; selected group exhibitions: 26 Young Sculptors (ICA) 1961 Deuxieme Biennale de Paris 1961, Sculpture Today & Tomorrow (Bear Lane Gallery Oxford) 1962, 3rd Int Biennale of Prints (Tokyo) 1962, Sculpture (Battersea Park) 1966, Chromatic Sculpture (Arts Cncl Cambridge) 1966, Expo '67 (Br Pavillion Montreal) 1967, Transatlantic Graphics (Camden Arts Centre) 1967, Leicestershire Collection (Whitechapel) 1967, Nagaoka Prize Exhibition (Nagaoka Museum Japan) 1967, Summer Exhibition (Museum of Modern Art Oxford) 1968, Prospect 68 (Dusselforf) 1968, Open Air Sculpture (Middleheim Antwerp) 1969, Br Sculpture out of the Sixties (ICA) 1970, 3 me Salon Internationale de Galeries Pilotes (Musee Cantal des Beaux Arts Lausanne and Musee d'Art Moderne de la Ville Paris) 1970, Rottweil Festival (Rottweil Germany) 1974, Print Biennale (Ljubliana Yugoslavia) 1975 1981 Inaugural Exhibition (Nat Museum of Art Singapore) 1976, Hayward Annual (Hayward Gallery) 1977, Int Biennale of Prints Tokyo 1979, Biennale of Euro Graphic Art Heidelberg Germany 1979, The First Exhibition (Nicola Jacobs Gallery) 1979, Sculpture for the Blind (Tate) 1981, Women's Art Show 1550-1950 (Notts Castle Museum) 1982, British Sculpture 1951-80 (Whitechapel) 1982, Group Show (Yorks Sculpture Park) 1984, Contemporary carving (Plymouth Arts Centre, touring) 1984-85, Beyond Appearance Castle Museum (Notts, touring) 198, Bradford Print Biennale 1986, Premio Internazionale Biella Per L'Incisione 1987 (Turin) 1987, Stoneworks (Powys Castle Welshpool) 1988; work in the collections of: Arts Cncl of GB,

Contemporary Arts Soc, IBM NY, Leics Educn Cncl, Middelheim Museum, Nagaoka Museum of Modern Art, Tate Gallery, Govt Art Collection Wakefield Art Gallery, Southampton Art Gallery, Atkinson Art Gallery Southport, Nat Museum of Art Singapore; *Style*— Ms Kim Lim; Waddington Galleries Ltd, 11 Cork St, London W1 (☎ 071 437 8611)

LIMB, Christopher; s of William Herbert Limb, of Lymm, and Dora *née* Clayton; *b* 12 March 1953; *Educ* Lymm GS, Univ of Liverpool (LLB); *m* 31 July 1976, Gilian May, da of John Ernest Heady, of Chester; 2 s (Timothy b 1984, Joseph b 1986); *Career* called to the Bar Gray's Inn 1975, practising Manchester; memb: Int Bar Assoc, Union International des Avocats; chm: Lymm-Meung Twin Town Soc, Lymm Rushbearing Ctee; co-organiser Lymm Jr Music Festival; memb Salford Choral Soc, Manchester Medico Legal Soc, North Cheshire Wine Soc; *Books* legal articles in New Law Jl; *Recreations* wine, music, French, my children; *Style*— Christopher Limb, Esq; 6th Floor Sunlight House, Quay St, Manchester M3 3LE

LIMB, Michael James; s of Jack Holmes Limb (d 1972), and Ada, *née* Farrow (d 1988); *b* 6 March 1933; *Educ* Woolverston Hall; *m* 1; 1 s (Michael David b 23 Sept 1956); m 2, 3 April 1969, Florence Sylvia, *née* McCormack; *Career* Regular Offr RAF 1951-68; RAC: gen sec, chm Speedway Contest Bd, vice chm RAC Br Motor Sports Cncl; dir of various cos; FIMI, FIBM; *Recreations* flying, sailing, motor sport; *Style*— Michael Limb, Esq; The Royal Automobile Club, 90 Pall Mall, London SW1Y 5HS (☎ 071 930 2345, fax 071 839 3271)

LIMB, Sue; da of Lewis Wilfred Limb, of South Woodchester, Glos, and Margaret Winifred, *née* Andrew; *b* 12 Sept 1946; *Educ* Pate's GS for Girls Cheltenham, Newnham Coll Cambridge (scholarship, BA); *m* 1, 1970 (m dis 1979), Roy Sydney Porter; m 2, 1984 (m dis 1991), Jan Vriend; 1 da (Elisabeth Susanna b 18 Feb 1985); *Career* res Cambridge 1968-70, clerk Halifax Building Soc 1970, kitchen asst Corpus Christi Cambridge 1971, teacher of English and drama 1971-75; writer and broadcaster 1976-; pubns: Captain Oates, soldier and explorer (biography, with Patrick Cordingley, 1982), Up the Garden Path (novel and radio and TV series, 1984), Love Forty (novel, 1986), The Wordsmiths at Gorsemere (book and radio series, 1987), Love's Labours (novel, 1989), Me Jane (teenage novel, 1989), Big Trouble (teenage novel, 1990), Bad Housekeeping (1990); columnist: Good Housekeeping 1986-, The Guardian (under name of Dulcie Domum) 1988-; numerous childrens books, journalism etc; Euro Parly candidate (Green) Cotswolds 1989; memb Green Pty; *Recreations* muck-raking, both literal and metaphorical; *Style*— Ms Sue Limb; c/o June Hall Literary Agency, 5th Floor, The Chambers, Chelsea Harbour, Lots Rd, London SW10 0XF (☎ 071 352 4233, fax 071 352 7356)

LIMBU, Capt Rambahadur; VC (1965); s of Tekbir Limbu (d 1949), and Tunimaya Limbu (d 1952); *m* 1, Tikamaya (d 1966); 2 s; m 2, 1967, Punimaya, da of Lachuman Rai, of Nepal; 2 s (and 1 s decd); *Career* VC for gallantry against Indonesians in Borneo; 10 Princess Mary's Own Gurkha Rifles 1957, Capt Dipakbahadur Gurung (Gurkha Tport Regt); HM The Queen's Gurkha Orderly Offr 1983-84; *Style*— Capt Rambahadur Limbu, VC; Ex 10th PMO Gurkha Rifles, HQ, Gurkha Reserve Unit, PO Box 420, Bandar Seri Begawan 1904, Brunei Darussalam

LIMERICK, 6 Earl of (I 1803); Patrick Edmund Pery; KBE (1983), DL (W Sussex 1988); also Baron Glentworth (I 1790; from 1834 the gs and h of 1 Earl was designated 'Viscount' Glentworth, now the style of the eldest s and h), Viscount Limerick (I 1800), and sits as Baron Foxford (UK 1815); s of 5 Earl of Limerick, GBE, CH, KCB, DSO, TD (d 1967), by his w Angela, GBE, CH, DStJ (da of Lt-Col Sir Henry Trotter, KCMG, CB, d 1981); *b* 12 April 1930; *Educ* Eton, New Coll Oxford; *m* 1961, Sylvia Rosalind, *qv*; 2 s (Viscount Glentworth, Hon Adrian b 1967), 1 da (Lady Alison b 1964); *Heir* s, Viscount Glentworth, *qv*; *Career* sits as Cons Peer in House of Lords, parly under sec state Dept of Trade and Indust 1972-74; Kleinwort Benson Ltd: dir 1967-72 and 1974-83, vice chm 1983-85, dep chm 1985-87; dir: Kleinwort Benson Gp plc 1982-89, T R Pacific Investment Trust plc 1976-, Brooke Bond Group plc 1981-84, The De La Rue Co plc 1983-; chm: Mallinson Denny Ltd 1979-81, BOTB 1979-83, govrs City of London Poly 1984-, Br Invisible Export Cncl 1984-, Polymeters Response Int Ltd 1988-, Pirelli UK plc 1989-; pres Inst of Export 1983-, vice pres Assoc of British C of Cs (pres 1974-77); tstee: City Parochial Fndn 1971-, Education 2000 1980-; pres: Anglo-Swiss Soc 1984-, Ski Club of Great Britain 1974-81, Alpine Ski Club 1985-87 (vice pres 1989-); *Recreations* skiing, mountaineering; *Style*— The Rt Hon the Earl of Limerick, KBE, DL; Chiddinglye, W Hoathly, E Grinstead, W Sussex (☎ 0342 810214); 30 Victoria Rd, London W8 (☎ 071 937 0537)

LIMERICK, Countess of; Sylvia Rosalind Pery; CBE (1991); er da of Brig Maurice Stanley Lush, CB, CBE, MC, and Diana Ruth, *née* Hill; *b* 7 Dec 1935; *Educ* St Swithun's Sch Winchester, Lady Margaret Hall Oxford; *m* 22 April 1961, 6 Earl of Limerick, *qv*; 2 s, 1 da; *Career* vice chm Fndn for the Study of Infant Deaths 1971-; pres: UK Ctee for UN Children's Fund 1972-79, Nat Assoc for Maternal and Child Welfare 1973-84; memb: Ctee of Mgmnt Inst of Child Health 1976-, cncl King Edward's Hosp Fund (ctee of mgmnt 1977-81 and 1985-89), Kensington Chelsea and Westminster Area Health Authy 1977-82; pres Health Visitors Assoc 1984-, chm Br Red Cross 1985-; Hon MA Univ of Oxford 1962, Hon DLitt CNAA 1990, Hon MRCP 1990; *Books* Sudden Infant Death: patterns, puzzles and problems (jtly, 1985); *Recreations* skiing, music; *Style*— The Rt Hon the Countess of Limerick, CBE; 30 Victoria Rd, London W8 5RG (☎ 071 937 0573); Chiddinglye, W Hoathly, E Grinstead, W Sussex RH19 4QT (☎ 0342 810214)

LIMERICK AND KILLALOE, Bishop of 1985-; Rt Rev Edward Flewett Darling; s of Ven Vivian W Darling, BD (Archdeacon of Cloyne, d 1965), and Honor Frances Garde, *née* Flewett (d 1984); *b* 24 July 1933; *Educ* Cork GS, Midleton Coll, St John's Sch Leatherhead, Trinity Coll Dublin (BA, MA); *m* 2 Aug 1958, (Edith Elizabeth) Patricia, da of Very Rev A W M Stanley Mann (Dean of Down, d 1968); 3 s (David b 1960, Colin b 1961, Philip b 1963), 2 da (Alison b 1966, Linda b 1968); *Career* curate: St Luke's Belfast 1956-59, St John's Orangefield Belfast 1959-62; incumbent St Gall's Carnalea Bangor Co Down 1962-72, rector St John's Malone Belfast 1972-85; *Books* A Child is Born (1966), Choosing the Hymns (1984), Irish Church Praise (ed); *Recreations* music, gardening; *Style*— The Rt Rev the Bishop of Limerick and Killaloe; Bishop's House, N Circular Rd, Limerick, Ireland (☎ 061 51532)

LINACRE, Sir (John) Gordon Seymour; CBE (1979), AFC (1943), DFM (1941); s of John James Linacre (d 1957), of Norton Woodseats, Sheffield; *b* 23 Sept 1920; *Educ* Firth Park GS Sheffield; *m* 1943, Irene Amy, da of Alexander Gordon (d 1946); 2 da; *Career* WWII RAF; Yorks Post Newspapers Ltd: md 1965-83, chm 1983-90, pres 1990-; dep chm United Newspapers Ltd 1983- (chief exec 1981-88), dir Yorkshire TV 1968-90, pres Fédération Internationale des Editeurs de Journaux et Publications 1984-88; former: chm and dir Press Assoc, pres Newspaper Soc; chm: Opera North, Leeds Trg and Enterprise Cncl 1989-, Univ of Leeds Fndn 1989-; kt 1986; *Recreations* golf, fishing, country walking; *Clubs* Alwoodley Golf; *Style*— Sir Gordon Linacre, CBE, AFC, DFM

LINACRE, Nigel Guy Thornton; s of Vivian Thornton Linacre, of Edinburgh, and Joan Linacre; *b* 21 Aug 1957; *Educ* George Heriot's Sch, Imberhorne Sch, Univ of Reading (BA); *m* 1979, Sue, da of Ronald Farish; 2 s (Thomas Edward Benedict b 30 Sept 1986, George Henry Michael b 20 Feb 1989), 1 da (Charlotte Lucy b 28 Nov 1982); *Career* account exec Charles Barker 1979-82, account mangr Collett Dickenson Pearce Financial 1982-85, advertising dir Boase Masimmi Pollit Business 1985-87, exec dir Collett Dickenson Pearce Financial 1987-89, dir Charles Barker 1989, md Charles Barker Advertising 1989; Parly candidate (C) Ealing Southall 1983; Freeman of Chippenham; MIPA 1990; *Books* Advertising For Account Handlers (1987); *Style*— Nigel Linacre, Esq; Charles Barker, 30 Farringdon St, London EC4A 4EA (☎ 071 634 1294, fax 071 236 0843)

LINAKER, Dr Barry David; s of Allan Lawrence Linaker (d 1973), and Gwendoline, *née* Higgs; *b* 7 April 1947; *Educ* Wigan GS, KCH Med Sch Univ of London (MB BS, MD); *m* 14 April 1973, Carol Yvonne, da of Lt Cdr John Michael Ogden, of 118 London Rd, Sunningdale, nr Ascot; 2 da (Emma b 1975, Amanda b 1979); *Career* MRC res fell and sr registrar in gastroenterology Univ Dept of Med Hope Hosp Manchester 1978-80, sr registrar in med Liverpool 1980-81, conslt physician and gastroenterlologist Warrington Dist Gen Hosp 1981-; author of papers in various jls especially on mechanisms of histamine stimulated secretion in rabbit ileal mucosa in gut; memb: Br Soc of Gastroenterology, Liverpool Med Inst, N Eng Gastro Soc, Merseyside and N Wales Physicians; memb BMA, FRCP 1989; *Recreations* sailing, clay pigeon shooting, golf, reading, travel; *Clubs* Budworth Sailing, Frodsham Golf; *Style*— Dr Barry Linaker; Warrington District General Hospital, Lovely Lane, Warrington, Cheshire WA5 1QG (☎ 0925 35911 ext 2411)

LINAKER, Lawrence Edward (Paddy); s of late Lawrence Wignall Linaker, and Rose, *née* Harris; *b* 22 July 1934; *Educ* Malvern; *m* 1963, (Elizabeth) Susan, *née* Elam; 1 s (Sam), 1 da (decd); *Career* Esso Petroleum 1957-63, dep chm and md M&G Gp 1988 (joined 1963), chm M&G Investment mgmnt 1987-; memb Cncl: RPMS 1977-89, Malvern Coll 1988-; memb governing body SPCK 1978-; FCA; *Recreations* music, wine and gardening; *Clubs* Athenaeum; *Style*— L E Linaker, Esq; Swyre Farm, Aldsworth, Cheltenham, Glos; M & G Group plc, Three Quays, Tower Hill, London EC3R 6BQ (☎ 071 626 4588, fax 071 623 8615, telex 887196)

LINCOLN, Sir Anthony Handley; KCMG (1965, CMG 1958), CVO (1957); s of John Bebrouth Lincoln, OBE (d 1938); *b* 2 Jan 1911; *Educ* Mill Hill Sch, Magdalene Coll Cambridge; *m* 1948, Lisette Marion, da of late A E Summers, of Buenos Aires; *Career* formerly cnsllr Br Embassy Copenhagen, ambass to Venezuela 1964-69; *Clubs* Brooks's, Reform; *Style*— Sir Anthony Lincoln, KCMG, CVO

LINCOLN, Hon Mr Justice; Hon Sir Anthony Leslie Julian; s of Samuel Lincoln; *b* 7 April 1920; *Educ* Highgate, Queen's Coll Oxford (MA); *Career* served WWII in Somerset LI and RA 1941-45; called to the Bar Lincoln's Inn 1949, QC 1968, rec of Crown Ct 1974-79, judge of the High Court of Justice family div 1979-; pres Restrictive Practices Court, chm Harrison Homes for the Elderly; kt 1979; *Style*— The Hon Mr Justice Lincoln; Royal Courts of Justice, Strand, London WC2

LINCOLN, (Fredman) Ashe; QC (1947); s of Reuben Lincoln (d 1954), of London, and Fanny, *née* Fredman (d 1977); *b* 30 Oct 1907; *Educ* Hoe GS Plymouth, Paterson HS USA, Haberdashers Aske's Sch, Exeter Coll Oxford (MA, BCL); *m* 5 Sept 1933, (Eileen) Sybil, da of Samuel Cohen, of London; 1 s (David Hamilton b 1937), 1 da (Roda b 1935); *Career* RNVR: Lt Mine Investigation 1939-42 (Lt Cdr 1941), Marine Commandos 1943- (Cdr 1944, Capt 1952); called to the Bar Inner Temple 1929, King's Counsel 1947-71, master of the Bench Inner Temple 1955, memb Bar Cncl (memb Exec Ctee and chm Ct Bldgs Ctee) 1957-61, rec Gravesend 1967, rec and dep judge Crown Ct 1971-79; pres: RNR Offrs Club, London Devonian Assoc; tstee: AMARC, BMCF; Liveryman City of London 1935, Liveryman Worshipful Co of Plaisterers 1935 (Master 1949-50); *Books* The Starra (1939), Secret Naval Investigator (1952); *Recreations* yachting; *Clubs* Athenaeum, Navy, MCC, RAC, Royal Corinthian Yacht, Bar Yacht; *Style*— Ashe Lincoln, Esq, QC; 9 King's Bench Walk, Temple, London EC4Y 7DX (☎ 071 353 7202 or 071 353 3909, fax 071 583 2030)

LINCOLN, 18 Earl of (E 1572); Edward Horace Fiennes-Clinton; er s of Edward Henry Fiennes-Clinton (ka 1916), and Edith Annie, *née* Guest (d 1965); suc his kinsman 10 and last Duke of Newcastle and 17 Earl of Lincoln (d 1988); *b* 23 Feb 1913; *m* 1, 1940, Leila Ruth, *née* Millen (d 1947); 1 s (Hon Edward Gordon), 1 da (Lady Patricia Elrick, *qv*); m 2, 3 Dec 1953, Linda Alice, *née* O'Brien; *Heir* s, Edward Gordon Fiennes-Clinton, *qv*; *Style*— The Rt Hon the Earl of Lincoln; 73 Picton Rd, Bunbury, W Australia 6230, Australia

LINCOLN, Frederick; s of F Lincoln, of Warlingham, Surrey, and Mary J, *née* Stevenson (d 1979); *b* 6 Oct 1927; *Educ* Croydon Poly, Regent St Poly, Sch of Architecture; *m* 30 Aug 1952, Frances Joan Ninette, da of Horace J Minshull, CBE (d 1963); 1 s (Paul b 1959), 1 da (Clare b 1957); *Career* chartered architect in private practice; formerly sr architect and asst to Sir William Atkins 1957-60 on Berkeley Nuclear Power Station; architect: Ford Tractor Plant Basildon 1962, SGS-Fairchild Falkirk 1966; CBI award; FRIBA; *Recreations* gardening, travel, vintage cars, industrial archaeology, France; *Clubs* VSCC; *Style*— Frederick Lincoln, Esq; Woldingham, Surrey (☎ 088 385 2223)

LINCOLN, His Hon Dr John Francis; AM; s of John Lincoln (d 1916); *b* 30 July 1916; *Educ* Newington Coll Aust, Balliol Coll Oxford; *m* 1952, Joan Alison, da of Harold Robert Lionel Scott (d 1977); 1 s, 1 da; *Career* Maj served India, Singapore, Palestine; called to the Bar Lincoln's Inn; DAAG 1946-47, acting judge Supreme Ct of NSW 1967, judge Dist Ct of NSW 1968-, dep chllr Macquarie Univ 1976-, chllr Dio of Newcastle NSW 1978-; former Mayor of N Sydney 1956-58, NSW state treas Lib Pty of Aust 1966-68; chm: Parole Bd of NSW 1984-, Electoral Dists Cmmrs NSW 1990-, N Sydney Community Hosp 1962-, Northolm GS; Hon LLD; Hon Rotarian 1988-, vice pres Order of Australia Assoc NSW 1988 (hon sec 1986-88); *Recreations* swimming; *Style*— His Hon Dr John Lincoln, AM; Stone Lodge, 30-34 Stanley St, St Ives NSW 2075, Australia

LINCOLN, 70 Bishop of (1072), 1986-; Rt Rev Robert Maynard Hardy; see founded from two more ancient ones (Lindisfarn at Sidnacester and Middle Angles at Leicester, united in one diocese under see of Leicester; the new entity was firstly removed to Dorchester and secondly, after the conquest, to Lincoln); patron of 154 livings and 21 alternately and by turns or jointly, the Canonries, Precentorship, Chancellor-ship, Sub-Deanery, and the Archdeaconries of Stow, Lincoln and Lindsey, also Prebendal stalls in the Cathedral; s of Harold Hardy, and Monica Mavie Hardy; *b* 5 Oct 1936; *Educ* Queen Elizabeth GS Wakefield, Clare Coll Cambridge (MA); *m* 1970, Isobel Mary, da of Charles Burch; 2 s, 1 da; *Career* deacon 1962, priest 1963, asst curate All Saints and Martyrs Langley Manchester 1962, fell and chaplain Selwyn Coll Cambridge 1965, vicar All Saints Borehamwood 1972, priest-in-charge Aspley Guise 1975, course dir St Albans Diocese ministerial trg scheme 1975, incumbent of United Benefice of Aspley Guise with Husborne Crawley and Ridgmont 1980, bishop suffragan of Maidstone 1980-86, bishop to HM Prisons 1985-; hon fell Selwyn Coll Cambridge 1986; *Recreations* walking, gardening, reading; *Style*— The Rt Rev the Bishop of Lincoln; Bishop's House, Eastgate, Lincoln LN2 1QQ (☎ 0522 534701)

LIND, Bernard J; s of Arthur Lind (d 1988), and Bella, *née* Sack (d 1956); *b* 8 Jan 1942; *Educ* Brandeis Univ Mass (BA), Columbia Univ Graduate Sch of Business NY (MBA); *m* 1, (m dis 1981), Patricia; 2 s (Carl b 1971, Evan b 1973); m 2, 21 May

1988, Sonia T, *née* Rossi; *Career* mangr of International money markets Merrill Lynch Pierce Finner & Smith NY 1965-74, sr vice pres and dep gen mangr Credit Industrial et Commercial NY 1974-83, exec vice pres and treas Midland Bank plc NY 1984-86, dir of gp market risk Midland Montagu Ltd London 1989-90 (fixed income dir 1987-89); dep gp treas National Westminster Bank 1990-, memb: Chicago Bd Trade, Chicago Mercantile Exchange; dir LIFFE; *Clubs* University, RAC; *Style*— Bernard J Lind, Esq; 59 Flood St, London SW3 5SU (☎ 071 351 6421); National Westminster Bank PLC, 135 Bishopsgate, London EC2M 3UR (☎ 071 375 4910)

LINDA, Lady Isobel Mackenzie; da of Countess of Cromartie (d 1962); *b* 1911; *m* 1947, Capt Oscar Linda; *Style*— The Lady Isobel Linda; Assynt House, Evanton, Ross (☎ 0349 830602)

LINDENBAUM, Dr David Edward; s of Dr Konrad Lindenbaum, of Hendon (d 1958), and Sybil Mary, *née* Thorpe (d 1972); *b* 7 July 1936; *Educ* St Paul's, Univ Coll Oxford (MA, BM, BCh), St Mary's Hosp London; *m* 4 March 1967, Kathleen Mary, da of Alec Davies Saxon (d 1962), of Wilmslow, Cheshire; 2 s (Roderic James Edward b 1972, Charles Peter b 1975), 1 da (Joanne Sarah b 1969); *Career* sr registrar Manchester Royal Infirmary, hon prosector RCS, res neurosurgical registrar Gt Ormond St Hosp for Sick Children, conslt radiologist Gen Hosp Northampton 1973-; fell Manchester Med Soc, memb Br Inst Radiology and Br Med Ultrasound Soc; DMRD 1969, FFR 1972, FRCR 1975; *Recreations* fly-fishing, trout and salmon, sailing; *Clubs* Royal Ocean Racing, Oxford Univ Yacht, Oxford Med Graduates; *Style*— Dr David Lindenbaum; The Coach House, Old Northamptonshire NN6 9RJ (☎ 0604 781214, 0604 34700); General Hospital, X-Ray Dept, Northampton NN1 5BD (☎ 0604 34700)

LINDESAY-BETHUNE, Hon John Martin; s of 14 Earl of Lindsay (d 1985), and Marjory (d 1988), da of late Arthur Graham Cross; *b* 27 Nov 1929; *Educ* Eton, Trinity Hall Cambridge; *m* 1, 1 Jan 1953 (m dis 1976), Enriqueta Mary Jeanne, da of Peter Maurice Jacques Koch de Gooreynd; 3 s, 1 da; m 2, 1977, Jean Maxwell, da of Brig Eric Brickman, and formerly w of Stephen John Younger; *Career* former Lt Scots Gds; md J Walter Thompson Gp Ltd 1975-81, chm Westminster C of C 1980-82; *Style*— The Hon John Lindesay-Bethune; Muircambus, Elie, Leven, Fife KY9 1HD (☎ 033 334 200)

LINDGREN, Hon Graham Alastair; s of Baron Lindgren (Life Peer, d 1971); *b* 25 July 1928; *Educ* Welwyn Garden City GS; *m* 1953, Gwendolyne Mary, da of late A W Miller, of Coleford, Glos; 1 s (Derek, b 1969); *Style*— The Hon Graham Lindgren; 43 Westly Wood, Welwyn Garden City, Herts (☎ 0707 326706)

LINDISFARNE, Archdeacon of; *see*: Bowering, Ven Michael Ernest

LINDLEY, Sir Arnold Lewis George; s of George Dilnot Lindley (d 1927), and Charlotte, *née* Hooley (d 1946); *b* 13 Nov 1902; *Educ* Woolwich Poly; *m* 1, 1927, Winifred (d 1962), da of Francis Cowling, of Somerset; 1 s, 1 da; m 2, 1963, Phyllis, da of Walter Burns, of Lincoln; *Career* chm GEC Ltd 1961-64 (vice chm 1959, md 1961-62); chm Engrg Indust Trg Bd 1964-74, vice chm Motherwell Bridge (Hldgs) Ltd 1965-84, dir General Advsrs Ltd; chm Cncl of Engrg Insts 1971-73, memb Design Cncl 1972-74; pres: Int Electrical Assoc 1963-65, IMechE 1968-69; conslt mechanical and electrical engr, conslt to Govt for various engrg projects; Hon DSc: City Univ 1969, Univ of Aston 1969, Univ of London 1970; kt 1964; *Recreations* golf; *Style*— Sir Arnold Lindley; Heathcote House, 18 Nab Lane, Shipley, W Yorks (☎ 0274 598484)

LINDLEY, Dr Bryan Charles; CBE (1982); s of Wing Cdr Alfred Webb Lindley (d 1988), of Lichfield, and Florence, *née* Pratten (d 1975); *b* 30 Aug 1932; *Educ* Reading Sch, UCL (BSc, PhD); *m* 2 May 1987, Dr Judith Anne Lindley, da of Robert Heyworth, of Bramhall; 1 s ((John) Julian b 1960); *Career* Nat Gas Turbine Estab 1954-57, Hawker Siddeley Nuclear Power Co Ltd 1957-59, International Research and Department Company Ltd and CA Parsons Nuclear Res Centre 1959-65, mangr R&D Div CA Parsons & Co Ltd 1965-68, chief exec and md ERA Technology Ltd (chm: ERA Patents Ltd, ERA Autotrack Systems Ltd) 1968-1979; dir: of technol Dunlop Holdings plc, Dunlop Ltd; chm: Thermal Conversions (UK) Ltd, Soilless Cultivation Systems Ltd, Dunlop Solaronics Div, Dunlop Bioprocesses Ltd 1979-85; dir technol and planning BICC Cables Ltd, chm Optical Fibres; dir: Thomas Bolton & Johnson Ltd 1985-88, RAPRA Technol Ltd 1985-; chief exec Nat Advanced Robotics Res Centre 1989-; visiting prof Univ of Liverpool 1989-; memb: ACARD 1980-86, Materials Advsy Gp DT1 1984; fell UCL 1979; FIMechE 1968, FIEE 1968, FInstP 1969, FPRI 1980; *Recreations* music, photography, walking, skiing, sailing; *Clubs* IOD; *Style*— Dr Bryan Lindley, CBE; 1 Edgehill Chase, Wilmslow, Cheshire, SK9 2DJ (☎ 0625 523323)

LINDLEY, (Raymond) Peter; s of Frederick George Lindley, and Edith Elizabeth, *née* Evans (d 1979); *b* 26 May 1929; *m* 1953, Lilian May, *née* Scales; 1 da; *Career* insur broker, ret; former dir: Reed Stenhouse UK Ltd 1969-85, Reed Stenhouse Ltd 1979-85; conslt to various cos and slrs; FCII; *Recreations* fly-fishing, genealogy, music; collecting porcelain; *Style*— Peter Lindley, Esq; Springrove House, Redwings Lane, Pembury, Tunbridge Wells, Kent (☎ 089 282 2172)

LINDLEY, Richard Howard Charles; s of Lt-Col (Herbert) Guy Lindley (d 1976), of Winchester, Hants, and Dorothea Helen Penelope Hatchell; *b* 25 April 1936; *Educ* Bedford Sch, Queens' Coll Cambridge (exhibitioner, BA, chm Film Soc); *m* 1976 (m dis 1986), Clare Fehrsen; 2 c (Thomas Paul Guy b 29 Dec 1977, Joanna Frances Eleanor b 12 April 1979); *Career* Nat Serv: 2 Lt Royal Hampshire Regt, served Malaya Emergency; prodr TV commercials Foote Cone and Belding 1960-62, reporter presenter and newscaster Southern TV Southampton 1963-64, reporter ITN (in Vietnam, Nigeria, Zimbabwe, Egypt, Israel) 1964-72; reporter and presenter: Panorama and Saturday Briefing BBC Current Affairs Gp 1972-88, This Week Thames TV 1989-; sr progs offr IBA 1988; *Recreations* friends, food, films; *Clubs* Royal Television Soc; *Style*— Richard Lindley; 46 Oak Village, London NW5 4QL (☎ 071 267 5870); c/o Thames TV, 30 Euston Rd, London NW1 3BB (☎ 071 387 9494, fax 071 388 7253)

LINDOP, Dr George Black McMeekin; s of George Lindop (d 1988); *b* 28 March 1945; *Educ* Hillhead HS Glasgow, Univ of Glasgow (BSc, MB ChB); *m* 22 Jan 1968, Sharon Ann, *née* Cornell; 2 s (Graeme Euan b 1975, Gavin Neil b 1978), 1 da (Amy Elizabeth b 1981); *Career* conslt in histopathology Ayrshire and Arran Health Bd 1976, sr lectr and hon conslt in histopathology Univ of Glasgow and Gtr Glasgow Health Bd; memb: Assoc of Clinical Pathologists 1979, American Soc for Hypertension 1984; FRCPath 1987 (MRCPath 1975); *Recreations* sport, music, cinema; *Clubs* Glasgow Golf; *Style*— Dr George Lindop; 8 Fifth Ave, Glasgow G12 0AT (☎ 041 339 8822); Dept of Pathology Western Infirmary, Glasgow G11 6NT (☎ 041 339 8822 ext 4390)

LINDOP, Dr Michael John; s of Donald Frederick Lindop, of Birmingham, and Phyllis Alice, *née* Burrows; *b* 29 July 1942; *Educ* King Edward Sch Birmingham, Gonville and Caius Coll Cambridge (MA), Guy's Hosp (MB, BChir); *m* 16 Aug 1968, Kari, da of Per Brachel (d 1955), of Oslo, Norway; 1 s (Tom b 1969), 3 da (Tanya b 1971, Michelle b 1973, Anne-Lise b 1978); *Career* sr registrar Westminster Hosp 1969-74, instr Univ of Washington Seattle USA 1973, conslt in anaesthesia and intensive care 1974-, currently dir anaesthesia servs Addenbrookes Hosp; examiner Coll of Anaesthetists, MO Howard Mallett Club Cambridge; memb: Intensive Care Soc, Anaesthetic Res Soc; fell Coll Anaesthetists 1971; *Books* contrib: Liver Transplantation (1987), Transplant Surgery (1988); *Recreations* racquet control, weed control; *Style*— Dr Michael Lindop; Addenbrookes Hospital, Cambridge CB2 1QQ (☎ 0223 217433, fax 0223 217223)

LINDOP, Sir Norman; DL (Hertford 1989); s of Thomas Cox Lindop, of Stockport, Cheshire, and May Lindop; *b* 9 March 1921; *Educ* Northgate Sch Ipswich, Queen Mary Coll London (MSc); *m* 1974, Jenny Caroline Quass; 1 s; *Career* chemistry lectr Queen Mary Coll 1946, asst dir examinations Civil Serv Cmmn 1951; sr lectr chemistry Kingston Coll of Technol 1953-57 (head of Chem and Geology Dept 1957-63); princ: SW Essex Tech Coll and Sch of Art 1963-66, Hatfield Coll of Technol 1966-69; dir Hatfield Poly 1969-82, princ Br Sch of Osteopathy 1982-90; chm: Hatfield Philharmonic Soc 1970-82, Ctee of Dirs of Polys 1972-74, Cncl for Professions Supplementary to Medicine 1973-81, Cncl of Westfield Coll London 1983-89, Home Office Data Protection Ctee 1976-78, DES Public Sector Validation Enquiry 1984-85, Br Library Advsy Cncl 1986-; chm Res Cncl for Complementary Med 1989-90; memb: US and UK Educnl Fulbright Cmmn 1971-81, SRC 1974-78, GMC 1979-84; fell: Queen Mary Coll London 1976, Hatfield Poly 1983, Coll of Preceptors; Hon DEd Cncl for Nat Academic Awards 1982; FRSA, FRSC kt 1973; *Clubs* Athenaeum; *Style*— Sir Norman Lindop, DL; 36 Queen's Road, Hertford, Herts

LINDOP, Prof Patricia Joyce; da of Elliot David Lindop (d 1973), of Burgess Hill, Sussex, and Dorothy, *née* Jones; *b* 21 June 1930; *Educ* Malvern, St Bartholomews Hosp Med Coll and Univ of London (BSc, MB BS, PhD, DSc, FRCP); *m* 6 May 1957, Gerald P R Esdale, s of Charles August Esdale (d 1949), of Sutton, Surrey; 1 s (Mark Elliott b 11 Aug 1958), 1 da (Patricia Michele b 11 Aug 1963); *Career* registered GP 1954, res and teaching posts in physiology and med radiobiology St Bartholomews Hosp Med Coll 1955-84, prof of radiation biology Univ of London 1970-84 (currently emeritus prof) ; UK memb Continuing Ctee of Pugwash Confs on Sci and World Affrs (asst sec gen 1961-71), chm and tstee Soc for Educn in the Applications of Sci 1968-, memb Royal Cmmn on Environment; Hon MRCR 1972, Hon APR 1984; *Publications* in field of radiation effects; *Clubs* Royal Society of Medicine; *Style*— Prof Patricia Lindop; 58 Wildwood Rd, Hampstead, London NW11 6UP (☎ 081 455 5860)

LINDQVIST, Andrew Nils Gunnar; s of Kjell Gunnar Lindqvist, of Nether Langleys, Tharston, Norwich, and Joan Bernice Kathleen, *née* Skingley; *b* 7 May 1943; *Educ* Gresham's, Trinity Hall Cambridge (MA); *m* 4 Sept 1971 (m dis), Sonia Frances, da of Sqdn Ldr Alfred Basil Charles, MBE (d 1984); 2 da (Hanna b 1980, Annika b 1982); *Career* called to the Bar 1968, memb area Legal Aid Ctee 1983; Friend and Volunteer First Mate Ocean Youth Club; *Recreations* sailing, tennis, hockey, languages; *Clubs* Norfolk (Norwich); *Style*— Andrew Lindqvist, Esq; Home Farm, Rumburgh, Halesworth, Suffolk 1P19 ONS (☎ 098685 467); Octagon House, 19 Colegate, Norwich NR3 1AT (☎ 0603 623 186, fax 0603 760 519)

LINDSAY, Col Alexander Thomas; s of the Hon James Louis Lindsay, of Pound House, Nether Cerne, Dorchester, Dorset, and the Hon Bronwen Mary, *née* Scott-Ellis; *b* 18 Dec 1936; *Educ* Eton, Magdalen Coll Oxford (MA); *m* 31 Dec 1966, (Jessie) Miranda Cecilia, da of Col John Anthony Tristram Barstow, DSO, TD, DL (d 1986); 3 s (James b 1969, Rory b 1970, Felix b 1973); *Career* cmmnd 17/21 Lancers 1956, CO Univ of Oxford OTC 1978-80, Armour Sch RAC Centre 1985-87, cdr Gunnery Sch RAC Centre 1987-; memb Br Olympic Rowing Team 1960; *Clubs* Cavalry and Guards; *Style*— Col Alexander Lindsay; East Farmhouse, Piddlehinton, Dorchester, Dorset (☎ 03004 458); Gunnery Sch, RAC Centre, Lulworth Camp, Wareham, Dorset (☎ 0929 462721 ext 4800)

LINDSAY, Lady Amabel Mary Maud Yorke; da of 9 Earl of Hardwicke (d 1974); *b* 2 April 1935; *m* 16 Dec 1955, Hon Patrick Lindsay (d 1986); 3 s, 1 da; *Style*— The Lady Amabel Lindsay; 12 Lansdowne Rd, London W11 3LW; Folly Farm, Hungerford, Berks

LINDSAY, Hon Mrs (Audrey Lavinia); *née* Lyttelton; da of 9 Viscount Cobham, KCB, TD (d 1949); *m* 21 June 1950, David Edzell Thomas Lindsay (d 1968); 1 s and 1 s decd, 1 da; *Style*— The Hon Mrs Lindsay; Poplar Cottage, Fore St Hill, Budleigh Salterton, Devon (☎ 039 54 5244)

LINDSAY, Hon Mrs (Bronwen Mary); *née* Scott-Ellis; da of 8 Baron Howard de Walden and (4 Baron) Seaford (d 1946); *b* 1912; *m* 1933, Hon James Louis Lindsay, *qv*, s of 27 Earl of Crawford and Balcarres; *Style*— The Hon Mrs Lindsay

LINDSAY, Lady Clare Rohais Antonia Elizabeth; *née* Giffard; da of 3 Earl of Halsbury, and his 2 w, Elizabeth Adeline Faith, da of late Maj Harry Crewe Godley, DSO; *b* 23 June 1944; *m* 27 Oct 1964, Col Oliver John Martin Lindsay, yr s of Sir Martin Alexander Lindsay of Dowhill, 1 Bt, CBE, DSO; 1 s (Mark (now Mark Giffard-Lindsay) b 1968), 2 da (Victoria (Mrs Gregory Wheatley) b 1967, Fiona b 1972); *Style*— The Lady Clare Lindsay; Brookwood House, Brookwood, nr Woking, Surrey GU24 0NX

LINDSAY, Crawford Callum Douglas; QC (1987); s of Douglas Marshall Lindsay, and Eileen Mary Lindsay; *b* 5 Feb 1939; *Educ* Whitgift Sch Croydon, St John's Coll Oxford (BA); *m* 1963, Rosemary Gough; 1 s, 1 da; *Career* barr 1961, rec SE circuit 1982-; *Style*— Crawford Lindsay, Esq, QC; 6 King's Bench Walk, Temple, London EC4Y 7DR (☎ 071 353 9901)

LINDSAY, Hon Erica Susan; da of 2 Baron Lindsay of Birker; *b* 1942; *Educ* Canberra HS Australia, Sch of Int Serv, American Univ Washington DC, LMH Oxford; *Style*— The Hon Erica Lindsay; 6812 Delaware St, Chevy Chase 15, Maryland, USA (☎ 656 4245); Gillbank, Boot, Holmrook, Cumberland

LINDSAY, Hugh; *see*: Hexham and Newcastle, Bishop of

LINDSAY, Hon James Francis; s and h of 2 Baron Lindsay of Birker; *b* 29 Jan 1945; *Educ* Canberra HS, Geelong GS Victoria, Bethesda-Chevy Chase HS, Univ of Keele, Univ of Liverpool; *Career* formerly lectr dept of physics Tunghai Univ Taichung Taiwan Repub of China; second sec Australian Embassy Santiago Chile 1973-76; first sec: Vientiane Laos 1979-80, Dhaka Bangladesh 1982-83, Caracas Venezuela 1986-89, Dept of Foreign Trade Canberra 1991-; *Recreations* hiking, mountaineering, tennis; *Style*— The Hon James Lindsay; Australian Foreign Service, Dept of Foreign Affairs, Canberra, ACT, Australia

LINDSAY, Sir James Harvey Kincaid Stewart; s of Arthur Harvey Lindsay (d 1970), and Doris Kincaid Lindsay (d 1944); *b* 31 May 1915; *Educ* Highgate Sch; *m* Marguerite Phyllis Boudville; 1 s, 1 da by previous m; *Career* int mgmnt conslt; formerly: chm and md The Metal Box Co of India Ltd, pres Assoc C of C and Indust of India, dir Int Progs Admin Staff Coll Henly 1969-80; tstee Inst of Family and Environmental Res 1971, dir Inst of Cultural Affrs Int Brussels (pres 1981-89), convenor Int Exposition of Rural Devpt 1981-85, dir Int Centre for Organisational Mgmnt 1988-; life memb All India Mgmnt Assoc; CBIM, FCInstM; kt 1966; *Recreations* music; *Clubs* East India, IOD; *Style*— Sir James Lindsay; Christmas Cottage, Lower Shiplake, Oxfordshire RG9 3JT (☎ 0734 402859)

LINDSAY, Hon James Louis; s of 27 Earl of Crawford and (10) Balcarres (d 1940); *b* 16 Dec 1906; *Educ* Eton, Magdalen Coll Oxford; *m* 26 April 1933, Hon Bronwen Mary Scott Ellis, *qv*, da of 8 Baron Howard de Walden; 3 s (Hugh John Alexander b 1934, Alexander Thomas b 1936, Stephen James b 1940), 1 da (Julia Margaret b 1941); *Career* formerly Maj KRRC, served WW II; contested Bristol SE 1950 and 1951, MP (C) N Devon 1955-59; *Style*— The Hon James Lindsay

LINDSAY, James Martin Evelyn; s and h of Sir Ronald Lindsay of Dowhill, 2 Bt; *b*

11 Oct 1968; *Educ* Shiplake Coll, RMA Sandhurst; *Career* 2 Lt Grenadier Guards 1989; *Recreations* tennis, squash; *Clubs* Cavalry and Guards'; *Style—* James Lindsay, Esq; Courleigh, Colley Lane, Reigate, Surrey RH2 9JO (☎ 0737 43290)

LINDSAY, 16 Earl of (S 1633); James Randolph Lindesay-Bethune; also Lord Lindsay of the Byres (S 1445), Lord Parbroath (S 1633), Viscount Garnock, and Lord Kilbirnie, Kingsburn and Drumry (both S 1703); s of 15 Earl of Lindsay (d 1989), by his 1 w, Mary, *née* Douglas-Scott-Montagu (*see* Hon Mrs Horn); *b* 19 Nov 1955; *Educ* Eton, Univ of Edinburgh (MA), Univ of California Davis; *m* 2 March 1982, Diana Mary, er da of Nigel Chamberlayne-Macdonald, LVO, OBE, of Cranbury Park, Winchester; 1 s (Viscount Garnock b 30 Dec 1990), 2 da (Frances Mary b 1986, Alexandra Penelope b 1988); *Heir* s, Viscount Garnock b 30 Dec 1990; *Career* landscape architect; tstee: Gardens for the Disabled, London Gardens Soc; pres Brighter Kensington and Chelsea Scheme, memb Advsy Panel Railway Heritage Tst; *Books* Garden Ornament (jtly); *Clubs* New (Edinburgh); *Style—* The Rt Hon the Earl of Lindsay; Lahill, Upper Largo, Fife KY8 6JE

LINDSAY, Prof (John) Kennedy; s of William Gray Lindsay (d 1966), of Ballycraigy, Newtownabbey, and Mary, *née* Kennedy; *b* 8 Sept 1924; *Educ* Trinity Coll Dublin (BA), Inst of Historical Res Univ of London, Univ of Edinburgh (PhD); *Career* univ teacher of S Carolina SC USA 1957-59 and memb Univ St Johns Newfoundland Canada 1959-60, memb academic staff Royal Military Coll of Canada 1960-61, i/c state papers room Historical Div Canadian Dept of External Affrs Ottawa Canada 1961-62, memb int team which estab Univ of Nigeria Nsukka Nigeria 1962-64, Canadian tech cooperation visiting prof Univ of W Indies 1964-69, memb ed bd Third World London 1970-71, MLA S Antrim NI Legislative Assembly 1973-74, ed Ulsterman newspaper 1975-76; legal conslt various cases Euro Cmmn on Human Rights Strasbourg incl: Black v UK, Orchin v UK, Br Ulster Pty v UK 1976-84, memb S Antrim constitutional convention 1976; owner: Dunrod Press UK 1979-, United Book Suppliers Wholesale 1981-; *Books* The British Intelligence Services in Action (1980); *Recreations* hiking; *Style—* Prof Kennedy Lindsay; 8 Brown's Road, Newtownabbey, Co Antrim BT36 8RN (0232 832362, fax 0232 848780, telex 9312132234 UN G)

LINDSAY, Dr (John) Maurice; CBE (1979), TD (1946); s of Matthew Lindsay (d 1969), of 32 Athole Gardens, Glasgow, and Eileen Frances, *née* Brock (1954); *b* 21 July 1918; *Educ* Glasgow Acad, Scottish Nat Acad of Music; *m* 3 Aug 1946, Aileen Joyce, da of Evan Ramsay Macintosh Gordon (d 1973); 1 s (Niall Gordon Brock b 1957), 3 da (Seona Morag Joyce b 1949, Kirsteen Ann b 1951, Morven Morag Joyce b 1959); *Career* poet, author, broadcaster, music critic and environmentalist; drama critic Scottish Daily Mail 1946-47, music critic The Bulletin 1946-60, ed Scots Review 1949-50; Border TV: programme controller 1961-62, prodn controller 1962-64, features exec and chief interviewer 1964-67; dir The Scottish Civic Tst 1967-83 (conslt 1983-), hon sec gen Europa Nostra 1982-, pres Assoc of Scottish Literary Studies 1988; Hon DLitt Glasgow 1982; Hon FRIAS; *Books* poetry: The Advancing Day (1940), Perhaps Tomorrow (1941), Predicament (1942), No Crown for Laughter: Poems (1943), The Enemies of Love: Poems 1941-45 (1946), Selected Poems (1947), Hurlygush: Poems in Scots (1948), At the Wood's Edge (1950), Ode for St Andrew's Night and Other Poems (1951), The Exiled Heart: Poems 1941-56 (1957), Snow Warning and Other Poems (1962), One Later Day and Other Poems (1964), This Business of Living (1969), Comings and Goings: Poems (1971), Selected Poems 1942-72 (1973), The Run from Life (1975), Walking Without an Overcoat: Poems 1972-76 (1977), Collected Poems (1979), A Net to Catch the Winds and Other Poems (1981), The French Mosquitoes' Woman and Other Diversions and Poems (1985), Requiem For a Sexual Athlete (1988), Collected Poems 1940-90 (1990); prose: A Pocket Guide to Scottish Culture (1947), The Scottish Renaissance (1949), The Lowlands of Scotland: Glasgow and the North (third edn, 1979), Robert Burns, The Man, His Work, The Legend (third edn, 1980), Dunoon: The Gem of the Clyde Coast (1954), The Lowlands of Scotland: Edinburgh and the South (third edn, 1979), Clyde Waters: Variations and Diversions on a Theme of Pleasure (1958), The Burns Encyclopaedia (fourth edn, 1989), Killochan Castle (1960), By Yon Bonnie Banks: A Gallimaufry (1961), Environment: A Basic Human Right (1968), Portrait of Glasgow (second edn, 1981), Robin Philipson (1977), History of Scottish Literature (1977), Lowland Scottish Villages (1980), Francis George Scott and the Scottish Renaissance (with Anthony F Kersting, 1980), The Buildings of Edinburgh (with Anthony Kersting, second edn, 1987), Thank You for Having Me: a personal memoir (with Dennis Hardley, 1983), Unknown Scotland (Dennis Hardley, 1984), The Castles of Scotland (1986), Count All Men Mortal - A History of Scottish Providence 1837-1987 (1987), Victorian and Edwardian Glasgow; Edinburgh Past and Present (with David Bruce, 1990), Glasgow (1989); other work: Poetry Scotland One, Two, Three (1943, 1945 and 1946), Sailing Tomorrow's Seas: An Anthology of New Poems (1944), Modern Scottish Poetry: An Anthology of the Scottish Renaissance 1920-45 (fourth edn, 1986) No Scottish Twilight: New Scottish Stories (with Fred Urquhart, 1947), Selected Poems of Sir Alexander Gray (1948), Poems, by Sir David Lyndsay, Poetry Scotland Four (with Hugh McDiarmid, 1948), Selected Poems of Marion Angus (with Helen Cruickshank, 1950), John Davidson: A Selection of his Poems (with Edwin Morgan and George Bruce, 1961), Scottish Poetry One to Six 1966-72 (with Edna Major and George Bruce), The Eye is Delighted: Some Romantic Travellers in Scotland (1970), Scottish Poetry Seven to Nine (with Alexander Scott and Robert Watson), A Book of Scottish Verse (with R L Mackie, 1974, 1976 and 1977), Scotland: An Anthology (1974, second edn, 1989), As I Remember (1979), The Discovery of Scotland (second edn, 1979), Scottish Comic Verse 1425-80 (1980), A Book of Scottish Verse (third edn, 1983), The Scottish Dog (with Joyce Lindsay, 1989), The Comic Poems of William Tennant (with Alexander Scott, 1989); *Recreations* enjoying compact disc collection, walking, sailing on paddle-steamers; *Style—* Dr Maurice Lindsay, CBE, TD; 7 Milton Hill, Milton, Dumbarton, Scotland G82 2TS (☎ 0389 62655)

LINDSAY, Col Oliver John Martin; yr s of Sir Martin Alexander Lindsay of Dowhill, 1 Bt, CBE, DSO (d 1981), and his 1 w, Joyce Emily, *née* Lindsay; *b* 30 Aug 1938; *Educ* Eton, RMA Sandhurst, Staff Coll Camberley, Nat Def Coll Latimer; *m* 27 Oct 1964, Lady Clare Rohais Antonia Elizabeth Giffard, da of 3 Earl of Halsbury; 1 s (Mark Oliver Giffard b 1968), 2 da (Victoria Louise Elizabeth Louise (Mrs Gregory Wheatley) b 1967, Fiona Emily Margaret b 1972); *Career* cmmnd Grenadier Gds 1958, served in W Africa, Cyprus, Hong Kong and Europe, and on staff in Rhodesia, Ottawa and London; memb Royal Co of Archers (Queen's Body Guard for Scotland); lectr (in particular on Far Eastern events 1940-45), historian and author; memb Bd of Govrs: Victoria League, Cwlth Tst 1988-90; FBIM 1990, FSA (Scot) 1990, FRHistS 1984; *Books* The Lasting Honour - The Fall of Hong Kong 1941 (1978), At the Going Down of the Sun - Hong Kong and South East Asia 1941-45 (1981), A Guard's General - the Memoirs of Sir Allan Adair (ed, 1986); *Recreations* tennis, writing; *Clubs* Boodle's, Royal Cwlth Soc; *Style—* Col Oliver Lindsay; c/o Child and Co, 1 Fleet Street, London EC4

LINDSAY, Penelope, Countess of; Penelope Georgina; *née* Crossley; er da of late Anthony Crommelin Crossley, MP; *b* 22 March 1928; *m* 1, 3 Oct 1951 (m dis 1969), Maj Henry Ronald Burn Callander, MC; 3 da (Sarah Alexandra Mary b 30 March 1952, Victoria b 2 Jan 1954, Emma Georgina b 30 March 1959); m 2, 9 June 1969, as his 2 w, 15 Earl of Lindsay (d 1989); *Style—* Penelope, The Countess of Lindsay; Combermere Abbey, Whitchurch, Shropshire SY13 4AJ; Coates House, Upper Largo, Fife KY8 6JF

LINDSAY, Robert Keith; s of Robert Lindsay (d 1978); *b* 15 Nov 1936; *Educ* Lancing, Magdalene Coll Cambridge; *m* 1961, Elisabeth, *née* Smith; 2 s, 1 da; *Career* dir Tennant Trading Ltd 1974-79, md New Metals and Chemicals Hldgs Ltd 1979-; CEng, FICemE; *Recreations* squash, gardening; *Clubs* Inst of Directors, Wilderness Squash; *Style—* Robert Lindsay, Esq; Russell House, Station Rd, Otford, Sevenoaks, Kent (☎ 09592 2352); Abbey Chambers, Highbridge St, Waltham Abbey, Essex (☎ 0992 711111)

LINDSAY, Hon Thomas Martin; MBE (1946); s of 1 Baron Lindsay of Birker, CBE (d 1952); *b* 5 March 1915; *Educ* Sidcot Sch, Edinburgh Univ; *m* 1, 1939 (m dis 1951), Denise Theresa, da of Gerald Albert Vaughan; 2 s, 1 da; m 2, 1951 (m dis 1961), Felicitas, da of Dr Martin Lange; 2 s; m 3, 1961, Erica, da of Maj Eric Thirkell-Cooper; 2 s; *Career* served 1939-45 War (despatches), Maj Sherwood Rangers; *Style—* The Hon Thomas Lindsay, MBE; 8 Avenue des Pinsons, 1410 Waterloo, Belgium

LINDSAY-FYNN, Adrian; s of Sir Basil Lindsay-Fynn (d 1988), and (Marion) Audrey Ellen, *née* Chapman (d 1991); *b* 12 April 1948; *Educ* Charterhouse; *m* 5 July 1974, Penelope Jean, da of Dennis Ward, of 4 Lyall Mews, London SW1; 3 s (James b 1975, Hugo b 1978, Alexander b 1981); *Career* farmer, landowner; dir: ALFCO Investmt Ltd 1983, Mortimer Machinery 1976, Carrollstown Estate Ltd 1974; *Recreations* shooting, sailing, tennis; *Clubs* Royal Irish Yacht; *Style—* Adrian Lindsay-Fynn, Esq; Carrollstown, Trim, Co Meath, Republic of Ireland (☎ Trim 31421, car 0860 333 783)

LINDSAY-FYNN, Nigel; s of Sir Basil Lindsay-Fynn (d 1988), and (Marion) Audrey Ellen, *née* Chapman (d 1991); *b* 4 May 1942; *Educ* Charterhouse, Oriel Coll Oxford (MA); *m* 12 May 1971, Heleen Vanda Mary, da of Bill Wilson-Pemberton, of London; 2 s (Piers b 1975, Charles b 1989), 2 da (Miranda b 1978, Eleanor b 1981); *Career* dir private family Cos (portfolio mgmnt and trusteeship); memb Cncl and Chief Steward Devon Co Agric Assoc, tstee Exeter Cathedral Preservation Tst, chm Exeter Nuffield Hosp; *Clubs* Buck's, Garrick, Kildare St, Univ Dublin, Royal Irish Yacht; *Style—* Nigel Lindsay-Fynn, Esq; Lee Ford, Budleigh Salterton, Devon EX9 7AJ (☎ 03954 5894, fax 03954 6219); 164 Campden Hill Rd, London W8 7AS (☎ 071 229 1684, fax 071 792 8969)

LINDSAY-HOGG, Sir Edward William; 4 Bt (UK 1905); s of Sir Lindsay Lindsay-Hogg, 1 Bt (d 1923), suc n, Sir William Lindsay-Hogg, 3 Bt, 1987; *b* 23 May 1910; *m* 1, 18 Nov 1936 (m dis 1946), Geraldine Mary, da of Edward Martin Fitzgerald; 1 s; m 2, 30 Oct 1957, Kathleen Mary, da of James Cooney, of Carrick-on-Suir, Co Tipperary, and wid of Capt Maurice Cadell, MC; *Heir* s, Michael Edward Lindsay-Hogg b 5 May 1940; *Clubs* St Stephen's Green (Dublin); *Style—* Sir Edward Lindsay-Hogg, Bt; Lista Correos, San Antonio Abad, Ibiza, Spain

LINDSAY-HOGG, Marie, Lady; Marie Teresa; *née* Foster; da of late John Foster, of St Helens, Lancashire; *m* 1; 4 s, 3 da; m 2, 1987, as his 2 w, Sir William Lindsay Lindsay- Hogg, 3 Bt (d 1987); 1 step da; *Style—* Marie, Lady Lindsay-Hogg; 84 Searles Close, Parkgate Rd, London SW11

LINDSAY-MacDOUGALL OF LUNGA, Colin John Francis; s of John Stewart Lindsay-MacDougall of Lunga, DSO, MC (ka 1943), and Shiela Marion, *née* Sprot; *b* 21 July 1939; *Educ* Radley; *m* 11 Feb 1961 (m dis 1979), Hon Frances Phoebe, da of Capt Hon Anthony Phillimore (ka 1943), of Cappid Hall, nr Henley on Thames, Oxfordshire; 3 s (James, Lucian, Aidan), 2 da (Antonia, Johanna); *Career* Nat Serv 2 Lt Queen's Own Hussars; landowner; *Recreations* sailing, riding, skiing, arts; *Clubs* Glasgow Art; *Style—* Colin Lindsay-MacDougall of Lunga; Lunga, Ardfern, Argyll (☎ 08 525 237); Lunga Estate, Argyll PA31 8QR (☎ 08 525 237, fax 085 25 639)

LINDSAY OF BIRKER, 2 Baron (UK 1945); The Rt Hon the Lord Michael Francis Morris Lindsay; s of 1 Baron Lindsay of Birker, CBE (d 1952); *b* 24 Feb 1909; *Educ* Gresham's, Balliol Coll Oxford; *m* 1941, Hsiao Li, da of Li Wen-chi, of the Chinese Army, of Lishih, Shansi; 1 s, 2 da; *Heir* s, Hon James Francis Lindsay; *Career* served with 18 Gp Army N China 1942-45; sinologist and economist; economics lectr at Yenching Univ Peking 1937; press attaché British Embassy Chunking 1940; visiting lectr Harvard Univ 1946-47, lectr Univ Coll Hull 1948-51, reader Australian Nat Univ Canberra 1951-59; former prof of far eastern studies American Univ Washington DC (now Prof Emeritus); *Style—* The Rt Hon the Lord Lindsay of Birker; 6812 Delaware St, Chevy Chase, Maryland 20815, USA (☎ 301 656 4245)

LINDSAY OF DOWHILL, Sir Ronald Alexander; 2 Bt (UK 1962), of Dowhill, Co Kinross; s of Sir Martin Lindsay of Dowhill, 1 Bt, CBE, DSO (d 1981) by 1 w, Joyce, da of Maj the Hon Robert Hamilton Lindsay, s of 26 Earl of Crawford; Sir Ronald is 23 in derivation from Sir William Lindsay of Rossie, 1 of Dowhill (b 1350) uncle of 1 Earl of Crawford. The coat of arms of Adam 5 of Dowhill d 1544 is shown in the Armorial of his Kinsman, Sir David Lindsay of the Mount, Lyon King of Arms. Adam had a Crown Charter of confirmation of his barony of Crambeth called Dowhill in 1541. Earlier such charters were in 1353 by David II, in 1397 by Robert III and in 1447 by James II. Dowhill Castle and the estates were sold by James 12 Laird in the 1740s. His three sons, Martin, James and William were involved in the losing side in the 1745 Jacobite Rising. The 1 Bt Sir Martin was Solihull's first MP (1945-62). He led the longest self-supporting sledge journey of 1050 miles across Greenland in 1934 (see Guinness Book of Records). In 1944-45 he cmd the 1 Bn The Gordon Highlanders in 16 ops in NW Europe. This Bn led the Siegfried line break through, not far from where in 1814 Sir Martin's ggf Col Martin Lindsay CB led the bayonet charge which broke through the French defences at Merxem when cmd the 78 Regt (the Seaforths); *b* 6 Dec 1933; *Educ* Eton, Worcester Coll Oxford (MA); *m* 1968, Nicoletta, yr da of Capt Edgar Storich (d 1985), Royal Italian Navy; 3 s (James b 1968, Hugo b 1970, Robin b 1972), 1 da (Lucia b 1974); *Heir* s, James Martin Evelyn Lindsay; *Career* Lt Grenadier Gds 1952-54; insur exec 1958-, dir Oxford Members' Agency Ltd 1989-; chm Baronets Tst 1990-; chm Standing Cncl of the Baronetage 1987-89; vice-chm Anglo-Spanish Soc 1985-; memb Queen's Body Gd for Scotland (Royal Co of Archers); FCII; *Style—* Sir Ronald Lindsay of Dowhill, Bt; Courleigh, Colley Lane, Reigate, Surrey RH2 9JJ (☎ 0737 243290)

LINDSAY-SMITH, Iain-Mór; s of Edward Duncanson Lindsay-Smith (d 1951); *b* 18 Sept 1934; *Educ* High Sch of Glasgow, Univ of London Extension Dip Course; *m* 1960, Carol Sara, da of Edward Philip Paxman (d 1948); 1 s (Sholto); *Career* cmmnd 1 Bn Cameronians (Scottish Rifles) W Germany 1953-55, 6/7 Bn 1955-63; journalist; Scottish Daily Record 1951-57, Daily Mirror 1957-60, features ed Daily Mail 1968-71 (foreign corr, foreign ed 1960-70), dep ed Yorkshire Post 1971-74, ed Glasgow Herald 1974-77, exec ed The Observer 1977-84; chm and publisher Lloyds List, chief exec and md Lloyds of London Press Ltd; dir: Lloyds of London Press Ltd, Lloyds of London Press Inc USA 1984-, Lloyds Maritime Info Servs Inc (USA), Lloyds of London Press (Far East) Ltd, Lloyds of London Press GmbM (Germany), Lloyds Maritime Info Servs Ltd; chm and chief exec Lloyds Info Servs, chm Lloyds of London Press Business Publishing, dir Lutine Pubns Ltd; dir: Mercury Theatre Colchester, Int Art and Antique Loss Register Ltd; memb: Ct Univ of Essex 1985-, Little Horkesley Parish Cncl 1986-, Little Horkesley PCC 1987; *Recreations* shooting (game and clays), highland bagpipes, gardening; *Clubs* Travellers'; *Style*— Iain-Mór Lindsay-Smith, Esq; Lloyds of London Press, 1 Singer St, London EC2A 4LQ (☎ 071 250 1500, telex 987321 Lloyds G)

LINDSELL, Charles Nicholas; s of Brig Robert Anthony Lindsell, MC, and Pamela Rosemary, *née* Cronk; *b* 31 Dec 1953; *Educ* Monkton Combe Sch; *m* 29 March 1980, Jill Penelope, da of Raymond Arthur Gransbury (d 1989); 1 s (David James b 1984), 1 da (Nicola Jane b 1986); *Career* fund mangr Phillips & Drew 1972-82, dir Henderson Administration Ltd 1987-88 (joined 1982), dep md Midland Montagu Asset Management 1988-; *Recreations* shooting, fishing, tennis, wine soc; *Style*— Charles Lindsell, Esq; Midland Montagu Asset Mgmnt, 10 Lower Thames St, London EC3R 6AE (☎ 071 260 9000)

LINDSEY, Alan Michael; s of Philip Stanley Lindsey, of Stanmore, Middx, and Doris Frederica Lindsey; *b* 7 Aug 1938; *Educ* Harrow HS, Orange Hill Co Grammar, LSE (BSc); *m* 3 Dec 1967, Dr Caroline Rachel Lindsey, da of Eli Gustav Weinberg; 1 da (Rebecca Adina b 2 Aug 1975); *Career* trained as CA Baker Sutton & Co (now pt of Ernst & Whinney) 1960-63; exec Corp Fin Dept Hill Samuel and NM Rothschild & Sons and fin exec International Timber plc 1963-72, sr investigation mangr Thornton Baker 1972-1980, in own practice Alan Lindsey & Co 1980-; author numerous articles in professional accounting magazines 1967-; memb: Ctee London Dist Soc of CAs 1979- (fndr ctee memb and past chm North London branch), Glyndebourne Festival Soc; FCA 1960 (memb Cncl 1988-); *Recreations* music (especially opera), theatre, cross country, skiing, mountain walking, swimming; *Clubs* LSE; *Style*— Alan Lindsey, Esq; Alan Lindsey & Co, 23 Gresham Gardens, London NW11 8NX (☎ 081 455 2882, fax 081 455 1214)

LINDSEY, Wing Cdr Ian Walter; OBE (1989); s of Walter Richard Lindsey (d 1966), of Bromley, and Christine, *née* Godsman (d 1981); *b* 7 May 1946; *Educ* Univ of Nottingham (BA, MPhil); *m* 1971, Janet, da of Sydney Hewitt; 2 s (Gordon b 1973, Robert b 1979), 1 da (Alison b 1972); *Career* cmmnd RAFVR(T) 1967, Flying Offr 1969, Flt Lt 1973, Sqdn Ldr 1983, Wing Cdr 1984, ret 1988, OC Herts/Bucks Wing ATC; mktg exec Williams and Glyns Bank 1971-75, sr lectr Harrow Coll 1975-77, conslt to Price Cmmn 1977-78, asst gen mangr TSB Trustcard Ltd 1978-83; dir: Save and Prosper Gp Ltd 1983-, Robert Fleming 1988-; treas ATC Central and E Region; FCIB 1980 (memb Central Cncl); *Recreations* flying; *Clubs* Halton House; *Style*— Wing Cdr Ian Lindsey, OBE; 3 Kinderscout, Leverstock Green, Herts HP3 8HW (☎ 0442 212 420); Save and Prosper Group Ltd, 1 Finsbury Ave, London EC2M 2QY (☎ 071 588 1717, fax 071 247 5006, telex 883838 SAVPRO G)

LINDSEY AND ABINGDON, 14 and 9 Earl of (E 1626 & 1682); Richard Henry Rupert Bertie; also Baron Norreys of Rycote (E 1572); s of Lt-Col Hon Arthur Michael Bertie, DSO, MC (d 1957), and Aline Rose, *née* Arbuthnot-Leslie (d 1948); suc cousin 13 Earl of Lindsey and (8 of) Abingdon 1963; *b* 28 June 1931; *Educ* Ampleforth; *m* 1957, Norah Elizabeth Farquhar-Oliver, da of late Mark Oliver, OBE, and Norah (d 1980), da of Maj Francis Farquhar, DSO, 2 s of Sir Henry Farquhar, 4 Bt, JP, DL; 2 s (Lord Norreys, Hon Alexander Michael Richard b 8 April 1970), 1 da (Lady Annabel Frances Rose b 11 March 1969); *Heir* s, Lord Norreys b 6 June 1958; *Career* sits as Cons Peer in House of Lords; served with Scots Gds 1950 and Royal Norfolk Regt 1951-52, Lt; insur broker and underwriting memb Lloyd's 1958; High Steward of Abingdon 1963; pres Friends of Abingdon 1982; co dir 1965; chm: Dawes & Henderson (Agencies) Ltd 1988, Anglo-Ivorian Soc 1974-77 (vice-pres 1978-); *Recreations* country pursuits; *Clubs* Pratt's, Turf, White's, Puffin's (Edinburgh); *Style*— The Rt Hon the Earl of Lindsey and Abingdon; Gilmilnscroft, Sorn, Mauchline, Ayrshire KA5 6ND (☎ 0290 51246); 3 Westgate Terrace, London SW10 9BT (☎ 071 480 7208)

LINDSLEY, David Middleton; s of Richard Middleton Lindsley (d 1960), of Valebrooke, Sunderland, Co Durham, and Ethel Muriel, *née* Greig; *b* 8 March 1936; *Educ* The Leys Sch Cambridge; *m* 20 Aug 1960, Elizabeth Anne Dickinson, da of Dr William Athelstane Dickinson Oliver (d 1964), of Belgrave, Coxhoe, Co Durham; 1 s ((David) James Middleton b 1971), 2 da ((Elizabeth) Suzanne Middleton b 1963, (Alice) Elspeth Middleton b 1967); *Career* slr, pres Sunderland Law Soc 1986-87; dir: Vedra Shipping Co Ltd 1976-, United and Gen Tst Ltd 1977-, Bright and Galbraith Ltd 1977-, Vale Trust Ltd 1977-; cdr Order of Merit SMO of Malta 1988; *Recreations* shooting; *Clubs* The Club (Sunderland); *Style*— David Lindsley, Esq; Springfield House, Fremington, Richmond, North Yorkshire (☎ 0748 84432); 52 John St, Sunderland, Tyne and Wear (☎ 091 5652421)

LINDUP, Dr Rhona; da of Gp Capt Lindup (d 1968), and Gladys, *née* Reffell (d 1966); *b* 15 April 1931; *Educ* Ancaster House Sch Bexhill-on-Sea, Royal Free Hosp Sch of Med London (MB BS); *Career* conslt radiotherapist and oncologist N Staffs Royal Infirmary Stoke-on-Trent; memb: N Staffs Field Club, Friends of Museum; vice pres Br Federation Univ Women; FRCR; *Recreations* hill walking, tennis, sport; *Clubs* Compden Hill Tennis; *Style*— Dr Rhona Lindup; 219 Seabridge Lane, Newcastle-under-Lyme, Staffs ST5 3LS (☎ 0782 618298); N Staffs Royal Infirmary, Stoke-on-Trent, Staffs (☎ 0782 49144)

LINE, Frances Mary (Mrs James Lloyd); da of Charles Edward Line, and Leoni Lucy, *née* Hendriks; *b* 22 Feb 1940; *Educ* James Allen's Girls' Sch; *m* 28 Nov 1972, James Richard Beilby Lloyd, s of James Beilby Lloyd; *Career* BBC: clerk typist 1957, sec in TV and radio 1959-67, prodr Radio 2 1967-73, sr prodr 1973-79, chief asst Radio 2 1979-83, chief asst Radio 4 1983-85, head of Music Dept Radio 2 1985-89, controller Radio 2 1990-; memb Cncl The Radio Acad; *Recreations* theatre, Sussex, happy snaps; *Clubs* The Rugby Club of London, Forum UK; *Style*— Miss Frances Line; BBC Radio 2, Western House, 99 Great Portland St, London W1A 1AA (☎ 071 927 4380, fax 071 436 5247)

LINE, Prof Maurice Bernard; s of Bernard Cyril Line (d 1978), of Bedford, and Ruth Florence, *née* Crane (d 1936); *b* 21 June 1928; *Educ* Bedford Sch, Exeter Coll Oxford (BA, MA); *m* 12 April 1954, Joyce, da of Walter Gilchrist (d 1953), of Paisley; 1 s (Philip b 1955), 1 da (Jill b 1957); *Career* sub librarian Univ of Southampton 1954-65, dep librarian Univ of Newcastle upon Tyne 1965-68; librarian: Univ of Bath 1968-71, Nat Central Library 1971-73; dir gen: lending div British Library 1974-85, sci tech and indust British Library 1985-88 (conslt 1988-); prof assoc Univ of Sheffield 1980-, visiting prof Univ of Loughborough 1987-; memb British Library Bd 1974-88; author of: 14 books and 260 articles in learned jls and 40 res reports; pres Library Assoc 1990; Hon DLitt Heriot Watt Univ 1980, Hon DSc Univ of Southampton 1988; FLA 1954, FIInfSci 1975, CBIM 1980, Hon FLA 1987, FRSA; *Recreations* tennis, walking, music listening, theatre; *Style*— Prof Maurice Line; 10 Blackthorn Lane, Burn Bridge, Harrogate, N Yorks HG3 1NZ (☎ 0423 872984, car 0423 872984)

LINEKER, Gary Winston; s of Barry Lineker, of 9 Coverdale Rd, The Meadows, Wigston, Leicester, and Margaret Patricia Morris, *née* Abbs; *b* 30 Nov 1960; *Educ* City of Leicester Boys GS; *m* 5 July 1986, Michelle Denise, da of Roger Edwin Cockayne, of 1 Brickman Close, Forest Farm, Forest East, Leicester; *Career* professional footballer, debut Leicester City 1979, transferred to Everton 1985, represented England in the 1986 World Cup Mexico (leading goal scorer) and 1990 World Cup Italy, FC Barcelona 1986-89, transferred to Tottenham Hotspur 1989; *Recreations* cricket, golf; *Clubs* MCC; *Style*— Gary Lineker, Esq; Tottenham Hotspur FC, White Hart Lane, 748 High Rd, Tottenham, London N17 0AP (☎ 081 808 8080, telex 295261)

LINES, David John Vincent; s of William Henry Lines, of Hayes, Kent, and Marjorie Florence Helen, *née* Wood (d 1973); *b* 9 Nov 1935; *Educ* City of London Sch, City of London Coll; *m* 8 April 1963 (m dis 1978), Patricia Ann, da of Charles Quested-Drayson (d 1975), of Addington, Surrey; 2 da (Deborah Karen Louise b 1967, Rebecca Sally Jane b 1970); *Career* indust chemist Standard Telephones and Cables 1952-59, conslt OW Roskill 1959-61, sales conslt Bary Wiggins (pt of BP) 1961-64, sales dir Reece Machinery Co 1964-; former hon chm Clothing Inst; chm: Br Assoc of Clothing Machinery Mfrs, Badminton Club and local soc club; Freeman: City of London 1959, Worshipful Co of Bakers; MInstPet, MBIM, MBInstPKG, FCTI; *Recreations* badminton, country dancing; *Clubs* Conservative; *Style*— David Lines, Esq; 113 Whyteleaf Rd, Caterham on the Hill, Surrey CR3 5EG (☎ 0883 46118); Reece (UK) Ltd, 6-7 Princes Court, 11 Wapping Lane, London E1 9DA (☎ 071 481 2835, fax 071 480 7485, telex 8876630

LINES, Richard Stuart; OBE (1991); s of Harold Thomas Lines, Wing Cdr RAF (d 1954), of Purley, and Mimi Kathleen Lee, *née* Bailey (d 1983); *b* 4 Aug 1936; *Educ* Seaford Coll Petworth Hants, RN; *m* 20 June 1959, Janet Marion Boyes, da of Percy Clifford Stronach; 2 s (Simon Richard b 1962, Timothy James b 1965); *Career* Air Crew Lt RN; chm and chief exec MTM plc 1986- and dir subsid and assoc cos (incl jt ventures with ICI plc 1967-78, mktg exec prior to 1967); chm bd of govrs Teeside Poly; *Recreations* golf, swimming, walking; *Style*— Richard Lines, Esq, OBE; MTM plc, Rudby Hall, Hutton Rudby, Yarm, Cleveland TS15 0JN (☎ 0642 701078, telex 58365, fax 0642 700667, car 0860 615625)

LINFORD, David; s of Albert Louis Linford, of Hatherton, Comberford Rd, Tamworth, Staffs (d 1976), and Olive Leonie, *née* Harston (d 1968); *b* 29 May 1934; *Educ* King Edward VII's Sch Bath, QEI GS Tamworth Staffs; *m* 29 Dec 1961, Barbara, da of Eric Whitehouse, of Woodend, Old Penkridge Rd, Cannock, Staffs; *Career* chm and md: F & E V Linford Ltd 1967- (and subsidiaries), Linford-Bridgeman Ltd 1985-; dir: Presco (Holdings) Ltd 1975-, Cannock and Burntwood Enterprise Agency Ltd, Staffordshire Training and Enterprise Cncl; *Recreations* hockey, int rotary, historic bldgs; *Style*— David Linford, Esq; The Kennels, Upper Longdon, Rugeley, Staffs (☎ 0543 491230); F & E V Linford Ltd, Park Rd, Cannock, Staffs (☎ 0543 466566)

LINFORD, Dr Susan Margaret Jane; da of Trevor Edwin Linford, and Hedy, *née* Belke; *b* 11 Sept 1953; *Educ* Cannock GS, Univ of Birmingham (MB ChB); *m* 30 June 1979, Dr Christopher Roy Barraclough, s of late William Barraclough; 2 da (Laura Susan Elizabeth b 14 Sept 1980, Evelith Margaret Jane b 16 Aug 1989); *Career* currently conslt psychiatrist Royal Shrewsbury Hosp Shelton; MRCPsych; *Style*— Dr Susan Linford; Royal Shrewsbury Hospital, Shelton, Bicton Heath, Shrewsbury, Shropshire SY3 8DN (☎ 0743 231122)

LING; *see*: de Courcy Ling

LING, Arthur George; s of George Frederick Ling (d 1957); *b* 20 Sept 1913; *Educ* Christ's Hosp, UCL; *m* 1939, Marjorie, da of Robert John Tall (d 1962); 1 s (Peter), 3 da (Anna, Judith, Frances); *Career* planning offr London CC 1943-55, sr lectr Dept of Town Planning Univ of London 1947-55, city architect and planning offr Coventry 1955-64, prof of architecture and planning Nottingham 1964-69, project mangr UN Habitat Project Physical Perspective Plan for Libya 1977-80; private practice Arthur Ling & Assocs Architects & Town Planners 1965-; vice-pres RIBA 1963-64, pres Royal Town Planning Inst 1968-69, pres Cwlth Assoc of Planners 1970-75; memb Sports Cncl 1967-71; fell UCL; *Books* Master Plan for Runcorn New Town, Urban and Regional Planning and Development in the Commonwealth; *Style*— Arthur Ling, Esq; The Old Rectory, Howell, Sleaford, Lincs (☎ 0529 60412)

LING, Maj-Gen Fergus Alan Humphrey; CB (1958), CBE (1964), DSO (1944), DL (1969); s of John Richardson Ling (d 1938), of Bath, and Mabel, *née* Pratchitt (d 1948); *b* 5 Aug 1914; *Educ* Stowe, RMC Sandhurst; *m* 20 March 1940, Sheelah Phyllis (d 1990), da of William Godfrey Molyneux Sarel (d 1950), of Berks; 2 s (Anthony b 1941, Philip b 1946), 3 da (Virginia b 1948, Elizabeth and Diana b 1950); *Career* cmd 2/5 Bn Queen's Royal Regt Italy 1944, DS Staff Coll Camberley 1951-53, cmd 5 Bn Queen's Royal Regt 1954-57, asst mil sec WO 1957-58, Cdr 148 Inf Bde (TA) 1958-61, Dep Adj-Gen Rhine Army 1961-65, Gen Offr cmd 54 E Anglian Div (TA) and Cdr E Anglian 1965-67, GOC Eastern Dist 1967-69, ret; dir: Caffin Holdings Ltd 1969-72, Lundi Appeal 1969; fndr admin dir Inst for the Study of Conflict 1970-72, def conslt ISC 1972-82; chm Surrey TAVR Assoc 1973-78, Col The Queen's Regt 1973-77 (Col 1969-73); vice Lord-Lieut Surrey 1973-82; chm SE TAVR Assoc 1978-79 (vice chm 1973-78); *Recreations* grandchildren, gardening; *Clubs* Royal Cwlth Soc; *Style*— Maj-Gen Fergus A H Ling, CB, CBE, DSO, DL; Mystole Coach House, nr Canterbury, Kent CT4 7DB (☎ 0227 738 496); Shepherd House, Netherwasdale, nr Seascale, Cumbria (☎ 0940 6312)

LING, Philip Henry; s of Dr Thomas M Ling, and Sylvia Margaret, *née* Burne; *b* 2 April 1946; *Educ* Downside New Coll Oxford (MA), London Business Sch (MSc); *m* 9 Sept 1969, Mary, da of W Hawley; 2 s (Sebastian b 1977, Alexander b 1983), 1 da (Harriet b 1974); *Career* dir Johnson & Firth Brown plc 1973-82, md Haden plc 1984-86 (London & Midland Industrials plc 1982-84), chm Haden Maclellan Holdings plc 1987- (Haleworth Holdings Ltd 1986-87); *Recreations* riding, skiing, reading; *Clubs* Lansdowne, Anabel's; *Style*— Philip Ling, Esq; Haleworth House, Tite Hill, Egham, Surrey TW20 0LT (☎ 07844 39791)

LING, Prof Robin Sydney Mackwood; s of William Harold Godfrey Mackwood Ling (d 1973), of Keighley, W Yorks, and Margaret Mona, *née* Price (d 1979); *b* 7 Sept 1927; *Educ* Shawnigan Lake Sch Vancouver Island Br Columbia, Univ of Oxford (MA, BM BCh), St Mary's Hosp London; *m* 18 Sept 1956, Mary, da of Capt W F Steedman, MC (d 1959); 2 da (Jennifer b 1959, Katherine b 1962); *Career* former conslt orthopaedic surgn: Royal Infirmary Edinburgh, Princess Margaret Orthopaedic Hosp Edinburgh; sr conslt orthopaedic surgn Princess Elizabeth Orthopaedic Hosp Exeter; hon prof of bio-engrg Univ of Exeter, past press Br Orthopaedic Assoc, pres Br Orthopaedic Res Soc 1979-80; visiting prof: Louisiana State Univ 1983, Univ of Arizona 1985, Chinese Univ of Hong Kong 1985, Univ of California 1986, Baylor Univ Texas 1986; memb: Int Hip Soc, SICOT; Lt Sir John Charnley Meml Lectr Univ of Liverpool 1986, Pridie Meml lectr Univ of Bristol 1987; pubns: incl numerous papers in leading med and scientific jls on hip surgery, implant fixation, properties of biomaterials; *Recreations* sailing; *Clubs* Royal Ocean Racing, Royal Dart YC, Royal Soc of Med; *Style*— Prof Robin S M Ling; Lod Cottage, The Lane, Dittisham, nr Dartmouth, Devon T96 0HB (☎ 080 422 451); 2 The Quadrant, Wonford Rd, Exeter EX2 4LE (☎ 0392 37070)

LING, Timothy Andrew; s of Edward Andrew Ling (d 1973), of Maidstone, Kent, and Muriel Garnett, *née* Harford; *b* 17 Sept 1948; *Educ* King's Sch Canterbury, Queen's Coll Oxford (MA); *m* 9 May 1981, Sarah Elizabeth, da of David James; 2 s (Edward David b 30 July 1983, Richard James b 19 Jan 1985), 2 da (Emma Sarah b 8 May 1987, Sarah Rebecca b 7 March 1990); *Career* Freshfields: articled clerk 1971-73, asst slr 1973-77, ptnr 1977-, head Corp Tax Dept 1985-; memb Law Soc (Revenue Law Ctee 1984-); contrib various taxation pubns 1975-; *Recreations* music, sailing; *Clubs* Royal Harwich Yacht, Orford Sailing; *Style*— Timothy Ling, Esq; Freshfields, Whitefriars, 65

Fleet St, London EC4Y 1HS (☎ 071 936 4000, fax 071 248 3487)

LINGAM, Dr Sundara; s of Thambu Sabaratnam, of Sri Lanka, and Vijayalaxsmi; *b* 3 April 1946; *Educ* St John's Coll Jaffna Sri Lanka, People's Friendship Univ Moscow, USSR (MD); *m* 12 June 1985, Susan Heather, da of Alex Reid, of Loughton, Essex; 1 da (Claire Anusha Laura b 1988); *Career* registrar neurology Hosp for Sick Children Gt Ormond St 1980-83, hon sr registrar developmental paediatrics Wolfson Centre Inst of Child Health 1985-88, conslt paediatrician 1988-; assoc ed World Paediatrics and Child Care; exec med dir Assoc for the Prevention of Disabilities; hon treas: Int Coll of Paediatrics, Int Acad of Paediatric Transdisciplinary Ed; MRCP, DCH, DRCOG, LMSSA; memb Br Paediatric Assoc; *Books* Manual on Child Development (1988), It's Your Life (1982), Case Studies in Paediatric Radiology (1985); *Recreations* sports, writing, creating models; *Style—* Dr Sundara Lingam; Beehives, 90 Hay Lane, Kingsbury, London NW9 0LG (☎ 081 200 8368); Princes Alexandra Hospital, Harlow, Essex CM20 1QX (☎ 0279 444455)

LINGARD, Brian Hallwood; s of Capt Abel Keenan Lingard, MC (d 1955), of Wanstead, London, and Elsie May Lingard, BEM; *b* 2 Nov 1926; *Educ* Stockport GS, Manchester Coll of Art, Sch of Architecture (Dip Arch); *m* 20 July 1949, Dorothy Gladys Lingard, da of Capt Herbert Clay (d 1978), of Bramhall, Cheshire; 2 s (Christopher b 1951, Timothy b 1953), 1 da (Rebecca b 1960); *Career* RN 1944-46; served: HMS Wolverine, Gibraltar 1944-45; radio engr 1946; architect; commenced private practice 1950; ptnr: Brian Lingard & Ptnrs 1972-90, Lingard & Styles Ptnrship (landscape architects) 1975-90, Gallery Lingard (architectural historians) 1982-90; prof awards incl: RIBA Regnl award (Wales), DOE and RIBA Housing medal (7 awards), Civic Tst (21 awards), The Times and RICS Conservation award (2 awards), Prince of Wales Conservation award (3 awards); chm Architects Benevolent Soc; ARIBA 1949, FRIBA 1957; *Books* The Opportunities for the Conservation and Enhancement of our Historic Resorts (1983); *Recreations* swimming, riding, tennis, old buildings; *Clubs* Carlton, RAC; *Style—* Brian Lingard; Plas Môr, Rhosneigr, Isle of Anglesey; 77 Cheyne Court, London SW3 (☎ 0407 810 728, 071 352 9288); Brian Lingard & Partners, 23 Trinity Square, Llandudno, Gwynedd; 50 Pall Mall, London SW1 (☎ 071 930 1645, fax 0407 811213)

LINGARD, Lady Caroline Flower; da of 16 Earl of Buchan (d 1984), and Christina, Countess of Buchan, *qv*; *b* 29 June 1935; *m* 26 Feb 1963, John Robin William Lingard; 2 da; *Style—* The Lady Caroline Lingard; Semley Grange, Shaftesbury, Dorset

LINGARD, James Richard; s of Walter Wadsworth Lingard, and Emily, *née* Watson; *b* 7 June 1936; *Educ* Dulwich, UCL (LLB); *m* 1, 7 Sept 1963, Maureen Winifred (d 1985), da of George Henry Ball; 3 s (Andrew b 1964, Peter b 1967, Christopher b 1971); m 2, 7 Oct 1989, Mary Teresa McFarran; *Career* slr Supreme Ct 1959-, ptnr Norton Rose 1972-, insolvency practitioner 1987-, dir Jt Insolvency Examination Bd 1988-; contrib Encyclopaedia of Forms and Precedents, past pres Insolvency Lawyers Assoc; memb: Cncl Soc of Practitioners of Insolvency, Law Soc Specialisation Commercial Casework Ctee; chm: City of London Law Soc Insolvency Sub Ctee (memb Banking Sub Ctee), Jt Law Soc Bar Banking Sub Ctee; Freeman City of London; memb Law Soc 1959; *Books* Corporate Rescues and Insolvencies (2 edn, 1989), Bank Security Documents (2 edn, 1988), Tolley's Commercial Loan Agreements (1990); *Recreations* writing, snooker; *Clubs* Law Soc; *Style—* James Lingard, Esq; Norton Rose, Kempson House, Camomile St, London EC3A 7AN (☎ 071 283 2434, fax 071 588 1181, telex 883652)

LINGENS, Michael Robert; s of Dr Friedrich Otto Lingens, of Stuttgart, W Germany, and Karin Weber; *b* 15 May 1957; *Educ* St Edmunds Sch Canterbury, Trinity Coll Oxford (MA); *Career* admitted slr 1982, ptnr Speechly Bircham, chm Bow Group 1984-85; cnclIr London Borough of Hammersmith and Fulham; Parly candidate (C) Bolsover 1987; *Books* The SDP - A Critical Analysis, Beveridge and The Bow Group Generation, Winning on Welfare; *Recreations* real tennis, rackets; *Clubs* Coningsby, The Queens, Carlton; *Style—* Michael Lingens, Esq; 8 Hauteville Court Gdns, Stamford Brook Ave, London W6 0YF (☎ (home) 081 748 4693, (business) 071 353 3290)

LINGWOOD, David Frederick; s of Frederick Joseph Lingwood, of Bedford, and Grace Anne, *née* Clark (d 1986); *b* 5 May 1946; *Educ* Royal GS Newcastle Upon Tyne, Univ of Newcastle; *Career* PA to md Theatres Consolidated, house mangr for Sadlers Wells Opera London Coliseum, gen mangr Watford Civic Theatre Tst, admin dir Unicorn Theatre, admin Actors Co, asst exec prodr Robert Stigwood Orgn; gen mangr: Mermaid Theatre London, Shaftesbury Theatre London; asst gen mangr Royal Albert Hall; theatre mangr: Duchess Theatre 1987, Queens Theatre 1987, London Palladium 1988-; *Recreations* music, theatre, swimming, gardening; *Style—* David Lingwood, Esq; 28 Ennismore Avenue, Chiswick, London W4 1SF (☎ 081 747 1441); London Palladium, Argyll St, London W1A 3AB (☎ 081 734 6846)

LININGTON, Richard; s of Reginald Friend Linington (d 1981), of Quex Farm, Birchington, Kent, and Gwendoline Florence Irene, *née* Amos (d 1986); *b* 31 March 1945; *Educ* Tonbridge, Birmingham Coll of Arts and Crafts (Dip Int Design); *m* 27 Sept 1969, (Hilary) Jane, da of Maj Ronald Jasper Lucas, of 3 The Green, Westington, Chipping Campden, Glos; 2 s (Noel b 1971, Ben b 1975); *Career* designer; interior designer R Seifert and Ptnrs 1967-69, designer for architect Stephen Garrett 1969-72, assoc with Austin Smith Lord Architects 1972-79, princ Hurley Linington McGirr Design Ptnrshp 1979-87, ptnr Bloomer Tweedale Architects 1988-; memb Int Rels Bd Chartered Soc of Designers, pres Int Fedn of Int Designers and Architects 1987-89; FCSD 1987; *Recreations* music, gardening; *Clubs* East India; *Style—* Richard Linington, Esq; The Old Rectory, Easthope, Much Wenlock, Shropshire TF13 6DN (☎ 074 636 626); Bloomer Tweedale, 20 Highfield Rd, Edgbaston, Birmingham B15 3DX (☎ 021 456 1984, fax 021 456 2991)

LINKLATER, Magnus Duncan; s of Eric Robert Linklater, CBE, TD, and Marjorie MacIntyre; *b* 21 Feb 1942; *Educ* Eton, Univ of Freiburg, Sorbonne, Trinity Hall Cambridge (BA); *m* 1967, Veronica, da of Lt-Col Michael Lyle, JP, DL, of Riemore Lodge, Dunkeld; 2 s (Alexander, Saul), 1 da (Freya); *Career* journalist: Daily Express Manchester 1964-69, Evening Standard (ed Londoner's Diary), The Sunday Times (ed Spectrum pages, ed Colour Magazine, asst ed News, exec ed Features) 1969-83, managing ed The Observer 1983-86; ed: The London Daily News 1986-87, The Scotsman 1988-; memb: Edinburgh Vision, Assoc of Br Eds, Int Press Inst; dep chm Scottish Daily Newspaper Soc; *Books* Hoax-The Howard Hughes Clifford Irving Affair (with Stephen Fay and Lewis Chester), Jeremy Thorpe - A Secret Life (with Lewis Chester and David May), The Falklands War (with the Sunday Times Insight team), Massacre - the story of Glencoe, The Fourth Reich-Klaus Barbie and the Neo-Fascist Connection (with Isabel Hilton and Neal Ascherson), Not with Honour - the inside story of the Westland Affair (with David Leigh), For King and Conscience - John Graham of Claverhouse, Viscount Dundee (with Christian Hesketh); *Recreations* cricket, fishing, book collecting; *Clubs* Caledonian, MCC, Press; *Style—* Magnus Linklater, Esq; The Scotman, 20 North Bridge, Edinburgh EH1 1YT (☎ 031 243 3207, fax 031 226 7420, telex 72255)

LINKLATER, Peter Stronach; s of Dr James Thomas Parker Linklater (d 1981), and Hilda Cuthbert, *née* Marr; *b* 7 Jan 1924; *Educ* Oundle, Clare Coll Cambridge; *m* 16 July 1949, Pauline Elizabeth, da of Duncan Hardwick (d 1955); 3 da (Catriona b 1950, Sarah b 1954, Victoria b 1957); *Career* Capt Scots Gds 1944-47, cmd Ceremonial Gd Nuremburg 1945; mangr patents and licensing Shell Int 1955-61; dir: Shell Chemical UK 1961-67, (personnel) Shell UK 1967-79; exec vice-chm Shell Res 1975-78; chm ed ctee Chemistry and Industry 1965-80; memb: CBI Cncl 1969-72, Employment Policy Ctee 1972-78, NEDO Ctee large construction sites 1970-78; chm: Friends of Lewes (Civic Soc) 1970-, The Windsor Meeting (biannual) at St George's House Windsor Castle 1980-, Careers Res and Advsy Centre Cambridge 1984-, World Conf Coop Educn Programme Edinburgh 1985; industl fell Churchill Coll Cambridge 1980-82 (industl advsr 1966-); indust memb: advsy ctee Adult and Continuing Educn 1978-84, advsy bd Res Cncls Post Graduate Awards 1981-83, Univ Grants Ctee Continuing Educn 1982-84; *Books* Education and the World of Work - Positive Partnerships (introduced and edited, 1987); *Recreations* opera, archaeology, walking; *Clubs* Garrick, Caledonian; *Style—* Peter S Linklater, Esq; The Gables, Southover High St, Lewes, E Sussex BN7 1JA (☎ 0273 473872); Birch Cottage, Aboyne, Aberdeenshire (☎ 0339 2251)

LINLEY, Viscount; *see* Royal Family section

LINLITHGOW, 4 Marquess of (UK 1902); Sir Adrian John Charles Hope; 12 Bt (NS 1698); also Earl of Hopetoun, Viscount Aithrie, Lord Hope (all S 1703), Baron Hopetoun (UK 1809), and Baron Niddry (UK 1814); o son of 3 Marquess of Linlithgow, MC (d 1987), and his 1 w Vivien, *née* Kenyon-Slaney (d 1963); *b* 1 July 1946; *Educ* Eton; *m* 1, 9 Jan 1968 (m dis 1978), Anne Pamela, eld da of Arthur Edmund Leveson, of Hall Place, Ropley, Hants; 2 s (Earl of Hopetoun b 22 May 1969, Lord Alexander b 3 Feb 1971); m 2, 1980, Peta Carol, da of Charles Victor Ormonde Binding, of Congresbury, Somerset; 1 s (Lord Robert b 17 Jan 1984), 1 da (Lady Louisa b 16 April 1981); *Heir* s, Earl of Hopetoun, *qv*; *Style—* The Most Hon the Marquess of Linlithgow; Hopetoun House, South Queensferry, West Lothian EH30 9SL; 123 Beaufort St, London SW3

LINNELL, David George Thomas; CBE (1987); s of George Linnell, and Marguerite, *née* Gardner; *b* 28 May 1930; *Educ* Leighton Park Sch Reading; *m* 11 March 1953, Margaret Mary, da of Robert John Paterson; 1 s (Mark David b 1955), 1 da (Claire Elizabeth b 1958); *Career* md Thomas Linnell and Sons Ltd 1964-75, chief exec Linfood Holdings Ltd 1975-81, chm Spar Food Hldgs 1975-79, pres Inst of Grocery Distribution 1980-82; chm: Eggs Authy 1981-86, Neighbourhood Stores PLC 1983-87, Brunning Group plc 1987-; FIGD 1977, CBIM 1978; *Clubs* Carlton; *Style—* David Linnell, Esq, CBE; The Old Rectory, Titchmarsh, Kettering, Northants

LINNELL, David Gerald; s of Rev Gerald Hislop Linnell (d 1944), and Enid Marion, *née* Anderson (d 1974); descendant of John Linnell, landscape artist (1792-1882); *b* 29 Dec 1934; *Educ* Christ's Hosp, Royal Tech Coll Salford; *m* 1985, Ann Nora, da of John Edwin Palmer; 2 s, 1 da by previous m and 1 step s, 1 step da; *Career* former chm and md Cableform Group Ltd 1973-86; former memb: NW Indust Devpt Bd, Electrical Engrg Sub Ctee of Machines and Power Ctee of Sci and Engrg Res Cncl 1985-87, Electrical Tech Ctee of Mech & Engrg Ctee of Electrical Engrg Regnl Bd 1980-84; md Cannon Materials Handling Ltd Liverpool; *Recreations* gardening, reading, photography, travel; *Style—* David Linnell, Esq; Heatherbank, 67 Gilbraltar Lane, Haughton Green, Manchester M34 1PY

LINNELL, Stuart Swain Goodman; s of Capt Eric Henry Goodman Linnell (d 1975), of Birmingham, and Dorothy Mary Swain (d 1974); *b* 22 Jan 1947; *Educ* Kings Norton GS Birmingham; *m* 1981, Susan Marie, da of Desmond Reginald Cleobury, of Coventry; 2 s (Nicholas Charles Goodman b 15 Feb 1983, Matthew Stuart b 4 July 1985); *Career* pt/t freelance broadcaster BBC Radio Birmingham 1970-74, sports ed Radio Hallam 1974-80, programme controller Mercia Sound 1983 (sports ed and afternoon presenter 1980), md Mercia Sound Ltd (formerly Midland Community Radio plc) 1986-; dir: Cable Advertising Sales (Coventry) Ltd 1986-87, Birmingham Broadcasting Ltd 1988-89, Midlands Radio Holdings plc 1988-89; memb: Assoc of Ind Radio Contractors Lab Rels Ctee 1987, Mercia TAP Agency Mgmnt Bd 1988, Bd of Govrs Coventry Poly 1988-, Bd of Govrs Woodlands Sch Coventry 1988-89, Coventry Common Purpose Cncl 1989-, City Links ctee (Coventry) 1990-; chm: Mercia FM Birthday Appeal Ctee 1987-, Mercia TAP Coventry Advsy Bd 1989-90, Mercia FM Walkathon Ctee 1989-; AIRC rep Sony Radio Award Ctee 1988-; tstee: Mercia Sound/Evening Telegraph Charity Snowball Tst 1988-, Midlands Radio Action Tst 1990-; *Recreations* watching Coventry FC, most sports (except ice-dancing!), studying the media, enjoying my family, winning at Trivial Pursuit; *Clubs* Coventry City Football (vice pres); *Style—* Stuart Linnell, Esq; Mercia Sound Ltd, Hertford Place, Coventry CV1 3TT (☎ 0203 633933, fax 0203 552055, telex 31413-MERCIA-G, car 0836 203389)

LINNETT, Mark Stuart; s of David Linnett, of Rugby, Warwickshire, and Patricia, *née* Lock (d 1987); *b* 17 Feb 1963; *Educ* Dunsmore GS, Hillmorton, Rugby; *m* 25 July 1987, Julie Anne, da of Jack Lorne; 1 s (David b 28 Aug 1987); *Career* Rugby Union prop forward Moseley RFC and England (1 cap); clubs: Rugby 1979-84, Moseley RFC 1984- (approx 200 appearances); 4 caps England Colts 1981-82, England U23 v Spain Twickenham 1986, 5 caps England B 1988-89; England debut v Fiji (scored try), 3 appearances (1 try) Barbarians, 20 caps Br Police, police officer W Midlands Police 1979-, Police Cadet Nat Discus and Shot champion 1980; *Recreations* anything to do with sport; *Style—* Mark Linnett, Esq; 98 Brookvale Rd, Olton, Solihull, West Midlands B91 7JA (☎ 021 708 2345); Moseley Rugby Football Club, Reddings Rd, Moseley, Birmingham (☎ 021 449 2149)

LINNETT, Michael John; s of Godfrey Samuel Johnston Linnett, of Worthing, Sussex, and Eileen Lilian, *née* Ward; *b* 11 Sept 1941; *Educ* Douai Sch, Gateway GS; *m* 9 Oct 1965, Joanna Judith, da of David Anthony O'Brien; 1 s (Toby James b 2 June 1972), 1 da (Victoria Louise b 6 March 1970); *Career* qualified asst then mangr Baker Bros Halford & Co 1967-73 (articled clerk, qualified chartered accountant 1965), co sec Karina Fashions Ltd 1966-67; ptnr: Thomson McLintock & Co 1974-87, KPMG Peat Marwick McLintock (following merger) 1987-; FCA (ACA 1965); *Recreations* squash, walking; *Style—* Michael Linnett, Esq; 507 Loughborough Rd, Birstall, Leicester LE4 4BJ (☎ 0533 674149); KPMG Peat Marwick McLintock, Peat House, 1 Waterloo Way, Leicester LE1 6LP (☎ 0533 471122, fax 0533 547626, car 0860 351250)

LINNETT, Dr Michael Joseph; OBE (1975); s of Joseph Linnett (d 1967), of Leicester, and Dora Alice Linnett; *b* 14 July 1926; *Educ* Wyggeston GS for Boys, St Bartholomew's Hosp; *m* 1950, Marianne Patricia, da of Aubrey Dibdin, CIE (d 1958); 2 da (and 1 s decd); *Career* house physician: St Bartholomew's Hosp 1949, Evelina Children's Hosp 1950; jr registrar St Bartholomew's 1955, GP 1957-; Apothecary to TRH The Prince and Princess of Wales 1983-91; chm of Cncl RCGP 1976-79, memb Medicines Cmmn 1976-, memb Ct of Assets Worshipful soc of Apothecaries; FRCGP; *Style—* Dr Michael Linnett, OBE; 82 Sloane St, London SW1X 9PA (☎ 071 245 9333); 37 Ashcombe St, London SW6 3AW (☎ 071 736 2487)

LINNETT, Simon John Lawrence; s of Prof John Wilfrid Linnett (d 1975), and Rae Ellen Fanny, *née* Libgott; *b* 14 Feb 1954; *Educ* The Leys Cambridge, Balliol Coll Oxford; *m* 28 Nov 1987, Penelope Jane, da of Sir Charles William Willink, Bt, of Highgate, London; *Career* NM Rothschild & Sons Ltd: joined 1975, mangr 1982, asst dir 1984, dir 1987, dir Exec Ctee 1989; *Recreations* environmental issues walking; *Style—* Simon Linnett, Esq; c/o N M Rothschild & Sons Limited, New Court, St

Swithin's Lane, London EC4P 4DU (☎ 071 280 5062)

LINSELL, Richard Duncan; s of Dr William Duncan Linsell, of Ipswich, and Margaret Sybil, *née* Burns; *b* 21 June 1947; *Educ* Mill Hill Sch, Jesus Coll Cambridge (MA); *m* 25 Oct 1985, Briony Margaret, da of Dr James Wright Anderton Crabtree, OBE, TD (Col and former QHP), of Devon; 1 da (Katherine Jemima Cory b 14 Oct 1987); *Career* admitted slr 1973, ptnr Rowe & Maw 1976-; memb: Law Soc, Int Bar Assoc; *Recreations* music, golf, walking; *Style—* Richard Linsell, Esq; 20 Black Friars Lane, London EC4V 6HD (☎ 071 248 4282, telex 262787, fax 071 248 2009)

LINTHWAITE, Peter John Nicholas; s of John Linthwaite, ISO, of Johannesburg, SA, and June Margaret Fiennes, *née* Nicoll; *b* 3 Dec 1956; *Educ* Bedford Modern Sch, New Coll Oxford (BA); *m* 18 Sept 1982, Gillian Deborah, da of Rei Oblitas, OBE, ED; *Career* vice pres Bank of America NT (SA, London and Hong Kong) 1978-86, Standard Chartered Bank Hong Kong 1986-87, dir Tranwood Earl and Co Ltd 1987-90, dir Murray Johnstone Developments Ltd; *Recreations* cricket, skiing, bridge, ballet; *Clubs* MCC, RAC; *Style—* Peter Linthwaite, Esq; 123 Sloane St, London SW1X 9BW (☎ 071 730 3412, fax 071 730 5770, car 0836 627509, telex 932016)

LINTON, Prof Alan Henry; s of Henry Miles Linton (d 1988), of Bristol, and Amelia Jane, *née* Parsley; *b* 29 Jan 1925; *Educ* St George GS Bristol, Univ of Bristol (BSc, MSc, PhD, DSc); *m* 4 April 1948, Muriel Hilda, da of George Reginald Speare (d 1988), of Bristol; 1 s (Stephen Paul b 10 May 1950), 1 da (Joy Esther b 10 July 1952, d 1974); *Career* biochemist Glaxo Laboratories 1945-46, prof of bacteriology Univ of Bristol 1983-90 (asst bacteriologist 1946-51, lectr 1951-63, sr lectr 1963-77, reader 1977-83, prof emeritus 1990-); memb Veterinary Products Ctee 1981-88 and 1990; FRCPath, Hon ARCVS; *Books* An Introduction to the Biology of Microorganisms, Microorganisms Function, Form and Environment, Microbes, Man and Animals, Disinfection in Veterinary and Farm Animal Practice, I Will Build My Church, Principles of Bacteriology, Virology and Immunology (ed and contrib 8 edn, Vol I); *Style—* Prof Alan Linton; 18 Romney Avenue, Bristol BS7 9TN (☎ 0272 515159)

LINTOTT, Sir Henry John Bevis; KCMG (1957, CMG 1948); s of late Henry John Lintott, RSA, and Edith, *née* Lunn; *b* 23 Sept 1908; *Educ* Edinburgh Acad, Univ of Edinburgh, Kings Coll Cambridge; *m* 1940, Margaret Orpen; 1 s, 1 da; *Career* entered Customs and Excise Dept 1932, Bd of Trade 1935-48, dep sec-gen OEEC 1948-56, dep under sec of state Cwlth Rels Office 1956-63, Br high cmmr in Canada 1963-68; co dir; *Style—* Sir Henry Lintott, KCMG; 12 Willow Walk, Cambridge (☎ 0223 312410)

LINTOTT, Robert Edward; s of Charles Edward Lintott (d 1981), and Doris Mary Lintott (d 1989); *b* 14 Jan 1932; *Educ* Cambridgeshire HS, Trinity Coll Cambridge (MA); *m* 26 July 1958, Mary Alice, da of Canon Frank Hope Scott (d 1971), of Hull; 3 s (Mark b 1959, John b 1961, Benedict b 1965); *Career* Nat Serv PO RAF 1951-52; Esso Petroleum Co/Esso UK 1955-86: dir logistics 1979-81, dir mktg 1981-83, md 1983-86; chief exec The Coverdale Organization plc 1987-; memb cncl: Royal Borough Windsor and Maidenhead 1987-91 (chm Leisure Servs Ctee 1988-91), Manchester Business Sch; chm: Exec Ctee Fndn for Mgmnt Educn, Oxford Summer Business Sch; CBIM, FInstPet; *Recreations* vintage motoring, cricket; *Clubs* RAF, MCC; *Style—* Robert Lintott, Esq; Huish Barton, Watchet, Somerset TA23 0LU (☎ 0984 402 08); La Queyrie Basse, Tremolat 24510, France; The Coverdale Organisation plc, Dorland House, 14-16 Regent St, London SW1 (☎ 071 925 0099, fax 071 491 7636, telex 295956 CTLCOVG)

LIPFRIEND, His Hon Judge Alan; s of Israel Lipfriend (d 1931), and Sarah Lipfriend (d 1970); *b* 6 Oct 1916; *Educ* Central Fndn Sch London, Queen Mary Coll London (BSc); *m* 1948, Adele Burke; 1 s; *Career* design staff Hawker Aircraft Ltd 1939-48; called to the Bar Middle Temple 1948, pres Appeal Tbnl (England and Wales) under Wireless and Telegraphy Act (1949) 1971-73, circuit judge 1973-, memb Parole Bd 1978-81; govr Queen Mary Coll 1981-89, govr and tstee Central Fndr Sch 1985-, fell Queen Mary Coll 1987; *Recreations* theatre, sport; *Clubs* RAC; *Style—* His Hon Judge Lipfriend; 27 Edmunds Walk, London N2 OHU (☎ 081 883 4420)

LIPKIN, Dr Malcolm Leyland; s of Dr Reuben Lipkin (d 1944), of Liverpool, and Evelyne, *née* Urding (d 1982); *b* 2 May 1932; *Educ* Liverpool Coll, RCM London, Univ of London (BMus, DMus); *m* 5 Aug 1968, Judith Eda, da of Jacob Frankel (d 1968), of Port Elizabeth, S Africa; 1 s (Jonathan b 21 Sept 1970); *Career* lectr in music Univ of Oxford Dept of Ext Studies 1967-75, lectr Univ of Kent at Canterbury Sch of Continuing Educn 1975-; composer; premieres incl: Piano Sonata no 3 (Gaudeamus Fndn Int Music Week Holland) 1951, Piano Sonata no 4 (Cheltenham Festival) 1955, Piano Concerto (Cheltenham Festival) 1959, Violin Concerto no 2 (Bournemouth Symphony Orch) 1963, Sinfonia di Roma Symphony no 1 (Royal Liverpool Philharmonic) 1966, Psalm 96 for chorus and orch (John Lewis Partnership cmmn) 1969, Clifford's Tower (Cheltenham Festival) 1980, Five Songs (BBC London) 1981, Harp Trio (Rye Festival) 1982, Naboth's Vineyard (Law Soc concerts) 1983, The Pursuit Symphony no 2 (BBC Philharmonic Manchester) 1983, Wind Quintet (BBC cmmn) 1986, Prelude and Dance in memory of Jacqueline du Pré (City of London Festival) 1988, Piano Sonata no 5 (Gt Comp Festival) 1989, Oboe Concerto (BBC cmmn) 1990; numerous recordings, broadcasts and performances worldwide; memb exec ctee Composers Guild of GB 1972-76; ARCM, LRAM; *Books* illustrated incl: Handel at Work (1963), A History of Western Music (1974), Casals and the Art of Interpretation (1976), The Nine Symphonies of Beethoven (1981), Tortelier, A Self-Portrait (1984), A Companion to the Concerto (1988); *Recreations* long country walks, travelling; *Style—* Dr Malcolm Lipkin; Penlan, Crowborough Hill, Crowborough, Sussex TN6 2EA (☎ 0892 652454)

LIPMAN, Dr Harald Martin; s of Dr Isaac Lipman (d 1955), and Dr Rachel Lipman, *née* Caplan (d 1964); *b* 10 Dec 1931; *Educ* City of London Sch, UCH (MB BS, DCH); *m* 19 April 1959, Nahid, da of Jacoub Sahim, of USA; 1 s (Marc b 1963), 1 da (Amanda b 1961); *Career* dir Small Wonder Ltd 1965-, med advsr Transcare Int 1977-87, conslt physician Repub of the Sudan 1980-87, regnl med advsr Br Embassy Moscow 1987-90; chm Moscow Med Assoc 1987-90, med advsr FCO; memb: GB-USSR Assoc, Iran Soc, Tibet Soc, Med Soc for study of Venereal Diseases; memb Worshipful Soc of Apothecaries, Freeman City of London; MRCGP, FRSM; *Recreations* skiing, tennis; *Clubs* City Livery; *Style—* Dr Harald Lipman; 43 Wimpole Street, London W1M 7AF

LIPPINCOTT, Hon Mrs (Caroline); yr da of Baron Seebohm, TD (Life Peer, d 1990), and Evangeline, *née* Hurst (d 1990); *b* 1940; *Educ* Oxford; *m* 1, 1962 (m dis 1967), Roger John Smith; m 2, 1974, Walter H Lippincott; 1 s (Hugh b 1982), 1 da (Sophie b 1978); *Career* writer; *Style—* The Hon Mrs Lippincott; 1 River Knoll Drive, Titusville, NJ 08560, USA

LIPSCOMB, Dr David John; s of John Francis Lipscomb (d 1986), and Dorothy *née* Waterhouse; *b* 19 Oct 1945; *Educ* Tonbridge, Guys Hosp London (MB BS); *m* 13 May 1972, Isobel Mary, da of Gordon Leslie May, OBE, of Walsall House, 40 The High St, Upnor, nr Rochester, Kent; 3 da (Katy b 2 Sept 1975, Sophie b 17 Jan 1977, Emily b 3 Oct 1982); *Career* sr registrar Addenbrooke's and Papworth Hosps Cambridge 1978-80, conslt physician Basingstoke Dist Hosp 1980-; contrib numerous articles on ultrasound of the pleura; memb: Br Thoracic Soc, BMA, HCSA; FRCP 1988; *Recreations* sailing, golf, skiing, tennis; *Style—* Dr David Lipscomb; High Bank House, Elm Road, Sherborne St John, Hampshire RG24 9HJ (☎ 0256 850 849); Basingstoke District Hospital, Aldermaston Rd; The Hampshire Clinic, Basing Rd, Basingstoke, Hampshire (☎ 0256 473202)

LIPSCOMB, (Edwin) Paul; s of Dr George Lipscomb (d 1979), and Kathleen A Lipscomb; *b* 9 Sept 1933; *m* 17 June 1961, Pauline Ann, da of Capt Henry John Farrell Palliser (d 1937); 1 s (Christopher John Farrell b 1962), 1 da (Catherine Ann Farrell b 1965); *Career* Nat Serv The Green Howards 1952-54, TA The Green Howards 1955-61, retd as Capt; CA Touche Ross & Co 1955-62; fin dir: Biscuits Belin France Nabisco 1962-64, Levitt & Sons France 1964-65; euro controller France Mead Corpn 1965-68, mangr fin controls Belgium HQ ITT Europe 1968-72, div dir London IHQ Rank Xerox 1972-75, exec vice pres Amsterdam and London Cinema Int Corpn 1975-82, fin controller BA 1982-85; gp dir Borthwicks plc 1985-89, JW Spear & Sons plc 1989-; tstee Fortune Centre for Riding Therapy; FCA, FBIM, AFST; *Recreations* travel, food & wine; *Clubs* Naval & Military; *Style—* Paul Lipscomb, Esq; Group Finance Director, JW Spear & Sons plc, Richard House, Enstone Rd, Enfield, Middx EN3 7TB (☎ 081 805 4848, fax 081 804 2426, telex 893746 SPEAR G)

LIPSCOMBE, Eric Richard; s of Eric Wilfred Lipscombe (d 1965), and Frances Selina Emma, *née* Cowdrey (d 1985); *b* 23 June 1938; *Educ* Churchers Coll Hants; *m* 5 March 1966, Rosemary Christine Frances, da of Maj Harold Ernest White (d 1978); 1 s (Guy b 1968), 2 da (Sophie b 1970, Emily b 1975); *Career* Nat Serv 1960-62, Asst Adj to Sch of Mil Engrg; vice pres Teradata Corp (USA), md Teradata Europe Ltd, chm Teradata UK Ltd; dir: Teradata Deutschland GMBH, Teradata France SA, Teradata Italia; non-exec chm: Euro Mktg Conslts, DPP (Hldgs) Ltd; fndr chm and md Computer Peripherals Ltd and subsidiaries 1979-84, dir Micro Business Systems plc 1984-86; Hants Rugby player, memb Richmond FC 1962-66; CEng, MICE; *Recreations* sport, music; *Clubs* East India; *Style—* Eric R Lipscombe, Esq; Bridgend House, Ockham, nr Ripley, Surrey (☎ 0483 222007); Teradata Europe Ltd, Alwyn House, 31 Windsor St, Chertsey, Surrey (☎ 0932 567777)

LIPSEY, David Lawrence; s of Lawrence Lipsey, and Penelope Lipsey; *b* 21 April 1948; *Educ* Bryanston Sch, Magdalene Coll Oxford (BA); *m* 1982, Margaret Robson; 1 da; *Career* journalist; res asst GMWU 1970-72, special advsr to Anthony Crosland MP 1972-77 (DOE 1974-76, FCO 1976-77), PM's Staff 10 Downing St 1977-79, journalist New Society 1979-80; econ ed Sunday Times 1982-86 (political staff 1980-82), ed New Society 1986-88, fndr and jt dep ed Sunday Correspondent 1988-90, assoc ed The Times 1990-; sec Streatham Lab Pty 1970-72, chm Fabian Soc 1981-82, memb Exec Ctee Charter for Jobs 1984-86; *Books* Labour and Land (1974), The Socialist Agenda: Crosland's Legacy (co-ed Dick Leonard, 1981), Making Government Work (1982); *Recreations* family life; *Style—* David Lipsey, Esq; 44 Drakefield Rd, London SW17 8RP (☎ 081 767 3268)

LIPTON, Prof Michael; s of Leslie Lipton (d 1977), and Helen, *née* Janssen; *b* 13 Feb 1937; *Educ* Haberdasher's Aske's, Balliol Coll Oxford (BA, MA), Mass Inst of Technol; *m* 9 Dec 1966, Merle, da of Charles Babrow (d 1979); 1 s (Emanuel b 1 March 1974); *Career* res offr with G Myrdal on Asian Drama 1960-61, fell All Souls Coll Oxford 1961-68 and 1982-84, fell of Inst of Devpt Studies and professorial fell Univ of Sussex 1971-77, 1979-87, 1990- (asst lectr 1961-62, lectr 1962-66, reader 1966-71), employment devpt advsr Govt of Botswana 1977-78, sr policy advsr World Bank 1981-82, prog dir consumption and nutrition prog Int Food Policy Res Inst Washington DC 1988-89; ed Jl of Devpt Studies 1968-80, chm Br Assoc for South Asian Studies 1985-87; numerous papers and pubns in jls; Hon DLitt Univ of Sussex 1982; *Publications* The Erosion of a Relationship: India and Britain since 1960 (with J Firn, 1975), Chess Problems: Introduction to an Art (with R Matthews and J Rice, 1962), Assessing Economic Performance (1968), The Crisis of Indian Planning (with P Streeten, 1968), Migration from Rural Areas: The Evidence from Village Studies (with J Connell, 1976), Why Poor People Stay Poor: Urban Bias and World Devt (1977), Botswana: Employment and Labour Use (1979), New Seeds and Poor People (1989), Aid to India: Does it Work? (with J Toye 1990); *Clubs* United Oxford & Cambridge Univ; *Style—* Prof Michael Lipton; Institute of Development Studies, University of Sussex, Brighton BN2 1EH (☎ 0273 678274, fax 0273 678420, telex 877997 IDSBTN G)

LIPTON, Stuart Anthony; s of Bertram Green, of London, and Jeanette Lipton; *b* 9 Nov 1942; *Educ* Berkhamsted Sch; *m* 16 June 1966, Ruth Kathryn, da of Harry Marks (d 1987), of London; 2 s (Elliot Steven b 17 March 1969, Grant Alexander b 20 Jan 1975), 1 da (Sarah Joanna b 15 June 1971); *Career* dir: Sterling Land Co 1971-73, First Palace Securities Ltd 1973-76; md Greycoat plc 1976-83, advsr to Hampton Site Co for Sainsbury Bldg Nat Gallery 1985; memb: Advsy Bd Dept of Construction Mgmnt Univ of Reading 1983-, Property Advsy Gp DOE 1986-, Mil Bldgs Ctee MOD 1987-, Cncl Br Property Fedn 1987-; tstee Whitechapel Art Gallery 1987-, cmmr Royal Fine Art Cmmn; memb: Cncl ICA 1986-, Bd Nat Theatre 1988-, Advsy Bd RA 1987, Governing Bd Imperial Coll 1987-; RIBA; *Recreations* architecture, crafts, art and technology, wine; *Style—* Stuart Lipton, Esq; Lansdowne House, Berkeley Square, London W1X 6BP (☎ 071 495 7575)

LIPWORTH, Sir (Maurice) Sydney; s of Isadore Lipworth (d 1966), of Johannesburg, SA, and Rae, *née* Sindler (d 1983); *b* 13 May 1931; *Educ* King Edward VII Sch Johannesburg, Univ of Witwatersrand Johannesburg (BCom, LLB); *m* 1957, Rosa, da of Bernard Liwarek (d 1943); 2 s (Bertrand, Frank); *Career* dep chm Allied Dunbar Assurance plc (formerly Hambro Life Assurance plc) 1984-88 (dir 1971-88, jt md 1980-84); chm: Allied Dunbar & Co plc, Allied Dunbar Unit Tsts plc 1985-88 (md 1983-85); dir: J Rothschild Holdings plc 1984-87, BAT Industries plc 1985-88; chm Monopolies and Mergers Cmmn 1988- (memb 1981-); tstee: Allied Dunbar Charitable Tst 1973, Philharmonia Orchestra 1982-, Royal Acad 1987-; govr Sadler's Wells Tst 1986-89; *Recreations* tennis, music, theatre; *Clubs* Queens, Reform; *Style—* Sir Sydney Lipworth; Monopolies and Mergers Commission, New Court, 48 Carey Street, London WC2A 2JT (☎ 071 324 1423)

LIRONI, Mark Creig; *b* 3 Oct 1937; *Educ* Bell Baxter HS Cupar, Edinburgh Coll of Art, Univ of Strathclyde Glasgow (Dip, TP); *m* 13 May 1961, Marjory; 2 s (Stephen b 1963, Graham b 1964), 2 da (Kathryn b 1966, Joanna b 1980); *Career* architect; fndr ptnr Cobban and Lironi (architects, planning conslts and engrs) 1973-; dir: Cobban & Lironi 1987-, Dumbarton Stabilisers Ltd 1987, Hotels Devpt Consortium Ltd 1985; 1984; Suil Scotland Ltd 1981; *Recreations* golf; *Clubs* Cathkin Braes GC; *Style—* Mark C Lironi, Esq; Cobban & Lironi, Park House, Park Circus Place, Glasgow G3 6AN (☎ 041 333 9466)

LIS, David George; s of Henry George Lis, of Penrith, Cumbria, and Irene Isabel Lis (d 1965); *b* 8 Feb 1950; *Educ* Queen Elizabeth GS Penrith Cumbria, Newcastle Upon Tyne Poly (HND); *m* 1, 10 June 1972 (m dis 1986), Patricia Ann, da of William Stredwick, of Yarm, N Yorks; 3 da (Emily b 1976, Katie b 1978, Sophie b 1981); m 2, Patricia Margaret, da of Ronald Teasdale (d 1980); 1 da (Stephanie b 1988), 1 step s (Ben b 1977), 1 step da (Nicola b 1980); *Career* investmt analyst NatWest Bank 1972-79; fund mangr: Carliol Investment Trust 1979-80, Target Unit Trust Managers 1980-84; investmt dir Baltic Trust Managers 1985, md Windsor Trust Managers and Windsor Investment Management 1985-90, dir Capital House Asset Management 1990-; *Recreations* golf, tennis, skiing, gardening; *Clubs* Lansdowne, Hadley Wood Golf; *Style—* David Lis, Esq; 57 Crescent West, Hadley Wood, Herts EN4 0EQ (☎

081 440 3469); Windsor House, 83 Kingsway, London WC2B 6SD (☎ 071 831 7373, fax 071 405 7472)

LISBURNE, 8 Earl of (I 1776); Capt John David Malet Vaughan; also Viscount Lisburne and Baron Fethard (I 1695); the eld s & h appears to have been styled Lord Vaughan since 1776; s of 7 Earl of Lisburne (d 1965); *b* 1 Sept 1918; *Educ* Eton, Magdalen Coll Oxford; *m* 1943, Shelagh, da of late T A Macauley, of Montreal, Canada; 3 s; *Heir* s, Viscount Vaughan; *Career* 2 Lt Welsh Gds 1939, Capt 1943, served 1939-45; barr Inner Temple; dir: British Home Stores plc 1961-87, S Wales Regnl Bd Lloyds Bank Ltd 1978-88, Nationwide Anglia Building Society (Welsh Bd), ret 1990; govr UCW; pres Wales Cncl for Voluntary Action; memb Exec Ctee AA 1981-88; *Clubs* Buck's, Pratt's, Turf; *Style*— The Rt Hon the Earl of Lisburne; Cruglas, Ystrad Meurig, Dyfed (097 45 230)

LISHMAN, Prof (William) Alwyn; s of George Hackworth Lishman (d 1984), and Madge Scott, *née* Young (d 1980); *b* 16 May 1931; *Educ* Houghton Le Spring GS, Univ of Birmingham (BSc, MB, ChB, MD, DPM, DSc, MRCP, Gaskell Gold medal Medico Psychological Assoc 1965); *m* 4 June 1966, Marjorie, da of Cecil Victor Loud (d 1987); 1 s (James William Michael b 1973), 1 da (Victoria Alison b 1971); *Career* Maj RAMC Wheatley Military Hospital Oxfordshire 1957-59; registrar in neurology United Oxford Hospitals 1959-60, registrar then sr registrar in pschiatry Maudsley Hospital London 1960-66, conslt psychiatrist Nat Hospital Queen Sq London 1966-67, sr lectr in psychological med Royal Postgrad Med Sch Hammersmith London 1967-69, conslt psychiatrist 1967-74 (Bethlem Royal Hospital, Maudsley Hospital), prof of neuropsychiatry Institute of Psychiatry London 1979- (reader 1974-79), visiting fell Green Coll Oxford 1983; dep chm Neurosciences Bd Medical Res Cncl 1976-77 (memb 1974-78); scientific advsr: DHSS 1979-82, Brain Res Tst 1986-; Chm Br Neuropsychiatry Assoc 1987-, civilian conslt RAF 1987, examiner and memb Bd of Examiners Univ of Oxford 1975-79; memb: Editorial Bds of numerous scientific journals, Experimental Psychology Soc 1975-, assoc of Br Neurologists 1979; guarantor of BRAIN 1984; FRCP 1972, FRCPsych 1972; *Books* Organic Pschiatry: The Psychological Consequences of Cerebral Disorder (1978, 2 edn 1987); *Recreations* organ, piano, harpsichord, travelling; *Style*— Prof Alwyn Lishman; 9 Elwill Way, Beckenham, Kent BR3 3AB; Institute of Psychiatry, De Crespigny Park, London SE5 8AF (☎ 071 703 5411)

LISLE, 7 Baron (I 1758); John Nicholas Horace Lysaght; s of Horace George Lysaght (d 1918), and Alice, da of Sir John Wrixon-Becher, 3 Bt; gs of 6 Baron (d 1919); *b* 10 Aug 1903; *m* 1, 1928 (m dis 1939), Vivienne (d 1948), da of Rev M Brew; m 2, 1939, Marie, da of A D Purgold, of Salop; *Heir* n, Patrick Lysaght; *Style*— The Rt Hon the Lord Lisle; 4 Bramerton St, London SW3

LISSER, Hon Mrs (June Lisette); *née* May; da of 2 Baron May (d 1950); *b* 1929; *Educ* St Paul's Girls' Sch; *m* 1958, Raymond Charles Lisser, o s of Henry Charles Lisser (d 1936), of Nottingham; 1 s (Aidan Charles b 1959); *Style*— The Hon Mrs Lisser; School House, Stanton, Broadway, Worcs WR12 7NE

LIST; *see*: Appleyard-List

LISTER, Anthony Charles Bramham; s of David Bramham Lister (d 1980), and Monica Joan, *née* Russell; *b* 31 Aug 1939; *Educ* Sutton Valence, Coll of Estate Mgmnt St Albans Grove London; *m* 1 June 1963, Susan Kitty, da of (Harold) Norman Funnell, of Great Paddock Farm, Challock, Ashford; 3 s (Giles Anthony Bramham b 12 Jan 1966, Timothy Norman Bramham (twin) b 12 Jan 1966, Guy Bramham b 16 Oct 1968); *Career* equity ptnr Geering and Colyer Chartered Surveyors 1972-82, Black Horse Agencies 1982-90, Keswick Holdings Ltd 1990; Freeman City of London 1961, Liveryman Worshipful Co of Leathersellers 1964 (Freeman 1961, 3 Warden 1988-89); AMBIM 1968, FRICS 1970; *Recreations* sheep farming, golf, sailing; *Clubs* Rye Golf, Whitstable Sailing; *Style*— Anthony Lister, Esq; Dean Court, Westwell, Ashford, Kent TN25 4NH (☎ 0233 712924); Keswick Holdings Ltd, Kent House, Station Rd, Ashford, Kent TN23 1PP (☎ 0233 640220)

LISTER, David; s of Frank Charles Lister (d 1973), of Grimsby, and Doris May Lister (d 1989); *b* 18 April 1930; *Educ* Humberston Fndn Sch Cleethorpes, Downing Coll Cambridge (BA, MA); *m* 6 Sept 1956, Margaret, da of Herbert Walter Crampin, OBE (d 1974), of Grimsby; 2 s (Richard b 1961, Mark b 1965), 1 da (Frances b 1958); *Career* Nat Serv RAF 1948-50; Wilkin and Chapman Solicitors Grimsby: articled clerk 1953, asst slr 1956, ptnr 1962-90; legal sec (formerly sec) Grimsby and Cleethorpes Church Extension Soc 1963-, chm S Humberside Marriage Guidance Cncl 1969-73, lay chm Grimsby and Cleethorpes Deanery Synod 1970-71; pres: Grimsby and Cleethorpes Law Soc 1979-80, Rotary Club Cleethorpes 1986-87; chm The Flag Inst 1983-, vice pres Br Origami Soc 1988- (chm 1972-75); memb Law Soc; *Recreations* heraldry and flags, paperfolding, study of playing cards, Arthurian literature and history, folklore, old roses, swimming; *Style*— David Lister, Esq; Candletrees, 21 Vaughan Avenue, Grimsby (☎ 0472 692033)

LISTER, Dr John; s of Thomas Lister (d 1967) of London, and Anna Rebecca Black (d 1987); *b* 8 Aug 1920; *Educ* St Paul's, St Johns Coll Cambridge (MD), St Bartholomews Hosp (MD); *m* 3 July 1943, Eileen Doris, da of Thomas Trafford (d 1945), of London; 3 s (Thomas Andrew b 1944, Ian Wilson b 1948 (d 1966), Robert William b 1953); *Career* RAMC 1944-47; conslt physician; King Edward VII Hosp Windsor 1953-84, post grad dean NW Thames Region (Univ of London) 1972-85, Lincre Fell RCP 1985-, numerous papers and diabetes melitus and post grad med educn, author of By The London Post column in the New England Jl of Med 1952-80; hon fell American Coll of Physicians 1983, FRCP; *Books* The Clinical Syndrome of Diabetes Mellitus (1959), By The London Post Collected essays 1985); *Recreations* golf, walking, writing; *Clubs* New (Edinburgh), Hon Co of Edinburgh Golfers; *Style*— Dr John Lister; Farm End, Burkes Rd, Beaconsfield, Bucks HP9 1PB (☎ 0494 674393)

LISTER, John Thomas; s of Albert William Lister (d 1978), of Cardiff, and Joan Trenear, *née* Tarr; *b* 26 Nov 1941; *Educ* Cardiff HS; *m* 1988, Mary; 2 s (Stephen b 29 July 1967, Andrew b 17 Sept 1975), 1 da (Victoria b 13 Nov 1979); *Career* athletics administrator; former athlete Wales 1959-70 and Cardiff Amateur Athletic Club; events competed at: 110m hurdles, decathlon, long jump, high jump (former Welsh record holder); hon treas: Cardiff Amateur Athletic Club 1968- (former pres and chm), AAA 1986-; memb Cncl BAAB, dir London Marathon; qualified CA 1964, dir and shareholder Euro Investments Ltd, chm Hicking Pentecost plc; *Recreations* athletics; *Style*— John Lister, Esq; 1 The Paddock, Lisvane, Cardiff CF4 5AY (☎ 0222 747734)

LISTER, Joseph; s of Joe Moon Lister (d 1965), and Ethel Macaulay; *b* 14 May 1930; *Educ* Cheltenham Coll; *m* Sheila May Lister; 1 s (Joseph Charles Lister b 9 July 1966); *Career* Nat Serv 1948-53 (played for Army Cricket XI and Combined Servs); became sec Worcestershire CCC 1956 (asst sec and player 1954-56), sec Yorkshire CCC 1971- (longest serving sec First-Class County Cricket)-; *Style*— Joseph Lister, Esq; Wyndley, Crag Lane, Huby, Leeds LS17 0BW (☎ 0423 734559)

LISTER, Dr (Herbert) Keith Norton; s of Maj Herbert Victor Lister (d 1934), of Saxon Lodge, Seaford, Sussex, and Kathleen, *née* Norton (d 1965); *b* 5 Dec 1922; *Educ* Eastbourne Coll, Queens' Coll Cambridge (BA, MA); *m* 1, 6 May 1950 (m dis 1979), Esther, da of Cdr Godfrey Wigram-Arkwright, DSO (d 1953), of Youngsbury, Ware, Herts; 2 s (John b 1954, Tom b 1956), 2 da (Jane (Mrs Allen) b 1951, Sarah b 1952); m 2, 25 June 1980, Caroline, da of Leslie Thomas Lawrence (d 1975), of Porlock, Somerset; 1 s (Christopher b 1982), 1 da (Lucie b 1979); *Career* med Capt and Temp Maj TA 1952; GP: Harlow Essex 1951-60, Minehead and Porlock Somerset 1960-83; asst surgn Minehead Hosp 1960; co MO Br Red Cross Essex Div 1952, fndr memb Ctee Pony Riding for the Disabled, chm Abbeyfield Porlock Soc, vice chm and govr St Dubricius Sch Porlock; memb ctee: St Margarets Hospice Taunton, Abbeyfield Withcare Taunton; published several articles on gardening 1985-89, subject of recent garden TV documentary and article in Country Living Magazine; MRCS, LRCP; memb: RHS, Int Camellia Soc, Int Dendrological Soc; *Recreations* gardening, tennis; *Style*— Dr Keith Lister; Chapel Knap, Porlock, Weir, Somerset TA24 8PA (☎ 0643 862364)

LISTER, Vicomtesse d'Orthez Moira; da of Maj JM Lister (d 1971), of SA, and Margaret Winifred, *née* Hogan (d 1951); *b* 6 Aug 1923; *Educ* Parktown Convent Johannesburg SA; *m* 23 Dec 1951, Jacques Gachassin-Lafite Vicomte d'Orthez s of Vicomte André d'Orthez (d 1924); 2 da (Chantal (Mrs d'Orthez-Burke) b 1954, Christobel b 1962); *Career* early theatrical appearances: Juliet, Desdemona, Olivia and Kate Hardcastle at the Shakespeare Memorial Theatre (toured Europe with the co when it was led by Sir John Gielgud, 1943-58); world tour with People In Love (one woman show 1958-59); appearances in Successful W End Prodns: Present Laughter (with Sir Noel Coward), Love of Four Colonels (with Peter Ustinov), The Gazebo, Devil May Care (with Ian Carmichael), Birthday Honours, Any Wednesday (with Dennis Price), Getting Married (1967); S African prodns: The Sleeping Prince, Bedtime Story (with Derek Nimmo); recent theatrical performances: Move over Mrs Markham, A Woman Named Anne, Twigs; film appearances : The Yellow Rolls Royce (with Rex Harrison), Seven Waves Away (with Tyrone Power), The Deep Blue Sea (with Vivien Leigh), The Double Man (with Yul Brynner); TV appearances: on top TV panel shows, and with Bob Hope and Maurice Shevalierm in her own comedy series The Very Merry Widow (written by Alan Melville), in her own series reading classic short stories, Simon and Laura, Major Barbara; nominated Best TV Actress of the Year for her performance in The Concert (1962), winner of The Variety of GB's Silver Heart Award for the Best Stage Actress (1971); *Books* The Very Merry Moira (1971); *Recreations* windsurfing, golf, swimming, writing, travel; *Style*— Miss Moira Lister

LISTER, Paul Kenneth; s of Eric Lister, of Yeovil, Somerset, and Molly Ada Patience; *b* 7 Aug 1952; *Educ* Birmingham Sch of Architecture (Dip Arch), Univ of Aston (BSc); *Career* ptnr Assoc Architects Birmingham 1984- (joined 1976), dir Assoc Architects Ltd London; fndr memb Birmingham Young Architects' Gp, memb Ctee Birmingham Architectural Assoc 1985-87 and 1988-; MRIBA 1979; *Style*— Paul Lister, Esq; Associated Architects, 35 St Pauls Square, Birmingham B3 1QX (☎ 021 233 2526, fax 021 200 1564, telex 265871 MONREF G MNU 520)

LISTER, Raymond George; s of Horace Lister (d 1971), and Ellen Maud Mary, *née* Arnold; *b* 28 March 1919; *Educ* Cambridge and County HS for Boys, St John's Coll Sch Cambridge; *m* 1947, Pamela Helen, da of Frank Bishop Brutnell; 1 s, 1 da; *Career* author, artist, co dir; dir: George Lister & Sons Ltd 1941-, John P Gray & Sons Ltd 1978-83; fell Wolfson Coll Cambridge; pres: Royal Soc of Miniature Painters Sculptors and Gravers 1970-80, Architectural Metalwork Assoc 1975-77; chm Bd of Govrs Fedn of British Artists 1976-80, a syndic Fitzwilliam Museum Cambridge 1981-89; Liveryman Worshipful Co of Blacksmiths' 1957- (memb Ct of Assts 1980-, Prime Warden 1989-90), Hon LittD Univ of Cambridge; *BooksPublications* The Letters of Samuel Palmer (1974), Prints and Printmaking (1984), Samuel Palmer and 'The Ancients' (1984), The Paintings of Samuel Palmer (1985), The Paintings of William Blake (1986), Samuel Palmer: His Life and Art (1987), Catalogue Raisonné of the Works of Samuel Palmer (1988), British Romantic Painting (1989); *Clubs* Athenaeum, Sette of Odd Volumes; *Style*— Dr Raymond Lister; Windmill House, Linton, Cambridge CB1 6NS (☎ 0223 891248)

LISTER, Prof (Margot) Ruth Aline; da of Dr Werner Bernard Lister, of Manchester, and Daphne, *née* Carter; *b* 3 May 1949; *Educ* Moreton Hall School, Univ of Essex (BA), Univ of Sussex (MA); *Career* dir Child Poverty Action Gp 1979-87 (legal res offr 1971-75, asst dir 1975-77, dep dir 1977-79), prof applied social studies Univ of Bradford 1987-; tstee Money Advice Tst; memb: mgmnt ctee Bradford CAB, Bradford Common Purpose, Bradford Fairweather Project; Hon LLD Univ of Manchester 1987; *Books* Supplementary Benefit Rights (1974), Welfare Benefits (1981), The Exclusive Society (1990), numerous pamphlets and chapters in books; *Recreations* walking, meditation, tai chi, reading, music, women's group; *Style*— Prof Ruth Lister; 26 Lynton Drive, Bradford BD9 5JT; Dept of Applied Social Studies, Univ of Bradford, W Yorks BD7 1DP (☎ 0274 733 466 ext 8258, fax 0274 305 340)

LISTER, Dame Unity Viola; DBE (1972, OBE 1959); da of Dr Arthur Sydney Webley (d 1931), and Viola, *née* Hockley (d 1938); *b* 19 June 1913; *Educ* St Helen's Blackheath, The Sorbonne; *m* 1940, Samuel William Lister, s of Victor Edward Lister (d 1954); *Career* memb London CC 1949-65 (dep chm 1963-64), int vice chm Euro Union of Women 1963-69, (memb Exec 1965-), memb Inner London Advsy Ctee on Appt of Magistrates; govr Royal Marsden Hosp 1957-83; chm: Horniman Museum 1967-, Women's Nat Advsy Ctee (Cons) 1966-69, Nat Union of Cons Unionist Assocs 1970-71; memb Exec: Euro Movement 1970-, Cons Gp for Europe 1970-; *Recreations* music, languages, walking, gardening, history; *Clubs* St Stephen's, Europe House; *Style*— Dame Unity Lister, DBE; 32 The Court Yard, Eltham, London SE9 5QE (☎ 081 850 7038)

LISTER-KAYE, Sir John Philip Lister; 8 Bt (UK 1812), of Grange, Yorkshire; s of Sir John Christopher Lister Lister-Kaye, 7 Bt (d 1982), by his 1 w, Audrey Helen (d 1979), da of Edwin James Carter, of Westbury on Trym, Glos; descended from Sir John Kaye, Knight, of Woodsome, Yorkshire living in 1066, and Sir John Kaye of Woodsome created Baronet in 1641 by Charles I, also Lord Mayor of York; This Baronetcy became extinct through illegitimacy in 1810 and Sir John Lister-Kaye of Grange was re-created Baronet in 1812 for services to George III; Sir John Lister-Kaye of Grange 3rd Baronet was groom-in-waiting to Edward VII; *b* 8 May 1946; *Educ* Allhallows Sch; *m* 1, 1972, Lady Sorrel Deirdre Bentinck, da of 11 Earl of Portland; 1 s, 2 da (twins); m 2, 17 Feb 1989, Mrs Lucinda Anne Baillie, eld da of Robin Law, of Withersfield, Suffolk; 1 da (Hermione Anne Lucinda Lorne b 27 Sept 1990); *Heir* s, John Warwick Noel Lister-Kaye b 10 Dec 1974; *Career* naturalist, author, lectr, farmer; dir of Aigas Field Centre Ltd 1977-, fndr dir Scottish Conservation Charity The Aigas Tst 1980-; chm Scottish Advsy Ctee RSPB 1986-; memb: Int Ctee The World Wilderness Fndn 1983, Scottish Advsy Ctee of Nature Conservancy Cncl 1990-91; chm NW Region Nature Conservancy Cncl for Scotland 1991- recipient of Wilderness Soc Gold Award for Conservation 1984; *Books* The White Island (1972), Seal Cull (1979), The Seeing Eye (1980); *Recreations* breeding horses and highland cattle; *Clubs* Farmers', Caledonian; *Style*— Sir John Lister-Kaye, Bt; Aigas House, Beauly, Inverness (☎ 0463 782729; Grange Estate Co Office, 782443)

LISTER-KAYE, Margaret, Lady; Margaret Isabelle; da of Lt-Col Barnaby Duke, TD, JP (d 1959), of Martinstown, Dorchester; *Educ* Sherborne Lady's Coll; *m* 1, 1940, late Rex Lovelace; 1 s (d 1981), 2 da; m 2, 1980, as his 2 w, Sir John Christopher Lister Lister-Kaye, 7 Bt (d 1982); 1 step s (Sir John Lister-Kaye, Bt), 1 step da; *Books* Where Have all the Cowslips Gone? Bishopsgate Press (one chapter);

Recreations hunting, sailing, gardening; *Style*— Margaret, Lady Lister-Kaye; Hawthorne Cottage, Rectory Rd, Piddlehinton, Dorchester, Dorset (☎ 030 04 229)

LISTON, (Edward) Robin; s of David Joel Liston, OBE (d 1990), and Eva Carole, *née* Kauffmann (d 1987); *b* 30 Oct 1947; *Educ* Bryanston, Mercersburg Acad PA USA, Univ of Kent (BA); *m* 6 July 1969 (m dis 1987), Judith Margaret, da of Frederick Tye, CBE; 2 da (Rebecca b 1970, Victoria b 1974); *Career* dist ed Kent Messenger 1969-70, asst ed Benn Bros 1970-72; assoc dir: Forman House PR Ltd 1972-79, Welbeck PR Ltd 1981-84; dir: Carl Byoir Ltd 1984-86, Hill & Knowlton Ltd 1986-88; jt md Buckmans PR 1988-; *Recreations* music, films, railways, suburban architecture; *Style*— Robin Liston, Esq; 26 Southern Rd, London, N2 9JG (☎ 081 883 7314); Buckmans Ltd, 1 Bedford St, London, WC2E 9HD (☎ 071 836 8866)

LISTOWEL, 5 Earl of (I 1822); William Francis Hare; GCMG (1957), PC (1946); also Baron Ennismore (I 1800), Viscount Ennismore and Listowel (I 1816, usually shortened to Viscount Ennismore when used as courtesy title for eldest s and h), and Baron Hare of Convamore (UK 1869, which sits as); s of 4 Earl (d 1931), by his w Hon Freda Vanden-Bempde-Johnstone (da of 2 Baron Derwent); er bro of Lord (1 Viscount) Blakenham and unc of Lord (3 Earl of) Iveagh; *b* 28 Sept 1906; *Educ* Magdalene Coll Cambridge; *m* 1, 1933 (m dis 1945), Judith, da of Raoul de Marffy-Mantuano, of Budapest; 1 da (Lady Grantley); m 2, 1958 (m dis 1963), Stephanie Sandra Yvonne, da of Sam Wise, of Toronto, and formerly w of Hugh Currie; 1 da; m 3, 1963, Pamela, da of Francis Day, of Croydon, and formerly w of John Read; 2 s, 1 da; *Heir* s, Viscount Ennismore; *Career* formerly Lt Intelligence Corps; memb LCC 1937-58; parly under-sec of state India Office 1944-45, also dep ldr House of Lords 1944-45 (Lab whip 1941-44); sec state: India 1947, Burma 1947-48; min state Colonial Affrs 1948-50, jt parly sec Min Agric & MAFF 1950-51; govr-gen Ghana 1957-60; chm Ctees House of Lords 1965-76; *Style*— The Rt Hon Earl of Listowel, GCMG, PC; 10 Downshire Hill, London NW3 (☎ 071 431 3327)

LITCHFIELD, Dame Ruby Beatrice; DBE (1981, OBE 1959); da of Alfred John Skinner and Eva Hanna, *née* Thomas; *b* 5 Dec 1912; *Educ* N Adelaide PS, PGC Glen Osmond SA; *m* 1940, Kenneth Litchfield (d 1976); 1 s; *Career* dir Festival City Broadcasters Ltd SA 1975-86, tstee Adelaide Festival Center Trust SA 1971-82, memb Bd of Govrs Adelaide Festival of Arts 1966-90 (memb Ctee 1960-), vice pres and bd memb Queen Victoria Maternity Hosp 1953-72 (life memb 1972), pres Sportswoman's Assoc 1969-74, mayoress of Prospect SA 1954-57, bd memb The Adelaide Repertory Theatre 1951-68 (life memb 1967), memb Div Cncl Red Cross Soc SA 1955-71, cncllr Royal Dist Bush Nursing Soc 1957-64; bd memb: Crippled Children's Assoc 1976-, Kidney Fndn 1968-, South Australia Housing Tst 1962-70, Telethon Channel 9 1961-86; cncl memb Sudden Infant Death Syndrome Res Fndn 1979-, hon life memb Spastic Paralysis Welfare Assoc Inc, memb Royal Cwlth Assoc; chm Bd of Carclew Youth Performing Arts Centre 1972-88, memb South Australian Davis Cup Ctee 1952, 1963 and 1968, memb SA Ctee Royal Academy of Dancing 1961-66, memb Bd Mary Potter Foundation, chm Mary Potter Fndn Appeal 1988; Queen's Silver Jubilee medal 1977, Advance Australia award 1985, South Australia Great award 1987; *Recreations* tennis (hardcourt tennis champion 1932-35); *Style*— Dame Ruby Litchfield, DBE

LITHERLAND, Robert Kenneth; MP (Lab) Manchester Central (by-election) Sept 1979-; s of Robert Litherland and Mary, *née* Parry; *b* 1930; *Educ* N Manchester HS for Boys; *m* 1953, Edna; 1 s, 1 da; *Style*— Robert Litherland, Esq, MP; 32 Darley Avenue, Didsbury, Manchester M20 8YD

LITHGOW, Sir William James; 2 Bt (UK 1925), of Ormsary, Co Argyll, DL (Renfrewshire 1970); s of Sir James Lithgow, 1 Bt, GBE, CB, MC, TD, JP, DL (d 1952); *b* 10 May 1934; *Educ* Winchester; *m* 1, 1964, Valerie Helen (d 1964), da of Denis Herbert Scott, CBE (d 1958); m 2, 1967, Mary Claire, da of Col F M Hill, CBE, of East Knoyle, Wilts; 2 s, 1 da; *Heir* s, James Frank Lithgow b 13 June 1970; *Career* industrialist and farmer; chm: Lithgows Ltd 1959-84 and 1988-, Hunterston Devpt Co Ltd 1987-, Scott-Lithgow Drydocks Ltd 1967-78, Western Ferries (Argyll) Ltd 1972-85; vice-chm Scott Lithgow Ltd 1968-78; dir: Bank of Scotland 1962-86, Landcatch Ltd 1981-, Lithgows Pty Ltd 1972-; memb: Br Ctee Det Norske Veritas 1966-, Exec Ctee Scottish Cncl Devpt and Indust 1969-85, Scottish Regnl Cncl of CBI 1969-76, Clyde Port Authy 1969-71, Bd Nat Ports Cncl 1971-78, W Central Scotland Plan Steering Ctee 1971-74, Gen Bd Nat Physical Labour 1963-66, Greenock Dist Hosp Bd 1961-66, Scottish Milk Mktg Bd 1979-83; chm Iona Cathedral Tstees Mgmnt Bd 1979-83, memb Cncl Winston Churchill Meml Tst 1979-83, hon pres Students Assoc, memb Ct Univ of Strathclyde 1964-69; Hon LLD Strathclyde 1979, memb Queen's Body Guard for Scotland (Royal Co of Archers); *Recreations* rural life, invention, photography; *Clubs* Oriental, Western, Royal Scottish Automobile (Glasgow); *Style*— Sir William Lithgow, Bt, DL; Ormsary House, by Lochgilphead, Argyllshire (☎ 08803 252); Drums, Langbank, Renfrewshire (☎ 0475 54 606)

LITMAN, Dr Gloria Klein; da of Emil Klein (d 1963), and Sadie Epstein (d 1982); *b* 10 April 1936; *Educ* Hunter Coll New York City (BA), North Texas State Univ (MSc), Univ of London (PhD); *m* 4 Dec 1954, Armand Charles Litman, s of Charles Louis Litman (d 1987); 2 s (David b 1957, Jonathan b 1960); *Career* sr lectr Inst of Psychiatry 1987, hon conslt psychologist Maudsley Hosp, clinical res psychologist Addiction Res Unit; *Recreations* bridge, yoga; *Style*— Dr Gloria Litman; 22 Stafford Terrace, London W8 7BH (☎ 081 937 9267)

LITTLE, Amanda Penelope Wyndham; da of Capt Alec Haines Little, CBE, of Hampshire, and Pamela, *née* Bolt; *b* 19 Jan 1948; *Educ* Winchester; *m* 7 Sept 1979, Kenneth William Elliott, s of John Attewell Elliott, of Notts; *Career* asst PR offr Milk Mktg Bd 1972-79; literary agent Bolt & Watson Ltd 1981-83, dir, pt owner and literary agent Watson Little Ltd 1983-; memb Assoc of Authors' Agents; *Recreations* singing, music, books; *Clubs* ACADEMY; *Style*— Ms Amanda Little

LITTLE, Lt-Col John Ernest; MC (1944), DL (Warwicks 1988); s of Noel Ernest Little (d 1954), of Lane House, Compton, Winchester, and Frances Catherine, *née* Eden (d 1974); *b* 8 June 1922; *Educ* Marlborough; *m* 23 May 1953, Nancy Elizabeth, da of Joseph William Smith; 1 s (William b 1958), 2 da (Catherine b 1955, Georgina b 1964); *Career* Royal Artillery 1940-67; memb Warwicks CC 1979-85 (chm Educn Ctee 1981-85), chm Stratford-upon-Avon Cons Assoc 1975-80; memb Cncl Univ of Warwick 1982- (chm: Careers Bd 1986-, Building Ctee 1987-); *Recreations* shooting, fishing; *Clubs* Army & Navy; *Style*— Lt-Col John Little, MC, DL; Newbold Pacey Hall, Warwick (☎ 0926 651270)

LITTLE, John Noel; s of Ronald Little (d 1974), and Margaret Elizabeth, *née* Thompson; *b* 25 Dec 1935; *Educ* Stockton-on-Tees GS; *m* 1961, Mavis, da of James Sydney Ord (d 1960); 1 s (Mark), 1 da (Elaine); *Career* Lloyds and Scottish plc 1957-84 (exec dir 1973-84), md Lloyds and Scottish Finance Ltd 1969-84; chm: Financial Houses Association 1980-82, Lease & Financial Services Ltd, Stortext (Scot) Ltd, J W Galloway Ltd, Randsworth Trust plc 1986-87, Lifecare International plc 1987-89; dir: Barry D Trentham Ltd, Hatrick-Bruce Ltd, Caledonian Trust plc; dep chm London Fiduciary Trust plc; FID; *Recreations* cricket, golf, bridge, watching rugby, swimming; *Clubs* RAC, Royal Burgess Golfing Soc, The Grange; *Style*— John N Little, Esq; Dunosdale, 22 Cammo Crescent, Edinburgh EH4 8DZ

LITTLE, Michael Robert; s of Robert William Little (d 1973), and Joan, *née* Brown; *b* 10 Sept 1949; *Educ* Tockington Manor, Blundells; *m* 1, 16 June 1973 (m dis 1977), Susan Elizabeth, da of Desmond Richard Bowden (d 1972), of Ranby Hall, Lincoln; m 2, 18 July 1985 (m dis 1990), Ellen Louise, da of Winston Walker, of Welford upon Avon, Warwickshire; 1 s (Henry Robert William b 7 April 1986); *Career* St Quintin Son and Stanley 1972-76; ptnr Molyneux Rose 1977-, chm Molyneux Rose Ltd 1987-; Master North Cotswold Hunt 1985-88; FRICS 1981, ACIArb 1980; *Recreations* hunting, shooting, squash; *Clubs* Royal Automobile, Lansdowne, Naval, IOD; *Style*— Michael Little, Esq; The Lydes, Toddington, Gloucestershire; (☎ 0242621 419); Pelican Wharf, 58 Wapping Wall, London E1 (☎ 071 702 2599); Molyneux Rose, 143 New Bond St, London W1Y 9FD (☎ 071 409 0130, fax 071 499 7636, car 0836 226975)

LITTLE, Nigel Stuart; s of Edward Little (d 1963), and Josephine Little; *b* 11 March 1954; *Educ* Queen Elizabeth I Sch (1563) Univ of London (BSc); *m* 17 May 1986, Fiona Mary, da of Henry Arthur Lee, of Foxes' Dale, Blackheath, London SE3; 1 s (Edward Oliver Henry b 11 Nov 1987); *Career* sales exec Kitkat & Aitken stockbrokers 1976-78, sr exec and head of Scot and Irish sales James Capel & Co stockbrokers 1978-88, dir and head of sales Morgan Stanley investmt bankers 1988-89 (princ of global firm) , dir Panmure Gordon & Co stockbrokers 1989-, dir Panmure Gordon Bankers Ltd 1989-; memb Royal Horticultural Soc, memb Borgia Club; Freeman City of London 1982; memb AIP 1979, memb Int Stock Exchange 1982, FBIM 1988; *Recreations* shooting, rugby union, motor sport, golf; *Style*— Nigel Little, Esq

LITTLE, Penelope Jane (Penny); da of Timothy Arnold Lincoln Little, of Harrogate, Yorks, and Rosemary Jill, *née* Livock (d 1969); *b* 25 Aug 1957; *Educ* Harrogate Coll, St James's Secretarial Coll; *Career* PR; jr sec then account exec Barbara Attenborough Associates 1977-80, PA then account exec Vernon Stratton Advertising 1981-82, UK press offr Habitat Designs Limited 1982-84; Camron Public Relations: sr account exec 1984-85, account mangr 1985-86, account dir 1986-88, dep md 1988-; *Style*— Ms Penny Little; Camron Public Relations, 7 Floral St, London WC2E 9DH (☎ 071 836 9843, fax 071 497 2753)

LITTLEALES, Paul Cade; s of Henry William Littleales (d 1986), of Sidmouth, Devon, and Marie Alice, *née* Cade (d 1984); *b* 8 Feb 1932; *Educ* Canford, Luton Poly; *m* 6 June 1962, Sallie Ann, da of Jack Thomas Joice (d 1968), of Fakenham, Norfolk; 2 s (Lawrence Henry b 1964, Andrew Paul b 1965); *Career* mech engr; chm and md: Trinity Motors Ltd 1962-84, Green's Garage Group 1968-84; fin and engrg consIt 1984-; memb Lloyds 1978-; *Recreations* riding, hunting; *Clubs* Eccentric; *Style*— Paul C Littleales, Esq; The Gate House, Limpsfield Common, nr Oxted, Surrey (☎ 0883 722104, fax 0883 722068)

LITTLECHILD, Prof Stephen Charles; s of Sydney Littlechild, of Wisbech, and Joyce, *née* Sharpe; *b* 27 Aug 1943; *Educ* Wisbech GS, Univ of Birmingham (BCom), Stanford Univ, Northwestern Univ, Univ of Texas at Austin (PhD), Univ of California at Los Angeles; *m* 1 Aug 1975, Kathleen (d 1982), da of Charles T Pritchard; 2 s (Harry b 1978, Richard b 1980), 1 da (Elizabeth b 1976); *Career* Harkness fell Univ of Stanford 1965-67, sr res lectr Graduate Centre for Mgmnt Studies Birmingham 1970-72, prof of applied econ Aston Univ 1973-75, prof of commerce and head Dept of Industl Econ and Business Studies Univ of Birmingham 1975-89; visiting prof: Univ of New York, Univ of Stanford, Univ of Chicago, Virginia Poly 1979-80; memb: Monopolies and Mergers Cmmn 1983-89, ACORD 1987-89; advsr UK Govt on privatisation of BT, water and electricity; dir gen Electricity Supply 1989-; *Books* Operational Research for Managers (1977), Fallacy of the Mixed Economy (1978), Elements of Telecommunications Economics (1979), Energy Strategies for the UK (with KG Vaidya, 1982), Regulation of British Telecoms Profitability (1983), Economic Regulation of Privatised Water Authorities (1986); *Recreations* genealogy; *Style*— Prof Stephen Littlechild; Office of Electricity of Regulation, Hagley House, Hagley Road, Birmingham B16 8QG (☎ 021 456 2100)

LITTLEFAIR, Henry George Peter (Harry); s of Bernard Littlefair, of York (d 1975), and Ellen Littlefair *née* Houghton (d 1961); *b* 6 Feb 1931; *Educ* Ratcliffe Coll, Leicester; *m* 9 Aug 1960, Mary Edith, da of Sydney Fryer Monkman, of York (d 1980); 2 s (Nicholas b 1962, Dominic b 1964); *Career* investmt mangr: vice chm Allied Dunbar Unit Tst 1986-; md: A D Unit Tst 1983-86 (dep md 1975-83); *Recreations* philately, music, chess, walking; *Style*— Harry Littlefair, Esq; 4 Fallowfield Close, Emmer Green, Reading, Berkshire RG4 8NQ (☎ 0734 475993); Allied Dunbar Unit Trusts plc, 9-15 Sackville Street, London W1X 1DE

LITTLEJOHN, Alan Morrison; s of Frank Littlejohn (d 1957), of 11 Grosvenor Rd, Jesmond, Newcastle upon Tyne, and Ethel Lucy, *née* Main (d 1970); *b* 17 Oct 1925; *Educ* Dame Allan's Boys' Sch Newcastle on Tyne, Kings Coll Univ of Durham (BSc), Lincoln Coll and Agric Econ Res Inst Oxford (Dip Agric Econ, BLitt); *m* 19 March 1955, Joy Dorothy Margaret, da of Frederick Till (d 1937), of 47 Balnacraig Avenue, Neasden, NW 10; 1 da (Sally Vanessa 21 Nov 1960); *Career* asst economist: agric econ dept King's Coll Univ of Durham 1945-47, agric econ dept Wye Coll Univ of London 1950-51; Shell Int Chemical Co 1951-67, head econ dept Agric Engrs Assoc 1968-73, dir gen Clay Pipe Dev Assoc 1973-77, dir Shipbuilders and Shiprepairers Ind Assoc 1977-89, dir Shipbuilders and Shiprepairers Assoc 1989-90; sec-gen UK Land and Hydrographic Survey Assoc 1980-90, dir Assoc High Pressure Water Jetting Contractors 1980-87; Chorleywood Parish Cncl 1979- (chm 1985-87); Three Rivers Dist Cncl: cncllr 1988-, chm Resources Ctee 1990-91; *Recreations* politics, gardening, photography; *Style*— Alan Littlejohn, Esq; 5 The Readings, Chorleywood, Herts WD3 5SY (☎ 0923 284420)

LITTLEJOHN, Alistair George; s of James Davidson Littlejohn (d 1970); *b* 17 Feb 1935; *Educ* Aberdeen GS, Univ of Aberdeen (BScEng); *m* 1962, Mairwen Lloyd, da of Capt Henry Lloyd Jones (d 1971); 1 s, 1 da; *Career* civil engr; dir Higgs and Hill Ltd; *Clubs* Eccentric, IOD; *Style*— Alistair Littlejohn, Esq; Harlyn, 14 Hempstead Lane, Potten End, Berkhamsted, Herts (☎ 0442 3706); Crown House, Kingston Road, New Malden, Surrey, KT3 3ST (☎ 081 942 8921)

LITTLEJOHN, Joan Anne; da of Thomas Littlejohn (d 1950), and Joan, *née* Wynn (Mrs Edward G Shepherd); *b* 20 April 1937; *Educ* Mary Datchelor Girls Sch, RCM, post-graduate study with Howells, Berkeley, Boulanger, Ruth Dyson & others; *Career* piano teacher Orpington GS 1958-59, freelance composer, poet, photographer, musicologist 1958-, admin staff RCM 1960-83, piano teacher Harrow 1972-73, asst to Br composers incl: Fricker, Howells, Hopkins, Poston, reassembled Howells Requiem 1980, collated his MS sketches 1983; fndr memb RCM staff assoc 1976, chm RCM NALGO and London Music Colleges NALGO 1978-81, vice chm RCM Local Jt Ctee 1978-81; creative works (music) incl: La Mascarade de Jean de la Fontaine, The Heights of Haworth, Poems from Palgrave, 4 Sea Songs (words by J M Ritchie), 4 Lieder von F Schnabel, London Street Cries (cmmnd by Beth Boyd), St Juliot Cornwall (words by Rachel Pearse), Dreams of Anubis, Settings of Blake Burns Shakespeare Hardy, choral scena The Bonny Earl of Murray (cmmnd by Antony Hopkins); Creative works (Poetry) incl: Poems for Free, In The Furrowed Field, Towards Exmoor, Bingo's Totleigh Diary, The Hearth, Hymn of the Interviewers, Grandad's Dinner, Autun, Legend; recording 90 tunes for The Queen Mother's 90th Year; memb: Devon Wildlife Tst, Woodland Tst, CPRE, Brontë Soc, British Roller

Canary Club, Rare Poultry Soc, PRS, Br Fedn Music Festivals, IBC Advsy Cncl; int life fell American Biographical Inst Res Assoc 1983; Highflyers List; World Decoration of Excellence Medallion from American Biog Inst 1989, first recipient IBC Medal Collection 1989 (for most distinguished biogs), recipient Howells' composing piano 1984; GRSM, LRAM; *Recreations* animals especially collies, canaries, rare poultry; *Style—* Miss Joan Littlejohn; Chanterhayes, Bow, nr Crediton, Devon EX17 6HR

LITTLEJOHNS, Cdre Douglas George; OBE (1984); s of Gordon Augustus Littlejohns, of Whittlesey, Cambs, and Margaret Goudie, *née* Smith; *b* 10 May 1946; *Educ* Borden GS, RNC Dartmouth, Univ of Reading (BSc); *m* 1, 14 Nov 1970 (m dis 1987), Fiona, *née* Hilton; 1 s (Andrew b 1974), 2 da (Imogen b 1978, Diana b 1979); m 2, 4 June 1988, Deborah Anne, da of Captain Angus Andrew Nicol (d 1971); *Career* CO: HMS Osiris 1975-76, HMS Sceptre 1981-83; Jt Serv Def Coll 1983-84, ops offr Flag Offr Submarines 1984-85, asst dir MOD 1985-87, CO HMS London 1987-89, PSO to CDS 1989-; Younger Bro Trinity House 1989, memb MENSA 1990; Freeman City of London 1988; AFIMA 1979, MNI 1988; *Recreations* cricket, riding, sailing, DIY, family; *Clubs* RUSI, Army and Navy, RN 1765 and 1785; *Style—* Cdre Douglas Littlejohns, OBE

LITTLEMORE, Christopher Paul; s of Frederick Percival Littlemore, of Dunchurch Rd, Rugby, and (Edith) Marie, *née* Clarkson; *b* 8 March 1959; *Educ* Rugby, Univ of Manchester (BA, BArch); *m* 28 July 1984, Jane Evelyn, da of Derek Chalk, of Poulton, Gloucestershire; 1 s (Andrew b 1987), 1 da (Katharine b 1989); *Career* architect Ellis Williams Partnership Manchester 1980-81; The Charter Partnership: architect Bedford Office 1983-87, assoc dir 1986, dir Bournemouth Office 1987-, Bd dir 1988; memb Midland Assoc of Mountaineers; RIBA 1984; *Recreations* mountaineering, golf, watercolour painting, music; *Clubs* Boscombe Golf; *Style—* Christopher Littlemore, Esq; The Charter Partnership Ltd, 2 St Stephens Court, 15-17 St Stephens Rd, Bournemouth BH2 6LA (☎ 0202 554625, fax 0202 294007, car 0836 260845)

LITTLER, Brian Oswald; s of William Oswald Littler (d 1958), of London, and Mavis Pricilla, *née* Copping; *b* 22 Nov 1942; *Educ* St Dunstans Coll, Kings Coll London (BDS, MB BS); *m* 19 Feb 1972, Susan Elizabeth, da of Arthur Stent, of Wonersh, Surrey; 1 s (Adam Oswald b 20 Oct 1975), 2 da (Elizabeth Ann b 30 May 1978, Bryony Susan Jane b 24 Oct 1984); *Career* conslt oral and maxillo facial surgn to: The London Hosp, Whipps Cross Hosp, St Margarets Hosp, Princess Alexandra Hosp Harlow, The London Independent Hosp, The Roding Hosp Redbridge; memb Inst of Advanced Motorists; FDSRCS 1969; *Recreations* sailing; *Style—* Brian Littler, Esq; Pentlowend, High Easter, Essex CM1 4RE (☎ 024 531 626); Whipps Cross Hospital, Whipps Cross Rd, London E11 1NR, (☎ 071 539 5522)

LITTLER, Sir (James) Geoffrey; KCB (1985, CB 1981); s of James Edward Littler (d 1961), of Manchester, and Evelyn Mary Taylor; *b* 18 May 1930; *Educ* Manchester GS, Corpus Christi Coll Cambridge (BA); *m* 20 Sept 1958, Shirley, da of Sir Percy William Marsh, CSI, CIE, of Dorchester-on-Thames, Oxfordshire; 1 s (Peter b 1967); *Career* civil servant: second perm sec (fin), HM Treasy 1983-88, joined Civil Serv in Colonial Office 1952, Treasy 1954: chm TR European Growth Trust plc, dep chm Maritime Transport Services Ltd; dir National Westminster Investment Bank Ltd; chm Working Party 3 of OECD 1985-88, Euro Community Monetary Ctee 1987-88; *Recreations* music, reading, travelling; *Clubs* Reform; *Style—* Sir Geoffrey Littler, KCB; National Westminster Bank Ltd, 135 Bishopsgate, London EC2M 3UR

LITTLER, George Gordon Clegg; s of George Clegg Littler, OBE, TD, of Ibiza Spain, and Barbara Noble Meidell-Andersen, *née* Gordon, of Bergen, Norway; *b* 1 May 1950; *Educ* Bradfield Coll, Coll of Law; *m* 1, 25 April 1981 (m dis 1986), Emma, da of Sir John Greville Stanley Beith, KCMG; m 2, 19 May 1990, The Hon Sarah, da of Viscount Long; *Career* slr: A J Sheffer & Co 1976-81, Simmons & Simmons ptnr 1985- (joined 1981) Law Soc; *Recreations* theatre, contemporary art, association football, fencing; *Clubs* Brooks's, The Lansdowne; *Style—* George Littler, Esq; Simmons & Simmons, 14 Dominion St, London EC2 (☎ 071 628 2020, telex 888562, fax 071 588 4129)

LITTLER, Hon Mrs (Sarah Victoria); da of 4 Viscount Long; *b* 1958; *m* 19 May 1990, George G Clegg Littler, er s of George Clegg Littler, and Frithjof Meidell-Andersen; *Career* art conslt ptnr of Long & Ryle Art International London; *Recreations* reading, travel; *Style—* The Hon Mrs Littler; 20 Oakley Gardens, London SW3 5QS

LITTLER, Lady; Shirley; da of Sir Percy Marsh, CSI, CIE (d 1969), of Dorchester-on-Thames, Oxon, and Joan Mary, *née* Beecroft (d 1972); *b* 8 June 1932; *Educ* Headington Sch Oxford, Girton Coll Cambridge (BA, MA); *m* 20 Sept 1958, Sir (James) Geoffrey Littler, KCB, *qv*; 1 s (Peter b 1967); *Career* princ HM Treasy 1960 (asst princ 1953), asst sec Prices and Incomes Bd (NBPI) 1969, sec to V and G Tbnl of Enquiry 1971, Home Office 1972; asst under sec of state: Broadcasting Dept Home Office 1978, Immigration and Nationality Dept Home Office 1981; dir gen of admin IBA 1990 (dir of admin 1983, acting dir gen of admin 1989, ret 1991); FRSA 1988, MRTS, RIPA; *Recreations* reading, history; *Style—* Lady Littler; c/o National Westminster Bank, 6 Torhill Street, London SW1H 9ND

LITTLER MANNERS, Judy; da of Sir Emile Littler (d 1984), and Lady Cora Littler, *née* Goffin; *b* 16 Oct 1952; *Educ* St Mary's Hall Brighton, Charters Towers Sch Bexhill-on-Sea, St Anne's Coll Oxford (MA); *m* 12 June 1982 (m dis 1990), David Peter Manners; 1 s (Max b 27 March 1983), 1 da (Marina b 6 Sept 1986); *Career* floor asst and asst floor mangr BBC Studio Mgmnt Dept 1975-78, prodn asst Drama in Europe Ltd and Derek Glynne Assocs 1978-79, producer MMA Presentations Ltd 1979-83, proprietor and chief exec Mum's The Word 1984-; dir: British Amalgamated Theatres Ltd 1985-, The Night Company Ltd 1985-, GR Productions Ltd 1985-; non-exec dir Stratagem Group plc (formerly London Entertainments plc), hon treas The Actors' Charitable Trust; tstee: The Emile Littler Actor's Charitable Tst, The Emile Littler Fndn; patron Theatre in Tst; *Recreations* theatre, tennis, skiing; *Clubs* Hurlingham; *Style—* Mrs Judy Littler Manners; Mum's the Word, 283 New King's Road, London SW6 4RD (☎ 071 731 7770, fax 081 877 1136)

LITTLETON, Hon Mrs (Aileen Mary); *née* Fitzherbert; er da of 14 Baron Stafford (d 1986); *b* 29 March 1953; *m* 1980, Antony Robin Walhouse Westby Littleton (changed his surname from Perceval to Littleton by Royal Licence 1971), son of Robert Westby Perceval, by his wife, Hon Joanna Ida Louise, da of 5 Baron Hatherton; 1 s (Thomas Alastair Westby b 1986), 2 da (Katrina Mary b 1983, Rosanna Sophie b 1989); *Style—* The Hon Mrs Littleton; Old Walls, Hannington, nr Basingstoke, Hants

LITTLETON, Hon Hestar Mary Modwena; da of 4 Baron Hatherton (d 1944); *b* 1912; *Career* 1939-45 with WTS/FANY; *Style—* The Hon Hestar Littleton; Pitt Manor Cottage, Winchester, Hants (☎ 0962 4898)

LITTLETON, Hon Jonathan Lloyd; s of 6 Baron Hatherton (d 1973), and his 2 w, Mary, Lady Hatherton, *qv*; *b* 17 July 1949; *m* 1970, Maxine Elizabeth, da of Alistair Brough Mills; 2 s (Alexander, Jonathan), 2 da (Rosalind, Melissa); *Style—* The Hon Jonathan Littleton; Eatonbrook House, Rushbrook, Church Stretton, Shropshire

LITTLETON, Hon Moonyeen Meriel; da of 6 Baron Hatherton (d 1973), and his 1 w, Nora Evelyn, *née* Smith (d 1955); *b* 1933; *Style—* The Hon Moonyeen Littleton; c/o Hassan Hafer St No 5, Saray El Qubba, Cairo, Egypt

LITTLETON, Hon Richard Brownlow; s of 6 Baron Hatherton (d 1973), and his 2 w, Mary, Lady Hatherton, *qv*; *b* 17 July 1949; *m* 1975 (m dis), Shirley Margaret Adamson; 1 s (Ian b 1981), 1 da (Kirsty 1985); partner from 1989, Linda Hoyland; *Career* Nat Tst warden i/c Aderley Estates and Hare Hill Estates; *Style—* The Hon Richard Littleton; Foresters Lodge, Nether Alderley, Macclesfield, Cheshire

LITTLEWOOD, Anthony George (Tony); s of George Kershaw Littlewood, of Sylvester House, Ashton-Under-Lyne, and Sarah, *née* Rogers; *b* 3 Oct 1949; *Educ* Audenshaw GS, Nottingham Univ (BPharm); *m* 11 Dec 1982, Nikola Ann, da of Lance James du Lys Mallalieu (d 1973); 3 s (Russell b 1984, Guy b 1986, Harry b 1988); *Career* pharmacist; chm and md George Hincliffe Ltd 1973-; chm: Northern (chemists) Ltd 1981-, Local Pharmaceutical Ctee 1989-, Tameside Family Health Servs Assoc 1990-; MRPharmS 1972, MBIM 1980; *Recreations* tennis, travel, (collecting) photographic, classic cars; *Clubs* Navel (Mayfair); *Style—* Anthony Littlewood, Esq; Wharmton Cottage, Wharmton Tower, Grasscroft OL4 4HL

LITTLEWOOD, Graham; s of Ernest Charles Littlewood (d 1960), and Ivy Lilian, *née* Masters (d 1978); *b* 19 Feb 1944; *Educ* Royal Liberty Sch Romford; *m* 30 Aug 1971, Marianne; 2 da (Catherine Ann b 22 March 1973, Jane Elizabeth b 9 June 1975); *Career* accountant; Bristow Burrell & Co 1960-67, Coopers & Lybrand 1967-69, gp fin controller Gazocean France 1969-71; ptnr: Keens Shay Keens & Co 1973, Pannell Kerr Forster 1978- (in charge auditing dept 1989-), Freeman City of London 1983; FCA 1966; *Recreations* golf, reading; *Clubs* East India; *Style—* Graham Littlewood, Esq; Pannell Kerr Forster, New Garden House, Hatton Garden, London EC1N 8JA (☎ 071 831 7393)

LITTLEWOOD, James; CB (1973); s of Thomas Littlewood (d 1930), of Royton, Lancs, and Sarah Jane, *née* Penhall (d 1967); *b* 21 Oct 1922; *Educ* Manchester GS, St John's Coll Cambridge (MA); *m* 9 Aug 1950, Barbara, da of Harry Shaw (d 1958), of Blackburn, Lancs; 2 s (David b 1955, Peter b 1957), 1 da (Pamela b 1953); *Career* enlisted Army 1942, cmmnd KORR, WWII serv India and Burma, transfd W Yorks Regt (later HQ 17 Indian Div 1945), Wingate's second campaign 1944, 17 Ind Div campaign 1945, Capt; Civil Serv: admin class 1947, HM Treasy 1947-67, seconded Cabinet Off 1955, transfd Dept for Nat Savings 1967, dir of savings 1972, ret 1981; *Recreations* golf, bridge; *Clubs* Utd Oxford and Cambridge Univ, Barton on Sea Golf; *Style—* James Littlewood, Esq, CB

LITTLEWOOD, John Nigel; s of George Littlewood, and Diana Mary, *née* Wallis; *b* 18 April 1935; *Educ* Lutterworth GS, Farnborough GS, New Coll Oxford (MA); *m* 29 Sept 1962, Rosemary Underwood; 2 s (William, Richard); *Career* Nat Serv RN 1954-56; ptnr Read Hurst-Brown Stockbrokers 1964-75 (joined 1959), ptnr Rowe & Pitman Stockbrokers 1975-86, dir S G Warburg Gp plc 1986-; independent govr City of London Poly 1989-; FSIA; *Recreations* cinema, gardening, golf, music, reading, writing; *Clubs* North Hants Golf; *Style—* John Littlewood, Esq; S G Warburg Group plc, 1 Finsbury Ave, London EC2M 2PA (☎ 071 606 1066)

LITTMAN, Helen Ruth; da of Anthony Frank Littman, and Valerie Ann, *née* Singer; *b* 25 July 1955; *Educ* Brighton and Hove GS for Girls, Eastbourne Coll of Art and Design, Camberwell Sch of Arts and Crafts (BA), St Martin's Sch of Art; *m* 15 Aug 1987, Colin Michael David, s of late Walter David; 1 s (Oliver Louis b 24 Feb 1989), 1 da (Isabelle Valentine Shelly b 14 Feb 1991); *Career* design dir English Eccentrics 1983- (designing hand-printed silk garments and scarves), external assessor Glasgow Sch of Art 1988-90, visiting lectr RCA; memb CNAA 1987-; *Books* English Eccentrics: The Textile Designs of Helen Littman (1991); *Recreations* theatre, music, finger painting, lego; *Style—* Ms Helen Littman; English Eccentrics, 9-10 Charlotte St, London EC2A 3DH (☎ 071 729 6233, fax 071 729 7891)

LITTMAN, Jeffrey James; s of Louis Littman (d 1981), of Edmonton, Middx, and Sarah (Sadie), *née* Coberman (d 1974); *b* 19 Feb 1943; *Educ* Latymer Sch Edmonton, St Catharine's Coll Cambridge (MA); *m* 20 March 1975, Sandra Lynne, da of David Kallman (d 1975), of NY; 2 da (Amanda, Léonie); *Career* ldr Mgmnt Gp Dept of Computing and Control Imperial Coll London; called to the Bar Middle Temple 1974; Midland and Oxford circuit; *Recreations* history; *Style—* Jeffrey Littman, Esq; 4 Verulam Buildings, Gray's Inn, London WC1R 5LW (☎ 071 405 6114, fax 071 831 6112)

LITTMAN, Mark; QC (1961); s of Jack Littman (d 1963), and Lilian, *née* Rose; *b* 4 Sept 1920; *Educ* Owens Sch, LSE (BSc), Queens Coll Oxford (MA); *m* 18 Sept 1965, Marguerite, da of Tyler Lamkin, of Monroe, Louisiana, USA; *Career* Lt RN 1941-46; called to the Bar Middle Temple 1947, in practice 1947-67 and 1979-, Master of Bench 1971, Master Treas Middle Temple 1988; dep chm Br Steel Corpn 1967-79; dir: RTZ, Burtons, Granada; former dir: Commercial Union, British Enkalon, Amerada Hess (US); memb Royal Cmmn Legal Servs 1976-79; *Clubs* Reform, Garrick, Oxford and Cambridge, Century (New York); *Style—* Mark Littman, Esq, QC; 79 Chester Square, London SW1 (☎ 071 730 2973); 12 Grays Inn Sq, London WC1 (☎ 071 405 8654)

LITVINOFF, Barnet; s of Max Litvinoff, and Rosa, *née* Michaelson, of London; *b* 23 Nov 1917; *m* 17 Dec 1940, Sylvia Litvinoff, *née* Roytman; 3 s (Adrian b 19 Aug 1949, Miles b 13 Dec 1950, Michael b 21 Aug 1946 (d 1949); *Career* RAMC and RAEC 1940-47, POW Italy and Germany 1942-45, author and journalist; *Books* Ben Gurion of Israel (1955), Road to Jerusalem (1964), A Peculiar People (1969), Another Time Another Voice (1971), Weizmann Last of the Patriachs (1976), The Letters and Papers of Chaim Weizmann, Baku to Baker St (jtly, 1984), The Burning Bush: Antisemitism and World History (1988); *Style—* Barnet Litvinoff, Esq; 28 Hollycroft Avenue, London NW3 7QL (☎ 071 435 7323)

LIU, David Tek-Yung; s of Pro Liu Tsu-Shya, of Sydney, Aust, and Mabel King, *née* Liang (d 1977); *b* 26 April 1941; *Educ* All Saints Bathurst NSW Australia, Univ of Sydney (MB BS), Univ of Sussex (MPhil); *m* 28 July 1976, Pamela Margaret, da of Arthur Heptinstall, of Surrey, England; 1 da (Natasha b 9 Sept 1981); *Career* res fell Univ of Sussex, lectr and res lectr Univ Coll London, sr lectr and hon conslt Univ of Nottingham 1989-, conslt Univ of Malaya 1989-; memb: Nottingham Charity Appeal for Pre-Natal Diagnosis, Birmingham and Midland Obstetric and Gynaecological Soc, jt MRC-RCOG Ctee Chorion Villus Sampling; FRCOG 1986; *Books* Thinking, Feeling (1987), Labour Ward Manual (1985), Chorion Villus Sampling (1987), Practical Gynaecology (1988); *Recreations* gardening, water sports, writing; *Clubs* Nottingham County Sailing; *Style—* David Liu, Esq; Department of Obstetrics & Gynaecology, City Hospital, Hucknall Road, Nottingham NG5 1PB

LIVELY, Penelope Margaret; OBE (1989); da of Roger Vincent Low, and Vera Maud Greer, *née* Reckitt; *b* 17 March 1933; *Educ* St Anne's Coll Oxford (BA); *m* 1957, Prof Jack Lively; 1 s (Adam), 1 da (Josephine); *Career* writer; children's books: Astercote (1970), The Whispering Knights (1971), The Wild Hunt of Hagworthy (1971), The Driftway (1972), The Ghost of Thomas Kempe (Carnegie Medal, 1974), The House in Norham Gardens (1974), Going Back (1975), Boy Without a Name (1975), A Stitch in Time (Whitbread Award, 1976), The Stained Glass Window (1976), Fanny's Sister (1976), The Voyage of QV66 (1978), Fanny and The Monsters (1978), Fanny and The Battle of Potter's Piece (1980), The Revenge of Samuel Stokes (1981), Fanny and the Monsters (three stories, 1983), Uninvited Ghosts (1984), Dragon Trouble (1984), Debbie and the Little Devil (1987), A House Inside Out (1987); non-fiction: The Presence of the Past (1976); fiction: The Road to Lichfield (1977), Nothing Missing but the Samovar (Southern Arts Literary Prize, 1978), Treasures of Time (Arts Cncl Nat Book Award, 1979), Judgement Day (1980), Next to Nature, Art (1982), Perfect

Happiness (1983), Corruption (1984), According to Mark (1984), Pack of Cards, stories 1978-86 (1986), Moon Tiger (Booker Prize, 1987), Passing On (1989); book reviews and short stories in numerous magazines, various TV and radio scripts; chm Soc of Authors (memb 1973-); memb: PEN 1985-, Arts Cncl Lit Panel; FRSL; *Style*— Ms Penelope Lively; c/o Murray Pollinger (Literary Agent), 222 Old Brompton Rd, London SW5 0B2 (☎ 071 373 4711)

LIVENS, Leslie John Philip; s of Lt Leslie Francis Hugh Livens (d 1981), of London, and Betty Livens; *b* 13 Dec 1946; *Educ* Wimbledon County Secdy Sch; *m* 3 Aug 1968, Carole Ann, da of Henry William Todd, of London; 1 s (Stephen b 1970), 1 da (Clare b 1972); *Career* ed and conslt ed Taxation Practitioner (Jl of Inst of Taxation) 1974-; former ed: Tax Planning International, Financial Times, World Tax Report, Review of Parliament; managing ed Butterworths Tax Books 1977-81, taxation conslt Rowland Nevill & Co (now Moores Rowland) 1981-83, ptnr Moores Rowland 1983-; ATII 1972, AITI 1983, MBAE 1989; *princ publications*: Moores & Rowland's Tax Guide (1982-87), Share Valuation Handbook (1986), Daily Telegraph Tax Guide (1987), Daily Telegraph Personal Tax Guide (1988); *Recreations* music, writing, walking, family; *Style*— Leslie Livens, Esq; Clifford's Inn, Fetter Lane, London EC4A 1AS (☎ 071 831 2345, fax 071 831 6123, telex 886504)

LIVERMORE, Karen; da of Joseph Livermore (d 1982), and Glenys, *née* Howard; *b* 12 Aug 1961; *Educ* Grays Sch, Thurrock Tech Coll; *Career* Drapers Record 1980-87, freelance journalist and stylist various cos and pubns for IPC Magazines and Sunday Mirror Magazine; fashion ed Daily Star 1989-; *Style*— Miss Karen Livermore; Daily Star, 245 Blackfriars Rd, London SE1 9UX (☎ 071 928 8000)

LIVERPOOL, Archdeacon of; *see*: Spiers, Ven Graeme Hendry Gordon

LIVERPOOL, 6 Bishop of (cr 1880) 1975-; Rt Rev David Stuart Sheppard; s of Stuart Sheppard (d 1937), and Barbara Sheppard (d 1983); *b* 6 March 1929; *Educ* Sherborne, Trinity Hall Cambridge (MA); *m* 1957, Grace, da of Rev Bruce Raymond Isaac; 1 da (Jenny); *Career* Nat Serv 2 Lt Royal Sussex Regt 1947-49; ordained: deacon 1955, priest 1956; curate St Mary's Islington 1955-57, warden and chaplain Mayflower Family Centre Canning Town 1957-69, bishop suffragan Woolwich 1969-75, bishop Liverpool 1975-; Hon LLD Univ of Liverpool 1981, Hon DTech Liverpool Poly 1987, Hon DUniv Cambridge 1990; *Books* Parson's Pitch (1964), Built as a City (1974), Bias to the Poor (1983), The Other Britain (Dimbleby Lecture, 1984), Better Together (with Archbishop Derek Worlock, 1988), With Christ in the Wilderness (with Archbishop Derek Worlock, 1990); *Recreations* painting, cricket (played for Sussex 1947-62, England 1950-63, Univ of Cambridge 1950-52), reading, gardening, music; *Style*— The Rt Rev the Bishop of Liverpool; Bishop's Lodge, Woolton Park, Liverpool L25 6DT Church House, 1 Hanover St, Liverpool L1 3DW (☎ 051 708 9480)

LIVERPOOL, Dean of; *see*: Walters, Very Rev (Rhys) Derrick Chamberlain

LIVERPOOL, 10 Archbishop of (RC, 1911 by Letters Apostolic 'Si qua est' of Pius X) 1976- Derek John Harford Worlock; also Metropolitan of Northern Province with Suffragan Sees, Hexham, Lancaster, Leeds, Middlesbrough, Salford and Hallam; s of Capt Harford Worlock and Dora, *née* Hoblyn; *b* 4 Feb 1920; *Educ* St Edmund's Coll Ware; *Career* ordained 1944, curate Kensington 1944-45, private sec to Archbishop of Westminster 1945-64, dean of Stepney 1964-65, bishop of Portsmouth 1965-76, translated Liverpool 1976, vice pres RC Bishops Conference of Eng and Wales 1978-; Hon LLD Univ of Liverpool 1981; Hon DTech Liverpool Poly 1987, hon fell Portsmouth Poly 1988, Hon DD Univ of Cambridge 1990; *Books* Seek Ye First (1950), Give Me Your Hand (1977), Better Together (1988), With Christ in the Wilderness (1990); *Style*— His Grace the Archbishop of Liverpool; Archbishop's House, 87 Green Lane, Mossley Hill, Liverpool L18 2EP (☎ 051 722 2379)

LIVERPOOL, 5 Earl of (UK 1905); Edward Peter Bertram Savile Foljambe; also Baron Hawkesbury (UK 1893) and Viscount Hawkesbury (UK 1905); s of Capt Peter George William Savile Foljambe (ka Italy 1944, gn of 4 Earl of Liverpool who d 1969 and who was ggs of half-bro of the nineteenth century PM), and Elizabeth Joan, *née* Flint (who m 2, Maj Andrew Gibbs, MBE, TD, *qv*); *b* 14 Nov 1944; *Educ* Shrewsbury, Perugia Univ Italy; *m* 29 Jan 1970, Lady Juliana Noel, *qv*, da of 5 Earl of Gainsborough; 2 s; *Heir* s, Viscount Hawkesbury; *Clubs* Turf, Pratt's; *Style*— The Rt Hon the Earl of Liverpool; Barham Court, Exton, Oakham, Rutland, Leics LE15 8AP (☎ 0572 812309)

LIVERPOOL, Countess of; Lady Juliana Mary Alice; *née* Noel; da of 5 Earl of Gainsborough; *b* 1949; *m* 1970, 5 Earl of Liverpool, *qv*; 2 s; *Style*— The Rt Hon the Countess of Liverpool; Barham Court, Exton, nr Oakham, Rutland

LIVERSEDGE, Richard Lorton; s of Lt-Col John Ridler Liversedge (d 1968), of Fawke House, Sevenoaks, Kent, and Grace Evelyn Liversedge (d 1982); *b* 31 Aug 1940; *Educ* Tonbridge, London Hosp Dental Sch (BDS), London Hosp Med Coll (MB BS); *m* 28 Oct 1972, Jennifer Jane, da of John Hurrel Robertson, of Johannesburg, SA; 1 s (Dominic b 1974), 2 da (Annabel b 1975, Belinda b 1979); *Career* registrar London Hosp 1970-72 (house surgn 1968-69), sr registrar Royal Dental Hosp and St Georges Hosp 1972-77; conslt maxillo-facial surgn: Middx Hosp 1977-89, Barnet Gp of Hosps 1977-; responsible for various surgical instrument innovations; winter sportsman (luge); winner Br Luge Champs 1971; Winter Olympics: represented GB Grenoble 1968, capt Sapporo 1972, capt Innsbruck 1976; pres Br Racing Toboggan Assoc 1972-; chm Med Ctee Fedn Internationale de Luge de Course 1972-, memb Med Ctee Br Olympic Assoc 1976-; Freeman City of London 1968, Liveryman Worshipful Co of Skinners 1977; FDSRCS (Ed) 1971, FDSRCS (Eng) 1972; *Recreations* Luge, cresta run, moto polo; *Clubs* St Moritz Tobogganing; *Style*— Richard Liversedge, Esq; Oak Cottage, 117 Flaunden, Hertfordshire HP3 0PB (☎ 0442 833 047); Flat 1, 43 Wimpole St, London W1M 7AF (☎ 071 935 7909)

LIVESAY, Vice Adm Sir Michael Howard; KCB (1989); s of William Lindsay Livesay (d 1982), of Bishop Auckland, Co Durham, and Margaret Elenora Chapman Steel (d 1974); *b* 5 April 1936; *Educ* Ackland Hall GS Middlesborough, RNC Dartmouth; *m* 8 Aug 1959, Sara, da of Dr Arthur Vivian House, of Bicester, Oxon; 2 da (Harriet b 1962, Georgia b 1964); *Career* joined RN 1952, trg appts 1954-57, cmmnd 1957, qualified aircraft direction specialist 1959, direction offr HMS Hermes and HMS Aisne, Fighter Direction Sch and 893 Naval Air Sqdn 1959-66; cmd: HMS Hubberston 1966-68, HMS Plymouth 1970-72; Capt 1975-77, Fishery Protection and Mine Counter Measures 1975-77, first CO HMS Invincible 1979-82, dir Naval Warfare 1982-84; Flag Offr Sea Trg 1984-85; asst chief Naval Staff 1986-88, Flag Offr Scotland and NI 1989, Second Sea Lord 1991; *Recreations* gliding, sailing, skiing, gardening, fishing, golf; *Clubs* Army and Navy, Royal Yacht Sqdn; *Style*— Vice Adm Sir Michael Livesay, KCB; c/o Naval Secretary, Old Admiralty Building, MOD, London SW1

LIVESEY, Dr Anthony Edward; s of Joseph Livesey (d 1976), of Gt Harwood Lancs, and Dorothy, *née* Birtwhisle; *b* 16 Jan 1953; *Educ* St Mary's Coll Blackburn Lancs, Univ of Dundee (BMSc, MB BCh); *m* 17 Oct 1974, Apolonia Marie, da of Jan Wachala, of Blackburn, Lancs; 2 s (Joseph John b 18 Jan 1980, David Michael b 12 Feb 1983); *Career* registrar psychiatry Manchester 1981-84, sr registrar child psychiatry Sheffield 1984-86, conslt adolescent psychiatry N Derbys DHA 1986-; treas Sheffield Branch Assoc Child Psychology and Psychiatry, vice chm Div Child Health N Derbys DHA; MRC Psych 1983, memb Assoc for Psychiatric Study Adolescents; *Recreations* cycling, distance running, wind surfing, photography; *Style*— Dr Anthony Livesey; 20 Conalan Avenue, Bradway, Sheffield S17 4PG (☎ 0742 360346); The Edmund Street Clinic, Edmund St, Chesterfield, Derbyshire (☎ 0246 451252)

LIVESEY, Bernard Joseph Edward; QC (1990); s of Joseph Augustine Livesey (d 1965), of Hatch End, Middx, and Marie Gabrielle, *née* Caulfield; *b* 21 Feb 1944; *Educ* Cardinal Vaughan Sch London, Peterhouse Cambridge (MA, LLB); *m* 25 Sept 1971, Penelope Jean, da of Samuel Walter Harper, of Slindon, W Sussex; 2 da (Sarah b 5 June 1973, Kate b 21 Aug 1977); *Career* called to the Bar Lincoln's Inn 1969, rec Crown Ct 1987; *Recreations* listening to music, gardening, bell ringing; *Style*— Bernard Livesey, Esq, QC; 2 Crown Office Row, Temple, London EC4 (☎ 071 353 1365)

LIVESEY, Geoffrey Colin; MBE (1968); *b* 21 Dec 1943; *m* 1969 (m dis 1982), Elisa Jane Pullen; 2 s; *Career* joined FCO 1962, second sec and vice-consul Abidjan 1977-81, vice-consul for Niger and Upper Volta 1981-83, first sec FCO 1983-; *Recreations* squash, tennis; *Style*— Geoffrey Livesey, Esq, MBE; 21 Villiers Rd, Kingston-upon-Thames, Surrey (☎ 081 541 0649); Foreign and Commonwealth Office, London SW1 (☎ 071 233 5412)

LIVESEY, Linda Ann; *née* Skelton; *Educ* (City and Guilds Construction Technicians Certificate, LIOB); *Career* architectural technician Tesco Stores Ltd Cheshunt 1974-78, architectural asst Giltspur Engineering Design 1979, project surveyor Bat Stores Holdings 1979-81, design projects co-ordinator D P Powell Shopfitters Ltd 1981-82, projects co-ordinator 1982-84, divnl dir Fitch RS Design Consultants 1984-; memb Assoc of Project Mangrs; *Style*— Mrs Linda Livesey; 51 Wroths Path, Loughton, Essex IG10 1SH (☎ 081 580 6765 and 071 278 7200)

LIVESEY, Robert; s of Stanley Livesey (d 1960), and Mable, *née* Heigh; *b* 23 Aug 1938; *Educ* Grace Ramsden GS, Huddersfield Coll of Technol; *m* 28 Oct 1961, Joan, da of Clifford Ledgard; 4 s (Stephen Alan b 1962, David Andrew b 1964, Graham Michael b 1967, Jonathan Robert b 1973); *Career* chartered measurement and control technologist; chm and fndr Chemitrol Process Equipment Ltd 1977-; Fisher Process Equipment Ltd 1972-77; MIMC; *Recreations* restoration of medieval buildings; *Style*— Robert Livesey, Esq; Chainhurst Farm, Hunton Rd, Marden, Kent; Cook Lubbock House, St Faith's St, Maidstone, Kent

LIVESEY, Rodger Charles; s of Roland Livesey; *b* 19 June 1944; *Educ* Downing Coll Cambridge (MA); *m* 29 May 1972, Pat; 2 s (Matthew b 1974, Graham b 1979), 1 da (Caroline b 1977); *Career* md Security Pacific Hoare Govett Ltd 1976-88, dep md Tokai International Ltd 1988-, chm W Hampton Ltd 1987-; Freeman City of London, Liveryman Worshipful Co of Actuaries; FIA; *Style*— Rodger Livesey, Esq; 60 West Common, Harpenden, Herts AL5 2LD (☎ 0582 767 527); Tokai International, 14 Finsbury Square, London (☎ 071 638 6030, fax 071 588 5875)

LIVINGSTON, Dorothy Kirby; da of Albert Paulus Livingston, of Ponteland, Northumberland, and Margaret Alice, *née* Kirby; *b* 6 Jan 1948; *Educ* Central Newcastle HS, St Hugh's Coll Oxford (MA); *m* 11 Sept 1971, Julian, s of Alfred Millar; 2 da (Katherine b 22 Jan 1983, 31 May 1986); *Career* Herbert Smith: articled Clerk 1970-72, slr 1972-80, ptnr 1980- memb: Law Soc 1979 City of London Slrs' Co 1979; memb Banking Law Sub Ctee City of London 1990; *Recreations* family, gardening, photography, history; *Style*— Mrs Dorothy Livingston; Herbert Smith, Exchange House, Primrose Street, London EC2A 2HS (☎ 071 374 8000, fax 071 496 0043)

LIVINGSTON, Air Vice-Marshal Graham; QHS (1985); s of Neil Livingston (d 1977), and Margaret Anderson, *née* Graham (d 1989), of Bo'ness, West Lothian; *b* 2 Aug 1928; *Educ* Bo'ness Acad, Univ of Edinburgh (MB, ChB, DPH, DIH); *m* 1, 11 Nov 1953 (m dis 1968), Catherine Law; 1 s (Graham b 1955), 2 da (Jennifer b 1957, Catriona b 1959, d 1961); m 2, 19 June 1970, Carol Judith Palmer; 1 s (David b 1972), 1 da (Sara Jane b 1971); *Career* RAF med offr, flying stations N Ireland 1952-4, SMO RAF El Hamra Abyad Egypt 1954-55; GP 1956-57; SMO: RAF Lindholme 1958-60, RAF Honington 1960-62; post grad Univ of Edinburgh 1962-63; sr med offr: RAF Laarbruch Germany 1963-66, RAF Coll Cranwell 1966-70; registrar RAF Hosp Cosford 1970, CO RAF IHMT Halton 1971, registrar TPMRAF Hosp Akrotiri Cyprus 1972-74; CO RAF Hosp: Cosford 1974-76, Wegberg Germany 1976-9; dep dir med personnel & orgn MOD 1979-80, Air Cdre 1980, dep PMO Strike Cmd 1981-3; PMO: RAF Germany 1983-4, RAF Support Cmd 1984-89; presently conslt occupational health physician NW Herts Health Authy 1989-; Air Vice-Marshal 1984; QHS 1985-89; MFCM 1974, MFOM 1981, FBIM 1986, MFPHM 1990; *Recreations* golf, skiing, caravanning; *Clubs* RAF, Ashridge GC; *Style*— Air Vice-Marshal Graham Livingston; c/o Lloyds Bank plc, Cox's and Kings Branch, PO Box 1190, 7 Pall Mall, London SW1Y 5NA

LIVINGSTON, Dr Martin Gerard; s of Arnold Louis Livingston, of 36 Broom Rd East, Newton Mearns, Glasgow, and Joyce, *née* Sternstein; *b* 19 May 1953; *Educ* Hillhead HS Glasgow, Univ of Glasgow (MB ChB, MD); *m* 4 July 1974, Hilary Monica, da of Dr Basil Green, of Glasgow; 1 s (Richard Jack b 1983), 1 da (Judith Fiona b 1985); *Career* psychiatry rotation Southern Gen Hosp and Leverndale Hosp 1978-79; Univ of Glasgow: lectr Psychological Med Dept 1979-83, sr lectr and hon conslt psychiatrist 1983-; pubns on: rehabilitation in psychiatry, psychological impact of head injury and epilepsy on patients and their relatives, drug treatments in psychiatry; regnl advsr on rehabilitation 1987-, chm Glasgow Psychiatric Speciality Ctee 1989-; MRCPsych 1980; *Books* Rehabilitation of Adults and Children with Severe Head Injury (contrib, 1989); *Recreations* reading, photography, classical music; *Style*— Martin Livingston, Esq; 15 Ayr Road, Whitecraigs, Glasgow G46 6SB (☎ 041 638 6868); Dept of Psychological Medicine, University of Glasgow, 6 Whittinghame Gardens, Great Western Rd, Glasgow G12 (☎ 041 334 9826); Gartnavel Royal General Hospitals, Great Western Rd, Glasgow G12 0YN (☎ 041 334 8122 ext 368)

LIVINGSTON, Roderick George; s of Hugh Livingston (d 1981), of Streetly, and Rhoda Margaret, *née* Mathieson; *b* 10 Dec 1944; *Educ* Shrewsbury, Univ of Aberdeen (BSc), Univ of Exeter (ADPA); *m* 23 Sept 1974, Willma, da of William Watt (d 1977), of Edinburgh; 2 s (Alastair b 1976, Michael b 1981); *Career* admin asst UCW Aberystwyth 1970-72 (graduate asst 1969-70) asst sec Univ of Dundee 1975-78 (sr admin asst 1972-75); Univ of Strathclyde: asst sec 1978-81, asst registrar 1981-85, sr asst registrar 1985-88, sr asst registrar and faculty offr 1988-; UCCA: memb Cncl of Mgmnt 1982-, memb Statistics Ctee 1986-, dir of co 1988- (1982-87), memb Exec Ctee 1988-; memb Scot Univs Cncl on Entrance 1987-90,Pubns and Schs Liaison Ctees; FSA Scot 1963, ACIS 1972; *Recreations* history, rowing; *Clubs* Lansdowne; *Style*— Roderick Livingston, Esq; 51 Strathblane Rd, Milngavie, Glasgow G62 8HA (☎ 041 956 3851); University of Strathclyde, McCance Building, 16 Richmond St, Glasgow G1 1XQ (☎ 041 552 4400 ext 2387, fax 041 552 0775, tlx 77472 UNSLIBG)

LIVINGSTON BOOTH, (John) Dick; OBE (1975); s of Julian Livingston Booth (d 1962), of Hadlow, Tonbridge, Kent, and Grace Marion, *née* Swainson (d 1962); *b* 7 July 1918; *Educ* Melbourne GS, Sidney Sussex Coll Cambridge (MA); *m* 1, 1 Nov 1941, Joan Ashley (d 1976), da of Ashley Tabrum, OBE (d 1952); 2 s (Timothy b 3 May 1943, Michael b 12 Dec 1946), 1 da (Fiona b 21 Feb 1960); m 2, Audrey Betty Hope Harvey, da of Sqdn Ldr James Haslett (ka 1916); *Career* War Serv 1940-43 T/Capt RA, instr 121 HAC OCTU RHA, RWAFF; Colonial Admin Serv Nigeria 1943-57, perm sec to Min of Local Govt E Nigeria 1956-57; dir Charities Aid Fndn 1957-81; charity conslt 1981-; chm: Europhil Tst 1986-90, Legislation Monitoring Serv for Charities 1981-; patron Int Standing Conf on Philanthropy 1987-; lay reader C of E

1955-83; FRGS 1949; *Books* Directory of Grant-Making Trusts (bi-annual 1968-), Charity Statistics (annual 1978-), Trusts and Foundations in Europe (1971), Report on Foundation Activity (1977); *Recreations* travel; *Clubs* Garrick, Royal Cwlth; *Style—* Dick Livingston Booth, Esq, OBE; Trulls Hatch IV, Rotherfield, E Sussex TN6 3QL (☎ 0892 853 205); 242 Bahia Dorada, Estepona, Malaga, Spain (☎ 010 34 052 801 226)

LIVINGSTONE, David Willmott; CBE; s of late George Blair Livingstone; *b* 3 Feb 1926; *Educ* Haberdashers' Aske's, Ch Ch Oxford; *m* 1950, Jane Margaret; 1 s, 3 da; *Career* Sub Lieut RNVR; dep chm and md Albright & Wilson Ltd (md 1972, dep chm and md 1977), dir IMI Ltd, vice-pres Chemical Industries Assoc (CIA), memb Econ Devpt for Chemical Industry, memb cncl CBI; life govr Birmingham Univ, hon tres-govr Fircroft Coll Birmingham; *Recreations* squash, golf, reading, music; *Clubs* Athenaeum, Edgbaston Priory, Edgbaston Golf; *Style—* David Livingstone, Esq, CBE; 87 Harborne Rd, Edgbaston, Birmingham (☎ 021 454 2087)

LIVINGSTONE, Prof Donald; s of Alexander Livingstone (d 1954), and Margaret, *née* Cattanach (d 1958); *b* 27 Sept 1924; *Educ* Eshowe Sch Zululand, Univ of Natal (BSc, MSc), Univ of Edinburgh (PhD); *m* 28 Dec 1949, Gertrude Mary, da of Richard Marie McElligott (d 1967); 2 s (Alasdair b 1954, Naill b 1966), 3 da (Catharine b 1951, Deirdre b 1957, Margaret b 1960); *Career* lectr and sr lectr Univ of Natal 1949-58, asst and assoc prof Univ of Michigan 1958-68, prof of pure mathematics Univ of Birmingham 1968-; various pubns in tech jls; memb Edinburgh Mathematical Soc 1948; LMS 1965; *Recreations* languages and cultures, natural history; *Style—* Prof Donald Livingstone; 64 Salisbury Road, Moseley, Birmingham B13 8JT (☎ 021 4493469), University of Birmingham, School of Mathematics and Statistics, PO Box 363, Birmingham B15 2TT (☎ 021 4146580)

LIVINGSTONE, Lady Elisabeth; Elisabeth Jeanne-Doreen; *née* Fox-Strangways; da of 8 Earl of Ilchester (d 1970), by his w Laure, *née* Mazaraki; *b* 22 Jan 1931; *m* 1, 1958 (m dis 1969), Peter Skelton; 1 da (Caroline); m 2, 1977, John Livingstone, s of Thomas Livingstone (d 1986), of Orchard Way, Woolavington, Somerset; *Career* french language tutor 1960-, interpreter Anglo-French Circle Torquay 1970-; princ of Personality and Modelling Course (Devon) 1982-; *Style—* The Lady Elisabeth-Doreen Livingstone; 1 St Anthony, Higher Woodfield Rd, Torquay, Devon

LIVINGSTONE, Ian; s of Donald Livingstone (d 1978), and Margaret Dunn Mackay, *née* Darling (d 1968); *b* 11 Oct 1933; *Educ* Univ of Sheffield (BA), Yale Univ (MA); *m* 8 Sept 1962, Grace Ida, da of Peter Watuwa (d 1983), of Mbale, Uganda; 1 s (John b 19 Nov 1966), 3 da (Shona b 19 June 1965, Edisa b 3 June 1973, Sia (twin) b 3 June 1973); *Career* dir economic res bureau Univ of Dares Salaam 1968-71, reader in economics Univ of Newcastle-upon-Tyne 1971-78, prof of devpt economics Univ of East Anglia 1978; *Books Monographs* West African Economics (1969), Economics and Development (1970), Economic Policy for Development (1971), Agricultural Economics for Tropical Africa (180), Economics for Eastern Africa (1980), Development Economics and Policy (1981), Irrigation Economics in Poor Countries (1982), Approaches to Development Studies (1982), Rural Development, Employment and Incomes in Kenya (1986), Economics for West Africa (1987), The Marketing of Cocoa and Copra in Papua New Guinea (1989), Dams, Drought and Development in Brazil (1990); *Recreations* squash; *Style—* Prof Ian Livingstone; 6 Rosslare, Norwich NR4 6AW (☎ 0603 55624), School of Development Studies, Univ of East Anglia, Norwich NR4 7TJ (☎ 0603 56161)

LIVINGSTONE, Ian Lang; s of John Lang Livingstone, of 23 Cunningham St, Motherwell, and Margaret Steele, *née* Barbour (d 1982); *b* 23 Feb 1938; *Educ* Hamilton Acad, Univ of Glasgow (BL); *m* 30 March 1967, Diane, da of Frank Hales, of 199 Inner Promenade, Lytham St Annes; 2 s (Andrew b 1968, Gordon b 1970); *Career* slr; dir: Motherwell Enterprise Tst 1983-, Scotland West Bd Tstee Savings Bank 1985, Glendale Homes (Strathclyde) Ltd, Bowmere Properties Ltd, Clydesdale Building Services Ltd; chm: Interchase Ltd, Motherwell Enterprise Devpt Co Ltd, Lanarkshire Development Agencies Ltd, Bowmere Properties Ltd, Hamilton and Dist Slrs Property Centre; Notary Public 1962; dir and chm Motherwell FC 1973-87; hon pres: Motherwell Cons Asoc 1981-, Motherwell Utd YMCA, Motherwell Co of St Andrew's Ambulance Corps; chm Cncl Motherwell Coll, hon slr Dalziel HS Memorial Tst; *Recreations* golf, music; *Clubs* Motherwell Cons; *Style—* Ian Livingstone, Esq; Roath Park, 223 Manse Rd, Motherwell ML1 2PY (☎ 0698 53750); Ballantyne & Copland, Solicitors, Torrance House, Knowetop, Motherwell (☎ 0698 66200, fax 0698 69387)

LIVINGSTONE, Jack; s of Harry Livingston, of Southport, and Ruth, *née* Kaye; *b* 27 April 1934; *Educ* Ackworth Sch, King's Coll London; *m* 5 June 1963, Janice Vivienne, da of Lt Sidney Jeffrey Manson, of Salford, Manchester; 1 s (Terence b 1966), 2 da (Joanna b 1964 d 1978, Vanessa b 1970); *Career* sr aircraftsman 2 Tactical Force RAF, served Germany; chm London Scottish Bank plc; memb Deposit Protection Bd; involved with: Jewish Blind Soc, Central Br Fund, Brookvale for the Mentally Handicapped; memb: Patrons and Assocs Manchester City Art Gallery, NW Ctee The Lord Taverners; *Recreations* tennis, bridge; *Style—* Jack Livingstone, Esq; London Scottish Bank plc, Arndale House, Arndale Centre, Manchester M4 3AQ (☎ 061 834 2861, fax 061 834 2536, car 0831 116397, telex 669004)

LIVINGSTONE, Ken; MP (Lab) Brent East 1987-; s of Robert Moffat and Ethel Ada Livingstone; *b* 17 June 1945; *Educ* Tulse Hill Comprehensive Sch, Philippa Fawcett Coll of Educn; *m* 1973 (m dis 1982), Christine Pamela Chapman; *Career* memb (Lab) GLC for Norwood 1973-77, Hackney North 1977-81, for Paddington 1981-86, leader GLC 1981-86; memb (Lab) NEC 1987-89; *Books* If Voting Changed Anything They'd Abolish It (1987), Livingstone's Labour (1989); *Style—* Ken Livingstone, Esq, MP; House of Commons, London SW1A 0AA

LIVINGSTONE, Marco Eduardo; s of Leon Livingstone, of London, and Alicia Arce, *née* Fernández; *b* 17 March 1952; *Educ* Univ of Toronto (BA), Courtauld Inst of Art (MA); *Career* asst keeper of Br Art Walker Art Gallery Liverpool 1976-82, dep dir Museum of Modern Art Oxford 1982-86, area ed 20th century The Dictionary of Art 1986- (dep ed 19th and 20th centuries 1987-), UK advsr to Art Life Ltd Tokyo 1989-; author of several pubns incl: Sheer Magic by Allen Jones (1979), David Hockney (1981, 2 edn 1987), Duane Michals (1985), R B Kitaj (1985), David Hockney: Faces (1987), Pop Art (1990); memb Soc of Authors 1980-; *Style—* Marco Livingstone, Esq; The Dictionary of Art, Macmillan Publishers Ltd, 4 Little Essex St, London WC2 (☎ 071 836 6633, fax 071 240 1075)

LIVINGSTONE-LEARMONTH, (Lestock Harold) George; s of Lestock Brian Livingstone-Learmonth, of Park Farm, Pinkney, Malmesbury, Wilts, and Nancy Douglas, *née* Roffey (d 1950); *b* 4 July 1942; *Educ* Radley, Univ of Edinburgh (BSc), Univ of Capetown (MBA); *m* 1, 4 June 1966 (m dis), Diana, da of Col C K Hill-Wood; 1 s (Alexander b 1969); m 2, 28 Sept 1973, Katherine, da of T R D Kebbell; 2 s (Edward b 1974, Maxwell b 1977); *Career* dir: Beralt Tin and Wolfram 1973-80, Ayer Hitam Tin 1976-77, Aokam Tin 1977-80, Tongkah Harbour 1977-78, Amalgamated Tin Mines of Nigeria 1977-80, Gopeng Consolidated 1978-80, New Court Natural Resources 1982-86; md: Hampton Gold Mining Areas plc 1980-86, Insituform Group Ltd 1987; fndr and chm Double II Communication Consultants 1989-; *Recreations* boxing, photography, choral singing, woodwork; *Clubs* Hurlingham, IOD; *Style—* George Livingstone-Learmonth, Esq; 23 Perrymead St, London SW6 3SN

LIVINGSTONE-LEARMONTH, John Christian; s of Lt-Col Lennox John Livingstone-Learmonth, DSO, MC (d 1988), and Nancy Winifred, *née* Wooler (d 1989); *b* 30 Oct 1950; *Educ* Eton, Univ of York (BA); *m* 13 Dec 1986, (Elizabeth) Fiona, da of A J Stewart-Liberty, MC, of The Lee, Buckinghamshire (d 1990); 1 s (Edward b 1988); *Career* SA mktg offr James Buchanan and Co 1975-83, sr ptnr Livingstone Communication 1987 chm Focus Communications 1991; Distinguished Visitor to Miami; *Books* The Wines of the Rhône (1978); *Recreations* the turf, fishing, association football, travel in S America, wine tasting and writing; *Clubs* Turf, Fox House; *Style—* John Livingstone-Learmonth, Esq; Focus Communications, Prince Rupert House, 9-10 College Street, London EC4 (☎ 071 248 5688, fax 071 248 5692)

LIYANAGE, Chris; s of Wilmot Porambe Liyanage (d 1971), and Valerie, *née* Rupasinghe; *b* 26 May 1939; *Educ* Royal Coll Colombo Sri Lanka, Univ of Ceylon (BSc), Univ of Surrey (MSc), Cranfield Sch of Mgmnt (MBA); *m* 6 July 1968, Dr Priya, da of Edmund Dias (d 1985), of Sri Lanka; 2 s (Priyantha b 31 Dec 1970, Rohantha b 28 Dec 1973), 1 da (Chrisanthi b 14 Nov 1971); *Career* Lt Ceylon Engrs Regt Sri Lankan Army 1964, Capt 1968; WS Atkins & Partners Epsom 1970-72, Santa Fe Engineering Ltd 1978-80, Worley Engineering Ltd 1980-85, Kvaerner Engineering A/S Norway 1985-88, project mangr Brown & Root Vickers Ltd 1989-; CEng, MICE, FIMarE, MBIM; *Recreations* squash, cricket, golf; *Clubs* RAC (Pall Mall and Woodcote); *Style—* Chris Liyanage, Esq; 19 Links Rd, Epsom, Surrey, KT17 3PP, (☎ 0372 721467); c/o Brown & Root Vickers Ltd, 125 High St, Colliers Wood, London SW19 2JR (☎ 081 540 8300, fax 081 543 1799 telex 8812671 BRRTLN G)

LLAMBIAS, Douglas Ernest John; s of Ernest Llambias (d 1943), and Hilda, *née* Peat (d 1984); *b* 13 Nov 1943; *Educ* De La Salle Sch London; *m* 25 June 1984, Renée; 1 s by previous m (Damian Heathcote Jotham b 1971); *Career* CA; taxation specialist Arthur Andersen 1968-70, chm Douglas Llambias Associate Ltd 1982- (md 1970), chm and chief exec Business Exchange Group 1984-, dir Murlen Ltd 1985-; memb Cncl ICA; *Recreations* badminton, wines; *Clubs* Reform, RAC; *Style—* Douglas Llambias, Esq; 21 John Adam St, London WC2N 6JG

LLANDAFF, Bishop of 1985-; Rt Rev Roy Thomas Davies; s of William Hubert John Davies (d 1967), and Dilys Hannah, *née* Thomas; *b* 31 Jan 1934; *Educ* St David's Coll Lampeter (BA), Jesus Coll Oxford (BLitt), St Stephen's House Oxford; *Career* ordained St David's Cathedral: deacon 1959, priest 1960; archdeacon of Carmarthen 1982-85, clerical sec The Governing Body Church in Wales 1983-85, consecrated bishop of Llandaff 1985; *Recreations* walking, reading; *Clubs* Cardiff and County; *Style—* The Rt Rev the Bishop of Llandaff; Llys Esgob, Cathedral Green, LLandaff, Cardiff, South Glamorgan CF5 2YE (☎ 0222 562400)

LLEWELLEN PALMER, Hon Mrs (Veronica); *née* Saumarez; da of late 5 Baron de Saumarez; *b* 1915; *m* 1945, Brig Anthony William Allen Llewellen Palmer, DSO, MC, King's Dragoon Gds (d 1990); *Career* VAD attached RAF 1940-43, ATS 1943-45; *Style—* The Hon Mrs Llewellen Palmer; Clos du Menage, Sark, Channel Islands

LLEWELLIN, Rt Rev (John) Richard Allan; *see*: St Germans, Bishop of

LLEWELLIN, (John) Stephen; s of John Charles Llewellin, of Guernsey, and Lilian, *née* Jenkins (d 1968); *b* 31 Oct 1938; *Educ* Cheltenham, Harper Adams Agric Coll; *m* 28 July 1961, Christine Irene, da of John Stanley Crewe (d 1955); 2 s (Richard b 1962, Peter b 1967); *Career* farmer and co dir; chm and md Little Haven Farms Ltd 1968-74; dir: Coastal Cottages Ltd, Celtic Sea Supply Base Ltd 1972-80, Barnlake Engineering Ltd 1972-80, Celtic Haven Ltd 1972-80; *Recreations* sailing, swimming; *Clubs* Lloyds of London; *Style—* Stephen Llewellin, Esq; Mill Race, Little Haven, Haverfordwest, Pembs SA62 3UH; Little Haven Farms Ltd, Fenton, Little Haven (☎ 0437 781 291)

LLEWELLIN DAVIES, Rev Dr Lawrence John David; s of Rev Canon Llewellin Davies (d 1948), of The Rectory, Narberth, Dyfed, and Elizabeth Anne, *née* Williams (d 1947); reverted surname to Llewellin Davies, the family name in the 18C, by deposition 1984; *b* 26 June 1916; *Educ* St David's Coll Sch Lampeter Dyfed, Jesus Coll Oxford (Schoolmaster Student 1967-68, BA, MA, Dip Ed), Univ of Bonn (DTheol); *m* 29 Dec 1949, Eileen May, da of late Harry Onion; 1 da (Elizabeth Anne (Mrs E A Kirby) b 1951); *Career* ordained St Davids Cathedral: deacon 1939, priest 1940; curate Narberth Dyfed 1939-48, officiating chaplain RAF 1942-44, chaplain Royal Marines Sch of Signalling 1944-46, chaplain RN Arms Depot Trecwn Dyfed 1947-48, TA CCF 1947-48, chaplain RAF (Extended Serv Cmmn) 1948-57, princ 2 Tactical Air Force Moral Leadership Sch Cologne W Germany 1953-57, dean of chapel and head Divinity Hall Herschel High Sch Slough 1959-80; sec gen: Schs Cncl for the Ordained Ministry 1970-80, BHS; FRSPB; *Books* The History of Early Hebrew Prophecy (1958), The Rich History of Mounton's Forgotten Sanctuary (1971); *Recreations* riding, gardening, protection of local environment; *Style—* The Rev Dr Llewellin Davies; Deans Lodge, Hollybush Hill, Stoke Poges, Slough, Berks SL2 4PZ (☎ 0753 662495)

LLEWELLYN *see also*: Seys Llewellyn

LLEWELLYN, Anthony David; s of William Henry Llewellyn (d 1977), of Rickmansworth, Herts, and Ida Elsie, *née* Davies (d 1980); *b* 23 March 1940; *Educ* Watford GS; *m* 23 May 1967, Jacqueline Hilary, da of William Frederick Curtis, of Croydon, Surrey; 2 da (Felicity b 1973, Lucinda b 1975); *Career* tax ptnr Touche Ross & Co CAs 1972-; memb Bd of Mgmnt and Fin and Gen Purposes Ctee LSHTM 1988-; ACIB 1963, FTII 1969, FCA 1977 (ACA 1970); *Recreations* tennis, skiing, bridge; *Style—* Anthony Llewellyn, Esq; Kingswood, Parkfield, Sevenoaks, Kent TN15 0HX; Touche Ross and Co, Friary Court, 65 Crutched Friars, London EC3N 2NP (☎ 071 480 7766, fax 071 480 6958)

LLEWELLYN, Dr (John) Anthony; s of George Armitage Llewellyn, of Ardsley, Yorks, and Hannah, *née* Jepson; *b* 18 June 1930; *Educ* Univ of Manchester (BSc), Univ of Leeds (MPhil), Univ of Lancaster (PhD); *m* 21 Feb 1957, Betty, da of William Masterton d (1980), of Barnsley, Yorks; 2 s (David Anthony b 2 Jan 1958, Stephen John b 5 July 1963), 1 da ((Margaret) Anne b 25 Aug 1959); *Career* computer systems design: English Electric Co, Ferranti Ltd, STC 1955-64; princ lectr Constantine Coll Middlesbrough 1964-69; sr lectr and head of dept Univ of Lancaster 1969-, author of various papers on theory of computer sci; Br int athlete in steeplechase 1957-, Br fell running champion super veteran category 1980, Euro 10,000m champion veteran category 1985; examiner and advsr Assoc Exammining Bd, assessor Nat HND and HNC; memb: BCS, BVA; *Books* Information and Coding (1987); *Recreations* athletics, road running, fell running; *Clubs* Walton Athletic, Lancaster and Manchester Athletic; *Style—* Dr Anthony Llewellyn; Computing Department, University of Lancaster, Lancaster, Lancs LA1 4YR (☎ 0524 65201, fax 0524 381707)

LLEWELLYN, Hon Lady (Christine Saumarez); da of 5 Baron de Saumarez (d 1969); *b* 1916; *m* 1944, Lt-Col Sir Henry (Harry) Morton Llewellyn, 3 Bt, CBE, DL, *qv*; *Career* serv WWII WRNS; *Style—* The Hon Lady Llewellyn; Ty'r Nant, Llanarth, Nr Raglan, Gwent NP5 2AR

LLEWELLYN, David St Vincent; s and h of Sir Harry Morton Llewellyn, 3 Bt, CBE, *qv*, and Hon Christine Saumarez, *qv*, yr da of 5 Baron de Saumarez; *b* 2 April 1946; *Educ* Eton, Aix-en-Provence; *m* 15 March 1980 (m dis 1987), Vanessa Mary, da of Lt Cdr Theodore Bernard Peregrine Hubbard; 2 da (Olivia b 1980, Arabella b 1983); *Career* ctee pres Club Royale of Geneva 1980-; *Recreations* foxhunting, wildlife preservation; *Clubs* Club Royal, Geneva; *Style—* David Llewellyn, Esq; 27 Hill Street, London W1 (☎ 071 493 1977, telex 881 3271 GECOMS-G)

LLEWELLYN, Prof David Thomas; s of Alfred George Llewellyn, of Gillingham, Dorset, and Elsie Elizabeth, *née* Frith; *b* 3 March 1943; *Educ* William Ellis GS, LSE (BSc); *m* 19 Sept 1970, Wendy Elizabeth, da of Henry Cecil James, MM (d 1973); 1 s (Mark b 15 Aug 1972, Rhys b 18 Dec 1978); *Career* economist: Unilever NV Rotterdam 1964-65, HM Treasy 1965-68; lectr Univ of Nottingham 1968-73, economist IMF Washington 1973-76, prof money and banking Loughborough Univ 1976- (head dept of economics 1980-); chm Loughborough Univ Banking Centre 1985-, conslt economist Butler Harlow Ueda 1989-; memb London Bd Halifax Building Soc 1986-; memb Ed Bd: Banking World 1984-, The Fin Journal 1989-; managing ed Chartered Inst of Bankers Occasional Res Papers Series; former conslt The World Bank, occasional memb Bank of England Panel of Academic Conslts; *Books* International Financial Integration (1980), Framework of UK Monetary Policy (1983), Regulation of Financial Institutions (1986), Evolution of British Financial System (1985), Reflections on Money (1990), Recent Developments in International Monetary Economics (1990); *Recreations* boating, cooking, DIY, gardening, travel; *Style—* Prof David T Llewellyn; 8 Landmere Lane, Ruddington, Nottingham NG11 6ND (☎ 0602 216 071); Dept of Economics, Loughborough Univ, Loughborough, Leics (☎ 0509 222 700, fax 0509 610 813, telex 34319)

LLEWELLYN, Sir David Treharne; 3 s of Sir David Richard Llewellyn, 1 Bt (d 1940), and Magdalene Anne, *née* Harries (d 1966); *b* 17 Jan 1916; *Educ* Eton, Trinity Coll Cambridge (MA); *m* 18 Feb 1950, Joan Anne, OBE, da of Robert Henry Williams; 2 s, 1 da; *Career* served 1939-45 War, fusilier Royal Fusiliers, Capt Welsh Gds NW Europe; MP (C) Cardiff North 1950-59, parly under sec of state Home Office 1951-52, resigned; former memb Broadcasting Cncl for Wales; journalist; kt 1960; *Books* Nye the Beloved Patrician, The Adventures of Arthur Artfully, The Racing Book of Quotations (jtly with Nick Robinson); *Style—* Sir David Llewellyn; The Glebe, Yattendon, nr Newbury, Berks

LLEWELLYN, David Walter; CBE (1983); s of Eric Gilbert Llewellyn, and Florence May Llewellyn; *b* 13 Jan 1930; *Educ* Radley; *m* 1, 1955 (m dis 1985), Josephine Margaret Buxton; 3 s; m 2, Tessa Caroline Sandwith; *Career* cmmnd RE 1952; jt md Llewellyn Mgmnt Servs Ltd and other cos in the Llewellyn Gp 1953-, industl advsr to Min of Housing and Local Govt 1967-68; pres Joinery and Timber Contractors' Assoc 1976-77; chm: Nat Contractors' Gp of Nat Fedn of Bldg Trade Employers 1977, Bldg Regulations Advsy Ctee 1977-85; dep chm Nat Bldg Agency 1977-82, Lloyd's underwriter 1978-, pres Chartered Inst of Bldg 1986-87; govr St Andrew's Sch Eastbourne 1966-78, tstee Queen Alexandra Cottage Homes Eastbourne 1973-; Master Worshipful Co of Tin Plate Workers (Wire Workers) 1985; *Recreations* the use, restoration and preservation of historic vehicles; *Clubs* Reform, The Devonshire (Eastbourne), Bentley Drivers; *Style—* David Llewellyn, Esq, CBE; Coopers Cottage, Chiddingly, nr Lewes, E Sussex (☎ 0825 872447); Walter Llewellyn & Sons Ltd, 16-20 South St, Eastbourne, East Sussex (☎ 0323 21300, telex 877213)

LLEWELLYN, Graham David; *b* 22 Sept 1921; *Career* gp chief exec Sotheby Parke Bernet 1982-83, gp sr vice-pres Sotheby Holdings Inc 1983-, advsy bd Sothbey Holdings Inc 1988-; *Style—* Graham D Llewellyn, Esq; Sotheby's, 34-35 New Bond St, London W1A 2AA (☎ 071 408 5423, telex 24454 SPBLON-G, fax 071 355 1317)

LLEWELLYN, Sir Henry Morton (Harry); 3 Bt (UK 1922), of Bwllfa, Aberdare, Glamorgan, CBE (1953, OBE Mil 1945), DL (Monmouthshire 1952); s of Sir David Richard Llewellyn, 1 Bt, (d 1940); suc bro, Sir Rhys Llewellyn, 2 Bt (d 1978); *b* 18 July 1911; *Educ* Oundle, Trinity Hall Cambridge (MA); *m* 1944, Hon Christine, *qv*, da of 5 Baron de Saumarez (d 1969); 2 s (David St Vincent and Roderic Victor, *qqv*), 1 da (Anna Christina); *Heir* s, David St Vincent Llewellyn; *Career* joined Warwickshire Yeo 1939, ME Staff Coll 1942, GSO2 8 Army 1943 (despatches twice), GSO1 21 Army Gp 1943-44; chm Davenco (Engineers) Ltd; pres: Whitbread Wales Ltd, dir Chepstow Racecourse Co Ltd, pres British Equestrian Fedn: British Show Jumping Assoc 1967-69; memb: Nat Hunt Ctee 1946- (steward 1948-50), Jockey Club 1969; Grand National (riding Ego): came 2 1936, 4 1937; chm Sports Council for Wales, vice-chm Civic Tst for Wales, chm Nationwide-Building Soc Wales; formerly chm: C L Clay & Co (Coal Exporters), Norths Navigation: Collieries Ltd, Welsh Regn B Eagle Star Insurance, Lloyds Bank reg B; dir TWW 1958-68; JP 1953-67, High Sheriff Monmouthshire 1966; memb UK Cncl World Wide Fund for Nature 1985-; fell Royal Inst for the Protection of Birds 1987; Grand Prix des Nations (Equestrian) Gold medal Olympic Games Helsinki 1952, Bronze medal London 1948, Royal Humane Soc medal 1956; *Style—* Sir Harry Llewellyn, Bt, CBE, DL; Ty'r Nant, Llanarth, nr Raglan, Gwent NP5 2A

LLEWELLYN, Lady Honor Morvyth Malet; *née* Vaughan; JP (Dyfed); da of 7 Earl of Lisburne (d 1965); *b* 1919; *m* 1943, Maj (William Herbert) Rhidian Llewellyn, MC, DL, *qv*; *Career* sub-visitor St David's Coll Lampeter 1964-85; *Style—* The Lady Honor Llewellyn, JP; 4 St Omer Rd, Guildford, Surrey GU1 2DB

LLEWELLYN, His Hon Judge John Desmond Seys; s of Charles Ernest Llewellyn (d 1957), and Hannah Margretta Llewellyn (d 1961); *b* 3 May 1912; *Educ* Cardiff HS, Jesus Coll Oxford (MA); *m* 1, 1939, Elaine (d 1984), da of Henry Leonard Porcher (d 1961); m 2, 1986, Joan, da of Reginald Holmes-Cuming, JP, of Plymouth; 3 s; *Career* served Capt RTR 1940-46; called to the Bar Inner Temple (in absence while on active serv) 1945, in practice Wales and Chester circuit 1947-71, dep chm Cheshire QS 1968-71, county ct judge 1971, circuit judge 1972; Parly candidate (Lib) Chester 1955 and 1956; *Recreations* travel, art, archaeology, English setters; *Clubs* Athenaeum (Liverpool); *Style—* His Hon Judge Seys Llewellyn; Little Chetwyn, Gresford, Clwyd (☎ 0978 852 419)

LLEWELLYN, Rev John Francis Morgan; LVO (1981); s of Canon David Leonard John Llewellyn (d 1966); *b* 4 June 1921; *Educ* King's Coll Sch Wimbledon, Pembroke Coll Cambridge, Ely Theol Coll; *m* 1955, Audrey Eileen, da of Frederick James Binks; *Career* served WWII; chaplain and asst master King's Coll Sch Wimbledon 1952-58, headmaster Cathedral Choir Sch and minor canon St Paul's Cathedral 1958-74, sacrist and warden of Coll of Minor Canons 1968-74, priest-in-ordinary to HM The Queen 1970-74 (dep priest-in-ordinary 1968-70 and 1974-), chaplain of the Chapel Royal of St Peter ad Vincula within HM Tower of London 1974-89; chaplain City of London Slrs Co 1974-89, sub-chaplain Order of St John of Jerusalem 1970-74, sr officiating chaplain 1974-; chaplain Worshipful Co of Builders Merchants 1986-; *Books* The Tower of London: Its Buildings and Institutions (contrib, 1978), The Chapels in the Tower of London (1987); *Clubs* Hawks (Cambridge), MCC; *Style—* The Rev John Llewellyn, LVO; Flat 1, Lavershot Hall, London Rd, Windlesham, Surrey GU20 6LE

LLEWELLYN, Sir Michael Rowland Godfrey; 2 Bt (UK 1959), of Baglan, JP (W Glamorgan 1984); s of Col Sir (Robert) Godfrey Llewellyn, 1 Bt, CB, CBE, MC, TD, JP, DL (d 1986); *b* 15 June 1921; *Educ* Harrow; *m* 1, 24 Sept 1946 (m dis 1951), Bronwen Mary (d 1965), da of Sir (Owen) Watkin Williams-Wynn, 8 Bt; m 2, 1 Dec 1956, Janet Prudence, da of Lt-Col Charles Thomas Edmondes, JP, DL, of Bridgend, Glamorgan; 3 da; *Career* Capt (Hon Maj) Grenadier Gds (Reserve); High Sheriff W Glamorgan 1980-81; pres: W Glamorgan Scout Cncl 1987-, W Glamorgan Branch SSAFA 1987-, Swansea Business Club 1985-88, Swansea Branch Br Legion 1987-, W Glamorgan Branch Magistrates Assoc 1988-, TA & VRA for Wales 1990-; chm W Glamorgan St John Cncl 1967-79 (vice pres 1979-88, pres 1988-); Lord Lt W Glamorgan 1987 (vice Lord Lt 1986, DL 1982); CStJ; *Recreations* shooting, gardening; *Style—* Sir Michael Llewellyn, Bt; Glebe House, Penmaen, nr Swansea, W Glamorgan SA3 2HH (☎ 0792 371 232)

LLEWELLYN, Maj-Gen (Richard) Morgan; OBE (1979, MBE 1976); s of Griffith Robert Poynz Llewellyn (d 1972), of Baglan Hall, Abergavenny, Gwent, and Bridget Margaret Lester, *née* Karslake (d 1980); *b* 22 Aug 1937; *Educ* Haileybury; *m* 24 Oct 1964, (Elizabeth) Polly Lamand, da of Lt-Col Francis Theodore Sobey, CBE, MC (d 1973), of Pine Lodge, Ilkley, Yorkshire; 3 s (Huw b 1967, Glyn b 1971, Robert b 1979), 2 da (Sally b 1967 d 1977, Kitty b 1981); *Career* cmmnd Royal Welch Fusiliers 1956, active serv in Malaya 1957 and Cyprus 1958-59, instr Army Outward Bound Sch 1962-63, Staff Coll 1970, mil asst to Chief of Gen Staff 1971-72, Bde Maj 39 Inf Bde 1974-76, cmd 1 Bn Royal Welch Fusiliers 1976-79, jr directing staff RCDS 1979-81, cmd Gurkha Field Force Hong Kong 1981-84, Col Gurhka Tport Regt 1984-, dir army staff duties MOD 1985-87, GOC Wales 1987-90, Col The Royal Welch Fusilers 1990-, Chief of Staff HQ UK Land Forces 1990-; chm: Army Mountaineering Assoc, Army Target Shooting; vice pres Operation Raleigh, memb Cncl Soldiers and Airman's Scripture Readers Assoc; FBIM; *Recreations* reading, hill walking, shooting; *Clubs* Army and Navy, Cardiff and County; *Style—* Maj-Gen Morgan Llewellyn, OBE; COS HQ, United Kingdom Land Forces, Wilton, Salisbury, Wilts SP2 0AG

LLEWELLYN, Maj (William Herbert) Rhidian; MC, DL (Dyfed); 4 s of Sir David Richard Llewellyn, 1 Bt, (d 1940); *b* 8 July 1919; *Educ* Eton, RMC; *m* 1943, Lady Honor, JP, *qv*, 2 da of 7 Earl of Lisburne (d 1965); *Career* Capt Welsh Gds 1941, served 1939-45 (despatches), Maj 1945; memb CC Cardiganshire 1961-70; High Sheriff 1967-68; memb: Welsh Hosps Bd 1964-70, Ct of Govrs Nat Library of Wales 1967-68, T&AF Assoc Cardiganshire 1961-68, Wales and Monmouthshire TA&AVR Assoc 1968-70, Cardiganshire Agric Exec Ctee 1968-72; *Style—* Maj Rhidian Llewellyn, MC, DL; 4 St Omer Rd, Guildford, Surrey GU1 2DB

LLEWELLYN, Roderic Victor (Roddy); 2 s of Sir Harry Llewellyn, 3 Bt, CBE, *qv*, and Hon Christine Saumarez, *qv*; *b* 9 Oct 1947; *Educ* Shrewsbury, Aix-en-Provence, Merrist Wood Agric Coll; *m* 1981, Tatiana, da of Paul Soskin (d 1975), film producer; 3 da (Alexandra b 1982, Natasha b 1984, Rose-Anna b 1987); *Career* landscape designer, designer of garden furniture and furnishings, author, journalist and presenter; gardening corr: (Daily) Star 1981-86, Oracle 1982-83, Mail On Sunday 1987-; gardening pres TV AM 1984; *Books* Town Gardens (1981), Beautiful Backyards (1985), Water Gardens (1987), Elegance and Eccentricity (1989); *Recreations* philately, jig-saw puzzles; *Style—* Roddy Llewellyn, Esq; Yew Tree House, Westbury, Nr Brackley, Northants NN13 5JR (☎ 0280 704440)

LLEWELLYN, Samson Evan (Sam); s of William Somers Llewellyn, of Leighterton, and Innis Mary, *née* Dorrien Smith; *b* 2 Aug 1948; *Educ* Eton, St Catherine's Coll Oxford (MA); *m* 1975, Karen Margaret Wallace; 2 s (William David b 1978, Martin Stephen b 1980); *Career* author; bass guitarist Spread Eagle 1971-72, ed Pan/Picador 1973-76, sr ed McClelland & Stewart Toronto Canada 1976-79; *books* Hell Bay (1980), The Worst Journey in the Midlands (1983), Dead Reckoning (1987), Great Circle (1987), Blood Orange (1988), Death Roll (1989), Deadeye (1990), Blood Knot (1991); *Recreations* sailing, building, accompanying Mrs Llewellyn on the guitar and banjo; *Clubs* The Academy; *Style—* Sam Llewellyn, Esq; Andrew Hewson, John Johnston, Clerkenwell House, 45-47 Clerkenwell Green, London EC1R 0HT (☎ 071 251 0125, fax 071 251 2172)

LLEWELLYN, Timothy David; s of Graham David Llewellyn, of Chislehurst, Kent, and Dorothy Mary Driver; *b* 30 May 1947; *Educ* St Dunstan's Coll, Magdalene Coll Cambridge; *m* 1, 8 Aug 1970, Irene Sigrid Mercy, da of Sigurd Henriksen, of Copenhagen, Denmark; 1 s (Kristian b 1975); m 2, 9 Sept 1978, Elizabeth, da of Prof Mason Hammond, of Cambridge, Mass, USA; *Career* md Sotheby's 1984- (dir 1974-); chm The Friends of the Courtauld Institute 1986-; Miny of Culture and Fine Arts of the People's Republic of Poland Order of Cultural Merit 1986; *Recreations* music, fishing, travel; *Clubs* Brooks's, Queen's; *Style—* Timothy D Llewellyn, Esq; 3 Cranley Mansion, 160 Gloucester Rd, London SW7 4QF (☎ 071 373 2333); Sotheby's, 34-35 New Bond St, London W1A 2AA (☎ 071 493 8080, telex 24454 SPBLON G)

LLEWELLYN JONES, His Hon Ilston Percival; s of Rev Louis Cyril Francis Jones (d 1968), and Gertrude Ann, *née* Edmunds (d 1974); *b* 15 June 1916; *Educ* St John's Sch Leatherhead; *m* 3, 1963, Mary Eveline; 1 s from earlier marriage (Nigel Llewellyn b 1943); *Career* cmmnd RA, WWII serv to 1942; admitted slr 1938, Slrs Dept New Scotland Yard 1942-48, Devon County prosecutor 1952-56, clerk N Devon Justices 1956-62, rec 1973-78, circuit judge 1978-88, Parole Bd 1975-79; *Recreations* golf, music; *Clubs* Burnham and Berrow Golf, Royal Porthcawl Golf; *Style—* His Hon Ilston P Llewellyn Jones; Stonecroft, The Hayes, Cheddar, Somerset BS27 3HP (☎ 0934 743524)

LLEWELLYN-JONES, John Everard; s of Dr John Llewellyn-Jones (d 1976), of Honan, W Mersea, Essex, and Dr Joan, *née* Hannaford; *b* 3 Aug 1943; *Educ* Allhallows Sch, Kings Coll London (BSc), Dept of Educn Univ of Cambridge; *m* 4 Jan 1969, Marianne, da of Leendert Been, of Friesland, Netherlands; 1 s (David b 1976), 1 da (Céline b 1974); *Career* biology master Soham GS, second year ldr City of Ely Coll, head of biology Chalvedon Sch, lectr Basildon Coll of Further Educn; meetings organiser and sec Basildon Natural History Soc, chm Friends of Southend Museums, memb Conchological Soc GB and Ireland, nature reserve warden Essex Naturalist Tst; *Books* Cambridge Vertebrate Cut-Out series: Fish, Amphibian, Reptile, Bird, Mammal (1984), An Introductory Study of some aspects of Pollution (1984), Body Plans, Animals from the Inside (1986), Biokeys (1988); *Recreations* badminton, natural history; *Style—* John Llewellyn-Jones, Esq; 22 Grasmere Rd, Thundersley, Essex SS7 3HF (☎ 0268 759268)

LLEWELLYN SMITH, Prof Christopher; s of John Clare Llewellyn Smith (d 1990), of W Bagborough, Somerset, and Margaret Emily Frances, *née* Crawford; *b* 19 Nov 1942; *Educ* Wellington, New Coll Oxford (BA, DPhil); *m* 10 Sept 1966, Virginia, *née* Grey; 1 s (Caspar Michael b 24 Jan 1971), 1 da (Julia Clare b 2 Nov 1968); *Career* Royal Soc exchange fell Lebedev Inst Moscow 1967-68, fell Theoretical Studies Div CERN Geneva 1968-70, res assoc Stanford Linear Accelerator Centre (SLAC) Stanford California 1970-72, staff memb Theoretical Studies Div CERN Geneva 1972-74; St John's Coll Oxford: fell 1974-, lectr 1974-80, reader 1980-87, prof 1987-, chm of physics 1987; FRS 1984; *Style—* Prof Christopher Llewellyn Smith, FRS; 3 Wellington Place, Oxford OX1 2LD (☎ 0865 57145); Clarendon Laboratory, Oxford (☎ 0865 272370/1, fax 0865 272400, telex 83154 CLAROX G)

LLEWELLYN SMITH, Dr Michael John; s of John Clare Llewellyn Smith (d 1990), and Margaret Emily Frances, *née* Crawford; *b* 25 April 1939; *Educ* Wellington, New Coll Oxford (BA), St Antony's Coll Oxford (DPhil); *m* 8 April 1967, Colette, da of Georges Gaulier (d 1979), of France; 1 s (Stefan Gregory b 1970), 1 da (Sophie Alexandra b 1971); *Career* cultural attaché Moscow 1973-75, first sec Br Embassy Paris 1976-77, cnsllr Athens 1980-83, head of Soviet Dept FCO 1985-87, min Paris Embassy 1988-; author; *Books* The Great Island - A Study of Crete (1965), Ionian Vision - Greece in Asia Minor 1919-22 (1983); *Clubs* Utd Oxford and Cambridge Univ; *Style—* Dr Michael Llewellyn Smith, CMG; Foreign and Commonwealth Office, King

Charles St, London SW1A 2AH

LLEWELLYN-SMITH, Elizabeth Marion; CB (1986); da of John Clare Llewellyn Smith (d 1990), of Bagborough, Somerset, and Margaret Emily Frances, *née* Crawford; *b* 17 Aug 1934; *Educ* Christ's Hosp, Girton Coll Cambridge (BA, MA); *Career* govt serv; Bd of Trade 1956, dep dir gen of Fair Trading 1982-87, dep sec DTI 1987-; dir European Investment Bank 1987-90; princ elect St Hilda's Coll Oxford 1990-; *Clubs* Utd Oxford and Cambridge Univ; *Style—* Miss Elizabeth Llewellyn-Smith, CB; 1 Charlwood Rd, Putney, London SW15 1PJ (☎ 081 789 1572); St Hilda's College, Oxford OX4 1DY (☎ 0865 276884)

LLEWELYN; *see*: Dillwyn-Venables-Llewelyn

LLEWELYN, Desmond Wilkinson; s of Ivor Llewelyn (d 1930), of Newport, Gwent and Mia, *née* Wilkinson (d 1942); *b* 12 Sept 1914; *Educ* Radley, RADA; *m* 16 May 1938, Pamela Mary, da of Charles William Rivers Pantlin (d 1978); 2 s (Ivor b 1949, Justin b 1952); *Career* actor; joined Artists Rifles 1939, OCTU RMC Sandhurst 1939-40, cmmnd Royal Welch Fusiliers 1940, joined 1 Bn 1940, POW Germany 1940-45; in repertory Oxford Playhouse 1939, first appearance on TV 1939; plays incl: Golden Eagle, Spiders Webb; TV incl Follyfoot; Films incl: Cleopatra, 14 James Bond films in the character of "Q"; *Recreations* gardening; *Clubs* Farmers; *Style—* Desmond Llewelyn, Esq; Linkwell, Old Town, Bexhill on Sea, East Sussex

LLEWELYN, Dr (David Evan) Huw; s of John Llewelyn, of Ammanford, Dyfed, and Catherine Jane, *née* Jones; *b* 1 Feb 1946; *Educ* Pontardawe GS, Univ of Wales; *m* 15 Feb 1969, Angela Mary, da of Norman John Williams; 1 s (Rhys Huw Gruffudd b 1980), 2 da (Rhian Eleri b 1974, Betham Mari b 1977); *Career* med registrar Univ Hosp of Wales, lectr med Bart's Med Coll, sr lectr med King's Coll Sch of Med and Dentistry; author of various books on the diagnostic process; RSM; *Recreations* squash, walking, rugby spectator; *Style—* Dr Huw Llewelyn; Department of Medicine, King's College School of Medicine & Dentistry, Bessemer Rd, London SE5 9PJ (☎ 071 2746222)

LLEWELYN, John William Howard; s of Maj Howard William Jones Llewelyn, MC (d 1987), of Llangynidr, Powys, and Gladys May Marshally; *b* 2 May 1939; *Educ* Harrow, Brasenose Coll Oxford; *m* 1, 18 March 1967, Priscilla Caroline, da of Thomas Arthur Rickard, of The Old Rectory, Rushock, Worcs; 2 s (Hugo b 1971, Benjamin b 1974), 2 da (Virginia b 1969, Joanne b 1979); m 2, 10 May 1984, Diana Mary, da of Timothy Hallinan (d 1970), of Co Cork; *Career* Lt The Shropshire Yeo 1961-66; slr 1966; asst dep coroner for Powys 1978-; under sheriff Brecknock 1979-85; *Recreations* fishing, shooting, sailing, golf, oenology; *Clubs* Cavalry and Guards'; *Style—* John W H Llewelyn, Esq; Lower Castleton, Clifford, Herefordshire (☎ 04973 591); 4 The Bulwark, Brecon, Powys (☎ 0874 4422, fax 0874 611303)

LLEWELYN DAVIES, Hon Harriett Lydia Rose; da of Baron Llewelyn-Davies (Life Peer, d 1981); *b* 1955; *Style—* The Hon Harriett Llewelyn Davies; 2 Carpenter's Yard, Park St, Tring, Herts

LLEWELYN-DAVIES OF HASTOE, Baroness (Life Peer UK 1967), of Hastoe, Co Hertford; (Annie) Patricia Llewelyn Davies; PC (1975); da of C P Parry, of Prenton, Cheshire; *b* 16 July 1915; *Educ* Liverpool Coll Huyton, Girton Coll Cambridge; *m* 3 June 1943, Baron Llewelyn-Davies (Life Peer, d 1981); 3 da (Hon Melissa (Hon Mrs Curling) b 1 June 1945, Hon Harriet Lydia Rose b 7 Jan 1955, Hon Rebecca (Hon Mrs Daniel Rea) b 21 Dec 1957); *Career* sits as Lab Peer in Lords; temp administrative civil servant 1940-51, Parly candidate (Lab) 1951-60; dir Africa Educnl Tst 1960-69, chm Bd of Govrs Gt Ormond St Hosp for Sick Children 1967-69 (memb 1955-69); a Baroness in waiting to HM The Queen 1969-70; oppn dep chief whip House of Lords 1972, oppn chief whip 1973-74, capt of The Gentlemen at Arms and govt chief whip 1974-79, oppn chief whip 1979-82, princ dep chm Ctees House of Lords 1982-86, chm Lords' Euro Communities Select Ctee 1982-86; chm Women's Nat Cancer Control Ctee 1972-74, dep speaker House of Lords 1986-; hon fell Girton Coll Cambridge 1978; *Style—* The Rt Hon the Lady Llewelyn-Davies of Hastoe, PC; Flat 15, 9-11 Belsize Grove, London NW3 4UU (☎ 071 586 4060)

LLOYD, Prof Alan Brian; s of Howard Brinley Lloyd (d 1989), of 30 Arnold Place, Tredegar, Gwent, and Doris Marian, *née* Walsh; *b* 24 Sept 1941; *Educ* Tredegar GS, Univ Coll Swansea (BA), Queen's Coll Oxford (MA, DPhil); *m* 1, 14 Aug 1965, Caroline Barclay (d 1984), da of The Hon Julius McDonald Greenfield, CMG, of 40 Berkeley Square, 173 Main Rd, 7700 Rondebosh, SA; 2 s (Julian b 14 Aug 1966, Duncan b 19 Nov 1967), 1 da (Katherine b 28 Feb 1970); m 2, 30 Nov 1985, Patricia Elizabeth, da of Patrick Cyril Ward, of 13 Chamberlain Rd, Llandaff North, Cardiff; *Career* Univ Coll Swansea: asst lectr 1967, sr lectr 1977, reader 1983, prof 1988; memb Ctee of Egypt Exploration Soc, sometime memb Cncl Hellenic Soc; FSA 1987; *Books* Herodotus Book II (1975-88); contrib: The Tomb of Hetepka (with G T Martin, 1978), Ancient Egypt (with B Trigger et al, 1983); Erodoto Le Storie Libro II (1989) Saqqara Tombs I (with W V Davies et al, 1984); *Style—* Prof Alan Lloyd; University College of Swansea, Singleton Park, Dept of Classics, Swansea SA2 8PP (☎ 0792 205678)

LLOYD, Angus Selwyn; s of Selwyn Lloyd (d 1935), of Great Dixter, Northiam, Sussex, and Elaine Mary, *née* Beck; *b* 12 July 1935; *Educ* Charterhouse; *m* 12 Jan 1961, Wanda Marian, da of Raymond Davidson, of 5 Devonshire Place, London W1; 3 s (James, Christopher, Richard), 2 da (Virginia, Philippa); *Career* Nat Serv 1954-55, 2 Lt 15/19 The Kings Royal Hussars (serv Malaya 1955); dir: Nathaniel Lloyd & Co (printers) 1956-63, Oscar & Peter Johnson Ltd (fine art dealers) 1963-81, Sealproof Ltd (textile proofing) 1973-; chm: Henri-Lloyd Ltd (textile mfrs) 1963-85, Craig-Lloyd Ltd (property) 1971-, Burlington Gallery Ltd (fine art/print dealers) 1979-, Burlington Paintings Ltd (fine art/picture dealers) 1984-; tstee: Albany Piccadilly 1967-, Charterhouse in Southwark 1962- (chm tstees 1979-82); Freeman: City of London, Worshipful Co of Stationers & Newspapermakers; *Recreations* golf; *Clubs* The Royal St Georges Golf (Sandwich) (capt 1985), The Berkshire (capt 1978), The Royal West Norfolk, The Royal and Ancient Golf (St Andrews), Swinley Forest, Walton Heath, The PGA Nat USA, Pine Tree Golf USA, The Honourable Co of Edinburgh Golfers; *Style—* Angus Lloyd, Esq; East Ct, Beech Ave, Effingham, Surrey (☎ 0372 458111); Burlington Paintings Ltd, 12 Burlington Gdns, London W1X 1LG (☎ 071 734 9984, fax 071 494 3770)

LLOYD, Rt Hon Lord Justice; Rt Hon Sir Anthony John Leslie; DL (E Sussex 1983); s of Edward John Boydell Lloyd, of Little Bucksteep, Dallington, Sussex; *b* 9 May 1929; *Educ* Eton, Trinity Coll Cambridge; *m* 1960, Jane Helen Violet, da of C W Shelford, of Chailey Place, Lewes, Sussex; *Career* Nat Serv 1 Bn Coldstream Gds 1948; called to the Bar Inner Temple 1955, QC 1967, attorney-gen to HRH The Prince of Wales 1969-77, High Ct judge (Queen's Bench) 1978-84, Lord Justice of Appeal 1984-; former memb Top Salaries Review Body, memb Criminal Law Revision Ctee 1981-, chm Civil Serv Security Appeals Panel 1982-, memb Parole Bd 1983-84; chm Glyndebourne Arts Tst 1975, dir RAM 1979-; chm Chichester Diocesan Bd of Fin 1972-76; kt 1978; *Style—* The Rt Hon Lord Justice Lloyd, DL; Ludlay, Berwick, E Sussex (☎ 0323 870204); 68 Strand-on-the-Green, London W4 (☎ 071 994 7790)

LLOYD, Anthony Joseph; MP (Lab) Stretford 1983-; *b* 25 Feb 1950; *Educ* Nottingham Univ, Manchester Business Sch; *m* Judith Lloyd; 1 s, 3 da; *Career* Univ lecturer, memb Trafford Dist Cncl 1979-84; *Clubs* West Indian Sports & Social, Stretford Ex-Servicemans, Stretford Trades & Labour; *Style—* Anthony Lloyd, Esq, MP; House of Commons, London SW1A 0AA

LLOYD, Barbara Christine; da of Francis Kenneth Lloyd, of the Bahamas, and Herta Erica, *née* Menzler (d 1984); *b* 17 Aug 1946; *Educ* Putney HS for Girls, École Le Grand Verger Lausanne Switzerland, École Lemania Lausanne Switzerland, French Lycée London, Le Fleuron Florence Italy, Oskar Kokoschka Summer Acad Salzburg Austria; *Career* Marlborough Galleries 1967-90; shorthand typist and switchboard operator rising to registrar Marlborough Gallery NY, dir Marlborough Graphics 1979- and subsequently Marlborough Fine Art London Ltd until 1990 (responsible for exhibitions incl: All FIAC exhibitions Grand Palais Paris, Bill Brandt- A Retrospective, Brassai Secret Paris of the 30s, Irving Penn, Still Lives, Avigdor Arikha, Raymond Mason, Therese Oulton, Travelling Mason Retrospective; full time photographer 1990-; tstee The Photographers Gallery London 1988-; *Books* The Colours of India (1988); *Recreations* looking at and collecting art, opera, music, photography, reading, tennis, enjoying life; *Clubs* Arts, Dover Street, Chelsea Arts; *Style—* Miss Barbara Lloyd

LLOYD, Barrie Otway; s of Arthur Balfour Lloyd (d 1963), and Elma Minnie, *née* Curnow; *b* 1 July 1940; *Educ* Fettes; *m* 18 Sept 1965, Ailsa Anne Grace, da of William Hector Stephenson; 1 s (James Rupert Samuel b 30 May 1972), 1 da (Kirstie Jane b 28 Feb 1969); *Career* admitted slr 1964, ptnr White & Leonard 1967-80, currently ptnr Masons; memb: City of London Slrs Co, Law Soc; *Recreations* cricket, golf, fishing, skiing; *Clubs* MCC, Worplesdon GC; *Style—* Barrie Lloyd, Esq; 4 Beech Lawn, Guildford, Surrey GU1 3PE; 10 Fleet St, London EC4Y 1BA (☎ 071 583 9990, fax 071 353 9745, telex 8811117)

LLOYD, (David) Bernard; s of George Edwards Lloyd, and Lilian Cahterine, *née* Thomas; *b* 14 Jan 1938; *Educ* Presteigne GS, Hereford HS; *m* 12 Oct 1968, Christine; 3 da (Claire b 1973, Joanne b 1975, Helen b 1975); *Career* Nat Serv RAPC; various posts in local govt fin; internal auditor UCL, accountant UCH Med Sch, sec RCOG 1976-82 (accountant 1971-76), sec Nat Inst of Agric Engrg 1982-86, sec RCP and Faculty of Occupational Med 1986-; govr Roundwood Jr Sch 1980-89 (chm 1985-88), memb Mgmnt Ctee St Albans CAB 1983- (chm 1990-), govr and chm Sir John Lawes Sr Sch 1986-87; FCCA 1977; *Recreations* walking, garden, local charity; *Style—* Bernard Lloyd, Esq; 29 Bloomfield Road, Harpenden, Hertfordshire AL5 4DD (☎ 0582 761292), Royal College of Physicians, 11 St Andrews Place, Regents Park, London NW1 4LE (☎ 071 935 1174, fax 071 487 5218)

LLOYD, Dr Brian Beynon; CBE (1983); s of David John Lloyd (d 1951), of Menai Bridge, Anglesey, and Olwen, *née* Beynon (d 1974); *b* 23 Sept 1920; *Educ* Newport HS, Winchester, Balliol Coll Oxford (BA, MA, DSc); *m* 1949, Reinhild Johanna, da of Dr Karl Wilhelm Engeroff (d 1951), of Bad Godesberg, W Germany; 4 s (Thomas, Martyn, Brian and Owen (twins)), 3 da (Megan and Olwen (twins), Lucy); *Career* registered as conscientious objector 1941, tech asst Oxford Nutrition Survey 1941 (res asst 1943-46), pres Jr Common Room Balliol 1941-42, chm Undergraduate Rep Cncl Univ of Oxford 1942; biochemist: SHAEF Nutrition Survey Gp Leiden Holland, Düsseldorf Germany 1945-46; Magdalen Coll Oxford: fell by examination in physiology 1948-52, by special election 1952-70, sr tutor 1963-64, vice pres 1967-68, emeritus fell 1970; chemist Laboratory of Human Nutrition, demonstrator and lectr in Physiology Univ of Oxford 1948-70, sr proctor 1960-61, dir Oxford Poly 1970-80, dir lut Nutrition Fndn 1990-; articles in physiological and biochemical jls on vitamin C, human respiration, blood gases, and exercise; memb Advsy Cncl on Misuse of Drugs 1978-81, visiting physiologist NY 1963, pres section I 1964-65, section X 1980, Br Assoc for the Advancement of Science (rep in Ceylon 1959, Russia 1964); chm: of govrs Oxford Coll of Technol 1963-69, CNAA Health and Med Servs Bd 1975-80, Oxford-Bonn Soc 1973-81, Oxford Mgmnt Club 1979-80, Health Educn Cncl 1979-82 (memb 1975-82), Oxford Gallery Ltd 1968-, Trumedia Study Oxford Ltd 1985-89, Trumedia Ltd, Pullen's Lane Assoc 1985; pres Oxford Poly Assoc 1984-89; *Books* Gas Analysis Apparatus (various Patents, 1960), The Regulation of Human Respiration (jt ed, 1962), Cerebrospinal Fluid and the Regulation of Respiration (jt ed 1965); *Recreations* klavarskribo, Correggio, analysis of athletic records, slide rules, ready reckoners, round tables, home computing; *Style—* Dr Brian B Lloyd, CBE; High Wall, Pullen's Lane, Oxford OX3 0BX (☎ 0865 63353)

LLOYD, Christopher; s of Nathaniel Lloyd, OBE (d 1933), of Great Dixter, Northiam, Rye, E Sussex, and Daisy, *née* Field (d 1972); *b* 2 March 1921; *Educ* Rugby, King's Coll Cambridge (MA), Wye Coll London (BSc); *Career* asst lectr in decorative hort Wye Coll 1950-54, fndr nursery in Clematis and unusual plants at family home Great Dixter 1954; author; Victoria Medal of Honour RHS, memb RHS; *Publications:* The Mixed Border (1957), Clematis (1965, revised 1977, revised with Tom Bennett 1989), Foliage Plants (1973), The Well Tempered Garden (1970), Shrubs and Trees for Small Gardens (1965), Gardening on Chalk and Lime (1969), Hardy Perennials (1967), The Well Chosen Garden (1985), The Adventurous Gardener (1985), The Year at Great Dixter (1987), The Cottage Garden (with Richard Bird 1990), Garden Flowers From Seed (with Graham Rice 1991); *Recreations* music, walking, entertaining friends at Great Dixter, cooking; *Style—* Christopher Lloyd; Great Dixter, Northiam, Rye, E Sussex TN31 6PH

LLOYD, Christopher; s of Rev Hamilton Lloyd, of Litchfield, Hants, and Suzanne, *née* Moon; *b* 30 June 1945; *Educ* Marlborough, ChCh Oxford (BA, MA, BLitt); *m* 7 Oct 1967, (Christine Joan) Frances, da of George Henry Reginald Newth (d 1978), of Whitchurch, Hants; 4 s (Alexander b 1970, Benedict b 1972, Oliver b 1973, Rupert b 1980); *Career* asst curator pictures ChCh Oxford 1967-68; dept Western Art Ashmolean Museum Oxford: print room asst 1968, departmental asst 1969, asst keeper 1972-88; surveyor of the Queen's pictures 1988-; fell Villa I Tatti Florence (Harvard Univ) 1972-73, visiting res curator early Italian painting Art Instit Chicago 1980-81; FRSA; *Books* Art and Its Images (1975), A Catalogue of the Earlier Italian Paintings in the Ashmolean Museum (1977), Camille Pissarro (1980), A Catalogue of the Drawings by Camille Pissarro in the Ashmolean Museum (1980), The Journal of Maria Lady Callcott 1827-28 (1981), Camille Pissarro (1981), Dürer to Cézanne: Northern European Drawings from the Ashmolean Museum (1982), Impressionist Drawings from British Collections (1986), Catalogue of Old Master Drawings at Holkham Hall (1986), Studies on Camille Pissarro (contrib, 1986), Woodner Collection Master Drawings (contrib, 1990), Henry VIII Images of A Tudor King (1990); *Recreations* real tennis, theatre, music; *Style—* Christopher Lloyd, Esq; 179 Woodstock Rd, Oxford OX2 7NB (☎ 0865 59133); The Royal Collection, Stable Yard House, St James Palace, London SW1A 1JR (☎ 071 930 4832)

LLOYD, Clive Hubert; AO (1985), OJ (1985), OR, OB (1986); s of Arthur Christopher Lloyd (d 1961), and Sylvia Thelma Lloyd; *b* 31 Aug 1944; *Educ* Fountain, Chatham HS Georgetown Guyana; *m* 11 Sept 1971, Waveney, *née* Benjamin; 1 s (Jason Clive b 15 June 1981), 2 da (Melissa Simone b 22 Feb 1974, Samantha Louise b 26 Jan 1976); *Career* clerk Georgetown Hosp 1960-66; cricketer; began career with Demarara CC Georgetown 1959, debut for Guyana 1963, first test match for the WI 1966, initial first class century 1966, played for Haslingden CC in the Lancs League 1967, first played for Lancs CCC 1969 (capt 1981-84 and 1986), capt WI 1974-78 and 1979-85; scored over 25,000 runs incl 69 centuries during career; dir Red Rose Radio plc 1987-, exec promotions offr Project Fullemploy 1987-; pt/t memb Cmmn for Racial Equality; memb: Sickle Cell Anemia Soc, Cwlth Soc for the Deaf; *Books* Living for Cricket (with Tony Cazier), Clive Lloyd the Biography (with Trevor McDonald); *Style—* Clive Lloyd, Esq, AO; Waverley, 296 Styal Rd, Meald Green, Cheadle, Cheshire; Harefield Home for the Elderley, Harefield Drive, Wilmslow, Cheshire (☎ 0625 522371, fax 061 437 8177)

LLOYD, Prof David; s of Frederick Lewis Lloyd (d 1961), of 16 Llanfair Rd, Penygraig, Rhondda, Glam, and Annie Mary, *née* Wrentmore; *b* 26 Nov 1940; *Educ* Porth Co GS for Boys, Univ of Sheffield (BSc, DSc), Univ of Wales Cardiff (PhD); *m* 5 April 1969, Margaret, da of Thomas John Jones, of Ynys Graianog, Ynys, Criccieth, Gwynedd; 2 s (Alun Lewis b 4 Aug 1970, Siôn Huw b 19 Sept 1973); *Career* MRC res fell Univ Coll of S Wales and Monmouth 1967-69 (ICI res fell 1964-67); Univ Coll Cardiff (now Univ of Wales Coll of Cardiff): lectr in microbiology 1969-76, sr lectr 1976, reader 1976-78, personal chair 1978-, head Dept of Microbiology 1982-87, established chair holder 1982-; memb: Biochemical Soc 1961, Ctee S Wales Cancer Res Campaign, Ctee of Welsh Scheme for Sci and Social Sci Res, Soc of Gen Microbiology 1980; *Books* The Mitochondria of Micro-organisms (1974), The Cell Division Cycle: Temporal Organization and Control of Cellular Growth and Reproduction (1982); *Recreations* music, cycling, tennis; *Style—* Prof David Lloyd; University of Wales College of Cardiff, Museum Ave, Cathays Park, Cardiff

LLOYD, David Alan; s of Dennis Herbert Lloyd, of Leigh-on-Sea, Essex, and Doris, *née* Renshaw; *b* 3 Jan 1948; *Educ* Southend HS; *m* 14 Dec 1972, Veronica Jardine, da of Maj Cochran Kirkwood MacLennan, MBE (d 1984); 1 s (Scott b 1975), 2 da (Camilia b 1979, Laura b 1981); *Career* tennis player, semi-finalist Wimbledon Doubles (with J Paish) 1973, Br Davis Cup Team 1973-82; opened: David Lloyd Slazenger Raquet Club Hestow 1982, David Lloyd Sports and Health Club Raynes Pk 1989, David Lloyd Sports and Health Club Finchley 1989; runs 4 tennis clubs (2 Spain, 2 Portugal), BBC Radio Commentator, ITV Tennis Commentator; launched Slater Tennis Fndn (sponsorship and coaching scheme for young players) with J Slater 1986; Freeman City of London 1985; *Recreations* golf; *Clubs* All England Lawn Tennis, Foxhills, Stage Soc; *Style—* David Lloyd, Esq; Appletree Cottage, 12 Leys Rd, Oxshott, Surrey KT22 OQE (☎ 0372 842150); David Lloyd Racquet Club, Southall Lane, Heston, Middx (☎ 081 573 0143)

LLOYD, David Mark; s of Maurice Edward Lloyd (d 1988), and Roma Doreen, *née* Morgan (d 1958); *b* 3 Feb 1945; *Educ* Felsted, Brentwood Sch Essex, BNC Oxford (MA); *m* 30 Oct 1982, Jana, da of Karel Tomas (d 1980); 1 s (Mark b 1983), 1 da (Katie b 1985), 1 step s (Tom b 1976); *Career* ed: The Money Programme 1980-82, Newsnight 1982-83, 60 Minutes 1983-84, Breakfast Time 1984-86; sr commissioning ed news and current affairs Channel 4 1986-; *Recreations* cricket, golf, music, photography; *Style—* David Lloyd, Esq; Channel 4, 60 Charlotte St, London W1 (☎ 071 927 8759)

LLOYD, Denys David Richard; s of Richard Norman Lloyd, of 7 Whitfield Hill, Kearsney, Dover, Kent, and Grace Enid, *née* Appleton; *b* 28 June 1939; *Educ* Brighton Coll, Trinity Hall Cambridge (MA), Univ of Leeds (MA); *Career* asst curate St Martin's Rough Hills Wolverhampton 1963-67, professed memb of the Community of the Resurrection Mirfield 1969, tutor Coll of the Resurrection Mirfield 1970-75, assoc lectr Dept of Theol and Religious Studies Univ of Leeds 1971-90, princ Coll of the Resurrection Mirfield 1984-90 (vice princ 1975-84); received into Roman Catholic Church 1990; *Recreations* walking, domestic architecture; *Style—* Denys Lloyd; Quarr Abbey, Ryde, Isle of Wight PO33 4ES

LLOYD, (Gabriel) Frederic Garnons; OBE (1969), JP (North Westminster 1969); s of Rev William Wellesley Gordon Lloyd (d 1947), of Blaen-y-Glyn, Merioneth, N Wales, and St Leonards-on-Sea, Sussex, and Minna Lucy Margaret, *née* Greenstreet (d 1958); *b* 1 July 1918; *Educ* Sandrock Hall Hastings, St Leonards Coll of Music; *m* 16 June 1945, Valerie, da of Rev John Buchanan Fraser (d 1944), of St Catharines, Nottingham; 2 s (William, Hugh); *Career* regnl dir Arts Cncl (N Midlands) 1943-50, dir Festival of GB Oxford 1950-51, gen mangr D'Oyly Carte Opera and Tst, gen mangr Savoy Theatre and dir Savoy Hotel Entertainments 1951-82, pres Theatre Mangrs Assoc 1967-70 (life vice-pres 1982); govr: Royal Academy of Music 1965 (chm 1980-84, vice pres 1984), Royal Gen Theatrical Fund 1960 (vice pres 1986), Sadler's Wells Theatre; chm Nottingham Co Music Ctee, warden Queens Chapel of the Savoy, convener Diocese of Moray Ross and Caithness; memb: Royal Choral Soc, Royal Philharmonic Orch, Scottish Opera Cncl, Malcolm Sargent Cancer Fund for Children, Central City Opera Denver USA; Freeman City of London 1961, Liveryman Worshipful Co of Musicians 1960; hon citizen: Denver 1953, Texas 1973; hon FRAM 1970, hon memb RCM 1976; *Books* The D'Oyly Carte Years (with Robin Wilson, 1984); *Recreations* music, gardening, fishing, reading; *Clubs* Garrick, MCC, Harvard (Boston USA); *Style—* Frederic Lloyd, Esq, OBE, JP; Blaen-y-Glyn, West Park, Strathpeffer, Ross-shire, Scotland 1V14 9BT (☎ 099 7 21429)

LLOYD, Prof Geoffrey Ernest Richard; s of William Ernest Lloyd (d 1975), of London, and Olive Irene Neville, *née* Solomon; *b* 25 Jan 1933; *Educ* Charterhouse, King's Coll Cambridge (BA, MA, PhD); *m* 14 Sept 1956, Janet Elizabeth, da of Edward Archibald Lloyd (d 1978), of Paris, France; 3 s (Adam b 1957, Matthew b 1962, Gwilym b 1963); *Career* Nat Serv Intelligence Corps 2 Lt/Actg Capt; Cambridge: fell King's Coll 1957-89, univ asst lectr classics 1965-67, univ lectr 1967-74, sr reader 1974-83, prof of ancient philosophy and sci 1983-; Bonsall prof Univ of Stanford 1981, Sather prof of classics California Univ (Berkeley) 1984, master Darwin Coll Cambridge 1989-; hon fell King's Coll Cambridge 1990; fell Royal Anthropological Soc 1970; FB 1983; *Books* Polarity and Analogy (1966), Aristotle The Growth and Structure of his Thought (1968), Early Greek Science (1970), Greek Science After Aristotle (1973), Hippocratic Writings (ed, 1978), Aristotle on Mind and the Senses (ed, 1978), Magic Reason and Experience (1979), Science Folklore and Ideology (1983), The Revolutions of Wisdom (1987), Demystifying Mentalities (1990); *Recreations* travel; *Style—* Prof Geoffrey Lloyd; 2 Prospect Row, Cambridge CB1 1DU (☎ 0223 355970)

LLOYD, Dr Geoffrey Gower; s of William Thomas Lloyd (d 1979), of Swansea, and Anne, *née* Davies; *b* 7 June 1942; *Educ* Queen Elizabeth GS Carmarthen, Emmanuel Coll Cambridge (BA, MB BChir, MD), Westminster Med Sch London, Inst of Psychiatry London (MPhil); *m* 19 Dec 1970, Margaret Hazel, da of Henry Doble Rose; 1 s (Richard Gower b 22 July 1977), 2 da (Alison Siân b 7 Nov 1972, Claire Rebecca b 16 July 1975); *Career* sr registrar Maudsley Hosp London 1974-76 (registrar 1970-73), lectr Inst of Psychiatry and King's Coll Hosp Med Sch London 1976-79; conslt psychiatrist: Royal Infirmary Edinburgh 1979-85, Royal Free Hosp London 1985-; ed Journal of Psychosomatic Research 1985-; FRSM 1977, FRCPE 1981, FRCPsych 1984, FRCP 1988; *Recreations* watching rugby football; *Style—* Dr Geoffrey Lloyd; 148 Harley St, London W1N 1AH (☎ 071 935 1207)

LLOYD, Herbert Merlin; TD; s of Leoline Oscar Lloyd (d 1945), of Elder House, Bridgend, Glamorgan, and Annie, *née* Tanner (d 1926); *b* 29 Oct 1912; *Educ* Bridgend Co GS, Cardiff Univ Coll, Open Univ (BA); *m* 30 Aug 1939, Dilys Bonnie, da of Idris Evan Davies (d 1957), of Austin Friars, Porthcawl, Glamorgan; 3 s (Jonathan Kendal b 29 Oct 1947, Brian Edwin b 9 March 1950, Peter Fraser b 19 Dec 1953); *Career* serv 77 Welsh HAA Regt 242 Battery TA 1937, cmmnd 1940, Air Def of GB, Staff Capt Far E 1942-45 (despatches), demob 1946; admitted slr 1937; former under sec Law Soc, former PR offr Port of London Authy, sr PR cnsllr Young & Rubicam 1975-76; md: Image Aust 1976-78, Compton Assocs (UK) Ltd 1978-80; sec: Wakefield and Tetley Tsts, Northcott Fndn, Tower Hill Improvement Tst; clerk All Hallows Devpt Fndn, chm Tidy Br Gp Tower Hill Project; fndr memb and vice chm: Cardiff Literary Soc 1946, Br Acad of Forensic Sci; fndr memb and tstee WWF, pres Inst of PR 1968-69, memb World Scout PR Ctee; Freeman City of London 1957, Liveryman Worshipful Co of Slrs 1957; memb Int Bar Assoc, FIPR, FRSA, fell Chartered Inst of Tport; *Books* Public Relations (1963), The Legal Limits of Journalism (1965); *Clubs* Reform, Highgate Golf; *Style—* Herbert Lloyd, Esq, TD; 49 Barnes Ct, Station Rd, New Barnet, Herts EN5 1QY (☎ 081 440 2087); Tower Hill Improvement Tst, 33B Station Rd, New Barnet, Herts EN5 1PH (☎ 081 441 7706)

LLOYD, Dame Hilda Nora; DBE (1951); da of late John Shufflebotham, of Birmingham; *b* 1891; *Educ* King Edward's Sch Birmingham, Birmingham Univ; *m* 1, 1930, Bertram Lloyd (d 1948); m 2, 1949, Baron Rose; *Career* emeritus prof of obstetrics and gynaecology Birmingham Univ and Utd Birmingham Hosp; pres Royal Coll of Obstetricians and Gynaecologists 1949-52; *Style—* Dame Hilda Lloyd, DBE; Broome House, Clent, Worcs

LLOYD, Prof Howell Arnold; s of John Lewis Lloyd (d 1971), of Llanelli, S Wales, and Elizabeth Mary, *née* Arnold (d 1986); *b* 15 Nov 1937; *Educ* Queen Elizabeth GS Carmarthen, Univ Coll of Wales (BA), Jesus Coll Oxford (DPhil); *m* Sept 1962, Gaynor Ilid, da of Moses John Jones, of Mold, N Wales; 3 s (Jonathan, Timothy, Christian), 2 da (Susanna, Rebecca); *Career* fell Univ of Wales 1961-62; Univ of Hull: asst lectr in history 1962-64, lectr 1964-73, sr lectr 1973-82, reader 1982-85, prof 1985-; FRHistS 1975; *Books* The Gentry of South-West Wales, 1540-1640 (1968), The Relevance of History (with Gordon Connell-Smith, 1972), The Rouen Campaign, 1590-92 (1973), The State, France and the Sixteenth Century (1983); *Recreations* walking, swimming; *Style—* Prof Howell A Lloyd; 23 Strathmore Avenue, Hull HU6 7HJ (☎ 0482 851146), Dept of History, The University of Hull, Hull HU6 7RX (☎ 0482 46311)

LLOYD, Sir Ian Stewart; MP (C) Havant 1983-; s of Walter John Lloyd (d 1973), and Euphemia Craig Lloyd (d 1971), of Natal, SA; descended from Tudor Trevor (d 1948) and his w, Angharad, da of Hywel Dda, King of Wales; *b* 30 May 1921; *Educ* Michaelhouse Natal, Witwatersrand Univ, King's Coll Cambridge, Admin Staff Coll Henley; *m* 1951, Frances Dorward, da of Hon William Addison, CMG, OBE, MC, DCM (d 1966), of Salisbury, Rhodesia; 3 s; *Career* SA Air Force 1941-45, RAFVR 1945-49; econ advsr Central Mining Corpn 1949, dir Bri Comin plc and gp econ advsr (former head Res Dept) British Commonwealth Shipping Co 1956-83; pres Cambridge Union; MP (C): Portsmouth Langstone 1964-74, Havant and Waterloo 1974-83; memb: UK delgn Cncl of Europe and WEU 1968-72, Select Ctee Sci and Technol 1970-79; chm: All-Pty Ctee on Info Technol 1979-87, Select Ctee on Energy 1979-89, Bd Parly Office for Sci and Technol 1988-; kt 1986; *Books* Rolls Royce: The Growth of a Firm (Vol I), The Years of Endurance (Vol II), The Merlin at War (Vol III); *Recreations* sailing (yacht 'Shelmalier'); *Clubs* Brooks's, Royal Yacht Sqdn; *Style—* Sir Ian Lloyd, MP; House of Commons, London SW1A 0AA

LLOYD, Illtyd Rhys; s of John Lloyd (d 1971), of Cwmafan, W Glamorgan, and Melvina Joyce, *née* Rees (d 1973); *b* 13 Aug 1929; *Educ* Port Talbot (Glan Afan) Co GS, Swansea UC Univ of Wales (BSc, MSc, DipEd, DipStat); *m* 1955, Julia, da of David John Lewis (d 1951), of Pontyberem, Dyfed; 1 s (Steffan), 1 da (Catrin); *Career* RAF (Educn Branch) 1951-54, Flt Lt; second maths master Howard Sch for Boys Cardiff 1954-57, head Maths Dept Pembroke GS 1958-59, dep headmaster Howardian HS 1959-63; Her Majesty's Inspectorate: HMI 1964-71, staff inspr 1972-82, chief inspr (Wales) 1982-90; memb: Family Health Servs Authy S Glamorgan 1990-, Cncl Baptist Union of Wales 1990-, Cncl CEWC (Cymru) 1990-; hon memb Gorsedd of Bards; hon fell Univ of Wales; *Recreations* walking; *Style—* Illtyd Lloyd, Esq; 134 Lake Rd East, Roath Park, Cardiff CF2 5NQ (☎ 0222 755296); Welsh Office, Cathays Park, Cardiff CF1 3NQ (☎ 0222 823431)

LLOYD, Baroness; Lady (Victoria) Jean Marjorie Mabell; *née* Ogilvy; da of 12 Earl of Airlie, KT, GCVO, MC, and Lady Alexandra Coke, da of 3 Earl of Leicester; *b* 21 Sept 1918; *m* 1942, 2 Baron Lloyd, MBE (d 1985, when the peerage became extinct); 2 da (and 1 s decd); *Style—* The Rt Hon The Lady Lloyd; Clouds Hill, Offley, Hitchin, Herts (☎ 046 276 350)

LLOYD, Jeffrey Hywel; s of Gwillym Hywel Lloyd (d 1966), of S Glamorgan, and Olwen Menai, *née* Williams (d 1978); *b* 9 June 1946; *Educ* Barry GS, UWIST (LLB); *m* 23 Oct 1976, Pauline Margaret, da of Benjamin Albert Jones, of Mountain Ash; 2 s (Adam b 1979, Simon b 1983); *Career* slr; *Recreations* walking, golf, chess; *Style—* Jeffrey H Lloyd, Esq; 39 Porth-y-Castell, Barry, S Glamorgan; 87A Holton Rd, Barry, S Glam (☎ 741919)

LLOYD, Jeremy William; s of Maj-Gen Richard Eyre Lloyd, CB, CBE, DSO, of Lymington, Hants, and Gillian, *née* Patterson; *b* 19 Dec 1942; *Educ* Eton, Pembroke Coll Cambridge (MA), Harvard Business Sch (MBA); *m* 2 Sept 1966, Britta Adrienne, da of Alfred de Schulthess, of Geneva, Switzerland; 1 s (Adrian b 1979), 3 da (Tara b 1971, Bettina b 1975, Antonia b 1985); *Career* called to the Bar Middle Temple; formerly with Hill Samuel & Co, subsid dir London & Co Securities Bank 1971-72, dir Manufacturers Hanover Property Services Ltd 1973-81, dir James Capel Bankers Ltd 1982-87, sr mangr Hong Kong & Shanghai Banking Corporation 1982-; *Recreations* tennis, skiing; *Style—* Jeremy Lloyd, Esq; Hong Kong & Shanghai Banking Corp, PO Box 199, 99 Bishopsgate, London EC2P 2LA (☎ 071 638 2366)

LLOYD, Jill Patricia; da of Peter Brown (d 1984), of Dublin, and Patricia Irene, *née* Tucker; *b* 2 Aug 1955; *Educ* Wallington HS, Univ of Warwick (BA), Courtauld Inst of Art (Phd), Free Univ Berlin; *m* 1989, Michael Henry Peppiatt, s of Edward George Peppiatt, s of Edward George Peppiatt; 1 da (Clio Patricia b 16 Feb 1991); *Career* lectr in art history Univ Coll London 1981-88, sr ed Arts International (Paris) 1989-90, ed-in-chief Art International (Paris) 1990-; reg contrib to: Art International, Art Monthly, Artscribe, The Burlington Magazine; articles on the early C20th and contemporary art; essays in exhibitions catalogues incl: Primitivism and Modernity, an Expressionist Dilemma (Royal Academy) 1985, Franz Xaver Messerschmidt Arnulf Rainer (ICA London) 1987, Gerhard Richter (Anthony D'Offay Gallery London) 1988, Bernhard Prinz (Serpentine Gallery London) 1988; awards: D&DA scholarship 1985, Br Cncl scholarship 1987, Paul Getty postdoctoral scholarship 1989; memb Int Art Critics' Arts; *Books* German Expressionism, Primitivism and Modernity (1991); *Recreations* theatre and cinema; *Clubs* RAC; *Style—* Dr Jill Lloyd; Art International, 77 Rue des Archives, 75003 Paris, France (☎ 010 33 1 48048454, fax 010 33 1 48048200)

LLOYD, John Andrew; s of Kenneth Lawrence Lloyd, JP, of Cheltenham, Glos, and Pamela Oriette, *née* Clarke; *b* 28 March 1951; *Educ* Cheltenham GS, Berks Coll of Educ, London Univ Inst of Educ; *m* 10 June 1989, Priscilla Jane, da of Charles Fennings-Mills (d 1986), widow of Flt Lt Michael Jennings (d 1987); 3 s (Guy b 1973, Peter b 1974, Ashley b 1976); *Career* teacher: Ashe Hall Sch Etwall Derbyshire 1972-74, Park Place Sch Henley Oxon 1974-79; press and pubns offr: Nat Children's Home 1980-83, Nat Assoc of Boys' Clubs 1983-88; freelance journalist and writer 1973-;

formerly polo corr: Daily Telegraph, The Independent UK; ed Polo Int; assoc Coll of Preceptors 1976; *Books* The Debrett Season (polo chapter, 1981), The Action Bunch Handbook (1983), The Polo Annual (1985), The Pimm's Book of Polo (1989), Debrett's Best of Britain (season chapter, 1990); *Recreations* swimming, theatre, reading; *Clubs* Wig and Pen; *Style*— John Lloyd, Esq; The Old School, 20B The Green, Calne, Wilts SN11 8DJ (☎ 0249 814888)

LLOYD, John David; s of John Alfred Lloyd (d 1981), and Lilian Mary, *née* Griffiths; *b* 1 Sept 1944; *Educ* SW Essex Sch of Art, London Coll of Printing (Dip AD); *m* 24 May 1975, Julia Patricia, da of Geoffrey Earnest Maughan; 1 s (Adam John b 17 June 1978), 2 da (Elinor Jane b 27 May 1980, Anna Carol b 20 Dec 1981); *Career* apprentice designer Edwin Jones & Sons (printers) 1960-64, graphic designer Allied International Designers 1968-75 (jt head Graphic Design 1972-75); corporate, identities incl: ABN Bank, Delta Group, Nicholas International, Meneba (Netherlands); currently chm and creative dir Lloyd Northover (fndr 1975); maj corporate identity progs for: BAA, Barclays de Zoete Wedd, Courtaulds, Dept of Employment, John Lewis, Nuclear Electric, Perkins Engines, Rover Group; other graphic design projects completed for RSC, Barclays Bank, Reuters; visiting lectr in typographic design London Coll of Printing 1970-72, chm Br Design Export Gp 1983-85, external assessor and course advsr Information Graphics Trent Poly 1984-89 and Media Design and Production London Coll of Printing 1989-; exhibitions Lloyd Northover at the Design Centre 1980-81, D&ADA 1981-83, Art Directors' Club of NY 1988; frequent speaker on design and identity mgmnt at confs and seminars; *Awards* winner Grand Prix in DBA/ Mktg Design Effectiveness Awards for Courtaulds corporate identity 1989; FCSD 1978, memb Designers and Art Dirs Assoc 1980; *Style*— John Lloyd, Esq; Lloyd Northover Ltd, 8 Smart's Place, London WC2B 5LW (☎ 071 430 1100, fax 071 430 1490)

LLOYD, John Eliot Fraser; s of Eliot Fraser Lloyd (d 1968), of London, and Bertha Mary, *née* Hackney (d 1989); *b* 17 Jan 1944; *Educ* Eton, Balliol Coll Oxford (BA), Manchester Business Sch (MBA); *m* 1, 18 Sept 1971 (m dis 1989), Penelope Anne, da of David Barrett Frost, of Essex; 1 s (Richard b 1981), 1 da (Harriet b 1978); m 2, 29 Sept 1989, Cathryn Gillian Knapp, da of John Nicholson, of Kent; *Career* trainee EMI 1965-69; Portals Hldgs: commercial dir Houseman (Burnham) 1974-76, md Zerolit Ltd 1976-78, md ops Portals Ltd 1978-85; md Portals Hldgs plc 1987- (gp corporate planner 1971-74, dep md 1985-87); *Recreations* music, skiing; *Style*— John Lloyd, Esq; Portals Hldgs plc, Laverstoke Mill, Whitchurch, Hants RG28 7NR (☎ 0256 892360, fax 0256 893398, telex 858059)

LLOYD, John Jeremy; s of Lt-Col Eric Martin Lloyd, OBE (d 1970), of Long Crendon, Bucks, and Margaret, *née* Lees (d 1979); *Educ* Manchester GS; *m* 1970 (m dis 1972), Joanna, da of Maj James Lumley; *Career* scriptwriter: Dickie Henderson Show, Are You Being Served, Allo Allo; writer and actor: Rowan and Martin's Laugh In; writer and performer: Wonderful World of Captain Beaky, The Woodland Gospels; actor: Those Magnificent Men in their Flying Machines, Doctor in Clover, A Very Important Person, Murder on the Orient Express, We Joined the Navy; stage actor: Robert and Elizabeth (musical); memb: Equity, Writers Guild of America; *Books* The Further Adventures of Captain Dangerfield, The Continuing Adventures of Captain Dangerfield, Captain Beaky vols 1 and 2, Captain Cat and the Carol Singers; *Recreations* classic car collector; *Clubs* Annabels; *Style*— John Lloyd, Esq

LLOYD, Dr John Walter; OBE (1988); s of Maj Joseph Howell Lloyd (d 1939), of Llandeilo, Dyfed, South Wales, and Kathleen May Zelie, *née* Nicholas (d 1986); *b* 26 Dec 1923; *Educ* Epsom Coll, The London Hosp; *m* 17 May 1969, Mary Frances, da of Flt Lt Stanley Rowland Lewis, of 4 Craigendarroch Walk, Ballater, Aberdeen; 3 s (Thomas Joe b 19 April 1971, William John Nicholas b 21 Aug 1972, John Henry b 24 Aug 1981), 1 da (Sarah Frances b 16 Aug 1974); *Career* Sqdn Ldr RAF med branch 1950-54 (MO i/c Air HQ Cyprus 1952-54), civilian MO RNCAF Germany 1954-56; conslt anaesthetist Radcliffe Infirmary Oxford 1962-89 (i/c intensive care 1962-66), dir Oxford Regnl Pain Unit 1970-89; inventor of techniques of cryoanalgesia 1976 and Barbotage of CSF; memb Int Assoc for Study of Pain 1970-, vice pres Intractable Pain Soc of GB and Ireland 1983- (chm 1983-85); memb Cncl for the Preservation of Rural England (Oxon); hon MA Oxon 1978; MRCS, LRCP, DA, FFARCS(Eng) 1960-, FRSM 1966-; *Books* Oxford Textbook of Medicine (contrib), Headache (contrib), Current Controversies in Neurosurgery (contrib), Techniques of Neurolysis (contrib); *Recreations* squash, vintage cars; *Clubs* RAF, Frewin (Oxford); *Style*— Dr John Lloyd, OBE; Gate House, Mill Street, Eynsham, Oxon OX8 1JU (☎ 0865 881477, 0865 515036); Bays Hill, Llandeilo, Dyfed, South Wales (☎ 0558 822561); 23 Banbury Road, Oxford (☎ 0865 616036)

LLOYD, John Wilson; s of Dr Ellis Lloyd, of Swansea (d 1964), and Dorothy Wilcoxon, *née* Smith; *b* 24 Dec 1940; *Educ* Swansea GS, Clifton, Christ's Coll Cambridge (BA, MA); *m* 25 March 1967, Buddug, da of Rev J D Roberts, of Caernarfon, Gwynedd; 2 s (Huw b 1972, Geraint b 1973), 1 da (Sarah b 1968); *Career* asst princ HM Treasy 1962-67 (private sec to Fin Sec 1965-67), princ successively HM Treasy, CSD and Welsh Off 1967-75 (private sec to Sec of State for Wales 1974-75), dep sec Welsh Off 1988- (asst sec 1975-82, under sec and princ establisment offr 1982-86, under sec Housing Health and Social Serv Gp 1986-88); *Recreations* golf, squash, swimming; *Style*— John Lloyd, Esq; Welsh Office, Cathays Park, Cardiff CF1 3NQ (☎ 0222 825111)

LLOYD, Prof Dame June Kathleen; DBE; da of Arthur Cresswell Lloyd MBE (d 1957), and Lucy Bevan, *née* Russell, BEM (d 1990); *b* 1 Jan 1928; *Educ* Royal Sch Bath, Univ of Bristol, (MB, ChB, MD), Univ of Durham (DPH); *Career* trg posts in medicine 1951-65 at Bristol, Oxford, Newcastle, Birmingham; Inst of Child Health London: sr lectr 1965-69, reader 1969-74, prof 1974-75; prof St George's Med Sch 1979-85; Nuffield prof of child health Univ of London 1985-; FRCP 1969, FRCPE 1990, FRCGP 1990; *Recreations* cooking, gardening; *Style*— Prof June Lloyd; Inst of Child Health, 30 Guilford St, London WC1N 1EH (☎ 071 242 9789)

LLOYD, Kerry Edward; s of Edward George Frederick Lloyd, of Portsmouth, and Olive Mary, *née* Whurr; *b* 24 May 1951; *Educ* Kingston Secdy Mod Sch Portsmouth, Portsmouth Coll of Art and Design (Dip Art and Design); *m* 1, 19 Sept (m dis 1985), (Barbara) Denise Mary, da of Donald Smaldon; 2 da (Rosy b 5 Sept 1976, Sophie b 6 Oct 1978); m 2, 21 Oct 1985, Melanie Jane, da of Lt Frederick Hind; *Career* dir and creative dir Golley Slater and Partners 1987-; *Recreations* sailing, walking, cooking; *Style*— Kerry Lloyd, Esq; The Mill House, Tintern, Chepstow, Monmouthshire NP6 6TQ; Golley Slater and Partners Ltd, 9-11 The Hayes, Cardiff (☎ 0222 388621)

LLOYD, Leslie Geoffrey; s of Geoffrey Llewellyn Lloyd, of Cradley, Worcs, and Rita Louise, *née* Palfrey; *b* 28 June 1940; *Educ* Worcester Royal GS; *m* 18 May 1968, Jenifer Elizabeth, da of Col Walter Sowden North CBE, of Rake, Hants; 2 s (Thomas b 1 Feb 1971, John b 25 June 1972), 1 da (Katharine b 10 Sept 1969); *Career* head of mgmnt servs Bank of Eng 1988- (joined 1957, asst chief cashier 1977-80, sr advsr Commodities and Futures Mkts 1980-84, The Auditor 1984-88); organist Milland Church Hamps; MBCS; *Recreations* music, philosophy; *Style*— Leslie Lloyd, Esq; The Loke, Rake, Liss, Hants; Bank of England, Threadneedle St, London EC2R

LLOYD, Lloyd; s of David Herbert Lloyd, and Rachel Dilys, *née* Davies; *b* 12 Feb 1950; *Educ* City of London Sch, Trinity Coll Cambridge, King's Coll London (LLM); *Career* called to Bar Gray's Inn 1973; cncl memb Hon Soc of Cymmrodorion; AIArb 1976; *Recreations* music, theology, art, travel, Welsh, literature; *Style*— Lloyd Lloyd, Esq; 3 Archery Fields House, Wharton St, London WC1X 9PN (☎ 071 837 4727); Queen Elizabeth Bldg, Temple, London EC4 (☎ 071 353 9153, fax 071 583 0126, telex 262762 INREM G)

LLOYD, Marion Evelyn; da of Capt Peter Gerald Charles Dickens, DSO, MBE, DSC (d 1987), and Mary Alice, *née* Blagrove; *b* 16 Oct 1952; *Educ* West Heath Sch Sevenoaks Kent; *m* 11 June 1977, Jonathan Salisbury Lloyd, s of Reginald Lloyd, of Acre Batch, Lower Wood, Allstretton, Shropshire; 2 s (Harry b 1983, Tom b 1986) 1 da (Poppy b 1980); *Career* ed Armada Children's Paperbacks (Wm Collins) 1974-86, ed dir Pan Children's Books 1986-89, conslt ed Pan Macmillan Children's Books 1990-; *Recreations* skiing, sailing, piano playing, video filming; *Style*— Mrs Marion Lloyd; 15 Sterndale Rd, London W14 0HT (☎ 071 603 9968)

LLOYD, Mark William; s of Keneth Charles Lloyd, of 16 Ivor St, Pontycymmer, Bridgend, Mid Glam, and Ivy, *née* Jones; *b* 5 Feb 1963; *Educ* Ynysawdre Comp Sch, Swansea Coll of Art, North Essex Sch of Art; *m* Joanna Caroline, da of Daniel James Peter Ryan; 1 da (Emily Elizabeth b 22 Oct 1989); *Career* designer Michael Peters & Partners 1984-87 (clients incl: Boots Co plc, NEDO, Campbells Soups, Fisons, Ross Electronics; work incl in Best of British Packaging 1988), designer, then sr designer, then asst creative dir Coley Porter Bell and Partners 1987- (clients incl: United Biscuits, DOE, Lego, Woolworths plc, Sainsbury's, Asda, Eden Vale, The Wellcome Foundation); *awards* Best American Foods Packaging CLIO (Masterchoice Pasta 1988, Masterchoice Olive Oil 1990), Packaging Section Br D&AD (A & P Tomato Ketchup 1989, Penguin Biscuits 1990), Design Effectiveness award Design Business Assoc (Master Choice Food Packaging); *Recreations* sport, film, theatre; *Style*— Mark Lloyd, Esq; Flat 6 Winscombe Hall, 19 Disraeli Rd, Ealing, London W5 5HS (☎ 081 840 2955); Coley Porter Bell, 4 Flitcroft St, London WC2H 8DJ (☎ 071 379 4355, fax 071 379 5164)

LLOYD, Michael Raymond; *b* 20 Aug 1927; *Educ* Architectural Assoc Sch of Architecture (AA Dip); *Career* chartered architect; dean and prof of architecture Faculty of Architecture Planning and Building Technol Kumasi Univ of Sci and Technol Ghana 1963-66; princ: Architectural Assoc Sch of Architecture 1966-71, Land Use Consultants London 1971-72; sr ptnr Sinar Associates Tunbridge Wells 1973-80; conslt head of sch Hull Sch of Architecture UK 1974-77, sr lectr Development Planning Unit Univ Coll London 1976-79 (pt/t 1974-76); visiting prof and critic: Sch of Architecture Univ of Baja California 1980, ITESO Guadalajara Mexico 1980; involved with workshop Columbian Assoc of Schs of Architecture Bogota 1980; tech offr Overseas Development Administration for Br Govt (advsr on higher educn to Univs of Central America) 1979-81; Norconsult International AS Oslo Norway 1981-: coordinating architect and planner Al Dora Township Baghdad Iraq for State Organization of Housing Government of Iraq 1981-83, exec cnslt for physical planning Buildings Div 1981-86, project mangr Al Qassim Comprehensive Regnl Development Plan for Miny of Municipal and Rural Affrs Kingdom of Saudi Arabia 1983-86, rector Bergen Sch of Architecture, sr conslt Development Gp on Third World Housing 1987-, currently exec architectural conslt for physical planning; extensive overseas work; author of: 14 papers on architectural and planning educn, 5 papers on housing, 7 reports for national govts, 2 books; external examiner Univs of: Edinburgh, Kuala Lumpur, Kumasi Newcastle, Zaria, Oslo; external examiner Polytechnics of Central London and Hull; visiting lectr: Baghdad, Bogota, Canterbury, Edinburgh, Enugu, Guadaljara, Guanajuato, Helsinki, Jyvaskyla, Kingston, Kuala Lumpur, Lund, Mexico City, Mexicali, Newcastle, Oslo, Oxford, Santiago, Trondheim, Valparaiso, Zaria, Zurich; extensive involvement with: International Union of Architects, UNESCO, Br Cncl; memb numerous professional ctees 1966-; memb Ct RCA 1968-80; memb: RIBA, Norwegian Architects' Assoc, AA; *Style*— Michael Lloyd, Esq

LLOYD, Sir Nicholas Markley; *b* 9 June 1942; *Educ* Bedford Modern Sch, St Edmund Hall Oxford (MA), Harvard Univ; *m* 1; m 2, 1979, Eve Pollard; 3 s, 1 da; *Career* dep ed Sunday Mirror 1980-82; ed Sunday People 1982-84, dir Mirror Gp 1982-84, ed News of the World Jan 1984-85, dir News Gp Newspapers 1985-; kt 1990; *Style*— Sir Nicholas Lloyd; News Group Newspapers, 30 Bouverie St, London EC4 (☎ 071 353 3030)

LLOYD, Patrick John; s of Edmund Commeline Lloyd (d 1936), of Pitsworthy, Exford, Som; *b* 20 March 1925; *Educ* Clifton, Magdalene Coll Cambridge (MA); *m* 1956, Margaret, da of Claude Douglas-Pennant (d 1955, gs of 1 Baron Penrhyn); 1 s (John Philip b 1960), 1 da (Phyllida Christian b 1957); *Career* Capt RA; wine merchant; master of wine 1961; *Recreations* hunting, shooting; *Style*— Patrick Lloyd, Esq; Valaford, West Anstey, South Molton, Devon EX36 3PW (☎ 039 84 258)

LLOYD, (George) Peter; CMG (1965), CVO (1983); er s of Sir Thomas Ingram Kynaston Lloyd, GCMG, KCB (d 1968), and Bessie Nora, *née* Mason; *b* 23 Sept 1926; *Educ* Stowe, King's Coll Cambridge; *m* 1957, Margaret, da of Dr Eugene Harvey, of Bermuda; 2 s, 1 da; *Career* served Lt KRRC 1945-48, dist offr Kenya 1951-60, colonial sec Seychelles 1961-66, chief sec Fiji 1966-70, def sec Hong Kong 1971-74, dep govr Bermuda 1974-81, govr Cayman Islands 1982-87; *Style*— Peter Lloyd, Esq, CMG, CVO; Watch House, 13 Fort Hamilton Dr, Pembroke, HM 19 Bermuda (☎ 2951301)

LLOYD, Peter Robert Cable; MP (C) Fareham 1979-; s of David Lloyd, and late Stella Lloyd; *b* 12 Nov 1937; *Educ* Tonbridge, Pembroke Coll Cambridge (MA); *m* 1967, Hilary Creighton; 1 s, 1 da; *Career* former mktg mangr Utd Biscuits, chm Bow Gp 1972-73; former ed Crossbow; sec Cons Parly Employment Ctee 1979-81, vice chm Euro Affrs Ctee 1980-81; PPS to Min of State NI 1981-82, memb Employment Ctee 1982, PPS; to Sec of State for Educn and Sci 1983-84; govt whip 1984-; lord cmmr of the Treasy Oct 1986-88; parly under sec: Dept of Social Security 1988-89, Home Office 1989-; *Style*— Peter Lloyd, Esq, MP; House of Commons, SW1

LLOYD, Reginald Arthur Harris; TD (1980, and clasp), DL (Shropshire 1979); s of Rev Richard Harris Lloyd (d 1952); *b* 24 Jan 1913; *Educ* Hull GS, Scarborough Coll; *m* 1946, Maureen, da of John Thelwall Salusbury (d 1946); 4 s, 1 da; *Career* Shropshire CC: cncllr 1961, vice chm 1977, chm 1981-85; head of office mgmnt Sun Alliance & London until 1973, ret; gen cmmr of taxes 1975-78; chm Bylaw (Ross) Ltd 1987; chm: Packwood Haugh Prep Sch Shropshire 1963-88, Shropshire Army Cadet League 1965-, W Mercia Police Authy 1989-, Church Stretton Sch; govr Shrewsbury Sch 1968-88; memb: Telford Devpt Corp 1977-89, Bell Concord Educnl Tst 1983-89, Bd of Tstees and Exec Bd Ironbridge Gorge Museum Tst 1985-; pres: Shropshire CPRE, Shropshire Assoc of Parish and Town Cncls 1984-, Shrewsbury and Atcham Cons Assoc 1988-; tstee Hereford Cathedral Appeal 1984-, memb Cncl W Midland Regnl Investmt Tst 1985-; *Recreations* riding, tennis, fishing; *Clubs* Carlton, MCC, Beaconsfield; *Style*— Reginald Lloyd, Esq, TD, DL; Acre Batch, Lower Wood, All Stretton, Shropshire SY6 6LG (☎ 069 45 233)

LLOYD, Sir Richard Ernest Butler; 2 Bt (UK 1960), of Rhu, Co Dunbarton; o s of Maj Sir (Ernest) Guy Richard Lloyd, 1 Bt, DSO, DL (d 1987), and Helen Kynaston, *née* Greg (d 1984); *b* 6 Dec 1928; *Educ* Wellington, Hertford Coll Oxford (MA); *m* 6 June 1955, Jennifer Susan Margaret, er da of Brig Ereld Boteler Wingfield Cardiff, CB, CBE (d 1988), of Easton Court, nr Ludlow, Shropshire; 3 s (Timothy b 12 April 1956,

Simon b 26 July 1958, Henry b 22 Feb 1965); *Heir* s, (Richard) Timothy Butler Lloyd b 12 April 1956; *Career* former Capt Black Watch, Mil Serv Malaya 1947-49; banker; exec then dir Glyn Mills & Co 1952-70, chief exec Williams & Glyn's Bank 1970-78; Hill Samuel Bank Ltd: dep chm 1978-80, dep chm and chief exec 1980-87, jt chm 1987-88, chm 1987-; Freeman City of London 1964, Liveryman Worshipful Co of Mercers 1965, memb Guild of Freemen of Shrewsbury 1978; CBIM, FCIB; *Recreations* fishing, gardening, walking; *Clubs* Boodle's; *Style*— Sir Richard Lloyd, Bt; Sundridge Place, Sundridge, Sevenoaks, Kent TN14 6DD (☎ 0959 63599); Hill Samuel Bank Ltd, 100 Wood St, London EC2P 2AJ (☎ 071 628 8011, fax 071 726 2818, telex 888822 HSAMUK)

LLOYD, Richard Hey; s of Charles Yates Lloyd (d 1969), and Ann, *née* Hey (d 1952); *b* 25 June 1933; *Educ* Rugby, Jesus Coll Cambridge; *m* 29 Dec 1962, (Teresa) Morwenna, da of Rev Oliver Leonard Willmott; 4 da (Emma b 1964, Julia b 1967, Catharine b 1969, Olivia b 1971); *Career* sub organist Salisbury Cathedral 1957-66; organist: Hereford Cathedral 1966-74, Durham Cathedral 1974-85; dep headmaster Salisbury Cathedral Sch 1985-88; *Recreations* reading, cricket, music, enjoying the countryside; *Style*— Richard Lloyd, Esq; Refail Newydd, Pentraeth, Anglesey LL75 8YF (☎ 024870 220)

LLOYD, Robert Andrew; CBE (1991); s of Inspr William Edward Lloyd (d 1963), and May, *née* Waples; *b* 2 March 1940; *Educ* Southend HS, Keble Coll Oxford (MA), London Opera Centre; *m* 22 Feb 1964 (m dis 1989), Sandra Dorothy, da of Douglas Watkins; 1 s (Marcus b 1965), 3 da (Anna b 1966, Candida b 1969, Alice b 1973); *Career* Instr Lt RN 1962-65; civilian tutor Bramshill Police Staff Coll 1966-68; freelance singer, writer and broadcaster; princ bass: Sadlers Well's Opera 1969-72, Royal Opera 1972-83; major opera appearances: Covent Garden, La Scala Milan, Metropolitan Opera, Paris Opera, Munich, Vienna, San Francisco; title role in Boris Godunov. (prodn by André Tarkovsky, Kirov Opera Leningrad), frequent broadcaster on radio and TV; films: Parsifal (Artificial Eye), 6 Foot Cinderella (BBC), Bluebeard's Castle (BBC, won 1989 Prix Italia); recordings and videos incl: Parsifal Don Carlos, Entführung aus dem Serial, Messiah, Dream of Gerontius, Damnation of Faust, Coronation of Poppea; memb Exec Ctee Musicians Benevolent Fund, pres Br Youth Opera; hon fell Keble Coll Oxford 1990; *Recreations* sailing, hill walking; *Clubs* Garrick; *Style*— Robert Lloyd, Esq, CBE; Harrison Parrott Ltd, 12 Penzance Place, London W11 (☎ 071 229 9166)

LLOYD, Robert Geoffrey; s of Robert Sydney Lloyd, MBE, of Llangefni, Gwynedd, and Joan Elizabeth, *née* Geerdts; *b* 20 April 1947; *Educ* Falcon Coll Rhodesia, Univ Coll Rhodesia; *Career* Capt Rhodesian Army 1973; sr registrar: Addenbrooke's Hosp Cambridge 1983-84, Norfolk and Norwich Hosp 1985-87; conslt in accident and emergency med Tameside Gen Hosp 1987-; memb Casuality Surgns Assoc; *Recreations* shooting, walking, reading; *Clubs* Anglesey Hunt; *Style*— Robert Lloyd, Esq; 12 Wellgate, Old Glossop, Derbyshire SK13 9RS (☎ 04574 69404); Tameside General Hospital, Ashton under Lyne, Lancashire OL6 9RW (☎ 061 330 8373)

LLOYD, Shirley; da of Trevor Emlyn Williams, of 1 Neville Rd, Porthcawl, Mid Glamorgan, and Elsie, *née* Jones (d 1974); *b* 7 Dec 1934; *Educ* Porthcawl Secdy Mod; *m* 12 Oct 1968, Robert David Lloyd, s of Robert Denis Lloyd, of 3 Fairfax Cres, Porthcawl, Mid Glamorgan; *Career* md: P E Thomas Ltd 1971-76 (dir 1966-71), P E Thomas (Porthcawl) Ltd 1976-82; dir P E Thomas (Precision) Ltd 1984-; divnl cmmr Girl Guides, sec Porthcawl Civic Festival Ctee; vice-pres: Porthcawl Disabled Gp, Porthcawl Rugby Club; memb Porthcawl Chamber of Trade; *Style*— Mrs Shirley Lloyd; P E Thomas (Precision), Glan Rd, Porthcawl CF36 5DF (☎ 065 671 3555)

LLOYD, Simon Croil; s of Lt-Col R C Lloyd, DSO, MC, TD (d 1972), of Denbigh, and Joan, *née* Tate (d 1980); *b* 10 March 1925; *Educ* Stowe; *m* 28 April 1951, Diana Nesta, da of Henry Robertson (d 1976), of Gwynedd; *Career* serv 1943-49 The Rifle Bde, Capt 1946; High Sheriff Denbighshire 1964; jt MFH Flint and Denbigh 1961-67 and 1985-; hon showyard dir Denbighshire and Flintshire Agric Soc 1962-; *Recreations* hunting, shooting, breeding and showing hunters; *Style*— Simon Lloyd, Esq; Garn, Denbigh, Clwyd LL16 5BW (☎ 074 574 610)

LLOYD, Hon Mrs (Thelma Margaret Leighton); *née* Seager; da of 1 Baron Leighton of St Mellons, CBE (d 1963); *b* 6 Nov 1923; *Educ* Queenswood Sch, Univ of London; *m* 1, 1951 (m dis 1981), Michael Edmonds; 1 s, 2 da; m 2, 1983, Joseph Evan Lloyd; *Career* magistrate 1962-68, psychiatric social worker; *Recreations* swimming, exploring, talking with friends; *Style*— The Hon Mrs Lloyd; Penarth, S Glam

LLOYD, Thomas (Tom); s of Thomas Lloyd (d 1969), and Dr Alice Margaret, *née* Ramsden; *b* 26 April 1946; *Educ* Wellington, Univ of Liverpool (BA); *m* 20 April 1974 (sep); 1 s (Owen Anthony b 14 Nov 1981), 1 da (Katherine b 22 Feb 1980); *Career* ed Fin Weekly 1983-; *Books* Dinosaur and Co Studies in Corporate Evolution (1984), Managing Knowhow (jtly, 1987), The Nice Company (1990); *Recreations* walking, reading, writing; *Style*— Tom Lloyd, Esq; 14 Greville St, London, EC1N 8SB (☎ 071 405 2288, fax 071 831 2625)

LLOYD, Thomas Owen Saunders; s of Maj John Audley Lloyd, MC, of Court Henry, Carmarthen, and (Mary Ivy) Anna, *née* Owen; *b* 26 Feb 1955; *Educ* Radley, Downing Coll Cambridge (MA); *m* 7 Nov 1987, (Christabel) Juliet Anne, da of Maj David Harrison-Allen (d 1976), of Cresselly, nr Pembroke; *Career* slr, author; chm Br Historic Bldgs Tst 1987- (tstee 1986); memb: Historic Bldgs Cncl for Wales, Nat Tst Ctee for Wales, Ctee Save Britain's Heritage; non-exec dir Dyfed Family Heath Servs Authy 1990-; *Books* The Lost Houses of Wales (1986); *Clubs* Lansdowne; *Style*— Thomas Lloyd, Esq; Freestone Hall, Cresselly, Kilgetty, Dyfed SA68 0SX (☎ 0646 651493)

LLOYD, Timothy Andrew (Andy); s of John Romer Lloyd (d 1979), of Whittington, Shropshire, and Gwen Mary, *née* Humphreys; *b* 5 Nov 1956; *Educ* Oswestry Boys HS, Dorset Inst of Higher Educn; *m* 17 Sept 1988, Gillian Nancy, da of Gordon Noel Upton; 1 da (Sophie Verity b 13 March 1987), 1 step da (Georgia Elizabeth Freeman b 19 May 1978); *Career* professional cricketer; Warwickshire CCC 1976-; first class debut 1977, awarded county cap 1980, capt 1988-, benefit 1990, 245 first class matches; England: 1 Test match v W Indies 1984 (retired hurt 10 not out after being struck on head by Malcolm Marshall delivery), 3 one day Ints v W Indies 1984; winner's medal Nat West Trophy 1989; schoolboy: capt co soccer team, winner various co table tennis titles; *Books* author of various soccer and cricket books for children; *Recreations* golf, horse racing, food and drink; *Style*— Andy Lloyd, Esq; Warwickshire CCC, County Ground, Edgbaston, Birmingham (☎ 021 446 4422, fax 021 446 4544)

LLOYD, Timothy Andrew Wigram; QC (1986); s of Thomas Wigram Lloyd (DR) d 1984 Margo Adela, *née* Beasley; *b* 30 Nov 1946; *Educ* Winchester, Lincoln Coll Oxford (exhibitioner, BA, MA); *m* 1978, Theresa Sybil Margaret, da of late Ralph Kenneth Holloway; *Career* called to the Bar Middle Temple 1970; *Books* Wurtzburg & Mills, Building Society Law (15 edn, 1989); *Recreations* music, travel; *Style*— Timothy Lloyd, Esq, QC; 11 Old Square, Lincoln's Inn, London WC2A 3TS (☎ 071 430 0341)

LLOYD, (Bertram) Trevor; s of Bertram Lloyd, of Scole Norfolk, and Gladys, *née* Baker; *b* 15 Feb 1938; *Educ* Highgate Sch, Hertford Coll Oxford (scholar, BA, MA), Clifton Theol Coll Bristol; *m* 30 June 1962, (Margaret) Eldey, da of Frederick Butler (d 1990); 3 s (Christopher 1967, Jonathan b 1969, Peter b 1972, d 1985), 1 da (Hilary Kemp 1965); *Career* curate Christ Church Barnet 1964-69, vicar Holy Trinity Wealdstone 1970-84, priest i/c St Michael and All Angels Harrow Weald 1980-84, vicar Trinity St Michael Harrow 1984-89, archdeacon of Barnstaple 1989-; area dean of Harrow 1977-82; memb: C of E Liturgical Cmmn 1981-, Gen Synod C of E, Cncl Scripture Union, Central Bd of Fin C of E, Gp for Renewal of Worship, Editorial Bd GROW-Alcuin; *publications* Informal Liturgy (1972), Institutions and Inductions (1973), The Agape (1973), Liturgy and Death (1974), Ministry and Death (1974), Lay Presidency at the Eucharist? (1977), Evangelicals Obedience and Change (1977), Anglican Worship Today (ed, 1980), Ceremonial in Worship (1981), Introducing Liturgical Change (1984), Celebrating Lent Holy Week and Easter (1985), Celebrating the Agape today (1986), The Future of Anglican Worship (1987); *Recreations* hill walking, photography, swimming, caravanning, making things from wood; *Style*— Ven Trevor Lloyd; Stage Cross, Whitemoor Hill, Bishop's Tawton, Barnstaple, Devon EX32 0BE (☎ 0271 75475)

LLOYD, Hon Mrs (Victoria Mary); *née* Ormsby-Gore; da of 5 Baron Harlech, KCMG, PC (d 1985); *b* 1946; *m* 1972, Julian Richard Leslie Lloyd; 1 s, 2 da; *Style*— The Hon Mrs Lloyd; The Glebe, Leixlip, Co Kildare, Republic of Ireland

LLOYD DAVIES, Dr Alan Trevor; s of Trevor L Davies (d 1962), of Reigate, Surrey, and Doris Madeleine, *née* Morris; *b* 30 Dec 1935; *Educ* King's Coll Choir Sch Cambridge, Malvern, King's Coll London, Westminster Med Sch and Univ of London (MB BS, MRCS, LRCP); *m* 4 April 1964, Rosalind Frances, da of Oliver Seadon Naylor, of Walton-on-Thames; 3 da (Ceri Henrietta b 1966, Sophie Sian b 1968, Megan Frances b 1972); *Career* house surgn: Westminster Hosp 1962, Redhill Gen Hosp 1963; res obstetrics offr St Teresa's Hosp 1964-65, civilian med practitioner 4 Field Ambulance 1965-68, GP 1968-, hosp practioner in geriatrics 1987-; former: pres Andover Rotary Club, sec Hants Branch Salmon and Trout Assoc; memb Waynflete Singers 1969, dir Goodworth Singers 1975-; memb BMA; *Recreations* fly fishing, game fishing, choral singing, golf; *Style*— Dr Alan Lloyd Davies; Godewirda, St Anns Close, Goodworth Clatford, Andover, Hants SP11 7RW (☎ 0264 352 983); 35 High Street, Andover, Hants (☎ 0264 361 424)

LLOYD-DAVIES, (John) Robert; CMG (1953); s of John Robert Lloyd-Davies (d 1971), of Muswell Hill, London, and Nellie Louise, *née* Wilson (d 1928); *b* 24 March 1913; *Educ* Highgate Sch, Oriel Coll Oxford (MA), Univ of Freiburg-im-Breisgau; *m* 1, 6 Feb 1943, Margery (d 1978), da of Maj William McClelland (d 1918); 1 s (Peter Russell b 18 Nov 1943), 1 da (Virginia Mary b 9 March 1947); m 2, 19 June 1982, Grace, *née* Williams, wid of Frederick Reynolds II, of Bethesda, USA; *Career* Lt RNVR 1942-45; sr civil servant and memb of HM Dip Serv; private sec to Sir Thomas Phillips, KCB (Employment Dept) 1940; Labour cncllr HM Embassies Paris 1956-60 and Washington DC 1972-73; princ Trg Serv Agency 1973-77; pt/t teacher: Working Men's Coll London 1970-, Inst for Learning in Retirement American Univ Washington DC 1987-; *Recreations* keyboard music (baroque and modern); *Clubs* Utd Oxford and Cambridge Univ; *Style*— Robert Lloyd-Davies, Esq, CMG; 59 Elm Park Court, Pinner, Middx HA5 3LL (☎ 081 866 9526)

LLOYD-DAVIES, (Reginald) Wyndham; s of Dr Allan Wyndham Lloyd-Davies (d 1974), of Branksome Park, Poole, Dorset, and Muriel Constance, *née* Martin; *b* 24 June 1934; *Educ* Rugby, Univ of London (MB, MS); *m* 1, 31 May 1958 (m dis 1981), Elizabeth Ann, da of Arthur Wesley Harding (d 1978); 2 da ((Susan) Vanessa b 1960, Fiona Caroline b 1964); m 2, 20 Aug 1983, Jill Black, da of Austin Hemingsley (d 1969); *Career* res urologist San Francisco Med Centre Univ of California 1969-70, conslt surgn Queen Victoria Hosp E Grinstead 1971-77, dep CMO Met Police 1983- (conslt surgn 1978-), sr conslt urologist St Thomas's Hosp 1986- (MRC res fell Dept of Surgery 1965, sr surgical registrar in urology 1966-69); numerous pubns on urological topics; Liveryman Worshipful Soc of Apothecaries 1974, Freeman City of London 1979; FRSM (memb Cncl 1975-87, vice-pres 1980, treas 1983-87; Urology Section: memb 1975-87, pres elect 1990, pres 1991-92), memb Br Assoc of Urological Surgns (memb Cncl 1980-83), FRCS (Eng); *Recreations* shooting, fishing, stalking; *Clubs* Carlton, Garrick; *Style*— Wyndham Lloyd-Davies, Esq; 53 Harley St, London W1N 1DD; Matthews Cottage, Kingham, Oxon (☎ 071 6314617)

LLOYD-DAVIS, Glynne Christian; s of Col G St G Lloyd-Davis (d 1956), and Daphne Mary, *née* Barnes; *b* 9 March 1941; *Educ* St Paul's, Ealing Tech Coll, Royal Sch of Mines (Univ of London); *m* 20 April 1963, Dorothy Helen, da of Michael O'Shea, of Aust; 1 s (Simon b 1966), 1 da (Sarah b 1964); *Career* chartered sec; asst sec The RTZ Corporation plc 1976, dir subsid cos; FCIS; *Recreations* reading, walking, sketching; *Clubs* Royal Overseas League; *Style*— Glynne Lloyd-Davis, Esq; Forge Cottage, Whitehill, Ospringe, Faversham, Kent; 6 St James's Square, London SW1Y 4LD (☎ 071 930 2399, telex 24639)

LLOYD-EDWARDS, Capt Norman; RD (1971, and Bar 1980); s of Evan Stanley Edwards (d 1986), of Cardiff, and Mary Leah, *née* Lloyd (d 1977); *b* 13 June 1933; *Educ* Monmouth Sch, Quakers Yard GS, Univ of Bristol (LLB); *Career* Capt RNR, CO HMS Cambria, S Wales Div RNR 1981-84; slr; ptnr Cartwright Adams & Black 1960-; memb Cardiff City Cncl 1963-87 (dep Lord Mayor 1973-74, Lord Mayor 1985-86); chapter clerk Llandaff Cathedral 1975-90, pres Friends of Llandaff Cathedral 1990-, memb BBC Cncl Wales 1987-90, chm Nat Res Trg Cncl 1984-, chm Cardiff Festival of Music 1981-89, pres S Glamorgan Scouts 1989-; chm: Wales Ctee Duke of Edinburgh Award 1980-, Glamorgan TA & VRA 1987-90; pres Cardiff Branch Nat Tst; Lord Lt S Glamorgan 1990- (Vice Lord Lt 1986); ADC to HM The Queen 1984; KStJ 1988 (OStJ 1983); Prior for Wales 1989; *Recreations* music, gardening, table talk; *Clubs* Army & Navy, Cardiff & Co, United Services Mess; *Style*— Capt Norman Lloyd-Edwards, RD; Hafan Wen, Llantrisant Rd, Llandaff, Cardiff CF5 2PU (☎ 0222 566107); 36 West Bute St, Cardiff (☎ 0222 465959, fax 0222 480006)

LLOYD GEORGE, Hon Robert John Daniel; s of 3 Earl Lloyd-George of Dwyfor; *b* 13 Aug 1952; *Educ* Eton, Univ Coll Oxford; *m* 1978, Kim, da of Carl Fischer of New York; 1 s (Richard b 1983), 1 da (Alice b 1987); *Style*— The Hon Robert Lloyd George

LLOYD GEORGE, Hon Timothy Henry Gwilym; s and h of, 3 Viscount Tenby; *b* 19 Oct 1962; *Educ* Downside, Univ Coll of Wales Aberystwyth; *Style*— The Hon Timothy Lloyd George; Triggs, Crondall, nr Farnham, Surrey

LLOYD GEORGE OF DWYFOR, 3 Earl (UK 1945); Owen Lloyd George; also Viscount Gwynedd (UK 1945); s of 2 Earl Lloyd George of Dwyfor (d 1968, s of the celebrated PM 1916-22) and his 1 w, Roberta, da of Sir Robert McAlpine, 1 Bt; *b* 28 April 1924; *Educ* Oundle; *m* 1, 1949 (m dis 1982), Ruth Margaret, da of Richard Coit (d 1960); 2 s, 1 da; m 2, 1982, (Cecily) Josephine (who m 1, 1957, as his 2 w, 2 Earl of Woolton, who d 1969; m 2, 1969 (m dis 1974), as his 2 w, 3 Baron Forres, who d 1978), er da of Sir Alexander Gordon Cumming, 5 Bt, MC (d 1939); *Heir* s, Viscount Gwynedd; *Career* Capt Welsh Gds 1942, serv 1944-45 in Italy; carried the sword at investiture of HRH The Prince of Wales, Caernarvon Castle 1969; underwriting memb of Lloyd's; memb Historic Buildings Cncl for Wales 1971-; pres Channel Tunnel Assoc; memb Ct Nat Museum of Wales; *Clubs* White's, Pratt's, City of London; *Style*— The Rt Hon the Earl Lloyd George of Dwyfor; 47 Burton Court, Chelsea, London SW3 4SL; Ffynone, Boncath, Pembrokeshire SA37 0HQ

LLOYD HUGHES, David; s of Trevor Lloyd Hughes, of 10a Kingsley Ave, Leeds, and Isabella Mary, *née* Buchan (d 1954); *b* 12 Aug 1941; *Educ* Leeds GS; *m* 1965, Jean Mary, da of William Kenny (d 1945); 1 s; *Career* fin dir and co sec Stylo plc and dir of each of its trading subsids; FCA; *Style*— David Lloyd Hughes, Esq; Stylo plc, Stylo House, Apperley Bridge, Bradford BD10 0NW (☎ 0274 617761, telex 517050, fax 0274 616111); 5 Hollin Gdns, Leeds LS16 5NL (☎ 0532 758478)

LLOYD-HUGHES, Sir Trevor Denby; s of Elwyn Lloyd-Hughes (d 1969), of Dwygyfylchi, Penmaenmawr, and Lucy, *née* Denby (d 1960); *b* 31 March 1922; *Educ* Woodhouse Grove Sch, Jesus Coll Oxford (MA); *m* 1, 9 May 1950 (m dis 1971), Ethel Marguerite Durward (decd), da of late John Ritchie, of Bradford; 1 s (Richard b 1954), 1 da (Katherine b 1951); m 2, 18 May 1971, Marie-Jeanne, da of Marcel Moreillon, of Geneva, Switzerland; 1 s (decd), 1 da (Annabelle b 1971), 1 adopted da (Nammon b 1969 in Thailand); *Career* asst inspr Taxes 1947-48; freelance journalist 1949; political corr: Liverpool Echo 1950, Liverpool Daily Post 1951-64; press sec to PM 1964-69, chief info advsr to Govt 1969-70, int conslt in public affrs 1971-; involved in many charitable, religious and environmental activities; chm Circle of Wine Writers 1972-73 (memb 1961); kt 1970; *Recreations* yoga, golf, travel, walking; *Clubs* Mossiman's (Belfry), Wellington; *Style*— Sir Trevor Lloyd-Hughes; Au Carmail, Labarrere, 32250 Montreal-du-Gers, France (☎ 010 33 62 29 45 31)

LLOYD JONES, David Elwyn; MC (1946); s of Daniel Lloyd Jones (d 1974), of Aberystwyth, and Blodwen, *née* Evans (d 1953); *b* 20 Oct 1920; *Educ* Ardwyn GS Aberystwyth, Univ Coll of Wales Aberystwyth (BA); *m* 23 July 1955, Mrs Elsie Winifred, wid of Dr Ian Gallie, da of Prof Robert Peers, CBE, MC (d 1972), of Nottingham; 1 steps; *Career* WWII OCTU 1941-42, cmmnd (Sandhurst) Indian Army 1942, served 1 Bn Assam Regt Burma Campaign 1942-46 (Maj 1945); Dept of Educn and Sci (formerly Miny of Educn): asst princ 1947-49, princ 1949-60, asst sec dep account gen 1961-68, under sec (head Higher and Further Educn Branch for Non Univ Sector) 1969-80, seconded princ private sec to Chllr of the Duchy of Lancaster 1960-61; Cncl memb: Royal Acad of Dancing 1980-, RCM 1981-, Froebel Educnl Inst 1981-; FRCM 1988; *Recreations* music, Indian history, playing golf, watching cricket; *Clubs* MCC, Roehampton, Royal Cwlth; *Style*— David E Lloyd Jones, Esq, MC; 5 Playfair Mansions, Queen's Club Gardens, London W14 9TR (☎ 071 385 0586)

LLOYD JONES, (Richard) David; s of Richard Francis Lloyd Jones (d 1976), and Hester, *née* Ritchie (d 1985); *b* 10 May 1942; *Educ* Edgeborough Sch, Bradfield Coll, Architectural Assoc (DipAA); *m* 1971, Linda Barbara, da of Duncan John Stewart; *Career* Stillman and Eastwick-Field Architects 1964, National Building Agency 1966-72; RMJM Ltd (previously Robert Matthew Johnson-Marshall & Partners): joined 1972, dir 1986, chm Design Group 1987; recent projects incl: Parkside Coventry for Parkside Devpt Co, HRH Prince of Wales' exhibition Vision of Britain at the Victoria and Albert Museum, Britain for HRH Prince of Wales, Barristers Chambers for Hon Members Gray's Inn, NFU Mutual and Avon Insurance Group HQ; RIBA 1968, FRSA 1990; *Recreations* sculpture, painting, tennis, dry stone walling, travelling; *Clubs* Architectural Assoc, Royal Soc of Arts & Science; *Style*— David Lloyd Jones, Esq; 24 Liston Rd, London SW4 ODF; 28 Ghammar St, Gharb, GO30, Malta; RMJM Ltd, 83 Paul St, London EC2A 4NQ (☎ 071 251 5588, fax 071 250 3131)

LLOYD JONES, Dr (John) Kenneth; s of Rev James Gwilym Jones (d 1978), and Margaret Olwen, *née* Thomas; *b* 2 June 1931; *Educ* Gonville and Caius Coll Cambridge, Guys Hosp Med Sch (MA, BM, BChir); *m* 23 April 1960, Rosalie Mary, da of Capt George Frederick Harry Harrison-Bloom (d 1982), of Gerrad's Cross, Bucks; 1 s (Huw b 1968), 1 da (Catrin b 1971); *Career* house offr Guys Hosp, registrar Lewisham Hosp Gp and Nat Heart Hosp, sr registrar King's Coll Hosp 1965-69, post-doctoral fell Univ of S California USA 1967-68, conslt in rheumatology and rehabilitation Trent Regnl Health Authy 1969-; chm Notts Ctee for the Employment of Disabled People, regnl chm Arthritis and Rheumatism Cncl, memb Central Notts Health Authy; FRCP 1977; *Books* Surgery of the Knee Joint (contrib, 1984), Copeman's Textbook of Rheumatology (contrib, 1986); *Recreations* gardening, music, photography; *Clubs* Royal Society of Medicine; *Style*— Dr J Kenneth Lloyd Jones; Sherwood, 10 Kirkby Road, Ravenshead, Nottingham NG15 9HF (☎ 0623 792717), Harlow Wood Orthopaedic Hosp, Mansfield, Notts NG18 4TH (☎ 0263 35431)

LLOYD-JONES, David Mathias; s of Harry Vincent Lloyd-Jones, and Margaret Alwyna, *née* Mathias; *b* 19 Nov 1934; *Educ* Westminster, Magdalen Coll Oxford (BA); *m* 23 May 1964, Anne Carolyn, da of Brig Victor Whitehead, of 2160 Lakeshore Dr, Montreal; 2 s (Gareth b 1966, Simon b 1968), 1 da (Vanessa b 1964); *Career* conductor; repetiteur with Royal Opera House Covent Garden 1959-60, chorus master and conductor New Opera Co 1961-64; freelance conductor engagements with: BBC, WNO, Scottish Opera; asst music dir Sadlers Wells ENO 1972-78, artistic dir Opera North 1978-90; ed original version of Mussorgsky's Boris Godunov 1974; published full score Gilbert and Sullivans' The Gondoliers 1983; trans: Eugene Onegin, Boris Godunov, The Queen of Spades, The Love of Three Oranges; Hon DMus Leeds; *Style*— David Lloyd-Jones, Esq; 9 Clarence Rd, Horsforth, Leeds (☎ 0532 584 490); 94 Whitelands House, Cheltenham Terrace, London SW3

LLOYD-JONES, His Hon David Trevor; VRD (1952); s of Trevor Lloyd-Jones (d 1933), of Holywell, and Ann, *née* Hughes Roberts (d 1977); *b* 6 March 1917; *Educ* Holywell GS; *m* 1, 1942 (m dis 1949), Mary Violet (d 1980), da of Frederick Barnardo, CIE, CBE; m 2, 1958, Anstice Elizabeth (d 1981), da of William Perkins; m 3, 1984 Florence Mary, da of William Fairclough, MM (d 1979); 1 s (Martyn), 2 da (Margaret, Ceridwen); *Career* WWII Lt Cdr RNVR Atlantic Pacific; called to the Bar Gray's Inn 1951; chm Caernarvonshire Quarter Sessions 1970-72 (dep chm 1960-66), HM circuit judge 1972-88; *Recreations* golf, music; *Clubs* Army and Navy, Royal Dornoch GC; *Style*— His Hon David Lloyd-Jones, VRD; 29 Curzon Park North, Chester

LLOYD-JONES, Prof Sir (Peter) Hugh Jefferd; s of Brevet Maj William Lloyd-Jones, DSO (d 1963, late Capt of Invalids Royal Hosp Chelsea), and Norah Leila, *née* Jefferd (d 1953); *b* 21 Sept 1922; *Educ* Westminster, Lycée Francais du Royaume Univ, Christ Church Oxford (MA); *m* 1, 30 July 1953 (m dis 1981), Frances Elizabeth, da of RHB Hedley; 2 s (Edmund b 1958, Ralph b 1960), 1 da (Antonia b 1962); m 2, 26 March 1982, Prof Mary Lefkowitz, da of Harold Rosenthal; *Career* 2 Lt Intelligence Corps, serv India 1942, Capt 1944, demob 1946; fell Jesus Coll Cambridge 1948-54, lectr Univ of Cambridge 1952-54 (asst lectr 1950-52), fell and EP Warren praelecter in Corpus Christi Coll Oxford 1954-60, regius prof Greek Univ of Oxford, student of Christ Church Oxford 1960-89; corresponding memb: Acad of Athens, American Acad of Arts and Scis, Rheinisch-Westfälische Akademie, Accademia di Letteratura Archelogia e Belle Arti Naples; Hon PhD Univ Tel Aviv 1982, Hon DH Chicago Univ 1970; *Books* The Justice of Zeus (1971, 2 edn 1983), Blood for the Ghosts (1982), Supplementum Hellenisticum (with P J Parsons 1983), Sophoclis Fabulae (with N G Wilson 1990), Sophoclea (1990), Academic Papers (1990); *Recreations* cats, remembering old cricket; *Clubs* Utd Oxford and Cambridge; *Style*— Prof Sir Hugh Lloyd-Jones; 110 Marlborough Rd, Oxford OX1 4LS; 15 West Riding, Wellesley, Massachusetts, 02181 (☎ USA 617 237 2212)

LLOYD-JONES, Mary; da of John Francis Elkington (d 1984), of Harrow-on-the-Hill, and Jennie Ada Sybil, *née* Tucker (d 1984); *b* 2 Aug 1931; *Educ* St Mary's Sch Baldslow St Leonards-on-Sea E Sussex, Hampstead Business and Secretarial Coll; *m* 2 May 1959, Col John Lloyd-Jones (d 1982), s of Capt Robert Lloyd-Jones (d 1959), of Ealing, London W5; 3 s (Jeremy b 1960, Adam b 1965, Tomas b 1968), 1 da (Vanessa b 1962); *Career* Guildford Borough Cncl: cncllr 1979-, mayoress 1986-87, dep mayoress 1987-88, mayor 1990-91; chm Housing and Health Ctee 1987-90 (vice chm 1983-87), tstee Yvonne Arnaud Theatre; memb Ct of Univ of Surrey, vice pres Guildford-Freiburg Soc; *Recreations* music, theatre, swimming, watching sport; *Clubs* Vanburgh Theatre (Guildford), Royal Aldershot Offrs; *Style*— Mrs Mary Lloyd-Jones; White Lodge, Wentworth Crescent, Ash Vale, Aldershot GU12 5LE (☎ 0252 26587); Associated Examining Board, Stag Hill House, Guildford GU2 5XJ (☎ 0483 506506 ext 2213, fax 0483 300152)

LLOYD-JONES, Rees Lloyd; s of Griff Jones (d 1968), of Pwllheli, N Wales, and Mary Louisa (d 1966); *b* 13 June 1925; *Educ* Pwllheli Sch, Univ of London (MB BS); *m* 1 May 1954, Elisabeth, da of Sir Henry Babington Smith (d 1921); 1 da (Emma Mary b 1957); *Career* RAF med branch 1948-50, conslt obstetrician and gynaecologist Middx Hosp 1961; memb Worshipful Soc of Apothecaries; memb: BMA; FRCS, FRCOG; *Recreations* gardening, walking, Bach; *Style*— Rees Lloyd-Jones, Esq; 44 Wimpole St, London W1 (☎ 071 487 4828)

LLOYD-JONES, Robert (Bob); s of Robert Lloyd-Jones (d 1950), of Caernarvon, N Wales, and Edith May, *née* Hughes (d 1954); *b* 30 Jan 1931; *Educ* Wrekin Coll, Queens' Coll Cambridge (MA), Harvard Business Sch; *m* 9 June 1958 (m dis 1977), Morny Downer; 2 s (Ashley Paul b 8 June 1961, Alasdair Guy b 12 Feb 1966), 1 da (Sarah Louise (Mrs Britton) b 14 Oct 1962); *Career* Lt RN 1956-59; patent attorney Shell International 1959-62, head legal and licensing BTR Industrial Ltd 1962-64, dir (Woolmark) International Wool Secretariat 1964-71, PA chm and export dir Schachenmayr Germany 1971-77; dir gen Br Textile Employers Assoc 1977-81, Retail Consortium 1981-83, dir gen Brick Devpt Assoc 1984-, dir Fedn Euro des Fabricants de Tuiles et de Briques 1984-; friend: Royal Acad, Tate Gallery; govr Cncl for Distributitive Trades 1982-84, fndr chm Nat Retail Trg Cncl 1982-84; FRSA; *Recreations* golf, tennis, squash, chess, travel, arts, reading, music; *Clubs* Lansdowne, Royal Birkdale, Rye, Liphook, Formby Golf, Royal Ascot Tennis, IOD; *Style*— R Lloyd-Jones, Esq; Newell Cottage, Winkfield, Windsor, Berks SL4 4SE (☎ 0344 883 054); Woodside House, Winkfield, Windsor, Berks SL4 2DX (☎ 0344 885651, fax 0344 890129, car 0860 363314)

LLOYD-JONES, (Glyn) Robin; s of William Rice Lloyd-Jones (d 1980), and Esme Frances, *née* Ellis; *b* 5 Oct 1934; *Educ* Blundell's, Selwyn Coll Cambridge (MA), Jordanhill Coll of Educ; *m* 30 July 1959, Sallie, da of Cdr John Hollocombe, RN (D 1981); 1 s (Glyn b 1962), 2 da (Kally b 1965, Léonie b 1969); *Career* educn advsr 1972-89; writer; pubns incl: Where the Forest and the Garden Meet (1980), Lord of the Dance (winner BBC-Arrow first novel competition, 1983), The Dreamhouse (1985); pres Scot Assoc of Writers 1981-87, vice pres Scot PEN Int; *Books* Assessment from Principles to Action (with Elizabeth Bray, 1985), Better Worksheets (1986), Argonauts of the Western Isles (1989); *Recreations* mountaineering, sea-canoeing, wind-surfing, photography; *Style*— Robin Lloyd-Jones, Esq; Cellulloyd Films Ltd & Eljay Management Services, 26 East Clyde St, Helensburgh G84 7PG (☎ 0436 72010, fax 0436 78978)

LLOYD LYONS, Bruno; s of Cyril Lloyd Lyons, and Kathleen Joan, *née* Webb; *b* 25 Jan 1942; *Educ* Henry Thornton GS; *m* 1, 1963 (m dis); 2 da (Sarah b 22 Aug 1972, Rebecca b 31 May 1969); m 2, 5 April 1986, Jennifer, da of Albert Cook; *Career* md Hartshorne Joyce Lloyd Lyons Ltd 1971-84, dir and dep chm Chetwynd Haddons Ltd 1984-89, chm Index Advertising Partnership Ltd 1989-90, vice chm Publicis Ltd 1990-; MIPA 1965; *Recreations* reading, opera, horse racing, skiing; *Style*— Bruno Lloyd Lyons, Esq; Publicis Ltd, 67 Brompton Rd, London SW3 1EF (☎ 071 823 9000, fax 071 823 8389, mobile 0860 718145)

LLOYD MOSTYN *see also*: Mostyn

LLOYD-MOSTYN, Dr Roger Hugh; s of Hugh Wynn Lloyd-Mostyn (d 1975), and Eileen Grace (decd); *b* 1 Dec 1941; *Educ* Lancing, Westminster Hosp Med Sch Univ of London; *m* 21 Jan 1967, Mary Frances, da of late Captain Edward Fothergill Elderton; 3 s (Christopher b 25 May 1968, James b 23 April 1970, David b 22 April 1981); *Career* house offr Westminster Hosp 1965-66, registrar Kings Coll Hosp 1970-73, sr registrar Queen Elizabeth Hosp 1973-76, conslt physician Mansfield 1976-; fndr and chm of local orgn for cardio-pulmonary resuscitation trg; memb: BMA, Br Diabetic Assoc; FRCP 1983; *Recreations* swimming, gardening, music; *Style*— Dr Roger Lloyd-Mostyn; Kings Mill Hospital, Sutton-in-Ashfield, Notts (☎ 0263 22515)

LLOYD OF HAMPSTEAD, Baron (Life Peer UK 1965), of Hampstead, London Borough of Camden; Dennis Lloyd; QC (1975); s of Isaac Lloyd (d 1975), co dir, of 22 Stourcliffe Close, London W1, and Betty, *née* Jaffa (d 1965); *b* 22 Oct 1915; *Educ* Univ Coll Sch, Univ Coll London (LLB), Gonville and Caius Coll Cambridge (BA, MA, LLD); *m* 15 Sept 1940, Ruth Emma Cecilia, da of late Carl Tulla; 2 da (Hon Naomi Katharine (Hon Mrs Hodges) b 1946, Hon Corinne Deborah (Hon Mrs Newman-Henderson) b 1951); *Career* serv RA 1939-41 and RAOC WWII, Capt DADOS, liaison offr Free French Forces in Syria and Lebanon; called to the Bar Inner Temple 1936; in practice in London 1937-39 and 1946-82; reader in English law Univ Coll London 1947-56 (Quain prof of Jurisprudence 1956-82, now emeritus); head of Dept of Law Univ Coll 1969-82; memb: Law Reform Ctee 1961-82, European Communities Ctee 1973-79 and 1984-89, Br Screen Advsy Cncl 1985-; chm: Nat Film and Television Sch 1970-88, Br Film Inst 1973-76 (govr 1968-76), Cncl of Univ Coll Sch 1971-79; fell: Univ Coll London, Ritsumeikan Univ Kyoto Japan 1978 (Hon LLD 1987); *Books* Unincorporated Associations (1938), Rent Control (2 edn, 1955), Public Policy (1953), Business Lettings (1956), Introduction to Jurisprudence (5 edn, 1985), Idea of Law (1964, revised edns 1968-87); *Recreations* painting, listening to music, modern Greek; *Clubs* Athenaeum, RAC; *Style*— The Rt Hon the Lord Lloyd of Hampstead, QC; Faculty of Laws, University College London, Endsleigh Gardens, London WC1

LLOYD PARRY, Eryl; s of Capt Robert Parry (d 1974), of Caernarfon, and Megan, *née* Lloyd (d 1962); *b* 28 April 1939; *Educ* Caernarfon GS, St Peter's Coll Oxford (BA, Dip Pub and Social Admin, MA); *m* 5 Aug 1967, Nancy Kathleen, da of Lt-Col Sir Richard Kenneth Denby (d 1986), of Ilkley; 3 s (Richard b 14 Jan 1969, Robert b 15 Dec 1970, Roland b 16 Jan 1979), 1 da (Helen b 16 May 1974); *Career* called to the Bar Lincoln's Inn 1966; in practice Northern Circuit 1966-, pt/t chm Industl Tbnls 1977, vice-pres Merseyside and Cheshire Rent Assessment Panel 1985; lay reader C of E, active memb Amnesty Int, memb Prayer Book Soc; *Recreations* amateur dramatics, playwriting, cricket, reading; *Clubs* Liverpool Bar Cricket, Ainsdale Sports, Southport Dramatic, Sussex Playwrights; *Style*— Eryl Lloyd Parry, Esq; 6 Stanley Ave, Birkdale, Southport, Merseyside PR8 4RU (☎ 0704 68163); Fruit Exchange Chambers, Victoria St, Liverpool L5 6QU (☎ 051 236 3778)

LLOYD PAYNE, Brett L; s of Allan James Lloyd Payne, and Sandra Margaret, *née* Lloyd; *b* 11 Dec 1966; *Educ* Luton Poly, Thames Poly; *m* 28 April 1990, Jacqueline Lesley, da of Sqdn Ldr Michael Hallam; *Career* CAD technician: Hobbs Architects 1983-86, ODEGW London 1986; systems mangr Turner Wright and PTS 1986-87, assoc ptnr and CAD systems mangr Melvin Lansley & Mark; *Recreations* walking, climbing, windsurfing, canoeing, cycling, mountain biking, paintballing, ju-jitsu; *Style*— Brett Lloyd Payne, Esq; 105A High St, Archway House, Berhamsted, Herts HP4

2DG (☎ 0442 862123, fax 0442 876217)

LLOYD-ROBERTS, George Edward; s of George Charles Lloyd-Roberts (d 1986), of Cheyne Place, London, and Catherine Ann, *née* Wright; *b* 21 March 1948; *Educ* Gordonstoun, Univ of London (MSc); *m* 2 Aug 1969, Elizabeth Anne, da of Horace Edward Kenworthy, of Cork, Eire; 1 s (Henry b 1977), 1 da (Sophie b 1975); *Career* underwriter GE Lloyd-Roberts Synd 55 at Lloyd's, Lloyds Non Marine Assoc 1986-, Lloyds Solvency and Security 1987-1989; *Recreations* running, riding, reading; *Style*— George Lloyd-Roberts, Esq; Lloyd's, Lime St, London (☎ 071 623 7100)

LLOYD-ROBERTS, Dr Robert Edmund; TD (1972); o s of Richard Lloyd Roberts (d 1939), of Pinner, Middx, and Margaret Sarah, *née* Evans (d 1987); representative of a cadet branch of the ancient house of Nannau, N Wales, derived from the Princes of Powys; *b* 22 July 1925; *Educ* Merchant Taylors', St Thomas's Hosp (MB BS, LRCP); *m* 2 July 1955, Elizabeth, yr da of Dr Mandale Byers (d 1923), of Mowhan House, Co Armagh, and St Anne's-on-Sea, Lancs (the Byers of Mowhan descend from the Byres of Coates, Scotland); 2 s (Richard b 1956, Meyrick b and d 1958), 2 da (Arabella b 1959, Sophia b 1963); *Career* Lt-Col RAMC RARO formerly TA, DADMS 44 (Home Counties) Divn TA 1962-67, CO 144 Field Ambulance RAMC(V) and SMO 44 Parachute Bde (V) 1969-73; hon treas Airborne Med Soc 1973-83; princ in gen med practice 1957-90; visiting med offr: Nunnery Fields Hosp 1957-90, Mount Hosp Canterbury 1985-89; med offr: Christ Church Coll 1962-90, St Edmund's Sch Canterbury 1986-90; chm War Pensions and Industl Injuries Med Bds DHSS, local med advsr Med Advsy Serv Civil Serv Dept; med examiner: insur cos, Br Red Cross Soc etc; in attendance on HH Pope John Paul II at his visit to Canterbury Cathedral 29 May 1982; memb: Br Geriatric Soc, Canterbury Police Advsy Ctee; former memb Dist Gen Practitioners Ctee, fndr The Welsh Registry 1990; FRSM, MRCSEng; OStJ 1967; *Recreations* history, heraldry, genealogy, membership of various socs; *Clubs* Army and Navy, Kent and Canterbury (Canterbury); *Style*— Dr R E Lloyd-Roberts, TD; Plas Glanafon, Talybont, Merioneth, Gwynedd; Longport House, 8 Longport, Canterbury, Kent CT1 1PE

LLOYD WEBBER, Andrew; s of William Southcombe Lloyd Webber, CBE (d 1982, dir London Coll Music, musical dir Westminster Central Hall London), and Jean Hermione, *née* Johnstone; *b* 22 March 1948; *Educ* Westminster, Magdalen Coll Oxford, RCM (FRCM); *m* 1, 24 July 1971 (m dis 1983), Sarah Jane Tudor, *née* Hugill; 1 s (Nicholas b 1979), 1 da (Imogen b 1977); m 2, 22 March 1984 (m dis 1990), Sarah, da of Grenville Geoffrey Brightman, of Bournemouth; m 3, Feb 1991, Madeleine Astrid, 2 da of Brig Adam Brampton Douglas Gurdon, CBE, *qv*; *Career* composer; *musicals* with lyrics by Tim Rice: Joseph and the Amazing Technicolour Dreamcoat 1968, Jesus Christ Superstar 1970 (revised 1973), Evita 1976 (stage version 1978); Jeeves (with lyrics by Alan Ayckbourn) 1975, Tell Me On a Sunday (with lyrics by Don Black) 1980, Cats (based on poems by T S Eliot) 1981, Song and Dance (with lyrics by Don Black) 1982, Starlight Express (with lyrics by Richard Stilgoe) 1984, The Phantom of the Opera (with lyrics by Richard Stilgoe and Charles Hart) 1986, Aspects of Love (with lyrics by Don Black and Charles Hart) 1989; prodr: Daisy Pulls It Off 1983, The Hired Man 1984, Lend me a Tenor (1986); *film scores* Gumshoe 1971, The Odessa File 1974; *compositions* Variations (based on A minor Caprice No 24 by Paganini) 1977, symphonis version 1986, Requiem Mass 1985; *awards* Tony awards: 3 in 1980, 2 in 1983, 1 in 1988; Drama Desk award: 1 in 1971, 2 in 1980, 1 in 1983, 2 in 1988; Grammy award: 2 in 1980, 1 in 1983, 1 in 1985; Grammy Living Legend award 1989, Triple Play award ASCAP 1988; honoured by City and Music Center of LA for outstanding contrib to the arts and world of music 1991; *Publications incl* Joseph and the Amazing Technicolour Dreamcoat (with Timothy Rice, 1982), The Complete Phantom of the Opera (1987); *Recreations* architecture; *Style*— Andrew Lloyd Webber, Esq; The Palace Theatre, Shaftesbury Ave, London W1V 8AY

LLOYD WEBBER, Julian; s of William Southcombe Lloyd Webber, CBE (d 1982), and Jean Hermione, *née* Johnstone; *b* 14 April 1951; *Educ* Westminster Under Sch, Univ Coll Sch, RCM; *m* 1, 1974 (m dis 1989), Celia Mary, *née* Ballantyne; m 2, 1 July 1989, Zohra Mahmud, *née* Ghazi; *Career* UK debut Queen Elizabeth Hall London 1972, USA debut Lincoln Centre NY 1980, debut with Berlin Philharmonic Orch 1984; has performed with all maj Br orchs and toured the USA, Germany, Holland, Africa, Bulgaria, Czechoslovakia, S America, Spain, Belgium, France, Scandinavia, Portugal and Australia; tour: Singapore and Japan 1986, Japan and Korea 1988, Singapore, Japan, Hong Kong, Taiwan 1990; has made first recordings of works by: Benjamin Britten, Frank Bridge, Frederick Delius, Gustav Holst, Joaquin Rodrigo, Ralph Vaughan Williams; Winner Best British Classical Recording for Elgar Cello Concerto 1987; ARCM; *Books Incl:* The Classical Cello (1980), The Romantic Cello (1981), The French Cello (1981), 6 pieces by Frank Bridge (1982), The Young Cellist's Repertoire Books 1, 2 & 3 (1984), Holst Invocation (1984), Vaughan Williams Fantasia on Sussex Folk Tunes (1984), Travels with My Cello (1984), Song of the Birds (1985), Recital Repertoire for Cellists (1986); *Recreations* turtle keeping, topography (especially Br), reading horror stories; *Style*— Julian Lloyd Webber, Esq; Patrick Garvey Management, 32 Big Wood Ave, Hove, E Sussex BN3 6FQ (☎ 0273 206623, fax 0273 208484)

LLOYD-WILLIAMS, Lt Cdr Huw Ceiriog; s of Tomos Lloyd-Williams (d 1963), of Derigaron, Tregaron, Dyfed, and Elizabeth, *née* Evans-Jones (d 1945); *b* 8 Feb 1928; *Educ* Tregaron Co Sch, Open Univ (BA); *m* 7 Dec 1968, (Celia) Anne, da of John Williams (d 1983), of Riverside, Tregaron; 2 s (Tomos b 1971, Daniel b 1972), 1 da (Laisa b 1973); *Career* joined RN 1944, Dartmouth Coll (Upper Yardsman) 1951-52, Greenwich 1952 (Sub Lt), Fleet Appts 1952-67, Staff Coll 1964, Flag Offr ME Staff 1963-65, Admty 1965-67, resigned 1967; Nationwide Building Society 1970-87: branch mangr Aberystwyth 1971-74, regnl mangr Wales 1974-87, memb Welsh Regnl Bd 1986-88; dep chm Corinthian Construction & Development Co 1987-; Parly candidate (Lib) Cardiganshire 1968-70; memb: Bd Housing Corporation 1983-88, Cncl Nat Museum of Wales, Cncl St Davids Univ Coll Lampeter; *Recreations* golf; *Clubs* Army and Navy, Radyr Golf; *Style*— Lt Cdr Huw Lloyd-Williams, RN; Plas Trefilan, Lampeter, Dyfed (☎ 0570 470 814); c/o Corinthian Construction & Development Co, Haywood House, Dunfries Place, Cardiff CF1 4BA (☎ 0222 378252, fax 0222 382380)

LLOYD-WORTH, Hon Mrs (Frances Patricia); da of 3 Baron Tollemache (d 1955); *b* 1908; *m* 1949 (m dis 1964), Charles Edward Lloyd-Worth; *Style*— The Hon Mrs Lloyd-Worth

LLOYDS, Jeremy William; s of Edwin William Lloyds, of SA, and Grace Cicely, *née* Cleaver; *b* 17 Nov 1954; *Educ* Blundell's; *m* 10 March 1989, Corné, da of Jan du Toit; *Career* professional cricketer; MCC young professional 1975-78; Somerset CCC: second eleven 1973-79, professional 1979-84, awarded county cap 1982; Gloucestershire CCC 1985-, awarded county cap 1985; overseas clubs represented incl: Toombull CC Brisbane, N Sydney CC, Preston CC Melbourne, Alberton CC Transvaal SA, Orange Free State SA, Fish Hoek CC SA; *Recreations* golf, music, watching motor racing, reading, gardening; *Style*— Jeremy Lloyds, Esq; c/o Gloucestershire CCC, Phoenix County Ground, Nevil Rd, Bristol BS7 9EJ (☎ 0272 245216)

LOACH, Kenneth Charles (Ken); s of John Loach (d 1973), of Nuneaton, and Vivien Nora, *née* Hamlin; *b* 17 June 1936; *Educ* King Edward VI Sch Nuneaton, St Peter's Coll Oxford (BA); *m* 17 July 1962, Lesley, da of William Leslie Ashton (d 1967); 3 s (Stephen b 1963, Nicholas b 1965, d 1971, James b 1969), 2 da (Hannah b 1967, Emma b 1972); *Career* film dir: Up The Junction 1965, Cathy Come Home 1966, Poor Cow 1967, Kes 1969, Family Life 1971, Days of Hope 1975, The Price of Coal 1977, The Gamekeeper 1979, Black Jack 1979, Looks and Smiles 1981, Which Side Are You On? 1984, Fatherland 1986, The View from the Woodpile 1988, Hidden Agenda 1990; Hon DLitt St Andrews; ACTT, memb Dirs' Guild GB; *Recreations* watching football; *Style*— Ken Loach, Esq; c/o Judy Daish Assoc, 83 Eastbourne Mews, London W2 6LQ (☎ 071 262 1101)

LOADER, Sir Leslie Thomas; CBE (1980); s of Edward Robert Loader (d 1963), of Southampton, and Ethel May, *née* Tiller (d 1966); *b* 27 April 1923; *Educ* Bitterne Park Sch, Bournemouth Coll, LSE; *m* 1, 27 April 1957, Jennifer Jane, *née* Pickering; 3 da (Melanie Susan (Mrs Loader-Pittams) b 18 Jan 1959, Katharine Lucy (Mrs Loader-Cledwyn) b 14 Oct 1961, Anna Victoria (Mrs Loader-Easton) b 10 Feb 1964); m 2, 26 Nov 1981, Elizabeth; *Career* cmmnd Regt (now Royal Hampshire Regt), active serv Italy; co chm (ret); cncllr (C) Southampton City Cncl 1947-59, Parly candidate (C) Southampton Itchen 1955, Nat Union Exec Cons Pty 1969-76; chm: Southampton Young Cons 1947, Southampton Itchen Cons Assoc 1964-70, Southampton Cons Fedn 1966-70, Wessex Area Cons Pty 1972-75 (vice chm 1969-72), Ctee Southampton Cncl 1952 (proposed sale of cncl houses to tenants 1949, Swaythling Housing Soc 1975-83 (pres), Wessex Body Scanner Appeal 1980-83; fndr chm and pres: Rotary Club of Bitterne, Woolston Housing Soc 1962-83; pres Eastleigh Cons Assoc; former memb: Southampton and SW Hants Health Authy, Ct of Govrs Univ Coll Southampton and Univ of Southampton; memb Southampton Harbour Bd 1950-56, tstee Wessex Med Sch Tst 1983-86, hon vice pres Wessex Area Cons Pty 1990; Freeman City of London, Liveryman Worshipful Co of Painter Stainers; kt 1987; *Books* various articles on politics and housing; *Clubs* Carlton; *Style*— Sir Leslie Loader, CBE; (☎ 04893 3551)

LOADER, Neil John; s of Charles Tyrle Loader (d 1986), of Chadwell Heath, and Emily Florence Loader; *b* 9 Sept 1929; *Educ* Brentwood Sch Essex; *m* 1 April 1960, Delphine Ann, da of Charles Stanley Dunlop (d 1986), of Brentwood; 2 s (Stuart b 1963, Phillip b 1964), 1 da (Susan b 1961); *Career* Nat Serv RNVR 1949-50; UK sales dir Monsanto Chems Ltd, md Loader Chemicals & Plastics Ltd 1973-; Freeman Worshipful Co of Needlemakers; *Recreations* golf, walking, bird watching; *Clubs* MCC, Old Brentwoods; *Style*— Neil Loader, Esq; 13 Headley Chase, Warley, Brentwood, Essex (☎ 0277 219 965); Loader Chemicals & Plastics Ltd, 2 Gresham Rd, Brentwood, Essex (☎ 0277 260 820, fax 0277 561 590, car 0836 622 805, telex 99337)

LOADES, Prof David Michael; s of Reginald Ernest Loades, and Gladys Mary, *née* Smith; *b* 19 Jan 1934; *Educ* Perse Sch Cambridge, Emmanuel Coll Cambridge (BA, MA, PhD, LittD); *m* 1, 18 Dec 1965 (m dis 1984), Ann Lomas, *née* Glover; m 2, 11 April 1987, Judith Anne, formerly Atkins; *Career* Nat Serv PO RAF 1953-55; lectr in political sci Univ of St Andrews 1961-63, reader Univ of Durham 1977-80 (lectr in history 1963-70, sr lectr 1970-77), prof of history Univ Coll N Wales 1980-; chief cmmr Wales S Scout Assoc; FRHistS 1967, FSA 1984; *Books* Two Tudor Conspiracies (1965), The Oxford Martyrs (1970), Politics and the Nation 1450-1660 (1974), The Reign of Mary Tudor (1979), The Tudor Court (1986), Mary Tudor: A Life (1989); *Recreations* scouting; *Style*— Prof David Loades, FSA; School of History and Welsh History, University College of North Wales, Bangor (☎ 0248 351151)

LOANE, (Simon Folliott) Warren Thomas Barton; DL (Co Fermanagh 1972); s of Simon Christopher Loane (d 1940), of Crocknacrieve, Enniskillen, NI, and Mildred Penelope Matilda, *née* Barton (d 1971); *b* 16 Aug 1920; *Educ* Portora Royal Sch; *m* 4 Aug 1955, (Heather Everina) Anne, da of Capt David Alexander Mackey (d 1986), of Crocknacrieve; 1 s (Charles b 14 Nov 1956), 1 da (Erica b 30 April 1959); *Career* farmer; dir and vice chm: Ulster Wools 1970-, Ulster Wool Group 1981-; dir Ulster Wool and Farm Supplies 1981- (chm 1981-89); exec memb Ulster Farmers' Union 1945-76 (cncl memb 1944-, fndr memb and former chm Fermanagh branch), fndr memb N Fermanagh Gp Ctee 1951 (chm 1951-76); chm: Ulster Wool Growers 1980- (memb 1959-), NI Regnl Ctee Br Wool Mktg Bd 1987- (memb 1959-); memb Cncl Royal Ulster Agric Soc 1969-73, tstee Agric Res Inst for NI 1963-86, dir UK Wool Growers Fedn 1977-83, chm Mgmnt Ctee Irvinestown and Dist Attested Sales 1982- (memb 1959-), memb Exec Ctee Ulster Agric Orgns Soc 1962-65; vice chm and fndn memb Western Educn and Library Bd 1973-85 (memb 1989-), chm Library and Info Servs Cncl NI 1983-85, memb Br Library Advsy Cncl 1984-85, Gen Synod Church of Ireland 1972- (memb Bd of Educn 1989); dist cmmr of Scouts 1957-62; govr Duke of Westminster HS 1975-; vice chm of govrs: Enniskillen Collegiate Sch 1983-90 (memb 1977-), Enniskillen HS 1982-90 (memb 1981-); memb: Enniskillen RDC 1965-67, Fermanagh CC 1967-73 (chm Planning Ctee 1968-73, fndr memb and chm Museum Ctee 1969-73), Fermanagh DC 1985- (chm Planning Ctee); vice pres (later pres) Ballinamallard Young Unionists 1963-73; memb: Exec Ctee Fermanagh Unionist Assoc 1981-, Fermanagh and S Tyrone Unionist Cncl 1981- (exec memb 1985-), Exec Ctee NI Assoc Educn and Library Bds 1984-85 and 1990-; *Recreations* outdoor pursuits, genealogy, local history; *Style*— Warren Loane, Esq, DL; Crocknacrieve, Enniskillen, NI (☎ 0365 81 214)

LOBANOV-ROSTOVSKY, Princess Roxane; *née* Bibica-Rosetti; da of Prince Raoul Bibica Rosetti and Dorothy, *née* Baroness Acton (*see* Princess Raoul Bibica Rosetti); *b* 3 Oct 1932; *Educ* St George's Ascot, Carlton Univ Ottawa; *m* 1956 (m dis 1980), Prince John Lobanov-Rostovsky, yr s of Prince Constantine Lobanov-Rostovsky, of Hove; 2 s (Prince Paul b 1956, Prince Dimitry b 1962), 1 da (Princess Helena b 1964); *Career* watercolourist and sculptor, memb Soc of Women Artists; *Style*— Princess Roxane Lobanov-Rostovsky; Swallowdale, 67 Woodruff Ave, Hove, Sussex BN3 6PJ

LOBB, Eric; s of William Hunter Lobb (d 1916), and Betsy, *née* Smerdon (d 1956); *b* 3 March 1907; *Educ* UCS Hampstead, Pembroke Coll Oxford (MA); *m* 1949 (m dis), Miss Denby; 1 s (Edward), 1 da (Alice); *Career* private HG; master bootmaker (family bootmaking business founded 1849); chm and md John Lobb Ltd; pres West End Master Bootmakers Assoc; holder Royal Warrants for: HM the Queen, HRH the Duke of Edinburgh, HRH the Prince of Wales; *Books* The Last Shall Be First, History of John Lobb, Bootmaker, by Brian Dobbs; *Recreations* small farming, laughter and the love of friends; *Clubs* Little Ship; *Style*— Eric Lobb, Esq; Newlands, Radlett, Herts WD7 8EH (☎ 0923 856311), 9 St James's St, SW1 A1ET (☎ 071 930 3664/5)

LOBB, Howard Leslie Vicars; CBE (1952); s of Hedley Vicars Lobb (d 1950); *b* 9 March 1909; *Educ* privately, Regent St Poly Sch of Architecture; *m* 1949, Charmian Isobel, da of Charles Oliver Callcott Reilly, MBE (d 1970); 3 s; *Career* sr ptnr Howard Lobb Ptnrship 1950-74, architect Br Pavilion Brussels Expo 1958, (Gold Medal award); architect for numerous schools, nuclear and oil fired stations, motorway service areas, offices, flats and other bldgs; chm Cncl for Architecture, Town planning and bldg res of The Festival of Br, and later controller of Construction of the South Bank Exhibition 1951; chm Architects' Benevolent Soc 1952-89 (vice pres), memb Cncl RYA 1977-80; chm Solent Protection Soc 1982-89; FRIBA, CEng, AIStructE, FRSA; *Recreations* sailing, model railways, painting; *Clubs* Royal Lymington Yacht, Tamesis (cdre 1954-57); *Style*— Howard Lobb, Esq, CBE; Shallows Cottage, Pilley

Hill, Pilley, Lymington, SO41 5QF (☎ 0590 677595)

LOBBENBERG, (John) Peter; s of Hans Lobbenberg (d 1955), and Annemarie, *née* Rabl (d 1971); *b* 12 Sept 1939; *Educ* Leighton Park Sch, Oriel Coll Oxford (MA); *m* 14 Dec 1969, Naomi, da of Ronald Green (d 1985); 1 s (David b 1971), 1 da (Anna b 1974); *Career* CA; sale practitioner, md JPL Portfolio Management Ltd, ptnr Clark Whitehill 1977-90, dir British Uralite plc 1984-88, chm Electronic Machine Co 1986-89; govr The Purcell Sch 1981-89; *Style—* Peter Lobbenberg, Esq; Peter Lobbenberg & Co, 74 Chancery Lane, London WC2A 1AA (☎ 071 430 9300, fax 071 430 9315)

LOBLE, George Frederick; JP (1967 Gateshead); s of Frederick Loble (d 1956), and Elsa, *née* Fried (d 1982); *b* 25 Sept 1926; *Educ* Rutherford Coll of Technol Newcastle upon Tyne, Regent St Poly London (HNC); *m* 12 April 1953, Eve Marion, da of Frederick Heinemann, of London; 1 s (Peter Frederick b 1958), 1 da (Monica Frances b 1955); *Career* chm and md Loblite Ltd 1965-; memb ctee of mgmnt of various local charities 1960-, chm Gateshead Cncl of Social Service 1965-75, govr Special Schools in Gateshead 1965-, tstee John Haswell Housing Tst 1965-80, pres Rotary Club of Gateshead 1968-69, tstee Rotary Club 50 Anniv Tst (Gateshead) 1971-; memb: Tech Ctees of Br Electrical Apparatus Mfrs Assoc 1976-, Tech Ctees of the Br Standards Inst 1980-; dep chm Juvenile Bench Gateshead; CEng, MIMechE, MIQA, FInstPet, MInstD, FRSA; *Recreations* mountain walking, skiing, photography, voluntary organisations; *Style—* George Loble, Esq, JP; 7 Howard house, 43 Elmfield Rd, Gosforth, Newcastle upon Tyne NE3 4BA; Loblite Ltd, Third Ave, Team Valley Trading Estate, Gateshead, Tyne & Wear NE11 0QQ (☎ 091 487 8103, fax 091 482 0270, telex 537358 LOBLIT G)

LOBO, Hon Sir Rogerio (Roger) Hyndman; CBE (1978, OBE 1972), JP; s of Dr P J Lobo and Branca Helena, *née* Hyndman; *b* 15 Sept 1923; *Educ* Escola Central Macao, Seminario de S Jose Macao, Liceu Nacional Infante Dom Henrique Macao, La Salle Coll Hong Kong; *m* 1947, Margaret Mary, *née* Choa; 5 s, 5 da; *Career* chm P J Lobo & Co Ltd Hong Kong 1950-; kt 1985 for public servs in Hong Kong; *Style—* Hon Sir Roger Lobo, CBE; Woodland Heights, E1, 2 Wongneichong Gap Rd, Hong Kong

LOCH, Hon Allegra Helen; da of 3 Baron Loch (d 1982), and his 4 w, Sylvia Barbara (who m 3, 1984, Richard G P Hawkins), da of Alexander Gordon Beauchamp Cameron, of Delmahoy, Midlothian, and formerly w of Christopher Beauchamp-Wilson; *b* 14 Oct 1982; *Style—* The Hon Allegra Loch

LOCH, 4 Baron (UK 1895); Spencer Douglas Loch; MC (1945); yr s of 2 Baron Loch, CB, CMG, DSO, MVO (d 1942), and Lady Margaret Compton, o da of 5 Marquess of Northampton; suc bro, 3 Baron Loch, 1982; *b* 12 Aug 1920; *Educ* Wellington, Trinity Coll Cambridge; *m* 1, 1948, Hon Rachel (d 1976), da of Baroness Lucas of Crudwell and Dingwall (9 and 12 holder of Baronies respectively) and Gp Capt Howard Lister Cooper, AFC, RAF; 1 da (and 2 s decd); m 2, 1979, Davina Julia, formerly w of Sir Richard James Boughey, 10 Bt, and da of FitzHerbert Wright and Hon Doreen, *née* Wingfield, only da of 8 Viscount Powerscourt; *Career* serv Maj Gren Gds NW Europe 1944-45; barr Lincoln's Inn 1948; *Clubs* Beefsteak, Cavalry and Guards'; *Style—* The Rt Hon the Lord Loch, MC; Lochluichart by Garve, Ross; Bratton House, Westbury, Wilts

LOCHHEAD, Robert; s of John Allan Lochhead, of Tockwith, N Yorks, and Gwendoline Alice, *née* Gibbs; *b* 26 July 1946; *Educ* West Bromwich GS; *m* 29 June 1968, Irene, da of Alfred Samuel Horton; 1 s (Alexander James b 9 March 1973); *Career* Serv RAF 1962-63; Leeds Permanent Building Society: trainee Birmingham and Walsall 1963-, first mgmnt appt Beeston Notts 1971-73, second mgmnt appt Derby 1973-78, mangr Head Office 1978-, mortgage advance mangr 1981-83, trg mangr 1983-86, asst gen mengr 1986, md Property Leeds (UK) Ltd 1987- (exec 1988-); FCBSI 1973 (ACBSI 1968); *Recreations* ornithology, reading, cycling; *Style—* Robert Lochhead, Esq; Property Leeds (UK) Ltd, Fitzwilliam House, Fitzwilliam St, Huddersfield HD1 5BB (☎ 0484 422445, fax 0484 422395, car 0860 526866)

LOCK, Barry David Stuart; s of John Albert Putnam Lock (d 1967), and Doris Nellie, *née* Amos (d 1975); *b* 28 July 1934; *Educ* Kings Sch Canterbury, Magdalen Coll Oxford (Mackinnon scholar, BCL, MA); *Career* admitted slr 1961; ptnr: Coward Chance 1964-87, Clifford Chance 1987-; City of London Slrs Co prize; *Recreations* music, the fine arts, collecting Chelsea and Derby porcelain; *Clubs* Athenaeum; *Style—* Barry Lock, Esq; 16 Morpeth Mansions, Morpeth Terrace, London SW1P 1ER (☎ 071 828 0491); Clifford Chance, Royex House, Aldermanbury Square, London EC2Y 7LD (☎ 071 600 0808)

LOCK, (George) David; s of George Wilfred Lock (d 1940), and Ann Elizabeth, da of Sidney Harold Biggs; *b* 24 Sept 1929; *Educ* Haileybury, Queens' Coll Cambridge (MA); *m* 1965, Ann Elizabeth, da of Sidney Harold Biggs; 4 s, 1 da; *Career* Br Tabulating Co Ltd (now ICL) 1954-59, Save & Prosper Gp Ltd 1959-69, American Express 1969-74, Private Patients Plan 1974-85 (md 1975-85); dir plan for active retirement Frizzell Insur and Fin Servs Ltd 1986-89; memb Bd of Mgmnt St Anthony's Hosp Cheam; dir: Home Concern for the Elderly 1985-, Hosp Mgmnt Tst 1985-; sec Frizzell Fndn 1988-; memb RSM; Freeman Worshipful Co of Barber Surgns; *Recreations* bridge, golf, music, entertaining, family activities; *Style—* David Lock, Esq; Buckhurst Place, Horsted Keynes, W Sussex RH17 7AH (☎ (0825) 790599)

LOCK, Lt Cdr Sir (John) Duncan; s of Brig-Gen F R E Lock, DSO; *b* 5 Feb 1918; *Educ* RNC Dartmouth; *m* 1947, (Alice) Aileen Smith (d 1982); 3 da; *Career* serv regular offr in RN 1931-58; WWII: Battle of the Atlantic, Norwegian and N African campaigns, Pacific War, Normandy and Anzio landings; farmed family estate in Somerset 1958-61; specialist in magnetic compasses Admty Compass Observatory 1961-83; memb: Lloyd's, Eton RDC 1967-74; chm: Bucks Branch RDC Assoc 1969-74, Bucks Dist Cncl 1985-87 (memb 1973-), Assoc of Dist Cncls of England and Wales 1974-79 (memb 1974-); Br rep Cncl of Local and Regnl Authys of Europe 1979-, Local Authys Mgmnt Servs and Computer Ctee 1981-1986, chm rep Body for England 1976-89; kt 1978; *Recreations* gardening, shooting; *Style—* Lt Cdr Sir Duncan Lock, RN; Fen Court, Oval Way, Gerrards Cross, Bucks SL9 8QD (☎ 0753 882467)

LOCK, (Thomas) Graham; *b* 19 Oct 1931; *Educ* Whitchurch GS, Univ Coll of South Wales & Monmouthshire (BSc), Coll of Technol Aston, Harvard Business Sch; *m* 24 July 1954, Janice Olive Baker; 2 da (Sian Kathrin b 10 March 1960, Sara Helen b 10 Sept 1961); *Career* Lucas Industs: joined 1956, geschaeftesfuhrer Girling Bremsen GmbH 1961-66, dir overseas operations Girling Ltd (UK) 1966-73; dir and gen mangr Lucas Servs Overseas 1973-79 (dir numerous gp cos overseas), chief exec Amalgamated Metal Corp 1983- (md in div 1979-83); Freeman City of London, Liveryman Worshipful Co of Gold and Silver Wyre Drawers; Reed Meml prize; CEng, FIM, CBIM; *Recreations* music, sailing, skiing; *Clubs* R N Sailing Assoc, Royal Southern Yacht, City Livery; *Style—* Graham Lock, Esq; The Cottage, Fulmer Way, Gerrards Cross, Buckinghamshire; Amalgamated Metal Corporation plc, Adelaide House, London Bridge, London EC4R 9DP (☎ 071 626 4521, telex London 888701, fax 071 623 6015)

LOCK, (Robert) Robin Christopher; s of Christopher Noel Hunter Lock (d 1949), and Lilian Mary, *née* Gillman (d 1966); *b* 14 Aug 1925; *Educ* Tonbridge, Gonville and Caius Coll Cambridge (BA, MA, PhD); *m* 1, July 1954 (m dis 1965), Jillian, *née* Amherst; 1 s (Martin b 1958), 2 da (Sheila b 1955, Diana b 1956); m 2, 14 Aug 1965, Ruth Margaret, *née* Pembrooke; 2 s (David b 1966, d 1987, Adrian b 1967); *Career* res fell Gonville and Caius Coll Cambridge 1951-54, sr princ scientific offr Aerodynamics Div NPL 1965-71 (joined 1954, princ scientific offr 1960), Aerodynamics Dept RAE Farnborough 1971-85; awarded Silver medal of RAes 1985, visiting prof of aerodynamics The City Univ 1985-, conslt at Engrg Sciences Data Unit Int 1985-; FIMA 1966, FRAes 1968, AFAIAA (America) 1971; *Books* Design of Aircraft Wings for Transonic Speeds (1985), Viscous Inviscid Interactions in External Aerodynamics (1987); *Recreations* listening to and playing music, gardening, swimming; *Style—* Robin Lock, Esq; 74 Ormond Ave, Hampton, Middlesex TW12 2RX

LOCK, Dr Stephen Penford; CBE (1991); s of Wallace Henry Lock (d 1968), and Edith Mary Bailey; *b* 8 April 1929; *Educ* City of London Sch, Queens' Coll Cambridge, St Bartholomew's Hosp (MA, MD, MSc); *m* 1955, Shirley Gillian, da of Edwin Walker; 1 s (decd), 1 da (Imogen); *Career* ed Br Med Journal; second offr class White Rose of Finland; *Recreations* trying to learn Russian and the harpsichord; *Clubs* Athenaeum; *Style—* Dr Stephen Lock, CBE; 115 Dulwich Village, London SE21 7BJ (☎ 081 693 6317); BMA House, Tavistock Square, London WC1H 9JR

LOCK-NECREWS, John Ernest; s of William Ernest Necrews (d 1982), and Mary Constance, *née* Lock (d 1987); *b* 30 Aug 1939; *Educ* Bridgend GS, Univ of Wales (Dip Arch); *m* 3 Jan 1978, Daphne, da of Maj Stanley Dickinson, of Cardiff; 1 s (Christian b 1979); *Career* CA; jt md Whinney Mackay-Lewis plc; architectural awards: Prince of Wales, Civic Tst, Times and RICS, Cardiff 2000, Lord Mayors civic award; guest speaker on architectural conservation UNESCO World Congress Basle 1983; chm Central Branch Soc of Architects Wales 1981-82 (cncl memb 1974-82); ARIBA, ACIArb, FFB; *Recreations* golf, skiing, painting; *Clubs* Carlton, Cardiff and Co, Royal Porthcawl Golf; *Style—* John E Lock-Necrews, Esq; Bishopsgate, Howells Crescent, Llandaff, Cardiff; Asta House, 55 Whitfield St, London W1 (☎ 071 636 6621)

LOCKE, Eur Ing (Harry) Brian; s of Henry William Locke (d 1982) of New Earswick, York, and Mary *née* Moore (d 1972); *b* 28 May 1924; *Educ* Bootham Sch York, Imperial Coll London; *m* 1, 19 Feb 1949, (m dis 1974), Margaret Beven, da of Thomas William King (d 1962), of Barnet; 1 s (Richard b 28 March 1961), 3 da (Sarah (Mrs Watson) b 1 July 1952, Frances b 20 Jan 1954, Judith b 22 April 1958); m 2, 3 Jan 1976, Marie Patricia Keegan; 1 step s (Michael b 18 July 1962); *Career* WWII serv Friends Ambulance Unit 1942-46; chem engr: Johnson Matthey Ltd 1948-49, Kestner Evaporator Ltd 1949-50, Miny of Power 1950-58, NCB 1958-65; mangr industl chemistry special projects and planning NRDC 1965-78, md Combustion Systems Ltd 1974-78; dir: Formed Coke Ltd 1975-78, Cadogan Conslts, Chartered Consulting Chem Engrs, Int Energy Mgmnt (process devpt technol transfer) 1978-; Electrolysis Energy Ltd 1979-83, Chemplant Stainless Ltd 1980-84, Locke Purandore Conslts (PVT) Ltd Bombay 1984-, special serv UN Agencies as coal and energy specialist 1980-, Cadogan Mgmnt Ltd 1984-90 (chm 1984-88), Cadogan Servs Ltd 1989-; received: Melchett award Design and Indust Assoc 1987, special award Inst Energy 1987; memb: Econ and Social Affrs Ctee UN Assoc, The Club of Rome, and Inst of Energy, CBI, exec The Watt Ctee on Energy (chm Fin and General Purposes Ctee), Low Grade Coal Ctee World Energy Conf, Br Standards Inst (chm Ctee Assessing Thermal Performance of Boilers); govr Paddington Coll, Chemical Engrg and Fuel Technol Dept Liaison Ctee Univ of Sheffield, Br Assoc Royal Instn, RSA; hon advsr Int Soc for Educn Info Japan, hon sec Assoc for Design and Technol Educn, pres elect Old Centralians The Imperial Coll Engrg Alumnus Assoc, fellowship City & Guilds of London Inst 1987; Freeman City of London 1984, Liveryman Worshipful Co of Engrs 1984; FIChemE 1948, FInstE 1953, FIGasE 1966, FIOD 1974, MConsE 1985, FCGI 1987, MBAE 1988; *Books* Industrial Fuel Efficiency (annually 1957-85), Modern Motoring Handbook (annually 1959-82), Coal (jtly, 1965), Energy Users Data Book (1985), Thermal Processing of Biomas for Energy (1990); *Recreations* Bentleys, Nat Tst, silver, origins of thought, engrg history; *Clubs* Athenaeum, Royal Automobile; *Style—* Eur Ing Brian Locke; Cadogan Consultants, The Court House, Bisley, Glos GL6 7AA (☎ 0452 770 010, fax 0452 770 058, telex 8950049 CADOGN G); Cadogan Consultants, 57 Cadogan St, London, SW3 2QJ (☎ 071 589 9778, fax 071 589 9778); Cadogan Consultants, London House, 53-54 Haymarket, London, SW1Y 4PR (☎ 071 925 0177, fax 071 930 4261, telex 8950049 CADOGN G)

LOCKE, John Howard; CB (1984); s of Percy John Howard Locke, and Josephine Alice, *née* Marshfield; *b* 26 Dec 1923; *Educ* Hymers Coll Hull, Queen's Coll Oxford (MA); *m* 1948, Eirene Sylvia Sykes; 2 da (Diana, Imogen); *Career* MAFF 1945-65; under sec: Cabinet Office 1965-66, Miny of Tport 1966-68, Dept of Employment and Productivity 1968-71; dep sec Dept of Employment 1971-74, dir Health and Safety Exec 1975-83; chm Nat Examination Bd in Occupational Safety and Health 1986-; *Recreations* mountain walking, gardening, opera; *Style—* John Locke, Esq, CB; 4 Old Palace Terrace, The Green, Richmond-on-Thames TW9 1NB (☎ 081 940 1830); Old Box Trees, East Preston, Sussex BN16 1JP (☎ 0903 785 154)

LOCKET, David Frank; s of late Frank Barton Locket, and Phyllis Jesie, *née* Lawson; *b* 29 June 1940; *Educ* Haileybury ISC, Battersea Coll of Technol; *m* 24 Sept 1966, (Ingegerd) Christina, da of Ake Bontell, of Sweden; 1 s (Martin Frank b 1970), 1 da (Annicka Louise b 1972); *Career* Savoy Hotel London, Strand Hotels London 1972-78, catering mangr Anchor Hotels London 1978-83; md LMS (conslts) Ltd 1983; memb ctee Veteran Car Club GB; clerk and chief exec to Master Innholders Assoc; Freeman City of London 1973; MCFA, FHCIMA; *Recreations* veteran cars, fishing, shooting, clocks; *Style—* David F Locket, Esq; Pinecrest, Northdown Rd, Woldingham, Surrey CR3 7AA (☎ 0883 653181)

LOCKETT, His Hon Judge Reginald; s of George Alfred Lockett and Emma, *née* Singleton; *b* 24 June 1933; *Educ* Ashton-in-Makerfield GS, Univ of Manchester, Univ of London; *m* 1959, Edna, *née* Lowe; 1 s, 1 da; *Career* admitted slr 1955, asst coroner Wigan 1963-70, registrar Dist and Co Ct Manchester 1970-81, rec Crown Ct 1978-81, circuit judge Northern Circuit 1981-; vice pres Boys Bde 1978- (dist pres NW 1973-90), lay reader C of E, co ed Butterworths Family Law Servs 1982-90, memb Co Ct Rule Ctee 1985-; *Style—* His Hon Judge Lockett; c/o Sessions House, Lancaster Rd, Preston

LOCKHART *see also*: Sinclair-Lockhart

LOCKHART; *see*: Macdonald Lockhart

LOCKHART, Brian Alexander; s of John Arthur Hay Lockhart, and Norah, *née* Macneil, of Quadrant Rd, Glasgow; *b* 1 Oct 1942; *Educ* Glasgow Acad, Glasgow Univ (BL); *m* 1967, Christine Ross, da of James B Clark, of Ayr; 2 s, 2 da; *Career* slr; ptnr Robertson Chalmers & Auld 1964-79; Sheriff: N Strathclyde 1979-81, Glasgow and Strathkelvin 1981-; *Recreations* fishing, golf, squash, family; *Clubs* Royal Scottish Automobile; *Style—* Brian Lockhart, Esq; 18 Hamilton Ave, Glasgow (☎ 041 427 1921); Sheriff Court, Glasgow (☎ 041 429 8888)

LOCKHART, (Harry) Eugene; s of Harry Eugene Lockhart, Sr, of Austin, Texas, USA, and Gladys Cummings Lockhart (d 1982); *b* 4 Nov 1949; *Educ* Univ of Virginia (BS, MBA)J; *m* 8 June 1974, Terry, da of Frederick Bon Jasperson, of Washington DC, USA; 1 s (Andrew Jasperson b 13 July 1977), 3 da (Julia Cummings b 9 Oct 1979, Victoria MacLaren b 15 Sept 1984, Charlotte Carson b 9 April 1987); *Career* md Nolan Norton and Co 1980-82, gp dir C T Bowring and Co 1982-85, md First Manhattan Bank 1985-87, chief exec ops and dir Midland Bank 1987-, dep chm Thomas Cook Gp, dir of Mastercard Int 1990; memb Royal Acad Advsy Bd; FCA; *Recreations* tennis, golf, running, skiing, photography, riding; *Clubs* St Georges Hill, Liphook, Vanderbilt; *Style—* H E Lockhart, Esq; 29 Kensington Gate, London W8 (☎ 071 584 3792); Road Farm, Churt, Surrey; Midland Bank plc, Poultry, London EC2 (☎ 071 260 7358)

LOCKHART, His Hon Judge Frank Roper; s of Clement Lockhart, of Braithwell, Yorks, and Betsy, *née* Roper (d 1981); *b* 8 Dec 1931; *Educ* King Edward VI GS Retford, Doncaster GS, Univ of Leeds (LLB); *m* 5 Aug 1957, Brenda Harriett, da of Cyril Johnson (d 1985), of Greenways, Woodlands, nr Doncaster; 1 s (John Michael Roper b 1961), 1 da (Jeanette Anne b 1959); *Career* slr; ptnr Jefferies Slrs 1965-88; chm: Soc Security Tbnls 1970-88, Industl Tbnls 1983; rec 1985, circuit judge 1988-; *Recreations* golf, rack, squash; *Style—* His Hon Judge Frank R Lockhart

LOCKHART, Geoffrey John Charles; s of George Arthur Lockhart (d 1961), of Christchurch, Hants, and Margaret Helen, *née* Sutton (d 1982); *b* 16 April 1926; *Educ* Truro Cathedral Sch; *m* 19 Feb 1960, Dodie Mary, da of John Walter Cooper (d 1958), of Brighton; 2 da (Juliet Caroline b 1963, Joanna Helen b 1964); *Career* CA; dir of several local family cos; sr ptnr: Bland Fielden 1982-89, Scrutton Bland 1989-90 (ptnr 1965); memb cncl ICAEW 1977-89, pres Assoc of Accounting Technicians 1985-86 (memb cncl 1980-89), chm of govrs St Mary's Sch Colchester 1970; FCA; *Recreations* cricket, golf, gardening, reading, sport generally; *Clubs* MCC; *Style—* Geoffrey Lockhart, Esq; Chandlers, Nayland, Colchester, Essex CO6 4LA (☎ 0206 262617); 18 Sir Isaacs Walk, Colchester CO1 1JL (☎ 0206 48811)

LOCKHART, Ian Stuart; s of Rev Prebendary Douglas Stuart Mullinger Lockhart (d 1983), and Hilda Mary, *née* Walker; *b* 9 Nov 1940; *Educ* Rugby, Clare Coll Cambridge (MA); *m* 30 Nov 1974, Rosanna, da of Capt Edward Hugh Cartwright; *Career* admitted slr 1967; ptnr: Peake & Co 1969-89, Charles Russell 1989-; dir Wynnstay Properties plc and assoc cos; govr St Mary's Sch Wantage; memb Ctee St Marylebone Almshouses, memb Ct of Assts Corpn of The Sons of The Clergy; Liveryman Worshipful Co of Tylers & Bricklayers 1974; *Clubs* Athenaeum; *Style—* Ian S Lockhart, Esq; 9 Marlborough Hill, London NW8 0NN; c/o Charles Russell, Hale Court, Lincoln's Inn, London WC2A 3UL (☎ 071 242 1031, fax 071 430 0388, telex 23521)

LOCKHART, James Duncan; s of James Jackson Lockhart (d 1974); *b* 3 Oct 1933; *Educ* HS of Glasgow, Univ of Glasgow; *m* 1964, Joyce, da of Harold Walter Oakley (d 1955); 2 da; *Career* Capt Army; md Tport Devpt Gp Ltd 1979-; *Style—* James Lockhart, Esq; c/o Transport Development Gp Ltd, Windsor House, 50 Victoria St, London SW1H 0NR

LOCKHART, John William; s of Sidney Samuel Lockhart (d 1978), and Winifred May, *née* Hillier (d 1943); *b* 20 May 1936; *Educ* Sir George Monoux GS, Coll of Estate Mgmnt; *m* Margaret Christine, da of Christopher Holder; 1 s (Charles David b 1962), 2 da (Anna Louise b 1963, Jane Elizabeth b 1965); *Career* Nat Serv RE 1958-59; surveyor; trainee Cuthbert Lake & Clapham 1952-53, Coll of Estate Mgmnt 1953-55, trainee CC Taylor & Son 1955-58; jt sr ptnr: Taylor Lockhart & Lang 1959-73, Michael Laurie & Ptnrs 1973-85; chm Morgan Grenfell Laurie 1988- (chief exec 1985-88); Freeman City of London 1991, memb The Worshipful Co of Chartered Surveyors 1991, FRICS 1958; *Recreations* tennis, golf, reading, music, horses; *Clubs* RAC, Hanbury Manor; *Style—* John Lockhart, Esq; Morgan Grenfell Laurie, Fitzroy House, 18-20 Grafton St, London W1X 4DD (☎ 071 493 7050k, fax 071 499 6279)

LOCKHART, Maj Simon Foster Macdonald; DL (1950); assumed surname of Lockhart, in lieu of Macdonald, by declaration 1946 on succeeding to estates of Lee, Carnwath and Dryden; s of John Ronald Moreton Macdonald (d 1921), of Largie Castle, Tayinloan, Argyllshire; *b* 1916; *Educ* Winchester, Magdalen Coll Oxford; *m* 1942, Ella Caitriona, da of Seton Gordon, of Upper Duntulm, Portree; 3 s, 1 da; *Career* served WWII with The Lovat Scouts, Italy (wounded), Maj 1946, Lanarkshire Yeo (TA) 1947-49; JP (1950 Lanarkshire); former dir Lawrie & Symington (Auctioneers) Ltd, Medwin Valley Sands, Largie Woodlands; *Books* Seven Centuries-A History of the Lockharts of Lee and Carnwath, To My Pocket-A Personal Cash Book of an 18th Century Scottish Laird; *Recreations* gardening; *Style—* Maj Simon Macdonald Lockhart, DL; Dunsyre House, Dunsyre, Lanark (☎ 089 981 260); Lee and Carnwath Estates, Estate Office, Carnwath, Lanark (☎ 0555 840 273)

LOCKHART-BALL, Hugh Frederick; s of Lt Cdr Alfred Ernest Ball, RN (d 1965), and Margaret Daphne, *née* Lockhart; *b* 18 April 1948; *Educ* Sedbergh, Birmingham Sch of Architecture, City of Birmingham Sch of Art and Design; *m* 1 April 1972 (m dis), Godelieve Antoinette; 1 s (Simon Hugh b 1976), 1 da (Amelia b 1979); *Career* architect; princ Lockhart-Ball Association 1981-, chm London Energy Group 1983-; memb Ctee UK Section of Int Solar Energy Soc 1984-, memb Cncl S London Soc of Architects 1979-, chm Tooting Traders Assoc 1986-; former pres Rotary Club of Tooting 1986; *Recreations* conserving energy, sketching, reading, photography, building, jazz and blues, wine and food; *Style—* Hugh Lockhart-Ball, Esq; 934 Garratt Lane, London SW17 0ND (☎ 081 767 6955, office 081 672 1056, fax 081 767 9401)

LOCKHART-MUMMERY, Christopher John; QC (1986); s of Sir Hugh Evelyn Lockhart-Mummery, KCVO (d 1988), of Duns House, Hannington, Basingstoke, Hants, and Elizabeth Jean, *née* Crerar (d 1981); *b* 7 Aug 1947; *Educ* Stowe, Trinity Coll Cambridge; *m* 4 Sept 1971, Hon Elizabeth Rosamund, da of Neil Patrick Moncrieff Elles, and Baroness Elles (Life Peer), of 75 Ashley Gardens, London; 1 s (Edward b 1975), 2 da (Clare b 1973, Alice b 1980); *Career* called to the Bar Inner Temple 1971; *Books* specialist ed: Hill and Redman's Law of Landlord and Tenant (1973); *Recreations* fishing, gardening, opera; *Style—* Christopher J Lockhart-Mummery, Esq, QC; 3a Lansdowne Rd, London, W8 7BS (☎ 071 229 9415); 2 Paper Bldgs, Temple, London, EC4 (☎ 071 353 5835, fax 071 583 1390)

LOCKHART-MUMMERY, Hon Mrs ((Elizabeth) Rosamund); *née* Elles; da of Baroness Elles (Life Peer), and Neil Patrick Moncrieff Elles; *b* 15 May 1947; *Educ* St Andrew's Univ (MA), Courtauld Inst, London Univ (MA); *m* 1971, Christopher John Lockhart-Mummery; 1 s, 2 da; *Style—* The Hon Mrs Lockhart-Mummery; 52 Argyll Rd, London W8 (☎ 071 937 1289)

LOCKHART-MURE, Thomas Ochterlony (Tom); s of Dr Thomas Valiant Lockhart-Mure (d 1925), and Isabella Dodds McGown (d 1941); *b* 25 Aug 1904; *Educ* Edinburgh Acad; *m* 18 July 1936, Sheila, da of John MacKinnon (d 1938); 3 s (Peter Thomas b 1941, John Kevin b 1945, James Edward b 1937, d 1965); *Career* Maj RASC serv Abyssinian Campaign (despatches); Cmd HQ Inspectorate of Mechanical Tport; ptnr Manchester Airways (A Barnstorming Co) 1923; dir: Kenyan Co rep General Motors Prods 1924-, Airspray Kenya; former pres: AA of E Africa, Areo Club of E Africa; conslt Caspair Air Charter; *Recreations* rugby, hockey, cricket; *Clubs* Mt Kenya Safari, Mombasa, Nairobi, Aero (E Africa); *Style—* Tom Lockhart-Mure, Esq; Thelwall, Winchelsea, East Sussex (☎ 0797 226269)

LOCKHART OF THE LEE, Angus Hew; recognised as Chief of the Name Lockhart by The Lord Lyon 1957; s of Maj Simon Foster Macdonald Lockhart of the Lee and Ella Catriona Gordon; *b* 17 Aug 1946; *Educ* Rannoch Sch Perths, N of Scotland Coll of Agric; *m* 1970, Susan Elizabeth, da of Hon William Normand (d 1967), s Baron Normand (Life Peer d 1962), and Hon Mrs William Norman *qv*; 1 s, 1 da; *Career* landowner; *Recreations* shooting, skiing, renovating cottages; *Clubs* New (Edinburgh); *Style—* Angus Lockhart of the Lee; Newholm, Dunsyre, Lanark ML11 8NQ (☎ 0968 82254); Lee and Carnwath Estates, Estate Office, Carnwath, Lanark (☎ 0555 840273)

LOCKLEY, Andrew John Harold; s of Archdeacon Dr Harold Lockley, of Quorn, Leicestershire, and Ursula Margarete, *née* Wedell (d 1990); *b* 10 May 1951; *Educ* Marlborough, Oriel Coll Oxford (Nolloth scholar, BA, MA); *m* 14 Sept 1974, Ruth Mary, da of (Laurence) John Vigor, of Bath, Avon; 2 s (Thomas Andrew b 1978, Philip Jonathan b 1981), 1 da (Naomi Jane Ursula b 1987); *Career* research scholar World Cncl of Churches 1973-75, articled clerk Messrs Kingsley Napley & Co London 1975-78, slr Messrs Young & Solon London 1979-80, slr Messrs Meaby & Co London 1980-82; Contentious Business The Law Soc: asst sec 1982-85, sec 1985-87; dir Legal Practice The Law Soc 1987-; memb: Cmmn of Efficiency in Criminal courts 1986-, CITCOM Advsy Ctee 1988-; dir Slrs Fin and Property Services Co Ltd 1988-; memb Law Soc 1979; *Books* Christian Communes (1976); *Recreations* growing fruit and vegetables, swimming, travel, cooking, reading; *Style—* Andrew Lockley, Esq; The Law Society, 50 Chancery Lane, London WC2A 1SX (☎ 071 242 1222, fax 071 831 0057, telex 261203)

LOCKWOOD, Arthur William; s of William Storm Lockwood (d 1971); *b* 11 May 1924; *Educ* Denstone Coll Staffs; *m* 1948, Heather, da of Maj William Rogerson, OBE, MC (d 1961); 1 s, 2 da; *Career* landowner and farmer; memb Lloyd's, chm Castle Hill Holdings Ltd; master Burton Hunt 1959-; *Recreations* hunting, yachting (yacht TSDY Island Fox); *Clubs* Carlton, RSrnYC; *Style—* Arthur Lockwood, Esq; Coach House, Spridlington, Lincoln (☎ 0673 61057); 6-7 Castle Hill, Lincoln (☎ 0522 22243)

LOCKWOOD, Baroness (Life Peer UK 1978), of Dewsbury, Co W Yorkshire; Betty; DL (W Yorks); da of late Arthur Lockwood; *b* 22 Jan 1924; *Educ* Eastborough Girls' Sch Dewsbury, Ruskin Coll Oxford; *m* 1978, Lt-Col Cedric Hall (d 1988), s of late George Hall; *Career* sits as Lab Peer in House of Lords; Yorks regnl women's offr Lab Pty 1952-67, chief woman offr and asst nat agent Lab Pty 1967-75, chm Equal Opportunities Cmmn 1975-83, chm EEC Advsy Ctee on Equal Opportunities for Women and Men 1982-83; pres Birkbeck Coll Univ of London 1983-89; memb: Advtg Standards Authy Cncl 1983-, Leeds Devpt Corpn 1988-; memb cncl: Univ of Bradford 1983- (pro-chllr 1988-), Univ of Leeds 1985-; hon fell: UMIST, Birbeck Coll; Hon DLitt Univ of Bradford, Hon DLL Univ of Strathclyde 1985; *Clubs* Soroptimist Int; *Style—* The Rt Hon the Lady Lockwood, DL; 6 Sycamore Drive, Addingham, Ilkley, W Yorks LS29 0NY (☎ 0943 831098)

LOCKWOOD, David Stuart; s of Capt Ronald Arthur Lockwood, of 21 Seawalls, Seawalls Rd, Sneyd Park, Bristol, and Rachael, *née* Bamforth; *b* 15 May 1945; *Educ* Guthlaxton GS Leicester, Cambridge Sch of Art, Sch of Architecture Leicester, RIBA (DipArch); *m* 1, 6 July 1968 (m dis 1974), Susan Margaret, *née* Mayne; m 2, 25 May 1978, Marion Janice, da of Walter Glen Page (d 1974), of Miller Ave, Ashfield, Sydney, Aust; *Career* Jr Leaders Regt RE 1960-63, RE 1963-66; architect; John Whisson and Ptnrs Newmarket 1966-67, Heaton and Swales Bury St Edmunds 1967-70, Gordon White and Hood Leicester 1973-74, Ivan P Jarvis and Assoc Leicester 1974-76, Cecil Denny Highton and Ptnrs London 1976- (assoc 1979, equity ptnr 1983); chm Acton Green Residents Assoc; memb: RIBA, ARCUK 1974; *Recreations* sailing, skiing, architecture, ballet, cycling, squash; *Clubs* RAC, Mudeford Sailing; *Style—* David Lockwood, Esq; 22 Montgomery Rd, Chiswick, London W4 (☎ 081 9957162); 11 Rushford Warren, Mudeford, Christchurch; Cecil Denny Highton, Chartered Architects, Axtell House, 23/24 Warwick St, London W1 (☎ 071 7346831, fax 071 7340508, car 0860 417244)

LOCKWOOD, Graham Henry; s of Henry George Lockwood, of Ipswich, and Doris Evelyn, *née* Dawson; *b* 16 June 1935; *Educ* Carlisle GS; *m* 20 Oct 1962, Eileen Joyce, da of Arthur Dawkes; 2 da (Elaine b 1967, Fiona b 1970); *Career* actuary; exec dir Eagle Star Group 1984- (gen mangr 1980-84); Freeman Worshipful Co of Actuaries; FIA 1964; *Recreations* music, squash, walking; *Style—* Graham Lockwood, Esq; Eagle Star Group, 60 St Mary Axe, London EC3A 8BA (☎ 071 929 1111, fax 071 626 1266)

LOCKWOOD, John William; s of Arthur William Lockwood, of The Coach House, Spridlington, Nr Lincoln, and Heather, *née* Rogerson; *b* 24 Aug 1954; *Educ* Uppingham, UMIST (BSc); *m* 28 May 1982, Judith Ann, da of Patrick Henry Dickinson, of Blyborough Hall, Gainsborough, Lincs; 1 s (George William b 5 March 1985), 1 da (Sarah Helen May b 2 Aug 1987); *Career* co dir: Castle Hill Holdings Ltd, Castle Square Developments Ltd, Castle Hill Developments Ltd, Castle Square Properties Ltd, Lockwood Estates Ltd, Lockwood Farms Ltd, Branston Packers Ltd; MFH Burton Hunt 1981-; churchwarden Cammeringham, chm Cammeringham Parish Cncl; *Recreations* hunting; *Style—* John Lockwood, Esq; Cammeringham Manor, Cammeringham, Nr Lincoln LN1 2SJ (☎ 0522 730342); 6/7 Castle Hill, Lincoln LN1 3AA (☎ 0522 522243, fax 0522 513483, car 0860 513450)

LOCKWOOD, Prof (Antony) Peter Murray; s of Sir John Francis Lockwood (d 1965), and Lady Marjorie Lockwood; *b* 12 March 1931; *Educ* St Pauls, Trinity Coll Cambridge (BA, MA, PhD); *m* 24 Aug 1957, Kathleen May, da of Robert Marshall (d 1989); 2 s (David b 1960, Roger b 1964), 1 da (Christine (Mrs Leigh-Jones) b 1958); *Career* Nat Serv 1950-51: cmmnd RA 1950, serv 42 LAA Regt; asst lectr Dept of Zoology Univ of Edinburgh 1957-59, res fell Trinity Coll Cambridge 1959-62, prof marine biology Univ of Southampton 1980- (lectr 1962-68, sr lectr 1968-72, reader 1972-80); hon zoological sec Soc for Experimental Biology 1969-73, chm Biological Cncl 1982-87 (hon sec 1976-80); memb: Bd Co of Biologists 1977-, Aquatic Life Scis Grants Ctee NERC 1978-80, Advsy Ctee on Int Oceanographic Affrs NERC 1980-87, Cncl of Europe Evaluation Sub Ctee on programme for postgrad trg 1984-; del to fourth ad hoc meeting on Trg Educn and Mutual Assistance UNESCO Cairo 1976 and Buenos Aires 1980, memb UNESCO interdisciplinary mission to Bahrain on AGU project 1983; FIBiol; *Books* Animal Body Fluids and Their Regulation (1963), Aspects of the Physiology of Crustacea (1968), The Membranes of Animal Cells (1971), The Physiology of Diving in Man and other Animals (with HV Hempleman, 1978); *Style—* Prof Peter Lockwood; 24 Merdon Ave, Chandlers Ford, Hants SO5 1EJ (☎ 0703 254268); Department of Oceanography, University of Southampton, Southampton SO9 5NH (☎ 0703 593640, telex 47661, fax 0703 593939)

LOCKYER, Bob; *b* 9 April 1942; *Career* dir and prodr dance progs BBC TV; asst to Margaret Dale (then sr dance prodr) and others; worked with choreographers incl: Ashton, MacMillan, Peter Wright and Birgit Cullberg; writer of ballet scenarios incl Corporal Jan (choreographed and directed by Peter Wright); dir and prodr dance progs incl: Royal Ballet (Les Noces (1978), Dance Masterclass with Sir Frederick Ashton on The Dream (1987), Sadler's Wells Royal Ballet now Birmingham Royal Ballet (Pineapple Poll (1979), Dance Masterclass with Peter Wright on Giselle (1987)), London Contemporary Dance Theatre (Stabat Mater (1979), Forest (1980), Cell (1983), Nympheas (1983), Mass for Man (BBC cmmn)), Rambert Dance Co (Pulcinella (1988), Soldat (1989), Four Elements (1991)); exec prodr (BBC TV): Heaven Ablaze in his Breast, Dance House; cmmnd and produced Points in Space 1986 (winner Festival Directors Diploma 1988 Prague Int TV Festival); dir Dance Video Course Aust Film TV and Radio Sch Sydney and various workshops Aust and NZ 1990; chm Dance UK (formerly Nat Orgn for Dance and Mime) 1982-; *Recreations* walking, collecting and cooking; *Style—* Bob Lockyer, Esq; Studio Five, St Albans Studios, South End Row, St Albans Grove, London W8 (☎ 071 937 1230)

LOCKYER-NIBBS, John Brian; s of Gerald Norman Henry Lockyer-Nibbs (d 1978), and Ella Nora Cook; *b* 1 July 1934; *Educ* St Paul's; *m* Diana, da of Bernard Murray Davis, of Cobham, Surrey; 2 da (Caroline Alison b 20 May 1963, Vanessa Anne b 16 Aug 1965); *Career* CA; ptnr Moss Dell & Co; cncllr Guildford Borough 1983-87, memb cncl Normandy Parish; FCA; *Recreations* horses in various activities; *Style—* John Lockyer-Nibbs, Esq; South Lodge, Westwood, Normandy, Guildford, Surrey (☎ 0483 811092); Welbeck House, High St, Guildford, Surrey (☎ 0483 503059, fax 0483 66761, telex 859643)

LODER, Hon Christina Anne; da of 3 Baron Wakehurst, *qv*, and Ingeborg Krumbholz-Hess (d 1977); *b* 13 Dec 1959; *Educ* Millfield, RCA London (MDes); *Clubs* No.2 Brydges Place; *Style—* The Hon Christina Loder; No.2 Brydges Place, Covent Garden, London WC1 (☎ 071 836 1436)

LODER, Edmund Jeune; s and h of Sir Giles Rolls Loder, 3 Bt; *b* 26 June 1941; *Educ* Eton; *m* 1966 (m dis 1971), Penelope Jane, da of Ivo Forde; 1 da; *Career* FCA; bloodstock breeder; *Style—* Edmund Loder, Esq; Eyrefield Lodge, The Curragh, Co Kildare

LODER, Sir Giles Rolls; 3 Bt (UK 1887), JP (Sussex), DL (W Sussex 1977); s of Capt Robert Egerton Loder (ka 1917); suc gf, Sir Edmund Giles Loder, 2 Bt, 1920; *b* 1914; *Educ* Eton, Trinity Coll Cambridge (MA); *m* 1939, Marie, only da of Capt Bertram Hanmer Bunbury Symons-Jeune (d 1963); 2 s; *Heir* s, Edmund Jeune Loder; *Career* serv 98 Surrey and Sussex Yeo Field Bde RA, 2 Lt 1935, Lt 1938; memb Horsham RDC 1947-68 (chm 1963-68), High Sheriff Sussex 1948-49; vice-pres Royal Horticulture Soc (VMH); *Recreations* horticulture, yachting; *Clubs* Royal Yacht Squadron (Cowes); *Style—* Sir Giles Loder, Bt, JP, DL; Ockenden House, Cuckfield, Haywards Heath, Sussex

LODER, Hon James David Gerald; s of 2 Baron Wakehurst, KG; *b* 1928; *Educ* Geelong C of E GS Victoria, Trinity Coll Cambridge; *Career* Coldstream Gds RARO; called to the Bar Inner Temple 1953; OStJ; *Style—* The Hon James Loder; 3l Lennox Gardens, London SW1

LODER, Hon Robert Beauclerk; CBE; s of 2 Baron Wakehurst, KG; *b* 24 April 1934; *Educ* Eton, Trinity Coll Cambridge (BA); *m* 1973, Josette, da of Joseph Bromovsky, of Otmanach, Pischeldorf, Karnten, Austria; 2 s (Jan, Nicolai), 1 da (Nell); *Career* farmer 1966-; dir: Transcontinental Servs Gp NV 1970-86 (formerly Esperanza Ltd), Precious Metals Tst 1981-; chm: Sheringham Hldgs Ltd 1982-, Mental Health Fndn 1982-; *Clubs* Beefsteak, Buck's; *Style—* The Hon Robert Loder, CBE; 14 Ladbroke Grove, London W11; Curtis Brown, 162-168 Regent St, London W1 (☎ 071 872 0331)

LODER, Hon Timothy Walter; s and h of 3 Baron Wakehurst, *qv*, and Ingeborg Krumbholz-Hess (d 1977); *b* 28 March 1958; *Educ* Millfield; *m* 1987, Susan E Hurst; *Style—* The Hon Timothy Loder; 26 Wakehurst Rd, London SW11 6BY

LODER-SYMONDS, Roderick Francis (Roddy); s of Brig Robert Guy Loder-Symonds, DSO, MC (ka 1945), of Three Chimneys, Heytesbury, Warminster, Wilts, and Mrs Merlin Audrey Houghton Brown, *née* Allen (d 1988); *b* 16 Nov 1938; *Educ* Radley, RAC Cirencester; *m* 20 July 1987, Caroline Anne, da of Cdr M F L Beebee (d 1988), of Womaston House, Presteigne, Radnorshire; 2 s (Robert b 31 Aug 1971, James b 28 May 1974), 1 da (Sacha b 19 Nov 1968); *Career* farmer Wellshead Farm Exford Somerset 1960-67, asst surveyor Knight Frank and Rutley 1962-72, ptnr Strutt & Parker 1976- (joined 1973); church warden Womenswold Church 1970-82; chm: Farmers Club 1976, Parish Cncl 1978-86, Canterbury Farmers Club 1982, Kent Branch CLA 1986-87; Bd memb Enteprise Agency E Kent 1985-, jt chm NFU/CLA Channel Tunnel Working Pty 1986-87; FRICS 1976; *Recreations* shooting and hunting; *Clubs* Farmers', Army and Navy; *Style—* Roddy Loder-Symonds, Esq; Denne Hill Farm, Womenswold, Canterbury, Kent CT4 6HD (☎ 0227 831203); Strutt & Parker, 2 St Margaret's St, Canterbury, Kent CT1 2TG (☎ 0227 451123, fax 0227 762509); 13 Hill St, London W14 8DL (☎ 071 627 7282)

LÖDERER, Karl; s of Karl Löderer, of Austraia, and Franziska, *née* Reschreiter; *b* 16 March 1939; *Educ* Realgymnasium Baden Bei Wien Vienna, Hotelfachschule Lower Austria; *m* June 1966, Margaret; 1 s (James b 3 March 1967), 1 da (Franziska Maria b 19 Aug 1969); *Career* chef; apprentice 1952-55 (Hotel de France Schottenring Vienna, Restaurant Kerzenstuberl, Hotel Europa Karntnerstr, Drei Husaren Franziskanerplatz), chef de parti Hotel de France Sark Channel Islands 1957, chef de cuisine 1958-59 (La Sablonnerie Lyons France, Restaurant Mereguy, Restaurant Andron, Restaurant St Nectaire Manoir des Viginets Cap d'Antibes), chef and ptnr La Frégate St Peter Port Guernsey 1960-66, chef de cuisine Gravetye Manor E Grinstead 1966-78, chef and proprietor Manley's Storrington 1978-; awarded one of first Michelin Rosettes in UK at Gravetye Manor, top awards in all major food and hotel guides during time at Gravetye and presently at Manley's, orgn memb Master Chefs of GB; memb of Steering Committee of master Chefs of GB 1984; *Recreations* opera goer, gardening, theatre; *Style—* Karl Löderer, Esq; Manley's, Manleys Hill, Storrington, West Sussex RH20 4BT (☎ 0903 742331)

LODGE, Dr Brian Robert William; s of Bertram Hugh Cleverly Lodge (d 1967), of 10 the Vale, Golders Green, London NW11, and Gwendolin Olive Theodosia, *née* Burford (d 1963); *b* 15 May 1925; *Educ* Univ Coll Sch Hampstead, London Hosp Med Sch (MRCS, LRCP); *m* 15 Dec 1954, Kathleen, da of Ernest Herbert Fox (d 1951), of Bunwell, Norfolk; *Career* temp conslt physician in geriatric med Utd Oxford Hosps and Oxford Regnl Hosp Bd 1965-71, conslt physician in geriatric and psychogeriatric med Leics Dist Health Authy 1971-, chm Specialist Planning Gp (elderly and severly mentally impaired) Mental Health Unit Leics Health Authy, memb Exec Ctee Age Concern Leics, vice chm MIND Hinckley Leics; memb: Exec Ctee Br Assoc for Services to the Elderly (BASE) 1988, Steering Gp for quadruple support for dementia Hinckley Leics Health Authy, Br Geriartrics Soc; Health and Social Serv Jl Jt Care Award 1983; FRSM; *Books* Coping With Caring Mind (1981), Living Well Into Old Age Kings Fund (jtly 1986), Handbook of Mental Disorders In Old Age (1988); *Recreations* walking, theatre, concerts, books; *Style—* Dr Brian Lodge; Carlton Hayes Hosp, Narborough, Leics LE9 5ES (☎ 0533 863481)

LODGE, Bubble; da of David Albert Ainley Lodge, of York and Judith Anne, *née* Pennicard; *b* 24 May 1964; *Educ* Queen Margaret's Sch Escrick Park York, Bretton Hall Coll W Bretton, Univ of Leeds (BA); *Career* admin and VIP host Nat Student Drama Festival Swansea 1985, co-organiser Nat Symposium of Youth Theatres Nottingham 1985, box office and co mangr Nat Student Theatre Co Edinburgh Festival 1985, first female asst mangr Stoll Moss Theatres (The London Palladium, Her Majesty's Theatre, Victoria Palace Theatre) 1986, house mangr The Globe Theatre, gen mangr The Theatre Comedy Co Ltd Shaftesbury Theatre 1988-91, administrator Everyman Theatre Cheltenham 1991-, exec dir Springboard Theatre Co 1988; teaching linguistically disadvantaged children 1982; Roteract Club 1982-84, external affrs office Bretton Hall Coll SU 1984-85; *Recreations* swimming, skiing, riding, dance, theatre, art, piano; *Clubs* The Ind Arts Club (hon memb); *Style—* Miss Bubble Lodge; Holmefield Court, Belsize Grove, London NW3 4TT; Rowancourt, Grantham Drive, York YO2 4TZ; The Everyman Theatre, Regent St, Cheltenham, Glos GL50 1HQ (☎ 0242 512515, fax 0242 224305)

LODGE, Prof David; s of Herbert Lodge, and Dorothy, *née* Moss; *b* 22 Sept 1941; *Educ* Weston Super Mare GS, Univ of Bristol (BVSc, PhD); *m* 15 Feb 1964, Susan, da of Sidney Hayling; 4 s (Marcus b 1964, Duncan b 1966, James b 1969, (Robert) Jolyon b 1971); *Career* jr fell and lectr dept veterinary surgery Univ of Bristol 1963-70, Wellcome Tst Fell dept of physiology Animal Health Tst 1970-74; post doctoral res fell Aust Nat Univ 1974-79; Royal Veterinary Coll London: sr lectr 1979-84, prof veterinary neuroscience 1984-89, prof vet physiology and head of veterinary basic sciences 1989; ed British Journal of Pharmacology, ed British Veterinary Journal; memb ctee Physiological Soc; MRCVS 1963, DVA 1969; *Books* Excitatory Amino Acid Transmission (1987), Excitatory Amino Acids in Health and Disease (1988); *Recreations* rugby, running, skiing, coaching junior sport; *Style—* Prof David Lodge; Dept of Veterinary Basic Sciences, Royal Veterinary College, Royal College St, London NW1 0TU (☎ 071 387 2898, fax 071 388 2342)

LODGE, Prof David John; s of William Frederick Lodge, and Rosalie Marie, *née* Murphy; *b* 28 Jan 1935; *Educ* St Joseph's Acad Blackheath, UCL (John Oliver Hobbes scholar, BA, MA, John Morley medal, Quain Essay prize), Univ of Birmingham (PhD); *m* 15 May 1959, Mary Frances, da of Francis Jacob (d 1969); 2 s Stephen David b 1962, Christopher Adrian b 1966), 1 da (Julia Mary b 1960); *Career* Nat Serv RAC 1955-57; asst British Cncl Overseas Students Centre London 1959-60; Dept of English Univ of Birmingham: asst lectr 1960-62, lectr 1961-72, sr lectr 1971-73, reader in English lit 1973-76, prof of modern English Lit 1976-87, hon prof of modern English lit 1987-; visiting assoc prof Univ of California Berkeley 1969, Henfield fell in Creative Writing UEA 1977, Whitney J Oates short term visiting fell Princetown Univ 1981, E J Pratt lectr Memorial Univ of St John's Newfoundland 1985, Lansdowne scholar Univ of Victoria BC 1986, Regents lectr Univ of California Riverside 1989; chm Booker Prize Judges 1989; has lectured and addressed conferences in Europe and further afield; FRSL 1976, hon fell UCL 1982; Novels: The Picturegoers (1960), Ginger You're Barmy (1965), The British Museum is Falling Down (1967), Out of the Shelter (1970), Changing Places: a Tale of Two Campuses (1975), How Far Can You Go (1980), Small World: an academic romance (1984), Nice Work (1988); non-fiction incl: Language of Fiction (1966), The Novelist at the Crossroads (1971), The Modes of Modern Writing (1977), Working With Structuralism (1981), Write On (1986), After Balhtin (1990); Stage and Screen: Between These Four Walls (with M Bradbury and J Duckett, 1963), Slap in the Middle (with M Bradbury, J Duckett and D Turner, 1965), Big Words - Small Worlds (Channel 4, 1987), Nice Work (BBC2 1989, Silver Nymph Award), The Writing Game (Birmingham Rep) 1990; *Style—* Prof David Lodge; Dept of English, University of Birmingham, Birmingham B15 2TT

LODGE, (John) Gordon; s of Abraham Gordon Lodge (d 1944), and Ivy, *née* Robertshaw; *b* 9 May 1944; *Educ* Bradford GS; *m* 3 Oct 1967, Diana Maureen, da of Nelson George Harrison, of 5 Langley Grove, Bingley, West York; 2 s (Alastair b 1973, James b 1977); *Career* Bradford & Bingley Bldg Soc: joined 1961, devpt mangr 1976-79, regnl mangr 1979-82, asst gen mangr personnel and trg 1982-87, gen mangr devpt of branch and agency network 1987-; pres Bradford GS, treas Shipley GC, govr Cottingley Sch, dir Beckfoot Estate Co; FBIM 1980-, memb Bldg Soc Inst 1964; *Recreations* golf, bridge, climbing, fell walking; *Clubs* Shipley Golf; *Style—* Gordon Lodge, Esq; Bradford & Bingley Building Soc, Main St, Bingley, West Yorks (☎ 0274 56 8111)

LODGE, Jane Ann; da of John Humphrey Lodge (d 1984), of York, and Marian, *née* Smith; *b* 1 April 1955; *Educ* Mill Mount GS York, Univ of Birmingham (BSc); *m* 2 July 1983, Anthony (Tony) John Borton, s of Reginal Aubrey Borton (d 1980), of Rugby; 1 s (John Aubrey b 1988); *Career* Touche Ross & Co Birmingham: trainee accountant 1973, qualified 1976 ptnr 1986; ctee memb Birmingham & W Midlands Soc of Chartered Accountants 1987-(chm Young Chartered Accountants Gp 1986-88); Univ of Birmingham: memb cncl 1986-, pres guild of graduates 1987-88, memb strategy planning and resources ctee 1987; ACA 1976; *Recreations* cookery, tapestry, golf; *Style—* Ms Jane Lodge; Touche Ross & Co, Kensington House, 136 Suffolk St, Queensway, Birmingham B1 1LL (☎ 021 631 2288, fax 021 631 4512, telex 338876 TRBHAM G)

LODGE, John Stuart; s of Edmund Roy Lodge (d 1961); *b* 30 April 1938; *Educ* Cranbrook Sch Sydney; *m* 1962, Peta, da of Sir Albert Robinson, KBE; 1 s, 2 da; *Career* Lt Far East 1958-59; int security specialist; *Recreations* hunting, tennis; *Clubs* Brooks's; *Style—* John Lodge, Esq; 20 Cadgan Lane, London SW1; Daglingworth Place, Cirencester, Glos GL7 7HU

LODGE, Oliver Raymond William Wynlayne; s of Oliver William Foster Lodge (d 1955), of Cud Hill House, Upton St Leonard's, Glos (s of late Sir Oliver Joseph Lodge, and Winifred, *née* Wynlayne (d 1922) only da of late Sir William Nicholas Atkinson; *b* 2 Sept 1922; *Educ* Bryanston, King's Coll Camb (MA); *m* 17 Oct 1953, Charlotte (d 1990), da of Col Arthur Davidson Young, CMG (d 1938), of St Margaret's, Twickenham; 1 s (Oliver b 1957), 2 da (Victoria b 1955, (Elizabeth) Lucy b 1960); *Career* Royal Fus 1942; called to the Bar Inner Temple 1945, practised Chancery Bar 1945-74, admitted *ad eundem* Lincoln's Inn 1949, bencher 1973, regnl chm Industl Tbnls 1980- (perm chm 1975-80); memb: Bar Cncl 1952-56 and 1967-71, Supreme Ct Rules Ctee 1968-71; gen cmmr of Income Tax Lincoln's Inn 1983-90; *Recreations* walking, reading history; *Clubs* Garrick, Bar Yacht; *Style—* Oliver Lodge, Esq; Southridge House, Hindon, Salisbury, Wilts; Central Office of the Industrial Tribunals, 93 Ebury Bridge Rd, London SW1 (☎ 071 730 9161)

LODGE, Robin Gregory; s of Roy Burgess Lodge, of Newton St, Margarets, Herefordshire, and Vera Karla, *née* Kotasova; *b* 8 March 1953; *Educ* Bedales Sch Petersfield Hampshire, Univ of Sussex (BA); *m* 2 June 1984, (Rosemary) Caroline, da of David Lester Hurford; 1 s (Henry David b 10 Aug 1988); *Career* report writer BBC Monitoring Serv Caversham Reading 1978-80, sub-ed then chief sub-ed Newsroom BBC External Servs Bush House London 1980-87, Moscow corr Reuters 1987-90, dip and E Europe corr Sunday Telegraph 1990- (formerly E Europe corr); *Recreations* food, wine, skiing, walking; *Style—* Robin Lodge, Esq; 34 Middleton Rd, London E8 (☎ 071 249 1051); The Sunday Telegraph, Peterborough Court, 181 Marsh Wall, London E14 9SR (☎ 071 538 7362, fax 071 538 1330)

LODGE, Sir Thomas; s of James Lodge (d 1936), of Sheffield; *b* 25 Nov 1909; *Educ* Univ of Sheffield; *m* 1940, Aileen (d 1990), da of James Corduff, of Co Donegal; 1 s, 1 da; *Career* medical practitioner (ret); conslt radiologist United Sheffield Hospitals 1946-74; clinical lectr Univ of Sheffield 1963-66; kt 1974; *Books* Recent Advances in Radiology (6 edn 1979); *Clubs* Royal Society of Medicine; *Style—* Sir Thomas Lodge; 46 Braemore Court, Kingsway, Hove, E Sussex BN3 4FG (☎ 0273 724371)

LODGE PATCH, Dr Ian Charles; s of Lt-Col Charles James Lodge Patch, MC, of Lahore, Pakistan, and Edith, *née* Jeffrey; *b* 7 Aug 1923; *Educ* Epsom Coll, London Hosp (MB BS, MD DPM); *m* 25 July 1959, Pauline, da of Arthur Eustace Ware; 2 s (Mark, John), 1 da (Emma); *Career* conslt psychiatrist: Springfield Hosp SW17, Hammersmith Hosp, St Charles Hosp; hon sr lectr Royal Post Grad Med Sch; examiner for membership of Royal Coll of Psychiatrists; FRCP 1971, FRCPsych 1971; *Recreations* water colour painting; *Style—* Dr Ian Lodge Patch; 152 Harley St, London W1 (☎ 091 935 2477)

LOEFFLER, Frank; s of Ernst Loeffler (d 1967), and Bianka Klein, *née* Breitmann; *b* 21 Jan 1931; *Educ* Mill Hill, Gonville and Caius Coll Cambridge, London Hosp Med Coll (MB BChir, FRCS, FRCOG); *m* 10 Aug 1958, Eva Augusta, da of Sir Ludwig

Guttmann (d 1981), of High Wycombe and Aylesbury; 1 s (Mark b 15 April 1961), 2 da (Clare b 13 Dec 1959, Juliet b 26 June 1964); *Career* conslt: Central Middlesex Hosp 1967-68, St Mary's Hosp W2 1968-, Queen Charlotte's Hosp 1983-; ed Br Jl of Obstetrics & Gynaecology 1973-80; memb Ctee on Safety of Medicines 1987-; memb Cncl RCOG 1987-90; FRCS 1959, FRCOG 1973; *Recreations* tennis, sailing, skiing; *Clubs* Aldeburgh Yacht, Royal Soc of Med; *Style*— Frank Loeffler, Esq; 86 Harley St, London W1N 1AE (☎ 071 486 2966); St Mary's Hospital, Praed St, London W2 (☎ 071 725 1045); Queen Charlotte's and Chelsea Hospital, Goldhawk Rd, London W6 (☎ 081 748 4666)

LOEHNIS, Anthony David; CMG (1988); s of Cdr Sir Clive Loehnis, KCMG, RN (ret), and Rosemary, da of Hon Robert Ryder (ka 1917, s of 2 Earl of Harrowby, KG, PC, and Lady Mary Cecil, da of 2 Marqess of Exeter); *b* 12 March 1936; *Educ* Eton, New Coll Oxford, Harvard Univ; *m* 7 Aug 1965, Jennifer, da of Sir Donald Anderson; 3 s; *Career* with FCO to 1966; Schroder Wagg 1967-80, exec dir Bank of England 1981-89 (assoc dir 1980-81), dir S G Warburg Gp plc and vice chm S G Warburg & Co Ltd 1989-; *Style*— Anthony Loehnis, Esq, CMG; Haughton House, Churchill, Oxon

LOEWE, Prof Raphael James; MC (1943); s of Herbert Martin James Loewe (d 1940), of Cambridge England, and Ethel Victoria, *née* Hyamson (d 1946); *b* 16 April 1919; *Educ* Dragon Sch Oxford, The Leys Sch Cambridge, St John's Coll Cambridge (MA); *m* 19 March 1952, Chloe, da of Mendel Klatzkin (d 1951), of London; 2 da (Elisabeth (Mrs Talbot) b 1953, Camilla b 1957); *Career* serv The Suffolk Regt, 142 Regt RAC N African and Italian Campaigns, wounded in action 1940-45; lectr in Hebrew Leeds 1949, Bye-fell Caius Coll Cambridge 1954, visiting prof Brown Univ Providence RI USA 1963-64, Goldsmid prof of Hebrew UCL until 1984 (formerly lectr then reader), author numerous articles in learned jls and presentation vols; elder Spanish and Portuguese Jews' Congregation London; past pres: Soc for Old Testament Study, Jewish Historical Soc of England; FSA, fell Royal Asiatic Soc; *Books* The Position of Women in Judaism (1966), Encylopaedia Judaica (contrib ed, 1971), Omar Khayyam (Hebrew version, 1982), The Rylands Haggadah (1988), Solomon ibn Gabirol (1989); *Recreations* travel, walking, translating English Latin & Hebrew poetry; *Style*— Prof Raphael Loewe, MC; 50 Gurney Drive, London N2 0DE (☎ 081 4555379)

LOEWENSTEIN-WERTHEIM-FREUDENBERG, Prince Rupert Ludwig Ferdinand zu; also Count von Loewenstein-Scharffeneck; s of Prince Leopold zu Loewenstein-Wertheim-Freudenberg (d 1974; of the family of mediatised Princes, title of Bavarian Prince conferred 1812, stemming from the morganatic marriage of Elector Palatine Friedrich I (d 1476) to Klara Tott, of Augsburg; Counts of HRE 1494, recreated Loewenstein-Scharffeneck 1875), and Countess Bianca Fischler von Treuberg; *b* 24 Aug 1933; *Educ* St Christopher's Letchworth, Magdalen Coll Oxford (MA); *m* 1957, Josephine Clare, da of Capt Montague Lowry-Corry (d 1977, gggs of 2 Earl Belmore) by his 1 w, Hon Mary Biddulph, yr da of 2 Baron Biddulph; 2 s (Prince Rudolf Amadeus b 1957, Prince Konrad Friedrich b 1958), 1 da (Princess Maria Theodora Marjorie b 1966); *Career* financial advsr, formerly merchant banker; Kt of San Gennaro, Kt of Honour and Devotion SMO Malta 1980, Bailiff Grand Cross of Justice Constantinian Order of St George; pres and chm Br Assoc; *Recreations* music; *Clubs* Beefsteak, Boodle's, Buck's, Portland, Pratt's, White's; *Style*— Prince Rupert zu Loewenstein-Wertheim-Freudenberg; Petersham Lodge, River Lane, Richmond, Surrey TW10 7AG (☎ 081 940 4442); Rupert Loewenstein Ltd, 2 King Street, London SW1Y 6QL (☎ 071 839 6454, fax 01 930 4032, telex 291367 FINANZ)

LOEWENTHAL, Lady; Anne June; da of James Stewart (d 1961), of Maitland, NSW, and Ethel, *née* Humphries (d 1987); *b* 1 Nov 1921; *Educ* Maitland Girls' HS, Library Sch Pub Library of NSW; *m* 1944, Sir John Loewenthal, CMG, ED, sometime prof and chm Univ of Sydney Surgery Dept (d 1979), s of A M Loewenthal, of Sydney (d 1945); 2 s (Andrew, Hugh), 2 da (Elspeth, Merran); *Career* Daily Telegraph Library 1940, Public Library of NSW 1941; VAD and Australian Army plc 1942-44; memb: Bd of Sydney Home Nursing Serv 1970-82, Divnl Cncl Red Cross Soc NSW 1982; vice chm NSW Div Red Cross Soc 1990-, hon life memb Aust Red Cross 1987; *Recreations* gardening, reading; *Clubs* Queens; *Style*— Lady Loewenthal; 82 Bendooley St, Bowral, NSW 2576 (☎ 010 6148 61 1172); 8/45 Wharf Rd, Birchgrove, NSW 2041 (☎ 010 612 810 1277)

LOFMARK, Prof Carl Johan; s of Carl Johan Lofmark (d 1958), and Florence Emily Parsonage (d 1988); *b* 4 July 1936; *Educ* Brockenhurst GS, King's Coll London (BA, AKC, MA, PhD); *m* 20 Aug 1960, Maureen Frances, da of Capt Richard James Hyde (d 1956); 1 s (Nils b 1969), 2 da (Astrid b 1964, Hilary b 1971); *Career* lectr Kings Coll London 1961-64, prof of German St David's Coll Lampeter 1972- (lectr 1964-72), many pubns on mediaeval German literature especially Wolfram von Eschenbach and Swedish (Hjalmar Söderberg); hon assoc Rationalist Press Assoc 1986; *Books* Rennewart in Wolfram's Willehalm (1972), Authority of the Source in MHG Poetry (1981), Hjalmar Söderberg: Short Stories (1987), Bards and Heroes (1989), Parzival and the Holy Grail (1990), What Is The Bible? (1990); *Style*— Prof Carl Lofmark; St David's University College, Lampeter, Dyfed SA48 7ED (☎ 0570 422351)

LOFT, Peter Hamilton; s of Flt Lt Leslie George Loft (d 1944), of Guildford, and Joyce Margaret, *née* Trigg; *b* 4 June 1941; *Educ* Eastbourne Coll; *m* 5 Dec 1964, Charlotte Mary, da of Richard Mason Pope, of Ketton, Rutland; 2 da (Amanda Jane b 1966, Katherine Charlotte b 1968); *Career* chm E Bowman & Sons Ltd 1980 (dir 1972, md 1973), dir Bowman (Oxon) Ltd 1982, chief exec Bowman (Cambs) Ltd 1988; memb Inst of Builders; *Recreations* sailing, skiing; *Clubs* West Anchor Sailing; *Style*— Peter Loft, Esq; 1 Wharf Road, Stamford, Lincs PE9 2DU (☎ 0780 55229), E Bowman & Sons Ltd, Cherryhold Rd, Stamford, Lincs PE9 2ER (☎ 0780 51015)

LOFTHOUSE, Geoffrey; JP (Pontefract 1970), MP (Lab) Pontefract and Castleford 1978-; s of Ernest Lofthouse (d 1935), and Emma Lofthouse (d 1944); *b* 18 Dec 1925; *Educ* Featherstone Primary and Secondary Schs, Whitwood Tech Coll, Leeds Univ; *m* 1946, Sarah (d 1985), da of Joesh Thomas Onions; 1 da; *Career* Manpower Office NCB 1964-70, personnel mangr NCB Fryston 1970-78; memb: Pontefract Borough Dist Cncl 1962-74, Wakefield Metropolitan Dist Cncl 1974-79; MIPM 1984; *Books* A Very Miner MP (autobiography 1986); *Recreations* rugby league, cricket; *Style*— Geoffrey Lofthouse, Esq, JP, MP; 67 Carlton Crest, Pontefract, W Yorkshire (☎ 0977 704 275); House of Commons, London SW1A 0AA (☎ 071 219 5133)

LOFTHOUSE, Reginald George Alfred; *b* 30 Dec 1916; *m* 1939, Ann Bernardine, *née* Bannan; 3 da; *Career* chief surveyor MAFF 1973-76, advsr Nature Conservancy Cncl 1978-82, vice chm Standing Conference on Countryside Sports 1988- (convener 1978-88); Bd of Govrs Coll of Estate Mgmnt 1963-85: memb 1963, chm 1972-77, res fell 1980-82, hon fell 1985; memb Cncl Univ of Reading, chm Advsy Ctee Centre for Agric Strategy 1982-; Freeman City of London 1976, Liveryman Worshipful Co of Loriners 1976; FRICS; *Clubs* Athenaeum, MCC; *Style*— Reginald Lofthouse, Esq; c/o College of Estate Management, Whiteknights, Reading, Berks (☎ 0734 861101)

LOFTHOUSE, Ronald William; s of William Lofthouse (d 1940), and Gladys Lofthouse (d 1985); *b* 13 Nov 1928; *Educ* Bootle GS, Bootle Tech Coll; *m* Rita, da of Richard Cooke (d 1944); 1 s (Neil b 8 July 1964), 1 da (Sandra b 13 March 1961); *Career* served MN, Lt (SP) RNVR 1951; trg advsr American Can C 1972-76 (works mangr 1966-72), md DKS Packaging 1979- (works dir 1976-79, chm 1990-); chm: Merseyside Trg Cncl, S Sefton C of C; dir S Sefton Enterprise Agency, vice chm Merseyside Training and Enterprise Cncl; FITD, FInstD; *Clubs* Conservative; *Style*— Ronald Lofthouse, Esq; 1 Rymers Green, off Old Town Lane, Freshfield, Formby (☎ 070 48 71889); 62-70 Litherland Rd, Bootle, Merseyside (☎ 051 922 2656, fax 051 933 0547, car 0836 272016, telex 628484)

LOFTHOUSE, Stephen; s of Harry Lofthouse (d 1980), and Janet) Mary Hume Scott, *née* Fraser; *b* 23 March 1945; *Educ* Tauntons GS, Univ of Manchester (BA, MA); *Career* res assoc Univ of Manchester 1968, lectr (later sr lectr) Manchester Poly 1969-72, lectr Manchester Business Sch 1972-75, dir Grade 10 Industs Assistance Cmmn Australia 1975, conslt Price Cmmn 1976-77, assoc Capel-Cure Myers 1977-83, sr exec James Capel and Co 1983-85, dir (later chm) James Capel Fund Managers (formerly James Capel International Asset Mgmnt Limited) 1985-; exec dir: James Capel Unit Trust Management Ltd 1988-, James Capel & Co Limited; non-exec dir Wardley Investmt Services Ltd 1988-; *Books* numerous articles published in acad and professional jls; *Style*— Stephen Lofthouse, Esq; 4 North Several, London SE3 0QR (☎ 081 318 7132); 7 Devonshire Square, London EC2M 4HV (☎ 071 626 0566, fax 071 621 0426, telex 9413578)

LOFTUS, Viscount; Charles John Tottenham; s and h of 8 Marquess of Ely; *b* 2 Feb 1943; *Educ* Trinity Coll Sch Port Hope Ont, Ecole Internationale de Genève, Toronto Univ (MA); *m* 1969, Judith Marvelle, da of Dr J J Porter of Calgary, Alberta, Canada; 1 adopted s (Andrew b 1973), 1 adopted da (Jennifer b 1975); *Heir* bro, Lord Timothy Tottenham, *qv*; *Career* head of Dept of French Strathcona-Tweedsmuir Sch Calgary, Alberta; *Style*— Viscount Loftus; 1424 Springfield Place SW, Calgary, Alberta, T2W OY1 Canada

LOFTUS, Ian William Townshend; s of Col Oliver St John Loftus (d 1980), of Hillcroft House, Hardington Mandeville, Somerset, and Edna Minnie Clare, *née* Davies (d 1986); *b* 4 July 1937; *Educ* Cheam Sch, Wellington, Univ of Cambridge (MA); *m* 9 May 1969, Elizabeth Antoinette, da of Harold Birchmore Harrison (d 1982), of Grove House, Utkinton, Tarporley, Cheshire; 1 s (Alexander b 1972); *Career* res scientist Shell (UK) 1961-66; bloodstock breeder; *Recreations* racing, tennis; *Style*— Ian Loftus, Esq; Bookham Stud, Bishopsdown, Sherborne, Dorset DT9 5PL (☎ 096 321 248)

LOFTUS, John Michael; s of Donald Loftus, of 4 Hemmant Way, Gillingham, Beccles, Suffolk, and Jean, *née* Hockney; *b* 4 Dec 1952; *Educ* Woodbridge Sch Suffolk, Univ of Sheffield (BSc); *m* 1988, Marilyn Vera; *Career* slr, NP, clerk to the Lowestoft Charity Bd 1987-, clerk to Gen Cmmrs of Taxes (Lowestoft Div) 1989-, ptnr Norton Peskett and Forward; cncllr Henstead Parish Cncl: parish Cncllr 1990-, church warden 1989-; *Recreations* running, gardening, cycling, camping, walking; *Style*— John Loftus, Esq; Keld House, The Street, Hulver, Beccles, Suffolk NR34 7UE (☎ 050 276 257); Norton Peskett & Forward, 148 London Road North, Lowestoft (☎ 0502 565146, fax 0502 515941)

LOGAN, Andrew David; s of William Harold Logan, of The Leys, Witney, Oxford, and Irene May, *née* Muddimer; *b* 11 Oct 1945; *Educ* Lord Williams's GS Thame, Burford GS Oxon, Oxford Sch of Architecture (Dip Arch 1970); *Career* sculptor and artist; Biba's Sculpture Garden Goldfield 1974, Exhibition Whitechapel Art Gallery 1976, Egypt Revisited Sand and Light Spectacular Super Tent Clapham Common 1978, Trigon-Graz Austria 1979, Goddesses Exhibition at Cwlth Inst London 1983, Henley Arts Festival; The Book Show, The Cylinder Gallery London 1984, Galactic Forest Exhibition, Functional Art Gallery, Los Angeles & Limelight Club New York 1985, Galactic Forest Exhibition Chicago, Daily Mail Ideal Home Exhibition Living Art Pavilion Arts Cncl, Glass Sculpture Exhibition Singapore 1986, Monuments & Music Exhibition, Botanical Gardens, Rome; designer: Wolfy, Ballet Rambert London 1987, Bastet, Sadler's Wells Royal Ballet 1988; jewellery and sculpture exhibited Moscow USSR 1989, Portraits new works (Glasshouse London) 1989, Wings Over Waves (Angela Flowers 1990, Untamed fashion Assembly jewellery incl in show Riga Latuia USSR; Andrew Logan's Alternative Miss World nos 1-7 1972-87; *Style*— Andrew Logan, Esq; The Glasshouse, Melior Place, London SE1 3QP; Doween, Rosscarbery, Co Cork, Ireland

LOGAN, David Brian Carleton; CMG (1991); s of Capt Brian Ewen Weldon Logan, RN, of Linchmere, Surrey, and Mary, *née* Fass; *b* 11 Aug 1943; *Educ* Charterhouse, Univ Coll Oxford (MA); *m* 4 March 1967, Judith Margaret, da of Walton Adamson Cole (d 1963); 2 s (Matthew b 1970, d 1988, James b 1976), 1 da (Joanna b 1968); *Career* Dip Serv 1965-; 3 sec (then 2 sec) Ankara 1965-69, private sec to Parly Under Sec of State for Foreign and Cwlth Affrs 1970-73, 1 sec UK Mission to the UN 1973-77, FCO 1977-82, cnsllr head of chancery and consul-gen Oslo 1982-85, head of Personnel Ops Dept FCO 1986-88; min and dep head of mission Moscow 1989-; sr assoc memb St Antony's Coll Oxford 1988-89; *Recreations* music, reading, sailing, tennis; *Clubs* Royal Ocean Racing, Roehampton; *Style*— David B C Logan, Esq, CMG; c/o Foreign and Commonwealth Office, King Charles St, London SW1

LOGAN, Sir Donald Arthur; KCMG (1977, CMG 1965); s of Arthur Alfred Logan (d 1967), and Louise Anne Bradley; *b* 25 Aug 1917; *Educ* Solihull; *m* 1957, Irène Jocelyne Angèle, da of Robert Everts, sometime Belgian Ambass to Madrid; 1 s, 2 da; *Career* served WWII RA; entered Dip Serv 1945: ambass Guinea 1960-62, cnsllr Paris 1964-70, ambass Bulgaria 1970-73, dep perm rep N Atlantic Cncl 1973-75, perm leader UK Delgn to UN Conf on Law of the Sea 1976-77, ldr UK Delgn to Conf on Marine Living Resources of Antarctica 1978-80; dir GB and E Europe Centre 1980-87; chm: St Clare's Coll Oxford 1984-, Jerusalem and East Mission Trust Ltd 1980-; *Clubs* Brooks's, RAC; *Style*— Sir Donald Logan, KCMG; 6 Thurloe St, London SW7 2ST (☎ 071 589 4010)

LOGAN, James; OBE (1988); s of John Logan, and Jean, *née* Howie; *b* 28 Oct 1927; *Educ* Robert Gordon's Inst Aberdeen; *m* 27 Dec 1958, Anne, da of Duncan Brand; 1 s (Jeremy b 1959), 1 da (Judith b 1961); *Career* sr scientific staff Macaulay Inst 1981, appeal admin Aberdeen Maritime Museum, dir Scot The What? revue co; fndr and chm Friends of Aberdeen Art Gallery and Museums, chm and dir Vol Serv Aberdeen, vice chm Scot Arts Cncl 1984-88, memb Arts Cncl GB 1984-88; CChem, MRIC; *Recreations* theatre going; *Style*— James Logan, Esq, OBE; 53 Fountainhall Rd, Aberdeen (☎ 0224 646914)

LOGAN, Joseph Andrew; s of late Joseph Baird Logan, of Aberdeen, and Hellen Dawson, *née* Wink; *b* 5 Nov 1942; *Educ* Hilton Academy Aberdeen; *m* 26 Sept 1964, Heather, da of late George Webster Robertson, of Aberdeen; 1 s (Marc Robertson b 1968), 1 da (Pamela Alison b 1971); *Career* sales mangr Newcastle Evening Chronicle 1969-77, asst md Evening Post (Luton) and Evening Echo (Watford) 1977-79; md: Peter Reed and Co 1982, Aberdeen Journals (sales mangr 1958-69, dep md 1982-83), Newcastle Chronicle and Jnl 1985-89 (exec asst 1976-77, asst md 1979-82), The Scotsman Publications Ltd 1989-; dir: Aberdeen Journals Ltd 1984, Newcastle Chronicle and Journals Ltd 1984-89, Warrington and Co 1984-89, Weekly Courier Ltd 1971-89, Thomson Regional Newspapers 1984-, The Scotsman Publications Ltd 1989-, Caledonian Offset Ltd 1989-, Central Publications Ltd 1989-, Thomson Scottish Organisation Ltd 1989-, Northfield Newspapers Ltd 1989-, Northern Rock Building Society Scotland 1989-; pres: Tyne and Wear News Trade Charity 1984-89, Border Newspaper Soc 1987-89; memb: Scottish Business in the Community 1989-, Scottish Business Award Trust Ltd 1989-, TAVR Liaison Ctee 1984-89, Bd Tyne and Wear C of C 1984-89, Bd of Business in the Community 1985-89, Br Airways Consumer Cncl

1986-89, Northumberland Coalition Crime 1988-89, Cncl Univ of Newcastle upon Tyne 1985-89; pres Scottish Daily Newspaper Soc 1990- (vice pres 1989-90); tstee: NE Civic Tst 1984-89, Univ of Newcastle upon Tyne Devpt Tst 1985-89; *Recreations* crossword, gardening, antiques; *Clubs* The Caledonian; *Style*— Joe Logan, Esq; Craigknowe, 197 Colinton Rd, Edinburgh (☎ 031 443 6727); The Scotsman Publications Limited, 20 North Bridge, Edinburgh EH1 1YT (☎ 031 225 2468, fax 031 225 5473)

LOGAN, Russell James Vincent Crickard; s of John Stuart Logan, of Kent, and Joan Ena, *née* Solly; *b* 5 Oct 1942; *m* 1978, Gillian Enid, da of Charles Redfern; *Career* studio mangr Forces Bdcasting Servs Cyprus 1960-62, freelance theatrical 1963-67; systems analyst IBM 1967-70, sr project mangr Twinlock Computer Services 1970-71, memb Bd Book Club Associates 1977-79 (fulfilment mangr 1971), fndr and sr ptnr Business Aid 1979-; chm and organiser annual BDMA Database Mktg Seminar 1986-, speaker trade confs and educn courses, advsr Br companies and charities; memb: BDMA, Crime Writers Assoc; chm Database Mktg Ctee 1986-; *Books* (all under pseudonym Russell James) Underground (1989), Daylight (1990), Payback (1991); *Recreations* criminal research, travel to unlikely places; *Style*— Russell Logan, Esq; Business Aid, Penrose House, 30 Sydenham Rd, Cheltenham, Glos GL52 6EB (☎ 0242 514992)

LOGAN, Stephen Andrew; s of Leslie Frank Logan (d 1983), and Celia, *née* Baker; *b* 4 Dec 1949; *Educ* Leyton Co GS; *m* 1 June 1974, Diane Beryl, da of John Henry Osbiston (d 1975); 1 s (Christopher b 1984), 1 da (Sarah b 1979); *Career* computer servs mangr Wiggins Teape Ltd 1986-; *Recreations* badminton, photography, restoring old houses; *Style*— Stephen Logan, Esq; Wiggins Teape Ltd, Gateway House, Basing View, Basingstoke, Hants RG21 2EE (☎ 0256 842020, telex 858031 WTBSTK G, fax 0256 840068, car 0836 231647)

LOGAN, Vincent Paul; *see*: Dunkeld, Bishop of

LOGAN-SALTON, Maurice Highton Ekegren; s of Ivor Logan Assheton-Salton, of Cornwall, and Tora Ulla Margaretha, *née* Ekegren; *b* 2 Feb 1952; *Educ* Canford Sch, Univ of Durham, Teesside Poly (Dip SW, CQSW); *Career* local authy social worker 1973-87, estates mangr Francome Ltd (nursing homes) 1988-; author Monday Club Policy Paper Juvenile Crime 1984; campaigner for reduction in custody for young offenders, supporter of CHEs (community homes with educn) and the equivalent trg of N Ireland and former List D Schs of Scotland as spokesman for Monday Club Law and Order Ctee 1984-, treas Univ of Durham Union Soc 1972-73; *Recreations* conservationist; *Style*— Maurice Logan-Salton, Esq; The Lodge, Llanarth Ct, Llanarth, Raglan, Gwent NP5 2YD (☎ 0873 840 200); 43 Falmouth Rd, Heaton, Newcastle upon Tyne NE6 5NS (☎ 091 2659992)

LOGERES; *see*: de Logeres

LOGIE, John Robert Cunningham; s of Norman John Logie, TD (d 1972), of Aberdeen, and Kathleen Margaret Cameron, *née* Neill; *b* 9 Sept 1946; *Educ* Robert Gordons Coll, Trinity Coll Glenalmond, Univ of Aberdeen (MB ChB, PhD); *m* 1981, Sheila Catherine, da of James Pratt Will (d 1957) of Peterhead; 1 s (David James Norman b 1989), 1 da (Joanna Catherine Neil b 1985); *Career* med trg Aberdeen Royal Infirmary 1970-81 (house offr, lectr, registrar, sr registrar), conslt gen surgn Raigmore Hosp Inverness 1981-; FRCS Ed 1974, FRCS 1975; *Recreations* gardening, railway matters, rugby refereeing; *Style*— John R C Logie, Esq; 20 Moray Park Ave, Culloden, Inverness IV1 2LS (☎ 0463 792090), Raigmore Hospital, Inverness (☎ 0463 234151)

LOGUE, Christopher; s of John Dominic Logue (d 1951), and Florence Mabel, *née* Chapman (d 1981); *b* 23 Nov 1926; *Educ* Portsmouth GS, Prior Park Coll Bath; *m* 1985, Rosemary Hill; *Career* writer, actor, Private Eye columnist; *Books* Ode to the Dodo: Poems 1953-78; War Music: an Account of Books 16-19 of Homer's Iliad (1988), Kings: an Account of Books 1 and 2 of Homer's Iliad (1991); ed: The Children's Book of Comic Verse (1979), The Bumper Book of True Stories (1981), The Oxford Book of Pseuds (1983), Sweet and Sour: an Anthology of Comic Verse (1983), The Children's Book of Children's Rhymes (1986); trans: Baal, The Seven Deadly Sins (1986), Bertold Brecht (1986); *Screenplays*: Professor Tucholsky's Facts (poem used as screenplay of animated film by Richard Williams, 1963), The End of Arthur's Marriage (music by Stanley Myers, dir Ken Loach, 1965), Savage Messiah (dir Ken Russell, 1972), Crusoe (with Walon Green, dir Caleb Deschanel, 1988); *Clubs* The Hotsy Totsy (Ghent); *Style*— Christopher Logue; 41 Camberwell Grove, London SE5 8JA (☎ 071 703 7853)

LOGUE, John Lindsay; s of Arthur Logue (d 1952), of Lytham House, Lytham St Annes, Lancs, and Mary Logue (d 1966); *b* 3 April 1930; *Educ* Manchester GS, Univ of Manchester; *m* 1967 (m dis 1977), Vivienne Louise, da of Patrick Wayland Warner (d 1970); 1 da (Lisa); *Career* engr, company dir and mgmnt conslt; chm and md SAP Ltd (engrg co); chm: Radiant Tube Ltd, BMK Carpets May 1982-; formerly dep md Bowyers Foot Gp; memb Worshipful Co of Pattenmakers; *Recreations* golf, sailing (yacht Vaquero), cricket; *Clubs* Royal Ocean Racing, Royal Thames Yacht, Royal Gourock Yacht, Royal Southern Yacht, St James's, Minchinhampton Golf; *Style*— John Logue, Esq; Amberley Court, Amberley, Glos GL5 5AE; Monkton Hall, Troon, Ayrshire; Eildon Hall, St Boswells, Roxburghshire, SAP Ltd, Chalford Industrial Estate, Brimscombe, Stroud, Glos (☎ 0453 884144); BMK Ltd, Kilmarnock, Ayrshire (☎ 0563 21100)

LOISEAU, Hon Mrs (Eliza); da of Baron Hutchinson of Lullington, *qv*; *b* 1941; *m* 1974, Pierre Loiseau; *Style*— The Hon Mrs Loiseau; Les Bouleaux, 2 Rue de Gazet, Seine Port, 77 France

LOKOLOKO, Sir Tore; GCVO (1982), GCMG (1977), OBE; s of Loko Loko Tore; *b* 21 Sept 1930; *Educ* Sogeri High Sch, Papua New Guinea; *m* 1950, Lalahaia Meakoro; 4 s, 6 da; *Career* govr-gen of Papua New Guinea 1977-83; *Style*— Sir Tore Lokoloko, GCVO, GCMG, OBE; Government House, Port Moresby, Papua New Guinea (☎ 010 675 25 9366)

LOMAS, Alfred; MEP (Lab) London NE 1979-; s of Alfred Lomas; *b* 30 April 1928; *Educ* St Pauls Elem Sch Stockport, various further educnl estabs; *Career* political sec London Co-op 1975-79; *Style*— Alfred Lomas, Esq, MEP; 28 Brookway, London SE3 9BJ (☎ 081 852 6689)

LOMAS, Derek Frank; s of Derek Edward James Lomas, of 3 Whitewood Cottages, Eynsford, Kent, and Pauline Lomas, *née* Clements; *b* 10 Oct 1960; *Educ* Dartford West Kent Secdy Boys Sch, Medway Coll of Art and Design (DATEC Dip in Photography); *Career* staff photographer Design Cncl Haymarket London 1984-86, photographer Waterlane Studios Richmond London 1986-89, freelance photographer (editorial photography, mainly still life work for magazines incl: Womans Jl, Options, Marie Claire, GQ) 1989-; *awards* AFAEP award for non-commissioned still-life 1989; memb AFAEP 1989; *Recreations* walking, cinema, cooking, photography; *Style*— Derek Lomas, Esq; Derek Lomas Photography, 69 Lambeth Walk, London SE11 6DX (☎ 071 735 0993)

LOMAS, Herbert; *b* 7 Feb 1924; *Educ* King George V Sch Southport, Univ of Liverpool (BA, MA); *Career* served WWII: King's Liverpool Reg attached to Queens 1943-44, Lance Corpl with Royal Warwickshire Dover, 2 Lt then Lt Indian Army 6 Btn Royal Garhwal Rifles (served Razmak Waziristan, Kohat NW Frontier Province) 1944-46; teacher of English Anargyrios Sch Spetsai Greece 1950-51, sr lectr Univ of Helsinki 1965 (lectr 1952-64); Borough Road Coll (later W London Inst of Higher Educn after merger with two other colls): pt/t lectr 1966-67, permanent lectr 1967-68, sr lectr 1968-72, princ lectr 1972-82; freelance writer and translator 1982-; Books: A Handbook of Modern English for Finnish Students (jtly, 1957), Chimpanzees are Blameless Creatures (1969), Who Needs Money (1972), Private and Confidential (1974), Public Footpath (1981), Territorial Song (1981), Fire in the Garden (1984), Letters in the Dark (1986), Contemporary Finnish Poetry (trans and ed) 1990; poetry and articles published in: London Magazine, Encounter, The Hudson Review, Ambit, The Tablet, London Lines; trans Medicine in Metamorphosis by Dr Martti Siirala; judge: Nat Poetry Competition 1989, Oxford union Poetry Competition 1989; *awards*: Poetry prize Guinness Poetry Competition 1961, runner-up prize Avon Fndn Poetry Competition 1980, Cholmondely award for Poetry 1982; memb Finnish Acad; *Style*— Herbert Lomas, Esq; North Gable, 30 Crag Path, Aldeburgh, Suffolk IP15 5BS

LOMAS, Jonathan; s of Grace Miriam Martha Hall, *née* Feesey (d 1988); *b* 30 April 1944; *Educ* Belmont Coll Bickington Devon, North Devon Coll Barnstaple, Poly SW (Dip Arch); *Career* qualified architect 1973; ptnr Dyer Feesey Wickham 1976, diocesan architect and eccleiastical architect-surveyor Diocese of Exeter 1988, cmmnd architect to the English Heritage 1988, architect to the Roman Catholic Diocese of Plymouth; conslt architect to the Nat Tst; memb: Exeter Diocesan Advsy Ctee 1980, Assoc for the Conservation of Historic Bldgs, Inst Archaeology Univ of London, Devonshire Assoc Cncl of Management Devon Historic Bldgs Tst; rep on historic bldgs and specialist in the repair of ancient bldgs Society for the Protection of Ancient Bldgs 1973 (memb); memb RIBA 1973, FRSA 1973; *Books* Devon's Traditional Buildings (contrib, 1980), The Buildings of England Series: Devon (contrib, 1989), Transactions of the Devonshire Association (contrib); *Recreations* archaeology and local history, photography, travel, surfing, gardening with a keen interest in Japanese Gardens, steam railways; *Style*— Jonathan Lomas, Esq; Sheraton Cottage, Old Sticklepath Hill, Barnstaple, North Devon EX31 2BG (☎ 0271 78752); Dyer Feesey Wickham (Architects), 14A Bridgeland St, Bideford, Devon EX39 2QE (☎ 0237 472448)

LOMAX, Prof Derek William; s of Robert Lomax (d 1985), of Birmingham, and Ada, *née* Marsh (d 1990); *b* 4 March 1933; *Educ* Thornleigh Coll Bolton, Merton Coll Oxford (BA, MA, DPhil); *Career* Nat Serv Gunner RA 1954-56; sr lectr Sch of Hispanic Studies Univ of Liverpool 1969-71 (asst lectr 1959-62, lectr 1962-69), prof of hispanic studies Univ of Birmingham 1972-90, emeritus prof of hispanic studies 1990-; memb Assoc of Hispanists of GB and Ireland 1959; *Books* La Orden de Santiago 1170-1275 (1965), Las Ordenes Militares en la Península Ibérica durante la Edad Media (1976), The Reconquest of Spain (1978), Fernão Lopes: The English in Portugal 1367-1387 (with R J Oakley, 1988), God and Man in Medieval Spain (with D Mackenzie, 1989); *Style*— Prof Derek Lomax; Dept of Hispanic Studies, Univ of Birmingham, Birmingham, B15 2TT (☎ 021 4146035)

LOMAX, Hon Mrs (Elizabeth Margaret); *née* Brand; da of 3 Viscount Hampden, GCVO, KCB, CMG (d 1958); *b* 1911; *m* 1935, Cecil Lomax (d 1988); 3 da; *Style*— The Hon Mrs Lomax; Codicote Mill, Hitchin, Herts (☎ 0438 820206)

LOMAX, Michael Acworth (Mike); s of Peter Francis George Lomax (d 1990), and Mary Rosamund Lomax; *b* 9 Jan 1943; *Educ* Downside Sch, Pembroke Coll Cambridge (BA); *m* (m dis); 2 s; *Career* grad trainee then mktg exec Foote Cone & Belding 1964-66, account exec Sharps Advertising 1966-69, account mangr McCann-Erickson 1969-70, Foster Turner & Benson 1970-75 (dir 1972-75), dir Streets Financial 1975-84, jt md Charles Barker City 1984-87, chief exec First Financial Advertising/PR 1989-90 (md 1987-89), dir First Corporate Communications Ltd 1990-; IPA: Finals tutor 1969-70, lectr Media Course 1970-71; memb: Media Representative Panel 1978-84, Mktg Panel 1984-85; memb LAUTRO Advtg and Product Disclosure Ctee 1989-, lectr on fin mktg topics for various bodies incl Mktg Centre Europe, Inst for Int Res and MINTEL; memb Nat Appeals Ctee Cancer Res Campaign 1974-90, nat chm Cancer Youth Action 1978-83, chm Mktg Ctee Cancer Res Campaign 1987-90; MIPA 1967; *Recreations* cricket, tennis, golf (capt Fin Advtg Golfing Soc 1989-90), hill walking, reading, opera; *Clubs* Scribes West Int; *Style*— Mike Lomax, Esq; First Corporate Communications Ltd, Drury House, 34 Russell St, London WC2B 5HA

LOMAX, Norman James Peter; s of Christine Mary Gillespie; *b* 13 Feb 1957; *Educ* St Brendons Coll Bristol; *partner* Susan Elizabeth Webber; 3 c (Phoebe b 7 May 1985, Poppy b 10 Aug 1987, Kit b 22 Aug 1990); *Career* photographer; formerly photographer's asst Bow St Studios London WC2, freelance photographer for int magazines (incl: Stern, Sports int, Figaro, Sunday Times magazine, Observer magazine), and numerous commercial clients 1979-90, sports and feature photographer Independent on Sunday 1990-; winner: Sports Photographer of the Year 1986, Golf Photographer of the Year 1986; *Recreations* fly-fishing, mountaineering, cycling, armchair sailing; *Clubs* Salisbury & District Angling; *Style*— Norman Lomax, Esq; Independent On Sunday, 40 City Rd, London EC1Y 2DB (☎ 071 253 1222)

LOMER, Richard Godfrey; MC; s of Lt-Col Godfrey Lomer, RHA, DSO (d 1952), and Mavis Mary, *née* Garrett (d 1979); inherited (1965) Ballinacor, Rathdrum, Co Wicklow from his c Capt W D O Kemmis, MC; *b* 22 April 1922; *Educ* Cranleigh Coll; *m* Patricia Katharine Mary, da of Sir Richard Lewis, KGMG, CB, CBE (d 1965); 2 s; *Career* WWII enlisted Royal Berks 1940, cmmnd Coldstream Guards served 1940-46, wounded Normandy (MC and despatches); recalled War Office (ERE list) 1950-56; qual slr 1949, sr ptnr Lomer & Co 1956-75; dir diverse cos; treas (then chm) Mulberry Housing Assoc; memb Mgmnt Ctee and tstee WWF; Wildfowl Tst; Merchant Taylor and Freeman City of London; *Recreations* conservation; *Style*— Richard Lomer, Esq; Manor Farm, Chantry, Frome, Somerset; Ballinacor Estates, Ballinacor, Rathdrum, Co Wicklow, Rep of Ireland

LONDESBOROUGH, Ann, Baroness; (Elizabeth) Ann; *née* Sale; da of late Edward Little Sale, ICS, and formerly w of late Thomas Chambers Windsor Roe, CBE; *b* 28 April 1916; *Educ* Headington Sch Oxford; *m* 15 June 1957, as his 2 w, 8 Baron Londesborough, TD (d 1968); 1 s (9 Baron); *Style*— The Rt Hon Ann, Lady Londesborough; 31 Lyttelton Rd, Droitwich, Worcs

LONDESBOROUGH, Jocelyn, Baroness; Jocelyn Helen; da of late Lt-Cdr Hugh Duppa Collins, RN; *m* 1952, as his 3 w, 7 Baron Londesborough (d 1967); *Style*— The Rt Hon Jocelyn, Lady Londesborough; Anchor Cottage, Bembridge, IOW (☎ 0983 872216)

LONDESBOROUGH, 9 Baron (UK 1850); Richard John Denison; s of 8 Baron Londesborough, TD, AMICE (d 1968, gs of Lord Albert Denison, *née* Conyngham, 2 s of 1 Marquess Conyngham), by his 2 w Ann; *b* 2 July 1959; *Educ* Wellington, Univ of Exeter; *m* 26 Sept 1987, Rikki, da of J E Morris, of Bayswater; *Heir* s, James Frederick b 4 June 1990; *Style*— The Rt Hon the Lord Londesborough; Edw Cottage, Aberedw, Powys

LONDON, Archdeacon of; *see*: Cassidy, Ven George Henry

LONDON, 130 Bishop of 1981-; Rt Rev and Rt Hon Graham Douglas Leonard; PC (1981); patron of one hundred and sixty livings and eighteen alternately with others, all Prebendal stalls, Archdeaconries of Londons, Middx, Hampstead, Hackney, Northolt and Charing Cross, the Precentorship, the Chancellorship and the Treasureship; the See of London has existed since the first introduction of Christianity into Britain. Restitutus, Bishop of London, was present at the Council of Arles in AD 314, and signed the decrees; s of Rev Douglas Leonard; *b* 8 May 1921; *Educ* Monkton Combe Sch, Balliol Coll Oxford, Westcott House Cambridge; *m* 1943, (Vivien) Priscilla, da of late Dr Swann; 2 s; *Career* served WWII Oxford & Bucks LI as Capt; ordained 1947, archdeacon Hampstead 1962-64, bishop suffragan of Willesden 1964-73, bishop of Truro 1973-81, delegate to fifth Assembly WCC Nairobi 1975; entered House of Lords 1977; chm Gen Synod Bd for Social Responsibility 1976-83, dean of HM's Chapel Royal 1981-, prelate Order of the British Empire 1981-; Gren lectr Westminster Coll Fulton Missouri 1987, Hensley Henson lectr Oxford Univ 1991-92; hon master of Bench of Middle Temple 1981-; chm: Churches Main Ctee 1981-, Jerusalem and Middle East Church Assoc 1981-, Bd of Educn and National Soc 1983-89; church cmmr; episcopal canon St George's Cathedral Jerusalem 1981-; memb Polys and Colls funding Cncl 1989-; hon fell Balliol Coll Oxford; Hon DD: Episcopal Theological Seminary Kentucky 1974, Westminster Coll Fulton Missouri 1987; Hon DCnL Nashotal House USA 1983, STD Siena Coll USA 1984, Hon LLD Simon Greenleaf Sch of Law USA 1987, Hon DLitt CNAA 1989; *Clubs* Athenaeum, Garrick; *Style*— The Rt Rev and Rt Hon the Lord Bishop of London; London House, 8 Barton St, London SW1 3NE (☎ 071 222 8661)

LONDON, John Frederick; s of Eric Horton London, MBE, of Bexhill-on-Sea, and Doris Emma, *née* Browning; *b* 17 Nov 1934; *Educ* Tonbridge; *m* 6 Oct 1962, Merrill Anne, da of Alfred Edward James Prior (d 1967), of Sevenoaks; 1 s (James b 8 Nov 1964), 2 da (Anne-Louise b 27 Oct 1967, Sally b 3 Aug 1969); *Career* Nat Serv 1953-54; Bank of England 1954-69, First Nat Bank of Boston London 1969-72; Quin Cope Ltd (formerly Gerald Quin Cope and Co Ltd) 1972-89: asst dir, dir, md; fin dir Royal Artillery Museums, chm and pres Sevenoaks and Dist Mental Health Assoc 1962-79, chm Sevenoaks Dist Scout Cncl 1971-88; memb: Sevenoaks UDC 1959-62 and 1963-74 (chm 1970-71), Sevenoaks Town Cncl 1974-, Major of Sevenoaks 1974-75 and 1988-89; vice-chm Sevenoaks Conservative Assoc; *Recreations* sailing; *Style*— John London, Esq; 18 Knole Way, Sevenoaks, Kent TN13 3RS (☎ 0732 456327)

LONDON, Malcolm John; s of Frederick Albert John London (d 1977), of Ruislip, Middx, and Cecily Maud, *née* Boyce (d 1978); *b* 27 July 1938; *Educ* Bishopshalt Sch, LSE (BSc); *m* m dis; *Career* ptnr Cork Gully 1969-80, ptnr Coopers & Lybrand Deloitte 1980-; hon treas: Royal Concert 1985-, Royal Musical Assoc 1981-; hon sec City Arts Tst 1973-, tstee Handel Inst 1987-, memb Cncl Insolvency Practitioners Assoc 1987-; Freeman City of London 1989, memb Worshipful Co of Musicians 1989; FCA (ACA 1964), memb Insolvency Practitioners Assoc 1979, FRSA 1989; *Books* Tolley's Liquidation Manual (jtly, 1989), Tax Implications of Liquidations, Receiverships, Administration Orders and Voluntary Arrangements (jtly, 1989); *Recreations* all performance and visual arts; *Style*— Malcolm London, Esq; Cork Gully, Shelley House, 3 Noble St, London EC2V 7DQ (☎ 071 606 7700, fax 071 606 9887)

LONEY, Francis Greville; s of Greville Groves Loney (d 1981), of Durban, S Africa, and Marjory Grace, *née* Redman; *b* 11 Dec 1936; *Educ* St Charles' Coll Pietermaritzburg S Africa, Regent St Poly; *Career* photographer; asst photographer to Robert Gibb, freelance 1966 - (Studio in Greek St Soho); photographic career has encompassed the entire spectrum of advtg and editorial photography incl: fashion, beauty, menswear, interiors, still life, celebrities, record sleeves, magazine covers, travel, theatre and the arts, press and society, landscapes, medical, portraits, children and animals, knitwear and charities, corporate; clients incl: Aquascutum, Pringle of Scotland, Int Wool Secretariat,DAKS Simpson, Austin Reed, N Peal, Easy Jeans, Stephen King, Beauty Without Cruelty, Ella Hosiery, Help a London Child, Irish Linen, Gordans Gin, Hamptons, Ladies Pride, The London Clinic, Cilla Black, Eartha Kitt, Des O'Connor, Ian Alberry; editotrial coverage ranging from Vogue to Woman's Weekly, the colour supplements and TV Times; *Recreations* looking after sons and heirs Jasper and Justin (pedigree blue Burmese cats); *Style*— Francis Loney, Esq; Sales Studio, Bardley House, Uxbridge, London W8 7AS (☎ 071 727 2382, fax 071 724 5012)

LONEY, Keith Edward; s of William Edward Loney (d 1977), of Yeovil, Somerset, and Marjorie Maud Rose Miles; *b* 16 Nov 1935; *Educ* King's Sch Bruton, Univ of London (LLB); *m* 1971, Valerie Elizabeth, da of Percy Arthur Stuttard (d 1977), of Purley, Surrey; *Career* Royal Signals 1954-57, Cyprus 1955-56; barr Lincoln's Inn 1972; memb: Inst of Chartered Accountants in England & Wales, Br Insur Assoc 1966-85 (asst sec 1971, dep sec 1975), Assoc of Br Insurers 1985 (dep chief exec 1987); vice pres Old Brutonian Assoc, memb Hon Artillery Co; Freeman City of London 1959, Liveryman The Worshipful Co of Butchers 1960; *Recreations* swimming, travel; *Clubs* Lansdowne; *Style*— Keith Loney, Esq; Aldermary House, 10/15 Queen St, London EC4N 1TT (☎ 071 248 4477, fax 071 489 1120, telex 937035)

LONG, Prof Adrian Ernest; s of Charles Long (d 1985), and Sylvia Evelyn Winifred, *née* Mills (d 1974); *b* 15 May 1941; *Educ* Royal Sch Dungannon, Queen's Univ of Belfast (BSc, PhD, DSc); *m* 18 March 1967, Elaine Margaret Long, da of James Thompson (d 1980); 1 s (Michael b 22 Feb 1971), 1 da (Alison b 18 Dec 1972); *Career* bridge design engr Toronto Canada 1967-68, asst prof Civil Engrg Dept Queen's Univ Kingston Canada 1968-71; Queens Univ Belfast: lectr Civil Engrg Dept 1971-75, prof of civil engrg 1976-77, prof and head Civil Engrg Dept 1977-89, dean of Faculty of Engrg 1988-, dir Sch of the Built Environment 1989-; visiting prof RMC Kingston Canada 1975-76, ed Jl of Engrg Structures; memb: Inst Civil Engrs (memb Cncl 1989-), Tport and Rd Res Lab; FICE 1982, FEng 1989, FIStructE 1989; *Recreations* walking, church activities; *Style*— Prof Adrian Long; Civil Engineering Dept, Queen's University, Belfast BT7 1NN (☎ 0232 245133 ext 4005, fax 0232 663754, telex QUBADM 74487)

LONG, Brian; s of Harry Long (d 1955), and Doris Long (d 1977); *b* 30 Aug 1932; *Educ* Hanson GS Yorks; *m* 29 Dec 1956, Joan Iris, da of Charles Eric Hoggard, of Huggate, Yorks; 2 s (Nigel b 10 Feb 1959, Gareth b 15 Jan 1962); *Career* qualified co sec 1953; International Computers and Tabulators Ltd 1955-65, joined Honeywell Ltd 1965, md Honeywell Information Systems Ltd 1978, memb Honeywell Advsy Cncl 1978, vice pres Honeywell Inc 1981; Honeywell Ltd: vice chm 1985, chief exec 1986; chm and chief exec Honeywell Bull Ltd (now Bull H N Information Systems Ltd) 1987, dir Bull SA of France 1987, chm Bull HN Information Systems Ltd 1990, chm Zenith Data Systems 1990; memb Bd Nat Computing Centre (NCC) 1970-71, memb Indust Ctee Help the Aged 1988; Freeman City of London 1987, memb Worshipful Co of Information Technologists 1987; FInstD 1970, CBIM 1987, MBCS 1987, FCIS 1988; FBCS 1989; *Recreations* golf, walking, music, theatre; *Clubs* RAC; *Style*— Brian Long, Esq; Bull H N Information Systems Ltd, Computer House, Great West Road, Brentford, Middx TW8 9DH (☎ 081 568 9191, fax 081 568 9191 ext 2305, telex 284534)

LONG, Hon Mrs (Anne) Cathrine); *née* Parnell; eldest da of 8 Baron Congleton, *qv*; *b* 1956; *Educ* St Mary's Calne, Trinity Coll of Music London; *m* 1980, (Michael) Robin Long; 2 s (Richard Per b 1981, Willum b 1984); *Style*— The Hon Mrs Long; Pear Tree Cottage, Ebbesbourne, Salisbury, Wilts

LONG, Christopher John; s of John Frederick Lawrence Long (d 1986), and Joan Ethel, *née* Murphy; *b* 16 Feb 1944; *Educ* Netteswell Comprehensive Sch Harlow, Queens' Coll Cambridge (MA); *m* 13 Dec 1969, Lesley Anne, *née* Hatcher, JP; 2 s (Stuart b 1976, Stephen b 1979), 1 da (Deborah b 1972); *Career* md CLA Ltd (Rutland Trust plc group) 1987-88, ptnr CJ Long & Co Management Consultants 1988- (Chartered Accountants 1981-), md Christopher Long & Associates Ltd 1984-87, dir Mutual of Omeha International Ltd 1986-87, vice pres Continental Illinois London 1981-84; mangr: Midland Bank International 1975-76, Finance for Shipping (3i) 1977-81; *Recreations* choral music, jazz, gardening; *Style*— Christopher Long, Esq; Alsa Wood House, Stansted, Essex CM24 8SU (☎ 0279 813111, fax 816564); 131 Finsbury Pavement, London EC2A 1AY (☎ 071 280 8496, fax 071 280 8415)

LONG, Christopher William; CMG (1986); s of late Eric Long, and May Long; *b* 9 April 1938; *Educ* King Edward's Sch Birmingham, Balliol Coll Oxford (Deakin scholar), Univ of Münster West Germany; *m* 1972, Patricia, da of Dennis Stanbridge; 2 s, 1 da; *Career* served RN 1956-58; HM Dip Serv 1963-: FO 1963-64, Jedda 1965-67, Caracas 1967-69, FCO 1969-74, Budapest 1974-77, Belgrade 1977, Cnsllr Damascus 1978-80, cnsllr and dep perm rep UK mission Geneva 1980-83, head of near East and N Africa Dept FCO 1983-85, asst under sec of State FCO 1985-88, HM ambass to Switzerland 1988-; *Style*— Christopher Long, Esq, CMG; British Embassy, Thunstrasse 50, 3005 Berne, Switzerland

LONG, Prof Derek Albert; s of Albert Long (d 1981), of Gloucester, and Edith Mary, *née* Adams (d 1983); *b* 11 Aug 1925; *Educ* Sir Thomas Rich's Sch Gloucester, Jesus Coll Oxford (MA, DPhil), Univ of Minnesota; *m* 8 Aug 1951, Moira Hastings, da of William Gilmore (d 1978), of Sheffield; 3 s (David b 1954, Richard b 1959, Andrew b 1962); *Career* fell Univ of Minnesota 1949-50, res fell spectroscopy Univ of Oxford 1950-55; Univ Coll Swansea 1956-66: lectr, sr lectr, reader in chemistry; Univ of Bradford: prof structural chemistry 1966-, chm Bd Physical Scis 1976-79, dir Molecular Spectroscopy Unit 1982-88; OECD travelling fell Canada and USA 1964, Leverhulme res fell 1970-71; visiting prof: Reims, Lille, Bordeaux, Paris, Bologna, Florence; chm second int conf on Raman spectroscopy Oxford 1970, co-dir NATO Advanced Studies Inst Bad Windsheim 1982, memb Italian-UK mixed cmmn for implementation of cultural convention 1985, vice chm Euro Laboratory for Non-Linear Spectroscopy Florence 1986-; fndr ed Jl of Raman Spectroscopy; hon Docteurès Sciences Reims 1979; FRCS, CChem; foreign memb Lincei Acad Rome 1979; *Books* Raman Spectroscopy (1977), Essays in Structural Chemistry (jt ed, 1971), Specialist Periodical Reports in Molecular Spectroscopy (jt ed vols 1-6, 1973-79), Non-Linear Raman Spectroscopy and its Chemical Applications (jt ed, 1982), Proceedings of the Eleventh International Conference on Raman Spectroscopy (jt ed, 1988), around 200 sci papers in learned jls; *Recreations* collecting antique woodworking tools, history of science, Pembrokeshire; *Clubs* Utd Oxford and Cambridge Univ; *Style*— Prof Derek A Long; 19 Hollingwood Rise, Ilkley, West Yorkshire LS29 9PW (☎ and fax 0943 608472), Three Houses, Roch, Nr Haverfordwest, Pembs, Dyfed, S Wales; Dept of Structural Chemistry, University of Bradford, W Yorkshire BD7 1DP (☎ 0274 733466, ext 8575, fax 0274 305340, telex 51309 UNIBFD G)

LONG, Gerald; *b* 22 Aug 1923; *Career* Intelligence Corps 1943-, posted ME 1943, cmmnd All-Arms Octu Acre, attached US army S of France invasion, served Number One Info Unit attached to Control Cmmn Germany, involved in activities connected with estab of free press, final rank Major, final post press offr N Rhine Westphalia; Reuters: corr in France Germany and Turkey 1950-60, asst gen mangr 1960-63, chief exec 1963-81, gen mangr 1963-73, md 1973-81; chm Visnews Ltd 1968-79, md Times Newspapers Ltd 1981-82, dep chm News International 1982-84; chm Exec Ctee Int Inst of Communications Ltd 1973-78, exec dir Journalists in Europe 1987-89, memb Design Cncl 1974-77; Commander Royal Order of the Phoenix (Greece) 1984, Grand Offr Order of Merit (Italy) 1973, Commander Order of Lion of Finland 1979, Commander's Cross, Order of Merit (Germany) 1983; FBIM 1978 (CBIM); *Recreations* cooking; *Style*— Gerald Long, Esq; 15 Rue d'Aumale, 75009 Paris, France (☎ 010 33 48 74 67 26); 51 Route De Caen, 14400 St Martin-Des-Entrées (☎ 010 33 31 92 47 12)

LONG, Hon Mrs (Jean); da of Baron Douglas of Cleveland (d 1978); *b* 1928; *m* 1952, Garry Long, FCIS; *Style*— The Hon Mrs Long; 8 The Avenue, Hatch End, Pinner, Middlesex

LONG, Jeremy Paul Warwick; s of Ronald Walter Long, of Warwick, and Gwendolen Dorothy Long; *b* 24 March 1953; *Educ* Warwick Sch, Exeter Coll Oxford (MA); *Career* former dep chief exec Mecca Leisure Gp (gp fin dir 1980), currently dir Brightreasons Ltd FCA; *Recreations* tennis, theatre, cinema, skiing; *Style*— Jeremy Long, Esq; Brightreasons Ltd, 74 Blackfriars Rd, London SE1 8HA (☎ 071 620 2577)

LONG, Hon John Hume; s of 3 Viscount Long; *b* 1930; *Educ* Harrow; *m* 1967 (m dis 1969), Averil Juliet, da of Henry Stobart; 1 da; *Style*— The Hon John Long; Flat 30 Eric Long Court, Eldene Rd, Dorcan, nr Swindon, Wilts; Swyre Farm Cottage, Aldsworth, Glos

LONG, John Richard; CBE (1987); s of Thomas Kendall Long (d 1968), and Jane, *née* Hall (d 1981); *b* 9 March 1931; *Educ* Kirkham GS; *m* 5 April 1952, Margaret Mary, da of John Edwin Thistlethwaite (d 1984); 1 s (Adrian b 1977), 2 da (Janet b 1953, Susan b 1955); *Career* entered Civil Service (Customs and Excise) as clerical offr 1947, resigned as under sec in Dept of Health 1988; mgmnt conslt specialising in health serv mgmnt, pharmaceutical indust and govt/indust relationships; *Recreations* gardening, current affairs, languages; *Clubs* Civil Serv; *Style*— John Long, Esq, CBE; 77 Prospect Rd, Farnborough, Hants GU14 8NT (☎ 0252 548525)

LONG, Martyn Howard; s of Victor Frederick Long, of Brighton, Sussex, and Dorothy Maud, *née* Lawrence; *b* 1 May 1933; *Educ* Univ Coll Sch London, Merrist Wood Agric Coll Surrey; *m* 4 Oct 1958, Veronica Mary Gascoigne, da of James Edward Bates (d 1952); 4 da (Helen b 1959, Maria b 1961, Samantha b 1965, Rosalind b 1969); *Career* Nat Serv RAF 1952-54; farmer 1949-85, dir of family firm; memb: W Sussex Area Health Authy 1973-77, S W Thames Regnl Health Authy 1980-81; chm: Mid-Downs Health Authy W Sussex 1981-, Nat Assoc of Health Authorities 1988-90 (former hon treas); vice-chm Nat Assoc of Health Authys and Tsts 1990- (chm Health Authy Ctee 1990-); chm E Grinstead Cons Assoc 1972-75; memb: E Sussex CC 1970-74, Cuckfield RDC 1972-74, W Sussex CC 1973-, Mid Sussex DC 1973-79, Assoc of CC's 1979-89, chm ACC Soc Servs 1982-88 (formerly vice chm), chm W Sussex CC 1989- (former chm Policy and Resources Ctee 1985-89); *Recreations* magic (assoc memb Inner Magic Circle with Silver Star); *Clubs* Farmers, Whitehall; *Style*— Martyn Long, Esq; Mid-Downs Health Authy, Haywards Heath, W Sussex (☎ 0444 441666)

LONG, Hon Mrs (Meriel Davina); *née* Edwardes; o da of Capt the Hon (Hugh) Owen Edwardes (d 1937), 2 s of 6 Baron Kensington; sis of 8 Baron and was raised to rank of Baron's da by Royal Warrant 17 May 1982; *b* 19 April 1935; *m* 1972, (David) Andrew Long; 2 s; *Style*— The Hon Mrs Long; Hill House, Filmore Hill, Privett, Alton, Hants GU34 3NX (☎ 073088 321)

LONG, Michael John; s of John Robert Long, and Annie Mabel, *née* Oates; *b* 15 March 1947; *Educ* King Edward VI GS East Retford, St John's Coll Cambridge (MA); *m* 23 Aug 1969, (Ursula) Christel, da of Alfred Kaempf (d 1944), of Wuerzburg, Germany; *Career* slr: Stephenson Harwood 1969-73, Donne Mileham & Haddock 1973-; The Law Soc: Cncl memb, final examiner; cncllr Hove Borough Cncl; senator JCI; Liveryman Worshipful Co of Solicitors; *Books* Some Aspects of the Family

Busines (with D T Sparrow, 1979); *Recreations* Scotland, Opera, theatre; *Clubs* United Oxford & Cambridge; *Style—* Michael Long, Esq; Donne Mileham & Haddock, Frederick Place, Brighton, E Sussex BN1 1AT (☎ 0273 29833, fax 0273 739764, telex 87107)

LONG, 4 Viscount (UK 1921); Richard Gerard Long; s of 3 Viscount Long, TD, JP, DL (d 1967); *b* 30 Jan 1929; *Educ* Harrow; *m* 1, 2 March 1957 (m dis 1984), Margaret Frances, da of Ninian Frazer; 1 s, 1 da (and 1 decd); m 2, 1984 (m dis 1990), Catherine Patricia Elizabeth Mier Woolf, da of Charles Terrence Miles-Ede, of Leicester; m 3, 19 June 1990, Helen Millar Wright Fleming-Gibbons; *Heir* s, Hon James Richard Long b 31 Dec 1960; *Career* The Wilts Regt 1947-49; pres Bath and Wilts Gliding Club, vice pres Wilts Royal Br Legion; oppn whip 1974-79, lord-in-waiting 1979-; *Recreations* shooting, gardening; *Style—* The Rt Hon the Viscount Long; House of Lords, London SW1

LONG, Dr Richard Glover; s of John Long (d 1978), of Higham, Kent, and Bridget, *née* Harrison; *b* 13 Aug 1947; *Educ* Canford Royal Free Hosp Sch of Med (MB BS, MD); *m* 12 Feb 1983, Anita Rosemary, da of Kenneth Eaton Wilson, of Aldridge, West Midlands; 1 s (Charles Matthew b 1983); *Career* hon sr registrar Hammersmith Hosp 1978-80, sr registrar St Thomas Hosp 1980-83, MRC travelling res fell San Francisco USA 1983, conslt gastroenterologist and clinical teacher Nottingham Hosp Med Sch 1983-; memb: Br Soc of Gastroenterology, American Gastroenterology Assoc, Med Res Soc; FRCP 1989; *Books* Radioimmunossay of Gut Regulatory Reptides (jt ed with S R Bloom, 1982); *Recreations* fly fishing; *Style—* Dr Richard Long; Coach House, Old Hall Drive, Widmerpool, Nottingham NG12 5PZ (☎ 06077 2467); City Hospital, Nottingham NG5 1PB (☎ 0602 691169); Park Hospital, Sherwood Lodge Drive, Arnold, Nottingham NG5 8RX (☎ 0602 670670)

LONG, (William Ivers) Roland; s of George Roland Long (d 1967), and Margaret, *née* Smith; *b* 18 Feb 1947; *Educ* Royal Belfast Acad Inst Belfast; *m* 17 April 1971, Jennifer Mary, da of Patrick Raymund Devin Carmichael (d 1985), of Bournemouth; 1 s (Jeremy b 1977), 1 da (Deborah b 1974); *Career* dir AV Browne Advertising 1967-72; chm: Armstrong Long Advertising Ltd 1972-83, The RLA Group Ltd 1984-; chm NI branch Inst of Marketing 1981-82; MInstM 1972, FBIM 1982, MIPA 1987; *Style—* Roland Long, Esq; The RLA Group Ltd, Burlington Arcade, Old Christchurch Rd, Bournemouth, Dorset BH1 2HZ (☎ 0202 297755, fax 0202 26149)

LONG, William Casson; s of Capt Clifford Long (d 1974), and Bessie, *née* Casson (d 1952); *b* 25 Aug 1923; *Educ* Sedbergh, St John's Coll Cambridge; *m* 14 June 1947, Joan Cantrill, da of Maj Norman Feather, MC (d 1971); 1 s (James Duncan Clifford b 1952), 1 da (Elspeth Jane Baty b 1949); *Career* 2 Lt RA 1942; Capt 1945, hon rank of Capt granted on demob 1947; Burma Cmd 14th Army 1944-46; CA in public practice 1952-88, memb Inst Taxation 1955, conslt Long and Co CA's, ACA 1951, FCA 1956, ATII 1955; *Recreations* gardening, fly-fishing, woodcarving, photography, ornithology, entomology, motor sport; *Clubs* Keighley RUFC, Kilnsey Anglers; *Style—* William Casson Long, Esq; 132 Banks Lane, Riddlesden, Keighley, W Yorks BD20 5PQ

LONG, William John; s of Maj Richard Samuel Long, of Mary's Cottage, Dunsbury Farm, Brook, Newport, IOW, and Mary, *née* Charrington; *b* 11 Nov 1943; *Educ* Woodbridge Sch; *m* 15 Jan 1969, Sarah Jane, da of Philip Barton Lockwood, of Le Domaine de Gavaisson, St Antonin-de-Var, 83150 Lorgues, France; 2 s (Samuel b 18 April 1974, John b 8 April 1979), 1 da (Jane b 6 Feb 1972); *Career* ptnr: Laing & Cruickshank 1973-79, Milton Mortimer & Co 1982-86; dir: Lockwoods Food Ltd 1977-82, National Investment Group plc 1986-, Capel-Cure Myers Capital Management Ltd 1990-; underwriting memb Lloyds; memb Earl Marshall's staff for state funeral of Sir Winston Churchill; MInstD, memb Int Stock Exchange; *Recreations* sailing, fishing, shooting and genealogy; *Style—* William Long, Esq; Coombe Fishacre House, Coombefishacre, Newton Abbot, Devon (☎ 0803 812242); The Registry, Royal Mint Court, London EC3N 4EY; 35 Southernhay East, Exeter EX1 1NX (☎ 0394 76244, fax 0392 72161)

LONGAIR, Malcolm Sim; *b* 18 May 1941; *Educ* Morgan Acad Dundee, Queen's Coll Univ of St Andrews (James Caird Travelling scholar), Univ of Cambridge (MA, PhD, James Clerk Maxwell scholar); *m* Deborah Janet; 1 s (Mark Howard b 13 Sept 1976), 1 da (Sarah Charlotte b 7 March 1979); *Career* Univ of Cambridge: demonstrator Dept of Physics 1970-75, offical fell and praelector of Clare Hall 1971-80, lectr Dept of Physics and visiting asst prof of Radio Astronomy California Inst of Technol Sept-Dec 1972, Interdisciplinary Scientists for the Hubble Space Telescope 1977-, visiting prof of Astronomy Inst for Advanced Study Princeton Sept-Dec 1978, exchange visitor to USSR Space Res Inst Moscow (on 6 occasions) 1975-79, regius prof of astronomy Univ of Edinburgh 1980-, dir Royal Observatory Edinburgh 1980-; visiting lectr: in astronomy and astrophysics Pennsylvania State Univ 1986-, Univ of Victoria Canada; Regents fellowship of the Smithsonian Instn at Smithsonian Astrophysical Observatory Harvard April-July 1990, Astronomer Royal for Scotland; memb: IUE Observatory Ctee 1975-78, Space Science Programme Bd 1985-88, Euro Space Agency Working Gp 1975-78, Anglo Australian Telescope Bd 1982-87; chm: Astronomy II (AII) Ctee 1979-80 (memb 1977-78), Millimetre Telescope Users Ctee 1979-83, Space Telescope advsy panel 1977-84, space Telescope Science Inst 1982-84; LLD Univ of Dundee 1982; fell: Royal Astronomical Soc, Royal Soc of Dundee; *Books* numerous public lectures; Observational Cosmology (co-ed JE Gunn M J Rees 1978), High Energy Astrophysics (1981), Theoretical concepts in Physics (1984), Alice and the Space Telescope (1989), The Origins of Our Universe (1990), author of numerous scientific papers; *Recreations* music, opera, art, architecture, golf; *Style—* Malcolm Longair, Esq; 41 Cluny Drive, Edinburgh, Scotland (☎ 031 447 9069); Royal Observatory, Blackford Hill, Edinburgh, Scotland EH9 3HJ (☎ 031 668 8260)

LONGBOTTOM, Charles Brooke; s of William Ewart Longbottom (d 1943); *b* 22 July 1930; *Educ* Uppingham; *m* Anita, da of Giulio Trapani; 2 da; *Career* called to the Bar Inner Temple, contested (C) Stockton on Tees 1955, MP (C) York 1959-66, pps to Chllr of Duchy of Lancaster 1961-63; chm: Austin & Pickersgill Shipbuilders Sunderland 1966-72, A & P Appledore Ltd 1970-78, Seascope Holdings Ltd 1970-82, Seascope Shipping Ltd 1970-86; dir: Henry Ansbacher Holdings plc, Henry Ansbacher & Co, Ansbacher Guernsey Ltd 1982-86, Kelt Energy plc, MC Shipping Inc; memb: Gen Advsy Cncl BBC 1965-75, Community Rels Cmmn 1968-70; pt/t memb Bd of Br Shipbuilders, chm Acorn Christian Healing Tst; *Style—* Charles Longbottom, Esq; 66 Kingston House North, Princes Gate, London SW7

LONGCROFT, James George Stoddart; s of Reginald Stoddart Longcroft (d 1969), and Annie Mary, *née* Thompson (d 1972); *b* 25 Oct 1929; *Educ* Wellington; *m* 4 s (Dominic b 1966, Christopher b 1971, Nicholas b 1975, Charles b 1990), 1 da (Juliet b 1970); *Career* sr ptnr Longcrofts CA; chm Tricentrol Ltd (oil exploration and prodn) 1979-81, Tricentrol plc 1981-88; Master Worshipful Co of Founders 1977-78; FCA, FInstPet, FBIM, FRSA; *Recreations* skiing, tennis; *Clubs* City of London, HAC; *Style—* James Longcroft, Esq; Chalet Tournesol, 3780 Gstaad, Switzerland (☎ 030 45416, fax 030 45418); Longcrofts Chartered Accountants, Longcroft House, Victoria Avenue, Bishopsgate, London EC2 (☎ 071 623 6626, fax 071 623 4997, telex 915074)

LONGDEN, Christopher John; s of John Stuart Longden, of Sheffield, Yorkshire, and Daisy, *née* Heath; *b* 22 March 1955; *Educ* Granville Coll Sheffield, Blackpool Coll; *m* 31 March 1978, Carol, da of Bryan Pettinger; 2 s (Benjamin b 6 July 1981, James b 15 Feb 1984), 1 da (Jennifer b 31 March 1985); *Career* trainee mangr British Transport Hotels 1974-77, food and beverage mangr Hotel L'Horizon Jersey CI 1977-81, mangr Gleddoch House Hotel & Country Club Langbank 1981-85, md Gleddoch Hotels (incl Gleddoch House, Gleddoch Golf Club and Houstoun House Broxburn) 1985-, Master Innholder 1986, Freeman City of London 1986; fell HCIMA 1974; *Recreations* yacht racing; *Style—* Christopher Longden, Esq; 15 Station Rd, Langbank, Renfrewshire (☎ 0475 54 757); Gleddoch Hotels Ltd, Gleddoch House, Langbank, Renfrewshire (☎ 0475 54 711, fax 0475 54 201)

LONGDEN, Sir Gilbert James Morley; MBE (Mil 1944); s of Lt-Col James Morley Longden, and Kathleen Morgan; *b* 16 April 1902; *Educ* Haileybury, Emmanuel Coll Cambridge (MA, LLB), Sorbonne; *Career* serv WWII with Durham LI, 2 Div and 36 Div in Burma Campaign; admitted slr 1927; sec ICI (India) Ltd 1930-38; contested (C) Morpeth 1945, MP (C) SW Herts 1950-74; UK del: Cncl of Europe 1953, XII and XIII Sessions of the UN 1957-58; kt 1972; *Books* A Conservative Philosophy (1947), One Nation (jtly 1950), Change is Our Ally (1954), A Responsible Society (1959), One Europe (1969); *Clubs* Brooks's, Hurlingham; *Style—* Sir Gilbert Longden, MBE; 89 Cornwall Gardens, London SW7 4AX (☎ 071 584 5666)

LONGDEN, (George) Howard; OBE (1991); s of George Longden (d 1958), and Doris, *née* Turner (d 1976); *b* 7 Feb 1930; *Educ* Varndean Co GS Brighton; *m* 25 Aug 1951, Margaret (d 1990), da of Frank Neve (d 1959); 1 s (Bruce b 1954), 1 da (Diane b 1957); *Career* local govt offical 1951-90; treas Southborough UDC 1965-67, dep borough treas Weston Super Mare Borough Cncl 1967-73, chief exec Hove Borough Cncl 1985-90 (borough treas 1973); fin advsr Assoc of Dist Cncls, memb Exec Ctee Assoc of Cncl Treasurers (former pres), sr vice pres Inst of Revenues Rating and Valuation (formerly Rating and Valuation Assoc), former pres Hove Rotary Club; memb IPFA 1965; *Books* Rating Law and Practice (contrib, 1985); *Recreations* watching cricket, philately; *Style—* Howard Longden, Esq, OBE; Meyner's Close, Hove, Sussex (☎ 0273 423173)

LONGE, Nicholas; s of late Lt Col Roland Bacon Longe, of Hasketon Lodge, Woodbridge, Suffolk, and Diana, *née* Hastings; *b* 20 March 1938; *Educ* St Peter's Court, Harrow; *m* 14 March 1970, Julia Victoria, da of Maj David Arthur Peel, MC (ka 1944); 2 s (William b 1972, David b 1975); *Career* Sub Lt RN 1957-59; farmer; PE Consulting Gp Ltd 1968-73, dir Brook House Investmts Ltd 1985-89; memb Apple and Pear Devpt Cncl 1979-89, dir Kingdom Mktg Scheme 1980-89 (chm 1980-82); chm: Museum of E Anglian Life, APDE Res Gp 1987-88; High Sheriff of Suffolk 1984-85; Freeman: City of London, Worshipful Co of Fruiterers; *Recreations* sailing, sport, reading; *Clubs* Naval and Military; *Style—* Nicholas Longe, Esq; Hasketon Manor, Woodbridge, Suffolk; Grange Farm, Hasketon, Woodbridge, Suffolk (☎ 047 335 610)

LONGFIELD, Richard Lewis; s of John Longfield, OBE, and Mary Lyon, *née* Waddell; *b* 2 Nov 1939; *Educ* Marlborough Coll, Trinity Coll Dublin (BA); *m* Felicity Laura, da of Alex Miller, of Straidarran, N Ireland; 1 s (Edward), 2 da (Onnalee, Shauna); *Career* oil co exec, head public affrs Shell UK oil; *Recreations* photography, golf, gardening, fishing; *Style—* Richard L Longfield, Esq; The Old Rectory, Weston Patrick, Hants; 11 Rousden St, Camden; Shell UK Ltd, Shell-Mex House, Strand, London WC2

LONGFORD, Countess of; Elizabeth; CBE (1974); da of late Nathaniel Bishop Harman, FRCS, and Katherine, *née* Chamberlain; *b* 30 Aug 1906; *Educ* Headington Sch Oxford, Lady Margaret Hall Oxford; *m* 1931, Hon Francis Pakenham, 7 Earl of Longford; 4 s, 3 da (1 da decd); *Career* author (as Elizabeth Longford and Elizabeth Pakenham); lectr for WEA and univ extension lectr 1929-35, contested (Lab) Cheltenham 1935, Oxford 1950, candidate for King's Norton Birmingham 1935-43, memb Rent Tbnl Paddington and St Pancras 1947-54, tstee Nat Portrait Gallery 1968-78; memb: Advsy Cncl V&A Museum 1969-75, Advsy Bd Br Library 1976-79; vice-pres London Library 1983-; Hon DLitt (Sussex 1970); FRSL; *Books* Jameson's Raid (reprinted 1982); *Biographies incl:* Victoria RI (James Tait Black Prize), Wellington (2 vols; Yorkshire Post Prize for vol I), The Royal House of Windsor, Churchill, Byron, Wilfrid Scawen Blunt, The Queen Mother, Elizabeth R (1983); other books: The Pebbled Shore (memoir, 1986), The Oxford Book of Royal Anecdotes (1989); *Style—* The Rt Hon the Countess of Longford, CBE; Bernhurst, Hurst Green, E Sussex (☎ 058 086 248); 18 Chesil Court, Chelsea Manor St, London SW3 (071 352 7794)

LONGFORD, 7 Earl of (I 1785); Francis Aungier Pakenham; KG (1971), PC (1948); also Baron Longford (I 1756), Baron Silchester (UK 1821), Baron Pakenham (UK 1945); sits as Baron Pakenham; s of 5 Earl of Longford, KP, MVO (ka 1915), by his w, Lady Mary Julia Child-Villiers (d 1933, da of 7 Earl of Jersey); suc bro, 6 Earl, 1961; *b* 5 Dec 1905; *Educ* Eton, New Coll Oxford; *m* 1931, Elizabeth, CBE (*see* Countess of Longford), da of Nathaniel Bishop Harman, FRCS; 4 s, 3 da (Lady Antonia Fraser/Pinter, Mrs Alexander Kazantzis, Lady Rachel Billington, and 1 da decd); *Heir* s, Thomas Pakenham; *Career* sits as Labour peer in Lords; lord-in-waiting to HM 1945-46, parly under-sec of state for War 1946-47, Chllr of Duchy of Lancaster 1947-48, min of Civil Aviation 1948-51, first lord of the Admty May-Oct 1951 and lord privy seal 1964-65, sec of state for the colonies 1965-66, again lord privy seal 1966-68; chm: Nat Youth Employment Cncl 1968-71, Sidgwick & Jackson 1970-80; *Style—* The Rt Hon The Earl of Longford, KG, PC; Bernhurst, Hurst Green, East Sussex (☎ 058 086 248); 18 Chesil Court, Chelsea Manor St, SW3 (☎ 071 352 7794)

LONGLAND, Sir John Laurence (Jack); eld s of Rev Ernest Harry Longland (d 1956), of Cambridge, and Emily Rose (d 1952), eld da of Sir James Crockett, of Dallington Lodge, Northampton; *b* 26 June 1905; *Educ* King's Sch Worcester, Jesus Coll Cambridge (MA); *m* 1934, Margaret Lowrey, da of Arthur Harrison (d 1936), of Durham (sr ptnr of Harrison and Harrison, builders of the organs of Westminster Abbey, Albert Hall, King's Coll Cambridge, Royal Festival Hall); 2 s, 2 da; *Career* by-fell Magdalene Coll Cambridge 1927-29, lectr Univ of Durham 1930-36, educn offr and later dir Community Serv Cncl for Durham Co 1936-40, dep educn offr Hertfordshire 1940-42, co-educn offr Dorset 1942-49, dir of educn Derbyshire 1949-70; broadcaster for 40 years; pres: Alpine Club 1974-76, Br Mountaineering Cncl, Climbers' Club, Cambridge Univ Mountaineering Club (memb Mount Everest Expdn 1933); devpt cmmr 1946-76, Royal Cmmn of Local Govt 1966-69, Countryside Cmmn 1966-72, vice chm Sports Cncl 1970-74; kt 1970; *Recreations* mountaineering, rugby, pole-vault (four times regnl champion); *Clubs* Savile, Alpine, Climbers', Achilles, Hawks; *Style—* Sir Jack Longland; Bridgeway, Bakewell, Derbyshire (☎ 062 981 2252)

LONGLEY, Adrian Reginald; s of Evelyn Longley (d 1956), and Mary Anastasia, *née* Thompson (d 1962); *b* 27 Sept 1925; *Educ* Winchester, Trinity Coll Cambridge (MA); *m* 14 Dec 1957, Sylvia Margaret, da of Capt George Keith Homfray Hayter (d 1968); 3 da (Anne b 1959, Joanna b 1960, Melissa b 1963); *Career* mil serv Rifle Bde (A/Capt) served M East 1944-47; admitted slr 1959; Freshfields 1959-69, White Brooks and Gilman 1970-72; legal advsr Nat Cncl for Voluntary Orgns 1972-90; memb: Goodman Ctee 1974-76, Cncl L'Orchestre du Monde (Orchestra of the World) 1988; tstee: Cyril Wood Meml Tst, Eurosphil Tst; UK contrib to Les Associations et Fondations en Europe: Régine Juridique et Fiscal 1990; *Recreations* music, walking, foreign travel; *Clubs* Royal Cwlth, Cavalry & Guards, MCC; *Style—* Adrian R Longley, Esq; 7 Kersley St, London SW11 4PR (☎ 071 223 7515); 26 Bedford Square, London WC1B 3HU (☎ 071 636 4066)

LONGLEY, Mrs Ann Rosamund; da of Jack Dearlove (d 1967), of Sevenoakes, Kent, and Rhoda, *née* Billing; *b* 5 March 1942; *Educ* Walthamstow Hall Sch, Univ of Edinburgh (MA); *m* 12 Dec 1964, Stephen R Longley (d 1979), s of Cedric J Longley (d 1987), of Histon; 1 s (Justin b 25 Oct 1965), 2 da (Catherine b 20 Aug 1968, Emma b 14 May 1970); *Career* teacher: Torak Coll Aust 1964-65, Choate Sch Conn USA 1968-73, Webb Sch California USA 1975-78; asst house mistress Penisula C of E Sch Victoria Aust 1966-67; headmistress: Vivian Webb Sch California USA 1981-84, Roedean 1984-; Fell ESU FRSA; *Recreations* tennis, swimming, fishing, walking; *Clubs* Univ (Los Angeles); *Style—* Mrs Ann Longley; Roedean House, Roedean Sch, Brighton, E Sussex BN2 5RQ (☎ 0273 603181)

LONGLEY, James Timothy Chapman; s of Alan Timothy Chapman Longley, of Haxby, nr York, and Avrill Ruth Nunn, *née* Midgley; *b* 21 May 1959; *Educ* Worksop Coll, Leeds Poly (BA); *m* 2 Sept 1989, Christina Susanne, da of Prof Dr Norman Denison, of Graz, Austria; *Career* CA; Finnie and Co 1980-83, Arthur Andersen and Co 1983-85, Creditanstalt-Bankverein 1985-88, Touche Ross and Co 1988-89; dir: Helo Ltd, Chapman Watson Ventures Ltd, Chapman Watson Finance Ltd, Longley Investments Ltd; ACA 1983; *Recreations* skiing, riding, tennis; *Clubs* Groucho; *Style—* James Longley, Esq; 53 Linver Rd, Fulham, London SW6 3RA (☎ 071 936 3000); Chapman Watson, 24-25 Cromwell Place, S Kensington, London SW7 2LD (☎ 071 581 1344, fax 071 581 1343)

LONGLEY, Michael; JP (1974); s of Sir Norman Longley, KBE, DL, of Crawley, W Sussex, and Dorothy Lillian, *née* Baker; *b* 23 July 1929; *Educ* Clifton, Brighton Tech Coll; *m* 24 Sept 1955, Rosemary, da of Walter Jackson (d 1968); 2 s (Julian Philip b 1957, James Christopher b 1959, d 1977); *Career* dir: James Longley Hldgs Ltd 1961-; chm: Longley Devpts 1961-, Romanbury Investmt Ltd 1961-, WG Boyce Ltd 1967-, James Longley and Co Ltd 1967-89, James Longley Enterprises Ltd 1976, Canningford Ltd 1978-, Longley Freeholds Ltd 1979-, Towgreen Ltd 1980-, Forum Crown 1980-, Longley Properties Ltd 1981, Canningford Investmts Ltd 1983-, Reigate Securities Ltd 1985-; Freeman City of London 1950, Liveryman Worshipful Co of Armourers and Brasiers 1963; FCIOB 1980; *Recreations* gardening, ornithology, natural history, property speculation; *Style—* Michael Longley, Esq, JP; Isle of Thorns, Lewes Rd, Chelwood Gate, Haywards Heath, West Sussex RH17 7DE; James Longley (Hldgs) Ltd, East Park, Crawley, West Sussex RH10 6AP (☎ 0293 561212 Ext 2230, direct line 0293 564230, fax 0293 564564)

LONGLEY, Peter; s of Sir Norman Longley, CBE, DL, and Dorothy Lilian Baker; *b* 28 July 1927; *Educ* Clifton; *m* 1954, da of Sidney Brittain (d 1974); 1 s (Robert b 1960), 2 da (Elizabeth b 1956, Alison b 1958); *Career* building contractor; dir: James Longley & Co Ltd 1961-87, James Longley (Holdings) Ltd 1969-; chm: Clayton House (Toc H) Crawley Ltd, The Longley Tst; dir: Brighton West Pier Tst, BEC Pension Tstees Ltd, Southern Industl History Centre; pres Crawley Boys' Club; vice pres Sussex Assoc of Boys' Clubs; Liveryman Worshipful Co of Armourers and Brasiers; FRSA, fell Chartered Inst of Bldg; *Style—* Peter Longley, Esq; Lackenhurst, Brooks Green, Horsham, W Sussex; Longley House, East Park, Crawley, W Sussex (☎ 0293 561212)

LONGMAN, Lady Elizabeth Mary; *née* Lambart; er da of Field Marshal 10 Earl of Cavan, KP, GCB, GCMG, GCVO, CBE (d 1946), and Joan, Countess of Cavan, DBE (d 1976); *b* 16 Oct 1924; *m* 1949, Mark Frederic Kerr Longman (d 1972), 5 s of late Henry Kerr Longman, of Wildwood, Pyrford, Surrey; 3 da; *Career* bridesmaid at wedding of HM The Queen 1947; dir The Fine Art Soc plc, tstee Harrison Homes; *Recreations* gardening; *Style—* The Lady Elizabeth Longman; The Old Rectory, Todenham, Moreton-in-Marsh, Glos; 1-58 Rutland Gate, London SW7 (☎ 071 581 1230); The Fine Art Society, 148 New Bond St, London W1

LONGMAN, Cncllr (James Edward) Ford; s of George Lewis Ernest Longman (d 1989), and Alice Lizzie Mary (d 1954); *b* 8 Dec 1928; *Educ* Watford GS, Birkbeck Coll London (BSc), Univ of Leeds; *m* 22 May 1954, Dilys Menai, da of Reginald Wilfred Richard Hunt (d 1972); 2 s (Jonathan b 1955, Richard b 1962), 3 da (Sarah b 1957, Rachel b 1960, Margaret b 1965); *Career* RAF Radar/Wireless Sch and Educn Branch 1947-49; Miny of Health, Bd of Control and Office Min for Sci 1949-62; hon sec Watford Cncl of Churches 1950-62, lay preacher; asst dir Joseph Rowntree Meml Tst, sec J R M Housing Tst, clerk to Joseph Rowntree Schs 1962-70; dir Yorks (Regnl) Cncl Social Serv 1970-75, sec seven other regnl bodies; hon sec Yorks Arts Assoc 1970-76, chm Yorks CSS 1967-70, sometime memb of ten Govt Ctees on Social Servs and Penal Matters (incl Ctee on Serv Overseas); Lord Chllr's Advsy Ctee on Crown Cts (NECCT), chm Bd HM Borstal Wetherby, conslt in social planning Govt of W Berlin and UNESCO, pioneered community devpt in Br, chm All-Pty Utd World Tst for Educn and Res, exec memb Nat Peace and NCSS, memb Yorks and Humberside Regnl Econ Planning Cncl (and three of its four working gps 1965-72); jt fndr: St Leonard's Housing Assoc, York Abbeyfield Soc, Regnl Studies Assoc, Community Devpt Tst 1968 (dir 1968-76); HM Inspr of Community Educn 1975-83; co cncllr N Yorks (dep ldr Lib Democrat Gp CC, shadow chm Social Services Ctee); Parly candidate (Lib/SDP Alliance) Selby 1987; memb: Soc of Friends (Quakers), Methodist Church, N Yorks Valuation Ct, NE Yorks C of C, Green Democrats, Lib Democrat Christian Forum; dep chm Ryedale Constituency Lib Democrats; *Recreations* painting, gliding, reading, renovating historic bldgs (with wife, restored Healaugh Priory 1981-86), writing; *Style—* Cncllr Ford Longman; Glebe House, Sheriff Hulton, York YO6 1PX (☎ 034 77683)

LONGMAN, Peter Martin; s of Denis Martin Longman, of Som, and Mary Joy, *née* Simmonds (d 1977); *b* 2 March 1946; *Educ* Huish's Sch Taunton, Univ Coll Cardiff (BSc), Univ of Manchester (Drama); *m* 22 May 1976, Sylvia June, da of John Lancaster Prentice, of E Sussex; 2 da (Tania Louise b 1978, Natalie Therese b 1981); *Career* housing arts offr Arts Cncl GB 1969-78 (Fin Dept 1968-69), dep dir Crafts Cncl 1978-83, dir and sec Museums & Galleries Cmmn 1990- (dep sec 1983-84, sec 1984-); sec working pty reports on: Trg Arts Admins Arts Cncl 1971, Area Museum Cncls and Servs HMSO 1984, Museums in Scot HMSO 1986; memb: Arts Centres Panel Gtr London Arts Assoc 1981-83, Bd of Caryl Jenner Prodns Ltd (Unicorn Theatre for Children) 1983-87, Cncl Textile Conservation Centre Ltd 1983-, co-opted Bd Scot Museums Cncl 1986-; FRSA 1989; *Recreations* discovering Britain, listening to music; *Style—* Peter Longman, Esq; Museums & Galleries Cmmn, 16 Queen Annes Gate, London SW1H 9AA (☎ 071 233 4200, fax 071 233 3686)

LONGMORE, Andrew Centlivres; QC (1983); s of Dr John Bell Longmore (d 1973), of Shrewsbury, and Virginia Albertina, *née* Centlivres; *b* 25 Aug 1944; *Educ* Winchester, Lincoln Coll Oxford (MA); *m* 17 Oct 1979, Margaret Murray, da of Dr James McNair (d 1980), of Milngavie, Glasgow; 1 s (James Centlivres b 1981); *Career* called to the Bar Middle Temple 1966; memb Bar Cncl 1982-85, chm Law Reform Ctee 1987-; *Books* MacGillivray and Parkington, Law of Insurance (co-ed, 6 edn 1975, 7 edn 1981, 8 edn 1988); *Recreations* fell-walking; *Style—* Andrew Longmore, Esq, QC; 7 Kings Bench Walk, Temple, London EC4 (☎ 071 583 0404)

LONGMORE, Prof Donald Bernard; s of Bernard George Longmore, of Wolverley, Sandown Rd, Sandwich, Kent, and Beatrix Alice, *née* Payne; *b* 20 Feb 1928; *Educ* Solihull Sch, Guys Hosp Med Sch (MB BS), Baylor Univ Texas, Univ of Texas, The London Hosp; *m* 2 April 1956, Patricia Christine Greig, da of Arthur Hardman Spindler (d 1984), of Bray on Thames, Berks; 3 da (Annabel b 1958, Juliet b 1959, Susan b 1962); *Career* Guy's Hosp: house appts 1953, jr lectr in anatomy 1954; surgical resident Baylor Univ Texas 1956-58, surgical registrar London Hosp 1958-59, sr registrar Middx Hosp 1960-61, lectr in surgery St Thomas' Hosp 1962-63, conslt Nat Heart Hosp 1963-83, dir Magnetic Resonance Unit Royal Brompton Hosp and Nat Heart Hosp 1983-, cardiac surgn and memb Britain's first heart transplant team, co fndr Coronary Artery Disease Res Assoc (CORDA) (memb bd of mgmnt), personal chair Univ of London; LRCP, FRCS, FRCSE, memb Br Inst Radiology; *Books* over 250 scientific pubns incl: Spare Part Surgery (1968), Machines in Medicine (1969), The Heart (1970), The Current Status of Cardiac Surgery (1975), Modern Cardiac Surgery (1978), Towards Safer Cardiac Surgery (1981); *Recreations* sailing, skiing; *Clubs* Royal Yacht Sqdn, Utd Hosps SC; *Style—* Prof Donald Longmore; Whitemayes, Chertsey Lane, Staines TW18 3LQ (☎ 0784 452436); Aldebaran, Flaine, France; Magnetic Resonance Unit, Royal Brompton Imaging Research, 30 Britten St, Chelsea SW3 6NN (☎ 071 351 5773, fax 071 351 4986)

LONGMORE, Lady Felicity Ann; da of 1 Earl Wavell; *b* 1921; *m* 1947, Maj Peter Maitland Longmore, MC, (RA); 1 s (and 1 s decd), 2 da; *Career* Co Cllr W Sussex 1981-; chm Social Services Ctee 1985-89; *Style—* The Lady Felicity Longmore; Bramleys, Funtington, Chichester

LONGMORE, Hon Mrs (Jean Mary); only da of 2 Baron Forres (d 1954), of Glenogil, Scotland; *m* 28 April 1941, Wing Cdr (William) James Maitland Longmore, CBE (d 1988), 2 s of Air Chief Marshal Sir Arthur Murray Longmore, GCB, DSO (d 1970); 3 da (Virginia, Carolyn, Jennifer); *Style—* The Hon Mrs Longmore; Cross Lane Cottage, Stake lane, Ashton, Bishops Waltham, Hants SO3 1FL (☎ 0489 892794)

LONGMORE, (Charles John) Nigel; DL (Herts 1971); s of Brig John Alexander Longmore, CB, CBE, TD, DL (d 1973), and Marguerite Madeleine, *née* Chapman Mathews; *b* 2 April 1933; *Educ* Harrow; *m* 1973 (m dis 1983), Celia Jane, *née* Walker; 1 da (Alexandra b 26 March 1975); *Career* admitted slr 1960; sr ptnr Longmores Hertford 1969; Dep Sheriff for Co of Herts 1960-69, Under Sheriff for Co of Herts 1969-; clerk to HM Cmmrs of Taxes for Hertford and Stevenage Divns 1965-, dep coroner 1986-; co cmmr, subsequently co cdr, now co pres St John Ambulance Bde for Herts; KStJ 1980, CStJ 1975, OStJ 1949; life govr Haileybury and Imperial Service Coll 1966-; pres Herts Agric Soc 1979-80; *Recreations* painting, shooting, fishing; *Clubs* Arts, Chelsea Arts; *Style—* Nigel Longmore, Esq, DL; Longmores, Solicitors, 24 Castle Street, Hertford SG14 1HP (☎ 0992 586781)

LONGRIGG, Roger Erskine; s of Brig Stephen Hemsley Longrigg, OBE, of Chancellor House, Tunbridge Wells (d 1979) and Florence Amy, *née* Anderson (d 1974); *b* 1 May 1929; *Educ* Bryanston Sch, Magdalen Coll Oxford (BA); *m* 20 July 1957, Jane Catherine, da of Capt Marcus Beresford Chichester, of Compton Chamberlyne, Wilts (d 1985); 3 da (Laura b 1958, Frances b 1961, Clare b 1963); *Career* entered army 1947, cmmnd Buffs 1948, demob 1949; joined TA 1952, Capt 1955; *Books* author of over 50 published books (pseudonyms incl Rosalind Erskine, Ivor Drummond, Laura Black, Domini Taylor); novels incl: High Pitched Buzz (1956), Daughters of Mulberry (1961), The Paper Boats (1965), The Desperate Criminals (1972), Bad Bet (1981), Mother Love (1983), Siege (1989); non fiction incl: The History of Horse Racing (1972), The History of Foxhunting (1975), The English Squire and His Sport (1977); *Recreations* trout fishing, painting; *Clubs* Brooks's, Pratt's; *Style—* Roger Longrigg, Esq; Orchard House, Crookham, Hampshire (☎ 0252 850333)

LONGSDON, Anthony Ernest Cross; s of Ernest Morewood Longsdon (d 1940), of Little Longstone, and Esther Chappé, *née* Cross (d 1956); family living at Little Longstone since 1507; *b* 12 March 1911; *Educ* Shrewsbury, Pembroke Coll Cambridge (BA); *m* 23 Sept 1936, Hilda Dearmer, da of John Cawley (d 1924), of Buxton; *Career* mining engr Trepca Yugoslavia 1933-36; civil engr J Mowlem 1936-46; farmer 1946-; *Recreations* fishing; *Style—* Anthony Longsdon, Esq; The Manor, Little Longstone, nr Bakewell, Derbyshire (☎ 062 987 215)

LONGSDON, Lt-Col (Robert) Shaun; s of late Wing Cdr Robert Cyril Longsdon, of Foxcote, Warwicks, and Evadne Lloyd, *née* Flower; *b* 5 Dec 1936; *Educ* Eton; *m* 19 Dec 1968, Caroline Susan, da of Col Michael Colvin Watson, OBE, MC, TD, of Barnsley, Gloucs; 3 s (James b 1971, Rupert b 1972, Charles b 1975), 1 da (Laura b 1983); *Career* reg Army Offr 1955-81; princ mil appts: Lt Col, mil asst (GSO1) to the Chief of Gen Staff 1975-77, CO 17/21 Lancers 1977-79, directing staff (GSO1 DS) NDC 1979-81; dir of mktg Knight Frank & Rutley 1981-; Ensign of the Queen's Body Gd of the Yeomen of the Guard 1985-, Col 17/21 Lancers 1988; govr RSC 1982-; *Recreations* field sports; *Clubs* White's, Cavalry and Guards, Pratt's; *Style—* Lt-Col Shaun Longsdon; Southrop Lodge, Lechlade, Glos GL7 3NU (☎ 036 785 284); 20 Hanover Square, London W1R 0AH

LONGSON, Geoffrey John; s of late Arthur Walter Longson, and late Mary Margaret, *née* Pratt; *b* 1 Aug 1935; *Educ* Tiffin Sch Kingston upon Thames, Guys Hosp Dental Sch (Open scholar, LDS, RCS (Eng), Newland Pedley prize), Univ of London BDS; *m* Aug 1959, Dianne Frances Isaac; 1 s (Mark Frazer), 1 da (Tanya Clare Marie); *Partner* Heather Jane Sutherland; 1 da (Olivia Jane Scott); *Career* dental surgn; in private practice Harley St and Fleet Hampshire; FRSM; fell: Int Acad of Implantology, Int Coll of Dentists; memb: American Acad of Gnathology, European Acad of Gnathology; *Style—* Geoffrey Longson, Esq; 130 Harley St, London W1N 1AH (☎ 071 636 6082, fax 071 935 2385, car 0836 690 207)

LONGSTAFF, Bernard; s of Joseph Longstaff (d 1980), of Wade House, Dewsbury, and Agnes Longstaff (d 1975); *b* 14 April 1939; *Educ* St Paulinus RC Sch Dewsbury, Dewsbury Tech Sch, Wakefield Tech Coll; *Career* md and chm Elco Power Plant Ltd (British Overseas Trade Bd's export award for small mfrg businesses 1982; Queen's Award for Export 1983); md S & B Longstaff Ltd; *Recreations* tennis, horses, farming, swimming; *Style—* Bernard Longstaff, Esq; Elco Power Plant Ltd, Station Rd, Tadcaster, N Yorks (☎ 0937 835834); Langdale House, York Rd, Malton, N Yorks (☎ 0653 5021)

LONGSTAFF, Wilfred; s of Thomas Longstaff (d 1980), and Phoebe Alice Calvert, *née* Rain; *b* 10 Dec 1931; *Educ* Tottenham Tech Coll, Northern Poly (Dip Arch); *m* 1 Aug 1959, Stephanie Maria, da of John Joseph Macken (d 1958); 2 s (Wilfred b 1960, David b 1961); *Career* RE Corpl served Cyprus and Egypt; chief architect Courage Eastern Ltd 1975-80, chartered architect in private practice 1983-; ARIBA, FFAS; *Recreations* golf; *Clubs* Goring & Streatley Golf; *Style—* Wilfred Longstaff, Esq; 7 Cambrian Way, The Orchard, Calcot, Reading, Berkshire RG3 7DD (☎ 0734 419152)

LONGUËIL; *see*: de Longuëil

LONGWELL, Dennis Charles; s of Charles Longwell, of San Diego, California, USA, and Viola, *née* Nelson; *b* 30 Aug 1941; *Educ* Evanston HS Evanston Illinois USA, Harvard Univ (BA), Stanford Business Sch Stanford USA (MBA); *m* 13 June 1964, Ashby, da of George Houghton Haslam, of Charlottesville, Virginia, USA; 2 s (John b 14 Sept 1970, David b 7 Dec 1972); *Career* US Army 1963-65: Lieut and ADC to Cmdg Gen Transportation Sch; The Chase Manhattan Bank: joined as credit trainee 1962, relationship mangr 1967, asst treas 1968, second vice pres 1969, vice pres 1970, asst sec to Mgmnt Ctee 1971, pres Chase Manhattan Bank of Centl NY (Syracuse) 1972-76, div exec Banks Corporate Industries Sector 1976, gp exec 1977, country mangr UK 1982, sr vice pres 1981, area exec for Europe Africa and M East; chm American Banks Assoc of London 1986-88, memb bd of govrs and managing cncl Ditchley Fndn; *Recreations* golf, sailing, boating, travel; *Clubs* Buck's, Annabel's, Harry's Bar, Sky Club of New York City; *Style—* Dennis Longwell, Esq; The Chase Manhattan Bank NA, Woolgate House, Coleman St, London EC2P 2HD (☎ 071 726 5200, fax 071 726 5909, telex 8813137)

LONGWILL, Col John Alexander Rankin; s of Matthew Rankin Longwill (d 1983), of Plymouth, and Winifred Lilian, *née* Sleath; *b* 5 Sept 1939; *Educ* Liverpool Coll, Liverpool Univ Med Sch (MB ChB), DTM and H London (DTM and H, DCH), RCOG London (DObst); *m* 5 Jan 1973, Say Fah, da of Shu Pi Chu (d 1965), of Singapore; 2 s (Toby b 1975, Andrew b 1979), 2 da (Sarah b 1973, Katie b 1977); *Career* British Army; cmmnd 1962, Capt RMO regular army Aden 1966-67; Maj SMO: Trucial Oman Scouts 1968-70, Anzuk FMC Singapore 1971-73, Minden BAOR 1974-77; Lt Col anaesthetist: BMH Belfast 1980, QEMH Woolwich 1980-83; detached anaesthetist: mine field surgical team Belize 1981, mil wing MPH Belfast 1982; cmdg offr BMG Falkland Islands 1983-84 (FMA), SMO Tutong Brunei 1984-87 (Royal Brunei Armed Forces, loan serv), Col SMO Hereford (HQ R Divn) BAOR 1987-; MRCGP 1971, BMA 1964; GSM Brunei 1985, Royal Brunei Armed Forces Jubilee Medal 1986; *Recreations* bloodhounds, photography, fishing; *Clubs* RAMC Mill Bank, The Bloodhound; *Style—* Col John Longwill; 8 Oxford Close, Bassingbourn, nr Royston, Hertfordshire SG8 5LL

LONGWORTH, Dr Ian Heaps; s of Joseph Longworth (d 1968), of Bolton, Lancs, and Alice, *née* Heaps (d 1961); *b* 29 Sept 1935; *Educ* King Edward VII Lytham, Peterhouse Cambridge (MA, PhD); *m* 27 Sept 1967, Clare Marian, da of Maurice Edwin Titford (d 1967), of Croydon; 1 s (Timothy b 1975), 1 da (Alison b 1978); *Career* Br Museum: asst keeper Dept of Br and Medieval Antiquities 1963-69, keeper Dept of Prehistoric and Romano British Antiquities 1973- (asst keeper 1969-73); memb Ancient Monuments Bd for England 1977-84, chm Area Archaeological Advsy Ctee for NW England 1978-79; vice pres Soc of Antiquaries 1985-88 (fell 1966, sec 1974-80); *Books* Durrington Walls - Excavations 1966-68 (with G J Wainwright, 1971), Collared Urns of the Bronze Age in GB and Ireland (1984), Prehistoric Britain (1985), Catalogue of the Excavated Prehistoric and Romano British Material in the Greenwell Collection (with I A Kinnes, 1985), Archaeology in Britain since 1945 (ed with J Cherry, 1986), Excavations at Grimes Graves Norfolk 1972-76 (contrib, 1988); *Clubs* MCC; *Style—* Dr Ian Longworth; 2 Hurst View Rd, S Croydon, Surrey CR2 7A6 (☎ 081 688 4960); Dept of Prehistoric and Romano-British Antiquities, British Museum, London WC1B 3DG (☎ 071 323 8293)

LONSDALE, 7 Earl of (UK 1807); Sir James Hugh William Lowther; 8 Bt (GB 1764); also Viscount and Baron Lowther (GB 1797); s of Viscount Lowther (d 1949, er s of 6 Earl); suc gf 1953; *b* 3 Nov 1922; *Educ* Eton; *m* 1, 1945 (m dis 1954), Tuppina Cecily (decd), da of late Capt C H Bennett; 1 s, 1 da; m 2, 1954 (m dis 1962), Hon Jennifer Lowther, da of late Maj the Hon Christopher William Lowther (himself s of 1 Viscount Ullswater); 1 s, 2 da; m 3, 1963, Nancy Ruth Stephenson, da of late Thomas Cobbs, of Pacific Palisades, Cal, USA; 1 s; m 4, 1975, Caroline Sheila, da of Sir Gerald Gordon Ley, 3 Bt, TD; 1 s, 1 da; *Heir* s, Viscount Lowther; *Career* served WWII 1939-45 RAC and as Capt E Riding Yeo (despatches); structural engr 1947-50, farmer, forester and dir of associated and local cos in Cumberland and Westmorland and of Border Television (now ret); memb The Sports Cncl 1971-74, English Tourist Bd 1971-75; pres Cumberland and Westmorland NPFA; CBIM, FRSA; *Clubs* Brooks's, Turf; *Style—* The Rt Hon the Earl of Lonsdale; Askham Hall, Penrith, Cumbria CA10 2PF (☎ 09312 208)

LOOKER, Roger Frank; *b* 20 Oct 1951; *Educ* Univ of Bristol (LLB); *Career* barr; dir Rea Brothers Ltd; *Recreations* rugby football; *Clubs* RAC, Harlequin Football (Chairman); *Style—* Roger Looker, Esq; Rea Brothers Ltd, Aldermans House, Aldermans Walk, London EC2M 3XR (☎ 071 623 1155, fax 071 623 2694)

LOOMES, Brian Robert; s of late Robert Loomes, and Dorothy, *née* Barratt; *b* 3 April 1938; *Educ* West Leeds HS, Univ of Leeds (BA); *m* 25 Jan 1966, Emily (Joy), da of late Robert Gartside, of Sheffield; 1 s (Robert b 1968); *Career* Civil Serv 1960-63, business 1963-66, self employed as dealer in antique clocks 1966-; fell Soc of Genealogists; *Books* 15 titles on antique clocks incl: White Dial Clocks (1974), Watch and Clock Makers of the World (1976), Complete British Clocks (1978), Grandfather Clocks and their Cases (1985) Antique British Clocks Illustrated (1991), Antique British Clocks: A Buyer's Guide (1991); *Recreations* horological research; *Style—* Brian Loomes, Esq; Calf Haugh Farmhouse, Pateley Bridge, via Harrogate, North Yorks (☎ 0423 711163)

LOOSEMORE, Sarah Jane; da of John Harrington Loosemore, of Cardiff, and Pamela Kay, *née* Bowyer; *b* 15 June 1971; *Educ* Bishop of Llandaff HS, New Coll Cardiff; *Career* professional tennis player; achievements incl: Junior Br Nat champion (under 14, under 16, under 18), Welsh Senior champion 1985, Senior Br Nat champion 1988, runner up Singapore Open 1990; represented Wales at sr level 1985-, represented GB Federation Cup 1990 (quarter-finalist); Welsh jr sports personality of the year 1985; *Recreations* hockey, golf, reading, music, theatre; *Style—* Miss Sarah Loosemore; The Abington Management Company Limited, 14 Old Park Lane, London W1Y 3LM (☎ 071 355 4464, fax 071 499 1154)

LOPES, Hon George Edward; yr s of 2 Baron Roborough, *qv*; *b* 22 Feb 1945; *Educ* Eton, RAC Cirencester; *m* 1975, Hon Sarah Violet Astor, da of 2 Baron Astor of Hever (d 1984); 1 s, 2 da; *Style—* The Hon George Lopes; Gnaton Hall, Yealmpton, Plymouth, Devon PL8 2HU

LOPES, Hon Henry Massey; s and h of 2 Baron Roborough; *b* 2 Feb 1940; *Educ* Eton; *m* 1, 1968 (m dis 1986), Robyn Zenda Carol, da of John Bromwich, of Point Lonsdale, Victoria, Aust; 2 s (Massey b 1969, Andrew b 1971), 2 da (Katie b 1976, Melinda b 1978); m 2, 1986, Sarah Anne Pipon, da of Colin Baker, of Peter Tavy, Devon; 2 da (Emily b 1987, Louisa b 1989); *Career* landowner; *Style—* The Hon Henry Lopes; Bickham House, Roborough, Plymouth (☎ 0822 852742)

LOPEZ, Paul Anthony; s of Anthony William Lopez, of Wolverhampton, and Lillian, *née* Rowley; *b* 22 Oct 1959; *Educ* Pendeford HS Wolverhampton, Univ of Birmingham (LLB); *m* 3 Nov 1984, Diana Douglas, da of Douglas Black (d 1982); *Career* called to the Bar Middle Temple 1982; memb: Family Law Bar Assoc, Birmingham Family Law Bar Assoc, Birmingham Medico-Legal Soc; *Recreations* horse riding, history, working; *Style—* Paul Lopez, Esq; 1 Canford Crescent, Codsall, Wolverhampton WV8 2AF (☎ 09074 7150); 9 Fountain Court, Steelhouse Lane, Birmingham B4 6DR (☎ 021 236 0863 0929, fax 021 236 6961)

LOPPERT, Max Jeremy; *b* 24 Aug 1944; *Educ* Hyde Park Sch Johannesburg, Univ of Witwatersrand Johannesburg (BA), Univ of York (BA); *m* Delayne, *née* Aarons; *Career* freelance music critic Venice and London 1972-76, teacher Oxford Sch Venice 1972, chief music and opera critic Financial Times 1980- (joined staff 1976), assoc ed Opera Magazine 1986-; memb Critics Circle London 1974; *Recreations* cooking, cinema, swimming, walking, in Richmond Park; *Style—* Max Loppert, Esq; Financial Times, 1 Southwark Bridge, London SE1 9HL; Opera, 1a Mountgrove Rd, London N5 2LU

LORAM, Vice Adm Sir David Anning; KCB (1979), LVO (1957); s of John Anning Loram (d 1969), and Jessie Eckford, *née* Scott (d 1961); *b* 24 July 1924; *Educ* RNC Dartmouth, King's Dirk; *m* 1, 1958 (m dis 1981), Fiona, *née* Beloe; 3 s; m 2, 1983 (m dis 1990), Diana, *née* Keigwin; *Career* RN: served WWII, ADC to Govr Gen NZ 1946-48, equerry to HM The Queen 1954-57, flag offr Malta and NATO Cdr SE Med and Cdr Br Forces 1973-75, Cmdt Nat Def Coll 1975-77, Dep Supreme Allied Cdr Atlantic 1977-80; a gentleman usher to HM The Queen 1982-; memb RN Cresta Team 1954-59, qualified helicopter pilot; *Recreations* fishing; *Style—* Vice Adm Sir David Loram, KCB, LVO; Sparkford Hall, Sparkford, Somerset BA22 7LD (☎ 0963 40834)

LORD, Alan; CB (1972); s of Frederick Lord; *b* 12 April 1929; *Educ* Rochdale, St John's Coll Cambridge (BA, MA); *m* Joan; 2 da; *Career* former cmmr and dep chm Inland Revenue, and second perm sec Treasury; dir Allied Breweries 1979-86, md Dunlop Hldgs 1980-84 (md Dunlop Int 1978-80), dir Bank of England 1983-86; dep chm and chief exec Lloyd's of London 1986-; *Style—* Alan Lord, Esq, CB; Mardens, Hildenborough, Tonbridge, Kent (☎ 0732 832268)

LORD, David Gerald; s of Lt Cdr Cuthbert Edward Lord, RN (ret), of Petersfield, Hants, and Nancy Muriel, *née* Gibson; *b* 14 Dec 1947; *Educ* Repton, Trinity Coll Dublin (BA); *m* 2 Sept 1978, (Diana) Jennifer, Herbert Louis Benjamin; 1 s (Benjamin Edward b 1979), 2 da (Philippa Katherine, Jessica Rachel); *Career* First Nat Bank Dallas 1971, Chase Manhattan Bank NA (London), exec dir Continental Illinois Ltd (Tokyo) 1974 (joined London office 1973, assoc dir 1980), md First Interstate Capital Mkts Ltd (formerly Continental Illinois) 1987- (joined 1984); *Recreations* sailing, skiing, golf; *Clubs* Boodle's Oriental; *Style—* David Lord, Esq; 30 Old Park Avenue, London SW12 (☎ 081 675 1700); The Coach House, Stanhoe Norfolk, 6 Agar St, London WC2 (☎ 071 379 5915, telex 947161)

LORD, Geoffrey; OBE (1989); s of Frank Lord (d 1978), of Rochdale, and Edith, *née* Sanderson; *b* 24 Feb 1928; *Educ* Rochdale GS, Univ of Bradford (MA); *m* 15 Sept 1955, Jean; 1 s (Andrew Nicholas b 1962), 1 da (Karen Janet b 1959); *Career* Midland Bank Ltd (AIB) 1944-58, Gtr Manchester Probation Serv 1958-77 (dep chief probation offr 1974-77), sec and treas Carnegie UK Tst 1977-; chm Pollock Meml Missionary Tst, pres Centre for Environmental Interpretation, vice pres The Selcare Tst; tstee: Home Start Consultancy, Charities Effectiveness Review Tst; chm Unemployed Voluntary Action Fund, sec and treas Adapt Fund; hon fell Manchester Poly 1987; FRSA 1985; *Books* The Arts and Disabilities (1981); *Recreations* arts; *Clubs* New (Edinburgh); *Style—* Geoffrey Lord, Esq, OBE; Carnegie United Kingdom Trust, Comely Park House, Dunfermline, Fife KY12 7EJ (☎ 0383 721445, fax 0383 620682)

LORD, Graham John; s of Harold Reginald Lord, OBE (d 1969), of Beira, Mozambique, and Ida Frances, *née* McDowall (d 1966); *b* 16 Feb 1943; *Educ* Falcon Coll Essexvale Bulawayo Rhodesia, Churchill Coll Cambridge (BA); *m* 12 Sept 1962 (m dis 1990), Jane, *née* Carruthers; 2 da (Mandy b 1963, Kate b 1966); *Career* ed Varsity Cambridge 1964; reporter: Cambridge Evening News 1964, Sunday Express 1965- (literary ed 1969-, launched Sunday Express Book of the Year Award 1987-); Lambourn parish cncllr 1983-87, vice chm Newbury Mencap 1982-88, chm Eastbury Poor's Furze Charity 1983-88, memb Sub Ctee W Berks Cons Assoc Exec 1985-88, cncllr Newbury DC 1985-87; *Books* Marshmallow Pie (1970), A Roof Under Your Feet (1973), The Spider and The Fly (1974), God and All His Angels (1976), The Nostradamus Horoscope (1981), Time Out Of Mind (1986); Return to Africa (1991); *Recreations* walking, tennis; *Clubs* Academy, Chelsea Arts; *Style—* Graham Lord, Esq; Sunday Express, 245 Blackfriars Rd, London SE1 9UX (☎ 071 922 7330)

LORD, His Honour Judge; John Herent; s of Sir Frank Lord, KBE, DL, JP (d 1974); *b* 5 Nov 1928; *Educ* Manchester GS, Merton Coll Oxford (MA); *m* 1959, June Ann, da of George Caladine (d 1969); 3 s; *Career* called to the Bar Inner Temple 1951; Jr Northern Circuit 1952, asst rec Burnley 1971, rec of Crown Ct 1972-78, circuit judge 1978-; *Recreations* photography, shooting, boating; *Clubs* Leander, St James's (Manchester); *Style—* His Honour Judge Lord; Three Lanes, Greenfield, Oldham, Lancashire (☎ 0457 872198)

LORD, John William; s of William James Lord (d 1970), and Bessie Maria, *née* Watkins; *b* 28 May 1931; *Educ* Gravesend GS for Boys; *m* 28 April 1956, Patricia Jane, da of Maj Frank Palmer (d 1979); 3 s (David b 1964, Richard b 1966, Peter b 1971); *Career* Nat Serv RAF 1953-55; articled clerk MacIntyre Hudson and Co 1948-53, qualified CA, audit mangr Evans Fripp Deed and Co 1955-57, tax mangr Midgley Snelling and Co 1957-60, sr ptnr Carley and Co 1983- (mangr 1961, ptnr 1962-); dir and sec Gravesend Masonic Hall Co Ltd; former: pres of Gravesend Chamber of Trade, chm Gravesend Round Table; memb Assoc of Ex Round Tablers; FCA 1953, ATII 1962; *Recreations* golf, tennis, gardening; *Clubs* Mid Kent Golf; *Style—* John Lord, Esq; Lark Rise, Pondfield Lane, Shorne, nr Gravesend, Kent DA12 3LD; 8 Overcliffe, Gravesend, Kent DA11 0HJ (☎ 0474 569032, fax 0474 320410)

LORD, Michael Nicholson; MP (C) Suffolk Central 1983-; s of John Lord, and Jessie, *née* Nicholson; *b* 17 Oct 1938; *Educ* Christs Coll Cambridge (MA); *m* 1965, Jennifer Margaret, *née* Childs; 1 s, 1 da; *Recreations* golf, sailing, trees; *Clubs* Farmers; *Style—* Michael Lord, Esq, MP; House of Commons, London SW1

LORD, Peter Herent; OBE (1991); s of Sir Frank Lord, KBE, of Oldham, and Rosalie Jeanette, *née* Herent; *b* 23 Nov 1925; *Educ* Manchester GS, St Johns Coll Cambridge, St Georges Hosp London (MChir); *m* 9 Aug 1952, Florence Shirley, *née* Hirst; 2 s (Frank Herent b 18 July 1954, Peter Herent b 21 Jan 1960), 2 da (Rozanne b 1 June 1953, Janine Herent (Mrs Railton) b 3 March 1957); *Career* Nat Serv, Capt RAMC 1953-54; house offr Christee Hosp Manchester 1952, sr registrar St George's Hosp 1956-63 (former registrar), H N Smith res fell RCP 1964, conslt surgn Wycombe Gen Hosp 1965-; memb Cncl RCS 1978- (vice-pres 1986-88); Past Master Worshipful Co of Barbers 1978; memb RSM; FRCS; *Recreations* sailing, sea fishing, photography; *Clubs* Leander; *Style—* Peter Lord, Esq, OBE; Holly Tree House, 39 Grove Rd, Beaconsfield, Bucks HP9 1PE (☎ 0494 67 4488); 14 Anchor Down, Solva, Pembrokeshire (☎ 0437 721 266)

LORD, Peter John; s of Godfrey Albert Lord, MBE (d April 1985), of Welwyn Garden City, and Rose, *née* Clark (d June 1983); *b* 1 Sept 1929; *Educ* Welwyn Garden City GS, The Architectural Assoc (AADipl); *m* 10 March 1956, (Dorothy) Shirley May, da of Reginald Munday (d 1973), of Hatfield; 1 da (Kathryn Jane b 8 Nov 1958); *Career* Nat Serv 1951-53, cmmnd RE and late AER; Austin-Smith: Lord (formerly J M Austin & Ptnrs): architect 1953-56, ptnr 1956, sr ptnr 1980; work incl: Warrington town plan, housing for LB Hillingdon and Warrington DC, offices for CEGB, Touche Ross and Deloittes, gallery shop and cafeteria for Br Museum, shops offices and warehouses for Heffers Booksellers and Stationers; awards: MOHLG, RIBA Nat and Regal, Civil Tst, NW Reg Energy; commendations: Civic Trust, Fiji Assoc of Architects; winner Albert Docks Casement Competition; hon memb: Industl Designers Soc of SA, Union Des Designers En Beligique; pres Int Cncl of Societies of Industl Design 1985-87; Freeman: City of London 1986, Worshipful Co of Chartered Architects 1986; memb: RIBA, PPCSD; FBIM, FRSA; *Books* Materials Handling in Factories and Warehouses (1963), The Concept of Professionalism in the Field of Design (1968), author of various articles in jls and magazines; *Recreations* fishing, horology, ornithology, photography; *Clubs* Arts; *Style—* Peter Lord, Esq; Sperberry Hill House, St Ippollitts, Herts SG4 7PA (☎ 0462 434297); Austin-Smith: Lord, 10-12 Carlisle Street, London W1V 5RF (☎ 071 734 6161, fax 071 439 2043, telex 267086 ASL G)

LORD, Richard Denyer; s of Arthur James Lord, and Daphne Anne, *née* Denyer; *b* 2

Jan 1959; *Educ* Stowe, Sidney Sussex Coll Cambridge (MA); *Career* called to the Bar Inner Temple 1981; *Books* Controlled Drugs: Law & Practice (1984); *Recreations* cricket; *Style—* Richard Lord, Esq; 12 Battishill St, London N1 1TE (☎ 071 359 7816); Brick Court Chambers, 15-19 Devereux Ct, London WC2R 3JJ (☎ 071 583 0777, fax 071 583 9401)

LORD, Richard Thomas Geoffrey; s of Sam Lord; *b* 29 March 1934; *Educ* Giggleswick Sch, Univ of Leeds; *m* 1959, Elizabeth Logie, *née* Forrester; 1 s, 2 da; *Career* chartered textile technologist; dir Scapa Group plc 1976-84 (joined 1955), Lancashire County Enterprises Ltd 1985-; business conslt; pres Chorley Cons Assoc 1988- (chm 1985-88); *Recreations* golf, local politics, old maps; *Clubs* District & Union (Blackburn), Pleasington Golf; *Style—* Richard Lord, Esq; Cuerden Lodge, Bamber Bridge, Preston PR5 6AU (☎ 0772 35326)

LORD, Rodney Arthur Lionel; s of Lionel Cornwallis Lord (d 1946), and Marjorie Agnes, *née* Webb-Jones; *b* 13 Jan 1946; *Educ* Christ's Hospital, Christ Church Oxford (MA); *m* 3 April 1971, Diana Mary, da of Neville Stanley Howarth, of Craglands, Clawthorpe, Burton, Carnforth, Lancs; 1 s (Simon b 1974), 1 da (Anna b 1977); *Career* fin writer Investors Review 1967-69, econs corr and columnist Daily Telegraph 1969-81, visiting res fell City Univ Business Sch 1981-82, special advsr HM Treasy 1983-86, econs ed The Times 1986-90, dir Privatisation International 1988-; *Books* Value for Money in Education (1984); *Recreations* sailing, music; *Style—* Rodney Lord, Esq; The Times, 1 Pennington St, London E1 9XN (☎ 071 782 5749, fax 071 782 5112, telex 262141)

LORENZ, Anthony Michael; s of Andre Lorenz (d 1986), and Mitzi Lorenz; *b* 7 Dec 1947; *Educ* Arnold House Sch, Charterhouse; *m* 1 Feb 1986, Suzanna Jane, da of Louis Solomon; 1 s (David Alexander b 5 June 1986), 1 da (Charlaine Alexandra b 15 Nov 1978); *Career* sr ptnr Baker Lorenz Estate Agents; former chm Fund-raising Ctee Multiple Sclerosis Soc; *Recreations* flying, polo, shooting, skiing; *Clubs* Hurlingham, Ham Polo; *Style—* Anthony Lorenz, Esq; 25 Hanover Square, London W1R 0DQ (☎ 071 409 2121, fax 071 493 3812, telex 894113)

LORETTO, Denis Crofton; s of Cecil Rupert Loretto, MM (d 1976), of Belfast, and Violet Florence, *née* Walker; *b* 7 April 1936; *Educ* Royal Belfast Academical Inst; *m* 17 March 1960, (Margaret) Wilma, da of William Alexander Campbell (d 1986), of Belfast; 1 s (Timothy 1961), 1 da (Angela b 1964); *Career* Cornhill Insur 1953-: branch underwriter Belfast 1953-59, head office underwriter London 1959-62, branch supt Belfast 1962-72, asst branch mangr Belfast 1972-74, branch mangr Belfast 1974-81, div mangr underwriting head off 1981-86, asst gen mangr Guildford 1986-; dir: Trafalgar Insur plc 1988, Br Reserve Insur Co Ltd 1988 (md 1989-), Cornhill Insur plc 1989, Allianz UK Ltd 1989, Allianz Legal Protection Insur Co Ltd 1989; memb The Northern Ireland Partnership; Belfast city cncllr 1977-81; FCII 1961; *Recreations* walking, photography; *Style—* Denis Loretto, Esq; 107 Lower Road, Fetcham, Leatherhead, Surrey KT22 9NQ (☎ 0372 453276); 57 Ladymead, Guildford, Surrey GU1 1DB (☎ 0483 68161, fax 0483 3009 52, telex 859383)

LORETTO, Prof Michael Henry; s of Carlo Claude Loretto (d 1963), of Caterham, Surrey, and Carrie, *née* Hill (d 1984); *b* 3 Dec 1930; *Educ* Caterham Sch, Univ of Sheffield (BMet); *m* 28 Aug 1955, Nita Margery, da of Henry Hill, of Neath, S Wales; 2 s (Peter b 1959, David b 1962), 3 da (Anne b 1963, Frances b 1965, Catherine b 1969); *Career* res offr CSIRO Melbourne Aust 1955-62 and 1963-66, visiting fell Cavendish Laboratory Cambridge UK 1962-63, prof and IRC dir Univ of Birmingham 1989- (lectr 1966-70, sr lectr 1970-80, head Sch of Metallurgy and Materials 1988-89); memb SERC Ctee: Inst of Metals, Inst of Physics; memb Cncl Birmingham Metallurgical Assoc (past pres); FIM, FInstP; *Books* Defect Analysis in Electron Microscopy (1976), Electron Beam Analysis of Materials (1983); *Recreations* music, walking; *Style—* Prof Michael Loretto; 54 Selwyn Rd, Edgbaston, Birmingham B16 0SW (☎ 021 454 3975); IRC in Materials for High Performance Applications, The University of Birmingham, Edgbaston, Birmingham B15 2TT (☎ 021 414 5214, fax 021 414 5232)

LORIMER, Sir (Thomas) Desmond; s of Thomas Berry Lorimer (d 1952), and Sarah Ann Lorimer; *b* 20 Oct 1925; *Educ* Belfast Tech HS; *m* 1957, Patricia Doris, da of Ernest Samways; 2 da; *Career* CA 1948, in practice 1952-74; sr ptnr Harmood Banner Smylie & Co Belfast 1960, chm Lamont Holdings plc 1973-; dir: Ruberoid plc 1972-88, Northern Bank Ltd (chm 1985-), Irish Distillers plc 1986-, Old Bushmills Distillery 1986-; chm: Industl Devpt Bd for NI 1982-86, Ulster Soc of CAs 1960, NI Housing Exec 1971-75; memb Review Body on Local Govt in NI 1970; fell Inst of CAs in Ireland (pres 1968-69); kt 1976; *Recreations* gardening, golf; *Clubs* Carlton, Royal Co Down Golf, Royal Belfast Golf; *Style—* Sir Desmond Lorimer; Windwhistle Cottage, 6A Circular Road West, Cultra, Holywood, Co Down BT18 0AT (☎ 02317 3323)

LORIMER, Hew Martin; OBE (1986); s of late Sir Robert Stodart Lorimer, KBE, and Violet Alicia, *née* Wyld; *b* 22 May 1907; *Educ* Loretto, Edinburgh Coll of Art; *m* 1936, Mary McLeod (d 1970), da of HM Wylie, of Edinburgh; 2 s, 1 da; *Career* sculptor; 7 allegorical figures for Nat Library of Scotland 1952-55, Our Lady of the Isles and South Uist 1955-57, St Francis Dundee 1957-59; representative of Nat Tst in Scotland (based in Fife); Dr Royal Scottish Acad; fell: Edinburgh Coll of Art 1934-35, Incorporation of Br Sculptors; Hon LLD Univ of Dundee 1983; *Recreations* music, travel, home; *Style—* Hew Lorimer, Esq, OBE; Kellie Castle, Pittenweem, Anstruther, Fife KY10 2RF (☎ 033 38 323)

LORIMER, Patrick James; s of Lt-Cdr J T Lorimer, DSO, DL, of the Upper Church, Barr, Girvan, Ayrshire, and Judith Eileen, *née* Hughes Onslow; *b* 1 Oct 1946; *Educ* Wellington, Magdalene Coll Cambridge (MA, DipArch); *m* 25 Sept 1976, (Julia) Caroline, da of Patrick Pringle (d 1974); 2 s (James b 7 May 1979, William b 23 Dec 1980), 1 da (Cressida b 14 April 1984); *Career* qualified architect 1972, fndr own practice ARP Architects London & Scotland 1974-; capt Ice Hockey Team Univ of Cambridge 1968; Freeman City of London, Liveryman Worshipful Co of Loriners 1979; memb RIBA, ARCUK; *Recreations* joinery and building; *Style—* Patrick Lorimer, Esq; Gemilston House, Kirkmichael, Maybolc, Ayrshire (☎ 0292 268181)

LORING, Anthony Francis; s of Brig Walter Watson Alexander Loring, CBE (d 1987), and Patricia Eileen, *née* Quirke; *b* 10 Oct 1954; *Educ* Ampleforth, Bedford Coll, Univ of London (BA); *Career* admitted slr 1979; res ptnr McKenna & Co in Bahrain 1988- (ptnr England 1988); memb Law Soc; *Recreations* tennis, bridge, skiing; *Style—* Anthony Loring, Esq; PO Box 5783, Manama, Bahrain (☎ 973 590403); McKenna & Co, PO Box 5783, Manama, Bahrain (☎ 973 271922, telex 8896, fax 972 259030)

LORNE, Marquess of; Torquhil Ian Campbell; only s and h of 12 Duke of Argyll; *b* 29 May 1968; *Career* page of honour to HM The Queen 1981-83; *Style—* Marquess of Lorne

LOSINSKA, Kathleen Mary (Kate); *née* Conway; OBE (1986); da of James Henry Conway (d 1941), and Dorothea Marguerite (d 1977); *b* 5 Oct 1924; *Educ* Selhurst GS; *m* 1942, Stanislaw Losinski, s of Franciszek Losinski and Helena Dekutowska (d 1949); 1 s (Julian); *Career* entered Civil Serv 1939, Office of Population Censuses and Surveys, memb Mgmnt Cncl of Civil Serv Unions (previously chm of Cncl), pres Civil and Public Servs Assoc; govr Ruskin Coll Oxford, memb Cncl Peace through NATO, cmmr Civil Serv Appeals Bd, vice chm Civil Serv Retirement Fellowship, Ctee of Mgmnt Civil Serv Benevolent Fund; work for: Christian Trade Union Movement, Solidarnosc Polish Trade Unions; memb Gen Cncl TUC; Nuclear Energy Review Cmmr (TUC); Cavalier Order Odrodzemia Polski 1987; *Recreations* journalism, writing, music, history, archaeology; *Clubs* Civil Service; *Style—* Mrs Kate Losinska, OBE; Ballinard, Herbertstown, Limerick, Republic of Ireland (☎ 010 35361 85229); 31 Dornton Rd, Balham, London SW12 9NB (☎ 071 673 0458)

LOSOWSKY, Prof Monty Seymour; s of Myer Losowsky (d 1936), and Dora, *née* Gottlieb; *b* 1 Aug 1931; *Educ* Coopers' Company's Sch, Univ of Leeds (MB ChB, MD, MRCP); *m* 15 Aug 1971, Barbara; 1 s (Andrew b 1978), 1 da (Kathryn b 1973); *Career* res fell Harvard Med Unit Mass 1961-62, reader in med Univ Dept of Med Leeds Gen Infirmary 1966-69 (lectr 1962-64, sr lectr 1964-66), prof of Med Univ Dept of Med St James's Univ Hosp Leeds 1969-, dean Faculty of Med Univ of Leeds 1989-; memb: Panel of Studies allied to Med Univ Grants Ctee 1982-88, Systems Bd Grants Ctee MRC 1984-88, Br Digestive Fndn Sci and Res Awards Ctee 1987-90, Scientific Advsy Ctee Br Nutrition Fndn 1987-, Yorkshire Regnl Health Authy 1989-90; Freeman City of London 1954; memb RSM, FRCP 1969; *Books* Malabsorption in Clinical Practice (1974), The Liver and Biliary System (1984), The Gut and Systemic Disease (1983), Advanced Medicine (1983), Clinical Nutrition in Gastroenterology (1986), Gut Defences in Clinical Practice (1986), Gastroenterology (1988); *Recreations* table tennis, watching cricket, medical memorabilia; *Style—* Prof Monty Losowsky; Southview, Ling Lane, Scarcroft, Leeds LS14 3HT (☎ 0532 892699); Dept of Medicine, St James's University Hospital, Leeds LS9 7TF (☎ 0532 433144, fax 0532 429722)

LOTEN, Alexander William; CB (1984); s of late Alec Oliver Loten, and late Alice Maud Loten; *b* 11 Dec 1925; *Educ* Churcher's Coll Petersfield, Corpus Christi Coll Cambridge (BA); *m* 1954, Mary Diana Flint; 1 s, 1 da; *Career* served WWII, RNVR 1943-46; engr: Rolls-Royce Ltd Derby 1950-54, Benham & Sons Ltd London 1954-58; Air Miny Work Directorate 1958-64; MPBW: sr engr 1964-70, superintending engr (mechanical design) 1970-75; pres CIBS 1976-77, under sec DOE 1981-85, dir Mechanical and Electrical Engrg Servs PSA 1981-85 (dir of works Civil Accommodation 1975-81); *Style—* Alexander Loten, Esq, CB; Mansers Farm, Nizels Lane, Hildenborough, Tonbridge, Kent TN11 8NX (☎ 0732 833204)

LOTHIAN, Lothian, Marchioness of; Antonella Reuss; *née* Newland; da of Maj-Gen Sir Foster Reuss Newland, KCMG, CB (d 1943), and Mrs William Carr (d 1986); *m* 1943, 12 Marquess of Lothian, *qv*; 2 s, 4 da; *Career* author, broadcaster, journalist; current affairs columnist Scottish Daily Express 1960-75, deviser and presenter of tv progs; vice pres Royal Coll of Nursing 1960-80, patron Nat Cncl of Women of GB, Ct patron RCOG, fndr and pres Woman of the Year Luncheon and Assoc; fndr: Health Festival Assoc, Valiant for Truth Media award; pres Order of Christian Unity, fell Inst of Journalists; *Recreations* swimming, walking, music; *Clubs* Arts, Reform; *Style—* The Marchioness of Lothian; 54 Upper Cheyne Row, London SW3 (☎ 071 352 4709); Tower Office, Jedburgh, Scotland (☎ 0835 64023)

LOTHIAN, Lt-Col James Lambert; s of Maj James Lothian (d 1970), and Nancy Lambert, *née* Mactaggart; *b* 21 Feb 1926; *Educ* Wellington, New Coll Oxford; *m* 1967, Jean Christine, da of Sir Arthur Clarke, KCMG, CBE (d 1967); 2 da (Sarah Jane b 1968, Katherine Susan b 1973); *Career* 2 Lt RA; served: India, Palestine, Egypt, Cyprus, Aden 1945-62, Staff Coll Camberley 1957; Lt-Col 1968 cmnd 42 Medium Regt RA 1968-70, Br instr W German Cmd and Staff Coll Hamburg 1970-73, ret 1975; PR dir Franklin Mint Limited 1982- (mangr 1975-82); German interpreter Civil Serv 1967; memb: Inst of Linguists 1973, Mail Order Sub Ctee of Ctee of Advertising Practice 1987, Bd Br Direct Marketing Assoc 1990; MBIB 1970; *Recreations* breeding dachshunds, cabinet making; *Style—* Lt-Col James Lothian; Hollymead, Leigh Rd, Hildenborough, Kent TN11 9AH (☎ 0732 838619); Franklin Mint Limited, 138 Bromley Rd, London SE6 2XG (☎ 081 697 8121, fax 081 698 4476)

LOTHIAN, 12 Marquess of (S 1701); Peter Francis Walter Kerr; KCVO (1983), DL (Roxburghshire 1962); also Lord Newbottle (S 1591), Lord Jedburgh (S 1622), Earl of Lothian, Lord Ker of Newbattle *(sic)* (both S 1631), Earl of Ancram (1633), Viscount of Briene, Lord Ker of Newbottle, Oxnam, Jedburgh, Dolphinstoun and Nisbet (all S 1701), and Baron Ker of Kersheugh (UK 1821); s of Capt Andrew William Kerr, JP, RN (d 1929), and cous of 11 Marquess (d 1940); *b* 8 Sept 1922; *Educ* Ampleforth, Ch Ch Oxford; *m* 1948, Antonella (fndr pres Women of the Year Luncheon), da of Maj-Gen Sir Foster Reuss Newland, KCMG, CB (d 1943), and Mrs William Carr, of Ditchingham Hall, Norfolk (d 1986); 2 s, 4 da; *Heir* s, Earl of Ancram, MP; *Career* Lt Scots Gds 1943; jt parly sec Miny of Health April-Oct 1964; a lord-in-waiting to HM the Queen 1972-73; chm of cncl Scottish Red Cross 1976-86; Lord Warden of the Stanneries and keeper of Privy Seal of Duke of Cornwall 1977-83; memb Royal Company of Archers (Queen's Body Guard for Scotland); FRSA; kt SMO Malta; *Recreations* music; *Clubs* Boodle's, Beefsteak, New (Edinburgh); *Style—* The Most Hon the Marquess of Lothian, KCVO, DL; 54 Upper Cheyne Row, London SW3; Ferniehirst Castle, Jedburgh, Roxburghshire (☎ 0835 64021); Melbourne Hall, Derby (☎ 033 16 2163)

LOTT, Dr Bernard Maurice; OBE (1966); s of William Alfred Henry Lott (d 1963), of Felpham, Sussex, and Margaret Florence, *née* Smith (d 1978); *b* 13 Aug 1922; *Educ* Bancroft's Sch Essex, Keble Coll Oxford (MA), Univ of London (MA, PhD), Univ of Edinburgh (Dip Applied linguistics); *m* 17 Sept 1949, Helena, da of Clarence Winkup (d 1944), of London; 2 s (Christopher b 1953 d 1983, David b 1956), 1 da (Carolyn b 1951); *Career* Petty Offr RN 1942-46; Br Cncl lectr in English Univ of Ankara and Gazi Inst Educn Turkey 1949-55, asst rep Br Cncl Finland 1955-57, prof of English and head of Dept Univ of Indonesia Jakarta 1958-61, dir studies Indian Central Inst of English Hyderabad 1961-66; Br Cncl: dep controller Educn Div London 1966-72, controller Eng Teaching Div 1972-75, rep Poland 1975-77; Eng Language Teaching Devpt Advsr 1977-79, course tutor Open Univ London 1979-87, lectr Applied Linguistics Central London Poly 1989-90, hon res fell UCL 1980-; memb: IATEFL 1967-, BAAL 1967-; *Books* New Swan Shakespeare (gen ed), A Course in English Language and Literature (1986), Macbeth (ed, 1958), Twelfth Night (ed, 1959), Merchant of Venice (ed, 1962), Hamlet (ed, 1968), King Lear (ed, 1974), Much Ado About Nothing (ed, 1977); *Style—* Dr Bernard Lott, OBE; 8 Meadway, London NW11 7JT (☎ 081 455 0918)

LOTT, David Charles; s of late Air Vice-Marshal (Charles) George Lott, CB, CBE, DSO, DFC, and Evelyn Muriel, *née* Little; *b* 8 May 1940; *Educ* Alhallows Sch, RAF Coll Cranwell; *m* 1, 5 June 1965 (m dis 1982), Elfriede; 2 s (Simon b 1966, Dieter b 1969); m 2, Kathryn Elizabeth; 1 da (Katie b 1986); *Career* RAF Coll Cranwell 1958-61, 17 Sqdn RAF Wildenrath 1961-64, ADC to AOC 23 Gp 1964-66, Hunter Pilot 208 54 Sqdn 1966-70, Deputy Flight Cdr 20 Sqdn Harriers 1970-74, Flight Cdr 1 Sqdn RAF Wittering 1974-78; Queens Commendation for Valuable Servs in the Air 1976; airline capt Britannia Airways; *Recreations* skiing, shooting, Jaguar cars; *Style—* Capt David Lott; c/o Britannia Airways, Newcastle Airport, Newcastle, Tyne and Wear

LOTT, Felicity Ann Emwhyla; CBE (1990); da of John Albert Lott, and Iris Emwhyla, *née* Williams; *b* 8 May 1947; *Educ* Pate's Girls GS Cheltenham, RHC Univ of London (BA), RAM (LRAM); *m* 1, 22 Dec 1973 (m dis 1982), Robin Mavesyn Golding; m 2, 19 Jan 1984, Gabriel Leonard Woolf, s of Alec Woolf; 1 da (Emily b 19 June 1984); *Career* opera singer, debut Magic Flute ENO 1975; princ appearances: ENO, Glyndebourne, Covent Garden, WNO, SNO, Paris, Brussels, Hamburg,

Chicago, Munich; recordings: EMI, Decca, Harmonia Mundi Chandos, Erato, Hyperion; sang at Royal Wedding 1986, patron New Sussex Opera; Hon DMus Univ of Sussex 1989; FRAM; *Recreations* reading, gardening; *Style—* Ms Felicity Lott, CBE; c/o Lies Askonas Ltd, 186 Drury Lane, London WC2B 5RY (☎ 071 405 1808)

LOUBET, Bruno Jean Roger; s of Clement Loubet, of Libourne Gironde France, and Mauricette, *née* Lacroix (d 1989); *b* 8 Oct 1961; *m* 27 Dec 1983, Catherine, da of Jacques Mougeol; 2 da (Laeticia b 4 Aug 1985, Laura Claire b 8 April 1987); *Career* lycée hotelier 1976-79; commis de cuisine: Hyatt Regency Brussels 1979-80, Restaurant Copenhague 1980-82; second maître Nat French Navy and chef to the Admiral TCD Ouragan 1982, commis chef Tante Claire London 1982; head chef: Gastronome one Fulham 1982-85, Manoir aux 4 saisons Gt Milton 1985-86; chef mangr Petit Blanc Oxford 1986-88, chef Four Seasons Restaurant Inn on The Park 1988-; *awards* Young Chef of The Year Good Food Guide 1985, Acorn award Caterer & Hotelkeeper 1988, Michelin star 1990; memb Académie Culinaire de France GB 1990-; *Style—* Bruno Loubet, Esq; Inn On The Park, Hamilton Place, Park Lane, London W1A 1AZ (☎ 071 499 0888, fax 071 499 5572)

LOUDON, George Ernest; *b* 19 Nov 1942; *Educ* Christlijk Lyceum Zeist Holland, Balliol Coll Oxford (BA), John Hopkins Univ Washington DC (MA); *m* Angela; 1 s (b 1972), 1 da (b 1970); *Career* fin analyst Lazard Freres & CIE Paris 1967-68, project mgmnt: Ford Foundation NY and Jakarta 1968-71, McKinsey & Co Amsterdam 1971-76; Amsterdam-Rotterdam Bank NV Amsterdam 1976-88 (memb Bd of mds responsible for: Investment Banking 1983-84, Treasury and Securities Trading 1984-86, Corporate and International Banking 1986-88 (gen mangr New Issue and Syndicate Dept 1976-83)); former dir: EBC Amro Bank Ltd, Banque Europeenne pour L'Amerique Latine, Netherlands Joint Custodian Institute, Leveraged Capital Holdings NV, Netherlandse Trust Maatschapij; former chm: Amsterdam Stock Exchange Pension Fund, Amro International Asia Ltd; former vice chm Amsterdam Stock Exchange, former treas Stichting 1688-1988, dir Midland Bank plc 1988-, chief exec Midland Montague 1988-; currently dir: Midland Montagu (Holdings) Ltd, Midland Bank International Finance Services Ltd, Samuel Montagu & Co Ltd, MBSA (France), Trinkaus und Burkhardt (Germany), Euromobiliare (Italy), Geveke NV (Holland), Oriental Art Magazine Ltd; chm: Policy Ctee Securities Indust Netheralnds Bankers Assoc, Assoc of Intermediaries in private placement market, Asiatic Art Soc; memb: Cncl of Japan Festival 1990, Acquisitions Ctee Museum of Modern Art of City of Amsterdam, Bd of Tstees Netheralnds Royal Coll of Art; treas SKIP fndn, govr Atlantic Coll; *Style—* George Loudon, Esq; Midland Bank plc, Poultry, London EC2P 2BX

LOUDON, James Rushworth Hope; s of Francis William Hope Loudon (d 1985), and Lady Prudence Katharine Patton, *née* Jellicoe; *b* 19 March 1943; *Educ* Eton, Magdalene Coll Cambridge (BA); *m* 17 May 1975, Jane Gavina, *née* Fryett; 2 s (Hugo John Hope b 1978, Alexander Guy Rushworth b 1980), 1 da (Antonia Louise Cameron b 1977); *Career* fin dir Blue Circle Industries plc 1987-; *Recreations* tennis, cricket, opera; *Clubs* MCC; *Style—* James Loudon, Esq; Olantigh, Wye, Ashford, Kent TN25 5EW (☎ 0233 812294); Blue Circle Industries plc, 84 Eccleston Square, London SW1 (☎ 071 828 3456)

LOUDON, Dr John Duncan Ott; OBE (1988); s of James Alexander Law Loudon (d 1931), of 10 Harrison Rd, Edinburgh, and Florence Ursula Marguerita, *née* Ott (d 1985); *b* 22 Aug 1924; *Educ* Wyggeston GS, Univ of Edinburgh (MB ChB); *m* 10 Sept 1963, Nancy Beaton, da of Alexander John Mann (d 1967), of Avoch, Rosshire; 2 s (Alasdair John b 7 April 1956, Richard Donald b 8 Oct 1957); *Career* RAF Med Branch 1948-50; conslt obstetrician and gynaecologist Eastern Gen Hosp Edinburgh 1960-87 (ret), sr lectr Univ of Edinburgh 1962-87; vice pres RCOG 1981-84, memb GMC 1986-; FRCS (Ed) 1954, FRCOG 1972 (memb 1956); *Recreations* golf, gardening, travel, food and drink; *Style—* Dr John Loudon, OBE; Ardbeg, 4 Kinnear Rd, Edinburgh EH3 5PE (☎ 061 552 1327)

LOUDON, Lady Prudence Katharine Patton; 5 da of Adm of the Fleet 1 Earl Jellicoe (d 1935), and Florence Gwendoline, *née* Cayzer (d 1964); *b* 30 Aug 1913; *Educ* N Foreland Lodge Broadstairs; *m* 22 Dec 1936, Francis William Hope Loudon (d 1985), s of James Hope Loudon (d 1952), of Olantigh, Kent; 1 s (James Rushworth Hope b 1943), 2 da (Katharine (Lady Wilkinson) b 1937, Annabella (Mrs I J Scott) b 1939); *Career* JP: London 1950-60, Kent 1963-76; chm Nat Cncl Unmarried Mother & Child 1958-68, former memb Cncl Univ of Kent, former govr Christ Church Coll Canterbury, past pres Kent Fedn Amenities Socs, chm Ashford Sch 1961-79, pres Friends of St Augustine's Hosp 1972-, acting chm Bd of Tstees Burrswood Kent 1981-82 (memb 1970-84); *Recreations* sketching; *Style—* The Lady Prudence Loudon; Little Olantigh, Wye, nr Ashford, Kent (☎ 0233 812916)

LOUDON, Prof Rodney; s of Albert Loudon (d 1965), and Doris Helen, *née* Blane (d 1980); *b* 25 July 1934; *Educ* Bury GS, Brasenose Coll Oxford (MA, DPhil); *m* 6 June 1960, Mary Anne, da of Eugene Philips; 1 s (Peter Thomas b 1964), 1 da (Anne Elizabeth b 1961); *Career* postdoctoral fell Univ of Calif Berkeley 1959-60, scientific civil servant RRE Malvern 1960-65, Bell Laboratories Murray Hill New Jersey 1965-66, prof of physics Essex Univ 1967- (reader 1966-67); visiting prof: Yale Univ 1975, Univ of Calif Irvine 1980, Ecole Polytechnique Lausanne 1985, Univ of Rome 1988, Univ Libre de Bruxelles 1990; chm Bd of Eds Optica Acta 1984-87; Thomas Young Medal and Prize Inst of Physics 1987; FRS 1987; *Books* The Quantum Theory of Light (1973, 2 edn 1983) Scattering of Light by Crystals (with W Hayes, 1978), Introduction to the Properties of Condensed Matter (with D J Barber, 1989); *Style—* Prof Rodney Loudon, FRS; 3 Gaston Street, East Bergholt, Colchester, Essex C07 6SD (☎ 0206 298550); Physics Department, Essex University, Colchester C04 3SQ (☎ 0206 872880, fax 0206 873598, telex 98440 UNILIB G)

LOUDOUN, Maj Gen Robert Beverley; CB (1973), OBE (1965); s of Robert Alexander Loudoun (d 1968), of Northwood, Middx, and Margaret Anne Homewood (d 1960); *b* 8 July 1922; *Educ* Univ Coll Sch London; *m* 1950, Audrey Olive, da of William Pearson Stevens (d 1976), of Dublin; 2 s (Steven, Robin); *Career* enlisted RM 1940, war serv Italy, Yugoslavia, post war serv Far East, Med, America, Caribbean, CO 40 Commando 1967-69, Brig UK Commandos 1969-71, Maj-Gen RM Trg 1971-75; chm Jt Shooting Ctee for GB 1977-82, dir Mental Health Fndn 1978-90; Rep Col Cmdt RM 1983-84, chm Br Yugoslav Soc 1989; Freeman City of London 1979, memb Guild of Freeman 1982-; *Recreations* sport (spectator); *Clubs* Army and Navy; *Style—* Maj Gen Robert Loudoun, CB, OBE; 2 Warwick Drive, Putney, London SW15 6LB (☎ 081 789 1826)

LOUGHBOROUGH, Archdeacon of; *see*: Jones, Ven (Thomas) Hughie

LOUGHBOROUGH, Derek Ralph; *b* 5 March 1927; *Educ* Clark's Coll; *m* 1 Sept 1951, Hazel Hilda; 2 s (Martin b 1959, Andrew b 1964); *Career* RN 1945-47; joined Sun Life Assurance Society 1943-77 (mangr 1969), sec PO Insurance Society 1977-87, dir Lautro Ltd 1986-; London Borough of Croydon: councillor 1974-, chm Educn Ctee 1978-88, Mayor 1988-89; ACII 1952, APMI 1977, MBIM 1977; *Recreations* walking, photography; *Style—* Derek Loughborough, Esq; 45 Cheston Ave, Croydon CRO 8DE (☎ 081 777 5583)

LOUGHLIN, Paul John; s of Terry Loughlin, of Liverpool Arms Public House, St Helens, and Christine Pilling; *b* 28 July 1966; *Educ* West Park HS St Helens (Capt first XV Rugby Union); *Career* rugby league football player; St Helens Rugby League FC: professional debut 1982, top goal kicker and point scorer in the rugby league 1986-87, played in 5 finals, Man of the Match John Player final 1988, played in Challenge Cup at Wembley on 2 occasions 2 GB under 19 caps, 2 GB under 21 caps, full GB debut against France 1987, toured Aust NZ and PNG 1988 (voted best tourist), 12 full GB caps; in top ten goal kick chart for past four years, most goals on a match 16, most points in a match 40 (v Carlisle 1986), Young Player of the Year 1987; *Style—* Paul Loughlin, Esq; 110 Old Road, Ashton in Makerfield, Wigan, Greater Manchester (☎ 0942 711823); St Helens RLFC, Dunriding Lane, St Helens, Merseyside (☎ 0744 23697)

LOUGHNAN, Kenneth Francis Manly; s of Col William F M Loughnan, MC, and Eileen Mary, *née* Manly; *b* 28 Feb 1925; *Educ* Beaumont Sch, Trinity Coll Oxford (MA); *m* 1973, Susan, da of Maj Geoffrey Huskisson, DSO, MC; 1 da (Grania b 1977); *Career* Lt 8 KRI Hussars 1945-47, Capt City of London Yeo 1952-57; admitted slr 1952, jt sr ptnr Triggs Turner Guildford; chm SCM Property & Investment Co Ltd; dir: Tindle Newpapers Ltd, County Sound plc, and others; chm St John Cncl for Surrey 1986-, CStJ; *Style—* Kenneth Loughnan, Esq; Old Langham Farm, Lodsworth, nr Petworth, W Sussex GU28 9DA (☎ 07985 453)

LOUGHRAN, James; s of James Loughran (d 1956), and Agnes, *née* Fox (d 1971); *b* 30 June 1931; *Educ* St Aloysius Coll Glasgow; *m* 1, 1961 (m dis 1983), Nancy Coggon; 2 s (Angus b 1965, Charles b 1966); m 2, 15 April 1985, Ludmila Navratil; *Career* conductor; First prize Philharmonia Competition 1961, assoc conductor Bournemouth Symphony Orch 1962-65; princ conductor: BBC Scottish Symphony Orch 1965-70, Hallé Orch 1971-83, Bamberg Symphony 1979-83; conductor of princ orchs of Europe, USA, Japan and Aust; recordings with: London Philharmonic, BBC Symphony, Philharmonia, Hallé and Scottish Chamber Orch (Gold Disc EMI 1983); Hon DMus Univ of Sheffield, FRSAMD, FRNCM; *Recreations* travel, walking, golf; *Style—* James Loughran, Esq; The Rookery, Bollington Cross, Macclesfield, Cheshire SK10 5EL

LOUGHREY, (Stephen Victor) Patrick; s of Eddie Loughrey (d 1979), and Mary, *née* Griffin; *b* 29 Dec 1955; *Educ* Loreto Coll Milford Donegal, Univ of Ulster (BA), Queen's Univ Belfast (MA, PGCE); *m* 4 July 1978, Patricia, da of Thomas Kelly (d 1984); 1 s (Stephen b 26 Dec 1980), 2 da (Joanne b 26 Feb 1982, Christine b 10 June 1984); *Career* teacher St Colm's HS Draperstown 1978-84, head of educnl bdcasting BBC NI 1988- (prodr 1984); memb: NI Curriculum Cncl, Hist Monuments Cncl, Advsy Ctee NI Arts Cncl; tstee Ulster Local History Tst Fund; *Books* Ordnance Survey of Ballinascreen (ed, 1981), The People of Ireland (ed, 1988); *Recreations* talking; *Style—* Patrick Loughrey, Esq; 7 The Willows, Coolshinney, Magherafelt, Northern Ireland (☎ 0648 33031, 0232 338442)

LOUGHTON, David Clifford; s of Clifford Loughton (d 1973) of Harrow, and Hazel Loughton; *b* 28 Jan 1954; *Educ* Roxeth Manor Sch Harrow Middlesex, Technical Colls in Harrow Watford and Southall; *m* 1986, Deborah, da of George Wellington; 1 s (Theodore David b 12 July 1990), 1 da (Georgina Anna b 12 July 1987); *Career* apprentice instrument technician Kodak Ltd 1970-74, asst hosp engr Hillingdon Area Health Authy 1974-76, hosp engr Herts Area Health Authy 1976-78, dir and gen mangr Ducost Ltd 1978-83, divnl mangr GEC Electrical Projects 1984-86, gen chief exec Walsgrave Hosp Coventry Health Authy 1986-; memb: Inst of Hosp Engrs, Inst of Plant Engrs; *Recreations* golf, water skiing, country pursuits; *Style—* David Loughton, Esq; Blacon Cottage, Norton Lindsey, nr Warwick, Warwickshire CV35 8JN (☎ 092 684 2070); Coventry Health Authority, Walsgrave Hospital, Clifford Bridge Rd, Coventry, W Midlands CV2 2DX (☎ 0203 602020, car 0831 213242)

LOULOUDIS, Hon Mrs (Madeleine Mary); *née* Dillon; 4 but 3 survg da (twin) of 20 Viscount Dillon (d 1979); *b* 29 Oct 1957; *m* 4 March 1989, Leonard Constantine Louloudis, o s of Constantine Louloudis; *Career* assist private sec to HRH The Princess Royal 1990-; *Style—* The Hon Mrs Louloudis; 17 The Porticos, 374 King's Rd, London SW3 (☎ 071 352 1584)

LOUSADA, Sir Anthony Baruh; s of Julian George Lousada (d 1945); *b* 4 Nov 1907; *Educ* Westminster, New Coll Oxford; *m* 1, 1937 (m dis 1960), Jocelyn, da of late Sir Alan Herbert, CH; 1 s, 3 da; m 2, 1961, Patricia, da of late Charles McBride, of USA; 1 s, 1 da; *Career* admitted slr 1933; Miny of Econ Warfare 1939-44; memb: Cncl Royal Coll of Art 1952-79 (hon fell 1957, sr fell 1967, vice chm 1960-72, treas 1967-72, chm 1972-79), Ctee Contemporary Art Soc 1955-71 (vice chm 1961-71), Cncl Friends of Tate Gallery 1958- (hon treas 1960-65, chm 1971-77); tstee Tate Gallery 1962-69 (vice chm 1965-67, chm 1967-69), conslt Stephenson Harwood (slrs) 1973-81 (ptnr 1935-73); kt 1975; *Recreations* painting, the arts, travel; *Clubs* Garrick; *Style—* Sir Anthony Lousada; The Tides, Chiswick Mall, London W4 (☎ 081 994 2257)

LOUSADA, Peter Allen; s of Air Cdre Charles Rochford Lousada, DL (d 1988), and Elizabeth, *née* Shaw; *b* 30 March 1937; *Educ* Epsom Coll; *m* 13 Oct 1962, Jane, da of Lt Col Donald Gillmor (d 1972); 2 s (Toby b 1963, James b 1965), 1 da (Sarah b 1965); *Career* Nat Serv, Flying Offr RAF, Canada & 61 Sqdn; vice pres Cadbury Beverages Europe 1987-, dir Schweppes International Ltd, Cadbury Beverages Ltd 1990-, non-exec chm Hydrophone Ltd 1990-; *Recreations* golf, fishing; *Clubs* RAF, Woburn Golf; *Style—* Peter A Lousada, Esq; Well Cottage, Bow Brickhill, nr Milton Keynes, Bucks MK17 9JU (☎ 0908 72186); Cilcambach, Eglyswen, Dyfed; 1-11 Hay Hill, London W1X 7LF (☎ 071 493 3961)

LOUSADA, Sandra Reignier; da of Sir Anthony Lousada, of The Tides, Chiswick Mall, London W4, and Jocelyn Herbert; *b* 29 June 1938; *Educ* St Pauls Girl Sch, Regent St Poly; *m* 1 Jan 1965, Brian Richards, son of Alexander Hodgson Richards; 1 s (Sam b 12 June 1966), 1 da (Polly b 17 May 1968); *Career* asst photographer Scaioni Studios 1956-59; freelance photographer 1959-63 (work for magazines incl: Queen Magazine, Tatler, Nova, Brides, Vogue, Elle (Paris), Marie Claire (Paris), Vanity Fair, Mademoiselle and Glamour Magazines (Conde Naste) NY; work for English Stage Co; work for films incl: The Lonliness of the Long Distance Runner, Tom Jones, The Charge of the Light Brigade; work incl all the pictures for the Aldeburgh Festival 1963); joined Whitecross Studios as one of a group of freelance photographers 1963-81 (worked for advtg agencies incl: J Walter Thompson, Ogilvy Benson & Mather Collett Dickinson and Pearce on projects incl Guinness, Andrex, Gas and ICI; work for magazines incl: Look Magazine (work in Japan, India and Russia), editorial work for Good Housekeeping, Vogue, Honey, Nova, Flair) Susan Griggs Agency 1981- (advertising clients incl Conran, Next, Azda, Marks and Spencer, Cow and Gate; portraits and editorial work for: Good Housekeeping, Brides, Tatler, Country Living, Marie Claire, Womans Journal; work for charities: Birthright, Great Ormond Street Hosp for Sick Children, Peper Harow Fndn); *awards* silver award AFAED 1988; *Style—* Ms Sandra Lousada; c/o Susan Griggs, 2B/101 Farm Lane, London SW6 1QJ (☎ 071 385 8112, fax 071 381 0935)

LOUSTAU-LALANNE, Bernard Michel; s of (Joseph Antoine) Michel Loustau-Lalanne, OBE (d 1982), of Mahé, Seychelles, and (Marie Therese) Madeleine Boullé (d 1974); *b* 20 June 1938; *Educ* Inns of Ct Sch of Law; *m* 15 March 1974 (m dis 1982), Debbie Temple-Brown; 1 da (Kate-Michele b 27 July 1975); *Career* asst inspr N Rhodesia Police 1962-64; called to the Bar Middle Temple London 1969; sr state counsel Attorney Gen's Office Seychelles 1972-76 (crown counsel 1970-72), Attorney Gen Seychelles 1976-78, High Cmmr for Seychelles London 1978-80, cwlth legal rep

Performing Right Soc 1980-90, sec gen Fédération Européene des Associations de Conseil en Organisation (FEACO) 1991-; memb: Hon Soc of the Middle Temple, Bar Assoc for Commerce Fin and Indust; *Style*— Bernard Loustau-Lalanne, Esq; Fedération Européene des Associations de Conseil en Organisation (F E A C O), 79 Ave de Cortenberg, B-1040 Brussels, Belgium (☎ 322 736 6000, fax 736 3008)

LOUTH, Baroness; Ethel May; da of Walter John Gallichen, of Jersey; *m* 1927, 15 Baron Louth (d 1950); *Style*— The Rt Hon Ethel, Lady Louth; Gardone Cottage, Hormfield Drive, St Brelade, Jersey, CI

LOUTH, 16 Baron (I 1541); Otway Michael James Oliver Plunkett; s of 15 Baron (d 1950); *b* 19 Aug 1929; *Educ* Downside; *m* 1951, Angela, da of William Cullinane, of Jersey; 3 s, 2 da; *Heir* s, Hon Jonathan Oliver Plunkett; *Style*— The Rt Hon the Lord Louth; Les Sercles, La Grande Piece, St Peter, Jersey

LOVAT, Sheriff Leonard Scott; s of Charles Lovat (d 1959), and Alice, *née* Hunter (d 1973); *b* 28 July 1926; *Educ* St Aloysius Coll Glasgow, Univ of Glasgow (BL); *m* 1960, Elinor Frances, da of Joseph Alexander McAlister (d 1979); 1 s (Andrew), 1 da (Judith); *Career* admitted slr 1948; in partnership 1955-59, asst to prof of Roman law Univ of Glasgow 1954-63, procurator fiscal depute Glasgow 1960, Cropwood fell Inst of Criminology Univ of Cambridge 1972, sr asst procurator fiscal of Glasgow and Strathkelvin 1976, Sheriff of S Strathclyde Dumfries and Galloway at Hamilton 1978-; *Recreations* music, mountaineering, bird-watching; *Clubs* Alpine; *Style*— Sheriff L S Lovat; 38 Kelvin Ct, Glasgow G12 0AE (☎ 041 357 0031); Sheriff Ct, Almada St, Hamilton (☎ 0698 282957)

LOVAT, Master of; Simon Augustine Fraser; s and h of 15 Lord Lovat, DSO, MC; *b* 1939; *Educ* Ampleforth; *m* 1972, Virginia, da of David Grose, of 49 Elystan St, SW3; 2 s, 1 da; *Career* Lt Scots Gds 1960; proprietor of around 190,000 acres made over to him by his father 1965; *Style*— Master of Lovat; Beaufort Castle, Beauly, Inverness-shire

LOVAT, 15 Lord (S 1458-64); Simon Christopher Joseph Fraser; DSO (1942), MC (1942), TD (1945), JP (Inverness-shire 1944), DL (1942); 24 Chief of Clan Fraser of Lovat; *de facto* 15 Lord, 17 but for the attainder; Baron Lovat of Lovat (UK 1837); s of 14 Lord Lovat, KT, GCVO, KCMG, CB, DSO, TD (d 1933), by his w Hon Laura Lister, da of 4 Baron Ribblesdale; er bro of Rt Hon Sir Hugh Fraser, MBE, MP (d 1984); bro-in-law of Sir Fitzroy Maclean, 1 Bt; bro-in-law and cous of 5 Earl of Eldon; *b* 9 July 1911; *Educ* Ampleforth, Magdalen Coll Oxford; *m* 1938, Rosamond, da of Sir Henry John Delves Broughton, 11 Bt (d 1942); 4 s, 2 da; *Heir* s, Master of Lovat; *Career* sits as Conservative in House of Lords; 2 Lt Lovat Scouts 1930, Brig 1944, served with Commandos 1941; jt parly under-sec of state Foreign Office 1945; Officier de la Légion d'Honneur, Croix de Guerre (France); Norwegian Cross; Order of Suvarov (Soviet Union); Papal Order of St Gregory with Collar; Kt Sov Mil Order of Malta; Hon LLD: Simon Fraser BC, Antigonish NS; OStJ, CStJ; *Style*— The Rt Hon the Lord Lovat, DSO, MC, TD, JP, DL; Balblair House, Beauly, Inverness-shire

LOVE, Prof Andrew Henry Garmany; s of Andrew Love (d 1976), of Ballymagee, Bangor, Co Down, and Martha, *née* Fleming (d 1981); *b* 28 Sept 1934; *Educ* Bangor Endowed Sch, Queens Univ Belfast (BSc, MB BCh, BAO, MD); *m* 29 May 1963, Margaret Jean, da of William Stuart Lennox (d 1987); 1 s (Anthony W G b 24 Oct 1967); *Career* Queens Univ Belfast: prof of gastroenterology 1977-83, dean of Faculty of Medicine 1981-86, prof of medicine 1983-; Ulster Boys Golf Champion 1952, Irish Amateur Golf Champion 1956; chm: Res Ctee Ulster Cancer Fndn, Central Med Advsy Ctee DHSS NI; memb: Bd of Govrs Campbell Coll, Eastern Health Social Servs Bd; pres Euro Assoc of Med Deans; FRCP 1973, FRCPI 1973; Gastroenterology, Tropical Diseases, Nutrition; *Recreations* riding, sailing; *Clubs* East India, Devonshire Sports, Royal Ulster Yacht; *Style*— Prof Andrew Love; The Lodge, New Rd, Donaghadee, Co Down BT21 ODU (☎ 0247 883507); Dept Medicine, Queen's University Belfast, Institute of Clinical Science, Grosvenor Road, Belfast BT12 6BJ (☎ 0232 240503 ext 2707, fax 0232 230788 ext 3020, telex 747578 QUB MEDG)

LOVE, Heather Beryl; da of the late John Sydney Love, and Joyce Margaret, *née* Cracknell; *b* 17 Nov 1953; *Educ* Mayfield Sch Putney; 1 s (Matthew Paul Hodges b 1982); *Career* IPC Magazines: publicity mangr 1980, gp publicity mangr 1981, assoc publisher 1985, publisher 1988, publishing dir (Woman's Journal, Marie Claire, Country Homes and Interiors) 1988-; memb Nat Small Bore Rifle Assoc; *Recreations* pistol shooting, interior design, workaholic; *Style*— Miss Heather Love; 2 Hatfields, London SE1 (☎ 071 261 5508, fax 071 261 4277)

LOVE, Dr Malcolm Barr; s of Malcolm MacFarlane Love, of Thornwood, 205 Alexandra Parade, Kirn Dunoon, Argyll, and Catherine Easdon, *née* Corson (d 1985); *b* 1 Nov 1929; *Educ* Worcester Royal GS, Univ of Birmingham; *m* 1961, Wendy Elizabeth *qv*, da of Eric Noble (d 1977), of Abbotsford, Fence, Lancs; 1 s (Richard b 19 Sept 1964), 2 da (Elizabeth b 14 Sept 1962, Caroline b 24 July 1966); *Career* formerly: Queen Elizabeth and Childrens' Hosp Birmingham, GP training Edinburgh; medical registrar: Gen Hosp Birmingham 1960-61, Brook Hospital Shooters Hill 1961-64; GP Ealing 1964-; FRSM 1965, MRCGP 1968; *Recreations* fishing, riding; *Clubs* Reform, Caledonian, Fly Fishers; *Style*— Dr M Barr Love; 337 Uxbridge Rd, London W3 (☎ 081 993 0982); 8 Upper Wimpole St, London W1M 7TD (☎ 071 935 6790)

LOVE, Prof Philip Noel; CBE (1983); s of Thomas Love, of Aberdeen, and Ethel, *née* Philip; *b* 25 Dec 1939; *Educ* Aberdeen GS, Univ of Aberdeen (MA, LLB); *m* 21 Aug 1963, Isabel Leah, da of Innes Mearns, of Aberdeen; 3 s (Steven b 1965, Michael b 1967, Donald b 1969); *Career* advocate in Aberdeen 1963; princ Campbell Connon & Co Slrs Aberdeen 1963-74 (conslt 1974-); Univ of Aberdeen: prof of conveyancing and professional practice of law 1974-, dean faculty of law 1979-82, vice princ 1986-90; memb Rules Cncl Ct of Session 1968-, vice pres Scottish Law Agents' Soc 1970, chm Aberdeen Home for Widowers' Children 1971-, local chm Rent Assessment Panel Scot 1972-, Hon Sheriff Grampian Highlands and Islands 1978-; Law Soc of Scot: memb 1963-, memb Cncl 1975-86, vice pres 1980-81, pres 1981-82; chm Grampian Med Ethical Ctee 1986-, pt/t memb Scottish Law Cmmn 1986-, pres Aberdeen GS Former Pupils' Club 1987-88, tstee Grampian and Islands Family Tst 1988-, memb Scot Univs Cncl on Entrance 1989-, govr Inst of Occupational Med Ltd 1990-, chm Magistrates of Scot Customer Advsy Gp 1990-, memb Butterworths Editorial Consultative Bd for Scot 1990-; FRS (Aberdeen); *Recreations* rugby (golden oldies variety now), keep fit; *Clubs* New (Edinburgh), Royal Scot (Aberdeen); *Style*— Prof Philip N Love, FRS; Univ of Aberdeen, King's Coll, Old Aberdeen AB9 2UB (☎ 0224 272414, fax 0224 272442, telex 73458 UNIABN G)

LOVE, Robert Malcolm; s of Robert Love, of Paisley, Scotland, and Mary, *née* Darroch; *b* 9 Jan 1936; *Educ* Paisley GS, Univ of Glasgow (MA), Washington Univ St Louis; *Career* short serv cmmn Flt Lt Educn Branch RAF 1959-62; actor and dir numerous English rep theatres 1962-66, prodr TV drama Thames TV 1966 -75; prodns incl: Public Eye, The Rivals of Sherlock Holmes, The Mind of Mr J G Reeder, Van der Valk, Frontier, Moody and Pegg; freelance TV prodr 1975-79, controller of drama Scottish TV 1979-; prodns incl: House on the Hill, Skin Deep, City Sugar, Northern Lights, Taggart, Extras, The Steamie, The Advocates; govr Scottish Theatre Co 1981-87, visiting lectr in media studies Univ of Stirling 1986-, vice chm BAFTA Scotland 1987-; memb RTS; *Recreations* music, theatre, foreign travel, books, railway history; *Style*— Robert Love, Esq; Scottish Television plc, Cowcaddens, Glasgow G2 3PR (☎ 041 332 9999, fax 041 332 6982)

LOVE, Wendy Elizabeth; da of Eric Noble (d 1977), of Fence, nr Burnley, and Phyllis, *née* Baldwin (d 1970); *b* 14 May 1930; *Educ* Crofton Grange Buntingford Herts, Royal Free Hosp Sch of Med (MB BS, MRCS, LRCP, FRCOG); *m* 1961, Dr Malcolm Barr Love *qv*, s of Malcolm MacFarlane Love; 1 s (Richard b 1964), 2 da (Elizabeth b 1962, Caroline b 1966); *Career* resident house posts Royal Free Hosp, Birmingham Maternity and Womens' Hosp 1960-61, Annie McCall res fell Royal Free Hosp 1962-64, gynaecologist and obstretrician Elizabeth Garrett Anderson Hosp 1964-89; memb: Br Fertility Soc 1975, Medical Womens' Fedn 1975, Menopause Soc 1990; *Recreations* fishing, embroidery; *Style*— Mrs Wendy Love; 8 Upper Wimpole St, London W1M 7TD (☎ 071 935 6790, fax 081 866 6339, car 0831 423815)

LOVEGROVE, Ross; s of Herbert William John Lovegrove, of 23 Dinas Road, Penarth, S Glamorgan, and Mary Eileen, *née* Lovegrove; *b* 16 Aug 1958; *Educ* St Cyres Comp Sch Penarth, Cardiff Coll of Art & Design, Manchester Poly (BA), RCA (MDes); partner, Miska Miller; 1 s (Roman S Lovegrove); *Career* designer: Allied International Designers London 1978-82, Frogdesign Germany 1983-84 (projects incl: Apple Computers, Sony Walkman, AHG Telefunken and Louis Vuitton Luggage), Knoll International Paris 1984, Atelier De Nimes 1984-86 (freelance projects for Cacharel and Dupont), fndr ptnr Lovegrove & Brown 1987-90, fndr Lovegrove Studio X 1990- (clients incl: Knoll International, BA, Porche Design, Louis Vuitton, Parker Pens, Cacharel, Puma, Carrera, Hermes and Berol Pens); winner: Oqqetti Per Domus award for the pocket disc camera and film cassette system 1984, first prize (product design) Creative Review Pantone Colour awards; work featured in various jls incl: Form, Design Week, L'Architecture D'Aujordhui, Elle, Harpers and Queen, Interior Design and Vogue; exhibitions incl: Designing for Britain or Abroad London 1985, Leading Edge Tokyo 1987, Mondo Materials California 1989-90, Synthetic Visions V & A London 1990; memb jury: Les 25 Objects Temoins des Annes 80 (for French product design) 1985, Interieur 90 Kortrijk Belgium 1990; *Style*— Ross Lovegrove, Esq; Lovegrove, Studio X, 81 Southern Row, London W10 5AL (☎ 081 968 0391, fax 081 968 0392)

LOVEJOY, Prof Derek Alfred Walter; s of J F Lovejoy (d 1952), and M Lovejoy (d 1975), *née* Stoner; *b* 16 Sept 1925; *Educ* St Olave's GS, Harvard Univ; *m* 5 Jan 1952, June, *née* Hotz; 1 s (Alan b 1956), 2 da (Davida b 1959, Vanessa b 1960); *Career* architect and townplanner; conslt: Derek Lovejoy and Partners (fndr sr ptnr), UN; prof of landscape architecture Univ of Sheffield ; Int Fedn of Landscape Architects: memb Grand Cncl 1956-83, sec gen 1960-68, first vice pres 1980-83, chm Int Ctee 1990; Inst of Landscape Architects: convenor and first chm PR Ctee, convenor and first chm Res Ctee, chm of examiners 1964-68, pres 1971-73; Dept of Transport: memb Landscape Advsy Ctee for Trunk Roads 1969-90, chm Lighting Sub Ctee 197-89, memb Service Area Sub Ctee 1971-81, Memb Urban Motorway Sub Ctee 1970-88; memb: Housing Awards Ctee Dept of the Environment 1970-80, Planning Ctee Cncl for the Protection of Rural England 1970-76, UK Cncl Euro Architectural Heritage Year (1975) 1973-75, Planning Ctee Social Sci Res Cncl 1974-76, Cncl The Building Conservation Tst 1975-, Ctee USA Transportation Bd 1980-, Tansportation Ctee Institution of Highways and Transportation; county cmmr Surrey for Enterprise Neptune Campaign The Nat Tst 1968-70, memb Cncl The Tree Council 1970- (chm 1980), chm Jt Cncl for Landscape Industs 1972, tstee The Queen's Trees 1976-80, former vice chm and hon life assoc Professional Institutions Conservation Cncl 1980, environment assessor for Dodoma Tanzania United Nations Environment Programme 1983, vice pres Tst for Urban Ecology; memb Panel XVth World Congress Mexico (The Road within the Environment) 1975; chief assessor for competitions RIBA 1975- (occasional regnl chm RIBA Architecture Awards), occasional chm Regnl Awards Civic Tst; memb: Worshipful Co of Constructors 1978, Worshipful Co of Architects 1988, Freeman City of London 1978; FRIBA 1952, PPILA 1952, FRTPI 1953, FRSA 1970, FIHT 1980; *Books* Land Use And Landscape Planning (1975 and 80); *Recreations* work, travel, music; *Clubs* Architecture, Athenaeum, Directors; *Style*— Prof Derek Lovejoy; 2 Burcott Rd, Purley, Surrey CR8 4AA (☎ 081 668 4237); Apartment 4, 150 Wapping High St, London E1 9XG (☎ 071 702 1268); 8-11 Denbigh Mews, Denbigh St, London SW1 (☎ 071 828 6392)

LOVELACE, 5 Earl of (UK 1838); Peter Axel William Locke King; also Lord King, Baron of Ockham (GB 1725), and Viscount Ockham (UK 1838); s of 4 Earl of Lovelace (d 1964, seventh in descent from the sis of John Locke, the philosopher), and his 2 w, Manon Lis (d 1990), da of Axel Sigurd Transo, of Copenhagen, and widow of Baron Carl Frederik von Blixen Finecke; *b* 26 Nov 1951; *Educ* privately; *Heir* none; *Style*— The Rt Hon the Earl of Lovelace; Torridon House, Torridon, Ross-shire (☎ 228)

LOVELL, Sir (Alfred Charles) Bernard; OBE (1946); s of Gilbert Lovell; *b* 31 Aug 1913; *Educ* Kingswood GS, Bristol Univ; *m* 1937, Mary Joyce Chesterman; 2 s, 3 da; *Career* served Telecommunications Res Estab MAP 1939-45; prof Radio Astronomy Manchester Univ 1951-80 (emeritus 1980-); fndr and dir Nuffield radio astronomy Laboratories Jodrell Bank 1945-81; pres: Royal Astronomical Soc 1969-71, British Assoc 1974-75; Master Worshipful Co of Church Musicians 1986-87; Cdr Order of Merit (Poland) 1975; FRS 1955; kt 1961; *Books Incl:* The Story of Jodrell Bank (1968), In the Centre of Immensities (1975), Emerging Cosmology (1981), The Jodrell Bank Telescopes (1985), Voice of the Universe (1987), Astronomer by Chance (1990); *Clubs* Athenaeum; *Style*— Sir Bernard Lovell, OBE, FRS; The Quinta, Swettenham, Cheshire (☎ 0477 71254); Jodrell Bank, Cheshire (☎ 0477 71321)

LOVELL, Dr Christopher Roland; s of Graham Ernest Lovell (d 1990), and Marion Gladys (d 1984); *b* 29 April 1950; *Educ* Bristol GS, Univ of Bristol (MD); *Career* sr registrar and tutor in dermatology Inst Dermatology London 1978-84, conslt dermatologist Bath Health Dist 1985-; memb: Dowling Club (formerly hon sec and hon pres); med advsy panel Nat Eczema Soc; memb: Br Assoc Dermatologists, Br Soc Rheumatology; MRCP, FRSM; *Recreations* cultivation and preservation of rare bulbs, music (mediaeval & renaissance recorder player); *Style*— Dr Christopher Lovell; Royal United Hospital, Combe Park, Bath BA1 3NG (☎ 0225 428331)

LOVELL, Mary Sybella; da of William George Shelton (d 1967), and Mary Catherine, *née* Wooley; *b* 23 Oct 1941; *Educ* Notre Dame Collegiate Liverpool, UCLA; *m* 14 Oct 1960 (m dis 1977), Clifford C Lovell; 1 s (Graeme Robert b 1961); *Career* fin controller Baron Instruments Ltd; dir and co sec; Yachting Provence 1976-78, Baron Computors & Security Ltd 1978-80; tech writer Tabs Ltd 1982-86; author; MFH New Forest 1988-89; MBIM 1973; *Books* A Hunting Pageant (1980), Cats as Pets (1981), Boys Book of Boats (1982), Straight on Till Morning (1986), The Splendid Outcast (ed 1987), The Sound of Wings (1989); *Recreations* foxhunting, flying, sailing, travel, reading; *Clubs* New Forest Hunt, Royal Over-seas League, Soc of Authors, Bournemouth Flying, MFHA; *Style*— Mrs Mary Lovell; Laura Cottage, Romsey Road, Lyndhurst, Hampshire (☎ 042 128 3371, fax 042 128 3074)

LOVELL-DAVIS, Baron (Life Peer UK 1974), of Highgate, in Greater London; Peter Lovell-Davis; s of William Lovell-Davis (d 1974), and Winifred Mary Lovell-Davis (d 1954); *b* 8 July 1924; *Educ* Christ's Coll Finchley, King Edward VI GS Stratford-on-Avon, Jesus Coll Oxford (BA, MA); *m* 1950, Jean, da of Peter Foster Graham (d 1948); 1 s (Hon Stephen Lovell b 1955), 1 da (Hon Catherine Ruth b

1958); *Career* sits as Labour peer in Lords; memb Bd Cwlth Devpt Corp 1978-84, London Consortium 1978-, md Central Press Features Ltd 1950-70; dir newspaper & printing cos 1950-70; chm: Davis & Harrison Ltd 1970-73, The Features Syndicate Ltd 1971-74; a lord in waiting to HM The Queen 1974-75, parly under-sec of state Dept of Energy 1975-76; chm: Lee Cooper Licensing Ltd 1983-90, Pettifor Morrow Assocs Ltd 1986-; memb Islington Dist Health Authy 1982-85, tstee Whittington Hosp Academic Centre 1980-, vice pres YHA 1978-; *Recreations* industrial archaeology, aviation, inland waterways, bird-watching, walking; *Style*— The Rt Hon the Lord Lovell-Davis; 80 North Rd, Highgate, London N6 4AA (☎ 081 348 3919)

LOVELOCK, Sir Douglas Arthur; KCB (1979, CB 1974); s of late Walter Lovelock, and Irene Lovelock; *b* 7 Sept 1923; *Educ* Bec Sch London; *m* 1961, Valerie Margaret Lane; 1 s, 1 da; *Career* joined Treasy 1949, asst under sec (personnel) MOD 1971-72 (previously with Minys of Technol and Aviation Supply), DTI 1972-74; dep sec: Trade, Indust, Prices & Consumer Protection Depts 1974-77; chm bd of Customs & Excise 1977-83, Civil Servs Benevolent Fund 1980-, first Church Estates Cmmr 1983-, govr Whitgift and Trinity schs 1986-; *Style*— Sir Douglas Lovelock, KCB; The Old House, 91 Coulsdon Rd, Old Coulsdon, Surrey (☎ 07375 55211)

LOVELOCK, Prof James Ephraim; CBE (1990); s of Tom Arthur Lovelock (d 1957); *b* 26 July 1919; *Educ* Strand Sch Brixton, Manchester, London; *m* 1942, Helen Mary (d 1989), da of David Manson Hyslop (d 1967); 2 s, 2 da; m 2, 14 Feb 1991, Sandra Jean Orchard (wid), da of Harley Beavers; *Career* scientist formerly staff memb Nat Inst for Med Res 1941-61, prof Baylor Coll of Med Texas 1961-64; pres Marine Biology Assoc 1986-; FRS; *Recreations* growing trees, mathematical puzzles; *Style*— Prof James Lovelock, CBE, FRS; Coombe Mill, St Giles on the Heath, Launceston, Cornwall

LOVERIDGE, Air Cdre David John; OBE (1981); s of Wing Cdr George Frederick Edmund Loveridge, OBE, of Melita, Middle Bourne, Farnham, Surrey, and Docie Annie, *née* West (d 1982); *b* 21 Oct 1937; *Educ* English Sch Cairo, Brockenhurst, RAF Coll Cranwell, RAF Staff Coll, Nat Def Coll; *m* 1 June 1983, Patricia (Poosie), da of Charles Perkins Garner (d 1971), of Burton Lazars, Melton Mowbray; 1 s (Simon b 1966), 1 da (Sarah b 1964); *Career* OC 230 operational conversion unit 1977-79, Wing Cdr Strike Attack MOD Air Plans 1979-82, Station Cdr RAF Gatow Berlin 1982-85, dep dir Air Force Plans MOD 1985-87, Air Cdre flying trg 1987-89, dir trg (G) (RAF) 1990-91; FRAeS, FBIM, MIPM; *Recreations* cycling, hill walking, sailing and flying; *Clubs* RAF, Royal Fowey Yacht; *Style*— Air Cdre David Loveridge, OBE; Bursar, St Paul's School, Lonsdale Road, Barnes, London SW13 9JT (☎ 081 748 5958)

LOVERIDGE, Sir John Henry; CBE (1964, MBE 1945); s of Henry Thomas Loveridge, and Vera Lilian Loveridge; *b* 2 Aug 1912; *Educ* Elizabeth Coll Guernsey, Caen Univ; *m* 1946, Madeleine Melanie, da of Eugene Joseph C M Tanguy; 1 s, 1 da; *Career* RAFVR 1954-59; called to the Bar Middle Temple 1950, advocate Royal Court of Guernsey 1951, bailiff of Guernsey 1973-82 (slr gen 1954-60, attorney-gen 1960-69, dep 1969-73), appeal judge Jersey 1974-82; KStJ 1980; kt 1975; *Clubs* Royal Guernsey Golf; *Style*— Sir John Loveridge, CBE; Kinmount, Sausmarez Rd, St Martin's, Guernsey, CI (☎ 0481 38038)

LOVERIDGE, Sir John Warren; JP (West Central Division 1963); s of Claude Warren Loveridge (d 1956), and Emilie Warren, *née* Malone (d 1954); *b* 9 Sept 1925; *Educ* St John's Coll Cambridge (MA); *m* 1954, Jean Marguerite, da of C E Chivers, of Devizes, Wilts; 3 s (Michael, Steven, Robert), 2 da (Amanda, Emma); *Career* head of family businesses; princ St Godric's Coll 1954-; farmer; Parly candidate (C) Aberavon 1951, contested Brixton (LCC) 1952; MP (C): Hornchurch 1970-74, Upminster 1974-83; memb: Parly Select Ctee on Expenditure, Gen Purposes Sub Ctee, Procedure Ctee; chm Cons Small Business Ctee 1979-83; memb Hampstead Borough Cncl 1953-59, treas and tstee Hampstead Cons Assoc 1959-74, pres Hampstead and Highgate Cons Assoc 1986-; vice pres: Gtr London Area Cons Assoc 1984-, Nat Cncl for Civil Protection (formerly Civil Def); pres Axe Cliff Golf; Liveryman Worshipful Co of Girdlers; FRAS, FRAgS, RIIA; kt 1988; *Books* Moving Forward: Small Businesses and the Economy (jt author), God Save the Queen (1981), Hunter of the Moon (1983), Hunter of the Sun (1984); *Recreations* painting, poetry, historic houses, shooting; *Clubs* Bucks, Carlton, Hurlingham; *Style*— Sir John Loveridge, JP; Bindon Manor, Axmouth, nr Seaton, Devon EX12 4AS; The White House, 82 Fitzjohn's Ave, London NW3

LOVETT, Ian Nicholas; s of Frederick Lovett, of Croydon, Surrey, and Dorothy Evelyn, *née* Stanley; *b* 7 Sept 1944; *Educ* Selhurst GS, Univ of Wales, (BA); *m* 3 May 1969, Patricia Lesley; 2 da (Emma b 1977, Sophie b 1979); *Career* md Dunbar Bank plc 1984-; FCIB 1982; *Recreations* cricket; *Clubs* MCC; *Style*— Ian N Lovett, Esq; Dunbar Bank plc, 9 Sackville St, London W1X 1DE (☎ 01 437 7844, telex 28300 ALLIED G)

LOVETT, Martin; OBE (1970); *b* 3 March 1927; *Educ* RCM; *m* 1950, Suzanne, *née* Rozsa; 1 s (Peter Sandor b 1955), 1 da (Sonia Naomi 1951); *Career* cellist of Amadeus Quartet 1947-1987; Hon DUniv York, Hon DMus London; memb: FRSA, Hon RAM; Grosses Verdienst Kreuz (Germany), Ehrenkreuz Fuer Kunst and Wissenschaft (Austria); prof RAM and Cologne Hochschule Für Musik; *Style*— Martin Lovett, Esq, OBE; 24 Redington Gdns, NW3 7RX (☎ 071 794 9898); 5 Coastal Rd, Angmering-On-Sea, W Sussex 1BN 1SJ (☎ 0903 786900)

LOVICK, Peter Alan; s of Peter George Lovick (d 1953), and Dora Evelyn, *née* Elvidge; *b* 23 Jan 1928; *Educ* City of London Coll; *m* 14 July 1961, Shirley Georgina, da of Edward Duffin (d 1956); 1 da (Susan Caroline b 1963); *Career* dir: Bleichroder Bing & Co Ltd (Lloyds brokers) 1965-69, Ropner Insurance Services 1969-72; Benfield Lovick Rees & Co Ltd: dir 1972-88, chm Underwriting Agencies Ltd 1980-89, chm Holdings Ltd 1984-88; dir: Bell & Clements Ltd 1984-, Benfield Bell & Clements Ltd 1985-; Liveryman Worshipful Co of Carmen; FCIB, FID; *Recreations* fine wine and food, MENSA, ecology, conservation; *Clubs* City of London; *Style*— Peter Lovick, Esq; 35 Chalkwell Esplande, Westcliff-on-Sea, Essex (☎ 0702 347041); Old Forge House, Thorington St, Stoke by Nayland, Suffolk (☎ 020637 255); 5M Portland Mansions, Chiltern St, London W1 (☎ 071 486 0198); Chesterfield House, 26-28 Fenchurch St, London EC3 (☎ 071 626 5432)

LOVICK, (Elizabeth) Sara; da of Charles Trevor Lovick, of St Albans, Herts, and Elizabeth Susan Hettie, *née* Phelps; *b* 3 Feb 1954; *Educ* North London Collegiate Sch Canons Edgware, Lady Margaret Hall Oxford (BA); *Career* admitted slr 1979; ptnr Cameron Markby Hewitt 1986-; Freeman Worshipful Co of Slrs 1989; memb: Law Soc, Common Law Inst of Intellectual Property; assoc memb: Chartered Inst of Patent Agents, The Inst of Trade Mark Agents; *Recreations* swimming, tennis, skiing, sailing, singing; *Clubs* Riverside Racquets; *Style*— Miss Sara Lovick; Cameron Markby Hewitt, Sceptre Court, 40 Tower Hill, London EC3N 4BB (☎ 071 702 2345, fax 071 702 2303, telex 925779)

LOVILL, Sir John Roger; CBE (1983), DL (E Sussex 1983); s of Walter Thomas Lovill and Elsie, *née* Page; *b* 26 Sept 1929; *Educ* Brighton Hove and Sussex GS; *m* 1958, Jacqueline, *née* Parker; 2 s, 1 da; *Career* chm exec cncl ACC 1983-86; kt 1987; *Style*— Sir John Lovill, CBE, DL; Narroway, Beddingham, nr Lewes, E Sussex

LOW; *see*: Morrison-Low

LOW, Alistair James; s of James Grey Low (d 1973), and Elsie Georgina, *née* Holden (d 1990); *b* 2 Aug 1942; *Educ* Dundee HS, Univ of St Andrews (BSc); *m* 30 Aug 1966, Shona Patricia, da of John Galloway Wallace, OBE, of Edinburgh; 2 s (John b 1970, Hamish b 1972), 1 da (Katharina b 1977); *Career* ptnr Duncan C Fraser and Co 1968-86, dir William M Mercer Fraser Ltd 1986-; chm Championship Ctee Royal & Ancient Golf 1986-88; FFA 1967; *Recreations* golf, skiing; *Clubs* Royal & Ancient Golf, Hon Co of Edinburgh Golfers, Gullane Golf, New (Edinburgh); *Style*— Alistair Low, Esq; Thornfield, Erskine Loan, Gullane, East Lothian; William M Mercer Fraser Ltd, Hobart House, 80 Hanover St, Edinburgh, Lothian (☎ 031 226 2477)

LOW, Prof (Donald) Anthony; s of late Canon Donald Low, and Winifred, *née* Edmunds; *b* 22 June 1927; *Educ* Haileybury ISC, Univ of Oxford (MA, DPhil); *m* 1952, Isobel Snails; 1 s, 2 da; *Career* lectr (later sr lectr) Makerere Coll Univ Coll of E Africa 1951-58, fell (then sr fell) in history Res Sch of Social Sciences ANU 1959-64, founding dean of Sch of African & Asian Studies and prof of history Univ of Sussex 1964-72, dir Res Sch of Pacific Studies ANU 1973-75, vice chllr ANU 1975-82; Univ of Cambridge: Smuts Prof of the History of the Br Cwlth 1983-, pres Clare Hall 1987-; PhD Cantab 1983; FAHA, FASSA; *Books* Buganda in Modern History (1971), Lion Rampant (1973), Congress and the Raj 1917-47 (1977); *Style*— Prof Anthony Low; Clare Hall, Cambridge

LOW, Hon Charles Harold Stuart; s and h of 1 Baron Aldington, KCMG, CBE, DSO, TD, PC; *b* 22 June 1948; *Educ* Winchester, New Coll Oxford, INSEAD; *m* 16 Sept 1989, Regine, da of late Erwin von Csongrady-Schopf; 1 s (Philip Toby Augustus b 1 Sept 1990); *Career* Citibank, dir Europe Grindlays Bank; gen mangr Deutsche Bank London; *Style*— The Hon Charles Low; 9L Warwick Square, London SW1; Deutsche Bank, 6 Bishopsgate, London EC2 (☎ 071 971 7509)

LOW, Ernest; s of Rev Eli Ernest Low (d 1978), of Melbourne, Australia, and Rose Anna, *née* Kwan (d 1983); *b* 19 Jan 1927; *Educ* St James's Sch Calcutta, Univ of Hong Kong (BSc), City and Guilds Coll, Imperial Coll London (DIC); *m* 5 Sept 1959 (m dis 1984), Elizabeth, da of Dr Christopher William Lumley Dodd (d 1972), of Haywards Heath, Sussex; 1 s (Christopher b 31 Jan 1961, d 7 Dec 1971), 1 da (Alison b 1 Oct 1962); *Career* sr engr: Wimpey Central Laboratory 1954-57, Binnie & Ptnrs 1957-59; mangr of Site Investigation Div Marples Ridgway Ltd 1959-70; ptnr Low and Parsons Brown 1969-77, Low and Ptnrs Hong Kong (conslt engrs) 1976-88, conslt 1986-; dep chm Civil Div Hong Kong Instn of Engrs 1978-80, chm Hong Kong Branch CIArb 1980-82; memb: Ctee on Arbitration of the Hong Kong Law Reform Cmmn 1980-82, Cncl CIArb 1988-; arbitrator on lists of: CIArb, pres Instn of Civil Engrs, pres Inst of Br Architects, Hong Kong Int Arbitration Centre, FIDIC, Euro Int Contractors, and others; Liveryman of the Worshipful Co of Painter Stainers 1973, Liveryman of the Worshipful Co of Arbitrators 1981; FICE 1968, FASCE 1969, FCIArb 1971, MConsE 1975; *Recreations* golf, oratorios, opera, reading; *Clubs* Carlton, Hong Kong; *Style*— Ernest Low, Esq; 7a Royal Court, 3 Kennedy Rd, Hong Kong (☎ 852 8206010, fax 852 8106223); 60 Carlton Mansions, Randolph Ave, London W9 1NR (☎ 071 925 0066, fax 071 930 8004)

LOW, Dr Francis McPherson; s of Sir Francis Low (d 1972), of High Gardens, Tekels Ave, Camberley, Surrey, and Margaret Helen *née* Adams; *b* 6 May 1928; *Educ* Aitcheson Coll Lahore, Gordonstoun, Univ of Cambridge (MA, MB BChir), Univ of London (DMRD); *m* 7 Sept 1957, Juliet Frances Clarice, da of Dr Kenneth James Langlands Scott (d 1970); 3 s (Jonathan b 1961, Andrew b 1965, Alasdair b 1967), 1 da (Juliette b 1960); *Career* short service cmmn RAF Med Branch 1956-58; Flying Offr 1956, Flt-Lt 1957, Sqdn Ldr 1958; med trg Cambridge and Barts Hosp 1948-54; specialist trg: Radcliffe Infirmary Oxford 1960-64, King's Coll Hosp Denmark Hill London 1964-66; conslt radiologist W Middx Univ Hosp 1966-, teacher Faculty of Med Univ of London 1980; Freeman City of London 1976, Liveryman Worshipful soc of Apothecaries 1979; BMA 1955, FRCR 1975, FFR 1965; *Recreations* gardening, breeding Siamese cats; *Clubs* Hawks; *Style*— Dr Francis Low; Department of Diagnostic Imaging, West Middlesex University Hospital Isleworth, Middx (☎ 081 565 5868)

LOW, Dr Norman Cranston; s of Dr Robert Cranston Low (d 1949), of Edinburgh, and Alice Armstrong, *née* Grant (d 1957); *b* 6 April 1924; *Educ* Edinburgh Acad, Univ of Edinburgh (MB ChB); *m* 20 Dec 1952, Pamela, da of Frank Albert Westbury Warwick, of Cardington and Shefford, Beds; 1 s (Simon b 1957), 3 da (Elizabeth b 1954, Harriet b 1958, Judith b 1962); *Career* house surgn Sir James Learmonth Royal Infirmary Edinburgh 1947-48, asst physician Royal Edinburgh Hosp 1948-49, RAMC 1949-52, sr house offr and registrar Royal Edinburgh Hosp, sr Hosp MO Rauceby Hosp Sleaford 1956-62, conslt psychiatrist Carlton Hayes Hosp Leicester 1962-89, visiting psychiatrist HM Prisons 1971-; DPM 1959, MRC Psych 1971, FRC Psych 1982; *Recreations* choir singing; *Clubs* Leicester Lions (pres); *Style*— Dr Norman Low; 28 Knighton Drive, Leicester LE2 3HB (☎ 0533 703550)

LOW, Roger L; s of Dr Niels L Low, of USA, and Mary Margaret Low; *b* 29 Jan 1944; *Educ* Columbia Coll, Columbia Univ (AB), Wharton Graduate Sch of Fin and Commerce, Univ of Pennsylvania (MBA); *m* 1967, Helen Webster, da of Bates W Bryan, of Lookout Mountain, Tennesse, USA; 1 s, 1 da; *Career* 1 Lt US Marine Corps, served Vietnam; Drexel Burnham & Co 1971-75, vice pres Salomon Bros 1975-81; md: Dean Witter Reynolds Overseas 1981-84, Bear Stearns & Co 1984-; *Recreations* marathon running, skiing; *Clubs* St Anthony Hall (NYC); *Style*— Roger L Low, Esq; Bear Stearns Int Ltd, 9 Devonshire Sq, London EC2M 4YL (☎ 01 626 5301)

LOW, William; CBE (1984), JP (1971); s of William Low (d 1957); *b* 12 Sept 1921; *Educ* Merchiston Castle Edinburgh; *m* 1949, Elizabeth Ann Stewart, *née* Sime; 2 s; *Career* Maj IA 1943-45; textile mfr, chm Dundee Industl Heritage Ltd 1984, Dundee Enterprise Tst, chm designate Scottish Enterprise Tayside Ltd; fell Scottish Cncl Devpt and Indust 1988; CBIM 1983; *Recreations* shooting, fishing, golf; *Clubs* Naval and Military, R & A St (Andrews); *Style*— William Low, Esq, CBE, JP; Herdhill Ct, Kirriemuir, Angus (☎ 0575 72215)

LOW-BEER, Dr Thomas Stephen; s of Walter Low-Beer (d 1954), and Alice Bettina, *née* Stadler; *b* 25 Feb 1932; *Educ* Gordonstoun, Univ of Oxford Med Sch (MA) Middx Hosp Med Sch (BM, BCh); *m* 3 Sept 1965, Ann, da of Alexander Smith (d 1990); 2 s (Daniel Walter b 17 June 1969, Jacob b 11 Dec 1971); *Career* Nat Serv RAMC 1950-52; res fell Duke Univ Med Center 1967-69, lectr in Med Univ of Bristol 1970-75, conslt physician and gastroenterologist Selly Oak Hosp Birmingham and sr clinical lectr Univ of Birmingham 1975-, conslt physician and gastroenterologist Wellington Hosp NZ 1985; author of contribs to several books; memb: Br Soc of Gastroenterology, American Gastroenterological Assoc, Br Assoc for Study of the Liver; tutor for visiting elective students Univ of Brimingham Med Sch; memb RSM, FRCP 1980; *Style*— Dr Thomas Low-Beer; Selly Oak Hospital, Birmingham B29 6JD (☎ 021 472 5313)

LOWBRIDGE, Roy Thomas; s of Thomas Eric Lowbridge, of 30 Kirk Balk, Hoyland, Barnsley, and Anni Sophie, *née* Sievers (d 1990); *b* 17 Oct 1950; *Educ* Kirk Balk Comp Hoyland, Barnsley Coll of Technol; *m* 25 Aug 1984, Caroline, da of John Pinder; 2 s (Thomas James b 7 April 1987, Joshua Alexander b 20 Feb 1989), 1 da (Amy Marie b 15 Feb 1985); *Career* engr; tech apprentice Newton Chambers Engineering Sheffield 1967-71, production and product devpt engr F Parramore Tools Sheffield 1972-77, jig and tool designer Record Tools Sheffield 1977-80, devpt mangr Ernest H

Hill Ltd Sheffield (design engr 1981-88); winner Br Design award 1990; *Recreations* playing guitar and piano; *Style*— Roy Lowbridge, Esq; c/o Ernest H Hill Ltd, Beta Works, Fitzwilliam St, Sheffield S1 3GX (☎ 0742 723019, fax 0742 730126)

LOWCOCK, Andrew Charles; s of Eric Lowcock, of Quarry Bank House, Styal, Wilmslow Cheshire, and Elizabeth, *née* Kilner; *b* 22 Nov 1949; *Educ* Malvern, New Coll Oxford (MA); *m* 1, 14 Aug 1976 (m dis 1985), Patricia Anne, da of Emlyn Roberts; m 2, 7 Sept 1985, Sarah Elaine, da of Robert Edwards, of Quinton Lodge, Ditchling, Sussex; 2 s (Robert Charles b 24 Feb 1988, Edward George b 23 Jan 1990); *Career* called to the Bar Middle Temple 1973, Northern circuit; *Recreations* music (princ timpanist Stockport Symphony Orchestra), cricket, theatre; *Clubs* Whicker Soc, Stockport Garrick Theatre; *Style*— Andrew Lowcock, Esq; 28 St John St, Manchester M3 4DJ (☎ 061 834 8418)

LOWE, Adam Charles Graham; s of Patrick Graham Lowe, of Grove Farm, Cold Aston, Bourton on the Water, Glos, and Susan Jean, *née* Huins; *b* 18 Feb 1959; *Educ* Dragon Sch Oxford, Radley, Ruskin Sch of Drawing Trinity Coll Oxford (BA, MA) RCA (MA); *m* 11 May 1989, Yuka Ishigaki, da of Tadashi Ishigaki, 1 s (Otto Gabriel); *Career* artist; solo exhibitions incl: Smith's Gallery London 1986, Pomeroy Purdy Gallery London 1989, Eastbourne Clark Gallery Florida 1990, Las Frutas (Pomeroy Paintings (Pomeroy Purdy Gallery London) 1991; gp shows incl: Ceramics (Somerville Coll Oxford) 1980, Selection from 1981 Degree Shows (Marley Gallery London) 1981, Young Figurative Painters (Fieldbourne Gallery London) 1982, Five Painters from the RCA (Consort Gallery Imp Coll London) 1984, Smith's Gallery 1984, RCA Degree Show 1985, Prelude (Kettles Yard Cambridge) 1985, 85 Show (Serpentine Gallery London) 1985, Leicester Schools Exhibition (Beaumont Hall Leicester) 1986, One Year On (ICA Fair, Olympia London) 1986, Young Masters (Solomon Gallery London) 1986, Six Artists (Groucho Club Soho) 1986, Opening Show and A Printed Image (Richard Pomeroy Gallery) 1987, Summer Show and Print Show (Pomeroy Purdy Gallery) 1988, Blasphemies, Ecstacies, Cries (The Serpentine Gallery London) 1989, School of London (Odette Gilbert Gallery) 1989, New Work by Gallery Artists (Pomeroy Purdy Gallery) 1990, Group Show (Colegio De Arquitectos de Malaga, Spain) 1990; work in collections: Atkinson Art Gallery, Southport Art Gallery, The Contemporary Art Soc; cmmns incl: Metropole, Parco Bongo and Takeo Kikuchi Building (Tokyo, Japan) 1986, cycle of paintings for interior of L'Arca di Now restaurant (Sapporo, Japan) 1988; *Style*— Adam Lowe, Esq; Pomeroy Purdy Gallery, Jacob Street Film Studios, Mill Street, London SE1 2BA (☎ 071 237 6062, fax 071 252 0118)

LOWE, David Alexander; QC (1984); s of David Alexander Lowe (d 1986), and Rea Sadie Aitchison, *née* Bridges; *b* 1 Nov 1942; *Educ* Pocklington Sch York, St John's Coll Cambridge (scholar and exhibitioner, MA); *m* 19 Aug 1972, Vivian Anne, da of Eric John Langley; 3 s (Alexander Vivian b 4 June 1976, Mungo James b 28 Aug 1977, Felix Henry b 3 July 1981), 2 da (Francesca Victoria b 16 April 1979, Octavia Lucia b 28 Nov 1983); *Career* called to the Bar Middle Temple 1965, in practice Chancery Bar 1966-; pt/t supervisor in real property and equity for Cambridge Colls 1964-69; memb Chancery Bar Assoc (former memb Ctee); *Recreations* fine arts and antiques, historic houses, restoration of listed buildings; *Style*— David Lowe, Esq, QC; Wilberforce Chambers, 3 New Square, Lincoln's Inn, London WC2A 3RS (☎ 071 405 5296, fax 071 831 6803)

LOWE, His Hon Judge; David Bruce Douglas Lowe; s of Douglas Gordon Arthur Lowe, QC (Olympic Gold Medallist 800m 1924 and 1928, d 1981), and Karen, *née* Thamsen; *b* 3 April 1935; *Educ* Winchester, Pembroke Coll Cambridge; *m* 1; 1 s, 1 da; m 2, 1978, Dagmar, da of Horst Bosse (d 1972); 1 s, 3 da; *Career* prosecuting counsel to Dept of Trade 1975-83, rec of the Crown Ct 1980-83, circuit judge S Eastern Circuit 1983-; *Recreations* tennis, music; *Clubs* Hawks (Cambridge); *Style*— His Hon Judge Lowe; The Crown Court at Middlesex Guildhall, Broad Sanctuary, London SW1P 3BB

LOWE, Air Chief Marshal Sir Douglas Charles; GCB (1977, KCB 1974, CB 1971), DFC (1943), AFC (1946); s of John William Lowe (d 1970); *b* 14 March 1922; *Educ* Reading Sch; *m* 1944, Doreen Elizabeth, da of Ralph Henry Nichols (d 1952); 1 s, 1 da (Frances, m 1974 Hon Christopher Russell Bailey, *qv*); *Career* entered RAF 1940, Air Vice-Marshal 1970, Air Marshal 1973, AOC 18 Gp 1973-75, Controller of Aircraft MOD 1975-82, ADC to HM The Queen 1978-83, Chief of Defence Procurement 1982-83; dir: Rolls Royce Ltd 1983, Royal Ordnance 1984-87; chm Mercury Communications Ltd 1984-85; *Style*— Air Chief Marshal Sir Douglas Lowe, GCB, DFC, AFC; c/o Lloyds Bank, 15 High Rd, Byfleet, Surrey

LOWE, Lady Elisabeth Olive; o da of 5 Earl Cairns, GCVO, CB (d 1989); *b* 1944; *m* 1965, Capt Martin Ralph Lowe; 1 s; *Style*— The Lady Elisabeth Lowe; Castle End, Ross-on-Wye

LOWE, Frank Budge; s of Stephen Lowe, and Marion Lowe; *b* 23 Aug 1941; *Educ* Westminster; *m* ; 1 s (Hamilton Alexander), 1 da (Emma Rose); *Career* Despatch Dept JWT 1960-62; account exec: Benton & Bowles London (previously in the US) 1964-67, Pritchard Wood 1967-68, Lintas 1968, SH Benson 1968-69; md Collett Dickenson Pearce 1972-79 (account exec 1969-72), fndr Lowe Howard-Spink London 1981, currently chm The Lowe Group plc; *Style*— Frank Lowe, Esq; The Lowe Group plc, Bowater House, 68-114 Knightsbridge, London SW1X 7LT (☎ 071 225 3434, fax 071 584 0336)

LOWE, Prof Gordon; s of Harry Lowe (d 1968), and Ethel, *née* Ibbetson (d 1989); *b* 31 May 1933; *Educ* RCS Imperial Coll London (BSc, ARCS, Govrs prize and Edmund White prize, PhD, DIC, Univ of Oxford (MA, DSc); *m* 1 Sept 1956, Gwynneth, da of Harold Hunter; 2 s (Antony Stephen Hunter b 1964, Richard Christopher b 1966); *Career* Univ of Oxford: univ demonstrator 1959-65, Weir Jr Res Fell Univ Coll 1959-61, official fell and tutor in organic chemistry Lincoln Coll 1962-, lectr Dyson Perrins Laboratory 1965-88, sub rector Lincoln Coll 1986-89, Aldrichian Praelector in chemistry 1988-89, prof of biological chemistry 1989-; memb: Molecular Enzymology Ctee Biochemical Soc 1978-84, Biochemistry and Biophysics Ctee SERC 1979-82, Advsy Panel biochemical Jl 1981-, Editorial Bd Bio-organic Jl 1983-, Oxford Enzyme Gp 1970-88, Oxford Centre for Moecular Sciences 1988-, Sectional Ctee 3 Royal Soc 1985-87; FRSC 1981, FRS 1984, FRSA 1986; Chm Medal for Enzyme Chemistry (RSC) 1983; *publications:* author of various reports and articles in learned jls; *Style*— Prof Gordon Lowe, FRS; 17 Norman Ave, Abingdon, Oxon OX14 2HQ (☎ 0235 523029); Dyson Perrins Laboratory, University of Oxford, South Parks Rd, Oxford OX1 3QY (☎ 0865 275649, fax 0865 275674); Lincoln College, Oxford OX1 3DR (☎ 0865 279782)

LOWE, Harry Frederick; OBE (1984); s of Harry Lowe (d 1963), Supt of Police, Kidderminster Dist, and Mary Jane Giles; *b* 31 May 1925; *Educ* Aston Univ (BSc); *m* 9 July 1948, Patricia Mary, da of Ernest Davies (d 1941); *Career* dir Brintons Ltd; former chm Brintons Telford Ltd; former dir Brintons Pty Ltd Australia; former memb Regnl & Nat Cncl CBI, former Govr Kidderminster Coll 1980-87; FTI, FIMechE, FIProdE; *Recreations* gardening; *Style*— Harry F Lowe, OBE; Brintons Ltd, PO Box 16, Kidderminster (☎ 0562 820000)

LOWE, Lady; Helen Suzanne; *née* Macaskie; da of Sandys Stuart Macaskie, slr; *m* 1971, as his 2 w, Sir Francis Lowe, 3 Bt (d 1986); *Style*— Lady Lowe; 4 New Sq, Lincoln's Inn, London WC2 (☎ 01 242 8508); Bagwich, Godshill, Isle of Wight

LOWE, Dr James Steven; s of James Stephen Lowe, of Leeds, and Mary Eileen, *née* Middleton; *b* 25 June 1955; *Educ* St Thomas Aquinas GS Leeds, Univ of Nottingham (BMedSci, BM BS, MRCPath); *m* 18 July 1979, Pamela Lynne, da of Robert Urie, of Garston Herts; 2 s (Nicholas b 1985, William b 1987); *Career* Reader in neuropathology and hon conslt neuropathology Trent RHA 1986-; memb Ed bd: for Neuropathology and Applied Neurobiology 1990-, for Jl of Pathology 1990-, for Neurodegeneration 1991-; memb: Pathological Soc of GB and Ireland, Neuropathological Soc, Int Acad of Pathologists, RCPath 1985; *Books* Histopathology (1985, 2 edn 1991), Pathology (ed, 1987), Clinical Dermatopathology (1990), Histology (1991); *Recreations* writing computer video games, midi music; *Style*— Dr James Lowe; Department of Pathology, Nottingham University Medical School, Queens Medical Centre, Nottingham NG7 2UH (☎ 0602 41269)

LOWE, John; s of William John Barry Lowe, of Danes Balk, Elkington, nr Sheffield, and Rita, *née* Grayson; *b* 18 Aug 1954; *Educ* City GS Sheffield, Univ of Nottingham (LLB); *m* 19 April 1980, Susan Lydia; 3 s (Thomas Frederick William b 21 Oct 1982, Henry George b 3 Aug 1984, Edwin Richard b 17 Sept 1986); *Career* called to the Bar Gray's Inn 1976; in practice NE circuit; *Style*— John Lowe, Esq; 50 Hotspur St, Tynemouth, N Shields, Tyne & Wear (☎ 091 258 2914); 12 Trinity Chare, Quayside, Newcastle upon Tyne NE1 1JP (☎ 091 232 1927, fax 091 232 7975)

LOWE, John; s of Frederick Lowe (d 1987), of New Tupton, Chesterfield, and Phyllis, *née* Turner (d 1988); *b* 21 July 1945; *Educ* Clay Cross Secondary Sch; *m* 30 July 1966, Diana, da of Jack Cuckson (d 1989), 1 s (Adrian b 14 April 1973), 1 da (Karen b 8 Feb 1975); *Career* professional darts player; England Capt; winner: fourteen world sponsorships, world champion, world masters, world cup singles, News of the World, ten times Br pentathlon; played over one hundred times for England, first player to do a perfect game of 501 on TV 1985; memb Lords Taveners; *Books* The Lowe Profile, The John Lowe Story, Darts John Lowe Way; *Recreations* golf, motor sport, gardening, darts; *Clubs* Matlock Golf, London Rugby; *Style*— John Lowe, Esq; 2A Chelverton Rd, Putney, London SW15 1RH (☎ 081 785 3622, fax 081 785 4568)

LOWE, John Evelyn; s of late Arthur Holden Lowe; *b* 23 April 1928; *Educ* Wellington, New Coll Oxford (MA); *Career* Sgt Instr RAEC 1947-49; Dept of Woodwork V & A Museum 1953-56, dep story ed Pinewood Studies 1956-57, asst to Dir V & A Museum (Dept of Caramics 1957-61); dir: City Museum and Art Gallery Birmingham 1964-69, Weald and Downland Open Air Museum 1969-74; prince West Dean Coll; lit ed Kansai Time Out 1983-88, visiting prof Br cultural studies Doshisha Univ Japan 1979-81 (full time 1982-); pres Midlands Fedn 1967-69; memb: Exec Ctee Midlands Arts Centre for Young People 1964-69, Cncl Br Sch Rome 1968-70, Crafts Advsy Ctee 1973-78; Hofer-Hecksher Bibliographical lectr Harvard 1974; tstee: Sanderson Art in Indust Fund 1968-, Edward James Fndn 1972-73, Idlewild Tst 1972-78; asst ed Collins Crime Club 1953-54, fndr ed Faber Furniture Series 1954-56; hon fell RCA 1988, FSA, FRSA; *Publications* Thomas Chippendale (1955), Cream Coloured Earthenware (1958), Japanese Crafts (1983), Into Japan (1985), Into China (1988), Corsica: A Traveller's Guide (1988), A Surrealist Life - Edward James (1991), author of various articles on applied arts, foreign travel, social history and Japan; *Recreations* Japan, music, travel, book-collecting, reading; *Style*— John Lowe, Esq, FSA; La Paillole Basse, Cours, 47360 Prayssas, France (☎ 53 68 86 45); 6-15 Daini Kume Mansion, 1-banchi, Nishikiraki-cho, Takano, Sakyo-ku, Kyoto, Japan (☎ 075 721 5948)

LOWE, (David) Mark; s of Capt Francis Armishaw Lowe, CBE, DSC, RN (d 1981), and Jean Christine, *née* Coates; *b* 17 June 1948; *Educ* Monkton Combe Sch, Univ of Kent (BA); *m* 15 Nov 1975, Christine Anne Elizabeth, da of Mostyn Thomas; 2 da (Rebecca b 22 Aug 1978, Jessica b 5 Nov 1981); *Career* admitted slr 1974; asst slr Kidd Rapinet Badge 1974-75, ptnr Kingsley Napley 1976-80, ptnr and head of Litigation Dept Field Fisher Waterhouse 1980-; fndr memb Euro Cncl LCIA 1987; memb: Association Internationale des Jeunes Avocats, Soc of Construction Law, Int Cultural Exchange; supporting memb The London Maritime Arbitrators Assoc; memb: British Polish Legal Assoc, Cwlth Lawyers' Assoc; ACIArb 1988; *Recreations* flying, music, squash, tennis; *Style*— Mark Lowe, Esq; The Coach House, Fernhill Lane, Hawley, nr Camberley, Surrey GU17 9HA (☎ 0276 35076); Field Fisher Waterhouse, 41 Vine St, London EC3N 2AA (☎ 071 481 4841, fax 071 488 0084, telex 262613 ADIDEM G)

LOWE, Neville Henry; s of Henry Lee Lowe (d 1974), and Dorothy, *née* Hesketh; *b* 28 Oct 1933; *Educ* Merchant Taylors', Law Soc's Sch of Law; *m* 30 March 1959, Ruth Margaret, da of James George Ernest Turner (d 1975); 1 s (Justin Henry b 1966), 1 da (Fiona Ruth b 1962); *Career* slr; ptnr Heckford Norton & Co Slrs (Letchworth, Royston and Stevenage) 1962-66, sr ptnr Mooring Aldridge & Haydon (Bournemouth and Poole), and Aldridge Myers until 1984, dist registrar of High Ct and County Ct Registrar (Bournemouth and Poole) 1984-91, dist judge 1991-; former memb Bd Western Orchestral Soc Ltd (Bournemouth Symphony Orchestra); pres Bournemouth & District Law Soc 1977-78; Freeman: Merchant Taylors' Co 1980-, City of London 1980-; *Recreations* squash, fishing, ancestral research, opera; *Style*— Neville H Lowe, Esq

LOWE, Peter Robert; s of George William Lowe, of Rayleigh, Essex, and Anne Elizabeth, *née* Tilyard (d 1984); *b* 13 Oct 1951; *Educ* Stratford GS, Univ of Newcastle-upon-Tyne; *m* 6 Dec 1986, Nicola Anne, da of Franciscus Gerardus van den Berg, of Ealing, London; 2 s (Thomas b 15 Nov 1987, Simon b 1 May 1989); *Career* BBC TV: film ed 1975-80, prodr 1980-86, exec prodr 1987-; *Recreations* the cinema; *Style*— Peter Lowe, Esq; BBC Television, Elstree Centre, Borehamwood, Herts (☎ 081 953 6100, fax 081 207 8042)

LOWE, Robson; s of John Boyd Lowe (d 1950); *b* 7 Jan 1905; *m* 1928, Winifred (d 1972); 2 da; *Career* philatelist (founded business 1920), publisher 1930-, auctioneer 1937- (merged with Christie's International 1980); ed The Philatelist 1933-89; chm Expert Ctee British Philatelic Assoc 1941-65, philatelic advsr National Postal Museum 1964-, pres Br Philatelic Fedn 1979-81, pres Postal History Soc 1986; exposed: 1937 Coronation forgeries, 1953 Sperati forgeries, 1980 Gee-Ma forgeries; *Books* Encyclopaedia of Empire Postage Stamps, Handstamps of the Empire, The British Postage Stamp, The Codrington Correspondence, The Lazara Correspondence, St Vincent (with J L Messenger), Waterlow Die Proofs (with Colin Fraser), 16th Century Letters to Grations Street London; *Recreations* postal history, postage stamps, writing; *Clubs* East India; *Style*— Robson Lowe, Esq; c/o East India Club, 16 St James's Square, London SW1 (☎ 071 930 1000); St Cross, Bodorgan Rd, Bournemouth (☎ 0202 55150); office: 10 King St, St James's, London SW1Y 6QT (☎ 071 930 5287, telex 895 0974)

LOWE, Rosemary Anne; *b* 12 March 1937; *Career* account exec: Voice & Vision PR 1966-72, Irving Strauss & Associates 1972-74; dir Golley Slater PR 1974-; *Style*— Ms Rosemary Lowe; Golley Slater Public Relations, 42 Drury Lane, London WC2B 5RN (☎ 071 240 5131, fax 071 379 4387)

LOWE, Ven Stephen Richard; *b* 3 March 1944; *Educ* Reading Sch, Birmingham Poly (BSc Univ of London), Ripon Hall Oxford; *m* Pauline Amy, *née* Richards; 1 s (Michael b 12 April 1969), 1 da (Janet b 7 Dec 1972); *Career* curate St Michael's Anglican Methodist Church Birmingham 1968-72, min in charge Woodgate Valley Conventional dist 1972-75, team rector East Ham 1975-88, hon canon Chelmsford Cathedral 1985-88, urban offr Chelmsford Diocesan 1986-88, archdeacon of Sheffield 1988-; chm Sheffield Anti Apartheid Res Centre; travelling fellowship Winston Churchill Meml Trust 1980; memb: NACRO Working Party into Juvenile Crime, Child Welfare Sub Ctee for Borough, House of Bishops' Review Gp, Borough Addictions Advsy Gp, Dept of Environment Working Party (produced report A Voice For Your Neighbourhood), Birmingham Community Rels Ctee; chm Newham Family Welfare Assoc, fndr Newham Branch of Samaritans; *Books* The Churches' Role in the Care of the Elderly (1969); *Style—* The Ven the Archdeacon of Sheffield; 23 Hill Turrets Close, Ecclesall, Sheffield S11 9RE (☎ 350191)

LOWE, Dr Stuart Shepherd; s of Ian William Shepherd Lowe, of Chalfont St Giles, and Margaret Isobella, *née* Reid; *b* 27 April 1954; *Educ* St Nicholas GS Northwood Middx, St Mary's Hosp Med Sch London (MB BS, LRCP); *m* 15 May 1976, Heather Donaldson, da of Thomas Oliver Donaldson Craig, of Surbiton, Surrey; 2 s (Matthew Shepherd, Simon Donaldson), 1 da (Emma Louise); *Career* sr house offr in anaesthetics Royal Sussex County Hosp Brighton 1978-79; rotation registrar in anaesthetics 1979-82: Charing Cross Hosp London, Nat Hosp for Nervous Diseases, Brompton Hosp London, Royal Surrey County Hosp Guildford; sr registrar in anaesthetics 1982-85: Addenbrooke's Hosp Cambridge, Papworth Hosp, W Suffolk Hosp; conslt in anaesthesia and intensive care W Suffolk Hosp 1985-; vice chm W Suffolk Scanner Appeal; memb: Intensive Care Soc, Assoc of Anaesthetists of GB and I; MRCS, FCAnaes 1981; *Recreations* tennis; *Style—* Dr Stuart Lowe; Intensive Care Unit, West Suffolk Hospital, Hardwick Lane, Bury St Edmunds, Suffolk IP33 2QZ (☎ 0284 763131)

LOWE, Sir Thomas William Gordon; 4 Bt (UK 1918); s of Sir Francis Reginald Gordon Lowe, 3 Bt (d 1986), and Franziska Cornelia Lanier, da of Siegfried Steinkopf; *b* 14 Aug 1963; *Educ* Stowe, LSE (LLB), Jesus Coll Cambridge (LLM); *Heir* bro, Christopher Francis b 1964; *Career* barr Inner Temple 1985, in practice at Chambers of Sir Graham Eyre, QC; *Style—* Sir Thomas Lowe, Bt; 8 Seymour Walk, London SW10; 8 New Square, Lincoln's Inn, London WC2A 3QP

LOWE-McCONNELL, Dr Rosemary Helen; da of Harold Newton Lowe, OBE (d 1970), of Liverpool, and Mary Birditt, *née* Bradford (d 1976); *b* 24 June 1921; *Educ* Howell's Sch Denbigh, Univ of Liverpool (BSc, MSc, DSc); *m* 31 Dec 1953, Richard Bradford McConnell (d 1986), s of Richard George McConnell (d 1942), of Ottawa; *Career* biologist, Freshwater Biological Assoc 1942-45, Overseas Res Serv at East African Fisheries Res Orgn Uganda 1947-53, freelance biologist in ecological studies of S American and African fishes based Br Museum (Natural History), UNDP FAO missions; memb: Tropical Gp Br Ecological Soc, Linnean Soc of London (formerly vice pres), Societas Internationalis Limnologiae; *Books* Speciation Tropical Environment (1969), Fish Communities in Tropical Freshwaters (1975), Ecological Studies in Tropical Fish Communities (1987); *Recreations* travel, bird and fish watching (natural history); *Clubs* Commonmwealth Soc; *Style—* Dr Rosemary Lowe-McConnell; Streatwick, Streat, nr Hassocks, West Sussex BN6 8RT (☎ 0273 890479)

LOWEIN, John Charles; CBE (1987); s of Authur Edmund Lowein (d 1950), of Cowes, IOW, and Kathleen Minnie, *née* Yates (d 1982); *b* 4 Feb 1924; *Educ* Pangbourne; *m* 24 March 1951, Pamela Fay, da of Thomas Christopher Ratsey (d 1965); 2 s (Miles, Robert), 1 da (Victoria); *Career* Midshipman RNR HMS Sheffield 1941-43, Sub Lt, Lt HMS King George V 1943-46, HMS Duke of York 1946-47; asst sec: TB Hall & Co Ltd 1949, Vacuum Oil Co Ltd 1950; Mobil Oil Co Ltd: credit and collections mangr 1952-59, exec asst NY 1959-62, planning and supply mangr Mobil Oil Co Ltd 1962-66, fin and planning dir 1966-68, mktg dir 1968-70, vice pres Mobil Sekiyu Tokyo 1970-74, planning dir europe Mobil Europe Inc 1974-78, exec vice pres europe 1978-80, chm and chief exec Mobil Oil Co Ltd 1980-87; chm IOW Devpt Bd 1988, tstee Jubilee Sailing Tst 1985; FCIS 1950; *Recreations* sailing; *Clubs* RYS, RNSA, ISC, DWSC, RAC; *Style—* John Lowein, Esq, CBE; 4 Colnebridge Close, Staines TW18 4RZ; 2 Melbourne Place, Queens Rd, Cowes, IOW; IOW Development Board, Samuel Whites Board Room, Medina Rd, Cowes, IOW (☎ 0983 200 222, fax 0983 297 242)

LOWELL, Lady Caroline Maureen; *née* Hamilton-Temple-Blackwood; er da of 4 Marquess of Dufferin and Ava (ka 1945); *b* 16 July 1931; *m* 1, 9 Dec 1953 (m dis 1957), Lucian Michael Freud, the painter, *qv*; m 2, 15 Aug 1959 (m dis), Israel Citkowitz (d 1974); 3 da (1 decd); m 3, 1972, Robert Lowell playwright and poet (d 1977); 1 s; *Books* fiction: Corrigan, Goodnight Sweet Ladies, For All that I Found There, The Stepdaughter, Great Granny Webster; cookery book: Darling, You Shouldn't Have Gone To So Much Trouble; reportage books: On The Perimeter, In The Pink; *Style—* The Lady Caroline Lowell; 80 Redcliffe Sq, London SW10

LOWEN, David Travers; s of Norman Frederick Lowen, of Southgate, London, and Beatrice, *née* Dannell; *b* 20 June 1946; *Educ* Queen Elizabeth's GS Barnet, Emmanuel Coll Cambridge (MA); *m* 23 May 1970, Jennifer, da of Sqdn Ldr Leonard Durston, of Tipton St John, Devon; 1 s (James Cybranet b 1 May 1973), 1 da (Amy Lys b 15 Jan 1976); *Career* prodr and ed; economist NatWest Bank 1967-68; Kent Messenger 1968-71, Southern Television 1971-74, Westward Television 1974-77, head of features Yorkshire Television 1977-, dir Sheffield Partnership Ltd, ITV rep CIRCOM Euro TV; memb: Yorks Ctee Lord's Taverners, Forty Club, Nat Cncl RTS (chm Yorks Ctee); *Books* Stay Alive (with Eddie McGee, 1979), Fighting Back: A Woman's Guide to Self-Defence (1983); *Recreations* cricket, birdwatching, horse racing; *Style—* David Lowen, Esq; Yorkshire Television, TV Centre, Leeds LS3 1JS (☎ 0532 438 283)

LOWENTHAL, Cecily; *Educ* SCEGGS Sydney NSW Aust (Betty Behan memb prize), Open Univ (BA); *m* Lawrence Lowenthal; 1 s (Andrew Simon b 15 May 1953), 1 da (Susan Elizabeth b 20 April 1951); *Career* freelance lectr and writer on art, Open Univ tutor 1985-86, guide Tate Gallery 1975; memb Exec Ctee: St John's Wood Soc 1960-, Contemporary Art Soc 1990-; fndr memb Patrons of New Art Tate Gallery, memb ICOM 1980-; *Recreations* photography, friends, my profession, travel; *Style—* Mrs Cecily Lowenthal

LOWER, Jonothan Amnest; s of Martin Amnest Lower, and Jane, *née* Noyes; *b* 20 May 1967; *Educ* Castle Sch Taunton; *Career* professional jockey; first ride 1985 as conditional jockey, winner Conditional Jockey's Championship 1987-88, best season 49 winners 1989-90; *Recreations* play squash, water ski all summer; *Style—* Jonothan Lower, Esq; 12 Denning Close, Newbarn Park, Galmington, Taunton, Somerset (☎ 0823 333221); Martin Pipe Racing Stables, Pond House, Nicholashayne, Wellington (☎ 0884 840715)

LOWIN, Rex James; s of Haydn Leslie Lowin (d 1971), and Madge Ruth, *née* Lamb; *b* 16 Nov 1945; *Educ* Luton GS, Imperial Coll London (BSc, MPhil, ARCS, DIC), Cranfield Sch of Management (MBA); *m* 20 July 1968, Susan Annette, da of Charles Thomas Gibbs (d 1982); 3 s (Simon b 1970, Guy b 1976, Julian b 1978), 1 da (Anastasia b 1972); *Career* md: Plessey Microwave Ltd 1983-88, Plessey Three-Five Group Ltd 1988-90; dir: Marplex SA (France) 1984-89, Pentagon Technical Services Ltd 1990-; chm: Lionmede Ltd 1990-, Northampton Signs Ltd 1990-; memb Cncl Northants C of C and Indust; *Style—* Rex Lowin, Esq; 19 Lower Rd, Milton Malsor, Northants NN7 3AW (☎ 0604 858605); Northampton Signs Ltd, Stour Rd, Weedon Rd Industrial Estate, Northampton NN5 5AA (☎ 0604 758198, fax 0604 759515)

LOWNDES, Rosemary Morley; da of Henry Vaughan Lowndes (d 1951), of Oxton, Cheshire, and Patricia, *née* Watts; *b* 20 Sept 1937; *Educ* Moreton Hall Shrops, Liverpool Coll of Art (BA); *m* 23 Oct 1975, Trevor Courtney Jones, s of William Jones (d 1978), of The White Lodge, Caversham, Berks; 1 s (Simon Geoffrey b 30 Oct 1977); *Career* graphic designer, writer and illustrator with Claude Kailer; 46 childrens books incl: Make Your Own World of Christmas, Make Your Own History of Costume, Make Your Own World of Theatre, Make Your Own Noah's Ark, Make Your Own Victorian House, The Market, An Edwardian Album; designer for china and stationery; oil-painting exhibitions incl one man shows in: Paris, Deauville, Honfleur, London, Oxford, Chicago; FCSD 1976; *Recreations* opera, ballet; *Style—* Miss Rosemary Lowndes; 132 Tachbrook St, London SW1 (☎ 071 834 5273)

LOWNIE, Andrew James Hamilton; s of His Hon Judge Ralph Hamilton Lownie, and Claudine, *née* Lecrocq; *b* 11 Nov 1961; *Educ* Fettes, Westminster, Magdalene Coll Cambridge (MA), Univ of Edinburgh (MSc); *Career* dir: John Farquharson Ltd literary agents 1986-88, Andrew Lownie literary agency 1988-; journalist; contrib: Spectator, The Times, Scotland on Sunday; tstee Iain MacLeod Award, former pres Cambridge Union Soc; *Books* A Literary Companion to Edinburgh, New-Revisionist Essays in American Espionage; *Recreations* music, outdoor pursuits; *Clubs* Travellers, Special Forces; *Style—* Andrew Lownie, Esq; 122 Bedford Court Mansions, Bedford Square, London WC1B 3AH (☎ 071 636 4917); 15-17 Heddon St, London W1R 7LF (☎ 071 734 1510, fax 071 287 5118)

LOWNIE, His Hon Judge Ralph Hamilton; s of James Hood Wilson Lownie (d 1961), of Edinburgh, and Jessie, *née* Aitken (d 1952); *b* 27 Sept 1924; *Educ* George Watson's Coll Edinburgh, Univ of Edinburgh (MA, LLB), Univ of Kent (PhD); *m* 12 Nov 1960, Claudine Theresa, da of Pierre Claude Lecrocq (d 1976), of Reims, France; 1 s (Andrew James Hamilton b 1961), 1 da (Solange Helen Hamilton b 1963); *Career* WWII RE 1943-47, served NW Europe; memb Faculty of Advocates 1959, called to the Bar Inner Temple 1962; practised privately as WS 1952-54, in Judicial and Legal Depts of Kenya Govt 1954-65, in Judicial Dept Bermuda Govt 1965-72, met stipendiary magistrate 1974-86, circuit judge 1986-; *Style—* His Hon Judge Lownie

LOWREY, Air Cmdt Dame Alice; DBE (1960), RRC (1954); da of William John Lowrey, and Agnes Lowrey; *b* 8 April 1905; *Educ* Yorkshire Training Sch, Sheffield Royal Hosp; *Career* joined PMRAFNS 1932; served in Iraq and Aden; princ matron HQ, Middle East Air Force and Far East Air Force 1956-58, HQ Home Command and Technical Training Cmmd 1958-59, Air Cmdt 1959, matron in chief PMRAFNS 1959-63 (ret), Offr Sister OStJ 1959; *Style—* Air Cmdt Dame Alice Lowrey, DBE, RRC; Oakwood House, Bupa Nursing Home, Old Watton Rd, Norwich, Norfolk NR4 7IP

LOWRIE, Anthony Carmel (Tony); s of Vincent Lowrie, of Rhodesia and SA (d 1988), and Gwendoline, *née* Stephens; *b* 24 March 1942; *Educ* Llewellyn HS N Rhodesia, RMA Sandhurst; *m* 1 Nov 1969, Liv Torill, da of Torbjon Ronningen; 1 s (Alexander Christian b 27 Jan 1975), 1 da (Louise Therese (twin) b 27 Jan 1975); *Career* Cadet Rhodesian Army 1960-62, 2 Lt Platoon Cdr Middx Regt, Lt Support Platoon Queen's Regt, Capt 10 PMO Gurkha Rifles cmdg support co, Maj 1/2 Gurkha Rifles cmdg C company; bd dir of Hoare Govett stockbrokers 1986- (trainee 1973, Devpt Asian Equity Sales, ptnr 1978-, dir of Hoare Govett Asia, head of SE Asia Devpt Singapore), chm Hoare Govett International Securities 1988-, bd dir Security Pacific Hoare Govett; dir: The SESDAQ Fund, The Scottish Asian Fund, The Thai Euro Fund, The Malaysian Emerging Companies Fund; non-exec dir: J D Weatherspoon, City Wine Bars; non-exec chm Superchalet Ltd; memb London Stock Exchange 1984; *Recreations* rugby, golf, tennis, skiing; *Clubs* Blackheath, Walton Health Golf, The Addington; *Style—* Tony Lowrie, Esq; 7 Orchard Drive, Blackheath, London SE3 (☎ 081 852 0652); Glassenbury Cottage, Cranbrook, Kent (☎ 0580 713148); Hoare Govett Ltd, Security Pacific House, 4 Broadgate, London EC2M 7LE (☎ 071 374 1256/071 601 0101, fax 071 256 9961, telex 297801)

LOWRY, (Edward) Frederick Blair; s of Henry Lowry (d 1973), and Evelyn Lowry (d 1970); *b* 27 Jan 1936; *Educ* Cambell Coll Belfast, Dublin Univ (BA, LLB); *m* 19 July 1961, (Flora) Elisabeth, da of Austin Fulton (d 1986); 3 s (David b 1963, John b 1966, Andrew b 1969), 1 da (Catherine b 1962); *Career* CA in practice 1965-67, co sec Ulster Hosiery Ltd 1967-70, dir Berks Int (UK) Ltd 1970-75; md: Lee Div of VF Corp (UK) Ltd 1975-81, Berks Hosiery (UK) Ltd 1982-89; chm Br Branded Hosiery Gp 1988-89; FCAI; *Recreations* golf, sailing, gardening, photography; *Style—* Frederick Lowry, Esq; Berkshire Hosiery (UK) Ltd, Donaghadee Rd, Newtownards, Belfast BT23 3QR (☎ and telex 0247 813 461, fax 0247 816 345)

LOWRY, Jean; da of George Fyfe (d 1961), of Langside, Histon, Cambridge, and Margaret, *née* Ferguson (d 1962); *b* 3 April 1912; *Educ* Perse HS for Girls Cambridge; *m* 29 July 1937, Martin Hofland Lowry, s of Prof Thomas Martin Lowry, CBE, FRS (d 1936), of Cambridge; 1 s (Martin Patrick b 17 March 1944), 1 da (Gillian Margaret b 8 June 1939); *Career* cncllr Hampstead Borough 1956-65, Mayoress of Hampstead 1964-65, JP for N Westminster 1968-83; tstee Wells and Campden Tst Hampstead 1966 (chm 1985-86); *Recreations* music, gardening, countryside pursuits, social work; *Style—* Mrs Jean Lowry

LOWRY, Sir John Patrick (Pat); CBE (1978); s of John McArdle Lowry; *b* 31 March 1920; *Educ* Wyggeston GS, LSE (BComm); *m* 1952, Sheilagh Davies; 1 s, 1 da; *Career* served WWII HM Forces, joined Engrg Employers Fedn (dir 1965-70); British Leyland 1970-81; chm ACAS 1981-87, mediator between govt and unions in NHS dispute 1982; former memb: UK employers delegn to ILO, ct of inquiry Grunwick dispute 1977; pres Inst of Personnel Mgmnt 1987-89; CPIM, CBIM; kt 1985; *Style—* Sir Pat Lowry, CBE; 31 Seaton Close, Lynden Gate, London SW15 3TJ (☎ 081 785 6199)

LOWRY, Her Hon Judge Noreen Margaret (Nina); *née* Collins; da of John Edmund Collins, MC (d 1971), of Sway, Hants, and Hilda Grace, *née* Gregory (d 1985); *b* 6 Sept 1925; *Educ* Bedford HS, Univ of Birmingham (LLB); *m* 1, 25 March 1950 (m dis 1962), Edward Lucas, s of late Edward Walker Gardner, of Preston, Lancs; 1 s (Stephen b 15 May 1956), 1 da (Sally b 2 Oct 1953); m 2, 24 April 1963, His Honour Judge Richard John Lowry *qv*; 1 da (Emma b 25 Nov 1964); *Career* called to the Bar Grays Inn 1948, practised as Miss Nina Collins, appointed Metropolitan Stipendiary Magistrate 1967, memb Criminal Law Revision Ctee 1975, appointed Circuit Judge 1976; *Recreations* theatre, travel; *Style—* Her Hon Judge Nina Lowry; Central Criminal Court, Old Bailey, London EC4M 7EH (☎ 071 248 3277)

LOWRY, His Hon Judge Richard John; QC (1968); s of Geoffrey Charles Lowry, OBE, TD (d 1974), of Ham, Surrey, and Margaret Spencer, *née* Fletcher-Watson (d 1976); *b* 23 June 1924; *Educ* St Edward's Sch Oxford, Univ Coll Oxford (BA, MA); *m* 24 April 1963, Her Honour Judge Noreen Margaret (Nina) *qv*, da of John Edmund Collins, MC (d 1971), of Sway, Hants; 1 da (Emma b 25 Nov 1964); *Career* enlisted RAF 1943, cmmnd and qualified as Pilot 1944, Gp Staff Offr 228 Gp India 1945, Fl Lt 1946; called to Bar Inner Temple 1949; bencher 1977, memb Bar Cncl 1965-69, dep chm Herts QS 1968, rec Crown Ct 1972-77, circuit judge 1977-, memb Home Office Advsy Ctee on Penal System 1972-77; *Recreations* theatre, swimming; *Clubs* Garrick, RAC, Vincent's, Leander; *Style—* His Hon Judge Richard Lowry, QC; Central Criminal Court, Old Bailey, London EC4M 7EH (☎ 071 248 3277)

LOWRY, Capt Robert Hugh; DL; s of Cdr R G Lowry, RN (d 1975), of Glasgdrummond, Annalong, Co Down, and Mary Langton, *née* Montgomery (d 1982); *b* 6 Oct 1932; *Educ* King's Sch Canterbury, RMA Sandhurst; *m* 11 Oct 1958, Angela Adine, da of Lt Cdr K Woods, RN (ka 1940); 2 s (Nicholas b 1961, Peter b 1964), 1 da (Joanna b 1969); *Career* cmmnd RIF 1954; served: Kenya 1954-55, ADC GOC NW Dist 1956-57, Tripoli 1959, Adj Armagh Depot 1959-60, Germany 1962-63; ret 1963; farmer of family estate since 1964; pres: Fivemiletown Branch Royal Br Legion, Clogher Valley Scouts Ctee, Clogher Valley Agric Soc, Bd of Ulster Tst for Nature Conservation; vice chm Fermanagh Harriers Hunt Club; memb of synod and church vestry; High Sheriff Co Tyrone 1987; *Recreations* riding, shooting; *Clubs* Naval and Military, 94 Piccadilly, Tyrone County (Omagh); *Style*— Capt Robert Lowry, DL; Blessingbourne, Fivemiletown, Co Tyrone, N Ireland (☎ 03655 21221)

LOWRY, Baron (Life Peer UK 1979), of Crossgar, Co Down; Robert Lynd Erskine Lowry; PC (1974), PC (NI 1971); s of William Lowry (Rt Hon Mr Justice Lowry, d 1949), and Catherine Hughes (d 1947), da of Rev R J Lynd, DD; *b* 30 Jan 1919; *Educ* Royal Belfast Academical Institution, Jesus Coll Cambridge (MA); *m* 1945, Mary Audrey (d 1987), da of John Martin (d 1979), of Belfast; 3 da (Hon Sheila Mary (Hon Mrs Corrall) b 1950, Hon Anne Lynd (Hon Mrs McCoubrey) b 1952, Hon Margaret Ina b 1956); *Career* served WWII N Africa Royal Irish Fusiliers 1940-46, Maj, Hon Col TA Bn; barr NI 1947, QC (NI) 1956, high court judge 1964; chm NI Constitutional Convention 1975; Lord Chief Justice of N Ireland 1971-88; Lord of Appeal in Ordinary 1988-; hon bencher: Middle Temple 1973, King's Inns Dublin 1973; hon fell Jesus Coll Cambridge; kt 1971; *Recreations* golf, showjumping; *Clubs* Royal and Ancient (St Andrews), MCC, Army and Navy; *Style*— The Rt Hon the Lord Lowry; White Hill, Crossgar, Co Down, NI (☎ 0396 830397); House of Lords

LOWRY, Roger Clarke; s of Henry Lowry (d 1972), and Evelyn Wilson Blair (d 1970); *b* 20 Sept 1933; *Educ* Campbell Coll Belfast, Queen's Univ Belfast (BSc, MB BCh, MRCP); *m* 3 April 1964, (Dorothy) Joan, da of David Smith (d 1976); 4 s (Kevin, Michael, Peter, Alan), 1 da (Julie); *Career* assoc prof of med Univ of Tennessee 1976-77, conslt physician Belfast City Hosp 1977- (1970-76); chm NI Chest Heart and Stroke Assoc 1980-, memb Br Thoracic Soc, involvement in interprovicial squash; memb BMA, FRCP 1980; *Recreations* golf, squash, tennis; *Clubs* Royal Co Down Golf, Royal Belfast Golf; *Style*— Roger Lowry, Esq; Milecross House, 49 Belfast Rd, Newtownards, Co Down BT23 4TR (☎ 0247 813284); Belfast City Hospital, Lisburn Rd, Belfast BT9 7AB (☎ 0232 329241 ext 2812)

LOWRY, Suzanne; da of C M Lowry, of Holywood, Co Down, NI, and Stella, *née* Davis; *Educ* Princess Gardens Sch Belfast, Trinity Coll Dublin (BA); ; 1 s (Max Patrick b 1976); *Career* journalist; reporter Belfast Telegraph 1969, diary reporter Daily Mail 1970-71, woman's ed and feature writer The Guardian 1971-77; ed: Living Pages The Observer 1977-80, Look Pages Sunday Times 1981-83; cultural features ed International Herald Tribune 1986-88, chief Paris corr Daily and Sunday Telegraph 1988-; *Books* The Guilt Cage (1980), The Young Fogey Handbook (1984), The Princess in the Mirror (1984); *Recreations* reading, gardening, and moving house; *Clubs* Groucho; *Style*— Miss Suzanne Lowry; Daily Telegraph, 4 Rue de Castiglione, 75001 Paris, France (☎ 010 33 1 4260 3885, fax 010 33 1 4261 5291)

LOWRY-CORRY, Frederick Henry; s of late Lt-Col Sir Henry Charles Lowry-Corry, and Betty, da of late Col Douglas Proby, who assumed surname Proby by Royal Licence 1904 in lieu of patronymic Hamilton (n of 1 Duke of Abercorn); *b* 23 Dec 1926; *Educ* Eton; *m* 1949, Hon Rosemary Diana Lavinia, da of 2 Viscount Plumer; 2 s; *Career* Lt RN (ret); *Style*— Frederick Lowry-Corry Esq; Edwardstone Hall, Boxford, Suffolk

LOWRY-CORRY, Hon Mrs (Rosemary Diana Lavinia); *née* Plumer; 3rd and yst da of 2 and last Viscount Plumer, MC (d 1944); *b* 29 Jan 1929; *m* 1949, Frederick Henry Lowry-Corry, *qv*; *Style*— The Hon Mrs Lowry-Corry; Edwardstone Hall, Boxford, Suffolk (☎ 210233)

LOWSLEY-WILLIAMS, David; TD (1971), JP (Gloucestershire 1967), DL (1974); s of Maj Philip Savile Lowsley-Williams, TD (d 1985) and Ida Moira Josephine, *née* Carroll-Leahy (d 1980); *b* 14 Aug 1933; *Educ* Eton, RAC Cirencester; *m* 14 April 1958, Rona Helena, da of Maj Angus McCorquodale (ka 1940, Coldstream Gds); 1 s (George b 1959), 2 da (Caroline b 1962, Joanna b 1963); *Career* Nat Serv 11 Hussars 1954-56, Royal Gloucestershire Hussars 1956-71, Wessex Yeo 1971-76 (CO 1973-76), SW Dist Staff 1976-79, Col TA, chm Gloucestershire TAVRA 1983-90; farmer, historic house owner, chm Tetbury NFU 1960-63, memb Cncl Historic Houses Assoc 1983-, steward Stratford on Avon Races, memb Gloucestershire Police Authy; *Recreations* golf, squash, skiing, travel; *Clubs* RAC; *Style*— David Lowsley-Williams, Esq, TD, JP, DL; Chavenage, Tetbury, Glos (☎ 0666 52329)

LOWSLEY-WILLIAMS, Lady (Caroline Moira) Fiona; *née* Crichton-Stuart; da of 5 Marquess of Bute (d 1956); *b* 1941; *m* 1959, Capt Michael Lowsley-Williams, 16/5 Lancers; 4 s; *Style*— The Lady Fiona Lowsley-Williams; Guadacorte, Estacion de San Roque, Cadiz, Spain

LOWSLEY-WILLIAMS, Hon Mrs (Olivia); *née* Bootle-Wilbraham; da of 6 Baron Skelmersdale, DSO, MC (d 1973), and Ann (d 1974), da of Percy Quilter and gda of Sir Cuthbert Quilter, 1 Bt; *b* 31 Dec 1938; *m* 29 July 1961 (m dis 1975), Anthony John Hoole Lowsley-Williams, 2 s of Maj Francis Saville Hoole Lowsley-Williams, 16/5 Lancers, and gs of Sir Paul Makins, 2 Bt, JP; 3 s (Richard b 1962, Sebastian b 1964, Benjamin b 1968); *Career* Interior Designer; *Style*— The Hon Mrs Lowsley-Williams; 24 Comyn Road, London SW11 1QD

LOWSON, Hon Lady (Ann Patricia); da of 1 Baron Strathcarron (d 1937); *b* 1919; *m* 1936, Sir Denys Colquhoun Flowerdew Lowson, 1 Bt (d 1975); 1 s (Sir Ian, *qv*), 2 da; *Career* OStJ; *Style*— The Hon Lady Lowson; Oratory Cottage, 33 Ennismore Gdns Mews, London SW7 1HZ

LOWSON, Sir Ian Patrick; 2 Bt (UK 1951), of Westlaws, Co Perth; s of Sir Denys Colquhoun Flowerdew Lowson, 1 Bt (d 1975), and Hon Lady Lowson, *qv*; *b* 4 Sept 1944; *Educ* Eton, Duke Univ USA; *m* 1979, Mrs Tanya Theresa H du Boulay, da of Raymond F A Judge; 1 s, 1 da; *Heir* s, Henry William Lowson b 10 Nov 1980; *Career* OStJ; *Clubs* Boodle's, Pilgrims, Brook (New York); *Style*— Sir Ian Lowson, Bt; 23 Flood St, London SW3

LOWSON, Prof Martin Vincent; s of Alfred Vincent Lowson (d 1961), of Wraysbury Bucks, and Irene Gertrude, *née* Thorp (d 1982); *b* 5 Jan 1938; *Educ* Kings Sch Worcester, Univ of Southampton (BSc, PhD); *m* 4 Nov 1961, (Roberta) Ann, da of Max Pennicutt, of Emsworth Hants; 1 s (Joff b 1965), 1 da (Sarah b 1967); *Career* apprentice Vickers Armstrongs 1955-60, res student and asst Univ of Southampton 1960-64, head of applied physics Wyle Laboratories Huntsville USA 1964-69, Rolls Royce Reader Loughborough Univ 1969-73, dir corp devpt Westland plc formerly Westland Helicopters Ltd 1979-86 (chief scientist 1973-79), prof aerospace engrg Univ of Bristol 1986-; author of articles on aerodynamics and acoustics; CEng, AFAIAA, FRAeSoc, FASA; *Recreations* research, squash, music; *Style*— Prof Martin Lowson; Department of Aerospace Engineering, University of Bristol, Bristol BS8 1TR (☎ 0272 303263, fax 0272 251154)

LOWTHER, Hon Mrs (Amanda Ursula Georgina); *née* Vivian; da of 4 Baron Swansea; *b* 22 Nov 1958; *m* 1985, Hugh William Lowther, o s of John Luke Lowther, CBE, *qv*; 1 s (Bertie b and d 1989), 1 da (Flora b 1988); *Style*— The Hon Mrs Lowther; Nortoft Grange, Guilsborough, Northants NN6 8QB

LOWTHER, Col Sir Charles Douglas; 6 Bt (UK 1824), of Swillington, Yorks; s of Sir William Guy Lowther, 5 Bt, OBE, DL (d 1982, himself 4 in descent from Sir John Lowther, 1 Bt, whose er bro was cr Earl of Lonsdale), and Grania, Lady Lowther, *qv*; *b* 22 Jan 1946; *Educ* Winchester; *m* 1, 1969 (m dis 1975), Melanie Pensee FitzHerbert, da of late Roderick Christopher Musgrave; m 2, 1975, Florence Rose, da of late Col Alexander James Henry Cramsie, OBE, of Ballymoney, Co Antrim; 1 s, 1 da (Alice Rose b 1979); *Heir* s, Patrick William Lowther b 15 July 1977; *Career* army offr; *Recreations* field sports, travel; *Clubs* Cavalry and Guards'; *Style*— Col Sir Charles Douglas Lowther, Bt

LOWTHER, Grania, Lady; Grania Suzanne; OStJ; yst da of Maj Archibald James Hamilton Douglas-Campbell, OBE (decd), of Blythswood, Renfrew, by his w, Hon Anna Leonora Beatrice, *née* Butler Massy, da of 5 Baron Clarina by his 2 w; *b* 1919; *m* 1939, Sir William Lowther, 5 Bt, OBE, DL, KStJ (d 1982); 1 s (6 Bt), 1 da (Grizelda b 1948, m 1968 Capt Timothy Bell, Scots Gds; 1 s and 1 da); *Style*— Grania, Lady Lowther; Erbistock Hall, nr Wrexham, Clwyd (☎ 0978 780144)

LOWTHER, Viscount; Hugh Clayton Lowther; s and h of 7 Earl of Lonsdale; *b* 27 May 1949; *m* 1971, Pamela Middleton; m 2, 1986, Angela Mary Wyatt; *Style*— Viscount Lowther; Lowther Estate Office, Lowther, Penrith, Cumbria CA10 2HH

LOWTHER, Hon Mrs Jennifer; *née* Lowther; raised to rank of a Viscount's da 1950; resumed her maiden name of Lowther 14 April 1989; 3 da (but 2 surviving) of Maj Hon Christopher Lowther (d 1935; er s of 1 Viscount Ullswater & f by his 1 w of 2nd Viscount), sometime MP Cumberland N, by his 2 w, Dorothy (da of Arthur Bromley Davenport and who had m 1 late Captain Samuel Loveridge; she subsequently m, as her 3 husb, 1936 (m dis 1951), Capt Hugh Cullen, MC, and m 4, 1958, Charles de Rougemont (d 1964)); *b* 11 June 1932; *m* 1, 1954 (m dis 1962), her 1 cous twice removed, 7 Earl of Lonsdale (she being his 2 w); 1 s (Hon William Lowther), 2 da (Ladies Miranda and Caroline Lowther, *qqv*); m 2, 1962 (m dis 1972), Flt Lt William Edward Clayfield, DFC, RAF; m 3, 1976 (m dis 1979), Rev Oswald Dickin Carter (d 1986); m 4, 1981 (having previously reverted to the name Hon Mrs Jennifer Lowther), James Cornelius Sullivan; *Style*— The Hon Mrs Jennifer Lowther; 19 Minister Yard, Lincoln LN2 1PY

LOWTHER, Col John Luke; CBE (1983), JP 1984); s of Col John George Lowther, CBE, DSO, MC, TD (d 1977), of Guilsborough Court, Northampton, and Lilah Challotte Sarah, *née* White (d 1976); 1st recorded Lowther Knight Sir Hugh Lowther 1250-1317; *b* 17 Nov 1923; *Educ* Eton, Trinity Coll Oxford (MA); *m* 21 Feb 1952, Jennifer Jane, da of Col J H Bevan, CB (d 1978); 1 s (Hugh b 1956), 2 da (Sarah b 1954, Lavinia b 1958); *Career* served Kings Royal Rifle Corps 1942-47, NW Europe Capt ; worked for Singer Machine Co USA 1949-51, md own manufacturing co 1951-60; dir Equitable Life Assurance Soc 1960-76; farmer 1960; Northants County Cncl 1970-84 (ldr of the Cncl 1977-81); High Sheriff 1971-, DL 1977, Hon Colonel The Royal Anglian Regt (Northamptonshire) 1986-89; Lord Lt and Custos Rotulorum of Northamptonsire 1984-; KStJ; *Recreations* shooting, countryman; *Clubs* Boodle's; *Style*— Col John Lowther, CBE, JP; Guilsborough Court, Northampton NN6 8QW (☎ 0604 740289)

LOWTHER, Hon Mrs Anthony; Lavinia; *née* Joyce; only child of Thomas H Joyce (decd), of San Francisco, USA; *m* 1958, Capt the Hon Anthony George Lowther, MBE, who d 1981 (raised to the rank of an Earl's son 1954), and yr bro of 7 Earl of Lonsdale; 1 s, 3 da; *Style*— Hon Mrs Anthony Lowther; Whitbysteads, Askham, Penrith, Cumbria

LOWTHER, Maurice James; s of James Lowther (d 1983), of Carnforth, Lancs, and Margaret Agnes Hind (d 1986); *b* 14 Sept 1926; *Educ* Lancaster Royal GS, Queen's Univ Belfast (BSc); *m* 1, 1 Nov 1947 (m dis 1976), Audrey Margaret, da of George Holmes (d 1979), of Belfast; 3 da (Anne, Valerie, Pamela); m 2, 1977, Dr Rachel Shirley Lloyd, da of Lt Cdr William F Hood (d 1980), of Handcross, Sussex; *Career* Capt RE 1944-48; md Newcastle and Gateshead Water Co 1971-86 (non exec dir 1988-90), non-exec dir Stanley Miller plc 1983-90; nat pres Inst of Water Engrs and Scientists 1980-81, nat chm Water Cos Assoc 1984-87, (vice pres 1987-); vice pres Water Aid (third world charity) 1991- (fndr dir 1981-91) chm Br Inst of Mgmnt Tyne and Wear 1973-75, govr Lancaster Royal GS 1982-; Freeman City of London, Liveryman Worshipful Co of Plumbers; Int Medal American Waterworks Assoc; FICE 1962, FIWES 1967, CBIM 1986; *Recreations* fell walking, angling, beekeeping; *Clubs* National, Northern Counties (Newcastle-upon-Tyne); *Style*— Maurice Lowther, Esq; The Old Schoolhouse, Wall Village, Hexham, Northumberland (☎ 043 481 660); Water Companies Assoc, Gt College St, Westminster

LOWTHER, Lady Miranda; *née* Lowther; er da of 7 Earl of Lonsdale, and his 2 w, Hon Jennifer Lowther (who later married Flt Lt William Edward Clayfield, DFC), younger da of late Hon Christopher William Lowther (only s of 1 Viscount Ullswater, PC, GCB); *b* 1 July 1955; *m* 1978, Martin Dunne; separated 1983 and resumed surname of Lowther by deed poll; *Career* carpenter; proprietor L M L Components; *Style*— The Lady Miranda Lowther; L M L Components, Beemill Garage, Ribchester, nr Longridge, Lancs (☎ 025 484 728)

LOWTHER, Hon Mrs Timothy; Susan Ann; *née* Smallwood; da of Capt Leonard Stephen Smallwood, of Jersey, CI, and Mrs Beryl Low, of Jersey; *m* 1977, as his 2 w, Hon Timothy Lancelot Edward Lowther (d 1984), yr s of 6 Earl of Lonsdale (d 1953), by his 2 w, Sybil Beatrix (d 1966), only child of late Maj-Gen Edward Feetham, CB, CMG, of Farmwood, Ascot; 1 da (Melinda Clare b 1978); *Career* social worker, ret; *Style*— The Hon Mrs Timothy Lowther; Ivystone House, Rue De La Croix, St Clements, Jersey, CI

LOWY, Kurt; s of Bedrich Lowy (d 1959), of London, and Marie, *née* Gutmann; *b* 28 Dec 1919, (North Czechoslovakia); *Educ* GS, Prague Univ Metallurgical Chemistry; *m* 4 Nov 1945, Blanche Ellaine, da of Isaac Pack (ka 1941); 3 da (Michele b 1948, Arlene b 1951, Stephanie b 1958); *Career* Sgt Home Guard and Anti-Aircraft Battery 1940-44; md Denham & Morely Overseas 1968-73; chm and md JVC (UK) Ltd 1973-83 (chm 1983-); *Clubs* IOD; *Style*— Kurt Lowy, Esq; 23 Cranbourne Gardens, London NW11 0HS (☎ 01 209 0181); JVC (UK) Ltd, Eldonwall Trading Estate, Priestley Way, London NW2 7BA (☎ 01 450 3282, fax 01 450 8218, telex 919215)

LOWY, Stanley Robert; MBE (1984), JP (1969); s of Frank Lowy (d 1969), of 74 Purley Bury Ave, Purley, Surrey, and Violet, *née* Rien (d 1982); *b* 20 May 1932; *Educ* Dulwich, Imperial Coll London (BSc); *m* 16 Oct 1954, Ann, da of Stanley Churchill Whitbread (d 1984), of Old Court, Ridgewood, E Sussex; 1 da (Gillian b 1956), 2 s (Richard b 1958, Edward b 1962); *Career* co dir: Unicorn Products Ltd 1958-, Gunn & Moore Ltd 1971-, Sports Feathers Ltd 1958-, Br Sports & Allied Industries Ltd 1963; chm: Croydon Bench 1980-82, SE London Magistrates Courts Ctee 1982-86, Croydon Magistrates Courts Ctee 1986-; pres Fedn of Br Mfrs of Sports and Games 1970-71, vice pres Euro Sports Trade Fedn 1975-85, tstee Sports Trade Benevolent Fund 1984-, memb Br Educn Cncl 1980-83; ACGI; *Recreations* gardening, hill walking, music; *Clubs* MCC; *Style*— Stanley Lowy, Esq, MBE, JP; The Coppice, Beech Ave, Sanderstead, Surrey CR2 0NL; Drimlee, Inveraray, Argyll (☎ 0499 2085); 119-121 Stanstead Rd, London SE23 1HJ (☎ 081 291 3344, fax 081 699 4008, telex 896124)

LOXAM, John Gordon; s of John Loxam (d 1986), of The Barn, Sellet Mill, Whittington, Carnforth, Lancs, and Mary Elizabeth, *née* Rigby (d 1966); *b* 26 April 1927; *Educ* Lancaster Royal GS, Royal (Dick) Veterinary Coll Edinburgh; *m* 7 June 1950, Margaret Lorraine, da of James Edward Smith (d 1970), of 20 Sharpes Ave, Lancaster, Lancs; 1 s (Richard b 1955, d 1977), 1 da (Stephanie b 1952); *Career* gen veterinary practice 1949-53; state veterinary serv MAFF; VO 1953, DVO 1963, DO Agric Devpt and Advsy Serv 1971, DRVO 1971, RVO 1976, ACVO 1979, DVFS 1983, ret 1986; BVA: memb Cncl 1959-71, chm Ctee 1963-67, hon sec Lincolnshire and Dist Div 1958-63; ASVO: hon sec 1963-66, pres 1966-67; sr vice pres COEs Standing Ctee on the welfare of animals kept for farming purposes 1979-80, elected to cncl of VBF 1986 (hon sec 1987-90, pres 1990), pres Old Lancastrians Club 1988-89; churchwarden All Saints Chelsworth 1990-, member Lavenham Deanery Synod 1990-, lay chairman Chelsworth PCC 1990-; MRCVS 1949; *Recreations* gardening, dog walking, golf, accommodating grand-daughters; *Clubs* Farmers, Stowmarket Golf (Suffolk); *Style—* John Loxam, Esq; Riverside, Chelsworth, Ipswich, Suffolk IP7 7HU (☎ 0449 740619)

LOXDALE, Peter Alasdair; s of Hector Alasdair Robert Loxdale, and Hilary Kathleen Ross, *née* Steen; *b* 21 Nov 1959; *Educ* Radley, Welsh Agric Coll Aberystwyth; *Career* farmer and land proprietor 1981-, dir Royal Oak Garages Ltd 1988-; chm Aberystwyth and Dist Rifle and Pistol Club 1984-, pres Llanilar and N Cardiganshire Agric Soc 1987-, pres Llanilar FC 1990-; vice chm Dyfed Exec Ctee CLA 1990-, Taxation Sub Ctee Country Landowners' Assoc 1990-; *Recreations* music, shooting; *Style—* Peter Loxdale, Esq; Castle Hill, Llanilar, Aberystwyth, Dyfed (☎ 097 47 202, mobile 0336 657439)

LOY, (Francis) David Lindley; s of Archibald Loy (d 1968), of Sheringham, Norfolk, and Sarah Eleanor, *née* Lindley (d 1967); *b* 7 Oct 1927; *Educ* Repton, CCC Cambridge (BA); *m* 28 Aug 1954, Brenda Elizabeth, da of William Henry Walker, of 11 Moorland Garth, Strensall, York; 3 da (Sarah b 1958, Alexandra b 1960, Phillida b 1967); *Career* RN 1946-8; called to the Bar Middle Temple 1952, in practice North Eastern Circuit 1952-72, rec Northern Circuit 1972; stipendiary magistrate: City of Leeds 1972-74, at Leeds 1974-; rec Crown ct N Eastern Circuit 1983-; chm Soc of Prov Stipendiary Magistrates 1990- (hon sec 1974-89); *Recreations* walking, reading, English history; *Clubs* Leeds; *Style—* David Loy, Esq; 4 Wedgewood Drive, Roundhay, Leeds LS8 1EF; 14 The Avenue, Sheringham, Norfolk; Magistrates Room, Town Hall, Leeds LS1 1NY (☎ 0532 459653)

LOYD, Christopher Lewis; MC (1943), JP (Berks 1950), DL (Berks 1954); s of Arthur Thomas Loyd, OBE, JP (d 1944), of Lockinge, Wantage, and Dorothy, *née* Willert (d 1966); *b* 1 June 1923; *Educ* Eton, King's Coll Cambridge (MA); *m* 13 Dec 1957, Joanna, da of Capt Arthur Turberville Smith Bingham, of Milburn Manor, Malmesbury, Wilts; 2 s (Thomas Christopher b 1959, James William b 1966), 1 da (Harriet Sara b 1962); *Career* served Capt Coldstream Gds 1942-46; chartered surveyor; High Sheriff of Berks 1961; tstee Wallace Collection 1973-90; FRICS 1955 (ARICS 1952); *Clubs* Boodle's, Jockey; *Style—* Christopher Loyd, Esq, MC, JP, DL; Lockinge, Wantage, Oxfordshire OX12 8QL (☎ 0235 833265)

LOYD, Sir Francis Alfred; KCMG (1965, CMG 1961), OBE (1954, MBE 1951); s of Maj A W K Loyd, Royal Sussex Regt; *b* 5 Sept 1916; *Educ* Eton, Trinity Coll Oxford (MA); *m* 1, 1946, Katharine (d 1981), da of Lt-Col S C Layzell, MC, of Kenya; 2 da; m 2, 1984, Monica, widow of Lt-Col C R Murray Brown, DSO, Royal Norfolk Regt; *Career* served WWII E Africa; dist offr Kenya 1939, private sec to Govr Kenya 1942-45, consul Mega Ethiopia 1945; Swaziland: dist cmmr 1947-55, provincial cmmr 1956, permanent sec govr's office 1962-63, HM Cmmr Swaziland 1964-68; dir London House for Overseas Graduates 1969-79; chm Oxfam Africa Ctee 1979-85; *Style—* Sir Francis Loyd, KCMG, OBE; 53 Park Rd, Aldeburgh, Suffolk (☎ 072 845 2478)

LOYD, Jeremy Charles Haig; s of Geoffry Haig Loyd, of Remenham House, Ocle Pychard, Herefordshire, and Patricia, *née* Maclean; *b* 4 July 1954; *Educ* Pangbourne Coll; *m* 6 Oct 1983, Sally, da of Duncan Robertson, TD, JP (d 1988), of Beadlam, Yorkshire; *Career* account exec Michael Rice and Co Ltd 1974-79; dir: RTI Productions Ltd 1976-80, Project Art Ltd 1978-; md Capital Radio; dir: First Oxfordshire Radio Co 1988-, Capital Radio Investments Ltd and Capital Enterprises Ltd 1989-, Wren Orchestra of London Ltd, Devonair Ltd; tstee Help a London Child; *Recreations* fishing, sailing; *Clubs* Flyfishers'; *Style—* Jeremy Loyd, Esq; Capital Radio, Euston Tower, London NW1 3DR (☎ 071 388 1288, fax 071 387 2345)

LOYD, Sir Julian St John; KCVO (1991, CVO 1979), DL (1983); s of Gen Sir Charles Loyd (d 1973), of Mettingham Pines, Bungay, Suffolk, and Moyra, *née* Brodrick (d 1982); *b* 25 May 1926; *Educ* Eton, Magdalene Coll Cambridge (MA); *m* 20 October 1960, Mary Emma, da of Sir Christopher Steel, of Southrop Lodge, Southrop, Lechlade, Glos (d 1973); 1 s (Charles b 1963), 2 da (Alexandra b 1961, Mary Rose b 1967); *Career* Coldstream Gds 1944-45; ptnr Savills 1955-64; Agent to HM The Queen at Sandringham 1964-91; FRICS 1958; *Recreations* fishing, shooting; *Clubs* Army and Navy; *Style—* Sir Julian Loyd, KCVO, DL; Perrystone Cottage, Burnham Market, King's Lynn, Norfolk (☎ 0328 730168)

LOYD, Peter Haig; s of Wilfrid Haig Loyd (d 1971), of 36 Chester Square, London SW1, and later of Oakhill, Seaview, IOW, and Emily Charlotte Eileen Loyd, MBE, *née* Oakeley (d 1978); *b* 9 Oct 1922; *Educ* Eton; *m* 1, 8 April 1950 (m dis 1957), Suzanne, da of late Eric McLeod Duncan, of The Croft, The Leigh, nr Cheltenham, Glos; 1 s (William b 6 June 1955), 2 da (Julie b 30 April 1952, Penelope b and d 8 May 1954); m 2, 26 Aug 1961, Rosemary Joan (Rosie), elder da of late Dr John Hay Moir, of Worplesdon, Surrey; 1 s (Anthony (Tony) b 5 Feb 1963), 1 da (Sophie b 10 June 1969); *Career* RM: probationary 2 Lt 1941, Lt 1943, Actg Capt 1943, Adj and Troop Cdr 42 Commando 1943-45, OC HMS Nigeria 1945-47, ADC Maj Gen Portsmouth 1947-49, Inf Trg Centre 1950-51, Capt and Troop Cdr 42 Commando 1952-53, seconded 1 Malay Regt 1955-56, ret 1957; plastics div ICI 1958-61, BTR Indust 1961-66, Industl Soc 1966-74, dir Br Inst of Mgmnt 1974-84; offshore yachtmaster 1976, neighbourhood watch area co-ordinator Hampstead Garden Suburb 1988-, vice chm Hampstead Garden Suburb Residents Assoc 1988; FMS 1966-84, FBIM 1974-, FIIM 1979-84; *Recreations* sailing, carpentry, DIY; *Clubs* Royal Naval Sailing Assoc; *Style—* Peter Loyd, Esq; 12 Meadway, Hampstead Garden Suburb, London NW11 7JS (☎ 081 455 4543)

LOYDEN, Edward; MP (Lab) Liverpool Garston 1983-; s of Patrick Loyden of Liverpool; *b* 3 May 1923; *Educ* Friary Elementary Sch, TUC educn courses, Nat Cncl of Lab Colls; *m* 1924, Rose Ann; 1 s, 2 da (1 da decd); *Career* former port worker and memb Mersey Docks and Harbour Bd (Marine) 1946-74, memb Liverpool: City Cncl 1960-74, CC Met 1973-; TGWU sponsored, MP (Lab) Liverpool Garston Feb 1974-1979; *Style—* Edward Loyden Esq, MP; 456 Queens Drive, Liverpool L4 8UA

LOYN, Prof Henry Royston; s of Henry George Loyn (d 1939), of Cardiff, and Violet Monica, *née* Thomas (d 1987); *b* 16 June 1922; *Educ* Cardiff HS, Univ of Wales (BA, MA, DLitt); *m* 14 July 1950, Patricia Beatrice, da of Capt Richard Selwyn Haskew, OBE (d 1959), of Harpenden and London; 3 s (Richard Henry b 1951, John Andrew b 1954, Christopher Edward b 1958); *Career* Univ Coll Cardiff: asst lectr 1946-49, lectr 1949-61, sr lectr 1961-66, reader 1966-69, dean 1968-70, prof 1969-74, established chair of medieval history 1974-77, dean 1975-76, fell 1981; prof and head of dept Westfield Coll London 1977-86 (vice princ 1980-86, fell 1989); pres: Cardiff Naturalists Soc 1975-76, Glamorgan History Soc 1975-77, Hist Assoc 1976-79; memb Ancient Monuments Bd for England 1982-84, pres Soc for Medieval Archaeology 1983-86, vice pres Soc of Antiquaries 1983-86; memb St Albans Abbey Res Ctee; FRHistS 1958, FSA 1968, FBA 1979; *Books* Anglo-Saxon England and The Norman Conquest (1962), Norman Conquest (1965), Norman Britain (1966), Alfred The Great (1967), A Wulfstan MS (1971), The Reign of Charlemagne (1975), The Vikings in Britain (1977), Medieval Britain (1977), The Governance of England Vol 1 (1984), The Middle Ages: A Concise Encyclopedia (ed 1989); gen intro to facsimile ed of Domesday Book (1987); *Recreations* natural history; *Clubs* Athenaeum; *Style—* Prof Henry Loyn; 25 Cunningham Hill Rd, St Albans, Herts AL1 5BX (☎ 0727 51456) Westfield College, University of London, Kidderpore Ave, London NW3 (☎ 071 435 7141)

LUARD, Hon Mrs (Philippa Mary Agnes Joan); da of 9 Viscount Chetwynd (d 1965); *b* 1930; *m* 1959, Maj John Anthony Hawtrey Luard; 1 s, 1 da; *Career* chm: Access and Rights of Way Policy Ctee, Br Horse Soc; *Style—* The Hon Mrs Luard; Maidenford, Goodleigh, nr Barnstaple, Devon EX32 7NG

LUBBOCK, Christopher William Stuart; 2 s of late Capt Rupert Egerton Lubbock, RN (3 s of Henry Lubbock, JP, DL, himself 2 s of Sir John Lubbock, 3 Bt and yr bro of 1 Baron Avebury); *b* 4 Jan 1920; *Educ* Charterhouse, BNC Oxford; *m* 1947, Hazel Gordon, *née* Chapman; 1 s, 1 da; *Career* WWII Lt RNVR 1939-45; Master of the Supreme Court of Judicature (1970-90); *Style—* Christopher Lubbock, Esq; New Barn House, Great Horkesley, Essex (☎ 0206 271207)

LUBBOCK, Hon Mrs (Helen Anne Boyd); yr da of 1 and last Baron Boyd-Orr, CH, DSO, MC (d 1971), and Elizabeth Pearson, *née* Callum; *b* 12 May 1919; *m* 7 July 1939, David Miles Lubbock, yr s of Maj Geoffrey Lubbock (himself n of 1 Baron Avebury), by his w Marguerite (wid of Sir Charles Tennant, 1 Bt, whose 2 w she was and by whom she was mother of (Margaret) Lady (w of 2nd Baron) Wakehurst, Baroness Elliot of Harwood, and the late (Nancy) Lady (w of 1 Baron) Crathorne); 3 s (Geoffrey b 1946, John b 1948, Kenneth b 1950), 1 da (Ann b 1941); *Career* sculptor; *Style—* The Hon Mrs Lubbock; Kapanda, Newton of Stracathro, Brechin, Angus DD9 7QQ (☎ 035 64 294)

LUBBOCK, John David Peter; s of Michael Ronald Lubbock, MBE (d 1989), and Diana Beatrix, *née* Crawley (d 1976); *b* 18 March 1945; *Educ* Radley, Royal Acad of Music (GRSM); *m* 12 Feb 1977 (sep), Eleanor *née* Sloan; 2 s (Daniel, Patrick); *Career* fndr and conductor Orchestra of St John's Smith Square, music dir Belfast Philharmonic Soc; *Recreations* tennis, racquets, Royal tennis; *Style—* John Lubbock, Esq; Coachmans Cottage, The Green North, Warborough Oxon OX9 8DN (☎ 086732 8210)

LUBBOCK, Hon Lyulph Ambrose Jonathan Mark; s and h of 4 Baron Avebury, *qv*, and his 1 w, Kina Maria, *née* O'Kelly de Gallagh; *b* 15 June 1954; *Educ* St Olave's GS, Univ of Birmingham (BSc); *m* 1977, Susan Carol, da of Kenneth Henry MacDonald, of Cliffsea Cottage, 10 Sunridge Close, Swanage, Dorset; 1 s (Alexander Lyulph Robert b 17 Jan 1985), 1 da (Vanessa Adelaide Felicity b 1983); *Career* local govt offr Computer Dept; *Recreations* golf, astronomy; *Style—* The Hon Lyulph Lubbock; 53 Worlds End Lane, Orpington, Kent

LUBBOCK, Hon Maurice Patrick Guy; 2 s of 4 Baron Avebury, *qv*, and his 1 w, Kina Maria, *née* O'Kelly de Gallagh; *b* 5 Nov 1955; *Educ* BSc; *m* 1982, Diana Rivia Tobin; *Career* ACGI, MIMechE, CEng; *Style—* The Hon Maurice Lubbock

LUBRAN, Jonathan Frank; s of Prof Michael Lubran, of LA, California, and Avril Roslyn, *née* Lavigne; *b* 27 April 1948; *Educ* Bedales, Univ of Chicago (BA), Cambridge (Dip, PhD); *Career* investmt advsr Crown Agents for Overseas Govts 1979-80; md: Royal Bank of Canada Investments Management International 1980-88, Bankers Trust Investment Management Ltd 1988-; former treas Crisis at Christmas, memb London Project Ctee Nat Art-Collections Fund 1977-88; *Recreations* opera, theatre, antiques, swimming, photography; *Clubs* Brooks's, Hurlingham; *Style—* Jonathan Lubran, Esq; 129 Studdridge St, London SW6 3TD (☎ 071 731 0048); Bankers Tst, 1 Appold St, London EC2A 2HE (☎ 071 726 4141, 01 982 2637, fax 01 982 3397, telex 883341)

LUCAS, Christopher Tullis; s of Philip Gaddesden Lucas, GM (d 1982), and Maise Hanson (d 1984); *b* 20 Dec 1937; *Educ* Winchester; *m* 14 July 1962, Tina, da of Dr Edward Colville; 2 da (Katherine b 1964, Suzannah b 1966); *Career* Nat Serv 1956-58; cmmnd 2 Lt 1956, 4/7 Royal Dragoon Guards; CA, Thomson McLintock and Co 1958-66 (articled 1958); chief exec ICEM 1966-72, IBA 1972-74, first md Radio Forth Edinburgh 1974-77; Royal Soc for the Encouragement of Arts Mfrs and Commerce: sec, chief exec, and non-exec dir RSA Examinations Bd; sec Faculty of Royal Designers for Industry; memb Inst CA of Scot; *Recreations* This and That; *Clubs* Garrick; *Style—* Christopher Lucas, Esq; 24 Montpelier Row, Twickenham TW1 2NQ (☎ 081 892 6584); Royal Society for the Encouragement of Arts, Manufactures & Commerce, 8 John Adam St, London WC2N 6EZ (☎ 071 930 5115, fax 071 839 5805)

LUCAS, (Henry) Cornel; s of John Lucas (d 1949), of London, and Mary Ann Elizabeth Lucas (d 1946); *b* 12 Sept 1923; *Educ* Regent St Poly, Northern Poly; *m* 30 Jan 1960, Jennifer Susan Lindem, da of Maj James Frederick Hilman, CBE (d 1974), of Loraine, St Ives, Cornwall; 3 s (Jonathan b 3 May 1961, Frederick b 29 Sept 1965, Linus b 5 March 1979), 1 da (Charlotte Rosie Linden b 29 May 1976); *Career* RAF Photographic Sch Farnborough 1941-46; Two Cities Films Denham Studios 1957-59, opened own film studio 1959, work in permanent collections of: Nat Portrait Gallery, Nat Museum of Photography, Film & Television Bradford, Royal Photographic Soc, Bath and Jersey Museum of Photography Jersey; FRPS, FBIPP; *Books* Heads and Tales (1988); *Recreations* music, painting, gardening; *Style—* Cornel Lucas, Esq; 2 Chelsea Manor Studios, Flood St, London SW3 (☎ 071 352 7344, fax 071 351 1983)

LUCAS, Sir Cyril Edward; CMG (1956); s of Archibald Lucas (d 1970); *b* 30 July 1909; *Educ* Hull GS, Univ of Hull; *m* 1934, Sarah Agnes, da of Henry Alfred Rose; 2 s, 1 da; *Career* head Dept of Oceanography Univ of Hull 1942-48; entered Civil Serv 1948; dir fishery research in Scotland Dept of Agric and Fisheries for Scotland 1948-70; memb: Cncl for Scientific Policy 1969-70, Natural Environment Res Cncl 1970-78; FRS; kt 1976; *Style—* Sir Cyril Lucas, CMG, FRS; 16 Albert Terrace, Aberdeen (☎ Aberdeen 0224 645568)

LUCAS, Brig Frederick John; CBE (1984); s of Frederick Victor Lucas (d 1977), of London, and Mary Lois, *née* Heath (d 1990); *b* 15 April 1932; *Educ* Credon Secdy Sch London, Scottish Business Sch Univ of Strathclyde (Dip Mgmnt Studies); *m* 8 Feb 1961, Virginia Isabella Elliott, da of James Robertson Hastie, of Invergordon; 3 s (Lance b 1962, Clive b 1963, Adam b 1964); *Career* cmmnd 1951, asst dir Royal Pioneers MOD 1979-81, dir Pioneers BAOR 1982-84, dir Army Pioneers 1983-85, Hon Col Cmdt Royal Pioneers 1988-; dist gen mangr Central Birmingham Health Authy 1985-86, dir Beacon Estates 1989; hon life memb Deutsche Angestellten-Gewerkschaft 1983; *Recreations* work; *Clubs* Lansdowne; *Style—* Brig Frederick Lucas, CBE; Old Swan House, King's Head St, Harwich, Essex CO12 3EE (☎ 0255 240 652)

LUCAS, Capt (Paul) Henry; s of Henry Lucas, and Alice Cowie; *b* 21 March 1962; *Educ* St George's Coll Zimbabwe; *Career* Capt QOH, Adjt RWxY; W Germany; involved property devpt Africa and Europe, fndr Ranchco Ranching; *Recreations* polo, downhill skiing; *Clubs* Cavalry and Guards'; *Style—* Capt Henry Lucas; c/o Lloyd's

Bank, 115 Victoria Road, Aldershot, Hampshire GU11 1JQ

LUCAS, Prof Ian Albert McKenzie; CBE (1977); s of Percy John Lucas (d 1970), and Janie Inglis Hamilton (d 1984); *b* 1 July 1926; *Educ* Clayesmore Sch, Univ of Reading (BSc), McGill Univ (MSc); *m* 20 Dec 1950, Helen Louise, da of Ernest Struban Langerman (d 1930), of SA; 1 s (Michael Ian b 27 Feb 1952), 2 da (Karen Elizabeth b 25 March 1953, Catherine Helen b 17 July 1967); *Career* lectr Harper Adams Agric Coll 1949-50, princ sci offr (formerly sci offr, then sr offr) Rowett Res Inst Aberdeen 1950-61, DSIR res fell Ruakura Res Station NZ 1957-58, prof of agric Univ Coll N Wales 1961-77, princ Wye Coll London 1977-88; memb: Br Soc of Animal Prodn, Agric Educn Assoc, RASE, Royal Welsh Agric Soc; hon memb Br Cncl 1987; FRAgS 1972, FIBiol 1978; *Recreations* sailing; *Clubs* Farmers; *Style—* Prof Ian Lucas, CBE; Valley Downs, Brady Rd, Lyminge, Folkestone, Kent CT18 8DU (☎ 0303 863 053)

LUCAS, Hon Ivor Thomas Mark; CMG (1980); 2 s of 1 Baron Lucas of Chilworth (d 1967); *b* 25 July 1927; *Educ* St Edward's Sch Oxford, Trinity Coll Oxford; *m* 1954, Christine Mallorie, twin da of Cdr A M Coleman, OBE, DSC, RN (d 1981); 3 s; *Career* served with RA; entered Dip Serv 1951, formerly dep high cmmr Kaduna Nigeria; cnsllr Copenhagen 1972-75, head Middle East Dept FCO 1975-79; ambass to: Oman 1979-81, Syria 1982-84; asst sec-gen Arab-Br C of C 1985-87; chm Management Bd Centre for Near and ME Studies SOAS 1987-90; memb Cncl Royal Soc for Asian Affrs 1988- (vice pres 1990-), memb Central Cncl Royal Over-Seas League 1988-, chm Anglo Omani Soc 1990-; *Books* Handbook to the Middle East (contrib, 1988), Politics and the Economy in Syria (contrib, 1991); *Recreations* music, cricket, tennis, scrabble; *Clubs* Commonwealth Tst, Royal Over-Seas League; *Style—* The Hon Ivor Lucas, CMG

LUCAS, Jeremy Charles Belgrave; s of Percy Belgrave Lucas, CBE, DSO, DFC, of London, and Jill Doreen, *née* Addison; *b* 10 Aug 1952; *Educ* Stowe, Pembroke Coll Cambridge (MA); *m* 4 Sept 1976, Monica Dorothea, *née* Bell; 2 s (Christopher b 1981, Timothy b 1984); *Career* slr Denton Hall and Burgin 1974-78; merchant banker Morgan Grenfell & Co Ltd 1978- (dir 1986-); *Recreations* tennis, golf; *Clubs* Royal West Norfolk Golf; *Style—* Jeremy Lucas, Esq; Morgan Grenfell & Co Ltd, 23 Great Winchester St, London EC2P 2AX (☎ 071 588 4545)

LUCAS, John Randolph; s of Ven Egbert de Grey Lucas (Archdeacon of Durham, d 1958), and Joan Mary, *née* Randolph (d 1982); *b* 18 June 1929; *Educ* Dragon Sch, Winchester, Balliol Coll Oxford (scholar, BA, John Locke Prize); *m* 17 June 1961, Helen Morar, da of Adm Sir Reginald Portal, KCB, DSO (d 1983), of Savernake Lodge, Marlborough; 2 s (Edward b 1962, Richard b 1966), 2 da (Helen b 1964, Deborah b 1967); *Career* fell: Corpus Christi Coll Cambridge 1956-59, Merton Coll Oxford 1953-56 and 1960-; memb Archbishop's Cmmn on Christian Doctrine; chm Oxford Consumer Gp; FBA 1988; *Books* The Principles of Politics (1964), The Concept of Probability (1970), The Freedom of the Will (1970), A Treatise on Time and Space (1973), Democracy and Participation (1976), Freedom and Grace (1976), On Justice (1980), Space Time and Causality (1985), The Future (1989), Spacetime and Electromagnetism (1990); *Style—* J R Lucas, Esq; Postmasters' Hall, Merton Street, Oxford OX1 4JE; Lambrook House, East Lambrook, South Petherton, Somerset TA13 5HW; Merton College, Oxford OX1 4JD (☎ fax 0865 276361)

LUCAS, Prof (William) John; s of Leonard Townsend Lucas, and Joan, *née* Kelly; *b* 20 June 1937; *Educ* Hampton GS, Univ of Reading (BA, PhD); *m* 30 Sept 1961, Pauline; 1 s (Ben b 28 June 1962), 1 da (Emma b 11 Dec 1964); *Career* asst lectr Univ of Reading 1961-74, visiting prof Univs of Maryland and Indiana 1967-68, reader in English studies Univ of Nottingham 1971-75 (lectr 1964-71, sr lectr 1971-75), dean Sch of Educn and Humanities Univ of Loughborough 1979-82 and 1988- (prof of English and drama and head of Dept 1977-88), Lord Byron visiting prof of English lit Univ of Athens 1984-85; advsy ed: Journal of European Studies, Victorian Studies, Critical Survey, Literature and History; gen and commissioning ed: Faber Critical Monograph, Merlin Press Radical Reprints; co-ed Byron Press 1965-82; reg contribs incl: Times Literary Supplement, Times Higher Education Supplement, London Review of Books, New Statesman & Soc, The Listener, Poetry Review, BBC (Radios 3 and 4), Essays in Criticism, Cahiers Victoriens & Edourdiens; *Books* incl: Tradition and Tolerance in 19th Century Fiction (with David Howard and John Goode, 1966), The Melancholy Man: A Study of Dickens, Arnold Bennett: A Study of his Fiction (1974), Modern English Poetry: from Hardy to Hughes (1986), Studying Grosz on the Bus: Poems (1989), England & Englishness 1990; contribs incl: Romantic Mythologies (1966), Moderns & Contemporaries (1985), Modern English Poetry (1986), Essays on Heaney (1989); poetry: About Nottingham (1971), A Brief Bestiary (1972), Chinese Sequence (1972), The Days of the Week (1983); *Style—* Prof John Lucas; 19 Devonshire Avenue, Beeston, Notts; Dept of English and Drama, Univ of Loughborough, Loughborough, Leics LE11 3TU (☎ 0509 222950)

LUCAS, Michael Stewart; s of William Lucas (d 1986), of Gt Totham, Essex, and Muriel Blanche, *née* Ginn; *b* 8 July 1947; *m* 1 Aug 1970, Letitia Marie, da of Thomas Ralph Auchincloss, of The Grange, Stanningfield, Bury St Edmunds, Suffolk; 2 s (Stewart, Charles), 2 da (Catherine, Antonia); *Career* dir Bristol Oil & Minerals plc 1986-88, chm BOM Hldgs plc 1988-, dir KCA Drilling plc 1987-90; FRICS 1969; *Style—* Michael Lucas, Esq; Rivenhall Park, Rivenhall, Essex

LUCAS, Nigel David; s of Joseph Lucas (d 1986), of Purley, Surrey, and Dorothy Mary, *née* Collier; *b* 14 May 1941; *Educ* Whitgift Sch, Westminster Hotel Sch; *m* 1, 19 Sept 1970, Linda Elisabeth (d 1979), da of Sidney Alfred Stanton (d 1972); 2 da (Sarah b 1973, Catherine b 1974); m 2, 5 May 1982, Janette Muriel, da of Harold Stanley Vian-Smith; 2 s (Matthew Peter b 12 Nov 1988, Andrew James (twin) b 12 Nov 1988); *Career* restaurateur and wine wholesaler; dir Castle Inn Ltd 1964-; memb: Hotel Catering and Institutional Mgmnt Assoc, Cookery and Food Assoc, memb Assoc Cullinaire Francaise; Freeman City of London 1983; *Recreations* family and home; *Style—* Nigel D Lucas, Esq; Withers, Chiddingstone, Edenbridge, Kent TN8 7AE (☎ 0892 870694); Castle Inn, Chiddingstone, Edenbridge, Kent TN8 7AH (☎ 0892 870247)

LUCAS, Peter William; s of William George Lucas, of Bradford Abbas, Dorset, and Jose Mabel, *née* House; *b* 12 April 1947; *Educ* Foster's Sch Sherborne, Harrow Coll (Dip M); *m* 10 June 1972, Gail da of John Small (d 1983), of Camberley, Surrey; 1 s (James Peter William b 1981), 2 da (Zoe b 1978, Joanna b 1984); *Career* mktg dir Lyons Tetley Ltd 1978-84, md Foodcare Ltd 1984-85, princ The Marketing Dept 1985-, managing ptnr Mappin Parry Lucas 1988- dir: Custom Management (UK) Ltd 1990-, Kingsbourne Ltd 1990-; chm Bd Govrs Watlington CPS; memb Mktg Soc 1980, MIGD 1985, FCIM 1987, F INST D 1989; *Recreations* shooting, gardening; *Style—* Peter Lucas, Esq; Clare Hill Cottage, Pyrton, Oxford OX9 5AX; 20 High Street, Watlington, Oxford OX9 5PY (☎ 049 161 3366, fax 049 161 2934, car 0836 288 621)

LUCAS, Hon Rachel Ann; da of 2 Baron Lucas of Chilworth; *b* 1963; *Educ* BA; *Career* public affrs political res 1986-88, foreign language teaching 1988-; *Recreations* travel; *Clubs* Royal Over-Seas League; *Style—* The Hon Rachel Lucas; c/o The Lord Lucas of Chilworth, House of Lords, London SW1A 0AA

LUCAS, Hon Simon William; s and h of 2 Baron Lucas of Chilworth; *b* 6 Feb 1957; *Educ* Univ of Leicester (BSc); *Career* computer systems engr, geophysicist (N and S America, Pakistan); *Style—* The Hon Simon Lucas; 1011 Beach Ave (2403), Vancouver, BC V6E 1T8, Canada

LUCAS, Stephen Ralph James; s and h of Sir Thomas Edward Lucas, 5 Bt; *b* 11 Dec 1963; *Educ* Wellington, Edinburgh Univ; *Style—* Stephen Lucas Esq

LUCAS, Susan Jane; da of Geoffrey Alan Lucas, and Margaret Jean, *née* Cheshire; *b* 10 May 1958; *Educ* Sir William Perkins GS for Girls, Royal Ballet Sch; *Career* ballet-dancer; roles at Royal Ballet incl: Girl in Two Pigeons, Aurora and Bluebird in Sleeping Beauty, title role in Giselle, Titania in The Dream, Poll and Blanche in Pineapple Poll, Ballerina in Petrushka, Lise in La Fille Mal Gardèe, Swanhilda in Coppelia; *Recreations* theatre, music, cinema; *Style—* Miss Susan Lucas; Royal Opera House, Covent Garden, London WC2 (☎ 071 240 1200)

LUCAS, Sir Thomas Edward; 5 Bt (UK 1887); s of Ralph John Scott Lucas (ka 1941), late Coldstream Gds, gs of 1 Bt, and Dorothy (d 1985), da of H T Timson; *b* 16 Sept 1930; *Educ* Wellington, Trinity Hall Cambridge; *m* 1, 1958, Charmian Margaret (d 1970), da of late Col James Stanley Powell; 1 s; m 2, 1980, Mrs Ann J Graham Moore; *Heir* s, Stephen Lucas; *Career* engr, scientist, management conslt, co dir 1952-; advsr EEC on int futures; FBIM, FRSA, MSPS; *Recreations* mountains, travel; *Clubs* Athenaeum, Ski Club of GB; *Style—* Sir Thomas Lucas, Bt; Sir T E Lucas & Partners (London), Shermans Hall, Dedham, Essex CO7 6DE (☎ 0206 323 506, telex 94011352)

LUCAS, Hon Timothy Michael; 2 s of 2 Baron Lucas of Chilworth; *b* 13 Sept 1959; *Educ* Lancing Coll, Univ of Surrey (BSc); *Style—* The Hon Timothy Lucas; Connaught Lodge, 59 Brownhill Rd, Chandlers Ford, Hants

LUCAS OF CHILWORTH, 2 Baron (UK 1946); Michael William George Lucas; s of 1 Baron Lucas of Chilworth (d 1967, sometime Lord in Waiting to George VI and parly sec to min of Transport), by his w Sonia (d 1979), da of Marcus Finkelstein, of Latvia; *b* 26 April 1926; *Educ* Peter Symonds Sch Winchester, Luton Tech Coll; *m* 1955, Ann-Marie, only da of Ronald Buck, of Southampton; 2 s, 1 da; *Heir* s, Capt Hon Simon William Lucas; *Career* sits as Cons peer in House of Lords; served with Royal Tank Regt 1943-47; pres: League of Safe Drivers 1976-80, Inst of Tport Admin 1980-83; vice pres Royal Soc for Prevention of Accidents 1980-; UK delegate N Atlantic Assembly 1981-83 and 1988-; memb: cncl Inst of Motor Industry 1971-75, RAC Public Policy Ctee 1981-83 and 1988- House of Lords Select Ctee Sci and Technol 1980-83, House of Lords Euro Communities Ctee 1987-; lord in waiting (govt whip) 1983-84; parly under sec of state Trade and Industry 1984-87; govr Churcher's Coll Petersfield 1984-; LAE, FIMI, FIOTA; *Style—* The Rt Hon the Lord Lucas of Chilworth

LUCAS OF CRUDWELL, Baroness (10 holder of E Barony of 1663) and Lady Dingwall (6 holder of S Lordship 1609); Anne Rosemary; *née* Cooper; da of Baroness Lucas also Lady Dingwall (d 1958, 12 holder of Lordship but for the attainder of 1715 whereby her ggggg unc, the Jacobite 2 Duke of Ormonde, was stripped of all Scottish and English honours) and Gp Capt Howard Lister Cooper (d 1972); co-heiress to Barony of Butler (abeyant since death in 1905 of her great unc, 7 and last Earl Cowper); *b* 28 April 1919; *m* 1950, Maj Hon Robert Jocelyn Palmer, MC, JP, s of 3 Earl of Selborne, CH, PC; 2 s, 1 da; *Heir* s, Hon Ralph Matthew Palmer; *Style—* The Rt Hon the Lady Lucas of Crudwell, and Dingwall; The Old House, Wonston, Winchester, Hants (☎ 0962 760323)

LUCAS-TOOTH, Hon Lady (Caroline); da of 1 Baron Poole, CBE, TD, PC; *b* 1934; *m* 1955, Sir (Hugh) John Lucas-Tooth, 2 Bt, *qv*; *Style—* The Hon Lady Lucas-Tooth; 44 Queens Gate Gdns, SW7; Parsonage Farm, East Hagbourne, Didcot, Berks

LUCAS-TOOTH, Sir (Hugh) John; 2 Bt (UK 1920); s of Sir Hugh Vere Huntly Duff Munro-Lucas-Tooth of Teananich, 1 Bt (d 1985), and Laetitia Florence, OBE (d 1978), er da of Sir John Ritchie Findlay, 1 Bt, KBE; *b* 20 Aug 1932; *Educ* Eton, Balliol Coll Oxford; *m* 1955, Hon Caroline Poole, er da of 1 Baron Poole; 3 da; *Heir* cousin, James Lingen Warrand b 6 Oct 1936; *Career* late Lt Scots Gds; dir of various cos including Lazard Investmts Ltd; *Clubs* Brooks's; *Style—* Sir John Lucas-Tooth, Bt; 21 Faroe Rd, London W14; Parsonage Farm, E Hagbourne, Didcot, Oxon

LUCE, Rt Hon Sir Richard Napier; MP (C) Shoreham 1974-, PC (1986); s of Sir William Luce, GBE, KCMG (d 1977), and Margaret (d 1989), da of Adm Sir Trevelyan Napier, KCB; *b* 14 Oct 1936; *Educ* Wellington, Christ's Coll Cambridge; *m* 5 April 1961, Rose Helen, da of Sir Godfrey Nicholson; 1 Bt, 2 s (Alexander b 1964, Edward b 1968); *Career* Nat Serv served Cyprus; dist offr Kenya 1960-62, former mangr Gallaher and Spirella Co (GB); Parly candidate (C) Hitchin 1970, MP (C) Arundel and Shoreham 1971-74, PPS to Min Trade and Consumer Affrs 1972-74, oppn whip 1974-75, oppn spokesman Foreign and Cwlth Affrs 1977-79; FCO: Parly under sec 1979-81, min state 1981-82 (resigned over invasion of Falkland Islands), re-appointed min state June 1983; min for the Arts and min of State Privy Cncl Office Sept 1985-July 1990; kt 1991; *Style—* The Rt Hon Sir Richard Luce, MP; House of Commons, London SW1

LUCIE-SMITH, (John) Edward McKenzie; s of John Dudley Lucie-Smith, MBE (d 1943), and Mary Frances Maud, *née* Lushington (d 1982); *b* 27 Feb 1933; *Educ* King's Sch Canterbury, Merton Coll Oxford (BA, MA); *Career* Nat Serv RAF Flying Offr 1954-56; worked in advtg 1956-66, poet art critic and freelance writer with contribs to The Times, Sunday Times, The Independent, The Mail on Sunday, The Listener, The Spectator, New Statesman, Evening Standard, Encounter, London Magazine, Illustrated London News; FRSL; *Books* A Tropical Childhood and Other Poems (1961), A Group Anthology (ed with Philip Hobsbaum, 1963), Confessions and Histories (1964), Penguin Modern Poets 6 (with Jack Clemo and George MacBeth, 1964), Penguin Book of Elizabethan Verse (ed, 1965), What is a Painting? (1966), The Liverpool Scene (ed, 1967), A Choice of Browning's Verse (ed, 1967), Penguin Book of Satirical Verse (ed, 1967), Towards Silence (1968), Thinking About Art (1968), Movements in Art since 1945 (1969), British Poetry since 1945 (ed, 1970), Art in Britain 1969-70 (with P White, 1970), A Primer of Experimental Verse (ed, 1971), French Poetry: The Last Fifteen Years (ed with S W Taylor, 1971), A Concise History of French Painting (1971), Symbolist Art (1972), Eroticism in Western Art (1972), The First London Catalogue (1974), The Well Wishers (1974), The Burnt Child (1975), The Invented Eye (1975), World of the Makers (1975), How the Rich Lived (with C Dars, 1976), Joan of Arc (1976), Work and Struggle (with C Dars, 1977), Fantin-Latour (1977), The Dark Pageant (1977), Art Today (1977), A Concise History of Furniture (1979), Super Realism (1979), Cultural Calendar of the Twentieth Century (1979), Art in the Seventies (1980), The Story of Craft (1981), The Body (1981), A History of Industrial Design (1983), Art Terms: an illustrated dictionary (1984), Art in the Thirties (1985), American Art Now (1985), The Male Nude: a Modern View (with Francois de Louville, 1985), Lives of the Great Twentieth Century Artists (1986), Sculpture Since 1945 (1987), The Self Portrait: a Modern View (Sean Kelly, 1987), Art in the 1980's (1990), Art Deco Painting (1990), Fletcher Banton (1990); *Recreations* the auction rooms; *Style—* Edward Lucie-Smith, Esq; c/o Rogers Coleridge & White, 20 Powis Mews, London W11

LUCK, Stewart Charles; s of Philip Charles Luck, of Northampton, and May Elizabeth, *née* Collins; *b* 5 Sept 1950; *Educ* Sywell C of E Sch, Overstone C of E Sch, Moulton Sch, Northampton Tech Coll; *m* 16 Aug 1980, Jane, da of Norman Bishop; 1 s (Henry Charles), 1 da (Aimee Elizabeth); *Career* progress offr Pianotorte

Supplies Ltd 1968-69, air traffic control asst London Heathrow 1969-70, flying instr Brooklands Aviation Sywell Airport 1970-71, commercial pilot Skycab Europe 1972, exec aircraft capt Ford Motor Co 1985- (first offr 1973-85); chm assoc of air display organisers and participants, memb Debden Parish Cncl; *Recreations* flying, gliding, water skiing, sailing, reading; *Clubs* Popular Flying Assoc, Historic Aircraft Assoc; *Style*— Stewart Luck, Esq; Kyalmai, Thaxted Rd, Debden, Saffron Walden, Essex CB11 3LW (☎ 0799 40866); Ford Motor Co, Air Transportation Dept, Stansted Airport, Essex

LUCKES, Richard James; s of Norman James Luckes, of Spain, and Phyllis Edna, *née* Perry; *b* 9 Dec 1945; *Educ* St George's Tunbridge Wells, Weston-super-Mare GS, Univ of Leeds (LLB); *m* 18 Oct 1969, Mary Penelope, da of Douglas Aldwyn Humphries, of Weston-super-Mare; 3 da (Anna b 1974, Julia b 1975, Sally (twin) b 1975); *Career* slr of Supreme Ct 1969-, NP 1980-; former memb Saffron Walden Round Table, tstee Saffron Walden Medics (formerly Accident Gp); memb: Univ of Leeds Law Graduates Assoc, Cambs and Dist Law Soc, Prov Notaries Soc, Slrs Benevolent Assoc; memb Law Soc, AIJA 1980; *Recreations* golf, tennis, motoring; *Clubs* Saffron Walden Golf, Saffron Walden Rotary; *Style*— Richard Luckes, Esq; 18 Hill St, Saffron Walden, Essex (☎ 0799 22636, fax 0799 513282)

LUCKETT, Nigel Frederick; s of George Ward Luckett (d 1958), of Wolverhampton, and Marjorie Phyllis, *née* Jefferey (d 1974); *b* 27 Aug 1942; *m* 18 Sept 1965, Janet Mary, da of late Albert Edward Sadler; 2 s (Richard Stephen b 18 Nov 1971, David Nigel b 6 Feb 1981); *Career* articled clerk Ridsdale Cozens & Purslow (accountants) Walsall, Birmingham Office Peat Marwick Mitchell & Co 1964-66; ptnr: Thomson McLintock & Co 1970 (joined 1966), KPMG Peat Marwick McLintock (upon merger) 1987-; memb Ctee Birmingham and West Midlands Soc of Chartered Accountants 1975-83; ATII 1966, FCA 1975 (ACA 1964); memb: Soc of Tech Analysts 1988, Br Acad of Experts 1991; *Recreations* golf, classical music, antiques, walking, the technical analysis of securities; *Style*— Nigel Luckett, Esq; Englefield House, 108 White Hill, Kinver, Stourbridge, West Midlands KPMG Peat Marwick McLintock, Peat House, 2 Cornwall St, Birmingham B3 2DL (☎ 021 233 1666, fax 021 233 4390)

LUCKHAM-DOWN, Melvyn Raymond; s of Sydney Claude Luckham-Down (d 1958), of The Glen, Plympton, Devon, and Florence Gard, *née* Oatey (d 1957); *b* 20 Aug 1926; *Educ* Plymouth Coll, Univ of London, Royal Dental Hosp (LDS, RCS); *m* 3 April 1954, Margaret Gwendoline, da of John Rees Davies (d 1950), of The Tonn, Llandovery, Wales; 2 s (John b 1956, Edwin b 1965), 1 da (Sarah b 1959); *Career* cmmnd Devonshire Regt 1944, Capt GSO3 Greece 1948, Maj RADC 1955-59; dental surgn and co dir; memb: Marine Biological Assoc, Fedn Dentaire Internationale; Freeman City of London 1977, Liveryman Worshipful Co of Wheelwrights; memb American Dental Assoc; *Recreations* fly fishing, golf, shooting, orchid growing; *Style*— Melvyn Luckham-Down, Esq

LUCKHOO, Hon Sir Edward Victor; QC (Guyana 1965); s of Edward Alfred Luckhoo, OBE (d 1965); bro of Sir Lionel A Luckhoo, *qv*, and Evelyn Maud, *née* Mungalsingh (d 1975); *b* 24 May 1912; *Educ* Queen's Coll Guyana, St Catharine's Coll Oxford (BA); *m* 1981, Maureen, da of John Mitchell Moxlow (resides in Yorkshire); *Career* called to the Bar Middle Temple 1936, chllr and pres Ct of Appeal Guyana 1968-77 ; high cmmr for Guyana to India and Sri Lanka 1977-83; chm: Customs Tariff Tbnl 1954-56, Judicial Serv Cmmn in Guyana 1968-76, Honours Advsy Cncl of Guyana 1970-76; pres Guyana Bar Assoc 19653-60; memb: Municipal Cncl of Georgetown 1946, Exec Bd UNESCO 1983-; rep Guyana: Caribbean Cncl of Legal Educn 1970-75, Cwlth Law Conf New Delhi 1977; Order of Roraima Guyana 1976; kt 1970; *Clubs* Georgetown Cricket; *Style*— Hon Sir Edward Luckhoo, QC; 17 Lamaha St, Georgetown, Guyana (☎ 58399); office: Whitehall Chambers, Croal Street, Georgetown (☎ 59232)

LUCKHOO, Hon Sir Joseph Alexander; s of Joseph Alexander Luckhoo, KC (d 1949), by his w Clara Irene Luckhoo (d 1966); *b* 8 June 1917; *Educ* Queen's Coll British Guyana, UCL (BSC); *m* 1964, Leila Patricia, da of David Dudistil Singh, of New Jersey, USA; 3 s, (Joseph b 1965, Philip b 1968, Jeremy b 1970), 1 da (Elizabeth b 1972); *Career* called to the Bar Middle Temple 1944, crown counsel Br Guyana 1949-53, legal draftsman Br Guyana 1953-55, additional puisne judge Br Guyana 1955-56, puisne judge Br Guyana 1956; chief justice: Br Guyana 1960-66, Guyana 1966-67; judge Ct of Appeal Jamaica 1967-76; reserve judge Bahamas Ct of Appeal 1978-81; Turks and Caicos Is Ct of Appeal: judge 1978-82, pres 1982-87; Bahamas Ct of Appeal: judge 1981-82, pres 1982-87; judge Belize Court of Appeal 1987-; ed Br Guyana Law Reports 1956-58, Br Guyana Section of West Indian Reports 1958-60, Jamaica section of West Indian Reports 1968-70; kt 1963; *Recreations* watching sport (principally tennis, baseball and hockey); *Style*— The Hon Sir Joseph Luckhoo; 31 Aldenham Crescent, Don Mills, Ontario M3A 1S3, Canada

LUCKHOO, Sir Lionel Alfred; KCMG (1969), CBE (1962), QC (Guyana 1954); s of Edward Alfred Luckhoo, OBE (d 1965); bro of Hon Sir Edward V Luckhoo, *qv*; *b* 2 March 1914; *Educ* Queen's Coll Guyana; *m* Sheila Chamberlin; 2 s, 3 da; *Career* called to the Bar Middle Temple 1940; MLC 1947-52, memb State Cncl 1953-54, MEC 1955-57, min without portfolio 1955-57; high cmmr for Guyana in the UK 1966-70; ambass for Guyana and Barbados to Paris Bonn and the Hague 1967-70; ambass of Guyana to Venezuela 1970-72; private law practice 1972- (holds record as world's most successful advocate with 236 successful defences in murder cases); *Style*— Sir Lionel Luckhoo, KCMG, CBE, QC; Lot 1, Croal St, Georgetown, Guyana

LUCKHURST, Prof Geoffrey Roger; s of William Thomas Victor Luckhurst (d 1970), and Hilda Mary, *née* Flood; *b* 21 Jan 1939; *Educ* Sir Joseph Williamson's Mathematical Sch Rochester, Univ of Hull, Univ of Cambridge; *m* 3 July 1965, Janice Rita, da of Colin Jack Flanagan, of Romsey, Hants; 2 da (Nicola Jane b 25 Jan 1970, Caroline b 15 July 1972); *Career* Univ of Southampton: lectr 1967-70, reader 1970-77, prof of chemistry 1977-, chem Dept of Chemistry 1990; FRSC 1982; *Style*— Prof Geoffrey Luckhurst; Department of Chemistry, The University, Southampton SO9 5NH (☎ 0703 593795, fax 0703 593781, telex 47661)

LUCKIN, (Peter) Samuel; s of Geoffrey Grimston Luckin (d 1986), of High Easter, nr Chelmsford, Essex, and Muriel Bessie, *née* Need (d 1962); *b* 9 March 1938; *Educ* Felsted Sch Essex; *Career* Nat Serv cmmnd Essex Regt 1956-58, platoon cdr BAOR; press aide for Rt Hon Edward Heath CCO 1960's, dep head PR for Brewers' Soc 1970's, Owner Sam Luckin Assoc Surrey 1980-, served on Bd of Mgmnt of Ashridge Mgmnt Coll Assoc 1982-85; memb IPR Cncl 1989-91 (chm Membership Ctee 1991-, memb Bd of Mgmnt 1991-), chm Residents Assoc, active with the Camberley Soc; FIPR 1990; *Recreations* swimming, jogging, theatre, mgmnt devpt, IPR events; *Clubs* Farmers Club, MCC; *Style*— Samuel Luckin, Esq; 13 Belmont Mews, Camberley, Surrey GU15 2PH (☎ 0276 61928)

LUCY; *see*: Fairfax-Lucy

LUCZYC-WYHOWSKA, Hon Mrs (Oriel Annabelle Diana Skeffington); da of 13 Visc Massereene and Ferrard; *b* 6 Feb 1950; *Educ* Downham, Tunbridge Wells Tutors, La Sorbonne; *m* 1971, Dominik Albin Thomas Luczyc-Wyhowska, s of Stanislaus Luczyc-Wyhowska, of Dalcove, Roxburgh; 2 da (Sofia b 1973, Kassia b 1980); *Style*— The Hon Mrs Luczyc-Wyhowska; Chilham Castle, Chilham, nr Canterbury, Kent (☎ 0227 730319)

LUDBROOK, Michael Sydney; *b* 31 Oct 1944; *m* 1 (m dis); 1 s (James Michael b 1982), 3 da (Claudia Jane b 1976, Gemma Elizabeth b 1977, Hannah Penelope b 1979); m 2, 31 March 1989, Sarah Louise, *née* Long; *Career* dir Mecca Dancing 1977; md: Mecca Leisure Ltd 1981, Warner Holidays 1985-87; jt md Mecca Leisure Group plc 1986, chm Mecca Int 1986; dir: Tiffany Productions Ltd 1986, Mecca Scotland; *Recreations* tennis; *Clubs* Groucho; *Style*— Michael S Ludbrook, Esq

LUDDINGTON, Sir Donald Collin Cumyn; KBE (1976), CMG (1973), CVO (1974); s of Norman John Luddington; *b* 18 Aug 1920; *Educ* Dover Coll, Univ of St Andrews (MA); *m* 1945, Garry Brodie, da of Alexander Buchanan Johnston; 1 s, 1 da; *Career* WWII served KOYLI and RAC; Hong Kong Govt 1949-73: dist cmmr 1969-71, sec for home affrs 1971-73; high cmmr Western Pacific 1973-74, govr Solomon Islands 1974-76, chm Public Servs Cmmn Hong Kong 1977-78, cmmr Ind Cmmn Against Corruption Hong Kong 1978-80, ret; *Style*— Sir Donald Luddington, KBE, CMG, CVO; The Firs, Little Lane, Easingwold, York

LUDDINGTON, Gary Anthony Cluer; s of Anthony William Davey Luddington, of Thurlestone, Devon, and Mae Luddington; *b* 20 Feb 1946; *Educ* Brockenhurst GS, Univ of Cambridge (MA); *m* 1, 1968; 1 s (Thomas James b 11 Jan 1972), 1 da (Victoria Louise b 31 July 1970); m 2, 1978, Diana Elizabeth Parkinson, *née* Turnbull; 1 step s (Rufus Joseph b 1972), 1 step da (Clair Elizabeth b 1966); *Career* brand mangr: Beecham 1968-70, Warner Lambert 1970-72; mktg mangr Mars Confectionery 1972-77, md ATV Licensing 1977-79, mktg dir Carlsberg UK 1979-82, md Letraset UK 1982-83, mktg dir Guinness Brewing 1983-87, world wide gp mktg dir Utd Distillers Gp 1987-89, exec dir Norman Broadbent Int 1989-; *Recreations* shooting, sailing, golf; *Style*— G Luddington, Esq; Norman Broadbent Int, 65 Curzon St, London (☎ 0491 579203)

LUDER, Dr Joseph; s of Abraham Luder (d 1969), of London, and Hannah, *née* Gershkovitch (d 1959); *b* 9 March 1923; *Educ* Parmiters Fndn Sch London, Guy's Hosp Med Sch (Open Jr Sci scholar, MB BS, MRCP, MD, DCH, Wooldridge meml prize in physiology, Golding-Bird Gold medal and prize in obstetrics and gynaecology); *m* 9 March 1952, Shirley June, da of Abraham Lishner; 2 s (Anthony Steven b 23 Nov 1953, Robert Irvan b 25 Dec 1956); *Career* Sqdn Ldr RAF Med Service UK and Singapore 1946-48; house physician and resident pathologist Guy's Hosp 1945; res med offr: Princess Louise Hosp for Children London 1949, Victoria Hosp for Children 1950-51; sr registrar Hosp for Sick Children Gt Ormond St 1952-57 (registrar 1951-52), seconded to Mulago Hosp Kampala and Makerere Univ Med Sch Uqanda Med Service 1954-56; conslt paediatrician: Royal Northern Hosp London 1957-83, City of London Maternity Hosp 1957-86, Spastics Soc 1959-83, West Herts Gp of Hosps 1960-64, Whittington Hosp London 1964-83; conslt i/c Watford Spastics Centre 1963-84, lectr at UCH Med Sch 1964-83; chm Med-Tech Ctee Int Games for Spastics 1978-88, visiting paediatrician Mother and Baby Unit Holloway Prison 1981-86, paediatric memb Dept of Health Vaccine Damage Tbnl 1987-; memb: BPA 1956, BMA 1957, RSM 1958-89; *Books* author of chapters in: Diagnosis and Treatment of Medical Diseases (1955), Diseases of Children in The Tropics and Sub-Tropics (1958); *Recreations* golf, canal boating, woodwork, music; *Style*— Dr Joseph Luder; Chatswood, 54 Galley Lane, Arkley, Barnet, Herts EN5 4AL (☎ 081 449 5311); Consulting Room, 152 Harley St, London W1N 1HH (☎ 071 935 3834)

LUDER, (Harold) Owen; CBE (1986); s of Edward Charles Luder (d 1981), and Ellen Clara, *née* Mason (d 1986); *b* 7 Aug 1928; *Educ* Sch of Architecture Regent St Poly, Sch of Architecture Brixton Sch of Bldg; *m* 1, 29 Jan 1951 (m dis 1989), Rose Dorothy (Doris), *née* Broadstock; 1 s (Peter Jonathan Owen b 6 Oct 1965, d 8 Dec 1965), 4 da (Jacqueline Kim b 3 May 1953, Kathryn Joy b 1954, Sara Jayne b 16 Oct 1966, Judith Amanda b 29 Jan 1968); m 2, 10 May 1989, Jacqueline Ollerton; *Career* Nat Serv RA 1946-48; qualified architect 1954, started own practice Owen Luder Ptnrship 1957, withdrew 1987 to develop new consultancy Communication In Construction; designed many bldgs UK and abroad 1954-87, environmental conslt NCB - Belvoir coal mines 1975-87; various awards incl: RIBA Bronze medallist 1963; pres: Norwood Soc 1981-, pres RIBA 1981-83 (hon treas 1975-78); vice pres Membership Communications 1989-90; columnist Building Magazine (Business Columnist of the Year 1985), contrib nat and tech press, radio and TV broadcaster; Arkansas Traveller 1971; ARIBA 1954, FRIBA 1967, PPRIBA 1983, FRSA 1984; *Recreations* writing, theatre, Arsenal FC, golf; *Clubs* RAC; *Style*— Owen Luder, Esq, CBE; 2 Smith Square, Westminster, London SW1P 3HS (☎ 071 222 4737); Owen Luder Consultancy, 2 Smith Square, Westminster, London SW1P 3HS (☎ 071 222 4737, fax 071 233 0428)

LUDLAM, Dr Christopher Armstrong; *b* 6 June 1946; *Educ* Univ of Edinburgh (BSc, MB ChB, PhD); *Career* res fell MRC Univ of Edinburgh 1972-75, sr registrar Univ Hosp of Wales Cardiff 1975-78, lectr haematology Univ of Wales 1979; Dept of Med Univ of Edinburgh 1980-: conslt haematologist, dir Edinburgh Haemophilia Centre, pt/t sr lectr; numerous publications on blood coagulation; FRCPE, FRCPath; *Style*— Dr Christopher Ludlam; Department of Haematology, Royal Infirmary, Edinburgh (☎ 031 229 2477, fax 031 228 2189)

LUDLOW, Christopher; s of Sydney Ludlow (d 1983), and Margaret Eleanor, *née* Barlee; *b* 7 Sept 1946; *Educ* King Edward VI Sch Macclesfield, London Coll of Printing (Dip AD); *m* 7 Sept 1969 (m dis 1980), Louise Frances Heather, da of Claude Duquesne Janitsch; 1 s (Edward b 1972); *Career* graphic designer; assoc Stevenson Ward Macclesfield 1971-, ptnr Gray Design Associate 1974-, princ Henrion Ludlow & Schmidt 1981; involvement in major corporate identities incl: Coopers & Lybrand, Amersham International, British Midland, London Electricity; conslt to cos incl: British Rail, KLM Royal Dutch Airlines, London Underground; organiser Annual Real World Student Seminar; articles in various design pubns, addressed American Soc Environmental Graphic Designers Detroit 1989; memb Cncl CSD; FCSD 1981; *Recreations* music, antique models; *Clubs* Zanzibar; *Style*— Christopher Ludlow, Esq; Henrion, Ludlow & Schmidt, 12 Hobart Place, London SW1W 0HH (☎ 071 235 5466, fax 071 235 8637)

LUDLOW, Lady Margaret Maud; *née* Abney-Hastings; da of Countess of Loudoun, *qv*, and her 3 husb, Peter Abney-Hastings; *b* 10 Feb 1956; *m* 1977, Brian Peter Ludlow; 2 s (Thomas William b 1983, Peter Arthur b 1987), 4 da (Kathleen Rose b 1981, Iona Clare (twin) b 1981, Alice Selina b 1985, Joy Elizabeth b 1990); *Style*— The Lady Margaret Ludlow

LUDLOW, Michael Basil; s of late George Rex Ludlow; *b* 1 Oct 1928; *Educ* Prior Park Coll Bath; *m* 1958, Anne, da of late William F P Bull; 1 s, 1 da (1 da decd 1987); *Career* md Devenish Redruth Brewery Ltd, dir J A Devenish plc (ret 1985); chm Falmouth Harbour Cmmrs; memb Cornwall Valuation Panel Appeal Ctee chm Assoc of Cornish Boys Club; *Recreations* sailing, gardening; *Clubs* Royal Cornwall Yacht; *Style*— Michael Ludlow, Esq; The Bluff, Restronguet Hill, Mylor, Falmouth, Cornwall TR11 5ST (☎ 0326 73785)

LUDLOW, Michael Richard; s of Sir Richard Robert Ludlow (d 1956), and Katharine Guthrie, *née* Wood; *b* 30 March 1933; *Educ* Rugby, Trinity Coll Oxford (MA); *m* 1, 6 Jan 1962 (m dis 1968), Prunella Evelyn Mary, *née* Truscott (now Mrs Clarke); 1 s (Richard Simon b 17 May 1964), 1 da (Anna Mary b 30 Nov 1966); m 2, 31 Oct 1969, Diane April, da of Rowland Wright, MBE (d 1960), of Bishops Park Rd, London; 2 da (Zehra Jane b 20 March 1972, Fiona Katharine b 30 Jan 1976); *Career* Nat Serv 1951-

52, jr under offr Royal Welsh Fus, cmmnd 2 Lt Queens Regt 1952, seconded to Sierra Leone Regt 1952 (trg offr), Lt N Staffs Regt TA 1952-54; admitted slr 1959, sr ptnr Beale & Co Slrs 1982- (ptnr 1965-82); cncl memb London Region CBI 1988-; Freeman: City of London 1987, Worshipful Co of Arbitrators 1987; FCIArb 1983, memb Law Soc 1959-; *Books* Fair Charges (1982); *Recreations* dreaming about past cricket, hockey and rugby exploits; *Clubs* Reform, Vincent's (Oxford), Grannie's Cricket; *Style*— Michael Ludlow, Esq; Garrick House, 27-32 King St, Covent Garden, London WC2E 8JD (☎ 01 240 3474, fax 01 240 9110, telex 912072)

LUDLOW, Peter Woods; s of Rev Richard Nelson Ludlow, of Bournemouth, and Dr Joyce Woods, MBE; *b* 20 Aug 1939; *Educ* Kingswood Sch Bath, Magdalen Coll Oxford (MA), Fitzwilliam House Cambridge (MA), Univ of Gottingen; *m* 18 April 1964, Carole Elizabeth, da of Charles Barfoot (d 1977); 2 s (Piers b 29 March 1968, Ivan b 9 Nov 1972), 1 da (Rachel b 9 Dec 1969); *Career* res fell Univ of Birmingham 1965-66, lectr in history QMC Univ of London 1966-76, and 1980-81, prof Euro Univ Inst Florence 1976-81, dir Centre for Euro Policy Studies Brussels 1981-, memb and raporteur Euro Community Asean High Level Working Pty 1985; RIIA, IISS London; *Books* The Making of the European Monetary System (1982), Beyond 1992 (1989), Towards a European Foreign Policy (with Henri Froment-Meurice, 1990); *Recreations* walking, skiing, tennis, music; *Style*— Peter Ludlow, Esq; 32 Ave De L'Hippodrome, 1050 Brussels (☎ 010 322 649 7867); Centre for European Policy Studies, Rue Ducale 33, B-1000 Brussels, Belgium (☎ 010 322 513 4080, fax 010 511 5960, telex 62818 CEPS B)

LUESLEY, Dr David Michael; s of Michael James Joseph Luesley, of Wakefield, Yorkshire, and Elizabeth Montogomery, *née* Aitken (d 1970); *b* 14 Feb 1952; *Educ* Queen Elizabeth GS Wakefield, Downing Coll Cambridge, Univ of Birmingham Med Sch (MA, MB Ch, MD); *m* 22 Dec 1972, Krystyna, da of Henryk Piotr Kopczynski (d 1973); *Career* sr lectr and hon conslt obstetrician and gynaecologist Dudley Rd Hosp Birmingham Univ of Birmingham; asst sec Br Soc for Colposcopy and Cervical Cytology, cncl memb Br Gynaecological Cancer Soc; MRCOG 1980; *Recreations* rugby football, travel, photography, painting; *Clubs* Moseley RUFC; *Style*— Dr David Luesley; Dudley Road Hosp, Maternity Department, Dudley Road, Birmingham (☎ 021 554 3801)

LUETCHFORD, Robert Sellick; s of William Luetchford (d 1984), and Roma, *née* Lawrence; *b* 29 March 1949; *Educ* Harrow Co GS, Pembroke Coll Oxford (MA); *m* 7 Nov 1990, Nicola Christine, da of Michael Gilbert; *Career* International Computers Ltd 1971-74 (systems engr, systems conslt), Sperry Univac (UK) Ltd 1974-77 (mainframe sales exec, sr sales exec), Plessy Co Ltd: mktg mangr Plessy Microsystems Ltd 1977-79, asst to dir Plessy Corp Staff 1979-81, dir of planning and business devpt Plessy Office Systems Ltd 1981-84; Prudential Bache Securities: head of electronics res 1984-86, vice pres 1986, sr vice pres Corp Fin 1986; md Marshall & Co (Brokers) Limited 1990- (dep chief exec 1986-90); *Recreations* opera, classical music, fly fishing; *Style*— Robert Luetchford, Esq; Upton Cottage, Upton, Hants (☎ 026 476 519); 29 Napier Terrace, London N1 (☎ 071 354 3629); Marshall & Co (Brokers) Limited, 13 Southampton Place, London WC1A 2AJ (☎ 071 404 4343, fax 071 404 5644)

LUFF, Peter James; s of Thomas Luff (d 1963), and Joyce, *née* Mills (d 1985); *b* 18 Feb 1955; *Educ* Licensed Victuallers' Sch Slough, Windsor GS, Corpus Christi Coll Cambridge (exhibitioner, MA); *m* May 1982, Julia Dorothy, da of Lt Cdr P D Jenks, RN; 1 s (Oliver Charles Henry b 10 Jan 1988), 1 da (Rosanna Amy b 29 Aug 1985); *Career* res asst to Rt Hon Peter Walker, MBE, MP 1977-80, head Private Office to Rt Hon Edward Heath, MBE, MP 1980-82, dir, asst md and md Good Relations Public Affairs Ltd 1980-87, special advsr to Sec of State for Trade and Indust 1987-89, sr conslt Lowe Bell Communications 1989-90, co sec Luff and Sons Ltd Windsor 1980-87, asst md Good Relations Ltd 1990-; Parly candidate (Cons) for Holborn and St Pancras Gen Election 1987, prospective Parly candidate (Cons) for Worcester 1990; tstee various charities, govr various schs, memb PCC, treas Deanery Synod; memb Routledge Soc of Friends; MIPR; *Recreations* steam railways, going to musicals and theatre, being with my family; *Clubs* RAC; *Style*— Peter Luff, Esq; Good Relations Ltd, 59 Russell Square, London WC1B 4HJ (☎ 071 631 3434, fax 071 631 1399)

LUFF, Richard William Peter; s of William Victor Luff (d 1962), and Clare, *née* Wieland (d 1968); *b* 11 June 1927; *Educ* Hurstpierpoint, Coll of Estate Mgmnt; *m* 1, 23 Sept 1950, Betty Hazel (d 1989), da of Alan Chamberlain (d 1970); m 2, 23 April 1990, Daphne Olivia Louise Andrews, da of Capt Philip Brough; *Career* Lt RA UK and India 1945-48; city surveyor Corp City of London 1975-84, dir British Telecom Pty 1984-87, memb Bd Cmmn for the New Towns 1987-, dep chm LRT Property Bd 1988- (memb 1987-); dir: Housing Standards Co 1988-, London Wall Litigation Claims Ltd 1988-; author of many articles in Antique Collector and Country Life; pres Local Authy Valuers Assoc 1978; pres: RICS 1982-83, Assoc Owners City Properties 1987-; Master Worshipful Co of Chartered Surveyors 1985-86; FRICS; *Books* Furniture in England, The Age of the Joiner (jtly); *Recreations* studying, lecturing, antique furniture, country houses; *Clubs* MCC; *Style*— Richard Luff, Esq; Blossoms, Broomfield Park, Sunningdale, Ascot, Berks SL5 0JT

LUFF, Robert Charles William; s of Robert Hill Luff (d 1955), and Ethel Maud Luff (d 1976); *b* 7 July 1914; *Educ* Bedford Modern Sch; *Career* served WWII Gordon Highlanders (India and Burma), Maj; underwriting memb Lloyd's 1961; life pres and tstee Cystic Fibrosis Res Tst, vice pres Nat Asthma Campaign; tstee: Brompton Hosp Adolescent and Adult Cystic Fibrosis Dept, Manton Charitable Tst, Gordon Highlanders Regtl Tst; pres: Br Scoliosis Res Fndn, Scarborough Ctee Br Heart Fndn, Scarborough Div St John Ambulance; dir: Cystic Fibrosis Res Investmt Tst 1981-85 (chm 1985-86), Hammersmith Palais Ltd 1955-61, European Sports Promotions Ltd Empress Hall 1952-60, Luff Light & Sound Ltd, Crucial Enterprises Ltd, Crucial Films Ltd; chm: Beryl Evetts & Robert Luff Animal Welfare Trust Ltd, Robert Luff Foundation Ltd (controlling Futurist Light & Sound Ltd), Robert Luff Ltd, Robert Luff Plays Ltd (controlling John Tiller Schs of Dancing); impresario responsible for the promotion of all the Black and White Minstrel Show presentations in the West End (recognised in the Guinness Book of Records as longest running musical prodn); FIOD; *Recreations* golf; *Clubs* RAC, Army and Navy, Highland Bde; *Style*— Robert Luff, Esq; 294 Earls Court Rd, London SW5 9BB (☎ 071 373 7003)

LUFFRUM, David John; s of Frederick George Luffrum (d 1970), and Gladys, *née* de Keyser; *b* 14 Dec 1944; *Educ* Latymer Upper Sch; *m* 20 May 1967, Christine, da of Albert Walker; 2 s (Daniel b 6 Feb 1969, Russell b 18 July 1972); *Career* gp accountant London Borough of Ealing 1967-70, asst treas Thames Conservancy Board 1971-73, Thames Water Authority 1974-89 (princ budget offr, asst fin dir, head of fin, fin dir), gp fin dir Thames Water plc 1989-; currently dir: TW Utilities Ltd, TW Enterprises Ltd, PWT Worldwide Ltd, Isis Insurance Co Ltd; IPFA 1967; *Recreations* golf, piano; *Style*— David Luffrum, Esq; 2 Bluebell Drive, Burghfield Common, Reading, Berks RG7 3EF (☎ 0734 833471); Thames Water plc, 14 Cavendish Place, London W1M 9DJ (☎ 071 636 8686, fax 071 436 6755, car 0836 532550)

LUFT, His Hon Arthur Christian; CBE (1988); s of Ernest Christian Luft (d 1962), and Phoebe Luft (d 1977); *b* 21 July 1915; *Educ* Bradbury Cheshire; *m* 1950, Dorothy, da of Francis Manley (d 1936); 2 s (Peter, Timothy); *Career* served RA and REME 1940-46; advocate Manx Bar 1940, HM Attorney Gen IOM 1973, HM Second Deemster (HC Judge) 1974, HM First Deemster, Clerk of the Rolls and dep govr IOM 1980-88; memb: Legislative Cncl of IOM 1988-, Dept of Local Govt and Environment 1988-; chm: Criminal Injuries Compensation Tbnl 1975-80, Prevention of Fraud Investmts Act Tbnl 1975-80, Licensing Appeal Ct 1975-80, Tynwald Ceremony Arrangements Ctee 1980-88, IOM Income Tax Cmmrs 1980-88; pres: Manx Deaf Soc 1975-, IOM Cricket Club 1980-; *Recreations* theatre, watching cricket, reading, gardening; *Clubs* Ellan Vannin, IOM Automobile; *Style*— His Hon Arthur C Luft, CBE; Leyton, Victoria Rd, Douglas, Isle of Man (☎ 0624 621048)

LUGG, (Herbert Kenneth) Michael; s of Reginald Lugg (d 1969), of Ryde, and Winifred Agnes, *née* Stuart; *b* 7 April 1934; *Educ* Ryde Sch Isle of Wight, Univ of London (BSc); *m* 22 July 1961, Valerie Dean, da of Maurice William Alfred Jacobs (d 1987); 1 da (Sarah b 1965); *Career* civil engr: agent Bridgwater Bros (PWC) 1962-64, engr Shell Mex & BP 1964-73, mangr of retail engrg BP Oil 1973-78, engrg mangr BP Oil 1978-; govr Ryde Sch 1987- (vice chm 1987); *Recreations* concerts, theatre going, classic sports cars, walking, gardening; *Style*— Michael Lugg, Esq; The Merrick, Tarn Rd, Hindhead, Surrey GU26 6TP (☎ 0428 606883); BP Oil, BP House, Breakspear Way, Hemel Hempstead, Herts HP2 4UL (☎ 0442 225719)

LUKE, Hon Mrs ((Oenone) Clarissa); *née* Chaplin; only da of 3 and last Viscount Chaplin (d 1981), and his 1 w, Alvilde, da of Lt-Gen Sir Tom Molesworth Bridges, KBE, KCMG, DSO, LLD (whose unc was Robert Bridges, the poet laureate); *b* 12 April 1934; *m* 1958, Michael Charles Deane Luke, yr s of Sir Harry Charles Luke, KCMG; 1 s (Igor b 1965), 3 da (Chloe b 1959, Oenone b 1960, Cressida b 1961); *Style*— The Hon Mrs Luke; Flat 6, 22 Eaton Sq, London SW1 (☎ 01 235 1841)

LUKE, Colin Rochfort; s of Donald Alfred Rochfort Luke, of Jersey, Channel Islands, and Mary Blanche, *née* Bennett; *b* 24 Jan 1946; *Educ* Bristol GS, Exeter Coll Oxford (MA, memb Univ fencing team, pres OU Film Soc, films ed Isis magazine); *m* 1, 1971 (m dis 1976), Sarah Moffat Hellings; m 2, 1978, Hon Felicity Margaret, da of Baron Crowther (Life Peer, d 1972); 2 s (Theodore Rochfort Luke b 1979, Hardey Rochfort b 1981), 1 da (Claudia Mary b 1983); *Career* BBC: joined as trainee film ed 1967, film and studio dirs course 1969, prodr/dir 1969-79; formed own co Wobbly Pictures Ltd 1977 (renamed Mosaic Pictures 1989), freelance film dir 1979-, dir Document Films Ltd 1982, formed Document Television Ltd 1987; progs for BBC 1969-79: The World About Us, The Romance of the Indian Railways (with James Cameron), A Desert Voyage (with Dame Freya Stark), Albion in the Orient (with Julian Pettifer), Black Safari, Take Six Girls-Israel, Taste for Adventure, Half Million Pound Magic Carpet, Diamonds in the Sky; freelance dir/prodr: Nature Watch (ATV/TV) 1980, Towards an Unknown Land (with Dame Freya Stark) 1981, The Arabs (Channel 4) 1981, Britain at the Pictures (BBC TV) 1983, Duneriders 1985-86, Heart of the Kremlin (ITV Network) 1991; freelance exec prodr: Assignment Adventure (channel 4 and worldwide) 1984-85, A Russia of One's Own (channel 4) 1987, The Great Australian Camel Race (channel 4) 1989, Dragon Flight (BBC) 1989, Passage Out of Paradise (channel 4) 1989, Nomads (channel 4) 1990; freelance dir: The Golden Road 1986-87, The Baltic Style 1987, An Affair in Mind (BBC TV) 1987-88; Freelance series ed: Voyager (Central TV/ITV Network) 1988-89, The World of Nat Geographic (Central TV) 1988-89; winner of numerous Adventure Film awards for Assignment Adventure, winner Best Film award at Le Plagne for Dragon Flight 1989; Freeman City of Louisville Kentucky 1963; fndr, memb: BAFTA, Dirs Guild of GB; memb: Prodr's Assoc, RTS 1990; *Recreations* family, travel, cinema, politics; *Clubs* BAFTA, Piccadilly, W1; *Style*— Colin Luke, Esq; Mosaic Pictures Ltd, 25 Westbourne Grove, London W2 4UA (☎ 071 229 1720, fax 071 792 9646); Document Films Ltd, 8-12 Broadwick St, London W1 (☎ 071 437 4526)

LUKE, 2 Baron (UK 1929); Ian St John Lawson-Johnston; KCVO (1976), TD (1949), JP (Beds 1939), DL (1938); s of 1 Baron Luke, KBE, JP (d 1943), and Hon Edith Laura (d 1941), da of 16 Baron St John of Bletso; *b* 7 June 1905; *Educ* Eton, Trinity Coll Cambridge; *m* 4 Feb 1932, Barbara, da of Sir FitzRoy Hamilton Anstruther-Gough-Calthorpe, 1 Bt, JP (d 1957); 4 s, 1 da; *Heir* s, Hon Arthur Charles St John Lawson-Johnston; *Career* life-pres Electrolux Ltd 1978-; chm: Gateway Building Society 1978-86, Bovril Ltd 1943-70; dir Ashanti Goldfields Corporation Ltd; former dir: Lloyds Bank, IBM UK; vice-pres Nat Playing Fields Assoc 1977- (late chm); chm Governing Body Queen Mary Coll Univ of London 1963-82, memb Int Olympic Ctee 1951-88 (hon memb 1988-); pres: Inst of Export 1973-83, London C of C 1952-55; late MFH Oakley Hunt; one of HM's Lts for City of London; CStJ; *Clubs* Carlton; *Style*— The Rt Hon Lord Luke, KCVO, TD, JP, DL; Odell Castle, Odell, Beds MK43 7BB (☎ 0234 720 240)

LUKE, Peter Ambrose Cyprian; MC (1944); s of Sir Harry Luke, KCMG (d 1969), and Joyce Evelyn, *née* Fremlin (d 1973); *Educ* Eton, Byam Shaw Sch of Art, Atelier Andre Lhote Paris; *m* 1, late Carola Peyton Jones; m 2, Lettice Grawshaw (m dis); 1 s (Harry d 1985), 1 da (Giana); m 3, 23 Nov 1963 (Mary Pamela) June, da of Lt-Col W V Tobin (d 1969); 2 s (Anthony, Ormody), 3 da (Anna, Oonagh, Rosario); *Career* WWII Rifle Bde 1939-46; served: Middle East, Italy, NW Europe; writer dramatist and dir; sub ed Reuters News Desk 1946-47, wine trade 1947-57; ABC TV: story ed 1958-62, ed The Bookman 1962-63, ed Tempo (arts programme) 1963-64; drama prodr BBC TV 1963-67; dir: Hadrian VII (Abbey Theatre Dublin) 1970, Edwards-Mac Liammoir (Dublin Gate Theatre Co) 1977-80, Rings for a Spanish Lady (Gaiety Theatre Dublin) 1978; writer of stage plays: Hadrian VII (Antionette Perry Award nomination 1968-69), Proxopera (adaption) 1979, Married Love 1985, Yerma by Federico Garcia Lorca (trans) 1987; produced TV play Silent Song (BBC TV, Prix Italia 1967); wrote and directed TV films: Anach Cuan (BBC TV) 1967, Black Sound-Deep Song (BBC TV) 1968; author TV plays: Small Fish are Sweet 1958, Pig's Ear with Flowers 1960, Roll on Bloomin' Death (with William Sanson) 1961, A Man on Her Back 1965, Devil a Monk Would Be 1966, Honour Profit and Pleasure 1985; hon memb Hermandad de Dos Hermanas Sevilla Spain; OStJ 1940; *Books* Sisyphus and Reilly (autobiography, 1972), Enter Certain Players Edwards - Mac Liammoir 1928-78 (ed, 1978), Paquito and the Wolf (1981), Telling Tales: selected short stories (1981), The Other Side of the Hill, a novel of the Peninsular War (1984), The Mad Pomegranate and the Praying Mantis, Adventure in Andalusia (1985); translated from Spanish: Yerma (by Federico Garcia Lorca), Rings for a Spanish Lady (by Antonio Gala, writer of many short stories); *Recreations* attending bull-fights, growing citrus fruit; *Style*— Peter Luke, Esq, MC; Calle San Sebastian, 2 Jimena de la Frontera, Prov de Cadiz, Spain

LUKE, (William) Ross; s of Maj Hamish Galbraith Russell Luke TD, JP (d 1970), and Ellen Robertson Boyd, *née* Mitchell; *b* 8 Oct 1943; *Educ* Stowe; *m* 16 May 1970, Deborah Jacqueline, da of Derek John Gordon; 3 da (Alison b 1973, Kirstene b 1974, Victoria b 1978); *Career* CA 1968; dir: The Mar Agency Ltd 1981, Ideal Securities Ltd 1985, R P M Securities Ltd 1989; hon sec London Scottish RFC 1988-; Met Police Commendation 1983; *Recreations* rugby football, squash; *Clubs* London Scottish Rugby FC; *Style*— Ross Luke, Esq; 105 Palewell Park, London SW14 8JJ (☎ 081 876 9228); 139 King St, London W6 9JG

LUM, Dr (Laurence) Claude; s of Samuel Lum (d 1954), and Florence, *née* Hill (d 1974); *b* 24 Jan 1916; *Educ* Adelaide HS, Univ of Adelaide (MB BS), Univ of Cambridge (MA); *m* 1, 1940, Mary Honora Carmody (d 1980); m 2, Cynthia Anne, da of Edward Stratemeyer Adams; 1 s (Edward Stratemeyer b 10 Jan 1987), 1 da (Claudia Stratemeyer b 17 Feb 1983); *Career* War Serv Aust Army Med Corps S W Pacific 1941-46; med and surgical house physician Royal Adelaide Hosp, med supt and flying doctor Alice Spring, 1946-47, asst supt (med) Royal Adelaide Hosp 1949-50, conslt physician Ipswich Chest Clinic and Br Legion Sanatorium Nayland 1950-59; Papworth Hosp: physician i/c cardio-pulmonary bypass 1959-65, conslt physician 1959-81, regnl conslt in respiratory physiology 1962-81; conslt physician W Suffolk and Newmarket Gen Hosps 1971-80; memb Cncl Nat Assoc of Clinical Tutors 1965-81 (vice pres 1973-81), ex officio memb Cncl for Post Graduate Med and Dental Educn 1974-76, vice pres RSM 1985-87; FRSM 1967, FRCP 1970 (MRCP 1948), FRACP 1973 (MRACP 1946); *Publications* Modern trends in psychosomatic medicine (contrib, 1976), Pseudo-allergic reactions (contrib, 1985), author of various papers on hyperventilation; *Recreations* ocean racing and cruising, water colour painting; *Clubs* Ipswich Art; *Style*— Dr Claude Lum; 30A Wimpole St, London W1M 7AE (☎ 071 486 1625)

LUMB, Geoffrey Norman; s of Norman Peace Lacy Lumb, OBE (d 1957), of Chidham, Bosham, Sussex, and Constance Ethel, *née* Bradley (d 1983); *b* 1 Jan 1925; *Educ* Marlborough, St Thomas's Hosp London (MB BS); *m* 11 March 1950, (Elinor) Alison, da of John Johnstone Duncan (d 1941), of Sunningdale; 2 s (Hugh b 1953, Roger b 1957), 1 da (Christine b 1951); *Career* WWII, Home Gd 1942-45, Nat Serv Flying Offr med branch RAF 1949, Flt Lt and actg Sqdn Ldr RAF Hosp St Athan 1950-51; jr hosp appts 1948-57: St Thomas's London, Guildford, Bath; sr registrar in urology 1959-64: United Bristol Hosps, Southmead Hosp; lectr in surgery Univ of Bristol 1964-65, conslt in urological surgery South Somerset Clinical Area 1965-, sr surgn Musgrove Park Hosp Taunton 1985-; memb Br Assoc Urological Surgns; FRSM; *Books* A Handbook of Surgical Diathermy (1978); *Recreations* golf, fly-fishing, travel, model railways; *Style*— Geoffrey Lumb, Esq; Kirkstall, 59 Kingsway, Fulland's Park, Taunton, Somerset TA1 3Y1 (☎ 0823 284802); Musgrove Park Hospital, Taunton, Somerset TA1 5DA (☎ 0823 333444 ext 2102)

LUMLEY, Henry Robert Lane; s of Edward Lumley Lumley (d 1960), and Kathleen Agnew, *née* Wills (d 1978); *b* 29 Dec 1930; *Educ* Eton, Magdalene Coll Cambridge (MA); *m* 7 Oct 1959, Sheena Ann, da of Air Vice-Marshal Somerled Douglas MacDonald, CB, CBE, DFC (d 1979); 2 s (Peter b 1960, Robert b 1965); 1 da (Julia (Mrs Scott McKay) b 1962); *Career* insur broker; chm Edward Lumley Holdings Ltd 1986 (joined 1974); dir: Edward Lumley & Sons Ltd, Lloyd's Brokers 1956-88, Lumley Corporation Ltd Aust 1974-89, chm Br Inst and Investmt Brokers Assoc 1990-, memb Cncl Insur Brokers Registration Cncl 1988-; *Clubs* East India; *Style*— Henry Lumley, Esq; 41 Tower Hill, London EC3N 4HA (☎ 071 488 3188, fax 071 488 3472)

LUMLEY, John Adrian; s of Thomas Lumley (d 1983), and Patience, *née* Henn Collins (d 1987); *b* 29 May 1942; *Educ* Eton, Magdalene Coll Cambridge (MA); *m* 14 June 1969, Catita, da of Hans Lieb (d 1959), of Algeciras, Spain; 1 s (Joshua b 1970), 2 da (Eliza b 1973, Olivia b 1981); *Career* dir Christie's (Christie, Manson & Woods Ltd) 1969 (joined 1964); memb Kent and E Sussex Regnl Ctee Nat Tst 1981-87; Liveryman Worshipful Co of Goldsmiths 1984; *Clubs* Brooks's; *Style*— John Lumley, Esq; Court Lodge, Egerton, Ashford, Kent (☎ 023 376 249); Christie's, 8 King St, London SW1 (☎ 071 839 9060)

LUMLEY, Richard Edward Walter; er s of Edward Lumley Lumley (d 1960), and Kathleen Agnew, *née* Wills (d 1978); respective fndrs of the Edward Lumley Hall at the RCS of England (opened by HM The Queen 1954), and of Kathleen Lumley Coll Univ of Adelaide S Aust (opened 1969); *b* 7 July 1923; *Educ* Eton; *m* 1953, Josephine Mary, da of Dr F Melville Harvey, MC (d 1935), of St Mary's Hosp Paddington and of Montevideo; 3 s (Edward d 1955, John, Christopher), 5 da (Sarah, Caroline, Astrid, Emma, Susan); *Career* served Coldstream Gds WWII Capt; underwriting memb of Lloyd's 1944-; chm: Edward Lumley & Sons Ltd 1980-85 (dir 1951-88, chm and md 1960-85), Edward Lumley & Sons (underwriting agencies) Ltd 1971-88, Edward Lumley Holdings Ltd 1974-85 (dir 1974-); dir Lumley Corporation Ltd Aust 1974-89; patron RCS of England, memb Cncl Br Aust Soc; *Recreations* family pursuits, walking in the country, skiing; *Clubs* Boodle's, Cavalry & Guards', East India & Devonshire, MCC, Berkshire Golf, Cook Soc; *Style*— Richard Lumley, Esq; Roundwood, Sunninghill Rd, Windlesham, Surrey GU20 6PP (☎ 0276 72337); 41 Tower Hill, London EC3N 4HA (☎ 071 488 3188)

LUMLEY, Viscount; Richard Osbert Lumley; s and h of 12 Earl of Scarbrough; *b* 18 May 1973; *Style*— Viscount Lumley

LUMLEY-SAVILE, Hon Henry Leoline Thornhill; s of 2 Baron Savile, KCVO (d 1931), and hp of bro, 3 Baron; *b* 2 Oct 1923; *Educ* Eton; *m* 1, 1946 (m dis 1951), Presiley June, da of Maj G H E Inchbald; 1 s; m 2, 1961, Caroline Jeffie (d 1970), da of Peter Clive; m 3, 1972, Margaret Ann (*née* Phillips), wid of Peter Bruce; 3 s (triplets b 1975); *Career* served with Grenadier Gds (wounded), demobilized 1947; *Clubs* White's; *Style*— The Hon Henry Lumley-Savile; 9 King's Road, Richmond, Surrey TW10 6NN

LUMSDEN, Alexander Sabine Courtenay; s of A L C Lumsden (d 1959), and Lillian K S Lumsden (d 1989); *b* 14 June 1921; *Educ* Malvern; *m* 1, 1943, Elisabeth Jean, da of Gp Capt B P H de Roeper, AFC, RAF; 1 da (Julia Frances Sabine b 1945); m 2, 1951, Elisabeth Vrena, da of late Sqdn Ldr W R Adkins; 1 s (Peter Alexander Courtenay b 1961), 1 da (Penelope Elisabeth Courtenay b 1956); m 3, 23 April 1969, Elizabeth Moncrieff, da of Lt-Col A R Cheale, TD (d 1940); *Career* War Service Flt Lt RAFVR 1939-46; asst sec BALPA 1948-53, route mangr Silver City Airways 1953-55, asst sec RAeS 1956-61, aviation sec Royal Aero Club of UK 1961-62, chief info offr Aerospace Info Dept Hawker Siddeley Int 1963-66, tech ed Interavia Geneva 1966-68, operations ed Aeroplane 1968, press offr and dep mangr press services BAC 1968-73; currently: aviation writer and PR conslt, professional photographer, ptnr Alec Lumsden Assocs; regular contributor to aviation magazines; MRAeS 1981; *Books* Wellington Special (1974), Combat Helicopters (co author 1985); *Recreations* music, writing; *Clubs* RAF; *Style*— Alexander Lumsden, Esq; The White House, Deptford, Wylye, nr Warminster, Wiltshire BA12 0QA (☎ 09856 292)

LUMSDEN, Sir David James; s of Albert Lumsden (d 1985), and Vera, *née* Tate (d 1980); *b* 19 March 1928; *Educ* Univ of Cambridge (MA, MusB, PhD); *m* 1951, Sheila Gladys, da of George Daniels; 2 s (Stephen, Andrew), 2 da (Jennifer, Jane); *Career* fell and organist New Coll Oxford 1959-76, princ Royal Scottish Acad of Music and Drama Glasgow 1976-82, Royal Acad of Music London 1982-; kt 1985; *Recreations* hill walking, reading, friends; *Style*— Sir David Lumsden; 47 York Terrace East, London NW1 4PT; Royal Acad of Music, Marylebone Rd, London NW1

LUMSDEN, Edward Gabriel Marr; s of Edward Gabriel Lumsden of Ferndown, Dorset, and Isobel, *née* Dyker; *b* 4 July 1946; *Educ* Hampton GS, Westminster Hotel Sch (Nat Dip in Hotelkeeping and Catering); *Career* area mangr Truman Taverns 1980-81, dir and gen mangr Arden Taverns 1981-83, tied trade dir Drybroughs of Scotland 1983-86, innkeeper dir Truman Ltd 1986, innkeeper ops dir Watney Co Reid & Truman 1986-88, innkeeper dir Watney Truman 1989-90, md TW Guest Trust Ltd 1991; FHCIMA, FCFA, FRSH, MBIM, MBII, FInstD; *Recreations* travel, gastronomy, the arts; *Style*— Edward Lumsden, Esq; Sunny Bank, North Side, Steeple Aston, Oxon OX5 3FE (☎ 0869 Aston 40546); 34 Kilburn High Rd, London NW6 5XY (☎ 071 372 6177)

LUMSDEN, Ian George; s of James Alexander Lumsden, MBE, of Bannachra, by Helensburgh, Dunbartonshire, and Sheila, *née* Cross; *b* 19 March 1951; *Educ* Rugby, Corpus Christi Coll Cambridge (BA), Edinburgh Univ (LLB); *m* 22 April 1978, Mary Ann, da of Maj Dr John William Stewart Welbon, of Cornwall; 1 s (Richard b 1984), 2 da (Sarah b 1986, Louise b 1989); *Career* ptnr Maclay Murray and Spens 1980- (trainee and asst slr 1974-78), asst slr Slaughter and May London 1978-80; memb Law Soc of Scotland, Royal Faculty of Procurators; *Recreations* golf, shooting; *Clubs* New (Edinburgh), Prestwick Golf; *Style*— Ian Lumsden, Esq; The Myretoun, Menstrie, Clackmannanshire FK11 7EB (☎ 0259 61453); Maclay Murray and Spens, 3 Glenfinlas St, Edinburgh EH3 6AQ (☎ 031 226 5196, fax 031 226 3174, 031 225 9610, telex 727238 VINDEX)

LUMSDEN, (George) Innes; s of George Lumsden, MM (d 1982), and Margaret Ann Frances, *née* Cockburn; *b* 27 June 1926; *Educ* Banchory Acad, Univ of Aberdeen (BSc); *m* 16 July 1958, Sheila, da of George Thomson (d 1965); 2 s (Graham b 1959, Richard b 1961), 1 da (Gillian b 1964); *Career* Geological Survey GB: geologist 1949-, dist geologist S Scotland 1970-, asst dir and sr offr Scotland 1980-; dir Br Geological Survey 1985- (dep dir 1982-85), ret 1987; chm: Recruitment Bds Civil Serv Cmmn 1988-, dirs W Euro Geological Surveys Standing Gp on Environmental Geology 1984-87 (sec 1988-); memb: Cncl Mgmnt Macaulay Inst Soil Res 1980-87, Engrg and Sci Advsy Ctee Derby Coll Higher Educn 1983-87, Geological Museum Advsy Panel 1985-87; FRSE 1967, MI Geol 1982; *Books* numerous papers on geological topics in official Geological Survey pubns and sci jls; *Recreations* music, theatre, sport, gardening; *Style*— G Innes Lumsden, Esq, FRSE; 15 Ockham Court, 24 Bardwell Rd, Oxford OX2 6SR (☎ 0865 57427)

LUMSDEN, James (Jimmy); s of Mike Lumsden, and Jean, *née* Murdoch; *b* 7 Nov 1947; *Educ* Kinning Park Secdy Sch Glasgow; *m* 20 Dec 1971, Valerie; 2 s (Michael James b 12 Sept 1972 d 18 Jan 1990, Jamie b 25 Aug 1974); *Career* professional football manager; player: Leeds Utd 1962-70, Southend Utd 1970-71, Morton 1971-73 and 1974-75 Cork Hibs 1973-74, St Mirren 1975-76, Clydebank 1976-79, Celtic 1979-82 (player-coach); asst mangr: Leeds Utd 1982-85, Rochdale 1986-87; mangr Bristol City 1990- (asst mangr 1988-90); Scot Div 2 Championship Clydebank 1976 (promoted to Premier Div 1977); *Recreations* horse-racing, music; *Style*— Jimmy Lumsden, Esq; Bristol City FC, Ashton Gate, Bristol (☎ 0272 632812, fax 0272)

LUMSDEN, Prof Keith Grant; s of Robert Sclater Lumsden (d 1964), of Bathgate, and Elizabeth, *née* Brow; *b* 7 Jan 1935; *Educ* The Academy Bathgate, Univ of Edinburgh (MA), Stanford Univ (PhD); *m* 21 July 1961, Jean Baillie, da of Capt Kenneth Macdonald, MC (d 1962), of Armadale; 1 s (Robert Alistair Macdonald b 1964); *Career* Stanford Univ: instr Dept of Econs 1960-63, assoc prof Graduate Sch of Business 1968-75 (asst prof 1964-67), prof econs Advanced Mgmnt Coll 1971-; res assoc Stanford Res Inst 1965-71, visiting prof econs Heriot-Watt Univ 1969, academic dir Sea Tport Exec Programme 1984-, currently affiliate prof econs INSEAD France; dir: Stanford Univ Conf RREE 1968, Econ Educn Project 1969-74, Behavioral Res Laboratories 1970-72, Capital Preservation Fund Inc 1971-75, Nielsen Engineering Research Inc 1972-75, Hewlett-Packard Ltd 1981-; currently dir The Esmée Fairbairn Res Centre; memb: American Econ Assoc Ctee on Econ Educn 1978-81, Advsy Cncl David Hume Inst 1984-; numerous articles in professional jls, creator of various softwear systems; *Books* The Free Enterprise System (1963), The Gross National Product (1964), International Trade (1965), Microeconomics: A Programmed Book (with R E Attiyeh and G L Bach, new edn 1981), Macroeconomics: A Programmed Book (with RE Attiyeh and GL Bach, new edn 1981), New Developments in the Teaching of Economics (ed, 1967); *Recreations* tennis, deep sea sports, fishing; *Clubs* Waverley Lawn Tennis and Squash, Dalmahoy Golf and Country; *Style*— Prof Keith Lumsden; 40 Lauder Road, Edinburgh EH9 1UE (☎ 031 667 1612); The Esmee Fairbairn Research Centre Heriot-Watt University, Riccarton, Edinburgh EH14 4AS (☎ 031 451 3090, fax 031 451 3002)

LUMSDEN-COOK, Anthony James; s of James Alexander Lumsden-Cook, MB, CHB, DLO (d 1977), of Durban, Natal, S Africa, and Mary Kathleen, *née* Bennion; *b* 23 Aug 1935; *Educ* Stowe, RAC; *m* 1, 1959 (m dis), Christine, da of Oswald Rissen (d 1958); 2 s (Mark Alexander Rowe b 28 Oct 1961, Sean Anthony b 6 June 1960), 1 da (Julie Clare b 16 July 1960); m 2, 3 Feb 1973, Carol Marie, da of Col Clinton Kearny, USAF (d 1976); 1 s (James Justin b 23 Oct 1975); *Career* serv HAC 1957-59; dir Swann & Everett Ltd 1967-72, md Alexander Howden & Swann 1973-76, chm Anthony Lumsden & Co 1977-84 (also chm of subsidiary cos), dir Wigham Poland Hldgs Ltd 1984-86, dep chm Sedgwick Marine Ltd 1985-86; proprietor Continental Villas and Sloan Travel 1987-, ptnr Lumsden Leche Ptnrship (int estate agents) 1987-; underwriting memb Lloyds 1959-; FBIM (1975), FCIB (1972); *Recreations* Concours D'Elegance cars, swimming; *Clubs* Caledonian RAC, Hurlingham, City of London Tanglin (Singapore), Singapore town; *Style*— Anthony Lumsden-Cook, Esq; 29 Pembroke Gardens Close, London W8 6HR (☎ 071 602 6381); 33 Great Tew, Oxon OX 75AL (☎ 060 883 444); Continental Villas, Eagle House, 58 Blythe Rd, Londn W14 OHA (☎ 071 371 1313, fax 071 602 4165, telex 918054 Villas G, car 0836 204 313)

LUMSDEN OF CUSHNIE, David Gordon Allen d'Aldecamb; Baron of Cushnie-Lumsden (Co of Aberdeen); s of Maj Henry Gordon Strange Lumsden (d 1969), of Nocton Hall, Lincs, and Sydney Mary, *née* Elliott (d 1985); *b* 25 May 1933; *Educ* Seafield Park Devon, Allhallows Devon, Bedford Sch, Jesus Coll Cambridge (MA); *Career* London Scottish TA; exec Br American Tobacco 1959-82 (served Belgian Congo, India, Rhodesia, Nyasaland, Ghana, Far East, Eastern Europe), co fndr Castles of Scotland Preservation Tst 1985, cncl memb The Royal Stuart Soc, memb Lloyds 1985, dir Heritage Procelain Ltd; Garioch Pursuivant of Arms 1986, FSA (Scot) 1984; Knight of Malta Honour and Devotion 1980, Knight of Justice Sacred Military Constantinian Order of St George 1978, Naples and Two Scicilies HQ Madrid 1978; *Books* The Muster Roll of Prince Charles Edward's Army 1745-46 (contrib 1984); *Recreations* shooting, polo, rowing, architectural history, Scottish history, heraldry; *Clubs* Brooks's, Pitt, Leander (Cambridge), Hidalgos (Madrid), Puffin's (Edinburgh); *Style*— David Lumsden of Cushnie; Leithen Lodge, Innerleithen, Peeblesshire EH44 6NW (☎ 0896 830297)

LUNAN, Dr (Charles) Burnett; s of Andrew Burnett Lunan, of Dalguise, Perthshire, and Jean Clarke, *née* Orr; *b* 28 Sept 1941; *Educ* Glasgow HS, Univ of Glasgow (MB ChB, MD); *m* 6 March 1973, Helen Russell, da of John Ferrie (d 1963); 2 s (Robert Ferrie b 1977, Donald John b 1979), 1 da (Kirsteen Burnett b 1974); *Career* lectr in obstetrics and gynaecology Univ of Aberdeen 1973-75, sr lectr in obstetrics and gynaecology Univ of Nairobi Kenya 1975-77, conslt in obstetrics and gynaecology Royal Infirmary and Royal Maternity Hosp Glasgow 1977-, WHO conslt in maternal and child health prog Bangladesh 1984-85 and 1988-89; vice pres Royal Medico-Chirurgical Soc of Glasgow 1990- (treas 1982-90); FRCOG 1983 (MRCOG 1970) FRCS 1985; *Recreations* gardening, photography, hill walking; *Style*— Dr Burnett Lunan; 1 Moncrieff Ave, Lenzie, Glasgow (☎ 041 776 3227); Royal Maternity Hosp, Rottenrow, Glasgow (☎ 041 552 3400)

LUNCH, John; CBE (1975), VRD (1965); s of Percy Valentine Lunch (d 1974), and Amy, *née* Somerville (d 1960); *b* 11 Nov 1919; *Educ* Roborough Sch Eastbourne; *m* 1943, Joyce Barbara (d 1989), da of Arnold Basil O'Connell Clerke (d 1959); 2 s; *Career* Lt Cdr RNR 1940-69 (ret), served WWII Crete, Malta convoys, N Africa, Sicily D-Day, Atlantic convoys; Col (TA) Engr and Tport Staff Corps RE 1971-; in business in City 1946-48; asst md Tokenhouse Securities Corp Ltd 1947, and dir several cos; Br Tport Cmmn, 1948-61, road and rail tport and ancillary businesses; PLA, 1961; dir of finance, also dir of commerce, 1966; asst dir-gen, responsible docks and harbour 1969; dir-gen PLA and bd memb 1971-76; chm: Comprehensive Shipping Gp 1973-75, Transcontinental Air Ltd 1973-75; cncl: memb ICAEW 1970-77, RNLI: memb ctee of mgmnt 1977- (vice-pres 1987-, pres Hayling Island Station 1978-88, fndr chm Manhood Branch 1976, hon art advsr 1981; Freeman City of London; court memb Worshipful Co of Watermen's 1976-; FCA, FCIT (memb 1973-76), FCIM, CBIM, FRSA, hon FIFF (pres 1972-73); *Recreations* sailing (yacht 'Lively'), art; *Clubs* Army and Navy, Itchenor Sailing; *Style—* John Lunch, Esq, CBE, VRD; Twittens, Itchenor, Chichester, W Sussex PO20 7AN (☎ 0243 512105); 97A York Mansions, Prince of Wales Drive, London SW11 4BN (☎ 071 622 8100)

LUND, Anthony Marling; s of Lt-Gen Sir Otto Lund, KCB, DSO (d 1956), and Margaret Phyllis Frances, *née* Harrison; *b* 24 Sept 1929; *Educ* Eton; *m* 1 Sept 1967, Sophie, da of Count Soumarokoff-Elston (d 1970), of London; 2 da (Tatiana b 1969, Anna Maria b 1970); *Career* 2 Lt 11 Hussars (PAO) 1948-49; assoc: Kuhn Loeb and Co NY 1952-59, Int Fin Corp Washington DC 1958-61; vice pres then ptnr/md: Kuhn Loeb and Co, Lehman Bros Kuhn Loeb Inc, Shearson Lehman Bros; chief exec EBC Amro Bank Ltd 1986-88; *Clubs* White's; *Style—* Anthony Lund, Esq; 10 Devonshire Square, London EC2 4HS (☎ 01 621 0101, fax 01 623 9309, telex 8811001)

LUND, Bryan; s of Capt Clifford Lund (d 1989), and Vera, *née* Miller (d 1975); *b* 15 April 1938; *Educ* Royal Liberty GS Havering Essex; *m* 18 April 1964, Diana, da of Ernest Wilshaw (d 1986); 2 s (Mark b 1965, Paul b 1968), 1 da (Deborah b 1975); *Career* articled FCA Hill Vellacott and Co 1954-59, Peat Marwick Cassleton Elliott (W Africa) 1960-62, gp audit mgr Touche Ross 1963-67, fin dir Norcros plc subsidiaries 1967-73, Euro Fin dir Morton Thiokol Incorporated Chicago 1973-82, gp finance dir: Borthwicks plc 1982-87, Wonderworld plc 1987-; Freeman: City of London 1982, Worshipful Co of CAs 1982-, Worshipful Co of Butchers 1984-; FCA 1960; *Recreations* golf, motoring, water-skiing; *Clubs* RAC, Northwood Golf (dir), Moor Park Golf; *Style—* Bryan Lund, Esq; Wonderworld plc, 11 Great Marlborough St, London W1A 3AF (☎ 071 434 1309, fax 071 439 3903)

LUND, Dr Charles Ames; s of (Henry) Charles Lund (d 1980), of Bebington, Cheshire, and (Sophia) Violet Iris, *née* Ames (d 1976); *b* 18 Aug 1942; *Educ* Birkenhead Sch, Univ of Liverpool (MB ChB), Univ of Aberdeen (Dip Psychotherapy); *m* 14 Feb 1968, Pauline, da of Arthur Morris Hunter, of Ponteland, Newcastle upon Tyne; 2 da (Sonia b 1969, Kathryn b 1974); *Career* sr house offr and registrar in psychiatry Sefton Gen Hosp Liverpool 1968-71 (house offr 1967-68), sr registrar in psychiatry Royal Southern Hosp Liverpool 1971-72; Univ of Aberdeen: Rowntree fell in psychotherapy 1972-73, lectr Mental Health Dept 1973-78; conslt psychotherapist Newcastle upon Tyne 1978-, dir of Newcastle Psychotherapy Course 1984-89, examiner for Membership Examination of RCPsych 1990-; author of pubns in psychotherapy trg and gp therapy; memb: Northern Assoc for Analytical Psychotherapist Scot Assoc of Analytical Psychotherapy, MBMA, FRCPsych 1987 (MRC Psych 1972); *Recreations* walking, gardening; *Style—* Dr Charles Lund; 92 Errington Rd, Darras Hall, Ponteland, Newcastle-upon-Tyne NE20 9LA (☎ 0661 72018); Regional Department of Psychotherapy, Claremont House, Royal Victoria Infirmary, Off Framlington Place, Newcastle-upon-Tyne NE2 4AA (☎ 091 232 5131)

LUND, Rodney Cookson; s of Arthur Lund (d 1975), and Doris, *née* Bond; *b* 16 June 1936; *Educ* Wallasey GS, Liverpool Univ (BCom); *Career* Lt RAPC 1957-59; Evans Medical 1959, Carreras Rothmans 1960-64, ptnr Urwick Orr & Ptnrs 1964-66 and 1969-73, md The Mace Voluntary Gp 1966-69, vice-chm Produce Importers Alliance 1966-69, exec dir Rank Radio Int 1973-75, exec dir British Sugar 1976-82, exec dir Woolworth Hldgs 1982-86; chm: Nat Bus Co 1986, chm Short Bros plc; CBIM; *Recreations* travel, opera, cooking; *Style—* R C Lund, Esq; 18 Billing Rd, Chelsea SW10 9UL (☎ 01 352 2641)

LUNGHI, Cherie Mary; da of Allessandro Lunghi (d 1989), of London, and Gladys Corbett Lee; *b* 4 April 1952; *Educ* Arts Educn Trust London, Central Sch of Speech and Drama; former partner, Roland Joffé; 1 da (Nathalie-Kathleen Lunghi-Joffé b 26 Aug 1986); *Career* actress; theatre: Irena in The Three Sisters and Lisa in Owners (Newcastle) 1973-74, Kate Hardcastle in She Stoops to Conquer (Nottingham Playhouse) 1974, Laura in Teeth 'n Smiles (Royal Ct Theatre) 1975, Holiday (Old Vic) 1987, Ruth in The Homecoming (Comedy Theatre) 1991; RSC 1976-80: Hero in Much Ado About Nothing, Perdita in The Winter's Tale, Cordelia in King Lear, Destiny, Bandits, Celia in As You Like It, Saratoga, Viola in Twelfth Night; TV incl: The Misanthrope (BBC) 1978, 'Tis Pity She's A Whore (BBC) 1979, The Manhood of Edward Robinson (Thames) 1981, The Praying Mantis (Channel 4) 1982, Desert of Lies (BBC) 1983, Huis Clos (BBC) 1984, Much Ado About Nothing (BBC) 1984, Letters From an Unknown Lover (Channel 4) 1985, The Monocled Mutineer (BBC) 1985, The Lady's Not For Burning (Thames) 1987, The Manageress (Channel 4) 1988 and 1989, Put on by Cunning (TVS) 1990; TV mini series: Master of the Game (US) 1983, Ellis Island (US) 1984, The Man Who Lived at The Ritz (US) 1988, The Strauss Dynasty (Austria) 1990; radio: Alice in Alice in Wonderland (BBC) 1965, Hedvig in The Wild Duck (BBC) 1965; films: Excalibur 1980, King David 1984, The Mission 1985, To Kill A Priest 1987; *Recreations* drawing and painting, going to the cinema and theatre, reading, walking, mothering; *Style—* Miss Cherie Lunghi; c/o Jonathan Bagley, ICM, Oxford St, London W1 (☎ 071 629 8080)

LUNN, Rt Rev David Ramsay; *see*: Sheffield, Bishop of

LUNN, Jonathan William Peter; s of Cecil Peter Lunn, and Eileen, *née* Smith; *b* 14 June 1955; *Educ* St John's Sch Leatherhead, Univ of Hull (BA), London Comtemporary Dance Sch; *m* 1979 (m dis 1985); *Career* dancer: Mantis 1980, Siobhan Davies & Dancers 1981, London Contemporary Dance Theatre 1981-; choreographer LCDT: Wild Life Dung 1986, Hang Up 1987, Bottom's Dream 1988, Shift 1988, Doppelgänger 1989, Goes Without Saying 1989; choreographer: LCDS Exchanges 1986, Love Let Loose 1987, Free Will 1988, Ballet Gulbenkian (Lisbon) Movimento Para Uma Tela 1988; *Style—* Jonathan Lunn, Esq; 17 Highbury Terrace, London N5 1UP (☎ 01 354 5108); LCDT, 16 Flaxman Terrace, London WC1 (☎ 01 387 0324)

LUNN, (George) Michael; s of John Lunn (d 1969), of Edinburgh, and May, *née* Hope (d 1971); *b* 22 July 1942; *Educ* Kelvinside Acad Glasgow, Univ of Glasgow (BSc), Heriot Watt Univ (Dip Brewing); *m* 27 Aug 1971, Jennifer, da of John Burgoyne, of Glasgow; 3 s (Stuart b 17 Jan 1974, Jamie b 27 July 1978, Alexander b 18 March 1981); 1 da (Victoria b 11 Jan 1976); *Career* Lt RNR 1956-66; chm and chief exec Whyte & Mackay Distillers Ltd Glasgow; chm Wm Muir Ltd, dir Cncl Scotch Whisky Assoc, memb Bd Glasgow Devpt Agency, fndr memb Glasgow Action Ctee, govr Kelvinside Acad Glasgow; *Recreations* golf, sailing, tennis; *Clubs* IOD (chm W Scot Branch), R & A Golf, Glasgow Gailes Golf; *Style—* Michael Lunn, Esq; Whyte & Mackay Distillers Ltd, Dalmore House, 296/298 St Vincent St, Glasgow G2 5XR (☎ 041 248 5771, fax 041 221 9667, telex 778552)

LUNN, Peter; CMG (1957), OBE (1951); s of Sir Arnold Lunn, the father of alpine ski racing, and Lady Mabel Northcote, sis of 3 Earl of Iddesleigh; *b* 15 Nov 1914; *Educ* Eton; *m* 1939, Hon Antoinette (d 1976), only da of 15 Viscount Gormanston; 3 s, 3 da; *Career* former Capt Br Ski Team; FO 1947-1972: served Vienna, Berne, Germany, Bonn, Beirut, FCO 1967-72; author; *Books* The Guinness Book of Skiing (1983); *Recreations* skiing; *Clubs* SCGB; *Style—* Peter Lunn, Esq, CMG, OBE; c/o The Ski Club of Great Britain, 118 Eaton Square, London SW1W 9AF

LUNNON, Raymond John; s of William John Lunnon (d 1960), of High Wycombe, and Eliza, *née* White (d 1981); *b* 31 Oct 1927; *Educ* Royal GS High Wycombe, Regent St Poly, Inst of Child Health Univ of London (MPhil); *m* 1953, Eileen Vera da of Conrad Charles Norman MacKinnon; 1 s (Adrian John MacKinnon b 10 Dec 1960), 1 da (Jane Melanie MacKinnon b 1 Sep 1967); *Career* RN: joined 1945, draughtsman 1947-48; mechanical and optical instrument draughtsman 1943-45, asst med photographer Inst of Opthalmology Univ of London 1948-52, lectr in clinical photography Inst of Dermatology St John's Hosp for Diseases of the Skin 1960 (head of Med Photography Dept 1952-66); dir of Med Illustration and sr lectr Inst of Child Health Univ of London 1966-89, The Hospitals for Sick Children Special Health Authy 1966-89; curator Museum and Archive Serv Hosps for Sick Children 1989-, freelance conslt in med and other fields of audio visual communication; author of various scientific articles; awarded combined Royal Med Coll s medal 1959, Lancet trophy 1961 and 1986, Silver medal BMA film competition 1972, Norman K Harrison Gold medal 1978; FRPS 1959, fell BIPP 1967, hon fell Inst of Med Illustrators 1988 (assoc 1969), hon FRPS 1989; OStJ 1987; *Recreations* painting, drawing, golf, St John Ambulance Bde (pres High Wycombe Div); *Style—* Raymond Lunnon, Esq; Museum & Archive Service, The Hospital for Sick Children, Great Ormond St, London WC1N 3JH (☎ 071 405 9200, 5920)

LUNT, Maj-Gen James Doiran; CBE (1964, OBE 1958); s of Brig Walter Thomas Lunt, MBE (d 1977), of Camberley, Surrey, by his w Archilles Cameron, *née* Dodd (d 1975); *b* 13 Nov 1917; *Educ* King William's Coll IOM, RMC Sandhurst; *m* 1940, Muriel Jessie, da of Albert Henry Byrt, CBE, of Bournemouth (d 1964); 1 s, 1 da; *Career* 2 Lt Duke of Wellington's Regt 1937; served: Burma Rifles 1939-42, Arab Legion 1952-55, Fedn Regular Army Aden 1961-64, chief of staff Contingencies Planning SHAPE 1968-70, Vice-Adj-Gen MOD 1970, Maj-Gen, ret 1972; Col 16/5 Queen's Royal Lancers 1975-80; fell and domestic bursar Wadham Coll Oxford 1973-83 (emeritus fell 1983-); author; FRGS, FRHistS; Hon MA Oxon; Order of Independence (Jordan) 1956, Order of South Arabia (1965); *Books Incl:* Charge to Glory (1961), From Sepoy to Subedar (1970), Imperial Sunset (1981), Glubb Pasha (1984), Hussein of Jordan (1989); *Recreations* writing, flyfishing; *Clubs* Cavalry and Guards', Flyfishers'; *Style—* Maj-Gen James Lunt, CBE; Hill Top House, Little Milton, Oxon OX9 7PU (☎ 0844 279242)

LURGAN, 5 Baron (UK 1839); Lt-Col John Desmond Cavendish Brownlow; OBE (1950); s of Capt the Hon Francis Cecil Brownlow (d 1932; 3 s of 2 Baron Lurgan); suc 1 cous, 4 Baron Lurgan, 1984; *b* 29 June 1911; *Educ* Eton; *Heir* none; *Career* Lt-Col Grenadier Gds, ret; *Style—* Lt-Col The Rt Hon the Lord Lurgan, OBE; Pennington House, Lymington, Hants

LURGAN, Baroness; (Florence) May Brownlow; *m* 1, Eric Cooper (decd), of Johannesburg, S Africa; m 2, 1979, 4 Baron Lurgan (d 1984); *Style—* The Rt Hon the Lady Lurgan; PO Box 18161, Dalbridge 4014, Natal, S Africa

LURY, Adam Thomas; s of Prof Dennis Albert Lury (d 1981), and Margaret Antoinette Goldie, of London; *b* 11 July 1956; *Educ* Simon Langton GS, St Catherine's Coll Oxford (BA); *partner*, Claire Crocker; *Career* account exec then account supervisor Wasey Campbell Ewald 1978-81; Boase Massimi Pollitt: planner 1981-84, appointed to Bd 1985, gp planning dir 1986-87; jt managing ptnr Howell Henry Chaldecott Lury 1987-; MIPA 1990; *Recreations* sculpture, consumer culture, Madonna fan; *Style—* Adam Lury, Esq; Howell Henry Chaldecott Lury, Kent House, 14-17 Market Place, Gt Titchfield St, London W1N 7AJ (☎ 071 436 3333)

LUSCOMBE, Prof David Edward; s of Edward Dominic Luscombe (d 1987), of 3 Ridgeview Rd, London, and Nora, *née* Cowell; *b* 22 July 1938; *Educ* Finchley Catholic GS, King's Coll Cambridge (BA, MA, PhD, LittD); *m* 20 Aug 1960, Megan, da of John Richard Phillips (d 1967); 3 s (Nicholas b 1962, Mark b 1964, Philip b 1968), 1 da (Amanda b 1970); *Career* fell King's Coll Cambridge 1962-64, fell, lectr and dir of studies in history Churchill Coll Cambridge 1964-72; Univ of Sheffield: prof of medieval history 1972-, head of Dept of History 1978-84 (1973-76), dean of Faculty of Arts 1985-87, pro vice chllr 1990-; vice pres Société Int L'Etude de la Philosophie Médiévale 1987-, pubns sec of the Br Acad 1990- (memb Cncl 1989-); FRHistS 1970, FSA 1984, FBA 1986; *Books* The School of Peter Abelard (1969), Peter Abelard's Ethics (1971); co-ed: Church and Government in the Middle Ages (1976), Petrus Abaelardus 1079-1142 (1980), D Knowles, The Evolution of Medieval Thought (1988); Cambridge Studies in Medieval Life and Thought (advsy ed 1983-88, gen ed 1988-); *Recreations* exercising a spaniel, cricket, swimming; *Style—* Prof David Luscombe, FSA; Department of History, The University, Sheffield S10 2TN (☎ 0742 768555, ext 6362, fax 07422 739826, telex 547216 UGSHEF G)

LUSCOMBE, Rt Rev Lawrence Edward; s of Reginald John Luscombe (d 1970), and Winifred Luscombe; *b* 10 Nov 1924; *Educ* Kelham Theol Coll, King's Coll London; *m* 1946, Dr Doris Carswell, da of Andrew Morgan; 1 da; *Career* served WW II Indian Army, India and Burma; formerly chartered accountant, ptnr Watson Galbraith CAs Glasgow 1952-63; ordained: deacon 1963, priest 1964; rector St Barnabas Paisley 1966-71, provost of St Paul's Cathedral Dundee 1971-75, bishop of Brechin 1975-90; hon canon Trinity Cathedral Davenport Iowa 1983-; Primus of the Scottish Episcopal Church 1985-90; memb: Educn Ctee Renfrew CC 1967-71, Court of Corpn of Sons of the Clergy 1985-, Tayside Regnl Health Bd 1989-; chm: Edinburgh Theol Coll 1985-90, governing body Glenalmond Coll 1987-; govr: Dundee Coll of Educn 1982-87, Lathallan Sch 1982-; OStJ; Hon LLD Univ of Dundee, Hon DLitt Geneva Theol Coll; FRSA, FSAScot; *Style—* The Rt Rev Lawrence Luscombe; Woodville, Kirkton of Tealing, by Dundee DD4 0RD (☎ 082 621 331)

LUSH, Christopher Duncan; CMG (1983); s of Eric Duncan Thomas Lush (d 1980); *Educ* Sedbergh, Magdalen Coll Oxford; *m* 1967, Marguerite Lilian, da of Frederick William Bolden (d 1975); *Career* barr 1953-59; asst legal advsr FO 1959-62, first sec West Berlin 1962-66, FO (later FCO) 1966-69, Amman 1969-71, cnsllr FCO 1971-73, Canadian Nat Def Coll 1973-74, Paris 1974-78, Vienna 1978-82, ambass to Cncl of Europe Strasbourg 1983-86, Euro Campaign for North South Awareness 1986-88, War Crimes Inquiry 1988; govr Br Inst of Human Rights 1988; *Clubs* Travellers'; *Style—* Christopher Lush, Esq, CMG; UK Delegation, 18 Rue Gottfried, Strasbourg, France (☎ 350078)

LUSH, Denzil Anton; s of Dennis John Lush and Hazel June, *née* Fishenden (d 1979); *b* 18 July 1951; *Educ* Devonport HS Plymouth, UCL (BA, MA), Coll of Law Guildford, CCC Cambridge (LLM); *Career* admitted slr 1978; ptnr Anstey Sargent & Probert Solicitors; author of numerous articles in learned jls, contrib Encyclopaedia of Forms and Precedents; licensed as reader (Wells Cathedral 1982) for utd benefice of E Harptree, W Harptree and Hinton Blewett (Diocese of Bath and Wells); memb Law Soc; *Recreations* supporting Plymouth Argyle FC and Somerset CCC; *Clubs* Exeter and County; *Style—* Denzil Lush, Esq; 3 Pennsylvania Park, Exeter, EX4 6HB; 5 Barnfield Crescent, Exeter EX1 1RF (☎ 0392 411221, fax 0392 218554)

LUSH, Peter Maurice; s of Bernard Simeon Lush, of Holmside, South Walk, Middleton-on-Sea, Sussex, and Judy Adele, *née* Markham; *b* 19 April 1939; *Educ* Brighton Coll; *m* 1 (m dis), Cynthia, *née* Leslie-Bredée; m 2 (m dis), Peggy, *née* Gough; m 3, 3 Oct 1964, Lyn, da of Eyre Fitzgerald Massy (d 1970); 1 s (Jonathan Charles b 11 July 1966), 1 da (Amanda Lyn Geraldine b 18 Aug 1967); *Career* account dir Ogilvy & Mather advtg agency 1958-72, jt md Knight Keeley Ltd 1972-74, conslt TCCB 1988- (PR and mktg mangr 1974-87); formed Peter Lush Ltd (PML) sports sponsorship and mktg conslts 1988; England cricket tour mangr: B team to Sri Lanka 1986, Aust (Ashes retained) 1986-87, World Cup in India and Pakistan 1987, Pakistan 1987, NZ 1988; Nehru Cup 1988, WI 1990, Aust and NZ 1990-91, Sussex jr squash champion 1957; *Recreations* cricket, golf; *Clubs* MCC, Old Brightonians, Sonning Golf; *Style—* Peter Lush, Esq; Dunmore, Holmemoor Dr, Sonning, Reading, Berks RG4 OTE (☎ 0734 693 735, fax 0734 693202); TCCB, Lord's Ground, London NW8 8QZ (☎ 071 286 4405, fax 071 289 5619, telex 24462 TCCB G)

LUSHINGTON, Sir John Richard Castleman; 8 Bt (GB 1791), of South Hill Park, Berkshire; s of Sir Henry Edmund Castleman Lushington, 7 Bt (d 1988); *b* 28 Aug 1938; *Educ* Oundle; *m* 21 May 1966, Bridget Gillian Margaret, o da of late Col John Foster Longfield, of Knockbeg, Saunton, N Devon; 3 s; *Heir* s, Richard Douglas Longfield Lushington b 29 March 1968; *Career* mgmnt trg consult, trading as MaST (Eastern), a memb of the MaST Orgn; *Style—* Sir John Lushington, Bt; The Glebe House, Henham, Bishops Stortford, Herts

LUSHINGTON, Pamela, Lady; Pamela Elizabeth Daphne; *née* Hunter; er da of late Maj Archer Richard Hunter, of Hare Hatch Grange, Twyford, Berks; *m* 2 Oct 1937, Sir Henry Edmund Castleman Lushington, 7 Bt (d 1988); 1 s (Sir John, 8 Bt, *qv*), 2 da (Caroline Elizabeth b 1942, Penelope Daphne b 1945); *Style—* Pamela, Lady Lushington; Carfax, Crowthorne, Berks (☎ 0344 2819)

LUSTIG, Lawrence Barry; s of Ralph Lustig, of London, and Shelia Jeanette, *née* Bloom; *b* 17 Sept 1956; *Educ* Chingford HS; *m* 29 June 1984, Carol Ann, da of Ronald William Corless; 1 s (Joe Lawrence b 2 June 1988), 1 da (Laura Elizebeth b 20 March 1986); *Career* trainee photographer SKR Photos Int 1972-74, photographer Sporting Pictures UK 1974-79, freelance photographer 1980-86, staff photographer Daily Star 1986-; major sporting events covered incl World Cup football and World title boxing contests; sports photographic awards from: Kodak, Ilford, BT; memb: NUJ, Assoc Int Press Sportees, Sports Writers' Assoc; fndr memb Fleet Street Sports Photographers' Assoc; *Recreations* football and boxing (non-participating); *Style—* Lawrence Lustig, Esq; The Daily Star, Express Newspapers, 245 Blackfriars Bridge Rd, London SE1 (☎ 071 928 8000, car 0831 237 035)

LUSTIG, Robin Francis; s of Fritz Lustig, and Susan, *née* Cohn; *b* 30 Aug 1948; *Educ* Stoneham Sch Reading, Univ of Sussex (BA); *m* 24 Feb 1980, Ruth, da of Dr W B Kelsey (d 1986), of London; 1 s (Joshua b 1982), 1 da (Hannah b 1985); *Career* journalist; Reuters: Madrid 1971-72, Paris 1972-73, Rome 1973-77; The Observer: news ed 1981-83, Middle East corr 1985-87, asst ed 1988-89; freelance journalist and broadcaster 1989-; *Books* Siege: Six Days at the Iranian Embassy (jtly, 1980); *Recreations* reading newspapers, children; *Style—* Robin Lustig, Esq; 124 Dukes Ave, London N10 2QB (☎ 081 883 3144)

LUSTY, Sir Robert Frith; s of late Frith Lusty, of Shrewsbury, and his w Winifred Hobbs; *b* 7 June 1909; *Educ* Soc of Friends Co-educnl Sch Sidcot; *m* 1, 1 Sept 1939, Joan Christie (d 1962), da of late Archibald Brownlie, of Glasgow; m 2, 7 Nov 1963, Eileen Mary, wid of Dr Denis Carroll, and da of late Dr George Phocian Barff; *Career* Messrs Hutchinson & Co 1928-35; co-fndr (with Michael Joseph) and editorial and prodn mangr of Michael Joseph Ltd 1936, resigned as vice-chm 1956; chm and md Hutchinson Publishing Group 1956-73, ret; govr BBC 1960-68 (vice-chm 1966-68); kt 1969; *Books* Bound to be Read (autobiography, 1975); *Style—* Sir Robert Lusty; Broad Close, Blockley, Moreton-in-Marsh, Glos GL56 9DY (☎ 0386 700335)

LUTHER, Barry; *b* 12 March 1946; *Career* fin dir Oxy Metal Industries 1979-82, Euro fin dir OMI Int Corpn 1982-85, chm and md OMI-IMASA UK Ltd 1985-; FCCA 1976; *Style—* Barry Luther, Esq; Meadowland, Sandhurst Rd, Wokingham, Berks RG11 3JD (☎ 0734 783148); Omi-Imasa (UK) Ltd, Forsyth Rd, Sheerwater, Woking, Surrey GU21 5RZ (☎ 0483 715971, fax 0483 728837, car 0860 281637, telex 859121)

LUTON, Elizabeth Mary; da of Alan David Luton, and Elaine Mary, *née* Harris; *b* 8 April 1958; *Educ* City of London Sch For Girls, The London Coll of Secs; *Career* sec and PA: Weatherall Green and Smith 1977-81, Longbarr Devpts Ltd 1981-82, Future Tech Systems Ltd 1982, devpt surveyor Longbarr Devpts Ltd 1982-84, dir The Rutland Gp 1984-; Freeman Worshipful Co of Painters and Stainers 1987; *Recreations* walking, reading, skiing, gardening, cooking; *Style—* Miss Elizabeth Luton; The Rutland Group, 11 Upper Brook St, London W1Y 1PB (☎ 01 499 6616, fax 01 408 1459, telex 23143 UBSLDN G)

LUTTMAN-JOHNSON, Hon Mrs (Barbara Amy); *née* Sclater-Booth; 2 da of 3 Baron Basing (d 1969); *b* 5 April 1926; *m* 27 April 1961, Peter Michell Luttman-Johnson; 1 s, 2 da; *Style—* The Hon Mrs Luttman-Johnson; Woodmancote, Lodsworth, Petworth, W Sussex

LUTTRELL, Lady Elizabeth Hermione; da of 12 Earl Ferrers (d 1954), and his w Hermione Justice (d 1969), da of A Noel Morley; *b* 3 Dec 1923; *Educ* Downe House; *m* 1959, John Fownes Luttrell (d 1985), s of Hugh Fownes Luttrell (d 1918); 1 s (Robert Hugh Courtenay Fownes b 1961); *Career* served with WRNS; held various secretarial posts until marriage; *Recreations* arts, architecture, gardening, travel, music; *Style—* The Lady Elizabeth Luttrell; Waterwynch, Itchen Abbas, nr Winchester, Hants SO21 1AX

LUTTRELL, Col (Geoffrey) Walter Fownes; MC (1945), JP (Somerset 1961); s of Geoffrey Luttrell (d 1957), of Dunster Castle (which until recently had been in the Luttrell family's possession from 1375), and Alys, da of Rear Adm Walter Bridges, of Trewalla, Victoria, Aust; *b* 2 Oct 1919; *Educ* Eton, Exeter Coll Oxford; *m* 1942, Hermione Hamilton, da of late Capt Cecil Gunston, MC (er bro of Sir Derrick Gunston, 1 Bt), and Lady Doris Hamilton-Temple-Blackwood, da of 2 Marquess of Dufferin and Ava; *Career* served with: 15/19 King's Royal Hussars 1940-46, N Somerset Yeo 1952, Lt-Col 1955, col 1987; Somerset: DL 1958, high sheriff 1960, vice Lord Lt 1968-78; Lord Lt 1978-; memb Nat Parks Cmmn 1962-66, liaison offr Miny Agric 1965-71; memb: SW Electricity Bd 1969-78, Wessex Regnl Ctee Nat Tst 1970-85; regnl dir Lloyds Bank 1972-83, memb University Grants Cmmn 1973-76, pres Royal Bath and West Show Soc 1982-83; Hon Col: 6 Bn Light Infantry 1977-87, Somerset ACF 1982-89; KStJ 1978; *Recreations* fishing, gardening; *Clubs* Cavalry and Guards'; *Style—* Col Walter Luttrell, MC, JP; Court House, East Quantoxhead, Bridgwater, Somerset TA5 1EJ (☎ 027 874 242)

LUTYENS, Mary; da of Sir Edwin Lutyens, OM, KCIE, PRA, the celebrated architect (particularly of New Delhi) and Lady Emily Lytton, da of 1 Earl of Lytton (s of the novelist Bulwer Lytton) and Edith, da of Hon Edward Villiers, yr bro of 4 Earl of Clarendon, the Victorian Foreign Sec; sis of Elisabeth Lutyens (decd), the composer, and aunt of 4 Viscount Ridley and Rt Hon Nicholas Ridley, MP, *qqv*; *b* 31 July 1908; *Educ* Queen's Coll London and abroad; *m* 1, 1930 (m dis 1945), Anthony Sewell (decd); 1 da (Amanda, b 1935, m John Pallant); m 2, 1945, Joseph Gluckstein Links, OBE, s of Calman Links; *Career* writer of fiction and of works on the Lyttons, Ruskin, Venice and Krishnamurti; FRSL; *Style—* Miss Mary Lutyens; 8 Elizabeth Close, Randolph Avenue, London W9 1BN (☎ 071 286 6674)

LUTYENS, Richard David; *b* 1 July 1948; *Educ* Rugby, St Edmund Hall Oxford; *m* 9 Oct 1971, Mary Ann July Phyllis; 3 da (Tanya b 1975, Alice b 1980, Camilla b 1985); *Career* exec dir SG Warburg and Co Ltd 1972-82, exec vice pres United Gulf Investment Co (Bahrain) 1982-84, vice pres Goldman Sachs International 1984-85, md: Merrill Lynch Europe Ltd 1985-88, Merrill Lynch Capital Markets (NY) 1985-88, Mercapital International BV, Eurosuez Capital Management Ltd Valgest SA; *Style—* Richard D Lutyens, Esq; 53 Clarendon Rd, London, W11 4JD (☎ 01 727 0577); Campbell Lutyens Hudson & Co Ltd, 4 Clifford St, London, W1X 1RB (☎ 071 439 7191, fax 071 437 0153, telex 21888 CAMLUT G)

LUX, Jonathan Sidney; s of Martin Lux, of 48 Shepherd's Hill, Highgate, London N6, and Ruth, *née* Swager (d 1983); *b* 30 Oct 1951; *Educ* Abbotsholme Sch Rochester Staffs, Univ of Nottingham (LLB), Aix-Marseille Université; *m* 3 Sept 1979, Simone, da of Shalom Itah, of Israel; 1 s (Adam b 14 Jan 1986), 2 da (Ruth b 24 April 1981, Danielle b 24 Sept 1983); *Career* admitted slr 1977; ptnr Ince & Co 1983- (asst slr 1977-73), admitted slr Hong Kong 1986; speaker at various maritime law confs and author of various articles 1983-; supporting memb London Maritime Arbitrators Assoc; memb Int Bar Assoc; Freeman of City of London, Liveryman of Worshipful Co of Solicitors; memb Law Soc 1977; *Books* The Law on Tug, Tow and Pilotage (jtly, 1982), The Law and Practice of Marine Insurance and Average (jtly, 1987); *Recreations* single seater motor racing (holder of RAC nat racing licence); *Style—* Jonathan Lux, Esq; 7 Holt Close, London N10 3HW (☎ 081 883 5704); Ince & Co, Knollys House, 11 Byward St, London EC3R 5EN (☎ 071 623 2011, fax 071 623 3225, telex 8944043 INCES G)

LUXMOORE, Rt Rev Christopher Charles; s of Rev William Cyril Luxmoore (d 1967), and Constance Evelyn, *née* Shoesmith (d 1979); *b* 9 April 1926; *Educ* Sedbergh, Trinity Coll Cambridge, Chichester Theological Coll; *m* 12 April 1955, Judith, da of Canon Verney Lovett Johnstone (d 1948); 4 s (Nicholas b 1956, Jonathan b 1957, Paul b 1960, Benedict b 1963), 1 da (Ruth b 1969); *Career* Army (The Green Howards) 1944-47, ADC to GOC-in-C Bengal and Assam 1946-47; ordained deacon 1952, ordained priest 1953, asst curate St John the Baptist Newcastle-on-Tyne 1952-55, vicar Newsham Blyth 1955-58, rector Sangre Grande Trinidad 1958-66, vicar Headingley Leeds 1967-81, memb Gen Synod 1975-81, hon canon Ripon 1981, canon residentiary of Chichester Cathedral 1981-84, bishop of Bermuda and dean of Bermuda Cathedral 1984-89, archdeacon of Lewes and Hastings 1989-91, provost Southern Div Woodard Corporation 1989-; *Recreations* music, church history, winemaking; *Style—* The Rt Rev Christopher Luxmoore; 42 Willowbed Drive, Chichester, West Sussex PO19 2JB (☎ 0243 784680)

LUXMOORE, Edmund; DL (Durham 1978); s of Allan Aylmer Luxmoore, DL (d 1969); *b* 21 Sept 1914; *Educ* Stowe, Trinity Coll Cambridge; *m* 1946, Diana Jean, MBE, da of John Methuen Coote, OBE (d 1967, 2 s of Sir Algernon Coote, 12 Bt); 2 s (Michael, *qv*, Richard), 1 da (Elizabeth Macdonald); *Career* Flt Lt RAF, Gibraltar and N Africa; slr (ret), Under Sheriff Co Durham and Co Cleveland (Durham deputy with his father 1937-65 and solely since 1965, and of Cleveland since formation); company dir, conslt 1989-; *Books* Deer Stalking (1980); *Recreations* shooting, fishing, stalking; *Clubs* Oxford and Cambridge, Durham County (chm), Yorkshire Fly Fishers'; *Style—* Edmund Luxmoore, Esq, DL; Staindrop Hall, Staindrop, Darlington, Co Durham (☎ 0833 60331); Crackenthorpe Hall, Appleby-in-Westmorland, Cumbria (☎ 0930 51409); Tom-Na-Moine, Roybridge, Inverness (☎ 039 781 558)

LUXMOORE, Michael John; s of Edmund Luxmoore, *qv*, of Staindrop Hall, Staindrop, Darlington, and Diana Jean, *née* Coote; *b* 5 April 1948; *Educ* Harrow, Trinity Coll Cambridge (MA); *m* 1, 28 April 1973 (m dis), Margaret Rosemary More-Nisbett; 2 s (Andrew b 1976, Jamie b 1979), m 2, 3 Dec 1988, Ann Dalrymple-Smith; *Career* admitted slr 1984; deputy under sheriff County of Durham; dir Middleton Hall Ltd 1984-; *Recreations* fell running; *Clubs* Swaledale Outdoor; *Style—* Michael Luxmoore, Esq; High Bank Hse, Fremington, Richmond, N Yorks DL11 6AS (☎ 0748 84361)

LYALL, Eric; CBE; s of late Alfred John Lyall, of Essex, and Alice Amelia, *née* Jackson (d 1982); *b* 12 May 1924; *Educ* Chigwell Sch, King's Coll Cambridge; *m* 1952, Joyce, da of late Sydney Edward Smith; 1 s (Alexander); *Career* formerly slr, ptnr Slaughter and May, former ptnr Guinness Mahon; chm: Rocla GB Ltd, Br Hartford Fairmont Ltd, Clark Nickolls & Coombs plc, Frewen Educnl Tst, Letchworth Garden City Corporation; dep chm Pearl Group plc; dir: AMP (UK) plc, Lockton Developments plc; gen cmmr of Income Tax; *Recreations* stamp collecting, tennis, medieval history; *Clubs* Oriental, City of London, MCC; *Style—* Eric Lyall, Esq, CBE; Riders Grove, Old Hall Green, Ware, Herts (☎ 0920 821370)

LYALL, Dr Fiona Jane; DL (Kincardine 1983); da of James Fraser (d 1984), and Christina Forbes (d 1983); *b* 13 April 1931; *Educ* Univ of Aberdeen (MB ChB, DPH); *m* 20 July 1957, Alan Richards Lyall, s of Alexander Lyall (d 1974); 1 s (Peter James Fraser b 9 Oct 1961), 1 da (Elizabeth Grace Hermione b 18 Oct 1958); *Career* GP Laurencekirk 1959-, dir Grampian TV plc 1980-; borough cncllr Laurencekirk, co cncllr Kincardineshire, regnl cncllr Grampian; *Recreations* skiing, Provincial Silver; *Style—* Dr Fiona Lyall, DL; Melrose Bank, Lawrencekirk, Kincardineshire AB3 1AL (☎ 05617 220)

LYALL, Gavin Tudor; s of Joseph Tudor Lyall, and Agnes Ann, *née* Hodgkiss (d 1989); *b* 9 May 1932; *Educ* King Edward VI Sch Birmingham, Pembroke Coll Cambridge (BA, MA); *m* 4 Jan 1958, Katharine Elizabeth, da of Alan Drummond Whitehorn, MA (d 1980); 2 s (Bernard b 1964, John b 1967); *Career* RAF pilot 1951-53; journalist Picture Post, BBC TV, Sunday Times until 1963; chm Crime Writers' Assoc 1966-67; memb Air Tport Users' Ctee 1979-85 (hon conslt 1985-); author; *Books* 11 thriller/espionage titles, incl: The Secret Servant (1980), The Conduct of Major Maxim (1982), The Crocus List (1985), Uncle Target (1988); *Recreations* model making, cartooning; *Clubs* RAF, Detection; *Style—* Gavin Lyall, Esq; 14 Provost Rd, London NW3 4ST (☎ 071 722 2308)

LYALL, Michael Hodge; s of Alexander Burt Lyall, of Glenrothes, and Isabella Campbell, *née* Paterson; *b* 5 Dec 1941; *Educ* Buckhaven HS, Univ of St Andrews (MB ChB), Univ of Dundee (ChM); *m* 25 Dec 1965, Catherine Barnett, da of James Thomson Jarvie (d 1986), of Leven; 3 s (Grant Alexander b 18 Oct 1966, Stuart James Jarvie b 24 Jan 1968, Ewan Mark Stephen b 28 July 1969); *Career* conslt surgn Tayside Health Bd 1975-, hon sr lectr Univ of Dundee 1975-; fell Assoc of Surgns of GB and I; FRCS 1970; *Recreations* reading, computing, rotary; *Clubs* Rotary of North Fife, Moynihan Chirurgical; *Style—* Michael Lyall, Esq; 26 Linden Avenue, Newport on Tay, Fife DD6 8DU (☎ 0382 543419); Ninewells Hospital & Medical School, Dundee (☎ 0382 60111)

LYBURN, Andrew Usherwood (Drew); s of Andrew Lyburn (d 1969), of Edinburgh, and Margaret Scott Glass (d 1988); *b* 16 Aug 1928; *Educ* Melville Coll, Univ of Edinburgh (MA); *m* 25 July 1958, Joan Ann, da of Eric Stevenson (d 1975), of Edinburgh; 3 s (Andrew b 1960, Colin b 1962, Iain b 1967), 1 da (Fiona b 1974); *Career* RAF Flying Offr Cyprus 1954-56; actuary; Scottish Widows Fund 1949-54 and

1956-57, Confed Life Toronto 1957-59; Standard Life: Montreal 1959-65, Edinburgh 1965-, gen mangr personnel 1989-; memb Occupational Pensions Bd 1982-, vice pres Faculty of Actuaries 1987-; chm: Cairn Petroleum Oil and Gas Ltd 1987-88, Melville Coll Tst 1983-86; FFA 1957, ASA USA 1957, FCIA Canada 1965, FPMI 1976; *Recreations* golf, gardening, squash, hill walking; *Clubs* Bruntsfield Links, Golfing Soc, Edinburgh, RAF London; *Style*— Drew Lyburn, Esq; 4 Cumlodden Ave, Edinburgh EH12 6DR (☎ 031 337 7580); 3 George St, Edinburgh EH2 2X2 (☎ 031 245 6142, fax 031 245 5830)

LYCETT, Andrew Michael Duncan; s of Peter Norman Lycett (d 1979), and Joanna Mary, *née* Day; *b* 5 Dec 1948; *Educ* Charterhouse, ChCh Oxford (MA); *m* 1981 (m dis 1989), Rita Diana Robinson; *Career* journalist and author; currently working for The Times and other newspapers and magazines; *Books* Gaddafi and The Libyan Revolution (with David Blundy, 1987); *Recreations* travel, reading, cricket; *Clubs* RAC; *Style*— Andrew Lycett, Esq; c/o The Times, 1 Pennington St, London E1 9XN (☎ 071 782 5000)

LYCETT, Maj Michael Hildesley Lycett; CBE (1987); s of Rev Norman Lycett (d 1963), of East Dean, Sussex, and Ruth Edith, *née* Burns-Lindow (d 1965); *b* 11 Dec 1915; *Educ* Radley, Merton Coll Oxford; *m* 1, 4 Feb 1944, Moira Patricia Margaret (d 1958), da of Maj Norman Martin, CBE; 1 da (Anthea Theresa b 6 June 1954); m 2, 12 Oct 1959, Lady (June) Wendy Pelham, da of 5 Earl of Yarborough, MC (d 1948); *Career* Maj Royal Scots Greys 1935-47; served: Palestine, Greece, Western Desert, Italy, Germany; md: Rhodesian Insurances Ltd 1949-61, Wright Deen Lycett Ltd Newcastle upon Tyne 1961-73, Lycett Browne-Swinburne & Douglas Ltd (chm 1973-76); chm L B S and D (underwriting agents) 1976, dir L B S and D (Cumbria) Ltd; Parly candidate (C) Consett Co Durham 1981 and 1983; London tstee Bernard Mizeki Schs 1961-(govr and first chm Exec Ctee 1959-61), chm Morpeth Div Cons Assoc 1966-72; MFH Tynedale Hunt 1975-77; pres Northumbria Euro Consituency, former memb Cons Nat Exec and GP Ctees, chm Cons Northern Area 1985-87; *Recreations* politics, field sports, looking things up, writing rhymes; *Clubs* Cavalry and Guards', Pratt's, Boodle's, Northern Counties; *Style*— Maj Michael Lycett, CBE; West Grange, Scots Gap, Morpeth, Northumberland NE61 4EQ (☎ 067 074 662)

LYCETT, Lady (June) Wendy; *née* Pelham; da of 5 Earl of Yarborough, MC (d 1948), and co-heiress to Baronies of Fauconberg and Conyers (*see* Lady Diana Miller); *b* 6 June 1924; *m* 12 Oct 1959, Maj Michael Hildesley Lycett CBE, late Royal Scots Greys, s of late Rev Norman Lycett; 1 da; *Career* late 3 offr WRNS, jt master Tynedale Hunt 1974-77; JP; *Clubs* Cavalry and Guards'; *Style*— The Lady Wendy Lycett; West Grange, Scots Gap, Morpeth, Northumberland NE61 4EQ (☎ 067 074 662)

LYCETT GREEN *see also*: Green

LYDDON, (William) Derek Collier; CB (1984); s of late Alfred Jonathan Lyddon, CBE, and Elizabeth Esther, *née* French (d 1942); *b* 17 Nov 1925; *Educ* Wrekin Coll, UCL; *m* 1949, Marian Louise Kaye, da of late Prof J K Charlesworth, CBE; 2 da; *Career* dep chief architect and planning offr Cumbernauld Devpt Corp 1962, chief architect and planning offr Skelmersdale Devpt Corp 1963-67, chief planning offr Scottish Devpt Dept 1967-85; pres Int Soc of City and Regnl Planners 1981-84; Hon DLitt Heriot Watt 1981; hon prof Heriot Watt Univ; hon fell: Univ of Edinburgh, Duncan Jordanstone Coll; chm: environment and planning ctee of Econ and Social Res Cncl 1986-87, Edinburgh Old Town ctee for conservation and renewal, mgmnt ctee Edinburgh Sch of Environmental Design; govr Edinburgh Coll of Art; *Style*— Derek Lyddon, Esq, CB; 38 Dick Place, Edinburgh EH9 2JB (☎ 031 667 2266)

LYDEKKER, Brig Richard Neville Wolfe; CBE (1976); s of Rev Neville Wolfe Lydekker (d 1956), of Sussex, and Sylvia Gwendolen, *née* Palmer (d 1970); descendant of Rev Gerrit Leydecker who presented the Petition of American Loyalists to King George III in 1782 before emigrating to England; *b* 7 May 1921; *Educ* Sherborne; *m* 25 March 1947, Margaret Julia Mary, da of Rev Canon Lionel Edward Lydekker (d 1973), of Bucks; 1 da (Elizabeth b 1955); *Career* cmmnd RA 1941, psc 1952, jssc 1959, serv WWII N Africa and Italy, cmd RA Regt Malaya and Borneo 1963-65, staff Strategic Reserve 1967-72, Dep QMG UK Land Forces 1972-74, dir MOD (Army Dept) 1974-76, ret; regnl organiser Army Benevolent Fund 1977-; *Recreations* field sports, cricket; *Clubs* Army and Navy; *Style*— Brig Richard Lydekker, CBE; Hatherden, nr Andover, Hants (☎ 0264 75 221); Bulford Camp, Salisbury, Wilts (☎ 0980 33371 ext 2337)

LYE, Richard Harold; s of Vincent Lye, and Agnes, *née* Ashurst; *b* 19 May 1947; *Educ* Bury GS, Univ of Manchester (BSc, MSc, MB ChB); *m* 15 Aug 1970, (Mary) Nanette, da of Dr John Randall Archibald; 5 s (Robert b 1973, James b 1974, Anthony b 1979, George b 1983, Matthew b 1986), 2 da (Helen (twin) b 1979, Catherine b 1988); *Career* conslt in neurosurgery 1982, sr lectr in neurosurgery Univ of Manchester 1985-; FRCS 1976; *Style*— Richard Lye, Esq; Department of Neurosurgery, Manchester Royal Infirmary, Oxford Road, Manchester M13 9WL (☎ 061 276 4565)

LYELL, Alastair Hew Roderick (Toby); s of Gp Capt Angus Chambers Lyell (d 1960), and Ida Angela Bryant, *née* Smith (d 1978); *b* 15 March 1926; *Educ* Radley; *m* 11 Feb 1967, Jane, da of Gen Richard Charles Woodroffe (d 1965), of Bembridge, Isle of Wight; 3 step s; *Career* WWII Capt Scots Gds Germany 1944-47 ; Lloyd's broker 1947, memb of Lloyd's 1955; Forestry Indust 1968-; cncl memb N E Royal Forestry Soc (past chm); memb: Timber Growers UK N Cncl, Int Dendrology Soc 1969-; *Recreations* fishing, shooting, arboriculture; *Clubs* White's, Pratt's; *Style*— Toby Lyell, Esq; Pallinsburn, Cornhill-on-Tweed, Northumberland TD12 4SG

LYELL, 3 Baron (UK 1914); Sir Charles Lyell; 3 Bt (UK 1894), DL (Angus); s of Capt 2 Baron Lyell, VC, Scots Guards (ka 1943, VC awarded posthumously), and Sophie, *née* Trafford (whose family, of Wroxham Hall, Norfolk were a cadet branch of the Traffords now represented by the de Trafford Bts), whose mother was Lady Elizabeth Bertie, OBE, yst da of 7 Earl of Abingdon; *b* 27 March 1939; *Educ* Eton, Ch Ch Oxford; *Heir* none; *Career* 2 Lt Scots Gds 1957-59; CA; oppn whip House of Lords 1974-79, a lord in waiting (Govt Whip) 1979-84; memb Queen's Body Guard for Scotland (Royal Co of Archers); Parly under sec of state NI Office 1984-89; *Clubs* White's, Pratt's, Turf; *Style*— The Rt Hon the Lord Lyell, DL; Kinnordy House, Kirriemuir, Angus (☎ 0575 72848); 20 Petersham Mews, Elvaston Place, London SW7 (☎ 071 584 9419)

LYELL, Hon Lady (Katharine); da of 1 Viscount Runciman, of Doxford (d 1949), and Hilda, *née* Stevenson (d 1956); *b* 1909; *Educ* St Leonard's Sch St Andrews, Girton Coll Cambridge; *m* 1, 23 Oct 1931, 4 Baron Farrer (d 1954); m 2, 24 Sept 1955, Sir Maurice Legat Lyell (d 1975); *Career* JP County of Hertford 1954-79, chm of Dacorum Magistrates 1976-79; *Recreations* nat hunt racing, hunting (Master of the Aldenham Harriers 1956-83); *Style*— The Hon Lady Lyell; Puddephats Farm, Markyate, Herts

LYELL, Malcolm Charles Alastair; s of Angus Chambers Lyell, MC (d 1960), of Church Farm House, Chippenham, Ely, Cambs, and Ida Angela Bryant, *née* Smith (d 1972); *b* 9 Jan 1922; *Educ* Westminster, Univ Coll of N Wales (BSc), Kings Coll London (BSc); *m* 22 April 1949, Mary Patricia Rosamunde, da of Douglas Horsford Wilmer (d 1973), of Hucklesbrook Cottage, Gorley, nr Fordingbridge, Hants; 2 da (Caroline b 1952, Harmony b 1955); *Career* TARO (invalided out 1941); dir Westley Richards 1948-56, md Westley Richards (Agency) Co 1956-60, md Holland & Holland 1960-84 (dep chm 1984-87, ret 1989); chm Buck's Club 1976-79, vice pres Br Assoc for Shooting and Conservation 1973-, memb Standing Conference on Countryside Sports 1978-; FRGS, FZS; Knight Commander of Order of the Star of Honour of Ethiopia (1987); *Recreations* big game shooting, fishing, gardening, photography; *Clubs* Buck's, Flyfishers', Shikar Club of GB; *Style*— Malcolm Lyell, Esq; The Old School House, Baverstock, nr Salisbury, Wilts SP3 5EN (☎ 0722 716462)

LYELL, Michael George Rudinge; s of George Drummond Lyell (d 1957), of Petersfield, Addington Park, Surrey, and Freda Adela, *née* Martin (d 1975); *b* 14 April 1924; *Educ* Charterhouse, Architectural Assoc London (Dip Arch); *m* 1, 26 Oct 1946 (m dis), Jean Mary Agnes, da of James Anderson (d 1950), of Mosside Park, Glasgow; 3 s (Nicholas b 1950, Jeremy b 1952, Jonathan b 1956), 1 da (Joanna b 1954); m 2, 30 Dec 1988, Berit, da of Harald Wildhagen (d 1980); *Career* RAF 1942-46, Flying Offr, Navigator/Wireless Operator; architect, sr ptnr Michael Lyell Assocs 1954-84 (conslt 1984); FRIBA, ARCUK; *Recreations* golf; *Clubs* Sunningdale Golf; *Style*— Michael Lyell, Esq; 78 Onslow Gardens, London SW7 3QB (☎ 071 373 0116); 16 Yeomans Row, London SW3 9AJ (☎ 071 589 7273, fax 071 225 2431, telex 917084 MILARC)

LYELL, Rt Hon Sir Nicholas Walter; PC (1990), QC (1980), MP (C) Mid-Bedfordshire 1983-; s of Hon Mr Justice Maurice Legat Lyell (d 1975), and his 1 w, Veronica Mary, *née* Luard (d 1950); *b* 12 Dec 1938; *Educ* Stowe, Ch Ch Oxford (MA), Coll of Law; *m* 2 Sept 1967, Susanna Mary, da of Prof Charles Montague Fletcher, CBE, MD, FRCP, FFCM, *qv*; 2 s (Oliver b 1 July 1971, Alexander b 8 Dec 1981), 2 da (Veronica b 8 May 1970, Mary-Kate b 5 March 1979); *Career* Nat Serv with RA 1957-59, 2 Lt 1957; with Walter Runciman & Co 1962- 64; called to the Bar Inner Temple 1965, bencher 1986; in private practice London 1965-86, rec of the Crown Ct 1985; MP (C) Hemel Hempstead 1979-83; jt sec Constitutional Ctee 1979, PPS to Attorney Gen 1979-86, Parly under sec of state (Social Security) DHSS 1986-87, Slr Gen 1987-; chm Soc of Cons Lawyers 1985-86 (vice chm 1982-85), vice chm BFSS 1983-86; Freeman City of London 1964, memb Worshipful Co of Salters; kt 1987; *Recreations* gardening, drawing, shooting; *Clubs* Brooks's; *Style*— The Rt Hon Sir Nicholas Lyell, QC, MP; 1 Brick Ct, Temple, London EC4Y 9BY (☎ 071 583 0777); House of Commons, London SW1A 0AA (☎ 071 219 3000)

LYELL, Baroness; Sophie Mary; da of Maj Sigismund William Joseph Trafford, JP, DL (d 1953), of Wroxham Hall, Norfolk, and Honinton Hall, Grantham, and Lady Betty Bertie, OBE (d 1987), da of 7 Earl of Abingdon (d 1928); *b* 10 Feb 1916; *m* 1938, 2 Baron Lyell, VC (ka 1943, serving with Scots Guards); 1 s (3 Baron, *qv*); *Career* cncllr Angus 1943-65; *Style*— The Rt Hon the Lady Lyell; Kinnordy, Kirriemuir, Angus DD8 5SR (☎ 0575 72848); 20 Petersham Mews, London (☎ 071 584 9419)

LYES, Jeffrey Paul; s of Joseph Leslie Lyes, of Daventry, Northants, and Rose Mary Anne, *née* Harris; *b* 19 April 1946; *m* 5 Oct 1968, Jan, da of John Armstrong, of Oxford; 2 da (Sarah b 1974, Julia b 1977); *Career* journalist United Newspapers 1963-69, news ed Heart of Eng Newspapers 1969-71, exec Hertford PR 1971-73, asst press and PR offr Thames Valley Police 1973-78; dir: Lexington Int PR 1978-81, Grenard Communications 1981-84 (dep md 1984), Good Relations Gp plc 1985-86, Good Relations Corporate Communications 1986-87; md Good Relations Technology 1985-86; chm Good Relations Ltd 1989- (md 1987-88); MIPR 1977, FBIM 1985, FInstD 1988; *Recreations* motor yacht cruising; *Style*— Jeffrey Lyes, Esq; Good Relations Ltd, 59 Russell Sq, London WC1B 4HJ (☎ 071 631 3434, fax 071 631 1399, telex 265903)

LYGO, Adm Sir Raymond Derek; KCB (1977); s of Edwin Lygo; *b* 15 March 1924; *Educ* Ilford Co HS, Clarke Coll Bromley; *m* 1950, Pepper Van Osten, of USA; 2 s, 1 da; *Career* served RN 1942-78, vice-chief and chief of Naval Staff 1975-78; with The Times 1940; Br Aerospace: md Hatfield/Lostock Div 1978-79, chief exec and chm Dynamics Gp 1980-82, memb Main Bd 1980, md 1983-86, chief exec 1986-89; chm Royal Ordnance 1987-88, chm various cos, dir James Capel Corporate Finance 1990-, non exec dir LET plc 1990-; Hon FRAeS, CBIM, FRSA, FPCL; *Clubs* RN & RAYC, RAC; *Style*— Adm Sir Raymond Lygo, KCB

LYGON, Hon Mrs Richard; Patricia Janet; *née* Norman; da of late Rev T K Norman; *m* 1939, Hon Richard Edward Lygon (d 1970), yr son of 7 Earl Beauchamp (d 1938); 2 da (Lettice Patricia Mary b 1940, Rosalind Elizabeth b 1946); *Style*— Hon Mrs Richard Lygon; Pyndar House, Hanley Castle, Worcester

LYLE, Hon Mrs (Elizabeth); *née* Sinclair; yr da of 1 Viscount Thurso, KT, CMG, PC (d 1970), of Thurso Castle, Caithness, and his w, Marigold, da of Col James Stewart Forbes; *b* 5 June 1921; *Educ* Kensington HS, Univ of Oxford; *m* 1942, Lt-Col Archibald Michael Lyle, yst s of Sir Archibald Lyle, 2 Bt; 4 da (Veronica b 1943, Janet b 1944, Diana b 1946, d 1972, Sarah b 1963); *Style*— The Hon Mrs Lyle; Riemore Lodge, Dunkeld, Perths (☎ 035 04 205)

LYLE, Sir Gavin Archibald; 3 Bt (UK 1929), of Glendelvine, Co Perth; s of Capt Ian Archibald de Hoghton Lyle (ka 1942), s of 2 Bt; suc gf, Col Sir Archibald Moir Park Lyle, 2 Bt, MC, TD, 1946; *b* 14 Oct 1941; *m* 1967 (m dis 1985), Susan Cooper; 5 s, 1 da; *Heir* s, Ian Abram Lyle b 25 Sept 1968; *Career* estate mangr; farmer; co dir; *Style*— Sir Gavin Lyle, Bt; Glendelvine, Caputh, Perthshire

LYLE, (Robert) Ian; s of Sgt Isaac Lyle (d 1954), of Edinburgh, and Margaret Mary, *née* Henderson; *b* 18 Aug 1949; *Educ* Heath Clark GS, Univ of Newcastle (BA), Cranfield Business Sch (MBA); *m* 10 June 1978, Leslie Mary, da of Reginald John Halcomb (d 1983), of Worcs; 2 da (Fiona Clare b 1987, Harriet Faith b 1989); *Career* Whitbread plc 1978-83, visiting prof Ohio USA 1980, md Mary Quant Ltd 1983-; dir: WWF, WFN; MBIM 1982, memb Mktg Soc; *Recreations* walking, cricket, squash; *Style*— Ian Lyle, Esq; Mary Quant Ltd, 3 Ives St, London SW3 2NE (☎ 071 584 8781, fax 071 589 9443, telex 923185 MQ LDN)

LYLE, Lt-Col (Archibald) Michael; DL (1961), JP (1950); s of Col Sir Archibald Moir Park Lyle, 2 Bt of Glendelvine, MC, TD, JP, DL (d 1946), of Glendelvine, Murthly, Perthshire, and Dorothy (d 1967), eld da of Sir James de Hoghton, 11 Bt; *b* 1 May 1919; *Educ* Eton, Trinity Coll Oxford (MA); *m* 18 July 1942, Hon Elizabeth Sinclair, da of 1 Viscount Thurso (d 1970), of Thurso Castle, Thurso, Caithness; 4 da (Veronica b 1943, Janet b 1944, Diana b 1946, d 1972, Sarah b 1963); *Career* Black Watch 1939-45 (wounded Normandy 1944, discharged with wounds 1946); Lt-Col The Scottish Horse RAC (TA) 1953-55; chm T & AF Assoc Perthshire 1959-64; memb Queen's Bodyguard for Scotland (The Royal Co of Archers); hon attaché Rome 1938-39; co cncllr: Perthshire 1945-74, Tayside Region 1974-79; vice Lord-Lt of Perth & Kinross 1984; chm Perth Coll of Further Educn 1981-; co dir, farmer; *Recreations* fishing, shooting, music; *Clubs* Royal Perth, Puffin's (Edinburgh), Brooks's, MCC; *Style*— Lt-Col Michael Lyle, DL, JP; Riemore Lodge, Dunkeld, Perthshire (☎ 03504 205)

LYLE, Robert Arthur Wyatt; s of Maj Robert David Lyle (d 1989), and Irene Joyce, *née* Francis (d 1984); nephew of Lord Wyatt of Weeford, *qv*; *b* 5 May 1952; *Educ* Eton, Oriel Coll Oxford (MA); *Career* registered insur broker; int business conslt; dir: Cornish Spring Water Co, Cornwall Light & Power, St Martin's Hotel, Premlina Ltd, BPL Holdings Ltd, Lim & Lyle PTE Singapore; tstee Lanlivery Tst; owner of Bonython Estate, which includes the Lizard Point, the most southerly outcrop of land in UK, one of the three hereditary Lords of the Lizard; Liveryman Worshipful Co of Glass Sellers; *Recreations* hurdles (co-owner of racehorses), travel, art and architecture; *Clubs* White's, MCC; *Style—* Robert Lyle, Esq; Bonython, Helston, Cornwall TR12 7BA (☎ 0326 240234, fax 0326 240478, car 0831 104888)

LYLES, John; CBE (1987), DL (West Yorkshire 1987); s of Percy George Lyles (d 1958), and Alice Maud Mary, *née* Robinson (d 1968); *b* 8 May 1929; *Educ* Giggleswick Sch, Leeds Univ (BSc); *m* 1953, Yvonne, da of G F Johnson (d 1954), of Waddesdon; 2 s (Jonathan, Christopher), 2 da (Jane, Anne); *Career* chm S Lyles plc, non exec dir Hillards plc 1984-87; High Sheriff West Yorkshire 1985-86; magistrate Dewsbury 1968-; chm Yorkshire and Humberside CBI 1983-85; *Recreations* gardening, travel, photography; *Style—* John Lyles, Esq, CBE, DL; c/o S Lyles plc, Jilling Ing Mills, Earlsheaton, Dewsbury, Yorks (☎ 0924 463161, telex 55303)

LYLES, Sam; CBE (1981); s of Percy George Lyles (d 1958), and Alice Maud Mary, *née* Robinson (d 1968); *b* 12 Sept 1920; *Educ* Giggleswick Sch; *m* 18 April 1945, Audrey Jean, da of Sir Walter Ward, CBE, JP (d 1959), of Lynn Wood, Alexandra Rd, Pudsey; 2 s (Jeremy b 1946, Timothy b 1951), 3 da (Veronica b 1953, Rosemary (twin) b 1953, Jenifer b 1946 d 1972); *Career* former non-exec dep chm S Lyles plc, formerly dir and chm S Lyles Sons and Co Ltd (carpet yarn mfrs); pres Dewsbury Constituency Con Assoc 1987, vice chm Batley & Spen Con Assoc; chm: Charles Jones Ct Batley, Royal Br Legion Housing Assoc; pres Dewsbury C of C 1958, fndr pres Dewsbury and Dist Jr C of C 1959; chm: Dewsbury and Dist Hosp Mgmnt Cmmn 1968, Kirklees Area Health Authy 1973-82, Kirklees Family Practitioner Ctee 1975-87, Dewsbury Dist Health Authy 1982-86; pres: Rotary Club of Dewsbury, Woollen Yarn Spinners Assoc; memb Wool Textile Delegation; *Recreations* travel; *Style—* Sam Lyles, Esq, CBE; Fieldhurst, Liversedge, W Yorks WF15 7DD (☎ 0924 402048)

LYMBERY, His Hon Judge Robert Davison; QC (1967); s of Robert Smith Lymbery (d 1981), of West Wittering, Sussex, and Louise, *née* Barnsdale (d 1968); *b* 14 Nov 1920; *Educ* Gresham's, Pembroke Coll Cambridge (MA); *m* 1952, Pauline Anne, da of Maj John Reginald Tuckett (d 1981), of Knebworth, Herts; 3 da (Carole, Sarah, Jane); *Career* served WWII 1940-46, cmmnd 1941 Maj Royal Tank Regt ME, Italy and Greece; called to the Bar Middle Temple 1949 (fndn exhibitioner Harmsworth law scholar), practised Midland Circuit 1949-71, rec Grantham 1965-71, chm Bedfordshire and Rutland Quarter Sessions, circuit judge 1971, master of the bench Middle Temple 1990; Freeman City of London 1983 (Common Serjeant 1990); *Recreations* various; *Clubs* Hawks (Cambridge); *Style—* His Hon Judge Lymbery, QC; c/o Central Criminal Ct, London EC4

LYMINGTON, Viscountess; Julia; *née* Ogden; only da of late W Graeme Ogden, DSC, and Sheila, *née* Faber; *m* 1, Peter Robin Kirwan-Taylor; m 2, as his 3 w, 1974, Viscount Lymington (d June 1984), s of 9 Earl of Portsmouth (d Sept 1984); 1 s (Charles), 2 da (Antonia, Laura); *Style—* Viscountess Lymington

LYMINGTON, Viscount; Oliver Henry Rufus Wallop; s and h of 10 Earl of Portsmouth, *qv*; *b* 22 Dec 1981; *Style—* Viscount Lymington

LYMPANY, Moura; CBE (1979); da of Capt John Johnstone, and Beatrice, *née* Limpenny; *b* 19 Aug 1916; *Educ* Belgium, England, Australia; *m* 1, 1944 (m dis 1950), Lt-Col Colin Defries; m 2, 1951 (m dis 1961), Bennet H Korn; 1 s (decd); *Career* pianist; first performance Mendelssohn's G Minor Concerto Harrogate 1929, won second prize Ysaye Int Pianoforte Competition Brussels 1938; performances given in USA Canada S America Aust NZ India Europe; records made for: EMI, Decca, Olympia, HMV; Cdr Order of Leopold Belguim, Medal of Cultural Merit Portugal 1989; *Style—* Miss Moura Lympany, CBE; 4 Boulevard Du Tenao, Monte Carlo, Monaco 66720, Rasigueres, France (☎ 010 33 93 30 73 29/010 33 68 29 05 47)

LYNAM, Desmond Michael; s of Edward Lynam, and Gertrude Veronica, *née* Malone; *b* 17 Sept 1942; *Educ* Varndean GS Brighton, Brighton Business Coll; *m* 1965 (m dis 1974), Susan Eleanor, *née* Skinner; 1 s (Patrick); *Career* in insurance and freelance journalism until 1967; local radio reporter 1967-69, reporter presenter and commentator BBC Radio 1969-78; presenter and commentator BBC TV Sport 1978- (incl Grandstand, Cwlth and Olympic Games, World Cup); TV Sports Presenter of the Year (TV and Radio Industries Club) 1985, 1986, 1988; Radio Times/Open Air Male TV Personality 1989; *Publications* Guide to Commonwealth Games (1986), 1988 Olympics (1988); *Style—* Desmond Lynam, Esq; c/o BBC TV, Kensington House, Richmond Way, London W14 0AX (☎ 081 895 6611)

LYNAM, Dr Graeme Grant; s of Leo Francis Lynam, of NZ, and Hazel Grace, *née* Frost; *b* 16 June 1955; *Educ* Papatoetoe HS, Univ of Otago (BDental Surgery); *m* Jennifer Shirley, da of John Snell; 1 s (Max Francis b 7 May 1990); *Career* dentist; private practice: Auckland NZ 1979-80, the Outback W Aust 1981; asst gen dental practitioner Leighton Buzzard Bedfordshire 1982, asst private dental practitioner West End 1984, in private practice 1984-; *Recreations* motorcycling in all forms, skiing, sailing; *Clubs* Professional and Exec Motorcyclist (chm); *Style—* Dr Graeme Lynam; 100 Harley St, London W1N 1AF (☎ 071 935 6030)

LYNCH, Alan Russell; s of Stanley Benjamin (d 1967), and Lilian Ivy Moffett (d 1976); *b* 29 Dec 1936; *Educ* Christ's Hosp Sch, Guy's Hosp Univ of London (BDS); *m* 29 Dec 1959, Margaret, da of Dr Theodore Parkman, of Hastings, Sussex; *Career* house surgn Queen Victoria Hosp E Grinstead 1962, gen dental practice 1963-72, assistenarzt Katharinen Hosp Stuttgart 1968, orthodontist in private practice 1972-; *Recreations* sailing, skiing, music, forestry; *Style—* Alan R Lynch, Esq; 78 Clifton Hill, London NW8 0JT; Pattendens Farm, Broad Oak Brede, nr Rye, E Sussex; 31 Queen Anne Street, London W1M 9FB (☎ 071 580 2786)

LYNCH, Barbara; da of Sgt Francis Vincent Lynch, of St Mary in the Marsh, Kent, and Maureen Dorothy, *née* Hartley; *b* 3 June 1953; *Educ* Simon Langton GS Canterbury, Univ of Essex (BA); *Career* sales mangr (braille and books) Royal Nat Inst for the Blind 1978-79, appeal dir Marie Stopes Centenary Appeal 1979-81, nat appeals dir The Samaritans 1981-86, devpt dir Scottish Opera 1986-; tstee Arches Charitable Tst; memb Inst Charity Fundraising Dirs 1981-; *Recreations* photography, opera, theatre; *Style—* Ms Barbara Lynch; 61 Inverness Terrace, London W2 3JT; 40 Derby St, Glasgow (☎ 041 334 3401); Scottish Opera, 39 Elmbank Crescent, Glasgow G2 (☎ 041 248 4567)

LYNCH, Dr Barry Andrew; s of Andrew Lynch, and Eileen, *née* O'Gara; *b* 20 Feb 1952; *Educ* Salford GS, Univ of St Andrews (BSc), Univ of Manchester (MB ChB); *Career* house offr Manchester Royal Infirmary and Univ Hosp of S Manchester 1977-78; BBC Wales: radio prodr 1978-82, TV prodr 1982-87, head of features and documentaries 1987-; health corr Radio Times 1989-; *Books* Don't Break Your Heart - All You Need to Know About Heart Attacks and How to Avoid Them (1987), The BBC Diet (1988), BBC Healthcheck (1989), The New BBC Diet (1990); *Style—* Dr Barry Lynch; BBC Broadcasting Hse, Llandaff, Cardiff CF5 2YQ (☎ 0222 572 888)

LYNCH, Lady; Leah Brigid; da of Thomas Joseph O'Toole (decd); *Educ* St Ann's Ladies Coll Victoria Aust, Coll of Occupational Therapy Univ of Melbourne Aust (Dip); *m* 1958, Rt Hon Sir Phillip Lynch, KCMG, PC (d 1984); 3 s; *Career* dir and co sec Denistoun Party Ltd 1983-; dir: Aarque Systems Party Ltd 1984-87, corporate PR Federal Pacific Hotels and Casinos 1988-; social sec Young Lib Movement 1956, Young Lib Rep on State Exec 1957; memb Bd of Dirs Micro-Surgery Unit St Vincent's Hosp Melbourne Aust; patron: Mt Eliza branch Save the Children Fund, Victoria Branch of Civilian Widows, Red Cross; *Recreations* art, gardening, tennis, golf, antiques collecting; *Clubs* Peninsula Golf, Daveys Bay Yachting; *Style—* Lady Lynch; 22 Cloverdale Ave, Toorak, Victoria 3142, Australia

LYNCH, Monte Allan; s of Lawrence Lynch, of 22 Wimbledon Rd, London, and Doreen, *née* Austin; *b* 21 May 1958; *Educ* Rydens Sch Walton-on-Thames Surrey; *partner*, Susan Low; 1 s (Louis), 1 da (Marissa); *Career* played for Surrey and S of Eng schs; Surrey CCC: joined 1977, first class debut v Northamptonshire 1977, county cap 1982; 3 one day International caps v W Indies 1988 (Edgbaston, Headingley, Lords); tourist with W Indies XI: Pakistan 1981-82, SA 1983-84; played for Guyana 1982-83 (winners Shell shield, Geddes/Grant Harrison Line trophy); 1000 runs in a season 7 times (personal record 1714 1985), 3 Benson & Hedges Gold awards, 1 Man of the Match Nat West trophy, 29 first class centuries; *Recreations* table tennis, football (broke leg playing for commentators XI in charity match); *Style—* Monte Lynch, Esq; The Fosters Oval, Surrey County Cricket Club, Kennington, London SE11 (☎ 071 582 6660)

LYNCH, Paul Dominic Anthony; s of James Alphusos Lynch (d 1986), and Kathleen Mary, *née* Jenkin (d 1976); *b* 7 Feb 1946; *Educ* St Bedes Coll, Univ of Manchester Med Sch; *m* 1969 (m dis 1989), Carol Angela Walker; 1 s (Rory Daniel b 14 April 1978), 2 da (Tara Grace b 12 Sept 1972, Camilla Alexandra b 11 March 1976); *Career* dental surgeon; various appts and gen practice, now in sole private practice (Harley St UK, France, Geneva), specialist in advanced restorative dental surgery; *Recreations* active in sports, the arts, Michelin 3 star restaurants; *Style—* Paul Lynch, Esq; 152 Harley St, London W1N 1HH (☎ 071 935 8762)

LYNCH, Prof Thomas Dawson; s of Andrew Lynch (d 1969), and Elizabeth Lynch, *née* Dawson (d 1961); *b* 14 June 1924; *Educ* Sacred Heart AC Glasgow; *m* 3 Feb 1951, Anne (d 1980), da of Charles Edward Dean (d 1965); 4 da (Anne b 1954, Elizabeth b 1955, Catherine b 1957, Frances b 1959), 2 s (Thomas b 1952, Michael b 1966); *Career* CA; ptnr Ernst & Whinney 1955-83; visiting prof Taxation Glasgow Univ 1982; dir: West Highland Woodlands 1983, Redburn Property Co Ltd 1983; lectr, author of articles and books on taxation; chm St Andrew's Hosp Airdrie Lanarkshire 1986-; *Recreations* forestry, gardening, walking, book collecting; *Clubs* Royal Scottish Automobile Glasgow, Royal Scots Edinburgh; *Style—* Prof Thomas D Lynch

LYNCH-BLOSSE, Elizabeth, Lady; Elizabeth; da of Thomas Harold Payne, of Welwyn Garden City; *m* 1950, Sir David Edward Lynch-Blosse, 16 Bt (d 1971); 1 s, 2 da; *Style—* Elizabeth, Lady Lynch-Blosse

LYNCH-BLOSSE, Gp Capt (Eric) Hugh; OBE (1952); s of Maj Cecil Eagles Lynch-Blosse (d 1966), and his 1 w Dorothy Delahaize, *née* Ouvry (d 1963); hp of kinsman, Sir Richard Hely Lynch-Blosse, 17 Bt; *b* 30 July 1917; *Educ* Blundell's, RAF Coll; *m* 1946, Jean Evelyn, da of Cdr Andrew Robertson Hair, RD, RNR (d 1965); 1 s (David), 1 da (Valerie), and 1 da decd (Fiona); *Career* served RAF 1935-67, POW 1941-45, Gp Capt; standards engr Rank Xerox 1969-74, sec Wyedean Tourist Bd and mangr Tourist Info Centre Ross on Wye 1974-80, ret; *Books* Wartime Memories from Newnham, Wings - and Other Things; *Clubs* RAF; *Style—* Gp Capt Hugh Lynch-Blosse, OBE; 17 Queens Acre, Newnham, Glos GL14 1DJ (☎ 0594 516 335)

LYNCH-BLOSSE, Sir Richard Hely; 17 Bt (I 1622), of Castle Carra, Galway; s of Sir David Edward Lynch-Blosse, 16 Bt (d 1971), and Elizabeth, *née* Payne; *b* 26 Aug 1953; *Educ* Welwyn Garden City, Royal Free Hosp Sch of Med Univ of London (MB BS, LRCP, MRCS); *m* 1976, Cara Lynne, only da of George Longmore Sutherland, of St Ives, Cambs; 2 da (Katy b 1983, Hannah b 1985); *Heir* kinsman, (Eric) Hugh Lynch-Blosse, OBE, *qv*; *Career* med practitioner, short serv cmmn with RAMC 1975; DRCOG, MRCGP; *Recreations* shooting, sailing, racquet sports; *Style—* Sir Richard Lynch-Blosse, Bt; The Surgery, Clifton Hampden, Oxon OX14 3EL

LYNCH-ROBINSON, Dominick Christopher; s and h of Sir Niall Bryan Lynch-Robinson, 3 Bt, DSC; *b* 30 July 1948; *m* 1973, Victoria, da of Kenneth Weir, of 37 Stokesay Rd, Sale, Manchester; 1 s (Christopher Henry Jake b 1 Oct 1977), 1 da (Anna Elizabeth Seaton b 19 July 1973); *Career* creative dir advertising agency; *Style—* Dominick Lynch-Robinson, Esq; Palmers Hill House, Burghclere, Newbury, Berks

LYNCH-ROBINSON, Sir Niall Bryan; 3 Bt (UK 1920), of Foxrock, Co Dublin, DSC (1941); s of Sir Christopher Henry Lynch-Robinson, 2 Bt (d 1958), and Dorothy Mary Augusta, *née* Warren (d 1970); *b* 24 Feb 1918; *Educ* Stowe; *m* 30 March 1940, Rosemary Seaton, er da of Capt Harold John Eller (d 1929); 1 s, 1 adopted da (Anthea Lucy b 1956); *Heir* s, Dominick Christopher Lynch-Robinson; *Career* Sub Lt RNVR 1939, Lt 1940; chm Leo Burnett Ltd 1969-78; memb Exec Ctee Nat Marriage Guidance Cncl 1960-1986; Croix de Guerre 1944; *Recreations* flyfishing, gardening, caravanning; *Style—* Sir Niall Lynch-Robinson, Bt, DSC; The Old Vicarage, Ampfield, Romsey, Hants SO51 9BQ

LYNDEN-BELL, Prof Donald; s of Lt-Col Lachlan Arthur Lynden-Bell, MC (d 1984), and Monica Rose, *née* Thring; *b* 5 April 1935; *Educ* Marlborough, Clare Coll Cambridge; *m* 1 July 1961, Ruth Marion, da of Dr D N Truscott, of Ely; 1 s (Edward Lachlan b 16 Dec 1968), 1 da (Marion Katharine b 10 April 1965); *Career* res fell Clare Coll and fell Cwlth (Harkness) Fund California Inst Technol and Mt Wilson and Palomar Observatories 1960-62, dir studies maths Clare Coll and asst lectr Univ of Cambridge 1962-65, SPSO Royal Greenwich Observatory Herstmonceux 1965-72, visiting prof Univ of Sussex 1970-72, dir Inst Astronomy Cambridge 1972-77 and 1982-87, prof astrophysics Univ of Cambridge and prof fell Clare Coll 1972-; pres: Cambridge Philosophical Soc 1982-84, RAS 1985-87 (Eddington Medal 1984); DSc Univ of Sussex 1987; foreign assoc US Nat Acad of Sci 1990; Brower Prize American Astronomical Soc 1990; FRS 1978; *Recreations* hill walking; *Style—* Prof Donald Lynden-Bell, FRS; 9 Storey's Way, Cambridge CB3 0DP (☎ 0223 354332); Inst of Astronomy (Cambridge University), The Observatories, Madingley Rd, Cambridge CB3 0DP (☎ 0223 337525, fax 0223 337523, telex 817297 ASTRON G)

LYNDON SKEGGS, Barbara Noel; MBE (1990), JP (1966), DL (1988); da of Philip Noel Rogers, of Hurstpierpoint, Sussex, and Beatrice, *née* Marillier; *b* 29 Dec 1924; *Educ* Queen Bertha's Sch Birchington Kent; *m* 1, 26 July 1943, (Griffith) Eric Carbery Vaughan Evans (d 1950), s of Brig-Gen Lewis Pugh Evans VC, CB, CMG, DSO, DL (d 1964); 2 s (Christopher b 5 Dec 1945, Roger b 23 June 1947); m 2, 8 April 1953, Michael Andrew Lyndon Skeggs, s of Dr Basil Lyndon Skeggs (d 1956); 2 da (Victoria (Mrs Bagge) b 28 April 1954, Marianne (Mrs Munro-Ferguson) b 11 Oct 1955); *Career* WRNS 1942-45; asst dir BRCS 1948-; Northumberland CC: co cncllr 1968-81, chm Health Ctee 1970-74, chm Soc Servs 1974-81; memb Guild of City Freeman 1973, vice chm Northumberland DHA 1989-90, FPC 1980-90, tax commissioner 1984; Freeman City of London 1973; *Recreations* a baker's dozen grandmother; *Style—* Mrs Barbara Lyndon Skeggs, MBE, JP, DL; Oakhall, Cornhill on Tweed, Northumberland TD12 4TH (☎ 089 082 250)

LYNDON-SKEGGS, Andrew Neville; s of Dr Peter Lyndon-Skeggs, of Valley House, Preston Candover, Hants, and June Angela, *née* Reid; *b* 10 Jan 1949; *Educ* Rugby, Magdalene Coll Cambridge; *m* 8 April 1972 (m dis); 2 da (Vanessa b 1975, Tessa b 1979); *Career* master and tstee Univ of Cambridge Drag Hunt 1968-71; chm Westbrook Property Developments Ltd; *Recreations* stalking, hunting, fishing, skiing, gardening; *Clubs* Travellers'; *Style—* Andrew Lyndon-Skeggs, Esq; Westbrook House, Holybourne, Alton, Hants (☎ 0420 83244/87539, fax 0420 89535/541542, car ☎ 0836 220633)

LYNE, Air Vice-Marshal Michael Dillon; CB (1968), AFC (1943, and two bars 1947

and 1955), DL (1973); s of Robert John Lyne (d 1943), and Ruth Walton, *née* Robinson (d 1952); *b* 23 March 1919; *Educ* Imperial Serv Coll, RAF Coll Cranwell; *m* 1943, Avril Joy, da of Lt-Col Albert Buckley, CBE, DSO (d 1965), of Liverpool; 2 s (Peter, Roderic), 2 da (Justine, Barbara); *Career* joined RAF 1937, Fighter Cmd 1939-43, ME 1943-46, Air Attaché Moscow 1961-63, Cmdt RAF Coll Cranwell 1963-64, Air Vice-Marshal 1965; pres: 54 Sqdn Assoc, Grantham Constituency Lib Democrats; vice pres: Old Cranwellian Assoc, RAF Gliding Assoc, RAF Motor Sport Assoc; *Recreations* photography, writing; *Clubs* RAF; *Style*— Air Vice-Marshal Michael Lyne, CB, AFC, DL; 9 Far Lane, Coleby, Lincoln LN5 0AH (☎ 0522 810468)

LYNE, Roderic Michael John; s of Air Vice-Marshal Michael Dillon Lyne, CB, AFC, of Far End, Far Lane, Coleby, Lincoln, and Avril Joy, *née* Buckley; *b* 31 March 1948; *Educ* Highfield Sch Liphook Hants, Eton, Univ of Leeds (BA); *m* 13 Dec 1969, Amanda Mary, da of Sir Howard Frank Trayton Smith, GCMG; 2 s (Jethro b 10 Nov 1971, Andrei b 31 May 1974), 1 da (Sasha b 7 Jan 1981); *Career* joined HM Dip Serv 1970, Br Embassy Moscow 1972-74, Br Embassy Senegal 1974-76; FCO: Eastern Europe and Soviet Dept 1976-78, Rhodesia Dept 1979, asst private sec to Foreign and Cwlth Sec 1979-82; UK mission to UN NY 1982-86, visiting res fell Royal Inst of Int Affrs 1986-87; head of chancery and head of Political Section Br Embassy Moscow 1987-90, head of Soviet Dept FCO 1990-; *Recreations* sport; *Style*— Roderic Lyne, Esq; Foreign and Commonwealth Office, King Charles Street, London SW1A 2AH

LYNK, Roy; OBE (1990); s of John Thomas Lynk (d 1950), and Ivy May Lynk (d 1980); *b* 9 Nov 1932; *Educ* Station Rd Higher Sch Notts, Univ of Nottingham (Cert Industl Rels); *m* 11 Nov 1978, Sandra Ann, da of William Watts (d 1949); 3 s (Roy b 28 May 1968, John b 29 Nov 1972, Mark b 31 Aug 1971), 3 da (Lorraine b 12 June 1960, Carol b 1 Dec 1961, Dawn b 2 Dec 1964); *Career* RN 1948-50, TA 1956-68; miner British Coal 1947-79; NUM Nottingham Area: branch sec Sutton Colliery 1958-79, full time official 1979-83, fin sec 1983-85, gen sec 1985; UDM: gen sec Nottingham Section 1985-, nat gen sec 1985-86, nat pres and sec 1987-; memb: St John Ambulance Bde 1968-80, Euro Coal and Steel Ctee 1987-; dist cncllr Ashfield 1972-80; *Recreations* playing golf, watching football; *Style*— Roy Lynk, Esq, OBE; Union of Democratic Mineworkers, Miners Offices, Berry Hill Lane, Mansfield, Notts NG18 4JU (☎ 0623 26094, fax 0623 642300)

LYNN, Bishop of 1986-; Rt Rev David Edward Bentley; s of William Edward Bentley (d 1980), of Gorleston, and Florence Maud Marion, *née* Dalgleish (d 1978); *b* 7 Aug 1935; *Educ* Gt Yarmouth GS, Univ of Leeds (BA), Westcott House Cambridge; *m* 5 Sept 1962, Clarice May, da of Reginald Lahmers (d 1964), of KirkBride, Isle of Man; 2 s (Simon b 1964, Matthew b 1966), 2 da (Katharine b 1963, Rachel b 1964); *Career* Nat Serv 1956-58, 2 Lt 5 Regt RHA; curate: St Ambrose Bristol 1960-62, Holy Trinity with St Mary Guildford 1962-66; rector: All Saints, Headley 1966-73, Esher 1973-86; rural dean Emly 1977-82; hon canon Guildford Cathedral 1980-86, chm Diocesan Cncl of Social Responsibility 1980-86, chm ACCM Candidates Cmmn 1987; *Recreations* music, sport, walking; *Clubs* MCC, Norfolk (Norwich); *Style*— The Rt Rev the Bishop of Lynn; The Old Vicarage, Castle Acre, King's Lynn, Norfolk PE32 2AA (☎ 0760 755 553)

LYNN, Jonathan Adam; s of Dr Robin Lynn, of London, and Ruth Helen, *née* Eban; *b* 3 April 1943; *Educ* Kingswood Sch Bath, Pembroke Coll Cambridge (MA); *m* 1 Aug 1967, Rita Eleonora Merkelis; 1 s (Edward b 19 Oct 1973); *Career* writer and dir; actor in repertory: Leicester, Edinburgh Bristol Old Vic, West End; TV and film actor: Barmitzvah Boy 1975, The Knowledge 1979, Outside Edge 1982, Diana 1984, Into The Night 1985, Three Men and A Little Lady 1990; artistic dir Cambridge Theatre Co 1977-81 (produced 42 prodns and directed over 20); London dir incl: The Glass Menagerie 1977, The Gingerbread Man 1977, The Unvarnished Truth 1978, Songbook 1979 (SWET and Evening Standard Awards for Best Musical, re-titled The Moony Shapiro Songbook for Broadway Prodn 1981), A Little Hotel On The Side (NT) 1984, Jacobowski and the Colonel (NT) 1986, Three Men on a Horse (NT, Olivier award for best comedy) 1987, Budgie 1988; company dir at NT 1986-87; TV writer incl: Yes Minister 1980-82, Yes Prime Minister 1986- (with co-author Anthony Jay received: BAFTA Writers award, Broadcasting Press Guild award (twice), Pye Television Writers award (twice), Ace award - best comedy writing on US cable TV, Special award from The Campaign For Freedom of Information); film scriptwriter: The Internecine Project 1974, Micks People (also dir) 1982, Clue (also dir) 1986, Nuns On The Run (also dir) 1989; TV dir: Smart Guys, Ferris Bueller (NBC TV pilots); Hon MA Univ of Sheffield; *Books* The Complete Yes Minister, Yes Prime Minister vols 1 and 2 (with Antony Jay), A Proper Man (1976); *Recreations* changing weight; *Style*— Jonathan Lynn, Esq; c/o Peters Fraser and Dunlop, Fifth Floor, The Chambers, Chelsea Harbour, Lots Rd, London SW10 0XF

LYNN, Maurice Kenneth; *b* 3 March 1951; *Educ* Thornleigh Salesian Coll, Magdalen Coll Oxford (William Doncaster open scholar, Heath Harrison travelling scholar, BA, MA); *Career* asst d'anglais École Normale Montpellier 1971-72; asst master: The Oratory Sch 1973-79, Radley Coll 1979-83; head of French Westminster Sch 1983-89, headmaster The Oratory Sch 1989-; *Recreations* soccer, cycling, swimming, acting; *Clubs* East India; *Style*— Maurice Lynn, Esq; The Oratory School, Woodcote, nr Reading RG8 0PJ (☎ 0491 680207)

LYNN, Prof Richard; s of Richard Lynn, and Ann Lynn; *b* 20 Feb 1930; *Educ* Bristol GS, King's Coll Cambridge (Passingham prize); *m* 1956 (m dis 1978), Susan Maher; 1 s, 2 da; m 2, 1989, Susan, *née* Hampson; *Career* lectr in psychology Univ of Exeter 1956-67; prof of psychology: Dublin Economic and Social Res Inst 1967-72, Univ of Ulster 1972-; awarded US Mensa award for Excellence (for work on intelligence) 1985 and 1988; *Books* Attention Arousal and the Orientation Reaction (1966), The Irish Braindrain (1969), The Universities and the Business Community (1969), Personality and National Character (1971), An Introduction to the Study of Personality (1972), The Entrepreneur (ed, 1974), Dimensions of Personality (ed, 1981), Educational Achievement in Japan (1987); author of various articles on personality, intelligence and social psychology; *Recreations* DIY; *Clubs* Northern Counties (Londonderry); *Style*— Prof Richard Lynn; Dunderg House, Coleraine Co, Londonderry

LYNN, Dame Vera Margaret; DBE (1975, OBE 1969); da of Bertram Welch, and Annie, *née* Martin; *b* 20 March 1917; *Educ* Brampton Rd Sch East Ham; *m* 1941, Harry Lewis; 1 da (Virginia Penelope Ann); *Career* singer; dir Channel Contemporary Radio; Forces' Sweetheart in WW II, toured Egypt, India, Burma 1944; over 12,000,000 copies of record Auf Wiederseh'n sold; pres Printers' Charitable Corpn 1980; *Recreations* gardening, painting, needlework, knitting; *Style*— Dame Vera Lynn, DBE

LYNTON, Prof Norbert Casper; s of Dr Paul Lynton (d 1974), and Amalie Christiane, *née* Lippert (d 1989); *b* 22 Sept 1927; *Educ* Douai Sch, Birkbeck Coll London (BA), Courtauld Inst (BA); *m* 1, 1 Oct 1949 (m dis 1968), Janet Mary, da of Henry Braid Irving; 2 s (Jeremy b 1957, Oliver b 1959); m 2, 3 May 1969, Sylvia Anne, *née* Towning; 2 s (Thomas b 1970, Peter b 1973); *Career* lectr history of art and architecture Leeds Coll of Art 1950-61, head of dept of art history and gen studies Chelsea Sch of Art 1961-70 (previously sr lectr), dir of exhibitions Arts Cncl of GB 1970-75, visiting prof of history of art Open Univ 1975, prof of history of art Univ of Sussex 1975-89 (dean of Sch of Euro Studies 1985-88), visiting tutor in painting RCA 1989-; London corr of Art Int 1961-66, art critic on The Guardian 1965-70, tstee Nat Portrait Gallery 1985-; chm of Visual Art and Crafts panel of SE Arts Assoc 1990-; memb Assoc of Art Historians 1977-; *Books* Paul Klee (1964), The Modern World (1968), The Story of Modern Art (2 edn, 1989), Looking at Art (1981), Looking into Paintings (jtly, 1985); *Style*— Prof Norbert Lynton; 28 Florence Rd, Brighton BN1 6DJ (☎ 0273 509478)

LYON, Prof Christina Margaret; da of Edward Arthur Harrison, of Liverpool, and Kathleen Joan, *née* Smith; *b* 12 Nov 1952; *Educ* Wallasey HS for Girls, UCL (LLB); *m* 29 May 1976, Adrian Pirrie Lyon, s of Alexander Ward Lyon, of London; 1 s (David Edward Arandall b 8 July 1985), 1 da (Alexandra Sophie Louise b 5 Jan 1984); *Career* slr Bell & Joynson Liscard Wallasey Merseyside 1975-77; lectr in law faculty: Univ of Liverpool 1977-80, Univ of Manchester 1980-86 (sub-dean 1986); head Sch of Law Univ of Keele 1988- (prof of law and head dept of law 1986-); Dr Barnardo's Res Fellowship 1987-89; ed Journal of Social Welfare and Family Law, pres N Staffs Relate Marriage Guidance 1987-, ind memb Merseyside Children's Secure Accommodation Panel 1988-; memb ESRC, memb Child Policy Review Gp NCB, tstee and dir IRCHIN; memb: Law Soc 1977, Soc of Pub Teachers of Law 1977; *Books* Cohabitation Without Marriage (1983), The Law of Residential Homes and Day Care Establishments (1984), Child Abuse (1990), Atkins on Minors (1990), Butterworths Family Law Encyclopaedia (1990); *Recreations* tennis, opera, theatre, foreign travel, writing; *Style*— Prof Christina Lyon; Dept of Law, Sch of Law, Univ of Keele, Keele, N Staffs ST5 5BG (☎ 0782 712794 ext 3713, fax 0782 613847, telex 36113 UNKLIB G)

LYON, Clive; s of Lt-Col Ivan Lyon DSO, MBE, The Gordon Highlanders (ka 1944), and Gabrielle Anna Georgina, *née* Bouvier (d 1978); *b* 12 Sept 1941; *Educ* Harrow, Selwyn Coll Cambridge (MA), RMC Cirencester; *m* 29 March 1967, Madeline Rosa Edith, da of Maj Herbert Frederick Brudenell Foster, TD, of Park House, Drumoak, Aberdeenshire; 2 s (Charles Henry b 1971, Francis James Edward b 1974); *Career* Subaltern Offr Gordon Highlanders 1964-67, active serv Borneo 1965-66; exec Consolidated Goldfields 1967-73; farmer 1975-88; *Recreations* reading, collecting books, walking; *Style*— Clive Lyon, Esq; The Old Rectory, Stanfield, Dereham, Norfolk (☎ 0328 700224)

LYON, Capt Donald Stewart; s of Alexander Lyon (d 1969), of London, and Dorothy Elizabeth, *née* Tomlinson (d 1986); *b* 27 June 1934; *Educ* Goring Hall, King Edward VII Nautical Coll, Univ of London; *m* 27 June 1956, Marie Pauline, da of Walter Alfred Greenfield (d 1980); *Career* MN Offr Shell (cadet to chief offr) 1951-62; Inchcape Group 1962-73: gen mangr (previously asst) ME, dir and vice pres jt venture Incape/Canadian Pacific Canada; Thorn EMI Group 1977-82: dir AFA Minerva Ltd, chm overseas cos within gp; md Voith Engrg Ltd 1982-, chm HFH Ltd 1990-; memb: Bahrain Soc, Anglo-Omani Soc; Freeman City of London 1974, Liveryman Honourable Co of Master Mariners; FInstD; *Recreations* squash; *Clubs* Special Forces, Oriental; *Style*— Capt Donald Lyon; Voith Engrg Ltd, 6 Beddington Farm Rd, Croydon, Surrey CR0 4XB (☎ 081 667 0333, fax 081 667 0403)

LYON, John Patrick; MBE (1991); s of Robert Lyon, of 3 Blockdown Grove, St Helens, and Jean Gertrude, *née* Wilson; *b* 9 March 1962; *m* 19 Jan 1980, Rita Mary, da of William Swift, of 6 Everton Grove, St Helens; 2 s (John Paul b 14 June 1980, Craig Michael b 3 Feb 1982), 1 da (Lisa Maire b 17 Nov 1984); *Career* boxer; ABA champion: light flyweight 1981-84, flyweight 1986-89 (total eight titles breaking 1890's record); Cwlth Games: Silver medal 1982, Gold medal 1986; capt England and GB boxing teams 1986-; *Clubs* Greenhall St Helens Amateur Boxing; *Style*— John Lyon, Esq, MBE; 10 Ashurst Drive, Blackbrook, St Helens, Merseyside WA11 9DW (☎ 0744 51300); Pilkington Glass, Watson St, St Helens, Merseyside (☎ 0744 69 6575)

LYON, Dr John Stuart; s of Edwin Lyon (d 1947), and Isobelle Lydia, *née* Malkin (d 1973); *b* 14 April 1932; *Educ* King's Coll Taunton, St John's Coll Cambridge, Westminster Med Sch London (MA, MB, BChir); *m* 4 Jan 1975, Christine Evelyn, da of John Edward Larner (d 1987); 1 s (Richard b 1977), 1 da (Annabelle b 1976); *Career* conslt psychiatrist Wessex RHA 1972; clinical teacher Univ of Southampton; memb ctees: RCPsych, Wessex RHA; involved with Mental Health Act Cmmn; memb: Mental Health Review Tbnls, Health Advsy Serv; pres Basingstoke MIND; clinical dir Adult Mental Health Basingstoke District; MRCPsych, FRCPsych, MRCP, FRCP; *Books* Breast Cancer Management (contrib, 1977), Die Erkrangungen der Weiblichen Brustdrusse (contrib, 1982); *Recreations* photography, DIY (of necessity!); *Clubs* Basingstoke and Deane Rotary; *Style*— Dr John Lyon; Basingstoke District Hospital, Basingstoke, Hants RG24 9NA (☎ 0256 473202)

LYON, Michael Edmund; s of Harry Limnell Lyon (d 1969), of Hillam Hall, S Milford, Yorks, and Lois Marjory, *née* Sharpe (d 1975); *b* 10 Oct 1916; *Educ* Uppingham; *m* 7 Jan 1947, Eliane Madeleine, *née* Lemmens; 1 s (Patrick b 1951); *Career* Capt Queens Own Yorks Dragoons: BEF 1939-40, MEF 1942 (POW 1942-45); chm and md Lyon & Lyon plc 1948-86; dir: Br Marine Mutual Insurance Association Ltd 1965-80, Yorks Tar Distillers 1969-75, Tees Towing Co Ltd 1970-84; JP (Pontefract) 1961-83, High Sheriff W Yorks 1976-77; govr The Kings Sch Pontefract 1970-86; Mayor The Merchants of the Staple of Eng 1978-79 (memb 1968-); ARINA; *Recreations* shooting, skiing, sailing; *Style*— Michael Lyon, Esq; Cedar House, Ackworth, W Yorks WF7 7EQ (☎ 0977 704910)

LYON, Maj Gen Robert; CB (1976), OBE (1964, MBE 1960); s of David Murray Lyon (d 1943), and Bridget, *née* Smith (d 1925); *b* 24 Oct 1923; *Educ* Ayr Acad; *m* 15 Jan 1951, Constance Margaret, da of Colin Gordon (d 1963); 1 s (David b 21 April 1953), 1 da (Melanie Jane (Mrs Manton) b 6 June 1957); *Career* cmmnd A & SH 1943; serv: Italy, Palestine, Egypt, Greece; transfrd and regular cmmn RA 1947, 19 Field Regt BAOR, 3 RHA Libya, F Sphinx Battery 7 Para RHA M E, instr Mons OCS,GSO 1 ASD 2 MOD 1962-65; CO 4 Light Regt: Borneo (despatches), UK, Germany; Brig CRA 1 Armd Div 1967-69, Imperial Def Coll 1970, dir operational requirements MOD 1971-73, Maj-Gen dir RA 1973-75, GOC SW Dist 1975-78, ret 1978; Col Cmdt RA 1976-; pres Army Hockey Assoc 1974-76; chm: Army Golf Assoc 1977-78, RA Cncl of Scotland 1984-; memb: Lothian Territorial Assoc 1980-, Offrs Assoc Scotland 1980-; bursar Loretto Sch 1979-; memb Exec Ctee: Ind Schs Bursars Assoc 1981-85, Ind Schs Info Serv (Scotland) 1988-; cmmr Queen Victoria Sch Dunblane 1984-; dir: Edinburgh Mil Tattoo plc 1988-, Braemar Civic Amenities Tst 1986-; memb Ctee Musselburgh Conservation Soc 1987-; MBIM 1978, FBIM 1981; *Recreations* golf, fishing, skiing, writing; *Clubs* New (Edinburgh), Hon Co of Edinburgh Golfers; *Style*— Maj Gen Robert Lyon, CB, OBE; Woodside, Braemar, Aberdeenshire (☎ 03383 667); Linkfield Cottage Musselburgh, E Lothian, (☎ 031 665 2380); Loretto Sch, Musselburgh, E Lothian, (☎ 031 605 2825)

LYON, (Colin) Stewart Sinclair; s of Col Colin Sinclair Lyon, OBE, TD (d 1967), and Dorothy Winstanley, *née* Thomason (d 1946); *b* 22 Nov 1926; *Educ* Liverpool Coll, Trinity Coll Cambridge (MA); *m* 9 Aug 1958, Elizabeth Mary Fargus, da of Oliver Fargus Richards (d 1946); 4 s (Richard b 1959, Julian b 1961, Ian b 1962, Alistair b 1963), 1 da (Catherine b 1962); *Career* chief exec Victory Insurance Co Ltd 1974-76, dir and chief actuary Legal and General Assurance Society Ltd 1976-85, gp chief actuary Legal and General Group plc 1985-87 (dir and gen fin mangr 1980-87); dir: Lautro Ltd 1987-, The Cologne Reinsurance Co Ltd 1987-, Aetna International (UK)

Ltd 1988-; vice pres Br Numismatic Soc 1971- (pres 1966-70); dir: Disablement Income Gp 1984-, City of Birmingham Touring Opera Ltd 1987-90; memb: Occupational Pensions Bd 1979-82, Inquiry into Provision for Retirement 1983-85; pres Inst of Actuaries 1982-84, tstee Ind Living Fund 1988-; Sanford Saltus Gold medallist (Br Numismatic Soc) 1974; Freeman City of London, memb Worshipful Co of Actuaries 1984; FIA 1954, FSA 1972; *Books* Coinage in Tenth-Century England (with C E Blunt and B H I H Stewart, 1989); *Recreations* numismatics, amateur radio, music; *Clubs* Actuaries; *Style*— Stewart Lyon, Esq, FSA; Cuerdale, White Lane, Guildford, Surrey GU4 8PR (☎ 0483 573 761)

LYON, Thomas Redshaw Spring (Tom); CBE (1978), TD (bar 1949 and 1955); s of Robert Lyon (d 1944), of Aberdeen, and Julia Gertrude, *née* Spring (d 1975); *b* 6 Nov 1919; *Educ* Tollington Sch; *m* 21 Sept 1954, Grace, da of Jesse Hedley Hayes, of Finchley; 1 da (Jane Elizabeth Redshaw b 1956); *Career* London Scottish (TA) 1938, cmmnd 1941, Staff Office Chitral 1942, Burma 1943, SS Office to Fin Dept Govt of India, war zones 1943-44, Bde Maj 8 Indian Div 1944-45, ret 1946; rejoined London Scottish 1947, 2 i/c 1959, chm Regtl Assoc; chm: various cos Clam-Brummer Group, NABM 1964, L&SE Region CBI 1966 (memb Cncl CBI 1965-), Smaller Firms Cncl CBI 1974-80; memb Metrication Bd 1976-80, vice pres Small Business Bureau; *Recreations* shooting, riding, swimming, country pursuits; *Clubs* Caledonian; *Style*— Tom Lyon, CBE, TD; Bedwell End, Essendon, Herts AL9 6HL (☎ 0707 261238); Clam-Brummer Ltd, Bradfield Rd, E16

LYON, Thomas Stephen; s of Clifford Alexander Lyon (d 1962), and Felicia Maria Maximiliana, *née* Rosenfeld; *b* 26 Nov 1941; *Educ* Univ Coll Sch, Wadham Coll Oxford (MA), LSE (LLM); *m* 1971, Judith Elizabeth Jervis, da of Joseph Globe, of Toronto, Canada; 3 s (Edmund b 1971, Charles b 1973, Roger b 1974); *Career* Woodham Smith Borradaile and Martin 1962-68, Berwin & Co 1968-70, Berwin Leighton 1970-; memb City Slrs Co; *Recreations* bicycling up hills, music; *Clubs* United Oxford and Cambridge Univs, Reform; *Style*— Thomas Lyon, Esq; 24 Denewood Rd, London N6 4AJ (☎ 081 340 0846); Fernlea, Redmire, Leyburn, N Yorks (☎ 0969 22776); Adelaide House, London Bridge, London EC4R 9HA (☎ 071 623 3144, fax 071 623 4416)

LYON, Victor Lawrence; s of Dr Jacqueline Beverley Lyon; *b* 10 Feb 1956; *Educ* Marlborough, Trinity Coll Cambridge (BA); *m* 4 Oct 1986, (Rosalind) Sara, da of Anthony Compton Burnett, of Winkfield, Berks; 1 s (Frederick James b 19 Feb 1990); *Career* called to the Bar Gray's Inn 1980; *Recreations* tennis, golf, swimming; *Style*— Victor Lyon, Esq; 4 Essex Ct, Temple, London EC4 9AJ (☎ 071 583 9191, telex COMCAS 888465, fax 071 353 3421)

LYON-SMITH, David; s of Dr George Lyon Lyon-Smith (d 1954), and Violet Mary, *née* Bovill (d 1974); *b* 19 Jan 1926; *Educ* Wellington, Christ's Coll Cambridge (BA); *m* 26 Aug 1961, Diana Caroline, da of Cdr Thomas Stanley Lane Fox-Pitt, OBE (d 1985), of Devon; 2 s (George Thomas b 1962, William Harry b 1964), 1 da (Katherine Diana b 1963); *Career* organist Christ's Coll Cambridge 1944, slr, chapter clerk Exeter Cathedral 1959-64, registrar of Archdeaconry of Exeter 1959-65; master: Stoke Hill Beagles 1952-63, E Devon Foxhounds 1963-66 and 1968-69; chm: Mid-Devon Hunt 1989-, All Hallows Sch 1989- (govr 1976-89); *Recreations* music, country sports; *Style*— David Lyon-Smith, Esq; Chapple, Gidleigh, Changford, Devon (☎ 064 749 2200)

LYON-DALBERG-ACTON, Hon Edward David Joseph; 4 s of 3 Baron Acton, CMG, MBE, TD (d 1989); *b* 4 Feb 1949; *Educ* Univ of York (BA), Univ of Cambridge (PhD); *m* 1972, Stella Marie, da of Henry Conroy, of 8 Stirling Rd, Bolton; 2 da; *Career* sr lectr in history Univ of Manchester; *Books* Alexander Herzen and the Role of the Intellectual Revolutionary (1979); Russia: the present and the past (1986), Rethinking the Russian Revolution (1990); *Recreations* tennis, bridge, racing; *Style*— The Hon Edward Lyon-Dalberg-Acton; 24 Moss Lane, Sale, Cheshire M33 1GD (☎ 061 973 0128); Dept of History, University of Manchester, Manchester M13 9PL (☎ 061 275 3115)

LYON-DALBERG-ACTON, Rev Hon John Charles; 2 s of 3 Baron Acton, CMG, MBE, TD (d 1989); *b* 26 Jan 1943; *Educ* Gregorian Univ Rome; *Career* prof of dogmatic theology Westminster Diocesan Seminary; *Style*— The Rev the Hon John Lyon-Dalberg-Acton; Westminster Diocesan Seminary, 28 Beaufort St, London SW3

LYON-DALBERG-ACTON, Hon John Charles Ferdinand Harold; o s and h of 4 Baron Acton, *qv*; *b* 19 Aug 1966; *Educ* Winchester, Balliol Coll Oxford; *Style*— The Hon John Lyon-Dalberg-Acton

LYON-DALBERG-ACTON, Hon Peter Hedley; 5 and yst s of 3 Baron Acton, CMG, MBE, TD (d 1989); *b* 27 March 1950; *Educ* Cirencester Agric Coll; *m* 1981, Annie Sinclair; 1 s (Simon); *Style*— The Hon Peter Lyon-Dalberg-Acton; Dancing Dicks, Witham, Essex

LYON-DALBERG-ACTON, Hon Robert Peter; 3 s of 3 Baron Acton, CMG, MBE, TD (d 1989); *b* 23 June 1946; *Educ* St George's Coll Salisbury S Rhodesia; *m* 1974, Michele Daniele, da of Henri Joseph Laigle, of Paris; 3 s (Christopher Richard Henri b 1977, Patrick John b 1979, William Benjamin b 1986); *Career* stud mangr; *Recreations* bridge, tennis; *Style*— The Hon Robert Lyon-Dalberg-Acton; Rutland House, Saxon Street, Newmarket, Suffolk; Dalham Hall Stud, Duchess Drive, Newmarket, Suffolk

LYONS, Bernard; CBE (1964), JP (Leeds 1960), DL (Yorks W Riding 1971); s of S H Lyons, of Leeds; *b* 30 March 1913; *Educ* Leeds GS; *m* 1938, Lucy, da of Wilfred Hurst, of Leeds; 3 s, 1 da; *Career* dir and chm and md UDS Gp Ltd 1954-82 (pres 1983-); memb Leeds City Cncl 1951-65; chm: Leeds Judean Youth Club 1955-70, Swarthmore Adult Educn Centre Appeal 1957-60, City of Leeds Audit Sub Ctee 1959-63, Yorks and NE Conciliation Ctee Race Relations Bd 1968-70; jt chm Leeds Branch Cncl of Christians and Jews 1955-60, hon life pres Leeds Jewish Rep Cncl 1960-; memb: Ct and Cncl Univ of Leeds 1953-58, Cmmn for Community Relations 1970-72, Govt Advsy Ctee on Retail Distribution 1970-76; Hon LLD Leeds 1973; *Books* The Thread is Strong (1981), The Narrow Edge (1985), The Adventures of Jimmie Jupiter (1988); *Recreations* farming, forestry, travel, writing; *Style*— Bernard Lyons, Esq, CBE, JP, DL; Upton Wood, Fulmer, Bucks SL3 6JJ (☎ 0753 66 2404); 2784 South Ocean Boulevard, Palm Beach, Florida 33480, USA (☎ 305 582 2227)

LYONS, Darryn Paul; s of Graham Fisher Lyons, of Australia, and Lorraine Dawn, *née* Trevor; *b* 19 Aug 1965; *Educ* Technical Sch Australia; *Career* formerly photographer: Geelong News, Geelong Advertiser; photographer The Daily Mail 1988- (final 4 nominee for News Photographer of the Year Br Press Awards for work from assignment in Timisoara Rumania 1989); third place Rothman's Australian Press Photographer of the Year Awards 1987; *Recreations* cricket, golf, sport; *Style*— Darryn Lyons, Esq; Daily Mail, Northcliffe House, 2 Derry St, Kensington, London W8 5TT (☎ 071 938 6000/6373, car 0831 580 354)

LYONS, Derek Jack; s of Leslie Albert Lyons (d 1950), and Vera Violet Lyons (d 1988); *b* 5 Dec 1943; *Educ* Cranleigh; *m* 26 Feb 1982, Philippa Kate; 1 s (Robert), 1 step s (Stewart), 1 step da (Charlotte); *Career* Union Discount Co of London plc 1961-70, A C Goode Group of Co's Melbourne 1970-71, exec dir Union Discount Co of London 1983-; *Recreations* sport, walking, travelling; *Clubs* Roehampton, Jesters; *Style*— Derek Lyons, Esq; Union Discount Company of London plc, 39 Cornhill, London EC3V 3NU (☎ 071 623 1020, fax 071 929 2110, telex 886434)

LYONS, Edward; QC (1974); s of Albert Lyons (d 1950), of Leeds, and Sarah, *née* Sellman; *b* 17 May 1926; *Educ* Roundhay Sch Leeds, Univ of Leeds (LLB); *m* 4 Sept 1955, Barbara, da of Alfred Katz (d 1972), of London; 1 s (John Adam b 1959), 1 da (Jane Amanda b 1961); *Career* served RA 1944-48, interpreter in Russian Br Control Cmmn Germany 1946-48; barr 1952, Crown Ct rec 1972-, bencher Lincoln's Inn 1983-; MP: (Lab) Bradford E 1966-74, Bradford W 1974-81, (SDP) Bradford W 1981-83; PPS Treasy 1969-70, chm PLP Home and Legal Affrs Gps 1977-79, Parly spokesman SDP Home and Legal Affrs 1981-83, memb SDP Nat Ctee 1984-89; *Recreations* history, walking, opera; *Style*— Edward Lyons, Esq, QC; 4 Primley Park Lane, Leeds LS17 7JR (☎ 0532 685351); 59 Westminster Gdns, Marsham St, London SW1P 4JG (☎ 071 834 1960); 4 Brick Court, Temple, London EC4Y 9AD (☎ 071 353 1492); 6 Park Sq, Leeds LS1 2NG (☎ 0532 459763)

LYONS, Gary; s of Michael John Lyons, and Diane Rosemary, *née* Mills; *b* 21 June 1968; *Educ* Essington St John's Secdy Sch, Cheslyn Hay High; *m* 31 March 1990, Debbie Lane, da of David William Watkins; *Career* National Hunt jockey; amateur jockney in Point to Points (100 rides and 2 winners) 1984-87, turned professional 1987 (400 rides and 44 winners to date); *Recreations* racing, sleep with a little bit of squash; *Style*— Gary Lyons, Esq; 27 Beech Pine Close, Hednesford, Cannock, Staffs (☎ 0543 876740); R Hollinshead, Lodge Farm, Upper Longdon, Nr Rugeley, Staffs (☎ 0543 490490)

LYONS, Sir (Isidore) Jack; CBE (1967); s of Samuel Henry Lyons (d 1958), of Leeds, and Sophia, *née* Niman; *b* 1 Feb 1916; *Educ* Leeds GS; *m* 21 Dec 1943, Roslyn Marion, da of Dr Jacob Rosenbaum; 2 s (David Stephen, Jonathon Edward), 2 da (Patricia Gail, Joanna Gaye); *Career* dir UDS Group 1955-80; chm: J E London Properties Ltd 1987, Natural Nutrition Co plc 1989-; chm LSO Trust 1961-91, life-tstee Shakespeare's Birthplace, memb Ct Univ of York; Freeman City of London; Hon DUniv York, hon FRAM; Kt 1973; *Recreations* tennis, swimming; *Style*— Sir Jack Lyons, CBE; 8 Ledbury Mews North, London W11 2AF (☎ 071 229 9481, fax 071 229 9229)

LYONS, Sir James Reginald; JP (Cardiff 1966); s of James Lyons (d 1968), and Florence Hilda Lyons (d 1951); *b* 15 March 1910; *Educ* Howard Gdns HS, Cardiff Tech Coll; *m* 1937, Mary Doreen, da of Thomas Alfred Fogg (d 1936); 1 s (Colin); *Career* served WW II Royal Tank Regt 1940-46; civil serv 1929-65; Cardiff City Cncl: cnllr 1949-58, Alderman 1958-74, Dep Lord Mayor 1966-67, Lord Mayor 1968-69; memb: Wales Tourist Bd 1951-72, BBC Wales; airport mangr Cardiff Airport 1954-75; chm and govr: De La Salle Sch, St Illtyds Coll 1955-, Univ Coll Cardiff 1955-70; local govt offr 1965-75, co dir 1977-; assessor under Race Rels Act 1976, pres Welsh Games Cncl, pres Cardiff Hort Soc 1962-; chm and dir Park Lodge Property Co; memb Norfolk Ctee 1968; holder of Silver Acorn for Scouts; OStJ, KCSG; kt 1969; *Recreations* rugby, all outdoor games; *Clubs* Cardiff Athletic; *Style*— Sir James Lyons, JP; 101 Minehead Ave, Sully, S Glamorgan, Wales CF6 2TL (☎ 0222 530403)

LYONS, Jeremy Nicholas Michael; s of Michael Joseph Lyons (d 1970), and Barbara Virginia Berry, *née* Van Den Bergh; *b* 20 Dec 1949; *Educ* Worth Abbey Sch Sussex, Sorbonne Paris; *Career* Lloyd's: broker 1971, memb 1978; currently dir Risk Investment, retained by Tyser and Co at Lloyds; memb: Game Conservancy Soc, Chelsea Cons Assoc, Lloyd's Wine Soc, Lloyd's Motor Club; Freeman: City of London 1981, Worshipful Co of Insurers 1982; *Style*— Jeremy Lyons, Esq; Lloyds, Lime St, London EC3 (☎ 071 623 6262, 071 623 7100, ext 4671, fax 071 621 9042, telex 883907)

LYONS, John; CBE (1986); s of Joseph Sampson Lyons (d 1989), and Henrietta, *née* Nichols (d 1984); *b* 19 May 1926; *Educ* St Pauls, Regent St Poly, Emmanuel Coll Cambridge (BA); *m* 25 March 1954, Molly; 4 c (Katherine Anna b 1958, Roderick Michael b 1960, Jane Rosalind b 1962, Matthew Jeremy b 1966); *Career* WWII RNVR 1944-46, Sub Lt Far Eastern Command; asst to mkt res mangr Vacuum Oil 1950; res offr: Bureau of Current Affrs 1951, PO Engrg Union 1952-57; dep gen sec IPCS 1966-73 (asst sec 1957-66); gen sec: Electrical Power Engrs Assoc 1973-, Engrs and Mangrs Assoc 1977-; memb: Exec Ctee Political and Econ Planning 1975-78, Nat Enterprise Bd 1976-79, Exec Ctee Industl Participation Assoc 1976-90, Cncl Policy Studies Inst 1978-81, Advsy Cncl for Applied R and D 1978-81, Court of Govrs LSE 1978-84, Bd of BT 1980-83, Engrg Cncl 1982-86 (fndr memb), Governing Body London Business Sch 1986-87; jt sec: Nat Jt Coordinating Ctee Electricity Supply Indust 1980-90, Nat Jt Negotiating Ctee Electricity Supply Indust 1980-86; sec Electricity Supply Trade Union Cncl 1976-; chm: NEDC Working Party on Indust Trucks 1977-80, TUC Energy Ctee 1988-; memb: TUC Gen Cncl 1983-, Wilton Park Acad Cncl 1989-, EC Econ and Social Ctee 1990-; FRSA 1980; *Recreations* family, gardening, reading, music, golf, chess; *Style*— John Lyons, Esq, CBE; Engrs and Mangrs Assoc, Station House, Fox Lane North, Chertsey, Surrey KT16 9HW (☎ 0932 564131, fax 0932 567707)

LYONS, Sir John; *b* 23 May 1932; *Educ* St Bede's Coll Manchester, Christ's Coll Cambridge (BA, Dip Ed, PhD, LittD); *m* 1959, Danielle Jacqueline Simonet; *Career* lectr in comparative linguistics SOAS of London 1957-61, lectr in gen linguistics Univ of Cambridge and fell Christ's Coll 1961-64, prof of gen linguistics Univ of Edinburgh 1964-76, prof of linguistics Univ of Sussex 1976-84 (pro vice chllr 1981-84), master Trinity Hall Cambridge 1984-; hon fell Christ's Coll Cambridge 1985-, hon memb Linguistic Soc of America 1978, Docteur des Lettres (Honoris Causa) Univ Cath de Louvain 1980; Hon DLitt: Univ of Reading 1986, Univ of Edinburgh 1988, Univ of Sussex 1990; FBA 1973; kt 1987; *Books* Structural Semantics (1963), Psycholinguistics Papers (ed with R J Wales, 1966), Introduction to Theoretical Linguistics (1968), Chomsky (1970), New Horizons in Linguistics (1970), Semantics 1 and 2 (1977), Language and Linguistics (1980), Language, Meaning and Context (1980), Natural Language and Universal Grammar (1991); *Style*— Sir John Lyons; Master's Lodge, Trinity Hall, Cambridge CB2 1TJ

LYONS, John Gerald; s of Arthur John Lyons (d 1977), and Elizabeth Caroline, *née* Braybrooke Webb (d 1973); *b* 14 Jan 1926; *Educ* WHSS Guildhall Schs of Music, RMC Sandhurst, City Univ (LR); *m* 1, 26 March 1949, Jean Hutcheon-Horne Smith (d 1980); 2 s (Russell b 11 May 1950, Stuart b 9 Oct 1951); m 2, 29 May 1983, Susan, da of Robert Cuffel; *Career* cmmnd Northamptonshire Regt Grenadier Gds; lectr and examiner in: physiological optics, anatomy, binocular vision, orthoptics, ocular pathology, ocular pharmacology; papers published and res in: fixation disparity, glaucoma and tonometry, binocular vision, visual inhibition and clinical studies; in practice at Chigwell and Whipps Cross Hosp Chigwell; Freeman City of London, Liveryman Worshipful Co of Spectacle Makers; SMSA, FBCO, FBOA, HD, DOrth, DCLP, FSMC, FAAO; *Recreations* offshore sailing, music (cello), astrophysics, anthropology; *Clubs* City Livery, CLYC; *Style*— John Lyons, Esq; 55 Romford Rd, Chigwell, Essex IG7 4QS (☎ 081 500 5402)

LYONS, John Trevor; s of Sir Rudolph Lyons, and Jeanette, *née* Dante; *b* 1 Nov 1943; *Educ* Leeds GS, Univ of Leeds (LLB); *m* 7 Sept 1969, Dianne Lucille, da of Geoffrey Saffer; 3 s (Alan b 1971, James b 1973, Benjamin b 1974); *Career* slr; ptnr J Lester Lyons & Falk; *Style*— John T Lyons, Esq; 140 Alwoodley Lane, Leeds LS17 7PP (☎ 0532 674575); Jubilee Chambers, The Headrow, Leeds LS1 2QS, (☎ 0532 450406, fax 0532 422169)

LYONS, Jonathon Edward; s of Sir (Isidore) Jack Lyons, CBE, *qv*; *b* 1 May 1951;

Educ Carmel Coll; *m* 30 Dec 1975, Miriam, da of Simon Djanogly (d 1977), of Geneva, Switzerland; 2 s (Jacob b 1976, Simon b 1980), 1 da (Deborah b 1983); *Career* exec sales Alexandra Ltd Leeds 1968-71, chief exec John David Mansworld Ltd 1971-89, ptnr International Investments Ltd 1978-, chief exec H Alan Smith Ltd 1983-85, dir JLC Ltd London 1986, jt chief exec JE London Properties Ltd 1988-, private investmt conslt Jonathon E Lyons & Co 1988-; dir: Britimpex Ltd Canada, Art Leasing Inc Canada; memb Ctee: Cons Industl Fund, RMC, RAM; jt chm Hyde Park Ctee Central Br Fund 1975-80; FInstD, memb FIMBRA; *Clubs* Carlton, IOD; *Style*— Jonathon E Lyons, Esq; 35 Loudoun Rd, St Johns Wood, London NW8 (☎ 071 624 7733); Chalet Emeraude, 1837 Chateau D'Oex, Switzerland; 38 Ledbury Mews North, Kensington, London W11 (☎ 071 229 9481, fax 071 229 9229, car phone 0836 200 683)

LYONS, (Andrew) Maximilian; s of Dennis John Lyons, CB, of Summerhaven, Gough Rd, Fleet, Hants, and Elizabeth Dora Maria, *née* Müller Haefliger; *b* 16 Jan 1946; *Educ* Queen Mary's GS Basingstoke, Brixton Sch of Bldg (Dip Arch); *m* 16 June 1983, Katherine Jane (Kate), da of Brig John Joseph Regan; 1 s (Shaun b 1984), 2 da (Rosalie b 1986, Charlotte b 1989); *Career* sr ptnr Lyons & Sleeman & Hoare architects 1974; winner of: Euro Architectural Heritage Award 1974, Br Cncl of Shopping Centres Award 1987, Euro Cncl of Shopping Centre Award 1988, City Heritage Award of London 1988, Silver Jubilee Cup RTPI 1988, other environmental and design awards; RIBA 1974; *Recreations* sailing, shooting, walking; *Style*— Maximilian Lyons, Esq; School Lane House, School Lane, Ewshot, Farnham, Surrey GU10 5BN (0252 850222); Old Threshing Barn, E Prawle, Kingsbridge, S Devon; 82 Park St, Camberley, Surrey GU15 3NY (☎ 0276 692266, fax 0276 692207)

LYONS, Hon Rodney Max; s of Baron Lyons of Brighton (Life Peer, d 1978), and Laurie Adele; *b* 27 May 1941; *Educ* St Paul's, Magdalen Coll Oxford (BA, post-grad CertEd); *m* 1963, Cory Frances, da of Dr William Owen Hassall, of the Manor House, Wheatley, Oxford; 1 s, 1 da; *Career* county advsr for English Devon LEA 1974-82, head of Dept of Arts and Humanities Exeter Coll 1982-86, dir of Coll Servs Exeter Coll 1986-88, princ Taunton's Coll Southampton 1989-; *Recreations* walking; *Style*— The Hon Rodney Lyons; Nursery Flat, Avington Park, Winchester, Hants (☎ 096278 676); Taunton's College, Highfield Rd, Southampton (☎ 0703 559651)

LYONS, Russell John Stewart; s of John Gerald Lyons, and Jean Hutcheon Horne, *née* Smith; *b* 11 May 1950; *Educ* Forest Sch, City Univ Graduate Sch (MBA); *m* 1, May 1970 (m dis 1986), Yvonne Noelly; 1 da (Caroline Jane b 26 Oct 1982); m 2, 1 June 1987, Margaret Roberta, da of Col George Lennie, MBE; *Career* dep md Nippon Int 1977, md Icon Int 1980, dir sales and mktg Torch Computers plc 1981 (fndr shareholder), chm Mgmnt Innovation Gp 1983-, md XAT software 1985; FCA 1973 and 1978, memb CMI 1975; *Recreations* sailing, waterskiing, riding, playing several musical instruments; *Clubs* Public Schs, East India; *Style*— Russell Lyons, Esq; Century House, Pluckley Rd, Charing, Kent (☎ 023371 3512); 9 New Rd, Rochester Kent (☎ 0634 814931, fax 0634 815878)

LYONS, Prof Terence John; s of Peter John Lyons, of Puddle Cottage, Puddle, nr Lanlivery, Bodmin, Cornwall, and Christobel Valerie, *née* Hardie; *b* 4 May 1953; *Educ* Univ of Cambridge (BA), Univ of Oxford (DPhil); *m* 30 Aug 1975, (Christina) Barbara, da of Joseph Epsom; 1 s (Barnaby b 1981), 1 da (Josephine b 1983); *Career* jr res fell Jesus Coll Oxford 1979-81, Hedrick visiting asst prof UCLA 1981-82, lectr in mathematics Imperial Coll of Sci and Technol 1981-85, head of Dept of Mathematics Univ of Edinburgh 1988- (Colin MacLaurin prof of mathematics 1985-); FRSE 1987; *Style*— Prof Terence Lyons; 11 West Savile Rd, Edinburgh EH16 5NG (☎ 031 667 3129); University of Edinburgh, Department of Mathematics, James Clerk Maxwell Building, The King's Buildings, Edinburgh EH9 3JZ (☎ 031 650 5061 ext 2942, fax 031 662 4712, telex 727442 UNIV G)

LYONS, Terence Patrick; s of Maurice Peter Lyons (d 1978), of Pevensey Bay, Sussex, and Maude Mary Elizabeth, *née* O'Farrell (d 1958); *b* 2 Sept 1919; *Educ* Wimbledon Coll, King's Coll London, LSE; *m* 11 June 1945, Winifred Mary, da of James Basil Ward Normile (d 1965), of Sutton, Surrey; 2 da (Moira Teresa b 16 Nov 1947, Celia Mary b 19 May 1952); *Career* Gunner RA and Offr Cadet IA 1940-41, 2 Lt Indian Armd Corps (attached RIASC) 1941-46, Capt 1942; head Staff Dept Unilever Ltd 1948-54, chief personnel offr Philips Industries (Croydon) 1954-60, gp personnel mangr Ilford Ltd 1960-66, dir of personnel Staveley Industries Ltd 1966-69, exec dir (personnel) Williams & Glyn's Bank 1969-82, dir Industl Trg Serv 1983-, conslt 1983-; pres IPM 1981-83; memb: CBI Educn Fndn Cncl 1974-86, MMC 1975-81, Open Univ Cncl 1980-90, MSC 1981-82; chm: CBI Manpower Servs Advsy Panel 1975-82, Fedn of London Clearing Bank Employers 1976-78, CBI Educn and Trg Ctee 1976-77; CIPM, FCIB; Hon MA Open Univ; *Books* The Personnel Function in a Changing Environment (second edn 1985); *Recreations* golf, sailing, bridge, music; *Clubs* Army and Navy, Wilderness Golf, Royal Eastbourne Golf, Chipstead Sailing, Riverhead Bridge; *Style*— Terence Lyons, Esq; Winter Ride, 2 Rosefield, Kippington Rd, Sevenoaks, Kent

LYONS, Thomas Colvill Holmes (Toby); s of Robert Henry Cary Lyons, of Cilwych Hse, Bwlch, Powys, and Dorothy Joan Garnons Lyons; *b* 8 March 1937; *Educ* Harrow, Oriel Coll Oxford (MA); *m* 1, 17 July 1965 (m dis 1971), Heather Mary Menzies Forbes; 1 s (David b 1968), 1 da (Sophia b 1966); m 2, 3 June 1972, (Gwendolin) Frances, da of Col W D Gosling, TD, DL; 2 da (Kate b 1975, Annabel b 1976); *Career* RWF 1956-58 (TA 1958-69); admitted slr 1965, Linklaters & Paines 1964-66, Allen & Overy 1966-69, md Minster Tst Ltd 1973; dir: Minster Assets plc 1976, Tillshare plc 1984, Monument Oil & Gas plc 1984; chm R & J Hadlee Fine Art plc 1985; Asst Worshipful Co of Tinplate Workers; memb Law Soc 1965; *Recreations* shooting, water sports, winter sports; *Style*— Toby Lyons, Esq; Hole Farm, Stansted, Essex CM24 8TJ

LYONS, Tony; s of Michael Lyons, of London, and Edith, *née* Morris; *b* 12 April 1947; *Educ* Tottenham GS, Univ of London (BA), Univ of Kent; *m* 30 July 1969, Alison, da of Simon MacLeod; 2 s (Matthew Simon b 30 Nov 1973, Frazer Alexander David b 3 Nov 1981), 1 da (Jessica Jane b 23 May 1976); *Career* dep ed Planned Savings 1969-71, journalist Sunday Telegraph 1971-78, journalist Sunday Telegraph 1971-78, dep city ed The Observer 1978-81, owner public house 1982-85, asst city ed Birmingham Post 1985-86, dir Buchanan Communications (formerly Binns Cornwall) 1986-; *Recreations* flying, fishing, fell walking, films, relaxing; *Style*— Tony Lyons, Esq; Buchanan Communications Ltd, 36 St Andrews Hill, London EC4V 5DE (☎ 071 489 1441, fax 071 248 3780)

LYONS, Hon William; s of Baron Lyons of Brighton (d 1978); *b* 1945; *m* 1963, Petra Deanna, da of William Tibble; *Style*— The Hon William Lyons; 15 Lower Town, Sampford, Peverell, Devon

LYSAGHT, Patrick James; s of late Horace James William Lysaght (bro of 6 Baron Lisle); hp to Barony of Lisle; *b* 1 May 1931; *Educ* Shrewsbury; *m* 1957, Mary Louise, da of late Lt-Col Geoffrey Riginald Devereux Shaw, and formerly w of Euan Guy Shaw-Stewart (now 10 Bt); 2 s, 1 da; *Career* late Lt Gren Gds; *Style*— Patrick Lysaght, Esq; 52 Wardo Ave, London SW6 6RE

LYSTER, Guy Lumley; DL (Essex 1975); s of Ronald Guy Lyster, OBE (d 1972), of Lances, Kelvedon, Essex, and Ada Erica, *née* Neal (d 1977); *b* 4 April 1925; *Educ* Winchester, Trinity Coll Cambridge (MA); *m* 10 May 1958, Gillian Rosemary, da of Michael Spencer Gosling (d 1979), of Parks Farm, Little Maplestead, Essex; 1 s (Anthony b 1960), 1 da (Sarah b 1961); *Career* Grenadier Gds 1943-47: served NW Euro 1945, Capt 1946; Strutt & Parker Coval Hall Chelmsford: chartered surveyor 1952, assoc ptnr 1958, ptnr 1969, dep sr ptnr 1979; Master E Essex Foxhounds 1983-, judge HIS Panel Ridden and In-Hand Hunters; Freeman City of London, Liveryman Worshipful Co of Salters 1955; FRICS 1961, FCAAV 1961; *Recreations* hunting, shooting, cricket; *Clubs* Cavalry and Guards'; *Style*— Guy Lyster, Esq, DL; Rayne Hatch House, Stisted, Braintree, Essex CM7 8BY (☎ 0787 472087); Strutt & Parker, Coval Hall, Chelmsford, Essex CM1 2QF (☎ 0245 258201, fax 0245 355299); Principal Office, 13 Hill St, London W1X 8DL

LYSTER, Peter Haggard; s of Lionel Charles Lyster (d 1980), of Apps, Stock, Essex, and Avice Dorothy, *née* Haggard (d 1986); bro of Rae Lionel Haggard Lyster, *qv*; *b* 17 Nov 1934; *Educ* Marlborough; *m* 1967, Gillian Barbara, da of Sir Arthur John Grattan-Bellew, CMG, QC (d 1985); 1 s (Thomas), 2 da (Grania, Anna); *Career* former 2 Lt 11 Hussars; former Capt City of London Yeo; ptnr Wedd Durlacher Mordaunt & Co 1962-86; memb: Stock Exchange 1956, Cncl of Stock Exchange; joint-master Meynell Foxhounds 1972-76; *Recreations* hunting, fishing; *Clubs* Cavalry and Guards'; *Style*— Peter Lyster, Esq; Little Chishill Manor, Royston, Herts (☎ 0763 838238)

LYSTER, Rae Lionel Haggard; s of Lionel Charles Lyster (d 1980), of Apps, Stock, Essex, and Avice Dorothy, *née* Haggard (d 1986); *b* 24 Aug 1931; *Educ* Bradfield, Trinity Coll Cambridge (BA); *m* 24 May 1958, Julia Elizabeth, da of Charles Humphrey Scott Plummer, of Mainhouse, Kelso, Roxburghshire; 1 s (Nicholas b 8 March 1959), 2 da (Amanda b 29 May 1961, Lucy b 23 May 1963); *Career* 2 Lt Royal Scots Greys (2 Dragoons) 1951-52, Capt Ayrshire (ECO) Yeo 1952-62; ptnr Cazenove & Co 1961-91; govr and hon treas Reed's Sch Cobham Surrey, chm and tstee The Perry Watlington Tst Essex; *Recreations* fishing, shooting, golf; *Clubs* Boodle's, City of London; *Style*— Rae Lyster, Esq; Malting Green House, Layer De La Haye, Colchester, Essex CO2 OJE; Cazenove & Co, 12 Tokenhouse Yard, London EC2R 7AN (☎ 071 588 2828, fax 071 606 9205, telex 886758)

LYTHALL, Basil Wilfrid; CB (1966); s of Frank Herbert Lythall (d 1969), of Kingswinford, Staffs, and Winifred Mary, *née* Carver (d 1953); *b* 15 May 1919; *Educ* King Edward's Sch Stourbridge, Ch Ch Oxford (MA); *m* 1942, Mary Olwen, da of Simon Dando (d 1980), of Wall Heath, W Midlands; 1 s (David); *Career* occasional res conslt; asst dir Physical Res Admlty 1957-58, dep chief scientist Admlty Surface Weapons Establishment 1958-60, first chief scientist Admlty Underwater Weapons Establishment 1960-64, chief scientist RN and memb Admlty Bd Def Cncl 1964-78, dep controller of Navy, Res and Devpt 1964-71, dep controller Establishments and Res Procurement Exec MOD 1971-78, dir Saclant ASW Res Centre La Spezia Italy 1978-81; tstee Nat Maritime Museum 1974-80, chm CORDA Policy Bd, Sema Gp 1985-89, tech advsr Monopolies and Mergers Cmmn 1989 and 1990; *Recreations* sculpting, music; *Style*— B W Lythall, Esq, CB; 48 Grove Way, Esher, Surrey KT10 8HL (☎ 081 398 2958)

LYTHGOE, Joseph; s of Adam Lythgoe (d 1946), of Wigshaw Grange, Culcheth, Warrington, and Mary Elizabeth, *née* Leather; *b* 11 Aug 1922; *Educ* Ashton-in-Makerfield GS; *m* 1, 1948 (m dis 1989), Catherine Crompton, *née* Brooks; 1 s (David b 1954); m 2, 1990, Dorothy Deighton; *Career* served RCS 1941-46; landowner; chm & md Adam Lythgoe Ltd fertilizer mfrs 1949-; chm Ches branch Cncl for the Protection of Rural Eng; *Recreations* restoration of rural economy, landscape conservation; *Clubs* Farmers', Warrington; *Style*— Joseph Lythgoe, Esq; Swinhoe Hse, Culcheth, Warrington WA3 4NH (☎ 092 576 4106)

LYTHGOE, (James) Philip; s of Sir James Lythgoe, CBE (d 1972), of Wilmslow, Cheshire, and Dorothy May, *née* Ashworth (d 1988); *b* 10 Nov 1926; *Educ* Bootham Sch, St John's Coll Cambridge (MA, MB BChir); *m* 22 Sept 1961, Anne, da of Redvers George Melvin (d 1964), of Leeds; 1 s (James b 1963), 1 da (Alison b 1967); *Career* Med Branch RAF 1950-52, sqdn ldr 1951-52; conslt surgn: Royal Preston Hosp 1964-, Chorley and Dist Hosp 1964-; fell Assoc of Surgns, memb Moynihan Chirurgical Club; FRCS 1957; *Recreations* gardening, hill walking; *Style*— Philip Lythgoe, Esq; 25 Devonshire Rd, Fulwood, Preston, Lancs (☎ 0772 774362); Royal Preston Hospital, Sharoe Green Lane, Fulwood, Preston, Lancs (☎ 0772 716565)

LYTTELTON, Hon (Nicholas) Adrian Oliver; s of 1 Viscount Chandos, KG, DSO, MC, PC (d 1972); *b* 1937; *Educ* Eton, Magdalen Coll Oxford; *m* 1960, Margaret, da of Sir Harold Hobson, CBE; 1 s, 1 da; *Career* prof of modern history: Reading Univ 1976-78, John Hopkins Univ Centre Bologna 1978-; fell: All Souls Coll Oxford 1960-69, St Antony's Coll Oxford 1969-75; *Style*— The Hon Adrian Lyttelton

LYTTELTON, Hon Christopher Charles; s of 10 Viscount Cobham, KG, GCMG, GCVO, TD, PC (d 1977), and Elizabeth Alison, *née* Makeig-Jones; *b* 23 Oct 1927; *Educ* Eton; *m* 1973, Tessa Mary, da of Col Alexander George Jeremy Readman, DSO (d 1973); 1 s (Oliver b 1976), 1 da (Sophie b 1978); *Career* chief exec NCL Investments Ltd (stockbrokers); *Recreations* gliding, cricket; *Clubs* MCC, Booker Gliding; *Style*— The Hon Christopher Lyttelton; 28 Abbey Gardens, London NW8 9AT; NCL Investments Ltd, 9-12 Basinghall St, London

LYTTELTON, Hon Matthew Peregrine Antony; s of 2 Viscount Chandos (d 1980), and hp of bro, 3 Viscount; *b* 21 April 1956; *Educ* Eton, Trinity Coll Cambridge; *Style*— The Hon Matthew Lyttelton; The Vine, Sherborne St John, Basingstoke, Hants

LYTTELTON, Hon Nicholas Makeig; 4 and yst s of 10 Viscount Cobham, KG, GCMG, GCVO, TD, PC (d 1977); *b* 3 Jan 1951; *Educ* Shiplake Court Oxon; *m* 1980, June Carrington; *Style*— The Hon Nicholas Lyttelton; 30 Paulton's Sq, London SW3

LYTTELTON, Hon Richard Cavendish; s of 10 Viscount Cobham, KG, GCMG, GCVO, TD, PC (d 1977); *b* 1949; *Educ* Eton; *m* 1971, Romilly, da of Michael Barker; 1 s (Thomas), 1 da (May); *Style*— The Hon Richard Lyttelton; 22 Baskerville Rd, London SW18

LYTTON, Lady Caroline Mary Noel; da of 4 Earl of Lytton, OBE (d 1985), and Clarissa, *née* Palmer; *b* 1947; *Educ* St Mary's Shaftesbury, Univ of Birmingham, Sir John Cass Sch of Art; *Career* arts admin and metalsmith; *Recreations* travel, reading; *Style*— Caroline Lytton; 113 Plimsoll Rd, London N4 2ED

LYTTON, Dowager Countess of; Clarissa Mary; *née* Palmer; da of Brig-Gen Cyril Eustace Palmer, CB, CMG, DSO; *m* 1946, 4 Earl of Lytton (d 1985); *Style*— The Rt Hon the Dowager Countess of Lytton; Garden Wing, Newbuildings Place, Shipley, nr Horsham, W Sussex RH13 7JQ

LYTTON, 5 Earl of (UK 1880); Sir John Peter Michael Scawen Lytton; also Viscount Knebworth (UK 1880), 18 Baron Wentworth (E 1529), and 6 Bt (UK 1838); s of 4 Earl of Lytton; *b* 7 June 1950; *Educ* Downside, Univ of Reading; *m* 1980, Ursula, da of Anton Komoly, of Vienna; 1 s (Viscount Knebworth b 7 March 1989), 1 da (Lady Katrina b 1985); *Heir* s, Philip Anthony Scawen, Viscount Knebworth b 7 March 1989; *Career* Inland Revenue Valuation Office 1975-81; Permutt Brown & Co 1982-86; Cubitt & West 1986-87; sole principal John Lytton & Co 1988-; FRICS; *Style*— The Rt Hon the Earl of Lytton; Estate Office, New Buildings Place, Dragons Green, Horsham, Sussex

LYTTON, Hon (Thomas) Roland Cyril Lawrence; s of 4 Earl of Lytton, OBE (d 1985); *b* 10 Aug 1954; *Educ* St Teresa's Minehead, Worth, Downside; *Career* farmer and engr; *Recreations* off-road racing; *Style*— The Hon Roland Lytton; Bratton Ct,

Minehead, Somerset

LYTTON COBBOLD, Hon Henry Fromanteel; eldest s and h of 2 Baron Cobbold (*qv*); *b* 12 May 1962; *m* 1987, Martha F, da of James Buford Boone, Jr, of Tuscaloosa, Alabama, USA; 1 da (Morwenna Gray b 16 Aug 1989); *Style*— The Hon Henry Lytton Cobbold

LYVEDEN, 6 Baron (UK 1859); Ronald Cecil Vernon; s of 5 Baron Lyveden (d 1973); *b* 10 April 1915; *m* 1938, Queenie Constance, da of Howard Ardern; 3 s; *Heir* s, Hon Jack Leslie Vernon; *Style*— The Rt Hon the Lord Lyveden; 20 Farmer St, Te Aroha, NZ (☎ 410)

M

M

MAAN, Bashir Ahmed; JP (1968), DL (Glasgow 1982); s of Chaudhry Sardar Khan Maan, of Village Maan, Gujranwala, Pakistan, and Hayat Begum Maan (d 1975); *b* 20 Oct 1926; *Educ* DB HS, Qila Didar Singh, Panjab Univ; *m* (m dis); 1 s (Tariq Hassan), 3 da (Rashda Begum, Hanna Bano, Aalya Maaria); *Career* involved in struggle of Pakistan 1943-47, organized rehabilitation of refugees from India in Maan and surrounding areas 1947-48; emigrated to UK, settled in Glasgow 1953; fndr sec Glasgow Pakistan Social and Cultural Soc 1955-65 (pres 1966-69), memb Exec Ctee Glasgow City Lab Pty 1969-70, vice chm Glasgow Community Rels Cncl 1970-75, cncllr Glasgow City Corp 1970-75, magistrate City of Glasgow 1971-74, vice chm Glasgow Corp Police Ctee 1974-75 (vice chm 1971-74); memb: Nat Road Safety Ctee 1971-74, Scot Accident Prevention Ctee 1973-75, BBC Immigrant Prog Advsy Ctee 1972-80; convenor Pakistan Bill Action Ctee 1973, Parly candidate (Lab) E Fife 1974, pres Standing Conference of Pakistani Orgns in the UK and Eire 1974-77, police judge City of Glasgow 1974-75, cncllr City of Glasgow DC 1975-84, dep chm Cmmn for Racial Equality 1977-80, memb Scot Gas Consumer Cncl 1978-81, baillie City of Glasgow 1980-84, memb Gtr Glasgow Health Bd 1981-, fndr chm Scot Pakistani Assoc 1984-, judge City of Glasgow District Cts, chm Strathclyde Community Relations Cncl 1986-, vice chm (chm Mgmnt Ctee) Glasgow Int Sports Festival Ltd 1987-89, govr Jordanhill Coll of FE 1987-; *Recreations* reading, golf; *Clubs* Douglas Park; *Style*— Bashir Maan, Esq, JP, DL; 8 Riverview Gardens, Flat 6, Glasgow G5 (☎ 041 429 7689)

MAAS, Robert William; s of Richard Felix Maas (d 1948), of London, and Hilda Rose, *née* Geitzen; *b* 13 Feb 1943; *Educ* Gunnerbury GS; *Career* articled clerk Godwin & Taylor 1959-65, tax ptnr Stoy Hayward 1970-77 (tax sr 1965-70), proprietor Robert Maas & Co 1977-83; tax ptnr: Casson Beckman 1983-87, Blackstone Franks & Co 1987-; Editorial Bd: Taxation, Tolley's Practical International Tax; contrib of articles to various magazines and jls, lectr on a wide variety of tax topics; memb: Tax Ctee ICAEW, Tax Ctee LSCA; chm Personal Tax Sub Ctee ICAEW, former chm Small Practioners Gp of Central London LSCA; ICAEW 1965, ATII 1965; *Publications* Tax Minimisation Techniques (4 edn, 1984), Taxation of Non-Resident Entertainers & Sportsmen (1987), Fringe Benefits (1987), Tax Planning for Entertainers (2 edn, 1987), Tolley's Property Taxes (3 edn, 1990), Tax Planning for the Smaller Business (1990), Tolley's Schedule E: Taxation of Employments 1990/91 (1990), Tolley's Anti-Avoidance Provisions (2 edn, 1991); *Recreations* reading, walking, drinking; *Clubs* Reform, St James's (Manchester); *Style*— Robert Maas, Esq; 76 Thirlmere Gardens, Wembley, Middlesex HA9 8RE (☎ 081 904 0432); Blackstone Franks & Co, Barbican House, 26-34 Old St, London EC1V 9HL (☎ 071 250 3300, fax 071 250 1402)

MABBUTT, Gary Vincent; s of Raymond William Mabbutt, of Bristol, and Avis Betty, *née* Blake (now Mrs Brown); *b* 23 Aug 1961; *Educ* Cotham GS Bristol; *Career* professional footballer; 147 appearances Bristol Rovers 1977-82 (debut v Burnley 1978); Tottenham Hotspur 1982-: debut v Luton Town 1982, capt 1987-, over 350 appearances; England caps: 11 youth (capt once), 7 under 21 (capt twice), 6 B (capt 4 times), 13 full 1983-88; capt Football League v League of Ireland 1990; honours: UEFA Cup winner's medal v Anderlecht 1984, FA Cup runners up medal v Coventry City 1987; *Books* Against All Odds (autobiography, 1990); *Style*— Gary Mabbutt, Esq; Tottenham Hotspur FC, 748 High Rd, Tottenham, London N17 OAP (☎ fax 0707 47399)

MABEY, Bevil Guy; CBE (1985); s of Guy Mabey (d 1951), and Madeline Johnson (d 1957); *b* 16 April 1916; *Educ* Tonbridge, Cambridge (MA); *m* 4 Oct 1947, June Penelope, da of Brig Cecil Herbert Peck, DSO, MC; 1 s (David b 1961), 5 da (Bridget Ann b 1949, Isabel Denise b 1950, Christine b 1954, Juliet b 1955, Fiona b 1965); *Career* cmmnd Royal Corps Signals 1939, RASC 1940-46, Maj, served France, N Africa, Italy, Yugoslavia, Greece; chm: Mabey Holdings Ltd, Mabey & Johnson Ltd, Mabey Hire Co Ltd, Fairfield-Mabey Ltd, Mabey Construction Co Ltd, Beachley Property Ltd; Freeman: City of London, Worshipful Co of Vintners; *Recreations* rowing, skiing, riding, golf, carpentry, bricklaying; *Clubs* Leander, London Rowing; *Style*— Bevil G Mabey, Esq, CBE; Mabey Holdings, Floral Mile, Twyford, Reading RG10 9SQ (☎ 0734 403921, telex 848 649 Mabey TG, fax 0734 403941)

MABEY, Richard Thomas; s of Thomas Gustavus Mabey (d 1963), and Edna Nellie, *née* Moore; *b* 20 Feb 1941; *Educ* Berkhamsted Sch, St Catherine's Coll Oxford (BA, MA); *Career* lectr social studies Dacorum Coll of Further Educn 1963-65, sr ed Penguin Books (Educn Div) 1966-73, freelance writer and broadcaster 1973-; contrib: BBC Wildlife, Sunday Times, Independent, Modern Painters, Sunday Telegraph, Country Living, Times, TES, Observer, Listener, Nature, New Scientist and other pubns; wrote and presented: The Unofficial Countryside (World About Us BBC2 1975), The Flowering of Britain (BBC2 1980), A Prospect of Kew (BBC2 1981), Back to the Roots (C4 1983), White Rock, Black Water (BBC2 1986); Times Educnl Supplement Information Books Award 1977, New York Acad of Sciences Childrens Book Award 1984, Whitbread Biography Award 1986; Leverhulme res fell 1983-84; memb: Cncl Botanical Soc of the British Isles 1981-83, Nature Conservancy Cncl 1983-86, Cncl Plantlife 1989-; pres London Wildlife Tst 1982-; dir: Common Ground 1988-, Learning through Landscapes Tst 1990-; *Books* incl: Street Flowers (1976), The Common Ground (1980), Oak and Company (1983), Gilbert White (1986), The Gardener's Labyrinth (ed, 1987), The Flowering of Kew (1988), Home Country (1990); *Recreations* walking, food; *Clubs* Groucho; *Style*— Richard Mabey, Esq; c/o Richard Scott Simon, 43 Doughty St, London WC1N 2LF

MABON, Rt Hon Dr (Jesse) Dickson; PC (1977); s of Jesse Dickson Mabon and Isabel Simpson, *née* Montgomery; *b* 1 Nov 1925; *Educ* schools in Cumbrae and Kelvinside; *m* 1970, Elizabeth Sarah, da of Major William Victor Zinn (sometime princ ptnr W V Zinn & Associates, consulting engrs); 1 s; *Career* formerly in coalmining industry, journalism (with Scottish Daily Record); MP (Lab and Co-op 1955-81, SDP 1981-83) Greenock 1955-74, Greenock and Port Glasgow 1974-83, fought Bute and N Ayrshire (Lab) 1951, Renfrewshire W (Lab and Co-op) 1955; jt Parly under sec Scotland 1964-67, min of state Scottish Office 1967-70, dep oppn spokesman Scotland 1970-72, min of state for Energy 1976-79; chm UK Labour Ctee for Europe 1974-76, Scottish PLP 1972-73 and 1975-76, fndr chm PLP Manifesto Gp 1974-76, pres European Movement 1975-76; memb: Cncl Europe 1970-72 and 1974-76, WEU Assembly 1970-72 and 1974-76; visiting physician Manor House Hosp London; fellow Faculty of History of Medicine, Soc of Apothecaries; FInstPet, FRSA; freeman City of London; *Style*— The Rt Hon Dr J Dickson Mabon; 57 Hillway, London N6 6AD

MAC-FALL, Nigel James; s of Thomas Coulson Mac-Fall (d 1970), and Sylvia Dorothy, *née* Harriss (d 1987); *b* 27 April 1948; *Educ* Sch of Three Dimensional Design Ravensbourne Coll of Art and Design (BA), Sch of Furniture Design RCA (MA); *m* 11 May 1974, Shirley Anne, da of Ernest Chubb; 2 s (Julian James Chubb b 9 Jan 1976, Oscar Alexander James b 18 May 1981), 1 da (Rosina Sylvia Anne b 7 July 1977), 1 adopted da (Elaine Anne b 16 Aug 1968); *Career* furniture and product designer Planning Unit Ltd design and consultancy 1972-75, sr designer Supplies Div Property Services Agency 1975-78, ptnr, dir and head Dept of Three Dimensional Design Minale Tattersfield & Partners Ltd int design consultancy 1978- (i/c: architecture, interiors, exhibition, product, furniture, signage, packaging, automotive; work incl: Heathrow Express, Hammersmith Station, BP Lubricants Packaging worldwide, Thorntons' Sweet Shops, Gucci Dining Room); *Recreations* family, swimming, cycling, sculpture, music, foreign travel; *Style*— Nigel James Mac-Fall, Esq; Minale Tattersfield & Partners Ltd, The Courtyard, 37 Sheen Rd, Richmond, Middlesex TW9 1AJ (☎ 081 948 7999, fax 081 948 2435)

MACADAM, (Elliott) Corbett; yr s of Sir Ivison Macadam, KCVO, CBE (d 1974), of Runton Old Hall, Cromer, Norfolk, and Caroline, *née* Corbett (d 1989); *b* 29 Aug 1942; *Educ* Eton, Trinity Coll Cambridge (BA), INSEAD Fontainebleau (MBA); *m* 17 Dec 1977, (Alexandra) Camilla, da of Maj Trevor Binny, of Little Wenham Hall, Colchester; 3 s (Harry b 1979, John b 1981, James b 1988); *Career* dir: Kleinwort Benson Ltd 1977-84 (mangr and other positions 1965-77), Baring Bros and Co Ltd 1984-89, md Banque Artil SA 1989-; *Clubs* Brooks's; *Style*— Corbett Macadam, Esq; 1 Rue de Villersexel, Paris, 75007, France; Banque Arjil, 7 Rue du Cirque, Paris, 75008, France (☎ 331 49 53 60 60)

McADAM, Dr Elspeth Katherine; da of Prof Sir Ian McAdam, of Plettenberg Bay, Cape Province, S Africa, and Hrothgarde, *née* Gibson; *b* 16 Oct 1947; *Educ* Kenya HS, Newnham Coll Cambridge (MA), Middx Med Sch; *m* 1970 (m dis 1981), Dr (John) David Seddon, s of Eric Seddon (d 1950); 2 s (Michael David Indra b 10 May 1974, James Alexander b 28 April 1976); *Career* conslt child and adolescent psychiatrist 1987-, tutor in systemic therapy training Kensington Consultation Centre and Roehampton Coll of Further Educn 1987-, dir Informetrics Computor Training and Consultancy; memb: Med Campaign Against Nuclear Weapons, Anti Aparthied Movement; MRCPsych 1982; *publications* author of articles on Cognitive Therapy with Children and Adolescents 1984-88, Working Systematically (1991); *Recreations* tennis, golf, ecology, bird watching, gardening; *Style*— Dr Elspeth McAdam

MCADAM, James; s of John Robert McAdam (d 1975), and Helen, *née* Cormack (d 1981); *b* 10 Dec 1930; *Educ* Lenzie Acad; *m* 4 Oct 1955, Maisie Una, da of Ernest James Holmes (d 1947); 2 da (Catherine Tryphena b 1956, Fiona Jane McAdam b 1961); *Career* Nat Serv RN 1949-50; J & P Coats Ltd: joined 1945, various overseas assignments 1953-61, fin dir Chile 1962-66, fin dir India 1966-70; fin dir Coats Patons (UK) 1972-75; Coats Patons plc: dir 1975, chief exec 1985, chm 1986; dep chm and chief ops offr Coats Viyella plc (merged company) 1986-, non-exec dir London PO 1985-87; dir Scottish Business in the Community 1986, memb Exec Ctee The Scottish Cncl Devpt & Indust 1989; FRSA, CBIM; *Recreations* theatre, gardening, travel; *Style*— James McAdam, Esq; Tara, 222 Thameside, Laleham Village, Nr Staines, Middlesex TW18 1UQ (☎ 0784 456970); Coats Viyella plc, 28 Savile Row, London W1X 2DD (☎ 071 734 4030, fax 071 437 2016, car 0836 214579)

MCADAM, Prof Keith Paul William James; s of Sir Ian William James McAdam, OBE, KBE, and (Lettice Margaret) Hrothgaarde, *née* Gibson (now Mrs Bennett); *b* 13 Aug 1945; *Educ* Prince of Wales Sch Nairobi Kenya, Millfield, Clare Coll Cambridge (MA, MB, BChir), Middx Hosp Med Sch; *m* 27 July 1968, Penelope Ann, da of Rev Gordon Charles Craig Spencer; 3 da (Karen, Ruth, Cheryl); *Career* house physician and house surgn Middx Hosp London 1969-70; sr house offr appts London: Royal Northern Hosp 1970-71, Brompton Hosp 1971-72, Royal Nat Hosp for Nervous Diseases 1972-73; lectr Inst of Med Res PNG 1973-75, Med Res Cncl travelling fellowship Nat Cancer Inst 1975-76, visiting scientist Nat Inst of Health Bethesda Maryland USA 1976-77, asst prof Tufts Univ Sch of Med Boston USA 1977-81, assoc prof New England Med Centre Boston USA 1982-84, Wellcome prof of tropical medicine London Sch of Hygiene and Tropical Med 1984-, physician Hosp for Tropical Diseases Bloomsbury & Islington Health Authy 1984-; memb Med Advsy Bds: Br Cncl 1988-, Br Leprosy Relief Assoc 1986-, Wellcome Trust 1985-90; chief med offr conslt advsr to NRC 1989-, expert advsr to House of Commons Soc Servs Ctee enquiry into AIDS 1987; FRSTM 1973, FRCP 1985, MRC 1988; *Recreations* cricket, squash, tennis, skiing; *Clubs* MCC; *Style*— Prof Keith McAdam; Oakmead, 70 Luton Lane, Redbourn, Herts AL3 7PY; Dept of Clinical Sciences, London Sch of Hygiene & Tropical Med, Keppel St, London WC1E 7HT (☎ 071 636 8636, fax 071 436 5389, telex 8953474)

MACADAM, Sir Peter; s of Francis Macadam (d 1981), of Buenos Aires, and Marjorie Mary, *née* Browne (d 1984); *b* 9 Sept 1921; *Educ* Buenos Aires Argentina, Stonyhurst; *m* 1949, Ann, da of Eric Methven Musson; 3 da; *Career* gp chm BAT Industries Ltd 1976-82 (joined 1946), dir National Westminster Bank plc 1978-84, chm Libra Bank plc 1984-90; pres Hispanic and Luso Brazilian Cncls (Canning House) 1982-87; Hon FBIM, FRSA; kt 1981; *Clubs* Naval & Military; *Style*— Sir Peter Macadam; Layham Hall, Layham, nr Hadleigh, Suffolk IP7 5LE (☎ 0473 822137); Libra Bank plc, 140 London Wall, London EC2

McAFEE, Patrick John; s of John McAfee, and Maud O'Donnell, *née* Lynas (d 1979); *b* 25 May 1940; *Educ* Portora Royal Sch, Trinity Coll Dublin (MA); *m* 2 March 1979, Jane Greer, da of Prof W L J Ryan, of Dublin; 1 da (Clare Jane b 1982); *Career* banker; dir Morgan Grenfell & Co Ltd 1973-; *Recreations* sailing, shooting; *Clubs* Royal St George Yacht; *Style*— Patrick J McAfee, Esq; c/o Morgan Grenfell & Co Ltd, 23 Gt Winchester St, London EC2P 2AX (☎ 071 588 4545)

MCALISTER, Michael Ian; s of S McAlister, CBE (d 1972), of Walton-on-Thames, Surrey, and Jessie Anne, *née* Smith; *b* 23 Aug 1930; *Educ* St John's Coll Oxford (MA); *m* 1, 4 July 1953 (m dis 1984), (Crystal) Patricia, da of John David Evans (d 1958), of

Sao Paulo, Brazil; 4 s (Richard b 1 June 1956, Peter b 5 Dec 1957, Sam b 29 July 1963, James b 17 March 1979), 3 da (Maureen b 9 June 1954, Carolyn b 25 Jan 1960, Emma b 19 May 1972); m 2, 2 June 1984, Elizabeth Anne, da of Louis Hehn, of Hatfield Peverel, Chelmsford, Essex; *Career* Nat Serv Army 1949-51, Acting-Capt Intelligence Corps 1951, (MI8) Austria (BTA 3); articled clerk Price Waterhouse & Co 1954-58, private and fin sec HRH Duke of Windsor KG 1959-61, md Ionian Bank Tstee Co 1961-69, chm Slater Walker Securities (Australia) 1969-72, pres Australian Stock Exchanges 1972-75, Knight Int plc Chicago 1975-78, corporate planning dir Cluff Resources plc 1979-89, chm Int Dynamics Ltd 1989-; chm Woking Cons Assoc 1967-68; ACA 1959, FCA 1969; *Recreations* carpentry, DIY, travel; *Clubs* RAC; *Style—* Michael McAlister, Esq; c/o International Dynamics Ltd, Imperial Coll, Exhibition Rd, London SW7 2BX (☎ 071 589 4548, fax 071 589 4538)

McALISTER, Maj-Gen Ronald William Lorne; CB (1977), OBE (1968, MBE 1958); s of Col Ronald James Frier McAlister, OBE (d 1963), of Edinburgh, and Mrs Nora Ford Collins, *née* Prosser; *b* 26 May 1923; *Educ* Sedbergh; *m* 25 Jan 1964, Sally Ewart, da of Dr Gordon King Marshall (d 1974), of Broadstairs, Kent; 2 da (Angela Frances b 15 May 1965, Caroline Jane b 14 Sept 1966); *Career* cmmnd 3 QAO Gurkha Rifles 1942, Adj 1/3 Gurkha Rifles Burma 1945 (despatches), 10 Gurkha Rifles 1948, Adj 2/10 Gurkha Rifles Malaya 1949-52 (despatches), instr Sch of Infantry Warminster 1952-55, Staff Coll 1956, Bde Maj Malaya 1957-58, Jt Serv Staff Coll 1961, asst sec Chiefs of Staff Ctee MOD 1962-64, CO 1/10 Gurkha Rifles 1965, Borneo 1966 (despatches), Hong Kong 1967, instr Jt Servs Staff Coll 1968, CO Berlin Infantry Bde 1968-71, Canadian Nat Def Coll 1971-72, exercise controller to UK Cs-in-C 1972-74, Maj Gen Bde of Gurkhas and Dep Cdr Hong Kong Land Forces 1975-77, ret 1977; bursar Wellesley House Prep Sch Broadstairs 1977-88; chm: Gurkha Brigade Assoc 1980-90, Buckmaster Memorial Home for Ladies Broadstairs 1983-; Capt Royal St Georges GC Sandwich 1989; *Books* Bugle and Kukri Vol 2(1986); *Recreations* golf, gardening; *Clubs* Army & Navy, Senior Golfers Soc; *Style—* Maj-Gen Ronald McAlister, CB, OBE; The Chalet, 41 Callis Court Rd, Broadstairs, Kent

McALISTER, William Harle Nelson; s of Flying Offr William Nelson (d 1940), and Marjorie Isobel, *née* McIntyre; *b* 30 Aug 1940; *Educ* St Edwards Sch Oxford, Univ Coll London (BA); *m* 1968 (m dis 1985), Sarah Elizabeth; 2 s (Daniel b 1969, Benjamin b 1977), 2 da (Leila b 1970, Alix b 1972); *Career* dir Almost Free Theatre 1968-72, dep dir Inter-Action Tst 1968-72, fndr dir Islington Bus Co 1972-77; dir: Battersea Arts Centre 1976-77, Sense of Ireland Festival 1980-; Bd dir London Int Theatre Festival 1983; chm: for the Arts IT 82 Ctee 1982, Recreational Tst 1972-; co fndr Fair Play for Children 1974-75, advsr Task Force Tst 1972-74; tstee: Circle 33 Housing Tst 1972-75, Moving Picture Mime Tst 1978-80, Shape (Arts for the Disadvantaged) 1979-81; govr Holloway Adult Educn Inst 1974-76; dir: ICA 1977-90, creative Res Ltd 1988-, Int House 1988, Performing Laboratories 1990-; memb: Ct RCA 1980-90; *Books* Community Psychology (1975), EEC and the Arts (1978); articles on arts policy; *Recreations* angling, tennis, travel; *Style—* William McAlister, Esq; 151c Grosvenor Ave, London N5 2NH (☎ 071 226 0205)

McALLISTER, Arthur George; s of John George McAllister (d 1971), of 54 Bramston Crescent, Coventry, and Ethel Mary McAllister (d 1962); *b* 31 July 1920; *Educ* Hull GS, St John's Coll York, Univ of Liverpool, Univ of Warwick (MEd); *Career* sports admin; rugby player RAF 1941-43, athlete E Hull Harriers 1935-40 and 1949-53; hon coach and sec Northern Counties Athletics Assoc 1954-69; chm Br Amateur Athletics Bd 1975-80 (chm UK Coaching Ctee 1972-75), pres AAA 1986- (chm Gen Ctee 1982-86); princ Nat Star Centre Cheltenham 1969-70, fndr princ Hereward Coll Coventry 1970-83; *Books* An Approach to the Further Education of the Physically Handicapped (with J Panckhurst, 1980); *Recreations* athletics, gardening, table tennis, walking; *Style—* Arthur McAllister, Esq; Amateur Athletic Association, Edgbaston House, 3 Duchess Place, Hagley Rd, Edgbaston, Birmingham B16 8NM (☎ 021 456 4050, fax 021 456 4061)

McALLISTER, John Brian; s of Thomas McAllister (d 1979), and Jane, *née* McCloughan; *b* 11 June 1941; *Educ* Royal Belfast Academical Instn, Queen's Univ Belfast (BA); *m* 1966, Margaret Lindsay, da of William Walker (d 1964), of Belfast; 2 da (Lynne b 1970, Barbara b 1972); *Career* civil servant 1964-; princ: Dept of Educn (NI) 1971 (asst princ 1968, dep princ 1969), NI Info Serv 1973; dep sec: Dept of Educn (NI) 1980 (asst sec 1976, sr asst sec 1978), Dept of Fin (NI) 1983; under sec DOE (NI) 1985, chief exec Industl Devpt Bd NI 1986 (dep chief exec 1985); *Recreations* family holidays, watching sport; *Clubs* NI Civil Serv; *Style—* John McAllister, Esq; c/o Industrial Devpt Bd for NI, IDB House, 64 Chichester St, Belfast, Northern Ireland BT1 4JX (☎ 0232 233233, telex 747025)

MCALLISTER, Stephen Drummond; s of Henry McAllister, of 20 Foxbar Road, Paisley, Renfrewshire, and Annie, *née* Gannon; *b* 16 Feb 1962; *Educ* Camphill HS Paisley; *Career* professional golfer; Scottish Masters 1987, Toyota Cup Denmark 1988, Atlantic Open Portugal 1990, Dutch Open 1990; amateur record: winner Lytham Trophy 1983, Scotland youth caps 1981-82, GB & Ireland youth cap 1982, 7 full Scotland caps 1983; memb Scotland Dunhill Cup team 1990; office clerk 1981-83; *Recreations* football, badminton, tennis, cars; *Style—* Stephen McAllister, Esq; c/o Monaghan Sports Management, 5 Lorraine Rd, Glasgow (☎ 041 339 4783)

McALLISTER, Victor Lionel; s of late Victor Lionel McAllister, and late Ethel Caroline McAllister; *b* 9 Oct 1941; *Educ* Sydney GS Aust, UCH (MB BS); *m* 22 April 1965, Pamela, da of Dr Denis Joel Johnson, MBE, TD (d 1982); 1 s (Peter Victor Lionel b 1970), 1 da (Karen Ann b 1967); *Career* conslt in admin charge neuroradiology Regnl Neurological Centre Newcastle Gen Hosp 1974-; invited lectr: Europe, India, Singapore, Aust; sec and treas Br Soc Neuroradiologists 1982-86, memb Euro Soc Neuroradiology; LRCP, MRCS, DMRD, FRCR; *Books* Subarachnoid Haemorrhage (1986), 60 pubns on all aspects neuroradiology; *Recreations* travel, badminton; *Clubs* Ponteland Lions, '62 (radiological); *Style—* Victor McAllister, Esq; Bermar, Horsley, Northumberland NE15 0NS (☎ 0661 85 3813); Dept of Neuroradiology, Newcastle General Hospital, Westgate Road, Newcastle upon Tyne NE4 6BE (☎ 091 273 8811 ext 22140, fax 091 272 2641)

MCALONAN, William Skilling; s of John McAlonan (d 1988), of Lanarks, and Margaret, *née* Black Skilling (d 1973); *b* 29 April 1929; *Educ* Wishaw HS, Nottingham Sch of Planning, Univ of Nottingham (MScEng); *m* 9 April 1955, Laura Elizabeth, da of Thomas Ralph Burrows; 1 s (David John b 18 June 1966), 2 da (Elsa Jane b 1 Nov 1958, Kirsten Emma b 2 March 1962); *Career* Nat Serv cmmnd RE 1954-56; apprentice civil engr Lanark CC 1947-52, asst Beeston and Stapleford UDC Notts 1952-54 and 1956-57, engr Leicester City Cncl 1957-59, sr engr Borough of Buxton Derbys 1959-61, asst city engr Nottingham 1961-69, dep city engr Stoke on Trent 1969-72, dep county surveyor Lanark CC 1972-75, dir of roads Strathclyde Region 1977-89 (dep dir 1975-77), conslt Babtie Shaw & Morton 1989-; dir: Strathclyde Buses Ltd 1989-, Mackenzie Construction Ltd 1989; chm Central & Southern Branch Inst of Highways and Transportation 1985-86, awarded AA Silver Medal 1986, visitor Tport Road Res Laboratory 1986-88, Br reporter Urban Roads PIARC Conf Brussels 1986, leader DTI Tech Mission to Aust and Japan 1988-; FIHT 1978, FICE 1979, FEng 1989; *Recreations* fishing, gardening, music; *Clubs* Royal Scottish Automobile; *Style—* William McAlonan, Esq; Brier Cottage, 88 Busby Road, Carmunnock, Glasgow G76 9BJ (☎ 041 644 1315); Babtie Shaw & Morton, Consulting Engineers, 95 Bothwell St, Glasgow G2 7HX (☎ 041 204 2511, fax 041 226 3109)

McALPINE, (Robert Douglas) Christopher; CMG (1967); s of Dr Archibald Douglas McAlpine, MBE (d 1981), and Elizabeth Meg, *née* Sidebottom (d 1941); *b* 14 June 1919; *Educ* Winchester, New Coll Oxford (MA); *m* 4 Dec 1943, Helen Margery Frances, da of Capt Astley Cannan(d 1934); 2 s (David b 1949, Robert b 1953), 2 da (Christine b 1944 d 1944, Sarah b 1946); *Career* WWII cmmnd Midshipman RNVR 1939, fighter pilot Fleet Air Arm 1941-44, demobbed as temp Lt 1946; Dip Serv 1946-69: FO 1946-47, asst private sec to Sec of State 1947-49, second sec (later first sec) Bonn High Cmmn 1949-52, FO 1952-54, Lima 1954-56, Moscow 1956-59, FO 1959-62, dep consul gen and cnsllr NYC 1962-65, cnsllr Mexico City 1965-68; ptnr and dir Baring Bros & Co Ltd 1969-79, non exec dir Horace Clarkson plc 1980-87; chm Tetbury Branch: Royal Br Legion, RNLI; cncllr Tetbury Town Cncl 1987-; Cdr Peruvian Order of Merit; *Recreations* sailing, tennis, golf; *Clubs* United Oxford & Cambridge Univ; *Style—* Christopher McAlpine, Esq, CMG

McALPINE, Hon David Malcolm; 3 and yst s of Baron McAlpine of Moffat (Life Peer and 5 Bt; d 1990); *b* 8 Oct 1946; *m* 1971, Jennifer Anne, da of Eric Hodges, of Chart Cottage, Fawley Green, Henley-on-Thames; 1 s (Robert Edward Thomas William b 1978), 2 da (Katherine Alexandra Donnison b 1972, Elizabeth Louise b 1973); *Career* dir Sir Robert McAlpine & Sons; *Style—* The Hon David McAlpine

McALPINE, Lady; Kathleen Mary; da of late Frederick Best; *m* 1, Charles Bantock Blackshaw; m 2, 1965, as his 2 w, Sir Thomas McAlpine, 4 Bt (d 1983); *see* McAlpine of Moffat, Baron); *Style—* Lady McAlpine; The Manor House, Stanford-in-the-Vale, nr Faringdon, Oxon

McALPINE, Kenneth; DL (Kent 1976); s of Sir Thomas Malcolm McAlpine, KBE (d 1967), and Maud Dees (d 1969); *b* 21 Sept 1920; *Educ* Charterhouse; *m* 1955, Patricia Mary, da of Capt Francis William Hugh Jeans, CVO, RN (d 1968); 2 s; *Career* WWII Flying Offr RAFVR; dir: Newarthill Ltd, Sir Robert McAlpine & Sons Ltd; High Sheriff Kent 1973-74; govr Royal Hosp of St Bartholomew 1972-74; owner Lamberhurst Vineyards; FRAeS; *Clubs* Royal Yacht Sqdn, Air Squadron; *Style—* Kenneth McAlpine Esq, DL; The Priory, Lamberhurst, Kent TN3 8DS

McALPINE, Sir Robin; CBE (1957); assumed forename of Robin in lieu of Robert by deed poll 1939; s of Sir (Thomas) Malcolm McAlpine, KBE (d 1967); *b* 18 March 1906; *Educ* Charterhouse; *m* 1, 1939, Nora Constance Perse (d 1966); m 2, 1970, Mrs Philippa Nicolson (d 1987), da of Sir Gervais Tennyson D'Eyncourt, 2 Bt (d 1971); *Career* chm: Sir Robert McAlpine & Sons (civil engrs) 1967-77, Newarthill Ltd 1972-77; pres Fedn of Civil Engrg Contractors 1966-71; racehorse breeder; kt 1969; *Style—* Sir Robin McAlpine, CBE; Aylesfield, Alton, Hants; 40 Bernard St, London WC1N 1LG

MCALPINE, Stewart; *b* 2 Jan 1937; *Career* chm 1960-: SMA Gp Ltd, Smedley McAlpine Ltd, IRB Group Ltd; dir: Airship Industries Ltd 1984-, City of London PR Group Plc 1988-, International Business Communications (Holdings) Plc 1987-88; dep md Barham Group Plc 1984-88; *Style—* Stewart McAlpine, Esq; Smedley McAlpine Ltd, 140 Camden St, London NW1 9PB (☎ 071 267 7070, fax 071 267 2707, car 0860 319 146)

McALPINE, Hon Sir William Hepburn; 6 Bt (UK 1918), of Knott Park, Co Surrey; eldest s of Baron McAlpine of Moffat (Life Peer and 5 Bt; d 1990), and his 1 w, Ella Mary Gardner, *née* Garnett (d 1987); *b* 12 Jan 1936; *Educ* Charterhouse; *m* 1959, Jill Benton, o da of Lt-Col Sir Peter Fawcett Benton Jones, 3 Bt, OBE (d 1972); 1 s (Andrew William b 1960), 1 da (Lucinda Mary Jane b 1964); *Heir* s, Andrew William McAlpine b 22 Nov 1960; *Career* Life Guards 1954-56; dir: Sir Robert McAlpine & Sons Ltd 1959-, Newarthill plc 1977-, Turner & Newall plc 1983-; chm Railway Heritage Tst 1985-; FRCE, FCIT; *Recreations* railway and transport preservation, horse racing; *Clubs* Garrick, Caledonian; *Style—* The Hon Sir William McAlpine, Bt; 40 Bernard St, London WC1N 1LG (☎ 071 837 3377, fax 071 837 5209)

McALPINE OF MOFFAT, Baroness; Nancy; *née* Garnett; da of James Gardner Garnett, of Vancouver, BC, Canada; *m* 1, Robert Hooper (decd); m 2, 15 Jan 1988, as his 2 w, Baron McAlpine of Moffat (Life Peer and 5 Bt; d 1990), widower of her sister Ella Mary Gardner Garnett; *Style—* The Rt Hon the Lady McAlpine of Moffat; Benhams, Fawley Green, nr Henley-on-Thames, Oxon RG9 6JG

McALPINE OF WEST GREEN, Baron (Life Peer UK 1984), of West Green in the Co of Hampshire; (Robert) Alistair; 2 s of Baron McAlpine of Moffat (Life Peer and 5 Bt, d 1990); *b* 14 May 1942; *Educ* Stowe; *m* 1, 1964 (m dis 1979), Sarah Alexandra, da of late Paul Hillman Baron, of 72 Bryanston Court, London W1; 2 da (Hon Mary Jane b 1965, Hon Victoria Alice b 1967); m 2, 1980, Romilly Thompson, o da of Alfred Thompson Hobbs, of Cranleigh, Surrey; 1 da (Skye b 1984); *Career* joined Sir Robert McAlpine & Sons Ltd 1958, dir George Weidenfeld Holdings Ltd 1975-83; vice pres: Friends of Ashmolean Museum 1969-, Gtr London Arts Assoc 1971-77; hon treas Conservative and Unionist Party 1975-90; vice-pres Euro League of Econ Cooperation 1975- (treas 1975-75); treas Euro Democratic Union 1978-; dir: ICA 1972-73, Theatre Investmt Fund 1981- (chm 1985-90); vice-chm Contemporary Arts Soc 1973-80; memb: Arts Cncl of GB 1981-82, Friends of V and A Museum 1976-, cncl British Stage Co 1973-75; tstee Royal Opera House Tst 1974-80; govr: Polytechnic of the South Bank 1981-82, Stowe Sch 1981-84; *Recreations* the arts, horticulture, aviculture, agriculture; *Clubs* Garrick, Carlton, Buck's, Beefsteak, Pratts, Weld (Perth, W Aust); *Style—* The Rt Hon the Lord McAlpine of West Green; House of Lords, Westminster, London SW1

MacANDREW, 3 Baron (UK 1959); Christopher Anthony Colin MacAndrew; er s of 2 Baron MacAndrew (d 1989); *b* 16 Feb 1945; *Educ* Malvern; *m* 1975, Sarah Helen, o da of Lt-Col Peter Hendy Brazier, of Nash Ct Farmhouse, Marnhull, Dorset; 1 s (Hon Oliver Charles Julian), 2 da (Hon Diana Sarah b 24 June 1978, Hon Tessa Deborah b 2 Aug 1980); *Heir* s, Hon Oliver Charles Julian MacAndrew b 3 Sept 1983; *Style—* The Rt Hon Lord MacAndrew; Hall Farm, Archdeacon Newton, Darlington (☎ 0325 462246)

MCANDREW, Ian Christopher; *b* 20 Feb 1953; *Educ* Univ of Cambridge (MA); *m* 26 Aug 1978, Geraldine Baker; 2 da (Cathryn b 12 Jan 1985, Madeleine b 12 March 1989); *Career* Coopers & Lybrand 1975-88, dir co sec and compliance offr British and Commonwealth Merchant Bank plc 1988-; FCA (ACA 1978); *Style—* Ian McAndrew, Esq; 3 Frank Dixon Close, London SE21 7BD (☎ 081 693 3592); British & Commonwealth Merchant Bank plc, 62 Cannon St, London EC4N 6AE (☎ 071 248 0900)

MacANDREW, Hon Nicholas Rupert; yr s of 2 Baron MacAndrew (d 1989); *b* 12 Feb 1947; *Educ* Eton; *m* 1975, Victoria Rose, da of George Patrick Renton, of Isington Close, Alton, Hants; 1 s, 2 da; *Style—* The Hon Nicholas MacAndrew; The Old Chapel, Greywell, Odiham, Hampshire RG25 1BS (☎ 0256 702390)

MCANDREW, Nicolas; s of Robert Louis McAndrew (1981), and Anita Marian, *née* Huband; *b* 9 Dec 1934; *Educ* Winchester; *m* 20 Sept 1960, Diana Leonie Wood; 2 s (Charles Gavin b 14 Jan 1962, Mark James b 16 Feb 1964), 1 da (Fiona Catherine Mary b 16 June 1968); *Career* Nat Serv 1 Bn The Black Watch 1953-55 (active serv Kenya); articled clerk Peat Marwick Mitchell & Co 1955-61, qualified chartered accountant 1961; S G Warburg & Co Ltd: investmt mangr 1962-69, chm Warburg

Investment Management 1975-78 (md 1969-75); md: NM Rothschild & Sons Ltd 1979-88, Rothschild Asset Management Ltd 1979-88, Murray Johnstone Ltd 1988-; memb Court of Assts Worshipful Co of Grocers (Master 1978-79); ASIA; *Recreations* fishing, shooting, gardening; *Clubs* White's, City of London, Western (Glasgow); *Style*— Nicolas McAndrew, Esq; Blairquhosh House, Blanefield, Glasgow G63 9AJ (☎ 0360 70232); Murray Johnstone Ltd, 7 West Nile St, Glasgow G1 2PX (☎ 041 226 3131, fax 041 204 0712)

McANDREW, Nicolas; s of Robert Louis McAndrew; *b* 9 Dec 1934; *Educ* Winchester; *m* 1960, Diana Leonie, *née* Wood; 3 c; *Career* Capt Black Watch (Army) Kenya 1954-55; CA; S G Warburg & Co Ltd 1961-78; md: NM Rothschild & Sons 1979-88, Murray Johnstone 1988-; memb Inst of CAs of Scotland 1962-; *Recreations* shooting, fishing, golf; *Clubs* White's City of London, Western (Glasgow), Swinley Forest Golf; *Style*— Nicolas McAndrew, Esq; Blairquhosh House, Blanefield, Stirlingshire (☎ 0360 70232); 36 Fabian Rd, London SW6 (☎ 071 381 1924, office 041 226 3131)

McARDELL, John David; s of Patrick John McArdell (d 1988), and Elizabeth Frances, *née* Powling; *b* 25 Dec 1931; *Educ* Haberdasher's Aske's; *m* 22 Aug 1959, Margaret Sylvia, da of George Lewis Cawley (d 1981); 2 da (Nicola Susan b 26 June 1964, Paula Frances b 19 Sept 1968); *Career* Nat Serv RAF Egypt 1950-52; dep md Ecclesiastical Insur Gp 1988- (mangr mktg and planning 1975-81, asst gen mangr 1985-88); dir: Aldwych Management Services Ltd Blaisdon Properties Ltd, REI Investment Ltd Ireland; memb: Insur Inst of London, Insur Golfing Soc of London; former pres Insur Inst of Gloucester, govr and dir Westonbirt Sch; Freeman: City of London 1981; Liveryman: Worshipful Co of Insurers, Worshipful Co of Marketers; ACII 1957, FInstD 1980, FBIM 1984, FCIM 1989, CI 1989; *Recreations* golf, bridge, rambling; *Clubs* IOD, City Livery, Wig and Pen; *Style*— John McArdell, Esq; Pen-Y-Bryn, Rodborough Common, Gloucs (☎ 045 387 3276); Beaufort House, Brunswick Rd, Gloucester (☎ 0452 28533, telex 43646)

McARDLE, Brian Thomas; s of John McArdle (d 1966), of Co Durham, and Mary, *née* McDonald; *b* 31 Jan 1948; *Educ* St Mary's Darlington, Univ of Newcastle upon Tyne (LLB); *m* 19 May 1973, Alison Jane, da of Edward William Knight, of Nottingham; *Career* slr; asst slr Molineux McKeag & Cooper Newcastle upon Tyne 1973-74; prosecuting slr: Northumbria Police Authy 1974-77, W Midlands Co Cncl 1977-86; chief crown prosecutor Inner London Crown Prosecution Serv 1987- (branch crown prosecutor 1986-87); memb: Prosecuting Slrs Soc 1974-86, Law Soc 1973-; *Recreations* skiing, photography, classical music, watching cricket; *Style*— Brian McArdle, Esq; Crown Prosecution Service, Inner London Area, 24th Floor, Portland House, Stag Place, London SW1E 5BH (☎ 071 828 9050, fax 071 976 5418)

McARDLE, Carrie Burnett; s of Denis James McArdle, of Lake Cottage, Rake Manor, Milford, Surrey, and Kathleen Burnett; *b* 7 June 1957; *Educ* St Catherines Sch, Bramley, Surrey; *Career* mangr publicity and promotions; ed: Tantivy Press, Thomas Yoseloff / AS Barnes Inc, Assoc Univ Presses 1977; ed promotions, Over 21 Magazine 1979-; asst and assoc ed Living Magazine 1983-, managing and dep editor Woman's Journal 1987-; *Recreations* reading, writing, walking, entertaining; *Style*— Carrie McArdle; 19 Dale Street, Chiswick, London WL1; Woman's Journal, IPC Magazines, Kings Reach Tower, Stamford Street, London SE1

McARDLE, Colin Stewart; *b* 10 Oct 1939; *Educ* Jordanhill Coll Sch Glasgow, Univ of Glasgow (MB ChB, MD); *m* June Margaret Campbell, *née* Merchant; 2 s (Peter Alexander b 1975, Alan Douglas b 1982), 1 da (Kirsten Anne b 1977); *Career* sr registrar in surgery Western Infirmary Glasgow 1972-75 (Nuffield res fell 1971-72); conslt surgn: Victoria Infirmary Glasgow 1975-78, Dept of Surgery Royal Infirmary Glasgow 1978-; author of papers on: breast, colon and stomach cancer, liver tumours, pain and postoperative pulmonary complications, shock, surgical sepsis and intensive care; FRCSEd 1968, FRCS 1969, FRCS Glasgow 1980, FRSM 1986; *Books* Surgical Oncology (1990); *Style*— Colin McArdle, Esq; 4 Collylinn Rd, Bearsden, Glasgow G61 4PN; University Department of Surgery, Royal Infirmary, Glasgow

MacARTHUR, Brian Roger; s of S H MacArthur (d 1971), of Ellesmere Port, Cheshire and Marjorie; *b* 5 Feb 1940; *Educ* Brentwood Sch, Helsby GS, Leeds Univ (BA MA (hon, Open); *m* 22 Aug 1975, Bridget da of Nicholas Rosevear Trahair of The Croft, South Milton, Kingsbridge, South Devon; 2 da (Tessa b 1976, Georgina b 1979); *Career* educn corr The Times 1967-70, ed The Times Higher Educ Supplement, 1971-76, exec ed The Times 1981-82, dep ed The Sunday Times 1982-84; ed: The Western Morning News 1984-85, Today 1985-86; exec ed Sunday Times 1987-; *Recreations* family, gardening, reading; *Clubs* Garrick; *Style*— Brian MacArthur, Esq; 50 Lanchester Road, London N6 4TA (☎ 081 883 1855); The Sunday Times, PO Box 481, Virginia Street, London E1 9BD (☎ 081 822 9801, fax 081 822 9658)

McARTHUR, (Allan Robin) Dayrell; s of Alan John Dennis McArthur (d 1988), of Combe Way, Bath, and Pamela Mary, *née* Henderson; *b* 28 June 1946; *Educ* Winchester; *m* 30 April 1977, Susan Diana, da of Christopher Cheshire, of Spain; 3 s (Alastair b 1979, Sam b 1981, Robert b 1985); *Career* Price Waterhouse 1965-69, McArthur Gp Ltd 1969- (md 1971, chm 1987); pres Nat Assoc of Steel Stockholders 1986-88, vice pres Club des Marchands de Fer 1989-; Master Soc of Merchant Venturers of Bristol 1989-; *Recreations* tennis, golf, cricket, rackets, music, theatre, skiing; *Clubs* MCC, Tennis & Rackets Assoc; *Style*— Dayrell McArthur, Esq; Moorledge Farm, Chew Magna, Bristol (☎ 0272 332357); McArthur Group Ltd, Foundry Lane, Fishponds Trading Estate, Bristol BS5 7UE (☎ 0272 656242, fax 0272 583536, telex 449189, car 0831 493786)

MacARTHUR, Ian; OBE (1988); yr s of Lt-Gen Sir William MacArthur, KCB, DSO (d 1964), and Marie Eugénie Thérèse, *née* Antelme; *b* 17 May 1925; *Educ* Cheltenham, Queen's Coll Oxford (MA); *m* 1957, Judith Mary, da of Francis Gavin Douglas Miller (d 1955); 4 s (Niall, Duncan, Ruaidhri, Gavin), 3 da (Jane, Anne, Lucy); *Career* serv with RN and RNVR 1943-46, Ordinary Seaman RN 1943, Lt RNVR 1946; MP (C) Perth and E Perthshire 1959-74; Lord Cmmr of the Treasy and Govt, Scottish whip 1963-64, oppn Scottish whip 1964-65, oppn spokesman on Scottish Affrs 1965-70, oppn front bench 1965-66 and 1969-70; vice chm Cons Pty in Scotland 1972-75; dir Br Textile Confedn 1977-89; former dir of admin J Walter Thompson Co Ltd; FRSA; Gold Cross of Merit Polish Govt in Exile 1971; King's Badge 1944; *Clubs* Naval, Puffin's (Edinburgh); *Style*— Ian MacArthur, Esq, OBE; 15 Old Palace Lane, Richmond, Surrey

MacARTHUR, Prof John Durno; s of Donald MacArthur (d 1936), of Harrow, Middlesex, and Isabel Norah, *née* Durno (d 1988); *b* 22 May 1934; *Educ* Reeds Sch, Caterham Sch, Univ of Reading, Univ of Oxford; *m* 11 July 1959, Anne Elliss, da of William Henry Hicks (d 1968), of Bexleyheath; 1 s (Andrew William b 1961), 2 da (Caroline Mary Anne b 1962, Juliet Claire b 1964); *Career* Nat Serv 1952-54, 2 Lt RASC 1953-54, serv Egypt; agric economist Kenya 1960-67, lectr UCNW Bangor 1967-72, prof agric and project econs Univ of Bradford 1988- (sr lectr 1972-87); conslt: IBRD, ODA, FAO, UNDP, UNIDO; fndr memb: SDP 1981, SLDP 1987 (Alliance candidate Elmet 1987); memb: Agric Econ Soc, Devpt Studies Assoc; *Books* Project Appraisal in Practice (co-author, 1976), Appraisal of Projects in Developing Countries (1988); *Recreations* golf, genealogy, bridge; *Style*— Prof John MacArthur; Development and Project Planning Centre, University of Bradford, Bradfor BD7 1OP (☎ 0274 733466, fax 0274 726918, telex 51309 UNIBFD G)

McARTHUR, Dr Thomas Burns (Tom); s of Archibald McArthur (d 1967), of Glasgow, and Margaret Dymock Dow, *née* Burns (d 1986); *b* 23 Aug 1938; *Educ* Woodside Secdy Sch Glasgow, Univ of Glasgow (MA), Univ of Edinburgh (MLitt, PhD); *m* 30 March 1963, Fereshteh, da of Habib Mottahedin, of Teheran, Iran; 1 s (Alan b 30 April 1970), 2 da (Meher b 11 Nov 1966, Roshan b 16 Nov 1968); *Career* 2 Lt offr instr RAEC 1959-62; educn offr: Depot the Royal Warks Regt, Depot the Mercian Bde; asst teacher Riland-Bedford Boys HS Sutton Coldfield Warks 1962-64, head of Eng Dept Cathedral and John Connon Sch Bombay India 1965-67, visiting prof Bharatiya Vidya Bhavan Univ of Bombay 1965-67, dir of studies Extra Mural Eng Language Courses Univ of Edinburgh 1972-79, assoc prof of Eng Université du Québec à Trois - Rivières Quebec Canada 1979-83; editor: English Today: The International Review of the English Language 1984-, The Oxford Companion to the English Language 1987-; conslt to: Collins, Longman, Chambers, Cambridge Univ Press, WHO, Henson Int TV (the Muppets), Govt of Quebec, Century Hutchinson, OUP; fndr memb and tutor Birmingham Yoga Club 1963, schs lectr and press offr Bombay Soc of Prevention of Cruelty to Animals (BSPCA) 1965-67, chm Scot Yoga Assoc 1977-79, co-chm Scots Language Planning Ctee 1978, memb Ed Bd International Journal of Lexicography 1988-, numerous broadcasts BBC Eng by Radio (World Serv); *Books* Building English Words (1972), Using English Prefixes and Suffixes (1972), Using Compound Words (1972), A Rapid Course in English for Students of Economics (1973), Using Phrasal Verbs (1973), Collins Dictionary of English Phrasal Verbs and Their Idioms (with Beryl T Atkins, 1974), Learning Rhythm and Stress (with Mohamed Heliel, 1974), Using Modal Verbs (with Richard Wakely, 1974), Times, Tenses and Conditions (with John Hughes, 1974), Languages of Scotland (ed with A J Aitken, 1979), Longman Lexicon of Contemporary English (1981), A Foundation Course for Language Teachers (1983), The Written Word: A Course in Controlled Composition (books 1 and 2, 1984), Worlds of Reference: Lexicography, Learning and Language from the Clay Tablet to the Computer (1986), Understanding Yoga: A Thematic Companion to Yoga and Indian Philosophy (1986), Yoga and the Bhagavad-Gita (1986), Unitive Thinking: A Guide to Developing a More Integrated and Effective Mind (1988); *Recreations* reading, television, walking, cycling, travel; *Style*— Dr Tom McArthur; 22-23 Ventress Farm Court, Cherry Hinton Rd, Cambridge CB1 4HD (☎ 0223 245934)

MACARTNEY, Sir John Barrington; 6 Bt (I 1799), of Lish, Armagh; s of John Barrington Macartney d 1951, and Selina, *née* Koch; and nephew of 5 Bt (d 1960); *b* 1917; *m* 1944, Amy Isobel Reinke; 1 s; *Heir* s, John Ralph Macartney *qv*; *Career* dairy farmer; *Style*— Sir John Macartney, Bt; 37 Meadow St, North Mackay, Queensland 4740, Australia

MACARTNEY, John Ralph; s and h of Sir John Barrington Macartney, 6 Bt; *b* 1945; *m* 1966, Suzanne Marie Fowler, of Nowra, NSW; 4 da; *Career* Petty Officer RAN (ret); teacher (head of dept) ACT Inst of TAFE; *Style*— John Macartney Esq; PO Box 589, Quean Beyan, NSW 2620, Australia

MACASKILL, John Harry; s of John Macaskill (d 1981), and Nancy Love, *née* Mills (d 1963); *b* 13 Feb 1947; *Educ* Oundle, Univ of Nottingham (BA); *m* 11 May 1974, Gwyneth June, da of Ralph Herbert Keith Evers, of Four Winds, Westward Ho, N Devon; 3 s (James b 6 Sept 1979, Robert b 1 Oct 1981, Sandy b 9 May 1985); *Career* ptnr Slaughter and May 1979- (articled clerk 1970-72, slr 1972-79); Freeman City of London 1985, Liveryman The City of London Solicitor's Co 1985; memb Law Soc 1972; *Recreations* walking, gardening, sheep dog trials; *Clubs* City Livery, RAC; *Style*— John H Macaskill, Esq; 35 Basinghall St, London EC2V 5DB (☎ 071 600 1200, fax 071 726 0038, telex 883486)

MACASKILL, Ronald Angus; s of Angus Duncan Macaskill, and Elsie Broadbridge, *née* Tosh; *b* 21 April 1947; *Educ* King's College Sch Wimbledon, King's Coll London (BSc, AKC), The City Univ (MSc); *m* 6 Aug 1977, Irmgard Elisabeth, da of Heinrich Matthias Hinterstein, of Poysdorf, Austria; 1 s (Roald Ian b 6 May 1990), 2 da (Elisabeth Ann b 6 Aug 1981, Alexandra Jane b 15 Apr 83); *Career* mktg exec: Dynamit Nobel (UK) Ltd 1969-71, Macaskill Group 1971- (dir 1975-); memb: Ctee Local Branch World Ship Soc, Farringdon Ward Club; sec Admty Ferry Crew Assoc, vice pres Rotary Club of Mitcham; Freeman City of London 1978, Liveryman Worshipful Co of Blacksmiths 1978 (sec Craft Ctee 1987-); MBIM 1970, FInstSMM 1979; *Recreations* skiing, swimming, ship modelling, photography; *Clubs* City Livery; *Style*— Ronald Macaskill, Esq; 41 The Gallop, Sutton, Surrey SM2 5RY (☎ 081 643 7743); Macaskill Engineering Ltd, Forval Close, Mitcham, Surrey CR4 4NE (☎ 081 640 7211, fax 081 640 9411, telex 885721 ASKMAC)

MACAULAY, Anthony Dennis; s of Dennis Macaulay, of Wakefield, W Yorks, and Frances, *née* Frain; *b* 15 Nov 1948; *Educ* Queen Elizabeth GS Wakefield, Keble Coll Oxford; *m* 8 Oct 1978, Dominica Francisca, da of Dr Henri Compernolle, of Bruges, Belgium; 1 s (Thomas b 29 March 1985), 2 da (Laura b 20 April 1983, Rosemary b 4 Oct 1987); *Career* admitted slr 1974; articled clerk/slr Biddle & Co 1971-75, asst slr Wilkinson Kimbers & Staddon 1975-77, ptnr Herbert Smith 1983- (asst slr 1977-83), sec to Panel on Take-overs and Mergers 1983-85; memb Law Soc; memb Worshipful Co of Slrs 1987; *Books* Butterworths Handbook of UK Corporate Finance (contrib 1988); *Recreations* tennis, skiing, music, cooking, family; *Clubs* Cumberland Lawn Tennis; *Style*— Anthony Macaulay, Esq; Watling House, 35 Cannon St, London EC4M 5SD (☎ 071 489 8000, fax 071 329 0426, telex 886633)

McAULAY, (John) Roy Vincent; QC (1978); s of Dr John McAulay, of West Wickham, Kent and Marty, *née* Kuni; *b* 9 Sept 1933; *Educ* Whitgift Sch, Queens' Coll Cambridge (MA); *m* 1970, Ruth Kathleen, da of Alexander Smith, of Sevenoaks Kent; 1 s (Gavin b 1972), 1 da (Charlotte b 1975); *Career* rec 1975, legal assessor to General Medical Council; *Style*— Roy McAulay, Esq, QC; 5 Montpelier Row, Blackheath, London SE3; office: 1 Harcourt Buildings, Temple, London EC4

MCAULEY, David Anthony; s of Donald Joseph McAuley, and Marion, *née* O'Neill; *b* 15 June 1961; *Educ* St Corngall's Secdy Sch, Larne Tech Coll; *m* 15 Sept 1983, Wendy, da of Omar Beggs; 1 da (Sacha b 12 June 1986); *Career* professional boxer; former memb St Agnes Club (amateur); amateur record: All-Ireland sr champion 1978-79, represented Ireland Euro Jr Championship 1979, 7 contests Ireland, Irish Flyweight champion 1980; turned professional 1983, won Br Flyweight title 1986 (relinquished title), challenged for WBA Flyweight title 1987 and 1988; Int Boxing Fedn Flyweight title: won v Duke McKenzie 1989, first defence 1989, second and third defences 1990; Br Boxing Bd of Control award for best contest (v Fidel Bassa) 1987, Texaco Sports Personality 1986, 1989, 1990; former employment: Kilroot Power Station 1978-83, chef 1983-89; *Recreations* clay pigeon shooting; *Style*— David McAuley, Esq; c/o B J Eastwood, Eastwood House, 2-4 Chapel Lane, Belfast (☎ 0232 238005)

MACAULEY, Hon Mrs (Diana Phyllis); *née* Berry; yst da of 1 Viscount Camrose (d 1954), and Mary Agnes, *née* Corns (d 1962); *b* 1924; *m* 7 April 1948, William Perine Macauley (d 1990), s of late Timothy Alfred Macauley, of Montreal, Canada; 3 s, 3 da; *Style*— The Hon Mrs Macauley; Ballyward House, Blessington, Co Wicklow

McAULIFFE, Prof Charles Andrew; *b* 29 Nov 1941; *Educ* Univ of Manchester (BSc, DSc), Florida State Univ (MS), Univ of Oxford (DPhil); *m* 1 April 1967, Margaret Mary; 1 s ((Charles) Andrew b 30 Nov 1977), 2 da (Amy Noelle b 15 Oct

1972, Juliette Hilda b 12 Dec 1975); *Career* prof of chemistry LIMIST; memb Dalton Div Cncl RSC 1990-; FRSC; *Books* Transition Metal Complexes of Phosphine, Arsoine and Antimony Ligands (with W Levason, 1978); *Style*— Prof Charles McAuliffe; The Coach House, 1 Pinewood, Bowdon, Cheshire WA14 3JG; Department of Chemistry, Umist, Manchester M60 1QD (☎ 061 200 2514, fax 061 200 4484, telex 666094)

MACAUSLAN, Harry Hume; s of John Mechan MacAuslan, and Helen Constance Howden, *née* Hume; *b* 2 Oct 1956; *Educ* Charterhouse, Univ of Manchester (BA); *m* 1981, Fiona Caroline, da of Brian Martin Boag; 2 s (Samuel Alexander b 9 Aug 1987, James Hume b 8 April 1989), 1 da (Clare Emily b 5 Jan 1985); *Career* advertising exec; mktg trainee De La Rue 1979-80; Bd dir J Walter Thompson 1989- (joined as graduate trainee 1980); *Style*— Harry MacAuslan, Esq; J Walter Thompson, 40 Berkeley Square, London W1X 6AD (☎ 071 499 4040)

MCAVOY, Michael Anthony; s of Lt-Col John McAvoy, and Gertrude, *née* Gradidge (d 1962); *b* 31 July 1934; *Educ* Beaumont Coll, Lincoln Coll Oxford; *m* 1963, June Anne, da of Robert Harper; 1 da (Annabel Jane b 1966); *Career* Young & Rubicam Ltd: joined 1957, md Planned Public Relations Ltd 1965, chm Planned Public Relations 1970, chm GLH Marketing Ltd 1970, dir Young & Rubicam Holdings 1970, vice president Young & Rubicam International 1971, vice chm Burson Marsteller Ltd 1979-81; fndr and ptnr McAvoy Wreford & Associates 1981-84, vice chm McAvoy Wreford Bayley Ltd 1986- (dir 1984), vice chm McAvoy Bayley Ltd 1990; fndr chm PR Consultants Assoc 1969-72; memb Int PR Assoc, FIPR; *Recreations* golf; *Clubs* RAC; *Style*— Michael McAvoy, Esq; McAvoy Bayley Ltd, 36 Grosvenor Gardens, London SW1W 0ED (☎ 071 730 4500)

McAVOY, Thomas McLaughlin; MP (Lab and Co-op) Glasgow Rutherglen 1987-; s of Edward McAvoy (d 1985), and Frances McLaughlin McAvoy (d 1982); *b* 14 Dec 1943; *Educ* St Columbkilles Jr Secdy Sch; *m* 1968, Eleanor Kerr, da of William Kerr, of 21 Burnhill St, Rutherglen, Glasgow; 4 s (Thomas b 1969, Michael b 1971, Steven b 1974, Brian b 1981); *Career* regnl cncllr Strathclyde 1982-87; *Style*— Thomas McAvoy, Esq, MP; 9 Douglas Avenue, Rutherglen, Glasgow

MacBAIN, Gordon Campbell; s of John Ritchie Gordon MacBain (d 1966), and Dora, *née* Campbell; *b* 29 April 1938; *Educ* HS of Glasgow, Univ of Glasgow (MB ChB); *m* 9 July 1964, Margaret Janet, da of George Drummond Tait Wilson, of 13 Torphin Rd, Colinton, Edinburgh; 1 s (John b 1971), 1 da (Katharin b 1966); *Career* conslt surgn Southern Gen Hosp Glasgow 1974, memb Bd of Dirs AMI Ross Hall Hosp Glasgow 1981; tstee: Forum Arts Soc, Martyrs Sch Glasgow 1983; FRCSEd 1966, FRCS Glasgow 1981; memb: BMA, Assoc of Surgns, Br Vascular Soc of GB and Ireland; *Recreations* music, golf; *Style*— Gordon MacBain, Esq; Cranford, 1 Bank Ave, Milngavie, Glasgow G62 8NG (☎ 041 956 3388); Southern General Hospital, Glasgow (☎ 041 445 2466)

McBAIN OF McBAIN, James Hughston; 22 Chief of Clan McBain (McBean); s of Hughston Maynard McBain of McBain (matriculated as Chief 1959, d 1977); *b* 1928; *Educ* Culver Mil Acad, Western Washington Coll, Univ of Arizona; *m* Margaret, *née* Stephenson; *Heir* s, Richard James b 1957; *Career* pres Scot Photo Shops Arizona 1962-; *Recreations* golf, Scottish history, Scottish country dancing; *Clubs* Royal Scottish Country Dance Soc; *Style*— James McBain of McBain; 7025 North Finger Rock Place, Tucson, Arizona 85718, USA

MacBEAN, Dr Ian Grant; CBE (1986); s of William Charles MacBean (d 1977), and Isabel Clara, *née* Haro; *b* 30 Sept 1931; *Educ* Highgate Sch, Imperial Coll London (PhD, BSc, DIC, ACGI); *m* 28 July 1956, Joan Annie, da of George Rowell (d 1989), of Alton, Hants; 3 da (Diane b 1961, Valerie b 1963, Judith b 1968); *Career* dir GEC plc, md GEC-Marconi Ltd; FEng, FIEE, CEng; *Recreations* golf, gardening, bridge, DIY; *Style*— Dr Ian MacBean, CBE; GEC-Marconi Ltd, The Grove, Stanmore, Middx (☎ 081 954 2311)

McBEATH, Hon Mrs; Janet Mary; *née* Blades; da of 1 Baron Ebbisham, GBE (d 1953); *b* 1916; *m* 1952, Rear Adm John Edwin Home McBeath, CB, DSO, DSC, DL (d 1982); 1 s, 1 da; *Style*— The Hon Mrs McBeath; Woodbury, 9 Annandale Drive, Lower Bourne, Farnham, Surrey GU10 3JD

MACBEATH, John Thomson; s of Angus Macbeath (d 1982), of Inverness, and Christina Robertson, *née* Thomson; *b* 27 May 1938; *Educ* Inverness Royal Acad, Univ of Edinburgh (MB ChB); *Career* registrar in anaesthesia Edinburgh Royal Infirmary 1966-69, Reckitt res fell in anaesthesia Univ of Salford 1969-71, sr registrar in anaesthesia NW Region 1971-73, conslt anaesthetist Salford Health Authy 1973-, hon lectr in anaesthesia Univ of Manchester 1983- (faculty and coll tutor 1983-90); memb: Ctee Section of Anaesthesia Manchester Med Soc 1986-89, Coll of Anaesthetists of GB, Assoc of Anaesthetists of GB and I, Manchester Med Soc; *Recreations* opera, classical music, running; *Style*— John Macbeath, Esq; Department of Anaesthesia, Hope Hospital, Eccles Old Rd, Salford M6 8HD (☎ 061 789 7373)

MACBETH, Dr Fergus Robert; s of Dr R G Macbeth, and Margaret, *née* Macdonald (d 1983); *b* 5 Jan 1948; *Educ* Eton, Merton Coll Oxford, King's College Hosp Med Sch London (MA, BM BCh, DM); *Career* conslt in radiotherapy and oncology 1988; FRCR 1987, FRCP Glasgow 1989; *Style*— Dr Fergus Macbeth; Beatson Oncology Centre, Western Infirmary, Glasgow G11 6NT (☎ 041 339 8822)

MACBETH, George Mann; s of George MacBeth, and Amelia Morton Mary, *née* Mann; *Educ* New Coll Oxford; *m* 1, 1955 (m dis 1975), Elizabeth Browell, *née* Robson; m 2, 1982 (m dis 1989), Lisa St Aubin de Téran; 1 s (Alexander b 1982); m 3, 1989, Penelope Ronchetti Church; 1 da (Diana b 1990); *Career* BBC 1955-76: prodr Overseas Talks Dept 1957, prodr Talks Dept 1958; ed: The Poets Voice 1958-65, New Comment 1959-64, Poetry Now 1965-76; Geoffrey Faber Memorial award (jointly) 1964, Cholmondely award (jointly) 1977; *Books* poems: A Form of Words (1954), The Broken Places (1963), A Doomsday Book (1965), The Colour of Blood (1967), The Night of Stones (1968), A War Quartet (1969), The Burning Cone (1970), Collected Poems 1958-70 (1971), The Orlando Poems (1971), Shrapnel (1973), A Poet's Year (1973), In the Hours Waiting For the Blood to Come (1975), Buying a Heart (1978), Poems of Love and Death (1980), Poems from Oby (1982), The Long Darkness (1983), The Cleaver Garden (1986), Anatomy of a Divorce (1988), Collected Poems 1958-82 (1989); prose poems, My Scotland (1975); prose: The Transformation (1975), The Samurai (1975), The Survivor (1977), The Seven Witches (1978), The Born Losers (1981), A Kind of Treason (1982), Anna's Book (1983), The Lion of Pescara (1984), Dizzy's Woman (1986); anthologies: The Penguin Book of Sick Verse (1963), Penguin Modern Poets VI (with J Clemo and E Lucie-Smith, 1964), The Penguin Book of Animal Verse (1965), Poetry 1900-1965 (1967), The Penguin Book of Victorian Verse (1968), The Falling Splendour (1970), The Book of Cats (1976), Poetry 1900- 1975 (1980), Poetry for Today (1984); children's books: Jonah and the Lord (1969), The Rectory Mice (1982), The Story of Daniel (1986); autobiography: A Child of the War (1987); *Recreations* Japanese swords; *Style*— George MacBeth, Esq; Moyne Park, nr Tuam, County Galway, Ireland

McBRATNEY, George; s of George McBratney (d 1977), of Comber, Co Down, NI, and Sarah Jane, *née* Bailie (d 1965); *b* 5 May 1927; *Educ* Coll of Technol Belfast, Northampton Coll for Advanced Technol, Univ of London (BSc), Queen's Univ Belfast (DipEd); *m* 5 Aug 1949, Margaret Rose Patricia (Trissie), da of the late John Robinson, of Melbourne, Aust; 1 s (Stephen George b 15 Aug 1954); *Career* apprentice fitter and draughtsman Harland and Wolff 1943-47, teacher Comber Trades Prep Sch 1947-54; Coll of Technol Belfast: lectr and sr lectr 1954-67, asst to princ 1967-69, vice princ 1969-84, princ 1984-89; chm Faculty of Educn Further Educn Advsy Ctee Univ of Ulster 1987-90; memb: NI Manpower Cncl, Cncl Lambeg Industl Res Assoc, Business and Technician Educn Cncl (London), Cncl NI branch IME; memb: CEng, FIMechE 1971 (chm NI branch 1984-86); *Books* Mechanical Engineering Experiments (with W R Mitchell vols I and II 1962, with T G J Moag, vol III 1964), Science for Mechanical Engineering Technicians (with T G J Moag 1966); *Recreations* gardening, reading, charitable work; *Style*— George McBratney, Esq; 16 Glencregagh Drive, Belfast BT6 ONL (☎ 0232 796123)

MCBRIDE, (William) Denis; s of William McBride, of Belfast, and Mary Jane, *née* Sloan; *b* 9 Sept 1964; *Educ* Belfast HS, Queens Univ Belfast; *m* 9 June 1990, Catriona (memb NI Volleyball Team), da of Michael Thomas Clarke; *Career* Rugby Union flanker Malone RFC and Ireland (8 caps); club: Queens Univ RFC 1983-87, Malone RFC 1987-; rep: Ulster Schs 1983, Ireland Schs 1983, Ulster U20 1984, Combined Provinces U21 1984, Ulster (debut v Connaught 1987); Ireland: debut v Wales 1988, toured France 1988, toured USA and Canada 1989; memb Irish Wolfhounds HK Sevens 1989; power station engr NI Electricity 1987-; *Recreations* athletics, cinema, most sports; *Style*— Denis McBride, Esq

McBRIDE, John Carlisle; s of Vice Adm Sir William McBride, KCB, CBE (d 1959), and Juanita, *née* Franco; *b* 11 March 1930; *Educ* Radley, RNC Greenwich; *m* Priscilla Reynolds; 2 s (Alexander b 1969, Nathaniel b 1971); *Career* reg cmmn RN 1948-55; mktg dir Sunday Times 1962-66, fndn Media Expenditure Analysis Ltd 1967; md: Hulton Technical Press 1973-82, AGB Publications 1982; dir: AGB Research plc 1982-89, Maxwell Business Communications Group Ltd 1989-; *Style*— John C McBride, Esq; 11 Chalcot Square, London NW1; AGB Publications Ltd, Audit House, Field End Road, Eastcote, Middx (☎ 081 868 4499)

McBRIEN, Michael Patrick; s of Leo Patrick McBrien (d 1969), and Elizabeth Rosemary, *née* Phillips; *b* 4 July 1935; *Educ* Stonyhurst Coll, St Thomas's Hosp, Univ of London (MB BS); *m* 11 July 1964, Tessa Ann Freeland, da of Col Richard Bayfield Freeland (d 1980), of Beccles, Suffolk; 2 s (James b 1968, Rowan b 1972), 1 da (Emma b 1966); *Career* registrar in surgery: Southampton Hosp, St Thomas' Hosp; sr registrar and lectr in surgery St Thomas' Hosp; sr conslt surgn: W Suffolk Hosp, Newmarket Hosp; Hunterian prof RCS, clinical teacher Univ of Cambridge; chm bd of govrs Moreton Hall prep Sch, memb bd of govrs St Edmund's Hosp; MS 1973; memb: BMA 1960-, RSM 1960; FRCS 1968; *Books* Postgraduate Surgery (1986); *Recreations* tennis, golf, squash, shooting, skiing, travel; *Clubs* RSM, MCC; *Style*— Michael McBrien, Esq; Stanton House, Norton, Bury St Edmunds, Suffolk IP31 3LQ (☎ 0359 30832); West Suffolk Hosp, Hardwick Lane, Bury St Edmunds, Suffolk (☎ 0284 763131)

McBRYDE, Prof William Wilson; s of William McBryde (d 1964), of Burntisland, Fife, and Marjory Wilson, *née* Husband; *b* 6 July 1945; *Educ* Perth Acad, Univ of Edinburgh (LLB), Univ of Glasgow (PhD); *m* 1, 4 Nov 1972 (m dis 1982), Elspeth Jean Stormont Glover; 1 s (Donald b 5 March 1976), 1 da (Eileen b 23 Feb 1974); m 2, 12 April 1986, Joyce Margaret, da of Rev James Marcus Gossip (d 1985), of Edinburgh; 1 da (Helen b 23 June 1988); *Career* apprentice with Morton Smart Macdonald & Milligan WS 1967-70; admitted slr 1969; court procurator Biggart Lumsden & Co Glasgow 1970-72, lectr in private law Univ of Glasgow 1972-76, sr lectr in private law Univ of Aberdeen 1976-87, specialist Parly advsr to House of Lords Select Ctee on Euro Communities 1980-83, dean Faculty of Law Univ of Dundee 1989-90 (prof of Scots law 1987-); dir Scot Univ Law Inst 1989-; memb: Scot Consumer Cncl 1984-87, Scot Advsy Ctee on Arbitration 1986-; *Books* Bankruptcy (Scotland) Act 1985 (1986), The Law of Contract in Scotland (1987), Petition Procedure in the Court of Session (2 edn, with N Dowie, 1988), Bankruptcy (1989); *Recreations* walking, photography; *Style*— Prof William McBryde; Faculty of Law, The University, Dundee DD1 4HN (☎ 0382 23181, fax 0382 26905, telex 76293)

MacCABE, Prof Colin Myles Joseph; s of Myles Joseph MacCabe, and Ruth Ward MacCabe; *b* 9 Feb 1949; *Educ* St Benedict's Sch Ealing London, Univ of Cambridge (BA, MA, PhD), Ecole Normale Supérieure; *m* 2 s, 1 da; *Career* univ asst lectr in English Univ of Cambridge and coll lectr and fell King's Coll Cambridge 1976-81, prof of English Univ of Strathclyde 1981-85 (chm Dept of English Studies 1982-84), visiting fell Griffith Univ Brisbane 1981 and 1984, memb English Teaching Advsy Ctee for Br Cncl 1983-85 (Br Cncl lectr Shanghai Foreign Language Inst 1984), chm John Logie Baird Centre for Res in TV and Film Univ of Strathclyde 1985 (founding dir 1983-85), visiting prof in Programme for Literacy Linguistics Univ of Strathclyde 1985-, Mellon visiting prof Univ of Pittsburgh 1985, head of prodn Br film Inst 1985-89, prof of English Univ of Pittsburgh 1986-, criticism ed Critical Quarterly 1987-, head of res Br Film Inst 1989-; *Books* James Joyce and the Revolution of The World (1979), Godard: Images, Sounds, Politics (1980), The Talking Cure: Essays in Psychoanalysis and Language (ed, 1981), James Joyce: New Perspectives (ed 1982), Theoretical Essays: film, linguistics, literature (1985), The BBC and Public Sector Broadcasting (jt ed, 1986), High Theory Low Culture: Analysing Popular Television and Film (ed, 1986), futures for English (ed, 1987), The Linguistics of Writing (jt ed,1988); *Recreations* eating, drinking, talking; *Style*— Prof Colin MacCabe; British Film Institute, Research Division, 21 Stephen Street, London W1P 1PL (☎ 071 255 1444)

McCABE, John; CBE (1985); s of Frank McCabe (d 1983), and Elisabeth Carmen, *née* Herlitzius; *b* 21 April 1939; *Educ* Liverpool Inst, Univ of Manchester (BMus), Royal Manchester Coll of Music (FRMCM), Hochschule für Musik Munich; *m* 1, (m dis 1973), Hilary Tann; m 2, 31 July 1974, Monica Christine, da of Jack Smith (d 1974); *Career* composer and pianist; res pianist Univ Coll Cardiff 1965-68, freelance music critic 1966-71, dir London Coll Music 1983-90; writer of operas, symphonies, concertos, choral and keyboard works, TV and film music; recent cmmnd works incl Rainforest II (Harrogate Festival 1987) and Fire at Durilgai (BBC Philharmonic Orch 1989); numerous recordings incl 16 record set complete piano works of Haydn; pres Inc Soc Musicians 1982-83, memb Hon Cncl Mgmnt RPS 1983-, chm Assoc Professional Composers 1985-86, memb Gen Cncl and Donations Ctee Performing Rights Soc 1985-88; vice pres: Malvern Music Club, Luton Music Club, Ruislip Gramophone Soc; memb: Wigmore Hall Board 1987-, Composers' Guild of GB, Mechanical Copyright Protection Soc, Nat Tst of Scotland, Musicians' Union, WWF; FLCM, FRCM, Hon RAM, FRNCM 1986, FTCL 1989; *Books* BBC Music Guide: Bartok's Orchestral Music (1974), Haydn's Piano Sonatas (1986); Gollancz Musical Companion (contrib, 1973), Novello Short Biography: Rachmaninov (1974); *Recreations* cinema, books, cricket, golf, (watching) snooker, bonfires (playing); *Style*— John McCabe, Esq, CBE; c/o Novello & Co Ltd (Music Publishers), 8 Lower James St, London W1 (☎ 071 287 5060, telex 95583 NOVELO G, fax 071 287 0816)

MacCABE, Michael Murray; s of Brian Farmer MacCabe, and Eileen Elizabeth Noel, *née* Hunter (d 1984); *b* 20 Nov 1944; *Educ* Downside, Lincoln Coll Oxford (1963-64); *m* 8 Aug 1969, Olga Marie (d 1985); 1 s (James Hunter b 1970), 1 da ((Alexandra) Kate b 1973); *Career* admitted slr 1969; managing ptnr: Freshfields 1985-90 (ptnr 1974-), Freshfields Paris 1981-84; dir Slrs Indemnity Mutual Insurance Association Ltd 1986-; memb Ctee City of London Slrs Co; FRSA; *Recreations* fishing, painting;

Style— Michael MacCabe, Esq; Freshfields, Whitefriars, Fleet St, London EC4

McCAFFER, Prof Ronald; s of John Gegg McCaffer (d 1984), and Catherine Turner, *née* Gourlay (d 1979); *b* 8 Dec 1943; *Educ* Univ of Strathclyde (BSc), Univ of Loughborough (PhD); *m* 13 Aug 1966, Margaret Elizabeth, da of Cyril Warner; 1 s (Andrew b 29 April 1977); *Career* design engr Babtie Shaw and Morton 1965-67; site engr: The Nuclear Power Gp 1967-69, Taylor Woodrow Construction 1969-70; Dept of Civil Engrg Univ of Loughborough: lectr 1970-78, sr lectr 1978-83, reader 1983-86, prof of construction mgmnt 1986-87, head of dept 1987-; FICE, FCIOB, MBIM; *Books* Worked Examples in Constrution Management (1986), Modern Construction Management (1989), Managing Construction Equipment (1991), Estimating and Tendering for Civil Engineering (1991); *Style*— Prof Ronald McCaffer; Dept of Civil Engineering, Loughborough University of Technology, Loughborough, Leicestershire LE11 3TU (☎ 0509 222600, fax 0509 610231, telex 0509 347282)

McCAFFREY, Sir Thomas Daniel (Tom); s of William P McCaffrey; *b* 20 Feb 1922; *Educ* Hyndland Secdy Sch, St Aloysius Coll Galsgow; *m* 1949, Agnes Campbell Douglas; 2 s, 4 da; *Career* served WWII RAF; Scottish Office 1948-61, chief info offr Home Office 1966-71, press sec 10 Downing St 1971-72, dir Info Servs Home Office 1972-74, head of News Dept FCO 1974-76, chief of staff to Rt Hon James Callaghan, MP 1979-80 (his chief press sec when he was PM 1976-79), chief asst to Rt Hon Michael Foot, MP 1980-; kt 1979; *Style*— Sir Tom McCaffrey; Balmaha, The Park, Great Bookham, Surrey (☎ 0372 54171)

McCALL, Christopher Hugh; QC (1987); s of Robin Home McCall, CBE, of Bernina, Northbrook Avenue, Winchester, and the late Joan Elizabeth, *née* Kingdon; *b* 3 March 1944; *Educ* Winchester, Magdalen Coll Oxford (BA); *m* 20 June 1981, Henrietta Francesca, 2 da of Adrian Leslie Sharpe, of Trebetherick, N Cornwall; *Career* called to the Bar Lincoln's Inn 1966, second jr counsel to Inland Revenue in chancery matters 1977-87, jr counsel to HM Attorney-Gen in charity matters 1981-87; jt hon treas Barristers' Benevolent Assoc 1981-86; *Recreations* mountains, music, travel; *Clubs* RAC, Leander; *Style*— C H McCall, Esq, QC; 29 Burgh Street, London N1 (☎ 071 226 4702); 7 New Square, Lincoln's Inn, London WC2A 3QS (☎ 071 405 1266)

McCALL, David Slesser; CBE (1988); s of Patrick McCall (d 1987), of Norwich, and Florence Kate Mary, *née* Walker; *b* 3 Dec 1934; *Educ* Robert Gordon Coll Aberdeen, Univ of Aberdeen; *m* 6 July 1968, (Lois) Patricia, da of Ernest Lonsdale Elder (d 1985), of Glasgow; *Career* Nat Serv RAF 1959-60; accountant Grampian TV Ltd 1961-68; Anglia TV Ltd: co sec 1968-76, dir 1970, chief exec 1976-86; fndr dir Channel 4 TV Co Ltd 1981-85; gp chief exec Anglia TV Gp plc 1986-, chm Independent TV Assoc 1986-88, dir Br Satellite Broadcasting Ltd 1987-90; hon vice-pres Norwich City FC 1988, dir Eastern Advsy Bd Nat West Bank 1988, pres Norfolk & Norwich C of C 1988-90 (vice pres 1984, dep pres 1986); MICAS 1958, FRTS 1988, CBIM 1988; *Recreations* golf, tennis, skiing, soccer, travel; *Clubs* Norfolk (Norwich); *Style*— David McCall, Esq, CBE; Woodland Hall, Redenhall, Harleston, Norfolk IP20 9QW (☎ 0379 854442); Anglia House, Norwich, Norfolk NR1 3JG (☎ 0603 615151, fax 0603 623081, telex 97424, car ☎ 0836 235 285)

McCALL, Hon Mrs; (Gillian Patricia Denman); da of 5 Baron Denman, CBE, MC; *b* 1944; *m* 1971, William K McCall; 2 s, 1 da; *Style*— The Hon Mrs McCall; Upper Old Park Farm, Farnham, Surrey

McCALL, John Armstrong Grice; CMG (1964); s of Rev Canon James George McCall (d 1954), of St Andrews, and Mabel Lovat Armstrong (d 1917); gggs of John McCall of Glasgow, one of fndrs of Thistle Bank in 1761; *b* 7 Jan 1913; *Educ* Glenalmond, Univ of St Andrews (MA), Univ of Cambridge; *m* 1951, Kathleen Mary, DL (Tweeddale 1987-), da of Arthur Clarke (d 1936); *Career* Colonial Admin Service (HMOCS) Nigeria 1936-67 (Class I 1956, Staff Grade 1958), chm Mid West Nigerian Corp 1966-67, asst chief admin offr East Kilbride Devpt Corp 1967-77, Scottish rep Exec Ctee Nigeria Br C of C 1977-88; memb: Panel Industl Tribunals (Scotland) 1972-74, Central Cncl Britain Nigeria Assoc 1983-; gen sec for Scotland Royal Overseas League 1978-80, sec West Linton Community Cncl 1980-83; *Recreations* golf, walking; *Clubs* Caledonian, Royal and Ancient (St Andrews), Royal Over-Seas League (hon life memb); *Style*— J A G McCall, Esq, CMG; Burnside, W Linton, Scotland EH46 7EW (☎ 0968 60488)

McCALL, John Kingdon; s of Robin Home McCall, CBE, of Winchester, and Joan Elizabeth, *née* Kingdon; *b* 28 July 1938; *Educ* Winchester; *m* 20 April 1963, Anne Margaret, da of Dr Harry Kirby Meller, MBE (d 1965); 2 s (Patrick b 1964, William b 1971), 1 da (Claire b 1966); *Career* slr; ptnr Freshfields 1969-, seconded to Head of Legal Dept The Br Nat Oil Corpn 1976-79, sr res ptnr Freshfields NY 1983-87, chm Int Bar Assoc's Section on Energy and Nat Resources Law 1988-90; memb: Law Soc, Int Bar Assoc; *Recreations* real tennis, road running, sea birds; *Clubs* Racquet and Tennis (NY); *Style*— John K McCall, Esq; Freshfields, Whitefriars, 65 Fleet St, London EC4Y 1HT (☎ 071 936 4000, fax 071 832 7001)

McCALL, Sir (Charles) Patrick Home; MBE (1944), TD (1946); s of Charles William Home McCall, CBE (d 1958), and Dorothy Margaret, *née* Kidd; *b* 22 Nov 1910; *Educ* St Edward's Sch Oxford; *m* 1934, Anne, da of late Samuel Brown, of Sedlescombe, Sussex; 2 s, 1 da; *Career* served WWII ADOS SEAC; admitted slr 1936; last clerk of the peace Lancs 1960-71, clerk of the CC 1960-72, clerk of the Lieutenancy Lancs 1960-74; kt 1971; *Recreations* gardening, walking, swimming, travel; *Style*— Sir Patrick McCall, MBE, TD; Auchenhay Lodge, Corsock, by Castle Douglas, Kirkcudbrightshire, Scotland DG7 3HZ (☎ 064 44 651)

McCALL, Robert Henry; s of William McCall (d 1937), and Anna Laurie (d 1937); *b* 15 Nov 1931; *Educ* Woodside Sr Secdy Sch Glasgow; *m* 4 Sept 1954, Grace, da of George Robinson (d 1958); 2 s (Laurie Allan b 1956, Roderick Robert b 1960); *Career* whisky broker and distiller; dir: Whyte & Mackay Distillers Ltd (parent company), Dalmore Whyte & Mackay Ltd, Whyte & Mackay Ltd, W & S Strong Ltd, Hay & Macleod Ltd, The Tomintoul-Glenlivet Distillery Ltd, Fettercairn Distillery Ltd, Jarvis Halliday & Co Ltd, Lycidas (109); *Recreations* golf, snooker, horse racing; *Clubs* Glasgow Golf; *Style*— Robert McCall, Esq; 20 Herries Rd, Glasgow, Scotland G41 4DF (☎ 041 423 4683); Whyte & Mackay Distillers Limited, Dalmore House, 296/298 St Vincent St, Glasgow G2 5RG (☎ 041 248 5771, fax : 041 221 1993)

McCALL, Robin Home; CBE (1976, OBE 1969); s of Charles William Home McCall, CBE (d 1958), of Chislehurst, Kent, and Dorothy Margaret, *née* Kidd (d 1966); *b* 21 March 1912; *Educ* St Edward's Sch Oxford, Law Soc Sch London; *m* 9 Oct 1937, Joan Elizabeth (d 1989), da of H F Kingdon (d 1922), of Woking; 2 s (John Kingdon, Christopher Hugh, QC, *qv*), 1 da (Elizabeth, (Mrs Peternal Wells), MBE); *Career* RAFVR 1941-46, Sqdn Ldr (D Day Normandy i/c 15083 Night Fighter GC Station), ret 1946; admitted slr 1935, town clerk City of Winchester 1948-72; sec AMA 1973-76, memb various govt ctees, govr St Swithuns Sch Winchester 1977-87, sole contrib "Local Government" Halsbury Laws of England (4 edn, 1980); Hon Freeman City of Winchester; *Recreations* gardens, mountains; *Clubs* Alpine; *Style*— Robin McCall, Esq, CBE; Bernina, Northbrook Ave, Winchester, Hants (☎ 0962854 101)

McCALL, William; s of Alexander McCall, and Jean Corbet, *née* Cunningham; *b* 6 July 1929; *Educ* Dumfries Acad, Ruskin Coll Oxford; *m* 3 Sept 1955, Olga Helen, da of William Brunton; 1 s (Martin b 1960), 1 da (Ruth b 1957); *Career* civil servant 1946-52, TUC 1954-58, gen sec Inst of Professional Civil Servants 1963-89 (asst sec 1958-63), vice chm Civil Serv Nat Whitley Cncl 1983 (memb 1963-89), hon treas Parly and Sci Ctee 1976-80, memb Ctee of Inquiry into Engrg Profession 1977-79, memb: (pt/t) Eastern Electricity Bd 1977-86, TUC Gen Cncl 1984-89, Ct Univ of London 1984-, Cncl Goldsmiths Coll 1989-, Pay and Employment Policy Ctee CVCP 1990-; *Style*— William McCall, Esq; Foothills, Gravel Path, Berkhamsted, Herts HP4 2PF (☎ 0442 864794)

McCALL-SMITH, Dr Alexander; s of Rodney Alexander McCall-Smith, of Trafalgar Cottage, Chart Sutton, Kent, and Daphne Evelyn, *née* Woodall (d 1979); *b* 24 Aug 1948; *Educ* Christian Brothers' Coll Bulawayo Zimbabwe, Univ of Edinburgh (LLB, PhD); *m* 4 Sept 1982, Dr Elizabeth Parry, da of Dr Richard Parry, of 12 Henderland Rd, Edinburgh; 2 da (Lucy Ishbel b 26 March 1984, Emily Rose b 15 Oct 1986); *Career* sr lectr in law Univ of Edinburgh 1988- (lectr 1974-88); visiting prof Southern Methodist Univ Dallas 1988; *Books* childrens' books: The White Hippo (1980), The Little Theatre (1981), The Perfect Hamburger (1982), On the Road (1987), Mike's Magic Seeds (1988), Alix and the Tigers (1988), Film Boy (1988), Uncle Gangster (1989), Suzy Magician (1990), Akimbo and the Elephants (1990), The Ice Cream Bicycle (1990), Jeffrey's Joke Machine (1990), The Five Lost Aunts of Harrier Bean (1990); legal books: Law and Medical Ethics (1984), Butterworths Medico Legal Encyclopaedia (1987); adult fiction: Children of Wax (1989); *Clubs* Scottish Arts; *Style*— Dr Alexander McCall-Smith; 16A Napier Rd, Edinburgh EH10 5AY (☎ 031 229 6083)

McCALLUM, Andrew Wilkie; s of Andrew Wilkie McCallam (d 1972), and Ella, *née* Bond; *b* 20 Oct 1936; *Educ* Allan Glen's Glasgow, Univ of Glasgow (MA); *m* 9 Feb 1962, Wendy, da of Edwin Hill; 1 s (Calum Andrew b 1967), 2 da (Mairi b 1962, Morag b 1964); *Career* lectr Glasgow Coll 1969-72, sr lectr James Watt Coll 1972-77, head of gen educn Falkirk Coll 1977-86, dep princ Aur Coll 1986-89; vice chm Scottish Youth Theatre 1982-; *Recreations* skiing, hill walking, music, theatre; *Style*— Andrew McCallum, Esq; John Wheatley College, 1346 Shettleston Rd, Glasgow (☎ 041 778 2426, fax 041 763 2384)

McCALLUM, Anthony Colin; s of Colin McCallum and Serena Enid, *née* Tylden; *b* 8 March 1947; *Educ* Radley; *m* 16 June 1972, Lady Charlotte Mary Cathcart, yr da of Maj-Gen 6 Earl Cathcart, CB, DSO, MC, *qv*; 2 s (Charles Colin b 1973, Anthony James b 1977), 1 da (Sophie Charlotte b 1975); *Career* Capt The Queen's Dragoon Gds 1966-76, served Aden, W Germany, Berlin, N Ireland, Argentina; dir: CT Bowring Reinsurance Ltd 1986, Guy Carpenter and Company Inc 1990-; insur broker and underwriter Lloyds; *Style*— Anthony McCallum, Esq; Week Green Farm, Froxfield, Petersfield, Hants; CT Bowring & Co, Tower Place, London EC3

McCALLUM, Hon Mrs (Celia Yvonne Lovett); *née* de Villiers; da of Baron de Villiers, of Wynberg, Cape Town, S Africa; *b* 7 Nov 1942; *Educ* Herschel Claremont Cape Town, Univ of Cape Town, Royal Northern Hosp London; *m* 1, 23 March 1968 (m dis 1978), Robin Hastings Sancroft Beck, s of (Harold) Hastings Beck, of St James, SA, and Mrs G G Denoon, of Rondebosch Cape Town, SA; 2 s, 1 da; m 2, 1979, Alan McCallum; 1 da; *Style*— The Hon Mrs McCallum

MacCALLUM, Prof Charles Hugh Alexander; s of Alister Hugh MacCallum (d 1955), of Perth, and Jessie MacLean, *née* Forsyth (d 1987); *b* 24 June 1935; *Educ* Hutchesons' GS Glasgow, Glasgow Sch of Architecture (BArch), MIT (MCP); *m* 27 Aug 1963, Andrée Simone, da of Rémond Jean René Tonnard (d 1986), of Brest, France; 2 da (Joëlle b 1964, Sophie b 1965); *Career* architect; Gillespie Kidd and Coia Glasgow 1957-67; Univ Coll Dublin Sch of Architecture: lectr 1970-73, exec dir 1973-74; private practice 1974-, chair of architectural design Univ of Wales 1985-; memb: Soc of Protection of Ancient Bldgs, Garden History Soc; commissaire of the bicentenary exhibition on Louis Viscontie Paris 1991; RIBA 1961, ARIAS 1986; *Recreations* gardening, watercolours; *Style*— Prof Charles MacCallum; 11A Charlbury Rd, Oxford OX2 6UT

McCALLUM, Lady Charlotte Mary; *née* Cathcart; yr da of 6 Earl Cathcart, CB, DSO, MC, *qv*; *b* 29 Oct 1951; *Educ* Woldingham; *m* 16 June 1972, Anthony Colin McCallum, *qv*; 2 s, 1 da; *Style*— The Lady Charlotte McCallum; Week Green Farm, Froxfield, Hants

McCALLUM, (Andrew) Graham Stewart; CBE (1975); s of H G McCallum (d 1975); *b* 1 April 1926; *Educ* Glenalmond, Pembroke Coll Oxford (MA); *m* 1952, Margaret; 1 da, 2 s; *Career* RAF 1944-47, Pilot Offr; pres John Swire & Sons (Japan) Ltd 1972-78, dir James Finlay plc 1979-, advsr to Bd John Swire & Sons Ltd 1988- (dir 1979-88); chm: British C of C in Japan 1975-76, Japan Assoc 1982-88; vice chm Japan Festival 1991; *Recreations* golf, tennis; *Clubs* Royal Ashdown Golf, Boodles; *Style*— Graham McCallum, Esq, CBE; Medleys Farm, High Hurstwood, nr Uckfield, E Sussex (☎ 082 581 2470); John Swire & Sons Ltd, 59 Buckingham Gate, London SW1

McCALLUM, Prof (Robert) Ian; CBE (1987); s of Charles Hunter McCallum (d 1958), and Janet Lyon, *née* Smith (d 1980); *b* 14 Sept 1920; *Educ* Dulwich, Guy's Hosp and Univ of London (MD, DSc); *m* 28 June 1952, Jean Katherine Bundy, da of Sir James Rögnvald Learmonth, KCVO, CBE (d 1967), of Edinburgh; 2 s (James b 1958, Andrew b 1966), 2 da (Helen b 1956, Mary b 1963); *Career* Rockefeller travelling fell USA 1953-54; Univ of Newcastle upon Tyne: reader in industl health 1962-81, prof of occupational health and hygiene 1981-85; conslt Inst of Occupational Med Edinburgh 1985-; chm Decompression Sickness Panel MRC 1982-85 (memb 1962-), ed Br Journal of Industl Med 1972-79, memb Advsy Ctee on Pesticides 1975-87; pres: Soc of Occupational Medicine 1979-80, Br Occupational Hygiene Soc 1983-84; hon conslt Br Army 1980-85, dean Faculty of Occupational Med RCP London 1984-86; FRCP London 1970, FFOM 1979, FRCPE 1985; *Recreations* gardening; *Clubs* RSM, Edinburgh Univ Staff; *Style*— Prof Ian McCallum, CBE; 4 Chessel's Court, Canongate, Edinburgh EH8 8AD (☎ 031 556 7977); Inst of Occupational Medicine, Roxburgh Place, Edinburgh EH8 9SU (☎ 031 667 5131)

MCCALLUM, Ian Stewart; s of John Blair McCallum (d 1972), and Margaret Stewart, *née* Hannah (d 1989); *b* 24 Sept 1936; *Educ* Kingston GS; *m* 1, 26 Oct 1957 (m dis 1984), Pamela Mary, da of James Herbert Shave; 1 s (Andrew Stewart b 12 Sept 1958), 2 da (Sheila Anne (Mrs Curling) b 8 July 1960, Heather Jean (Mrs Drury) b 26 June 1963); m 2, 15 Sept 1984, Jean, da of Patrick Wittingstall Lynch, of 95 Oakwood Rd, Bricket Wood, Herts; 2 step da (Michelle b 6 Feb 1971, Donna b 8 May 1974); *Career* Highland LI 1954-56, Eagle Star Insurance Co Ltd 1953-54 and 1956-58, FE Wright & Co 1958-63, M Clarkson Home Ltd 1963-68, currently exec sales mangr Save & Prosper Group Ltd (joined 1968); Mayor Woking Borough Cncl 1976-77 (ldr 1972-76 and 1978-81, dep ldr 1981-84); hon vice pres Woking Cons Assoc 1976-, chm Assoc of DCs 1979-84 (ldr 1976-79); pres Woking Swimming Club 1977-84; vice chm: UK Steering Ctee on Local Authy Superannuation 1974-84, Standing Ctee Local Authys & the Theatre 1977-81, The Sports Cncl 1980-86; memb: Consultative Cncl on Local Govt Fin 1975-84, Local Authys Conditions of Serv Advsy Bd 1978-84, Cncl for Business & the Community 1981-84, Audit Cmmn 1983-86, Health Promotion Res Tst 1983-; LIA; *Recreations* swimming, jogging, walking, reading; *Style*— Ian McCallum, Esq; 5 Minters Orchard, Maidstone Rd, St Marys Platt, nr Sevenoaks, Kent TN15 8QJ (☎ 0732 883653); Save & Prosper Group Ltd, Alhambra House, 27 Charing Cross Rd, London (☎ 071 839 4631)

McCALLUM, John (Ian); s of Hugh McCallum (d 1978), of Old Kilpatrick,

Dunbartonshire, and Agnes Falconer Wood, *née* Walker (d 1983); *b* 13 Oct 1920; *Educ* Allan Glen's Sch Glasgow, Univ of Glasgow (BSc); *m* 19 June 1948, Christine Peggy (d 1989), da of Thomas Edwin Sowden (d 1973), of Paignton, Devon; 2 s (Hugh b 1951, Angus b 1953); *Career* asst lectr in naval architecture and marine engineering Univ of Glasgow 1943-44; Lloyd's Register of Shipping: ship surveyor Newcastle-upon-Tyne 1944-49, ship surveyor Glasgow 1949-53, sr ship surveyor with roving trouble-shooting cmmn (London HQ) 1953-60; recalled to John Brown & Co Clydebank (his apprenticeship co) as chief naval architect and tech dir 1960-70; chief designer of QE2, Kungsholm (now Sea Princess) and other large ships; recalled to Lloyd's Register of Shipping London as chief ship surveyor 1970-81 (supervising design approval, construction, maintenance, repair, research and development of 11,700 ships in all maritime nations); conslt naval architect 1981-; author of over 40 technical papers in learned jls; Freeman City of London 1975, Liveryman Worshipful Co of Shipwrights 1975 (memb Educn Ctee 1976-); FEng 1977, FRINA (past chm, now vice-pres), FICE (life fell 1978), 1 cncl memb Smeatonian Soc of Civil Engrs 1979, life fell SNAME (NY) 1981, medallist of ATMA Paris 1978, MIES 1962; over 40 technical papers in learned journals; *Recreations* golf, piano, crayon painting; *Clubs* Caledonian Westminster Business; *Style—* Ian McCallum, Esq; Dala, Garvock Drive, Kippington, Sevenoaks, Kent TN13 2LT (☎ 0732 455462)

MACCALLUM, Dr Norman Ronald Low; s of Neil Maccallum (d 1956), and Janet Jane, *née* Aitkenhead (d 1983); *b* 18 Feb 1931; *Educ* Allan Glen's Sch, Univ of Glasgow (BSc, PhD); *m* 23 June 1964, Mary Bentley, da of William Alexander (d 1977); 1 s (Andrew b 22 Aug 1971), 2 da (Moira b 24 July 1967, Catriona b 12 July 1969); *Career* Nat Serv RN 1955-57, Sub Lt RNVR 1956-61; Dept Mechanical Engrg Univ of Glasgow: lectr 1957-61 and 1962-72, sr lectr 1972-82, reader 1982-; performance engr Rolls-Royce Ltd 1961-62, conslt engr to various co's 1963-, expert witness in legal cases 1967-; numerous contribs to jls and confs; elder in local church Trinity Cambuslang (now Trinity St Paul's Cambuslang) 1967- (session clerk 1979-); FIMechE 1979 (memb 1968); *Recreations* singing; *Clubs* Royal Scottish Automobile; *Style—* Dr Norman Maccallum; 43 Stewarton Drive, Cambuslang, Glasgow, Scotland G72 8DQ (☎ 041 641 3402); Dept of Mechanical Engineering, University of Glasgow, Glasgow G12 8QQ (☎ 041 339 8855 ext 4320, fax 041 330 4343)

McCALMONT, Hugh Dermot; s of Maj Dermot Hugh Bingham McCalmont, MC (d 1968), of Mount Juliet, Thomastown, Co Kilkenny, and June Patteson, *née* Nickalls (d 1983); *b* 23 Jan 1942; *Educ* Uppingham; *m* 19 Aug 1963, Gillian Mary, da of Andrew Levins Moore, of Yeomanstown, Naas, Co Kildare; 1 s (Jamie b 20 June 1968), 1 da (Zara b 28 July 1964); *Career* asst trainer to Bryan Marshall, Tom Jones and Paddy O'Gorman, leading amateur rider in England, Ireland and Kenya 1959-64, proprietor to D Gilbert and Sons Saddlers Newmarket (Royal Warrant Holder to HM The Queen 1964-74), md Bloodstock and Gen Insurance 1968-74, fndr memb Bloodstock and Racehorse Industs Consideration 1974, breeder of race horses; memb Race Horse Owners Cncl 1977-; Freeman: City of London 1966, Worshipful Company of Saddlers; *Recreations* hunting, shooting, gardening, horseracing; *Clubs* Turf, Jockey, Rooms; *Style—* Hugh McCalmont, Esq; St Agnes Cottage, Bury Rd, Newmarket, Suffolk CB8 7BT (☎ 0638 662072); Yeomanstown Lodge, Naas, Co Kildare; Tramuntana, Sa Coma, Andraitx, Mallorca (☎ 010 3471 671199)

McCALMONT, Michael Robert; s of Maj Dermot Hugh Bingham McCalmont (d 1968), of Mount Juliet, Thomastown, Co Kilkenny, Eire, and June Patteson, *née* Nickalls (d 1983); *b* 13 June 1946; *Educ* Maidwell Hall, Eton; *m* 8 Oct 1977, Harriet Jane, da of Maj-Gen John Myles Brockbank, CBE, MC, DL, of Manor House, Steeple Langford, Salisbury, Wilts; 1 s (Arthur James b 15 Feb 1984), 1 da (Katherine Rose b 3 June 1981); *Career* md Bingham Land Co Ltd 1972-; *Recreations* riding, shooting, skiing; *Style—* Michael McCalmont, Esq; 16 Bramerton St, London SW3 5JX; Winton House, Hampstead Norreys, Newbury, Berks RG16 0TF (☎ 0635 201538)

McCANCE, (John) Neill; s of Henry Bristow McCance, CBE (d 1977), and Francis May McCance (d 1976); the family has been involved in banking and the linen industry in NI since early eighteenth century; John McCance was MP for Belfast 1835; *b* 6 Aug 1928; *Educ* Radley, Lincoln Coll Oxford MA; *Career* barr Inner Temple; stockbroker with Vickers da Costa Ltd 1954-86; memb: Stock Exchange 1955, Cncl of Stock Exchange 1982-84 (Cncl's Membership, Settlement Servs and Disciplinary Ctees); dir Worldwide Special Fund; dep chm Allside Asset Management Co Ltd 1986; *Recreations* shooting, fishing, travel, music; *Clubs* Brooks's, 1900; *Style—* Neill McCance, Esq; Flat 8, 6 Tedworth Sq, London SW3 4DY; Allside Asset Management Co Ltd, 7 Old Park Lane, London W1Y 3LJ (☎ 071 629 2714, telex 295554)

McCANN, Christopher Conor; s of Noel McCann, and Katharine Joan, *née* Sultzberger; *b* 26 June 1947; *Educ* Downside, Clare Coll Cambridge (MA); *m* 1 June 1974, Merlyn Clare Winbolt, da of Dr Francis Lewis, of Osborne House, Falloden Way, Bristol; 1 s (Edward), 2 da (Kate, Eleanor); *Career* Price Waterhouse and Co 1969-73, asst dir Barclays Merchant Bank 1973-82, sr vice pres Barclays Bank plc NY 1983-87; dir: County Natwest Ventures Ltd 1987-, County Natwest Ltd 1987-; non exec dir: Aynsley Group Ltd 1988-, Redifon Holdings Ltd 1988-, Maritime Transport Services Ltd 1990-, British Air Ferries 1990-; FCA 1969, ACIB 1978; *Recreations* skiing, sailing, travel; *Style—* Christopher McCann, Esq; 10 Lonsdale Sq, London N1 1EN (☎ 071 607 8546); The Old Rectory, Ibberton, Dorset; County Natwest Ltd, 135 Bishopsgate, London EC2M 3UR (☎ 071 375 5102, fax 071 375 6262, telex 882121)

MCCANN, Michael Denis; s of Walter McCann, of The Cottages, Toft-Newton, Lincs, and May, *née* Tindall; *b* 31 March 1948; *Educ* Greatfields Sch Yorks, Hull Univ (BSc); *m* 28 June 1975, Anne Jennifer, da of Wing-Cdr Alan James Bannister (ret), of Nightingale Cottage, Rickmansworth, Herts; 1 da (Penelope Olivia); *Career* gp treas: Grand Met plc 1988-, Trafalgar House plc 1986-88, Ford Motor Co Ltd 1983-86, Ford of Europe Inc 1970-83; dir: Grand Met Fin plc 1988-, Grand Met Investmts Ltd 1988-, Grand Met Int Fin plc 1988-, Grand Met Hotel and Catering Ltd 1988-, Cappoquin Securities Ltd 1988-, Rachel Securities 1988-, Stag Insur Co Ltd, City Corp Treas Cnslts Ltd; Fell Assoc of Corp Treasurers 1983; *Recreations* shooting, fishing, rugby; *Clubs* RAC; *Style—* Michael McCann, Esq; Giffords Farm, Rettendon, Essex (☎ 0261 710 383); 11-12 Hanover Square, London W1A 1DP (☎ 071 629 7488, fax 071 408 1246, car 0860 746870, telex 299606)

McCANN, Peter Toland McAree; CBE (1977), JP (1967), DL (1977); s of Peter Toland McAree McCann, MSM (d 1943), of Glasgow, and Agnes Kennedy, *née* Waddell (d 1978); *b* 2 Aug 1924; *Educ* St Mungo's Acad Glasgow, Univ of Glasgow (BL); *m* 25 Nov 1958, Maura Eleanor Ferris, JP, da of Patrick Ferris (d 1959), of Causeway End, Lisburn, NI; 1 s (Peter Toland McAree b 13 Oct 1968); *Career* admitted slr 1947; cnclir Glasgow 1961, magistrate Glasgow 1962-66, Lord Provost of Glasgow 1975-77; NP, OStJ 1977; Medal of King Faisal Saudi Arabia 1976, three Golden Swords and one Silver Sword Saudi Arabia 1975-77; *Recreations* model soldiers, model aeroplanes, model railway, history, music; *Style—* Peter McCann, Esq, CBE, JP, DL; Craig-en-Ross, Queen Mary Ave, Crosshill, Glasgow; Peter T McCann & Co, Solicitors, 90 Mitchell St, Glasgow (☎ 041 221 1429 2725)

McCARRAHER, Hon Mrs (Belinda Jane); *née* Siddeley; only da of 3 Baron Kenilworth (d 1981); *b* 11 Jan 1950; *Educ* Downham Sch; *m* 1, 1971 (m dis 1974), Christopher Aston James; m 2, 1982, David Ian McCarraher, step s of His Hon Judge McCarraher, VRD, *qv*; 1 da (Tara Louise b 30 Dec 1989); *Career* gift shop owner in Richmond; *Recreations* relaxing with friends, holidaying in France; *Style—* The Hon Mrs McCarraher; Silver Coppers, College Road, Epsom, Surrey (☎ 0372 720601)

McCARRAHER, His Hon Judge David; VRD (1964); s of Colin McCarraher (d 1960); *b* 6 Nov 1922; *Educ* King Edward VI Sch Southampton, Magdalene Coll Cambridge; *m* 1950, Betty, *née* Haywood (d 1990); 2 da (Vera, Jane), 1 step s (*see* Hon Mrs McCarraher), 1 step da (Anne); *Career* WWII Indian Ocean NW Europe, Capt RNR 1969, CO Solent Div (HMS Wessex) 1969-72, ADC to HM The Queen 1972-73; called to the Bar Lincoln's Inn, ad eundum Western Circuit 1948-52, admitted slr 1955, rec Crown Ct 1979-84, circuit judge 1984-; *Recreations* family, golf, sailing; *Clubs* Stoneham Golf, Royal Naval Sailing Assoc, Naval; *Style—* His Hon Judge McCarraher, VRD; Guildhall Broad St, Bristol BS1 2HL

McCARTER, Keith Ian; s of Maj Peter McCarter (d 1971), of Edinburgh, and Hilda Mary, *née* Gates; *b* 15 March 1936; *Educ* The Royal HS of Edinburgh, Edinburgh Coll of Art; *m* 5 Jan 1963, Brenda Maude Edith, da of James A Schofield (d 1974), of Langley, Bucks; 1 s (Andrew Keith b 1968), 1 da (Alix-Jane b 1966); *Career* Nat Serv RA 1954-56; sculptor; primarily involved in architectural and landscaped situations; numerous cmmns incl: Ordnance Survey HQ Southampton 1967, Lagos Nigeria 1974, Wingate Centre City of London 1980, Goodmans Yard City of London 1982, 1020 19th Street Washington DC 1983, American Express Bank City of London 1984, Guys Hosp NCC London 1986, Royal Exec Park NY 1986, Evelyn Gdns London 1987, London Docklands 1988, Midland Bank London 1989, Vogans Mill London 1989, Moody Gardens Galveston Texas USA (with Sir Geoffrey Jellicoe); works in private collections world-wide; FRSA 1970; *Recreations* music, literature, beachcombing; *Clubs* Farmers; *Style—* Keith McCarter, Esq; Ottermead, Church Rd, Great Plumstead, Norfolk NR13 5AB (☎ 0603 713001)

McCARTHY, Daniel Peter Justin; TD (1978, and Bar 1984); s of Thomas Joseph McCarthy, GM, of Bootle, and Margaret Mary Josephine, *née* Bowden; *b* 4 July 1939; *Educ* St Mary's Coll Crosby, Univ of Aberdeen (MB ChB), Coll of Law London; *m* 1977, Dr Bronwen Elizabeth Knight Teresa, da of Richard Knight Evans, of Wimbledon; 5 s (Oliver, Richard (twins), Simon, Philip, Nicholas); *Career* cmmnd 3 Bn The Gordon Highlanders 1964, MO 4 (V) Bn Royal Green Jackets 1982-, Maj RAMC (TA); called to the Bar Inner Temple 1978; med practitioner; HM dep coroner: City of London 1979-88, Inner W London 1980-; divnl surgn St John Ambulance, med offr Royal Home and Hosp at Putney 1986-91; Freeman City of London 1975, Liveryman Worshipful Soc of Apothecaries 1974; kt Sovereign Military Order of Malta 1985; FSA Scot; Cross of Merit with Swords (pro meritor melitensi) 1988; *Recreations* running, jumping, standing still; *Clubs* Cavalry and Guards, Green Jackets; *Style—* Dr D P J McCarthy, TD, FSA; 23 Grandison Road, London SW11 6LS; 328 Clapham Rd, London SW9 9AE (☎ 071 622 2006)

McCARTHY, David; s of John Francis McCarthy, of 2 Watercall Ave, Styvechale, Coventry, Warwickshire, and Ivy Eileen, *née* Davies; *b* 27 Jan 1942; *Educ* Ratcliffe Coll Syston Leics, Univ of Birmingham (LLB); *m* 2 s (Gavin Stephen b 19 Feb 1972, Nicholas James b 17 May 1974); *Career* slr articled with Wragge & Co, Birmingham; joined Coward Chance 1976 (ptnr 1978), ptnr Clifford Chance; dir: Mithras Ltd, Mithras Nominees Ltd, St George's Hill Residents Assoc Ltd; memb City of London Law Soc Co Law Sub Ctee; *Recreations* fly fishing, tennis, cricket, books; *Clubs* Richmond Cricket, St George's Hill Tennis, Loch Achonachie Angling; *Style—* David McCarthy, Esq; La Pineta, East Rd, St George's Hill, Weybridge, Surrey; Royex House, Aldermanbury Sq, London EC2V 7LD (☎ 071 600 0808)

MacCARTHY, Fiona; da of Lt-Col Gerald MacCarthy (d 1943), and Yolande, *née* de Belabre; *b* 23 Jan 1940; *Educ* Wycombe Abbey Sch, Oxford Univ (MA); *m* 19 Aug 1966, David, s of Colin Mellor (d 1969); 1 s (Corin b 1966), 1 da (Clare b 1970); *Career* dir of exhibitions: Homespun Highspeed (Sheffield City Art Galleries) 1979, Omega Workshops (Decorative Arts of Bloomsbury Crafts Cncl) 1984, Eye For Indust (V & A Museum) 1987; hon fell RCA London 1989, Royal Soc of Arts Bicentenary Medal 1987; *Books* All Things Bright and Beautiful (1972), The Simple Life: C R Ashbee in the Cotswolds (1981), British Design since 1880 (1982), Eric Gill (1989); *Style—* Ms Fiona MacCarthy; The Round Building, Hathersage, Sheffield S30 1AZ (☎ 0433 50220)

MCCARTHY, John; *b* 8 May 1965; *Educ* Pembroke Secdy Modern Sch, Amersham Coll of Higher Educn, Barnet Coll of Higher Educn (and Middx Poly, HND in graphic design); *Career* jr designer The Red Box Design Co 1985-86, sr designer Creative Direction Ltd 1986-87, fndr and creative princ dir J M Design House Ltd 1987-91, ptnr and dir (head of design) The Creative Direction Partnership Ltd 1991-; winner Br Design award (for extensive work on Autoroute Plus, packaging and print support) 1990; *Recreations* classic cars, music, restaurants; *Style—* John McCarthy, Esq; The Creative Direction Partnership Ltd (Trading as Creative Direction), 16-17 Little Portland St, London W1 (☎ 071 436 7565, fax 071 636 5833)

McCARTHY, Rory Clement; s of Michael Joseph McCarthy, of Gable Lodge, The Bishop's Ave, London N2 0BA, and Marcia, *née* Cortoubelides; *b* 25 June 1960; *Educ* St Benedict's Sch; *m* 6 June 1987, Elizabeth Lucy, da of Keith Elliot Way, of Little Brook, Mid-Holmwood Lane, Dorking, Surrey; 1 s (Cameron Michael Gildart b 23 March 1989); *Career* institutional sales exec W I Carr Sons and Co 1984-86, mangr Swiss Bank Corpn Int 1987-88, exec dir and head of global sales Asia Equity (UK) Ltd (formerly First Pacific Securities (UK) Ltd) 1988-; world record holder for: greatest descent by hang glider 34500 feet 19 June 1984, greatest freefall parachute altitude by a civilian 33400 feet from 35600 feet; memb Br Parachuting Assoc; *Recreations* hot air ballooning, aerobatics, skydiving; *Clubs* Raffles, Mark's Annabel's; *Style—* Rory McCarthy, Esq; 5 Hambledon Place, Dulwich, London SE21 7EY (☎ 071 229 3426); Asia Equity (UK) Ltd, Sun Court, 66-67 Cornhill, London EC3V 3NB (☎ 071 929 4026, fax 929 782 0328, telex 928380 FPSEC G, car 0836 249493)

McCARTHY, Terence David; s of Patrick Terence McCarthy and Sheila Mary, BA, *née* Jackson (d 1989); *b* 5 May 1954; *Educ* Haileybury, Oxford Univ (MA); *Career* managing editor The Coat of Arms; Bluemantle Pursuivant of Arms 1983-; Freeman City of London; divnl pres Essex St John Ambulance; *Recreations* painting, reading, generally trying to avoid ignorance in the arts; *Clubs* Norfolk; *Style—* Terence McCarthy, Esq, Bluemantle Pursuivant of Arms; The Old Vicarage, Cornish Hall End, Finchingfield, Essex (☎ 079 986 368); College of Arms, Queen Victoria St, London EC4V 4BT (☎ 071 236 2749/071 248 2762)

McCARTHY, Thomas Martin; s of Patrick McCarthy (d 1977), of Cappoquin, Co Waterford, Eire, and Helena, *née* Tobin (d 1979); *b* 6 March 1954; *Educ* St Anne's Cappoquin Co Waterford, Univ Coll Cork; *m* 22 July 1982, Catherine, da of T J Coakley, of Mallow, Co Cork; 1 s (Neil Patrick b 13 July 1988), 1 da (Kate Inez b 30 March 1985); *Career* librarian Cork City Libraries 1978-; former ed Poetry Ireland Review, currently poetry ed Stet Magazine; US lectr tour for Irish American Cultural Inst 1990, writer-in-res Combined Univs of Minneapolis St Paul US 1990; poet and author of: The First Convention (1978), The Sorrow-Garden (1981), The Non-Aligned Storyteller (1984), Seven Writers in Paris (1989); novel Without Powers (1991), awarded: Patrick Kavanagh 1977, Alice Hunt Bartlett prize 1981, annual literary award American-Irish Fndn 1984; hon fell Univ of Iowa 1978-79; memb: Bd of Dirs, Poetry of Ireland Soc; *Recreations* gardening, spreading political gossip; *Style*— Thomas McCarthy, Esq; Carrigbrack, Lovers Walk, Montenotte, Cork, Ireland (☎ 021 503738); Anvil Press Poetry, 69 King George St, London SE10 8PX

McCARTHY, Baron (Life Peer UK 1975), of Headington in the City of Oxford; William Edward John McCarthy; s of Edward McCarthy; *b* 30 July 1925; *Educ* Holloway Court Sch, Ruskin Coll, Merton Coll and Nuffield Coll Oxford (MA, DPhil); *m* 1957, Margaret, da of Percival Godfrey; *Career* formerly worker in men's outfitters and clerk; lectr in industrial rels Univ of Oxford, res dir Royal Cmmn on Trade Unions and Employers Assocs 1965-68, fell Nuffield Coll Univ of Oxford and Oxford Mgmnt Centre 1969-, chm Railway Staff Nat Tribunal 1974-86; dir Harland & Wolff Ltd 1976-86, special cmmr Equal Opportunities Cmmn 1977-79; oppn spokesman (Lords) Employment 1983-; *Recreations* theatre, ballet, gardening; *Clubs* Reform; *Style*— The Rt Hon the Lord McCarthy; 4 William Orchard Close, Old Headington, Oxford (☎ 0865 62016)

MacCARTHY MOR, The; Terence Francis McCarthy; Chief of the Name and Head of the ancient Irish Royal House of Munster (51st generation in unbroken male line descent from King Eoghan Mor (d AD 192) and heir of line of King Donal VII MacCarthy Mor (d 1596); in all this dynasty reigned for a period in excess of 1400 years); eldest surv s of The MacCarthy Mor, and Harriet, eldest da of The Maguire of Fermanagh; suc to the Chiefship 1980; *b* 1957; *Educ* privately, The Queen's Univ Belfast (BA 1980, MA 1982); *Career* dir: Genealogical Services Ulster Historical Fndn 1983-86, Ulster Pedigrees 1986-90; rep for Ireland of Int Cmmn for Orders of Chivalry; patron Royal Clan MacCarthy Soc; chm Royal Clan MacCarthy Tst; holder of several foreign orders including: Gd Offr of Skanderbeg (conferred by HM King Leka I of the Albanians), Kt Cdr St Maurice and St Lazarus (conferred by HRH Crown Prince Victor Emmanuel of Italy), Kt of Justice Sacred Military Order of Constantine St George of Naples (conferred by HRH the Duke of Calabria), Order of St Michael of the Wing (House of Bragança, Portugal, conferred by HRH the Duke of Bragança); memb Royal Ulster Academy Assoc 1991; *Books* One Thousand Royal and Noble Ancestors of the House of MacCarthy Mor (1988), The New Dictionary of Heraldry (all Irish sections 1988), numerous articles on heraldry, genealogy and Irish history; *Recreations* painting, writing, travel, music; *Style*— The MacCarthy Mor; El Minzah, 85 rue de la Liberté, Tangier, Morocco

MCCARTNEY, Dr Alison Caroline Elliott; da of Maj Bernard William Elliott (d 1969), and Jean Florence, *née* Baker; *Educ* Ashford Girls GS, Canterbury Tech Coll, Girton Coll Cambridge (BA, MA), St Bartholomew's Hosp (MB BChir); *m* 27 June 1975, Peter Russell, s of Ernest McCartney, of 4 Robin Hill, Dundrum, Co Down; 1 s (Max Elliot b 17 Aug 1986), 1 da (Alexandra Mary b 29 May 1984); *Career* house surgn ENT dept St Bartholomew's Hosp 1975, house physician Prince of Wale's Hosp Tottenham 1976, registrar in histopathology St Stephen's Hosp Chelsea 1977-79 (sr house offr 1976-77), sr lectr and hon conslt pathologist Charing Cross Hosp Med Sch 1982-85 (lectr and hon sr registrar in histopathology 1979-82), sr lectr in histopathology Inst of Ophthalmology and hon conslt histopathologist Moorfields Eye Hosp 1985-; various reviews: British Journal of Ophthalmology, Journal of Clinical Pathology, Journal of Paediatric Ophthalmology and Genetics, Ophthalmic Research, Eye; memb: Acad Cncl 1986-, Res Ctee 1987, Ctee of Mgmnt 1988, Br Assoc of Ocular Pathology 1983-, Assoc of Clinical Pathologists; JP Inner London Bench 1981-83; elected: to Euro Ophthalmic Pathology Soc 1988, Assoc memb American Acad of Ophthalmology 1989; memb RSM, MRCPath 1981; FCOphth 1988; *Books* Immunology of the Eye (contrib, 1989); *Recreations* reading, singing, cooking; *Style*— Dr Alison McCartney; 23 Belitha Villas, London N1 1PE; Department of Pathology, Institute of Ophthalmology, 17-25 Cayton St, London EC1V 9AT; Moorfields Eye Hospital, City Rd, London EC1 (☎ 071 387 9621 ext 280, fax 071 250 3207, telex Eyestute Kincross London)

McCARTNEY, Gordon Arthur; s of Arthur McCartney (d 1987), and Hannah, *née* Seel; *b* 29 April 1937; *Educ* Grove Park GS Wrexham; *m* 1, 23 July 1960 (m dis 1987), Ceris Isobel Davies; 2 da (Heather Jane b 11 April 1963, Alison b 6 Dec 1965); m 2, 26 March 1988, Wendy Ann Vyvyn, da of Sidney Titman; *Career* admitted slr 1959, chief exec Delyn Borough Cncl Clwyd 1974-81, sec Assoc of DCs 1981-, co sec Local Govt Int Bureau 1988-, dir Nat Tport Tokens Ltd 1984-; *Recreations* music, gardening, cricket; *Clubs* Middx CCC, Northants CCC; *Style*— Gordon McCartney, Esq; 33 Duck Street, Elton, Peterborough, Cambs PE8 6RQ (☎ 0832 280659); 203 Frobisher House, Dolphin Sq, London SW1 (☎ 071 630 8207); 26 Chapter St, London SW1 8NZ (☎ 071 233 6868, fax 071 233 6551)

McCARTNEY, (James) Paul; MBE (1965); s of late James McCartney, of Liverpool, and late Mary Patricia, *née* Mohin; *b* 18 June 1942; *Educ* Liverpool Inst; *m* 13 April 1969, Linda Louise, da of Lee Eastman, of New York City; 1 s (James b 1977), 1 da (Mary b 1969), 2 step da (Stella b 1961, Heather b 1962); *Career* musician and composer; joined first group, the Quarrymen, and started writing songs with John Lennon 1956; formation of the Beatles 1960; first Beatles recordings issued in Germany 1961: Please Please Me gave group their first British No 1, She Loves You cemented their success 1963; first triumphant American tour 1964; Royal Command Performance and release of first film A Hard Day's Night 1964; single I Want to Hold Your Hand became the biggest selling British single ever, with worldwide sales of 15,000,000; release of second film Help 1965; last ever Beatles public performance in San Francisco Aug 1966; release of Sergeant Pepper's Lonely Hearts Club Band album, as well as Penny Lane/Strawberry Fields Forever 1967; formation of Apple Corps 1968; release of third film, the cartoon Yellow Submarine and their only double album, The Beatles (The White Album) 1968; group played live for the last time together on the roof of the Apple building in London 1969; fourth and final film, Let It Be, released 1970; dissolution of Apple sees the break-up of the Beatles; formed MPL group of cos and released debut solo album McCartney 1970; released second solo album Ram and formed Wings 1971; returned to live work 1972; appeared in own TV special James Paul McCartney 1973; Wings toured UK and Australia 1975; Wings first American tour resulted in a triple album Wings Over America 1976; Mull of Kintyre became best selling single ever in UK and received Ivor Novello award for this achievement 1977; released a new album London Town, and a compilation Wings Greatest Hits 1978; honoured by the Guinness Book of Records with a Triple Superlative Award, for sales of 100,000,000 albums, 100,000,000 singles and as holder of 60 gold discs, making him the most successful popular music composer ever 1979; presented with a unique Rhodium Disc by the Minister of the Arts; released Wings Rockshow film from 1976 US tour 1981; released acclaimed Tug of War album 1982; Pipes of Peace album released 1983; Give My Regards to Broad Street released 1984; performed Let It Be at Bob Geldof's Live Aid concert to 1.5 billion people 1985; released 15th solo album Press To Play and returned to concert stage for special Royal Command concert The Prince's Trust, in the presence of TRH The Prince and Princess of Wales 1986; Flowers in the Dirt LP and tour 1990; winner numerous Grammy awards Nat Acad of Recording Arts and Scis USA incl Lifetime Achievement award 1990; winner Ivor Novello award: for Int Achievement 1980, for Int Hit of the Year 1982 (Ebony and Ivory), for Outstanding Contribution to Music 1989; PRS special award for unique achievement in popular music; Freeman City of Liverpool 1984; Hon DUniv Sussex 1988; *Style*— Paul McCartney, Esq, MBE; c/o MPL Communications Ltd, 1 Soho Square, London W1V 6BQ

McCAUGHREAN, Geraldine Margaret; da of Leslie Arthur Jones (d 1980), of Enfield, Middx, and Ethel, *née* Thomas; *b* 6 June 1951; *Educ* Enfield Co Sch for Girls, Christ Church Coll of Educn Canterbury (BEd); *m* 23 Nov 1988, John, s of William McCaughrean (d 1964), of Aughton, Lancs; 1 da (Ailsa b 12 Dec 1989); *Career* Thames Television Ltd 1970-77, staff writer Marshall Cavendish Partworks Ltd 1977-89 (sec, sub-ed); freelance writer 1989-; Whitbread Book of the Year (Childrens Novel) for A Little Lower than the Angels 1987, Carnegie Medal and Guardian Children's Fiction Award for A Pack of Lies 1988, first radio play produced 1991; *Books* 1001 Arabian Nights (1982), The Canterbury Tales (1984), A Little Lower than the Angels (1987), A Pack of Lies (1988), The Maypole (1989), St George and the Dragon (1989), El Cid (1989), Fire's Astonishment (1990), Vainglorg (1991); *Style*— Ms Geraldine McCaughrean; Oxford University Press (childrens), Walton Rd, Oxford OX2 6DP (☎ 0865 56767)

MCCAVE, Prof (Ian) Nicholas; s of T T McCave (d 1941), and G M Langlois; *b* 3 Feb 1941; *Educ* Elizabeth Coll Guernsey, Hertford Coll Oxford (BA, MA, DSc), Brown Univ Providence USA (PhD); *m* 3 April 1972, Susan Caroline Adams, da of G de P Bambridge; 3 s (Thomas b 1973, Robert b 1975, Geoffrey b 1978), 1 da (Elise b 1981); *Career* NATO res fell Netherlands Inst voor Onderzoek der Zee 1967, reader Sch of Environmental Sci UEA 1976 (lectr 1969), visiting scientist Woods Hole Oceanographic Institution 1978-86, Woodwardian prof of geology Univ of Cambridge 1985-, fell St Johns Coll Cambridge 1986; chm Cmmn on Marine Geology of the Int Union of Geological Scis, memb Sci Ctee on Oceanic Res; FGS 1963; *Books* The Benthic Boundary Layer (ed, 1976); *Style*— Prof Nicholas McCave; Dept of Earth Sciences, University of Cambridge, Downing St, Cambridge (☎ 0223 333400)

MCCLATCHEY, Dr Samuel Jones; s of Thomas McClatchey (d 1946), and Emily, *née* Jones (d 1975); *b* 13 June 1916; *Educ* Royal Belfast Academical Inst, Queens Univ Belfast (MB BCh, BAO, DPH, MFCM, Univ Athletic blue); *m* 2 April 1942, Patricia Kathleen (d 1981), da of Frederick Allen (d 1948); 3 da (Judith b 5 Sept 1944, Diana b 8 March 1948, Lindsay b 16 May 1951); *Career* WWII Sqdn Ldr RAF, station MO Northolt 1943-44, Sqdn MO 137 Sqdn 2 TAF Normandy landings 1944-45, sr MO RAAE Boscombe Down 1945-46; MO of health New Windsor 1950-74 (presented at Ct Windsor Castle 1952), community physician and MO environmental health East Berks 1975-86; currently: med referee to Crematoria, mangr Mental Health Cmmn to Cardinal Clinic Windsor; hon treas Soc Community Med 1976-83; memb: Royal Br Legion, RNLI; parish cncllr; memb BMA, MFCM; *Recreations* yachting, ocean cruising; *Clubs* Pathfinder (RAF), Leander, Windsor Constitutional, RFYC; *Style*— Dr Samuel McClatchey; Cluain-na-Slige, Thames St, Sonning-on-Thames, Berkshire (☎ 0734 693 197)

McCLEAN, Professor (John) David; s of Maj Harold McClean (d 1983), of Prestbury, Cheshire, and Mabel, *née* Callow (d 1981); *b* 4 July 1939; *Educ* Queen Elizabeth GS Blackburn, Magdalen Coll Oxford (BA, BCL, MA, DCL); *m* 10 Dec 1966, Pamela Ann, da of Leslie Arthur Loader (d 1959), of Yeovil, Somerset; 1 s (Michael b 1969), 1 da (Lydia b 1972); *Career* Univ of Sheffield: lectr 1961-68, sr lectr 1968-73, prof 1973-; visiting lectr Monash Univ 1968 (visiting prof 1978); lay vice pres Sheffield Diocesan Synod 1982-; memb: Gen Synod 1970-, Crown Appts Cmmmn 1977-87; vice chm House of Laity 1979-85 (chm 1985-); *Books* Legal Context of Social Work (1975, 2 edn 1980), Recognition of Family Judgments in the Commonwealth (1983); co-author: Criminal Justice and the Treatment of Offenders (jtly, 1969), Defendants in the Criminal Process (1976), Shawcross and Beaumont on Air Law (4 edn 1977), Dicey and Morris, the Conflict of Laws (10 edn 1980, 11 edn 1987); *Recreations* detective fiction; *Clubs* RCS; *Style*— Prof David McClean; 6 Burnt Stones Close, Sheffield S10 5TS (☎ 0742 305794); Faculty of Law, The University, Sheffield S10 2TN (☎ 0742 768555, ext 6754)

McCLEAN, Richard Arthur Frank; s of Donald Stuart McClean (d 1959), and Marjory Cathleen, *née* Franks; *b* 5 Dec 1937; *Educ* Marlborough; *m* 29 Aug 1959, Janna, da of Eric Constantine Doresa; 1 s (Paul b 23 Sept 1962); 2 da (Lucinda b 27 June 1961, Philippa b 23 July 1966); *Career* Financial Times: joined Advertising Dept 1955, advertising dir 1974, appointed to the Bd 1977, mktg dir 1979, md Marketing, md Europe 1981, dep chief exec 1983; dir: Financial Times Group Ltd 1984, FT Business Information Ltd 1984, St Clements Press Ltd 1981, The Financial Times (Europe) Ltd 1978, Westminster Press Ltd 1986; *Recreations* golf, tennis; *Clubs* Garrick, Royal St Georges Golf; *Style*— Richard McClean, Esq; Catherinehams, Grove Heath, Ripley, Surrey (☎ 0483 224050); The Financial Times Ltd, Bracken House, 10 Cannon St, London EC4P 4BY (☎ 071 248 8000)

McCLEARY, Benjamin Ward; s of George William McCleary, of Asheville, N Carolina, and Nancy, *née* Grim; *b* 9 July 1944; *Educ* St Mark's Sch, Princeton Univ (AB); *m* 1, 6 May 1967 (m dis 1977), Deirdre Stillman Marsters; 1 s (Benjamin Pierce b 6 May 1970), 1 da (Katherine Chase b 1 Sept 1972); m 2, 15 Oct 1983, Jean, da of Henry G Muchmore, of New Vernon, NJ, USA; *Career* Lt US Navy 1966-69; vice pres Chemical Bank 1969-81, sr vice pres Lehman Brothers 1981-84, md Shearson Lehman Brothers 1984-89, ptnr McFarland Dewey & Co 1989-; *Recreations* sailing, skiing; *Clubs* Dunes; *Style*— Benjamin W McCleary, Esq; 114 E 90th Street, New York NY 10128 (☎ 212 831 5461); Mcfarland Dewey & Co, 230 Park Ave, NY 10169 (☎ 212 867 4949)

McCLELLAN, Anthony; CBE (1991); s of James McClellan (d 1941), and Violet Mary, *née* Heenan (d 1974); *b* 12 April 1925; *Educ* Sedbergh, Clare Coll Cambridge; *m* 14 Jan 1958, Marie-Jose Alberte, da of Maurice Marie-Edouard Joriaux (d 1963); 1 s (James-Edward b 1 Dec 1961), 1 da (Beatrice Georgina Marguerite b 20 Aug 1963); *Career* RN Y Scheme 1943-44, transferred Army 1944, cmmnd KOSB, seconded 2 King Edward VII Own Gurkhas (The Sirmoor Rifles) 1945, demob as Capt 1947; HMs Colonial Serv 1947, admin and JP N Nigeria 1949, ADC to Govr of Nigeria 1952, dist offr and magistrate Sarawak 1954, called to the Bar Inner Temple 1958, legal appts in commerce and indust 1959-73, princ legal advsr Cmmn of Euro Communities 1989-90 (legal advsr 1974), returned to practice at the Bar Oct 1990; author of articles in legal jls; memb: Euro Cncl LCIA, Richmond and Barnes Cons Assoc; life memb Univ of Cambridge Cons Assoc; memb: BACFI, CIArb; *Recreations* formerly polo, rugby and skiing, currently reading and travel; *Clubs* East India, Sirmoor, Sarawak Assoc; *Style*— Anthony McClellan, Esq, CBE; 5 Paper Buildings (European Law Chambers) Temple, London EC4Y 7HB (☎ 071 583 9275, fax 071 583 1926, telex LDE 415

McCLELLAN, Col Sir (Herbert) Gerard Thomas; CBE (1979, OBE 1960), TD (1955), JP (City of Liverpool 1968), DL (Merseyside 1974, Lancs 1967-74); s of late George McClellan and Lillian, *née* Fitzgerald; *b* 24 Sept 1913; *m* 1939, Rebecca Ann Nancy (d 1982), da of Michael Desforges; 1 s (Anthony George), 3 da (Mary Colette, Ann Winifred (Mrs Walsh), Petra Clare (Mrs Plant)); *Career* served WWII Loyal (N Lancs) Regt, Royal Regt of Artillery, London Irish Rifles RUR, served M East, N Africa, Italy (wounded, despatches), cmd 626 (Liverpool Irish) HAA Regt (RA, TA), 470 (3 W Lancs) RA TA 1955-60, County Cmdt W Lancs Army Cadet Force 1961-66; vice chm and md: Vernons Tst Corpn, Vernons Finance Corpn, Vernons Insur Brokers; dir Vernons Orgn; md Competition Mgmnt Servs 1977-82; ret 1982; chm

Intro Merseyside Ltd 1988-; dir: JS Mortgage Corpn plc 1986-, Richmond Storage and Transit Co (UK) Ltd 1990, Richmond Freight Services Ltd 1990-; memb: TAVR Assoc W Lancs 1955-66 (vice-chm 1966-68), N W England & IOM 1968-70 (vice-chm 1970-75, chm 1975-79); former memb Liverpool City Cncl (Childwall Ward); govr: Archbishop Whiteside SM - St Brigid's High Sch, 1961-; Christ's Coll Liverpool 1962-69; St Mary's (Little Crosby) RC Primary Sch 1986-90, Sandown Coll Liverpool 1989-91; chm: Liverpool (Liverpool European) Cons Constituency Cncl 1978-84, Merseyside West European CCC 1984-85 (pres 1985-90); vice pres: Merseyside County Soldiers Sailors & Airmens Assoc 1975-, Churchill Cons Club, Wavertree 1976-, The Liverpool Sch of Tropical Med 1987-; memb: North West Area Cons Assoc 1971-90, The Nat Union of Cons and Unionist Exec Ctee 1982-87, Mabel Fletcher Tech Liverpool 1969- (chm Govrs 1971-86); pres: Wavertree Cons Assoc 1967-76 (chm 1962-67), Garston Cons Assoc 1979-90, Halewood Cons Club 1981-88, Crosby Cons Assoc 1986-89 (chm 1989-91); High Sheriff Merseyside 1980-81; FInstAM; kt 1986; *Clubs* Athenaeum (Liverpool), Army & Navy; *Style—* Col Sir Gerard McClellan, CBE, TD, JP, DL; 10 Ince Blundell Hall, Ince Blundell, Liverpool L38 6JN (☎ 051 9292269)

McCLELLAN, John Forrest; s of John McClellan (d 1978), of Caledonian Place, Aberdeen, and Hester, *née* Niven (d 1954); *b* 15 Aug 1932; *Educ* Aberdeen GS, Univ of Aberdeen (MA); *m* 22 Dec 1956, Eva Maria, da of Otto Pressel (d 1967), of Churchfields, 37 The Ridgeway, Fetcham, nr Leatherhead, Surrey; 3 s (James b 1957, Nicholas b 1960, Tommy b 1963), 1 da (Rose b 1965); *Career* Nat Serv Army 1954-56, 2 Lt Gordon Highlanders 1955-56, seconded to Nigeria Regt Royal West African Frontier Force 1955-56; entered Civil Serv 1956; Scottish Educn Dept: asst princ 1956-59, princ 1960-68, asst sec 1969-77; Scottish Office: private sec to Perm Under Sec of State 1959-60, asst under sec of state 1977-80; civil serv fell Univ of Glasgow 1968-69, under sec Indust Dept for Scotland 1980-85, ret Civil Serv 1985; dir Scottish Int Educn Tst 1986-; memb Mgmnt Ctee Hanover Housing Assoc Scotland 1986-; hon fell Dundee Inst of Technol 1988; *Books* Then a Soldier (1991); *Recreations* walking, vegetable gardening; *Clubs* Royal Scots; *Style—* John McClellan, Esq; Grangeneuk, West Linton, Peeblesshire EH46 7HG (☎ 0968 60502); 22 Manor Place, Edinburgh (☎ 031 225 1113)

McCLELLAND, Dr (David) Brian Lorimer; s of William Lorimer McClelland (d 1982), of Painswick, and Elizabeth McClelland (d 1973); *b* 12 May 1944; *Educ* Calday Grange GS Cheshire, Univ of Edinburgh (BSc, MB ChB), Univ of Leiden (PhD); *m* Elizabeth Jean Steven, da of Alistair Rae (d 1980); 3 s (Tom, Ailis, Ralph), 1 da (Lucy); *Career* dir SE Scot Blood Transfusion Service 1979-, sr lectr Dept of Med Univ of Edinburgh 1977-; memb various blood transfusion related ctees; FRCPE, MRCPath; *publications:* author of numerous med and scientific publications; *Style—* Dr Brian McClelland; Blood Transfusion Service, Royal Infirmary, Edinburgh EH3 9HB (☎ 031 229 2585, fax 031 229 1069)

McCLELLAND, Prof (William) Grigor; s of Arthur McClelland (d 1966), of Newcastle upon Tyne, and Jean, *née* Grigor (d 1966); *b* 2 Jan 1922; *Educ* Leighton Park Sch, Balliol Coll Oxford (MA); *m* 1946, Diana Avery, da of William Harold Close, of Hampstead; 2 s, 2 da; *Career* md Laws Stores Ltd 1949-65 and 1978-85 (chm 1966-85), sr res Balliol Coll 1962-65, dir Manchester Business Sch 1965-77, prof of business admin Univ of Manchester 1967-77; ed: Quakers Visit China 1957, Journal of Management Studies 1963-65; dep chm Nat Computing Centre 1966-68; chm: Washington Devpt Corp 1977-88, EDC for the Distributive Trades 1980-84 (memb 1965-70), Tyne Tees Telethon Tst 1988-, Tyne and Wear Fndn 1988-; memb: Friends Ambulance Unit 1941-46, Consumer Cncl 1963-66, Econ Planning Cncl (Northern Region) 1965-66, IRC 1966-71, NEDC 1969-71, SSRC 1971-74, Northern Industl Devpt Bd 1977-86; tstee: Joseph Rowntree Charitable Tst 1956- (chm 1965-78), Anglo-German Fndn for the Study of Indust Soc 1973-79, Millfield House Fndn 1976-; govr: Nat Inst of Econ and Social Res, Leighton Park Sch 1952-60 and 1962-66; MBA Univ of Manchester, Hon DCL Univ of Durham; FIGD; CBIM; *Books* Studies in Retailing (1963), Costs and Competition in Retailing (1966), And a New Earth (1976); *Recreations* walking, tennis, skiing; *Style—* Prof Grigor McClelland; 66 Elmfield Rd, Gosforth, Newcastle upon Tyne NE3 4BD

McCLELLAND, Dr (William) Morris; s of James McClelland, of Moodage, Tanderagee, Co Armagh, N Ireland, and May, *née* Johnstone; *b* 22 June 1945; *Educ* Portadown Coll Queen's Univ Belfast (MB BcH, BAO); *m* 14 Aug 1969; Margaret Christine, da of David Joseph Robinson, of Ballynagarrick, Gilford, Co Down, N Ireland; 1 s (Jamie b 4 April 1978), 2 da (Joanna b 7 May 1972, Sarah b 15 Jan 1976); *Career* dir NI Blood Transfusion Serv 1980-, conslt haematologist Royal Victoria Hosp Belfast 1980-; conslt advsr: to chief med offr NI 1986-, to Overseas Devpt Admin 1988-; FRC Path; *Style—* Dr Morris McClelland; 103 Osborne Park, Belfast BT9 7JQ ☎ 0232 666724; N Ireland Blood Transfusion Service, 89 Durham St, Belfast BT12 4GE (☎ 0232 321414, fax 0232 4390017)

McCLELLAND, Dr Richard (stage name Richard Leech); s of Herbert Saunderson McClelland (d 1953), of 18 Palmerston Park, Dublin, and Isabella Frances, *née* Leeper (d 1963); *b* 24 Nov 1922; *Educ* Haileybury, Trinity Coll Dublin (BA, BAO, MB BCh); *m* 1, 28 Jan 1950, Helen Hyslop, *née* Uttley (d 1971); 2 da (Sarah Jane b 15 Jan 1952, Eliza b 3 June 1954); *m* 2, 27 June 1975, (Margaret) Diane, *née* Pearson; *Career* house surgn and house physician Meath Hosp Dublin 1946; actor; theatre incl: All My Sons 1948, The Lady's Not for Burning 1949, Relative Values 1950, No Other Verdict 1954, Uncertain Joy 1955, Subway in the Sky 1956, A Man for All Seasons 1960, Dazzling Prospect 1961, Cider with Rosie 1963, The Rt Hon Gentleman 1964, Horizontal Hold 1967, The Cocktail Party 1968, Whose Life Is It Anyway (Savoy Theatre) 1979-81; TV incl: Jane Eyre, The Gold Robbers, The Doctors, Barchester Chronicles, Smiley's People; films incl: Dam Busters, A Night to Remember, Ice Cold in Alex, The Young Churchill, Gandhi, A Handful of Dust, The Shooting Party; wrote column Doctor in the Wings in World Medicine 1968-83; dir Rocks Country Wines Ltd 1985-; *Books* How To Do It (1979), TCD Anthology (1945); *Recreations* bricklaying, cinematography, gardening; *Clubs* Garrick; *Style—* Dr Richard McClelland; 27 Claylands Rd, London SW8 1NX (☎ 01 735 1678); Loddon Park Farm, Twyford, Berks; Rocks Country Wines Ltd, Loddon Park Farm, New Bath Rd, Twyford, Berks (☎ 0734 342 344)

McCLENAGHAN, Lt-Col (Frank) Worsfold; JP (Hants 1954), DL (Hants 1972); s of Rev George Richard McClenaghan (d 1950), of Stockton Hall, Beccles, Suffolk, and Amy Margaret, *née* Mayo (d 1926); *b* 6 July 1910; *Educ* Marlborough, Clare Coll Cambridge (MA), Yale Univ USA; *m* 12 Dec 1945, Elizabeth, da of Allon Dawson (d 1928), of Leathley Grange, Otley, Yorks; 2 da (Elizabeth b 1946, Virginia b 1950); *Career* Gunner RA (TA) 1938, cmmnd 2 Lt 1939, Capt 1941, Maj 1942, Lt-Col 1943; farmer; High Sheriff Hants and IOW 1971; *Recreations* shooting; *Clubs* Special Forces, Hampshire (Winchester), Elizabethan (New Haven USA); *Style—* Lt-Col Worsfold McClenaghan, JP, DL; Westfield House, Highclere, Newbury, Berks (☎ 0635 253067)

MACCLESFIELD, Archdeacon of; *see*: Gaisford, Ven John Scott

MACCLESFIELD, 8 Earl of (GB 1721); George Roger Alexander Thomas Parker; JP (Oxon 1955), DL (1965); also Lord Parker, Baron of Macclesfield, Co Chester (GB 1716) and Viscount Parker (GB 1721); s of 7 Earl of Macclesfield (d 1975), and Lilian Joanna Vere, *née* Boyle (d 1974); *b* 6 May 1914; *Educ* Stowe; *m* 18 June 1938, Hon Valerie Mansfield, o da of 4 Baron Sandhurst, OBE (d 1964); 2 s; *Heir* s, Viscount Parker; *Career* Lt RNVR, served WWII; *Style—* The Rt Hon the Earl of Macclesfield, JP, DL; Shirburn, Watlington, Oxon

MACCLESFIELD, Countess of; Hon Valerie; *née* Mansfield; da of 4 Baron Sandhurst, OBE (d 1964); *b* 25 Dec 1918; *m* 18 June 1938, 8 Earl of Macclesfield; *Career* chm CC Oxon 1970; CStJ 1990; *Style—* The Rt Hon The Countess of Macclesfield; Shirburn Castle, Watlington, Oxon

MCCLEVERTY, Prof Jon Armistice; s of John Frederick McCleverty (d 1948), and Agnes Elder, *née* Melrose (d 1973); *b* 11 Nov 1937; *Educ* Aberdeen GS, Fettes Coll Edinburgh, Univ of Aberdeen (BSc), Imperial Coll Univ of London (PhD); *m* 29 June 1963, Dianne Margaret, da of Ian William Barrack (d 1955); 2 da (Ashley b 1967, Roslyn b 1971); *Career* post doctoral fell (Fulbright scholar) MIT USA 1963-64, lectr and reader dept of chemistry Univ of Sheffield 1964-80; prof of Inorganic Chemistry: Univ of Birmingham 1980-90, Univ of Bristol 1990-; SERC: memb chm ctee 1988-93 (chm 1990-93), chm Inorganic Chemistry Sub-Ctee 1988-90, memb Sci Bd 1990-93; chm Ctee of Heads of Univ Chemistry Depts 1989-91; memb Royal Soc of Chemistry, memb American Chem Soc; *Recreations* gardening, jazz, travel, food and wine; *Style—* Prof Jon McCleverty; School of Chemistry, University of Bristol, Cantocks Close, Bristol BS8 1TS

McCLINTOCK, Nicholas Cole; CBE (1979); s of Col Robert Singleton McClintock, DSO (d 1969), of Brakey Hill, Godstone, Surrey, and Mary Howard, *née* Elphinstone (d 1965); *b* 10 Sept 1916; *Educ* Stowe, Trinity Coll Cambridge (BA, MA); *m* 3 Sept 1953, Pamela Sylvia, da of Maj Rhys Clavell Mansel (d 1968), of Smedmore, Corfe Castle, Dorset; 2 s (Alexander b 1959, Michael b 1960), 2 da (Sylvia b 1954, Elizabeth b 1962); *Career* WWII cmmnd RA 1938-45 served Dunkirk, cmd 1 Field Batty final Burma Campaign 1945; Col admin serv 1946-62; Northern Nigeria: private sec to Govr 1949-50, clerk to Exec Cncl Northern Region 1950-53, actg res Kano Province and res Bornu Province 1958-62; KStJ 1968 (sec gen Order of St John 1968-81); sec Dorset Historic Churches Tst 1984-, chm Aidis Tst 1988-; Freeman City of London 1981; *Clubs* Army & Navy; *Style—* Nicholas McClintock, Esq, CBE; Lower Westport House, Wareham, Dorset (☎ 0829 553252)

McCLINTOCK-BUNBURY, Hon Pamela Rosemary; da of 4 Baron Rathdonnell (d 1959); *b* 30 July 1948; *Educ* Lawnside Gt Malvern Worcs, Millfield; *Career* sculptor, painter; *Style—* The Hon Pamela McClintock-Bunbury; Calle Marbella 4, Benehavis, Malaga, Spain

McCLUNE, Rear Adm (William) James; CB (1978); s of James McClune, MBE (d 1952); *b* 20 Nov 1921; *Educ* Foyle Coll, Queen's Univ Belfast, Univ of Birmingham (MSc); *m* 1953, Joan Elizabeth Symes, da of Albert Prideaux (d 1952); 1 s (James), 1 da (Bridget); *Career* radar offr RNVR 1941-47, CSO (engrg) to C-in-C Fleet 1976-78; chm of tstees Royal Sailors' Rests; chm: Christian Alliance Housing Assoc, Mgmnt Ctee RNLI; *Recreations* sailing; *Clubs* Royal Cwlth Soc, Royal Naval and Royal Albert Yacht; *Style—* Rear Adm James McClune, CB; Harlam Lodge, Lansdown, Bath, Avon (☎ 0225 311748); 7 Theed St, London SE1 (☎ 071 928 2720)

McCLURE, Brian David; s of Walter James McClure, of Belfast, and Margaret, *née* Thompson; *b* 24 Sept 1946; *Educ* Methodist Coll Belfast, Clare Coll Cambridge (BA); *Career* admitted slr 1970; called to the Bar Grays Inn 1976; ACIArb 1990; *Recreations* tennis; *Clubs* Cumberland Lawn Tennis, Hampstead; *Style—* Brian McClure, Esq; 12 Gray's Inn Square, Gray's Inn, London WC1R 5JP (☎ 071 404 486618654, fax 071 831 0713, telex 252633 ref: M3011)

McCLURE, Wing Cdr Charles George Buchanan; AFC (1944), AE (1944), DL (1976); s of Judge George Buchanan McClure (d 1955, cmmr at Old Bailey), and Doris Elizabeth, *née* Tydd; *b* 20 April 1916; *Educ* Winchester, Trinity Coll Oxford, de Havilland Tech Sch; *m* 1943, Helen Margaret Gilloch, da of Maj John Whyte, MBE; 1 s, 1 da; *Career* test pilot RAE 1941 (tested whittle WZB 1943) Wing Cdr RAF 1945, chief test pilot RAE Farnborough 1945-46, ops offr Miny of Civil Aviation 1946, head of flight Cranfield Coll of Aeronautics 1949; prof of flight Cranfield Inst of Technol 1973, ret 1981; CEng, FRAeS; *Recreations* golf, gardening; *Clubs* RAF, Leander; *Style—* Wing Cdr Charles McClure, AFC, AE, DL; The Shrubbery, Aspley Guise, Milton Keynes MK17 8HE (☎ 0908 583126)

McCLURE, Prof John; s of Richard Byrne McClure (d 1949), of Omagh, Co Tyrone, and Isabella McClure (d 1983); *b* 2 May 1947; *Educ* Queen's Univ Belfast (BSc, MD, BCh, BAO); *m* 26 June 1970, Sheena Frances, da of Alfred Henry Tucker (d 1973), of Belfast; 3 da (Sarah b 26 Oct 1971, Katy 13 Dec 1975, Emma 30 Jan 1978); *Career* trg posts in pathology Queen's Univ Belfast 1972-78, clinical sr lectr (also specialist and sr specialist tissue pathology) Inst of Med and Veterinary Sci and Univ of Adelaide S Aust 1978-83; Univ of Manchester: sr lectr and hon conslt histopathology 1983-87, Procter Prof of Pathology and head Dept Pathological Scis 1987-; memb Rochdale Health Authy; MRCPath 1977, FRCPath 1989; *Style—* Prof John McClure; Department of Pathological Sciences, The Medical School, University of Manchester, Oxford Rd, Manchester M13 9PT (☎ 061 275 5300)

MCCLURE, Neil James; s of Kenneth James McClure, of Wymondham, Norfolk, and Marjorie Joan, *née* Bacon; *b* 9 June 1953; *Educ* King Edward VI Sch Norwich, Grey Coll Durham (BA); *m* Helen Ruth, *née* Beeley; 1 s (Thomas James), 1 da (Rebecca Ruth); *Career* Coopers and Lybrand 1974-79, Williams Glyn & Co 1979-80, corp fin mangr Phillips and Drew 1980-85, regnl corp fin dir Saatchi and Saatchi Co plc 1985-86, gp fin dir FKB Gp plc 1986-89, gp chief exec The Birkdale Gp plc 1989-; ACA; *Recreations* reading, wine, golf; *Clubs* Royal Over-Seas League, Groucho; *Style—* Neil McClure, Esq; Rotherfield House, Colliers Lane, Peppard Common, Henley on Thames, Oxfordshire RG9 5LT (☎ 04917 535); The Birkdale Group plc, 52-54 Broadwick St, London W1V 1FF (☎ 071 287 3650, fax 071 734 0813)

McCLURE FISHER, David Anthony; s of Douglas McClure Fisher, of Northwood, Middx, and Mary Margaret, *née* Haley; *b* 4 March 1939; *Educ* Tonbridge; *m* 30 Dec 1961, Lesley Carol, da of William Henry Chester-Jones (d 1971); 1 s (Duncan b 1964), 1 da (Joanna b 1968); *Career* md: Hogg Automotive Insurance Services Ltd 1984-, Greyfriars Administration Services Ltd 1984-, Hogg Insurance Brokers Ltd; dir Hogg Group plc 1990-; FCII, FInstD, FCIS, FBIIBA, MIMI; *Recreations* golf, bridge; *Clubs* Moor Park Golf; *Style—* D A McClure Fisher, Esq; 1 Station Hill, Reading, Berks (☎ 0734 391221, car 0831 407222)

McCLUSKEY, Hon David Francis; s of Baron McCluskey, QC (Life Peer); *b* 1963; *Educ* St Augustine's HS, Napier Coll Edinburgh; *m* July 1989, Katherine Elizabeth Marion Douglas; *Career* software engr; *Recreations* canoeing, golf; *Clubs* Edinburgh Univ Staff; *Style—* The Hon David McCluskey

McCLUSKEY, Baron (Life Peer UK 1976), of Churchill in District of City of Edinburgh; John Herbert McCluskey; QC (Scotland 1967); s of Francis John McCluskey (d 1961), of Edinburgh; *b* 12 June 1929; *Educ* St Bede's GS Manchester, Holy Cross Acad Edinburgh, Edinburgh Univ (Vans Dunlop Scholar, MA, LLB); *m* 1956, Ruth, da of Aaron Friedland, of Manchester; 2 s (Hon (John) Mark b 1960, Hon David Francis b 1963), 1 da (Hon Catherine Margaret b 1962); *Career* advocate 1955, advocate-depute 1964, sheriff princ of Dumfries and Galloway 1973-1974, slr gen for Scotland 1974-79, senator of the Coll of Justice in Scotland 1984; BBC Reith lectr 1986; Hon LLD Dundee 1989; *Books* Law, Justice and Democracy (1987); *Style—* The

Rt Hon the Lord McCluskey; Ct of Session, Parliament Square, Edinburgh (☎ 031 225 2595); 5 Lansdowne Crescent, Edinburgh EH12 5EQ (☎ 031 225 6102)

McCLUSKEY, Hon (John) Mark; s of Baron McCluskey, QC (Life Peer), of Edinburgh, and Ruth, *née* Friedland; *b* 21 July 1960; *Educ* George Watson's Coll, Univ of Aberdeen, The Napier Coll; *m* 1986, Judith Karen, *née* Fernie; 1 s (Scott John b 29 Dec 1989), 1 da (Kate Louise b 2 Jan 1988); *Career* contract's exec: GEC Ferranti Defence Systems Ltd, Display Systems Div South Gyle Edinburgh; *Recreations* golf, swimming; *Style*— (The Hon) Mark McCluskey (does not use courtesy title of Honourable); 20 Redford Avenue, Edinburgh EH13 0BU (☎ 031 314 8148)

McCOLGAN, Elizabeth; *née* Lynch; da of Martin Lynch, of Dundee, and Elizabeth, *née* Fearn; *b* 24 May 1964; *Educ* St Vincent de Paul PS, St Saviour's HS Dundee, Ricks Coll Idaho, Univ of Alabama; *m* 3 Oct 1987, Peter Conor McColgan, s of Thomas McColgan, of Strabane, NI, 1 da (Eilish Karen b Nov 25 1990); *Career* sports devpt offr Dundee DC; Gold Medallist 10000m Cwlth Games 1986, Silver Medallist World and Country Championships 1986, Silver Medallist 10000m 1988, UK 5000m champion 1988, Grand Prix winner 3000 and 5000m 1988, Silver Medallist Olympic Games 1988; Cwlth Games 1990: Bronze Medallist 3000m, Gold Medallist 10000m; Silver Medallist 3000m Indoor World Championships; world record holder 5000m and 10000m on roads, Euro 10000m record holder, Br and Scottish 5000m and 10000m record holder; granted Freedom of Tuscaloosa Alabama 1986; *Recreations* cooking, cinema, crosswords, my dogs; *Style*— Mrs Elizabeth McColgan; Formentera, Husbandtown Monikie, Dundee, Scotland (☎ 082 623 506); 353 Clepington Rd, Dundee, Scotland (☎ 0382 231 41); Woodtree House, Arbroath, Scotland

McCOLL, Ian; CBE (1983); s of John McColl (d 1947), of Glasgow, and Sarah Isabella McColl (d 1968), of Bunessan, Isle of Mull; descends from the McColls of Mull; *b* 22 Feb 1915; *Educ* Hillhead HS Glasgow; *m* 1968, Brenda, da of Thomas McKean (d 1949), of Glasgow; 1 da (Elaine b 1970); *Career* served RAF WWII in air crew Coastal Cmd 202 Sqdn (despatches 1945); chm Scottish Express Newspapers Ltd 1975-82, dir Express Newspapers 1971-82; ed: Daily Express 1971-74, Scottish Daily Express 1961-71 (joined 1933); former memb: Press Cncl, Gen Assembly Bd of Pubns; vice pres Newspaper Press Fund 1981-; contested (Lib) Dumfries-shire 1945, Greenock 1950; former session clerk Sandyford-Henderson Meml Church of Scotland and former memb Presbytery of Glasgow and Synod of Clydesdale; chm: media div Cwlth Games (Scotland) 1986, Saints and Sinners Club of Scotland 1981; *Style*— Ian McColl, Esq, CBE; 12 Newlands Rd, Glasgow G43 2JB

McCOLL OF DULWICH, Baron (Life Peer UK 1989); Ian McColl; s of Frederick George McColl (d 1985), of Dulwich, and Winifred Edith, *née* Murphy (d 1984); *b* 6 Jan 1933; *Educ* Hutchesons' GS Glasgow, St Paul's, Univ of London (MB BS, MS); *m* 27 Aug 1960, Dr Jean Lennox, da of Arthur James McNair, FRCS, FRCOG (d 1964), of London; 1 s (Dr Hon Alastair James b 25 July 1961), 2 da (Dr Hon Caroline Lennox b 19 Aug 1963, Hon Mary Alison b 9 Oct 1966); *Career* surgn to St Bartholomew's Hosp London and sub dean Med Coll 1967-71, prof of surgery at Guy's Hosp 1971-, dir surgery Guy's Hosp 1985-, chm Dept of Surgery United Med and Dental Schs of Guy's and St Thomas's Hosps 1987-; hon conslt surgn to British Army 1984-, pres Mildmay Mission Hosp 1985-, vice chm Disablement Services Authority 1987-; Freeman City of London, Liveryman of Worshipful Cos of: Apothecaries 1979, Barber Surgeons 1986; memb Cncl RCS Eng; FRCS, FACS, FRCSE; *Books* Intestinal Absorption in Man (jtly, 1975), NHS Data Book (jtly, 1983); *Recreations* forestry; *Clubs* Athenaeum; *Style*— The Rt Hon Lord McColl of Dulwich; Dept of Surgery, Guy's Hospital, London SE1 9RT (☎ 071 955 4466, 071 407 4084)

McCOMB, Dr Janet Mary; da of Samuel Gerald McComb, of 3 New Forge Grange, Belfast, and Mary Clarke; *b* 22 Aug 1951; *Educ* Queen's Univ of Belfast (MB BCh, BAO, MD); *Career* clinical and res fell: Harvard Med Sch and Massachusetts Gen Hosp 1983-86, conslt cardiologist Univ of Newcastle upon Tyne 1986- (sr lectr 1986-90); memb: Br Cardiac Soc, Br Pacing and Electrophysiology Gp; MRCP; *Style*— Dr Janet McComb; Cardiac Department, Freeman Hospital, Newcastle upon Tyne NE7 7DN (☎ 091 284 3111, fax 091 213498)

McCOMBE, Mary; da of James Driscoll (d 1979), of Caldicot, Gwent, and Sarah Jane, *née* Pritchard; *b* 20 Sept 1942; *Educ* Rhymney GS Gwent; *m* 1, 3 Aug 1963, Martin, s of Spencer C W Barnes, of Cambridge, Cambs; 2 s (Simon b 1964, Matthew b 1966); m 2, 6 June 1980, Robert Kenneth Johnston, s of John Claude McCombe (d 1978), of Cardiff, S Glamorgan; *Career* md The Mary McCombe Staff Bureau 1982-, currently dir Child Care at Work; pres Bristol Business Ladies Club, memb Cncl Bristol C of C; MInstD; *Style*— Mrs Mary McCombe; Little Hill House, Ham Lane, Wraxall, Bristol BS19 1LA (☎ 0272 856348); The Mary McCombe Staff Bureau, Northcliffe House, Colston Ave, Bristol BS1 4NA (☎ 0272 277467, fax 0272 226359, car 0836 618810)

McCOMBE, Richard George Bramwell; QC (1989); s of Barbara Bramwell McCombe, *née* Bramwell (d 1969); *b* 23 Sept 1952; *Educ* Sedbergh, Downing Coll Cambridge (MA); *m* 1 (m dis 1986), m 2, 1986, Carolyn Sara, da of Robert Duncan Birrell, of Chart Rising, Ballards Lane, Limpsfield, nr Oxted, Surrey; 1 s (Duncan b 4 Apr 1987), 1 da (Tamara b 20 Nov 1989); *Career* called to the Bar Lincoln's Inn 1975; first jr counsel to Dir Gen of Fair Trading 1987-89 (second jr counsel 1982-87); sec London section Old Sedberghian Club; memb: Senate Inns of Ct and Bar Cncl 1981-86, Bar Cncl Ctees 1986-89 (chm Young Barristers Ctee 1983-84); *Recreations* various sporting interests, travel; *Clubs* RAC, MCC, London Scottish FC, Harlequin FC; *Style*— Richard McCombe, Esq, QC; 13 Old Square, Lincoln's Inn, London WC2A 3UA, (☎ 071 404 4800 fax 071 405 4267)

McCONNACHIE, (John Sneddon) Iain; s of John Meek McConnachie, of Sale, Greater Manchester, and Charlotte Sneddon, *née* Christie (d 1984); *b* 11 March 1956; *Educ* Sale GS, Lymm GS, Oxford Poly (HND), Huddersfield Poly (Dip MKtg Studies); *m* 9 June 1979, Shirley Diane, da of Norman George Burgess (d 1983); 1 da (Sara Anne b 2 Feb 1985); *Career* mkting asst Zockoll Group 1977-78, asst advertising mangr Baxter Travenol 1978-79, American Express 1979-88 (mkting exec, mktg mangr mktg dir), vice pres sales and mktg Chase Manhattan Bank 1988-; MInst M 1989; *Recreations* golf, photography, shooting; *Clubs* West Hove Golf; *Style*— Iain McConnachie, Esq; 55 Dorney Court, Carrara Wharf, Fulham, London SW6 3UE (☎ 071 384 2343); Chase Manhattan Bank, 3 Shortlands, Hammersmith, London W6 8RZ (☎ 081 747 4510, fax 081 747 4158)

McCONNELL, Prof (James) Desmond Caldwell; s of Samuel David McConnell (d 1976), of Magheragall, NI, and Cathleen, *née* Coulter; *b* 3 July 1930; *Educ* Wallace HS Lisburn, Queen's Univ Belfast (BSc, MSc), Univ of Cambridge (MA, PhD); *m* 14 July 1956, Jean Elspeth, da of John Jackson Ironside (d 1975), of Wimborne, Dorset; 1 s (Craig b 1 July 1957), 2 da (Deirdre b 19 May 1959, Elspeth b 3 Nov 1960); *Career* Univ of Cambridge: demonstrator in Mineralogy 1955-60, lectr in mineralogy 1960-72, fell Churchill Coll 1962-82, reader in mineralogy 1972-82, Schlumberger/Cambridge res head of rock physics dept 1983-86, extraordinary fell Churchill Coll 1983-87; prof of physics and chemistry of minerals Univ of Oxford 1986-; FRS 1987; *Books* Principles of Mineral Behaviour (with Andrew Putnis, 1980); *Recreations* choral singing, vernacular architecture; *Style*— Prof Desmond McConnell, FRS; 8 The Croft, Old Headington, Oxford OX3 9BU (☎ 0865 69100); Dept of Earth Sciences, Parks Rd, Oxford (☎ 0865 272 043)

McCONNELL, Hon Mrs; Hon Elizabeth Millicent; da of 2 Viscount Selby (d 1923); *b* 1917; *m* 1948, Clarence Henry Quentin McConnell (d 1972); 1 s, 1 da; *Style*— The Hon Mrs McConnell; PO Box 43148, Nairobi, Kenya

McCONNELL, John; s of Donald McConnell, (d 1982), and Enid, *née* Dimberline (d 1967); *b* 14 May 1939; *Educ* Borough Green Secdy Mod Sch Kent, Maidstone Coll of Art Kent (Nat Dip); *m* 1 March 1963, Moira Rose, da of William Allan Macgregor; 1 s (Sam b 20 Feb 1966), 1 da (Kate b 1 Feb 1969); *Career* designer; own practice 1963-74, co-fndr Face Photosetting 1967; dir: Pentagram 1974, Faber and Faber 1983, Clarks of England Inc 1987; D and A D President's Award for outstanding contrib to design 1985; ed Pentagram Papers 1975-; memb: PO Stamp Advsy Ctee, CNAA; *Books* Living By Design (jtly, 1978), Ideas on Design (jtly, 1986); *Recreations* cookery, home restoration; *Clubs* Groucho; *Style*— John McConnell, Esq; 40 Bassett Rd, London W10 9JL (☎ 081 969 2014); Pentagram Design Ltd, 11 Needham Rd, London W11 2RP (☎ 071 229 3477, fax 071 727 9932, telex 8952000 PENTA G)

McCONNELL, Rt Hon Robert William Brian; PC (N Ireland 1964); s of Alfred Edward McConnell (d 1963), 2 s of Sir Robert John McConnell, 1 Bt; *b* 1922; *Educ* Sedbergh, Queen's Univ Belfast (BA, LLB); *m* 1951, Sylvia Elisabeth Joyce, da of late Samuel Agnew; 2 s, 1 da; *Career* called to the Bar NI 1948, MP (U) S Antrim, min home affrs NI Govt 1964-66, NI Parly 1951-68; pres Industl Ct 1968-88, vice chm Eur Movement in NI 1987-; *Style*— The Rt Hon Robert McConnell; 50 Glenavy Rd, Lisburn, Co Antrim

McCONNELL, (Walter) Scott; OBE (1989); s of Robert Wight McConnell, and late Agnes Reid, *née* Mathieson; *b* 7 April 1936; *Educ* Kilmarnock Acad, Royal Tech Coll Glasgow (PhC); *m* 1 April 1964, Elizabeth Janet, da of late William Ramsay; 1 s (Robbie b 1969), 3 da (Beth b 1965, Morag b 1967, Katie b 1972); *Career* Nat Serv 1959-61; ptnr R W McConnell & Son 1962-, currently chm Ayrshire Pharmaceuticals Ltd (fndr dir 1964-); memb: Pharmaceutical Soc 1958, local review ctee HM Prison Dungavel 1976- (former chm); chm Pharmaceutical Gen Cncl Scotland 1983-86 (memb 1968-), FRPharmS 1986; *Recreations* golf, curling; *Style*— Scott McConnell, Esq, OBE; Braehead of Priestgill, Strathaven, Lanarkshire ML10 6PS (☎ 0357 21218); Invererne, Whiting Bay, Brodick, Isle of Arran KA27 8QH (☎ 07707 344); R W McConnell & Son, 27 Mauchline Rd, Hurlford, Kirlmarnock, Ayrshire KA1 5AB (☎ 0563 25393)

McCORKELL, Col Michael William; OBE (1964), TD (1954), JP (1980); s of Capt B F McCorkell (d 1957), of Templeard Culmore, Co Londonderry, and Eileen Miller (d 1984); *b* 3 May 1925; *Educ* Aldenham; *m* 1950, Aileen Allen (OBE 1975), da of Lt-Col E B Booth, of Darver Castle, Dundalk, Co Louth (d 1962); 3 s (John b 1952, David b 1955, Barry b 1959); 1 da (Mary b 1951); *Career* 16/5 Lancers 1943-47; Maj North Irish Horse 1951, Lt-Col 1961 cmd North Irish Horse TA, ret 1964, TAVR Col NI 1971-74, Bt-Col 1974; Pres TA & VR 1977-88; ADC to HM The Queen 1972, High Sheriff 1961, Lord Lieut Co Londonderry 1975 (DL 1962); *Recreations* fishing, shooting; *Clubs* Cavalry and Guards; *Style*— Col Michael W McCorkell, OBE, TD, JP; Ballyarnett, Londonderry, N Ireland (☎ 0504 351239)

McCORKELL, (Henry) Nigel Pakenham; s of Capt Barry Henry McCorkell (d 1948), and Nina Florence Kendal, *née* Gregory; *b* 9 Jan 1947; *Educ* Wellington, City of London Poly; *m* 12 Sept 1973, Lesley Joan, da of Ernest Rowley, of Southwold, Suffolk; 1 s (Marcus b 1981), 2 da (Clare b 1975, Emma b 1977); *Career* CA; trained Thornton Baker 1968-72; fin dir: KCA International plc 1977-78, FR Group plc 1981-83, Meggitt PLC 1983-, The Microsystems Group plc 1984-88 (non-exec); asst divnl dir Nat Enterprise Bd 1979-81; FCA; *Recreations* golf, skiing, fishing; *Clubs* MCC; *Style*— Nigel McCorkell, Esq; Farrs House, Cowgrave, Wimborne, Dorset BH21 4EL (☎ 0202 841141, fax 0202 842478)

MacCORKINDALE, Simon Charles Pendered; s of Gp Capt Peter Bernard MacCorkindale, OBE, and Gilliver Mary, *née* Pendered, of 8 Pettitts Lane, Dry Drayton, Cambridge; *b* 12 Feb 1952; *Educ* Haileybury; *m* 1, 10 July 1976 (m dis), Fiona Elizabeth Fullerton, o da of Brig Bernard Victor Hilary Fullerton, RAPC; m 2, 5 Oct 1984, Susan Melody (*see* Susan George), da of Norman Alfred George, of 5 Acacia Ave, Wraysbury, Berks; *Career* actor, prodr writer and dir; *films* incl: Juggernaut (1974), Road to Mandalay (1977), Death on the Nile (1977), The Riddle of the Sands (1978), The Quatermass Conclusion (1978), Cabo Blanco (1979), The Sword and the Sorcerer (1982), Jaws 3D (1982-83), Stealing Heaven (prodr 1987), That Summer of White Roses (prodr and writer 1988); films for TV incl: Jesus of Nazareth (1975), Quatermass (1978), Visitor from the Other Side (1980), The Manions of America (1980-81), Falcon's Gold (1982), Obsessive Love (1984), Sincerely Violet (1986); TV series: Manimal (1983), Falcon Crest 1984-86, Counterstrike (1990); dir: Amy International Productions Inc 1984-, Amy International Productions Ltd 1986-; memb: dirs Guild of America, Screen Actors Guild, British Actors Equity, American Equity, Acad of Motion Pictures Arts and Scis, The British Acad of Film & TV Arts; *Recreations* tennis, skiing, music, writing, photography; *Clubs* St James; *Style*— Simon MacCorkindale, Esq; Amy International Productions Ltd, Greentiles, 2A Park Ave, Wraysbury, Staines, Middx TW19 5ET (☎ 0784 483131/3288)

MCCORMACK, Rev Father Arthur Gerard; s of Frank McCormack (d 1940), of Liverpool, and Elizabeth, *née* Ranard (d 1949); *b* 16 Aug 1911; *Educ* St Francis Xavier Coll Liverpool, Training Coll at St Joseph's Missionary Soc, Univ of Durham (BA); *Career* ordained priest 1936, Mill Hill missionary to Cameroon W Africa 1940-48, invalided home; advsr to superior Gen Mill Hill Missionaries 1963, attended II Vatican Cncl Rome as expert on population and devpt of developing countries 1963-65, co fndr Vatican Cmmn for Justice and Peace 1965, special advsr to Sec Gen World Population Conf Bucharest 1974, dir Population and Devpt Office Rome 1973-76, conslt UN Fund for Population Activities 1975-; Freeman City of Cagayan di Oro Philippines; *Books* People, Space, Food (1960), Christian Responsibility and World Poverty (ed, 1963), World Poverty and the Christian (1963), Poverty and Population (1964), The Popluation Problem (1970), The Population Explosion and Christian Concern (1964), The Multinational Investment: Boon or Burden for the Developing Countries (1980); *Recreations* reading, driving; *Style*— The Rev Father Arthur McCormack; St Joseph's College, Lawrence St, Mill Hill, London NW7 4JX (☎ 081 959 8493, 081 959 8254)

MacCORMACK, Prof Geoffrey Dennis; s of Capt Douglas Muns MacCormack (d 1946), and Kathleen Edith, *née* Peacock; *b* 15 April 1937; *Educ* Parramatta HS Sydney, Univ of Sydney (BA, LLB), Univ of Oxford (MA, DPhil); *m* 25 June 1965, Sabine Gabriele, da of Alfred Oswalt, of Frankfurt; 1 da (Catherine b 3 May 1970); *Career* prof of Jurisprudence Univ of Aberdeen 1971-; *Recreations* walking; *Style*— Prof Geoffrey MacCormack; Department of Jurisprudence, University of Aberdeen, Aberdeen (☎ 0224 272418)

McCORMACK, Most Rev John; *see*: Meath, Bishop of

McCORMACK, Mark Hume; s of Ned Hume McCormack, and Grace Wolfe McCormack; *b* 6 Nov 1930; *Educ* Princeton Univ, William and Mary Coll (BA), Yale Univ Law Sch; *m* 1, 1954, Nancy Breckenridge; 2 s (Breck b 11 Dec 1957, Todd b 2 July 1960), 1 da (Leslie b 21 March 1966); m 2, 1 March 1986, Helen Elizabeth Nagelsen; *Career* Specialist 3 cl Mil Police Corp; admitted Ohio Bar 1957; assoc in Arter Hadden Wykoff & Van Duzer 1957-63 (ptnr 1964); fndr pres (currently chm and chief exec) Int Mgmnt Gp 1962- (handles personalities in int entertainment and sporting world, also handled the Pope's visit to Great Britain 1982); commentator for televised golf; *Books* The World of Professional Golf (1967, 24 edn 1990), Arnie: The Evolution of a Legend (1967), The Wonderful World of Professional Golf (1973), What They Don't Teach You at Harvard Business School (1984), The Terrible Truth About Lawyers (1987), Success Secrets (1989); *Recreations* golf, tennis; *Clubs* Royal and Ancient Golf (St Andrews), Sunningdale Golf, Wentworth (Virginia Water), Annabel's; *Style*— Mark McCormack, Esq; International Management Gp, Pier House, Strand on the Green, Chiswick, London W4 3NN (☎ 01 994 1444, fax 01 994 9606, telex 267486)

MACCORMICK, Iain Somerled MacDonald; s of John MacDonald MacCormick (d 1961), of Glasgow, and Margaret Isobel, *née* Miller; *b* 28 Sept 1939; *Educ* Glasgow HS, Univ of Glasgow (MA); *m* 1, 31 March 1964 (m dis 1986), Micky Trefusis, da of Thomas Cogan Elsom (d 1974), of Inverness; 2 s (Angus b 1965, Duncan b 1966), 3 da (Marion b 1968, Annabel b 1970, Susan b 1976); m 2, 14 Sept 1988, Chardle Story; *Career* Capt Queen's Own Lowland Yeo (TA) 1957-67; asst princ teacher of history and econs Oban HS 1965-74; MP (SNP) Argyll 1974-79; sr nat account mangr British Telecommunications plc 1982-86; cncllr Argyll and Bute Dist Cncl 1979-80, press offr SDP Scot 1982-84; *Recreations* rugby, sailing, local history; *Clubs* Brooke's; *Style*— Iain MacCormick, Esq; Le Bourg, St Pierre Tarentaine, 14350 Le Beny-Bocage, Calvados (☎ 31 19 67 74)

MCCORMICK, John; s of Joseph McCormick (d 1977), and Roseann, *née* McNamara (d 1976); *b* 24 June 1944; *Educ* St Michael's Acad Irvine, Univ of Glasgow (MA, MEd); *m* 4 Aug 1973, Jean Frances, da of William Gibbons, of Kirkintillock, Glasgow; 1 s (Stephen b 1980), 1 da (Lesley Anne b 1978); *Career* teacher St Gregory's Secdy Sch Glasgow 1968-70, educn offr BBC Sch Broadcasting Cncl for Scotland 1970-75, sr educn offr Scotland 1975-82, sec and head of info BBC Scotland 1982-87, sec of the BBC 1987-; memb: Glasgow Children's Panel 1972-77, visiting ctee Glenochil Young Offenders Instn 1979-85; vice-chm Youth-at-Risk Scotland 1985-; *Style*— John McCormick, Esq; BBC, Broadcasting House, London W1A 1AA (☎ 071 927 5090, fax 071 580 9455)

MacCORMICK, Prof (Donald) Neil; s of John MacDonald MacCormick, and Margaret Isobel, *née* Miller; *b* 27 May 1941; *Educ* HS Glasgow, Univ of Glasgow (MA), Balliol Coll Oxford (BA, MA), Univ of Edinburgh (LLD); *m* 6 Nov 1965 (m dis 1988), (Caroline) Karen Rona, da of Archibald Craig Barr (d 1973), of Garrachorran, Argyll; 3 da (Janet b 1966, Morag b 1969, Shena b 1971); *Career* lectr law St Andrews Univ and Queen's Coll Dundee 1965-67, fell Balliol Coll Oxford 1967-72, regius prof public law nature and nations Univ of Edinburgh 1972-; pres Soc Public Teachers of Law 1983-84; memb: Broadcasting Cncl Scotland 1985-89, Nat Cncl Scottish Nat Pty 1989- (and 1978/84, 1985-86); Juris Doctor hc Univ of Uppsala Sweden 1986, FRSE 1986, FBA 1986; *Books* The Scottish Debate (ed, 1970), Lawyers In Their Social Setting (ed, 1976), Legal Reasoning and Legal Theory (1978), HLA Hart (1981), Legal Right and Social Democracy (1982), An Institutional Theory of Law (with Ota Weinberger, 1986), The Legal Mind (ed with P Birks, 1986), Enlightenment, Rights and Revolution (ed with Z Barkowski, 1989); *Recreations* piping, hill walking, sailing; *Clubs* Staff (Edinburgh); *Style*— Prof Neil MacCormick, FRSE; 9 Warrender Park Terrace, Edinburgh EH9 1JA (☎ 031 229 7758); Centre for Criminology and the Social and Philosophical Study of Law, Faculty of Law, Univ of Edinburgh EH8 9YL (☎ 031 667 1011 ext 2260, fax 031 662 4902, telex 721442 UNIVED G)

McCORMICK, Sean Robert; s of Lt-Col Robert McCormick, of Windsor, Berks, and Letitia *née* Worsley; *b* 1 May 1950; *Educ* Alexandra GS Singapore, Chard Sch Somerset; *m* 22 Nov 1977, Zandra, da of Frederick William Hollick; 1 s (Liam b 1978), 1 da (Katy b 1984); *Career* Actg Pilot Offr RAF, aircrew trg RAF Henlow; assoc dir broadcast buying mangr Leo Burnett advertising agency 1970-76, sr media mangr R H Kirkwood & Co advertising agency 1976-78, dep md BBDO UK formerly SJIP/BBDO (previously media dir and ptnr SJIP advertising agency 1978-84), ptnr and bd account dir Horner Collis & Kirwan 1984, fndr ptnr Juler McCormick West 1987, chm Good Business Ltd, communications devpt dir Gears Gross plc; *Recreations* motor racing, go karting, rugby, cricket, family life; *Clubs* BARC, RAC; *Style*— Sean McCormick, Esq; Windyridge, High Park Avenue, East Horsley, Surrey KT24 5DF; 110 St Martin's Lane, London WC2N 4DY (☎ 01 240 7100, fax 01 240 5500, mobile tel 0836 236883)

McCORQUODALE, Alastair; er (but sole surviving) s of Maj Kenneth McCorquodale, MC, TD (himself 1 cous of 1 and last Baron McCorquodale of Newton); *b* 5 Dec 1925; *Educ* Harrow; *m* 1947, Rosemary, er da of Maj Herbert Broke Turnor, MC, JP, DL and Lord of the Manors of Stoke Rochford, Little Ponton and Colsterworth (gs of Lady Caroline, *née* Finch Hatton, eld da 10 Earl Winchilsea, by his w Lady Enid, *née* Vane, er da of 13 Earl of Westmoreland, CBE, JP, and wid of Hon Henry Vane, eld s of 9 Baron; 1 s (Neil b 10 April 1951, *m* Lady Sarah, *née* Spencer), 1 da (Mrs Geoffrey Van Cutsem, *qv*); *Career* chm McCorquodale & Co Ltd; dir: Br Sugar Corpn Ltd, McCorquodale & Blades Tst Ltd, McCorquodale (Scotland) Ltd, Guardian Royal Exchange Assur 1983-; *Style*— Alastair McCorquodale, Esq; McCorquodale & Co Ltd, 15 Cavendish Sq, London W1M GHT (☎ 071 637 3511)

McCORQUODALE, Hon Mrs ((Charlotte) Enid); da of 1 Baron Luke, KBE (d 1943), and Laura (d 1942); *b* 13 Oct 1910; *m* 1933, George McCorquodale (d 1979), s of Norman McCorquodale (d 1937); 1 s (Hamish, *qv*), 3 da (Mrs Hugh Wilbraham b 1935, Mrs Simon Biddulph (*see* Peerage Baron Buddulph), Mrs Charles Barnett); *Style*— The Hon Mrs McCorquodale; The Old Rectory, Hethe, nr Bicester, Oxfordshire OX6 9ES

McCORQUODALE, Hamish Norman; s of George McCorquodale (d 1979), and the Hon Mrs Charlotte Enid McCorquodale, *qv*; *b* 6 Feb 1945; *Educ* Harrow, AMP Harvard; *m* 27 July 1985, Mary Anne, da of Capt Peter Cookson, of Pennshill, Lower Slaughter, Cheltenham, Glos; 1 s (Malcolm George b 3 Oct 1989), 1 da (Caroline b 31 Aug 1987); *Career* md: Aeroprint Ltd (part of IBF Group Brazil) 1990-, Garamond Ltd 1989-90; fin dir Hambro Countrywide plc 1987-89, dir McCorquodale plc 1982-86; ACA 1968, FCA 1978; *Recreations* shooting, fishing, deer stalking; *Clubs* Boodle's, Pratt's; *Style*— Hamish McCorquodale, Esq; The Old Rectory, Hethe, nr Bicester, Oxon (☎ 0869 277218); Gatehouse Way, Aylesbury, Bucks HP19 3DD (☎ 0296 85131)

McCORQUODALE, Ian; s of Hugh McCorquodale, MC (d 1963), and Barbara Cartland, *qv*; bro of Countess Spencer, *qv*; *b* 11 Oct 1937; *Educ* Harrow, Magdalene Coll Cambridge; *m* Anna, *née* Chisholm; 2 da; *Career* former commercial and export mangr Br Printing Corp; chm: Debrett's Peerage Ltd, Corporate Broking Servs Ltd, Media Investmts Ltd; ptnr Cartland Promotions 1976-; dir Royal Exchange Art Gallery; *Recreations* fishing, shooting, gardening, tennis; *Clubs* Boodle's, White's; *Style*— Ian McCorquodale, Esq; 112 Whitehall Ct, London SW1

McCORQUODALE, Lady (Elizabeth) Sarah Lavinia; *née* Spencer; da (by 1 m) of 8 Earl of Spencer, MVO, JP, DL, *qv*; sis of HRH The Princess of Wales (*see* Royal Family); *b* 19 March 1955; *Educ* West Heath Sevenoaks, Le Vieux Chalet Château d'Oex Switzerland; *m* 1980, Neil Edmund McCorquodale, s of Alastair McCorquodale, *qv*, and Rosemary, *née* Turnor, da of Lady Enid Vane (da of 13 Earl of Westmorland); 1 s (George b 1984), 2 da (Emily b 1983, Celia b 1989); *Style*— The Lady Sarah McCorquodale; Stoke Rochford, Grantham, Lincs

McCOSH, Prof Andrew MacDonald; s of Rev Andrew McCosh (d 1970), of Dunblane, Scotland, and Margaret, *née* MacDonald (d 1968); *b* 16 Sept 1940; *Educ* Edinburgh Acad, Univ of Edinburgh (BSc), Univ of Harvard (DBA); *m* 17 July 1965, Anne, da of Nicholas Rogers (d 1981), of Tenterden, Kent; 3 da (Alison Christine b 1970, Linda b 1970, Susan b 1972); *Career* assoc prof of accounting Univ of Michigan 1966-71; prof: of mgmnt accounting Manchester Business Sch 1971-85, of the orgn of industry and commerce Univ of Edinburgh 1986-; MBA Manchester 1976; CA Scott Inst 1963; *Books* Practical Controllership (1973), Management Decision Support Systems (1978), Developing Managerial Information Systems (1983), Organisational Decision Support Systems (1988); *Recreations* fishing, climbing, golf; *Clubs* Caledonian; *Style*— Prof Andrew McCosh; University of Edinburgh, 50 George Sq, Edinburgh EH8 9JY (☎ 031 667 1011, fax 031 668 3053, telex 727442)

McCOSH OF HUNTFIELD, Lt Cdr Bryce Knox; JP (Lanark); s of Robert McCosh of Hardington, OBE, MC, WS, JP (d 1959), and Agnes Dunlop Knox; *b* 30 March 1920; *Educ* Loretto; *m* 1948, Sylvia Mary (Lady of the Manors of Dacre, Dalemain and Barton, Patterdale and Martindale in the Co of Cumberland), da of Edward William Hasell of Dalemain, JP, DL (d 1972); 3 s; *Career* Lt Cdr RNVR; WWII 1939-46 served: Atlantic, Channel, Dieppe, Far East; formerly with Linen Thread Co, dir W J Knox Ltd and others, sr ptnr SM Penney & Macgeorge stockbrokers (Glasgow, Edinburgh and London) 1956-76, hon pres Cncl Thistle Fndn; formerly: chm Thistle Tst, dir Target Trust Managers (Scotland) Ltd, Rachan Investments Ltd; ret farmer; memb Royal Co of Archers (Queen's Body Guard for Scotland), chm Biggar Museum Tst, Church of Scot Session Clerk; *Recreations* shooting; *Style*— Lt Cdr Bryce McCosh of Huntfield, JP; Huntfield Estate Office, Biggar ML12 6NA, Scotland (☎ 0899 20208); Dalemain Estate Office, Dacre, Penrith, Cumbria CA11 OHB (☎ 076 8486450)

McCOUBREY, Hon Mrs (Anne Lynd); *née* Lowry; 2 da of Baron Lowry, PC (Life Peer), *qv*; *b* 1952; *m* 1980, Neville McCoubrey, QGM; 1 s, 2 da; *Style*— The Hon Mrs McCoubrey

McCOWAN, Rt Hon Lord Justice; Rt Hon Sir Anthony James Denys McCowan; PC (1989); s of John McCowan, MBE, of Georgetown, Br Guiana; *b* 12 Jan 1928; *Educ* Epsom, BNC Oxford; *m* 1961, Sue, da of Reginald Harvey, of Braiseworth Hall, Tannington, Suffolk; 2 s, 1 da; *Career* called to the bar Gray's Inn 1951, QC 1972, rec Crown Ct 1972-81, judge of the High Ct (Queen's Bench) 1981-89, presiding judge SE Circuit 1986-89 (ldr 1978-81), Lord Justice of Appeal 1989-, bencher Gray's Inn 1980; memb: Parole Bd 1982-84, Crown Ct Rule Ctee 1982-88; *Style*— The Rt Hon Lord Justice McCowan; c/o Royal Courts of Justice, Strand, London WC2A 2LL

McCOWAN, David William Cargill; s of Sir David James Cargill McCowan, 2 Bt (d 1965); hp of bro, Sir Hew Cargill McCowan, 3 Bt; *b* 28 Feb 1934; *m* ; 1 s (David b 1975), 1 da; *Style*— David McCowan, Esq

McCOWAN, Sir Hew Cargill; 3 Bt (UK 1934); s of Sir David James Cargill McCowan, 2 Bt (d 1965); *b* 26 July 1930; *Heir* bro, David William Cargill McCowan; *Style*— Sir Hew McCowan, Bt; Marbelo, Malviera da Serra, Cascais, Portugal

McCOWEN, Hon Mrs (Philippa Ursula Maud); *née* Baillie; 2 da of 3 Baron Burton by his 1 w; *b* 1951; *m* 1980, Ian McCowen; 2 s (Ewan b 1981, Christopher Richard b 1983); *Style*— The Hon Mrs McCowen; Polwarth Manse, Greenlaw, Berwickshire

McCOY, Hugh O'Neill; s of Hugh O'Neill McCoy, and Nora May, *née* Bradley; *b* 9 Feb 1939; *Educ* Dudley GS, Univ of London; *m* Margaret Daphne, da of Robert John Corfield; *Career* currently dir: Horace Clarkson plc, Holman Wade Insurance Group, Victoria (Hong Kong) Shipbrokers Ltd; currently dep chm H Clarkson & Co Ltd; vice pres and pres elect Inst Chartered Shipbrokers; memb Lloyds; Freeman City of London, Liveryman Worshipful Co of Shipwrights; FICS; *Style*— Hugh McCoy, Esq; Horace Clarkson plc, 12 Camomile St, London EC3A 7BP (☎ 071 283 9020, fax 071 283 5260)

McCOY, Sylvester; s of Percy James Kent-Smith (d 1943), and Molly Sheridan (d 1969); *b* 20 Aug 1943; *Educ* Blair's Coll Aberdeen, Dunoon GS; *m* Agnes, da of Tenn Verkaik; 2 s (Sam Kent-Smith b 19 Feb 1976, Joe Kent-Smith b 6 Nov 1977); *Career* actor; theatre incl: Ken Campbell's Roadshow, theatre workshop with Joan Littlewood, title role in The Pied Piper (NT), Feste in Twelfth Night (Leicester), Tranio in The Taming of The Shrew and Pompey in Anthony and Cleopatra (Haymarket), Stephano in The Tempest (Ludlow Festival), Puck in Benjamin Britten's A Midsummer Night's Dream (WNO), Asdak in Caucasian Chalk Circle (Young Vic), Androcles in Androcles and the Lion, Stan Laurel in Gone With Hardy (London and Toronto), Burt in I Miss My War, Satie in Adrian Mitchell's Satiesday Night, Bix in Hoagy Bix and Wolfgang Beethoven Bunkhaus, all the other parts in Can't Pay Won't Pay (Criterion), Pinnochio in Abracadabra (Lyric), Samuel in Pirates of Penzance (Drury Lane), Genie in Aladdin (Palace Theatre Manchester), The Devil in Temptation (Westminster Theatre), Good Robber in Babes in the Wood (Cambridge Arts), Count in Rajad Bolt's trans of Marriage of Figaro (Watford); TV incl: Vision On (BBC), Tizwoz (Central TV), Big Jim and The Finger Club (BBC), Eureka (BBC), Starstrider (Granada), Dr Who (BBC), What's Your Story (BBC), Last Place on Earth (ITV); radio incl: Big Jim and the Figaro Club, The Shiver Show, Play For Radio 3; films incl: Dracula, The Secret Policeman's Ball, 3 Kinds of Heat; played Spoons with London Concert Orch at Barbican Hall; *Recreations* contemplating cycling, walking and yachting; *Clubs* Groucho; *Style*— Sylvester McCoy, Esq; Michael Ladkin Personal Management, 11 Southwick Mews, London W2 1JG (☎ 071 402 6644)

McCRACKEN, John Strachan; CBE (1986); s of Robert Ralston McCracken (d 1959), and Susan Dorian Strachan; *b* 5 July 1930; *Educ* Beath HS, Univ of Edinburgh (BSc); *m* 1, 1954, Margaret Boswell Smith (d 1984), da of George Allan Buchan (d 1961); 2 da (Margaret b 1955, Suzanne b 1957), 1 s (Ralston b 1959); m 2, 1988, Moira Ann, da of late Eric Stein, of Westchester, USA; *Career* Lt RN 1953-56; IBM UK Ltd 1956; dir: IBM Scotland and N England 1980-85, Int Business Machines Ltd 1980-86, Scot Endeavour Trg 1983-85, Scot Nat Orch 1985-, Scott Lithgow Ltd 1984-88, IBM Communications 1985-89, IBM UK Ltd 1986-89, Ewbank Preece 1988-, Pan World Travel 1989-; memb: Bd Scot Devpt Agency 1980-86, BR (Scotland) 1984-89; chm Exec Cncl Scot Business in the Community 1982-86; tstee: Nat Museums of Scot 1985-, Soc of Scot Artists 1984-; memb Cncl: Edinburgh Festival 1985-, Scot Enterprise Fndn 1981-85, Scot Graduate Enterprise 1981-85; *Recreations* golf, art, music, cricket; *Clubs* Caledonian, Bruntsfield Links, MCC, New (Edinburgh); *Style*— John S McCracken, Esq, CBE; 23 Clarendon Street, London SW1 (☎ 071 630 6561); Big Canoe, Ga 30143, USA (404 268 3439)

McCRAE, Ian Robert; s of John McCrae (d 1974), of Auchen Castle, Beattock, Dumfriesshire, and Marion Isabella, *née* Provan-Logan (d 1962); *b* 13 May 1932; *Educ* The HS of Glasgow, The Scottish Hotel Sch; *Career* personnel dir Waldorf Hotel London 1960-64, gen mangr Excelsior Hotel Manchester 1964-66, proprietor Auchen Castle Hotel Beattock Dumfriesshire 1966-76; conslt to Nat Tst for Scotland 1980-87; chm: British SPAS Fedn, Ross & Cromarty Tourist Bd, Ross & Cromarty Heritage Soc; Highland memb Nat Tst for Scotland; supporter of charities Malcolm Sargeant Cancer Fund for Children; memb: Incorpn of Wrights Glasgow, The Grand Antiquity Soc Glasgow; *Recreations* music, walking, gardening; *Style*— Ian McCrae, Esq; Eden

Cottage, Jamestown, Strathpeffer, Ross-shire IV14 9ER (☎ 0997 21934)

McCRAE, Dr (William) Morrice; s of William Boyd McCrae (d 1982), of Kilmarnock, and Jean Alexandra, *née* Morrice; *b* 11 March 1932; *Educ* Kilmarnock Acad, Univ of Glasgow (MB ChB); *m* 28 Mar 1987, Jennifer Jane, da of John Graham (d 1985), of Aberdour, Fife; *Career* Capt RAMC 1955-57; lectr in child health Univ of Glasgow (hall fell in med), conslt physician Royal Hosp for Sick Children Edinburgh 1965, hon sr lectr Univ of Edinburgh, pubns on genetics and eastroenterology; FRCPE, FRCP Glasgow; *Recreations* gardening, history; *Clubs* New, Scottish Art; *Style—* Dr Morrice McCrae; Seabank House, Aberdour, Fife KY3 1TY (☎ 0383 860452)

McCRAE, William; s of James Farrell McCrae, and Rose Ann, *née* McGeachie; *b* 10 Oct 1934; *Educ* Holyrood Sr Secdy Sch Glasgow, Univ of Glasgow (BSc, Phd); *m* 15 April 1966, Carole Elizabeth, da of Henry Douglas Rose (d 1984); 2 da (Catherine Alexandra b 1971, Jennifer Elaine b 1973); *Career* Glasgow Univ Air Sqdn (RAFVR), Student Pilot Offr 1957-59; res chm Lederle Labs Pearl River USA 1961-64, ICI fell and NATO fell Univ of Cambridge 1964-66, res chm and admin Syntex Labs Palo Alto USA 1966-71, dep gen mangr licensing Wilkinson Match plc, dir technol transfer PA Management Consultants Ltd 1978-80, conslt NEB and Celltech 1980-81, co-fndr and non exec dir Bioclone Ltd, co-fndr and md Cambridge Life Sciences plc 1981-88; fndr and dir: Fieldguild Ltd, Abington Associates; tech and commercial conslt to the healthcare indust 1988-; *Recreations* golf; *Style—* William McCrae, Esq; 19 Meadow Walk, Great Abington, Cambridge CB1 6AZ (☎ 0223 892294)

McCRAITH, Hon Mrs (Philippa Mary Ellis); *née* Robins; da of 1 and last Baron Robins (d 1962); *b* 19 Sept 1923; *m* 16 Feb 1946, Col Patrick James Danvers McCraith, MC, TD, DL, s of late Sir Douglas McCraith, of Normanton Grange, Notts; 1 s, 1 da; *Style—* The Hon Mrs McCraith; Cranfield House, Southwell, Notts

McCREA, Sir William Hunter; s of Robert Hunter McCrea (d 1956), of Chesterfield, and Margaret, *née* Hutton (d 1963); *b* 13 Dec 1904; *Educ* Chesterfield Sch, Trinity Coll Univ of Cambridge (MA, PhD, ScD), Göttingen Univ; *m* 1933, Marian Nicol Core, da of Thomas Webster, JP (d 1939), of Edinburgh; 1 s (Roderick), 2 da (Isabella, Sheila); *Career* WWII Flt Lt RAFVR (trg branch) 1941-45, temp princ experimental offr Admty 1943-45; prof of mathematics: Queen's Univ Belfast 1936-44, Royal Holloway Coll London 1944-66; prof of astronomy Univ of Sussex 1966-72 (emeritus prof 1972-); pres: Royal Astronomical Soc 1961-63, Mathematical Assoc 1973-74; Freeman City of London 1988; kt 1985; FRS 1952; *Books* Relativity Physics (1935), Analytical Geometry of Three Dimensions (1942), Physics of the Sun and Stars (1950), Royal Greenwich Observatory (1975); *Recreations* walking, travel; *Clubs* Athenaeum; *Style—* Sir William McCrea; 87 Houndean Rise, Lewes, Sussex BN7 1EJ (☎ 0273 473296); Astronomy Centre, Univ of Sussex, Brighton BN1 9QH (☎ 0273 606755, telex 877159 BHVTXS G)

McCREA, Rev Dr (Robert Thomas) William; MP (UDUP) Mid-Ulster 1983-; s of Robert Thomas McCrea, and Sarah Jane, *née* Whann; *b* 6 Aug 1948; *Educ* Cookstown HS, Theological Hall Free Press Church of Ulster; *m* 25 June 1971, Anne Shirley, da of George McKnight (d 1983), of Rathfriland, Co Down; 2 s (Ian b 1976, Stephen b 1978), 3 da (Sharon b 1973, Faith b 1979, Grace b 1980); *Career* memb NI Assembly 1982-85; dist cncllr 1973- (chm 1977-81); gospel singer (recording artist) received 2 silver, 2 gold and 1 platinum disc for record sales; dir Daybreak Recordings Co; Hon Dr of Divinity 1989; *Recreations* riding; *Style—* The Rev Dr William McCrea, MP; 10 Highfield Road, Magherafelt, Co Londonderry, N Ireland BT45 5JD (☎ 0648 32664, fax 0648 32035)

McCREDIE, Ian Forbes; OBE (1984); s of John Henry McCredie, and Diana, *née* Harris; *b* 28 Dec 1950; *Educ* Harvey GS, Churchill Coll Cambridge (MA); *m* 20 March 1976, (Katharine) Lucy, da of Sir Robert John Frank, 3 Bt (d 1987), of Reading; 1 s (James b 1981), 1 da (Alexandra b 1983); *Career* diplomat; Br Embassy Copenhagen 1985-89; *Recreations* squash, jazz, food and drink; *Style—* Ian McCredie, Esq, OBE

McCRICKARD, Don; s of Peter McCrickard (d 1975), and Gladys Mary McCrickard (d 1982); *b* 25 Dec 1936; *Educ* Hove GS, LSE, Univ of Malaya; *m* 7 May 1960, Stella May, da of Walter Edward Buttle (d 1984); 2 da (Sarah Jane b 1961, Lucy Gail b 1965); *Career* chief exec UK (later Far East) American Express Co 1975-83, chief exec United Dominions Trust Ltd; chm: UDT Bank Ltd, Swan National Ltd, Barnet Enterprise Trust Ltd 1986-; dir Hill Samuel Group plc 1987-; chief exec: TSB Bank plc 1989-, gp chief exec TSB Group plc 1990-; *Recreations* golf, tennis, theatre; *Clubs* RAC; *Style—* Don McCrickard, Esq; 25 Milk St, London EC2V 8LU (☎ 071 606 7070)

MacCRINDLE, Robert Alexander; QC; s of Fergus R MacCrindle (d 1965), of Ayrs, and Jean, *née* Hill (d 1976); *b* 27 Jan 1928; *Educ* Girvan HS, King's Coll London (LLB), Gonville and Caius Coll Cambridge (LLM); *m* 1959, Pauline Dilys, da of Mark S Morgan, of Berks; 1 s (Guy), 1 da (Claire); *Career* Flt Lt RAF 1948-50; called to the Bar Gray's Inn 1952, memb Bar of Hong Kong; conseil juridique, ptnr Shearman & Sterling NY; memb Royal Cmmn on Civil Liability; fell of American Coll of Trial Lawyers; *Recreations* golf; *Clubs* Univ (NY); *Style—* R A MacCrindle, Esq, QC; 88 Ave de Breteuil, 75015 Paris (☎ 33 1 4567 1193); 12 Rue d'Astorg 75008 Paris (☎ 33 1 4471 1717)

McCRINDLE, Sir Robert Arthur; MP (C) Brentwood and Ongar 1974-; s of late Thomas Arthur McCrindle, of Girvan, Ayrs; *b* 1929; *Educ* Allen Glen's Coll Glasgow; *m* 1953, Myra, da of James P Anderson, of Glasgow; 2 s; *Career* dir: Langham Life Assurance Co 1972-76, Worldmark Travel Ltd 1978-82, Hogg Robinson plc 1987-, M & G Assurance Group; chm: Cometco Ltd 1972-78, City Bond Storage plc, Parly Aviation Gp; MP (C) Billericay 1970-74, PPS to Min of State Home Office 1974, advsr to Br Caledonian Airways, conslt to Br Insur and Investmt Brokers Assoc; memb Select Ctees on: Trade and Indust 1983-87, Tport 1988-; *Style—* Sir Robert McCrindle, MP; 26 Ashburnham Gdns, Upminster, Essex (☎ 040 22 27152)

McCRORY, Glenn George; s of Brian McCrory, of Annfield Plain, Stanley, Co Durham, and Gloria, *née* Barrass; *b* 23 Sept 1964; *Educ* St Patrick's Dipton Co Durham, St Bede's Lanchester; *m* 1 June 1985, Amanda Teresa, da of Andrew Walsh, of Annfield Plain, Co Durham; 1 s (Joseph b 24 Oct 1990), 1 da (Victoria b 24 Nov 1985); *Career* boxer; nat jr champion (middleweight), young England rep (light- heavy, undefeated British Cwlth Cruiserweight Champion, IBF World Cruiserweight Champion; professional boxing mangr; boxing commentator for BBC, ITV, Sky; made acting debut 1990; memb Equity; Boxing News Prospect of Year 1985, Boxer of Year 1989, NE Sports Personality 1989; *Recreations* sport, acting, reading; *Style—* Glenn McCrory, Esq; 18-21 Station Rd, Stanley, Co Durham (☎ 0207 234064)

MCCRUM, Michael William; s of late Capt C R McCrum, RN, and Ivy Hilda Constance, *née* Nicholson; *b* 23 May 1924; *Educ* Sherborne, Corpus Christi Coll Cambridge (scholar, BA, MA); *m* 1952, Christine Mary Kathleen, da of Sir Arthur Fforde, GBE; 3 s, 1 da; *Career* WWII RN 1943-45 (Sub Lt RNVR 1943); asst master Rugby Sch 1948-50 (lower bench master 1949-50); Corpus Christi Coll Cambridge: fellow 1949, second tutor 1950-51, tutor 1951-62, master 1980-; headmaster: Tonbridge Sch 1962-70, Eton 1970-80; vice chllr Univ of Cambridge 1987-89; Univ of Cambridge: memb Council of the Senate 1955-58 and 1981-89, memb Gen Bd of Faculties 1957-62 and 1987-89, memb Fin Bd 1985-89, chm Faculty Bd of Educn 1981-86, memb Bd of Extra-Mural Studies 1982-86; chm: HMC 1974, Jt Educnl Tst 1984-87, GBA 1989- (dep chm 1982-89), Cathedrals Fabric Cmmn 1990-; memb Governing Body Schools Cncl 1969-76; govr: Bradfield Coll 1956-62, Eastbourne Coll 1960-62, King's Sch Canterbury 1980-, Sherborne Sch 1980-, Oakham Sch 1981-85, United World Coll of the Atlantic 1981-, Rugby Sch 1982-; tstee: King George VI and Queen Elizabeth Fndn of St Catherine's Cumberland Lodge 1983-, Nat Heritage Meml Fund 1984-90; Hon Freeman Worshipful Co of Skinners 1980; Hon DEd Victoria BC 1989; Comendador de la Orden de Isabel la Catdlica (Spain) 1988; *Books* Select Documents of the Principates of the Fluvian Emperors AD 68-96 (with A G Woodhead, 1961), Thomas Arnold - Headmaster (1989); *Clubs* Athenaeum, United Oxford & Cambridge University, East India, Devonshire, Sports and Public Schools, Hawks (Cambridge); *Style—* Michael McCrum, Esq; The Master's Lodge, Corpus Christi College, Cambridge CB2 1RH (☎ 0223 338029)

McCRUM, (John) Robert; s of Michael William McCrum, of Cambridge, and Christine Mary Kathleen, *née* fforde; *b* 7 July 1953; *Educ* Sherborne, Corpus Christi Coll Cambridge (scholar, MA), Univ of Pennyslvania (Thouron fell); *m* 1979 (m dis 1984), Olivia Timbs; *Career* reader Chatto & Windus 1977-79, ed in chief Faber & Faber 1990- (ed dir 1979-89); books: In The Secret State 1980, A Loss of Heart 1982, The Fabulous Englishman 1984, The Story of English (non fiction, 1986), The World is a Banana (for children, 1988); for The Story of English: Peabody Award 1986, Emmy 1987; *Style—* Robert McCrum, Esq; Faber & Faber Ltd, 3 Queen Square, London W1CN 3AU (☎ 071 465 0045)

McCRYSTAL, Damien Peter Adam Doyle; s of Cal C McCrystal, of 94 Totteridge Lane, London N20, and Stella Maris, *née* Doyle; *b* 23 March 1961; *Educ* Christ's Coll Finchley; *Career* dep ed: Advertiser North London GP, PR Week; city corr London Evening Standard, asst city ed Today, city ed The Sun, presenter What the Papers Say, columnist Punch; *Style—* Damien McCrystal, Esq; 2 Grove Park, Camberwell, London SE5 (☎ 071 733 7100)

McCUBBIN, Very Rev David; s of David McCubbin (d 1977), of Greenock, Strathclyde, and Annie Robertson Cram, *née* Young (d 1965); *b* 2 Nov 1929; *Educ* Finnart Sch Greenock, Greenock Acad, King's Coll London (AKC), S Boniface Coll Warminster; *Career* ordained Wells Cathedral: deacon 1955, priest 1956; curate Christ Church Frome 1955-57, curate Glastonbury Parish Church 1957-60; rector: Holy Trinity Dunoon 1960-63, St Peter's Kirkcaldy 1963-70, Wallsend Parish Church 1970-79; surrogate Diocese of Newcastle 1970-79; rector: St John's Aberdeen 1979-81, St Bride's Kelvinside Glasgow 1981-87; provost and first canon Cumbrae Cath 1987-, rector St Andrew's Millport 1987-, canon St John's Cath Oban 1987-, synod clerk Diocese of Argyll and The Isles 1988-; ed: Agryll & The Isles Diocesan Gazette 1960-63, Glasgow & Galloway Diocesan Gazette 1981-85; chm: Govrs Wallsend C of E Sch 1970-79, mangrs Wallsend C of E First Sch 1970-79, Prayer Book Soc (Scotland) 1988-; *Recreations* reading, music, walking; *Style—* The Very Rev the Provost of Cumbrae Cathedral; The College Millport, Millport, Isle of Cumbrae KA28 0HE (☎ 0475 530 353)

McCUBBIN, Henry Bell; MEP (Lab) N E Scot 1989-; s of late Henry McCubbin and Agnes McCubbin; *b* 15 July 1942; *Educ* Allan Glen's Sch Glasgow, Open Univ (BA Soc Sci); *m* Katie Mary, da of Malcolm Campbell, of Isle of Harris; 3 da; *Career* film cameraman: BBC TV 1960-77, Grampian TV 1977-89; dir Dundee Repertory Theatre 1985; memb: CND, Friends of the Earth; *Recreations* theatre, the arts, hill walking; *Style—* Henry McCubbin, Esq, MEP; 58 Castle Street, Broughty Ferry, Dundee DD5 2EJ (☎ 0328 730773)

McCUBBIN, Ronald Andrew (Ron); s of Niblock McCubbin (d 1968), of Glasgow, and Margaret, *née* Hughes (d 1971); *b* 27 May 1935; *Educ* Whitehill Secdy Sch, Univ of Strathclyde (Dip in Mgmnt Studies); *m* 4 Oct 1962, Elizabeth Connery, da of late William K Wilson; 2 s (Colin William b 29 May 1966, Alan Ronald b 13 May 1969); *Career* Nat Serv RASC 1953-55; Stewarts & Lloyds Ltd: clerical asst Steel Records Dept 1950-53, Wages Dept 1955-60, asst cashier 1960-64, PA to Gen Mangr 1964-69, cashier 1969-70; British Steel Corporation; pensions offr 1970-72, sec Manual Grades Superannuation Scheme 1972-81, sec Staff and Manual Grades Superannuation Schemes 1981, currently sec British Steel Pension Scheme; assoc Pensions Mgmnt Inst 1976; *Recreations* golf; *Clubs* Windyhill Golf; *Style—* Ron McCubbin, Esq; Secretary, British Steel Pension Scheme, Central Pensions Office, Box 22, Motherwell Lanarkshire ML1 1SX (☎ 0698 66211, fax 0698 75040)

McCUE, Ian Roderick; s of John McCue, and Frances Mary, *née* Quantrill; *b* 24 May 1937; *Educ* Gravesend Tech Sch, SE London Tech Coll (HNC); *m* 1 April 1961, Stella Kathleen, da of Henry Battle; 1 s (Sean decd), 2 da (Jane b 1964, Sara b 1965); *Career* electrical engr; student apprentice Siemen Brothers Ltd 1953-59, co-fndr md Sarasota Automation Ltd 1966; dir: Sarasota Automation Inc USA 1978-90 (also pres), CEO Sarasota Technology plc 1982-88, Peek plc 1987-90; chm McCue plc 1990-; FBIM, FID; *Recreations* power boating, flying (private pilot's license), photography; *Clubs* The Field (Florida, USA); *Style—* Ian R McCue, Esq; Parsonage Barn, Compton, Hampshire SO21 2AS (☎ and fax 0962 713049)

McCULLAGH, Dr Anthony Graham; s of Dr Graham Patterson McCullagh (d 1957), and Margaret Janet, *née* Dick; *b* 5 July 1947; *Educ* King's Coll Choir Sch Cambridge, Epsom Coll, Queen's Coll Cambrige (BA), St Bart's Hosp London (MB BCh); *m* 29 May 1971, Lucy Ann, da of George Horace Alphonse Pearce, of Eastbourne; 1 s (Edward b 1985), 1 da (Hannah Margaret b 1983); *Career* princ in GP Lakeside Health Centre Thamesmead London SE2 1980-, clinical lectr in GP Guys Hosp London 1980-, forensic med examiner (police surgn) 1987-; memb: local med ctee Greenwich and Bexley 1986, Post Grad Educn Sub Ctee 1989, SE London Trainer Selection Ctee for GPs 1989; Freeman Worshipful Soc of Apothecaries; BMA; *Books* Endocrinology, common medical diseases in practice (jtly, 1985); *Recreations* sailing; *Clubs* Frobisher SC; *Style—* Dr Anthony McCullagh; Lakeside Health Centre, Thamesmead, London SE2 9UQ (☎ 081 310 3281)

McCULLOCH, Hon Mrs (Cecily Mary Clare); *née* Cornwallis; el da of 3 Baron Cornwallis, OBE, DL (by his 2 w); *b* 23 Oct 1954; *m* 1980, Ian McCulloch; 3 s (Ruari b 1982, Rohan b 1984, Fiennes b 1989), 1 da (Skye b 1987); *Style—* The Hon Mrs McCulloch; c/o 25b Queen's Gate Mews, London SW7

MCCULLOCH, James Russell; s of Dr John McCulloch, of 27 Langside Drive, Newlands, Glasgow, and Laura Patricia, *née* Russell; *b* 19 Nov 1954; *Educ* Glasgow Acad, Univ of Stirling (BA); *m* 16 Oct 1980, Sally Lindsay, da of Benjamin Butters; 3 da (Lindsay Anne b 17 July 1984, Victoria Jayne b 6 June 1986, Caroline Fiona b 12 April 1989); *Career* CA; articled clerk Coopers & Lybrand Glasgow 1976-79, audit mangr Coopers & Lybrand Houston Texas USA 1980-82, ptnr Speirs & Jeffrey 1985- (joined 1982); memb Stock Exchange 1985; memb Merchant House of Glasgow 1990; MICAS 1979; *Recreations* golf, squash, tennis, skiing; *Clubs* Glasgow Academical, Royal Scottish Automobile, Pollok Golf; *Style—* James McCulloch, Esq; 16 Calderwood Rd, Newlands, Glasgow G43 2RP (☎ 041 637 1892); Speirs & Jeffrey Ltd, 36 Renfield St, Glasgow G2 1NA (☎ 041 248 4311, fax 041 221 4764)

MacCULLOCH, Dr Malcolm John; s of William MacCulloch (d 1976), of Macclesfield, Cheshire, and Constance Martha, *née* Clegg; *b* 10 July 1936; *Educ* Kings Sch Macclesfield, Univ of Manchester (MB ChB, DPM, MD); *m* 1, 14 July 1962 (m dis 1975), Mary Louise, da of Ernest Sutcliffe Beton (d 1987), of Norwich; 1 s (Thomas

Alistair b 1965), 1 da (Louise Elizabeth Mary b 1968); m 2, 24 Sept 1975, Carolyn Mary, da of Sqdn Ldr (William) Alan Walker Reid, of London; 2 da (Sarah Caroline b 1976, Sophie Isabel 1978); *Career* conslt child psychiatrist Cheshire 1966-67, lectr in child in psychiatry and subnormality Univ of Birmingham 1967-70, sr lectr psychiatry Univ of Liverpool 1970-75, sr princ med offr DHSS London 1975-79, med dir Park Lane Hosp Liverpool 1979-89, conslt WHO 1977-79, visiting prof of forensic psychiatry Toronto 1987-89, advsr in forensic psychiatry Ontario Govt 1987-89, sr res psychiatrist Ashworth Hosp Liverpool 1989-; author of numerous pubns in professional jls; FRCPsych 1976; *Books* Homosexual Behaviour: Therapy and Assessment (1971), Human Sexual Behaviour (1980); *Recreations* music, golf, horse riding, inventing; *Style*— Dr Malcolm MacCulloch; 10 Abbotsford Rd, Blundellsands, Merseyside L23 6UX (☎ 051 924 4989)

McCULLOCH, Rt Rev Nigel Simeon; *see*: Taunton, Bishop of

McCULLOCH, Robert Brownlie; s of Robert McCulloch (d 1969); *b* 13 Dec 1939; *Educ* Victoria Drive and Hyndland Schs, Univ of Glasgow; *m* 1964, Lilias Stewart; 1 s, 1 da; *Career* CA; co sec Smith & McLaurin Ltd 1966-71, plant accountant Leyland Nat Co Ltd 1971-73, sec and chief accountant Bridon Engineering Ltd 1973-76, fin dir GTE Sylvania (UK) Ltd and princ subsids 1976-85, mfrg controller Euro Lighting Div GTE Sylvania Inc (USA) 1982-84, fin dir and co sec Carter & Parker Ltd and subsids 1985-; FBIM, FInstD; *Recreations* tennis, badminton, gardening; *Style*— Robert McCulloch, Esq; 27 Dalesway, Tranmere Park, Guiseley, W Yorks (☎ 0943 79080, office 0943 72264, telex 51234 WENDY G)

McCULLOUGH, John; s of Henry Christie McCullough, of Belfast, and Jessie, *née* Niven (d 1978); *b* 23 March 1949; *Educ* Model Sch Belfast, Portsmouth Poly (MSc, PhD); *m* 25 Mar 1971, Geraldine Mabel, da of Gerald Thomas Gardner, of Belfast; 1 s (Alexander b 1982), 2 da (Katherine b 1979, Eleanor b 1985); *Career* conslt engr (various appts in NI, England and Scotland), ptnr Hancox & Ptnrs 1982-88, dir Rendel Hancox Ltd 1988-; chm Scottish region Inst of Energy 1984-85; CEng 1980, FInstE 1983, FIMechE 1986, EurIng 1988; *Recreations* music, walking, swimming; *Clubs* Royal Overseas League; *Style*— Dr John McCullough; Kinnoul, Kilmacolm, PA13 4DZ (☎ 050587 2895); Rendel Hancox Ltd, 42 Kelvingrove St, Glasgow G3 7RZ (☎ 041 332 4153, fax 041 331 1285, telex , 778913 HANCOX G)

McCUNN, Peter Alexander; CBE (1980); s of Alexander McCunn (d 1958), and Ida May, *née* Bailey (d 1938); *b* 11 Nov 1922; *Educ* Mexborough GS, Univ of Edinburgh; *m* 1 Feb 1943, Margaret, da of George William Prescott (d 1981); 3 s (Robert Alexander b 10 Nov 1948, Gerald Peter b 25 March 1950, Neil Andrew b 9 Jan 1952, d 1981); *Career* WWII enlisted and cmmnd W Yorks Regt 1942, served Royal Norfolk Regt 1942-44, wounded Normandy 1944, Capt S Lancs Regt 1944-46; Cable and Wireless: joined 1947, exec dir 1969, md and dep chm 1977-81, dep chm 1981-82, ret 1982 continuing pt/t until 1984; dir External Communications Ltd: Nigeria 1969-72, Sierra Leone 1969-72, Trinidad and Tobago 1972-77, Jamaica International 1972-77; dir: Cable and Wireless Hong Kong Ltd 1981-84, Mercury Communications Ltd 1981-84; *Recreations* music, gardening, reading, crosswords; *Clubs* Exiles Twickenham, Phyllis Court Henley; *Style*— Peter McCunn, Esq, CBE; 14 Lime Walk, Pinkneys Green, Maidenhead, Berks (☎ 0628 24308)

McCUSKER, Sir James Alexander; *b* 2 Dec 1913; *Educ* Perth Modern Sch W Aust; *m* Mary, *née* Martindale; 3 children; *Career* WWII 1939-45 Sgt 1 Armd Div; Cwlth Bank of Aust (sr branch mangr in Perth until 1959, chm State Ctee of Inquiry into Rates and Taxes 1980), fndr Town and Country Permanent Bldg Soc 1964 (chm 1964-83); fell Aust Inst of Valuers; kt 1983 for servs to the financial and housing industries; *Style*— Sir James McCusker; 195 Brookdale St, Floreat Park, W Australia 6041

McCUTCHEON, Dr (William) Alan; s of William John McCutcheon (d 1978), of Bangor, Co Down, NI, and Margaret Elizabeth, *née* Fullerton (d 1987); *b* 2 March 1934; *Educ* Royal Belfast Academical Inst, Queen's Univ of Belfast (BA), pt/t univ study (MA, PhD); *m* 30 June 1956, Margaret, da of John Craig (d 1974), of Belfast, NI; 3 s (Patrick b 23 Feb 1961, Conor b 4 May 1963, Kevin b 21 Sept 1965); *Career* geography teacher Royal Belfast Academical Inst 1956-62, dir Survey of Indust Archaeology for Govt of NI 1962-68, keeper of technol and local history Ulster Museum Belfast 1968-77, dir Ulster Museum 1977-82, visiting teacher Glenalmond Coll 1984 and 1986, teacher (geography specialist) Ditcham Park Sch Petersfield Hants 1986; chm Historic Monuments Cncl NI 1980-85; memb: Malcolm Ctee on Regnl Museums in NI 1977-78, jt ctee Industl Archaeology NI 1981-85, Indust Archaeology Ctee Cncl for Br Archaeology 1981-85; FRGS 1958, FSA 1970, MRIA 1983; *Books* The Canals of the North of Ireland (1965), Railway History in Pictures-Ireland (Vol 1, 1970, Vol 2 1971), Wheel and Spindle - Aspects of Irish Industrial History (1977), The Industrial Archaeology of Northern Ireland (1980); contrib to many others, author of numerous articles and papers in professional jls; *Recreations* music, reading, poetry, travel, photography, swimming, hill walking; *Style*— Dr Alan McCutcheon; 3 Coxes Meadow, Petersfield, Hampshire GU32 2DU (☎ 0730 65366)

McDERMID, Ven Norman George Lloyd Roberts; s of Rev Lloyd Roberts McDermid (d 1975), of Greystones, Bedale, and Annie, *née* Harrison (d 1966); *b* 5 March 1927; *Educ* St Peter's York, St Edmund Hall Oxford (BA, MA), Wells Theol Coll; *m* 29 July 1953, Vera, da of Albert John Wood (d 1967), of Park View, Kirkby Overblow, Harrogate; 1 s (Nigel Lloyd b 1957), 3 da (Katherine Jane b 1954, Helen Sarah b 1959, Angela Mary b 1963); *Career* RN 1944-47; curate of Leeds 1951-56, vicar of Bramley Leeds 1956-64, rector Kirkby Overblow 1964-80, rural dean Harrogate 1977-83, vicar Knaresborough 1980-83, hon canon of Ripon Cathedral 1972-, archdeacon of Richmond 1983-; stewardship advsr: Ripon diocese 1964-76, Bradford & Wakefield diocese 1973-76; church cmmr 1978-83; memb: C of E Pensions Bd 1972-79, Bd Assets Ctee and Gen Purposes Ctee 1978-83, Exec Ctee Central Bd of Fin 1985-, Redundant Churches Fund 1977-89; chm: House of Clergy Ripon Diocese 1982-, Ripon Diocesan Bd of Finances 1988-; *Recreations* church buildings, investment, gardens; *Clubs* Nat Lib; *Style*— The Ven the Archdeacon of Richmond; 62 Palace Road, Ripon, Yorks (☎ 0765 4342)

MCDERMID, Rev Canon Richard Thomas Wright; s of Rev Lloyd Roberts McDermid (d 1975), and Annie McDermid (d 1966); *b* 10 Oct 1929; *Educ* St Peter's Sch York, Univ of Durham (BA, Dip Theol, MA); *m* 1 Aug 1956, Joyce Margaret, da of Frederick Barclay Pretty, of 18 Cavendish Ave, Harrogate; 1 s (Mark b 1962), 4 da (Gillian b 1957, Rachel b 1960, Sarah b 1964, Ruth b 1965); *Career* Nat Serv Intelligence Corps 1947-50; curate Seacroft Leeds 1955-61, vicar St Mary Hawkesworth Wood Leeds 1961-70, vicar Christ Church Harrogate 1970-, chaplain Harrogate Dist Hosp 1975-88, hon canon Ripon Cathedral 1983-, chaplain to HM The Queen 1986-; chm of govrs St Aiden's HS Harrogate 1973-86, chm Ripon Diocesan Bd of Educn 1983-86, memb Advsy Ctee for the Care of Churches 1986-; *Style*— The Rev Canon Richard McDermid; Christ Church Vicarage, 11 St Hilda's Rd, Harrogate, N Yorks HG2 8JX (☎ 0423 883390)

MACDERMOT, Brian Hugh; s of Francis Charles MacDermot (d 1975), of Paris, and Elaine Orr MacDermot (d 1974); *b* 2 Dec 1930; *Educ* Downside, New Coll Oxford (MA); *m* 23 March 1985, Georgina Maria, da of Dayrell Gallwey, of Rockfield House, Tramore, Co Waterford; 1 s (Thomas Patrick b 16 March 1986), 1 da (Elaine Francesca b 19 Nov 1987); *Career* Lt Irish Guards 1952-55; memb Stock Exchange 1959-90, currently assoc Panmure Gordon and Co (formerly ptnr 1964-76), chm Mathaf Gallery Ltd; numerous contribs in jls; tstee: St Gregory Charitable Tst, Downside Sch; former vice pres RAI, former cncl memb RGS; Master Worshipful Company of Bowyers 1984-86; FRGS, FRAI; *Books* Cult of the Sacred Spear (1972); *Recreations* squash, tennis; *Clubs* Brooks's; *Style*— Brian MacDermot, Esq; Clock House, Rutland Gate, London SW7 1NY; Mathaf Gallery Ltd, 24 Motcomb St, London SW1X 8JV

MACDERMOT, Niall; CBE (1990, OBE Mil 1944), QC (1963); s of Henry MacDermot, KC (d 1955), of Dublin, and Gladys, *née* Lowenadler (d 1962); *b* 10 Sept 1916; *Educ* Rugby, Corpus Christi Coll Cambridge, Balliol Coll Oxford; *m* 1, 1940 (m dis 1966), Violet, *née* Maxwell; 1 s (John b 1947); m 2, Aug 1966, Ludmila, *née* Benvenuto; *Career* Nat Serv Intelligence Corps 1939-45; Lance Corpl Frane 1939-40, war office 1941-43, Normandy planning staff 1944, Lt-Col i/c counter intelligence 21 Army Gp Normandy to Hamburg; called to the Bar Inner Temple 1946; dep chm Beds Quarter Sessions 1962, rec of Newark 1963-64, QC 1963, master of the bench Inner Temple 1970, rec Crown Ct 1972-74; politician; Lab MP Derby 1962-70 (N Lewisham 1957-59), fin sec Treasy 1964-67, Minister of State for Planning and Land 1967-68; tstee Tate Gallery 1969-76, sec gen Int Cmmn of Jurists 1970-90, chm Geneva Special NGO Ctee for Human Rights 1973-86 (vice chm 1986-); *Style*— Niall MacDermot, Esq, CBE, OBE, QC; 34 Avenue Weber, 1208 Geneva, Switzerland (☎ 010 4122 735 40 86)

McDERMOTT, Dermot St John; s of Lionel St John McDermott (d 1981), and Margaret Isabel, *née* Axworthy (d 1984); *b* 4 July 1939; *Educ* Douai Sch, Balliol Coll Oxford (MA), Cornell (MBA); *m* 1, 16 Feb 1963, Sally Ann Hay, da of Gp Capt Arthur Hay Donaldson, DSO, DFC (d 1980); 2 da (Georgina b 1964, Arabella b 1968); m 2, 20 Dec 1984, Helen, da of George Dennis Leinster, of Madrid; *Career* dir: Esso Nederland BV 1980-83, Esso UK plc 1985-87, Trafalgar House plc 1987-; chm Cunard Line Ltd 1988-; *Style*— Dermot McDermott, Esq; 1 Berkeley St, London W1A 1BY (☎ 071 499 9020)

MacDERMOTT, The Rt Hon Lord Justice; Hon Sir John Clarke; er s of Baron MacDermott, MC, PC (Life Peer, d 1979), and Louise Palmer, *née* Johnston; *b* 9 May 1927; *Educ* Campbell Coll Belfast, Trinity Hall Cambridge (BA), Queens Univ Belfast; *m* 1953, Margaret Helen, da of Hugh Dales (d 1935); 4 da (Helen b 1954, Anne b 1956, Janet b 1958, Gillian b 1959); *Career* called to the Bar Inner Temple and NI 1949, QC (NI) 1964, judge of High Ct NI 1973, Lord Justice of Appeal 1987; kt 1987; *Recreations* golf; *Clubs* The Royal Belfast Golf; *Style*— The Rt Hon Lord Justice MacDermott; 6 Tarawood, Holywood BT18 0HS; The Royal Courts of Justice, Belfast

MacDERMOTT, Baroness; Louise Palmer; o da of Rev John Corry Johnston, of Dublin; *b* 7 March 1902; *Educ* Dublin HS, Trinity Coll Dublin; *m* 26 June 1926, Baron MacDermott, MC, PC (d 1979); 2 s (Rt Hon Lord Justice MacDermott *qv*, Rev Hon Robert *qv*), 2 da; *Style*— The Rt Hon Lady MacDermott; Glenburn, 8 Cairnburn Rd, Belfast BT4 2HR

McDERMOTT, Patrick Anthony; MVO (1972); s of Patrick J McDermott, of Belfast (d 1966), and Eileen, *née* Lyons; *b* 8 Sept 1941; *Educ* Clapham Coll London; *m* 1, 1963 (m dis), Patricia Hunter-Naylor; 2 s (Jeremy b 1967, Justin b 1970); m 2, 1976, Christa, da of Emil Herminghaus, of Krefeld, W Germany; 2 s (Nicholas b 1977, Christian b 1981); *Career* joined FO 1960, Mexico City 1963, attaché UK delgn to UN 1966, vice consul Belgrade 1971, FO 1973, second sec Bonn 1973, first sec Paris 1976, FO 1979, HM consul gen W Berlin 1984-88, FO 1988-90, cnsllr Paris 1990-; Freeman City of London 1986; *Recreations* clocks, gardening; *Style*— Patrick McDermott, Esq, MVO; c/o Foreign Office, Downing St, London SW1A 2AH

MACDIARMID, Hon Mrs; (Lucinda Mary Joan); *née* Darling; da of 2 Baron Darling; *b* 23 Dec 1958; *m* 4 Sept 1982, Rory P A Macdiarmid, o s of late Col Peter Macdiarmid; 2 s (George b 1985, Fergus b 1987); *Style*— The Hon Mrs Macdiarmid; 69 Haldon Rd, London SW18 5QF

MCDONAGH, Noel Hilary; s of Maj Patrick J McDonagh (d 1978), of Dublin, and Susan Frances, *née* Fennell (d 1981); *b* 25 Dec 1931; *Educ* Coll of Technol Bolton St Dublin; *m* 1959, Moira, *née* Hannon; 2 s (Mark b 1961, Brian b 1963), 1 da (Hilary b 1968); *Career* jr asst Padraig Mulcahy 1953-55; sr asst: A F Whelan 1955-58, Padraig Mulcahy 1958-61; sr ptnr Mulcahy McDonagh and Partners 1972 (ptnr 1961); chm and sr ptnr: The MMP Partnership (London), Mulcahy McDonagh and Partners (Dublin); speaker and author of many papers for confs courses and seminars, author of govt reports, occasional lectr Univ Coll Dublin; Coll of Technol Bolton St: chm Surveying and Bldg Advsy Ctee 1970-80, external examiner to Construction Econs Dip Course 1985-88, occasional lectr; advsr Trinity Coll Dublin, memb Editorial Advsy Bds Irish Journal of Environmental Science and Construction Management and Economics; memb Irish Nat Building Elements Ctee 1970-87 (chm 1982-87); Int Cncl for Building Res Studies and Documentation: memb Working Cmmn 52 1973-79, chm Int SfB Devpt Gp 1975-88, memb Info Study Gp 1980-81 (co-author of report), chm Working Cmmn 74 1980-88, chm ad hoc Long Range Planning Gp 1983-85, bd memb 1983-86; Republic of Ireland Branch RICS: hon sec 1966-69, chm QS Div 1966-67, chm 1970-72; memb Quantity Surveyors Divnl Cncl RICS London 1974- (pres QS Div 1990-91); memb various ctees and Cncl Soc of Chartered Surveyors in Republic of Ireland since fndn, chm organisation for Third World Self Help Devpt 1984-; *Recreations* reading, music, Third World development; *Clubs* Fitwilliam LTC, Royal Zoological Soc of Ireland, Royal Dublin Soc; *Style*— Noel McDonagh, Esq; Varradene, Bird Avenue, Clonksea, Dublin 14, Republic of Ireland (☎ 0001 697442); Mulcahy McDonagh & Partners, 164 Lower Rathmines Rd, Dublin 6, Republic of Ireland (☎ 0001 973393, fax 0001 960521)

MACDONALD, Alexander; s of John Macdonald, and Agnes, *née* Watson; *b* 17 March 1948; *Educ* Kinning Park Sch; *m* 7 June 1968, Christine, da of Roy Dunes; 2 s (Nicholas b 20 Jan 1973, Kristopher b 10 July 1980), 1 da (Lisa b 21 Nov 1971); *Career* footballer: St Johnstone 1965-68, Rangers 1968-80; player mangr Heart of Midlothian 1980-; achievements: Scot v Switzerland 1976, Euro Cup Winners' Cup Winners medal 1971, 4 Leauge Cup Winners medals, 4 Scottish Cup Winners medals, 3 League Championship medals; *Recreations* wild birds, golf; *Style*— Alexander Macdonald, Esq; Heart of Midlothian FC, Tynecastle Park, Edinburgh (☎ 031 337 6132, fax 031 346 0699, telex 72694)

MacDONALD, Sheriff Alistair Archibald; s of James MacDonald (d 1984), and Margaret, *née* McGibbon (d 1947); *b* 8 May 1927; *Educ* Broughton Sch Edinburgh, Univ of Edinburgh (MA, LLB); *m* 1949, Jill, da of Sir Robert Russell (d 1972); 1 s (Ian b 1957), 1 da (Catriona b 1964); *Career* serv Army 1945-48; called to the Scottish Bar 1954; Sheriff of Grampian Highland and Islands at Lerwick and Kirkwall, DL of Shetland; Kt of the Equestrian Order of the Holy Sepulchre of Jerusalem; *Clubs* Royal Northern; *Style*— Sheriff Alistair MacDonald; West Hall, Ness of Sound, Lerwick, Shetland; 110 Nicolson St, Edinburgh; Sheriff Courts, Lerwick, Shetland

MACDONALD, His Hon Judge Angus Cameron; s of Hugh Macdonald, OBE (d 1971), of Ravensden, Bedford, and Margaret Cameron, *née* Westley; *b* 26 Aug 1931; *Educ* Bedford Sch, Trinity Hall Cambridge (MA); *m* 1956, Deborah Anne, da of John Denny Inglis, DSO, MC and Bar, JP (d 1976), of Oban, Argyll; 3 da (Deborah, Sarah,

Fiona); *Career* Lt RA (TA) 1951-57; barr Gray's Inn 1955, resident magistrate Nyasaland Govt 1957-60, crown counsel and sr state counsel Nyasaland/Malawi Govt 1960-67, practised NE Circuit 1967-79; *Recreations* singing, shooting, fishing; *Clubs* Northern Counties (Newcastle upon Tyne); *Style*— His Hon Judge Angus Macdonald; Blàran, Kilninver, by Oban, Argyll (☎ 085 22 246)

MACDONALD, Angus David; s of Surgn Capt Iain MacDonald, CBE (d 1976), of Strathtay, Perthshire, and Molly, *née* Barber (d 1983); *b* 9 Oct 1950; *Educ* Portsmouth GS, Jesus Coll Cambridge (MA), Univ of Edinburgh (BEd); *m* 10 April 1976, Isabelle Marjory, da of Maj John Ross, of Connel; 2 da (Mairi Catriona b 1982, Eilidh Iona b 1983); *Career* asst teacher Alloa Acad 1972-73, asst teacher Edinburgh Acad 1973-82, asst teacher King's Sch Paramatta NSW 1978-79, dep princ George Watson's Coll 1982-86 (head of geography 1982), headmaster Lomond Sch 1986-; *Recreations* outdoor recreation, piping, sport, gardening; *Style*— Angus Macdonald, Esq; Ashmount, 8 Millig St, Helensburgh (☎ 0436 72472); Lomond School, 10 Stafford St, Helensburgh (☎ 0436 72476)

MACDONALD, Angus John; s of Colin Macdonald (d 1966), and Jean, *née* Livingstone; *b* 20 Aug 1940; *Educ* Allan Glen's Sch Glasgow; *m* 7 Sept 1963, Alice; 2 da (Jean b 1965, Rowan b 1967); *Career* dir of progs Granada TV 1985-90 (prodr, presenter and dir 1967-85), md Scottish Television 1990-; fndr chm Edinburgh Int TV Festival 1977, viewers' ombudsman on Channel 4 Right to Reply programme 1982-, visiting prof film and media studies Univ of Stirling, govr Nat Film and TV Sch; FRSA, FInstD; author; *Books* Victorian Eyewitness, Early Photography; *Recreations* visual arts, music, literature, sport; *Clubs* Reform, RAC, Glasgow Art; *Style*— Angus Macdonald, Esq; Scottish television, Cowcaddens, Glasgow G2 3PR (☎ 041 332 9999)

MACDONALD, Angus Stewart; CBE, DL; *Educ* Conon Primary Sch, Gordonstoun; *m* 2 June 1969, Janet Ann, da of Air Cdre Duncan Somerville; 3 s (Angus, Stewart, Duncan); *Career* dir Scottish English and Welsh Wool Growers, chm Reith & Anderson Dingwall; dir: Grampian TV plc, Wonderland Wool Ltd, Wool Growers (GB) Ltd; chm Gordonstoun Sch, Aberlour Sch; memb Bd: British Wool Market Bd, Highlands and Islands Enterprise; Crown Estate cmmr; The Queen's Body Guard for Scotland (Royal Co of Archers); FRAgs; *Style*— Angus Macdonald, Esq, CBE, DL; Torgorm, Conon Bridge, Dingwall, Ross-shire IV7 8DN (☎ 0349 61365, fax 0349 61362)

MACDONALD, Angus William; s of William MacDonald, of Isle of Lewis, and Mary Ann; *b* 18 Feb 1951; *Educ* Nicolson Inst Stornoway, Strathclyde Univ Glasgow; *m* 3 July 1987, Joyce, da of Duncan Munro (d 1986), of Stornoway; *Career* slr, ptnr Macdonald Maciver & Co Notary Public (Scotland) 1987; chm Gaelic Drama Assoc 1985-; *Recreations* amateur drama; *Style*— Angus W MacDonald, Esq; 14A Cross St, Stornoway, Isle of Lewis (☎ 0851 2685); 20 Francis St, Stornoway, Isle of Lewis (☎ 0851 4343)

MACDONALD, Hon Mrs; (Margaret) Anne; *née* Boot; 3 da of 2 and last Baron Trent, KBE (d 1956), and Margaret Joyce, *née* Pyman; *b* 31 July 1920; *m* 1, 29 June 1940 (m dis 1948), Maj John Edward Jocelyn Davie, MC, Derbys Yeo, yr s of late Lt-Col Bertie George Davie, of Stanton Manor, Rowsley, Derbys; 1 s (Simon b 1941), 1 da (Mrs Robin d'Abo); m 2, 12 May 1949, Air Vice-Marshal Somerled Douglas Macdonald, CB, CBE, DFC (d 1979), s of late Dr David Macdonald, of Kilmichael, Glen Urquhart, Inverness; *Style*— Hon Mrs Macdonald; Thane, Kintbury, Berks (☎ 0488 58067)

McDONALD, Antony Rycroft; s of Alastair McDonald, of Weston-Super-Mare, Avon, and Cicely Elaine, *née* Hartley; *b* 11 Sept 1950; *Educ* Monkton Coombe Sch Bath, Central Sch of Speech and Drama, Manchester Poly Sch of Theatre, Univ of Manchester; *Career* asst dir The Community and Schs; Co of The Welsh Nat Opera and Drama Co 1974-76; design work incl: Let's Make an Opera (Welsh Nat Opera) 1978, Jessonda (Oxford Univ Opera Soc) 1980, War Crimes (Inst of Contemporary Art) 1981, Degas (Ian Spink Dance Group, later filmed by C4) 1981, Dances from the Kingdom of the Pagodas (Royal Danish Ballet) 1982, Secret Gardens (Mickery Theatre Amsterdam) 1982, Insignifigance (Royal Court) 1982, Mrs Gauguin, Hedda Gabler (Almeida Theatre) 1984, Tom and Viv (Royal Court 1984, Public Theatre NY 1985), Orlando (Scottish Opera) 1985, Midsummer Marriage (Opera North), Bosendorfer Waltzes (Second Stride, Munich New Dance Festival) 1986, Dancelines (C4) 1986, A Streetcar Named Desire (Crucible Theatre Sheffield) 1987, The Trojans (WNO, Opera North and Scottish Opera) 1987, Billy Budd (ENO) 1988, Hamlet (RSC) 1988, Mary Stuart (Greenwich Theatre) 1988, Heaven Ablaze in his Breast (Second Stride), As You Like It (Old Vic) 1989, Beatrice and Benedict (ENO) 1990, Berenice (Royal Nat Theatre) 1990, Mad Forest (Royal Court and Nat Theatre Bucharest) 1990, Richard II (RSC) 1990, Benvenuto Cellini (Netherlands Opera) 1991, Lives of the Great Poisoners (Second Stride) 1991; *Style*— Antony McDonald, Esq; Loesje Sanders, 82 Mercers Rd, London N19 (☎ 071 272 8295, fax 071 272 3455)

McDONALD, Air Marshal Sir Arthur William Baynes; KCB (1958, CB 1949), AFC (1935), DL (Hants 1965); s of Dr William Maclauchlan McDonald (d 1950), of Antigua, WI, and Hilda Ellen, *née* Edwards (d 1960); *b* 14 June 1903; *Educ* Antigua GS, Epsom Coll, Peterhouse Cambridge (MA); *m* 1928, Mary Julia, da of Dr Ronald Gray, of Hindhead, Surrey; 2 s, 2 da; *Career* joined RAF 1924, serv WWII (despatches four times), Gp Capt 1941, Air Cdre 1943, Air Vice-Marshal 1952, Air Marshal 1958, C-in-C Pakistan Air Force 1956, AOC-in-C Tech Trg Cmd 1958, air memb for personnel 1959-61, ret 1962; CEng, FRAeS; *Recreations* sailing (represented GB in 1948 Olympics; yachts: Bachante, Mollymawk); *Clubs* RAF Sailing Assoc (Adm), RAF, Royal Lymington Yacht; *Style*— Air Marshal Sir Arthur McDonald, KCB, AFC, DL; 9 Daniell's Walk, Lymington, Hants (☎ 0590 673843)

MACDONALD, Charles Adam; s of Alastair Cameron Macdonald, of Redlands Rd, Glasgow, and Jessie Catherine, *née* McCrow; *b* 31 Aug 1949; *Educ* The Glasgow Acad, New Coll Oxford (MA), Cncl of Legal Educn; *m* 17 June 1978, Dinah Jane, da of Ronald Manns, of Lattice Cottage, Backsideans, Wargrave, Berkshire; 3 da (Kate, Anna, Elspeth); *Career* called to the Bar Lincoln's Inn 1972, practising in maritime and commercial Law; memb Commercial Bar Assoc, supporting memb London Maritime Arbitrators Assoc; *Recreations* family life, squash, food and wine; *Style*— Charles Macdonald, Esq; Tye House East, Hartfield, East Sussex TN7 4JR (☎ 0892 770 451); 2 Essex Court, Temple, London EC4Y 9AT (☎ 071 583 8381, telex 8812528 ADRIOT G, fax 071 353 0998)

MACDONALD, Dr (Isabelle Wilma) Claire; da of William Garland (d 1972), of Glasgow, and Barbara Sutherland, *née* MacDonald; *b* 6 Feb 1951; *Educ* Hutchesons Girls GS, Univ of Glasgow (BSc, MB ChB); *m* 28 April 1977, David John MacDonald, s of Alastair MacDonald, of 4 Crown Gardens, Glasgow; 2 da (Jennifer b 21 Aug 1979, Elizabeth b 6 Dec 1982); *Career* Victoria Infirmary Glasgow: house offr in surgery 1975-76, registrar in pathology 1977-79, sr registrar 1979-81; house offr in medicine Stirling Royal Hosp 1976, sr house offr in pathology Western Infirmary Glasgow 1976-77, lectr in pathology Univ of Aberdeen 1981-84, conslt histopathologist and chm of div Pontefract Gen Infirmary 1984-; chm Wakefield and Pontefract div BMA; MRCPath 1982; *Recreations* swimming, reading; *Clubs* Caledonian Soc, Con; *Style*— Dr Claire Macdonald; Pathology Dept, Pontefract General Infirmary, Pontefract, W Yorks WF8 1PL (☎ 0977 600600)

MCDONALD, David Cameron; s of James Fraser Macdonald, OBE (d 1977), and Anne Sylvia Hutcheson; *b* 5 July 1936; *Educ* St Georges Sch Harpenden, Newport GS; *m* 1, 14 Feb 1968 (m dis 1980), Melody Jane, da of Ralph Vernon Coles, of Portland, Maine, USA; 2 da (Nancy Anne b 1969, Jessica Jean b 1972); m 2, 11 Nov 1983, Sally Anne Robertson, da of William Rodger, of Invercargill, NZ; 1 s (Hamish William b 1984), 1 da (Laura Mary Clare b 1987); *Career* Nat Serv 2 Lieut RA 1954-56, articled clerk then slr Slaughter and May 1956-64, dir and dep chm Hill Samuel & Co Ltd 1964-77 and 1979-80, chief exec and chm Antony Gibbs Holdings 1980-83, sr UK advsr Crèdit Suisse First Boston 1983-; dir: Coutts & Co 1980-, Sears plc 1981-, Bath & Portland Group plc (chm 1982-85), Merivale Moore plc 1985-, Pittard Garnar plc (chm 1985-); dir gen Takeover Panel 1977-79, chm Issuing Houses Assoc 1975-77, advsr to Sec of State for Trade and Indust on Upper Clyde shipbuilding crisis 1971; *Recreations* family, country pursuits, music; *Style*— David Mcdonald, Esq; United Kingdom House, 2A Great Titchfield St, London W1 (☎ 071 322 4000)

MACDONALD, David Cameron; s of James Fraser Macdonald, OBE, of Umtali, Zimbabwe, and Anne Sylvia, *née* Hutcheson; *b* 5 July 1936; *Educ* St George's Sch Harpenden, Newport GS; *m* 1, 1968, Melody Jane, da of Ralph Vernon Coles; 2 da (Nancy b 1969, Jessica b 1972), m 2, 1983, Sally Anne, da of William Rodger, of Invercargill, NZ; 1 s (Hamish b 1984) 1 da (Laura b 1987); *Career* 2 Lt RA Germany 1954; slr Slaughter & May 1961, dir Hill Samuel & Co Ltd 1968 (dep chm 1979, dir Hill Samuel Gp), chm and chief exec Antony Gibbs 1980, sr advsr Credit Suisse First Boston 1983, advsr to HM Govt on Upper Clyde Shipbuilding Crisis 1971; chm: Issuing Houses Assoc 1975-77, Bath and Portland Gp plc 1983-85, Pittard Garnar plc 1984-; dir gen Panel on Takeovers and Mergers 1977-79; dir: Coutts and Co 1980-, Sears plc 1981-, Merivale Moore plc 1985-; memb Br Tourist Authy 1971-82, tstee of London City Ballet Tst 1982-1987; *Recreations* fishing, music; *Style*— David Macdonald, Esq; Sweetapples Farmhouse, Martin Fordinbridge, Hants (☎ 072 589 368); 2A Great Titchfield Street, London W1 (☎ 071 322 4954)

McDONALD, David Wylie; CMG (1978); s of William McDonald (d 1956), of 16 Pitkerro Road, Dundee, and Rebecca Wilkinson, *née* Wylie (d 1964); *b* 9 Oct 1927; *Educ* Harris Acad Dundee, Sch of Architecture Dundee Coll of Art (DA); *m* 3 July 1951, Eliza (Betty) Roberts, da of David Low Steele (d 1955), of 56 Loons Road, Dundee; 2 da (Mairi Stewart (Mrs Bailey) b 22 Nov 1955, Fiona Margaret (Mrs Byrne) b 31 May 1959); *Career* mil serv Black Watch (RHR); architect with Gauldie Hardie Wright & Needham Dundee 1953, architect architectural office Public Works Dept Hong Kong 1955 (sr architect 1964, chief architect 1967, govt architect 1970, princ govt architect 1972); dir: bldg devpt 1973, public works 1974; sec for lands and works 1981 (ret 1983); memb Cwlth Pty Assoc; former chm: Town Planning Bd, Devpt Progress Ctee, Lands and Works Conf; former memb: Legislative Cncl, Fin Ctee, Public Works Sub Ctee, Public Works Priorities Ctee, Land Devpt Policy Ctee, Hong Kong Housing Authy; former dir: Mass Tport Railway Corpn, Hong Kong Ind Estate Corpn, Ocean Park Ltd; former memb Cncl: Hong Kong Red Cross, Girl Guides Assoc, MENSA, Hong Kong Housing Soc; tstee Scottish Tst for the Physically Disabled, memb Ctee Margaret Blackwood Housing Assoc; Lorimer Meml prize 1950, City Corpn Design prize 1953, Silver Jubilee medal 1977; DA Univ of Dundee; FHKIA, RIBA, ARIAS; *Recreations* drawing, painting, calligraphy; *Clubs* Hong Kong (chm 1977), Royal Hong Kong Jockey; *Style*— David Wylie McDonald, Esq, CMG; Northbank, Backmuir of Liff, by Dundee DD2 5QT (☎ 0382 580483)

MACDONALD, Dr Eleanor Catherine; MBE; da of Frederick William Macdonald (d 1959), and Frances Catherine, *née* Glover (d 1958); *b* 1 Sept 1910; *Educ* Woodford Sch Croydon, Univ of London (BA); *Career* WWII MOI and Security Serv 1939-45; fencing prof 1939 (1st woman to become Maître d'Armes de L'Académie d'Epée de Paris); Unilever: dir several subsid cos 1947-69; princ owner mgmnt and trg consultancy 1969-; author of numerous articles on staff devpt; fndr: Women in Mgmnt, 300 Gp; Hon DUniv Bradford 1989; memb RIIA, RSA; *Books* incl: Live by Beauty, The Successful Secretary, Nothing by Chance; *Recreations* gardening, bird watching; *Style*— Dr Eleanor Macdonald, MBE; 4 Mapledale Ave, Croydon, Surrey CR0 5TA (☎ 081 654 4659)

MACDONALD, Hon Mrs (Elspeth Ruth); yst da of 2 Baron Craigmyle (d 1944), and Lady Margaret Cargill, *née* Mackay (d 1958), eldest da of 1 Earl of Inchcape, GCSI, GCMG, KCIE; *b* 17 Feb 1921; *m* 12 Sept 1945, Archibald James Florence Macdonald, JP (d 1983), er s of late Dr G B D Macdonald, of The Oaks, 61 Frognal, NW3; 2 s (Michael b 1947, Ian b 1950); *Style*— The Hon Mrs Macdonald; 22 Heath Drive, Hampstead, London NW3

MACDONALD, Euan Ross; s of Iain Somerled Macdonald (d 1958), and Elisabeth Barbara Perfect, *née* Warmington; *b* 8 April 1940; *Educ* Marlborough, Univ of Cambridge (BA Econ), Graduate Sch of Business Columbia Univ NY (MBA); *m* March 1965, (Jacqueline) Anne Gatacre; 4 s (Iain Graham b 23 Oct 1966, Russell Ross b 19 May 1969, James Curtis (twin) b 19 May 1969, Dougal Evelyn b 7 May 1974); *Career* Lazard Brothers & Co Ltd 1963-74, first gen mangr International Financial Advisers Kuwait 1974-82, dir gen Ifabanque SA Paris 1979-82, head Overseas Advsy Div S G Warburg & Co Ltd 1988- (dir 1982-); work in Black Africa, India, Caribbean, Latin America and Eastern Europe carrying out fin and advsy contracts with sovereign and private sector clients; memb Worshipful Co of Clothworkers; *Style*— Euan Macdonald, Esq; S G Warburg & Co Ltd, 2 Finsbury Avenue, London EC2M 2PA (☎ 071 860 0378, fax 071 860 0105, telex 937011)

MacDONALD, Prof (Simon) Gavin George; s of Simon MacDonald (d 1967), of 34 Moat St, Edinburgh, and Jean Hogarth, *née* Thompson (d 1974); *b* 5 Sept 1923; *Educ* George Heriot's Sch, Univ of Edinburgh (MA), Univ of St Andrews (PhD); *m* 22 Oct 1948, Eva Leonie, da of Kurt Austerlitz (d 1929), of Breslau, Germany; 1 s (Neil b 1950), 1 da (Carolyn b 1954); *Career* jr sci offr RAE Farnborough 1943-46; lectr Univ of St Andrews 1948-57; sr lectr: Univ Coll of the WI 1957-62, Univ of St Andrews 1962-67; Univ of Dundee 1967-73: dean of sci 1970-73, vice princ 1974-79, prof physics 1974-88; chm Bd of Dirs: Dundee Rep Theatre 1975-89, Fedn of Scottish Theatres 1978-80; convener Scottish Univ Cncl on Entrance 1976-82 (dep convener 1972-76, memb 1970); UCCA: convener Tech Ctee 1979-83, dep chm and convenor Fin and Gen Purposes Ctee 1983-89, convenor Stat Ctee 1989-; FInstP 1958, FRSE 1973; *Books* Problems in General Physics (1967), Physics for Biology and Premedical Students (1970, 1975), Physics for the Life and Health Sciences (1975); *Recreations* bridge, golf, writing; *Clubs* Royal Commonwealth; *Style*— Prof Gavin MacDonald, FRSE; 10 Westerton Ave, Dundee DD5 3NJ (☎ 0382 78692)

MACDONALD, His Hon George Grant; s of Patrick Thompson Tulloch MacDonald (d 1966), and Charlotte Primrose, *née* Rintoul (d 1978); *b* 5 March 1921; *Educ* Kelly Coll Tavistock, Bristol Univ (LLB); *m* 1967, Mary Dolores, *née* Gerrish; *Career* RN 1941-46, Lt RNVR Western Approaches Corvettes, Frigates, and Minesweeping; barr 1947, Western circuit; dep chm Dorest QS 1969, rec of Barnstaple 1971, circuit judge 1972-87, ret; *Recreations* sailing, chess, bridge; *Clubs* Clifton (Bristol); *Style*— His Hon George MacDonald; Flat 1, Minterne House, Dorchester, Dorset DT2 7AX

MACDONALD, 8 Baron (I 1776); Godfrey James Macdonald of Macdonald; JP (1976), DL (1986); Chief of the Name and Arms of Macdonald; s of 7 Baron Macdonald, MBE (d 1970); 3 Baron m 1803 Louisa Maria La Coast, natural da of HRH Duke of Gloucester (issue b before m succeeded to Bosville MacDonald, Bt *qv*); *b* 28

Nov 1947; *Educ* Belhaven Hill Sch Dunbar, Eton; *m* 14 June 1969, Claire (Glenfiddich's 1982 Writer of the Year), eld da of Capt Thomas Noel Catlow, CBE, RN; 1 s (Hon Godfrey Evan Hugo Thomas b 24 Feb 1982), 3 da (Hon Alexandra Louisa b 1973, Hon Isabella Claire b 1975, Hon Meriel Iona b 1978); *Heir* s, Hon Godfrey Macdonald of Macdonald; *Career* pres Royal Scottish Country Dance Soc 1970-73, memb Inverness CC 1970-75, tstee and memb Exec Ctee Clan Donald Lands Tst 1970-, vice convener Standing Cncl of Scottish Chiefs 1974-, memb of Skye and Localsh Dist Cncl 1975-83 (chm Fin Ctee 1979-83), chm Skye and Lochalsh Local Health Cncl 1978-80; memb Highland Health Bd 1980-89; *Clubs* New (Edinburgh); *Style—* The Rt Hon Lord Macdonald; Kinloch Lodge, Isle of Skye (☎ 047 13 214)

MacDONALD, Dr (Donald) Gordon; RD (1976, and Bar 1986); s of Donald MacDonald (d 1981), of Milngavie, and Thelma Gordon, *née* Campbell (d 1975); *b* 5 July 1942; *Educ* Kelvinside Acad Glasgow, Univ of Glasgow (BDS, PhD); *m* 21 May 1966, Emma Lindsay (Linda), da of William Lindsay Cordiner (d 1961), of Coatbridge; 2 s (Lindsay b 1969, Alastair b 1972), 1 da (Katharine b 1968, d 1989); *Career* joined RNR 1959, CO HMS Graham 1982-86; currently Capt and Sr Offr Naval Control of Shipping; visiting assoc prof of oral pathology Univ of Illinois Chicago 1969-70, expert in forensic dentistry 1971-, hon conslt in oral pathology Glasgow 1974-, reader in oral med and pathology Univ of Glasgow 1982- (sr lectr 1974-82); sec Assoc of Head and Neck Oncologists of GB 1983-87, speciality rep for oral pathology RCPath 1988-, pres Br Soc for Oral Pathology 1988-91; MRCPath 1971, FRCPath 1985, FDSRCPS Glasgow 1986; *Books* Colour Atlas of Forensic Dentistry (1989); *Recreations* Royal Naval Reserve, golf; *Clubs* Commonwealth Trust; *Style—* Dr D Gordon MacDonald, RD; Dept of Oral Medicine and Pathology, Glasgow Dental Hospital and School, 378 Sauchiehall St, Glasgow G2 3JZ (☎ 041 332 7020)

MacDONALD, Hamish Neil; s of John MacDonald (d 1977), of Glasgow, and Marion McKendrick, *née* Cuthbert; *b* 17 Aug 1933; *Educ* Glasgow HS, Univ of Glasgow (MB ChB), Univ of Leeds (PhD); *m* 16 Aug 1968, Rosemary Paterson, da of John Paterson (d 1982), of Campbeltown, Argyllshire; 1 s (Alasdair James b 13 Jan 1978), 1 da (Fiona Ann b 13 Jan 1978); *Career* Lt then Capt RAMC 1959-62, GSM (1960); asst res Hosp for Women of Maryland Baltimore USA 1963-64, res registrar Glasgow Royal Maternity Hosp 1964-66, sr registrar and tutor United Leeds Hosps 1966-68, conslt obstetrician gynaecologist and lectr United Leeds Hosps and Univ of Leeds 1968-72, conslt obstetrician gynaecologist and sr clinical lectr St James's Univ Hosp and Univ of Leeds 1972-; med memb Dist Mgmnt Bd Leeds Eastern Health Authy; memb: Incorporation of Hammerman of Glasgow, Grand Antiquity Soc, Gynaecological Visiting Soc of GB and Ireland; FRCOG; *Recreations* reading, walking, swimming, tennis; *Clubs* Chapel Allerton Lawn Tennis and Squash; *Style—* Hamish MacDonald, Esq; St James's University Hospital, Beckett St, Leeds, West Yorkshire LS9 7TF (☎ 0532 433144)

MACDONALD, Hugh John; *b* 31 Jan 1940; *Educ* Univ of Cambridge (MA, PhD); *Career* lectr in music: Univ of Cambridge 1966-71, Univ of Oxford 1971-80, visiting prof of music Indiana Univ 1979, Gardiner prof of music Univ of Glasgow 1980-87, Avis Blewett prof of music Washington Univ St Louis 1987-; FRCM; awarded Szymanowski medal of Poland; *Books* Skryabin (1978), Berlioz (1982); *Style—* Prof Hugh Macdonald; Department of Music, Washington University, St Louis, MO 63130, USA (☎ 314 889 5581, fax 314 889 5799)

MACDONALD, Prof Ian; s of Ronald Macdonald, CBE, MC (d 1983), and Amy Elizabeth, *née* Stutz (d 1965); *b* 22 Dec 1921; *Educ* Lancaster Royal GS, Univ of London and Guy's Hosp (MB BS, PhD, MD, DSc); *m* 1, 2 Feb 1946 (m dis 1980), Nora Patricia; 2 s (Graham b 1949, Peter b 1952), 1 da (Helen b 1961); m 2, 10 Aug 1980, Rose Philomena; *Career* RAMC 1946-48; Guy's Hosp: prof of applied physiology 1967-89, head Dept of Physiology 1977-89; memb Food Additives & Food Advsy Ctee MAFF 1977-86, pres Nutrition Soc 1980-83, vice pres Br Nutrition Fndn 1989- (chm 1985-87), chm joint WHO/FAO Expert Ctee on Dietary Carbohydrates 1980, memb Med Sub Ctee Br Olympic Assoc 1986-89, Cncl London Sports Med Inst; Freeman: City of London 1967, Worshipful Co of Apothecaries 1967; FIBiol; memb American Soc of Clinical Nutrition; *Books* ed: Effects of Carbohydrates on Lipid Metabolism (1973), Metabolic Effects of Dietary Carbohydrates (1986), Sucrose (1988); *Recreations* walking, DIY; *Style—* Prof Ian Macdonald; Hillside, Fountain Dr, London SE19 1UP (☎ 081 670 3055)

MacDONALD, Ian Alexander; QC (1988); s of Ian Wilson Macdonald (d 1989), of Gullane, E Lothian, and Helen, *née* Nicholson (d 1990); *b* 12 Jan 1939; *Educ* Glasgow Acad, Cargilfield Sch Edinburgh, Rugby, Clare Coll Cambridge (MA, LLB); *m* 1, 20 Dec 1968 (m dis 1977), Judith Mary, da of William Demain Roberts of Stockport, Cheshire; 2 s (Ian b 3 July 1970, Jamie b 25 Sept 1972); m 2, 12 Oct 1978 (m dis 1990), Jennifer, da of Roy Hall, of Grimsby, S Humberside; 1 s (Kieran b 17 Oct 1979); *Career* called to the Bar Middle Temple 1963, Astbury scholar 1962-65, lectr in law Kingston Poly 1968-72, sr legal writer and res conslt Income Data Servs 1974-80, pres Immigration Law Practitioners' Assoc 1984-, memb Editorial Advsy Bd Immigration and Nationality Law and Practice Journal; memb: SE Circuit, Euro Law Assoc, Criminal Bar Assoc, Admin Law Bar Assoc; chm: Ind Inquiry into Racial Violence in Manchester Schs 1987-88, Inquiry into Funding of Caribbean House Hackney 1989-90; *Books* Race Relations and Immigration Law (1969), Race Relations - The New Law (1977), The New Nationality Act (with NJ Blake 1982), Immigration Law and Practice (third edn 1991), Murder in the Playground (1990); *Recreations* swimming, squash, watching football, reading; *Clubs* Cumberland Lawn Tennis; *Style—* Ian Macdonald, Esq, QC; 2 Garden Court, Temple, London EC4Y 9VL (☎ 071 353 1633, fax 071 353 4621)

MACDONALD, Ian Crawford; s of Lt Cdr Henry Crawford Macdonald, RN, DSC, (d 1928), of London, and Olive, *née* Darling (d 1971); *b* 29 Aug 1923; *Educ* Stowe, Trinity Hall Cambridge (MA); *m* 22 June 1963, Anna Elizabeth Carlisle, da of Col Arthur Boyce, DSO, of Eye, Suffolk; 3 s (Angus b 24 June 1964, Neil b 10 Oct 1967, James b 2 Dec 1969), 1 da (Kate b 28 Dec 1965); *Career* Nat Serv Lt RNVR served destroyers, E coast convoys, Dieppe raid, Russian convoys, Far E Malaya landings 1941-46; asst res land agent Powis Castle Estates Welshpool Montgomeryshire 1949-51, res agent GEH Palmer Esq Priors Ct Estate Newbury Berks 1954-60, res agent Maj RN Macdonald-Buchanan Cottesbrooke Estate, Northants 1951-53, advsy land serv MAFF 1961, res agent AA Hall Esq Cricket St Thomas Estate Chard Somerset 1962-66, managing own property 1966-; memb Country Landowners Assoc: chm Avon and Somerset branch 1979-81, memb HQ Ctees on agric land use and water, rep on NFU, memb Working Pty on Straw Burning, cncl rep for Environmental Conservation Youth Ctee, former chm CLA Wessex Water Ctee; memb Somerset customer consultative Ctee Wessex Water Authy, memb Wells constituency Party Ctee NFU, memb Royal Bath and W Agric Soc (fndr and former chm Conservation Ctee), cncllr Mendip DC (former chm Environmental Health and Housing Ctee and Health Ctee), former chm Mendip Disabled Advsy Gp, dir Radio Somerset Ltd; memb: Castle Housing Soc Yeovil, Customer Serv Ctee Wessex OFWAT 1990-; High Sheriff of Somerset 1991-; FRICS 1954 (assoc 1948, qualified assoc 1951); *Recreations* skiing, sailing, shooting; *Clubs* Naval & Military; *Style—* Ian Macdonald, Esq; Higher Hill Farm, Butleigh, Glastonbury, Somerset BA6 8TW (☎ 045 822 3252)

MACDONALD, Prof Ian Grant; s of Douglas Grant Macdonald (d 1964), and Irene Alice, *née* Stokes; *Educ* Winchester, Trinity Coll Cambridge (BA, MA), Oxford Univ (MA); *m* 31 July 1954, Margaretha Maria Lodewijk, da of René Van Goethem (d 1982); 2 s (Alexander b 1955, Christopher b 1957), 3 da (Catherine b 1959, Helen b 1959, Nicola b 1963); *Career* Nat Serv Rifle Bd 1947-49; asst princ and prin MOS 1952-57, asst lectr Univ of Manchester 1957-60, lectr Univ of Exeter 1960-63, fell and tutor in mathematics Magdalen Coll Oxford 1963-72, Fielden prof of pure mathematics Univ of Manchester 1972-76, prof of pure mathematics Queen Mary Coll Univ of London 1976-87, Emeritus 1987; FRS 1979; *Books* Algebraic Geometry: Introduction to Schemes (1968), Introduction to Commutative Algebra (with M F Atiyah, 1969), Spherical Functions on a Group of p-adic type (1972), Symmetric Functions and Hall Polynomials (1979); *Style—* Prof I G Macdonald; 8 Blandford Avenue, Oxford OX2 8DY (☎ 0865 515373); School of Mathematical Sciences, Queen Mary College, London E1 4NS (☎ 071 975 5438)

MACDONALD, Ian Hamish; OBE (1972); *b* 30 Dec 1926; *Educ* Inverness Royal Acad, Inverness Technical HS; *m* 1962, Patricia, da of James Lace; 1 da (Katie Fiona b 7 Jan 1967); *Career* memb: Industl Soc 1984-87, Design Cncl 1985-88; currently memb: Design Cncl Scot, SCDI, Scot Cncl Fndn, Clan Donald Lands Tst, NEP, SSEB (now Scot Power); memb Ct Univ of Edinburgh; FIB Scot, CBIM, RSA; *Recreations* bridge, fishing, walking; *Clubs* New (Edinburgh) Oriental, Highland, Royal and Ancient, Hong Kong; *Style—* Ian Macdonald, Esq, OBE; Minewood Cottage, 11 Abercromby Drive, Bridge of Allan FK9 4EA (☎ 0768 832894); IF, 24 Moray Place, Edinburgh EH3 6DA (☎ 031 2256869)

McDONALD, Prof (William) Ian; s of William Allan Chapple McDonald (d 1962), of Christchurch, NZ, and Helen, *née* Leithead; *b* 15 March 1933; *Educ* St Andrew's Coll Christchurch NZ, Univ of Otago NZ (BMedSci, MB ChB, PhD); *Career* res fell Harvard Univ 1965-66; conslt physician: Nat Hosps of Queen Sq and Maida Vale 1966- (hon 1974-), Moorfields Eye Hosp 1969- (hon 1974); prof of clinical neurology Inst of Neurology London 1974-; res prof Univ of Düsseldorf 1990; memb ed bd: Brain (ed 1991-), Euro Archives for Psychiatry and Neurological Scis 1981-, Clinical Visual Scis 1986-; memb: Med Res Advsy Ctee Multiple Sclerosis Soc, cncl Action Res for the Crippled Child, cncl Assoc Br Neurologists, Neurosciences Bd MRC, Sci Advsy Panel Nat Fund for Res into Crippling Diseases, cncl Royal Coll of Physicians, UK Delgn COMAC Biology Ctee on Med and Pub Health Res of EEC; Liveryman Worshipful Soc Apothecaries 1988; FRACP 1968, FRCP 1972, FCOphth 1989; *Books* Diseases of the Nervous System (with A K Asbury and G McKhann, 1986), Multiple Sclerosis (with D H Silberberg, 1986); *Recreations* music; *Clubs* Garrick; *Style—* Prof Ian McDonald; Institute of Neurology, Queen Square, London WC1N 3BG (☎ 071 829 8758, fax 071 278 5069)

MacDONALD, Hon Mrs (Jacaranda Fiona); yr da of 2 Viscount Craigavon (d 1974); *b* 8 Jan 1949; *m* 1972 (m dis 1982), Dudley Francis MacDonald; 1 s (Toby James Francis b 1975), 1 da (Rose Carole b 1978); *Style—* The Hon Mrs Macdonald; 23 Kelso Place, London W8 (☎ 071 937 6056)

MACDONALD, Dr James Stewart; s of Kenneth Stewart Macdonald (d 1959), of Mauritius and Perthshire, and Mary Janet, *née* McRorie; *b* 11 Aug 1925; *Educ* Sedbergh, Univ of Edinburgh (MB ChB, DMRD); *m* 19 Oct 1951, Dr Catherine Wilton Drysdale, da of John Drysdale, CBE (d 1979), of Kuala Lumpur, Malaya and Perthshire; 2 s (Kenneth John Stewart, Murdo James Stewart); *Career* RAMC Maj 2 i/c 23 Para Field Ambulance 1952; asst radiologist St Thomas's Hosp London 1959-62; Royal Marsden Hosp: conslt radiologist 1962-85, vice chm Bd of Govrs 1975-82 (memb Bd 1967-82), dir Diagnostic X-ray Dept 1978-85; hon sr lectr Inst of Cancer Res 1966-85, teacher in radiology Univ of London 1966-85; contrib to numerous books and scientific jls on radiology of cancer; memb: Ctee of Mgmnt Inst of Cancer Res 1969-82, London Ctee Ludwig Inst for Cancer Res 1971-85; appeals sec Duke of Edinburgh's Award Scheme (Perth and Kinross) 1986-88, chm Timber Growers UK (E of Scotland) 1988-; memb: BMA, Br Inst of Radiology; FRSM, FRCPE, FRCR; *Recreations* field sports; *Clubs* Army & Navy; *Style—* Dr J S Macdonald; Darquhillan, Gleneagles, Auchterarder, Perthshire PH3 1NG (☎ 0764 62476)

MACDONALD, Hon Mrs (Joan Marguerite); *née* Lord; da of 1 and last Baron Lambury (d 1967), and Ethel Lily, *née* Horton; *b* 10 July 1927; *m* 1, 4 April 1951 (m dis 1965), Miles Lucas Breeden, s of late Carl Breeden; 1 s (Guy b 1953), 1 da (Gail b 1956); m 2, 1966, Angus James Macdonald; *Style—* The Hon Mrs Macdonald; 113 Century Court, St John's Wood Rd, NW8

MacDONALD, John; s of Robert Ross MacDonald (d 1956), of Helensburgh, and Marion Crooks, *née* McMurtrie (d 1977); *b* 1 Feb 1921; *Educ* McLaren HS Callander; *m* 26 Sept 1945, Margaret Owen, da of Maurice Owen Keats Jones (d 1970), of Kidmore End; 1 s (Gavin b 1949), 1 da (Sheila b 1947); *Career* pilot RAFVR 1939, nightfighters 1940, flying instructor 1942, Sqdn Ldr AM D of Nav 1944; air traffic control offr MCA 1946, dep dir Air Traffic Ops NATS 1973, dir ATS Ltd 1977; parish cncllr Dorset; Master Guild of Air Traffic Control Offrs 1962; *Books* Sheep and Actors USA (1981); *Recreations* swimming, riding, walking, skiing, flying own aircraft; *Style—* John MacDonald, Esq; Long Acres, Huntick Rd, Lytchett Matravers, Poole, Dorset BH16 6BB (☎ 0202 622693)

MacDONALD, John Grant; s of John William MacDonald (d 1985), of 14 Park Ct, Bishopbriggs, Glasgow, and Jessie, *née* Grant; *b* 20 May 1933; *Educ* Allan Glen's Sch Glasgow, Univ of Strathclyde; *m* 30 March 1968, Ione Margaret, da of Melvyn Philip Bremer, JP (d 1977), of Lake Farm, Waverley, NZ; 1 da (Fiona b 5 March 1970); *Career* Nat Serv RAF 1959-61 serv Malaya and Singapore; worked in London with Sir Basil Spence 1961-65, registered architect 1963, worked with Garner Preston & Strebel 1965-66, directorate of devpt DOE 1966-73, private practice 1973-; chm Andover Town Twinning Assoc 1977-78, pres Andover Chamber of Trade Commerce and Indust 1978-79, chm Central Hants Branch RIBA 1987-89; ARIBA 1965; *Recreations* sailing; *Style—* John MacDonald, Esq; Thorsby, 2 Humberstone Rd, Andover, Hants SP10 2EJ (☎ 0264 51277), Russell Hse, 40 East St, Andover, Hants SP10 1ES (☎ 0264 24068)

MACDONALD, John Grant; CBE (1989, MBE 1962); s of John Nicol MacDonald (d 1969), and Margaret, *née* Vasey (d 1977); *b* 26 Jan 1932; *Educ* George Heriot's Sch, NDC Latimer; *m* 5 Feb 1955, Jean, da of John Kenneth Kyle Harrison (d 1972); 1 s (Iain b 1959), 2 da (Margaret, Fiona); *Career* HM Armed Forces 1950-52; HM FS now Dip Serv 1949-: Berne 1954-59, third sec Havana 1960-62, second then first sec (commerce) Lima 1966-71, Parly clerk FCO 1972-75, first sec (commerce) and head of Trade Promotion Section Washington 1975-79, head of Chancery Dhaka 1980-81, head of Chancery and HM Consul Bogota 1981-84, cnsllr FCO 1985-86, HM ambassador to Paraguay 1986-89, HM ambass to Panama 1989-; *Recreations* travel, photography, swimming; *Clubs* Naval and Military, Royal Over-seas League; *Style—* John G MacDonald, Esq, CBE; c/o Foreign and Commonwealth Office, London SW1A 2AH

MACDONALD, Sir Kenneth Carmichael; KCB (1990), CB (1983); s of William Thomas Macdonald, and Janet Millar Macdonald; *b* 25 July 1930; *Educ* Hutchesons' GS, Univ of Glasgow (MA); *m* 1960, Ann Elisabeth Pauer; 1 s, 2 da; *Career* MOD: second perm sec 1988-90, dep under sec of state (procurement exec) 1980-84, dep under sec of state (Resources and Progs) 1985-88; *Recreations* golf; *Style—* Sir

Kenneth Macdonald, KCB; c/o Barclays Bank, 357-366 The Strand, London WC2R 0NX

MCDONALD, Kevin; s of Patrick McDonald (d 1966), and Teresa Mary McDonald (d 1976); *b* 20 Oct 1933; *Educ* Mexborough Schofield Tech Coll (City & Guilds Plumbing Sanitary and Domestic Engr); *m* 22 Jan 1988, Donna Bridget, *née* Nunn; 1 s (Michael Francis b 14 March 1988); *Career* dir Hepworth Iron Co 1966-72; fndr chm and md: Bartol Plastics Ltd 1965-72, Macdee Plastics 1973-75, Polypipe plc 1980-; *Recreations* shooting, motor sport, fishing; *Clubs* Annabel's; *Style—* Kevin McDonald, Esq; Polypipe plc, Broomhouse Lane, Doncaster, S Yorkshire DN12 1S (☎ 0709 770000, fax 0709 770001, telex 547353)

McDONALD, Dr (Edward) Lawson; s of late Charles Seaver McDonald, of London, and late Mabel Deborah, *née* Osborne; *b* 8 Feb 1918; *Educ* Felsted, Clare Coll Cambridge, Middx Hosp, Harvard Univ; *m* 1953 (m dis 1972), (Ellen) Greig, *née* Rattray; 1 s (James b 16 June 1956); *Career* WWII Surgn Lt RNVR served N Atlantic and Normandy campaigns 1943-46; asst Med Dept Peter Bent Brigham Hosp Boston Mass and res fell Harvard Univ 1952-53, Rockefeller travelling fell 1952-53, asst dir Inst of Cardiology Univ of London 1955-61; conslt cardiologist: London Hosp 1960-78, Nat Heart Hosp 1961-83, King Edward VII Hosp for Offrs London 1968-88, King Edward VII Hosp Midhurst 1970-; hon conslt cardiologist Nat Heart Hosp 1983-; memb: Bd of Govrs Nat Heart and Chest Hosps 1975-82, Cncl Br Heart Fdn 1975-83; advsr Malaysian Govt; visiting lectr: Univs and Cardiac Socs in Europe, N and S America, China and USSR; St Cyres lectr 1966, Charles A Berns Meml lectr Albert Einstein Coll of Med NY 1973, 5 World Congress of Cardiology Souvenir Orator and Lectr's Gold medallist 1977; int fell Cncl on Clinical Cardiology American Heart Assoc; memb: Br Cardiac Soc, Assoc of Physicians GBI, American Heart Assoc, Italian Soc of Cardiology, Pakistan Cardiac Soc, Revista Portuguesa de Cardiologia; fell American Coll of Cardiology; FRCP; Order of the Crown of Jahore 1980; *Books* Medical and Surgical Cardiology (jtly, 1969), Very Early Recognition of Coronary Heart Disease (ed, 1977); *Recreations* art, skiing, mountain walking, sailing; *Style—* Dr Lawson McDonald; 9 Bentinck Mansions, Bentinck St, London W1M 5RJ (☎ 071 935 0868/ 7101)

MACDONALD, (Donald) Lewis; s of Donald Macdonald, of Brue, Isle of Lewis, and Catherine, *née* Maclean; *b* 22 Sept 1942; *Educ* Clydebank HS, Univ of Glasgow (BSc), Chelsea Coll of Sci and Technol; *m* 22 Aug 1969, Christina MacMillan (Christine), da of Donald Roderick Martin, of Lurebost, Isle of Lewis; 3 da (Kay b 1972, Nina b 1974, Anne b 1978); *Career* Cadet Pilot RAFVR Univ of Glasgow Air Sqdn 1960, cmmnd actg Pilot Offr 1963, sr student 1964; quality assurance mangr Racal-BCC Wembley 1973-74 (prodn planning mangr 1968-73), prodn mangr Racal Datacom Salisbury 1974-78, prodn dir Racal Consec Salisbury 1978-82, md Racal Acoustics Wembley & Watford 1982-90; memb: Lond NW Euroconstituency Businessmen Club, The Europa Club, Lapwing Flying Gp Denham Aerodrome; MIEE 1974; *Recreations* oil painting, photography, amateur radio, flying, cycling; *Style—* Lewis Macdonald, Esq; Lincoln Lodge, Chalfont Lane, Chorleywood, Rickmansworth, Herts; Racal Acoustics Ltd, Waverley Industrial Park, Hailsham Drive, Harrow, Middlesex (☎ 44 (0) 1 4277727, fax 44(01)1 427 0350)

McDONALD, Hon Mrs; (Margaret Joan); da of Baron Fraser of Lonsdale (d 1974); *b* 1920; *m* 1939, Arthur Edward McDonald; *Style—* THe Hon Mrs McDonald; Tal Marruxa, Safi, Malta

MACDONALD, Michael Stanley; s of Stanley Roche Macdonald (d 1958), and Elsie Roche, *née* Nichols; *b* 12 Sept 1923; *Educ* Churchers Coll Petersfield, Cranleigh; *m* 27 Sept 1947, Cynthia Mary, da of Horace Winstone Harrison (d 1959); 1 s (Martin Stanley Harrison b 1951), 2 da (Michele Annette Cynthia (Mrs Foot) b 1949, Penelope Mary (Mrs Hughes) b 1952); *Career* WWII RAF 1941-46, AC2 wireless operator, cmmnd PO (Intelligence), served in India and Burma 1942-45, Flt Lt ADC to AOC Malaya 1945-46; md: Taylors Eagle Brewery and Austine Cravers 1946-51, Carlsberg Sales Ltd 1951-74, Carlsberg Distributors Ltd 1974-81; Carlsberg Brewery Ltd: sales dir 1981-85, md 1985-88, non-exec dir 1988-; church warden St Winifreds Harrogate 1964-74; JP: City of Manchester 1965-71, Harrogate 1971-74; chm Canterbury Diocesan Bd of Fin 1990, memb Archbishop's Cncl 1990; Freeman City of London, Liveryman Worshipful Co of Distillers; Knight of the Danebrau (Denmark); *Recreations* golf, tennis, swimming, gardening; *Clubs* RAF; *Style—* Michael Macdonald, Esq; Carlsberg Brewery Ltd, Bridge St, Northampton NN1 1PD (☎ 0604 234333)

MACDONALD, Morag (Mrs Walter Simpson); da of Murdoch Macdonald Macdonald, of Glasgow, and Isobel, *née* Black; *b* 8 Feb 1947; *Educ* Bellahouston Acad Glasgow, Univ of Glasgow (LLB), Coll of Law London; *m* 12 Nov 1983, Walter Freeman Simpson, s of Vivian Simpson, OBE (d 1973); 1 da; *Career* called to the Bar Inner Temple 1974; The Post Office: joined 1968, various posts in telecommunications and corporate HQ 1969-79, PA to MD Girobank 1980-81, seconded to DTI 1982, sec PO 1985- (dep sec 1983-85); memb Cncl and Mgmnt Ctee Indust and Parly Tst; memb Hon Soc The Inner Temple 1971, FRSA 1990; *Recreations* walking, embroidery; *Style—* Ms Morag Macdonald; 30 St James's Square, London SW1Y 4PY (☎ 071 389 8030, fax 071 389 8035)

MCDONALD, Neal Angus; s of Ian Angus McDonald, of Alban House, Holly Hill Lane, Sarisbury Green, Hants, and Gwynfa Rose, *née* Neal; *b* 22 July 1963; *Educ* St Mary's Coll Bitterne, Royal Naval Engrg Coll Manadon, UCL (BSc, MSc); *Career* yachtsman; memb UK (RYA) youth team helming 420 class 1978-80; memb GB World Championship team: 420 class Aust 1981, 505 class Germany 1985 and Canada 1990, FD class Holland 1988 and USA 1990; crewed winner 505 class Nat Championships 1986, helmed runners up Int 14 class Nat Championships 1986, helmed third place Int 14 class World Championships Japan 1987, winner Prince of Wales Cup and Int 14 class Nat Championships 1988, crewed for Roger Yeoman in Flying Dutchman class 1988, competed in Olympic Games Seoul 1988, built own Int 14 boat 1989, winner USA Nat Championships and Int 14 World Championships 1989 (bro Duncan crewed in all 420 and Int 14 events), bowman aboard Gestetner in Aust 1989-90 (runners up 18' Skiff class World Championships) helmed runners up one design 14 class Ziploc San Francisco event 1990, bowman aboard Remington Pitney Bowers in Aust 1990-91 (runners up 18' Skiff class Nat Championships); Silk Cut helmsman of the year 1989; Royal Corps of Naval Constructors 1980-89; *Style—* Neal McDonald, Esq; Alban House, Holly Hill Lane, Sarisbury Green, Hants SO3 6AG (☎ 048957 2371)

McDONALD, Dr Oonagh; MP (Lab) Thurrock July 1976-; da of Dr McDonald; *b* 21 Feb 1938; *Educ* Roan Sch for Girls Greenwich, E Barnet GS, King's Coll London (PhD); *Career* former philosophy lectr Bristol Univ, sociology lectr, schoolmistress; Parly candidate (Lab): Glos S Feb and Oct 1974; pps to chief sec treasy 1977-79; memb: Lab NEC industl policy sub-ctee 1976-, finance and econ affrs sub-ctee 1978-; oppn front bench spokesman: Defence and Disarmament 1981-Nov 1983, Treasy and econ affrs Nov 1983-; *Style—* Dr Oonagh McDonald, MP; House of Commons, SW1A 0AA (☎ 01 219 3415/01 940 5563)

MACDONALD, Peter Cameron; DL (West Lothian 1987-); s of Sir Peter George MacDonald, WS, JP, DL (d 1983), of 18 Hermitage Drive, Edinburgh, and Lady Rachel Irene, *née* Forgan; *b* 14 Dec 1937; *Educ* Loretto, East of Scotland Coll of Agric (Dip Agric); *m* 2 Aug 1974, Barbara Helen, da of David Ballantyne, of Peebles; 2 step s (David Drimmie b 1964, Patrick Drimmie b 1967); *Career* farmer 1961-; dir J Dickson & Son Gunmakers 1968-; Scottish Landowners Fedn: memb Cncl 1976-, convener 1985-88, chm Countryside Review Gp 1988, vice pres 1989; memb: Cncl Blackface Sheepbreeders Assoc 1970-74, Pentland Hills Rural Land Mgmnt Gp 1977-84, West Lothian Countryside Advsy Ctee, West Lothian Regn Countryside Ctee 1978-81, Forth River Purification Bd 1979-87; dir Royal Highland Agric Soc of Scotland 1985, Pentland Hills Advsy Ctee; vice chm: Pentland Hills Regnl Park Consultative Ctee 1987-89, Pentland Hills Regional Park Advsy Ctee 1989-; *Recreations* fishing, shooting, golf; *Clubs* Hon Co of Edinburgh Golfers; *Style—* Peter Macdonald, Esq, DL; Colzium Farm, Kirknewton, Midlothian EH27 8DH (☎ 0506 880607)

McDONALD, Hon Lord; Robert Howat McDonald; MC (1944); s of Robert Glassford McDonald (d 1965), of Paisley, Renfrew; *b* 15 May 1916; *Educ* John Neilson Inst Paisley, Glasgow Univ (MA, LLB); *m* 1949, Barbara, da of John Mackenzie, of Ross-shire; *Career* served WWII Maj NW Europe, KOSB (despatches); advocate 1946, QC 1956, Sheriff Ayr & Bute 1966-71, pres Industl Tbnl Scotland 1971-73, senator Coll Justice (Scottish Lord of Session with title Lord McDonald) 1973-89; *Clubs* New (Edinburgh); *Style—* The Hon Lord McDonald, MC; 5 Doune Terrace, Edinburgh

MACDONALD, Vice Adm Sir Roderick Douglas; KBE (1978, CBE 1966); s of late Douglas Macdonald, and Marjorie; *b* 25 Feb 1921Java; *Educ* Fettes; *m* 1, 1943 (m dis 1980), Joan, da of Adm of the Fleet Sir Algernon Usborne Willis, GCB, KBE, DSO; 2 s (and 1 s decd); m 2, 1980, (Cynthia) Pamela Mary, da of Humphrey Ernest Bowman, CMG, CBE (d 1965), and sis of Paul Humphrey Armytage Bowman, *qv*; formerly w of Rear Adm Josef Bartosik, CB, DSC, RN; *Career* entered RN 1939, served WWII, served Cyprus 1957 (despatches), cmd Naval Forces Borneo 1965-66 (CBE), Vice Adm 1976, ADC to HM The Queen 1973, COS to C-in-C Naval Home Cmd 1973-76, COS Allied Naval Forces S Europe 1976-79; artist with regular one-man exhibitions London and Edinburgh 1979-; vice-pres 1976-85 and fell Nautical Inst; pres: Skye Highland Games, Skye Piping Soc, Inverness Sea Cadet Unit; tstee Clan Donald Lands Trust; yr bro Trinity House; *Recreations* gardening, sailing; *Clubs* Caledonian, Royal Naval Sailing Assoc, Royal Scottish Pipers Soc; *Style—* Vice Adm Sir Roderick Macdonald, KBE; Ollach, Braes, Isle of Skye, Scotland

MACDONALD, Roderick Francis; QC; s of Finlay Macdonald (d 1991), and Catherine, *née* Maclean; *b* 1 Feb 1951; *Educ* St Mungo's Acad Glasgow, Univ of Glasgow (LLB Hons); *Career* admitted advocate 1975, advocate-depute (crown counsel 1987-, home advocate-depute (sr crown counsel) 1990-; *Style—* Roderick MacDonald, QC; 6A Lennox Street, Edinburgh EH4 1QA (☎ 031 332 7240); Advocates' Library, Parliament House, Edinburgh EH1 1RF (☎ 031 226 5071, fax 031 225 3642, telex 727856 FACADVG)

MACDONALD, Ronald Robert; s of George Macdonald, of 1 Burton Cres, Leeds, and Anne, *née* Chapman (d 1972); *b* 31 Dec 1927; *Educ* Hutchesons Boys GS, Univ of Glasgow (MB ChB, MD), Royal Coll of Obstetricians and Gynaecologists (MRCOG, FRCOG), Royal Coll of Surgeons Edinburgh (FRCSE); *m* 17 Feb 1962, Joan, da of James Albert Raper, of Glebe Cottage, Burton Cres, Leeds; 1 s (Robert Duncan b 1966), 1 da (Anne b 1963); *Career* Sqdn Ldr med branch RAF 1952-55 (despatches 1954); Hall fell Dept of Obstetrics and Gynaecology Univ of Glasgow 1958-60, sr lectr Dept of Obstetrics and Gynaecology Univ of Leeds 1962-, conslt obstetrician and gyaecologist Leeds 1963-; memb BMA; *Books* Scientfic Basis of Obstetrics and Gynaecology (ed 3 edn, 1985), European Journal of Obstetrics and Gynaecology (Br ed); *Recreations* golf, photography; *Clubs* Perinatal; *Style—* Ronald Macdonald, Esq; Glebe House, 5 Shaw Lane, Leeds LS6 4DH (☎ 0532 789 471); The General Infirmary, Leeds

MACDONALD, Hon Mrs (Rosemary); *née* Brooke; da of 1 Viscount Alanbrooke, KG, GCB, OM, GCVO, DSO (d 1963), and Jane Mary Richardson (d 1925); *b* 25 Oct 1918; *m* 13 July 1945, Capt Ronald Alastair Macdonald, RA, s of Robert MacDonald, of Liverpool; 2 s (Alastair b 1947, Ian b 1952), 1 da (Janey b 1949); *Style—* The Hon Mrs Macdonald; Deepleigh Barn, Deepleigh Lane, Langley Marsh, Wivemiscombe, Somerset TA4 2UU

MacDONALD, Dr Stuart Beamish; s of Angus Beamish MacDonald (d 1980), of Beamish Lodge, Lanarkshire, Scotland, and Morag Doris Ethel, *née* Campbell; *b* 8 April 1947; *Educ* Herriot Sch Edinburgh , Univ of Edinburgh (LLB), Univ of Virginia USA (LLM, SND); *m* 8 Jan 1976, Rosalind Cynthia, da of Peter Smith, of Plymouth House, 21 Kewyatta St, Narobi, Kenya; *Career* admitted slr 1979; ptnr Clyde & Co (joined 1978); memb Cons Pty; memb Law Soc 1976; *Recreations* fox hunting, debating; *Clubs* RAC; *Style—* Dr Stuart MacDonald; Clyde & Co, 51 Eastcheap, London EC3M 1UP (☎ 071 623 1244, telex 884886, fax 071 623 5427, car 0836 275126)

MACDONALD, Trevor John; s of Francis John MacDonald, of 31 Orchard Gardens, Hove, E Sussex, and Violet Eveleigh, *née* Taverner; *b* 15 April 1933; *Educ* Brighton Hove and Sussex GS, Hertford Coll Oxford (MA); *Career* Nat Serv Bombardier RA 1955-57; with Br Iron and Steel Fedn 1957-67 (until nationisation), Br Steel Corp 1967-88 (until privatisation), asst to chm Br Steel plc 1988-; reader C of E; *Style—* Trevor MacDonald, Esq; 31 Orchard Gardens, Hove, E Sussex (☎ 0273 771228); British Steel plc, 9 Albert Embankment, London SE1 7SN (☎ 071 735 7654, fax 071 387 1142, telex 916061)

MacDONALD-BARKER, Anthony William; s of William Hector MacDonald-Barker, of Croxley Green, Herts, and Sylvia Gwendoline Ada, *née* Rollings; *b* 18 May 1943; *Educ* Merchant Taylors'; *Career* chemicals trader LS Raw Materials Ltd 1972-75, sales mangr Pharmaceutical Div Intercity Chemicals Ltd 1976-77, sales dir Harbottle (Pharmaceuticals) Ltd 1978- (specialising import export trade with China); FIEx 1984; *Recreations* most sports especially cricket (player), football (spectator), horseracing (owner in syndicate), music, travel, philately; *Clubs* Old Merchant Taylors' Soc; *Style—* Anthony MacDonald-Barker, Esq; 29a Chingford Ave, Chingford, London E4 6RJ (☎ 081 529 6054); Harbottle (Pharmaceuticals) Ltd, Seabright House, 72-76 River Rd, Barking, Essex IG11 0DY (☎ 081 594 4074/9617, fax 081 591 8563, telex 897933/897788)

MACDONALD-BUCHANAN, (Alexander) James; s of Maj Sir Reginald Narcissus Macdonald-Buchanan, KCVO, MBE, MC, DL (d 1981), and Hon Catherine Buchanan (d 1987), o da of 1 Baron Woolavington; bro of Capt John Macdonald-Buchanan, *qv*; *b* 21 April 1931; *Educ* Eton; *m* 26 April 1960, Elizabeth Vivian, da of Hon Hugh Adeane Vivian Smith, MBE (d 1978) (3 s of 1 Baron Bicester), of Souldern Manor, Bicester, Oxon; 4 s (Hugh b 1961, James b 1963, Nicholas b 1967, (Charles) Alexander b 1970); *Career* Nat Serv Capt Scots Gds; dir: Macdonald-Buchanan Tstees Ltd, James Buchanan & Co Ltd, Colonial Mutual Life Assurance Society Ltd; High Sheriff Northants 1972; *Clubs* White's, Turf, Pratt's, Jockey; *Style—* A J Macdonald-Buchanan, Esq; Strathconon, Muir of Ord, Ross-shire (☎ 09977 245)

MACDONALD-BUCHANAN, Capt John; MC (1945), DL (Northants 1978); s of Sir Reginald Macdonald-Buchanan, KCVO, MBE, MC, DL (d 1981), and Hon Catherine Buchanan (d 1987), da of 1 Baron Woolavington; bro of Alexander Macdonald-Buchanan, *qv*; *b* 15 March 1925; *Educ* Eton, RMC; *m* 1, 3 Nov 1950 (m dis 1969), Lady Rose Fane, o da of 14th Earl of Westmorland (d 1948); 1 s (Alastair b 1960), 2 da (Fiona b 1954, Serena b 1956); m 2, 1969, Jill Rosamonde, o da of Maj-Gen Cecil Benfield Fairbanks, CB, CBE (d 1980), and former w of Maj Jonathan Salusbury-Trelawney (ggs of Sir William S-T, 10 Bt); 2 da (Kate b 1970, Lucy b 1972); *Career* 2 Lt Scots Gds 1943, served 1944-45 NW Europe, Malaya 1948-50, Capt 1948, ret 1952; High Sheriff Northants 1963-64; sr steward of Jockey Club to 1982 (steward 1969-72), memb Horserace Betting Levy Bd 1973-76; *Clubs* Turf, White's; *Style—* Capt John Macdonald-Buchanan, MC, DL; Cottesbrooke Hall, Northamptonshire NN6 8PQ (☎ 060 124732); 22 Cadogan Place, London SW1 (☎ 071 235 8615)

MACDONALD BURNS, Dr David C; s of Lt-Col Evan MacDonald Burns (d 1956), and Enid, *née* Reynolds; *b* 24 Feb 1937; *Educ* Malvern Univ of London (MB BS); *m* 9 Nov 1964, Janet, da of Dr John Smallpiece; 1 s (Richard), 1 da (Katherine); *Career* Royal Signals 1955-57; conslt venereologist Royal Free Hosp and HMP Holloway 1973-85, sr conslt STD Royal Free Hosp Hampstead Health Authy 1985-; hon sec Hampstead Div BMA, fndr memb Int AIDS Soc, librarian ATDC (Austins 1930-39), former vice pres and sec Harveian Soc London; MRCS, LRCP, MRCOG, FRCOG; *Books* contrib: Gynaecological Enigmata (1981), Primary Care in Obstetrics and Gynaecology (1991); *Recreations* pre-war Austins, single malts, turn keys; *Clubs* Steering Wheel; *Style—* Dr David MacDonald Burns; The Harley Specialists Gp, 139 Harley St, London W1N 1DJ (☎ 01 224 3303 fax 01 224 2583)

MacDONALD-EVANS OF DENOVAN, Capt, 23 Laird of Denovan Victor James; s of Arthur Edward MacDonald-Evans, and Mabel, *née* Skinner; *b* 10 May 1945; *Educ* Darroch Sch, Univ of Edinburgh; *m* 5 April 1968, Ann, da of William Baird, of Edinburgh; *Career* 13/18 Hussars 1967-70, cmd Pay Office BAOR 1970-71, Scottish Inf Depot 1971-74, RAPC Depot 1974-77, 24 Regt RCT 1977-79, 3 Para Regt 1979-82, RAPC Depot 1982-84, KOSB 1984-87, 28 Signal Regt 1987-90, RPO Glasgow 1990-; memb Guild of Barons & Ancient Scottish Courts; FSA(Scot)F FRSA, memb: Inst of Admin Mgmnt, Inst of Supervisory Mgmnt; *Recreations* game shooting, heraldry, fishing; *Clubs* Muthaiga (Nairobi); *Style—* Capt Victor MacDonald-Evans of Denovan, FSA; RPO Glasgow, Kentigern House, 64 Brown St, Glasgow G2 8EX

MACDONALD OF BOISDALE, Andrew Ivor Alexander; s of The Capt of Clanranald, and Jane Primrose, *née* Campbell-Davis; *b* 17 June 1965; *Educ* Ampleforth, Univ of Buckingham (BSc), Central Arts Sch; *Career* dir Boisdale Wines; fndr Venture for Adventure, adventure yacht chartering in Scandinavia, Med, Atlantic, Canary Isles, Barbados, won first place in yacht class Antigua to Azores; currently mgmnt conslt Alexander Proudfoot; *Recreations* yacht racing, bagpipes, stained glass; *Clubs* Turf, Western (Glasgow), Hamble River Sailing; *Style—* Andrew Macdonald of Boisdale, Esq; 16 Moleton Terrace, London SW1; Wester Lix, Killin, Perthshire

MACDONALD OF CLANRANALD, Ranald Alexander; *see*: Clanranald, Capt of

MACDONALD OF GWAENYSGOR, 2 Baron (UK 1949); Gordon Ramsay Macdonald; s of 1 Baron, KCMG, PC (d 1966), and Mary, *née* Lewis (d 1967); *b* 16 Oct 1915; *Educ* Upholland GS, Manchester Univ; *m* 6 May 1941, Leslie Margaret, da of John Edward Taylor, of Rainford, Lancs; 3 da; *Heir* none; *Career* served 1940-46 with RA, Maj GSO; joined Bd of Trade 1946; UK trade cmmr Australia 1947-53; md Tube Investments (Export) Ltd 1953-64; chief exec UK Operations Hayek Engineering (AG Zurich), Ferro Metal & Chemical Co, Satra Consultants (UK); *Style—* The Rt Hon Lord Macdonald of Gwaenysgor; c/o House of Lords, London SW1

MACDONALD OF MACDONALD, Hon (Alexander Donald) Archibald; yr s of 7 Baron Macdonald, MBE (d 1970); *b* 3 Sept 1953; *Educ* Eton, Magdalene Coll Cambridge; *Style—* The Hon Archibald Macdonald of Macdonald; Armadale House, Isle of Skye, Scotland

MACDONALD OF SLEAT; *see*: Bosville Macdonald

MACDONALD OF TOTE, Maj John Lachlan; DL; s of Col Kenneth Lachlan Macdonald of Tote and Skeabost, DSO (d 1938), and his 2 wife, Margaret Elinor, *née* Caldwell; *b* 22 Dec 1919; *Educ* Ampleforth, Trinity Coll Cambridge; *m* 2 June 1961, Mary Imogen, o da of Richard Gerald Micklethwait, TD, of Ardsley House, Barnsley, Yorks; 2 s, 1 da; *Heir* s, Charles Lachlan b 9 July 1964; *Career* served in Lovat Scouts and GHQ Liaison Regt in Faroes, N Africa and Europe 1939-46; dir Electro Devices Ltd 1962-84; memb CC Inverness 1955-64, govr N of Scotland Agric Coll 1959-61; *Clubs* New (Edinburgh); *Style—* Maj John Macdonald of Tote, DL; Tote House, Skeabost Bridge, Isle of Skye (☎ 047 032203); 50 Chelsea Park Gardens, London SW3 (☎ 071 352 1925)

MACDONALD ROSS, George; s of John MacDonald Ross, CBE, of London, and Helen Margaret, *née* Wallace; *b* 11 Nov 1943; *Educ* Mill Hill Sch, St Catharine's Coll Cambridge (MA); *m* 24 June 1974, (Margaret) Lynne Ross, da of Elwyn Chubb, of Cardiff; *Career* asst lectr in philosophy Univ of Birmingham 1969-72; Univ of Leeds: res fell in history and philosophy of sci 1972-73, lectr in philosophy 1973-88, sr lectr 1988, head of Dept of Philosophy 1990-; chm Nat Ctee for Philosophy; memb: Ctee Br Soc for the History of Philosophy, Cncl Royal Inst of Philosophy, Ctee Leibniz-Gesellschaft; pres Leibniz Assoc; pres Leibniz Assoc; *Books* Leibniz (1984); *Recreations* conviviality, bricolage, walking; *Style—* George MacDonald Ross, Esq; 10 Ashwood Villas, Leeds LS6 2EJ (☎ 0532 755 961); Department of Philosophy, The University, Leeds LS2 9JT (☎ 0532 333 283, fax 0532 333 265, telex 556 473 UNILDS G)

MacDONELL OF GLENGARRY, Air Cdre (Aeneas Ranald) Donald; CB (1964), DFC (1940); Hereditary 22 Chief of Glengarry, 12 Titular Lord MacDonell; eld s of Maj Aeneas Ranald MacDonell of Glengarry, CBE (d 1941), of Swanage, Dorset (*see* Burke's Landed Gentry, 18 edn, vol III), and Dorah Edith, *née* Hartford (d 1935); *b* 15 Nov 1913; *Educ* Hurstpierpoint Coll, RAF Coll Cranwell; *m* 1, 14 Oct 1940 (m dis 1972), Diana Dorothy (d 1980), da of Lt-Col Henry Richard Keane, CBE (d 1938), of Belleville House, Cappoquin, Co Tipperary; 2 s ((Aeneas) Ranald Euan (Younger of Glengarry) b 1941, (Colin) Patrick b 1946), 1 da (Lindsay Alice (Mrs Brian Cuthbertson) b 1947); m 2, 9 March 1973, Lois Eirene Frances, da of Rev Gerald Champion Streatfeild (d 1988), of Winchester, Hants; 1 s (James Donald of Scotus b 1974), 1 da (Penelope Lois b 1976); *Career* cmmd Pilot Offr RAF 1934, No 54 (F) Sqdn 1934-36, seconded to Fleet Air Arm 1936 (Fleet Fighter Pilot); Flying Instr 1938, Sqdn Ldr Air Min 1939, Offr Cmdg No 64 Spitfire Sqdn 1940-41, POW 1941-45, War Cabinet Off (Wing Cdr) 1946-47, Chief Flying Instr RAF Coll Cranwell 1949-50; Air Cdre, Air Attaché Moscow 1956-58; Cmdt No 1 Initial Trg Sch 1959-60; dir Mgmnt and Work Study MOD 1960-64; ret 1964; mangr operational res, Constructors John Brown 1964-67; personnel mangr CITB 1967-73; head of Industl Dept Industrial Soc 1973-77; ptnr John Courtis & Ptnrs 1977-80; ret; memb Standing Cncl of Scottish Chiefs; tstee: Clan Donald Lands Tst, Finlaggan Tst, Invergarry Castle Tst; vice pres Ross & Cromarty Branch of Soldiers', Sailors' and Airmens' Families Assoc; MBIM, FIWSP; *Recreations* bird watching, reading, writing; *Clubs* RAF; *Style—* Air Cdre Donald MacDonell of Glengarry, CB, DFC; Elonbank, Castle St, Fortrose, Ross-shire IV10 8TH (☎ 0381 20121)

MCDONNELL, David Croft; JP; *b* 9 July 1943; *m* 9 Nov 1967, Marieke; 3 da (Emma, Sarah-Jane, Sophia); *Career* Bryce Hanmer & Co (became Thornton Baker 1964 then Grant Thornton 1971): articled clerk 1959-64, ptnr 1972, nat managing ptnr 1989; ACA 1965; *Recreations* sailing, motor racing (spectating), walking, mountaineering; *Style—* David McDonnell, Esq, JP; Grant Thornton, Grant Thornton House, Melton St, London NW1 2EP (☎ 071 383 5100, fax 071 383 4715)

McDONNELL, His Hon Denis Lane; OBE (Mil) 1945; s of David John Joseph McDonnell (d 1938), and Mary Nora, *née* Lane (d 1970); *b* 2 March 1914; *Educ* Christian Bros Coll Cork, Ampleforth, Sidney Sussex Coll Cambridge (MA); *m* 10 Sept 1940, Florence Nina, da of Lt-Col Hugh Thomas Ryan, DSO (d 1936), of Cork; 4 da (Margaret b 1943, Aileen b 1946 (decd), Patricia b 1948, Clare b 1957), 1 s (Hugh b 1949, decd); *Career* WWII RAFVR 1940-45 served in UK and Europe, Wing Cdr; called to the Bar Middle Temple 1936, practised 1938-40 and 1946-67, bencher 1965, co ct judge 1967-71, circuit judge 1972-86; hon sec cncl HM Circuit Judges 1979-83 (pres 1985); FCIArb; *Recreations* golf, gardening; *Clubs* Pildown Golf, Rye Golf, Woking Golf, Royal Cinque Ports Golf; *Style—* His Hon Denis L McDonnell, OBE

McDONNELL, Hon Hector John; s of 8 Earl of Antrim (d 1977), and Angela, Countess of Antrim (d 1984); *b* 1 March 1947; *Educ* Eton, Christ Church Oxford; *m* 1969 (m dis 1974), Catherine Elizabeth, da of Ronald Chapman, of Buttermilk Hall, Brill, Bucks; 1 s (Colquitto Angus b 1972), 1 da (Hannah b 1971); *Career* painter, exhibited London, Dublin, Paris, Vienna, Brussels, Belfast, Madrid, Munich, Stuttgart, Lyons (one-man shows); won Darmstädter Kunstpreis 1978, maj retrospective in Matildenhöhe, Darmstadt 1981; master of Hounds 1966-69; *Publications* Ballad of William Bloat (1982), The Ould Orange Flute (1983), The Night Before Larry was Stretched (1984), A Tibetan Sketchbook (1987), Chinese Journey (1986), A Journey to Tsaparang (1990); *Recreations* bloodsports, travelling; *Style—* The Hon Hector McDonnell; The Old Rectory, Glenarm, Co Antrim (☎ 0574 841 554)

McDONNELL, Hon James Angus; MBE (1946); s of 7 Earl of Antrim (d 1932); *b* 1917; *Educ* Eton; *m* 1939, Jeanne Irene, da of Col Stanley Leonard Barry, CMG, CBE, DSO, MVO, DL, JP (*see* Baronetage Barry); 1 s (Sorley James b 1940), 1 da (Louisa b 1946); *Career* 2 Lt 5 Bn Royal Norfolk Regt 1939; *Style—* The Hon James McDonnell; 36 Farley Ct, Melbury Rd, London W14

McDONNELL, Prof James Anthony Michael (Tony); s of Michael Francis McDonnell, of Madeley, Nr Crewe, Cheshire, and Vera Phyllis, *née* Redding (d 1987); *b* 26 Sept 1938; *Educ* St Joseph's Coll Stoke on Trent, Univ of Manchester (BS, PLD); *m* 22 July 1961, Jean Mary, da of George Gordon (d 1976); 2 s ((Benedict) Michael b 27 Feb 1965, Roger James b 1 June 1971), 1 da (Louise Anne b 21 Aug 1962); *Career* res asst Nuffield Radio Ast Labs 1964-65, post-doctoral res assoc NASA Goddard Spaceflight Centre USA 1965-67; Univ of Kent: lectr in physical electronics 1967-72, sr lectr in electronics 1972-77, reader in space sciences 1977-85, prof of space physics and head of space sci 1985; contrib to Planetary Science in Europe JAM McDonnell (Planetary and Interstellar Dust) 1980; various chapters of Advanced Space Res incl: Progress in Planetary Exploration 1981, Recent Researches into Solid Bodies and Magnetic Fields in the Solar System 1982, Cosmic Dust and Space Debris 1986; organiser and orater of welcome address Comet Nucleus Sample Return ESA Cornerstone Workshop Canterbury 1986; memb Ctee Space Astronomy and Radio Div SERC 1979-81; memb: UK Halley Watch Steering Ctee (later CHUKCC) 1983-87, space sci prog Br Nat Space Centre 1988-; COSPAR: memb and sec Panel 3 C 1973-79, memb Sub-cmmn B1 ISC B 1982-86, exec memb ISC B 1984-88, chm ISC B 1988-, memb Organising Ctee IAU Cmmn 22 1979; memb: meteoroid shield design workshop ESA Comet Halley Mission 1981, ESA Lunar Polar Workshop 1981; govr workshop on planetology European Sci Fndn 1981, chm Organisation Ctee Symposium 6 COSPAR/IAU/IUTAM 1982, discipline specialist Int Hally Watch 1983, memb ESA/NASA primative bodies study team 1984; conslt: space station design USRA 1985, Comet nucleus sample return CNSR 1985-87, CAESAR assessment study 1986, UESTA phase A 1987; memb: Solar System Working Gp 1988-90, Rosetta Mission definition team ESA 1988; FRAS, FBIS 1987; *Books* Cosmic Dust (ed and co-author with John Wiley, 1978); *Recreations* tennis, woodwork; *Style—* Prof Tony McDonnell; Unit for Space Sciences, Physics Laboratory, University of Kent, Canterbury, Kent CT2 7NR (☎ 0227 459616, fax 0227 762616, telex 965449)

McDONNELL, John Beresford William; QC (1984); s of Beresford Conrad McDonnell (d 1960), and Charlotte Mary, *née* Caldwell (d 1981); *b* 26 Dec 1940; *Educ* City of London Sch, Balliol Coll Oxford (MA), Harvard Law Sch (LLM); *m* 3 Feb 1968, Susan Virginia, da of Wing Cdr Hubert Mortimer Styles, DSO (d 1942), and Audrey Elizabeth (now Lady Richardson); 2 s (Conrad b 1971, William b 1973), 1 da (Constance b 1975); *Career* first sec Dip Serv, asst private sec to Sec of State 1970, Cons Res Dept 1966-69; fell: Hackness, American Political Sci Assoc Congressional 1964-66; *Recreations* sculling; *Clubs* London Rowing; *Style—* John McDonnell, Esq, QC; 20 Brompton Square, London SW3 2AD (☎ 071 584 1498); office: 1 New Square, Lincoln's Inn, London WC2A 3SA (☎ 071 405 0884, fax 071 831 6109, telex 295257 NITPIK G)

MacDONNELL, John Graham Randal; s of John Patrick Randal MacDonnell (d 1964), of Ilfracombe, and Vera Fuggle; *b* 15 Nov 1955; *Educ* Thames Valley GS, King Edward VI Sch Witley Surrey, Ealing GS, Newcastle upon Tyne Poly (BA); *m* Barbara Anne, da of William McBride, of Glasgow; 1 s (Graham Patrick Randal); *Career* film ed BBC Scotland 1983-90 (joined 1979); programmes incl: Campus 1983, The Smith Boys (Centenary of the Boys Brigade) 1983, A Kick Up The 80's 1984, The Visit 1984-88, Laugh - I Nearly Paid My Licence Fee 1985, The Master of Dundreich 1985, Naked Video 1986; BBC Scotland: Tutti Frutti (1987 BAFTA nomination, Kodak award), Arena - Byrne About Byrne 1988, The Justice Game 1989, Your Cheatin' Heart 1989-; freelance film ed 1990- (recently completed The Black Velvet Gown for Worldwide International Television/Tyne Tees); *Recreations* cinema, galleries, photography, television, reading, swimming, music; *Clubs* BBC; *Style—* John MacDonnell, Esq; 10 Ferndale Drive, Summerston, Glasgow G23 5BU (☎ 041 946 5810)

McDONNELL, Hon Randal Alexander St John; s and h of 9 Earl of Antrim; *b* 2 July 1967; *Style—* The Hon Randal McDonnell

McDONNELL OF THE GLENS, The Count Randal Christian Charles Augustus Somerled Patrick; s of The Count and 24 Chief Robert Jarlath Hartpole Hamilton McDonnell of the Glens (d 1984), of 5 Longford Terr, Monkstown, Dublin, and his 2 w, The Countess McDonnell of the Glens, *née* Una Kathleen Dolan; descent from Ian Mor McDonnell, 2 s of John Lord of the Isles and Margaret, da of King Robert II of Scotland, who m Heiress of the Glens, of Antrim, *see* Burke's Peerage Antrim, E (who descended from a yr s of 5 Chief in the female line), and Irish Family Records 1976; f suc kinsman the 23 Chief (ka 1941); 19 Chief cr Bt 1872, dsp 1875; *b* 19 Aug 1950; *Educ* Stonyhurst, Trinity Coll, Dublin and the King's Inns, Dublin; *Heir* bro, Count Peter Martin Ignatius Laurence David Colla Hamilton McDonnell; *Career* 25 chief Clandonald S of Antrim; officially recognised Chief of the Name by the Chief Herald of Ireland (Gaelic patronymic "McIan Mor") Lord of the Glens of Antrim; Count of the Holy Roman Empire (which title, created in the preceeding generation passed to the heirs male of the 1st Count in 1766); memb bd of govrs Irish Quarter Horse Soc; kt SMOM (1971); *Recreations* opera, ballet, rugby, polo, parties, history; *Style—* The Count Randal McDonnell of the Glens; Harlochstown House, Ashbourne, County Meath, Ireland (☎ 351993)

MACDONOGH, Jeremy Felix; s of Sqdn Ldr Redmond Joseph Macdonogh (d 1986), of Chelsea, and Elizabeth, *née* Zirner-Bacon; *b* 14 April 1949; *Educ* Gonville & Caius Coll Cambridge, Rome Univ; *m* 31 March 1982, Helen Alice Elizabeth, da of Paul

Edward Seale, of Bristol; 1 s (Felix Augustus Maximilian b 1982); *Career* sr broker C T Bowring & Co Ltd 1974-79, business devpt Swiss Re SA 1979-82, dir Team Success & Co Ltd 1982-86, area mangr Manchester Exchange Investmt Bank 1986-87, mangr Reuters Ltd 1987-91, dir of strategic mktg Europe Knight-Ridder Unicom Ltd 1991-; playwright Flight of Fancy (1981); *Recreations* writing, opera, travel, reading, theatre, wine; *Clubs* Wig and Pen; *Style*— Jeremy Macdonogh, Esq; 96-98 Clarendon Rd, London W11 2HR (☎ 071 727 3042); Knight-Ridder Unicom, 72-78 Fleet St, London EC4 (☎ 071 353 1020)

McDONOUGH, David Fergus; s of Alan James McDonough, of 34 Milnthorpe Rd, Eastbourne, Sussex, and Shirley Davis; *b* 7 June 1953; *Educ* Stowe, Merton Coll Oxford (MA); *m* 1978, Caroline Eugénie, *née* Axford; *Career* personal asst to md Dundee Combex Marx 1975-79, md McDonough Assocs Ltd 1979-90, sr conslt Lowe Bell Consultants 1990-; fndr and chm The October, chm Appeals Ctee Queen Elizabeth's Fndn for the Disabled; Freeman: City of London, Worshipful Co of Merchant Taylors; *Recreations* politics, reading, theatre, golf; *Clubs* Bucks; *Style*— David McDonough, Esq; 21 Helix Gardens, London SW2 2JJ (☎ 081 671 4973); Lowe Bell Consultants, 7 Hertford St, Mayfair, London W1Y 7DY (☎ 071 495 4044, fax 071 629 1279, car 0831 327526)

McDOUGALL, Alexander Francis Sebastian; s of Capt Ian Alexander McDougall, RM (d 1984), of Emsworth, Hants, and Dr Margaret Joan, *née* Francis (d 1982); *b* 20 Nov 1960; *Educ* Portsmouth GS, Chichester Coll; *m* 30 Aug 1986, Deborah Sara, da of Vincent Christopher Finn, of Lavant, West Sussex; 2 s (Maximilian b 27 May 1988, Hamish Finn b 19 July 1990); *Career* dir: Harborn Ltd 1986, N R Resources SDNBHD 1987, Senikah SDNBHD 1987, Harborn France Sarl 1987, Pacol Ltd (Group) 1988, Pacol Futures Ltd 1988, Pacol Rubber & Latex 1988, Pacol Harborn Rubber Ltd 1990, The Poloshop Ltd 1990; *Recreations* water and snow skiing, tai chi, collector of veteran cars; *Clubs* RAC, Emsworth SC; *Style*— Alexander McDougall, Esq; Croft Cottage, Almshouse Common, Petworth Rd, Haslemere, Surrey (☎ 0428 643692); Pacol Harborn Rubber Ltd, Allum House, 1 St Thomas Street, London SE1 9RY (☎ 071 407 4400, fax 071 403 3487, telex 888 712/3)

MacDOUGALL, Sir (George) Donald Alastair; CBE (1945, OBE 1942); s of Daniel Douglas MacDougall (d 1929), and Beatrice Amy Miller (d 1954); *b* 26 Oct 1912; *Educ* Shrewsbury, Balliol Coll Oxford (MA); *m* 1, 1937 (m dis 1977), Bridget Christabel, da of George Edward Bartrum; 1 s, 1 da; m 2, 1977, (Laura) Margaret, da of George Edward Linfoot, and formerly w of Robert Lowe Hall (later Baron Roberthall, d 1988); 2 step da; *Career* economist; fell: Wadham Coll Oxford 1945-50 (hon fell 1964-), Nuffield Coll 1947-64 (hon fell 1967-); Winston Churchill's Statistical Branch 1939-45 and 1951-53; econ dir NEDO 1962-64, dir gen Dept of Econ Affairs 1964-69, head Govt Econ Serv and chief econ advsr HM Treasury 1969-73, chief econ advsr CBI 1973-84; pres Royal Econ Soc 1972-74; Hon LLD Univ of Strathclyde, Hon LittD Univ of Leeds, Hon DSc Aston Univ; FBA; kt 1953; *Books Incl:* The World Dollar Problem (1957), Studies in Political Economy (2 vols, 1975), Don and Mandarin: Memoirs of an Economist (1987); *Recreations* fishing; *Clubs* Reform; *Style*— Sir Donald MacDougall, CBE; 86A Denbigh St, Westminster, London SW1V 2EX (☎ 071 821 1998)

McDOUGALL, Douglas Christopher Patrick; s of Patrick McDougall (d 1950), and Helen McDougall (d 1980); *b* 18 March 1944; *Educ* Edinburgh Acad, ChCh Oxford (MA); *m* 4 June 1986, Hon Carolyn Jane, da of Baron Griffiths, MC, PC (Life Peer), *qv*; 2 da (Fiona Maria b 1987, Mary Helen b 1990); *Career* investmt mangr and ptnr Baillie Gifford & Co 1969 (sr ptnr 1989-); non-exec dir: IMRO 1987-, Provincial Group plc 1989-, Baillie Gifford Japan Trust PLC 1989-, Baillie Gifford Technology PLC 1989-; memb: Investmt Ctee Univ of Cambridge 1985-, Exec Ctee Institutional Fund Mangrs Assoc 1989-; *Clubs* Brooks's, New (Edinburgh), City of London, Hon Co of Edinburgh Golfers; *Style*— Douglas McDougall, Esq; Linplum House, Haddington, E Lothian EH41 4PE (☎ 062 081242); Baillie Gifford & Co, 10 Glenfinlas St, Edinburgh EH3 6YY (☎ 031 225 2581, fax 031 225 2358)

MacDOUGALL, Lady; (Laura) Margaret; *née* Linfoot; da of George Edward Linfoot (d 1970), and Laura Edith, *née* Clayton (d 1925); *b* 27 Aug 1910; *Educ* Sheffield HS, High Storrs GS, Somerville Coll Oxford (MA); *m* 1, Dec 1932 (m dis 1968), Robert Lowe Hall, later Baron Roberthall (Life Peer, d 1988); 2 da (Hon Felicity Margaret (Hon Mrs Skidmore) b 1936, Hon Anthea Mary (Hon Mrs Wilkinson) b 1939); m 2, 1977, Sir (George) Donald Alastair MacDougall, *qv*; *Career* economist; US Govt Office of Price Admin 1941-44, UNNRA Planning Div Washington DC Sydney and London 1944-45; lectr Lincoln Coll Oxford 1946-47, lectr 1947-49 then fell and tutor Somerville Coll Oxford 1949-75, univ lectr in Economics 1949-75; visiting prof: MIT USA 1961-62, Univ of Stirling 1984-87 (Hon Prof 1987-), conslt Nat Econ Devpt Office (NEDO) 1962-87, economic conslt Distillers' Co plc 1978-84; memb: Treasury Purchase Tax Ctee 1954, Inter-departmental Ctee on Economics and Social Research 1957-58, Gaitskell Independent Cooperative Cmmn 1958, Min of Agric Ctee on Remuneration of Milk Distributors in UK 1962, Reith Ind Cmmn on Advertising 1964, Covent Garden Market Authy Advsy Ctee 1972, Distributive Trades Industrial Trng Bd's Research Ctee 1972, Economic Devpt Ctee (EDC) for Distributive Trades 1963-87, Monopolies and Mergers Cmmn 1973-76, various wages cncls; Hon LLD Nottingham 1979, hon fell Somerville Coll Oxford; *Books* Effect of War on British Retail Trade (1943), Distributive Trading: an economic analysis (1954), Distribution in Great Britain and North America (1961), The Small Unit in Retail Trade (1972); *Recreations* fishing; *Style*— Lady MacDougall; 86a Denbigh Street, London SW1V 2EX (☎ 071 821 1998); Appletree Cottage, The Chase, Dedham Heath, Colchester, Essex CO7 6BX (☎ 0206 322814)

MACDOUGALL, Patrick Lorn; s of James Archibald Macdougall, W S (d 1982), and Valerie Jean, *née* Fraser; *b* 21 June 1939; *Educ* Schools in Kenya, Millfield, Univ Coll Oxford; *m* 1, 24 June 1967 (m dis 1982), Alison Noel, da of Herbert Charles Offer, M C, of Alderley Edge, Cheshire; 2 s (Alasdair William Lorn b 1970, Thomas Hugh James b 1972); m 2, 15 April 1983, Bridget Margaret, da of Peter Scott Young (d 1988); 3 da (Laura Margaret Valerie b 1984, Nicola Elizabeth Bridget b 1987, Vanessa Emily Hope b 1990); *Career* called to the Bar Inner Temple 1962, mangr NM Rothschild & Sons 1967-70, chief exec Amex Bank (formerly Rothschild Intercontinental Bank) 1977-78 (exec dir 1970-77), exec dir Jardine Matheson Holdings 1978-85, chm and chief exec Chartered West LB Ltd (formerly Standard Chartered Merchant Bank) 1990- (chief exec 1985-89); FCA 1967, FRSA 1988; *Recreations* skiing, golf, opera, bridge; *Clubs* RAC, Hurlingham, Sotogrande C C (Spain), SHEK O C C (Hong Kong); *Style*— Patrick Macdougall, Esq; 40 Stevenage Road, London SW6 6ET (☎ 071 736 3506); Chartered West LB Ltd, 33-36 Gracechurch St, London EC3V OAX (☎ 071 623 8711)

MCDOWALL, David Buchanan; s of Angus David McDowall (d 1957), and Enid Margaret, *née* Crook; *b* 14 April 1945; *Educ* Monkton Combe Sch, RMA Sandhurst, St John's Coll Oxford (MA, MLitt); *m* 19 April 1975, Elizabeth Mary Risk, da of Dr John McClelland Laird; 2 s (Angus b 1977, William b 1979); *Career* Subaltern RA 1965-70; Br Cncl (Bombay, Baghdad & London) 1972-77, UNRWA 1977-79; writer (for adults and children); *Books* Lebanon - A Conflict of Minorities (1983), The Kurds (1985), The Palestinians (children's book 1986), The Palestinians (Minority Rights Gp 1987), The Spanish Armada (1988), An Illustrated History of Britain (1989), Palestine and Israel: The Uprising and Beyond (1989), Britain in Close-up (1991); *Style*— David McDowall, Esq; 31 Cambrian Rd, Richmond, Surrey TW10 6JQ (☎ 081 940 3911)

MacDOWALL, Dr David William; s of William MacDowall (d 1944), of West Derby, Liverpool, and Lilian May, *née* Clarkson (d 1961); *b* 2 April 1930; *Educ* Liverpool Inst HS, Corpus Christi Coll Oxford (BA, MA, DPhil), Br Sch at Rome; *m* 21 June 1962, Mione Beryl, da of Ernest Harold Lashmar (d 1969), of Hinderton, Berkhamsted, Herts; 2 da (Sophie b 1965, Tara b 1968); *Career* Royal Signals: 2 Lt 1951-53, 2 Lt (TA) 1953, Lt (TA) 1956; asst keeper Dept Coins and Medals Br Museum 1956-60, princ Miny Educn 1960-65; Univ Grants Ctee: princ 1965-70, asst sec 1970-73; master Univ Coll and hon lectr classics ancient history and oriental studies Univ of Durham 1973-78; dir N London Poly 1980-85 (asst dir 1979), chm Soc S Asian Studies 1983-; conslt: OECD 1962 (also 1964 and 1966), UNESCO 1977 and 1978; hon treas: Royal Numismatic Soc 1966-73, Br Archeological Assoc 1989-; memb Editorial Bd Numismatic Chronicle 1966-, hon sec Soc Afghan Studies 1972-82; Barclay Head Prize Ancient Numismatics Univ of Oxford 1953 and 1956, Medallist Associacion Numismatica Espanola 1964, Nelson Wright Medallist Numismatic Soc India 1974; corresponding memb Istituto Italiano per il Medio ed Estremo Oriente 1986; FRNS 1952, FRAS 1958, FSA 1960; *Books* Coin Collections Their Preservation Classification and Presentation (1978), The Western Coinages of Nero (1979); *Recreations* travel, antiquities, photography, natural history, genealogy; *Clubs* Athenaeum; *Style*— Dr David MacDowall, FSA; Admont, Dancers End, Tring, Herts HP23 6JY

McDOWALL, Keith Desmond; CBE (1988); s of William Charteris McDowall (d 1941), of Croydon, Surrey, and Edna Florence, *née* Blake (d 1988), of Banstead, Surrey; *b* 3 Oct 1929; *Educ* Heath Clark Sch Croydon Surrey; *m* 1, 1957 (m dis 1985), Shirley Margaret Russell Astbury; 2 da (Clare Hamilton (Mrs Reid), Alison Ross (Mrs Dodson); m 2, 30 April 1988, Brenda Dean, *qv*; *Career* Nat Serv RAF 1947-49; journalist 1946-55, journalist Daily Mail 1955-67 (indust ed London 1962-67); dir of info 1969-78: Bd of Trade, Dept of Econ Affrs, Home Office, Dept of Housing and Local Govt, N Ireland Office, Dept of Employment; dep dir gen CBI 1986-88 (dir of info 1981-86); conslt on public affrs and govt rels 1988-; *Recreations* sailing, golf; *Clubs* Reform, Medway Yacht, South Herts Golf; *Style*— Keith McDowall, Esq, CBE; 2 Malvern Terrace, Islington, London N1 1HR

MCDOWALL, Kenneth; s of Andrew McDowall, and Sarah, *née* McCann; *b* 29 July 1963; *Educ* Kingsbridge Secdy Sch; partner, Elizabeth Barr; *Career* professional footballer; former player Partick Thistle, currently St Mirren; Scot Cup Winners' medal St Mirren 1987; *Recreations* golf, swimming, table tennis, tennis; *Style*— Kenneth McDowall, Esq; St Mirren FC, Love Street, Paisley PA3 2EG (☎ 041 889 2558)

MacDOWEL, Hon Mrs (Angela Christine); *née* Hazlerigg; da of 2 Baron Hazlerigg, MC, and Patricia, *née* Pullar; *b* 22 Dec 1946; *m* 31 May 1969, Timothy Effingham MacDowel, o son of Lt-Col Horace St George MacDowel, of Fulbrook House, Burford, Oxon; 2 s; *Style*— The Hon Mrs MacDowel; The White Cottage, Duncar Road, Gullane, East Lothian, Scotland EH31 2EG

MacDOWELL, Prof Douglas Maurice; s of Maurice Alfred MacDowell (d 1973), and Dorothy Jean, *née* Allan (d 1980); *b* 8 March 1931; *Educ* Highgate Sch, Balliol Coll Oxford (MA); *Career* classics master: Allhallows Sch 1954-56, Merchant Taylors' 1956-58; reader in Greek and Latin Univ of Manchester 1970-71 (asst lectr 1958-61, lectr 1961-68, sr lectr 1968-70), prof of Greek Univ of Glasgow 1971-; *Books* Andokides: On the Mysteries (1962), Athenian Homicide Law (1963), Aristophanes: Wasps (1971), The Law in Classical Athens (1978), Spartan Law (1986), Demosthenes: Against Meidias (1990); *Style*— Prof Douglas MacDowell; Dept of Classics, University of Glasgow, Glasgow G12 8QQ (☎ 041 339 8855)

McDOWELL, Sir Eric Wallace; CBE (1982); s of Martin Wallace McDowell (d 1968), of Belfast, and Edith Florence, *née* Hillock (d 1974); *b* 7 June 1925; *Educ* Royal Belfast Academical Inst; *m* 24 June 1954, Helen Lilian, da of William Montgomery (d 1951), Belfast; 1 s (Martin b 11 Nov 1959), 2 da (Kathleen b 24 Jan 1958, Claire b 25 March 1964); *Career* WWII serv 1943-46; qualified CA 1948; ptnr Wilson Hennessey & Crawford 1952-73, sr ptnr in Belfast Deloitte Haskin & Sells 1980-85 (ptnr 1973-80); dir: NI Transport Holding Co 1971-74, Spence Bryson Ltd 1986-89, TSB Bank Northern Ireland plc 1986-, Capita Northern Ireland Ltd; memb: Advsy Ctee NI Central Investmt Fund for Charities 1975- (chm 1980-), NI Econ Cncl 1977-83, Industl Devpt Bd for NI 1982- (chm 1986-), Broadcasting Cncl for NI 1983-86; memb: Exec Ctee Relate Marriage Guidance 1981-, Presbyterian Church in Ireland (trustee 1983-), Abbeyfield Belfast Soc (treas 1986-), Bd Govrs Royal Belfast Academical Inst 1959- (chm 1977-86), Cncl Inst of CAs Ireland 1968-77 (pres 1974-75); Hon DSc Econ Queen's Univ of Belfast 1989; FCA 1957; kt 1990; *Recreations* current affairs, music & drama, foreign travel; *Clubs* Ulster Reform (Belfast), Royal Overseas; *Style*— Sir Eric McDowell, CBE; Beechcroft, 19 Beechlands, Belfast BT95HU (☎ 0232 668 771)

McDOWELL, Sir Henry McLorinan; KBE (1964, CBE 1959); s of John McDowell, and Margaret Elizabeth Bingham; *b* 10 Dec 1910; *Educ* Witwatersrand Univ, Queen's Coll Oxford, Yale Univ; *m* 1939, Norah Douthwaite; 1 s, 1 da; *Career* served WWII 1 Bn N Rhodesia Regt; entered Colonial Serv 1938, sec Fed Treasy Rhodesia and Nyasaland 1959-63; chm Zimbabwe Bd Barclays Bank Int 1969-79; chllr Rhodesia/Zimbabwe Univ 1971-82; *Style*— Sir Henry McDowell, KBE; 2 Donne Ct, Burbage Rd, London SE24

McDOWELL, Johanna Susan; da of Vincent Bernard Lena (d 1979), and Ethel Florence, *née* Watkins; *b* 31 Jan 1952; *Educ* Olton Ct Convent Solihill, Twickenham Coll of Technol; *Career* advtg exec; bd dir Brookes & Vernons 1986-, lectr in advtg; *Recreations* bridge, theatre, dinner parties; *Clubs* Edgbaston Priory; *Style*— Mrs Johanna McDowell; 22 South St, Harborne B17 0DB; Brookes & Vernons, 109 Hagley Rd, Edgbaston (☎ 021 455 9481)

McDOWELL, (Charles William) Michael; *b* 11 Feb 1928; *Educ* Huntingdon GS, UCL (BSc); *m* Audrey Diana; 1 s (Robert), 3 da (Sally Ann (Mrs Muir), Julie (Mrs Lloyd), Marion (Mrs Cook)); *Career* Public Works Dept Tanganyika 1951, sr engr Howard Humphreys & Sons 1958-62 (res engr 1954-56), dep res engr London CC 1956-58, princ and fndr M McDowell & Ptnrs 1963, sr ptnr M McDowell Co Partnership 1976-88, princ Engrg Disputes Servs 1988-, cncllr London Borough of Sutton 1968-74; IPHE: chm Met Centre 1972; memb Cncl 1973-87, pres 1982-83; memb Cncl IWEM 1987-88, dir Water Pollution Control Fedn 1986-89, dir Ciria 1988-90, chm Br Standard Clay Pipes; memb and leader: Euro Standards Delgn on Clay Pipes Sewerage, Euro Standards Delgn on Small Sewerage Treatment Works; delegate Euro Standards Delgn on Sewerage and drainage; Freeman City of London 1980, memb Worshipful Co of Paviors 1980, Master Guild of Water Conservators 1988-90; FICE 1955, FIPHE 1956, FIHT 1958, FCIArb 1963, Hon FIWEM 1988; *Recreations* veteran athletics; *Clubs* Ranelagh Harriers and Veterans Athletic, City Livery, United Wards; *Style*— Michael McDowell, Esq; 13 Gilhams Ave, Banstead, Surrey SMY 1QL (☎ 081 394 1573, fax 081 394 1864)

MacDUFF, Alistair Geoffrey; s of Alexander MacDonald MacDuff (d 1985), and Iris Emma, *née* Gardner; *b* 26 May 1945; *Educ* Ecclesfield GS nr Sheffield, LSE (LLB), Univ of Sheffield (LLM); *m* 27 Sept 1969, Susan Christine, da of Ronald David Kitchener, of Salthouse, Norfolk; 2 da (Karen b 1971, Jennifer b 1972); *Career* called to the Bar Lincoln's Inn 1969, rec Crown Ct 1987; former chm local ward of Lib Party; *Recreations* golf, association football, collecting (and drinking) wine; *Clubs* Hendon GC, Economicals AFC; *Style*— Alistair MacDuff, Esq; The Owls, 84 Northumberland Rd, New Barnet, Herts (☎ 081 449 1816); Devereux Chambers, Devereux Court, London WC2 (☎ 071 353 7534, fax 071 353 1724)

MACDUFF, Earl of; David Charles Carnegie; s and h of 3 Duke of Fife, *qv* (*see* Peerage, Royal Family Section); *b* 3 March 1961; *Educ* Eton, Pembroke Coll Cambridge (MA), RAC (MBA); *m* 1987, Caroline Anne, o da of Martin Bunting; 1 s (Hon Charles Duff Carnegie b 1 July 1989); *Heir* s, Hon Charles Duff Carnegie; *Career* stockbroker; formerly with Cazenove & Co and Bell Lawrie Ltd; memb Worshipful Co of Clothworkers, Freeman of City of London 1987; *Style*— Earl of Macduff

MacECHERN, Gavin MacAlister; s of Dugald MacAlister MacEchern, and Diana Mary, *née* Body; *b* 7 March 1944; *Educ* Tonbridge; *m* 9 Nov 1972, Sarah Alison, da of late Eric Walker; 3 da (Georgina b 1976, Tanya b 1978, Christina b 1981); *Career* admitted slr 1967; fndr shareholder and dir Arlington Securities plc 1980-; *Recreations* hunting, skiing, shooting, tennis; *Clubs* Brooks's, Royal Southern Yacht; *Style*— Gavin MacEchern, Esq; Burdocks, Fairford, Glos; Arlington Securities plc, 1 Brewer's Green Buckingham Gate, London SW1

McELHERAN, John; s of Joseph Samuel McElheran (d 1971), and Hilda, *née* Veale (d 1986); *b* 18 Aug 1929; *Educ* Archbishop Holgate's GS York, St Edmund Hall Oxford (BA); *m* 1956, Jean Patricia, da of Fred Durham, of Woodham Walter, Essex (d 1967); 1 s (Richard b 1960), 2 da (Alison b 1962, Catherine b 1964); *Career* ptnr Leathes Prior & Son Norwich 1962-67 (asst slr 1959-62), sr legal asst Land Cmmn Newcastle-Upon-Tyne 1967-71, asst slr DTI and successor depts 1974-83 (sr legal asst 1971-74), under sec (legal) MAFF 1983-89; *Recreations* photography; *Clubs* Civil Service; *Style*— John McElheran, Esq; 12 Bedern, York Y01 2LP

McELROY, Vernon William; s of Stanley Cowan McElroy (d 1980), and Emily McElroy, *née* Clark (d 1980); *b* 28 March 1934; *Educ* James Watt Tech Sch Smethwick Staffs; *m* 1, 1957 (m dis), Dorothy, da of late Robert Audin; 2 da (Julie b 1963, Susan b 1969); m 2, 1975, Sylvia Evelyn, da of late Lewis Hodge; 2 s (Niall b 1978, Iain (twin) b 1978); *Career* Nat Serv Lt RE and Intelligence Corps 1958-60; chartered surveyor and chartered town planner; ptnr Goddard & Smith 1965-71, property controller The Rank Orgn 1971-75 (md Rank Property Devpts 1971-73, jt md Rank City Wall 1973-75); dir: estate mgmnt Cambridge Univ 1975-87, Aquila Investmts Ltd 1984-, Foxhollow Ltd 1976-; property dir Unex Gp 1987-; fell St Johns Coll Cambridge 1977-87, cncl memb and treas Cambridge Forum for the Construction Indust 1980-; *Recreations* DIY, local affairs; *Clubs* Dartmouth House, 1970; *Style*— Vernon McElroy, Esq; Foxhollow, 15 High St, Orwell, Royston, Herts SG8 5QN (☎ 0223 207707); UNEX House, Church Lane, Stetchworth, Newmarket, Cambridge CB8 9TN (☎ 063876 8144)

McENERY, John Hartnett; s of Maurice Joseph McEnery (d 1934), and Elizabeth Margaret, *née* Maccabe (d 1958); *b* 5 Sept 1925; *Educ* St Aloysius Coll Glasgow, Univ of Glasgow (MA); *m* 24 Sept 1977, (Lilian) Wendy, da of George Reginald Gibbons (d 1976); *Career* WWII RA 1943-47 (Staff Capt HQ Burma Cmd 1946-47); Civil Serv 1949-64; first sec UK Delgn to NATO Paris 1964-66, cnsllr Br Embassy Bonn 1966-69, regnl dir (under sec) Yorks and Humberside Region DTI 1972-76, under sec (Concorde and nat compensation div) DTI 1977-81; author, conslt and conceptual analyst 1981-; *Books* Manufacturing Two Nations (1981), Towards a New Concept of Conflict Evaluation (1985), Epilogue in Burma 1945-48 (1990); *Recreations* travel, military history; *Clubs* Hurlingham; *Style*— John McEnery, Esq; 56 Lillian Road, London SW13 9JF (☎ 081 748 8658)

McENERY, Peter Robert; s of Charles McEnery (d 1981), and Ada Mary Brinson McEnery; *b* 21 Feb 1940; *m* 1978; 1 da; *Career* actor; roles incl: Rudge in Next Time I'll Sing to You (Criterion 1963), Konstantin in The Seagull (Lyric 1964), Edward Glover in Made in Bangkok (Aldwych 1986), Trigolin in The Seagull (Lyric 1975); dir: Richard III (Nottingham 1971), The Wound (Young Vic 1972); films: Tunes of Glory (1961), The Victim (1961), The Moonspinners (1963), Entertaining Mr Sloane (1970); TV: Clayhanger (1976), The Aphrodite Inheritance (1979), The Jail Diary of Albie Sachs (1980), Japanese Style 91982), The Collectors (1986), The Mistress (1986); assoc artist with RSC; *Recreations* steam railway preservation, skiing; *Style*— Peter McEnery, Esq

McEVOY, David Dand; QC (1983); s of David Dand McEvoy (d 1988), of Stevenston, Ayrshire, and Ann Elizabeth, *née* Breslin; *b* 25 June 1938; *Educ* Mount St Mary's Coll, Lincoln Coll Oxford (BA); *m* 6 April 1974, Belinda Anne, da of Lt-Col Thomas Argyll Robertson, OBE, of Pershore, Worcs; 3 da (Alice b 1978, Louise b 1979, Isabella b 1984); *Career* 2 Lt The Black Watch (RHR) 1957-59, served Cyprus 1958; called to the Bar Inner Temple 1964, dep circuit judge 1977, rec Crown Ct 1979-; *Recreations* racing, golf, fishing; *Clubs* Caledonian, Blackwell Golf; *Style*— David McEvoy, Esq, QC; Chambers Court, Longdon, Tewkesbury, Glos GL20 6AS (☎ 068 481 626); 2 Fountain Court, Steelhouse Lane, Birmingham 4 (☎ 021 236 3882)

McEVOY, Air Chief Marshal; Sir Theodore Newman; KCB (1956, CB 1951), CBE (1945, OBE 1941); s of Rev Cuthbert McEvoy (d 1944), of Watford, Herts, and Margaret Kate, *née* Ulph; *b* 21 Nov 1904; *Educ* Haberdashers' Aske's, RAF Coll Cranwell; *m* 17 Sept 1935, Marian Jane Benson, da of William A E Coxon (d 1956); of Cairo; 1 s, 1 da; *Career* joined RAF 1923, served WWII, AOC 61 Gp 1947-50, ACAS (trg) 1951-53, COS AAFCE 1956-59, Air ADC to HM The Queen 1959-62, air sec Air Miny 1959-62, ret; *Recreations* calligraphy, glass engraving, gardening; *Clubs* RAF; *Style*— Air Chief Marshal Sir Theodore McEvoy, KCB, CBE; Hurstwood, West Drive, Aldwick Bay Estate, Bognor Regis PO21 4LZ

McEWAN, Surgn Capt Alan; OBE (1977); s of Norman McEwan (d 1972), of Darnick, Melrose, and Ethel Maud, *née* Stanley (d 1983); *b* 20 Dec 1928; *Educ* Dollar Acad, Edinburgh Univ (LRCP, LRCS, LRFPS); *m* 29 March 1963, Caroline Mary, da of Lt-Col Roderick Dillwyn Sims (d 1965), 2 s (Angus b 1964, Alistair b 1967); *Career* RN 1957, Royal Naval Hosp Haslar 1957-59, MO HMS Troubridge 1959-61, Infectious Disease Unit RN Hosp Haslar 1961-62, RA Med Coll Millbank 1962-63, Fleet MO S Atlantic and S American on C-in-C Staff Cape Town S Africa, Admty Med Bd London 1965-67; Base MO: HMS Tamar Hong Kong 1965-67, Polaris Base HMS Neptune Faslane Scotland 1969-72, HMS Tamar Hong Kong 1972-73, staff of med dir gen London 1973-75, staff of med, dir gen dep dir med personnel and advsr in gen practice to RN 1975-77, dir of postgrad studies Inst of Naval Med Alverstoke Hants 1977-79, Surgn Capt 1977, voluntary ret 1979; OStJ 1977; res MO HM Tower of London 1979; med advsr: Financial Times 1980-, Booker plc 1980-, Int Wool Secretariat 1980-, Goldman Sachs 1981-, Channel Four TV 1981-, Charles Barker Group 1985-, Total Oil Marine 1985-, John Swire & Sons Ltd; memb Scottish Int Rugby Squad 1954-55 (played for Univ of Edinburgh, Melrose, Cooptimists, South & Scotland); hon med advsr SSAFA HQ London, memb Exec Ctee Forces Help Soc & Lord Roberts Workshops, med examiner in first aid St John Ambulance; former memb: Med Cncl Hong Kong 1967-69 and 1972-73, Gen Practice Advsy Ctee, Postgrad Cncl for Med Educn England and Wales 1974-79; Freeman City of London 1980, Liveryman Worshipful Co of Curriers 1980; FRSM 1973, MFCM 1977, FRCGP 1978, fell Med Soc of London 1980; *Recreations* golf, cricket, rugby; *Clubs* White's, Army & Navy, Berkshire GC, MCC, London Scottish RFC; *Style*— Surgn Capt Alan McEwan, OBE; HM Tower of London EC3 (☎ 071 481 1880); 8 Wellington Rd, Hampton Hill, Middx (☎ 081 977 6170); 107 Harley St, London W1 (☎ 071 935 9463)

McEWAN, Geraldine; da of Donald McKeown, and Norah, *née* Burns; *b* 9 May 1932; *Educ* Windsor County Girls' Sch; *m* 1953, Hugh Percival Cruttwell, *qv*; 1 s (Greg), 1 da (Claudia); *Career* actress; RSC 1956, 1958 and 1961, Nat Theatre Co 1965-71, 1980-81 and 1983-84, A Lie of The Mind Royal Court Theatre 1987, Lettice and Lovage Globe Theatre 1988-89; TV: The Prime of Miss Jean Brodie 1977, L'Elegance 1982, The Barchester Chronicles 1983, Mapp and Lucia 1985-86, Oranges are Not the Only Fruit 1990; dir: As You Like It for the Renaissance Co Phoenix Theatre 1988, Treats at the Hampstead Theatre Club 1989 film: Henry V 1989, Prince of Thieves 1991; *Style*— Geraldine McEwan; c/o Marmont Management Ltd, 302-308 Regent St, London W1

McEWAN, Ian Russell; s of Maj David McEwan, of Ash, Hants, and Rose Violet Lilian Moore; *b* 21 June 1948; *Educ* Woolverstone Hall Sch, Univ of Sussex (BA), Univ of E Anglia (MA); *m* 1982, Penelope Ruth, da of Dennis Allen, of Lewes, Sussex; 2 s (William b 1983, Gregory b 1986), 2 step da (Polly b 1970, Alice b 1972); *Career* author; began writing 1970; Hon DLitt Sussex 1989; FRSL 1982; *Books* First Love, Last Rites (1975), In Between The Sheets (1978), The Cement Garden (1978), The Comfort of Strangers (1981), The Imitation Game (1981), Or Shall We Die? (1983), The Ploughman's Lunch (1985), The Child in Time (1987), The Innocent (1990); films: Last Day of Summer (1984), Sour Sweet (1989); *Style*— Ian McEwan, Esq; c/o Jonathan Cape, 20 Vauxhall Bridge Road, London

McEWAN, Dr John Alexander; s of Duncan Watson McEwan (d 1980), of Bexhill-on-Sea, E Sussex, and Dr Mary McEwan, *née* Buck (d 1956); *b* 5 Feb 1929; *Educ* Sherborne, Univ of Cambridge (MA), The London Hosp (MB BChir); *m* 23 Aug 1958, Ishbel Margaret Maxwell, da of James Black (d 1973), of Strathclyde; 1 s (Ewan Duncan b 15 April 1960), 1 da (Islay Mary b 9 June 1962); *Career* Nat Serv, RAF med offr Egypt and Cyprus 1954-56; GP Southwark 1957-89, conslt in family planning KCH 1974-, dir of GP studies KCH Med Sch 1976-81, jt dir Dept Reproductive Med KCH 1989; memb: Clinical and Scientific Advsy Ctee Nat Assoc of Family Planning doctors 1983-, Camberwell Health Authy 1986-90; chm: Brook Advsy Centres, Jt Ctee on Contraception RCOG and RCGP; memb: BMA, RSM, NAFPD; FRCGP 1977; *Books* Handbook of Contraceptive Practice - DHSS (1974), Planning or Prevention (with P C L Diggory, 1976); *Recreations* sailing (medium distance cruising); *Clubs* Cruising Association; *Style*— Dr John McEwan; 9 Nathan House, Reedworth St, London SE11 4PG (☎ 071 582 7346); Dept of Reproductive Med, 6th Floor New Ward Block, King's College Hospital, Denmark Hill, London SE5 9RS (☎ 071 326 3423)

MacEWAN, Nigel Savage; s of Nigel Savage, and Ellen, *née* Wharton; *b* 21 March 1933; *Educ* Yale (BA), Harvard (MBA); *m* 12 Feb 1972, Alison Montgomery, *née* Jones; 1 s (Nigel), 3 da (Alison, Pamela, Elizabeth); *Career* served USN 1955-57; assoc: Morgan Stanley & Co NYC 1959-62, White Weld & Co NYC 1962-63; vice pres R S Dickinson and Co Charlotte North Carolina 1963-68, chm Financial Consultants International Ltd Brussels 1965-68, pres and dir White Weld & Co NYC 1968-78, sr vice pres then dir Merrill Lynch Pierce Fenner and Smith NYC 1978-87, pres and chief exec offr Kleinwort Benson N America Incorporated NYC 1987 (latterly dir); pres and dir: Kleinwort Benson Holdings Incorporated, Kleinwort Benson Ltd, Kleinwort Benson Group plc; chm: Merrill Lynch Capital Partners Incorporated 1985-87, NY Gp Securities Indust Assoc 1975-76, Sharps Pixley Inc, Va Trading Corp; former dir: Supermarkets General, Amstar, Cellu-Craft, Sun Hung Kai International Ltd, Merrill Lynch International Ltd, Credit Suisse Whiteweld; adj prof business admin Univ of NY 1973-75, pres Tokeneke Tax Dist Darien 1978-80 (latterly treas), memb Securities Indust Assoc (chm NY Gp 1975-76); *Clubs* Links, Yale, Tokeneke, Midbrook, Bond (NY), NY Yacht, Mill Reef; *Style*— Nigel S MacEwan, Esq; Shennamere Rd, Darien, CT 06820 (☎ 203 655 9184); Kleinwort Benson Ltd, PO Box 560, 20 Fenchurch St, London EC3P 3DB

McEWAN, Prof Peter James Michael; s of Gp Capt James Albert Newlyn McEwan, OBE (d 1965), and Violet Kathleen, *née* Rose (d 1985); *b* 16 Nov 1924; *Educ* Highgate Sch, Univ of Edinburgh (MA, PhD); *m* 1 Aug 1949, Dorothy Anne Wilson Turnbull, da of Rev R W Turnbull (d 1968), of Kirkmichael Manse, Parkgate, Dumfries; 2 s (Malcolm Peter Stuart b 1952, Rhoderick b 1957), 1 da (Feona b 1950); *Career* sr pres Student's Rep Cncl Univ of Edinburgh 1948-49, co-fndr Scottish Union of Students, res fell Rhodes Livingstone Inst 1959-62, fndr 60 Gp (multifacial assoc Southern Rhodesia), visiting prof Univ of NY 1963-64, dir Centre for Social Res Univ of Sussex 1968-73, co-fndr McEwan Gallery 1973, fndr and ed-in-chief social sci and med 1966-; chm: planning ctee, Int Conf on Soc and Med; lib candidate Caithness and Sunderland 1952, conslt WHO; *Books* The Study of Africa (with R B Sutcliffe), Readings in African history (3 vols), Industrial Organisations and Health; *Recreations* breeding ornamental water fowl, music, chess & bridge, hill walking; *Style*— Prof Peter McEwan; Glengarden, Ballater, Aberdeenshire AB3 5UB (☎ 03397 55429); Eilean Horisdale, Badachro, by Achnasheen, Wester Ross, NB

McEWAN, Robin Gilmour; QC; s of Ian Gilmour McEwan (d 1976), and Mary McArthur Bowman McEwan; *b* 12 Dec 1943; *Educ* Paisley GS, Univ of Glasgow (LLB, PhD); *m* 1973, Sheena, da of Stewart Francis McIntyre (d 1974); 2 da (Stephanie b 1979, Louisa b 1983); *Career* Sheriff of Lanark 1982-88, Sheriff of Ayr 1988-; *Recreations* golf; *Clubs* New (Edinburgh), Hon Co of Edinburgh Golfers, Prestwick Golf; *Style*— Robin McEwan, Esq, QC; Sheriff Ct, Ayr KA7 1DR (☎ 268474)

McEWEN, Lady; Brigid Cecilia; *née* Laver; only da of James Laver, CBE (d 1975), and Veronica Turleigh, actress; *m* 1954, Sir Robert Lindley McEwen, 3 Bt (d 1980); 2 s (4 and 5 Bts), 3 da (and 1 da decd); *Style*— Lady McEwen; Polwarth Crofts, Greenlaw, Berwickshire TD10 6YR

McEWEN, Cecilia; *née* Countess von Weikersheim; da of HSH Franz, 2 Prince (*Fürst*, Austrian cr of Emperor Franz Josef 1911 for Carl 2 Baron von Bronn, s of HSH Prince Carl of Hohenlohe-Langenburg (*see* Burke's Royal Families of the World Vol 1, Mediatized Section) and Marie Dorothea, *née* Grathwohl, *suo jure* Baroness von Bronn) Weikersheim, of Fox House, Faringdon, Oxon (d 1983), and HSH Princess Irma zu Windisch- Graetz (d 1984); *b* 28 Oct 1937; *m* 1960, Alexander Dundas McEwen (b 16 May 1935, formerly Queen's Own Cameron Highlanders), 4 s of Sir John McEwen, 1 Bt, JP, DL; 2 s (Alexander b 1962, Hugo b 1965), 1 da (Sophie b 1961); *Career* Dame of the Order of Knights of Malta; MFH Eglinton Ayrshire Scotland; *Style*— Mrs Alexander McEwen; Bardrochat, Colmonell, Ayrshire KA26 05G

McEWEN, Sir John Roderick Hugh; 5 Bt (UK 1953), of Marchmont, Co Berwick, and Bardrochat, Co Ayr; yr s of Sir Robert Lindley McEwen, 3 Bt (d 1980) and Lady (Brigid) McEwen, *qv*; suc bro, Sir James Francis Lindley, 4 Bt, 1983; *b* 4 Nov 1965; *Educ* Ampleforth, UCL; *Heir* cousin, Adam Hugo McEwen, b 9 Feb 1965; *Style*— Sir John McEwen, Bt; Polwarth Crofts, Greenlaw, Duns, Berwickshire

McEWEN, John Sebastian; 6 s of Sir John Helias Finnie McEwen, 1 Bt (d 1962), of Marchmont, Berwickshire, Scotland, and Bridget Mary, *née* Lindley (d 1971); *b* 29 July 1942; *Educ* Eton, Trinity Coll Cambridge (MA); *m* 1975, Gillian Josephine, da of Dennis Martin Heeley; 2 s (David b 2 Nov 1977, Duncan Dundas b 3 May 1979);

Career dep ed Studio International 1972-75, art critic The Spectator 1975-83, contributing ed Art in America 1985-, art critic The Sunday Telegraph 1990-; memb: Visual Arts Advsy Ctee Br Cncl 1983-89, Govt Arts Ctee 1984-88; *Publications* Howard Hodgkin: Forty Paintings 1973-84 (with David Sylvester, 1984); *Clubs* Beefsteak, Garrick; *Style*— John McEwen, Esq; 74 St Augustine's Road, London NW1 (☎ 071 485 4386, fax 071 284 4846)

MCEWEN, Prof Keith Alistair; s of George Charles McEwen (d 1979), and Marjorie Anne, *née* Field; *b* 11 Dec 1944; *Educ* Dr Challoner's GS Amersham, Pembroke Coll Cambridge (MA, PhD); *m* 20 May 1986, Ursula, da of Maximilian Steigenberger (d 1983); *Career* lectr in physics: Univ of Copenhagen 1970-73, Univ of Salford 1973-81; seconded as sr lectr to Institut Laue-Langevin Grenoble 1981-86, prof of experimental physics at Birkbeck Coll Univ of London 1986-; CPhys, FInstP 1989; *Recreations* music, walking, skiing; *Style*— Prof Keith McEwen; Department of Physics, Birkbeck College, University of London, Malet St, London WC1E 7HX (☎ 071 631 6310, fax 071 436 8918)

MACEY, Rear Adm David Edward; CB (1984); s of Frederick William Charles Macey (d 1978), of Strood, Kent, and Florence May, *née* Macey (d 1986); *b* 15 June 1929; *Educ* Sir Joseph Williamson's Mathematical Sch Rochester, Britannia RNC Dartmouth; *m* 1, 1958, Lorna Therese (d 1976), er da of His Hon Judge Oliver William Verner (d 1957); 1 s (Hugo), 1 da (Anna); m 2, 1982, Fiona Beloe, o da of Vice Adm Sir William Beloe, KBE, CB, DSC (d 1966); 3 step s; *Career* RNC Dartmouth, Midshipman 1948, cruisers carriers and destroyers 1950-63, Cdr 1963, American Staff Coll 1964, Cdr RNC Dartmouth 1970, Capt 1972, Directorate Naval Plans 1972-74, RCDS 1975; dir: RN Staff Coll 1976-78, Naval Manpower 1979-81; ADC to HM the Queen 1981, Rear Adm 1981, Dep Asst Chief of Staff (Ops) Staff of the Supreme Allied Cdr 1981-84, ret; receiver gen Canterbury Cathedral 1984-, gentleman usher of the Scarlet Rod 1985-90; sec and registrar Order of the Bath 1990-; *Recreations* walking, cricket, cooking; *Clubs* MCC; *Style*— Rear Adm David Macey, CB; Petham Oast, Garlinge Green, Canterbury, Kent CT4 5RT (☎ 0227 70291); The Receiver General, Cathedral House, The Precincts, Canterbury, Kent CT1 2EG (☎ 0227 762862)

MACEY, Air Vice-Marshal Eric Harold; OBE (1975); s of Harold F Macey (d 1989), and Katrina Macey (d 1981); *b* 9 April 1936; *Educ* Shaftesbury GS; *m* 1957, Brenda Ann, da of Frederick Tom Spencer Bracher (d 1983); 1 s (Julian b 1958); 1 da (Sharon b 1963); *Career* AOC and Cmdt RAF Coll Cranwell 1985-87, asst chief Def Staff (policy and nuclear) 1987-89, dir gen of trg RAF 1989-; *Style*— Air Vice-Marshal Eric Macey, OBE; Ministry of Defence, Adastral House, Theobalds Rd, London (☎ 071 430 7290)

MACEY, Roger David Michael; s of Eric Hamilton Macey, and Margaret Maria, *née* Newman; *b* 15 Nov 1942; *Educ* St Mary's Coll Ireland; *m* 18 April 1970, Julie Elizabeth, da of John Everard Mellors, of Mount Eliza, Melbourne, Aust; 2 s (Jonathan b 20 April 1972, Giles b 25 May 1976); *Career* dir: Wm Brandts Sons & Co (insur) Ltd 1972-76, P S Mossé & Ptnrs Ltd 1977-83, Macdonagh Boland Group 1989; non exec dir: J Jackson & Partners Ltd 1975-76, P S Mossé Life & Pensions 1977-83, George Miller Underwriting Agencies Ltd 1977-86; md Macey Williams Ltd 1976-, chm Macey Williams Insurance Services Ltd, memb Lloyds 1974-; *Recreations* shooting, golf, tennis, horse racing; *Clubs* Carlton, Turf, City of London; *Style*— Roger Macey, Esq; 2 Gonville House, Manor Fields, Putney, London SW15 (☎ 081 788 9864); Macey Williams Ltd, 10 New St, London EC2M 4TP (☎ 071 623 4344, fax 071 929 0414, car 0836 579696, telex 896618)

McFADYEAN, Colin; s of Sir Andrew McFadyean (d 1974), and Dorothea Emily, *née* Chute; gs of Sir John McFadyean (d 1941), pres RVC and fndr of modern veterinary science; *b* 21 Sept 1914; *Educ* Rugby, Brasenose Coll Oxford; *m* 1, 1940 (m dis 1960), Marion, da of Herbert Gutmann (d 1942); 2 da (Andrea b 1949, d 1983, Melanie b 1950); m 2, 16 June 1960, Mary, formerly w of Sir Basil Bartlett, 2 Bt (d 1985), and da of Sir Ian Malcolm, KCMG (d 1944); *Career* WWII Lt Cdr RNVR 1939-45; admitted slr 1946, ptnr Slaughter and May 1951-82; chm Section on Business Law at Int Bar Assoc 1974-76; dir: Charles Ede Ltd 1970-, David Carritt Ltd 1974-, Artemis Fine Arts Ltd 1974-; *Recreations* travel, gardening; *Style*— Colin McFadyean, Esq; 30 Queen's Grove, London NW8 6HJ (☎ 071 722 4728)

McFADYEAN, Colin William; s of Capt Angus John McFadyean, MC (ka 1944), and Joan Mary Irish; *b* 11 March 1943; *Educ* Plymouth Coll, Bristol GS, Loughborough Coll of Educn (DLC), Univ of Keele (Advanced Dip Ed); *m* 29 Aug 1970, Jeanette Carol, da of James A T Payne; 1 s (Ian Robert b 1974); *Career* rugby player, sports commentator, PE teacher 1965-67 (lectr 1967-72, sr lectr 1972-74), dep dir Nat Sports Centre Lilleshall 1974-78, chief coach Jubilee Sports Centre Hong Kong 1979-82, housemaster Dulwich Coll 1983-85, dir gen Nat Playing Fields Assoc 1985-87, Croydon Educn Authy 1988-90, dir coaching Bristol FC (Rugby Union) 1990-; memb Hong Kong Cncl for Recreation and Sport 1980-82; *Recreations* golf, tennis; *Clubs* Br Sportsman's, England Rugby Internationals, Moseley Football (vice pres); *Style*— Colin McFadyean, Esq; c/o Bristol FC, The Memorial Ground, Filton Ave, Horfield, Bristol

MCFADYEN, Jock; s of James Lachlan McFadyen, of 2 Carlogie Rd, Carnoustie, Angus, and Margaret, *née* Owen; *b* 18 Sept 1950; *Educ* Renfrew HS, Chelsea School of Art (BA, MA); *m* 1971 (m dis 1989), Carol Ann, da of Albert Hambleton; 1 s (James b 29 July 1972); *Career* pt/t lectr Slade Sch of Art 1980-; 25 solo exhibitions since 1978 incl: Acme Gallery, Blond Fine Art, National Gallery, Scottish Gallery, Camden Arts Centre; many mixed exhibitions in Europe and USA incl: Hayward Annual, John Moore's, Royal Academy, British Art Show, New British Painting (USA), British Cncl Foreign Touring Show; works in 18 public museums incl: National Gallery (residency), V & A, Imperial War Museum, Kunsthalle Hamburg, Manchester, Birmingham, Glasgow; cmmns incl: Arts Cncl purchase, National Gallery residency, Imperial War Museum Eastern Europe Project; *Recreations* Poodles, Motorcycles; *Clubs* Vintage Japanese Motorcycle; *Style*— Jock McFadyen, Esq; 31 Turners Road, London E3 4LE (☎ 071 515 7890)

McFADZEAN, Hon (Gordon) Barry; s of Baron McFadzean (Life Peer); *b* 14 Feb 1937; *Educ* Winchester, Christ Church Oxford; *m* 1, 1968 (m dis 1982), Julia Maxine, da of Sir Max Dillon, of Sydney, NSW, Aust; 2 da; m 2, 1984, Diana Rosemary, yst da of late Sam Waters, of Norfolk; *Career* Nat Serv 2 Lt RA 1955-57; CA 1963; dir of various merchant banks 1964-85, exec dir S G Warburg & Co Ltd (Merchant Bankers) 1975-78, exec chm Corporate Advsy Partnership Ltd 1986-; *Recreations* music, theatre; *Clubs* Boodle's, City of London, Melbourne (Melbourne), Australian (Sydney); *Style*— The Hon Barry McFadzean; c/o The Butlers Wharf Building, London SE1 2YE (☎ 071 357 7673)

McFADZEAN, Baron (Life Peer UK 1966), of Woldingham, Co Surrey; William Hunter McFadzean; KT (1976); s of Henry McFadzean (d 1918), of Reyburn, Stranraer, Wigtownshire, and Agnes Wylie Hunter (d 1960); *b* 17 Dec 1903; *Educ* Stranraer Acad and HS, Univ of Glasgow; *m* 1933, Eileen, da of Arthur Gordon, of Blundellsands, Lancs; 1 s (Hon Barry b 1937), 1 da (Hon Mrs Donald b 1942), 1 adopted da (Mrs Riehl b 1941); *Career* BICC: dir 1945-73, chm 1954-73, hon life pres; chm BIC Construction Co Ltd 1952-64, dir and chm BIC (Submarine) Cables Ltd 1954-73, dir and dep chm Canada Life Assur Co of GB Ltd 1971-82 (dir 1982-84); dir: Canada Life Assur Co (Canada) 1969-79 (hon dir), Canadian Imperial Bank of Commerce 1967-74 (dir emeritus, int advsy cncl memb 1976-83), Midland Bank Ltd 1959-81 (dep chm 1968-77), Midland Bank Trust Co Ltd 1959-67; dep chm Nat Nuclear Corpn Ltd 1973-80; dir and dep chm: RTZ/BICC Aluminium Hldgs Ltd 1967-73, Canada Life Unit Trust Managers Ltd 1971-82 (dep chm 1982-84); chm Standard Broadcasting Corpn (UK) Ltd 1972-79 (hon life pres 1979-86, dir Canada 1973-80); dir and chm Home Oil (UK) Ltd 1972-78 (dir Canada 1972-78), chm Scurry Rainbow (UK) Ltd 1974-78; pres: FBI 1959-61, Br Electrical Power Convention 1961-62; memb: Ct Br Shippers' Cncl 1964 (pres 1968-71), Advsy Ctee for Queen's Award to Indust 1965-67 (chm Review Ctee 1970); fndr chm: Export Cncl for Europe 1960-64, Br Nat Export Cncl 1964-66 (pres 1966-68); Cdr Order of Dannebrog Denmark 1964 (Grand Cdr 1974), Grande Oficial da Ordem do Infante Dom Henrique Portugal 1972; kt 1960; *Recreations* gardening, golf, travel; *Clubs* MCC, Carlton; *Style*— The Rt Hon the Lord McFadzean, KT; 16 Lansdown Crescent, Bath BA1 5EX (☎ 0225 335487); 114 Whitehall Court, London SW1A 2EP (☎ 071 930 3160)

McFADZEAN OF KELVINSIDE, Baron (Life Peer UK 1980), of Kelvinside in the Dist of City of Glasgow; Francis Scott McFadzean; s of Francis Findlay McFadzean; *b* 26 Nov 1915; *Educ* Univ of Glasgow, LSE; *m* 1, 1938, Isabel McKenzie (d 1987), da of James Beattie; 1 da (Hon Felicity Carmen Francesca b 1946, m Baron Marsh, *qv*); m 2, 20 April 1988, Sonja Lian Hoa Nio, *née* Khung, of Indonesia; *Career* War Serv 1940-45 (Col), Malayan Govt 1945; Bd of Trade 1938, (treas 1939), Colonial Devpt Corp 1949, md Royal Dutch/Shell 1964-76, chm Shell Transport and Trading 1972-76 (dir 1964-86); chm: Shell International Marine Ltd 1966-76, Shell Canada Ltd 1970-76, Shell Petroleum Co Ltd 1972-76 (dir 1964-86); dir: Shell Oil Co 1972-76, Beecham Group Ltd 1974-86, Coats Patons Ltd 1979-; chm: Br Airways 1976-79, Rolls Royce Ltd 1980-83; Cdr Netherlands Order of Orange Nassau 1975; hon fell LSE; kt 1975; *Style*— The Rt Hon the Lord McFadzean of Kelvinside; House of Lords, London SW1

MCFALL, John; MP (Lab) Dumbarton 1987; *b* 31 Jan 1920; *Educ* Paisley Coll of Technol (BSc), Open Univ (BA), Strathclyde Business Sch (MBA); *Career* Educn Dept Strathclyde Regnl Cncl 1974-87: asst teacher, asst princ teacher, princ teacher of guidance, asst head teacher; educn convener Scot Gp of Lab MPs 1987-89, exec memb Parly Gp for Energy Studies 1987-, memb Select Ctee on Def 1988-, oppn front bench whip with responsibility for Trade and Indust Foreign Affairs and Euro Community; fell Indust and Parly Tst (attachment with Royal Bank of Scotland), memb Br Irish Inter-Parliamentary Body; *Style*— John McFall, Esq, MP; 14 Oxhill Road, Dumbarton G82 4PG

McFALL, John; MP (Lab) Dumbarton 1987-; s of John McFall, and Jean McFall; *b* 14 Oct 1944; *Educ* St Patrick's Sch, Paisley Coll of Technol (BA), Open Univ (BA), Strathclyde Business Sch (MBA); *m* 1969, Joan, *née* Ward; 3 s (John, Gerald, Kevin), 1 da (Elaine); *Career* Strathclyde Regnl Cncl Educn Dept: asst teacher 1974-76, asst princ teacher 1976-79, princ teacher of guidance 1979-83, asst head teacher 1983-87; educn convenor Scottish Gp of Lab MPs' 1987-89; memb Exec Parly Gp for Energy Studies 1987-, Select Ctee on Def 1988-; oppn front bench whip with responsibility for trade & indust, Foreign Affrs and Euro Community, fell Indust and Parl Tst (attachment with Royal Bank of Scotland); *Recreations* golf, running, reading; *Style*— John McFall, Esq, MP; 14 Oxhill Rd, Dumbarton G82 4PG (☎ 0389 31437); House of Commons, London SW1A 0AA (☎ 071 219 3521)

McFARLAND, Anthony Basil Scott; er s and h of Sir John Talbot McFarland, 3 Bt, TD; *b* 29 Nov 1959; *Educ* Marlborough, Trinity Coll Dublin (BA); *m* 28 Oct 1988, Anne Margaret, 3 da of Thomas Kennedy Laidlaw, of Gernonstown Slane, Co Meath; 1 da (Amelia Elizabeth b 13 Sept 1990); *Career* exec: Ladbroke Group plc, Thompson T Line plc, Price Waterhouse; dir: Lanes (Business Equipment) Ltd, J T McFarland Holdings; ACA; *Recreations* tennis, rugby, skiing; *Style*— Anthony McFarland, Esq; 31 Walham Grove, London SW6

McFARLAND, Sir John Talbot; 3 Bt (UK 1914), of Aberfoyle, Co Londonderry, TD; s of Sir Basil Alexander Talbot McFarland, 2 Bt, CBE, ERD (d 1986), and Annie Kathleen, *née* Henderson (d 1952); *b* 3 Oct 1927; *Educ* Marlborough, Trinity Coll Oxford; *m* 5 March 1957, Mary Scott, da of Dr Scott Watson (d 1956), of Carlisle Place, Londonderry; 2 s (Anthony Basil Scott, Stephen Andrew John b 23 Dec 1968), 2 da (Jane (Mrs Gailey) b 11 Dec 1957, Fiona Kathleen b 1 Feb 1964); *Heir* s, Anthony Basil Scott b 29 Nov 1959; *Career* Capt RA (TA), Capt (RCT) 1962; memb Londonderry Co Borough Cncl 1955-69, High Sheriff Co Londonderry 1958, DL Londonderry 1962-82 (resigned), High Sheriff City of The Co of Londonderry 1965-67; memb North West HMC 1960-73, jt chm Londonderry & Foyle Coll 1976; chm: Lanes Business Equipment Ltd, J T McFarland Holdings; *Recreations* golf, shooting; *Clubs* Kildare and Univ, Northern Counties; *Style*— Sir John McFarland Bt, TD; Dunmore House, Carrigans, Lifford, Co Donegal, Republic of Ireland; Lanes Business Equipment Ltd, 51/53 Spencer Rd, Londonderry, N Ireland (☎ 0504 47326)

MACFARLANE, Dr Alan Donald James; s of Maj Donald Kennedy Macfarlane (d 1976), and Iris, *née* Rhodes James; *b* 20 Dec 1941; *Educ* Dragon Sch, Sedbergh, Worcester Coll Oxford (MA, DPhil), LSE (MPhil), SOAS (PhD); *m* 1, 1966 (m dis), Gillian Ions; 1 da (Katharine b 1970); m 2, 1981, Sarah, *née* Tarring; *Career* Univ of Cambridge: lectr in social anthropology 1975-81, reader in hist anthropology 1981-, fell King's Coll 1981- (sr res fell 1971-74); FRHistS 1967, FRAI 1970, FBA 1986; *Books* Witchcraft in Tudor and Stuart England (1970), The Family Life of Ralph Josselin (1970), Resources and Population (1976), The Diary of Ralph Josselin (ed, 1976), Reconstructing Historical Communities (1977), The Origins of English Individualism (1978), The Justice and the Mare's Ale (1981), A Guide to English Historical Records (1983), Marriage and Love in England (1986), The Culture of Capitalism (1987); *Recreations* gardening, second-hand book hunting, filming; *Style*— Dr Alan Macfarlane; 25 Lode Road, Lode, nr Cambridge CB5 9ER (☎ 0223 811976); King's College, Cambridge

MACFARLANE, Anne Bridget; da of Dr D W Griffith (d 1969), and Dr Grace Griffith (d 1971); *b* 26 Jan 1930; *Educ* Univ of Bristol (LLB); *m* 15 Feb 1957, J D Macfarlane; 2 da (Jessica, Deborah); *Career* admitted slr 1954; H M Land Registry 1966-75, registrar Bromley County Court 1975-82, Master Court of Protection 1982-; contrib Atkins Court Forms 1983; *Recreations* collecting Victorian tiles; *Clubs* Law Soc; *Style*— Mrs A B Macfarlane; Stewart House, 24 Kingsway, London WC2B 6JH (☎ 071 269 7178, fax 071 831 0060)

MACFARLANE, Sir George Gray; CB (1965); s of John Macfarlane (d 1938), and Mary Knox Macfarlane (d 1933); *b* 8 Jan 1916; *Educ* Airdrie Acad, Univ of Glasgow (BSc), Dresden Technische Hochschule (DrIng); *m* 1941, Barbara Grant, da of Thomas Thomson (d 1947); 1 s, 1 da; *Career* scientist; Telecom Res Estab Malvern 1939-60, dep dir Nat Physical Laboratory 1960-62, dir Royal Radar Estab 1962-67, res controller Miny of Technol 1967-71, controller R & D Estabs and Res MOD 1971-76; memb: Bd PO 1978-81, Bd of Tstees Imperial War Museum 1978-86, NEB 1980-82, NRDC 1981-82, Br Technol Group 1982-85, Bd BT 1981-87; kt 1971; *Recreations* walking, gardening; *Clubs* Athenaeum; *Style*— Sir George Macfarlane, CB; Red Tiles, Orchard Way, Esher, Surrey (☎ 0372 63778)

McFARLANE, Harry William; s of Harry McFarlane (d 1986), and Ann Crammond, *née* Rew; *b* 21 July 1929; *Educ* Univ of St Andrews; *m* 4 Jan 1960, Zlata, da of Cedomir Dzinovic (d 1970); *Career* med branch RAF 1954-62, RAMC Vol 1979-; house surgn Royal Infirmary Huddersfield 1952-53, demonstrator in anatomy and lectr in physiology Univ of St Andrews 1956-59, surgical registrar Royal Infirmary Dundee 1959 (casualty offr 1953, house physician 1953-54, sr house offr in surgery 1954), surgical registgrar Aberdeen Gp of Hosps 1959-61, lectr in otorhinolaryngology Univ of Aberdeen 1963-65 (registrar in otorhinolaryngology 1961-62, sr registrar 1963-65); conslt otorhinolaryngologist: Derby Gp of Hosps 1965-, Royal Sch for The Deaf Derby 1965-, Midlands Asthma and Allergy Res Assoc 1970-, Br Army 1983-; med examiner industl deafness DHSS 1974- (med examiner war pensions 1970-); examiner Midlands Inst of Otolaryngology 1966, auditor Derby Med Soc 1972-76 (treas 1968-72), bd memb and rep for Euro Soc for Ear Nose and Throat Advances in Children 1980, chm of res ctee Midlands Asthma and Allergy Res Assoc 1985 (chm of ethical ctee 1970); memb: Aberdeen Medico-Chirurgical Soc 1965, S Otolaryngological Soc 1963, Regnl Hosp Conslts and Specialists Assoc 1966, Midlands Visiting Gp in Otolarymgology 1968, Euro Working Gp in Paediatric Otolaryngology 1975, Nottingham Medico-Legal Soc 1987; MB ChB 1952, FRCS 1961, FRCSEd 1961, FRSM 1966, FBIM 1985, fell Joseph Soc 1987, FICS 1988, MInstD 1988; *Recreations* sailing, skiing, hillwalking; *Clubs* Rotary; *Style*— Harry McFarlane, Esq; 110 Whitaker Rd, Derby DE3 6AP (☎ 0332 45174); Ear Nose and Throat Dept, Derbyshire Royal Infirmary, London Rd, Derby DE1 2QY (☎ 0332 47141)

MACFARLANE, Iain; s of David Macfarlane (d 1984), of Giffnock, Glasgow, and Jean Gibson, *née* Condie; *b* 6 Sept 1932; *Educ* Jordanhill Coll Sch Glasgow; *m* 2 Sept 1960, Sheila Marian, da of Alexander James Ironside (d 1980), of Giffnock, Glasgow; 1 s (Ranald b 1964 d 1990), 1 da (Heather b 1962); *Career* sales mangr The Wrigley Co Ltd UK 1968-70; md: The Wrigley Co (EA) Ltd Nairobi Kenya 1974-78 (mktg mangr 1970-73), Wrigley Taiwan Ltd Taipei Taiwan 1978-79; area gen mangr (int) Wm Wrigley Jr Co Chicago USA 1981- (mktg mangr 1979-81); chm Confectioners Benevolent Fund (Cornwall and Devon branch), memb Buckland Monarchorum Parish Church Devon; MIOD 1988; *Recreations* golf, bird shooting; *Clubs* Yelverton Golf; *Style*— Iain Macfarlane, Esq; The Wrigley Co Ltd, Estover, Plymouth, Devon PL6 7PR, (☎ 0752 701107, fax 0752 778850, telex 45543)

MCFARLANE, Dr James Sinclair; CBE (1986); s of John Mills McFarlane (d 1959), and Hannah, *née* Langtry (d 1969); *b* 8 Nov 1925; *Educ* Manchester GS, Emmanuel Coll Cambridge (MA, PhD); *m* 31 March 1951, Ruth May, da of William Wallace Harden (d 1974); 3 da (Mary b 1952, Lucy b 1954, Joanna b 1959); *Career* ICI Ltd 1949-53, tech mangr and sales dir Henry Wiggin & Co Ltd 1953-69, chm and md Smith-Clayton Forge Ltd (GKN) 1969-76, md Garringtons Ltd (GKN) 1976-77, main bd dir GKN plc 1979-82, dir gen Engrg Employers' Fedn 1982-89; CEng, FIM, CBIM; *Recreations* music; *Clubs* United Oxford and Cambridge Univ, Caledonian; *Style*— Dr James McFarlane, CBE; The Ct House, Atch Lench, Evesham, Worcs WR11 5SP (☎ 0386 870225)

MACFARLANE, Sir James Wright; JP (Renfrew 1940), DL (Renfrew 1962); s of James Colquhoun Macfarlane, OBE, of Braehead, Glasgow; *b* 2 Oct 1908; *Educ* Allan Glen's Sch Glasgow, Royal Coll of Sci and Technol, Univ of Glasgow (PhD); *m* 1937, Claire, da of George Ross, of Glasgow; *Career* Lt-Col TA (ACF) ret; dir Macfarlane Engrg Co 1926-73, md Cathcart Investmt Co 1964-85; convenor County of Renfrew 1967-73, pres Assoc of CC in Scotland 1969-71; memb: Royal Commission of the Police 1970-71, Holroyd Dept Ctee on the Fire Serv; kt 1973; *Style*— Sir James Macfarlane, JP, DL; 2 Sandringham Court, Newton Mearns, Glasgow, Scotland G77 5DT

MCFARLANE, John; s of John McFarlane, of Dumfries, Scotland, and Christina Campbell (d 1976); *b* 14 June 1947; *Educ* Dumfries Acad, Univ of Edinburgh (MA), Cranfield Sch of Mgmnt (MBA); *m* 31 Jan 1970, Anne, da of Rev Fraser Ian MacDonald Dumfries (d 1983), of Scotland; 3 da (Kirsty b 14 March 1976, Rebecca b 17 March 1979, Fiona b 18 March 1983); *Career* Ford Motor Co 1969-74; Citicorp 1975-: md Citicorp Scrimgeour Vickers Ltd 1988, head Citicorp/Citibank (UK, Ireland and Channel Is) 1990, chief exec Citicorp Investment Bank Ltd, dir Citicorp Insurance Holdings Ltd; dir: The Int Stock Exchange, The Securities Assoc; dir Blackhealth Concert Halls; memb: Ct Cranfield Inst of Technol, Cncl Orchestra of St John; *Recreations* Scottish affairs, music; *Style*— John McFarlane, Esq; Citibank NA, PO Box 199, Cottons, Hays Lane, London SE1 2QT (☎ 071 234 2351, fax 071 234 5413, telex 885171/886004)

MACFARLANE, John Caldwell; CBE (1990); *b* 5 Dec 1930; *Educ* Glasgow Acad, Univ of Strathclyde (Formerly RCST); *m* Anita, *née* Beard; 2 s, 1 da; *Career* CEng; chm: Cummins (UK) Ltd, Cummins Engine Co Ltd; dir Lloyds Register Quality Assurance Ltd 1985; memb English Industl Estates Corp; chm: Barnard Castle Sch 1987, NHS Prescription Pricing Authy 1989; Queens Award CECL; Darl Div, Dav Div; FEng, CBIM; *Recreations* golf, skiing, swimming; *Clubs* RAC, RSAC, Caledonian; *Style*— John C Macfarlane, Esq, CBE; Cummins Engine Co Ltd, Yarm Rd, Darlington, Co Durham DL1 4PW (☎ 0325 460606)

MACFARLANE, Jonathan Stephen; s of William Keith Macfarlane (d 1987), and Pearl Hastings, *née* Impey; *b* 28 March 1956; *Educ* Charterhouse, Oriel Coll Oxford (MA); *m* 7 May 1983, Johanna Susanne, da of John Mordaunt Foster (d 1988); 1 s (David b 1988), 1 da (Laura b 1990); *Career* admitted slr 1980; ptnr Macfarlanes 1985-; *Clubs* Leander; *Style*— Jonathan Macfarlane, Esq; 10 Norwich St, London EC4A 1BD (☎ 071 831 9222, fax 071 831 9607, telex 296381)

MACFARLANE, (David) Neil; MP (Cons) Sutton and Cheam Feb 1974-; s of Robert and Dulcie Macfarlane, of Yelverton, S Devon; *b* 7 May 1936; *Educ* Bancroft's Sch London; *m* 1961, June Osmond, er da of John King, of Somerset; 2 s, 1 da; *Career* Lt 1 Bn Essex Regt 1955-58, Capt RA 265 LAA TA 1959-69; Essex cricketer 1952-56, Capt YA XI; Shell Mex & BP 1959-74; dir: RMC plc, Bradford & Bingley Bldg Soc, Zetters plc; chm The Golf Fund plc; Parly candidate: East Ham North 1970, Sutton & Cheam (by-election) 1972; sec: Cons Greater London membs, Cons sports ctee, Cons energy ctee; memb all-pty select ctee Sci and Technol; Parly under-sec state: DES 1979-81, Sport 1981-85, DOE 1981-85; dep Arts Min 1979-81; capt Parly Golfing Soc, vice pres PGA European Tour; govr Sports Aid Fndn 1985-90; kt 1988; *Books* Politics and Sport (1986); *Recreations* golf; *Clubs* MCC, Essex CCC, Huntercombe Golf, Wentworth Golf, Harlequins RFC, Sunningdale Golf, Walton Heath Golf; *Style*— Sir Neil Macfarlane, MP; 48 Benhill Ave, Sutton, Surrey (☎ 081 642 3791); c/o House of Commons, London SW1A 0AA (☎ 071 219 3404)

MACFARLANE, Nicholas Russel; s of John Macfarlane, DL, and Pamela, *née* Laing; *b* 21 Feb 1952; *Educ* Cheam Sch, Radley, Univ of Lancaster (BA); *m* 25 July 1987, Elisabeth Anne, da of W David Crane, of Hallaughton; 1 s (James b 7 Sept 1989); *Career* admitted slr 1977; ptnr Faithfull Owen & Fraser 1980 (amalgamated with Durrant Piesse 1985), currently ptnr specialising in intellectual property law Lovell White Durrant (amalgamated with Durrant Piesse 1988); Freeman Worshipful Co of Slrs; memb: Law Soc, Patent Slrs Assoc; *Recreations* fishing, shooting; *Clubs* City of London; *Style*— Nicholas Macfarlane, Esq; Lovell White Durrant & Ptnrs 21 Holborn Viaduct, London EC1A 2DY (☎ 01 236 0066, telex 887122 LWD G, fax 01 248 4212)

MACFARLANE, Sir Norman Somerville; s of Daniel Robertson Macfarlane (d 1985), and Jessie Lindsay, *née* Somerville (d 1975); *b* 5 March 1926; *Educ* High Sch of Glasgow; *m* 1953, Marguerite Mary, da of John Johnstone Campbell, of 17 Norwood Drive, Whitecraigs; 1 s (Hamish), 4 da (Fiona, Gail, Marjorie, Marguerite); *Career* cmmnd RA; chm and md Macfarlane Gp (Clansman) plc; chm: United Distillers plc, United Distillers UK (formerly Arthur Bell Distillers plc), American Tst plc, The Fine Art Soc plc; deputy chm Guinness plc; dir: Clydesdale Bank plc, Gen Accident Fire & Life Assurance Corp plc, Edinburgh Fund Managers plc; dir: Glasgow C of C 1976-79, Scottish Nat Orch 1977-82, Third Eye Centre 1978-81; former pres: Company of Stationers of Glasgow, Stationers Assoc of GB and Ireland, Glasgow HS Club; former memb Royal Fine Art Cmmn for Scotland, memb Scot CBI Cncl 1975-81, pres Royal Glasgow Inst of the Fine Arts 1976-87, govr Glasgow Sch of Art 1976-87, memb Bd Scot Devpt Agency 1979-87, memb Glasgow Univ Ct 1980-88, vice chm Scot Ballet 1983-87; Scot patron The Nat Arts Collections Fund, chm of govrs The HS of Glasgow; tstee: Nat Heritage Memorial Fund, The Nat Galleries of Scot; chm Glasgow Action, hon vice pres Glasgow Bn Boys Bde; underwriting memb Lloyd's of London; Hon FRIAS 1984; Hon LLD: Strathclyde 1986, Glasgow 1988; Hon RSA 1987, Hon RGI 1987; kt 1982; *Clubs* Royal Scottish Automobile, Glasgow Art, Glasgow Golf, New (Edinburgh); *Style*— Sir Norman Macfarlane; 50 Manse Road, Bearsden, Glasgow; office: Macfarlane Gp (Clansman) plc, Sutcliffe Rd, Glasgow G13 1AH (☎ 041 959 3396)

MacFARLANE, Peter Froude; s of Archibald Macfarlane (d 1958), and Edith Decima Macfarlane; *b* 3 July 1938; *Educ* Woodhouse GS; *m* 29 Oct 1960, Dianne Jennifer, da of Charles Hotton; 2 da (Sarah Elizabeth b 1965, Claire Fiona b 1970); *Career* CA; sr auditor Coopers & Lybrand Nigeria 1961-65, asst GP accountant Int Computers UK 1965-66, fin mangr (later dir) Kimberley-Clark UK USA Holland and Germany 1966-69, int controller and md BL Nigeria 1969-79 (treas London 1969-79); Rolls Royce 1979-: treas, dir industl and marine, dir corp devpt, dir fin; FCA, FCT; *Recreations* tennis, sailing; *Clubs* Royal Southern Yacht; *Style*— Peter Macfarlane, Esq; The Old Curatage, Birch Green, Nr Hertford, Herts SG14 2LR (☎ 0992 583467); Rolls-Royce plc, 65 Buckingham Gate, London SW1E 6AT (☎ 071 222 9020, fax 071 233 1733, telex 918091, car 0836 645693)

MACFARLANE, Dr Peter Wilson; s of Robert Barton Macfarlane (d 1965), of Glasgow, and Dinah, *née* Wilson; *b* 8 Nov 1942; *Educ* Hyndland Secondary Sch Glasgow, Univ of Glasgow (BSc, PhD); *m* 8 Oct 1971, Irene Grace, da of James Muir (d 1975), of Kirkintilloch; 2 s (Alan b 1974, David b 1977); *Career* Univ of Glasgow: asst lectr in med cardiology 1967-70, lectr 1970-74, sr lectr 1974-80, reader 1980-; author and ed of various books and proceedings, res interest computers in electrocardiography, princ author of electrocardiogram analysis programme marketed worldwide; sec Int Cncl on Electrocardiology, memb Br Cardiac Soc 1974; FBCS 1976, CEng 1990; *Books* An Introduction to Automated Electrocardiogram Interpretation (1974), Computer Techniques in Clinical Medicine (1985), Comprehensive Electrocardiology (1989); *Recreations* jogging, playing the violin; *Style*— Dr Peter Macfarlane; 12 Barrcraig Rd, Bridge of Weir, Strathclyde PA11 3HG (☎ 0505 614443); University Department of Medical Cardiology, Royal Infirmary, 10 Alexandra Parade, Glasgow G31 2ER (☎ 041 552 3535 ext 5082, fax 041 552 4683)

MACFARLANE, Maj-Gen William Thomson (Bill); CB (1981); s of James MacFarlane (d 1966), and Agnes Boylan (d 1970); *b* 2 Dec 1925; *m* 16 July 1955, Dr Helen Dora Macfarlane, da of The Rev Leonard Nelson Meredith (d 1976); 1 da (Christina b 22 July 1957); *Career* served Europe, Near, Middle and Far East theatres 1946-1981; Cdr 16 Parachute Bde Signal Sqdn 1961-63, mil asst to C in C Far East Land Forces 1964-66, Cdr 1 Div HQ and Signal Regt Germany 1967-70, Cabinet Offr Secretariat 1970-72, Cdr Corps Royal Signals Germany 1972-73, dir PR (Army) 1973-75, chief of staff UK Land Forces 1975-78, chief jt services liaison offr Br Forces Germany 1978-81, Col Cmdt Royal Signals 1980-85, ret; co dir, conslt, lectr; ops dir Hong Kong Resort Co Ltd 1981-84, chm Citicare Co Ltd 1984; *Recreations* golf; *Clubs* Naval and Military, Piccadilly; *Style*— Maj-Gen William Macfarlane, CB; Colts Paddock, Aveley Lane, Farnham, Surrey; Sion Coll, Victoria Embankment, London EC47 0DN

McFARLANE OF LLANDAFF, Baroness (Life Peer UK 1979), of Llandaff in Co of South Glamorgan; Jean Kennedy McFarlane; da of James McFarlane (d 1963); *b* 1 April 1926; *Educ* Howell's Sch Llandaff, Bedford and Birkbeck Colls London Univ (MA, BSc); *Career* dir of educn Inst of Advanced Nursing Educn London 1969-71, sr lectr in nursing Dept of Social and Preventive Medicine Manchester Univ 1971-73, sr lectr and head dept of nursing Manchester Univ 1973-74, chm English National Bd for Nursing, Midwifery and Health Visiting 1980-83, prof and head Dept of Nursing Manchester Univ 1974; and memb with War Graves Cmmn (former memb Royal Cmmn on NHS); Hon DSc Ulster 1981, Hon DEd (CNAA) 1984; SRN, SCM, FRCN; *Books* The Proper Study of the Nurse (1970), The Practice of Nursing Using the Nursing Process(1982); *Recreations* photography, walking, music, travel; *Clubs* Royal Cwlth; *Style*— The Rt Hon the Lady McFarlane of Llandaff; 5 Dovercourt Ave, Heaton Mersey, Stockport, Cheshire; Department of Nursing, Univ of Manchester, Manchester M13 9PT

MacFARQUHAR, Prof Roderick Lemonde; s of late Sir Alexander MacFarquhar; *b* 2 Dec 1930, Lahore; *Educ* Fettes, Keble Coll Oxford (BA), Harvard Univ (AM), LSE (PhD); *m* 1964, Emily Jane, da of Dr Paul W Cohen, of New York; 1 s (Rory b 1971), 1 da (Larissa b 1968); *Career* Nat Serv 2 Lt; China specialist Daily Telegraph 1955-61, ed The China Quarterly 1959-68, reporter BBC's Panorama 1963-64, co presenter BBC World Servs 24 Hours 1972-74 and 1979-80, prof of govt Harvard Univ 1984-, dir Fairbank Centre for E Asian Res Harvard Univ 1986-, Leroy B Williams prof of history and political science 1990-; fell: Res Inst on Communist Affairs and E Asian Inst Columbia 1969, Royal Inst of Int Affairs 1971-74, Woodrow Wilson Int Centre for Scholars Washington DC 1980-81, Leverhulme Res, Force Fndn Res Grant, Rockefeller Fndn Res Grant; MP (Lab) 1974-79; *Recreations* reading, travel, listening to music; *Style*— Prof Roderick MacFarquhar; 378 Broadway, Cambridge, MA 02139, USA

McFERRAN, (John) Christopher Herdman; JP (1989); s of Lt-Col John Rowan Addison McFerran, DL, JP (d 1969), of Camus, Strabane, Co Tyrone, and Iona Mary McFerran, OBE, *née* Herdman; *b* 16 April 1937; *Educ* St Edward's Sch Oxford; *m* 15 June 1963, Elizabeth Murray, da of Cdr Ian Murray Nicoll Mudie, MBE, RN (d 1985), of Chilbolton, Hants; 1 s (Nicholas John Mudie b 28 July 1971), 1 da (Sarah Frances Mary (Mrs Jenkinson) b 9 Oct 1966); *Career* Lt Northern Irish Horse (TA) 1956-62, TARO 1962; proprietor and md Carpex (NI) Ltd Belfast 1972-90, co dir Herdman's Ltd Sion Mills 1980-; govr Rockport Prep Sch Craigavad 1974-; memb Textile Inst 1967-; *Recreations* sailing; *Clubs* Royal North of Ireland Yacht; *Style*— Christopher McFerran, Esq, JP; The Priory, Marino, Holywood, Co Down BT18 0AH (☎ 02317 3108)

MCFETRICH, (Charles) Alan; s of Cecil McFetrich, OBE (d 1988), of 8 Belle Vue Drive, Sunderland, Tyne & Wear, and Kathleen Margaret, *née* Proom; *b* 15 Dec 1940; *Educ* Oundle, Magdalene Coll Cambridge (MA); *m* 1, 25 March 1970 (m dis 1989); 2 s (Daniel Ross b 1974, Nicholas William (twin) b 1974), 1 da (Anna Louise b 1973); m 2, 3 Aug 1990, Janet Elizabeth Henkel, *née* Munro; *Career* student accountant Graham Proom & Smith 1959-61 and 1964-66; CA 1966; Deloitte Haskins & Sells: joined 1966, consIt 1968-73, consIt ptnr 1973-80, seconded under sec industl devpt unit Dept Indust 1981-82, ops ptnr 1983-84, managing ptnr UK 1985-89; managing ptnr Coopers & Lybrand Deloitte 1990-; IMC 1969, FCA 1976; *Recreations* gardening, theatre, reading; *Clubs* Gresham; *Style—* Alan McFetrich, Esq; Coopers & Lybrand Deloitte, Plumtree Court, London EC4A 4HT (☎ 071 583 5000, fax 071 822 4652, telex 887470)

McGAHERN, Francis Jude Anthony (Frank); s of Francis McGahern (d 1977), and Susan, *née* McManus (d 1944); *b* 4 Nov 1943; *Educ* Presentation Coll; *m* Jan 1965, Mary Ellen, da of Michael Maher; 1 s (Mark b 20 Aug 1968), 3 da (Monica b 1 Oct 1965, Rachael b 12 Jan 1974, Rebecca b 12 Aug 1975); *Career* accountant; trainee Albright & Wilson (Chemicals) 1960-70, The Gas Cncl 1970-72; BBC 1972-: Engrg Cost Accountant, head of engrg fin and costing servs, head of fin central servs, radio, chief accountant; fell Chartered Inst of Mgmnt Accountants (memb 1970); *Recreations* reading, swimming, home DIY, dinghy sailing; *Style—* Frank McGahern, Esq; BBC Radio, Room 4107, Broadcasting House, London W1A 1AA (☎ 071 927 4893, fax 071 580 5780, telex 265781, car 0860 455206)

MCGAHERN, John; s of Francis McGahern, and Susan, *née* McManus; *b* 12 Nov 1934; *Educ* Presentation Coll Carrick-on-Shannon, St Patrick's Dublin, Univ Coll Dublin; *m* 3 Feb 1973, Madeline; *Career* res fell Univ of Reading 1969-72, visiting prof Colgate Univ USA 1970-91, Br Northern Arts fell Univ of Newcastle upon Tyne and Univ of Durham 1974-76, visiting fell Univ of Dublin 1988; Hon LittD Univ of Dublin 1991; memb: Irish Acad of Letters, AOSDANA; Chevalier de L'Ordre des Arts et des Lettres 1989; *Books* The Barracks (1963), The Dark (1965), Nightlines (1971), The Leavething (1975), Getting Through (1978), The Pornographer (1980), High Ground (1985), Amongest Women (1990); *Style—* John McGahern, Esq; Faber and Faber, 3 Queen Square, London WC1 3NAU

McGAIRL, Stephen James; s of John Lloyd McGairl (d 1979), of Chichester, and Lucy Hudson; *b* 18 Feb 1951; *Educ* Chichester HS, Worcester Coll Oxford (BA, MA); *m* 24 May 1975, Madeleine, da of Christopher William Talbot Cox (d 1964), of Sidlesham; 4 s (Sam b 1977, Thomas b 1978, Joe b 1983, George b 1986); *Career* Legal and Parliamentary Dept GLC 1974-77, admitted slr 1976; Freshfields: joined 1977, ptnr 1984, moved to Paris office 1986; admitted Conseil Juridique 1988; memb: Law Soc, City of London Slrs Co, Société Française de Droit Aèrien; *Pubns* contrib: Air Finance Annual, Leasing Digest, Aircraft Investor, memb Ed Bd Central European Finance and Business; *Recreations* sailing, opera, classic cars; *Clubs* Cercle de l'Union Interalliee, Chichester Yacht; *Style—* Stephen McGairl, Esq; 14 Ave Gourgaud, 75017 Paris (☎ 331 4766 5159, fax 331 4766 1063, telex 648363)

McGAREL GROVES, Anthony Robin; s of Col Robin Jullian McGarel Groves, OBE, of Lymington, Hampshire, and Constance Morton, *née* Macmillan; *b* 7 Sept 1954; *Educ* Eton, Univ of Bath (BSc); *m* 16 Dec 1978, Ann Candace, da of Jack Dawes, of Ross on Wye, Herefordshire; *Career* CA Deloitte Haskins and Sells 1981; currently working as sr investmt mangr The Kuwait Investmt Office; *Recreations* shooting, skiing, theatre, bridge, politics; *Clubs* Lansdowne, Ski; *Style—* Anthony R McGarel Groves, Esq; Clapton Revel, Wooburn Moor, Buckinghamshire HP10 0NH; St Vedast House, 150 Cheapside, London EC2 6ET

McGARRIGLE, Colin Sinclair; s of Dr Robert Percival McGarrigle (d 1976), of York, and Mrs Jessie Elizabeth, *née* Altman (d 1988); *b* 15 Aug 1941; *Educ* Radley, Trinity Coll Dublin (MA), Univ of Leeds (Graduate Cert Educn); *m* 1, 3 Sept 1966 (m dis 1975), (Jennifer) Julia Leila, da Lt-Col K E Boome (d 1974), of Geneva, Switzerland; 1 s (Giles b 1970), 2 da (Sophie b 1967, Tessa b 1974); m 2, Morag Muriel Ferguson Cowling, da of John Wiley (d 1969), of Hartlepool; *Career* 2 Lt The Green Howards 1965; headmaster Bramcote Sch Scarborough 1968-83, headmaster Queen Margaret's Sch Escrick York 1983-; memb Yorks Gentlemens CC; IAPS 1968, SHA 1983, GSA 1983; *Recreations* golf, jazz, gardening; *Clubs* Knights of the Campanile; *Style—* Colin McGarrigle, Esq; Wold Cottage, Langton Rd, Norton, Malton, N Yorkshire (☎ 0635 692026); Queen Margaret's Sch, Escrick Park, York YO4 6EU (☎ 0904 87261)

McGARRITY, James Forsyth; CB (1981); s of James McGarrity (d 1977), and Margaret, *née* Davidson (d 1976); *b* 10 April 1921; *Educ* Bathgate Acad, Glasgow Univ (MA, BSc, MEd); *m* 1951, Violet Smith Gunn, da of John Philp (d 1957); 1 s (Forsyth), 1 da (Gillian); *Career* 5 Lt (A) RNVR 1943-46; HM sr chief inspr of schs (Scotland) 1973-81; *Recreations* golf, gardening, bridge; *Style—* James McGarrity Esq, CB; 30 Oatlands Park, Linlithgow (☎ 0506 84 3258)

MCGARVEY, Alan; s of William Johnson McGarvey (d 1967), and Rosina, *née* Plane; *b* 22 June 1942; *Educ* Wallsend GS, Univ of Newcastle upon Tyne (BSc), Cranfield Sch of Mgmnt (MBA); *m* 11 Sept 1967, Eileen; *Career* CA; Parsons 1958-64, Rio Tinto Zinc Ltd 1968-71, Decca Group 1972-76, MK Electric Ltd 1976-78, NEB 1978-82, GLEB 1982-86, GMED 1987-90; memb Bd Northern Chamber Orchestra, chair Medlock Primary Sch; UK memb Centre for Devpt of Indust (EEC-ACP) Brussels; *Recreations* would-be sculptor, part way chef; *Style—* Alan McGarvey, Esq; 11 Old Hall Mews, Old Hall Lane, Bolton BL1 7PW (☎ 0204 40141, fax 0204 40723)

McGAVIGAN, James Bartholomew; s of William McGavigan (d 1964), and Sarah, *née* Bradley (d 1978); *b* 24 Aug 1945; *Educ* St Patrick's High Coatbridge, Univ of Glasgow (MB ChB); *m* 10 Jan 1968, Moira Shaw, da of Hector Douglas Shaw, of 2 Hay Burn St, Glasgow; 2 s (Stuart William b 1968, Andrew Douglas b 1972); *Career* consIt microbiologist 1977-80; memb postgrad ctees Univ of Glasgow, chm W of Scot Microbiology Gp, tstee W of Scot Surgical Infection Study Gp; memb: Assoc of Clinical Pathologists, Assoc of Med Microbiologist; MRCPath 1977; *Books* Notes on Medical Microbiology (contrib, 1980); *Recreations* golf, classic car restoration; *Style—* James McGavigan; Microbiology Dept, Royal Infirmary, Livilands, Stirling (☎ 0786 73151)

McGAVIN, Dr Clive Roderick; s of Donald Burns McGavin, and Cynthia, *née* Scott, JP (d 1989); *b* 9 Feb 1945; *Educ* Eton, Trinity Coll Cambridge (MA, MB BChir, MD); *m* 4 Aug 1973, Rachel Elizabeth, da of John Barnes, CBE (d 1975); 3 da (Lucy b 1974, Ruth b 1976, Kate b 1980); *Career* consIt physician specialising in respiratory med and occupational lung disorders Plymouth Health Authy 1978; FRCP; *Style—* Dr Clive McGavin; Dostabrook, Horrabridge, Yelverton, Devon (☎ 0822 854577); Dr Clive McGavin, Plymouth Chest Clinic, Freedom Fields Hospital, Plymouth PL4 7JJ (☎ 0752 834139)

McGEACHIE, Daniel (Dan); s of David McGeachie (d 1969), of Arbroath, and Jessie McGeachie; *b* 10 June 1935; *Educ* Arbroath HS; *m* 16 Jan 1962, Sylvia, *née* Andrew; 1 da (Fiona b 1964); *Career* Nat Serv 1953-55; journalist Scotland and Fleet St 1955-60, foreign corr (Africa) Daily Express 1960-65, parly corr then dip and political corr Daily Express 1965-75, UK political advsr to Conoco 1975-77, dir and gen mangr Govt and Public Affrs Conoco (UK) Ltd; cncl memb Indust and Parliament Tst, memb Parly Energy Studies Gp; *Clubs* Reform; *Style—* Dan McGeachie, Esq; 27 Hitherwood Drive, Dulwich, London SE19 1XA (☎ 081 670 5546); Conoco (UK) Ltd, Park St, London W1Y 4NN (☎ 071 408 6608)

McGEE, Darryll St John; s of Henry John McGee (d 1966), and Jessie Adelene, *née* Guvv (d 1976); *b* 15 Nov 1939; *Educ* Emanuel Sch, King's Coll Cambridge (BA); *m* 12 Sept 1979, Christine Mary, da of Arthur Castle; 3 s (Daeron, Charles, Tim); *Career* bd memb: Finicisa SA Portugal 1981-86, Nurel SA Spain 1981-86, ICI Fibres 1981-88; chm Cantex Fabrics Ltd 1981-86; memb: Nuffield Hosp Local Advsy Ctee, N Yorks Indust Advsy Panel, bd of govrs Harrogate Int Festival; *Recreations* skiing, sailing, tennis; *Style—* Darryll McGee, Esq; ICI plc, Chemicals & Polymer, The Heath, Runcorn, Cheshire WA7 4QF (☎ 0928 514 444)

McGEE, Prof James O'Donnell; s of Michael McGee (d 1981), and Bridget Gavin (d 1982); *b* 27 July 1939; *Educ* Univ of Glasgow (MB ChB, PhD, MD), Univ of Oxford (MA); *m* 26 August 1961, Anne McCarron Lee, da of Patrick Lee, of 55 Edgam Drive, Cardonald, Glasgow; 1 s (Damon-Joel b 1969), 2 da (Leeanne b 1962, Sharon b 1964); *Career* lectr then sr lectr in pathology Univ of Glasgow 1967-75, distinguished visiting scientist Roche Inst of Molecular Biology Nutley NJ USA 1989 (Med Res Cncl travelling fell 1969-70, visiting scientist 1970-71 and 1981), prof and head Nuffield Dept of Pathology and Bacteriology Univ of Oxford 1975-, fell Linacre Coll Oxford 1975-, assoc fell Green Coll Oxford 1981-; memb: Cancer Res Campaign UK 1978-, Ctee on Safety of Meds Med Div UK 1984-90; MRCPath 1973, FRCPath 1986, FRCP 1989; *Books* Biopsy Pathology of Liver (1980, 2 edn 1988), In Situ Hybridisation: Principles and Practice (1990), Oxford Textbook of Pathology (vols 1 and 2, 1991); *Recreations* talking with my family, swimming; *Style—* Prof James O'D McGee; 17 Cadogan Park, Woodstock, Oxon OX7 1UW (☎ 0993 811556); University of Oxford, Nuffield Department of Pathology & Bacteriology, John Radcliffe Hospital, Headington, Oxford OX3 9DU (☎ 0865 220549, fax 0865 220078)

MCGEECHAN, Ian Robert; s of Robert Matthew McGeechan (d 1969), and Hilda, *née* Shearer; *b* 30 Oct 1946; *Educ* Moor Grange HS, West Park HS, Allerton Grange Comp, Carnegre Coll of Physical Educn; *m* 9 Aug 1969, Judy Irene, da of Thomas Fish; 1 s (Robert James b 5 Nov 1978), 1 da (Heather Jane b 17 Aug 1983); *Career* Rugby Union national coach and former fly-half Scotland (32 caps); clubs: Headiingley FC 1965-82 (300 appearances, capt 1972-73), Barbarians RFC 1973-78, Yorks CCC 1963-68 (played for second XI); Scotland: debut v NZ 1972, tour NZ 1975 (1 test appearance), capt 1977 and 1979, final game v France 1979, asst coach 1985-88, national coach 1988-, coached Grand Slam winning team 1990; British Lions: toured SA 1974 (4 tests, won series 3-1), toured NZ 1977 (4 tests), coach on tour of Aust 1989 (won series 2-1); head of Games Moor Grange HS 1968-72, head of Humanities and Year Gp ldr Fir Tree Middle Sch 1972-90, PR mangr Scottish Life Assurance Company 1990-; Rugby Writers: Rubert Cherry Trophy 1989, Pat Marshall Trophy 1990; Rugby World Coach of the Year 1989 and 1990, Br Inst of Sports Coaches Coach of the Year 1990; *Books* Scotlands Grand Slam (with Ian Robertson and M Cleary); *Recreations* caravaning, hill walking, family life, sailing; *Style—* Ian McGeechan, Esq, OBE; Scottish Rugby Union, Murrayfield, Edinburgh EH12 5PJ (☎ 031 337 9551, fax 031 313 2810)

MCGEOCH, Vice Adm Sir Ian Lachlan Mackay; KCB (1969, CB 1966), DSO (1943), DSC (1943); s of L A McGeoch of Dalmuir; *b* 26 March 1914; *Educ* Pangbourne, Univ of Edinburgh (MPhil); *m* 1937, Eleanor Somers, da of Rev Canon Hugh Farrie; 2 s, 2 da; *Career* joined RN 1932; Flag Offr: Scotland and NI 1968-70, Submarines 1965-67; Adm pres RNC Greenwich 1964-65; memb: Royal Co Archers (Queen's Body Guard for Scotland) 1969-, Cncl White Ensign Assoc; tstee Imperial War Museum 1977-87; ed The Naval Review 1973-80, dir Naval Forces 1980-83; dir Midar Systems Ltd; *Books* with Gen Sir John Hackett: The Third World War: a Future History (1978), The Third World War; The Untold Story (1982), An Affair of Chances (1991); *Clubs* Royal Yacht Sqdn, Army & Navy; *Style—* Vice Adm Sir Ian McGeoch, KCB, DSO, DSC; Southerns, Castle Hedingham, Halstead, Essex CO9 3DG

MCGEOUGH, Brian Thomas; s of John Anthony McGeough (d 1990), of Cannock, Staffordshire, and Edna Laura, *née* Davis; *b* 1 Nov 1933; *Educ* St Chads Coll Wolverhampton, Trinity Hall Cambridge (BA); *m* 25 June 1960, Philippa Ann, da of Bernard Vincent James; 1 s (John b 1962), 2 da (Sarah b 1961, Judith b 1965); *Career* Nat Serv 2 Lt RASC (now RCT) 1952-54, TA Serv South Staffordshire Regt; admitted slr 1960, ptnr Denton Hall Burgin & Warrens (formerly Warrens) 1963-; treas Henry Smiths Charity 1989-; *Recreations* tennis, riding, books, music, pictures; *Clubs* Athenaeum; *Style—* Brian McGeough, Esq; Denton Hall Burgin & Warrens, 5 Chancery Lane, Clifford's Inn, London EC4A 1BU (☎ 071 242 1212)

MCGEOUGH, Prof Joseph Anthony; s of Patrick Joseph McGeough (d 1982), of Stevenston, Ayrshire, and Gertrude, *née* Darroch (d 1975); *b* 29 May 1940; *Educ* St Michael's Coll Irvine, Univ of Glasgow (BSc, PhD), Univ of Aberdeen (DSc); *m* 12 Aug 1972, Brenda, da of Robert Nicholson, of Blyth, Northumberland; 2 s (Andrew b 1974, Simon b 1977), 1 da (Elizabeth b 1975); *Career* res demonstrator Univ of Leicester 1966, sr res fell Queensland Univ 1967, res metallurgist International R & D Ltd 1968-69, sr res fell Univ of Strathclyde 1969-72; Univ of Aberdeen: lectr 1972-77, sr lectr 1977-80, reader in engrg 1980-83; regius prof in engrg and head Dept Mechanical Engrg Univ of Edinburgh 1983-; industl fell Sci and Engrg Res Cncl Royal Soc 1987-89; chm Coll Cncl Dyce Acad 1980-83, memb Tech Advsy Ctee Scot Centre Agric Engrg 1987-, hon pres Lichfield Sci and Engrg Soc 1988-89, chm Edinburgh and SE Scot Panel Inst Mechanical Engrs 1988-, hon vice pres Univ of Aberdeen Athletics Assoc 1981-; various Scot Co AAA and universities Athletic Championship awards; FRSE, FIMechE, FIProdE, MIM, companion Inst Chem Engrs; *Books* Principles of Electrochemical Machining (1974), Advanced Methods of Machining (1988), section on Nonconventional Machining: Encyclopaedia Britannica (1987); *Recreations* walking, athletics; *Style—* Prof Joseph McGeough, FRSE; 39 Dreghorn Loan, Colinton, Edinburgh EH13 0DF (☎ 031 441 1302); Dept of Mechanical Engineering, University of Edinburgh, King's Buildings, Edinburgh EH9 3JL (☎ 031 661 1081 ext 3350, fax 031 667 7938, telex 727442 UNIVED G)

McGEOWN, Prof Mary Graham; CBE (1985); da of James Edward McGeown, of Prospect Hall, Aughagallon, Lurgan, NI, and Sarah Graham, *née* Quinn; *b* 19 July 1923; *Educ* Lurgan Coll, Queen's Univ Belfast (MB, BAO, MD, PhD); *m* 1 Sept 1949 (Joseph) Maxwell Freeland (decd), s of Herbert Freeland (d 1982); 3 s (Peter b 1956, Mark b 1957, Paul b 1961); *Career* house physician Royal Victoria Hosp Belfast 1947-48, house offr Royal Belfast Hosp for Sick Children 1948; asst lectr: biochemistry Queen's Univ Belfast 1949-50, pathology Queen's Univ Belfast 1950-55; grantee MRC 1953-56, res fell Royal Victoria Hosp Belfast 1956-58, consIt nephrologist Belfast Hosps 1962-88, physician in admin charge renal unit Belfast City Hosp 1968-88, chm UK Transplant Mgmnt Ctee 1983-; med advsr to NI Kidney Res Fund 1972-88 (patron 1988-), prof fell Queen's Univ 1988-; memb: American Soc Artificial Internal Organs, Ulster Med Soc (pres 1986-87), Assoc Physicians Br and Ireland, American Soc Artificial Internal Organs, Int Soc Nephrology, S African Renal Assoc; pres Irish Nephrological Soc 1990-; hon memb: Renal Assoc (pres 1983-86, hon treas 1986-89), Ulster Med Soc (pres 1986-87), Assoc Physicians Br and Ireland, Br Transplantation Soc (chm Supervisory Ctee on Organ Transplantation), American Soc Artificial Internal Organs, SA Renal Assoc, Euro Dialysis and Transplant Assoc, Euro Renal Assoc; Hon Dsc New Univ of Ulster 1983; FRCP, FRCPE, memb Royal Cwlth Soc; author of numerous articles and chapters on calcium metabolism, kidney diseases treatment, kidney transplantation; *Books* Clinical Management of Electrolyte Disorders (1983); *Recreations* gardening, genealogy; *Style—* Prof Mary McGeown, CBE; 14 Osborne Gardens, Belfast BT9 6LE (☎ 0232 669 918); Dept Medicine, Univ Floor Tower, Belfast City Hospital, Belfast BT9 7AB (☎ 0232 329 241 ext 2963)

McGHIE, James Marshall; QC (1983); s of James Drummond McGhie (d 1970), and

Jessie Eadie Bennie (d 1975); *b* 15 Oct 1944; *Educ* Perth Acad, Univ of Edinburgh; *m* 1968, Ann Manuel, da of Stanley Gray Cockburn (d 1982); 1 s (Angus b 1975), 1 da (Kathryn b 1983); *Career* advocate Scots Bar; advocate-depute 1983-86; pt/t chm Med Appeal Tbnls 1987; *Style—* James M McGhie, Esq, QC; 3 Lauder Rd, Edinburgh (☎ 031 667 8325); Parly House, Edinburgh (☎ 031 226 2881)

McGIBBON, Lewis; s of Lewis McGibbon (d 1973), of Newcastle-upon-Tyne, and Norah Rebecca, *née* Duggan; *b* 8 Oct 1931; *Educ* Wallsend GS; *m* 12 Sept 1955, Pauline, da of John Walter Haywood (d 1977), of Newcastle-upon-Tyne; 2 s (David b 21 June 1957, Keith b 16 Oct 1961), 2 da (Susan (Mrs King) b 20 Aug 1960, Gillian b 31 July 1965); *Career* Nat Serv RAF 1955-57; CA; Church & Co Ltd 1960-65, ptnr Grant Thornton 1965-70; currently self employed non-exec dir and chm various cos; former local Magistrate, memb Northampton Health Authy, ctee memb Northants Golf (former ctee memb Northants CCC); FCA 1959, played cricket for Northumberland CCC 1950-56 and Northamptonshire 1957-59 (against Australian Cricket XI 1956); *Recreations* golf, bridge; *Style—* Lewis McGibbon, Esq; Green Close, Church Brampton, Northampton

MacGILLIVRAY, Dr (Barron) Bruce; s of John Alexander MacGillivray (d 1940), of SA, and Doreene Eleanore, *née* Eastwood (d 1974); *b* 21 Aug 1927; *Educ* Kings Edward VII Sch Johannesburg, Univ of Witwatersrand (BSc), Univ of Manchester, London Univ (MB, BS); *m* 7 Jan 1955, Ruth Marjorie, da of Albert Valentine (d 1965), of Cheshire; 2 s (John Bruce b 1955, Robert Alexander b 1962), 1 da (Carol Susan b 1957); *Career* house surgn and house physician Manchester Royal Inf 1953-56, res med offr Stepping Hill and Stockport Infirmary 1957-59, registrar and sr registrar Nat Hosp for Nervous Diseases 1959-64, res fell UCLA 1964-65, conslt physician neurology and neurophysiology Royal Free Hosp 1965-, conslt neurophysiology Nat Hosp for Nervous Diseases 1971-; Univ of London: dean Royal Free Hosp Sch of Med 1974-89, memb Senate 1980-89, pro vice chllr med 1985-87; memb Cncl Sch of Pharmacy 1976-; author various scientific pubns on neurophysiology, brain death and med computing; memb: Camden and Islington Area Health Authy 1976-82, NE Thames Regnl Health Authy 1982-86, Ctee Vice Chllrs and Princs 1982-87; FRSM, FRSA, FRCP; *Recreations* flying, wood turning, photography; *Style—* Dr Bruce MacGillivray; 18 St Johns Ave, Putney, London SW15 2AA (☎ 081 788 5213); Royal Free Hosp, Dept of Clinical Neurophysiology, Hampstead, London NW3 2QG (☎ 071 794 0500)

MacGILLIVRAY, Neil; s of John MacGillivray, JP (d 1972), of Camuscross, Isle Ornsay, Isle of Skye, and Flora, *née* MacLeay; *b* 27 Nov 1939; *Educ* Dingwall Acad, Univ of Edinburgh (MB ChB); *m* 21 Sept 1969, Gay, da of John Oram (d 1989), of Thornton Cleveleys, Lancs; 1 s (Iain), 1 da (Dede); *Career* house physician Royal Infirmary Edinburgh 1965-66, sr house offr St Georges Hosp 1968-69, registrar Royal Infirmary Glasgow 1970-71, sr registrar Manchester Hosps 1972-75, conslt otolaryngologist Victoria Hosp Blackpool and Lytham Hosp 1975-; FRCSEd 1972; memb: BMA, HCSA, RSM, N of E Orl Soc; *Recreations* golf, skiing, travel; *Clubs* Royal Lytham and St Annes Golf; *Style—* Neil MacGillivray, Esq; Skippool Cottage, Breck Rd, Poulton-le-Fylde, Lancs; Fylde Coast Hospital, St Walburgas Rd, Blackpool, Lancs FY3 8BP (☎ 0253 34188)

McGILLYCUDDY OF THE REEKS, The (Mac Giolla Chuda); Richard Denis Wyer McGillycuddy; suc 1959; s of John Patrick, The McGillycuddy of The Reeks (d 1959), and Elizabeth Margaret, The Madam McGillycuddy of The Reeks; *b* 4 Oct 1948; *Educ* Eton, Aix en Provence; *m* 1984, Virginia Lucy, eld da of Hon Hugh Waldorf Astor, of Folly Farm, Sulhamstead, Reading, Berks, *qv*; 2 da (Tara b 1985, Sorcha b 1989); *Heir* cousin, Donough McGillycuddy b 1939; *Career* chm: Chelsea Green Ltd 1981-84, Figurehead Ltd 1981-83; *Recreations* motor-racing, reading; *Clubs* Pratt's; *Style—* The McGillycuddy of the Reeks

McGIVERN, Eugene; s of James McGivern (d 1981), of Belfast, NI, and Eileen, *née* Dickie; *b* 15 Sept 1938; *Educ* St Colman's Sch, St Mary's GS Belfast; *m* 1 Feb 1960, Teresa, da of Owen Doran, of Lurgan, NI; 2 s (Christopher b 1963, Nicholas b 1971), 1 da (Annette b 1961); *Career* Inland Revenue: joined 1955, on secondment sec to Min of State (now Baroness White, *qv*) Welsh Office 1967-69, under sec 1986- (asst sec 1973); chm Mgmnt Ctee Cwlth Assoc of Tax Admins 1982-86, chm John Fisher Sch Purley 1985-86 (govr 1979-); *Recreations* reading, gardening (if unavoidable); *Style—* Eugene McGivern, Esq; c/o Board of Inland Revenue, Somerset House, Strand, London (☎ 071 438 6622)

MCGLADDERY, Joseph Raymond; s of Joseph McGladdery (d 1946), and Margaret McGladdery (d 1983); *b* 28 May 1927; *Educ* Methodist Coll Belfast, Queens Univ Belfast (BSc); *m* 31 March 1967, Ann Pitcairn, da of John Reekie (d 1982); 1 s (Joseph John); *Career* involved construction Carrington Power Station nr Manchester 1949 and i/c various projects NI 1950-58, a dep chief engr Durgapur Steelworks in W Bengal 1959-60, rep London consltss i/c of first major construction project in Danakil Desert Ethiopa 1961-62; fndr McGladdery & Ptnrs 1962-; FIEI 1970, FICE 1973, MConsE 1974, FCIArb 1974, FIStructE 1975, FIHT 1975, FIWEM 1987, Eur Ing 1989; *Style—* Joseph McGladdery, Esq; The Cottage, 43A Malone Park, Belfast BT9 6NL (☎ 0232 669 734); McGladdery and Partners, Consulting Civil and Structural Engrs, 64 Malone Avenue, Belfast BT9 6ER (☎ 0232 660682)

McGLASHAN, John Reid Curtis; CBE (1974); s of John Adamson McGlashan (d 1961), and Emma Rose May, *née* Curtis (d 1986); *b* 12 Dec 1921; *Educ* Fettes, Christ Church Oxford (Rugby Blue); *m* 9 Aug 1947, Dilys Bagnall, da of Oliver Buxton Knight (d 1950); 1 s (John b 1949), 2 da (Jill b 1951, Julie b 1955); *Career* RAF Bomber Cmd 1940-45 (POW 1941-45); HM Dip Serv 1953-79: Baghdad 1955-57, Tripoli 1963-65, Madrid 1968-70, cnsllr FCO 1970-79, ret; *Style—* John McGlashan, Esq, CBE; Allendale, Clayton Rd, Selsey, W Sussex PO20 9BD (☎ 0243 602 019)

MacGLASHAN, Maureen Elizabeth; da of Kenneth MacGlashan (d 1967), and Elizabeth, *née* Elliott; *b* 7 Jan 1938; *Educ* Luton Girls HS, Girton Coll Cambridge (BA, LLM); *Career* Dip Serv 1961-: third sec (later second sec) HM Embassy Tel Aviv 1964-67, first sec and head of chancery E Berlin 1973-75, UK rep EEC Brussels 1975-77, Home Civil Serv 1977-82, cnsllr HM Embassy Bucharest 1982-85, asst dir Res Centre for Int Law Cambridge 1986; cnsllr HM Embassy Belgrade 1990, head of Western Euro Dept FCO 1991-; ASIL 1986, ILA (Br Section) 1986, BIICL; *Style—* Miss Maureen MacGlashan; 5 Cranmer Rd, Cambridge CB3 9BL

McGLASHAN, Prof Maxwell Len; s of Leonard Day McGlashan (d 1969), of Greymouth, NZ, and Margaret Cordelia, *née* Bush (d 1985); *b* 1 April 1924; *Educ* Greymouth NZ Schs, Canterbury Univ Coll Christchurch NZ (BSc, MSc), Univ of Reading (PhD, DSc); *m* 15 Jan 1947, Susan Jane, da of Col Hugh Edward Crosse, MC, OBE, of Patoka, Hawkes Bay, NZ (d 1962); *Career* sr lectr in chemistry Canterbury Univ Coll NZ 1953 (asst lectr 1946-48, lectr 1948-53), reader in chemistry Univ of Reading 1961-64 (Sims Empire Scholar 1949-52, lectr 1954-61), prof of physical chem Univ of Exeter 1964-74, prof of chem and head Dept of Chem UCL 1974-89, emeritus prof Univ of London 1989-; ed Journal of Chemical Thermodynamics 1969; Cmmn on Physicochemical Symbols Terminology and Units: memb 1963-65, vice chm 1965-67, chm 1967-71; memb: Metrication Bd 1969-80, Comité Consultatif des Unités (Metre Convention) 1969-; chm Interdivisional Ctee on Nomenclature and Symbols Int Union of Pure and Applied Chemistry 1971-76 external memb Br Gas Res Ctee 1979-, tstee Ramsay Meml Fellowships Tst 1982- (chm Advsy Cncl 1975-89); FRSC 1962; *Books* Physicochemical Quantities and Units (2 edn, 1971), Chemical Thermodymanics (1979); *Recreations* alpine climbing, theatre; *Clubs* Athenaeum, Swiss Alpine; *Style—* Prof Maxwell McGlashan; Patoka, Fairwarp, Uckfield, E Sussex (☎ 082 571 2172); Dept of Chemistry, Univ Coll London, 20 Gordon St, London WC1H 0AJ (☎ 071 380 7451, fax 071 380 7463)

McGONIGAL, Christopher Ian; s of Maj H A K McGonigal, MC (d 1963), of Beverley, E Yorks, and Cora, *née* Bentley (d 1946); *b* 10 Nov 1937; *Educ* Ampleforth, CCC Oxford (MA); *m* 28 Sept 1961, (Sara) Sally Ann, da of Louis David Mesnard Fearnley Sander (d 1975); 3 s (Dominic b 1962, Gregory b 1967, Fergus b 1969), 1 da (Alice b 1964); *Career* slr 1965; Coward Chance: asst slr 1965-68, ptnr 1969-87, sr litigation ptnr 1972-79, sr resident ptnr ME 1979-83, sr litigation ptnr 1983-87; slr Hong Kong 1981, jt sr litigation ptnr Clifford Chance 1987-; asst rec 1989-; memb Lamberhurst Local History Soc; Freeman Worshipful Co of Slrs 1972; *Recreations* local history, gardening, walking; *Style—* Christopher McGonigal, Esq; Sandhurst Farm, Clayhill Road, Lamberhurst, Kent TN3 8AX (☎ 0892 890595); Clifford Chance, Blackfriars House, 19 New Bridge Street, London (☎ 071 353 0211, fax 071 489 0046, telex 887847)

McGONNIGILL, Hon Mrs (Jean Brown) Kirkwood; da of 1 Baron Kirkwood, PC (d 1955); *b* 1917; *m* 1943, William Henderson McGonnigill; 3 da; *Career* town cncllr; *Style—* The Hon Mrs McGonnigill; Dryleaze, Wotton-under-Edge, Glos

McGOUGH, Roger Joseph; *b* 9 Nov 1937; *Educ* St Mary's Coll Liverpool, Hull Univ (BA, Cert Ed); *Career* poet; fell of poetry Univ of Loughborough 1973-75, writer-in-residence Western Aust Coll of Advanced Educn Perth 1986; memb Exec Cncl The Poetry Soc 1989-; *Poems* In the Glassroom (1976), Holiday on Death Row (1979), Summer with Monika (1978), Waving at Trains (1982), Melting into the Foreground (1986), Selected Poems (1989); *Childrens* The Great Smile Robbery (1983), Sky in the Pie (1983), The Stowaways (1986), Noah's Ark (1986), Nailing the Shadow (1987), An Imaginary Menagerie (1988), Helen Highwater (1989), Counting by Numbers (1989), Blazing Fruit (1990), The Lighthouse That Ran Away (1991), You At The Back (1991); *Clubs* Chelsea Arts (chm 1984-86); *Style—* Roger McGough, Esq; c/o Peter, Fraser & Dunlop, 5th Floor, The Chambers, Chelsea Harbour Lots Rd, London SW10 0XF

MCGOWAN, Bruce Henry; s of Henry McGowan (d 1948), and Nora Heath, *née* Godwin (d 1963); *b* 27 June 1924; *Educ* King Edward's Sch Birmingham, Jesus Coll Cambridge (MA, CertEd); *m* 1947, Beryl McKenzie, da of Alfred Heath Liggitt; 1 s (Stuart Henry b 21 March 1949), 3 da (Alison Catherine b 10 July 1951, Sheila Jane (Mrs Joseph Curran) (twin) b 11 July 1951, Bridget Helen (Mrs Richard Simpson) b 9 July 1955); *Career* served RA (India and Burma) 1943-46; asst master King's Sch Rochester 1949-53, sr history master Wallasey GS 1953-57; headmaster: De Aston Sch Market Rasen Lincs 1957-64, Solihull Sch 1964-73, Haberdashers' Aske's Sch Elstree 1973-87; chm Church Schs Co Ltd 1987-; Page scholar English-Speaking Union 1961; memb: Church Assembly C of E 1963-70, Public Schs Cmmn 1968-70; chm: Boarding Schs Assoc 1967-69, Headmasters' Conf 1985; Freeman City of London 1987, Liveryman Haberdashers' Co 1987; FRSA; *Recreations* walking, swimming, foreign travel, music, theatre; *Clubs* East India, English-Speaking Union; *Style—* Bruce McGowan, Esq; 57 Oxford St, Woodstock, Oxford OX7 1TJ (☎ 0993 811811); Church Schools Co Ltd, 1A Doughty St, London WC1N 2PH (☎ 071 404 3134)

McGOWAN, Dowager Lady; Carmen; da of Sir (James) Herbert Cory; *m* 1937, 2 Baron McGowan (d 1966); 3 s, 2 da; *Style—* The Rt Hon the Dowager Lady McGowan; Bragborough Hall, Daventry, Warwickshire (☎ 0788 890210)

McGOWAN, Hon Mrs; (Arabella) Charlotte; *née* Eden; da of Baron Eden of Winton (Life Peer); *b* 1 Aug 1960; *m* 1983, Hon Mungo McGowan, *qv*; 1 s, 1 da; *Style—* The Hon Mrs McGowan; Bragborough Hall, Daventry, Northants

MCGOWAN, Prof David Alexander; s of George McGowan, MBE (d 1979), of Portadown, Co Armagh, and Annie Hall, *née* Macormac; *b* 18 June 1939; *Educ* Portadown Coll, Queen's Univ Belfast (BDS, MDS), Univ of London (PhD); *m* 21 June 1968, (Vera) Margaret, da of James Macauley, of Closkelt, Co Down; 1 s (Andrew), 2 da (Anna, Marion); *Career* lectr in dental surgery Queens Univ Belfast 1968, sr lectr in oral and maxillofacial surgery London Hosp Med Coll 1970-77, dean of dental educn Univ of Glasgow 1990- (prof of oral surgery 1977-, postgrad advsr in dentistry 1977-90); dean of the Dental Faculty RCPSG, memb Gen Dental Cncl, former memb Cncl BAOMS; FDSRCS 1964, FFDRCSI 1966, FDSRCPSG 1978; *Books* An Atlas of Minor Oral Surgery (1989); *Recreations* music, dog-walking; *Style—* Prof David McGowan; Glasgow Dental Hospital & School, 378 Sauchiehall St, Glasgow G2 3JZ (☎ 041 332 7020)

McGOWAN, Hon Dominic James Wilson; s of 2 Baron McGowan (d 1966); *b* 26 Nov 1951; *Educ* Bradfield Coll; *Style—* The Hon Dominic McGowan; Bragborough Hall, Braunston, Daventry, Northants

McGOWAN, Frankie (Mrs Peter Glossop); *Educ* Notre Dame HS, Poly of Central London; *m* 27 March 1971, Peter Glossop; 1 s (Tom b 28 Dec 1973), 1 da (Amy b 8 May 1977); *Career* journalist and feature writer; Evening News 1970-73, freelance 1983-85, co-ordinating ed Woman's Journal 1985-86, asst ed Sunday Mirror 1986-87, launch ed and ed New Woman 1988-90, ed-in-chief and relaunch ed People Magazine; *Recreations* family life; *Style—* Ms Frankie McGowan; c/o People Magazine, Mirror Group Newspapers Ltd, Orbit House, 1 New Fetter Lane, London EC4A 1AR (☎ 071 822 3483, fax 071 822 3829)

McGOWAN, Baroness; Lady Gillian Angela; *née* Pepys; da of late 7 Earl of Cottenham; *b* 1941; *m* 1962, 3 Baron McGowan; 1 s, 2 da; *Style—* The Rt Hon the Lady McGowan

McGOWAN, 3 Baron (UK 1937); Harry Duncan Cory McGowan; s of 2 Baron McGowan (d 1966), and Carmen, da of Sir Herbert Cory, 1 Bt, JP, DL; *b* 20 July 1938; *Educ* Eton; *m* 1962, Lady Gillian Angela Pepys, da of 7 Earl of Cottenham (d 1968); 1 s, 2 da; *Heir* s, Hon Harry John Charles McGowan b 23 June 1971; *Career* ptnr Panmure Gordon & Co 1971-; *Clubs* Boodle's; *Style—* The Rt Hon the Lord McGowan; 12 Stanhope Mews East, London SW7 (☎ 071 370 2346); Highway House, Lower Froyle, Alton, Hants (☎ 0420 22104)

MacGOWAN, Hon Mrs (Jane Alice Camilla); *née* Casey; da of Baron Casey, KG, GCMG, CH, DSO, MC, PC (Life Peer, Govr-Gen of Australia 1965-69, d 1976), and Ethel, AC (d 1983), da of Maj-Gen Sir Charles Snodgrass Ryan, KBE, CB, CMG; *b* 7 Oct 1928; *m* 12 March 1955 (m dis 1981), Murray Wynne MacGowan, s of Clifford Glover MacGowan, of Melbourne; 1 s, 3 da; *Style—* The Hon Mrs MacGowan; 5 Darley Pla, Darlinghurst, NSW 2021, Australia

McGOWAN, John Peter; s of Peter McGowan, of Motherwell, Scotland, and Jean, *née* Findlay; *b* 3 June 1943; *Educ* OLHS, Scottish Coll of Commerce; *m* 1964, Rebecca, da of John Cox (d 1986), of Holytown, Scotland; 1 s (J Paul b 1971), 1 da (Mhairi b 1967); *Career* md AAF Ltd, chm and chief exec Wheway plc; *Recreations* golf; *Clubs* RAC, 1837; *Style—* John P McGowan, Esq; Lantern House, Naunton Beauchamp, Pershore, Worcestershire WR10 2LQ; 214 Hagley Road, Edgbaston, Birmimgham, B16 9PH (☎ 021 456 3634, fax 021 456 3810, telex 336159)

McGOWAN, Hon Mungo Alexander Cansh; s of 2 Baron McGowan (d 1966), and Carmen, *née* Cory; *b* 10 Dec 1956; *Educ* Eton, RAC; *m* 1983, Hon (Arabella)

Charlotte, *qv*, da of Baron Eden of Winton (Life Peer); 1 s (James Alexander Cory b 21 June 1985), 2 da (Laura Charlotte Iona b 8 May 1987, another b 7 Feb 1991); *Career* landowner; *Style—* The Hon Mungo McGowan; Bragborough Hall, Daventry, Northants

McGRADY, Alexander Hughes; TD (1946); s of Clement Alexander McGrady (d 1947), of Dundee, and Kate Giffen, *née* Fairweather (d 1952); *b* 14 April 1916; *Educ* Merchiston Castle Edinburgh; *m* 3 April 1946, (Vivian) Jytte, da of Gunnar Victor Hartmann (d 1957), of Copenhagen; 1 s (Hamish b 1950), 2 da (Susan (Mrs Coles) b 1947, Lou (Hon Mrs Michael Howard) b 1952); *Career* 2 Lt 76 (Highland) Field Regt RA TA 1939 served BEF France and Belgium 1940, seconded RAF 1942; Flt Lt 26 Sqdn RAF 1944-45 served: Normandy, Holland, Germany (despatches 3 times); Capt: 276 (Highland) Field Regt RA TA 1947, 666 (Scottish) Air OP Sqdn RAuxAF 1950; Bell & Sime plc (Formerly Bell & Sime Ltd): joined 1933, dir 1947-81, md and alternate chm 1951-81, ret 1981; *Recreations* motoring; *Clubs* Bentley Drivers; *Style—* Alexander McGrady, Esq, TD; Brackenbrae, West Ferry, Dundee DD5 1RX (☎ 0382 79732)

MCGRADY, Edward Kevin; MP (SDLP) Down South 1987-; s of late Michael McGrady, of Downpatrick, and Lillian, *née* Leatham; *b* 3 June 1935; *Educ* St Patrick's Downpatrick; *m* 6 Nov 1959, Patricia, da of Willia Swail; 2 s (Jerome, Conaill), 1 da (Paula); *Career* ptnr MB McGrady & Co CA and insur brokers; Downpatrick Urban Dist Cncl: cncllr 1961-73, chm 1964-73; Down Dist Council: cncllr 1973-, chm 1974, 1976, 1978, ret 1989; memb South Down: 1973-74, 1987-, NI Convention 1975, NI Assembly 1982-86; min co-ordination NI Exec 1974; SDLP: first chm 1970-72, chief whip 1975-; chm: Down Regnl Museum 1981-, Jobspace NI Ltd 1985-; FCA, ACA; *Recreations* gardening, walking, ancient monuments, choral music; *Style—* Edward McGrady, Esq, MP; Constituency Office, 14A Scotch St, Downpatrick, Co Down, N Ireland (☎ 0396 612 882)

MCGRAIL, Prof Sean Francis; *b* 5 May 1928; *Educ* Univ of Bristol (Harry Crook Scholar, BA), Univ of London Inst of Archaeology, Univ of London (PhD), Campion Hall Oxford (MA), Univ of Oxford (DSc); *m* 28 July 1955, (Ursula) Anne Yates; 1 s (Hugh Fergus b 29 Jan 1958), 3 da (Frances Joanna b 26 May 1956, Mary Ursula b 9 March 1960, Catherine Clare b 29 March 1963); *Career* RN: cadet to Lt Cdr (qualified as Master Mariner) 1946-68, pilot Fleet Air Arm 1952-68 (cmd 849 Sqdn 1962-63); National Maritime Museum: asst keeper (archaeology) Dept of Ships 1972, head Dept of Archaeology of Ships 1973-76, chief archaeologist and head Archaeological Res Centre 1976-86 (dep keeper 1976-80, keeper 1980-86); prof maritime archaeology Inst of Archaeology Univ of Oxford 1986-; memb Cncl: Prehistoric Soc 1980-83, Soc of Antiques 1983-86; memb: Dept of Tport Advsy Ctee on Historic Wrecks 1975-, Exec Ctee Mary Rose Tst 1980-86, Egyptian Antiques Orgn's Ctee on Establishment of a Nat Maritime Museum in Alexandria 1985-86, Academic Advsy Ctee of States of Guernsey Ancient Monuments Ctee 1985-; vice chm Tst for Preservation of Oxford Coll Barges 1987-, excavations on prehistoric and medieval sites (Norway, Denmark, Orkney, Ireland, Britain) 1974-; FSA 1981, MIFA 1983; *Books* Sources and Techniques in Boat Archaeology (ed, 1977), Logboats of England and Wales (1978), Medieval Ships and Harbours in Northern Europe (ed, 1979), Rafts, Boats and Ships (1981), Aspects of Maritime Archaeology and Ethnography (1984), Ancient boats in NW Europe (1987), Seacraft of Prehistory (ed 2 edn, 1988), Maritime Celts, Frisians and Saxons (1990), National Maritime Museum Archaeological Series (ed 1977-86); *Style—* Prof Sean McGrail, FSA; Institute of Archaeology, 36 Beaumont Street, Oxford OX1 2PG (☎ 0865 278240)

McGRATH, Anthony Charles Ormond; s of Patrick Anthony Ormond McGrath, MC, TD (d 1988), of Southwater, Sussex, and Eleanor Mary Howard, *née* Horsman; *b* 10 Nov 1949; *Educ* Worth Abbey Sch, Univ of Surrey (BSc); *m* 20 July 1974, Margaret Mary, da of Capt William Arthur Usher, RN (d 1959), of Painswick; 1 s (Thomas b 21 Aug 1978), 1 da (Philippa b 20 Nov 1980); *Career* Deloitte Haskins & Sells 1971-76, Baring Brothers & Co Ltd 1976-, (dir 1984-); non-exec dir W & FC Bonham & Sons Ltd 1987-90, non-exec memb Br Standards Inst Quality Assurance Bd 1986-; FCA 1974; *Style—* Anthony McGrath, Esq; Baring Brothers & Co Ltd, 8 Bishopsgate, London EC2N 4AE (☎ 071 280 1040, fax 071 283 4209)

MCGRATH, Brian Henry; CVO (1988); s of William Henry McGrath, and Hermione Gioja; *b* 27 Oct 1925; *Educ* Eton; *m* 1959, Elizabeth Joan Bruce, *née* Gregson-Ellis (d 1977); 2 s, 1 step s; *Career* served Irish Guards 1943-46, Lt; Cannon Brewery Co 1946-48; Victoria Wine Co: joined 1948, dir 1949, chm 1960-82; chm Grants of St James's Ltd, dir Allied Breweries Ltd (later Allied-Lyons plc) 1970-82, chm Broad Street Securities 1983-, treas to Duke of Edinburgh 1984- (asst private sec, then private sec 1982-); *Recreations* golf, tennis, shooting; *Clubs* Boodle's, White's; *Style—* Brian McGrath, Esq, CVO

McGRATH, Capt John Neilson; s of John McGrath (d 1977), of Aberdare, Mid Glamorganshire, and Agnes Louisa Jones (d 1989); *b* 16 May 1941; *Educ* St Benedict's Sch Ealing, Univ Coll Cardiff (BSc, Phd), RNC Greenwich (MSc); *m* 14 April 1970, Zena Gladys, da of Norman William Haysom, of Fareham, Hants; 2 s (James 1971, Paul 1973); *Career* Lt 1967, Lt Cdr 1971, Cdr 1979, Capt 1986 trg cdr career Trg HMS Sultan 1979-82, head of materials tech RNEC 1982-86, Capt 1986, head of manpower computer systems HMS Centurion 1987-89, dean RNEC Manadon Plymouth 1990-; Welsh épée champion 1965, Welsh foil champion 1970; vice chm Grange Gp of Schs 1979-82; memb: Technician Educn Cncl Maritime Studies Ctee 1979-82, Devon Sci and Technol Regnl Orgn 1984-86; CEng, MIM 1975, FIMarE 1988; *Recreations* fencing, gardening, book collecting; *Style—* Capt John McGrath; The Dean, Royal Naval Engineering College, Manadon, Plymouth PL5 3AQ (☎ 0752 553740 ext 81255, fax 0752 553740 ext 81282)

McGRATH, John Peter; s of John Francis McGrath (d 1986), and Margaret McCann (d 1985); *b* 1 June 1935; *Educ* Alyn GS Mold Clwyd, St John's Coll Oxford; *m* 1962, Elizabeth, da of Sir Hector Ross MacLennan (d 1978); 2 s (Finn b 1966, Daniel b 1968), 1 da (Kate b 1979); *Career* playwright, theatre dir, writer of screen plays for TV and films, TV dir; artistic dir: 7:84 Theatre Co England, 7:84 Theatre Co Scotland; Over 36 plays performed and many published; writer of over 20 film screenplays and TV plays; poems and songs published and performed; *Style—* John McGrath, Esq; c/o Margaret Ramsay, 14A Goodwins Ct, St Martins Lane, London WC2 (☎ 071 240 0691)

McGRATH, Dr Patrick Gerard; CB (1981), CBE (1971); s of Patrick McGrath (d 1960), of Glasgow, and Mary, *née* Murray (d 1924); *b* 10 June 1916; *Educ* St Aloysius' Coll Glasgow, Univ of Glasgow (MB ChB), Univ of Edinburgh (Dip Psych); *m* 1949, Helen Patricia O'Brien, 3 s (Patrick, Stephen, Simon), 1 da (Judith); *Career* Lt-Col RAMC (Emergency Cmmn), served in UK, Gibraltar, India, Burma, China, Malaya, Maj 2i/c, 80 Ind Para FLD AMB 1944-45; Hon Lt-Col RAMC; registered med practitioner and conslt psychiatrist; physician supt Broadmoor Hosp 1956-81; contrib to various books on forensic psychiatric subjects; R C Psych: fndn fell 1971, vice pres 1978-80, hon fell 1981; memb: Mental Health Review Tbnl 1960-84, Parole Bd 1982-85; *Recreations* golf, bridge; *Clubs* RSM, East Berks Golf; *Style—* Dr Patrick McGrath, CB, CBE; 18 Heathermount Drive, Crowthorne, Berks RG11 6HN

McGRATH, Peter William; s of Maj William Patrick McGrath (d 1960), of Salisbury Wilts, and Winifred Clare Fill (d 1966); *b* 19 Nov 1931; *Educ* Boroughmuir Sch Edinburgh, London Univ (BSc); *m* 20 March 1954, Margaret Irene, da of Leonard S Page (d 1973), of Hartley Wintney, Hants; 1 s (Nicholas John), 3 da (Jennifer, Caroline, Melanie); *Career* Nat Serv RA 1950-51; fin mangr Ford (Germany) 1967-69, controller of fin BR bd 1969-72, fin dir Nat Freight Corp 1972-77, fin and systems dir Truck and Bus Div BL 1977-78, md Leyland Int 1978, chm and md BL Components Ltd 1978-80, gp md Rotaflex plc 1980-82, UK ops dir Stone Int Ltd 1982-86, vice chm Emess plc 1987-; *Recreations* sailing, opera; *Clubs* Medway Yacht; *Style—* Peter McGrath, Esq; St Leonard's Forest House, Horsham, W Sussex RH13 6HX (☎ 0293 835 19); 20 St James St, London SW1 (☎ 01 321 0127, fax 01 925 2734, car 0836 701 175)

MCGRAW, Mark Robertson; s of Allan McGraw, of Gourock, and Jean Davin Robertson McGraw; *b* 5 Jan 1971; *Educ* Gourock HS; *Career* professional footballer; Greenock Morton: joined 1987, debut 1989, 12 appearances; transferred to Hibernian for a fee of £175,000 Feb 1990-; *Recreations* golf, listening to music; *Style—* Mark McGraw, Esq; Hibernian FC, Easter Road Stadium, Albion Rd, Edinburgh EH7 5QG (☎ 031 661 2159)

MacGREEVY, Hon Mrs (Catriona Mary); *née* Shaw; da of 3 Baron Craigmyle; *b* 30 Oct 1958; *m* 7 June 1986, Dr Brian Irial Patrick MacGreevy, s of late Dr Brian MacGreevy; 2 s (Ivor Alexander Patrick b 1987, Hubert Donald Brian b 1989), 1 da (b 1991); *Style—* The Hon Mrs MacGreevy; Fernshaw Rd, London SW10 OTB

MacGREGOR, Alastair Rankin; s of Alexander MacGregor, and Anna, *née* Neil; *b* 23 Dec 1951; *Educ* Glasgow Acad, Univ of Edinburgh, New Coll Oxford (MA); *m* 21 Feb 1982, Rosemary Alison, da of Ralph Trevor Kerslake; 1 s (James b 13 June 1984), 1 da (Martha b 5 Jan 1989); *Career* called to Bar Lincoln's Inn 1974, in practice London; *Style—* Alastair MacGregor, Esq; One Essex Court, Temple, London EC4Y 9AR (☎ 071 583 200, fax 071 503 0118, telex 889109 ESSEX G)

McGREGOR, Rev Alistair Gerald Crichton; QC (1982), WS (1965); s of James Reid McGregor, CB, CBE, MC (formerly Capt and perm under-sec of state at WO, d 1985), and Dorothy Janet, *née* Comrie (d 1979); *b* 15 Oct 1937; *Educ* Charterhouse, Pembroke Coll Oxford (BA), Univ of Edinburgh (LLB), New Coll Univ of Edinburgh (BD); *m* 7 Aug 1965, Margaret Dick, da of David Jackson Lees, of 22 Primrose Bank Rd, Edinburgh; 2 s (James b 1969, Euan b 1973), 1 da (Elizabeth b 1970); *Career* Nat Serv Intelligence Corps 1956-58; admitted slr 1965, advocate 1967; standing jr counsel to: Queen's and Lord Treasurer's Remembrancer 1976, Scot Home and Health Dept 1978, Scot Devpt Dept 1979; clerk to Ct of Session Rules Cncl 1974, temporary sheriff 1984-86; minister N Leith Parish Church Edinburgh 1987-; sec Barony Housing Assoc Ltd 1973-83; chm: Family Care Inc 1983-88, Discipline Ctee of Potato Mkting Bd; dir Apex (Scot) Ltd 1989-, Church of Scot Elder 1967-86; memb Faculty of Advocates 1967; *Recreations* squash, tennis, swimming; *Clubs* Edinburgh University Staff, Edinburgh Sports; *Style—* The Rev Alistair McGregor, QC, WS; 22 Primrose Bank Rd, Edinburgh EH5 3JG (☎ 031 551 2802); 1A Madeira Place, Leith, Edinburgh 6 (☎ 031 553 7378)

McGREGOR, Dr Angus; s of Dr William Hector Scott McGregor (d 1989), of Mickleton, Glos, and Dr Olwen May Richards (d 1967); *b* 26 Dec 1926; *Educ* Solihull Sch, Univ of Cambridge (MA, MD), Univ of Liverpool (DPH); *m* 14 Apr 1951, May Bridget, da of Peter Burke (d 1967), of Birr, Ireland; 1 da (Catherine b 1963); *Career* RAMC: Lt 1951, Capt 1952, GP 1953, asst MOH Chester 1954-56, dep MOH: Swindon 1957, Hull 1958-65; MOH and Port MO Southampton 1965-74, dist community physician E Dorset 1964-79, regnl MO W Mids RHA 1979-88, ret 1988; visiting prof Univ of Keele 1988-; FFCM 1973, FRCP 1986, FRSA 1986; *Books* Disciplining and Dismissing Doctors in the NHS (with T Bunbury, 1988), and contributions to various med jls; *Recreations* piano; *Clubs* Royal Over-Seas League; *Style—* Dr Angus McGregor; 4 Meon Close, Upper Quinton, Stratford upon Avon CV37 8SX (☎ 0789 720863)

McGREGOR, Donald Malcolm William; s of Donald E McGregor, of Langley, Bucks, and Amy, *née* Smee (d 1947); *b* 16 Sept 1932; *Educ* Southall Tech Coll; *m* 2 Nov 1957, Jean Margaret, da of Raymond Joseph Loveday (d 1965); 2 s (Robert b 1963, Stuart b 1968); *Career* radar fitter RAF 1950-55; BBC: joined 1955, head of Studio Engrg Servs TV 1980-86, head of resources Current Affairs Prodn Centre 1986-87, dep gen mangr resources news and current affairs 1987-90, broadcasting conslt 1990-; *Recreations* swimming, fishing, walking; *Style—* Donald McGregor, Esq; 69 Huntercombe Lane North, Slough, Berks SL1 6DX (☎ 0628 605473); BBC, Television Centre, Wood Lane, London W12 7RJ (☎ 081 576 1129, fax 081 743 7055, telex 265781)

McGREGOR, Gp Capt Douglas Rodric Howe; s of Air Marshal Sir Hector McGregor, KCB, CBE, DSO (d 1973), of Old Bosham, W Sussex, and Lady McGregor, *née* Jean Martin; *b* 29 Aug 1942; *Educ* Haileybury, RAF Coll Cranwell; *m* 7 Aug 1965, Jillian Mary, da of Wing Cdr George Frederick Edmund Loveridge, OBE, of Farnham, Surrey; 1 s (Stephen b 29 Nov 1970), 1 da (Clare b 14 Aug 1972); *Career* memb RAF Aerobatic Team 1966, Br Def Staff Washington 1980-83, CO RAF Brawdy 1984-86, cmd Allied Air Forces Central Europe 1986-89; MRAeS 1974; *Recreations* sailing, philately, music; *Clubs* RAF; *Style—* Gp Capt Douglas McGregor; Bulls Cottage, Old Bosham, West Sussex PO18 8LS (☎ 0243 572263); HQ 1 Group, RAF Upavon, Pewsey, Wilts

MACGREGOR, Sir Edwin Robert; 7 Bt (UK 1828), of Savile Row, Middlesex; s of Sir Robert James McConnell Macgregor, 6 Bt (d 1963); *b* 4 Dec 1931; *Educ* Univ of British Columbia; *m* 1, 1952 (m dis 1981), Margaret Alice Jean, da of Arthur Peake, of Haney, BC, Canada; 2 s (1 decd), 2 da; m 2, 1982, Helen Linda Herriott; *Heir* s, Ian Grant Macgregor; *Career* dep min of Crown Lands, Provincial Govt BC Canada; *Style—* Sir Edwin Macgregor, Bt; 6136 Kirby Rd, RR3, Sooke, BC V0S 1NO, Canada

McGREGOR, Dr Gordon Peter; s of William Arthur Kenney McGregor (d 1976), of Horfield, Bristol, and Mary Aloysius, *née* O'Brien (d 1978); *b* 13 June 1932; *Educ* St Brendan's Coll Bristol, Univ of Bristol (BA), Univ of Africa (MEd), Univ of Sussex (DPhil); *m* 10 Aug 1957, Jean Olga, da of William Henry Thomas Lewis (d 1984), of New Tredegar, Gwent; 3 da (Clare b 1958, Helen b 1962, Fiona b 1963); *Career* Flying Offr RAF (Educn Branch) 1953-56; asst master: Worcester Coll for the Blind 1956-59, Kings Coll Budo Uganda 1959-63, lectr in English language Makerere Univ Uganda 1963-66; Univ of Zambia: sr lectr in educn 1966-68, reader and head of Dept of Educn 1968-69, prof of educn 1970; princ: Bishop Otter Coll Chichester Sussex 1970-80, Univ Coll of Ripon and York St John 1980-; writer for: Times Higher Education Supplement, Church Times, Univs Quarterly, PNEU Journal; memb: Nat Cmmn UNESCO 1983-86, Voluntary Sector Consultative Cncl for Higher Educn 1985-88, Bd of Nat Advsy Body for Higher Educn 1986-88; memb: York Dist Health Authy 1982-86, Ct Univ of York, Ct Univ of Hull; Hon DLitt Ripon Coll Wisconsin USA 1986; FRSA 1976; *Books* King's Coll, Budo The First Sixty Years (1967), Educating the Handicapped (1967), English for Education? (1968), Teaching English as a Second Language (1970), English in Africa (1971), Bishop Otter College and Policy for Teacher Education, 1839-1980 (1981), A Church College for the 21st Century? 150 Years of Ripon and York St John (1991); *Recreations* literature, theatre, music, swimming, travel, writing; *Style—* Dr Gordon McGregor; Hollyhocks, High St, Selsey,

West Sussex (☎ 0904 623 745); The University College of Ripon and York St John, Lord Mayor's Walk, York YO3 7EX (☎ 0904 656 771)

MacGREGOR, Prof Graham A; s of Prof A B McGregor (d 1964), and Sybil, *née* Hawkey (d 1974); *b* 1 April 1941; *Educ* Marlborough, Trinity Hall Cambridge (MA, MB BChir), Middx Hosp; *m* 2 Nov 1968, Christiane, da of Maurice Bourquin (d 1956), of Switzerland; 1 s (Christopher b 6 Sept 1973), 2 da (Annabelle b 16 Nov 1970, Vanessa b 3 April 1972); *Career* dir Blood Pressure Unit (former sr lectr) Charing Cross and Westminster Med Sch 1979-89, prof of cardiovascular medicine and dir Blood Pressure Unit St George's Hosp Med Sch 1989-; FRCP 1982; *Books* Salt Free Diet Book (1985), Hypertension in Practice (1987); *Style*— Prof Graham MacGregor; Blood Pressure Unit, Dept of Medicine, St George's Hosp Med School, Cranmer Terrace, London SW17 0PE (☎ 081 784 2793, fax 081 682 2564)

McGREGOR, Harvey; QC (1978); s of William Guthrie Robertson McGregor, and Agnes, *née* Reid; *b* 25 Feb 1926; *Educ* Inverurie Acad, Scarborough Boys' HS, Queen's Coll Oxford (BA, BCL, MA, DCL) Univ of Harvard (Dr of Juridical Sci); *Career* Nat Serv 1944-48, Flying Ofr; called to the Bar Inner Temple 1955, bencher 1985, Bigelow teaching fell Univ of Chicago 1950-51, visiting prof NY Univ and Rutgers Univ 1963-69, conslt to Law Cmmn 1966-73, author of articles in legal jls; memb ed bd Modern Law Review 1986- (memb ed ctee 1967-86); dep ind chm London Theatre Cncl 1971-, tstee Oxford Union Soc 1977-, pres Harvard Law Sch Assoc of UK 1981-, fell Winchester Coll 1985-; *Books* McGregor on Damages (15 edn, 1988), International Encyclopaedia of Comparative Law (contrib, 1972), articles in legal journals; *Recreations* music, theatre, travel, sailing; *Clubs* Garrick; *Style*— Harvey McGregor, Esq, QC; The Warden's Lodgings, New College, Oxford OX1 3BN (☎ 0865 279555 fax 0865 279590); Gray's Inn Chambers, Gray's Inn, London WC1R 5JA; 4 Paper Buildings, Temple, London EC4Y 7EX (☎ 071 353 3366, fax 071 353 5778)

McGREGOR, Prof Sir Ian Alexander; CBE (1968, OBE 1959); s of John McGregor (d 1945), of Cambuslang, Lanarkshire, and Isabella, *née* Taylor (d 1974); *b* 26 Aug 1922; *Educ* Rutherglen Acad, and St Mungo Coll of Med, Glasgow (LRCPE, LRCSE, LRFPS Glas); *m* 30 Jan 1954, Nancy Joan, da of Frederick Herbert Small (d 1968), of Mapledurham, Oxfordshire; 1 s (Alistair b 1956), 1 da (Lesley b 1957); *Career* Capt RAMC 1946-48, served Palestine (despatches); scientific staff MRC 1949-84; Human Nutrition Res Unit 1949-53, dir MRC Laboratories Gambia W Africa 1954-73, head Laboratory for Tropical Community Studies Nat Inst for Med Res 1974-77, dir MRC Laboratories Gambia 1978-80, MRC external staff at Univ of Liverpool 1981-84, visiting prof Univ of Liverpool at Liverpool Sch of Tropical Med; memb: WHO Advsy Panel of Malaria 1960-, MRC Tropical Med Res Bd 1975-77 and 1981-83, Cncl of Liverpool Sch of Tropical Med 1982-; pres Royal Soc of Tropical Med and Hygiene 1983-85, chm WHO Expert Ctee on Malaria 1985-89; memb Cncl Royal Soc 1985-87 (chm Med Sciences Res Ctee 1988-, chm Ctee for Sci in Developing Countries 1988-), memb Ed Bd Annals of Tropical Paediatrics 1989; Chalmers medal of Royal Soc Tropical Med and Hygiene 1963, Stewart Prize in Epidemiology of BMA 1971, Darling Fndn medal and prize of WHO 1974, Laveran medal of Soc de Pathologie Exotique de Paris 1983, Glaxo prize for Med Writing 1989; Fred Soper lectr American Soc of Tropical Med and Hygiene 1983, Heath Clark lectr London Sch of Hygiene and Tropical Med 1983-84 (memb Ct of Govrs 1987-), Henry Cohen History of Med Lecture Univ of Liverpool 1989; hon memb: American Soc of Tropical Med and Hygiene 1984, Br Soc for Parasitology 1988-; Hon LLD Univ of Aberdeen 1983, Hon DSc Univ of Glasgow 1984; MRCP, FRCP, FFCM, FRS, FRSE, Hon FRCP&S (Glasgow); kt 1982; *Publications* Malaria - The Principles and Practice of Malariology (ed jtly, 1988); *Recreations* ornithology, fishing, travel; *Clubs* Royal Society of Medicine; *Style*— Prof Ian McGregor, CBE; The Glebe House, Greenlooms, Hargrave, Chester CH3 7RX (☎ 0829 40973); Liverpool Sch of Tropical Medicine, 3 Pembroke Place, Liverpool L3 5QA (telex 627095 UNIPLG)

MacGREGOR, Ian George Stewart; s of Charles MacGregor (d 1979), and Mary Brown, *née* Wallace (d 1978); *b* 29 Dec 1924; *Educ* Bell-Baxter Sch Fife, Univ of St Andrews, Univ of Edinburgh (MA, MEd), New York Univ (fellowship); *Career* asst princ Miny of France NI 1947-50, fellowship in educnl psychology New York Univ 1953-54, teacher Buckhaven High Sch Fife 1954-55 (1952-53), princ admin asst Edinburgh Educn Dept 1955-59, asst dir of educn Aberdeenshire 1959-64, sr dep dir of educn W Lothian 1964-70, rector Bathgate Acad 1970-88, ptnr MacGregor and Ptnrs 1988-; Scot HQ cmmr The Scout Assoc, memb Univ Ct Univ of Edinburgh, memb Ctee Glasgow and West of Scotland Outward Bound Assoc; FBIM; *Recreations* hill walking, photography, philately; *Clubs* Scottish Arts (Edinburgh), New Golf (St Andrews), Rotary (Bathgate); *Style*— Ian MacGregor, Esq; 20 Stewart Ave, Bo'ness, West Lothian EH51 9NL (☎ 0506 822462, fax 0506 847700)

MACGREGOR, Ian Grant; s & h of Sir Edwin Robert Macgregor, 7th Bt; *b* 22 Feb 1959; *Style*— Ian Macgregor Esq

MacGREGOR, Sir Ian Kinloch; s of Daniel MacGregor and Grace, *née* Maclean; *b* 21 Sept 1912; *Educ* George Watson's Coll Edinburgh, Hillhead High Sch Glasgow, Glasgow Univ (BSc); *m* Sibyl, *née* Spencer; 1 s (Ian), 1 da (Elizabeth (Mrs Bates)); *Career* chm and chief exec Amax Inc 1966-77 (hon chm 1977-82), dep chm BL Ltd 1977-80, ptnr Lazard Frères & Co New York 1978-88, pres Int C of C 1978, chm and chief exec Br Steel Corp 1980-83, chm NCB 1983-86; chm: Trusthouse Forte Inc 1988-, Hunter Print plc, Goldcrest Gp; tstee Glasgow Univ Tst; Hon DL, DEng, DSc, AIMMPE; Chev Legion d'Honneur (France) 1974; kt 1986; *Books* The Enemies Within (1986); *Recreations* fishing, gardening, reading, golf; *Clubs* RAC, Brooks's, Caledonian; *Style*— Sir Ian MacGregor; Castleton House, by Lochgilphead, Argyll PA31 8RU (☎ 0546 2185); 33/44 Brewer Street, London W1R 3HP (☎ 071 437 8696); 230 Park Avenue, New York, NY 10169 (☎ 0101 2129167473)

McGREGOR, Dr James Stalker; *b* 30 Oct 1927; *Educ* Dumfries Acad, Royal Tech Coll Glasgow (ARTC), Glasgow Univ (BSc, CEng); *m* 1953, Iris; 1 s; *Career* chm Honeywell Ltd 1981-, md Honeywell Control Systems Ltd 1971-87, chm Honeywell advsy cncl 1981-; Hon LLD Strathclyde Univ, MIMechE, CBIM; *Recreations* golf; *Style*— Dr James McGregor, Esq; Honeywell House, Charles Sq, Bracknell, Berks (☎ 0344 424555, telex 847064))

MACGREGOR, Joanna Clare; da of Alfred MacGregor, of North London, and Angela, *née* Hughes; *b* 16 July 1959; *Educ* South Hampstead Sch for Girls, New Hall Cambridge (BA), Royal Acad of Music (recital dip, Gold medallist), Van Cliburn Inst Texas (masterclasses with Jorge Bolet); *m* 1986, Richard Williams; *Career* pianist; appeared as soloist with RPO, LSO, Eng Chamber Orch (tours to Bermuda and USA incl Carnegie Hall), BBC Symphony Orch, BBC Orch Scot, City of London Sinfonia, Nat Youth Orch (prom 1990), London Mozart Players; Br Cncl tours: Senegal, Sierra Leone, Zimbabwe, The Phillipines, Norway; premiered works by Br composers incl: Michael Finnissy, Gary Carpenter, Alasdair Nicolson, Hugh Wood; recordings incl: American Piano Classics (1989), Satie Piano Music, Britten Piano Concerto (with Eng Chamber Orch and Stuart Bedford), Barber/Ives Sonatas; composer Br music for theatre and tv prodns incl: Cheek By Jowl, Oxford Stage Co, C4; author of fantasy play based on Erik Satie's Writings (BBC Entry Prix d'Italia 1990, Sony awards entry 1991), radio presenter for BBC Radio 3; *Style*— Ms Joanna MacGregor; David Sigall, Ingpen and Williams, 14 Kensington Court, London W8 5DN (☎ 071 937 5158, fax 071 938 4175)

MacGREGOR, Rt Hon John Roddick Russell; OBE (1971), PC (1985), MP (C) S Norfolk Feb 1974-; s of late Dr N S R MacGregor, of Shotts; *b* 14 Feb 1937; *Educ* Merchiston, Univ of St Andrews, King's Coll London; *m* 1962, Jean Dungey; 1 s, 2 da; *Career* univ admin 1961-62; former chm: Fedn of Univ Cons & Unionist Assocs, Bow Gp; first pres Cons and Christian Democratic Youth Community, currently with New Society and Hill Samuel (dir 1973-79); special asst to PM 1963-64, CRD 1964-65, head of Ldr of Oppn's Private Office 1965-68, oppn whip 1977-79, lord cmmr Treasy 1979-81, Parly under sec Trade and Indust with responsiblity for small businesses 1981-83, min state Agric Fisheries and Food 1983-85, chief sec Treasy 1985-87, min of Agric Fisheries and Food 1987-July 1989, sec of state for Educn July 1989-Nov 1990, Lord Pres of the Council and Leader of the Commons Nov 1990-; *Recreations* opera, gardening, travel, conjuring; *Style*— The Rt Hon John MacGregor, OBE, MP; House of Commons, London SW1A 0AA

MACGREGOR, His Hon John Roy; s of Charles George McGregor, of Jamaica and New York (d 1914); and Amy Lilla Isabelle, *née* Green (d 1962); *b* 9 Sept 1913; *Educ* Bedford Sch; *Career* WWII RA 1939-46, served ME (POW), RA (TA) and SAS (TA) 1950-61, Maj; called to the Bar Gray's Inn 1939, dep chm Cambs QS 1967-71, rec 1972-74, legal assessor to Gen Optical Cncl 1972-74, hon rec Margate 1972-79, circuit judge 1975-87; vice pres Clan Gregor Soc; *Clubs* Special Forces; *Style*— His Hon John Macgregor; Nether Gaulrig, Yardley Hastings, Northampton NN7 1HD (☎ 060 129 861)

MacGREGOR, (Robert) Neil; s of Alexander Rankin MacGregor, and Anna Fulton Scobie, *née* Neil; *b* 16 June 1946; *Educ* Glasgow Acad, New Coll Oxford, Ecole Normale Supérieure Paris, Univ of Edinburgh, Courtauld Inst of Art; *Career* memb Faculty of Advocates Edinburgh 1972, lectr in history of art and architecture Univ of Reading 1976, ed Burlington Magazine 1981-86, dir Nat gallery 1987-; *Style*— Neil MacGregor, Esq; The National Gallery, Trafalgar Sq, London WC2N 5DN (☎ 071 839 3321)

McGREGOR, Peter; s of Peter McGregor (d 1977), of Altafearn, Kames, Argyll, and Margaret Thomson, *née* McAuslan; *b* 20 May 1926; *Educ* Cardiff HS, Univ of Birmingham, LSE (BSc); *m* 4 Sept 1954, Marion Edith Winifred, da of Herbert Thomas Downer (d 1974), of Cardiff; 1 s (Iain Peter b 1955), 1 da (Fiona Janet b 1958); *Career* mangr Ferranti Ltd 1950-74, gen mangr Power Div 1970-74; dir: Industrie Elettriche di Legnano (Italy) 1970-74, Oxford Univ Business Summer Sch 1972 (memb Steering Ctee 1974-79); sec gen Anglo-German Fndn for the Study of Industrial Soc 1974-80, industl dir (dep sec) Nat Econ Devpt Office 1980-84, dir gen Export Gp for Constructional Industs 1984-, assoc dir Corp Renewal Assocs Ltd 1988-; former industl advsr to the Lib Pty, memb Konigswinter Conf Steering Ctee 1975-90, hon treas Anglo-German Assoc 1978-; FRSA, FIEE, CEng, FBIM, MCIM, Companion IProdE; *Recreations* gardening, walking, listening to music, sailing, reading; *Clubs* Caledonian; *Style*— Peter McGregor, Esq; EGCI, Kingsbury House, 15/17 King St, St James's, London SW1Y 6QU (☎ 071 930 5377)

MACGREGOR, Susan Katriona (Sue); da of Dr James McWilliam MacGregor, of Cape Town, and Margaret, *née* MacGregor; *b* 30 Aug 1941; *Educ* Herschel Sch Cape Town; *Career* programme presenter S African Broadcasting Corp 1962-67, BBC radio reporter (World at One, PM, World this Weekend) 1967-72; presenter BBC Radio 4: Woman's Hour 1972-87, Today 1985-, Conversation Piece (occasional series); Around Westminster BBC TV 1990; dir Hemming Publishing Ltd; FRSA; *Recreations* theatre, cinema, skiing; *Style*— Ms Sue MacGregor; c/o BBC, London W1A 1AA (☎ 071 927 5566)

McGREGOR, Hon William Ross; eld s of Baron McGregor of Durris (Life Peer); *b* 1948; *Educ* Haberdashers' Aske's Sch, Univ Coll London; *m* 1981 (separated 1987), Ann Holmes, da of Archibald MacGregor, of Fife, and wid of Matthew Johnson, of Edinburgh; 1 s (William Oliver James); *Style*— The Hon William McGregor; 6, Dura Park, Woodside, Glenrothes, Fife KY7 5EF

MACGREGOR-HASTIE, Prof Roy Alasdhair Niall; Japanese Name: Rekishi Inochi; s of Allan John Macgregor-Hastie (d 1972), and Winifreda Alexandra, *née* Simonska Walewska (d 1972); *b* 28 March 1929; *Educ* New Coll RMA Sandhurst, Univ of Manchester (BA), Univ of Iowa (MFA), Univ of Hull (MEd, PhD); *m* (m dis); 1 da (Cynthia Tamara b 1951), 2 s (Alasdair Niall b 1961, Robert Allan John b 13 Oct 1973); *Career* foreign correspondent (E Eur) Redatorial Brasil 1953-57 (Tokyo 1950-53, 1957-58 and 1966-68); reporter: and editor This Week ARTV 1958-60, ATV, Westward TV series, communist affrs Sunday Express 1959-64; UPI special projects 1964-65, European bureau chief RB 1965-66; sr lectr Hull Coll of Higher Educn 1968-77 (Humberside Poly), sabbatical US Hill Fndn Scholar 1971-72, prof mod Euro history Univ of Perugia 1977-80, prof Dept of Continuing Educn San Jose State Univ USA 1980-84, dean American Grad Sch in Euro 1984-86, prof Social History Osaka Gakuin Univ 1986-; memb: SNP, PEN, Mensa Japan; pres Brit Assoc for Romanian Studies (former sec), hon fell Univ of Iowa; *Books biography and history*: The Man from Nowhere (1960), The Red Barbarians (1961), Pope John XXIII (1962), Pope Paul VI (1966), The Throne of Peter (1967), The Day of the Lion - a History of Fascism (1964), Getting it Right (1990), Never to be Taken Alive (1985), Nell Gwyn (1987), History of Western Civilsation (1989); *travel*: The Compleat Migrant (1962), Dont Send Me to Omsk (1964), Signor Roy (1967), Africa (1968); *art history*: Picasso (1988); *poetry and criticism*: A Case for Poetry (1960), Interim Statement (1962), Eleven Elegies (1969), Frames (1972), The Great Transition (1975), Poems for Our Lord and Lady (1976), Poeme (1980); *UNESCO collection of rep works*: Eminescu, The Last Romantic (1972), Anthology of Contemporary Romanian Poetry (1969, 2 edn 1977, 3 edn 1982), Anthology of Bulgarian Poetry (1978), Eminescu Centennial Commem Volume (1989); *politics*: The Mechanics of Power (1966); *novels in translation*: The Gypsy Tribe (Nobel Prize short list, 1974); *Recreations* cooking, gardening; *Clubs* Reform, Chelsea Arts, Savage; *Style*— Prof Roy Macgregor-Hastie; Osaka Gakuin University, Department of International Studies, Kishibe, Suita, Osaka 564 Japan (☎ 06 381 8434, fax 078 308 3691)

McGREGOR OF DURRIS, Baron (Life Peer UK 1978), of Hampstead in Greater London; Oliver Ross McGregor; s of late William McGregor; *b* 25 Aug 1921; *Educ* Worksop Coll, Univ of Aberdeen, LSE; *m* 1944, Nellie, da of Harold Weate, of Manchester; 3 s (Hon William Ross b 1948, Hon Alistair John b 1950, Hon Gregor Weate b 1952); *Career* sits as SDLP peer in House of Lords; chm: Forest Philharmonic Orchestra, Advertising Standards Authy 1980-91, Press Complaints Commission 1991-; pres: Nat Cncl for One Parent Families, Nat Assoc of Citizens Advice Bureaux 1981-87; prof of social instns Univ of London 1964-85, head of Dept of Sociology Bedford Coll 1964-77, jt dir Rowntree Legal Research Unit 1966-85, dir Centre for Socio-Legal Studies Univ of Oxford 1972-75, fell Wolfson Coll Oxford 1972-75; ind tstee Reuters 1984-, chm Reuters Founders Share Co 1987-; hon fell LSE 1977-, Hon LLD Univ of Bristol 1986; *Clubs* Garrick; *Style*— The Rt Hon Lord McGregor of Durris; Far End, Wyldes Close, London NW11 7JB (☎ 081 458 2856); Press Complaints Commission, 1 Salisbury Square, London EC4Y 8AE

MacGREGOR OF MacGREGOR, Brig Sir Gregor; 6 Bt (GB 1795), of Lanrick, Co Perth; 23 Chief of Clan Gregor; s of Capt Sir Malcolm MacGregor of MacGregor, 5

Bt, CB, CMG, JP, DL, RN (d 1958), and Hon Gylla Rollo, OBE (d 1980), sis of 12 Lord Rollo; *b* 22 Dec 1925; *Educ* Eton; *m* 8 Feb 1958, Fanny, o da of Charles Hubert Archibald Butler, of Newport, Essex, sometime High Sheriff for that county; 2 s; *Heir* s, Capt Malcolm Gregor Charles MacGregor of MacGregor, yr; *Career* Scots Gds, served 1939-45, Palestine 1947-48, Malaya 1950-51, Borneo 1965; Staff Coll Course 1960; Jt Servs Staff Coll 1965; cmd 1 Bn Scots Gds 1966-69, Br Liaison Offr US Army Inf Centre 1969-71, Col 'A' Recruiting HQ Scotland 1971, Lt-Col cmdg Scots Gds 1971-74; def and mil attaché Br Embassy Athens 1975-78, cmd Lowlands 1978-80, ADC to HM The Queen 1979; Grand Master Mason of Scotland 1988-; memb Royal Co of Archers (Queen's Bodyguard for Scotland); *Clubs* Pratt's, New (Edinburgh); *Style*— Brig Sir Gregor MacGregor of MacGregor, Bt; Bannatyne, Newtyle, Angus PH12 8TR (☎ 082 85 314)

MacGREGOR of MacGREGOR, YOUNGER, Capt Malcolm Gregor Charles; s and h of Brig Sir Gregor MacGregor of MacGregor, 6 Bt, and Fanny MacGregor of MacGregor, *née* Butler; *b* 23 March 1959; *Educ* Eton; *m* 8 Oct 1988, Cecilia Margaret Lucy, er da of Sir Ilay Campbell of Succoth, 7 Bt; *Career* Capt Scots Gds, serv Hong Kong, NI, UK; *Recreations* travel, photography, tennis; *Style*— Malcolm MacGregor of MacGregor, younger; Bannatyne, Newtyle, Angus PH12 8TR (☎ 08285 314)

McGRIGOR, Sir Charles Edward; 5 Bt (UK 1831), of Campden Hill, Middx; DL (Argyll and Bute); s of Lt-Col Sir Charles Colquhoun McGrigor, 4 Bt, OBE (d 1946), and Amabel Caroline, *née* Somers-Cocks (d 1977); Sir James McGrigor, 1 Bt, KCB, was dir-gen Army Med Dept for thirty-six years and three times Lord Rector of Marischal Coll Aberdeen; *b* 5 Oct 1922; *Educ* Eton; *m* 7 June 1948, Mary Bettine, da of Sir Archibald Charles Edmonstone, 6 Bt (d 1954), of Duntreath Castle, Blanefield, Stirlingshire; 2 s (James b 19 Oct 1949, Charles b 7 Aug 1959), 2 da (Lorna b 18 Feb 1951, Kirsty b 3 Feb 1953); *Heir* s, James Angus Rhoderick Neil McGrigor; *Career* 2 Lt Rifle Bde 1942, Capt 1943, served in N Africa and Italy (despatches); ADC to HRH The Duke of Gloucester, KG 1945-47 (Australia and England); memb Royal Co of Archers (Queen's Body Guard for Scotland); Exon of the Queen's Body Guard of Yeomen of the Guard 1970-85; vice-pres, a dep chm and memb Ctee of Mgmnt RNLI; convenor Scottish Lifeboat Cncl; *Recreations* fishing, gardening; *Clubs* New (Edinburgh); *Style*— Sir Charles McGrigor, Bt, DL; Upper Sonachan, by Dalmally, Argyll (☎ 08663 229)

McGRIGOR, James Angus Rhoderick Neil; s and h of Sir Charles Edward McGrigor, 5 Bt; *b* 19 Oct 1949; *m* Caroline, da of late Jacques Roboh, of Paris; 2 da (Sibylla b 1988, Sarah b 1989); *Career* memb Royal Company of Archers (Queen's Body Guard for Scotland); *Recreations* fishing, shooting, travel, music, cinema; *Clubs* Turf, Chelsea Arts; *Style*— James McGrigor, Esq; Ardchonnel House, by Dalmally, Argyll PA33 1BW; 12 Upper Cheyne Row, London SW3

MCGROUTHER, (Duncan) Angus; *b* 3 March 1946; *Educ* Univ of Glasgow (MB ChB, MD), Univ of Strathclyde (MSc); *Career* Cruden med res fell Bioengineering Unit Univ of Strathclyde 1972-73, sr registrar in plastic surgery Canniesburn Hosp Glasgow 1976-78 (registrar 1975-76), assistentartz Klinikum rechts der Isar Munich 1978, hon clinical lectr Univ of Newcastle upon Tyne 1978-80; conslt plastic surgn: Northern RHA Shotley Bridge Gen Hosp 1979-80, Canniesburn Hosp Glasgow 1981-89; asst ed Journal of Hand Surgery 1987; examiner in anatomy Royal Coll of Physicians and Surgns of Glasgow; Br Assoc of Plastic Surgns: memb 1978, sec Sr Registrars Travelling Club 1978-79, memb Educn and Res Ctee 1982-84 (chm 1988-), memb Editorial Bd Br Journal of Plastic Surgery 1981-83, memb Cncl 1986-89; Br Soc for Surgery of the Hand: memb 1980, memb Cncl 1983-85, memb Editorial Bd 1983-85; Int Fedn of Socs for Surgery of the Hand: memb Flexor Tendon Injuries Ctee, memb Res Ctee, chm Dupuytren's Disease Ctee; chm Div of Plastic and Maxillofacial Surgery 1986-, chair plastic and reconstructive surgery UCL (newly created, funded by Phoenix Appeal) 1989-; FRCS 1973, FRCS Glasgow 1973; *Publications* contrib: Cleft Lip and Palate, Oral Surgery (1986), Microanatomy of Dupuytren's Contracture, Dupuytren's Disease (1986), Dupuytren's Disease, Methods and Concepts in Hand Surgery (1986), Surgery of the Thumb (with D A C Reid, 1986), Principles of Hand Surgery (with F D Burke and P Smith, 1989); author of numerous papers on hand and limb reconstructive surgery; *Recreations* skiing; *Style*— Prof D Angus McGrouther; Department of Plastic and Reconstructive Surgery, University College London, The Rayne Institute, University St, London WC1E 6JJ

McGUCKIAN, John Brendan; s of Brian McGuckian (d 1967), of Ardverna, Cloughmills, Ballymena, and Pauline, *née* McKenna; *b* 13 Nov 1939; *Educ* St McNissis Coll Garrontower, Queen's Univ of Belfast (BSc); *m* 22 Aug 1970, Carmel, da of Daniel McGowan, of Pharis, Ballyveeley; 2 da (Breige b 1977, Mary Pauline b 1989), 2 s (Brian b 1972, John b 1981); *Career* chm Cloughmills MFG Co 1967-; dir: Ulster TV plc 1970- (chm 1990-), Munster & Leinster Bank 1972-, Allied Irish Bank plc 1976-, Harbour GP Ltd 1978-, Aer Lingus plc 1979-84, Unidare plc 1987-, Irish Ferries plc 1988-; memb Derry Devpt Cmmn 1968-71; Laganside Corp 1988-, chm Int Fund for Ireland 1990-; pro chllr Queens Univ Belfast 1990-; *Style*— John B McGuckian, Esq; Ardverna, Cloughmills, Ballymena (☎ 0265 63 692); Lisgoole Abbey, Culkey, Enniskillen; 1 Ballycregagh Rd, Cloughmills, Ballymena (☎ 0265 63 692, fax 0265 63 754, telex 747603)

MCGUCKIAN, Maeve Therese Philomena (Medbh); da of Hugh Albert McCaughan, of Belfast, and Margaret, *née* Fergus; *b* 12 Aug 1950; *Educ* Fortwilliam Convent GS Belfast, Queen's Univ Belfast (open scholar, BA, MA, Dip Ed, TC); *m* June 1977, John McGuckian, s of John McGuckian; 3 s (John Lian b 23 April 1980, Hugh Oisin b 6 July 1982, Fergus Joseph Gregory b 20 March 1985), 1 da (Emer Mary Charlotte Rose b Aug 1989); *Career* teacher of Eng Fortwilliam Convent Belfast and St Patrick's Coll Belfast, writer in residence Queen's Univ Belfast, lectr in Eng St Mary's Trg Coll Belfast, visiting fell Univ of Calif Berkeley 1991; writer, pubns incl: Single Ladies (1980), Portrait of Joanna (1980), The Flower Master (1982), Venus and the Rain (1984), On Ballycastle Beach (1987), Two Women - Two Shores (1988); *awards* winner Nat Poetry Competition, Alice Hunt Bartlett award, Rooney prize for lit, Gregory award 1980, Irish memb Aosdana, winner Cheltenham poetry prize; memb: Cultural Rels Ctee (Dublin), Eng Soc Queen's Univ Belfast; *Style*— Mrs Medbh McGuckian; Henry Raddie, c/o Downview Avenue, Antrim Rd, Belfast TB15 4EZ

McGUFFIN, Prof Peter; s of Capt William Brown McGuffin, RD, of Uladh Seagrove Manor Rd, Seaview, IOW, and Melba Martha, *née* Burnison; *b* 4 Feb 1949; *Educ* Leeds Univ Med Sch (MB ChB), Univ of London (PhD); *m* 11 July 1972, Dr Anne Elizabeth Farmer, da of Alfred Lesly Farmer; 1 s (Liam b 1976), 2 da (Catrina b 1975, Lucy b 1978); *Career* house offr then registrar St James Univ Hosp Leeds 1972-77, registrar then sr registrar Bethlem Royal and Maudsley Hosp London 1977-79, MRC fell and lectr Inst of Psychiatry London 1979-82, visiting fell Washington Univ of St Louis MO 1981-82, MRC sr clinical fell, hon conslt and sr lectr Inst of Psychiatry and KCH London 1982-86, prof and head of dept of psychological med Univ of Wales Coll of Med; hon sec of res ctee Mental Health Fudn, memb sci ctee Assoc of Med Res Charities; FRCP 1988 (MRCP 1976), FRC Psych 1990 (MRC Psych 1978); *Books* The Scientific Principles of Psychopathology (with Shanks and Hodgson, 1984), A Psychiatric Catechism (with Greer, 1987), Schizophrenia: The Major Issues (with Bebbington, 1988); *Clubs* Lisvane Tennis; *Style*— Prof Peter McGuffin; Dept of Psychological Medicine, University of Wales College of Medicine, Heath Park, Cardiff CF4 4XN (☎ 0222 755944)

McGUFFOG, John Lee; s of Capt Donald McGuffog, of Rose Cottage, Little Bookham St, Little Bookham, Surrey, and Ethel Mary, *née* Lee; *b* 18 Aug 1945; *Educ* Wallington GS; *m* 1, 1971 (m dis 1976), Patricia Anne White; m 2, 6 March 1978, Penelope Jayne, da of Philip Gordon Lee, of Selve Cottage, Monksilver, Somerset; 1 da (Charlotte b 21 Feb 1979); *Career* surveyor 1963-, qualified chartered auctioneer 1968, chief surveyor Leonard W Cotton & Ptnrs 1969; Mann & Co (estate agents): joined 1972, dir 1975, chm commercial div 1985; main bd dir Countrywide Surveyors Ltd 1988-; memb Cranleigh and Dist Round Table 1978-86; memb City Owls (promoted by Worshipful Co of Chartered Surveyors); ARVA 1969, FRICS 1976, ACIArb 1979; *Recreations* fishing; *Clubs* Fernfell; *Style*— John McGuffog, Esq; Hillfield, Amlets Lane, Cranleigh, Surrey; Countrywide Surveyors Ltd, Cavendish House, Goldsworth Rd, Woking, Surrey (☎ 04862 22256, fax 0483 756 229, car 0836 263 823)

McGUINNESS, Anne Marie; da of Roland McGuinness, of 1 Cooldarragh Park North, Belfast BT14 6TL, and Eileen, *née* Fitzpatrick; *b* 29 Oct 1954; *Educ* St Dominic's HS Belfast, Queens Univ Belfast (MB BCh, BAO); *m* 10 March 1984, James William Park, s of James Boyd Park (d 1989), of Challis Lane, Braintree, Essex; 1 s (Oscar Boyd b 1988); *Career* sr house offr in accident and emergency Queen's Univ Belfast 1980-81, former registrar in surgery Royal Victoria Hosp Belfast (jr house offr 1979) and Ulster Hosp Dundonald Belfast, registrar in surgery Ards Hosp Newtownards Co Down 1982-84, conslt Royal Free Hosp 1987-; memb: BMA 1979, CSA 1986, Br Trauma Soc 1989; FMS (London) 1986, FRCS (Ed) 1983; *Recreations* swimming, music, art; *Style*— Miss Anne McGuinness; Accident & Emergency Dept, Royal Free Hospital, Pond St, London NW3 2QG (☎ 071 794 0500)

McGUINNESS, Maj-Gen Brendan Peter; CB (1986); s of Bernard McGuinness; *b* 26 June 1931; *Educ* Mount St Mary's Coll, Staff Coll Camberley, RCDS; *m* 1968, Ethne Patricia Kelly; 1 s, 1 da; *Career* Borneo (despatches 1966), Brig RA 1975, GOC Western Dist 1983-86; govr City Technol Coll Kingshurst, dir Engrg Employers' Assoc W Midlands; *Style*— Maj-Gen B P McGuinness, CB; The Old Rectory, 14 Whittington Rd, Worcester WR5 2JU

McGUINNESS, Dennis; s of William McGuinness, of Glasgow, and Jane Ross Henderson, *née* Hannah; *b* 20 Nov 1943; *Educ* Holyrood Secdy Sch; *m* 15 Sept 1964, Maureen Campbell, da of Andrew Gaughan (d 1972); 1 s (Dennis William Andrew b 1965), 2 da (Annjanette b 1966, Elaine b 1968); *Career* chm: Bremner plc, Carswell Ltd; chm Child and Family Tst; memb Stock Exchange 1973-; *Recreations* golf, swimming, football, horse racing; *Clubs* Bonnyton Golf; *Style*— Dennis McGuinness, Esq; The Rannoch, Peel Rd, Thorntonhall, Glasgow G74 5AG; Carswell Ltd, Stock Exchange House, 7 Nelson Mandela Place, Glasgow G2 1BU (car ☎ 0836 705248)

McGUINNESS, James Joseph; *see*: Nottingham, Bishop of (RC)

MACH, David Stefan; s of Joseph Mach, of Methil, Fife, Scotland, and Martha, *née* Cassidy; *b* 18 March 1956; *Educ* Buckhaven HS, Duncan of Jordanstone Coll of Art Dundee (Duncan of Drumfork travelling scholar, Dip in Art, Post Dip in Art, Pat Holmes Meml prize, SED minor and major prizes), RCA (MA, Royal Coll drawing prize); *m* 25 Aug 1979, Lesley June, da of William Ronald White; *Career* professional sculptor 1982-; exhibitions incl: British Sculpture '83 (Hayward Gallery London) 1983, Fuel for the Fire (Riverside Studio London) 1986, Int Iron Sculpture Symposium (Kitakyushu Japan) 1987, A Hundred and One Dalmations (Tate Gallery London) 1988, Five Easy Pieces (Barbara Toll Fine Art NY) 1989, Here to Stay (The Tramway Glasgow) 1990, Out of Order (Kingston-upon-Thames Surrey) 1990; video Clydedale Classic (Channel 4) 1980; one of two Br reps at Sao Paolo Biennale 1987, one of three Scottish reps at Venice Biennale 1990; nominated for Turner prize 1988; *Recreations* television, film, music; *Clubs* Chelsea Arts; *Style*— David Mach, Esq; 64 Canonbie Rd, Forest Hill, London SE23 3AG (☎ 081 699 1668)

MacHALE, Joseph Patrick; s of Seamus Joseph MacHale, and Margaret Mary, *née* Byrne (d 1982); *b* 17 Aug 1951; *Educ* Ampleforth, Queen's Coll Oxford (MA); *m* 28 Feb 1981, Maryann, da of Rear Adm David Dunbar-Nasmith, CB, DSC; 3 s (Henry b 1983, Martin b 1986, Thomas b 1990), 1 da (Laura b 1985); *Career* Price Waterhouse 1973-78, qualified CA 1976; joined JP Morgan Inc 1979, sr vice pres Morgan Guaranty Tst 1986-, md JP Morgan Securities Inc 1989; FCA 1978; *Clubs* Brooks's; *Style*— Joseph MacHale, Esq; 11 Red Coat Lane, Greenwich, CT 06830, USA

McHARDY, David Keith; s of Charles Stuart McHardy (d 1956), and Mary Isabella, *née* Laverick; *b* 29 Aug 1950; *Educ* Lord Wandsworth Coll Long Sutton Hampshire, PCL Univ of London (LLB); *m* Barbara Lillian, da of Donald Farley (d 1956); 2 s (Alexander b 27 Sept 1981, Nicholas b 31 July 1984); *Career* admitted slr 1978; ptnr Hutchins & Co 1979-; Slrs Family Law Assoc: chm Legal Aid Working Pty 1987-89 (memb 1985-89), nat chm 1989-91; memb Legal Aid Area Ctee Legal Aid Bd; memb Law Soc; *Recreations* golf, West Essex Golf; *Style*— David McHardy, Esq; 21 Chiltern Way, Woodford Wells, Essex IG8 0RQ (☎ 081 504 6440); Hutchins & Co, 85 Lower Clapton Rd, London E5 0NP (☎ 081 986 3911, fax 081 986 8252)

McHARDY, Dr (George Jamieson) Ross; s of Lt-Col William Sinclair McHardy (d 1940), of Linlithgow, W Lothian, and Esther George, *née* Ross; *b* 17 Nov 1930; *Educ* Wellington, Brasenose Coll Oxford (MA, MSc, BM BCh), Middx Hosp Med Sch, Johns Hopkins Univ Baltimore; *m* 17 Aug 1968, Dr Valentine Urie Dewar, da of Dr John Dewar (d 1968), of St Andrews, Fife; 2 s (Robert b 31 Jan 1970, Ian b 26 Jan 1972), 1 da (Margaret b 10 April 1974); *Career* Nat Serv Flt Lt RAF med branch 1959-60, High Altitude Res Unit RAF Inst Aviation Med Farnborough; house appts Middx Hosp London 1957-58, med registrar Middx and Hammersmith Hosp 1961-63, tutor in med Royal Postgrad Med Sch 1964-65, USPHS fell Johns Hopkins Univ Sch of Hygiene Baltimore 1965-66, conslt clinical respiratory physiologist Lothian Health Bd 1966-, conslt physician City Hosp Edinburgh 1966-, sr lectr (pt/t) Dept of Med Univ of Edinburgh 1966-; med advsr Fit for Life Campaign Scottish Sports Cncl 1977, pres Scottish Thoracic Soc 1986-88; chm: Educn Ctee Br Thoracic Soc 1986-89, Lothian Area Med Ctee 1988-, chm SE Regnl Ctee Postgrad Med Educn 1988-; memb: Med Appeals Tbnls, Cncl Br Lung Fndn 1990; memb RSM FRCP 1973, FRCPE 1970; *Books* Basic Techniques in Human Respiration and Metabolism (jtly, 1967); contrib: Davidson's Textbook of Medicine (10 edn, 1971-), Clinical Physiology (5 edn, 1984); sci papers on applied respiratory physiology and respiratory med in med jls; *Recreations* sailing, skiing, fishing; *Style*— Dr Ross McHardy; 6 Ettrick Rd, Edinburgh, Scotland EH10 5BJ (☎ 031 229 9026); Respiratory Medicine Unit, City Hospital, Greenbank Drive, Edinburgh EH10 5SB (☎ 031 447 1001 ext 3210)

MCHARDY-YOUNG, Dr Stuart; s of John McHardy-Young (d 1974), of Twickenham, Middx, and Violet Collin; *b* 20 Feb 1936; *Educ* St Paul's, Guy's Hosp Univ of London (MD, MB BS), Stanford Univ California USA; *m* 9 Sept 1961, Margaret Elizabeth, da of William Alan Cash (d 1949), of Eaglescliffe, Co Durham; 1 da (Catherine b 19 April 1978); *Career* post doctoral fell Stanford Univ Med Sch California 1967-68, sr lectr and hon conslt physician Guy's Hosp Med Sch 1970-72; conslt physician and endocrinologist: Central Middx Hosp 1972-, Royal Nat Throat Nose and Ear Hosp 1973-, Royal Masonic Hosp London 1982-; subdean St Mary's Hosp Med Sch London 1983-88; hon clinical sr lectr UCL 1973-; memb Br Diabetic Assoc, chm NW Thames

Regnl Med Manpower Cmmn (memb Central Ctee), former univ memb Brent Health Authy; memb: BMA, RSM; *Recreations* golf, travel; *Clubs* Royal Mid-Surrey Golf; *Style—* Dr Stuart McHardy-Young; 20 Belmont Rd, Twickenham, Middx TW2 5DA; 2 Hillview, Uplopers, Bridport, Dorset; 106 Harley St, London W1 (☎ 071 935 2797); Central Middlesex Hospital, London NW10

MACHARG, (John) Maitland; s of Walter Simpson Macharg (d 1945), of Glasgow, and Isabella Ure Elder, *née* Orr (d 1979); *b* 22 May 1928; *Educ* Glasgow HS, Strathallan Sch, Univ of Glasgow (MA); *m* 10 July 1961, Madeline, da of Sidney Yates (d 1979), of Weeke, Winchester; 2 s (Walter b 1962, Richard b 1964), 1 da (Mary Anne b 1965); *Career* Nat Serv 1947-49, 2 Lt RAEC BAOR; gen mangr and actuary Scottish Provident Institute 1970-88, dir Scottish Provident 1981-88, chm The Associated Scottish Life Office 1980-82; FFA 1954 (pres 1985-87), CBIM 1987; *Recreations* golf, skiing, gardening, hill walking; *Clubs* New (Edinburgh), Caledonian, Murrayfield GC; *Style—* Maitland Macharg, Esq; Champery, 215 Braid Rd, Edinburgh EH10 6NY (☎ 031 447 4105)

McHARG, Bt-Col William Wilson; OBE (1960), MC (1944), TD (1954), DL (Ayr 1970); s of Alexander McHarg (d 1956); *b* 29 Aug 1918; *Educ* Irvine Royal Acad, Univ of Glasgow; *m* 1947, Janet, *née* Gommer; 1 s, 1 da; *Career* Maj MEF, CMF, TA 1938-46 and 1947-61, Col; slr; racecourse mangr and clerk of the course; *Clubs* Ayr County; *Style—* Bt-Col William McHarg, OBE, MC, TD, DL; 29 Earls Way, Doonfoot, Ayr, Ayrshire KA7 4HF (☎ 0292 41350)

MACHELL, Dr Richard John; s of Richard Greville Kenneth Machell (d 1951), of Plymouth, and Muriel, *née* Harvey; *b* 3 Sept 1946; *Educ* Queen's Coll Taunton, Univ of London (MB BS, LRCP); *m* 10 May 1969, Elizabeth Joan Walter, da of John Ambrose Walter Reed (d 1950), of Feniton, Devon; 1 s (Jonathan b 9 May 1970), 2 da (Claire b 28 May 1971, Isabel b 12 April 1977); *Career* house offr Guy's Hosp 1969-70, sr house offr Univ of Southampton Hosps 1970-73, registrar Addenbrookes Hosp Cambridge 1973-76, lectr in medicine Univ of Cambridge 1976-80, conslt physician and gastroenterologist The Royal Cornwall Hosp 1980-; memb Br Soc of Gastroenterology 1977, chm Cornwall Gastrointestinal Cancer Appeal 1987-; Hon MA Univ of Cambridge 1977; MRCS, FRCP 1990; *Books* Cimetidine in the 1980s (1981); *Recreations* tennis, wind surfing, gardening; *Clubs* BSG; *Style—* Dr Richard Machell; The Royal Cornwall Hospital, Treliske, Truno, Cornwall (☎ 0872 74242)

MACHIN, David; s of Lt Cdr Noel Percy Machin, RN, ret, of Las Palmas, Canary Islands (d 1977), and Joan Evelyn Hildige (d 1959); *b* 25 April 1934; *Educ* Sunningdale Sch Berks, Eton, Trinity Coll Cambridge (MA); *m* 8 June 1963, Sarah Mary, da of Col William Alfred Chester-Master, DL, of Norcote House, Cirencester, Glos (d 1963); 2 da (Georgina b 1964, Alice b 1966); *Career* Nat Serv 1952, 2 Lt Welsh Gds served UK & Egypt; publisher's ed and literary agent William Heinemann Ltd and Gregson & Wigan Ltd 1957-68, ptnr A P Watt & Son 1968-70, dir Jonathan Cape Ltd 1970-78, gen sec Soc of Authors 1978-81, md The Bodley Head Ltd 1981-87; under treas elect Gray's Inn 1989-, vice chm Hammersmith Democrats 1988-89; *Recreations* reading, walking; *Clubs* Garrick; *Style—* David Machin; 4 South Square, Gray's Inn, London WC1R 5HP (☎ 071 831 3859)

MACHIN, Edward Anthony; QC (1973); s of Edward Arthur Machin (d 1958), of Finchley, London, and Olive Muriel, *née* Smith (d 1980); *b* 28 June 1925; *Educ* Christ's Coll Finchley, New Coll Oxford (BCL, MA); *m* 1953, Jean Margaret, da of Reginald McKanna (d 1972), of Epsom; 2 s (Timothy, Christopher), 1 da (Anna); *Career* Vinerian law scholar 1950, Tancred student 1950, Cassel scholar 1951; called to the Bar Lincoln's Inn 1951; rec Crown Ct 1976-90, judge Cts of Appeal of Jersey and Guernsey 1988; *Recreations* music, sailing (Kasta Loss), languages; *Clubs* Bar Yacht; *Style—* Anthony Machin, Esq, QC; Strand End, Strand, Topsham, Exeter (☎ 0392 87 7992); 1 Paper Buildings, Temple, London EC4 (☎ 071 583 7355)

MACHIN, (George) Ian Thom; s of Rev George Seville Machin (d 1950), of Heaton Moor, Stockport, Cheshire, and Mary Dunsmore Brown, *née* Thom (d 1981); *b* 3 July 1937; *Educ* Silcoates Sch Wakefield, Jesus Coll Oxford (MA, DPhil); *m* 2 April 1964, Dr Jane Margaret Pallot, da of Reginald Charles Pallot (d 1971), of Jersey, CI; 2 s (Jonathan b 1965, Raoul b 1969), 1 da (Anna b 1967 d 1981); *Career* asst lectr then lectr in history Univ of Singapore 1961-64, lectr in mod history Univ of St Andrews 1964-67, prof of Br history Univ of Dundee 1989- (lectr in mod history 1967-75, sr lectr 1975-82, reader 1982-89); treas Dundee branch Historical Assoc 1981-; FRHist S 1965; *Books* The Catholic Question in English Politics 1820 to 1830 (1964), Politics and the Churches in Great Britain 1832 to 1868 (1977), Politics and the Churches in Great Britain 1869 to 1921 (1987); *Recreations* the arts, hill-walking, swimming, learning languages; *Style—* Prof Ian Machin; 50 West Rd, Newport on Tay, Fife DD6 8HP (☎ 0382 543371); Dept of Modern History, The University, Dundee DD1 4HN (☎ 0382 23181 ext 4514)

MACHIN, Stephen James; s of Maj John Machin, of Sheffield, Yorks, and Edna, *née* Young; *b* 9 Nov 1954; *Educ* King Edward VII Sch Sheffield, Univ of Cambridge (MA, LLB); *m* 27 March 1978, Michaela, da of Oskar Maximillian Tomasch, of Vogau, Austria; 1 s (Alexander Peter b 22 April 1980), 1 da (Susannah Helan b 22 April 1982); *Career* admitted slr 1980; slr of Supreme Ct 1980, ARII 1982, ptnr Ashurst Morris Crisp 1987-; *Recreations* cricket, golf, squash, Sheffield Wednesday FC, music, playing piano; *Clubs* Tilford CC; *Style—* Stephen Machin, Esq; Ashurst Morris Crisp, Broadwalk House, 5 Appold St, London EC2A 2HA (☎ 071 638 1111, fax 071 972 7900, telex 887067, car 0831 420352)

McHUGH, Christopher John Patrick (Chris); s of Stanley Thomas McHugh, and Ann Agnes McHugh, *née* Maher; *b* 3 April 1945; *Educ* St John's RC Sch, City of Bath Tech Coll; *m* 9 Jan 1971, Frances Merla, da of Harry Stewart Townsend; 1 s (Daniel Thomas b 1972), 3 da (Georgina Ann b 1973, Annabel Carolyn b 1976, Claudia Jane b 1984); *Career* sr ptnr Chris McHugh & Co Financial Servs, dir St Lawrence Tst Ltd; *Recreations* most sports, horses, show jumping; *Clubs* BSJA, Conservative Assoc; *Style—* Chris McHugh, Esq; Burnt Ash House, Cirencester Road, Chalford, Stroud, Glos GL6 8PE; Willow Court, Beeches Green, Stroud, Glos GL5 8BJ (☎ 04536 70606, telex 43198 SWAGGY, fax 04536 70600)

McHUGO, (Christopher) Benedict; s of Christopher Lawrence McHugo (d 1987), and Doris May, *née* Bellringer; *b* 11 July 1949; *Educ* John Fisher Sch Purley, Wadham Coll Oxford (MA); *Career* Peat Marwick Mitchell 1971-76 (qualified CA 1974), called to the Bar Middle Temple 1978, Br Insurance Assoc 1980-85, corp taxation mangr Assoc of Br Insurers 1988; memb: The Catenian Assoc, BACFI; FCA (ACA 1974); *Recreations* travel, languages, cooking; *Style—* Benedict McHugo, Esq; Association of British Insurers, Aldermary House, Queen St, London EC4N 1TT (☎ 071 248 4477, fax 071 489 1120)

McHUGO, John Herbert Augustine; s of Christopher Lawrence McHugo (d 1987), of Coulsdon, Surrey, and Doris May, *née* Bellringer; *b* 13 July 1951; *Educ* John Fisher Sch Purley, Wadham Coll Oxford (MA, MLitt), The American Univ in Cairo (MA); *Career* admitted slr 1982; slr of the Supreme Court 1982, conslt (currently ptnr) Trowers & Hamlins 1984; author of various articles in legal pubns and learned jls; *Recreations* mountain walking, reading, writing, learning languages; *Clubs* Comrades of the Great War (Coulsdon); *Style—* John McHugo; 4 Bisenden Rd, Croydon, Surrey CR0 6UN; Trowers & Hamlins, 6 New Square, Lincoln's Inn, London WC2A 3RP (☎ 071 831 6292, fax 071 831 8700, telex 21422)

McILROY, Hon Mrs (Elizabeth Mary); da of 2 Baron Rochester; *b* 1951; *m* 1974, Thomas Meredith McIlroy; 3 s, 1 da; *Style—* The Hon Mrs McIlroy

McILROY, Harry Alexander; Baron di Novara; *b* 17 May 1940; *Educ* Swinton Coll; *m* 1971, Winifred; 1 s (Nicholas Henry Christopher), 1 da (Catherine Harriet); *Career* chm and owner Unico Gp Ltd; memb Int Financial Futures Exchange (Bermuda), underwriting memb of Lloyd's; Freeman City of London, Liveryman: Worshipful Co of Basketmakers, Worshipful Co of Marketers; FRSA, FInstM; *Clubs* Carlton, City Livery, E India; *Style—* Harry McIlroy, Esq

MCILROY, Ian; *b* 28 Dec 1947; *Educ* Glasgow Sch of Art (DA); *m* Diane Elizabeth, *née* Murray; 1 s (Sean b 30 June 1983); *Career* worked for: J & P Coats and William Collins 1972-79, Tayburn Design Group 1979-81; formed McIlroy Coates 1981; recent clients incl: Kwik-Fit, The Nat Galleries of Scotland, The Design Cncl, The Clydesdale Bank; awards incl: Design Annual award of excellence 1984, D & ADA 1980, 1982, 1983, 1990, Br Letterhead Awards 1981 and 1985, Scottish Designer of the Year runner up 1984, Scottish Annual Repost prize 1988 and 1989; visiting lectr in graphic design Duncan of Jordanstone Coll of Art Dundee; memb: CSD 1980, D & ADA 1980; *Style—* Ian McIlroy, Esq; McIlroy Coates Ltd, 10 Bernard St, Leith, Edinburgh EH6 6PP (☎ 031 555 1342, fax 031 555 1343)

MCILVANNEY, William Angus; s of William Angus McIlvanney (d 1955), and Helen Crawford, *née* Montgomery; *b* 25 Nov 1936; *Educ* Kilmarnock Acad, Univ of Glasgow; *m* 1961 (m dis 1982), Moira Watson; 1 s (Liam b 1969), 1 da (Siobhan b 1967); *Career* asst teacher of English 1960-68, housemaster 1968-70, princ teacher of Eng 1971-72, asst headmaster 1972-78; writer; novels: Remedy is None (1966), A Gift From Nessus (1968), Docherty (1975), Laidlow (1977), The Papers of Tony Veitch (1983), The Big Man (1985); poetry: The Longships in Harbour (1970), Landscapes and Figures (1973), These Words: Weddings and After (1983), In Through the Head (1988); short stories Walking Wounded (1989); Geoffrey Faber Meml award 1966, Scot Arts Cncl publication award 1968, Whitbread prize 1975, Silver Dagger award 1977 and 1983, The People's prize Glasgow Herald 1990; *Style—* William McIlvanney, Esq; Vivienne Schuster, John Farquharson and Curtis Brown, 162-68 Regent St, London

McILWAIN, Alexander Edward; CBE (1985); s of Edward Walker McIlwain (d 1974), of Aberdeen, and Gladys Edith, *née* Horne; *b* 4 July 1933; *Educ* Aberdeen GS, Univ of Aberdeen (MA, LLB); *m* 14 July 1961, Moira Margaret, da of William Kinnaird (d 1951), of Aberdeen; 3 da (Karen b 5 March 1963, Shona b 6 Feb 1967, Wendy b 17 March 1969); *Career* Lt RCS 1957-59; dist prosecutor Hamilton 1975-76 (burgh prosecutor 1967-75), dean Soc of Slrs Hamilton and Dist 1981-83, Hon Sheriff of S Strathclyde Dumfries and Galloway at Hamilton 1981- (temp Sheriff 1984-); sr ptnr Leonards (slrs) Hamilton 1984-, WS 1985-; sec Lanarkshire Scout Assoc 1967-81, chm Lanarkshire Scout Area 1981-, memb Lanarkshire Health Bd 1981-, hon memb American Bar Assoc 1983-, pres Law Soc of Scotland 1983-84, memb Central Advsy Ctee on JP's 1985-, chm Legal Aid Central Ctee 1985-87; memb: Scout Cncl 1986-, Supreme Ct Ctee Scottish Legal Aid Bd 1987-; SSC 1966; *Recreations* gardening, reading, listening to music; *Clubs* New (Edinburgh); *Style—* A E McIlwain, Esq, CBE; 7 Bothwell Rd, Uddingston, Glasgow (☎ 0698 813368); Leonards, 133 Cadzow St, Hamilton, Strathclyde (☎ 0698 457313)

MACILWAINE, Bruce Rodney; *b* 6 April 1945; *Educ* Salton Valence Sch Kent; *Career* Bank of London and South America (BOLSA): int pre-trainee 1963-66, int mgmnt trainee 1967-69, account mangr 1969-70; mangr CIA Financiera de Londres Argentina 1970-71; Lloyds Bank International (formed after Lloyds Bank acquired BOLSA): banking offr rising to vice pres NY and Chicago 1971-76, vice pres and mangr Corp Foreign Exchange & Money Markets NY 1977-78, vice pres & mangr Pittsburgh 1979-82, princ mangr Japan 1982-86; chief mangr Office of the Dir International Banking Division (formed after merger with Lloyds Bank International) Lloyds Bank London 1986-89, md Manchester Exchange & Investment Bank 1989-; *Recreations* scuba diving, skiing, riding, exercise, travel; *Style—* Bruce MacIlwaine, Esq; 4 Peel Street, Kensington, London W8 7PD (☎ 071 727 5182, office 071 356 2103)

MacILWAINE, David Robin; s of Robin MacIlwaine, and Anne MacIlwaine (d 1967); *b* 16 Dec 1947; *Educ* Rydens Sch Walton upon Thames, Univ of Leicester (BA); partner, Rose Gray; 1 s (Dante MacIlwaine Gray b 1973), 3 step c (Hester Gray b 1963, Lucy Gray b 1964, Ossie Gray b 1965); *Career* Christies Contemporary Art 1986-89, sculpture and painting dir Berkeley Square Gallery 1989-; *Recreations* sculpting; *Style—* David MacIlwaine, Esq; Berkely Square Gallery, 23A Bruton St, London W1X 7DA (☎ 071 493 7939, fax 071 493 7798)

McILWRAITH, Dr George Robert; s of Alexander Herd McIlwraith (d 1971), of Ruislip, Middx, and Kathleen Joan, *née* Heaton; *b* 15 July 1941; *Educ* Merchant Taylors', Univ of St Andrews (MB ChB); *m* 24 July 1982, Isabel Margaret, da of Harry Jack Manwaring (d 1988), of Collier St, Marden, Kent; 1 s (Harry Alexander b 1987); *Career* various jr appts in UK hosps; asst prof of internal med Pulmonary Div Univ of Michigan Med Sch USA 1979-80, conslt physician Maidstone Dist Hosps 1981-; author of pubns, chapters, papers and articles on cardiological and respiratory med matters; memb: Br Thoracic Soc, Br Geriatric Soc; FRCP 1988; *Style—* Dr George McIlwraith; Noah's Ark Farmhouse, East Sutton Rd, Headcorn, Ashford, Kent TN27 9PS (☎ 0622 891278); The Maidstone Hospital, Hermitage Lane Barming, Maidstone, Kent (☎ 0622 729000)

MCINALLY, James Edward (Jim); s of Archibald McInally, of Glasgow, and Agnes, *née* Adamson; *b* 19 Feb 1964; *Educ* St Margaret Mary's Secdy Sch; *m* 15 June 1985, Alison; 1 da (Laura b 21 Feb 1988); *Career* professional footballer; 4 appearances Celtic, 12 appearances on loan Dundee, 42 appearances Nottingham Forest, 5 appearances Coventry City; currently over 200 appearances Dundee Utd; Scotland caps: 16 youth, 1 under 21, 4 full; *Recreations* golf, watching movies; *Style—* Jim McInally, Esq; Dundee United FC, Tannadice Park, Dundee (☎ 0382 833166)

McINDOE, Lady Felicity Aileen Ann; *née* Stopford; 3 da of 8 Earl of Courtown, OBE, TD, DL (d 1975) (but sole da by his 2 w Rt Hon Patricia, Countess of Courtown; *b* 17 Dec 1951; *m* 1, 1977 (m dis 1981), Leslie Edward Archer-Davis; resumed name Stopford; m 2, 1982, (John) Andrew Barr McIndoe; 1 s (Harry b 1985); *Style—* The Lady Felicity McIndoe; 9 Franche Court Rd, London SW17 (☎ 081 946 9872)

McINDOE, William Ian (Bill); CB (1978); s of John McInoe, MM (d 1982); *b* 11 March 1929; *Educ* Sedbergh, Corpus Christi Coll Oxford; *m* 1, 1954, Irene Armour Mudie (d 1966); 3 c; m 2, 1971, Jamesanna Smart, *née* MacGregor; *Career* Nat Serv 2 Lt RHA 1951-53; HM Dip Serv: joined 1953, served in Canberra and Salisbury 1956-62, private sec to Sec of State 1962-63, private sec to Sec of Cabinet then asst sec Cabinet Office 1963-66, Scottish Office 1966-76 (under sec 1971); dep sec: Cabinet Office 1976-79, DOE 1979-86; dep chm Housing Corp 1986-90; *Recreations* golf; *Clubs* New (Edinburgh); *Style—* Bill McIndoe, Esq, CB; Speedyburn House, Station Rd, Gifford, E Lothian EH41 4QL (☎ 062 081 363)

MCINNERNY, Tim; s of William Ronald McInnerny, and Mary Joan, *née* Gibbings; *b* 18 Sept 1956; *Educ* Marling Sch Stroud Glos, Univ of Oxford (BA); *Career* actor;

theatrical performances incl: Lorenzaccio Story (Edinburgh Festival), Freddie in Pygmalion (Glasgow Citizens Theatre), Lyssipus in The Maid's Tragedy (Glasgow Citizens Theatre), Derek in Once A Catholic (Leicester Haymarket), Keith in Local Affairs, Laertes in Hamlet, Sir Benjamin in School for Scandal (Leicester Haymarket), Paul in Valued Friends (Hampstead Theatre), Frankenfurter in The Rocky Horror Show (Piccadilly Theatre); Royal Exchange Manchester: Clitandre in The Misanthrope, Gately in PVT Wars, Charlie in The Detective Story, Billy Bibbett in One Flew Over The Cuckoos Nest, Mick in The Caretaker, Orsino in Twelfth Night, The Kid in The Unseen Hand, Roy in Lone Star; NT: Waiter in The Government Inspector, Andrew May in Pravda, Hamlet in Hamlet; TV appearances incl: Black Adder, Blackadder II, Blackadder Goes Forth, Edge of Darkness, Sherlock Holmes, A Very British Coup, Shadow of the Noose, August Saturday, The Comic Strip Presents; films: John Morgan in Wetherby, Sven in Erik The Viking; *Recreations* acting; *Style—* Tim McInnerny, Esq; Sally Hope, Hope & Lyne, 108 Leonard Street, London EC2A 4RH (☎ 071 739 6200, fax 071 739 4101)

MacINNES, Archibald; CVO (1977); s of Duncan MacInnes (d 1987), of Gourock, and Catherine, *née* MacDonald (d 1970); *b* 10 April 1919; *Educ* Kirkcudbright Acad, Royal Tech Coll Glasgow; *m* 10 June 1950, Nancey Elizabeth (d 1976), da of Alec Blyth (d 1958), of Wivenhoe; 1 s (Duncan John b 1955), 2 da (Morag Catherine b 1951, Fiona Margaret b 1960); *Career* Scotts Shipbuilding and Engrg Co Greenock 1938-45, HMOCS Nigeria 1945-59; WO: cmd works offr Gibraltar 1959-63, supt engr Southern Cmd Wilton 1963-64; supt engr MPBW Bristol 1964-68, cmd works offr DOE Germany 1968-72, dir London Region PSA 1972-79, under sec 1973, conslt planning inspr DOE 1980-89; CEng, FIMechE, FBIM; *Recreations* fishing, shooting, golf, rugby supporter; *Clubs* Civil Service, Salisbury RFC, High Post Golf; *Style—* Archibald MacInnes, Esq, CVO; New House, Lower Rd, Homington, Salisbury SP5 4NG (☎ 072 277 336)

McINNES, Prof Edward; s of Rev William McInnes, and Sophia, *née* O'Hara; *b* 5 July 1935; *Educ* Renfrew HS, Greenock Acad; *m* 4 July 1964, Jean Robertson, da of David Kilgour; 1 s (Iain William b 26 Oct 1972), 3 da (Katharine Margaret b 11 Aug 1965, Alison Jane b 5 Dec 1967, Fiona Elizabeth b 23 March 1969); *Career* asst lectr in German King's Coll London 1961-62; Univ of Edinburgh: asst lectr in German 1962-64, lectr 1964-73, reader 1973-74; prof of German: Univ of Strathclyde 1974-79, Univ of Hull 1979-; *Books* German Today (with A J Harper, 1967), German Social Drama 1840-1900: From Hebbel to Hauptmann (1976), J M R Lenz: Die Soldaten (1977), Das Deutsche Drama des 19 Jahrhunderts (1983), Ein Ungeheures Theater, The Drama of the Sturm und Drang (1987), German in Society (1989), The Critical Reception of Charles Dickens in Germany 1837-1870 (1990), J M R Lenz: Der Hofmeister (1991), Sozialgeschichte der deutschen Literatur (with G Plumpe et al, 1991); *Recreations* reading theology, walking the dog, supporting Hull City; *Style—* Prof Edward McInnes; University of Hull, Cottingham Rd, Hull (☎ 0482 46311)

MacINNES, Hamish; OBE (1980), BEM (1965); s of Duncan MacInnes, of Gourock, Renfrewshire (d 1987), and Catherine, *née* MacDonald (d 1967); *b* 7 July 1930; *Educ* Gatehouse of Fleet Public Sch; *Career* writer, mfr, advsr on films and mountain rescue; designer: mountain rescue stretchers (used internationally), first all metal ice axe, terodactyl climbing tools; dep ldr Everest SW Face Expedition 1975 (taken part on 20 other expeditions to various parts of the world), special advsr to BBC and feature films in many countries, hon pres Search and Rescue Dog Assoc, former pres Alpine Climbing Gp, ldr Glencoe Mountain Rescue Team, hon memb Scottish Mountaineering Club; Hon DSc Univ of Aberdeen 1988, hon dir Leishman Res Laboratory; Hon LLD Univ of Glasgow; *Style—* Hamish MacInnes, Esq, OBE, BEM; Achnacone, Glencoe, Argyll (☎ 08552 258)

McINNES, Sheriff John Colin; QC (1989); s of Ian Whitton McInnes (d 1976), of Cupar, Fife, and Lucy Margaret, *née* Wilson; *b* 21 Nov 1938; *Educ* Cargilfield Sch Edinburgh, Merchiston Castle Sch Edinburgh, Brasenose Coll Oxford (BA), Univ of Edinburgh (LLB); *m* 6 Aug 1966, Elisabeth Mabel, da of Hugh Royden Neilson, of Kelso, Roxburghshire; 1 s (Ian b 1969), 1 da (Iona b 1972); *Career* 2 Lt 8 RTR 1956-58, Lt Fife and Forfar Yeo Scottish Horse TA 1958-64; advocate in practice Scottish Bar 1963-72, dir R Mackness & Co Ltd 1963-70, tutor Univ of Edinburgh 1964-72, chm Fios Group Ltd (continental quilt manufacturers) 1970-72; memb Ct Univ of St Andrews 1983-91, chm Fife Family Conciliation Serv 1988-90, vice pres Security Serv Tbnl 1989-; Sheriff: Lothians and Peebles 1973-74, Tayside Central and Fife 1974-; *Books* Divorce Law and Practice in Scotland; *Recreations* fishing, shooting, skiing, photography; *Style—* Sheriff John McInnes, QC; Parkneuk, Blebocraigs, Cupar, Fife KY15 5UG; Sheriff Court, Cupar, Fife (☎ 0334 52121); Sheriff Court, Perth (☎ 0738 20546)

MacINNES, Keith Gordon; CMG (1984); s of Kenneth Lionel MacInnes, CBE (d 1989), and Helen, da of Sir (Archibald) Douglas Gordon, CIE (d 1966); *b* 17 July 1935; *Educ* Rugby, Trinity Coll Cambridge (MA); *m* 1, 1966 (m dis 1980), Jennifer Anne Fennell; 1 s (Alexander b 1970), 1 da (Francesca b 1968); m 2, 9 March 1985, Hermione Ann Felicity Pattinson, 2 step s (Kyle b 1968, Rupert b 1970); *Career* diplomat; ambass to the Philippines; *Recreations* bridge, chess, golf, tennis; *Clubs* Manila Polo, Manila Golf and Country; *Style—* Keith MacInnes, Esq, CMG; c/o FCO (Manila), King Charles St, London SW1A 2AH

MCINROY, Alan Roderick; s of Charles Alan McInroy (d 1932), of St Mary's Tower, Birnam, Perthshire, and Marjory, *née* Walford (d 1981); *b* 6 June 1920; *Educ* Loretto, Hertford Coll Oxford; *m* 6 Jan 1966, Daphne Eileen Wells, da of Sir Eric Weston (d 1976), of The Manor, Moreton Pinkney, Northants; *Career* RA served ME 1940-42, Italy (POW) 1942-43, Germany (POW) 1943-45, Palestine 1946-48; ptnr Scott-Moncrieff Thomson & Shiells CA 1953-59, mangr American Trust Ltd 1959-69, md Edinburgh Fund Managers plc 1969-84; chm: McInroy & Wood Ltd 1986-, First Tokyo Index Tst plc, Edinburgh Oil & Gas plc; dir Noble Grossart Holdings Ltd; chm Haddington Citizens Advice Bureau 1983-88; memb Soc Investmt Analysts 1963; MICA 1951; *Recreations* golf, music; *Clubs* New (Edinburgh), Hon Co of Edinburgh Golfers, Club de Golf Valderrama (Spain); *Style—* Alan McInroy, Esq; Muirfield Green, Gullane, East Lothian EH31 2EG (☎ 0620 842175)

MACINTOSH, Alexander James; s of Edward Hyde Macintosh, CBE (d 1970) of Rebeg House, Kirkhill, Inverness-Shire, and Doreen O'Hara *née* Cross; *b* 5 Oct 1931; *Educ* Stowe, Trinity Coll Cambridge (MA); *m* 12 June 1965, Jane Wigham, da of Michael Finch Wigham Richardson (d 1988), of Downton, Wiltshire; 2 s (Jonathan b 1968, Marcus b 1970); *Career* cmmnd Seaforth Highlanders 1950; numerous directorships incl: Cunard Steam Ship Co plc and subsidiaries 1985-, Associated Container Transportation Ltd and subsidiaries 1985-, The Port of London Authority 1980-, Ellerman Group Ltd 1987-, Heavylift Cargo Airlines Ltd 1985-, Gen Cncl of British Shipping Ltd 1987-, British Shipping Federation Ltd 1987-, Ben Line Containers Ltd 1987-, H E Moss & Co Ltd 1987-; *Recreations* country pursuits; *Style—* Alexander Macintosh, Esq; 29 Richborne Terrace, London SW8 1AS (☎ 01 735 4399); Cunard Ellerman Ltd, 12-20 Camomile Street, London EC3A 7EX (☎ 071 283 4311, fax 071 283 1767, telex 884771/2); Station Farm, South Leigh, Near Witney, Oxfordshire OX8 6XJ (☎ 0993 704492)

McINTOSH, (Alastair) Bruce; s of Robert Ian Fanshawe McIntosh (d 1988), of Budleigh Salterton, Devon, and Jane, *née* Rought; *b* 25 Feb 1958; *Educ* Winchester, Cambridge Univ (MA); *Career* SG Warburg Group plc 1984-89, dir John Govett and Co Ltd 1989-90; *Style—* Bruce McIntosh, Esq; 7 Steeles Rd, London NW3 4SE (☎ 071 586 6643)

MCINTOSH, David A; *b* 10 March 1944; *Career* admitted slr Supreme Ct of Eng and Wales 1969, sr ptnr Davies Arnold Cooper 1976- (ptnr 1969-); memb: Jt Working Ctee of Senate of the Bar and Law Soc (made recommendations to Lord Chllr on proposed US/UK Reciprocal Enforcements Convention and allied jurisdictional matters), Law Soc's Working Pty (made recommendations in context of Lord Chllr's Review of Civil Justice with regard to personal injury litigation), Int Bar Assoc (sec Ctee S On Consumer Affairs, Advertising, Unfair Competition and Products, Liability, chm Disaster Litigation Worldwide Prog Strasbourg 1989), Soc of Eng and American lawyers, US Int Assoc of Defence Counsel and of its Excess and Reinsurance Product Liability and Toxic and Hazardous Substances Litigation Ctees, Def Res and Trial Lawyers Assoc of America; Int assoc memb American Bar Assoc, ACIArb; author of numerous pubns in learned jls; *Style—* David McIntosh, Esq; Davies Arnold Cooper, 6-8 Bouverie St, London EC4V 8DD

MCINTOSH, David Angus; s of Robert Angus McIntosh, of Scotland, and Monica Joan Sherring, *née* Hillier; *Educ* Selwood Co Sch Frome Somerset; *m* 14 Sept 1968, Jennifer Mary, da of Jack Dixon, of Mill Hill, London; 2 da (Sarah Alison b 1973, Louise b 1978); *Career* clerk Ames Kent & Rathwell Somerset, articled clerk Davies Arnold Cooper 1964, admitted slr 1968, sr ptnr Davies Arnold Cooper 1976 (ptnr 1968); served on various Law Soc Working Parties concerned with Reform and Admin of Civil Law; Freeman City of London, Liveryman Blacksmiths Co; memb Law Soc of England and Wales, Int Bar Assoc, Int Assoc of Def Cncl, CIArb; *Books* regular contributor to legal, insurance, and pharmaceutical journals; *Recreations* golf, fitness; *Clubs* Chigwell Golf, Barbican Health and Fitness Centre, City Livery; *Style—* David McIntosh, Esq; Spareleaze Lodge, 1 Spareleaze Hill, Loughton, Essex; 12 Bridewell Place, London EC4V 6AD (☎ 071 353 6555, fax 071 353 0574, telex 262894)

MACINTOSH, Dr Farquhar; CBE (1982); s of John Macintosh (d 1938), of Elgol, Isle of Skye, and Kate Ann, *née* Mackinnon (d 1975); *b* 27 Oct 1923; *Educ* Portree HS Skye, Univ of Edinburgh (MA), Univ of Glasgow (DipEd); *m* 19 Dec 1959, Margaret Mary Inglis, da of James Inglis Peebles (d 1965); 2 s (John James, Kenneth Donald), 2 da (Ann Mary, Ailsa Kate); *Career* joined RN 1944, cmmnd Sub Lt RNVR 1944, serving in the Far East; teacher of history Greenfield Jr Secdy Sch Hamilton 1951-52, history master Glasgow Acad 1953-59, princ teacher of history Inverness Royal Acad 1959-62, headmaster Portree HS 1962-66, rector Oban HS (headmaster) 1967-72, rector Royal HS Edinburgh 1972-89; regular contributor: The Times Scottish Educnl Supplement, The Scotsman, The Glasgow Herald; memb: Skye Hosps Bd of Mgmnt 1963-66, Oban Hosps Bd of Mgmnt 1968-72, Aberdeen Coll of Educn Governing Body 1961-66, Jordanhill Coll of Educn Glasgow 1967-72 (chm 1970-72), Highlands and Islands Devpt Consultative Cncl 1965-82 (chm Educn Sub Ctee 1968-82); sec Gaelic Soc of Inverness 1960-62; chm: Scot Assoc for Educnl Mgmnt and Admin 1980-83, Scot Examination Bd 1977-90, Sch Broadcasting Cncl Scot 1980-85; DLitt Heriot Watt Univ 1980, FEIS Conferred by Educnl Inst of Scotland 1970; memb: Educ Inst of Scot, Headmasters' Conference, Headmasters' Assoc of Scot, Scot History Soc, An Comunn Gaidhealach; *Recreations* hill-walking, sea-fishing, Gaelic; *Clubs* Rotary (Murrayfield-Cramond), East India; *Style—* Dr Farquhar Macintosh, CBE; 12 Rothesay Place, Edinburgh EH3 7SQ (☎ 031 225 4404)

McINTOSH, Hon Francis Robert; er s of Baron McIntosh of Haringey (Life Peer), *qv*; *Educ* Highgate Wood Sch London, London Coll of Furniture; *m* Tamsin Jane, *née* Hardman; *Style—* The Hon Francis McIntosh

McINTOSH, Ian Alexander Neville; s of Alexander McIntosh (d 1990), of Heaton, Bradford, W Yorks, and Marie Josephine, *née* Lester; *b* 24 Sept 1938; *Educ* Bradford GS, Univ of Edinburgh (MA); *m* 26 June 1965, Gillian Mary Sophia, da of Harold John Cropp (d 1984); 1 s (Angus b 15 June 1975), 1 da (Fiona b 3 June 1971); *Career* CA; Armitage & Norton 1959-63, Coopers & Lybrand 1963-69, Samuel Montagu & Co Ltd 1969- (dir 1972-, dep chief exec 1989-); memb Quotations Ctee of Int Stock Exchange; Liveryman Worshipful Co of Goldsmiths; FCA 1963; *Recreations* golf, tennis; *Clubs* MCC, Mid Herts Golf, RAC; *Style—* Ian McIntosh, Esq; Samuel Montagu & Co Ltd, 10 Lower Thames St, London EC3R 6AE (☎ 071 260 9301, fax 071 623 5512)

McINTOSH, Vice Adm Sir Ian Stewart; KBE (1973, MBE 1941), CB (1970), DSO (1944), DSC (1942); s of Alexander James McIntosh (d 1973), of Melbourne, Aust; *b* 11 Oct 1919; *Educ* Geelong GS; *m* 1943, Elizabeth Rosemary, da of Albert Henry Rasmussen, of Aalesund, Norway; 3 s (1 da decd); *Career* joined RN 1938, Capt 1959, Rear Adm 1968, dir-gen Weapons (Naval) MOD 1969-70, Vice Adm 1970, dep CDS (Operational Requirements) MOD 1970-73, ret; conslt Alexander Hughes and Assocs 1973-78; *Style—* Vice Adm Sir Ian McIntosh, KBE, CB, DSO, DSC; 19 The Crescent, Alverstoke, Hants

McINTOSH, Kinn Hamilton; MBE (1988); da of Robert Aeneas Cameron McIntosh (d 1978), and Violet Jessie, *née* Kinnis (d 1988); *b* 20 June 1930; *Educ* Waverley Sch Huddersfield Yorkshire, Greenhead HS; *Career* detective novelist as Catherine Aird; asst treas World Assoc of Girl Guides and Girl Scouts 1978-84, chm UK Fin Ctee Girl Guides Assoc 1983-87, chm Crime Writers Assoc 1990-; Hon MA Univ of Kent at Canterbury 1985; *Books* The Religious Body (1966), A Most Contagious Game (1967), The Complete Steel (1969), Henrietta Who? (1968), A Late Phoenix (1971), His Burial Too (1973), Slight Mourning (1975), Parting Breath (1978), Some Died Eloquent (1979), Passing Strange (1981), Last Respects (1982), Harms's Way (1984), A Dead Liberty (1986), The Body Politic (1990); *Recreations* bridge; *Clubs* The English-Speaking Union; *Style—* Miss Kinn McIntosh, MBE

McINTOSH, Hon Philip Henry Sargant McIntosh; s of Baron McIntosh of Haringey (Life Peer), *qv*, and Naomi Ellen Sargant (*see* Prof Naomi McIntosh); *b* 1964; *Educ* Highgate Wood Sch London, Kingston Poly (BA); *Career* pres Kingston Polytechnic Students Union 1987-88; *Style—* The Hon Philip McIntosh

McINTOSH, Sir Ronald Robert Duncan; KCB (1975, CB 1968); s of Thomas Steven McIntosh, and Christina Jane McIntosh; *b* 26 Sept 1919; *Educ* Charterhouse, Balliol Coll Oxford; *m* 1951, Doreen Frances, only da of Cdr Andrew MacGinnity, of Frinton-on-Sea, Essex; *Career* served MN WWII; joined BOT 1947, under sec 1963-64, dep under sec of state DEA 1966-68, dep sec Cabinet Office 1968-70; dep sec: Employment 1970-72, Treasy 1972-73; dir gen NEDO and memb NEDC 1973-77; chm APV plc 1982-89 (dep chm 1981); dir: S G Warburg, Foseco, London & Manchester Gp; chm Br Food Consortium for the USSR 1989-; memb Cncl CBI 1980-90; Hon DSc (Aston) 1977; FRSA, CBIM; *Style—* Sir Ronald McIntosh, KCB; 24 Ponsonby Terrace, London SW1 P4QA (☎ 071 821 6106)

MCINTOSH, Thomas Lee; s of John Christian McIntosh (d 1967), of Washington DC, and Mildred White (d 1953); *b* 3 Dec 1938; *Educ* Juilliard Sch of Music (BSc, MSc); *m* 30 Sept 1982, Miranda Harrison Vincent, da of Vincent Booth Reckitt (d 1975), of Otley, Yorks; *Career* conductor and music dir London City Chamber Orch 1973-; artistic dir: E Anglian Summer Music Festival 1978-, Penang Malaysia Music Festival 1986 and 1987, Opera Anglia 1989-; contributing ed eighteenth century symphonic music for Garland Symphony Series; Arrangements for Orch of the following: Valentine

Waltzes (George Antheil), Rag Suite (various composers), Flower Rag Suite (Scott Joplin); FRSA; *Recreations* gardening, theatre; *Clubs* Cwlth Tst; *Style—* Thomas McIntosh, Esq

McINTOSH OF HARINGEY, Baron (UK 1982), of Haringey in Gtr London; Andrew Robert McIntosh; s of Prof Albert William McIntosh, and Helena Agnes (Jenny), *née* Britton (d 1989); *b* 30 April 1933; *Educ* Haberdashers' Aske's, Hampstead Sch, Royal GS High Wycombe, Jesus Coll Oxford (MA), Ohio State Univ; *m* 1962, Naomi Ellen Sargant (*see* Lady McIntosh), da of Thomas Sargant, OBE, JP (d 1988), of London N6, and previously w of Peter Joseph Kelly; 2 s (Hon Francis Robert b 1962, Hon Philip Henry Sargant b 1964); *Career* memb Hornsey Borough Cncl 1963-65, memb Haringey Borough Cncl 1964-68; chm: Market Res Soc 1972-73, Assoc for Neighbourhood Cncls 1974-80; memb GLC for Tottenham 1973-83, ldr GLC oppn 1980-81; House of Lords: chm Computer Sub Ctee 1984-, princ (Lab) oppn spokesman on environment 1987- (on educ and sci 1985-87); dep chm IFF Research Ltd 1988- (md 1965-81, chm 1981-88), chm SVP UK Ltd 1983-; chm Fabian Soc 1985-86; *Style—* The Rt Hon the Lord McIntosh of Haringey; 27 Hurst Avenue, London N6 5TX (☎ 081 340 1496)

McINTOSH OF HARINGEY, Baroness; Prof Naomi Ellen Sargant; da of Tom Sargant, OBE, JP (d 1988), of London N6; *b* 10 Dec 1933; *Educ* Friends Sch Walden, Bedford Coll London Univ; *m* 1, 1954, Peter Joseph Kelly; 1 s (David); m 2, 1962, Andrew Robert McIntosh (Baron McIntosh of Haringey, *qv*); 2 s (Francis, Philip); *Career* pro vice-chllr Student Affairs The Open Univ 1974-78, prof of applied social res 1978-81; chm Nat Gas Consumers Cncl 1977-80; memb: Nat Consumer Cncl 1978-, Cmmn on Energy and Environment 1978-; pres Nat Soc for Clean Air 1981-; sr commissioning ed (education) Channel Four TV 1981-89; *Recreations* gardening, photography; *Style—* The Rt Hon the Lady McIntosh of Haringey; 27 Hurst Avenue, London N6 5TX (☎ 081 340 1496, fax 081 348 4641)

MACINTYRE, Angus Donald; s of Maj Francis Peter Macintyre, OBE (d 1944), and Evelyn Mary Josephine, *née* Synnott (d 1956); *b* 4 May 1935; *Educ* Wellington, Hertford Coll Oxford, St Antony's Coll Oxford (MA, DPhil); *m* 5 Sept 1958, Joanna Musgrave, da of Sir Richard Harvey, 2 Bt (d 1978), of Chisenbury Priory, Pewsey, Wilts; 2 s (Benedict Richard Pierce, Magnus William Lachlan), 1 da (Katherine Cressida Eve); *Career* Lt Coldstream Gds 1953-55; official fell and tutor in modern history Magdalen Coll Oxford (univ lectr 1963-, vice pres 1981-82, actg pres 1987), ed English Historical Review 1978-86; chm Thomas Wall Tst 1971-, govr Wolverhampton GS 1985-, govr Magdalen Coll Sch Oxford 1987-; FRHistSoc 1972; *Books* The Liberator: Daniel O'Connell and the Irish Parlimentary Party (1965), Daniel O'Connell: Portrait of a Radical (contrib, 1984), Magdalen College and the Crown (contrib, 1988); *Recreations* cricket, book collecting; *Clubs* MCC; *Style—* Angus Macintyre, Esq; 8 Linton Rd, Oxford; Achaglachgach, By Tarbert, Argyll; Magdalen College, Oxford

MACINTYRE, Charles Edward Stuart; s of John Macintyre (d 1978), and Mary, *née* Agnew; *b* 13 Feb 1932; *Educ* Priory GS Shrewsbury; *m* 28 June 1956, Barbara Mary, da of William Abley (d 1959); 3 da (Sarah (Mrs Garratt) b 10 April 1957, Ruth b 30 March 1958, Jane b 23 May 1963); *Career* dir and gen mangr Heart of England Building Soc 1983-; pres Coventry Centre Building Soc's Inst; FCBSI 1969; *Recreations* sport; *Style—* Charles Macintyre, Esq; Merrywood, Hampton-on-the-Hill, Warwick CV35 8QR (☎ 0926 492766); Heart of England Building Soc, 22-26 Jury St, Warwick CV34 4ET (☎ 0926 496111)

McINTYRE, Donald Conroy; CBE (1985, OBE 1975); s of George McIntyre, and Hermyn, *née* Conroy; *b* 22 Oct 1934; *Educ* Mount Albert GS New Zealand, Auckland Teachers Trg Coll, Guildhall Sch of Music London; *m* 29 July 1961, Jill Redington, da of Norton Mitchell, DFC (d 1989), of Barnstaple, Devon; 3 da (Ruth Frances b 1965, Lynn Hazel b 1967, Jenny Jane b 1971); *Career* princ bass: Sadler's Wells Opera 1960-67, Royal Opera House Covent Garden 1967-, annual appearances at Bayreuth Festival 1967-81; roles incl: Wotan and Wanderer (Der Ring), Dutchman (Der Fliegende Hollander), Telramund (Logengrin), Barak (Die Frau ohne Schatten), Pizzaro (Fidelio), Golaud (Pelleas et Melisande), Kurwenal (Tristan and Isolde), Gurnemanz, Klingsor and Amfortas (Parsifal), Heyst (Victory), Jochanaan (Salome), Macbeth, Scarpia (Tosca), The Count (Marriage of Figaro), Nick Shadow (The Rake's Progress), Hans Sachs (Die Meistersinger), Doctor (Wozzeck), Cardillac (Cardillac Hindemith), Balstrode (Peter Grimes), Rocco (Fidelio), Kasper (Don Freishutz), Sarastro (Magic Flute); recordings incl: Pelleas et Melisande, Oedipus Rex, Il Trovatore, Ring, Parsifal, Damnation de Faust, Messiah; Fidelio Medal Oct 1989; *Recreations* swimming, tennis, farming, walking; *Style—* Donald McIntyre, Esq, CBE

McINTYRE, Prof (James) Eric; s of John Charles McIntyre, MC, MBE (d 1965), and Henrietta Mary, *née* Mitchell (d 1988); *b* 7 May 1928; *Educ* Morrison's Acad Crieff, Univ of St Andrews (BSc); *m* 14 Sept 1957, Pauline, da of George Brocklehurst (d 1984); 1 s (Neil b 1959); *Career* res offr and res mangr ICI Fibres 1952-77, prof of textile industs 1977-; dean Faculty of Engrg Univ of Leeds 1987-89; FRSC 1977, FTI 1977, FPRI 1986, CEng 1988; *Books* The Chemistry of Fibres (1971); *Recreations* walking, golf; *Style—* Prof Eric McIntyre; Department of Textile Industries, The University of Leeds, Leeds LS2 9JT (☎ 0532 333731, fax 0532 333704, telex 556473 UNILDS G)

MACINTYRE, Prof Iain; s of John MacIntyre (d 1954), of Tobermory, Mull, and Margaret Fraser Shaw (d 1967), of Stratherick, Inverness; *b* 30 Aug 1924; *Educ* Jordanhill Coll Sch Glasgow, Univ of Glasgow (MB ChB), Univ of London (PhD, DSc); *m* 14 July 1947, Mabs Wilson, da of George Jamieson (d 1951), of Largs, Ayrshire; 1 da (Fiona Bell b 1953); *Career* Royal Post Grad Med Sch: prof endocrine chemistry 1967-82, chm Academic Bd 1986-89, dir Dept of Chemical Pathology and Endocrine Unit 1982-89, emeritus prof and sr res fell Dept of Med 1989-; conslt chem pathologist Hammersmith and Queen Charlottes Hosps; memb: Hammersmith and Queen Charlottes Health Authy 1982-90, Br Postgraduate Fedn Central Academic Cncl 1983-89, Bd of Studies in Med Univ of London, Bd of Studies in Pathology Univ of London; vice pres Eng Chess Assoc; Gairdner Int award Toronto 1967, Hon MD Turin Univ 1985; MCRPath (fndr memb) 1963, MRCP 1969, FRCPath 1971, FRCP 1977; *Recreations* tennis, chess; *Clubs* Athenaeum, Queen's, Hurlingham; *Style—* Professor Iain MacIntyre; Great Broadhurst Farm, Broad Oak, Heathfield, Sussex TN21 8UX (☎ 0435 883 515, fax 0435 883 611); Dept of Chemical Pathology, Royal Postgraduate Medical School, Du Cane Rd, London W12 0NN (☎ 081 740 3227, fax 081 740 6680)

McINTYRE, Ian; s of Donald McIntyre, BEM (d 1952), of Glasgow, and Jessie, *née* Macgillivray Roberton (d 1982); *b* 4 July 1921; *Educ* Hyndland Sch Glasgow, Open Univ (BA); *m* 25 Nov 1943, Joyce, da of Benjamin Pugh Davies (d 1967), of Haverfordwest; 1 s (Bruce b 1946), 2 da (Lesley Joanne b 1950, Lindsay Clare b 1952); *Career* RA TA 1938, Capt RA 1943 (mentioned in despatches 1945); Br Linen Bank 1937, md S Pension Tstees Ltd 1952, chief exec Noble Lowndes-Partners Ltd 1978 (joined 1951, dir 1968), dir Hill Samuel Gp; chm The Br Fedn of Music Festivals, Hammerman Trades House Glasgow; Freeman Worshipful Co of Musicians; FPMI 1976; *Recreations* reading, walking, golf; *Clubs* Caledonian, RAC; *Style—* Ian McIntyre, Esq; The British Federation of Music Festivals, Festivals House, 198 Park Lane, Macclesfield, Cheshire SK11 6UD (☎ 0625 28297)

McINTYRE, Ian James; s of Hector Harold McIntyre (d 1978), of Inverness, and Annie Mary Michie (d 1979); *b* 9 Dec 1931; *Educ* Prescot GS Lancs, St John's Coll Cambridge (BA, MA, pres Cambridge Union), Coll of Europe Bruges; *m* 24 July 1954, Leik Sommerfelt, da of Benjamin Vogt (d 1970), of Kragero, Norway; 2 s (Andrew James, Neil Forbes), 2 da (Anne Leik, Katharine Elspeth); *Career* Nat Serv cmmnd Intelligence Corps; writer and broadcaster; BBC: current affrs talks prodr 1957-59, ed At Home and Abroad 1959-60, mgmnt trg organiser 1960-61, bdcasting contract 1970-76; controller: Radio 4 1976-78, Radio 3 1978-87; assoc ed The Times 1989-90; prog servs offr ITA 1961-62, dir of info and res Scot Cons Central Office Edinburgh 1962-70; Parly candidate Roxburgh, Selkirk and Peebles (Cons) gen election 1966; *Books* The Proud Doers (1968), Words (1975); *Recreations* walking, swimming, gardening; *Clubs* Cambridge Union, Beefsteak; *Style—* Ian McIntyre, Esq; Spylaw House, Newlands Avenue, Radlett, Herts WD7 8EL (☎ 0923 853532)

McINTYRE, Very Rev Prof John; CVO (1985); s of John Clark McIntyre, of Bathgate, and Annie McIntyre; *b* 20 May 1916; *Educ* Bathgate Acad, Edinburgh Univ (MA, BD, DLitt); *m* 1945, Jessie, da of William Buick, of Coupar, Angus; 2 s, 1 da; *Career* ordained 1941, min Fenwick Parish 1943-45, prof of systematic theol St Andrews Coll Sydney 1946-56 (princ 1950-56), prof Divinity Edinburgh Univ 1956-86, princ warden Pollock Halls of Residence 1960-71, princ New Coll and dean Faculty of Divinity Edinburgh Univ 1968-74, acting princ and vice-chllr Edinburgh Univ 1973-74 and 1979, dean Order of Thistle 1974-89; chaplain to HM The Queen in Scotland 1975-86, extra chaplain 1974-75 and 1986-, moderator Gen Assembly of Church of Scotland 1982; Hon DHL College of Wooster Ohio 1983, Hon DD Glasgow Univ 1961, Dr (honoris causa) Edinburgh Univ 1987; *Books* St Anselm and His Critics (1954), The Christian Doctrine of History (1957), On the Love of God (1962), The Shape of Christology (1966), Faith, Theology and Imagination (1987); *Style—* The Very Rev Prof John McIntyre, CVO; 22/4 Minto St, Edinburgh EH9 1RQ (☎ 031 667 1203)

McINTYRE, Keith Thomas; s of Gordon Leslie McIntyre, of 20 Riversdale Rd, Edinburgh, and Sheila, *née* McDonald; *b* 22 Dec 1959; *Educ* Trinity Acad Secdy Sch Edinburgh, Dundee Coll of Art (Drumfolk travelling scholar, Farquar Reid travelling scholar), Barcelona Paper Workshop; *m* 30 Dec 1983, Sheenagh Margaret Patience; 1 s (Lewis Cathcart b 22 Oct 1987); *Career* artist; solo exhibitions: Shore Gallery Leith 1982, 369 Gallery Edinburgh 1984 and 1986, Compass Gallery Glasgow 1985, Pittenweem Arts Festival Fife 1985, Raab Galerie Berlin 1987, Raab Gallery London 1988, The Paintings for Jock Tamson's Bairns (Tramway Theatre Glasgow and Raab Gallery London) 1990; group exhibitions incl: Saltire Soc Edinburgh 1982, Clare Hall Cambridge 1984 and 1986, Five Contemporary Scottish Artists (Leinster Fine Art London) 1985, Open Circle (Schweinfurt Exhibition Germany) 1986, De Brakke Gallery Amsterdam 1987, The Lion Rampant: New Scottish Painting and Photography (Artspace San Francisco) 1988, Scottish Myths (Sc Gallery Edinburgh) 1990, Galerie Bureaux & Magasins Ostend Belgium 1991; public collections incl: Aberdeen Art Gallery, BBC, Dundee Coll of Commerce, Sc Nat Gallery of Modern Art, W Sussex CC; arts projects incl: visual dir Jock Tamson's Bairns (Tramway Theatre Glasgow) 1989-90, jt film venture (with Timothy Neat and John Berger) 1990; pt/t teacher in fine art Glasgow Sch of Art 1984-89; awards: Hospitalfield scholar Arbroath 1981, RSA Carnegie 1982, RSA William Gillies 1983, Elizabeth Greenshields 1983; *Style—* Keith McIntyre, Esq; Raab Gallery, 6 Vauxhall Bridge Rd, London SW1V 2SD (☎ 071 828 2588, fax 071 976 5041)

McINTYRE, Malcolm; s of Stanley Archibald Lovell McIntyre, of Purley, Surrey, and Mary, *née* MacGregor; *b* 28 May 1934; *Educ* Roke Sch; *m* 17 May 1958, Avis Joan, da of Robert Leonard Winwood (d 1968), of New Malden, Surrey; 2 s (Simon Timothy b 1959 d 1962, Paul Timothy b 1963), 2 da (Clair Louise b 1961, Kate Lucy b 1965); *Career* PA to Maj-Gen Robert Urquhart GOC in C Br Troops Austria 1952-54; journalist and ed 1954-70; jt md Kingsway PR (later Saatchis) 1970-83, md and owner Malcolm McIntyre Consultancy 1984-; UK rep Champagne industry's governing body 1984-; *Books* Home Extensions; *Recreations* golf; *Clubs* RAC, Lords Taverners; *Style—* Malcolm McIntyre, Esq; Crusader House, 14 Pall Mall, London SW1 (☎ 071 839 1461, fax 071 925 2206, telex 917700 MALMACG)

MACINTYRE, Malcolm Valentine Strickland; s of Donald George Frederick Wyville Macintyre, RN, DSO, DSC (d 1981), and Monica Josephine Clifford Rowley, da of Roger Walter Strickland (descended in the sr line of Strickland of Sizergh Castle, Westmorland); f Capt Donald Macintyre was famous U-boat hunter in WWII, f's great uncle Lt-Gen Donald Macintyre raised the 4th Gurkhas and won VC, ggf Gen John Macintyre also served in Indian Army in Madras Artillery; gf Maj-Gen Donald Macintyre served in 2nd and commanded 4th Gurkhas; *b* 5 Nov 1942; *Educ* Ampleforth; Luton Coll of Technol (HND Mechanical Engineering); *m* 22 Feb 1969, Lesley Winifred, da of Leslie Donald Brown (d 1961); 1 s (Donald Malcolm Macintyre 1970); *Career* appointed dir Plysu plc 1981; *Recreations* dog breeding and training; *Style—* Malcolm V S Macintyre; Cedarbrook, Lower Dean, Huntingdon, Cambs, PE18 0LL; Plysu plc, Woburn Sands, Bucks (☎ 0908 582311)

McINTYRE, Michael Mackay (Mike); MBE (1988); s of Prof (William) Ian Mackay McIntyre, CBE, of Shandon, Helensburgh, Strathclyde, and Ruth Dick, *née* Galbraith; *b* 29 June 1956; *Educ* Hermitage Acad Helensburgh Strathclyde, Univ of Glasgow (BSc); *m* 29 Aug 1980, Caroline Maria, da of Gerald Albert Abraham, of Stert, nr Devizes, Wilts; 1 s (Angus b 28 Jan 1985), 1 da (Gemma b 24 June 1987); *Career* yachtsman; International Finn Class: British Champ 1981, 1983, 1984, Euro Champ 1984, 7 Olympic Games 1984; Int Star Class: British Champ 1988, Olympic Gold medalist 1988; AMIEE; *Style—* Mike McIntyre, Esq, MBE; 21 West Dean, nr Salisbury, Wilts SP5 1JB (☎ 0794 409 60); Orbitel Mobile Communications Ltd, The Keytech Centre, Ashwood Way, Basingstoke, Hants (☎ 0256 843 468, fax 0256 843 207, car 0836 707 848)

McINTYRE, Prof Neil; s of John William McIntyre (d 1986), of Ferndale, Mid Glamorgan, and Catherine, *née* Watkins; *b* 1 May 1934; *Educ* Porth Co Sch for Boys, King's Coll London (BSc), King's Coll Hosp Med Sch (MB BS, MD); *m* 3 Sept 1966, Wendy Ann, da of Wing Cdr Richard Kelsey (ret), of Southwold, Suffok; 1 s (Rowan b 1969), 1 da (Waveney b 1968); *Career* MRC travelling fellowship Mass Gen Hosp and Harvard Med Sch USA 1966-68, hon conslt Royal Free Hosp; Royal Free Hosp Sch of Med: sr lectr in med 1968-73, reader in med 1973-78, clinical sub-dean 1976-80, prof of med 1979-83, prof and chm Dept of Med 1983-; sec MRS 1972-77; Freeman City of London, Liveryman Worshipful Soc of Apothecaries; FRCP 1972; *Books* The Problem Orientated Medical Record (1979), Lipids and Lipoproteins (1990), Clinical Hepatology (1991); *Recreations* golf, photographing medical statues; *Clubs* Athenaeum; *Style—* Prof Neil McIntyre; 20 Queenscourt, Wembley, Middx HA9 7QU (☎ 081 902 2751); Department of Medicine, Royal Free Hospital, Pond St, London NW3 2QG (☎ 071 794 0500 ext 3969, fax 071 435 0186)

McINTYRE, Patrick; s of Patrick Owen McIntyre (d 1986), of Winnipeg, Manitoba, Canada, and Elizabeth May, *née* Gair (d 1985); *b* 18 June 1936; *Educ* St Paul's Coll Winnipeg, Open Univ (BA); *m* 27 June 1957, Margaret Inger (d 1990), da of Robert Jarman (d 1954); 1 s (Patrick), 1 step s (David), 1 step da (Hilary Patricia); *Career* Royal Winnipeg Ballet 1946-56, American Ballet Theatre 1957-58, West End Theatre (West Side Story) 1958-60, Ten West End prodns 1960-83, num feature films and TV series 1960-83, house mangr Old Vic Theatre 1983-; direction and choreography: RSC

Stratford, LA Light Opera, Gaiety Theatre Dublin, Br prov theatres; memb: AGMA, AGVA, Actra, American and Br Equity; *Recreations* walking, reading, travel; *Style—* Patrick McIntyre, Esq; Old Vic Theatre, Waterloo Rd, London SE1 8NB (☎ 071 9282651, fax 071 2619161)

McINTYRE, Dr Robert Douglas; s of John Ebenezer McIntyre (d 1961), of Edinburgh, and Catherine Campbell, *née* Morison (d 1961); *b* 15 Dec 1913; *Educ* Hamilton Acad, Daniel Stewart Coll, Univ of Edinburgh (MB ChB), Univ of Glasgow (DPH); *m* 11 Sept 1954, Letitia Sarah, *née* MacLeod; 1 s (John Douglas b 21 Sept 1959); *Career* area conslt chest physician Stirlingshire 1951-79, hon conslt Stirling Royal Infirmary 1978-; Scot Nat Pty: MP Motherwell & Wishaw 1945, chm 1948-56, pres 1958-80; Parly candidate: Motherwell & Wishaw 1950, Perth and E Perthshire 1951, 1955, 1959, 1964, West Stirlingshire 1966, 1970, Stirling Burgh's (by election 1971 gen election Feb and Oct 1974), Euro election Mid Scotland & Fife 1979; memb Univ Ct Univ of Stirling 1967-75 and 1979-88 (chllrs assessor 1979-88), memb Stirling Town Cncl 1957-75 (hon treas 1958-64), provost 1967-75; Hon DUniv Univ of Stirling; Freeman Royal Burgh of Stirling, fell Scot Cncl; *Recreations* sailing; *Clubs* Scottish Arts, Stirling County; *Style—* Dr Robert McIntyre; 8 Gladstone Place, Stirling (☎ 0786 73456)

MacINTYRE, Robert Hamilton (Sandy); s of Robert Hamilton MacIntyre (d 1964), of 4 Bede House, Manor Fields, London, and Doris, *née* Bateman (d 1978); *b* 2 March 1932; *Educ* St Pauls; *m* 3 March 1956, Jean-Anne, da of James Pizzey (d 1975); 2 s (Robert b 1965, Richard b 1967), 2 da (Lisbeth-Anne b 1959, Amanda b 1961); *Career* mil serv Sgt RAPC; ptnr MacIntyre Hudson (CA), dir Surrey Building Society; former chm W Wickham Round Table; FCA; *Recreations* motoring, motor sport, swimming; *Clubs* Leander Rowing, Thames Rowing; *Style—* Sandy MacIntyre, Esq; 87 Copse Ave, West Wickham, Kent BR4 9NW; 26/28 Ely Place, London EC1N 6RL (fax 071 405 4786)

MACINTYRE, William Ian; s of Robert Miller Macintyre, CBE, of Charnwood, Maresfield Park, Uckfield, E Sussex, and Florence Mary, *née* Funnell; *b* 20 July 1943; *Educ* Merchiston Castle Sch, Univ of St Andrews (MA); *m* 2 Sept 1967, Jennifer Mary, da of Sir David Bruce Pitblado, KCB, CVO, of 23 Cadogan St, London SW1; 1 s (Jonathan b 13 Sept 1974), 2 da (Emma b 22 March 1969, Victoria b 6 Dec 1971); *Career* BP Co Ltd 1965-72, ECGD 1972-73, DTI 1973-77 (seconded ICFC 1977-79); Dept Energy: asst sec Gas Div 1979-1983, dir gen Energy Efficiency Office 1983-87, under sec Electricity Div 1987-, under sec Electricity Div B 1988-; govr: Shene Sch 1982-86, East Sheen Primary Sch; *Style—* William Macintyre, Esq; Dept of Energy, 1 Palace St, London SW1E 5HE (☎ 071 238 2181)

McIVOR, Rt Hon (William) Basil; PC (1971), OBE (1991); s of Rev Frederick McIvor (d 1968), and (Elizabeth) Lilly, *née* Dougan (d 1972); *b* 17 June 1928; *Educ* Methodist Coll Belfast, Queen's Univ Belfast (LLB), Lincoln's Inn; *m* 3 Jan 1953, (Frances) Jill (*qv*), da of late Cecil Reginald Johnston Anderson, of Lisburn, NI; 2 s (Jonathan, Timothy), 1 da (Jane); *Career* called to the Bar NI 1950, presiding magistrate 1974, MP (Ulster Unionist) Larkfield NI Parly 1969, min of Community Relations NI 1971-72, memb (UU) for S Belfast, NI Assembly 1973-5, min Educ NI 1974; govr Campbell Coll 1975- (chm 1983); fndr memb and chm: Fold Housing Assoc NI 1976-, govrs and dirs of Lagan Coll (the first purposely designed integrated RC and Protestant Sch in NI) 1981-; *Recreations* music, gardening, golf; *Clubs* Royal Overseas League; *Style—* The Rt Hon Basil McIvor, OBE; Larkhill, 98 Spa Road, Ballynahinch, Co Down (☎ 0238 563534)

McIVOR, Ian Walker; s of William Walker McIvor, of Worsley, Manchester (d 1986), and Susannah, *née* Glover (d 1990); *b* 19 Jan 1944; *Educ* Worsley HS, Bolton Inst, London Univ (LLB); *m* 16 Sept 1969, Patricia Wendy, da of Harry Blackhurst Swift, of Caerphilly, South Wales; 1 s (Andrew Walker b 1977), 4 da (Helen b 1970, Rachel b 1971, Caroline b 1974, Joanne b 1984); *Career* AVR 2 Kings Regt OTC 1966-68; barr Inner Temple 1973, head of Chambers 1977-; memb Catenian Assoc; *Recreations* golf, swimming, walking, DIY; *Clubs* Heald Green and Didsbury Golf; *Style—* Ian McIvor, Esq; 38 Framingham Rd, Brooklands, Sale, Cheshire M33 3SG (☎ 061 962 8205); Courtletts House, 38 King St West, Manchester (☎ 061 833 9628)

MCIVOR, Dr James; s of James McIvor, of 12 Wemyss Cresent, Tronn, Ayrshire, and Ann Donaldson, *née* Hunter; *b* 23 Sept 1936; *Educ* Glasgow Acad, Univ of Glasgow (BDS, MB ChB, FDS RCS, FRCR, Odontological Soc Prize, Ure Prize in surgery), Br Med Students Tst travelling scholarship to Duke University North Carolina USA; *m* 1966 (m dis 1988), Elizabeth Ann Gibbon; 1 s (Martin James b 4 Feb 1972), 1 da (Claire Elizabeth b 14 June 1975); *Career* jr house offr Glasgow Royal Infirmary 1963-64; registrar in oral surgery: Eastman Dental Hosp London 1964-65, Queen Mary's Hosp Roehampton 1965-66; registrar in radiology: Westminster Hosp London 1966-67, Kings Coll Hosp London 1968-69; conslt radiologist Hillingdon Hosp Uxbridge Middlesex 1970-76, conslt radiologist Charing Cross Hosp 1976-, in private radiological practice Harley St 1980-, head of X-Ray Dept Inst of Dental Surgery 1985-; author or jt author over 30 scientific papers in med jls 1962-; memb Editorial Bd three med jls, chm DDR Examination Bd RCR 1990-; fell Cardiovascular and Interventional Radiological Soc of Europe 1986-; *Books* Dental and Maxillo - Facial Radiology (1986), Short Practice of Surgery (contrib, 1984), Diagnostic Radiology (contrib, 1988); *Recreations* fringe theatre, moderate exercise, gossip; *Style—* Dr James McIvor; 39 Rosedew Road, London W6 9ET (☎ 081 748 7853); 86 Harley St, London W1N 1AE (☎ 071 580 3623); Charing Cross Hosp, Fulham Palace Rd, London W6 8RF (☎ 081 846 1234); Institute of Dental Surgery, Gray's Inn Rd, London WC1 8LD

McIVOR, (Frances) Jill; da of Cecil Reginald Johnston Anderson (d 1956), of Lisburn, Co Antrim, and Frances Ellen, *née* Henderson (d 1978); *b* 10 Aug 1930; *Educ* Lurgan Coll, Queen's Univ Belfast (LLB); *m* 1953, Rt Hon William Basil McIvor, *qv*; 2 s (Jonathan, Timothy), 1 da (Jane); *Career* Queen's Univ Belfast: asst librarian (law) 1954-55, tutor in legal res Law Faculty 1965-74; editorial staff NI Legal Quarterly 1966-76, librarian Dept of Dir of Public Prosecutions 1977-79; memb Gen Dental Cncl 1979-91, chm Lagan Valley Regnl Park Ctee 1984-89 (memb 1975-89); memb: N Ireland IBA 1980-86, Ulster Countryside Cmmn 1984-89, Fair Employment Agency 1984-89, Lay Panel Juvenile Ct 1976-77, GDC 1979-91, Fair Employment Cmmn 1990-91; called to the Bar NI 1980; memb: Bd Cooperation North 1987-90, NI Advsy Ctee Br Cncl 1987-91, Home Sec's Advsy Panel on Community Radio 1985-86; chm: Ulster NZ Tst 1987-, Bd of Visitors Queen's Univ Belfast 1988-, EGSA (Educnl Guidance Serv for Adults) 1988-89; memb and dep chm Radio Authy 1990-; NI Ombudsman 1991-; *Publications* Irish Consultant, Manual of Law Librarianship (contrib, 1976), Elegantia Juris: selected writings of F H Newark (ed, 1973), Chart of the English Reports (new edn, 1982); *Recreations* gardening; *Clubs* Royal Overseas League; *Style—* Mrs Jill McIvor; Larkhill, 98 Spa Road, Ballynahinch, Co Down (☎ 0238 563534)

MACK, Prof Alan Osborne; s of Arthur Joseph Mack (d 1957), and Florence Emily, *née* Norris; *b* 24 July 1918; *Educ* Westbourne Park Sch, Univ of London, Royal Dental Hosp (LDS, FDS, RCS), Durham Univ (MDS); *m* 19 June 1943, Marjorie Elizabeth, da of Charles Edward Westacott; 2 s (Peter John b 1945, Ian Robert b 1948), 1 da (Susan Elizabeth (Mrs Shinaco) b 1953); *Career* Flt Lt RAF Dental Branch 1943-47; civil conslt in prosthetic dentistry RAF 1978-88; house surgn Royal Dental Hosp 1942-43, demonstrator Royal Dental Hosp 1948 (asst dir and sr lectr 1949-56), prof of dental prosthetics Univ of Durham 1956-67 (Univ of London 1967-81); examiner RCS Univs of: Manchester 1957, Leeds 1961, Glasgow 1961, Liverpool 1965, London 1965, Edinburgh 1968, Lagos Nigeria 1970, Singapore and Khartoum 1977, Benghazi 1978; examination visitor for Gen Dental Cncl, advsr Univ of Malaya, memb Bd of Faculty RCS 1959, pres Br Soc for Study of Prosthetic Dentistry 1963, pt/t conslt Stoke Mandeville Hosp and John Radcliffe Hosp 1976, visiting prof Univ of Singapore 1981; memb BDA 1942-; *Books* Full Dentures (1971); *Recreations* gardening, pottery; *Style—* Prof Alan Mack; Home Farm, London Rd, Aston Clinton, Bucks HP22 5HG (☎ 0296 630 522)

MACK, Anthony George; s of Anthony Mack, of Old West Gate, Aldwick Bay Estate Bognor, Sussex, and Joyce Agnes, *née* Smith; *b* 10 Dec 1948; *Educ* Imberhorne Sch; *m* 17 Feb 1979, Sally Frances, da of Frank Frederick Legg, of Sussex; 2 s (Alastair b 1981, Freddy b 1986), 1 da (Holly b 1982); *Career* Air London International plc (formerly Air London Ltd): dir 1970, md 1979, chm and md 1989; FFA, AMRAeS; *Recreations* sailing, squash, skiing; *Clubs* Castle Rock Yacht; *Style—* Anthony Mack, Esq; Air London International plc, Mack House, Aviation Court, Gatwick Rd, Crawley, Sussex RH10 2GG (☎ 0293 549555, fax 0293 36810, telex 87671)

MACK, Hazel Mary; da of Peter Nevard Perkins, of 6 Keswick Ave, Loughborough, Leics, and Elizabeth, *née* Walker; *b* 4 April 1952; *Educ* Loughborough HS for Girls, Univ of Exeter (BA); *m* 19 May 1977, Brian Mack, s of Frank Mack (d 1982); *Career* co sec Morgan Grenfell 1987-90 (joined 1980), exec dir Professional and Fin Risks Div Willis Faber & Dumas Limited 1990-; ACIS; *Recreations* cooking, gardening, fly fishing, swimming; *Style—* Mrs Hazel Mack; Pounce Hall Cottage, Sewards End, nr Saffron Walden, Essex CB10 2LE (☎ 0799 27740); Ten Trinity Square, London EC3P 3AX (☎ 071 975 2329, fax 071 488 8223, telex 882141 WILLIS G)

MACK, Keith Robert; s of David Stanley Mack (d 1986), and Dorothy Ivy, *née* Bowes (d 1989); *b* 2 March 1933; *Educ* Edmonton Co Sch; *m* 23 Jan 1960, Eileen Mary, da of William Owen Cuttell (d 1978); 2 s (Barry b 1962, Bevin b 1964), 4 da (Penny b 1966, Hazel b 1967, Heather (twin) b 1967, Beth b 1970); *Career* RAF Pilot 1951-58; civilian air traffic control offr Scot and Oceanic Air Traffic Control Centre 1960-67, RAF Staff Coll Bracknell 1968, Nat Air Traffic Servs (NATS) HQ 1969-71, ATC watch supervisor Scot ATCC 1972-73, CAA chief offr Cardiff Airport 1974, NATS HQ, 1975-76, ATC watch supervisor London ATCC 1977, NATS dep dir of control (airspace policy) 1978-79, Superintendent London ATCC 1980-82, dep controller NATS 1983-84, gp dir and memb bd CAA controller Nat Air Traffic Servs 1985-88, dir gen Euro Orgn for the Safety of Air Navigation 1989-; *Recreations* cycling, walking, photography, music; *Style—* Keith R Mack, Esq; Director General, European Organisation for the Safety of Air Navigation, 72 rue de la Loi, 1040 Brussels, Belgium (☎ 010 32 2 7293500)

McKAIG, Adm Sir (John) Rae; KCB (1973), CBE (1966); s of Sir John Bickerton McKaig, KCB, DSO (d 1962); *b* 24 April 1922; *Educ* Loretto; *m* 1945, Barbara Dawn, da of Dr Frank Marriott, MC; 2 s, 1 da; *Career* joined RN 1939, served WWII, Rear-Adm 1968, Asst Chief Naval Staff Ops Requirements 1968-70, Vice-Adm 1970, Flag Offr Plymouth & Port Adm Devonport, Cdr Central Sub Area E Atlantic & Cdr Plymouth Sub Area Channel 1970-73, Adm 1973, UK mil rep to NATO 1973-75, ret 1976; memb Royal Patriotic Fund Corpn 1978-, dep chm and chief exec Gray Mackenzie & Co 1980-86, exec dir Inchcape plc 1981-86, dir Assoc of Leading Visitor Attractions 1989-; *Recreations* sailing, shooting, fishing; *Clubs* RYS Army and Navy; *Style—* Adm Sir Rae McKaig, KCB, CBE; Hill House, Hambledon, Hants

McKANE, Christopher Hugh; s of Leonard Cyril McKane, MBE, of The Old Bakehouse, Ampney St Peter, Cirencester, Glos, and (Eleanor) Catharine, *née* Harris; *b* 13 July 1946; *Educ* Marlborough, New Coll Oxford (MA); *m* 31 Oct 1970, Anna Rosemary, da of George Paul Henshell (d 1984); 3 da (Camilla b 1977, Sophie b 1979, Felicity b 1981); *Career* journalist; The Oxford Times 1968-71, The Birmingham Post 1971-74; The Times: joined 1974, chief home sub ed 1982-86; The Independent: dep home ed 1986-88, picture ed 1988; *Recreations* bonsai, wine, running; *Style—* Christopher McKane, Esq; The Independent, 40 City Rd, London EC1Y 2DB (☎ 071 253 1222)

McKANE, Prof William; s of Thomas McKane (d 1964), and Jemima, *née* Smith (d 1957); *b* 18 Feb 1921; *Educ* Univ of St Andrews (MA, Football blue), Univ of Glasgow (MA, PhD, DLitt); *m* 3 July 1952, Agnes Mathie, da of James Howie (d 1973), of South Fergushill, Ayrshire; 3 s (Tom b 15 May 1953, James b 8 July 1956, William b 4 May 1966), 2 da (Ursula b 22 Jan 1959, Christina b 20 March 1963); *Career* RAF 1941-45; sr lectr in Hebrew Univ of Glasgow 1965 (asst lectr 1953); Univ of St Andrews: prof of Hebrew and Oriental languages 1968-90 (emeritus prof 1990-), dean Faculty of Divinity 1973-77; foreign sec Soc for Old Testament Study 1981-86 (pres 1978), princ St Mary's Coll St Andrews 1982-86; Burkitt medal of Br Acad for distinguished work in biblical studies 1985; Min Church of Scot; DD (Honoris Causa) Univ of Edinburgh 1984; FRAS 1957, FBA 1980, FRSE 1983; *Books* I and II Samuel (1963), Prophets and Wise Men (1965), Proverbs: A New Approach (1970), Jeremiah 1-25 International Critical Commentary (1986), Studies in the Patriarchal Narratives (1979), Selected Christian Hebraists (1989); *Recreations* walking incl hill walking; *Clubs* Royal and Ancient (St Andrews); *Style—* Prof William McKane; 51 Irvine Cres, St Andrews, Fife KY16 8LG (☎ 0334 73797); St Mary's Coll, St Andrews, Fife KY16 9JU (☎ 0334 76161)

MACKANESS, John Howard; er s of Alfred James Mackaness (d 1964), of Little Billing, Northampton, and Florence May, *née* Pepper (d 1964); family history from 1465 recorded College of Arms; granted armorial bearings 1960; *b* 11 Oct 1915; *Educ* Oakham Sch, Wye Coll, Univ of London; *m* 28 Sept 1940, Marjorie, da of Cecil Stanley Andrews (d 1953); 4 s (Sam *qv*, James *qv*, Simon b 5 Feb 1949, Mark *qv*); *Career* fndr and life pres Mixconcrete (Holdings) plc; dir: A J Mackaness Ltd, Billing Aquadrome Ltd; gen cmmr Income Tax 1965-69; memb Northants CC 1961-70; master of Pytchley Hunt 1968-71, Royal Warrantholder as Maker and Supplier of Charcoal to HM The Queen; landowner; *Books* Boughton Hall (1969), 600 Years with the Mackaness Family in Northamptonshire (1982); *Recreations* hunting, shooting, walking, travel; *Style—* John Mackaness, Esq; The Dower, Boughton Hall, Northampton (☎ 0604 843221); Rudding Arch, Harrogate (☎ 0423 879604)

MACKANESS, Mark; 4 and yst s of John Howard Mackaness, of The Dower, Boughton Hall, *qv*; *b* 20 Jan 1952; *Educ* Oundle, RAC Cirencester; *m* 1985, Nicola Louise, da of William Henry Lax, of Kirkby Chase, Kirkby Overblow, Harrogate, N Yorks; *Career* land agent; dir: A J Mackaness Ltd, Billing Fin Ltd, Billing Aquadrome Ltd, Neaveford Ltd, Rudding Park Ltd, Rudding House Ltd, Wavermace Developments Ltd; FRICS; *Recreations* skiing, shooting; *Clubs* Farmers'; *Style—* Mark Mackaness, Esq; Park House, Follifoot, Harrogate, N Yorks; Rudding Park, Follifoot, Harrogate, N Yorks HG3 1DU (☎ 0423 872228)

MACKANESS, Sam; eldest s of John Howard Mackaness, of The Dower, Boughton, Northampton, and Marjorie, *née* Andrews; descended from John Mackernes, of Thingdon (later Finedon), Northants, whose will was dated 14 Oct 1515 (*see* Burke's Landed Gentry, 18 Edn, vol II, 1969); *b* 17 March 1943; *Educ* Oundle, Lycée Jaggard Switzerland, Shuttleworth Agric Coll; *m* 4 May 1968, Karen Marie, o da of Cecil

Featherstone, of Poplars House, Rothersthorpe, Northampton; 1 s (Paul b 8 April 1972), 1 da (Shena b 26 May 1969); *Career* chm A J Mackaness Ltd; dir Billing Finance Ltd; md Billing Aquadrome Ltd; dir: Pershore Central Markets Ltd, Rudding House Ltd; *Recreations* shooting, fishing, skiing; *Clubs* Farmers'; *Style*— Sam Mackaness, Esq; Preston Deanery Hall, Northampton NN7 2DX (☎ 0604 870913); Billing Aquadrome Ltd, Little Billing, Northampton NN3 4DA (☎ 0604 408181)

MACKANESS, Simon Peter; s of John Mackaness, of The Dower, Boughton Hall, Northampton, and Marjorie, *née* Andrews; *b* 5 Feb 1949; *Educ* Oundle; *m* 22 Sept 1979, Judith Mary, da of Gordon Everatt; 2 s (Matthew Gordon b 13 June 1981, Nicholas John b 8 March 1984); *Career* Peat Marwick McLintock 1969-74, Cawoods Holdings Limited 1974-80, A J Mackaness Limited 1980-; chm Yorks Inland Branch of the British Holiday and Home Park Assoc, memb Yorks Ctee CLA; FCA; *Recreations* coursing, skiing; *Style*— Simon Mackaness, Esq; Rudding House Limited, Rudding Park, Follifoot, Harrogate, North Yorkshire HG3 1JH (☎ 0423 871350, fax 0423 872286)

MACKARNESS, Simon Paul Richard; TD (1980); s of Peter John Coleridge Mackarness, TD, of Petersfield, Hants, and Torla Frances Wedd, *née* Tidman; *b* 10 Sept 1945; *Educ* Portsmouth GS, Univ of Bristol (BA); *m* 9 Dec 1978, Diana, da of Dr Lewis MacDonald Reid, MC (d 1978); 1 s (Daniel b 1982), 1 da (Louise b 1981); *Career* Capt Royal Signals on RARO; admitted slr 1970, sr ptnr Mackarness & Lunt; memb Law Soc; *Recreations* amateur dramatics, motorcycling; *Style*— Simon Mackarness, Esq, TD; 16 High Street, Petersfield, Hants (☎ 0730 65111, fax 0730 67994)

MACKAY, Hon Alan John Francis; 2 s of 2 Earl of Inchcape (d 1939), by his 1 w, Joan (d 1933), da of Rt Hon Lord Justice Moriarty; *b* 6 Sept 1919; *Educ* Eton, Trinity Coll Cambridge; *m* 1, 3 Jan 1945 (m dis 1946), Janet Mary, yst da of Frederick Wallis, of Elvendon Priory, Goring-on-Thames; m 2, 30 June 1948 (m dis 1953), Sonia Cecilia Helen, yst da of Capt James Richard Tylden, of Milstead Manor, Kent, and Lady Tower, of Sway, Hants; 2 da (Siobhan b 1949, Kristina b 1951); m 3, 7 July 1955, Countess Lucie Catinka Christiane Julie, only da of Count Curt Ludwig Haugwitz-Hardenberg-Reventlow, of Korinth, Fyn, Denmark, and former w of late John Patrick Douglas-Boswell; 3 step s; *Career* served with: Cameronians 1939-40, Mercantile Marine 1941-46; *Clubs* Naval & Military, Union (Sydney), Royal Sydney Golf, Eccentric, Lansdowne; *Style*— Hon Alan Mackay; Enterkine, Annbank, Ayrshire (☎ 0292 520223); Fairybridge, Oughterard, Co Galway, Ireland (☎ 091 82223); Skyttegaarden, Korinth, 5600 Faaborg, Fyn, Denmark (☎ 09 65 10 03)

MACKAY, Baron (and Hon) Alexander William Rynhard; 2 s of 12 Lord Reay (d 1921), and Baroness Maria Johanna Bertha Christina Van Dedem (d 1932); *b* 7 Dec 1907; *Career* dir Bank of the Netherlands; *Style*— Baron Alexander Mackay; De Lindelaan, 76 Schapendrift, Blaricum (NH), Netherlands

MACKAY, Capt Alistair Stuart; s of William Mackay (d 1985), of Surrey, and Myra, *née* Freer; *b* 26 Oct 1954; *Educ* Emanuel Sch London, Oxford Air Trg Sch; *m* 7 July 1983; 2 da (Fiona Victoria, Morag Rachel); *Career* RAF cmmn Gen Duties Branch; airline captain; memb Aberdeen Mountain Rescue Assoc, mountain advsr to Scout Assoc; Freeman: City of London 1984, Worshipful Co of Air Pilots and Air Navigators 1980; FBIM, FInstD, MRIN; *Recreations* mountaineering, fishing, shooting; *Clubs* RAF; *Style*— Capt Alistair Mackay; Upper Walden, Horsewood Rd, Bridge of Weir, Renfrewshire, Scotland; Caprice, 25 Westhall Park, Warlingham, Surrey (☎ 0505 612909)

McKAY, Allen; JP, MP (Lab) Barnsley W and Penistone 1983-; s of Fred McKay (d 1980), and Martha Anne McKay; *b* 5 Feb 1927; *Educ* Hoyland Kirk Balk Secdy Mod Sch; *m* 1949, June, da of Clifford Simpson (d 1964); 1 s; *Career* clerical and steel works 1941-45, mineworker 1945-47, mining electrical engr 1947-65, asst manpower offr NCB Barnsley 1966-78 (industl res trainee 1965-66); JP Barnsley 1971, MP (Lab) for Penistone 1978-83, oppn whip 1982; *Style*— Allen McKay, Esq, JP, MP; 24 Springwood Rd, Hoyland, Barnsley, S Yorks S74 0AZ (☎ 0226 743418); House of Commons, London SW1 (☎ 071 219 4026)

MacKAY, Andrew James; MP (C) Berks E 1983-; s of Robert James MacKay, and Olive Margaret MacKay; *b* 27 Aug 1949; *Educ* Solihull; *m* 1975, Diana Joy Kinchin; 1 s, 1 d; *Career* ptnr Jones MacKay & Croxford Estate Agents 1974-; MP (C) Birmingham Stechford March 1977-79; dir Birmingham Housing Industs Ltd 1975-83; PPS to Tom King (Sec of State for NI) 1986-; sec of Cons Parly Foreign Affairs Ctee 1984-86, sec of state for Defence 1989; *Recreations* golf, squash; *Clubs* Berks Golf, Aberdoury Golf; *Style*— Andrew MacKay, Esq, MP; House of Commons, London SW1 (☎ 071 219 4109)

McKAY, Sheriff Archibald Charles; s of Patrick McKay, of Agolagh, Co Antrim (tenant of Sir George White, the hero of Ladysmith) (d 1957), and Catherine, *née* McKinley (d 1962); *b* 18 Oct 1929; *Educ* Knocknacarry Co Antrim, St Aloysius' Glasgow, Univ of Glasgow (MA, LLB); *m* 1956, Ernestine Maria Theresa, da of Ernest Tobia, of Glasgow (d 1934); 1 s (Timothy), 3 da (Frances, Ernestine, Oonagh); *Career* Nat Serv Lt RASC 1955-56; Sheriff 1978, Sheriff of Glasgow and Strathkelvin 1979-; *Recreations* flying light aircraft, motor cycling, amateur radio, tennis; *Style*— Sheriff Archibald McKay; 96 Springkell Gardens, Pollokshields, Glasgow G41 4EL

MacKAY, Hon Mrs (Cynthia); *née* Vansittart; da of 1 Baron Vansittart (d 1957); *b* 31 Dec 1922; *Educ* Heathfield, Ascot; *m* 1, 9 Jan 1942 (m dis 1954), Frederick Crocker Whitman, s of Malcolm D Whitman; 3 s, 1 da; m 2, 25 Nov 1955, Edward Hart MacKay, s of Dr Edward Hart Mackay; 2 s; *Style*— The Hon Mrs MacKay; 2655 Clay St, San Francisco, California 94115, USA (☎ 415 346 5625)

MACKAY, Dominic; *b* 12 Oct 1928; *Educ* HNC Electrical Engrg, Dip in Mgmnt Studies; *Career* signal instr HM Forces 1943-49; electrical engrg apprentice BEA 1949-51, quality engr AV Roe & Co 1951-59, reliability engr DeHavilland 1959-60; Honeywell: quality engr 1960-62, assembly mangr 1962-66, prodn mangr 1966-71, dir of prodn 1971-74; TMC Ltd: gen mangr 1974-79, ops dir 1979-84, md 1984-86; unit gen mangr 1987-: Glasgow Royal Infirmary, Stobhill Gen Hosp Unit, Greater Glasgow Health Bd; FIIM; *Recreations* music, reading; *Style*— Dominic Mackay, Esq

MACKAY, Prof Donald Iain; s of William MacKay (d 1980), and Rhona, *née* Cooper; *b* 27 Feb 1937; *Educ* Dollar Acad, Univ of Aberdeen; *m* 31 July 1961, Diana Marjory, da of Maj George Raffan (d 1980); 1 s (Donald Gregor b 1969), 2 da (Deborah Jane b 1964, Paula Clare b 1967); *Career* prof of political economy Univ of Aberdeen 1971-76, fell Heriot Watt Univ 1981- (prof of econs 1976-81); chm Piedon 1975-; dir: Adan and Company 1984-, Grampian Holdings 1987-; econ conslt to Sec of State for Scot 1971-; memb: Sea Fish Indust Authy 1981-87, S of Scot Electricity Bd 1985-88, Scot Econ Cncl 1985-; govr NIESR; FRSE 1987; *Books* Geographical Mobility and the Brain Drain (1970), Local Labour Markets and Wage Studies (1970), Labour Markets Under Different Employment Conditions (1971), Men Leaving Hull (1971), The Political Economy of North Sea Oil (1975), British Employment Statistics (1977); *Recreations* tennis, golf, bridge, chess; Newfield, 14 Gamekeeper's Road, Edinburgh EH4 6LU (☎ 031 336 1936); Pieda, 10 Chester St, Edinburgh EH3 7RA (☎ 031 225 5737, fax 031 225 5196)

MACKAY, Donald Scrimgeour (Don); s of Archibald Mackay (d 1984), of 41 Scott St, Perth, Scotland, and Mary Elizabeth, *née* Wells; *b* 19 March 1940; *Educ* Perth Acad, Perth HS, Dundee Trades Coll; *m* 19 June 1965, Patricia Anne, da of David Miller; 2 s (Craig Scrimgeour b 13 Oct 1966, Murray Graham b 26 Feb 1970); *Career* profesional football manager; player: 40 appearances Jeanfield Swifts 1958-59, 125 appearances Forfar Athletic 1959-62, 320 appearances Dundee Utd 1962-72, 18 appearances Southend Utd 1972-74; coach: Bristol City 1974-78, Norresundby Denmark 1978-80; mangr: Dundee 1980-83, Coventry City 1984-86, reserve team Glasgow Rangers 1986-87, Blackburn Rovers 1987-; honours: Danish Div 4 Championship Norresundby, runners up Bells League Cup Dundee 1981, Full Members Cup Blackburn Rovers 1987, Div 2 play offs Blackburn Rovers 1988, 1989, 1990; mangr of the month: Dundee 1981, Blackburn Rovers 6 times 1987-90; motor mechanic 1961-62 (apprentice 1956-61), qualified referee, coach Scot Football Assoc; *Recreations* golf, swimming, cricket, family; *Style*— Don Mackay, Esq; Blackburn Rovers FC, Ewood Park, Nuttall St, Blackburn, Lancs (☎ 0254 55432, fax 0254 671042)

MACKAY, Baron Donald Theodore; s of Baron Daniel Mackay (d 1962, s of Baron Theodoor Mackay, unc of 12 Lord Reay, and Baroness Juliana Anna van Lynden, da of Baron Constantijn van Lynden), and his 1 w, Helene, *née* Hommel; British subject; *b* 23 Feb 1910; *m* 1, 6 Dec 1939 (m dis 1945), Jonkvrouwe Alexandra Frederica, da of Jonkheer Bonifacius Christiaan de Savornin Lohman; m 2, 26 Sept 1945 (sep 1978), Kathleen, da of Percy Shaw Pearce; 1 s (Baron Niall Mackay b 1956, m 1985, Jennifer Mary, da of Hugh Butcher; 1 s (Baron Calum Hugh Mackay b 1989)), 1 da (Baroness Moira Mackay b 1952); *Career* Lt-Cdr (executive) Royal Netherlands Navy, served WWII with RN (submarines); LRCP, LRCS Edin, LRFP&S Glas 1951; *Style*— Baron Donald Mackay; Tigh a Chnuic, 15 Kentulavig, Leverburgh, Isle of Harris, Outer Hebrides PA83 3TX (☎ 085 982 301)

MACKAY, Sir (George Patrick) Gordon; CBE (1962); s of Rev Adam Mackay, BD (d 1931), and Katie Forrest, *née* Lawrence (d 1918); *b* 12 Nov 1914; *Educ* Univ of Aberdeen (MA); *m* 1954, Margaret Esmé, da of Christopher John Martin (d 1948); 1 s, 2 da; *Career* gen mangr East African Railways and Harbours 1961-64; World Bank: 1965-71, consultant 1971-73, dep dir 1974-75, dir 1975-78; memb Bd of Crown Agents 1980-82; OStJ 1964; kt 1966; *Recreations* golf; *Clubs* Nairobi; *Style*— Sir Gordon Mackay, CBE; Well Cottage, Sandhills, Brook, Surrey GU8 5UP (☎ 042 879 2549)

McKAY, Graham; s of Tom McKay (d 1985), of St Bees, Cumbria, and Dora Frances, *née* Graham (d 1950); *b* 11 July 1935; *Educ* Whitehaven GS, King's Coll London (LLB); *m* 24 Feb 1968, Christine Taylor, da of Charles Elijah Farnworth, of St Bees, Cumbria; 1 s (James Graham b 1973), 1 da (Sarah Louise b 1971); *Career* admitted slr 1959, cmmr for oaths 1966, chm Social Security Appeals Tbnls 1971; pres W Cumbria Law Soc 1985; memb Law Soc 1959; *Recreations* music; *Style*— Graham McKay, Esq; Abbey House, St Bees, Cumbria CA27 0DY (☎ 0946 822462); PO Box 1, 44 Duke St, Whitehaven, Cumbria CA28 7NR (☎ 0946 692194, fax 0946 62686)

MACKAY, Dr (Edward) Hugh; s of Hector Mackay (d 1971), of Rugby, Warwickshire, and Marjorie Rose, *née* Rolfe; *b* 10 Aug 1941; *Educ* Lawrence Sheriff Sch Rugby, Univ of Bristol (MB ChB); *m* Sept 1962, Valerie, da of Albert Cyril Ellenger (d 1961); 2 s (Andrew b 1965, Colin b 1968); *Career* registrar in pathology Frenchay Hosp Bristol 1970-72, clinical tutor in pathology Radcliffe Infirmary Oxford 1972-78, conslt histopathologist Leicester Gen Hosp 1978-; pres Leicestershire and Rutland Div BMA; memb: RSPB, Leicester Caledonian Soc; FRCPath 1986, memb ACP 1989; *Recreations* trout fishing, bird watching, sketching; *Clubs* Leicester Med Soc; *Style*— Dr Hugh Mackay; 68 Leicester Rd, Markfield, Leicestershire LE6 0RE (☎ 0530 243770); Leicester General Hospital, Gwendolen Rd, Leicester LE5 4PW (☎ 0533 490490)

MACKAY, Ian Munro; s of Henry Mackay (d 1983), and Annabel Clark, *née* Fraser; *b* 14 Sept 1947; *Educ* Golspie HS, Univ of Edinburgh (B Com); *m* 12 June 1970, Maureen Craig; 2 s (Adam b 1978, Grant b 1980), 2 da (Holly b 1973 d 1977, Rowan b 1975); *Career* CA; Inverness Office Ernst & Young 1973-76 (qualified Edinburgh Office 1973), mangr Shair & Co CAs Abu Dhabi and Dubai 1976-79, fndr of own firm of CAs 1979; Hon Sheriff Dornoch Ct 1985, vice pres Sutherland Curling Province, sec Dornoch Curling Club, treas and auditor local clubs and charities; memb Inst of CAs Scot 1973; *Recreations* curling, golf, garden, local history; *Style*— Ian Mackay, Esq; An Cala, 4 Sutherland Rd, Dornoch, Sutherland IV25 3SX (☎ 0862 810333); Anvil House, Main St, Golspie, Sutherland KW10 (☎ 04083 3160)

MACKAY, Ian Stuart; s of Rev Gordon Ernest Mackay, of Adelaide, Aust, and Sylvia Viola Dorothy, *née* Spencer (d 1975); *b* 16 June 1943; *Educ* Kearsney Coll Bothas Hill Natal SA, Univ of London (MB BS); *m* 1, 11 May 1968 (m dis), Angela; 1 s (Angus b 1971), 1 da (Fiona b 1972); m 2, 4 Sept 1981, Madeleine Hargreaves, *née* Tull; 1 da (Antonia b 1982), 1 step da (Charlotte b 1971); *Career* conslt ENT Surgn Charing Cross Hosp and Brompton Hosp, hon sr lectr in rhinology Inst of Laryngology and Otology, hon sr lectr Cardiothoracic Inst Univ of London; jt ed Scott-Brown's Otolaryngology: Rhinology Volume, contrib on rhinoplasty to Smith's Operative Surgery; hon treas Euro Acad Facial Surgery, asst sec Br Assoc of Otolaryncologists; memb RSM, FRCS; *Style*— Ian S Mackay, Esq; The Traverse, Bull Lane, Gerrards Cross, Bucks; 55 Harley Street, London W1N 1DD (☎ 071 580 5070)

MACKAY, Hon Mrs (Iona Héloïse); da of Baron Tanlaw (Life Peer); *b* 1960; *m* 1978 (m dis 1988), Stephen P Hudson; *Style*— The Hon Iona Mackay

MACKAY, Hon James; o s of Baron Mackay of Clashfern (Life Peer); *b* 1958; *Educ* Cambridge Univ (MA), Edinburgh Univ (MB, ChB); *m* 15 Feb 1991, Marion E, da of J E McArthur, of Edinburgh; *Career* medicine, hon regnl and res fell Univ Dept of Clinical Surgery Univ of Edinburgh; *Style*— Dr the Hon James Mackay; 123 Nicolson Street, Edinburgh, EH8 9ER

MACKAY, Hon James Jonathan Thorn; yr s of 3 Earl of Inchcape and his 1 wife Aline Thorne (Pixie), *née* Pease; *b* 28 May 1947; *Educ* Eton, Trinity Coll Cambridge (MA); *m* 1970, Mary Caroline, er da of Peter Joyce, of Becklands Farm, Whitchurch-Canonicorum, Dorset; 1 s, 1 da; *Style*— The Hon James Mackay; 34A Dorset Square, London NW1 6QJ

McKAY, Sir James Wilson; JP (Edinburgh 1972), DL (Edinburgh 1972); s of John McKay; *b* 12 March 1912; *Educ* Dumfermline HS, Portobello Secdy Sch Edinburgh; *m* 1942, Janette K A Urquhart; 3 da; *Career* served WW II Lt RNVR; insur broker; md John McKay (Insur) Ltd Edinburgh; Lord Lt of City of Edinburgh 1969-72, Lord Provost of Edinburgh 1969-72; kt 1971; *Style*— Sir James McKay, JP, DL; 11 Cammo Gdns, Edinburgh, Scotland EH8 8EJ (☎ 031 339 6755)

MACKAY, Dr John; s of William Mackay (d 1952), of Nottingham, and Eliza, *née* Kellock (d 1952); *b* 23 June 1914; *Educ* Mundella Sch Nottingham, Univ Coll Nottingham, Merton Coll Oxford (BA, DPhil); *m* 7 Aug 1952, Margaret, da of Alexander John Ogilvie (d 1937), of Edinburgh; 2 s (William b 1953, Andrew b 1960), 2 da (Elspeth b 1955, Mary b 1957); *Career* ordinary and able seaman RN 1940-42, Sub Lt RNVR 1942-45, temp instr Lt RN 1945-46; travelling sec Student Christian Movement 1936-38, English lectr St John's Diocesan Trg Coll York 1938-40 and 1946, res Merton Coll Oxford 1946-48, asst master Merchant Taylors' Sch Crosby 1948-54, second master Cheltenham Coll 1954-60, headmaster Bristol GS 1960-75; chm HMC 1970; *Recreations* gardening, reading, watching cricket; *Clubs* East India; *Style*— Dr John Mackay; The Old Post Office, Tormarton, Badminton, Avon GL9 1HU (☎ 0454

21243)

McKAY, Dr John Henderson; CBE (1987), DL (Edinburgh 1988); s of Thomas Johnstone McKay (d 1956), of 16 Letham Grove, Pumpherston, Midlothian, and Patricia Madeleine, *née* Henderson (d 1986); *b* 12 May 1929; *Educ* West Calder HS, Open Univ (BA, PhD); *m* 8 Feb 1964, Catherine Watson, da of William Middleton Taylor (d 1968), of 21 Crewe Grove, Edinburgh; 1 s (Ewen b 1969), 1 da (Charis b 1965); *Career* Nat Serv RA 1950-52, gunner UK and Far East; Customs & Excise 1952-85; Lord Provost of Edinburgh 1984-88, JP Edinburgh 1984, Lord Lt Edinburgh 1984-88; chm Edinburgh Int Festival Soc 1984-88, co-chm Edinburgh Mil Tattoo 1984-88; cnclr Royal Caledonian Hort Soc 1974-77 and 1984-88 (vice pres, sec and treas 1988-); Hon DUniv Edinburgh 1989; *Recreations* golf, gardening; *Clubs* Lothianburn Golf; *Style—* Dr John McKay, CBE, DL; 2 Buckstone Way, Edinburgh EH10 6PN (☎ 031 445 2865)

MACKAY, John Jackson; s of Jackson MacKay (d 1964), and Jane, *née* Farquharson; *b* 15 Nov 1938; *Educ* Univ of Glasgow (BSc, Dip Ed); *m* 1961, Sheena, da of James Wagner (d 1963); 2 s, 1 da; *Career* former head Maths Dept Oban HS; MP (C): Argyll 1979-83, Argyll and Bute 1983-87; PPS to George Younger as Sec of State for Scotland 1982; Parly under sec of state Scot Office with responsibility for: Health and Social Work 1982-85, Health Social Work and Home Affrs 1985-86, Educn Agric and Fisheries 1986-87; chief exec Scot Cons Pty 1987-90, chm Sea Fish Industry Authority 1990-; *Recreations* fishing, sailing; *Style—* John MacKay, Esq; Innishail, 51 Springkell Drive, Pollokshields, Glasgow G41 4EZ (☎ 041 427 5356)

MACKAY, Lady Lucinda Louise; *née* Mackay; did not assume husband's surname on marriage; da of 3 Earl of Inchcape and Aline, *née* Pease (now Thorn Roe), da of Sir Richard Pease, 2 Bt (d 1970), of Richmond, Yorks; *b* 13 Dec 1941; *Educ* Chatelard Sch, Univ of Edinburgh (MA), Edinburgh Coll of Art, Central Sch of Art and Design; *m* 8 April 1983 (m dis 1987), Sheriff David Wilson Bogie, s of Robert Bogie (d 1978), of Edinburgh; *Career* formerly schoolmistress in comprehensive sch; portrait painter; exhibitions in London and Edinburgh; *Books* Poems (1980), Lucidities (1989); *Recreations* Scrabble, poetry, bridge, theatre, letter writing, skiing, looking for spoonerisms, riding, philosophy, music, making friends, dancing (classical, ballet, ballroom, Scottish), sewing, embroidery, home cooking, arranging flowers, languages; *Clubs* Edinburgh Univ Staff, Royal Over Seas League, The Sloane, Scottish Arts; *Style—* Lady Lucinda Mackay; c/o The Scottish Arts Club, 24 Rutland Sq, Edinburgh 1

MACKAY, Neil Douglas Malcolm; s of Gp Capt Malcolm Bruce Mackay (d 1971), and Josephine Mary, *née* Brown (d 1965); *b* 28 Aug 1939; *Educ* Loretto; *m* 10 May 1969, Frances Sarah, da of Lt-Col Claude Dudgeon van Namen, of Gaunt Cottage, Wargrave, Berks; 2 s (Loudon b 1971, Rory b 1982), 2 da (Kirsty b 1973, Lorna b 1976); *Career* Lt RA BAOR; merchant banker; Lazard Bros & Co Ltd: asst dir 1974, exec dir 1979, md 1987-; Indust Reorganisation Corporation 1967-68; non-exec dir of cos incl: Trident Group Printers Ltd 1974-79, R & AG Crossland Ltd 1975-78, Hadson Oil (UK) Ltd 1981-86, Hadson Petroleum International plc 1981-86, Aaronite Group plc 1983-86; *Recreations* bridge, tennis; *Clubs* Hurlingham; *Style—* Neil D M Mackay, Esq; 21 Moorfields, London EC2P 2HT (☎ 071 588 2721)

MACKAY, Prof Norman; s of Donald Mackay (d 1937), of Glasgow, and Catherine, *née* Macleod (d 1957); *b* 15 Sept 1936; *Educ* Govan HS, Univ of Glasgow (MB ChB, MD); *m* 10 Feb 1961, (Grace) Violet, da of Charles McCaffer (d 1959), of Kilwinning; 2 s (Ronald b 8 Sept 1967, Donald b 30 Dec 1970), 2 da (Susan b 28 July 1962, Violet b 24 July 1964); *Career* hon conslt physician Victoria Infirmary Glasgow 1989- (conslt 1973-89), dean of postgrad med and prof of postgrad med educn Univ of Glasgow 1989-; hon sec: RCPSGlas 1973-83, Conf of Royal Med Colls and Faculties in Scot 1982-; pres Southern Med Soc 1989-90; FRCP, FRCPE; *Recreations* soccer, golf, gardening; *Style—* Prof Norman Mackay; 4 Erskine Ave, Dumbreck, Glasgow G41 5AL (☎ 041 427 0900); Department of Postgraduate Medical Education, The University, Glasgow (☎ 041 339 3786, fax 041 330 4526)

MACKAY, Peter; s of John Swinton Mackay, of Kinloch, Perthshire, and Patricia May, *née* Atkinson (d 1976); *b* 6 July 1940; *Educ* Glasgow HS, Univ of St Andrews (MA); *m* 29 Aug 1964, Sarah White, da of Reginald White Holdich, of Cherry Burton, East York; 1 s (Andrew), 2 da (Elspeth, Sally); *Career* teacher Kyogle HS NSW Aust 1962-63, asst princ Scottish Office 1963, princ private sec to Sec of State of Scotland Rt Hon Gordon Campbell MC and Rt Hon William Ross MBE 1973-75, head Manpower and Orgn Div SO 1975-78, Nuffield Travelling fell (Canada, Aust, NZ) 1978-79, head Local Govt Div SO 1979-83, seconded dir Scotland Manpower Servs Cmmn 1983-85; under sec: Dept of Employment 1985-86, Scottish Educn Dept 1987-89 (responsible for further and higher educn arts and sport); princ estab offr Scot Office 1989, sec Indust Dept for Scot 1989-; *Recreations* high altitudes and latitudes, climbing, sea canoeing, sailing, tennis; *Clubs* Clyde Canoe, Lothian Sea Kayak; *Style—* Peter Mackay, Esq; 6 Henderland Rd, Edinburgh EH12 6BB (☎ 031 337 2830); New St Andrews House, Edinburgh EH1 3TA (☎ 031 244 4602, fax 031 244 4785)

MACKAY, Hon (Shona) Ruth; da of Baron Mackay of Clashfern (Life Peer); *b* 1968; *Educ* St Margaret's Sch Edinburgh; *Career* veterinary student; *Style—* The Hon Ruth Mackay; 19/11 East Parkside, Edinburgh EH16 5XN

MACKAY, Shena; da of Benjamin Carr Mackay, of London, and Morag, *née* Carmichael; *b* 6 June 1944; *Educ* Tonbridge Girls' GS, Kidbrooke Comp; *m* 1964 (m dis), Robin Francis Brown; 3 da (Sarah Frances b 11 March 1965, Rebecca Mary b 21 Aug 1966, Cecily Rose b 15 May 1969); *Career* author; awarded: Arts Cncl grants 1970s, travelling scholarship Soc of Authors 1986, Fawcett prize 1987; memb: ALCS, The Writers' Guild; *Books* Dust Falls on Eugene Schlumberger (1964), Toddler on the Run (1964), Music Upstairs (1965), Old Crow (1967), An Advent Calendar (1971), Babies in Rhinestones (1983), A Bowl of Cherries (1984), Redhill Rococo (1986), Dreams of Dead Women's Handbags (1987); *Style—* Ms Shena Mackay; Rogers Coleridge & White Ltd, 20 Powis Mews, London W11 1JN (☎ 071 221 3717, 071 229 9084)

McKAY, William Robert; s of William Wallace McKay (d 1987), of Edinburgh, and Margaret Halley Adamson, *née* Foster; *b* 18 April 1939; *Educ* Trinity Acad Leith, Univ of Edinburgh (MA); *m* 28 Dec 1962, Margaret Muriel, da of Eric Millard Bellwood Fillmore, OBE, of Bexhill on Sea, Sussex; 2 da (Catriona b 4 March 1967, Elspeth (Mrs Sagar) (twin) b 4 March 1967); *Career* dept of the clerk of the House of Commons 1961-, clerk Scot Affrs Ctee 1971-74 and 1979-81, sec House of Commons Cmmn 1981-84, princ clerk fin ctees 1985-87, interim clerk designate Scot Assembly 1978, sec Public Accounts Cmmn 1985-87; jt clerk Br-Irish Inter-Parly Body 1989-, Clerk of the Jnls 1987-; *Books* Erskine May's Private Journal 1883-86 (ed, 1984), Mr Speaker's Secretaries (1986), Clerks in the House of Commons 1363-1989 a Biographical List (1989), Observations, Rules and Orders (ed, 1989), The Northern Whig, George Mackay 3rd Lord Reay and the Jacobites (1991); *Recreations* living on Coll; *Style—* William McKay, Esq; 26 Earl St, Cambridge CB1 1JR; Lochan a'Bhaigh, Isle of Coll, Argyll; House of Commons, London SW1A 0AA

MACKAY-LEWIS, Hon Mrs (Virginia Charlotte Angela); *née* Campbell; da of 3 Baron Colgrain, and his 1 w Veronica Margaret, *née* Webster; *b* 19 Oct 1948; *m* 1973, Maj Jonathan Charles Mackay-Lewis; 2 s (James Edward b 1978, George Mungo Pyne b 1984), 1 da (Gemma Elizabeth b 1977); *Style—* Hon Mrs Mackay-Lewis; Gattertop, Leominster, Herefordshire HR6 0JY

MACKAY OF CLASHFERN, Baron (Life Peer UK 1979), of Eddracchillis in the District of Sutherland; James Peter Hymers Mackay; PC (1979); s of James Mackay (d 1958); *b* 2 July 1927; *Educ* George Heriot's Sch Edinburgh, Univ of Edinburgh, Trinity Cambridge; *m* 1958, Elizabeth Gunn Hymers, da of D D Manson; 1 s (Hon James b 1958), 2 da (Hon Elizabeth Janet (Hon Mrs Campbell) b 1961, Hon Shona Ruth b 1968); *Career* advocate 1955, QC Scot 1965; sheriff principal Renfrew and Argyll 1972-74, vice dean Faculty of Advocates 1973-76, dean 1976-79; cmmr Northern Lighthouses 1975-84, pt/t memb Scottish Law Cmmn 1976-79, dir Stenhouse Holdings Ltd 1976-78, memb Insur Brokers' Registration Cncl 1978-79; Lord Advocate of Scotland 1979-84, Lord of Session 1984-85, Lord of Appeal in Ordinary 1985-89, Lord Chllr Oct 1987-; Hon LLD: Dundee 1983, Edinburgh 1983, Strathclyde 1985, Aberdeen 1987, St Andrews 1988, Cambridge 1989; Hon Dr of Laws Coll of William and Mary 1989, hon fell: Trinity Coll Cambridge 1989, Girton Coll Cambridge 1989, Inst Taxation 1983; fell Int Acad of Trial Lawyers 1979, FRSE 1984, hon FICE 1989; *Clubs* New (Edinburgh); *Style—* The Rt Hon the Lord Mackay of Clashfern, PC; House of Lords, London SW1R 0PW

McKEAN, Charles Alexander; s of John Laurie McKean, of Glasgow, and Nancy Burns, *née* Lendrum; *b* 16 July 1946; *Educ* Fettes Coll Edinburgh, Univ of Bristol (BA); *m* 18 Oct 1975, Margaret Elizabeth, da of Mervyn Yeo, of Cardiff; 2 s (Andrew Laurie b 1978, David Alexander b 1981); *Career* ed London Architect 1970-75; RIBA: London regnl sec 1968-71, Eastern regnl sec 1971-79, projects offr Community Architecture and Industl Regeneration 1977-79; sec and treas RIAS 1979-, architectural corr Scotland on Sunday 1988-90 (The Times 1977-83); memb Exhibitions Panel Scottish Arts Cncl 1980-83, dir Workshops and Artists Studios Ltd 1980-85, sec to the RIAS Hill House Tst 1979-82, tstee Thirlestane Castle Tst 1983-, memb Environment and Town Planning Ctee The Saltire Soc 1984-85, memb Advsy Cncl for the Arts in Scotland 1985-88; currently memb Cncl: Architectural Heritage Soc of Scotland and Charles Rennie Mackintosh Soc; Architectural Journalist of the Year 1979 and 1983, Bldg Journalist of the Year, RSA Bossom Lecture 1986; hon memb The Satire Soc 1990; FRSA 1978, FSA Scot 1983, Hon FRIBA 1990; *Books* London 1981 (1970), Modern Buildings in London 1965-75 (with Tom Jestico, 1975), Living over the Shop (1976), Battle of Styles (with David Atwell, 1976), Funding the Future (1977), Fight Blight (1977), An Outine of Western Architecture (jtly, 1980), Architectural Guide to Cambridge and East Anglia since 1920, Edinburgh - an illustrated architectural guide (1982), Dundee - an illustrated introduction (with David Walker, 1984), Stirling and the Trossachs (1985), The Scottish Thirties (1987), The District of Moray (1987), Central Glasgow (with David and Dr Frank Walker), Banff and Buchan (1990), For a Wee Country (1990); *Clubs* Scottish Arts; *Style—* Charles McKean, Esq; 10 Hillpark Rd, Edinburgh EH4 (☎ 031 226 2753); The Royal Incorporation of Architects in Scotland, 15 Rutland Sq, Edinburgh EH1 2BE (☎ 031 229 7205)

McKEAN, Douglas; CB (1977); s of Alexander McKean (d 1962), of Enfield, and Irene Emily, *née* Ofverberg (d 1980); *b* 2 April 1917; *Educ* Merchant Taylors', St John's Coll Oxford (MA); *m* 6 June 1942, Anne, da of Roger Clayton (d 1954), of Riding Mill, N'mberland; 2 s (Robert b 1944, Andrew b 1948); *Career* Civil Serv: princ WO 1947-49, HM Treasy 1949-77 (asst sec 1956-62, under sec 1962-77, loan to DOE 1970-72); dir Agric Mortgage Corp 1978-87; dep sec Central Bd of Fin C of E 1978-83, tstee Irish Sailors and Soldiers Land Tst 1980-, govr Whitelands Coll Roehampton 1984-89, churchwarden parish church of St Andrew Enfield 1987-; *Books* Money Matters - A Guide to the Finances of The Church of England (1987); *Recreations* mountain walking; *Clubs* Utd Oxford and Cambridge Univ; *Style—* Douglas McKean, Esq, CB; The Dower House, Forty Hill, Enfield, Middlesex EN2 9EJ (☎ 081 363 2365)

MCKEAN, Lorne; da of Lt Cdr J A H McKean, RN (d 1981), and Beatrice Blance Mowbray *née* Bellairs; *b* 16 April 1939; *Educ* Elmhurst Ballet Sch, Guildford Art Sch, Royal Acad Schs; *m* 7 Nov 1964, Edwin John Cumming, s of Edwin Russell; 2 da (Rebecca b 21 Jan 1966, Tanya b 25 April 1968); *Career* sculptor; public and large works include: A A Milne memorial London Zoo Bear Club, Shearwaters Richmond, Arctic Terns Chester Business Park, Willoughby House Fountain Richmond, Girl and the Swan Reading, Herons Thames Water Authy Reading, Osprey Fountain Greenwich Connecticut USA, Great Swan Great Swan Alley EC2, Swan Fountain Horsham; equestrian and horse sculptures: H R H Prince Philip on his polo pony, HM The Queens personal Silver Wedding gift to her husband, Prince Charles on polo pony Pans Folly, John Pinches International Dressage Trophy, Galoubet French show jumping stallion, Pony series for Royal Worcester Porcelain, racehorses Troy and Snurge; portraits include: The late Lord Salisbury (Hatfield House), Sir Michael Redgrave, The late HRH Prince William of Gloucester, The Earl of Lichfield televised for portrait series, HM The Queen Drapers Hall and RHHT; FRBS 1968; *Recreations* animals; *Style—* Miss Lorne McKean; Lethendry, Polecat Valley, Hindhead, Surrey GU26 6BE (☎ 0428 605655)

McKEAN, Roderick Hugh Ross (Roddy); *b* 13 March 1956; *Educ* The HS of Dundee, Univ of Edinburgh (LLB); *Career* articled clerk W & J Burness, WS 1978-80; admitted slr 1980; asst slr: Maclay Murray and Spens 1980-84, Lovell White & King 1984-88; ptnr Lovell White Durrant 1988-; memb: Law soc, Law Soc of Scotland; *Recreations* skiing, tennis, yachting, riding; *Style—* Roddy McKean, Esq; Lovell White Durrant, 65 Holborn Viaduct, London EC1A 2DY (☎ 071 236 0066, fax 071 248 4212, telex 887122)

McKEE, Dr Angus Hugh; s of William Bissett McKee, of Glasgow, and Alice, *née* Ingram; *b* 12 Feb 1946; *Educ* Buckhaven HS, Univ of Edinburgh (BSc, MB ChB); *m* 18 Oct 1980, Ruth Fraser, da of Alec McBain (d 1978), of Douglas, Lanarkshire; *Career* sr registrar in anaesthetics (former sr house offr, registrar) W Infirmary Glasgow 1972-77, conslt anaesthetist Stobhill Hosp Glasgow 1977-; church elder and covenanter ldr W Glasgow New Church; fell Coll of Anaesthetists 1974; *Recreations* hill walking, preaching; *Style—* Dr Angus McKee; 526 Anniesland Rd, Glasgow G13 1YA (☎ 041 954 1992); Stobhill General Hospital, Balornock Rd, Glasgow (☎ 041 558 0111)

McKEE, Maj Sir (William) Cecil; ERD (1945), JP (Belfast 1957); s of W B McKee; *b* 13 April 1905; *Educ* Methodist Coll, Queen's Univ Belfast; *m* 1932, Florence Ethel Irene Gill; 1 da; *Career* served WW II RA; estate agent; Lord Mayor of Belfast 1957-59; Hon LLD Queen's Univ Belfast; KStJ; kt 1959; *Style—* Maj Sir Cecil McKee, ERD, JP; 250 Malone Rd, Belfast, N Ireland (☎ 0232 666979)

McKEE, Ian Arthur; MBE (1973); s of Rev John McKee (d 1960), of 37 Lyford Rd, London, and Irene Mary, *née* Sainsbury (d 1962); *b* 14 April 1916; *Educ* Taunton Sch, Trinity Coll of Music; *m* 21 Aug 1954, Jessie Stephen, da of Edward Poole; 1 s (James b 27 Aug 1965), 1 da (Melissa b 23 Nov 1963); *Career* cmmnd KOSB 1942, Capt 1943 QM and Adj 5 Northants Regt; J Curwen & Sons Ltd 1934, educn mangr Hutchinson & Co 1950, educn rep Methuen and Co Ltd 1954, mangr educn dept Methuen Publishers 1958, chm Educn Publishers Exhibition Ctee 1965-68, sales dir Methuen Educnl Ltd 1966, chm Book Devpt Cncl Overseas Exhibition Ctee 1972-76, vice chm Methuen Educnl Ltd 1974-83, Educnl Publishers Supplies Ctee conslt 1983- (memb 1970-82); hon sec 78 Div Battleaxe Club 1947-, life govr Taunton Sch 1940-, vice chm Hants Branch Mental Health Fndn 1987-, memb Winchester Co Music Festival Ctee

1978-; *Style*— Ian McKee, Esq, MBE; 5 Park Ave, Winchester, Hants SO23 8DJ (☎ 0962 860992)

McKEE, (George) Kenneth; CBE (1972); s of Frederick Charles McKee (d 1958), of Ilford, Essex, and Alice Theodora, *née* Nicholson (d 1953); *b* 5 Jan 1906; *Educ* Chigwell Sch Essex, St Bartholomew's Hosp Coll; *m* 1, July 1932 (m dis 1952), Sylvia Blanch, da of Joseph Bird (d 1950), of Lewisham; 1 s (Michael b 22 Aug 1933), 1 da (Theodora b 8 Jan 1935); m 2, 8 Jan 1954, (Elizabeth Rosemary) Diana; 1 da (Belinda b 6 April 1955); *Career* Nat Serv Maj RAMC duration of WWII; res surgn St Bartholomew's Hosp 1930-32; Norfolk and Norwich Hosp: conslt orthopaedic surgn 1939-59, sr conslt orthopaedic surgn 1959-71, res orthopaedic surgn 1971-76; author of numerous articles on orthopaedics especially on hip replacement; Hon ScD Univ of Cambridge 1975; FRSM 1930, FRCS 1934, fell Br Orthopaedic Assoc 1936-; *Books* Biomaterials (1982), Total Hip Replacement - Past, Present and Future; *Recreations* golf, skiing, sailing; *Clubs* Royal Norfolk and Norwich Golf; *Style*— Kenneth McKee, Esq, CBE; Christmas Cottage, The Green, Tacolneston, Norwich NR16 1EA (☎ 050 841 500); Flat 3, 81 Newmarket Rd, Norwich NR2 2HN (☎ 0603 623968)

McKEE, Dr William James Ernest; QHP (1987); s of John Sloan McKee (d 1974), of Pontefract, Yorks, and Annie Emily *née* McKinley (d 1971); *b* 20 Feb 1929; *Educ* Queen Elizabeth's Wakefield, Trinity Coll Cambridge (BA, MA, MB BChir, MD, LRCP, MRCS), Queen's Coll Oxford, The Radcliffe Infirmary; *m* Josée, da of Francis James Tucker (d 1975), of Cardiff; 3 da (Jennifer b 1958, Katherine b 1963, Fiona b 1971); *Career* Nat Serv RAF Educn Serv 1947-49; clinical and res hosp appts 1952-61, community med appts with London RHB 1961-69, sr admin MO Liverpool RHB 1969-74; regnl MO: Mersey RHA 1974-76, Wessex RHA (regnl med advsr) 1976-89; contrib to med jls on various subjects; memb: Hunter Working Pty on the Future Arrangements for Med Admin and Public Health in the NHS 1972-73, Sec of State's Advsy Ctee on the Application of Computing Sci to Med and the NHS 1973-76; chm Jt Liason Ctee for Health Serv Boundary Reorganisation in Met Co of Merseyside 1974; memb: Cncl for Postgrad Med Educn (Eng and Wales) 1975-85, Bd of Faculty of Med Univ of Southampton 1976-89; chm Working Pty to Review Health Serv Policy for the Mentally Handicapped in Wessex 1978, memb DHSS Advsy Ctee on Med Manpower Planning 1982-85, chm Eng Regnl Med Offrs 1984-86, UK med rep to Hosp Ctee of the EEC 1985-89, memb DHSS Jt Planning Advsy Ctee 1985-89, head UK delgn to Hosp Ctee of EEC 1988 and 1989, conslt various State Bds and Depts of Health 1989-; FFCM 1972; *Recreations* fly fishing, golf; *Style*— Dr William McKee, QHP; Morningdale, 22A Bereweeke Ave, Winchester, Hants SO22 6BH (☎ 0962 861369)

MacKELLAR, Jean Elizabeth; da of Edward Gosset Green-Emmott (d 1976), and Violet Mary, *née* Turner (d 1973) *see* Burke's Landed Gentry 18 edn Vol II, Green Emmott of Emmott Hall; Lady of the Manor of Rawdon; *b* 17 Jan 1935; *Educ* Hatherop Castle; *m* 14 Sept 1962, Maj Peter Malcolm Kerr MacKellar, s of Lt-Col John Gray MacKellar, DSO, OBE, DL (d 1975); 1 s (Peter Douglas Edward Emmott b 1967), 1 da (Kathryn Mary Emmott b 1964); *Style*— Mrs Peter MacKellar; Eden House, Warren Rd, Liss, Hants (☎ 0730 895 191)

McKELLEN, Sir Ian Murray; CBE (1979); s of Denis Murray McKellen (d 1964), of Bolton, Lancs, and Margery Lois, *née* Sutcliffe (d 1952); *b* 25 May 1939; *Educ* Wigan GS, Bolton Sch, St Catharine's Coll Cambridge (BA); *Career* actor and dir; first professional appearance A Man For All Seasons (Belgrade Theatre Coventry) 1961, first London appearance A Scent of Flowers (Duke of York's) 1964, Nat Theatre at the Old Vic 1966, Recruiting Offr in Chips with Everything (Cambridge Theatre Co) 1968, revived Richard II and Edward II at Edinburgh Festival with Br and Euro tour (incl Mermaid and Piccadilly Theatres) 1969-70, Hamlet Br and Euro tours and Cambridge Theatre 1971; fndr memb Actors' Co 1971-73; performances incl: Ruling The Roost, 'Tis Pity She's a Whore (Edinburgh Festival) 1972, Knots, The Wood Demon (Edinburgh Festival) 1973; RSC performances incl: Dr Faustus (Edinburgh Festival) 1974, King John (Aldwych) 1975, Romeo and Juliet, The Winter's Tale and Macbeth (Plays and Players award 1976) Stratford 1976-77, Pillars of the Community (SWET Award 1977), The Alchemist (SWET award 1978) Aldwych and RSC Warehouse 1977-78, Iago in Othello (Evening Standard and Plays and Players awards) The Other Place Stratford 1989; RSC touring company (also artistic dir): Twelfth Night, Three Sisters, Is There Honey Still for Tea?, Ashes (Young Vic) 1975, Words, Words, Words (solo recital, Edinburgh Festival and Belfast Festival) 1979, Every Good Boy Deserves Favour, Bent (SWET award 1979) Royal Court and Criterion 1979, Amadeus New York (Tony Award) 1980-81, Cowardice (Ambassadors) 1983; Nat Theatre: Venice Preserv'd, Coriolanus (Evening Standard award) 1984-85, Wild Honey (Laurence Olivier award, Plays and Players award) 1986-87, Henceforward (Vaudeville) 1988-89; assoc dir NT 1985- (produced and acted in): The Duchess of Malfi, The Real Inspector Hound, The Critic, The Cherry Orchard, Bent 1990, Kent in King Lear 1990, title role Richard III 1990; one-man USA and UK tour Acting Shakespeare 1987; films incl: Priest of Love, Plenty, Scandal (1988); TV: Walter 1982, Walter and June 1983, Countdown to War 1989; pres Marlow Soc 1960-61, memb Cncl Equity 1971-72, hon fell St Catharine's Coll Cambridge 1982, Hon DLitt Univ of Nottingham 1989; kt 1991; *Style*— Sir Ian McKellen, CBE; James Sharkey Associates, 15 Golden Square, London W1R 3AG (☎ 071 434 3801/6, telex 295 251 ISA Long)

McKELVEY, Air Cdre John Wesley; CB (1969), MBE (1944); s of Capt John Wesley McKelvey, of Enfield, Middx (d 1939), and Emily Francis Louisa, *née* Milsted (d 1976); *b* 25 June 1914; *Educ* Enfield Central Sch, RAF Aircraft Apprentice; *m* 13 Aug 1938, Eileen Amy, da of John Charles Carter, of Enfield (d 1968); 2 s (John b 1943, d 1969, Michael b 1944); *Career* fighter cmd 1932-38, cmmnd 1941 (Eng branch), served Egypt, Syria, Iraq, Bomber Cmd 1939-45, OC Air Miny Manpower Res Unit 1945-47, OC Air Miny Servicing and Devpt Unit 1947-49, RAF Staff Coll 1949; engr duties: FEAF 1949-52, HQ Bomber Cmd 1952-54; Jt Servs Staff Coll Latimer 1954, OC no 60 Maintenance Unit 1954-56; sr tech SO: HQ no 19 GP 1956-57, Task Force Grapple Christmas Is 1957-59; sr air SO HQ no 24 gp 1959-62, dep dir of intelligence (tech) 1962-64, dir aircraft and asst attache def res devpt Br Embassy Washington DC 1964-66, AO Wales and Cmdt RAF St Athan 1966-69, ret 1969; sec appeals RAF Benevolent Fund 1970-79; MRAeS 1967, CEng 1968; *Recreations* bowls, gardening; *Clubs* RAF; *Style*— Air Cdre John McKelvey, CB, MBE; Inchmerle, 19 Greensome Drive, Ferndown, Winbourne, Dorset BH22 8BE (☎ 0202 894464)

McKELVEY, William; MP (Lab) Kilmarnock and Loudoun 1983-; *b* 1934,July; *Educ* Morgan Acad, Dundee Coll of Technol; *m* ; 2 s; *Career* former full-time union official, memb Dundee City Cncl, joined Lab Pty 1961, MP Kilmarnock 1979-1983; sponsored by AUEW; *Style*— William McKelvey, Esq, MP; 41 Main Street, Kilmaurs, Ayrshire

MCKELVIE, Dr James Donald; s of Donald McKelvie (d 1964), of Kildown, Isle of Arran, and Mary Anne, *née* Macleod; *b* 17 Nov 1955; *Educ* Strathallan Sch, Univ of St Andrews (MA), Univ of Strathclyde (DAcc), Nat Univ of Ireland (MB ChB, BAO, LRCSI, LRCPI); *Career* doctor; trained in gen med and back pain Glasgow Royal Infirmary 1986, Yale Hosp Clwyd 1989, physician London Scottish RFC; memb OStJ 1986; *Recreations* swimming; *Clubs* RSAC, Western Baths Glasgow; *Style*— Dr James McKelvie; 69 Marley St, London W1N 1DE (☎ 071 224 6247)

MCKENNA, Charles; s of John George McKenna (d 1987), and Bernadette, *née* Conney; *b* 9 April 1954; *Educ* St Bede's GS Lanchester Co Durham, Univ of Durham (BA); *m* 30 May 1986, Alison Jane, da of John Fearn, of Abercych, S Wales; *Career* admitted slr 1978; ptnr Allen & Overy 1985- (articled clerk, asst slr 1978-85, seconded as legal advsr in quotations dept The Stock Exchange 1981-82); Freeman Worshipful Co of Slrs 1986; memb Law Soc 1975; *Recreations* sport, travel; *Style*— Charles McKenna, Esq; Allen & Overy, 9 Cheapside, London EC2V 6AD (☎ 071 248 9898, fax 071 236 2191, telex 8812801)

McKENNA, David; CBE (1967, OBE 1946, MBE 1943); s of Rt Hon Reginald McKenna (d 1943), and Pamela Margaret, *née* Jekyll (d 1943); *b* 16 Feb 1911; *Educ* Eton, Trinity Coll Cambridge (BA, MA); *m* 4 April 1934, Lady Cecilia Elizabeth Keppel, da of 9 Earl of Albemarle, MC (d 1979); 3 da (Miranda (Mrs John Villiers) b 10 Aug 1935, Primrose (Mrs Christopher Arnander) b 9 May 1937, Sophia b 11 June 1944); *Career* WWII RE Capt 1939, Maj 1942, Lt-Col 1944 Transportation Serv Iraq, Turkey, India, Burma; London Passenger Tport Bd: 1934-39, 1946-55, asst gen mangr Southern Region BR 1955-61, chief commercial offr HQ 1962, gen mangr S Region 1963-68, memb bd BR 1968-76 (pt/t memb bd 1976-78); dir Isles of Scilly Steamship Co 1976-; chm: govrs of Sadlers Wells 1962-76, Bach Choir 1968-76 (memb 1934-76); memb Dover Harbour Bde 1969-80, vice pres RCM 1980 (memb Cncl 1946); FRCM, FCIT (pres 1972); Commandeur de l'Ordre Nationale du Mérite (France) 1974; *Recreations* music; *Clubs* Brooks's, Royal Cornwall Yacht; *Style*— David McKenna, Esq, CBE; Rosteague, Portscatho, Truro, Cornwall TR2 5EF (☎ 087258 346)

MCKENNA, John Michael; s of John Maurice McKenna (d 1961), of Purley, Surrey, and Gladys Mary, *née* Staker (d 1965); *b* 28 Aug 1929; *Educ* Purley GS, Imperial Coll London (BSc, ACGI, MSc, DIC); *m* 22 Aug 1959, Evelyn Mary, da of Thomas Cunney (d 1964), of Aclare, Co Sligo, Ireland; *Career* Nat Serv 2 Lt RE 1948-50; Binnie & Ptnrs 1953-66 (graduate engr rising to head Fndn Dept Mangla Dam Project Pakistan), sr engr Soil Mechanics Ltd 1967-69, individual conslt and geotechnical engr specialising in site investigation and design of earth and rock fill dams 1969-; currently memb 10 Dam Review Bds; FICE 1967 (MICE 1958), FIWE 1968 (MIWE 1959), FGS 1968, FASCE 1969 (MASCE 1959), FIWEM 1987; *Recreations* fly-fishing, golf; *Style*— John McKenna, Esq; 47 The Park, St Albans, Herts AL1 4RX (☎ 0727 860862, fax 0727 47724)

MCKENNA, Virginia Anne (Mrs William Travers); da of Terence Morell McKenna (d 1948), and Anne-Marie Oakeley, *née* Dennis; *b* 7 June 1931; *Educ* Herschel Capetown SA, Herons Ghyll Horsham, Central Sch of Speech and Drama; *m* 1, (m dis 1957), Denholm Elliot; m 2, 19 Sept 1957, William Inglis Lindon Travers, s of William Halton Lindon Travers, *qv*, (d 1966); 3 s (William Morrell Lindon b 4 Nov 1958, Justin McKenna Lindon b 6 March 1963, Daniel Inglis Lindon b 27 Feb 1967), 1 da (Louise Annabella Lindon b 6 July 1960); *Career* actress; theatre: season Old Vic 1955-56, The Devils 1961, Beggars Opera 1963, A Little Night Music 1976, The King and I (SWET award for best musical actress), Hamlet (RSC) 1984; films: The Cruel Sea 1952, Carve Her Name With Pride (Belgian Prix Femina) 1957, Born Free (Variety Club award for best actress) 1964, Ring of Bright Water, A Town Like Alice (Academy award for best actress); TV: Romeo and Juliet (Best Actress award ITV) 1955, Passage to India 1965, The Deep Blue Sea 1974, Cheap in August; fndr dir Zoo Check Charitable Tst 1984; patron: Elizabeth Fitzroy Homes, Slade Centre, Dorking Operatic Soc, World Family, Dorking Hospice Homecare, Crusade; pres Beauty Without Cruelty UK; Freeman City of Houston Texas 1966; *Books* On Playing with Lions (with Bill Travers), Some of my Friends have Tails, Beyond the Bars (jt ed and jt author), Headlines from the Jungle (anthology of verse, co-ed, 1990); *Recreations* reading, travelling, gardening; *Style*— Miss Virginia McKenna; Zoo Check Charitable Tst, Coldharbour, Surrey RH5 6HA (☎ 0306 712 091)

MACKENZIE; *see*: Muir Mackenzie

MACKENZIE, Sir (Alexander George Anthony) Allan; 4 Bt (UK 1890), of Glen Muick, Aberdeenshire; s of Capt Allan Keith Mackenzie (ka 1916), by Hon Alexandra L E, da of 1 Viscount Knollys, GCB, PC, and nephew of 3 Bt, DSO, MVO (d 1944); *b* 4 Jan 1913; *Educ* Stowe; *m* 24 Aug 1937, Marjorie, da of A F McGuire, of Alberta, Canada; 4 da; *Heir* cousin, James William Guy Mackenzie; *Career* memb Royal Canadian Mounted Police 1932-37; page of honour to King George V; enlisted Calgary Highlanders 1939, Lt Seaforth Highlanders of Canada 1941, Capt Black Watch of Canada, ret 1961; *Style*— Sir Allan Mackenzie, Bt; RRI, Cobble Hill, Vancouver Island, BC, Canada

MACKENZIE, Angus Alexander; s of Kenneth Mackenzie (d 1958), of Drumine, Gollanfield, Inverness-shire, and Christina, *née* Mackinnon (d 1966); *b* 1 March 1931; *Educ* Inverness Royal Acad, Univ of Edinburgh; *m* 31 March 1959, Catherine, da of Murdo Maclennan (d 1971), of Sand Gairloch Ross-shire; 1 da (Margaret Jane b 1960); *Career* Nat Serv RAF 1955-57; qualified CA 1955, own practice 1961-; currently: sr ptnr Angus Mackenzie & Co Inverness, local dir Eagle Star Insurance Co Ltd, dir PLM Helicopters Ltd; chm Highland Gp Riding for the Disabled Assoc, sec and treas Highland Field Sports Fair, chm Highland Club Inverness; MICAS 1955; *Recreations* shooting, stalking, hill walking, and gardening; *Clubs* Highland Inverness; *Style*— Angus Mackenzie, Esq; Tigh-An-Allt, Tomatin, Inverness-shire (☎ 08082 270); Redwood, 19 Culduthel Rd, Inverness (☎ 0463 235353, fax 0463 235171)

MACKENZIE, Lady Anne Mildred Ismay; *née* FitzRoy; o da of 10 Duke of Grafton (d 1970), and his 1 wife Lady Doreen Maria Josepha (d 1923), 2 da of 1 Earl Buxton, GCMG; *b* 7 Aug 1920; *m* 19 April 1947, Maj Colin Dalzell Mackenzie, MBE, MC, DL, *qv*; 2 s, (Alastair d 1951, Philip), 3 da (Caroline, Laura, Harriet); *Recreations* gardening; *Clubs* Turf, Lansdowne; *Style*— The Lady Anne Mackenzie; Farr House, Inverness; The Gardens, Ashby St Mary, Norwich NR14 7AZ

MACKENZIE, Brig Charles Baillie; DSO (1944), OBE (1950); s of Theodore Charles Mackenzie (d 1951), of Druim, Inverness, and Margaret Irvine, *née* Wilson (d 1962); *b* 29 Dec 1909; *Educ* Fettes, RMC Sandhurst; *m* 18 March 1938, Nancy Veronica (d 1962), da of George Francis Dalziel, WS, of Sydney Lodge, Whitehouse Loan, Edinburgh; 1 s (Angus b 1951), 2 da (Anne (Mrs Lawrie) b 1939, Biddy (Mrs Lewis) b 1940); *Career* cmmnd Queen's Own Cameron Highlanders 1930, Lt 1942; WWII serv: 1 Liverpool Scottish, 5 Scottish Parachute Bn, HQ 1 Airborne Div, HQ 44 Indian Airborne Div; WO (Dept of Air), 4/5 Camerons (TA), Col WO (AG2), Brig 154 Highland Bde (TA) 1954-57, dep cdr Lowland Div 1957-59; sec City of Glasgow TA Assoc and Lowland TAVR Assoc 1959-74; *Recreations* fishing, shooting; *Clubs* Western (Glasgow); *Style*— Brig Charles Mackenzie, DSO, OBE; 16 Grendon Court, Snowdon Place, Stirling (☎ 0786 50618)

MACKENZIE, Charles William Taaffe Munro; s of John Hugh Munro Mackenzie and Eileen Louise Agate *née* Shanks; *b* 3 Feb 1956; *Educ* Eton, Trinity Coll Oxford (MA); *m* 17 July 1981, Emma, da of Thomas Liddell, of Dormans Corner, Racecourse Rd, Dormansland, Surrey; 2 s (Charles Alexander Munro b 1983, Kenneth Thomas Munro b 1986), 1 da (b 1990); *Career* dir London and Northern Gp plc 1985-87, currently dir Scot English and Euro Textiles plc; *Recreations* music, travel; *Style*— Charles Mackenzie, Esq; Essex Hall, Essex Street, London WC2

McKENZIE, Dr Christopher Gurney; s of Benet Christopher McKenzie (d 1984), and Winifred Grace, *née* Masterman (d 1984); *b* 3 Jan 1930; *Educ* Douai Sch, Univ of London (MB BS); *m* 12 Oct 1963, Barbara Mary Kinsella, da of James Quirk (d 1983);

2 s (James b 1966, Richard b 1972), 1 da (Caroline b 1964); *Career* nat serv in Dental branch RAF (Flt Lt) 1953-55; Maj RAMC (Sr Specialist Surgery) 1967-70; conslt Clinical Oncology Hammersmith Hosp, sr lectr Royal Postgrad Med Sch 1974-; hon conslt: St Mary's Hosp Paddington, the Central Middlesex Hosp; LDS, memb RCS 1951, FRCS 1962, DMRT 1972, FRCR 1974; *Books* author of many articles and chapters on med subjects; *Recreations* sailing, opera; *Clubs* Cruising Assoc; *Style—* Dr Christopher G McKenzie; 61 Mount Avenue, Ealing W5 1PN (☎ 081 997 3452); Dept of Clinical Oncology, Hammersmith Hospital (☎ 081 740 3061)

MACKENZIE, Colin John; s of John Mackenzie, and Edith Vanan, *née* Murray; *b* 18 Jan 1955; *Educ* Craigbank Sch, Stow Coll Glasgow; *m* 26 March 1982, Hazel, da of Frank Neil Walker; 1 s (Struan b 22 May 1986), 1 da (Kirsty b 20 April 1984); *Career* md: Hifi Corner (Edinburgh) Ltd 1972-, Hifi Corner (Glasgow) Ltd 1984-, James Kerr & Co Ltd 1986; dir: Eastaura Ltd 1983-89, Bill Hutchinson Hifi Ltd 1983-85; chief exec Hifi Experience plc 1988-89 (dir 1985-), mgmnt conslt Kerr, Mccosh Ltd 1988-90; memb Mgmnt Ctee Br Audio Dealers Assoc 1987 and 1990-91, organiser annual Scot Hifi Exhibition 1976-, PRO Tranent and Elphinstone Community Cncl, chm Tranent Infant Sch Bd 1990 and 1991; *Style—* Colin MacKenzie, Esq; Westbank House, Westbank Farm, nr Macmerry, E Lothian (☎ 0875 613 409); Unit 2, 172 The Lane, Easter Rd, Edinburgh (☎ 031 652 1885, fax 031 652 1436)

MACKENZIE, Colin Scott; DL (Western Isles 1975); s of Colin Scott Mackenzie (d 1971), of Stornoway, and Margaret Sarah Tolmie; inter alia celebrated 100 yrs (unbroken) in 1984 as Public Prosecutors in Stornoway; *b* 7 July 1938; *Educ* Nicolson Inst Stornoway, Fettes, Univ of Edinburgh (BL); *m* 1966, Christeen Elizabeth Drysdale, da of William McLauchlan (d 1968), of Tong, Isle of Lewis; *Career* admitted slr 1960; procurator fiscal Stornoway 1969-, clerk to the Lieutenancy 1974-, dir Harris Tweed Assoc Ltd 1979, Vice Lord-Lt Western Isles 1984-; memb Cncl Law Soc of Scotland 1985-, kirk elder 1985; convener Church and Nation Ctee Presbytery of Lewis 1990; *Recreations* fishing, boating, travel; *Clubs* RSAC (Glasgow), New (Edinburgh); *Style—* C Scott Mackenzie, Esq, DL; Park House, Matheson Rd, Stornoway (☎ 0851 2008, office 0851 3439)

MCKENZIE, Dr Dan Peter; s of William Stewart McKenzie, and Nancy Mary McKenzie; *b* 21 Feb 1942; *Educ* Westminster, King's Coll Cambridge (BA, MA, PhD); *m* 5 June 1971, Indira Margaret; 1 s (James Misra b 3 April 1976); *Career* Univ of Cambridge: sr asst in res 1969-75, asst dir of res 1975-79, reader in tectonics 1979-84, prof of earth scis Dept of Earth Scis; Hon MA Univ of Cambridge 1966; memb Royal Soc 1976, foreign assoc US Nat Acad of Scis 1989; Balzan Prize of Int Balzan Fndn (with F J Vine and O H Matthews, 1981), Japan Prize Sci and Technol Fndn of Japan (with W J Morgan and X Le Pichon, 1990); *Publications* author of various papers in learned journals; *Recreations* gardening; *Style—* Dr Dan McKenzie; Bullard Laboratories, Madingley Road, Cambridge CB3 0EZ

MACKENZIE, Rear Adm David John; CB (1983); s of David Mackenzie (d 1950), and Alison Walker, *née* Lawrie; *b* 3 Oct 1929; *Educ* Cargilfield Sch Edinburgh, RNC; *m* 1965, Ursula Sybil, da of Cdr Ronald Hugh Balfour, RN; 2 s (David, Alastair), 1 da (Rachel); *Career* joined RN cadet 1943-47, Midshipman 1947-48, Sub Lt 1950-51, Lt 1951-59, Lt Cdr 1959-65, promoted Cdr 1965, exec offr HMS Glamorgan 1965-67, Cdr Sea Trg 1967-70, CO HMS Hermione 1971, promoted Capt 1972, CO HMS Phoenix 1972-74, Capt F8 HMS Ajax 1974-76, dir Naval Equipment 1976-78; CO HMS: Blake 1978-79, Hermes 1979-80; promoted Rear Adm 1981; Flag Offr Gibraltar 1981-83; ret 1983; dir Atlantic Salmon Trust 1985-, vice pres and fell Nautical Inst; memb Royal Co of Archers (Queen's Bodyguard for Scotland); *Recreations* shooting, fishing; *Clubs* New (Edinburgh); *Style—* Rear Adm John Mackenzie, CB; Atlantic Salmon Tst, Moulin Pitlochry, Perthshire (☎ 0796 3439)

McKENZIE, Justice Donald Cameron Moffat; s of John McKenzie (d 1975), of Perth, and Jessie Cameron Creelman, *née* Moffat (d 1989); *b* 3 March 1934; *Educ* St Ninian's Cathedral Sch, Balhousie Boys' Sch, Perth Commercial Sch; *m* 29 June 1967, Patricia Janet, da of Ernest Russell Hendry (d 1974), of Dundee; 2 da (Alison b 1968, Evelyn b 1972); *Career* accountant Trinity Coll Glenalmond 1966-70, bursar Corp of High Sch Dundee 1970-80; co cncllr, magistrate, social work convener, health convener of Perth 1971-75; co cncllr Perth and Kinross 1971-75, justice District Court 1975, estate factor of Pitlochry Estate Tst 1980; govr Dundee Coll of Educn, dir R Dundee Instn for Blind; capt Soc of High Constables; memb: Justices Ctee, Prison Visiting Ctee; OStJ (1978); FInst AA (1976); FBIM; *Recreations* rifle shooting, cricket, music; *Style—* Justice Donald McKenzie; Balnacraig, Moulin, Pitlochry, Perths (☎ 0796 2591, Pitlochry Estate Office ☎ 0796 2114)

MCKENZIE, Duke Roger; s of Dudley McKenzie, and Daphney, *née* Barnett; *b* 5 May 1963; *Educ* Heathclarke HS Purley; *m* 22 July 1989, Diane Jean, da of John Fagan; *Career* professional boxer; debut Wembley Arena 2 round ko's v Charlie Brown Nov 1982, 27 fights, 17 Ko's, 2 defeats; represented: Young England v Sweden and Hungary, London ABA v Sweden; ABA semi-finalist 1978, Br Flyweight champion 1985 (ko Danny Flynn, Royal Albert Hall), Euro Flyweight champion 1986 (ko Charlie Magri Wembley Arena); Int Boxing Fedn World Flyweight champion Oct 1988 - June 1989: won title v Rolando Bohlo 11 round ko Wembley Grand Hall 1988, retained title v Tony Delvca Royal Albert Hall 1989, lost title v Dave McCauley on points Wembley Arena 1989; messenger Nestle Co Croydon 1989-; *Recreations* horse riding, reading, charity football, cooking; *Style—* Duke McKenzie, Esq; c/o 60-66 Wardour St, London W1 (☎ 071 734 1041)

MacKENZIE, Rt Hon (James) Gregor; PC (1977), JP (Glasgow 1957); o s of James MacKenzie (d 1984), and Mary, *née* Wood (d 1972); *b* 15 Nov 1927; *Educ* Queen's Park Sch, Royal Tech Coll, Univ of Glasgow Sch of Social Studies; *m* 15 Aug 1958, Joan Swan, o da of John Campbell Provan (d 1981); 1 s (Derek Gregor Provan b 25 Feb 1960), 1 da (Gillian Elizabeth Jean (Mrs Gordon Martin) b 30 Oct 1961); *Career* joined Lab Pty 1944; Parly candidate (Lab): Aberdeenshire E 1950, Kinross and Perth 1959; MP Rutherglen 1964-87, PPS to Rt Hon James Callaghan 1965-70, shadow oppn spokesman Posts and Telecommunications 1970-74, min of state for Industry 1975-76 (Parly under sec 1974-75), min of state Scottish Office 1976-79; memb: Ctee of Privileges House of Commons 1983-87, House of Commons Ctee on Sound Broadcasting 1985-87; *Style—* The Rt Hon Gregor MacKenzie; 8 Buchanan Drive, Newton Mearns, Glasgow G77 6HT (☎ 041 639 4997)

MACKENZIE, (James William) Guy; s of Lt-Col Eric Dighton Mackenzie, CMG, CVO, DSO (d 1972), and Elizabeth Kathrine Mary, *née* Innes; hp of cousin, Sir (Alexander George Anthony) Allan Mackenzie, 4 Bt, CD; *b* 6 Oct 1946; *Educ* Stowe; *m* 1972, Paulene Patricia Simpson; 1 da; *Style—* Guy Mackenzie Esq; 1 Molerun, Pheasant Drive, High Wycombe, Bucks

MACKENZIE, Vice Adm Sir Hugh Stirling; KCB (1966, CB 1963), DSO (1942, and bar 1943), DSC (1945); 3 s of Dr Theodore Charles Mackenzie (d 1951), of Inverness; *b* 3 July 1913; *Educ* Cargilfield Sch, RNC Dartmouth; *m* 10 Aug 1946, Helen Maureen, er da of Maj John Edward Mountague Bradish-Ellames (d 1984); 1 s, 2 da; *Career* RN: joined 1927, served WWII submarines, Capt 1951, Rear Adm 1961, Flag Offr Submarines 1961-63, Chief Polaris Exec 1963-68, Vice Adm 1964, ret 1968; chm: Navy League 1969-74, Atlantic Salmon Tst 1979-83 (dir 1969-79); CBIM; *Recreations* the country; *Clubs* Naval and Military; *Style—* Vice Adm Sir Hugh Mackenzie, KCB, DSO, DSC; Sylvan Lodge, Puttenham, nr Guildford, Surrey (☎ 0483 810 368)

MACKENZIE, Lady Jean; *née* Leslie; da of 20 Earl of Rothes (d 1975); *b* 26 Aug 1927; *m* 26 April 1949, Roderick Robin Mackenzie, s of Capt Roderick Kilgour Mackenzie (d 1937); *Style—* The Lady Jean Mackenzie; Kingfisher House, Ampfield, Hants

MACKENZIE, John; s of late Roderick Mackenzie, and Margaret, *née* Maclean; *b* 5 June 1940; *Educ* Inverness Royal Acad; *m* 9 Dec 1978, (Nicola) Jane, *née* Boughey; 1 s (Cosmo b 24 June 1983), 1 da (Octavia b 11 April 1980); *Career* Standard Chartered plc: joined 1958, posted to ME, served Asia, Europe and N America, chm various subsids, area gen mangr Hong Kong; dir: Standard Chartered Holdings Ltd 1989-, Chartered Financial Holdings Ltd 1989-, Standard Chartered Bank 1989-, Standard Chartered Bank Africa plc 1990-, Chartered Trust plc 1990-; gp exec dir Standard Chartered plc 1989-; held government appts Hong Kong, chm Hong Kong Assoc of Banks 1987-88; FCIB; *Style—* John Mackenzie, Esq; Standard Chartered plc, 1 Aldermanbury Square, London EC2V 7SB (☎ 071 280 7088, fax 071 280 7236)

MACKENZIE, John Alexander Hugh Munro; s of John Mackenzie of Mornish, *qv*, and Eileen Louise Agate, *née* Shanks; *b* 16 Aug 1953; *Educ* Eton, Corpus Christi Coll Oxford; *Career* called to the Bar 1976; dir: Tace plc 1981-, Scottish Eng and Euro Textiles plc 1983-; chm and md Sloane Graphics Ltd 1987-; dir: London and Northern GP plc 1985-87, Kenneth Mackenzie (Hldgs) Ltd 1988-, Justunit Ltd 1988-; Freeman: City of London 1975, Worshipful Co of Merchant Taylors; *Recreations* racing, reading, all field sports, opera; *Clubs* Vincent's (Oxford); *Style—* John Mackenzie, Esq; 21 Upper Mall, London W6 9TA (☎ 081 748 5139); Essex Hall, Essex St, London WC2R 3JD (☎ 071 836 9261, fax 071 836 4859)

McKENZIE, John Cormack; s of William Joseph McKenzie and Elizabeth Frances Robinson; *b* 21 June 1927; *Educ* St Andrew's Coll, Trinity Coll Dublin (MA, MAI), Queen's Univ Belfast (MSc); *m* 1954, Olga Caroline; 3 s, 1 da; *Career* civil engr: McLaughlin & Harvey, Sir Alexander Gibb & Ptnrs 1946-48; asst lectr Queen's Univ Belfast 1948-50, Edmund Nuttal Ltd 1950-82 (dir 1967-82), chm Nuttall Geotechnical Services Ltd 1967-82, md Thomas Telford Ltd 1982-90; sec: Inst of Civil Engrs 1982-90, Cwlth Engrs Cncl 1983-; foreign sec Fellowship of Engrs 1990, sec gen WFEO 1987-, vice pres Register of Engrs for Disaster Relief, dep chm UK Ctee Int Decade for Natural Disaster Relief; FEng, FICE, FIEAus, FIEI; *Publications* Research into some Aspects of Soil Cement (1952), Engineers: Administrators or Technologists? (1971), Civil Engineering Procedure (3 edn, 1979); *Recreations* philately, collecting ancient pottery, climbing; *Clubs* Athenaeum; *Style—* John McKenzie, Esq; The Fellowship of Engineering, 2 Little Smith St, London SW1P 3DL (☎ 071 233 0054)

McKENZIE, Prof John Crawford; s of Donald Walter McKenzie (d 1978), and Emily Beatrice, *née* Stracey; *b* 12 Nov 1937; *Educ* LSE (BSc), Bedford Coll (M Phil), Inst of Educn (PGCE); *m* 5 Aug 1960, Ann; 2 s (Simon Andrew b 28 Feb 1964, Andrew John b 10 March 1966); *Career* princ: Ilkley Coll 1978, Bolton Inst of Higher Educn 1981; rector: Liverpool Poly 1984, The London Inst 1986-; visiting prof Univs of London and Newcastle; dir various cos; *Books* Changing Food Habits (ed, 1964), Our Changing Fare (ed, 1966), The Food Consumer (ed, 1987); *Recreations* collecting antiquarian books; *Clubs* Athenaeum, Chelsea Arts; *Style—* Prof John McKenzie; The London Institute, 388-396 Oxford Street, London W1R 1FE (☎ 071 491 8533)

MCKENZIE, Julia (Mrs Jerry Harte); da of Albion James Jeffrey McKenzie (d 1970), of Enfield, Middx, and Kathleen, *née* Rowe; *b* 17 Feb 1942; *Educ* Tottenham Co Sch, Guildhall Sch of Music and Drama; *m* 1972, Jerry Harte, s of Carl Harte; *Career* actress; *Theatre* incl: Cowardy Custard, Miriam in Outside Edge, Lily Garland in On the Twentieth Century, Hobson's Choice, Schweyk in the Second World War, Miss Adelaide in Guys and Dolls (Nat Theatre, winner Best Actress Variety Club and The Soc of West End Theatre Awards 1982), Sally in Follies, The Witch in Into the Woods; West End and NY performances incl: Company, Promises Promises, Name, Side by Side by Sondheim; Alan Ayckbourn plays incl: Norman Conquests, Ten Times Table, Woman in Mind (winner Best Actress London Evening Standard Awards 1986); *TV* Fame is the Spur, Dear Box Number, Those Glory Glory Days, Blott on the Landscape, Absent Friends, Hotel du Lac, Hester in Fresh Fields (now French Fields, voted Favourite Comedy Performer TV Times Viewers' Poll 1985, 1986, 1987 and 1989); *films* incl: Gillian in Shirley Valentine; theatre dir: Stepping Out (Duke of York's Theatre), Steel Magnolias (Lyric Theatre), Just So (Watermill Theatre Newbury), Merrily We Roll Along (staged concert, 1988); FGSM 1985; *Style—* Ms Julia McKenzie; c/o April Young, 6 St Catherine's Mews, Milner St, London SW3 (☎ 071 584 1274)

McKENZIE, Julia Kathleen; da of Albion James Jeffrey McKenzie (d 1970), of Enfield, Middx, and Kathleen Maudie, *née* Rowe; *b* 17 Feb 1942; *Educ* Tottenham Co Sch, Guildhall Sch of Music and Drama; *m* 9 Sept 1972, Jerry Harte (formally Gerald Carl Hjert), s of Carl Hjert (d 1983), of USA; *Career* actress; has made over 25 West End appearances notably: Guys and Dolls (SWET Award Best Actress), Woman in Mind (Evening Standard Best Actress), Follies (Critics Award Best Actress), Into The Woods; TV series incl: Fresh Fields (2 Awards), French Fields 1989 and 1990, numerous plays and musical specials; dir: Stepping Out, Steel Magnolias; govr Res Into Ageing; hon fell Guildhall Sch of Music and Drama 1984; *Books* Clothes Line (1988); *Recreations* cooking; *Style—* Miss Julia McKenzie; c/o April Young, The Clockhouse, 6 St Catherine's Mews, Milner St, London SW3 2PU (☎ 071 584 1274)

MACKENZIE, Lady (Sibell Anne) Julia; *née* Mackenzie; has resumed use of maiden name; er da of 4 Earl of Cromartie, MC, TD (d 1989), and his 1 w, Dorothy, *née* Downing; *b* 15 Feb 1934; *m* 1, 16 June 1953 (m dis 1961), Francis Edward Lascelles-Hadwen, er s of late Edward Hubert Lascelles Hadwen, Levant Consular Service; 1 s (James Brian Mackenzie b 1957), 1 da (Georgina Frances b 1959); m 2, 1974, Apputhurai Jeyarama Chandran; 1 da (Anita Anne Dorothy b 1977); *Style—* The Lady Julia Mackenzie; c/o Casle Leod, Strathpeffer, Ross and Cromarty, Scotland

MacKENZIE, Kenneth John; s of Capt John Donald MacKenzie (d 1967), of Milngavie, Dunbartonshire, and Elizabeth Pennant Johnston, *née* Sutherland (d 1985); *b* 1 May 1943; *Educ* Birkenhead Sch, Pembroke Coll Oxford (BA, MA), Stanford Univ California (AM); *m* 3 Sept 1975, Irene Mary, da of William Ewart Hogarth (d 1947), of Mayfield, Paisley, Renfrewshire; 1 s (John b 1977), 1 da (Mary b 1979); *Career* asst princ Scot Home & Health Dept 1965-70, private sec to Jt Parly Under Sec of State Scot Office 1969-70; princ: Regnl Devpt Div Scot Office 1970-73, Scot Educn Dept 1973-77; Civil Serv fell: Downing Coll Cambridge 1972, Dept of Politics Univ of Glasgow 1974-75; princ private sec to Sec of State for Scotland 1977-79; asst sec: Scot Econ Planning Dept 1979-83, Scot Office Fin Div 1983-85; princ fin offr Scot Office 1985-88; under sec Scot Home and Health Dept 1988-; session clerk St Cuthbert's Parish Church Edinburgh 1979-91; hon pres Edinburgh Civil Serv Dramatic Soc 1989-; *Clubs* National Liberal; *Style—* Kenneth MacKenzie, Esq; Scottish Office, St Andrew's House, Edinburgh EH1 3DE (☎ 031 244 2133)

McKENZIE, Michael; s of Robert McKenzie, of Brighton, and Kitty Elizabeth, *née* Regan (d 1985); *b* 25 May 1943; *Educ* Varndean GS Brighton; *m* 19 Sept 1964, Peggy Dorothy, da of Thomas Edward William Russell, of Heathfield, E Sussex; 3 s (Justin Grant b 31 May 1968, Gavin John b 28 April 1971, Jamie Stuart b 14 Jan 1977); *Career* called to the Bar Middle Temple 1970, dep clerk of the peace Middx Quarter Sessions

1970-72, dep courts admin Middx Crown Court 1972-73, courts admin NE Circuit (Newcastle) 1974-79, clerk of the Central Criminal Court 1979-84, dep circuit admin SE circuit 1984-86, asst registrar Court of Appeal Criminal Div 1986-88, Queens Coroner and Attorney and Master of the Crown Office; registrar: of Criminal Appeals, of Courts Martial Appeal Court 1988-; Freeman City of London 1979; FRSA 1990; *Recreations* Northumbrian stick dressing, fell walking, shooting; *Style—* Master McKenzie; Royal Cts of Justice, Strand, London WC2A 2LL (☎ 071 936 6108, fax 071 936 6900)

MACKENZIE, Michael Philip Uvedale Rapinet; s of Brig M R Mackenzie, DSO (d 1985), of Mayfield, Sussex, and Vivienne, *née* Price; *b* 1937; *Educ* Downside, Lincoln Coll Oxford; *m* 1966, Jill, da of Charles Foweraker Beckley, of Chislehurst, Kent; 1 s (William b 1966), 1 da (Elizabeth b 1970); *Career* United Biscuits plc 1966-86; prodn dir of various businesses 1974-83, md DS Crawford Bakeries 1983-86; DG Food and Drink Fedn; FRSA 1988; *Clubs* Travellers; *Style—* Michael Mackenzie, Esq; Ebony Cottage, Ebony, nr Tenterden, Kent TN30 7HT; Food & Drink Federation, Catherine St, London WC2B 5JJ

MACKENZIE, Robert Stephen; s of Brig Frederick Stephen Ronald Mackenzie, OBE (d 1981), and Daphne Margaret, *née* Jickling; *b* 12 Nov 1947; *Educ* Radley, RMA Sandhurst; *m* 24 Mar 1973, Amanda Clare, da of Lt Cdr Richard John Beverley Sutton; 1 s (Rupert b 1982), 1 da (Emily b 1977); *Career* serv Queens Royal Irish Hussars; Allied Lyons 1978, md Hall and Woodhouse and Badger Inns 1984 (dir 1983); *Recreations* riding; *Style—* Robert Mackenzie, Esq; Northfield House, Todber, Sturminster, Newton, Dorset (☎ 0258 820269); Badger Inns, The Brewery, Blandford, Dorset (☎ 0258 451462, fax 0258 459528, car 0865 239741)

MACKENZIE, Sir Roderick Mcquhae; 12 Bt (NS 1703), of Scatwell, Ross-shire; s of Capt Sir Roderick Edward François McQuhae, CBE, DSC (d 1986); *b* 17 April 1942; *Educ* Sedbergh, King's Coll London, St George's Hosp (MB BS, MRCP (UK), FRCP (C), DCH); *m* 1970, Nadezhda (Nadine), da of Georges Frederick Leon Schlatter, Baron von Rorbas, of Buchs-K-Zurich, Switzerland; 1 s (Gregory Roderick McQuhae b 1971), 1 da (Nina Adelaida b 1973); *Heir* s Gregory; *Style—* Sir Roderick Mackenzie, Bt; 2431 Udell Rd, Calgary NW, Alberta, Canada

McKENZIE, Sally; da of Eric Hodge, of 37 Gwynant Cres, Lakeside, Cardiff, and Sylvia, *née* Evans; *b* 31 May 1966; *Educ* Cardiff HS, South Glamorgan Inst of Higher Educn (HND); *m* 27 March 1989, Neil McKenzie, s of Roderick McKenzie, of 28 Crystal Wood Rd, Heath, Cardiff; *Career* cyclist; Br 500m sprint champion 1983, 20km points race champion Goodwill Games Moscow 1986, first place 30km points race World Championships 1988 (seventh place 3000m pursuit 1987), nineth place 80km road race Olympic Games 1988; won nine Br titles and a record between 1983 and 1989; *Style—* Mrs Sally McKenzie; 79 Traherne Drive, St Fagans, Cardiff (☎ 0222 596720)

McKENZIE, Dr Sheila Agnes; da of Capt Raymond K McKenzie (d 1980), of Dollar, Scotland, and Agnes Muirhead, *née* Steel (d 1978); *b* 5 June 1946; *Educ* Dollar Acad, Univ of Edinburgh; *Career* conslt paediatrician Rush Green Hosp Romford Essex; regnl paediatric advsr Br Paediatric Assoc (RCP); FRCP (and Edinburgh) 1989; *Recreations* hill-walking, cultivation of old roses, study of 17 century Dutch culture; *Style—* Dr Sheila McKenzie; 69 Gordon Rd, London E18 1DT (☎ 081 505 7481); Rush Green Hospital, Romford, Essex (☎ 0708 46066)

MACKENZIE-GREEN, John Garvie; s of Jack Green (d 1990), of Malvern, Worcs, and Moira, *née* Garvie; *b* 28 April 1953; *Educ* Malvern, Guilford Law Sch; *m* 1976, Tessa Mary, *née* Batten; 2 s (Henry, William), 1 da (Claire); *Career* dir Fielding Insurance Holdings 1976-86, dir CE Heath plc 1986- (gp md 1990-), chm Heath Fielding Insurance Broking 1986-; MBIBA; *Recreations* sailing, skiing, rural gardening, shooting; *Clubs* Lloyds, HAC, Royal Western; *Style—* John Mackenzie-Green, Esq; C E Heath plc, 150 The Minories, London EC3 (☎ 071 488 2488)

MACKENZIE OF GAIRLOCH; *see*: Inglis of Glencorse

MACKENZIE OF MORNISH, John Hugh Munro; s of Lt-Col John Munro Mackenzie of Mornish, DSO, JP, Military Knight of Windsor (d 1964), of Henry VIII Gateway, Windsor Castle and Etheldreda Henrietta Marie, *née* Taaffe (d 1965); The Mornish branch of the Mackenzie Clan are direct male descendants of the ancient feudal Barons of Kintail, chiefs of the Mackenzie Clan through the Mackenzies of Gairloch and the Mackenzies of Letterewe; *b* 29 Aug 1925; *Educ* Edinburgh Acad, Loretto, Trinity Coll Oxford (MA), Hague Academy of Int Law, Inns of Ct Law Sch, McGill Univ Montreal; *m* 20 June 1951, Eileen Louise Agate, da of Alexander Shanks, OBE, MC (d 1965); 5 s (John b 1953, Charles b 1956, Kenneth b 1961, d 1984, Cristin b 1959, James b 1966), 1 da (Catriona b 1952); *Career* served Army 1942-47, Capt The Royal Scots (Royal Regt); War Serv: Europe, 1 KOSB, A Co, 9 Bde, 3 Inf Div (despatches, certs of gallantry), Far E HQ Allied Land Forces SE Asia and HQ Ceylon Army Cmd, Staff Capt Mil Sec's Branch; HM Guard of Honour Balmoral 1946, HQ 3 Auto Aircraft Div 1946-47, GSO III; Harmsworth law scholar Middle Temple 1950, called to the Bar Middle Temple 1950; trainee Utd Dominions Tst, legal asst Estates Dept ICI Ltd 1951; Hudson's Bay scholar 1952-53; buyer ICI 1953-54, co sec and legal advsr Trubenised (GB) Ltd and Assoc Cos 1955-56, gp devpt offr Aspro-Nicholas Ltd 1956-57, Knitmaster Holdings 1957, formed Grampian Holdings Ltd (mangr and sec) 1958 (md 1960), dep chm and md London and Northern Gp Ltd 1962; chm: Tace plc 1967-, Scottish English and European Textiles plc 1969-, London and Northern Group plc 1962-87, Pauling plc 1976-87, Goring Kerr plc 1983-; eight Queen's Awards for Export won by gp cos; FRSA, FBIM, memb Worshipful Co of Farmers; *Recreations* opera, bridge, shooting, fishing, field sports; *Clubs* Royal Automobile, Royal Scots (Edinburgh), New (Edinburgh); *Style—* John Mackenzie of Mornish; Mortlake House, Vicarage Rd, London SW14 8RN; Scaliscro Lodge, Uig, Isle of Lewis; Shellwood Manor, Leigh, Surrey; Scottish English & European Textiles plc, and Tace plc, Essex Hall, Essex Street, London WC2R 3JD (☎ 071 836 9261)

McKENZIE SMITH, Ian; s of James McKenzie Smith (d 1977), of Aberdeen, and Mary, *née* Benzie (d 1989); *b* 3 Aug 1935; *Educ* Robert Gordon's Coll Aberdeen, Gray's Sch of Art Aberdeen (DA), Hospitalfield Coll of Art Arbroath; *m* 3 April 1963, Mary Rodger, da of John Fotheringham (d 1990); 2 s (Patrick John b 8 Aug 1966, Justin James b 4 Feb 1969), 1 da (Sarah Jane b 5 Jan 1965); *Career* educn offr Cncl of Industl Design Scottish Ctee 1963-68, dir Aberdeen Art Gallery and Museums 1968-89, city arts offr City of Aberdeen 1989-; work in permanent collections: Scottish Nat Gallery of Modern Art, Scottish Arts Cncl, Arts Cncl of NI, Contemporary Art Soc, Aberdeen Art Gallery and Museums, Glasgow Art Gallery and Museums, Abbott Hall Art Gallery Kendal, Huntarian Museum Glasgow, Nuffield Foundation, Carnegie Tst, Strathclyde Educn Authy, Lothian Educn Authy, Royal Scottish Acad, DOE; memb: Scottish Arts Cncl, Scottish Museums Cncl, Nat Heritage Scottish GP, Scottish Sculpture Workshop; govr: Edinburgh Coll of Art, Robert Gordon Inst of Technol Aberdeen; Hon LLD Aberdeen 1991; RSA 1987 (dep pres 1990-91, treas 1990-), PRSW 1981-88, FRSA 1973, FSS 1984, FMA 1988, FSA Scotland 1970; *Clubs* Royal Northern (Aberdeen); *Style—* Ian McKenzie Smith, Esq, FSA; 70 Hamilton Place, Aberdeen (☎ 0224 644531); City Arts Department, St Nicholas House, Aberdeen (☎ 0224 276276, fax 0224 648256)

MACKENZIE-STUART, Baron (Life Peer UK 1988), of Dean in the City and County of Edinburgh; Alexander John Mackenzie Stuart; s of Prof Alexander Mackenzie Stuart, KC (d 1935), and Amy Margaret, er da of John Reid Dean, of Aberdeen; *b* 18 Nov 1924; *Educ* Fettes, Sidney Sussex Coll Cambridge (BA, hon fell 1977), Univ of Edinburgh (LLB); *m* 1952, Anne Burtholme, da of late John Sidney Lawrence Millar, WS, of Edinburgh; 4 da (Hon Amanda Jane (Hon Mrs Hay) b 29 April 1954, Hon Katherine Anne b 13 June 1956, Hon Laura Margaret b 27 March 1961, Hon Judith Mary (Hon Mrs Aspinall) b 14 May 1964); *Career* served RE 1942-47 (T/Capt 1946); admitted Faculty of Advocates 1951, QC (Scot) 1963, Keeper of the Advocates Library 1970-72; Standing Jr Counsel: Scottish Home Dept 1956-57, Inland Revenue in Scotland 1957-63; Sheriff-Princ of Aberdeen, Kincardine and Banff 1971-72, a senator of the College of Justice in Scotland (as Hon Lord Mackenzie Stuart) 1972-73, judge of the Court of Justice European Communities Luxembourg 1972-84 (pres 1984-88); govr Fettes Coll 1962-72; hon bencher: Middle Temple 1978, King's Inn Dublin 1983; hon memb Soc of Public Teachers of Law 1982, hon prof Collège d'Europe Bruges 1974-77; Hon DUniv Stirling 1973; Hon LLD: Exeter 1978, Edinburgh 1978, Glasgow 1981, Aberdeen 1983, Cambridge 1987, Birmingham 1988; awarded: Grand-Croix de l'Ordre Grand-Ducal de la Couronne de Chêne Luxembourg 1988, Prix Bech for servs to Europe 1989; *Books* Hamlyn Lectures: The European Communities and the Rule of Law (1977); articles in legal publications; *Recreations* collecting; *Clubs* Athenaeum, New (Edinburgh); *Style—* The Lord Mackenzie-Stuart; 7 Randolph Cliff, Edinburgh EH3 7TZ; Le Garidel, Gravières, 07140 Les Vans, France

MACKENZIE-WELTER, Lady Gilean Frances; *née* Blunt Mackenzie; da of 4 Earl of Cromartie, by his 1 w, Dorothy Porter, da of G B Downing, of Kentucky, USA; *b* 25 Feb 1936; *m* 3 Oct 1959 (m dis 1973), René Eugene Welter, o s of late Prof Georges F Welter, of Montreal, Canada, Consul-Gen for Luxembourg; 1 s (Michael b 1964), 1 da (Nadine b 1960); *Career* public relations conslt and advsr on fund-raising for charities; fndr Scots Int; *Style—* The Lady Gilean Mackenzie-Welter; 52 South Edwardes Sq, London W8

McKEOWN, Dean Russell; s of Samuel Rothwell McKeown, of Lewis, E Sussex, and Maureen, *née* Hill; *b* 5 Feb 1960; *Educ* Sir Charles Lucas Sch Colchester; *m* 13 March 1987, Catherine, da of Eric Bell; 3 da (Lauren b 6 Dec 1984, Hayley b 7 Oct 1987, Francesca b 2 April 1990); *Career* professional jockey 1984-; apprentice: Peter Robinson 1976-78, Patrick Haslam 1978-81, William Hastings-Bass 1981-83, Bill O'Gorman 1983-84; achievements as apprentice: Crown Plus Two champion 1981, 22 winners in England, 3 winners in Kenya incl Kenya Guineas; major wins as professional: William Hill Cambs 1987 (Balthus) and 1989 (Rambo's Hall), John Smith's Magnet Cup 1988 (Bashful Boy), Queen Mary Stakes), Royal Ascot 1990 (On Tiptoes, Queen Alexandra Stakes Royal Ascot 1990 (Regnl Reform), Cartier Premier Challenge 1990 (Sir Harry Hardman); leading jockey for the Queen with 8 wins 1989, leading northern jockey with 88 wins 1990 (10th in England), over 400 winners worldwide (incl 24 in India 1990); *Style—* Dean McKeown, Esq; The Stables, Old Vicarage Lane, Monk Fryston, Leeds, West Yorkshire LS25 5EA (☎ 0977 681247)

McKEOWN, Dermot William; s of Ronald Hubert McKeown, of Dungannon, and Rosemary, *née* McMorran; *b* 16 Aug 1954; *Educ* Royal Sch Dungannon, Univ of Edinburgh (MB ChB); *m* 23 July 1976, (Margaret Janet) Laurie, da of (Samuel) Clinton, of Strathaven; 1 s, 2 da; *Career* Anaesthetics: SHO, registrar, sr Edinburgh 1978-84, sr anaesthesia and intensive care Flinders Med Centre SA 1985, conslt anaesthetist Royal Infirmary of Edinburgh 1986-; FFARCS 1981; *Style—* Dermot McKeown, Esq; 3 Merchiston Gardens, Edinburgh, Scotland EH10 5DD (☎ 031 337 5967)

McKEOWN, John Wilson; s of John McKeown, and Sarah, *née* Black; *b* 17 April 1950; *Educ* Royal Belfast Academic Inst, Christ's Coll Cambridge (MA); *m* Lynn Fennah; 1 s (Christopher William John b 7 Aug 1983), 1 da (Rachel Sara Louise b 2 April 1978); *Career* dir Ind Coope Ltd, md Ind Coope & Allsopp Ltd, md Ansells Ltd; *Recreations* sport, politics; *Style—* John McKeown, Esq; 1 Swithland Lane, Rothley, Leicester (☎ 0533 302480); Ansells Ltd, Aldridge Rd, Perry Barr, Birmingham B42 2TZ (☎ 021 344 4507)

McKERN, Leo Reginald; AO 1983; s of Norman Walton McKern (d 1969), of Sydney, and Vera Martin (d 1971); two McKern bros migrated to Sydney from Limerick (McKern printing works) in 1864; *b* 16 March 1920; *Educ* Sydney Technical HS; *m* 9 Nov 1946, Joan Alice (Jane Holland, actress), da of late Joseph Southall; 2 da (Abigail b 1955, Harriet b 1964); *Career* engrg apprentice 1935-37, served AIF (Corp Engrs) 1940-42; actor: first appearance Metropolitan Theatre Sydney (amateur) 1943, arrived England 1946; stage work incl: Love's Labour's Lost, She Stoops to Conquer, Hamlet, Old Vic New Theatre 1949; Feste in Twelfth Night (re-opening of Old Vic Theatre 1950), Bartholomew Fair, Henry V 1951, Merry Wives of Windsor, Electra, The Wedding, King Lear; Shakespeare Memorial Theatre Australian and NZ tour 1953: Iago in Othello, Touchstone in As You Like It, Glendower and Northumberland in Henry IV Pt 1; Stratford Season 1954: Ulysses in Troilus and Cressida, Grumio in Taming of the Shrew, Quince in A Midsummer Night's Dream, Friar Lawrence in Romeo and Juliet; Toad in Toad of Toad Hall (Prince's Theatre 1954), Big Daddy in Cat on a Hot Tin Roof (Aldwych 1958); dir The Shifting Heart (Duke of York's 1959), Rollo (title role, Strand 1959) , the Common Man in A Man for all Seasons (Globe 1960), Thomas Cromwell in A Man for all Seasons (Anta Theatre, NY 1961); last season at Old Vic 1962-63: Peer Gynt, The Alchemist, Othello; Volpone (title rôle), Garrick 1971; Melbourne Theatre Co 1971, Adelaide Festival (best actor); Shylock in The Merchant of Venice (Oxford Playhouse 1973), Uncle Vanya (title role, Royal Exchange Manchester 1978), Crime and Punishment, Rollo 1980, Boswell for the Defence 1989-90 (London, Melbourne, Sydney, Hong Kong Festival), best performance Victorian Green Room Award; has appeared in over 30 films, incl: Murder in the Cathedral, A Man for all Seasons, Ryan's Daughter, The French Lieutenant's Woman, Travelling North; TV appearances incl: King Lear, Monsignor Quixote, Rumpole of the Bailey (series 1977-, best TV series award 1984), The Master Builder; best actor award Montreal Film Festival 1987; *Books* Just Resting (memoirs, 1983); *Recreations* sailing, photography, travel; *Style—* Leo McKern, Esq, AO; Barclays, 211/213 Banbury Rd, Oxford OX2 7HH; Richard Hatton, Hatton & Bradley, 18 Jermyn St, London SW1Y 6HN (☎ 071 439 2971)

MACKERRAS, Sir (Alan) Charles MacLaurin; CBE (1974); s of Alan Patrick Mackerras (d 1973), and Catherine Brearcliffe (d 1977); *b* 17 Nov 1925; *Educ* Sydney GS Aust, NSW Conservatorium of Music Aust, Acad of Music Prague; *m* 1947, Helena Judith, da of Frederick Bruce Wilkins (d 1961); 2 da; *Career* musician; staff conductor Sadler's Wells Opera 1948-54, princ conductor BBC Concert Orch 1954-56, first conductor Hamburg State Opera 1966-70, musical dir ENO 1970-77, princ guest conductor ENO 1978-, chief conductor Sydney Symphony Orch 1982-85, chief guest conductor Royal Liverpool Philharmonic Orch 1985-87, musical dir Welsh Nat Opera 1987-; Hon Dr of Music Univ of Hull 1990; FRCM 1987; kt 1979; *Style—* Sir Charles Mackerras, CBE; 10 Hamilton Terrace, London NW8 9UG (☎ 071 286 4047)

McKERRON, Dr Colin Gordon; s of Sir Patrick Alexander Bruce McKerron, KCMG (d 1964), and Marjorie Kennedy, *née* Rettie (d 1975); *b* 8 Sept 1934; *Educ* Rugby, London Univ (MB BS); *Career* RAMC 1960-62; travelling fell John Hopkins Hosp Baltimore USA 1966-67; conslt physician: Kings Coll Hosp 1969-85, Greenwich Health

Dist 1975-85; hon conslt physician King's Coll Hosp; former examiner in med RCP; regnl advsr RCP (SE Thames Regnl Health Authy) 1979-82; FRCP 1972; *Books* papers on thyroid disease, endocrinology and med educn; *Recreations* gardening, walking, music; *Clubs* Lansdowne; *Style*— Dr Colin G McKerron; Brook Cottage, Dennington, Woodbridge, Suffolk IP13 8JH (☎ 072875 209); 148 Harley St, London W1 (☎ 071 637 4177)

McKERROW, Colin William; s of Maj William Henry McKerrow, MC (d 1976), and Phyllis Mary Livingstone, *née* Robinson; *b* 22 Jan 1934; *Educ* The Downs Colwall, Eastbourne Coll; *Career* trainee Royal Insurance Co plc 1951-58, stockbroker 1958-; dir Derby County FC plc 1983; memb Stock Exchange 1966-; *Recreations* football, cricket, bridge, travel and wine; *Clubs* MCC, Hurlingham, Caledonian and Kent CC; *Style*— Colin McKerrow, Esq; 6 Thornton Road, Wimbledon, London SW19 4NE (☎ 081 946 6195); Laing & Cruickshank Investment Management Services, Floor 2, Broadwalk House, 5 Appold St, London EC2A 2DA (☎ 071 588 2800, fax 071 374 0066, telex 9419248)

MACKESON, Hon Lady (Camilla Margaret); *née* Keith; da of Baron Keith of Castleacre (Life Peer); *b* 7 March 1947, (twin); *m* 22 July 1968 (m dis 1972), Sir Rupert Henry Mackeson, 2 Bt; *Style*— The Hon Lady Mackeson; 5 Pembroke Gardens, London W8; Apt 36E, 1365 York Ave, New York 10021, USA

MACKESON, Sir Rupert Henry; 2 Bt (UK 1954), of Hythe Co, Kent; s of Brig Sir Harry Ripley Mackeson, 1 Bt (d 1964); *b* 16 Nov 1941; *Educ* Harrow, Trinity Coll Dublin (MA); *m* 22 July 1968 (m dis 1972), Hon Camilla Margaret, da of Baron Keith of Castleacre; *Career* Capt RHG, ret 1968; author of numerous books as Rupert Collens; *Style*— Capt Sir Rupert Mackeson, Bt; 12-14 High Rd, London N2

MACKESON-SANDBACH, Ian Lawrie; s of Capt Lawrie Mackeson-Sandbach (d 1984), of Caerllo, Llangernyw, Clwyd, and Geraldine, *née* Sandbach; *b* 14 June 1933; *Educ* Eton, Univ of New Brunswick; *m* 6 May 1967, Annie Marie, da of J M G Van Lanschot (d 1983), of S'Hertogen Bosch, Netherlands; 4 da (Antoinette b 1969, Sara b 1970, Louise b 1973, Megan b 1976); *Career* Lt Welsh Gds emergency reserve 1952-57; md France Fenwick Ltd 1969-75, dir Demerara Co Ltd 1969-76, chief exec Ernest Notcutt Group Ltd 1976-82, chm Hafodunos Farms Ltd 1982; chm Crown Estate Paving Cmmn 1983 (cmmr 1974); Provost Grand Master N Wales 1990; memb Inst Fire Engrs 1960; *Recreations* shooting, fishing; *Clubs* Boodles, Pratts, Royal St Georges (Sandwich); *Style*— Ian Mackeson-Sandbach, Esq; 20 Hanover Terrace, Regents Park, London NW1 4RJ; Maesol, Llangernyw, Clwyd; Sir John Lyon House, 5 High Timber St, Upper Thames St, London EC4V 3LE (☎ 071 248 4931, fax 071 402 6390)

MACKEY, Prof James Patrick; s of Peter Mackey (d 18 Nov 1976), and Esther Josephine, *née* Morrissey; *b* 9 Feb 1934; *Educ* Mount St Joseph Coll, Nat Univ of Ireland (BA), Pontifical Univ Maynooth (LPh, BD, STL, DD), Queen's Univ Belfast (PhD); Univs of: London, Oxford, Strasbourg; *m* 25 Aug 1973, (Hanorah) Noelle, da of Nicholas Alphonsus Quinlan, of City View, Leamy St, Waterford, Ireland; 1 s (James b 28 Jan 1976), 1 da (Ciara b 9 Oct 1974); *Career* Queens Univ Belfast 1960-66 (asst lectr and lectr in philosophy 1963-66), lectr in theology St John's Coll Waterford 1966-69, visiting assoc prof Catholic Univ of America 1968, Univ of San Francisco 1969-79 (assoc prof and prof of systematic and philosophical theology 1973-79), visiting prof Univ of California Berkley 1974, Thomas Chalmers prof of theology Univ of Edinburgh 1979- (dean Faculty of Divinity 1984-88), visiting prof Dartmouth Coll NH USA 1989; writer and presenter: The Hall of Mirrors (Channel Four) 1984, Perspectives (BBC Belfast) 1986-87, The Gods of War (Channel Four) 1987; memb Catholic Theologic Soc GB; *Books* The Modern Theology of Tradition (1962, 1963), Life and Grace (1966), Tradition and Change in the Church (1968), Contemporary Philosophy of Religion (1968), Morals, Law and Authority: Sources and Attitudes in the Church (ed, 1969), The Church, Its Credibility Today (1970), The Problems of Religious Faith (1972), Jesus the Man and the Myth (1979), The Christian Experience of God as Trinity (1983), Religious Imagination (ed, 1986), Modern Theology: A Sense of Direction (1987), New Testament Theology in Dialogue (with JDG Dunn, 1987), An Introduction to Celtic Christianity (ed, 1989); *Recreations* sailing; *Clubs* Edinburgh Univ, Saint Brendan's Cruising; *Style*— Prof James Mackey; 10 Randolph Crescent, Edinburgh EH3 7TT (☎ 031 225 9408); Clonea, Dungarvan, Co Waterford, Ireland; Faculty of Divinity, University of Edinburgh, New College, Mound Place, Edinburgh EH1 2LX (☎ 031 225 8400)

McKIBBIN, Prof Brian; s of William McKibbin (d 1971), and Elizabeth, *née* Wilson (d 1984); *b* 9 Dec 1930; *Educ* Roundhay Sch Leeds, Univ of Leeds (MB ChB, MD), Univ Coll Oxford, Univ of Illinois (MS); *m* Pamela Mary, da of John Charles Francis Pask (d 1965); 2 s (Alexander b 1964, Hugh b 1967); *Career* Nat Serv Capt RAMC 1957-58; sr lectr and head Dept of Orthopaedics Univ of Sheffield 1966-72, prof of traumatic and orthopaedic surgery Univ of Wales Coll of Med 1972-; pres: Br Orthopaedic Res Soc 1973-75, Br Orthopaedic Assoc 1987-88; memb Cncl RCS; FRCS 1960; *Books* Recent Advances in Orthopaedics (vol 2, vol 3, 1979, vol 4, 1981); *Style*— Prof Brian McKibbin; Dept of Orthopaedics, Cardiff Royal Infirmary, Newport Rd, Cardiff (☎ 0222 494855)

McKICHAN, Duncan James; OBE (1990); s of John James McKichan, OBE (d 1973), and Alice Annie, *née* Middleton (d 1930); *b* 28 July 1924; *Educ* George Watson's Coll Edinburgh, Solihull Sch, Downing Coll Cambridge, Univ of Glasgow (BL); *m* 30 Sept 1959, Leila Campbell, da of Very Rev John Annand Fraser, MBE, TD, DD (d 1985); 2 da (Susan b 1960, Alison b 1963); *Career* WWII RNVR 1943-46; admitted slr 1950, ptnr Maclay Murray & Spens 1952, dean Royal Faculty of Procurators in Glasgow 1983-86, Hon Consel for Canada in Scotland, NI and N England 1986; memb Law Soc of Scotland 1950; *Books* Drafting and Negotiating Commercial Leases in Scotland (jtly); *Recreations* walking, swimming, sailing, skiing, gardening; *Clubs* Western Glasgow, Royal Northern and Clyde Yacht; *Style*— Duncan McKichan, Esq, OBE; Invermay, 7 Queen St, Helensburgh G84 9QH (☎ 041 248 5011, fax 041 248 5819, telex 77474)

MACKIE, Charles Gordon; TD (1945), DL (1985); s of Capt Charles Gordon Stewart Mackie, OBE (d 1965), of St Ann's, by Brechin, Angus, and Gertrude Irvine Mackie (d 1946); *b* 19 March 1916; *Educ* Harrow, St John's Coll Oxford (MA); *m* 5 May 1945, Margaret Georgina (Peggy), da of Maj Frederick Ernest Koebel, DSO (d 1940), of Chudleigh, Devon; 1 s (Alexander b 1946), 2 da (Mary b 1953, Sally b 1958); *Career* cmmnd 2 Lt 7 Bn Argyll and Sutherland Highlanders 51 Highland Div TA 1938, served France 1939-40 (wounded, despatches), Capt 1941, 8 Army 1941-42; serv: N Africa, Sicily, Italy; Europe 1944 (wounded), invalided out 1945; Stewarts & Lloyds 1937-67: trainee 1937-39, mangr London City office 1953; asst md Stanton Ironworks Ltd (subsid) 1956, md Stanton & Staveley Ltd (subsid) 1962, chm and md Stanton & Staveley Ltd; dir: Stewarts & Lloyds 1964-67, Tubes Div British Steel Corporation 1967-78; chm: Shanks & McEwan Ltd 1978-81, Booth International Ltd 1979-82; treas Univ of Nottingham 1982- (cncl memb 1962-); gen cmmr of income tax 1960-91; High Sheriff Nottinghamshire 1977-78; OStJ 1967; *Recreations* shooting, fishing, skiing, golf; *Clubs* Carlton; *Style*— Charles Mackie, Esq, TD, DL

MACKIE, Clive David Andrew; s of David Hugh Mackie (d 1978), of Hampton Court, and Lilian Edith, *née* Claughton (d 1990); *b* 29 April 1929; *Educ* Tiffin Sch Kingston-on-Thames; *m* 20 Dec 1953, Averil Mary Amy, da of John Alfred Ratcliff (d 1974); 1 s (Duncan b 1957), 3 da (Louise b 1958, Rosalind b 1963, Nina b 1967); *Career* CA; dir Grundy Gp Teddington 1961-67, dir and sec D Sebel & Co Ltd 1967-70, asst sec Poly of the S Bank 1970-73, sec gen Inst of Actuaries 1983- (dep sec 1973-78, sec 1978-83); FCA, FSS; *Recreations* music (post 1780), cricket, carpentry, countryside; *Clubs* Reform, Kent CCC; *Style*— Clive Mackie, Esq; Withermere, Burwash, E Sussex TN19 7HN (☎ 0435 882427); Staple Inn Hall, London WC1V 7QJ (☎ 071 242 0106, fax : 071 405 2482)

MACKIE, David Lindsay; s of Alastair Cavendish Lindsay Mackie, CBE, DFC, of London, and Rachel, *née* Goodson; *b* 15 Feb 1946; *Educ* Ardingly Coll, St Edmund Hall Univ of Oxford (BA, MA); *m* 1, 13 Feb 1971 (m dis 1986), 2 s (James b 1974, Edward b 1976), 1 da (Eleanor b 1978); m 2, 6 Dec 1989, Phyllis, da of Robert Gershon of NYC; *Career* admitted slr 1971, ptnr Allen & Overy 1975-, asst Crown Court 1988; chm Product Liability Advertising and Unfair Competition Ctee Int Bar Assoc 1987-; *Books* Products Liability - An International Manual of Practice (jtly, 1988); *Recreations* climbing; *Clubs* Roehampton; *Style*— David Mackie, Esq; Allen & Overy, 9 Cheapside, London EC2V 6AD (☎ 071 248 9898, fax 071 236 2192, telex 8812801)

MACKIE, (William) Denis Grenville; s of (William) Grenville Mackie, of The Lodge, Lissanoure, Loughguile, Cloughmills, Co Antrim, and Constance Beatrice, *née* Rodden (d 1981); *b* 10 Sept 1934; *Educ* Shrewsbury; *m* 23 April 1960, Susannah, da of Bernard Dixon (d 1983), of Pampisford Place, Pampisford, Cambs; 2 s (Alastair b 15 March 1963, Peter (twin) b 15 March 1963), 1 da (Caroline b 1961); *Career* dir: James Mackie and Sons Ltd Belfast (and Hldgs) 1968-77, Robert Mccalmont and Co Ltd Belfast 1968-83; md Lissanoure Farms Ltd Co Antrim 1969-, non-exec dir Strand Spinning Co Belfast 1977-90; memb: Co Antrim Jury Bursay Ctee, BASC NI Advsy Cncl 1990; High Sheriff Co Antrim 1979; *Recreations* skiing, country pursuits, sailing; *Clubs* Ulster Reform (Belfast), Royal NI Yacht; *Style*— Denis Mackie, Esq; Lissanoure, Loughguile, Cloughmills, Co Antrim, NI (☎ 02656 41471)

MACKIE, Hon George Yull; 3 and yst s of Baron John-Mackie (Life Peer); *b* 19 April 1949; *Style*— The Hon George Mackie; The Bungalow, Harold's Park Farm, Nazeing, Essex

MACKIE, Gordon; s of Lavens Mathewson Mackie (d 1966), and Marion Klara Gabrielle, *née* Dorndorf; Mackie family is a sect of MacKay (Clan Aodh); *b* 1 Jan 1937; *Educ* Merchiston Castle; *m* 1, 18 July 1963, Elizabeth Ann, da of Cecil Gordon Falloon, of Millicent House, Sallins, Co Kildare; 1 s (Timothy Gordon b 1965); 2 da (Catriona Ann b 1964, Grania Esther b 1967); m 2, 23 Aug 1985, Ruth Alison, da of Hubert Allan Hall, of 33 Lislunnan Rd, Kells, Co Antrim; 2 da (Alexandra Helen b 1987, Sarah Margot b 1988); *Career* chm and chief exec James Mackie and Sons Ltd 1981 (dir 1968), with Inpendent International Textile Consultancy 1989-; CIMechE 1982; FRSA 1984; *Recreations* aviation, sub-aqua, skiing, shooting, apiculture; *Style*— Gordon Mackie, Esq; Ladyhill, 18 Ladyhill Rd, Antrim, Co Antrim BT41 2RF (☎ 08494 63051)

MACKIE, James Campbell Stephen; s of Prof John Duncan Mackie, CBE, MC, LLD (d 1978), and Cicely Jean, *née* Paterson (d 1976); *b* 1 Oct 1926; *Educ* Charterhouse, New Coll Oxford (MA); *m* 1951, Margaret Pamela Daphne Moore, da of late Maj Hugh King, Seaforth Highlanders, MC; 4 s (Alexander b 1952, Hugh b 1956, Simon b 1960, Tobias b 1964), 1 da (Miranda b 1962); *Career* serv RM 1944-47, cmmnd NW Europe 1946; HM Overseas Civil Serv 1951-59, Malaya (asst sec PM's, Dept); dir Corn Exchange Co 1975-80; dir gen Grain & Feed Trade Assoc 1972-91; sec: Liverpool Cotton Assoc 1960-65, Cattle Food Trade Assoc 1965-72; chm Grayswood Branch of Cons and Unionist Assoc 1965-73 and 1976-83 (Farnham Div 1973-76); pres: SW Surrey Cons Assoc 1988 (vice chm 1984), Haslemere Branch Cons Assoc 1987-; vice pres Haslemere Hockey Club 1988-; Freeman City of London 1990, memb Worshipful Co of Arbitrators 1990; *Recreations* photography, tennis, hockey, history, antiques, dogs, reading, travelling; *Clubs* Caledonian, Farmers'; *Style*— James C S Mackie, Esq; Weald Mount, Hill Rd, Haslemere, Surrey GU27 2JP

MACKIE, Hon John Maitland; s of Baron John-Mackie (Life Baron); *b* 1944; *m* 1, Marion Halliday; m 2, 1984, Janet Ann Hart; 1 da (Louise b 1985); *Style*— The Hon John Mackie; 52 Lucas Lane, Hitchin, Herts SG5 2LT

MACKIE, Sir Maitland; CBE (1965), JP (Aberdeen 1959); s of Maitland Mackie and bro of Baron Mackie of Benshie and of Baron John-Mackie; *b* 16 Feb 1912; *Educ* Aberdeen GS, Aberdeen Univ; *m* 1, 1935, Isobel Ross (d 1960); 2 s, 4 da; m 2, 1963, Pauline M Turner; *Career* farmer 1932-; Lord Lt Aberdeenshire 1975-87, chm Jt Advsy Ctee Scot Farm Bldgs Investigation Unit 1963-75, Aberdeen Milk Mktg Bd 1965-82, Peterhead Bay Management Company 1975-86, memb Bd Scot Cncl Devpt and Indust 1975-82; chm: Oil Policy Ctee 1975-82 (Aberdeen Branch), Aberdeen Cable Services Ltd 1983-87; OStJ 1977; *Style*— Sir Maitland Mackie, CBE, JP; High Trees, Inchmarlo Rd, Banchory (☎ 03302 4274)

MACKIE, Neil; s of William Fraser Mackie (d 1979), of Hilton Cottage, King's Gate, Aberdeen, and Sheila Roberta, *née* Taylor (d 1973); *b* 11 Dec 1946; *Educ* Aberdeen GS, Royal Scot Acad of Music and Drama, RCM (fndn scholar); *m* 1973, Kathleen Mary, da of William Livingstone (d 1972); 2 da (Alison Kathleen b 1980, Elinor Sheila b 1983); *Career* int opera singer (tenor); many cmmnd works by Scot composers; recorded with: EMI, Decca, Philips, Chandos, Unicorn-Kanchana, Accent, Abbey Records, EMI Serenade for Tenor; Horn and Strings - Scottish Chamber Orchestra voted runner up solo voice recording of the year 1989 Gramophone; prof of singing RCM 1985-; Gulbenkian fellowship; London debut: recital Wigmore Hall 1972, concert Eng Chamber Orch under Raymond Leppard 1973; world premières incl Unpublished Songs by Britten, Three Auden Settings by Hans Werner Henze; works especially written by Peter Maxwell Davies for him: The Martyrdom of St Magnus (title role), The Lighthouse (role of Sandy), Into the Labyrith (solo cantata for tenor and orch), A Solstice of Light; OStJ; *Recreations* reading, charity work and occasional gardening; *Clubs* Athenaeum; *Style*— Neil Mackie; 70 Broadwood Avenue, Ruislip, Middlesex HA4 7XR (☎ 0895 632115); Lies Askonas Ltd, 186 Drury Lane, London WC2B 5RY (☎ 071 405 1808, fax 071 242 1831)

MACKIE, Dr Peter Howard; s of Dr Lawrence Percival Mackie (d 1988), of Wellesbourne, Warwick, and Elizabeth Bates, *née* Pedlow; *b* 13 Oct 1947; *Educ* Cheltenham Coll, Hertford Coll Oxford Univ (MA, BM, BCh); *m* 14 July 1973, Joanna Jane, da of John Henry McGhee, TD (d 1987), of Kineton Warwick; 4 da (Sarah b 1975, Julia b 1978, Diana b 1980, Rachel b 1986); *Career* house physician Harefield Hosp 1973, house surgn Cheltenham Gen Hosp 1973-74, sr house offr and registrar Bristol Royal Infirmary 1974-76, hon tutor Univ of Bristol 1974-76, res registrar Queen Elizabeth Hosp Birmingham 1976-77, lectr Dept of Immunology Univ of Birmingham 1977-79, sr registrar haematology John Radcliffe Hosp Oxford 1979-82, conslt haematologist E Berks Dist 1982-; hon sec E Berks Div BMA, memb Cncl Windsor and Dist Organists' Assoc; memb: Ctee Parents' Assoc Dr Challoner's HS Amersham, Ancient Soc of Coll Youths 1970; MRCP 1978, MRCPath 1981; *Recreations* music, bellringing, gardening; *Style*— Dr Peter Mackie; Westbury, Duffield Lane, Stoke Poges, Bucks SL2 4AH (☎ 0753 645510)

MacKIE, Prof Rona; da of Prof J Norman Davidson, FRS (d 1972), of Bearsden, Glasgow, and Morag, *née* McLeod; *b* 22 May 1940; *Educ* Laurel Bank Sch, Univ of

Glasgow (MB, ChB, MD); *m* 18 Sept 1962, Euan Wallace MacKie, s of Iver Eachaan MacKie; 1 s (Douglas b 1965), 1 da (Alison b 1963); *Career* hon conslt dermatologist Gtr Glasgow Health Bd 1978- (conslt dermatologist 1973-78), prof of dermatology Univ of Glasgow 1978-; memb BBC Sci Consultative Ctee, memb Gtr Glasgow Health Bd, vice-pres Nat Eczema Soc; FRCP Glasgow 1978, FRSE 1983, FRCPath 1984, FRCP London 1985, FIBiol 1988; *Books* Clinical Dermatology - An Illustrated Textbook (1981), Eczema and Dermatitis (1983), Malignant Melanoma (ed, 1983), Current Perspectives in Immunodermatology (ed, 1984), Milne's Dermatopathology (ed, 1984), Clinical Dermatology An Illustrated Textbook (1986), Skin Cancer (1989); *Recreations* skiing, music especially opera, gardening; *Style—* Prof Rona MacKie; University of Glasgow, Dept of Dermatology, Anderson College Building, 56 Dumbarton Rd, Glasgow G11 6NU (☎ 041 339 8855 ext 4006, fax 041 330 4008, telex 777070 UNIGLA)

MACKIE, Sheila Gertrude (Mrs R Fenwick-Baines); da of James Watt Bell Mackie (d 1968), and Edna Irene, *née* Watson (d 1989); *b* 5 Oct 1928; *Educ* Durham HS, King Edward VII Sch of Art Newcastle upon Tyne, Univ of Durham (BA); *m* 3 Aug 1967, Robert Fenwick-Baines, s of Albert Baines; 1 s (James Alastair b 1970), 1 da (Anneliese b 1969); *Career* head Dept of Art Consetts Sch 1950-82, occasional lectr Sunderland Coll of Art and lectr numerous art socs, artistic advsr Bertam Mills Circus 1950s-60s; artist and illustrator; pubns incl: Adventure in Glides Garden (with Terri Le Guerre, 1979), The Great Seasons (with David Bellamy, 1980), The Mouse book (with David Bellamy, 1982), Lindisfarne - the Cradle Island (with Magnus Magnusson, 1984), Beowulf (with Magnus Magnusson and Julian Glover, 1987), The Wanderer (with Michael Cronin and Charlton Heston, 1989); work in Royal Collection, exhibited RA and RSA; shows in London and provinces; *Style—* Miss Sheila Mackie; Hoddington Oaks, Spa Grounds, Shotley Bridge, Consett, Co Durham DH8 0TN (☎ 0207 503 065)

MACKIE, (John) Stuart; s of Norman Frederic Mackie (d 1956), of Halifax, and Mary, *née* Rushworth (d 1976); *b* 12 March 1933; *Educ* Sowerby Bridge GS, Univ of Sheffield (Dip Arch); *m* 3 Aug 1957, Elsie, da of William Breeden, of Ashton under Lyne; 1 s (Robin Jonathan b 1964), 1 da (Amanda Lauren b 1958); *Career* RE 1955-57, serv Germany and Cyprus; chartered architect, md private practice; chm RIBA: Teeside Branch 1975-76, Northern Regn 1978-79, Housing Advsy Gp 1982-; memb Cncl: Aruck 1982-89, RIBA 1981-; sec Teeside Civic Soc, dir Cleveland Bldgs Preservation Tst; *Recreations* travel, photography; *Style—* Stuart Mackie, Esq; 15 Spring Hill, Welbury, Northallerton, N Yorks (☎ 060 982 453); Wilson & Womersley Ltd, 2 Vaughan Street, Linthorpe Road, Middlesbrough (☎ 0642 232333)

MACKIE OF BENSHIE, Baron (Life Peer UK 1974), of Kirriemuir, Co Angus; George Yull Mackie; CBE (1971), DSO (1944), DFC (1944), LLD (1982); s of Maitland Mackie, OBE, LLD and bro of Baron John-Mackie and Sir Maitland Mackie; *b* 10 July 1919; *Educ* Aberdeen GS, Aberdeen Univ; *m* 1, 1944, Lindsay Lyall (d 1985), da of Alexander Sharp, OBE, Advocate, of Aberdeen; 3 da (Hon Lindsay Mary (Hon Mrs Rusbridger) b 1945, Hon Diana Lyall (Hon Mrs Hope) b 1946, Hon Jeannie Felicia (Hon Mrs Leigh) b 1953) (and 1 s decd); m 2, 29 April 1988, Jacqueline, widow of Andrew Lane; *Career* serv WWII Bomber Cmd; farmer 1945-; chm Mackie Yule & Co, Caithness Glass Ltd 1966-85; Caithness Pottery Co, Benshie Cattle Co; rector Univ of Dundee 1980-83; MP (Lib) Caithness & Sutherland 1964-66; Parly candidate (Lib): Angus S 1959, (for Euro Parl) Scotland NE 1979; chm Scot Lib Pty 1965-70; chm Land & Timber Services Ltd 1986-88; Lib spokesman House of Lords: Devolution, Agriculture, Scotland, Indust; memb: Parly Assembly Cncl of Europe 1986-, Western Euro Union 1986-; pres Scottish Lib Pty until 1988 (became SLD); *Recreations* golf, tennis, shooting; *Clubs* Garrick, Farmers', RAF, Nat Lib; *Style—* Rt Hon Lord Mackie of Benshie, CBE, DSO, DFC; Cortachy House, by Kirriemuir, Angus (☎ 0575 4229)

MACKILLIGIN, Robert Guy Walter; MC (1944, and bar 1945); s of late Hector Rennie Mackilligin; *b* 11 Oct 1918; *Educ* Charterhouse, Camborne Sch of Mines; *m* 1949, Daphne Gwendoline, *née* Cooper; 3 da; *Career* serv WWII 51 Highland Div RA 1939-46; petroleum engr Shell International Petroleum Co Ltd 1946-53, mangr Shell International Co Ltd 1954-73, exec dir Bisichi Mining plc 1974-, chm Dragon Markets Ltd 1984-; *Recreations* genealogy, gardening, ornithology; *Style—* Robert Mackilligin, Esq, MC; Walnut Tree Cottage, Woodlands, Pembury Rd, Tunbridge Wells (☎ 0892 30392, 071 236 3539)

McKILLOP, Prof James Hugh; s of Dr Patrick McKillop (d 1979), of Coatbridge, and Dr Helen Theresa McKillop, *née* Kilpatrick; *b* 20 June 1948; *Educ* St Aloysius' Coll Glasgow, Univ of Glasgow (BSc, MB ChB, PhD); *m* 17 Aug 1973, Caroline Annis, da of Charles Allen Oakley, CBE, of Glasgow; 2 da (Beth b 1977, Jenny b 1981); *Career* Harkness fellowship Stanford Univ 1979 and 1980, Muirhead prof of med Univ of Glasgow 1989 (lectr 1977-82, sr lectr 1982-89); treas Scottish Soc of Experimental Med 1982-87; Br Nuclear Med Soc: cncl memb 1985-, hon sec 1988-90, pres 1990-; vice chm ARSAC Ctee Dept of Health 1989- (memb 1988-); FRCPG 1985, FRCPE 1990; *Books* Atlas of Technetium Bone Scans (with D L Citrin, 1978), Imaging in Clinical Practice (with A G Chalmers and P J Robinson, 1988); *Recreations* cricket, opera, reading; *Clubs* Royal Soc of Med; *Style—* Prof James McKillop; 10 Kirklee Circus, Glasgow G12 0TW (☎ 041 339 7000); University Department of Medicine, Royal Infirmary, Glasgow G31 2ER (☎ 041 552 4014, fax 041 552 4014)

McKIMMIE, John Hedley; s of Dr John McKimmie (d 1983), and Dr Patricia Lucy Frances, *née* Heaton; *b* 25 April 1948; *Educ* Gordonstoun, Univ of Glasgow; *m* 10 July 1971, Jacqueline Ann; 1 s (Andrew b 1977), 1 da (Rosie b 1975); *Career* CA; chm and chief exec Parkway Gp plc 1987-89, fin dir WCRS Group 1982-87; *Recreations* family, golf, hockey, animals; *Clubs* West Hill Golf, Woking Hockey; *Style—* John H McKimmie, Esq; Windlecote House, Heath House Rd, Worplesdon Hill, nr Woking, Surrey GU22 0RD (☎ 04867 3153)

MACKINLAY, Col Hamish Grant; LVO 1979; s of James Johnstone Mackinlay (d 1988), of Tillicoultry, Clackmannanshire, and Margaret Keir, *née* Grant; *b* 11 March 1935; *Educ* Dollar Acad, RMA Sandhurst; *m* 25 Jan 1964, Elizabeth (Elspeth) Paul Gray, da of The Rev Peter Bryce Gunn (d 1979), of Ancrum, Roxburghshire; 1 s (Jamie b 1966), 1 da (Diana b 1969); *Career* cmmnd RCS 1955, sr seconded offr State of Qatar 1976-79, SO Army Staff Duties MOD 1979-82, dep head Mil Mission to HRH the Crown Prince of Saudi Arabia 1982-86, def and mil attaché Cairo 1986-88, Col Def Signal Staff MOD 1989, dep govr (security) HM Tower of London 1989-; FBIM; *Clubs* Naval and Military, Royal Cwlth Soc; *Style—* Col Hamish Mackinlay, LVO; Office of the Deputy Govr (Security), HM Tower of London, London EC3N 4AB (☎ 071 709 0765)

McKINLAY, William James Alexander; s of William Waddell McKinlay, and Mary Theresa, *née* Mullin; *Educ* St Ambrose HS Coatbridge; *m* 1 July 1989, Donna Irene, da of William Reid; *Career* professional footballer; over 108 appearances Dundee Utd 1986-, debut Hibernian 1986; Scotland caps: schoolboy, under 16, under 17, under 18, 6 under 21 1984-85; Scot Young Player of the Year 1989; *Recreations* snooker, music; *Style—* William McKinlay, Esq; Dundee Utd FC, Tannadice Park, Tannadice St, Dundee (☎ 0382 833166)

MacKINLAY MacLEOD, Michael John; s of John MacKinlay MacLeod, of Worcs, and Dorothy Rule, *née* MacFarlane (d 1975); *b* 2 Oct 1935; *Educ* Eton, Pembroke Coll Cambridge, RAC Cirencester; *m* 1, 17 May 1958 (m dis 1966), Sandra Elizabeth, da of late Lt-Col Alister Maynard, MBE; 3 s (Torquil b 1959, Jocelyn b 1961, Caspar b 1963); m 2, 14 Feb 1967, Pamela Dawn, da of late Hugh Nicholas Charrington; 1 s (Euan b 1970), 2 da (Emma b 1967, Iona b 1971); *Career* Lt Grenadier Gds, Capt Ayrshire (ECO) Yeomanry; shipping Baltic Exchange London, Redheads Tyne; ship mangr H Hogarth and Sons Glasgow; antiques business London & Broadway Worcs; farmer Scotland and Worcs, branch chm CLA 1987; govr Worcs Coll of Agriculture; memb: Agric Land Tribunal (Midlands Area), W Midlands Agric Forum; AICS; *Recreations* shooting; *Clubs* Pratt's, Farmer's, Union & County (Worcs); *Style—* Michael MacKinlay MacLeod, Esq; The Old Vicarage, Overbury, Tewkesbury, Glos GL20 7NT (☎ 038689 510)

MCKINNELL, Ian Hayes; s of Neil Hayes McKinnell (d 1990), of Newcastle-upon-Tyne, and Olga, *née* Smith; *b* 6 Nov 1954; *Educ* Penistone GS Yorkshire, Barnsley Sch of Art and Crafts, Faculty of Art & Design Brighton Poly (BA Hons); partner, Elizabeth Heaney; *Career* photographic technician for various cos in Brighton and Newcastle 1976-79, exhibition designer Dove Cottage Trust Grasmere Cumbria 1980-81, self-employed photographer 1981-; solo exhibitions: Still Life (Spectro Arts Centre Newcastle-upon-Tyne and tour) 1980, Recent Work (Special Photographers Co Gallery London and tour) 1990; gp exhibitions incl: Br Int Print Biennale Bradford, Northern Young Contemporaries Manchester, 6th and 7th Assoc of Photographers Tour, Royal Photographic Soc's Annual Exhibition Bath 1990, Against the Grain Camerawork London 1990; memb Assoc of Photographers 1987; *Books* One Day and 1/30th of a Second in Edinburgh (1979); *Recreations* travel, work; *Style—* Ian McKinnell, Esq; 9 Bristol House, 80a Southampton Row, London WC1B 4BB (☎ 071 631 3017, fax 071 404 2026)

MACKINNON, Alastair Marr; s of Hector Allan MacKinnon (d 1990), of Aberdeen, Scotland, and Edith Patterson, *née* Marr; *b* 25 Feb 1960; *Educ* Glenrothes HS Fife, Univ of Edinburgh (LLB, BD), Dartmouth Coll New Hampshire USA; *Career* asst St Cuthbert's Parish Church and St Johns Scottish Episcopal Church Edinburgh 1985-87, dir St Cuthbert's Educn Centre 1985-87, tutor in Christian Ethics and Practical Theology Univ of Edinburgh 1988-89; freelance journalist and writer: Scottish corr Church Times London 1990-, religious affairs corr Scotland on Sunday 1990-, Crucible, Theology; conslt to Centre for Theology and Public Issues Univ of Edinburgh; *Recreations* modern visual art, cooking, badminton; *Clubs* Univ of Edinburgh Staff; *Style—* Alastair MacKinnon, Esq

McKINNON, (David) Douglas; s of John McKinnon (d 1957), and Margaret Douglas (d 1963); *b* 18 July 1926; *Educ* Stirling HS, Univ of Glasgow (BSc); *m* 1960, Edith June, da of Edward Fairful Kyles (d 1942); 1 s, 2 da; *Career* asst maths dept Univ of Glasgow 1946-48, pres Faculty of Actuaries 1979-81, memb Cncl Int Actuarial Assoc 1972-89 (UK sec 1975-89); gen mangr and actuary Scottish Mutual Assurance Society 1982-90 (formerly dep gen mangr and dir 1981-); pres Falkirk Bn the Boys Bde 1972-77, vice chm Church of Scotland Tst 1984-89, memb Church of Scotland Assembly Cncl 1987-, chm Assoc Scottish Life Offices 1988-89, memb Bd Assoc of Br Insurers 1988-90; FFA, FIMA; *Recreations* golf; *Clubs* Western (Glasgow); *Style—* Douglas McKinnon Esq; Kinburn, 4 Carronvale Rd, Larbert, Stirlingshire FK5 3LZ (☎ 0324 562373); Scottish Mutual Assur Soc, 109 St Vincent St, Glasgow G2 5HW (☎ 041 248 6321, telex 777145)

MACKINNON, Hon Mrs (Patricia Ann); *née* Souter; da and co heiress of 25 Baron Audley; *b* 10 Aug 1946; *m* 1969, Carey Leigh Mackinnon; 1 s, 1 da; *Style—* The Hon Mrs Mackinnon; Holts Crest, Fordcombe, Tunbridge Wells, Kent

MACKINNON, Hon Mrs; (Patricia Clare); da of 1 Baron Glentoran, OBE, PC (d 1950); *b* 1919; *m* 1940, Lt Cdr Adam McLeod Mackinnon, RN; 2 s, 3 da; *Style—* The Hon Mrs Mackinnon; The Cottage Inn, Maidens Green, Winkfield, Windsor, Berks

McKINNON, Warwick Nairn; s of His Hon Judge Neil Nairn McKinnon (d 1988), of Purley, Surrey, and Janetta Amelia, *née* Lilley; *b* 11 Nov 1947; *Educ* King's Coll Sch Wimbledon, Christ's Coll Cambridge (MA); *m* 29 July 1978, Nichola Juliet, da of David Alan Lloyd, of Limpsfield, Surrey; 1 s (Rory b 1981), 1 da (Kirsty b 1982); *Career* called to the Bar Lincoln's Inn 1970; ad eundum SE Circuit; *Recreations* cricket, golf, opera; *Style—* Warwick McKinnon, Esq; Queen Elizabeth Buildings, Temple, London EC4Y 9BS

MacKINNON OF MacKINNON, Madam; Anne Gunhild MacKinnon; da of Alasdair Neil Hood MacKinnon of MacKinnon (d 1983), 37 Chief of Clan Fingon (MacKinnon); suc father as 38 Chief; *b* 13 Feb 1955; *Educ* Badminton Sch Bristol, St Loyes Sch of Occupational Therapy (Dip of Occupational Therapy); *m* 1981, Allan; 2 s (Andrew b 1982, Robert b 1985); *Career* occupational therapist Somerset Hosps and Social Services 1976-90; *Style—* Madam MacKinnon of MacKinnon; 16 Durleigh Rd, Bridgwater, Somerset TA6 7HR

MacKINNON OF MacKINNON, Lt-Col Ian Kroyer; yr s of Cdr Arthur Avalon MacKinnon of MacKinnon, OBE, RN (d 1964), 36 Chief of Clan MacKinnon, of Charity Acre, Pilgrims Way, Hollingbourne, Kent, and Gunhild, *née* Kroyer (d 1946); er bro Alasdair Neil Hood MacKinnon, 37 Chief of Clan MacKinnon (d 1983); *b* 8 Oct 1929; *Educ* Wellington, RMA Sandhurst; *m* 1 Jan 1955, Joanna Eileen, er da of Capt Sir Robert William Stirling-Hamilton, 12 Bt, JP, DL (d 1982); *Career* cmmnd Queen's Own Cameron Highlanders 1950; served with 1 Bn in: Tripoli, Canal Zone, Austria 1950-53; Depot Camerons Inverness 1953-56, 1 Bn in Malaya, Aden and Dover 1956-59, Adjt 4/5 Bn Queen's Own Cameron Highlanders (TA) Inverness 1959-61, staff appt HQ Land Forces Hong Kong 1961-63, Trg Maj Univ of St Andrews 1964-65, 1 Bn Queen's Own Highlanders (Seaforth and Camerons) Osnabrück and Berlin 1965-66, staff appt HQ Highland Div and Dist Perth 1966-68, 1 Bn Queen's Own Highlanders (2 i/c) Edinburgh and Sharjah 1968-71, HQ BAOR DAMS 1971-73, staff appt HQ Dir of Inf Warminster 1973-76, Lt-Col 1976, cmd Scottish Inf Depot Bridge of Don Aberdeen 1976-79, cmdt Stanford Trg Area Thetford Norfolk 1979-84, ret 1984; regnl sec Norfolk and Suffolk CLA 1985-; fndr chm: Breckland Group, Norfolk Naturalists' Tst; memb Norfolk Centre Ctee The Nat Tst; *Recreations* shooting, gardening; *Style—* Lt-Col Ian MacKinnon of MacKinnon; Little Breck House, 4 Trenchard Crescent, Watton, Norfolk IP25 6HR (☎ 0953 883139)

MACKINTOSH, Dr Alan Finlay; s of Dr Finlay George Mackintosh (d 1989), and Eileen Ormsby, *née* Johnson; *b* 10 Jan 1948; *Educ* Oundle, King's Coll Cambridge (BA), Westminster Med Sch (MD BChir); *m* 16 Feb 1974, Susan Patricia, da of Col Claude Hugo Macdonald Hull (d 1979); 1 s (Nicholas b 14 April 1982), 1 da (Clare b 18 April 1979); *Career* med registrar: Brighton 1975-76, King's Coll Hosp London 1976-77; sr cardiology registrar Cambridge 1978-81, conslt cardiologist St James' Univ and Killingbeck Hosp Leeds 1981-, lectr Univ of Leeds 1981-; treas Br Cardiovascular Intervention Soc; FRCP; *Books* The Heart Disease Reference Book (1984), Case Presentations Heart Disease (1985); *Recreations* horse racing, tennis, opera; *Style—* Dr Alan Mackintosh; 15 Charville Gardens, Shadwell, Leeds LS17 8JL (☎ 0532 737293); St James' Univ Hosp, Beckett St, Leeds LS9 7TP (☎ 0532 433144)

MACKINTOSH, Anthony Robert Kilgour (Tony); s of Philip Kilgour Mackintosh, of Five Ashes, Sussex, and Beryl Ada, *née* Brodie; *b* 15 June 1943; *Educ* Brighton Hove and Sussex GS, Hertford Coll Oxford (MA); *m* 21 Oct 1967, Barbara Dorothy, da of

Thomas Fox; 3 s (Julian b 1970, Alastair b 1971, Jonathan b 1975); *Career* exec Br Petroleum Co 1965-71; dir: Wood Mackenzie & Co Ltd 1984-86 (ptnr 1976-84, oil analyst 1972-76), Hill Samuel Bank Ltd 1986-89, Laing and Cruickshand 1990-; *Recreations* chess, bridge, golf, reading; *Clubs* Utd Oxford and Cambridge Univ, Highgate Golf; *Style*— Tony Mackintosh, Esq; 3 North Hill, London N6 (☎ 081 340 4984); Laing and Cruickshank, Broadwalk House, 5 Appold St, London EC2A 2DA (☎ 071 588 4000, fax 071 588 0290)

MACKINTOSH, Colin Edward; s of Colin Mayne Mackintosh (d 1974), and Mary Victoria, *née* Pitcairn; *b* 10 Jan 1936; *Educ* Melville Coll Edinburgh, Univ of Edinburgh (MB ChB); *m* 1965 (m dis 1984); 2 da (Sarah b 29 June 1969, Celia b 1 March 1973); *Career* house surgical and physican appts Leith Hosp and Edinburgh Royal Infirmary 1959-62, surgical sr house offr and registrar Kirkaldy Hosp and Edinburgh Royal Infirmary 1962-64, registrar then sr registrar in diagnostic radiology Nat Hosp for Nervous Diseases Royal Free Hosp 1964-70, visiting assoc prof of radiology Univ of Southern Calif 1970-71, conslt radiologist Royal Free Hospital 1971- contrib to British Journal of Hospital Medicine 1976-82, fndr of London Imaging Centre (first computerised tomogram clinic in the W End 1980), first person to run a private mobile CT scanner 1982; Rohan Williams medal; FRSM, FRCR; *Recreations* riding, music; *Style*— Colin Mackintosh, Esq; 50 Harley Street, London W1N 1AD (☎ 071 255 1859)

MACKINTOSH, Colin Richard; s of Euan Bracebridge Mackintosh (d 1979), of Birmingham, and Enid Mary Lucy, *née* Harris; *b* 19 June 1953; *Educ* Blackfriars Llanarth, George Dixon GS Birmingham, Univ of Birmingham (LLB); *m* 18 June 1977, Jani Elizabeth Mary, da of Kenneth Townsend; 3 da (Elizabeth b 1980, Lucy b 1982, Alice b 1987); *Career* called to the Bar Inner Temple 1976; M & O Circuit; memb Hon Soc of the Inner Temple; *Recreations* reading, hill walking, fishing, family; *Style*— C R Mackintosh, Esq; 3 Fountain Court, Steelhouse Lane, Birmingham B4 6DR (☎ 021 236 5854)

MACKINTOSH, Lady Fiona Eve Akua; *née* Hare; da of 5 Earl of Listowel, GCMG, PC, and his 2 w, Stephanie Sandra Yvonne, *née* Wise; *b* 24 Feb 1960; *m* 5 Sept 1987, Christopher G D Mackintosh, s of Charlach Mackintosh, of Calgary, Alberta, Canada; 1 da (Anna Frances b 14 Dec 1988); *Style*— The Lady Fiona Mackintosh; Box 30093, 6455 Macleod Trail, Calgary, Alberta T2H OAO, Canada

MACKINTOSH, Hon Graham Charles; s of 2 Viscount Mackintosh of Halifax (d 1980), and Gwynneth *née* Gledhill hp of bro, 3 Viscount; *b* 12 March 1964; *Educ* The Leys Sch, Univ of Newcastle upon Tyne (BSc), Coll of Estate Mgmnt, Univ of Reading; *Career* surveyor; *Recreations* cricket, golf, tennis, swimming, hockey, squash; *Clubs* E India, MCC, Artist's, Morton's, Annabels; *Style*— The Hon Graham Mackintosh; 32A Queen's Gate Mews, Kensington, SW7 5QN

McKINTOSH, His Hon Judge Ian Stanley; s of Herbert Stanley McKintosh (d 1975), of Cranford Ct, Chester; *b* 23 April 1938; *Educ* Leeds GS, Exeter Coll Oxford (MA); *m* 2 Sept 1967, (Alison) Rosemary, da of Kenneth Blayney Large, of Inglenook Cottage, Erlestoke, Wilts; 2 s (Edward b 1970, William b 1975), 1 da (Alexandra b 1972); *Career* serv RAF UK and Germany 1957-59; admitted slr 1966, Slrs Dept New Scotland Yard 1966-68, private practice 1969-88, dep circuit judge 1976-81, rec Crown Ct 1981-88, circuit judge 1988-; chm Swindon Branch of Stonham Housing Assoc, memb of Stonham Housing Assoc, memb of SW Legal Aid Area Local Gen and Area Appeals Ctees 1970-89; *Recreations* family, cricket, sailing, rowing, talking; *Clubs* MCC, XL; *Style*— His Hon Judge McKintosh; c/o The Courts of Justice, Edward St, Truro, Corwall

MACKINTOSH, Lady; (Mary) Yolande Bickford; JP (W Sussex 1968), DL (W Sussex 1982); only da of Leonard William Bickford Smith (3 s of Sir George John Smith, VD, JP, DL), and Anna Greta, *née* Huth (d 1986); *b* 21 June 1919; *Educ* Downe House, London Univ (BSc); *m* 1, Dr John Clegg (decd); 1 s, 2 da; m 2, 1962, as his 2 w, Capt Sir Kenneth Lachlan Mackintosh, KCVO, RN (d 1979), sometime Yeoman Usher of The Black Rod and sec to the Lord Great Chamberlain, also Serjeant-at-Arms House of Lords; 1 step s (and 2 step s decd), 1 step da; *Style*— Lady Mackintosh, JP, DL; The Garden House, Slinfold, Horsham, W Sussex

MACKINTOSH OF HALIFAX, 3 Viscount (UK 1957); Sir (John) Clive Mackintosh; 3 Bt (UK 1935); s of 2 Viscount Mackintosh of Halifax, OBE, BEM (d 1980, whose f was head of the Mackintosh confectionery manufacturers), by his 2 w, Gwynneth, *see* Viscountess Mackintosh of Halifax; *b* 9 Sept 1958; *Educ* The Leys Sch, Oriel Coll Oxford (MA); *m* 1982, Elizabeth, only da of late D G Lakin, and Mrs F E G Melener, of Esher; 2 s (Hon Thomas Harold George b 1985, Hon George John Frank b 24 Oct 1988); *Heir* s, Hon Thomas Harold George Mackintosh b 8 Feb 1985; *Career* CA with Price Waterhouse; pres Oxford Univ Cons Assoc 1979; sits as Cons in House of Lords; ACA; *Recreations* cricket, golf, bridge; *Clubs* Carlton, MCC; *Style*— The Rt Hon the Viscount Mackintosh of Halifax; House of Lords, SW1

MACKINTOSH OF HALIFAX, Gwynneth, Viscountess; Gwynneth Charlesworth; da of late Charles Gledhill, of Halifax; *m* 1956, as his 2 w, 2 Viscount Mackintosh of Halifax, OBE, BEM (d 1980); 2 s (3 Viscount, Hon Graham Mackintosh); *Style*— The Rt Hon Gwynneth, Viscountess Mackintosh of Halifax; The Old Hall, Barford, Norwich NR9 4AY (☎ 060 545 271)

MACKINTOSH OF MACKINTOSH, The; Lt Cdr Lachlan Ronald Duncan; OBE (1972), JP, DL (Inverness-shire 1965), RN; 30 Chief of the Clan Mackintosh; s of Vice Adm Lachlan Donald Mackintosh of Mackintosh, CB, DSO, DSC (d 1957); *b* 27 June 1928; *Educ* Elstree, RNC Dartmouth; *m* 1962, Mabel Cecilia Helen (Celia), da of Capt Hon John Bernard Bruce, RN (d 1971); 1 s (John b 1969), 2 da (Louisa b 1962, Bridget b 1966) (and 1 da decd); *Heir* s, John Lachlan, b 1969; *Career* Flag Lt to First Sea Lord 1951, specialised in communications 1954, served on HMY Britannia 1957, ret 1963; chm Highland Exhibitions Ltd 1964-84; vice pres Scottish Cons and Unionist Assoc 1969-71, CC Inverness-shire 1970-75, Vice Lt 1971-85, regnl cllr Highland Region 1974-, Lord Lt Lochaber Inverness, Badenoch & Strathspey 1985-; *Clubs* Naval & Military, Highland (Inverness); *Style*— The Mackintosh of Mackintosh, OBE, JP, DL, RN; Moy Hall, Tomatin, Inverness (☎ 080 82 211)

MCKIRDY, John Langlands; s of Alexander Watson McKirdy (d 1972), of 24 Fyvie Ave Glasgow, and Agnes, *née* Langlands; *b* 13 Sept 1931; *Educ* Queens Park Sch Glasgow; *m* 28 Sept 1955, Isobel Fawkes, da of Andrew Brownlee; 4 da (Susan Janet b 14 Nov 1956, Fiona Ann b 27 Oct 1957, Lesley Jane b 14 May 1960, Alison Lynn b 10 Dec 1962); *Career* Nat Serv RAF 1951-53; agency inspr Scottish Amicable 1955-60 (actuarial student 1948-55), life supt Yorkshire Insurance Co 1960-63; Noble Lowndes & Partners Glasgow: joined as conslt 1963, regnl life dir Scot 1967, regnl life dir London 1969, memb Bd 1972, asst new business dir Noble Lowndes Personal Fin Servs 1973, new business dir 1976, dep md 1978, md 1979, dep chief exec Noble Lowndes & Partners Ltd 1987, dep chm 1990-; Bd appts: chm Noble Lowndes Personal Fin Servs, dir Noble Lowndes NZ and Aust; dep chm Br Insur and Investmt Brokers' Assoc, chm Fin Servs Ctee BIIBA (memb Cncl); *Recreations* golf, bridge; *Clubs* RAC, Tandridge Golf; *Style*— John McKirdy, Esq; Noble Lowndes & Partners Limited, Norfolk House, Wellesley Rd, Croydon CR9 3EB (☎ 081 686 2466, fax 081 681 1458)

MCKISSOCK, Sir Wylie; OBE (1946); s of Alexander Cathie McKissock; *b* 27 Oct 1906; *Educ* City of London Sch, London Univ (MB, MS), St George's Hosp (MS); *m* 1934, Rachel Madeline, da of Leonard Martin Jones; 1 s, 2 da; *Career* consulting neurological surgn in London 1936-71: Nat Hosp WC1, Hosp for Sick Children Great Ormond St, Queen Square Hosp, St George's Hosp; surgn i/c: EMS Head Centre, Atkinson Morley's Hosp, Leavesden Hosp 1939-45; MS, FRCS, FRSM, Hon FRCR; kt 1971; *Style*— Sir Wylie McKissock, OBE; Camus na Harry, Lechnaside, Gairloch, Wester Ross (☎ 044 583 224)

MACKLEN, Victor Harry Burton; CB; s of Harry Macklen (d 1965), of Brighton, Sussex, and Annie Clara, *née* Hayward (d 1972); *b* 13 July 1919; *Educ* Varndean Secdy Sch Brighton, King's Coll London (BSc); *m* 22 Sept 1950, Scylla Ursula Irene, da of Henry Hope Fellows (d 1924); *Career* Capt Army Operational Res Gp 1943, Capt GHQ Cairo 1943-44, special Operational Res Gp WO and Air Miny 1944, Maj sci advsr staff WO 1944-45, Lt Col GSO1 Sci 2 WO 1945-49; princ sci offr: Sci 2 WO 1949, Operational Res Section HQ BAOR 1950-54; dep chief sci offr Chief Sr Advr's Staff MOD 1958-60 (sr princ sci offr 1954-58), head of Tech Secretariat Reactor Gp UKAEA 1960-64, dep dir Tech Ops Reactor Gp UDAEA 1964-67, asst chief sci advsr (Nuclear) MOD 1967-69, dep sec and dep chief advsr Projects and Nuclear MOD 1969-79, special advsr to Chm Dynamics Gp BAe 1980-81, personal advsr to Chm BT 1981-87; chm Hartlip Parish Cncl 1983-, pres Sittingbourne and Milton Regis Branch Royal Br Legion; FRSA; *Clubs* Army and Navy; *Style*— Victor Macklen, Esq, CB; Stepp House, The Street, Hartlip, Sittingbourne, Kent ME9 7TH (☎ 0795 842 591)

MACKLEY, Frank Rainsford; yr s of Capt John Thomas Mackley (d 1960), of Kingsmead, Maudlyn Lane, Steyning, W Sussex, and Louise Matilda, *née* Brown (d 1930); *b* 13 Nov 1923; *Educ* Shoreham GS, Brighton Tech Coll; *m* 18 Jan 1947 (m dis 1965), Peggy, da of Walter Hamblin (d 1957), of Hangleton Road, Hove, East Sussex; 2 s (b March 1949, b Nov 1950); *Career* port construction and repair gp RE HQ No 5 1942-47; articled pupil civil and structural engrg 1939-42, engrg asst 1947-50, res engr West Africa 1950-53, sr asst engr 1953-56, contracts mangr and engr 1956-60, chief design engr 1960-62, dir chief engr and consulting engr 1962-81, co chm 1981-; chm: Southern assoc ICE 1971-72, Maritime & Waterways Engrg Bd ICE 1976 (1977, 1981), Piling Gp 1976-77; memb Cncl ICE 1974-77 and 1981-83; author of sundry tech papers incl Amphibious Air Cushion Duo Platforms to ICE (awarded Webb prize 1974 and S G Brown award Royal Society 1976); FICE 1956, FInstW 1961, MIWEM 1963, memb Société des Ingénieurs et Scientifiques de France 1965, FCI Arb 1971, FEng 1984, FRSA 1986; *Books* Piles & Foundations (contrib, 1981); *Style*— Frank Mackley, Esq; 34 Anzac Close, Peacehaven, East Sussex BN10 7SY; No 177, Alle 10, Domaine Marin de Grimaud, 83310 Grimaud, Var, France; Bankside House, Small-Dole, Henfield, West Sussex BN5 9XQ (☎ 0273 492212, fax 0273 494328)

MACKLEY, Ian Warren; CMG (1989); s of Harold William Mackley (d 1973), and Marjorie Rosa Sprawson, *née* Warren; *b* 31 March 1942; *Educ* Ardingly Coll; *m* 1, 9 Nov 1968 (m dis 1988), Jill Marion, da of Frank Saunders (d 1955); 3 s (Jonathan b 1970, Nicholas b 1973, Christopher b 1983); m 2, Jan 1989, Sarah Anne, da of John Churchley; 1 da (Elizabeth b 1989); *Career* FO: entered 1960, third sec Br Embassy Saigon 1963, asst private sec Min of State 1967; second sec 1968, Br High Cmmn Wellington NZ 1969, first sec 1972; FCO 1973, Br High Cmmn New Delhi 1976, FCO 1980, seconded to ICI 1982; cnsllr 1984, dep head UK Delgn to CDE Stockholm, chargé d'affaires Br Embassy Kabul Afghanistan, dep high cmmr Canberra 1989; pres and capt Kabul Golf and Country Club; *Recreations* golf; *Style*— Ian W Mackley, Esq, CMG; c/o FCO, King Charles St, London SW1A 2AH

MACKLIN, David Drury; CBE (1989); s of (Laurence) Hilary Macklin, OBE (d 1969), of Wendens Ambo, Essex and Alice Dumergue, *née* Tait (d 1977); *b* 1 Sept 1928; *Educ* Felsted, St John's Coll Cambridge; *m* 23 July 1955, Janet, da of Alastair MacNaughton Smallwood (d 1985), of Uppingham; 4 s (Alan Drury, Simon Andre, Alastair Jeremy, Adrian Roger); *Career* asst slr: Coward Chance and Co 1954-56, Warwicks CC 1956-61, Devon CC 1961-67 (asst clerk 1967-69); dep clerk Derbys CC 1969-73; chief exec: Lincs CC 1973-79, Devon CC 1979-88, ret 1988; *Recreations* golf, sailing, bird watching; *Clubs* Hawks, Exeter Golf and Country; *Style*— David Macklin, Esq, CBE; Randolls, Victoria Rd, Topsham, Exeter, Devon EX3 0EU (☎ 0392 873 160)

MACKLIN, Peter Richard (Charlie); s of Lt-Col P H Macklin, OBE (d 1976), and Joan Elizabeth, *née* Butcher, of Springfield, Hazlebury Bryan, Sturminster Dorset; *b* 1 April 1946; *Educ* Wellington, Durham Univ (BA); *m* 21 Aug 1971, Pamela Adele, da of A F Plant Jr, of Washington DC, USA; 3 s (Andrew b 1974, Jonathan b 1977, Christopher b 1981); *Career* slr Clifford Turner 1971-76, ptnr Freshfields 1979- (departmental managing ptnr Property Dept 1986-); memb cncl Br Property Fedn; memb Worshipful Co of Slrs; memb Law Soc; *Recreations* family, opera, exploration; *Clubs* Maldon Golf; *Style*— Peter Macklin, Esq; 53 Matlock Way, New Malden, Surrey KT3 3AT (☎ 081 942 5033); Whitefriars, 65 Fleet St, London EC4Y 1HT (☎ 071 936 4000, fax 071 248 3487/8/9, telex 889292)

MACKRELL, Judith Rosalind (Mrs S P Henson); da of Alexander George Mackrell, of Surrey, and Margaret Elizabeth, *née* Atkinson; *b* 26 Oct 1954; *Educ* Sutton HS, Univ of York (BA), Univ of Oxford (DPhil); *m* Simon Peter Henson, s of Peter Henson; 1 s (Frederick Juan b 12 Feb 1990); *Career* pt/t lectr in English literature: Oxford Poly, Lincoln and St Anne's Coll Oxford, City Lit London 1981-85; freelance dance writer 1984- (work published in Vogue, Tatler, Dance Theatre Journal), dance corr The Independent 1986-; broadcastings incl: Dance International BBC TV, South Bank Show, Radio 3, Radio 4 and World Service; *Books* British New Dance (1991); *Recreations* family, travel, reading, playing violin badly, music, attending dance classes for hacks; *Style*— Ms Judith Mackrell; 73 Greenwood Road, London E8 1NT (☎ 071 249 5553)

MACKRELL, Keith Ashley Victor; s of Henry George Mackrell (d 1967), of Romsey, Hants, and Emily Winifred Jesse Mackrell (d 1972); *b* 20 Oct 1932; *Educ* Peter Symonds Sch Winchester, LSE BSc (Ecm); *m* 20 Feb 1960, June Yvonne, *qv*; 1 s (Ashley b 1961), 3 da (Elliot b 1956, Kim b 1958, Lee b 1961); *Career* RAF Flying Offr 1953-55; dir: Cope Allman Int 1977-86, Shell Int 1977-, Private Investmt Corp for Asia (PICA) 1980-84; memb Int Advsy Cncl East-West Centre Honolulu 1985; MICD 1977, CBIM; *Clubs* Hurlingham; *Style*— Keith Mackrell, Esq; 34 Inner Park Rd, Wimbledon, London SW19 6DD (☎ 081 788 7826); Shell International Petroleum Co Ltd, Shell Centre, London SE1 7NA (☎ 071 934 5226, fax 071 934 4284)

MACKSEY, Kenneth John; MC (1944); s of Henry George Macksey (d 1949), and Alice Lillian, *née* Nightingall (d 1972); *b* 1 July 1923; *Educ* Goudhurst Sch for Boys; *m* 22 June 1946, (Catherine Angela) Joan, da of Thomas Henry Little (d 1967); 1 s (Andrew b 1949), 1 da (Susan b 1947); *Career* enlisted RAC 1941, cmmnd from Sandhurst 141 Regt RAC (The Buffs), transferred RTR 1946, various regtl and staff, appts Army Staff Coll 1956, ret Maj 1968; mil historian; dep ed Purnell's History of the Second and First World War, conslt Canadian Army with task of writing tactical instructional manuals in form of novels; Clash series 1981-; fndr and vice chm Beaminster Sports Assoc, memb Beaminster Town Cncl 1973-84, vice chm Dorset Local Cncls Assoc 1983-85; *Books* incl: The Shadow of Vimy Ridge, Afrika Korps, Guinness Book of Tank Facts and Feats, The Guinness History of Land Warfare, Kesselring: the Making of the Luftwaffe, The Tanks 1945-75, History of the Royal Armoured Corps 1914-75, First Clash, The Guinness History of Sea Warfare, The

Tank Pioneers, Guderian Panzer-General, Technology in War, Godwin's Saga, Military Errors of World War II, Tank Versus Tank; *Recreations* umpiring ladies hockey; *Style*— Kenneth Macksey, Esq, MC; Whatley Mill, Beaminster, Dorset DT8 3EN (☎ 0308 862321)

MACKWORTH, Cdr Sir David Arthur Geoffrey; 9 Bt (GB 1776), RN (ret); s of Vice Adm Geoffrey Mackworth, CMG, DSO (d 1952), 5 s of 6 Bt; suc n, Sir Harry Llewellyn Mackworth, 8 Bt, CMG, DSO, 1952; *b* 13 July 1912; *Educ* Farnborough Sch Hants, RNC Dartmouth; *m* 1, 1941 (m dis 1971), Mary Alice, da of late Harry Grylls; 1 s; m 2, 1973, Beryl Joan, former w of late E H Sparkes, da of late Pembroke Henry Cockayn Cross; *Heir* s, Digby John Mackworth; *Career* joined RN 1926, served HMS Eagle and HMS Suffolk 1939-45, Cdr 1948; naval advsr to Dir of Guided Weapon R & D Miny of Supply 1945-59, ret 1956; *Clubs* Royal Naval (Portsmouth), Royal Ocean Racing, Royal Naval Sailing Assoc, Royal Yacht Sqdn; *Style*— Cdr Sir David Mackworth, Bt, RN; 36 Wittering Rd, Hayling Island, Hants (☎ 0705 464085)

MACKWORTH, Digby John; s and h of Sir David Arthur Geoffrey Mackworth, 9 Bt; *b* 2 Nov 1945; *Educ* Wellington; *m* 1971, Antoinette Francesca, da of Henry James McKenna, of Ilford, Essex; *Career* former Lt, AAAC in Malaysia and Vietnam; with Iranian Helicopters Ltd; *Style*— Digby Mackworth, Esq; PO Box 2898, Tehran, Iran

MACKWORTH-PRAED, Humphrey Winthrop; MBE (1988); s of Lt-Col Cyril Winthrop Mackworth-Praed, OBE (d 1974), of Castletop, Burley, Ringwood, Hants, and Edith Mary Henrietta (d 1990), *née* Stephenson Clarke; *b* 30 Nov 1919; *Educ* Eton, Trinity Coll Cambridge; *m* 3 June 1947, Penelope, da of Maj Gen RHD Tompson, CB, CMG, DSO (d 1937); 2 s (Nicolas b 1951, Mark b 1955), 3 da (Sheila b 1948, Margaret b 1949, Vanessa b 1959); *Career* WWII, Euro Theatre, RE capt 1942, Maj 1945 (despatches twice); memb London Stock Exchange 1947-72, sr ptnr Francis & Praed 1966-72; conservation offr Nat Tst Southern Region 1972-84, ecology conslt 1985-; chm: Regnl Advsy Ctee SE England Conservancy Forestry Cmmn 1980-85 (memb 1967-85), Surrey Wildlife Tst 1983-86 (memb 1963-), Nat Tst Headley Heath Local Mgmnt Ctee 1985-89 (memb 1953-), Bedgebury Pinetum Advsy Ctee 1985- (memb 1974-); FRES 1938; *Books* Conservation Pieces (1991); *Recreations* conservation and forestry; *Clubs* Travellers; *Style*— Humphrey Mackworth-Praed, Esq, MBE

MACKWORTH-YOUNG, Lady Eve(lyn); *née* Leslie; da of 20 Earl of Rothes (d 1975), and Beryl, Countess of Rothes (*née* Dugdale); *b* 11 March 1929; *m* 1949, (Gerard) William Mackworth Mackworth-Young (d 1984), s of Gerard Mackworth Mackworth-Young (d 1965); 4 da; *Style*— The Lady Eve Mackworth-Young; Fisherton Mill, Fisherton de la Mere, Warminster, Wilts BA12 0PZ (☎ 098 56 246)

MACKWORTH-YOUNG, Lady Iona Sina; *née* Lindsay; da of 29 Earl of Crawford and (12 of) Balcarres; *b* 10 Aug 1957; *Educ* Univ of Edinburgh (MA); *m* 1983, Charles Gerard Mackworth-Young, s of Sir Robin Mackworth-Young, GCVO, *qv*; 2 da (Rose Bettina Natalie b 1987, Constance Ruth Sina b 1990); *Career* art historian; asst curator: Exhibitions Print Room Windsor Castle 1982-84, Drawing Dept Fogg Art Museum 1984-86; *Recreations* paper marbling, bookbinding; *Style*— The Lady Iona Mackworth-Young; 18 The Chase, London SW4 0NH

MACKWORTH-YOUNG, Sir Robert Christopher (Robin); GCVO (1985, KCVO 1975, CVO 1968, MVO 1961); s of Gerard Mackworth-Young, CIE (d 1965; s of Sir (William) Mackworth Young, KCSI, himself 3 s of Sir George Young, 2 Bt, by Susan, da of William Mackworth-Praed and sis of Winthrop MP, the MP and poet); *b* 12 Feb 1920; *Educ* Eton, King's Coll Cambridge; *m* 1953, Helen Rosemarie, da of Werner Charles Rudolf Aue (d 1978), of Menton, France; 1 s (Charles Gerard, m Iona, *qv*, da of 29 Earl of Crawford); *Career* serv RAFVR as Sqdn Ldr UK, ME, Normandy; Foreign Serv 1948-55; dep librarian Windsor Castle 1955-58, librarian and asst keeper The Queen's Archives 1958-85, librarian emeritus to HM The Queen 1985-; *Recreations* music, skiing, electronics; *Clubs* Roxburghe; *Style*— Sir Robin Mackworth-Young, GCVO; c/o Baring Bros & Co Ltd, 8 Bishopsgate, London EC2

MACLACHLAN, Alistair Andrew Duncan; s of Alexander Syme MacLachlan (d 1974), and Amy Louise Pennington, *née* Anderson; *b* 14 March 1946; *Educ* Perth Acad, Univ of Strathclyde (BA); *m* 9 Aug 1968, Alison Mary Simpson, da of James Love, of Dundee; 2 s (Laurie b 3 July 1975, Greg b 26 June 1977); *Career* asst rector Keith GS 1974-78 (princ teacher of business studies and economics 1971-74); rector: Elgin HS 1978-82, Forres Acad 1983-; memb Ctee Scottish Squash Rackett Assoc, sometime chm Elgin Squash Club, exec sec and treas Keith Show; *Recreations* music, reading, keeping fit, coaching squash; *Style*— Alistair MacLachlan, Esq; 82 Duncan Drive, Elgin IV30 2NH (☎ 0343 542193); Forres Acad, Burdsyard Rd, Forre, IV36 0DG (☎ 0309 72271)

McLACHLAN, Gordon; CBE (1967); s of Gordon McLachlan (d 1946), of Leith, and Mary Thomson, *née* Baird; *b* 12 June 1918; *Educ* Leith Acad, Univ of Edinburgh (BComm); *m* 17 Feb 1951, (Monica) Mary, da of Nevill Alfred Malcolm Griffin; 2 da (Katrina Mary (Kirstie) b 19 March 1958, Tessa Anne b 17 Dec 1961); *Career* RNVR 1939-46, gunnery specialist 1943-46; accountant Edinburgh Corp 1946-48 (apprentice 1935-39), NW Met Regnl Hosp Bd 1948-53, asst dir of fin Nuffield Fndn 1953-55, sec accountant ed Nuffield Prov Hosp Tst 1955-86; memb various official ctees of Miny Health; memb Inst of Med of the Nat Acad of Sciences Washington DC 1974-, hon fell RCGP 1978; Hon LLD Birmingham 1977; FCA 1947; *Recreations* reading, theatre, rugby football; *Clubs* Caledonian; *Style*— Gordon McLachlan, Esq, CBE; 95 Ravenscourt Rd, London W6 0UJ (☎ 081 748 8211)

McLACHLAN, John James; s of William McLachlan (d 1980), of Birkenhead, and Helen, *née* Duffy; *b* 28 Aug 1942; *Educ* Rock Ferry High GS Cheshire; *m* 24 Sept 1966, Heather Joan, da of George Smith (d 1975), of Heswall; 1 s (Alexander b 4 Jan 1975), 1 da (Deborah b 19 Feb 1972); *Career* mgmnt accountant Norwest Construction 1966-67, investmt analyst Martins Bank Trust Co 1967-69, investmt res mangr Barclays Bank Trust Co 1969-71, dep investmt mangr 1971-74, investmt mangr British Rail Pension Fund 1974-83, dir pensions investmt 1983-84, investmt mangr Reed International plc 1984-88, investmt mangr and dir United Friendly Insurance plc 1988-; former chm Investmt Ctee Nat Assoc of Pension Funds; former memb: Panel on Take Overs and Mergers, Institutional Shareholders Ctee; non-exec dir: Iceland Frozen Foods Holdings, Investment Management Regulatory Organisation; FCA, AMSIA, FRSA; *Recreations* squash, watching cricket and soccer, collecting Wisdens; *Style*— John McLachlan, Esq; United Friendly Insurance plc, 42 Southwark Bridge Rd, London SE1 9HE (☎ 071 928 5644, fax 071 261 9077, telex 8813953)

McLACHLAN, Peter John; OBE (1983); s of Rev Dr H J McLachlan, of Sheffield, and Joan Dorothy Hall (d 1979); gf Dr H McLachlan, historian, author of many historical books, prof of Hellenistic Greek at Univ of Manchester; *b* 21 Dec 1936; *Educ* Magdalen Coll Sch, Queen's Coll Oxford (MA); *m* 1965, Gillian Mavis, da of John Christopher Lowe (d 1985); 2 da (Heather b 1967, Fiona b 1969); *Career* admin trainee Miny of Fin NICS 1959-62, admin Nat Youth Orchestra of GB 1962-65 and 1966-70, PA to chm of IPC 1965-66, Cons Res Dept 1970-72, exec dir Watney & Powell Ltd 1972-73, Unionist memb S Antrim in NI Assembly 1973-75, gen mangr S H Watterson Engineering 1975-77, jt md Ulster Metalspinners Ltd 1976-77, projects mangr Peace by Peace Ltd 1977-79, sec Peace People Charitable Tst 1977-79, chm Community of The Peace People 1978-80; fndr chm: NI Fedn of Housing Assocs 1976-78, Belfast Improved Houses Ltd 1975-81 (memb Ctee 1975-); memb: Ctee Lisnagarvey Housing Assoc Ltd 1977-, The Corrymeela Community 1975-, Admin Cncl Royal Jubilee Tsts 1975-82, NI Projects Tst 1977-87; chm NI Peace Forum 1980-82; vice chm: NI Hospice Ltd 1981-, Gulbenkian Advsy Ctee on Community Work 1978-81; gen sec Belfast Voluntary Welfare Soc 1980-86, dir Bryson House 1986-, memb Cncl Children's Community Holidays 1982-85, memb Exec Ctee NI Children's Holiday Scheme 1982-85, chm Dismas House 1983-87 (memb Ctee 1983-89), presenter BBC Street Corner (Community Action programme) 1983-86; memb: Min's Advsy Ctee on Community Work 1982-84, Min's Advsy Ctee on Personal Social Services 1984-88, Exec Ctee NI Chest Heart & Stroke Assoc 1982-85, Bd of Visitors HM Prison Maghaberry 1986 (dep chm 1987-89, chm 1989); tstee: Buttle Tst 1987-, Anchor Tst 1987-, Victoria Homes Tst 1989-; hon sec NI Fedn Victims' Support Scheme 1983-, vice chm Victim Support UK 1988-90 (memb Cncl 1987-), hon treas Lisburn VSS 1986-89, fndr Ctee memb NI Conflict and Mediation Assoc 1986-, dir Belfast Community Radio Ltd 1989-; UK Eisenhower fell 1986; *Recreations* piano playing, singing, mountain walking, conservation; *Style*— Peter McLachlan, Esq, OBE; 82 Moira Road, Hillsborough, Co Down, N Ireland BT26 6DY (☎ 0846 683497); Bryson House, 28 Bedford St, Belfast BT2 7FE (☎ 0232 325835)

MacLACHLAN, Simon; MBE (1983); s of Geoffrey Cheasty MacLachlan (d 1965), of Ipswich, and Violet Edith Gasgoigne, *née* Hicks; *b* 17 Dec 1934; *Educ* Downside Sch; *m* 11 May 1963, Julie, da of John Mannering (d 1985), of River House, River, Kent; 2 s (Justin b 1964, Luke b 1965), 2 da (Martha b 1968, Hannah b 1972); *Career* 2 Lt Queens Own Royal West Kent Regt 1953-55, seconded 5 Bn Kings African Rifles 1953-54 (served in Kenya, despatches), Lt 4/5 BN Queens Own Royal West Kent Regt (TA) 1955-62; admitted slr 1959, ptnr Clifford-Turner 1964, assigning ptnr Co Dept 1980-87, ptnr Clifford Chance 1987-, vice chm Ctee on Securities Int Bar Assoc 1986-; chm New Islington and Hackney Housing Assoc 1983; tstee: Circle 33 Housing Tst 1978-, George V Playing Fields Sissinghurst; memb: Law Soc 1959-, Int Bar Assoc 1979-; *Books* Life After Big Bang (1987); *Recreations* gardening, tennis; *Clubs* RAC; *Style*— Simon MacLachlan, Esq, MBE; Sissinghurst Place, Sissinghurst, Cranbrook, Kent TN17 2JP; Royex House, Aldermanbury Sq, London EC2 (☎ 071 600 0808, fax 071 600 1064, telex 887847)

McLACHLAN, Stuart Munro; QC (1982); s of Dr Ian McLachlan, of Solihull, and Dr Margaret Quinn (MB ChB); *b* 26 Feb 1951; *Educ* Solihull Sch, Mercersburg Acad Pennsylvania USA, Univ of Nottingham (LLB), Cncl of Legal Educn; *Career* sch teacher 1977-79;called to the Bar Gray's Inn 1982, in chambers of F Ashe Lincoln; *Recreations* scuba diving, walking, photography, music; *Style*— Stuart McLachlan, Esq, QC; 66 Dumbarton Road, London SW2 5LU (☎ 081 671 6744); 9 King's Bench Walk, Temple, London EC4 (☎ 071 353 7202)

MACLACHLAN, Dr Thomas Kay; s of Dr Thomas Kay Machlachlan, and Dr Sarah Hodgson Nelson, MBE; *b* 21 Jan 1932; *Educ* Rugby, Univ of London (DPM), Univ of Edinburgh (MB ChB); *m* 7 May 1966 (Mary) Elizabeth, da of John Calvert, OBE; 1 s (Roderick b 2 April 1974), 2 da (Anne b 2 April 1968, Mary b 26 April 1971); *Career* Nat Serv 2 Lt HLI; conslt psychiatrist Med Res Cncl Population Cytogenetics Unit 1968-69, dir Child Guidance Servs Worcestershire 1969-71, conslt child psychiatrist Family Consultation Clinic Cambridge 1971-, assoc lectr Univ of Cambridge Med Sch 1972-; Hon MA Univ of Cambridge 1972; FRCP, MRCPsych; *Recreations* golf, people, art, antiques; *Clubs* Gog Magog Golf; *Style*— Dr Thomas Maclachlan; 17 West End, Whittlesford, Cambridge (☎ 0223 832359); Family Consultation Clinic, 3 Benet Place, Cambridge CB2 4LX (☎ 0223 66501)

MACLACHLAN OF MACLACHLAN, Madam; Marjorie Susan Mary; Lady of the Barony (territorial) Strathlachlan, Chief of the Clan of Maclachlan; da of John Maclachlan of Maclachlan, 23 of that Ilk (d 1942); *b* 1920; *Educ* Oxenfoord Castle, Abbots Hill; *m* 1948, George Styles Rome, *qv* (assumed surnmane of Maclachlan); 3 s, 3 da; *Heir* s, Euan John Rome-Maclachlan, yr of Maclachlan b 1949; estate mangr and farmer on Maclachlan estate; *Style*— Madam Maclachlan of Maclachlan; Castle Lachlan, Strathlachlan, Strachur, Cairndow, Argyll

MCLAREN, Dr Anne; *b* 26 April 1927; *Educ* Univ of Oxford (MA, DPhil); *m* 1952, Donald Michie; 1 s (Jonathan b 1957), 2 da (Susan b 1955, Caroline b 1959); *Career* memb Scientific Staff of Agric Res Cncl's Unit of Animal Genetics Edinburgh 1959-74, dir Mammalian Devpt Unit MRC 1974-; memb: Govt Ctee on Human Fertilisation and Embryology 1982-84, Voluntary (Interim) Licensing Authy for Human Fertilisation and Embryology 1985-91, Human Fertilisation and Embryology Authy 1990-; FRS 1975, FRCOG 1987; memb Polish Academy of Sciences 1988; *Books* Mammalian Chimeras (1976), Germ Cells and Soma (1981); *Style*— Dr Anne McLaren; MRC Mammalian Development Unit, 4 Stephenson Way, London NW1 2HE

McLAREN, Hon (Henry) Charles; s and h of 3 Baron Aberconway, *qv*; *b* 26 May 1948; *Educ* Eton, Sussex Univ (BA); *m* 1981, Sally Ann, yr da of late Capt Charles Nugent Lentaigne, RN, of Hawkley Place, Hawkley, Liss, Hants, and formerly w of Philip Charles Bidwell; 1 s (Charles Stephen b 27 Dec 1984), 1 da (Emily b 1982), and 1 step s (Alex b 1975); *Style*— The Hon Charles McLaren; Sailing Barge Repertor, St Mary's Churchyard, London SW11

McLAREN, Hon Christopher Melville; s of 2 Baron Aberconway, CBE (d 1953); *b* 1934; *Educ* Eton, King's Coll Cambridge; *m* 1973, Jane Elizabeth, da of James Barrie; 1 s (Robert Melville b 1974), 1 da (Lara Jane Christabel b 1976); *Career* business conslt; chm Systems C Holdings Ltd; chm Southbank Poly Bd of Govrs; *Recreations* gardening, walking; *Style*— The Hon Christopher McLaren; 31 Upper Addison Gardens, London W14 8AJ

MACLAREN, Deanna; *née* Bullimore; *b* 4 Feb 1944; *m* 1, 1965, Patrick Alexander Moffat Maclaren; m 2, 1974, Michael Dennis Godfrey; m 3, 1987, Nicholas Kent; *Career* author, journalist, broadcaster, and public speaker; *Books* Little Blue Room (1974), The First of all Pleasures (1975), Dagger in the Sleeve (1979), Your Loving Mother (1983); non-fiction: The Single File, How to Live Alone, and Like It; *Recreations* tennis, opera, gardening; *Clubs* Network; *Style*— Ms Deanna Maclaren; 22 Cromwell Ave, Highgate, London N6 5HL

MACLAREN, Derek Anthony Ewen; s of late John Ewen Maclaren; *b* 19 Jan 1925; *Educ* Cranbrook, Sydney Univ; *m* 1951, Pamela Ann, da of Harold Miller; 2 s, 1 da; *Career* Sub-Lt Royal Australian Navy 1943-47; dir: PA Consulting Services Pty Ltd 1966-70, PA Int Consulting Services Ltd 1971-1985, PA Hldgs Ltd 1982-85, Critchley Ltd 1984-, CSL Ltd 1987-89; chm: PA Computers and Telecommunications 1976-83, Imperial Software Technol Ltd 1984-88, Videologic 1985-; Stock Exchange: memb Information Services Bd 1987-89, memb Trading Markets Managing Bd 1990-; memb: Computing Servs Assoc Cncl 1975-76, CSERB 1976-78; memb advsy bd: Information Systems & Technol for the Post Office 1986-88, BR 1985-90, Syntech 1986-; FIMC; *Recreations* history, Tudor architecture, skiing; *Style*— Derek Maclaren, Esq; The Manor House, West Coker, Somerset (☎ 093 586 2646); Flat 3, 13 Wetherby Gardens, London SW5 0JW (☎ 071 373 8330)

McLAREN, (George William) Derek; s of Thomas George McLaren, of Eldon Lee, Ormiston Gardens, Melrose, Scotland, and Davina Siddis (d 1982); *b* 21 Nov 1934; *Educ* Galashiels Acad; *m* 1, 7 June 1958 (m dis 1987), Marjory Watt, da of Robert McInnes (d 1981), of Edinburgh; 2 s (Roger b 1960, Angus b 1962), 1 da (Fay (Mrs

Thom) b 1964); m 2, 12 Aug 1988, Waltraud, da of Fritz Loges (d 1975), of W Germany; *Career* Nat Serv RAMC 1953-55; mangr Theodore Hamblin Ltd 1963-68, md Silhouette Fashion Frames Ltd 1975-; chm: Optical Frame Importers Assoc 1980, Optical Info Cncl 1988-; memb Cncl: Fedn of Mfrg Opticians, Assoc of Br Dispensing Opticians; involved with Fight for Sight Charity; Freeman City of London 1980, Liveryman and Court Asst Worshipful Co of Spectacle Makers 1982; FBDO 1956, FInstD 1981, MBIM 1980; *Recreations* gardening, antique restoring, reading; *Clubs* City Livery; *Style—* Derek McLaren, Esq; 25 Dartmouth Park Ave, London NW5 1JL (☎ 071 485 2467); Silhouette Fashion Frames Ltd, 333 High Rd, London N22 4LE (☎ 081 889 9997, fax 081 889 2782, telex 24795)

MACLAREN, Lady Edith Huddleston; *née* Abney-Hastings; da of Countess of Loudoun (d 1960); co-heiress to the Baronies of Botreaux, Stanley and Hastings; *b* 1925; *m* 1947, Maj David Kenneth Maclaren; 2 s; *Style—* The Lady Edith Maclaren; Ard Daraich, Ardgour, by Fort William, Inverness-shire PH33 7PA (☎ 08555 248)

MacLAREN, Iain Ferguson; s of Dr Patrick Duncan MacLaren (d 1967), of 3 Minto St, Edinburgh, and Sheenac MacInnes, *née* Ferguson; *b* 28 Sept 1927; *Educ* The Edinburgh Acad, Fettes Coll, Univ of Edinburgh (MB ChB); *m* 23 June 1967, Fiona Barbara, da of George Mills Heptonstall (d 1945), of Wood Ditton, Newmarket, Cambridgeshire; 1 s (Patrick b 1972), 1 da (Catriona b 1970); *Career* Nat Serv Capt RAMC and RMO 1 Bn XX The Lancashire Fusiliers 1950-52; fell in surgical res Hahnemann Med Coll and Hosp Philadelphia Pennsylvania USA; conslt surgn: Deaconess Hosp Edinburgh 1967-85, The Royal Infirmary Edinburgh 1974-, Leith Hosp Edinburgh 1985-87; hon clinical teacher Dept of Clinical Surgery Univ of Edinburgh 1970-; chm Scottish Triple Qualification Bd of Mgmnt 1984-89, vice pres RCS(Ed) 1983-86 (memb Cncl 1972-, hon sec 1972-77); Liveryman Worshipful Soc of Apothecaries of London 1989; FRCSEd 1955, FRCS 1960; *Recreations* music, reading; *Clubs* New (Edinburgh); *Style—* Iain MacLaren, Esq; 3 Minto Street, Edinburgh EH9 1RG (☎ 031 667 3487); The Royal Infirmary, Lauriston Place, Edinburgh (☎ 031 229 2477)

McLAREN, Hon Michael Duncan; s of 3 Baron Aberconway, *qv*; *b* 29 Nov 1958; *Educ* Eton, Christ's Coll Cambridge; *m* 1985, Caroline Jane, er da of Air Chief Marshal Sir (William) John Stacey, KCB, CBE (d 1981), of Winchester, and his w, Frances Jean, da of Prof Lawrence William Faucett, of USA; 1 s (Angus John Melville b 1987); *Career* called to the Bar Middle Temple; *Recreations* travel, music, gardening; *Style—* The Hon Michael McLaren; 1 Maids of Honour Row, The Green, Richmond, Surrey (☎ 081 940 5968)

McLAREN, Robin John Taylor; CMG (1982); s of Robert Taylor McLaren (d 1981), of Richmond, Surrey, and Marie Rose, *née* Simond; *b* 14 Aug 1934; *Educ* Ardingly Coll Sussex, St John's Coll Cambridge (MA); *m* 5 Sept 1964, Susan Ellen (Sue), da of Wilfrid Byron Hatherly (d 1988), of Little Rissington, Glos; 1 s (Duncan b 1973), 2 da (Emma b 1965, Jessica b 1966); *Career* Nat Serv Sub Lt RN 1953-55; FO 1958-, Chinese language student Hong Kong 1959-60, third sec Peking 1960-61, FO 1962-64 (asst private sec to Lord Privy Seal 1963-64), second (later first sec) Rome 1964-68, asst political advsr Hong Kong 1968-69, FCO 1970-75 (dep head Western Orgns Dept 1974-75), cnsllr and head Chancery Copenhagen 1975-78; FCO: head Hong Kong and Gen Dept 1978-79, head Far Eastern Dept 1978-81; political advsr Hong Kong 1981-85, HM ambass to Philippines 1985-87, asst under sec of state Asia 1987-90, dep under sec of state 1990-; *Recreations* music, walking; *Clubs* United Oxford and Cambridge Univ, Hong Kong (Hong Kong); *Style—* Robin McLaren, Esq, CMG; c/o FCO, King Charles St, London SW1A 2AH (☎ 071 270 2214)

McLAREN, Lady Rose Mary Primrose; *née* Paget; da of 6 Marquess of Anglesey, GCVO (d 1947); *b* 1919; *m* 1940, Hon John Francis McLaren (d 1953); 2 da (Victoria (Mrs Jonathan Taylor) b 1945, Harriet (Mrs Hugh Geddes) b 1949); *Style—* The Lady Rose McLaren; Old Bodnod, Eglwysbach, Colwyn Bay, North Wales LL28 5RF

McLAREN, Hon Mrs; (Rosemary Jean); da of 2 Baron Kinross, KC; *b* 1910; *m* 1, 1934 (m dis 1958), Alec M Mitchell; 1 s, 3 da; m 2, 1958, Robert Monteath McLaren (d 1969); *Style—* The Hon Mrs McLaren; 7B Gloucester Square, Edinburgh EH3

MacLAREN of MacLAREN, The; Donald MacLaren of MacLaren and Achleskine; s of late Donald MacLaren of MacLaren; suc his father 1966 as Chief of Clan Labhran; *b* 1954; *m* 1978, Maida Jane, da of late Robert Paton Aitchison, of Markinch, Fife; 3 s (Donald b 1980, Florian Robert b 1981, Louis James Douglas b 1984); 1 da (Iona Margaret b 1987); *Heir* Donald MacLaren, yr of MacLaren; *Style—* The MacLaren of MacLaren

McLAUGHLIN, Eleanor Thomson; JP (1975); da of Alexander Craig, and Helen , *née* Thomson; *b* 3 March 1938; *Educ* Broughton Sch; *m* 1959, Hugh McLaughlin; 1 s (Michael b 8 Dec 1967), 2 da (Eleanor b 26 Aug 1961, Maureen b 7 Jan 1963); *Career* memb (Lab) Edinburgh DC 1974- (dep chm 1984-88), Lord Provost and Lord Lieutenant of Edinburgh 1988-; chm: Edinburgh Festival Soc 1988-, Edinburgh Military Tattoo Ltd 1988-; *Recreations* Shetland lace knitting, gardening, alpine plants; *Style—* Mrs Eleanor McLaughlin, JP; 28 Oxgangs Green, Edinburgh EH13 9JS (☎ 031 445 4052); Edinburgh District Council, City Chambers, High St, Edinburgh EH1 1PL (☎ 031 225 2424, fax 031 220 1494)

MacLAURIN, Sir Ian Charter; s of Arthur George MacLaurin (d 1989), and Florence Evelina, *née* Bott (d 1970); *b* 30 March 1937; *Educ* Malvern; *m* 25 March 1960, Ann Margaret, da of Edgar Ralph Collar (d 1968); 1 s (Neil Ralph Charter b 1966), 2 da (Fiona Margaret (Mrs Archer) b 1962, Gillian b 1964); *Career* Nat Serv RAF Fighter Cmd 1956-58; Tesco PLC: first co trainee 1959, memb Bd 1970, md 1973, chm 1985; non-exec dir: Enterprise Oil PLC 1984-90, Guinness PLC 1986; pres Inst of Grocery Distribution 1989, govr Sports Aid Fndn; memb Save The Children Fund Commerce and Indust Ctee; Freeman City of London 1981, memb Worshipful Co of Carmen 1982; Hon DPhil Univ of Stirling 1987; memb IOD 1984, FRSA 1986, FInstM 1987; kt 1989; *Recreations* golf; *Clubs* MCC, RAC; *Style—* Sir Ian MacLaurin; Tesco PLC, Tesco House, Delamare Road, Cheshunt, Waltham Cross, Herts EN8 9SL (☎ 0992 32222, fax 0992 30794)

MACLAURIN, Robert Allister Charles; s of (Allister) James Maclaurin, and Mary, *née* Boniface; *b* 12 June 1961; *Educ* Edinburgh Coll of Art; *Career* artist; solo exhibitions incl: Mercury Gallery Edinburgh 1987, 369 Gallery Edinburgh 1989, Berkeley Square Gallery London 1990, The Fruitmarket Gallery Edinburgh 1991; gp exhibitions incl: Cultural Exchange Exhibition (Akademie der Bildenden Kunst, Munich) 1984, Scottish Young Contemporaries (touring exhibition) 1984-85, Hunting Group Art Prizes Exhibition (The Mall Galleries, London) 1986, The Smith Biennial (Stirling Art Gallery and Museum) 1987, New Scottish Painting (Art in General, NY) 1988, Fruitmarket Open Exhibition Edinburgh 1988-89, Chicago International Art Exposition 1988-89, Athena Awards Exhibition (Barbican Art Gallery, London) 1988-89, Contemporary Scottish Art in Cambridge (Clare Hall, Cambridge) 1989, International Weeks of Painting (touring exhibition of Yugoslavia) 1989-90, Scottish Art Since 1900 (Scottish Nat Gallery of Modern Art Edinburgh, Barbican Art Gallery London) 1989-90, Painting the Forth Bridge (369 Gallery, Edinburgh and tour) 1990, Benjamin Rhodes Gallery London 1990; work in the collection of: Edinburgh City Art Centre, Contemporary Art Soc, Scottish Nat Gallery of Art, Allied Breweries, St Catharine's Coll Cambridge, G T Management, Fleming's Bank, Coopers and Lybrand, Arthur Young, Phillips Petroleum (London), The Standard Life Assurance Company, Private Banking Trust, McKenna and Co, Scottish Art Cncl; *awards* John Kinross scholar RSA Florence 1984, Turkish Govt scholar 1984-85, Br Cncl travel grant 1988, Scottish Arts Cncl bursary 1988; *Style—* Robert Maclaurin, Esq; The Benjamin Rhodes Gallery, 4 New Burlington Place, London W1X 1SB (☎ 071 434 1768/9, fax 071 287 8841)

McLAY, Alastair John; s of David Bird McLay (d 1964), of Dundee and Troon, Ayrshire, and Nora Oakeshott, *née* Henderson; *b* 7 May 1928; *Educ* Fettes, Univ of St Andrews (BSc); *m* 19 March 1954, Augusta Michie (Lolo), da of James Neilson (d 1948), of Malaysia and Gullane, E Lothian; 1 s (James b 1956); *Career* Nat Serv RAF 1951-53, Flying Offr 54 Sqdn; consulting engr; ptnr Clarke Nicholls & Marcel London 1966-81, conslt A J McLay & Partners Glasgow 1990- (sr ptnr 1981-90); deacon convener Trades House of Glasgow 1979-80; Freeman: City of Glasgow 1949, Incorporation of Skinners Glasgow (deacon 1973); CEng 1955, FICE 1977, MConsE 1977; *Recreations* golf; *Clubs* Glasgow Golf, Royal and Ancient Golf; *Style—* Alastair McLay, Esq; 7 Pk Circus Place, Glasgow G3 6AH (☎ 041 332 1984, fax 041 332 8614)

MACLAY, Hon Angus Grenfell; s of 2 Baron Maclay, KBE (d 1969); *b* 11 Aug 1945; *Educ* Winchester, RAC Cirencester; *m* 1, 1970, Hon (Elizabeth) Victoria Baillie (d 1986), da of 3 Baron Burton; 2 s (Robert, Fergus), 1 da (Sarah); m 2, 18 Dec 1990, Jane Elizabeth Angela, da of late Lt-Col Alistair Monteith Gibb, R Wilts Yeo, and formerly w of 13 Marquess of Huntly; *Recreations* shooting, skiing; *Style—* The Hon Angus Maclay; Gledswood, Melrose, Roxburghshire (☎ 089682 2234)

MACLAY, Hon David Milton; 2 s of 2 Baron Maclay, KBE (d 1969), and Nancy Margaret, *née* Greig; *b* 21 March 1944; *Educ* Winchester; *m* 29 Nov 1968, Valerie, da of late Lt-Cdr J P Fyfe, of Kinkell, St Andrews, Fife; 1 s; *Style—* The Hon David Maclay; 12 Langton St, London SW10

MACLAY, Hon Mrs Walter; Dorothy; da of late William Lennox, WS, of Edinburgh, and Georgina Mary Lennox (d 1947); *b* 21 Oct 1901; *Educ* Harrogate Coll; *m* 26 April 1928, Hon Walter Symington Maclay, CB, OBE, MD (d 1964), 4 s of 1 Baron Maclay (d 1951); 3 s, 1 da; *Style—* The Hon Mrs Walter Maclay; 40 Kensington Sq, London W8 5HP

MACLAY, 3 Baron (UK 1922); Sir Joseph Paton Maclay; 3 Bt (UK 1914); s of 2 Baron Maclay, KBE (d 1969); *b* 11 April 1942; *Educ* Winchester; *m* 1976, Elizabeth, da of George Buchanan, of Pokataroo, NSW; 2 s, 1 da; *Heir* s, Hon Joseph Paton Maclay b 6 March 1977; *Career* md: Denholm Maclay Ltd 1970-83, Triport Ferries Mgmnt 1975-83, Denholm Maclay Offshore Ltd 1976-83; dir: Milton Shipping 1970-83, Br Steamship Short Trades Assoc 1976-83, N of England Protection & Indemnity Assoc 1978-83; md Milton Timber Servs Ltd 1984-89, chm Scottish branch Br Sailors Soc 1979-81, vice-chm Glasgow Shipowners & Shipbrokers Benevolent Assoc 1982-83; DL Renfrewshire 1986-; *Recreations* gardening, fishing; *Clubs* Western; *Style—* The Rt Hon Lord Maclay; Duchal, Kilmacolm, Renfrewshire (☎ 050 587 2255)

MACLAY, Nancy, Baroness; Nancy Margaret; da of Robert C Greig, of Hall of Caldwell, Uplawmoor, Renfrewshire; *m* 1936, 2 Baron Maclay, KBE (d 1969); 3 s, 2 da (1 decd); *Style—* The Rt Hon Nancy, Lady Maclay; Milton, Kilmacolm, Renfrewshire (☎ 050 587 2131)

McLEAN, Prof André Ernest Michael; s of Dr Fritz Fraenkel (d 1943), of Mexico, and Hildegard Maria, *née* Leo; *b* 5 Jan 1931; *Educ* Christ's Hosp, Univ of Oxford, UCL (BM BCh, PhD); *m* Oct 1956, Dr Elizabeth Kathleen Hunter, da of Donald Hunter (d 1978); 2 s (Thomas b 1958, Adam b 1960), 2 da (Angela b 1961, Martha b 1965); *Career* Colonial Med Serv 1960-63; assoc prof Chicago Med Sch 1964-65, memb scientific staff MRC Jamaica and Carshalton 1965-67, prof of toxicology Univ of London 1980-; author of papers on human malnutrition and relation between diet and toxicity of drugs and chemicals; chm Br Toxicology Soc 1987-88, former memb ctees on food additives and pesticides, memb Ctee on Safety of Medicines for Dept of Health; FRCPath; *Recreations* ski mountineering, gardening; *Style—* Prof André McLean; Toxicology Laboratory, Department Clinical Pharmacology, University College London, University St, London WC1 (☎ 071 380 9676)

McLEAN, (Douglas) Brian; s of Ronald Alexander McLean, of The Bungalow, Burgham Farm, nr Felton, Morpeth, Northumberland, and Gwendoline McLean; *b* 5 Dec 1953; *Educ* Strathalian Sch Perthshire, Dundee Coll of Commerce (Dip Business Studies); *m* 18 June 1983, Angela, da of Bennet Dodd, of Blaydon, Tyne and Wear; 2 da (Jessica b 1985, Stephanie b 1986); *Career* professional racehorse trainer, breeder and prodr of thoroughbreds, int 3 day event rider 1976-78, ptnr in family farming bloodstock and devpt business; memb and player Newcastle Gosforth RFC; *Recreations* family, rugby; *Style—* Brian McLean, Esq; Burgham Farm, nr Felton, Morpeth, Northumberland (☎ 0670 787314)

MACLEAN, Charles Andrew Bourke; s of Sir Robert Maclean, KBE, DL, *qv*, of South Branchal Farm, Bridge of Weir, Renfrewshire, and Vivienne Neville Bourke; *b* 31 Jan 1945; *Educ* Harrow, Trinity Coll Dublin (MA); *m* 1972, Moya Clare, da of Cdr T A Pack-Beresford, MBE, RN, of The Tansey, Baily, Co Dublin, Eire (d 1981); 1 s (Robert b 1979), 2 da (Tara b 1975, Georgina b 1976); *Career* dep chm and chief exec Stoddard Holdings plc 1982-87, currently dep md The Gates Rubber Co Ltd; *Recreations* forestry, shooting, skiing; *Clubs* Western (Glasgow); *Style—* Charles Maclean, Esq; Carruth, Bridge of Weir, Renfrewshire PA11 3SG (☎ 0505 87 2189); The Gates Rubber Co Ltd, Edinburgh Road, Heathhall, Dumfries, Dumfriesshire DG1 1QA (☎ 0387 51311, fax 0387 68937, telex 778785)

McLEAN, Colin; CMG (1977), MBE (1964); s of late Dr L G McLean; *b* 10 Aug 1930; *Educ* Fettes, St Catharine's Coll Cambridge; *m* 1953, Huguette Leclerc; 1 s, 1 da; *Career* Dip Serv 1964, cnsllr Oslo 1977-81, head Trade Rels and Export Dept FCO 1981-83, high cmmr Uganda 1983-86, UK perm rep to Cncl of Europe (with rank of ambass) 1986-; *Style—* Colin McLean, Esq, CMG, MBE; c/o FCO, King Charles St, London SW1

MACLEAN, David John; MP (C) Penrith and The Border 1983-; s of John Maclean, and Catherine Jane Maclean; *b* 16 May 1953; *Educ* Fortrose Acad, Univ of Aberdeen (LLB); *m* 1977, Jay(alaluna) Dawn, *née* Gallacher; *Career* Lt 2/51 Highland (V) 1976-79; *Style—* David Maclean Esq, MP; House of Commons, London SW1A OAA (☎ 071 219 6494)

MACLEAN, Sir Donald Og Grant; s of Maj Donald Og Maclean, OBE, MC (d 1974), of Dalnabo, Crieff, and Margaret, *née* Smith (d 1972); *b* 13 Aug 1930; *Educ* Morrison's Acad Crieff, Heriot-Watt Univ; *m* 11 Jan 1958, Muriel (d 1984), da of Charles Giles (d 1972), of Newcastle upon Tyne; 1 s (Donald b 1962), 1 da (Fiona b 1960); *Career* Nat Serv RAMC 1952-54; ophthalmic optician (optometrist) in practise 1963-: Edinburgh, Newcastle upon Tyne, Perth, Ayr; chm: Ayr Constituency Assoc (C) 1971-75, W of Scotland Area Cncl SCUA 1977-79; pres SCUA 1983-85, vice chm Scottish Cons Pty 1989- (dep chm 1985-89), elder Church of Scotland, former memb Local Transport Users Consultative Ctee, former chm SW Scotland AOP and Local Optical Ctee, former pres W Highland Steamer Club; Freeman City of London 1987, Liveryman Worshipful Co of Spectacle Makers 1986; FBOA, FBCO; kt 1985; *Recreations* photography, reading; *Clubs* Royal Scottish Automobile (Glasgow); *Style—* Sir Donald Maclean; Dun Beag II, Woodend Rd, Alloway, Ayrshire; J Rusk (Opticians), 59 Newmarket St, Ayr KA7 1LL (☎ 0292 262530)

MACLEAN, Baroness; (Joan) Elizabeth; er da of Capt Francis Thomas Mann, Scots Guards (d 1964), and Enid Agnes, *née* Tilney (d 1976); *b* 30 May 1923; *m* 7 June 1941, Baron Maclean, KT, GCVO, KBE, PC (Life Peer and 11 Bt) (d 1990); 1 s (Hon Sir Lachlan, 12 Bt), 1 da (Hon Mrs Barne); *Style*— Elizabeth, The Lady Maclean; Wilderness House, Hampton Court Palace, East Molesey, Surrey KT8 9AR (☎ 081 943 4400)

McLEAN, Sir Francis Charles; CBE (1953, MBE 1945); s of Michael McLean; *b* 6 Nov 1904; *Educ* Birmingham Univ (BSc); *m* 1930, Dorothy Blackstaffe; 1 s, 1 da; *Career* chief engr Psychological Warfare Div SHAEF 1943-45, dir of engrg BBC 1963-68 (dep chief engr 1952-60, dep dir 1960-63), chm BSI Telecommunications Industry Standards Ctee 1960-77, dir Oxley Devpts 1961-; kt 1967; *Style*— Sir Francis McLean, CBE; Greenwood Copse, Tile Barn, Woolton Hill, Newbury, Berks (☎ 0635 253583)

MACLEAN, Gordon Hector; s of Lt-Col Norman George Maclean (d 1975), ex Cmmr of Colonial Police, and Katherine Emily, *née* Scott (d 1977); *b* 30 June 1932; *Educ* Bedford Sch, Univ of the Witwatersrand and Johannesburg (BArch 1955); *m* 5 Sept 1959, Heather (d 1984), da of Donald Graham (d 1983); 2 s (Angus b 1960, Donald b 1962), 1 da (Jane b 1965); *Career* architect; sr ptnr Murray Ward & Partners (chartered architects); FRIBA 1970 (ARIBA 1957); *Recreations* music, philately; *Style*— Gordon Maclean, Esq; 12B Daleham Gardens, Hampstead, London NW3 (☎ 071 431 2975); Murray Ward & Partners, 1 Heddon St, Piccadilly, London W1 (☎ 071 439 9774, telex 21530, fax 071 494 3250)

MACLEAN, Vice Adm Sir Hector Charles Donald; KBE (1962), CB (1960), DSC (1941), JP (Norfolk 1963), DL (Norfolk 1977); s of Capt Donald Charles Hugh Maclean, DSO, Royal Scots (d 1909), and Gwendoline Katherine Leonora, *née* Hope (ggggda of 1 Earl of Hopetoun); *b* 7 Aug 1908; *Educ* Wellington; *m* 1933, Opre, da of late Capt William Geoffrey Vyvyan, Royal Welsh Fus; 1 s, 2 da; *Career* joined RN 1926, served WWII, Rear Adm 1958, Vice Adm 1960, ret 1962; *Style*— Vice Adm Sir Hector Maclean, KBE, CB, DSC, JP, DL; Deepdale Old Rectory, Brancaster Staithe, King's Lynn, Norfolk (☎ 048 521 210281)

MCLEAN, Hector John Finlayson; s of Dr Murdoch McLean (d 1965), and Dr Edith Muriel Finlayson, *née* McGill (d 1985); *b* 10 Feb 1934; *Educ* Dulwich, Pembroke Coll Cambridge (BA); *m* 19 Dec 1959, Caroline Elizabeth, da of Leslie Lithgow (d 1961); 1 s, 2 da; *Career* Nat Serv 2 Lt KOSB 1953-55; ICI 1958-87: personnel Dyestuffs Div 1959-72, personnel mangr Organics Div 1972-74, business area mangr Polyurethanes 1974-75, dir Agric Div 1975-86; sec Archbishops' Appts 1987-, non-exec chm People & Potential 1987-; memb: Cncl Univ of Newcastle 1985-87, Chemical and Allied Products ITB 1979-82, Northern Regnl Cncl CBI 1981-85, Exec Ctee North of Eng Devpt Cncl 1978-83; dir Cleveland Enterprise Agency, tstee NE Civic Tst 1978-88, govr Teesside Poly 1978-82; FIPM; *Recreations* music (esp choral), travel, gardening, walking; *Clubs* Utd Oxford and Cambridge Univ; *Style*— Hector McLean, Esq; Fielden House, Little College St, Westminster, London SW1P 3SH (☎ 071 233 0393, fax 071 233 1104)

MACLEAN, Iain Donald; s of Donald Maclean, and Leokadia, *née* Osko; *b* 2 Aug 1949; *Educ* Milton Sch, Goldsmith's Coll London; *m* 16 Aug 1975, Briony Susan Aldersey, da of Cdr Noel Hugh Aldersey Taylor, RN (ret); 3 s (Andrew James Donald b 1977, James Hugh Alexander b 1983, Hector Charles Bellasis b 1990), 1 da (Iona Felicity Odette b 1980); *Career* controller J Walter Thompson 1970-74, sculptor 1974-75, copywriter Harrison Cowley Advertising 1975-76, mktg mangr The Franklin Mint 1977-78, mktg dir Spink 1978-82, assoc creative dir Ogilvy Mather Direct 1983-85, creative dir Dewar Coyle Maclean 1986-89 (fndr 1986), creative conslt Ogilvy & Mather 1989-90; currently: fndr and creative dir Maclean Collectibles and ptnr Leybourne Brown Maclean; winner of 15 awards for creativity in: UK, Europe, USA; memb: Hartfield and Withyhall Hort Soc, Hartfield Cons Assoc, NSPCC, Coleman's Hatch Church; *Recreations* advertising, writing, sculpture, painting, gardening; *Style*— Iain Maclean, Esq; Hill House, Upper Hartfield, E Sussex (☎ 0342 82 2429); Leybourne Brown Maclean, Baird House, 15-17 Cross St, London EC1N 8UN (☎ 071 430 0805, fax 071 831 8521)

MCLEAN, James Yuille (Jim); s of Thomas McLean, of Ashgillhead Rd, by Larkhall, Lanarkshire, and Annie, *née* Yuille; *b* 2 Aug 1937; *Educ* Larkhall Acad; *m* Doris, da of Robert Aitken; 2 s (Colin Thomas b 21 Sept 1962, Gary Robert b 10 Oct 1968); *Career* professional football manager; former player: Hamilton Academical, Clyde, Dundee FC, Kilmarnock; former coach Dundee, mangr Dundee Utd 1972- (chm 1989-); former rep Glasgow Select; Scot League Cup 1980 and 1981, runners up UEFA Cup 1987; former joiner; *Recreations* golf, bowls, tennis; *Style*— Jim McLean, Esq; Dundee Utd FC, Tannadice Park, Dundee (☎ 0382 832202, fax 0382 89398)

McLEAN, John Alexander Lowry; QC (1974); s of John McLean (d 1969), and Phoebe Jane Bowditch (d 1975); *b* 21 Feb 1921; *Educ* Methodist Coll, Queen's Univ Belfast (LLB); *m* 1950, Diana Elisabeth (d 1986), da of S B Boyd Campbell, MC (d 1971); 1 s (Simon), 2 da (Jane, Sara); *Career* served WWII Intelligence Corps 1943-47, NW Europe 1944-45, Rhine Army 1945-47; barr NI 1949; asst sec NI Supreme Ct and private sec to LCJ of NI 1956-66, perm sec NI Supreme Ct 1966 (princ sec to LCJ 1979-), clerk of the Crown for NI 1966, under treas Inn of Ct of NI 1966; chm Wages Cncls; FRSA; *Clubs* Royal Cwlth Soc; *Style*— John A L McLean, Esq, QC; 24 Marlborough Park South, Belfast BT9 6HR (☎ 0232 667330); Lifeboat Cottage, Cloughey, Co Down BT22 1HS (☎ 024 77 71313); Royal Courts of Justice, Belfast (☎ 0232 235111)

MACLEAN, Maj John Kenneth Charles; s of Alan Murdoch Maclean (d 1981), and Muriel Jeanette, *née* McAdam; *b* 11 Jan 1945; *Educ* Eastbourne Coll, Univ of Leicester; *m* 26 July 1980, Diana Clare, da of Maj-Gen B Aubrey Coad (d 1980), of Nurstead House, Devizes; 2 s (Christopher Charles Aubrey b 1982, William Alan Hamilton b 1986); *Career* cmmnd RCS 1966, Troop Cdr Germany, Singapore 1966-71, cmd Royal Signals Motor Cycle Display Team 1972-73, Regtl cmd Staff Appt 1973-78, cmd 63 SAS Signal Sqdn V 1979-82; MOD appt 1982-84, dir of marketing Unisys Corp; Freeman Worshipful Co of Info Technologists; *Books* Military Computer Market Europe (1987); *Recreations* tennis, sailing; *Clubs* Royal Ocean Racing; *Style*— Maj John Maclean; Georgian House, Eastbridge, Crondall, Surrey (☎ 0252 850 699); Unisys Europe Africa Division, Bakers Ct, Bakers Rd, Uxbridge MX (☎ 0895 37 137)

MACLEAN, John Robert; DL (Moray 1987); s of Cdr Hugh Chapman Maclean, JP, DL, RN (d 1973), of Westfield House, and Sylvia Louise Radford, *née* Boase; *b* 24 May 1951; *Educ* Blairmore Sch, Milton Abbey Sch; *m* 12 Jan 1979, da of Evelyn Hubert-Powell (d 1985), of Mayfield, Sussex; 1 s (Hugh Charles b 8 May 1984), 2 da (Charlotte Louise b 19 Jan 1982, Anastasia Mary b 18 Sept 1986); *Career* Mons Offr Cadet Sch 1971, cmmnd Queens Own Highlanders, served Germany, NI and Canada 1971-73, trg offr Scottish Int Depot Edinburgh 1973-75, served Germany, Belize, UK and NI 1975-77, ret Lt 1977; chm Elgin Branch Earl Haig Fund; memb Ctee: Highland Branch Scottish Landowners Fedn, Moray War Veterans; memb Royal Co of Archers (Queens Bodyguard of Scotland); *Recreations* shooting, tennis, golf, farming; *Clubs* Army and Navy; *Style*— John Maclean, Esq, DL; Westfield House, nr Elgin, Moray, Highlands (☎ 0343 547308)

McLEAN, John Talbert; s of Talbert McLean, of Arbroath, and Dorothy, *née* Gladhill; *b* 10 Jan 1939; *Educ* Arbroath HS, Univ of St Andrews, Courtauld Inst Univ of London (BA); *m* 1964, Janet Alison, da of Edward Backhouse Norman; *Career* teacher of art history: pt/t Chelsea Sch of Art 1966-74, UCL 1974-78; teacher of painting Winchester Coll of Art 1978-82, visiting tutor in painting at many art schs in GB, Canada and USA; solo exhibitions incl: Talbot Rice Art Centre (Univ of Edinburgh) 1975, House Gallery London 1978, Nicola Jacobs Gallery London 1980, Art Placement Saskatoon Canada 1981, Art Space Galleries Aberdeen 1982, Byck Gallery Louisville Kentucky USA 1983, Martin Gerrard Gallery Edmonton Canada 1984, Talbot Rice Art Centre (Univ of Edinburgh) 1985, Dept of Architecture (Univ of Edinburgh) 1986, Kapil Jariwala Gallery London 1987, Jariwala-Smith Gallery NY USA 1988, Francis Graham Dixon Gallery London 1988 and 1989, Edinburgh Coll of Art 1989; paintings in pub collections incl: Tate Gallery, Scot Nat Gallery of Modern Art, Art Cncl of GB, Scot Arts Cncl, Br Cncl, DOE, Federated Union of Black Artists S Africa; paintings in corporate collections worldwide; maj work incl cmmn for three large paintings for Pollock Hall Univ of Edinburgh 1971; *awards* Arts Cncl award 1974, Arts Cncl Maj award 1980, Br Cncl Travel award 1981 and 1984; *Recreations* looking at art and architecture, travel, walking, concert-going, reading; *Style*— John McLean, Esq; Francis Graham-Dixon Gallery, 17-18 Great Sutton St, London EC1V ODN (☎ 071 250 1962, fax 071 490 1069)

MACLEAN, Maj Hon Sir Lachlan Hector Charles; 12 Bt (NS 1631); 28 Chief of Clan Maclean; o s of Baron Maclean, KT, GCVO, KBE, PC (Life Peer and 11 Bt, d 1990), and (Joan) Elizabeth, *née* Mann; *b* 25 Aug 1942; *Educ* Eton; *m* 1966, Mary Helen, eldest da of William Gordon Gordon, of Lude, Blair Atholl, Perthshire; 2 s (Malcolm Lachlan Charles b 1972, Andrew Lachlan William b 1979), 2 da (Emma Mary b 1967, Alexandra Caroline b 1975), and 1 da decd; *Heir* s, Malcolm Lachlan Charles Maclean b 1972; *Career* Maj Scots Gds (ret); *Style*— Maj The Hon Sir Lachlan Maclean, Bt; Arngask House, Glenfarg, Perthshire

MACLEAN, Lowry Druce; s of Ian Albert Druce Maclean, and Diana Futvoye, *née* Marsden-Smedley (d 1979); *b* 22 July 1939; *Educ* Eton, Pembroke Coll Cambridge (MA); *m* 1966, Anne Francis, da of Henry Crawford (d 1967), of USA; 2 s, 1 da; *Career* dir: Karastan Inc 1970-72, John Crossley & Sons Ltd 1972-79, Wesleyan & Gen Assur Soc 1987-, John Smedley Ltd 1989-; chm Tomkinsons plc 1986- (gp chief exec 1979-); *Clubs* Lansdowne; *Style*— Lowry Maclean, Esq; The Pound, Old Colwall, Gt Malvern, Worcs (☎ 0684 40426); Tomkinsons plc, PO Box 11, Duke Place, Kidderminster, Worcs (☎ 0562 820006)

McLEAN, Peter Standley; CMG (1985), OBE (1965); s of Maj William McLean (d 1961), and Alice, *née* Standley; *b* 18 Jan 1927; *Educ* King Edward's Sch Birmingham, Wadham Coll Oxford (MA); *m* 23 Jan 1954, Margaret Ann, da of Richard Henry Minns (d 1967); 2 s (Iain b 1957, Alistair b 1964), 2 da (Fiona b 1955, Catriona b 1962); *Career* Lt 15/19 King's Royal Hussars 1946-48; permanent sec for planning Uganda 1963-65 (joined Colonial Serv Uganda 1951), asst sec ODA FCO 1975-79 (memb 1965-87, princ 1965-75), min and perm rep to UN Food and Agric Orgn Rome 1980-85; *Recreations* water-colour painting, watching sport; *Style*— Peter McLean, Esq, CMG, OBE; 17 Woodfield Lane, Ashtead, Surrey KT21 2BQ (☎ 0372 278 146)

MacLEAN, Ranald Norman Munro; QC (1977); The Hon Lord MacLean; s of John Alexander MacLean, of Duart, 12 Eriskay Rd, Inverness, and Hilda Margaret Lind, *née* Munro; *b* 18 Dec 1938; *Educ* Fettes, Univ of Cambridge (BA), Univ of Edinburgh (LLB), Yale Univ (LLM); *m* 21 Sept 1963, Pamela, da of Prof Allan Dawson Ross, of London (d 1982); 3 s (Fergus Ranald b 1970, Donald Ross b 1972, 1 s decd); 1 da (Catriona Joan b 1967); *Career* called to Scottish Bar 1964, advocate-depute 1972-75, home advocate-depute 1979-82; memb: Cncl on Tbnls 1985-90 (chm Scottish Ctee), Scottish Legal Aid Bd 1986-90; senator of the Coll of Justice 1990; *Recreations* hill walking, Munro collecting; *Clubs* Scottish Arts, New (Edinburgh); *Style*— Ranald N M MacLean, Esq, QC; 12 Chalmers Crescent, Edinburgh EH9 1TS (☎ 031 667 6217); Court of Session, Parliament Square, Edinburgh

MACLEAN, Sir Robert Alexander; KBE (1973), DL (Renfrewshire 1970); s of Andrew Johnston Maclean, JP (d 1924); *b* 11 April 1908; *Educ* Glasgow HS; *m* 1938, Vivienne Neville, da of Capt Bertram Walter Bourke, JP (ka 1915), and half sis of Eileen, Countess of Mount Charles; 2 s, 2 da; *Career* CA; chm Scottish Ctee Cncl of Industl Design 1949-58, regnl controller (Scot) Bd of Trade 1944-46; memb: Export Cncl for Europe 1960-64, Br Nat Export Cncl 1966-70; chm: Scottish Industl Estates Corp 1955-72, Scottish Exports Ctee; pres Glasgow C of C 1956-58, chm Cncl of Scottish C of C 1960-62, pres Assoc of British C of C 1966-68, dir Norwich Union Insurance Group, hon pres Stoddard Carpets Ltd and assoc cos; Hon LLD Glasgow Univ 1973; CStJ 1975; FRSA, CBIM; kt 1955; *Recreations* golf, fishing; *Clubs* Carlton; *Style*— Sir Robert Maclean, KBE, DL; South Branchal Farm, Bridge of Weir, Renfrewshire PA11 3SJ

McLEAN, (John David) Ruari; CBE (1973), DSC (1943); s of John Thomson McLean (d 1962), of Stranraer, and Isabel Mary Ireland (d 1958); *b* 10 June 1917; *Educ* Dragon Sch Oxford, Eastbourne Coll; *m* 1945, Antonia Maxwell, da of Dr Henry George Carlisle, MD, of Heswall; 2 s (David, Andrew), 1 da (Catriona); *Career* RNVR served Atlantic, SE Asia as Ordinary Seaman, sub Lt, then Lt 1940-45; typographer; fndr ptnr Rainbird McLean Ltd 1951-58, hon typographic advsr HM Stationery Office 1966-80; tstee Nat Library of Scot 1981; Croix de Guerre (France) 1941; *Books* Modern Book Design (1958), Victorian Book Design (1963, revised edn 1972), Magazine Design (1969), Jan Tschichold, Typographer (1975), Manual of Typography (1980), The Last Cream Bun (1984), Benjamin Fawcett, Engraver and Colour Printer (1988), Nicolas Bentley drew the pictures (1990); *Clubs* New (Edinburgh), Double Crown (pres 1971); *Style*— Ruari McLean, Esq, CBE, DSC; Pier Cottage, Carsaig, Isle of Mull PA70 6HD (☎ 06814 216)

MACLEAN, (Richard) Ruari Willard; s of Alexander David Willard Maclean, of London, and Diana Elizabeth Carolyn, *née* Solomon; *b* 27 Sept 1961; *Educ* Dulwich, S Glamorgan Inst of HE Cardiff; *m* 7 March 1987, Cindy Louise, da of William Anthony Dale; 2 c (Molly Cara Louise b 11 Sept 1987, Drew Frederick Willard b 16 March 1989); *Career* Rugby Union Centre and full-back Moseley FC and Scotland; clubs: S Glamorgan Inst RFC 1981-84 (110 appearances), Old Alleynians, Gloucester RFC 1985-89 (102 appearances), Llanelli RFC, Newport RFC, Moseley FC 1989-; rep: Welsh Colleges (won Br Colls Cup 1982), Welsh Students Rugby League (capt 1984), Anglo-Scots, Capt Scotland B 1991 (debut 1987, 4 caps); Scotland: tour Zimbabwe 1988, tour Japan 1989; physical educn teacher Cheltenham GS 1984-89; head of Dept: Crypt GS Glos 1989-90, Tudor Grange Sch 1990-; *Recreations* home brew, graphic design, children, enjoying life; *Style*— Ruari Maclean, Esq; Moseley RFC, The Reddings, Reddings Rd, Moseley, Birmingham B13 8LW (☎ 021 449 2149); Tudor Grange School, Dingle Lane, Solihull B91 3PD (☎ 021 704 1867)

MACLEAN, Hon Mrs (Sarah Elizabeth Cameron); eldest da of 3 Baron Rowallan; *b* 5 April 1949; *m* 17 April 1968, (Lachlan) Roderick Maclean, er s of Maj Gordon Maclean, of London; 2 da; *Style*— The Hon Mrs Maclean; 8 Elthiron Rd, London SW6

MACLEAN, Lady Sarah Elizabeth Jane; *née* Finch-Knightley; da of 11 Earl of Aylesford; *b* 14 July 1950; *Educ* Abbot's Hill Hemel Hempstead; *m* 1974, Angus Nigel Garnet Maclean, s of Maj Lachlan Gordon Maclean, MC, 11 of Hynish; 2 s (Angus Charles, Ian Andrew); *Style*— The Lady Sarah Maclean; c/o Child & Co, Fleet St,

London EC4

MACLEAN, William James; s of John MacLean (d 1962), Master Mariner, of Harbour House, Inverness, and Mary Isabella, *née* Reid (d 1978); *b* 12 Oct 1941; *Educ* Inverness Royal Acad, HMS Conway, Grays Sch of Art Aberdeen (DA); *m* 18 Aug 1968, Marian Forbes, da of David Leven, of Upper Greens, Auchtermuchty, Fife, Scotland; 2 s (John b 1973, David b 1981), 1 da (Miriam b 1971); *Career* schoolteacher (art) Fife County 1970-79; lectr fine art Dundee Coll of Art 1981-; numerous exhibitions in UK and abroad; works in public collections incl: British Museum, Fitzwilliam Museum Camb, Scottish National Gallery of Modern Art Edinburgh, Kelvingrove Art Gallery Glasgow; memb SSA, Assoc Royal Scot Acad 1978, FSA Scot 1981; Scottish Educnl Tst Award 1973, Scottish Art Cncl Visual Arts Award 1979, Royal Scottish Acad Gillies Award 1988; *Style*— William Maclean, Esq, FSA; Runkel-Hue-Williams Gallery, 6-8 Old Bond Street, London W1X 3TA (☎ 071 495 7917, fax 071 495 0179)

MACLEAN-BRISTOL, Hon Mrs (Lavinia Mary); da of 9 Baron Hawke (d 1985); *b* 15 June 1945; *Educ* Hatherop Castle, Queensgate London; *m* 1965, Maj Nicholas Maclean Verity Bristol, eld s of late Arnold Charles Verity Bristol; 3 s; *Career* admin Project Tst 1973-; *Clubs* Army & Navy; *Style*— The Hon Mrs Bristol; Breacachadh Castle, Isle of Coll, Argyll (☎ 087 93 378)

MACLEAN-BRISTOL, Maj Nicholas Maclean Verity; s of Arnold Charles Verity Bristoi (d 1984), of The Forester's Cottage, Wotton, Surrey, and Lillias Nina, *née* Francis-Hawkins; *b* 25 May 1935; *Educ* Wellington, RMA Sandhurst; *m* 2 April 1965, The Hon Lavinia Mary Hawke, da of The Lord Hawke of Towtan (d 1985), of Faygate Place, Faygate, Sussex; 3 s (Charles Bladen b 1967, Alexander Stanhope b 1970, Larchlan Neil b 1974); *Career* 2 Lt KOSB 1955, Malaya 1955-58, Lt 1957, ADC GOC 52(L) Inf Div and Lowlarsh Dist 1958-60, Berlin 1960-61, Capt 1961, Aden 1962-64, Radfan 1964, Borneo 1965, GSO3 18 Inf Bde, GSO3 MOD (AT2) 1966-68, Maj 1968, Trg Maj 1 51 Highland 1970-72; proprietor Breacachadh Builders and Contrators 1983-; dir The Project Tst 1972- (fndr 1968, dir 1968-70, vice chm 1970-72), jt fndr soc West Highland and Island Historical Res Ltd 1972; FSA (Scot); *Books* Hebridean Decade: Mull, Coll and Tiree 1701-1771 (1982), The Life of Coll in 1716 (1989); *Recreations* farming, hebridean history, wine; *Clubs* Army & Navy, New (Edinburgh); *Style*— Maj Nicholas Maclean-Bristol, FSA; Breacachadh Castle, Isle of Coll, Argyll PA78 6TB (☎ 08793 353); The Project Trust, Isle of Coll, Argyll (☎ 08793 444, fax 08793 357, telex 77732 GG)

MACLEAN OF DOCHGARROCH, yr, The Very Rev Allan; s of Rev Donald Maclean, of Dochgarroch, of Hazelbrae House, Glen Urquhart, and Loraine, *née* Calvert; *b* 22 Oct 1950; *Educ* Dragon Sch, Trinity Coll Glenalmond, Univ of Edinburgh, Cuddesdon Coll Oxford, Pusey House Oxford; *m* 29 Jan 1990, Anne Cameron Cavin, wid of David Lindsay (d 1983); 1 step s (David Lindsay b 1983); *Career* ordained: deacon 1976, priest 1977; chaplain St Mary's Cathedral Edinburgh 1976-81, rector Holy Trinity Dunoon 1981-86, examining chaplain to Bishop of Argyll and the Isles 1983-, provost St John's Cathedral Oban 1986-; vice pres Clan Maclean Assoc 1982-; editor: Clan Maclean 1975-85, Argyll and the Isles 1984-; *Books* Telford's Highland Churches (1989); *Recreations* topography, history, genealogy, architecture; *Clubs* New, Puffins (both Edinburgh); *Style*— The Very Rev the Provost; The Rectory, Ardconnel Terrace, Oban, Argyll PA34 5DJ (☎ 0631 62323); 3 Rutland Sq, Edinburgh EH1 2AS (☎ 031 228 6036)

MACLEAN OF DUNCONNEL, Sir Fitzroy Hew Maclean; 1 Bt (UK 1957), of Dunconnel, Co Argyll; CBE (Mil 1944); 15 Hereditary Keeper and Captain of Dunconnel; s of Maj Charles Maclean, DSO (whose paternal grandmother was Elizabeth, ggda of 5 Duke of Beaufort, while his paternal great grandmother was da of 2 Earl of Hopetoun); *b* 11 March 1911; *Educ* Eton, King's Coll Cambridge; *m* 1946, Hon Veronica, *née* Fraser, 2 da of 14 Lord Lovat and wid of Lt Alan Phipps (gggs of 1 Earl of Mulgrave, f of 1 Marquess of Normanby); 2 s; *Heir* s, Charles Maclean, yr of Dunconnel; *Career* Brig cmdg Br Mil Mission to Yugoslav Partisans 1943-45; formerly with Foreign Serv, Queen's Own Cameron Highlanders and SAS (Hon Col 23 Special Air Serv Regt Vols 1984-88); MP (C) Lancaster 1941-59, Bute and N Ayrshire 1959-74, Parly under sec and fin sec WO 1954-57; Croix de Guerre France, Order of Kutuzov USSR, Partisan Star 1 Class Yugoslavia, Yugoslav Order of Merit 1969, Order of the Yugoslav Star with Ribbon 1981; *Clubs* White's, Pratt's, Puffin's (Edinburgh), New (Edinburgh); *Style*— Sir Fitzroy Maclean of Dunconnel, Bt, CBE; Strachur House, Argyll (☎ 036 986 242)

MACLEAN OF DUNCONNEL, Hon Lady (Veronica Nell); da of 15 Lord Lovat (and 17 but for the attainder) KT, GCVO, KCMG, CB, DSO, TD (d 1933); *b* 1920; *m* 1, 1940, Lt Alan Phipps, RN (d 1943); 1 s, 1 da; m 2, 1946, Brig Sir Fitzroy Hew Royle Maclean, 1 Bt, CBE, *qv*; 2 s; *Style*— The Hon Lady Maclean of Dunconnel; Strachur House, Argyll

MACLEAN, YR OF DUNCONNEL, Charles Edward; s and h of Sir Fitzroy Hew Maclean of Dunconnel, 1 Bt, CBE, *qv*; *b* 31 Oct 1946; *Educ* Eton, New Coll Oxford; *m* 1986, Deborah, da of Lawrence Young, of Chicago; 2 da (Margaret Augusta b 1986, Katharine Augusta b 1988); *Books* Island on the Edge of the World, The Wolf Children, The Watcher; *Style*— Charles Maclean, yr of Dunconnel; Inverglen, Strathur, Argyll

MACLEARY, Prof Alistair Ronald; s of Donald Herbert MacLeary (d 1984), of Inverness, and Jean Spiers, *née* Leslie (d 1973); *b* 12 Jan 1940; *Educ* Inverness Royal Acad, Coll of Estate Mgmnt, Edinburgh Coll of Art (Dip TP), Univ of Strathclyde (MSc); *m* 6 May 1967, Mary-Claire Cecilia (Claire), da of James Leonard (d 1976), of Livingston; 1 s (Roderic b 1976), 1 da (Kate b 1984); *Career* asst Gerald Eve & Co chartered surveyors 1962-65, asst to dir Murrayfield Real Estate Co Ltd 1965-67, asst to partners Wright and Partners Surveyors 1967-76, MacRobert prof of land economy Univ of Aberdeen 1976-89; memb: Lands Tbnl Scotland 1989-, Natural Environment Rs Cncl 1988-, Govt Ctee of Inquiry into the Aquisition and Occupancy of Agricultural Land (The Northfield Ctee 1977-79); pres planning and devpt div RICS 1984-85; chm: Bd of Educn Cwlth Assoc Surveying and Land Econ 1980-90, Watt Ctee on energy Working Gp on Land Resources 1977-79; FRICS, FRTPI, FRSA, MBIM; *Books* Property Investment Theory (with N Nanthakumeran, 1988), National Taxation for Property Management and Valuation (1990); *Recreations* golf, shooting, skiing, hill walking; *Clubs* Royal Northern & Univ (Aberdeen), Royal Aberdeen Golf; *Style*— Prof Alistair MacLeary; St Helens, St Andrews Rd, Ceres, Fife KY15 5NQ (☎ 033 482 8862); Lands Tribunal for Scotland, 1 Grosvenor Crescent, Edinburgh

McLEAVY, Hon Frank Waring; s of Baron McLeavy (Life Peer); *b* 1925; *Educ* Wirral GS, Liverpool Univ, Leeds Univ; *m* 1954, Verena, da of Emil Lüsher, of Unterkulm, Switzerland; *Style*— The Hon Frank McLeavy

McLEAVY, Hon Mrs Douglas; Janet Elizabeth; da of Harry Ogden; *b* 14 Jan 1934; *Educ* Bingley GS, St Osyth's Coll; *m* 1958, Hon Douglas John McLeavy (d 1969), s of Baron McLeavy (Life Peer, d 1975); 1 s (Mark b 1969), 1 da (Ruth b 1964); *Career* school mistress; *Style*— The Hon Mrs Douglas McLeavy; 40 Ruskin Drive, Morecambe, Lancs

McLEAVY, Baroness; Mary; *née* Waring; da of late George Waring, of Rock Ferry, Birkenhead; *m* 1924, Baron McLeavy (Life Peer, d 1976); *Style*— The Rt Hon The Lady McLeavy; 9 Sheridan Terrace, Whitton Ave West, Northolt, Middx

MACLEAY, Very Rev John Henry James (Ian); s of James Macleay (d 1932), and Charlotte Isabella, *née* Kilgour (d 1932); *b* 7 Dec 1931; *Educ* Trinity Coll Glenalmond, St Edmund Hall Oxford (MA); *m* 14 Jan 1970, (Jane) Jean Speirs, da of James Cuthbert (d 1964); 1 s (James b 1971), 1 da (Mairi b 1971); *Career* ordained: deacon 1957, priest 1958; curate: St John's E Dulwich 1957-60, St Michael's Inverness 1960-62 (rector 1962-70), priest i/c St Columba's Grantown-on-Spey with St John the Baptist Rothiemurchus 1970-78, rector St Andrew's Fort William 1978, canon Inverness Cathedral 1977-78, canon Oban Cathedral and synod clerk Dio of Argyll and the Isles 1980-87, dean of Argyll 1987-; *Recreations* reading, fishing, visiting old buildings; *Style*— The Very Rev the Dean of Argyll; St Andrew's Rectory, Parade Rd, Fort William PH33 6BA (☎ 0397 702979)

MacLEHOSE OF BEOCH, Baron (Life Peer UK 1981), of Beoch in the District of Kyle and Carrick and of Victoria in Hong Kong; Sir (Crawford) Murray MacLehose; KT (1983), GBE (1976, MBE (Mil) 1946), KCMG (1971, CMG 1964), KCVO (1975), DL (Ayr and Arran 1983); s of Hamish A MacLehose, and Margaret Bruce, *née* Black; *b* 16 Oct 1917; *Educ* Rugby, Balliol Coll Oxford; *m* 1947, Margaret Noël, da of Sir (Thomas) Charles Dunlop, TD, JP, DL (d 1960), of Doonside, Ayrshire, and Elfrida, *née* Watson (whose mother was Ernestine, da of Ernest Slade and gda of Gen Sir John Slade, 1 Bt); 2 da (Hon Mrs Wedgwood, Hon Mrs Sandeman, *qqv*); *Career* serv WWII as Lt RNVR; joined Foreign Serv 1947 (later FO, then FCO, also seconded to CRO), served Hankow, FO, Prague, Wellington, Paris; princ private sec to Foreign Sec 1965-67; ambass: Vietnam 1967-69, Denmark 1969-71; govr and C-in-C Hong Kong 1971-82 (political advsr with rank of cnsllr 1959-63); dir Nat Westminster Bank 1983-88; chm: Scottish Tst for the Physically Disabled, Margaret Blackwood Housing Assoc, SOAS; pres GB China Centre; Hon LLD: Univ of York, Univ of Strathclyde; KStJ 1972; *Clubs* Athenaeum, New (Edinburgh); *Style*— The Rt Hon the Lord MacLehose of Beoch, KT, GBE,KCMG,KCVO,DL; Beoch, Maybole, Ayrshire (☎ 0655 83114)

McLEISH, Alexander; s of Alexander N McLeish (d 1981), and Jane (Jean), *née* Wylie; *b* 21 Jan 1959; *Educ* Barrhead HS, John Neilson HS Paisley; *m* 8 Dec 1980, Jill Moira, da of Daniel Taylor, of 348 North Anderson Drive, Aberdeen; 2 s (Jon Alexander b 28 May 1981, Jamie Daniel b 6 Aug 1985), 1 da (Rebecca Lisa b 7 July 1989); *Career* professional footballer; Aberdeen FC, Scot Nat Team; capped 75 times, won all domestic hons Aberdeen FC, Euro Cup winners medal, Super Cup winners medal, five Scot Cup wins, two League Cup wins, three championship winners medals; involved in local charities; *Books* Don of an Era (1988); *Recreations* tennis, cinema, golf; *Style*— Alexander McLeish, Esq; Aberdeen Football Club, Pittodrie Stadium, Aberdeen

MCLEISH, David James Dow; s of David James McLeish (d 1972), and Margaret Scott Lawrie MacFarlane (d 1972); *b* 3 Feb 1936; *Educ* HS of Stirling; *Career* actuarial student rising to asst actuary Scottish Mutual Assurance Soc 1953-68; Godwins Ltd: dir 1969-74, md 1975-82, chm and md 1983-87, chm 1988-; chm 1988-: Godwins Inc, Godwins Overseas Inc, Godwins International Holdings Inc (also chief exec); dir: Frank B Hall (Holdings) plc 1975-, Frank B Hall (UK) Ltd 1990-; pres Soc of Pension Conslts 1982-84, memb Occupational Pensions Bd 1984-87; Freeman City of London, memb Worshipful Co of Actuaries; FFA 1964, FPMI 1976, ASA 1980, FRSA 1987, memb American Acad of Actuaries 1989; *Recreations* music, tennis, golf, curling; *Style*— David McLeish, Esq; Godwins International Holdings Inc, 549 Pleasantville Rd, Briarcliffe Manor, NY 10510 (☎ 011 44 914 747 2002, fax 011 44 914 742 3239)

MCLEISH, Kenneth; s of John McLeish, of Victoria, Canada, and Stella, *née* Tyrrell; *b* 10 Oct 1940; *Educ* Bradford GS, Worcester Coll Oxford (BMus, MA); *m* 30 May 1967, Valerie; 2 s (Simon b 27 Dec 1968, Andrew b 9 Sept 1970); *Career* schoolmaster 1963-75 incl posts at: Watford GS 1963-68, Bedales Sch 1969-73; author and translator; *over 70 publications include* for adults: The Theatre of Aristophanes (1980), Penguin Companion to the Arts in the 20th Century (1984), Listener's Guide to Classical Music (jtly with V McLeish, 1985), Shakespeare's Characters (1987, 2 edn 1991), Bloomsbury Good Reading Guide (1988 - biannually), Good Reading Guide to Murder (jtly with V McLeish, 1990); for children: Oxford First Companion to Music (jtly with V McLeish, 1979), Children of the Gods (1984), Collins Illustrated Encyclopaedia of Famous People (jtly with V McLeish, 1990); trans widely, performed on stage tv and radio: The Serpent Son (BBC TV 1979), Philoctetes (Cheek by Jowl, 1988), Electra (RSC London, 1990), Peer Gynt (Royal Nat Theatre, 1990); reviewer Sunday Times, broadcaster; *Recreations* listening to music, gardening; *Style*— Kenneth McLeish, Esq; c/o A P Watt Ltd, 20 John St, London WC1N 2DR (☎ 071 405 6774)

MACLEISH, Martin; s of Cyril Hubert MacLeish (d 1986), and Kathleen Josephine, *née* McCoy; *b* 1 Sept 1955; *Educ* St Ignatius Coll Enfield Middx; *m* 18 April 1981, Shirley Teresa, da of Sidney Gilbert Rodrigues, of Sydney, Aust; 2 s (Mark b 8 March 1983, Michael b 18 Feb 1986); *Career* fndr dir Kensington Pubns Ltd int reference book and magazine publishers for: UN, Cwlth Secretariat; author: VIP Guide to London 1989-90 (3 other edns), The Australian Bicentenary 1788-1988, The Commonwealth Ministers Reference book 1989-90; *Recreations* tennis, golf, travel; *Style*— Martin Macleish, Esq; Kensington Publication Ltd, 1 Gt Cumberland Place, London W1H 7AL (☎ 071 630 5596, fax 071 872 0197, telex 936012)

MCLELLAN, Prof David Thorburn; s of Robert Douglas McLellan (d 1973), and Olive May, *née* Bush; *b* 10 Feb 1940; *Educ* Merchant Taylor's, St John's Coll Oxford (BA, MA, DPhil); *m* 1 July 1967, Annie, da of André Brassart; 2 da (Gabrielle b 8 Nov 1968, Stephanie b 8 May 1970); *Career* Univ of Kent: lectr 1966-70, sr lectr in politics 1970-75, prof of political theory 1975; visiting prof State Univ of NY 1969, visiting fell Indian Inst of Advanced Study Simla 1970; *Books* The Young Hegelians and Karl Marx (1969), Marx before Marxism (1970), Karl Marx: The Early Texts (1971), Marx's Grundrisse (1971), The Thought of Karl Marx (1971), Marx (1971), Karl Marx: His Life and Thought (1973), Engels (1977), Karl Marx: Selected Writings (1977), Marxism after Marx (1980), Karl Marx: Interviews and Recollections (1983), Marx: The First Hundred Years (ed, 1983), Karl Marx: The Legacy (1983), Ideology (1985), Marxism: Selected Texts (ed, 1987), Marxism and Religion (1987), Simone Weil: Utopian Pessimist (1990), Unto Caesar: The Political Relevance of Christianity (1991); *Style*— Prof David McLellan; 13 Ivy Lane, Canterbury, Kent CT1 1TU (☎ 0227 463579); Eliot College, University of Kent, Canterbury, Kent CT2 7NS (☎ 0227 764000)

MACLELLAN, Ian David; s of Maj Henry Crawford Maclellan, MBE, TD, of Walton-on-the-Hill, Surrey, and Daphne Loya, *née* Taverner; *b* 21 Feb 1948; *Educ* Sherborne, Cranfield Business Sch (MBA); *m* 29 Aug 1974, Maja Ursula, da of Dr Hans Schaschek, of Weinheim, W Germany; 1 s (Henry b 1983), 1 da (Kirstin b 1980); *Career* public co dir; jt md Ibstock Johnsen plc, dir Glen Gery Corp USA, chm Price & Pierce Group Ltd; FCA; *Recreations* shooting, tennis; *Style*— Ian D Maclellan, Esq; Wormleighton Grange, nr Leamington Spa, Warwickshire CV33 0XJ (☎ 029577 334); Lutterworth House, Lutterworth, Leics (☎ 04555 3071)

MacLELLAN, Maj-Gen (Andrew) Patrick Withy; CB (1981), CVO (1989), MBE (1964); s of Kenneth MacLellan (d 1981), and Rachel Madeline, *née* Withy (d 1979); *b* 29 Nov 1925; *Educ* Uppingham; *m* 1954, Kathleen Mary, da of Capt Robert

Armstrong Bagnell (d 1969), of Hindhead; 1 s (Ian), 2 da (Fiona, (twin) Diana); *Career* cmmnd Coldstream Gds 1944; serv Palestine, N Africa, Egypt, Germany, DAA and QMC 4 Gds Bde Gp 1958-59, mil asst to Chief of Def Staff (Adm of the Fleet Earl Mountbatten of Burma) 1961-64, instr Staff Coll Camberley 1964-66, GSO1 (plans) Far East Cmd 1966-67, CO 1 Bn Coldstream Gds 1968-70, Col GS Near East Land Forces 1970-71, Cdr 8 Bde 1971-72, RCDS 1973, dep cdr and COS London Dist 1974-77, pres Regular Cmmns Bd 1978-80; govr and keeper of the Jewel House HM Tower of London 1984-89, memb Ct of Common Cncl City of London 1989-; Freeman: City of London, Worshipful Co of Watermen and Lightmen of the River Thames; Liveryman Worshipful Co of Fletchers; Chevalier de la Légion d'Honneur 1960; *Clubs* White's, Pratt's; *Style*— Maj-Gen Patrick MacLellan, CB, CVO, MBE; c/o Bank of Scotland, 38 Threadneedle St, London EC2P 2EM

MacLELLAN, Sir (George) Robin Perronet; CBE (1969), JP (Dunbartonshire 1973); s of George Aikman MacLellan (d 1966); *b* 14 Nov 1915; *Educ* Ardvreck Sch Crieff, Clifton, Ecole de Commerce Lausanne; *m* 1941, Margaret (d 1990), da of Dr Berkeley Robertson (d 1941); 1 s; *Career* WWII Sgt-Maj RA (invalided out 1941); mfr then export salesman then chm George MacLellan Holdings 1964-76, dep chm British Airports Authority 1965-74; dir: Scottish National Trust plc 1970-85, Nationwide Building Society 1971-84, British Tourist Authority 1974-80; memb Advsy Bd BR (Scot) 1976-81, dep chm Nat Tst for Scot 1980-85, chm Scot Tourist Bd 1974-80, chm Bield (Sheltered Housing Tst) 1983-87, dir Edinburgh Branch Melville Retirement Homes Ltds 1984-87; pres The Old Cliftonian Soc 1983-85; hon FRCPS (Glasgow), hon fell RIAS 1988; kt 1980; *Recreations* angling, swimming, keeping friendships in good repair; *Clubs* Western (Glasgow), RNVR (Glasgow); *Style*— Sir Robin MacLellan, CBE, JP; 11 Beechwood Court, Bearsden, Glasgow, Scotland G61 2RY (☎ 041 942 3876)

McLELLAND, (James) Forrest; TD (1953), JP (1970); s of James Forrest McLelland (d 1942), of Northfield, Bearsden, Glasgow, and Janet MacDairmid, *née* Carmichael (d 1978); *b* 13 Nov 1919; *Educ* Glasgow Acad, Fettes; *m* 15 June 1979, Helen Elizabeth (d 1985), da of late George Mailer; *Career* WWII Maj TA UK Western Desert, Italy 1939-46; chm Browntee plc 1980-85, pres Timber Res and Devpt Assoc 1985-, chm Glasgow North Ltd; chm Glasgow Academical Club 1969-71, elder New Kilpatrick Parish Church 1987-, dir of ceremonies Priory of Scotland, chm govrs Glasgow Academy 1985-90; KStJ 1988 (OStJ 1985); deacon Incorporation of Wrights in Glasgow 1959; FIWSc; *Recreations* rugby football, walking; *Clubs* Western (Glasgow), RNVR (Glasgow), St John's House; *Style*— Forrest McLelland, Esq, TD, JP; 34 Coloquhoun Dr, Bearsden, Glasgow G61 4NQ (☎ 041 942 5959)

McLENNAN, Peter Robert; s of Jack McLennan (d 1985), and Dorothy, *née* Walker; *b* 8 March 1946; *Educ* Edmonton Co GS, Middx Poly, Enfield Coll; *m* 29 July 1972, Vivien Joy, da of Kenneth William West; *Career* md: Metal Supplies Ltd 1982-, Boustead Industs Ltd 1986-; dir Boustead plc; memb Wicken Bonhunt PCC; *Recreations* gardening, architecture, travel; *Style*— Peter McLennan, Esq; Wicken Hall Cottage, Wicken Bonhunt, Saffron Walden, Essex (☎ 0799 41121); Sete Ouintas, Querenca, Loule, Portugal; Boustead plc, 14-15 Conduit St, London W1R 9TG (☎ 071 491 7674, fax 071 493 6647, car 0860 579550)

MACLENNAN, Robert Adam Ross; MP (Lab until 1981, when joined SDP) Caithness & Sutherland 1966-; s of Sir Hector Maclennan (d 1978), by his 1 w, Isabel, *née* Adam; *b* 26 June 1936; *Educ* Glasgow Acad, Balliol Coll Oxford, Trinity Coll Cambridge, Columbia Univ NY; *m* 1968, Helen, wid of Paul Noyes, and da of Judge Ammi Cutter, of Cambridge, Mass; 1 s, 1 da, 1 step s; *Career* called to the Bar 1962; PPS to Cwlth Affrs Sec 1967-69 and to Min without Portfolio 1969-70, additional oppn spokesman Scottish Affrs 1970-71, Def 1971-72, Parly under-sec Prices and Consumer Protection 1974-79, memb Commons Public Accounts Ctee 1979-; oppn spokesman on Foreign Affrs 1979-80; SDP spokesman: Agric 1981-87, on Home & Legal Affrs 1983-87; elected ldr of the SDP 1987-88, Lib Dem spokesman Home Affrs 1988-; *Recreations* theatre, music, books, 2800 square miles of constituency; *Clubs* Brooks's; *Style*— Robert Maclennan, Esq, MP; House of Commons, London SW1A 0AA (☎ 071 219 6553)

MacLENNAN, Prof William Jardine; s of Alexander MacLennan (d 1975), and Mary Sinclair Angus (d 1986); *b* 11 Feb 1941; *Educ* Hutchesons' Boys GS, Univ of Glasgow (MB ChB, MD); *m* 9 Aug 1969, Fiona Hannah, da of Hugh Campbell, of 17 Sommerville Drive, Mount Florida, Glasgow; 2 s (Peter b 1974, Richard (twin) b 1974); *Career* jr hosp and univ post in Glasgow 1964-71, sr lectr in geriatric med Univ of Southampton 1971-80, sr lectr then reader in geriatric med Univ of Dundee 1980-86, prof of geriatric med Univ of Edinburgh 1986-; chm of tstees Dementia Servs Devpt Centre Stirling, memb Cncl for professions Supplementary to Medicine; FRCP (Glasgow, Edinburgh, London); *Books* The Elderly (with A N Shephard and I H Stevenson, 1984), Bone Disease in the Elderly (with C R Paterson, 1984), Medical Care of the Elderly (with M R P Hall and M D W Lye, 2 edn, 1986), Metabolic and Endocrine Problems in the Elderly (with N R Peden, 1989), Old Age (1990); *Recreations* reading, hillwalking, model ship building; *Style*— Prof William MacLennan; 26 Caiystane Ave, Fairmilehead, Edinburgh (☎ 031 445 1755); Dept of Geriatric Medicine, City Hospital, Greenbank Drive, Edinburgh (☎ 031 447 1001)

MacLENNAN OF MacLENNAN, Ruairidh Donald George; 35 Chief of Clan MacLennan; o s of Ronald George MacLennan of MacLennan (d 1989), 34 Chief of Clan MacLennan, and Margaret Ann, *née* MacLennan; *b* 1977; *Educ* Inverness Royal Acad Fettes; *Career* head chorister St Andrew's Episcopal Cathedral Inverness; *Recreations* canoeing, fishing; *Style*— The MacLennan of MacLennan; The Old Mill, Dores, Inverness IV1 2TR

McLEOD, Dr Andrew Alasdair; s of Andrew Frederick McLeod, OBE, of Bathford, Nr Bath, Somerset, and Janet Mary, *née* Comline; *b* 21 Jan 1948; *Educ* King Edward's Sch Bath, St Catharine's Coll Cambridge (BA, MA, MB BChir, MD), FRCP; *m* 3 Sept 1983, Sharon, da of Wallace Redpath, of 29 Beechways, Appleton Park, Cheshire; 1 da (Anna Louise b 26 May 1989); *Career* assoc faculty med Duke Univ Med Centre 1983 (Br Heart Fndn and American Heart Assoc fell 1981-83), conslt cardiologist King's Coll and Dulwich Hosps 1984-88, conslt cardiologist and physician Poole Gen Hosp Dorset 1988-; memb: Cncl Action on Smoking and Health, Rehabilitation Ctee Coronary Prevention Gp, Br Cardiac Soc; FRCP; *Recreations* golf, sailing, classical guitar, music; *Clubs* Parkstone Yacht, Parkstone Golf; *Style*— Dr Andrew McLeod; Poole Gen Hosp, Longfleet Rd, Poole, Dorset BH15 2JB (☎ 0202 675100 ext 2572)

MACLEOD, Sheriff Angus; CBE (1967); s of Alexander MacLeod (d 1945), of Glendale, Isle of Skye, and Flora, *née* MacPherson (d 1962); *b* 2 April 1906; *Educ* Hutchesons Boys GS Glasgow, Univ of Glasgow (MA, LLB); *m* 25 June 1936, (Jane) Winifred (d 1977), da of Sir Robert Bryce Walker, CBE, DL, JP; 3 s (Donald Ian Kerr b 1937, Neil Alistair b 1942, Euan Roderick b 1944); *Career* admitted slr 1929, qualified asst legal practice Glasgow 1929-34; depute fiscal 1934-42: Dunfermline, Glasgow, Edinburgh (sr depute Edinburgh); procurator fiscal: Dumfries 1942-52, Aberdeen 1952-55, Edinburgh 1955-71; hon Sheriff Edinburgh 1972, temp Sheriff Scot 1973-77; chm VAT Appeals Tbnl 1974-77; memb: (fndr memb) Cncl Law Soc Scot 1967-73, Grant Ctee Sheriff Ct 1963-67; pres: PTA, Dumfries Acad 1949-50, Maxwellton Bowling Club Dumfries 1948-49; memb Stair Soc 1948- (memb Cncl 1958-61); *Recreations* reading; *Style*— Sheriff Angus MacLeod, CBE; 7 Oxford Terrace, Edinburgh EH4 1PX (☎ 031 332 5466)

MACLEOD, Dr Calum Alexander; s of Rev Lachlan Macleod (d 1966), of Glenurquhart, and Jessie Mary Morrison (d 1970); *b* 25 July 1935; *Educ* Nicolson Inst Stornoway, Glenurquhart Sch, Univ of Aberdeen (MA, LLB); *m* 21 July 1962, Elizabeth Margaret, da of David Davidson (d 1973), of Inverness; 2 s (Allan b 1966, David b 1968), 1 da (Edythe b 1972); *Career* Nat Serv 2 Lt RAEC; ptnr Paull & Williamsons (advocates) Aberdeen 1964-80; chm: Aberdeen Petroleum plc 1982-, Harris Tweed Association 1984-, Abtrust Scotland Investment Co plc 1986-, Britannia Life 1990-; dep chm: Grampian TV plc 1982-, Scottish Eastern Investment Trust plc 1988-; dir Aberdeen Bd Bank of Scotland 1980-; chllr's assessor Univ of Aberdeen 1979-90; chm: Robert Gordon's Coll 1981-, Satro North Scot 1986-; memb: White Fish Authy 1973-80, North of Scot Hydro-Electric Bd 1976-84; Highlands and Islands Devpt Bd 1984-; vice chm Scot Cncl of Ind Schs 1988-; Hon LLD Univ of Aberdeen 1986; memb Law Soc of Scotland 1958, FInstD 1982; *Recreations* golf, music, travel, reading; *Clubs* Royal Northern, Royal Aberdeen Golf, Nairn Golf; *Style*— Dr Calum MacLeod; 6 Westfield Terrace, Aberdeen AB2 4RU (☎ 0224 641614); Royfold House, Hill of Rubislaw, Anderson Dr, Aberdeen AB2 6GZ (☎ 0224 208110, fax 0224 208120)

McLEOD, Sir Charles Henry; 3 Bt (UK 1925), of The Fairfields, Cobham, Surrey; s of Sir Murdoch Campbell McLeod, 2 Bt (d 1950), and Susan, *née* Whitehead (d 1964); *b* 7 Nov 1924; *Educ* Winchester; *m* 5 Jan 1957, Anne Gillian (d 1978), 3 da of late Henry Russell Bowlby, of London; 1 s, 2 da; *Heir* s, James Roderick Charles McLeod; *Style*— Sir Charles McLeod, Bt; Coombe Green Cottage, Lea, Malmesbury, Wiltshire

McLEOD, Prof David; s of Norman McLeod (d 1985), and Anne, *née* Heyworth; *b* 16 Jan 1946; *Educ* The GS Burnley Lancs, Univ of Edinburgh (MB ChB, BSc); *m* 16 Dec 1967, Jeanette Allison; 1 s (Euan b 1972), 1 da (Seona b 1974); *Career* conslt ophthalmic surgn Moorfields Eye Hosp 1978-88, conslt advsr in ophthalmology to the RAF 1984-, prof of ophthalmology Univ of Manchester 1988-, hon conslt ophthalmic surgn Royal Eye Hosp Manchester 1988-; FRCS 1974, FCOphth 1988; *Recreations* walking, golf; *Clubs* Bramall Park Golf Bramhall Cheshire; *Style*— Prof David McLeod; Willowtrees, Ladybrook Rd, Bramhall, Cheshire SK7 3LZ (☎ 061 485 2013); Royal Eye Hospital, Oxford Rd, Manchester M13 9WH (☎ 061 276 5620)

MACLEOD, Air Vice-Marshal Donald Francis Graham; CB (1977); s of Alexander Macleod (d 1967), of Stornoway, Isle of Lewis, Scotland, and Isabella Macleod (d 1975); *b* 26 Aug 1917; *Educ* Univ of St Andrews (LDS); *m* 1 Nov 1941, Marjorie Eileen, da of late William Davidson Gracie, of Glamis Rd, Dundee, Scotland; 1 s (Ronald b 1944), 1 da (Gael b 1947); *Career* joined Dental Branch RAF as Flying Offr 1942, serv W Africa (Apapa, Lagos) 1943-44, Cranwell 1944, Harley St London 1945; RAF Hosps: Cosford 1945-50, Aden 1950-52, Wroughton 1952-59; specialist in oral surgery RAF Hosps: Wroughton 1955-59, Wegberg Germany 1959-62, Ely Cambs 1962-65; Gp-Capt conslt RAF Hosp Aden 1965-67, conslt oral surgery RAF Hosp Ely 1967-72, Air Cdre princ dental offr Strike Cmd 1972-73, Air Vice-Marshal dir RAF dental branch 1973-76; private practice 1940-41, Aberdeen Public Health Authy 1941-42; Ely and Dist Probus Soc: fndr memb 1982, vice-chm 1982, chm 1983; Royal Humane Soc Resuscitation Award 1937; QHDS 1972; FDS, memb RCS(Ed) 1955; *Recreations* golf, gardening, outdoor pursuits; *Clubs* Royal Worlington & Newmarket Golf; *Style*— Air Vice-Marshal D F G Macleod, CB; 20 Witchford Rd, Ely, Cambs CB6 3DP (☎ 0353 663164)

MACLEOD, Dr Donald MacRae; s of Allan Martin MacLeod, of Glen Hse, Carloway, Isle of Lewis, and Margaret MacLeod; *b* 19 Oct 1956; *Educ* Nicolson Inst Stornoway, Univ of Aberdeen (MB, ChB); *m* 19 April 1986, Moira Catherine, da of Thomas Anderson, of Marykirk; 1 s (Allan b 1987), 1 da (Alice b 1989); *Career* lectr London Hosp Med Coll 1986-88, visiting assoc Duke Univ Med Centre Durham N Carolina USA 1988-89, conslt anaesthetics Aberdeen Royal Infirmary 1989-; hon sr lectr Univ of Aberdeen; FFARCSI 1986; *Recreations* sailing, golf; *Clubs* Banff Sailing, Royal Aberdeen Golf; *Style*— Dr Donald MacLeod; Hansville, 44 Gilbert Rd, Bucksburn, Aberdeen; Aberdeen Royal Infirmary, Aberdeen, Scotland

MacLEOD, Duncan James; CBE (1986); s of Alan Duncan MacLeod, of Skeabost, Isle of Skye (ka Sicily 1943), and Joan Nora Paton, *née* de Knoop; *b* 1 Nov 1934; *Educ* Eton; *m* 14 June 1958, Joanna, da of Samuel Leslie Bibby, CBE, DL, of Villans Wyk, Headley, Surrey (d 1985); 2 s (Alan Hamish b 1959, Charles Alasdair b 1961), 1 da (Davina b 1965); *Career* CA 1958; ptnr Brown Fleming & Murray (now Ernst & Young) 1960-89; dir: Bank of Scotland 1973-, Scottish Provident Institute 1976-, The Weir Group plc 1976-, Harry Ramsden's plc 1989-, Motherwell Bridge Holdings Ltd 1990-; memb: Scot Industl Devpt Advsy Bd 1980- (chm 1989-), Scot Tertiary Educn Advsy Cncl 1985-87; *Recreations* golf, shooting, fishing; *Clubs* Western (Glasgow), Prestwick Golf, Royal and Ancient, MCC; *Style*— Duncan J MacLeod, Esq, CBE; Monkredding House, Kilwinning, Ayrshire KA13 7QN (☎ 0294 52336); George Hse, 50 George Sq, Glasgow G2 1RR (☎ 041 552 3456, fax 041 553 1812)

MacLEOD, Ewan Douglas; s of Douglas Hamilton MacLeod (d 1970), of Park Close, Melbury Rd, London W8, and Lesley Frances Ronaldson (d 1978); *b* 13 Nov 1936; *Educ* Rugby, Trinity Coll Cambridge (MA); *Career* Nat Serv, 2 Lt 2 Bn 7 DEO Gurkha Rifles in HK and Malaya 1955-57 (GSM Malaya 1956); asst architect 1964-68, started private architectural practice 1968-; ARIBA 1965; *Recreations* drawing, painting, opera, music, Italy, France; *Style*— Ewan MacLeod, Esq; 86 Lyndhurst Way, London SE15 5AQ (☎ 071 703 1989, fax 071 708 4830)

McLEOD, Fraser Neil; s of James McLeod, of 67 Tolmers Rd, Cuffley, Herts, and Mary, *née* Yuill; *b* 13 July 1951; *Educ* Hertford GS, St Bartholemews Hosp Med Coll (MB BS); *m* 16 April 1983, Angela Mary, da of Thomas Campbell, of 2A Woodcote Drive, Purley, Surrey; 1 s (David Paul Christopher b 13 Feb 1989); *Career* lectr in obstetrics and gynaecology and pioneer in test tube baby devpt Royal Free Hosp 1981-83, sr registrar in obstetrics and gynaecology Southmead Hosp Bristol 1983-85, conslt obstetrician and gynaecologist Frenchay and Southmead Hosps Bristol 1985-; local tres BMA, examiner RCOG; MRCOG 1980, MRCS; *Recreations* golf; *Clubs* Berkshire Golf, Henbury Golf; *Style*— Fraser McLeod, Esq; 7 Percival Rd, Clifton, Bristol BS8 3LE (☎ 0272 741 396)

McLEOD, Capt (William) Hamish Hendry; OBE (1977), RN; s of Maj William McLeod, of Mayford, Surrey, and Isabella Loan, *née* Archibald; *b* 1 Jan 1932; *Educ* Jordanhill Coll Sch Glasgow, RNC Dartmouth; *m* 27 July 1957, Anne, da of Cdr Richard Burnaby Cooper, RN (d 1969); 1 s (Angus b 1962), 1 da (Jane b 1959); *Career* RNC Dartmouth 1949; served Korea and Malaya 1950-52; HM submarines 1953-61; in cmd: HMS Wiston 1963-64, HMS Matapan 1972-74; exec offr HMS Ark Royal 1976-78, Capt 1979, NA Br Embassy Sultanate of Oman 1980-82; Capt of Port and Queen's Harbour Master: Rosyth 1982-85, Plymouth 1985-87; appt dir Marine Emergency Ops DTp 1988, responsible for HM Coastguard and Marine Pollution Control Unit UK, chm UK Search and Rescue Ctee 1988-; Yr Bro Trinity House 1989-; memb Nautical Inst 1983; *Recreations* revolver target shooting; *Clubs* New (Edinburgh), Naval and Mil; *Style*— Capt Hamish McLeod, OBE, RN; Marine Directorate, DTp, Sunley House, 90/93 High Holborn, London WC1V 6LP (☎ 071 405 6911 ext 3132, fax 071 831 7681, telex 8812048 MARINF G)

MACLEOD, Hon Mrs (Hermione Jane); *née* McClintock-Bunbury; da of 4 Baron

Rathdonnell (d 1959); *b* 11 Aug 1943; *m* 1988, Callum Macleod, of New Zealand; *Style*— The Hon Mrs Macleod; 34 Newell St, Pt Chevalier, Auckland, New Zealand

MACLEOD, Prof Iain Alasdair; s of Donald MacLeod (d 1976), of Achiltibuie, Rosshire, and Barbara Mary, *née* Mackenzie (d 1977); *b* 4 May 1939; *Educ* Lenzie Acad, Univ of Glasgow (BSc, PhD); *m* 18 Nov 1967, Barbara Jean, da of Allen Daven Booth (d 1973), of Salmon Arm, Br Columbia, Canada; 1 s (Alastair b 1976), 1 da (Mairi b 1975); *Career* structural engr: Crouch and Hogg Glasgow 1960-62, H A Simons Vancouver Canada 1966-67; structural res engr Portland Cement Assoc USA 1967-69, lectr Dept of Civil Engrg Univ of Glasgow 1969-73 (asst lectr 1962-66); prof, head of Dept of Civil Engrg, Paisley Coll of Technol 1973-81; prof of structural engrg Univ of Strathclyde 1981-; vice pres Inst StructE 1989-90, memb Standing Ctee on Structural Safety; FIStructE, FICE; *Books* Analytical Modelling of Structural Systems (1990); *Recreations* sailing, mountaineering, skiing; *Style*— Prof Iain MaCleod; Dept of Civil Engineering, University of Strathclyde, 107 Rottenrow, Glasgow G4 0NG (☎ 041 552 4400 ext 3275, fax 041 552 2891)

McLEOD, Sir Ian George; JP (1977); s of George McLeod; *b* 17 Oct 1926; *Educ* Kearsney Coll Natal, Natal Univ; *m* 1950, Audrey; 2 da; *Career* md EDP Servs Computer Bureau 1964-; memb bd SE Electricity Bd 1983-; chm: Croydon Central Cons Assoc 1973-76, Greater London Area Conservatives 1981-84; memb Nat Union Exec Ctee Conservative Pty 1974-84; ACIS; kt 1984; *Clubs* Carlton, MCC; *Style*— Sir Ian McLeod, JP

McLEOD, James Roderick Charles; s and h of Sir Charles Henry McLeod, 3 Bt; *b* 26 Sept 1960; *m* 20 Jan 1990, Helen M, er da of Capt George T Cooper, OBE, RN, of Lilliput, Poole, Dorset; *Style*— James McLeod, Esq

MACLEOD, Dr John Alasdair Johnston; DL (Western Isles 1979-); s of Dr Alexander John Macleod, OBE (d 1979), of Lochmaddy, and Dr Julia Parker, *née* Johnston (d 1989); *b* 20 Jan 1935; *Educ* Lochmaddy Sch, Nicolson Inst Stornoway, Keil Sch Dumbarton, Univ of Glasgow (MB ChB); *m* 4 Nov 1972, Lorna, da of Dr Douglas Ian Ferguson, of The Cottage, Station Rd, Winterbourne Down, nr Bristol; 2 s (Alasdair Ian b 1974, Torquil John b 1979), 1 da (Elizabeth Jane b 1975); *Career* Temp Actg Sub Lt RNVR 1957-59; jr hosp posts Glasgow and London 1963-70, RMO and sr registrar Middx London 1970-72, GP Isle of N Uist 1973-, examing offr DHSS 1973-, med offr Lochmaddy Hosp 1974-, Admty surgn and agent 1974-, local med offr 1974-; non-exec dir Olscot Ltd 1969-; visiting prof Dept of Family Med Univ of N Carolina; memb: N Uist Highland Gathering, N Uist Angling Club, Scandinavian Village Assoc; sec Western Isles Local Med Ctee 1977-; author of various articles and papers on isolated gen practise within the NHS; memb Western Isles Advsy Ctee on JPs 1985-; memb BMA; MRCGP, FRSM; *Recreations* promoting Western Isles, time-sharing, arboriculture, writing; *Clubs* RNVR (Scotland), Highland; *Style*— Dr John A J Macleod, DL; Tigh-na-Hearradh, Lochmaddy, Isle of N Uist, Western Isles PA82 5AE (☎ 08763 224)

MACLEOD, John Francis Matheson (Jeff); s of Dr Ian Matheson Macleod (d 1963), of Inverness, and Annie Frances, *née* Sime (d 1977); *b* 24 Jan 1932; *Educ* Inverness Royal Acad, George Watson's Coll, Univ of Edinburgh (MA, LLB); *m* 15 April 1958, Alexandra Catherine, da of late Donald Macleod, of Tarbert Harris; 1 s (Ian Diarmid Skene b 1959); *Career* in practice as slr Scotland; dean Faculty of Slrs of the Highlands, memb Cncl Law Soc of Scotland; formerly chm: Highland Region of Scottish Lib Pty, Crofters Cmmn 1978-86; vice-chm Broadcasting Cncl for Scotland; Parly candidate (Lib): Moray & Nairn 1964, Western Isles 1966; *Clubs* Royal Scots (Edinburgh); *Style*— Jeff Macleod, Esq; Bona Lodge, Aldourie, by Inverness; Messrs Macleod & MacCallum, Solicitors, 28 Queensgate, Inverness (☎ 0463 239 393, fax 0463 222 879)

MacLEOD, Hon John Maxwell Norman; s of Baron MacLeod of Fuinary, MC (Life Peer) and h to father's Btcy only; *b* 23 Feb 1952; *Educ* Gordonstoun; *Style*— The Hon John MacLeod; Fuinary Manse, Loch Aline, Morven, Argyll

MCLEOD, Michael Alastair; s of Robert David McLeod (d 1976), of Surrey, and Iris Mary, *née* Hocking; *b* 19 Jan 1935; *Educ* Falmouth GS, Christ Coll Brecon; *m* 1957, Joan Patricia Joyce, da of Phillip Charles Mitchell; 2 da (Anne b 23 Aug 1959, Fiona b 29 July 1964); *Career* trainee JH Snellgrove & Partners Cornwall 1951-57, Langdon & Every: asst Singapore 1957-58, office mangr Kuala Lumpur 1958-61, assoc Kuala Lumpur 1961-63, ptnr Kuala Lumpur 1963-69, ptnr London 1970-88; jt sr ptnr Davis Langdon & Everest 1988-, sr ptnr Davis Langdon Arabian Gulf 1988- (dir associated cos in Italy, Aust, Germany 1988-); FRICS 1966 (ARICS 1957); *Recreations* golf, sailing, gardening, music; *Style*— Michael McLeod, Esq; Davis Langdon & Everest, Princes House, Kingsway, London WC2B 6TP (☎ 071 497 9000, fax 071 497 8858)

MacLEOD, Rev Murdo Allan; s of John MacLeod, DCM (d 1971), of Glendale, Isle of Sleye, and Christina MacLeod (d 1972); *b* 5 Sept 1926; *Educ* Inverness Royal Acad, Univ of Edinburgh (MA), Free Church of Scotland Coll Edinburgh; *m* 11 Sept 1954, Nancie Margaret, da of Frank Johnstone (d 1981), of Westcliff-on-Sea, Essex; 2 s (John b 1955, Donald b 1959), 2 da (Ruth b 1957, Catherine b 1963); *Career* ordained min Free Church of Scotland 1955; min of free Church of Scot: Tabert Argyllshire 1955-63, London 1963-70; dir and gen sec Christian Witness to Israel 1970-, int pres Lausanne Consultation on Jewish Evangelism 1983-, moderator Free Church of Scotland Gen Assembly 1984; *Books* contrib to: Hold Fast Your Confession (1962), International Bible Encyclopedia (4 volumes, 1979), Illustrated Bible Dictionary (3 volumes 1980), Witness of the Jews to God (1982), Twentieth Century Encyclopedia of Religious Knowledge (1991); *Recreations* antique furniture, photography, walking; *Style*— The Rev Murdo MacLeod; 11 St Martins Drive, Eynsford, Dartford DA4 0EY (☎ 0322 863277); 44 Lubbock Rd, Chislehurst, Kent BR7 5JX (☎ 081 467 2296, fax 081 295 1586)

MACLEOD, Nigel Ronald Buchanan; QC (1979); s of Donald Macleod (d 1956), and Katie Ann Buchanan Macleod; *b* 7 Feb 1936; *Educ* Wigan GS, Ch Ch Oxford (MA, BCL); *m* 1966, Susan Margaret; 1 s (Alasdair b 1968), 1 da (Victoria b 1972); *Career* Nat Serv RAF 1954-56; called to the Bar Gray's Inn 1961, asst cmmr Boundary Cmmn for England 1981-84, rec Crown Court 1981-; *Recreations* walking, dinghy sailing; *Style*— Nigel Macleod, Esq, QC; The Start, Start Lane, Whaley Bridge, Derbyshire (☎ 0663 732732); 127 Santa Monica, Av du Pacifique, Cap d'Agde, Herault, France; 2 Paper Buildings, Temple, London EC4 (☎ 071 353 5835, fax 071 583 1390, telex 885358 TEMPLE G)

MacLEOD, Sheriff Princ Norman Donald; QC (Scot 1986); s of Rev John MacLeod, of Edinburgh, and Catherine Mullen, *née* Macritchie (d 1939); *b* 6 March 1932; *Educ* Mill Hill, George Watson's Boys' Coll, Edinburgh Univ, Oxford Univ; *m* 1957, Ursula Jane, da of George Herbert Bromley, of Inveresk, Midlothian (d 1982); 2 s (Ian b 1959, Patrick b 1963), 2 da (Catriona b 1960, Johanna b 1964); *Career* passed advocate 1956, Colonial Serv dist offr and crown counsel 1957-64, sheriff of Lanarkshire at Glasgow (subsequently sheriff of Glasgow and Strathkelvin) 1967-86; sheriff princ of Glasgow and Strathkelvin 1986-; visiting prof Strathclyde Univ; *Recreations* gardening, sailing; *Style*— Sheriff Princ Norman D MacLeod, QC; Calderbank, Lochwinnoch, Renfrewshire PA12 4DJ (☎ 0505 843 340); Sheriff Principal's Chambers, Sheriff Court of Glasgow and Strathkelvin, 1 Carlton Place, Glasgow G5 9DA (☎ 041 429 8888)

McLEOD, (Harris) Norman Grimstone; s of Earnest Alexander Brown McLeod, of Bulawayo, Zimbabwe, and Mary, *née* Hopkins; *b* 27 March 1941; *Educ* St George's Coll Harare Zimbabwe, Royal Agric Coll Cirencester Glos; *m* 2 May 1970, Penelope Mary, da of William Plender (1976); 3 s (Magnus b 27 Feb 1975, Alastair b 13 March 1977, John b 4 Jan 1983), 2 da (Fiona b 18 April 1973, Harriet b 22 May 1986); *Career* KOYLI 1962-67; stockbroker Seccombe Marshall & Campion Agency Brokers Ltd; chm Int League for the Protection of Horses, govr St Philips Sch London; memb Stock Exchange 1980; ACIS; *Recreations* horses, shooting, reading; *Style*— Norman McLeod, Esq; Seccombe Marshall & Campion Agency Brokers Ltd, 7 Birchin Lane, London EC3V 9DE

McLEOD, Robert; s of Robert Frew McLeod (d 1973), and Marion McLeod; *b* 1 Oct 1928; *Educ* Alloa Academy and Royal Tech College (Glasgow); *m* 1954, Agnes Myrtle, da of David George; 1 s, 1 da; *Career* dep chm Scottish Bus Gp 1979-89; (md 1987-88), Scot Bus Gp 1987; *Recreations* gardening, travel, golf; *Style*— Robert McLeod, Esq; Rozelle, 4 Briarhill Ave, Dalgety Bay, Fife KY11 5UR (☎ 0383 823 200)

MacLEOD, Sir (Hugh) Roderick; s of Neil MacLeod, and Ruth, *née* Hill; *b* 20 Sept 1929; *Educ* Bryanston, St John's Coll Cambridge; *m* 1958, Josephine Seager Berry; 2 s, 1 da; *Career* chm and chief exec Lloyd's Register of Shipping 1983-; dir: Lloyd's Register Technical Services Inc, Lloyd's Register Industrial Services (Insurance) Inc, Lloyd's Register Inspection Ltd, Lloyd's Register (Overseas) Ltd, Lloyd's Register Espana SA, Lloyd's Register of Shipping (ASBL) Belgium, Rontgen Technische Dienst, Lloyd's Register of Shipping Trust Corporation Ltd, The Monks Investment Trust plc, Murray Enterprise plc; jt md Ben Line Steamers 1964-82, dir Scottish Equitable Life Assurance Society, chm British Railways (Scottish) Board 1980-82, pt/t memb British Railways Board 1980-86; kt 1989; *Recreations* outdoor pursuits, music; *Style*— Sir Roderick MacLeod; 14 Dawson Place, London W2; Lloyd's Register of Shipping, 71 Fenchurch St, London EC3 (☎ 071 709 9166)

McLEOD, Thomas Symington; s of Prof James Walter McLeod, OBE, FRS (d 1978), and Jane Christine, *née* Garvie (d 1953); *b* 5 Oct 1919; *Educ* Leeds GS, Trinity Hall Cambridge (MA); *m* 12 Aug 1941, Marion Boyd, da of Duncan McNicol Thomson (d 1951); 2 s (Hugh b 1944, Peter b 1946), 2 da (Alison b 1950, Elizabeth b 1954); *Career* served WWII 1941-45 Capt RM, Africa, Italy, France, Belgium, Holland (despatches); chartered electrical engr, tech mangr The Plessey Co plc 1952-79, dir Design Technol 1979-85; memb Cncl and chm Social Security Ctee CBI 1974-81; chm: Tech and Vocational Educn Initiative Dorset 1986-; CEng, FIEE 1958; *Books* The Management of Research, Development and Design in Industry (1 edn 1969, 2 edn 1988), Research and Development, Industrial (Encyclopedia Britannica, 15 edn); *Recreations* golf, fly fishing, bridge, chess, skiing; *Style*— Thomas McLeod, Esq; Little Woolgarston Cottage, Corfe Castle, Dorset (☎ 0929 480536)

MACLEOD, Hon Torquil Anthony Ross; s of Baroness Macleod of Borve (Life Peer), *qv*, and late Rt Hon Iain Macleod, MP; *b* 20 Feb 1942; *Educ* Harrow; *m* 1967 (m dis 1973), (Elizabeth) Meriol, da of Brig Arthur Pelham Trevor, DSO (d 1984); 1 s (Iain b 1970); *Style*— The Hon Torquil Macleod; c/o Barclays Bank, 77 Gloucester Rd, London SW7

McLEOD-BAIKIE, Ian; s of David George McLeod-Baikie (d 1963), and Winifred May, *née* McNicol; *b* 13 Dec 1921; *Educ* Private and Perth Acad, Univ of Glasgow, Glasgow Royal Infirmary; *m* 27 Aug 1949, Sylvia Rosemary, da of John Smith, MBE (d 1978), of Lancs; *Career* conslt orthopaedic surgn, ret 1984; hon conslt surgn St Anthony's Hosp and Holy Cross Hosp; chm: Pembs Branch Cncl for Protection of Rural Wales, Coomb Cheshire Home; FRSM; *Recreations* gardening, sailing, photography, history; *Clubs* Naval; *Style*— Ian McLeod-Baikie, Esq; The Forge, Landshipping, nr Norberth, Pembrokeshire SA67 8BG (☎ 0834 891279)

MACLEOD MATTHEWS, Alistair Francis; OBE (1970), JP (Bucks 1971); s of Capt Reginald Francis Macleod Matthews; *b* 12 April 1921; *Educ* St Paul's, Christ Church Oxford; *m* 1956, Elizabeth Marina Addenbrooke, da of Lt-Col Gordon Spencer Marston, DSO, MC, (RE), of Chalfont St Giles; 2 s; *Career* served as Lt-Col Gen Staff Med; former asst gen mangr BP; dir: Br Gas Corpn 1975-84, Volvo Petroleum UK Ltd, Leyland Bus Gp; memb: Royal Institution, Scottish Industl Devpt Bd 1972-87; companion Inst of Gas Engrs; former High Sheriff Bucks; *Recreations* shooting, fishing, historical research; *Clubs* Royal Scottish Automobile; *Style*— Alistair Macleod Matthews, Esq, OBE, JP; 29 Carlisle Place, London SW1 (☎ 01 828 2032); Achnacarnin, Culkein, Sutherland (☎ 057 15 262); The Manor House, Chenies, Herts (☎ 02 404 2888)

MACLEOD OF BORVE, Baroness (Life Peer UK 1971), of Borve, Isle of Lewis; Evelyn Hester Macleod; *née* Blois; JP (Middx 1955), DL (Gtr London 1977); da of Rev Gervase Vanneck Blois (d 1961, yst s of Sir John Blois, 8 Bt, DL), and Hon Hester Pakington, da of 3 Baron Hampton; *b* 19 Feb 1915; *Educ* Lawnside Gt Malvern; *m* 1, 1937, Mervyn Charles Mason (ka 1940), s of Alwyne Humfrey-Mason, JP, formerly of Foxley Manor, Malmesbury and Necton Hall Norfolk; m 2, 1941, Rt Hon Iain Norman Macleod, PC, MP (d 1970), s of Dr Norman Macleod, of Isle of Lewis; 1 s (Hon Torquil Anthony Ross b 1942), 1 da (Hon Diana Hester (Hon Mrs Heimann) b 1944); *Career* sits as Cons in House of Lords; memb IBA 1972-76; chm: Nat Gas Consumers Cncl 1972-77, Nat Assoc League of Hosp Friends 1976-85 (pres 1985-89); memb Parole Bd 1977-81; govr Queenswood Sch 1977-85; pres Nat Assoc of Wids 1976-; co-fndr and pres of charity of single homeless Crisis at Christmas; tstee Attle Meml Fndn 1980-90; *Recreations* family, music, conservation; *Style*— The Rt Hon the Baroness Macleod of Borve, JP, DL; Luckings Farm, Coleshill, Amersham, Bucks (☎ 0494 725158)

MacLEOD OF GLENDALE, Donald Alexander; er s of Col Colin Sherwin MacLeod of Glendale, OBE, TD (d 1977), of Kilchearan, South Oswald Rd, Edinburgh, and Margaret Drysdale Robertson, *née* Campbell (d 1987); head of a cadet branch descended from Iain Borb MacLeod, 6 Chief of MacLeod (d c 1442), which acquired Glendale in the 17 cent (*see* Burke's Landed Gentry, 18 edn, vol I, 1965); *b* 23 Jan 1938; *Educ* Edinburgh Acad, Pembroke Coll Cambridge (BA); *m* 10 Dec 1963, Rosemary Lilian Abel, da of Abel Edward Randle (d 1951), of Gnosall, Staffs; 2 s (Rory b 1965, Alasdair b 1971), 2 da (Katrina b 1967, Fiona b 1970); *Career* 2 Lt Queen's Own Cameron Highlanders 1956-58; entered FO 1961, Br Embassy Rangoon 1962-66, private sec to Min of State Cwlth Office 1966-69, 1 sec Br High Cmmn Ottawa 1969-73, FCO 1973-78, head of chancery Br Embassy Bucharest 1978-81, commercial cnsllr Br High Cmmn Singapore 1981-84, dep high cmmr Br High Cmmn Barbados 1984-87, head of protocol dept, FCO 1987-89 (ret); *Recreations* hill walking; *Style*— Donald MacLeod of Glendale; Kinlochfollart, by Dunvegan, Isle of Skye IV55 8WQ

MacLEOD OF MacLEOD, John; s of Capt Robert Wolrige-Gordon, MC; officially recognised in the name of MacLeod of MacLeod, Yr, by decree of Lyon Court 1951; suc maternal grandmother Dame Flora MacLeod of MacLeod, DBE, 1976, as Chief of Clan MacLeod; *b* 10 Aug 1935; *Educ* Eton; *m* 1, 1961, Drusilla Mary, da of Sebastian Shaw, actor; m 2, 1973, Melita, da of Duko Kolin, of Sofia, Bulgaria; 1 s (Hugh b 1973), 1 da (Elena b 1977); *Heir* s, Hugh Magnus b 1973; officially recognised in the name of MacLeod of MacLeod, Yr, by decree of Lyon Ct 1951; *Style*— John MacLeod of MacLeod; Dunvegan Castle, Isle of Skye

MacLEOD-SMITH, Alastair MacLeod; CMG (1956); s of Robert Arthur Smith (d

1950), and Catherine Ethel Welsh, *née* Kellner (d 1977); *b* 30 June 1916; *Educ* Wells House Malvern Wells, Ellesmere Coll Salop, Queen's Coll Oxford (BA); *m* 18 Aug 1945, Ann, da of George Francis Langdale Circuitt (d 1966); 1 s (Geoffrey Langdale b 1953), 1 da (Catherine Amanda b 1955); *Career* Colonial Admin Serv: Nigeria 1939-49, econ and fin advsr Windward Islands 1949-52, fin sec Western Pacific High Cmmn 1952-57, fin sec Sierra Leone 1957-61; jt dir Selection Trust 1975-80 (joined 1961), ret; conslt National Westminster Bank 1980-82; *Recreations* golf; *Clubs* United Oxford and Cambridge Univ, Knole Park Golf (Sevenoaks); *Style*— Alastair MacLeod-Smith, Esq, CMG; Roughetts Lodge, Coldharbour Lane, Hildenborough, Kent TN11 9JX (☎ 0732 833239)

McLINTOCK, (Charles) Alan; s of Charles Henry McLintock (d 1947), and Charlotte Alison, *née* Allan (d 1971); *b* 28 May 1925; *Educ* Rugby; *m* 1955, Sylvia Mary, da of George Foster Taylor (d 1968); 1 s, 3 da; *Career* CA; sr ptnr K M G Thomson McLintock 1982-87 (ptnr 1954-87); chm: Woolwich Equitable Building Soc, Ecclesiastical Insurance Group plc, Govett Atlantic Investment Trust plc, Govett Strategic Investment Trust plc, AJ's Family Restaurants Ltd; dir: M & G Group plc, Church Urban Fund; chm governing body Rugby Sch 1988- (vice chm 1984-88, memb 1973); memb Court Univ of London 1987-; *Recreations* music, family life; *Clubs* Army and Navy; *Style*— Alan McLintock, Esq; The Manor House, Westhall Hill, Burford, Oxon (☎ 099 382 2276); 74/78 Finsbury Pavement, London EC2A 1JD (☎ 071 638 3722)

McLINTOCK, Hon Mrs (Carla Ann); da of Adm of the Fleet Baron Hill-Norton, GCB (Life Peer); *b* 14 Nov 1943; *Educ* St Mary's Sch Calne; *m* 1, 1966, Christopher Thomas Jowett; 2 s; m 2, 1974, Thomson Graeme McLintock, MBE, s of Charles Henry McLintock, OBE (d 1946); *Style*— The Hon Mrs McLintock; Old Beith House, Milland, Liphook, Hampshire (☎ 042876 589)

McLINTOCK, Jean, Lady; Jean; da of late Robert Traven Donaldson Aitken, of Newcastle, New Brunswick, Canada; *m* 1929, Sir Thomson McLintock, 2 Bt (d 1953); *Style*— Jean, Lady McLintock; 38 Orrok Park, Edinburgh EH16 5UW

MCLINTOCK, Sir Michael William; 4 Bt (UK 1934), of Sanquhar, Co Dumfries; s of Sir William Traven McLintock, 3 Bt (d 1987); *b* 13 Aug 1958; *Style*— Sir Michael McLintock, Bt; 8 Grove Place, Dixons Hill Rd, Welham Green, Herts AL9 7DG

McLOUGHLIN, Kevin; *b* 17 July 1952; *Educ* Xaverian Coll, Univ of Sheffield (MA); *m* 16 Dec 1978, Sheila Mary McLoughlin; 1 s (Daniel b 27 July 1980), 1 da (Jessica b 14 Sept 1984); *Career* admitted slr 1978, memb Law Faculty Bd Univ of Sheffield, slr Dibb Lupton and Broomhead; *Style*— Kevin McLoughlin, Esq; 98 Riverdale Road, Ranmoor, Sheffield S10 3FD (☎ 0742 307350); Dibb Lupton Broomhead, Fountain Precinct, Balm Green, Sheffield S1 1RZ (☎ 0742 760351, telex 0742 547566, fax 0742 700568)

MCLUCAS, William Philip; s of James McLucas, of South Queensferry, and Jean Violet, *née* Stobie (d 1986); *b* 12 Feb 1955; *Educ* Daniel Stewarts Coll Edinburgh, Scottish Coll of Textiles Galashiels (SHND); *m* 25 March 1976, Blyth Agnes, da of late Thomas Russell McLaren; 1 s (James Thomas William b 19 June 1982), 1 da (Camilla Charlotte Blyth b 28 July 1984); *Career* investmt analyst Scottish Amicable Life Assurance Soc 1967-77, moneybroker UDISCO Brokers Ltd 1977-78, stockbroker Laurence Prust & Co (London) 1978-80, stockbroker Jackson Graham Moore & Ptnrs (Sydney) 1980-84, md Waverley Asset Management Ltd 1984-; memb: Assoc of Mining Analysts 1981, Scottish Young Business Group 1990-; *Recreations* skiing, sailing, travel; *Style*— William McLucas, Esq; Waverley Asset Management Limited, 13 Charlotte Square, Edinburgh EH2 4DJ (☎ 031 225 1551, fax 031 225 1550, portable 0836 638912)

McLURE, Donald Niven Allen; s of Alexander McLure (d 1934), and Helen Russell McLure; *b* 20 March 1926; *Educ* Dollar Acad, Brasenose Coll Oxford (MA); *m* 1956, Rosemary, da of James E Mardon (d 1973); 4 da; *Career* Capt RA (attached Indian Mountain Artillery) India 1943-47; dir: Beecham Group plc 1957-86, London Buses Ltd 1986-, United Distillers plc 1987-89; dep chm Wessex Water Authy 1986-; chm: Arthur Bell and Sons plc 1986-89, Int Laboratories Ltd 1986-89, European Brands Group Ltd 1988-, Burns Stewart Group Ltd 1988-; memb: Gen Advsy Cncl of Independent Broadcasting Authy 1986-, Cncl of Inc Soc of Br Advertisers 1976- (former pres); vice pres Propriety Assoc of GB 1981-; FInstM; *Clubs* Lansdowne; *Style*— Donald McLure, Esq; Woodpeckers, Alleyns Lane, Cookham Dean, Berks SL6 9AD

MACLURE, Sir John Robert Spencer; 4 Bt (UK 1898), of The Home, Whalley Range, nr Manchester, Co Palatine of Lancaster; s of Lt-Col Sir John Maclure, 3 Bt, OBE (d 1980), and Elspeth King, *née* Clark (d 1991); *b* 25 March 1934; *Educ* Winchester; *m* 26 Aug 1964, Jane Monica, da of late Rt Rev Thomas Savage, Bishop of Zululand and Swaziland; 4 s; *Heir* s, John Mark Maclure b 27 Aug 1965; *Career* 2 Lt KRRC 2 Bn BAOR 1953-55, Lt Royal Hants Airborne Regt TA; asst master Horris Hill 1955-66 and 1974-78; teacher: NZ 1967-70, St Edmund's Hindhead 1971-74; headmaster Croftinloan Sch 1978-; Dip IAPS; *Clubs* MCC, Royal and Ancient Golf, Royal Perth Golfing Soc; *Style*— Sir John Maclure, Bt; Croftinloan School, Pitlochry, Perthshire (☎ 0796 2057); Wild Goose Cottage, Gooseham, Morwenstow, Bude, N Cornwall (☎ 028883 584)

MACLURE, (John) Mark; s and h of Sir John Robert Spencer Maclure, 4 Bt, and Jane Monica, *née* Savage; *b* 27 Aug 1965; *Educ* Winchester; *Career* stockbroker; *Recreations* cricket, soccer, tennis, squash, shooting, swimming; *Clubs* Lansdowne; *Style*— Mark Maclure, Esq; 205 Queenstown Rd, Battersea, London SW8 (☎ 071 622 9660); Croftinloan, Pitlochry, Perthshire; Wild Goose Cottage, Gooseham, Morwenstow, Bude, N Cornwall

MACLURE, (John) Stuart; CBE (1982); s of Hugh Seton Maclure (d 1967), of Highgate, London, N6, and Berth Lea, *née* Hodge (d 1948); *b* 8 Aug 1926; *Educ* Highgate Sch, Christ's Coll Cambridge (MA); *m* 8 Sept 1951, (Constance) Mary, da of Alfred Ernest Butler, of Fulbrook, Burford, Oxon (d 1962); 1 s (Michael b 1952), 2 da (Mary b 1957, Clare b 1962); *Career* Sub Lt RNVR 1946-47; ed trainee The Times 1950, reporter The Times Educnl Supplement 1951-54; ed: Education 1954-69, The Times Educnl Supplement 1969-89; JRMT Distinguished visiting fell Policy Studies Inst 1989-90; hon fell: Sheffield Poly Westminster Coll, Coll of Preceptors; FRSA; *Books* Educational Documents England and Wales 1816 to present day (ed, 1965-86), A Hundred Years of London Education (1970), Educational Development and School Building 1945-1973 (1984), Education Re-Formed (1988); *Recreations* golf, bridge; *Clubs* MCC; *Style*— Stuart Maclure, Esq, CBE; 109 College Rd, Dulwich, London SE21 7HN (☎ 081 693 3286)

MCLYNN, Francis James (Frank); *b* 29 Aug 1941; *Educ* John Fisher Sch Purley, Wadham Coll Oxford (open scholar, BA, MA), UCL Inst of Latin American Studies (MA, PhD); *Career* author; asst dir Bogota and Colombia Br Cncl 1969-71 (joined 1968), Parry fell Buenos Aires Argentina 1971-72, Alistair Horne res fell St Anthony's Coll Oxford 1987-88, now full time author; books: France and The Jacobite Rising of 1745 (1981), The Jacobite Army in England (1983), The Jacobites (1985), Invasion: From The Armada To Hitler (1987), Charles Edward Stuart (1988), Crime and Punishment in Eighteenth Century England (1989), Stanley: The Making of An African Explorer (1989), Burton: Snow Upon The Desert (1990), Of No Country (1990), Stanley: Sorcerer's Apprentice (1991), From The Sierras To The Pampas (1991); Cheltenham prize for literature 1985; FRHistS 1987, FRGS (1987); *Style*— Frank McLynn, Esq; Andrew Lownie, 15-17 Heddon St, London W1R 7LF (☎ 071 734 1510, fax 071 287 5118)

McMAHON, Anthony Gordon; s of George John McMahon (d 1973), of London, and Ivy, *née* Butler (d 1952); *b* 29 June 1935; *Educ* Kilburn GS; *m* 27 Dec 1958, Gillian Margaret, da of Capt Albert Dockerill, of Stanstead Mountfitchett, Essex; 2 s (Sean b 1960, Christopher b 1964); *Career* Nat Serv RAF 1953-55; HM Dip Serv (former Foreign Serv) 1956-57, Ankara and Beirut 1958, Moscow 1959-60, Antwerp 1960, Br pro-consul Düsseldorf 1961-71, HM vice consul Karachi 1975-79, HM consul W Berlin 1979-82, first sec FCO 1982-85 (memb 1967-68 and 1971-74), HM consul gen Bilbao 1985-; *Recreations* cricket, tennis, flat racing; *Clubs* Fellowship; *Style*— Anthony McMahon, Esq; British Consulate-General, Alameda de Urquijo 2-8, 48008 Bilbao, Spain (☎ 010 344 415 7600, telex 32446 BRBIL E, fax 010 344 415 7632)

McMAHON, Sir Brian Patrick; 8 Bt (UK 1817); s of Sir (William) Patrick McMahon, 7 Bt (d 1977); *b* 9 June 1942; *Educ* Wellington, Wednesbury Tech Coll (BSc); *m* 1981, Kathleen Joan, da of late William Hopwood; *Heir* bro, Shaun Desmond McMahon; *Career* AIM; *Style*— Sir Brian McMahon, Bt; 157B Wokingham Road, Reading, Berks RG6 1LP

MACMAHON, Brian Sean; s of Gerard MacMahon (d 1962), of Dublin, and Mary, *née* Coughlan; *b* 3 April 1938; *Educ* Terenure Coll Dublin; *m* 1, 18 Sept 1961 (m dis 1977), Una Mary, da of Bernard Egan (d 1953), of Dublin; 2 s (Gerard b 1965, Cormac b 1967), 2 da (Cara b 1962, Niamh b 1964); m 2, 17 Dec 1983, Colleen Jean, da of Harry Harbottle, of Bristol; *Career* Irish Pensions Tst Dublin 1955-72, pension fund mangr Allied-Lyons Pension Fund 1973-82, gp pensions exec BET plc 1982-; memb cncl Pensions Mgmnt Inst 1981-85, vice chm Nat Assoc of Pension Funds 1989-90 (cncl memb 1983-); *Recreations* golf, cricket, theatre; *Clubs* Bristol and Clifton Golf; *Style*— Brian MacMahon, Esq; BET plc, Stratton House, Piccadilly, London W1X 6AS (☎ 071 629 8886, fax 071 499 5118, telex 299573 BETCL G)

McMAHON, Sir Christopher William (Kit); *b* 10 July 1927; *Educ* Melbourne GS, Univ of Melbourne, Magdalen Coll Oxford; *m* 1, 1956, Marion Kelso; 2 s; m 2, 1982, Alison Braimbridge; *Career* fell and economics tutor Magdalen Coll Oxford 1960-64; Bank of England: advsr 1964, advsr to the govrs 1966-70, exec dir 1970-80, dep govr 1980-86; Midland Bank plc: gp chief exec 1986-91, dep chm 1986-87, chm 1987-91; chm Midland Montagu Holdings; dir: Hong Kong and Shanghai Banking Corp 1987-, Eurotunnel 1987-; hon fell UCNW; FInstM; kt 1986; *Style*— Sir Kit McMahon; Midland Bank plc, Poultry, London EC2P 2BX (☎ 01 260 8000)

MacMAHON, Dr Douglas Graham; s of Kenneth Graham Macmahon (Sqdn Ldr), and Stella Miriam, *née* Coster; *b* 1 Jan 1951; *Educ* Latymer Upper Sch, King's Coll Hosp Univ of London (MB BS); *m* 5 Jan 1974, Pauline Angela, da of Roger Mitchell; 2 s (Richard Graham b 3 June 1978, Michael James b 18 May 1980); *Career* conslt physician (special responsibility for the elderly) 1979; special interests: the elderly, Parkinson's disease, strokes, diabetes; sr registrar John Radcliffe Hosp and Radcliffe Hosps Oxford, registrar Stoke Mandeville, sr house offr Portsmouth, house surgn Portsmouth, house physician King's Coll Hosp; memb Exec Ctee Br Geriatrics Soc, memb RCP Geriatrics Ctee; MRCS, LRCP 1973, MRCP 1976; *Books* Care of the Elderly (dep ed); *Style*— Dr Douglas MacMahon; Alma Manor, 66 Highertown, Truro, Cornwall TR1 3QD (☎ 0872 72260); Barncoose Hospital, Illogan Highway, Redruth, Cornwall TR15 3ER (☎ 0209 213021, fax 0209 212980)

McMAHON, Linda Ann; da of Richard Burtonshaw Martin, and Mary Ann Smith, *née* Paterson; *b* 12 June 1954; *m* 29 July 1989, Gerald John McMahon, s of James McMahon; *Career* fencer; memb Br Fencing Team 1977-; competitor Olympic Games: Moscow 1980, LA 1984, Seoul 1988; competitor 9 World Championships (finalist 1982), Bronze medallist Euro Championships 1983; Br Champion: 1976, 1982, 1983, 1985, 1987; memb Amateur Fencing Assoc; *Style*— Mrs Linda McMahon; 83 Perham Rd, London W14 9SP (☎ 071 385 7442, fax 071 381 6382, telex 8956058 CLPRG)

McMAHON, Shaun Desmond; s of Sir (William) Patrick McMahon, 7 Bt (d 1977); h to Btcy of bro, Sir Brian Patrick McMahon, 8 Bt; *b* 29 Oct 1945; *Educ* Wellington Coll; *m* 1971, Antonia Noel, da of Antony James Adie, of Rowington, Warwicks; *Style*— Shaun McMahon Esq; 28 Mathew Rd, Claremont, Cape Town, S Africa

MacMANAWAY, Maj (James) Peter Alexander; ERD (1943); s of Lt-Col Richard Thomas Ringwood MacManaway, OBE (d 1945), of 7 Warren Fields, Stanmore, Middx, and Zelma Norah Kathleen MacManaway (d 1985); *b* 26 Dec 1919; *Educ* Imperial Service Coll Windsor (now rejoined with Haileybury); *m* 3 Nov 1945, Joyce, da of Harold Tout Tilley (d 1940), of Haileybury, Purley Way, Purley, Surrey; 2 da (Rosemary b 30 Oct 1948, Heather b 18 March 1950); *Career* serv: BEF in France and Belgium, Dunkirk 1939-40, UK Counter Invasion Duties 1940-42, 1 Army N Africa, Italy and Austria 1942-48, UK 1948-50, Korea 1950-52, BAOR Germany 1952-55, Suez Operation 1956, UK 1957-59; Supplementary Cmmn 1938-44, Reg Cmmn 1944, promoted Major 1945; area mangr Planned Giving Ltd 1959-64, dir Joint Anglican Missionary Exhibition (Task 6) 1964-68, mktg and purchasing offr National Westminster Bank 1968-80, fin offr Trident Trust 1980-81, The Duke of Edinburgh's Award Int Head Office 1981-85; memb Dunkirk Veterans Assoc; Freeman City of London 1982, Liveryman Worshipful Co of Carmen 1982; King Leopold III; *Recreations* bowls & snooker; *Clubs* City Livery, Sion Coll (London), Drive Bowls (Hove), Past Rotarians (Hove & Brighton), The Hove, Hove Probus, Civic Soc (Hove); *Style*— Maj Peter MacManaway, ERD; 16 St Aubyns, Hove, E Sussex BN3 2TB (☎ 0273 29 289)

McMANNERS, Prof the Rev John; s of Rev Canon Joseph McManners (d 1975), and Ann Marshall (d 1979); *b* 25 Dec 1916; *Educ* Univ of Oxford (BA), Univ of Durham (Dip Theol), Univ of Oxford (D Litt); *m* 27 Dec 1951, Sarah Carruthers, da of George Errington (d 1956); 2 s (Joseph Hugh b 9 Dec 1952, Peter John b 9 Jan 1958), 2 da (Helen b 28 Feb 1955, Ann b 22 June 1961); *Career* WWII 2 Lt Royal Northumberland Fusiliers 1940; First Bn Royal Northumberland Fusiliers: platoon cdr, co second in cmd, adjutant; Maj GSO II 210 Br Liaison Unit (Greek Mission) 1943; fell and chaplain St Edmund Hall Oxford 1948-56, prof of hist Univ of Tasmania 1956-59, prof of european history Univ of Sydney 1959-66, professorial fell All Souls Coll Oxford 1965-66, prof of history Univ of Leicester 1967-72, Regius Prof of ecclesiastical history and Canon of Christchurch Univ of Oxford 1972-84, fell and chaplain All Souls Coll Oxford 1984-, directeur d'Études associé École Pratique des Hautes Études Paris 1980-81; Wolfson Literary prize 1981; tstee Nat Portrait Gallery 1970-78, Doctrine Commn of C of E 1978-82; Univ of Durham (D Litt 1984); fell Aust Acad of Humanities 1970, FRHistS 1956, FBA 1978; Offr of the Royal Order of King George I of the Hellenes; *Books* French Ecclesiastical Society under the Ancien Regime: a Study of Angers (1960), Lectures on European History 1789-1914: Men, Machines and Freedom (1966), The French Revolution and the Church (1969), Church and State in France 1870-1914 (1972), Death and The Enlightenment (1981), Oxford Illustrated History of Christianity (1990); *Recreations* tennis; *Style*— Prof the Rev John McManners; All Souls College, Oxford OX1 4AL (☎ 0865 279 368)

MCMANUS, Francis Joseph; s of Patrick McManus (d 1962), and Celia Mullen; *b* 16 Aug 1942; *Educ* Queen's Univ Belfast (BA, DipEd); *m* 11 Aug 1971, Carmel Veronica, da of Anthony Doherty (d 1977); 2 s (Ronan b 14 Feb 1978, Myles b 3 July 1984), 1

da (Emer b 2 Oct 1972); *Career* teacher; MP (Ind/Unity) Fermanagh and South Tyrone 1970-74, co-fndr Irish Independence Party 1977; slr Queens Univ Belfast 1978-; *Books* Ireland - The Future, Fermanagh Facts (jtly); *Style*— Francis McManus, Esq

MacMANUS, His Hon; John Leslie Edward; TD (1945), QC (1970); s of Edward Herbert MacManus (d 1979), of Hove, and Hilda Smith, *née* Colton (d 1962); *b* 7 April 1920; *Educ* Eastbourne Coll; *m* 18 July 1942, Gertrude Mary Frances (Trudy), da of Bernard Koppenhagen (d 1952); 2 da (Frances Mary Theresa b 6 July 1950, Georgina Anne b 6 Oct 1956); *Career* TA 1939, RA 1939-45, served M East, Italy, Crete, Yugoslavia, Maj 1945; called to Bar Middle Temple 1947, dep chm E Sussex QS Sessions 1965-71, co ct judge 1971, circuit judge 1972, ret 1990; *Recreations* gardening, travel; *Style*— His Hon John MacManus, TD, QC; c/o Circuit Administrator, South Eastern Circuit, 18 Maltravers St, London WC2R 3EU

McMANUS, Richard Brian; s of Michael Mansley McManus (d 1982), and Margaret, *née* Davison; *b* 15 March 1956; *Educ* Huddersfield New Coll, Jesus Coll Oxford (BA), INSEAD (MBA); *m* 9 Sept 1978 (m dis 1983), Susan Mary; *Career* mgmnt conslt: Proctor & Gamble 1977-80 (mktg), Johnson & Johnson 1980-82 (business devpt), INSEAD 1982-83 (MBA), BCG 1984-86; md: First Res 1987-, First Europe 1988-; *Recreations* skiing, cycling, theatre, travelling; *Clubs* Beaujolais, IOD; *Style*— Richard McManus, Esq; 44 Upham Pk Rd, Chiswick (☎ 081 994 1980); business: (☎ 081 747 4054, fax 081 747 3969)

McMASTER, Paul; s of Dr James McMaster (d 1987), of Liverpool, and Sarah Lynne McMaster; *b* 4 Jan 1943; *Educ* Liverpool Coll, Univ of Liverpool (M ChB), Univ of Cambridge (MA); *m* Aug 1969, Helen Ruth, da of Derek Bryce; 2 s (Michael Robert b 1971, Richard Benjamin b 1978), 1 da (Amanda Helen b 1974); *Career* conslt surgn; sr lectr dept of surgery Cambridge 1976-80, tutor Trinity Hall Cambridge 1978-80, dir transplant surgery Queen Elizabeth Hosp Univ of Birmingham 1980-; memb: Nat and Int Transplantation Soc, Euro Soc Organ Transplantation; FRCS 1970; *Style*— Paul McMaster, Esq; 13 St Agnes Road, Moseley, Birmingham B13 (☎ 021 449 5600); The Liver Unit, The Queen Elizabeth Hospital, University of Birmingham, Edgbaston, Birmingham (☎ 021 472 1311, fax 021 414 8133)

MCMASTER, Peter; s of Peter McMaster (d 1965), and Ada Nellie, *née* Williams (d 1966); *b* 22 Nov 1931; *Educ* Kelvinside Acad Glasgow, Royal Mil Coll of Sci Shrivenham; *m* 23 Dec 1955, Catherine Ann, da of William Rosborough (d 1968); 1 s (Peter), 1 da (Morag); *Career* Mil Serv: Royal Mil Acad Sandhurst 1950-52, RE 1952-70, ret Maj; called to the Bar Middle Temple 1969; dir gen Ordnance Survey 1985- (joined 1970); visiting prof Kingston Poly; memb Cncl Br Cartographic Soc; memb RGS, FRICS 1971, FIIM 1990; *Recreations* foreign travel, walking; *Style*— Peter McMaster, Esq; Hillhead, Stratton Rd, Winchester, Hampshire SO23 8JQ (☎ 0962 862684); Ordnance Survey, Romsey Rd, Maybush, Southampton, Hampshire SO9 4DH (☎ 0703 792559, fax 0703 792404, telex 477843)

McMASTER, Stanley; s of Fredwin Raymond McMaster, and Irene Maud, *née* Bunting; *b* 23 Sept 1926; *Educ* Campbell Coll Belfast, Trinity Coll Dublin (MA, BCom); *m* 25 March 1959, (Verda) Ruth, da of late R S Tynan, of Co Down, NI; 2 s (Robert b 25 Dec 1959, Patrick b 23 Aug 1965), 2 da (Caroline b 28 Dec 1960, Catherine b 30 Nov 1962 d 1968, Jane b 23 Oct 1968); *Career* called to the Bar Lincoln's Inn 1953, MP (UU) Belfast East 1959-74; various political and legal ctees; *Recreations* shooting, golf; *Style*— Stanley R McMaster, Esq; New Court, Temple, London EC4

MCMEEHAN, David Robert; s of Robert James McMeehan, and Ethel Doris, *née* Miller; *b* 21 April 1944; *Educ* ortsmouth GS, Portsmouth Poly (DipArch); *Career* architect specialising in design mgmnt and team leadership; various private practices (incl own) 1970-74; Property Services Agency Dept of the Environment: architect and project mangr 1975-86, advsr on briefing systems 1975-86, design team leader and supervising offices for a major special hospital redevpt 1978-86, project mangr Design Standards Office 1986; mangr design and construct Higgs and Hill plc 1986-88, ptnr Building Design Partnership 1988- (design team mangr Royal Opera House devpt, job mangr St Nicholas Centre Sutton); memb: Architects Registration Cncl UK, RIBA, Assoc of Project Mangrs; *Recreations* cross country skiing, aimless wandering, dodging squash balls; *Clubs* Nat Tst; *Style*— David McMeehan, Esq; 3 Sheepwalk Mews, The Ridgway, Wimbledon, London SW19 4QL (☎ 081 947 5369)

McMICHAEL, Prof Andrew James; s of Sir John McMichael, of 2 North Square, London, and Sybil Eleanor, *née* Blake (d 1965); *b* 8 Nov 1943; *Educ* St Paul's, Gonville and Caius Coll Cambridge (BA, MA), St Mary's Hosp Medical School (MB B Chir); *m* 12 Oct 1968, Kathryn Elizabeth, da of Capt Alexander Alfred Cross, MBE, of The Old Smithy Cottage, Whittonditch, Ramsbury, Wiltshire; 2 s (Hamish b 1973, Robert b 1982), 1 da (Fiona b 1971); *Career* MRC clinical res prof of immunology Nuffield Dept of Medicine Univ of Oxford 1982- (Wellcome sr fell in clinical science 1977-79, lectr 1979-82), fell Trinity Coll Oxford 1982-; memb: Scientific ctee Cancer Res Campaign 1986-88, Systems Bd MRC 1987-, AIDS steering ctee MRC 1988-; FRCP 1985; *Books* Monoclonal Antibodies in Clinical Medicine (ed 1981), Leucocyte Typing III, White Cell Differentiation Antigens (ed 1987); *Recreations* windsurfing, walking, reading; *Style*— Prof Andrew McMichael; Institute of Molecular Medicine, John Radcliffe Hospital, Oxford (☎ 0865 752336)

McMICHAEL, Sir John; s of James McMichael (d 1933), and Margaret, *née* Sproat; *b* 25 July 1904; *Educ* Kirkcudbright Acad, Univ of Edinburgh (MD); *m* 1, 1942, Sybil Eleanor (d 1965), da of Francis Blake; 4 s; m 2, 1965, Dr Sheila M Howarth, wid of Prof E P Sharpey-Schafer; *Career* emeritus prof of med Univ of London; served on: MRC 1949-53, Wellcome Trust 1960-77, Univ Grants Med Advsy Ctee 1964-72; dir British Post-grad Medical Federation 1966-71, chm Cncl British Heart Foundation 1966-72, pres World Congress of Cardiology 1970; FRS, FRCP, FRCPE; kt 1965; *Style*— Sir John McMichael; 2 North Square, London NW11 7AA (☎ 081 455 8731)

McMICHAEL, Hon Dr (Paquita Mary Joanna); *née* Florey; da of Baron Florey (Life Peer) (d 1968); *b* 26 Sept 1929; *m* 1955, John McMichael, s of Dr Gerald Joseph Wylde McMichael (d 1958), of 255 Woodstock Rd, Oxford, and Farchynys Fach, Bontddu, Merioneth; 2 s (1 decd); *Style*— The Hon Dr McMichael; 12 Craigleith Gdns, Edinburgh EH4 3JW

MCMICHAEL-PHILLIPS, (William) James; s of William James Phillips (d 1982), of Edinburgh, and Mary Jane, *née* Sneddon (d 1983); *b* 17 March 1934; *Educ* George Heriot's Sch Edinburgh; *m* 1, 12 Aug 1957, Fleming (d 1981), da of James Mckinnel McMichael (d 1982), of Lochmaben, Dumfriesshire; 2 s (Scott b 1961 d 1961, James b 1962), 1 da (Danielle b 1966); m 2, 4 Oct 1982, Laura Teresa, da of Valtiero Bertonesi, of La Spezia, Italy; *Career* cmmnd RA 1952-54, cmmnd RA (TA) 1954-57; dir 1969-72: John Newbould & Son Ltd Bradford, Arthur Davy & Son Ltd Sheffield, Sunblest Bakeries Ltd Sheffield; regnl gen mangr Associated Dairies Ltd Leeds 1972-78; currently dir: Sorbie Cheese Co Ltd (chm 1981-82 and 1985-86), Galloway Cheese Co Ltd, Associated Co-op Ltd, Southern Co-op Dairies Ltd, United Co-op Dairies Ltd; gp gen mangr Milk Group Co-op Wholesale Society Ltd, vice chm English Butter Marketing Co Ltd (chm 1988-89); vice pres EEC Advsy Ctee on Milk and Milk Products 1982-, pres Dairy Trade Fedn 1987-89 (vice pres 1982-91); MCIM 1960; *Recreations* badminton, reluctant gardener; *Style*— James McMichael-Phillips, Esq; Co-Operative Wholesale Soc Ltd, Milk Group, PO Box 53, New Century House, Manchester M60 4ES (☎ 061 834 1212, fax 061 832 0430, telex 667046)

McMICKING, Maj David John; LVO (1966); s of Maj-Gen Neil McMicking, CB, CBE, DSO, MC, DL (d 1963), of Eastferry, Dunkeld, Perthshire, and Margaret Winifred, *née* Landale (d 1989); *b* 29 April 1939; *Educ* Eton, RMA Sandhurst, Univ of Strathclyde (MSc); *m* 6 June 1970, Janetta Ellen Dorothea, da of Lt-Col Douglas Alwyn Charles Wood-Parker, OBE, DL (d 1968), of Keithick, Coupar Angus, Perthshire; 1 s (Alexander b 6 April 1981), 1 da (Susannah b 12 Jan 1978); *Career* cmmnd Black Watch 1960, Equerry to HM Queen Elizabeth The Queen Mother 1963-66, Adj Black Watch 1968-70, Staff Offr MOD 1970-72, Co Cdr Black Watch in Hong Kong 1972-73, ret 1973; business exec personnel John Menzies 1973-86, md Somerton Guns; life memb: Nat Tst for Scotland, Nat Arts Collection Fund, RSPB, Br Assoc for Shooting and Conversation, Scottish Wildlife Tst, Br Deer Soc; exec memb: Earl Haig Fund, Offrs Assoc Scotland; memb: Queens Bodygaurd for Scotland (Royal Co of Archers), Worshipful Co of Merchants of Edinburgh 1984, FBIM 1982, MIPM 1985; *Recreations* shooting; *Clubs* Whites, Pratts, New (Edinburgh); *Style*— Maj David McMicking, LVO; 10 Albert Terrace, Edinburgh EH10 5EA (☎ 031 447 6192); Needs, Alyth, Blairgowrie, Perthshire; Somerton Guns Ltd, West St, Somerton, Somerset TA11 7PS (☎ 0458 73732, fax 0458 72065)

MACMILLAN, Hon Adam Julian Robert; s of Viscount Macmillan of Ovenden (Rt Hon Maurice Macmillan, d 1984), and Katharine, Viscountess Macmillan of Ovenden, *qv*; *b* 21 April 1948; *Educ* Eton, Univ of Strasbourg; *m* 1982, Sarah Anne Mhuire, yr da of late Dr Brian MacGreevy, of London; 2 da (Sophia Elizabeth Katherine b 1985, Alice Charlotte Rose b 1987); *Style*— The Hon Adam Macmillan

MACMILLAN, Dr Alexander Ross; s of Donald Macmillan (d 1975), and Johanna, *née* Ross (d 1973); *b* 25 March 1922; *Educ* Tain Royal Acad; *m* 17 June 1961, Ursula Miriam, da of Edwin Grayson (d 1975); 2 s (David b 1964, Niall b 1966), 1 da (Alexandra b 1962); *Career* WWII Corpl RAF 1942-46 (despatches 1945); banker 1938-87; chief gen mangr Clydesdale Bank plc 1971-82 (dir 1974-87); dir: Caledonian Applied Technol plc 1982-87, Highland North Sea Ltd 1982-, Highland Deephaven 1982-, John Laing plc 1982-86, Radio Clyde plc 1982-, Scottish Development Finance Ltd 1982-, Martin Black plc 1983-85, Kelvin Technol Development 1984-, First Northern Corporate Finance Ltd 1983-87, Wilsons Garage Co (Argyll) Ltd 1987-, Wilsons Fuels Ltd 1987-, EFT Gp plc 1987-, Balmoral Gp Ltd 1988-, North of Scotland Radio Ltd 1989-, Nemoquest Ltd 1990-; chm Nat House Building Cncl (Scot) 1982-1988; dir HS of Glasgow 1979-, memb Court Univ of Glasgow 1980- (Hon Dr Univ of Glasgow 1989); FIB (Scot) 1942, CBIM 1980; *Recreations* golf; *Clubs* Killermont Glasgow; *Style*— Dr Alexander R Macmillan; 16 Ledcameroch Rd, Bearsden, Glasgow G61 4AB (☎ 041 942 6455, 041 943 0606)

McMILLAN, (William) Bill; s of Edward McMillan (d 1975), of Ayrshire, and Agnes Conway (d 1979); *b* 11 Jan 1929; *Educ* Ayr Acad, Royal Tech Coll, Univ of Glasgow; *m* 1, 26 Aug 1950 (m dis), Sheila Hallett; 2 s (Ian William b 1955, Neil David b 1960); m 2, Moira, da of Austin Damer; 1 da (Hannah Katy b 30 Nov 1988); *Career* joined Standard Telephones & Cables (ITT) 1955 as researcher (later press relations mangr), PR mangr Br Standards Inst 1963-65, princ scientific offr Miny of Technol 1965-68, mangr public affrs Assoc of Br Pharmaceutical Indust; dir of information: Chemical Indust Assoc 1973-83, UK Atomic Energy Authy 1983-88; sec gen Assoc Européenne des Producteurs d'Acides Gras (APAG) Brussels; *Books* numerous tech articles in New Scientist and elsewhere, The Role and Place of the Chemical Industry in Europe (cmmnd by UN 1982); FRSM; *Recreations* music, skiing; *Style*— Bill McMillan, Esq; 36 Hill House Close, Turners Hill, W Sussex RH10 4YY (☎ 0342 716315); APAG, 250 Avenue Louise, Bte 111, B-1050 Bruxelles (☎ 02 648 82 90)

MACMILLAN, Hon David Maurice Benjamin; s of Viscount Macmillan of Ovenden (Rt Hon Maurice Macmillan, d 1984), and Katharine, Viscountess Macmillan of Ovenden, *qv*; *b* 1957; *Educ* Harrow; *Clubs* Brooks, Turf; *Style*— The Hon David Macmillan; Flat 3, 12 Bramham Gardens, London SW5

McMILLAN, Rev Monsignor Donald Neil; s of Daniel McMillan (d 1942), and Mary Cameron, *née* Farrell (d 1951); *b* 21 May 1925; *Educ* St Brendan's Coll Bristol, Prior Park Coll Bath, Oscott Coll Sutton Coldfield; *Career* Army Chaplain 1951-81: BAOR 1961-63, 1966-68, 1975-77, Middle East 1956-59, 1968-70, E Africa 1961, Far East 1952-55, Princ RC Chaplain and Vicar Gen (Army) MOD 1977-81; ordained priest Diocese of Clifton 1948; curate: Bath 1948-49, Gloucester 1949-51, Taunton 1951; parish priest: St Augustine's Gloucester 1981-85, St Teresa's Bristol 1985-86, St Nicholas Winchcombe 1986-; Prelate of Honour 1977; *Recreations* walking, reading; *Clubs* Army and Navy, Challoner; *Style*— The Rev Monsignor Donald McMillan; St Nicholas Presbytery, Chandos St, Winchcombe, Glos GL54 5HX (☎ 0242 602412)

MACMILLAN, Dr (John) Duncan; s of Prof William Miller Macmillan (d 1974), and Mona Constance Mary, *née* Tweedie, of Dorchester on Thame, Oxon; *b* 7 March 1939; *Educ* Gordonstoun, Univ of St Andrews (MA), Univ of London (Academic Dip), Univ of Edinburgh (PhD); *m* 5 June 1971, Vivien Rosemary, da of Canon W T Hinkley, of Alnwick, Northumberland; 2 da (Christina Rachel b 1973, Annabel Kate b 1976); *Career* Dept of Fine Art Univ of Edinburgh: lectr 1974-83, sr lectr 1983-88, reader 1988-; curator Univ of Edinburgh Galleries & Collections 1988-; chm Scottish Soc for Art History, memb Euro Community Ctee for Cultural Cooperation, univ rep Scottish Museums Cncl, memb Univ Museums Gp; *Books* Gavin Scobie (1984), Painting in Scotland: The Golden Age (1986), Scottish Art 1460-1990 (1990); *Recreations* walking; *Style*— Dr Duncan Macmillan; 20 Nelson Street, Edinburgh, Scotland EH3 6LJ (☎ 031 556 7100); Talbot Rice Gallery, The University of Edinburgh, Old College, S Bridge, Edinburgh (☎ 031 667 1011, fax 031 667 7938, telex 27442 UNIVED P)

MACMILLAN, Sir (Alexander McGregor) Graham; s of James Orr Macmillan (d 1961), of Glasgow, and Sarah Dunsmuir, *née* Graham (d 1952); *b* 14 Sept 1920; *Educ* Hillhead HS Glasgow; *m* 1947, Christina Brash, da of Robert Brash Beveridge, of Glasgow; 2 s (Alistair b 1948, Donald b 1956), 2 da (Janie b 1950, Catriona b 1955); *Career* govr Leeds GS 1968-75, dir Scot Cons Pty 1975-84, dir M & P Financial Services 1984-88 (chm 1986-88), chm Mid Anglian Enterprise Agency 1986 (govr 1987, chm 1988); exec sec YorCan Communications Ltd 1989-; memb Tport Users' Consultative Ctee for Eastern England 1987-; kt 1983; *Recreations* fishing, watching cricket and rugby; *Clubs* St Stephen's Constitutional; *Style*— Sir Graham Macmillan; 46 Crown St, Bury St Edmunds, Suffolk IP33 1QX (☎ 0284 704443)

McMILLAN, Dr John Alexander; s of Col Alec McMillen (d 1989), and May, *née* Sowden (d 1983); *b* 10 Nov 1930; *Educ* King's Sch Canterbury, St Thomas' Hosp Univ of London (MB BS, DPath); *m* 1, 4 Sept 1954 (m dis 1972), Ann Latham, da of Clifford Braithwaite (d 1979); 2 s (Richard b 15 May 1958, David b 17 Aug 1961), 1 da (Margaret West b 10 Sept 1956); m 2, 19 Oct 1973, Joan Lilian, da of Percy Shave (d 1986); *Career* Capt RAMC 1957-60, lectr in pathology St Thomas Hosp London 1960-64, conslt Greenwich Dist Hosp 1964-68, coslt cytopathologist Portsmouth and SE Hants Health dist 1968-; MRCS, LRCP, FRCPath, BMA 1954, Assoc Clinical Pathologists 1960, BR Soc Clinical Cytology 1968; *Recreations* sailing, photography; *Clubs* Brading Haven Yacht, Cruising Assoc; *Style*— Dr John McMillan; 60 Somervell Drive, Fareham, Hampshire PO16 7QW (☎ 0329 234675); Queen Alexandra Hospital, Portsmouth, Hampshire PO6 3LY (☎ 0705 379451)

MacMILLAN, Sir Kenneth; *b* 11 Dec 1929; *m* 1974, Deborah Williams; *Career* choreographer; former dancer Royal Ballet; princ choreographer Royal Ballet 1977-; works incl: Romeo and Juliet, The Song of The Earth, Manon, Elite Syncopations, Mayerling, Gloria, Isadora; kt 1983; *Style*— Sir Kenneth MacMillan; c/o Royal Opera House, Covent Garden, London WC2

MACMILLAN, Marie Alpine; JP; da of William Jones (d 1987), of 30 Matheson Rd, Stornoway, and Mary Ann, *née* Maciver (d 1988); *b* 26 April 1924; *Educ* Hyndland Sch Glasgow, West of Scotland Commercial College; *m* 14 Aug 1947, Ian Macleod Macmillan, s of John Macmillan (d 1980); 1 s (Iain b 1948), 1 da (Moira (Mrs Cook) b 1950); *Career* memb Electricity Consulate Cncl 1974-; chm: Western Isles Health Bd 1979- (memb 1973-), Electricity Consultative Ctee; memb: Supplementary Benefit Appeals Tbnl, Nat Insurance Appeals Tbnl, Justices Ctee; *Recreations* reading, sewing; *Clubs* Royal Scottish Automobile Glasgow; *Style*— Mrs Marie Macmillan, JP; 22 Matheson Road, Stornoway, Isle of Lewis (☎ 0851 2760); Western Isles Health Board, South Beach St, Stornoway, Isle of Lewis

McMILLAN, Dr Nigel Charles; s of Ian McInnes McMillan (d 1980), and Joan Muriel McMillan, *née* Winchester; *b* 13 May 1950; *Educ* Loretto, Univ of Glasgow (MB ChB); *m* 24 March 1976, Linda Jean Douglas, da of Sqdn Ldr Archibald McDougall, of 2c, 2 Hutcheson Ct, Giffnock, Glasgow; 1 s (Christopher b 1978), 1 da (Lorna b 1981); *Career* GP S Glasgow 1976-78, conslt radiologist to Western Infirmary Glasgow 1983- (registrar then sr registrar in radiology 1978-83), conslt radiologist to Gartnavel Gen Hosp Glasgow 1983-; FRCR 1982; *Recreations* choral music, golf, skiing; *Style*— Dr Nigel McMillan; 5 Woodburn Road, Glasgow, Scotland G43 2TN (☎ 041 637 1441)

MACMILLAN, Roderick Alan Fitzjohn; s of John Armour Macmillan (d 1939), and Margery Babington O'Cock, *née* Hill (d 1975); *b* 2 May 1928; *Educ* Winchester, New Coll Oxford (MA); *m* 27 Sept 1952, Brenda Courtenay, da of Courtenay Walter Snook (d 1986); 2 s (Jeremy b 1957, Bruce b 1963), 1 da (Sally b 1954); *Career* RA 1946-48, 2 Lt 1947; elected memb Lloyds 1965, dir Leslie & Godwin (Underwriting) Ltd 1973-1985; active underwriter: Syndicate 80 1973-88, Syndicate 843 1977-86; dir RAF Macmillan & Co Ltd 1976-; chm Rickmansworth & West Hyde Branch Royal Br Legion 1986-; Liveryman Worshipful Co of Insurers 1982, Freeman Worshipful Co of Watermen and Lightermen 1989; ACII 1952, FIOD 1986; *Recreations* golf, rowing (Olympic Games 1952); *Clubs* City of London, Beaconsfield GC, Thames RC; *Style*— Roderick Macmillan, Esq; 14 The Readings, Chorleywood, Rickmansworth, Herts WD3 5SY; RAF Macmillan & Co Ltd; Octavian Group, 1 Aldgate EC3M 4BY (☎ 071 265 0071, fax 071 481 1631)

MACMILLAN, Rev William Boyd Robertson; s of Robert Macmillan (d 1953), and Annie Simpson, *née* Machattie (d 1989); *b* 3 July 1927; *Educ* Royal HS Edinburgh, Univ of Aberdeen (MA, BD); *m* 22 Aug 1962, Mary Adams Bisset, da of Donald Bisset Murray (d 1974); *Career* RN 1946-48; parish min: St Andrews Bo'ness 1955-60, Fyvie 1960-67, Bearsden (South) 1967-78, St Mary's Dundee 1978-; moderator Presbytery of Dumbarton 1976-77, convenor Bd of Practice and Procedure and convenor of Assembly Arrangements C of S 1984-88, chaplain in ordinary to HM the Queen in Scotland 1988-; moderator-designate Gen Assembly of the Church of Scotland (to take office May 1991); chaplain: Dundee DC, Guildry Incorpn of Dundee, HS of Dundee; sr chaplain Sea Cadet Corps; memb: Exec Cncl Scottish Veterans' Assoc, Scottish Church Soc, Church Serv Soc; Hon LLD Univ of Dundee 1990; *Recreations* golf, stamp collecting, reading; *Style*— The Rev William Macmillan; Manse of Dundee, 371 Blackness Rd, Dundee DD2 1ST, (☎ 0382 69406); Dundee Parish Church (St Mary's), Nethergate, Dundee DD1 4DG, (☎ 0382 26271)

MACMILLAN OF MACMILLAN AND KNAP, George Gordon; s of Gen Sir Gordon Holmes Alexander MacMillan, KCB, KCVO, CBE, DSO, MC (d 1986), of Finlaystone, Langbank, Renfrewshire, and Marian, *née* Blakiston-Houston, OBE; *b* 20 June 1930; *Educ* Eton, Trinity Coll Cambridge (MA), Univ of Strathclyde; *m* 2 Sept 1961, (Cecilia) Jane, da of Capt Arthur Rushworth Spurgin, IA (d 1934); 3 s (Arthur Gordon b 29 July 1962, Richard Anthony b 30 Dec 1963, d 1985, Malcolm James b 30 June 1967); *Career* teacher Wellington Coll 1953-63, lectr in religious knowledge Trinity Coll Toronto 1963-64, lectr in religious studies Bede Coll Durham 1965-74; currently self-employed and owner of small estate with historic house and garden open to the public; memb Cncl of Mgmnt Quarrier's Village Renfrewshire, elder Langbank Church of Scotland; *Recreations* garden-tending, making small structures; *Style*— George MacMillan of MacMillan and Knap; Finlaystone, Langbank, Renfrewshire PA14 6TJ (☎ 047 554 285)

MACMILLAN OF OVENDEN, Katherine, Viscountess of; Hon Dame Katharine Margaret Alice Macmillan; *née* Ormsby-Gore; DBE (1974); da of 4 Baron Harlech, KG, GCMG, PC (d 1964); *b* 4 Jan 1921; *m* 1942, Rt Hon Maurice Victor Macmillan, PC, MP, (Viscount Macmillan of Ovenden, d 1984), s of 1 Earl of Stockton, *qv*; 3 s (and 1 s decd), 1 da; *Career* vice-chm Cons Pty 1968-71; *Style*— Katharine, Viscountess Macmillan of Ovenden, DBE; 9 Warwick Sq, London SW1 (☎ 01 834 6004)

McMILLAN-SCOTT, Edward Hugh Christian; MEP (C) York 1984; s of Walter Theodore Robin McMillan-Scott, and Elizabeth Maud Derrington Hudson; *b* 15 Aug 1949; *Educ* Blackfriars Sch Llanarth Raglan Mon, Blackfriars Sch Laxton Corby, Exeter Tech Coll; *m* 1972, Henrietta Elizabeth Rumney, da of Richard Derrington Mogridge Hudson, of Bristol Avon; 2 da (Lucinda b 1973, Arabella b 1976); *Career* tour dir in Europe, Africa, USSR 1968-75; private exec then Parly conslt 1976-84, political advsr Falkland Islands Govt London Off 1983-; *Clubs* St Stephens Constitutional; *Style*— Edward McMillan-Scott, MEP; Wick House Farm, Wick, Pershore, Worcs WR10 3NU; European Parliament, 97 Rue Belliard, Brussels 1040, Belgium

McMINN, Alexander (Alex); JP (Merseyside 1972); s of William Edward Blanchard McMinn, and Sara, *née* Bird; *b* 12 Dec 1932; *Educ* Liverpool Collegiate Sch, Inst of Med Laboratory Sciences Liverpool Univ Centre; *m* 18 Aug 1956, Kathleen Frances, da of Arthur Rannard; 2 da (Helen b 1961, Fiona b 1964); *Career* princ lectr in med scis Liverpool Poly 1968-72; educn advsr: WHO Geneva 1972-84, UN Econ Cmmn for Europe 1984-85; exec dir Int Assoc for Med Scis 1982-88; chief exec: Health Manpower Servs Ltd 1984-88, Athena Trg Int 1988-; chm Vocational Guidance Assoc UK 1985-; dir: Diagnostic Servs Ltd and Copass Int Ltd 1984-, Merseyside Vocational Servs 1985-, Heriot Business Servs Ltd 1987-; hon sr lectr dept of int community health Liverpool Sch of Tropical Med 1985-, conslt in health care Univ of N Carolina USA, conslt in med educn for numerous govts and int orgns 1972-, cncl memb Univ Coll of Ajman UAE 1988-, educn and trg advsr St John's Ambulance Assoc; memb: tst Merseyside Christian Youth Camps 1970-, educn and trg ctee Merseyside Chamber of Trade 1986-; FRSM, MIBiol 1964, CBiol, fell Inst of Med Laboratory Scis 1955; Medal of the Cncl of Europe; *Books* Training Medical Laboratory Technicians (1975), Design of Competency Based Curricula for Health Workers (1984); *Recreations* watersports, playing organ; *Clubs* Athenaeum (Liverpool); *Style*— Dr Alex McMinn, JP; 10 St Bedes Close, Old Mill Hill, Ormskirk, Lancs; Athena Training International, Mast House, Derby Rd, Merseyside L20 1EA (☎ 051 933 6072, 051 944 1559, car 0836 251351, telex 626273 HERIOT G)

McMULLEN, Fergus John; s of John Christopher McMullen, of Westmill, nr Buntingford, Herts, and Cecily Rose, *née* Pearson-Rogers; *b* 2 Nov 1958; *Educ* Harrow, RAC Cirencester; *m* 4 Sept 1982, Clare Margaret, da of Maj Ivan Straker, of Edinburgh; 2 s (Rory James b 6 July 1985, Hugo George b 4 June 1987); *Career* sales and mktg exec The Hertford Brewery (family owned and run business); memb Br Field Sports Assoc; *Recreations* shooting, fishing, cricket, golf; *Style*— Fergus McMullen, Esq; Flint Cottage, Wendens Ambo, Saffron Walden, Essex CB11 4UL (☎ 0799 412 69); The Hertford Brewery, 26 Old Cross, Hertford, Herts (fax 0992 500 729)

McMULLEN, John Christopher; s of Capt O J G McMullen, of May St Farm House, Gt Chrishall, Herts, and Muriel Mary, *née* Chew (d 1979); *b* 16 Aug 1932; *Educ* Harrow; *m* Cecily Rose, da of Gp Capt H W Pearson-Roger, of The Lodge Tostock, New Bury St Edmunds, Suffolk; 2 s (James b 24 Oct 1956, Fergus b 2 Nov 1958); *Career* chm McMullen & Sons Ltd 1979-; High Sheriff Herts 1982-83; *Recreations* fishing, shooting, golf, classical; *Style*— John McMullen, Esq; McMullen & Soles Ltd, The Brewery, Herts (☎ 0992 584770, fax 0992 550757, car 0836 247693)

McMURRAY, Dr Cecil Hugh; s of Cecil Edwin McMurray, and Margaret Napier, *née* Smyth; *b* 19 Feb 1942; *Educ* Royal Belfast Academical Inst, Greenmount Agric Coll, Queen's Univ Belfast (BSc, BAgr), Univ of Bristol (PhD); *m* 3 Jan 1967, (Isabel) Ann, da of C A Stuart, of Belfast; 2 s (Alan, Trevor), 1 da (Rebecca); *Career* res fell Harvard Univ Cambridge Mass USA 1970-72, head of biochemistry Vet Res Labs Dept of Agric for NI 1972-84; joint appt as prof of food and agric chemistry Queens Univ Belfast and dep CSO Dept of Agric for NI 1985-88, CSO Dept of Agric for NI 1988-; assessor: AFRC, Priorities Bd for Agric and Food UK; memb Technol Bd for NI, tstee Agric Res Inst for NI; Salzburg fell 1983; FRSC 1981, FIFST 1987; *Publications* contrib: CIBA Fndn Symposia number 79 copper also number 101 Biology of Vitamin E, Trace Elements of Man and Domestic Animals Vol 5, and 6 Int Conference on Production Disease of Farm Animals, Selenium in Biology and Medicine; *Recreations* photography, walking; *Style*— Dr Cecil McMurray; 25 Sheridan Drive, Helen's Bay, Co Down, Northern Ireland BT19 1LB (☎ 0247 853655); Department of Agriculture for Northern Ireland, Dundonald House, Upper Newtownards Rd, Belfast BT4 3SB (☎ 0232 650111, fax 0232 656697, telex 74578 DEPAGR-G)

McMURRAY, David Bruce; CFM (1974); s of James McMurray, CBE (d 1950), and Kathleen Mary, *née* Goodwin; *b* 15 Dec 1937; *Educ* Loretto, Pembroke Coll Cambridge (BA, MA); *m* 25 Aug 1962, Antonia Alexandra, da of Lt Cdr A D S Murray (d 1988); 3 da (Georgina b 1963, Philippa b 1968, Suzannah b 1973); *Career* Nat Serv 1956-58, 2 Lt the Royal Scots 1957-58; asst master: Stowe Sch 1961; Fettes Coll: asst master 1964, head of English Dept 1968, house master 1972; headmaster: Loretto 1976, Oundle 1984-; memb Edinburgh Festival Cncl 1981-84; FRSA 1989; *Recreations* golf, diving, theatre; *Clubs* MCC, East India, Devonshire, Sports & Public Sch; *Style*— David McMurray, Esq, CFM; Cobthorne, West St, Oundle, Peterborough PE8 4ER (☎ 0832 272251); Oundle Sch, Oundle, Peterborough PE8 4EN (☎ 0832 273536 fax 0832 74448)

McMURTRIE, (Robert) Peter Lax; VRD; s of Donald Scott Anderson McMurtrie (d 1962), and Margaret Isobel Stratton McMurtrie (d 1962); *b* 24 March 1926; *Educ* Marlborough, St John's Coll Cambridge (MA); *m* 1953, Margaret Jane, da of Lt-Col Lancelot Edwin Lax Wright; 3 da; *Career* Lt Cdr RNVR 1943-46; md: Fractional HP Motors Ltd 1964-67, Hills (Patents) Ltd 1967-74, Southern Instrument Holdings 1974-76, Consumer & Video Holdings Ltd 1976-78; chm: Imhof-Bedco Standard Products Ltd, Imhof-Bedco Special Products Ltd 1976-82, I-B Precision Engineering Ltd 1978-82, Skinners (Electro-Platers) Ltd 1978-82, I-B Gerard SA (France) 1978-82; dir Plantation Holdings 1978-79, non exec dir Phicom Ltd 1982-87 (dir 1979-82); chm and chief exec offr: Elbar Industry plc 1983-85, Viewplan plc 1987-88; non exec dir Intergrad 1983-88, non exec chm Scientex Ltd 1986-87, non exec dir Interexec 1988-, non exec chm Munro Corporation 1989; vice chm Hertfordshire Cons, lay memb Slrs Disciplinary Tbnl Law Soc 1986-, dir Christian Children's Fund of GB 1987-; *Recreations* shooting, gardening, countryside; *Clubs* Naval; *Style*— R P L McMurtrie, Esq, VRD; St Ibbs Bush, nr Hitchin, Herts (☎ 0462 432146)

McMURTRIE, Gp Capt Richard Angus; DSO (1940), DFC (1940); s of Radburn Angus McMurtrie (d 1961), of Edinburgh, and Ethel Maud, *née* Wilkins (d 1927); *b* 14 Feb 1909; *Educ* Newcastle upon Tyne Royal GS, RAF Staff Coll, RN War Coll Greenwich; *m* 1, 2 Nov 1931, Gwenyth Mary (d 1958), da of Rev Herbert James Philpott (Lt-Col); m 2, 1963, Laura, da of William H Gerhardi, of Smolensk; *Career* 2 Lt 72 Bde RA (TA) Newcastle upon Tyne 1927-29, PO RAF No 2 FTS Digby 1930, No 2 AC Sqdn Manston 1931-32, Flying Offr 1932, No 442 Flight HMS Furious (later 822 Sqdn 1933-), RAF Cranwell (E & W Sch) 1933-35, Flt Lt 1935, Flying Boat Pilot's course RAF Calshot 1935-36 (No 201 Flying Boat Sqdn 1938), Sqdn Ldr Cmd No 2 Recruits Sub-depot RAF Linton-on-Ouse until 1939, 2 i/c No 269 (GR) Sqdn RAF Abbotsinch, WWII (despatches thrice), RAF Wick and Iceland, Wing Cdr i/c Sqdn 1940, HQ18 GP 1941, CO RAF Sumburgh 1942-43, Gp Capt 1942, Coastal Cmd 1943, Tport Cmd Air Miny Whitehall HQ 1944, Station Cdr RAF Stoney Cross Hants 1945, fndr No 61 Gp RAF Reserve Cmd 1946, Br Jt Servs Mission Washington DC 1946-49, Cmd Cardington 1949-52, HQ No 1 Gp RAF 1952-54, HQ Supreme Cmd Atlantic NATO 1954-56, HQ Coastal Cmd Northwood 1957-59, ret 1959; *Recreations* sailing; *Clubs* RAF Yacht (hon life memb), Royal Cornwall Yacht; *Style*— Gp Capt Richard A McMurtrie, DSO, DFC; Rose in Vale Farm, Constantine, Falmouth TR11 5PU (☎ 0326 40338)

MACNAB, Brig Sir Geoffrey Alex Colin; KCMG (1962, CMG 1955), CB (1951); s of late Brig-Gen Colin Macnab, CMG, and Beatrice Bliss; *b* 23 Dec 1899; *Educ* Wellington, RMC Sandhurst; *m* 1930, Norah Cramer-Roberts (d 1981); *Career* first cmmn Royal Sussex Regt 1919, instr Small Arms Sch Hythe 1925-28, Staff Coll Camberley 1930-31, Capt Argyll and Sutherland Highlanders 1931, GSO 3 WO 1933-35, BM 10 Inf Bde 1935-38, mil attaché Prague and Bucharest 1938-40, served WWII (despatches 1940), campaigns Western Desert, Greece, Crete, Brig 1944, mil mission Hungary 1945, DMI ME 1945-47, mil attaché Rome 1947-49, Paris 1949-54, Gold SO at coronation of HM Queen Elizabeth 1952, ret 1954; sec Govt Hospitality Fund 1957-68, local pres Royal Br Legion; *Clubs* MCC, Army and Navy; *Style*— Brig Sir Geoffrey Macnab, KCMG, CB; Stanford House, Stanford, Ashford, Kent (☎ 030 381 2118)

McNAB, John Stanley; s of Alice Mary, *née* Sawyers; *b* 23 Sept 1937; *m* 1, (m dis 1977), Carol; 2 da (Lesley Anne b 12 Oct 1965, Jacqueline Carol Davey b 19 July 1968); m 2, 30 Jan 1980, Jacqueline; *Career* Nat Serv RE 1956-58; Port of London Authority: joined as jr clerical offr 1954, various acountancy appts rising to docks accountant Upper Docks 1971, md PLA (Thames) Stevedoring Ltd (formerly Thames Stevedoring (1965) Ltd) 1973, dir Upper Docks 1974, exec dir manpower (formerly jt dir) 1978, dir docks ops 1982-83, dir Tilbury 1983-87; currently dir: Port of London Authy (chief exec Port of Tilbury) 1987-, Forty Two Berth Tilbury Ltd, 44 Berth Ltd, Tilbury Cargo Handling Ltd, Tilbury Grain Handling Ltd, Port of Tilbury Grain Handling Ltd, Port Documentation Services Ltd, Tilbury Plant Services Ltd, Tilbury Container Engineering Services Ltd; chm London Port Employers Assoc 1978-89, memb Nat Dock Lab Bd 1978-89; former memb: Exec and Mgmnt Ctees Nat Assoc of Port Employers, Nat Jt Cncl for Port Tport Indust; govt Thurrock Tech Coll (chm Fin and Gen Purposes Ctee); Freeman: City of London 1988, Worshipful Co of Watermen and Lightermen of the River Thames 1989; FCCA, MBIM; *Recreations* walking, swimming, tennis, DIY; *Style*— John McNab, Esq; Port of Tilbury, Leslie Ford House, Tilbury, Essex RM18 7EH (☎ 0375 852427, fax 0375 855106, telex 995170, car 0831 499837)

MACNAB, Hon Mrs (Sarah Margaret); da of 10 Lord Polwarth, TD; *b* 1944; *m* 1977, John Alexander Hamish Macnab of Barravorich; 2 da; *Style*— The Hon Mrs Macnab; 16 Cupar Rd, London SW11 4JW

MACNAB OF MACNAB, Hon Mrs (Diana Mary); *née* Anstruther-Gray; er da of Baron Kilmany, PC, MC, JP, DL (Life Peer d 1985), and Monica Helen Anstruther-Gray, OBE, JP, *née* Lambton (d 1985); *b* 16 June 1936; *m* 11 April 1959, James Charles Macnab of Macnab (The Macnab, *qv*); 2 s (James William Archibald b 1963, Geoffrey Charles b 1965), 2 da (Virginia Mary (Mrs Fyffe) b 1960, Katharine Monica b 1968); *Career* chm Scotland's Gardens Scheme; *Style*— The Hon Mrs Macnab of Macnab; West Kilmany House, Cupar, Fife KY15 4QW (☎ 082 624 247)

MACNAB OF MACNAB (THE MACNAB), James Charles Macnab of Macnab; 23 Chief of Clan Macnab; eldest s of Lt-Col James Alexander Macnabb, OBE, TD (d 1990, *de jure* 21 Chief), of Bramerton St, Chelsea, and his 1 w, Ursula, *née* Barnett (d 1979); suc great unc, Archibald Corrie Macnab of Macnab, CIE (*de facto* 22 Chief) 1970; *b* 14 April 1926; *Educ* Radley, Ashbury Coll Ottawa; *m* 11 April 1959, Hon Diana Mary Anstruther-Gray (*see* Hon Mrs Macnab of Macnab); 2 s, 2 da; *Heir* s, James William Archibald Macnab of Macnab, yr, b 22 March 1963; *Career* RAF 1944, Scots Gds 1944-45, Lt Seaforth Highlanders 1945-48, Capt Seaforth Highlanders (TA) 1960-64; asst then dep supt Fedn of Malaya Police 1948-57; mangr and owner Kimiel Estate and farms 1957-78, exec Hill Samuel Investment Services Ltd (Scot) 1982-; memb: Western Dist Cncl of Perthshire 1961-64, Perth and Kinross Jt County Cncl 1964-75, Central Regnl Cncl 1978-82; memb Royal Co of Archers (Queen's Bodyguard for Scotland); JP Perthshire 1968-75 and Stirling 1975-86; *Clubs* New (Edinburgh), Puffin's (Edinburgh); *Style*— The Macnab; West Kilmany House, Kilmany, Cupar, Fife KY15 4QW (☎ 082 624 247 and 527)

MACNAE, Dr John; s of John McNae (d 1962), of Straiton, Ayrshire, Scotland, and Agnes Smith McNae; *b* 20 April 1930; *Educ* Kirkcudbright Acad, Univ of Edinburgh (MB ChB); *m* 1, March 1965, Barbara Rose (d 1986), da of William Small; 1 s (Angus John b 30 Oct 1966), 1 da (Fiona Ruth b 22 Nov 1967); m 2, 6 Oct 1990, Kate, da of Mentz Darre Lodrup (d 1968), of Oslo, Norway; *Career* Nat Serv Capt to Maj RAMC 1954-56 (Suez Canal); Royal Infirmary Edinburgh: house surgn accident & emergency 1952-53, house surgn March 1953-Oct 1953; demonstrator in anatomy Univ of Edinburgh Oct 1953-Feb 1954, house surgn Longmore and Astley Ainslie Hosp Edinburgh 1956-57, registrar in plastic surgery Bangour Hosp Broxburn Edinburgh 1957-58, registrar in gen surgery Royal Infirmary Perth 1958-62, asst orthopaedic surgn Keighley Yorkshire 1962-70, gen practice Bingley Yorkshire 1971-72, conslt accident & emergency med The Accident Service Norfolk & Norwich Hosp 1972-90, memb Casualty Surgns Assoc, chm Int Trauma Fndn; *Style*— Dr John Macnae; The Coach House, Low Rd, Mettingham, Bungay, Suffolk NR35 1TP (☎ 0986 892216, fax 0986 895332); 79 Newmark Rd, Norwich, Norfolk NR2 2HW (☎ 0603 625959); 152 Harley St, London W1N 1HH (☎ 071 936 2477)

MACNAGHTEN, Angus Iain Jacques; s of Capt Angus Charles Rowley Stewart Macnaghten, Lt Black Watch (ka 1914); collateral branch of the Macnaghten Baronets of Bushmills House Co Antrim, and Hazel, *née* Irwin (d 1956); *b* 29 May 1914; *Educ* Eton, Trinity Coll Cambridge (BA); *m* 1 May 1957, Daphne (d 1984), da of Horace Nettleship Soper (d 1956); 1 adopted da (Fiona (Mrs Asquith) b 1962); *Career* served in Intelligence Corps 1940-46, Maj (despatches); Gold Staff Offr at Coronation of HM Queen Elizabeth II; served in British Cncl 1946-67; author; *Recreations* gardening, walking; *Style*— Angus Macnaghten, Esq; New Mile Cottage, Ascot, Berks SL5 7EX (☎ 0990 21081)

MACNAGHTEN, Magdalene, Lady; Magdalene; da of late Edmund Fisher; *m* 1926, Sir Antony Macnaghten, 10 Bt (d 1972); *Style*— Magdalene, Lady Macnaghten; Dundarave, Bushmills, Co Antrim

MACNAGHTEN, Sir Patrick Alexander; 11 Bt (UK 1836), of Bushmills House, Co Antrim; s of Sir Antony Macnaghten, 10 Bt (d 1972); *b* 24 Jan 1927; *Educ* Eton, Trinity Coll Cambridge; *m* 1955, Marianne, da of Dr Eric Schaefer, of Cambridge; 3 s; *Heir* s, Malcolm Francis Macnaghten; *Career* ret project mangr Cadbury Schweppes plc; *Style*— Sir Patrick Macnaghten, Bt; Dundarave, Bushmills, Co Antrim, NI BT57 8ST

MACNAGHTEN, Robin Donnelly; s of Sir Henry Pelham Wentworth Macnaghten (d 1949); *b* 3 Aug 1927; *Educ* Eton, King's Coll Cambridge; *m* 1961, Petronella Gertrude Anne Card; 2 adopted s, 1 adopted da; *Career* asst Mackinnon Mackenzie & Co Bombay 1949-54, house master Eton Coll 1965-74 (asst master 1954-65), headmaster Sherborne Sch 1974-88; author; *Recreations* gardening, walking; *Clubs* Royal Western India Turf; *Style*— Robin Macnaghten Esq; Prospect House, Tisbury, Wilts (☎ 0747 870355)

McNAIR, Archibald Alister Jourdan (Archie); s of Donald McNair (d 1975); *b* 16 Dec 1919; *Educ* Blundell's; *m* 1954, Catherine Alice Jane, da of John Fleming (d 1947), of Barraghcore, Kilkenny, Ireland; 1 s (Hamish Lindsay), 1 da (Camilla Margaret); *Career* chm: Mary Quant Group 1955-88, Thomas Jourdan plc 1971-88, TPI Corp plc 1988-90; dir City & Capital Hotels plc 1986-; *Recreations* fruit farming, chess, carving wood; *Clubs* Turf; *Style*— Archie McNair, Esq; c/o Coutts & Co, 440 Strand, London WC2N 5LJ

McNAIR, Douglas Fenn Wyndham; s of A W McNair, CSI, OBE (d 1965), and Elizabeth Eva Dawn, *née* Griffith (d 1965); *b* 29 Jan 1914; *Educ* Cheltenham, Christ's Coll Cambridge (MA); *m* 15 April 1944, Rosemary Dew, da of Capt A E Monro, RN (d 1958); 2 s (Duncan b 1945, Bruce b 1946), 2 da (Rosamund b 1952, Anne b 1956); *Career* F Perkins Ltd (diesel engine mfrs): joined 1935, service mangr 1946- 51, export sales dir 1951-60, dep mktg dir 1962-63; dir Perkins Outboard Motors Ltd and Perkins Gas Turbines 1960-62; Charles Churchill Ltd tube investmts 1963-76: md V L Churchill & Co Ltd, divnl dir T I machine tool div, chief exec tport serv equipment operation; MIEx 1955-62, CEng, MSAE, FIMechE 1964; *Recreations* classic car restoration and use; *Clubs* Caledonian; *Style*— Douglas McNair, Esq; Beaworthy House, Beaworthy, Devon EX21 5AB (☎ 0409 221 501)

McNAIR, 3 Baron (UK 1955); Duncan James McNair; s of 2 Baron McNair (d 1989); *b* 26 June 1947; *Educ* Bryanston; *m* ; 1 s (Hon Thomas John); *Heir* s, Hon Thomas John McNair; *Style*— The Rt Hon the Lord McNair; House of Lords, Westminster, London SW1

McNAIR, Prof Philip Murray Jourdan; s of Donald McNair (d 1975), of The Old Grammar Sch, Cirencester, Gloucs, and Janie Grace, *née* Jourdan (d 1970); *b* 22 Feb 1924; *Educ* Blundell's, Christ Church Oxford (MA, DPhil), Univ of Cambridge (PhD); *m* 3 Feb 1948, May, da of Arthur Thomas Aitken (d 1926), of Edinburgh; 1 da (Philippa (Pippa) b 1949); *Career* WWII 1942-48 Queen's Royal Regt, Claims Cmmn, RAEC; served: Italy, Austria, Belgium, Germany; lectr in Italian: Univ of Leeds 1954-61, Bedford Coll London 1961-63, Cambridge Univ 1963-74 (fell Darwin Coll 1965-74, dean Darwin Coll 1965-69, emeritus fell 1990-); visiting prof Univ of California (Berkeley) 1970, Serena prof and head of Dept of Italian Univ of Birmingham 1974-89 (emeritus prof 1989-), Barlow lectr on Dante Univ of London 1979; hon pres Birmingham Univ Christian Union 1980-89, church warden St John's Church Harborne Birmingham 1978-81 (elder 1978-88), lay chm Edgbaston Deanery Synod Diocese of Birmingham 1978-87, hon pres Dante Alighieri Soc (Birmingham) 1976-89, govr Malvern Coll 1977-86; *Books* Peter Martyr in Italy: An Anatomy of Apostasy (1967, Italian edn 1971); *Recreations* music, painting, foreign travel, gardening; *Style*— Prof Philip McNair; Linnett Hill, 213 Huntingdon Rd, Cambridge CB3 0DL

McNAIR, Hon William Samuel Angus; s of 2 Baron McNair (d 1989); *b* 1958; *Style*— The Hon William McNair

McNAIR SCOTT, Hon Mrs (Camilla Birgitta); *née* Davidson; da (twin) of 2 Viscount Davidson by 1 w; *b* 17 Feb 1963; *m* 14 May 1988, Simon Guthrie McNair Scott, *qv*, s of Thomas McNair Scott; *Style*— The Hon Mrs McNair Scott; 47 Winchester Street, London SW1V 4NY

McNAIR SCOTT, Simon Guthrie; s of Thomas Michael McNair Scott, of St Peter, Jersey, CI, and Susannah, *née* Hodges; *b* 12 May 1960; *Educ* Eton, Univ of Exeter (BA); *m* 14 May 1988, The Hon Camilla Birgitta McNair Scott, *née* Davidson, da of The Viscount Davidson, of Chichester, Sussex; *Career* film and TV freelance location mangr 1982-; film credits incl: Mona Lisa 1986, The Fourth Protocol 1986, Nightbreed 1989; TV credits inc: Porterhouse Blue 1987, Traffik 1989, Jeeves and Wooster 1990; *Recreations* golf, surfing; *Clubs* Lansdowne, Brooks's; *Style*— Simon McNair Scott, Esq; 47 Winchester St, London SW1V 4NY (☎ 071 828 2633)

McNAIR-WILSON, Sir (Robert) Michael Conal; MP (C) Newbury 1974-; s of Dr Robert McNair Wilson; bro of Sir Patrick McNair-Wilson, MP, *qv*; *b* 12 Oct 1930; *Educ* Eton; *m* 1974, Deidre Elizabeth, wid of Court Granville, and eldest da of Philip Debell Tuckett, of Ludbrook, Buckland Monachorum, Devon; 1 da; *Career* 2 Lt Royal Irish Fus 1948, serv Jordan, Suez Canal, Gibraltar; farmer Hants 1950-53; dir Sidney-Barton Ltd (public rels consltS) 1961-79, currently pub affrs conslt Shandwick Public Affairs; MP (C) Walthamstow E 1969-74, chm Cons Aviation Ctee 1972-74, dep chm All Pty Air Safety Gp 1979-, PPS to Min of Agric 1979-83, memb Select Ctee on Members' Interests, Educn Sci and the Arts; pres Nat Fedn of Kidney Patient Assoc 1989-; kt 1988; *Recreations* gardening, riding; *Style*— Sir Michael McNair-Wilson, MP; House of Commons, London SW1

McNAIR-WILSON, Patrick Michael Ernest David; MP (C) New Forest 1968-; s of Dr Robert McNair-Wilson, of Lyndhurst, Hants; bro of Sir (Robert) Michael McNair-Wilson, MP, *qv*; *b* 28 May 1929; *Educ* Eton; *m* 1953, Diana Evelyn Kitty Campbell, da of Hon Laurence Methuen-Campbell (d 1970, s of 3 Baron Methuen); 1 s, 4 da; *Career* conslt; MP (C) for Lewisham W 1964-66, PPS to Min for Tport Indust DOE 1970-74, oppn front bench spokesman on energy 1974-76, chm Jt Lords and Commons Select Ctee on Private Bill Procedure 1987-; kt 1989; *Recreations* pottery, photography; *Style*— Sir Patrick McNair-Wilson, MP; House of Commons, London SW1

McNALLY, Lt Cdr Gordon Louis; VRD; s of William McNally (d 1988), of Bexhill on Sea, Sussex, and Alice Lina, *née* Allbutt (d 1987); *b* 26 June 1924; *Educ* St Mary's Commercial Sch Hornsey; *m* 1, 4 Jan 1947 (m dis 1982), Marie Alice Doreen, *née* Upton; 2 s (Graham b 1947, Ross b 1958), 2 da (Alison b 1952, Heather b 1956); m 2, 31 May 1985, Sylvia Anne-Marie, da of Idris Henry Lowe, of Perth, W Aust; *Career* Lt Cdr RNVR and RNR 1943-71, served HM Ships N Sea, Atlantic, Pacific, Ceylon, organised repatriation Far E Allied POWs and internees; md Yuills Ltd 1965 (joined 1940, co sec 1954, md Exchange Travel subsid Yuills Ltd 1958); pioneered: tourism Malta Gibraltar and Cyprus 1960, lowering Aust NZ-UK air fares and formed ANZEFA which was first to charter Boeing 747 1965-67; chm Exchange Travel Group 1972, purchased Exchange Travel Group from Yuills Ltd 1972, pioneered franchising in travel industry 1984; memb Nat Cncl ABTA 1965-72; ind Parly candidate: Hastings and St Leonards 1979, Hastings and Rye 1983; fell Inst Travel and Tourism 1965, CBIM 1985; *Recreations* swimming, exotic horticulture, walking; *Style*— Lt Cdr Gordon McNally, VRD; Exchange Travel (Holdings) Ltd, Exchange House, Parker Rd, Hastings, E Sussex TN34 3UB (☎ 0424 423571, fax 0424 420515, telex 957153)

McNALLY, Jack Reginald Moore; MBE (1963), JP (Fife 1965); *b* 15 Dec 1916; *m* 1939, Lena; *Career* Lt Home Guard; author; engr Dental Mfg, Telephone Mfg Co; with Sunvic Controls Ltd, Electrothermal Engrg Ltd; md Beckman Instruments Ltd 1963-76 (chm 1976-80), dir Beckman Int Operations; chm: Beckman Instruments (Hldg) Ltd 1970-80, Scientific Documentation Centre Ltd 1960-, Vivian Industries Ltd 1960-, Triad Tech & Indust Servs Ltd 1980-, Kineticon Ltd 1983; memb: CBI (London) Regnl Devpt and Euro Ctee, Fife Region Health Bd 1975-85, Glenrothes Devpt Corpn Bd 1975-85; pastmaster Worshipful Co Scientific Inst Makers (London); Queen's Award to Industry (Export) 1975; FSCCM, FIWM, FBIM, FAEEE, FInstD, FRSA; *Clubs* City Livery, RAC; *Style*— Jack McNally, Esq, MBE, JP

McNALLY, Kevin Robert; s of Robert Gerard McNally, of Wedmore, Somerset, and Margaret June, *née* Spering; *b* 27 April 1956; *Educ* Central GS Birmingham, RADA (Ronson award, Bancroft award); ptnr Stevie Harris; 1 step s (Peter), 1 da (Rachel b 7 Nov 1988); *Career* actor; *theatre incl* Birmingham Repertory Theatre 1972-73, Not Quite Jerusalem and Prayer For My Daughter (Drama Sch, Royal Ct); NT 1979-80: Lark Rise, The Passion, Dispatches, The Iceman Cometh, Loose Ends (Hampstead Theatre), Pistols and Airbase (The Arts), Andromache (Old Vic), Scenes from an Execution (with Almeida Co); West End theatre incl: Extremities (Duchess), Glen Garry Glen Ross (Mermaid), Hidden Laughter (Vaudeville); *TV incl* for BBC: Commitments, Poldark, I Claudius, Duchess of Duke Street, Diana, This Air, Dream Baby, Tygo Read, The Common Pursuit; Bad Sister (Channel 4), Praying Mantis (Channel 4), A Brother's Tale (Granada), The Contract (YTV), The Paradise Run (Thames TV), Hard Cares (Central TV), Act of Will (Tyne Tees TV), Jekyll and Hyde (LWT); *films incl* The Spy Who Loved Me, The Long Good Friday, Inside Man, Enigma, The Antagonists, Not Quite Jerusalem, Berlin Affair, Cry Freedom, The Hangover; writes for TV under name Kevin Sperring with ptnr Bernard Dempsey; *Recreations* golf, Guinness and videoing the children; *Clubs* Carlton Snooker, Groucho's; *Style*— Kevin McNally, Esq; Eric L'Epine Smith & Carney, 10 Wyndham Place, London W1 (☎ 071 724 0739)

McNALLY, Peter Joseph Deane; s of Gp Capt Patrick John McNally, of Marlow, Bucks, and Mary Deane, *née* Outred; *b* 16 March 1933; *Educ* Stonyhurst; *m* 1, 1956 (m dis 1960), Mary B Gardiner; 1 da (Joanna b 1957); m 2, 3 March 1969, Edmée Maria, da of Egon Carmine del Sasso, of Estaplatz, Vienna, Austria; 2 s (Alexis b 1970, Markus b 1972); *Career* CA 1955-; exec dir: LWT (Holdings) plc 1976-, LWT 1972-; past dir Hutchinson Ltd and Independant TV Publications Ltd 1973-89; chm: Company of Designers plc 1987-, Arcadian Internationl plc 1986, The Listner Ltd; non-exec dir Claridge Group Ltd 1973-; underwriter at Lloyd's; FCA; *Recreations* fishing, shooting, skiing, tennis, bridge; *Clubs* RAC, Hurlingham; *Style*— Peter McNally, Esq; 1 Elthiron Rd, London SW6; Kent House, London SE1 (☎ 071 261 3148); Saxon Hall, Upper Lamborne, Berks

McNALLY, Thomas; s of John Patrick McNally (d 1982), and Elizabeth May McNally (d 1982); *b* 20 Feb 1943; *Educ* Coll of St Joseph Blackpool, UCL (BSc); *m* 1, 28 Aug 1970, Eileen Isobel, da of Thomas Powell, of Dumfries, Scot; m 2, Juliet, da of George Lamy Hutchinson, of Swansea, S Wales; 1 s (John b 15 June 1990); *Career* asst gen sec the Fabian Soc 1966-67, vice pres NUS 1966-67, int sec Lab Party HQ 1969-74 (researcher 1966-77); political advsr: to Foreign and Cwlth Sec 1974-76, to PM (head of Political office 10 Downing St) 1976-79; public affrs advsr to GEC, Pilkington, Granada Retailers; head of pub affrs Hill and Knowlton 1987; MP (Lab) for Stockport South 1979-83, memb Select Ctee Indust and Trade 1979-83, joined SDP 1981, ed exec Lib Democrats 1987-; *Recreations* watching sport, reading political biographies; *Style—* Thomas McNally, Esq; Hill and Knowlton, 5-11 Theobalds Rd, London WC1X 8SH (☎ 071 413 3050, fax 071 413 3113, telex 264100 HILNOL G)

MACNAMARA, James Justin (JJ); TD (1989); s of (Patrick) Carroll Macnamara, of Invercharron House, Ardgay, Sutherland, and Avril Thompson, *née* Thompson-Schwab; *b* 28 Oct 1956; *Educ* Stowe, New Coll Oxford (BA); *m* 6 July 1985, Baroness Marcelle Alpheda-Maria von Schoenberg, da of Baron Witold von Schoenberg, of Newhall House, Newhall, Naas, Co Kildare, Ireland; *Career* Lt The Royal Scots Dragoon Gds 1978-80, Capt HQ (Westminster Dragoons) Sqdn The Royal Yeo 1980-; asst mangr Price Waterhouse 1980-85; gp fin dir: Onslow Boyd Gp 1985-89, The SPS Consultancy Gp plc 1989-90, Reliance Security Services Ltd 1990-; Liveryman Worshipful Co of CAs in Eng and Wales; ACA 1983; *Recreations* TA, shooting, beagling; *Clubs* Cavalry & Gds, City of London; *Style—* JJ Macnamara, Esq, TD

McNAMARA, John Francis; s of Francis McNamara (d 1978), of Nolton, Lancs, and Olivia, *née* Whittingham (d 1982); *b* 18 July 1945; *Educ* Worsley-Wardley GS, Univ of Leeds; *m* 19 Dec 1981, Olwen, da of Richard Fellows, of Altrincham, Cheshire; 1 s (James Declan b 23 Oct 1983), 1 da (Katherine Jane b 16 March 1985); *Career* sr MO Br Nuclear Fuels Risley Nuclear Power Centre 1979-83, occupational health physician City of Salford 1983-87, conslt physician in occupational med Mersey RHA 1986-, conslt occupational physician to Cheshire Co Ambulance Serv; memb: BMA 1971, Soc of Occupational Med 1977, Chester and N Wales Med Soc 1986, Cncl Assoc of Nat Health Occupational Physicians 1986; LRCP 1970, MRCS 1970, MRCGP 1975, MRCP 1979 (collegiate memb London and Edinburgh 1979), MFOM (RCP) 1983; *Books* The patient with Respiratory Problems (contrib, 1989); *Recreations* bridge, swimming, walking, history, scripophily; *Style—* Dr John McNamara; Upway, Parkhill Road, Hale, Altrincham, Cheshire WA15 9JX (☎ 061 980 5054); Occupational Health Unit, Leighton Hospital, Crewe, Cheshire (☎ 0270 255141); Occupational Health Unit, Countess of Chester Hospital, Chester

McNAMARA, (Joseph) Kevin; MP (Lab) Hull North 1983-; s of Patrick McNamara, of Liverpool; *b* 5 Sept 1934; *Educ* St Mary's Coll Crosby, Hull Univ (LLB); *m* 1960, Nora, da of John Jones, of Warrington; 4 s, 1 da; *Career* former lectr in law Hull Coll of Commerce and head History Dept St Mary's GS Hull; MP: Hull North 1966-74, Kingston-upon-Hull Central 1974-83; sec of state for econ affrs 1967-69, PPS to min without portfolio 1969-70, chm PLP NI Gp 1974-79, oppn front bench spokesman Def and Disarmament 1982-87; shadow Sec of State for NI 1987; sec TGWU Parly Gp, vice pres League Against Cruel Sports; *Style—* Kevin McNamara Esq, MP; 145 Newland Park, Hull, East Yorkshire HU5 2DX (☎ 0482 448170)

McNAUGHT, His Hon Judge; John Graeme; s of Charles William McNaught (d 1955), and Isabella Mary McNaught (d 1969); *b* 21 Feb 1941; *Educ* King Edward VII Sch Sheffield, Queen's Coll Oxford (MA); *m* 1966, Barbara Mary, da of George Rufus Smith (d 1961); 2 s, 1 da; *Career* called to the Bar Gray's Inn 1963; in practise Western circuit, rec 1981-87, circuit judge 1987-; *Style—* His Hon Judge McNaught; Ryton Hse, Lechlade, Glos (☎ 0367 52286)

McNAUGHTAN, David Pringle; s of late James McNaughtan, of Glasgow, and Helen Duff, *née* Pringle; *b* 6 March 1950; *Educ* High Sch of Glasgow, Univ of Strathclyde (BA); *m* 26 June 1980, Anne Patricia, da of late Michael Joseph Harrington, of St John's Hosp, St John's Hill, London; 1 s (James Alexander b 1984), 1 da (Eleanor Rose b 1985); *Career* investmt banker: Deltec Securities (UK) Ltd 1981 (merged 1988), Deltec Banking Corporation Ltd 1986, May & Hassell plc 1985 (resigned 1986), Deltec Panamerican Trust Co Ltd 1988-; *Recreations* gardening; *Clubs* City of London, Travellers'; *Style—* David P McNaughtan, Esq; PO Box N-3229 Nassau, Bahamas (☎ 809 327 8071); Deltec House, PO Box N-3229 Lyford Cay-Nassau-Bahamas (☎ 809 362 4549, fax 809 362 4623)

MACNAUGHTON, Hon Mrs (Elizabeth Margaret); da of 3 Baron Wrenbury, and Penelope Sara Frances, *née* Fort; *b* 31 May 1964; *Educ* St Andrews Sch Eastbourne, St Leonards-Mayfield Sch Mayfield, UMIST; *m* 30 April 1988, Capt Andrew Murray Macnaughton, The Argyll and Sutherland Highlanders, elder s of R M Macnaughton, of Edinburgh; *Career* devpt scientist Corporate Res Div Amersham Int plc, transferred to Life Sciences Business Div 1989; *Recreations* reading, walking, country life, travel; *Style—* The Hon Mrs Macnaughton; Corner Cottage, 1 The Strand, Quainton, nr Aylesbury, Bucks HP22 4AS

McNAUGHTON, John Ewen; OBE (1985), JP; s of Alastair McNaughton (d 1968), and Anne Corries Campbell (d 1967); *b* 28 May 1933; *Educ* Cargilfield, Loretto; *m* 4 Sept 1956, Jananne Ogilvy, da of Lt-Col Percy Ewen Clunes Honeyman (d 1945); 2 s (Malcolm b 1957, Allan b 1959), 2 da (Carolyn b 1961, Fiona b 1964); *Career* farmer; memb: Panel of Agric Arbiters 1973-, Red Deer Cmmn 1975-, Br Wool Mktg Bd 1975-, Nat farmers Union of Scot, Scottish Agric Arbiters Assoc; chm: Scotch Quality Beef and Lamb Assoc 1981-, formerly of Nat Sheep Assoc; elder Church of Scot; FRAgS; *Recreations* yachting and stalking; *Clubs* Farmers'; *Style—* John McNaughton, Esq, OBE, JP; Inverlochlarig, Balquhidder, Lochearnhead, Perthshire FK19 8PH (☎ 087 74 232, Fax 087 74 695)

MacNAUGHTON, Hon Mrs (Liza Jane); *née* Pearson; da of 3 Viscount Cowdray; *b* 30 March 1942; *Educ* Cheltenham Ladies' Coll, Brondesbury-at-Stocks, Paris, Madrid, California State Univ Hayward (BA); *m* 1967, Malcolm MacNaughton; 1 s, 1 da; *Style—* The Hon Mrs MacNaughton; 1302 Canada Rd, Woodside, Calif 94062, USA

MACNAUGHTON, Sir Malcolm Campbell; KB (1986); s of James Hay Macnaughton (d 1951), and Mary Robieson, *née* Hogarth (d 1954); *b* 4 April 1925; *Educ* Glasgow Acad, Univ of Glasgow (MB ChB, MD); *m* 26 April 1955, Margaret-Ann, da of William Boyd Galt, of Glasgow; 2 s (Graham b 1958, Torquil b 1964), 3 da (Jane b 1960, Gillian b 1965, Jennifer (twin) b 1965); *Career* Capt RAMC 1949-51; lectr in obstetrics and gynaecology Univ of Aberdeen 1957-61, sr lectr Univ of St Andrews 1961-66, hon sr lectr Univ of Dundee 1966-69, prof emeritus and sr res fell Dept of Obstetrics and Gynaecology 1990- (Muirhead prof 1969-90); memb Warnock Ctee 1982-84, govr Glasgow Acad and Laurel Bank Sch; memb Incorportaion of Fleshers Glasgow 1944; LLD Univ of Dundee 1988; FRCOG (pres 1984-87), FRCP Glasgow, FRSE 1984; *Books* Combined Text Book of Obstetric Gynaecology (1976), Medical Gynaecology (1984); *Recreations* fishing, golf, walking; *Clubs* Glasgow Academical; *Style—* Sir Malcolm Macnaughton, KB, FRSE; 15 Boclair Road, Bearsden, Glasgow G61 2AF (☎ 041 942 1909); Department of Obstetrics & Gynaecology, Queen Elizabeth Building, 10 Alexandra Parade, Glasgow G31 2ER (☎ 041 552 3535)

McNAY, Michael George; s of Harold Edward McNay (d 1978), of Darlington, Co Durham, and Eleanora McNay, *née* Yanischek (d 1989); *b* 7 March 1935; *Educ* Lawrence Royal Mil Sch India, Queen Elizabeth GS Darlington Co Durham, Balliol Coll Oxford; *m* 1, 1957 (m dis 1972), Marian Alison Milne; 1 s (Ross b 1956), 1 da (Lois b 1963); m 2, 1974, Susan Pilkington; 1 da (Anna b 1979); *Career* reporter Bedfordshire Times 1958-62, sub ed Oxford Mail 1962-63; The Guardian 1963-: sub ed 1963, northern arts critic 1964-70, ed arts page 1970-75, dep features ed 1975-78, asst ed (i/c design) 1978-; *Books* East Malling: Portrait of a Kentish Village (1980), Red Guide to Kent (1989); *Recreations* cooking; *Style—* Michael McNay, Esq; The Guardian, 119 Farringdon Rd, London EC1R 3ER (☎ 071 278 2332)

MacNEACAIL OF MacNEACAIL AND SCORRYBREAC, Iain (formerly Ian Norman Carmichael Nicolson of Scorrybreac); Chief of the Highland Clan MacNeacail; recognised by the Lord Lyon in the name Iain MacNeacail of MacNeacail and Scorrybreac 18 May 1988; eldest s of late Norman Alexander Nicolson of Scorrybreac; *b* 19 June 1921; *Educ* Scotch Coll Tasmania; *m* 1946, Pamela Savigny, da of Philip Oakley Fysh; 1 s; *Heir* s, Philip John Lyne Nicolson; *Career* served WW II 1939-45; grazier and company dir; *Style—* Iain MacNeacail of MacNeacail and Scorrybreac; PO Box 420, Ballina, NSW 2478, Australia

MACNEAL, Alastair Rauthmell; s of Torquil Duncan Feracher Macneal, DL (d 1973), of Lossit, Machrihanish, Campbeltown, Argyll, and Joan Gladys, *née* Rauthmell (d 1986); *b* 28 June 1927; *Educ* Eton, Trinity Coll Oxford (MA); *m* 24 Sept 1960, Patricia Louise, da of Lt-Col John Kenneth MacFarlan, OBE, DL (d 1987), of East Hall Farm, Blackford, Nr Yeovil, Somerset; 1 s (Hector Lorne MacFarlan b 1961), 3 da (Mary Louise Loring b 1963, Ailsa Helen b 1967, Isla Tania (twin) b 1967); *Career* cmmnd 60 Rifles 1946-48, Maj TA Queen Victoria Rifles 1950-58; C T Bowring & Co: joined 1950, asst dir 1960, dir 1966; exec dir C T Bowring Charities Co 1968, dir English and American Insurance Co 1968; tstee Constable Fund HM Tower of London 1979-90; memb Lloyds 1953-; *Recreations* gardening, fishing, shooting; *Clubs* City University, Royal Green Jackets London; *Style—* Alastair Macneal, Esq; The Old Rectory, Compton Pauncefoot, Nr Yeovil, Somerset BA22 7EL (☎ 0963 40668)

McNEAL, Hon Mrs (Julia); da of Baroness Gaitskell (Life Peeress, d 1989); *b* 1939; *Educ* Somerville Coll Oxford; *m* 1969, George Peter McNeal; *Style—* The Hon Mrs McNeal; 35 Newstead Rd, London SE12

MCNEANY, Kevin Joseph; s of Bernard Joseph McNeany, of Keady, Co Armagh, and Mary Christina, *née* McDonnell; *b* 10 April 1943; *Educ* St Patricks Coll Armagh, Queens Univ Belfast (BA), Univ of London, Univ of Manchester; *m* 1 Aug 1968 (m dis 1985), Christine, da of Stephen McNulty; 2 s (Matthew Ciaron b 1970, Myles Anthony b 1986); *Career* teacher: St Pauls Sch Lurgan Co Armagh 1964-66, Corpus Christi Sch Leeds 1966-68; lectr: Kitson Coll Leeds 1968-70, Southport Tech Coll 1970-73, Wythenshawe Coll Manchester 1973-77; co-fndr (with Christine McNeany) 1972, md and chief exec Nord Anglia Education plc (formerly Nord-Anglia International) 1977-; *Recreations* walking, cycling, tennis; *Style—* Kevin McNeany, Esq; Ridge Park, 32 Bramhall Park Rd, Bramhall, Cheshire SK7 3JN (☎ 061 439 2563); 10 Eden Place, Cheadle, Cheshire SK8 1AT (☎ 061 491 4191, fax 061 491 4409)

McNEE, Sir David Blackstock; QPM (1975); s of John McNee; *b* 23 March 1925; *Educ* Woodside Sr Secdy Sch Glasgow; *m* 1952, Isabella Hopkins; 1 da; *Career* dep chief constable Dunbartonshire 1968-71; chief constable: Glasgow 1971-75, Strathclyde 1975-77; cmmr Metropolitan Police 1977-82; memb Air Safety Review Ctee Br Airways 1982-87, advsr to chm Br Airways 1982-87; dir: Clydesdale Bank 1982-, Fleet Holdings 1983-86, Trusthouse Forte 1983-, Control Technology (UK) Ltd 1986; chm: Integrated Security Systems 1985-90, Clyde Publishing Ltd 1987-89; non-exec chm Scottish Express Newspapers 1983-; pres: Nat Bible Soc of Scotland, Royal Life Saving Soc UK 1982-89; hon vice pres Boys' Bde, patron Scottish Motor Neurone Disease Assoc; Freeman City of London; FBIM; CStJ; kt 1978; *Clubs* Caledonian, Naval (life memb); *Style—* Sir David McNee, QPM; Scottish Express Newspapers, Park House, Park Circus Place, Glasgow 3

MACNEE, (Daniel) Patrick; s of Daniel Macnee (d 1952), of Lambourn, Berks, and Dorothea Mary Henry, BEM (d 1985, niece of 13 Earl of Huntingdon); *b* 6 Feb 1922; *Educ* Summerfields, Eton; *m* 1, Nov 1942 (m dis 1956), Barbara Douglas; 1 s (Rupert b 1947), 1 da (Jennifer b 1950); m 2, April 1965 (m dis 1968), Kate Woodville; m 3, Feb 1988, Baba Sekerley, *née* Majos de Nagyzsenye; *Career* served WWII 1942-46: Sub-Lt HMS Alfred (Offrs' Trg Sch nr Brighton) 1942, Royal Naval Coll Greenwich 1943,1 MTB Flotilla 1943, 1 Lt 1944, demobbed 1946; Long Service Medal, Atlantic Medal; actor; films incl: The Life and Death of Colonel Blimp 1942, Hamlet 1948, The Elusive Pimpernel 1950, Scrooge 1951, Battle of the River Plate 1956, Les Girls 1957, Incense for the Damned (US: Bloodsuckers) 1970, Mr Jericho 1970, Matt Helm 1975, King Solomon's Treasures 1976, Sherlock Holmes in New York 1976, Battlestar Galactia 1979, The Sea Wolves 1980, The Howling 1981, This is Spinal Tap 1983, A View to a Kill 1984, Shadey 1984, Waxworks 1988, The Chill Factor 1988, The Lobster Man From Mars 1988; TV incl: The Avengers 1960-69, Alfred Hitchcock presents, Dial M For Murder, Thriller, Columbo, For The Term of his Natural Life; over 150 stage appearances; Kinky Boots recorded with Honor Blackman 1964 (reached no 5 in the Top 40 singles Dec 1990); memb: Palm Springs Youth Centre, Palm Springs Opera Guild; Freedom of Filey Yorks 1962, Freedom of City of Macon Georgia 1985; Variety Club of GB Jt TV Personality of the Year Award (with Honor Blackman) 1963, Straw Hat Award (NY) 1975, Golden Camera Award (Berlin), Air Safety Award From the Administrator of the Federal Airway Administration (Washington DC); *Books* Blind In One Ear (autobiography) 1988; *Recreations* tennis, reading, conversing with friends, swimming, walking; *Style—* Patrick Macnee, Esq; Michael Whitehall Ltd, 125 Gloucester Rd, London SW7 4TE

McNEECE, John; s of Francis McNeece (d 1967), and Mary Frances, *née* Ferguson (d 1990); *b* 27 Oct 1939; *Educ* Glasgow Sch of Art (DA); *m* 1, 1964 (m dis), Margaret Josephine Fleming; 2 s (Adrian b 1965, Mark b 1968); m 2, 6 May 1980, Norma Margaret; *Career* interior designer to architects: Keppie Henderson & Ptnrs 1963-64, J L Gleave & Ptnrs 1964-65; currently chm John McNeece Ltd (ptnr and dir 1963-); nat design award Br Inst of Interior Designers 1988; memb Rotary club London; Freeman: City of London 1989, Worshipful Co of Gardeners 1989; FCSD 1970, FBID 1970; *Recreations* shooting, golf, swimming, music; *Clubs* Caledonian; *Style—* John McNeece, Esq; John McNeece Ltd, 2 Holford Yard, Cruickshank St, London WC1X 9HD (☎ 071 837 1225, fax 071 837 1233)

McNEIL, Lady; Barbara Jessie; da of Percy Stuart Turner (d 1944), and Laura Beatrice Cowley (d 1967); *b* 7 Jan 1915; *Educ* Wimbledon Sch; *m* 1939, Sir Hector McNeil, CBE (d 1978); 1 s, 1 da; *Career* fndr pres Motor Neurone Disease Assoc; *Recreations* gardening, tapestry, foreign languages; *Style—* Lady McNeil; Bramber, St George's Hill, Weybridge, Surrey (☎ 0932 848484)

MACNEIL OF BARRA, The; Ian Roderick Macneil of Barra; 46 Chief of Clan Macneil; s of Robert Lister Macneil of Barra, of Kisimul Castle, Isle of Barra (d 1970), and Kathleen Gertrude Metcalf Macneil (d 1933); *b* 20 June 1929; *Educ* Scarborough Sch, Vermont Univ (BA), Harvard Univ (LLB); *m* 1952, Nancy Carol, da of James Tilton Wilson, of Ottawa, Canada; 2 s, 1 da (and 1 s decd); *Heir* s, Roderick Macneil, yr of Barra b 1954; *Career* Lt US Army 1951-53, Army Res 1950-69; prof Cornell Law Sch Ithaca NY 1959-72 and 1974-76, visiting prof Faculty of Law Univ Coll Dar-es-Salaam Tanzania 1965-67, visiting prof of law Duke Univ 1970-71, prof of law and memb Centre For Advanced Studies Univ of Virginia 1972-74, Ingersoll prof of law Cornell 1976-80; visiting fell: Univ of Oxford 1979, Univ of Edinburgh 1978 (1979 and 1987); Wigmore prof of law Northwestern Univ 1980-, Braucher visiting prof of law Harvard Univ 1988-89; author; *Recreations* tennis; *Clubs* New; *Style—* The Macneil of

Barra; Kisimul Castle, Isle of Barra (☎ 087 14 300); 357 E Chicago Avenue, Chicago, Illinois 60611, USA

McNEILE, Hon Mrs (Henrietta Cecilia Imogen); da of 2 Viscount Ingleby; *b* 1961; *m* 27 Oct 1990, James J P McNeile, er s of Rory J McNeile, of Nonsuch, Bromham, Wilts; *Style*— The Hon Mrs McNeile

MACNEILE DIXON, Hon Mrs (Daphne Cecil Rosemary); da of 1 Baron Harmsworth (d 1948); *b* 1901; *m* 1, 14 March 1928 (m dis 1937), Capt Colin David Brodie; m 2, 12 May 1938, Lt-Col Harold Macneile Dixon, RASC; 2 da; *Style*— The Hon Mrs Macneile Dixon; Lagham Manor, South Godstone, Surrey

McNEILL, Cameron Alastair; s of Albert William McNeill, of Newbury, Berks, and Elizabeth, *née* Kelly; *b* 25 March 1958; *Educ* Christ's Hosp, Pembroke Coll Oxford (BA); *Career* dir: Barclays De Zoete Wedd Ltd 1986-89, Barclays De Zoete Wedd Capital Mkts Ltd 1986-89, Ebbgate Holdings Ltd 1986-89; md Oxford Tech Systems Ltd 1986- (dir 1983), exec dir Fuji International Finance Ltd 1991-; memb Ad Hoc Swaps Ctee Bank of Eng 1988-89; *Clubs* United Oxford and Cambridge Univ; *Style*— Cameron McNeill, Esq; c/o Messrs Druces and Attlee, Salisbury House, London Wall, London EC2M 5PS (☎ 071 638 9271)

McNEILL, Prof John; s of Thomas McNeill (d 1972), of Edinburgh, and Helen Lawrie, *née* Eagle (d 1984); *b* 15 Sept 1933; *Educ* George Heriot's Edinburgh, Univ of Edinburgh (BSc, PhD); *m* 1, 29 July 1961 (m dis 1990), Bridget Mariel, da of Paul Winterton; 2 s (Andrew Thomas b 1964, Douglas Paul b 1966); m 2, 6 April 1990, Dr Marilyn Lois James; *Career* asst lectr then lectr Dept of Agric Botany Univ of Reading 1957-61, lectr Dept of Botany Univ of Liverpool 1961-69, sr res sci biosystematics Res Inst Agric Canada Ottawa 1977-81 (res sci 1969-77), prof and chm Dept of Biology Univ of Ottawa Canada 1981-87, Regius Keeper Royal Botanic Garden Edinburgh 1987-89; dir Royal Ontario Museum Toronto Canada 1990- (assoc curatorial dir 1989-90); author of numerous sci papers and reports; pres: Biological Cncl of Canada 1986-87 (vice-pres 1984-86), Canadian Cncl of Univ Biology Chairmen 1984-85 (vice-pres 1983-84); exec memb Int Union of Biological Sci 1985-88, admin of fin Int Assoc of Plant Taxonomy 1987- (cncllr 1981-87); memb 15 sci socs; *Books* Phenetic and Phylogenetic Classification (ed with V H Heywood, 1964), Grasses of Ontario (with W G Dore, 1980), The Genus "Atriplex" in Canada (with I J Bassett et al, 1983), International Code of Botanical Nomenclature (adopted 1981, jt ed, 1983), International Code of Botanical Nomenclature (adopted 1987, jt ed, 1988), Preliminary Inventory of Canadian Weeds (with C W Crompton, A E Stahevitch and W A Wojtas, 1988); *Style*— Prof John McNeill; Royal Ontario Museum, 100 Queen's Park, Toronto, Ontario M5S 2C6, Canada (☎ 010 1 416 586 5639, fax 010 1 416 586 8044)

McNEILL, Maj-Gen John Malcolm; CB (1963), CBE (1959, MBE 1942); s of Brig-Gen Angus John McNeill, CB, CBE, DSO, TD (d 1950), of Acre, Palestine, and Lilian Vaughan Barron (later Findlay); *b* 22 Feb 1909; *Educ* Imperial Serv Coll Windsor, RMA Woolwich; *m* 24 Nov 1939, Helen Barbara Christine, da of Col C H Marsh, DSO; 2 da (Sheila b 1940, Jean b 1944); *Career* 2 Lt RA 1929; WWII served: Western Desert, Sicily, Italy, NW Europe, Burma; cmd 1 regt RHA 1948-51, student Imperial Def Coll 1952, dep sec Chiefs of Staff Ctee MOD 1953-55, cmd 2 Div RA 1955-58, cmdt Sch of Artillery 1959-60, Cdr Br Army Staff and mil attaché Washington DC 1960-63, Col Cmdt RA 1964-74, princ staff offr to Sec of State for Cwlth Rels 1964-69, ADC to HM the Queen 1958-60; *Recreations* field sports; *Clubs* Army and Navy, English Speaking Union; *Style*— Maj-Gen John McNeill, CB, CBE; Hole's Barn, Pilton, Shepton Mallet, Somerset BA4 4DF (☎ 074989 212)

McNEILL, Peter Grant Brass; s of William Arnott McNeill (d 1973), and Lillias Philips, *née* Scrimgeour (d 1980); *b* 3 March 1929; *Educ* Hillhead HS Glasgow, Morrison's Acad Crieff, Univ of Glasgow (MA, LLB, PhD); *m* 1959, Matilda Farquhar; 1 s (Angus), 3 da (Christian, Morag, Katrina); *Career* called to the Bar Scotland 1956; Hon Sheriff Substitute of Lanarkshire and of Stirling, Clackmannan and Dumbarton 1962, standing jr counsel to Scottish Devpt Dept (Highways) 1964, advocate depute 1964; Sheriff of: Lanarkshire (later Glasgow and Strathkelvin) at Glasgow 1965, Lothian and Borders at Edinburgh 1983; chm: Scottish Legal History Gp 1990-, Cncl Stair Soc 1990-; *Books* Balfour's Practices (ed, 1962-63), An Historical Atlas of Scotland c400-c1600 (jt ed, 1975), Adoption of Children in Scotland (2 edn, 1986); legal and historical articles in: Juridicial Review, Scots Law Times, Glasgow Herald, Encyclopaedia Britannica; *Recreations* legal history, gardening, bookbinding; *Style*— Dr Peter G B McNeill, QC; c/o Sheriff Court, Lawnmarket, Edinburgh EH1 2NS (☎ 031 226 7181)

McNEILLY, Dr (Robert) Henry; s of Maurice Knight McNeilly (d 1985), of Ballymena, Co Antrim, N Ireland, and Elizabeth, *née* Nevin; *b* 26 Jan 1940; *Educ* Ballymena Acad, Queens Univ of Belfast (MB BCh, BAO), Univ of London (MD, FFCM); *m* 30 May 1976, (Philippa) Jane, da of Douglas Quartley Watson, of The Corner, Thursley, Surrey; 1 s (James Henry b 1981), 1 da (Sarah Elizabeth b 1979); *Career* princ in gen practice 1967-71, postgrad student London 1971-73; community physician: NI 1973-75, Oxford RHA 1976-82; dir United Med Enterprises 1982-85, vice pres Nat Med Enterprise (Europe) 1985-86, dir Private Patients Plan Ltd 1986-; memb BMA; *Recreations* tennis, gardening, collecting; *Clubs* RAC; *Style*— Dr Henry McNeilly; PPP Medical Centre, 99 New Cavendish St, London W1 (☎ 071 637 8941, fax 071 636 7918)

MCNEISH, Prof Alexander Stewart; s of Dr Angus Stewart McNeish (d 1964), and Minnie Howieson, *née* Dickson; *b* 13 April 1938; *Educ* Glasgow Acad, Univ of Glasgow (MB ChB), Univ of Birmingham (MSc); *m* 4 March 1963, Joan Ralston, da of William Hamilton (d 1970); 2 s (Alistair Stewart b 1964, Iain Alexander b 1968), 1 da (Fiona Hamilton b 1966); *Career* fndn prof of child health Univ of Leicester 1976-80; Univ of Birmingham: Leonard Parsons prof of paediatrics and child health and dir Inst of Child Health 1980-' dean Faculty of Medicine and Dentistry 1987-; memb: GMC 1985-, Central Birmingham Health Authy 1987-91, pres Euro Soc for Paediatric Gastroenterology and Nutrition 1984-87; FRCP 1974, FRCP (Glas) 1981; *Recreations* golf, music, gardening; *Clubs* Athenaeum, Blackwell Golf, Southerness Golf; *Style*— Prof Alexander McNeish; 128 Westfield Rd, Edgbaston, Birmingham B15 3JQ (☎ 021 454 6081); Drumbuie, Kirkbean, Dumfries and Galloway; The Medical School, University of Birmingham, Vincent Drive, Birmingham B15 (☎ 021 414 4044)

McNICOL, Prof George Paul; s of Martin Wilkinson McNicol (d 1956), and Elizabeth Straiton, *née* Harper (d 1973); *b* 24 Sept 1929; *Educ* Hillhead HS Glasgow, Univ of Glasgow (MD, PhD); *m* 1959, Susan Moira, da of Gilbert Benjamin Ritchie (d 1969); 1 s, 2 da; *Career* hon conslt physician Makerere Univ Coll Med Sch Nairobi 1965-66, appts in Glasgow Teaching Hosps and Univ of Glasgow 1952-81, chm Bd Faculty of Med Univ of Leeds 1978-81, prof of med and hon consulting physician Leeds Gen Infirmary 1971-81, princ Univ of Aberdeen 1981-; memb Local Aberdeen Bd Bank of Scotland 1983-, chm of Govrs Rowett Res Inst 1981-; chm Med Advsy Ctee Ctee of Vice-Chllrs and Princs 1985- (memb Cncl 1989-); memb Ctee for Int Co-op in Higher Educn (CICHE) Br Cncl 1985-, memb Cncl Assoc of Cwlth Univs 1988-; Hon DSc Wabash Coll Indiana 1989; FRSE, FRSA, FRCP, FRCPG, FRCPE, FRCPath, Hon FACP; *Recreations* skiing, sailing; *Clubs* Caledonian, Athenaeum; *Style*— Prof George McNicol; Chanonry Lodge, 13 The Chanonry, Old Aberdeen AB2 1RP; Univ of Aberdeen, Regent Walk, Aberdeen AB9 1FX (☎ 0224 272134, fax 0224 488605, telex 73458 UNIABN G)

MACNICOL, Ian Duncan Robertson; s of Maj Duncan Cowan MacNicol (d 1969), and Ethel Margaret, *née* Blanch (d 1976); *b* 25 Aug 1943; *Educ* Fettes, Royal Agric Coll Cirencester; *m* 11 May 1974, Adel Jean, da of Richmond Noel Richmond-Watson, of Wakefield Lodge, Potterspury, Northants; 2 s (Charles b 1 Sept 1980, George b 9 Feb 1983), 2 da (Arabella b 24 Aug 1976, Catherine b 6 June 1978); *Career* current dir: GC & FC Knight Ltd, Yeovil Livestock Auctioneers, Dorchester Livestock Market, Barnham Broom plc, Raynham Workshops; former tstee Game Conservancy, former chm Norfolk branch CLA; currently: chm taxation ctee CLA (memb cncl), memb cncl Royal Agric Soc, chm bd govrs Astley Primary Sch, chm bd govrs Beeston Hall Sch, chm Stody Parish Cncl; FRICS; *Recreations* country pursuits; *Clubs* White's, Farmer's; *Style*— Ian MacNicol, Esq; Stody Lodge, Melton Constable, Norfolk NR24 2EW (☎ 0263 860 254); Stody Estate Office, Melton Constable, Norfolk (☎ 0263 860 572)

MacNICOL, Malcolm Fraser; s of Rev Robert (Roy) Simpson Macnicol (d 1986), of Edinburgh, and Eona Kathleen; *b* 18 March 1943; *m* 30 Sept 1972, Anne Morag; 2 s (Sean Malcolm Fraser b 1979, Calum Alexander Ruaridh b 1983), 1 da (Sarah Anne Marie b 1977); *Career* conslt orthopaedic surgn, sr lectr; treas: RCSE(d), Special Advsy Ctee in Orthopaedic Surgery; memb: Shaw Report team, Br Orthopaedic Assoc, Br Assoc for Surgery of the Knee; *Books* Basic Care of The Injured Hand (1984), Aid To Orthopaedics (1984), The Problem Knee (1986); *Recreations* tennis, squash, painting; *Clubs* Scottish Arts; *Style*— Malcolm Macnicol, Esq; 10 Bright's Crescent, Edinburgh EH9 2DD, Scotland (☎ 031 667 6609); Princess Margaret Rose, Orthopaedic Hosp, Edinburgh (☎ 031 445 4123)

MCNISH, Althea Marjorie; da of Joseph Claude McNish (d 1964), of Port of Spain, and Margaret Bourne (d 1977); *Educ* educated Port of Spain by father and others, London Coll of Printing (NDD (Special), Illustration prize), Central Sch of Art and Crafts, Royal Coll of Art (DesRCA); *m* 20 Aug 1969, John Saul Weiss, s of Woolf Weiss, of London; *Career* freelance designer 1957-; exhibitions incl: Inprint 1964-71, Design Cncl USA and Sweden 1969, London 1970 and 1975-80, USA 1972, Design-In (Amsterdam) 1972-74, The Way We Live Now (V & A London) 1978, Indigo Lille 1981-82, Cwlth Festival Art Exhibition (Brisbane) 1982, Designs for British Dress and Furnishing Fabrics (V & A London) 1986, Make or Break (Henry Moore Gallery London) 1986, Surtex NY 1987, Ascher (V & A London) 1987; commissioned by Ascher and Liberty's 1957, designs for mfrs worldwide 1957-; visiting lectr: Central Sch of Art and Crafts and other colls and polys 1960-, USA 1972, Italy, W Germany and Yugoslavia 1985-; advsy tutor furnishing and surface design London Coll of Furniture 1972-90, external assessor for educnl and professional bodies incl CSD and CNAA 1966-, memb jury for Leverhulme scholarships 1968; judge: Portuguese textile design competition Lisbon 1973, Living Design Awards 1974; Carnival Selection Panels Arts Cncl of GB 1982-83; designer: special features Daily Mail Ideal Home Exhibition 1966-78, for sec gen of the Cwlth 1975, bedlinen collection Courtaulds 1978, for BR Bd 1978-81, for London Office of High Cmmr of Trinidad and Tobago 1981, for Fede Cheti Milan 1987-, murals and hangings for passenger liners Nordic Empress 1990 and Monarch of The Seas 1991; advsr on exhibition design for Govt of Trinidad and Tobago Cwlth Inst 1982-84; memb: Bd Design Cncl 1974-81, Selection Panels for Design Awards and Design Index 1968-80, Selection Panel Jubilee Souvenir 1976 and Royal Wedding Souvenir 1981, CNAA Fashion and Textiles Design Bd 1975-78, Governing Body Portsmouth Coll of Art 1972-81, London Local Advsy Ctee IBA 1981-90, Formation Ctee ILEA London Inst 1985; CSD: assessor and examiner 1966-, vice pres 1977-78, memb Cncl and Ctees 1958-90; FCSD, FSIA 1968 (MSIA 1960); Chaconia Gold medal of the Repub of Trinidad and Tobago 1976; *Publications* textile designs produced in many countries 1957- and published in many jls and books incl: Decorative Art, Studio Books (1960, '61 and '62), Designers in Britain (1972), Did Britain Make It, Design Council (1986), Fabrics and Wallpapers (1986), Ascher (1987), Black Art Profiles (1991); *Recreations* skiing, travelling, music, gardening; *Clubs* Soroptimist; *Style*— Ms Althea McNish; 142 West Green Rd, London N15 5AD (☎ 081 800 1686)

MACNIVEN, Hugh Campbell; s of Hugh MacNiven, MBE (d 1960), of Glasgow, and Georgina May, *née* Fraser; *b* 24 April 1942; *Educ* Glasgow Acad, Univ of Glasgow (MA); *m* 2 May 1966, Jacqueline, da of Georges Stanislaus Suder; 2 da (Isabelle b 1970, Catriona b 1974); *Career* dir Butler Dennis & Garland Ltd 1976, md The Publicity Department 1981; FInstD; *Recreations* opera, book collecting; *Style*— Hugh MacNiven, Esq; 2 Fairfield Villas, Henrietta Road, Bath, Avon BA2 6LT (☎ 0225 466062); The Publicity Department, 2 Fairfield Villas, Henrietta Rd, Bath BA2 6LT (☎ 0225 466062, fax 0225 448708)

MACNULTY, Christine Avril; da of William Arthur Ralph (d 1975), of The Brook House, Egerton, Lancs, and Marjorie Holland, *née* Hale; *b* 22 April 1945; *Educ* Bolton Sch, Univ of London, George Washington Univ; *m* 26 Aug 1972, (William) Kirk MacNulty Jr, s of Brig-Gen William K MacNulty; *Career* systems analyst Plessey Radar Ltd 1967-69, sr memb staff International Research & Technology Corporation 1969-72, ptnr Many Futures 1972-76, conslt Progs Analysis Unit 1976-78, program mangr Europe Strategic Environment Centre SRI International 1978-82, conslt Int Res Inst on Social Change 1982-84; md Taylor Nelson Applied Futures 1984-88, chief exec Applied Futures Ltd 1988-; lectr: American Management Assoc, Univ of Bradford, Admin Staff Coll, Ashridge Management Coll, Brunel Univ, The Industl Soc; memb: Cncl The Fndn for Adaptation in Changing Environments, Inst for Transitional Dynamics; FRSA 1989; *Books* Industrial Applications of Technological Forecasting (jtly, 1971), The Future of the UK 2010 (jtly), author of numerous articles on scenario devpt, social change and forecasting; *Recreations* sailing, cooking, philosophy, psychology, comparative mythology; *Style*— Mrs Christine MacNulty; Yacht Kantele, Brighton Marina, Brighton, East Sussex BN2 5UF; Applied Futures Ltd, Windsor House, 83 Kingsway, London WC2B 6SD (☎ 071 242 0486, fax 071 242 0503)

McNULTY, Lady Sarah Lillian; *née* Lowry-Corry; da of 7 Earl Belmore (d 1960); *b* 31 March 1945; *Educ* Manor House Armagh N Ireland, Florence Italy; *m* 1979, Gary McNulty; *Style*— The Lady Sarah McNulty; 4131 County Rd 103, Carbondale, 81623 Colorado, USA

McPARTLIN, Sheriff Noel; s of Michael Joseph McPartlin, of Galashiels (d 1955), and Ann, *née* Dunn (d 1978); *b* 25 Dec 1939; *Educ* Galashiels Acad, Univ of Edinburgh (MA, LLB); *m* 10 July 1965, June Anderson, da of David Anderson Whitehead, of 14 Lennox Avenue, Stirling (d 1961); 3 s (Simon b 1970, Guy b 1972, Donald b 1982), 3 da (Alison b 1966, Diana b 1967, Julia b 1979); *Career* slr 1964-76, advocate 1976; Sheriff: Grampian Highland and Islands at Peterhead and Banff 1983-85, Elgin 1985-; *Recreations* country life; *Clubs* Elgin; *Style*— Sheriff McPartlin; Sheriff Court, Elgin

McPETRIE, Sir James Carnegie; KCMG (1966, CMG 1961), OBE (1953); s of James Duncan McPetrie (d 1948); *b* 29 June 1911; *Educ* Madras Coll St Andrews, St Andrews Univ (MA), Jesus Coll Oxford (MA); *m* 1941, Elizabeth Howie; 1 da; *Career* served WWII RA; called to the bar Middle Temple 1938; legal advsr: Colonial Off 1960-66, Cwlth Off 1966-68, Foreign and Cwlth Off 1968-71, ret; temp memb legal staff DOE 1972-75; chm UNESCO Appeals Bd 1973-79; *Style*— Sir James McPetrie, KCMG, OBE; 52 Main St, Strathkinness, St Andrews, Fife, Scotland KY16 9SA (☎

033 485235)

McPHAIL, Bruce Dugald; s of Dugald Ronald Macphail; *b* 1 May 1939; *Educ* Haileybury, Balliol Coll Oxford, Harvard Business Sch; *m* 1, 1963, Susan Mary (d 1975), da of late Col T Gregory, MC, TD; 3 s; m 2, 1983, Caroline Ruth Grimston, o da of Capt Tatlock Hubbard, MC, RA, and former w of David Dangar Henry Honywood Curtis-Bennett; *Career* dir Sterling Guarantee Tst 1969-74, md Town & City Properties Ltd 1976-; FCA; *Style—* Bruce McPhail, Esq; 13 West Heath Rd, London NW3 (☎ 071 435 9412)

MACPHAIL, Sheriff; Iain Duncan; QC (Scotland, 1989); s of Malcolm John Macphail (d 1988), of Edinburgh, and Mary Corbett Duncan (d 1973); *b* 24 Jan 1938; *Educ* George Watson's Coll, Univ of Edinburgh (MA), Univ of Glasgow (LLB); *m* 1970, Rosslyn Graham Lillias, da of Edward John Campbell Hewitt, TD, of Edinburgh; 1 s (David b 1973), 1 da (Melissa b 1977); *Career* admitted to Faculty of Advocates 1963, practising barr Scotland 1963-73, Faulds Fell in law Univ of Glasgow 1963-65; lectr in evidence and procedure: Univ of Strathclyde 1968-69, Univ of Edinburgh 1969-72; extra advocate-depute 1973; Sheriff of: Glasgow and Strathkelvin (formerly Lanarkshire) 1973-81, Tayside, Central and Fife at Dunfermline and Alloa 1981-82, Lothian and Borders at Linlithgow 1982-88, Edinburgh 1988-; memb: Scottish Law Cmmn 1990-, Assoc for the Study of Delinquency 1978-81; *Books* The Law of Evidence of Scotland (1979), Evidence (1987), Sheriff Court Practice (1988); *Recreations* music, theatre, reading, writing; *Clubs* New (Edinburgh); *Style—* Sheriff I D Macphail, QC; Scottish Law Commission, 140 Causewayside, Edinburgh EH9 1PR (☎ 031 6688 2131)

MACPHAIL, Ian Angus Shaw; s of Robert Shaw MacPhail (d 1938), and Edith Hadden (d 1968); *b* 11 March 1922; *Educ* Grays Sch of Art Aberdeen (Dip Graphic Design); *m* 1, 1943 (m dis 1948), Armorel Davie; 1 da (Diana); m 2, 12 March 1951, Michal Hambourg, da of Mark Hambourg; *Career* RAF 1940-43; Asst music controller ENSA 1944-46, asst music dir Arts Cncl 1946-52, publicity dir Dexion Ltd 1952-58, dir Greenway Advsy Serv 1958-60, PR conslt Brewers Soc 1960-61, DG World Wildlife Fund (UK) 1961-67, chief info offr Arthur Guinness Son & Co Ltd (conslt in communications) 1968-79; broadcaster BBC Far Eastern Serv, Euro co-ordinator Fund for Animal Welfare, govr Brathay Hall Tst; hon PR advsr: Fauna Preservation Soc, Nat Assoc for Gifted Children; former chm PR Ctee Royal Soc for the Prevention Accidents; ed: You and the Theatre, You and the Opera, English Music 1200-1750, Dexion Angle, Good Company, World Wildlife News; lectr to: publicity and Rotary Clubs, schs, tech colls, univs, HM Prisons and borstals, womens socs; graphic designer (responsible for prodn supervision of publicity): eight Coronation concerts at the Royal Festival Hall, third congress Int Assoc of Gerontology, jt metallurgical soc's meeting in Europe, house-style and literature World Wildlife Fund, first world conf on Gifted Children; Orden den Sol Cdr (Order of the Sun Peru) 1985, Kt Order of the Gold Ark (Netherlands); MSIA, FIPR 1970; *Books* You and the Orchestra (1948), Birdlife of Britain and Europe (1977); *Recreations* ornithology, music, poetry; *Clubs* Savile, Wig and Pen; *Style—* Ian MacPhail, Esq; 35 Boundary Rd, St John's Wood, London NW8 0JE (☎ 071 624 3535, telex 957 471 IFAW SXG, fax 071 624 9358)

McPHEE, George McBeth; s of late George Hugh McPhee, and Daisy, *née* Clyne; *b* 11 Nov 1937; *Educ* Woodside Sch, Royal Scot Acad of Music, Univ of Edinburgh (BMus); *m* 22 July 1961, Margaret Ann, da of Robert Scotland (d 1951); 1 s (Colin b 1964), 2 da (Catriona b 1966, Susan b 1969); *Career* asst organist St Giles' Cathedral Edinburgh 1959-63, dir of music Paisley Abbey 1963-, lectr in music Royal Scot Acad of Music and Drama 1963-; numerous performances, recordings, broadcasts and appearances; special commissioner Royal Sch of Church Music, examiner Assoc Bd Royal Schs of Music, chm Paisley Int Organ Festival; memb ISM 1965; *Recreations* golf; *Clubs* Royal Troon Golf; *Style—* George McPhee, Esq; 17 Main Road, Castlehead, Paisley PA2 6AJ (☎ 041 889 3528); Royal Scottish Academy of Music and Drama; 100 Renfrew St, Glasgow (☎ 041 332 4101)

MACPHERSON, Alexander Calderwood (Sandy); Sheriff (South Strathclyde Dumfries and Galloway at Hamilton, 1978); s of Alexander MacPherson (d 1982), and Jean McCulloch, *née* Calderwood; *b* 14 June 1939; *Educ* Glasgow Acad, Univ of Glasgow (MA, LLB); *m* 1963 (m dis 1985), Christine Isobel, *née* Hutchison; 2 s (Alan b 1965, Duncan b 1967); m 2, 1990, Marian Claire, *née* Hall; *Career* admitted slr 1962; in practice until 1978, pt/t asst Law Faculty Univ of Glasgow 1962-66, pt/t lectr Law Faculty Univ of Strathclyde 1966-78; chm Glasgow N and E branch Multiple Sclerosis Soc 1973-87; *Recreations* bagpipe playing, psychotherapy, the theatre; *Clubs* RSAC (Glasgow), Glasgow Art, Royal Scot Pipers' Soc; *Style—* Sheriff A C Macpherson; Hamilton Sheriff Court, Hamilton, Lanarks ML3 6AA (☎ 0698 282 957)

MACPHERSON, Hon Mrs (Alexandra Grace); *née* Baring; 2 da of 5 Baron Northbrook (d 1990); *b* 4 Feb 1957; *Educ* St Mary's Sch Wantage; *m* 1981, (Philip) Strone Stewart Macpherson, s of late Brig George Philip Stewart Macpherson, OBE, TD, of The Old Rectory, Aston Sandford, Bucks; 1 s (Philip Strone Alexander Stewart b 1985), 2 da (Temora Anne b 1988, Clementina Grace b 1989); *Style—* The Hon Mrs Macpherson; Woodmancott House, Woodmancott, nr Winchester, Hants SO21 3BN

MACPHERSON, Angus John; s of Lt Archibald Norman Macpherson, RN, of Commonwood, Bearsted, Kent, and Joan Margaret, *née* Backhouse; *b* 17 March 1953; *Educ* Stowe, Pembroke Coll Cambridge (MA); *m* 14 Aug 1982, Anne Louise Felicity, da of Capt Edward Morton Barford, of Lilac Cottage, Bowlhead Green, Godalming, Surrey; 1 s (William Archibald b 19 March 1988), 2 da (Eloise Isobel b 5 Jan 1985, Myrtle Maud b 30 Jan 1991); *Career* called to the Bar Inner Temple 1977, in practice SE circuit; *Recreations* tennis, Scottish history, cooking; *Clubs* Lansdowne; *Style—* Angus Macpherson, Esq; 44 Kyrle Rd, London SW11 (☎ 071 228 3816); 1 Harcourt Buildings, Temple, London EC4 (☎ 071 353 2214)

MACPHERSON, Archibald Ian Stewart; s of Sir (Thomas) Stewart Macpherson, CIE (d 1949), and Helen, *née* Cameron (d 1976); *b* 10 Aug 1913; *Educ* Edinburgh Acad, Fettes, Univ of Edinburgh (MB ChB, ChM, capt of rugby, cricket, fencing), Columbia Univ New York; *Career* RAMC 1942-47, Maj surgical specialist 1943-45, Lt-Col and offr i/c surgical div 31 BGH 1946, served in N Africa, Sicily, Italy, Austria, hon conslt surgn to Army in Scotland 1976-81; Univ of Edinburgh: Crichton res scholar 1940-42, clinical tutor 1940-42 and 1947-52, sr lectr 1954-78; Rockefeller fell Columbia Presbyterian New York 1948-49; conslt surgn: Royal Edinburgh Infirmary 1954-78, Royal Edinburgh Hosp 1954-78, Leith Hosp 1958-66; pres Vascular Surgical Soc 1976-77, vice pres RCSE 1976-79 (memb Cncl); Scot cricket int 1934-35; chm Clan Macpherson Assoc 1969-73 (currently hon vice pres), pres Graduates' Assoc Univ of Edinburgh 1972-75, chief Gaelic Soc of Inverness 1984-85; vice pres: Royal Celtic Soc, Clan Chattan Assoc; FRCSE 1940, FRSE 1962, memb Vascular Surgical Soc 1964, hon memb Surgical Res Soc; *Books* The Spleen (1973); *Recreations* golf, fishing, highland history; *Clubs* New (Edinburgh), Hon Company of Edinburgh Golfers; *Style—* Archibald Macpherson, Esq, FRSE; 18 Grange Terr, Edinburgh EH9 2LD (☎ 031 667 1169); Speyville, Newtonmore, Inverness-shire PH20 1AR (☎ 05403 224)

MACPHERSON, Donald Charles; s of Donald Hugh Macpherson (d 1947), of Calcutta, India, and Hilda Mary, *née* Pulley (d 1952); *b* 3 Jan 1932; *Educ* Winchester; *m* 3 May 1962, Hilary Claire, da of Lt-Col Norman Standish, MBE (d 1988), of Port Elizabeth, SA; *Career* Nat Serv 2 Lt Black Watch 1950-52; mangr Thomson & Balfour Ltd 1952-57, sr ptnr Fielding Newson Smith & Co 1985 (joined 1957, ptnr 1961), md County Nat West Ltd 1989 (exec dir 1986-89), dir Nat West Investment Bank 1989; *Recreations* collecting, ballet, opera; *Style—* Donald Macpherson, Esq; 28 Campden Hill Square, London W8 7JY (☎ 071 727 8292); County Nat West Ltd, 135 Bishopsgate, London EC2M 3UR (☎ 071 375 6189/90/91)

MACPHERSON, Ewen Cameron Stewart; s of G P S Macpherson (d 1981), and Elizabeth Margaret Cameron, *née* Smail; *b* 19 Jan 1942; *Educ* Fettes Coll Edinburgh, Queens' Coll Cambridge (MA), London Business Sch (MSc); *m* 1982, Laura Anne, da of 5 Baron Northbrook, *qv*; 2 s (James b 25 Oct 1983, George b 27 Nov 1985); *Career* rep Massey-Ferguson (Export) Ltd 1964-68, various appointments ICFC 1970-, dir 3i Group plc (Investors in Industry and subsids) 1989- (memb Exec Ctee 1985-); *Recreations* gardening, sailing, vintage motor cars; *Clubs* City of London, Caledonian; *Style—* Ewen Macpherson, Esq; The Old Rectory, Aston Sandford, nr Aylesbury, Bucks HP17 8LP (☎ 0822 291335); 91 Waterloo Rd, London SE1 8XP (☎ 071 928 3131, fax 071 928 0058)

MACPHERSON, (John Hannah) Forbes; CBE (1983); s of John Hannah Macpherson (d 1942), of Glasgow, and Anne Hicks, *née* Watson (d 1976); *b* 23 May 1926; *Educ* Glasgow Acad, Merchiston Castle Sch; *m* 1959, Margaret Graham, da of Robert Roxburgh (d 1957), of Glasgow; 1 s (John b 1972); *Career* Sub Lt RNVR 1943-47; apprentice chartered accountant Wilson Stirling & Co (subsequently Touche Ross & Co) 1947-49 (ptnr 1956), ret 1986; chm: Glasgow Jr C of C 1965, Scot Industl Estates Corp 1972, Irvine Devpt Corp 1976, Glasgow Opportunities Enterprise Tst 1983, Scot Mutual Assur Soc 1985, Glasgow Action 1985; pres Glasgow C of C 1980, dir TSB Gp plc 1985; chm: TSB Bank Scotland 1984, Scot Business in the Community 1985, Scot Met Property plc 1986; memb: Prince and Princess of Wales Hospice, Merchants House of Glasgow, The Scot Civic Tst; govr Merchiston Castle Sch 1988; OStJ 1980; *Recreations* travel, gardening, reading; *Clubs* East India, Western (Glasgow), RNVR (Scotland); *Style—* Forbes Macpherson, Esq, CBE; 16 Collylinn Rd, Bearsden, Glasgow G61 4PN (☎ 041 942 0042); TSB Bank Scotland plc, Henry Duncan House, 120 George St, Edinburgh EH2 4TS (☎ 031 225 4555)

MACPHERSON, Ian; s of William Rodger (ka 1940), and Isobel, *née* Laing (d 1976); *b* 25 March 1936; *Educ* Morrison's Acad Crieff; *m* 6 Aug 1960, Margaret (Greta); 1 s (Ian b 24 Aug 1969), 1 da (Karen b 20 Aug 1966); *Career* CA 1961, ptnr W Greenwell & Co 1967-73, dir various cos 1973-76, vice pres Mfrs Hanover Tst 1976-79, dep chief exec Br Linen Bank 1982-88 (dir 1979-88), chm and chief exec Watson & Philip plc 1989; non-exec chm: Low & Bonar PLC, Martin Currie Unit Trusts Ltd; non-exec dir: Amalgamated Foods Ltd, Securities Trust of Scotland Ltd; memb Ct Univ of Dundee; *Recreations* golf, reading, gardening; *Style—* Ian Macpherson, Esq; c/o Watson & Philip plc, Blackness Rd, Dundee DD1 9PU (☎ 0382 27501, fax 0382 22065)

MACPHERSON, Hon Ian David Patrick; s and h of 2 Baron Strathcarron; *b* 31 March 1949; *Style—* The Hon Ian Macpherson; 28 Hornton St, London W8 4NR (☎ 071 376 0130); Otterwood, Beaulieu, Hants SO42 7YS (☎ 0590 612334)

MACPHERSON, Prof Ian Richard; s of George Macpherson (d 1974), of Aberdeen, and Violet Alice Macpherson (d 1974); *b* 4 Jan 1934; *Educ* Aberdeen GS, Univ of Aberdeen (MA), Univ of Manchester (PhD); *m* 7 Aug 1959, Sheila Constance, da of Capt John Turner (d 1949), of Heaton Mersey; 2 s (David John b 21 Feb 1962, Peter Jeremy b 24 Jan 1964); *Career* temp lectr Univ of Manchester 1959-60; lectr Univ of Wales at Aberystwyth 1960-64; Univ of Durham: lectr 1964-72, sr lectr 1972-75, reader 1975-80, prof of Spanish 1980-; visiting prof Univ of Wisconsin Madison 1970-71; pres: Assoc of Hispanists of GB and I 1986-88, Br-Spanish Mixed Cmmn 1986-; corresponding memb The Hispanic Soc of America 1986; Comendador de la Orden de Isabel la Catolica Spain 1986; *Books* Juan Manuel; Libro de los estados (with R B Tate, 1974), Spanish Phonology: Descriptive and Historical (1975), Juan Manuel Studies (1975), The Manueline Succession: The Poetry of Don Juan Manuel II and Dom Joao Manuel (1979), Juan Manuel: A Selection (1980), Federico Garcia Lorca: Yerma (with Jacqueline Minett, 1987), The Age of the Catholic Monarchs 1474-1516: Literary Studies in Memory of Keith Whinnom (with Alan Deyermond, 1989); *Recreations* books, tennis, bridge, Europe; *Style—* Prof Ian Macpherson; Dept of Spanish and Italian, The University, Elvet Riverside, New Elvet, Durham DH1 3JT (☎ 091 374 2915, fax 091 374 3740)

McPHERSON, James Alexander Strachan; CBE (1982); s of Peter John McPherson (d 1953), and Jeannie Geddie, *née* Strachan (d 1969); *Educ* Banff Acad, Univ of Aberdeen (MA, BL, LLB); *m* 4 Aug 1960, Helen Marjorie, da of Capt Jack Perks, CBE, DSC (d 1973), of Kibworth, Beauchamp, Leics; 1 s (Ewan John b 1961), 1 da (Lesley Anne b 1963); *Career* Nat Serv cmmnd Lt RA 1952-54; sr ptnr Alexander George & Co slrs Macduff, memb Macduff Town Cncl and Banff CC 1958-75, convener Banff CC 1970-75, provost of Macduff 1972-75, chm Public Protection Ctee Grampian Regnl Cncl 1974-86 (memb Cncl 1974-90); Lord-Lt of Grampian Region 1987-, Hon Sheriff Grampian Highland and Islands at Banff 1972-; govr Scottish Police Coll 1974-86; memb: Grampian Health Bd 1974-82, Police Advsy Bd for S 1974-86, Post Office Users Nat Cncl for Scot 1976-80; FSAScot; *Recreations* reading, sailing, swimming; *Clubs* Town and County (Banff); *Style—* James McPherson, Esq, CBE; Dun Alastair, Macduff, Banffshire (☎ 0261 32377); 24 Shore St, Macduff, Banffshire (☎ 0261 32201, fax 0261 32350)

McPHERSON, Dr James Paton (Pat); OBE (1987); s of David Robb McPherson (d 1974), of Dundee, and Georgina Watt, *née* Dunbar (d 1969); *b* 9 July 1916; *Educ* Dundee HS; *m* 7 March 1942, Muriel Stewart, da of Stewart Finlay Anderson (d 1948), of Dundee; *Career* RAF Air Sea Rescue 1941-46; chm: Wright Health Group Ltd, Walter D Watt and Co Ltd, Drug Development (Scot) Ltd; dir: Abbey National Building Soc (Scottish bd) 1981-87, Dundee Indust Assoc; govr of fin and memb Ct Univ of Dundee, vice chm Tenorus Tayside; former pres Rotary Club of Dundee, memb Ctee The Malcolm Sargent Cancer Fund for Children (Dundee Ctee), memb Bobby Jones Memorial Tst; JP, Cmmr of Taxes; LLD Univ of Dundee 1986; MInstD; *Recreations* golf; *Clubs* Rosemount, Gleneagles Golf; *Style—* Dr Pat McPherson, OBE; Mylnfield House, Invergowrie, Dundee, Scotland DD2 5EH (☎ 082 622 360); Wright Health Group Ltd, Kingsway West, Dundee, Scotland DD2 3QD (☎ 0382 833 866, fax 0382 811 042, telex 76443)

MACPHERSON, Hon Mrs (Laura Anne); *née* Baring; eldest da of 5 Baron Northbrook (d 1990); *b* 12 June 1952; *m* 1982, Ewen Cameron Stewart Macpherson, eldest s of late Brig George Philip Stewart Macpherson, OBE, TD, of The Old Rectory, Aston Sandford, Bucks; 2 s (James Francis Stewart b 1983, George Malcolm Stewart b 1985); *Style—* The Hon Mrs Macpherson; The Old Rectory, Aston Sandford, nr Aylesbury, Bucks

MACPHERSON, Hon Mrs (Sarah Catherine); *née* Conolly-Carew; yr da of 6 Baron Carew, CBE; *b* 6 Nov 1944; *m* 5 March 1966, Ian Arthur Cluny Macpherson, s of late Maj Arthur Clarence Macpherson, of N Devon; 1 s, 2 da; *Style—* The Hon Mrs Macpherson; Bratton Farm, Chittlehampton, North Devon EX37 9QH (☎ 07694 231)

MACPHERSON, (Ronald) Thomas Stewart; CBE (1967), MC (1943, and 2 bars 1944 and 1945), TD (1960), DL (Gtr London 1972); 5 s of Sir (Thomas) Stewart Macpherson, CIE (d 1949), of Newtonmore, Inverness-shire, and Helen (d 1976), er da of Rev Archibald Borland Cameron, of Edinburgh; bro of 1 Baron Drumalbyn, cous of 15 Earl of Kinnoull and 2 Baron Strathcarron, *qqv*; *b* 4 Oct 1920; *Educ* Cargilfield, Fettes Coll, Trinity Coll Oxford (MA); *m* 1953, Jean Henrietta, yst da of David Butler-Wilson, of Alderley Edge, Cheshire; 2 s, 1 da; *Career* Queen's Own Cameron Highlanders 1939, cmmnd serv WWII: Scot Commando, parachutist (POW 1941-43), Maj 1943 (despatches); Mallinson-Denny Group 1980-82 (joined William Mallinson & Sons Ltd 1948, md Mallinson-Denny 1967-81); former chm cos in Aust and USA; dir: Transglobe Expedition Ltd 1976-83, Brooke Bond Group 1981-82, Birmid Qualcast plc 1982-88 (chm), Scot Mutual Assur Soc 1982-, NCB 1983-86, C H Industrials plc 1983-, Cosmopolitan Textile Co Ltd 1983- (chm); memb: Cncl CBI (past chm London and SE Region, memb Pres's City Advsy Bd), Ctee on Invisible Exports 1982-85, Scot Cncl for Devpt and Indust, Steering Bd Univ of Strathclyde 1980-85; chm: Cncl London C of C 1980-82 (vice pres 1982-), Allstate Reinsurance Co Ltd 1983-, Employment Conditions Abroad Ltd, Owl Creek Investments plc 1989-, Keller Group plc 1990-; memb Nat Employers Liaison Ctee for Vol Res Forces 1986; dir: New Scotland Insurance 1986-, TSB Scotland 1986-; chm Boustead plc 1986-, London advsr Sears Roebuck & Co 1984-, chm Assoc of British C of C 1986-88, memb Int Advsy Bd Bain & Co 1987-; govr Fettes Coll, pres Achilles Club 1981; memb Royal Co of Archers (Queen's Bodyguard for Scotland); High Sheriff Gtr London 1983-84; memb Worshipful Co of Dyers (Prime Warden 1985-86); Chev de la Légion d'Honneur, Croix de Guerre (2 palms and star); FRSA, FBIM; *Recreations* fishing, shooting, outdoor sport, squash, modern languages, Univ of Oxford and London Scot rugby player, Univ of Oxford and Mid-Surrey hockey player, Oxford blue athletics (and Scot Int); *Clubs* Hurlingham, MCC; *Style—* Thomas Macpherson, Esq, CBE, MC, TD, DL; 27 Archery Close, London W2 2PN (☎ 071 262 8487); Balavil, Kingussie, Inverness-shire (☎ 054 0661 470)

MACPHERSON-FLETCHER OF BALAVIL, Allan William; s of Rev John Fletcher (d 1990), of Edinburgh, and Elizabeth, *née* Stoddart (d 1966); nephew of Mrs H E Brewster-Macpherson of Balavil (d 1990); assumed additional surname of Macpherson 1990; *b* 27 July 1950; *Educ* Trinity Coll Glenalmond, Univ of Aberdeen (BSc); *m* 30 Oct 1976, Marjorie, da of George Daniel (d 1984), of Aberdeen; 1 s (James b 1979), 1 da (Elizabeth-Anne b 1978), 3 step s (Antony Sherlock b 1965, Michael Sherlock b 1966, Nicholas Sherlock b 1973); *Career* mangr McLaren Marine Queensland Aust 1973-75, proprietor Balavil Estate 1975-, dir Badenoch Land Mgmnt Ltd 1975-, mangr Bell-Ingram Sporting Dept 1987-89, sporting estate conslt Hamptons 1989-; dir Hamptons East Midlands Northern and Scottish region; dir and govr Butterstone Sch Hldgs Ltd 1988-; memb: Northern Meeting Soc, Scottish Landowners' Fedn, Game Conservancy, Kingussie Sheep Dog Trial Assoc; memb Lloyds 1983; *Recreations* shooting, stalking, fishing, skiing, sailing, travel, wine; *Clubs* The Highland; *Style—* Macpherson-Fletcher of Balavil; Balavil, Kingussie, Inverness-shire (☎ 0540 661 413); 10 Glencairn Crescent, Edinburgh; 13 Sandend, Portsoy, Banffshire; 6 Arlington St, St James's, London SW1 (☎ 071 493 8222, fax 071 491 3541)

MACPHERSON OF CLUNY (AND BLAIRGOWRIE), Hon Mr Justice; Hon Sir William Alan Macpherson of Cluny (Cluny Macpherson); TD (1965), QC (1971); 27 Chief of the Clan Macpherson; s of Brig Alan David Macpherson of Cluny-Macpherson, DSO, MC (d 1969), and Catherine Richardson Macpherson (d 1967); *b* 1 April 1926; *Educ* Wellington Coll, Trinity Coll Oxford (MA); *m* 27 Dec 1962, Sheila McDonald, da of Thomas Brodie (d 1979), of Edinburgh; 2 s (Alan Thomas b 8 Oct 1965, James Brodie b 5 June 1972), 1 da (Anne b 10 Nov 1963); *Heir* s, Alan Macpherson, yr of Cluny b 1965; *Career* Capt Scots Gds 1944-47, Lt-Col 21 SAS Regt (TA) 1962-65, Hon Col 21 SAS 1983-90; barr Inner Temple 1952, bencher 1978; Crown Ct rec 1971; judge of the High Ct of Justice (Queen's Bench Div) 1983; presiding judge Northern Circuit 1984-88; hon memb Northern Circuit 1987; memb Royal Co of Archers (Queen's Body Guard for Scotland) 1977, Brig 1989; govr Royal Scottish Corpn (vice pres 1989); pres London Scottish Football Club 1972-79; kt 1983; *Recreations* golf, fishing, rugby football; *Clubs* Caledonian, Special Forces, Highland Soc of London (pres 1991), London Scottish Football (pres 1972-79), Blairgowrie Golf, Denham Golf; *Style—* The Hon Mr Justice Macpherson of Cluny, TD, QC; Royal Courts of Justice, Strand, London WC2

MACPHERSON OF DRUMOCHTER, 2 Baron (UK 1951); (James) Gordon Macpherson; JP (Essex 1961); s of 1 Baron (d 1965), and Lucy (d 1984), da of Arthur Butcher; *b* 22 Jan 1924; *Educ* Wells House Malvern, Loretto; *m* 1, 1947, (Dorothy) Ruth (d 1974), da of Rev Henry Coulter (decd), of Bellahouston, Glasgow; (1 s decd), 2 da; m 2, 1975, Catherine Bridget, only da of Dr Desmond MacCarthy, of Brentwood; 1 s, 2 da (Hon Jennifer b 1976, Hon Anne b 1977); *Heir* s, Hon James Anthony Macpherson b 27 Feb 1979; *Career* served with RAF 1941-46; memb: Cncl of London C of C 1958, Exec Ctee of W India Ctee 1959 (dep chm 1971, chm 1973); fndr chm and patron Br Importers Confedn 1972-; chm Godron Macrobin (Insur) Ltd; chm and md of Macpherson, Train and Co Ltd, Food and Produce Importers and Exporters; chm A J Macpherson & Co Bankers; memb Cncl E Euro Trade Cncl 1969-72; chief Scottish Clans Assoc London 1972-74; Freeman: City of London 1969, Worshipful Co of Butchers 1969; memb Essex Magistrates' Cts Ctee 1974-75, dep chm Brentwood Bench 1972; govr Brentwood Sch 1970-, hon game warden for the Sudan 1974; landowner (10,000 acres grouse, deer and salmon, with 1000 farming); Fell Royal Entomological Soc, FZS, FRSA; *Recreations* shooting, fishing, orchids; *Clubs* Boodle's; *Style—* The Rt Hon the Lord Macpherson of Drumochter, JP; Kyllachy, Tomatin, Inverness-shire (☎ 08082 212); Macpherson House, 69-85 Old St, London EC1 (☎ 071 253 9311)

MACPHERSON OF PITMAIN, (Michael) Alastair Fox; 17 Sr Chieftain of Clan Macpherson; s of Stephen Marriott Fox (d 1971), of Surrey, and Margaret Gertude Macpherson of Pitmain; *b* 17 Dec 1944; *Educ* Haileybury, Magdalene Coll Cambridge (BA Law); *m* 10 June 1972, Penelope Margaret, da of Frederick William Birkmyre Harper (d 1977), of Oxon; 2 s (Alexander b 1976, Charles b 1980), 1 da (Isabella b 1973); *Heir* s, Alexander Macpherson, yr of Pitmain; *Career* admitted slr 1971; ptnr Ashurst Morris Crisp slrs of Broadwalk House 1974; non-exec dir: Smith & Nephew plc 1986-, Johnson Fry plc 1987-89, Thomas Jourdan plc 1987-; *Recreations* golf, cricket, fishing, ballet; *Clubs* Oxford and Cambridge, Hurlingham; *Style—* Alastair Macpherson of Pitmain, Esq; 58 Luttrell Ave, Putney, London SW15 6PE (☎ 071 788 1812); Achara House, Duror of Appin, Argyll (☎ 063 174 262)

MACPHIE, Maj-Gen Duncan Love; s of Donald Macphie (d 1967), of Glasgow, and Elizabeth Adam, *née* Gibson; *b* 15 Dec 1930; *Educ* Hutchesons' Sch Glasgow, Univ of Glasgow (MB ChB); *m* 11 July 1957, Isobel Mary (Mollie), da of Archibald James Jenkins (d 1985), of Stirling; 1 s (Ruary James b 26 March 1964), 2 da (Moruen Elizabeth b 29 May 1959, Catriona Mary b 24 Oct 1966); *Career* RMO TRS 1958-61, RMO 3RHA 1963-66, CO BMH Bharan and SMO British Gurkha L of C 1970-72, CO 24 Field Ambulance RAHC 1972-74, CO BMH Munster 1974-76, ADMS 4 Armoured Div 1976-80, ADG AMDI MOD 1980-83, CO QEMH Woolwich 1983-85, Chief Med Plans Branch SHAPE 1985-87, Cdr Med BAOR 1987-90, ret as Maj-Gen; QHS 1985-90; OStJ; BMA; *Recreations* gardening, reading, classical music, rugby - watching; *Style—* Maj-Gen Duncan Macphie; c/o The Royal Bank of Scotland, Kirkland House, Whitehall, London

MACPHIE, (Charles) Stewart; s of Charles Macphie (d 1970), and Hilda Gladys, *née* Marchant (d 1978); *b* 22 Sept 1929; *Educ* Rugby; *m* 12 April 1958, Elizabeth Margaret Jill, da of Charles George Michael Pearson (d 1977); 1 s (Alastair b 1961), 1 da (Fiona b 1959); *Career* chm Macphie of Glenbervie, dir Grampian Enterprise, former dir N of Scotland Hydro Electric Co; farmer; ptnr Glenbervie Home Farm; memb Scottish Cncl of CBI 1981-87, chm of govrs Oxenfoord Castle Sch Midlothian, govr Rowlett Res Inst, former chm Bakery and Allied Trades Assoc, former memb Cncl Food Mfrg Res Assoc Leatherhead; tstee Kincairdineshire Jubilee Tst, former pres of appeal Bakers Benevolent Assoc; *Recreations* estate management, travel, reading, theatre; *Clubs* New (Edinburgh), Caledonian; *Style—* Stewart Macphie, Esq; Glenbervie, Kincardineshire (☎ 056 94 226); Macphie of Glenbervie, Glenbervie, Kincardineshire (☎ 056 94 641, fax 05694 677, telex 73589)

McQUAID, Dr James; s of James McQuaid (d 1981), and Brigid, *née* McDonnell (d 1988); *b* 5 Nov 1939; *Educ* Christian Brothers Sch Dundalk, Univ Coll Dublin (BEng), Jesus Coll Cambridge (PhD), Nat Univ of Ireland (DSc); *m* 17 Feb 1968, Catherine Anne, da of Dr James John Hargan (d 1988), of Rotherham; 2 s (James Benedict b 1968, Martin Hargan b 1971), 1 da (Fiona Catherine b 1969); *Career* graduate engr apprentice Br Nylon Spinners Ltd 1961-63; Safety in Mines Res Estab: sr res fell 1966-68, sr sci offr 1968-72, princ sci offr 1972-78; dir Safety Engrg Laboratory 1980-85 (dep dir 1978-80), res dir Health and Safety Exec 1985-; CEng, MIMechE 1972, FIMinE 1986; *Recreations* model engineering, ornamental turning, industrial archaeology; *Clubs* Athenaeum; *Style—* Dr James McQuaid; 61 Pingle Rd, Sheffield, S Yorks S7 2LL (☎ 0742 365349); Health and Safety Executive, Broad Lane, Sheffield, S Yorks S3 7HQ (☎ 0742 768141)

MACQUAKER, Donald Francis; CBE (1991); s of Thomas Mason Macquaker (d 1979), of Brae of Auchendrane by Ayr, and Caroline Bertha Floris Macquaker (d 1983); (gf Sir Thomas, fndr Royal Samaritan Hosp for Women Glasgow); *b* 21 Sept 1932; *Educ* Winchester, Trinity Coll Oxford (MA), Univ of Glasgow (LLB); *m* 9 Jan 1964, Susan Elizabeth, da of William Archibald Kay Finlayson (d 1969); 1 da (Diana b 1965), 1 s (Charles b 1968); *Career* farmer, landowner and slr; ptnr T C Young & Son Glasgow 1957-; memb (later vice chm) bd of mgmnt Royal Maternity Hosp 1965-74; chm: Gtr Glasgow Health Bd 1983-87 (convenor Fin Ctee 1973-83), Common Servs Agency Scot Health Serv 1987-; dir Lithgows Ltd 1987-; *Recreations* shooting, fishing, gardening; *Clubs* Western (Glasgow), Western Meeting (Ayr), Leander (Henley); *Style—* Donald Macquaker, Esq, CBE; Blackbyres, by Ayr KA7 4TS (☎ 0292 41088); 30 George Square, Glasgow G2 1LH

McQUARRIE, Sir Albert; s of Algernon Stewart McQuarrie (d 1955), and Alice Maud Sharman (d 1961); *b* 1 Jan 1918; *Educ* Highlanders Acad Greenock, Greenock HS, Univ of Strathclyde; *m* 1945, Roseleen (d 1986), da of Hugh McCaffery (d 1960); 1 s (Dermot Hugh Hastings, producer/dir Scottish TV); m 2, 1989, Rhoda A, da of Noel Gall (d 1988); *Career* HM Forces 1939-45; chm and md A McQuarrie & Son (GB) Ltd 1946-87, conslt Bredero plc 1979-, chm and chief exec Sir Albert McQuarrie & Associates Ltd 1987-; dir: Westminster House plc, Hunterston Development Co Ltd 1989; former MP (C): East Aberdeenshire 1979-83, Banff and Buchan 1983-87; hon patron NE Jr FA; Freeman City of Gibraltar 1982; kt 1987; *Recreations* golf, bridge, soccer, horticulture; *Clubs* The Lansdowne, Troon Marine; *Style—* Sir Albert McQuarrie; Crimond, 11 Balcomie Crescent, Troon, Ayreshire KA10 7AR (☎ 0292 316462)

MacQUEEN, Dr Hector Lewis; s of John MacQueen, of Edinburgh, and Winifred, *née* McWalter; *b* 13 June 1956; *Educ* George Heriots Sch Edinburgh, Univ of Edinburgh (LLB, PhD); *m* 29 Sept 1979, Frances Mary, da of Robert Young, of Dalkeith; 2 s (Patrick b 1984, Jamie b 1987), 1 da (Sarah b 1982); *Career* assoc dean faculty law Univ of Edinburgh 1987-90 (lectr 1979-); *Books* ed New Perspectives in Scottish Legal History (ed 1984), Centenary: Heriots FP Cricket Club 1889-1989 (1989), Copyright, Competition and Industrial Design (1989); *Recreations* cricket, things Scottish, walking; *Clubs* Edinburgh Univ Staff, Heriots FP Cricket; *Style—* Dr Hector MacQueen; 37 Falcon Ave, Edinburgh EH10 4AL (☎ 031 447 3043); Univ of Edinburgh, Dept of Scots Law, Old Coll, South Bridge, Edinburgh EH8 9YL (☎ 031 650 2060, fax 031 662 4902, telex 727442 UNIVED G)

MCQUEEN, John; s of R. Leonard George McQueen, and Mira Milstead, *née* Birch; *b* 20 May 1942; *Educ* Rugby, Trinity Coll Cambridge, St Thomas's Hosp Med Sch (MA, MB BChir); *m* Dorothy, da of Gilbert Dyke; 5 da (Katy b 1968, Deborah b 1971, Philippa b 1977, Sarah b 1984, Laura b 1987); *Career* sr registrar Queen Charlotte Hosp and Chelsea Hosp, currently conslt obstetrician gynaecologist Bromley Health Authy; author of various papers on obstetrics, gynaecology and the menopause; memb Int Menopause Soc; FRCS 1972, FRCOG 1985 (memb 1973); *Recreations* travel, golf; *Clubs* London Obstetric, Gynaecological Soc; *Style—* John McQueen, Esq; Downs View, Heritage Hill, Keston, Kent BR2 6AU (☎ 0689 859058); Beckenham Hospital, Croydon Rd, Beckenham, Kent BR3 3QL (☎ 081 650 0125)

MACQUEEN, Professor John; s of William Lochhead Macqueen (d 1963), of 92 Hermiston Rd, Springboig, Glasgow, and Grace Palmer, *née* Galloway (d 1983); *b* 13 Feb 1929; *Educ* Hutchesons' GS, Univ of Glasgow (MA), Christ's Coll Cambridge (BA, MA); *m* 22 June 1953, Winifred Wallace, da of Wallace McWalter (d 1979), of 114 Maxwellton Road, Calderwood, East Kilbride; 3 s (Hector b 1956, Angus b 1958, Donald b 1963); *Career* PO, Flying Offr RAF 1954-56; asst prof Washington Univ St Louis Missouri USA 1956-59; Univ of Edinburgh: lectr 1959-63, Masson prof 1963-71, dir Sch of Scottish Studies 1969-88, prof of Scottish lit 1971-88, endowment fell 1988-; Hon DLitt Nat Univ of Ireland 1985; *Books* St Nynia (1961, revised edn 1990), Robert Henryson (1967), Ballattis of Luve (1970), Allegory (1970), Progress and Poetry (1982), Numerology (1985), The Rise of the Historical Novel (with W W MacQueen, 1988), Scotichronicon 3 and 4 (1989), Humanism in Renaissance Scotland (ed, 1990); *Recreations* walking, reading, music, casual archaeology; *Clubs* Scottish Arts, University Staff (Edinburgh); *Style—* Professor John MacQueen; 12 Orchard Toll, Edinburgh EH4 3JF; Slewdonan, Damnaglaur, Drummore, Stranraer, Wigtownshire DG9 9QN (☎ 031 332 1488); School of Scottish Studies, University of Edinburgh, 27 George Square, Edinburgh EH8 9LD (☎ 031 667 1011)

MCQUIGGAN, John; MBE (1955); s of John McQuiggan (d 1937), of Liverpool, and Sarah Elizabeth, *née* Sim (d 1960); *b* 24 Nov 1922; *Educ* St Edward's Coll Liverpool; *m* 17 June 1950, (Doris)Elsie, da of Gilbert Henry Hadler (d 1973), of Bromley; 3 s (Anthony b 8 March 1956, Simon b 21 July 1959, David b 29 April 1963), 1 da (Sarah b 13 Sept 1961); *Career* Dominions Office 1940-42, CRO 1947-50, admin offr Canberra 1950-54, 2 sec and consul Lahore and Dacca 1954-57, 1 sec (inf) Lahore and Peshawar 1957-58, dep dir UK info serv 1958-61; dir Br Info servs: E Nigeria 1961-64, Uganda 1964-69 (1 sec Kigali Rwanda); FCO London 1969-73, HM Consul Chad (London based) 1970-73, dep high cmmr Lusaka Zambia 1973-76; ret (own request) HM Dip Serv 1976; princ John McQuiggan Assoc 1976-78 and 1987-, exec dir UK S Africa Trade Assoc 1978-86, dir-gen Br Indus Ctee on S Africa 1986; numerous contribs to trade and econ jls; FIOD, MIPR; *Recreations* tennis, carpentry, craftwork (wood), music; *Clubs* Royal Overseas League London; *Style—* John McQuiggan, Esq, MBE; 7 Meadowcroft, Bickley, Kent BR1 2JD (☎ 081 467 0075)

MacRAE, (Alastair) Christopher Donald Summerhayes; CMG; s of Dr Alexander

MacRae, and Dr Grace MacRae; *b* 3 May 1937; *Educ* Rugby, Lincoln Coll Oxford, Harvard; *m* 1963, Mette Willert; 2 da; *Career* served RN 1956-58, joined CRO 1962; served: Dar es Salaam 1963-65, ME Centre for Arab Studies Lebanon 1965-67, Beirut 1967-68; FCO 1968-70; first sec and head of chancery: Baghdad 1970-71, Brussels 1972-76; (granted temp leave from FCO) Euro Cmmn Brussels 1976-78; ambass: Gabon 1978-80, (non-res) Sao Tomé and Principé 1979-80; head W Africa Dept FCO 1980-83, ambass Chad (non-res) 1982-83, political cnsllr and head of chancery Paris 1983-87, min head of Br Interests Section Swedish Embassy Tehran 1987, under sec Cabinet Office 1988-91, high cmmr Nigeria 1991; *Clubs* Royal Commonwealth Soc; *Style*— Christopher MacRae, Esq, CMG; FCO, King Charles St, London SW1

McRAE, Frances Anne; *née* Cairncross; da of Sir Alec (Alexander Kirkland) Cairncross, KCMG, *qv*; *b* 30 Aug 1944; *Educ* Laurel Bank Sch Glasgow, St Anne's Coll Oxford (MA), Brown Univ Rhode Island USA (MA); *m* 1971, Hamish McRae, qv; 2 da; *Career* staff memb: The Times 1967-69, The Banker 1969, The Observer 1970-73, The Guardian (economics corr 1973-81, ed women's page 1981-84), Br ed The Economist 1984-89, environmental ed The Economist 1989; memb Economics Ctee SSRC 1972-76, Newspaper Panel Monopolies Cmmn 1973-80, Cncl Royal Economic Soc 1980-85, Inquiry into Br Housing 1984-85; hon tres Nat Cncl for One Parent Families 1980-83, tstee Kennedy Meml Tst 1974-89, non exec dir Prolific Gp 1988-89; *Books* Capital City (with Hamish McRae, 1971), The Second Great Crash (with Hamish McRae, 1973), The Guardian Guide to the Economy (1981), Changing Perceptions of Economic Policy (1981), The Second Guardian Guide to the Economy (1983), Guide to the Economy (1987); *Recreations* childcare; *Style*— Mrs Hamish McRae; 6 Canonbury Lane, London N1 2AP (☎ 071 359 4612)

MCRAE, Hamish Malcolm Donald; s of Donald McRae (d 1980) Barbara, *née* Budd; *b* 20 Oct 1943; *Educ* Fettes Coll Edinburgh, Trinity Coll Dublin (BA); *m* 10 Sept 1971, Frances, da of Sir Alexander Kirkland (Alec) Cairncross, KCMG, gv; 2 da (Isabella Frances b 28 July 1977, Alexandra Barbara Mary b 5 Dec 1979); *Career* graduate trainee Liverpool Post 1966-67, The Banker 1967-72 (asst ed, dep ed), ed Euromoney 1972-75, fin ed The Guardian 1975-89, business and city ed The Independant 1989-; Harold Wincott Young Fin Journalist of the Year 1971, Harold Wincott Fin Journalist of the Year 1979; *Books* Capital City: London as a Financial Centre (with Francis Cairncross, 1973, current edn 1991), The Second Great Crash; how the oil crisis could destroy the world economy (with Nihon Keisai Shimbun, 1975) Japan's Role in the Emerging Global Securities Market (1985); *Recreations* skiing and walking; *Style*— Hamish McRae, Esq; Business & City Editor, The Independent, 40 City Rd, London EC1Y 2DB (☎ 071 956 1674, fax 071 956 1580)

McRAE, Hamish Malcolm Donald; s of Donald Barrington McRae (d 1980), and Barbara Ruth Louise (Jasmine), *née* Budd; *b* 20 Oct 1943; *Educ* Fettes, Trinity Coll Dublin (BA); *m* 20 Sept 1971, Frances Anne, *qv*, da of Sir Alexander Kirkland Cairncross, KCMG, of Oxford; 2 da (Isabella b 1977, Alexandra b 1979); *Career* dep ed The Banker 1971-72, ed Euromoney 1972-74, fin ed The Guardian 1975-89; ed business and city news and asst ed The Independent 1989-; Fin Journalist of the Year 1979; *Books* Capital City: London as a Financial Centre (with Frances Cairncross, 1971); *Recreations* walking, skiing; *Style*— Hamish McRae, Esq; 6 Canonbury Lane, London N1 2AP (☎ 071 359 4612); The Independent, 40 City Rd, London EC1 (☎ 071 956 1674)

MACRAE, James Norman; s of Col William Donald Macrae, MC, TD, and Mary Robertson, *née* Crowther; *b* 5 July 1940; *Educ* Loretto; *m* 1 Oct 1977, Miranda Jane, da of Sir Dugald Leslie Lorn Stewart of Appin, KCVO, CMG (d 1984); *Career* 15 (Scot) Bn The Para Regt 1959-65 and 1967-69, 21 SAS Regt (Artists Rifles) 1965-67, 23 SAS Regt 1975-77, (A/Maj) 3/51 Highland Volunteers 1986-; CA; dir Arbuckle Smith & Co Ltd 1971-76, gp fin dir and co sec Arbuckle Smith Group 1976-; *Recreations* riding, yachting, skiing, TA, amateur stage; *Clubs* Royal Northern and Clyde Yacht; *Style*— James N Macrae, Esq; Burnside Cottage, Gartocharn, Dunbartonshire G83 8SD (☎ 038 983 430); Arbuckle Smith & Co Ltd, 91 Mitchell St, Glasgow G1 3LS (☎ 041 248 5050, telex 778212)

MacRAE, (Merelina) Mary Phyllis; DL (Suffolk 1984); er da of Capt (John) Duncan George MacRae (d 1966), and Lady Phyllis MacRae (d 1990); *b* 20 Aug 1922; *Educ* Downham, Brilliamont Lausanne; *Career* served in ATS 1942-46; dir MacRae Farms Ltd; chm Suffolk CC 1984-86, pres Suffolk Agric Assoc 1987; *Style*— Miss Mary MacRae, DL; Hatchery House, Little Mill Lane, Barrow, Bury St Edmunds, Suffolk IP29 5BT (☎ 0284 810442, business ☎ 0284 810300)

McRAE, (Stuart) Neil; s of Max Harvey McRae, and Vivienne Blanche Rosemary, *née* Lewin; *b* 23 June 1939; *Educ* Diocesan Coll Cape Town SA; Univ of Witwatersrand (BA); *m* 24 June 1961, Joyce Rowena, da of Arthur Breeze-Carr (d 1968); 3 da (Fiona Jane b 1965, Louise Mary b 1967, Caroline Anne b 1970); *Career* md Reader's Digest Assoc Ltd 1986-, dir Reader's Digest: (Ireland) Ltd, AB Sweden; dir: Drive Pubns Ltd, Nine Colt Ltd, Periodical Publishers Assoc 1987-, Save the Children Fund (Sales) Ltd 1987- pres Assoc of Mail Order Publishers 1986; *Recreations* squash, tennis, dinghy sailing; *Clubs* Lansdowne; *Style*— Neil McRae, Esq; Readers Digest Association Ltd, Berkeley Square, London W1X 6AB (☎ 071 629 8144)

MACRAE, Neill Roderick; s of Maj I D K MacRae, DL (d 1979), of Druidaig Lodge, Letterfearn, and Annie Frances Ayliffe Neill (d 1943); *b* 13 Dec 1943; *Educ* Belhaven Hill Sch, Gordonstoun; *m* 20 Nov 1982, Miranda Dorothy Gertrude Aubrey, da of Patrick George Talbot Whitehead, of Easter Essenside, Ashkirk, Selkirkshire; 1 s (Ian b 1984), 1 da (Antonia b 1985); *Career* civilian flying instructor RAF 1972-76; overseer Australian Estates Co Ltd 1963-66; dir: Totaig Sea Foods 1970-80, Eagle Aviation 1980-89, Aquapure 1989; 13 in Observer Round Britain 2 handed yacht race 1979, and co inventor Haggis Hurling; *Recreations* shooting, fishing, flying, yacht racing; *Clubs* Royal Highland Yacht, BASC, BMAA, BBAC; *Style*— Neill Macrae, Esq; Totaig, Letterfearn, Kyle, Ross-Shire; Ashieburn Farm, Ancrum, Roxburghshire

MacRAE, Hon Mrs (Susan Mary); *née* Southwell; da of 6 Viscount Southwell (d 1960); *b* 1926; *m* 1951, Keith Francis MacRae; 2 s; *Style*— The Hon Mrs MacRae; 27 Dennis Rd, Slacks Creek, via Brisbane

MCRAE, Prof Thomas Watson; s of Thomas Watson McRae (d 1977), of Edinburgh, and Catherine Hawthorn, *née* Galloway (d 1972); *b* 16 Sept 1932; *Educ* Royal HS Edinburgh, LSE (BSc); *m* 26 March 1960, Helen Elizabeth, da of Emlyn Thomas (d 1956), of Peterborough; 1 s (Paul David Watson b 19 July 1963), 2 da (Julie Clare b 21 Dec 1961, Cathleen Margaretta b 26 Feb 1966); *Career* Nat Serv Lt KAR Kenya and Uganda 1955-57; sr auditor Price Waterhouse London 1957-58, systems analyst and lectr IBM Career London 1958-61, PD Leake res fell LSE 1961-63, lectr in accounting and fin Univ of Hull 1963-65, lectr Manchester Business Sch 1965-69, prof of business admin Witwatersrand Univ Business Sch Johannesburg SA 1969-71, prof of fin Univ of Bradford Mgmnt Centre 1972-; memb Bank of England Ctee on Training for the Fin Insts 1973-75; memb of ICAS 1955; *Books* Introduction to Business Computers Programming (1966), Analytical Management (1969), Computor and Accounting (1972), Foreign Exchange Management (1981), The Uses of Statistical Sampling in Internal Auditing (1983); *Recreations* microcomputing, travel, hill-walking; *Style*— Prof Thomas McRae; 109 Grove Road, Ilkley, West Yorkshire (☎ 0943 607071); Bradford University Management Centre, Emm Lane, Bradford, W Yorks (☎ 0274 542299, fax 0274 546866, telex 51309 UNIBFD G)

MACREADY, Sir Nevil John Wilfrid; 3 Bt (UK 1923), of Cheltenham, Co Gloucester; CBE (1983); s of Lt-Gen Sir Gordon Nevil Macready, 2 Bt, KBE, CB, CMG, DSO, MC (d 1956); *b* 7 Sept 1921; *Educ* Cheltenham, St John's Coll Oxford; *m* 1949, Mary, da of Sir (John) Donald Balfour Fergusson, GCB (d 1963); 1 s, 3 da; *Heir* s, Charles Nevil Macready; *Career* served RA 1942-47, Staff Capt 1945; BBC Euro Serv 1947-50, md Mobil Oil Co Ltd 1975-85; pres: Royal Warrant Holders' Assoc 1979-80, Inst of Petroleum 1980-82; chm: Crafts Cncl 1984-91, Horseracing Advsy Cncl 1986-; tstee V & A Museum 1985-; *Clubs* Boodle's, Naval and Military, Jockey (Paris); *Style*— Sir Nevil Macready, Bt, CBE; The White House, Odiham, Hants RG25 1LG (☎ 0256 70 2976)

MacROBERT, (John Carmichael Thomas) Michael; s of John MacRobert (d 1947), of Lismore, Millikenpark, Renfrewshire, and Jessie Simpson, *née* MacCuaig; *b* 26 April 1918; *Educ* Rugby, Univ of Cambridge (MA), Univ of Glasgow (LLB); *m* 16 Sept 1947, Anne Rosemary, da of Kenneth MacKay Millar, of Hill House, Paisley; 1 s (David John Carmichael b 1953), 2 da (Fiona Garwood b 1949, Susan Walker b 1951); *Career* 80 Field Regt RA TA, 125 OCTU Filey 1939, 2 Lt 10 Field Regt RA BEF 1940, India 1942, Egypt 1943, Assam and Burma 1944 (despatches), 80 Field Regt 1946 BAOR, 402 anti-tank Regt RA TA (402 A & SH Mortar Regt 1947); slr; ptnr MacRoberts (formerly MacRobert Son & Hutchison) 1948, cncl memb Law Soc of Scot 1965-77, Hon Sheriff 1969, ret 1987; chm Paisley Cons Assoc, hon pres Paisley South Cons Assoc, cncl Nat Tst for Scot, memb Clyde Estuary Amenity Cncl, hon vice pres Scot Civic Tst, hon sec Paisley Abbey Surroundings Ctee; *Recreations* sailing, country sports; *Clubs* Western (Glasgow); *Style*— Michael MacRobert, Esq; Failte Colintraive, Argyll (☎ 070084 239); 21 Carriage Hill, Paisley

MacRORY, Avril; da of Patrick Simon MacRory, of Dublin, Ireland, and Elizabeth, *née* Flynn; *b* 5 April 1956; *Educ* Sion Hill Dublin, Univ Coll Dublin (BA); *m* 9 Sept 1983, Valentine John Griffin, s of Valentine John Griffin (d 1987), of Dublin, Ireland; 1 s (Sam b 31 March 1985); *Career* TV prodr and dir Radkio Telefis Eireann (RTE) 1979-86, head of variety 1986-88, commissioning ed Channel 4 TV 1988-; fndr memb Centre for Performing Arts Dublin; memb ITPA 1985, bd memb IM2 1989; *Recreations* music, cinema, sailing; *Clubs* United Arts, Dublin, Affiliated Chelsea Arts; *Style*— Mrs Avril MacRory; Channel Four TV Plc, 60 Queen Charlotte St, London WIP 2AX (☎ 071 631 4444, fax 071 580 2618)

MACRORY, Henry David; s of Sir Patrick Macrory, of Walton-on-the-Hill, Surrey, and Lady Marjorie Elizabeth, *née* Lewis; *b* 15 Dec 1947; *Educ* Westminster, Univ of Kent (BA); *m* 4 April 1972, Janet Carolyn, da of Henry James Potts; 1 s (David b 1985), 2 da (Julia b 1978, Caroline b 1980); *Career* reporter Kent Messenger 1969-72; Sunday Express 1972-: reporter 1972-79, political columnist 1979-83, asst ed 1983-, exec ed 1990-; *Style*— Henry Macrory, Esq; Sunday Express, Ludgate House, 245 Blackfriars Rd, London SE1 (☎ 071 928 8000, fax 071 620 1656)

MACRORY, Sir Patrick Arthur; s of Lt-Col F S N Macrory, DSO, DL (d 1956); *b* 21 March 1911; *Educ* Cheltenham, Trinity Coll Oxford (MA); *m* 1939, Elizabeth, da of Rev J F O Lewis (d 1960); 3 s; *Career* serv WWII; called to the Bar Middle Temple 1937; joined Unilever 1947 (sec 1956, dir 1968, ret 1971); memb NI Devpt Cncl 1956-64, gen treas Br Assoc for Advancement of Sci 1960-65, chm Review Body on Local Govt in NI 1970; memb ctee: Inquiry into Indust Representation 1971-72, Preparation of Legislation 1974-75; chm Confedn of Ulster Socs 1974 (pres 1980-83); dep pres Cncl Cheltenham Coll 1980-83; kt 1972; *Style*— Sir Patrick Macrory; Amberdene, Walton-on-the-Hill, Tadworth, Surrey (☎ 073 781 3086)

MACRORY, Richard Brabazon; s of Sir Patrick Macrory, of Walton-on-the-Hill, Surrey, and Marjorie Elizabeth, *née* Lewis; *b* 30 March 1950; *Educ* Westminster, Ch Ch Oxford (MA); *m* 6 Oct 1979, Sarah Margaret, da of Bernard Christian Briant, CVO, of Aldeburgh, Suffolk; 2 s (Sam b 1980, Robert b 1983); *Career* called to the Bar Grays Inn 1974; legal advsr FOE Ltd 1975-78, lectr in environmental law and policy Imperial Coll Centre for Environmental Technol 1980-89, assoc dir Journal of Environmental Law 1989- (ed in chief 1988-), reader in environmental law Univ of London 1989; articles in legal and specialist jls; memb Cncl UK Environmental Law Assoc (first chm 1986-88), specialist advsr House of Commons select ctee on the environment, standing counsel Cncl for Protection of Rural England; memb: environmental advsy bd Shanks & McEwan Ltd, UK Nat Advsy Gp on Eco-labelling; dir Merchant-Ivory Film Prodns Ltd; FRSA 1984-; *Books* Nuisance (1982), Water Law: Principles and Practice (1985), Water Act 1989 (1989); *Recreations* reading, board games, films; *Style*— Richard MacRory, Esq; Centre for Environmental Technology, Imperial Coll of Science Technology and Medicine, 48 Princes Gardens, London SW7 (☎ 071 589 5111, fax 071 581 0245); European Law Chambers, Hamilton House, 1 Temple Ave, London EC4Y 0HA

McSHANE, Ian David; s of Henry McShane, of Manchester, and Irene, *née* Cowley; *b* 29 Sept 1942; *Educ* Stretford GS Leeds, RADA; *m* 30 Aug 1980, Gwendolyn Marie, da of Claude Humble; 1 s (Morgan b 7 July 1974), 1 da (Kate b 18 April 1970); *Career* actor; films incl: The Wild and the Willing 1962, The Battle of Britain 1968, If its Tuesday this must be Belgium 1969, Villain 1971, Sitting Target 1972, Exposed 1984, Torchlight 1986; theatre (West End): The Glass Menagerie 1965, Loot 1966, The Promise 1967 (also on Broadway); theatre (Los Angeles): As You Like It 1979, Betrayal 1983, Inadmissable Evidence 1985; TV: Jesus of Nazareth, Wuthering Heights, Disraeli, Whose Life Is It Anyway?, Lovejoy, Dallas, War and Remembrance, The Letter, Evergreen, Perry Mason, Columbo; memb: BAFTA, Acad of Motion Picture Arts and Sciences; *Style*— Ian McShane, Esq; Duncan Heath Associates Ltd, Paramount House, 162-170 Wardour St, London

MacTAGGART, Lady; Irene; da of late Ferdinand Richard Holmes Meyrick; *b* 2 Aug 1914; *m* 1, 1939 (m dis 1954), 6 Earl of Craven (d 1965); 1 da; m 2, 1961, Sir Andrew MacTaggart (d 1978); *Style*— Lady Irene MacTaggart; Box 17, Balgowan, Natal, South Africa

MACTAGGART, Sir John Auld; 4 Bt (UK 1938), of Kings Park, City of Glasgow; s of Sir Ian (John) Auld Mactaggart, 3 Bt (d 1987), and Lady Belhaven and Stenton (*see* Belhaven and Stenton, Lord); *b* 21 Jan 1951; *Educ* Shrewsbury, Trinity Coll Cambridge; *m* 1977 (m dis 1990), Patricia, da of late Maj Harry Alastair Gordon, MC; *Heir* bro, Philip Auld Mactaggart b 26 Feb 1956; *Career* chartered surveyor; chm: Central and City Holdings, Western Heritable Investment Co Ltd; dir of property cos; dir Scottish Ballet; FRICS; *Clubs* Annabel's, Argyllshire Gathering; *Style*— Sir John Mactaggart, Bt; Ardmore House, Ardtalla Estate, Islay, Argyll; 55 St James's St, London SW1A 1LA (☎ 071 491 2948, fax 071 629 0414)

MacTAGGART, Dr Kenneth Dugald; s of Iain MacTaggart, of Bem, Glasgow, and Isabel Paton, *née* Dow; *b* 15 April 1953; *Educ* Allan Glen's Sch Glasgow, Paisley Coll of Technol (BA), Univ of Aston (PhD); *m* 16 March 1985, Caroline, da of Henry McNicholas, of Finchley, London; 1 da (Laura Ann b 1989); *Career* doctoral res Univ of Aston 1976-80;publisher and ed Export Times London 1983-84 (asst ed 1980-83), ed Property International London 1984-87, dir Inc Newsletters London 1987-88, sr economist Highlands and Islands Devpt Bd 1988-; memb Nat Tst Scot, Mountain Bothies Assoc; chm Old Astonians Mountaineering Club; memb Br Assoc of Picture Libraries and Agencies 1985; *Books* Technical Innovation in Industrial Production

(1984); *Recreations* piano, photography, mountaineering, reading; *Clubs* TAF, Glasgow; *Style*— Dr Kenneth MacTaggart; The Sutors, 28 Broadstone Park, Inverness IV2 3LA (☎ 0463 233717); Highlands & Islands Development Board, Bridge House, 20 Bridge St, Inverness IV1 1QR (☎ 0463 244278, fax 0463 233717, telex 75267)

MacTAGGART, Air Vice-Marshal William Keith; CBE (1976, MBE 1956); s of Duncan MacTaggart (d 1947), of Islay, and Marion Winifred, *née* Keith (d 1988); *b* 15 Jan 1929; *Educ* Aberdeen GS, Univ of Aberdeen (BSc); *m* 1, 30 July 1949 (m dis 1977), Christina Carnegie, da of James Geddes (d 1974), of Aberdeen; 1 s (Alan b 26 May 1954), 2 da (Carol b 24 March 1950, Shelagh b 23 April 1952); m 2, 9 Sept 1977, Barbara Smith Brown, da of Adm Stirling P Smith (d 1977); 1 step da (Carolyn b 12 June 1957); *Career* cmmnd RAF 1949, Engr Offr/Pilot 1949-70, Gp Capt and OC RAF Newton 1971, Air Cdre and dir of air armament MOD (PE) 1973, RCDS 1977, Air Vice-Marshal and vice pres Ordnance Bd 1978 (pres 1978-80); dep chm Tomash Holdings Ltd 1980-84, md MPE Ltd 1984-, ret 1989; CEng 1965, FIMechE 1973, FRAeS 1974, FBIM 1978; *Recreations* music, travel, reading; *Clubs* RAF; *Style*— Air Vice-Marshal W MacTaggart, CBE; Croft Stones, Lothmore, Helmsdale, Sutherland KW8 6HP

MacTHOMAS OF FINEGAND, Andrew Patrick Clayhills; o s of Capt Patrick Watt MacThomas of Finegand (d 1970), and Elizabeth Clayhills-Henderson, of Invergowrie, Angus; suc f 1970 as 19 Chief of Clan MacThomas; *b* 28 Aug 1942; *Educ* St Edward's Sch Oxford; *m* 1985, Anneke Cornelia Susanna, o da of Mr and Mrs A Kruyning-van Hout, of Heesch, The Netherlands; 1 s (Thomas b 1987), 1 da (Amy b 1989); *Heir* s, Thomas David Alexander MacThomas, yr of Finegand; *Career* public affairs, Barclays Bank; memb Standing Cncl of Scottish Chiefs; pres Clan MacThomas Soc; FSA (Scot); *Recreations* Travel, promoting the clan; *Style*— Andrew MacThomas of Finegand, FSA; c/o Clan MacThomas Society, 19 Warriston Ave, Edinburgh EH3

MACVE, Prof Richard Henry; s of Alfred Derek Macve, of Buckhurst Hill, Essex, and Betty Lilian, *née* Simmons; *b* 2 June 1946; *Educ* Chigwell Sch Essex, New Coll Oxford (scholar, MA), LSE (MSc); *m* 28 July 1973, Jennifer Jill, da of Leslie Charles Wort; 2 s (Thomas Charles b 25 March 1980, Arthur James b 5 March 1985), 1 da (Joanna Catherine b 16 Sept 1977); *Career* Peat Marwick Mitchell London 1968-74 (articled clerk, sr accountant, asst mangr), internal auditor seconded to MOD 1973-74, lectr in accounting LSE 1974-78, Julian Hodge prof of accounting and head of Dept of Accounting Univ Coll of Wales Aberystwyth 1978-, visiting assoc prof of accounting Rice Univ Houston Texas 1982-83; memb Cncl ICAEW 1986-, chm Conf of Profs of Accounting 1990-; ICAEW (first place intermediate examination 1969, second place final pt one 1970, first place final pt two 1971); FCA 1979 (ACA 1972); *Publications* A Conceptual Framework for Financial Accounting and Reporting (1981), A Survey of Lloyd's Syndicate Accounts (2 edn, 1991), Accounting for Marketable Securities in The Financial Services Industry (1991); *Recreations* sailing, mountain walking; *Clubs* Royal Over-seas League, Aberystwyth Sea Angling and Yacht; *Style*— Prof Richard Macve; Bronwydd, 3 Trefor Rd, Aberystwyth, Dyfed SY23 2EH (☎ 0970 624586); Department of Accounting, The University College of Wales, Aberystwyth SY23 3DY (☎ 0970 622201, fax 0970 617172)

McVITTIE, John Bousfield; s of Brig Arthur Bousfield McVittie , OBE (d 1976), and Valerie Florence, *née* Crichton; *b* 9 April 1943; *Educ* Radley, Selwyn Coll Cambridge (MA), Stanford Business Sch (MBA); *m* 4 Sept 1971, Jane Elizabeth, *née* Hobson; 2 da (Clare, Amy); *Career* md Privatbanken Ltd 1984-87, sr vice-pres and gen mangr First Interstate Bank of California 1987-89, md John Charcol Commercial 1989-; Freeman: City of London 1969, Worshipful Co of Clothworkers 1974; *Recreations* skiing, tennis; *Clubs* Queens, Pembroke Tennis (hon sec); *Style*— John McVittie, Esq; 72 Scarsdale Villas, London W8 6PP (☎ 071 937 8926); 195 Knightsbridge, London SW7 1RE (☎ 071 589 8926)

McWATTERS, George Edward; s of Lt-Col George Alfred McWatters, 81 Pioneers, IA (d 1955), and Ellen Mary Christina, *née* Harvey (d 1977), gd of John Harvey, the Bristol wine merchant; *b* 17 March 1922; *Educ* Clifton; *m* 1, 7 Dec 1946, Margery Neilson (d 1959), da of David Neilson Robertson; m 2, 23 July 1960, Joy Anne Matthews; 1 s (Christopher George b 19 Aug 1962); *Career* joined Royal Scots 1940, cmmnd 14 Punjab Regt 1941, served NW Frontier, ret as T/Maj 1946; Vintners Scholar 1947; chm: John Harvey & Sons 1956-66, John White Footwear (subsequently Ward White Group plc) 1967-82, HTV West 1969-88, HTV Ltd 1986-88; dir: Martins Bank 1960-70, corp affrs HTV Group; memb: Ctee AA 1962-89, Grand Cncl CBI 1970-82; chm: Appeal Ctee Avon Wildlife Tst 1982, St John Cncl Avon 1983; vice-chm Bristol & West Building Society 1985-; govr Clifton Coll 1958- (pres Old Cliftonian Assoc 1989), chm Bishop of Bristol's Urban Appeal 1989; city cllr Bristol 1949-53, JP Bristol 1960-67, JP Marylebone 1969-71, High Sheriff Cambs 1979; master Soc of Merchant Venturers Bristol 1986-87; Hon Freeman: City of Bristol 1947, City of London 1948, Worshipful Co of Vintners 1948, Worshipful Co of Patternmakers 1976; *Recreations* swimming, walking; *Clubs* Buck's, MCC; *Style*— George McWatters, Esq; Burrington House, Burrington, Bristol BS18 7AD (☎ 0761 62294, fax 0761 63100, car 0860 502662)

McWATTERS, Dr the Hon Veronica; *née* Stamp; da of 2 Baron Stamp (d 1941), and Katharine, Baroness Stamp (d 1985); *b* 25 May 1934; *Educ* Queenswood Sch Hatfield, Royal Free Hosp Med Sch London; *m* 1961, Richard Alfred Hugh McWatters, s of Sir Arthur Cecil McWatters, CIE (d 1966); 1 s, 2 da; *Career* doctor (MRCS, LRCP), former house offr Royal Free Hosp and Stamford and Rutland Hosp; pt/t GP Bristol; *Recreations* bee keeping; *Clubs* Br Bee Keepers Assoc; *Style*— Dr the Hon Veronica McWatters; The Grove, Dundry, Bristol, Avon BS18 8JG (☎ 0272 641334)

MCWHINNIE, Prof William Robin; s of William Clark McWhinnie (d 1961), and Mary Gabrielle, *née* Birch; *b* 10 July 1937; *Educ* Chislehurst and Sidcup GS, QMC (BSc, PhD, DSc); *m* 19 Jan 1961, Vinitha Lilamani, da of Prof Joseph Lionel Christie Rodridgo, CMG (d 1972); 2 s (Dr Sean Lakshman William b 1964, Neil Rohan Clark b 1965); *Career* Aquinas Univ Coll Sri Lanka 1960-62, Queen Elizabeth Coll Univ of London 1962-67; Aston Univ: reader 1967-73, prof 1973-, pro vice chllr 1974-76, dir of univ relations 1987-88; author of over 150 scientific papers; CChem FRSC, FRSA; *Recreations* the arts (especially opera); *Style*— Prof William McWhinnie; 22 Widney Manor Road, Solihull, West Midlands B92 3JQ (☎ 021 359 3611 ext 4738); Department of Chemical Engineering and Applied Chemistry, Aston University, Aston Triangle, Birmingham B4 7ET (☎ 021 359, fax 021 359 4094, telex 336997 UNIAST G)

MACWHIRTER, Iain; s of Robert Archibald MacWhirter, and Christina, *née* McKean; *b* 24 Sept 1952; *Educ* George Heriots' Sch Edinburgh, Univ of Edinburgh; *m* 9 June 1984 (m dis 1989), Susan Elaine; *Career* researcher BBC Scot 1978-80, prodr current affrs for TV 1985-86 (reporter 1980-83), Scot political corr for Radio 1986-89, Scot Parly corr for TV 1989-; *Recreations* climbing, classic cars, conversation; *Style*— Iain Macwhirter, Esq; 19 Grosvenor Crescent Lane, Glasgow G12 9AB (☎ 041 339 8103); BBC Scotland Broadcasting House, Queen Margaret Drive, Glasgow (☎ 041 330 2210, fax 041 334 0614, car 0860 518462)

McWHIRTER, Norris Dewar; CBE (1980); s of William McWhirter; er twin brother of Ross McWhirter (killed 1975), Norris's co-fndr and ed of Guinness Book of Records (1954-86); *b* 12 Aug 1925; *Educ* Marlborough, Trinity Coll Oxford (MA); *m* 1957, Carole (d 1987), da of George Eckert; 1 s, 1 da; *Career* dir: Gieves plc 1972-, McWhirter Twins Ltd, Guinness Superlatives Ltd 1954- (md 1954-76); former sports (athletics) correspondent Observer and Star, BBC Olympic commentator (radio 1952-56, TV 1960-72); co presenter: Record Breakers (with Roy Castle) BBC 1972-, Guinness Hall of Fame (with David Frost) 1986-; chm: Freedom Assoc 1983-, Hampden Trust; tstee: Police Convalescent and Rehabilitation Tst, Ross McWhirter Fndn, Res Fndn for Study of Terrorism; memb Judging Panel Young Citizens Awards; pres: Wiltshire Branch RNLI, Nat Union of Track Statisticians; Parly candidate (C) Orpington 1964 and 1966, memb Sports Cncl 1970-74; *Books* Guinness Book of Records (280 edns in 33 languages 65 million sales), Dunlop Book of Facts (1964-73), Guinness Book of Answers, Ross- Story of a Shared Life; *Recreations* family tennis, skiing, hunting in libraries, watching athletics and rugby; *Clubs* Caledonian, Achilles, Vincent's (Oxford); *Style*— Norris McWhirter, Esq, CBE; c/o Guinness Publishing Ltd, 33 London Rd, Enfield, Middlesex EN2 6DJ (☎ 081 367 4567)

McWHIRTER, Prof Robert; CBE (1963); s of Robert McWhirter (d 1944), of Ballantrae, Ayrshire, Scotland, and Janet Ramsay, *née* Gairdner (d 1947); *b* 8 Nov 1904; *Educ* Univ of Glasgow (MB ChB), Cambridge Univ (DMRE); *m* 26 June 1937, Susan Muir, da of William Mac Murray (d 1938), of 40 Kelvinside Gardens, Glasgow; 1 s (William b 18 May 1939); *Career* cancer res fell Holt Radium Inst Manchester 1933-34, chief asst X-ray Dept St Bartholomews Hosp London 1934-35, prof of med radiology Univ of Edinburgh 1946-70 (lectr 1935-46); pres: Radiology Section RSM 1956-57, Scottish Radiological Soc 1957-58, Medical and Dental Defence Union 1959-90, Radiotherapists Visiting Club 1965-69, RCR 1966-69; chm: Standing Cancer Ctee Scottish Health Servs Cncl 1962-70, Nat Soc Cancer Relief Scotland 1963-70; conslt adviser Organsiation of Radiotherapy Servs (govts of Australia, S Africa, Nigeria, Rep of Ireland); awards incl: Liston Victoria Jubilee Prize RCS Edinburgh 1941, Twinning Meml medal Royal Coll of Radiologists 1943, Fndn lecture Mayo Clinic USA 1948, Caldwell Meml Lecture Montreal, America, Roentgen Ray Soc 1963; hon memb American Radium Soc 1948, hon fell RCR of Australia 1954, hon memb American Coll of Radiologists 1964, hon FFR RCS Ireland 1967; hon memb Radiological Soc: France 1967, Italy 1968; FRCS 1932, FRCR 1939, FRCP 1965, fell Royal Soc of Edinburgh; *Books* British Surgical Practice (contrib vol 2, 1948), British Practice in Radiotherapy (contrib, 1955), Frontiers of Radiotherapy (contrib, 1970); *Recreations* ornithology and golf; *Clubs* Edinburgh Univ Staff, Bruntsfield Links GC; *Style*— Prof Robert McWhirter, CBE; 2 Orchard Brae, Edinburgh EH4 1NY (☎ 031 332 5800)

MCWILLIAM, (Frederick) Edward; s of Dr William Nicholson McWilliam, of Banbridge, Co Down, Ireland; *b* 30 April 1909; *Educ* Campbell Coll Belfast, Slade Sch of Fine Art; *Career* serv RAF WWII UK and Far East; sculptor; memb of staff Slade Sch of Fine Art Univ of London 1947-66, memb Art Panel Arts Cncl 1960-68; solo exhibitions incl: London Gallery 1939, Hanover Gallery 1949, 1952, 1956, Waddington Galleries 1961, 1963, 1966, 1971, 1973, 1976, 1979, 1984, Dawson Gallery Dublin, Felix Landau Gallery LA; retrospective exhibtions: Belfast Dublin and Londonderry 1981, Warwick Arts Tst 1982, Tate Gallery 1989, New Art Centre 1989, Mayor Gallery; open-air exhibitions: London, Antwerp, Arnhem, Paris; work incl in Br Cncl touring exhibitions to: USA, Canada, Germany, S America; fell UCL 1972, Hon DLit Belfast 1964; RA 1990; *Style*— F E McWilliam, Esq; 8A Holland Villas Rd, London W14 8BP

McWILLIAM, Prof George Henry; s of George McWilliam (d 1948), of Wallasey, Cheshire, and Mary May, *née* Dickson (d 1963); *b* 11 June 1927; *Educ* Oldershaw GS, Univ of Leeds (BA), Pavia Univ, Univ of Dublin (MA); *m* 1, 9 April 1955 (m dis), Jennifer Magdalen, *née* Hobson, da of Bouverie Hoyten, of Penzance; 2 s (Paul b 1956, Edwin b 1963), 1 da (Laura b 1958); m 2, 14 Sept 1989, Eileen Elizabeth, da of Oscar Charmant (d 1975), of Gerrards Cross; 1 s (Jonathan Paul Henry b 1968), 2 da (Joanna Catherine Elizabeth b 1970, Rachel Lucy Mary b 1972); *Career* RAF 1945-48; asst lectr Univ of Leeds 1954-55, Bedford Coll Univ of London 1955-58; lectr in charge Dept of Italian Trinity Coll Dublin 1958-66 (promoted to reader 1963 and elected FTCD), reader in Italian Univ of Kent at Canterbury 1966-72, assoc prof in Italian Univ of Leicester 1986- (prof and head of Dept of Italian 1972-86, emeritus prof 1986); memb and former treas Soc for Italian Studies; memb: Assoc of Teachers of Italian, Ancient Monuments Soc; Silver medal for serv to Italian culture Italian govt 1965; *Books* Two Plays by Ugo Betti (1965), Three Plays on Justice by Ugo Betti (1964), Boccaccio's Decameron (1972), Shakespeare's Italy Revisited (1974); *Recreations* bowls, foreign travel, Satellite Communications, computing; *Style*— Prof George McWilliam; Lewins, Lewins Road, Chalfont St Peter, Bucks SL9 8SA (☎ 0753 888175); Department of Italian, University of Leicester, Leicester LE21 7RH (☎ 0533 522655)

MacWILLIAM, Very Rev (Alexander) Gordon; s of Andrew George MacWilliam (d 1940), of Conwy, Gwynedd, and Margaret, *née* Davies; *b* 22 Aug 1923; *Educ* Queen Elizabeth GS, Univ of Wales (BA), Univ of London (BD, PhD); *m* 28 June 1951, Catherine Teresa, da of John Bogue, of Britannia Terrace, Valley, Holyhead, Gwynedd; 1 s (Andrew John b 1957); *Career* minor canon Bangor Cathedral 1949-55, rector Llanfaethlu Gwynedd 1955-58, head Dept of Theol Trinity Coll Carmarthen 1958-74, head Sch of Society Studies 1974-84, visiting prof Central Univ of Iowa USA, dean of St Davids Cathedral 1984-; ret 1990; *Recreations* travel, classical music; *Style*— The Very Rev Gordon MacWilliam; The Deanery, Haverfordwest, Dyfed (☎ 0437 720202)

McWILLIAM, Jillian; MBE (1988); da of Herbert McWilliam, of Preston, Lancs, and Mabel Harwood, *née* Harrison; *b* 17 Nov 1946; *Educ* Ashton-on-Ribble Secdy Sch, Elizabeth Gaskell Coll (DipEd); *m* 28 Sept 1979, Geoffrey Michael Lee, s of Percy John Lee (d 1977), of Flamstead, Herts; *Career* mktg dir Bejam 1987-88, PR dir Iceland Frozen Foods plc 1989-, currently broadcaster; memb Inst Home Economics; *Books* 7 cookery books on freezing and microwave cooking; *Recreations* cooking, reading, gardening; *Style*— Miss Jillian McWilliam, MBE; Adelaide Cottage, Common Rd, Studham, nr Dunstable, Beds (☎ 0582 873 214); Iceland Frozen Foods plc, Honeypot Lane, Stanmore, Middx (☎ 081 952 8311, fax 081 952 3577, telex 21776 ICELAND)

McWILLIAM, John David; MP (Lab) Blaydon 1979-; s of Alexander McWilliam, and Josephine McWilliam; *b* 16 May 1941; *Educ* Leith Acad, Heriot Watt Univ, Napier Coll of Science and Technol; *m* 1965, Lesley Mary Catling; 2 da; *Career* engr Post Office, treas City of Edinburgh 1973-74, cmmr Local Authy Accounts in Scotland 1974-78; memb: Bd of Scottish Cncl for Technical Educn 1973-80, Mr Speaker's Panel of Chairman 1987-; *Style*— John McWilliam, Esq, MP; House of Commons, London SW1

McWILLIAMS, Dr Donald Michael; s of Owen John (d 1974), of Dublin, and Josephine, *née* Murphy (d 1981); *b* 23 June 1929; *Educ* Blackrock Coll Dublin, Prior Park Coll Bath, Trinity Coll Dublin (MA, MB BCh, BAO, BA); *m* 12 Aug 1956 (m dis 1976), (Josephine) Valerie Mary, da of Ronald Shepherd, OBE; 2 s (Michael Owen b 1957, (Ronald) Nigel b 1957), 1 da (Wendy Jane b 1958); m 2, 15 June 1978, Anne Norah, *née* Oldershaw; *Career* conslt anaesthetist Royal Berkshire Hosp 1961- (sr registrar 1959-61); memb and chm: Social Serv Berkshire CC, E Berkshire AHA 1982-; memb: RSM, Assoc of Anaesthetists; FFARCS; *Recreations* ornithology, porcelain, music; *Clubs* Royal St George Yacht, Phyllis Court; *Style*— Dr Donald McWilliams; Portland Cottage, 63 Northfield End, Henley-on-Thames, Oxon RG9 2JJ (☎ 0491 575444); Royal Berkshire Hosp, Reading, Berks (☎ 0734 875111); East Berkshire Health Authority, Frances House, St Frances Rd, Windsor, Berks (☎ 0753 859221)

MADDEN, Anne; *Educ* Chelsea Sch of Art; *m* Louis le Brocquy; 2 s; *Career* artist; solo exhibitions: Leicester Galleries London 1959, 1961 and 1967, Dawson Gallery Dublin 1960, 1964, 1968, 1970 and 1974, New Gallery Belfast 1964, New Art Centre 1970, 1972, 1974, 1978 and 1990, Oxford Gallery Oxford 1970, Gimpel Weitzenhoffer Gallery NY 1970, Demarco Gallery Edinburgh 1971, Ulster Museum Belfast 1974, Galerie Darthea Speyer Paris 1976 and 1979, Taylor Galleries Dublin 1979, 1982 and 1987, The Arts Cncl of NI Belfast 1979, Galerie Le Dessin Paris 1978 and 1980, Fondation Maeght Saint-Paul France 1983, The Bank of Ireland Dublin 1984, Wexford Arts Centre Ireland 1984, Galerie Maeght Barcelona 1985, Galerie Joachim Becker Cannes 1985, Armstrong Gallery NY 1986, Galerie Jeanne Bucher Paris 1989, The Kerlin Gallery Dublin 1990, R H A Gallagher Gallery Dublin 1991; gp exhibitions: The Mirror and the Square (Burlington Galleries London) 1951, The Irish Exhibition of Living Art (Dublin) 1952, Art '65 (American Express Pavillion NY World Fair) 1965, Quatriéme Biennale de Paris (representing Ireland) 1965, Modern Irish Painters (CIE Ulster Museum Belfast) 1966, Modern Irish Painting (Helsinki, Gothenburg, Norrköping, Stockholm) 1969, An Oireachtas (Dublin) 1970 and 1988, The 8th International Biennial Exhibition of Prints (Tokyo) 1973, Irish Directions (touring) 1974-75, ICA (Boston Mass) 1974-75, Salon de Montrouge (Paris) 1982, ROSC 84 (Dublin) 1984, CNAC (Nice) 1985, A Propos de Dessin (Galerie Adrian Maeght Paris) 1987, Prestige du Fonds Regional d'Art Contemporain (Provence France) 1989, Modern Masters (Musée Jacquemart André Paris) 1989, The Nat Self Portrait Collection (Crawford Municipal Art Gallery Cork and Nat Gallery Dublin) 1990, Les Abstractions Autour des Années 1970-80, Museum of Modern Art and Contemporary Art Nice 1990; public collections possessing work incl: Contemporary Arts Society London, The Gulbenkian Fndn Portugal, The Arts Council of Ireland, The Arts Council of NI, The Arts Council of GB, The Hugh Lane Municipal Gallery of Modern Art Dublin, The J H Hirshhorn Museum and Sculpture Garden Washington D C, Contemporary High Arts Society, Musée d'Art Moderne de la Ville de Paris, La Fondation Maeght France, Musée Picasso Antibes, Musée d'Art Moderne et d'Art Contemporain; *Style*— Ms Anne Madden; c/o New Art Centre, 41 Sloane Street, London SW1X 9LU

MADDEN, Adm Sir Charles Edward; 2 Bt (UK 1919), of Kells, Co Kilkenny; GCB (1965); s of Adm of the Fleet Sir Charles Edward Madden, 1 Bt, GCB, OM, GCVO, KCMG (d 1935), and Constance Winifred (d 1964), yst da of Sir Charles Cayzer, 1 Bt, of Gartmore; *b* 15 June 1906; *m* 1942, Olive (d 1989), da of late George Winchester Robins, of Caldy, Ches; 1 da (Roseann); *Heir* n, Peter John Madden b 1942; *Career* joined RN 1920, WWII served HMS Warspite (despatches) and HMS Emperor (despatches); chief of Naval Staff NZ 1953-55, naval ADC to HM The Queen 1955, C-in-C Plymouth 1959-62, Adm 1961, C-in-C Home Fleet and Eastern Atlantic 1963-65, ret 1965; chm Royal Nat Mission to Deep Sea Fishermen 1971-81, tstee Nat Maritime Museum 1968 (chm 1972-77), chm Standing Cncl of the Baronetage 1975-77; Vice Lord Lt (Gtr London) 1969-82; *Clubs* Arts; *Style*— Adm Sir Charles Madden, Bt, GCB; 21 Eldon Rd, London W8 (☎ 071 937 6700)

MADDEN, Maxwell Francis (Max); MP (Lab) Bradford West 1983-; s of George Francis Leonard Madden, and Rene Frances Madden; *b* 29 Oct 1941; *Educ* Lascelles Secdy Mod Sch, Pinner GS; *m* 1972, Sheelagh Teresa Catherine, *née* Howard; *Career* journalist: E Essex Gazette, Tribune, Sun, Scotsman; Br Gas Corpn press and info offr; MP (Lab) Sowerby Feb 1974-79; dir of publicity Lab Pty 1979-, front bench oppn spokesman Health and Social Security 1983-84; *Recreations* fishing; *Style*— Max Madden, Esq, MP; House of Commons, London SW1A 0AA

MADDEN, Michael; s of John Joseph Madden (d 1978), and Mary Ann, *née* Donnelly; *b* 14 Jan 1937; *Educ* St Illtyds Coll Cardiff Wales, LSE (BSc); *m* 27 Feb 1960, Patricia Margaret, da of Charles Gaspa, of Cliftonville, Kent; 2 s (Simon Jude b 1960, Stephen Paul b 1964), 1 da (Alison Maria b 1962); *Career* asst gen mangr Moscow Narodny Bank Ltd 1966-68 (economic advsr 1959-66), gen mangr First Nat Fin Corpn Ltd 1968-70, md Exim Credit Mgmnt Consits Ltd 1971-76, exec dir Standard Chartered Merchant Bank Ltd 1977-86, dir Standard Chartered Merchant Bank Hldgs 1984-86, md Standard Chartered Merchant Bank Ltd 1986, gen mangr Standard Chartered Bank 1987-88, chief exec Standard Chartered Export Fin Ltd 1987-88; non exec dir and dep chm Int Bank of W Africa (Fin) Ltd; non-res conslt: 1BRD (World Bank) Washington, FAO (Investmt Centre) Rome, UNCTAD Geneva; *Recreations* rugby football, gardening, writing; *Clubs* Reform, Overseas Bankers; *Style*— Michael Madden, Esq; 16 Wolsey Rd, Moor Park, Herts HA6 2HW (☎ 09274 26767)

MADDEN, Michael; s of Harold Madden (d 1956), and Alice Elizabeth, *née* Grenville (d 1968); *b* 12 Feb 1936; *Educ* King Edward VII Sch Sheffield; *m* 1, 30 Jan 1960 (m dis 1977), (Elaine) Marion, da of Ernest Will (d 1985); 2 s (Peter Richard b 22 Dec 1960, Andrew David b 13 Dec 1961), 1 da (Kathryn Jane b 5 Oct 1966); *Career* Miny of Tport & Civil Aviation 1955-63; Miny of Agric Fisheries & Food: asst princ 1963, asst private sec to Min 1966-67, princ Land Improvement Div and Tropical Foods Div 1967-73, asst sec 1973-85, under sec Mgmnt Services Gp 1985-90, currently under sec Flood Defence Plant Protection & Agric Resource Policy Gp; *Recreations* walking, wine, music, friends; *Clubs* Farmers'; *Style*— Michael Madden, Esq; Ministry of Agriculture, Fisheries & Food, 3 Whitehall Place, London SW1A 2HH (☎ 071 270 8099)

MADDISON, Prof Peter John; s of John Maddison, of 14 Nant Rd, London, and Renee, *née* Lemmesurier; *b* 12 Dec 1945; *Educ* St Albans Sch, Pembroke Coll Cambridge, Bart's Med Sch (MA, MB BChir, MD); *m* 17 Feb 1968, Merle Chadburn, da of Denby Bamford, CBE, of Station Farmhouse, Little Barrow, Cheshire; 1 s (Christopher); *Career* fell in rheumatology and immunology Stake Univ of New York at Buffalo 1974-77, asst prof of med 1977-79, conslt rheumatologist Royal Nat Hosp for Rheumatic Diseases Bath 1979-88; Univ of Bath: prof of bone and joint med 1988-, dean Sch of Postgraduate Med 1989; res dir Bath Inst of Rheumatic Diseases, res and educn dir Royal Nat Hosp for Rheumatic Diseases 1991-; author of 130 scientific articles, reviews and chapters; med sec of the Arthritis and Rheumatism Cncl, advsy bd memb of Nat Osteoporosis Soc; tstee: REMEDI, Bath Inst of Rheumatic Diseases; FRCP 1986, memb British Soc of Rheumatology; *Books* Rheumatological Medicine (with P A Dieppe, M Doherty and D G Macfarlane, 1985), The Skin In Rheumatic Diseses (with C L Lovell and G Campion, 1989); *Recreations* cooking, cricket, golf, modern literature; *Style*— Prof Peter Maddison; Woodbury House, 29 Bloomfield Rd, Bath BA2 2AD (☎ 0225 334413); The Royal National Hosp For Rheumatic Diseases, Upper Borough Walls, Bath BA1 lRL (☎ 0225 465941)

MADDISON, Roger Robson; s of Ralph Robson Maddison (d 1943), and Ethel Daisy, *née* Smith; *b* 15 July 1929; *Educ* Dulwich Coll, Cambridge Univ (MA); *m* 1, 1954 (m dis 1975), Christine Elizabeth, *née* Fulljames; 2 s (Patrick James Robson b 1959, Timothy Paul Robson b 1963), 1 da (Vivien Mary b 1956); m 2, Sara Caroline, da of Arthur Geoffrey Howland-Jackson, MBE; *Career* slr; sr ptnr Knapp-Fishers (Westminster) 1980-83; sr ptnr Baldocks (Guildford) 1984-; memb Law Soc; *Recreations* golf, tennis, music, gardening; *Clubs* Worplesdon GC, St George's Hill LTC; *Style*— Roger Maddison, Esq; Rydal House, East Horsley, Surrey (☎ 048 65 2377); 59 Quarry St, Guildford, Surrey (☎ 0483 573 303)

MADDOCK, Thomas Patrick; s of John Henry Maddock, of The Chase, High Knott, Arnside, Cumbria, and Julia, *née* Murphy; *b* 5 March 1942; *Educ* Downside; *m* 15 July 1972, Carmen, da of Royston St Noble (d 1971), of Barcelona, Spain; 2 s (Royston b 1975, William b 1978); *Career* Lt Duke of Lancaster's Own Yeo (TA); owner and dir The Tom Maddock Gallery Barcelona 1968-, dir Charles Maddock Ltd; *Recreations* riding, tennis, swimming; *Clubs* Real Club de Polo (Barcelona), Sloane; *Style*— Thomas Maddock, Esq; Ganduxer 136, 2o2a 08022 Barcelona, Spain; Casanova, Vilanova del Valles, Prov de Barcelona, Spain; The Chase, High Knott Rd, Arnside, Cumbria (☎ 343 418 3975); TOM MADDOCK Gallery, Aribau 306, 08006 Barcelona, Spain (☎ 343 201 2687, fax 343 203 3512)

MADDOCKS, Fiona Hamilton; da of William Hunter Maddocks, and Dorothy Christina, *née* Hill; *b* 1 June 1955; *Educ* Blackheath HS London, Newnham Coll Cambridge (MA); *m* 1989, Robert James Cooper, s of John Samuel Pontifex Cooper Cooper; 1 da (Arabella Phoebe Hamilton); *Career* teacher of Eng lit Istituto Orsoline Cortina D'Ampezzo Italy 1978, art publisher Medici Soc 1979, news trainee rising to sr prodr LBC 1980-82, ed Comment (Channel 4) 1982, reg contrib to The Times 1983-86, asst commissioning ed Music (Channel 4) 1985, journalist and pre-launch music ed and feature writer Independent 1986-; freelance writer various pubns, TV and radio; assoc Newnham Coll 1985-, exec memb Soc for Promotion of New Music 1990; patron Newnham Coll Appeal 1990-; *Recreations* playing chamber music; *Style*— Ms Fiona Maddocks; The Independent, 40 City Rd, London EC1Y 2DB (☎ 071 956 1651)

MADDOCKS, Sir Kenneth Phipson; KCMG (1958, CMG 1956), KCVO (1963); s of Arthur P Maddocks (d 1957); *b* 8 Feb 1907; *Educ* Bromsgrove Sch, Wadham Coll Oxford; *m* 1, 1951, Elnor Radcliffe (d 1976), da of Sir E John Russell, OBE, FRS (d 1965); m 2, 1980, Patricia Josephine, *née* Hare Duke, wid of Sir George Mooring, KCMG; *Career* HMOCS; civil sec Northern Region Nigeria 1955-57, dep govr 1957-58, actg govr Northern Region Nigeria 1956 and 1957, govr and C-in-C Fiji 1958-63, dir and sec East Africa and Mauritius Assoc 1964-69; KStJ; *Recreations* gardening; *Clubs* Royal Cwlth Soc; *Style*— Sir Kenneth Maddocks, KCMG, KCVO; 11 Lee Rd, Aldeburgh, Suffolk IP15 5HG (☎ 0728 453443)

MADDOCKS, Rt Rev Morris Henry St John; s of Rev Canon Morris Arthur Maddocks (d 1953), and Gladys Mabel, *née* Sharpe; *b* 28 April 1928; *Educ* St John's Sch Leatherhead, Trinity Coll Cambridge, Chichester Theol Coll; *m* 1955, Anne, da of late William Oliver Miles; *Career* Nat Serv 2 Lt RASC; curate: St Peter's Ealing 1954-55, St Andrew's Uxbridge 1955-58; vicar: Weaverthorpe Helperthorpe and Luttons Ambo 1958-61, St Martin-on-the-Hill Scarborough 1961-71; suffragan bishop of Selby 1972-83; hon asst bishop: Diocese of Bath and Wells 1983-87, Diocese of Chichester 1987-; chm of Churches Cncl for Health and Healing 1982-85 (joint chm 1975-82), advsr to the Archbishops of Canterbury and York for the Miny of Health and Healing 1983-; joint fndr (with wife) of Acorn Christian Healing Tst; FRSM 1988; *Books* The Christian Healing Ministry (1981), The Christian Adventure (1983), Journey to Wholeness (1986), A Healing House of Prayer (1987), Twenty Questions About Healing (1988); *Recreations* walking, gardening, music; *Clubs* Army and Navy; *Style*— The Rt Rev Morris Maddocks; St Mary's, Burrswood, Groombridge, nr Tunbridge Wells, Kent TN3 9PY (☎ 0892 863637 ext 221); Acorn Christian Healing Trust, Whitehall Chase, Bordon, Hampshire GU35 OAP (☎ 0420 478121/2)

MADDOCKS, Dr Peter Dobell; s of Thomas Frederick Maddocks (d 1976), and Enid Margaret Dobell Newton, *née* Colson; *b* 16 Feb 1935; *Educ* Berkhamstead Sch, Univ of London, Middlesex Hosp Med Sch (MB, BS, MRCP, DPM); *m* 6 June 1959, Dr (Williamina Thelma) Astrid, da of Dr William Frederick Twining McMath; 4 s (Mark b 1961, Jeremy b 1962, William b 1965, Giles b 1967); *Career* sr house offr St Lukes Woodside Hosp, casualty med offr Middlesex Hosp, med registrar Sr Helier Hosp Carshalton, sr registrar St Thomas' Hosp, conslt psychiatrist Wexham Park Hosp; memb: Slough Dist Assoc for Mental Health, Maidenhead Assoc for Mental Health; regnl advsr to Oxford RHA, hon sec Chiltern and Thames Valley div RCPsych; FRCPsych 1984 (MRCPsych 1972, memb Cncl); *Recreations* travel, windsurfing; *Style*— Dr Peter Maddocks; 47 Alma Rd, Windsor, Berks (☎ 0753 851551); Dept of Psychiatry, Wexham Park Hosp, Slough, Berks (☎ 0753 34567)

MADDOX, John Royden; s of A J Maddox, of Swansea, and M E Maddox; *b* 27 Nov 1925; *Educ* Gowerton Boys Co Sch, ChCh Oxford, Kings Coll London; *m* 1, Nancy Fanning (d 1960); 1 s, 1 da; m 2, 1960, Brenda Power, *née* Murphy; 1 s, 1 da; *Career* asst lectr then lectr theoretical physics Univ of Manchester 1949-55, sci corr The Guardian 1955-64, affiliate Rockfeller Inst NY 1962-63, asst dir Nuffield Fndn and co-ordinator Nuffield Fndn sci teaching project 1964-66, md Macmillan Jls Ltd 1970-72, dir Macmillan & Co Ltd 1968-73, chm Maddox Ltd 1972-74, dir Nuffield Fndn 1975-80; memb: Royal Cmmn on Environmental Pollution 1976-78, Genetic Manipulation Advsy Gp 1976-80, Br Library Advsy Cncl 1976-81, Cncl on Int Devpt 1977-79; chm cncl Queen Elizabeth Coll 1980-85, memb cncl King's Coll London 1985-; *Books* with Leonard Beaton: The Spread of Nuclear Weapons (1962), Revolution in Biology (1964), The Doomsday Syndrome (1972), Beyond The Energy Crisis (1975); *Clubs* Athenaeum; *Style*— John Maddox, Esq; 9 Pitt St, London W8 (☎ 071 937 9750); Macmillan Magazines Ltd, 4 Little Essex St, London WC2R 3LF (☎ 071 836 6633)

MADDRELL, Geoffrey Keggen; s of Capt Geoffrey Douglas Maddrell (d 1975), of Port Erin, IOM, and Barbara Mary Maddrell; *b* 18 July 1936; *Educ* King Williams Coll Isle of Man, Corpus Christi Coll Cambrige (MA), Columbia Univ New York (MBA); *m* 12 Oct 1964, Winifred Mary Daniel, da of Frank Dowell Jones (d 1984), of St Asaph, Clwyd; 2 s (Paul b 1965, Michael b 1971), 1 da (Siân b 1966); *Career* Lt Parachute Regiment 1955-57; Shell Int Petroleum 1960-69; dir Bowater Corp 1978-86; chief exec Tootal Gp plc 1986-; *Recreations* running, golf; *Clubs* Rowany Golf; *Style*— Geoffrey Maddrell, Esq; Summerhill, 16 Meadlay, Esher, Surrey (☎ 0372 68694); Tootal Group plc, Spring Gardens, Manchester (☎ 061 831 7777)

MADDRELL, (Alan) Lester; s of Capt Stanley Taubman Maddrell, of Colby, IOM, and Sylvia, *née* Leece; *b* 20 Feb 1944; *Educ* King William's Coll IOM; *m* 26 March 1966, Diana Mary, da of Arthur Fallows Tate (d 1984), of Douglas, IOM; 2 s (Richard b 1975, Alan b 1976), 2 da (Tania b 1974 (decd), Stephanie b 1987); *Career* admitted slr 1971-; dep co prosecuting slr Gloucs 1977-80, HM coroner for the Cheltenham Dist of Gloucs; *Recreations* family; *Style*— Lester Maddrell, Esq; 70 Bournside Rd, Cheltenham GL51 5AH; Lester Maddrell & Co, 25 Imperial Square, Cheltenham GL50 1QZ (☎ 0242 514 000, fax 0242 226 575)

MADEL, (William) David; MP (C) S W Bedfordshire 1983-; s of William R Madel (d 1975), and Eileen Madel; *b* 6 Aug 1938; *Educ* Uppingham, Keble Coll Oxford (MA); *m* 1971, Susan Catherine, da of Lt Cdr Hon Peter Carew, RN (ret); *Career* advertising exec; memb Bow Gp Cncl 1966-67; MP (C) Bedfordshire South 1970-83, PPS to jt Parly under-secs of state Def 1973-74, pps to min of state for Def 1973-74, chm Cons Parly Educn 1983-85; *Style*— David Madel, Esq, MP; 120 Pickford Rd, Markyate, Herts

MADEN, Prof (Barry) Edward Howorth; s of Lt Harold Maden, of Windermere, and

Kathleen, *née* Cope; *b* 5 Nov 1935; *Educ* Uppingham, Cambridge (MA, MB BChir, PhD); *m* 16 July 1960 (m dis 1989), Regina, da of Reginald Cheers (d 1957); 1 s (Christopher b 1961), 1 da (Jill b 1963); *Career* res assoc Albert Einstein Med Coll NY 1967-69, lectr Dept of Biochemistry Univ of Glasgow 1969-72; Univ of Liverpool: sr lectr, reader 1976-83, Johnston prof of biochemistry 1983; visiting scientist Dept of Embryology Carnegie Instn of Washington Baltimore USA 1977-78; contrib: Journal of Molecular Biology, Biochemical Journal and Nature; tstee Drummond Trust for Nutrition; FRSE 1978; *Books* contrib to: Cell Biology in Medicine (1972), Ribosomes (1974), Transmethylation (1978), Classic Rock (1978), The Cell Nucleus (vol 10, 1982), The Nucleolus (1983), Chromatography and Modification of Nucleosides (part b, 1989); *Recreations* mountaineering; *Clubs* Alpine, Climbers, Scottish Mountaineering; *Style*— Prof Edward Maden, FRSE; 25 Gwydrin Rd, Liverpool L18 3HA (☎ 051 722 0290); Univ of Liverpool, Dept of Biochemistry, PO Box 147, Liverpool L69 3BX (☎ 051 794 4350, fax 051 708 6502, telex 627095 UNILPEL G)

MADGWICK, Sandra Elizabeth; da of Kenneth Edward Madgwick, and Shirley Anne, *née* Cross; *b* 7 March 1963; *Educ* The Royal Ballet Sch; *Career* ballet dancer; performances: Royal Ballet Sch and 60 birthday anniversary of Sir F Ashton, La Fille Mal Gardee (Lise), Petipa's The Sleeping Beauty (Aurora), Peter Wright's Coppetia (Swanhilda), David Bintley's Hobsons Choice (Vicky Hobson), Sir Frederick Ashton's The Two Pigeons (Girl), David Bintley's The Snow Queen (Gerd), Sir Kenneth MacMillan's Quartet; *Style*— Miss Sandra Madgwick; The Royal Opera House, Floral St, London (☎ 071 240 1200)

MADOC, Ruth Llewellyn (Mrs John Jackson); *b* 16 April 1943; *Educ* RADA; *m* John Jackson; 1 s (Rhys), 1 da (Lowri); *Career* actress; began career with Black and White Minstrel Show; tv credits incl: Gladys Pugh in Hi-De-Hi, Hunters Walk, Lloyd George, The Morecambe and Wise Show, Blankety Blank, Give Us A Clue, Whose Baby, Tell the Truth, Through the Keyhole; subject of This is Your Life 1984; theatre work incl: Man of La Mancha (Piccadilly Theatre), Under Milk Wood, Irma in Irma La Douce, Letty in Something's Afoot, Mixed Feelings, Maria in Twelfth Night (Regent's Park Open Air Theatre), Bless the Bride (Sadlers Wells Theatre) 1988, Touch and Go (Opera House Jersey) 1988, Rose in Gypsy, Helen in A Taste of Honey (Grand Theatre Swansea), Find the Lady (Salisbury, Eastbourne and Jersey) 1990, guest appearance in Night of a Hundred Stars (London Palladium) 1990; pantomine work incl: principal boy in pantomine nationwide, Babes in the Wood 1987, Robinson Crusoe (Theatre Royal Plymouth) 1988; film credits incl: Fiddler on the Roof, The Prince and the Pauper, Under Milk Wood; three appearances in Royal Variety Shows, numerous guest appearances for charity nationwide; *Style*— Ms Ruth Madoc; Madoc Entertainments, Hawk Group Ltd, Blundell House, Torrington Ave, Coventry CV4 9GU (☎ 0203 46628, fax 0203 469393, car 0836 724039)

MADOCKS, John Edward; CBE (1965, MBE 1956), DL (Notts 1978); s of Sidney George Robert Madocks (d 1935); *b* 14 March 1922; *Educ* King Edward VI Sch Lichfield, Univ of Birmingham; *m* 1945, Jessica Kinross, da of Andrew Davidson (d 1939); 1 s, 1 da; *Career* served WWII, Europe and ME, Maj; perm sec HMOCS 1946-65; bursar Univ of Nottingham 1967-87; dir ATV Network Ltd 1979-81, chm East Midlands Bd Central Independent Television 1982-; memb Regnl Bd BR (London Midland) 1979-90; memb: E Midlands Economic Planning Cncl 1975-79, Prince's Youth Business Tst, Nottingham Devpt Enterprise; chm Notts Economic Planning Forum 1980-82, nat chm and vice pres Assoc of Br Chambers of Commerce 1980-82, co rep Royal Jubilee Tsts 1976-86; pres: Nottinghamshire Hospice, East Midlands Quality Club; High Sheriff of Nottinghamshire 1988-89; *Recreations* books, pictures, sport; *Clubs* Royal Cwlth; *Style*— John Madocks, Esq, CBE, DL; 7 Middleton Cres, Beeston, Nottingham (☎ 0602 256592)

MAFFEI, Waldo; s of Waldo Maffei Sr, and Cathrine, *née* Garbar; *b* 4 Oct 1955; *Educ* Rice Univ (BArch), Univ of Harvard (MArch); *Career* architect; dir Hanscomb Davies Maffei London; *Clubs* Harvard, New York Athletic; *Style*— Waldo Maffei, Esq; 25 Central Park West, New York, NY 10023, USA; 28 Ocean Ave, Hyannis Port, MA 02647, USA; 45 Rockefeller Plaza, New York, NY 10020, USA (☎ 010 12123074008, fax 010 12123076592)

MAFFEY, Hon Christopher Alan; s of 2 Baron Rugby (d 1990), and Margaret, *née* Bindley; *b* 20 Feb 1955; *Educ* Malvern; *m* 1, 1977 (m dis 1981), Barbara Anne, yr da of Guthrie Stewart, of Auckland, NZ; m 2, 1982, Kathryn, er da of Viv Rutherfurd, of Waiuku, NZ; 2 s (Aaron John b 1983, Leigh Alan b 1984); *Career* farmer; pres Manukau Peninsula Play Centre; *Recreations* fishing, building; *Clubs* Awhitu Social Club; *Style*— The Hon Christopher Maffey; Hamiltons Rd, RD4, Waiuku, New Zealand

MAFFEY, Hon Mark Andrew; yst s of 2 Baron Rugby (d 1990), and Margaret, *née* Bindley; *b* 7 June 1956; *Educ* Harrow, Ecole de Commerce Neuchâtel Switzerland; *m* 16 July 1983, Angela Mary, da of Derek J Polton, of The Pennies, Draycote, Rugby; 1 s (Thomas Henry b 1988), 1 da (Georgina Louise b 1986); *Career* gen mgmnt; Liveryman Worshipful Co of Saddlers; *Recreations* shooting, fishing; *Style*— The Hon Mark Maffey; Grove Farm Flat, Frankton, Rugby, Warwicks

MAFFEY, Hon Selina Penelope; er da of 2 Baron Rugby (d 1990), and Margaret, *née* Bindley; *b* 15 Nov 1952; *Educ* Hawnes Sch Beds; 1 s (Tamas Henry b 1990), 1 da (Angelica Helena b 1986); *Career* farmer, tropical fruit and cattle, landowner; *Style*— The Hon Selina Maffey; McDougal Road, Julatten, Queensland 4880, Australia

MAFFEY, Hon Simon Chelmsford Loader; s of 1 Baron Rugby, GCMG, KCB, KCVO, CSI, CIE (d 1969); *b* 1919; *Educ* Rugby; *m* 1949 (m dis 1962), Andree Norma, da of George Middleton; 1 da; *Career* Lt Coldstream Gds 1937, served 1939-42, served MN 1942-45; *Style*— The Hon Simon Maffey

MAGAN, George Morgan; s of Brig William Morgan Tilson Magan, CBE, and Maxine, *née* Mitchell; *b* 14 Nov 1945; *Educ* Winchester; *m* 1972, Wendy Anne, da of Maj Patrick Chilton, MC; 2 s (Edward b 1975, Patrick b 1984), 1 da (Henrietta b 1977); *Career* merchant banker; dir: J O Hambro Magan & Co Ltd, Asprey plc, WCRS Gp plc, CCA Pubns plc; govr Hawtrey's Sch; FCA; *Clubs* Royal Yacht Squadron, Turf, Boodle's; *Style*— George Magan, Esq; J O Hambro Magan & Co Ltd, 30 Queen Anne's Gate, London SW1 (☎ 071 222 2020); St Michael's House, Nr Tonbridge, Kent

MAGAURAN, Denise Mary; da of Wilfrid Magauran (d 1964), and Dr Iris Mary Magauran; *b* 8 Nov 1940; *Educ* Convent of the Sacred Heart Woldingham Surrey, Charing Cross Hosp Med Sch (MB BS); *Career* house physician house surgn and sr house offr in ophthalmology: Royal Free Hosp, Manchester Eye Hosp, Bart's Hosp; clinical asst: Bart's Hosp, Moorfields Eye Hosp, W Ophthalmic Hosp; registrar St James's Hosp Balham, sr registrar St Paul's Eye Hosp Liverpool, Hayward Fellowship as asst surgn St John Ophthalmic Hosp Jerusalem, conslt ophthalmologist Gloucester Health Authy 1974; visiting ophthalmologist St Helena; actively involved in: Royal Cwlth Soc of the Blind, ODA; OStJ 1973; LRCP, MRCS 1963, DO 1966, FRSM, FRCS 1971, FCOphth 1989; *Books* Ocular Injuries Caused by Airgun Pellets - An Analysis of 105 Cases (jtly, 1973), Unilateral Spontaneous Hyphaemata (1973), The Effect of Thiopentone and Fazadinium on Intraocular Pressure (jtly, 1979); *Recreations* travel, tapestry, swimming, walking; *Clubs* local leisure; *Style*— Miss Denise Magauran; The Cottage, 89 London Road, Gloucester GL1 3HH (☎ 0452 23238); The Gloucester Clinic, Denmark Rd, Gloucester GL1 3HH (☎ 0452 423601, fax 0452 306602)

MAGEE, Bryan; s of Frederick Magee; *b* 12 April 1930; *Educ* Christ's Hosp, Lycée Hôche Versailles, Keble Coll Oxford (MA), Yale; *m* 1954 (m dis), Ingrid Söderlund; 1 da; *Career* writer, critic, and broadcaster; formerly: columnist The Times, drama critic The Listener; music critic for numerous pubns 1959-, hon sr fell in the history of ideas King's Coll London 1984-, lectr in philosophy Balliol Coll Oxford 1987-88; visiting fell All Souls Coll Oxford 1987-88, pres Univ of Edinburgh Philosophy Soc 1987-88, hon fell QMC 1988, fell Royal Philharmonic Soc 1990, visiting scholar Wolfson Coll Oxford 1991-93, cncl memb Ditchley Fndn 1982- (govr 1979-); Parly candidate (Lab) Mids Beds 1959 and 1960, MP Leyton (Lab until 1982, Ind Lab 1982, SDP 1982-83); judge: Evening Standard Opera Award 1973-84, Laurence Olivier Opera Award 1990-91; silver medallist RTS 1978, pres Critics Circle 1983-84 (cncl memb 1975-); *Books* Crucifixion and Other Poems (1951), Go West Young Man (1958), To Live in Danger (1960), The New Radicalism (1962), The Democratic Revolution (1964), Towards 2000 (1965), One in Twenty (1966), The Television Interviewer (1966), Aspects of Wagner (1968 and revised, ed 1988), Modern British Philosophy (1971), Popper (1973), Facing Death (1977), Men of Ideas (1978), The Philosophy of Schopenhauer (1983), The Great Philosophers (1987); *Recreations* music, theatre, travel; *Clubs* Beefsteak, Brooks's, Garrick, Savile; *Style*— Bryan Magee, Esq; 12 Falkland House, Marloes Rd, London W8 (☎ 071 937 1210)

MAGEE, Christopher Douglas; s of Douglas David Magee, of Farnham, Surrey, and Eva Mary, *née* Pope; *b* 3 Nov 1945; *Educ* George Abbott Sch Guildford, Guildford Coll of Technol, Univ of Reading (OND, HND, MSc); *m* 4 May 1985, Carol Elizabeth, da of Alan Boocock, of Bispham, Blackpool, Lancs; 2 da (Laura Victoria b 27 May 1986, Sarah Eve b 7 April 1988); *Career* mangr Jeddah W S Try Int Ltd 1979, commercial exec W S Try Ltd 1984, gen mangr Barlow Turnkey Contracts Ltd 1986, md George Kemp Stroud & Co Ltd 1989 (dir 1988); memb Ctee CIOB Guildford Centre (chm 1987); FCIOB 1981, FBIM 1982; *Recreations* keeping fit, squash, photography; *Clubs* Hart Health and Fitness; *Style*— Chris D Magee, Esq; 45 Abbots Ride, Farnham, Surrey GU9 8HZ (☎ 0252 723743); George Kemp Stroud & Co Ltd, Elms Rd, Aldershot, Hampshire GU11 1LL (☎ 0252 20339, fax 0252 333924, car 0860 234744)

MAGENTA, Duchesse de; Hon Amélie Margaret Mary; da of Capt Humphrey Drummond of Megginch, MC, and Baroness Strange, *qqv*; *b* 2 July 1963; *Educ* Heathfield, Dundee Coll of Commerce, London Poly; *m* 4 May 1990, as his 2 w, Philippe, 4 Duc de Magenta, 8 Marquis de MacMahon, s of Maurice, 3 Duc de Magenta, 7 Marquis de MacMahon (d 1954); 1 da (Pélagie b 24 June 1990); *Recreations* winemaking, gardening; *Style*— La Duchesse de Magenta; Megginch Castle, Errol, Perthshire; Château de Sully, 71360 Epinac, Saone-et-Loire, France

MAGGS, Air Vice-Marshal William Jack; CB (1967), OBE (1943); s of Frederick Wilfrid Maggs (d 1959), and Hilda Lilian Marguerite Maggs (d 1914); *b* 2 Feb 1914; *Educ* Bristol GS, St John's Coll Oxford (MA); *m* 1940, Margaret Grace, da of Thomas Liddell Hetherington (d 1975); 1 s, 1 da; *Career* joined RAF 1939, Air Vice-Marshal 1967; served WWII in UK, N Africa, Sicily, Italy; sr staff offr RAF Maintenance Cmd 1967-69; official fell and domestic bursar Keble Oxford 1969-77, emeritus fell Keble Coll 1981-; govr Bristol GS 1979; *Recreations* golf, gardening; *Clubs* RAF; *Style*— Air Vice-Marshal William Maggs, CB, OBE; No 7 The Spindlers, Church St, Old Kidlington, Oxford OX5 2YP (☎ 086 75 3139)

MAGINNIS, Ken Wiggins; MP (Ulster Unionist) Fermanagh and S Tyrone 1983-; s of Gilbert Maginnis (d 1974), of Dungannon, and Margaret Elizabeth Wiggins (d 1984); *b* 21 Jan 1938; *Educ* Royal Sch Dungannon, Stranmills TTC Belfast; *m* 1961, Joy, da of Herbert Moneymore (d 1976); 2 s (Stewart b 1963, Steven b 1971), 2 da (Gail b 1964, Grainne b 1969); *Career* UDR 1970-81 (cmmnd 1972, Maj), princ sch teacher 1966-82; memb: Dungannon DC 1981-, NI Assembly 1982-86; chm Security & Home Affrs Ctee 1983-86; memb Select Ctee: on Def 1983-86, on Armed Forces Bill 1991; pty spokesman on security Ulster Unionist Pty; *Clubs* Army & Navy; *Style*— Ken Maginnis, Esq, MP; House of Commons, London SW1

MAGNUS, Alan Melvyn; s of Norman Alexander Magnus, and Mimi, *née* Folkson; *b* 31 Aug 1938; *Educ* Sir George Monoux GS, Worcester Coll Oxford (MA), Coll of Law; *m* 25 Nov 1962, Judith Sophia, da of Sidney Sack (d 1987); 2 s (Adrian b 1963, Brian b 1966), 1 da (Tina b 1968); *Career* admitted slr 1964; head co and commercial branch legal dept NCB 1973-87; ptnr D J Freeman & Co Slrs 1987-; jt treas Reform Synagogues of GB 1988-91; memb: City of London Slrs Co 1988, Law Soc 1963; Freeman City of London 1988; *Recreations* scuba diving, opera, ballet, music; *Style*— Alan M Magnus, Esq; 84 Holders Hill Rd, Hendon, London NW4 1LN (☎ 081 346 1941); D J Freeman & Co, 43 Fetter Lane, London EC4A 1NA (☎ 071 583 4055, 071 583 2373, fax 071 353 7377, telex 894579)

MAGNUS, Sir Laurence Henry Philip; 3 Bt (UK 1917), of Tangley Hill, Wonersh, Co Surrey; s of Hilary Barrow Magnus, TD, QC (d 1987), and Rosemary Vera Anne, *née* Masefield; suc unc, Sir Philip Magnus-Allcroft, 2 Bt (d 1988); *b* 24 Sept 1955; *Educ* Eton, Christ Church Oxford; *m* 1983, Jocelyn Mary, eldest da of Robert Henry Foster Stanton; 2 s (Thomas Henry Philip b 1985, Edmund Robert Hilary b 1991), 1 da (Iona Alexandra b 1988); *Heir* s, Thomas Henry Philip Magnus b 1985; *Career* exec dir Samuel Montagu & Co Ltd merchant bankers; memb Bow Gp; *Recreations* fishing, reading, hill walking; *Style*— Sir Laurence Magnus, Bt; 66 Archer House, Vicarage Crescent, London SW11 3LG

MAGNUS, Samuel Woolf; QC (1964); s of Samuel Woolf Magnus (d 1910), and Elizabeth, *née* Sachs (d 1958); *b* 30 Sept 1910; *Educ* privately, UCL (BA), Sch of Slavonic Studies; *m* 7 June 1938, Anna Gertrude, da of Adolph Shane (d 1958), of Cardiff; 1 da (Patricia Ruth (Mrs Anthony Morris) b 11 Feb 1943); *Career* WWII 1939-46, cmmnd RAOC served Egypt and Palestine; called to the Bar Gray's Inn 1937, in practice London 1937-59, ptnr legal firm N Rhodesia 1959-64, legal conslt 1964; MP: N Rhodesia 1964, Zambia 1964-68; puisne judge Zambia High Court 1968, justice of appeal Zambia 1971, cmmr Compensation Cmmn 1977-83; Parly candidate (Lib) Central Hackney 1945, treas Assoc of Liberal Lawyers, memb Cncl London Lib Pty, pres N Hendon Lib Assoc 1959; chm Law Parly and Gp Ctee Bd of Deputies of Br Jews 1979-83, memb Exec Ctee Friends of Westminster Hosp, pres Westminster E Rotary Club 1980; FCIArb 1987; *Books* Companies Act 1947 (with M Estrin, 1947), Companies: Law and Practice (with M Estrin, 1948, 1978, supplement 1981), Advertisement Control (with A M Lyons, 1949), Magnus on Leasehold Property (Temporary Provisions Act) 1951, (1951), Magnus on Landlord Tenant Act 1954 (1954), Magnus on Housing Repairs and Rents Act 1954 (1954), Knight's Annotated Housing Acts 1958 (with F E Price, 1958), Magnus on Housing Finance (with Tovell, 1960), Companies Act 1967 (with M Estrin, 1967), Magnus on the Rent Act 1968 (1968), Magnus on Business Tenancies (1970), Magnus on the Rent Act 1977 (1978), Butterworths Company Forms Manual (1988); *Style*— Samuel Magnus, Esq, QC; 33 Apsley Hse, Finchley Rd, St John's Wood, London NW8 0NX (☎ 071 586 1679)

MAGNUS-ALLCROFT, Lady; Jewell; *née* Allcroft; o da of Herbert John Allcroft (d 1911), of Stokesay Court, and Margaret Jane (who m 2, 1917, Brig-Gen John Guy Rotton, CB, CMG, and d 1946), o da of Gen Sir William Russell, 2 Bt, CB; *b* 26 Jan 1907; *m* 14 July 1943, Sir Philip Montefiore Magnus-Allcroft, 2 Bt, CBE (d 1988);

Career Welfare Offr ATS 1943-45; co vice-chm Br Legion Women's Section; *Clubs* Ladies' Carlton, Shropshire County; *Style—* Lady Magnus-Allcroft; Stokesay Ct, Onibury, Shropshire SY7 9BD (☎ 058 477 372)

MAGNUSSON, Magnus; Hon KBE (1989); s of Sigursteinn Magnússon (d 1982), of Edinburgh, and Ingibjorg, *née* Sigurdardóttir (d 1983); *b* 12 Oct 1929; *Educ* The Edinburgh Acad, Jesus Coll Oxford (MA); *m* 30 June 1954, Mamie, da of John Baird (d 1945), of Rutherglen, Glasgow; 2 s (Siggy b 1961, d 1973, Jon b 1965), 3 da (Sally b 1955, Margaret b 1959, Anna b 1960); *Career* journalist and broadcaster; Scot Daily Express 1953-61, asst ed The Scotsman 1961-68; presenter many BBC TV and radio progs incl: Mastermind, Chronicle, Tonight, Mainly Magnus, BC: The Archaeology of the Bible Lands, Vikings!, Pebble Mill at One, Living Legends, Personal Pursuits, Current Account, All Things Considered, Landlord or Tenant - A View of Irish History; rector Univ of Edinburgh 1975-78, fndr chm Scot Churches Architectural Heritage Tst 1978-85, chm Ancient Monuments Bd for Scot 1981-89, tstee Nat Museums of Scot 1985-89, pres RSPB 1985-90, memb UK ctee for Euro Year of the Environment 1987, chm Nature Conservancy Cncl for Scot 1991-, chm designate Scottish Natural Heritage; Hon DHc Univ of Edinburgh 1978, Hon DUniv Univ of York 1981; FSA Scot 1974, FRSE 1980, FRSA 1983, Hon FRIAS 1987; Knight of the Order of the Falcon Iceland 1975, Knight Cdr 1986; *Books* Introducing Archaeology (1972), Viking Expansion Westwards (1973), Viking Hammer of the North (1976), BC: The Archaeology of the Bible Lands (1977), Vikings! (1980), Treasures of Scotland (1981), Lindisfarne (1984), Iceland Saga (1987), Chambers Biographical Dictionary (ed, 1990); *Recreations* reading, wildlife; *Style—* Magnus Magnusson, Esq, KBE, FSA, FRSE; Blairskaith House, Balmore-Torrance, Glasgow G64 4AX (☎ 0360 20226)

MAGONET, Rabbi Dr Jonathan David; s of Capt Alexander Philip Magonet (d 1978), and Esther, *née* Slonims (d 1972); *b* 2 Aug 1942; *Educ* Westminster, Middlesex Hosp Med Sch Univ of London (MB BS), Leo Baeck Coll (Rabbinic ordination), Univ of Heidelberg (PhD); *m* 10 May 1974, Dorothea Elsa Martha, da of Gerhardt Foth; 1 s (Gavriel b 4 May 1978), 1 da (Avigail b 28 April 1981); *Career* lectr and head of Dept of Bible Studies Leo Baeck Coll 1974-85, princ Leo Baeck Coll 1985-, scholar in residence Dept of Jewish Educn Univ of Tel Aviv 1990-91; memb Editorial Bd: European Judaism 1978-, Christian-Jewish Relations 1987-; *Books* Form and Meaning: Studies in Literary Techniques in the Book of Jonah (1976), Forms of Prayer: Vol 1 Daily and Sabbath Prayerbook (co-ed with Lionel Blue, 1977), Forms of Prayer: Voll III Days of Awe Prayerbook (co-ed with Lionel Blue, 1985), The Guide to the Here and the Hereafter (co-ed with Lionel Blue, 1988), A Rabbi's Bible (1991); *Style—* Rabbi Dr Jonathan Magonet; Leo Baeck College, 80 East End Rd, London N3 2SY (☎ 081 349 4525, 081 349 0694)

MAGORIAN, Michelle Jane; da of William Magorian, and Gladys Freda Evans (d 1975); *b* 6 Nov 1947; *Educ* Kilbreda Coll Victoria Aust, Convent of the Cross Hants, Rose Bruford Coll of Speech and Drama, L'Ecole Internationale de Mime Paris; *m* 18 Aug 1987, Peter Keith Venner, s of Albert Keith Venner; 1 s (Thomas b 5 March 1989); *Career* performing in rep 1970-, one woman show touring Italy and UK 1980; memb: Soc of Authors, PEN, Equity; *Books* Goodnight Mister Tom (1981), Back Home (1985, made into a TV film in 1989), Waiting For My Shorts To Dry (1989), Who's Going to Take Care of Me? (1990); short stories incl four anthologies; *Recreations* swimming, sailing, dance, reading; *Style—* Ms Michelle Magorian

MAGUIRE, Dr Anne; da of Richard Patrick Maguire (d 1971), and Ruth Alice, *née* Glencross (d 1963); *b* 2 March 1921; *Educ* London Sch of Med for Women Royal Free Hosp (MB BS), CG Jung Inst Zurich (Dip/Analyt Psychol); *Career* dermatological trg St John's Hosp for Diseases of the Skin Guy's Hosp and Univ Coll Hosp 1956-57, conslt physician for diseases of the skin E Lancs Gp of Hosps 1964-84, private practice Harley St and Blackburn; author of various papers; Ratclyffe Crocker Travelling Fellowship Univ Coll Hosp 1964; FRCP, FRSM; memb: Br Assoc of Dermatologists, St John's Dermatological Soc, Int Assoc of Internal Med, Int Assoc for Analytical Psychologists; *Style—* Dr Anne Maguire; 17 Wellington St, St John's, Blackburn BB1 8AF (☎ 0254 59910); 22 Harley St, London W1 (☎ 071 637 0491)

MAGUIRE, Air Marshal Sir Harold John; KCB (1966, CB 1958), DSO (1946), OBE (1949); s of Michael Maguire, of Maymooth, Ireland, and Harriette, *née* Warren; *b* 12 April 1912; *Educ* Wesley Coll, Trinity Coll Dublin; *m* 1940, Mary Elisabeth, da of George Wild, of Dublin; 1 s, 1 da; *Career* joined RAF 1933, served WWII, Gp Capt 1950, Air Cdre 1958, Air Vice-Marshal 1960, SASO Far East Air Force 1962-64, asst CAS (Intelligence) 1964-65, dep CDS (Intelligence) 1965-68, Air Marshal 1966, ret RAF 1968; dir-gen Intelligence MOD 1968-72; dir Commercial Union Assur Co 1975-82 (political and economic advsr 1972-79); Freeman City of London 1978, Liveryman Worshipful Guild of Airpilots and Navigators 1978; chm cncl of Offrs' Pension Soc 1974-84; *Clubs* RAF; *Style—* Air Marshal Sir Harold Maguire, KCB, DSO, OBE; c/o Lloyds Bank, 6 Pall Mall, London SW1

MAGUIRE, Robert Alfred; OBE (1983); s of Arthur Maguire (d 1950), of London, and Rose Lilian, *née* Fountain (d 1986); *b* 6 June 1931; *Educ* Bancroft's, The Architectural Assoc Sch of Arch (AA Dip); *m* 1, 6 Aug 1955 (m dis 1978), Robina Helen, da of Robert Finlayson; 4 da (Susan b 1956, Rebecca b 1958, Joanna b 1960, Martha b 1963); m 2, 26 Oct 1982, Alison Margaret, da of George Marshall Mason, of Henley-on-Thames; *Career* bldgs ed Architects' Jl 1954-59, private architectural practice 1956-, ptnr Robert Maguire and Keith Murray 1959-89; chm: Maguire & Co 1989-, Maguire and Co International 1990-; most important works incl: St Pauls' Church Bow Common London 1959 (listed Grade II Star), Trinity Coll Oxford extensions 1965, student village, Stag Hill Ct Univ of Surrey 1969; comp winners incl: extensions Magdalen Coll Oxford 1975, Kindertagesstatte Berlin-Kreuzberg 1983, extensions Pembroke Coll Oxford 1986, visitor centre Chepstow Castle 1986, extensions Worcester Coll Oxford 1988; also bldgs in Cathedral Precinct for King's Sch Canterbury 1975-86; Surveyor of the Fabric to St George's Chapel Windsor Castle 1975-87, head of Dept of Architecture Oxford Poly 1976-86; churchwarden St Lawrence's Church S Weston Oxon; RIBA 1953, FRSA 1984; *Books* Modern Churches of the World (1963); *Recreations* sailing, growing sub-tropical fruits; *Style—* Robert Maguire, Esq, OBE; South Weston Cottage, South Weston, Tetsworth, Oxon OX9 7EF (☎ 084 428 262); Cortijo Pepe Pedro, Pago de Sarja, Competa, Malaga, Spain; 104 High St, Thame, Oxon OX9 3DZ (☎ 084 421 7373, fax 084 421 6846); 21 St John's Rd, Richmond, Surrey TW9 2PE

MAHAFFY, Sarah Georgiana; da of Rupert Mahaffy, of London, and Victoria, *née* Ponsonby; *b* 21 July 1952; *Educ* Francis Holland Sch, St Hughe's Coll Oxford (BA); *m* W H Barker; 1 s (Charles); *Career* ed asst Methuen Educational 1974-75; Macmillan Publishers: copywriter 1975-76, mktg exec 1976-78, ed 1978-80, publisher for Humanities 1980-84; estab own Co Baker Mahaffy 1984-86, fndr and md Boxtree 1986-; *Recreations* theatre, food, reading, my family; *Style—* Miss Sarah Mahaffy; 28 Cassland Rd, London E9 7AN; The Old Rectory, Scremby, nr Spilsby, Lincs; Boxtree, 36 Tavistock St, London WC2E 7PB (☎ 071 379 4666, fax 071 836 6741)

MAHAPATRA, Dr Sasi Bhusan; s of late Nila Kantha Mahapatra, and late Moti; *b* 2 Nov 1935; *Educ* BC HS Ranpur Orissa India, Ravenshaw Coll Cuttack Orissa India, SCB Med Coll and Utkal Univ Orissa India (MB BS, DPM); *m* 1 Oct 1963, Maureen Rose, da of late William Henry Piggott; 1 s (Timothy Martin), 2 da (Sonjeeta Krishna, Rachelle Elizabeth); *Career* house offr and house surgn SCB Med Coll Cuttack Orissa 1958-59, med offr Manmunda Health Centre Orissa India 1959-61; sr registrar in psychiatry 1964-66: Runwell Hosp Wickford Essex (sr house offr and registrar 1961-64), St Clements Hosp, The London Hosp; conslt psychiatrist Univ of Leeds 1976- (lectr 1966-70, sr lectr and hon consIt 1970-76), sr clinical lectr St James's Univ Hosp 1976-, dir psychiatry servs Leeds Eastern Health Authy 1986-90, med dir Harrogate Clinic 1990-; memb N Yorks AHA 1971-76, sub dean RCPsych 1977-82; chm: NE Div RCPsych 1984-88, Sub Ctee of Overseas Psychiatry Trainees 1976-84; FRCP 1982, FRCPsych; *Books* Antidepressive Drugs - Side Effects of Drugs (1972), Deafness and Mental Health (1972), Psychosomatic Aspects of Coronary Artery Disease - Psychosomatic Medicine (1973), Problems of Language in Examinations for Foreign Psychiatrists (1974), Short Term Effects of Antidepressive Drugs and Placebo (1975), Schizophrenic Language (ed, 1976), Handbook for Psychiatric Inceptors and Trainees (ed, 1980); *Recreations* cricket, gardening, sailing, music, skiing, photography; *Style—* Dr Sasi Mahapatra; Woodlands Grange, Woodlands Drive, Apperley Bridge, Bradford BD10 0NX (☎ 0532 506854); Dept of Psychiatry, St James's Univ Hosp, Beckett St, Leeds LS9 7TF (☎ 0532 433144 ext 5519); Glebe House, 5 Shaw Lane, Leeds 6 (☎ 0532 789472)

MAHER, Stephen Francis; s of Francis John Maher, of Harrow, Middlesex, and Bridget Rita, *née* Dillon; *b* 19 Feb 1961; *Educ* The John Lyon Sch Middlesex, Balliol Coll Oxford (exhibitioner, MA, Coolidge Pathfinder award); *m* 23 Sept 1989, Sarah Jane, da of Adrian George Beckett; *Career* graduate account trainee Allen Brady & Marsh Ltd 1983; account mangr: ABM 1984-86, Abbott Mead Vickers SMS Ltd 1986-88; account dir AMV 1988-89, Bd account dir Simons Palmer Denton Clemmow & Johnson Ltd 1990- (account dir 1989-90); *Recreations* soul music, guitar playing, reading, travel, skiing, football, photography, film, corgi/dinky car collecting; *Style—* Stephen Maher, Esq; Simons Palmer Denton Clemmow & Johnson Ltd, 19-20 Noel St, London W1V 3PD (☎ 071 287 4455, fax 071 734 2658)

MAHER, Terence; s of John Maher (d 1954), and Bessie Maher; *b* 20 Dec 1941; *Educ* Burnley GS, Univ of Manchester (LLB); *m* 4 Sept 1965 (m dis 1983); 2 da (Catherine Helen b 1971, Elizabeth Jane b 1972); *Career* met stipendiary magistrate 1983-, chm Inner London Juvenile Ct, rec of the Crown Ct; memb editorial bd Journal of Criminal Law; *Recreations* reading, walking, travel; *Clubs* Frewen (Oxford); *Style—* Terence Maher, Esq; Horseferry Road Magistrates Court, Horseferry Road, London WC1

MAHER, Terence Anthony (Terry); s of Herbert Maher (d 1978); *b* 5 Dec 1935; *Educ* Xaverian Coll Manchester; *m* 1960, Barbara, da of Dr Franz Greenbaum (d 1961); 3 s (Nicholas b 1960, Anthony b 1962, Jeremy b 1964); *Career* fndr, chm and chief exec Pentos plc; dir various subsid and associated cos; *Recreations* skiing, reading, walking, tennis; *Style—* Terry Maher, Esq; 33 Clarence Terrace, London NW1 4RD; Pentos plc, New Bond St House, 1 New Bond St, London W1Y 0SB (☎ 071 499 3484, fax 071 629 9413)

MAHLER, Prof Robert Frederick; s of Dr Felix Mahler (d 1959), of London, and Olga, *née* Lowy (d 1989); *b* 31 Oct 1924; *Educ* Edinburgh Acad, Univ of Edinburgh (BSc, MB ChB); *m* 13 June 1951, Maureen, da of Horace Calvert (d 1963), of Dublin; 2 s (Graeme, Brian); *Career* Sqdn Ldr RAF Med Branch 1949-51; res fell Harvard Univ 1956-58, reader Guy's Hosp London 1958-66; prof: Univ of Indiana 1962-63, Univ of Wales 1966-79; visiting prof Stockholm 1976-77, physician Clinical Res Centre Harrow 1979-90; ed Jl of RCP 1987; FRCP (London) 1963, FRCP (Edinburgh) 1963; *Recreations* opera, theatre, music, watching rugby; *Clubs* RSM; *Style—* Prof Robert Mahler; Royal Coll of Physicians, St Andrews Place, Regents Park, London NW1 4LE (☎ 071 935 1174)

MAHON, Sir (John) Denis; CBE (1967); s of John FitzGerald Mahon (d 1942), 4 s of Sir W Mahon, 4 Bt, and Lady Alice Evelyn Browne (d 1970), da of 5th Marquess of Sligo; *b* 8 Nov 1910; *Educ* Eton, Ch Ch Oxford (MA); *Career* art historian; tstee Nat Gallery 1957-64 and 1966-73, memb Advsy Panel Nat Arts Collection Fund 1975; specialist on 17th century painting in Italy and has notable collection; has long campaigned for fiscal measures to encourage support from private individuals for art galleries and museums; author of numerous articles, especially on Caravaggio and Poussin in art historical periodicals incl: Apollo, The Art Bulletin, The Burlington Magazine, Gazette des Beaux Arts, Art de France, Commentari, Paragone, Zeitschrift für Kunstwissenschaft; collaborated in compilation of catalogues raisonnés of many exhibitions incl: Artists in 17th Century Rome (London 1955), Italian Art in Britain (Royal Academy 1960), L'Ideale Classico dei Seicento in Italia (Bologna 1962), Omaggio al Guercino (Cento 1967); memb Ctee of the Biennial Exhibitions at Bologna Italy; awarded: medal for Benemeriti della Cultura 1957, Archiginnasio d'Oro City of Bologna 1968, Serena medal for Italian Studies Br Acad 1972; elected Academico d'Onore Clementine Acad Bologna 1964, corr fell Accad Raffaello Urbino (1968), Deputazione di Storia Patria per le provincie di Romagna (1969), Ateneo Veneto (1987); Hon Citizen Cento (1982), Hon DLitt Newcastle 1969; FBA 1964; kt 1986; *Books* Studies in Seicento Art and Theory (1947), Mostra dei Carracci, Catalogo critico dei Disegni (1956, 1963), Poussiniana (1962), Catalogues of the Mostra del Guercino (Dipinti 1968, Disegni 1969), The Drawings of Guercino in the Collection of HM The Queen at Windsor Castle (with N Turner, 1989); contrib: Actes of Colloque Poussin (1960), Friedlaender Festschrift (1965), Problemi Guardeschi (1967), I Dipinti del Guercino (consIt to Luigi Salerno, 1988); *Style—* Sir Denis Mahon, CBE; 33 Cadogan Square, London SW1X 0HU (☎ 071 235 7311, 071 235 2530)

MAHON, Sean Patrick Lauriston; s of John Patrick Mahon (d 1983), of Sheffield, and Peggy Lauritson, *née* Bines (d 1977); *b* 16 April 1946; *Educ* Ratcliffe Coll Leics; *m* 14 Sept 1968, Pauline Kathleen, da of Eric Vincent Starling; 1 s (Sean Ciaran b 15 June 1971), 3 da (Victoria Amanda b 4 Oct 1972, Siobhan Katherine b 3 April 1975, Anne Marie b 1 Nov 1983, d 1 Jan 1985); *Career* articled clerk Smith Holloway and Clarke Sheffield 1964-69, CA qualified 1969; Coopers & Lybrand (now Coopers & Lybrand Deloitte) Chartered Accountants Sheffield: joined 1969, secondment to Montreal and Chicago 1973-74, ptnr Sheffield 1976, memb Nat Audit Ctee 1983, memb Audit Bd (following merger) 1989, ptnr i/c Sheffield 1989-; chm: Sheffield CAs Students Soc 1979-84, Sheffield CAs Tech Advsy Ctee 1982-87; memb: Accreditation Bd ICAEW 1982-88, Tech Advsy Ctee ICAEW 1984-87; pres: Sheffield & Dist Soc of CAs 1990-91, Irish Soc of Sheffield & District 1982-87; memb Univ of Sheffield Careers Advsy Bd 1982-88, chm Fin Ctee Boys Clubs of S Yorks 1984-; capt: Sheffield RFC Colts, Yorks Rugby Colts; England U21 trialist; FCA (ACA 1969); *Recreations* fishing trout, salmon and pike in Ireland, clay pigeon shooting; *Clubs* Lansdowne, Sheffield, Abbeydale RFC, Abbeydale Golf; *Style—* Sean Mahon, Esq; 41 Stumperlowe Crescent Rd, Sheffield S10 3PR (☎ 0742 304069); Coopers & Lybrand Deloitte, Chartered Accountants, 1 East Parade, Sheffield S1 2ET (☎ 0742 729214, fax 0742 752573, car 0860 628787)

MAHON, Suzanne, Lady; Suzanne; *née* Donnellan; da of late Thomas Donnellan, of Pirbright, Surrey; *m* 1958, as his 2 w, Sir George Edward John Mahon, 6 Bt (d 1987); 1 da (Sarah Caroline b 1959); *Style—* Suzanne, Lady Mahon; 16 St James' Terrace, Winchester, Hants SO22 4PP (☎ 0962 863615)

MAHON, Col Sir William Walter; 7 Bt (UK 1819), of Castlegar, Co Galway; s of Sir George Edward John Mahon, 6 Bt (d 1987), and his 1 w, Audrey Evelyn (d 1957), da of Walter Jagger; *b* 4 Dec 1940; *Educ* Eton; *m* 20 April 1968, Rosemary Jane, yr da of late Lt-Col Michael Ernest Melvill, OBE, of The Old Manse, Symington, Lanarkshire; 1 s, 2 da (Annabel Jane b 1970, Lucy Caroline b 1972); *Heir* s, James William Mahon b 29 Oct 1976; *Career* Irish Gds 1960-; *Recreations* shooting, badge collecting; *Clubs* Army and Navy; *Style*— Col Sir William W Mahon, Bt; c/o Lloyd's Bank, 147 High Street, Guildford, Surrey GU1 3AG

MAHONEY, Eric; s of John Mahoney (d 1948), and Dorothy Maxey, *née* Appleby; *b* 2 April 1945; *m* 1 June 1968, Iris; 1 s (Simon b 1970), 2 da (Jane b 1973, Lucy b 1979); *Career* md Br Credit Tst Ltd 1986-, dir Bank of Ireland Br Hldgs Ltd, exec dir Citibank Savings 1986- (business dir 1984); FBIM; *Recreations* horse racing, golf; *Clubs* RAC; *Style*— Eric Mahoney, Esq; British Credit House, High St, Slough, Berks (☎ 0753 73211, car tel 0836 297810)

MAHONY, David Arthur; *b* 10 Feb 1944; *Educ* Hatfield Sch, Univ of York (BA), London Business Sch (MSc); *m* 2 Jan 1977, Adrienne Mahony, da of Capt Iain Kerr (d 1944); 1 s (Iain James Albert), 2 da (Catriona Jane, Antonia Brickell); *Career* chm: Barwell International Ltd, Cavendish Automation Ltd, Applied Holographics plc, Parker Baines Group Ltd; dep chm Harland Simon Group plc; dir: Holdres Technology plc, SIRA Ltd; FRSA 1980; *Recreations* shooting, fishing, golf; *Clubs* Carlton; *Style*— David Mahony, Esq; 41 Towerhill, London EC3N 4HA (☎ 071 480 5000)

MAHONY, Capt Dominic John Grehan; s of Cdr John Grehan Mahony, RN, of Alverstoke, Hampshire, and Josephine Diana, *née* Foulds; *b* 26 April 1964; *Educ* Millfield, LSE (BSc), RMA Sandhurst; *Career* cmmd Lt LG 1987, Troop Ldr CVR Windsor 1987-89, 2 i/c MBT Sqdn BAOR 1990, currently capt; Br under 20 epée fencing champion 1984, Br jr under 21 modern pentathlon champion 1984-85, Br epée team champion 1983-85, Br Univ epée champion 1984, Br epée champion 1986, Army epée champion 1984-85, 1987 and 1990, Servs epée champion 1987-88 and 1990; modern pentathlon: World Bronze team medallist 1987, Olympic Bronze team medallist 1988, Army/Inter Services champion 1989; Br modern tetrathlon champion 1990; Combined Servs Sportsman of the Year 1988; *Clubs* Cavalry and Guards, Epée; *Style*— Capt Dominic Mahony; Hyde Park Barracks, Knightsbridge, London

MAHONY, Stephen Dominic Patrick; s of Dermot Cecil Mahony, of Sundays Well, Cork, Ireland, and Kate, *née* O'Neill; *b* 3 March 1956; *Educ* Ampleforth, Univ of Oxford (MA); *m* 15 July 1983, Lucinda Margaret Ann, da of Maj Donald Struan Robertson, of Winkfield, Windsor, Berks; 1 s (Dermot b 16 Nov 1988), 1 da (Caroline b 3 May 1987); *Career* Citibank NA 1977-82; exec dir Swiss Bank Corp International Ltd 1982-88 (exec dir 1986-88); head of eurosecurities and swaps capital markets gp Istituto Bancario San Paolo di Torino London 1989-; *Recreations* the arts, books, bottles; *Clubs* Chelsea Arts; *Style*— Stephen Mahony, Esq; Broadclose House, Babcary, Somerton, Somerset TA11 7ED (☎ 045822 3318); Istituto Bancario San Paolo di Torino, 9 St Paul's Churchyard, London EC4M 8AB (☎ 071 489 0254)

MAHOOD, Prof Molly Maureen; da of James Mahood, CBE, ISO (d 1950), of London, and Violet Maud, *née* Daintry (d 1949); *b* 17 June 1919; *Educ* Surbiton HS, King's Coll London (MA); *Career* asst lectr in English King's Coll London 1943-46, fell and tutor St Hugh's Coll Oxford 1948-54, prof of English Univ of Ibadan Nigeria 1954-63, prof of literature Univ of Dar-es-Salaam Tanzania 1963-67, prof of English literature Univ of Kent at Canterbury 1967-79 (emeritus prof 1979-); active memb Green Party; *Books* Poetry and Humanism (1950), Shakepeare's Wordplay (1957), Joyce Cary's Africa (1964), The Colonial Encounter (1976); *Recreations* walking, swimming; *Clubs* PEN; *Style*— Prof M M Mahood; Rutherford College, University of Kent

MAHY, Dr Brian Wilfred John; s of Wilfred John Mahy (d 1966), of Guernsey, CI, and Norah Lilian, *née* Dillingham (d 1968); *b* 7 May 1937; *Educ* Elizabeth Coll Guernsey, Univ of Southampton (BSc, PhD), Univ of Cambridge (ScD, MA); *m* 1, 27 Aug 1959 (m dis 1986), Valerie Elaine, da of John Victor Pouteaux, of Guernsey; 2 s (Alex b 1964, Tim b 1966), 1 da (Penny b 1970); m 2, 29 Oct 1988, Penny Mary, da of Robert William Cunningham (d 1987), of Swansea, S Wales; *Career* Univ of Cambridge: asst dir of res in virology 1965-80, Huddersfield lectr in special pathology 1980-84, fell Wolfson Coll 1966-84; dir: Animal Virus Res Inst 1984-89, Div of Viral and Rickettsial Diseases Centers for Disease Control Atlanta USA 1989; *Recreations* violin, gardening; *Style*— Dr Brian Mahy; Steele Cobb House, 2632 Fox Hills Drive, Decatur, Ga 30033, USA (☎ 404 7280564); Division of Viral & Rickettsial Diseases, Centers for Disease Control, 1600 Clifton Rd, Atlanta, Ga 30333, USA (☎ 404 6393574, fax 404 6393163)

MAIDEN, (James) Dennis; s of James William Maiden (d 1971), of Parkgate, Yorkshire, and Elsie, *née* Brotherton (d 1982); *b* 28 June 1932; *Educ* Wath-upon-Dearne GS; *m* 4 June 1953, Irene, da of Benjamin Harris (d 1976), of Rotherham, Yorkshire; 1 s (Jonathan b 1962), 1 da (Sally b 1959); *Career* engrg conslt Husband and Co 1958-63, chief engr British Shoe Corporation 1963-67; CITB: devpt mangr 1967-73, gen mangr 1973-76, dir of trg 1976-85, chief exec 1985-90, dir gen designate Fedn of Master Builders 1990, tstee the Leonard Cheshire Fndn; pres: Norfolk Outward Bound Assoc, Kings Lynn branch BIM; Freeman City of London 1988, Freeman Worshipful Co of Constructors 1988, Liveryman Worshipful Co of Plumbers 1989; CEng, MIMechE 1960, CBIM 1966, MIPM 1969, FFB 1987; *Recreations* golf, gardening, theatre; *Clubs* RAC, The Norfolk, Hunstanton Golf; *Style*— Dennis Maiden, Esq; Micklebring, Church Lane, Bircham, King's Lynn, Norfolk PE31 6QW (☎ 048 523 336); 203 Gilbert House, Barbican, London (☎ 071 588 6019); Federation of Master Builders, 14-15 Great James St, London WC1N 3DP (☎ 071 242 7583, fax 071 404 0296)

MAIDEN, Robert Mitchell; *b* 15 Sept 1933; *Career* The Royal Bank of Scotland plc: supt of Branches London 1974-76, treas 1976-77, chief accountant 1977-81, gen mangr fin control 1981-82, exec dir 1982-86, md 1986; dir Lothian and Edinburgh Enterprises Ltd; govr Napier Poly Edinburgh; FBIM Scotland (vice pres); *Recreations* music, golf, reading, hill walking; *Clubs* New (Edinburgh); *Style*— Robert Maiden, Esq; The Royal Bank of Scotland plc, 42 St Andrew Square, Edinburgh EH2 2YE (☎ 031 556 8555, fax 031 557 6140, telex 72230 RBSCOT)

MAIDMENT, Francis Edward (Ted); s of Charles Edward, and late Olive Mary Maidment; *b* 23 Aug 1942; *Educ* Pocklington Sch York, Jesus Coll Cambridge (scholar); *Career* housemaster Lancing 1975-81 (asst master 1965-81); headmaster: Ellesmere Coll Shropshire 1982-88, Shrewsbury 1988-; *Recreations* singing, medieval history, modest tennis; *Style*— Ted Maidment, Esq; Shrewsbury School, Shropshire SY3 9BA (☎ 0743 4537)

MAIDMENT, Dr (Charles) Geoffrey Haylock; s of Dr John Charles Haylock Maidment, of Harleston, Norfolk, and Mary Helen, *née* Drysdale; *b* 30 June 1948; *Educ* Haileybury, London Hosp Med Coll, Univ of London (MD); *m* 16 Nov 1974, Dr Rosamond Anne Kay, da of (Harold) Kay Jones, of Reigate, Surrey; 2 da (Rachel b 13 Mar 1980, Alice b 12 Nov 1982); *Career* conslt physician Wexham Park Hosp Slough and King Edward VII Hosp Windsor, hon sr lectr and conslt physician Royal Postgrad Med Sch Hammersmith Hosp 1985-; memb RSM, MRCP; *Recreations* music, walking, squash; *Style*— Dr Geoffrey Maidment, Wexham Park Hosp, Slough, Berks SL2 4HL (☎ 0753 234567)

MAIDMENT, Dr Susan Rachel; da of Peter Elman, of Jerusalem, Israel, and Frances, *née* Tuckman; *b* 15 Feb 1944; *Educ* South Hampstead HS for Girls, LSE (LLB, LLM), Univ of Keele (LLD); *m* 16 Aug 1969, Dr Richard Anthony Maidment, s of Harold St Clair Maidment (d 1971), of London; 1 s (Adam b 1973), 2 da (Alice b 1971, Eleanor b 1980); *Career* called to the Bar Lincoln's Inn 1968, lectr law Univ of Bristol 1967-70, sr lectr law Univ of Keele 1970-84, practising barr 1984-; *Books* Child Custody and Divorce (1984); *Style*— Dr Susan Maidment; 36 Gondar Gardens, London NW6 1HG (☎ 071 794 1630); 1 King's Bench Walk, Temple, London EC4 (☎ 071 583 6266)

MAIDSTONE, Viscount; Daniel James Hatfield Finch Hatton; s and h of 16 Earl of Winchilsea; *b* 7 Oct 1967; *Style*— Viscount Maidstone

MAIDSTONE, Rt Rev David James Smith; Bishop of 1987-; s of Stanley James Smith (d 1965), and Gwendolen Emie, *née* Nunn (d 1960); *b* 14 July 1935; *Educ* Hertford GS, King's Coll London (AKC), St Boniface Coll Warminster; *m* 2 Dec 1961, Mary Hunter, da of Eric John Moult (d 1970); 1 s (Christopher Michael b 16 Sept 1966), 1 da (Rebecca Clare b 9 Feb 1965); *Career* asst curate: All Saints Gosforth 1959-62, St Francis High Heaton 1962-64, Longbenton 1964-68; vicar: Longhirst with Hebron 1968-75, St Mary Monkseaton 1975-81, Felton 1982-83; archdeacon of Lindisfarne 1981-87, bishop to HM Forces 1990-; *Recreations* walking, reading science fiction; *Style*— The Rt Rev the Bishop of Maidstone; Bishop's House, Pett Lane, Charing, Ashford, Kent TN27 ODL (☎ 023 371 2950)

MAILE, Nigel Kingsley; s of David G Maile, of Canterbury, Kent, and Suzanne Mary, *née* Derham; *b* 4 Sept 1955; *Educ* Mill Hill Sch, Hatfield Poly; *m* 19 Oct 1985, Julia Eileen, da of Cdr John E Hommert of Rowland Castle, Hants; *Career* chartered accountant Spicer & Oppenheim 1977-82, fin dir Bartle Bogle Hegarty (advtg agency) 1982-; ACA 1982; *Recreations* golf, walking, motorcycling; *Style*— Nigel Maile, Esq; Manor Way, Potters Bar, Herts (☎ 0707 55622); Bartle Bogle Hegarty Ltd, 24-27 Great Pulteney St, London W1R 3DB (☎ 071 734 1677, fax 071 437 3666)

MAIN, Rev Prof Alan; TD (1982); s of James Emslie Walker Main, and Mary Ann Ross, *née* Black; *b* 31 March 1936; *Educ* Robert Gordon's Coll Aberdeen, Univ of Aberdeen (MA, BD, PhD), Union Theol Seminary NY (STM); *m* 30 July 1960, Anne Louise, da of Alexander Swanson, of Thurso, Caithness (d 1959), 2 da (Katherine b 1 April 1964, Lesley Anne b 20 Dec 1965); *Career* cmmnd chaplain RACHD 1971, with 153(H) Artillery Support Regt RCT(v) 1971-; parish minister Chapel of Garioch Aberdeenshire 1963-70, chaplain Univ of Aberdeen 1970-80, prof of practical theology Christs Coll Aberdeen 1980-; sr advsr in religious bdcasting Grampian TV 1977-87; chm: Grampian Marriage Guidance Cncl 1978-82, Cruse 1980-84, NE Cncl on Disability 1982-85; memb Assembly Cncl Church of Scotland 1982-87; *Books* Worship Now II (ed, 1989); *Recreations* golf, music; *Style*— The Rev Prof Alan Main, TD; Kirkfield, Barthol Chapel, Inverurie, Aberdeenshire AB51 8TD (☎ 06514 602); Department of Practical Theology, Faculty of Divinity, King's College, University of Aberdeen (☎ 0224 272380/5)

MAIN, Prof Brian George McArthur; s of George McArthur Main, of Buckhaven, Fife, and Margaret Welsh, *née* Currie; *b* 24 Aug 1947; *Educ* Univ of St Andrews (BSc), Univ of California Berkeley (MBA, MA, PhD); *m* 4 July 1980, June Marks, da of James S Lambert; 2 s (Christopher b 23 June 1985, Simon b 4 July 1988); *Career* prodn planning assoc and mangr Eli Lilly 1970-72, reader in economics Univ of Edinburgh 1983-87 (lectr 1976-83); prof of economics: Univ of St Andrews 1987-91, Univ of Edinburgh 1991; memb Cncl Scottish Economic Soc 1982-; *Recreations* running, fishing; *Style*— Prof Brian Main; Univ of Edinburgh, Dept of Economics, Edinburgh, Scotland EH8 9JY (☎ 031 667 1011, fax 031 668 3053)

MAIN, Rev Canon David Murray; s of James Main (d 1969), of Birkenhead, and (Isabel) Rhoda Main (d 1989); *b* 8 Oct 1928; *Educ* Wrekin Coll, Univ Coll Oxford (MA), St Deiniol's Library Hawarden; *Career* Nat Serv RE 1947-49, 2 Lt 1948-49, Offr Shrewsbury Sch CCF 1952-65, CO with rank of Maj 1959-65; asst master Shrewsbury Sch 1952-73 (housemaster 1965-73); ordained: deacon 1973, priest 1974; curate St Margaret's Newlands Glasgow 1973-75; rector: All Saint's Challoch with St Andrew's Newton Stewart 1975-79, Holy Trinity Kilmarnock 1979-; canon St Mary's Catholic Glasgow 1985; *Books* A Course in Nuclear Physics (1961); *Recreations* music, walking; *Style*— The Rev Canon David Main; The Parsonage, 1 Dundonald Rd, Kilmarnock, Ayrshire KA1 1EQ (☎ 0563 23577)

MAIN, His Hon Judge John Roy Main; QC (1974); s of Alfred Charles Main (d 1968); *b* 21 June 1930; *Educ* Portsmouth GS, Hotchkiss Sch USA, BNC Oxford; *m* 1955, Angela de la Condamine, da of Robert William Home Davies (d 1970); 2 s, 1 da; *Career* Lt RNR; called to the Bar Inner Temple 1954; memb Special Panel Tport Tbnl 1970-76, dep chm IOW Quarter Sessions 1971, rec Crown Court 1972-76, circuit judge 1976-; *Recreations* walking, gardening, music; *Style*— His Hon Judge Main, QC; 4 Queen Anne Drive, Claygate, Surrey KT10 0PP (☎ 0372 466380)

MAIN, Kathleen Anne (Kate); da of John Blackburn Main, and Elizabeth Aitken, *née* Milne; *b* 23 Oct 1959; *Educ* Sutton HS GPDST, Univ of Durham (BA); *Career* grad admin trainee Surrey CC 1981-84, princ admin educn ACC 1990- (sr admin 1986-90, admin asst policy and fin 1984-86); assoc memb ICSA (memb educn admins panel); *Recreations* music, opera, ballet; *Style*— Miss Kate Main; Eaton House, 66A Eaton Square, London SW1W 9BH (☎ 071 235 1200, fax 071 235 8458)

MAIN, Sir Peter Tester; ERD (1964); s of Peter Tester Main (d 1977), of Aberdeen, and Esther Paterson, *née* Lawson (d 1968); *b* 21 March 1925; *Educ* Robert Gordon's Coll Aberdeen, Univ of Aberdeen (MB ChB, MD); *m* 1, 13 May 1952, Dr Margaret Fimister (d 1984), da of Thomas William Tweddle (d 1952); 2 s (Lawson Fimister b 16 Feb 1953, Gerald Peter b 5 Oct 1957), 1 da (Jennifer Marjory (Mrs Shilton) b 26 June 1955); m 2, 13 Dec 1986, May Hetherington Anderson, *née* McMillan; *Career* Lt-Col RAMC (AER); The Boots Co: joined 1957, dir of res 1968, dir 1973-85, vice-chm 1980-81, chm 1981-85; dir: W A Baxter & Sons Ltd 1985-, John Fleming & Co Ltd 1985-89; govr Henley Mgmnt Coll 1983-86; memb: NEDC 1984-85, Scottish Health Servs Policy Bd 1985-88; chm Inveresk Research International 1986-89; dir Scottish Devpt Agency 1986-, memb Univ of Aberdeen Devpt Tst 1987-, chm Grantown Heritage Tst 1987-; Hon LLD Aberdeen 1986; FRCPE 1982, CBIM 1978; kt 1985; *Recreations* fishing, shooting, Scottish music; *Clubs* Naval & Military; *Style*— Sir Peter Main, ERD; Lairig Ghru, Dulnain Bridge, Grantown-on-Spey, Highland PH26 3NT (☎ 047 985 264)

MAINDS, Allan Gilfillan; s of Capt George Gordon Gilfillan Mainds, and Helen Northgate, *née* Woodhouse; *b* 15 Dec 1945; *Educ* Berkhampsted Sch; *m* 17 July 1982 (m dis 1987), Hon Veronica Mary Addington, da of Viscount Sidmouth; *Career* admitted slr 1972; called to the Bar Inner Temple 1977; *Recreations* flying light aircraft and gliding, rowing and sculling; *Clubs* London Rowing; *Style*— Allen Mainds, Esq; The Chapel of Ease, Bishopstone, Aylesbury, Bucks (☎ 0296 748 752); 1 Kings Bench Walk, Temple, London EC4Y 7DB (☎ 071 353 8436)

MAINES, (James) Dennis; s of late Arthur Burtonwood Maines, and Lilian Maines, *née* Carter; *b* 26 July 1937; *Educ* Leigh GS, City Univ (BSc); *m* 15 Oct 1960, Janet Enid, da of late Percy Kemp; 3 s (Stephen, Christopher, Daniel); *Career* joined RSRE (formerly RRE) Malvern 1956: scientific offr 1960, head Guided Weapons Optics and Electronics Gp 1981, head Microwave and Electro-optics Gp 1983; head sensors electronic warfare and guided weapons ARE Portsdown 1984, dep dir (weapons) RAE

1986, dir gen guided weapons and electronics MOD (PE) 1988; FIEE, CEng; *Books* Surface Wave Filters (contrib 1977), more than 30 pubns in learned jls; *Recreations* sailing, cricket, squash, painting, gardening, car restoration; *Style—* Dennis Maines, Esq; MOD (PE), c/o Ministry of Defence, Whitehall, London SW1A 2HB

MAINGARD DE LA VILLE-ES-OFFRANS, Sir (Louis Pierre) Rene; CBE (1961); s of Joseph René Maingard de la Ville-es-Offrans (d 1956), and Véronique, *née* Hugnin (d 1969); *b* 9 July 1917; *Educ* St Joseph's Coll, Royal Coll of Mauritius, Business Trg Corp London; *m* 1946, Marie Hélène Françoise, da of Sir Philippe Raffray, CBE, QC (d 1975); 3 da (Catherine, Anne, Sophie); *Career* served WWII RAF Fighter Cmd 131 and 165 Sqdn 1939-45; chm De Chazal du Mée Assocs Ltd, chm and md Rogers & Co Ltd 1948-82; chm: Colonial Steamships Co Ltd 1948-, Mauritius Steam Navigation Co Ltd 1964, Mauritius Portland Cement Co Ltd 1960-, Mauritius Molasses Co Ltd 1968-, New Mauritius Dock Co Ltd 1948-, Utd Docks Ltd 1960-; dir: Mauritius Commercial Bank Ltd 1956-, The Anglo-Mauritius Assur Soc Ltd; consul for Finland in Mauritius 1957-83, Order of the White Rose Finland 1973; kt 1982; *Recreations* golf, fishing, boating; *Clubs* Dodo, Mauritius Turf; *Style—* Sir René Maingard de la Ville-ès-Offrans, CBE; De Chazal Du Mée Associates Ltd, PO Box 799, Port Louis, Mauritius (☎ 010 230 08 7923, telex 4417 COLYB)

MAINI, Sir Amar Nath; CBE (1953, OBE 1948); s of Nauhria Ram Maini, of Nairobi; *b* 31 July 1911; *Educ* Govt Indian Sch Nairobi, LSE, Middle Temple; *m* 1935, Ram Saheli Mehra (d 1982); 2 s; *Career* first mayor of Kampala 1950-55, min Commerce and Indust Uganda 1958-61, speaker E African Central Legislative Assembly 1961-67, dep chm Kenya Broadcasting Corp 1962-63; formerly: advocate High Cts of Uganda and Kenya, pres Central Cncl Indian Assocs Uganda, dep chm Uganda Electricity Bd; kt 1957; *Clubs* The Reform; *Style—* Sir Amar Maini, CBE; 55 Vicarage Rd, E Sheen, London SW14 8RY (☎ 081 878 1497)

MAINWARING, Richard Charles; s of Henry Charles Richard Mainwaring, and Ann Findley, *née* Hobbs; *b* 4 June 1953; *Educ* Avonhurst Sch Bristol; *m* 15 Nov 1980, Josephine Ann, da of Kenneth Wiltshire; *Career* Br barefoot waterskiing speed record 72 mph 1978 (entry in Guiness Book of Records still current); most successful Euro and Br barefoot waterskier ever: 6 times Euro champion (1983, 1984, 1985, 1986, 1987 and 1989), 7 times Br champion 1984-90, capt Br Barefoot Waterski Team 1985-88, currently Br record holder slalom and tricks events, ranked 11 in world; Br rep Euro Waterski Cncl, Freedom Tell City Indiana (USA tour 1979); *Clubs* Keuka Waterski; *Style—* Richard Mainwaring, Esq; 11 Arlington Row, Bibury, Gloucestershire GL7 5NJ (☎ 0285 74423)

MAIR, Alexander; MBE (1968); s of Charles Meston Mair (d 1968), and Helen, *née* Dickie (d 1969); *b* 5 Nov 1922; *Educ* Skene Central Sch, Sch of Accountancy Glasgow; *m* 7 Aug 1953, Margaret Isobel Gowans, da of John Rennie (d 1955); *Career* RAC 1943-47, 3 Carabiniers 1944-47, served in India and Burma; chief accountant Bydand Industrial Holdings 1956-60; Grampian TV: co sec 1961-70, dir 1967, chief exec 1970-87; dir: ITN 1978-87, TV Times 1975-87; chm: RGIT Survival Centre Ltd 1988-, Clifton Collier Advertising Ltd 1987-; pres: Aberdeen C of C 1989-91, Royal Northern and Univ Club 1984-85; chm Aberdeen Int Football Festival 1981-90; memb: Aberdeen Airport Users Ctee 1978-, Working Gp Grampian Initiative 1987-90, Aberdeen 2000 Gp 1987-90; ACMA, FRTS, FRSA; *Recreations* skiing, golf, gardening; *Clubs* Royal Northern and University (Aberdeen), Royal Aberdeen Golf; *Style—* Alexander Mair, Esq, MBE; Ravenswood, 66 Rubislaw Den South, Aberdeen AB2 6AX (☎ 0224 317619)

MAIR, Antony Stefan Romley; s of John Mair, MBE (d 1971), of Hill House, Surley Row, Caversham, Berks, and Marie Justine Antoinette, *née* Bunbury; *b* 27 Dec 1946; *Educ* Reading Sch, Magdalen Coll Oxford (BA, MA); *Career* slr; chm Mgmnt Ctee Holman Fenwick and Willan 1987-88 (joined 1976, ptnr 1979), ptnr Stephenson Harwood 1988-; govr St Stephen's RC Sch Shepherds Bush London; memb: Br Horse Soc, Law Soc, IBA, UIA; Freeman City of Oxford 1975; *Recreations* dressage, gardening; *Style—* Antony Mair, Esq; One St Paul's Churchyard, London EC4 (☎ 071 329 4422, fax 071 606 0822, telex 886789 SHSPC G)

MAIR, Prof (William) Austyn; CBE (1969); s of Dr William Mair (d 1968), of London, and Catharine Millicent, *née* Fyfe (d 1966); *b* 24 Feb 1917; *Educ* Highgate Sch, Clare Coll Cambridge (BA, MA); *m* 15 April 1944, Mary Woodhouse, da of Rev Christopher Benson Crofts (d 1956); 2 s (Christopher b 1945, Robert b 1950); *Career* RAF (Tech Branch) cmmnd Pilot Offr 1940, released from serv Sqdn Ldr 1946, attached to Royal Aircraft Estab 1940-46; dir Fluid Motion Laboratory Univ of Manchester 1946-52, Francis Mond prof of aeronautical engrg Univ of Cambridge 1952-83 (head of Engrg Dept 1973-83), fell Downing Coll 1953-83 (hon fell 1983-), emeritus prof of aeronautical engrg 1983-; Hon DSc Cranfield 1990; FRAeS 1952, FEng 1984; *Clubs* United Oxford & Cambridge Univ; *Style—* Prof Austyn Mair, CBE; 74 Barton Rd, Cambridge CB3 9LH (☎ 0223 350137)

MAIR, Colin James Robertson; s of Prof Alexander William Mair (d 1928), of Edinburgh, and Elizabeth Mackay Bisset, *née* Williams (d 1951); *b* 21 Dec 1919; *Educ* The Edinburgh Acad, Univ of Edinburgh (MA); *m* 1, 13 June 1942 (m dis 1983), Catherine Barbara, da of James Finlay, of Edinburgh; 1 s (Colin b 4 Aug 1953), 1 da (Anne b 3 Aug 1943); *m* 2, 24 July 1987, Susan Margaret Janetta, *née* Clark; *Career* Nat Serv cmmnd 2 Lt E Lancs Rgt 1940, Lt, then Capt 1942, Instr 76 Div Battle Sch 1943-45, posted to King's Regt Liverpool, demobbed 1946; housemaster Edinburgh Acad 1953-58 (on staff 1948-58), cmd CCF for four years, rector Kelvinside Acad Glasgow 1958-80; memb Headmasters Conf, tstee Buttle Tst (chm Scot distribution ctee of same), lay memb disciplinary ctee of Inst of Chartered Accountants of Scot; *Recreations* rugby, cricket, golf, reading, walking; *Clubs* The Edinburgh Academicals, Kelvinside Academicals, Scottish Wayfarers; *Style—* Colin Mair, Esq; 131 Clyde St, Carluke, Lanarkshire ML8 5BG (☎ 0555 70716)

MAIR, Hon Mrs (Elizabeth Smith); da of 1 Baron Kirkwood, PC (d 1955); *b* 1908; *m* 1944, John Archibald Dugald Mair, ARIBA; 1 s, 2 da; *Style—* The Hon Mrs Mair; Shieldaig, 12 Iain Rd, Bearsden, Dunbartonshire

MAIRANTS, Ivor; s of Solomon Mairants (d 1933), of London, and Sara Thema, *née* Kopa (d 1975); *b* 18 July 1908; *Educ* Raine's Foundation Sch London; *m* 18 Oct 1931, Lily, da of Aaron Schneider (d 1962), of London; 1 s (Stuart b 1938), 1 da (Valerie b 1933); *Career* guitarist; Roy Fox's Band 1932-37, Ambrose's Band 1938-43, Geraldo's Orchestra 1940-52, guitar conslt to Boosey and Hawkes Ltd 1950-60, estab Central Sch of Dance Music London 1950-59, Mantovani's Orchestra 1963-77, Manuel and His Music of the Mountains 1962-78, Melody Maker poll winner 1944-46 (1950-51 and 1953-54); memb: Musician's Union, Performing Right Soc, Br Acad of Song Writers Composers and Authors, Guitar Fndn of America; Freeman: City of London 1987, Worshipful Co of Musicians 1989; memb Guild of Freemen 1989; Fell Inst of Arts and Letters Switzerland 1957; composer of numerous guitar works; subject of Focus on Ivor Mairants (Zodiac cassette, 1990); *Books* My Fifty Fretting Years (autobiography, 1980); *Recreations* swimming, travel, walking; *Clubs* Esquire; *Style—* Ivor Mairants, Esq; 4 Hollies End, Mill Hill Village, London NW7 2RY (☎ 081 959 3136); Ivor Mairants Musicentre, 56 Rathbone Pl, London W1P 1AB (☎ 071 636 1481/2)

MAIRS, Raymond John; s of David Mairs, of Co Antrim, and Susan Elizabeth, *née* Colvin (d 1978); *b* 15 Aug 1951; *Educ* Ballyclare HS, Queen's Univ Belfast (BSc, Dip Arch); *m* 6 Aug 1976, Carol Jean Ruth, da of Neville Arthur Ginn, of Co Antrim; 3 da (Rachel Ruth b 1981, Rebecca Ann b 1985, Jessica Elizabeth b 1989); *Career* architect, fish farmer; private practice 1978, ptnr Mairs & Wray 1979-; memb RSUA Housing Ctee 1985-86; chm: Br Trout Assoc 1988-90, Euro Gp of Fédération Européenne de la Salmoniculture 1988-; rapporteur Agric Working Gp of Fisheries Advsy Ctee to Euro Cmmn 1989, memb Health Promotion Agency N Ireland 1990-; *Style—* Raymond J Mairs, Esq; Glen Oak House, Crumlin BT29 4BW (☎ 08494 23172); Mairs & Wray Architects, 1 Nutts Corner Rd, Crumlin BT29 4BW (☎ 08494 52975)

MAIS, Sir (Robert) Hugh; s of Robert Stanley Oliver Mais (d 1947), and Edith Catherine, *née* Ashley (d 1974); *b* 14 Sept 1907; *Educ* Shrewsbury, Wadham Coll Oxford (MA); *m* 1938, Catherine (d 1987), da of James Pearson Pattinson (d 1945); 1 s; *Career* served WWII RAF, Wing Cdr; called to the Bar Inner Temple 1930; chllr of the Diocese of Manchester 1948-71, Carlisle 1950-71, Sheffield 1950-71; co court judge: W London 1958-60, Marylebone 1960-71; dep chm Berks QS 1964-71, cmmr of assizes SE Circuit 1964 and 1967, Oxford Circuit 1968 and 1969, NE Circuit 1971, bencher Inner Temple 1971, High Court judge (Queen's Bench) 1971-82, ret; memb Winn Ctee Personal Injuries Litigation; hon fell Wadham Coll Oxford 1971; kt 1971; *Recreations* fishing, golf; *Style—* Sir Hugh Mais; Ripton, Streatley-on-Thames, Berks (☎ 0491 872397)

MAIS, Hon Jonathan Robert Neal; yr s of Baron Mais, GBE, ERD, TD (Life Peer); *b* 1954; *Educ* Hurstpierpoint, City of London Coll of Commercial Law; *m* 1978, Frances Louise, da of late Robert Mark Barrington Brown; 2 s (Joel Robert Barrington b 7 Aug 1979, Duncan Jonathan Christopher b (twin) 7 Aug 1979); *Style—* The Hon Jonathan Mais; Farthings, 5 Pound Lane, Topsham, Exeter, Devon EX3 ONA

MAIS, Baron (Life Peer UK 1967), of Walbrook, City of London; (Alan) Raymond Mais; GBE (1973, OBE 1944), ERD (1958), TD (1944), JP (City of London 1962), DL (Kent 1976, Co of London subsequently Gtr London 1951-76); s of late Capt Ernest Mais, of Mornington Court, Kensington; *b* 7 July 1911; *Educ* Banister Court Hants, Coll of Estate Mgmnt Univ of London; *m* 1936, Lorna Aline, da of Stanley Aspinall Boardman, of Addiscombe, Surrey; 2 s (Hon Richard Jeremy Ian b 1945, Hon Jonathan Robert Neal b 1954), 1 da (Hon Angela Clare (Hon Mrs Beckman) b 1946); *Career* 2 Lt Royal West Kent Regt 1929, RE 1931-70; dir Royal Bank of Scotland 1969-81, chm Peachey Property Corp 1977-81; formerly: with Richard Costain, chm Trollope & Colls; alderman Walbrook Ward 1962-81, Lt City of London 1963, Sheriff 1969-70, Lord Mayor of London 1972-73 (first Lab Lord Mayor), Cmmr of Income Tax 1972-81, sitting as Lib peer in House of Lords 1981- (formerly Lab); memb: Court of City Univ 1973, Cwlth Scholars Cmmn 1978, Govt Ctees for Works and Bldgs Emergency Orgn; pres London C of C & Indust 1975-78, past pres London Master Builders' Assoc, vice pres Inst of Structural Engrs; Freeman: Worshipful Co of Marketors 1977 (Master 1983-84), Worshipful Co of Cutlers (Master 1966-67), Worshipful Co of Pavior's (Master 1974-75); Hon DSc Univ of Ulster, Hon DSc City Univ; FICE, FIStructE, FRICS, KStJ; *Style—* The Rt Hon Lord Mais, GBE, ERD, TD, JP, DL; Griffins, Sundridge Ave, Bromley, Kent (☎ 081 460 9896)

MAIS, Hon Richard Jeremy Ian; s of Baron Mais, OBE (Life Peer), *qv*; *b* 2 Nov 1945; *Educ* Cumnor House Sch, Stowe, Ewell Tech Coll; *m* 17 June 1972, Janice, da of Ralph Dean, of Hurley, Berks; 1 s (Alexander b 1975), 2 da (Vanessa b 1977, Lydia b 1981); *Career* property developer; with Higgs & Hill Ltd 1963-69, J M Jones & Sons Ltd 1969-71, Lyon Group Ltd 1971-75; md Clarke Nickolls & Coombs plc 1975-; chm: Becontree Estates Ltd, Altbarn Properties Ltd, CNC Properties Ltd, CNC Developments Ltd, CNC Benfleet Ltd, Philpot Managment Ltd, Beacontree Plaza Ltd, CNC Delaware Inc, CNC California Investments Inc; vice chm St Pancras Housing Assoc; Freeman of the City of London 1968, Liveryman of Worshipful Co of Cutlers 1968; MCIOB 1980, FIOD 1984; *Recreations* motor racing, sailing, skiing, badminton; *Clubs* Br Automobile Racing; *Style—* The Hon Richard Mais; 79 Seal Hollow Road, Sevenoaks, Kent TN13 3RY (☎ 0732 454886); Clarke, Nickolls & Coombs plc, 33 High Street, Sunninghill, Ascot, Berks SL5 9NR (☎ 0344 28721, fax 0344 28711, car 0836 230248)

MAISEY, Prof Michael Norman; *b* 10 June 1939; *Educ* Caterham Sch Surrey, Guy's Hosp Med Sch (BSc, MB BS, MD); *m* 2 c; *Career* Guy's Hospital: house physician March 1964, casualty offr June 1964, house surgeon 1964-65; sr house offr in Medicine New Cross Hosp 1965; house physician in: chest diseases Brompton Hosp, rheumatology Hammersmith Hosp; registrar: (locum) in Neurology Brook Gen Hosp 1967, in Gen Med Guy's Hosp 1969-70 (endocrinology and radioisotopes 1967-69); fell Nuclear Medicine John Hopkins Hosp USA 1970-72; Guy's Hosp: sr registrar gen med 1970-72, conslt physician in nuclear Med and endocrinology 1973-83, clinical dir Radiological Service, conslt physician in nuclear med, conslt physician to Thyroid Centre; prof of radiological sciences United Med & Dental Schs of Guy's and St Thomas's Hosps, hon conslt in nuclear medicine and endocrinology to the Army, memb Guy's Hosp Unit Mgmnt Bd, examiner Soc of Radiographers Diploma in Nuclear Medicine 1976-, pres British Nuclear Medicine Soc 1978-80 (sec 1976-78), visiting prof Nuclear Medicine Toronto 1976, chm SAC (Nuclear Medicine) of JCHMT 1982-84, visiting exchange prof John Hopkins Hosp Baltimore 1985-, visiting lectr Forces Inst of Cardiology Pakistan 1987, visiting prof Shanghai Univ Hosp 1988; memb: Scientific Ctee on Euro Nuclear Med Congress 1989, UMDS Guy's & St Thomas's Hospital PET Managerial Ctee, Ed Bd Nuclear Medicine Communications and Euro Jl of Nuclear Med; memb: BIR, British Nuclear Medicine Soc, Euro Nuclear Med Soc, American Soc of Nuclear Med, Thyroid Club, EORTC Thyroid Cancer Gp; FRCR, FRCP, MRCP, MRCS, LRCP; *Books* Nuclear Medicine - A Clinical Introduction (1980), An Altas of Normal Skeletal Santigraphy (with J J Plarsagan, 1985), An Altas of Nuclear Medicine (with I Fogelman, 1988), Clinical Nuclear Medicine (ed with K E Britton, D L Gilday, 1983), numerous articles in various learned jls; *Style—* Prof Michael Maisey; Guy's Hospital, St Thomas Street, London SE1 9RT

MAISNER, Air Vice-Marshal Alexander (Aleksander); CB (1977), CBE (1969), AFC (1955); s of Henryk Maisner (d 1943), and Helene Anne, *née* Brosin (d 1959); *b* 26 July 1921; *Educ* High Sch and Lyceum Czestochowa Poland, Warsaw Univ; *m* 1946, Mary, da of O R Coverley (d 1958); 1 s, 1 da; *Career* War Serv Polish Artillery and Polish AF, joined RAF 1946, DSD RAF Staff Coll, CO RAF Seletar, asst Cmdt RAF Coll Cranwell, ret as dir gen Personnel Mgmnt 1977; personnel exec Reed Int Ltd 1977-82; govr Shiplake Coll 1978-; pres of Polish AF Assoc 1982-; dir Indust and Parly Tst 1984-1987; Cmdr's Cross with Star, Order of Polonia Restituta 1990; *Recreations* reading, gardening; *Clubs* RAF; *Style—* Air Vice-Marshal Alexander Maisner, CB, CBE, AFC; c/o Lloyds Bank, 1 Reading Rd, Henley-on-Thames, Oxon RG9 1BR

MAITLAND, Colin Neil; s of Col Otis Edward Maitland, MBE (d 1977), of Surrey, and Margaret Joan, *née* Haslehurst (d 1955); *b* 7 July 1940; *Educ* Old Buckenham Hall Norfolk, Embley Park Romsey Hants, Univ of Southampton; *m* 30 Sept 1967, Judy, da of Col Howard Watson Wright; 2 s (Mark Otis b 1976, Sam Ragen b 1980), 1 da (Kate Margaret b 1978); *Career* offr RM 1958-69 (45 Commando 1959-61, Cdr Trg Sch 1962-63, ADC 1965-69); NOP 1969-70, Louis Harris 1970-71, res dir Leo Burnett LPE 1971-73; md: Eyes Can 1973-83, ISIS Research 1984-; chm Embley Park Sch 1969; *Books* New Product Launch Planner (1988); *Style—* Colin Maitland, Esq

MAITLAND, David Henry; CVO (1988); s of George Maitland (d 1959), of London, and Mary Annie, *née* Levy (d 1977); *b* 9 May 1922; *Educ* Eton, King's Coll Cambridge; *m* 21 June 1955, Judith Mary, da of Patrick Hugh Gold (d 1976), of London; 3 da (Jessica b 1957, Lucy b 1957, Rebecca b 1964); *Career* served 1 Bn Oxford and Bucks LI 1943-47, Capt and Adjt 1945-47; chief exec Save & Prosper Group 1965-81, chm Unit Tst Assoc 1973-75, memb City Capital Market Ctee 1974-84; tstee Lord Mayor Treloar Coll 1984-; memb: Cncl of Duchy of Lancaster 1977-87, Bethlem Royal Hosp SHA 1982-90, Maudsley Hosp SHA 1982-90, Royal Cmmn for 1851 Exhibition 1983-; chm Inst of Psychiatry 1985-90; FCA 1950; *Recreations* golf, gardening; *Clubs* City of London; *Style*— David Maitland, Esq, CVO; St Paul's House, Upper Froyle, nr Alton, Hants

MAITLAND, Sir Donald James Dundas; GCMG (1977, CMG 1967), OBE (1960); s of Thomas Douglas Maitland, and Wilhelmina Sarah Dundas; *b* 16 Aug 1922; *Educ* George Watson's Coll Edinburgh, Univ of Edinburgh (MA); *m* 1950, Jean Marie, da of Gordon Young (d 1969); 1 s, 1 da; *Career* served WWII ME India and Burma in Royal Scots and Rajputana Rifles; served Foreign Serv (later Dip Serv) 1947-80: in Amara, Baghdad, dir MECAS Lebanon 1956-60, Cairo, head News Dept FO 1965-67, princ private sec 1967-69, ambass Libya 1969-70, chief press sec 10 Downing St 1970-73, ambass and perm UK rep UN 1973-74 and EEC 1975-79, dep under-sec FCO 1974-75, dep perm under-sec FCO 1979-80, perm under-sec Dept Energy 1980-82, ret 1982; govt dir Britoil 1983-85, dir Slough Estates 1983-; chm: UK Ctee World Communications Year 1983, Ind Cmmn for World-Wide Telecommunications Devpt 1983-85 Christians for Europe 1984-; memb Cwlth War Graves Cmmn, advsr to Br Telecom 1985-86, dir Northern Engineering Industries 1986-89, dep chm IBA 1986-89; chm Health Educn Authy 1989-; kt 1973; *Recreations* hill-walking, music; *Style*— Sir Donald Maitland, GCMG, OBE; Murhill Farm House, Limpley Stoke, Bath BA3 6HH (☎ 0225 723157)

MAITLAND, Lady Elizabeth Sylvia; da of Viscount Maitland (ka 1943); *b* 1943; *Career* granted 1953, title, rank and precedence of an Earl's da which would have been hers had her father survived to succeed to Earldom of Lauderdale; *Style*— The Lady Elizabeth Maitland; 11 Boundary Close, Woodstock, Oxford OX7 1LR

MAITLAND, Helena, Viscountess; Helena Ruth; *née* Perrott; da of Col Sir Herbert Charles Perrott, 6 and last Bt, CH, CB (d 1922), and Ethel Lucy, *née* Hare (d 1939); *b* 14 Aug 1912; *m* 29 Oct 1936, Ivor Colin James, Viscount Maitland (s and h of 15 Earl of Lauderdale, ka 1943 predeceasing his f); 3 da (Lady Mary Biddulph, Lady Anne Eyston, Lady Elizabeth Maitland, all raised to rank of Earl's da); *Career* OStJ; *Recreations* fishing, gardening; *Style*— Helena, Viscountess Maitland; Flat E, 34 Cadogan Square, London SW1 (☎ 071 584 9920); Park House, Makerstoun, nr Kelso, Roxburghshire (☎ 057 36 248)

MAITLAND, Viscount; Ian Maitland; The Master of Lauderdale; s and h of 17 Earl of Lauderdale; *b* 4 Nov 1937; *Educ* Radley, Brasenose Oxford (MA); *m* 27 April 1963, Ann Paul, da of Geoffrey B Clarke, of London; 1 s, 1 da; *Heir* s, Master of Maitland; *Career* Lt RNR 1963-73; has held various appts in mfrg industry, regnl mangr Middle East Nat Westminster Bank Ltd 1975-; memb The Queen's Body Guard for Scotland (Royal Co of Archers); *Recreations* sailing, photography; *Clubs* Royal Ocean Racing, New (Edinburgh), Overseas Bankers; *Style*— Viscount Maitland; 150 Tachbrook St, London SW1V 2NE

MAITLAND, The Master of; Hon John Douglas Peter Maitland; s and h of Viscount Maitland; *b* 29 May 1965; *Educ* Emanuel Sch, Radley, Durham Univ (BSc); *Style*— The Master of Maitland

MAITLAND, Gp Capt John Edward; s of Air Vice-Marshal Percy Eric Maitland, CB, CBE, MVO, AFC (d 1985), and Alison Mary, *née* Kettlewell; *b* 1 April 1933; *Educ* Clifton, RAF Coll Cranwell; *m* 3 June 1961, Janet Rachel (Jan), da of late William Dunham Todd; 1 da (Julia Rosemary b 1966); *Career* cmmnd 1953, RAF pilot on fighters, tport and helicopters, Staff Coll Camberley 1964, Sqdn Ldr 1961, Wing Cdr 1968, Gp Capt 1980, currently CO Jt Airmiss Section (investigating all UK airmisses) and chm Jt Airmiss Working Gp; memb Berkshire Ctee Salmon and Trout Assoc; Upper Freeman Guild of Air Pilots and Air Navigators; *Recreations* fishing (mainly for trout), shooting, gardening; *Clubs* RAF; *Style*— Gp Capt John Maitland; OC Joint Airmiss Section, Hillingdon House, Uxbridge, Middx UB10 0RU (☎ 0895 76120)

MAITLAND, Lady; Lavender Mary Jex; da of late Francis William Jex Jackson, of Kirkbuddo, Forfar; *m* 1951, Maj Sir Alexander Keith Maitland, 8 Bt (d 1963); *Style*— Lady Maitland; Burnside, Forfar, Angus

MAITLAND, Lady (Caroline Charlotte) Militsa; da of 17 Earl of Lauderdale; *b* 18 Nov 1946; *Educ* Queen's Gate Sch London, SS Mary and Anne Abbots Bromley Rugeley, Lycée Français de Londres, Univ of London; *Career* teacher 1970-77; *Recreations* song and dance; *Style*— The Lady Militsa Maitland; 12 St Vincent St, Edinburgh (☎ 031 556 5692)

MAITLAND, Neil Kenneth; s of Col John Kenneth Maitland, MBE, MC, DL, JP (d 1972), of Hertingfordbury, Herts, and Jean Redman, *née* Collingridge, MBE; *b* 26 Dec 1929; *Educ* Sedbergh Sch Canada, Winchester Coll; *m* 21 Jan 1961, Gillian (d 1988), da of Gerald Leonard Forstern Bird, (d POW 1944); 1 s (James b 1962), 1 da (Elizabeth b 1968); *Career* Nat Serv 2 Lt RA 1948-49; md Ridgways Ltd Tea & Coffee Merchants 1968; Master Worshipful Co of Girdlers 1979-80, chm London Fedn of Boys' Clubs 1983-, dir Inst of Child Health; *Recreations* golf, gardening; *Clubs* Royal Ashdown Forest GC, Army and Navy; *Style*— Neil K Maitland, Esq; Barnsden House, Duddleswell, nr Uckfield, Sussex TN22 3DB (☎ 082 572 2426)

MAITLAND, Lady (Helen) Olga; *née* Maitland; elder da of 17 Earl of Lauderdale, *qv*; *b* 23 May 1944; *Educ* Sch of St Mary and St Anne Abbots Bromley, Lycée Francais de Londres; *m* 19 April 1969, Robin William Patrick Hamilton Hay, s of William Reginald Hay, of Mapperley, Nottingham; 2 s (Alastair b 1972, Fergus b 1981), 1 da (Camilla b 1975); *Career* former trainee reporter with Fleet St News Agency, Blackheath and Distict Reporter; former sec Br Embassy Mexico City; journalist Sunday Express 1967-, reporter and columnist; memb Islington S and Finsbury Cons Assoc (memb Exec Ctee Chelsea Young Cons 1960, YC rep on Brompton Ward); memb Bow Gp 1970-, fndr and chm Families for Def 1983; chm Br Red Cross Westminster Christmas Fair 1983-; memb Euro Union of Women; nominated UN Media Peace Prize 1983; vice chm WHY Campaign Against Offensive Weapons 1987-, conslt ILEA Holborn & St Pancras; Parly candidate (C) Bethnal Green & Stepney 1987; fndr and chm Conserve 1990; patron: Stoke Park Tst for Handicapped, Rainbow Tst Holidays for the Disabled; *Publications* Peace Studies in Our Schools (contrib, 1985), Political Indoctrination in Our Schools (contrib, Margaret Thatcher: the First Ten Years (1989); *Recreations* theatre, travel painting; *Style*— The Lady Olga Maitland; 21 Cloudesley St, London N1 (☎ 071 837 9212); Mill Farm, Wighton, Wells-Next-the-Sea, Norfolk (☎ 032 872 666); Sunday Express, Fleet St, London EC4 (☎ 071 353 8000 ext 3678, 071 353 1656)

MAITLAND, Pelham Harper; s of Gordon Pelham Maitland (d 1975), and Ada Mary, *née* Harper (d 1976); *b* 17 Nov 1929; *Educ* Downs Sch Colwall Hereford, Leighton Park Sch Reading, London external (LLB); *Career* admitted slr 1952, Trowers and Hamlins 1956- (ptnr 1964-), currently conslt revenue law and tst matters; sec UK Clan Maitland Ctee; *Recreations* basset hounds, national heritage, modern languages, classical music; *Style*— Pelham Maitland, Esq; Messrs Trowers & Hamlins, 6 New Square, Lincoln's Inn, London (☎ 071 831 6292, fax 071 831 8700, telex 21422)

MAITLAND, Sir Richard John; 9 Bt (UK 1818), of Clifton, Midlothian; s of Maj Sir Alexander Maitland, 8 Bt (d 1963; sixth in descent from Gen Hon Sir Alexander Maitland, 1 Bt, 5 s of 6 Earl of Lauderdale); *b* 24 Nov 1952; *Educ* Rugby, Univ of Exeter, Edinburgh Sch of Agriculture; *m* 1981, Carine, er da of J St G Coldwell, of Somerton, Oxford, by his w Mrs R A Rooney, of Llandovery; 1 s (Charles b 1986), 1 da (Alice Emma b 1983); *Heir* s, Charles Alexander b 1986; *Career* farmer; memb Royal Co of Archers (Queen's Body Guard for Scotland); *Recreations* skiing, shooting, fishing, travel; *Style*— Sir Richard Maitland, Bt; Burnside, Forfar, Angus

MAITLAND, Hon Mrs (Rosemary Ethel Coupar); JP (Glos 1973); yr da of 1 and last Baron Abertay (d 1940), and Baroness Abertay (d 1983); *b* 26 Jan 1931; *Educ* Crofton Grange, Brillant Mont Lausanne Switzerland; *m* 1952, John Stuart Maitland, s of Lt-Col John Kenneth Maitland, MC, TD, JP, DL; 3 s (John Andrew Charles b 1954, Robin Neil b 1958, Angus Kenneth b 1963), 1 da (Fiona Romaire b 1961); *Style*— The Hon Mrs Maitland, JP; The Grange, Park Lane, Stancombe, Dursley, Glos GL11 6AY

MAITLAND, Rev the Hon Sydney Milivoye Patrick; s of 17 Earl of Lauderdale, *qv*; *b* 23 June 1951; *Educ* Eton, Edinburgh Univ (BSc), Strathclyde Univ (DipTP); *m* 1974, (Dorothy) Eileen, da of A R Bedell, of Kirbymoorside, N Yorks; *Career* town planner; made deacon in Scottish Episcopal Church 1986, ordained priest in Scottish Episcopal Church 1987, hon priest-in-charge, St Georges Sandbank St Maryhill Glasgow; MRTPI; *Recreations* sailing, photography; *Clubs* Loch Ard SC; *Style*— The Rev the Hon Sydney Maitland; 14 Kersland St, Glasgow G12 8BL

MAITLAND BIDDULPH, Hon William Ian Robert; yr s of 4 Baron Biddulph (d 1988), bro and hp of 5 Baron, *qv*; *b* 27 March 1963; *Educ* Loretto; *Career* wine merchant; *Recreations* shooting, fishing, tennis, hockey, walking, cooking, wine making, gardening; *Style*— The Hon William Maitland Biddulph

MAITLAND-CAREW, Hon Gerald Edward Ian; DL (Roxburgh, Ettrick and Lauderdale 1990); yr s of 6 Baron Carew, CBE, *qv*; name changed to Maitland-Carew by deed poll 1971; *b* 28 Dec 1941; *Educ* Harrow; *m* 1972, Rosalind Averil, da of Lt-Col Neil Hanning Reed Speke, MC; 2 s, 1 da; *Career* 2 Lt 15/19 Hussars 1961, Capt 1965, formerly ADC to GOC 44 Div Dover, Castle; memb the Queens Body Guard for Scotland, The Royal Co of Archers 1978; elected memb the Jockey Club 1987, chm Lauderdale Hunt 1979-; *Clubs* Cavalry, New; *Style*— The Hon Gerald Maitland-Carew, DL; Thirlestane Castle, Lauder, Berwickshire

MAITLAND PARKS, Hon Sarah Caroline; da of Viscount Maitland; *b* 1964; *Educ* St Paul's Girls' Sch, Trevelyan Coll Durham (BA); *m* 5 Nov 1988, Stuart George Parks; *Style*— The Hon Sarah Maitland Parks

MAITLAND-ROBINSON, Hon Mrs (Susannah Jane); *née* Henderson; da of 3 Baron Faringdon; *b* 1963; *m* 1986, Aidan James Maitland-Robinson, s of Joseph Maitland-Robinson (d 1989), of St Lawrence, Jersey; 1 s (Joseph Charles b 1989), 2 da (Joanna Alice b 1987, Sarah Florence b 1990); *Style*— The Hon Mrs Maitland-Robinson

MAITLAND SMITH, Geoffrey; s of Philip John Maitland Smith (d 1989), of Ramsden Heath, Billericay, Essex, by his w Kathleen, *née* Goff; *b* 27 Feb 1933; *Educ* Univ Coll Sch London; *Career* chartered accountant; chm Sears plc 1985- (chief exec 1978-88, dir 1971-), dir Asprey & Co 1980- (the Bond Street jewellers, in which Sears has a 25 percent stake); chm: Br Shoe Corp 1985-, Selfridges 1985-, Garrard & Co 1985-90, Mappin & Webb 1985-90; dir: Courtaulds plc 1983-90, Imperial Gp plc 1984-86, Central Ind Television plc 1983-85, Midland Bank plc 1986-, Hammerson Property Investment and Development Corporation plc 1990-; chm: Mallett plc 1986-89; chm of Cncl of Univ Coll Sch London 1987; hon vice pres Inst of Marketing 1987-; memb: Fin Reporting Cncl 1990-, Royal Acad Advsy Bd 1986-, Fin Devpt Bd NSPCC 1985-89, Industry and Commerce Gp The Save The Children Fund 1989-; Freeman Worshipful Co of Gardeners; *Recreations* opera; *Clubs* Cripplegate Ward; *Style*— Geoffrey Maitland Smith, Esq; 40 Duke St, London W1A 2HP (☎ 071 408 1180)

MAITLAND-TITTERTON, Col (ret) David Henry Sandford Leslie; s of Maj David Maitland-Titterton, TD (d 1989), of Herald Marchmont, Moberty, Airlie, and Mary Etheldritha Audrey Leslie (d 1988); *b* 4 Jan 1933; *Educ* Campbell Coll Belfast, MONS OCS, RMA Sandhurst, JSSC; *m* 23 April 1963, Rinalda Malvina, da of Sqdn Ldr The Hon Greville Baird (ka 1941); 1 s (Rupert Seymour Aulin Leslie b 1965), 1 da (Shân Gelda Jane b 1968); *Career* 2 Lt NIH (TA) 1952, 2 Lt 12 L 1954, GSOI US Army Armour Sch Fort Knox 1968, CO 9/12 Royal Lancers 1972, GSOI Br Army Trg Team Sudan 1974, GSOI (PE) 1977, CO Kuwait Liaison Team 1978, Col M3 (MOD) 1981, Defence Naval Military and Air Attache Damascus and Beirut 1985-86, COS (Army) HQ 1 Gp 1986, ROI Chief Range Safety Inspection Team (Army) 1989-; memb: NVET, CPRE, BHAS 1989; Order of Two Niles Sudan 1980; *Recreations* country pursuits, history, engineering; *Clubs* Naval and Military; *Style*— Col David Maitland-Titterton; Rimes Gigot, Baughurst, Hants RG26 5LW (☎ 0734 81 5098)

MAITLAND-MAKGILL-CRICHTON; *see*: Crichton

MAITLIS, Peter Michael; s of Jacob J Maitlis (d 1987), and Judith, *née* Ebel (d 1985); *b* 15 Jan 1933; *Educ* Hendon Co GS, Univ of Birmingham (BSc), Univ of London (PhD, DSc); *m* 19 July 1959, Marion da of Herbert Basco (d 1977); 3 da (Niccola b 1963, Sally b 1965, Emily b 1970); *Career* asst lectr Univ of London, 1956-60, Fulbright fell Cornell Univ 1960-61, res fell Harvard Univ 1961-62; McMaster Univ Hamilton Canada: asst prof 1962-64, assoc prof 1964-67, prof 1967-72; prof of inorganic chem Univ of Sheffield 1972-, fell Alfred P Sloan Fndn (USA) 1968-70, EWR Steacie Prize (Canada) 1971, RSC Medallist (UK) 1981, Tilden lectr 1979, Sir Edward Frankland lectr (UK) 1984; various offices in RSC (pres Dalton Div 1984-86), chm Serc Chemistry Ctee 1985-88 memb BBc Sci Consultative Gp FRS, FRSC; *Books* The Organic Chemistry of Palladium (Vols 1 & 2 1971); res paper in various chemistry jls; *Recreations* travel, tending fruit, overworking; *Style*— Prof Peter Maitlis, FRS

MAJOR, Christopher Ian; s of Edward Richard Major, of Friar's Cliff, Dorset and Audrey Yvonne, *née* Beardmore; *b* 14 June 1948; *Educ* Kingston GS, Wadham Coll Oxford (MA); *m* 19 Aug 1972, Susan Fenella, da of Harry Morrison Kirton (d 1984); *Career* slr 1973; ptnr: Lovell, White & King 1979-88, Lovell White Durrant 1988-; memb Worhsipful Co Slrs 1974; memb: Law Soc of England & Wales - 1973, Int Bar Assoc 1979, American Bar Assoc 1981, American Arbitration Assoc 1981; *Recreations* tennis; *Style*— Christopher Major, Esq; 73 Cheapside, London EC2V 6ER (☎ 071 236 0066, fax 071 236 0084, telex 919014)

MAJOR, Dr Edward; s of Morgan Major, of Castell House, Llangynwyd, Bridgend, Mid Glamorgan, and Nancy, *née* Jenkins; *b* 26 Nov 1948; *Educ* Maesteg GS, London Hosp Med Coll (MB BS); *m* 9 March 1974, Heather Gillian, da of Christopher Bevil Spiller, of 23 Tavistock Rd, Swansea; 2 s (Euan Thomas, Huw Edward), 1 da (Sarah Ann); *Career* sr registrar Hosp for Sick Children Gt Ormond St 1979, sr lectr and conslt in anaesthetics London Hosp 1979-84 (sr registrar 1978-79), conslt in anaesthesia and intensive therapy Morriston Hosp Swansea 1984-; chm of Intensive Care Soc 1989- (cncl memb 1984-, meetings sec 1987-89); memb: Coll of Anaesthetists, Assoc of Anaesthetists; *Books* Hazards and Complications of Anaesthesia (ed with T H Taylor, 1987); *Recreations* sailing; *Clubs* Mumbles Yacht; *Style*— Dr Edward Major; Heddfan, 23 Tavistock Road, Sketty, Swansea SA2 0SL; Intensive Therapy Unit, Morriston Hospital, Swansea SA6 6NL (☎ 0792 703472)

MAJOR, The Rt Hon John; PC (1987), MP (C) Huntingdon 1983- (Huntingdonshire 1979-83); s of Thomas Major (d 1963), actor (real name Abraham Thomas Ball), and his 2 w, Gwendolyn Minnie, *née* Coates (d 1970); *b* 29 March 1943; *Educ* Rutlish GS; *m* 1970, Norma Christina Elizabeth, da of Norman Johnson (ka 1945); 1 s (James b 1975), 1 da (Elizabeth b 1972); *Career* sr exec Standard Chartered Bank plc 1965-79; joined Conservative Party 1960, various offices Brixton Cons Assoc 1960-69 (chm 1970-71), memb Lambeth Borough Cncl 1968-71 (chm Housing Ctee 1970-71); parly candidate (C) St Pancras N (Camden) 1974 (both elections); dir Warden Housing Assoc 1974-82, jt sec Cons Parly Party Environment Ctee 1979-81, parly conslt Guild of Glass Engravers 1979-83, pres Eastern Area Young Conservatives 1983-85; PPS to Mins of State Home Office 1981-83, asst govt whip 1983-84, a lord cmmr of the Treasury 1984-85, parly under sec of state for Social Security DHSS 1985-86, min of state for Social Security and the Disabled 1986-87, chief sec to the Treasury June 1987-July 1989, sec of state for Foreign and Cwlth Affairs July-Oct 1989, Chancellor of the Exchequer Oct 1989-Nov 1990, Prime Minister, First Lord of the Treasury and Min for the Civil Service 28 Nov 1990-; AIB; *Recreations* reading, watching opera, cricket and rugby; *Clubs* Carlton; *Style—* The Rt Hon John Major, MP; 10 Downing Street, London SW1A 2AA

MAJUMDAR, Bish; s of Pran Kumar Majumdar (d 1949), of Calcutta, and Sudha, *née* Sengupta; *b* 20 Jan 1944; *Educ* Univ of Calcutta (MB, BS), Univ of London (DLO); *m* 19 Jan 1979, Sutapa Majumdar, da of Kalyan Sengupta (d 1954); 2 da (Selina b 26 Jan 1983, Mita b 27 Nov 1985); *Career* registrar: Dept ENT Surgery Univ Hosp of Wales 1974-76, Dept ENT surgery W Infirmary Glasgow 1976-78; sr registrar: Sheffield Hosps 1978-80, Univ Hosps Nottingham 1980-82; conslt ENT surgn Derbys Royal Infirmary 1982-; memb: Portmann Fndn (Bordeaux), Euro Acad of Rhinology, Otolaryngolgy Res Soc, Br Assoc of Otolaryngology, Midland Inst of Otology, Euro Acad of Facial Surgery; FRCSEd 1976, FRCS 1978, FRSM; *Recreations* swimming, golf, travel; *Style—* Bish Majumdar, Esq; 478 Burton Rd, Derby DE3 6AL (☎ 0332 371209); Derbyshire Royal Infirmary, Dept of Otolaryngology, London Rd, Derby (☎ 0332 47141)

MAKA, (Lady) Isabella Augusta; da of 6 Earl of Gosford, OBE; does not use courtesy title of Lady; *b* 17 Jan 1950; *m* 1979, Tevita T Maka; 3 s (Charles Nicholas b 1980, Toby Manu b 1985, James Alipate b 1989); *Style—* Mrs Maka; PO Box 1234, Nuku' Alofa, Tonga

MAKEPEACE, Dr Alan Rutherford; s of Andrew Rutherford Makepeace, of Bristol, and Alice, *née* Green; *b* 13 Dec 1949; *Educ* Univ of London (BSc, MB BS); *m* 12 Aug 1972, Penelope Jane, da of Henry Brown, of Cambridge; 2 da (Zoe b 12 June 1975, Clare b 10 Jan 1979); *Career* conslt oncologist; memb BMA, FRCS 1981, FRCSEd 1981, FRCR 1985; *Style—* Dr Alan Makepeace; The Maycroft, 24 Williams Way, Radlett, Herts; Department of Radiotherapy, Mount Vernon Hospital, Northwood, Middx (☎ 0895 78011)

MAKEPEACE, John; OBE (1988); s of Harold Alfred Smith (d 1967), of Woad House, Fenny Compton, Leamington Spa, Warwicks, and Gladys Marjorie, *née* Wright; *b* 6 July 1939; *Educ* Denstone Coll Staffs; *m* May 1963 (m dis 1978), Ann, da of William Sutton; m 2, 3 Dec 1984, Jennifer Moores, da of Harry Brinsden; *Career* teacher Birmingham Educn Authy 1959-62, dir Farnborough Barn Ltd (subsequently John Makepeace Ltd) 1963-; dir: The Parnham Tst (charitable educnl tst) 1977-, Sch for Craftsment in Wood 1977-, Hooke Park Coll 1989-; memb Crafts Cncl 1972-77; Liveryman Worshipful Co of Furniture Makers 1977, tstee Victoria and Albert Museum 1988-90; FCSD 1975, FBIM 1986; *Clubs* Royal Overseas League, Farmers; *Style—* John Makepeace, Esq, OBE; Parnham House, Beaminster, Dorset DT8 3NA (☎ 0308 862204)

MAKER, Daljit Singh; s of late Kishan Singh Maker (d 1961), and Daya Kaur Maker; *b* 21 Jan 1954; *Educ* Brighton Coll; *Career* fund mangr James Capel Stockbrokers 1974-78; dir: Savory Milln Stockbrokers (fund mangr 1978-84, ptnr 1984), Parrish Stockbrokers 1988; memb Int Stock Exchange; *Recreations* squash, tennis, skiing; *Clubs* Hampstead Cricket; *Style—* Daljit Maker, Esq; Parrish Stockbrokers, 4 London Wall Buildings, London Wall EC2 (☎ 071 638 1282)

MAKEY, Arthur Robertson; s of Arthur Frank Makey (d 1968), of Dover, and Lily, *née* Findlay (d 1964); *b* 3 June 1922; *Educ* Dover GS, King's Coll London, Charing Cross Hosp Med Sch (MB BS, MS); *m* 19 March 1947, Patricia Mary, da of lion Victor Cummings (d 1984), of Canford Cliffs, Dorset; 2 s (David b 1949, John b 1955), 1 da (Margaret b 1951); *Career* RAFVR Med Serv, served in India 1946-48; hon emeritus conslt cardiothoracic surgn: Charing Cross Hosp 1955-89, W Middx Univ Hosp 1975-89, Colindale Hosp 1967-85; civil conslt thoracic surgery RAF 1985-, sr examiner in surgery Univ of London 1968-86; chm ct of examiners RCS 1980; external examiner in surgery: Univ of Malaysia 1981 and 1982, Univ of Khartoum 1985; official visitor for RCS and RCP Univ of Khartoum 1984; contrib chapters in med books; FRCS; *Recreations* golf, music, gardening; *Clubs* Royal Midsurrey Golf; *Style—* Arthur R Makey, Esq; 2 Beverley Close, Barnes, London SW13 0EH (☎ 081 876 7347); Charing Cross Hospital, London W6 8RF (☎ 081 846 1149)

MAKGILL, Hon Diana Mary Robina; CVO (1990, LVO 1983, MVO 1971); da (by 1 m) of 12 Viscount of Oxfuird, *qv*; *b* 4 Jan 1930; *Educ* Strathcona Lodge Sch Vancouver Island BC Canada; *Career* ceremonial offr Protocol Dept FCO 1961-90, protocol conslt 1990-; vice chm Women of the Year Luncheon; memb Int Ctee: Operation Raleigh 1990-, Action on Addiction 1990-; hon steward of Westminster Abbey 1978-; Freedom of the City of London 1989; Jubliee Medal 1977; Order of Star of Afghanistan 1971, Order of the White Rose of Finland 1969, Order of the Sacred Treasure of Japan 1971, Order of Al Kawkab of Jordan 1966; *Recreations* riding, reading, gardening; *Style—* The Hon Diana Makgill, CVO; Clouds Lodge, E Knoyle, nr Salisbury, Wilts SP3 6BE (☎ 0747 830260); 15 Iverna Court, Iverna Gdns, London W8 6TY (☎ 071 937 2234)

MAKGILL CRICHTON MAITLAND, Maj John David; s of Col Mark Edward Makgill Crichton Maitland, CVO, DSO, DL, JP (d 1972), of The Island House, Wilton, Salisbury, Wilts; *b* 1925; *Educ* Eton; *m* 1, 1954, Jean Patricia (d 1985), da of Maj-Gen Sir Michael Creagh, KBE, MC (d 1970), of Salisbury, Wilts; 1 s, 1 da; m 2, 1987, Mary Ann Vere Curzon, *née* Ogilvy, widow of Capt James Quintin Curzon (d 1986); *Career* Gren Gds 1944-57, Temp Maj 1952, ret 1957 as Capt (Hon Maj); Lord-Lieut Renfrewshire 1980- (DL 1962, Vice-Lord Lieut 1972); *Clubs* Turf, Puffins, MCC; *Style—* Maj J D M Makgill Crichton Maitland; Houston House, by Johnstone, Renfrewshire PA6 7AR (☎ 0505 612 545)

MAKIN, (Norman) Christopher; s of Windsor Makin, of Huddersfield, and Kathleen Mary, *née* Dyson; *b* 7 July 1943; *Educ* King James GS Huddersfield; *m* 9 Aug 1969, Gillian, da of Eric Reginald Mitton; 1 da (Rebecca Jane b 3 May 1977); *Career* chartered accountant; with Henry Shaw & Co then H N Bostock & Co; sr ptnr and sole practitioner Charles F Beer & Co 1973- (ptnr 1971-), practice merged with Revell Ward Chartered Accountants 1987; chm Huddersfield Youth Brass Ensemble, princ double bass Leeds Symphony Orch; FCA 1969, FBIM 1978, MBAE 1990; *Style—* Christopher Makin, Esq; Well Cottage, 39 Water Royd Lane, Mirfield, West Yorkshire WF14 9SF (☎ 0924 495888); Revell Ward, Chartered Accountants, Airedale House, 77 Albion St, Leeds LS1 5HT (☎ 0532 451483, fax 0532 426124, car 0836 635676)

MAKIN, John Beverley; s of William Makin (d 1983), of Ottershaw, Surrey, and Helen, *née* Southern (d 1980); *b* 28 Feb 1937; *Educ* Kingston GS; *m* 6 Oct 1969, Alicia Jane, da of Gordon Edward Fairclough, of Weybridge, Surrey; 3 s (Andrew b 1975, Alex b 1980, Stephen b 1983); *Career* assoc ed Motoring News 1960, ed Cine Camera 1960-63 (formerly asst ed), Parker PR 1963-67, chm IH Publications 1967-77 (formerly md), dep chief exec Adgroup 1977-81, dir Dewe Rogerson 1982-; memb Br Assoc of Industl Eds 1966 (nat chm 1973-74, fell 1976, chm of senate 1984-87); *Books* A Management Guide to House Journals (1970); *Recreations* cooking, bridge, golf; *Clubs* RAC; *Style—* John Makin, Esq; Easter Cottage, Wrens Hill, Oxshott, Surrey (☎ 0372 843 516); Dewe Rogerson Ltd, 3 1/2 London Wall Buildings, London Wall, London EC2M 5SY (☎ 071 638 9571)

MAKINS, Hon Christopher James; s and h of 1 Baron Sherfield, GCB, GCMG; *b* 23 July 1942; *Educ* Winchester, New Coll Oxford; *m* 1975, Wendy Cortesi; *Career* HM Dip Serv 1964-74; fell All Souls' Coll Oxford 1963; *Style—* The Hon Christopher Makins; 3034, P St NW, Washington DC, USA

MAKINS, Hon Dwight William; s of 1 Baron Sherfield, GCB, GCMG, and Alice, *née* Davis; *b* 2 March 1951; *Educ* Winchester, Christ Church Oxford; *m* 1983, Penelope Jane, da of Donald R L Massy Collier; *Career* dir: King & Shaxson plc, Wistech (Hldgs) plc; md John Govett & Co 1985-88; *Recreations* shooting; *Style—* The Hon Dwight Makins; Beaurepaire Ho, Sherborne St John, Basingstoke, Hants

MAKINS, Jean, Lady; Jean; MBE; da of Capt Lord Arthur Vincent Hay (decd); *m* 1932, Lt-Col Sir William Vivian Makins, 3 Bt (d 1969); *Style—* Jean, Lady Makins, MBE; Malthouse Cottage, 56 The Dean, Alresford, Hampshire SO24 PBD

MAKINSON, Jeremy David; s of Alan Makinson, of Moorcot, Nicky Lane, Mellor, nr Blackburn, and Dorothy Mary, *née* Holden; *b* 31 Jan 1959; *Educ* St Augustines RC Sch Whalley, St Mary's RC Coll Blackburn; *m* 27 July 1986, Carol Ann, da of Frederick Mercer; 1 s (James Alistair b 11 April 1990), 1 da (Laura Jane b 3 March 1988); *Career* photographer's asst Paul Deaville Photography Blackburn 1977, portrait and wedding photographer J G Farnworth Studio Darwen 1980, proprietor The Jeremy Makinson Studio (specialising in wedding work and portraiture) 1985-; lectr throughout Europe for Fuji Professional Film; five solo painting exhibitions 1974-81, Wedding Photographer of the Year 1987; FRSA 1985, FBIPP 1989, fell Master Photographers Assoc; *Recreations* game fishing, bird painting and watching, travel, good food; *Style—* Jeremy Makinson, Esq; The Jeremy Makinson Studio, Jubilee Mill, Logwood Street, Blackburn, Lancashire BB1 9TU (☎ 0254 583080, fax 0254 680433)

MAKOWER, Peter; s of Anthony Makower, (d 1984), of London, and Sylvia Evelyn, *née* Chetwynd; *b* 12 Sept 1932; *Educ* Westminster, Trinity Coll Cambridge (MA), The Poly Regent St (Dip Arch), UCL (Dip Town Planning); *m* 20 Aug 1960, Katharine, da of John Howarth Paul Chadburn, MBE, of London; 2 s (Andrew b 1961, Timothy b 1965), 1 da (Mary b 1963 (d 1979)); *Career* RE 1951-56, architect and town-planner on staff of Frederick Gibberd & Ptnrs 1959-82 and Chapman Taylor Ptnrs 1982-85, in practice as Peter Makower Architects and Planners 1985-; FRIBA; MRTPI; *Style—* Peter Makower, Esq; Peter Makower Architects and Planners, 32 Tideway Yard, Mortlake High St, London SW14 8SN (☎ 081 392 1488, fax 081 878 1807)

MALAND, David; s of Rev Gordon Albert Maland (d 1978), and Florence Maude, *née* Bosence; *b* 6 Oct 1929; *Educ* Kingswood Sch Bath, Wadham Coll Oxford; *m* 23 March 1953, Edna, *née* Foulsham; 2 s (Oliver b 1957, Nicholas b 1959); *Career* Nat Serv, Flying Offr RAF 1951-53; asst master Brighton GS 1953-56, sr history master Stamford Sch 1957-66, headmaster Cardiff HS for Boys 1966-68, headmaster Denstone Coll 1969-78, high master Manchester GS 1978-85; called to the Bar Gray's Inn 1986; memb Ctee of Headmasters Conference 1977-79 and 1982-84; *Books* Europe in the Seventeenth Century (1966), Culture and Society in Seventeenth Century France (1971), Europe in the Sixteenth Century (1975), Europe at War 1600-1650 (1981); *Clubs* East India, Devonshire Sports and Public Schools; *Style—* David Maland, Esq; Windrush, Underhill Lane, Westmeston, nr Hassocks, East Sussex (☎ 07918 4783); 1 Garden Court, Temple, London (☎ 071 353 5524, fax 071 583 2029)

MALCOLM, Alastair Richard; s of late Colin Ronald Malcolm; *b* 20 Oct 1947; *Educ* Eton, New Coll Oxford; *m* 1971, Elizabeth Anne, da of Edward Wilfred George Joicey-Cecil; 2 s; *Career* barr Inner Temple 1971; *Recreations* shooting, country pursuits; *Style—* Alastair Malcolm, Esq; Hart Hill Farm, Woodfalls, Salisbury, Wilts

MALCOLM, Hon Mrs (Annabel Mary Adelaide); *née* Norrie; da of 1 Baron Norrie, GCMG, GCVO, CB, DSO, MC (d 1977); *b* 23 Dec 1945; *Educ* Downham Herts, Blois France; *m* 16 April 1988, Ian R Malcolm, s of late C R Malcolm, of Newent, Glos; *Style—* The Hon Mrs Malcolm; 124 Swan Court, Chelsea Manor St, SW3

MALCOLM, Sir David Peter Michael; 11 Bt (NS 1665), of Balbedie and Innertiel, Co Fife; s of Maj Sir Michael Albert James Malcolm, 10 Bt (d 1976); *b* 7 July 1919; *Educ* Eton, Magdalene Coll Cambridge (BA); *m* 6 June 1959, Hermione, da of Sir David Home, 13 Bt; 1 da; *Heir* kinsman, Col James William Thomas Malcolm; *Career* Scots Gds 1939-46, Maj; CA; former dir James Capel & Co; former memb: Stock Exchange 1956-80, Stock Exchange Cncl 1971-80, memb Queen's Bodyguard for Scotland (Royal Co of Archers); *Clubs* New (Edinburgh), Hon Co of Edinburgh Golfers; *Style—* Sir David Malcolm, Bt; Whiteholm, Whim Road, Gullane, Scotland

MALCOLM, Dugald; CMG (1966), CVO (1964), TD (1945); s of Maj-Gen Sir Neill Malcolm, KCB, DSO (d 1953), and Angela Malcolm (d 1930); *b* 22 Dec 1917; *Educ* Eton, New Coll Oxford (MA); *m* 22 June 1957, Patricia Anne, wid of Capt Peter Atkinson Clarke (killed 1944), da of late Gilbert Gilbert-Lodge; 2 da (Anne (Mrs Carpenter) b 1943, Helen (Mrs Whittow) b 1962); m 2, Margaret Roy, da of Rev R P R Anderson (d 1989); *Career* Argyll & Sutherland Highlanders (Territorial Cmmn) 1939, discharged wounded 1945; HM Dip Serv: Lima, Bonn, Seoul 1945-57, HM Vice-Marshal of the Dip Corps 1957-65, ambass Luxembourg 1966-70, Panama 1970-74; Min Holy See 1975-77; Freeman Worshipful Co of Fishmongers; *Clubs* Boodle's, Brooks's, Travellers; *Style—* Dugald Malcolm, Esq, CMG, CVO, TD

MALCOLM, George John; CBE (1965); s of George Hope Malcolm, and Johanna, *née* Brosnahan; *b* 28 Feb 1917; *Educ* Wimbledon Coll, Balliol Coll Oxford (MA, BMus), RCM; *Career* musician; master of the cathedral music Westminster Cathedral 1947-59 (trained unique boys' choir for which Benjamin Britten wrote Missa Brevis), now mainly harpsichordist pianist and conductor; winner Cobbett medal Worshipful Co of Musicians 1960; hon fell Balliol Coll Oxford 1966; Hon DMus Sheffield 1978; hon RAM 1961, FRCM 1974, Hon FRCO 1988; Papal Knight of the Order of St Gregory the Great 1970; *Style—* George Malcolm, Esq, CBE; 99 Wimbledon Hill Rd, London SW19 7QT; c/o Harold Holt Ltd, 31 Sinclair Rd, London W14 0NS (☎ 071 603 4600, fax 071 603 0019, telex 22339 Hunter G)

MALCOLM, Kathleen, Lady; Kathleen; da of late Cdr George Jonathan Gawthorne, RN, and formerly w of James Melvin; *m* 1947 (as his 2 w), Maj Sir Michael Albert James Malcolm, Scots Guards, 10 Bt (d 1976); *Clubs* Cavalry and Guards'; *Style—* Kathleen, Lady Malcolm; 11 Onslow Square, London SW7 3NJ

MALCOLM, (Thomas) Neil Carmichael; s of Robert Malcolm (d 1983), and Janet Irene, *née* Carmichael; *b* 1 Sept 1938; *Educ* HS of Stirling, Univ of Glasgow; *m* 30 Sept 1967, Kay Donnet, da of John Donnet Anderson; 1 s (Colin b 1977), 2 da (Susan b 1968, Victoria b 1971); *Career* CA; sr ptnr Macfarlane Gray 1967-; memb Tax Practice Ctee Inst of CAs of Scotland; treas: Allan Park South Church of Scotland

1971-, Stirling GC 1977-; FCCA, FSAS; *Recreations* golf, squash, tennis, hill walking; *Clubs* Stirling Golf, Stirling Lawn Tennis and Squash, Stirling and County, Rotary of Stirling; *Style—* T N C Malcolm, Esq; 26 Snowdon Place, Stirling FK8 2JN (☎ 0786 75975); 6 Viewfield Place, Stirling FK8 1NR (☎ 0786 51745)

MALCOLM-BROWN, Tessa; da of Bernard Dixon (d 1983), of Pampisford, Cambridge, and Olive Marie, *née* Watts; *b* 23 July 1937; *Educ* Chatelard Sch Les Avants Montreux Switzerland; *m* 26 July 1958 (m dis 1979), James Anthony Gerard Malcolm-Brown, s of William Isbister Malcolm-Brown, of Harpenden; 3 s (Charles Barry b 13 Dec 1961, Guy James b 15 Nov 1963 (decd), Mark b 19 May 1965); *Career* dir: Dixon Int Ltd 1979, Dixon Int Gp Ltd 1984, Sealmaster Ltd 1968, SK Bearings Ltd 1979, The Dixon Malt Co Ltd 1979 (chm and md all cos 1984); md and chm Intumescent Seals Ltd 1980-; *Recreations* breeding arabian horses, carriage driving, piano; *Clubs* Br Driving Soc (horse carriages), Arab Horse Soc, Br Morgan House Soc and American Morgan Horses; *Style—* Mrs Tessa Malcolm-Brown; Pampisford Court, Pampisford Cambridge (☎ 0223 832795); Pampisford, Cambridge (☎ 0223 832851, telex 81664 Dixon G, fax 837215)

MALDEN, Aubrey Dicken; s of Peter James Malden, of Chiswick, London, and Marie Roselyn, *née* Clarke; *b* 7 Nov 1949; *Educ* Fowey Sch Cornwall, Ealing Sch of Art London; *m* 24 Sept 1983, Veronika Susan, da of Horst Max Schneider (d 1979), of Johannesburg, SA; *Career* fndr memb Craton Lodge & Knight New Product Development Consultancy London 1973-79, gp head of J Walter Thompson Brussels 1979-80, creative dir and memb Bd Ogilvy & Mather Brussels 1980-82 Johannesburg 1982-87, creative dir and memb Bd Ash Gupta Communications; Clio awards for TV work, radio & print work, other awards for print, TV, and Radio; involved in Prince's Tst Charity, memb The Creative Forum; *Recreations* rugby, squash, fishing; *Style—* Aubrey Malden, Esq; Ash Gupta Communications, 9 Coates Crescent, Edinburgh EH3 7AL (☎ 031 225 9587, fax 031 225 9588, telex 72346); 8 Rosehall Place, Haddington, Scotland

MALDEN, Viscount; Frederick Paul de Vere Capell; s and h of 10 Earl of Essex; *b* 29 May 1944; *Educ* Skerton Boys' Secdy Sch, Lancaster Royal GS, Didsbury Coll of Educn, N Sch of Music; *Career* acting head teacher Marsh Co Jr Sch 1974-77; head teacher Cockerham C of E Sch 1979-81; i/c pastoral care curriculum devpt and music Skerton Co Primary Sch Lancaster 1981-, dep head teacher Skerton CP Sch 1990-; patron Morecambe Philharmonic Choir; LLCM (TD), ALCM, FRSA, ACP; *Recreations* classical music; *Style—* Viscount Malden; Lindisfarne, Pinewood Avenue, Brookhouse, Lancaster, Lancs

MALE, David Ronald; s of Ronald Male (d 1963), of Worthing, and Gertrude, *née* Simpson (d 1946); *b* 12 Dec 1929; *Educ* Aldenham; *m* 6 June 1959, Mary Louise, da of Rex Powis Evans, of St Albans; 1 s (James b 1964), 2 da (Sarah b 1962, Charlotte b 1966); *Career* Nat Serv 2 Lt RA 1948-49; memb: Bd Dirs Building Centre 1970-80, Govt Construction Panel 1973-74; RICS: memb Gen Cncl 1976-, pres quantity surveyors Divnl Cncl 1977-78, pres 1989-90; sr ptnr Gardiner & Theobald 1979-(ptnr 1960), chm Commercial Buildings Steering Group 1984-88; govr Aldenham Sch 1974-, memb Econ Devpt Cncl for Bldg 1982-86; MCC: memb Ctee 1984-, chm Estates Sub Ctee 1984-; pres Old Aldenhamian Soc 1986-89; Church cmmr 1989-; Freeman City of London 1961, Liveryman Worshipful Co Painter-Stainers 1961-, Master Worshipful Co of Chartered Surveyors 1984-85 (memb Ct 1977-90); ARICS 1954, FRICS 1964; *Recreations* opera, ballet, lawn tennis, real tennis, golf; *Clubs* Boodle's, Garrick; *Style—* David Male, Esq; Pollards Farm, Kinsbourne Green, Harpenden, Herts AL5 3PE; 6 Bowland Yard, Kinnerton St, London SW1X 8EE; 49 Bedford Square, London WC1B 3EB (☎ 071 637 2468, fax 071 636 3185, car 0860 544 601, telex 24410)

MALEK, David William; s of John Stephen Malek, of Montreal, Canada, and Brenda Josephine, *née* Carley; *b* 14 May 1964; *Educ* St Pius X HS Ottawa Canada, Nat Ballet Sch of Canada (scholar), Royal Conservatory, Banff Sch of Arts; *Career* actor; leads in film and TV incl: Road to Avonlea, Sing, Jeff in the Garden, Moondog in the Beginning; featuring in The Sinatra Suite; theatre credits incl: Alex in Aspects of Love (Prince of Wales Theatre London), Marius in Les Miserables (Royal Alexandra Theatre Canada), Munkestrap, Plato, Alonzo, Macavity, Skimbleshanks, Coricopat and Pouncival in Cats (Canada), Paris in Adriana Le Couveur (Canada Opera Co), Riff in West Side Story (Banff Sch of Arts Canada), featured in Idominao (Canada Opera Co), Og in Finian's Rainbow (Pius Theatre Guild Canada), Joseph in Joseph's Amazing Technicolour Dream Coat (Pius Theatre Guild Canada), Smirnov in The Boor (Pius Theatre Guild Canada); *Style—* David Malek, Esq; 32 Glenloch Rd, London; Bellsize Park, 23 Sammon Ave, Toronto, Ontario, Canada; Mark Hudson Ltd, 420 The Strand, London (☎ 071 240 8851, fax 071 379 0089); Michael Oscars, 59 Berkley St, Toronto, Canada

MALET, Sir Harry Douglas St Lo; 9 Bt (GB 1791), of Wilbury, Wilts; JP; s of Sir Edward William St Lo Malet, 8 Bt, OBE (d 1990), and (Maria Johana) Benedicta (d 1979), da of Baron Wilhelm von Maasburg, of Vienna; *b* 26 Oct 1936; *Educ* Downside, Trinity Coll Oxford; *m* 28 Aug 1967, Julia Gresley, da of Charles Harper, of Perth, W Australia; 1 s (Charles Edward St Lo); *Heir* s, Charles Edward St Lo Malet b 30 Aug 1970; *Career* late Queen's Royal Irish Hussars; *Style—* Sir Harry Malet, Bt, JP; Wrestwood, RMB 184, Boyup Brook, W Aust 6244, Aust

MALET, Dr (Baldwyn) Hugh Grenville; s of Col George Edward Grenville Malet, OBE (d 1952), and Gwendolin Illiffe, *née* Gibbon; *b* 13 Feb 1928; *Educ* Wellington, King's Coll Cambridge (MA, PhD); *m* June 1958, Kathleen Patricia (d 1983), da of Arthur Morris, of Whitby, Cheshire; 1 s (Durand David b 12 Jan 1965), 1 da (Pheobe Jane b 2 Oct 1962); *Career* served in army educn and intelligence Italy and Palestine 1945-48; dist cmmr Sudan Political Serv 1951-55, Shell Co (incl Egypt) 1956-58, dir of studies Brasted Theological Coll 1962-73, lectr and hon lectr local history Univ of Salford 1973-; freelance author and broadcaster, ed Nat Christian News; an authority on aspects of inland waterway history (author of numerous articles); pres W Somerset Village History Soc, memb various ctees incl Somerset Archaeology and Natural History Soc; Freeman City of London 1953, Liveryman Wax Chandlers' Co 1969; *Publications incl* Bridgewater - The Canal Duke (3 edn, 1990), Voyage in a Bowler Hat (2 edn, 1985); *Recreations* local and family history, fishing, poetry; *Clubs* Lansdowne; *Style—* Dr Hugh Malet; c/o National Westminster Bank, Williton, Somerset

MALET, Hon Mrs (Margaret Cherry); da of 2 Baron Wigram, MC; *b* 24 April 1942; *m* 1972, Lt-Col Greville J W Malet, OBE; 1 s (Charles b 1976), 1 da (Henrietta b 1978); *Style—* The Hon Mrs Malet; The Walled House, Hatherop, Cirencester, Glos GL7 3NA

MALIA, (John) David; s of Austin Patrick Malia, of 10 Croft Park, Tarbert, Loch Fyne, and Hilda Elizabeth, *née* Mallan (d 1974); *b* 31 Jan 1947; *Educ* St Cuthbert's GS; *m* 1 (m dis 1982), Marie; 1 s (Aidan b 12 Dec 1976); m 2, 20 Sept 1986, Agnes, da of James O'Brien (d 1966); *Career* chm BUMA Engineering Co Ltd 1981 (dir 1973, jt md 1975, md 1979), chm Tosson PC; memb Northumbria Tourist Bd; *Recreations* viniculture, opera, photography, golf; *Style—* David Malia, Esq; The Pele Tower, Whitton, Rothbury, Northumberland NE65 7RL (☎ 0669 20410); BUMA Engineering Co Ltd, Robson St, Newcastle upon Tyne NE6 1NB (☎ 091 2659088, fax 091 2651259, telex 537886 BUMA G)

MALICKI, Janusz Maciej; s of Malicki Marian (d 1970), of Poland, Naleczow, and Malicka Helena, *née* Majdylo (d 1971); *b* 11 Aug 1929; *Educ* Secdy Sch Naleczow, Merchant Secdy Sch Lublin, Central Sch of Planning and Statistics (MSc); *m* 27 Nov 1955, Irena Wanda, da of Wolski Konstanty (d 1939), of Jablonowo, Poland; 1 s (Donald b 1960), 1 da (Maryla (Mrs Ostrowska) b 1956); *Career* various positions Nat Bank of Poland 1950-63, expert Int Bank for Econ Co-operation Moscow 1964-68, dir of dept Bank Handlowy W Warszawie SA Warsaw 1968-72, mangr int rels Int Bank for Econ Co-operation 1973-75, md and gen dir Int Investmt Bank Moscow 1976-81, dir and gen mangr Bank Handlowy N Warsawie SA London 1985 (vice pres Bd of Mgmnt Warsaw 1981-85); memb: Overseas Bankers Club, Lombard Assoc; Polonia Restituta, Knight's Cross, Cross of Merit Gold Class, Cross of Merit Silver Class; *Style—* Janusz Malicki, Esq; Bank Handlowy W Warszawie SA, 4 Coleman St, London EC2R 5AS (☎ 071 606 7181, fax 071 726 4902, telex 8811681)

MALIK, Rex Henri Charles; s of Rev Marcus Abraham Malik (d 1964), of Hasanpur India and Oxford, and Henriette, *née* Benoist; *b* 2 July 1928; *Educ* City of Oxford HS; *m* 1, 1962 (m dis 1967) Diana Chalmers; 2 s (Nicholas Rex b 1963, Marcus Henri b 1964); m 2, 1969, Gillian Frances Gardner, da of George Smith, of Welwyn Garden City; *Career* RAF 1946-48, IAF 1948-52; journalist 1955-, worked for Times Newspapers and others, tv writer and reporter 1964-, industrial corr Southern TV 1964-65, first articles on computing published 1956 (Europe's first computer journalist); first regular radio computing-affairs broadcaster (BBC New Worlds) 1966-72, first broadcast enquiry into social and political consequences of computing (BBC Third Programme) 1969, originator and reporter world's first tv series about computing (Computers in Business) BBC 1971; conslt/ commentator world's first general computer education tv series (The Computer Programme) 1981-82; ptnr: Malik and Malik (Futures) Consultancy 1984-, Malik and Hubbard (editorial conslts) 1989-, ed InterMedia 1989-; fndr memb Real Time Club 1968; memb Worshipful Co of Info Technologists 1987 (hon archivist), Freeman City of London; *Books* incl: What's Wrong with British Industry (1964), And Tomorrow the World?...Inside IBM (1974), The Viewdata Revolution (with Sam Fedida, 1978); *Recreations* swimming, collecting books; *Clubs* Savile; *Style—* Rex Malik, Esq; 107 North End Rd, London NW11 7TA (☎ 081 458 3993, 071 455 8090)

MALIM, Christopher John; CBE (1969); s of Frederick Blagden Malim (d 1966, Master Haileybury Coll 1911-21, and Wellington 1921-37), and Amy Gertrude, *née* Hemmerde (d 1960); *b* 14 Sept 1911; *Educ* Wellington, Corpus Christi Coll Oxford (MA); *m* 1, 30 Nov 1939, Naomi, da of Waldemar Max de Paula (d 1972); 2 s (Adrian b 1941, Andrew b 1943); m 2, 20 Jan 1959, Audrey, da of Quiller Orchardson Gilbey Gold (d 1972); m 3, 24 May 1975, Barbarie, da of Col W E C Terry (d 1959); *Career* 1 Bn (43) Oxon and Bucks LI 1940, WO 1941, GSO2 PM Jt Planning Staff 1942-43, GSO1 plans HQ SE Asia Cmd 1943-45, Col 1945; chm: Moorfields Eye Hosp 1957-69 (govr 1955-69), Pantechnicon (Seth Smith Bros Ltd) 1976-86; chm: Hampstead Garden Suburb Tst 1967-69, London Post-Grad Ctee 1968-69; govr London Hosp 1970-78; memb: Cncl King Edward's Hosp Fund for London 1969-, Borough of Kensington 1953-59, Cncl Law Soc 1959-68; dir Westminster Fire Office (Sun Alliance W End Branch) 1960-83, tstee Wellington Coll Tst Funds 1979-; Master Worshipful Co of Scriveners 1990 (memb Ct 1989); FRSA 1968; *Recreations* music, real tennis, country life; *Clubs* Carlton, MCC; *Style—* Christopher Malim, Esq, CBE; 45 Whitelands House, Cheltenham Terrace, London SW3 (☎ 071 730 3520); Shepherds Cottage, Greys Green, Henley-on-Thames, Oxon (☎ 049 17 235)

MALIM, Rear Adm Nigel Hugh; CB (1971), LVO (1960), DL (1987); s of John Charles Malim, MBE (d 1957), and Brenda Stirling, *née* Robinson (d 1973); *b* 5 April 1919; *Educ* Weymouth Coll, RN Engrg Coll Plymouth, RNC Greenwich; *m* 6 Sept 1944, Moonyeen Maureen Ogilby, da of Capt William Edmund Maynard, DLI (d 1926); 2 s (Jeremy b 1945, Timothy b 1957), 1 da (Marquita b 1953); *Career* special entry cadet RN 1936, HMS Manchester 1940-42, HMS Norfolk 1942-43, HMS Jamaica 1945-47, staff RNEC 1948-50, HMS Triumph 1954-56, Admty 1956-58 (1951-54), HM Yacht Britannia 1958-60, dist overseer Scotland 1960-62, dep dir Marine Engrg 1962-65, IDC 1966, Capt RNEC 1967-69, CSO (T) to C in C Western Fleet 1967-69; md Humber Graving Dock & Engineering Co Ltd 1972-82, chm Association Western Euro Shiprepairers 1982-86; Lincoln Cathedral: memb Preservation Cncl 1985, chm Fabric Cncl 1985; *Recreations* gardening, sailing; *Clubs* RNSA, Royal Ocean Racing; *Style—* Rear Adm Nigel Malim, CB, LVO, DL; The Old Vicarage, Caistor, Lincoln LN7 6UG (☎ 0472 851 275)

MALIN, Dr Stuart Robert Charles; s of Cecil Henry Malin (d 1968), and Eleanor Mary, *née* Howe; *b* 28 Sept 1936; *Educ* Royal GS High Wycombe, King's Coll London (BSc), Univ of London (PhD, DSc); *m* 30 March 1963, Irene, da of Frederick Alfred Saunders (d 1989), of Polegate, Sussex; 2 da (Jane b 1966, Rachel b 1969); *Career* Royal Greenwich Observatory Herstmonceux: asst experimental offr 1958-61, scientific offr 1961-65, sr scientific offr 1965-70 , princ scientific offr 1970-76; Cape observer Radcliffe Observatory SA 1963-65, visiting scientist Nat Center Atmospheric Res USA 1969; Inst Geological Scis Herstmonceux and Edinburgh: sr princ scientific offr (individual merit) 1976-81, head Geomagnetism Unit 1981-82; Green Scholar Scripps Inst Oceanography USA 1981, visiting prof Dept of Physics and Astronomy UCL 1983-; head: Dept of Astronomy and Navigation Nat Maritime Museum 1982-88, Mathematics Dept Dulwich Coll 1988-; assoc ed Quarterly Jl of The Royal Astronomical Soc 1988-; pres Jr Astronomical Soc, vice pres Maidstone Astronomical Soc, churchwarden St Margaret's Church Lee; FRAS 1961, FInstP 1971, CPhys 1985; *Books* The Greenwich Meridian (with C Stott, 1984), Spaceworks (with C Stott, 1985), The Planets (1987), Stars Galaxies and Nebulae (1989), The Story of the Earth (1991); *Recreations* croquet, clocks; *Clubs* RAS; *Style—* Dr Stuart Malin; 30 Wemyss Rd, Blackheath, London SE3 0TG (☎ 071 318 3712); Dulwich Coll, Dulwich, London SE21 7LD (☎ 071 693 5271)

MALINS, Humfrey Jonathan; MP (C) Croydon NW 1983-; s of Rev Peter Malins, and Lilian Joan Malins, of Greenwich; *b* 31 July 1945; *Educ* St John's Sch Leatherhead, Brasenose Coll Oxford (MA); *m* 1979, Lynda Ann; 1 s (Harry b 1985), 1 da (Katherine b 1982); *Career* slr; PPS to Home Office Min 1987-; *Recreations* rugby football, golf, gardening; *Clubs* Vincents (Oxford), W Sussex GC; *Style—* Humfrey Malins, Esq, MP; Highbury, Westcott Street, Westcott, Surrey (☎ 0306 885554); work: Old Gun Court, North St, Dorking, Surrey (☎ 0306 881256)

MALLABY, Sir Christopher Leslie George; KCMG (1988); s of Brig A W S Mallaby, CIE, OBE (ka 1945), and Margaret Catherine, *née* Jones; *b* 7 July 1936; *Educ* Eton, King's Coll Cambridge (BA); *m* 1961, Pascale, da of Francois Thierry-Mieg, of Paris; 1 s (Sebastian b 1964), 3 da (Emily b 1967, Julia b 1971, Charlotte b 1972); *Career* entered HM Dip Serv 1959, Moscow Embassy 1961-63 and 1975-77, first sec Berlin 1966-69; dep dir Br Trade Devpt Office (NY) 1971-74; head of: Arms Control & Disarmament Dept FCO 1977-79, E Euro and Soviet Dept 1979-80, Planning Staff 1980-82; min Bonn 1982-85, dep sec Cabinet 1985-87, ambass to Fed Repub of Germany 1988-; *Recreations* fishing, reading, travel; *Clubs* Brooks's, Beefsteak; *Style—* Sir Christopher Mallaby, KCMG; c/o Foreign Commonwealth Office , London SW1

MALLABY, Lady; Elizabeth Greenwood; *née* Brooke; da of Hubert Edward Brooke, and Helen Honey; *b* 12 Nov 1911; *m* 1, J W D Locker, OBE (decd); m 2, 1955, Sir (Howard) George (Charles) Mallaby, KCMG, OBE (d 1978); *Recreations* painting, gardening; *Style*— Lady Mallaby; Mill End, Dunwich Rd, Bylthburgh, Suffolk IP19 9LY (☎ 050 270 273)

MALLALIEU, Ann; QC (1988); da of Sir William Mallalieu (d 1980), and Lady Mallalieu, *née* Tinn; *b* 27 Nov 1945; *Educ* Holton Park Girls GS Wheatley Oxon, Newnham Coll Cambridge (MA, LLM); *m* 1979, Timothy Felix Harold Cassel, QC, s of Sir Harold Cassel, Bt, QC; 2 da (Bathsheba b 1981, Cosima b 1984); *Career* first woman pres Cambridge Union Soc 1967; called to the Bar Inner Temple 1970, rec 1985-; *Recreations* horses, sheep, reading poetry; *Style*— Miss Ann Mallalieu, QC; Studdridge Farm, Stokenchurch, Bucks HP14 3XS; 6 Kings Bench Walk, Temple, London EC4 (☎ 071 583 0410)

MALLALIEU, Huon Lancelot; s of Sir Edward Lancelot Mallalieu, QC, MP (d 1979), and Betty Margaret Oxley, *née* Pride; *b* 11 Aug 1946; *Educ* Dragon Sch Oxford, Harrow, Trinity Coll Oxford (MA); *m* 11 Dec 1982, Fenella Jane, *née* Rowse; 1 s (Joshua, b 25 Sept 1990), 1 da (Ilaira b 4 June 1988); *Career* cataloguer for Christies 1969-73; writer and journalist 1973-; contrib: The Times, Country Life, The Sunday Telegraph, The Antiques Trade Gazette; ed Watercolours and Drawings Magazine 1986-, property ed Country Life 1989-90; Saleroom Writer Country Life 1990-; memb Ctee two maj antique fairs; *Books* Crome, Cotman and The Norwich School (1974), The Dictionary of British Watercolour Artists (3 vols 1976, 1979, 1990), How To Buy Pictures (1984), Understanding Watercolours (1985); *Recreations* helicopters, writing novels; *Style*— Huon Mallalieu, Esq; 100 Mortimer Rd, London N1 4LA

MALLARD, Prof John Rowland; s of John Edward Mallard (d 1947), of Northampton, and Margaret Gwendoline, *née* Huckle (d 1958); *b* 14 Jan 1927; *Educ* Northampton Town and County Sch, Univ Coll Nottingham (BSc), Univ of Nottingham (PhD, DSc); *m* 6 June 1958, Fiona MacKenzie Murdoch, da of Robert Murdoch Lawrence (d 1934), of Aberdeen; 1 s (John b 1959), 1 da (Katriöna b 1964); *Career* asst physicist Liverpool Radium Inst 1951-53, head of Dept of Physics Hammersmith Hosp 1958-63 (physicist 1953-58), reader in med physics Postgrad Med Sch and St Thomas's Hosp Med Sch London 1963-65, prof of med physics Univ of Aberdeen 1965-, hon dir of med physics Grampain Health Bd; Julio Palacios lectr Lisbon 1974, Silvanus Thompson Medal Br Inst Radiologists 1981 (Barclay Prize 1976), Otto Glasser Lectr Cleveland USA 1982, Royal Soc Wellcome Fndn Prize and Gold Medal 1984, Free Enterprise Special Award Aims for Industry 1984, George Van Hevesy Medal Euro Soc for Nuclear Med 1985, Award of Euro Workshop of Nuclear Magnetic Resonance in Med 1987, Commemoration lectr Univ of Osaka Japan 1987, Sr Scientist Award of Merit Int Union of Physical and Engrg Scis in Med 1988; memb Sec of State for Scotland Equipment Res Ctee 1973-77 (bio-engrg study gp 1969-72, bio-med res ctee 1973-77), memb MRC bds 1975-86, chm UK Ctee for Med Physics 1975-88 (sec 1965-75); memb: UK Nat Ctee for Bio-Physics 1977-85, admin of Radioactive Substances Advsy Ctee DHSS 1982-85, cmmr Int Cmmn of Radiation Units and Measurements 1985; hon fell Australian Coll of Physical Scis applied to Med; hon memb: RCR 1966, Br Nuclear Med Soc; FInstP (C Phys) 1960, FIEE (CEng) 1962, FRSE 1972, FRCPath 1974, FIPSM 1951 (pres 1970-73), BES 1975 (pres 1975-78); *Books* contrib: Radioisotopes in Medical Diagnosis (1971), Progress in Nuclear Medicine (1972), NMR Imaging (1983), Modern Microscopies (1989); *Recreations* handicrafts; *Style*— Prof John Mallard; 121 Anderson Drive, Aberdeen (☎ 0224 316204); Dept of Bio-Medical Physics & Bio-Engineering, University of Aberdeen and Grampian Health Bd, Foresterhill, Aberdeen AB9 2ZD (☎ 0224 681818 ext 52499, fax 0224 685645, telex 73458 UNIABN G)

MALLET, John Valentine Granville; s of Sir Victor Alexander Louis Mallet, GCMG, CVO (d 1969), and Christiana Jean (Peggy), *née* Andreae (d 1984); bro of Philip Louis Victor Mallet, *qv*; *b* 15 Sept 1930; *Educ* Winchester, Balliol Coll Oxford (BA); *m* 6 Sept 1958, Felicity Ann, da of (Philip Thurstane Richard) Ulick Basset, of Beaupré, Glamorgan; 1 s (Hugo Thurstane Victor Ulick b 1962); *Career* Nat Serv Intelligence Corps, temp Lt Trieste Security Office 1949-50; Ceramics and Works of Art Dept Sotheby & Co 1955-62; keeper Dept of Ceramics V & A 1976-89 (asst keeper 1962-76, sec Advsy Cncl 1967-73); Prime Warden Ct of Assts Fishmongers Co 1983-84 (memb of Ct 1970-); memb: Exec Ctee Nat Art Collection Fund 1989-, Wissenschaftlicher Beirat of the Ceramica-Stiftung (Basel) 1990-; FRSA, FSA; *Books* various articles and reviews on ceramics; *Recreations* tennis; *Clubs* Brooks's; *Style*— John Mallet, Esq

MALLET, Hon Mrs (Laura); *née* Aitken; da of Sir Max Aitken, 2 Bt, DSO, DFC (d 1985; 2 Baron Beaverbrook who disclaimed title 1964), by his 3 w, Violet, da of Sir Humphrey de Trafford, 4 Bt, MC; sis of 3 Baron Beaverbrook; *b* 18 Nov 1953; *m* 1984, David Victor Mark Mallet, s of Sir Victor Mallet, GCMG, CVO (d 1969); 1 s (David Sonny Victor Maxwell b 1984); *Style*— The Hon Mrs Mallet; Oakwood Farm, Oakwood, nr Chichester, Sussex

MALLET, Philip Louis Victor; CMG (1980); s of Sir Victor Alexander Louis Mallet GCMG, CVO (d 1969), and Christiana Jean, *née* Andreae (d 1984); descended from Jacques Mallet du Pan, chronicler of the French Revolution; *b* 3 Feb 1926; *Educ* Winchester, Balliol Coll Oxford (BA); *m* 1953, Mary Moyle Grenfell, da of Rev Granville William Borlase (d 1953); 3 s (James, Stephen, Victor); *Career* HM Dip Serv (ret); high cmmr Guyana, non-res ambass Suriname 1978-82; *Clubs* Brooks's; *Style*— Philip Mallet, Esq, CMG; Wittersham House, Wittersham, Kent TN30 7ED (☎ 0797 270238)

MALLETT, Dr Bernard Louis James; s of Bernard Remi James Mallett (d 1946), and Dorothy Ella Jane, *née* Ovenden (d 1983); *b* 23 Sept 1924; *Educ* Colston Sch, Guys Hosp Med Sch (MB BS Hons, DPM); *m* 1, 24 July 1948, Vera Louise (d 1985), da of Sydney George Pateman (d 1967); 1 s (Richard b 1956); m 2, 1 March 1987, Beryl Mary, da of James Cunliffe Ashworth (d 1955); 2 s (Simon b 1958, Peter b 1961), 1 da (Sarah b 1956); *Career* WWII RNVR Sub-Lt on HMS Norfolk, Vivien and Zenith 1942-46; house surgn physician and registrar Guy's Hosp 1952-57, sr registrar prof Unit of Maudsley Hosp 1957-60, Nuffield res rell Guy's 1960-62, conslt psychiatrist Fairfield Hosp 1963-73, sr conslt psychiatrist and head of dept Lister Hosp 1973-89, memb Mental Health Tbnls of Oxford and N W Thames 1972-; memb and sec Rotary Club of Hitchin; MRCS 1952, MRCP 1956, FRSM 1957; memb Med Res Soc 1960, FRCPsych 1983, memb Medico-Legal Soc 1989; *Recreations* fell walking, photography, bridge; *Style*— Dr Bernard Mallett; The Tilehouse, 27 Tilehouse Street, Hitchin, Herts SG5 2DY (☎ 0462 432659)

MALLETT, Prof Michael Edward; s of Edward Campbell Mallett, of Little Roods, Gamblesby, nr Penrith, Cumbria, and Mary Florence, *née* Thompson; *b* 14 July 1932; *Educ* St Edwards Sch Oxford, Worcester Coll Oxford (BA, MA, DPhil); *m* 3 June 1961, Patricia Berenice, da of Ivor George Sullivan (d 1955); 2 s (Lucien b 1976, Cyprian b 1978); *Career* Nat Serv RA 1951-52, 2 Lt 1952; asst prof in history Univ of Manitoba 1960, asst dir and librarian Br Sch at Rome 1962, prof of history Univ of Warwick 1978 (lectr 1967, sr lectr 1971, reader 1974); memb Exec Ctee Venice in Peril Fund; FRSL 1970, FR Hist S 1977; *Books* The Florentine Galleys in the 15th Century (1967), The Borgias (1969), Mercenaries and Their Masters: Warfare in Renaissance Italy (1974), The Military Organisation of a Renaissance State: Venice 1400-1617 (with J R Hale, 1984), Lettere di Lorenzo de' Medici, vols V and VI (1990); *Style*— Prof Michael Mallett; 2 Lansdowne Circus, Leamington Spa, Warwickshire CV32 4SW (☎ 0926 425529); Department of History, University of Warwick, Coventry CV4 7AL (☎ 0203 523487)

MALLETT, Michael John; s of Albert William Mallett (d 1972); *b* 14 Dec 1931; *Educ* Devonport HS Plymouth, Penzance; *m* 1956, Joan Barbara, *née* Ayre; 1 s, 2 da; *Career* ptnr Noel Lewis & Co Liverpool 1957-60; James Neill Hldgs Ltd: sec 1960, dir corp devpt 1970, dep chief exec 1974; chm: Ayre Mallett & Co Ltd 1960-, Radio Hallam Ltd 1979-90, Girobank plc (NE Regnl Bd), Yorks Radio Network plc 1987-90, Andionics Ltd 1987-90, Coated Electrodes Int 1988-90; chm and chief exec Neill Tool Gp Ltd 1981, chm and md Neill Tools 1981-83, exec dir James Neill Hldgs plc 1983-84, dep chm TT Gp plc 1984-; chm: Record Holdings plc 1985-, Rediffusion (Singapore) Private Limited 1989-, Rediffusion Communication Private Ltd 1989-, Rediffusion Tours (S) Private Ltd 1989-, Hotelevision Singapore Private Limited 1989-; dir: Unishelf Ventures Ltd 1984-, Viking Radio Ltd 1987-90, Bradford Community Ltd 1987-90, Sheffield Academic Press Ltd 1988-, Yorkshire Venture Capital Ltd 1989; chm: Yorks and Humberside Regnl Cncl CBI 1979-81, Nat Cncl CBI 1979-, Econ and Fin Policy Ctee CBI 1982-88, Accounting Standards Ctee 1982-89, Sheffield Dist Soc Chartered Accountants (pres 1986-87); Master Co of Cutlers in Hallamshire 1978-79; FCA; *Recreations* riding, reading; *Style*— Michael Mallett Esq; 106 Ivy Park Rd, Sheffield, S Yorks S10 3LD (☎ 0742 305166)

MALLICK, Dr Netar P; s of Dr Bhawani Mallick (d 1964), of Blackburn, Lancs, and Shanti Devi, *née* Talwar (d 1986); *Educ* Queen Elizabeth Sch Blackburn, Univ of Manchester (BSc, MB ChB); *m* 11 July 1960, Mary, da of Albert Wilcockson (d 1977), of Brough, E Yorkshire; 3 da (Andrea b 1964, Naomi b 1966, Paula b 1968); *Career* conslt physician Dept of Renal Med Manchester Royal Infirmary 1973 (sr lectr med 1972-73); vice chm Blackburn Hyndburn Ribble Valley Health Authy 1985-90; pres: Manchester Lit and Philosophical Soc 1985-87, Renal Assoc of GB and I 1989-; chm Registry Ctee Euro Renal Assoc 1991-; FRCP 1976; *Books* Renal Disease in General Practice (1979), Case Presentations in Renal Medicine (1983); *Style*— Dr Netar Mallick; Department of Renal Medicine, Manchester Royal Infirmary, Oxford Rd, Manchester M13 9WL (☎ 061 276 4111)

MALLIN, Rev Canon Stewart Adam Thomson; s of George Garner Mallin (d 1976), of Melville View, Lasswade, Midlothian, and Elizabeth, *née* Thomson, (d 1949); *b* 12 Aug 1924; *Educ* Lasswade Secdy Sch, Coates Hall Theol Coll Edinburgh; *Career* ordained: deacon 1961, priest 1962; precentor Inverness Cathedral 1961-64, itinerant priest for the Diocese 1964-68, priest i/c St Peter and The Holy Rood Thurso and rector St John the Evangelist Wick 1968-77, canon Inverness Cathedral 1974, rector St James the Great Dingwall and St Anne's Strathpeffer 1977, dean Moray Ross and Caithness 1983-91 (synod clerk 1981-83), hon canon Inverness Cathedral and res priest St Paul's Strathnairn 1991-; memb: Co of the Servants of God, St John Assoc of Scotland Highland Branch, Rotary Club of Dingwall (former pres); hon memb Royal Br Legion Thurso Caithness (Communication USA Caithness) Unit 1971-77; exec memb Ross and Cromarty Cncl (on Alcohol, of Voluntary Serv); chaplain Dingwall Acad; *Recreations* gardening, music, travel; *Style*— The Rev Canon Stewart Mallin; St Paul's Parsonage, Croachy, Strathnairn, Inverness IV1 2UB (☎ 080 83 397)

MALLINCKRODT, George William; s of Arnold Wilhelm von Mallinckrodt, and Valentine, *née* von Joest; *b* 19 Aug 1930; *Educ* Schule Schloss Salem, Hamburg Business Sch; *m* 31 July 1958, Chairmaine Brenda, *née* Schroder; 2 s (Philip b 26 Dec 1962, Edward b 29 June 1965), 2 da (Claire b 11 Aug 1960, Sophie b 8 Aug 1967); *Career* merchant banker; Agfa AG (Munich) 1948-51, Münchmeyer & Co (Hamburg) 1951-53, Kleinwort Sons & Co (London) 1953-54, J Henry Schroder Banking Corporation (New York) 1954-55 and 1957-60, Union Bank of Switzerland (Geneva) 1956-57, J Henry Schroder Wagg & Co Limited (formerly J Henry Schroder & Co) 1960-; dir: Allianz of America Inc 1978-84, Banque Privee de Gestion Financiere 1980-83, Multitrading International Ltd 1982-84, J Henry Schroder Banking Corporation 1984-86, Schroders Australia Holdings Ltd (Sydney) 1984-, Wertheim Schroder Holdings Inc (NY) 1986-, Wertheim Schroder & Co Inc (NY) 1986-, Euris SA (Paris) 1987-, Schroder International Merchant Bankers Ltd 1988-, Siemens plc 1989-; chm: Schroders plc 1984-, J Henry Schroder Bank AG Zurich 1984-, and chief exec offr J Henry Schroder Bank & Trust Company 1984-86; memb: Euro Advsy Ctee McGraw-Hill Inc 1986-89, City Advsy Cncl CBI 1990-; pres German YMCA London, vice pres German YMCA London, vice pres German Chamber of Indust & Commerce UK, dir Euro Arts Fndn; memb: Br N American Ctee, City Advsy Cncl CBI 1990-; FRSA, CBIM; Verdienstkreuz am Bande des Verdienstordens (GFR) 1986, Verdienstkreuz 1 Klasse des Verdienstordens (GFR) 1990; *Clubs* River (NY); *Style*— George Mallinckrodt, Esq; Schroders plc, 120 Cheapside, London EC2V 6DS (☎ 071 382 6000, fax 071 382 6878, telex 885029)

MALLINSON, Anne Mary; da of David Butler Wilson, MC (d 1961), of Alderley Edge, Cheshire, and Dorothy Catherine, *née* Bunn; *b* 20 Aug 1930; *Educ* Acton Reynold Shropshire, Edinburgh Coll of Domestic Sci; *m* 4 June 1955, Terence Stuart Mallinson, s of Col Sir Sidney Mallinson, DSO, OBE, MC, JP, DL (d 1981), of Woodford Green, Essex; 3 s (Lawrence Stuart b 4 Sept 1957, Michael David Stuart b 22 April 1959, Roland Arthur Stuart b 13 July 1966), 1 da (Sheila Mary Anne b 24 May 1961); *Career* memb Westminster City Cncl 1974-; magistrate: N Westminster 1966-89, City of London 1969-88; Lord Mayor of Westminster 1986-87, Westminster rep London Tourist Bd 1980-85; memb: Paddington & North Kensington DHA 1983-85, Governing Cncl London Institute 1989-, chm Tower Hamlets DHA 1988-90; chm Bd of Govrs St James and St Michael's C of E Primary Sch 1988- (memb 1975-), govr Marlborough Coll 1974-87; chm: Beauchamp Lodge Settlement 1981-86, Tstees The Montisori Coll 1988-; govr St Mary Hosp 1985-; Freeman: City of London 1968, Worshipful Co of Gardeners 1987; Order GDR 1987, Commendatore Republica Italiana 1988, Dame Chevalier de L'Ordre des Coteaux de Champagne 1987-; *Recreations* hill walking, design, gardening, meeing people; *Clubs* Aldeburgh Yacht, English Speaking Union; *Style*— Mrs Terence Mallinson; 28 Albion St, London W2 2AX (☎ 071 262 1717, fax 071 706 2266)

MALLINSON, Anthony William; s of Stanley Tucker Mallinson, of Bury St Edmunds, Suffolk (d 1955), and Dora Selina, *née* Burridge (d 1960); f was 2 s of Sir William Mallinson, 1 Bt, of Walthamstow, the fndr of William Mallinson & Sons Ltd, timber merchants, now part of the Mallinson-Denny Group; *b* 1 Dec 1923; *Educ* Marlborough, Gonville and Caius Coll Cambridge (BA, LLM); *m* 30 April 1955, Heather Mary, da of Thomas Arthur Mansfield Gardiner (d 1950); *Career* Army 1943-47, Maj RA Europe and India; admitted slr 1951; sr ptnr Slaughter and May 1984-86 (ptnr 1957-86); dir: Stratton Investment Trust plc 1986, Morgan Grenfell Asset Management Ltd 1986; slr to Worshipful Co of Fishmongers 1964-86, chm Cinematograph Films Cncl 1973-76, hon legal advsr Accounting Standards Ctee 1982-86, memb Cncl Section on Business Law Int Bar Assoc 1984-90, memb London Bd Bank of Scotland 1985, memb Exec Ctee Essex CCC 1986; *Recreations* sport watching (principally cricket), reading; *Clubs* MCC; *Style*— Anthony Mallinson, Esq; 15 Douro Place, London W8 5PH (☎ 071 937 2739)

MALLINSON, Dr Christopher Mels; s of Lawrence Mallinson (d 1960), and Thea

Ruth, *née* Bergmann (d 1990); *b* 29 Oct 1935; *Educ* Cheltenham, King's Coll Cambridge (VIII Henley), Guy's Hosp; *m* 1966, Helen Gillian, da of J Noel Bowen; 1 s (William b and d 1977), 2 da (Polly Jane b 1973, Sarah (twin) b and d 1977); *Career* house physican Guy's Hosp, house surgn W Middlesex Hosp, sr house offr Guy's Neurosurgical Unit, registrar then sr registrar Guy's Hosp, res fell Pennsylvania USA; conslt physician and clinical tutor Greenwich Dist Hosp, lectr in physiology Guy's Hosp Med Sch 1969-79, conslt physican Lewisham Hosp 1979; fndr memb and memb Ctee Pancreatic Soc of GB and Ireland (pres 1987-88), pres Gastroenterology Sub Ctee European Union of Med Specialists, memb Br Soc of Gastroenterology 1965; FRCP 1973; *Books* Food Allergy (contrib, 1988), Baso Symposium on Biliary Tract & Pancreatic Cancer (contrib, 1990); *Recreations* garden design, painting, opera, conversation; *Clubs* Garrick; *Style—* Dr Christopher Mallinson; 134 Harley St, London WC1 (☎ 071 935 4849)

MALLINSON, Michael Heathcote; s of Reynold Heathcote Mallinson (d 1970), of Skateshill Farm, Chalford, Glos and Beatrice Maud *née* Butt (d 1978); *b* 17 Sept 1934; *Educ* Marlborough; *m* 9 Aug 1958, Audrey, da of Lt-Col Frank Clifford Arnold, of Hillcrest, 11A Avenue Rd, Belmont, Surrey; 1 s (Matthew Frank Heathcote b 1964); *Career* RA 1953-55, 2 Lt 1954; chartered surveyor Prudential Assur Co 1955-80, property dir and chief surveyor Prudential Portfolio Mangrs Ltd 1985- (jt chief surveyor 1981-85); pres of the Br Property Fedn 1989-90 (memb 1984-); memb: Cmmn for the New Towns 1986-, Property Advsy Gp to the DOE 1985-88; govr South Bank Poly 1986-; dir: Property and Professional Services Ltd 1990-, Small Business Property Investment (London) Ltd; FRICS 1960; *Recreations* music, gardening, walking; *Style—* Michael Mallinson, Esq; Chelston, Guildford Rd, Chobham, Surrey (☎ 09905 8720); Princeton House, 271/3 High Holborn, London WC1V 7EE (☎ 071 548 6620, fax 071 548 6999, telex 8811 419)

MALLINSON, Sir William John; 4 Bt (UK 1935), of Walthamstow, Co Essex; s of Sir (William) Paul Mallinson, 3 Bt (d 1989), and his 1 w, Eila Mary, *née* Guy; *b* 8 Oct 1942; *Educ* Charterhouse; *m* 1968 (m dis 1978), Rosalind Angela, da of Rollo Hoare; 1 s (William James), 1 da (Kate Sophia b 1972); *Heir* s, William James Mallinson b 22 April 1970; *Style—* Sir William Mallinson, Bt; 1 Hollywood Mews, London SW10 9HU

MALLON, Rt Rev Monsignor Joseph Laurence; s of John Mallon, and Mary, *née* O'Neill; *b* 8 Aug 1942; *Educ* St Nathy's Coll, St Kieran's Coll; *Career* ordained priest Diocese of Salford 1966; curate: St Joseph's Bury 1966-67, St Anne's Stretford 1967-73; RAChD: commissioned 1973, various postings UK and overseas as sr chaplain 1982-89 (chaplain 1973-82), princ RC chaplain and vicar general (Army) MOD 1989-; Prelate of Honour 1989; *Recreations* recreational mathematics, bridge, The Times crossword, owns a set of golf clubs (a squash racquet and some fishing rods) but has the strength of character to overcome guilt feelings about their non use; has reservations about: dog owners, children in groups of more than three, curry lunches; *Style—* The Rt Rev Monsignor Joseph Mallon; 1 Minorca Avenue, Deepcut, Camberley, Surrey GU16 6TT (☎ 0252 835768); Ministry of Defence, Bagshot Park, Bagshot, Surrey GU19 5PL

MALLON, Seamus; MP (SDLP Newry & Armagh 1986-); s of Francis Patrick Mallon (d 1969), of Markethill, Armagh, and Jane, *née* O'Flaherty (d 1965); *b* 17 Aug 1936; *Educ* Abbey GS Newry, St Mary's Coll of Educn Belfast; *m* 22 June 1964, Gertrude Cora, da of Edward Cush, of 1 Moy Rd, Armagh; 1 da (Orla b June 1969); *Career* headmaster St James' PS Markethill 1960-73; memb: Armagh DC 1973-, NI Assembly 1973-74, NI Convention 1975-76, Irish Senate 1982, New Ireland Forum 1983-84, House of Commons Select Ctee on Agric 1986, Br-Irish Inter-Parly Body 1990-; Humbert Summer Sch Peace Prize 1988; *Recreations* golf, angling, landscape painting; *Clubs* Challoner; *Style—* Seamus Mallon, Esq, MP; 5 Castleview, Markethill, Armagh (☎ 0861 551 555); House of Commons, Westminster SW1A 0AA (☎ offices: 071 219 3000, 0861 526 800, 0396 679 33)

MALLOWS, Surgn Rear Adm (Harry) Russell; s of Harry Mallows (d 1953), of Martock Somerset, and Amy, *née* Law (d 1941); *b* 1 July 1920; *Educ* Wrekin Coll, Christ's Coll Cambridge (MA, MD), Univ of London (DPH); *m* 1942, Rhona Frances, da of William Christopher Wyndham-Smith, of Patagonia, Argentina; 1 s (Richard), 2 da (Robin, Bryony); *Career* RN, serv Home Med and Far E Cmds 1946-77; house physician Wellhouse Hosp Barnet and Royal N Hosp Holloway, sr med advsr Shell International Petroleum Co Ltd 1977-85; QHP 1974-77; FFOM, FFPHM, DIH; CStJ 1976; *Recreations* music, travel; *Style—* Surgn Rear Adm Russell Mallows; Chesters, 1 Shear Hill, Petersfield, Hants GU31 4BB

MALMESBURY, Bishop of 1983-; Rt Rev Peter James Firth; s of Atkinson Vernon Firth (d 1952), of Stockport, Cheshire, and Edith, *née* Pepper (d 1967); *b* 12 July 1929; *Educ* Stockport GS, Emmanuel Coll Cambridge (BA, MA, DipEd), St Stephens House Oxford; *m* 27 Aug 1955; Felicity Mary, da of late Longworth Allan Wilding, of Oxford; 2 s (Julian b 8 Jan 1961, Matthew b 10 Aug 1966), 3 da (Gabriel 23 Oct 1958, Susannah b 12 Nov 1962, Linda Hennessy (fostered since 1974) b 17 Feb 1967); *Career* asst curate St Stephens Barbourne Worcs 1955-58, priest i/c Ascension Church Malvern Link 1958-62, rector St George's Abbey Hey Gorton Manchester 1962-66, asst prodr Religious Progs BBC Manchester 1966-67, sr prodr and organiser Religious Progs BBC Bristol Network Centre 1967-83; winner Int Radio Award Seville Festival 1975; chm Public Enquiry into Swindon Rail Closure 1985 (with John Garnett and Lord Scanlon); *Books* Lord of the Seasons (1978); *Recreations* photography, music, TS Eliot, Manchester Utd; *Style—* The Rt Rev the Bishop of Malmesbury; 7 Ivywell Rd, Bristol BS9 1NX (☎ 0272 685 931)

MALMESBURY, 6 Earl of (GB 1800); William James Harris; TD (1944) and two clasps, JP (Hants 1950), DL (Hants 1983); also Baron Malmesbury (GB 1788) and Viscount Fitzharris (GB 1800); s of 5 Earl of Malmesbury, JP, DL (d 1950, gn of 3 Earl, who d 1889, having been sec of state for foreign affrs and Lord Keeper of the Privy Seal); 1 Earl was last to be created in the GB Peerage (three days before the Union with Ireland), he had previously been sent in 1794, as a special envoy to Brunswick, to negotiate the marriage between Princess Caroline and the future George IV; *b* 18 Nov 1907; *Educ* Eton, Trinity Coll Cambridge (MA); *m* 1932, Hon Diana Claudia Patricia (Maria) Carleton (d 1990), da of 2 and last Baron Dorchester, OBE (d 1963); 1 s (James), 2 da (Sylvia, Nell); *Heir* s, Viscount FitzHarris; *Career* serv Royal Hampshire Regt (TA); a gold staff offr at Coronation of King George VI; surveyor; chm Hants CLA 1954-56, personal liaison offr Min of Agric SE Region 1958-64, chm Hants Agric Exec Ctee 1959-67, dir Mid Southern Water Co 1961-78; Official Verderer of the New Forest 1966-74; Jp Hants 1949-82, DL 1957-60, Vice Lord Lt Southampton Co 1960-73, Lord Lt and Custos Rotulorum of Hants 1973-83; Hon Col 65 Signal Regt 1959-66 and Hon Col 2 Bn Wessex Regt 1970-73; Master Worshipful Co of Skinners 1952-53; KStJ; ARICS; *Recreations* rural life, sailing, working and training labradors, travel; *Clubs* Royal Yacht Sqdn (vice cdre 1971-78); *Style—* The Rt Hon the Earl of Malmesbury, TD; Greywell Hill, nr Basingstoke, Hants RG25 1DB (☎ 0256 702033)

MALONE, Andrew Grant Scott; s of Desmond Noel Scott Malone, and Kathleen Helena Murray Malone; *b* 10 Oct 1967; *Educ* Inverkeithing HS; *Career* reporter with D C Thomson Ltd (working for Dundee Courier, Sunday Post and Evening Telegraph) 1984-87, press offr The Scot Office (working for the Scot Prison Serv) 1988-89, duty news ed Radio Forth 1989-90, educn corr and gen news and feature duties Scotland on Sunday 1990-; memb NUJ; *Recreations* fly-fishing, squash, reading; *Style—* Andrew Malone, Esq; 7 Marchmont Crescent, Edinburgh, Lothian (☎ 031 228 5537); Scotland on Sunday, 20 North Bridge, Edinburgh EH1 1YT (☎ 031 243 3560, fax 031 220 2443, car 0836 364828)

MALONE, Carole-Anne; da of James Lesley Malone, of Newcastle upon Tyne, and Patricia, *née* McIlroy; *b* 14 Oct 1954; *Educ* St Joseph's GS; *Career* journalist; trainee Shields Weekly News Tyne and Wear; chief reporter: The Sunday Sun (regnl newspaper), The Journal Newcastle; The Daily Star: reporter Manchester 1983-88, reporter London 1988, woman's ed and columnist 1989-; *Style—* Ms Carole Malone; Express Newspapers, Ludgate House, 245 Blackfriars Rd, London SE1 9UX (☎ 071 922 7458, fax 071 922 7962)

MALONE, Christopher Kevin; s of Stanley Malone (d 1973), and Beryl Marguerite, *née* Fletcher (d 1982); *b* 20 June 1947; *Educ* St John's Coll Southsea; *m* 7 July 1973, Pamela Ann, da of James W Bird, of 57 Southbrook Rd, Havant; 1 s (Timothy James b 1978), 1 da (Rebecca Suzanne b 1980); *Career* CA; with own practice, ptnr Malone Rudling & Co; chm Portsmouth Area CAs 1979-81, memb Dist Soc Southern Soc of CAs 1979-; FCA, FCIS, FCMA, MBCS, MBIM; *Style—* Christopher K Malone, Esq; 91 Red Barn Lane, Fareham, Hants PO15 6HE (☎ 0329 288 060)

MALONE, Hon Mr Justice; Hon Sir Denis Eustace Gilbert; s of Sir Clement Malone, OBE, QC; *b* 24 Nov 1922; *Educ* St Kitts-Nevis GS, Wycliffe Coll Glos, Lincoln Coll Oxford (BA); *m* 1963, Diana, *née* Traynor; *Career* serv RAF 1942-46; barr Middle Temple 1950, slr-gen Barbados 1958-61; puisne judge: Belize 1961-65, Trinidad and Tobago 1966-74; chief justice Belize 1974-79, puisne judge Bahamas 1979-; *Style—* The Hon Mr Justice Malone; c/o The Supreme Court, P O Box N8167, Nassau, Bahamas

MALONE, (Peter) Gerald; s of Peter Andrew Malone and Jessie Robertson Ritchie Malone, of Glasgow; *b* 21 July 1950; *Educ* Aloysius Coll, Glasgow Univ (MA, LLB); *m* 1981, Anne Scotland, da of William Blyth, of Edinburgh; 1 s (Andrew Blyth b 24 Aug 1990), 1 da (Jane); *Career* slr; MP (C) Aberdeen S 1983-87; PPS to Parly Under Secs of State Dept of Energy 1985, asst govt whip 1986-87; *Recreations* opera, music; *Clubs* Royal Northern & Univ, Glasgow Arts; *Style—* Gerald Malone, Esq; 32 Albyn Lane, Aberdeen (☎ 0224 571779)

MALONEY, Michael Anthony Gerard; s of Gp Capt Gerard Maloney, of London, and Pamela Maloney; *b* 19 June 1957; *Educ* Ampleforth, LAMDA; *Career* actor; theatre incl: Hal in Henry IV parts 1 and 2 (RSC), Romeo in Romeo and Juliet (RSC), Derek in Berek (RSC), Taking Steps (Lyric Theatre), Benjamin Britten in Once in a While the Odd Thing Happens (Nat Theatre), Peer Gynt in Peer Gynt (Cambridge), Two Planks and a Passion (Greenwich); films: Dauphin in Henry V, Rosencrantz in Hamlet, Leonardo in La Maschera, Truly Deeply Madly, Ordeal By Innocence, Sharma and Beyond; tv: Dominic in What if it's Raining (C4), Starlings (BBC, first prize Monte Carlo), William Boot in Scoop (LWT), Telfords Change (BBC), The Bell (BBC), Falkland in The Rivals (BBC), Relatively Speaking (BBC); jt winner Alec Clunes award LAMDA; *Style—* Michael Maloney, Esq; Markham & Froggatt, 4 Windmill St, London W1 (☎ 071 636 4412)

MALPAS, Prof James Spencer; s of Tom Spencer Malpas (d 1972); *b* 15 Sept 1931; *Educ* Sutton Co GS, St Bart's Hosp Univ of London, Univ of Oxford; *m* 1957, Joyce May, da of Albert Edward Cathcart (d 1962); 2 s; *Career* Flt Lt RAF; prof of med oncology St Bart's Hosp Univ of London, dir Imperial Cancer Res Fund Unit of Med Oncology, conslt physician St Bart's Hosp, dean Med Coll 1969-72; asst registrar RCP 1975-80, vice pres Med Coll 1987; *Recreations* skiing, sailing, history, painting, travel; *Style—* Prof James Malpas; 36 Cleaver Square, London SE11 4EA (☎ 071 735 7566)

MALPAS, Maurice Daniel Robert; s of Daniel Malpas, of Townhill, Dunfermline, Fife, and Annie Clements Millar, *née* McKenzie; *b* 3 Aug 1962; *Educ* Queen Anne HS, Dundee Coll of Technol (BSc); *m* 2 June 1984, Maria Divito, da of Scott Robertson Johnston, of Dunfermline; 1 s (Darren b 1987), 1 da (Zoe b 1990); *Career* professional footballer Dundee Utd FC; Premier League Champions 1983; runners up: UEFA Cup 1987, Scot Cup 1988 (previously 1985 and 1987); Scot caps: full 39, U21 9; memb Scotland's Squad for 1986 World Cup Mexico and 1990 World Cup Italy; *Recreations* DIY, golf; *Style—* Maurice Malpas, Esq; Tannadice Park, Tannadice St, Dundee, Angus (☎ 0382 832202)

MALPAS, (John) Peter Ramsden; s of A H Malpas (d 1942), and E N Malpas, *née* Gledhill; *b* 14 Dec 1927; *Educ* Winchester, New Coll Oxford (MA); *m* 10 May 1958, Rosamond Margaret, da of R J Burn (d 1984), of Chiswick, London; 3 s (Simon b 1959, David b 1962, Johnny b 1965); *Career* Lt RB served India and UK 1946-48; commercial asst Imperial Chemical Industries 1951-55, Chase Henderson & Tennant Stockbrokers 1956-58; Paribas Quilter Securities (formerly Quilter Goodson, previously Quilter & Co): joined 1959, dep sr ptnr and chm 1983-87; dir Penny & Giles International 1988; hon treas Royal Hosp and Home Putney, memb Ctee Friends of Templeton Coll Oxford, tstee Devpt Tst for Young Disabled; memb Stock Exchange 1961-88; *Recreations* skiing, walking, sailing, the arts; *Clubs* Carlton, Itchenor SC, SCGB (memb Cncl); *Style—* Peter Malpas, Esq; 48 Berwyn Rd, Richmond, Surrey TW10 5BS (☎ 081 878 2623); Penny and Giles International, 8 Airfield Way, Christchurch, Dorset

MALPAS, Robert; CBE (1976); s of Cheshyre Malpas (d 1962), and Louise Marie Marcelle, *née* Boni (d 1984); *b* 9 Aug 1927; *Educ* Taunton Sch, St Georges Coll Buenos Aires, King's Coll Univ of Durham (BSc); *m* 30 June 1956, Josephine, da of Leslie James Dickenson (d 1982); *Career* main bd dir ICI 1975-78, pres Halcon International Corporation USA 1978-82, memb Bd and md BP plc 1983-89, chm PowerGen (one of successor cos to CEGB) 1989-90; non exec dir: BOC plc, Eurotunnel, Baring plc, Repso S A (Spain); chm LINK (the DTI business HEI initiative), pres Soc of Chem Indust 1988-89, sr vice pres Fellowship of Engrg; memb Cncl of Indust and Higher Educn; hon doctorate: Univ of Surrey 1986, Univ of Loughborough 1985; fell N London Poly 1988; FEng, FIMechE, FIChemE, FIMatH; Order of Civil Merit (Spain) 1968; *Recreations* music, sport, opera; *Clubs* RAC London, Mill Reef (Antigua), The River (New York); *Style—* Robert Malpas, Esq, CBE; 2 Belgrave Mews West, London SW1X 8HT (☎ 071 235 3924)

MALTBY, Colin Charles; s of George Frederick Maltby, MC, and Dorothy Maltby; *b* 8 Feb 1951; *Educ* George Heriot's Sch Edinburgh, King Edward's Sch Birmingham, Christ Church Oxford (MA, MSc); *m* 1983, Victoria Angela Valerie, da of Paul Guido Stephen Elton; 1 s (Matthew b 1989), 2 da (Lorna b 1976, Katherine b 1986); *Career* pres Oxford Union 1973; chm Fedn of Cons Students 1974-75; merchant banker; dir: Kleinwort Benson (ME) EC 1983-84, Kleinwort Benson Investmt Mgmnt Ltd 1984-, Banque Kleinwort Benson SA 1985-, Kleinwort Benson Group plc 1989-; chief exec Kleinwort Benson Investment Management Ltd 1988-; *Recreations* curiosity; *Style—* Colin Maltby, Esq; 51 Addison Ave, London W11; 10 Fenchurch St, London EC3

MALTBY, John Newcombe; CBE (1988); s of Air Vice-Marshal Sir Paul Copeland Maltby, KCVO, KBE, CB, DSO, AFC, DL (d 1971), and Winifred Russell, *née* Paterson; *b* 10 July 1928; *Educ* Wellington, Clare Coll Cambridge; *m* 28 July 1956, Lady Sylvia Veronica Anthea Harris, er da of 6 Earl of Malmesbury, TD; 1 s (William John b 5 Sept 1959), 2 da (Caroline Jane b 14 May 1957, Sophia Louise b 11 Nov

1963); *Career* chm: Burmah Oil plc 1983-90, Dover Harbour Board 1989-, UKAEU 1990-; non-exec dir Harrisons & Crosfield plc; pt/t bd memb UK Atomic Energy Authy; *Recreations* history, sailing, gardening; *Clubs* Naval and Military, Brooks's; *Style—* John Maltby, Esq, CBE; Broadford House, Stratfield Turgis, Basingstoke, Hants RG27 0AS; UKAEA, 11 Charles II St, London SW1Y 4QP (☎ 071 389 6549)

MALTBY, Lady Sylvia Veronica Anthea; *née* Harris; da of 6 Earl of Malmesbury, TD; *b* 17 May 1934; *Educ* Croft House Dorset; *m* 1956, John Newcombe Maltby, CBE, s of late Air Vice-Marshal Sir Paul Copeland Maltby, KCVO, KBE, CB, DSO, AFC, DL; 1 s, 2 da; *Style—* The Lady Sylvia Maltby; Broadford House, Stratfield Turgis, Basingstoke, Hants

MALTHOUSE, Eric James; s of James William Malthouse (d 1961), of 13 Heol Stradling, Whitchurch, Cardiff, and Florence Dorothy, *née* Alder (d 1971); *b* 20 Aug 1914; *Educ* King Edward VI Sch Aston, Birmingham Coll of Arts and Crafts; *m* 24 July 1942, Anne May, da of late William Gascoigne, of High Row, Haswell, Durham; 1 s ((Jonathan) Paul Gascoigne b 14 June 1952), 2 da (Penelope b 19 May 1944, Diana b 29 April 1948); *Career* WWII serv RAC 1940-42 (invalided out); artmaster Salt High Schs Saltaire Shipley 1938-43, asst lectr (later sr lectr) Cardiff Coll of Art 1944-73; artist; exhibited first painting Royal Birmingham Soc of Artists 1931; mural paintings at: Wales Gas Helmont House, Penlyan Hostel Univ Coll Cardiff, L G Harris & Co Ltd Bromsgrove; exhibitions incl: Ten Year Retrospective 1959, Growth of Two Paintings 1963, New Vision Gallery (paintings) 1965, AIA (small paintings) 1969, Bangor Art Gallery (paintings and prints) 1970, Oxford Gallery 1971, Exeter Univ 1975, A Family Affair Sherman Theatre 1981; work in collections incl: Nat Museum of Wales, Welsh Art Cncl, Swansea Art Gallery, Newport Art Gallery, Bath Art Gallery, Bristol Art Gallery, V & A, Univ of Cardiff, Univ of Aberystwyth, Univ of Swansea, Univ of Exeter, Univ of Glasgow, Oxford CC, Glamorgan CC, Somerset CC; fndr memb: S Wales Gp 1949, Watercolour Soc Wales 1959; fndr 56 Gp Wales 1956 (resigned 1970); Welsh Arts Cncl Prize for best designed book Ancestor Worship by Emyr Humphreys 1971; memb Print Makers Cncl 1971, RWA; *Recreations* gardening, walking, jazz, chamber music, opera; *Style—* Eric Malthouse, Esq; 56 Porth-Y-Castell, Barry, South Glamorgan CF6 8QE (☎ 0446 749380)

MALTWOOD, Derek Ryder; s of Ryder Gardyne Maltwood (d 1988), and Nancy Kathleen, *née* Lewis (d 1983); *b* 2 May 1938; *Educ* Radley, Pembroke Coll Cambridge; *m* 1, 27 Sept 1965, Lesley; 1 s (Bruce b 1968), m 2, 16 Sept 1972, Margaret; 1 s (Damien b 1975); *Career* dir Stock Group CI; chm Jersey Branch IOD 1984-87, dep for St Mary 1987; memb Stock Exchange 1968; *Recreations* gardening, travel, DIY; *Clubs* United, IOD, RAC; *Style—* Deputy Derek R Maltwood; Greenfields, Rue de Bel Air, St Mary, Jersey, Chanel Islands (☎ 0534 65392); 1 James St, St Helier, Jersey, Channel Islands (☎ 0534 30400)

MALVERN, 3 Viscount (UK 1955); Ashley Kevin Godfrey Huggins; s of 2 Viscount Malvern (d 1978); *b* 26 Oct 1949; *Heir* unc, Hon (Martin) James Huggins; *Style—* The Rt Hon the Visount Malvern

MALVERN, John; s of Harry Ladyman Malvern, CBE (d 1982), of Cookham, and Doreen, *née* Peters; *b* 3 Oct 1937; *Educ* Fettes, Univ of London (BSc), London Hosp (MB BS); *m* 10 July 1965, Katharine Mary Monica, da of Hugh Guillebaud (d 1958), of Marlborough; 1 s (James b 1977), 2 da (Susan b 1966, Joanna b 1969); *Career* conslt obstetrician Queen Charlottes Hosp 1973, conslt gynaecologist Chelsea Hosp for Women and hon sr lectr Inst of Obstetrics and Gynaecology 1973-; pres Obstetrics and Gynaecology Section RSM; examiner: RCOG, Central Midwives Bd, Univs of London, Liverpool, Manchester, Benghazi, Colombo, Khartoum; memb: Central Manpower Ctee 1981-84, Cncl RCOG 1977-83 and 1987-; chm: Blair Bell Res Soc, Int Continence Soc (fndr memb), Academic Gp Inst of Obstetrics and Gynaecology 1986-88; pres Queen Charlotte's Hosp Dining Club; Liveryman Worshipful Soc of Apothecaries; FRCSEd, FRCOG, FRSM; *Books* The Unstable Bladder (ed with Freeman, 1989), The Textbook of Obstetrics (contrib 1989), various pubns on urogynaecology and obstetrics; *Recreations* wine tasting, Chinese ceramics, travel; *Clubs* RSM, Hurlingham; *Style—* John Malvern, Esq; 30 Roedean Crescent, Roehampton, London SW15 5JU (☎ 081 876 4943); 84 Harley St, London W1 (☎ 071 636 2766)

MALVERN, Viscountess; Patricia Margery; da of Frank Renwick-Bower, of Durban; *m* 1949, 2 Viscount Malvern (d 1978); *Style—* The Rt Hon Viscountess Malvern; c/o Standard Bank, Cecil Sq, Salisbury, Zimbabwe

MAMBA, HE Senator Hon George Mbikwakhe; GCVO (hon, 1987); s of Ndzabatebelungu Mamba, of Swaziland and gs of Chief Bhokweni, and Getrude Mtwalose, *née* Thwala; *b* 5 July 1932; *Educ* Betani Misson Sch, Newhaven Misson Sch, Cambridge Inst of Educn, Nairobi Univ; *m* 1960, Sophie Sidanda, da of Johanes Mapamula Nsibande (d 1987); 3 s (Ndumiso b 1961, Subusiso b 1963, Phuthumile b 1964), 2 da (Pholile b 1967, Muzi b 1971); *Career* head teacher Makhonza Mission Sch 1956-60, teacher Kwaluseni Central Sch 1961-66, head teacher Enkamheni Central Sch 1966-67, insp of Schs 1969-71, welfare/aftercare offr 1971-72, cnsllr Swaziland High Cmmn Nairobi 1972-77; High Cmmr London 1978-; field cmnr Swaziland Boy Scots Assoc 1967-68, chief cnsllr of Order of Sobhuza II 1987; *Style—* HE Senator Hon George Mamba; 64 Aylestone Ave, London NW6 7AB (☎ 081 459 3372); Swaziland High Commission, 58 Pont St, London SW1

MAMUJEE, Dr Abdullah; s of Mulla Mamujee Nurbhai (d 1947), and Khatijabai, *née* Alibhai (d 1942); *b* 10 Oct 1934; *Educ* Univ of Poona (MB, BS); *m* 15 Dec 1966, Dr Nalini Mamujee, da of Vaikunth Gopal Shanbhag (d 1980); 1 s (Salil b 5 Nov 1969), 1 da (Anila b 10 June 1968); *Career* surgical registrar Ashford Hosp Middx, surgical registrar Poplar Hosp London, conslt and sr lectr in surgery Univ of Dar es Salaam Tanzania, conslt and head of Accident and Emergency Dept Ipswich Hosp 1978, chm Cncl of Racial Equality, memb Bd of Visitors Hollesly Bay Young Offenders Inst, memb Rotary Club; RSM, BMA; FRCSEd; *Recreations* reading, writing; *Style—* Dr Abdullah Mamujee; Springfields, 151 The Street, Rushmere St Andrew, Ipswich, Suffolk IP5 7DG (☎ 0473 723970); Accident and Emergency Dept, Ipswich Hospital, Heath Rd, Ipswich, Suffolk (☎ 0473 712233)

MANASSEI DI COLLESTATTE, Hon Mrs Susan Barbara; *née* Addington; da of 7 Viscount Sidmouth; *b* 1945; *m* 1, 1965 (m dis 1975), Count John Paul James Alessandro Camillo Manassei di Collestatte, s of Count Alessandro Manassei di Collestatte and Lady Maryel de Wichfield, *née* Drummond, da of 16 Earl of Perth and Hon Angela Constable-Maxwell, da of 11 Lord Herries of Terregles; 1 s, 1 da; m 2, 1990, Anthony Andrew Ward Kimpton, s of Col Anthony Charles Ward Kimpton, and Hon Mrs Kimpton, *née* Hazlerigg (*see Lord Hazlerigg*); *Style—* The Hon Mrs A A W Kimpton; Bullen House, Ledbury, Herefordshire HR8 2JE

MANATON, John Westacott; s of William Alfred Westacott Manaton, and Linda Maud, *née* Townsend; *b* 10 Jan 1926; *Educ* Dulwich, Downing Coll Cambridge; *m* 23 June 1951, Mavis June, da of Frederick George Langton (d 1959), of Dartford, Kent; 1 da (Gillian Clare b 15 May 1964); *Career* Fleet Air Arm RN 1945-47; Lt Inns of Court Regt and 3/4 Co of London Yeo (Sharpshooters) TA; Royal Exchange Assurance 1947-51, Legal & General Assurance Society Ltd 1951-56, Canada Life Assurance Co Ltd 1956-59, Scottish Provident Institution 1959-63, pensions mangr National Mutual Life Association of Australasia Ltd 1964-67, gen mangr (UK) Swiss Life Insurance and Pension Co 1967-89, chm Westacott & Manton Ltd 1977-90; Freeman City of London 1980, Liveryman Worshipful Co of Actuaries 1980; AIA 1968, FPMI 1976; *Recreations* sailing (yachtmaster); *Clubs* United Oxford and Cambridge Univ, Little Ship, RNSA, Alleynian SS; *Style—* John Manaton, Esq; 2 Blair Drive, Sevenoaks, Kent TN13 3JR (☎ 0732 458528); Westacott & Manaton Ltd, 6 Stoneydeep, Twickenham Rd, Teddington, Middx TW11 8BL (☎ 081 943 1653)

MANCE, Jonathan Hugh; QC (1982); s of Sir Henry Stenhouse Mance (d 1981), and Lady Joan Erica Robertson, *née* Baker; *b* 6 June 1943; *Educ* Charterhouse, Univ Coll Oxford (MA); *m* 26 May 1973, Ms Mary Howarth Arden, QC, da of Lt-Col Eric Cuthbert Arden (d 1973); 1 s (Henry b 1982), 2 da (Abigail b 1976, Jessica b 1978); *Career* barr; *Recreations* tennis, music, languages; *Clubs* Cumberland LTC; *Style—* Jonathan Mance Esq, QC; 7 King's Bench Walk, Temple, London EC4Y 7DS (☎ 071 583 0404, telex 88791 KBLAW, fax 071 583 0950)

MANCERA, Rafael Joaquin; s of Rafael Mancera, of Mexico City, and Guadalupe de Arrigunaga de Mancera; *b* 19 Aug 1956; *Educ* Universidad Iberoamericana, Northwestern Univ (MBA); *m* 3 July 1982, Katherine, da of Vaden Fitton, of Hamilton Ohio, USA; 1 s (Eduardo b 1988), 2 da (Katherine b 1985, Luisa b 1987); *Career* vice pres Banco Nacional de Mexico 1977-85, dep md Int Mexican Bank Ltd 1985- (seconded by Banco Nacional de Mexico); *Recreations* squash, classical music; *Style—* Rafael Mancera, Esq; 29 Gresham St, London EC2V 7ES (☎ 071 600 0880, fax 071 600 9891, telex 881 1017)

MANCHESTER, Duchess of; Andrea; da of Cecil Alexander Joss, of Durban; *m* 1, G J W Kent; m 2, 1978, as his 2 w, 11 Duke of Manchester (d 1985); *Career* memb of Lloyd's; *Recreations* riding, breeding and owning racehorses, writing, photography, conservation of game worldwide; *Clubs* Jockey Club of Kenya, Muthaiga Country; *Style—* Her Grace Andrea, Duchess of Manchester; PO Box 24667, Karen, Kenya

MANCHESTER, 12 Duke of (GB 1719); Angus Charles Drogo Montagu; also Baron Kimbolton (E 1620) and Earl of Manchester (E 1626, cr three days after Charles I's coronation); s of 10 Duke, OBE (d 1977; himself tenth in descent from the 2 Earl of Manchester, a Parly Cdr in the Great Rebellion, being Cromwell's immediate superior at Marston Moor) and his 1 w, Nell; suc bro, 11 Duke (d 1985); *b* 9 Oct 1938; *Educ* Gordonstoun; *m* 1961 (m dis 1970), Mary Eveleen, da of Walter Gillespie McClure, of Geelong, Vic, Australia; 2 s, 1 da; m 2, 1971 (m dis 1985), Diane Pauline, da of Arthur Plimsaul, of Wimborne, Dorset; m 3, 27 Jan 1989, Mrs Ann-Louise Bird, da of Dr Alfred Butler Taylor, of Cawthorne, S Yorkshire; *Heir* s, Viscount Mandeville; *Career* business conslt; pres and patron The Duke's Tst; *Recreations* golf; *Style—* His Grace the Duke of Manchester; House of Lords, Westminster, London SW1

MANCHESTER, Elizabeth, Duchess of; Elizabeth; da of Samuel C Fullerton, of Miami, Oklahoma; *m* 1, W W Crocker; m 2, 1969, as his 2 w, 10 Duke of Manchester (d 1977); *Style—* Her Grace Elizabeth, Duchess of Manchester; PO Box 303, Pebble Beach, California 93953, USA; Ca Vendramin, 13 Giudecca, 30123 Venice, Italy (☎ 5207 746)

MANCHESTER, 9 Bishop of (cr 1847) 1979-; Rt Rev Stanley Eric Francis Booth-Clibborn; s of Eric Booth-Clibborn and Lucille Booth-Clibborn; *b* 20 Oct 1924; *Educ* Highgate Sch, Oriel Coll Oxford (MA), Westcott Ho Cambridge; *m* 1958, Anne Roxburgh, da of late Prof W R Forrester; 2 s, 2 da; *Career* serv WWII RA and Royal Indian Artillery, temp Capt; curate of Heeley, Diocese of Sheffield, of the Aercliffe Parishes; trg offr Christian Cncl Kenya 1956-63, ed-in-chief E African Venture Christian Papers (Target and Lengo) 1963-67, ldr Lincoln City Centre Team Miny 1967-70, vicar of Great St Mary's Cambridge 1979, moderator of Movement for the Ordination of Women in C of E to 1982; entered House of Lords 1985; memb Int Affairs Ctee Br Cncl of Churches 1968-79, leader BCC Delgn to Namibia 1982, chm Namibia Communications Centre, pres St Ann's Hospice 1979; hon fell Manchester Poly 1989; *Recreations* tennis, reading, listening to music; *Clubs* Royal Cwlth Soc; *Style—* The Rt Rev the Bishop of Manchester; Bishops Ct, Bury New Rd, Manchester M7 OLE (☎ 061 792 2096/1779)

MANCROFT, 3 Baron (UK 1937); Sir Benjamin Lloyd Stormont; 3 Bt (UK 1932); s of 2 Baron Mancroft, KBE, TD (d 1987); *b* 16 May 1957; *Educ* Eton; *m* 20 Sept 1990, Emma L, eldest da of Tom Peart, of Kensington; *Heir* none; *Style—* The Rt Hon the Lord Mancroft; House of Lords, London SW1

MANDELSON, Hon Mrs (Mary Joyce); da of Baron Morrison of Lambeth (Life Peer; d 1965); *b* 1921; *m* 1, 1941 (m dis 1948), Horace Williams (afterwards The Hon Horace Williams), s of Baron Williams of Barnburgh (Life Peer); m 2, 1948, George Mandelson (d 1988); 2 s; *Style—* The Hon Mrs Mandelson; 12 Bigwood Rd, London NW11

MANDER, Sir Charles Marcus; 3 Bt (UK 1911), of the Mount, Tettenhall, Co Stafford; s of Maj Sir Charles Mander, 2 Bt, TD, JP, DL (d 1951), and Monica Claire, *née* Cotterell (d 1963); *b* 22 Sept 1921; *Educ* Eton, Trinity Coll Cambridge; *m* 1945, Maria Dolores Beatrice, da of Alfred Brödermann (d 1923) of Hamburg; 2 s, 1 da; *Heir* s, Charles Nicholas Mander; *Career* served WWII, Capt Coldstream Gds; dir: Mander Bros Ltd 1948-58, Headstaple Ltd 1976, Arlington Securities (chm 1976-82, dep chm 1982-83); chm London & Cambridge Investments Ltd; underwriting memb of Lloyd's; High Sheriff Staffs 1962; Liveryman Worshipful Co of Fishmongers; *Recreations* yachting, shooting, music; *Clubs* Boodle's, Royal Thames Yacht; *Style—* Sir Charles Mander, Bt; Little Barrow, Moreton-in-Marsh, Glos (☎ 0451 30265); 6 Greville Ho, Kinnerton St, London SW1 (☎ 071 235 1669)

MANDER, David Charles; s of Alan Mander, of 5 Charlecote, Warwicks, and Muriel Betty, *née* Whitemann (d 1975); *b* 16 April 1938; *Educ* Wrekin Coll Salop, Univ of Birmingham (LLB); *m* (m dis); 2 s (Philip James b 1964, Nicholas David b 1967), 1 da (Charlotte Louise b 1972); *Career* slr; sr ptnr Mander Hadley & Co Solicitors; dir Warwicks Law Soc Ltd 1969-; memb Cncl: Warwicks Law Soc (sec 1969-72), Birmingham Law Soc 1972-80; memb Cncl The Law Soc for constituency of: W Midlands W Mercia and Welsh Marshes 1980-89, Coventry and Warwickshire 1989-; chm: Coventry Diocesan Tstees 1985-, Law Soc Indemnity Insur Ctee 1986-87; dir Solicitors Indemnity Fund Ltd 1987- (chm 1987-89); Freeman City of Coventry; *Recreations* golf, fell walking; *Clubs* The Law Soc; *Style—* David C Mander, Esq; Whitestitch House, Great Packington, Nr Meriden, Warwickshire CV7 7JW (☎ 0676 22362); Mander Hadley & Co, 1 The Quadrant, Coventry CV1 2DW (☎ 0203 631212, fax 0203 633131, telex 312290)

MANDER, John; VRD (1964); s of Thomas Goddard Mander, OBE, JP (d 1959), of 10 Park Lane, Sheffield, and Edith Alice Ruth, *née* Bland (d 1987); *b* 5 Aug 1924; *Educ* Dean Close Sch Cheltenham, Emmanuel Coll Cambridge (MA, MB BChir); *m* 24 July 1957, Mary Josephine (d 1968), da of Cornelius Clifford (d 1961), of Ballard, Tralee, Co Kerry; 2 s (Philip b 1960, Brian b 1964), 2 da (Jane b 1961, Maria (Mrs Coveney) b 1962); *Career* Surgn Lt RNVR 1949, lectr in aviation med Gosport 1950-51, Surgn Lt Cdr 1965, ret 1977-; house offr 1948-54: UCH, Queen Charlotte's Hosp, Soho Hosp for Women; registrar St Thomas' Hosp 1955-56, sr registrar Chelsea Hosp for Women and Queen Charlotte's Hosp 1956-60, clinical asst Royal Marsden Hosp and St Paul's Hosp, conslt obstetrician and gynaecologist York 1960-; FRSM, FRCS 1958, FRCOG 1969; *Recreations* sailing, tennis, walking, crosswords; *Clubs* Naval,

Yorkshire, Island Cruising; *Style—* John Mander, Esq, VRD; 99 Station Rd, Upper Poppleton, York (☎ 0904 794447); 28 High Petergate, York (☎ 0904 632983)

MANDER, His Hon Judge Michael Harold; s of Elisha Harold Mander, of Cumberland (d 1984), and Ann, *née* Moores (d 1960); *b* 27 Oct 1936; *Educ* Workington GS, Queen's Coll Oxford (MA); *m* 6 Aug 1960, Jancis Mary, da of The Rev Charles William Dodd (d 1974), Eaton Constantine; *Career* RA 2nd Lt 1955-57; slr 1963-72; called to the Bar Inner Temple 1972; in practise Birmingham 1972-85, asst rec 1982-85; dep chm of Agric Lands Tbnl 1983-85; CJ 1985-; *Recreations* life under the Wrekin; *Clubs* Wrekin Rotary (hon memb); *Style—* His Honour Judge Michael Mander; Garmston, Eaton Constantine, Shrewsbury, SY5 6RL (☎ 0952 510288)

MANDER, Michael Stuart; s of James Charles Stuart Mander (d 1974), and Alice Patricia Mander (d 1964); *b* 5 Oct 1935; *Educ* Tonbridge, Hackley NY; *Career* dir: International Thomson Organisation plc 1983-86, Thomson Directories 1983-; chm and chief exec: Thomson Information Services Ltd 1985-86, Hill Samuel & Co Ltd 1987-, chm Market Analysis and Information Database Systems Ltd 1988-, dir South News plc 1989, chm Jicnars 1990-; memb Cncl IOD 1976; *Recreations* sailing, skiing, golf; *Clubs* Royal Southern Yacht, Royal Wimbledon Golf; *Style—* Michael Mander, Esq; 41 Rivermill, Grosvenor Rd, London SW1V 3JN (☎ 071 821 9651); Hill Samuel & Co Ltd, 100 Wood St, London EC2P 2AJ (☎ 071 628 8011)

MANDER, (Charles) Nicholas; s and h of Sir Charles Marcus Mander, 3 Bt; *b* 23 March 1950; *Educ* Downside, Trinity Coll Cambridge (scholar MA); *m* 1972, Karin Margareta, da of Gustav Arne Norin (d 1985), of Stockholm; 4 s (Charles Marcus b 1975, Benedict b 1977, Hugo b 1981, Fabian b 1987), 1 da (Sarra b 1973); *Career* co dir (various publishing, educnl, land and overseas property devpt cos); farming, holiday cottages and forestry; Lloyd's underwriter 1972; fndr ptnr of Mander Portman Woodward (private tutors) in Kensington 1973; Liveryman Worshipful Co of Fishmongers; proprietor of Owlpen, a Tudor manor house and garden 1974-; fndr dir Alan Sutton Publishing Ltd 1976-86; *Recreations* humane letters and arts, conversation, conservation, dreaming; *Clubs* Boodle's; *Style—* Nicholas Mander, Esq; Owlpen Manor, nr Dursley, Gloucs GL11 5BZ (☎ 0453 860261, fax 0453 860819); Finca La Katria, Mijas, Málaga

MANDUCA, Charles Victor Sant; s of Victor John Sant Manduca (d 1989), and Ethel Florence, *née* Johnson (d 1960); *b* 21 Nov 1954; *Educ* Harrow, UCL (LLB); *Career* admitted slr 1979; ptr Lovell White Durrant (formerly Durrant Piesse) 1983-; Freeman Worshipful Co of Slrs 1988; memb: Law Soc, London Slrs Litigation Assoc; *Recreations* golf, gardening, antique clocks; *Clubs* Wentworth Golf, Landsdown; *Style—* Charles Manduca, Esq; 65 Holborn Viaduct, London EC1A 2DY (☎ 071 236 0066, telex 887122, fax 071 248 4212, 071 236 3602, 071 236 0084)

MANDUCA, HE John Alfred; s of Capt Philip Dei Conti Manduca (d 1984), and Emma, *née* Pullicino (d 1968); *b* 14 Aug 1927; *Educ* St Edwards Coll Malta; *m* 20 April 1954, Sylvia, da of Eric Parnis (d 1930), of Malta; 2 s (Martin b 7 Feb 1956, Anthony b 16 Nov 1962), 2 da (Anne b 11 Jan 1955, Louise b 23 Aug 1958); *Career* serv 11 HAA Regt Royal Malta Artillery 1952-55, Cmmnd 1953; Allied Malta Newspapers Ltd 1945 (dep ed 1953-62), Malta corr The Daily Telegraph and The Sunday Telegraph 1946-62, joined Malta Bdcasting Authy 1962 (chief exec 1963-68), dir and mangr The Malta TV Serv Ltd 1968-71, md Redifusion Gp of Cos Malta 1971-76, chm Tourist Projects Ltd 1976-, DG Confedn of Private Enterprise 1983-87, High Cmmr for Malta in London 1987, ambass to Norway, Sweden, Denmark 1988; chm Malta Branch Inst of Journalists 1957 (1959, 1961), memb Bd Govrs St Edwards Coll 1966-75, chm Hotels and Catering Estab Bd 1970-71, hon treas Malta branch Inst of Dirs 1975; *Books* Tourist Guide to Malta and Gozo (1967), Tourist Guide to Harbour Cruises (1974), Connoisseur's Guide to City of Mdina (1975), Malta Who's Who (gen ed 1978); *Recreations* collecting melitensia, current affairs, gardening; *Clubs* Traveller's, Royal Overseas League, Casino Maltese (Malta); *Style—* His Excellency Mr John Manduca; The Maltese Embassy, The High Commissioner for Malta in London, 16 Kensington Sq, London W8 5HH (☎ 071 938 1210, fax 071 937 8664, telex 261102 MLT LDNG)

MANDUCA, Paul Victor Sant; s of Victor Sant Manduca (d 1989), and Elisabeth, *née* Johnson (d 1960); *b* 15 Nov 1951; *Educ* Harrow, Hertford Coll Oxford (MA); *m* 1982, Dr Ursula, da of Edmund Vogt, of Jollenbeck, nr Bielefeld, W Germany; 2 s (Mark b 1983, Nicholas b 1988); *Career* vice chm Touche Remnant Hldgs 1987-89 (chm 1989-); dir TR Smaller Cos IT plc 1987-; md TR Industrial and Gen plc 1987-88; dir Clydesdale IT 1987-88, chm TR High Income plc 1989-; Freeman of the City of London 1988, Liveryman Worshipful Co of Bakers 1989; *Recreations* golf, squash; *Clubs* Wentworth, Lansdowne; *Style—* Paul Manduca, Esq; 54 Brompton Square, London SW3 2AG (☎ 071 584 3987); Mermaid House, 2 Puddle Dock, London EC4 (☎ 071 236 6565, fax 071 248 9756, telex 885703)

MANEY, Richard John; s of Richard J Maney, of Orange Park, Florida, USA, and Sarah Jane, *née* Cook; *b* 1 July 1947; *Educ* The Berkshire Sch Sheffield Mass USA, Washington & Jefferson Univ (BA), Univ of Pittsburgh (MS); *m* Irena Bruna, da of Alphonso Sumberac; *Career* May Company Department Stores Pittsburgh 1973-77 (trainee, asst buyer), sr vice pres and gen mangr Associated Drg Goods Department Stores Newark NJ 1979-83 (vice pres and merchandise mangr 1977-79); sr vice pres and gen merchandise mangr: Dillards Department Stores St Louis 1983-86, Lord & Taylor Department Store NY 1986-88; md Harvey Nichols 1988-; *Recreations* tennis, golf, classical music; *Clubs* Queens, Vanderbilt Racquet, Marks, Mosimanns; *Style—* Richard Maney, Esq; Harvey Nichols & Company Ltd, 109-125 Knightsbridge, London SW1X 7RJ (☎ 071 235 5000, fax 071 235 8560)

MANFORD, Bruce Robert James; s of John Julian Manford, of Braemar, Church Rd, Stanmore, Middlx HA7 4AG, and Ruth, *née* Heldmann; *b* 21 March 1957; *Educ* Haberdashers' Aske's, Keele Univ (BA); *Career* admitted slr 1981; ptnr Lawrence Graham 1988-; memb: Law Soc 1981, Royal Inst Public Admin 1977; *Style—* Bruce Manford, Esq; Lawrence Graham, 190 Strand, London WC2R 1JN

MANGEOT, Fowke Jean André; s of André Louis Mangeot (d 1970), of 21 Cresswell Place, London SW10, and Olive Summerley Rede, *née* Fowke (d 1969); *b* 18 April 1911; *Educ* Westminster; *m* 20 Nov 1954, (Erica) June Leslie, da of Gp-Capt Eric Mackay Murray, DSO, MC (d 1954), of Inches, Battledown, Cheltenham, Glos; 1 s (Andrew Rede Fowke b 15 Nov 1955), 1 da (Louise Rose Everest b 18 July 1958); *Career* Home Gd 1942-44; Price Waterhouse & Co: articled clerk 1928-33, qualified CA 1933-38; mgmnt conslt Prodn Engrg Ltd 1938-47, commercial dir Dowty Equipment Ltd 1949-69 (chief accountant 1947-49), jt md Elliot-Flight Automation Ltd 1962-70, fin dir GEC Avionics Ltd 1970-76; hon treas Aldeburgh GC; ACA 1933, AIPE 1948, companion Royal Aeronautical Soc 1953, FCA 1960; *Recreations* squash, tennis, sailing, golf, reading; *Clubs* Rye GC, Aldeburgh Golf; *Style—* Fowke Mangeot, Esq; The Crows Nest, North End Ave, Thorpeness, Leiston, Suffolk IP16 4PD (☎ 0728 452042)

MANGHAM, Maj-Gen (William) Desmond; CB (1978); s of Lt-Col William Patrick Mangham (d 1973), and Margaret Mary, *née* Donnachie (d 1965); *b* 29 Aug 1924; *Educ* Ampleforth; *m* 1960, Susan, da of Col Henry Brabazon Humfrey (d 1964); 2 s (Mark b 1962, Benedict b 1971), 2 da (Catherine b 1965, Marie b 1966); *Career* 2 Lt RA 1943, served India, Malaya 1945-48, BMRA 1 Div Egypt 1955, staff HQ ME, Cyprus 1956-58, instr Staff Coll Camberley and Canada 1962-65, OC 3 Regt RHA 1966-68, Cdr RA 2 Div 1969-70, RCDS 1971, COS 1 Br Corps 1972-74, GOC 2 Div 1974-75, VQMG MOD 1976-79; Col Cmdt: RA 1979; RHA 1983; dir of the Brewers' Soc 1979-90; memb: Fndn Ctee Gordon's Sch, Advsy Governing Body Ampleforth Coll; *Recreations* shooting, golf; *Clubs* Army & Navy; *Style—* Maj-Gen Desmond Mangham, CB; Redwood House, Woolton Hill, Nr Newbury, Berks (☎ 0635 253460)

MANGNALL, Richard Anthony; JP (S Westminster 1986); s of Col (Anthony) Derek Swift Mangnall, OBE, TD, of Bradley Court, Chieveley, Berks, and Lady (Cynthia) Mary Fitzgerald, *née* Foster; *b* 27 Nov 1942; *Educ* Douai Abbey Berks; *m* 25 March 1975, Maureen Patricia, da of Lawrence Donnelly (d 1965), of Delhi, India; *Career* Sant & Co Loss Adjusters 1962-74, chm Tyler & Co (Adjusters) Ltd 1989- (ptnr 1974-); elected underwriting memb of Lloyds 1978, pres The Insurance Adjusters Assoc 1987-89 (assoc 1967, fell 1972), memb Lime St Ward Club; Freeman: City of London 1989, Worshipful Co fo Fletchers 1989; FIAA; *Recreations* sailing; *Clubs* Royal London Yacht, Royal Ocean Racing, Royal Southern Yacht; *Style—* Richard Mangnall, Esq, JP; 23 Queens Gate Gardens, London SW7 5LZ; Villa Gardenia, 53 Ave de la Mer, Eze sur Mer, AM France; 152 Commercial St, London E1 6NU (☎ 071 377 0282, fax 071 377 6355, telex 264017, car 0860 242 966)

MANGOLD, Thomas Cornelius (Tom); s of Dr Fritz Mangold (d 1957), and Dorothea Stephanie Mangold (d 1986); *b* 20 Aug 1934; *Educ* Dorking GS; *m* 3 da (Sarah b 1965, Abigail b 1975, Jessica b 1979); *Career* served RA BAOR; Sunday Mirror 1958-62, Daily Express 1962-64; reporter: BBC TV News 1964-70, BBC TV current affrs and several investigative documentaries 1970-76; tv reporter BBC TV Panorama 1976-; *Books* The File on the Tsar (co-author, 1976), The Tunnels of Cu Chi (co-author 1985), Cold Warrier (1991); *Recreations* reading, writing, playing blues harmonica; *Style—* Tom Mangold, Esq; c/o BBC TV, Lime Grove, London W12 7RJ (☎ 081 743 8000)

MANGRIOTIS, Hon Mrs (Anne Margaret); da of Maj Sir Arthur Lindsay Grant, 11 Bt (ka 1944), and Baroness Tweedsmuir of Belhelvie (Life Peeress d 1978); *b* 1937; *Educ* Lady Margaret Hall Oxford; *m* 1965, Nicolas Mangriotis; 2 s; *Style—* The Hon Mrs Mangriotis; 24 Amity Grove, London SW20 OLJ

MANHIRE, Dr Adrian Ross; s of Kenneth Croyden Manhire, of Norwich, and Ida, *née* Fielding; *b* 28 March 1945; *Educ* City of Norwich Sch, King Edward VI Sch Norwich, Univ of London (MB BS, BSc); *m* 13 Nov 1982, Eileen Margaret, da of Walter Le May, DFC, of Bishopton, Renfrewshire; *Career* conslt radiologist City Hosp Nottingham 1984-; MRCP 1976, FRCR 1983, memb MENSA 1981; *Recreations* skiing, squash, badminton, photography; *Style—* Dr Adrian Manhire; 21 Troutbeck Crescent, Bramcote, Nottingham NG9 3BP (☎ 0602 222475); Department of Radiology, City Hospital, Nottingham (☎ 0602 691169)

MANKIEWICZ, Joseph Leo; s of Prof Frank Mankiewicz (d 1941), and Johanna, *née* Blumenau (d 1943); *b* 11 Feb 1909; *Educ* Columbia Univ (BA), Yale; *m* 1, 1939, Rosa Stradner (d 1958); 2 s, (1 s by previous m); *m* 2, 1962, Rosemary Helen Joan, da of Hubert John Matthews, Archdeacon of Hampstead 1950-62 (d 1971); 1 da (Alexandra Kate); *Career* writer, film dir 1929-; pres Screen Dirs Guild (1950); first awards for both direction and screenplay Motion Picture Academy 1949 and 1950, screen dir awards 1949 and 1950, Br Film Academy 1950, NY Critics award 1950; dir La Bohème for Metropolitan Opera 1952; films incl: Philadelphia Story, Woman of the Year, Julius Caesar, Keys of the Kingdom, A Letter to Three Wives, All About Eve, Suddenly Last Summer, Guys and Dolls, Sleuth; *Retrospectives* Cinémathèque Française (1967), Br Film Institute (1960 and 1982); *author* All About Eve (screenplay, 1951), More About All About Eve (colloquy, 1972), Erasmus award City of Rotterdam 1984, D W Griffith award, Dirs Guild of America 1986, Alexander Hamilton medal Columbia Coll NYC 1986, Golden Lion award Venice Film Festival 1987, Retrospective Hommage Cinémathèque Français 1987, Cinématèque Municipale Retrospective City of Luxembourg 1987; Cdr Order of Merit (Italy) 1965; assoc fell Yale Univ; Chev de la Legion d'Honneur (France) 1988; *Recreations* theatrical history, golf, travel; *Clubs* Bedford GC and Tennis (NY); *Style—* Joseph Mankiewicz, Esq; 491 Guard Hill Rd, RFD 1, Bedford, New York 10506, USA

MANKIN, Robert Michael; s of James William Mankin (d 1969), of Coventry, and Margaret Florence, *née* Lewin; *b* 21 Nov 1936; *Educ* The Coventry Sch; *m* 29 Sept 1968, Megan Christine, da of Arthur Samuel Frank Langridge, of Bournemouth; 1 s (James b 1977), 1 da (Elizabeth b 1972); *Career* CA 1959 (RSA silver medal 1956); dir: Bridport Gundry plc 1978-81, Datafit Ltd 1985-, Dillon Technol Ltd 1985-, Microscribe Ltd 1986-, March Med plc 1987-, Curran Gp Ltd 1987-, Cotton Commercial Ltd 1988-, David Lunan Ltd 1986-87, Percell Gp Ltd 1985-87; *Recreations* walking, reading, crosswords, social events; *Style—* Robert Mankin, Esq; Oaklawn, 1 Childs Hall Close, Gt Bookham, Leatherhead, Surrey KT23 3QE (☎ 0372 57838, car ☎ 0836 239 539)

MANLEY, Brian William; s of Gerald William Manley (d 1950), of Eltham, London, and Ellen Mary, *née* Scudder (d 1965); *b* 30 June 1929; *Educ* Shooters Hill GS, Univ of London, Woolwich Poly (BSc), Imperial Coll (DIC); *m* 1 May 1954, Doris Winifred, da of Alfred Dane (d 1966), of Eltham, London; 1 s (Gerald b 1958), 1 da (Susan b 1955); *Career* RAF 1947-49; Mullard Res Laboratories 1954-68, commercial gen mangr Mullard Ltd 1971-75; md: Pye Business Communications Ltd 1975-77, TMC Ltd 1977-82, Philips Data Systems Ltd 1979-82; gp md Philips Business Systems 1980-83, chm and md MEL Def Systems 1983-86, dir for telecommunications def electronics and res Philips Electronic & Assoc Industs Ltd 1983-87; chm: AT&T Network Systems (UK) Ltd 1986-89, Pye Telecommunications Ltd 1984-87, BYOPS Communications Ltd 1989-; managing ptnr Manley Moon Assocs 1988-, pres Telecommunications Engrg & M/rg Assoc 1985-86, dep pres Inst of Electrical Engrs 1989-; memb: cncl Inst of Manpower Studies 1986-, exec ctee Nat Electronics Cncl 1986-88, NEDO ctee Info Technol 1982-85, police scientific devpt ctee Home Office, Cncl Univ of Loughborough 1988-, Cncl Univ of Sussex 1970-, Cncl Engrg Trg Authy 1990-; chm thames Industl Liaison Bd 1990-; represented England in swimming 1947-50; FInstP 1967, FIEE 1974, FEng 1984, FIProdE 1990, FCGI 1990; *Recreations* swimming, walking, gardening; *Style—* Brian Manley, Esq; Hopkins Crank, Ditchling Common, Sussex BN6 8TP (☎ 0444 233734); Manley Moon Associates, St John's Innovation Centre, Carling Rd, Cambridge CB4 4WS (☎ 0223 421033)

MANLEY, Bruce; s of Maj William Arthur Reginald Ivor Manley (d 1973), of Bacton, Hereford, and Gwendoline Deidamia, *née* Trewhella; *b* 1 Oct 1940; *Educ* Downside; *m* 1, 28 Oct 1968 (m dis 1975), Alison Dudley Ward; 2 s (Edward b 1969, Dominic b 1970); *m* 2, 18 Nov 1978, Charlotte Mary Frances, da of Cdr John Harford Stanhope Lucas-Scudamore, DL, RN, of Kentchurch Court, Hereford, and Lady Evelyn Patricia Mary, *née* Scudamore-Stanhope, da of 12 Earl of Chesterfield; 1 s (Harry b 1979); *Career* md Bacton Stud and farms; dir Probiotics Int Ltd; *Recreations* horseracing; *Style—* Bruce Manley, Esq; The Old Rectory, Bacton, Hereford HR2 OAP; Bacton Stud, Bacton, Hereford HR2 OAP (fax 0981 240 840)

MANLEY, Ivor Thomas; CB (1984); s of Frederick Stone and Louisa Manley; *b* 4 March 1931; *Educ* Sutton HS Plymouth; *m* 1952, Joan Waite; 1 s, 1 da; *Career* entered Civil Serv 1951; princ: Miny of Aviation 1964-66, Miny of Technol 1966-68; private sec to: Rt Hon Anthony Wedgwood Benn 1968-70, Rt Hon Geoffrey Rippon

1970; princ private sec to Rt Hon John Davies 1970-71, asst sec Dept of Trade and Industry 1971-74, princ estab offr Dept of Energy 1974-78, under sec Atomic Energy Div 1978-81; dep sec Dept of Energy 1981-87, Dept of Employment 1987-; memb UKAEA 1981-86; *Style*— Ivor Manley, Esq, CB; 28 Highfield Ave, Aldershot, Hants GU11 3BZ (☎ 0252 22707)

MANN, Alexander Rupert; s and h of Sir Rupert Edward Mann, 3 Bt; *b* 6 April 1978; *Style*— Alexander Mann, Esq

MANN, David Francis Chadwick; s of William Frank Mann (d 1969), of London, and Clara Mann (d 1971); *b* 10 June 1924; *Educ* Alleyn's Sch Dulwich, LSE (MSc); *m* 8 May 1947, Daphne, da of Sidney Bonny (d 1958), of Rochester, Kent; 2 s (Michael b 1950, Robert b 1952), 1 da (Margaret b 1950); *Career* Capt RAEC 1943-47, Army Emergency Reserve of Offrs 1947-69; ICI Ltd 1947-64, Milk Mktg Bd 1964-84 (dir of Admin, personnel and admin dir, latterly gp personnel dir); vice pres Inst of Admin Mgmnt 1971- (chm 1969-71), chm of employers Nat Jt Cncl for the Dairy Indust 1977-84, jt UK rep to ILO meeting on food industs 1978, memb Industl Tbnls for England and Wales 1983-; memb: Cncl Exec and Fin Ctees Industl Soc 1967-84 (chm Tstees Pension Fund 1984-), CBI SE Cncl 1980-84, Surrey Area Manpower Bd 1982-85, Merton and Sutton Health Authy 1986-90, Cncl Swedenborg Soc 1971-89 (former pres and chm); FInstAM 1960 (chm 1969-71), FBIM 1977, FIPM 1982; *Books* Effective Adminstration (1967); *Recreations* walking, writing; *Clubs* Athenaeum, Nat Lib; *Style*— David Mann, Esq; Ashdown, Four Acres, Cobham, Surrey KT11 2EB (☎ 0932 862391)

MANN, David William; s of William James Mann (d 1966), of Trimley Saint Mary, Suffolk, and Mary Ann, *née* Bloomfield (d 1987); *b* 14 June 1944; *Educ* Felixstowe County GS, Jesus Coll Cambridge (BA, MA); *m* 29 June 1968, Gillian Mary, da of Rev David Emlyn Edwards (d 1978), of Felixstowe, Suffolk; 2 s (Richard b 1972, Edward b 1975); *Career* computing systems conslt; CEIR (UK) Ltd (now SD-Scicon plc) 1966-69, joined Logica plc on its formation 1969 (mangr conslt 1971, mangr Advanced Systems Div 1972, dir Advanced Systems Gp 1976), md Logica Ltd 1979 (chm 1982), dep md and head of ops Logica plc 1986 (md 1987); memb Cncl Br Computer Soc, memb Co of Info Technologists; CEng; *Recreations* gardening, walking, skiing, golf; *Style*— David Mann, Esq; Theydon Copt, Forest Side, Epping, Essex CM16 4ED; 64 Newman Street, London W1A 4SE (☎ 071 637 9111, fax : 071 637 0719)

MANN, Dr Felix Bernard; s of Leo William Mann (d 1956), and Caroline Lola Mann (d 1985); *b* 10 April 1931; *Educ* Shrewsbury, Malvern, Christ's Coll Cambridge, Westminster Hosp; *m* 1986, Ruth Csorba von Borsai; *Career* doctor; fndr Med Acupuncture Soc (pres 1959-80); *Books* Acupuncture; the Ancient Chinese Art of Healing (2 edn, 1971), The Meridians of Acupuncture (1964), Atlas of Acupuncture (1966), Acupuncture; cure of many diseases (1971), Scientific Aspects of Acupuncture (1977), Textbook of Acupuncture (1987); *Recreations* walking in the countryside; *Clubs* RSM; *Style*— Dr Felix Mann; 15 Devonshire Place, London W1N 1PB (☎ 071 935 7575)

MANN, Dr (Frederick) Francis Alexander; CBE 1980; s of Richard Mann and Ida *née* Oppenheim; *b* 11 Aug 1907; *Educ* Univs of: Geneva, Munich, Berlin (Dr Jur), London (LLD); *m* 1933, Eleonore *née* Ehrlich (d 1980); 1 s 2 da; *Career* asst Berlin Faculty of Law 1929-33, int law conslt London 1933-46, admitted slr 1946; conslt Herbert Smith & Co 1984- (ptnr 1957 - 83); memb: Legal Div Allied Control Cncl Berlin 1946, Lord Chllrs Standing Ctee on Place of Payment Cncl of Europe 1968-71; lectr: Acad of Int Law at the Hague (1959, 1964, 1971 and 1984), Univs in England, Austria, Belgium, Germany, Switzerland, Japan, and USA; hon prof: Univ of Birmingham 1985-87, Univ of Bonn 1960-; fell Br Acad 1974, hon Dr Jur: Kiel 1978, Zürich 1983; hon DCL Oxford 1989, Alexander von Humboldt prize 1984; Grand Cross of Merit W Germany 1977 (with Star 1982); *Books* The Legal Aspect of Money (1938, 1953, 1971, 1982), Studies in International Law (1973), Foreign Affairs in English Courts (1986), Further Studies in International Law (1990), numerous articles on int law and monetary law in Eng and foreign jls; *Recreations* music, walking; *Clubs* Athenaeum; *Style*— Dr Francis Mann, CBE; Flat 4, 56 Manchester St, London W1 M5PA (☎ 071 487 4735)

MANN, Geoffrey Horton; s of Stanley Victor Mann (d 1986), of Coventry, and Dorothy, *née* Horton (d 1964); *b* 12 May 1938; *Educ* Warwick Sch, Univ of Liverpool (BArch), RIBA (MCD); *m* 28 Dec 1963, Meg, da of Francis Richard Evans, of Denton, Manchester; 4 da (Katherine b 1964, Clare b 1966, Rachel b 1968, Shelley b 1972); *Career* architect; W S Hattrell & Ptnrs Manchester 1963-70, equity ptnr Renton Howard Wood Levin Ptnrship 1980- (joined 1970); responsible for commercial bldgs incl Beaufort House and St Katharine's Dock; memb: Friends of the Earth, Coventry City FC, leukaemia res charities, Bodmin & Wenford Railway; memb: ARCUK 1965; ARIBA 1965; *Recreations* Coventry City FC, railways; *Clubs* Coventry City; *Style*— Geoffrey Mann, Esq; 41 Charles St, Berkhamsted, Herts (☎ 0442 864 707), 13 Shelton St, London WC2; Saughtree Railway Station, Roxburghshire; Renton Howard Wood Levin Partnership, 77 Endell St, London WC2 (☎ 071 379 7900, fax 071 836 4881, telex 896691 TLXIR G Renhow, car 0831 327663

MANN, (Francis) George; CBE (1983), DSO (1942), MC (1941); s of Capt Francis Thomas Mann (d 1964; 3 s of Sir Edward Mann, 1 Bt who was chm of Mann Crossman & Paulin, and of Brandon's Putney Brewers), and Enid Agnes, *née* Tilney; *b* 6 Sept 1917; *Educ* Eton, Pembroke Coll Cambridge (BA); *m* 1949, Margaret Hildegarde, *née* Marshall Clark; 3 s (Simon, Richard, Edward), 1 da (Sarah); *Career* served WWII Scots Gds (wounded); dir: Mann Crossman and Paulin, Watney Mann, Watney Mann and Truman Brewers 1946-77; non-exec dep chm Extel Group 1980-87 (dir 1977-87); Middx CCC: first played 1937, capt 1948-49, pres 1983-91; captained England: SA 1948-49 NZ 1949; chm: Test and County Cricket Bd 1978-83, Cricket Cncl 1983; *Clubs* MCC (pres 1984-85); *Style*— George Mann, Esq, CBE, DSO, MC; Great Farm House, West Woodhay, Newbury, Berks RG15 0BL (☎ 04884 243)

MANN, Cdr Graham Hargrave; s of Cdr Edgar H Mann (d 1969), and Wenonah Mann; *b* 26 June 1924; *Educ* RNC Dartmouth; *m* 1959, Carol Mary, da of Victor Leslie Seyd; 3 da; *Career* joined RN 1941; served: Atlantic, Arctic, Med, Korea; Capt HMS Crossbow 1960-62, ret Cdr 1962; head Private Client Dept and ptnr Grieveson Grant & Co stockbrokers 1967-1986, conslt Binder Hamlyn Chartered Accountants; *Recreations* yachting (helmsman 1958 Americas Cup Challenger 'Sceptre'; Olympic Yachting Teams: 1956, 1960, 1964), book collecting; *Clubs* Royal Yacht Sqdn, Royal Lymington Yacht, Royal Sailing Assoc; FRGS 1990; *Style*— Cdr Graham Mann, RN; 30, Stanley Rd, Lymington, Hampshire SO41 9SG (☎ 0590 74271); 138 Rivermead Court, London SW6 3SA (☎ 071 736 2263)

MANN, Jessica D E; da of Dr F A Mann, CBE, of London, and Eleonore, *née* Ehrlich (d 1980); *b* 13 Sept 1937; *Educ* St Paul's, Newnham Coll Cambridge (MA), Univ of Leicester (LLB); *m* 1 July 1959, Prof A Charles Thomas, CBE, s of D W Thomas (d 1959), of Cornwall; 2 s (Richard b 1961, Martin b 1963), 2 da (Susanna b 1966, Lavinia b 1971); *Career* writer and journalist; memb: Carrick DC 1972-78, Cornwall AHA 1976-78, Industl Tbnls 1977-, SW RHA 1979-84, Med Practices Ctee 1982-87, Cornwall FPC 1985-88; *Books* A Charitable End (1971), Mrs Knox's Profession (1972), The Only Security (1973), The Sticking Place (1974), Captive Audience (1975), The Eighth Deadly Sin (1976), The Sting of Death (1978), Deadlier than the Male (1981), Funeral Sites (1982), No Man's Island (1983), Grave Goods (1985), A Kind of Healthy Grave (1986), Death Beyond The Nile (1988), Faith Hope and Homicide (1991); *Style*— Ms Jessica Mann; Lambessow, St Clement, Cornwall TR1 1TB (☎ 0872 72980)

MANN, John Frederick; s of Frederick Mann (d 1972), and Hilda Grace *née* Johnson; *b* 4 June 1930; *Educ* Poole and Tavistock GS, Univ of Oxford (MA), Univ of Birmingham; *m* 30 July 1966, Margaret, da of Herbert Frederick Moore, of Bridlington, Yorks; 1 s (David John b 6 Dec 1971), 1 da (Susan Margaret b 6 March 1970); *Career* Nat Serv RAF 1949-50; asst educn offr Essex CC 1965-67, dep educn offr Sheffield City Cncl 1967-78, sec Schools Cncl for Curriculum and Examination 1978-83, dir of educn London Borough of Harrow 1983-88, educn conslt London Boroughs of Harrow and Camden 1988-; JP Sheffield Bench; memb: Nat Tst, Br Educn Mgmnt and Admin Soc; hon fell: Sheffield City Poly 1979, Coll of Preceptors 1986; FBIM, FRSA; *Books* Education (1979), Chapters in Education Administration (1988), Life & Death of Schools Council (1985); *Recreations* local history, theatre, writing; *Style*— John Mann, Esq; 109 Chatsworth Rd, London NW2 4BH (☎ 081 459 5419)

MANN, Joseph Anthony; s of Joseph Mann (d 1988), and Olive May, *née* Burrows; *b* 14 Aug 1949; *Educ* Allan Wilson Tech HS Harare Zimbabwe; *m* 10 Jan 1987, Adrienne Joy, da of late Geoffrey Tufnail; 1 s (Benjamin Joseph b 19 Nov 1988); *Career* Nat Serv Rhodesian Army 1968; photographic technician Univ of Rhodesia 1969-70, photographer Rhodesia Herald 1970-72, sports photographer Sporting Pictures (UK) Ltd 1973-86, freelance sports photographer for various nat dailies 1986-87, staff sports photographer Daily Telegraph 1987-; maj assignments incl: The World Cup 1982 1986 and 1990, Olympics 1984 and 1988, most maj British sporting events 1973-; winner The Whitbread/Rugby World Best Rugby Picture of the Year 1988; *Recreations* spending time with family, reading, music, sport; *Style*— Joseph Mann, Esq; The Daily Telegraph, 181 Marsh Wall, London E14 9SR (☎ 071 538 7385)

MANN, Rt Hon Lord Justice; Sir Michael; QC (1972); s of Adrian Mann, CBE; *b* 9 Dec 1930; *Educ* Whitgift, King's Coll London (LLB, PhD); *m* 1, 1957, Jean, *née* Bennett; 2 s; m 2, 22 Dec 1989, Audrey, *née* Umpleby, widow of Lt Cdr H Umpleby, RN; *Career* called to the Bar Gray's Inn 1953; bencher 1980, pt/t legal asst FO 1954-56; law lectr LSE 1957-64 (asst lectr 1954-57), jr counsel Land Cmmn 1967-71, Crown Ct recorder 1979-82, high ct judge 1982-88, Lord Justice of Appeal 1988-; inspr Vale of Belvoir Coal Inquiry 1979-80; fell Kings Coll 1984; kt 1982; *Books* (ed jtly) Dicey, Dicey & Morris, Conflict of Laws (7 edn 1957, 8 edn 1967 to 10 edn 1980); *Clubs* Athenaeum; *Style*— The Rt Hon Lord Justice Mann; Royal Courts of Justice, London WC2A 2LL

MANN, Rt Rev Michael Ashley; KCVO (1989); s of late Herbert George Mann, and Florence Mary *née* Kelsey, MBE (d 1950); *b* 25 May 1924; *Educ* Harrow, RMC Sandhurst, Wells Theol Coll, Harvard Business Sch (AMP); *m* 25 June 1949, Jill Joan (d 1990), da of Maj Alfred Jacques (d 1960), of Thanet; 1 s (Capt Philip Ashley Mann, 1 Queen's Dragoon Gds, b 1 Aug 1950 ka 1975), 1 da (Dr Elizabeth Mann b 22 Aug 1950); *Career* 1 King's Dragoon Gds, served Italy 1943-44, Greece 1944-45, ME 1945, Palestine 1945-46, Capt 1945, Maj 1945; Colonial Admin Serv Nigeria 1946-55; ordained 1957, curate Newton Abbot 1957-59; vicar: Sparkwell 1959-62, Christ Church Port Harcourt 1962-67; dean Port Harcourt Social and Industl Project 1963-67, home sec Missions to Seamen 1967-69, canon Norwich Cathedral 1969-73 (vice-dean 1971-73), Bishop of Dudley 1973-76; Dean of Windsor, Domestic Chaplain to HM The Queen, Register of the Order of the Garter 1976-89; Prelate of the Ven Order of St John of Jerusalem 1990-; dep chm Tstees: Imperial War Museum, Army Museums Ogilby Tst; cmmr Royal Hosp Chelsea 1983-90, chm Friends Nat Army Museum, govr Harrow Sch (chm 1980-88); CBIM; KStJ; *Books* A Particular Duty, A Windsor Correspondence, And They Rode On, China 1860, Some Windsor Sermons, Survival or Extinction; *Recreations* military history; *Clubs* Cavalry and Guards; *Style*— The Rt Rev Michael Mann, KCVO; Lower End Farm Cottage, Eastington, Northleach GL54 3PN (☎ 0451 60 767)

MANN, Patricia (Mrs Pierre Walker); *née* Mann; da of Charles Alfred Mann (d 1986), of Westcliff-on-Sea, Essex, and Marjorie Lilian, *née* Heath; *b* 26 Sept 1937; *Educ* Clifton HS for Girls, Bristol; *m* 23 June 1962, Pierre George Armand Walker, s of Lt Thomas George Walker (d 1969), of Paris and London; 1 da (Lucy b 26 June 1965); *Career* ed Consumer Affrs 1974-, vice pres International J Walter Thompson Co Ltd 1981- (joined 1959), head of external affrs J Walter Thompson Gp (UK) 1981-; dir: Woolwich Building Society 1983-, UK Centre Econ and Environmental Devpt 1984-, Valor plc 1985- (now Yale & Valor plc); govr CAM Educnl Fndn 1971-77; memb: Cncl Advertising Standards Authy 1973-86, Cncl Nat Advertising Benevolent Soc 1973-77, Awards Nomination Panel Royal TV Soc 1974-78, Cncl Brunel Univ 1976-86 (memb Ct 1976-); govr Admin Staff Coll Henley 1976-; MMC 1984-; memb: Food Advsy Ctee 1986-, Gas Consumers Cncl 1986- (Nat Gas Consumer Cncl 1981-86), Kingman Ctee Enquiry Teaching of English 1987, EEC Commerce and Distribution Ctee 1989-; FIPA 1966, FCAM 1979, CBIM 1986, FRSA 1989; *Recreations* word games; *Clubs* Reform, Women's Advertising London; *Style*— Miss Patricia Mann; J Walter Thompson Co Ltd, 40 Berkeley Square, London W1X 6AD (☎ 071 449 4040, fax 071 493 8432 and 071 493 8418, telex 22871 JWT LDN 6)

MANN, (Thomas) Richard Edward; s of Thomas Conrad Mann, and Eileen Olive Mary, *née* Barrett (d 1979); *b* 6 May 1936; *Educ* Malvern Coll, Universite de Grenoble; *m* 28 April 1962, Josephine, da of Joseph Rex Pearson; 2 s (James b 1963, Andrew b 1964); *Career* brewery dir: Tamplins 1963-69, Mann Crossman and Paulin 1965-69, Watney Combe Reid 1968-69; dir: Watney Mann (London and Home Cos) Ltd 1969-77, Watneys (London) Ltd 1969-78; md: Watneys Southern Ltd 1969-81, Grand Metropolitan Community Servs Tst 1981-; *Recreations* skiing, golf, gardening, game shooting; *Clubs* Ski Club of GB, Seaford GC; *Style*— Richard Mann, Esq; Litlington Place, Litlington, Nr Polegate, E Sussex (☎ 0323 870330); Grand Metropolitan Community Servs Ltd, 64-65 North Rd, Brighton (☎ 0273 570170)

MANN, Dr Robert John; s of Robert William Mann, of Pewsey, Wiltshire, and Margaret, *née* Longley; *b* 2 Oct 1949; *Educ* The Perse Sch Cambridge, Corpus Christi Coll Cambridge, Guys Hosp (MA, MB BChir); *m* 2 Aug 1975, Patricia Margaret, da of Lionel Francis William Bowen, of Titchfield Hampshire; 1 s (William b 1978), 1 da (Naomi b 1980); *Career* registrar dermatology Queens Med Centre Nottingham 1978-80, sr registrar dermatology Bristol Royal Infirmary 1980-82, conslt dermatologist Swindon Health Dist 1982-; MRCP, memb Br Assoc of Dermatologists 1987; *Recreations* music; *Style*— Dr Robert Mann; 10 West Manton, Marlborough, Wiltshire SN8 4HN (☎ 0672 512840); Princess Margaret Hospital, Okus Rd, Swindon, Wiltshire SN1 4JU (☎ 079353 6231)

MANN, Sir Rupert Edward; 3 Bt (UK 1905), of Thelveton Hall, Thelveton, Norfolk; s of Edward Charles Mann, DSO, MC (d 1959), and great nephew of Sir John Mann, 2 Bt (d 1971); *b* 11 Nov 1946; *Educ* Malvern; *m* 1974, Mary Rose, da of Geoffrey Butler, of Cheveley Cottage, Stetchworth, Newmarket, Suffolk; 2 s (Alexander, William); *Heir* s, Alexander Rupert Mann; *Career* farmer; *Clubs* Norfolk, MCC; *Style*— Sir Rupert Mann, Bt; Billingford Hall, Diss, Norfolk (☎ 0379 740314)

MANN, Dr William Neville; s of William Frank Mann (d 1969), and Clara, *née*

Chadwick (d 1971); *b* 4 April 1911; *Educ* Alleyn's Sch, Guys Hosp Med Sch Univ of London (MB BS, MD, MRCP); *m* 1 March 1957, Pamela Mary Everson, da of Howard Everson Chasteney (d 1947); 2 s (Charles, Stephen), 4 da (Alexandra, Georgina, Lucy, Susan); *Career* temp Lt-Col RAMC, served Middle East, Indian Ocean 1940-45; hon visiting physician John Hopkins Hosp Baltimore USA 1947; physician to: HM Household 1954-64, HM The Queen 1964-70, King Edward VII Hosp for Offrs 1965-76; consulting physician emeritus Guys Hosp 1976 (house physician demonstrator of pathology and med registrar 1935-39, physician 1946-76); hon fell Med Artists Assoc; Hon Dr H L John Hopkins Univ Baltimore 1986; FRCP 1947 (sr censor and vice pres 1969-70); *Books* The Medical Works of Hippocrates (jtly, 1950), Clinical Examination of Patients (jtly, 1950), Conybeare's Textbook of Medicine 16 edn (ed, 1975); *Clubs* Garrick; *Style*— Dr William Mann; 90 Alleyn Rd, London SE21 8AH

MANNERS, Crispin Luke; s of Norman Donald Manners, of 3 Hatch End, Windmill Field, Windlesham, Surrey GU20 6QB and Noeline Mary, *née* Blake; *b* 2 Aug 1957; *Educ* Ranelagh GS Bracknell Berkshire, Bedford Coll London (BSc); *m* 18 Aug 1979, Judith Ann, da of Peter Simpson; 2 s (Matthew b 1 July 1981, Philip b 12 May 1985); *Career* salesman CPC UK Limited 1978-80; The Argyll Consultancies: exec asst to Chm 1980, account dir 1984, md 1987, chief exec 1989-; MIPR, MInstD; *Recreations* golf, football, coaching cub scouts, rugby; *Style*— Crispin Manners, Esq; The Argyll Consultancies, Manhattan House, 140 High Street, Crowthorne, Berkshire RG11 7AU (☎ 0344 779000, fax 0344 779555)

MANNERS, Prof Gerald; s of George William Wilson Manners (d 1964), and Louisa Hannah, *née* Plumpton (d 1979); *b* 7 Aug 1932; *Educ* Wallington Co GS, St Catharine's Coll Cambridge (MA); *m* 1, 11 July 1958 (m dis 1982), Anne, *née* Sawyer; 1 s (Christopher Winslow b 24 Oct 1962), 2 da (Carolyn Jarvis b 16 Jan 1961, Katharine b 26 April 1967); m 2, 11 Dec 1982, Joy Edith Roberta, *née* Turner; 1 s (Nicholas Robert b 12 May 1985); *Career* Nat Serv Flying Offr RAF 1955-57; Univ Coll Swansea: lectr in geography 1957-67; UCL: reader in geography 1967-80, prof of geography 1980-; visiting scholar Resources for the Future INC Washington DC 1964-65, visiting fell Harvard-MIT Jt Center for Urban Studies 1972-73, Location of Offices Bureau 1970-80, SE Econ Planning Cncl 1971-79; specialist advsr to House of Commons Select Ctee on Energy 1980-; chm: Govrs Sadler's Wells Fndn 1986- (govr 1978-), Estate Ctee City Parochial Fndn 1987- (memb Central Governing Body 1977); FRGS, MIBG, FRSA, FBIEE; *Books* Geography of Energy (1964), South Wales in the Sixties (1964), Changing World Market for Iron Ore (1971), Spatial Policy Problems of the British Economy (1971), Minerals and Man (1974), Regional Development in Britain (1974), Coal in Britain (1981), Office Policy in Britain (1986); *Recreations* music, dance, theatre, walking; *Style*— Prof Gerald Manners; 105 Barnsbury St, London N1 1EP (☎ 071 607 7920); University College London, Gower St, London WC1E 6BT (☎ 071 387 7050)

MANNERS, Lord John; s of 9 Duke of Rutland (d 1940); *b* 1922; *Educ* Eton, New Coll Oxford; *m* 1957, Mary Diana, da of Lt-Col L Geoffrey Moore, DSO (decd); 1 s, 2 da; *Career* 2 Lt Life Gds 1941; High Sheriff Leics 1973-74; *Clubs* Pratt's, White's; *Style*— The Lord John Manners; Haddon Hall, Derbyshire (☎ 062 981 2014); Reservoir Cottage, Knipton, Grantham, Lincs (☎ 0476 870225)

MANNERS, Hon John Hugh Robert (Willie); s and h of 5 Baron Manners, *qv*; *b* 5 May 1956; *Educ* Eton; *m* 8 Oct 1983, Lanya Mary Patrica (Lala), da of late Dr H E Heitz, and Mrs Ian Jackson, and step da of Ian Jackson; 1 da (Harriet Frances Mary b 29 July 1988); *Career* admitted slr 1980; ptnr Macfarlanes 1986-; *Recreations* riding, shooting; *Clubs* Pratt's; *Style*— The Hon Willie Manners; 14 North Ripley, Avon, nr Christchurch, Dorset (☎ 0425 72249); 10 Norwich Street, London EC4A 1BD (☎ 071 831 9222, fax 071 831 9607)

MANNERS, 5 Baron (UK 1807); John Robert Cecil Manners; s of 4 Baron Manners, MC, JP, DL (d 1972, himself ggs of 1 Baron, who was in his turn 5 s of Lord George Manners-Sutton, 3 s of 3 Duke of Rutland, KG), by his w Mary, twin da of Rt Rev Lord William Gascoyne-Cecil, DD, 65 Bishop of Exeter and 2 s of 3 Marquess of Salisbury, the Cons PM; *b* 13 Feb 1923; *Educ* Eton, Trinity Oxford; *m* 1949, Jennifer Selena, da of Stephen Fairbairn (whose w Cynthia was gggda of Sir William Arbuthnot, 1 Bt); 1 s, 2 da; *Heir* s, Hon John Hugh Robert Manners; *Career* joined RAFVR, Flying offr 1942, Fl Lt 1944; slr to Supreme Ct 1949; Official Verderer of the New Forest 1983-; *Clubs* Brooks's; *Style*— The Rt Hon The Lord Manners; Sabines Avon, Christchurch, Dorset BH23 7BQ (☎ 0425 72317)

MANNERS, Baroness; Mary Edith; da (twin) of the Rt Rev Lord William R Gascoyne Cecil, Bishop of Exeter (d 1936); *b* 1900; *m* 1921, 4 Baron Manners, MC (d 1972); 3 s, 1 da; *Style*— The Rt Hon Mary, Lady Manners; 1 Cranwell Close, Bransgore, Christchurch, Hants BH23 8HY

MANNERS, Hon Richard Neville; 2 s of 4 Baron Manners (d 1972); *b* 1924; *Educ* Eton; *m* 1945, Juliet Mary, da of Col Sir Edward Hulton Preston, 5 Bt, DSO, MC (decd); 3s, 1 da; *Style*— The Hon Richard Manners; Cromer Hall, Norfolk

MANNERS, (Arthur Edward) Robin; s of Arthur Geoffrey Manners, and Betty Ursula Joan, *née* Rutter (d 1972); *b* 10 March 1938; *Educ* Winchester, Trinity Hall Cambridge; *m* 22 Oct 1966, Judith Mary, da of Lt-Col Francis William Johnston, MBE, of The Old Steading, Berkhamsted, Hertfordshire; 2 s (George b 1968, Richard b 1970); *Career* 2 Lt 10 Royal Hussars 1956-58, Maj Staffordshire Yeo 1958-68; Bass plc: joined 1961, dir 1983; md Bass Brewers 1989; *Recreations* golf, tennis, shooting, gardening, skiing; *Clubs* Cavalry and Guards'; *Style*— Robin Manners, Esq; The Old Croft, Bradley, Stafford ST18 9EF

MANNERS, Lord Roger David; s of 9 Duke of Rutland (d 1940), and Kathleen, *née* Tennant (d 1989); *b* 1925; *m* 1965, Finola St Lawrence, only da of T E Daubeney; 2 da; *Career* 2 Lt Grenadier Gds 1944; *Clubs* Pratt's, White's; *Style*— The Lord Roger Manners; Marsh End Farm, Heddington, Calne, Wiltshire

MANNERS, Hon Thomas Jasper; s of 4 Baron Manners, MC (d 1972); *b* 1929; *Educ* Eton; *m* 1955, Sarah, er da of Brig Roger Peake, DSO, OBE (d 1959), of Little Missenden, Bucks; 3 s; *Career* dir: Scapa Group, Lazard Bros, Legal & General Group, Mercantile Credit, Davy Corporation, Govett Oriental Investment Trust; *Recreations* shooting, fishing; *Clubs* White's, Pratt's; *Style*— The Hon Thomas Jasper Manners; The Old Malt House, Ashford Hill, Newbury, Berks; 9 Cadogan Sq SW1

MANNING, (Everard Alexander) Dermot Niall; s of Col Frederick Everard Beresford Manning, Indian Med Serv (d 1987), and Elizabeth Robina, *née* Webber; *b* 20 Feb 1949; *Educ* Rossall Sch Lancs, The Middx Hosp Med Sch London (MB BS); *m* 1 Aug 1981, Ann Ming Choo, da of Pak Shoon Wong, of Kuala Lumpur, Malaysia; 1 s (Edward b 1985), 1 da (Catherine b 1988); *Career* registrar in obstetrics and gynaecology St Helier Hosp Surrey 1981-83, The Middx Hosp London 1983-85; sr registrar obstetrics and gynaecology The Middx Hosp and Central Middx Hosp London 1985-87, conslt and clinical dir obstetrics and gynaecology Parkside Health Authy and hon clinical sr lectr St Mary's Hosp Med Sch 1987-; dist tutor Parkside Health Authy and RCOG, NW Thames RHA Advsy Ctee Obstetrics and Gynaecology, Br Soc for Colposcopy and Cervical Pathology FBI; MRCOG 1982, forum memb RSM 1985; *Recreations* photography, gemmology and jewellery, antique furniture; *Clubs* Wine Soc; *Style*— Dermot Manning, Esq; Central Middlesex Hospital, Action Lane, Park Royal, London NW10 7NS (☎ 081 9655733 ext 2410, 081 453 2410)

MANNING, Prof Geoffrey; CBE (1986); s of Ruby Frances, *née* Lambe; *b* 31 Aug 1929; *Educ* Tottenham GS, RCS Imperial Coll London (BSc, Phd, ARCS, DIC); *m* 9 Sept 1951, Anita Jacquline; 2 s (Howard b 3 March 1953, Ian b 25 March 1956), 1 da (Karen b 20 Dec 1959); *Career* Nat Serv Sgt Educn Corps RAF 1948-49; asst lectr in physics Royal Coll of Science 1953-55; res physicist: English Electric Company 1955-56, Canadian Atomic Energy Agency 1956-58, California Inst of Technol 1958-59; princ scientific offr AERE 1959-66; Rutherford Laboratory: sr princ scientific offr 1966-69, dep dir 1969-79, head High Energy Physics Div 1969-75 (dep head 1968-69), head Atlas Computing Div 1975-79; project leader Construction of the Spallation Neutron Source 1977-81, dir Rutherford in Rutherford Appleton Laboratories 1979-81, computing co-ordinator SERC 1980-84, dir Rutherford Appleton Laboratory 1981-86, chm Active Memory Technology 1986-; memb: Ordnance Survey Sci and Technol Advsy Ctee 1986-89, Bd of Visitors Physics Dept Imperial Coll London 1987-, Civil Service Individual Merit Promotion Panel 1988-89, Systems Architecture Ctee DTI/SERC (chm Parallel & Novel Architecture Sub Ctee) 1988-; visiting prof Dept of Physics & Astronomy UCL 1987; author of over 40 articles in scientific jls; FInstP 1985, MBCS 1989; *Recreations* squash, skiing, golf; Active Memory Technology Ltd, 65 Suttons Park Ave, Reading RG6 1AZ (☎ 0734 661111, fax 0734 351 395, car 0860 366 862)

MANNING, Dr Geoffrey Lewis; s of Issac Harold Manning (d 1960), and Florence Hilda, *née* Tomlin (d 1983); *b* 21 Sept 1931; *Educ* Rossall Sch Fleetwood Lancs, Univ of Birmingham (BDS, MB ChB); *m* 15 Sept 1978, Patricia Margaret (Maggie), da of Frederick Wilson (d 1986), of Trentham; 1 da (Kate Elizabeth b 27 Aug 1980); *Career* Nat Serv, Capt RADC Wuppertal BAOR Germany 1954-56; house offr N Staffs Royal Infirmary 1961-63; sr registrar in oral surgery 1964-68: Central Middx Hosp, Mount Vernon Hosp Northwood Middx; exchange res Parkland Memorial Hosp Dallas 1967, conslt oral surgn N Staffs Hosp 1968-; dir Stoke City FC 1984- (MO 1987-), chm Med Advsy Ctee 1985-, memb N Staffs DHA 1985-; fell: Br Assoc of Oral and Maxillo-facial Surgns, Oral Surgery Club of GB (pres 1986); FDSRCS(Eng) 1964, FRCS(Ed) 1986; *Recreations* squash, gardening; *Clubs* Trentham Golf Staffordshire, British Pottery Manufacturers Fedn; *Style*— Dr Geoffrey Manning; Grove House, King St, Newcastle, Staffs (☎ 0782 614174)

MANNING, Graham Ralph; s of James William Manning (d 1974), of Chelmsford, Essex, and Daisy Maud, *née* Warren; *b* 4 June 1943; *Educ* Chelmsford Tech HS; *m* 29 Sept 1966, Barbara, da of Cyril Alfred Burrough (d 1979), of Bradford; 2 s (James 1973, John 1978), 1 da (Joanne 1971); *Career* trainee CA Longcrofts 1960-66, qualified CA 1966, supervisor Deloitte Haskins & Sells Montreal 1966-69, ptnr Buzzacott & Co 1970-79 (mangr 1969-70); ptnr: McNally Manning & Co Ipswich 1979-83, Manning Hilder & Girling Ipswich 1983-; memb ICEAW; *Recreations* sailing, books, paintings; *Style*— Graham Manning, Esq; 16a Falcon St, Ipswich IP1 1SL (☎ 0473 2599 84, fax 0473 2599 88)

MANNING, Dr Jane Marian; OBE (1990); da of Gerald Manville Manning (d 1987), of Norwich, and Lily, *née* Thompson (d 1989); *b* 20 Sept 1938; *Educ* Norwich HS, Royal Acad of Music (GRSM, LRAM, ARCM), Scuola Di Canto Cureglia Switzerland; *m* 24 Sept 1966, Anthony Edward Payne, s of Edward Alexander Payne (d 1958), of London; *Career* int career as soprano concert singer; London debut 1964, more than 250 world premieres, regular appearances in leading halls and festivals, Brussels Opera 1980, Scottish Opera 1978, numerous tours of Aust, NY debut 1981, first BBC broadcast 1965 (over 300 since), numerous recordings incl Messiaen Song Cycles; visiting prof Mills Coll Oakland California: 1981, 1983, 1986; visiting lectr: Harvard Univ, Stanford Univ, Princeton Univ, Yale Univ, Univ of York, Univ of Cambridge, Univ of Durham; vice pres Soc for the Promotion of New Music, chm Nettlefold Festival Tst, fndr and artistic dir Jane's Minstrels ensemble 1988, memb Ctee Musicians Benevolent Fund; received special award composers Guild of GB 1973; Hon DUniv York 1988; memb ISM, SPNM, FRAM 1984; *Books* New Vocal Repertory (1986); *Recreations* cinema, ornithology, reading; *Style*— Dr Jane Manning, OBE; 2 Wilton Square, London N1 3DL (☎ 071 359 1593); 7 Park Terrace, Upperton Rd, Tillington, nr Petworth, W Sussex

MANNING, Patrick John Mannes (Paddy); s of Col Francis James Manning, TD, of Heathstock Cleeve, Wiveliscombe, Somerset, and Sarah Margaret, *née* Jenkins; *b* 16 July 1940; *Educ* Downside, RMA Sandhurst; *m* 19 April 1986, Sally Gail, da of Maj Jeremy Green, of Bickmarsh Hall, Bideford on Avon, Warwicks; 1 s (Francis James Daniel b 5 March 1990), 1 da (Charlotte b 1987); *Career* Lt 4/7 Royal Dragoon Gds 1961-64, Royal Yeo 1965-72; stockbroker Laurence Keen & Gardner 1965-70; dir: Charles Barker City Ltd 1970-80, of PR McCann Erickson 1981-84, St James PR Ltd 1984-; hon PR advsr The Br Cwlth Ex-Servs League; MIPR 1974; *Recreations* shooting, opera; *Clubs* Cavalry and Guards; *Style*— Paddy Manning, Esq; Inglewood, Lower Wardington, Banbury, Oxfordshire; 49 Breer St, London, SW6 3HE; St James Public Relations, 63 St Martins Lane, London, WC2N 4JS (☎ 071 379 5646, fax 071 379 5951)

MANNING-COX, Andrew Richard; s of Frederick Cox, of Kinver, Staffs, and Beatrice Maud, *née* Brown; *b* 23 April 1956; *Educ* Peter Symonds' Sch Winchester, Univ of Cambridge (MA); *m* 31 Oct 1987, Janet Elaine, da of Eric Binns, of Bramhall, Cheshire; *Career* admitted slr 1980; ptnr Wragge & Co 1985; sec Birmingham Branch Cambridge Soc; memb Law Soc 1980; *Recreations* riding, walking, country pursuits; *Style*— Andrew Manning-Cox, Esq; Wragge & Co, Bank House, 8 Cherry St, Birmingham B2 5JY (☎ 021 632 4131, fax 021 643 2417, telex 338728 WRAGGE G, car 0831 297086)

MANNINGHAM-BULLER, Hon James Edward; er s and h of 2 Viscount Dilhorne; *b* 20 Aug 1956; *Educ* Harrow, Sandhurst; *m* 4 May 1985, Nicola Marion, eldest da of Sven Mackie (d 1986); 1 s (Edward John b 25 Jan 1990); *Career* Capt Welsh Gds 1976-84; Lloyd's Broker: Stewart Wrightson Surety and Specie Ltd 1984-86, Gibbs Hartley Cooper Ltd 1986-89; insur conslt Heritage Insurance Services; *Recreations* shooting, skiing; *Clubs* Pratt's; *Style*— The Hon James Manningham-Buller; Ballymote House, Downpatrick, Co Down

MANNINGHAM-BULLER, Hon Mervyn Reginald; s of 2 Viscount Dilhorne (d 1989); *b* 1962; *m* 7 Oct 1989, Lucy, da of George Thurstan; *Style*— The Hon Mervyn Manningham-Buller; 126 Hurlingham Rd, London SW6 3NF

MANNINGS, William Anthony; s of William Edward Mannings (d 1965), of Claverton Down, Bath, and Helena Mary, *née* Stoffels (d 1961); *b* 2 Sept 1930; *Educ* King Edward Sch Bath; *m* 1 June 1957, June, da of Albert Edward Hill (d 1955), of Bath; *Career* Nat Serv Fleet Air Arm RN 1948-50; chm G Mannings and Sons Ltd 1965-, ptnr JW Knight and Son 1965-, dir Fred Daw Garden Centre Trowbridge 1980- (Bath 1975), chm Lloyd Blackmore Ltd 1984-; chm Bath Investment and Building Society 1984-; govr King Edwards Sch Bath 1983-, pres Bath Golf Club 1988-90 (capt 1962); FFB; *Recreations* golf; *Clubs* Bath Golf; *Style*— William Mannings, Esq; Byfield, Winsley, Bradford on Avon, Wilts BA15 2HW (☎ 0225 722220); Oxford House, Combe Down, Bath, Avon (☎ 0225 837 955, fax 0225 834 385)

MANNION, Noel Patrick Stephen; s of Tom Mannion, of Balliwaside, Co Galway, and Bridie, *née* Morrisey; *b* 12 Jan 1963; *Educ* St Josephs Coll Ballinasloe; *Career*

Rugby Union No 8 and flanker Lansdowne RFC and Ireland (12 caps); club: Ballinasloe RFC, Drumoyne RFC (Aust), Corinthians RFC (winner 3 Connacht Sr Cups and 1 Sr League title), Lansdowne RFC, Barbarians RFC (debut v Newport 1988), Wolfhounds RFC; rep: Connacht 1985-, Ireland U25 (1 cap), British Isles (v Rest of Europe); Ireland: debut v Western Samoa 1988, Five Nations v France 1989, tour Canada 1989; *Recreations* all sport, music, films, reading; *Style*— Noel Mannion, Esq; c/o Lansdowne RFC, Lansdowne Rd, Dublin 4 (☎ 081 689 292)

MANNION, Rosa; da of Patrick Anthony Mannion, of 16 Moorside Rd, Crosby, Liverpool, and Maria, *née* MacGregor; *b* 29 Jan 1962; *Educ* Seafield GS Crosby Liverpool, Royal Scottish Acad of Music and Drama (BA, RSAMD), with Patricia Boyer Kelly; *m* 13 July 1985, Gerard McQuade, s of Michael McQuade, of Cardonald, Glasgow; *Career* opera singer; debut L'Elisir d'Amore Scottish Opera 1984, princ Soprano Scottish Opera 1984-86, Buxton Festival 1986 and 1987; debut: Edinburgh Festival with Scottish Nat Orch 1985, ENO as Sophie in Der Rosenkavalier 1987, Glyndebourne Festival as Konstanze in Die Entführung aus dem Serail (sung first performance at 5 hours notice) 1988, Wigmore Hall 1988; winner Scottish Opera Int Singing Competition 1988, finalist Luciano Pavarotti Singing Competition 1985; *Recreations* tennis, swimming, cooking; *Style*— Ms Rosa Mannion; 23 Prospect Place, Epsom, Surrey (☎ 0372 723937); Lies Askonas, 186 Drury Lane, London (☎ 071 405 1809/1808)

MANS, Keith Douglas Rowland; MP (C) Wyre 1983-; s of Maj Gen Rowland Spencer Noel Mans, CBE, of Ivy Bank Cottage, Vinegar Hill, Off Barnes Lane, Milford on Sea, Hants, and Violet Mans, *née* Sutton; *b* 10 Feb 1946; *Educ* Berkhamsted Sch, RAF Coll Cranwell, Open Univ (BA); *m* 19 Aug 1972, Rosalie Mary, da of J McCann (d 1977), of 22 Ullet Rd, Liverpool; 1 s (David, b 9 Sept 1982); 2 da (Louise, b 5 Nov 1980, Emma b 6 May 1986); *Career* former Flt Lt RAF; serv UK, Germany, Malta, Cyprus and Malaya; formerly central buyer for electronics for John Lewis Ptnrship; former dep ldr New Forest DC (dist cncllr 1983-87); memb House of Commons Select Ctee on the Environment, sec Cons Aviation Ctee; sch govr 1984-87; memb Royal United Servs Inst for Def Studies 1965; *Recreations* flying; *Clubs* Army and Navy, RAF; *Style*— Keith D R Mans, Esq, MP; House of Commons, London SW1A 0AA (☎ 071 219 6334/3436)

MANS, Maj-Gen Rowland Spencer Noel; CBE (1971, OBE 1966, MBE 1956); s of Thomas Frederick Mans (d 1954), of Bispham, Lancs, and May Frances, *née* Seigenberg (d 1975); *b* 16 Jan 1921; *Educ* Surbiton GS, RMC Sandhurst; *m* 6 Jan 1945, Veeo Ellen, da of Frank Sutton (d 1951), of Southampton; 3 s (Keith b 1946, Mark b 1955, Lance b 1957); *Career* WWII Queens Royal Regt and Kings African Rifles 1939-45, Maj served: E Africa, Madagascar, Palestine, ME, Far East, Canada; Queen's Royal Regt 1939-76, regtl and staff appts 1945-69, Col, Cdr Aldershot A/GOC SE Dist, Brig, Dir Personnel Servs 1972-73, Dir Mil Assistance Office 1973-76, Maj-Gen, Col Queen's Regt 1978-83; conslt Stewart Wrightson (now Willis) 1976-, mil advsr Def Manufacturers Assoc 1976-, UK assoc Burdes Law Ltd (USA) 1988-, articles for jls in UK and USA; co cncllr Hants 1984-89, pres New Forest Cons Assoc 1984-87; Freeman City of London; Knight Cdr: Dannebrog (Denmark) 1983, Orange & Nassau (Netherlands) 1983; *Books* Canada's Constitutional Crisis (1978); *Recreations* writing, gardening; *Clubs* Army and Navy, Royal Lymington YC; *Style*— Maj-Gen Rowley Mans, CBE; Ivy Bank Cottage, Vinegar Hill, Milford-on-Sea, Hants (☎ 0590 643982)

MANSEL, Rev Canon James Seymour Denis; KCVO (1979, MVO 1972); s of Edward Mansel (d 1941), of 17 Clarendon Square, Leamington, and Muriel Louisa Mansel (d 1956); *b* 18 June 1907; *Educ* Brighton Coll, Exeter Coll Oxford (MA); *m* 1942, Ann Monica Waterhouse (d 1974), 1 da; *Career* sub dean HM Chapels Royal, dep clerk of the Closet, sub almoner and domestic chaplain to HM The Queen 1965-79, extra chaplain to HM The Queen 1979-, canon and prebendary of Chichester Cathedral 1971-81, canon emeritus 1981-, asst priest St Margarets Westminster 1980, priest vicar Westminster Abbey 1983-88; JP City of Winchester 1950-56, Inner London Cmmn 1964; CStJ; *Clubs* Athenaeum; *Style*— The Rev Canon James Mansel, KCVO, FSA; 15 Sandringham Ct, Maida Vale, London W9 1UA (☎ 071 286 3052)

MANSEL, Maj John Clavell; DL (Dorset 1974); s of Maj Rhys Clavell Mansel (d 1969), of Ropley Manor, Hants, and Sylvia Nina, *née* Campbell (d 1944); *b* 9 Jan 1917; *Educ* Eton, Ch Ch Oxford (MA); *m* 11 Aug 1945, Damaris Joan, da of Robert Hyde Hyde-Thomson (d 1970), of 36 Victoria Rd, London W8; 2 s (Richard b 1949, Philip b 1951), 1 da (Lavinia b 1946); *Career* enlisted 1 Bn RB 1938, 2 Motor Trg Bn and 10 RB 1939-41, 1 RB W Desert 1941-42, Capt 1942, HQ Persia Area and RAF Levies Iraq 1943-44, 10 RB Italy 1944-45, Staff Coll 1945-46, Maj 1946, GHQ MELF and HQ BTE 1946-49, 1 RB BAOR 1949-51, served UK regimentally and on staff 1951-58, ret 1958; pres: Dorset Wildfowlers Assoc 1970-87, Corfe Castle Branch S Dorset Cons Assoc 1974-, Corfe Castle Branch Royal Br Legion 1977-, Wareham Dist Twinning Assoc 1978-88; chm Dorset Historic Churches Tst 1974-84, memb for Kimmeridge of Wareham and Purbeck Dist Cncl 1958-74; High Sheriff of Dorset 1968-69, JP Wareham Div 1961-82 (chm 1980-82); *Recreations* general country living, occasional shooting; *Style*— Maj John Mansel, DL; The Old Parsonage, Kimmeridge, Wareham, Dorset BH20 5PE (☎ 0929 480722)

MANSEL, Sir Philip; 15 Bt (E 1622), of Muddlescombe, Carmarthenshire; s of Sir John Philip Ferdinand Mansel, 14 Bt (d 1947); *b* 3 March 1943; *Educ* Grosvenor Coll Carlisle, Carlisle GS; *m* 24 Aug 1968, Margaret, da of Arthur Docker; 1 s, 1 da (Nicol); *Heir* s, John Philip Mansel b 19 April 1982; *Career* fell Inst of Sales Mgmnt; md Eden-Vale Engrg Co Ltd; *Style*— Sir Philip Mansel, Bt; 4 Redhill Drive, Fellside Park, Whickham, Newcastle upon Tyne

MANSEL LEWIS, David Courtenay; JP (1969); s of Charlie Ronald Mansel Lewis (d 1960), and Lillian Georgina (d 1982), da of Sir Courtenay Warner, 1 Bt; *b* 25 Oct 1927; *Educ* Eton, Keble Coll Oxford (MA); *m* 1953, Lady Mary, *qv*; 1 s, 2 da; *Career* Welsh Gds 1946-49, Lt 1948 RARO; High Sheriff Carmarthenshire1965, DL 1971, Lord Lt Camarthenshire 1973-74, HM Lt Dyfed 1974-79, Lord Lt Dyfed 1979-; KStJ; *Recreations* sailing (yacht 'Nandhi'), music; *Clubs* RYS, Lansdowne, Cruising Assoc; *Style*— David Mansel Lewis, Esq, JP, HM Lord Lt of Dyfed; Stradey Castle, Llanelli, Dyfed SA15 4PL (☎ 0554 774626); 53 New Rd, Llanelli, Dyfed (☎ 0554 773059)

MANSEL LEWIS, Lady Mary Rosemary Marie-Gabrielle; *née* Montagu-Stuart-Wortley; OBE (1983), JP (1974); da of 3 Earl of Wharncliffe (d 1953), and Lady Maud Lilian Elfrida Mary (d 1979), eldest da of 7 Earl Fitzwilliam; goddaughter of Princess Royal (decd); *b* 11 June 1930; *Educ* Heathfield; *m* 1953, David Courtenay Mansel Lewis, *qv*; 1 s (Patrick Charles Arhchibald b 1953), 2 da (Catherine Maud Leucha b 1956, Annabel Lillian Elfrida b 1962); *Clubs* assoc memb Royal Yacht Sqdn, Lansdowne; *Style*— The Lady Mary Mansel Lewis, OBE, JP; Stradey Castle, Llanelli, Dyfed SA15 4PL (☎ 0554 774626)

MANSELL, Gerard Evelyn Herbert; CBE (1977); s of Herbert Goodinge Mansell, of Paris (d 1968), and Anne Marie Lintz (d 1985); *b* 16 Feb 1921; *Educ* Lycée Hoche Versailles, Lycée Buffon Paris, Ecole Libre des Sciences Politiques Paris, Chelsea Sch of Art London (Nat Dip in Design); *m* 1956, Diana Marion, da of Roland Crichton Sherar, of Burnham Market, Norfolk; 2 s; *Career* WWII 1940-46 (despatches), Royal Norfolk Regt and Durham LI, served Western Desert, Sicily, NW Europe; intelligence staff offr 50 Div and 8 Corps (Maj); joined BBC Euro Serv 1951, controller Radio 4 and music programme BBC 1965-69, dir of programmes Radio BBC 1970-71, md external bdcasting BBC 1972-80, dep DG BBC 1977-80; chm: Communications Advsy Ctee UK Nat Cmmn for UNESCO 1983-85, Friends of UNESCO 1986-87, CNAA, Br Ctee for Journalists in Europe 1977, Int Cncl for Journalists in Europe 1977-, Jt Advsy Ctee for Trg of Radio Journalists 1981-87, New Hampstead Garden Suburb Tst 1984-90; govr Falmouth Sch of Art and Design 1988-; memb Franco-British Cncl 1990-; French Croix de Guerre 1944; FRSA; *Books* Tragedy in Algeria (1961), Let Truth be Told (1982); *Style*— Gerard Mansell, Esq, CBE; 46 Southway, London NW11 6SA

MANSELL, Nigel Ernest James; OBE (1991); *b* 8 Aug 1953; *Educ* Hall Green Bilateral, Matthew Bolton Poly, Solihull Tech Coll, N Birmingham Poly (HND); *m* 19 April 1975, Rosanne Elizabeth, da of Walter Denis Perry; 2 s (Leo James b 4 Jan 1985, Greg Nigel b 8 Nov 1987), 1 da (Chloe Margaret b 16 Aug 1982); *Career* motor racing driver; began car racing 1976, Winner Br Fusegear Championship 1977, memb Unipart March Dolomite Formula 3 team 1979, memb Ralt-Honda Formula 2 team 1980; formula 1: first grand prix Austria 1980, memb Lotus team 1981-84, memb Canon Williams team 1985-88 and 1991-, memb Farrari team 1989-90; achievements incl: driven in 149 grand prix, first win Grand Prix of Europe Brands Hatch 1985, total 16 wins, 15 pole positions, runner up World Drivers' Championship 1986 and 1987; records held: 16 fastest laps on various circuits, 15 consecutive front row grid positions 1987; BBC Sports Personality of the Year 1986, Br Racing Drivers' Club award 1989; former laboratory technician then prodn mangr Lucas Aerospace, former sr sales engr Tractor Div Girling; *Recreations* flying both planes and helicopters, golfing, shooting, running, cycling, swimming, Red Arrows; *Style*— Nigel Mansell, Esq, OBE; c/o Sue Membery, Shute Field, Oakridge Lane, Sidcot, nr Winscombe, Avon BS25 1LZ (☎ 0934 843101, fax 0934 843609)

MANSELL-JONES, Richard Mansell; s of Arnaud Milward Jones, of Carmarthen (d 1964), and Winifred Mabel, *née* Foot (d 1978); n of Prof P Mansell-Jones (ed of the Oxford Book of French Verse); *b* 4 April 1940; *Educ* Queen Elizabeth's Carmarthen, private tuition, Worcester Coll Oxford (MA); *m* 30 June 1971, Penelope Marion, da of Maj Sir David Henry Hawley, 7 Bt (d 1988); *Career* CA, memb Stock Exchange; dir: Brown Shipley & Co Ltd 1974-88 (dep chm 1984-88), Brown Shipley Hldgs plc 1984, Barr & Wallace Arnold Tst plc 1984, Heim Gallery (London) Ltd; chm J Bibby & Sons plc 1988 (dep chm 1987, dir 1978); non-exec dir Robert Bruce Fitzmaurice Ltd, Madison Trust Ltd, Barlow Rand Ltd, Rand Mines; *Recreations* art, music; *Clubs* Overseas Bankers, Oriental; *Style*— Richard Mansell-Jones, Esq; 16 Stratford Place, London W1N 9AF (☎ 071 629 6243)

MANSELL-MOULLIN, Michael; s of Sqdn Ldr Oswald Mansell-Moullin (d 1964), and Mary Bagott Mansell-Moullin, *née* Green; *b* 8 Oct 1926; *Educ* St Edwards Sch Oxford, Jesus Coll Cambridge (MA, DIC); *m* 17 May 1969, Marion Elizabeth, da of Capt R L Jordan RN (d 1988); 1 s (David b 1972), 1 da (Jenny Melissa b 1976); *Career* Capt RE India & Pakistan 1944-49; chief hydrologist Binnie & Ptnrs (Consulting Engrs) 1959-69, conslt hydrologist UK and Int 1970-; fndr and pres-elect Br Hydrological Soc 1983-85; *Publications* contrib leading scientific jls on water resources and hydrological subjects; companion ICE, MIWEM, FRGS; *Recreations* sailing, hill walking, woodwork; *Clubs* Bosham Sailing; *Style*— Michael Mansell-Moullin, Esq; Old Hatch, Lower Farm Rd, Effingham, Surrey KT24 5JL (☎ 0372 452 672)

MANSER, (Peter) John; s of Lt-Col Peter Robert Courtney Manser (d 1944), and Florence Delaplaine, *née* Ismay (d 1983); *b* 7 Dec 1939; *Educ* Marlborough, Univ of Grenoble; *m* 31 May 1969, Sarah Theresa Stuart (Tessa), *née* Todd; 2 da; *Career* CA; Brown Fleming & Murray 1959-66, dir Robert Fleming & Co Ltd 1967-75, md Jardine Fleming & Co Ltd 1975-79, chief exec Save & Prosper Gp Ltd 1979-88, dir Robert Fleming Hldgs 1988-, chief exec Robert Fleming gp; memb: Securities and Investmts Bd, Cncl Cancer Res Campaign; dir Cancer Cards Ltd; Freeman City of London, Liveryman Worshipful Co of Grocers; FCA 1976; *Recreations* gardening, shooting, walking; *Clubs* Boodle's, City of London, MCC; *Style*— John Manser, Esq; 51 Hamilton Terrace, London NW8 9RG (☎ 071 286 7595); Robert Fleming Holdings Ltd, 25 Copthall Ave, London EC2R 7DR (☎ 071 638 5858, fax 071 588 7219, telex 297451)

MANSER, Michael John; s of Edmund George Manser (d 1971), and Augusta Madge, *née* Bonell (d 1987); *b* 23 March 1929; *m* 1953, Dolores Josephine, da of Isadore Bernini; 1 s (Jonathan), 1 da (Victoria); *Career* Nat Serv RE, Staff Capt; chartered architect; pres RIBA 1983-85; memb: Cncl RSA, Nat Tst; architectural awards: Civic Tst Award, Civic Tst Commendation, Euro Heritage Year Award, DOE Commendation for Good Design in Housing, Steel Award Commendation, RIBA Award Commendation; architectural journalism, radio and tv; RIBA, Hon FRAIC; *Recreations* home, garden, books, music, walks, boats (Amadeus); *Clubs* Brooks's; *Style*— Michael Manser, Esq; Morton House, Chiswick Mall, London W4 2PS; Manser Assocs, Bridge Studios, Hammersmith Bridge, London W6 9DA

MANSER, Paul Robert; s of Bob Manser, and Margaret, *née* Rubinstein; *b* 27 March 1950; *Educ* Eltham Coll, Univ of Warwick (BA); *m* 28 July 1972, Lindy, da of Harry Myers; 2 s (Nicolas b 19 June 1981, Edward b 18 Feb 1983); *Career* slr: ptnr Berwin Leighton 1981-86, ptnr Hammond Suddards 1988-89, ptnr Clyde & Co 1988-; memb Law Soc; *Recreations* tennis, photography, music, books; *Style*— Paul Manser, Esq; 62 Crooms Hill, London SE10 8HG; Clyde & Co, 51 Eastcheap, London EC3M 1JP (☎ 071 623 1244, fax 071 623 5427, telex 884886)

MANSERGH, Capt Michael Cecil Maurice; s of Adm Sir Maurice James Mansergh, KCB, CBE (d 1966), Ch of Staff to Allied Naval C-in-C, Expeditionary Force for invasion of Normandy (responsible for naval planning 'Overlord'), 5 Sea Lord, C-in-C Plymouth, by his wife, Violet Elsie (d 1983), da of late Bernard Hillman; ggs of James Mansergh (d 1905), Pres Inst of Civil Engrs; *b* 12 Aug 1926; *Educ* RNC Dartmouth, psc and War Coll; *m* 10 March 1956, Margaret Jean, da of Bernard Howell Cameron Hastie (d 1981); 2 s (Robert b 1957, Michael b 1959), 1 da (Penelope b 1963); *Career* RN 1940, serv WWII supporting Russian convoys 1944, HMS Berwick, Far East and Pacific Fleets 1944-45, HMS Howe, Quality, Illustrious, qualified gunnery and air weapons; serv: HMS Mauritius, Jutland, Agincourt, Triumph, Centaur, Peregrine (RNAS Ford), Heron (RNAS Yeovilton), Fulmar (RNAS Lossiemouth) 1957-58; 2 in cmd 1966-68; Naval Staff MoD 1968-69, Capt 1969, Naval Asst to Ch of Fleet Support 1969, Queen's Harbourmaster Plymouth 1972-73, cmdg offr Gunnery Sch HMS Excellent 1974-76, ADC to HM The Queen 1978; vice-pres Admty Interview Bd 1976-79, Naval asst to Naval Sec 1979-82; FBIM 1970, FRHS; *Recreations* gardening, swimming, golf, rough shooting; *Clubs* Army and Navy, Lyme Regis Golf; *Style*— Capt Michael Mansergh, CBE, RN; Cothayes, Whitchurch Canonicorum, Bridport, Dorset DT6 6RH (☎ Chideock 89261)

MANSFIELD, Colin Eric; Emergency Reserve Decoration (1958); s of Donald Haddon Mansfield (d 1979) of Bishops Stortford and Doris Lydia *née* Hallett (d 1981); *b* 28 May 1929; *Educ* Bishops Stortford Coll, Northampton Poly; *m* 8 Feb 1956, Mary Winifred; 2 s (David Jonathon b 1959, Peter James b 1967), 2 da (Joanna Mary b 1961, Sarah Jane b and d 1966); *Career* Maj RE 1957-65, dir Trollope & Colls Ltd 1972-86 (md 1985-86), md Trollope & Colls Mgmnt 1981-4 (dep chm 1986-89); Freeman City of London; memb Carpenters Co; pres The Concrete Soc 1987-88; *Recreations* church work, golf, drama, gardening; *Style*— Colin Mansfield, Esq; 1 Dane O'Coys Rd, Bishops Stortford, Herts (☎ 0279 654520)

MANSFIELD, David James; s of Wilfred Victor Leonard Mansfield (d 1972), and Helen, *née* Preston; *b* 12 Jan 1954; *m* 15 Sept 1979, Alison Patricia, da of Gerald Frederick Hedley Pullin; 1 s (James William Robert b 1983), 1 da (Clare Amy Frances b 1986); *Career* sales and sr mktg exec Scottish and Grampian TV 1977-80, mktg gp head and gen sales mangr Scottish TV 1981-84; Thames TV: mktg controller 1985-87, sales and mktg controller 1987-90, dep sales dir 1990-; *Recreations* fly fishing, contemporary music, art deco china; *Style*— David Mansfield, Esq; 16 Sudbrooke Rd, London SW12 8TG; Thames Television plc, 149 Tottenham Court Rd, London W1P 9LL (☎ 071 387 9494, telex 25286, fax 071 388 7587)

MANSFIELD, Gp Capt Eric Arthur; s of Edward Arthur Mansfield (d 1980), and Violet Mary, *née* Ricketts (d 1973); *b* 14 April 1932; *Educ* Southend HS, Univ of Cambridge (MA), RAF Tech Coll, Univ of Southampton (MSc); *m* 2 Jan 1954, Marion, da of Alfred Charles Byrne (d 1975); 1 s (Russell b 27 Jan 1956), 1 da (Penelope b 10 June 1958); *Career* apprentice RAF 1949, cmmnd 1953, pilot wings 1958, jr appts fighter and bomber units, MOD 1963, HQ SAC (USAF) 1966, HQ Strike Cmd 1969, RAF Cottesmore 1972, HQ RAF Germany 1974, HQ 18 GP 1978, MOD 1981, HQ AfSouth 1984, HQ RAF Support Cmd 1986; dir public affrs Assoc of Consulting Engrs 1989-; Freeman City of London; CEng, MRAeS; *Recreations* squash, skiing, rough shooting, photography, philately; *Clubs* RAF; *Style*— Gp Capt Eric Mansfield; 33 Chalgrove End, Stoke Mandeville, Buckinghamshire (☎ 0296 613792); Alliance House, 12 Caxton St, Westminster, London SW1H OQL (☎ 071 222 6557, fax 071 222 0750)

MANSFIELD, Vice Adm Sir (Edward) Gerard Napier; KBE (1974), CVO (1981); s of Vice Adm Sir John Maurice Mansfield, KCB, DSO, DSC (d 1949), and Alice Talbok Napier (d 1979); *b* 13 July 1921; *Educ* RNC Dartmouth; *m* 1943, Joan Worship, da of Cdr John Byron, DSC, and Bar (decd); 2 da; *Career* joined RN 1935, serv WWII, Capt 1959, Rear Adm 1969, sr naval memb Directing Staff IDC 1969-70, Flag Offr sea Trg 1971-72, Vice Adm 1972, Dep Supreme Allied Cdr Atlantic 1973-75, ret; chm Assoc of RN Offrs' Cncl 1975-86; memb Admin Cncl Royal Jubilee Tsts 1978-82, chm Operation Raleigh 1984-89; *Recreations* golf, gardening; *Clubs* Army and Navy; *Style*— Vice Adm Sir Gerard Mansfield, KBE, CVO; White Gate House, Heath Lane, Ewshot, Farnham, Surrey GU10 5AH (☎ 0252 850325)

MANSFIELD, Hon Guy Rhys John; s and h of 5 Baron Sandhurst, DFC; *b* 3 March 1949; *Educ* Harrow, Oriel Coll Oxford (MA); *m* 1976, Philippa St Clair, da of late Digby Everard Verdon-Roe, of Le Cannet, France; 1 s (Edward James b 12 April 1982), 1 da (Alice Georgina b 4 Feb 1980); *Career* barr Middle Temple 1972; *Recreations* cricket; *Clubs* Leander, MCC; *Style*— The Hon Guy Mansfield; 1 Crown Office Row, London EC4Y 7HH

MANSFIELD, Michael; QC; s of Frank Le Voir Mansfield (d 1960), of London, and Marjorie, *née* Sayer (d 1977); *b* 12 Oct 1941; *Educ* Highgate Sch, Univ of Keele (BA); *m* 28 Sept 1965, Melian, da of Lt Cdr Bordes; 3 s (Jonathan, Leo, Keiran), 2 da (Anna, Louise); Mr Michael Mansfield also has issue by Yvette Vanson; 1 s (Frederic); *Career* called the Bar Gray's Inn 1967, estab chambers Tooks Ct 1984; memb TGWU, hon memb NUM; *Style*— Michael Mansfield, Esq, QC; 14 Tooks Ct, Cursitor St, London (☎ 071 405 8828)

MANSFIELD, Prof Peter; s of Sidney George Mansfield (d 1966), of 87 Kemble House, Lambeth, London, and Rose Lilian, *née* Turner (d 1985); *b* 9 Oct 1933; *Educ* William Penn Sch Dulwich and Peckham, QMC London (BSc, PhD); *m* 1 Sept 1962, Jean Margaret, da of Edward Francis Kibble (d 1972), of Peckham, London; 2 da (Sarah Jane b 1967, Gillian Samantha b 1970); *Career* Nat Serv RASC 1952-54; res assoc Univ of Illinois USA 1962-64; Univ of Nottingham 1964-79: lectr, sr lectr, reader; sr res visitor Max Planck Inst for Med Res Heidelberg Germany 1971-72, prof of physics Univ of Nottingham 1979-, pres Soc of Magnetic Resonance in Med 1987-88, fell QMC, London 1987; gold medal Soc of Magnetic Resonance in Med 1982, gold medal and prize Royal Soc Wellcome Fndn 1984, Duddell medal and prize Inst of Physics 1988, Sylvanus Thompson medal Br Inst of Radiology 1988, Euro Workshop Trophy Euro Soc of Magnetic Resonance in Med and Biology 1988, Antoine Béclère medal for Radiology 1989, Royal Soc Mullard medal 1990; FRS 1987; *Books* NMR Imaging in Biomedicine (with P G Morris, 1982); *Recreations* languages, walking, DIY; *Style*— Prof Peter Mansfield; 68 Beeston Fields Drive, Bramcote, Notts; Dept of Physics, Univ of Nottingham, Univ Pk, Nottingham NG7 2RD (☎ 0602 484848, ext 2830, fax 0602 229 792, telex 37346 UNINOT G)

MANSFIELD, Sir Philip Robert Aked; KCMG (1984, CMG 1973); s of Philip Theodore Mansfield (d 1975); *b* 9 May 1926; *Educ* Winchester, Pembroke Coll Cambridge; *m* 1953, Elinor, da of Dr Burtis Russell MacHatton (d 1959), of USA; 2 s (Adrian, Humphrey); *Career* WWII Lt Grenadier Gds 1944-47; Sudan Political Serv Equatoria Province 1950-55; Dip Serv: Addis Ababa, Singapore, Paris, Buenos Aires; cnsllr and head Rhodesia Dept FCO 1969-72, Royal Coll Def Studies 1973, cnsllr and head of chancery 1974-75, dep high cmmr Nairobi 1976, asst under sec of state FCO 1976-79, ambass and dep perm rep to the UN 1979-81, ambass to the Netherlands 1981-84; conslt: Rank Xerox, BPB Industs; *Recreations* birdwatching, tree planting, cooking; *Clubs* Royal Cwlth Soc; *Style*— Sir Philip Mansfield, KCMG; Gill Mill, Stanton Harcourt, Oxford, (☎ 0993 702554)

MANSFIELD, Prof Roger; s of Arthur George Mansfield (d 1985), and Edith, *née* Leggett (d 1985); *b* 18 Jan 1942; *Educ* Kingston GS, Gonville and Caius Coll Cambridge (BA), Wolfson Coll Cambridge (MA, PhD); *m* 24 July 1969, Helene Marie Louise, da of Rene Rica, of Quimper, France; 2 da (Marie-Anne b 1972, Stephanie b 1977); *Career* student apprentice and res engr Stewarts and Lloyds Ltd Corby 1960-66; FME teaching fell Dept of Engrg Univ of Cambridge 1966-68, visiting lectr Yale Univ 1968-69, sr res offr London Business Sch 1969-73, lectr in industl sociology Imperial Coll 1973-76, prof of business admin Univ of Wales Cardiff Business Sch 1976-; head of dept: Business Admin and Accountancy UWIST 1977-85, Business and Economics UWIST 1985-87; dir Cardiff Business Sch 1987-, dep princ UWIST 1985-88; dep chm Cncl of Univ Mgmnt Schs, vice chm Br Acad of Mgmnt, memb Cncl Inst of Welsh Affrs, dir S Glamorgan Trg and Enterprise Cncl 1989-; memb Br Acad of Mgmnt; *Books* Managers in Focus: the British Manager in the Early 1980s (with M J F Poole, 1981), Organizational Structures and National Contingencies (1983), Frontiers of Management Research and Practice (1989); *Recreations* gardening; *Clubs* Cardiff and County; *Style*— Prof Roger Mansfield; 64 Bishops Road, Whitchurch, Cardiff CF4 1LW (☎ 0222 617381); Cardiff Business School, University of Wales, Aberconway Building, Colum Drive, Cardiff CF1 3EU (☎ 0222 874417, fax 0222 874419, telex 497368)

MANSFIELD AND MANSFIELD, 8 Earl of (GB 1776 and 1792); William David Mungo James Murray; JP (Perth and Kinross 1975), DL (1980); also Lord Scone (S 1605), Viscount Stormont (S 1621), Lord Balvaird (S 1641); hereditary keeper of Bruce's Castle of Lochmaben; s of 7 Earl of Mansfield, JP, LL (d 1971, whose family were long the owners of Robert Adam's neo-classical Kenwood; Lord Mansfield is sixth in descent from the bro of the celebrated Lord Chief Justice and 1 Earl who was Alexander Pope's 'silver-tongued Murray'), and Dorothea (d 1985), da of Hon Sir Lancelot Carnegie, GCVO, KCMG, (2 s of 9 Earl of Southesk, by his 2 w); *b* 7 July 1930; *Educ* Wellesley House, Eton, ChCh Oxford; *m* 19 Dec 1955, Pamela Joan, da of Wilfred Neill Foster, CBE; 2 s (Viscount Stormont, Hon James b 7 June 1969), 1 da (Lady Georgina b 10 March 1967); *Heir* s, Viscount Stormont, *qv*; *Career* Nat Serv Lt Scots Gds 1949-50 (Malaya); called to the Bar 1958; practising barrister until 1971; dir Gen Accident Fire & Life Assurance Corpn and numerous cos 1972-79 and 1985-; oppn front bench spokesman in the House of Lords 1975-79; min of state: Scottish Office 1979-83, NI Office 1983-84; First Crown Estate Cmmr and chm 1985-; memb Br Delgn to Euro Parliament 1973-75; Hon Sheriff Perth 1974; chm Historic Houses Assoc Scotland 1976-79; pres: Scottish Assoc of Boys' Clubs 1976-79, Fédération des Associations de Chasse de l' Europe 1977-79, Royal Scottish Country Dance Soc 1977-; *Clubs* Turf, White's, Pratt's, Beefsteak; *Style*— The Rt Hon the Earl of Mansfield and Mansfield, JP, DL; Scone Palace, Perthshire PH2 6BE (☎ 0738 51115)

MANSFIELD COOPER, Sir William; s of late William Ellis Cooper, and late Georgina Caroline Cooper; *b* 20 Feb 1903; *Educ* Univ of Manchester; *m* 1936, Edna Mabel, da of late Herbert Baker; 1 s (Christopher); *Career* Univ of Manchester: asst lectr and lectr 1938-49, registrar 1945-52, prof of industl law 1949-70, vice chllr 1956-70, emeritus prof 1970-; CStJ 1970; kt 1963; *Recreations* gardening, bird watching; *Clubs* Athenaeum; *Style*— Sir William Mansfield Cooper; Flat 32, The Chestnuts, West St, Godmanchester, Cambs

MANSON, Alexander Reid; CBE (1989); s of Capt Alexander Manson (d 1965), of Kilblean, Oldmeldrum Inverurie, Aberdeenshire, and Isobel, *née* Reid, MBE (d 1985); *b* 2 Sept 1931; *Educ* Robert Gordons Coll Aberdeen, N of Scotland Coll of Agric (Dip Ag); *m* 29 May 1957, Ethel Mary, da of Robert Philip (d 1980), of Hillfoot, Strichen; 1 s (Alexander b 1961), 2 da (Anne b 1958, Lesley b 1960); *Career* fndr chm Aberdeen Beef & Calf Ltd 1962, chm Buchan Meat Producers Ltd 1982 (joined 1968), pres Scot Agric Orgn Soc Ltd 1986-89, vice pres Fedn of Agric Co-operatives (UK) Ltd 1990-, chm Scot Beef Devpts Ltd 1990-; tstee Plunkett Fndn Oxford 1977-; memb: Meat & Livestock Cmmn 1986-, Williams Ctee Bd of Enquiry 1989; chm Oldmeldrum Sports Ctee 1971-75 (memb 1955-82), memb Oldmeldrum Town Cncl 1960-65; *Recreations* golf, shooting and conservation, bird watching; *Clubs* Farmers, Royal Northern and Univ; *Style*— Alexander Manson, Esq, CBE; Kilblean, Oldmeldrum, Inverurie, Aberdeenshire AB5 ODN (☎ 065 122 226); Buchan Meat Ltd, Markethill, Turriff, Aberdeenshire AB5 7HW (☎ 0888 63751, fax 0888 62751, car telephone 0836 700 694, telex 73328)

MANSON, Finian Paul Louis; s of Stephen Louis Manson, of 66 Burnaby Gardens, London, and Grainne Caitlin Manson (Dempsey); *b* 8 March 1950; *Educ* Chiswick GS, Poly of the South bank, Cranfield Business Sch MBA, FCCA; *Career* chm and md Thomas Christy Ltd; dir: Michael Denham Ltd, Medicam Laboratories Ltd, Marna Christina Ltd, Thomas Christy (SA) Ltd, Thomas Christy (Australia) Ltd, Christy Cosmetics Ltd, Christy (GB) Ltd; *Style*— Finian Manson, Esq; Christy Estate, North Lane, Aldershot, Hants GU12 4QP (☎ 0252 29911, telex 858196)

MANSON, Ian Stuart; s of David Alexander Manson (d 1973), of Halifax, Calderdale, and Elsie May, *née* Newton (d 1985); *b* 15 March 1929; *Educ* Heath GS Halifax, Clare Coll Cambridge (BA); *m* 11 Sept 1957, Pamela, da of John Horrocks-Taylor (d 1949), of Halifax; 3 s (Andrew b 1959, Simon b 1962, David b 1964); *Career* Nat Serv 1948-49; asst prosecuting slr: Bradford 1956-57, Birmingham 1960-66; prosecuting slr: Southampton 1957-58, Portsmouth 1958-60, W Mids Police Authy 1966-74; chief prosecuting slr W Mids CC 1974-86, Chief Crown Prosecutor W Mids 1986-1989; ex-warden Kings Norton Parish Church, pres Soc Yorkshirefolk in Birmingham, memb Birmingham Medico-Legal Soc; former pres Prosecuting Slrs Soc Eng and Wales, cncl memb Birmingham Law Soc; memb: The Law Soc 1976, Birmingham Law Soc 1978; *Recreations* reading, music, gardening; *Style*— Ian Manson, Esq; The McLaren Building, Dale End, Birmingham B4 7NR (☎ 021 233 3133, fax 021 233 2499)

MANT, John; OBE (1986); s of Charles Arthur Mant (d 1969), of Bath, and Hilda Ada Louise, *née* Landor (d 1969); *b* 23 May 1920; *Educ* King Edward VI Sch Bath; *m* 2 Jan 1943, Barbara Joan (d 1989), da of William George Wolfe (d 1968), of Bath; 1 s (Charles b 1951), 3 da (Elizabeth b 1948, Sarah b 1955, Helen b 1962); *Career* HM Army 1940-46: Home Forces 1940-42, Middle East and Sicily 1943, France, Belgium, Holland and Germany 1944-45, Capt; admitted slr 1949, ptnr in private practice 1953-86, conslt Withy King and Lee Slrs Bath 1986-88; memb House of Laity Gen Synod of the C of E 1975-80, pres Bath Law Soc 1979-80, Assoc of South Western Law Soc 1982, govr Salisbury and Wells Theol Coll 1982-90; pres Wansdyke Constituency Cons Assoc 1986-89 (fndr chm 1983-85); *Recreations* gardening, walking, foreign travel; *Style*— J C B Mant, OBE; Bassett Barn, Claverton, Bath, Avon BA2 7BG (☎ 0225 469692)

MANTEL, Hilary Mary (Mrs Gerald McEwen); da of Henry Thompson (took name of step f, Jack Mantel), and Margaret Mary, *née* Foster; *b* 6 July 1952; *Educ* Harrytown Convent Romiley Cheshire, LSE, Univ of Sheffield (B Jurisprudence); *m* 1972, Gerald McEwen, s of Henry McEwen; *Career* film critic The Spectator 1987-90, writer of columns and criticism in a wide range of newspapers and magazines 1987-; judge Booker Prize 1990; author of short stories; *novels* Every Day is Mother's Day (1985), Vacant Possession (1986), Eight Months on Ghazzah Street (1988), Fludd (1989); Shiva Naipaul Meml prize 1987, Winifred Holtby prize 1990, Cheltenham Festival Lit prize 1990, Southern Arts Lit prize 1991; assoc London Coll of Music 1968, FRSL 1990; *Recreations* watching cricket; *Style*— Hilary Mantel; Bill Hamilton A M Heath & Co, 79 St Martins Lane, London WC2N 4AA (☎ 071 836 4271, fax 071 497 2561)

MANTELL, Brian Stuart; s of Sidney Mantell (d 1988), of Chigwell, Essex, and Anne, *née* Goldstein (d 1981); *b* 14 Jan 1935; *Educ* Co HS Ilford, Univ of London (MB BS, MRCP); *m* 15 Aug 1971, Dr Janet Mantell, da of Maurice Share (d 1963), of Kingston Surrey; 1 s (David b 1974), 1 da (Rachel b 1977); *Career* conslt in Radiotherapy and Oncology: The Royal London Hosp 1970-, London chest Hosp 1971-; memb BMA, treas Radiotherapists Visiting Soc of GB and Scandinavia; RSM 1961, FFR 1967, FRCR 1975, FRCP 1990; *Recreations* reading, swimming, travel; *Clubs* RSM; *Style*— Dr Brian Mantell; The London Hospital, London E1 1BB (☎ 071 377 7690); 10 Ferrings, College Rd, Dulwich, London SE21 7LU (☎ 081 693 8141)

MANTERFIELD, Kenneth Charles; s of Charles Harold Manterfield (d 1974), of Corzon Park, Calne, Wilts, and Hilda Mary, *née* Ricketts (d 1941); *b* 6 June 1925; *Educ* King Edward VII GS Sheffield, Queens' Coll Cambridge; *m* 16 June 1951, Brenda Milner, da of late Arthur Milner Lusby, of Orchard Cottage, The Quay, Blakeney, Norfolk; 1 s (Robert b 1953), 1 da (Rosamund (Mrs Williams) b 1958); *Career* RAF, trg RCAF Air Navigation Sch Winnipeg Canada, aircrew cadet 1943, navigator and PO 1945, air traffic controller and flying offr RAF Mauripiur Karachi India 1946, sr air traffic control and Flt-Lt RAF Palam Airport New Delhi India 1947, demobbed 1947; CA; audit mangr Camm Metcalfe Best & Co Sheffield 1951-54, asst sec and gp accountant C & T Harris (Calne) Ltd Wilts 1954-59, chief accountant R Silcock & Sons Ltd Liverpool 1959-63, gp controller of electronics Plessey Co plc Ilford Essex 1970-73 (chief internal auditor 1963-70), fin exec staff Plessey Ilford Essex 1973-80; corp fin advsr: Bank of England Printing Works Debden Essex 1983-85 (accountant 1980-83), Venture Technol Ltd Abingdon 1985-88; chief exec Chazem Prods Newcastle 1988-; former memb Jt Review Bd Advsy Ctee CBI and HM

Treasy; sidesman St John's Church Buckhurst Hill Essex, auditor Woodford Music Soc; memb: Nat Tst Woodford Centre, Choral Fndn St Peter Ad Vincula HM Chapel Royal Tower of London; Liveryman Worshipful Co of CAs; FCA 1951 (cncl memb 1975-81 and 1983); *Recreations* walking, music, ornithology, gardening, golf; *Style—* Kenneth Manterfield, Esq; 3 The Drive, Buckhurst Hill, Essex IG9 5RB (☎ 081 504 1005); Spectrum House, 20-26 Cursitor St, London EC4A 1HY (☎ 071 405 2088)

MANTHORP, Rev (Brian) Robert; s of Alan Roy Manthorp (d 1972), of Framlingham, Suffolk, and Stella, *née* Butcher; *b* 28 July 1934; *Educ* Framlingham Coll Suffolk, Pembroke Coll Oxford (BA, MA), Westcott House Cambridge, Coll of Teachers of the Blind (Dip); *m* 8 Aug 1954, Jennifer Mary, da of Vernon Rosewarne Caradine (d 1985), of East Preston, Sussex; 3 s (Christopher b 1955, Stephen b 1958, Jonathan b 1964), 1 da (Helen b 1963); *Career* Instr Lt RN 1955-58; ordained priest Guildford 1961; asst master and chaplain Charterhouse Surrey 1958-65, head of English and housemaster Lawrence Coll Murree W Pakistan and Aitchison Coll Lahore W Pakistan 1965-70, head of English Oakbank Sch Keighley W Yorks 1970-73; headmaster: Holy Trinity Sch Halifax W Yorks 1973-80, Worcester Coll for the Blind 1980-; chm of govrs Bishop Perowne HS Worcs 1986-89, vice chm Warnock Ctee Ind Schs Jr Cncl 1982-; fell Coll of Preceptors 1985; *Books* Fifty Poems for Pakistan (1971); *Recreations* sport, sketching; *Clubs* East India; *Style—* The Rev Robert Manthorp; The Brew House, High St, Chipping, Campden, Glos; The Principal's House, Worcester College for the Blind, Worcester WR5 2JX (☎ 0905 763 933)

MANTON, Dr Donald John; *b* 23 Feb 1926; *Educ* Cheltenham GS, St Mary's Hosp Med Sch (MB BS, FRCR); *m* 6 Feb 1960, Patricia Maud, *née* Beasley; 1 s (Simon Paul b 1967), 1 da (Catherine Elizabeth b 1964); *Career* registrar in radiology Hammersmith Hosp 1958-60, sr registrar Charing Cross Hosp 1960-64; conslt radiologist: East Birmingham Hosp 1964-67, Farnham and Frimley Park Hosps 1967-; memb W Surrey and North East Health Authy 1984-89; memb: BMA 1952, BIR, RCR 1960, RSM 1970, BMUS, BMNS 1972; *Books* Building and Extending a Radiology Department (with E J Roebuck and G L Fordham, 1988); *Recreations* masonry; *Style—* Dr Donald Manton; 43 Oast House Crescent, Farnham, Surrey GU9 0NP (☎ 0252 721051); Frimley Park Hospital, Camberley, Surrey GU16 5UJ (☎ 0276 692777)

MANTON, 3 Baron (UK 1922); Joseph Rupert Eric Robert Watson; DL (Humberside 1980); s of 2 Baron Manton, JP (d 1968), by his 1 w Alethea (d 1979, da of Col Philip Langdale, OBE, and gggda of 17 Baron Stourton); *b* 22 Jan 1924; *Educ* Eton; *m* 1951, Mary Elizabeth, twin da of Maj T D Hallinan (decd); 2 s, 3 da; *Heir* s, Hon Miles Ronald Marcus Watson; *Career* joined Army 1942, Lt Life Gds 1943, transferred 7 (QO) Hussars 1951, Capt, ret 1956; sr steward Jockey Club 1982-85, former Jockey Club representative on Horserace Betting Levy Bd 1970-75, former gentleman rider (won 130 Nat Hunt races and Point to Points 1947-64); landowner, farmer, race horse owner; *Clubs* Jockey, White's; *Style—* The Rt Hon the Lord Manton, DL; Houghton Hall, Sancton, York (☎ 0430 873234)

MANWARING, Michael John; s of Randle Gilbert Manwaring, of Newick, Sussex, and Betty, *née* Rout; *b* 7 Sept 1946; *Educ* Christ Coll Brecon, Imperial Coll London (BEng); *m* Dec 1977, Annabelle, da of Praxidus Fernandes; 3 da (Nina Joanna b 12 May 1980, Lara Sophia b 13 Oct 1983, Maya Louise b 15 Sept 1986); *Career* KMP Partnership Ltd: joined 1969, dir 1976, client services dir 1978, dep md 1982-84; dep chm WCRS 1989- (client services dir 1985-); memb Inst of Practitioners in Advertising 1990; *Recreations* tennis, photography, Indian culture/art; *Clubs* MCC, Glyndebourne, Queens Tennis; *Style—* Michael Manwaring, Esq; WCRS, 41-44 Great Queen St, London WC2B 5AR (☎ 071 242 2800, fax 071 831 4126)

MANWARING, Randle Gilbert; s of George Ernest Manwaring (d 1939), of London, and Lilian, *née* Gilbert; *b* 3 May 1912; *Educ* Univ of London, Univ of Keele (MA); *m* 9 Aug 1941, Betty Violet, da of Herbert Percy Rout (d 1986), of Norwich; 3 s (David b 1944, Michael b 1946, Christopher b 1949), 1 da (Rosemary b 1942); *Career* joined RAFVR 1940, cmmnd RAF 1941, cmd various sqdns RAF Regt as founding offr 1943-45, Wing Cdr all units of RAF Regt in Burma (approx 3,500 men) 1945, demob Wing Cdr 1945; dir (later md) CE Heath & Co Ltd 1964-71, first md CE Heath Urquhart & Co Ltd 1966-71; dir: Excess Life Assurance Co 1967-75, Excess Insurance Co 1975-78; vice chm Midland Bank Insurance Services Ltd 1974-77 (first md 1972-74); chm govrs: Luckley - Oakfield Sch 1972-83, Northease Manor Sch 1972-84; chm Uckfield Probus Club 1989-90, pres Soc of Pension Consits 1968-70, dep chm Corp of Insur Brokers 1970-71; memb: Chichester Deanery and Diocesan Synods, Bishop's Cncl; Churchwarden St Peter-Upon-Cornhill, reader Dio of Chichester 1968-, vice pres Crusaders Union; FSS 1970, FPMI 1971; *Books* The Heart Of This People (1954), A Christian Guide to Daily Work (1963), Run Of The Downs (1984), From Controversy To Co-Existence (1985), 10 Volumes of Poetry Culminating In Collected Poems (1986), The Good Fight (1990), A Study of Hymnwriting and Hymnsinging in the Christian Church (1991); *Recreations* music, reading, following cricket; *Clubs* RAF, MCC; *Style—* Randle Manwaring, Esq; Marbles Barn, Newick, East Sussex BN8 4LG (☎ 082572 3845)

MAPLES, John Cradock; MP (C) Lewisham W 1983-; s of Thomas Cradock and Hazel Mary Maples; *b* 22 April 1943; *Educ* Downing Coll Cambridge, Harvard Business Sch; *m* 1986, Jane; *Career* economic sec to the Treasury 1990-; *Style—* John Maples, Esq, MP; House of Commons, London SW1A 0AA (☎ 071 219 6373)

MAPLESON, Prof William Wellesley; s of Francis Mapleson (d 1959), of Amersham, Bucks, and Amy Kathleen, *née* Parsons (d 1968); *b* 2 Aug 1926; *Educ* Dr Challoner's GS Amersham Bucks, Univ Coll Durham (BSc, PhD, DSc); *m* 10 July 1954, Gwladys Doreen, da of William Horatio Wood (d 1981), of Cardiff; 1 s (Roger b 1963), 1 da (Jenny b 1955); *Career* Nat Serv instr in radar Flying Offr RAF 1947-49; prof of physic of anaesthesia Coll of Med Univ of Wales 1973-(lectr 1952-65, sr lectr 1965-69, reader 1969-73); memb Health Care Ctee 46 Br Standards Inst; Faculty medal of Faculty of Anaesthetics RCS 1981, Pask Certificate of Honour AAGBI 1972; hon memb Brazilian Soc of Anaesthesiology 1983; FInstP, FIPSM, FRSM; *Books* Automatic Ventilation of the Lungs (jtly, 3 edn, 1980); *Recreations* theatre-going, walking; *Style—* Prof William Mapleson; Dept of Anaesthetics, University of Wales College of Medicine, University Hospital of Wales, Cardiff CF4 4XW (☎ 0222 742096, fax 0222 747203)

MAPPLE, Andrew (Andy); s of Roy Boardman Mapple, of Preston, and Janet, *née* Marquis; *b* 3 Nov 1962; *Educ* Carr Hill HS Kirkham Lancs; *m* 17 Oct 1987, Deena, *née* Brush (the water skier); *Career* professional water skier; began competing 1976, memb Br team 1981; Gold medal Slalom World Championships 1981-82, current slalom world champion, world professional slalom champion 1987-, US Masters champion 6 times; world record holder slalom 1989-, world professional record holder; memb Team O'Brien; *Recreations* golf, motorsports, cycling, triathlon, cars; *Style—* Andy Mapple, Esq; c/o Mr & Mrs Roy Mapple, Marsh Garage, Lytham Rd, Clifton, Preston, Lancs PR4 0XE (☎ 0772 632233)

MAR, Lady Janet Helen of; da of 30 Earl of Mar; *b* 31 Jan 1946; *Educ* Univ of St Andrews, Univ of Kent; *m* 1969, Lt Cdr Laurence of Mar (formerly Laurence Duncan McDiarmid Anderson, of Winton Castle, E Lothian) recognized in surname of Mar by warrant of Lord Lyon 1969; 2 da (Elizabeth b 1970, Catherine b 1971); *Style—* The Lady Janet of Mar; c/o Midland Bank, 26 Biggin Street, Dover, Kent CT16 1BJ; Princes Ct, Brompton Rd, SW3

MAR, Countess of (31 holder of S Earldom *ab initio*, before 1114); Margaret; *née* of Mar; also Lady Garioch (an honour originally held together with the ancient territorial Earldom of Mar; holder of Premier Earldom of Scotland by date (the oldest peerage in the Br Isles); the predecessors of the original Earls of Mar were Mormaers of Mar in pre-feudal Scotland, long before the term 'Earl' came to be used; maintains private offr-of-arms (Garioch Pursuivant); da of 30 Earl of Mar (d 1975), and Millicent Mary Lane, *née* Salton; *b* 19 Sept 1940; *Educ* Lewes County GS for Girls Sussex; *m* 1, 1959 (m dis 1976), Edwin Noel of Mar (recognised in surname 'of Mar' by Warrant of the Lord Lyon 1969), s of Edwin Artiss; 1 da (Lady Susan Helen, Mistress of Mar, b 31 May 1963); m 2, 1976, John (also recognised in the surname 'of Mar' by Warrant of Lord Lyon 1976), s of Norman Salton; m 3, 1982, John Henry Jenkin, MA(Cantab), LRAM, FRCO, ARCM, s of William Jenkin, of Hayle, Cornwall; *Heir* da, Mistress of Mar; *Career* holder of Premier Earldom of Scotland; British Telecom sales superintendent until 1982; patron Dispensing Doctors' Assoc; lay memb Immigration Appeals Tbnl; patron Worcester Mobile Disabled Group; chm ENACT; *Recreations* gardening, painting, interior decoration, pig and goat keeping; *Style—* The Rt Hon the Countess of Mar; St Michael's Farm, Great Witley, Worcester WR6 6JB

MAR, Mistress of; Lady Susan Helen; *née* of Mar; da of Countess of Mar in her own right (31 holder of S Earldom) by her 1 husb Edwin Artiss (later 'of Mar'); *b* 31 May 1963; *Educ* Kidderminster HS for Girls, Christie Coll Cheltenham; *Style—* Mistress of Mar; 72 Oakwood Rd, London NW11 (☎ 081 455 3111)

MAR AND KELLIE, 13 and 15 Earl of (S 1565, 1619); John Francis Hervey Erskine; JP (Clackmannanshire 1971); also Lord Erskine (S 1426), Baron Erskine of Dirletowne (*sic* as stated by The Complete Peerage, S 1604), and Viscount of Fentoun and Lord Dirletoun (S 1619, whereby Lord Mar and Kellie is premier Viscount of Scotland); also Hereditary Keeper of Stirling Castle; s of Lord Erskine, GCSI, GCIE (d 1953), and Lady Marjorie Hervey (d 1967), (er da of 4 Marquess of Bristol); suc gf, 12 Earl, KT, 1955; *b* 15 Feb 1921; *Educ* Eton, Trinity Cambridge; *m* 24 April 1948, Pansy Constance, OBE, CStJ, JP, da of Gen Sir Andrew Nicol Thorne, KCB, CMG, DSO (d 1970); 3 s, 1 da; *Heir* s, Lord Erskine; *Career* serv 1939-45 War, Maj 1950, ret 1954; chm T and AF Assoc Clackmannanshire 1961-68; scottish rep peer 1958-63; co cncllr (1955-75); chm Forth Conservancy Bd 1957-68; Lord-Lt Clackmannanshire 1966- (DL 1954, Vice-Lt 1957-66); elder Church of Scotland 1958-; memb Royal Co of Archers (Queen's Body Guard for Scotland); farmer; KStJ 1966; *Clubs* New (Edinburgh); *Style—* The Rt Hon the Earl of Mar and Kellie, JP; Claremont House, Alloa, Clackmannanshire FK10 2JF (☎ 0259 212020)

MAR AND KELLIE, Countess of; Pansy Constance; OBE (1984), JP (1971); da of Gen Sir Andrew Thorne, KCB, CMG, DSO (d 1970), and Hon Margaret Douglas Pennant (d 1967), da of 2 Baron Penrhyn; *b* 16 Dec 1921; *Educ* privately; *m* 24 April 1948, 13 and 15 Earl of Mar and Kellie, *qv*; 3 s, 1 da; *Career* serv WWII, subaltern ATS, UK; chm: Youth-at-Risk Advsy Gp 1968-, Scottish Standing Conference Voluntary Youth Orgns 1978-81 (SCANVYO); hon pres Girls' Bde Scotland 1979-90, pres UK Ctee UNICEF 1979-84, pres JMB Devpt Trg 1985-87, Scottish chm Int Year of the Child (IYC) 1979; elder of the Church of Scotland 1977-; CStJ 1983 (OStJ 1977); *Recreations* walking, family outings; *Clubs* New (Edinburgh), Univ Women's; *Style—* The Rt Hon the Countess of Mar and Kellie, OBE, JP; Claremont House, Alloa, Clackmannanshire FK10 2JF (☎ 0259 212020)

MARA, Rt Hon Ratu Sir Kamisese Kapaiwai Tuimacilai; GCMG (1983), KBE (1969, OBE 1961), PC (1973); *b* 13 May 1920; *Educ* Sacred Heart Coll NZ, Otago Univ NZ, Wadham Coll Oxford (MA); *m* 1951, Adi Lady Lala Mara; 3 s, 5 da; *Career* MLC Fiji 1953-, MEC 1959-61, prime minister of Fiji 1970-, hereditary high chief of the Lau Islands; *Style—* The Rt Hon Ratu Sir Kamisese Mara, GCMG, KBE; 6 Berkeley Crescent, Domain, Suva, Fiji

MARA, Prof Timothy Nicholas (Tim); *b* 27 Sept 1948; *Educ* Epsom and Ewell Sch of Art (fndn course), Wolverhampton Poly (DipAD, Stowells Trophy, BA Art award), RCA (Major Travelling scholar, MA, New Contemporaries award); *Career* artist; lectr in printmaking: Nat Coll of Art & Design 1976-78, Brighton Poly 1978-79; princ lectr in printmaking Chelsea Sch of Art London 1980; visiting lectr 1976- (numerous art schs and colls incl RCA, Slade, Ruskin, Central, Newcastle Poly); external examiner: Nat Coll of Art & Design Dublin 1983-87, Falmouth Sch of Art 1984-87, Staffordshire Poly 1988-91, Glasgow Sch of Art 1988-91, Limerick Coll of Art 1990-; artist in residence Br Sch at Rome 1984; solo exhibitions: Birmingham Arts Lab 1974, ICA London 1976, Project Arts Centre Dublin 1977, Wolverhampton Municipal Art Gallery 1977, Nuffield Gallery Southampton Univ 1978, Thumb Gallery 1980, David Hendrik's Gallery Dublin 1981, Oxford Gallery 1986, Angela Flowers Gallery London 1988, Drumcroon Arts Centre Wigan 1988, The Black Prints (Flowers East) London 1990, The Graphic Studio Dublin Eire 1991; numerous gp exhibitions incl (most recently): The Ties That Bind, The Family in Contemporary Art (Univ of Strathclyde Glasgow and tour) 1987-88, Open Print Competition (Bankside Gallery, London) 1988, Leicestershire CC Exhibition Loughborough 1988, Figuratively Speaking (Bankside Gallery London) 1989, Angela Flowers 20 Year Anniversary Exhibition (Barbican Arts Centre) 1989-90; work exhibited in numerous international exhibitions; prints in the collections of: V&A Museum, Arts Cncl of GB, Br Cncl, Tate Gallery, Brooklyn Museum NY, Nat Art Gallery Wellington NZ, Wakefield Art Gallery Bath, Rank, Zerox, BBC, J Walter Thompson, Collet Dickinson and Pearce; *Clubs* Chelsea Arts; *Style—* Prof Tim Mara; Royal College of Art, Kensington Gore, London SW7 2EU (☎ 071 584 5020 ext 253)

MARAN, Prof Arnold George Dominic; s of John Maran (d 1969), of Edinburgh, and Hilda, *née* Mancini (d 1984); *b* 16 June 1936; *Educ* Daniel Stewarts Coll Edinburgh, Univ of Edinburgh (MB ChB); *m* 25 April 1962, Anna Marie Terese; 1 s (Charles Mark Damien b 1965), 1 da (Dr Nicola Jane b 1963); *Career* prof of otolaryngology Univ of Edinburgh; author of over 100 scientific papers; hon sec RCSE(d), pres laryngology section RSM; FRCS 1963, FACS 1974, FRCP 1988; *Books* Clinical Otolaryngology (1964), Head and Neck Surgery (1969), Clinical Rhinology (1990); *Recreations* music, golf, travel; *Clubs* New (Edinburgh), Royal & Ancient Golf (St Andrews); *Style—* Prof Arnold Maran; 15 Cluny Drive, Edinburgh, Scotland (☎ 031 447 8519); 2 Double Dykes Rd, St Andrews (☎ 03347 2939); 14 Moray Place, Edinburgh (☎ 031 225 8025)

MARANGOS, Anthony C; s of John Anthony Marangos, and Peggy D, *née* Swinden; *b* 9 July 1943; *Educ* Stone Ho, Cheltenham Coll; 1 s (Nicholas b 1972), 2 da (Natacha b 1987, Alexandra b 1987); *Career* served HAC 2 Lt; md: Laura Ashley 1974-81, ACM Marketing 1981-84, Cartier Ltd 1984; Young and Rubican; chm and md Herbert Johnson Ltd 1990-; memb Cncl: French C of C, Bond St Assoc, Goldsmith; Freeman City of London; *Recreations* riding, tennis, clocks; *Clubs* Brooks, RTYC; *Style—* Anthony Marangos, Esq; Herbert Johnson Ltd, 30 New Bond Street, London W1 (☎ 071 494 1405)

MARANZANO, Alexander Mario (Alex); s of Michele Luciano Maranzano, and Iole, *née* Iannamico; *b* 27 Nov 1943; *Educ* Royal Coll of Art (MD), Camberwell Coll of Art (Nat Dip in Design); *m* 14 Sept 1968, Rosemary Jean, da of Dennis Norman Licence; 3 s (Damian Paul b 27 Sept 1970 d 1989, Michael Anthony b 15 May 1976, James

William b 25 May 1979), 1 da (Sonia Elisa b 13 May 1972); *Career* designer; Minale Tattersfield & Partners Ltd: joined 1968, ptnr and dep md 1983, md 1988-; gold award for Fox Corp Identify Design NY 1976, silver award Designers and Arts Dirs Club London for Heathrow Subways 1978, designed Central TV Symbol 1982, most outstanding graphics silver for PO applied design 1984, designed concept for Br Airports Exhibition currently in Museum of Modern Art NY; memb Exec Ctee Designers and Art Dirs Club 1985-87; FCSD; *Style—* Alex Maranzano, Esq; Minale Tattersfield & Partners Ltd, The Courtyard, 37 Sheen Rd, Richmond, Surrey TW9 1AJ (☎ 081 948 7999, fax 071 731 7768, telex 8953130)

MARCELL, Philip Michael; s of Stanley Marcell (d 1972), and Mabel Isobel Thomas, *née* Coe; *b* 21 Aug 1936; *Educ* Wimbledon Coll, Britannia RNC Dartsmouth, RNC Greenwich, Univ of London (LLB), Cambridge (postgrad res); *m* 22 Dec 1962, Lucina Mary, da of Capt Ernest May (d 1978); 1 s (Andrew b 1967), 3 da (Susannah b 1964, Virginia b 1965, Harriet b 1973); *Career* RN cadet BRNC Dartmouth 1952-54, Midshipman 1955, Sub Lt 1956, Lt 1958, Lt Cdr 1966, Cdr 1972; dir Jardines Insurance Brokers 1980 (co sec 1978-), chief exec American Reinsurance Co (UK) Ltd 1983; chm: Continental Reinsurance London (Continental Reinsur Corp (UK) Ltd, Unionamerica Insurance Co Ltd) 1986-; memb exec ctee Reinsurance Offices Assoc 1985-; Freeman Worshipful Co of Chartered Secs and Admins; FIFA 1977, MBIM 1978, FCIS 1987; *Recreations* squash, sailing; *Clubs* Utd Oxford & Cambridge; *Style—* Philip Marcell, Esq; Weavers End, Church Lane, Haslemere, Surrey GU27 2BJ (☎ 0428 651421); 77 Gracechurch Street, London EC3 ODA (☎ 071 548 5952, fax 071 929 3160, telex 883148)

MARCH, Sir Derek Maxwell; KBE (1988, CBE 1982, OBE 1973); s of Frank George March, (d 1963), of Plymouth, and Vera Winifred, *née* Ward (d 1989); *b* 9 Dec 1930; *Educ* Devonport HS for Boys, Birkbeck Coll London; *m* 4 June 1955, Sally Annetta, da of Alfred Riggs (d 1964), of Walsall, Staffs; 1 s (Michael b 1956), 2 da (Judith b 1957, Sarah b 1959); *Career* Nat Serv RAF 1949-51; joined HM Dip Serv 1949, Foreign Office 1951, Br Embassy Bonn 1955, HM vice consul Hanover 1957, asst trade cmmr Salisbury 1959, HM consul Dakar 1962, first sec Foreign Office 1964, first sec Rawalpindi 1968, first sec Peking 1971, first sec Foreign and Cwlth Office 1974, cnsllr Dept of Trade 1975, sr Br trade cmmr Hong Kong 1977, cnsllr DOI 1982, Br High Cmmr Kampala 1986, ret 1990; *Recreations* cricket, golf, reading history; *Clubs* East India, MCC, Hong Kong; *Style—* Sir Derek March, KBE; Soke House, The Soke, Alresford Hants SO24 9DB (☎ 0962 732558)

MARCH, Peter Reginald; s of Edwin Charles March (d 1987), of Bristol, and Alice Gladys, *née* Cave (d 1988); *b* 23 March 1940; *Educ* Bristol GS, Redland Coll, Univ of Bristol (ACE, DipEd); *m* 25 Aug 1962, Christine Ann, da of Ernest William Clark (d 1979), of Poole, Dorset; 2 s (Andrew b 1965, Daniel b 1972), 2 da (Alison b 1967, Rachel b 1974); *Career* contrib ed Aircraft Illustrated 1968-; Careers Res and Advsy Centre 1972, princ careers advsr Co of Avon 1974-87, managing ed RAF Benevolent Funds IAT Publishing 1987-; ed: Air Display International 1987-, RAF Yearbook, USAFE Yearbook, RAF Action Special 1988-; aviation correspondent HTV West 1989-, mangr RAF Benevolent Fund IAT, memb West of England Educn Ctee HTV; dir: Bristol and Wessex Aeroplane Club, Disabled Flyers Gp; *Books* 17+ Decisions - Your Choice Beyond School, Military Aircraft Markings (1978), Preserved Aircraft (1980), Your Choice at 16+ (1986); *Recreations* private flying, photography; *Clubs* Bristol & Wessex Aeroplane; *Style—* Peter March, Esq; PO Box 46, Westbury-on-Tyrm, Bristol BS9 1TF (☎ 0272 685193, fax 0272 683928)

MARCH, Prof Philip Vincent; s of Arthur Philip March (d 1965), of Gwent, and Violet Ethel, *née* Webb (d 1966); *b* 16 Aug 1929; *Educ* Univ of Birmingham (BSc, PhD); *m* 17 Sept 1955, Margaret Jean, da of William Hall Lewis, of Solihill; 2 s (Peter b 1956, David b 1957), 1 da (Rosemary b 1959); *Career* Nat Serv RAF 1947-49; lectr in physics Univ of Glasgow 1956-62; Westfield Coll London: lectr in physics 1962-65, reader in physics 1965-71, prof of physics 1971-84; dean of sci Royal Holloway and Bedford New Coll 1988- (prof of physics 1984-); FInstP; *Recreations* skiing, squash, opera, travel; *Style—* Prof Philip March; Royal Holloway and Bedford New Coll, Egham Hill, Egham, Surrey (☎ 0784 434455)

MARCH AND KINRARA, Earl of; Charles Henry Gordon Lennox; o s and h of 10 Duke of Richmond and (4 Duke of) Gordon, *qv*; *b* 8 Jan 1955; *Educ* Eton; *m* 1976 (m dis 1989), Sally, da of late Maurice Clayton, and Mrs Dennis Irwin; 1 da (Lady Alexandra b 1985); *Style—* Earl of March and Kinrara; Goodwood, Chichester, Sussex

MARCH PHILLIPPS DE LISLE, Hon Mrs (Aubyn Cecilia); *née* Hovell-Thurlow-Cumming-Bruce; da of 8 Baron Thurlow, KCMG; *b* 1958; *Educ* Westonbirt School, Univ of Exeter; *m* Frederick March Phillipps de Lisle; 2 s (James b 1987, Ralph b 1989); *Career* mktg conslt; *Recreations* reading, skiing, theatre, stalking, painting; *Style—* The Hon Mrs Frederick March Phillips de Lisle; 2 St Stephen's Terrace, London SW8

MARCHANT, Graham Leslie; s of Leslie Marchant (d 1989), and Dorothy, *née* Wood; *b* 2 Feb 1945; *Educ* King's Sch Worcester, Selwyn Coll Cambridge (MA); *Career* admin: Actor's Co 1973-75, Tricycle Theatre 1983-84; gen mangr English Music Theatre 1975-78, gen admin Opera North 1978-82, md Playhouse Theatre Co 1984-86, dir arts coordination Arts Cncl GB 1986-89, head of site improvement South Bank Centre 1989-; *Recreations* gardening, reading; *Style—* Graham Marchant, Esq; 142 Elsley Road, Battersea, London SW11 5LH (☎ 081 960 6914); South Bank Centre, Royal Festival Hall, London SE1 8XX (☎ 071 921 0936, fax 071 928 0063, telex 929 226 SBB G)

MARCHANT, Philip Lester; s of Frederick Marchant (d 1984), of Theydon Bois, Essex, and Marjorie Marchant, *née* Fuller; *b* 7 Sept 1944; *Educ* King's Coll Taunton; *m* 30 Nov 1968, Helen Shirley, da of Stanley Lawrence Middleton, of Melbourne, Australia; 3 s (Simon b 1972, James b 1974, Robert b 1979); *Career* co dir: Marchant Manufacturing Co Ltd 1975-, Castle St Devpts Ltd 1981-, Haverhill Trg Servs Ltd 1986-; *Recreations* golf; *Clubs* IOD; *Style—* Philip L Marchant, Esq; Camps Hall, Castle Camps, Cambridgeshire CB1 6TP (☎ 079 984265); Marchant Manufacturing Co Ltd, Piperell Way, Haverhill, Suffolk CB9 8QW (☎ 0440 705351)

MARCHWOOD, 3 Viscount (UK 1945); Sir David George Staveley Penny; 3 Bt (UK 1933); also Baron Marchwood (UK 1937); s of 2 Viscount Marchwood, MBE (d 1979), and Pamela, *née* Colton Fox; *b* 22 May 1936; *Educ* Winchester; *m* 1964, Tessa Jane, da of Wilfred Francis Norris, of Chiddingfold, Surrey; 3 s (Hon Peter, Hon Nicholas b 1967, Hon Edward b 1970); *Heir* s, Hon Peter George Worsley Penny b 8 Oct 1965; *Career* 2 Lt, Royal Horse Gds (The Blues) in UK and Cyprus 1955-57; former dir of various cos in Cadbury Schweppes Gp; md Moët & Chandon (London) Ltd; dir other cos in Moët Hennessy Gp; *Recreations* cricket, shooting, racing; *Clubs* White's, Twelve, MCC; *Style—* The Rt Hon the Viscount Marchwood; Filberts, Aston Tirrold, nr Didcot, Oxon (☎ 0235 850386); 5 Buckingham Mews, London SW1 (☎ 071 828 2678)

MARCKUS, Hon Mrs (Rachel); *née* King; o da of Baron King of Wartnaby (Life Peer); *b* 1945; *m* 1, 1968 (m dis 1974), Michael Gibson; m 2, 1980 (m dis 1985), Guy Henry René Bondonneau, of Paris; m 3, 1987, Melvyn Marckus; *Style—* The Hon Rachel Marckus; 25 Waterford Road, London SW6 2DJ

MARCOW, Hon Mrs (Hannah Olive); da of 1 Baron Marks of Broughton (d 1964); *b* 1918; *m* 1, 1941 (m dis 1959), Dr Alec Lerner; 1 s (Joel David b 1942, m 1982 Deborah, da of C Travers, of Woking), 2 da (Diana b 1947, Maureen b 1952); m 2, 1960, Gerald William Harold Marcow; *Style—* The Hon Mrs Marcow

MARCUS, Frank Ulrich; s of Frederick James Marcus (d 1963), of London, and Gerda, *née* Marcuse (d 1981); *b* 30 June 1928; *Educ* Bunce Ct Sch Kent and Shropshire, St Martins Sch of Art; *m* 8 July 1951, Jacqueline Ruth, da of Philip Silvester (d 1979), of London; 1 s (Paul b 1954), 2 da (Joanna b 1956, Julia b 1961); *Career* playwright and critic; plays: The Formation Dancers (1964), The Killing of Sister George (1965), Cleo (1965), Studies of the Nude (1966), Mrs Mouse Are You Within (1968), Notes on a Love Affair (1971), Beauty and the Beast (1975); numerous other plays for TV and Radio; translations of: Schnitzler, Molnar, Hauptmann, Kaiser; drama critic: London Magazine 1965-68, Sunday Telegraph 1968-78; TV critic on Plays Internat 1983-, former memb Drama Panel of Arts Cncl; memb Soc of Authors, hon life memb Critics Circle; *Recreations* cats; *Style—* Frank Marcus, Esq; 8 Kirlegate, Meare, Glastonbury, Somerset BA6 9TA (☎ 045 86 398); c/o Margaret Ramsay Ltd, 14 Goodwins Court, St Martins Lane, London WC2N 4LL (☎ 071 240 0691)

MARCUS, Martin Alan; s of Sydney Marcus; *b* 12 Jan 1948; *Educ* Wanstead Co HS; *m* 1971, Cheryl Natalie, da of Dr Benjamin Green; 2 s; *Career* dep chm and jt md Queens Moat Houses plc; tstee and treas British SLE Aid Gp; FCA; *Recreations* golf, tennis, table tennis; *Clubs* Abridge Golf, Woodford Golf, Woodford Wells Crostyx and Tennis; *Style—* Martin Marcus, Esq; Queens Moat Houses plc, Queens Court 9-17, Eastern Rd, Romford, Essex, RM1 3NG

MARCUS, Steven David; s of Gerald Marcus, of Bushey, Herts, and Joan Kasmir; *b* 5 Oct 1951; *Educ* Merchant Taylors', Univ of Nottingham (BSc); *m* 5 Sept 1979, Madeleine, da of Godfrey Lee; *Career* Grant and Partners 1973-76 (jr negotiator, sr negotiator), Jones Lang Wootton 1976-78, assoc Allsop & Co 1978-84, currently exec dir Druce & Co (ptnr 1984); FRICS (prof assoc 1979); *Style—* Steven Marcus, Esq; Druce & Co, 21 Manchester Square, London W1A 2DD (☎ 071 486 1252, fax 071 486 9366)

MAREK, Dr John; MP (Lab) Wrexham 1983-; *b* 24 Dec 1940; *Educ* King's Coll London (BSc, PhD); *m* 1964, Anne, da of R H Pritchard; *Career* lectr in applied mathematics Univ Coll Wales Aberystwyth 1966-83; *Style—* Dr John Marek, MP; House of Commons, London SW1A 0AA (☎ 071 219 6347)

MARFFY, Hon Mrs (Pelline Margot); *née* Lyon-Dalberg-Acton; eldest da of 3 Baron Acton, CMG, MBE, TD (d 1989); *b* 24 Dec 1932; *m* 30 June 1953, Laszlo de Marffy von Versegh, s of Elemer de Marffy von Versegh; 7 s (1 decd), 1 da; *Style—* The Hon Mrs Marffy; Ealing Farm, PO Box 29, Umvukwes, Zimbabwe

MARGADALE, 1 Baron (UK 1964); John Granville Morrison; TD (1944), JP (Wilts 1936), DL (Wilts 1983); s of Hugh Morrison, MP, JP, DL (d 1931), and Lady Mary Leveson-Gower (d 1934, 2 da of 2 Earl Granville by his 2 w Castalia, yst da of Walter Campbell of Islay); *b* 16 Dec 1906; *Educ* Eton, Magdalene Coll Cambridge; *m* 1928, Hon Margaret Esther Lucie Smith, JP (d 1980), da of 2 Viscount Hambleden (d 1928); 3 s (James, Charles, Peter, *qqv*), 1 da (Mary, *qv*); *Heir* s, Maj Hon James Ian Morrison, TD, DL; *Career* served WWII with Royal Wilts Yeo (M East), Hon Col Royal Wilts Yeo, RAC (TA) 1960-72 and Royal Yeo; Cmdt Yeomanries until 1972; master South and W Wilts foxhounds 1932-65; High Sheriff Wilts 1938, DL Wilts 1950-69, Lord Lt Wilts 1969-81; MP (C) Salisbury 1942-64, chm 1922 Ctee 1955-64, pres Br Field Sports Soc 1980-; KStJ; *Recreations* hunting, shooting, fishing, racing; *Clubs* Pratt's, White's, Turf, Jockey; *Style—* The Rt Hon the Lord Margadale, TD, JP, DL; Eallabus, Bridgend, Islay, Argyll (☎ 049 681 223); Fonthill Ho, Tisbury, Salisbury, Wilts SP3 5SA (☎ 0747 870202); 55 Westminster Gardens, London

MARGESSON, 2 Viscount (UK 1942); Francis Vere Hampden Margesson; s of 1 Viscount, PC, MC (d 1965, whose mother was Lady Isabel Hobart-Hampden, JP, 3 da of 7 Earl of Buckinghamshire); *b* 1922; *Educ* Eton, Trinity Coll Oxford; *m* 1958, Helena Backstrom, of Oulu, Finland; 1 s, 3 da; *Heir* s, Capt the Hon Richard Francis David Margesson, Coldstream Guards; *Career* late ADC to Govr Bahamas, dir Thames & Hudson Publications Inc of N Y; Sub-Lt RNVR 1942-45; info offr Br Consulate-Gen N Y 1964-70; *Style—* The Rt Hon the Viscount Margesson; Ridgely Manor, Box 245, Stone Ridge, New York, NY 12484, USA

MARGESSON, Capt Hon Richard Francis David; s and h of 2 Viscount Margesson; *b* 25 Dec 1960; *Educ* St Paul's Sch New Hampshire USA, Eton, Exeter Univ; *m* 15 Dec 1990, Wendy Maree, da of James Hazelton, of Kempsey, NSW, Australia; *Career* cmmnd Coldstream Guards 1983; *Style—* Capt the Hon Richard Margesson; Cheney Cottage, 7 Glovers Lane, Middleton Cheney, Oxon OX17 2NU

MARGETSON, Sir John William Denys; KCMG (1986, CMG 1979); s of The Very Rev W J Margetson (d 1946), and Marian, *née* Jenoure (d 1937); *b* 9 Oct 1927; *Educ* Blundell's, St John's Coll Cambridge (MA); *m* 1963, Miranda, da of Sir William Coldstream; 1 s (Andrew b 1965), 1 da (Clare b 1967); *Career* Lt Life Gds 1947-49; dist offr Tanganyika Colonial Serv 1951-60 (private sec to Govr 1956-57); Dip Serv 1960-87: The Hague 1962-64, speech writer for sec Rt Hon George Brown MP 1966-68, head of chancery Saigon 1968-70, seconded to Cabinet Secretariat 1971-74; head of chancery UK Delgn to NATO 1974-78, ambass Vietnam 1978-80, seconded to MOD as sr civilian instr Royal Coll of Def Studies 1980-82, ambass and dep perm rep UN NY 1983-84, pres UN Tsteeship Cncl 1983-84, ambass Netherlands 1984-87; dir John S Cohen Fndn 1988-, chm Royal Sch of Church Music 1988-, chm Foster Parents Plan (UK) 1988-90, chm Yehudi Menuhin Sch 1990-, patron Suffolk Int Trade Gp 1988-90, jt pres Suffolk and SE Cambridgeshire 1992 Club 1988-90; *Recreations* music, the arts; *Clubs* Brooks's; *Style—* Sir John Margetson, KCMG; c/o Coutts & Co, 1 Old Park Lane, London W1Y 4BS

MARGO, David Philip; s of Gerald Margo, of 4 The Grove, Bexleyheath, Kent, and Rene, *née* Goldstein; *b* 14 May 1951; *Educ* Chislehurst and Sidcup GS for Boys; *m* 14 Nov 1976, Lezley Susan, da of Maurice Kaye, of 43 Bath Hill Court, Bournemouth, Dorset; 1 s (Alexi Nicholas b 1981), 2 da (Jodi Rochelle b 1980, Kerri Mirian b 1984); *Career* admitted slr 1975; ptnr Saunders Sobell Leigh & Dobin; memb Law Soc; *Recreations* bridge, swimming; *Style—* David Margo, Esq

MARGRETT, David Basil; s of Basil Stanley Margrett, of Yelverton, Devon, and Kathleen Hilda Nellie, *née* Hayter; *b* 25 Oct 1953; *Educ* Plymouth Poly; *m* 15 March 1985, Pauline Annette, da of Donald Lowe; 1 s (Charles); *Career* dir Lowndes Lambert UK Ltd 1982 (md 1986), dir Lowndes Lambert Gp Ltd 1987; ACII; *Style—* David Margrett, Esq; 98 Priory Gardens, Highgate, London N6 5QT; Lowndes Lambert House, 53 Eastcheap, London EC3P 3HL (☎ 071 283 2000, fax 071 283 1927)

MARGRIE, Victor Robert; CBE (1984); s of Robert Margrie, of London, and Emily Miriam, *née* Corbett; *b* 29 Dec 1929; *Educ* Southgate Co GS, Hornsey Sch of Art (now Middx Poly, NDD, ATD); *m* 1955, Janet, *née* Smithers; 3 da (Joanna b 19 Oct 1959, Kate b 26 Dec 1961, Miriam b 10 Sept 1963); *Career* own workshop 1952-71, pt/t teaching London Colls of Art and Design 1952-56, head of ceramics and sculpture Harrow Sch of Art 1956-71 (fndr studio pottery course 1963); solo exhibitions Crafts Centre of GB (now Contemporary Applied Arts): 1964, 1966, 1968; prof RCA 1984-85; studio potter, critic and teacher 1985-; external advsr: Dept of Ceramics Bristol Poly 1987-, Goldsmiths' Coll London Univ 1989-; memb Bd Studies in Fine Art Univ of

London 1989; memb Faculty of Visual Arts Banff Centre for the Arts Alberta 1988-, sec Crafts Advsy Ctee 1971-77, dir Crafts Cncl 1977-84; memb: Advsy Cncl Victoria and Albert Museum 1979-84, Ctee for Art and Design CNAA 1981-84, Fine Art Advsy Ctee Br Cncl 1983-86, UK Nat Cmmn UNESCO 1984-85; govr Loughborough Coll of Art and Design 1984-, memb Craft Initiative Gulbenkian Fndn 1985-89; memb: Craftsmen Potters Assoc 1960-89, Int Acad of Ceramics 1971, FCSD 1975; *Books* contrib: Europaischt Keramik Seit 1950-79 (1979), Oxford Dictionary of Decorative Arts (1975), Lucie Rie (1981); *Recreations* cooking; *Style—* Victor Margrie, Esq, CBE; Bowlders, Doccombe, Moretonhampstead, Devon TQ13 8SS (☎ 0647 40264)

MARIO, Ernest; *b* 12 June 1938; *Educ* Rutgers Coll of Pharmacy (BSc), Univ of Rhode Island Kingston (MA, PhD); *m* ; 3 s; *Career* Squibb Corp Princeton New Jersey: vice pres of manufacturing US Pharmaceutical Div ER Squibb & Sons 1977, vice pres and gen mangr Chemical Div 1979, pres Chemical Div and Engrg Div and sr vice pres ER Squibb & Sons 1981, chm and chief exec offr Squibb Medical Products 1983, memb Parent Bd 1984; Glaxo Holdings plc: pres and chief operating offr Glaxo Inc US 1986, memb Bd April 1988, chm and chief exec offr Glaxo Inc (with responsibility for Glaxo Canada Inc and Glaxo Latin America incl July 1988, chief exec 1989; chm US Nat Fndn for Infectious Diseases, vice chm American Fndn for Pharmaceutical Educn, memb N Carolina Inst of Med, former chm President's Cncl American Lung Assoc; tstee Duke Univ, memb Business Sch Bd of Visitors Univ of N Carolina, memb President's Cncl Univ of Rhode Island; tstee Fndn: Univ of Rhode Island, Rutgers Univ pharmacy fac advsr: Coll of Pharmacy Rutgers Univ; *Style—* Dr Ernest Mario; Glaxo Holdings plc, Lansdowne House, Berkeley Square, London W1X 6BP (☎ 071 493 4060, fax 071 408 0228, telex 25456)

MARJORIBANKS, Sir James Alexander Milne; KCMG (1965, CMG 1954); s of Rev Thomas Marjoribanks of that Ilk, DD (d 1947); *b* 29 May 1911; *Educ* Edinburgh Acad, Univ of Edinburgh (MA), Univ of Strasbourg; *m* 1936, Sonya Patricia Stanley Alder (d 1981); 1 da; *Career* HM Dip Serv 1934-71: asst under sec of state FCO 1962-65, ambass to EEC Euro Atomic Energy Community and ECSC 1965-71; dir The Distillers Co 1971-76; chm Scot in Europe 1979-90; vice-pres Scottish Cncl (devpt and indust) 1971-83; governing memb Inveresk Res Fndn 1979-89; Europe Medal 1973; *Recreations* mountaineering; *Clubs* Scot Mountaineering, New (Edinburgh); *Style—* Sir James Marjoribanks, KCMG; 13 Regent Terrace, Edinburgh, Scotland EH7 5BN (☎ 031 556 3872); Lintonrig, Kirk Yetholm, Kelso, Roxburghshire, Scotland TD5 8PH (☎ 057 382 384)

MARK, Jan Marjorie; da of Colin Dennis Brisland, and Marjorie, *née* Harrow; *b* 22 June 1943; *Educ* Ashford County GS, Canterbury Coll of Art; *m* 1 March 1969 (m dis 1989), Neil John Mark; 1 s (Alexander b 1974, Isobel b 1969); *Career* writer; freelance 1975-, writer fell Oxford Poly 1982-84; books: Thunder & Lightnings (1976), The Ennead (1978), Divide and Rule (1979), Aquarius (1982), Feet (1983), Handles (1984), Zeno Was Here (1987), Enough is Too Much Already (1988), A Can of Worms (1990); Penguin/Guardian award 1975, Library Assoc Carnegie medal 1976 and 1983, Rank/ Observer award 1982, Angel award for fiction 1983 and 1987; *Recreations* gardening; *Style—* Ms Jan Mark; 98 Howard St, Oxford OX4 3BG (☎ 0865 727702); c/o Murray Pollinger, 222 Old Brompton Rd, London SW5 0BZ (☎ 071 373 4711, fax 071 373 3775)

MARK, (John) Richard Anthony; s of John Mark, and Dorothy, *née* White; *b* 20 Jan 1946; *Educ* Clifton, Magdalene Coll Cambridge (MA); *m* 1, 30 Sept 1972 (m dis 1979), Angela Mary, da of Jeffrey Holroyd; 1 s (James b 1975), 1 da (Clare b 1973); m 2, 31 March 1983, Diane Virginia, *née* Roberts; 1 da (Isabel b 1985); *Career* Peat Marwick Mitchell & Co 1967-73, Br Linen Bank 1973-77, Carolina Bank Ltd (now Panmure Gordon Bankers Ltd) 1977-; FCA 1970; *Style—* Richard Mark, Esq; 108 Somerset Rd, London SW19 (☎ 081 947 1496); Panmure Gordon, 14 Moorfields Highwalk, London EC2 (☎ 071 638 4010)

MARK, Sir Robert; GBE (1977), QPM (1965); s of John Mark (d 1962); *b* 13 March 1917; *Educ* William Hulme's GS Manchester, Univ of Oxford (MA); *m* 1941, Kathleen Mary, da of William Leahy (d 1977); 1 s (Christopher), 1 da (Christina); *Career* served WWII RAC, Maj, NW Europe 1942-47; chief constable Leicester 1957-67, cmmr London Metropolitan Police 1972-77 (dep cmmr 1968-72); dir Phoenix Assurance Co 1977-85, chm Forest Mere Ltd 1978-, dir Control Risks Ltd 1979-87; Dimbleby TV Lecture 1973; govr and memb Admin Bd Corps of Commissionaires 1977-86; KStJ 1977; Hon LLM Leicester 1967, Hon DLitt Loughborough 1976; Hon LLD: Manchester 1978, Liverpool 1978; kt (1973); *Publications* Policing a Perplexed Society (1977), In the Office of Constable (1978); *Style—* Sir Robert Mark, GBE, QPM; Esher, Surrey KT10 8LU

MARKER, William Bennett; s of William Marker (d 1983), of Greenock, and Jean, *née* Hamilton (d 1980); *b* 5 Feb 1928; *Educ* Ulverston GS, Wadham Coll Oxford (MA), Univ of Durham (MEd); *m* 29 Aug 1959, Anne Margaret, da of George Manthorpe (d 1975), of Blaydon; 1 s (Alasdair b 1964), 1 da (Alison b 1962); *Career* Flying Offr RAF Educn Branch 1949-52; sr history master Queen Elizabeth Sch Kirkby Lonsdale 1958-67, schoolmaster fell Univ of Hull 1967, asst princ Jordanhill Coll 1976-86 (lectr 1967-72, princ lectr 1972-75), field offr Scot Ctee for Staff Devpt in Educn 1987-; memb: Nat Ctee for Inservice Training of Teachers 1976-85, Scot Cncl for the Validation of Courses for Teachers 1983-86; *Recreations* hill-walking, theatre-going; *Clubs* fell and rock climbing; *Style—* William Marker, Esq; 2 Huntly Drive, Bearsden, Glasgow G61 3LD (☎ 041 942 6756)

MARKHAM, Betty, Lady; (Frederica) Betty Cornwallis Crawford; da of late Hon Christian Edward Cornwallis Eliot, OBE; *m* 1942, as his 3 w, Sir Charles Markham, 2 Bt (d 1952); *Style—* Betty, Lady Markham; P O Box 583, Mbabane, Swaziland

MARKHAM, Sir Charles John; 3 Bt (UK 1911), of Beachborough Park, Newington, Kent; s of Sir Charles Markham, 2 Bt (d 1952); *b* 2 July 1924; *Educ* Eton; *m* 1949, Valerie, da of Lt-Col E Barry-Johnston, of Kenya; 2 s, 1 da; *Heir* s, (Arthur) David Markham; *Career* served 1943-47, Lt 11 Hussars (despatches); MLC Kenya 1955-60; KStJ; *Style—* Sir Charles Markham, Bt; PO Box 15096, Nairobi, Kenya (☎ 891 182)

MARKHAM, (Arthur) David; s and h of Sir Charles John Markham, 3 Bt; *b* 6 Dec 1950; *m* 1977, Carolyn, da of Capt Mungo Park, of The Lodge, Carraig Breac, Baily, Co Dublin; 2 da; *Style—* David Markham Esq; PO Box 42263, Nairobi, Kenya

MARKHAM, Frederick Charles Theodore; s of The Rev Canon Gervase William Markham, of Penrith, Cumbria, and Barbara Mary, *née* Dalzell Banks; *b* 6 July 1949; *Educ* Winchester, Trinity Coll Cambridge (MA), Univ of Lancaster (MA); *m* 25 Sept 1976, Suzanna Pauline, da of Major Ian Steel, MC, of Kirkwood, Lockerbie Dumfriesshire; 3 s (Gervase b 1978, Arthur b 1980, Francis b 1986), 1 da (Diana b 1982); *Career* Hoare Govett Ltd: Stockbroker 1973-76, funding conslt 1978-80; mktg dir Survival Aids Ltd 1980-87, chm and md Travelling Light 1987-; cncllr Eden DC 1989, memb Fin and Gen Purposes Ctee County Landowners Assoc 1989; FRGS 1980, FInstD 1985; *Recreations* shooting, architecture, family life; *Clubs* Lansdowne; *Style—* Frederick Markham, Esq; Morland House, Morland, Penrith, Cumbria CA10 3AZ (☎ 09314 488, fax 09314 555)

MARKHAM, (Arthur) Geoffrey; s of Col Frank Stanley Markham (d 1978), of Huddersfield, and Emma Woodhouse, *née* Spurr (d 1983); *b* 27 Sept 1927; *Educ* Giggleswick Sch, Univ of Leeds (LLB); *m* 26 Sept 1959, Patricia, da of John James Holliday (d 1935) of Barnsley, Yorks; 1 s (Jonathan b 1962), 1 da (Sarah b 1966); *Career* admitted slr 1949, sr ptnr Raley and Pratt Barnsley 1967-89, conslt Raleys Barnsley 1990-; chm Soc Security Appeal Tribunal 1981-; historian; memb Law Soc 1949-; *Books* Woolley Hall, The Historical Development of a Country House (1979); *Recreations* reading, writing, music, freemasonry, gardening; *Style—* Geoffrey Markham, Esq; Petwood House, Woolley, Wakefield WF4 2JJ (☎ 0226 382495); 5 Regent St, Barnsley S70 2EF (☎ 0226 733777, fax 0226 731829)

MARKHAM, Rev Canon Gervase William; s of Algernon Augustus Markham, Bishop of Grantham (d 1949), of Stoke Rectory, Grantham, and Winifred Edith, *née* Barne; *b* 7 Nov 1910; *Educ* Bramcote Sch Scarborough, Winchester, Trinity Coll Cambridge (MA); *m* 29 Aug 1945, Barbara Mary Dalziel, da of Rev Bennet Banks (d 1953), of Barnham Broom Rectory, Norwich; 1 s (Frederick b 6 July 1949), 2 da (Victoria (Mrs Singh) b 10 July 1952, Frances (Mrs Dennys) b 8 Feb 1954); *Career* Chaplain to the Forces 1940-45, 8 Army N Africa 1942, Sicily 1943, Normandy 1944; schoolmaster Bishop Gobat Sch Jerusalem 1932-34, student Westcott House Cambridge 1934-36; ordained (Durham Cathedral): deacon 1936, priest 1937; curate Bishopwearmouth Parish Church Sunderland, domestic chaplain to Bishop of Durham 1939; vicar: St Stephen's Burnley 1945, Grimsby 1952, Morland 1965-84; hon canon: Lincoln Cathedral 1955, Carlisle Cathedral 1972; fndr: Morland Choristers' Camps, Morland Festival of Village Choirs; *Recreations* book collecting, gardening, dry stone-walling; *Style—* The Rev Canon Gervase Markham; Garden Flat, Morland House, Morland, Penrith, Cumbria (☎ 09314 654)

MARKHAM, Richard; s of Charles Roberts Markham, of Grimsby, and Marion Edna, *née* Willows; *b* 23 June 1952; *Educ* Wintringham GS Grimsby, RAM London; *Career* pianist; London début as soloist with Eng Chamber Orch conducted by Raymond Leppard at Queen Elizabeth Hall 1974, has toured internationally with David Nettle (Nettle-Markham Piano Duo), also with Raphael Wallfisch (cello) and Burlington Piano Trio; solo and piano duo performances at: Royal Festival Hall, Royal Albert Hall, Barbican Hall and at princ festivals incl BBC proms; recordings incl: Kabalevsky with Raphael Wallfisch (cello) 1976; Stravinsky: The Rite of Spring and Petrushka 1984, Holst: The Planets 1985, Dyson: The Blacksmiths (with RCM Chamber Choir and RPO, 1987), Elgar: From the Bavarian Highlands and Holst: Folksongs 1987, Delius and Grainger 1988, Bernstein arranged Nettle and Markham: Scenes from West Side Story 1988, Gershwin arranged Grainger: Fantasy on Porgy and Bess 1988, Bennett: Four Piece Suite 1988, Rossini: Petite Messe Solennelle (with soloists Field, Owens, Barham, Tomlinson and CBSO chorus, 1990), South of The Border: Latin American Songs with Jill Gomez (with two pianos and NPO, 1990), Saint-Saens: Carnival of The Animals (with Aquarius, 1991); *awards* Nora Naismith scholarship 1969-72, prizewinner Geneva Int Competition 1972, Countess of Munster Musical Tst awards 1973 and 1974, Frederick Shinn fellowship 1975, Gulbenkian Fndn fellowship 1976-78; ARAM 1983; *Recreations* travelling, theatre, playing cards, naturism; *Clubs* ISM, RAM, LGS; *Style—* Richard Markham, Esq; 99 John Ruskin St, London SE5 0PQ (☎ and fax 071 708 3341)

MARKHAM, (Frank) Richard Gordon; s of Maj Sir Frank Markham, MP, DL (d 1975), of Leighton Buzzard, Beds, and Lady Frances, *née* Lawman; *b* 18 March 1939; *Educ* Bedford Modern Sch, Nat Foundry Coll; *m* 27 Sept 1969, Hazel Jean, da of PF Martin, of Dunstable, Beds; 1 da (Katharine Frances Elizabeth b 10 Sept 1978); *Career* apprentice Foundry Equipment Ltd 1957-64, ptnr Markham Robinson Planning Conslts 1964-85, land mangr Black Horse Agencies Estate Agents 1985-88, ptnr Malcolm Reay & Co Estate Agents 1988-; cncllr Leighton-Linslade UDC (chm Planning Ctee 1964-74, vice-chm 1974-75), chm South Beds DC 1975-76 (chm Planning Ctee 1975), vice chm Planning Ctee South Oxfordshire Cncl 1985 (memb 1984-); *Recreations* driving of horses, golf; *Style—* Richard Markham, Esq; Home Farm, Henton, Chinnor, Oxford OX9 4AH (☎ 0844 51369); Malcolm Reay & Co, Ipsden House, Oxford Rd, Stokenchurch, Bucks H14 3SX (☎ 024 026 4273, fax 024 026 5219)

MARKHAM, Sarah Anne Judith; da of Leonard Markham, of Tithe Farm, Renhold, Bedfordshire, and Margaret Elizabeth, *née* Joyce; *b* 25 July 1962; *Educ* Bedford HS, Oxford and County; *Career* Shuttleworth Coll staff 1981-88, Christie's Old Master picture Dept 1988-; *Recreations* riding, scuba diving, squash, travelling, wildlife conservation; *Clubs* The Farmers'; *Style—* Miss Sarah Markham; Tithe Farm, Renhold, Bedfordshire MK41 OLX (☎ 0234 771364); Christie's, 8 King St, St James's, London SW1Y 6QT (☎ 071 389 2531, fax 071 389 2209)

MARKING, Giles; s of Frank I Marking, of Lynch Farm, Corfe Castle, Wareham, Dorset, and Anne, *née* Percival; *b* 26 Dec 1947; *Educ* Duncan Hall Norfolk, Architectural Assoc Sch of Architecture (AA Dipl), Univ of Washington (M Arch); *m* 11 Sept 1971 (Margaret Judith) Stacy, da of Canon R Patteson Stacy-Waddy, of Manormead, Hindehead, Surrey; 1 da (Havana b 3 March 1972); *Career* designer Francisco and Jacobus NY 1967-68, film designer Maizin Wycoff NY 1968-70, graphic designer Inst Contemporary Arts 1971-74, lectr in architecture Univ of Washington 1975-76, visiting prof Univ Metropolitana Mexico City 1980, md (Environments) Fitch RS London 1976-; D and ADA 1986, ICSC 1987; *Books* Emergency Housing in Peru - Architectural Design; *Recreations* travel, sheep farming, India and cricket; *Style—* Giles Marking, Esq; 5 Mercer St, Covent Gdn, London WC2 (☎ 071 240 2345); The Manor, Toller Whelme, Beaminster, Dorset; 31 Rue Du Mitan-Four, Seillans, Var, France

MARKING, Sir Henry Ernest; KCVO (1978), CBE (1969), MC (1944); s of Isaac Marking; *b* 11 March 1920; *Educ* Saffron Walden GS, UCL; *Career* served WWII Sherwood Foresters (N Africa, ME, Italy); admitted slr 1948; asst slr BEA 1949 (chief exec 1964-72, chm 1971-72); memb bd: BOAC 1971-72, BA 1971-80 (md 1972-76, dep chm 1972-77); chm: Br Tourist Authy 1977-85 (memb bd 1969-77), Carreras Rothmans 1979-85, Rothmans (UK) Ltd 1985-86; dir Barclays International Ltd 1978-86, memb bd Rothman Int plc 1979-; CRAeS, FCIT, FBIM; *Clubs* Reform; *Style—* Sir Henry Marking, KCVO, CBE, MC; 6A Montagu Mews North, London W1H 1AH

MARKOVA, Dame (Lilian) Alicia Marks; DBE (1963, CBE 1958); da of Arthur Tristman Marks and Eileen Barry; *b* 1 Dec 1910; *Career* Diaghilev's Russian Ballet Co 1925-29, Rambert Ballet Club 1931-34, Vic-Wells Ballet Co 1933-35, Markova-Dolin Ballet Co 1935-37, Ballet Russe de Monte Carlo 1938-41, Ballet Theatre USA 1941-46, co fndr and prima ballerina Festival Ballet 1950-51, Br prima ballerina assoluta; guest prima ballerina: La Scala, Milan 1956, Buenos Aires 1952, Royal Ballet 1953 and 1957, Royal Danish Ballet 1955, Festival Ballet 1958 and 1959; guest appearances at Metropolitan Opera House New York 1952, 1953-54, 1955, 1957, 1958; vice pres Royal Acad of Dancing 1958-, dir Metropolitan Opera Ballet 1963-69; guest prof: Royal Ballet Sch 1973-, Paris Opera Ballet 1975, Australian Ballet Sch 1976; prof of Ballet and Performing Arts College-Conservatory of Music Univ of Cincinnati 1970-; govr Royal Ballet 1973-; pres: London Ballet Circle 1980-, English Nat Ballet and Sch 1989-; BBC series Markova's Ballet Call 1960, Masterclass BBC2 1980; Queen Elizabeth II Coronation award, Royal Acad of Dancing 1963; Hon DMus: Leicester 1966, East Anglia 1982; prof Yorkshire Ballet Seminars 1975-; pres: All England Dance Competition 1983-, London Festival Ballet 1986-, Arts Educnl Schs 1984-; *Books* Giselle and I (1960), Markova Remembers (1986); *Style—* Dame Alicia

Markova, DBE; c/o Royal Ballet School, London W14

MARKS, Hon Mrs; (Adrianne Barbara Ellis); da of Baron Stone, MB (Life Peer) (d 1986), and Beryl Florence, *née* Bernstein (d 1989); *b* 1934; *m* 1957, Clive M Marks; *Style*— The Hon Mrs Marks; 39 Farm Ave, London NW2

MARKS, Bernard Montague; OBE (1984); s of Alfred Marks (d 1942), and Elizabeth Marks (d 1972); *b* 11 Oct 1923; *Educ* Highgate, Imperial Coll London; *m* 11 Oct 1956, Norma Delphine, da of Jack Renton (d 1972); 2 s (Nicholas b 1952, Stephen b 1959); *Career* md (later chm) Alfred Marks Bureau Group of Cos 1946-84, life pres 1984-; memb Equal Opportunities Commn 1984-85, vice chm (later chm) Fedn of Personnel Services 1965-69 and 1973-82; *Recreations* bridge, golf, skiing; *Clubs* St George's Hill Golf; *Style*— Bernard Marks, Esq, OBE; Leyfield House, Onslow Road, Burwood Park, Walton-On-Thames, Surrey KT12 5AY

MARKS, David Norman; s of Alex Marks, of London, and Edna, *née* Dufman; *b* 13 Feb 1953; *Educ* Orange Hill GS Edgware Middx, LSE (BSc); *m* 22 June 1975, Selina Rachael, da of Michael Sharpe, of London; 2 s (Daniel b 1980, James b 1982); *Career* accountant; Arthur Andersen & Co 1974- (tax ptnr 1984); FCA 1978, ATII 1979; *Books* Practical Tax Saving (jtly, 1984), Tax Digest on Share Incentive Schemes for Institute of Chartered Accountants in England and Wales (1989); *Recreations* theatre, music; *Style*— David Marks, Esq, Arthur Anderson & Co, 1 Surrey St, London WC2R 2PS (☎ 01 438 3429 fax 01 831 1133); Arthur Andersen & Co, 1 Surrey St, London WC2R 2PS (☎ 071 438 3429, fax 071 831 1133)

MARKS, Geoffrey Robert; s of Nathan Marks (d 1985), and Lily, *née* Bargroff; *b* 22 Dec 1941; *Educ* Arnold Sch Blackpool, Lancaster Gate Coll of Law London (G H Charlesworth scholar, George Hadfield prize); *m* 1967, Rachel, *née* Stemmer; 2 s (Daniel Richard b 1971, John Edward b 1974), 1 da (Karen Ilana b 1969); *Career* articled clerk then ptnr A H Howarth & Co Manchester (later Howarth Goodman & Co) 1964-74; ptnr: Maurice Rubin & Co 1974-85, Halliwell Landau 1985-; former co cncllr then chm Mgmnt Ctee Gtr Manchester CC (now abolished); memb Law Soc 1963; *Recreations* the study of ancient and contemporary Hebrew, politics, theatre, family, friends; *Clubs* Manchester Anglers Assoc; *Style*— Geoffrey Marks, Esq; Hilton House, Bland Rd, Prestwich, Manchester M25 8WL (☎ 061 773 6092); Halliwell Landau, St James's Court, Brown St, Manchester M2 2JF (☎ 061 835 3003, fax 061 835 2994, car 0836 648294)

MARKS, Prof Isaac; s of Morris Norman Marks (d 1979), of Cape Town, and Anna Marks (d 1981); *b* 16 Feb 1935; *Educ* Univ of Cape Town (MB ChB, MD), Univ of London (DPM); *m* 14 Oct 1957, Shula, da of Chaim Winokur (d 1957), of Cape Town; 1 s (Rafi b 1965), 1 da (Lara b 1963); *Career* prof of experimental psychopathology Int of Psychiatry London, conslt psychiatrist Royal Bethlem Maudsley Hosp London; pres Assoc of Behavioural Clinicians; former chm: Br Assoc of Behavioural Psychotherapy, European Assoc of Behavioural Therapy; FRCPsych 1971; *Books* inter alia: Living with fear (1978), Fears Phobias and Rituals (1987); *Recreations* theatre, gardens, hiking; *Style*— Prof Isaac Marks; Institute of Psychiatry, London SE5 8AF (☎ 071 703 5411 ext 3365, fax 071 703 5796)

MARKS, Dr John Henry; s of Lewis Myer Marks (d 1960), and Rose, *née* Goldbaum (d 1986); *b* 30 May 1925; *Educ* Tottenham Co GS, Univ of Edinburgh (MB ChB, MD, DObstRCOG); *m* 17 June 1954, Shirley Evelyn, da of Alic Nathan, OBE (d 1988); 1 s (Richard), 2 da (Helen, Laura); *Career* Capt RAMC 1949-51; house physician and surgn Wembley Hosp 1948-49, sr house offr obstetrics St Martin's Hosp Bath 1951-52; clinical asst dermatology: Barnet Gen, Mount Vernon, Wat Gen Hosps; trainee asst 1952-53, asst GP 1953-54, GP Borehamwood 1954-89; chm Cncl BMA 1984-90; memb Herts CC Health Ctee, chm Herts Exec Cncl 1971-74; memb: GMC 1979-84 and 1989-, Standing Med Advsy Ctee 1984-90; MRCGP 1959, FRCGP 1975; *Recreations* modern British postal stamps, medical politics, walking, gardening; *Style*— Dr John Marks; Brown Gables, Barnet Lane, Elstree, Herts WD6 3RQ (☎ 081 953 7687); 10 Harley St, London WIN 1AA (☎ 071 636 504)

MARKS, Jonathan Clive; s of Geoffrey Jack Marks of Remenham Court, Henley-on-Thames, and Patricia Pauline, *née* Bowman; *b* 19 Oct 1952; *Educ* Harrow, Univ Coll Oxford (BA); *m* 18 Dec 1982, Sarah Ann, da of Gerald FG Russell, OBE, of Worcs; 1 s (David b 1986), 1 da (Freya b 1988); *Career* called to the Bar Inner Temple 1975; in practice Western circuit, visiting lectr in advocacy Univ Malaya Kuala Lumpur 1985, 1989 and 1990, visiting lectr in advocacy Univ of Mauritius 1988; fndr memb SDP 1981, Euro Parly candidate for Cornwall and Plymouth 1984; Parly candidate: Weston-Super-Mare 1983, Falmouth and Camborne 1987; memb Lib Democrat Ctee for England 1988-89; Freeman: City of London 1975, Worshipful Co of Pattenmakers; *Recreations* skiing, tennis, theatre, food, wine, travel; *Clubs* RAC; *Style*— Jonathan Marks, Esq; 30 Slaidburn St, London SW10 (☎ 071 351 3425); 4 Pump Ct, Temple, London EC4Y 7AN (☎ 071 353 2656, fax 071 583 2036, telex 8813250 REFLEX G)

MARKS, Paul; s of Sidney Marks, OBE, of Brecon House, The Close, Totteridge; *b* 16 Sept 1935; *Educ* Acton GS; *m* 1960, Patricia Susan; 2 children; *Career* chm M Y Hldgs plc (packaging materials); vice pres English Table Tennis Association, vice chm Br Toy & Hobby Manufacturers Assoc; *Recreations* tennis, table tennis; *Style*— Paul Marks, Esq; 48 Regents Park Road, Primrose Hill, London NW1 7SX

MARKS, Pauline; da of Jacob Noskeau, (d 1984), and Bessie, *née* Zenftman (d 1971); *b* 20 Oct 1935; *Educ* S Hampstead HS; *m* 2 May 1954, Martin Marks, s of Samuel Sidney Marks; 1 s (Stephen Harold b 17 Aug 1964), 1 da (Alison Rachel (Mrs Hirsch) b 24 Nov 1961); *Career* md Pauline Marks Direct Mktg; chm: BT 1 Int Telmarketing Conf, Telecom Aust Int Telemarketing Conf, Audiotext plc 1985; MInstM; *Books* The Telephone Marketing Book (1984), Telephone Marketing Handbook (1989); *Recreations* reading, family; *Clubs* IOD; *Style*— Mrs Pauline Marks; 3 Oldfield Mews, London N6 (☎ 081 341 4633); Pembroke House, Campsbourne Rd, London N8 (☎ 081 341 5656, fax 01 340 3269, car tel 0836 215046)

MARKS, Dr Richard Charles; s of Maj William Henry Marks (d 1982), and Jeannie Eileen, *née* Piggott (d 1979); *b* 2 July 1945; *Educ* Berkhamsted Sch, QMC (BA), Courtauld Inst of Art, Univ of London (MA, PhD); *m* 19 July 1970, Rita, da of Charlie Spratley; *Career* researcher Corpus Vitrearum Ctee Br Acad 1970-73 (currently Ctee memb), asst keeper Dept Medieval and Later Antiquities Br Museum 1973-79, keeper Burrell Collection and asst dir Glasgow Museums and Art Galleries 1979-85, dir Royal Pavilion Art Gallery and Museums Brighton 1985-; chm Gp Dirs of Museums; memb Cncl: Soc of Antiquaries, Chichester Diocesan Advsy, Conservation Sub-Ctee on Stained Glass Care of Churches, Beds Hist Records Soc; Liveryman Worshipful Co of Glaziers 1990; fell Soc of Antiquaries 1977; *Books* British Heraldry (jtly, 1978), The Golden Age of English Manuscript Painting (jtly, 1980), The Burrell Collection (jtly, 1983), Burrell Portrait of a Collector (1983 and 1988), The Glazing of the Collegiate Church of the Holy Trinity Tattershall (1984), The Souvenir Guide to the Burrell Collection (1985), Sussex Churches and Chapels (jtly, 1989); *Recreations* opera, parish churches, travelling in the Levant, cricket, rowing; *Clubs* MCC, Clydesdale Rowing, Bedford Rowing; *Style*— Dr Richard Marks; 14 Hampton Place, Brighton, E Sussex BN1 3DD; 38 High St, Wing, nr Leighton Buzzard, Beds LU7 0NR; Royal Pavilion, Art Gallery and Museums, Brighton, E Sussex BN1 1UE (☎ 0273 603005, fax 0273 779108)

MARKS, Prof Ronald; s of late Isadore Marks, and Jessie Marks; *b* 25 March 1935; *Educ* St Marylebone GS, Guy's Hospital Med Sch (BSc, MB BS); *m* 1 (m dis 1978); 2 da (Louise Anne b 17 March 1962, Naomi Suzanne b 1 Jan 1965); m 2, 11 Nov 1978, Hilary, *née* Venmore; *Career* MO short service cmmn 1960, med div Queen Alexander Mil Hosp 1961-63, specialist in dermatology Br Mil Hosp Munster W Germany 1963-65; sr lectr Inst of Dermatology and conslt dermatologist St John's Hosp for Diseases of the Skin London 1971-73; Univ of Wales Coll of Med Cardiff: sr lectr in dermotology Dept of Med 1973, reader 1977, personal chair in dermatology 1980, established chair in dermatology 1990; hon conslt in dermatology Univ Hosp of Wales 1973; lit award Soc of Cosmetic Chemists NY USA 1985; hon chm Br Assoc of Univ Teachers of Dermatology, hon chm Skin Charity to Advance Res, hon pres Int Soc for Bioengineering and the Skin; Freeman City of Besancon 1983; FRCP 1977 (memb 1964), FRCPath 1985 (MRCP 1980); *Books* Common Facial Dermatoses (1976), Investigative Techniques in Dermatology (ed, contrib, 1979), Psoriasis (1981), Acne (1984), Skin Diseases in Old Age (1987), Acne and Related Disorders (jt ed, contrib, 1989); *Recreations* visual art of the 19th and 20th centuries, playing squash; *Style*— Prof Ronald Marks; Department of Medicine, University of Wales College of Medicine, Heath Park, Cardiff CF4 4XN (☎ 0222 755944 ext 2885, fax 0222 762314)

MARKS, Prof Shula Eta; da of Chaim Winokur (d 1957), of Cape Town, and Frieda, *née* Sack; *b* 14 Oct 1938; *Educ* Univ of Cape Town (BA), Univ of London (PhD); *m* 31 March 1957, Issac Meyer Marks, s of Moses Nahman Marks (d 1979), of Cape Town; 1 s (Rafi b 26 Jan 1965), 1 da (Lara b 22 Jan 1963); *Career* Univ of London: lectr in history of Africa jtly at Inst of Cwlth Studies and SOAS 1963-76, reader in history of Southern Africa 1976-84, dir Inst of Cwlth Studies 1983-, prof of cwlth hist 1984-; conslt WHO 1977-80, chair World Univ Southern African Scholarships Ctee 1981-, govr Inst of Devpt Studies Univ of Sussex 1988-, memb Advsy Cncl on Public Records 1989-; *Books* Reluctant Rebellion: An Assessment of the 1906-08 Disturbance in Natal (1970), Economy and Society in Preindustrial Society (jtly, 1980), Industrialisation and Social Change in South Africa (jtly, 1982), The Politics of Race, Class and Nationalism in Twentieth Century South Africa (jtly, 1987); *Recreations* theatre, cinema; *Style*— Prof Shula Marks; Institute of Commonwealth Studies, 27-28 Russell Square, London WC1B 5DS (☎ 071 580 5876, fax 071 255 2160, telex 262284 Ref 3284)

MARKS, Hon Simon Richard; only s and h of 2 Baron Marks of Broughton; *b* 3 May 1950; *Educ* Eton, Balliol Coll Oxford; *m* 1982, Marion, only da of Peter F Norton, of the Azores; 1 s (Michael b 13 May 1989), 2 da (Miriam b 1983, Susannah b 1986); *Heir* s, Michael Marks; *Style*— The Hon Simon Marks; c/o Michael House, Baker St, London W1

MARKS, Prof Vincent; s of Lewis Myer Marks (d 1960), of London, and Rose, *née* Goldbaum (d 1987); *b* 10 June 1930; *Educ* Tottenham Co Sch, Brasenose Coll Oxford, St Thomas Med Sch; *m* 10 Feb 1957, Averil Rosalie, da of Maurice Sherrard (d 1965), of London; 1 s (Lewis b 27 Jan 1961), 1 da (Alexandra b 9 Sept 1959); *Career* sr lectr chemical pathology Univ of London 1961, conslt chemical pathologist Epsom 1962-70; chm: Guildhay Antisera Ltd 1984, Food and Veterinary Laboratories Ltd 1986; head Dept of Biochemistry Univ of Surrey 1986-89 (prof of clinical biochemistry 1970, dean Faculty of Sci); vice pres RCPath 1989-, pres Assoc of Clinical Biochemists 1989-; FRCPE 1957, FRCPath 1963, FRCP 1969, FIFST 1987; *Books* Scientific Foundations of Clinical Biochemistry Vol 1 and 2 (1978 and 1983), Hypoglycaemia (2 edn 1981); *Recreations* conversation; *Style*— Prof Vincent Marks; University of Surrey, Guildford GU2 5XH (☎ 0483 571281, fax 0483 576978)

MARKS OF BROUGHTON, 2 Baron (UK 1961); Michael Marks; s of 1 Baron Marks of Broughton, sometime chm and jt md Marks & Spencer (d 1964), by his w Miriam, sis of Joseph Edward Sieff (Hon Pres of M & S), and late Baron Sieff (Life Peer), who m (the first) Lord Marks of Broughton's sis) and aunt of Baron Sieff of Brimpton; *b* 27 Aug 1920; *Educ* St Paul's, CCC Cambridge; *m* 1, 1949, Ann Catherine (m dis 1958), da of Maj Richard James Pinto, MC; 1 s, 2 da; m 2, 1960, Helene (m dis 1965), da of Gustav Fischer; *Heir* s, Hon Simon Richard Marks; *Style*— The Rt Hon Lord Marks of Broughton; Michael House, Baker St, W1

MARLAND, Prof (Peter) Michael; CBE (1977); s of Albert Marland (d 1977), of London; *b* 28 Dec 1934; *Educ* Christs Hosp, Sydney Sussex Coll Cambridge (BA, MA); *m* 1, 1955, Eileen (d 1968), 4 s (Edgell b 1956 d 1990, Oliver b 1959, Timothy b 1962, Benjamin Peter b 1967), 1 da (Folly b 1956); m 2, 1972 (m dis 1977), Rose; m 3, 11 Feb 1989, Linda; *Career* teacher: Der Halephagen Oberschule Hamburg 1957-58, Simon Langston GS Canterbury 1958-61; head of eng Abbey Wood Sch London 1961-64, head of eng then dir of studies Crown Wood Sch London; headmaster: Woodberry Down Sch London 1971-79, North Westminster Sch (London's first multi-campus fd sch) 1980-; chm: Nat Textbook Reference Library, Royal Opera House Advsy Cncl, AIDS and the Tutor Working Pty; memb: Ethical Implications of AIDS Study Gp, Inst of Med Ethics, Technol Educn Project, Educn and Human Devpt Ctee ESRC, Cwth Inst Educn Ctee, Faculty of Community Med, Nat Assoc of Arts in Educn City of Westminster Arts Coll; *Books* Education for the Inner City (1980), Departmental management (1981), Sex Differentiation and Schooling (1983), Meetings and Partings (1984), Short Stories for Today (1984), School management Tasks (1985), New directions in Pastoral Care (1985), The Tutor and the Tutor (1990), numerous other stories and papers; *Recreations* reading, music; *Style*— Prof Michael Marland, CBE; 22 Compton Terrace, London N1 2UN; North Westminster Community School, Marylebone Lower House, Penfold Street, London NW1 6RX

MARLAND, Paul; MP (C) Gloucestershire W 1979-; s of Alexander Marland by his w Elsa May Lindsey; *b* 19 March 1940; *Educ* Gordonstoun, Trinity Coll Dublin; *m* 1 1965 (m dis 1983), Penelope Anne Barlow; 1 s, 2 da; m 2, 1984, Caroline Anne Rushton; *Career* farmer; worked with Hopes Meal Windows 1964, London Press Exchange 1965-66; jt PPS to Hon Nicholas Ridley as fin sec Treasy and Jock Bruce-Gardyne as econ sec to Treasy, 1981-83, PPS to Rt Hon Michael Jopling as Min of Agric 1983-1986; memb Agricultural Select Ctee 1986-, chm Cons Backbench Agric Ctee 1990; *Clubs* Boodles; *Style*— Paul Marland Esq, MP; Ford Hill Farm, Temple Guiting, Cheltenham, Glos (☎ 045 15 232)

MARLAND, Ross Crispian; s of John Marland (d 1988), and Sylvia, *née* Norris; *b* 17 Aug 1940; *Educ* Stamford Sch, RNC Dartmouth, UCL (LLM, Dip Air and Space Law); *m* 23 Oct 1965, (Daphne Mary) Virginia, da of Brig William Hugh Denning Wakely (d 1979); 1 s (Timothy b 27 July 1970), 1 da (Lavinia b 22 Sept 1974); *Career* graduated RNC Actg Sub Lt 1961, No 1 Flying Trg Sch HMS Heron 1961-63, transfd RAF PO 1963, No 2 Air Navigation Sch 1963, No 1 Advanced Navigation Sch flying offr 1964, visual bombing course Canberra OCU 1964-65, Flt Lt No 3 Sqdn Germany 1966-70, jt servs warfare course 1968, Radar Navigation and Bombing Sch Vulcan OCU 1970, 50 Sqdn UK 1970-73, Jr Cmd and Staff Sch 1973, Flt Cdr Jt Air Reconnaisance and Intelligence Centre 1973-79; called to the Bar Inner Temple 1975, in practice 1979-81; dir: Int Insur Servs Ltd 1981-87, Airclaims Insur Servs Ltd 1987-; memb: Bar Assoc Commerce Finance and Indust, Aust Aviation Law Assoc; memb ctee: Asia Pacific Lawyers Assoc, Air Law Gp; memb: Royal Aeronautical Soc, Air Law Gp; lectr Chartered Inst Insur Studies; memb Huntingdon Cons Club; MRIN 1973, MRAeS 1982, ACIArb 1984; *Recreations* salmon fishing, equestrian sports; *Clubs* RAF; *Style*— Ross Marland, Esq; 84 East Hill, Wandsworth, London SW18 2HG (☎ 081 870 6893); Winterfold, The Village, Orton Longeville, Peterborough, Cambs; Airclaims Insur

Services Ltd, Cardinal Point, Newall Rd, Heathrow Airport (London), Hounslow TW6 2AS (☎ 081 897 1066, fax 081 897 0300, telex 934679)

MARLAR, Robin Geoffrey; s of Edward Alfred Geoffrey Marlar, MBE (d 1976), and Winifred, *née* Stevens; *b* 2 Jan 1931; *Educ* Magdalene Coll Cambridge (BA); *m* 1, 1955, Wendy, da of J S Dumeresque; 2 s (John b 1957, James b 1964), 4 da (Sarah b 1959, Kate b 1962, Anna-Jane b 1966, Tammy b 1968); m 2, 1980, Gillian, da of Baron Taylor of Hadfield (Life Peer), *qv*; *Career* fndr Marlar Int (head hunters) 1971; cricket corr Sunday Times 1970-; Capt Univ of Cambridge Cricket 1953, Sussex 1955-59; Parly Candidate (C) Bolsover 1959, Leicester NE (by-election) 1962; *Books* History of Cricket, English Cricketers Trip to USA 1859, Decision against England; *Recreations* sport, music, gardening; *Clubs* Garrick, MCC; *Style*— Robin Marlar, Esq; Brantings Hay, Chilworth, Guildford GU4 8RE (☎ 0483 898912)

MARLBOROUGH, 11 Duke of (E 1702); John George Vanderbilt Henry Spencer-Churchill; JP (Oxon 1962), DL (1974); also Baron Spencer (E 1603), Earl of Sunderland (E 1643), Baron Churchill of Sandridge (E 1685), Earl of Marlborough (E 1689), Marquess of Blandford (E 1702), Prince of the Holy Roman Empire (1704), and Prince of Mindelheim (1705, cr of the Emperor Joseph); s of 10 Duke of Marlborough (d 1972), by his 1 w, Hon Alexandra Cadogan, CBE, da of Viscount Chelsea and gda of 5 Earl Cadogan, KG; *b* 13 April 1926; *Educ* Eton; *m* 1, 1951, Susan Mary (m dis 1960, she m 1962 Alan Cyril Heber-Percy), da of Michael Charles St John Hornby, of Pusey House, Berks, by his w Nicolette (da of Capt Hon Cyril Ward, MVO, RN, 5 s of 1 Earl of Dudley); 1 s, 1 da (and 1 s decd); m 2, 1961, Mrs Tina (Athina) Livanos (m dis 1971, she d 1974), da of Stavros G Livanos, of Paris, and formerly w of Aristotle Onassis (decd); m 3, 1972, (Dagmar) Rosita (Astri Libertas), da of Count Carl Ludwig Douglas (decd); 1 s (Lord Edward b 1974), 1 da (Lady Alexandra b 1977) (and 1 s decd); *Heir* s, Marquess of Blandford; *Career* proprietor of Blenheim Palace, said to be England's largest domestic bldg and one of the masterpieces of Sir John Vanbrugh; formerly Capt Life Gds to 1953; chm: Martini & Rossi Ltd 1979-, London Paperweights Ltd; pres: Thames and Chilterns Tourist Bd 1974-, Oxon Assoc Boys' Clubs, Oxon CLA 1978-; former Oxon ccllr; memb House of Lords Bridge Team in match against Commons 1982; dep pres Nat Assoc Boys' Clubs; pres: Sports Aid Fndn (Southern Area) 1981; Oxfordshire Branch SSAFA 1977; Oxford United Football Club 1975; hon vice-pres Football Assoc 1959; cncl memb Winston Churchill Memorial Tst 1966-; *Clubs* White's, Portland; *Style*— His Grace the Duke of Marlborough, JP, DL; Blenheim Palace, Woodstock, Oxon (☎ 0993 811666); 1 Shepherd's Place, Upper Brook St, London W1 (☎ 071 629 7971)

MARLER, Christopher John Sydney; s of Maj Leslie Sydney Marler, OBE, TD (d 1981), of Bolebec House, Whitchurch, Bucks , and Doris Marguerite, *née* Swaffer, JP; *b* 22 Feb 1932; *Educ* Stowe, RAC Cirencester; *m* 22 Sept 1957, Shirley Carolyn, da of Lewis Edward van Moppes (d 1983), of Theale, Berks; 1 s (James Christopher Sydney b 1962), 2 da (Julie Carolyn b 1959, Serena Rose b 1965); *Career* pedigree cattle breeder and zoo owner; chm Whaddon Estates Ltd (property and investmt co); Liveryman Worshipful Co of Merchant Taylors' 1955, Freeman City of London 1955; FZS, FLS; *Recreations* racing, travel, animal photography; *Style*— Christopher Marler, Esq; Overbrook House, Weston Underwood, Olney, Bucks (☎ 0234 711451)

MARLER, David Steele; OBE (1985); s of Steele Edward Marler (d 1961), and Dorothy Eliza, *née* Vickery; *b* 19 March 1941; *Educ* Brighton Hove & Sussex GS, Merton Coll Oxford (open postmastership, BA, MA); *m* 17 Aug 1963, Belinda Mary, da of Harold William Handisyde (d 1974); 2 s (Blake David b 1964, Edmund Henry b 1968); *Career* British Council: joined 1962, seconded to SOAS 1962-63, asst rep Bombay 1963, regnl offr India 1967, dep rep Ethiopia 1970, rep Ibadan 1974, dir Policy Research Dept 1977, rep Cyprus 1980, seconded to SOAS 1984, Nat Univ Singapore 1985, rep China 1987, controller Asia Pacific & Americas Div 1990-; *Recreations* sailing, flying, walking, reading; *Clubs* Changi Sailing (Singapore), Cyprus Aero; *Style*— David Marler, Esq, OBE; The British Council, 10 Spring Gardens, London SW1A 2BN (☎ 071 389 4786, fax 071 839 6347, telex 8952201 BRICON G)

MARLER, Dennis Ralph Greville; s of Greville Sidney Marler (d 1952), and Ivy Victoria, *née* Boyle (d 1977); *b* 15 June 1927; *Educ* Marlborough; *m* 11 June 1952, Angela, da of Harold Cann Boundy, of Putney; 1 s (Timothy b 1957), 1 da (Melanie b 1955); *Career* Lt 2 Bn Royal Lincs Regt 1945-48, served in Palestine (MELF); chm Capital & Counties plc 1985-90 (md 1969-85); pres Br Property Fedn 1983-84; Freeman of City of London, memb Ct Worshipful Co of Merchant Taylors'; FRICS 1969, CBIM, FRSA; *Recreations* reading, golf, travel; *Clubs* Royal Thames Yacht, St Stephen's, Roehampton, St Enodoc Golf; *Style*— Dennis Marler, Esq; 13 Whaddon House, William Mews, London SW1X 9HG (☎ 071 245 6139)

MARLING, Sir Charles William Somerset; 5 Bt (UK 1882), of Stanley Park and Sedbury Park, Co Gloucester; s of Lt-Col Sir John Stanley Vincent, 4 Bt, OBE (d 1977); *b* 2 June 1951; *Educ* Harrow; *m* 1979, Judi P, adopted da of Thomas W Futrille, of Sunningdale; 3 da (Georgina b 1982, Aimy b 1984, Laura Beatrice b 1990); *Clubs* White's, Chelsea Arts; *Style*— Sir Charles Marling, Bt; The Barn, The Street, Eversley, Hants

MARLOW, Antony Rivers (Tony); MP (C) Northampton N 1979-; s of late Maj Thomas Keith Rivers Marlow, MBE, RE, and late Beatrice Nora, *née* Hall; *b* 17 June 1940; *Educ* Wellington, RMA Sandhurst, St Catharine's Coll Cambridge; *m* 1962, Catherine Louise Howel, *née* Jones; 3 s, 2 da; *Career* served Army 1958-69; mgmnt conslt 1969-79; *Clubs* Spencer Working Mens; *Style*— Tony Marlow Esq, MP; House of Commons, London SW1A 0AA

MARLOW, David Ellis; *b* 29 March 1935; *m* Margaret; 1 da (Jenny); *Career* CA; articled clerk for practice assoc with (and now part of) Peat Marwick & Mitchell; 3i Group plc: joined Leicester office 1960, former mangr Brighton and Manchester offices, former asst gen mangr for South East Regn (incl London), dir 1976, chief exec 1988-; memb: Slrs Disciplinary Tribunal, CBI's Econ and Fin Policy Ctee, Taverners' Tst; memb Cncl King Edward VII Hosp Midhurst; *Recreations* playing tennis, playing the piano and the organ, scrambling in the Alps; *Style*— David Marlow, Esq; The Platt, Elsted, Midhurst, W Sussex GU29 0LA; 3i Group plc, 91 Waterloo Rd, London SE1 8XP (☎ 071 928 3131, fax 071 928 0058, telex 917844)

MARLOW, Kingsley Hamnett; s of Walter Marlow RN (d 1930), and Nora Marlow, *née* Bakewell; *b* 6 June 1930; *Educ* Western Park Sch Leicester, Leicester Polytechnic (BA); *m* 1977, Mary Mackinnon, da of Harold Noel Hamilton Barlow Waldie, Maj (ret), of Langholm, Dumfriesshire, Scotland (d 1985); *Career* man dir EX-Cell-O Corp 1983- (finance dir and co sec 1974-82, co sec and financial controller 1964-74); dir: Ex-Cell-O Mulhead Ltd 1984-, LETG Ltd 1978-81, Pure-Pak Ltd 1972-84; govr Charles Keene Coll of FE Leicester 1980-83; companion British Inst of Mgmnt 1983- (memb cncl 1981-83, memb finance ctee 1980-83, chm East Midlands Branch Area Ctee 1980-83); memb: E Midlands Regnl Bd BIM 1984-, Nat Economic Devpt Office Professional Mgmnt Ctee 1985-, BR Assoc for Shooting and Conservation, Inland Waterways Assoc; *Recreations* fishing, shooting, woodword, philatelist, numismatist, gardening; *Style*— Kingsley Marlow, Esq; Ex-Cell-O Corporation, PO Box 133, Hastings Rd, Leicester LE5 OHT (☎ 0533 768181)

MARLOW, Hon Mrs (Teresa); *née* Sackville-West; da (by 1 m) of 6 Baron Sackville; *b* 1954; *m* 1979, (Alastair) Rupert Marlow, s of Capt C N Marlow, RN, of Greenhill House, Upper Westwood, Wilts; 1 s (Sebastian b 1985), 2 da (Julia 1982, Rebecca b 1983); *Style*— The Hon Mrs Marlow

MARMOT, Michael Gideon; s of Nathan Marmot, of Sidney, Australia, and Alice, *née* Weiner; *b* 26 Jan 1945; *Educ* Univ of Sydney Australia (BSc, MB BS), Univ of California Berkeley (MPH, PhD); *m* 8 Sept 1971, Alexandra, da of Bernard Ferster; 2 s (Andre b 1982, Daniel b 1986); *Career* Univ of Sydney: student fell in cardiovascular pharmacology 1965-66, res med offr Royal Prince Alfred Hosp 1969, fell in thoracic med 1970, travelling fell Postgraduate Med Fndn 1971-72; lectr Dept of Biomedical and Environmental Health Sciences Univ of California Berkeley 1975-76, sr lectr (formerly lectr) in epidemiology London Sch of Hygiene and Tropical Med 1976-85; UCH and Middlesex Sch of Med: prof 1985-, fell Faculty of Public Health Med (formerly Faculty of Community Med) 1989 (memb 1984); prof of epidemiology London Sch of Hygiene and Tropical Medicine 1990-; memb: Medical Aspects of Food Policy Ctee Dept of Health, Br Heart Fedn; memb coronary Prevention Gp; *Books* Mortality of Immigrants to England and Wales (1984); *Style*— Prof Michael Marmot; 23 Dartmouth Park Avenue, London NW5 (☎ 071 485 6341); Dept of Community Medicine, UCMSM, 66-72 Gower Street, London WC1E 6EA (☎ 071 380 7602, fax 071 380 7608)

MAROWITZ, Charles; s of Harry Julius Marowitz, of Lithuania, and USA, and Tillie, *née* Rosencrantz; *b* 26 Jan 1934; *Educ* UCL, Central Sch Speech and Drama, London Acad Music and Dramatic Art, Sorbonne; *m* 1, 1976 (m dis 1980), Julia; m 2, 14 Dec 1982, Jane Windsor, da of Rear Adm David John Allsop, RN, of Ipswich; *Career* US Army 1952-54; dir In-Stage 1958-62, co-dir RSC Experimental Gp 1966-67, co-artistic dir London Traverse Co 1967-68, artistic dir Open Space Theatre 1968-801, assoc dir LA Theatre Center 1982-89, artistic dir Malibu Stage Co 1990-, West Coast corr The Times 1980-, drama critic LA Herald Examiner 1989, West Coast Theatre Columnist Theatre Week Magazine 1989-; memb: International PEN, Sons of Judas Macabelas, Schmendrick Soc of Gtr LA County, Dramatists Guild, The Writers Guild of America; Order of the Purple Sarh (Denmark) 1974; *Books* Method as Means (1964), Confessions of a Counterfeit Critic (1973), The Marowitz Shakespeare (1980), Sex Wars (1986), Prospero's Staff (1987), Burnt Bridges (1990); *Recreations* balling; *Clubs* Raymond Revuebar; *Style*— Charles Marowitz, Esq; 7 St Anne's Terrace, London NW8; 305 Sequit Drive, Malibu, Calif 90265, USA (☎ 0101 213 456 8170)

MARPER, (William) John; s of Ronald Marshall Marper, of Saltburn, and Caroline, *née* Jarville; *b* 9 Dec 1946; *Educ* Sir William Turners Sch; *m* 12 Dec 1976, Maureen Ann, da of Henry Pullen, of Eastbourne; *Career* CA; Charles Barker Gp 1972-77, vice pres Citicorp 1977-85, dir ANZ Merchant Bank 1985-89; FCA, memb Stock Exchange; *Recreations* tennis, English lit; *Style*— John Marper, Esq; 1 Balloon St, Manchester M60 (☎ 061 832 3456)

MARPLES, Baroness; Ruth; da of F W Dobson, JP, FSA (decd), of Nottingham; *m* 1956, as his 2 w, Baron Marples, PC (Life Peer) (d 1978); *Style*— The Rt Hon Lady Marples; 33 Eccleston St, London SW1

MARQUAND, Prof David Ian; s of Rt Hon Hilary Marquand, PC (d 1972), and Rachel Eluned, *née* Rees; *b* 20 Sept 1934; *Educ* Emanuel Sch, Magdalen Coll Oxford, St Antony's Coll Oxford, Univ of California Berkeley; *m* 12 Dec 1959, Judith Mary, da of Dr Morris Reed, of London; 1 s (Charles b 1962), 1 da (Ruth b 1964); *Career* Nat Serv RAF 1952-54; leader writer The Guardian 1959-62, res fell St Antony's Coll Oxford 1962-64, lectr in sch of social studies Univ of Sussex 1964-66; MP (Lab) Ashfield 1966-67; PPS to: Min of Works 1966-67, Min of Overseas Devpt 1969-79; Br delegate to Cncl of Europe and WEU Assemblies 1970-73, chief advsr European Cmmn Brussels 1977-78; prof of contemporary hist and politics Univ of Salford 1978-; jt ed The political Quarterly 1987-; chm High Peak SDP 1981-82 and 1987-88, pres High Peak SLD 1988-; memb: Nat ctee SDP 1981-88, Policy ctee SLD 1988-; FRHistS 1986; *Books* Ramsay MacDonald (1977), Parliament for Europe (1979), European Elections and British Politics (with David Butler, 1981), John MacKintosh on Parliament and Social Democracy (ed, 1982), The Unprincipled Society (1988); *Recreations* walking, listening to music; *Style*— Prof David Marquand; 2 Buxworth Hall, Buxworth, Stockport, Cheshire SK12 7NH (☎ 06633 2319); Dept of Politics and Contemporary History, Univ of Salford, M5 4WT (☎ 061 736 5843)

MARQUIS, James Douglas; DFC (1945); s of James Charles Marquis, ISM (d 1983), and Jessica Amy, *née* Huggett (d 1988); *b* 16 Oct 1921; *Educ* Shooters Hill Sch Woolwich; *m* 8 Jan 1945, Brenda Eleanor, da of Robert Reyner Davey, of Blackpool, Lancashire; 2 s (Peter b 1947, David b 1953); *Career* RAF 1941-46, Pilot Offr 1942, Flying Offr 1943, Sqdn Navigation Offr 177 Sqdn 1943-44, Flt Lt 1944, Gp Navigation Offr 224 Gp 1944, Navigation Offr AHQ Malaya 1945-46, Sqdn Ldr 1945 (RAF First Class Navigation Warrant 1945); local govt 1946-56, New Town devpt 1957-81; md Irvine Development Corporation 1972-81; *Recreations* growing bonsai, water colour painting; *Clubs* Scot Bonsai Assoc; *Style*— James Marquis, Esq, DFC; Vibelyng, 3 Knoll Park, Ayr KA7 4RH (☎ 0292 42212)

MARR, Prof Geoffrey Vickers; s of John Marr (d 1971), and Florrie, *née* Vickers; *b* 30 Jan 1930; *Educ* Darlington Queen Elizabeth GS, Univ of Manchester (BSc, DSc), Univ of Reading (PhD); *m* 3 July 1954, Jean, da of John Robert Tebb; 2 s (Peter John b 1956, Richard Nigel b 1961), 1 da (Kathryn Janet b 1959); *Career* fell Dept of Physics Univ of Western Ontario 1954-57, lectr Dept of Physics McGill Univ Montreal 1957-59, physicist Atomic Power Div English Electric 1959-61, lectr and reader in physics J J Thomson Laboratory Univ of Reading 1961-81; Univ of Aberdeen: prof of natural philosophy and head of Dept of Physics 1981-89, prof (pt/t) Dept of Engrg 1989-1990, Emeritus prof 1990; current res interests incl photoionization of molecules, physics of thin films, synchrotron radiation source (in association with Aberdeen Engrg Physics and Daresbury SERC); FInstP 1963, CPhys 1986, FRSE 1986, FRSA 1988; *Books* Photoionization Processes in Gases (1967), Plasma Spectroscopy (1968), Handbook on Synchrotron Radiation Vol 2 (ed, 1987); *Recreations* walking, painting, beekeeping; *Style*— Prof Geoffrey Marr; The Long House, Low Row, nr Richmond, N Yorks DL11 6NE (☎ 0748 86452); Dept of Engineering, Fraser-Noble Building, Aberdeen University, Aberdeen AB9 2UE (☎ 0224 272495, fax 0224 487048, telex 73458 UNIABN G)

MARR, John; s of Harry Needham Marr, of Manchester, and Harriet Constance, *née* Portwood; *b* 7 March 1946; *Educ* Doncaster GS; *m* 15 April 1972, Caroline Anne, da of David Cowan, of Stockport; 1 s (Richard b 23 March 1985), 2 da (Victoria b 18 Oct 1978, Jessica 3 Feb 1981); *Career* accountant Mather and Platt 1964-69, investmt mangr Co Operative Insur Soc 1969-73; Charterhouse Tilney (formerly Tilney and Co) Stockbrokers: res investmt analyst 1973-, dir 1986; underwriter Lloyds of London 1987; ACIS 1969, ASIA 1970, FCCA 1970, memb Stock Exchange 1976; *Recreations* squash, cricket, vintage cars; *Clubs* Liverpool Racquet, Yorks County Cricket; *Style*— John Marr, Esq; Sea Lawn, 14 Westcliffe Rd, Birkdale, Southport PR8 2BN (☎ 0704 68283); Charterhouse Tilney, Royal Liver Building, The Pier Head, Liverpool L3 1NY (☎ 051 236 6000, fax 051 236 6000 ext 273)

MARR, (Sir) Leslie Lynn; (2 Bt, UK 1919, of Sunderland, Co Palatine of Durham); does not use title; s of Col John Lynn Marr, OBE, TD (decd), s of 1 Bt; suc gf, Sir James Marr, 1 Bt, CBE, JP; *b* 14 Aug 1922; *Educ* Shrewsbury, Pembroke Coll Cambridge (MA); *m* 1948 (m dis 1956), Dinora Delores Mendelson; 1 da (adopted); m

2, 1962, Lynn Heneage; 2 da (Joanne b 1963, Rebecca b 1966); *Heir* kinsman, Allan James Marr, CBE; *Career* Pilot Offr RAF 1942, Flight Lt; artist (painter and draughtsman); *Publications* 'From my Point of View' (1978); *Style—* Leslie Marr, Esq

MARR, Lindsay Grigor David; s of Grigor Wilson Marr (d 1986), and Linda Grace, *née* Sergeant; *b* 14 Sept 1955; *Educ* The Perse Sch, Gonville and Caius Coll Cambridge (BA, MA); *Career* slr 1981; Freshfields: articled clerk 1979-81, asst slr 1981-87, ptnr 1987-; Freeman City of London Slrs Co 1988; memb The Law Soc; *Recreations* reading, music, golf, squash; *Style—* Lindsay Marr, Esq; 39 Broad Lane, Hampton, Middlesex TW12 3AL (☎ 081 979 0517); Whitefriars, 65 Fleet St, London EC4Y 1HS (☎ 071 936 4000, fax 071 832 7001)

MARR-JOHNSON, Hon Mrs (Diana Julia); *née* Maugham; da of 1 Viscount Maugham (d 1958); *m* 1932, Kenneth Marr-Johnson (d 1986); 3 s (Frederick b 1936, Simon b 1938, William b 1945); *Books* seven novels; *Style—* The Hon Mrs Marr-Johnson; Flat 3, 14 Onslow Sq, London SW7 3NP

MARR-JOHNSON, Frederick James Maugham; s of Kenneth Marr-Johnson (d 1986), and Hon Diana Julia, *née* Maugham, da of 1 Viscount Maugham; *b* 17 Sept 1936; *Educ* Winchester, Trinity Hall Cambridge (MA); *m* 26 March 1966, Susan, da of Maj R P H Eyre, OBE (d 1982); 1 s (Thomas b 30 Sept 1966), 1 da (Rachel b 27 May 1969); *Career* Nat Serv RN 1955-56, midshipman RNVR; called to the Bar Lincoln's Inn 1962, rec 1986-; *Recreations* sailing, skiing; *Style—* Frederick Marr-Johnson, Esq; 59 Perrymead St, London SW6 3SN (☎ 071 731 0412); Farrar's Building, Temple, London EC4Y 7BD (☎ 071 583 9241, fax 071 583 0090)

MARRACK, Rear Adm Philip Reginald; CB (1979); s of Capt Philip Marrack, RN (d 1955), and Annie Kathleen, *née* Proud; *b* 16 Nov 1922; *Educ* Eltham Coll, RNEC; *m* 1954, Pauline Mary, da of Charles Haag (d 1938); 2 da (Claire, Philippa); *Career* war serv Atlantic and Mediterranean, Naval Offr, 8 appointments at sea in surface ships and submarines, 5 other appointments in shore estabs and MOD, ret 1981; dir: Naval Ship Production MOD 1974-77, Dockyard Production and Support MOD 1977-81; specialist in engrg and submarines; *Recreations* trout and salmon fishing, viticulture; *Style—* Rear Adm Philip Marrack, CB; c/o Barclays Bank, Princess St, Plymouth

MARRE, Lady; (Romola) Mary; *née* Gilling; CBE (1979); da of Aubrey John Gilling (d 1952), of Chelmsford, Essex, and Romola Marjorie, *née* Angier (d 1989); *b* 25 April 1920; *Educ* Bedford Coll for Women, Univ of London (BA); *m* 24 Dec 1943, Sir Alan Samuel Marre, KCB (d 1990); 1 s (Andrew), 1 da (Kate); *Career* served ATS 1942-45, Jr Cdr, psychologist No 41 (ATS) WOSB; asst principal (temp) Miny of Health 1941-42, organiser W Hampstead Citizens' Advice Bureau 1962-65, dep gen sec Camden Cncl of Social Service 1965-73, advsr on community health cncls to DHSS 1974-75, chm advsy gp on hosp services for children with cancer in N Western Region 1979; memb: Milk Marketing Bd 1973-82, Lord Chancellor's Advsy Ctee on Legal Aid 1975-80, (later chm) BBC and IBA Central Appeals Advsy Ctee 1980-86; chm Volunteer Centre 1973-78, dep chm Royal Jubilee Tsts 1981-89, tstee City Parochial Fndn 1975- 89 (vice chm 1989-); memb Cncl: Charity Projects 1984-, Middx Hosp Ethics Ctee 1988-; chm: Ctee on Future of Legal Profession 1986-88, Cmmn of Enquiry into Human Aids to Communication 1990-; pres: Barnet Voluntary Service Cncl, Disablement Assoc in Borough of Barnet; *Recreations* gardening, embroidery, enjoying meeting friends, family life; *Style—* Lady Marre, CBE; 44 The Vale, London NW11 8SG (☎ 081 458 1787)

MARRETT, Dr (Henry) Rex; s of Dr Henry Norman Marrett (d 1961), and Florence Dering, *née* Mathew-Lannowe (d 1944); *b* 25 Oct 1915; *Educ* Felsted, St Bartholomews Hosp (DA); *m* 25 Oct 1940 (Diana) Jacqueline, da of Philip Henry Marsh; 2 s (Norman b 1942, Roger b 1944); *Career* WWII Lt RAMC 1943, Capt 1944, Maj 1944-46, specialist anaesthetist Euro Campaign with Field Surgical unit, inventor of the Marrett Anaesthetic Apparatus at the request of the Army 1945; jr anaesthetist St Bartholomews Hosp 1941-43, conslt anaesthetist Coventry 1947-79, inventor Medrex Apparatus for Dental Anaesthesia; fndr memb Hickman Anaesthic Soc; hon memb: History of Anaestesia Soc, Assoc Dental Anaesthists; Essex Co Hockey colours 1939, capt Coventry Golf Club 1974, MRCS, LRCP FFARCS; memb: RSM, Assoc of Anaesthetists; *Recreations* engineering, golf, gardening; *Style—* Dr Rex Marrett; 7A The Firs, Kenilworth Rd, Coventry CV5 6QD (☎ 0203 674706)

MARRIAN, Lady Emma Clare; da of 6 Earl Cawdor; *b* 15 March 1958; *m* 1983, David Marrian, s of Peter Marrian, of Nairobi; 2 s (Jack Alexander Wolf b 1985, Hunter James b 1988); *Style—* The Lady Emma Marrian; 15 Callow St, London SW3

MARRIOTT; *see*: Smith-Marriott

MARRIOTT, Hon Mrs (Dinah Lilian); yst da of Hon William Douglas-Home and Baroness Dacre, *qqv*; *b* 22 Jan 1964; *m* 28 Oct 1989, Harry J Marriott, 2 s of John Marriott, of Great Milton, Oxfordshire; *Style—* The Hon Mrs Marriott

MARRIOTT, Martin Marriott; s of Rt Rev Philip Selwyn Abraham, The Bishop of Newfoundland, Canada (d 1956), and Elizabeth Dorothy Cicely (d 1975); *b* 28 Feb 1932; *Educ* Lancing, New College Oxford (MA); *m* 10 Nov 1956, Judith Caroline Guerney, da of Lt-Col Michael Ronald Lubbock, MBE, of Toronto, Canada; 1 s (Charles), 2 da (Virginia (Mrs O'Coner), Rebecca); *Career* educn officer RAF 1956-59; teacher: Heversham GS 1959-66, Haileybury College 1966-76; headmaster Canford Sch 1976-; chm: Headmasters' Conf 1989, Steering Ctee of the Bloxham Project 1985-91; *Recreations* sailing, royal tennis, walking, gardening; *Clubs* East India; *Style—* Martin Marriott, Esq; The Headmaster's House, Canford School, Wimborne, Dorset BH21 3AD (☎ 0202 882411, fax 0202 881009)

MARRIS, David Drummond; s of Adam Denzill Marris, CMG (d 1983); *b* 5 May 1942; *Educ* Winchester; *m* 1978, Clare Katrina, *née* Mayers; *Career* 2 Lt 3 Green Jackets, The Rifle Bde; banker; dir Barclays Bank Ltd Manchester 1977-82 (Chelmsford 1973-77); Caribbean dir Barclays Int 1982-83; Barclays Bank plc: sr Caribbean dir 1983-87, regnl dir Luton 1987-; *Recreations* country pursuits, sailing, music; *Clubs* Boodle's; *Style—* David Marris, Esq

MARRON, (Joseph) Ronald; s of Joseph Marron, Acklam, Middlesborough, Cleveland, and Elsie Marron, *née* Harding; *b* 20 Jan 1935; *Educ* St Richards RC; *m* 1955, Audrey, da of Thomas Dowson, of Cleveland County Cleveland; 3 s (Ronald, Craig, Jason), 3 da (Carol, Susan, Tracy); *Career* gen sec Assoc Metal Workers Union; *Style—* Ronald Marron, Esq; 92 Deansgate, Manchester 3

MARS-JONES, Hon Mr Justice; Hon Sir William Lloyd; MBE (1945); s of Henry Mars Jones, of Denbighshire; *b* 4 Sept 1915; *Educ* Denbigh Co Sch, Univ Coll of Wales at Aberystwyth (LLB), St John's Cambridge (BA); *m* 1947, Sheila Cobon; 3 s; *Career* WWII Lt Cdr RNVR; barr 1941, QC 1957, dep chm Denbighshire QS 1962-68; rec: Birkenhead 1959-65, Swansea 1965-68, Cardiff 1968-69; high ct judge (Queen's Bench) 1969-, presiding judge Wales & Chester circuit 1971-75; inspector Home Off inquiry into allegations against Metropolitan Police Offrs 1964, memb Home Sec's advsy cncl on Penal System 1966-68; pres N Wales Arts Assoc 1976-, treas Gray's Inn 1982; pres: Univ Coll of N Wales Bangor 1983-, Univ Coll of Wales Aberystwyth Old Students Assoc 1987-88, London Welsh Tst 1989-; Hon LLD Univ Coll Wales; kt 1969; *Style—* The Hon Mr Justice Mars-Jones, MBE; Royal Courts of Justice, Strand, London WC2

MARSDEN, Andrew Guy; s of Flt Lt Geoffrey Ansdell Marsden, DFC, of Egmont House, Darley, Harrogate, N Yorks, and Margaret Jean, *née* Furniss; *b* 6 Aug 1953; *Educ* Monkton Combe Sch, Pembroke Coll Oxford (MA); *Career* called to the Bar Middle Temple 1975, memb S E circuit; in practice: Colchester, Norwich, Ipswich 1977-; patron Acorn Villages Mistley Home for Mentally Handicapped, organist Church of Holy Innocents Lamarsh Essex, memb Kelvedon Singers; *Recreations* historical vocal recordings, architecture, singing; *Clubs* United Oxford and Cambridge; *Style—* Andrew Marsden, Esq; Little Gables, Lamarsh, Bures, Suffolk (☎ 0787 227054); 53 North Hill, Colchester, Essex (☎ 0206 572756, fax 0206 562447); 3 Princes St, Ipswich, Suffolk, Wensum Chambers, Wensum St, Norwich; 4 Paper Buildings, Temple, London EC4

MARSDEN, Andrew Kendall; s of Frank Marsden, of 22 Moorhead Terrace, Shipley, Yorks, and Jeane Mary, *née* Kendall; *b* 24 May 1948; *Educ* Woodhouse Grove Sch, Univ of Leeds; *m* 20 March 1976, Alberta (Abe), *née* Flynne; 2 da (Stephanie Jane b 1980, Jenny Kay b 1984); *Career* conslt accident and emergency med Pinderfields Gen Hosp Wakefield 1979, chm Resuscitation Cncl UK 1984-88, dep chief med offr St John Ambulance Assoc 1988-; author pubns on accident and emergency med; memb Bd Immediate Med Care, RCSE, sr police surgn (expert in medico legal case reporting); chm: Ambulance Serv Steering Gp on Extended Trg W Yorkshire, Accident and Emergency Records Computer User Gp; memb Exec Ctee Casualty Surgns' Assoc; memb: Br Assoc Immediate Care, Emergency Med Res Soc, Assoc Police Surgns GB, RSM, World Assoc Emergency and Disaster Med; *Books* Care Of The Acutely Ill And Injured (1982), Save A Life - An Instructors Guide (1986), Textbook Of Accident & Emergency Medicine (1989), Resuscitation For The Citizen (1989); *Recreations* fell walking, music; *Clubs* Domus Medica (RSM); *Style—* Andrew Marsden, Esq; 3 Richmond Rd, St Johns, Wakefield WF1 3LA (☎ 0924 377739); Pinderfields Gen Hosp, Accident and Emergency Dept, Aberford Rd, Wakefield WF1 4DG (☎ 0924 375 217 ext 2316, fax 0924 372 079)

MARSDEN, Sir Nigel John Denton; 3 Bt (UK 1924), of Grimsby, Co Lincoln; s of Sir John Denton Marsden, 2 Bt (d 1985); *b* 26 May 1940; *Educ* Ampleforth; *m* 1961, Diana Jean, da of Air Marshal Sir Patrick Hunter Dunn, KBE, CB, DFC, *qv*; 3 da (Lucinda Ann b 1962, Rose Amanda b 1964, Annabel Juliet b 1968); *Heir* bro, Simon N L Marsden Esq, *qv*; *Career* self employed gardener; *Recreations* walking, family, countryside pursuits; *Style—* Sir Nigel Marsden, Bt; 1 Grimsby Rd, Waltham, Lincs

MARSDEN, Paul Anthony; s of Lewis Marsden (d 1967), and Edith Lily Cheshire; *b* 19 Feb 1934; *Educ* Huddersfield Coll, Univ of Leeds (BSc); *m* 1 Oct 1955, Brenda, da of Ralph Shaw (d 1977); 1 s (Jonathan Mark b 1961 d 1990), 2 da (Julie Helen b 1958, Hilary Susan b 1959); *Career* RNVR (non commissioned) 1953-55; Nat Serv RN (rank Sub Lt RNVR) 1955-57: served Hydrographic Branch RN, active serv Suez 1956, serv in home waters with coastal forces based on HMS Hornet; served on reserve 1957-67; ICI: joined Engrg Dept 1955, mechanical engrg apprentice Richardsons-Westgarth 1957-58, res on gas liquid systems 1958-60, boiler plant engr 1960-62, mangr Billingham Power Station 1962-64, seconded to Canadian Industries Ltd 1964-66, prodn mangr (Building Products) 1966-69, works mangr of Engrg Works 1969-72, gen mangr Billingham Site 1972-74, gen mangr Engrg 1974, dep chm Agric Div 1980-86 (dir 1974-80), md ICI Fertilizers 1987-; served Construction Indust Little NEDY; govr local sch, involved with local civic socs; FIMechE 1982, FEng 1982, FRSA; *Recreations* sailing, golf, walking, model engineering; *Style—* Paul Marsden, Esq; ICI Fertilizers, PO Box 1, Billingham, Cleveland TS23 1LB (☎ 0642 522138, fax 0642 523201, telex 587443)

MARSDEN, Rear Adm Peter Nicholas; s of Dr James Pickford Marsden (d 1977), and Evelyn Holman (d 1970); *b* 29 June 1932; *Educ* Felsted; *m* 12 Oct 1956, Jean Elizabeth, da of Cdr J H Mather, DSO, VRD, RNVR (d 1957); 2 s (James b 1957, Jonathan b 1960), 1 da (Joanna b 1963); *Career* RN 1950-88, Dir Fleet Supply Duties Div MOD 1980-81, Cdre Admty Interview Bd 1983-85, sr naval memb directing staff RCDS 1985-88, exec dir 21 Century Trust 1989-; *Recreations* beagling, golf; *Style—* Rear Adm Peter Marsden; c/o National Westminster Bank, Standishgate, Wigan, Lancs WN1 1UJ

MARSDEN, Prof Philip Law; s of Arthur Beeton Marsden, and Dorothy, *née* Whitely; *b* 14 Feb 1924; *Educ* Univ of Birmingham (BSc), Univ of Leeds (PhD); *m* 22 June 1946, Doreen Iris, da of Frederick George Mounty; 2 s (Simon b 1953, Andrew b 1957 d 1983), 1 da (Jane b 1950); *Career* jr scientific offr Telecommunications Res Estab Malvern 1944-46, scientific offr Nat Physics Laboratory Teddington 1946-47; Univ of Leeds: asst lectr 1948-51, lectr 1951-54, sr lectr and reader 1964-68, prof 1968-69, currently emeritus prof; hon sec Edward Boyle Meml Tst; FInstP, CPhys, FRAS; *Recreations* astrophysics, gardening, walking, computing; *Style—* Prof Philip Marsden; 18 Park Crescent, Leeds LS8 1DH (☎ 0532 662671); Physics Department, University of Leeds, Leeds LS2 9JT (☎ 0532 333869)

MARSDEN, Simon Neville Llewelyn; yr s of Sir John Denton Marsden, 2 Bt (d 1985); hp of bro, Sir Nigel John Denton Marsden, 3 Bt, *qv*; *b* 1948; *Educ* Ampleforth, Sorbonne; *m* 1, 1970 (m dis), Catherine Thérèsa, da of Brig James Charles Windsor-Lewis, DSO (decd); m 2, 1984, Caroline Stanton; 1 s (Teige Orlando Denton b 25 Dec 1990), 1 da (Skye Atlanta b 24 Feb 1988); *Career* author and photographer; collections in: V & A, Getty Museum California; *Books* In Ruins (The Once Great Houses of Ireland) (1980), The Haunted Realm (Ghosts, Witches and other Strange Tales) (1986), Visions of POE (1988), Phantoms of the Isles (1990); *Style—* Simon Marsden, Esq; The Presbytery, Hainton, Lincoln LN3 6LR

MARSDEN, (James) Stuart; s of James Herbert Marsden (d 1969), and Constance Hilda Naylor (d 1970); *b* 20 Dec 1930; *Educ* William Hulmes Sch Manchester; *m* 22 June 1957, Eileen Kinloch Wilkinson, da of Reginald Wilkinson (d 1928), of Ormskirk; 1 s (Richard James Nicholas b 16 July 1961), 1 da (Jill Karen (Mrs Walsh) b 14 March 1958); *Career* Nat Serv RAF, FLying Offr 1950-52; Barclays Bank 1948-50; articled to W H Robinson Manchester 1952, British Waterways 1955-57, currently practice chm Edmund Kirby Architects and Surveyors (joined 1957), dir Property Agents International Ltd; chm Merseyside & Isle of Man Branch RICS 1980; memb: Cncl Merseyside C of C & Indust, Ctee of Management Merseyside Improved Houses; chm: Environmental and Public Affrs Ctee, Merseyside Improved Houses Harbour Housing Assoc, MCCI; memb Ctee: Merseyside Civic Soc, Heswall Soc, Dale Farm for the Mentally Handicapped (chm 1985); FRICS 1957; *Recreations* sailing, skiing, tennis, gardening; *Style—* Stuart Marsden, Esq; Edmund Kirby, India Buildings, Water St, Liverpool L2 0TZ (☎ 051 236 4552, fax 051 236 4024)

MARSDEN, Hon Mrs (Vere Mary); da of Hon Conrad Adderley Dillon (d 1901), and sister of 19 Viscount Dillon, CMG, DSO (d 1946); *m* 1911, Reginald Edward Marsden (d 1960); 3 s, 3 da; granted 1934, title, rank and precedence of a Viscount's da, which would have been hers had her father survived to succeed to Viscountcy of Dillon; *Style—* The Hon Mrs Marsden; Bishopsgate Pla, Englefield Green, Egham, Surrey (☎ 0784 3034)

MARSDEN, William; s of Christopher Alexander Marsden (d 1989), of The Vineyard, Saffron Walden, Essex, and (Margaret) Ruth, *née* Kershaw (d 1970); *b* 15 Sept 1940; *Educ* Winchester, Lawrenceville Sch USA, Trinity Coll Cambridge (MA), Univ of London (BSc); *m* 19 Sept 1964, Eileen Ursula (Kaya) Collingham; 1 s (Thomas Alexander b 16 Jan 1970), 1 da (Inge Katharine b 29 July 1966); *Career* third sec UK Delgn to NATO Paris 1964-66, second sec Rome Embassy 1966-69, seconded asst to gen mangr Joseph Lucas Ltd 1970, first sec and cultural attaché Moscow Embassy 1976-79, asst head Euro community dept FCO 1978-81, cnsllr UK Representation to the EEC Brussels 1981-85, head E African dept FCO and cmmr Br Indian Ocean Territory 1985-88, ambass to Costa Rica (concurrently non-resident ambass to nicaragua) 1989-; Freeman: City of London 1967, Worshipful Co of Grocers 1967; MBIM; *Style*— William Marsden, Esq; c/o Foreign and Commonwealth Office, London SW1A 2AH

MARSH, Alan James; s of James Alfred Leonard Marsh, of Castlemain, Avondale Rd, St Leonards-on-Sea, Sussex, and Grace Maud, *née* Weller (d 1985); *b* 26 Aug 1929; *Educ* Colfes GS, Ch Ch Oxford (MA); *m* 1, 28 Dec 1957 (m dis 1984), Ingrid Hilma Elizabet, da of Nils Areskog (d 1977), of Kalmar, Sweden; 1 s (Neil b 4 Aug 1959), 1 da (Caroline b 27 Oct 1961); m 2, Joanna Maud, da of Brig Bertram Edward Lionel Burton, CBE (d 1976), of Uckfield, Sussex; *Career* Lt 4 RTR 1952-54; Metal Box Co 1954-61, mangr Corporate Strategy Div PA Int Mgmnt Consits 1961-71, gp fin dir Revertex Chemicals Ltd 1971-80, exec dir Midland Montagu Ventures 1980-89, chm Aegis Corp Strategy Ltd 1989-; Freeman City of London, Liveryman Worshipful Co of Gold and Silver Wire Drawers; FCMA 1966, FCT 1978, MIMC 1963; *Recreations* sailing, golf; *Clubs* United Oxford and Cambridge Univ, Royal Corinthian YC; *Style*— Alan Marsh, Esq; Flat 8, 11 Lindfield Gardens, Hampstead, London NW3 6PX (☎ 071 435 8427); 7 The Belvedere, Burnham-on-Crouch, Essex; 10 Lower Thames St, London EC3R 6AE (☎ 071 794 0616, fax 071 794 0618, car 0836 582 815)

MARSH, Alan John Scott; s of Reginald John Marsh, MA, Cantab, and Vera Kathleen Marsh; *b* 1 Nov 1936; *Educ* Charterhouse and Coll Estate Mgmt London; *m* 3 Nov 1962, Pamela Mary, da of Albert Edward White, of Eastbourne; 2 da (Caroline b 1963, Nicola b 1965); *Career* md and chief exec Toyota (FB) Ltd 1986-; md IMC Belgium 1984-85; gen sales mangr Austin Morris Div 1974-75, Fleet Sales dir Leylandcars 1975-77, regnl dir Leyland Int 1977-78, dir Service Rover Triumph 1978-79, sales and marketing dir Toyota (FB) Ltd 1979-84; *Recreations* motoring, sport, sailing; *Style*— Alan Marsh, Esq; Toyota (FB) Ltd, The Quadrangle, Redhill, Surrey RH1 1PX (☎ 0737 768585)

MARSH, Alexander James; s of James Robertson Marsh, of London, and Clara, *née* Rakos (d 1984); *b* 18 Jan 1946; *Educ* Univ Coll Sch London (BSc), Univ of Newcastle upon Tyne (BSc); *m* 29 June 1968, Elspeth Mary Russell, da of Joseph Russell Cameron of Newcastle upon Tyne; 3 s (Nicholas b 1971, Alasdair b 1974, Stephen b 1980); *Career* Swan Hunter Shipbuilders Ltd: gen mangr Wallsend Shipyard 1976-80, shipbuilding dir 1980-83, dir 1980-, dep md 1983-84, md 1984-86, jt md 1986-87, chief exec 1987-89; chief exec Swan Hunter Ltd 1987-(jt md 1986-87), dir Maravia International Ltd 1987-, chm Swan Hunter International Ltd 1989-; memb Cncl NE Coast Inst Engrs and Shipbuilders 1987-; MRINA 1974, MIMarE 1974, CEng 1976; *Recreations* vintage sports cars, sailing, travel, wine, sheep farming; *Style*— Alexander Marsh, Esq; Swan Hunter Ltd, Wallsend, Newcasle upon Tyne NE28 6EQ (☎ 0912 628921, fax 091 234 0707, telex 53151)

MARSH, Dr Barbara Elizabeth; JP (Shropshire 1969); da of John Watson (d 1965), of St Helens, Lancs, and Elizabeth, *née* Burrows (d 1987); *b* 3 July 1931; *Educ* Cowley Girls GS, Univ of London (BSc), Univ of Birmingham (PhD); *m* 1 April 1958, (George) Eric Marsh, s of Richard George Marsh, of Newport, Shropshire; 3 s (Andrew b 1958, Stephen b 1961, Piers b 1963), 1 da (Fiona b 1967); *Career* demonstrator Kings Coll Newcastle 1956-57, lectr St Helen Tech Coll 1957-58, teacher Adams GS Newport 1959-60, non-exec memb: Bd Midlands Electricity Bd 1984-89, Shropshire Health Authy 1990-; memb: Cncl on Tbnls 1977-84, Roskill Ctee on Fraud 1984-86, W Mercia Police Authy 1989-; vice chm Shropshire CC 1981-85 (cncllr 1964-), memb Exec Assoc of CC, former chm Area Manpower Bd for Shropshire, vice pres Nat Inst of Adult Continuing Educn, memb Industl Tbnl, dep church warden St Nicholas Church Newport; *Recreations* dabbling; *Style*— Dr Barbara Marsh, JP; Middle Farm, Chetwynd Aston, Newport, Shropshire

MARSH, (Graham) Barrie; s of Ernest Heaps Marsh (d 1983), of 102 Victoria Court, Birkdale, Southport, and Laura Greenhalgh, *née* Bancher; *b* 18 July 1935; *Educ* Loughborough GS, Univ of Liverpool (LLB); *m* 5 April 1961, Nancy, da of Leslie Herbert Smith (d 1984), of 146 Cropston Rd, Anstey, Leicester; 1 s (Peter James b 1962), 2 da (Susan Nancy b 1964, Caroline Judith b 1966); *Career* Nat Serv with RASC 1957-59; admitted slr 1957; pres Liverpool Publicity Assoc 1980; chm: Merseyside Chamber of Commerce and Indust 1984-86, Radio City plc 1988-; nat chm Young Slr Gp Law Soc 1975; pres: Liverpool Law Soc 1978-79, Slrs Disciplinary Tbnl 1988-; Belgian Consul in Liverpool; FRIA; *Books* Employer and Employee (3 edn, 1989); *Recreations* hill walking, golf, bird watching; *Clubs* Liverpool Racquet, Anglo-Belgian (London); *Style*— Barrie Marsh, Esq; Calmer Hey, Benty Heath Lane, Willaston, South Wirral L64 1SA (☎ 051 327 4863); Mace & Jones, 19 Water St, Liverpool L2 0RP (☎ 051 236 8989, fax 051 227 5010)

MARSH, Brian Peter; s of Albert Edward Marsh (d 1980), and Maud Elisabeth, *née* Holman; *b* 28 Feb 1941; *Educ* Sutton Valence Sch; *m* Aleksandra Barbara, *née* Waclawik; 1 s (Rupert b 1973), 2 da (Natalie b 1976, Antonia b 1988); *Career* chm Nelson Hurst & Marsh (Hldgs) Ltd and 40 other cos 1979-89; sr tstee Marsh Christian Tst; *Recreations* swimming, writing; *Clubs* Authors; *Style*— Brian P Marsh, Esq; Flat 7, 30 Onslow Gardens, London SW7 (☎ 071 584 6056); 1 Seething Lane, London EC3

MARSH, Caroline Elizabeth; da of A J Marsh, of Lindfield Gardens, Hampstead, London, and Ingrid Areskog, of Flemmingatan 60 IV, 11245 Stockholm, Sweden; *b* 27 Oct 1961; *Educ* Felixstowe Coll, Godolphin and Latymer Sch, Hammersmith and W London Coll, Middx Hosp Sch of Physiotherapy (Dip Physiotherapy); *Career* sec Allen Brady & Marsh Ltd 1980-81; physiotherapist Middx Hosp 1984-86, sr physiotherapist Daly Physiotherapy Services 1986-87; self-employed sole physiotherapist: Medical Express Clinic 1987-88, Central Sch of Ballet 1987-, The Danceworks Clinic 1987-90; currently ptnr at Central London Injuries Clinic; attending physiotherapist to: The Kirov Ballet Co, The Bolshoi Ballet Co, Northern Ballet Co, Rambert Dance Co, numerous W End Musicals; pt/t work incl: Crystal Palace Nat Sports Centre, Cannons Sports Club, London Marathon 1986, Marks & Spencer plc; lectr in sports and dance injuries to various orgns; author of various published articles; teacher of jazz keep fit and body conditioning classes; memb: Central London Branch Chartered Soc of Physiotherapy 1985-87, Med Advsy Panel Nat Orgn of Dance and Mime; *Recreations* professional jazz classes, singing and music, art and theatre, sports; *Style*— Miss Caroline Marsh; Central London Injuries Clinic, Ground Floor Suite, 27 Weymouth St, London W1N 3FJ (☎ 071 636 4890)

MARSH, David John; s of Harry Cheetham Marsh, of Solihull Warwickshire (d 1979), and Florence, *née* Bold; *b* 2 Nov 1936; *Educ* Leeds GS, Merton Coll Oxford (MA); *m* 26 May 1962, Hilary Joy, da of Edwin Leslie Pitt, of Tetbury, Glos; 1 s (Nigel b 1966), 2 da (Carole b 1963, Rowena b 1965); *Career* admitted slr 1961, ptnr Wragge & Co Slrs 1963-, dir Marla Tube Fittings Ltd 1965-, dir and sec Fownes Hotels plc 1985-; memb Law Soc 1961; *Recreations* sport, travel, wine, food; *Clubs* Midland Sporting; *Style*— David Marsh, Esq; Lenchwick House, Lenchwick, nr Evesham, Worcs WR11 4TG (☎ 0386 442451); Wragge & Co, Bank House, 8 Cherry St, Birmingham B2 5JY (☎ 021 632 4131, fax 021 643 2417, telex 338728 WRAGGE G)

MARSH, Dr David Max; s of Joseph Richard james Maximilian Marsh (d 1985), and Dorothy, *née* Pemberton; *b* 29 April 1934; *Educ* King George V Sch Southport, Gonville and Caius Coll Cambridge (BA, MB BChir); *m* 7 Nov 1959, Jennifer Margaret, da of Robert Samuel Heaton (d 1977); 2 s (Simon b 24 Nov 1960, Nigel b 4 July 1962), 1 da (Fiona b 25 Jan 1964); *Career* GP 1961-, employment med advsr Health and Safety Exec 1973-; English golf champion 1964 and 1970, English int golf 1956-72, capt England golf 1968-71, capt GB golf 1973-75; chm Rules of Golf Ctee Royal Ancient Golf Club 1988-90, dir Everton GC; pres: Lancashire Union of Golf Clubs 1985, Eng Golf Union 1988; MFOM; *Recreations* golf, soccer; *Clubs* Southport and Ainsdale Golf, Formby Golf, Royal and Ancient (Capt 1990-91), Ormskirk Golf, Royal Worlington and Newmarket Golf, Royal Over-Seas League; *Style*— Dr David Marsh; 26 Blundell Drive, Southport, Merseyside PR8 4RG (☎ 0704 65639); 63 Henlow Ave, Kirkby, Liverpool L32 9RN (☎ 051 549 2212)

MARSH, Eric Morice; s of Frederick Morice Marsh (d 1970), of Carnforth, Lancs, and Anne, *née* Leigh; *b* 25 July 1943; *Educ* The Abbey Sch Fort Augustus Inverness-shire Scotland, Courtfield Catering Coll Blackpool, Lancs (Nat Dip Hotelkeeping & Catering); *m* 2 Sept 1968, Elizabeth Margaret, da of John (Jack) Lowes, of Macclesfield, Cheshire; 2 s (Andrew Paul b 4 Aug 1969, Christopher Simon b 5 July 1974), 2 da (Erika Louise b 26 Oct 1971, Lucy Anne b 4 Aug 1982); *Career* student Hotel Sch 1960-63, stagiare George V Hotel Paris 1964-65, trainee The Dorchester 1965-68, asst mangr Royal Lancaster 1969-73, dir and gen mangr Newling Ward Hotels Ltd 1973-75, tenant Cavendish Hotel Chatsworth Estate 1975-; md: Paludis Ltd (trading as Cavendish Hotel) 1975-, Cavendish Aviation; pt/t lectr Sheffield Poly, occasional contribs to professional pubns; memb Catholic Church Fin Ctee, Co-ordinator Ctee Neighbourhood Watch; memb Ctee: Br Aerobatics Assoc, Br Hotels Restaurants & Caterers Assoc; memb Inst of Advanced Motorists, MinstM; *Recreations* collection of fine art, aviation (aerobatics), distance running; *Style*— Eric Marsh, Esq; Cavendish Hotel, Baslow, Derbys DE4 1SP (☎ 024 658 2311); Paludis Ltd, Baslow, Derbys DE4 1SP (☎ 024 658 2311, fax 024658 2312, car 0836 587 690, telex 547150 CAVTEL G)

MARSH, Baroness; Hon Felicity Carmen Francesca; da of Baron McFadzean of Kelvinside (Life Peer); *b* 26 April 1946; *Educ* St Paul's Girls' Sch, SOAS (BA in Japanese); *m* 1979, as his 3 w, Baron Marsh, *qv*; *Career* investment analyst/portfolio mangr Robert Fleming 1974-79, asst vice pres Rowe Price-Fleming Int Inc 1979-81, dir Mannington Mgmnt Servs Ltd 1982-; *Books* Japanese Overseas Investment - The New Challenge (1983), Japan's Next Export Success: The Financial Services Industry (1986); *Recreations* oriental antiques, classic cars, windsurfing, photography; *Style*— The Rt Hon Lady Marsh; Lloyds Bank Ltd, South Bank Branch, 2 York Rd, London SE1

MARSH, Francis Patrick (Frank); s of Horatio Septimus Marsh, of Leeds, Yorks, and Violet Mabel Constance, *née* Murphy; *b* 15 April 1936; *Educ* Gonville and Caius Coll Cambridge (BA, MB BChir, MA), London Hosp Med Coll Univ of London (MRCP); *m* 31 Aug 1963, Pamela Anne Campbell, da of Richard Campbell Bradbury (d 1963), of London; 1 s (Nicholas b 1966), 2 da (Penelope b 1964, Alexandra b 1971); *Career* The Royal London Hosp: house offr 1960-61, registrar in med 1963-65, res fell Med Unit Med Coll 1965-67, lectr Med Coll 1967-70, sr lectr in med 1970-, conslt physician 1971-, dean of med studies Med Coll 1990-; SHO Kent and Canterbury Hosp 1961-62, registrar in med Royal Free Hosp 1962-63; chm NE Thames Regnl Med Advsy Ctee; memb: Jt Formulary Ctee Br Nat Formulary, Special Advsy Ctee on Renal Disease, Jt Ctee on Higher Med Trg, Euro Renal Assoc, BR Transplant Soc; memb RSM, FRCP 1976; *Books* incl: Urology (contrib, 1976), Price's Textbook of Medicine (contrib, 1978), Oxford Textbook of Medicine (contrib, 1982, 1987), Postgraduate Nephrology (ed, 1985), Hutchisons Clinical Methods (contrib, 1989), Drugs and the Kidney (contrib, 1990); *Recreations* music, sailing, skiing; *Clubs* Blizard; *Style*— Dr Frank Marsh

MARSH, Frederick Oliver; *b* 13 Sept 1925; *Educ* Regent St Poly (Dip Mgmnt Studies); *Career* Capt Royal Berks Regt, demobbed 1948; chm and md Winton-Smith (Foods) Ltd 1964-74, princ Marsh Business Servs 1974-; mktg conslt: UN Agency (ITC UNCTAD GATT) 1978-86, Helsinki Sch of Econs 1984-; vice chm Royal Aero Club 1977-82, vice pres Fedn Aeronautique Internationale 1982-, pres Europe Airports; Br Air Racing champion 1972, winner Duke of Edinburgh Trophy for Formula Air Racing 1972 and 1976; FAI Tissandier Dip 1978, OM World Aerospace Educn Orgn 1985, Royal Aero Silver medal 1989; Liveryman Worshipful Co of Butchers 1962; FBIM 1970; *Books* The Market for New Foods and Beverages in Europe (1986, re-written 1988); *Recreations* air sport, painting, travel, Scottish dancing; *Clubs* Naval & Mil, Royal Aeronautical; *Style*— Frederick Marsh, Esq; 17 Albany Court, Palmer St, London SW1H 0AB (☎ 071 233 3123, fax 071 233 3123)

MARSH, Gordon Victor; s of The Venerable Wilfred Carter Marsh (d 1931), of Devil's Lake, North Dakota, USA, and Rosalie Marsh (d 1947); *b* 14 May 1929; *Educ* The Coll and Cwlth GS's Swindon Wilts, Keble Coll Oxford (MA), Sloan Business Sch Cornell Univ USA; *m* 13 June 1959, Millicent, da of Christopher Thomas Rowsell (d 1959); 1 s (Richard Marsh b 1960), 1 da (Susan Marsh b 1961); *Career* RAF PO personnel selection branch 1947-49; dep sec United Cardiff Hosps 1960-65, dep sec and house govr St Georges Hosp 1965-72, admin and sec Bd of Govrs UCH 1972-74, area admin Lambeth Southwark and Lewisham Area Health Authy (teaching) 1974-82, dep health serv cmmr for Eng Scot and Wales 1982-89; memb of the Police Complaints Authority 1989-, chm Trelawn Mgmnt Ctee of Richmond Fellowship 1970-83; memb: Advsy Bd Coll of Occupational Therapists 1974-, various working parties concerned with med ethics; wandsman and hon sec of congregation St Paul's Cathedral, memb Cncl NAHA 1979-82, vice chm Assoc of Chief Admins of Health Authys 1980-82; memb RSM, FIHSM 1964; *Recreations* gardens and gardening, music; *Clubs* United Oxford and Cambridge Universities; *Style*— Gordon Marsh, Esq; Springwater, St Lucian's Lane, Wallingford OX10 9ER (☎ 0491 36 660); Police Complaints Authority, 10 Great George St, London SW1P 3AE (☎ 071 273 6484)

MARSH, Honoria Diana; da of Arthur E Marsh (d 1942), and Letitia Octavia, *née* Perkin (d 1989); *b* 13 Feb 1923; *Educ* privately; *Career* WRNS (special duties) 1942-45; artist, author, glass engraver, lectr and book reviewer; glass engravings incl: The Life-Boat Goblet (Gulbenkian Museum Lisbon) 1964, Chateau-Lafite-Rothschild Centenary Goblet (Banque Rothschild Paris) 1967-68, Churchill Goblet 1968, RAF Goblet (RAF Museum Hendon) 1976, Mountbatten Memorial Goblet (Mountbatten Museum Hants) 1980-81; several London and provincial exhibitons (first living artist to exhibit a group of pictures in Nat Portrait Gallery 1972), work illustrated in numerous art books and magazines; contrib articles various magazines incl: Connoisseur, Antique Collector, Literary Review; memb Cons Party 1945-; memb Master Glass Painters 1950; *Books* Shades from Jane Austen (written and illustrated, 1975); *Recreations* good food, good wine, good friends, good books, an addicted cruciverbalist, watching polo all summer; *Style*— Miss Honoria Marsh; Windwhistle Farm, Winterborne Kingston, nr Blandford Forum, Dorset DT11 9AZ (☎ 0929 472 136)

MARSH, Capt John; CBE (1977); s of Arthur Frank Marsh (d 1953), of Cheam, Surrey, and Doris Evelyn, *née* Dabbs; *b* 23 Aug 1932; *Educ* Epsom Coll, St Johns Coll Cambridge (MA); *m* 12 April 1958, Margaret Hilda, da of Eric William Beresford

Brailey (d 1977), of Fremington, Devon; 2 s (Jonathon b 1961, Nigel b 1964); *Career* cmmnd RN 1954, Cdr 1968, Staff of Saclant Norfolk, UA, USA 1972, HMS Ark Royal 1975, RN Sch of Meteorology and Oceanography 1977, Capt 1978, Staff of Saceur Belgium 1979, Staff of Cincfleet Northwood and UK 1982, dir naval oceanography and meteorology MOD London 1985, Chief Naval Instr Offr 1986; dir Int Toga Project Office World Meteorological Orgn Geneva Switzerland 1987; vice-chm Royal Br Legion Swiss Branch; memb: Anglo Swiss Club of Geneva, Br Residents Assoc; *Recreations* bridge, music, walking; *Style—* Capt John Marsh, CBE; World Meteorological Orgn, CP No 2300, CH 1211, Geneva 2, Switzerland (☎ 010 41 22 730 8225)

MARSH, Prof John Stanley; s of Stanley Albert Marsh (d 1973), and Elsie Gertrude, *née* Powell (d 1969); *b* 5 Oct 1931; *Educ* George Dixon GS Birmingham, St John's Coll Oxford (MA); *m* 20 Sept 1958, Kathleen Edith, da of Eric Arthur Casey (d 1982); 1 s (Peter b 1967), 1 da (Christine b 1969); *Career* Nat Serv RAF 1950-52; Univ of Reading 1956-77: res economist, lectr, sr lectr, reader, prof agric economics 1984-, dean agric 1986-89, dir centre for agric strategy; Univ of Aberdeen prof agric economics 1977-84; author of numerous articles and pubns on agric related topics; sec Agric Economics Soc 1969-84; memb: Potato Mktg Bd 1979-84, EDC Food and Drink Mfrg; FRSA 1978-, ARAgS 1990; *Books* A Preliminary Study of the Small Dairy Farm and the Small Farm Scheme (1960), The National Association of Corn and Agricultural Merchants and the Merchant's Future (1967), A Future for European Agriculture (jtly, 1971), CAP: UK Priorities, European Opinion (1976), L'Ordre Alimentaire Mondial (contrib, 1982), The Human Food Chain (contrib, 1989); *Recreations* photography, caravanning; *Clubs* Farmer's, Royal Cwlth; *Style—* Prof John Marsh; 15 Adams Way, Earley, Reading, Berks RG6 2UT (☎ 0734 868434); Department of Agricultural Economics and Management, University of Reading, 4 Earley Gate, Whiteknights Rd, P O Box 237, Reading, Berkshire RG6 2AR (☎ 0734 318970, telex 847813 RULIBG, fax 0734 314404)

MARSH, June Margaret; da of Frederick John Palmer (d 1981), of Cheshunt, Hertfordshire, and Ivy Margaret, *née* Tate; *b* 3 July 1948; *Educ* King Harold Sch Waltham Abbey Essex, London Coll of Fashion; *m* Graham John Marsh, s of late Frederick John Marsh; *Career* res asst: Planning Unit Interior Designers 1968-69, Sampson/Fether architects/design conslts 1970-73; fashion ed: Woman's Own 1974-78, Evening News 1979-80, TV Times 1980-81; ed Browns magazine 1980-81, fashion and beauty ed Options 1981-86, tutor St Martin's Sch of Art 1986-; contrib ed: Sunday Times, Times, Evening Standard, Vogue, Observer, Sunday Express Magazine, New Woman, Company magazine; fashion ed and Women's page ed Country Life 1989-91, contrib fashion ed The Daily Telegraph 1991, involved in advtg campaigns for Mulberry Co and Ballantynes; memb NUJ; *Recreations* reading, theatre, music, cinema, gardening, interior design, travelling, writing, painting, cooking; *Style—* Mrs June Marsh; Country Life Magazine, IPC Magazines, Kings Reach Tower, Stamford St, London SE1 (☎ 071 261 6603, fax 071 261 5139); 6 Hyde Vale, Greenwich, London SE10 8QH

MARSH, Laurie Peter; s of Davis Marsh; *b* 23 Oct 1930; *Educ* Perse Sch, Univ of Cambridge; *m* 1961 (m dis); 1 s, 2 da; *Career* md LP Marsh Properties Ltd 1958-, John Laurie & Co Ltd 1961-64, jt md English Property Corporation 1965-70, chm and chief exec Intereuropean Properties Ltd (formerly Tigon Group) 1969-, merged with Assoc Communications Corporation 1979, dir ACC 1979-; chm and chief exec: Laurie Marsh Group, Soundalive Holdings & US Subsid, Laurie Marsh Consultants Ltd, and others 1980-; *Recreations* travel, theatre, music, literature; *Style—* Laurie Marsh, Esq; Laurie Marsh Group Ltd, 30 Grove End Rd, London NW8 9LJ (☎ 071 289 6081); 244 East 48th St, New York 10017

MARSH, Prof Leonard George; s of Ernest Arthur Marsh, and Anne Eliza, *née* Bean; *b* 23 Oct 1930; *Educ* Ashford GS, Borough Road Coll London Inst of Educn, Univ of Leicester, Univ of York; *m* 20 Aug 1953, Ann Margaret, da of Thomas Francis Gilbert (d 1979); 1 s (David Richard b 1964), 1 da (Carol Ann b 1956); *Career* lectr St Paul's Coll Cheltenham 1963-65, princ lectr and head Postgrad Primary Educn Dept Goldsmith Coll London 1965-74, princ Bishop Grosseteste Coll Lincoln 1974-; visiting lectr: Bank St Coll NY, Virginia Cwlth Univ; former conslt OECD Portugal, educnl conslt Teacher Trg Project Botswana 1981, specialist tour India for Br Cncl; memb: Gen Advsy Cncl IBA 1977-82, N Lincs AHA 1984-90; chm Nat Assoc for Primary Educn 1981-83; Hon FCP; *Books* Let's Explore Mathematics Books 1-4 (1964-67), Children Explore Mathematics (1967, 3 edn 1969), Exploring the Metric World (1970), Let's Discover Mathematics Books 1-5 (1971-72), The Guinness Mathematics Book (1980), Alongside the Child in the Primary School (1970), Being a Teacher (1973); *Recreations* photography, theatre going, films; *Style—* Prof Leonard Marsh; Bishop Grosseteste College, Lincoln LN1 3DY (☎ 0522 527347, fax 0522 530243)

MARSH, Prof Paul Rodney; s of Harold Marsh, of Bournemouth, Dorset, and Constance, *née* Miller; *b* 19 Aug 1947; *Educ* Poole GS, LSE (BSc), London Business Sch (PhD); *m* 13 Sept 1971, Stephanie Beatrice, da of Mark Simonow, of London; *Career* systems analyst: Esso Petroleum 1968-69, Scicon 1970-71, London Business Sch 1974-; Bank of England res fell 1974-85, dir Sloan Fellowship Prog 1980-83; Centre for Mgmnt Devpt: dir, non exec dir 1984-, prof of mgmnt & fin 1985-, memb Governing Body 1986-, faculty dean 1987-, dep princ 1989-; non exec dir M+G Investmt Mgmnt 1989-; author of numerous pubns on corporate fin and investmt mgmnt in: Journal of Finance, Journal of Financial Economics, Managerial Finance, Harvard Business Review, Journal of the Institute of Actuaries, Research in Marketing, The Investment Analyst, Long Range Planning; memb CBI task force on City-Indust relationships 1986-88; exec ctee memb Br Acad of Mgmnt 1986-89; memb: Euro Fin Assoc, American Fin Assoc; *Books* Cases in Corporate Finance (1988), Managing Strategic Investment Decisions (1988), Accounting for Brands (1989), The HGSC Smaller Companies Index (1990); *Recreations* gardening; *Style—* Prof Paul Marsh; 52 Vivian Way, London N2 0HZ (☎ 071 444 6462); London Business Sch, Sussex Place, Regents Park, London NW1 4SA (☎ 071 262 5050, fax 071 724 7875, telex 27461 LONDISKOL)

MARSH, Peter Dudley; s of Dudley Graham Marsh (d 1969), of Canterbury, and Norah Marion *née* Wacher (d 1974); *b* 16 Feb 1926; *Educ* Dulwich, St John's Coll Hurstpierpoint, Univ of Edinburgh, Sch of Architecture Canterbury Coll of Art; *m* 1, 18 Aug 1949, June, *née* Saxby (d 1969); 2 s (Richard b 1957, Jonathan b 1961), 1 da (Anne Crouch b 1953); m 2, 23 May 1970, Valerie, da of Charles Alfred Williams (d 1983); 1 s (Henry b 1977); *Career* architect in private practice 1952-, Surveyor to the Fabric Canterbury Cathedral 1969-; chm: Canterbury Branch RIBA 1969, Cathedral Architects Assoc 1984-87; pres Rotary Club of Dover 1970, memb Tech Sub Ctee Euro Cathedrals Assoc 1986-, chm Fabric Advsy Ctee Rochester Cathedral, Canterbury Conservation Advsy Ctee; govr Kent Inst of Art and Desig; Freeman City of London, Liveryman Worshipful Co of Masons 1978; memb EASA, ARIBA 1953, FSA 1982; *Recreations* bee keeping; *Style—* Peter Marsh, Esq, FSA; Little Watersend, Temple Ewell, Dover, Kent CT15 7EP (☎ 0304 822022)

MARSH, Baron (Life Peer UK 1981), of Mannington, Co Wilts; Richard William Marsh; PC (1966); s of William Marsh, of Belvedere, Kent; *b* 14 March 1928; *Educ* Jennings Sch Swindon, Woolwich Poly, Ruskin Coll Oxford; *m* 1, 1950 (m dis 1973), Evelyn Mary, da of Frederick Andrews, of Southampton; 2 s (Hon Andrew b 1950, Hon Christopher b 1960); m 2, 1973, Caroline Dutton (d 1975); m 3, 1979, Hon Felicity Carmen Francesca McFadzean, o da of Baron McFadzean of Kelvinside (Life Peer), *qv*; *Career* health servs offr Nat Union of Public Employees 1951-59; memb Clerical and Admin Whitley Cncl for Health Serv 1953-59; MP (L) Greenwich 1959-71; memb Nat Exec Fabian Soc; jt parly sec Miny of Labour 1964-65, Miny of Technol 1965-66, Miny of Power 1966-68; chm: Br Railways Bd 1971-76, Br Iron and Steel Consumers' Cncl to Jan 1983, Lee Cooper Licensing Services, Lee Cooper plc 1982-88, Newspaper Publishers Assoc 1976-90, (pt/t) TV-AM 1983-84, Mannington Management Services Ltd, Lopex plc, Laurentian Holding plc 1989-, Laurentian Life 1989, China and Eastern Investment Trust (Hong Kong) 1987-; dir: BAII Holdings Co 1986, Imperial Life of Canada (Toronto) 1984, Laurentian Group Corporation (Montreal); kt 1976; *Clubs* Reform, Buck's; *Style—* The Rt Hon the Lord Marsh, PC; Laurentian Financial Group plc, Laurentian House, Barnwood, Gloucester GL4 7RZ (☎ 0452 371371, fax 0452 612509, telex 43521)

MARSH, Robin Lewis; s of Charles Edward Marsh (d 1969), of Westminster London, and Elsie May, *née* Peckham (d 1986); *b* 20 July 1939; *Educ* Henry Thornton Sch London, Christ's Coll Cambridge (MA); *m* 26 Oct 1963, Suzette Fay, da of Frederick William Cockerton (d 1988), of Petersfield, Hants; 1 s (Charles Timothy Cockerton b 1980), 3 da (Claire Louise Cockerton b 1965, Annabel Lucy Cockerton b 1968, Camilla Sophie Cockerton b 1972); *Career* CA; articled clerk Fuller Wise Fisher 1958-60 and 1963-65; md Br Rare Earth Ltd 1966-69; chm and chief exec: CT Gp Ltd 1970-85, Wills Gp plc 1985-87; chm Marsh & Co Ltd 1987-; non exec dir various cos; memb Ctee: Cons, Bramley Sch, Residents Assoc; Freeman City of London 1968, Liveryman Worshipful Co Butchers 1969; FCA 1975 (ACA 1964), FRGS, FInstD; *Recreations* shooting, fishing, skiing, antique map collecting, travel, golf; *Style—* Robin Marsh, Esq; Marsh & Co Ltd, PO Box 47, Tadworth, Surrey KT20 7SZ (☎ 073 781 2920, fax 073 781 3113)

MARSH, Roger Edward; s of Albert Edward Marsh (d 1980), of Bickley, Kent, and Maud Elizabeth, *née* Holman; *b* 5 March 1945; *Educ* Sutton Valence Sch, Cranbrook USA; *m* 12 Sept 1968 (m dis 1989), Susan Louise, da of Alfred Gabriel Chase, of Bexhill-On-Sea; 1 s (Nicholas b 22 Feb 1971); m 2, Maryanne, da of Peter Flack, of Ingatestone; *Career* entered Lloyd's 1963 with Sir Wm Garthwaite Ins, elected underwriting memb Lloyd's 1966; Tyser & Co: ptnr 1975 (sr ptnr 1988), various directorships within gp (UK & overseas); memb St Helen's PCC Bishopsgate 1981-84, chm Lloyd's Wine Soc; *Recreations* wine, books (antiquarian), music, shooting, tennis, cricket; *Clubs* City Univ, MCC, Harlequins FC, Les Ambassadeurs; *Style—* Roger Marsh, Esq; Peel Arms Cottage, 53 Peel St, London W8 7PA (☎ 071 243 0441); Tyser & Co, Ellerman House, 12/20 Camomile St, London EC3 (☎ 071 623 6262)

MARSHALL; *see*: Johnson-Marshall

MARSHALL, Alan John; JP; s of Arthur Edward Marshall, ISO, and Hilda May, *née* Sloss (d 1988); *b* 31 Dec 1927; *Educ* William Morris Central Sch; *m* 2 Sept 1950, Dorothy Margaret, da of Arthur Vernon, of Highams Park; 1 s (Chistopher Alan b 1957), 1 da (Caroline Jane b 1955); *Career* Nat Serv RAF; keeper Guildhall City of London 1970-80; magistrate Inner London Bench 1975-, cncllr Epping Forest DC 1982-86; pres Essex Co Bowls 1991; Freeman City of London, Liveryman Worshipful Co of Scriveners; *Recreations* flat green bowls; *Clubs* Bread Street Ward; *Style—* Alan Marshall, Esq, JP; The Keeper, The Guildhall, London

MARSHALL, Dr Alan Ralph; s of Ralph Marshall (d 1931), of London, and Mabel, *née* Mills; *b* 27 July 1931; *Educ* Beckenham Tech Sch, London Univ (AcDipEd), Eastern Washington Univ (M Ed), London Univ (M Phil), Stanford Univ California (MA); *m* 19 Feb 1959, Caterina, da of Luigi Gattico (d 1971), of Pallanza Italy; 1 s (Roy Luigi b 1966), 1 da (Dilva b 1961); *Career* RAF Air Photographic Intelligence 1950-51; teaching posts in Eng and USA 1954-62, sr lectr Shoreditch Coll Surrey 1962-68, visiting prof Eastern Washington State Coll 1964-65, field dir Sch Cncl Project Technol 1970-71, course team chm Open Univ 1972-75; DES: HM Insp 1977-82, HM Staff Inspr Secdy Educ 1983-85, HM Chief Insp Teacher Educn 1985-; Hon PhD Nottingham Poly; FRSA; *Books* School Technology in Action (Ed, 1975), International Dictionary of Education (with Page & Thomas, 1977-), Giving Substance to a Vision (1990); *Recreations* theatre, travel, reading; *Style—* Dr Alan Marshall; Educational Consultant, 98 Wheathampstead Rd, Harpenden, Herts AL5 1JB

MARSHALL, Albert Selwyn; MBE (1968); s of Albert Marshall (d 1978), of Barrow, Bury St Edmunds, Suffolk, and Ethel, *née* Andrews; *b* 26 Sept 1934; *Educ* Dartford West Co Sch; *m* 1, 19 March 1960, Joan Margaret (d 1985), da of Victor Percy Lashwood, of Sussex; 1 s (Trevor Keith b 19 June 1961), 1 da (Julie Carina b 8 Aug 1963); m 2, 19 July 1988, Marion Rose, *née* Wilmott; *Career* diplomat: FO 1955-61, communications offr UK mission to UN NY 1961-64, archivst Br Embassy Prague 1964-65, immigration offr Br High Cmmn Kingston Jamaica 1965-68, FCO 1968-72, admin offr Br Embassy Addis Ababa Ethiopia 1972-75, Br vice consul Belgrade Yugoslavia 1976-77, HM vice consul Tokyo Japan 1977-81, FCO 1981-86, first sec Br Embassy Washington USA 1986-90, HM consul Br Embassy Tel Aviv Israel 1990-; *Recreations* ice skating, gardening, cycling, cricket; *Style—* Albert Marshall, Esq, MBE; 4 Tansy Close, Merrow Park, Guildford, Surrey GU4 7XN (☎ 0483 478115); British Embassy, 192 Hayarkon St, Tel Aviv, Israel 63405 (☎ 03 2491781)

MARSHALL, Alexander Badenoch; *b* 31 Dec 1924; *Educ* Glenalmond, Worcester Coll Oxford (MA); *m* 1961, Mona; 2 s, 1 da; *Career* served WWII RNVR; chm Commercial Union Assurance Co plc 1983-90; chm: Bestobell plc 1979-85, The Maersk Co Ltd 1986-, RBC Holdings (UK) Ltd 1988-; vice chm The Boots Co plc, dir Royal Bank of Canada; *Style—* Alexander Marshall, Esq; The Maersk Co Ltd, Westminster Tower, 3 Albert Embankment, London SE1 7SP (☎ 071 537 3333)

MARSHALL, Alfreda, aka Fredda Brilliant; da of Mordechai Marshall (d 1946), of Melbourne, Aust, and Roselle Wartezki (d 1947); *b* 7 April 1908; *Educ* Gymnasium Poland; *m* 1935, Herbert P J Marshall (prof emeritus), s of P C Marshall (d 1957); *Career* actress and singer USA 1930-33, sculptress 1932-, actress and script writer London 1937-50; works as sculptress incl Nehru, Krishna Menon, Paul Robeson, Herbert Marshall, Mahatma Gandhi (a maquette of which is in The Queen's Collection, St George's Chapel, Windsor), Indira Gandhi, Carl Albert, Sir Maurice Bowra, Duncan Grant, Lord Elwyn-Jones, Sir Isaac Hayward, Tom Mann, Dr Delyte Morris; exhibitions in London incl Royal Acad, Royal Watercolour Soc, Whitechapel Art Gallery, India House, St Paul's Cathedral, etc; other exhibitions in Melbourne, Moscow, New Delhi, Bombay and Washington; FRSA; *Books* Biographies in Bronze (1986), Women in Power (1987); *Recreations* singing, composing, lyricist; *Style—* Ms Fredda Brilliant; 1204 Chautauqua St, Carbondale, Illinois 62901, USA (☎ 618 549 4569)

MARSHALL, Dr Alistair Graeme; s of Alan Francis Marshall (d 1955), and Edna Janet, *née* Houlker; *b* 28 Dec 1943; *Educ* Univ of Otago NZ (BSc, MB ChB); *m* 1 Jan 1985, Margaret Ann, da of William Crane, of Wauchope, NSW, Aust; 1 da (Geraldine Jane b 6 Nov 1987); *Career* conslt anaesthetist The London and London Chest Hosps 1983-; treas Aust and NZ Med and Dental Assoc; memb RSM, FFARCS; *Books* Hazards and Complications of Anaesthesia (contrib, 1987); *Recreations* gardening; *Style—* Dr Alistair Marshall; The Anaesthetic Dept, The London Hospital, Whitechapel, London E1 (☎ 071 3777793)

MARSHALL, Sir Arthur Gregory George; OBE (1948), DL (Cambs 1968); s of David Gregory Marshall, MBE (d 1942), and Maude Edmunds, *née* Wing (d 1931); *b* 4 Dec 1903; *Educ* Tonbridge, Jesus Coll Cambridge (MA, Athletics blue); *m* 1931, Rosemary Wynford (d 1988), da of Marcus Dimsdale (d 1918); 2 s, 1 da; *Career* chm and md Marshall of Cambridge (Engrg) 1942-89 (joined Garage Co of Marshall (Cambridge) Ltd 1926, established Aircraft Co now Marshall of Cambridge (Engrg) Ltd 1929-), life pres Marshall of Cambridge (Holdings) Ltd 1990; High Sheriff of Cambs and Isle of Ely 1967-70; chm Aerodrome Owners Assoc 1964-65; memb: Air Cadet Cncl 1951-59 and 1965-76, Advsy Cncl on Technol 1967-70; Hon Old Cranwellian 1979, Companion of RAeS 1980, hon fell Univ of Cambridge 1990; Olympic Team Reserve 1924; Order of Istiqlal 1st Class (Jordan) 1990; kt 1974; *Recreations* flying; *Clubs* RAF, Hawks (Cambridge); *Style*— Sir Arthur Marshall, OBE, DL; Horseheath Lodge, Linton, Cambridge CB1 6PT (☎ 0223 891318); Marshall of Cambridge (Engrg) Ltd, Airport Works, Newmarket Rd, Cambridge CB5 8RX (☎ 0223 61133, telex 81208)

MARSHALL, Arthur Stirling-Maxwell; CBE (1986, OBE 1978); s of Victor Stirling-Maxwell Marshall (d 1941), of Edinburgh, and Jeannie Theodora, *née* Hunter (d 1971); *b* 29 Jan 1929; *m* 1, 25 Dec 1955, Eleni (d 1969), da of Panagiotis Kapralos (d 1946), of Athens, Greece; 1 s (John b 1958), 2 da (Jeannie b 1956, Anna b 1957); m 2, 14 Aug 1985, Cheryl Mary, da of Desmond Hookens, of Madras, India; 1 da (Christina b 1988), 1 step s (Lionel b 1974), 2 step da (Suzanne b 1972, Margaret b 1973); *Career* FO 1959, ME Centre for Arab Studies Lebanon 1959-61, political offr Bahrain 1961-64, registrar HBM Ct for Bahrain 1961-64, attache Br Embassy Athens 1964-67, second sec Br Embassy Rabat Morocco 1967-69, first sec Br High Cmmn Nicosia Cyprus 1970-75 (formerly second sec), first commercial sec Br Embassy Kuwait 1975-79, dep Br high cmmr Southern India 1979-83, cnsllr Br Embassy Kuwait 1983-85, Br ambass People's Democratic Repub of Yemen 1986-89, ret 1989; *Recreations* nature, music; *Clubs* Oriental; *Style*— Arthur Marshall, Esq, CBE; 147 Highbury Grove, London N5 1HP

MARSHALL, (Herbert) Brian; s of Charles Ridings Marshall, MBE (d 1974), of 151 Thorne Rd, Doncaster, and Phyllis Enid Marshall; *b* 2 March 1935; *Educ* Bradfield, Univ of Leeds (LLB); *m* 1 Feb 1964, Jillian Lloyd, da of Owen Tunnicliffe (d 1972), of Wildwood, Bawtry Rd, Bessacarr, Doncaster; 1 s (Timothy Noel b 2 Jan 1965), 1 da (Juliet Anne Lloyd b 24 Feb 1967); *Career* admitted slr 1959, NP, clerk to the Tax Commissioners Conisborough Div; chm Doncaster Racecourse Club; memb Law Soc; *Recreations* horse racing, snooker, travel; *Clubs* St Georges (Doncaster); *Style*— Brian Marshall, Esq; Canterbury, 19 St Wilfrids Rd, Bessacarr, Doncaster, South Yorkshire DN4 6AA (☎ 0302 535366); Hill House Chambers, 7 Regent Terrace, South Parade, Doncaster, South Yorkshire DN1 2EJ (☎ 0302 366831, fax 0302 329718)

MARSHALL, Christopher James; s of Geoffrey Gordon Marshall, and Mary Beatrice, *née* Try (d 1986); *b* 24 Sept 1959; *Educ* John Lyon Sch Harrow, Univ of Reading (BA), Goldsmith's Coll London (MMus); *m* 31 Aug 1985, Wendy Jane, da of Leslie Thompson; 1 s (William James b 1987); *Career* BBC 1981-; sr prodr Music Dept Radio Three 1988- (prodr 1985-88); *Recreations* reading, 20th century fiction, cooking; *Style*— Christopher Marshall, Esq; BBC, Broadcasting House, London W1A 1AA (☎ 071 927 4880)

MARSHALL, Sir Colin Marsh; s of Marsh Edward Leslie Marshall, and Florence Mary Marshall; *b* 16 Nov 1933; *Educ* Univ Coll Sch Hampstead; *m* 1958, Janet Winifred, da of John Cracknell; 1 da; *Career* Orient Steam Navigation Co 1951-58; Herts Corporation: joined as mgmnt trainee (Chicago and Toronto) 1958, gen mangr (Mexico) 1959-60, asst to Pres (NY) 1960, gen mangr (UK) 1961-62; Avis Inc: regnl mangr and vice pres (Europe 1964-66, Europe and ME 1966-69, worldwide 1965-71), exec vice pres and chief operating offr (NY), pres 1975, chief exec 1976, co chm 1979 (following takeover by Norton Simon Inc of which he became exec vice pres 1979); dir and dep chief exec Sears Holdings plc 1981-83, chief exec and Bd memb BA 1983-; Bd memb: Midland Bank Group, BTA, Grand Metropolitan plc, American C of C (London); vice pres: Advtg Assoc, CIM; memb: Cncl IOD, Exec Ctee IATA, New York Stock Exchange Listed Advsy Ctee; Bd dir Br American C of C; tstee: Duke of Edinburgh Cwlth Study Conf, Prince's Youth Business Tst; vice chm World Travel and Tourism Cncl; kt 1987; *Recreations* tennis, skiing; *Clubs* Queen's; *Style*— Sir Colin Marshall; Head Office, Speedbird House, PO Box 10, London Airport (Heathrow), Hounslow, Middx TW6 2JA (☎ 081 759 5511, telex 8813983)

MARSHALL, David; MP (Lab) Glasgow, Shettleston 1979-; *b* 7 May 1941; *Educ* Larbert, Denny and Falkirk High Schs, Woodside Sr Secondary Sch; *m* 1968, Christina; 2 s, 1 da; *Career* joined Lab Pty 1962, memb TGWU, former Lab Pty organiser for Glasgow, vice chm Gtr Glasgow Passenger Tport Authy, regnl cncllr Strathclyde 1974-79 (chief whip, chm Manpower Ctee), vormer chm Manpower Ctee of the Convention of Scottish Local Authorities (COSLA), former memb LACSAB; memb: Select Ctee Scottish Affairs 1981-83, Select Ctee Tport 1983- (chm 1987-); sec Scottish Labour MPs 1981-; chm PLP Tport Ctee 1987-; put Solvent Abuse (Scotland) Act 1983 through Parl; *Recreations* music, gardening; *Style*— David Marshall, Esq, MP; 32 Enterkin St, Glasgow G32 7BA (☎ 041 778 8125); House of Commons, London SW1A 0AA (☎ 071 219 5134)

MARSHALL, (Andrew) David Michael Creagh; s of Andrew Harold Marshall (d 1970), of London, and Brenda Medlicott, *née* Massy; *b* 6 Sept 1954; *Educ* King's Coll Sch Wimbledon, Merton Coll Oxford (MA); *m* 19 March 1983, Jill Francesca, da of Laurence Duval Merreywether, of Harrogate; 1 s (Andrew b 1988), 1 da (Cicely b 1987); *Career* called to the Bar Lincoln's Inn 1981; cncl memb Soc for Computers and Law 1987-; *Style*— David Marshall, Esq; 3 Paper Buildings, Temple, London EC4Y 7EU (☎ 071 583 1183, fax 071 583 2037)

MARSHALL, Sir Denis Alfred; s of late Frederick Herbert, and Winifred Mary Marshall; *b* 1 June 1916; *Educ* Dulwich; *m* 1, 1949, Joan Edith, *née* Straker (d 1974); 1 s; m 2, 1975, Jane, *née* Lygo; *Career* WWII cmmnd XX The Lancashire Fusiliers 1939, served India and Burma (Maj) 1940-45, slr 1937; ptnr Barlow Lyde & Gilbert 1949-83 (conslt 1983-); memb: Cncl Law Soc 1966-86 (vice-pres 1980, pres 1981-82), Insur Brokers Registration Cncl 1979-, Criminal Injuries Compensation Bd 1982-90; memb Cncl FIMBRA 1986-90; kt 1982; *Recreations* sailing (yacht 'Turtledove of Mersea'); *Clubs* Naval and Military, Lloyd's Yacht, Royal Dart Yacht; *Style*— Sir Denis Marshall; Redways, Warfleet Rd, Dartmouth, South Devon TQ6 9BZ; Beaufort House, 15 St Botolph St, London EC3A 7NJ, (☎ 071 247 2277, telex 887249 G)

MARSHALL, Dr Enid Ann; da of Rev John Marshall (d 1945), of Whitehills, Banff, and Lizzie, *née* Gilchrist (d 1975); *b* 10 July 1932; *Educ* Whitehills Jr Secdy, Banff Acad, Bell-Baxter Sch Cupar, Univ of St Andrews (MA, LLB, PhD); *Career* apprentice slr Pagan & Osborne WS Cupar 1956-59, lectr in law Dundee Coll of Technol 1959-72, ed Arbitration Section The Journal of Business Law 1976-, reader in business law Univ of Stirling 1977- (lectr 1972-74, sr lectr 1974-77), ed Scottish Law Gazette 1984-; chm Social Security Appeal Tbnl Stirling and Falkirk 1984-; memb: Law Soc of Scotland 1959, Scot Law Agents Soc 1960; FRSA 1984, ARICS 1986, ACIArb 1988; *Books* incl: The Companies (Floating Charges and Receivers) (Scotland) Act 1972 (1972), Scottish Cases on Contract (1978), Scottish Cases on Agency (1980), Scottish Cases on Partnerships and Companies (1980), General Principles of Scots Law (1971, 5 edn 1991), Scots Mercantile Law (1983), Gill on Arbitration 3 edn (ed, 1983), Oliver and Marshall's Company Law (11 edn 1991); *Recreations* animal welfare, veganism; *Style*— Dr Enid Marshall; 24 Easter Cornton Rd, Stirling FK9 5ES (☎ 0786 78865); Edenbank, 1 Dermoch Drive, Dunblane, Perthshire FK15 9JH (☎ 0786 823117); University of Stirling, Stirling FK9 4LA (☎ 0786 73171, fax 777557 STUNIV G, int fax 44 736 63000, telex 0786 63000)

MARSHALL, Ernest Harold; s of Ernest Marshall (d 1931), of Chadwell Heath, and Annie Beatrice, *née* Lefever (d 1967); *b* 29 Nov 1924; *Educ* Rayleigh Sr, Shrewsbury, Univ of Bonn, Univ of Tehran; *m* 21 July 1954, Christine Louise Harrad (d 1957), of Thundersley, Essex; 2 s (Ian b 22 July 1960, Nicholas b 16 Dec 1964); *Career* RAF Polish Sqdn 1942-47; dir Sedgwick Group 1960-81, underwriter Lloyd's 1969-, conslt 1981-, dir SE Essex Tech Coll 1989-; St John's Ambulance: pres Rayleigh Div 1984-, vice pres Essex 1990-, memb Cncl Essex 1986-; pres Rochford Constituency Cons Assoc 1986-89; OStJ 1988; Freeman City of London 1980, Liveryman Worshipful Co of Insurers 1981-, hon prof Tehran Univ 1976; vice pres Insurance Inst London 1978-, memb IBRC 1981-, memb CIB 1974-81; Pilsudski medal (Poland) 1944; *Books* Construction and Erection Insurance (1978 and 1985), Directors and Officers (1986); *Recreations* travel, fine arts; *Clubs* Rochford Westminster; *Style*— Ernest Marshall, Esq; Beverley Lodge, Great Wheatley Road, Rayleigh, Essex SS6 7AP (☎ 0268 775156, fax 0268 776919)

MARSHALL, Dr Geoffrey; s of Leonard William Marshall (d 1953), and Kate, *née* Turner (d 1961); *b* 22 April 1929; *Educ* Arnold Sch Blackpool, Univ of Manchester (BA, MA), Univ of Glasgow (PhD); *m* 10 Aug 1957, Patricia Anne Christine, da of Edward Cecil Woodcock (d 1988), of Oxford; 2 s (David b 1962, Stephen Edward b 1967); *Career* res fell Nuffield Coll Oxford 1955-57, fell and praelector The Queen's Coll Oxford 1957-, Andrew Dixon White visiting prof Cornell Univ 1985-, delegate OUP 1987-; memb Oxford City Cncl 1964-74, Sheriff City of Oxford 1970-71; FBA 1970; *Books* Parliamentary Sovereignty and the Commonwealth (1957), Police and Government (1965), Constitutional Theory (1971), Constitutional Conventions (1986), Ministerial Responsibility (1989); *Recreations* squash; *Style*— Dr Geoffrey Marshall; The Queen's College, Oxford

MARSHALL, Geoffrey Wyndham; s of Wyndham J Marshall, of Reepham, Norfolk, and the late Gwendoline May Burdick Marshall; *b* 5 March 1937; *Educ* KES Birmingham, Jesus Coll Oxford, Harvard Business Sch (MBA); *m* 1960, Sally Rose, da of the late Thomas Barton Gerard; 2 s (Andrew b 1965, Julian b 1969), 1 da (Miranda b 1964); *Career* shoemaker; dir: Somervell Brothers Ltd 1972-75, Bally Shoe Factories (Norwich Ltd) and Bally Shoe Co Ltd 1975-, Bally London Shoe Co Ltd 1979- (chm 1990-), Russell and Bromley Ltd 1984-, Paper Chain East Anglia Ltd 1987-; gp md Bally Group UK Ltd 1979-89 (chief exec 1990-) exec vice chm Bally International AG Zurich 1990-, chm Bally Canada Inc Toronto 1989-, dir Bally Inc NY 1989-; chm Norwich Enterprises Agency Tst 1981-84; pres: Norwich and Norfolk C of C and Indust 1981-83, Norwich Footwear Mfrs Assoc 1983-84, Br Footwear Manufacturers Fedn 1987-88; Trade Warden Worshipful Co of Pattenmakers 1984-86 (Renter Warden 1987-88, Upper Warden 1988-89, Master 1989-90); chm Theatre Royal Norwich Tst 1985-90; dir Norfolk and Waveny Trg and Ent Cncl 1989-90; *Recreations* theatre, music, travel, skiing, house and garden; *Clubs* United Oxford and Cambridge Univ, City Swiss, Anglo-Swiss; *Style*— Geoffrey Marshall, Esq; Salle Place, Salle, Reepham, Norfolk NR10 5SF (☎ 0603 870638); Bally House, 27-29 Beach St, London W2R 3LB (☎ 071 287 2266, fax 071 734 2433)

MARSHALL, Dr (Frank) Graham; s of Frank Marshall, of Knole Hall, Knyverton Rd, Bournemouth, *née* Barker; *b* 28 March 1942; *Educ* W Bridgford GS, Univ of Birmingham (BA), Univ of Nottingham (PhD); *m* 10 July 1965, Patricia Anne, da of Thomas Leonard Bestwick, of Nottingham; 2 s (Stephen James b 1967, David Edward b 1971), 1 da (Anne-Marie b 1969); *Career* RS and Radar Estab (MOD) Malvern 1969-80; cnsllr Sci and Technol Br Embassy Tokyo 1980-82; md Plessey Res Roke Manor Romsey 1982-87; tech dir: Plessey Naval Systems Ltd, Templecombe 1987-; FIEE; *Recreations* country hobbies, electronic projects; *Style*— Dr Graham Marshall; Wilkinthroop House, Templecombe, Somerset BA8 0DH (☎ 0935 442566 ,telex 46108)

MARSHALL, Graham Robert; s of Robert Marshall, of Peebles, and Jean Grainger, *née* Whitson; *b* 23 May 1960; *Educ* Currie HS, Jordanhill Coll; *m* 29 Dec 1983, Anne Irene, da of Robert McMorran; 1 da (Kirsty Anne b 10 July 1988), 1 s (Callum Robert b 14 July 1990); *Career* Rugby Union flanker Selkirk RFC and Scotland (3 caps); clubs: Jordanhill RFC (now Hillhead-Jordanhill) 1979-82, Wakefield RFC 1982-88, Selkirk RFC 1988-; Scotland: debut v Aust 1988, toured Japan 1989, toured NZ 1990; physical educn teacher Darton HS Barnsley 1982-88, head of physical educn Selkirk HS; *Recreations* all sports; *Style*— Graham Marshall, Esq; c/o Selkirk RFC, Philiphaugh, Selkirk, Borders

MARSHALL, Prof (Ian) Howard; s of Ernest Ewart Marshall (d 1977), and Ethel, *née* Curran; *b* 12 Jan 1934; *Educ* Dumfries Acad, Aberdeen GS, Univ of Aberdeen (MA, BD, PhD), Univ of Cambridge (BA), Univ of Göttingen; *m* 25 March 1961, Joyce Elizabeth, da of Frederick John Proudfoot (d 1971); 1 s (Neil), 3 da (Morag, Aileen, Alison); *Career* asst tutor Didsbury Coll Bristol 1960-62, methodist min Darlington 1962-64, prof of New Testament Univ of Aberdeen 1979- (lectr 1964-70, sr lectr 1970-77, reader 1977-79), dean Faculty of Divinity Univ of Aberdeen 1981-84; *Books* Eschatology and the Parables (1963, 1978), Pocket Guide to Christian Beliefs (1963, 1978, 1989), The Work of Christ (1969), Kept by the Power of God (1969, 1975), Luke: Historian and Theologian (1970, 1989), The Origins of New Testament Christology (1976), New Testament Interpretation (ed 1977, 1979), The Gospel of Luke (New International Greek Testament Commentary, 1978), I Believe in the Historical Jesus (1977), The Epistles of John (New International Commentary on the New Testament, 1978), Acts (1980), Last Supper and Lord's Supper (1980), Biblical Inspiration (1982), 1 and 2 Thessalonians (1983), Christian Experience in Theology and Life (ed, 1988), Jesus The Saviour (1990); *Recreations* reading, walking, gardening, music; *Style*— Prof I Howard Marshall; Department of New Testament, University of Aberdeen, Aberdeen AB9 2UB (☎ 0224 272388, fax 0224 487048, telex 73458)

MARSHALL, Hugh; *Educ* S E Essex Tech Coll Barking (Dip Graphics NDD Illustration (SL), Illustration prizes), RCA (Royal Scholar, ARCA), travelling scholarship Germany 1957; *Career* illustrator/designer 1960-; designer and ed audio-visual film strips for an American co 1969-73, designer poster Bulls Blood Wine 1976-78, cmmnd to produce new symbols for Blue Circle Cement 1984 (shortlisted BBC Design awards 1987), designer exhibits for Museum of Natural Science Taiwan and King David Tower Jerusalem; pt/t lectr: illustration/graphics tutor Southend Sch of Art 1958-68, deviser first year design syllabus Sch of Photography Paddington Coll 1979-80, visiting lectr Barnet Coll 1980-81 (conslt lectr and advsr on industl contact 1983-84), lectr and deviser first year course on type/sign/symbol Canterbury Coll of Art 1981-87 (produced feasibility study for MA course 1986), visiting lectr Croydon Coll of Art 1986-87, external tutor Central Sch of Art 1987-88, visiting lectr Art Dept Richmond on Thames Coll 1987-89, short course leader in graphic design Kingston Poly 1990-; conslt to ASB Gallery on the Herbert Bayer exhibition (and compiler press release) 1985, ed/designer RCA Soc Newsletter 1985-; lectr on the Bauhaus, modern graphics and typography, conductor of instructional tours at various colls and for Friends of the V & A; exhibitons: Brno Czechoslovakia 1986 and 1990, Vancouver Canada 1986, Paperpoint London 1986, Berthold Centre Toronto 1988-89, Self Image Israel Museum Jerusalem 1989; awards: Silver medal IGI of America (for drawings for Rank Xerox) 1986, Studio Magazine awards (for designs for the Wine Soc 1988, for exhibition work in Jerusalem 1989), 12 Biennale of Graphic Design 1986, 14 Biennale of Graphic Design 1990; memb: Art & Architecture 1985, Design and Indust Assoc 1985, Soc for the Protection of Ancient Bldgs 1985-, Liaison Panel Croydon Coll (chaired by Martin Lambie-Nairn) 1988-90; served on Membs Ctee ICA 1971-74, fndr FORUMS for Assoc of Illustrators 1975; CSD: fell 1984, memb Graphics Gp Panel 1985-, appointed to Educ and Trg Bd 1986-88; *Books* Art Directing Photography (1989); *Style*— Hugh Marshall, Esq; 36 Stanhope Gardens, London SW7 5QY (☎ 071 373 2890)

MARSHALL, Ian; *b* 27 May 1947; *Educ* Univ of Edinburgh (MA); *Career* accountant Peat Marwick Mitchell 1970-74, gp accountant Thomas Tilling 1974-76, head of planning TSB Group 1981-86 (head of finance 1976-81), fin dir Ogilvy & Mather Ltd 1986-89, gen mangr Bain Clarkson Ltd 1989-; FCA; *Style*— Ian Marshall, Esq; Bain Clarkson Ltd, Bain Clarkson House, 15 Minories, London EC3N 1NJ (☎ 071 481 3232)

MARSHALL, James; MP (Lab) Leicester S Oct 1974-; *b* 13 March 1941; *Educ* Sheffield City GS, Leeds Univ; *m* 1962, Shirley, da of W Ellis; 1 s, 1 da; *Career* oppn spokesman Home Affrs 1982-, asst govt whip 1977-79, fought Leicester S Feb 1974 Gen Election, Harborough 1970 Gen Election; former memb Leeds & Leicester Cncls; *Style*— James Marshall Esq, MP; Flat 15, The Woodlands, 31 Knighton Rd, Leicester (☎ 708237)

MARSHALL, James Charles; s of James Charles Marshall (d 1964), of London, and Beatrice Fanny, *née* Wingrove (d 1984); *b* 29 July 1923; *m* 1, 1942 (m dis 1971), Violet Elizabeth, da of Samuel Wheeler Dover; 1 s (Terry b 15 March 1944); m 2, 1975 (m dis 1982), Irene, *née* Philips; 1 da (Victoria b 18 Aug 1971); m 3, 27 July 1985, Nancy Elizabeth, da of George William Noel Kilpin, of Aspley Guise; *Career* professional musician and singer, then drummer, dance, band leader and drum teacher 1949-60; md: Jim Marshall & Son 1960-63, J & T Marshall Ltd 1963-66, Jim Marshall Prods Ltd 1964-, Marshall Music 1966-80; mfr of Marshall Amplification and winner Queens award for Export Achievement 1984; chm: Variety Club of GB Youth Clubs Ctee, Variety at Work; vice pres: London Fedn of Boys Clubs, Variety Club of GB, Bucks Assoc of Boys Clubs; pres Bedfordshire Youth Assoc, ctee memb MacIntyre Homes Milton Keynes; *Style*— James Marshall, Esq; Jim Marshall Products Ltd, Denbigh Rd, Bletchley, Milton Keynes MK1 1DQ (☎ 0908 375411, fax 0908 376118, telex 826483 MARAMP)

MARSHALL, (John) Jeremy Seymour; s of Edward Pope Marshall (d 1983), of Truro, Cornwall, and Nita Helen, *née* Seymour; *b* 18 April 1938; *Educ* Sherborne, New Coll Oxford (MA); *m* 20 July 1962, Juliette Anne, da of (Archibald) Donald Butterley (d 1957), of Leicester; 1 s (Simon b 1965), 2 da (Sarah b 1964, Anna b 1971); *Career* Nat Serv Lt Royal Signals 1956-58; Wiggins Teape 1962-64, Riker Laboratories 1964-67, CIBA Agrochems 1967-71, Hanson 1971-87; md: Dufaylite Developments Ltd 1971-76, SLD Olding Ltd 1976-79; chief exec: Lindustries Ltd 1979-86, Imperial Foods Ltd 1986-87, BAA plc 1987-89, De La Rue plc 1989- dir First Stansted Assured Properties plc; FBIM,FCIT; *Recreations* tennis, squash, skiing; *Clubs* Army and Navy, RAC; *Style*— Jeremy Marshall, Esq; Willow House, Bourn, Cambridge CB3 7SQ; De la Rue plc, 3-5 Burlington Gardens, London W1 (☎ 071 734 8020)

MARSHALL, Prof John; CBE; s of James Herbert Marshall, and Bertha, *née* Schofield; *b* 16 April 1922; *Educ* Thornleigh Coll Bolton, Univ of Manchester (MB ChB, MD, DSc); *m* 9 Oct 1946, (Margaret) Eileen, da of Albert Hughes (d 1937), of Unionville, Pennsylvania, USA; 2 s (Michael John, Christopher John), 3 da (Patricia Mary, Mo Lin Cecilia, Catherine Ann); *Career* Lt-Col RAMC 1949-51; sr lectr Univ of Edinburgh 1954-56; Univ of London: reader in neurology 1956-71, prof 1971-87, dean Inst of Neurology 1982-87, emeritus prof 1987; chm Attendance Bd 1982- (memb 1978-); memb: Assoc of Br Neurologists 1954, Assoc of Physicians 1956; Auenbrugger medal Univ of Graz (1983); *Books* Management of Cerebrovascular Disease (1965), Planning for a Family (1965), The Infertile Period (1969); *Recreations* walking, gardening; *Style*— Prof John Marshall, CBE; 203 Robin Hood Way, London SW20 0AA (☎ 081 942 5509)

MARSHALL, Capt John Andrew; LVO (1979); s of The Rt Rev Guy Marshall, MBE (d 1979), and Dorothy Gladys, *née* Whiting (d 1975); *b* 14 Dec 1937; *Educ* St John's Sch Leatherhead Surrey, RNC at Dartmouth and Manadon; *m* 15 Jan 1966, Vivien Mary, da of Kenneth James Robertson, DSC (ka 1943); 1 s (Rory Jerome), 2 da (Peta Sophie, Morva Anna); *Career* RN served HMS Ulster 1958-59, HMS Albion 1963-65, HMS Dolphin 1965, HMS Cachalot 1965-68, RNC Dartmouth 1968, RNC Greenwich 1968-69, HMS Renown 1970-72, HMS Forth and HMS Defiance 1972-74, Royal Dockyard Devonport 1974-77, Royal Yacht 1977-79, naval attaché Moscow 1984-85, MOD 1979-82, 1985-88 and 1990-91, Capt RNEC 1988-90; CEng, FIMechE, FIMarE; *Recreations* sailing, estate, garden design, management; *Style*— Capt John Marshall, LVO, RN; 3 Park Street, Bath, Avon (☎ 0225 427750)

MARSHALL, John Anthony; s of Charles Joseph Marshall, of Warwick, and Jean Edith, *née* Leeson; *b* 13 Jan 1953; *Educ* Myton Sch Warwick, Mid-Warwickshire Coll of FE Leamington Spa, UEA (BA), Univ of Essex; *Career* freelance journalist Gay News 1981-83, ed Gay Times 1983-; *Books* contrib: Homosexuality: Power and Politics (1980), The Making of the Modern Homosexual (1981), Prejudice and Pride (1983); *Style*— John Marshall, Esq; 2A Bonny St, London NW1 9PG (☎ 071 267 2674); Gay Times, 283 Camden High St, London NW1 7BX (☎ 071 482 2576, fax 01 284 0329)

MARSHALL, John Leslie; MP (C) Hendon South 1987; s of Prof William Thomas Marshall (d 1975), of Glasgow, and Margaret Ewing Marshall; *b* 19 Aug 1940; *Educ* Glasgow Acad, Univ of St Andrews (MA); *m* 1978, Susan Elizabeth, da of David Spencer Mount, JP, of The Dower House, Petham, Kent; 2 s (William b 1979, Thomas b 1982); *Career* lectr in economics Univ of Aberdeen 1966-70; stockbroker, ptnr Carr Sebag & Co 1979-1982; Kitcat & Aitken: assoc memb 1982-83, ptnr 1982-83, ptnr 1983-86, dir investment res 1986-90; conslt Carr Kitcat & Aitken 1990; MEP (EDG) London N 1979-89; PPS: to Min of State for Social Security 1989-90, to Sec of State for Social Security 1990-; ACIS; *Recreations* spectator sports, theatre, bridge; *Clubs* Carlton, Middlesex Cricket; *Style*— John Marshall Esq, MP; House of Commons, London SW1A 1AD (☎ 071 219 6327)

MARSHALL, Margaret Anne (Mrs Graeme Davidson); *née* Marshall; *b* 4 Jan 1949; *Educ* Stirling HS, Royal Scottish Acad of Music and Drama; *m* 25 March 1970, Graeme Griffiths King Davidson; 2 da (Nicola b 19 Nov 1974, Julia b 29 Dec 1977); *Career* int opera singer; First prize Munich Int Festival 1974; concert appearences: Florence, Covent Gdn, Hamburg, Koln, Frankfurt, La Scala, Milan, Vienna, Salzburg; numerous recordings; *Recreations* skiing, squash, tennis, cooking, golf; *Clubs* Gleneagle Country; *Style*— Miss Margaret Marshall; Woodside, Gargunnock, Stirling FK8 3BP (☎ 0786 86633); c/o Harold Holt, 31 Sinclair Rd, London W14 0NS (☎ 01 603 4600, fax 01 603 0019, telex 22339 HUNTER)

MARSHALL, Mark Anthony; CMG (1991); s of Prof T H Marshall (d 1981), of Cambridge, and Nadine, *née* Hambourg; *b* 8 Oct 1937; *Educ* Westminster, Trinity Coll Cambridge (BA); *m* 29 Aug 1970, Penelope Lesley, step da of George Seymour (d 1987), of Powick, Worcester; 2 da (Charlotte Dorothea b 1973, Frances Margaret b 1975); *Career* Dip Serv 1958-; cnsllr: Tripoli 1979-80, Damascus 1980-83; ambass Yemen Arab Republic 1987-; *Recreations* golf, fell walking; *Style*— Mark Marshall, Esq, CMG; c/o Foreign & Commonwealth Office, London SW1

MARSHALL, Michael John; DL (Cambridgshire 1989); s of Sir Arthur Gregory George Marshall, and Rosemary Wynford Dimsdale; *b* 27 Jan 1932; *Educ* Eton, Jesus Coll Cambridge (MA, rowing Blue); *m* 1, 1960 (m dis 1977), Bridget Wykham Pollock; 2 s, 2 da; m 2, 1979, Sibyl Mary Walkinshaw, *née* Hutton; 2 step s; *Career* RAF pilot 1949-52; joined Marshall of Cambridge (Eng) Ltd 1955, dep chm and md Marshall (Cambridge) Ltd 1964, chm and chief exec Marshall of Cambridge Gp of Cos; memb Eastern Electricity Bd 1971-77; chm: Civilian Ctee 104 (City of Cambridge) Squadron ATC 1975- (memb 1970-), chm Cambs Manpower Ctee 1980-83; pres Cambridge Soc for the Blind 1989-; rowed for GB European Championships 1955; High Sheriff of Cambridgeshire 1988; Freeman the City of London, Liveryman Guild of Air Pilots and Air Navigators; FRAeS, FIMI, VP of IMI; memb Inst Engrg; *Recreations* flying, sailing, countryside; *Clubs* RAF, Hawks; *Style*— Michael Marshall, Esq, DL; Swaffham Prior House, Cambridge CB5 0LD

MARSHALL, Michael Leicester John; s of Sir James Marshall, JP, DL (d 1977), and Rebecca Mary, *née* Gotley (d 1966); *b* 26 May 1924; *Educ* Eastbourne Coll, Coll of Estate Mgmnt; *m* 6 June 1959, Tessa Rosemary, da of Charles Miles Skerrett-Rogers (d 1972); 2 s (Julian b 24 April 1960, Thomas b 1 July 1964), 1 da (Antonia b 6 June 1961); *Career* Maj 5 Royal Gurkha Rifles (FF); active serv: Arakan 1943-44 (wounded), Kohima 1944, Burma 1944-45; Capt 4 Bn Queens Regt TA 1947-50, ret; chartered surveyor; sr ptnr Chestertons, receiver Church Cmmrs for England, surveyor Royal Masonic Sch for Boys, hon surveyor Charterhouse Sch; memb Court of Assts Corp of Sons of the Clergy (former sr treas); memb Court Worshipful Co of Tylers and Bricklayers (Master 1986-87); Lambeth Degree MA Oxon 1989; FRICS 1952; *Recreations* gardening, walking; *Clubs* Army and Navy, MCC; *Style*— Michael Marshall, Esq; East Brabourne House, Brabourne, Ashford, Kent TN25 5LR (☎ 030 381 2112)

MARSHALL, Sir (Robert) Michael; MP (C) Arundel Feb 1974-; s of Robert Ernest Marshall (d 1988) and Margaret Mary (d 1983), of Hathersage, Derbyshire; *b* 21 June 1930,Sheffield; *Educ* Bradfield Coll, Harvard Univ (BA), and Stanford Univ; *m* 1972, Caroline Victoria Oliphant, da of Alexander Oliphant Hutchison (d 1973), of Upper Largo, Fife; 2 step da; *Career* BBC cricket commentator 1954-69; mangr Calcutta Branch United Steel (India) Ltd 1954-58 and md (Bombay) 1960-64; commercial dir Workington Iron & Steel Co Ltd 1964-67, md Head Wrightson Export Co Ltd 1967-69, mgmnt conslt Urwick Orr & Partners Ltd 1969-74; Parly under sec of state for Industry 1979-81, Parly advsr to Br Aerospace and Cable & Wireless 1981-; Hon DL New England Coll 1982; kt 1990; *Books* author/editor of 7 books incl Jack Buchanan, Gentleman and Player; *Recreations* cricket commentating, golf, theatre, writing and travel; *Clubs* Garrick, Lord's Taverners, R & A, MCC, Goodwood Golf; *Style*— Sir Michael Marshall, MP; Old Inn House, Slindon, Arundel, W Sussex; House of Commons, London SW1A 0AA (☎ 071 219 4046)

MARSHALL, Nigel Bernard Dickenson; s of Norman Dickenson Marshall (d 1958), of The Old Rectory, Lea, Gainsborough, and (Gertrude) Olga, *née* Pumfrey (d 1991); *b* 9 April 1935; *Educ* Rugby, Queens' Coll Cambridge (MA, LLM); *Career* ptnr: Underwood and Co slrs London 1964-90, Miller and Co slrs Cambridge 1969-88; sole practitioner 1990-; clerk: St Edward's Parochial Charity Cambridge 1967-90, The Great St Mary's Charity Camabridge 1967-71, The Wray Jackenett Merrill & Elic Charity Cambridge 1971-72; sec Cambridge and District Trade Protection Assoc 1967-86; *Recreations* gardening; *Clubs* United Oxford and Cambridge Univ, Univ of Cambridge Pitt, Oriental; *Style*— Nigel Marshall, Esq; The Old Rectory, Lea, Gainsborough, Lincs; 50 Rawlings Street, London SW3

MARSHALL, Noel Hedley; CMG (1986); s of Dr Arthur Hedley Marshall, CBE, of Styvechale Coventry, and Margaret Louise, *née* Longhurst (d 1987); *b* 26 Nov 1934; *Educ* Leighton Park Sch, Lawrenceville Sch NJ USA, St John's Coll Cambridge; *Career* Foreign (later Dip) Serv: third sec Br Embassy Prague 1959, FO 1961, second sec Br Embassy Moscow 1963, CRO 1965, first sec (tech asst) Br High Cmmn Karachi 1966 and Rawalpindi 1967, charge d'affaires Br Embassy Ulan Bater 1967, Rawalpindi 1968, FCO 1970, first sec (press) UK Representation to Euro Communities 1974, NATO Def Coll Rome 1977, cnsllr UK delegation conf on Disarmament Geneva 1978, head N American Dept FCO 1982, dip serv inspr 1985, min Br Embassy Moscow 1986-; *Recreations* offshore sailing, the theatre; *Clubs* Royal Ocean Racing; *Style*— Noel Marshall, Esq, CMG; c/o FCO, King Charles Street, London SW1A 2AA

MARSHALL, Sir Peter Harold Reginald; KCMG (1983, CMG 1974); s of Reginald Henry Marshall; *b* 30 July 1924; *Educ* Tonbridge, Corpus Christi Coll Cambridge; *m* 1, 1957, Patricia Rendell Stoddart (d 1981); 1 s, 1 da; m 2, 16 Sept 1989, Judith, *née* Miller, wid of E W F Tomlin; *Career* diplomat; asst dir Treasy Centre for Admin Studies 1964-66, cnsllr UK Mission Geneva 1966-69, cnsllr and head of chancery Paris 1969-71, head of Fin Relations Dept FCO 1971-73, asst under sec of state FCO 1973-75, UK rep to Econ and Social Cncl of UN 1975-79, ambass and UK perm rep to Office of UN and other int orgns Geneva 1979-83, dep cwlth sec-gen (Econ) 1983-88; hon fell Corpus Christi Coll Cambridge; chm Cwlth Tst (and Royal Cwlth Soc) 1989-, pres Queen Elizabeth House Oxford 1990-, memb Bd of Govrs English Speaking Union 1984-90, tstee King George VI and Queen Elizabeth Fndn of St Catharine's 1986-; memb Cncl: Overseas Devpt Inst 1989-, VSO 1990-; memb Exec Ctee Pilgrims of GB; *Clubs* Travellers'; *Style*— Sir Peter Marshall, KCMG; Commonwealth Trust, Commonwealth House, 18 Northumberland Ave, London WC2N 5BJ (☎ 071 930 6733)

MARSHALL, Peter Izod; s of Charles Marshall (d 1987), of Buxton, Derbyshire, and Gwendoline Anne, *née* Parker (d 1989); *b* 16 April 1927; *Educ* Buxton Coll; *m* 4 Aug 1955, Davina Mary, da of Ernest Hart (d 1980), of Grappen Hall, Cheshire; 1 s (David Bruce b 4 Feb 1960), 1 da (Helen Elizabeth (Mrs Le Houx) b 21 Feb 1957); *Career* commercial dir EMI Electronics Ltd 1962-67, fin dir Norcros plc 1967-77, dir and dep chief exec Plessey Co plc 1977-87, chm Ocean Transport and Trading plc 1987-; memb Jarrett Ctee on Br Univs; LRAM 1945, FCA 1955, CBIM 1986, FIOD 1986; *Recreations* music, swimming, golf; *Clubs* Les Ambassadeurs, Wentworth (Surrey); *Style*— Peter Marshall, Esq; Moyns, Christchurch Rd, Virginia Water, Surrey (☎ 09904 2118); 47 Russell Sq, London WC1B 4JP (☎ 071 636 6844, fax 071 636 0289, telex 291689)

MARSHALL, Sir Robert Braithwaite; KCB (1971, CB 1968), MBE (1945); s of Alexander Halford Marshall, and Edith Mary, *née* Lockyer; *b* 10 Jan 1920; *Educ* Sherborne, CCC Cambridge; *m* 1945, Diana Elizabeth Westlake; 1 s, 3 da; *Career* WWII served FO; chm Nat Water Cncl 1978-82, fndr and first chm Wateraid Tst 1981-82 (currently memb Cncl); second perm sec Dept of Environment 1973-78, indust sec DTI as second perm sec 1970-73 (dep sec 1966-70, under sec 1964-66);

served Ministries: Works, Aviation, Power Technology; private sec to sec of Cabinet 1950-53; chm Liberal Party's Trade & Indust Panel 1984-86; *Style*— Sir Robert Marshall, KCB, MBE; 1 Shatcombe Uploders, Bridport, Dorset (☎ 030885 348)

MARSHALL, Roger Michael James; s of James Edward Frederick Marshall (d 1979), and Jeanne, *née* Warren; *b* 20 Aug 1948; *Educ* Truro Sch, LSE (BSc); *m* 4 May 1974, Margaret Elizabeth Marshall, da of John MacPherson, of The Manor House, Abbotskerswell, Devon; 2 da (Charlotte Emily b 1977, Anabelle Verity b 1978); *Career* articled to Price Waterhouse 1970, CA 1973, ptnr with Price Waterhouse 1981-; FCA; *Recreations* sailing, bridge, reading, skiing; *Style*— Roger Marshall, Esq; Price Waterhouse, 32 London Bridge St, London SE1 9SY

MARSHALL, Roy Edwin; s of John Archibald Marshall (d 1950), of Coverley Plantation Barbados, and Hilda Verne Green (d 1983); early settlers in Barbados; *b* 25 April 1930; *Educ* Lodge Sch St John's Barbados; *m* 1954, Shirley Marjorie, da of Lionel Butterworth (d 1938), of Poynton, Cheshire; 3 da (Shelley, Debra, Joanne); *Career* played first class cricket (Barbados v Trinidad) aged 15 years; toured: England 1950, Aust and NZ 1951-52 with the W Indies; played cricket for Hampshire 1953-72 (Capt 1966-70), scored 1000 in a season 18 times (6 times over 2000), scored more runs (35,725) than any non-qualified English cricketer; *Books* Test Outcast; *Recreations* cricket, golf; *Clubs* Cricketers (London), MCC, Hampshire CCC, Somerset CCC, Lords Taverners; *Style*— Roy Marshall, Esq; 7 Compass Hill, Taunton, Somerset TA1 4EF (☎ 0823 256821)

MARSHALL, HE Sir (Oshley) Roy; CBE (1968); s of Fitz Roy Marshall, and Corene Carmelita Marshall; *b* 21 Oct 1920; *Educ* Harrison Coll Barbados, Pembroke Coll Cambridge, Univ Coll London; *m* 1945, Eirwen Lloyd; 1 s, 3 da; *Career* vice chllr Univ of Hull 1979-85, head of enquiry into immigration serv for Cmmn on Racial Equality until 1981; called to the Bar 1947, prof of law, head Dept of Law Univ of Sheffield 1956-69 (visiting prof 1969-79), prof of law and dean of Law Faculty Univ of Ife Nigeria 1963-65, vice chllr Univ of WI 1969-74; chm Cwlth Educn Liaison Ctee 1974-81 and Cwlth Legal Cooperation Ctee 1975, vice-chm Governing Body Cwlth Inst 1980-81, memb Police Complaints Bd 1977-81; chm: Cwlth Standing Ctee on Student Mobility 1982-, Bd of Govrs Hymers Coll 1985-89; exec chm Cncl for Educn in the Cwlth 1980-, chm Review Ctee on the Cave Hill Campus of the Univ WI 1986, constitutional commn on the Turks and Caicos Islands 1986, memb Bd of Govrs The Commonwealth of Learning 1989-; High Commissioner for Barbados in London 1989-; kt 1974; *Clubs* Royal Cwlth Soc; *Style*— His Excellency Sir Roy Marshall, CBE; Iverta, Burten Shaw Rd, Thames Ditton, Surrey KT7 OTP (☎ 081 398 1873)

MARSHALL, Sally Christine; da of Maj John Trevor Marshall (d 1985), of Nottingham Broadstone, Dorset, and Marjorie Kathleen, *née* Cooke; *b* 19 Oct 1949; *Educ* Mountford House West Hallam Derbys, Clifton Hall Nottingham, Univ Coll of Wales Aberystwyth (BSc); *Career* investmt mangr Hill Samuel 1972-80; Henderson Admin Gp 1980-; dir Henderson Admin Ltd, dep md Henderson Pension Fund Mgmnt Ltd; Freeman City of London; memb: Nat Assoc Pension Funds; *Recreations* golf, skiing, tennis, travel; *Clubs* Roehampton, Broadstone GC, Dorset; *Style*— Miss Sally Marshall; 4 Putney Common, London SW15 1HL; Henderson Pension Fund Management Ltd, 3 Finsbury Avenue, London EC2M 2PA (☎ 071 638 5757)

MARSHALL, Sally Rose; da of Thomas Barton Gerard (d 1988), of Newburgh, Lancs, and Clara Margery, *née* Salisbury (d 1985); *b* 2 Nov 1938; *Educ* Brentwood Sch Southport, Lady Margaret Hall Oxford (BA); *m* 27 Aug 1960, Geoffrey Wyndham Marshall, s of Wyndham Joseph Marshall, of Reepham, Norfolk; 2 s (Andrew Gerard b 7 Aug 1965, Julian Geoffrey b 18 July 1969), 1 da (Miranda Lucy b 2 March 1964); *Career* dep ldr Norfolk CC 1987-88 (memb and chm libraries and recreation ctee); memb Library and Info Servs Cncl, chm Assoc of Co Cncls Recreation Ctee; *Recreations* gardening, reading, antique restoration, local politics; *Style*— Mrs Sally Marshall; Salle Place, Salle, Reepham NR10 5S7 (☎ 0603 870638)

MARSHALL, Stuart Walter; s of Walter Clement Marshall, and Elsie Vera, *née* Hawkins; *b* 9 Sept 1935; *Educ* Beckenham and Penge GS; *m* 5 Aug 1961, Patricia Ann, da of Hugh Lawrence Bentley; 1 s (Adrian b 1967), 1 da (Anne b 1970); *Career* Coutts & Co: joined 1952, dep head branch 1981-86, head Mgmnt Serv Div 1986-90, dir 1989, head Commercial Banking 1990-; memb Cncl and hon treas Invalid Childrens Aid Nationwide, tstee WALK Fund, govr Colfe's Sch; FCIB; *Recreations* fishing, shooting, skiing, opera, gardening; *Style*— Stuart Marshall, Esq; Chelsfield, Kent; Coutts & Co, 440 Strand, London WC2R 0QS (☎ 071 379 6262); Coutts & Co, 27 Bush Lane, Cannon Street, London EC4R 0AA (☎ 071 623 3434)

MARSHALL, Valerie Margaret; da of Ernest Knagg; *b* 30 March 1945; *Educ* Brighton, Hove HS, Girton Coll Cambridge, London Graduate Sch of Business Studies; *m* 1972, Alan Roger Marshall; 1 s, 1 da; *Career* financial controller Industrial and Commercial Finance Corpn 1970-79, memb investment exec Scottish Development Agency 1979-, Monopolies and Mergers Cmmn 1977-, Scottish Design Cncl 1974-77; *Recreations* music, ballet, drama, golf; *Style*— Mrs A R Marshall; Valhalla, Garth Estate, by Fortingall, Perthshire; Kilmore, 16 Dalkeith Ave, Dumbreck Glasgow (☎ 041 427 0096)

MARSHALL, Dr William Jasper; s of Edward Alwyn Marshall (d 1986), of Tenterden, Kent, and Lorna Alice, *née* Jeffery (d 1988), of Bromley, Kent; *b* 1 April 1944; *Educ* St Dunstan's Coll, St Catherine's Coll Oxford (MA), Univ of London (PhD, MB BS, MSc); *m* 2 da (Eleanor Ruth b 24 Nov 1970, Harriet Lorna Mary b 13 Aug 1973); *Career* sr lectr and hon conslt chemical pathology King's Coll Sch of Med and Dentistry 1980-; MRCP 1979, MRCPath 1980, memb BMA; *Books* Illustrated Textbook of Clinical Chemistry (1988), Clinical Chemistry, an Illustrated Outline (1991); *Recreations* writing, gardening, DIY; *Clubs* Players Theatre; *Style*— Dr William Marshall; Dept of Clinical Biochemistry, King's College School of Medicine and Dentistry, London SE5 9PJ (☎ 071 274 6222, fax 071 737 7434)

MARSHALL-CLARKE, Geoffrey; s of Colin Marshall Clarke, of Rowan Drive, Kilburn, Derbyshire, and Irene, *née* Allsop; *b* 2 Oct 1952; *Educ* Swanwick Hall GS, Univ of Nottingham (LLB); *m* 25 Oct 1975, Susan Joy, da of Kenneth Norman Sansom, of Pentire Crescent, Newquay, Cornwall; 1 s (Alexander b 18 June 1985), 1 da (Holly b 18 July 1987); *Career* graduate trainee Boots The Chemist 1973-75, brand mangr Ranks Hovis McDougall 1975-76, mktg mangr Br Aluminium 1976-78, md Print Promotions and Publicity 1978-82, chm Koster Marshall-Clarke plc 1982-; fndr memb SDP, memb Lib Democrats; memb: IOD 1980, Inst of Mgmnt 1984, The Mktg Soc 1988, SPCA Ctee 1988-90; *Recreations* golf, squash, reading, music; *Clubs* Y; *Style*— Geoffrey Marshall-Clarke, Esq; Lye Green Cottage, Lycrome Rd, Lye Green, nr Chesham, Bucks (☎ 0494 774465); Koster Marshall-Clarke Group plc, Netherfield, Gravel Path, Berkhamsted, Herts HP4 2PF (☎ 0442 875941, fax 0442 866459, car 0836 72002, telex 825442)

MARSHALL OF GORING, Baron (Life Peer UK 1985), of South Stoke, Co Oxfordshire; Sir Walter Charles Marshall; CBE (1973); s of late Frank Marshall, and Amy, da of Edgar Pearson, of Wales; *b* 5 March 1932; *Educ* Birmingham Univ; *m* 1955, Ann Vivienne, da of late Ernest Vivian Sheppard, of Cardiff; 1 s (Hon Jonathan Charles Walter b 1963), 1 da (Hon Victoria Ann (Hon Mrs Burrill) b 1959); *Career* AERE Harwell: scientific offr 1954-57, gp leader solid state theory 1959-60, head Theoretical Physics Univ 1960-66, dep dir 1966-68, dir 1968-1975; res physicist: Univ of California 1957-58, Harvard 1958-59; chm: Advsy Cncl Res and Devpt Fuel and Power 1974-77, Offshore Energy Technol Bd 1975-77, UKAEA 1981-82 (dep chm 1975-81, memb 1972-82), CEGB 1982-89, World Assoc of Nuclear Operators 1989-; chief scientist Dept of Energy 1974-1977; ed Oxford Int Series of Monographs on Physics 1966-; Maxwell medal 1964, Glazebrook medal 1975; Hon DSc City Univ 1982, Hon DSc Salford, Foreign Assoc Nat Acad Engrg USA; fell Royal Swedish Acad Engrg Scis, FRS 1971, FBIM; kt 1982; *Style*— The Rt Hon Lord Marshall of Goring, CBE, FRS; 262A Fulham Rd, London SW10 9EL (☎ 0491 875017)

MARSHALL OF LEEDS, Baroness; Mary Marshall; *née* Barr; JP (City of Leeds 1964); da of Robert Barr (d 1961), of Shadwell House, Shadwell, Leeds, and Edith, *née* Midgeley (d 1964); *b* 11 Sept 1915; *Educ* Calder Girls' Sch Seascale Cumberland, Yorkshire Coll of Housecraft (Dip Domestic Sc); *m* 2 Aug 1941, Baron Marshall of Leeds (Life Peer, d 1990); 2 da (Hon Angela Hermione (Hon Mrs Widdows) b 1944, Hon Virginia Mary (Hon Mrs Learmond) b 1949); *Career* voluntary serv with Red Cross and YWCA; dir Oswalds Hotel Ltd 1955-; formerly dir: Yorkshire Ladies Hostels Ltd, Yorkshire Ladies Cncl of Educn; hon sec City of Leeds NSPCC for 12 years, now patron; patron Leeds Save the Children Fund; *Style*— The Rt Hon Lady Marshall of Leeds, JP; Holtby, York YO1 3UA

MARSHALL OF RACHAN AND GLENHOVE, Henry Bruce (Harry); DL (Tweeddale 1984); s of Maj James Rissik Marshall, TD, JP, DL, QC (d 1959), of Baddinsgill, W Linton, Peeblesshire, and Eileen Margaret, *née* Bruce (d 1976); *b* 19 Oct 1924; *Educ* Rugby, Trinity Coll Oxford, Univ of Edinburgh (BSc); *m* 19 Sept 1951, Catriona Mary Mackenzie, da of Maj Alfred Badenoch, TD, of Edinburgh; 1 s (Gavin b 30 May 1955), 1 da (Elspeth (Mrs Fleming) b 24 May 1953); *Career* served in army 1945-48, 2 Lt Queen's Own Cameron Highlanders 1946, Lt 1947; memb Queen's Bodyguard for Scotland (Royal Co of Archers) 1958; avionic engr with Ferranti Ltd 1952-76; farmer/estate mangr 1971-; elder St Andrew's Church W Linton; *Recreations* shooting, photography; *Clubs* Tweeddale Shooting; *Style*— Harry Marshall of Rachan and Glenhove, DL; Baddinsgill, West Linton, Tweeddale (☎ 0968 60683)

MARSHAM, Lady Anne Rhoda; o da of Lt-Col Hon Reginald Hastings Marsham, OBE (d 1922) (2 s of 4 Earl of Romney); raised to the rank of an Earl's da 1976; *b* 7 June 1909; *Career* served 1939-45 war as Section Offr, WAAF; Kenya Police Reserve 1952-60; *Style*— The Lady Anne Marsham; c/o The Rt Hon the Earl of Romney, Wensum Farm, West Rudham, King's Lynn, Norfolk

MARSHAM, Julian Charles; JP; s of Col Peter Marsham, MBE (s of Hon Sydney Marsham, yst s of 4 Earl of Romney), and Hersey, da of Maj Hon Richard Coke (3 s of 2 Earl of Leicester, KG, JP, DL, by his 2 w, Hon Georgina Cavendish, da of 2 Baron Chesham); hp of kinsman, 7 Earl of Romney; *b* 28 March 1948; *Educ* Eton; *m* 1975, Catriona, da of Robert Christie Stewart CBE, TD (nephew of Sir Christopher Lighton, 8 Bt, MBE); 2 s (David b 1977, Michael b 1979), 1 da (Laura b 1984); *Career* land agent; farmer; *Recreations* shooting, fishing, silviculture, gardening; *Style*— Julian Marsham, Esq, JP; Gayton Hall, King's Lynn, Norfolk (☎ 055 386 259, estate off 055 386 292)

MARSLAND, Christopher John; s of Jack Ronald Marsland (d 1975), of Westerlands, Valley Prospect, Newark, Notts, and Victoria Irene, *née* Lees; *b* 18 Feb 1940; *Educ* Strathallan Sch Pertshire, Univ of Manchester; *m* 1 May 1969, Carole, da of John Alexander Elliott (d 1981), of Bingham, Notts; 1 s (David b 1976), 2 da (Vikki b 1961, Helen b 1974); *Career* graduate trg scheme Wiggins Teape 1961-64; Br Shoe Corps Ltd 1965-88: work study engr Factories Div 1965-67, transferred to head office (head of mgmnt servs, salary admin); Warehouse: chief exec 1976, distribution dir 1977-84, retail ops dir 1985-86, md 1987-88; currently dir: Sears plc, Br Shoe Corp Ltd, BSC Footwear Supplies Ltd, Dolcis Ltd, Freeman Hardy & Willis Ltd, Lilley & Skinner Ltd, Saxone Shoe Co Ltd, Trueform Ltd, Zephyr Sports Ltd, Hoogenbosch Schoenen BV; govr Colston Basset Sch; *Recreations* golf, shooting, equestrian sports; *Style*— Christopher Marsland, Esq; Tanglewood, Colston Bassett, Notts NG12 3FB (☎ 0949 468); British Shoe Corporation Ltd, Sunningdale Rd, Leicester LE3 1UR (☎ 0533 320 202, fax 0533 320 210, car 0836 277 373, telex 0533 34493)

MARSLAND, Prof David; s of Ernest Marsland, of Leavesden Green, Herts, and Fay, *née* Savoury; *b* 3 Feb 1939; *Educ* Watford GS, Christ's Coll Cambridge (BA, MA), LSE, Brunel Univ (PhD); *Career* dept of sociology Brunel Univ 1964-88: lectr, sr lectr, dir postgrad studies, prof assoc; prof social res West London Inst of Higher Educn 1989-; asst dir The Social Affairs Unit London 1981-; memb: social scis bd UNESCO 1983-86, social scis ctee CNAA 1987-, EC Social Res Assoc; formerly hon gen sec Br Sociological Assoc 1987-; memb: BSA (1964), SRA (1985), MBIM (1987); *Books* Seeds of Bankruptcy: Sociological Bias Against Business and Freedom (1988), Cradle to Grave: Comparative Perspectives on the State of Welfare (1989), Changes in Education: Rescue and Reform (1989); *Recreations* reading and writing poetry, anti-communism; *Clubs* Arts; *Style*— Prof David Marsland; W London Inst, 300 St Margaret's Rd, Twickenham, Middx (☎ 081 891 0621)

MARSTON, (Jeffery) Adrian Priestley; s of Maj J E Marston, DSO, MC (d 1945), and Doreen, *née* Norris (d 1980); *b* 15 Dec 1927; *Educ* Marlborough, Magdalen Coll Oxford (MA, DM, MCh); *m* 17 July 1951, Sylvie; 2 s (John b 24 Feb 1960, Nicholas b 4 Jan 1963), 1 da (Joanna b 24 Sept 1954); *Career* Nat Serv Lt RAMC, then Capt 1954-57; surgical registrar and sr registrar St Thomas's Hosp 1960-65, sr lectr in surgery The Middx Hosp Med Sch 1965-; conslt surgn: The Middx Hosp 1968-, Royal Northern Hosp 1970-85, UCH 1985-; memb Cncl and vice pres RCS, vice chm NCEPOD; pres: Vascular Surgical Soc of GB and Ireland 1985, Assoc of Surgns of GB and Ireland 1986; Hon MD Université de Nice 1986; FRCS 1958; *Books* Intestinal Ischaemia (1976), Contemporary Operative Surgery (1979), Visceral Artery Reconstruction (1986), Splanchnic Ischaemia and Multiple Organ Failure (1989); *Recreations* literature, languages, travel, music; *Clubs* Hurlingham, RAC; *Style*— Adrian Marston, Esq; 82 Harley St, London W1N 1AE (☎ 071 637 0977)

MARSTON, David Charles; s of Reginald Charles Moor Marston, and Catherine Ann, *née* Romanes; *b* 22 March 1955; *Educ* Shrewsbury, Univ of Newcastle on Tyne (BA); *Career* Coopers & Lybrand Deloitte 1976-80 (articled clerk, accountant), under sec Auditing Practices Ctee ICAEW 1980-82, audit mangr Grant Thornton 1982-84, Citicorp Group 1984- (fin controller of various subsids, UK group compliance offr Citibank NA); memb Fin Reporting Ctee ICAEW 1990-; Liveryman Worshipful Co of Gardeners 1980; FCA 1979; *Recreations* tenor in church choir, group scout leader; *Style*— David Marston, Esq; Citibank NA, 336 Strand, London WC2 (☎ 071 438 1562)

MARSTON, Dr Geoffrey; s of Arthur Marston (d 1982), of Newark, Notts, and Mabel, *née* Binns; *b* 17 March 1938; *Educ* Magnus GS Newark Notts, UCL (LLB, LLM, PhD); *Career* mgmnt trainee Assoc Br Maltsters Export Co Ltd 1960-62, project offr Australian public serv Canberra 1962-67, sr lectr in Law Australian Nat Univ of Canberra 1967-70, attaché de recherches Graduate Inst of Int Studies Geneva 1970-73, fell Sidney Sussex Coll and lectr in Law Cambridge Univ 1973-; *Books* The Marginal Seabed: United Kingdom Legal Practice (1981); *Recreations* mountain walking, beachcombing, photography, traditional jazz; *Clubs* Athenaeum; *Style*— Dr Geoffrey Marston; Sidney Sussex College, Cambridge CB2 3HU (☎ 0223 338800, fax 0223 338884)

MARSTON, James Leslie; s of John Kenneth Marston (d 1982), and Jeanie, *née*

Cranmer (d 1984); *b* 30 Jan 1944; *Educ* Rothesay Acad I of Bute; *m* (m dis 1988); 1 s (Craig b 1976), 1 da (Natalie b 1979); *Career* tax mangr Roffe Swayne and Co 1969-73, sr ptnr McColl and Crow 1985- (ptnr 1974); chm Chartered Fin Gp plc 1987-; memb Inst Curative Hypnotherapists; involved charity work for disabled; racehorse owner; composer numerous published songs; FCA, FCCA, ATII, FInstD; *Recreations* music, sports, travel; *Style*— J L Marston, Esq; Tudor Court, Heatherlands Rd, Chilworth, Hants (☎ 0703 768140); 1-3 The Avenue, Southampton SO1 2SE (☎ 0703 335211, fax 0703 331205, car 0860 719773)

MARSTON, Hon Mrs (Vanessa Mary); *née* Cawley; da of 3 Baron Cawley; *b* 30 Dec 1951; *Educ* Downe House; *m* 1971, Dr John Anthony Marston, s of Donald Marston, of Br Embassy, Beirut; 4 da (Cicely b 1973, Emma b 1975, Camilla b 1977, Annabel b 1979); *Style*— The Hon Mrs Marston; Gorwell House, Barnstaple, N Devon (☎ 0271 23202)

MARTEL, Maj Charles Peter; s of Lt-Gen Giffard le Quesene Martel, KCB, KBE, DSO, MC, (d 1958), and Maud Martel, *née* McKenzie (d 1982); of Huguenot descent Arms registered at Coll of Arms; *b* 6 June 1923; *Educ* Wellington, RMA Sandhurst; *m* 19 Oct 1957, Susan Carole, da of J R Ropner, Esq, of The Limes, Dalton, N Yorks; 3 da (Carole b 1959, Virginia b 1964 (d 1971), Sarah b 1973), 1 s (Nicholas b 1961); *Career* regular army offr; Maj 1942-45: 5 Royal Inniskillen Dragoon Gds, wounded Europe 1944; memb Lloyd's of London 1956-; memb Worshipful Co Gunmakers, Freeman City of London 1971; *Recreations* shooting, bridge; *Clubs* Pratt's, Turf, Beefsteak, Cavalry and Guards'; *Style*— Maj Charles Martel

MARTELL, Vice Adm Sir Hugh Colenso; KBE (1966, CBE 1957), CB (1963); s of Engr Capt Albert Arthur Green Martell, DSO (d 1951), and Susie, da of Williams Colenso; *b* 6 May 1912; *Educ* Edinburgh Acad, RNC Dartmouth; *m* 1, Marguerite Isabelle, da of Sir Dymoke White, 2 Bt; m 2, Margaret, da of Maj A R Glover (d 1979); *Career* joined RN 1926, serv WWII (despatches), Russian Convoys and Pacific, Capt 1952, ADC to Her Majesty, Overall Operational Cdr Nuclear Tests in Montebellos NW Australia 1957, Rear Adm 1962, Dir Gen Naval Recruiting 1964-65, Admiral Cmdg Reserves, Vice Adm 1965, Chief Allied Staff NATO Forces Mediterranean 1965-67, ret; dir: Derritron Electronics Ltd, Reslosound Ltd, City and Military Personnel Conslts and Dirs Secs Ltd; chm Bury Manor Schs Tst Ltd; govr: Dorset House Sch, Manor House Sch; *Recreations* yachting; *Clubs* Royal Naval, RN Sailing Assoc; *Style*— Vice Adm Sir Hugh Martell, KBE, CB

MARTEN, Lt Cdr George Gosselin; LVO (1985, MVO 1950), DSC (1942); s of Vice Adm Sir Francis Arthur Marten (d 1950), and Phyllis Raby, *née* Morgan; *b* 28 Dec 1918; *Educ* RNC Dartmouth; *m* 25 Nov 1949, Hon Mary Anna, *née* Sturt, OBE, DL, da of 3 Baron Alington (ka 1940); 1 s (Napier b 1959), 5 da (Victoria b 1950, Charlotte b 1952, Georgina b 1953, Amabel b 1954, Sophia b 1962); *Career* served in destroyers WWII, in cmd HMS Wilton 1943-45 (despatches 3 times); equerry to HM King George VI 1948-50, High Sheriff of Dorset 1962; *Recreations* forestry, bloodstock breeding; *Clubs* Turf; *Style*— Lt Cdr George Marten, LVO, DSC; Crichel, Wimborne, Dorset

MARTEN, (Richard) Hedley Westwood; s of Capt Lewis Westwood Marten (ka 1944), and Kathleen, *née* Ogston (d 1988); *b* 24 Jan 1946; *Educ* Winchester, Magdalene Coll Cambridge (MA); *m* 30 July 1971 (m dis 1983), Fiona Mary, da of George William Carter Sinclair, of 12 Sussex Square, London; 2 s (Benedict b 9 Sept 1976, Alexander b 24 July 1978), 1 da (Laura b 19 April 1973); *Career* called to the Bar Lincoln's Inn 1966; practice at Chancery Bar 1968-; Chancery Bar rep Bar Cncl 1990-; *Recreations* music, cricket; *Clubs* Brooks's; *Style*— Hedley Marten, Esq; 40 Sutherland Place, London W2 (☎ 071 229 3254); 3 New Square, Lincoln's Inn, London WC2 (☎ 071 405 5577, fax 071 404 5032)

MARTEN, Hon Mrs (Mary Anna Sibell Elizabeth); OBE (1980), DL (Dorset 1989); da of 3 Baron Alington (d 1940), and Lady Mary Ashley Cooper (d 1936), da of 9 Earl of Shaftesbury; *m* 25 Nov 1949, Lt Cdr George Gosselin Marten, LVO, DSC, s of late Sir Francis Arthur Marten, KBE, CB, CMG, CVO; 1 s, 5 da; *Career* tstee Br Museum 1985-; High Sheriff of Dorset 1989; *Style*— The Hon Mrs Marten, OBE, DL; Crichel, Wimborne, Dorset

MARTIN, Prof Alan Douglas; s of Frederick Charles Martin (d 1979), and Emily May, *née* Berkley (d 1990); *b* 4 Dec 1937; *Educ* Eltham Coll, UCL (BSc, PhD); *m* 4 April 1964, Rev Penny Elizabeth Martin, da of William Eric Leggett Johnson, BEM (d 1985); 1 s (Robert b 4 April 1967), 2 da (Rebecca b 30 March 1966, Rachel b 23 March 1974); *Career* res assoc: Univ of Illinois 1962-63, Rutherford Laboratory 1963-64; Univ of Durham: lectr, sr lectr, reader, prof 1964-; CPhys, FInstP; *Books* Elementary Particle Theory (with T D Spearman, 1970), Quarks and Leptons (with F Halzen, 1984), Hadron Interactions (with P D B Collins, 1984), Particle Physics and Cosmology (jtly, 1989); *Recreations* tennis, walking, music; *Style*— Prof Alan Martin; 26 Telford Close, High Shincliffe, Durham DH1 2YJ (☎ 091 386 1742); Dept of Physics, University of Durham, Durham City DH1 3LE (☎ 091 374 2162, fax 091 374 3749)

MARTIN, Alan Frederick Joseph Plunkett; s of Dr Hugh Thomas Plunkett Martin, of 30 Buckingham Mansions, Bath Rd, Bournemouth, and Sylvia Mary, *née* Gilbert; *b* 22 Aug 1951; *Educ* Realgymnasium Basel Switzerland, Univ of Basel; *m* 19 May 1979, Rita Maria, da of Walter Gasser, of Rorschach, St Gall, Switzerland; 3 da (Stephanie b 1980, Felicity b 1983, Dominique b 1986); *Career* Swiss Bank Corp: Basel 1975-77 and 1979-80, NY 1981; Credit Commercial de France Paris 1978, SBCI Swiss Bank Corporation Investment Banking Ltd London 1981- (exec dir 1986); *Recreations* family, music, gardening, skiing, photography; *Style*— Alan Martin, Esq; 36 Cumberland Drive, Esher, Surrey KT10 OBB (☎ 081 398 6215); Swiss Bank House, 1 High Timber St, London EC4V 3SB (☎ 071 329 0329, fax 071 329 8700, telex 887434)

MARTIN, Alan Gould; s of Arthur Herbert Martin (d 1962), of Hale, Cheshire, and Cecil Muriel (d 1980), da of John Gould, of Stafford; *b* 19 Jan 1920; *Educ* Monkton Combe Sch; *m* 21 Nov 1953, Barbara Goodier, da of John Goodier Haworth, of Bowdon; 2 s (John Goodier b 1954, Peter Michael b 1957); *Career* served WWII RN 1940-46, navigator Med destroyers, attached Royal Hellenic Navy 1943; dir: Boydell Bros Ltd 1966-, Nat and Provincial Bldg Soc 1970-87, Industl and Commercial Fin Corp Ltd 1976-81; W Yorks Ind Hosp plc 1980-87, Rainford Venture Capital Ltd 1989-, Robert Glew & Co Ltd 1981-89, Yorks Chemicals plc 1981-90 (chm 1984), Hillards plc 1982-87, Land Instruments Int Ltd 1982-; chm: Singleton Birch Ltd 1979-, Frank Horsell Gp plc 1980-85; govr St Aidans Sch Harrogate N Yorks; FCA 1947; Hellenic Distinguished Serv Medal 1943; *Recreations* idleness; *Clubs* Leeds; *Style*— Alan G Martin, Esq; Huby House, Strait Lane, Huby, Leeds LS17 0EA (☎ 0423 734254)

MARTIN, Col Sir (Robert) Andrew St George; KCVO (1988), OBE (1959, MBE 1949), JP (1985); s of Maj William Francis Martin (ka 1915), and Violet Anne Philippa Wynter (d 1963), of The Poplars, Mountsorrel, Leics; *b* 23 April 1914; *Educ* Eton, RMC Sandhurst, Staff Coll Camberley; *m* 1950, Margaret Grace Martin, JP, da of John V Buchanan, (d 1966); 1 s (Robert); *Career* cmmn Oxford Bucks LI 1934-38, ADC to Govr-Gen of SA 1938-40, served WWII, UK 1940-44, NW Europe (despatches) 1944-45, Malaya 1946-49, Cyprus 1957-59, BAOR 1951-55, mil sec to Govr-Gen Aust 1955-57, cmmnd 1 Green Jackets 1957-59, Bde Col Green Jackets Bde 1959-62, CRLS HQ Western Cmd 1962-65, Lord-Lt and Custos Rotulorum Leics 1965-89; Hon LLD Univ of Leicester 1984, Hon DTech Univ of Loughborough 1988; Order of Orange Nassau 1950; KStJ 1966; landowner; *Recreations* hunting, shooting, gardening; *Clubs* Army and Navy, MCC; *Style*— Col Sir Andrew Martin, KCVO, OBE, JP; The Brand, Woodhouse Eaves, Loughborough, Leicestershire LE12 8SS (☎ 0509 890269)

MARTIN, Barrie Stuart Meredyth; s of James William Meredyth Martin of Mayfield, E Sussex and formerly of Shanghai and Hong Kong, and Joyce Stuart, *née* Bidwell; *b* 18 Aug 1941; *Educ* Shanghai Br Sch, St John's Beaumont, Beaumont Coll, Trinity Coll Dublin (BA, LLB); *Career* articled clerk to Sir Charles Russell Bart, ptnr Charles Russell and Co, asst slr Sprott and Sons, sr ptnr J M Rix and Kay slrs; memb Law Soc; *Recreations* tennis, travel; *Clubs* The Sloane; *Style*— Barrie Martin, Esq; J M Rix and Kay, 84 High St, Heathfield, East Sussex TN21 8JG (☎ 04352 5211, fax 04352 6822); Postmill House, Argos Hill, Rotherfield, E Sussex TN6 3QF

MARTIN, Brian; s of James Martin, of 5 Hillfoot Rd, Airdrie, Lanarks, and Anne Martin; *b* 24 Feb 1963; *Educ* St Margarettes Secdy Sch; *m* 9 Aug 1985, Anne, da of Frank Kelly; 1 s (Ryan b 7 May 1987), 1 da (Jacqueline b 8 Oct 1990); *Career* professional footballer; Shotts Jrs 1981-85, Falkirk 1985-87, Hamilton Academical 1987-88, St Mirren 1988-; 4 Scotland jr caps; won promotion to Premier League Falkirk 1986 and Hamilton Academical 1988; player of the year awards Falkirk and St Mirren; *Recreations* golf, hill walking; *Style*— Brian Martin, Esq; St Mirren FC, St Mirren Park, Love Street, Paisley PA3 2EG (☎ 041 889 2558

MARTIN, Brian William; s of Cecil William, of Southend on Sea, Essex, and Annie Elizabeth, *née* Bradley (d 1986); *b* 26 June 1937; *Educ* Southend HS, Hertford Coll Oxford (MA, DipEd), Univ of Leicester (PhD); *m* 22 Dec 1965, Margaret Louise, da of Kenneth Maidment, of Oxford and Auckland, NZ; 2 s (Barnaby b 1972, Felix b 1974), 2 da (Sophie b 1971, Laura b 1980); *Career* cmmnd RAEC 1958-60; head of English Magdalen Coll Sch Oxford (housemaster and archivist) 1961-, examiner Oxford and Cambridge Schs Examination Bd 1965-; lectr in modern English lit: New Coll Oxford 1974-76, Pembroke Coll 1976-83; tutor Oxford and Berkeley Univ prog 1971-78, tutor and lectr Univ of Massachusetts Oxford prog 1980-85, res lectr Hertford Coll Oxford 1985; book critic and occasional columnist The Times, book critic Daily Telegraph and Spectator 1980-, various contribs to learned jls; vice pres Eng Schs Hockey Assoc 1970; *Books* John Keble: Priest, Professor and Poet (1976), John Henry Newman his life and work (1982, revised edn 1990), John Henry Newman (ed 1986), volume 4 Nineteenth Century Macmillan Anthology of English Literature (ed 1989); *Recreations* lawn tennis, real tennis; *Clubs* Theological Wine; *Style*— Brian Martin, Esq; 4 Chalfont Road, Oxford OX2 6TH

MARTIN, Cary John; s of John Martin, of 13 Woodlands Rd, Manchester, and Joan Molly Wilson, *née* Skinner; *b* 22 Aug 1956; *Educ* William Hulme's GS Manchester, Univ of Birmingham (MA, BA), Christ Coll Cambridge; *m* 23 Sept 1978, Ruth Lillian, da of Arthur Henry George Amy, of 17 Charnhill Drive, Bristol; *Career* exec Mori 1979-85, dep chief exec Dewe Rogerson 1989-(joined 1985); hon res fell UCL; *Books* A Demotic Land Lease from Philadelphia (2 ed 1986); *Recreations* Egyptology; *Style*— Cary Martin, Esq; 14 Collingham Place, London SW5 0P2 (☎ 071 373 6773); Dewe Rogerson, 31/2 London Wall Buildings, London Wall, London EC2M 5SY (☎ 071 638 9571, fax 071 628 3444)

MARTIN, Charles Edmund; s of Flt Lt Charles Stuart Martin,£RAFVR (ka 1944), of Newcastle upon Tyne, and Sheila, *née* Richardson; *b* 19 Sept 1939; *Educ* Lancing, Selwyn Coll Cambridge (MA), Univ of Bristol (PGCE); *m* 6 Aug 1966, Emily Mary, da of Ernest Franklin Bozman, MC (d 1968), of Cambridge; 1 s (Joseph Ernest), 1 da (Charlotte Mary); *Career* VSO Sarawak 1958-59, asst master Leighton Park Sch Reading 1964-68, sixth form master and day housemaster Sevenoaks Sch Kent 1968-71, dep headmaster and head of English Pocklington Sch York 1971-80; headmaster: King Edward VI Camp Hill Boys Sch Birmingham 1980-86, Bristol GS 1986-; memb: HMC 1986, SHA 1980; *Recreations* walking, beekeeping, travel; *Clubs* E India, Public Schs; *Style*— Charles Martin, Esq; The Grammar Sch, Univ Rd, Bristol BS8 1SR (☎ 0272 736 006)

MARTIN, Christopher John William; s of William Joseph Martin (d 1942), of Potters Bar, and Kathleen Emily Martin (d 1982); *b* 13 Feb 1939; *Educ* Seaford Coll, KCL (LLB), Merton Coll Oxford; *m* 29 June 1963, Felicity Mary, da of Gp Capt Alfred Weston (d 1985), of Kilkenny; 2 s (Dominic b 1964, Jonathon b 1970), 1 da (Diana b 1966); *Career* account exec Lintas in London and Barcelona 1961-64; BBC TV 1964; documentary prodr, dir and ed Omnibus, ed Arts Features, ed Design and Architecture; films incl: A Life of Christ with Malcolm Muggeridge, Triumph of the West with John Roberts, A Vision of Britain and The Earth in Balance with HRH The Prince of Wales; chm Art and Architecture 1984-; *Recreations* walking; *Style*— Christopher Martin, Esq; BBC TV, Kensington House, Richmond Way, London W14 0AX (☎ 071 895 6776, fax 749 9259)

MARTIN, David; s of Edward Sydney Morris Martin, of Exeter, and Dorothy Mary, *née* Cooper; *b* 11 Feb 1952; *Educ* Worthing HS for Boys, St John's Coll Cambridge; *Career* ptnr Herbert Smith 1986-(tax slr 1979-, asst slr 1979-86); memb Religious Soc of Friends; *Recreations* reading, walking; *Style*— David Martin, Esq; 26 Pied Bull Court, Bury Place, London WC1A 2JR (☎ 071 831 6086); Herbert Smith, Exchange House, Primrose St, London EC2A 2HS (☎ 071 374 8000, fax 071 496 0043, telex 886633)

MARTIN, Rev Prof David Alfred; s of Frederick Martin (d 1979), and Rhoda Miriam, *née* Davey (d 1981); *b* 30 June 1929; *Educ* Richmond and E Sheen GS, Westminster Coll Oxford (Dip Ed), LSE (BSc, PhD); *m* 1, 12 April 1953 (m dis 1957), Daphne Sylvia (d 1973), da of Arthur Treherne (d 1970); 1 s (Jonathan Paul b 25 March 1956); m 2, 30 June 1962, Bernice, da of Frederick William Thompson (d 1956); 2 s (Izaak David b 4 May 1965, Magnus Aidan b 25 Jan 1971), 1 da (Jessica Heloïse b 8 April 1963); *Career* Nat Serv 1948-50; sch teaching 1952-59, lectr Univ of Sheffield 1961-62, prof LSE 1971-88 (lectr 1962-67, reader 1967-71), prof emeritus 1989-; Scurlock prof Southern Methodist Univ Dallas 1986-90; visiting prof: King's Coll London 1989-90, Univ of Boston 1991; pres Int Assoc for Sociology of Religion 1975-83; ordained deacon 1983, priest 1984; hon asst Guildford Cathedral 1983- (non-stipendiary priest 1984); vice-pres: Prayer Book Soc 1980-, London Soc for Study of Religion 1974-; select preacher Univ of Cambridge; fell Japanese Soc for the Promotion of Sci 1978-79; memb: UK UNESCO Ctee 1982-83, UK Advsy Ctee Encyclopaedia Britannica 1986-; chm Cncl for Academic Autonomy 1988-90; *Books* Pacifism (1965), A Sociology of English Religion (1967), The Religious and the Secular (1971), A General Theory of Secularization (1978), The Breaking of the Image (1980), Tongues of Fire (1990); *Recreations* piano accompaniment; *Style*— The Rev Prof David A Martin; Cripplegate Cottage, 174 St John's Rd, Woking, Surrey (☎ 04862 762134); LSE, Aldwych, London, WC2 (☎ 071 405 7686, fax 071 242 0392, telex 24655 BLPES G)

MARTIN, David John Pattison; MP (C) Portmouth South 1987-; s of John Besley Martin, CBE (d 1982), and Muriel, *née* Pattison; *b* 5 Feb 1945; *Educ* Kelly Coll Tavistock, Fitzwilliam Coll Cambridge (BA); *m* 8 Jan 1977, Basia Constance, da of Tadeusz Dowmvnt; 1 s (Henry b 1985), 4 da (Naomi b 1978, Melissa b and d 1980, Francesca 1981, Charis b 1983); *Career* barr Inner Temple, practised 1969-76; dir Martins Caravan Co and assoc co; govr Drummer Acad USA; *Recreations* music, golf; *Clubs* Hawks; *Style*— David Martin, Esq, MP

MARTIN, David McLeod; s of Allan McLeod Martin (d 1976), and Jessie McCurdie, *née* Harris (d 1974); *b* 30 Dec 1922; *Educ* Govan HS, Glasgow Sch of Art (Dip Art); *m* 30 July 1951, Isobel Agnes Fowlie, da of George Frances Fowlie Smith (d 1972); 4 s (Brian b 4 Aug 1954, Allan b 26 Sept 1956, Kenneth b 21 July 1960, Derek b 30 Sept 1966); *Career* WWII Sgt 1943-46; teacher and princ teacher Hamilton GS 1973-83; painter 1983-; annual exhibitions: RSA, RSW, RGI (RA 1984); numerous group shows; one man shows: Glasgow, Edinburgh, Perth, Greenock & Stone Gallery Newcastle, Lynne Stern Assoc London; work in private and public collections incl: The Fleming Collection London, The Earl of Moray, Lord Goold, Sir Norman MacFarlane, Lady MacKay, Scottish Arts Cncl; work cmmnd by Lord Bute for Bute Fabrics, special award of merit Robert Colquhoun Meml art prize Kilmarnock 1974, prizewinner Friends of the Smith Gallery Stirling 1981, Mary Marshall Brown Award RSW 1984, EIS Purchase Prize 1986, prizewinner Hamilton museum exhibiton 1988; cncl memb RGI, cncl memb RSW (past vice president); memb: SSA (1949), RSW (1961), RGI (1981), Paisley Arts Inst (1984); *Recreations* gardening, period ship modelling, music; *Style*— David Martin, Esq; The Old Schoolhouse, 53 Gilmour St, Eaglesham, Glasgow G76 0LG (☎ 03553 3308)

MARTIN, David Norman; s of Norman Henry Edward Martin, of Angmerins, Sussex, and Joyce Elizabeth Martin; *b* 27 Aug 1948; *Educ* Tulse Hill Sch London SW2; *Career* sales dir Shubette of London Gp 1971-78, owner and dir Whole Meal Vegetarian Cafe 1978-; *Recreations* golf, tennis; *Clubs* Purley Downs GC, Surrey Tennis and Country Club; *Style*— David Martin, Esq; 14 Oakfield Gdns, Dulwich Wood Ave, London SE19 1HF (☎ 081 670 0137); 1 Shrewsbury Rd, Streatham, London SW16 2AS (☎ 081 769 0137)

MARTIN, David Selby; s of Archibald Western Martin (d 1966), of Broadstairs, Kent, and Magdelene Martin (d 1971); *b* 26 March 1926; *Educ* Bradfield Coll, The Leys, Univ of Manchester (BSc, BArch); *m* 24 Sept 1982, Cunita Amanda Egerton, da of Lt-Col Hugh Michael Allen Knight, MC, DL, of The Parsonage, Talkin, nr Brampton, Carlisle; 1 da (Serena b 7 Aug 1985); *Career* Capt and adjutant RE 1948 (joined in 1945, served in Egypt); qualified as architect 1959, founded private paractice 1963, Caroe & Partners 1970- (now Caroe & Martin); memb: Cncl Salmon and Trout Assoc, Fisheries Ctee British Field Sports Soc, Regnl Rivers Advsy Ctee NRA; RIBA 1958; *Recreations* fishing, gardening, conservation; *Clubs* Flyfishers'; *Style*— David Martin, Esq; 12 Limerston Street, London SW10 0HH (☎ 071 352 5399); West Cottage, Station Rd, Bishopsbourne, nr Canterbury, Kent CT3 5JB; Caroe & Martin, 1 Greenland Place, London NW1 0AP (☎ 071 267 9348)

MARTIN, David Weir; MEP (Lab) Lothians 1984; s of William Martin and Marion Weir; *b* 26 Aug 1954; *Educ* Liberton HS, Heriot Watt Univ (BA); *m* 1979, Margaret Mary, *née* Cook; 1 s (Kevin), 1 da (Claire); *Career* former stockbroker's asst and animal rights campaigner; memb Lab Pty 1975-, Lothian regnl cncllr Inch/Gilmerton 1982, won Lothians' Euro seat (Lab) 1984 (re-elected 1989), ldr Br Lab Gp 1987-88, vice-pres Euro Parl 1989; memb: Tport and Gen Workers Union, Scot CND, Fabian Soc, Anti-Apartheid Movement, Tribune Gp MEPS; memb Parly: Inst Ctee, Regnl Ctee, Social Ctee, Delgn Aust and NZ; vice-pres Nat Playbus Assoc, memb bd govrs Road Indust Trg Bd Livingston MOTEC, memb ctee Scot Soc for Prevention of Vivisection, dir St Andrew Animal Fund, ex-officio memb W Lothian Econ Devpt Cncl; *Books* Traditional Industl Regions of the European Community (report), Bringing Common Sense to the Common Market - A Left Agenda for Europe (pamphlette, 1988), Chap The Democratic Deficit in A Claim of Right for Scotland (ed Owen Dudley Edwards), European Union and the Democratic Deficit (pamphlet, 1990); *Recreations* reading, sport; *Style*— David Martin, Esq, MEP; Ruskin House, 15 Windsor St, Edinburgh EH5 5LA (☎ 031 557 0936, fax 031 557 5671)

MARTIN, Prof Derek Humphery; s of Alec Gooch Martin (d 1986), of Eastbourne, and Winifred, *née* Humphery; *b* 18 May 1929; *Educ* Hitchin GS, Eastbourne GS, Univ of Nottingham (BSc, PhD); *m* 7 July 1951, Joyce Sheila, da of William Samuel Leaper (d 1973), of Eastbourne; 1 s (Richard Jonathan b 1960), 1 da (Elizabeth Jane b 1962); *Career* prof of physics Queen Mary Coll London 1967- (lectr 1954-63, reader 1963-67); Athlone Press 1973-83, IOP Publications Ltd 1985-; ed Advances in Physics 1974-85; senator Univ of London 1980-87, hon sec Inst of Physics 1984-; memb: Royal Greenwich Observatory Estab Ctee 1977-80, Br Nat Ctee for Radioscience 1983-88, Ct Univ of Essex 1986-, Br Nat Ctee for Physics 1987-90; Metrology award of the Nat Physical Laboratory 1983; FInstP 1965, CPhys 1985; *Books* Magnetism in Solids (1967), Spectroscopic Techniques (1967); *Clubs* Athenaeum; *Style*— Prof Derek Martin; Hermanus, Hillwood Grove, Brentwood, Essex, (☎ 0277 210546); Queen Mary and Westfield College, Mile End Rd, London E14 NS

MARTIN, Edward Charles; *b* 2 Sept 1932; *Educ* Alderman Newton's GS Leicester 1941-44, Henry Mellish GS Nottingham 1944-48, Nottingham Coll of Art and Design (pt/t); *m* 1958, Audrey Elizabeth, *née* Eite; 1 da (Alison Wendy b 1967); *Career* Nat Serv 1950-52 Prov Marshal Branch RAF Police; Marshall and Co Ltd (photographers and printers) 1948-50, Nottingham Coll of Art and Crafts, studio and location asst Vogue Studios London 1954-55, F R Logan Ltd Birmingham 1955-57, teacher Birmingham Coll of Art and Crafts 1956-57, lectr in photography Birmingham Coll of Art and Crafts Birmingham Poly 1957-74 (head of Sch of Photography 1967-74), course ldr Trent/Derby Dip Course in Creative Photography 1974-; sec: IBP E Midlands Gp Assts and Students Gp 1949-50, Nottingham Coll of Art and Crafts Students Union 1950-52, IBP W Midlands Gp 1956-70, Communication Studies Course Devpt Ctee Trent Poly 1974-75; chm: Soc for Photographic Educn UK 1973-74, Creative Arts Course Devpt Ctee Trent Poly 1974-76, Assoc Examining Bd Photography Advsy Ctee 1987-89 (memb 1983-89); memb: Assoc Teachers of Photography (fndr) 1963, Mgmnt Ctee Soc Photographic Educn UK 1973-80, EEC Working Pty on Photographic Educn Brussels 1969; vice chm Assoc Examining Bd Visual Arts Advsy Ctee 1987-89; numerous papers on photography; memb NUJ, FBIPP; *Recreations* garden designing and maintenance; *Style*— Edward Martin, Esq; Lambley Lane, Burton Joyce, Nottinghamshire NG14 5BN; Dept of Visual Arts, Nottingham Polytechnic, Burton St, Nottingham NG1 4BU (☎ 0602 486479, fax 0602 486403, telex 377534 Polnot G)

MARTIN, Geoffrey Haward; CBE (1986); s of Ernest Leslie Martin (d 1967), of Colchester, and Mary Hilda, *née* Haward (d 1987); *b* 27 Sept 1928; *Educ* Colchester Royal GS, Merton Coll Oxford (MA, DPhil), Univ of Manchester; *m* 12 Sept 1953, Janet Douglas, da of Douglas Hamer, MC (d 1981), of Sheffield; 3 s (Christopher b 1957, Patrick b 1963, Matthew b 1963), 1 da (Sophia b 1961); *Career* prof of history Univ of Leicester (formerly Univ Coll of Leicester) 1973-82 (lectr 1952-66, reader 1966-73), keeper of Public Records 1982-88, visiting prof Carleton Univ Ottawa 1958-59 and 1967-68, visiting res fell Merton Coll Oxford 1971, sr visiting fell Loughborough Univ of Technol 1987-, distinguished visiting prof of history Univ of Toronto 1989-, res fell Merton Coll Oxford 1990-, res prof Univ of Essex 1990-; chm: Br Records Assoc 1981-, Cwlth Archivists Assoc 1984-88; hon visiting fell Sch of Library Archive and Info Studies UCL; memb Royal Cmmn on Historical Monuments (England) 1987-, miembro Distinguido del Sistema Nacional de Archivos Mexico 1988, govr Museum of London 1989-; vice pres: Cumberland and Westmorland Archaeological Soc, Essex Archaeological Soc; Hon DUniv Essex 1989; FSA 1975, FRHistS 1958 (vice pres 1984-88), FRSA 1987; *Books* The Town: A Visual History (1961), The Royal Charters of Grantham (1963), Bibliography of British and Irish Municipal History (with Sylvia McIntyre, 1972), Ipswich Recognizance Rolls (1973); *Recreations* fell-walking, gardening; *Clubs* Utd Oxford and Cambridge Univ, RCS; *Style*— Prof G H Martin, CBE, FSA; Flat 27, Woodside House, Wimbledon, London SW19 7QN (☎ 081 946 2570)

MARTIN, (Thomas) Geoffrey; s of Thomas Martin (d 1973), Belfast, NI, and Sadie Adelaide, *née* Day; *b* 26 July 1940; *Educ* Newry GS, Queen's Univ Belfast; *m* 6 July 1968, Gay Madeleine Annesley, da of Herbert Annesley Brownrigg, of Bognor Regis; 1 s (Thomas), 3 da (Blue Bell, Poppy, Gabriella); *Career* pres NUS 1966-68, dir Shelter 1972-73, dip staff Cwlth Secretarial 1973-79; head: Euro Cmmn office NI 1979-85, Pres and Info Serv EC SE Asia 1985-87, External Relations Euro Cmmn Office London 1987-; *Recreations* running; *Clubs* Travellers'; *Style*— Geoffrey Martin, Esq; 64 Mortlake Rd, Kew, Richmond TW9 4AS (☎ 081 876 3714); 8 Storeys Gate, London SW1 4AS (☎ 071 222 8122)

MARTIN, Prof Geoffrey Thorndike; s of Albert Thorndike Martin (d 1947), and Lily, *née* Jackson (d 1964); *b* 28 May 1934; *Educ* Palmer's Sch, Grays Thurrock, UCL (BA), CCC Cambridge, Christ's Coll Cambridge (MA, PhD); *Career* Lady Wallis Budge Res fell in Egyptology Christs Coll Cambridge 1966-67; UCL: lectr in Egyptology 1970-78, reader in Egyptian archaeology 1978-87, prof of Egyptology (Ad Hominem) 1987, Edwards prof of Egyptology 1988; field dir jt Egypt Exploration Soc and Leiden Museum exp in Egypt 1975-, memb Ctee Egypt Exploration Soc, corresponding memb German Archaeological Inst 1982; FSA 1975; *Books* Egyptian Administrative and Private-Name Seals (1971), The Royal Tomb at El-Amarna (vol 1 1974, vol 2 1989), The Tomb of Hetepka (1979), The Sacred Animal Necropolis at North Saqqara (1981), Canopic Equipment in the Petrie Collection (with V Raisman, 1984), Scarabs, Cylinders, and other Ancient Egyptian Seals (1985), The Tomb Chapels of Paser and Raia (1985), Corpus of Reliefs of the New Kingdom (vol 1 1987), Excavations in the Royal Necropolis at El-Amarna (with A El-Khouly, 1987), The Memphite Tomb of Horemheb (1989), The Hidden-tombs of Memphis (1991); *Recreations* travel, English history, book collecting; *Style*— Prof Geoffrey Martin; Department of Egyptology, University College London, Gower St, London WC1E 6BT (☎ 071 387 7050)

MARTIN, George Henry; CBE (1988); s of Henry Martin (d 1967), and Bertha Beatrice, *née* Simpson (d 1948); *b* 3 Jan 1926; *Educ* St Ignatius Coll, Bromley County Sch, GSM; *m* 1, 1 March 1948 (m dis 1966), Sheena Rose, *née* Chisholm; 1 s (Gregory Paul b 1957), 1 da (Alexis Jane b 1953); m 2, 24 June 1966, Judy, da of late Maj Kenneth Lockhart Smith; 1 s (Giles Henry Blake b 1969), 1 da (Lucie Annabel b 1967); *Career* Fleet Air Arm 1944-46; BBC (6 months) 1950, EMI 1950-65, record Prodr and head of Parlophone Records, fndr and chm Air Studios (merged with Chrysalis 1974) 1965-, main bd dir Chrysalis plc 1985-, fndr Air Studios Montserrat BWI 1979; original sponsor Br Sch for Performing Arts, professional patron Salford Coll for Performing Arts; Hon DMus Berklee Coll of Music Boston Mass 1989; *Books* All You Need Is Ears (1979), Making Music (1983); *Recreations* music, design, boats, snooker; *Clubs* Oriental; *Style*— George Martin, Esq, CBE; Air Studios, Lyndhurst Hall, Lyndhurst Rd, Hampstead (☎ 071 431 4040, fax 071 794 0623)

MARTIN, Glenn Philip; s of Walter Philip, and Eileen Denton, *née* Savage; *b* 11 Feb 1949; *Educ* Kings Coll Sch Wimbledon, Wadham Coll Oxford (BA); *m* 4 July 1970, Beryl, da of Albert Darby, of Sale; 3 s (Christopher, Alastair, Nicholas), 1 da (Sarah); *Career* dir banking ops Swiss Bank Corpn 1990 (assoc dir 1988); *Recreations* squash, tennis; *Clubs* City Swiss, Overseas Bankers; *Style*— Glenn Martin, Esq; 14 Langham Dene, Kenley, Surrey CR8 5BX (☎ 081 668 9674); Swiss Bank House, 1 High Timber St, London EC4V 3SB (☎ 071 711 2694, fax 071 329 8700)

MARTIN, Harold Raymond (Harry); s of Lt Frederick Sidney Martin, DSM (d 1925), of Appledore, N Devon, and Blanche, *née* Hookway (d 1958); *b* 2 June 1920; *Educ* Bideford GS; *m* 4 Sept 1950, Pamela Mary, da of William Henry Baron; 1 s (Denys Raymond b 1954), 1 da (Susan Rosalind b 1951); *Career* WWII RA served: BEF France 1939-40, Western Desert 1940-41 (POW Italy 1941-43, Germany 1943-45); National Provincial Bank 1937-68; National Westminster Bank 1968-80; chief mangr stock office services 1968-69, chief mangr 15 Bishopsgate London 1969-80; hon gen sec Nat Honey Show 1980-89; Freeman City of London 1966, Liveryman Worshipful Co of Scriveners 1966; FCIB 1967 (ACIB 1948); *Recreations* beekeeping, music, swimming; *Style*— H R Martin, Esq; Gander Barn, Southfields Rd, Woldingham, Surrey (☎ 0883 653152)

MARTIN, Ian; s of Frank Martin, of 26 Burscough Crescent, Sunderland, and Joyce, *née* Turnock; *b* 13 June 1953; *Educ* Monkwearmouth GS Sunderland, Univ of Leeds (BSc); *m* 1975, Joyce, da of Raymond Wright; 2 s (Christopher David b 29 Nov 1982, Richard Andrew b 18 April 1990), 1 da (Rebecca Helen b 6 Sept 1984); *Career* articled clerk then audit sr Price Waterhouse 1975-79, brewery accountant Vaux Brewery Ltd 1979-81, chief accountant Blayneys (subsid of Vaux) 1981-83, devpt accountant International Paint (Courtaulds Coatings) 1983-86; fin dir: Blayneys 1986-89, Celluware Ltd 1989-; chm Tyne and Wear Soc of CAs 1990-91 (sec 1986-90); FCA (1988, ACA 1978), CIMA 1988; *Recreations* golf, soccer, music, theatre, reading; *Style*— Ian Martin, Esq; 37 Beechwood Terrace, Thornhill, Sunderland SR2 7LY (☎ 091 5671202); Celluware Limited, Derwent St, Blackhill, Consett, Co Durham DH8 8LY (☎ 0207 503751, fax 0207 507873)

MARTIN, Ian James; *b* 14 June 1952; *Educ* Univ of Essex (BA); *m* Theresa Mary; 1 s (Maximillian Joseph b May 1988), 1 da (Kerenia May b Aug 1981); *Career* Arthur Andersen and Co (London and S America) 1973-85; fin dir: County NatWest then NatWest Investment Bank 1985-87, Baring Securities Ltd 1987-; numerous articles and speaking engagements; The Securities Association Ltd 1988-: dir, memb Capital Ctee, memb Exec Ctee, chm Int Policy Ctee; FCA (memb: Business Law Ctee, Banking Ctee); *Books* Accounting In The Foreign Exchange Market (1987); *Style*— Ian Martin, Esq; Baring Securities Ltd, Lloyds Chambers, 1 Portsoken St, London E1 8DF (☎ 071 621 1500, fax 071 528 7691)

MARTIN, Ian Robert; s of William Otway Martin (d 1985), of Wallington, and Marion Weir, *née* Gillespie (d 1976); *b* 29 Dec 1935; *Educ* Wallington Co Sch, Ch Ch Oxford (BA, MA); *m* 1 Aug 1964, Susan, da of Neville Joseph Mountfort, of Olton, Solihull; 3 s (Andrew, Roger, Alan), 1 da (Sally); *Career* Nat Serv RN 1954-56; worked on current affrs and feature progs incl Face to Face BBC TV 1959-68; Thames TV: exec prodr documentaries 1968-70, ed This Week 1971, exec produc features 1972-75, controller features educn and religion 1976-85, head of documentaries 1986-87, head of music and arts 1988-; exec producer many maj documentaries and specials incl: St Nicolas (1977), The Gospel According to St Mark (1979), Swan Lake (1980), Br fund-raising Telethon (1980), Rigoletto (1982), The Mikado (1987), Jessye Normans Christmas Symphony (1987), Martin Luther King - The Legacy (1988), In From the Cold? Richard Burton (1988), Twelfth Night (1988), Xerxes (1989), The Midsummer Marriage (1989), The Tailor of Gloucester (1989), Una Stravaganza dei Medici (1990); chm of govrs Isleworth & Syon Sch, memb Kensington Area Synod; BAFTA (former chm TV and Awards Ctees); *Books* From Workhouse to Welfare (1969); *Recreations* collecting puzzles and quotations; *Style*— Ian Martin, Esq; 83 Wood Lane, Isleworth, Middx TW7 5EG (☎ 081 560 4584); Thames TV, 306-316 Euston Rd, London NW1

(☎ 071 387 9494, fax 071 388 9386, telex 22816)

MARTIN, Janet Hazel; da of James Henry Wilkinson, of Dorchester, Dorset, and Florence Daisy, *née* Steer; *b* 8 Sept 1927; *Educ* Dorchester GS, S Dorset Tech Coll; *m* 15 Aug 1951, Kenneth (Peter) Martin, s of Leonard Henry Martin, of Steepleton, nr Dorchester; 1 s (Timothy b 4 June 1960), 1 da (Judith (Mrs Thomson) b 2 July 1957); *Career* PA NHS 1949-56, freelance interviewer various res insts 1967-86, residential social worker (children with special needs) SW Hants Social Servs 1976-78, social servs offr Test Valley Social Servs 1978-86, residential care mangr (elderly and frail) 1986-87, psychosexual cnsllr (Aldermoor Clinic) NHS 1981-84, housing warden (elderly) Test Valley Social Servs 1988-; memb: Wessex Psychotherapy Soc, Salisbury Arts Centre, Thomas Hardy Soc; lay memb Press Cncl 1973-78; *Recreations* books, buildings; *Style—* Mrs Janet Martin; Hunters Lodge, Linden Avenue, Dorchester, Dorset (☎ 0305 269839)

MARTIN, (Patricia) Jean; *née* Smith; da of Thomas Gregory Smith, of Clifton, Bristol, and Amy Rose, *née* Tyley; *m* April 1963, Michael Graham Martin; *Career* md Audio Televisual Communications, fndr dir MJM Communications 1970-, her work is concerned with the skills of spoken communications, listening and advising on approximately 1000 business presentations each year; clients incl: BIM, Ashbridge Mgmnt Coll, Br Tport Staff Coll, Nat West Bank, AERE Harwell; worked for multinationals in Paris, Brussels, Rome, Madrid, Copenhagen, Dublin; first conslt to offer trg to business and professionals to "Meet The Media"; TV acclimatisations for Cons Pty Central Office, Price Waterhouse, Northcliffe Newspaper Gp, Ciba Geigy; assoc memb of faculty Ashridge Mgmnt Coll 1983-85; LRAM, LGSM; *Recreations* gardening, cooking; *Style—* Mrs Jean Martin; Holmwood, 63 Downton Rd, Salisbury, Wilts SP2 8AT (☎ 0722 245 89)

MARTIN, Jeremy Tobin Wyatt; s of Albert Wyatt (Toby) Martin (d 1986), and Joan Elizabeth, *née* Hallett (d 1982); *b* 27 March 1943; *Educ* Sherborne, Downing Coll Cambridge (MA); *m* 17 May 1969, Penelope Ann, da of Ronald Owen Jenkins, of Guildford; 2 da (Amanda Juliet b 1972, Sally Wyatt b 1974); *Career* admitted slr 1967; dir: Daniel Thwaites plc 1978, Strikegold Ltd, Longstop, Showlag Management Ltd; chm Manuplastics Ltd; memb: Macular Disease Soc, Law Soc; *Recreations* gardening, walking; *Style—* Jeremy Martin, Esq; Beechfield, 54 Warren Rd, Guildford GU1 2HH (☎ 0483 62934); Trowers & Hamlins, 6 New Square, Lincoln's Inn, London WC2A 3RP (☎ 071 831 6292, fax 071 831 8700, telex 21422)

MARTIN, Jessica Cecelia Anna Maria Thérèse; da of Placido Martin, of London, and Mary Bernadette, *née* Maguire; *b* 25 Aug 1962; *Educ* St Michael's Convent GS London, Westfield Coll Univ of London (exhibitioner, BA); *Career* actress; pantomime: Cinderella (De Montfort Hall Leicester 1985, The Palace Manchester 1987), Aladdin (The Grand Wolverhampton) 1986, The Wizard of Oz (Theatre Royal Plymouth) 1988; theatre: nat tour with Rory Bremner 1987, Babes in Arms (Open Air Theatre Regents Park) 1988, Me and My Girl (Adelphi Strand) 1989-91; TV: Spitting Image 1985, Copycats 1985, And There's More 1985, Bobby Davro on the Box 1985, Bobby Davro's IV Weekly 1986, Summertime Special 1986, Tarby and Friends 1986, Royal Variety Show 1987, Bobby Davro's Christmas Annual 1987, Dr Who 1988, A Night of a Hundred Stars 1990; awarded scholarship UCLA; *Style—* Miss Jessica Martin; Sara Randall, Saraband Associates, 265 Liverpool Rd, London N1 (☎ 071 609 5313/4)

MARTIN, John Cecil; s of Cecil Walter Martin (d 1939), of School House, Lydd, Kent, and Mabel Emma, *née* Harvey (d 1957); *b* 14 Jan 1927; *Educ* Simon Langton GS Canterbury Kent, De Havilland Aeronautical Tech Sch Hatfield Herts; *m* 1, 15 Aug 1953 (m dis 1979), Marjorie Stella, da of Frank Simpson (d 1989); 1 s (Roderick b 7 Feb 1958), 1 da (Helen b 14 Aug 1954); m 2, 29 May 1980, Barbara Jean, *née* Watkins; *Career* chief design engr (equipment and furnishings) Hawker Siddeley Aviation Hatfield 1967-80; BAe 146: dep project designer 1980-82, project designer 1982-87, chief designer 1987-88, chief design engr 1988-89; chief designer special projects airlines dir Bae 1989, aviation conslt BP International Ltd 1989-, ind aviation conslt 1989-; CEng, FRAeS 1970; *Recreations* watching cricket, music, woodwork, gardening; *Clubs* Kent CCC; *Style—* John C Martin, Esq; White Timbers, 89a Sandpit Lane, St Albans, Herts AL1 4BJ

MARTIN, Vice Adm Sir John Edward Ludgate; KCB (1972, CB 1968), DSC (1943); s of Surgn Rear Adm W L Martin, OBE; *b* 10 May 1918; *Educ* RNC Dartmouth; *m* 1942, Rosemary Deck; 2 s, 2 da; *Career* RN: served in WWII, Capt 1957, Cdr Br Forces Caribbean Area 1962-63, Rear Adm 1966, Flag Offr ME 1966-67 (despatches), Cdr Br Forces Gulf 1967-68, dir gen Personnel Servs and Trg (Navy) 1968-70, Vice Adm 1970, Dep Supreme Allied Cdr Atlantic 1970-73, ret; Lt Govr and C-in-C of Guernsey 1974-80; FNI (pres 1975-78); *Style—* Vice Adm Sir John Martin, KCB, DSC; c/o Army and Navy Club, 36 Pall Mall, London SW1

MARTIN, John Hadlow; JP (Macclesfield) 1979-; s of Norman Hadlow Martin (d 1988), of Sidmouth, Devon, and Irene Priscilla, *née* Thomas; *b* 11 Aug 1931; *Educ* Minchenden Sch N London, Univ of Liverpool; *m* 13 July 1957, (Winifred Elizabeth) Myfanwy, da of Osborn Vernon Whitley Jones (d 1986), of Deganwy, N Wales; 3 s (Timothy b 1960, Nicholas b 1962, Julian b 1964); *Career* Capt RADC 1959-62, dental specialist BMH Singapore; lectr Univ of St Andrews 1962-70, conslt dental surgn Edinburgh 1970-72, conslt orthodontist Leighton Hosp Cheshire 1972-, visiting conslt IOM 1980-, hon lectr Univ of Liverpool 1980-; memb: BDA, BSSO, EOS; FDSRCS, DOrth; *Recreations* sailing; *Clubs* RYA, NWCC; *Style—* John Martin, Esq, JP; Leighton Hospital, Crewe, Cheshire (☎ 0270 255141 ext 2240)

MARTIN, John Joseph Charles; s of Benjamin Martin, and Lucille Martin; *b* 25 Nov 1940; *Educ* Latymer Upper; *m* 1979, Frances, *née* Oster; 1 s (James b 1982), 1 da (Lucy b 1980); *Career* Illustrated Newspapers 1960-63, Planned Public Relations 1963-68, Martin Dignum Assocs 1969, chm Welbeck Golin/Harris Communications Ltd 1988 (joined 1969-, dir 1972, chief exec 1984); MIPR; *Recreations* painting, tennis; *Style—* John Martin, Esq; 53 Hampstead Way, Hampstead Garden Suburb, London NW11 (☎ 081 455 8482); Welbeck Golin/Harris Communications Ltd, 43 King St, Covent Garden, London WC2E 8RJ (☎ 071 836 6677, fax 071 836 5820, telex 263291)

MARTIN, (Leonard) John; VRD (1969); s of Leonard A Martin (d 1983), and Anne Elizabeth, *née* Scudamore (d 1975); *b* 20 April 1929; *Educ* Ardingly Coll; *m* 3 March 1956, Elisabeth Veronica, da of David Samuel Jones, MBE (d 1968); 1 s (Christopher John b 15 July 1958), 1 da (Rosemary Elisabeth Scudamore b 12 May 1960); *Career* Nat Serv Navy 1949-50, Sub Lt RNVR, ret Lt Cdr RNR 1975; actuary R Watson & Sons 1952-: qualified actuary 1954, ptnr 1957, sr ptnr 1983-; vice-pres Inst of Actuaries 1986-88; chm: Assoc of Conslt Actuaries 1985-87, Occupational Pensions Jt Working Gp 1986-87, Consultative Gp of Actuaries in EEC 1988-; dep chm Occupational Pensions Bd 1988-; Liveryman: Guild of Air Pilots and Navigators, Worshipful Co of Actuaries; FIA 1954, FPMI 1958, FSS 1958; *Recreations* singing, sailing and flying; *Clubs* Naval; *Style—* John Martin, Esq, VRD; R Watson & Sons, Watson House, London Rd, Reigate, Surrey (☎ 0737 241144, fax 0737 241496, telex 946070)

MARTIN, Sir John Miller; KCMG (1952), CB (1945), CVO (1943); s of Rev John Martin (d 1927), and Edith Godwin Martin (d 1945); *b* 15 Oct 1904; *Educ* Edinburgh Acad, Corpus Christi Coll Oxford (MA); *m* 1943, Rosalind Julia, da of Sir David Ross, KBE (d 1971); 1 s; *Career* entered Civil Serv 1927, (Dominions Office) seconded to Malayan Civil Serv 1931-34, sec of Palestine Royal Cmmn 1936, princ private sec to the Prime Minister 1941-45, asst under sec Colonial Off 1945-56, dep under-sec of state Colonial Office 1956-65, Br high cmmr Malta 1965-67, ret; hon fell CCColl Oxford; KStJ; *Style—* Sir John Martin, KCMG, CB, CVO; The Barn House, Watlington, Oxford OX9 5AA (☎ 049 161 2487)

MARTIN, Prof John Powell; s of Bernard Davis Martin (d 1986), and Grace Edith Martin (d 1976); *b* 22 Dec 1925; *Educ* Leighton Park Sch Reading, Univ of Reading (BA), LSE (Dip Soc Admin), Univ of London (PhD); *m* 1, 11 July 1951 (m dis 1981), Sheila Isabel, da of Stuart Feather (d 1985); 3 s (Andrew b 1953, Lawrence b 1955, Stuart b 1957); m 2, 16 Sept 1983, Joan Margaret, *née* Higgins; *Career* lectr LSE 1952-59, asst dir of res Inst of Criminology Cambridge 1960-66, fell King's Coll Cambridge 1964-67; Univ of Southampton: prof of sociology and social admin 1967-87, prof of social policy 1987-89, res prof 1989-; academic adviser Police Trg Cncl and Police Staff Bd of Govrs 1990-; memb and vice chm Bd of Visitors HM Prison Albany 1967-78; memb: IOW Health Authy 1974-90, Jellicoe Ctee on Bds of Visitors 1974-75, Hants Probation Ctee 1975-; *Books* Social Aspects of Prescribing (1957), Offenders as Employees (1962), The Police: A Study in Manpower (with Gail Wilson, 1969), The Social Consequences of Conviction (with D Webster, 1971), Violence and the Family (ed, 1978), Hospitals in Trouble (1984), Licensed to Live (with J B Coker, 1985); *Recreations* sailing, DIY, photography; *Clubs* Lymington Town Sailing; *Style—* Prof John Martin; 4 Furzedown Rd, Southampton SO2 1PN (☎ 0703 552 795); Dept of Sociology and Social Policy, University of Southampton SO9 5NH (☎ 0703 595 000, fax 0703 593 939, telex 47661)

MARTIN, John Sinclair; CBE (1977); s of Joseph Heber Martin, JP (d 1974), of Ely, Cambs, and Mary Sinclair, *née* McDade; *b* 18 Sept 1931; *Educ* Leys Sch Cambridge, St Johns Coll Cambridge (BA, DipAg, MA); *m* 2 July 1960, Katharine Elisabeth, da of Rev George Barclay (d 1953), of Glasgow; 3 s (William b 1961, David b 1963, Robert b 1965), 1 da (Clare b 1967); *Career* farmer; chm Ely Local Branch NFU 1963, memb Gt Ouse River Authy 1970-74; chm: Anglian Water Gt Ouse Drainage Ctee 1984-89, NRA Anglian Regnl Flood Def Ctee 1989-; memb Bd Anglian Water 1988-89, vice pres Assoc of Drainage Authys 1986-, chm Regnl Panel MAFF 1981-86, memb ARC 1968-78; High Sheriff of Cambs 1985; *Recreations* fell walking; *Clubs* Farmers'; *Style—* John Martin, Esq, CBE; Denny Abbey, Waterbeach, Cambridge (☎ 0223 860282)

MARTIN, John Vandeleur; s of Col Graham Vandeleur Martin, MC, of Devizes, Wilts, and Margaret Helen, *née* Sherwood; *b* 17 Jan 1948; *Educ* Malvern, Pembroke Coll Cambridge (MA); *m* 7 Dec 1974, Stephanie Johnstone, da of Maj Michael Johnstone Smith, MC, of Bedford; 2 s (Timothy b 1979, Nicholas b 1985), 1 da (Josephine b 1983); *Career* called to the Bar Lincoln's Inn 1972, in practice Northern circuit; Freeman City of London 1969, Liveryman Worshipful Co of Drapers 1973; *Recreations* opera, walking; *Style—* John Martin, Esq; Wilberforce Chambers, 3 New Square, Lincoln's Inn, London WC2A 3RS (☎ 071 831 6803, fax 071 831 6803)

MARTIN, John William; s of John Joseph William Martin, and Doris May, *née* Bowden; *b* 6 Aug 1935; *Educ* City of London Sch; *m* 26 March 1988, Murielle Fernande, da of Mr Davis; *Career* actuarial student Clerical Med and Gen Assurances 1954-64, asst actuary Local Govt Offrs Insur Assoc 1964-65, dep investmt mangr central fin bd C of E 1965-70, investmt mangr Br Steel Pension Fund 1970-81, chm American Property Tst 1978-, gen mangr invesmts BP 1981-; tstee Walker Ground Southgate, Liveryman Worshipful Co Actuaries 1983; fell Inst Actuaries 1964; *Recreations* skiing, squash, tennis, opera ballet; *Style—* John Martin, Esq; 89 The Ridgeway, Cuffley, Herts (☎ 0707 872 492); Britannic House, Moor Lane, London EC2 (☎ 071 920 7388, fax 071 920 3736)

MARTIN, Jonathan Arthur; s of Arthur Martin (d 1977), of Gravesend, Kent, and Mabel Gladys, *née* Bishop (d 1969); *b* 18 June 1942; *Educ* Gravesend GS, St Edmund Hall Oxford (BA); *m* 4 June 1967, Joy Elizabeth, da of Cecil William Fulker, OBE (d 1970), of Rickmansworth, Herts; 2 s (Stewart John Edmund b 1969, Andrew Robert Jonathan b 1972); *Career* BBC: gen trainee 1964-65, prodn asst Sportsview and Grandstand 1965-69, prodr Sportsnight 1969-74, ed Sportsnight and Match of the Day 1974-79; exec prodr: Wimbledon Tennis Coverage 1979-81, Grand Prix 1977-80, Ski Sunday 1978-80; managing ed Sport 1980-81, head of Sport TV 1981-87, head of Sport and Events Group TV 1987-; *Recreations* watching sport, watching television, golf, skiing; *Style—* Jonathan Martin, Esq; Arkle, Valentine Way, Chalfont St Giles, Bucks HP8 4JB (☎ 02407 4855); BBC Television, Kensington House, Richmond Way, London W14 (☎ 081 895 6174)

MARTIN, Judy Gordon; da of Kenneth Robert Lockhart Smith (d 1978), of Green Tye, Much Hadham, Herts, and Iris Opal Gordon, *née* Blake (d 1979); *b* 13 Nov 1928; *Educ* Bedford Sch, St James Secretarial Coll; *m* 24 June 1966, George Henry Martin, CBE, s of Henry Martin; 1 s (Giles b 9 Oct 1969), 1 da (Lucie b 9 Aug 1967); *Career* EMI Abbey Rd Studios 1948, sec to Oscar Preuss 1948-55, PA to George Martin, head Parlophone Records 1955-65, fndr memb Air Records 1965, ret to raise family 1967, co-fndr Air Studios Montserrat 1969; memb Hyde Park Christian Business and Professional Gp; *Recreations* gardening, reading, travel; *Clubs* Oriental; *Style—* Mrs George Martin

MARTIN, June Eileen; da of Edward William Martin (d 1983), and Vera Cecelia, *née* Hayes; *b* 13 June 1948; *Educ* Pontypridd Girls GS, Banger Sch for Girls, Hatfield Poly (BSc); *Career* business conslt ICL 1972-81, mgmnt conslt Ernst & Whinney 1981-87, dir P E Int 1987-; *Recreations* small bore rifle shooting; *Style—* Miss June Martin; P E Int, Wick Rd, Egham TW20 0HW (☎ 0784 434411)

MARTIN, Jurek; *b* 22 Feb 1942; *Educ* Royal GS Worcester, Hertford Coll Oxford (BA); *m* ; 1 da; *Career* editor; FT: NY bureau chief 1970-72, foreign news ed 1973-75, US ed Washington DC 1975-81; visiting fell Univ of South Carolina 1981-82, ed Europe magazine Washington DC 1981-82; FT: Far East ed Tokyo 1982-86, foreign ed FT London 1986-; broadcaster: BBC World Service, Voice of America, numerous radio and TV stations in US; *Recreations* eating, drinking, tennis, golf, Sumo wrestling and the modern Japanese diet, baseball; *Style—* Jurek Martin, Esq; Foreign Editor, The Financial Times, Number One, Southwark Bridge, London SE1 9HL (☎ 071 873 3291, fax 071 407 5700)

MARTIN, Kit; s of Prof Sir John Leslie Martin, of The Barns, Church St, Gt Shelford, nr Cambridge, and Sadie, *née* Speight; *b* 6 May 1947; *Educ* Eton, Jesus Coll Cambridge (MA, DipArch); *m* 1, 24 Oct 1970 (m dis 1978), Julia Margaret, da of Dr Peter Dennis Mitchell, of Bodmin, Cornwall; m 2, 15 Sept 1980, Sally Martin, da of Sqdn Ldr Edwin Hector Gordon Brookes, AFC (d 1947), of Laxton, Northants; *Career* ptnr Martin & Weighton 1969-76, chm Lucca Wines Ltd 1974; responsible for rescue restoration and conversion of important listed bldgs incl: Dingley Hall, The Hazells, Gunton Park, Cullen House, Keith Hall, Callaly Castle, Tyninghame House; pubns incl: The Country House To Be or Not To Be; memb Historic Bldgs Cncl for Scotland 1987-; *Recreations* skiing, squash, private flying, landscape gardening; *Style—* Kit Martin, Esq; Gunton Park, Hanworth, Norfolk NR11 7HJ (☎ 0263 761202)

MARTIN, Prof Laurence Woodward; DL (Tyne and Wear 1987-); s of Leonard Martin (d 1983), and Florence Mary, *née* Woodward (d 1987); *b* 30 July 1928; *Educ* St Austell GS, Christ's Coll Cambridge (MA), Yale (MA, PhD); *m* 18 Aug 1951, Betty, da of William Parnall (d 1958); 1 s (William Martin b 1962), 1 da (Jane Martin b 1959); *Career* Flying Offr RAF 1948-50; instr political sci Yale Univ 1955-56, asst prof of political sci MIT 1956-61, assoc prof of Euro diplomacy sch of Advanced Int Studies Johns Hopkins Univ 1961-64, Woodrow Wilson prof of int politics Univ of Wales 1964-68 (dean Faculty of Social Sci 1966-68), prof of war studies King's Coll London 1968-77, vice chllr Univ of Newcastle upon Tyne 1978-90; dir: Royal Inst of Int Affrs 1990-, Tyne Tees TV Ltd; *Books* The Anglo-American Tradition in Foreign Affairs (with Arnold Wolfers, 1956), Peace without Victory: Woodrow Wilson and British Liberalism (1958), Neutralism and Non-Alignment (1963), The Sea in Modern Strategy (1966), America and The World (jtly 1970), Arms and Strategy (1973), Retreat from Empire (jtly 1973), Strategic Thought in the Nuclear Age (ed 1979), The Two-Edged Sword: Armed Force in the Modern World (1982), Before The Day After (1985), The Changing Face of Nuclear Warfare (1987); *Style*— Prof Laurence Martin, DL; Director, Royal Inst of Int Affrs, Chatham House, St James Square, London SW1Y 4LE (☎ 071 930 2233, fax 071 839 3593)

MARTIN, Prof Sir (John) Leslie; s of late Robert Martin, of Manchester; *b* 17 Aug 1908; *Educ* Univ of Manchester (MA, PhD); *m* 1935, Sadie, da of Dr Alfred Speight; 1 s, 1 da; *Career* practising architect; architect to LCC 1953-56 (dep architect 1948-53), prof of architecture Univ of Cambridge 1956 (emeritus prof 1973-); Slade prof of fine arts Oxford 1965-66, visiting prof Yale 1973-74, Lethaby prof RCA 1981, emeritus fell Jesus Coll Cambridge 1976 (fell 1956, hon fell 1973); bldgs designed for: Univs of Cambridge, Oxford, Leicester, Hull, RSAMD Glasgow; Gallery of Modern Art Gulbenkian Fndn, Lisbon; scheme design Royal Concert Hall Glasgow; Royal Gold Medallist RIBA 1973; Hon LLD: Univ of Leicester, Hull, Manchester; Hon DUniv Essex; Hon FRSAMD Glasgow; Cdr Order of Santiago da Espada Portugal; RA 1986; FRIBA; kt 1957; *Clubs* Athenaeum; *Style*— Prof Sir Leslie Martin; The Barns, Church St, Great Shelford, Cambridge CB2 5EL (☎ 0223 842399)

MARTIN, Lionel; s of Max Rosenthal, and Renée, *née* Marks; *b* 9 Aug 1950; *Educ* Quintin Sch; *m* 20 July 1975, Carole, da of Michael Packer; 3 da (Carly b 1978, Jojo b 1981, Lily b 1987); *Career* CA; ptnr Martin Greene Ravden; ACA 1973, FCA 1983, FCCA 1983; *Recreations* tennis, music (incl professional writing); *Clubs* The David Lloyd Slazenger Racquet; *Style*— Lionel Martin, Esq; 55 Loudoun Rd, St John's Wood, London, NW8 0DL (☎ 071 625 4545, fax 071 625 5265, car 0836 209 962, telex 21338 MARTIN G)

MARTIN, Michael Charles; s of Charles Stanley Martin (d 1979), and Muriel, *née* Mudd (d 1965); *b* 7 April 1933; *Educ* Malvern, Univ of Loughborough (BSc); *m* 1, 2 May 1964 (m dis 1988), Katharine Valentine, da of Thomas Arthur Saul, of Skegness, Lincs; 1 s (Charles Thomas b 3 May 1967), 1 da (Arabella Katharine b 15 March 1966); m 2, 26 Sept 1988, Helen Gillard, *née* Coleman (d 1988); *Career* 2 Lt REME 1956-58, serv Germany; chm CS Martin Group of Cos, dep chm Louis Newmark plc, former chm Leicester branch IOD and Inst of Prodn Engrs, memb Leicester C of C; govr Sports Aid Fndn E Midlands, pres Leics Lawn Tennis Assoc 1985-88, hon sec and treas Soc of Lawn Tennis Referees; Liveryman Worshipful Co of Makers of Playing Cards 1967, Worshipful Co of Framework Knitters: Liveryman 1962, memb Ct of Assts 1977, Master 1988-89; FInstD 1961, CEng 1968, MIProdE 1968, CBIM 1987; *Recreations* tennis, rugby referee, holiday golf, sailing; *Clubs* RAC, Army & Navy; *Style*— Michael Martin, Esq; The Paddocks, Hungarton, Leics LE7 9JY (☎ 053 750 230); CS Martin Hldgs Ltd, Martin House, Gloucester Crescent, Wigston, Leics LE8 2YL (☎ 0533 773399, fax 0533 787090, telex 34526)

MARTIN, Dr Michael Frederick Roy; s of Frederick Roy Martin, of Bournemouth, and Elisie Winifred Martin; *b* 29 March 1949; *Educ* Clifton, Jesus Coll Cambridge (MB BCh), St Bartholomews Hosp Med Sch; *m* 18 Aug 1973, Ann Teresa, da of Joseph O'Neill (d 1974); 1 s (Andrew Michael b 24 Oct 1987), 3 da (Gemma b 7 Aug 1975, Leana b 11 Nov 1977, Rebecca b 16 May 1981); *Career* house offr St Bartholomew's Hosp 1973, md registrar Royal Cornwall Hosp Leeds 1977, sr registrar in rheumatology Leeds 1980, conslt rheumatologist St James's Leeds 1984, author of papers on prostaglandin E in various peripheral vascular diseases 1979-85; memb: Nat Tst, Royal Northern Horticultural Soc, Nat Heritage; MRCP 1978, memb Br Soc for Rheumatology 1980; *Recreations* sailing, squash, marathon running, gardening; *Clubs* Ripon Sailing, Harrogate Squash and Hockey; *Style*— Dr Michael Martin; 26 Duchy Rd, Harrogate, N Yorkshire HG1 2ER (☎ 0423 509307); St James's University Hospital, Beckett St, Leeds LS9 7TF (☎ 0532 433144)

MARTIN, Michael John; MP (Lab) Glasgow, Springburn 1979-; s of Michael Martin, and Mary Martin; *b* 3 July 1945; *Educ* St Patrick's Boys Sch Glasgow; *m* 1965, Mary McLay; 1 s, 1 da; *Career* Rolls Royce (Hillington) AUEW shop steward 1970-74, trade union organiser 1976-79; PPS to Rt Hon Denis Healey 1981-, memb Mr Speaker's Panel of Chairmen; *Style*— Michael Martin, Esq, MP; 144 Broomfield Rd, Balornock, Glasgow G21 3UE

MARTIN, Millicent; da of William Martin (d 1970), of Florida, and Violet, *née* Bedford (d 1946); *b* 8 June 1934; *Educ* Heath Park HS, Italia Conti Stage Sch; *m* 26 Sept 1977, Marc Alexander; *Career* actress and singer; recent theatre work incl: 42nd Street New York (also Los Angeles and Las Vegas) 1981-85, Two Into One (opposite Tony Randell) USA 1987, Follies Shaftesbury Theatre London 1988-89, Shirley Valentine (westport and US Tour 1990-91); tv incl: Downtown Los Angeles 1986, LA Law Los Angeles 1987, Hardball Los Angles 1989; *Recreations* cooking, swimming, dancing; *Style*— Miss Millicent Martin; Connecticut & NYC

MARTIN, Paul Charles; JP; s of Charles Francis Martin, of Edinburgh, and Elizabeth Angus, *née* Hislop; *b* 10 May 1958; *Educ* Royal HS of Edinburgh, Univ of Edinburgh (MA); *Career* dir Edinburgh Festival Soc Ltd 1980-85, cncllr Edinburgh City Cncl 1980-, Parly Candidate (C) E Edinburgh 1983, dir Lowland Housing Society Ltd 1983-, gen sec Br Youth Cncl Scot 1984-87, leader Cons Gp Edinburgh City Cncl 1984-, asst dir CBI Scot 1987-88, dir Systech Mktg Ltd 1988-; memb Exec Ctee XIII Cwlth Games 1983-87, vice chm Scot Cons Candidates Assoc; prospective Parly candidate (C) Central Edinburgh 1990-; *Recreations* field Sports; *Style*— Paul Martin, Esq, JP; City Chambers, High St, Edinburgh EH1 1PN (☎ 031 225 2424, fax 031 556 0710)

MARTIN, Hon Mrs (Penelope Christina); *née* Plowden; da of Baron Plowden (Life Peer); *b* 1941; *Educ* St Mary's Convent Ascot, New Hall Cambridge; *m* 1, 1965 (m dis 1975), Christopher Roper; m 2, 1981, Rees, s of Leslie Martin, of Te Awa Ave, Napier, NZ; 1 s (Henry b 1984); *Style*— The Hon Mrs Martin; 43 Lansdowne Gardens, London SW8 (☎ 071 720 5736)

MARTIN, Maj Gen Peter Lawrence de Carteret; CBE (1968, OBE 1964); s of late Col Charles de Carteret Martin; *b* 15 Feb 1920; *Educ* Wellington, Sandhurst; *m* 1, 1949 (m dis), Elizabeth Felicia, da of the late Col C M Keble, OBE; 1 s, 1 da; m 2, 1973, Valerie Elizabeth, nee Brown; 2 step s; *Career* DPS (Army) 1971-74, Col the 22 (Cheshire) Regt 1971-78, Col Cmdt Mil Provost Staff Corps 1972-74; head of admin Smith & Williamson 1976-86; chm Lady Grover's Hospital Fund for Offrs' Families 1975-85 (vice-pres 1985, pres 1989); memb: Nat Exec Ctee Forces Help Soc 1975-, Gen Ctee Ex-Servs Mental Welfare Soc 1977-; servs liaison offr Variety Club of GB 1976-86, dir Utd Womens Homes Assoc 1981-, nat vice pres Normandy Veterans Assoc 1989; *Recreations* golf, skiing, walking, reading; *Clubs* Army & Navy; *Style*— Maj-Gen Peter Martin, CBE; 17 Station St, Lymington, Hants (☎ 0590 672 620)

MARTIN, (Roy) Peter; MBE (1970); s of Walter Martin (d 1959), and Annie Mabel, *née* Cook (d 1966); *b* 5 Jan 1931; *Educ* Highbury Co Sch, Birkbeck Coll London (BA, MA), Univ of Tübingen; *m* 1, 31 March 1951 (m dis 1960), Marjorie Patricia Anne Peacock; m 2, March 1960 (m dis 1977), Joan Drumwright; 2 s (Adam b 1963, James b 1964); m 3, 11 April 1978, Catherine Mary Sydee; *Career* Nat Serv RAF educn branch 1949-51; Br Cncl: offr 1960-83, cultural attaché Br Embassy Budapest 1972-73, cultural cnsllr Br Embassy Tokyo 1979-83; freelance author 1983-; memb: BAFTA, Crime Writers' Assoc, Mystery Writers of America, and other socs; *Books* Japanese Cooking (with Joan Martin, 1970); (as James Melville): The Wages of Zen (1979), The Chrysanthemum Chain (1980), A Sort of Samurai (1981), The Ninth Netsuke (1982), Sayonara, Sweet Amaryllis (1983), Death of a Daimyo (1984), The Death Ceremony (1985), Go Gently Gaijin (1986), The Imperial Way (1986), Kimono For A Corpse (1987), The Reluctant Ronin (1988), A Haiku for Hanae (1989); A Tarnished Phoenix (1990), The Bogus Buddha (1990); *Recreations* music, books; *Clubs* Travellers', Detection; *Style*— Peter Martin, Esq, MBE; c/o Curtis Brown, 162-168 Regent St, London W1R 5TB

MARTIN, Philip Charles; s of C A Martin (d 1991), and Margaret Elsie, *née* Allison (d 1984); *b* 19 Oct 1948; *Educ* Forest Hill Sch; *Career* RAF 1968-75, cmmnd 1969; Heidelberg Graphic Equipment Ltd, Booker McConnel plc, Lambart Computing Ltd, Sphinx Ltd, md N Europe computer systems div Encore Computer (UK) Ltd (former Gould Electronics Ltd); *Clubs* Royal Air Force, RAF Yacht, Cruising Assoc; *Style*— Philip Martin, Esq; Derwent House, 8 Derwent Cl, Tangmere, Chichester West Sussex PO20 6FQ (☎ 0243 531929)

MARTIN, Richard Alfred; s of Alfred Martin (d 1986), and Margaret Emma, *née* Portch; *b* 30 June 1946; *Educ* Wandsworth GS; *m* 20 Sept 1969, Judith Ann, da of Leslie Frederick Green, of London; 1 s (Steven b 1979), 2 da (Joanne b 1972, Claire b 1975); *Career* trainee dealer William H Hart & Co 1965-66, business devpt exec Castrol Ltd 1966-71, market devpt mangr Courage Ltd 1971-73, chief exec Improvements Gp plc 1973-; chm: Mktg Improvements Res Ltd, Mktg Improvements Learning Ltd 1973-; church warden St Dunstan with St Thomas Willesden Episcopal Area; memb Mktg Soc; *Recreations* the theatre, reading, tennis, chess; *Style*— Richard Martin, Esq; Marketing Improvements Group plc, 17 Ulster Terrace, Regents Park Outer Circle, London NW1 4PJ (☎ 071 487 5811, fax 071 935 4839, telex 299 723 MARIMPG)

MARTIN, Richard Graham; s of Horace Frederick Martin MC (d 1974), and Phyllis Jeanette Graham Martin, *née* Macfie (d 1984); *b* 4 Oct 1932; *Educ* Sherborne, St Thomas's Hosp; *m* 1957, Elizabeth, da of Harold Savage; 2 s, 1 da; *Career* vice chm and chief exec Alled-Lyons plc (dir 1981); *Style*— Richard Martin, Esq; Allied-Lyons plc, 24 Portland Place, London W1N 4BB (☎ 071 323 9000)

MARTIN, Richard Henry Bolam; s of Leonard Geoffrey Cadoux Martin, of St John's Cottage, Chester, and Rosemary Janet, *née* Bolam; *b* 19 Nov 1955; *Educ* Uppingham, Univ Coll Cardiff (BSc); *Career* corporal CCF; called to the Bar Inner Temple 1978; chm S Branch Stafford Lab pty; *Recreations* skiing, toad sexing; *Style*— Richard Martin, Esq; Rowchester Chambers, 4 Rowchester Court, Whittal St, Birmingham (☎ 021 236 1951)

MARTIN, Richard Lionel; TD (1965); s of Alfred John Martin (d 1948), and Ellen Mary, *née* Warren (d 1981); *b* 18 June 1932; *Educ* Churchers Coll Petersfield, Architectural Assoc Sch of Architecture London; *m* 13 Sept 1958, Gillian Mary, da of Lesley Vivian Taylor, of Weybridge, Surrey; 3 s (Nigel Peter b 1962, Richard John b 1964, David James b 1966); *Career* Nat Serv 1950-52, Royal Hampshire Regt: cmmnd 2 Lt 1951 served 1 Bn, TA (V), promoted Lt 1952 serv 4 TA Bn and 4/5 (TA) Bn, promoted Capt 4/5 (TA) 1954; Capt 4/5 (TA) Bn Cameronian Scot Rifles 1964-67, ret 1967; London CC Architects Dept 1957-63 (worked on Crystal Palace Sports Centre and Queen Elizabeth Concert Hall Haywood Gallery), Scott Brownrigg & Turner Architects and Planning Conslts 1963-, ptnr SBT Advsy Servs 1986-; Structural Steel Design Award 1972; Freeman City of London 1978, Liveryman Worshipful Co Arbitrators 1981; RIBA 1961, ARIAS 1964, FCIArb 1973, FFB 1976, MSCL 1985, MBAE 1988, FBAE 1990; *Recreations* classical music; *Clubs* Wig and Pen; *Style*— Richard Martin, Esq, TD; Colesons, South Hay, Binsted, Hants (☎ 04203 3237); SBT Advsy Servs Conslt Architects, 10-13 King St, London WC2E 8HZ (☎ 071 836 2091, fax 071 831 1231, telex 25897)

MARTIN, Robert Logan (Roy); QC (1988); s of Robert Martin, MC, of The Willows, Crosbie Wood, Paisley, and Janet Johnstone, *née* Logan; *b* 31 July 1950; *Educ* Paisley GS, Univ of Glasgow (LLB); *m* 9 Nov 1984, Fiona Frances, da of John Roxburgh Bingham Neil, of 39 Richmond Ave, St Ives, NSW, Aust; 1 s (John Neil Robert b 12 Aug 1987), 1 da (Camilla Nancy Neil b 25 Sept 1988); *Career* slr 1973-76, admitted to Faculty of Advocates 1976, memb Sheriff Courts Rules Cncl 1981-84, standing jr counsel to Dept of Employment (Scotland) 1983-84, advocate-depute 1984-87, admitted to Bar of NSW 1987, called to the Bar Lincoln's Inn 1990; hon sec Wagering Club 1982-91; *Recreations* shooting, skiing; *Clubs* New (Edinburgh); *Style*— Roy Martin, Esq, QC; Hardengreen House, by Eskbank, Dalkeith, Midlothian (☎ 031 660 5997); Advocate's Library, Parliament House, Edinburgh (☎ 031 226 5071)

MARTIN, Roger John Adam; s of Geoffrey Richard Rex Martin, of The Green, Winchmore Hill, London (d 1985), and Hazel, *née* Matthews; *b* 21 Jan 1941; *Educ* Westminster, BNC Oxford, (BA); *m* 24 Aug 1972, Alison Ann Veronica Cornwell, da of Air Vice-Marshal Robert Sharp, Washington DC, USA (d 1956); 1 s (Adam b 1974); *Career* HM Dip Serv 1964-66, resigned; served Jakarta 1966-67, Saigon 1968-70, Geneva 1975-79, head of ME/N Africa Branch DTI 1981-83, dep high cmmr Harare 1983-86; Wells City Cnsllr 1987, dir Somerset Tst 1988-; *Books* Southern Africa: The Price of Apartheid (1988); *Recreations* climbing, sailing, lecturing, opera; *Clubs* Royal Cwlth Soc; *Style*— Roger J A Martin, Esq; Coxley House, Upper Coxley, Wells, Somerset (☎ 0749 72180)

MARTIN, Ronald Kerr; *Educ* (BSc, MSc); *Career* dir The Distillers Co 1982-, chm of the gp's Scotch Whisky Prodn Ctee July 1982-; chm of two subsidiaries of Distillers' Co: Scottish Grain Distillers July 1982-, Scottish Malt Distillers July 1982- (previously md); FIChemE; *Style*— Ronald Martin, Esq; The Distillers Co plc, 32-34 Melville St, Edinburgh EH3 7HD (☎ 031 225 7843)

MARTIN, Stanley William Frederick; LVO (1981); s of Stanley Martin (d 1976), of Walmer Kent, and Winifred Rose Kilburn (d 1976); *b* 9 Dec 1934; *Educ* Bromley GS, Univ Coll Oxford (MA); *m* 3 Sept 1960, Hanni Aud, da of Aage Valdemar Johannes Hansen (d 1957), of Copenhagen, Denmark; 1 s (Nicholas b 1962), 1 da (Birgit b 1964); *Career* mil serv 2 Lieut RASC 1953-55; entered CRO 1958, asst private sec to Sec of State 1959-62; first sec: Canberra 1962-64, Kuala Lumpur 1964-67; Planning Staff and Personnel Dept FCO 1967-70, seconded to CSD (CSSB) 1970-71, asst marshal Dip Corps 1972-81, first asst marshal Dip Corps 1981-, assoc head Protocol Dept FCO 1986-; visiting prof Dip Acad PCL 1987-; Freeman City of London 1988; FRSA 1985; contrib to JL of Orders and Medals Res Soc; *Recreations* collecting books and ms, hist res and writing, walking; *Clubs* Royal Over Seas League; *Style*— Stanley Martin, Esq, LVO; Protocol Department, Foreign & Commonwealth Office, London SW1A 2AH (☎ 071 210 6390)

MARTIN, Stephen Alexander; s of James Alexander Martin of Bangor, Co Down, NI, and Mamie, *née* Weir; *b* 13 April 1959; *Educ* Bangor GS, Univ of Ulster (BA); *m* 13 April 1987, Dorothy Esther Elizabeth, da of William Edwin Armstrong, of Belmont, Belfast; *Career* hockey player; Bronze medallist World Champions Trophy 1984, Bronze medallist Olympic Games 1984 (Los Angeles), Silver medallist World Champions Trophy 1985, Gold medallist Olympic Games 1988 (Seoul); 65 Caps GB 1983-88, 122 Caps Ireland 1980-90, played Ulster 1980-90; memb Programme Ctee NI Inst of Coaching 1985-88, memb Ulster Branch IHU; *Recreations* hockey, golf; *Clubs* Holywood 87 Hockey, Donaghadee GC; *Style*— Stephen Martin, Esq; 5 Garranard Manor, Circular Rd, Belfast BT4 2RC (☎ 0232 763735)

MARTIN, Stephen Graham Balfour; s of Graham Hunter Martin (d 1985), and Ragna, *née* Balch-Barth; *b* 21 Oct 1939; *Educ* Tonbridge; *m* 27 Nov 1976, Elizabeth Mary, da of Dennis John Ward, of Chatteris; 1 s (Diccon Carl Henry b 1967), 1 da (Charlotte Louise Elizabeth b 1978); *Career* chm and md: Intermail Holdings Ltd, Home Shopping Club Ltd; dir: Fineline Printing Ltd, Strategic Mktg Databases Ltd, Common Cause Ltd; FIWC, Dip DM; *Recreations* fishing, shooting, gardening, collecting watercolours and oils; *Clubs* In & Out, Fly-fishers; *Style*— Stephen Martin, Esq; Manor Farm Chilton Foliat, Hungerford, Berks; Intermail Ltd, 10 Fleming Rd, Newbury, Berks (fax 0635 41678)

MARTIN, Timothy Charles (Tim); s of Godfrey Martin (d 1975), of Findon, Sussex, and Nancy Cordelia, *née* Orrom; *b* 17 May 1951; *Educ* Worthing HS, King's Coll Cambridge (BA, MA); *m* 31 March 1984, Sarah, da of Arthur James Moffett, FRCS, of Cooksey Green, Worcs; 2 s (Alexander Dods b 19 Aug 1985, Charles Murray b 15 Jan 1988); *Career* admitted slr 1977; Allen and Overy 1975-79, dir (corp fin) Hill Samuel and Co 1986-87 (joined 1979); dir (corp fin) Barclays de Zoete Wedd Ltd 1988-; *Recreations* tennis, gardening, opera; *Clubs* Hurlingham, Lansdowne; *Style*— Tim Martin, Esq; Barclays de Zoete Wedd Ltd, Ebbgate House, Swan Lane, London EC4 (☎ 071 623 2323, fax 071 929 3846)

MARTIN, Trevor John Lloyd; s of William Gideon Martin (d 1973), of Hastings, Sussex, and Anna Jeanette, *née* Suters; *b* 21 March 1927; *Educ* Hastings GS, Chichester HS, King's Coll Cambridge (MA); *m* 12 Jan 1955, Anne Mary, da of Maj Robert Alured Denne (d 1969), of Villars-sur-Ollon, Switzerland; 2 s (William b 1966, Henry b 1967), 1 da (Marianne (Mrs Lee) b 1964); *Career* educn offr RAF Stradishall 1948, RAF Mildenhall 1949 (Flying Offr), placed on reserve 1950; asst master Papplewick Sch Ascot 1951; Shellmex and BP Ltd: joined 1956, head of retail planning 1967, regnl mangr BP Midland Region 1968; Br Petroleum Co Ltd: automotive branch mangr 1972, Retail Div mangr 1974, mktg coordinator 1975, mangr Mktg Servs and Lubricants 1978, ret 1982; fndr: Lindsell Chairs (a specialist antique business) 1982, Edwardian Chairs Ltd 1983, Late Victorian Chairs Ltd 1983, Chair Restorations Ltd 1984, Sedilia Victoriana 1985; visiting lectr UMIST 1980-81; ctee memb Chamber of Trade Coggeshall Essex, treas Village Hall Fund Lindsell Essex; memb: Royal Br Legion Coggeshall Branch, Cripplegate Ward Club; Freeman City of London 1974, Liveryman Worshipful Co of Carmen 1974; *Recreations* history, book collecting, rough gardening, carpentry; *Clubs* Utd Oxford & Cambridge, City Livery; *Style*— Trevor Martin, Esq; The Glebe House, Great Dunmow, Essex CM6 3QN (☎ 0371 84222); 11 Market Hill, Coggeshall, Essex CO6 1TS (☎ 0376 562766)

MARTIN, Dr Vivian Max; s of Martin Martin, of Melbourne, Australia, and Rachel, *née* Godfrey; *b* 9 Oct 1941; *Educ* Monash Univ Aust (MB BS), RCP (MRCP); *m* Dec 1967, Penelope Georgina, da of Leon Samuels; 2 s (Simon James b 9 Nov 1971, Nicholas Giles b Dec 1973); *Career* jr RMO Launceston Gen Hosp Tasmania 1968, sr RMO Sutherland Dist Hosp Sydney 1969-70, sr RMO Queen Victoria Meml Hosp Melbourne 1970-71; SHO Royal Free Hosp 1972-73, registrar Whittington Hosp 1973-76; sr registrar UCH 1976-81; conslt rheumatologist: St Albans City Hosp 1981-82, QEII Hosp 1981-82, Welwyn Garden City 1981-82, Cromwell Hosp 1982-, UCH 1983-84; in private rheumatological practice (Devonshire Place) 1982-, conslt physician PPP Med Centre 1985-; memb: BMA, RSM, Br Soc for Rheumatology, RCP, Int Back Pain Soc; *Publications* author of articles in various learned journals; *Style*— Dr Vivian Martin; 38 Devonshire Place, London W1N 1PE (☎ 071 486 2365, fax 071 580 3612); Cromwell Hospital, Cromwell Rd, London SW5 0TU (☎ 071 370 4233, fax 071 370 4063)

MARTIN, William Edward (Bill); s of Joseph Edward Martin (d 1987), of Upminster, Essex, and Pamela Maud, *née* Ruse; *b* 10 March 1951; *Educ* Beal Essex, Univ of Exeter (BA), Univ of Wales (MSc); *m* 28 Aug 1976, Yvette Mary, da of James Geard McBrearty (d 1976); 1 s (Samuel b June 1978), 1 da (Anna b May 1980); *Career* economist DTI 1973-81, advsr Central Policy Review Staff Cabinet Office 1981-83, Phillips & Drew 1983-; advsr Treasy and Civil Serv Select Ctee 1986-; memb Royal Economics Society; *Books* The Economics of the Profits Crisis (ed 1981); *Recreations* skiing; *Style*— Bill Martin, Esq; 80 Mount Crescent, Brentwood, Essex CM14 5DD (☎ 0277 262 047); UBS Phillips & Drew, Broadgate, London

MARTIN, William Wylie Macpherson (Bill); s of Ian Alistair Macpherson (d 1985), of Glasgow, and Lettia, *née* Wylie; *b* 9 Nov 1938; *Educ* Glasgow; *m* Janet Mary, da of Maj Bruce Anthony Olley (d 1981); 1 s (Angus), 3 da (Meran, Alison, Melanie); *Career* songwriter: Puppet on a String, Congratulations, My Boy, The Water Babies, Shangalang and 50 other top ten songs; music publisher: Sky, Van Morrison, Bay City Rollers, BA Robertson, Bill Connolly; record producer: Billy Connolly, Bay City Rollers, Elkie Brooks; Freeman: City of London 1981, City of Glasgow 1987; Liveryman Worshipful Co of Distillers; *Recreations* golf; *Clubs* RAC, Annabels, 100, St George's Hill; *Style*— Bill Martin, Esq; 12 Floor, 93 Albert Embankment, London SE1 7TY (☎ 071 582 7622, fax 0932 248749)

MARTIN-BATES, James Patrick; JP (1961); s of Robert Martin-Bates, JP (d 1950); *b* 17 April 1912; *Educ* Glenalmond, Worcester Coll Oxford (MA); *m* 1939, Dorothy Clare, da of Prof James Miller (d 1962), of Kingston, Ontario, Canada; 1 s, 2 da; *Career* md PE Management Group 1938-61, princ Admin Staff Coll 1961-72; dir: WS Atkins Group 1970-86, WS Atkins Ltd, Averys 1970-77, Charringtons Industrial Holdings 1972-77, Hutchinson 1958-78; chm Atkins Holdings Ltd 1987-89; memb Cncl BIM 1974, chm Cncl Univ of Buckingham 1977-87 (Hon DUniv); High Sheriff of Bucks 1974-75; Burnham meda; FCIS, CBIM; *Recreations* golf, fishing; *Clubs* Caledonian (London), Royal & Ancient St Andrews; *Style*— James Martin-Bates Esq, JP; Ivy Cottage, Fingest, nr Henley-on-Thames Oxon RG9 6QD (☎ 049 163 202)

MARTIN-BIRD, Col Sir Richard Dawnay; CBE (1971, OBE 1953), TD (1950), DL (Cheshire 1974); s of Richard Martin Bird and Mildred, *née* Yates; *b* 19 July 1910; *Educ* Charterhouse; *m* 1935, Katharine, da of Sir Arthur Selborne Jelf, CMG; 1 s (and 1 decd), 3 da; *Career* 8 Ardwick Bn, The Manchester Regt (TA) 1936-53, Lt-Col cmdg 1947-53, later Hon Col, Regtl Cllr The King's Regt 1967-, former ADC to HM The Queen, High Sheriff Greater Manchester 1976-77, chm TA&VR Assoc Lancs, Cheshire and IOM, later TA&VRA for New England and IOM 1968-75, chm and jt md Yates Brothers Wine Lodges Ltd Manchester, pres Wine and Spirit Assoc of GB 1978-79; DL Lancs 1964-74, kt 1975; *Style*— Col Sir Richard Martin-Bird, CBE, TD, DL; Stockinwood, Chelford, Cheshire SK11 9BE (☎ 0625 523)

MARTIN-JENKINS, Christopher Dennis Alexander; s of Lt-Col Dennis Frederick Martin-Jenkins, TD, of Cranleigh, Surrey, and Dr Rosmary Clare, *née* Walker; *b* 20 Jan 1945; *Educ* Marlborough, Cambridge (BA, MA); *m* 1971, Judith Oswald, da of Charles Henry Telford Hayman (d 1952), of Brackley; 2 s (James b 1973, Robin b 1975), 1 da (Lucy b 1979); *Career* BBC sports broadcaster 1970-, cricket corr 1973-80 and 1984-91, ed The Cricketer 1981-91 (dep ed 1967-70), cricket corr Daily Telegraph 1991; played cricket for Surrey 2 XI and MCC; *Books* author of 12 books on cricket; *Recreations* cricket, golf, tennis; *Clubs* MCC; *Style*— Christopher Martin-Jenkins, Esq; Cricket Correspondent, Daily Telegraph, 181 Marsh Wall, London E14 9SR

MARTIN-JENKINS, David Dennis; s of Dennis Frederick Martin-Jenkins, TD, of Maytree House, Woodcote, Guildford Rd, Cranleigh, Surrey, and Dr Rosemary Clare Walker; *b* 7 May 1941; *Educ* Kingsmead, Meols, St Bede's Eastbourne, Marlborough; *m* 24 June 1967, Anthea, da of Arthur Milton de Vinny (d 1983); *Career* dir: JW Cameron and Co Ltd 1972-82, Elerman Lines plc 1974-82, Tollemache and Cobbold Breweries Ltd 1976-82; chm: MN Offrs Pension Fund Investmt ctee 1976-82, Primesight Ltd 1984-; dir: Nat Home Loans Holdings plc 1985-, Nat Morgage Bank plc 1990-, Capital and Regnl Properties plc 1986-; tres Lurgashall PCC; FCA 1965, FCT 1979; *Recreations* sport (Tranmere Rovers and Liverpool FC's), politics (Lib Democrat), hill walking (climbed Mount Mera (21200ft) Nepal 1986), the countryside; *Clubs* Lancashire CCC; *Style*— David Martin-Jenkins, Esq; Jobson's Cottage, Jobson's Lane, Haslemere, Surrey GU27 3BY (☎ 042 878 294)

MARTIN-JENKINS, Dennis Frederick; TD (1945); s of Frederick Martin Jenkins (d 1941), and Martha Magdalene, *née* Almeida; *b* 7 Jan 1911; *Educ* Marlborough; *m* 1937, Rosemary Clare, da of Dr Robert Alexander Walker, of Northants; 3 s (David, Christopher, Timothy); *Career* RA 1939-45, serv UK and Europe, Lt-Col; chm: Gen Cncl of Br Shipping for UK 1963, Ellerman Lines Ltd 1967-80 (md 1967-76), Int Chamber of Shipping 1971-77; Merchant Navy Offrs Pension Trustees Ltd 1971-81; pres Chamber of Shipping of UK 1965; memb: Mersey Docks and Harbour Bd, Port of London Authy, Nat Dock Lab Bd, Br Tport Docks Bd; Prime Warden Worshipful Co of Shipwrights 1981; *Recreations* golf, gardening; *Clubs* United Oxford & Cambrdige University, Woking Golf, Thurlestone Golf; *Style*— Dennis Martin-Jenkins, Esq, TD; Maytree House, Woodcote, Guildford Rd, Cranleigh, Surrey GU6 8NZ (☎ 0483 276278)

MARTIN-JENKINS, Timothy Dennis (Tim); s of Lt-Col Dennis Frederick Martin-Jenkins, TD, and Dr Rosemary Clare Martin-Jenkins; *b* 26 May 1947; *Educ* Marlborough, Univ of Cambridge (MA), Harvard (MBA); *Career* dir Ellerman Lines Ltd 1978-82, chm Ellerman Commercial Holdings Ltd 1980-82, md Pacific Holdings Inc; *Recreations* golf, tennis, music; *Clubs* Royal Hong Kong Golf, Woking Golf, Hawks, Hurlingham, Shek O, Hong Kong, Thurlestone Golf, Chung Shan Golf; *Style*— Tim Martin-Jenkins, Esq; Pacific Holdings Inc, 50 Stubbs Rd, Hong Kong

MARTIN-QUIRK, Howard Richard Newell; s of George Donald Martin, of Dorset, and Nelly Katie, *née* Newell; *b* 8 Aug 1937; *Educ* Lancing, Christs Coll Cambridge (MA), UCL (BSc Arch, MSc); *m* 1, 4 Jan 1964, Sally Anne (d 1976), da of Ernest Davies, of London; *m* 2, 1 Oct 1976, Mary Teresa, da of Dudley C Quirk, JP; 1 s (Inigo b 1989); *Career* architect & architectural historian, author, sr tutor Kingston Poly Sch of Architecture 1970-, ptnr Martin Quirk Assoc 1983-, chief oenologist Chiddingstone Vineyards Ltd 1984-; *Recreations* music, chess, squash rackets, gardening, wine; *Clubs* Architectural Assoc, Soc of Architectural Historians, Victorian Soc, Wagner Soc, EVA; *Style*— Howard Martin-Quirk, Esq; Sorrel, Vexour Farm, Chiddingstone, Edenbridge, Kent TN8 7BB (☎ 0892 870439); Kingston Polytechnic (☎ 549 081 6151, MQA 8780010/0892 870439)

MARTIN SMITH, Julian Roland; MC (1943); s of Everard Martin Smith (d 1938), of Codicote Lodge, Hitchin, Herts, and Violet Mary Martin Smith, MBE, *née* Hambro (d 1966); *b* 7 June 1916; *Educ* Eton; *m* 1 Nov 1934, Susan Mary, da of Maj Philip Pearson Gregory (d 1952), of Queen Ann Cottage, Windsor; 2 s (Andrew b 1952, Jonathon b 1959); *Career* Maj Welsh Guards 1939-46; dir Smith St Aubyn 1951, Ashdown Investment Trust 1951-86, sr ptnr Rowe & Pitman 1967-79 (ptnr 1949), Philip Hill Investment Trust 1977-86, Hambros Bank 1979-86, River Plate & Son Investment Trust 1979-, chm East Holdings 1986-89; High Sheriff Hertfordshire 1976; *Recreations* golf, shooting; *Clubs* White's, Pratt's; *Style*— Julian Martin Smith, Esq, MC; c/o River Plate & General Investment Trust, 197 Knightsbridge, London SWY (☎ 071 225 1044)

MARTINDALE, Air Vice-Marshal Alan Rawes; CB (1984); s of late Norman Martindale, and late Edith, *née* Rawes; *b* 20 Jan 1930; *Educ* Kendal GS, Univ Coll Leicester (BA); *m* 1952, Eileen Alma Wrenn; 3 da; *Career* cmmnd RAF 1951, dep dir Supply Mgmnt MOD Harrogate 1971-72 (dir 1974-75), Cmd Supply Offr RAF Germany 1972-74, RCDS 1976, Air Cdre Supply and Movements RAF Support Cmd 1977, dep gen mangr NATO Multi-Role Combat Aircraft Mgmnt Agency 1978-81, dir Supply Policy (RAF) MOD 1981-82, dir gen Supply (RAF) 1982-84; dist gen mangr Hastings Health Authy 1985-90, census area mangr S Kent and Hastings 1990-91; *Recreations* gardening, skiing; *Clubs* RAF; *Style*— Air Vice-Marshal Alan Martindale, CB; Taylors Cottage, Mountfield, Robertsbridge, E Sussex TN32 5JZ

MARTINDALE, Prof Andrew Henry Robert; s of Rev Henry Martindale (d 1946), and Augusta Celia, *née* Burn (d 1981); *b* 19 Dec 1932; *Educ* Westminster, New Coll Oxford (BA, MA), Courtauld Inst of Art (Academic Dip History of Art); *m* 19 June 1959, Jane Primrose, da of Malcolm Archibald Brooke, of Crouch, Kent; *Career* Nat Serv Royal Signals 1951-53 (cmmnd 2 Lt E Cmd Signals Regt 1952), Princess Louise Kensington Regt TA 1953-57 (resigned with rank of Lt); res asst to Nikolaus Pevsner 1958-59, lectr Courtauld Inst of Art London Univ 1959-65, prof visual arts UEA 1974- (sr lectr in history of art 1965-74); UEA: conslt in art history and fine art Arts Sub Ctee Univ Grants Ctee 1978-89, Univ Funding Cncl 1989-; memb Conservation Ctee Cncl for Care of Churches 1979-; FBA 1958, FRAI 1958, FSA 1968, FRSA 1977; *Books* Man and the Renaissance (1966), Gothic Art (1967), The Rise of the Artist (1972), The Triumphs of Caesar by Andrea Mantegna (1979), Heroes Ancestors, Relatives and the Birth of the Portrait (1988), Simone Martini (1988), The Vanishing Past: Studies in Medieval Art Liturgy and Metrology presented to Christopher Hohler (jt ed and contrib 1981); contrib to: Burlington Magazine, Archaeologia, Jl Br Archaeological Assoc; *Recreations* travel, gardening, visiting bookshops; *Style*— Prof Andrew Martindale; University of East Anglia, School of Art History and Music, Norwich NR4 7TJ (☎ 0603 56161)

MARTINDALE, Richard John; s of Eric Martindale (d 1970), of Hindley, nr Wigan, and Margaret Joyce, *née* Whiteside; *b* 25 Oct 1950; *Educ* Bolton Sch, Univ of Sheffield (LLB); *m* 5 Aug 1971, Jackie Avril, da of Philip Watkin Edwards; 4 s (Nicholas Jolyon b 16 April 1977, Timothy George b 8 Aug 1978, Alastair James b 16 July 1982, Justin Matthew b 31 Aug 1984); *Career* Hill Dickinson Davis Campbell (formerly Hill Dickinson & Co) Liverpool: articles until 1974, ptnr 1979, specialist in commercial law; chief examiner in shipping law RSA 1980-84; memb Law Soc 1974-, Slrs Euro GP; *Recreations* music, in particular choral singing, reading, dinghy sailing, walking; *Style*— Richard Martindale, Esq; Hill Dickinson Davis Campbell, Pearl Assurance House, Derby Square, Liverpool L2 9XL (☎ 051 236 5400, fax 051 236 2175)

MARTINEAU, David Nicholas Nettlefold; s of Frederick Alan Martineau (d 1990) of Valley End House, Chobham, Surrey, and Vera Ruth, *née* Naylor; *b* 27 March 1941; *Educ* Eton, Trinity Coll Cambridge (MA, LLB); *m* 20 Jan 1968, Elizabeth Mary, da of Maurice James Carrick Allom, of Gibbons Place, Ightham, Kent; 1 s (Luke b 27 March

1970), 1 da (Alice b 8 June 1972); *Career* called to the Bar Inner Temple 1964, rec 1986 (asst rec 1982); memb Nat Exec Ctee Cystic Fibrosis Res Tst 1989-; *Recreations* skiing, water skiing, windsurfing, walking; *Clubs* Hawks, MCC; *Style—* David Martineau, Esq; 37 Bedford Gardens, London, W8 7EF (☎ 071 727 7825); 2 Garden Ct, Temple, London, EC4Y 9BL (☎ 071 353 4741)

MARTINEAU, (Alan) Denis; s of Col Sir Wilfrid Martineau, MC, TD (d 1964), of 30 Rotton Park Rd, Edgbaston, Birmingham and Upper Coscombe, Temple Guiting, nr Cheltenham, Glos, and Elvira Mary Seton, *née* Lee Strathy (d 1982); *b* 5 April 1920; *Educ* Rugby, Trinity Hall Cambridge (BA, MA); *m* 5 July 1952, Mollie, da of John Lewis Davies, MBE (d 1987), of St Brides Major, Glamorgan; 3 s (Jeremy b 1955, Peter b 1956, Charles b 1961); *Career* Army 1940-46, cmmnd Royal Warwickshire Regt 1941, served as Capt in ME, N Africa and Italy; admitted slr 1950; ptnr Ryland Martineau & Co 1954-84, NP; memb Birmingham City Cncl 1961- (Lord Mayor 1986-87); dir: City of Birmingham Symphony Orch (chm 1968-74), Birmingham Repertory Theatre, Birmingham Botanical Gardens; chm: Cncl of Order of St John W Mids, Birmingham Civic Soc, George Henry Collins Charity; pres Birmingham Bach Soc; vice pres: Birmingham Festival Choral Soc, SENSE in the Midlands; vice patron Birmingham Co Royal Br Legion; memb: Law Soc 1952, Soc of Provincial Notaries 1965; OStJ 1988; *Recreations* music, Birmingham history, the country, watching sport; *Style—* Denis Martineau, Esq; 10 Vicarage Rd, Edgbaston, Birmingham B1S 3ES (☎ 021 454 0479); Pike Cottage, Upper Coscombe, Temple Guiting, Glos

MARTINEAU, (Elizabeth) Jane; da of Rupert William Hammond, CBE (d 1986), of Sussex, and Camille Sylvia, *née* Longmore; *b* 27 March 1951; *Educ* Cheltenham Ladies Coll; *m* 7 Aug 1982, John Denis Martineau, s of Charles Herman Martineau, of Fife; 2 s (Robert b 1985, Edward b 1987); *Career* admitted slr 1974; currently ptnr Clyde & Co; memb Law Soc; *Recreations* walking, tennis; *Style—* Mrs Jane Martineau; Clyde & Co, 51 Eastcheap, London EC3 (☎ 071 623 1244, fax 071 623 5425, telex 884886)

MARTINEAU, Jeremy John; s of Capt Denis Martineau, of Birmingham, and Mary Rena, *née* Davies; *b* 16 Sept 1955; *Educ* Rugby, Trinity Hall Cambridge (MA); *Career* slr 1981, asst slr Freshfields London 1981 (articled clerk 1979-81), ptnr Ryland Martineau Birmingham 1985-87 (asst slr 1981-84), ptnr Martineau Johnson Birmingham 1987-; sec Inst of Fiscal Studies Midlands Regn, tstee Feeney Tst; memb Law Soc 1981; *Recreations* various sports, photography, foreign travel, music; *Style—* Jeremy Martineau, Esq; 43 Kingscote Rd, Edgbaston, Birmingham B15 3LA (☎ 021 454 1493); Martineau Johnson, St Philips House, St Philips Place, Birmingham B3 2PP (☎ 021 200 3300, fax 021 200 3330, telex 339793 RYLMAR G)

MARTLEW, (Margaret) June; MBE (1974); da of George Martlew (d 1966), and Mary Jane, *née* Gaskell (d 1987); *b* 20 June 1935; *Educ* Wigan Mining and Tech Coll, Carlisle Tech Coll; *Career* HM Dip Serv 1963-; Bonn 1963-66, Kinshasa Congo 1966-68, Amman 1970-79, sec Belize 1971-73; pa to govr: Buenos Aires 1975-76, Santiago 1977-79, East Berlin 1980-82; FCO London 1982-86: pa to asst under sec, transferred to exec stream 1984; Belize 1986-89, vice consul, Prague 1990; *Recreations* golf, tennis, painting, walking; *Clubs* Carlisle Golf (Carlisle); *Style—* Miss June Martlew, MBE; c/o Foreign & Commonwealth Office, King Charles St, London SW1

MARTON, Capt Christopher; s of Henry Brooks Marton (d 1978), and Eileen, *née* Moon (d 1980); *b* 18 Aug 1939; *Educ* Eccles HS, Liverpool Tech Coll (Masters Cert of Competency); *m* 14 Jan 1969, Margaret Christine, Marton, da of Henry Clarence Broughton (d 1972); 2 s (Andrew Christopher b 1 June 1969, Robert Charles b 3 Oct 1971); *Career* apprentice MN 1956-60, MN Offr 1960-72; master: hydrographic survey ship 1972-73, offshore supply vessels 1973-74; marine surveyor and conslt 1974-; cncl memb: Naval Club London, PCC; Freeman: City of London 1981, Worshipful Co of Loriners 1982; *Recreations* cricket, shooting, squash, gardening; *Clubs* Lighthouse, Rugby, Lancs CCC; *Style—* Capt Christopher Marton; 10 Church Green, Milton Ernest, Bedford NK44 1RH; Noble Denton & Associates Ltd, Noble House, 131 Aldersgate St, London EC1A 4EB (☎ 071 606 4901, fax 071 606 5035, telex 885 802)

MARTONMERE, 2 Baron (UK 1964) John Stephen Robinson; s of Hon Richard Anthony Gasque Robinson (d 1979), and Hon Mrs (Wendy Patricia) Robinson, *qv*; gs of 1 Baron Martonmere, GBE, KCMG, PC (d 1989); *b* 10 July 1963; *Educ* Lakefield Coll Sch, Seneca Coll; *Heir* bro, David Alan Robinson b 15 Sept 1965; *Style—* The Rt Hon Lord Martonmere; 382 Russell Hill Rd, Toronto, Ontario, Canada M4V 2V2 (☎ 416 485 3077)

MARTYN, (Anthony) Nigel; s of Alfred Horace Martyn, of St Austell, Cornwall, and Delphia June, *née* Marks; *b* 11 Aug 1966; *Educ* Penrice Comp St Austell; *m* 17 Aug 1987, Amanda Tamblyn, da of Christopher Edwin Bailey; *Career* professional footballer; Bristol Rovers 1987-89 (debut Aug 1987 v Rotherham, 124 appearances); Crystal Palace 1989-: joined for a fee of £1m, debut Nov 1989 v Tottenham Hotspur, over 70 appearances; England: 11 under 21 caps, 3 B Caps; FA Cup Loser's medal v Manchester Utd 1990; office clerk Smith and Treffry Coal Merchants 1983-87, plastics mixer Holmbush Plastics 1987; *Recreations* golf, cricket, most other sports; *Style—* Nigel Martyn, Esq; Crystal Palace Football Club, Selhurst Park, London SE25 (☎ 081 653 4462)

MARTYN, (Charles) Philip; s of James Godfrey Martyn (d 1970), of London, and Kathleen Doris, *née* Crawford; *b* 17 July 1948; *Educ* St Dunstans Coll London, Exeter Univ (LLB); *Career* slr: Coward Chance London 1972-77 (articled clerk 1970-72), Clifford Turner 1977-79; jt gen mangr Sumitomo Bank Ltd London 1988- (legal advsr 1979-84, sr mangr 1984-86, dep gen mangr 1986-88); tstee: N London Rudolf Steiner Sch, Waldorf Sch London; cncl memb Anthroposophical Soc GB; memb Law Soc; *Recreations* studying Rudolf Steiner's work, green politics, gardening, Bach, green economics; *Style—* Philip Martyn, Esq; The Sumitomo Bank Ltd, Temple Ct, 11 Queen Victoria St, London EC4N 4TA (☎ 071 236 7400, fax 071 236 0049)

MARTYN, Master (Charles) Roger Nicholas; s of Rev Charles William Martyn, of Aylsham, Norfolk, Clerk in Holy Orders (d 1956), and Doris Lilian, *née* Batcheller (d 1989); *b* 10 Dec 1925; *Educ* Charterhouse, Merton Coll Oxford (MA); *m* 24 Sept 1960, Helen Ruth, da of Samuel Frank Everson, of Camberley, Surrey (d 1981); 1 s (Nicholas b 1963, Christopher b 1965); 1 da (Sarah b 1962); *Career* 60 Rifles KRRC 1944-47; admitted slr 1952; ptnr: Sherwood & Co (Parly agent) 1954-60, Lee Bolton & Lee 1961-73; master of the Supreme Ct 1973-; *Recreations* sailing, walking, horology, book-binding; *Clubs* Thames Barge, Salcombe Yacht; *Style—* Master Roger Martyn; Royal Courts of Justice, Strand, London WC2A 2LL

MARTYN-HEMPHILL, Hon Charles Andrew Martyn; s of 5 Baron Hemphill; *b* 8 Oct 1954; *Educ* Downside, Univ of Oxford; *m* 1985, Sarah J F, eld da of Richard Lumley, of Roundwood, Windlesham, Surrey; 1 s (Richard Patrick Lumley b 17 May 1990), 2 da (Clarissa b 1986, Amelia b 1988); *Career* dir Morgan Grenfell International Fund Management; *Recreations* sailing, skiing, shooting, hunting; *Style—* The Hon Charles Martyn-Hemphill; 78 Streathbourne Rd, London SW17 8QY

MARTYR, Peter McCallum; s of John Walton Martyr, and Jean Wallace Robertson, *née* McCallum; *b* 31 March 1954; *Educ* Clifton, Univ of Wales (LLB); *m* 27 May 1978, Carol Frances, da of Donald Edgar Busby; 1 s (Luke b 26 Dec 1985), 1 da (Laura b 7 Nov 1988); *Career* admitted slr 1979, ptnr Norton Rose 1985- (specializing in int and marine litigation); Freeman Worshipful Co Solicitors 1979; *Recreations* swimming, collector's motor cars, music; *Style—* Peter Martyr, Esq; The Lodge, 44 Teddington Park, Teddington (☎ 081 977 6079); Norton Rose, Kempson House, Camomile St, London EC3A 7AN (☎ 071 283 2434, fax 071 588 1181)

MARU, Rajesh Jamnadass; s of Jamnadass Maru, and Prabhavati, *née* Galoria; *b* 28 Oct 1962; *Educ* Rooks Heath HS Harrow, Pinner Sixth Coll; *Career* professional cricketer; North London Poly 1975-79, Brondersbery 1980-83, Middlesex CCC 1980-83, Hampshire CCC 1984- (awarded county cap 1986); England: schs under 15 1977-78 (capt 1978), 2 Test matches Young England v W Indies 1979-80, 3 Test matches Young England v India 1980; represented MCC v Middlesex 1986; County Championship and Gillette Cup medals Middlesex 1980; best bowling figures for 1989 (8 for 41 v Kent), most promising English schoolboy Cricket Soc 1978, Hampshire young player of the year 1986; coaching: Nat Coaching Assoc qualified cricket coach, coached in NZ 1985-87, ran private coaching sch 1988, coach to W of England Schs under 14 1990; *Recreations* golf, squash, swimming, tennis, badminton; *Style—* Rajesh Maru, Esq; Hampshire CCC, Northlands Rd, Southampton, Hampshire (☎ 0703 333788)

MARVIN, John Charman; s of Robert George Marvin (d 1979), and Vera Emily, *née* Charman (d 1988); *b* 18 March 1933; *Educ* Christ's Hosp, King's Coll Cambridge (MA); *m* 29 March 1958, Wendy (d 1989), da of Matthew Raeside (d 1976); 2 s (Timothy b 1964, Matthew b 1968), 1 da (Hilary b 1961); *Career* Nat Serv RNVR Lt 1954-56; Reserve Lt Cdr 1956-69; dir ICI Plastics Div 1956-83; md Hickson Int plc 1983-89, dep chm Whitecroft plc 1990-; Health & Safety Cmmr 1990-; *Recreations* sailing, windsurfing, tennis (real); *Style—* John C Marvin, Esq

MARWICK, Prof Arthur John Brereton; s of William Hutton Marwick, and Maeve Cluna, *née* Brereton; *b* 29 Feb 1936; *Educ* George Heriot's Sch Edinburgh, Edinburgh Univ (MA, DLitt), Balliol Coll Oxford (BLitt); unmarried; 1 da; *Career* asst lectr in history Univ of Aberdeen 1959-60, lectr in history Univ of Edinburgh 1960-69, prof of history Open Univ 1969-, dean and dir of studies in arts Open Univ 1978-84, visiting prof in history State Univ of NY at Buffalo 1966-67, visiting scholar Hoover Inst and visiting prof Stanford Univ 1984-85, directeur d'études invité l'Ecole des Hautes Etudes en Sciences Sociales Paris 1985, visiting prof Rhodes Coll Memphis Tennessee 1991; FRHistS; *Books* The Explosion of British Society (1963), Clifford Allen (1964), The Deluge (1965, 2 edn 1991), Britain in the Century of Total War (1968), The Nature of History (3 edn, 1989), War and Social Change in the Twentieth Century (1974), The Home Front (1976), Women at War 1914-1918 (1977), Class: image and reality in Britain, France and USA since 1930 (1980, 2 edn 1990), Illustrated Dictionary of British History (ed 1980), British Society since 1945 (1982, 2 edn 1990), Britain in Our Century (1984), Class in the Twentieth Century (ed 1986), Beauty in History: society politics and personal appearance c 1500 to the present (1988), Total War and Social Change (ed, 1988), The Arts, Literature and Society (ed, 1990), Culture in Britain since 1945 (1991); *Clubs* Open Univ Football and Tennis; *Style—* Prof Arthur Marwick; 67 Fitzjohns Ave, Hampstead, London NW3 6PE

MARWICK, Sir Brian Allan; KBE (1963, CBE 1954, OBE 1946), CMG (1958); s of James Walter Marwick (d 1931), and Elizabeth Jane, *née* Flett (d 1957); *b* 18 June 1908; *Educ* Univ of SA (BA), Univ of Cape Town (MA), CCC Cambridge; *m* 1934, Riva Lee (d 1988), da of Maj Harry Claud Cooper (d 1959); 2 da (Sally, Tessa); *Career* entered Colonial Serv 1925; first asst sec: Swaziland 1947-48, Basutoland 1949-52; dep resident cmmr and govt sec Basutoland 1952-55, admin sec high cmmr Basutoland Bechuanaland Protectorate Swaziland 1956, resident cmmr then HM cmmr Swaziland 1956-64; perm sec: Miny of Works and Town Planning Bahamas 1965-68, Miny of Educn and Culture Bahamas 1968-71; *Books* The Swazi-An Ethnographic Account of the Natives of the Swaziland Protectorate (1940, 2 edn 1966); *Recreations* gardening; *Style—* Sir Brian Marwick, KBE, CMG; Sea Bank, Shore Rd, Castletown, Isle of Man (☎ 0624 823782)

MARWOOD, Roger Paul; s of Kenneth Ian Marwood (d 1988), Blanche Greenberg (d 1980); *b* 23 July 1947; *Educ* Cheltenham GS, Univ of London (MB BS, MSc, Water Polo double purple); *m* 21 Feb 1976, Suzanne Christine, da of Francis Brown; 1 s (Joseph Roger George b 31 Oct 1984), 2 da (Rebecca Alice Georgina b 25 March 1978, Sophie Christine Blanche b 30 Dec 1979); *Career* sr registrar in obstetrics and gynaecology St Mary's Hosp 1980-82 (registrar 1975-80); conslt: in obstetrics and gynaecology Westminster Hosp 1982-, gynaecologist to King Edward VII Hosp 1985-; memb Worshipful Co of Apothecaries 1985; memb RSM, FRCOG 1989 (MRCOG 1977); *Books* contrib to numerous Jls on clinical obstetrics and gynaecology; *Recreations* opera, skiing, pinball machines, swimming; *Style—* Roger Marwood, Esq; 80 Harley St, London W1; Westminster Hospital, Dean Ryle St, SW1

MARYON DAVIS, Dr Alan Roger; s of Cyril Edward Maryon Davis, of Osterley, Middx, and Hilda May, *née* Thompson; *b* 21 Jan 1943; *Educ* St Paul's, St John's Coll Cambridge (MA, MB BChir) St Thomas' Hosp Med Sch, LSHTM (MSc); *m* 14 March 1981, (Glynis) Anne, da of Dr Philip Trefor Davies (d 1970) of Hartlepool; 2 da (Jessica b 1983, Elizabeth b 1985); *Career* med conslt, writer and broadcaster; clinical med 1969-74, community and preventive med 1974-, chief MO Health Educn Cncl 1984-87, hon sr lectr in community med St Mary's Hosp Med Sch 1985- 89, hon specialist in community med Paddington and N Kensington Health Authy 1985-88, conslt in public health med W Lambeth Health Authy 1988-, hon sr lectr in public health med Utd Med and Dental Schs Guy's and St Thomas' Hosps 1988-; BBC Radio 4 series: Action Makes the Heart Grow Stronger 1983, Back in 25 Minutes 1984, Not Another Diet Programme 1985, Cancercheck 1988; BBC TV series: Your Mind in Their Hands 1982, Save a Life 1986, Bodymatters 1985-89; regular med columnist for Woman magazine; MRCP 1972, FFCM 1986; *Books* Family Health & Fitness (1981), Bodyfacts (1984), Diet 2000 (with J Thomas, 1984), How to Save a Life (with J Rogers, 1987), Pssst a Really Useful Guide to Alcohol (1989); *Recreations* relaxing in the Dales, singing in the group Instant Sunshine; *Style—* Dr Alan Maryon Davis; 4 Sibella Rd, London SW4 6HX (☎ 071 720 5659); West Lambeth Health Authority, St Thomas's Hospital, London SE1 7EH (☎ 071 928 9292)

MASCHLER, Thomas Michael; s of Kurt Leo Maschler; *b* 16 Aug 1933; *Educ* Leighton Park; *m* 1970, Fay Goldie (the writer on restauarants Fay Maschler), da of Arthur Coventry (d 1969); 1 s (Benjamin Joseph b 1974), 2 da (Hannah Kate b 1970, Alice Mary b 1972); *Career* publisher; chm Jonathan Cape 1970- (editorial dir 1960, md 1966); prodn asst André Deutsch 1955, ed MacGibbon & Kee 1956-58, fiction ed Penguin Books 1958-60; *Recreations* tennis, skiing; *Style—* Thomas Maschler Esq; 15 Chalcot Gardnes, London NW3 4YB (☎ 071 586 3574)

MASDIN, Dr (Edward) Guy; s of Frank Masdin (d 1987), and Marjorie Mary, *née* Clark (d 1980); *b* 9 May 1936; *Educ* Ecclesfield GS, Univ of Sheffield (BSc, PhD, res paper prize, memb univ first XI cricket); *m* 21 June 1958, Beryl Monica, da of George Barnes; 2 s (Robert Howard b 1962, Philip Carr b 1970), 2 da (Kay Judith b 1964, Linda Ruth b 1966); *Career* res div head Shell Research Ltd 1966-73 (res engr 1960-63 res gp ldr 1963-66), tech mktg mangr Shell Coal International 1973-81, head res planning and coordination Shell International Petroleum Co 1981; dir: Shell Research Ltd 1981-, Shell Recherches 1981-; past pres Inst of Energy; memb: Cncl Inst of Chem Engrs, Ct and Cncl Univ of Reading, Nat Assoc of Cricket Coaches; tstee Wokingham Cricket Club; FInstE, FIChemE, FBIM, FEng; *Recreations* golf, gardening, cricket; *Clubs* Berks CCC; *Style—* Dr Guy Masdin; 2 Maktins Drive,

Wokingham, Berkshire RG11 1NY (☎ 0734 785880); Shell Centre, London SE1 7NA (☎ 071 934 3272)

MASEFIELD, Sir Peter Gordon; s of Dr (William) Gordon Masefield, CBE, JP, MRCS, LRCP, DPM, sometime Hon Gen Sec BMA, by his w Marian Ada, da of Edmund Lloyd-Owen, of New York; Sir Peter's gf was 2 cousin of John Masefield, Poet Laureate 1930-67; *b* 19 March 1914; *Educ* Westminster, Chillon Coll Switzerland, Jesus Coll Cambridge; *m* 1936, Patricia Doreen, da of Percy Rooney; 3 s, 1 da; *Career* former pilot, aircraft designer and aviation journalist; advsr to Lord Privy Seal (Lord Beaverbrook) and sec War Cabinet Ctee on Post War Civil Air Tport 1943-45, first civil air attaché Br Embassy Washington DC 1945-47, dir gen of long term planning and projects Miny of Civil Engrg 1947-48; md: BEA 1949-55, Bristol Aircraft Ltd 1955-60; dir Beagle Aviation Finance Ltd 1962-71; chm: Beagle Aircraft Ltd 1968-70 (md 1960-68), Project Management Ltd 1972-; dir: Worldwide Estates Ltd 1972-89, Nationwide Building Society 1973-80; jt dep chm Caledonian Airways Group 1978- (dep chm British Caledonian Airways 1972-87), currently dir London Transport (memb 1973, chm 1980-82); chm Br Airports Authy 1965-71, past pres Inst of Road Tport Engrs; memb numerous aviation socs incl pres: Duxford Aviation Soc 1970-, Assoc of Br Aviation Consits 1979-, Croydon Airport Soc; memb Cncl Royal Aero Club (chm Aviation Ctee 1960-65, chm 1968-70); past pres numerous charitable tsts; chm: Brooklands Museum Tst 1987-, Bd of govrs Reigate GS 1979-; govr Ashridge Mgmnt Coll 1981-; Hon DSc Cranfield 1977, Hon DTech Loughborough 1977; Freeman City of London, Liveryman Guild of Air Pilots and Air Navigators; hon fell: American Inst of Aeronautics and Astronautics, Canadian Aeronautics and Space Inst; Hon FRAeS, FCIT, CIMechE, CBIM, CEng; kt 1972; *Books* To Ride the Storm (1982); *Recreations* reading, writing, gardening; *Clubs* Athenaeum, Royal Aero, Nat Aviation (Washington); *Style*— Sir Peter Masefield; Rosehill, Doods Way, Reigate, Surrey RH2 0JT (☎ 0737 242396)

MASEFIELD, (John) Thorold; CMG (1986); s of Dr Geoffrey Bussell Masefield, and (Mildred) Joy Thorold, *née* Rogers; *b* 1 Oct 1939; *Educ* Dragon Sch Oxford, Repton, St John's Coll Cambridge (MA); *m* 18 Aug 1962, Jennifer Mary, da of Rev Dr Hubert Carey Trowell, OBE; 2 s (Nigel Anthony b 26 March 1964, Roger Francis b 24 Dec 1970), 2 da (Sally Clare b 18 Dec 1966, Helen Rachel b and d Aug 1968); *Career* Dip Serv: joined Cwlth Relations Off 1962; private sec to Permanent Under Sec 1963-64, second sec Br High Cmmn Kuala Lumpur 1964-65, second sec Br Embassy Warsaw 1966-67, FCO 1967-69, first sec UK delgn to disarmament conf Geneva 1970-74, dep head policy planning staff FCO 1974-77, dep head Far Eastern Dept FCO 1977-79, cnsllr and consul gen Br Embassy Islamabad 1979-82, head of Personnel Serv Dept FCO 1982-85, head of Far Eastern Dept FCO 1985-87, Br High Cmmr Utd Republic of Tanzania 1989-; fell Center for Int Affairs Harvard Univ 1987-88, memb Civil Serv Selection Bd 1988-89; *Recreations* fruit and vegetables; *Clubs* Royal Cwlth; *Style*— Thorold Masefield, Esq, CMG; c/o FCO, London SW1A 2AH

MASEFIELD, Hon Mrs (Veronica Margery); da of 8 Baron Hawke (d 1939), and Francis Alice Wilmer; *b* 30 Jan 1915; *m* 1940, Jack Briscoe Masefield, s of George Henry Masefield; 1 da (Delphinia (Mrs Richard James Fairfax Hall) b 1947); *Style*— The Hon Mrs Masefield; Down Lodge, East Harting, Petersfield, Hants (☎ 073 085 291)

MASERI, Prof Attilio; s of Adriano Maseri, and Antonietta Maseri; *b* 12 Nov 1935; *Educ* Cividale (Udine) Licenza Liceo Classico, Med Sch of Padua (MD), postgrad bds in cardiology and nuclear med, Med Sch Univ of Pisa; *m* 30 July 1960, Countess Francesca Maseri Florio di Santo Stefano; 1 s (Filippo); *Career* Univ of Pisa: intern Med Clinic 1960-62, Euratom Res Fell 1962-65, asst prof Dept of Med 1967-70, Docenza in Patologia Medica 1968, Aiuto Istituto Patologia Medica 1970-79, prof of Cardiopulmonary Pathophysiology 1970-79, prof of patologia Speciale Medica 1977-79, Cattedra di Fisiopatologia Cardiocircolatoria 1979; res fell: Columbia Univ NY 1965-66, John Hopkins Univ 1966-67; head Coronary Res Gp Laboratory of Clinical Physiology of Nat Res Cncl Pisa 1970-79, Sir John McMichael Prof of Cardiovascular med Royal Postgrad Med Sch Univ of London 1979-, dir cardiology Hammersmith Hosp 1979-; visiting professorships incl: Mount Sinai Sch of Med NY 1977, Cedars-Sinai Med Center LA 1984, Vanderbilt Univ Nashville 1986, Baylor Coll of Medicine Houston 1991; memb Ed Bd Circulation and Jl of the American Coll of Cardiology; FRCP, FACC; memb: Assoc of Physicians of GB & Ireland, Med Res Soc, Br Cardiac Soc, Italian Soc of Cardiology, American Heart Assoc (hon fell Cncl on Clinical cardiology 1982), Academic Cncl Inst of Sports Med; foreign memb Royal Acad of Med Belgium; George von Heresy Prize for Nuclear Med (World Congress of Nuclear Med Tokyo) 1974, James B Herrick Heart Award (Int Congress of Cardiovascular Diseases Las Vegas) 1979, lifetime memb John Hopkins Soc of Scholars 1980, commendatoré (Italy) 1990; *publications:* author of numerous book chapters and articles in learned jls, ed of various books of proceedings; *Recreations* tennis, skiing, sailing; *Clubs* Queens; *Style*— Prof Attilio Maseri; Cardiovascular Research Unit, Hammersmith Hospital, Ducane Rd, London W12 0NN (☎ 081 740 3263, fax 081 740 8373)

MASHAM OF ILTON, Baroness (Life Peer UK 1970), of Masham in N Riding, Co Yorkshire; Susan Lilian Primrose Cunliffe-Lister (Countess of Swinton); da of Maj Sir Ronald Norman Sinclair, 8 Bt, and Reba Inglis, later Mrs R H Hildreth (d 1985); *b* 14 April 1935; *Educ* Heathfield Ascot, London Poly; *m* 8 Dec 1959, 2 Earl of Swinton, *qv* (works under title Lady Masham of Ilton); 1 s, 1 da (both adopted); *Career* sits as Independent peer in House of Lords; pres N Yorks Red Cross 1963, patron 1989; pres Yorks Assoc for Disabled; memb Bd Visitors for Wetherby Borstal 1963 (now Young Offenders Inst); pres Spinal Injuries Assoc, late memb Peterlee and Newton Aycliffe Corpn; vice pres: Coll of Occupational Therapists Action for Dysphasic, Hosp Saving Assoc; patron of Disablement Income Group, Adults (DIA), tstee of Spinal Res Tst; memb: Parly All Pty Disablement Gp Drug Misuse Ctee (vice chm), Penal Affairs Gp; vice chm Parly AIDS Ctee; memb Winston Churchill Tst; patron Yorks Faculty of GPs; memb: Yorks RHA, Family Health Services Authy N Yorks 1990-, Gen Advsy Cncl of BBC; chm: Home Office Ctee on Young People, Alcohol and Crime, Phoenix House (Drug Rehabilitation Centres), Cncl London Lighthouse; Hon MA (York, Leeds, Ulster and Open Univs), hon fell Royal Coll of GPs; *Recreations* swimming, breeding Highland ponies, gardening; *Style*— The Rt Hon the Baroness Masham of Ilton; Dykes Hill House, Masham, Ripon, Yorks HG4 4NS (☎ 0765 89241); 46 Westminster Gardens, Marsham St, London SW1P 4JG (☎ 071 834 0700)

MASKALL, Michael Edwin; s of Leslie George Maskall (d 1968), and Alice Rose, *née* Hare (d 1984); *b* 26 Oct 1938; *Educ* Brentwood Public Sch; *m* (m dis 1987); 2 s (Andrew James b 6 March 1963, Jake Alexander b 17 April 1971), 2 da (Louise Claire b 6 March 1963, Michelle Amanda b 30 Sept 1965); *Career* CA 1961; ptnr i/c int tax and trade Price Waterhouse 1985 (ptnr 1976-); FCA 1971; *Books* International Taxation Management And Strategy (1985), European Trends In Taxation Towards 1992 (1988); *Recreations* skiing, model making; *Clubs* Pickwick (Orsett, Essex); *Style*— Michael Maskall, Esq; Price Waterhouse, New City Court, 20 St Thomas St, London SE1 9RP (☎ 01 939 8000, telex)

MASKELL, John Michael; s of Horace Maclean Maskell (d 1985), and Kathleen Muriel, *née* Hatton; *b* 26 March 1942; *Educ* Winchester, Peterhouse Cambridge (MA, LLB); *m* 6 Aug 1966 (m dis 1982), Elisabeth Joan (d 1986), da of Montagu Ralph Threlkeld Edwards (d 1983); 1 s (Paul Nicholas John b 18 Oct 1973), 1 da (Jane Elisabeth b 26 March 1971); *Career* admitted slr 1966; ptnr Norton Rose 1971-; chm London Arbitrators Assoc Supporting Membs 1980-84, pres Aldgate Ward Club 1986-87; Freeman Worshipful Co Slrs; Memb Law Soc, ACIArb; *Recreations* bridge, war games, music; *Style*— John Maskell, Esq; Jacksons Farm, Maltings Lane, Witham, Essex (☎ 0376 51 3388); Norton Rose, Kempson Hse, PO Box 570, Camomile St, London EC3A 7AN (☎ 071 283 2434)

MASKELL, Miles Gerald; s of Capt Gerald Nye Maskell, MC (d 1970), of Cape Town, SA, and Faith Gertrude, *née* Saunders; *b* 2 Oct 1936; *Educ* Diocesan Coll Cape Town, Le Rosey Rolle Switzerland, Magdalene Coll Cambridge; *Career* asst to chm John Harvey & Sons Ltd (Bristol) 1959-60, advertising sales rep Time Inc 1960-63, sales dir Domtar Ltd 1963-74, chm and princ shareholder Green's Ltd 1974-87, jt md and shareholder Quorom Ventures Ltd 1988-89, md and shareholder Anglo-French Properties Ltd 1990-; Liveryman Worshipful Co of Vintners; *Recreations* golf, bridge; *Clubs* White's, Swinley Forest Golf; *Style*— Miles Maskell, Esq

MASKREY, Stephen William; s of Jack Maskrey, of Broxburn, West Lothian, and Ann Murray, *née* Dickson; *b* 16 Aug 1962; *Educ* Broxburn Acad, Coatbridge Tech Coll, West Lothian Coll; partner, Susanne Cherie, da of Michael Duffin; *Career* professional footballer; Falkirk 1983-84, 58 appearances East Stirlingshire 1984-86, 43 appearances Queen of the South 1986-87, over 130 appearances St Johnstone 1987-; honours: promotion to Div 1 Queen of the South 1986 and St Johnstone 1988, Div 1 Championship St Johnstone 1990; *Recreations* angling, golf; *Style*— Stephen Maskrey, Esq; St Johnstone FC, McDiarmid Park, Crieff Rd, Perth (☎ 0738 26961)

MASON, Anita Frances; da of Osbert Roy Campbell Mason, of Tavistock, Devon, and Edith Rosalyn Beryl, *née* Hann; *b* 30 July 1942; *Educ* Red Maids' Sch Bristol, St Hilda's Coll Oxford (MA); *Career* writer; books: Bethany (1981), The Illusionist (1983), The War Against Chaos (1988), The Racket (1990); *Recreations* large projects; *Style*— Ms Anita Mason; Jennifer Kavanagh, 39 Camden Park Rd, London NW1 9AX (☎ 071 482 3676, fax 071 482 6684)

MASON, Air Vice-Marshal (Richard) Anthony; CB (1988), CBE (1982); s of William Mason (d 1971), and Maud, *née* Jenkinson (d 1978); *b* 22 Oct 1932; *Educ* Bradford GS, St Andrew's Univ (MA), Univ of London (MA); *m* 17 Nov 1956, Margaret Sneddon da of Alexander McNab Stewart, MBE, of Burntisland, Fife; 2 da (Alice Lindsay b 21 Sept 1957, Pamela Anne b 17 Aug 1959, d 1985); *Career* RAF: commissioned 1956, USAF War Coll 1971, RAF Staff Coll 1972; dir: Defence Studies 1976-82, (Ground) Personnel 1982-84; Air Sec 1986-89 (dep 1985-86); Leverhulme Airpower res dir Fndn for Int Security 1989-, memb Bd Brassey UK Ltd 1989, visiting sr fell Univ of Birmingham 1989-; external doctoral examiner in Defence Studies 1986-: Univ of Oxford, Univ of Cambridge, Univ of London; res fell: Soviet Studies Centre RMA Sandhurst, Mosher Defence Inst Texas; memb Advsy Bd Smithsonian Inst Washington DC; pres Cheltenham Branch RAF ASSOC 1987; memb: IISS 1966, RUSI 1966; *Books* History of RAF Staff College (1972), Readings in Airpower (1978), Airpower in the Next Generation (1979), The Royal Air Force Today and Tomorrow (1982), Airpower in the Nuclear Age (1983/5), British Airpower in the 1980's (1984), War in the Third Dimension (1986), The Soviet Air Force (1986), Airpower: an Overview of Roles (1987), To Inherit the Skies (1990); *Recreations* music, squash, gardening; *Clubs* RAF; *Style*— Air Vice-Marshal R A Mason, CB, CBE; Foundation for International Security, The Rookery, Adderbury, Oxon OX17 3NA (☎ 0295 810993, fax 0994 813244)

MASON, David; s of George Edward and Florence Kate Mason, of Northborough, Peterborough; *b* 3 Nov 1944; *Educ* Deacon's GS Peterborough, RAC Cirencester (MRAC, NDA); *m* 1970, Shirley Ann, da of John James Adams (d 1962), of Grimsby; 2 s, 1 da; *Career* trials offr Rotherwell Plant Breeders 1968-72, cereal trials co-ordinator N American Plant Breeders 1973-75; dir Rothwell Plant Breeders 1975-79, md Mickerson RPB Ltd 1979-; *Recreations* gardening, family, shooting; *Clubs* Farmers'; *Style*— David Mason, Esq; Glebe House, Southdale, Caistor, Lincoln LN7 6LS; Nickerson RPB Ltd, JNRC, Rothwell, Caistor, Lincoln (☎ 0472 89 471, telex 52072)

MASON, David Arthur; *b* 13 May 1946; *Career* social worker 1966-70, sr social worker Hounslow 1970-72, unit organiser Birmingham FSU 1972-75, area mangr Birmingham 1975-81; divisional dir of social servs: Warwickshire 1981-84, dir of social servs: Knowsley MBC 1985-87, Liverpool 1987-; memb Central Cncl for Educn and Trg in Social Work; *Style*— David Mason, Esq; Social Services Department, 26 Hatton Garden, Liverpool L3 2AW (☎ 051 225 3779, fax 051 225 3916)

MASON, Prof David Kean; CBE (1987); s of George Hunter Mason (d 1983), of Glasgow Rd, Paisley, and Margaret MacCulloch Kean (d 1975); *Educ* Paisley GS, Glasgow Acad, Univ of St Andrews (LDS, BDS), Univ of Glasgow (MB ChB, MD); *m* 3 June 1967, Judith Anne, da of John Campbell Armstrong (d 1979), of Belfast, NI; 2 s (Michael b 1971, Andrew b 1979), 1 da (Katie b 1974); *Career* hon conslt dental surgn Gtr Glasgow Health Bd 1965-, dean dental educn Univ of Glasgow 1980- (prof oral med 1967-); pres Gen Dental Cncl 1989-; *Recreations* golf, tennis, gardening, enjoying countryside pleasures; *Clubs* Royal and Ancient Golf, St Andrews; *Style*— Prof David Mason, CBE; Greystones, Houston Rd, Kilmacolm, Renfrewshire, PA13 (☎ 050 587 2001); Glasgow Dental Hospital and School, 378 Sauchiehall St, Glasgow G2 3JZ (☎ 041 332 7020)

MASON, Donald David; s of Robert Mason, of Upton Wirral, and Mary, *née* Davies; *b* 25 June 1938; *Educ* Ruthin Sch N Wales, Fitzwilliam House Cambridge (MA, LLM); *m* 28 Sept 1963, Joyce, da of George Henry Griffiths; 1 s (Ian Stuart b 1 July 1970), 1 da (Susan Caroline b 22 Jan 1966); *Career* Batesons & Co Liverpool (merged with Alsop Stevens 1967, now Alsop Wilkinson): articled clerk 1960-63, asst slr 1963-67, ptnr 1967-; chm Liverpool Sch of Tropical Med; memb: Law Soc 1963, Liverpool Law Soc 1963; *Recreations* reading, music, rugby league (listening and watching); *Clubs* Lyceum (Liverpool); *Style*— Donald Mason Esq; Alsop Wilkinson, India Buildings, Liverpool L2 0NH (☎ 051 227 3060, fax 051 236 9208)

MASON, Hon Mrs (Elizabeth); *née* Eden; da of 7 Baron Auckland (d 1955); *b* 1928; *Educ* Brondesbury; *m* 1954, Maj Frederic Edward Isdale (Robin) Mason; 2 s, 1 da; *Style*— The Hon Mrs Mason; Reed Hall, Holbrook, nr Ipswich, Suffolk (☎ 0473 328327)

MASON, Sir Frederick Cecil; KCVO (1968), CMG (1960); s of Ernest Mason (d 1966), and Sophia Charlotte, *née* Dodson (d 1953); *b* 15 May 1913; *Educ* City of London Sch, St Catharine's Coll Cambridge (BA); *m* 1941, Karen, da of Christian Rorholm (d 1968), of Denmark; 2 s, 1 da (and 2 da decd); *Career* entered Consular Serv 1935; serv: Antwerp, Paris, Belgian Congo, Faroes, Panama, Chile, Oslo, FO, Bonn, Athens, Tehran; head Econ Rels Dept FO 1960-64, under sec Miny of Overseas Devpt and Cwlth Rels Office 1965-66; ambass: Chile 1966-70, to UN Geneva 1971-73, ret; dir New Ct Natural Resources 1973-83, UK memb Int Narcotics Control Bd 1974-77, chm Anglo-Chilean Soc in London 1979-83; *Recreations* ball games, walking, bird watching, painting, singing; *Clubs* Canning; *Style*— Sir Frederick Mason, KCVO, CMG; The Forge, Church St, Ropley, Hants SO24 0DS (☎ 096 277 2285)

MASON, George Verrinder; s of George Ashton Frederick Mason (d 1945), of

Enfield, Middx, and Elsie Dorothy, *née* Verrinder; *b* 25 June 1930; *Educ* Ardingly Coll; *m* 15 Sept 1956, Josephine Elizabeth, da of Stanley Northcott, of Bishop's Lydeard, Somerset; 3 s ((George) Stephen b 1960, Richard Henry b 1964, James Robert b 1967), 1 da (Sally Elizabeth b 1958); *Career* Nat Serv 2 Lt RASC 1953-55; admitted slr 1953, ptnr Laytons 1960-68, sr ptnr Braby & Waller 1981-(ptnr 1968-81); pres Rickmansworth Hockey Club; memb Law Soc 1953; *Recreations* hockey, watching cricket, fishing; *Clubs* MCC; *Style*— George Mason, Esq; Juniper House, Harefield Rd, Rickmansworth, Herts WD3 1PB (☎ 0923 776 732); Braby & Waller, 82 St John St, London EC1M 4DP (☎ 071 250 1884, fax 071 250 1749, telex 889264)

MASON, Harvey Christopher; *b* 22 Dec 1932; *Educ* Rothesay Acad, Univ of Glasgow (MB ChB), London (DTM & H); *m* 27 Dec 1957, Rosemary Elizabeth; 2 s (Christopher b 27 Feb 1960, Jon b 8 July 1962), 1 da (Allie b 5 June 1965); *Career* serv in Korea, W Germany Cyprus; cmd advsr in GP BAOR 1977-80 and 1985-87, dir of Army GP 1988-; Hon Surgn HM the Queen 1989; memb: BMA, RSM; Montefiore medal 1971; OStJ 1987; FMS London, FRCGP (1977, MRCGP 1972); *Recreations* food, wine, opera, reading, cats; *Style*— Brig Harvey Mason; Mytilus House, 75 Brown St, Salisbury, Wilts SP1 2BA (☎ 0722 337705); Dept of General Practice, Royal Army Medical College, Millbank, London SW1 4RJ (☎ 071 930 4466 ext 8209)

MASON, Prof Haydn Trevor; s of Herbert Thomas Mason (d 1973), of New Hedges, nr Tenby, Dyfed, and Margaret Ellen, *née* Jones (d 1973); *b* 12 Jan 1929; *Educ* Greenhill GS Tenby, Univ Coll of Wales Aberystwyth (BA), Middlebury Coll Vermont USA (AM 1951), Jesus Coll Oxford (DPhil); *m* 1, 5 Feb 1955 (m dis 1982), Gretchen; 1 s (David b 24 March 1961), 1 da (Gwyneth b 8 April 1964); m 2, 14 Sept 1982, Adrienne Mary, da of Alfred Barnes, of Sutton Coldfield; 1 step da (Kate b 26 Nov 1968); *Career* Nat Serv 1951-53, 2 Lt RASC 1952; instr in French Princeton Univ USA 1954-57, lectr Univ of Newcastle 1960-63, reader Univ of Reading 1965-67 (lectr 1964-65), prof Univ of E Anglia 1967-79, prof Université de Paris-III Sorbonne Nouvelle 1979-81, prof Univ of Bristol 1981-; pres: Assoc of Univ Profs of French 1981-82, Soc of French Studies 1982-84, Br Soc for Eighteenth Century Studies 1984-86, Int Soc for Eighteenth Century Studies 1991- (vice-pres and pres-elect 1987-); chm Bd of Dirs Voltaire Fndn Univ of Oxford 1989- (dir 1977-); Officier dans L'Ordre des Palmes Académiques 1985, Médaille d'Argent de la Ville de Paris 1989; *Books* Pierre Bayle and Voltaire (1963), Voltaire (1975), Voltaire: A Biography (1981), French Writers and their Society 1715-1800 (1982), Cyrano de Bergerac: L'Autre Monde (1984); ed: Marivaux: Les Fausses Confidences (1984), Voltaire: Zadig and Other Tales (1971), Essays Presented in Honour of W H Barber (with R J Howells, A Mason and D Williams, 1985), Myth and its Making in the French Theatre: studies presented to W D Howarth (with E Freeman, M O'Regan and S W Taylor, 1988), The Impact of the French Revolution on European Consciousness (with W Doyle, 1989); *Recreations* walking, crosswords, gardening; *Style*— Prof Haydn Mason; French Dept, University of Bristol, 19 Woodland Rd, Bristol BS8 1TE (☎ 0272 303416, fax 0272 735767)

MASON, Ian Douglas; s of Lawrence Wrangham Mason, of Rhu-Na-Dee, Deeview Rd South, Cults, Aberdeen, and Elaine Mary Brown, *née* Cooper; *b* 31 July 1949; *Educ* Rannoch Sch, Ealing Coll (BA); *Career* called to the Bar Lincoln's Inn 1978; fell Sch of Econ Sci; *Recreations* sailing, skiing, Shakespearian theatre; *Clubs* National Liberal; *Style*— Ian Mason, Esq; Upper Woodroffe House, Chiswick Mall, Chiswick, London W4 (☎ 081 995 9089); Mitre Court Chambers, Temple, London EC4Y 7BP (☎ 071 353 9394, fax 071 353 1488)

MASON, Sir (Basil) John; CB (1973); s of John Robert Mason (d 1937); *b* 18 Aug 1923; *Educ* Fakenham GS, Univ Coll Nottingham (BSc, DSc); *m* 1948, Doreen Sheila Jones; 2 s (Barry b 1955, Nigel b 1962); *Career* serv WWII Flt-Lt RAF; prof of cloud physics Imp Coll London 1961-65, dir gen Meteorological Office 1965-83; perm rep of the UK at the World Meteorological Orgn 1965-83 (memb Exec Ctee 1966-75 and 1977-83), treas and sr vice pres The Royal Soc 1976-86, pro chllr Univ of Surrey 1980-85, dir UK/Scandinavian Acid Rain Prog 1983-; pres: Br Assoc 1982-83, UMIST 1986-, Nat Soc for Clean Air and Environmental Protection 1989-; memb Advsy Bd Res Cncls 1983-86, chm Coordinating Ctee for Marine Sci and Technol 1987-; FRS; kt 1979; *Recreations* music, walking, foreign travel; *Style*— Sir John Mason, CB; 64 Christchurch Rd, East Sheen, London SW14 7AW (☎ 081 876 2557)

MASON, Sir John Charles Moir; KCMG (1980, CMG 1976); o s of Charles Moir Mason, CBE (d 1967), and Madeline Mason; *b* 13 May 1927; *Educ* Manchester GS, Peterhouse Cambridge (MA); *m* 1954, Margaret Newton, da of Noel David Vidgen (d 1971); 1 s, 1 da; *Career* Lt XX Lancashire Fusiliers 1946-48, Capt Royal Ulster Rifles Korea 1950-51; HM Foreign Serv 1952, third sec FO 1952-54, sec & private sec to Ambass Br Embassy Rome 1954-56; second sec: Warsaw 1956-59, FO 1959-61, first sec (commerical Damascus 1961-65), first sec & asst head of dept FO 1965-68, dir Trade Devpt and dep consul-gen New York 1968-71, head Euro Integration Dept FCO 1971-72, seconded as under sec ECGD 1972-75, asst under sec state (econ) FCO 1975-76, ambass to Israel 1976-80, Br high cmmr to Australia 1980-84; chm: Lloyds Bank NZA, Sydney 1985-90, Thorn EMI (Australia) 1985, VSEL (Australia) 1985, Spencer Stuart Bd of Advice, Sydney 1985, Prudential Corporation Australia 1987, Prudential Finance 1987-90, Prudential Funds Management 1987, Lloyds International 1987-90, Multicon 1987, North Shore Heart Research Fndn 1987; dir: Wellcome (Australia) 1985-90, Fluor Daniel (Australia) 1985, Pirelli Cables Australia 1987, Churchill Meml Tst 1985, Nat Bank of New Zealand 1985-90; *Clubs* Athenaeum, Union (Sydney), Melbourne; *Style*— Sir John Mason, KCMG; 147 Dover Rd, Dover Heights, NSW 2030, Australia

MASON, John Harold; s of Albert Leonard Mason, of Blackheath, and Agnes Jane, *née* Smith (d 1956); *b* 10 Sept 1932; *Educ* Westminster City Sch; *m* 25 July 1959, Monica, da of Thomas Stevenson (d 1949), of Ravenstone; 3 s (Felix b 1962, Guy b 1964, Toby b 1966), 1 da (Tina b 1960); *Career* RAOC 1951-53, cmmnd 1952, serv Germany and Belgium; The Hongkong and Shangahi Banking Corp 1954-86 serv: London, Hong Kong, Cambodia, Vietnam, Japan, Philippines, India, Singapore, and Brunei 1954-76, mangr Thailand 1976-78, rep Hongkong Bank Gp in Aust and gen mangr Hongkong Fin 1979-80, area mangr Brunei 1980-83, chief exec offr Japan 1984-86, ret; chm: Banks Assoc of Brunei 1980-83, Personnel Standing Ctee (memb Gen Ctee) Inst of Foreign Bankers Japan 1984-86; ind trg conslt; *Recreations* sailing, choral singing, psychotherapy, campanology, walking; *Clubs* Oriental, Naval, Royal Lymington Yacht, Royal Hong Kong Yacht, Royal Hong Kong Jockey, Hong Kong; *Style*— John Mason, Esq; Birchcroft, 29 Westfield Rd, Lymington, Hants SO41 9QB (☎ 0590 678084)

MASON, John Muir; MBE (1987); s of James William Mason, Sheriff Clerk, of Wigtown (d 1962), and Tomima Watt, *née* Muir (d 1972); *b* 21 Jan 1940; *Educ* Kirkwall GS, Orkney, Douglas Ewart HS Newton Stewart, Univ of Edinburgh (BL); *m* 25 Jan 1967, Jessica Hilary Miller, da of John Groat (d 1981) of Stronsay, Orkney Islands; 1 s (James Muir Angel b 1969), 2 step s (Peter John Chalmers b 1960, Rognvald Inkster Chalmers b 1963); *Career* slr; sr ptnr Waddell & Mackintosh Slrs Troon, md J D C Pubns Ltd, dir private cos; princ conductor and musical dir The Strings of Scotland and The Scottish Fiddle Orchestra; chm The Rev James Currie Memorial Tst, life govr Imp Cancer Res Fund, tstee Niel Gow Memorial Tst; *Recreations* music, history; *Style*— John Mason, Esq, MBE; 27 Victoria Dr, Troon, Ayrshire (☎ 0292 312796); 36 West Portland St, Troon, Ayrshire (☎ 0292 312222)

MASON, Keith Edward; s of Arthur Ernest Mason (d 1982), and Nellie Louise, *née* Hawkes; *b* 3 May 1943; *Educ* Westminster GS; *m* 11 Feb 1964 (m dis 1988) Jacqueline Claire, da of Robert W Mitcham; 3 s (Sean b 9 March 1965, Nicholas b 11 Feb 1967, Stuart b 24 March 1974), 1 da (Jacqueline b 22 Aug 1968); *Career* asst mangr admin Bank of London and S America 1971-72, head of data processing Lloyds and Bolsa Int 1972-73; C Hoare & Co: head of data processing 1974-77, head of accounts 1977-83, mangr admin 1983-87, gen manr 1987-; *Recreations* rowing, reading, music; *Clubs* London Rowing, Stewards Enclosure Henley; *Style*— Keith Mason, Esq; 119 Kenilworth Court, Lower Richmond Rd, Putney, London SW15 1WA (☎ 01 788 3434), C Hoare & Co, 37 Fleet St, London EC4P 4DQ (☎ 081 353 4522, fax 081 353 4521, telex 24622)

MASON, Prof (John) Kenyon French; CBE (1973); s of Air Cdre John Melbourne Mason, CBE, DSC, DFC (d 1955), and Alma Ada Mary, *née* French (d 1983); *b* 19 Dec 1919; *Educ* Downside, Univ of Cambridge (MA, MD), Univ of Edinburgh (LLD); *m* 14 Jan 1943, Elizabeth Hope, (d 1977), da of Trevor Latham, (d 1960) 2 s (Ian b 1944, Paul b 1947); *Career* RAF: Sqdn MO 1943-47, pathologist trg 1948, conslt in pathology and offr i/c Dept of Aviation and Forensic Pathology RAF Inst of Pathology 1955-73, ret Gp Capt 1973; regius prof of forensic med Univ of Edinburgh 1973-, ret 1985, pres Br Assoc in Forensic Med 1982-84; hon fell Faculty of Law Univ of Edinburgh 1985-; King Haakon VII Freedom Medal (Norway) 1945; FRCPath; *Books* Forensic Medicine for Lawyers (2 ed 1983), Law and Medical Ethics (2 ed co-author 1987), Butterworths Medico-legal Encyclopaedia (co-author 1987), Human Life and Medical Practice (1988), Medico-legal Aspects of Reproduction and Parenthood (1990), The Courts and the Doctor (co-author 1990); *Clubs* RAF; *Style*— Prof Kenyon Mason, CBE; 66 Craiglea Dr, Edinburgh EH10 5PF (☎ 031 447 2301); Faculty of Law, Old College, South Bridge, Edinburgh EH8 9YL (☎ 031 650 2051)

MASON, Hon Mrs (Kristina Elizabeth); da of Baroness Robson of Kiddington (Life Peeress 1974), and late Sir Lawrence Robson; *b* 1946; *m* 1967, Dr Iain McLaren Mason; 3 da (Laura b 1971, Tanya b 1973, Fiona b 1977); *Career* dir: Brackley Sawmills Ltd, Oxford Gallery Ltd; *Style*— The Hon Mrs Mason; 17 Crick Rd, Oxford, OX2 6QL

MASON, Michael Aidan; s of Kenneth Albert Mason, of Emsworth, Hants, and Marjorie Evelyn, *née* Edwards; *b* 5 March 1947; *Educ* Lancing, St Edmund Hall Oxford (MA); *Career* news ed Gay News 1972-81, presenter Bookshelf LBC Radio 1975-76, dir Kenneth Mason Publications 1976-, co-fndr and ed Capital Gay 1981-; Freeman Worshipful Co of Skinners; *Books* Dinghy Sailing (1966); *Style*— Michael Mason, Esq; Stonewall Press Ltd, 38 Mount Pleasant, London WC1X 0AP (☎ 071 278 3764); Kenneth Mason Publications, Dudley House, North St, Emsworth, Hants

MASON, Monica Margaret; da of Richard Mason, and Mrs E Fabian; *b* 6 Sept 1941; *Educ* Johnannesburg, Royal Ballet Sch; *m* 1968, Austin Bennet; *Career* Royal Ballet Co: joined 1958, princ dancer 1968, asst to Sir Kenneth Macmillan 1980, asst to princ Choreographer 1980-84, princ repetiteur 1985, asst to dir 1988-, asst dir 1991-; *Style*— Miss Monica Mason

MASON, His Hon (George Frederick) Peter; QC (1963); s of George Samuel Mason (d 1966), of Keighley, and Florence May Mason (d 1965); *b* 11 Dec 1921; *Educ* Lancaster Royal GS, St Catharine's Coll Cambridge (BA, MA); *m* 1, 30 Dec 1950 (m dis 1977), Faith Maud, *née* Bacon; 2 s (Jonathan b 18 Nov 1952, Michael b 1 April 1962), 3 da (Pippa b 25 July 1951, Melodie b and d 1957, Alison b 17 Oct 1960); m 2, 6 March 1981, Sara Lilian, da of Sir Robert Ricketts, 7 Bt, of Forwood House, Minchinhampton, Glos; *Career* WWII cmmnd 78 Medium Regt RA (Duke of Lancaster's Own Yeomanry), Staff Capt RA 13 Corps ME and Italy; barr 1947, dep chm Agric Land Tbnl W Yorks and Lancs 1962, dep chm West Riding Qtr Sessions 1965; rec of York 1965; circuit judge 1970-87, sr judge Snaresbrook Crown Ct 1974-81, sr judge Inner London Crown Ct 1983-87; Freeman City of London 1977, Liveryman Worshipful Wax Chandlers Co 1981; FCIArb 1986, lay memb Cncl Assoc of Futures Brokers and Dealers 1987; *Recreations* golf, cycling in foreign parts, music; *Clubs* Athenaeum, Hawks (Cambridge); *Style*— His Honour Peter Mason, QC; Lane Cottage, Amberley, Glos GL5 5AB (☎ 0453 872412, fax 0453 878557); 11 King's Bench Walk, Temple, London EC4 (☎ 071 353 3337, fax 071 583 2190)

MASON, Richard Graham; s of Arthur Ernest Mason (d 1988), and Catherine Mary, *née* Boakes (d 1964); *b* 21 June 1944; *Educ* Wilson's GS Camberwell London SE5; *m* 2 Sept 1967, Lynda Miriam Mary, da of Frederick William Tothill (d 1983); 1 s (Andrew Philip b 1970), 1 da (Karen Elizabeth b 1973); *Career* Bank of England: Exchange Control Dept 1965-79, sec City EEC Ctee 1980-84, sec City Capital Markets Ctee 1980-84, sec City Taxation Ctee 1980-82; exec dir British Invisibles 1984- (sec and treas 1982-84); treas: Chertsey PCC 1969-82 and 1987-89, Chertsey Jt Church Cncl 1980-87, Runnymede Deanery Synod 1989-, Bread Street Ward Club 1989-; memb: CBI Export Promotion Ctee 1984-89, London C of C Int Trade Ctee 1984-, Br Tourist Authy Devpt Ctee 1984-, Guildford Diocesan Bd of Fin 1989-; ACIB 1966, MIEx 1987; *Books* author of various articles on invisible exports; *Recreations* walking, church fin; *Clubs* Overseas Bankers; *Style*— R G Mason, Esq; Betoncroft, 21A Abbey Rd, Chertsey, Surrey KT16 8AL (☎ 0932 564 773); Windsor House, 39 King St, London EC2V 8DQ (☎ 071 600 1198, fax 071 606 4248, telex 941 3342 BIEG)

MASON, The Ven Richard John; s of Vice Adm Frank Trowbridge Mason, KCB (d 1988), of 114 High St, Hurstpierpoint, W Sussex, and Dora Margaret, *née* Brand; *b* 26 April 1929; *Educ* Shrewsbury; *Career* clerk in Holy Orders, asst curate Bishop's Hatfield Herts 1958-64, domestic chaplain to the Bishop of London 1964-69, vicar of Riverhead Kent 1969-73, vicar of Edenbridge Kent 1973-83, archdeacon of Tonbridge 1977-, min of St Luke Sevenoaks 1983-; *Recreations* watching cricket; *Style*— The Ven Richard Mason; St Luke's House, 30 Eardley Rd, Sevenoaks, Kent TN13 1XT (☎ 0732 452462)

MASON, Roger James; s of Philip Talbot Mason (d 1965), of Solihull, and Monica Beryl, *née* Mangham (d 1986); *b* 12 July 1937; *Educ* Solihull Sch, Univ of Birmingham (LLB); *m* 26 Oct 1967, Merle Ann (NP), da of George William Hill, of Rugby; *Career* admitted slr 1962; in private practice 1962-, Notary Public practice 1967-, cmmr for oaths 1968-; memb: W Midland Rent Assessment Ctee 1980-, W Midland Rent Tbnl 1980-, W Midland Leasehold Valuation Tbnl 1981-; memb The Notaries Soc 1967-, FCIArb 1975; *Recreations* buying land, making home made jam, thinking; *Clubs* Vintage Motor Cycle, Morgan Three Wheeler; *Style*— Roger Mason, Esq; The Close, Beausale, Warwick CV35 7PD (☎ 0926 484424); Biddle, Mason & Co, Stowe House, 1688 High St, Knowle, Solihull, W Midlands B93 OLY (☎ 0564 776127)

MASON, Prof Sir Ronald; KCB (1980); s of David John Mason (d 1950) and Olwen, *née* James; *b* 22 July 1930; *Educ* Quakers Yard, Univ of Wales (BSc), Univ of London (PhD, DSc); *m* 1, 1952, Pauline Pattinson; 1 s (decd), 3 da; m 2, 1979, Elizabeth Rosemary, da of Maj Theodore Walpole Grey-Edwards; *Career* prof of inorganic chemistry Univ of Sheffield 1963-71, prof of chemistry Univ of Sussex 1971-, pro vice-chllr Univ of Sussex 1977-78, chief sci advsr MOD 1977-83; Advsy Bd Res Cncls 1977-83; SRC 1971-75; many visiting professorships in USA, Canada, France, Israel, NZ, Aust; dep chm Hunting Engineering Ltd 1985-87 (chm 1987-88), visiting prof Int

Relations Univ Coll of Wales 1985-, pres BHRA 1987-; dir Thom UK Holdings 1987-90; chm: BHR Group 1989-, B Ceram Res Ltd 1990- (dir 1988); chm Eng Tech Ctee DTI 1990-; FRS; *Recreations* cooking and stirring; *Clubs* Athenaeum; *Style*— Prof Sir Ronald Mason, KCB, FRS; Chestnuts Farm, Weedon, Bucks HP22 4NH; BHR Group Cranfield, Beds MK43 0AJ (☎ 0234 750422); Univ of Sussex, Falmer, Brighton, E Sussex (☎ 0273 606755)

MASON, Rowland Hill Berkeley (Bill); s of Dr Edward Daniel Mason (d 1968), and Elsie Anne, *née* Berkeley (d 1967); *b* 9 Nov 1915; *Educ* Greshams, Christ's Coll Cambridge (BA, MA); *m* 18 Oct 1941, (Ailsa) Sarah, da of Walter James Kershaw (d 1936), of Moseley, Birmingham; 1 s (Nick b 27 Jan 1944), 3 da (Sarah b 4 Aug 1945, Melanie b 17 Sept 1948, Serena b 3 Sept 1953); *Career* Shell Film Unit 1941-56, chm Berkeley & Co Ltd 1968- (memb Bd 1936-), fndr Bill Mason Films Ltd 1970; winner numerous int awards incl Montagu Trophy Guild of Motoring Writers 1962-, memb Gen Selection Ctee Nat Film Archive 1965-70, chm Awards Selection Ctee Br Film Acad 1970, commodore Dell Quay Sailing Club 1975-78; memb: Br Film Acad 1949-86, Guild of Motoring Writers; *Clubs* Savile, Vintage Sports Car, Bentley Drivers, Della Mille Miglia; *Style*— Bill Mason, Esq; Bill Mason Films Ltd, Orchard House, Dell Quay House, Chichester, West Sussex PO20 7EE (☎ 0243 783558); Berkeley & Co Limited, Stafford Park 18, Telford, Shropshire TF3 3AW

MASON, Stephen Maxwell; s of Harold Geoffrey Mason (d 1986), and Ursula, *née* Habermann; *b* 19 May 1949; *Educ* Bradford GS, Gonville and Caius Coll Cambridge (MA); *m* 26 March 1976, Judith Mary, da of Hebbert, of 2 Manley Rd, Ilkley; 2 da (Fiona b 1979, Nicola b 1985), 1 s (Alistair b 1981); *Career* slr; ptnr Mason Bond, Leeds, sec Bradford Law Centre Mgmnt Ctee, author of articles on package holiday law including Don't Shoot the Tour Operator (1983), Holiday Damages the Gravy Train Slows Down (1987); *Recreations* writing, travel by train; *Clubs* Law Soc; *Style*— Stephen Mason, Esq; Abbey House, Park Row, Leeds LS1 5NG (☎ 0532 424444, telex 556681, fax 0532 467542)

MASON, (John) Stuart; s of late Wilfred Mason, and Elizabeth L, *née* Meehan; *b* 17 April 1952; *Educ* Burnley Tech HS; *m* 26 June 1976, Valerie; 2 da (Rachel Jayne b 9 June 1983, Danielle Clare b 17 May 1986); *Career* lab technician gas development engineering 1970-73; photographer: Burnley Express 1973-83, Sunday Express 1983-; memb NUJ; *Recreations* sampling quality ales; *Clubs* GUANO; *Style*— Stuart Mason, Esq; 20 Mosedale Drive, Manor Park Farm, Ightenhill, Burnley, Lancs BB12 8UJ (☎ 0282 58878); Sunday Express, Great Ancoats St, Manchester (☎ 061 236 2112, car 0831 237082)

MASON, Sydney; s of Jack Mason (d 1936); *b* 30 Sept 1920; *m* 1945, Rosalind, da of Woolf Victor (d 1975); *Career* mangr Land Securities plc 1943-49, md Hammerson Property Investment & Development Corporation plc 1949- (chm 1958-); advsr Royal Acad of Arts, memb Archbishop of Canterbury's Church Urban Fund Ctee; memb Ct Worshipful Co of Masons; FSVA; *Recreations* painting, in oils and acrylics; *Clubs* Naval, Royal Thames Yacht, City Livery; *Style*— Sydney Mason, Esq; 100 Park Lane, London W1Y 4AR (☎ 071 629 9494)

MASON, Terence Harold; s of Harold Henry Mason, of Walsall, W Mids, and Winifred May, *née* Sadler; *b* 7 July 1941; *Educ* Queen Mary's GS Walsall; *m* 25 Sept 1971, Beryl, da of Albert Ernest Hughes, of Claverley, Shrops; *Career* articled clerk Herbert Pepper & Rudland Chartered Accountants Walsall 1957-64, audit mangr Peat Marwick Mitchell CAs Birmingham 1964-66, gp fin dir Tarmac Plc Wolverhampton 1986- (other fin posts 1966-86); memb Ironbridge Gorge Museum Dept Tst; FCA 1964, RSA 1987; *Recreations* golf, theatre, arts; *Style*— Terence Mason, Esq; Stratton Ct, Long Common, Claverley, Shropshire (☎ 07466 577); Tarmac plc, Hilton Hall, Essington, Wolverhampton WV11 2BQ (☎ 0902 307 407, fax 0902 307 408, telex 338544)

MASON, Timothy Ian Godson; s of Ian Godson Mason, of Alverstoke Hants, and Muriel Marjorie Berkeley, *née* Vaile; *b* 11 March 1945; *Educ* St Alban's Sch Washington DC USA, Bradfield Coll Berks, ChCh Oxford (BA, MA); *m* 1975, Marilyn Ailsa, da of Frederic George Williams (d 1969), of Wellington, NZ; 1 s (Giles b 1982), 1 da (Grace b 1979); *Career* asst admin Oxford Playhouse 1966-67, asst to Peter Daubeny World Theatre Season London 1967-69; admin: Ballet Rambert 1970-75, Royal Exchange Theatre Manchester 1975-77; dir: Western Aust Arts Cncl 1977-80, Scottish Arts Cncl 1980-90; conslt to Arts Cncl and Office of Arts and Libraries; *Recreations* arts, family; *Style*— Timothy Mason, Esq; 30 Chatsworth Way, London SE27 9HN

MASON, William Ernest; CB (1983); s of Ernest George Mason, and Agnes Margaret Mason, *née* Derry; *b* 12 Jan 1929; *Educ* Brockley GS, LSE (BSc); *m* 1959, Jean; 1 s, 1 da; *Career* Miny of Food 1949-54; MAFF 1954: princ 1963, asst sec 1970, under sec 1975, Fisheries sec 1980, dep sec (Fisheries and Food) 1982-89; dir Allied-Lyons plc 1989-; conslt to food and drink industs; *Recreations* music, reading, gardening; *Clubs* Reform; *Style*— William Mason, Esq, CB; 82 Beckenham Place Park, Beckenham, Kent BR3 2BT (☎ 081 650 8421)

MASON-HORNBY, Anthony Feilden; s of Capt Paul Randle Feilden Mason (d 1944), of The Cedars, Sandhurst, Berks, and Joyce Madeline, *née* Wigan (d 1984); assumed additional name and arms of Hornby by Royal Licence 15 Sept 1987, under terms of will of late Edmund Geoffrey Stanley Hornby (d 1923); *b* 9 March 1931; *Educ* Eton, RAC Cirencester (dip Estate Mgmnt); *m* 11 June 1960, Cecily Barbara, da of Lt-Col Henry Gordon Carter, MC, DL (d 1966), of Tan-y-Bryn, Bangor, N Wales; 2 s (Francis b 1961, Christopher b 1963), 1 da (Catherine b 1964); *Career* landowner 1966-; warden and co-founder of Ogwen Cottage Mountain Sch 1959-64, Br Mountaineering Cncl Guide 1961-64; fndr and dir The Westmorland Singers 1974, chm tstees St John's Hospice Lancaster 1980-; MRAC; *Recreations* climbing, shooting, singing; *Clubs* Climbers', Westmorland LAG INJ; *Style*— Anthony Mason-Hornby, Esq; Dalton Hall, Burton, (☎ 0524 781228)

MASON OF BARNSLEY, Baron (Life Peer UK 1987), of Barnsley, S Yorkshire; Roy Mason; PC (1968); s of late Joseph Mason, of Carlton, nr Barnsley; *b* 18 April 1924; *Educ* Carlton and Royston Elementary Schs, LSE; *m* 1945, Marjorie, da of Ernest Sowden, of Royston, W Riding; 2 da (Hon Susan Ann (Hon Mrs Duke) b 1947, Hon Jill Diane (Hon Mrs Martin) b 1955); *Career* former coal miner 1938-53; MP (Lab) Barnsley 1953-83, Barnsley Central 1983-87; oppn spokesman Def and Post Office 1960-64; min of state BOT 1964-67; min Def Equipment 1967-68, postmaster-gen 1968, min Power 1968-69; pres BOT 1969-70; oppn spokesman Civil Aviation Shipping Tourism Films & Trade 1970-74; sec of state: Def 1974-76, NI 1976-79; oppn spokesman Agric Fish & Food 1979-; former NUM official; chm Yorks Gp Labour MPs Miners Gp of Labour MPs; *Style*— The Rt Hon Lord Mason of Barnsley, PC; 12 Victoria Ave, Barnsley, S Yorks

MASSAM, (Arthur) David Wright; s of Arthur Greenwood Massam, (d 1989), of Southport, Lancashire, and Emily, *née* Wright (d 1945); *b* 18 Nov 1934; *Educ* King George V Sch Southport, Univ of London (LLB); *m* 1957 (m dis 1970), Angela, da of Joseph Smith (d 1985), of Southport, Lancashire; 1 s (Nigel b 1961), 1 da (Melinda b 1958); *Career* Nat Serv RAMC 1956-58; exec dir DataPharm Pubns Ltd 1980-, sec Assoc of the Br Pharmaceutical Indust 1982- (joined 1970); memb: Advsy Cncl on Misuse of Drugs, Standing Pharmaceutical Advsy Ctee, Poisons Bd; fell Royal Ctee Poisons Bd; memb of the Hon Soc of the Inner Temple 1968, Fell of the Royal Pharmaceutical Soc of GB 1980; *Recreations* history, reading; *Clubs* Reform; *Style*— David Massam, Esq; 80A Westbury Road, Finchley, London N12 7PD (☎ 081 446 1037); The Association of the British Pharmaceutical Industry, 12 Whitehall, London SW1A 2DY (☎ 071 930 3477, fax 071 930 3290, telex 298916 ABPI G)

MASSER, Patrick Kenneth (Pat); s of Arnold Kenneth Masser, of 44 Shipton Rd, York, and Muriel Olive, *née* Benson (d 1985); *b* 19 Feb 1931; *Educ* St Olives Sch York, St Peters Public Sch York; *m* 28 March 1964, Margaret Joan Boyle, da of Alexander Moig, of Cupar, Fife; *Career* trainee hotel mangr BT Hotels 1951-57 (The Midland Hotel Manchester, Gleneagles Scotland, Lotti Hotel Paris, Charing Cross London); asst mangr: Great Western Royal Hotel London 1957-58, Midland Hotel Manchester 1958-60; staff mangr Gleneagles Hotel Scotland 1960-62; mangr: North British Hotel Edinburgh 1962-64, Adelphi Hotel Liverpool 1964-66; gen mangr: Queen's Hotel Birmingham 1966, Lockalsh Hotel Kyle of Lochalsh 1967, Royal Victoria Hotel Sheffield 1968-73, Adelphi Hotel Liverpool 1973-75; ops mangr BT Hotels Ltd London 1975-77; gen mangr: North British Hotel Glasgow 1977-82, Savoy Hotel Blackpool 1985-88, Ruskin Hotel Blackpool 1988-90; md Associated Business Consultants 1991-; govr: Sheffield Poly, Glasgow Coll of Food Technol, Liverpool Coll of Craft & Catering, Blackpool & Fylde Coll, Ayr Tech Coll; Master Innholder 1977, Winston Churchill fellowship 1987; Freeman City of London 1978; FHCIMA, BHRCA; memb: RIPH&H, Cookery & Food Assoc, Northern Guild of Toastmasters, Guild of Sommeliers, La Chaine de Rotisseurs, NW Tourist Bd; *Recreations* cricket, rugby, athletics, swimming; *Clubs* RAC, London & Scotland Yorkshire County Cricket, ST Annes Conservative; *Style*— Pat K Masser, Esq; 155 Clifton Drive, Starr Gate, Blackpool FY4 1RU (☎ 0253 47864); Associated Business Consultants, Hotel & Catering, 155 Clifton Drive, Starr Gate, Blackpool FY4 1RU (☎ 0253 47864, fax 0253 752687)

MASSEREENE AND FERRARD, 13 & 6 Viscount (I 1660 & 1797); John Clotworthy Talbot Foster Whyte-Melville Skeffington; DL (Co Antrim 1957); also Baron of Loughneagh (I 1660), Baron Oriel of Collon (I 1790), and Baron Oriel of Ferrard (UK 1821, which sits as); patron of one living; s of 12 (& 5) Viscount, DSO, JP, DL (d 1956, himself ggs of Harriet, w of 2 Viscount Ferrard, and Viscountess Massereene in her own right; Harriet's f was the 4 & last Earl of Massereene; the Viscountcy of Massereene (but not that of Ferrard) is the only Irish Peerage heritable by a female, and Jean Barbara Ainsworth, JP (d 1937), da of Sir John Stirling Ainsworth, MP; *b* 23 Oct 1914; *Educ* Eton; *m* 15 March 1939, Annabelle Kathleen, er da of late Henry David Lewis, of Combwell Priory, Hawkhurst; 1 s, 1 da; *Heir* s, Hon John David Clotworthy Whyte-Melville Skeffington, *qv*; *Career* Lt Black Watch SR 1933-36 and 1939-49 WWII invalided, served invasion, small vessels pool RN 1944; sits as Cons peer in House of Lords; driver leading Br car Le Mans Grand Prix 1937, gold staff offr Coronation of HM The Queen 1953, Peers memb Inter-Parly Union Delgn to Spain 1960, jt chm Cons Peers Ctee (IUP, now The Cons Peers Ctee) House of Lords 1965-70, for IUP; promoted and ran 1st scheduled air serv Glasgow, Oban, Isle of Mull; memb parly delegation to Malawi 1976, an original pioneer in commercial development of Cape Canaveral USA, presented operetta Countess Maritza at Palace Theatre London; former dir Aviation & Shipping Ltd, chm Sunset & Vine plc (TV), former chm Ferrard Holdings Ltd; former chm: London Scottish Clas Assoc, Victoria League for Kent; former pres Kent Hotels & Restaurants Assoc and other socs, MFH Ashford Valley Foxhounds 1953-54, vice pres Animal Welfare Year 1976-77, memb Deer Ctee Br Field Sports Soc, pres Monday Club 1981-; Freeman City of London, memb Worshipful Co of Shipwrights; Cross Cdr Order of Merit SMOM; *Books* The Lords (1973); *Recreations* sailing - (yacht 'Benmore Lady'); *Clubs* Royal Yacht Sqdn, Turf, Carlton, Pratt's, House of Lords YC (former cdre); *Style*— The Rt Hon the Viscount Massereene and Ferrard, DL; Chilham Castle, Canterbury, Kent (☎ 0227 730319); Knock, Isle of Mull, Argyll (☎ 06803 356)

MASSEY, Alan; s of Herbert Massey (d 1988), of Reading, Berks, and Ada Alice, *née* Mort (d 1975); *b* 28 Sept 1935; *Educ* Bolton Sch, Univ of Manchester (BSc); *m* 4 Oct 1964, Merril Ann, da of Brian Upton, of Meir Heath, Staffs; 1 s (Brian James b 1969), 1 da (Sarah b 1967); *Career* freelance TV newsreader BBC and Granada 1958-60; Holland & Hannen and Cubitts Ltd 1960-68, Richard Costain Ltd 1968-69, APC International 1969-, md Project Management International plc 1969-; pres CIOB 1990; govr Shiplake Coll and Abbey Sch Reading; FCIOB 1980, FRSA 1983, FBIM 1981; *Recreations* golf, hockey, cricket; *Clubs* MCC, Oriental, Berkshire CCC, Huntercombe Golf (capt 1989-90); *Style*— Alan Massey, Esq; Tall Trees, Chalkhouse Green, Reading, Berkshire RG4 9AD (☎ 0734 723778); The Lodge, Harmondsworth, West Drayton, Middx (☎ 081 897 1121, fax 081 897 9486, telex 935 186, car 0836 608763)

MASSEY, Charles Trevor; s of Roland Massey (d 1973), of Sunnymeade, Higham, nr Barnsley, S Yorkshire, and Vera, *née* Hemmingway; *b* 3 May 1934; *Educ* Queen Elizabeth GS Wakefield, Univ of Leeds (BSc); *m* Enid, da of William Cyril Herbert (d 1972); 2 s (Brynnen David b 1960, Adrian Paul b 1962), 1 da (Angela Dawn b 1963); *Career* mining engr; British Coal (formerly NCB): colliery mangr 1969-72, prodn mangr 1972-74, chief mining engr Doncaster Area 1974-77, dep dir S Yorkshire Area 1977-81 (N Yorkshire Area i/c Selby Project 1981-85), head Tech Dept 1985-; memb Int Ctee of Coal Res, dir IEA Coal Res, vice pres Inst of Mining Engrs 1990-91; FIMinE, fell Fellowship of Engrs; *Recreations* gardening, bee keeping; *Style*— Trevor Massey, Esq; Vissitt Manor, Hemsworth, Pontefract, West Yorkshire WF9 4PN (☎ 0977 611388); British Coal Corporatiobn, Eastwood Hall, Eastwood, Nottinghamshire NG16 3EB (☎ 0773 531313 ext 32670, fax 0773 531313 ext 32643, telex 378474 BCEAST G)

MASSEY, Daniel Raymond; s of Raymond Hart Massey (d 1983), and Adrianne Allen, *née* Whitney; *b* 10 Oct 1933; *Educ* King's Coll Cambridge (MA); *m* 1 (m dis), Adrienne Corri; 1 da (Alice Linden Pearl b 1977); m 2, (m dis), Penelope Wilton; *Career* actor; served 2 Lt Scots Guard 1951-53; theatre incl: The Happiest Millionaire (Cambridge Theatre) 1958, Make Me and Officer (Haymarket), The School for Scandal (Haymarket), The Rivals, The Importance of Being Earnest (Haymarket), Bloomsbury (Phoenix Theatre), Don Juan Comes Back From The War (Nat Theatre), Macbeth (Nat Theatre), Man and Superman (SWET award for actor of the year 1981), Twelfth Night (RSC), Measure for Measure (RSC), The Time of Your Life (RSC), Follies (Shaftesbury Theatre); TV incl: The Golden Bowl, Roads to Freedom, Good Behaviour (BBC), Intimate Contact (Central), Inspector Morse, G.B.H. (C4); films incl: Girls At Sea 1957, The Queen's Guard 1960, Go To Blazes 1962, Moll Flanders 1966, Star 1968 (best supporting actor Hollywood Golden Globe Award 1968), The Cat and the Canary 1978, Escape to Victory 1981; *Recreations* golf, gardening, classical music; *Style*— Daniel Massey, Esq; c/o Julian Belfrage Associates, 68 St James's St, London SW1 (☎ 071 491 4400)

MASSEY, Doreen Elizabeth; da of Jack Hall (d 1989), of Darwen, Lancs, and Mary Ann, *née* Sharrock (d 1973); *Educ* Darwen GS, Univ of Birmingham (BA, DipEd, vice pres Student Union, Hockey and Cricket blues), Univ of London (MA); *m* Dr Leslie Massey, s of James York Massey, of Conisbrough, Yorks; 3 c (Elizabeth Caitlin b 1969, Owen John b 1971, Benjamin James b 1973); *Career* family planner; grad serv overseas Gabon 1962-63, Springside Sch Philadelphia USA 1967-69, Pre-Sch Play Group Assoc 1973-77, Walsingham Sch 1977-83, advsr Inner London Educn Authy 1983-85, mangr Young People's Prog Health Educn Authy 1985-87, dir The Family

Planning Assoc 1989- (dir of educn 1987-89); memb numerous voluntary orgns, primary and secdy sch govr; *Books* Sex Educn: Why, What and How (1988); *Recreations* theatre, cinema, opera, reading, vegetarian cookery, walking, yoga; *Style*— Mrs Doreen E Massey; Family Planning Association, 27-35 Mortimer Street, London W1N 7RJ (☎ 071 631 0555, fax 071 436 3288)

MASSEY, Hon Mrs (Lavinia); *née* Bootle-Wilbraham; da of 6 Baron Skelmersdale (d 1973); *b* 1937; *m* 1969, Robert Brian Noel Massey; 2 s; *Style*— The Hon Mrs Massey; Waterstone House, Waterstone Close, Itchenor, nr Chichester, W Sussex

MASSEY, Dr Roy Cyril; s of Cyril Charles Massey (d 1966), of Birmingham, and Beatrice May, *née* Morgan (d 1987); *b* 9 May 1934; *Educ* Moseley GS Birmingham, Univ of Birmingham (BMus); *m* 22 Feb 1975, Ruth Carol Craddock, da of Frederick George Grove (d 1958), of Fron-y-Gog, Machynlleth, Montgomeryshire; *Career* organist: St Alban's Conybere St Birmingham 1953-60, St Augustine's Church Edgbaston Birmingham 1960-65, Croydon Parish Church 1965-68; warden Royal Sch of Church Music Addington Palace Croydon 1965-68, conductor Birmingham Bach Soc 1966-68, organist and master of the choristers Birmingham Cathedral 1968-74, dir of music King Edward's Sch Birmingham 1968-74, organist and master of the choristers Hereford Cathedral 1974-, conductor Three Choirs Festival and Hereford Choral Soc 1974-; memb Cncl: CO, Royal Sch of Church Music; fell St Michael's Coll Tenbury 1979-88; chm: Hereford Concert Soc, Hereford Competitive Music Festival; DMus (Cantuar) 1991, FRSCM 1972, FRCO 1956, ARCM 1954; *Recreations* the countryside, walking the dog on the Malvern hills, motoring; *Clubs* Conservative (Hereford); *Style*— Dr Roy Massey; 14 Coll Cloisters, Cathedral Close, Hereford HR1 2NG (☎ 0432 272011); The Cobbles, Stretton Grandison, Ledbury, Herefordshire HR8 2TW

MASSEY, Rupert John Candide; s of Zenke Stefan, of Warsaw, Poland, and Sonia Mary Massey (d 1978); *b* 21 Nov 1945; *Educ* Clayesmore Sch Dorset, Balliol Coll Oxford (BA); *m* 6 Jan 1984, Kate Miranda, da of Philip Rae-Scott, of Richmond Surrey; 3 s (Thomas Jack b 14 Dec 1985, Jacob Jonathan b 23 Aug 1988, Joel Peter (twin) b 23 Aug 1988); *Career* warden youth and community centre S London 1968-72, called to the Bar Inner Temple 1972, barr-at-law; broadcasting journalist; contrib to: Granada TV, Capital Radio, BBC Radio 4, Thames ITV and Nat Press; performer and actor: Clockwise 1986, Intimate Contact Zenith 1987, Life Story BBC TV 1987, Battalion 1988; guest speaker Cranworth Law Soc Downing Coll Cambridge 1991, hon legal and policy advsr Nat Fedn of Self Employed and Small Businesses, tstee Ben Bryant Tst; memb: NUJ, Br Equity, BAFTA; ACTT, hon memb Soc of Inner Temple London; *Recreations* deep sea sailing/cruising, all water sports, youth & community work, work with young offenders, psychology; *Clubs* Cruising Assoc; *Style*— Rupert Massey, Esq; 141 Sheen Road, Richmond upon Thames, Surrey (☎ 081 940 3672); Eaton House, 4 Eaton Rd, Branksome Park, Poole, Dorset BH13 6DG (☎ 0202 766301); 6 Kings Bench Walk, The Temple, London EC4Y 7DR (☎ 071 583 0695, 071 353 4931, fax 071 353 1726)

MASSEY, William Greville Sale; s of Lt Col Patrick Massey, MC, of Arawai House, Liss, Hants, and Bessie Lee, *née* Byrne (d 1978); *b* 31 Aug 1953; *Educ* Harrow, Hertford Coll Oxford (BA); *m* 2 Dec 1978, Cecilia D'Oyly, da of Daniel Edmund Awdry, TD, DL, of The Old Manor, Beanacre, Melksham, Wilts; 2 s (Patrick William Edmund b 31 July 1983, Richard Daniel Hugh b 8 May 1985); *Career* called to the Bar Middle Temple 1977; memb: Chancery Bar Assoc, Revenue Bar Assoc; *Books* Potter and Monroe's Tax Planning with Precedents (jtly, 9 edn), Encyclopaedia of Forms and Precedents (contrib); *Recreations* skiing, gardening, bookbinding, chess; *Style*— William Massey, Esq; 4 Pump Court, Temple, London EC4Y 7AN (☎ 071 583 9770, fax 071 353 6366)

MASSIE, Allan Johnstone; s of Alexander Johnstone Massie, of Banchory, Aberdeenshire, and Evelyn Wilson, *née* Forbes; *b* 16 Oct 1938; *Educ* Drumtochty Castle, Glenalmond, Trinity Coll Cambridge (BA); *m* 22 June 1983, Alison Agnes Graham, da of Robert Scott Langlands, of Kelso, Roxburghshire; 2 s (Alexander, Louis), 1 da (Clauda); *Career* sch master Drumtochty Castle 1960-71, TEFL Rome 1972-75; author, journalist and playwright; princ fiction reviewer The Scotsman 1975-, TV critic The Sunday Standard 1981-83; columnist: Glasgow Herald 1985-88, Sunday Times Scotland 1987-; plays incl: Quintet in October, The Minstrel and The Shirra 1989; winner: Frederick Niven Prize for the Last Peacock 1981, Fraser of Allander Award Critic of the Year 1982, Scottish Arts Cncl Book Awards 1982 and 1986, The Scotsman, Scottish Book of the Year 1990; memb Scottish Arts Cncl 1989; FRSL 1982; *Books* Change and Decay in All Around I See (1978), The Last Peacock (1980), The Death of Men (1981), The Caesars (1983), Portrait of Scottish Rugby (1984), One Night in Winter (1984), Augustus (1986), Bryon's Travels (1987), A Question of Loyalties (1989), Glasgow (1989); *Recreations* reading, watching rugby, cricket, walking the dogs; *Clubs* Academy, Selkirk RFC; *Style*— Allan Massie, Esq; Thirladean House, Selkirk TD7 5LU (☎ 0750 20393)

MASSIMO OF ROCCASECCA DEI VOLSCI, Prince (Title of Papal and Italian Royal Decree 31 March 1932) Stefano Shaun Francesco Filippo Gabriel Charles James; Don Stefano, Prince of Roccasecca dei Volsci; s of Prince Vittorio Massimo and his 2 wife Dawn Addams, the film actress; *b* 10 Jan 1955,London; *Educ* Collegio San Giuseppe de Merode Rome, Collegio alla Querce Florence; *m* 1973, Atalanta Edith, da of Maj Ivan Foxwell, *qv*, and Lady Edith Sybil, *née* Lambart, gda of 9 Earl of Cavan, KP, PC, DL; 3 s (Don Valerio b 1973, Don Cesare b 1977 Don Tancredi b 1986); *Heir* Don Valerio Massimo; *Career* photographer; *Clubs* Circolo degli Scacchi, (Rome); *Style*— Prince Massimo of Roccasecca dei Volsci; c/o National Westminster Bank, Bloomsbury Way, London WC1A 2TS

MASSY, Hon David Hamon Somerset; s and h of 9 Baron Massy; *b* 4 March 1947; *Educ* St George's Coll Weybridge; *Career* serving with Merchant Navy; *Style*— The Hon David Massy

MASSY, 9 Baron (I 1776); Hugh Hamon John Somerset Massy; s of 8 Baron (d 1958); *b* 11 June 1921; *Educ* Clongowes Wood Coll, Clayesmore Sch; *m* 1943, Margaret Elizabeth, da of John Flower (decd); 4 s, 1 da; *Heir* s, Hon David Hamon Somerset Massy; *Career* serv 1940-45 War, Private RAOC; *Style*— The Rt Hon the Lord Massy; 88 Brooklands Rd, Cosby, Leicester

MASSY-BERESFORD, Michael James; s of Brig Tristram Hugh Massy-Beresford (d 1987), and Helen Lindsay, *née* Lawford (d 1979); *b* 10 April 1935; *Educ* Eton, Jesus Coll Cambridge (BA), RMCS (MSc); *Career* Oxford and Bucks LI 1955-59, Royal Green Jackets 1959-81; dir Miltrain Ltd 1981-; *Recreations* water sports, bicycling; *Style*— Michael Massy-Beresford, Esq; 11 Charleville Mansions, Charleville Rd, London W14 9JB (☎ 071 385 1983)

MASTER, (Humphrey) Simon Harcourt; s of Humphrey Ronald Master, of Thetford, Norfolk, and Rachel Blanche, *née* Plumbly (d 1989); *b* 10 April 1944; *Educ* Ardingly, Univ de La Rochelle; *m* 3 May 1969, Georgina Mary, da of Sir Brian Caldwell Cook Batsford, of Winchelsea, East Sussex; 2 s (Nicholas Harcourt b 1973, Matthew Harcourt b 1976); *Career* sr ed: Pan Books Ltd 1966-69, B T Batsford Ltd 1969-70; Pan Books Ltd: editorial dir 1970-73, publishing dir 1973-79, managing dir 1980-87; chief exec Random House UK Ltd 1987-89, exec vice pres int Random House Inc 1989-91, dep chm Random Century Group 1989-, exec chm Arrow Books 1990-, dir HMSO 1990-; memb Cncl Publishers Assoc 1989-; *Recreations* reading, golf, classic cars, gardening; *Clubs* Groucho, Sherborne Golf; *Style*— Simon Master, Esq; 13 Patten Rd, London SW18 3RH (☎ 081 874 2204); Random Century House, 20 Vauxhall Bridge Rd, London SW1V 2SA (☎ 071 973 9000, fax 071 233 6115)

MASTERMAN, Crispin Grant; s of Osmond Janson Masterman (d 1988), of Gerrards Cross Bucks, and Anne, *née* Bouwens; *b* 1 June 1944; *Educ* St Edwards Sch Oxford, Univ of Southampton (BA); *m* 3 Jan 1976, Margaret Elizabeth Clare, da of Robert Fletcher (d 1967), of Cardiff; 1 s (Kerrin b 25 Oct 1979), 2 da (Claudia b 21 Sept 1977, Laura b 9 Aug 1982); *Career* cmmd RAFVR 1967 PO; called to the bar 1971, currently rec 1988; govr Llysfaen Sch Cardiff; *Recreations* athletics, aviation, automobiles; *Style*— Crispin Masterman, Esq; 28 South Rise, Llanishen, Cardiff, South Glamorgan CF4 5RH (☎ 0222 754072); 34 Park Place, Cardiff CF1 3TN (☎ 0222 382731)

MASTERS, Sheila Valerie (Mrs Barry Noakes); da of Albert Frederick Masters, of Eltham, London, and Iris Sheila, *née* Ratcliffe; *b* 23 June 1949; *Educ* Eltham Hill GS, Univ of Bristol (LLB); *m* 3 Aug 1985, (Colin) Barry Noakes, s of Stuart Noakes, of Brenchley; *Career* KPMG Peat Marwick McLintock: joined 1970, ptnr 1983-, ptnr in charge Pub Sector Practice 1986-; seconded to: HM Treasy as accounting/ commercial advsr 1979-81, Dept of Health as fin dir on NHS Mgmnt Exec 1988; elected to: London Soc of CAs 1984, Cncl ICAEW 1987; appointed to Ctee of Enquiry MAFF 1988; FCA, ATII; *Books* Tolley's Stamp Duties (1980); *Recreations* skiing, horse-racing, opera, early classical music; *Style*— Ms Sheila Masters; Spyways, High St, Goudhurst, Kent TN17 1AL (☎ 0580 211 427, fax 0580 212244); Peat Marwick McLintock, Blackfriars, London EC4V 3PD (☎ 071 236 8000, fax 071 248 6552)

MASTERSON, (Margaret) Valerie (Mrs Andrew March); CBE; da of Edward Masterson, and Rita McGrath; *Educ* Holt Hill Convent, studied in London and Milan on scholarship with Edwardo Asquez; *m* 1965, Andrew John March; 1 s ((Edward) Jason b 13 May 1969), 1 da (Caroline Louisa b 13 Aug 1973); *Career* opera and concert singer; debut Landestheater Salzburg; appearances with D'Oyly Carte Opera, Glyndebourne Festival Opera, ENO, Royal Opera House Covent Garden; appearances with princ opera houses incl: Paris, Aix En Provence, Toulouse, Munich, Geneva, Barcelona, Milan, San Francisco, Chile; leading roles in: La Traviata, Le Nozze di Figaro, Manon, Faust, Alcina, Die Entfhrung, Julius Ceasar, Rigoletto, Romeo and Juliet, Carmen, Count Ory, Mireille, Lousie, Idomeneo, Les Dialogues des Carmelites, The Merry Widow, Xerxes, Orlando; recordings incl: La Traviata, Elisabetta, Regina d Inghilterra, Der Ring des Nibelungen, The Merry Widow, Julius Caesar Scipione, several Gilbert and Sullivan; broadcasts regularly on radio and tv; vice pres Br Youth Opera; *Recreations* tennis, swimming, ice skating; *Style*— Ms Valerie Masterson, CBE; Music International, 13 Ardilaun Rd, Highbury, London N5 2QR

MASUDA, Yosuke; s of Kazuo Masuda (d 1957), of Tokyo, and Miyoko, *née* Hameda (d 1983); *b* 27 April 1946; *Educ* Waseda Sch, Waseda Univ Tokyo (BSc), QMC London (LLB); *m* 16 Feb 1975, Yuriko, da of Yoshiaki Ohnari, dir of Miny of Int Trade and Indust Tokyo; 1 s (Christopher Toshihiro b 1977), 2 da (Alison Nobuko b 1980, Margaret Takako b 1988); *Career* structural engr Kumagai Gumi Co Ltd 1969, asst project mangr Hong Kong Mass Transit Railway 1976-79, md Kumagai Gumi UK Ltd 1985, assoc dir Kumagai Co Ltd Tokyo 1988; called to the Bar Middle Temple 1984; memb: Japanese C of C UK, Anglo Japanese Assoc; fell QMC London; memb Japanese Inst of Civil Engrs; *Books* Pneumatic Caisson Design (1975); *Recreations* theatre, travel, classical music, fishing, riding; *Clubs* Reform; *Style*— Yosuke Masuda, Esq; The Lawn, 109 Camlet Way, Hadley Common, Herts (☎ 081 449 0272); 8 St James Sq, London SW1 (☎ 071 925 0066, fax 071 930 8004)

MATANLE, David John Link; s of Leslie William Matanle, of Crediton, Devon, and Dorothy Ellen, *née* Palfreman (d 1968); *b* 22 April 1933; *Educ* Queen Elizabeth's Sch Crediton Devon; *m* 19 Sept 1959, (Margaret) Jean, da of George Edward Clifford (d 1959), of Bristol; 2 da (Ann b 16 Dec 1963, Helen b 15 July 1965); *Career* Nat Serv RAF 1951-53; Purser Orient Line 1954-60, accountant P & O 1960-66, accountant and asst sec Gibbards Ltd 1966-68, co sec Braithwaites plc 1968-72; dir: John Perring Ltd 1972-83, Manor Distribution Servs Ltd 1988-; dir and co sec Cullens Stores plc 1983-88; sec: Bookham CC 1978-84, Bookham Sports Assoc 1979-84; govr Coll for the Distributive Trades 1981-83, chm Educn Ctee Nat Assoc of Furnishers 1981-83; Freeman City of London 1979, memb Worshipful Co of Furnituremakers 1979; FCIS 1966, MBIM 1973; *Recreations* sports, music, walking; *Style*— David Matanle, Esq; 43 Eastwick Pk Ave, Gt Bookham, Surrey KT23 3LZ (☎ 0372 454385)

MATES, Lt-Col Michael John; MP (C) E Hants 1983-; s of Claude Mates; *b* 9 June 1934; *Educ* Salisbury Cathedral Sch, Blundell's, King's Coll Cambridge; *m* 1, 1959 (m dis 1980), Mary Rosamund Paton; 2 s, 2 da; m 2, 1982, Rosellen, da of W T Bett, of West Wittering, W Sussex; 1 da; *Career* army offr 1954-74 (Royal Ulster Rifles, Queen's Dragoon Gds RAC, Maj 1967, Lt-Col 1973); vice-chm: Cons NI Ctee 1979-81 (sec 1974-79), Cons Home Affrs Ctee 1979-87 (chm 1987-88); chm: All Party Anglo-Irish Gp 1979-, Select Ctee Def 1987- (memb 1979-); sec 1922 Ctee 1987-88; MP (C) Petersfield Oct 1974-1983; Liveryman Worshipful Co of Farriers' 1975 (Master 1986); *Style*— Lt-Col Michael Mates, MP; House of Commons, London SW1A 0AA

MATHER, Sir (David) Carol Macdonell; MC (1944); s of Loris Emerson Mather, CBE (d 1975) and Leila Gwendoline, *née* Morley; yr bro of Sir William Mather, *qv*; *b* 3 Jan 1919; *Educ* Harrow, Trinity Coll Cambridge; *m* 1951, Hon Philippa Selina Bewicke-Copley, da of 5 Baron Cromwell, (*see* Hon Lady Mather); 1 s (Nicholas), 3 da (Selina, Rose, Victoria); *Career* joined Welsh Gds 1940, WWII served Commandos, SAS, LO to Montgomery Palestine 1946-48; AMA Athens 1953-56, WO 1957-61, Mil Sec E Cmd 1961-62, ret as Lt-Col 1962; CRD 1962-70, Parly candidate Leicester NW 1966, MP (C) Esher 1970-87, oppn whip 1975-79; Lord Cmmr of the Treasy 1979-81, vice chamberlain of HM's Household 1981-83, comptroller 1983-86; memb Cncl RGS, memb Ctee Nat Tst; kt 1987; *Clubs* Brooks's; *Style*— Sir Carol Mather, MC; Oddington House, Moreton-in-Marsh, Glos

MATHER, Graham Christopher Spencer; er s of Thomas Mather, and Doreen Mather; *b* 23 Oct 1954; *Educ* Hutton GS, New Coll Oxford (Burnet Law scholar, MA); *m* 18 Sept 1981, Fiona Marion McMillan, er da of Sir Ronald Bell, QC, MP (d 1982); 1 s (Oliver b 20 June 1987); *Career* slr Cameron Markby 1978- (conslt 1986-); IOD: asst to DG 1980-83, head of Policy Unit 1983-86; Inst of Econ Affrs: dep dir 1987, gen dir 1987-; radio and tv broadcaster, contributor to The Times and various jls; memb: MMC 1989-, Westminster City Cncl 1982-86, cncl Small Business Res Tst, econ Advsy Ctee Cncl for Charitable Support, HM Treasy Working Pty on Freeports 1983; Parly candidate (C) Blackburn 1983; *Clubs* Oxford and Cambridge; *Style*— Graham Mather, Esq; 2 Lord North St, London SW1P 3LB (☎ 071 799 3745, fax 071 799 2137)

MATHER, Howard Stephen Gilchrist; s of T Mather, and M D Mather; *b* 10 July 1957; *Educ* Hutton GS, New Coll Oxford; *Career* admitted slr 1982; ptnr corporate fin and co law Simmons & Simmons 1986-; *Recreations* antiquarian book collecting, chess, oriental travel (FRGS); *Style*— Howard Mather, Esq; Simmons & Simmons, 14 Dominion St, London EC2M 2RJ (☎ 071 628 2020, fax 071 588 4129, telex 888562 SIMMON G)

MATHER, John Williamson; s of John Williamson Mather (d 1979), of Coatbridge, Scotland, and Janet Murdoch, *née* McIntyre; *b* 30 Sept 1929; *Educ* Coatbridge Secdy

Sch, Univ of Glasgow, Inst of Chartered Accountants of Scotland; *m* 1, 5 Dec 1954 (m dis), Jean; 1 da (Elizabeth b 8 Feb 1961); m 2, 4 Dec 1971, Mavis, da of William Henry Horne, of Burley Lane Farm, Ashe, Basingstoke, Hants; *Career* joined Portals Holdings plc (fin controller 1966-69, md Portals Ltd 1969-72, md Portals Holding plc 1972-86, appointed special projects dir 1987), ret; *Recreations* badminton, tennis, fell walking; *Style*— John W Mather, Esq; Burley Lane Farm, Ashe, Basingstoke, Hants RG25 3AG (☎ 0256 770267); Portals Holdings plc, Laverstoke Mill, Whitchurch, Hants (☎ 025 682 2360)

MATHER, Prof Paul Michael; s of Albert Mather (d 1953), of Bolton, Lancs, and Catherine, *née* Faulkner (d 1980); *b* 27 Jan 1944; *Educ* Thornleigh Coll Bolton, Selwyn Coll Cambridge (BA, MA), Univ of Nottingham (PhD); *m* 3 Jan 1970, Rosalind Mary, da of Roland Trench-Smith (d 1986), of Axminster, Devon; 4 s (Charles b 1971, William b 1974, James b 1976, John Paul b 1981), 1 da (Tamsin b 1972); *Career* lectr Univ of Manchester 1969, prof of geographical info systems Univ of Nottingham 1988 (lectr 1970, sr lectr 1981), dep dir Inst of Engrg Surveying and Space Geodesy chm The Remote Sensing Soc 1989-; *Books* Computational Methods of Multivariate Analysis (1976), Computers in Geography (1976), Computer Processing of Remotely-Sensed Images, Computer Applications in Geography (1991) (1987) Computer Applications in Geography (1991); *Recreations* working; *Style*— Prof Paul Mather; 33 Willow Road, W Bridgford, Nottingham NG2 7AY (☎ 0602 235469); Dept of Geography, The University, Nottingham NG7 2RD (☎ 0602 484848, telex 37346, fax 0602 420825)

MATHER, Hon Lady (Philippa Selina); *née* Bewicke-Copley; o da of 5 Baron Cromwell, DSO, MC (d 1966); *b* 5 Dec 1925; *m* 13 Jan 1951, Sir (David) Carol MacDonell Mather, MC, *qv*; 1 s, 3 da; *Style*— The Hon Lady Mather; Oddington House, Moreton-in-Marsh, Glos

MATHER, Sir William Loris; CVO (1986), OBE (1957), MC (1945), TD (and 2 Clasps 1949), DL (Cheshire 1963); s of Loris Emerson Mather, CBE (d 1976), and Gwendoline Leila, *née* Morley (d 1976); elder bro of Sir Carol Mather, MC, *qv*; *b* 17 Aug 1913; *Educ* Oundle, Trinity Coll Cambridge (MA); *m* 1937, Eleanor, da of Prof R H George (d 1979), of Providence, Rhode Island; 2 s, 2 da; *Career* serv WWII, Cheshire Yeo and IRTR, ME, Western Desert, Italy, Belgium, Holland, Germany, instr Staff Coll Camberley 1943-44, cmd Cheshire Yeo 1954-57, Dep Cdr 23 Armd Bde TA 1957-60, Col; chm: Mather & Platt Ltd 1960-78, CompAir Ltd 1978-83, Neolith Chemical Co Ltd 1983-87, Advanced Mfrg Technol Centre 1985-88; dir: Dist Bank, National Provincial Bank and Nat Westminster Bank 1960-84 (chm Northern Bd), Br Steel Corpn (regnl dir) 1968-73, Manchester Ship Canal Co 1970-85, Wormald Int Ltd 1977-78, Imperial Continental Gas Assoc 1980-83; chm: NW Econ Planning Cncl 1968-75, IOD 1979-82; pres: Manchester C of C and Indust 1964-66, Br Pump Makers Assoc 1977-79, Manchester Guardian Soc for Protection of Trade 1971-85, Gtr Manchester E Scouts 1972-, Br Mech Engrg Confedn 1974-79, Assoc of Colls of Higher and Further Educn 1975-76, Manchester Univ Inst of Sci and Technol 1976-85, Civic Tst for the NW 1980-90 (chm 1961-80), Econ League for the NW 1982-, Manchester YMCA 1982- (chm 1958-82); memb Cncl Duchy of Lancaster 1977-85; High Sheriff Cheshire 1969-70, Vice Lord-Lt Cheshire 1975-90; hon fell Manchester Coll of Art and Design 1967, hon fell UMIST 1986, hon memb Town Planning Inst 1977; Hon DEng Liverpool 1980, Hon LLD Manchester 1983; CEng, CBIM, FRSA; kt 1968; *Recreations* field sports, golf; *Clubs* Leander; *Style*— Sir William Mather, CVO, OBE, MC, TD, DL; Whirley Hall, Macclesfield, Cheshire SK10 4RN (☎ 0625 422077)

MATHER-JACKSON, Lady; (Evelyn) Mary; er da of Lt-Col Sir Henry Kenyon Stephenson, 1 Bt, DSO, of Hassop Hall, Bakewell; *m* 1923, Sir Anthony Mather-Jackson, 6 Bt, JP, DL (d 1983); 3 da; *Style*— Lady Mather-Jackson; Archway House, Kirklington, Newark, Notts (☎ 0636 2070)

MATHERS, James Irvine; s of James Cuthbert Mather, of 4 Dalhousie Gdns, Bishopbriggs, Glasgow, and Jean Benton, *née* Cobb; *b* 26 Sept 1947; *Educ* Lenzie Acad, Univ of Strathclyde (BSc, DMS); *m* 12 July 1970, Janis Chalmers, da of Douglas Bell (d 1959), of Glasgow; 1 s (Craig b 1973), 1 da (Lynne b 1975); *Career* analyst and programmer Singer Sewing Machines 1968-74, sr systems analyst Hepworth Tailoring 1974-79, sr systems analyst Consolidated Pneumatic Tool Co 1979-80; Hydro Electric: systems mangr 1980-89, computer ops mangr 1989-; elder Church of Scot; MBIM 1988; *Style*— James Mathers, Esq; 68 Newburgh Drive, Bridge of Don, Aberdeen (☎ 0224 820606); Hydro Electric, Ashgrove Road West, Aberdeen AB9 2NY (☎ 0224 692671)

MATHERS, Baroness; Jessie Newton; da of George Graham, JP, of Peebles and Edinburgh (decd); *m* 1940, as his 2 w, 1 and last Baron Mathers, Kt, PC, DL (d 1965); *Style*— The Rt Hon Lady Mathers; 50 Craiglea Drive, Edinburgh 10 (☎ 031 4477 555)

MATHESON, Alasdair Burnett; OBE (1991); s of Chief Constable Alexander John Matheson, MBE (d 1963), of Aberdeen, and Elizabeth Rose, *née* Burnett; *b* 18 June 1940; *Educ* Aberdeen GS, Univ of Aberdeen (MB ChB); *m* 15 July 1969, Moira, da of William Salmond MacFarlane (d 1975), of Friockheim; *Career* Aberdeen Royal Infirmary: house offr in med and surgery 1964-65, sr registrar 1975-77, conslt in accident and emergency care 1977-; lectr in physiology Univ of Newcastle upon Tyne 1966, demonstrator in anatomy Univ of Aberdeen 1967, registrar in surgery Cumberland Infirmary Carlisle 1970-73; med memb Royal Med Benevolent Fund Aberdeen, treas Aberdeen Medico-Chirurgical Soc, dep chm Scot Ctee Hosp Med Servs, vice chm Grampian Area Ctee Hosp Med Servs; FRCSEd 1972; *Books* Pys's Surgical Handicraft (contrib edn 21, 1984); *Recreations* trout fishing, curling, model engrg, architecture; *Style*— Alasdair Matheson, Esq, OBE; The Accident and Emergency Dept, Aberdeen Royal Infirmary, Foresterhill, Aberdeen AB9 2ZB (☎ 0224 681818)

MATHESON, Andrew Malcolm Hugh; o s of Capt Alexander Francis Matheson, RN (d 1976), and Frances Mary, *née* Heywood-Lonsdale; *b* 30 June 1942; *Educ* Gordonstoun, RAC Cirencester; *m* 1972, Judith Helen Mackay, da of (Aldred) Ian Mackay Baldry; 3 s (Alexander b 1974, Hamish b 1976, Philip b 1979); *Career* Gren Gds 1962-66; asst chief cmmr for Scotland (Scout Assoc); ARICS 1970; *Style*— Andrew Matheson, Esq; Brahan, Dingwall, Ross-shire

MATHESON, Duncan; QC (1989); *Educ* Trinity Coll Cambridge (MA, LLM); *Career* called to the Bar Inner Temple 1965; rec Crown Ct 1985, in practice SE Circuit; *Style*— Duncan Matheson, Esq, QC; 1 Crown Office Row, Temple, London EC4Y 7HH (☎ 071 353 1801, fax 071 583 1700)

MATHESON, Maj Fergus John; yr s of Gen Sir Torquhil George Matheson, 5 Bt, KCB, CMG (d 1963), and Lady Elizabeth Matheson, da of 8 Earl of Albemarle; hp to Btcy of bro, Sir Torquhil Alexander Matheson of Matheson, 6 Bt; *b* 22 Feb 1927; *Educ* Eton; *m* 17 May 1952, Hon Jean Elizabeth Mary, *née* Willoughby *qv*, da of 11 Baron Middleton, KG, MC; 1 s (Maj Alexander Matheson, Coldstream Gds b 1954, m 1983, *see* Michael Oswald, CVO), 2 da (Elizabeth Angela Matilda b 1953, Fiona Jean Lucia b 1962); *Career* serv 1 and 3 Bns Coldstream Gds 1945-64: Palestine, N Africa, Germany, Adjt Mons OCS 1952-55, RARO Coldstream Gds 1964-; one of HM Bodyguard of Hon Corps of Gentlemen at Arms 1979-; *Clubs* Army & Navy; *Style*— Maj Fergus Matheson; Hedenham Old Rectory, Bungay, Norfolk NR35 2LD (☎ 050 844 218)

MATHESON, Hamish Clive Duncan; s of Maj James Matheson, of 66 Ouse Lea, Clifton, York, and Elizabeth Crawford, *née* Donaldson; *b* 6 Oct 1953; *Educ* Archbishop Holgates York, Univ of Liverpool (BSc); *m* 29 Oct 1977, Patricia Ewid Mary Matheson; 3 s (Benjamin James, Andrew George, Daniel Crawford); *Career* social work Scotland 1974-75, copywriter Dorlands 1978, creative dir Wagner Advtg 1982-; memb Writers Guild; *Recreations* film, reading, swimming; *Style*— Hamish Matheson, Esq; Hazel Bank, Miwster Rd, Busbridge, Godalming; 6 Queens Rd, Upper Hale, Farham, Surrey; Hickley's Ct, Farham, Surrey (☎ 0252 737 040)

MATHESON, Hon Mrs (Jean Elizabeth Mary); JP (1976); da of 11 Baron Middleton, KG, MC (d 1970), and Angela Florence Alfreda (d 1978); *b* 26 Jan 1928; *m* 1952, Maj Fergus John Matheson, *qv*; 1 s, 2 da; *Clubs* Army & Navy; *Style*— The Hon Mrs Matheson, JP; Hedenham Old Rectory, Bungay, Norfolk NR35 2LD (☎ 050 844 218)

MATHESON OF MATHESON, Maj Sir Torquhil Alexander; 6 Bt (UK 1882), of Lochalsh, Co Ross, DL (1987 Somerset); s of Gen Sir Torquhil George Matheson, 5 Bt, KCB, CMG (d 1963), and Lady Elizabeth Keppel, ARRC (d 1986), o da of 8 Earl of Albemarle, GCVO, CB, VD, TD; *b* 15 Aug 1925; *Educ* Eton; *m* 1954, Serena Mary Francesca, o da of Lt-Col Sir (James) Michael Peto, 2 Bt, of Barnstable; 2 da (Eleanor Mary Francesca b 1955, Isobel Sophia (Mrs William Craven) b 1957); *Heir* bro, Maj Fergus John Matheson; *Career* serv WWII with 5 Bn Coldstream Gds; 3 Bn Palestine 1945-48 (despatches), Libya and Egypt 1950-53; Maj 1959, seconded KAR (Kenya) 1961-64, ret 1964; Wiltshire Regt (TA) 1965-67; farmer; one of HM Body Guard of the Hon Corps of Gentleman at Arms 1977-, Clerk of Cheque and Adjutant 1990; succeeded as Chief of Clan Matheson 1975; FSA Scot 1989; *Clubs* Army & Navy, Leander; *Style*— Maj Sir Torquhil Matheson of Matheson, Bt, DL; Standerwick Court, Frome, Somerset BA11 2PP

MATHEW, HSH Princess Olga Romanoff, Mrs Thomas; *née* HSH Princess Olga Romanoff; da of HH Prince Andrew of Russia (eld s of HIH The Grand Duke Alexander, 4 s of HIH The Grand Duke Mikhail, 4 s of Tsar Nicholas I of Russia) by his 2 w, Nadine, da of Lt-Col Herbert McDougall, of Belgravia; *b* 8 April 1950; *m* 1975, Thomas Mathew, 2 s of Francis Mathew, formerly with The Times; 2 s (Nicholas b 1976, Francis Alexander b 1978), 1 da (Alexandra b 1981); *Style*— HSH Princess Olga Romanoff, Mrs Thomas Mathew; Welford House, nr Rugby, Northants

MATHEW, John Charles; QC (1977); s of Sir Theobald Mathew, KBE, MC (d 1964), of 7 Cranley Mansions, London SW7, and Phyllis Helen, *née* Russell (d 1982); *b* 3 May 1927; *Educ* Beaumont; *m* 6 Sept 1952, (Jennifer) Jane, da of Reginald Bousfield Lagden, OBE, MC (d 1944), of Calcutta; 2 da (Sally (Mrs Jamieson) b 14 March 1956, Amanda b 13 Oct 1958); *Career* RN 1945-47; called to the Bar Lincoln's Inn 1949; jr prosecuting counsel to Crown at Central Criminal Ct 1959 (sr Prosecuting Counsel 1964), bencher of Lincoln's Inn 1972; *Recreations* golf, tennis, bridge, backgammon; *Clubs* Garrick; *Style*— John Mathew, Esq, QC; 47 Abingdon Villas, London W8 6XA (☎ 071 937 7535); 5 Paper Buildings, Temple, London EC4 (☎ 071 583 6117, fax 071 353 0075, telex 8956431 ANTON G)

MATHEW, Theobald David; s of Robert Mathew (d 1954), and Joan Alison, da of Sir George Young, Bt, MVO; *b* 7 April 1942; *Educ* Downside Abbey, Balliol Coll Oxford (MA); *Career* Green staff offr at Investiture of HRH Prince of Wales 1969, Rouge Dragon Pursuivant of Arms 1970, Windsor Herald of Arms 1978-; dep treas College of Arms; OStJ 1986; *Recreations* sailing, cricket, music, sketching; *Clubs* Athenaeum, MCC, Middlesex CCC, Royal Harwich Yacht; *Style*— Theobald Mathew, Esq; 76 Clifton Hill, London NW8 0JT (☎ 071 624 8448)

MATHEWS, Dr John Alan; s of Henry Alexander Mathews, and Dora, *née* Apley; *b* 19 June 1934; *Educ* Haberdashers' Aske's, Jesus Coll Cambridge, Guy's Hosp Med Sch (MD); *m* 14 July 1957, Wendy, da of Jack Dewhurst; 1 s (Colin David b 1960), 2 da (Gillian Anne b 1962, Catherine Jane b 1972); *Career* conslt physician dept of rheumatology St Thomas' Hosp London 1970-; sometime sec: Heberden Soc, Br Assoc for Rheumatology and Rehabilitation, Rheumatology and Rehabilitation Section RSM; FRCP; *Style*— Dr John A Mathews; 6 Longwood Drive, Roehampton, London SW15 5DL (☎ 081 789 7831); Department of Rheumatology, St Thomas' Hospital, London SE1 7EH (☎ 071 928 9292 ext 2084); Churchill Clinic, 80 Lambeth Rd, London SE1 7PW (☎ 071 928 5633)

MATHEWS, Michael Robert; s of George Walter Mathews, of London, and Betty, *née* Willcox; *b* 3 Nov 1941; *Educ* Uppingham, King's Coll Cambridge (hon scholar, MA); *m* 19 March 1966, Ann Rosemary, da of David Watson Gieve, OBE; 2 s (Robert George b 12 Oct 1969, Stephen Charles b 1 Jan 1973), 1 da ((Caroline) Lucy b 27 Aug 1975); *Career* Coward Chance (became Clifford Chance 1987): articled clerk 1963-66, asst slr 1966-71, ptnr 1971-; Broderig prize Law Soc 1966, City of London Solicitors Co prize 1966; Liveryman City of London Solicitors Co; memb: Law Soc, Ctee City of London Law Soc; *Recreations* walking, watching good cricket; *Style*— Michael Mathews, Esq; Clifford Chance, Royex House, Aldermanbury Square, London EC2V 7LD (☎ 071 600 0808, fax 071 726 8561)

MATHEWSON, Dr George Ross; CBE; s of George Mathewson, of Perth, by his w Charlotte Gordon, *née* Ross; *b* 14 May 1940; *Educ* Perth Acad, Univ of St Andrews (BSc, PhD), Canisius Coll Buffalo NY (MBA); *m* 1966, Sheila Alexandra Graham, da of Eon Bennett (d 1975), Bridge of Earn, Perth; 2 s; *Career* asst lectr Univ of St Andrews 1964-67; with Bell Aerospace (Buffalo, NY) in res and devpt and avionics engrg 1967-72, joined ICFC Edinburgh 1972, area mangr Aberdeen 1974, asst gen mangr and dir 1979; chief exec and memb Scottish Devpt Agency 1981-87; dir strategic planning and development The Royal Bank of Scotland Gp plc 1987 (dep gp chief exec 1990); Hon LLD Dundee 1983; FRSE, CEng, MIEE, CBIM; *Recreations* rugby, golf, business; *Clubs* New (Edinburgh); *Style*— Dr George Mathewson, CBE, FRSE; 29 Saxe Coburg Place, Edinburgh EH3 5BP; The Royal Bank of Scotland Gp plc, 42 St Andrew Square, Edinburgh EH2 2YE (☎ 031 523 2672)

MATHIAS, Julian Robert; s of Anthony Robert Mathias (d 1973), and Cecily Mary Agnes, *née* Hughes; *b* 7 Sept 1943; *Educ* Downside, Univ Coll Oxford (MA); *Career* mangr Hill Samuel and Co Ltd 1964-71, ptnr Buckmaster and Moore 1971-81, dir Foreign and Colonial Management Ltd 1981-; *Recreations* wine tasting, bridge, golf, shooting; *Clubs* Boodle's, City of London, Berkshire Golf; *Style*— Julian Mathias, Esq; Foreign and Colonial Management Ltd, Exchange House, Primrose St, London EC4A 2NY (☎ 071 628 8000, fax 071 628 8188, telex 886197, 8811745)

MATHIAS, Dr Peter; CBE (1984); s of John Samuel Mathias (d 1960), and Marion Helen, *née* Love; *b* 10 Jan 1928; *Educ* Colston's Hosp, Jesus Coll Cambridge (BA, MA), Harvard; *m* 5 April 1958, (Elizabeth) Ann, da of Robert Blackmore (d 1979), of Bath; 2 s (Sam b 3 March 1959, Henry b 15 May 1961), 1 da (Sophie b 25 July 1964); *Career* Univ of Cambridge: history lectr 1955-68, res fell Jesus Coll 1952-55, fell and dir history studies Queens' Coll 1955-68 (tutor 1957-68), sr proctor 1965-66; Chichele prof of econ history Univ of Oxford 1969-87 (fell All Souls Coll); LittD (Oxon) 1985, DLitt (Cantab) 1987; The master Downing Coll Cambridge 1987-; hon treas Econ History Soc 1967-88, curator Bodleian Library 1972-87, pres Int Econ History Assoc 1974-78 (hon pres 1978-), vice pres Int Inst of Econ History Datini Prato Italy, vice pres Royal Historical Soc 1975-80, hon treas Br Acad 1979-89; chm: Int Advsy Ctee

Univ of Buckingham 1979-84, Advsy Panel Hist Med Wellcome Tst 1980-88; memb: Advsy Bd Res Cncls 1983-89, Round Table Cncl of Indust and Higher Educn 1989-, Econ History Soc 1951- (pres 1989-), Academia Europeae 1989-, Humanities and Social Scis Advsy Cncl Br Library 1990-; pres Business Archives Cncl 1984- (vice-pres 1980-84, chm 1967-72); visiting prof: Toronto Univ 1961, Delhi Univ 1967, California Univ Berkeley 1967, Pennsylvania Univ 1972, Virginia Univ (Gildersleeve prof) Columbia 1972, John Hopkins Univ 1979, Natal Univ 1980, Australian National Univ 1981, Geneva Univ 1986, Leuven Univ 1990; memb syndicate Fitzwilliam Museum Cambridge 1987-; Hon Litt D (Univ of Buckingham 1985), Hon D Litt (Univ of Birmingham 1988); chm Friends of Kettle's Yard 1990; fell Royal Hist Soc 1972, FBA 1977; *Books* The Brewing Industry in England 1700-1830(1959), English Trade Tokens(1962), Retailing Revolution(1967), The First Industrial Nation(1969, 1983), The Transformation of England(1979), Science and Society (ed and contrib, 1972); *Recreations* travel; *Clubs* United Oxford and Cambridge Univ; *Style*— Dr Peter Mathias, CBE; The Master's Lodge, Downing College, Cambridge CB2 1DQ (☎ 0223 334 868)

MATHIAS, Prof William (James); CBE (1985); s of James Hughes Mathias (d 1969), of Llwynbedw, Whitland, Dyfed, and Marian, *née* Evans (d 1980); *b* 1 Nov 1934; *Educ* Whitland GS, Univ Coll of Wales Aberystwyth (BMus, DMus), RAM (FRAM, LRAM); *m* 17 Sept 1959, (Margaret) Yvonne, da of Mervyn Collins (d 1967); 1 da (Rhiannon b 10 Oct 1968); *Career* lectr in music Univ Coll N Wales Bangor 1959-68, sr lectr in music Univ of Edinburgh 1968-69, prof and head of music dept Univ Coll N Wales Bangor 1970-88; freelance composer and conductor 1988-; pres Incorporated Soc of Musicians 1989-90; vice pres: Br Arts Festivals Assoc 1988-, Royal Coll of Organists 1985; artistic dir N Wales Music Festival 1972-; govr: Nat Museum of Wales 1973-78, Nat Youth Orchestra of GB 1985-; memb: Welsh Arts Cncl 1974-88 (chm Music Ctee 1982-88), Music Advsy Ctee Br Cncl 1974-83, Br Section ISCM 1976-80, BBC Central Music Advsy Ctee 1979-86, Welsh Advsy Ctee Br Cncl 1979-90, Cncl Composers' Guild of GB; pubns incl: Piano Concerto No 2 1964, Piano Concerto No 3 1970, Harpsichord Concerto 1971, Harp Concerto 1970, Clarinet Concerto 1976, Horn Concerto 1984, Organ Concerto 1984, Oboe Concerto 1990; orchestral compositions incl: Symphony No 1 1969, Festival Overture 1973, Celtic Dances 1974, Vistas 1977, Vivat Regina (for brass band) 1978, Requiescat 1979, Dance Variations 1979, Symphony No 2 (Summer Music) (cmmnd by Royal Liverpool Philharmonic Soc) 1983, Ceremonial Fanfare (for two trumpets) 1983, Anniversary Dances (for centenary of Univ Coll Bangor) 1985, Carnival of Wales 1987, Threnos 1990, Symphony No 3 1991; chamber compositions incl: String Quartet 1970, String Quartet 2 1981, String Quartet 3 1986, Violin Sonata 2 1984, Capriccio for flute and piano 1971, Wind Quintet 1976, Concertino 1977, Zodiac Trio 1977, Clarinet Sonatina 1978; choral and vocal compositions incl: A Vision of Time and Eternity (for contralto and piano) 1972, This Worlde's Joie 1974, Ceremony after a Fire Raid 1975, The Fields of Praise (for tenor and piano) 1977, A Royal Garland 1977, Shakespeare Songs 1980, Songs of William Blake (for mezzo-soprano and orchestra) 1980, Rex Gloriae (four Latin motets) 1981, Lux Aeterna 1982, The Echoing Green 1985, O Aula Nobilis (for opening of orangery at Westonbirt Sch by TRH Prince and Princess of Wales) 1985, Veni Sancte Spiritus (Hereford Three Choirs Festival) 1985, Gogoneddawg Arglwydd (for Nat Youth Choir of Wales) 1985, Jonah (A Musical Morality) 1988, Learsongs 1989, World's Fire 1989; numerous organ compositions; anthems and church music incl: O Sing unto the Lord 1965, Make a Joyful Noise 1965, Missa Brevis 1974, Arise Shine 1978, Let the People Praise Thee O God (anthem composed for the wedding of the Prince and Princess of Wales) 1981, Missa Aedis Christi-in memoriam William Walton 1984, Salve Regina 1986, As Truly as God is our Father 1987; opera: The Servants (libretto by Iris Murdoch) 1980; fell Univ Coll of Wales Aberystwyth 1990; Hon DMus Westminster Choir Coll Princeton USA 1987, Bax Soc Prize 1968, John Edwards Meml Award 1982; *Clubs* Athenaeum, Cardiff and Co; *Style*— Prof William Mathias, CBE; Y Graigwen, Cadnant Rd, Menai Bridge, Anglesey, Gwynedd LL59 5NG (☎ 0248 712 392)

MATHIESON, Ian Douglas; s of Robert James Mathieson (d 1958), of Harrow, and Violet Lilian, *née* Jones (d 1981); *b* 1 Oct 1942; *Educ* Harrow Weald GS, Coll of Estate Mgmnt Univ of London (BSc), UCL (DipTP); *m* 19 Aug 1967, Lesley, da of Jack Stanley Glass, of Pinner; 2 s (Mark James b 1973, John Robert b 1977); *Career* chartered surveyor in local govt and private practice until 1973, md Commercial Union Properties Ltd 1984- (property investmt mangr 1974-80, dir 1980-), dep md Commercial Union Asset Mgmnt Ltd 1987-; memb Wycombe Dist Health Authy 1983-; memb Teesside Devt Corp 1990-; Freedom City of London 1986; ARICS 1967, FRICS 1975; *Clubs* RAC, Overseas League; *Style*— Ian Mathieson, Esq; Schomberg Ho, 80-82 Pall Mall, London SW1Y 5HF (☎ 071 283 7500, ext 3558, fax 071 930 3844)

MATHIESON, Jeffery George; OBE (1988); s of Walter Douglas Mathieson, OBE, MC (d 1983), of Middleton Thatch, Freshwater, IOW, and Florence Winifred, *née* Burley (d 1988); *b* 17 Feb 1925; *Educ* Whitgift Sch Croydon; *m* 16 Sept 1961, Patricia (d 1988), da of Fredrick Murton Faers (d 1975); 2 da (Jacqueline b 31 May 1963, Ann b 12 Sept 1966); *Career* RAF 1943-47, navigator/wireless operator (Air Crew); asst valuer Corporation of Birmingham 1952-54, asst estates offr Basildon Development Corporation 1954-59; Corporation of London: asst estates offr 1959-63, princ asst estates offr 1963-79, dep city surveyor 1979-90; conslt St Quintin Chartered Surveyors London 1990-; Freeman City of London 1970, Liveryman Worshipful Co of Chartered Surveyors 1982; FRICS 1976; *Recreations* golf, gardening, cooking; *Style*— Jeffery Mathieson, Esq, OBE; 2 Sandown Close, Tunbridge Wells, Kent TN2 4RL (☎ 089282 2839)

MATHIESON, Kenneth Alasdair; s of Ronald Alexander Mathieson, of Salisbury, Wilts, and Sheila Mary Browning, *née* Harris, of E Grafton, Marlborough, Wilts; *b* 22 Sept 1945; *Educ* King Alfred Sch Wantage, Univ of Bath (BSc, BArch); *m* 13 June 1970 (m diss), Rosemary, da of Kenneth Faire, Swindon, Wilts; *Career* founded Mathieson Cox Assocs 1975, left 1984 to concentrate on own property devpts; formed West Hendred Properties 1983; RIBA; *Recreations* food, wine (have own wine bar), photography, travel; *Clubs* Mensa (Oxford branch); *Style*— Kenneth A Mathieson, Esq; 10 High St, Highworth, Wilts (☎ 0793 763025); Silver St, Bourton, Oxfordshire; Calle Alsabini 56, Figurettes, Ibiza, Spain; The Old Pumphouse, Cnwc Y Llo Rd, Builth Wells, Powys

MATHIESON, William Allan Cunningham; CB (1970), CMG (1955), MBE (1945); s of Rev William Miller Mathieson (d 1935), of Scotland, and Elizabeth Cunningham, *née* Reid (d 1957); *b* 22 Feb 1916; *Educ* Dundee HS, Univ of Edinburgh (MA), King's Coll Cambridge; *m* 18 May 1946, Elizabeth Frances, da of Henry Marvell Carr, RA, RP (d 1970), of London; 2 s (Alexander b 1947, Rhoderick Henry b 1951); *Career* RA 1940-45, Maj Europe; Colonial Office 1939-45, asst sec 1949, cnsllr colonial affrs, Br Mission to the UN New York 1951-54, head E Africa Dept Colonial Office 1955-58, min of educn Labour and Lands Govt of Kenya 1958-60, under sec Dept of Tech Co-Operation 1961-64, min of Overseas Devpt 1964, dep sec 1968-75, sr conslt UN Devpt Prog New York 1976-81, memb Exec Bd UNESCO 1968-74; memb Bd of Tstees Int Wheat and Maize Improvement Centre Mexico 1976-86, memb and chm Bd of Tstees Int Serv for Nat Agric Res The Hague 1979-84, memb Governing Cncl Int Centre of Insect Physiology and Ecology Nairobi 1983-89; hon fell African Acad of Sciences 1989; *Recreations* gardening, angling, photography, archaeology, travel; *Style*— William Mathieson, Esq; 13 Sydney House, Woodstock Rd, Bedford Park, London W4 1DP (☎ 081 994 1330)

MATILAL, Prof Bimal Krishna; s of Hara Krisna Matilal (d 1978), of Joynagar-Mazilpur, 24 Parganas, W Bengal, India, and Parimal, *née* Chakrbarti; *b* 1 June 1935; *Educ* Scot Church Coll Calcutta, Univ of Calcutta (BA, MA), Univ of Harvard (AM, PhD); *m* 8 May 1958, Karabi, da of Dr Krishna Kumar Chatterjee (d 1985), of 8-2 Ganesh Banerjee Lane, Calcutta 700031, India; 1 s (Tamal b 18 Feb 1961), 1 da (Anvita b 16 May 1972); *Career* Univ of Toronto Canada: asst prof 1965-67, assoc prof 1967-71, prof of Indian philosophy 1971-76, Spalding prof of eastern religions and ethics and fell All Souls Coll Oxford 1976-; visiting assoc prof Univ of Pa USA 1969-70; visiting prof: Univ of California Berkeley 1979-80, Univ of Chicago 1983-84; fndr ed Journal of Indian Philosophy; memb: American Oriental Soc, APA, ASSR, IABS, RAS; *Books* The Navyanyaya Doctrine of Negation (1965), Logic, Language and Reality (1985, 1990), Perception (1986, 1991), Yukti Niti O Dharma (1987), The Word and The World (1990); *Recreations* gardening; *Style*— Prof Bimal Matilal; All Souls College, Oxford OX1 4AL (☎ 0865 279344, fax 0865 279 378)

MATSON, Malcolm John; s of Gp Capt Jack Norman Matson, of Hinton Wood, Bournemouth, and Wynne Ruth, *née* Parker; *b* 4 Oct 1943; *Educ* Strodes Sch, Trinity Coll of Music, Univ of Nottingham (BA), Harvard (MBA); *m* 13 Sept 1969 (m dis 1988), Judith Helen Welby, da of Arthur Kenneth Colley (d 1986); 2 s (Thomas Daniel Blandford b 5 Feb 1975, Henry Samuel Quarrington b 21 Dec 1977), 1 da (Cecilia Elspeth Adean b 26 Feb 1980); *Career* J Walter Thompson 1966-69, Winston Churchill fell 1969, mgmnt conslt 1972-84, non-exec chm Silverbrands Ltd 1976-, gen comm mangr Westland Helicopters Ltd 1978-81, dir Assoc Helicopter Conslts 1983-, conslt MMG Patricof (venture capital) 1982-84, fndr and chm Nat Telecable Ltd 1984-, memb Cncl PITCOM (Parly Inf Techno Ctee); Freeman City of London 1967, Liveryman and Under Warden Worshipful Co of: Coopers 1967, Glass Sellers 1988; FBIM 1982; *Recreations* music, motor cycling, thinking, walking; *Clubs* Lansdowne; *Style*— Malcolm Matson, Esq; Minster Cottage, Yetminster, Dorset DT9 6LF (☎ 071 490 1348, fax 071 490 0702)

MATSON, Richard Tullis; s of Robert Lancelot Matson (d 1986), of The Twemlows, Whitchurch, Shropshire, and Helen Rosemary, *née* Hanson; *b* 24 Sept 1942; *Educ* Uppingham, Royal Agric Coll Cirencester; *m* 9 May 1964, Petronella Vyvyan Anne, da of Lt-Col RFP Eames, TD (d 1987), of Cotley, Chard, Somerset; 2 s (Edward, Tullis), 1 da (Sarah); *Career* farmer and stud owner; hon treas and vice pres Royal Agric Soc of England, steward and memb Cncl at Light Horse Breeding Soc, govr Harper Adams Agric Coll; *Recreations* hunting, shooting, stalking; *Clubs* Farmer's; *Style*— Richard Matson, Esq; Twemlows Hall, Whitchurch, Shropshire SY13 2EZ (☎ 0948 3239, fax 0948 3239, car 0860 526 768)

MATTHEW, Christopher Charles Forrest; s of Leonard Douglas Matthew (d 1984), of Wells-next-the-Sea, Norfolk, and Doris Janet Matthew (d 1988); *b* 8 May 1939; *Educ* King's Sch Canterbury, St Peter's Coll Oxford (MA); *m* 19 Oct 1979, Wendy Mary, da of Kenneth Henry Whitaker (d 1987), of Tilford House, Tilford, Surrey; 2 s (Nicholas b 1980, William b 1982), 1 step da (Charlotte b 1970); *Career* journalist; columns incl: Punch, Vogue, The Daily Telegraph, The Observer; radio 4: chm Something to Declare, The Travelling Show, presenter Points of Departure, presenter Invaders; publications incl: The Times Travel Guide (ed 1972-74), A Different World: Stories of Great Hotels (1974), Diary of a Somebody (1978), Loosely Engaged (1980), The Long-Haired Boy (1980, adapted for TV as A Perfect Hero), The Crisp Report (1981), Three Men in a Boat (annotated edn with Benny Green 1982), The Junket Man (1983), How to Survive Middle Age (1983), Family Matters (1987); *Recreations* skiing, sailing, walking in the country with a dog; *Clubs* Garrick, Aldeburgh Yacht; *Style*— Christopher Matthew, Esq; 35 Drayton Gardens, London SW10 9RY (☎ 071 373 5946)

MATTHEW, Dr (Henry) Colin Gray; s of Henry Johnson Scott Matthew, and Joyce Mary, *née* McKendrick; *b* 15 Jan 1941; *Educ* Sedbergh, ChCh Oxford (MA, DPhil); *m* 17 Dec 1966, Sue Ann, da of Clarence William Curry, of Indianapolis, USA; 2 s (David Hamish Curry b 26 April 1968, Oliver James Gray b 25 July 1973), 1 da (Lucy Ellyn b 21 Nov 1969); *Career* educn offr (IIA) Tanzanian CS 1963-66, lectr in Gladstone studies ChCh Oxford 1970-76, student of ChCh Oxford 1976-78, fell and tutor in modern history St Hugh's Coll Oxford 1978-; literary dir Royal Historical Soc 1984-89; FRHistS 1973; *Books* The Liberal Imperialists (1973), The Gladstone Diaries, Vols 3-11 (1974-90), Gladstone 1809-1874 (1986); *Recreations* second hand book buying, fishing; *Style*— Dr Colin Matthew; St Hugh's College, Oxford (☎ 0865 274900)

MATTHEW, Philip Gregory; s of William Percival Matthew (d 1956), and Winifred Edith, *née* Wilding; *b* 7 Nov 1940; *Educ* St Dunstan's Coll; *m* (m dis); *Career* articled clerk Cooper & Cooper London 1958-63, qualified CA 1964 (Robert Fletcher prize and Plender prize ICAEW 1961), ptnr Martin & Acock 1974- (joined 1964); former chm S Norfolk Liberal Democrats; FCA (ACA 1964), FCCA 1981; *Recreations* politics , photography; *Clubs* MENSA; *Style*— Philip Matthew, Esq; Martin & Acock, 2 The Close, Norwich, Norfolk NR1 4DJ (☎ 0603 612311, fax 0603 613210)

MATTHEW-WALKER, Robert; s of Samuel Walker (d 1964), of Eltham, and Mary Elizabeth Walker; *b* 23 July 1939; *Educ* St Olaves's GS, Goldsmith's Coll, London Coll of Music, London Coll of Printing; *m* 27 Dec 1969, Lynn Sharon, da of Kenneth Herbert Alfred Andrews (d 1981), of Bromley, Kent; 1 s (Paul b 1971); *Career* Nat Serv RASC 1959-62; private composition study with W Darius Milhaud Paris 1962-63, co sec Thom and Cook Ltd 1963-70, head of Classical Dept CBS Records UK 1971-74, dir mktg CBS Records 1974, dir of masterworks Europe CBS 1974-75, head of Classical Dept RCA Records 1975-78, fndr Chandos Records Ltd 1979-80, fndr Phoenix Records 1982-87, ed Music and Musicians Int 1984-88; dir classical music: Filmtrax plc 1986-88, AVM Records (UK) 1988-90, Allied West Entertainments Ltd 1989-; md: Grayways Ltd 1989-, Alfred Lengnick & Co Ltd 1989-; first performances of compositions incl: Sonata for String Orch Tehran Orch 1976, Piano Trio Cardiff Festival 1978, Sinfonia Solemnis RNCM 1981, Sinfonia Magna For Organ Cologne Cathedral 1984, Christ On The Road to Emmaus City of London Festival 1988; prodr of over 120 records, awarded Grand Prix Du Disque of Academie Charles Cros Paris for Sonatas for String Quartet by Brian Ferneyhough 1980; memb: PRS, Critics Circle; *Books* Rachmaninoff - His Life and Times (1980), Muhammad Ali - His Fights In The Ring (1978), Elvis Presley - A Study in Music (1979), Simon and Garfunkel (1984), David Bowie - Theatre of Music (1985), Madonna (1989), Heartbreak Hotel - The Life and Music of Elvis Presley (1989), The Authentic Gershwin (1989), Edvard Grieg (1990), The Keller Column (1990), The Symphonies of Robert Simpson (1990), Rachmaninoff's Piano Music (1991), A Composer and the Gramophone - Alun Hoddinott on Record (1991); *Recreations* history, boxing; *Clubs* National Liberal; *Style*— Robert Matthew-Walker; 1 Exford Road, London SE12 9HD (☎ 081 857 1582); Alfred Lengnick & Co Ltd, 7-8 Greenland Place, London NW1 0AP (☎ 071 267 9736, fax 071 485 5133)

MATTHEWMAN, His Hon Judge; Keith Matthewman; QC (1979); s of Lt Frank Matthewman (d 1976), and Elizabeth, *née* Lang (d 1985); *b* 8 Jan 1936; *Educ* Long

Eaton GS, UCL (LLB); *m* 1962, Jane, da of Thomas Maxwell (d 1957); 1 s; *Career* called to the Bar Middle Temple 1960; commercial asst (Int Div) Rolls Royce Ltd 1961-62; in practice at the Bar 1962-83 (Midland Circuit, later Midland-Oxford Circuit), rec Crown Ct 1979-83, circuit judge Midland and Oxford 1983-; memb: Heanor UDC 1960-63, Ctee of the Cncl of Her Majesty's Circuit Judges 1984-89, Notts Probation Ctee 1986-; *Recreations* gardening, reading; *Clubs* Beeston Fields Golf; *Style—* His Hon Judge Matthewman, QC; Nottingham Crown Ct, Nottingham

MATTHEWS, Dr Aubrey Royston; s of Douglas Royston Matthews and Phyllis Mary Matthews; *b* 14 Nov 1931; *Educ* Queen Elizabeth's Hosp Bristol, Univ of Bristol; *m* 1960, Hazel, *née* Ellis; 3 children; *Career* Shell International Petroleum Ltd: Venezuela 1958-62, Trinidad 1962-66, USA 1967-68, UK 1968-73, Netherlands 1973-74; dir Dr Colin Phipps & Partners Ltd (conslts) 1974-79, tech dir Clyde Petroleum plc 1979-; *Recreations* opera, cricket, theatre; *Clubs* Reform, MCC; *Style—* Dr Aubrey Matthews; Folly End, Cook's Folly Rd, Sneyd Park, Bristol (☎ 0272 683282); Clyde Petroleum plc, Coddington Ct, Coddington, Ledbury, Herefordshire HR8 1JL (☎ 053 186 811, telex 35320)

MATTHEWS, Dr Colin Herbert; s of Herbert Henry Matthews (d 1975), of London, and Elsie Lilian; *b* 13 Feb 1946; *Educ* Univ of Nottingham (BA, MPhil), Univ of Sussex (DPhil); *m* 29 Oct 1977, Belinda Mary, da of Maj-Gen R E Lloyd, CB, CBE, DSO, of Lymington; 1 s (Daniel b 1978), 2 da (Jessica b 1972, Lucy b 1980); *Career* lectr Univ of Sussex 1971-72 and 1976-77; more than sixty compositions since 1968 incl: orchestral Fourth Sonata (1974), Night Music (1977), Landscape (1981), Cello Concerto (1984), Monody (1987), Cortége (1989); received S Nat Orchestra Ian Whyte award 1975 and Park Lane Gp Composer award 1983; dir Holst Estate and Fndn 1973-, memb Cncl and Exec Soc for Promotion of New Music 1981-, tstee Britten Pears Fndn and dep chm Britten estate 1983-, memb Exec Cncl Aldeburgh Fndn 1984-, patron Musicians against Nuclear Arms 1986-; *Style—* Dr Colin Matthews; c/o Faber Music Ltd, 3 Queen Square, London WC1N 3AU (☎ 071 278 7436, fax 071 278 3817, telex 299633 FABER G)

MATTHEWS, Col Denis Holman; s of Ben Matthews (d 1970), of Dorset, and Susan, *née* Holman (d 1983); *b* 18 May 1922; *Educ* Downside, Univ of London, London Hosp (MRCS, LRCP); *m* 4 April 1961, Ann Margaret, da of Capt Maurice Symington, OBE (d 1975), of Oporto; 1 s (Mark b 1962), 2 da (Emma b 1963, Georgina (twin) b 1963); *Career* Capt Rifle Bde 1942-46, regular cmmn Royal Horse Guards (The Blues), Sugn Maj RMO Royal Horse Guards and Household Cavalry Regt 1957-65, Lt Col RAMC DADMS Southern Cmd 1965-67; ADMS: M East Cmd 1967, Home Co's Dist 1968; CO: 15 Fd Ambulance 1969-71, Catterick Mil Hosp 1971-74; Col ADMS London Dist and HQ Household Div 1974-77, ret 1977; Capt of Invalids Royal Hosp Chelsea 1985; Confrater Abbey of St Gregory the Great Downside 1939; *Style—* Col Denis Matthews; Stud House, Pimperne, Nr Blandford, Forum, Dorset (☎ 0258 453415)

MATTHEWS, Dr Geoffrey Vernon Townsend; OBE (1986); s of Geoffrey Tom Matthews (d 1943), of Northwood, Middx, and Muriel Ivy Matthews (d 1984); *b* 16 June 1923; *Educ* Bedford Sch, Christ's Coll Cambridge (MA, PhD); *m* 1, 6 July 1946 (m dis 1961), Josephine, da of Col Alured Charles Lowther O'Shea Bilderbeck, of Bexhill-on-Sea; 1 s (Vincent Anthony b 1951), 1 da (Rosalind Josephine b 1953); m 2, 2 Jan 1964 (m dis 1978), Janet, da of William Kear, of Sevenoaks; m 3, 26 Jan 1980, Mary Elizabeth, da of William Evans, of Vancouver; 1 s (Alexander William Geoffrey b 1983), 1 da (Catriona Elizabeth b 1981); *Career* Flt Lt and Sci Offr RAFVR 1943-46, serv operational res sections (Bomber Cmd, SE Asia Cmd, Air Miny); dep dir and dir of res and conservation Wildfowl Tst Slimbridge 1955-88, special lectr Univ of Bristol 1956-88, hon professorial fell Univ Coll Cardiff 1970-90, dir Int Waterfowl Res Bureau 1969-88, author of numerous papers on bird migration/orientation and wetland and waterfowl conservation; vice pres Br Ornithologists Union 1972-74 (union medal 1980), pres Assoc for the Study of Animal Behaviour; memb: Advsy Ctee on Birds Nature Conservancy Cncl, Anglo-Soviet Environmental Protection Agreement, Severn Barrage Ctee Dept of Energy 1978-81; chm Environmental Advsy Panel Severn Tidal Power Gp 1987-89, memb many other ctees; corr fell: American Ornithologists Union 1969, Swiss Soc for Bird Study 1975; RSPB medal 1990; FIBiol; Officier De Orde Van De Gouden Ark (Netherlands, 1987); *Books* Bird Navigation (1955, 2 ed 1968), also author of chapters in a number of multi-authored books; *Recreations* listening to music, collecting bird stamps, collecting fossils, DIY; *Clubs* Victory; *Style—* Dr Geoffrey Matthews, OBE; Uplands, 32 Tetbury St, Minchinhampton, Stroud, Glos GL6 9JH (☎ 0453 884 769)

MATTHEWS, Jeffery Edward; s of Henry Edward Matthews (d 1960), and Sybil Frances, *née* Cooke (d 1951); *b* 3 April 1928; *Educ* Alleyn's, Brixton Sch of Building (NDD); *m* 12 Sept 1953, (Sylvia Lilian) Christine, da of Cecil Herbert William Hoar (d 1974), 1 s (Rory b 1956), 1 da (Sarah Jane b 1958); *Career* graphic designer J Edward Sander 1949-52, pt/t tutor 1952-55, lettering and calligraphy assessor SIAD 1970-; designs for the PO: decimal 'To Pay' labels 1971, font of numerals for definitive stamps 1981, new range of colours for stamps 1987; stamps: United Nations 1965, British Bridges 1968, definitives for Scotland, Wales, NI and IOM 1971, Royal Silver Wedding 1972, 25th Anniversary of the Coronation 1978, London 1980, 80th Birthday of the Queen Mother 1980, Christmas 1980, Wedding of Prince Charles and Lady Diana Spencer 1981, Quincentenary of the College of Arms 1984, 60th Birthday of the Queen 1986, Wedding of Prince Andrew and Sarah Ferguson 1986, Order of the Thistle Tercentenary of Revival 1987, 150th Anniversary of The Penny Black 1990; also: first day covers, postmarks, presentation packs, souvenir books and posters; designer of film Picture to Post 1969; other work includes: title banner lettering and coat of arms Sunday Times 1968, cover design and lettering for official programme Royal Wedding 1981, The Royal Mint commemorative medal Order of the Thistle 1987, official heraldry and symbols HMSO, hand-drawn lettering COI, calligraphy, packaging, promotion and book binding designs, logotypes, brand images and hand-drawn lettering; for various firms incl: Unicover Corp USA, Harrison & Sons Ltd, Metal Box Co, DRG, Reader's Digest Association Ltd, Encyclopaedia Britannica International Ltd, ICI, H R Higgins (Coffee-Man) Ltd; work exhibited in A History of Bookplates in Britain and at V & A Museum 1979; Citizen & Goldsmith of London (Freedom by Patrimony) 1949; FCSD 1978, FRSA 1987, AIBD 1951; *Books* Designers In Britain (contrib 1964, 1971), 45 Wood-Engravers (contrib, 1982), Royal Mail Year Book (contrib, 1984, 1986, 1987); *Recreations* furniture restoration, playing the guitar, gardening, DIY; *Style—* Jeffery Matthews, Esq

MATTHEWS, Prof John; CBE (1990); s of John Frederick Matthews (d 1973), of Aylesbury, Bucks, and Catherine Edith, *née* Terry (d 1979); *b* 4 July 1930; *Educ* Royal Latin Sch Buckingham; *m* 20 Feb 1982, Edna Agnes Luckhurst, da of Charles Ernest Stratton, of Southwark, London; 2 da (Jane Katherine b 1956, Shirley Rose b 1959); *Career* scientific offr GEC Res Laboratories 1951-59; Nat Inst of Agric Engrg 1959-84: head of Tractor and Cultivation Dept 1967-82, asst dir of mktg 1982-84; dir AFRC Inst of Engrg Res 1984-90; former pres Inst of Agric Engrs; chm Governing Body Luton Coll of Higher Education 1989-; FInstP, FIAgrE, FEngS, FRAgS, memb ASAE, CEng 1980, CPhys 1984; Eur Ing; *Clubs* Lions International; *Style—* Eur Ing Prof John Matthews, CBE; Church Cottage, Tilsworth, Leighton Buzzard, Beds LU7 9PN (☎ 0525 210204)

MATTHEWS, Prof John Burr Lumley (Jack); s of Dr John Lumley Matthews (d 1971), of Leamington Spa, and Susan Agnes, *née* Burr (d 1990); *b* 23 April 1935; *Educ* Warwick Sch, St John's Coll Oxford (MA, BSc, DPhil); *m* 28 July 1962, Jane Rosemary, da of Eric Goldsmith (d 1946); 1 s (Roderic John b 1964), 2 da (Susan Jane b 1966, Eleanor Mary b 1971); *Career* Nat Serv 15/19 King's Royal Hussars 1953-55 (served Germany and Malaya); sr scientific offr Oceanographic Laboratory Edinburgh 1964-67, visiting prof Univ of Br Columbia 1977-78, prof of marine biology Univ of Bergen Norway 1978-84 (sr lectr 1967-78), dir and sec Scottish Marine Biological Assoc 1988- (dep dir 1984-88), dir Dunstaffnage Marine Laboratory NERC 1989-; memb Ctee for Scotland Nature Conservancy Cncl 1989-90 (memb Bd SW Region 1991-), tstee Int Sch Bergen; FRSE 1988, FRSA 1989; *Books* Freshwater on the Sea (jt ed), author of numerous scientific articles in professional jls; *Recreations* gardening, country winemaking; *Style—* Prof Jack Matthews, FRSE; Grianaig, Rockfield Rd, Oban, Argyll PA34 5DH (☎ 0631 62734); Dunstaffnage Marine Laboratory, PO Box 3, Oban, Argyll PA34 4AD (☎ 0631 62244, fax 0631 65518)

MATTHEWS, Dr John Chester; s of Leonard Matthews (d 1967), and Olive Madeline, *née* Chester (d 1969); *b* 1 May 1920; *Educ* Gresham's Sch Holt, Guy's Hosp London (LMSSA, LDS); *m* 28 Feb 1954, Ann Barbara, da of John Dudley Paine Hunt, of The Cottage, Knowsley Way, Hildenboroygh, Kent; 2 s (Richard Chester b 1957, Peter John Gunn b 1958), 1 da (Susan Ann b 1956); *Career* Guy's Hosp London: med 1939-45, dental surgery 1950-53; SMO Princess Alice Meml Hosp Eastbourne 1945, naval surgn MN 1945-50, asst dental surgn Chichester and Wimpole St London, princ dental surgn Bath and Somerset 1954-75; graphologist 1982-; MRCS 1945, LRCP 1945, LDSRCS 1953; *Recreations* classical music, graphological analysis, laughing; *Clubs* Br Med Assoc, Br Inst of Graphology; *Style—* Dr John Matthews; Bell Cottage, 20 Bell St, Shaftesbury, Dorset SP7 8AE (☎ 0747 51668)

MATTHEWS, Dr John Duncan; CVO (1989); s of Joseph Keith Matthews (d 1956), of Grayrigg, Tyrells Wood, Surrey, and Ethel, *née* Chambers (d 1978); *b* 19 Sept 1921; *Educ* Shrewsbury, Univ of Cambridge (BA), Univ of Edinburgh (MB ChB); *m* 12 Oct 1945, Constance Margaret, da of Dr James Moffat (d 1975), of Glendevon, West Cornforth, Co Durham; 2 s (Graeme b 1948, Christopher b 1952); *Career* RAMC: 1946-48, TA 1951-62, Col TARO; conslt physician Royal Infirmary Edinburgh 1956-86, hon sr lectr Univ of Edinburgh 1956-86, private practice 1956-88, CMO Scottish Provident Inst 1970-88, vice pres RCPEd 1982-85; chm and memb various NHS and BMA ctees, played cricket for Scotland 1951-58; Holyroodhouse: High Constable 1961-, Moderator of High Constables and Guard of Hon 1987-89; FRCPE; *Recreations* fishing, erstwhile cricket, golf; *Clubs* Edinburgh Medical Angling, Grange Cricket, Luffness Golf; *Style—* Dr John Matthews, CVO; 3 Succoth Gardens, Edinburgh EH12 6BR (☎ 031 337 2636)

MATTHEWS, John Waylett; s of Lt Percy Victor Matthews (d 1970), and Phyllis Edith, *née* Waylett; *b* 22 Sept 1944; *Educ* Forest Sch; *m* 27 May 1972, Lesley Marjorie, da of Alastair Herbert Menzies Halliday; 2 s (Jonathan b 1975, Edward b 1977), 1 da (Anna b 1981); *Career* Dixon Wilson & Co 1962-69, N M Rothschild and Sons 1969-71, dir Co Natwest Ltd 1971-, non-exec dir Perry Gp plc 1979-, dep chm and dep chief exec offr Beazer plc 1982-; FCA; *Recreations* golf, squash, hockey, tennis, bridge; *Clubs* Crail Golf, Chigwell Golf; *Style—* John Matthews, Esq; 52 Ollards Grove, Loughton, Essex (☎ 081 508 9060); Beazer plc, City Tower, Level 8, 40 Basinghall St, London EC2V 5VE (☎ 071 588 6079, fax 071 588 9367)

MATTHEWS, Kenneth Joseph (Ken); MBE; s of Joseph Harold Matthews, (d 1988), of Sutton Coldfield, West Midlands, and Florence, *née* Brain (d 1984); *b* 21 June 1934; *Educ* Moor End Lane Secdy Modern Sch Birmingham; *m* 12 Aug 1962, Sheila Iris, da of Harry James Eyre; 1 s (Ian Kenneth b 10 July 1966); *Career* former international athlete; Royal Sutton Coldfield Walking Club 1955; 10 AAA titles 2 miles and 7 miles; 16 major appearances incl: Gold medal 20 km walk World Walking Championships Lugano 1961 and 1963, Gold medal 20 km walk Euro Championships Belgrade 1962, Gold medal 20 km walk Olympic Games Tokyo 1964 (also competed Rome 1960); records: world 5 mile walk 1960, world 10 mile walk 1964, Br 6 to 15 miles 1964, Br and Cwlth 20 km 1964, Br and Cwlth 1 hour walk 1964, UK 2 hour walk 1964, UK and Cwlth 7 mile walk 1964; *Recreations* cycle time trials; *Style—* Ken Matthews, Esq, MBE

MATTHEWS, Maj-Gen Michael; CB (1984), DL (Hampshire 1991); s of William Matthews (d 1984), of Byways, Chagford, Devon, and Marjorie Hilda Matthews; *b* 22 April 1930; *Educ* Kings Coll Taunton, RMA Sandhurst (psc); *m* 1955, Elspeth Rosemary, da of late Sir John Maclure, 3 Bt, OBE; 2 s (Graeme, James), 2 da (Nichola, Julie); *Career* cmmnd RE 1951; dir Personal Servs (Army) 1980, engr-in-chief (Army) 1983, sec to TA Cncl 1986; memb RCDS, Companion Inst of Civil Engrs, FBIM; *Clubs* Army & Navy, MCC; *Style—* Maj-Gen Michael Matthews, CB, DL; c/o Lloyds Bank, Chagford, Newton Abbot, Devon

MATTHEWS, Michael Gough; s of late Cecil Gough Matthews, and Amelia Eleanor Mary Matthews; *b* 12 July 1931; *Educ* Chigwell Sch, RCM; *Career* pianist; RCM: dir Junior Dept and prof of piano 1972-75, registrar 1975, vice dir 1978-84, dir 1985-; dip of honour and prize Chopin Int Piano Competition 1955, Italian Govt scholarship 1956, Chopin fellowship Warsaw 1959; dir Assoc Bd of the Royal Schs of Music, tstee The Countess of Munster Musical Tst; memb: Governing Ctee Royal Choral Soc, Nat Youth Orchestra, Royal Philharmonic Soc, Mgmnt Bd London Int String Quartet Competition, Exec Ctee Incorporated Soc of Musicians, Music Study Group EEC, Comité d'Honneur Presence de L'Art Paris; vice pres: Royal College of Organists, Nat Youth Choir, Herbert Howells Soc; Hon FLCM 1976, Hon RAM 1979; ARCO, ARCM, FRCM 1972, FRSAMD 1986, Hon GSM, FRSA; *Recreations* gardening; *Clubs* Athenaeum; *Style—* Michael Gough Matthews, Esq; c/o RCM, Prince Consort Rd, London SW7 2BS

MATTHEWS, Neil Howard; s of Howard Matthews, and Gwyneth Thompson, *née* Davies; *b* 2 Aug 1948; *Educ* Duffryn GS, Port Talbot Welsh Sch of Architecture Cardiff (BSc, BArch); *m* 29 July 1972, Averil Susan, da of Ronald Abbott (Flt-Offr RAF), of 132 Bolgoed Rd, Pontardulais, W Glam; 1 da (Lydia Dee Matthews b 1978), 1 s (Jack Timothy Rhys Matthews b 1986); *Career* architect and developer; princ Neil H Matthews Assoc; md: ASA Project Management Ltd 1983, Jabbeam Ltd 1985, Mitre UNK Ltd 1985-, Holwell Property Co 1986, Rhodethorn Developments Ltd, Croftstone Ltd 1987; played rugby: Bridgend, Glam Wanderers, Llanelli; Aberawn 11/21 swimmer of the year BLDSA (selected GB team Scheld Holland School championships), Wales 11/21 water polo team 1967, John Williams prizwinner WSA 1972; RIBA; *Recreations* squash, swimming; *Style—* Neil Matthews, Esq; Frongelli House, Llanedi, Pontarducais SA4 1YR (☎ 0792 883251); 2 Station Rd, Pontarducais

MATTHEWS, Sir Peter Alec; Hon AO (1980); s of Maj Alec Matthews; *b* 21 Sept 1922; *Educ* Vancouver, Oundle; *m* 1946, Sheila Bunting; 4 s, 1 da; *Career* serv WWII, Maj RE; dir: Vickers Australia 1971-, Lloyds Bank 1974-, Br Electric Traction 1976-, Sun Alliance & London Insur 1979-, Lloyds and Scottish 1983-; chm: Lloyds Bank (Central London Regional Bd) 1978-, Pegler-Hattersley 1979 (dir 1977-), Engrg Industs Cncl 1980-, Vickers 1980-84 (md 1970-79); pres Engrg Employers' Fedn 1982-84; memb IOD; hon fell Univ Coll London 1982; FBIM, FRSA; kt 1975; *Style—*

Sir Peter Matthews, AO; Ladycross House, Dormansland, Surrey RH7 6NP (☎ 034287 650)

MATTHEWS, Sir Peter Jack; CVO (1978), OBE (1974), QPM (1970), DL (Surrey 1981); s of Thomas Matthews; *b* 25 Dec 1917; *Educ* Blackridge Public Sch W Lothian; *m* 1944, Margaret, da of Cecil Levett; 1 s; *Career* WWII, Flt Lt and pilot RAF; with Met Police 1937-65 (seconded to Cyprus 1955), chief constable Surrey 1968-82 (E Suffolk 1965-67, Suffolk 1967-68); chm Home Office Standing Ctee on Police Dogs 1978-; int pres Int Police Assoc 1966-70 (Br pres 1964-70), pres Assoc of Chief Police Offrs (Eng and Wales) 1976 (seconded to Royal Hong Kong Police 1981), i/c Br Study Team in Singapore 1982; lectures of major incident procedures given to police forces: Royal Hong Kong, Singapore, Royal Bahamas, Canada, USA; also lectured to: BMA, BASICS, Airline Trg Assocs, International Military Services Ltd; specialist advsr Def Select Ctee House of Commons 1983-; ACPO rep of Interpol 1977-80; hon memb BASICS; CBIM; kt 1981; *Clubs* RAF; *Style*— Sir Peter Matthews, CVO, OBE, QPM, DL

MATTHEWS, Peter Jeffrey; s of Arthur Robert Matthews (d 1977), of Wembley, Middlesex, and Rosina Louise, *née* Saulez (d 1984); *b* 29 July 1942; *Educ* Ealing Tech Coll, Ealing Sch of Art (DipAD); *m* 2 April 1977, Caroline, da of Maj John Harvey Moore, OBE, ISO, of Kemp Town, Brighton, Sussex; 1 s (Ross b 1978), 1 da (Chloë b 1980); *Career* craftsman demonstrator RCA 1962-65, sr lectr Wimbledon Sch of Art 1966-; exhibitions: RWS Gallery London 1961, British Printmakers in the 60s touring USA 1966, Galerie Unicorn Copenhagen 1978, Ljubljana Print Biennale 1985, British Prints State Publishing Gallery Moscow 1989, Int Print Biennale Varna Bulgaria 1989; public collections: V and A Museum London, Bibliotheque Royale Brussels, Br Cncl, Albertina Museum Vienna; fell Royal Soc of Painter-Etchers 1985; *Clubs* Royal Soc of Painter-Etchers; *Style*— Peter Matthews, Esq; 1 Manor Road, London SW20 9AE; Beinn Griam, Stathy, By Thurso, Caithness; Wimbledon School of Art, Merton Hall Rd, Wimbledon, London SW19 (☎ 081 540 0231)

MATTHEWS, Richard Bonnar; CBE (1971), QPM (1965); s of Charles Richard Matthews (d 1960), of Dudley House, Marine Parade, Worthing, and Beatrice Alexandra, *née* Bonnar (d 1975); *b* 18 Dec 1915; *Educ* Stowe; *m* 1 Jan 1943, Joan Emily, da of Basil Worsley (d 1978), of The Pound, Henstridge, Somerset; 2 da (Miranda b 22 Jan 1944, Rosemary b 23 Dec 1946); *Career* WWII serv Lt RNVR 1939-45; Met Police 1936-, asst chief constable E Sussex 1954-56; chief constable: Cornwall and Isles of Scilly 1956-64, Warwickshire 1964-76; chm Traffic Ctee Assoc of Chief Police Offrs 1973-76, memb Williams Ctee on obscenity and film censorship 1977-79, chm Bds for Civil Serv cmmn 1979-85; *Recreations* fishing, skiing, gardening; *Clubs* Naval; *Style*— Richard Matthews, Esq, CBE, QPM; Smoke Acre, Great Bedwyn, Marlborough, Wiltshire SN8 3LP (☎ 0672 870 584)

MATTHEWS, Sir Stanley; CBE (1957); s of Jack Matthews; *b* 1 Jan 1915; *Educ* Wellington Sch Hanley; *m* 1, 1935 (m dis 1975), Elizabeth Hall, da of J Vallance; 1 s, 1 da; m 2, 1975, Mila (Gertrud Winterova); *Career* played association football with Stoke City FC 1931-47, Blackpool FC 1947-61 (FA Cup 1953), Stoke City FC 1961-65; gen mangr Port Vale FC 1965-68; played 88 times for England; kt 1965; *Clubs* Nat Sporting; *Style*— Sir Stanley Matthews, CBE; Idle House, Marsaxlokk, Malta (☎ 71068)

MATTHEWS, Baron (Life Peer UK 1980), of Southgate in the London Borough of Enfield; Victor Collin Matthews; s of A and J Matthews; *b* 5 Dec 1919; *Educ* Highbury; *m* 1942, Joyce Geraldine, *née* Pilbeam; 1 s (Hon Ian V); *Career* serv WWII RNVR; chm and chief exec Express Newspapers Ltd 1977-85; gp md Trafalgar House Ltd 1968-77, dep chm 1973-85, gp chief exec 1977-83; chm: Cunard Steam-Ship Co Ltd 1971-83, Cunard Cruise Ships Ltd 1978-83, Cunard Line Ltd 1978-83, Fleet Publishing Int Hldgs Ltd 1978-81, Eastern Int Investmt Tst Ltd 1974-81, The Ritz Hotel (London) Ltd 1976-83; dir: Associated Container Transportation (Aust) Ltd 1972-82, Cunard Crusader World Travel Ltd 1974-85, Racecourse Hldgs Tst Ltd 1977-85, Associated Communications Corpn Ltd 1977-82, Goldquill Ltd 1979-83, Darchart Ltd 1980-83, Garmaine Ltd 1980-83; chm: Ellerman Lines 1983-85; Evening Standard Co Ltd 1980-85, Fleet Hldgs plc 1982-85, Trafalgar House Devpt Hldgs 1970-83; Trafalgar House Constr Hldgs 1977-83; FCIOB, FRSA, CBIM FCIOB, FRSA, CBIM; *Clubs* MCC, RAC; *Style*— The Rt Hon the Lord Matthews; Waverley Farm, Mont Arthur, St Brelade, Jersey, CI

MATTHEWS-MAXWELL, Maj Christopher Ranulph George; TD (1979 and Clasp 1985); 26 Lord of Mounton and Lord of the Manor of Cophill; formerly patron of two livings; s of Lt-Col Alastair Arthur Charles Matthews-Maxwell, 25 Lord of Mounton (d 1958), and Georgina Muriel, *née* Reay (d 1953); *b* 28 June 1945; *Educ* King's Sch, Skerry's Coll, Newcastle Poly; *m* 1983, Bronwen Nicola Grendon, *née* Grendon-Jones (late Maj QARANC); *Career* cmmnd Royal Northumberland Fusiliers 1967, transferred to T&AVR 1970, Maj 1980, HAC 1981; chartered sec and farmer, owner of Mounton and Cophill Estates, chm S Northumberland Area YFC 1970-71; memb: Centre for Mgmnt in Agric, BIM Management Group North, Northern MBA Working Gp 1986-88; govr RNLI, memb Serv Ctee Northumberland Health and Family Health Service Authys; memb: Northumberland Regnl Ctee for Employment of Disabled Persons, Sr Med Appts Ctee Northern RHA, Occupational Pensions Advsy Serv; Hospitaller Order of St John of Jerusalem 1983; Freeman City of London, Liveryman Worshipful Co of Meadmakers; FCIS, CDipAF, DipMM, MIPM, MBIM, FRSA; *Recreations* hunting, shooting, skiing, sailing, equestrian sports; *Clubs* Constitutional, Royal Overseas League, Prince Albert Brussels; *Style*— Maj Christopher Matthews-Maxwell, TD; Royal Bank of Scotland, Grey St, Newcastle upon Tyne

MATTISON, John Eric; s of Alfred James Mattison (d 1973), of Lingwood, Norfolk, and Mildred Edith, *née* Temperley (d 1974); *b* 12 Aug 1940; *Educ* City of Norwich Sch, LSE (BSc); *m* March 1964, Margaret Jane, da of Patrick Malervy; 3 s (John Patrick b 17 March 1965, James Gerard b 24 July 1966, Nicholas Frank b 30 Nov 1970); 2 da (Sally Jane b 22 March 1968, Catherine Temperley b 5 Sept 1975); *Career* fin journalist 1962-70: Investors' Chronicle, Evening Standard, Sunday Times; dir: McLeish Associates 1970-80, Lopex Public Relations 1980-85, Hill & Knowlton 1985-88; chief exec Burson-Marsteller Financial 1988-; Freeman Borough of Alnwick Northumberland 1956; *Books* Bluffer's Guide to Finance (1968); *Recreations* golf, sailing; *Style*— John Mattison, Esq; Burson-Marsteller Financial, 24-28 Bloomsbury Way, London WC1A 2PX (☎ 071 831 6262, fax 071 430 1052)

MATTOCK, John Clive; s of Raymond Jack Mattock, of 10 Brownlands Rd, Sidmouth, E Devon, and Eva Winifred Zoë, *née* Ward; *b* 21 Jan 1944; *Educ* Dartford GS; *m* 1985, Susan, da of Richard Clulow, of 97 Upper Mealines, Harlow, Essex; 2 s (Anthony b 1986, Christopher b 1988); *Career* stockbroker, ptnr Fiske and Co 1975-88; dep chm: Carlisle Group plc 1985-90, Peak Tst Ltd 1988, Corporate Services plc 1989; dir: Stalwart Assurance Group plc 1986-89, Takare plc 1986-89; FCA 1967; *Recreations* tennis, country pursuits; *Clubs* Bexley Lawn Tennis (vice pres), Cannons; *Style*— J C Mattock, Esq; Chippens Bank House, Hever, Kent; Mill-enium Publications Ltd, 57 Grosvenor St, London W1 (☎ 071 629 9544)

MATTOCK, Prof John Nicholas; s of Gilbert Arthur James Mattock (d 1970), of Horsham, Sussex, and Margaret Kathleen, *née* Gale; *b* 6 Jan 1938; *Educ* Christ's Hosp, Pembroke Coll Cambridge (BA, MA, PhD); *Career* Drapers res fell Pembroke Coll Cambridge 1963-65, prof of Arabic and Islamic studies Univ of Glasgow 1987- (lectr 1965, sr lectr 1976); pres UEAI 1990-; memb BRISMES (fell 1973); *Books* Arabic Technical and Scientific Texts (6 vols, 1965-78); *Recreations* food and wine, tennis, golf; *Clubs* Royal and Ancient Golf (St Andrews); *Style*— Prof John Mattock; Dept of Arabic and Islamic Studies, University of Glasgow, Glasgow G12 8QQ (☎ 041 339 8855 ext 5586, fax 041 330 4808, telex 777070 UNIGLA)

MAUCHLINE, Lord; Michael Edward Abney-Hastings; assumed by deed poll 1946 surname of Abney-Hastings; s of Countess of Loudoun, *qv*, and (first husb) Capt Walter Strickland Lord; h to Earldom of mother; *b* 22 July 1942; *Educ* Ampleforth; *m* 1969, Noelene, da of W J McCormack; 2 s, (Hon Simon Abney-Hastings b 1974, Marcus William b 1981), 3 da (Hon Amanda Louise b 1969, Hon Lisa b 1971, Hon Rebecca (twin) b 1974); *Heir* s, Hon Simon Abney-Hastings b 1974; *Style*— Lord Mauchline; 74 Coreen St, Jerilderie, NSW 2716, Australia

MAUD, Hon Humphrey John Hamilton; CMG (1982); s of Baron Redcliffe-Maud (Life Peer); *b* 17 April 1934; *Educ* Eton, King's Coll Cambridge, Nuffield Coll Oxford; *m* 1963, Maria Eugenia Gazitua; 3 s; *Career* Nat Serv Coldstream Gds 1953-55; instr in Classics Univ of Minnesota 1958-59; joined FO 1959; served: Madrid 1961-63, Havana 1963-65, FCO 1966-67, seconded to Cabinet Off 1968-69, Paris 1970-74, at Nuffield Coll Oxford studying economics 1974-75, head Financial Rels FCO 1975-79, min Madrid 1979-82, ambass Luxembourg 1982-85, asst under-sec of state (int economic affairs and trade rels) FCO 1985-; *Recreations* music; *Clubs* Utd Oxford and Cambridge Univ; *Style*— The Hon Humphrey Maud, CMG

MAUDE, Hon Charles John Alan; s of Baron Maude of Stratford-upon-Avon (Life Peer); *b* 1951; *Educ* Abingdon, Corpus Christi Coll Cambridge; *Career* writer and designer; *Style*— The Hon Charles Maude; Flat 2, 8 Maresfield Gdns, London NW3 5SU (☎ 071 794 6955)

MAUDE, Hon (Robert) Connan Wyndham Leslie; s and h of 8 Viscount Hawarden; *b* 23 May 1961; *Educ* St Edmund's Sch Canterbury, RAC Cirencester; *Career* farming, including vineyards; *Recreations* shooting, motorcycling, indoor cricket, skiing; *Style*— The Hon Connan Maude; 2 Dene Cotts, Adisham Rd, Wingham, Canterbury, Kent CT3 1NU

MAUDE, Hon Francis Anthony Aylmer; MP (C) N Warwickshire 1983-; s of Baron Maude of Stratford-upon-Avon (Life Peer) and Barbara Elizabeth Earnshaw, *née* Sutcliffe; *b* 4 July 1953; *Educ* Abingdon Sch, Corpus Christi Coll Cambridge (BA); *m* 1984, Christina Jane, yr da of A Peter Hadfield, of Copthorne, Shrewsbury; 1 s (Henry Peter Angus b 10 Sept 1990), 2 da (Julia Elizabeth Barbara b 26 Dec 1986, Cecily Mary Anne b 1988); *Career* barr in chambers of Sir Michael Havers, QC, MP; financial sec to the Treasy 1990-; *Recreations* skiing, cricket, music, opera; *Style*— The Hon Francis Maude, MP; House of Commons, London SW1A 0AA

MAUDE, Hon Henry Cornwallis; yr s of 7 Viscount Hawarden (d 1958), and Marion, *née* Wright (d 1974); *b* 3 March 1928; *Educ* Marlborough, Worcester Coll Oxford (MA); *m* 8 Aug 1964, Elizabeth Georgina, o da of David McNaught Lockie, of Grasse, France; 2 s, 2 da; *Career* schoolmaster, farmer; High Sheriff of Kent 1989-90; *Recreations* swimming, reading, gardening; *Style*— The Hon Henry Maude; Wingham Well House, Wingham, Canterbury, Kent

MAUDE OF STRATFORD-UPON-AVON, Baron (Life Peer UK 1983), of Stratford-upon-Avon, Co Warwicks; Sir Angus Edmund Upton Maude; TD, PC (1979); only child of Col Alan Hamer Maude, CMG, DSO, TD (d 1979), and Dorothy, *née* Upton (d 1960); *b* 8 Sept 1912; *Educ* Rugby, Oriel Coll Oxford (BA 1933, MA 1945); *m* 1946, Barbara Elizabeth Earnshaw, o da of John Sutcliffe; 2 s (Hon Charles John Alan b 1951, Hon Francis Anthony Aylmer b 1953), 2 da (Hon Elizabeth Jane (Hon Mrs Spurrier) b 1946, Hon Deborah Gervaise (Hon Mrs Hayter) b 1948); *Career* serv WWII RASC; author and journalist; fin journalist: The Times 1933-34, Daily Mail 1935-39; MP (C) Ealing S 1950-57 (resigned pty whip in protest over withdrawal from Suez), MP (Ind Cons) 1957-58, fought Dorset by-election 1962, MP (C) Stratford-upon-Avon 1963-83; ed Sydney Morning Herald 1958-61; dir Cons Political Centre 1951-55, chm CRD 1975-79, dep chm Cons Pty 1975-79; *Style*— The Rt Hon the Lord Maude of Stratford-upon-Avon, TD, PC; Old Farm, South Newington, nr Banbury, Oxon (☎ 0295 720464)

MAUDE-ROXBY, Richard Gay; s of John Henry Maude-Roxby; *b* 7 June 1947; *Educ* Dauntseys Sch; *m* 1971, Lynda Helena Marjorie, *née* Sanders; 3 c; *Career* dir: buying and mktg Budgen Limited 1978-82, Budgen Ltd 1982-86, Booker Food Services 1986-89, Booker Cash & Carry 1989-; non-exec dir: Honeysuckle Foods Ltd, Cameron Choat & Ptnrs; *Recreations* shooting, fishing; *Style*— Richard Maude-Roxby, Esq; Charmandean, Green Lane, Prestwood, Great Missenden, Bucks (☎ 024 06 2566)

MAUDSLAY, Hon Mrs (Arabella Bridget Rachel); *née* Jauncey; da of Baron Jauncey of Tullichettle (Life Peer) and his 1 w, Jean, *née* Cunninghame Graham; *b* 14 April 1965; *m* 22 July 1989, James Maudslay, s of Maj Sir Rennie Maudslay, GCVO, KCB, MBE (d 1988); *Style*— The Hon Mrs Maudslay; 84 Muncaster Rd, London SW11 6NU

MAUDSLAY, John Rennie; s of Maj Sir Rennie Maudslay, GCVO, KCB, MBE (d 1988), and Jane Ann, *née* McCarty; *b* 26 May 1953; *Educ* Eton; *m* 12 April 1986, Alexandra, da of Dr William Lothian, of Shoreham, Kent: 2 da (Georgina b 1987, Sophia b 1989); *Career* memb of Lloyd's 1979; ptnr Barder & Marsh 1988; Freeman of City of London, Liveryman of Worshipful Co of Mercers 1980; *Recreations* shooting, fishing; *Clubs* White's; *Style*— John Maudslay, Esq; 3 Orbel St, London SW11 3NX (☎ 071 228 7908); Barder & Marsh, River House, 119-121 Minories, London EC3N 1DR (☎ 071 709 0219)

MAUGHAN, Air Vice-Marshal Charles Gilbert; CB (1976), CBE (1970), AFC (1960); s of Charles Alexander (d 1964), of London, and Magdalene Maria, *née* Tacke (d 1979); *b* 3 March 1923; *Educ* Sir George Monoux GS, Harrow Co Sch; *m* 14 June 1947, Pamela Joyce, da of late Cecil Wicks, of London; 1 s (David b 24 Nov 1953), 1 da (Susan b 12 July 1950); *Career* Fleet Air Arm (Swordfish, Albacore, Seafire) 1942-46, joined RAF 1949, CO 65 Sqdn (Hunter) 1958, Won Daily Mail Air Race London-Paris 1959, CO 9 Sqdn (Vulcan) 1964; Station Cdr: RAF Honnington (Victor) 1964, RAF Waddington (Vulcan) 1965; Gp Capt Opns HQ Bomber Cmd 1967, Air Attache Bonn 1970, AI Admin Strike Cmd 1974, Sr ASO Strike Cmd 1975, ret RAF 1978; gen sec Royal Br Legion 1978-83, inspr on panel of ind insprs DOE and Tport 1983-; tstee Katherine Lady Berkeley Sch; Chevalier Legion d'Honneur France 1960; *Recreations* walking, travel, theatre; *Style*— Air Vice-Marshal Charles Maughan, CB, CBE, AFC; Whitestones, Tresham, Wotton under Edge, Gloucs GL12 7RW (☎ 0666 890272)

MAUGHFLING, David John; s of Frank Rosewarne Maughfling (d 1990), of Cornwall, and Alice Ann, *née* Hooper (d 1957); *b* 25 Sept 1938; *Educ* Truro Cathedral Sch; *m* 16 July 1968, Peggy Elizabeth Frances, da of Harold Hollis (d 1979), of Glos; 1 s (Edward b 1972), 1 da (Morwenna b 1970); *Career* ptnr Little & Co 1966-; FICA 1973 (assoc memb 1963); *Recreations* jazz music, ceramics, genealogy; *Clubs* Cheltenham Graduates, Gloucester Lunch; *Style*— David J Maughfling, Esq; 181 Leckhampton Rd, Cheltenham, Glos GL53 0AD (☎ 0242 513542); Little & Co, 45 Park Rd, Gloucester GL1 1LP (☎ 0452 308966)

MAULEVERER, Peter Bruce; QC (1985); s of Maj Algernon Arthur Mauleverer, of Arncliffe, Springfield Rd, Poole, Dorset (d 1979), and Hazel Mary, *née* Flowers (d 1983); *b* 22 Nov 1946; *Educ* Sherborne, Univ of Durham (BA); *m* 7 Aug 1971, Sara, da of Dr Michael Hudson-Evans, of Yew Tree Place, St Maughans, Monmouth, Gwent; 2 s (Edward b 1972, Barnaby b 1974), 2 da (Harriet b 1977, Clementine b 1982); *Career* called to the Bar Inner Temple 1969, rec Crown Ct 1985; hon sec gen Int Law Assoc 1986; *Recreations* sailing, skiing; *Style*— Bruce Mauleverer, Esq, QC; 4 Pump Ct, Temple EC4Y 7AN (☎ 071 353 2656, fax 071 583 2036)

MAUND, Rt Rev John Arthur Arrowsmith; CBE (1975), MC (1946); s of Arthur Arrowsmith Maun (d 1945), Frenchlands, Lower Broadheath, Worcester, and Dorothy Jane, *née* Armstrong (d 1911); *b* 19 Oct 1909; *Educ* Worcester Cathedral King's Sch, Univ of Leeds (BA); *m* (Catherine) Mary, da of Frederick Joseph Maurice (d 1932), of Laleham, Middx; *Career* chaplain to the Forces, The Kaffrarian Rifles SA 1940-46; asst Parish of All Saints with St Lawrence Evesham 1933-36; asst priest: Parish of All Saints Blackheath 1936-38, Pretoria Native Mission 1939-40; chaplain to the Forces 1940-46; priest i/c St Peter's Lady Selborne Pretoria 1946-50, bishop of Basutoland (now Lesotho) 1950-76, anglican chaplain to Hengrave Community Bury-St-Edmunds 1977-83, chaplain Beauchamp Community Newland and hon asst bishop of Worcester 1983-; *Recreations* horse riding, bridge, gardening, ornithology; *Style*— The Rt Rev John Maund, CBE, MC; Warden's Lodge, The Beauchamp Community, Newland, Malvern, Worcs (☎ 0684 568072)

MAUNDER, Prof Leonard; OBE (1977); s of Thomas George Maunder (d 1975), and Elizabeth Ann Maunder, *née* Long (d 1985); *b* 10 May 1927; *Educ* Bishop Gore GS Swansea, Univ Coll Swansea (BSc), Univ of Edinburgh (PhD), MIT (ScD); *m* 1958, Moira Anne, da of Edwin George Hudson (d 1977); 1 s (David), 1 da (Joanna); *Career* instr and asst prof MIT 1950-54, Aeronautical Res Lab US Air Force 1954-56, lectr Univ of Edinburgh 1956-61; Univ of Newcastle upon Tyne: prof of mech engrg 1967- (prof of applied mechanics 1961), dean of Faculty of Engrg 1973-78; chm: SRC/DTI Working Pty for the Teaching Co Scheme 1981-, SRC Engrg Bd 1976-80, Advsy Cncl on R & D Dept of Energy 1981-; memb: NRDC 1976-81, Cncl Br Technol Gp 1981-; dep chm Newcastle Hosps Mgmnt Ctee 1971-73, memb Newcastle Dist Health Authy; pres: Int Fedn for the Theory of Machines & Mechanisms 1976-79, Engrg Br Assoc for the Advancement of Sci 1980; vice pres Inst of Mech Engrs 1976-81; Christmas lectr Royal Inst 1983; memb Advsy Cncl on Sci Technol 1987-; *Books* Gyrodynamics and its Engineering Applications (with R N Arnold, 1961), Machines in Motion (1986), numerous papers in the fields of applied mechanics; *Style*— Prof Leonard Maunder, OBE; Stephenson Bldg, The Univ of Newcastle upon Tyne NE1 7RU (☎ 0632 2328511, telex 53654)

MAUNDERS, Prof Keith Terrence; s of Roy Keith Maunders, of Newport, Gwent, and Hilda Violet, *née* Brett; *b* 11 Sept 1939; *Educ* Newport High Sch, Univ of Hull (BSc); *m* 26 July 1969, Julie, da of James E Mantle, of Leeds; 2 da (Helen b 1976, Hannah b 1980); *Career* prof of: business fin and accounting Univ of Leeds 1978-89, accounting Univ of Hull 1989-; visiting prof: Univ of Texas 1985, Univ of Sydney 1986, Aust Nat Univ 1989; gen sec Br Accounting Assoc; FCCA; *Books* Accounting Information Disclosure and Collective Bargaining (1977), Corporate Social Reporting (1987); *Recreations* birdwatching; *Style*— Prof Keith Maunders; Dept of Accounting, University of Hull, Hull HU6 7RX (☎ 0482 466391, fax 0482 466377, telex 592530 UNIHUL G)

MAUNDRELL, John William; s of Rev Canon Wolseley David Maundrell, of Stonegate, Wadhurst, East Sussex and Barbara Katharine, *née* Simmons (d 1985); *b* 27 Sept 1955; *Educ* Winchester, Courtauld Inst of Art London (BA); *m* 31 Oct 1987, Hazel, da of Francis Walter Monck; 1 da (Alexandra Katharine b 30 Sept 1989); *Career* articled clerk Deloitte Haskins & Sells 1979-82, qualified chartered accountant 1982, asst dir County Bank Ltd/County Nat West 1986-87 (joined 1982), dir Gilbert Eliott Corporate Finance Ltd 1989-90 (asst dir 1987-89), dir Rea Brothers Limited 1991-; FCA (ACA 1982); *Recreations* mountaineering, squash, swimming, gardening; *Style*— John Maundrell, Esq; Tanglewood, 6 Hall Close, Henham, nr Bishop's Stortford, Hertfordshire CM22 6AU; REA Brothers Limited, Alderman's House, Alderman's Walk, London EC2M 3XR (☎ 071 623 1155, fax 071 623 2694)

MAUNSELL, Michael Brooke; s of Capt Terence Augustus Ker Maunsell, RN (d 1972), of Walton on Thames, Surrey, and Elizabeth, *née* Brooke (d 1974); *b* 29 Jan 1942; *Educ* Monkton Combe Sch, Gonville and Caius Coll Cambridge (MA, LLB); *m* 1, 7 Aug 1965 (m dis 1986), Susan Pamela, da of George Cruickshank Smith (d 1969), of Attenborough, nr Nottingham; m 2, 8 Aug 1986, (Caroline) Harriet, da of Prof Geoffrey Sharman Dawes, CBE, of Oxford; *Career* slr; ptnr: Lovell White & King 1971-88, Lovell White Durrant 1988-; tstee Highgate Cemetary Charity 1988-; Liveryman Worshipful Co of Slrs 1980; memb Law Soc 1967; *Recreations* walking, watching birds, travelling; *Style*— Michael Maunsell, Esq; Lovell White Durrant, 65 Holborn Viaduct, London EC1A 2DY (☎ 071 236 0066, fax 071 248 4212, telex 887122)

MAURICE, Brian Armstead; s of Norman Brocklehurst Maurice, OBE (d 1975), and Dorothy, *née* Armstead (d 1966); *b* 27 July 1928; *Educ* Oundle, Trinity Hall Cambridge (BA, MA, MChir); *m* 13 Sept 1958, Marjorie Anne, da of Ernest Frederick Sammons (d 1985); 2 s (Adrian b 1959, Christopher b 1965), 1 da (Laura b 1961); *Career* Nat Serv Flying Offr MO 2FTS Hullavington 1954, Flt Lt surgn RAF Hosp St Athan 1955; former surgical registrar Warwick Hosp; former sr surgical registrar: St Thomas' Hosp (house surgn, lectr in anatomy, registrar), KCH; conslt surgn Kent and Sussex Hosp Tunbridge Wells; now ret; surgical tutor RCS; memb: Cncl of Hosp Conslts and Specialist Assoc, Registered Homes Tbnl; Freeman: City of London 1955, Worshipful Co of Barbers 1987; Master Worshipful Co of Playing Card Makers 1970 (Freeman 1956); FRCS 1958; *Books* Surgery for General Practioners (1988); *Recreations* golf, bridge, koi keeper; *Clubs* City Livery, Santa Cristina Golf; *Style*— Brian Maurice, Esq

MAURICE, Clare Mary; *née* Rankin; da of Antony Colin Deans Rankin, of Peacock Cottage, Manton, Marlborough, Wiltshire, and Barbara, *née* Vernon; *b* 25 Feb 1954; *Educ* Sherborne Sch for Girls, Univ of Birmingham (LLB); *m* 20 Dec 1980, Ian James Maurice, s of Douglas Creyke Maurice (d 1968); 2 da (Anna b 10 Mar 1987, Kate b 8 Oct 1989); *Career* admitted slr 1978, ptnr Allen & Overy 1985 (articled 1976, asst slr 1978); *Recreations* theatre, travel; *Clubs* Reform; *Style*— Mrs Ian Maurice; 33 Norland Square, London W11 4PU (☎ 071 221 0962); Allen & Overy, 9 Cheapside, London EC2V 6AD (☎ 071 248 9898, fax 071 236 2192)

MAURICE, Hon Mrs (Pamela Mary Violet); JP (Wilts 1951); eldest da of Baron Goddard, GCB (Life Peer, d 1971; Lord Chief Justice of Eng 1946-58), and Marie Linda (d 1928), da of Sir Felix Schuster, 1 Bt; *b* 28 Dec 1907; *Educ* St Paul's; *m* 1934, James Burdett (d 1979), s of Col George Thelwall Kindersley Maurice, CMG, CBE (d 1950, late AMS); 1 s (Martin Thelwall Rayner b 1938), 1 da (Rosanagh Mary Goddard (Mrs Simon Anthony Evans) b 1935); *Style*— The Hon Mrs Maurice, JP; Batt's Farm, Wilton, Marlborough, Wilts SN8 3SS (☎ 0672 870287)

MAURICE, Dr Rita Joy; da of Albert Newton Maurice (d 1944), and Florence Annie, *née* Dean (d 1971); *b* 10 May 1929; *Educ* East Grinstead Co Sch, UCL (BSc, PhD); *Career* lectr in economic statistics UCL 1951-58; statistician then chief statistician Miny of Health and Central Statistical Office 1959-72; head of Econs and Statistics Div DTI 1972-77; dir of statistics Home Office 1977-89; memb Cncl Royal Statistical Soc 1976-82; *Style*— Dr Rita Maurice

MAURICE-WILLIAMS, Robert Stephen; s of Dr Hubert Cecil Maurice-Williams, OBE (d 1981), of Southampton, and Eileen Florence, *née* Lauder; *b* 14 June 1942; *Educ* Winchester, Pembroke Coll Cambridge (BA, MA, MB BChir), St Thomas' Hosp Med Sch; *m* 9 Sept 1968, Elizabeth Anne, da of Dr Swithin Pinder Meadows, of Harley St, London; 1 s (Julian Robert Cecil b 1979), 3 da (Francesca Clare Louise b 1971, Harriet Elizabeth Anne b 1974, Vanessa Christine Alice b 1982); *Career* registrar in neurosurgery Guy's Maudsley Neurosurgical Unit 1971-73, sr registrar in neurosurgery St Bartholomew's Hosp 1973-77, conslt neurosurgn Brook Hosp 1977-80, sr conslt neurosurgn The Royal Free Hosp 1980-; papers on surgery and physiology of the central nervous system; memb Cncl Soc of Br Neurological Surgns, assoc ed British Journal of Neurosurgery, fell Hunterian Soc 1980 FRCS 1971, FRCP 1990 (MRCP 1973); *Books* Spinal Degenerative Disease (1981), Subarachnoid Haemorrhage (1988); *Recreations* walking; *Clubs* The Athenaeum, Pitt (Cambridge); *Style*— Robert Maurice-Williams, Esq; Royal Free Hosp, Regnl Neurosurgical Unit, London NW3 2QG (☎ 071 794 0500 ext 3356/3357); 134 Harley St, London W1N 1AM (☎ 071 935 4698)

MAVOR, Air Marshal Sir Leslie Deane; KCB (1970, CB 1964), AFC (1942), DL (N Yorks 1976); s of William David Mavor (d 1943); *b* 18 Jan 1916; *Educ* Aberdeen GS; *m* 1947, June Lilian, da of Lt-Col Cyril Henry Blackburn (decd); 4 s; *Career* cmmnd RAF 1937, AOC 38 Gp 1964-66, Asst Chief of Air Staff (Policy) 1966-69, AOC-in-C RAF Trg Cmd 1969-72, ret 1973; princ Home Office Home Def Coll 1973-80; co-ordinator of Voluntary Effort in Civil Def 1981-84; FRAeS; *Recreations* shooting, fishing, golf, gliding; *Clubs* RAF, Yorkshire; *Style*— Air Marshal Sir Leslie Mavor, KCB, AFC, DL; Barlaston House, Alne, Yorks (☎ 034 73 412)

MAVOR, Michael Barclay; CVO (1983); s of William Ferrier Mavor, of 10 Greenriggs Ave, Melton Park, Newcastle upon Tyne, and Sheena Watson, *née* Barclay; *b* 29 Jan 1947; *Educ* Loretto, St John's Coll Cambridge (MA); *m* 20 Aug 1970, (Jane) Elizabeth, da of Albert Sucksmith (d 1958), of Lima, Peru; 1 s (Alexander b 31 Oct 1981), 1 da (Veronica b 5 Oct 1977); *Career* Woodrow Wilson fell Northwestern Univ Evanston Illinois USA 1969-72, asst master Tonbridge 1972-78, course tutor for The Open Univ 1974-76; headmaster: Gordonstoun 1979-90, Rugby Sch 1990-; *Recreations* fishing, golf, painting, theatre; *Clubs* Hawks'; *Style*— Michael Mavor, Esq, CVO; Rugby School, Rugby, Warwickshire CV22 5EH (☎ 0788 543465, fax 0788 569124)

MAVROGORDATO, Peter; s of Nicolas Mavrogordato and Nol, *née* Dineen (d 1989); *b* 5 April 1943; *Educ* Elstree, Eton, RAC Cirencester; *m* Hosanna, da of Paul Henry Mills Richey DFC; *Career* chartered surveyor; ptnr Warmingtons 1971-; FRICS; *Recreations* everything; *Clubs* Bucks; *Style*— Peter Mavrogordato, Esq; Pavenham, Bedfordshire (☎ 02302 3661, fax 02302 2625)

MAVROSKOUFIS, Filippos; s of Simeon Mavroskoufis, of Thessaloniki, Greece, and Leontia, *née* Vassilakaki; *b* 15 Aug 1952; *Educ* Thessaloniki HS Greece, Dental Sch Avistotelion Univ of Thessaloniki (DDS), Univ Coll London (MSc, PhD), Univ of Lund Malmö Sweden; *m* 25 May 1985, Janice Gibson, da of John Sailes Clark; 1 s (Simeon b 30 July 1985), 1 da (Antigoni b 15 July 1989); *Career* Univ Coll Hosp: registrar Prosthetics Dept Dental Sch 1977-78, registrar Community Med Dept 1978-79, involved in teaching of prosthetic dentistry and treating of patients Dental Sch 1977-83; in general practice: pt/t 1981-83, full-time 1983-; in Harley St 1988-; presented 3 scientific papers to Dental Confs of Euro Prosthodontic Assoc, published 6 scientifc papers in Dental Journals of Europe and America; memb: Br Soc for study of Prosthetic Dentistry 1977, Euro Prosthodontic Assoc 1977, General Dental Practitioners Assoc 1989, Hellenic Soc of Professional People and Scientists in GB, Hellenic Med Soc in GB; *Recreations* basketball, swimming, stamp collection, cooking, debating; *Clubs* YMCA; *Style*— Dr Filippos Mavroskoufis; 68 Uplands Rd, London N8 9NJ (☎ 081 348 1370); 44 Harley St, London W1N 1AD (☎ 071 255 1492)

MAW, (John) Nicholas; s of Clarence Frederick Maw (d 1967), and Helen, *née* Chambers (d 1950); *b* 5 Nov 1935; *Educ* Wennington Sch Wetherby Yorks, RAM; *m* Nov 1960 (m dis 1975), Karen Graham; 1 s (Adrian Lindsay), 1 da (Natasha Helen von Sternberg); *Career* tutor in composition: RAM 1962-64, Univ of Exeter 1972-74; visiting prof of composition: Yale Univ USA 1984, 1985 and 1989, Boston Univ USA 1986; prof of music Milton Avery Graduate Sch for the Arts Bard Coll USA 1990; Midsummer Prize City of London 1980; memb and ex-chm Assoc of Professional Composers; FRAM 1973; composer of operas, symphonic works, instrumental, chamber and choral music; *Style*— Nicholas Maw, Esq; c/o Faber Music, 3 Queen Square, London WC1N 3AU (☎ 071 278 7436)

MAWBY, Trevor John Charles; s of George Albert Mawby (d 1983), of London, and Kathleen Ellen, *née* Clegg; *b* 19 Feb 1949; *Educ* Eastfield HS, Bristol Poly; *m* 5 Sept 1970, Susan Patricia, da of Eric Tippins (d 1960), of Bath; 2 s (James b 1977, Thomas b 1982); *Career* CA qualified 1971; Walter Lawrence plc: gp fin dir 1980-84, dep md 1984-85, chief exec 1985-; dir Walter Lawrence Properties Ltd; chm: Walter Lawrence Construction Ltd, Walter Lawrence Homes Ltd, Tricom Supplies Ltd, Rock Asphalte Ltd, Nat Flooring Co Ltd, Walter Lawrence Mgmnt Ltd; FCA, CBIM; *Recreations* theatre, golf, reading; *Style*— Trevor Mawby, Esq; 18 Luard Rd, Cambridge CB2 2PJ (☎ 0223 210841); Walter Lawrence plc, Lawrence House, Pishiobury, Sawbridgeworth, Herts CM21 OAF (☎ 0279 725001, fax 0279 725004)

MAWDSLEY, Jack; s of Evan Mawdsley, of Stamford, Lincs, and Ellen, *née* Whitaker (d 1989); *b* 29 Nov 1938; *Educ* Bolton Sch Lancs, Longton HS Stoke-on-Trent, Royal Sch of Mines Univ of London (BSc); *m* 29 July 1961, (Christine) Gillian, da of Alfred Maurice Smith, of Wolverhampton; 1 s (Tristan b 16 May 1966), 1 da (Larret b 20 Feb 1965); *Career* chartered engr, main bd dir Tarmac plc 1987 (regnl dir 1976, md 1985, chief exec 1986); pres Tarmac France SA 1990-; non-exec dir (BR London Midland Bd) 1987-89; chm: Nat Jt Industl Cncl (Roadstone) 1981-86, BACMI Indust Trade Assoc 1988-90; chm Govrs: Thomas Telford Sch 1990-, City Technol Coll 1990-; CEng MIME 1963, FIMM 1965, FIQ 1985; *Recreations* game fishing, golf, opera, walking, bird watching; *Style*— Jack Mawdsley, Esq; Tarmac Quarry Prods Ltd, Millfields Rd, Ettingshall, Wolverhampton WV4 6JP (☎ 0902 353 522, fax 0902 353 980, car tel 0860 350 522, telex 339 825)

MAWHINNEY, Brian Stanley; MP (C) Peterborough 1979-; s of Stanley Mawhinney; *b* 26 July 1940; *Educ* Royal Belfast Academical Inst, Queen's Univ Belfast (BSc), Univ of Michigan (MSc), London Univ (PhD); *m* 1965, Betty Louise Oja; 2 s, 1 da; *Career* asst prof of radiation res Univ of Iowa 1968-70; lectr and sr lectr Royal Free Hosp Sch of Med 1970-84; memb: MRC 1980-83, Gen Synod 1985-90; contested (C) Stockton-on-Tees Oct 1974; PPS to: Min of State Treasury (Barney Hayhoe) 1982-84, Sec of State Employment and NI (Tom King) 1984-86, Parly Under Sec of State 1986-90; min of state N Ireland 1990-; pres Cons Trade Unionists 1987-90; *Style*— Dr Brian Mawhinney, MP; House of Commons, London SW1A 0AA (☎ 071 219 6205)

MAWREY, Richard Brooks; QC (1986); s of Philip Stephen Mawrey, of Benson, Oxon, and Alice Brooks, *née* Blezard; *b* 20 Aug 1942; *Educ* Rossall Sch, Magdalen Coll Oxford (Eldon law scholar, BA, MA), Gray's Inn (Albion Richardson scholar); *m* 18 Sept 1965, Gillian Margaret, da of Francis (d 1985); 1 da (Eleanor Frances b 1977); *Career* barr; called to the Bar Gray's Inn 1964; lectr in law: Magdalen Coll Oxford 1964-65, Trinity Coll Oxford 1965-69; rec Crown Court 1986- (asst rec 1982-86); *Books* Computors and the Law (1988); *Recreations* opera, history, cooking; *Style*—

Richard B Mawrey, Esq, QC; 2 Harcourt Buildings, Temple, London EC4Y 9DB (☎ 071 583 9020, fax 071 583 2686)

MAWSON, David; OBE (1990), JP (Norwich 1972), DL (Norfolk 1986); s of John William Mawson (d 1964), of Keri Keri, NZ, and Evelyn Mary *née* Bond; *b* 30 May 1924; *Educ* Merchant Taylor's Sch Sandy Lodge, Wellington Coll NZ, Auckland Univ NZ, Kingston-upon-Thames Coll of Art; *m* 1951, Margaret Kathlyn, da of Charles Joseph Norton (d 1942), of Norwich, Norfolk; 1 s (Iain), 1 da (Diana); *Career* architect 1953- (to Norwich Cathedral 1977-90), conslt Feilden & Mawson 1990- (ptnr 1956-90); vice pres: Norfolk Soc (CPRE) 1976- (chm 1971-76), Br Assoc of Friends of Museums 1989- (chm 1973-89); chm Friends of Norwich Museums 1985-; fndr pres World Fedn of Friends of Museums 1975-81; pres: Norfolk Club 1986, Norfolk Assoc of Architects 1977-79 (memb 1952-); hon treas Heritage Co-ordination Gp 1980-86, memb Ctee of Nat Heritage 1973-, fndr and chm Norfolk Gardens Tst 1988-; FSA, RIBA; *Recreations* yachting, photography; *Clubs* Norfolk (Norwich); *Style—* David Mawson, Esq, OBE, JP, DL; Gonville Hall, Wymondham, Norfolk NR18 9JG (☎ 0953 602166)

MAWSON, Dr David Charles; s of Richard Mawson, and Alice Margaret, *née* Greenhalgh; *b* 8 April 1947; *Educ* Aldenham, UCH London (MB BS, DPM); *m* 3 Oct 1970, Mina Mawson; 2 s (Benjy b 1971, Ben b 1977), 1 da (Laura b 1980); *Career* conslt forensic psychiatrist Broadmoor Hosp and sr lectr Inst Psychiatry 1981-86; med dir: Moss Side Hosp 1986-89, AMI Stockton Hall 1989-; author of chapters and articles on general and forensic psychiatry; MRCPsych 1976, FRCPsych 1989; *Style—* Dr David Mawson; AMI Stockton Hall Psychiatric Hosp, Stockton-on-The-Forest, Nr York YO3 9UN (☎ 0904 400500, fax 0904 400354)

MAWSON, Desmond Leonard; s of Leonard Mawson (d 1947), and Amelia *née* Huxley (d 1985); *b* 26 Dec 1923; *Educ* Firth Park GS Sheffield, Rotheram Tech Coll; *m* 27 Dec 1944, Eva, da of Henry Boulton (d 1971); 1 da (Lynne b 1949); *Career* WWII navigator RAF (Flt Sgt); serv 1942-46: Europe, Middle E, Burma, India; chm and chief exec Ross Catherall Group plc 1987- (md 1968-85, chm and md 1985-87); main bd dir Vickers plc 1989; memb IOD, MInstP; *Recreations* golf, walking; *Clubs* IOD; *Style—* Desmond L Mawson, Esq; Sherwood, Aughton Lane, Aston, Sheffield (☎ 0742 872201); Ross Catherall Group plc, Forge Lane, Killamarsh, Sheffield (☎ 0742 488882, fax 0742 475999)

MAX, Robert Ian; s of Michael G Max, and Wendy, *née* Segal; *b* 7 Feb 1968; *Educ* St Paul's Sch Barnes, RAM (GRSM, DipRam, LRAM), RNCM (post graduate dip), Julliard Sch New York USA; *Career* cellist; winner: Euro Music for Youth Cello Competition Brussells 1984, Int Young Concert Artists Tst competition (strings section) 1989; recitals and concert performances in UK Germany Austria and Belgium 1984-89; as cellist of Barbican Piano Trio: recording for ASV released March 1988 (subsequently signed long term contract), toured Denmark France Italy USA and UK 1989-90, broadcasts incl BBC Radio 3 and French TV for BBC World Service; former pres RNCM, memb Ctee Music Aid, conductor Hampstead Garden Suburb Youth Music Centre, plays Saveuse Stradivanus Cello of 1726; *Recreations* cooking Indian food, reading, walking, opera, skiing; *Style—* Robert Max, Esq; 5 Asmuns Hill, London NW11 6ES (☎ 081 458 2839)

MAXEY, Peter Malcolm; CMG (1982); *b* 26 Dec 1930; *Educ* Bedford Sch, CCC Cambridge; *m* 1, 1955 (m dis 1978), Joyce Diane Marshall; 2 s, 2 da; m 2, 1978, Christine Irene Spooner; *Career* entered Foreign Serv 1953, seconded to Lazard Bros 1971-72, cnsllr CSCE Delgn Geneva 1973, head UN Dept FCO 1974-77, cnsllr Dublin 1977, loaned to Cabinet Off as under-sec 1978-81, ambass GDR 1981-84, ambass & dep perm rep to UN (New York) 1984-; *Style—* Peter Maxey Esq, CMG; UK Mission to UN, 845 Third Avenue, New York, NY 10022, USA; c/o Foreign and Cwlth Off, London SW1

MAXLOW-TOMLINSON, Paul Christian; s John Maxlow-Tomlinson, and Margot Maude, *née* Muhlenkamp; *b* 24 Oct 1931; *Educ* Cranleigh, Trinity Coll Dublin, Wadham Coll Oxford (MA); *m* 28 June 1969, Anne, da of Charles Trench Stewart; 1 s (Charles Henry b 29 July 1974), 1 da (Claudia Lucy b 6 March 1972); *Career* cmmnd Queens Royal W Surrey Regt 1950-52; Mercantile Credit Co: Zimbabwe 1956-62, London 1962-63, NI 1963-64; admitted slr 1971; sr ptnr Stones (joined 1972); chm Ski Club of GB 1982-87 (memb Cncl 1978-82); memb: Devon Probation Ctee 1983-86, Exec Cncl Br Acad of Forensic Scis 1987-, Legal Ctee Federation Internationale de Ski Berne 1988; fndr memb and chm Oakfields Project (ex-prisoners' hostel in Exeter); memb Law Soc; *Recreations* skiing, shooting, fishing; *Clubs* Ski Club of GB (London); *Style—* Paul Maxlow-Tomlinson, Esq; Stones Slrs, Northernhay Place, Exeter EX4 3QQ (☎ 0392 51501, fax 0392 57007)

MAXMIN, Dr (Hiram) James; s of Henry W Maxmin, of 527 Manor Rd, Elkins Park 17, Penna, USA, and Louise, *née* Strousse (d 1977); *b* 26 Sept 1942; *Educ* Cheltenham HS, Grinnell Coll Iowa (BA), Fitzwilliam Coll Cambridge, Kings Coll London (PhD); *m* 9 July 1968, Dr Jacqueline S Maxmin, da of L P Viden, 3 s (Peter b 29 Nov 1972, Jonathan b 7 June 1977, Ben b 21 April 1983), 1 da (Kate b 3 Feb 1971); *Career* trainee Unilever Ltd 1968-69, Lever Bros 1969-71, dir Unilever Orgn 1971-73, mktg dir Volvo Concessionaires UK 1975-78, jt chm and md Volvo UK 1978-83, dir Thorn EMI plc 1983-, chm and chief exec Thorn Home Electronics 1983-, pres Thorn EMI inc (USA) 1983-; lectr at business coll, fund raiser Fitzwilliam Coll Cambridge, involved in local educn initiatives; SMMT (offr), FIMI 1983, CBIM 1985; *Recreations* rugby, fishing, swimming; *Style—* Dr James Maxmin; 16A Alexander Sq, London SW3 2AX; 110 Marlborough St, Boston, Mass, 02116 (USA); Lake View Farm, Morang Cove Rd, Nobelboro, Damiscrotta, Maine (USA); Thorn EMI plc, 4 Tenterden St, Hanover Sq, London W1R 9AH (☎ 06284 75441, 617 367 0111, fax 06284 75356, 617 267 1407 (OGA)); Thorn-EMI Inc, 38 Newbury St, Boston, Mass 02116

MAXTON, John Alston; MP (Lab) Glasgow, Cathcart 1979-; s of John Maxton, and Jenny Maxton; *b* 5 May 1936; *Educ* Lord Williams' GS Thames, Univ of Oxford; *m* Christine Maxton; 3 s; *Career* joined Lab Pty 1970; oppn spokesman: health, local govt and housing in Scotland 1985-87, Scotland 1987-; memb: Scottish Select Ctee 1981-83, Public Accounts Ctee 1983-84; *Style—* John Maxton, Esq, MP; House of Commons, London SW1

MAXTONE GRAHAM, James Anstruther (Jamie); s of Anthony James Oliphant Maxtone Graham (d 1971), of Cultoquhey, and Joyce Anstruther (d 1953) (author of Mrs Miniver); *b* 10 May 1924; *Educ* Eton, Gordonstoun; *m* 1, 1952 (m dis 1972), Diana Evelyn, da of Thomas Lowe Macgregor (d 1953), of Edinburgh; 2 s (Robert Oliphant b 1955, Anthony James b 1958), 1 da (Mary Alma b 1953); m 2, 1972 (m dis 1976), Diana Irene, *née* Pilcher; *Career* Lt Scots Gds 1942-47; farmed in Perthshire until 1962; freelance writer 1962-78 (mainly sporting subjects for American magazines), proprietor 39 Steps (smallest restaurant in Britain) 1976-80, world's biggest dealer in vintage fishing tackle 1979-; *Books* Eccentric Gamblers (1975), The Best of Hardy's Anglers' Guides (1982), To Catch a Fisherman (1984), Fishing Tackle of Yesterday: A Collector's Guide (1989); *Recreations* fly-fishing, bridge, cooking, travel, collection of vintage fishing tackle; *Style—* Jamie Maxtone Graham, Esq; Lyne Haugh, Lyne Station, Peebles, Scotland EH45 8NP (☎ 07214 304, fax 07214 214, car 0836 246923)

MAXTONE GRAHAM, Robert Mungo; s of Anthony James Oliphant Maxtone Graham (d 1971), of Cultoquhey, Crieff, Perthshire, and Joyce Anstruther (d 1953, 'Jan Struther' author of 'Mrs Miniver'); the Maxtone of Cultoquhey line is traced back to 1410 (see Burke's LG, 18 edn, Vol III, 1972); *b* 6 May 1931; *Educ* USA, Stowe, Trinity Coll Cambridge (MA), Univ of Edinburgh; *m* 1962, Claudia Eva Elizabeth Page-Phillips, da of Frederick Tannert (d 1980), of 238a Southlands Rd, Bickley, Kent; 1 da (Ysenda b 1962), and 1 step da (Livia b 1958); *Career* Nat Serv cmmnd Scots Gds 1949-51 served Malaya; advocate of the Scots Bar 1957, legal assoc Royal Town Planning Inst, town planning conslt, fndr and proprietor Malthouse Arcade Hythe Kent; *Recreations* genealogy, book-collecting, photography; *Style—* Robert Maxtone Graham, Esq; 6 Moat Sole, Sandwich, Kent (☎ 0304 613270); 8 Atholl Crescent Lane, Edinburgh 3 (☎ 031 228 3338); 55 rue des Teinturiers, Avignon, France (☎ 90865292)

MAXWELL, Alastair William; s of William James Maxwell (d 1929), of Kirkcaldy, Scotland, and Mary, *née* Bruce; *b* 30 Sept 1927; *Educ* Geo Watsons Coll Edinburgh, Univ of Edinburgh (MB ChB); *m* 23 April 1960, Celia Margaret, da of Robert Jenkinson (d 1983), of Waverton Hall, Cumbria; 1 s (Simon b 1962), 1 da (Virginia b 1963); *Career* surgn Lt RNVR 1951-53; conslt obstetrician and gynaecologist Nottingham and Newark 1963-; FRCSEd 1957, FRCOG 1972; *Recreations* golf, hill walking, running; *Style—* Alastair Maxwell, Esq; Little Acre, 4 Strathkinnes High Rd, St Andrews, Scotland; 11 Regent St, Nottingham NG1 5BS (☎ 0602 473772); 7 Windmill Rd, St Andrews, Scotland

MAXWELL, Lady Avena Margaret Clare; *née* Stanhope; da of 11 Earl of Harrington; *b* 29 March 1944; *m* 1969, Adrian J Maxwell, s of Maj James Maxwell, of Buckby; 2 da (Sacha b 1974, Kerry b 1978); *Style—* The Lady Avena Maxwell; South Lodge, Carrick-on-Suir, Co Tipperary, Ireland

MAXWELL, (Wellwood George) Charles; s of Maj George Cavendish Maxwell, of Four Acre House, West Green, Hartley Wintney, Hants, and Margaret, *née* Bishop; *b* 27 June 1952; *Educ* Stowe; *m* 15 Sept 1977, Anne, da of Rear Adm Bryan Cecil Durant, CB, DSO, DSC (d 1983); 1 s (George b 4 April 1981), 1 da (Eloise b 18 Nov 1983); *Career* dir: Finsbury Distillery Co 1981 (md 1986), JE Mather & Sons Ltd 1983, Matthew Clark & Sons (Holdings) plc 1988; Freeman City of London 1974, memb Worshipful Co of Distillers 1974; *Recreations* shooting, motor racing, rough gardening, wine, music, stamp collecting; *Clubs* Cavalry Guards, BARC; *Style—* Charles Maxwell, Esq; Squirrels, Kennel Lane, Frensham, Surrey; Matthew Clark & Sons (Hldgs) plc, The Clockhouse, London Rd, Guildford (☎ 0483 34411, fax 0483 303482)

MAXWELL, Cdr (John) David; DL (Co Down 1988), RN; s of Capt Thomas K Maxwell RN (d 1972); *b* 21 June 1929; *m* 1,1954, Georgiana Angela, 27 Baroness de Ros (d 1983); 1 s (28 Baron de Ros, *qv*), 1 da (Hon Diana Maxwell, *qv*); m 2, 1984, Patricia Carolyn Coveney, *née* Ash; *Career* High Sheriff Co Down 1981; *Style—* Cdr David Maxwell, DL, RN; Old Ct, Strangford, Co Down, N Ireland

MAXWELL, Donald; s of Kenneth M MacAlpine, of Perth, Scotland, and Margaret MacAlpine; *b* 12 Dec 1948; *Educ* Perth Acad, Univ of Edinburgh (MA); *Career* baritone; Scottish Opera 1976-82: debut 1977, John Noble bursary, title-role in Barbiere di Siviglia, Sharpless in Madama Butterfly, Enrico in Lucia di Lammermoor, Zurga in Les Pecheurs de Peries, Ipparco in L'Egisto, Shiskov in From the House of the Dead, WNO 1982-85; roles incl: Renato in Un Ballo in Maschera, Shishkov, Marcello in La Boheme, Don Carlos in Ernani, Rigoletto, Iago in Otello, The Count in Le Nozze di Figaro, title-role in Falstaff; freelance 1985-, Royal Opera House debut 1987; performances at Royal Opera House incl: The English Archer in The King Goes Forth to France (Br premiere), The Herald in Lohengrin, Kothner in Die Meistersinger von Nurnberg, Alidoro in La Cenerentola, Gunther in Gӧtterdämerung; ENO: Yeletsky in The Queen of Spades, title-role in Il Barbiere di Siviglia, Wozzeck, Leander in L'Armour des Trois Oranges; Opera North: Riccardo in I Puritani Germont in La Traviata, Escamillo in Carmen, Pizarro in Fidelio, title-role in Der Fliegende Hollander, Scarpia in Tosca; numerous appearances in UK festivals and in foreign operas; regular contribs to radio and tv operas; memb Music Box; recordings incl: Carmina Burana, Kismet, Amahl and The Night Visitors, Bitter Sweet, The Student Prince, Le Nozze di Figaro, Noye's Fludde, The Song of Norway; *Recreations* railways, travel; *Style—* Donald Maxwell, Esq; Music International, 13 Ardilaun Rd, Highbury, London N5 2QR (☎ 071 359 5183, fax 071 226 9792)

MAXWELL, (Charles) James Stuart; s of Charles Chalmers Maxwell, and Mary Stuart, *née* Sheppard; *Educ* Marlborough House Kent, Sherborne; *m* 9 April 1983, Joanna Augustine Lewis, da of H J L Osbourn; 1 s (Charles Thomas Osbourn b 21 April 1987), 1 da (Lucy Stuart Osbourn b 29 Sept 1988); *Career* journalist: Haymarket Publishing Ltd 1975-78, Daily Mail 1978; sr conslt: Comark Europe Brussels 1979-80, Shandwick 1980-82, dir Shale Gornall (SGL) Ltd 1982-83, md Scope: Communications Management 1983-; Scope voted Best Small PR Consultancy in UK (PR Week Awards) 1987 and 1988; Freeman City of London, memb Worshipful Co of Merchant Taylors; memb Devpt Ctee PRCA 1990, MInstD; *Recreations* cricket, tennis, shooting, gun dog training; *Clubs* MCC, Hurlingham; *Style—* James Maxwell, Esq; 16 Caldervale Rd, London SW4 (☎ 071 720 9826); Scope:Communications Management, Tower House, 8-14 Southampton St, London WC2E 7HA (☎ 071 379 3234, fax 071 240 7729)

MAXWELL, John Frederick Michael; s of late Lt Frederic Michael Maxwell (RIN), of Sidcup, Kent, and Mabel Doreen, *née* Turner; *b* 20 May 1943; *Educ* Dover Coll, New Coll Oxford (MA); *m* 1, 1964 (m dis 1986), Jennifer Mary; 1 s (Edward b 1967) 1 da (Alice b 1966); m 2, 1 Sept 1986, Jayne Elizabeth, da of George Douglas Hunter (d 1984), of Birmingham; *Career* called to the Bar Inner Temple 1965, Midland and Oxford Circuit; chm: Johnstone House Tst (Samye Ling Tibetan Centre Eskdalemuir Dumfriesshire, Karma Kagyu Tst, Birmingham Karma Ling Buddhist Centre); tstee Rokpa Tst (aid to Tibetan Refugees); *Recreations* music, yachting; *Clubs* Royal Yachting Assoc, Old Gaffers Assoc, Gravesend Sailing; *Style—* John Maxwell, Esq; Grey Walls, 1131 Warwick Rd, Solihull, W Midlands B91 3HQ (☎ 021 705 2670); 4 Fountain Ct, Steelhouse Lane, Birmingham B4 6DR (☎ 021 236 3476)

MAXWELL, Kevin Francis Herbert; s of (Ian) Robert Maxwell, MC, *qv*, and Elizabeth, *née* Meynard; *b* 20 Feb 1959; *Educ* Marlborough Balliol Coll Oxford (MA); *m* 5 May 1984, Pandora Deborah Karen, da of John Warnford-Davis; 1 s (Edward Robert Meynard b 1986), 3 da (Matilda Anne Zoe b 1984, Eloïse Tamara b 1988, Chloe Genevieve Skye b 1989); *Career* chm Oxford United Football Club 1987-, vice chm MacMillan Inc 1988-, jt md Maxwell Communication Corporation 1988-; tstee New Sch NY; *Recreations* football, water colour painting; *Style—* Kevin Maxwell, Esq; Headington Hill Hall, Oxford OX3 0BU; 8-10 New Fetter Lane, London EC1 (☎ 071 353 0246)

MAXWELL, Sir Michael Eustace George; 9 Bt (Ns 1681), of Monreith, but does not yet appear on the Official Roll of the Baronetage; o s of Maj Eustace Maxwell (d 1971), and Dorothy Vivien (Dodo), *née* Bellville; suc u, Sir Aymer Maxwell, 8 Bt, 1987; *b* 28 Aug 1943; *Educ* Eton, Univ of London; *Heir* unascertained; *Career* chartered surveyor; currently: running Montieth Estate and holiday accomodation, devpt surveyor Eagle Star Properties; ARICS; *Style—* Sir Michael Maxwell, Bt; Monreith House, Port William, Newton Stewart, Scotland DG8 9LB (☎ 098 87 248);

c/o Eagle Star, 22 Arlington St, London SW1 (☎ 071 929 1111); 56 Queensmill Rd, London SW6 (☎ 071 385 6163)

MAXWELL, Hon Lord; Peter Maxwell; s of Cdr Desmond Herries Maxwell, RN, of Munches, Dalbeattie, Kirkcudbrightshire; *b* 21 May 1919; *Educ* Wellington, Balliol Oxford, Edinburgh Univ; *m* 1941, Alison, da of James Readman; 1 s, 2 da (and 1 s decd); *Career* served WWII Capt A & SH & RA Normandy; advocate Scotland 1951, QC 1961, sheriff princ Dumfries & Galloway 1970-73, senator Coll Justice (Lord of Session) 1973-88; chm Scottish Law Cmmn 1982-88; *Style*— The Hon Lord Maxwell; 19 Oswald Rd, Edinburgh EH9 2HE

MAXWELL, Sir Robert Hugh; KBE (1961, OBE 1942); s of William Robert Maxwell; *b* 2 Jan 1906; *m* 1935, Mary Courtney Jewell; 2 s; *Career* Cdr Order of George I of Greece, Order of Merit Syria; *Clubs* Athens; *Style*— Sir Robert Maxwell, KBE; Ct Hay, Charlton Adam, Somerton, Somerset (☎ 045 822 3269)

MAXWELL, (Ian) Robert; MC (1945); s of Michael and Ann Hoch; *b* 10 June 1923; *Educ* self-educated; *m* 1945, Elisabeth, *née* Meynard; 3 s (and 1 s decd), 4 da (and 1 da decd); *Career* serv WWII (MC); in German section FO (head of Press Section Berlin) 1945-47; publisher: Daily Mirror, Daily Record, Sunday Mail, Sunday Mirror, The People, Sporting Life 1984-, Sporting Life Weekender, Maygar Hirlap, Moscow News (english edn); publisher and ed in chief The European 1988-, fndr and publisher Pergamon Press (Oxford, NY and Paris) 1949-; chm: Mirror Gp Newspapers Ltd, Pergamon AGB plc, Maxwell Pergamon Publishing plc, Maxwell Macmillan Pergamon Int Publishing, Mirror Colour Print Ltd (formerly The Br Newspaper Printing Corp plc) 1983-, Br Cable Servs (Rediffusion Cablevision) 1984-, Pergamon Media Tst plc 1986-, MTV Europe 1987-, Maxwell Communication Corp Inc NY 1987-, The Macmillan Fndn 1988-, Berlitz Int Ltd 1988-, Scitex Corp Ltd Israel 1988-, Thomas Cook Travel Inc 1989-, Official Airline Guides Inc 1989-; chm and chief exec: Maxwell Communication Corp plc, Macmillan Inc 1988-; dir: SelecTV plc 1982-, Central TV plc 1983-, The Slrs Law Stationery Soc plc 1985-, Mirrorvision 1985-, Clyde Cablevision Ltd 1985-, Philip Hill Investmt Trust 1986-, Reuters Holdings plc 1986-, TFI 1987-, Maxwell Media Paris 1987-, Maxwell Consumer Publishing and Communications Ltd 1989-, Maxwell Business Communications Group Ltd 1989-; pres State of Israel Bonds (UK) Ltd 1988-; memb Cncl Newspaper Publishers Assoc 1984-; chm: GB-Sasakawa Fndn 1985-, Derby Football Club 1987-, Nat Aids Tst Fundraising Gp 1987-; tstee Int Centre for Child Studies; co-prodr films: Mozart's Don Giovanni (Salzburg Festival) 1954, Bolshoi Ballet 1957, Swan Lake 1968; prodr DODO the Kid from Outer Space (children's TV series) 1968; MP (Lab) Buckingham 1964-70; chm: Lab Nat Fund Raising Fndn 1960-69, Lab Working Party on Science Technol and Indust 1963-64; memb Cncl of Europe 1968 (vice chm Ctee on Science and Technol), contested (Lab) Buckingham 1974 (twice), treas The Round House Tst Ltd (formerly Centre 42) 1965-83; Kennedy fell Harvard Univ 1971, hon memb Acad of Astronautics 1974, memb Club of Rome 1979- (exec dir Br gp); memb: senate Univ of Leeds 1986-, Bd of Tstees Poly Univ of NY 1987-; Hon Dr of Science: Moscow State Univ 1983, Poly Univ of NY 1985; Hon Dr of Law Univ of Aberdeen 1988, fell Imperial Coll London 1988; Dr Honoris Causa: Adama Mickiewicza Univ Poland 1989, L'Universite Du Quebec A Trois-Rivieres 1989; Hon Dr of Laws Temple Univ Philadelphia USA 1989, Hon Dr Bar-Ilan Univ Israel 1989, Hon Dr of Letters Plymouth Univ 1989; Prism award Centre for Graphic Arts Mgmnt and Technol NY Univ 1989, World of Difference award The Anti-Defamation League NY 1989; Royal Swedish Order of the Polar Star (Officer 1st Class) 1983, Bulgarian People's republic Order Stara Planina (1st Class) 1983, Cdr Order of Merit with Star Polish People's Republic 1986, Order of the White Rose of Finland (1st Class) 1988, Officier de L'Ordre des Arts et des Lettres Republique Francaise 1989; *Publications* The Economics of Nuclear Power (1965), Public Sector Purchasing (1968), Man Alive (jt author, 1968), Leaders of the World Series (gen ed, 1980-); *Recreations* chess, football; *Style*— Robert Maxwell, Esq, MC; Holborn Circus, London EC1A 1DQ (☎ 071 353 0246); Headington Hill Hall, Oxford OX3 0BB (☎ 0865 794141); 866 Third Avenue, New York, NY 10022 (☎ 212 702 2000)

MAXWELL, Dr Robert James; JP (1971); s of Dr George Barton Maxwell, MC (d 1972), and Cathleen Maxwell, *née* Blackburn; *b* 26 June 1934; *Educ* Leighton Park Sch Reading, New Coll Oxford (BA, MA), Univ of Pennsylvania (MA), LSE (PhD); *m* 1960, Jane, da of Geoffrey FitzGibbon, JP, of Dursley Gloucestershire; 3 s (Patrick, Benedict, Geoffrey), 2 da (Catherine, Favell); *Career* Lt Cameronians (Scot Rifles) 1952-54; asst mangr Union Corp 1958-66, princ McKinsey and Co 1966-75, admin Special Tstees for St Thomas' Hosp London 1975-80, sec King Edward's Hosp Fund for London 1980-, chm Leighton Park Sch Reading; govr Nat Inst of Social Work, London Sch of Hygiene and Tropical Medicine (chm of the Ct), United Med and Dental Sch, Florence Nightingale Museum Tst (vice chm); *Recreations* walking, poetry; *Clubs* Brooks's; *Style*— Dr Robert Maxwell, JP; Pitt Court Manor, N Nibley, Dursley, Glos (☎ 0453 542942); 14 Palace Ct, London W2 4HT (☎ 071 727 0581)

MAXWELL, Hon Simon Kenlis; s of Lt-Col Hon Somerset Arthur Maxwell, MP (d of wounds 1942); *b* 12 Dec 1933; *Educ* Eton; *m* 1964, Karol Anne, da of Maj-Gen G E Prior-Palmer, CB, DSO; 2 s, 1 da; granted 1959, title, rank and precedence of a Baron's s which would have been his had his father survived to succeed to Barony of Farnham; *Style*— The Hon Simon Maxwell; The Dower House, Westcote, Kingham, Oxon

MAXWELL DAVIES, Sir Peter; CBE (1981); s of Thomas Maxwell Davies and Hilda Maxwell Davies; *b* 8 Sept 1934; *Educ* Leigh GS, Univ of Manchester (MusB 1956), Royal Manchester Coll of Music; *Career* composer; studied with Goffredo Petrassi in Rome 1957, dir of music Cirencester GS 1959-62, fndr and co-dir (with Harrison Birtwistle) The Pierrot Players 1967-70, fndr and artistic dir Fires of London 1971-87, fndr and dir St Magnus Festival Orkney Islands 1977, dir of music Dartington Hall Summer Sch of Music 1980-85; pres School's Music Assoc 1983; *Works include* operas: Taverner (1970), The Martyrdom of St Magnus (1976), The Two Fiddlers (1978, opera for children), The Lighthouse (1979), chamber opera), Cinderella (1980, opera for children); two ballets incl Salome; four orchestral symphonies; FRNCM 1978, Hon RAM 1978; Hon DMus Edinburgh 1979, Manchester 1983, Bristol 1984, Open Univ 1986; Hon LLD: Aberdeen 1981, Warwick 1986; kt 1987; *Style*— Sir Peter Maxwell Davies, CBE; c/o Mrs Judy Arnold, Flat 3, 50 Hogarth Rd, London SW5 (☎ 071 370 1477)

MAXWELL-HYSLOP, Robert John (Robin); MP (C) Tiverton Nov 1960-; s of late Capt A H Maxwell-Hyslop, GC, RN, of Prideaux House, Par, Cornwall; *b* 6 June 1931; *Educ* Stowe, ChCh Oxford (MA); *m* 1968, Joanna Margaret, er da of late Thomas McCosh, of Pitcon, Dalry, Ayrshire; 2 da; *Career* Capt TARO RA; Rolls-Royce Aero Engines 1954-1960; Parly candidate N Derby (C) 1959; chm Br - Brazilian Parly Gp; gp memb: Trade and Indust Select Ctee 1971-; Standing Orders Ctee 1977-, Procedure Select Ctee 1978-; *Style*— Robin Maxwell-Hyslop, Esq, MP; 4 Tiverton Road, Silverton, Exeter, Devon

MAXWELL-IRVING, Alastair Michael Tivey; s of Reginald Tivey (d 1977), of Warwickshire, and Barbara Annie Bell Irving (d 1988); *b* 1 Oct 1935; *Educ* Lancing Coll, Univ of London (BSc (Eng)); *m* 21 Sept 1983, Esther Mary, da of Rev James Hamilton, of Auchterhouse, Angus; *Career* chartered engr: English Electric Co 1960-64, Annandale Estates 1966-69, Weir Pumps Ltd 1970- (Commercial Manager 1990-); antiquarian and archaeologist; hon asst Royal Cmmn on Ancient and Historical Monuments Scotland; memb: Dumfries and Galloway Antiquarian Soc, Stirling Field and Archaeological Soc, Antiquarian Horological Soc (memb Scottish Ctee); fndr memb and sec BIM Central Scotland 1975-79, community cncllr Blairlogie 1984-; CEng (1973), MIEE (1972), MBIM (1974), AMICE (1970), FSA Scot (1967); *Books* The Irvings of Bonshaw (1968), The Irvings of Dumfries (1968), Early Firearms and their Influence of the Military And Domestic Architecture of the Borders (1974), Cramalt Tower, Historical Survey and Excavations 1977-79 (1982), Borthwick Castle, Excavations 1979 (1982), Hoddom Castle, a Reappraisal of its Architecture and Place in History (1989); *Recreations* architecture and history of the Border towers of Scotland, archaeology, family history and genealogy, art and architecture of Tuscany, horology, heraldry, photography, gardening; *Style*— Alastair Maxwell-Irving, Esq; Telford House, Blairlogie, Stirling, Falkirk FK9 5PX (☎ 0259 61721); Weir Pumps Ltd, Alloa, Clackmannanshire FK10 1NR (☎ 0259 722100)

MAXWELL-LAWFORD, Nicholas Anthony; OBE 1986; s of Capt F Maxwell-Lawford MBE (k rail accident 1937), of Achimota Coll Accra, Gold Coast, and Ruth Claire, *née* Jerred; *b* 8 Nov 1935; *Educ* Stonyhurst Coll, GWEBI Coll of Agric, S Rhodesia (Dip AG), Harvard Business Sch; *m* 8 Sept 1962, Mary Susan, da of Richard Fauconburg Bellasis (d 1984) of Rioki, Kiambu, Kenya; 1 s (Richard b 1965), 3 da (Helena b 1967, Frances b 1970, Antonia b 1973); *Career* Nat Serv Devonshire Regt 1955 and seconded KAR 1955-56, ADC & private sec to HE The Govr of Nyasaland Sir Robert Armitage, KCMG, MBE, 1959-61; joined Barclays Bank Ltd: various appts 1961-69, local dir for branches local head office 1969-73, local dir Lombard St local head office 1973-75, asst gen mangr Barclays Bank International 1976, res dir Barclays Bank SA (Paris) 1977, regnl dir SW Regnl Office 1987-, dir Fauconbury (Holdings) Ltd; Paris: Freeman City of London 1965, Liveryman Drapers Co 1968; Kt of Grace and Devotion Sov order of Malta 1977, City of Paris medal in Silver-Gilt 1986; *Style*— Nicholas Maxwell-Lawford, Esq, OBE; The Old Rectory, Buckerell, Honiton, Devon, EX14 OEJ

MAXWELL OF KIRKCONNELL, Francis Patrick; s of Robert William Maxwell-Witham (d 1961), and Bettina Margaret Grierson, *née* Melross, family enlarged Kirkconnell House in 1760 with first bricks used in Scotland; *b* 7 June 1954; *Educ* Downside; *m* 16 July 1983, Nicola Mary, da of Edward Henry Lovell, of 24 Hendrick Ave, London SW12; 4 da (Georgiana b 1985, Bettina b 1986, Merlin b 1988, Clementina b 1990); *Recreations* shooting, curling, choral singing, genealogy, history; *Style*— Francis Maxwell of Kirkconnell; Kirkconnell, New Abbey, Dumfries DG2 8HL (☎ 038 785 276)

MAXWELL-SCOTT, Lady; Deirdre Moira; da of late Alexander McKechnie; *m* 8 June 1963, Sir Michael Fergus Constable Maxwell-Scott, 13 Bt (d 1989); 2 s (Sir Dominic James, 14 Bt, Matthew Joseph b 1976), 1 da (Annabel Jane b 1973); *Style*— Lady Maxwell-Scott; 10 Evelyn Mansions, Carlisle Place, London SW1 (☎ 071 828 0333); Dennett Cottage, Bembridge, Isle of Wight

MAXWELL-SCOTT, Sir Dominic James; 14 Bt (E 1642), of Haggerston, Northumberland; er s of Sir Michael Fergus Constable Maxwell-Scott, 13 Bt (d 1989), and Deirdre Moira, *née* McKechnie; *b* 22 July 1968; *Heir* bro, Matthew Joseph Maxwell-Scott b 1976; *Style*— Sir Dominic Maxwell-Scott, Bt; 10 Evelyn Mansions, Carlisle Place, London SW1 (☎ 071 828 0333); Dennett Cottage, Bembridge, Isle of Wight

MAXWELL-SCOTT, Dame Jean Mary Monica; DCVO (1984, CVO 1969); da of Maj-Gen Sir Walter Maxwell-Scott, 1 and last Bt, CB, DSO, DL (d 1954), and Mairi, *née* MacDougall ggggda of Sir Walter Scott; *b* 8 June 1923; *Educ* Couvent des Oiseaux Westgate-on-Sea; *Career* VAD Red Cross nurse 1941-46; lady-in-waiting to HRH Princess Alice Duchess of Gloucester 1959-; *Clubs* New Cavendish; *Style*— Dame Jean Maxwell-Scott, DCVO; Abbotsford, Melrose, Roxburghshire TD6 9BQ

MAXWELL-SCOTT, Mrs Patricia Mary; OBE (1972); da of Maj-Gen Sir Walter Joseph Maxwell-Scott, 1 Bt, CBE, DSO (d 1954), of Abbotsford, Melrose, and Mairi, *née* Macdougall (d 1924); ggggda of Sir Walter Scott; resumed her maiden name in the Court of Session Edinburgh 1953; *b* 11 March 1921; *Educ* Convent of Les Oiseaux Westgate-on-Sea Kent; *m* 8 Sept 1944 (separated), Sir (Harold Hugh) Christian Boulton, 4 Bt, *qv*; *Career* pres: Roxburgh Branch BRCS, Border Branch Save the Children Soc, Border Branch Spartie Soc; Hon Sheriff of Selkirk 1971-; *Recreations* reading, travelling; *Style*— Mrs Patricia Maxwell-Scott, OBE; Abbotsford, Melrose, Roxburghshire TD6 9BQ (☎ 0896 2043)

MAY, Hon Mr Justice; Sir Anthony Tristram Kenneth May; s of Dr Kenneth Sibley May (d 1985), and Joan Marguérite, *née* Oldaker (d 1985); *b* 9 Sept 1940; *Educ* Bradfield, Worcester Coll Oxford (MA); *m* 4 May 1968, Stella Gay, da of Rupert George Pattisson (d 1976); 1 s (Richard b 1974), 2 da (Charmian b 1971, Lavinia b 1972); *Career* called to the Bar Inner Temple 1967; QC 1979; rec 1985, bencher Inner Temple 1985; cmmr Savings and Investment Bank Public Enquiry Isle of Man 1990; Judge of the High Court (Queen's Bench Divn) 1991-; chm Guildford Choral Soc; kt 1991; *Publications* Keating on Building Contracts (5 edn, 1991); *Recreations* gardening, music, books; *Style*— The Hon Mr Justice May; Royal Courts of Justice, Strand, London WC2A 2LL

MAY, Prof Brian Albert; s of Albert Robert May (d 1986), and Eileen, *née* May; *b* 2 June 1936; *Educ* Faversham GS, Univ of Aston (BSc); *m* 2 Aug 1961, Brenda Ann, da of Norman Smith; 3 s (Christopher b 15 March 1964, Timothy b 1965, Jeremy b 1967); *Career* Nat Serv Craftsman REME Kenya and Malaya 1954-56; design engr Massey Ferguson 1962-63; Silsoe Coll: lectr and sr lectr 1963-72, head Dept of Agric Engrg 1972-75, head of coll 1976-87; prof agric engrg Cranfield Inst of Technol 1975- (dean of faculty 1976-), head Cranfield Rural Inst 1987-; ed The Agricultural Engineer 1970-75; chm Br Agric Educn and Trg Servs 1984-86, pres Inst Agric Engrs 1984-86, dir Br agric Export Cncl 1985-88, memb Br Cncl Agric and Veterinary Advsy Ctee 1985-, dir Bd Br Soc for Res in Agric Engrg; MIMechE, FIAgrE, FRAgs, MASAE, FEng; *Books* Power on the Land (1975); *Recreations* reading, photography, people; *Clubs* Farmers; *Style*— Prof Brian May; Fairfield, Greenway, Campton, Beds (☎ 0462 813451); Cranfield Rural Institute, Silsoe Campus, Silsoe, Beds (☎ 0525 61527, telex 265871 MONREF G EUM 300)

MAY, Brian William; s of Donald Richard Vincent May, and Phoebe Louise, *née* Flain; *Career* dir St James Press Ltd (holding co of AZ Worldwide Hotel Guides) 1977-89, fndr publisher A-Z series which became the hotel directory with largest circulation in the world; fund raiser RSPB; *Recreations* climbing, tennis, sailing, ornithology; *Style*— Brian May, Esq; 39 Alleyn Rd, Dulwich, SE21 8AD (☎ 081 670 0221); Suite 112, 156 Blackfriars Rd, London SE1 (☎ 071 721 7077)

MAY, David Oliver; s of John Oliver May (d 1960), and Joan, *née* Harrison; *b* 1 March 1935; *Educ* Wellington, Southampton Univ; *m* March 1960, Baroness Catherine, da of Baron Van Den Branden De Reeth (d 1966); 2 s (Brian, Dominic), 1 da (Georgia); *Career* Nat Serv Sub Lt RN 1954-55; chm: Berthon Boat Co Ltd, Lymington Marina Ltd, Newmil Garage, Lymington Marine Garage, Nat Boat Shows 1986-88; tstee Br Marine Inds Fedn 1988; dir: Vi-Tal Hosp Prods Ltd, Imatronic Ltd, Transatlantic Capital Ltd; Liveryman Worshipful Co of Shipwrights; FRINA 1964, CEng; *Recreations* yacht racing, sailing, shooting; *Clubs* Royal Thames YC, Royal Ocean Racing, RN, Royal Lymington YC, Royal London YC, Island Sailing; *Style—* David Oliver May, Esq; The Shipyard, Lymington, Hants

MAY, Derwent James; s of Herbert Alfred May (d 1982), and Nellie Eliza, *née* Newton (d 1959); *b* 29 April 1930; *Educ* Strodes Sch Egham, Lincoln Coll Oxford (MA); *m* 22 Sept 1967, Yolanta Izabella, da of Tadeusz Sypniewski, of Lodz, Poland (d 1970); 1 s (Orlando James b 1968), 1 da (Miranda Izabella b 1970); *Career* theatre and film critic Continental Daily Mail Paris 1952-53, lectr English Univ of Indonesia 1955-58, sr lectr in English lit Univs of Warsaw and Lodz Poland 1959-63, ldr writer TLS 1963-65, lit ed The Listener 1965-86, lit and arts ed The Sunday Telegraph 1986-90, contrib of nature notes to The Times 1981-, ed Élan (the arts magazine of the European) 1990-; memb Booker Prize Jury 1978, memb Hawthornden Prize Ctee 1987-; *Books* The Professionals (1964), Dear Parson (1969), The Laughter in Djakarta (1973), A Revenger's Comedy (1979), Proust (1983), The Times Nature Diary (1983), Hannah Arendt (1986); ed: Good Talk: An Anthology from BBC Radio (1968), Good Talk 2 (1969), The Music of What Happens: Poems from The Listener 1965-80 (1981); *Recreations* birdwatching, opera; *Clubs* Beefsteak; *Style—* Derwent May, Esq; 201 Albany St, London NW1 4AB (☎ 071 387 0848); The European, 5 New Fetter Lane, London EC4A 1AP (☎ 071 822 3975)

MAY, Douglas; *b* 24 April 1931; *Career* ed-in-chief Bedford Div Westminster Press 1967-73, md and chief exec Cheshire Co Newspapers 1975-87 (md designate 1973-74); dir: Piccadilly Radio plc Manchester 1975-, Signal Radio Stoke-on-Trent 1982-; conslt Messenger Group Warrington 1987-; chm Guild of Br Newspaper Eds London and Home Counties Region 1970; pres: North West Newspaper Soc 1982-83, Newspaper Society Cncl London 1982-87; *Style—* Douglas May, Esq; Pilgrim's Latch, Eype, Nr Bridport, Dorset DT6 6AL (☎ 0308 25595); c/o Messenger Group, Newspaper House, Sankey St, Warrington WA1 1NH

MAY, Douglas Anthony Roland; s of late Roland John May, of Guildford, Surrey, and late Amy Doreen, *née* Hall; *b* 14 Nov 1940; *Educ* Woking Boys GS; *m* 1, 30 Dec 1961 (m dis 1979) Jill Margaret Toothill; 1 s (Timothy b 1968), 1 da (Joanna b 1971); m 2, 6 Oct 1979, Jacqueline Diane, da of Sydney Albert Norman Humphries; 2 s (Oliver b Oct 1981, Thomas b 1982); *Career* Legal and General Assur Soc Ltd 1961-68, Crawfurd Beck and Amos Ltd 1968-71, Graham How and Co Insur Brokers Ltd 1971-81 (life pensions dir 1972, md 1976-82), md Hinton Hill Life and Pensions Conslts 1982-88, chm of all fin servs Hinton Hill Gp 1988-91, md Pendleton May Financial Services Ltd 1951-; dir: Pendleton May Insurance Brokers Ltd, Retirement Planning Services Ltd 1984, St Pancras Building Society 1991-; leader Guildford Borough Cncl 1982-87 (memb 1973-); chm Yvonne Arnaud Theatre Tst 1983-88 (tstee 1976-), chm Yvonne Arnaud Theatre Mgmnt Ltd (dir 1979-); ACII, FBIIBA; *Recreations* breeding and showing Jacob sheep; *Clubs* Vanbrugh; *Style—* Douglas May, Esq; Monkshatch Cottage, Compton, Guildford, Surrey GU3 1DL (☎ 0483 810229); Pendleton May Financial Services Ltd, 101 Woodbridge Rd, Guildford, Surrey GU1 4PY (☎ 0483 39922, fax 0483 37552, car 0836 226180)

MAY, Douglas James; QC (1989); s of Thomas May (d 1977), of Edinburgh, and Violet Mary Brough, *née* Boyd; *b* 7 May 1946; *Educ* George Heriot's Sch Edinburgh, Univ of Edinburgh (LLB); *Career* advocate Scot 1971; temp sheriff 1990; Parly candidate (C): Edinburgh E 1974, Glasgow Cathcart 1983; capt Scot Univs Golfing Soc 1990; memb Faculty of Advocates; *Recreations* golf, photography, travel, concert going; *Clubs* Bruntsfield Links Golfing Soc; *Style—* Douglas May, Esq, QC; Advocates Library, Parliament House, Edinburgh (☎ 031 226 5071)

MAY, Evelyn Jane; da of Henry May (d 1980), and Jane Bonner, *née* Brown; *b* 16 Jan 1955; *Educ* Glasgow HS for Girls, Univ of Glasgow (BDS), Univ of Wales (MScD), FDRCS (Glasgow), DOrthRCS; *Career* postgrad student in orthodontics Welsh Nat Sch of Med Cardiff 1981-83, registrar in orthodontics Ragimore Hosp Inverness 1983-84, sr registrar in orthodontics Glasgow Dental Hosp 1984-88 (house offr, then sr house offr 1977-81), conslt Middlesbrough Gen Hosp 1988-; memb: Br Soc for the Study of Orthodontics, Conslt Orthodontics Gp, BDA, Craniofacial Soc of GB; *Style—* Miss Evelyn May; 27 Tameside, Stokesley, North Yorkshire; Middlesbrough General Hospital, Ayresome Green Lane, Middlesbrough, Cleveland TS5 5AZ (☎ 0642 850222 ext 316)

MAY, Geoffrey John; s of James Ebrey Clare May (d 1986), of London, and Eleanor Isobel, *née* Tate; *b* 7 May 1948; *Educ* Eltham Coll London, Fitzwilliam Coll Cambridge (MA, PhD); *m* 5 Jan 1974, Sarah Elizabeth, da of Stanley George Felgate (d 1986), of Warrington; 2 s (Timothy b 1976, Daniel b 1980); *Career* Chloride Group plc 1974-82, Hawker Siddeley Group 1982-90, and 1991-, dir Tungstone Batteries Ltd 1982-88, dir and gen mangr Hawker Fusegear Ltd 1988-90, dir Caporo Industries plc, md Barton Abrasives Ltd 1990-91, dir Res and Devpt Hawker Batteries Ltd 1991-; CEng 1978, FIM 1987; *Recreations* skiing, gardening, walking; *Style—* Geoffrey May, Esq; Troutbeck Hse, 126 Main St, Swithland, Loughborough, Leics LE12 8TJ (☎ 0509 890547); Hawker Batteries Ltd, Market Harborough, Leics LE16 9E2 (☎ 0858 410900, fax 0858 410505, telex 34305 TUNGST G)

MAY, Hon Jasper Bertram St John; s and h of 3 Baron May; *b* 24 Oct 1965; *Educ* Harrow; *Style—* The Hon Jasper May

MAY, Rt Hon Sir John Douglas; PC (1982); s of E A G May (d 1942), of Shanghai; *b* 28 June 1923; *Educ* Clifton, Balliol Coll Oxford (MA); *m* 1958, Mary, da of Sir Owen Morshead, GCVO, KCB, DSO, MC; 2 s, 1 da; *Career* served WWII Lt (SpSc) RNVR; called to the Bar Inner Temple 1947, master of the Bench 1972, QC 1965, rec of Maidstone 1971, ldr SE Circuit 1971, high ct judge (Queen's Bench) 1972-82, presiding judge Midland & Oxford Circuit 1973-77, lord justice of appeal 1982-89, appointed conduct Inquiry into Guildford and Woolwich Bombings 1989; memb Parole Bd 1977-80 (vice chm 1980); chm: Inquiry into Prison Servs 1978-79, Univ Commissioners 1989; kt 1972; pres Clifton Coll 1987-; *Clubs* Vincents' (Oxford); *Style—* The Rt Hon Sir John May; Lindens, Sturminster Newton, Dorset DT10 1BU (☎ 0258 73321)

MAY, 3 Baron (UK 1935); Sir Michael St John May; 3 Bt (1931); s of 2 Baron (d 1950), by his 2 w Ethel; *b* 26 Sept 1931; *Educ* Wycliffe Coll, Magdalene Cambridge; *m* 1, 1958 (m dis 1963), Dorothea Catherine Ann, da of Charles McCarthy; m 2, 1963, Jillian Mary, da of Albert Edward Shipton; 1 s, 1 da (Hon Miranda b 17 Oct 1968); *Heir* s, Hon Jasper Bertram St John May b 24 Oct 1965; *Career* late Lt Royal Corps of Signals; *Style—* The Rt Hon the Lord May; Gautherns Farm, Sibford Gower, Oxfordshire

MAY, (William) Nigel; s of Flt Lt (William) David May, of 70 Chaldon Way, Coulsdon, Surrey, and (Evelyn) Christine, *née* Pike; *b* 24 May 1950; *Educ* Whitgift Sch, Univ of Nottingham (BA), Univ of Cambridge (Dip); *Career* called to the Bar Inner Temple 1974; currently working in criminal practice, prosecution and def, grade three prosecutor for Crown Prosecution Serv; fndr memb of present chambers in 1984, nominated by Attorney Gen to prosecute for HM Customs & Excise; *Recreations* reading, skiing, walking, music; *Style—* Nigel May, Esq; 3 Gray's Inn Square, London WC1 (☎ 071 242 6476)

MAY, Phillip Stephen; s of Sidney May, of Llanelli, and Maida, *née* Jones; *b* 1 July 1956; *Educ* Llanelli GS, Univ Coll Swansea, Univ Coll Wales Aberystwyth; *m* 11 Aug 1979, Ann Elizabeth, da of Roy Jenkins; 2 s (Owen Stephen b 11 June 1974, David Phillip b 11 Sept 1975); *Career* Rugby Union Flanker Llanelli RFC and Wales (6 caps); debut Llanelli 1974 (capt 5 seasons, 512 appearances); Wales: debut v Eng 1988, memb Triple Crown winning team 1988, toured NZ 1988; teacher, area accounts mangr Crown Berkley Brewery (formerly Harp sales rep); *Recreations* reading, horse racing; *Style—* Phillip May, Esq; Llanelli RFC, Football Ground, Stradey Park, Llanelli, Dyfed (☎ 0554 774060); Crown Berkley Brewery, Gilbert Rd, Llanelli, Dyfed (☎ 0554 777714, fax 0443 237096)

MAY, Phineas Leopold; s of Aron May (d 1937), and Miriam, *née* Franklin (d 1938); *b* 9 May 1906; *Educ* Haberdashers' Askes, Vernon House Sch, London Sch of Cartooning, Central Sch of Arts & Crafts; *m* 2 Nov 1941, Vivienne Beatrice, da of Myer Lewis; 1 s (Edmund Michael b 1952), 1 da (Adrienne (Mrs Harris) b 1948); *Career* cmmnd Army 1940, demob as Capt 1945; cartoonist, hon custodian The Jewish Museum of London, organiser Centenary Exhibition of The United Synagogue at Christies, Loyal Addresses to The Royal Family on all occasions; special constable 1926-39; memb: cncl of Ben Uri Art Gallery, Jewish Book Cncl; *Books* Cartoon History and Anglo Jewry (1983), Cartoonist: Jewish Joke Book (3 vols by Michael Dines, 1986); *Recreations* art, cartooning; *Style—* Phineas May, Esq; 22 Marlow Court, Willesden Lane, London NW6 7PS

MAY, Prof Robert McCredie; s of Henry Wilkinson May, of Sydney, Australia; *b* 8 Jan 1936; *Educ* Sydney Boys' Sch, Sydney Univ (BSc, PhD); *m* 3 Aug 1962, Judith, da of Jerome Feiner, of New York, USA; 1 da (Naomi Felicity b 25 March 1966); *Career* Gordon Mackey lectr in applied mathematics Harvard Univ 1959-61 and 1966, prof of physics Sydney Univ 1962-72, prof of astrophysics California Inst of Technol 1967; prof of plasma physics: UKAEA Lab Culham 1971, Magdalen Coll Oxford 1971, Inst for Advanced Study Princeton 1972, King's Coll Res Centre Cambridge 1976; visiting prof Imperial Coll London 1975-88, Class of 1877 prof of zoology Princeton Univ 1973-88, Royal Soc res prof Oxford Univ and Imperial Coll London 1988-; memb: NRC, Sci-Advsy Cncl for WWF (US) 1978, Int Whaling Cmmn 1978-82, US Marine Animals Cmmn 1979-, governing bd Soc of Conservation Biologists 1985-88, advsy bd Inst for Sci Info 1986-; tstee: British Museum Natural History 1989-94, WWF (UK) 1990-93; Rockefeller scholar Italy 1986; Hon Degrees Univs of London 1989 and Uppsla 1990; FRS 1979, fell American Acad of Arts and Sci 1977; *Books* Stability and Complexity in Model Ecosystems (1973, 2 edn 1974), Theoretical Ecology: Principles and Applications (ed 1976, 2 edn 1981), Population Biology of Infectious Diseases (ed with R M Anderson, 1982), Exploitation of Marine Communities (ed, 1984), Perspectives in Ecological Theory (ed with J Roughgarden and S A Levin, 1989); *Recreations* running, tennis; *Clubs* Athenaeum; *Style—* Prof Robert May, FRS; Department of Zoology, University of Oxford, South Parks Rd, Oxford OX1 3PS (☎ 0865 271170, fax 0865 310447)

MAY, Roger; s of Fred May (d 1967), and Agnes Doreen, *née* Abrahams (d 1971); *b* 12 June 1931; *Educ* High Storrs GS Sheffield; *m* 1, 14 March 1953 (m dis 1973); 2 s (Paul b 1958, Jonathan b 1962); m 2, 1973, (Margaret) Yvonne; *Career* slr; former justices' clerk: Barry, Cowbridge, Penarth; dep High Ct and Co Ct registrar; memb Law Soc; *Recreations* photography, travel; *Style—* Roger May, Esq; Hillcrest, Quarhouse, Brimscombe, Stroud, Gloucestershire; Frome House, London Rd, Stroud, Gloucestershire

MAY, Simon Philip Walter; s of Walter May (d 1963), and Marianne Louise, *née* Leidtke; *b* 9 Aug 1956; *Educ* Westminster, ChCh Oxford (MA); *Career* Euro affrs advsr to Rt Hon Douglas Hurd MP 1977-79, foreign affrs advsr to Rt Hon Edward Heath 1979-83, memb Cabinet of Vice Pres EEC Cmmn 1983-85, co fndr Action Ctee Europe 1985-86; dir: Northern Telecom Europe 1986-88, Axiom Advisors Ltd; chief exec Mondiale Ltd 1988-; memb Cncl Centre for World Devpt Educn 1981; *Books* The European Armaments Market and Procurement Cooperation (1988); *Recreations* music, walking; *Style—* Simon May, Esq; 129 Riverview Gardens, London SW13 9RA (☎ 081 748 6920); 117 Belmont Rd, Maidenhead, Berks SL6 6LG (☎ 0628 35317, fax 0628 36894, car 0831 323502)

MAY, Stephen Charles; s of Paul May, CBE, and Dorothy Ida, *née* Makower (d 1961); *b* 5 Sept 1937; *Educ* Berkhamsted Sch, ChCh Oxford (MA); *m* 2 June 1977, Jeannette de Rothschild (d 1980), da of Frederick Ernest Bishop (d 1940); *Career* Nat Serv 2 Lt RA 1956-58; John Lewis Partnership: joined 1961-, md Edinburgh 1973-75, md Peter Jones 1975-1977, dep dir of personnel 1977-78, dir of personnel 1978-; *Recreations* skiing, tennis, travel; *Clubs* Vanderbilt; *Style—* Stephen May, Esq; The John Lewis Partnership, 171 Victoria St, London SW1E 5NN (☎ 071 828 1000, ext 6130, telex 9419911/2 Jonel G)

MAY, Walter Anthony Holland; MC (1945); s of Bertram May (d 1959), of Falmouth, Cornwall, and Alice Kathleen, *née* Kent (d 1965); *b* 15 Dec 1919; *Educ* Shrewsbury, Loughborough Engrg Coll (Dip Eng), MIT Boston USA; *m* 10 Jan 1942, Wendy, da of Eric G Attenborough (d 1969), of Letchmore Heath, Herts; 1 s (Michael Walter b 1950), 2 da (Rosemary Elizabeth b 1942, Veronica Kathleen b 1945); *Career* 2 Lt RE TA 1938, 54 div 249 Field Co RE 1939, Maj SME 1943-44, 14 Field Sqdn RD 1944-45, acting CRE Gds Armd Div 1945; George Kent Ltd: personnel mangr 1947-51, exec dir 1951-84, fin dir 1955-63, dep md 1963-71; md Int Div Brown Boveri Kent Plc 1971-81, dir BECENTA Ltd 1986; non-exec dir: ABB Kent (Holdings) Plc 1984-, Luton Int Airport Ltd 1988-; chm: BIMCAM 1966-67, Luton & Dist Employment Ctee 1961-76, Eastern Regnl Industl Savings Ctee 1968-78; pres Mid-Anglian Engrg Employers Assoc 1979-82, memb Policy Ctee Engrg Employers Fedn 1980-86, Mgmnt Bd Engrg Employers Fedn 1979 (ret 1989), memb Eastern Regnl Cncl CBI 1985-; involved in local politics over many years; FBIM, IOD; *Recreations* tennis, golf; *Style—* Walter May, Esq; Guelders, Lower Gustard Wood, Herts AL4 8RS (☎ 0582 833080); ABB Kent (Hldgs) plc, Biscot Rd, Luton, Beds LU1 3AE (☎ 0582 31255, fax 0582 421115, telex 825066 ABBKENT G)

MAYALL, David William; s of Arthur William Mayall, of Derby, and Pamela, *née* Bryant; *b* 19 July 1957; *Educ* Repton, Univ of Cambridge (MA); *m* 22 June 1985, Wendy Madeleine, da of Peter Black of Douglas, of IOM; 1 s (James b 13 April 1988), 1 da (Sophie b 31 May 1990); *Career* called to the Bar Gray's Inn 1979; *Recreations* bridge, tennis, golf; *Style—* David Mayall, Esq; 5 Rookfield Close, London N10 (☎ 081 444 1683); 1 Verulam Bldgs, Gray's Inn, London WC1R 5LQ (☎ 071 242 7646)

MAYALL, Sir (Alexander) Lees; KCVO (1972, CVO 1965), CMG 1964); s of Alexander Mayall (d 1943); *b* 14 Sept 1915; *Educ* Eton, Trinity Coll Oxford; *m* 1, 1940 (m dis 1947), Renee Eileen Burn; 1 da; m 2, 1947, Hon Mary Hermione, *qv*, da of 4 Baron Harlech, KG, GCMG, PC (d 1964); 1 s, 2 da; *Career* served Armed Forces 1940; entered Dip Serv 1939; cnsllr: Tokyo 1958-61, Lisbon 1961-64, Addis Ababa 1964-65; HM Vice-Marshal of Dip Corps 1965-72, ambass Venezuela 1972-75, ret; *Books* Fireflies in Amber, A Memior (1989); *Style—* Sir Lees Mayall, KCVO, CMG; Sturford Mead, Warminster, Wilts (☎ 037 388 219)

MAYALL, Hon Lady (Mary Hermione); *née* Ormsby-Gore; da of 4 Baron Harlech KC, GCMG, PC (d 1964); *b* 1914; *m* 1, 1936 (m dis 1946), Capt Robin Francis Campbell, DSO, s of Rt Hon Sir Ronald Hugh Campbell, GCMG (decd); 2 s; m 2, 1947, Sir Alexander Lees Mayall, KCVO, CMG, *qv*; 1 s, 2 da; *Style—* The Hon Lady Mayall; Sturford Mead, Warminster, Wilts (☎ 037 388 219)

MAYBURY, Neil Martin; s of Leonard Albert Maybury, of 34 Gilmorton Close, Harborne, Birmingham, and Kathleen Margaret, *née* Howse (d 1982); *b* 25 Aug 1943; *Educ* King Edwards Sch Birmingham, Univ of Birmingham (LLB); *m* 10 May 1980, Sally Elizabeth, da of Kenneth Carroll, of 50 Rosemary Hill Rd, Streetly, W Midlands; 2 s (Thomas Charles b 1983, Toby George b 1985), 1 da (Natasha Poppy b 1987); *Career* admitted slr 1969; asst slr Clifford-Turner & Co London 1969-72, ptnr Pinsent Co 1975-; dir Glenarn Investments Ltd, sec Wemtech Ltd; memb: Cncl Soc for Computers and Law 1979-88, Fedn Against Software Theft Legal Advsy Gp; memb technol ctee: Birmingham C of C, Birmingham Law Soc; memb Law Soc; *Books* Guide to The Electronic Office (with Keith James, 1988); *Recreations* tennis, squash, gardening, classic cars, skiing, opera; *Clubs* Edgbaston Priory, Wig & Pen, Edgbaston Golf; *Style—* Neil Maybury, Esq; Pinsent & Co, Post and Mail House, 26 Colmore Circus, Birmingham B4 6BH (☎ 021 200 1050, fax 021 200 1040)

MAYBURY, Air Cdre Peter Lawrence; s of Lysander Montague Maybury (d 1971), of Portsmouth, and Florence Edna, *née* Kaines (1989); *b* 10 Aug 1928; *Educ* Sherborne, Univ of Cambridge, UCH (MA, MB BChir); *m* 18 Sept 1954, Helen Lindsay Livingstone, da of Daniel Wills (d 1946), Res Cmmn Central Johore; 2 da (Nicola Helen b 1956, Karen Peta b 1958); *Career* qualified med practitioner 1952; joined RAF Med Branch 1954, Air Cdre served UK, RAF Germany, Libya, Cyprus; dep princ med offr HQ RAF Germany 1967-70, cmdg health and med offr HQ Strike Cmd 1975-78, dep dir health and res MOD 1978-80 (dir 1980-82), ret 1982; RAF Central Med Estab London: sr med offr, dep pres Central Med Bd 1982-; FFCM, FFPHM, MFOM; *Recreations* gardening, walking, sailing; *Clubs* RAF; *Style—* Air Cdre Peter Maybury; Puddledock Garden, Clay Hall Lane, Acton, Sudbury, Suffolk (☎ 0787 77092); Central Medical Establishment, RAF Kelvin House, Cleveland St, London (☎ 071 836 4651)

MAYCOCK, Peter Duncan; s of David George Maycock, and Adrienne Elaine, *née* Barry; *b* 11 Aug 1967; *Educ* Daniel Stewarts and Melville Coll Edinburgh, Plymouth Coll, Bristol Poly; *Career* canoeist; represented GB jr and sr level in Flat Water Kyake Racing; memb GB sr team 1989: Bosbaan Int Regatta Holland, Duisburg Int W Germany, Nottingham Int and World Championships, Ploudiu Bulgaria; memb GB sr team 1990: Mecheln Belgium, Pre-Worlds Paris Regatta, Duisburg Int Regatta W Germany; K4 Nat Champion 500m 1990; ACIB, memb Br Canoe Union; *Style—* Peter Maycock, Esq; 57 Teignmouth Rd, Teignmouth, Devon TQ14 8UR (☎ 06267 73887)

MAYER, Dr Christopher Norman; s of George Emanuel Mayer, of Bath, Avon, and Margaret, *née* Jones; *b* 30 Aug 1954; *Educ* City of Bath Boys Sch Avon, Welsh Nat Sch of Med Cardiff (MB BCh); *m* 12 Sept 1981, Joanna Paget, da of Michael James Lock, of Arundel, Sussex; 3 da (Alice b 25 July 1984, Annabel b 9 Feb 1986, Felicity b 30 July 1988); *Career* sr registrar Dept of Psychiatry St Georges Hosp London 1983-86, conslt psychiatrist and psychiatric tutor W Suffolk Hosp Bury St Edmunds 1986-; pubns incl papers on anorexia nervosa; TV appearances incl: The Purchase and Importation of Camels from North Africa (BBC 2), The Crisis of British Public Conveniences (Channel 4); psychiatric advsr and patron W Suffolk Relate (was Marriage Guidance Cncl); MRCPsych 1983; *Recreations* digging, self-promotion, wine, literature; *Style—* Dr Christopher Mayer; Cattishall Farmhouse, Great Barton, Bury St Edmunds, Suffolk IP31 2QT (☎ 028487 340); West Suffolk Hospital, Hardwick Lane, Bury Bury St Edmunds, Suffolk IP33 2QZ (☎ 0284 763131)

MAYER, Thomas (Tom); CBE (1985); s of Hans Mayer (d 1967), and Jeanette, *née* Gumperz (d 1956); *b* 17 Dec 1928; *Educ* Kings Sch Harrow, Regent St Poly (BSc); *m* 1975, Jean Patricia, da of John Ernest Frederick Burrows, of 6 Boyne Rd, Dagenham; 1 s (Peter), 1 da (Helen); *Career* md Marconi Communications Systems Ltd 1969-81, chm and md Thorn EMI Electronics Ltd 1981-86, dir Soc of Br Aerospace Cos Ltd 1984-90, chief exec Thorn EMI Technology Group 1986-89, chm Thora EMI Electonics 1986-90; dir: Babcock Thorn 1986-90, Thorn EMI plc 1987-90, Devonport Management Ltd 1990-, Electron House plc 1991-; chm: Eldbury Ltd 1990-, Holmes Protection Group Inc 1990-; memb Nat Electronics Cncl; FEng, FIEE, FRSA, FRTS; *Clubs* RAC, Whiteleaf Golf; *Style—* Tom Mayer, Esq, CBE; 1590 AD, Burton Lane, Monks Risborough, Bucks HP17 9JF

MAYER, William Edgar; s of John William Mayer, of Old Colwyn, nr Wales, and Adelaide Gertrude, *née* Saunders; *b* 1 July 1910; *Educ* Epworth Coll N Wales; *m* 1, 1933, Margaret Elizabeth Cowell, da of Richard Greaves (d 1938), of Polperro, Cornwall; 1 s (Peter); m 2, 1945, Evelyn, da of Bertram Hayes (d 1966), of Chorley, Lancs; 1 s (Christopher b 1960), 1 da (Hilary b 1951); *Career* chartered architect; asst architect New Works Div (Min of Works 1945); artist: has given many exhibitions at various galleries, theatres, academies (UK) national winner of the 1000 TV Times Great Outdoors painting competition 1978; memb Soc of Geneologists; FRIBA, FRSA; *Recreations* genealogy, painting; *Clubs* Royal Soc of Arts, Adelphi (London); *Style—* William E Mayer, Esq; Stone Cottage, 145 Town Lane, Whittle-le-Woods, Chorley, Lancs PR6 8AG (☎ 02572 62068); The Studio, 145 Town Lane, Whittle-le-Woods, Chroley, Lancs PR6 8AG (☎ 02572 62068)

MAYHEW, Audrey Louise; da of George Ernest Mayhew (d 1969), of London, and Wilhelmina Louise, *née* Brandt (d 1977); *b* 20 Jan 1925; *Educ* North London Collegiate Sch, Girton Coll Univ of Cambridge (MA); *Career* actg headmistress (former dep headmistress) Lewes Girls' GS, dep headmistress Ealing Girls' GS, headmistress St Elphin's Sch Darley Dale Matlock Derbys; memb: AAM, AHM, Kent and E Sussex Girtonians Assoc; *Recreations* Greek and Roman Studies, music, oil painting, gardening, foreign travel; *Clubs* Country Gentlemen's Assoc; *Style—* Miss Audrey Mayhew; Haslemere, Mushroom Field, Kingston, Lewes, E Sussex BN7 3LE (☎ 0273 474 374)

MAYHEW, Baron (Life Peer UK 1981), of Wimbledon, Greater London; Christopher Paget Mayhew; s of Sir Basil Edgar Mayhew, KBE, and Dorothea, da of Stephen Paget and gda of Sir James Paget, 1 Bt, whereby His Lordship is 2 cous of the present (4) Bt, Sir Julian (Gentleman Usher to HM), and Paul Paget, the architect, also great nephew to a brace of Bishops (Francis, sometime Bp of Oxford, and Henry, sometime Bp of Chester); *b* 12 June 1915; *Educ* Haileybury, Ch Ch Oxford (MA); *m* 1949, Cicely Elizabeth, da of George Ludlam; 2 s (Hon David Francis b 1951, Hon (Christopher) James b 1959), 2 da (Hon Teresa Ruth b 1953, Hon Judith Emily Ann b 1955); *Career* served Surrey Yeo RA WWII, Maj (despatches); MP (L): S Norfolk 1945-50, Woolwich E (subsequently Greenwich, Woolwich E) 1951-74 (when resigned from Labour Pty and joined Libs); MP (Lib) July-Oct 1974, Parly candidate (Lib) for Bath 1974 & 1979, min of Def (RN) 1964-66, Lib Spokesman for Def 1974-; Euro Parly candidate (Lib): Surrey as prospective MEP 1979, London SW Sept 1979; chm ME Int (Publishers), ANAF Fndn; *Books* Men Seeking God, Britain's Role Tomorrow, Party Games, Publish It Not, The Middle East Cover Up, Time to Explain; *Recreations* golf, music; *Clubs* National Liberal; *Style—* The Rt Hon the Lord Mayhew; 39 Wool Rd, London SW20 (☎ 081 946 3460)

MAYHEW, Hon David Francis; er s of Baron Mayhew (Life Peer), *qv*; *b* 31 July 1951; *Educ* St Paul's, ChCh Oxford (BA PPE, BA Theol, MA); *m* 1979, Elizabeth Helen, da of Lt-Col Pusinelli, of Chinagarth, Thornton-le-Dale, N Yorks; 3 da (Jessica Elizabeth b 1980, Nicola Helen b 1981, Hannah Ruth b 1986); *Career* careers offr, area sec TOC H; *Recreations* windsurfing, golf, gardening, politics; *Style—* The Hon David Mayhew; The White House, Whickham View, Newcastle upon Tyne NE15 6SY (☎ 091 274 3757)

MAYHEW, Hon (Christopher) James; yr son of Baron Mayhew (Life Peer); *b* 8 Dec 1959; *Educ* St Paul's, King's Coll London (BSc); *m* 2 March 1985, Deborah Ann, o da of Martin John Lewis, of Hong Kong; 1 da (Emily Rose b 23 Dec 1989); *Career* md Mayhew & Mayhew Ltd; *Recreations* golf; *Style—* The Hon James Mayhew; 34 Morden Road, Wimbledon, London SW20 3BR; Le Passons, Quettreville-sur-Seine, 50660 France

MAYHEW, Hon Judith Emily Ann; yr da of Baron Mayhew (Life Peer); *b* 1955; *Career* professional muscian; *Style—* The Hon Judith Mayhew; 3 Shelton Rd, Merton Park, London SW19

MAYHEW, Kenneth (Ken); s of Albert Chadwick Mayhew (d 1967), and Alice, *née* Leigh; *b* 1 Sept 1947; *Educ* Manchester GS, Worcester Coll Oxford (MA), LSE (MSc); *m* 1 (m dis 1982), Margaret, *née* Humphreys; 1 da (Rowena Kate b 1978); m 2, 15 Dec 1990, Gillian Alexandra, da of Arthur Alexander McGrattan, of Belfast; *Career* economist; economic asst HM Treasy 1970-72; res offr: Queen Elizabeth House Oxford 1972, Inst of Econs Oxford 1972-81; fell Pembroke Coll Oxford 1976-, econ dir NEDO 1989-90; assoc ed Oxford Review of Economic Policy; *Books* Pay Policies for the Future (ed with D Robinson, 1983), Improving Incentives for the Low Paid (ed with A Bowen, 1990); *Recreations* travel, literature; *Clubs* Reform; *Style—* Ken Mayhew, Esq; 49 Hamilton Rd, Oxford OX2 7PY (☎ 0865 510977); Pembroke College, Oxford OX1 1DW (☎ 0865 276434, fax 0865 276418)

MAYHEW, Lionel Geoffrey; s of Geoffrey Dixon Mayhew (d 1963), of Speldhurst, Tunbridge Wells, Kent, and Bertha Irene, *née* Short (d 1929); *b* 5 Dec 1916; *Educ* Eton, Trinity Coll Oxford (MA); *m* 19 Oct 1939, Beatrice, da of Thomas Vowe Peake (d 1956), of The Grange, Rawnsley, Cannock, Staffs; 1 s (David Lionel b 20 May 1940), 3 da (Jane Barbara (Mrs Thomas) b 28 March 1943, Bridget Ann (Mrs Martin) b 2 Dec 1944, Rosamund Betty (Mrs Weaver) b 29 June 1949); *Career* RMC Sandhurst 1939-40, cmmnd Royal Leics Regt 1940, joined 2/5 (later 7) Bn, transferred Intelligence Corps 1943, served with SHAEF and in Air Miny (particularly concerned with German Secret Weapons V1 & V2), WO (GSO 2) MI 14 (H), demobbed Maj 1946; stockbroker; London Stock Exchange 1947-49; Liverpool Stock Exchange 1949: joined 1949, memb 1955, memb Ctee 1963 (chm Ctee 1971-74); memb SE Cncl 1975-78, sr ptnr Neilson Hornby Crichton & Co 1978-86, Neilson Milnes 1986-87, ret; chm City of Chester Cons Assoc 1960-65; Chester Grosvenor Nuffield Hosp: chm Fund Raising Ctee 1971-74, chm Med Advsy Ctee 1974-81; Liveryman Worshipful Co of Gold and Silver Wyre Drawers 1949 (memb of Ct 1968, Master 1979); *Recreations* shooting, stalking, gardening; *Clubs* RAC, Racquet Club (Liverpool); *Style—* Lionel G Mayhew, Esq; The Oast House, Isington, Alton, Hants

MAYHEW, Hon Mrs (Margaret Louise); 3 da of Baron Brock (Life Peer; d 1980); *b* 8 May 1936; *Educ* Malvern Girls' Coll; *m* 1962 (m dis 1988), (John Alexander) Simon Cary Mayhew, eldest son of Maj John de Perigault Gurney Mayhew, S Staffs Regt; 2 da (Ella b 1963, Matilda b 1965); *Style—* The Hon Mrs Mayhew; c/o Wright, Webb Syrett, 10 Soho Square, London W1V 6EE

MAYHEW, The Rt Hon Sir Patrick Barnabas Burke; PC (1986), QC (1972), MP (C) Tunbridge Wells 1974-; s of (Alfred) Geoffrey Horace Mayhew, MC (d 1985), of Sevenoaks Weald, Kent, and Sheila Margaret Burke, *née* Roche; *b* 11 Sept 1929; *Educ* Tonbridge, Balliol Coll Oxford (MA); *m* 15 April 1963, Jean Elizabeth, 2 da of John Gurney, *qv*, of Walsingham Abbey, Norfolk; 4 s (James b 1964, Henry b 1966, Tristram b 1968, Jerome b 1970); *Career* served 4/7 Royal Dragoon Gds, Capt (Nat Serv and AER); bencher Middle Temple 1982 (barr 1956); Parly candidate (C) Camberwell and Dulwich 1970, vice chm Cons Home Affrs Ctee and memb Exec 1922 Ctee 1976-79, Parly under sec Employment 1979-81, min of state Home Office 1981-83, SG 1983-87, AG 1987-; pres: Tonbridge and Tunbridge Wells Dist MENCAP, Tunbridge Wells Constitutional Club, Kilndown CC; vice pres: Tunbridge Wells RFC, Goudhurst CC; kt 1983; *Recreations* sailing, country pursuits; *Clubs* Pratt's, Beefsteak, Garrick, Tunbridge Wells Constitutional; *Style—* The Rt Hon Sir Patrick Mayhew, QC, MP; House of Commons, London SW1A 0AA

MAYHEW-SANDERS, Sir John Reynolds; s of Jack Mayhew-Sanders (d 1982); *b* 25 Oct 1931; *Educ* Epsom Coll, RNC Dartmouth, Jesus Coll Cambridge; *m* 1958, Sylvia Mary, da of George S Colling (d 1959); 3 s, 1 da; *Career* RN 1949-54; chm John Brown & Co Ltd 1978-83 (chief exec 1975-83, dir 1972-83), Overseas Project Bd 1980-83; non-exec dir: Rover Gp plc 1980-88, Dowty Gp plc 1982-86; memb: Cncl of Engrg Employers' Fedn 1977-80, BOTB 1980-83, BBC Consultative Gp Industl & Business Affrs 1981-83, chm Heidrick & Struggles 1985-87, chief exec Samuelson Gp plc 1987-88; formerly with Mayhew-Sanders CAs and with PE Consulting Gp Ltd; pres Br-Soviet C of C 1983-88; govr Sadler's Wells Fndn 1983-89, dir Sadler's Wells Tst, chm New Sadler's Wells Opera Co; FCA; kt 1982; *Recreations* fishing, shooting, music, astronomy, the gardening; *Style—* Sir John Mayhew-Sanders; Earlstone House, Burghclere, Newbury, Berkshire (☎ 063 527 288)

MAYNARD, Prof Alan Maynard; s of Edward Joseph Maynard, of W Kirby, Wirral, Merseyside, and Hilda Marion, *née* McCausland; *b* 15 Dec 1944; *Educ* Calday Grange GS W Kirby Merseyside, Univ of Newcastle upon Tyne, Univ of York (BPhil); *m* 22 June 1968, Elizabeth Mary, da of Kevin Joseph Shanahan, of Edinburgh; 2 s (Justin b 11 Feb 1970, John b 24 Oct 1971), 2 da (Jane b 31 July 1974, Samantha b 8 Nov 1976); *Career* asst lectr and lectr in economics Univ of Exeter 1968-71, currently prof of economics and dir Centre for Health Economics Univ of York (lectr in economics 1971-76, sr lectr and dir Graduate Prog in Health Economics 1976-83); visiting lectr: Italy, NZ, Sweden, over 150 articles in jls; memb: York Health Authy 1982-, ESRC 1983-86 (memb Human Behaviour and Devpt Ctee 1988-), Health Servs Res Ctee MRC 1986-, chm Evaluation Panel for Fourth Med and Health Res Prog Euro Commn 1990; memb: Royal Econ Soc, Soc for the Study of Addiction, Royal Society of Medicine; *Books* Health Care in the European Community (1976), Public Private Mix for Health (ed with G McLachlan, 1982), Controlling Legal Addictions (ed with D Robinson and R Chester, 1989), Preventing Alcohol and Tobacco Problems (ed with P Tether, 1990), Competition in Health Care: Reforming the NHS (ed, with A J Cuzyer and J Posnett); *Recreations* reading, walking, current affairs and cricket; *Clubs* RSM, Royal Cwlth Soc; *Style—* Prof Alan Maynard; 86 East Parade, Henworth, York YO3 7YH (☎ 0904 425051); Centre for Health Economics, University of York, York YO1 5DD (☎ 0904 433645, fax 0904 433644)

MAYNARD, (Henry) Charles Edward; s of Henry Maynard, of Coleshill, Bucks, and Diana Elizabeth, *née* Lee; *b* 10 Feb 1941; *Educ* Bryanston, Imperial Coll London (BSc); *m* 17 March 1984, Susan Marjorie, da of Edward George Hedges Barford; 2 da (Catherine Anna b 1 May 1986, Rebecca Jane b 28 April 1989); *Career* ptnr Moores Rowland CA's 1969 (ptnr i/c London Office 1979-85, vice chm Moores Rowland Int 1987-); memb Worshipful Co of CA's in England and Wales; FCA 1962; *Recreations* golf, tennis, skiing, sailing, Victorian watercolours; *Clubs* Hurlingham, Royal West Nofolk GC; *Style—* Charles Maynard, Esq; Moores Rowland, Cliffords Inn, Fetter Lane, London EC4 1AS (☎ 071 831 2345, fax 071 831 6123)

MAYNARD, Edwin Francis George (Frank); s of Edwin Maynard, and Nancy Frances, *née* Tully; *b* 23 Feb 1921; *Educ* Westminster, ME Staff Coll; *m* 1, May 1945

(m dis 1962), Patricia Baker; 1 s (John Edwin b 1947), 1 da (Ann b 1948); m 2, Feb 1963, Anna Maria McGettrick; 2 s (Gareth b 1964, James b 1966); *Career* Royal Fusiliers 1939-40, cmmnd 4/8 Prince of Wales Own Punjab Regt, Capt 1941 ME & Burma HQ 17 Indian Div 43 45, Maj GSO II (I) 1945, Instr Intelligence Sch India 1946; BBC French Serv 1948, FO 1949, consular & oriental sec Jedda 1950, 1 sec Benghazi 1952, FO 1954, commercial sec and supt Consul Bogota 1956, 1 sec Info Khartoum 1959, FO 1960, Baghdad 1962, fndr dir Dip Serv Language Centre 1966, cncllr Aden 1967, commercial cncllr New Delhi 1968-72, commercial min Buenos Aires 1972-76, Chargé d'Affaires 1974-75, dep high cmmr Calcutta 1976-80; business conslt and dir; memb local Cons Soc; *Recreations* shooting, fishing, languages, gardening; *Clubs* Brooks's, Circulo de Armas Buenos Aires, Bengal; *Style—* Frank Maynard, Esq; Littlebourne Court, Littlebourne, Canterbury, Kent

MAYNARD, Prof Geoffrey Walter; s of Walter F Maynard, and Maisie, *née* Bristow; *b* 27 Oct 1921; *Educ* Univ of London, LSE (BSc), Univ of Wales (PhD); *m* 1949, Marie Lilian, *née* Wright; 2 da (Joanna b 1956, Victoria b 1961); *Career* taught at several univs in UK and USA; at various times conslt: FCO, World Bank, Harvard Univ Devpt Advsy Serv; held advsy posts to number of developing countries incl Argentina and Liberia; ed Bankers' Magazine 1968-72, dep chief econ advsr HM Treasy 1976-77 (under sec 1972-74), vice pres and dir of econs Europe and Middle East Chase Manhattan Bank 1977-86 (econ conslt 1974), econ conslt Investcorp International Ltd 1986-; memb Econ Affrs Ctee Econ and Soc Res Cncl 1982-85, govr Inst of Development Studies Univ of Sussex 1984-; *Books* princ books incl: Economic Development and the Price Level (1961), A World of Inflation (jtly, 1976), The British Economy Under Mrs Thatcher 1979-87 (1988); *Recreations* walking; *Clubs* Reform; *Style—* Prof Geoffrey Maynard; Flat 219, Queens Quay, 58 Upper Thames St, London EC4

MAYNARD, John David; s of Albert William Henry Maynard (d 1968), of Surrey, and Ellen Hughes-Jones (d 1970); *b* 14 May 1931; *Educ* Whitgift Sch, Charing Cross Hosp London (MB BS, Gold medal Clinical Medicine and Surgery); *m* 1, 13 Aug 1955 (m dis 1971), Patricia Katharine, da of C W F Gray (d 1985), of Sutton, Surrey; 2 s (Andrew b 1959, Nicholas b 1962), 2 da (Sarah b 1956, Julia b 1962); m 2, 23 June 1972, Gillian Mary, da of H F Loveless, of Milford-on-Sea, Hampshire; 1 s (Timothy b 1976); *Career* Capt RAMC 1954; sr conslt surgn Guy's Hosp London 1967-, curator Gordon Museum Guy's Med Sch 1969-, teacher Univ of London 1963-; surgical tutor: RCS 1967-76, Guy's Hosp Med Sch 1967-76; sr examiner of surgery Univ of London 1962-85, examiner of surgery Soc of Apothecaries 1962-70, lectr in anatomy London Hosp 1958-59; memb The Chelsea Clinical Soc 1962-, chm The Salivary Gland Tumour Panel England 1970-, hon conslt surgn St Luke's Hosp for the Clergy 1990-, late Hunterian prof RCS 1963; Liveryman The Worshipful Soc of Apothecaries 1962; scientific FZS 1956; FRSM 1958 fell: The Hunterian Soc 1985, Assoc of Surgeons 1967; FRCS; memb: Med Soc of London 1961-, BMA 1954; author of various papers on diseases of salivary glands; *Books* Surgery (jtly, 1974), Surgery of Salivary Glands in Surgical Management (1984, 1988), Contemporary Operative Surgery (1979); *Recreations* golf, mountaineering, photography; *Clubs* Carlton; *Style—* John D Maynard, Esq; 14 Blackheath Park, London SE3 9RP (☎ 081 852 6766); Mountsloe, Frogham, Fordingbridge, Hants SP6 2HP (☎ 04255 3009); Guy's Hosp, London SE1 9RT (☎ 071 955 4359); 97 Harley St, London W1N 1DF (☎ 071 935 4988)

MAYNARD, Air Chief Marshal Sir Nigel Martin; KCB (1973, CB 1971), (CBE 1963), (DFC 1942), (AFC 1947); s of Air Vice-Marshal Forster Herbert Martin Maynard, CB, AFC (d 1976); *b* 28 Aug 1921; *Educ* Aldenham; *m* 1946, Daphne, da of Griffith Llewellyn (d 1972); 1 s, 1 da; *Career* served WWII RAF, Gp Capt 1958, ADC to HM The Queen 1961-65, Air Cdre 1965, Air Vice-Marshal 1968, Cmdt Staff Coll Bracknell 1968-70, Air Cdr Far East 1970-71, Air Marshal 1972, Dep C-in-C Strike Cmd 1972, C-in-C RAF Germany and Cdr 2 Allied Tactical Air Force 1973-76, Air Chief Marshal 1976, C-in-C Strike Cmd 1976-77, ret; *Recreations* travel; *Clubs* Naval and Military, RAF, MCC; *Style—* Air Chief Marshal Sir Nigel Martin, KCB, CBE, DFC, AFC; Manor House, Piddington, Bicester, Oxon (☎ 0844 238270)

MAYNARD, Richard Lacey; s of Henry Maynard, of Coleshill, Bucks, and Diana Elizabeth, *née* Lee; *b* 4 Oct 1946; *Educ* Bryanston, Univ of London (BSc); *m* 27 May 1972, Jacqueline Nina, da of Eric Hodges, of Chart Cottage, Fawley, nr Henley, Oxon; 1 s (William b 1988), 1 da (Susannah b 1980); *Career* chm and md Nationcrest plc (involved in construction, employment agencies and retailing); *Recreations* racing, tennis, squash, skiing; *Style—* Richard Maynard, Esq; Grimms Hill Lodge, Grimms Hill, Gt Missenden, Bucks (☎ 02406 2465); Nationcrest plc, International House, Ethorpe Cresent, Gerrards Cross, Bucks (☎ 0753 888369, fax 0753 880434, car 0860 364832)

MAYNE, Prof David Quinn; s of Leslie Harper Mayne (d 1963), and Jane Theresa, *née* Quin; *b* 23 April 1930; *Educ* Christian Brothers Coll Boksburg SA, Univ of The Witwatersrand SA (BSc, MSc), Univ of London (PhD, DSc); *m* 16 Dec 1954, Josephine Mary, da of Joseph Karl Hess (d 1968); 3 da (Susan Francine (Mrs Leung) b 9 March 1956, Maire Anne b 16 July 1957, Ruth Catherine b 18 April 1959); *Career* lectr Univ of the Witwatersrand 1950-54 & 1957-59, R & D engr Br Thomson Houston Co; Rugby 1955-56, reader Imperial Coll London 1967-71 (lectr 1959-67), res fell Harvard 1971-, prof Imperial Coll 1971-(head electrical eng dept 1984-88);FIEE 1980, FIEEE 1981, FRS 1985, FEng 1987; *Books* Differential Dynamic Programming (1970); *Recreations* walking; *Style—* Prof David Mayne; 123 Elgin Crescent, London W11 2JH (☎ 071 229 1744); Dept Electrical Engineering, Imperial College, London SW7 2BT (☎ 071 589 5111 ext 5113)

MAYNE, Hon Mrs (Helena Stewart); yr da of Baron Keith of Avonholm (Life Peer, d 1964), and Jean Maitland, *née* Bennett; sister of Baron Keith of Kinkel, *qv*; *b* 28 May 1919; *m* 1943, Gerald Outram Mayne (d 1980), s of John Fitzgerald Mayne, MD, of Itchen Abbas, Winchester; has issue; *Style—* The Hon Mrs Mayne; 47B Fairdene Road, Coulsdon, Surrey CR3 1RG

MAYNE, James Edward Mosley; s of Rupert Eric Mosley Mayne; *b* 16 July 1944; *Educ* Wellington Coll, Pembroke Coll Oxford; *m* 1970, Patricia Ann Mary, *née* Mayer; 1 s, 2 da; *Career* barr; chm: Habit Precision Engineering plc 1979-89, Wymanor Investments Ltd 1976-, Flextech plc 1986-89; *Recreations* historical research, shooting, fishing, skiing; *Clubs* United Oxford and Cambridge Univ, Boodles; *Style—* James Mayne Esq; The Manor House, Wycomb, Melton Mowbray, Leics

MAYNE, John Fraser; CB (1986); s of John Leonard Mayne (d 1982), and Martha Laura, *née* Griffiths; *b* 14 Sept 1932; *Educ* Dulwich, Worcester Coll Oxford (BA); *m* 10 May 1958, Gillian Mary, da of Leonard Arthur Key (d 1955); 1 s (Jonathan Leonard b 1964), 1 da (Catharine Hilary b 1965); *Career* Nat Serv RTR Subaltern 1951-53; Air Miny 1956-64, HM Treasy 1964-67, Cabinet Office and Central Policy Review Staff 1970-73, MOD Aus Air Staff 1976-78 (asst private sec to Sec of State 1968-70, private sec to Sec of State 1975-76), princ establishments and fin offr NI Office 1979-81, dir gen of mgmnt Audit MOD 1981-83, dep sec Cabinet Office MPO 1984-86, princ establishments and fin offr DH 1986-90 (DHSS 1986-89); management conslt; memb Cncl RUSI 1986-89; Freeman City of London 1983; FBIM 1981, FIPM 1984; *Recreations* music, fell walking, cooking, work; *Clubs* Utd Oxford and Cambridge Univ; *Style—* John Mayne, Esq, CB; c/o Holt's, Royal Bank of Scotland, Kirkland House, Whitehall SW1A 2EB (☎ 071 828 5059)

MAYNE, Very Rev Michael Clement Otway; s of Michael Ashton Otway Mayne (d 1933), and Sylvia Clementina, *née* Lumley Ellis; *b* 10 Sept 1929; *Educ* Kings' Sch Canterbury, Corpus Christi Coll Cambridge (BA, MA); *m* 16 Oct 1965, Alison Geraldine, da of Henry Erskine McKie (d 1985); 1 s (Mark b 1968), 1 da (Sarah b 1966); *Career* Nat Serv Pilot Offr RAF 1949-51; asst curate St John the Baptist Harpenden 1957-59, domestic chaplain to Bishop of Southwark 1959-65, vicar Norton Letchworth 1965-72, head religious progs BBC Radio 1972-79, vicar Great St Mary's (Univ Church) Cambridge 1979-86, dean Westminster 1986-, dean Order of the Bath; chm Govrs Westminster Sch, memb Cncl St Christophers Hospice; *Books* Prayers for Pastoral Occasions (1982), Encounters (ed, 1985), A Year Lost and Found (1987); *Recreations* theatre, reading novels and poetry, bird watching; *Style—* The Very Rev the Dean of Westminster; The Deanery, Deans Yard, Westminster Abbey, London SW1P 3PA (☎ 071 222 2953)

MAYNE, Dr Richard John; s of John William Mayne (d 1975), of London, and Kate Hilda Mayne, *née* Angus; *b* 2 April 1926; *Educ* St Paul's Sch London, Trinity Coll Cambridge (MA, PhD); *m* 1, 1954, Margaret Ellingworth Lyon; m 2, 1970, Jocelyn Mudie, da of William James Ferguson, of London; 2 da (Zoë, Alice); *Career* official of the Euro Communities 1956-63, PA to Jean Monnet 1963-66, dir Federal Tst 1971-73, head of UK Offices Commn of The Euro Communities 1973-79, co ed Encounter 1985-; *Books* The Community of Europe, The Recovery of Europe, The Europeans, Postwar, The Atlantic Challenge, Western Europe (ed), Federal Union: The Pioneers, The Memoirs of Jean Monnet (trans), Europe: A History of its People (trans); *Recreations* travel, fellwalking, sailing (Flying Falcon); *Clubs* Groucho, Les Misérables (Paris); *Style—* Dr Richard Mayne; Albany Cottage, 24 Park Village East, Regent's Park, London NW1 7PZ (☎ 071 387 6654); Encounter, 44 Great Windmill St, London W1V 7PA (☎ 071 434 3063)

MAYNE, Dr Stewart; s of Dr Gerald Outram Mayne (d 1980), of Coulsdon, Surrey, and Hon Helena Stewart, *née* Keith; *b* 25 Aug 1947; *Educ* Welsh Nat Sch of Med (BSc, MB BCh); *m* 30 Oct 1971, Diane, da of Harold Henry Charles Anger, of Aberdare, Glamorgan; 2 s (Alastair b 1976, James b 1985), 1 da (Sally b 1974); *Career* conslt haematologist Derby City Hosp; FRCPath; *Style—* Dr Stewart Mayne; 21 Trowels Lane, Derby, Derbyshire DE3 3LS (☎ 0332 31007); Derby City Hospital, Uttoxeter Rd, Derby DE3 3NE (☎ 0332 40131)

MAYNE, William; s of William Mayne, and Dorothy, *née* Fea (d 1964); *b* 16 March 1928; *Career* writer 1950-; author of ca 90 stories for children; Library Assoc medal 1957; *Recreations* baking, typesetting; *Style—* William Mayne, Esq; c/o David Higham Associates, 5-8 Lower John St, Golden Square, London W1R 4HA

MAYO, Hon Mrs (Christine Mary); *née* Plumb; yr da of Lord Plumb (Life Peer), *qv*; *b* 1950; *m* 1973, Benjamin John Mayo; 3 da (Katharine Elizabeth b 1977, Sarah Louise b 1979, Stephanie Caroline b 1983); *Style—* The Hon Mrs Mayo; The Garth, Kirkby Lane, Great Broughton, N Yorks

MAYO, Col (Edward) John; OBE (1976); s of Rev Thomas Edward Mayo, JP (d 1973), of Axminster Devon, and Constance Muriel, *née* Knibb; *b* 24 May 1931; *Educ* Kings Coll Taunton; *m* 1961, Jacqueline Margaret Anne, MBE (d 1985), da of Brig Charles Douglas Armstrong, CBE, DSO, MC (d 1985); 1 s (Charles); *Career* cmmd RA 1951, served in Malta, N Africa, Malaya, W Germany; cmdt 17 Trg Regt and Depot RA 1972-75, Col Gen Staff HQ BAOR 1979-83, ret; dir gen Help the Aged 1983-; tstee: Helpage India 1985, Helpage Kenya 1985, Helpage Sri Lanka 1986; FRSA; *Recreations* gardening, fine arts, travel, swimming; *Clubs* Army and Navy, MCC, Special Forces; *Style—* Col John Mayo; Sehore House, Tekels Ave, Camberley, Surrey (☎ 0276 29653); Help the Aged, St James's Walk, Clerkenwell, London EC1 (☎ 071 253 0253)

MAYO, John William; s of Malcolm Guy Mayo (d 1968); *b* 8 Oct 1920; *Educ* St Paul's; *m* 1959, Susan Margaret; 3 s, 1 da; *Career* Capt RA (UK, Ceylon, India); admitted slr 1947; Linklaters & Paines slrs: joined 1947, ptnr 1952, sr ptnr 1980-85; S G Warburg & Co Ltd 1985-; Hon FRCGP 1979; *Recreations* bridge, golf; *Clubs* Royal Wimbledon Golf, Hunstanton Golf, Ealing RFC; *Style—* John Mayo, Esq; 38 Marryat Rd, Wimbledon, London SW19 5BD (☎ 081 946 1537); The Mill Cottage, Ringstead, Hunstanton, Norfolk (☎ 048 525 391); S G Warburg & Co Ltd, London EC2M 2PA (☎ 081 860 0950)

MAYO, Peter Dereck Buckpitt; s of Leonard George Mayo (decd Wellington, NZ, date unknown), and Margery Muriel, *née* Buckpitt (d 1986); *b* 2 Oct 1920; *Educ* Colfes GS, Kings Coll Dental Hosp (LDS); *m* 14 April 1945, Mary, da of John Macnamara (d 1950), of O'Connell St, Kilkee, Co Clare, Ireland (d 1940); 2 s(David b 1946, Christopher b 1959), 1 da (Felicity b 1951); *Career* surgn Lt (D) RNVR 1945-48, RNB Chatham, Royal Marines Deal, HMS Hornet Gosport, HMS Excellent Whale Island Portsmouth; W Suffolk Deniac Ctee, dental rep on W Suffolk Health Ctee, Opthalitic and Disciplinary Ctees, vice chm Bd of Visitors HMP Highpoint 1986- (chm 1987); RCS; *Recreations* swimming, gardening, horse racing; *Style—* Peter Mayo, Esq; Maythorpe, Malting End, Wickhambrook, Newmarket, Suffolk (☎ 0440 820 313)

MAYO, 10 Earl of (I 1785); Terence Patrick Bourke; also Baron Naas (I 1776) and Viscount Mayo (I 1781); s of Hon Bryan Longley Bourke (d 1961), and nephew of 9 Earl (d 1962); *b* 26 Aug 1929; *Educ* St Aubyns Rottingdean, RN Coll Dartmouth; *m* 1952, Margaret Jane Robinson, da of Gerald Harrison, DL (d 1954); 3 s; *Heir* Lord Naas; *Career* Lt RN 1952, served Suez 1956; Solo Aerobatic Displays, Farnborough 1957; md Irish Marble Ltd Merlin Park Galway; memb Lib Pty 1963-65, stood for Dorset S as Lib candidate 1964; memb Gosport Borough Cncl 1961; *Clubs* Naval and County Galway; *Style—* The Rt Hon the Earl of Mayo; Doon House, Maam, Co Galway, Eire

MAYOR, Hugh Robert; QC (1986); s of George Mayor, Esq, of 9 Greyfriars Crescent, Fulwood, Preston, and Grace Mayor; *b* 12 Oct 1941; *Educ* Kirkham GS, St John's Coll Oxford (MA), Univ of Leicester (MA); *m* 1970, Carolyn Ann, da of Gp Capt Dennis Raymond Stubbs RAF, DSO, DFC, OBE, of Pond Farm, Sutton, Norfolk (d 1973); 1 s (Nicholas Dennis Robert b 1973), 1 da (Sally Jane b 1975); *Career* called to the Bar Gray's Inn 1968, in practice Midland and Oxford circuit, rec 1982; *Recreations* sailing, tennis; *Style—* Hugh R Mayor, Esq, QC; The Grange, Slawston, Leics (☎ 085 889 200); 2 Dr Johnson's Buildings, Temple (☎ 071 353 5371)

MAYOR, (Frederick) James; s of Fred Hoyland Mayor (d 1973), and Pamela Margaret, *née* Colledge; *b* 20 March 1949; *Educ* Charterhouse; *m* 1978, Viviane Martha Cresswell, da of John Leigh Reed; 2 da (Louisa Harriett Cresswell b 1981, Alice Marina Pamela b 1984); *Career* asst: Galerie Louise Leiris Paris 1968, Perls Galleries NY 1968, Impressionist Painting Dept Sothebys's London 1969, i/c Contemporary Painting Dept Barke-Bernet Inc NY 1969-72; chm The Mayor Gallery Ltd London 1980- (md 1973-); *Recreations* cooking, painting and gardening; *Clubs* Bucks, The Travellers (Paris), The Jockey Club of GB; *Style—* James Mayor, Esq; The Mayor Gallery Ltd, 22A Cork Street, London W1X 1HB (☎ 071 734 3558, fax 071 494 1377)

MAYOR, Susan; da of Fred Hoyland Mayor (d 1973), and Pamela Margaret, *née* Colledge; *b* 1 March 1945; *Educ* French Lycée London; *m* 9 July 1975, Prof J Mordaunt Crook, s of Austin Mordaunt Crook (d 1967); *Career* Christies 1964- (dir

1984); memb Ctee: Costume Soc 1975, Fan Circle Int 1975-; *Books* Collecting Fans (1980), Letts Guide to Collecting Fans (1991); *Recreations* travelling; *Style—* Miss Susan Mayor; 55 Gloucester Ave, London NW1 7BA (☎ 071 485 8280); Christie's South Kensington, 85 Old Brompton Rd, London SW7 3LD (☎ 071 581 7611, fax 071 584 0431, telex 922061)

MAYORCAS, Joseph David; s of M J Mayorcas (d 1986), of Barnes, London, and Lilian, *née* Valins; *b* 2 Dec 1937; *Educ* Latymer Upper; *m* 6 Oct 1973, Caroline Marguerite, da of Basil Rogers, of Kew, Surrey; 3 da (Claire b 1974, Miranda (twin) b 1974, Alice b 1980); *Career* dir for 30 years of Mayorcas Ltd (dealing in antique textiles and tapestries); *Recreations* opera, theatre, cinema, keeping fit; *Style—* Joseph David Mayorcas, Esq; 52 Grove Park Gardens, London W4 3RZ; 38 Jermyn Street, London SW1Y 6DN

MAYS, Colin Garth; CMG (1988); s of William Albert Mays (d 1982), and Sophia May Mays, *née* Pattinson (d 1972); *b* 16 June 1931; *Educ* Acklam Hall Sch, St John's Coll Oxford (BA); *m* 1956, Margaret Patricia, da of Philemon Robert Lloyd, and Gladys Irene Lloyd, *née* Myers, of Marske by Sea Cleveland; 1 s (Nicholas b 1964); *Career* HM Dip Serv: FO 1955-56, Sofia 1956-58, Baghdad 1958-60, UK Delgn to the Conf of the 18 Nation Ctee on Disarmament Geneva 1960, Bonn 1960-65, FCO 1965-69, Prague 1969-72, FCO (head of Info Admin Dept 1974-) 1972-77; commercial cnsllr Bucharest 1977-80, seconded to PA Management Consultants Ltd 1980-81, overseas inspr Dip Serv 1981-83; Br high cmmr: Seychelles 1983-86, The Bahamas 1986-; Liveryman Worshipful Co of Painter Stainers; *Recreations* sailing, travel; *Clubs* Travellers; *Style—* Colin Mays, Esq, CMG; c/o FCO, King Charles St, London SW1A 2AH

MAYS-SMITH, (Robert) Martin; s of Lt-Col Robert Shankland Mays-Smith, MBE (d 1980), of Randolphs, Iden, Rye, Sussex, and Brenda Mary Hilda, *née* Rickett; *b* 17 Nov 1930; *Educ* Eton, Trinity Coll Cambridge; *m* 22 June 1963, Jennifer Joan (d 1989), da of Capt Eustace Makins (d 1968), of Wood Farm, Little Fransham, Dereham, Norfolk; 3 da (Kate b 6 March 1964, Henrietta b 17 Jan 1966, Arabella b 10 July 1970); *Career* Irish Guards 1949-51; Bank of England 1954-63, local dir Oxford Barclays Bank 1968-69 (joined 1963); md: William Brandt & Sons & Co Ltd 1969-72, Nat & Grindlays Bank 1970-72; dir: A L Sturge Holdings Ltd, Kleinwort Benson Ltd 1972-89 (banking dir 1972-84, head of Banking Div 1984-87), Kleinwort Benson Gp plc 1988-89; chm: Empire Stores Group plc, dir First Nat Fin Corpn, Australian Mutual Provident London Bd, Morland & Co; memb: Norwich & Peterborough Building Soc; Governing Body of Ripon Coll Cuddesdon, Cncl of Mgmnt GAP, govr May House GS for the Deaf; Liveryman Worshipful Co of Clothworkers; FCIB 1983; *Recreations* life in the country especially fishing, music especially opera; *Clubs* Fly Fishers, Leander; *Style—* Martin Mays-Smith, Esq; Beedon House, Beedon, Newbury, Berkshire RG16 8SW (☎ 063528 233); Kleinwort Benson Ltd, 20 Fenchurch St, London EC3P 3DB (☎ 071 623 8000)

MEACHER, Michael Hugh; MP ((Lab) Oldham W 1970-); s of George Hubert Meacher (d 1969), of Berkhamsted, Herts; *b* 4 Nov 1939; *Educ* Berkhamsted Sch, New Coll Oxford; *m* 1, 1962 (m dis 1987), Molly Christine, da of William Reid, of Grayshott, Surrey; 2 s, 2 da; m 2, 1988, Lucianne, da of William Craven, of Gerrards Cross, Bucks; *Career* joined Lab Pty 1962, sec Danilo Dolci Tst 1964, lectr in social admin Univ of York 1966-69 and LSE 1970; parly under sec state: Dept of Indust 1974-75, DHSS 1975-76, Dept of Trade 1976-79; memb Treasy Select Ctee 1980-83, chm Select Ctee on Lloyd's Bill 1982, defeated Lab dep leadership election 1983, elected to shadow cabinet 1983, memb NEC Oct 1983-; front bench oppn spokesman: Health and Social Security 1983-87, Employment 1987-89, Social Security 1989-; author; *Books* Taken for a Ride (1972), Socialism with a Human Face (1982); *Style—* Michael Meacher, Esq, MP; 5 Cottenham Park Rd, London SW20

MEAD, Anthony Frederick John; s of Frederick James Mead (d 1978), of Carshalton, Surrey, and Doris Kathleen, *née* Sharratt (d 1990); *b* 4 May 1941; *Educ* Trinity Sch Croydon, Univ of Hull (BSc); *m* 29 July 1972, Alison Margaret, da of George Melvin Ward; 2 s (Christopher Frederick James b 9 Dec 1976, Andrew Melvin John b 31 Dec 1978), 1 da (Katharine Mary Louise b 1 July 1981); *Career* articled clerk Lewis Bloom & Co 1963-66, sr mangr Coopers & Lybrand Deloitte 1967-78, internal auditor AFIA Worldwide Insurance 1978-79, ptnr and insur indust specialist Rowley Pemberton Roberts & Co (became Pannell Kerr Forster 1981) 1980- (mangr 1979-80); FCA 1967; *Recreations* family, sch govr; *Style—* Anthony Mead, Esq; Pannell Kerr Forster, New Garden House, 78 Hatton Garden, London EC1N 8JA (☎ 071 831 7393, fax 071 405 6736)

MEAD, Anthony John; RD (1986); s of James Reginald Mead, JP (d 1984), and Muriel Violet, *née* Johnston; *b* 3 Feb 1942; *Educ* Wrekin Coll; *m* 25 March 1988, June, da of Sydney Thomas Farrington, DFC (d 1981); *Career* RNR Lt 1971, Lt Cdr 1979; CA; articles Foster and Stephens Birmingham 1960-64, Touche Ross and Co Birmingham 1964-65, ptnr Daffern and Co Coventry 1965-75, princ Mead and Co Kenilworth and Kingswear 1976-; memb Cncl Univ of Warwick 1984-87, tstee Charitable Tst 1961; FCA; *Recreations* offshore sailing; *Clubs* Royal Naval Sailing Assoc, Royal Dart Yacht; *Style—* Anthony J Mead, Esq

MEAD, Brian Leonard; s of Leonard William Mead, of 93 Meadway, Ilford, Essex, and Lillian Elizabeth, *née* Crick; *b* 12 March 1944; *Educ* Mayfield Boys Sch; *m* 1, 18 Aug 1972 (m dis 1986), Faith Margaret, da of Harold Scholes, of Manchester; 1 da (Elizabeth b 1983); m 2, 13 May 1989, Mandy-Elizabeth, da of Lt Cdr Keith Alexander Broach, RN; *Career* slr; Jackson Pixley & Co ACs: articles 1962-67, admitted slr 1967, mangr 1968-70; sr mangr Mann Judd CAs 1971-73, assoc gp fin dir Green Shield Training Stamp Co Ltd 1973-78, gp fin dir Cray Electronics Holdings plc 1979-; cdre Little Ship Club London 1982-85; FCA 1967, MInstD 1980; *Recreations* sailing, yacht racing, cruising; *Clubs* Royal Southern, Little Ship, RYA; *Style—* Brian Mead, Esq; The Haven, 5 Sylvan Lane, Hamble, Southampton, Hampshire (☎ 0703 456 101); Cray Electronics Holdings Plc, Cray Manor, 12 Manor Ct, Fareham, Hampshire

MEAD, Prof Denys John; s of Edwin Ewart Mead (d 1983), of S Woodford, London, and Daisy Edith Mead (d 1962); *b* 15 Jan 1926; *Educ* Bancroft's Sch, Coll of Aeronautics Cranfield Beds (DCAe, DSc); *m* 27 March 1954, Rosemary Winifred, da of Samuel George Lidstone (d 1967), of Cheam, Surrey; 2 s (Peter b 1955, John b 1957); *Career* structural engr De Havilland Aircraft Co 1946-49, dynamics engr Supermarine Aircraft Co 1951-52, prof of structural dynamics Univ of Southampton 1985- (lectr, sr lectr, reader 1952-85); *Books* Noise and Acoustic Fatigue in Aeronautics (with E J Richards, 1968); *Recreations* photography, forest walking; *Style—* Prof Denys Mead; Dept of Aeronautics and Astronautics, University of Southampton, Southampton Hants (☎ 0703 552314, fax 0703 593939, telex 47661)

MEAD, Janet Mabel; da of Frank William Mead (d 1983), and Peggy Gertrude Florence Lyne, *née* Martin; *b* 4 July 1942; *Educ* St Martin-in-the-Fields HS, Univs of Barcelona, Madrid and Grenoble (various language and translators diplomas, Dip CAM); *Career* personal mgmnt Petroleos Mexicanos Paris 1965-68, PRO for Ted Bates Advertising Agency Paris 1968-72, travelled extensively in S America 1972-73, corporate communications mangr HB Maynard Inc 1973-76, marketing services mangr Thomas Ness Ltd 1976-80, gen mangr Retailine Research Ltd 1980-82, md Assoc Research Ltd 1982; dir: Penarvon plc 1983, Retail Audits Ltd 1981; *Recreations* theatre, travel, running, painting, talking; *Clubs* Zonta Int London II (fndr memb); *Style—* Miss Janet Mead; Assoc Research Ltd, Banderway House, 158-162 Kilburn High Rd, London NW6 (☎ 071 328 3213)

MEAD, Richard Barwick; s of Thomas Gifford Mead, MBE, of 4 Wyndham Lea, W Chiltington, W Sussex, and Joyce Mary, *née* Barwick; *b* 18 Aug 1947; *Educ* Marlborough, Pembroke Coll Cambridge (MA); *m* 25 June 1971, Sheelagh Margaret, da of James Leslie Thom, of Holly Cottage, Stoke St Milborough, Ludlow, Shropshire; 2 s (Timothy b 1973, Rupert b 1977), 1 da (Nicola b 1975 d 1976); *Career* audit supervisor Arthur Young 1969-73, corporate fin exec Brandts Ltd 1973-75, dir and head Corporate Fin Dept Antony Gibbs and Sons 1975-83, dir corporate fin Credit Suisse First Boston Ltd 1983-85, ptnr and nat dir corporate fin Ernst & Young 1985-; FCA 1972; *Recreations* gardening, history, music, family; *Style—* Richard Mead, Esq; Shambles, Watts Cross, Hildenborough, Tonbridge, Kent TN11 9NB (☎ 0732 832 858); Ernst & Young, Rolls House, 7 Rolls Buildings, Fetter Lane, London EC4A 1NH (☎ 071 928 2000, fax 071 405 2147, telex 888604)

MEADE, Eric Cubitt; s of William Charles Abbott Meade (d 1970), and Vera Alicia Maria, *née* Cubitt (d 1981); *b* 12 April 1923; *Educ* Ratcliffe Coll Syston Leics; *m* 2 July 1960, Margaret Arnott, da of Archibald McCallum; 2 s (Vincent b 20 April 1961, Christopher b 5 April 1963), 1 da (Veronica b 11 Feb 1965); *Career* WWII Hampshire Regt 1942-46, served N Africa, Italy (cmmnd in field), Capt 1944 (POW 1944-45); CA 1947, sr ptnr Deloitte Haskins & Sells 1982-85 (joined 1949, ptnr 1958-85); chm: Parly Law Ctee 1974-76, Investigation Ctee 1976-77, Consultative Ctee of Accountancy Bodies Ethics Ctee 1977-83; memb Audit Cmmn 1986-89, lay member Slrs Complaints Bureau 1985-89; FCA (memb Cncl 1969-79); *Recreations* tennis, bowls; *Clubs* Hurlingham; *Style—* Eric Meade, Esq; 56 Hurlingham Court, Ranelagh Gardens, London SW6 3UP (☎ 071 736 5382)

MEADE, Richard John Hannay; OBE (1974); s of John Graham O'Mahoney Meade, JP, DL, of The Glyn Farm, Chepstow, Gwent, and Phyllis Brenda, *née* Watts; *b* 4 Dec 1938; *Educ* Lancing, Magdalene Coll Cambridge; *m* 11 May 1977, Angela Dorothy, da of Lt Charles Richard Farquhar, MC, DL (d 1980), of Cubley Lodge, Ashbourne, Derbyshire; 3 s (Charles b and d 1979, Harry b 1983), 1 da (Lucy b 1985); *Career* Nat Serv 1958-60, cmmnd 11 Hussars (Prince Albert's Own); competed internationally for 25 years in Three-day Eventing; rep GB: four Olympic Games, five World Championships, six Euro Championships 1963-82; Olympics: team gold Mexico 1968, team gold Munich 1972, individual gold 1972; World Championships: individual silver Burghley 1966, individual silver Punchestown 1970, team gold Punchestown 1970, team silver Burghley 1974, team gold Luhmühlen 1982; Euro Championships: team silver Moscow 1965, team gold Punchestown 1967, team gold Burghley 1971, team bronze Kiev 1973, team gold Horsens Denmark 1981; also rep GB at alternative Olympics Fountainbleau 1980, won Burghley 1964, Badminton 1970 and 1982, memb Three-Day Event Ctee Int Equestrian Fedn 1977-80 (memb Bureau), pres Br Equestrian Fedn; church warden St James's Church W Littleton; Yeoman Worshipful Co of Saddlers 1972, Hon Freeman Worshipful Co of Loriners 1975; *Books* Fit for Riding (1984); *Recreations* shooting, skiing; *Style—* Richard Meade, Esq, OBE

MEADE, Lady Sophia Catherine Gathorne-Hardy; da of 4 Earl of Cranbrook, CBE; *b* 1936; *m* 1957, Simon Robert Jasper Meade; *Style—* Lady Sophia Meade

MEADE-KING, Richard Oliver; s of (William) Oliver Meade-King (d 1971), and Ellen Collins, *née* Sherlock; *b* 30 Jan 1926; *Educ* Radley, Jesus Coll Cambridge (BA); *m* 22 Dec 1951, Hilary Scott, da of Charles Woodhouse (d 1968); 1 s (Charles) 1 da (Tessa (Mrs Mackenzie)); *Career* Sub Lt Fleet Air Arm RNVR 1944-46; Binnie Deacon and Gourley Consulting Engrs 1949-58: asst research engr Sillent Valley Water Tunnel Project, surveyor of potential hydro electric sites Nigeria, designer sewerage and surface water drainage Lusaka; English China Clays 1958-86, dir ECCI 1967-86; memb Bd of ECC subsidiaries incl: chm ECC Carbonates, chm Fordiman Sales Ltd, dep chm Anglo American Clays Inc and Kaolin Australia, dir for ops of co's in Japan Brazil Portugal Spain France and Italy, ret 1986; fndr chm W Country Ventures Ltd (ret 1986); former memb Plymouth Cattwater Harbour Cmmrs, memb Fowey Harbour Cmmrs; *Style—* Richard Meade-King, Esq; Penellick, Par, Cornwall

MEADEN, Sonia Irene; da of Marshal Coneley, of Puerto De La Cruz, Tenerife, and Irene, *née* Bowles; *b* 27 Nov 1936; *Educ* Oswetry Girls HS Salop, Kidderminster GS Worcs; *m* 1, 1954 (m dis 1960), Henry Charles; 2 da (Gail b 1956, Deborah b 1959); m 2, 1962 (m dis 1964), Raymond Peagram; m 3, 1966, Brian Meaden, s of Thomas Meaden (d 1982); 2 da (Emma b 1969, Cass b 1972); *Career* nat vice pres and first lady Br Amusement Catering Trades Assoc 1987- (nat chm and first lady 1985-87), chm and first lady Nat Amusement Cncl 1987-, dir and first lady Amusement Trades Exhibition 1988; memb George Thomas Fellowship, tstee The Grand Order of Lady Ratlings, chm BACTA Charitable Tst; *Recreations* boating, theatre, travel; *Style—* Mrs Sonia Meaden; 84 Marylebone High St, London W1 (☎ 071 935 8381); Carousel Warren Rd, Minehead, Somerset TA24 5BG (☎ 0643 2707, fax 0643 7508)

MEADES, Jonathan Turner; s of John William Meades (d 1981), of Salisbury, Wilts, and Margery Agnes, *née* Hogg; *b* 21 Jan 1947; *Educ* Kings Coll Taunton, Univ of Bordeaux, RADA; *m* 1, 15 Sept 1980 (m dis), Sally Dorothy Renée, da of Raymond Brown; 2 da (Holly b 7 May 1981, Rose (twin) b 7 May 1981); m 2, 1 June 1988, Frances Anne, da of Sir William Bentley; 1 da (Eleanor Lily b 31 Dec 1986); *Career* journalist, writer and tv presenter 1971-; contrib to: Books and Bookman, Time Out, Curious, The Observer, Architects Jl, Sunday Times, Harpers & Queen, Literary Review, Tatler, A La Carte, The Times, The Independent, Sunday Correspondent, Evening Standard, magazines in Canada and USA; ed Event 1981-82, pt/t memb editorial staff Tatler 1982-87; tv series incl: The Victorian House (1987), Abroad in Britain (1990); *Books* This is Their Life (1979), An Illustrated Atlas of The World's Buildings (1980), Filthy English (1984), Peter Knows What Dick Likes (1989); awards: Glenfiddich Restaurant Writer of The Year 1986 and 1990, runner up Critic of the Year UK Press Awards 1989; *Recreations* buildings, mushrooms, sloth; *Clubs* Academy, Groucho's; *Style—* Jonathan Meades, Esq; c/o Peters Fraser and Dunlop, 503-4 The Chambers, Chelsea Harbour, London SW10

MEADOW, Prof (Samuel) Roy; s of Samuel Tickle Meadow (d 1980), of Wigan, Lancs, and Doris Marion, *née* Peacock (d 1984); *b* 9 June 1933; *Educ* Wigan GS, Bromsgrove, Worcester Coll Oxford (BA, MA), Guy's Hosp Med Sch (BM BCh); *m* 1 Sept 1962 (m dis 1974), Gillian Margaret, da of Sir Ian Maclennan, KC, MG (d 1985), of Richmond; m 2, 14 Aug 1978, Marianne Jane, *née* Harvey; 1 s (Julian Robert Ian b 1963), 1 da (Anna Jane b 1965); *Career* Lt RA 1951-53; jr med posts 1960-67, sr res fell MRC Inst Child Health Birmingham 1967-68; St James' Univ Hosp Leeds: sr lectr and conslt paediatrician 1970-80, inaugural prof and head of Dept of Paediatrics and Child Health 1980-; ed Archives of Disease in Childhood 1979-87; published reports Meadows Syndrome One 1968 and Meadows Syndrome Two (Munchausen Syndrome By Proxy) 1977; memb and chm Assoc Child Psychology and Psychiatry 1983-84, memb Ctee Safety of Med 1987-90, chm Academic Bd Br Paediatric Assoc; MRCP, FRCP, DRCOG; *Books* Lecture Notes on Paediatrics (1973), Bladder Control and Enuresis (1973), The Child and His Symptons (1978), Recent Advances in Paediatrics (ed, 1983-86), ABC of Child Abuse (ed, 1989); *Recreations* Gardening; *Style—* Prof Roy Meadow; Weeton Grange, Weeton, Leeds LS17 0AP (☎ 0423 734234); Dept of

Paediatrics & Child Health, Univ of Leeds, St Jame's Univ Hosp Leeds LS9 7TF (☎ 0532 433144 ext 5657)

MEADOWS, Prof Bernard William; s of William A F Meadows, and Ethel; *b* 19 Feb 1915; *Educ* Norwich Sch, Norwich Sch of Art, RCA; *m* 1939, Marjorie, *née* Payne; 2 da (Julia, Anthea); *Career* sculptor 1947-; lectr Chelsea Sch of Art 1947-60, emeritus prof RCA 1980- (prof of sculpture RCA 1960-80); works incl in the collections of: V&A, British Museum, Metropolitan Museum NY, Guggenheim Museum NY, Tate Gallery; various public and private collections in Europe and America; memb Royal Fine Art Commission 1971-76, ARCA 1947; *Style—* Prof Bernard Meadows; 34 Belsize Grove, London NW3 4TR (☎ 071 722 0772)

MEADOWS, Prof (Arthur) Jack; s of Flt Sgt Arthur Harold Meadows (d 1971), and Alice, *née* Elson (d 1962); *b* 24 Jan 1934; *Educ* New Coll Oxford (MA, DPhil), UCL (MSc); *m* 6 Dec 1958, (Isobel) Jane Tanner, da of Stanley Charles Bryant (d 1937); 1 s (Michael b 1962), 2 da (Alice b 1960, Sally b 1962); *Career* Nat Serv Lt Intelligence Corps 1952-54; Univ of Leicester 1966-86: lectr, sr lectr, prof 1972-, head Depts Astronomy and History of Sci; head Primary Communications Res Centre 1976-86, head Office Humanities Communication 1983-86, prof and head Dept Library and Info Studies Univ of Loughborough 1986-; author of sixteen books and approximately 150 res papers; memb Br Library Advsy Ctees; FInstP 1983, FLA 1989, FInfSc 1987; *Recreations* sleeping; *Style—* Prof Jack Meadows; 47 Swan St, Seagrave, Leics LE12 7NL (☎ 0509 812557); Department of Library and Information Studies, Loughborough University of Technology, Loughborough, Leics LE11 3TU (☎ 0509 223058, fax 0509 223053)

MEADOWS, Dr John Christopher; s of Dr Swithin Pinder Meadows, and Doris Steward, *née* Noble; *b* 25 March 1940; *Educ* Westminster, Univ of Cambridge (BA, MB BChir, MD); *m* 9 July 1966, Patricia, da of the late John Appleton Pierce, of IOM; 2 s; *Career* former conslt neurologist St George's Hosp, conslt neurologist King Edward VII Hosp, hon neurologist Newspaper Press Fund; FRCP; *Recreations* gardening, walking, travelling, reading; *Style—* Dr John C Meadows; c/o 143 Harley St, London W1N 1DJ (☎ 071 935 1802)

MEADOWS, William Robert; DL (Somerset)1989; s of William de Warenne Meadows (d 1974), of Norfolk, and Marianne Alice *née* Stokes (d 1930); *b* 10 Aug 1926; *Educ* Sherborne, Corpus Christi Coll Cambridge; *m* 8 Nov 1960, Alison Rosemary, da of Sir Austin Anderson (d 1973), of Surrey; 1 s (William b 1972), 2 da (Victoria b 1962, Marianne b 1963); *Career* Lt RM Commandos 1944-47, served Europe, Far East; glass engraver and lectr; memb Baltic Exchange 1951-68; Somerset CC: chm Educn Ctee 1981-83, chm 1983-85; chm: Exmoor Nat Park Ctee 1987-89, Somerset Co Cadet Ctee 1987-90; *Recreations* gardening, painting, fishing; *Style—* William R Meadows, Esq, DL; The Old House, Milverton, Taunton, Somerset TA4 1LR

MEADWAY, (Richard) John; s of Norman Pardey Meadway (d 1957), of Arundel, Sussex, and Constance, *née* Parker; *b* 30 Dec 1944; *Educ* Collyer's Sch Horsham, Peterhouse Cambridge (MA), Univ of Edinburgh (PhD), Univ of Oxford (MA); *m* 23 March 1968, Dr Jeanette Valerie, da of Stephen George Partis (d 1984), of Long, Clawson, Leics; 2 da (Eleanor Anne b 1974, Margot Elizabeth b 1977); *Career* asst princ Miny of Technol 1970, private sec to Min for Trade and Consumer Affrs 1973-74, princ Dept of Prices and Consumer Protection 1974-76, private sec to PM 1976-78; asst sec: Dept of Trade Int Trade Policy Div 1979-83, DTI Vehicles Div 1983-86, DTI Mgmnt Servs Div 1987-89; under sec DTI Overseas Trade Div 2 1989-; *Recreations* reading, travel; *Clubs* Reform; *Style—* John Meadway, Esq; Department of Trade and Industry, 1-19 Victoria Street, London SW1H 0ET (☎ 071 215 5000)

MEAGER, Hon Mrs; (Joan Beryl); da of 5 Baron Henley; *b* 1893; *m* 1914, Kildare Stucley Meager; 1 s, 1 da; *Style—* The Hon Mrs Meager; 117 Brighton Rd, Worthing, Sussex

MEAKIN, Christopher Rolf; s of Benet Garth Meakin, of Spalding, Lincs, and Jean Mary, *née* Platt (d 1978); *b* 25 Sept 1949; *Educ* East Grinstead GS, Cambridgeshire HS for Boys; *m* 1969, Patricia Ann, da of late Gordon Slarks; 2 da (Vanessa Mary b 6 Sept 1972, Hannah Elizabeth b 18 April 1975); *Career* trainee reporter: Sussex Express, Sussex County Herald, East Grinstead Observer 1967-71, asst PR offr then press offr Volkswagen (GB) Ltd (employed by in-house consultancy Philip Stein Associates) 1971-74, princ features writer Yorkshire Evening Press 1974-77, account dir then creative dir Connors Publicity Ltd Cambridge (now Nicklin Advertising Cambridge Ltd) 1977-89, md Nicklin Advertising Cambridge Ltd 1989-; MIPR 1988; *Recreations* music, vintage vehicles; *Style—* Christopher Meakin, Esq; 39 Hall Drive, Hardwick, Cambridge CB3 7QN (☎ 0954 211154); Nicklin Advertising Cambridge Ltd, Meadowcroft, Church St, Cambridge CB4 1EL (☎ 0223 314545, fax 0223 324611, car 0831 153739)

MEAKIN, Henry Paul John; s of Wing Cdr Henry John Walter Meakin, DFC (d 1989), of 9 Glanmore Rd, PO Chisipiti, Harare, Zimbabwe, and Elizabeth Wilma, *née* Fairbairns; *b* 2 Jan 1944; *Educ* Plumtree Sch Rhodesia; *m* 2 Jan 1971, Vicki Lynn, da of Maurice James Bullus (d 1990), of Hilltop Hall, Pannal, Harrogate, N Yorks; 2 s (Oliver b 1975, Harry b 1980), 1 da (Katie b 1972); *Career* exec dir Pensord Press Ltd 1970-74; chm: Aspen Communications 1979-85 (md 1975-78), Aspen Communications PLC 1985-; dir: Wiltshire Radio plc 1981-85, GWR Radio 1985-87; chm GWR Gp plc 1988-; FRSA; *Recreations* tennis, golf, music; *Style—* Henry Meakin, Esq; Aspen Communications PLC, 18 Thomas St, Cirencester, Gloucs GL7 2AX (☎ 0285 652176, fax 0285 656620)

MEALE, (Joseph) Alan; MP (Lab) Mansfield 1987-; s of Albert Henry Meale (d 1986), and Elizabeth, *née* Catchpole; both parents trade union shop stewards; *b* 31 July 1949; *Educ* Ruskin Coll Oxford; *m* 15 March 1983, Diana, da of Lt Cdr John Gillespy, RN (ret); *Career* nat employment devpt offr (Home Office funded) 1977-79, asst to Ray Buckton (gen sec ASLEF) 1979-83, Parly and political advsr to Michael Meacher MP 1983-87; vice chm Employment Ctee PLP 1987-; memb: Parly Select Ctee Home Affrs, War Pensions Bd 1990-; *Books* author and ed various publications; *Recreations* reading; *Clubs* Mansfield Lab; *Style—* Alan Meale, Esq, MP; 4 Welbeck St, Mansfield, Notts; House of Commons, London SW1A 0AA

MEANEY, Sir Patrick Michael; s of Joseph Francis Meaney (d 1953), and Ethel Clara Meaney (d 1966); *b* 6 May 1925; *Educ* Wimbledon Coll, Northern Poly; *m* 1967, Mary June, da of Albert William Kearney (d 1986); 1 s (Adam b 1968); *Career* served HM Forces 1941-47; md Thomas Tilling plc 1973-83 (dir 1961-83); dir: Cable & Wireless plc 1978-84, ICI plc 1981-; chm: Rank Orgn 1983- (dir 1979-), A Kershaw & Sons plc 1983-; dep chm: Midland Bank plc 1984- (dir 1979), Horserace Levy Bd 1985-, MEPC plc, Tarmac plc 1990-; dir: Metropolitan and County Racecourse Holders Ltd 1985-, Racecourse Tech Serv Ltd 1985-; Int Adv CRH plc 1985; pres Inst of Mktg 1981-; memb: Cncl London C of C 1977-82, Conference Bd 1982-87, Br N American Ctee 1979-, CBI 1979-90, Advsy Bd World Econ Forum 1979, Royal Society of Arts 1987-, Br Exec Serv Overseas 1987-, Stock Exchange Listed Cos Advsy Ctee 1987-, President's Ctee Advertising Assoc 1987-, kt 1981; *Recreations* sport, music, education; *Clubs* British Sportsmans, Harlequin Football; *Style—* Sir Patrick Meaney; 6 Connaught Place, London W2 (☎ 071 706 1111, telex 263549)

MEANS, Hon Mrs (Juliet Evelyn Mary); *née* Deedes; eldest da of Baron Deedes (Life Peer), *qv*; *b* 1948; *m* 7 April 1990, Robert Dale Means, eldest s of Robert Means, of Blythe, California, USA, and Mrs Clyda Holbrook, of Hemet, California, USA; *Style—* The Hon Mrs Means; 1707 E St, Eureica, CA 95501, USA

MEARA, Dr Robert Harold; s of Robert Meara (d 1935), of Gwent, and Anne Davies (d 1958); *b* 8 Dec 1917; *Educ* Jones' Haberdashers Sch Pontypool, St Catharine's Coll Cambridge (MA); *m* 18 Feb 1943, Mair, da of William Jones (d 1958), of Glamorgan; 1 s (Jolyon b 1956), 2 da (Jennifer b 1944, Imogen b 1955); *Career* dermatologist; emeritus conslt physician: Middx Hosp London, St John's Hosp for Diseases of the Skin; former hon dermatologist to Br Army; *Recreations* music, walking, bridge, travel; *Clubs* RSM; *Style—* Dr Robert H Meara; 34 Channings, Kingsway, Hove, E Sussex (☎ 0273 733809)

MEARS, Rt Rev John Cledan; *see*: Bangor, Bishop of

MEARS, Patrick Michael; s of Alex Benjamin Albert Mears, of Henley-on-Thames, and Moira Denise, *née* Buzetti; *b* 19 Jan 1958; *Educ* Henley GS, LSE (LLB); *m* 27 Aug 1983, Carol Lucia (d 1987), da of Carl William Anders (d 1968), of Rochester, NY; 1 da (Elizabeth Helen Carol b 8 Sept 1987); *Career* admitted slr 1982; ptnr Allen & Overy 1988; Freeman Worshipful Co of Slrs; memb Law Soc; *Recreations* bridge, squash, theatre; *Clubs* Dulwich Squash Rackets; *Style—* Patrick Mears, Esq; Allen & Overy, 9 Cheapside, London EC2V 6AD (☎ 071 248 9898, fax 071 236 2192)

MEARS, Roger Malcolm Loudon; s of Dr K P G Mears, of Vancouver Island, Canada, and Dr Eleanor, *née* Loudon, of Sleaford, Lincs; *b* 15 Feb 1944; *Educ* City of London Sch, Corpus Christi Coll Cambridge (MA, DipArch); *m* 4 Nov 1978, Joan Adams, da of William Archer Speers, of Brooklyn Heights, NY; 3 da (Emily b 1981, Rebecca b 1983, Jessica b 1986); *Career* architect with own practice and particular interest in historic bldgs; *Recreations* music (viola player), watermills and milling; *Style—* Roger Mears, Esq; 2 Compton Terrace, London N1 2UN (☎ 071 359 8222)

MEATH, 14 Earl of (I 1627); Anthony Windham Normand Brabazon; also Baron Ardee (I 1616), and Baron Chaworth (UK 1831), in which title he sits in House of Lords; s of 13 Earl, CB, CBE (d 1949), by his w Lady Aileen Wyndham Quin (da of 4 Earl of Dunraven); *b* 3 Nov 1910; *Educ* Eton, RMC Sandhurst; *m* 30 July 1940, Elizabeth Mary, da of Capt Geoffrey Vaux Salvin Bowlby, Royal House Gds (ka 1915); 2 s, 2 da; *Heir* s, Lord Ardee; *Career* ADC to Govr Bengal 1936, Capt Grenadier Gds 1938, Maj 1941, wounded 1943, ret 1946; *Style—* The Rt Hon the Earl of Meath; Killruddery, Bray, Co Wicklow, Ireland

MEATH, Michael Smith; s of John Smith, and Bridget Fagan, of Liss, Oldcastle, Co Meath; *b* 6 June 1940; *Educ* St Finian's Coll Mullingar, Lateran Univ Rome; *Career* ordained 1963, Bishop of Meath 1990-; *Style—* The Most Rev the Bishop of Meath; Bishop's House, Dublin Road, Mullingar, Co Westmeath, Ireland (☎ 044 48841/42038, fax 044 43020)

MEDAWAR, Nicholas Antoine Macbeth; s of late Antoine Nicholas Medawar, and Annie Innes Logietulloch, *née* Macbeth; *b* 25 April 1933; *Educ* Keswick Sch, Trinity Coll Dublin (BA, LLB); *m* 1, 1962 (m dis 1977), Joyce Catherine, *née* Crosland-Boyle; 1 s (Anthony Crosland b 1962), 1 da (Zohara Dawn b 1966 (decd)); m 2, 1977, Caroline Mary, *née* Collins; *Career* Nat Serv 1957-59 Cyprus; barr Gray's Inn 1957, QC 1984, rec 1985; *Recreations* walking; *Style—* Nicholas Medawar, Esq; 4 Paper Buildings Temple London, EC4 7EX (☎ 071 583 0816, fax 071 353 4979)

MEDD, (William) Gordon; s of William Thomas Medd (d 1959); *b* 30 Dec 1920; *Educ* Scarborough HS, Univ of Liverpool; *m* 1943, Joan, *née* Fenwick; 1 s; *Career* served 1941-46 Parachute Regt, Capt; biochemist, biscuit mfr; dir Assoc Biscuit Mfrs 1967-82, O P Chocolate 1973, W & R Jacob (Dublin) 1976; regnl councillor CBI 1975-81; *Recreations* golf; *Clubs* Scarborough NC; *Style—* Gordon Medd, Esq; Highmoor Croft, Hutton Buscel, Yorks (☎ 0723 863486)

MEDDINGS, Hon Mrs (Susan Jane); *née* Delfont; er da of Baron Delfont (Life Peer), *qv*; *b* 10 April 1947; *Educ* Millfield; *m* 1982, Mark Derek Meddings (a film special effects technician), s of Derek Meddings; 1 s, 1 da; *Career* stills photographer (films and television); *Style—* The Hon Mrs Meddings; 34 Hamilton Gdns, St John's Wood, London NW8

MEDFORTH-MILLS, Dr (Leslie) Robin; s of Cyril Mills, and Nora, *née* Medforth; *b* 8 Dec 1942; *Educ* Univ of Durham (BA, PhD); *m* 24 Sept 1983, HRH Princess Helen of Roumania, *qv*, 2 da of HM King Michael of Roumania, GCVO; 1 s (Nicholas Michael de Roumanie b 1 April 1985), 1 da (Elisabetta Karina de Roumanie b 4 Jan 1989); *Career* third world devpt conslt: Nigeria 1964-67, Sudan 1967-71, Ghana 1971, Sierra Leone 1972-74, Sudan (Int Lab Orgn) 1974-81, UN Fund for Population Activities 1981-87; sr res fell Centre for Overseas Res and Devpt Univ of Durham 1987-90; conslt UN Children's Fund (UNICEF) Geneva 1987-; *Recreations* genealogy, antique silver, calligraphy; *Clubs* Athenaeum; *Style—* Dr Robin Medforth-Mills; Flass Hall, Esh Winning, Durham DH7 9QD (☎ 091 373 0466, fax 091 373 2466)

MEDHURST, Brian; s of Eric Gilbert Medhurst (d 1983), by his w Bertha May (d 1989); *b* 18 March 1935; *Educ* Godalming GS, Trinity Coll Cambridge (MA); *m* 1960, Patricia Anne, da of Bernard Charles Beer (d 1982); 2 s, 1 da; *Career* The Prudential Assurance Co Ltd: investmt mangr 1975-80, jt chief investmt mangr 1981-82, gen mangr 1982; md: Int Div Prudential Corporation plc, Prudential Property Services; dir: Prudential Nominees Ltd 1981-, Prudential Assurance Co Ltd 1981-, St Helens Trust Ltd 1985- (chm), Prudential Corporation Canada 1985-, Prudential Life of Ireland Ltd 1985-, Maricourt Ltd 1985-, Jackson National Life Insurunce Co 1986-, Brooke Holdings Inc 1986; Brooke Life Insurance Co 1986-, Chrissy Corporation 1986-, Prudential Corporation Australia 1988-, Emeric Insurance Co 1988-, Prudential Vita Spa 1990-, Prudential Corporation Asia Ltd 1989-; chm Br Insur Assoc Investmt Protection Ctee until 1982, memb Cncl Inst of Actuaries 1982-87 (fell 1962-), Prudential Assurance Co Singapore (Pte) Ltd 1990-, The Ombudsman for Corporate Estate Agents Company Limited 1990-; *Recreations* squash, golf, piano duets, tree felling; *Clubs* North Hants Golf, Royal Aldershot Offrs'; *Style—* Brian Medhurst, Esq; Prudential Corporation, 1 Stephen St, London W1P 2AP (☎ 071 548 3500)

MEDLAND, Prof Anthony John (Tony); s of Reginald George (d 1989), of Newton Abbot, Devon, and Phyllis Mary, *née* Battershill (d 1989); *b* 13 July 1940; *Educ* Highweek Sch Newton Abbot, Torquay Tech Coll, Brunel Coll Action (Dip Technol); *m* 5 June 1965, Beryl Denise, da of David Gynn (d 1974), of Forestgate, London; 1 s (Paul David b 1972), 1 da (Clare Catherine b 1969); *Career* patent engr Westland Aircraft Ltd 1963-64 (gen engrg apprenticeship 1957-63), stress engr Westland Helicopters Ltd 1963-64, post grad res student UCL 1964-67, sr res and devpt engr (mechanical) Cambridge Consultants Ltd 1967-70, MOD/SRC res fell Hatfield Poly, sr res and devpt engr PATS Centre Int 1977-78, prof in computer aided design Brunel Univ 1985-90 (lectr and sr lectr 1978-85); MIMechE 1973, FIMechE 1990; *Books* The Computer-Based Design Process (1986), CADCAM in Practice (with Piers Burnett, 1986), Principles of CAD - A Coursebook (with G Mullineux, 1988); *Style—* Prof Tony Medland; Department of Manufacturing and Engineering Systems, Brunel University, Kingston Lane, Uxbridge, Middlesex UB8 3PH (☎ 0895 74000 ext 2943, fax 0895 32806)

MEDLAND, David Arthur; s of James William Medland (d 1986), and Merle Ermyntrude, *née* Rotchell; *b* 23 Sept 1946; *Educ* St Paul's Sch Darjeeling India; *m* 20 Oct 1973 (m dis 1979), Patricia Ann, da of Timothy Wood (d 1971); 1 stepson (Christopher James b 25 Dec 1968); *Career* CA; Robson Rhodes 1965-: asst mangr

1973, mangr 1974, sr mangr 1976, ptnr 1979; ACA 1971, FCA 1979; *Books* The Unlisted Securities Market - A Review; *Recreations* pianist, theatre, sport; *Style*— David A Medland, Esq; Robson Rhodes, 186 City Rd, London EC1V 1NU (☎ 071 251 1644, fax 071 250 0801, telex 885734)

MEDLAND, Peter; s of Gerald Berthold Medland (d 1931), and Rowena, *née* Grant (d 1931); *b* 5 Dec 1927; *Educ* Taunton Sch; *m* 25 March 1962, Ann, da of Reginald Newman (d 1969); 1 s (Graham b 1968); *Career* MN 1942-53 (ret as Capt); various exec posts local govt 1955-85; dir and regnl mangr Wessex Holdings 1987-89, chm Westwise Properties Ltd 1989; dir: Western Challenge Housing Assoc, Hengistbury Housing Assoc, Trafalgar Housing Assoc; ABIM 1973, MIMunBM 1974, FInstD 1989; *Clubs* Naval, Sloane, Lions; *Style*— Peter Medland, Esq; Chineburlai, Long St, Sherborne, Dorset (☎ 0935 816 819)

MEDLEY, (Edward) David Gilbert; s of Cecil Rhodes Medley, of 2 Westside, Allington, Salisbury, Wilts, and Edith Sarah, *née* Dear; *b* 18 May 1935; *Educ* Univ of Southampton (BSc), Univ of London (BDS); *m* 30 Aug 1968, Elizabeth Beatrice, da of Alex Pennington, of Greenhill Cottage, Dimmocks Lane, Sarratt, Herts; 2 da (Jocelyn Sarah Rosalind b 1971, Sarah Elizabeth Jane b 1974); *Career* dental surgn gen practice 1967-71, Winchester AHA 1971-; fndr memb and dir Dental Sci Advancement Fndn; chm Salisbury Med Soc 1985-86; memb Winchester: Dist Jt Consultative Ctee, Dist Dental Advsy Ctee, Community Jt Advsy Ctee; accredited rep Br Dental Assoc; parish cnsllr Grateley Parish Cncl; MIBiol, MRCS, CBiol, LDS; *Recreations* flying, jazz, sailing, badminton; *Clubs* Concorde; *Style*— David Medley, Esq; The Rookery, Grateley, Andover, Hants (☎ 026 488 641)

MEDLEY, George Julius; OBE (1989); s of Brig Edgar Julius Medley, DSO, OBE, MC (d 1972), and Norah, *née* Templer; *b* 2 Aug 1930; *Educ* Winchester, Wye Coll Univ of London (BSc, full purple for Athletics 1951), London Business Sch; *m* 4 Sept 1952, Vera Frances, da of George Brand (d 1980); 1 s (Patrick Jonathan Julius b 1956), 1 da (Alexandra Isobel Frances b 1957); *Career* fruit farmer 1952-56, mangr Chemical Dept Harrisons & Crosfield Colombo 1956-63 (mercantile asst 1956-58), dir Fisons (Ceylon) Ltd 1958-63, tech devpt mangr Tata Fison Industries Ltd (Bangalore) 1963-64, gen mangr Tata Fison Industries Ltd (Bombay) 1964-68, sales mangr Western Hemisphere Fisons International Ltd (London) 1968-70, overseas mangr Fisons Agrochemical Div (Cambridge) 1970-72, md Glaxo Laboratories India Ltd 1973-77 (dep md 1972-73); dir World Wide Fund for Nature UK 1978-; tstee: Farming & Wildlife Trust Ltd 1983-, Falklands Islands Fndn 1984-; memb Bd Int Inst Environment & Dept 1989-, founding memb Inst of Charity Fundraising Mangrs 1983- (chm 1984-86), chm London Business Sch Alumni Assoc 1970-72, vice pres Orgn Pharmaceutical Producers of India 1973-77; FRSA 1989, FBIM 1977, fell Inst Charity Fundraising Mangrs 1988; *Books* Long Range Planning (contrib, 1987); *Recreations* gardening, DIY; *Style*— George Medley, Esq, OBE; Hoddinotts House, Tisbury, Wilts SP3 6QQ (☎ 0747 870677); WWF-World Wide Fund for Nature - UK, Panda House, Weyside Par, Godalming, Surrey GU7 1XR (☎ 0483 426444, fax 0483 426409)

MEDLEY, Peter; s of Tom Medley (d 1982), and Doris, *née* Smith (d 1957); *b* 22 Aug 1935; *Educ* Southcoates HS Hull, Hull Municipal Tech Coll; *m* 14 June 1958, Stella, da of Frederick Carnaby Robertson (d 1946); 1 s (Simon Andrew (Sam) b 21 Feb 1965), 1 da (Jennifer Kate b 27 Aug 1967); *Career* RE 1953-55; Caxton Press (W Africa) Ltd and McCorquodale and Co (W Africa) Ltd 1963-79 (md of both 1974-79), divnl dir books and magazines McCorquodale & Co Ltd 1980-86; chm: Norton-Opax Book Printing Ltd 1986-89, Bowater Book Printing Division 1989-; chm Waveney and Yare Housing Assoc 1984-, co fndr Nigeria Printers & Publishers Assoc 1976; fell Inst of Printing, memb Inst Indust Mangrs; *Recreations* sailing, dinghy racing; *Style*— Peter Medley, Esq; The White House, The Causeway, Boxford, Suffolk (☎ 0787 210836); Bowater Book Printing Division, 16 Mason Rd, Cowdray Centre, Colchester, Essex (☎ 0206 45582, fax 0206 572637)

MEDLEY, (Charles) Robert Owen; CBE (1982); *b* 19 Dec 1905; *Educ* Gresham's, Slade Sch of Fine Art London and Paris; *Career* artist; public collections: Tate Gallery, Victoria and Albert Museum, Walker Art Gallery Liverpool, Contemporary Art Soc, City Inns Leeds Arts Cncl, Nat Gallery of Ontario, City Art Gallery NY; expositions: retrospective at Whitechapel 1963, retrospective at Museum of Mod Art Oxford 1984, numerous other galleries in GB and abroad 1927-89; sr RA 1986; *Books* The Ascent to Calvary: Painters on Painting (1969), Robert Medley - 'Drawn from Life'- A Memoir (1983); *Style*— Robert Medley, Esq, CBE

MEDLICOTT, Michael Geoffrey; s of late Geoffrey Henry Medlicott, of Hythe, Kent, and late Beryl Ann, *née* Burchell; *b* 2 June 1943; *Educ* Downside, Lincoln Coll Oxford (MA); *m* 8 Sept 1973, Diana Grace, da of Brian Fife Fallaw, of Gosforth, Northumberland; 1 s (Oliver), 3 da (Charlotte, Annabel, Flora); *Career* dir Europe P & O 1983-86 (gen mangr fleet 1975-80, gen mangr Europe 1980-83), md P & O Air Holidays 1980-86, dir P & O Travel 1980-84, md Swan Hellenic 1983-86, chief exec Br Tourist Authority 1986-; memb: Cncl of Mgmnt Passenger Shipping Assoc 1983-86, Bd of Mgmnt Heritage of London Tst 1986-, Br Travel Educn Tst 1986-, Tidy Britain Gp 1986-; FRSA; *Recreations* philately, gardening, tennis; *Style*— Michael Medlicott, Esq; Thames Tower, Blacks Rd, London W6 (☎ 081 846 9000)

MEDLYCOTT, Sir Mervyn Tregonwell; 9 Bt (UK 1808), of Ven House, Somerset; s of late Thomas Anthony Hutchings Medlycott (d 1970), 2 s of Sir Hubert Medlycott, 7 Bt, of Edmondsham House, Dorset, and Cecilia Mary Eden, da of late Maj Cecil Harold Eden, of Cranborne, Dorset; suc unc, Sir Christopher Medlycott, 8 Bt (d 1986); *b* 20 Feb 1947; *Career* genealogist; fndr Somerset and Dorset Family History Soc 1975 (hon sec 1975-77, chm 1977-84, pres 1986-); memb: Assoc of Genealogists and Record Agents (AGRA), Historic Houses Assoc; FSG; *Clubs* East India, Devonshire, Sports and Public Schools; *Style*— Sir Mervyn Medlycott, Bt; The Manor House, Sandford Orcas, Sherborne, Dorset (☎ 096 322 206)

MEDWAY, Lord; (John) Jason Jasper Gathorne-Hardy; s and h of 5 Earl of Cranbrook; *b* 26 Oct 1968; *Educ* Woodbridge Sch, Pembroke Coll Oxford (BA); *Career* artist; *Recreations* drawing, painting, hiking, cycling; *Style*— Lord Medway; 7 Woodfall Street, Chelsea, London SW3 4DJ (☎ 071 730 2980); Great Glemham House, Great Glemham, Saxmundham IP17 1LP (☎ 072 878543)

MEDWAY, Sarah Dorothea; da of Michael David Hilborne-Clarke, of Germany, and Margaret, *née* Lythell; *b* 9 July 1950; *Educ* Sutherland House Sch Cromer, ICA London (Dip in History of Modern Art), Chelsea Sch of Art, Heatherley's Sch of Fine Art; *m* 19 Dec 1974, David Ian Medway, s of Murray Medway, JP; 1 s (Adam Murray b 12 May 1977); *Career* shoe designer Medway Shoes (London and branches) 1974-84; patron of new art Tate Gallery 1985- (memb Acquisitions Sub-Ctee 1990-91; *Recreations* arts, poetry, film, theatre, ballet, skiing, swimming, tennis; *Clubs* Vanderbilt, RAC, Hurlingham, Groucho, Annabel's, Harry's Bar, Tramps; *Style*— Mrs Sarah Medway

MEDWIN, Michael Hugh; adopted s of Dr Mary Jeremy, OBE, and Ms Clopton-Roberts; *b* 18 July 1927; *Educ* Canford, Inst Fischer Montreux Territet Lac Leman Switzerland; *m* 1960 (m dis 1970), M B Sunny Back; *Career* theatre, TV, film actor and prodr; theatre credits incl: Man and Superman, The Rivals, Love for Love, Duckers and Lovers, Alfie, St Joan of the Stockyards, Weapons of Happiness, Volpone (NT), What The Butler Saw, Lady from the Sea, There's a Girl in my Soup, The Division Belle; TV credits incl: The Army Game, The Love of Mike, Three Live Wires, Shoestring, The Ronnie Corbett Show, Minder, Boon; film credits incl: The Courtneys of Curzon Street, Boys in Brown, An Ideal Husband, Charlie Moon, The Steel Helmet, Man on the Beach, Twenty Four Hours to Kill, The Longest Day, Rattle of a Simple Man, Countess of Hong Kong; fndr ptnr (with Albert Finney) Memorial Films Limited 1965-; plays produced by Michael Medwin incl: Spring and Port Wine 1965, A Day In The Death of Joe Egg 1967, Joe Egg 1968, Forget-Me-Not Lane 1972, Chez Nous 1974; films produced by Michael Medwin incl: Charlie Bubbles 1966, If.... 1968, Spring and Port Wine 1969, Gumshoe 1971, O Lucky Man 1972, Alpha Beta 1973, Law and Disorder 1974, Memoirs of a Survivor 1981; plays co-produced with Robert Fox incl: Another Country, Interpreters, Orphans; currently dir David Pugh Ltd; winner: Evening Standard Drama Desk award Best Play of the Year Joe Egg 1968, Best Commedy of the Year Privates on Parade 1978 (co-prodr); *Recreations* golf, skiing; *Clubs* The Turf, Royal & Ancient Golf, Sunningdale Golf; *Style*— Michael Medwin, Esq; c/o Lou Coulson, 37 Berwick St, London W1 (☎ 071 734 9633)

MEE, Bertie; OBE (1983); s of Edwin Mee (d 1951), and Gertrude, *née* Wylde (d 1955); *b* 25 Dec 1918; *Educ* Highbury Sch Nottingham; *m* 26 March 1949, Doris, da of Jess Leonard Edwards (d 1960); 2 da (Beverley b 1959, Allyson b 1961); *Career* Sgt RAMC 1939-46, tutor Army Sch of Physiotherapy 1940-42; rehabilitation offr NHS 1947-60; Arsenal FC: physiotherapist 1960-66, mangr 1966-76 (UEFA Cup Winners 1970, Football League Championship and FA Cup Double 1971-); dir Watford FC 1977-, chm Milas Gp of Cos (health care); memb: Aspire Spinal Injury Charity, Olympic Fin Servs Charity; pres FA Remedial Med Soc, vice pres Football League Exec Staffs Assoc, memb cncl Inst Sports Med; Freeman: City of London, Worshipful Co of Fan Makers; MCSP 1942; *Recreations* reading, music, spectator-sports; *Clubs* City Livery Club, Bishopsgate Ward; *Style*— Bertie Mee, Esq, OBE; 120 Friars Walk, Southgate, London N14 5LH (☎ 081 368 3607)

MEECHIE, Brig Helen Guild; CBE (1986); da of John Strachan Meechie, of Walderslade, Kent, and Robina Guild, *née* Robertson (d 1980); *b* 19 Jan 1938; *Educ* Morgan Acad Dundee, Univ of St Andrews (MA); *Career* cmmnd WRAC 1960, served UK, Cyprus and Hong Kong 1961-76, UK and Germany 1977-82, dir WRAC 1982-86, ADC to HM The Queen 1986 (hon ADC 1982-86), Hon Col Tayforth Univs OTC 1986-91, memb RCDS 1987, dir Army Serv Conditions 1988-89, dep DG Personnel Servs Army 1989-91; govr Royal Sch Hampstead, memb Cncl Union Jack Club; memb Nat Exec Ctee Forces Help Soc and Lord Roberts Workshops; Freeman City of London 1983; Hon LLD Univ of Dundee 1986; CBIM 1986; *Recreations* golf, gardening, music, travel; *Style*— Brigadier Helen Meechie, CBE; Ministry of Defence, Empress State Building, Lillie Rd, London SW6 1TR (☎ 071 1244 ext 2581, fax 2425)

MEEHAN, (Tony) Anthony Edward; s of the late Edward Joseph Meehan, of 8 Highburgh Rd, Glasgow, and Mary, *née* Whelan; *b* 24 Aug 1943; *Educ* St George's Maida Vale London; *m* 24 Oct 1975, Linda Jane, da of John Alexander Portugal Stone, of Vancouver Island, BC; 1 s (Michael Anthony b 1980), 1 da (Claire Louise b 1982); *Career* md Tony Meehan and Assocs Ltd 1976-, chief exec and md TMA Communications 1985-, former chm IPR Scottish Gp 1987-89 (chm Educn Ctee 1984-87 vice chm 1985-87); *Clubs* Royal Over-Seas League, The Western, Scottish Society of Epicureans; *Style*— Tony Meehan, Esq; Moorhouse, Old Mugdock Rd, Strathblane, Stirlingshire (☎ 041 339 9305, fax 041 339 7165)

MEEK, Charles Innes; CMG (1961); s of Charles Kingsley Meek, DSc (d 1965), and Margery Helen, *née* Hopkins (d 1960); ggf Gen Sir Thomas Gordon was one of well-known twins with identical careers, the other Gen Sir John Gordon; *b* 27 June 1920; *Educ* Magdalen Coll Oxford (MA); *m* 1947, Nona, da of Charles Corry Hurford (d 1955); 2 s (Innes, Kingsley), 1 da (Sheena); *Career* 2 Lt A and SH 1940-41; Colonial Admin Serv Tanganyika 1941, head of The Civil Serv 1961, perm sec to PM, sec to The Cabinet, chm White Fish Authy 1973 (chief exec 1962), ret 1982; chm Nautilus Conslts 1986-88; *Recreations* travel, bridge, The Spectator crossword; *Clubs* Royal Over-Seas League; *Style*— Charles Meek Esq, CMG; Mariteau Cottage, German St, Winchelsea, Sussex TN36 4ES (☎ 0797 226408)

MEEK, Dr Harold Alan; s of Philip Meek (d 1966), of Southport, and Rita, *née* Sugarman (d 1970); *b* 2 June 1922; *Educ* Manchester GS, Univ of Manchester (BA), Queen's Univ Belfast (PhD); *m* 1, 1943, Irene (d 1972), da of Paul Schlesinger (d in Nazi Holocaust), of Berlin; 1 da (Marion b 1944); m 2, 1973, Beatrice, da of Isaac Jackson (d 1949), of Dublin; *Career* RN 1941-46; ancient monuments architect Govt of NI 1955-67, sr lectr in architecture Queens Univ Belfast 1973-85 (lectr 1967-73), area ed 15-18 century Euro architecture The Dictionary of Art Macmillan Publishers 1989-; memb Historic Bldgs Cncl for NI 1973-82; FRIBA 1970; Cavaliere dell'Ordine al Merito della Repubblica Italiana Italy 1966; *Books* Guarini and his Architecture (1988); *Recreations* astronomy, attending Jewish weddings; *Clubs* Civil Service, Manchester University Union; *Style*— Dr Harold Meek; The Dictionary of Art, Macmillan Publishers Ltd, 4 Little Essex St, London WC2R 3LF (☎ 071 836 6633, telex 262024)

MEEK, Prof John Millar; CBE (1975); s of Alexander Meek (d 1972), of W Kirby, Wirral, and Edith, *née* Montgomery (d 1976); *b* 21 Dec 1912; *Educ* Monkton Combe Sch Bath, Univ of Liverpool (BEng, DEng), Univ of California Berkeley; *m* 18 July 1942, Marjorie, da of Bernard Ingleby (d 1957), of Sale, Cheshire; 2 da (Rosalind b 1945, Sara b 1947); *Career* res engr Met-Vickers Electrical Co Ltd Trafford Park 1934-38 and 1940-45, prof electrical engrg Univ of Liverpool 1946-78; pres IEE 1968-69, memb IBA 1969-74; Hon DSc Univ of Salford 1971; FIEE 1954, FInstP 1956; *Books* The Mechanism of the Electric Spark (1941), Electrical Breakdown of Gases (1953), High-Voltage Laboratory Technique (1953); *Recreations* golf, gardening, theatre; *Style*— Prof John Meek, CBE; 4 The Kirklands, W Kirby, Wirral (☎ 051 625 5850)

MEEK, Marshall; CBE (1989); s of Marshall Meek (d 1955), of Auchtermuchty, Fife, and Grace Robertson, *née* Smith (d 1970); *b* 22 April 1925; *Educ* Bell Baxter HS Cupar Fife, Univ of Glasgow (BSc); *m* 2 March 1957, Elfrida Marjorie, da of William George Cox (d 1946), of Purley, Surrey; 3 da (Hazel Valerie b 1960, Ursula Katherine b 1962, Angela Judith b 1966); *Career* chief naval architect and dir Ocean Transport & Trading Ltd 1967-78 (joined 1953), head of ship technol British Shipbuilders 1979-85, dep chm British Maritime Technology 1985-86, visiting prof in naval architecture: Univ of Strathclyde 1972-83, UCL 1983-86; JP Liverpool 1977-78; past pres NE Coast Inst of Engrs & Shipbuilders 1984-86, pres RINA 1990-; memb: Panel of Nautical Assessors DOT, Tech Ctee Lloyd's Register of Shipping; chm Northumberland Branch Gideons Int 1988; hon RDI (RSA) 1986; FRINA, FIMarE, FEng, FRSA; *Books* contrib numerous tech papers to learned jls; *Recreations* garden; *Clubs* Caledonian; *Style*— Marshall Meek, Esq, CBE; Redstacks, Tranwell Woods, Morpeth, Northumberland NE61 6AG; (☎ 0670 517 221)

MEERS, Dr John Laurence; s of Laurence Wilfred Victor Lord Meers, of 343 Victoria Ave, Southend-on-Sea, Essex, and Elizabeth Audrey, *née* Hooker; *b* 4 Feb 1941; *Educ* Westcliff HS Essex, Univ of London (BSc, PhD); *m* 1, 1961 (m dis 1982), Pamela Mary, *née* Milsom; 1 s (Ian), 1 da (Jennifer); m 2, 1985; *Career* res and devpt dir John and E Sturge Ltd 1978-87; dir: Glumamates Ltd 1981-87, Sturge Chemicals Ltd 1981-87; md Sturge Enzymes 1982-84 (tech dir 1979); memb: Biotechnol

Directorate Sci and Engrg Res Cncl, Fauna and Flora Preservation Soc, Rare Breeds Survival Tst; chief exec Enzymatix Ltd 1987-; pres Enzymatix Incorporated; chm Ryedale Constituency SDP; *Recreations* preservation of rare breeds of farm-stock; *Clubs* Europe House, Fauna and Flora Preservation Soc; *Style*— Dr John Meers; 9 Willow Walk, Cambridge CB1 1LA (☎ 0223 65393); Enzymatix Ltd, Cambridge Science Park, Milton Rd, Cambridge CB4 2QT (☎ 0223 420430)

MEGAHEY, Leslie; s of Rev Thomas Megahey (d 1975), and Beatrice, *née* Walton; *b* 22 Dec 1944; *Educ* Elm Grove Belfast, King Edward VI Lichfield, Pembroke Coll Oxford; *Career* dir, writer prodr of film drama and documentary; ed Omnibus 1979-81; prodns incl: Schalcken the Painter 1979, Cariani and the Courtesans 1987, Duke Bluebeard's Castle 1988; head of music and arts BBC TV 1988-; *Style*— Leslie Megahey, Esq; c/o Peters Fraser & Dunlop, The Chambers, Chelsea Harbour, London SW10 OXF (☎ 071 376 7676, fax 071 352 7356)

MEGAHY, Thomas; MEP (Lab) SW Yorks 1979-; s of Samuel Megahy, and Mary Megahy; *b* 16 July 1929; *Educ* Wishaw HS, Ruskin Coll Oxford, Coll of Educn (Tech) Huddersfield, Univ of London (BSc, Dip Econ and Political Sci, Dip FE Leeds); *m* 1954, Jean, *née* Renshaw; 3 s; *Career* former railway worker and lectr; vice pres Euro Parl 1987-89, vice pres Euro Parl Gulf States Delgn; memb: Social Affrs Ctee, Employment and the Working Environment Ctee, Tport and Tourism Ctee; *Style*— Thomas Megahy, Esq, MEP; 6 Lady Heton Grove, Mirfield, W Yorks WF14 9DY

MEGARRY, Rt Hon Sir Robert Edgar; PC (1978); s of Robert Lindsay Megarry, OBE, LLB (d 1952), of Belfast and Croydon, Surrey, and Irene Marion (d 1929), da of Maj-Gen Edgar Clark; *b* 1 June 1910; *Educ* Lancing, Trinity Hall Cambridge (MA, LLD); *m* 1936, Iris, da of Elias Davies, of Neath, Glamorgan; 3 da; *Career* slr 1935-41; Miny of Supply: princ 1940-44, asst sec 1944-46; called to the Bar Lincoln's Inn 1944; book review ed and asst ed Law Quarterly Review 1944-67; asst reader in equity Inns of Ct 1946-51 (reader 1951-67), memb Lord Chllr's Law Reform Ctee 1952-73, QC 1956, bencher Lincoln's Inn 1962 (and treas 1981), High Ct judge 1967-85, vice chllr High Ct Chancery Div 1976-81, vice chllr Supreme Ct 1982-85; the visitor: Univ of Essex 1983-90, Clare Hall Cambridge 1984-88; chm: Friends of Lancing Chapel 1969-, Cncl of Law Reporting 1972-87, Comparative Law Section of Br Inst of Int and Comparative Law 1977-88; memb Advsy Cncl on Public Records 1980-85, pres Lancing Club 1974-; Hon LLD: Hull, Nottingham, London, The Law Soc of Upper Canada; FBA 1970; kt 1967; *Books* The Rent Acts (1939), Miscellany-At-Law (1955), The Law of Real Property (with Prof H W R Wade, QC, 1957), Lawyer and Litigant in England (The Hamlyn Lectures, 1962), A Second Miscellany-At-Law (1973); *Recreations* heterogeneous; *Style*— The Rt Hon Sir Robert Megarry; 5 Stone Buildings, Lincoln's Inn, London WC2A 3XT (☎ 071 242 8607); Institute of Advanced Legal Studies, Charles Clore House, 17 Russell Square, London WC1B 5DR (☎ 071 637 1731)

MEGAW, Rt Hon Sir John; CBE (1956), TD (1951), PC (1969); 2 s of Hon Mr Justice Megaw (d 1947), of Belfast; *b* 16 Sept 1909; *Educ* Royal Academical Inst Belfast, St John's Coll Cambridge, Harvard Law Sch; *m* 1938, Eleanor Grace Chapman; 1 s, 2 da; *Career* served WWII, Col RA; called to the Bar Gray's Inn 1934, QC (1953, NI 1954), rec Middlesbrough 1957-61, high ct judge (Queen's Bench) 1961-69, pres Restrictive Practices Ct 1962-68, lord justice of appeal 1969-80, chm Ctee of Inquiry into Civil Serv Pay Dispute 1981-82; last judge to pass death sentence (1964, later commuted to life imprisonment); Hon LLD Queen's Univ 1968, Hon DSc Univ of Ulster 1990; hon fell St John's Coll Cambridge, Legion of Merit (US) 1946; kt 1961; *Style*— The Rt Hon Sir John Megaw, CBE, TD; 14 Upper Cheyne Row, London SW3

MEGSON, Raymond James; s of Roderick Kevin Megson, and Margaret Elizabeth, *née* Welsh; *b* 4 Sept 1945; *Educ* North Sydney HS, Douglas Ewart HS, Univ of Edinburgh (LLB); *m* 11 Oct 1976, Kim Frances, da of Norman McCreadie; 3 s (Jason b 1977, Calum b 1983, Gregor b 1985), 1 da (Paula b 1978); *Career* slr, SSC, NP, memb Criminal Law Ctee Law Soc of Scotland, former pres The Faculty of Procurators of Midlothian; former rugby player at centre: Edinburgh Wanderers, Scottish Co-optimists, Edinburgh Dist; rugby referee Scottish Int Panel: Eng v Japan 1986, Wales v Eng 1987, Ireland v Wales 1988, Ireland v Italy 1988, Namibia v France 1990, Italy v Holland 1990, Italy v Romania 1990, Wales v England 1991; *Recreations* golf, rugby, tennis; *Clubs* Edinburgh Wanderers, Mortonhall Golf, Mortonhall Tennis; *Style*— Raymond J Megson, Esq; 22 Cluny Drive, Edinburgh (☎ 447 2343); Grindlay St Ct, Edinburgh (☎ 228 2501, fax 228 5554)

MEHIGAN, Patrick Joseph; s of Patrick Denis Mehigan (d 1965), of Dublin, and Johanna, *née* Scully (d 1971); *b* 1 Aug 1924; *Educ* Catholic Univ Sch Dublin, UCD (BEng); *m* 17 Sept 1957, Eithne, da of Comdt Daniel Vincent Horgan, of Lansdowne Hotel, Pembroke Rd, Dublin; 2 s (Declan, Brian), 3 da (Sinead, Caoileann, Caralosa); *Career* chm Nicholas O'Dwyer and Ptnrs consulting engrs 1970- (trainee engr 1945-47, asst engr 1948-54, sr engr 1956-57, ptnr and dir 1961-), res engr Waterville Water Supply Scheme 1947-48, sr res engr North Dublin Water Supply 1954-56, sr engr and section leader Howard Humphreys and Sons Consulting Engrs London 1957-61; hon sec Marist Boys Club 1951-57 and 1961-87 (later Marist Boys Home for Homeless Boys), dir of Rehabilitation Inst 1975- (Ireland's largest charity); dir Dublin and Central Properties Public Quoted Co 1975-80, memb Exec Ctee FIDIC 1976-81; FIEI 1957, FICE 1961, FIWEM 1962; *Recreations* golfing, sailing; *Clubs* Milltown GC, Royal Irish YC; *Style*— Patrick Mehigan, Esq; 6 de Vesci Terrace, Dun Laoghaire, Co Dublin (☎ and fax 0001 801432); Nicholas O'Dwyer and Partners, Consulting Engrs, Carrick House, Dundrum Centre, Dublin 14 (☎ 0001 984499, fax 0001 984957, telex 30350 NOD E1)

MEHTA, Dr Atul Bhanu; *b* 14 Jan 1954; *Educ* Battersea GS, Jesus Coll Cambridge (MA, MB BChir), King's Coll Hosp Univ of London (MD, MRCP, MRCPath); *m* 23 May 1981, Kokila; 1 da (Avani b 6 Sept 1986); *Career* Royal Postgrad Med Sch and Hammersmith Hosp 1981-86: registrar, sr registrar, MRC res fell; conslt haematologist Royal Free Hosp 1986-; author of various res papers on haematological diseases and their treatment; *Style*— Dr Atul Mehta; Dept of Haematology, Royal Free Hospital, Pond St, London NW3 2QG (☎ 071 794 0500 ext 3264, fax 071 431 4537)

MEHTA, Pravin Shantilal; s of Shantilal B Mehta, of Bhavnagar, India, and Kanchan Mehta; *b* 23 March 1944; *Educ* Univ of Gujarat India (BCom, BA, LLB, MLW); *m* 19 Oct 1968, Merunissa, da of Abdul Azis Lalani; 1 s (Meenaz b 2 Dec 1970); *Career* accounts mangr Assoc Servs Ltd 1965-68, chief accountant later co sec and chief dealer Commodity Analysis 1968-78; trading dir GNI Ltd 1978-; ACIS, MBIM; *Recreations* astrology; *Clubs* Durbar, Royal Over-Seas League; *Style*— Pravin Mehta, Esq; Glen House, 34D Oakleigh Park South, London N20 (☎ 081 446 3554); GNI Limited, Colechurch House, No 1 London Bridge Walk, London SE1 (☎ 071 407 2773/071 378 7171, fax 071 407 3848, car 0860 266936)

MEHTA, Dr (Sukhdev) Thomas; s of Dr Ramji Das Mehta (d 1956), of New Delhi, India, and Basanti Devi Mehta (d 1976); *b* 8 July 1927; *Educ* Univ of Calcutta (MB BS); *m* 20 Sept 1964, Pauline Phyllis; 1 s (Anil b 1965), 1 da (Anita Jane b 1968); *Career* conslt anaesthetist Burnley Gp of Hosps 1968-; author of articles on anaesthetics and related topics; examinership Pt III F C Anaesthetics of GB and Ireland, chm Extended Training Advsy Body Lancashire Ambulance Serv, memb NW Royal Higher Awards Ctee, fell Overseas Doctors Assoc 1986; memb: Assoc of Anaesthetics of GB and Ireland, Intensive Care Soc, Intractable Pain Soc, History of Anaesthesia Soc; FFARCS; *Books* A Concise Guide to Treatment of Cardiac Arrest (1984); *Recreations* research, photography, reading; *Style*— Dr Thomas Mehta; Burnside, 11 Reedley Drive, Burnley, Lancashire BB10 2QZ (☎ 0282 63515); Consultant Anaesthetist, Department of Anaesthetics, Burnley General Hospital, Casterton Ave, Burnley, Lancs BB10 2PQ (☎ 0282 25071 ext 2454)

MEHTA, Zubin; *Educ* Vienna Musikakademie (studied with Hans Swarawsky); *Career* conductor; debut Vienna 1958, asst conductor Royal Liverpool Philharmonic Orchestra, music dir for life Israel Philharmonic Orchestra (recent tour Soveit Union); music dir: Montreal Symphony 1960-64, Los Angeles Philharmonic 1961-78, NY Philharmonic Orchestra 1978- (longest ever holder of post, has conducted over 1000 pub concerts); recent work incl: Live from Lincoln Centre (for TV), Pension Fund Concert (with Daniel Barenboim), New Year's Eve Concert (with June Anderson), Mozart Bicentennial Celebration, Salute to Carriegie Hall (with Isaac Stern) 1990; tours with NY Philharmonic incl: Argentina and the Dominican Repub 1978, Europe 1980 and 1988, US and Mexico 1981, S American 1982, US 1983, Asia 1984 and 1989, Europe and Israel 1985, Latin America 1987, Soviet Union 1988 (incl jt concert in Gorky Park Moscow with State Symphony Orchestra of Soviet Miny of Culture); advsr to Maggio Musicale Fiorentino (recently conducted Don Giovanni), frequent guest conductor for maj orchestras and opera cos; numerous recordings with NY Philharmonic incl: Mahler's Symphony No 5, Holst's The Planets, Sibelius Symphony No 2 and Finlandia, Stravinsky's La Sacre du Printemps and Symphony in Three Movements, Gershwin collection (incl Rhapsody in Blue, An American in Paris, excerpts from Porgy and Bess), Paine's Symphonies Nos 1 and 2, Overture to As You Like It, Dvořák's Violin Concerto (with Midori), Domingo at the Philharmonic; recordings with Berlin Philharmonic incl: Richard Strauss' Alpine Symphony, Bartók's Concerto for Orchestra, Miraculous Mondarin Suite and Violin Concertos Nos 1 and 2 (with Midori); recordings with Israel Philharmonic incl: Chopin's Piano Concertos Nos 1 and 2 (with Murray Parahia), Fauře Schoenberg and Sibelius settings of Pelléas et Mélisande; *awards* winner first prize Int Conductors Competition Liverpool 1958, Padma Bhusham (Order of the Lotus) of Indian Govt, Gold medal from Pope Paul VI, commendation from PM Golda Meir for contrib to the cultural life of Israel, Commendatore Repub of Italy 1976, Nikisch Ring (bequeathed to him by Karl Boehm), Vienna Philharmonic Ring of Honor; hon citizen of Tel Aviv; *Style*— Zubin Mehta, Esq; Lies Askonas Ltd, 186 Drury Lane, London WC2B 5RY (☎ 071 405 1808, fax 071 242 1831, telex 265914 ASKONA G)

MEHTAR, Shaheen; da of Maj-Gen Mohammed Anis-Ur-Rehman Khan, of Pakistan, and Keneez Khan; *b* 19 Sept 1948; *Educ* Presentation Convent, St Mary's HS, Punjab Univ (MB BS); *m* 24 April 1971, Moosa Mehtar, s of Ismail Mehtar (d 1984); 1 s (Omar b 1972); *Career* sr registrar UCH 1975-79; conslt microbiologist: N Middx Hosp 1979-, Manor House Hosp 1989-91 visiting lectr Univ of Philippines 1988; FRCPath 1990 (MRCPath 1978); *Style*— Mrs Shaheen Mehtar; North Middlesex Hospital, London N18 1QX (☎ 081 807 1748)

MEIKLE, Alan; CBE (1987); s of Malcolm Coubrough Meikle, MC (and Bar) (d 1947), of Wick Grange, Pershore, Worcs, and Mary Alma, *née* Fletcher (d 1985); *b* 22 March 1928; *Educ* St Michael's Coll Tenbury Wells, Pangbourne Coll Berks, Birmingham Sch of Architecture (Dip Arch); *m* 1, 30 Aug 1958, Marjorie Joan (d 1981), da of Arundel Spencer Clay (d 1982); 2 s (Stewart b 1959, Robert b 1960), 1 da (Grace b 1963); m 2, 22 Oct 1988, Barbara Joan Zienau, *née* Warland; *Career* midshipman RNR 1945-46; furniture designer Herts CC 1952-55, asst architect Notts CC 1955-71, co property offr Hereford and Worcs CC 1982-88 (co architect 1971-82); designer of sports centres, schools, libraries and other pub bldgs; advsr Audit Cmmns: DES, NEDO; head Clients' Advsy Serv RIBA 1989- (vice pres 1980-81, memb Cncl 1977-83), chm Assoc Heads of Co Property Depts 1986; RIBA 1953; *Recreations* sailing, sculpture, furniture design; *Style*— Alan Meikle, Esq, CBE; 22 Orchard Way, Leigh, Worcester, WR6 5LF (☎ 0386 32957)

MEINERTZHAGEN, Daniel; s of Louis Meinertzhagen, gs of Daniel Meinertzhagen, who settled in London from Bremen 1826; ancestor Johann von Meinertzhagen, Cllr of Cologne 1464-76, the Meinertzhagens stemming from a Hanseatic patrician family which sat regularly in the ruling cncls of the free imperial cities of Cologne (1402-1683) and Bremen (1696-1803) and which received hereditary honours in 1683 (nobility for all members following Cologne custom of according this to families whose heads held the Lord Mayorship), 1748 (Kt of HRE for Obercassel line), 1764 (Prussian recognition) and 1769 (Countship of HRE, now extinct); bro of Luke (d 1984) and Sir Peter, unc of Nicholas Meinertzhagen, *qqv*; *b* 2 March 1915; *Educ* Eton, New Coll Oxford; *m* 1940, Marguerite, da of A Leonard; 2 s; *Career* served WWII as Wing Cdr RAFVR; former chm Lazard Bros and Co Ltd merchant bankers; chm: Royal Insur Co 1974-, Alexanders Discount Co; dir: Costain Gp, Tozer Kemsley and Millbourn Hldgs, Brixton Estate; *Clubs* White's; *Style*— Daniel Meinertzhagen Esq; Bramshott Vale, Liphook, Hants (☎ 723243)

MEINERTZHAGEN, Nicholas Neil; only s of Luke Meinertzhagen (d 1984, late sr ptnr Cazenove and Co), and Sheila Cameron, da of late Neil Cameron Macnamara, CBE; nephew of Daniel and Sir Peter, *qv*; *b* 26 Aug 1943; *Educ* Eton, New Coll Oxford, Univ of Aix-en-Provence; *m* 1, 1966 (m dis 1978), Erzsébet Sarolta, da of János von Kenyeres, Capt Royal Hungarian Hussars, and Countess Eva Toldalagi de Nagy Ertse (Erzsébet m 1979 Count Ferdinand von und zu Trauttmansdorff-Weinsberg of the mediatised princely house); 2 da; m 2, 1980, Princesse Anne de Polignac, docteur-ès-sciences, er da of Prince Edmond de Polignac (first cous of 7 Duc de Polignac and 2 cous of HSH Prince Rainier III of Monaco), and Ghislaine Brinquant, desc of 3 consec Generals Durand de Villers; 1 da; *Career* antiquarian bookseller; former memb London Stock Exchange, assoc Cazenove and Co 1969; *Clubs* St Johann's (Vienna); *Style*— Nicholas Meinertzhagen, Esq; 82 Ritherdon Rd, London SW17 8QG (☎ 081 672 2288); 22, rue de l'Elysée F-75008 Paris (☎ 010 33 1 4265 52 62)

MEINERTZHAGEN, Sir Peter; CMG (1966); yst s of Louis Ernest Meinertzhagen (d 1941), and Gwynedd, da of Sir William Llewellyn, GCVO, PRA; yr bro of Daniel, *qv*, and Luke (d 1984), unc of Nicholas, *qv*; *b* 24 March 1920; *Educ* Eton; *m* 1949, Dido, da of late (William) Jack Pretty, of Cranleigh, Surrey; 1 s (Simon b 1950), 1 da (Tana (Mrs Knyvett)); *Career* serv WWII Maj Europe and Far East (despatches); gen mangr Cwlth Devpt Corp 1973-85; appointed bd Booker Tate Ltd 1988; Croix de Guerre; kt 1980; *Clubs* Muthaiga Country (Nairobi); *Style*— Sir Peter Meinertzhagen, CMG; Mead House, Ramsbury, Wilts SN8 2QP (☎ 0672 20715)

MEIR, John Thomas; JP (1976); s of John Thomas Meir (d 1939), of Burslem, Stoke-on-Trent, and Maria, *née* Hilton (d 1985); *b* 24 Feb 1935; *Educ* Watlands Co Secdy Sch (Dip); *m* 26 Dec 1955 (m dis), Ivy (d 1965), da of Edward Roberts, of Newcastle, Staffs; 1 da (Lesley b 1961); *Career* RAMC 1953-56; relief signalman BR; co cnllr Staffs 1972-, dep ldr Newcastle-under-Lyme Borough Cncl 1972; memb: Assoc of CCs 1981, Police Negotiating Bd 1982-; offr Boys Bde, vice chm Staffs Educn Ctee; *Recreations* football, cricket; *Style*— John T Meir, Esq, JP; 6 Silverton Close,

Bradwell, Newcastle, Staffordshire, ST5 8LU (☎ 0782 660 947)

MEIRION-JONES, Prof Gwyn Idris; s of Maelgwyn Meirion-Jones, of Manchester (d 1989), and Enid, *née* Roberts (d 1962); *b* 24 Dec 1933; *Educ* N Manchester GS, King's Coll London (BSc, MPhil, PhD); *m* 1 April 1961, Monica, da of George Havard, of Winchester (d 1961), and Marion, *née* Milson (d 1976); *Career* Nat Serv RAF 1954-56; schoolmaster 1959-68, lectr in geography Kingston Coll of Technol 1968; City of London Poly (formerly Sir John Cass Coll): sr lectr in geography 1969, head of geography 1970-89, prof 1983-89, Leverhulme res fell 1985-87, emeritus prof 1989-; author and conslt on historic bldgs; author of papers on scientific, archaeological and ethnological jls; Ancient Monuments Soc: cncl memb 1974-79 and 1983-, hon sec 1976-79, vice pres 1979-, ed 1985-; memb Royal Cmmn on the Historical Monuments of England 1985-, pres Surrey Domestic Bldgs Res Gp 1986-91, ed Medieval Village Res Gp 1978-86; hon corr memb Société Jersiaise 1980-, corr memb Compagnie des Architectes en Chef des Monuments Historiques 1989-; FSA 1981; *Books* La Maison Traditionnelle (1978), The Vernacular Architecture of Brittany (1982), Châteaux in Brittany (1991); *Recreations* food, wine, music, walking, swimming; *Clubs* Athenaeum; *Style*— Prof Gwyn Meirion-Jones, FSA; 11 Avondale Rd, Fleet, Hampshire GU13 9BH (☎ and fax 0252 614300)

MEJIA, Virginia Anne; da of Maj Edward Tyler, of Hedsor Farm House, Wooburn Green, Bucks, and Philippa Fitzalan Howard; *b* 16 Oct 1941; *Educ* St Mary's Convent South Ascot Berks; *m* 29 Oct 1965, Carlos J Mejia, s of Pedro Mejia, of Cali, Colombia; 1 s (Carlos-Felipe b 31 Dec 1967), 2 da (Mariana b 30 March 1971, Elenita b 1 Dec 1975); *Career* decorative antiques dealer; *Style*— Mrs Virginia Mejia; 26 Mallord Street, London SW3 6DU (☎ 071 352 9659)

MELCHETT, 4 Baron (UK 1928); Sir Peter Robert Henry Mond; 4 Bt (UK 1910); s of 3 Baron Melchett (d 1973, gs of 1 Baron, better known as Sir Alfred Mond, first chm of ICI and min of Health 1921-22); *b* 24 Feb 1948; *Educ* Eton, Pembroke Coll Cambridge, Keele Univ; *Career* sits as Lab peer in House of Lords; at LSE and Addiction Res Unit 1973-74; a lord in waiting (govt whip) 1974-75, Parly under-sec of state DOI 1975-76, min of state NI Office 1976-79; chm: Working Pty on Pop Festivals 1975-76, Community Indust 1979-85, Greenpeace UK 1986-88; pres Ramblers' Assoc 1981-84; exec dir Greenpeace UK 1988-; *Style*— The Rt Hon the Lord Melchett; The House of Lords, London SW1

MELDON, Hon Mrs; ((Dorothy) Albreda); da of Gen Sir Robert C A Bewicke-Copley, KBE, CB (d 1923), and sis of 5 Baron Cromwell, DSO; *m* 1926, Lt-Col Philip Albert Meldon, DSO, RA, MA (d 1942); *Style*— The Hon Mrs Meldon; 7 Editha Mansions, Edith Grove, SW10

MELDRUM, Keith Cameron; s of Dr Walter James Meldrum (d 1971), and Eileen Lydia, *née* Freckelton; *b* 19 April 1937; *Educ* Uppingham, Royal Sch of Veterinary Studies Univ of Edinburgh (B Veterinary Med and Surgery, Dip Veterinary State Med); *m* 1, 3 March 1962, (m dis 1980), Rosemary Ann, da of Maj Jack Aikman Crawford (d 1988); 2 s (James Aikman b 1966, Andrew William b 1968), 1 da (Janet Marina b 1964); m 2, 11 Aug 1982, Vivien Mary; *Career* in gen practice as veterinary surgn Scunthorpe Lincs 1961-63, chief veterinary offr MAFF Tolworth 1988- (Oxford 1963-72, divnl veterinary offr Tolworth 1972-75), divnl veterinary offr Leamington Spa 1975-78, dep regnl veterinary offr Nottingham 1978-80, regnl veterinary offr Tolworth 1980-83, asst chief veterinary offr 1983-86, dir of veterinary field serv 1986-88); MRCVS; *Recreations* competitive target rifle shooting, outdoor activities; *Clubs* North London Rifle, Farmers'; *Style*— Keith Meldrum, Esq; Ministry of Agriculture, Fisheries and Food, Government Buildings, Hook Rise South, Tolworth, Surbiton, Surrey KT6 7NF (☎ 081 330 8050, telex 22203 AHSURB, fax 081 330 6872)

MELFORD, David Austin; OBE (1990); s of Austin Melford (d 1971), of London, and Jessie, *née* Winter (d 1971); *b* 16 Oct 1927; *Educ* Hall Sch Hampstead, Charterhouse, Clare Coll Cambridge (MA, PhD, ScD); *m* 3 Sept 1955, Amanda Patricia, da of Leonard Farrar (Cdr RN, d 1959); 1 s (Mark Austin b 29 April 1969), 1 da (Clare Amanda b 14 June 1973); *Career* Nat Serv 1946-48: The Queens Royal Regt, cmmnd 2 Lieut Royal Signals; asst site rep Woodall-Duckham Co 1949, TI fell Cavendish Laboratory Cambridge 1955-57; TI Group: res scientist TI Research Laboratories 1957-68, design and devpt Scanning Electron Probe Microanalyser, chief metallurgist and head of Metallurgy Div 1968-79, dir of res and dep gen mangr 1979-87; materials res conslt 1987-; memb Cncl and memb Standing Ctee on Engineering Fellowship of Engineering; Inst of Metals: sr vice pres, memb Cncl, memb Exec Ctee; SERC: FEng assessor on Cncl, memb Engrg Bd, memb Materials Cmmn; former: chm Materials Advsy Ctee DTI, memb NDT Exec Ctee ECSC, memb Materials Ctee SERC; author of numerous contribs to learned jls esp jl of Inst of Metals; FEng, FIM, MInstP; *Recreations* writing, instrument making, gardening and the pursuit of trout; *Clubs* MCC; *Style*— David Melford, Esq, OBE; Clare College, Cambridge

MELGUND, Viscount; Gilbert Timothy George Lariston Elliot-Murray-Kynynmound; s and h of 6 Earl of Minto, MBE; *b* 1 Dec 1953; *Educ* Eton (BSc); *m* 30 July 1983, Diana Barbara, da of Brian S L Trafford, of Tismans, Rudgwick, W Sussex; 3 s (Gilbert b 1984, Lorne b and d 1986, Michael b 1987); *Heir* s, Hon Gilbert Francis Elliot-Murray-Kynynmound b 15 Aug 1984; *Career* Lt Scots Gds 1972-76; memb Royal Co of Archers; ARICS; *Clubs* White's; *Style*— Viscount Melgund

MELHUISH, Ralph John; s of Thomas Melhuish (d 1985), and Maud Estella, *née* Fletcher; *b* 15 May 1933; *Educ* Chipping Sodbury GS, Univ of Bristol (BSc); *m* 27 July 1956, Margot Martha, da of Kurt Leopold Patschull (d 1960); 1 s (Ralph Thomas Kurt b 1962); *Career* Flying Offr Engrg Branch RAF 1956-60; student apprentice then serv engr Bristol Aero Engine Co 1952-56, PA to chm, mangr machine shop and contracts mangr Distington Engineering Co 1960-64, mgmnt conslt Mead Carney and Co 1964-67, prodn engr and dir manufacturing Rank Precision Industries 1967-70, chief exec Transformer and Switchgear Divs Aberdare Holdings 1970-74, gen mangr and prodn dir Porth Textiles 1974-76, md Switchgear and Transformer Business Unit Babcock International 1977-85, chm and md Ottermill Ltd 1985-; memb Bd Electrical Installation Equipment Mfrs Assoc; MIMechE, FRSA; *Recreations* genealogy; *Clubs* RAF; *Style*— Ralph Melhuish, Esq; Ottermill Ltd, Ottery St Mary, Devon (☎ 0404 812131)

MELIA, Dr Terence Patrick; s of John Melia (d 1975), and Kathleen, *née* Traynor (d 1984); *b* 17 Dec 1934; *Educ* Sir John Deanes GS Northwich, Univ of Leeds (PhD); *m* 21 May 1976, Madeline, da of Arthur Carney (d 1975); 1 da (Alexandra b 1980); *Career* tech offr ICI Ltd 1961-64, lectr and sr lectr Univ of Salford 1964-70, princ N Lindsey Coll of Technol 1970-74; HM Inspr of Schs 1974-: regnl staff inspr NW 1982-84, chief inspr higher educn 1985-; FRSC, CChem; *Recreations* golf, gardening; *Clubs* Berhamsted Golf; *Style*— Dr Terence Melia; Dept of Education and Science, Elizabeth House, York Rd, London SE1 7PH (☎ 071 934 9842)

MELLAART, James; s of Jacob Herman Jan Mellaart (d 1972), of Kasteel Mheer, Holland, and Apollonia Dingena, *née* Van Der Beek (d 1934); *b* 14 Nov 1925; *Educ* Gymnasiums The Hague and Maastricht Holland, UCL (BA); *m* 23 April 1954, (Meryem) Arlette, da of Kadri Cenani, OBE (d 1984), of Istanbul; 1 s (Alan b 1955); *Career* archaeologist; asst dir Br Inst of Archaeology Ankara Turkey 1959-61 (scholar and fell 1951-58), specialist lectr Istanbul Univ 1961-63, lectr in anatolian archaelogy Inst of Archaelogy Univ of London 1964-; excavations: Beycesultan (with S Lloyd) 1954-59, Hacilar 1957-60, Çatal Hüyük 1961-63 and 1965; FSA 1964, FBA 1980; *Books* Beycesultan (excavation reports with Seyton Lloyd, Vol I 1962, Vol II 1965), Earliest Civilisations of The Near East (1965), The Chalcolithic and Early Bronze Ages in The Near East and Anatolia (1966), Çatal Hüyük, A Neolithic Town in Anatolia (1967), Excavations at Hacilar (1970), The Neolithic of the Near East (1975), The Archaeology of Ancient Turkey (1978), The Goddess from Anatolia, II, Çatal Hüyük and Anatolian Kilms (1989); *Recreations* music (Baroque and Gaelic), Celtic and Turkish Art, Geology, Ancient History; *Style*— James Mellaart, Esq; 12-13 Lichen Court, 79 Queen's Drive N4 2BH (☎ 081 802 6984); Institute of Archaeology, University of London, University College, 31-34 Gordon Sq, London WC1H OPY (☎ 071 387 7050 ext 4478)

MELLANBY, Prof Kenneth; CBE (1953, OBE 1944); s of Prof Alexander Lawson Mellanby (d 1951), of Bridge of Weir, Renfrewshire, and Anne Warren, *née* Maunder (d 1963); *b* 26 March 1908; *Educ* Barnard Castle Sch, King's Coll Cambridge (BA, ScD), Univ of London (PhD); *m* 1, 1933 (m dis 1948), Helen Neilson; 1 da (Jane b 13 July 1938); m 2, 15 April 1949, Jean Louie, da of Robert Copeland (d 1965), of Clitheroe, Lancs; 1 s (Alexander b 15 May 1950); *Career* WWII Sqdn Ldr CO Sheffield Univ Air Sqdn RAFVR 1939-43, Maj RAMC 1943 attached SACSEA Kandy Serv Assam, Burma; res worker London Sch of Hygiene and Tropical Med (Wandsworth fell) 1930-36, Sorby fell Royal Soc 1937-45 (interrupted by WWII), reader in med entomology London Univ 1945-47, fndr-princ Univ of Ibadan Nigeria 1947-53, head Entomology Dept Rottamsted Experimental Station 1955-62, fndr-dir Monts Wood Experimental Station 1961-74, ed Int Journal Enviromental Pollution 1974-88, currently enviromental conslt; hon prof Univs of: Leicester, Cardiff, PCL; pres: Cambridge Cncl for the Protection of Rural England, Bedfordshire and Huntingdonshire Wildlife Tst; Hon DSc Univs of: Ibadan, Bradford, Leicester, Essex, Sheffield; pres Inst of Biology 1971; *Books* Scabies (1943), Human Guinea-pigs (1945), The Birth of Nigeria's University (1958), Pesticides and Pollution (1967), The Mole (1971), The Biology of Pollution (1972), Can Britain Feed Itself (1975), Talpa The Story of a Mole (children's book, 1976), Farming and Wildlife (1981), Waste and Pollution (1991), The DDT Story (1991); *Clubs* Atheneum; *Style*— Prof Kenneth Mellanby, CBE; 38 Warkworth St, Cambridge CB1 1EG (☎ 0223 328 733)

MELLAR, Gordon Hollings; s of George Herbert Mellar (d 1962), and Gladys, *née* Hollings (d 1990); *b* 15 Oct 1935; *Educ* High Storrs GS Sheffield, Trinity Coll Cambridge (MA); *m* 17 Aug 1963, Ann Mary, da of Herbert Bates (d 1961); 1 s (Toby b 21 March 1972), 1 da (Sadie b 8 June 1969); *Career* Nat Serv cmmnd RAF (pilot trg) 1954-56, Flying Offr (pilot) No 616 S Yorks Sqdn RAUXAF 1956-57; dir Centrax Ltd 1977- (mechanical engr 1959-, dep md Gas Turbine Div 1976-); marker and referee Newton Abbot Squash Club; memb: Mid Devon Road Club, Newton Abbot Photographic Club; FIMechE; *Recreations* squash, cycling, photography, golf; *Style*— Gordon Mellar, Esq; Centrax Ltd, Newton Abbot, Devon TQ12 4SQ (☎ 0626 53342, 0626 52251, fax 0626 52250, telex 42935 CENTRX G)

MELLERS, Prof Wilfrid Howard; OBE (1982); s of late Percival Wilfrid Mellers, and Hilda Maria, *née* Lawrence; *b* 26 April 1914; *Educ* Leamington Coll, Downing Coll Cambridge (BA, MA); *m* 1, 1940 (m dis), Vera Muriel, da of late Gustavus Hobbs; m 2, March 1950 (m dis), Peggy Pauline Lewis; 3 da (Judith, Olivia Caroline, Sarah); m 3, 17 July 1980, Robin Stephanie Hildyard, *née* Spicer; *Career* tutor and supervisor Downing Coll Cambridge 1945-48, staff tutor in music Extra Mural Dept Univ of Birmingham 1948-60; visiting prof of music: Univ of Pittsburgh USA 1960-63, City Univ 1981-, Univ of Keele 1981-; emeritus prof Univ of York 1982 (founding head of Dept of Music 1964-81), former visiting prof of music at numerous American Univs, currently Andrew Mallon visiting prof Tulane Univ USA; author of numerous pubns in reference books and encyclopaedia; fell Sonneck Soc USA 1984; Hon DPhil City Univ London 1981; FGSM 1981; *Books* Music and Society (1956), Music in the Making (1951), Music in a New Found Land: Themes and Developments in the History of American Music (1964), Twilight of the Gods: the Beatles in Retrospect (173), Beethoven and the Voice of God (1983), Vaughan Williams and the Vision of Albion (1989); *Style*— Prof Wilfrid Mellers, OBE; Oliver Sheldon House, 17 Aldwark, York YO1 2BX (☎ 0904 638686)

MELLING, John Kennedy; s of John Robert Melling (d 1948), of Westcliff-on-Sea, Essex, and Ivy Edith May, *née* Woolmer (d 1982); *b* 11 Jan 1927; *Educ* Thirsk Sch Westcliff, Westcliff HS for Boys; *Career* CA; dramatic and literary critic, lectr, author, broadcaster, playwright and historian; memb Ctee Crime Writers' Assoc 1985-88, int life vice-pres American Fedn of Police, UK rep Criminal Investigators Assoc USA, awarded Knight Grand Cross Order of St Michael the Archangel of the Nat Assoc of Police USA; govr Corp of the Sons of the Clergy; Master Worshipful Co of Poulters 1980-81; FCA, FFB, FRSA, FTII, MCFA; *Books* Discovering Lost Theatres, Discovering London's Guilds and Liveries (fourth edn), Murder Done To Death, The Gilded Cage (play); *Recreations* reading, collecting theatre and crime ephemera; *Clubs* City Livery; *Style*— John Melling, Esq; 85 Chalkwell Ave, Westcliff-on-Sea, Essex SS0 8NL (☎ 0702 76012); 9 Blenheim St, New Bond St, London W1Y 9LE (☎ 071 499 2519/7249)

MELLING, Joseph Anthony (Joe); s of John Gerard Melling (d 1989), of Preston, Lancashire, and Monica, *née* Clifton; *b* 18 June 1946; *Educ* Preston Catholic Coll; *m* Patricia Mary, da of Thomas Gornall; 3 da (Sarah Louise b 28 Oct 1973, Jane Elizabeth b 9 May 1975, Louisa Clare b 9 May 1979); *Career* journalist; acting sports ed Blackburn Times 1967, sport and news reporter Lancashire Evening Post 1968 (trainee news reporter 1965); Daily Express: sport sub ed Manchester 1969, NE area sports writer 1972-78, Midlands sports reporter 1978-80, dep chief football writer 1980-83; football ed Mail On Sunday 1986- (chief football writer 1983); Sports Reporter of the Year (1986), special award of distinction for coverage of Hillsborough disaster; chm Football Writers' Assoc 1987; *Books* United To Win (biography of Ron Atkinson, 1984), Kerry (biography of Kerry Dixon, 1986); *Recreations* walking, gourmet eating, wine collecting; *Style*— Joe Melling, Esq; Mail On Sunday, Northcliffe House, 2 Derry St, Kensington, London (☎ 071 938 7075, fax 071 937 4115, car 0836 273030)

MELLINGER, Lucas Emmanuel Matthias; s of Dr Frederick Mellinger (d 1970), of Los Angeles, USA, and Eva, *née* Schlesinger (d 1959); *b* 9 July 1921; *Educ* Bunce Court Sch, Northern Poly (DipArch); *m* 27 Sept 1957 (m dis 1987), Janet Elizabeth, da of Sidney Kybert (d 1964); 1 s (Simon b 1964), 1 da (Karina b 1959); *Career* Corpl RE 1940-46; architect, planning conslt, design conslt; planning offr Notts Co Cncl 1948-50, chief tech and res asst Wells Wintemute Wells Coates 1950-53, in private practice 1953-; former conslt to: Br Film Inst, Cinematograph Exhibitors' Assoc, Film Prodn Assoc; architect of exhibitions, trade fairs and restaurants incl: Hatchetts (Piccadilly), The Sands (Bond St), Dukes (Duke St), Xenon Nightclub (Piccadilly); conslt to housing assocs and charitable tsts, church Authys, Leisure Indust; patentee of furniture sets, assemblies for sedentary work and window fitting; three times winner RIBA Int Design award; FRIBA, FRTPI, FCSD; *Recreations* armchair philosophy, politics; *Clubs* Private; *Style*— Lucas E M Mellinger, Esq; 60 Richmond Hill Court, Richmond, Surrey TW10 6BE (☎ 081 940 8255); 4 Kew Green, Richmond, Surrey TW9 3BH (☎ 081 948 5437/8)

MELLIS, Capt David Barclay Nairne; DSC (1941), RN; s of Rev David Barclay Mellis Mellis (d 1961), of 2 Belgrave Place, Edinburgh, and Margaret Blaikie, *née* MacKenzie (d 1970); *b* 13 June 1915; *Educ* RNC Dartmouth, RNC Greenwich; *m* 13 April 1940, Anne Patricia, da of Lt-Col Walter Stuart Wingate-Gray, MC (d 1977); 1 s (Patrick b 1943), 2 da (Matilda b 1941, Charlotte b 1952); *Career* RN: cadet 1929, midshipman 1933, Sub Lt 1935; served HMS: Malaya 1932, York 1934, Gallant 1936-37; Lt 1937, navigation specialist 1938, Persian Gulf and China HMS Bideford 1938-39; served HMS: Malcolm, Worcester and Mackay (Portsmouth and Harwich) 1940-41, Manchester 1942, Rotherham (Eastern Fleet) 1942-43, memb Staff Cdre D Eastern Fleet 1943-45, Lt Cdr 1945, memb Staff HMS Dryad 1945-47, Fleet Navigating Offr East Indies HMS Norfolk 1947-49, First Lt HMS Dryad 1949-51, Cdr 1951, in cmd HMS Redpole 1951-52, Admty 1952-54, in cmd HMS St Kitts 1954-55, 2 i/c and Exec Offr Centaur 1955-56, memb Staff C-in-C Med as Asst Capt of the Fleet Suez War 1956-58, Capt 1958, JSSC 1958, Br Naval Attaché Athens and Tel Aviv 1959-61, in cmd HMS Puma Captain 7 Frigate Sqdn (S Atlantic and S America) 1961-63, in cmd HMS Dryad 1963-65, COS to C-in-C Med and as COMEDSOUEAST (Nato appt) 1965-67, Cdre 1965-67, ret 1967; comptroller Duart Castle Mull 1967-68, Admty Approved Master (Warship Trials) 1969-79; jt fndr: Royal Naval Pipers Soc 1951, Royal Naval Club Argyll 1969; hon vice pres Argyll and Bute Cons and Unionist Assoc; Cdre Western Isles Yacht Club 1975-81, tstee Royal Highland Yacht Club; younger brother Trinity House, elder Church of Scotland; *Recreations* sailing, fly fishing, bridge, arguing; *Clubs* New (Edinburgh), Royal Scottish Pipers Soc; *Style*— Capt David Mellis, DSC, RN; High Water, Aros, Isle of Mull, Argyll PA72 6JG (☎ 0680 300 370)

MELLIS, Margaret; da of David Barclay Mellis (d 1961), and Margaret, *née* MacKenzie (d 1970); *b* 22 Jan 1914; *Educ* Queen Margarets PNEU Sch Edinburgh, Edinburgh Coll of Art (DA, MacLaine Watters medal for colour, Andrew Grant postgrad award, travelling scholar, fellowship 2 years); *m* 1, 1938, Adrian Stokes (the writer), s of Durham Stokes; 1 s (Telfec b 1940); m 2, Francis Davison (the collagist), s of George Davison; *Career* artist; studied in Paris Spain and Italy, worked Euston Road Sch London, lived and worked St Ives Cornwall then Cap d'Antibes France, currently based Suffolk; solo exhibitions: AIA Gallery London 1958, Scottish Gallery Edinburgh b 1959, UEA 1967, Bear Lane Gallery Oxford 1968, Grabowski Gallery London 1969, Richard Demarco Gallery Edinburgh 1970, Univs of Stirling and Exeter 1970, Basil Jacobs Gallery London 1972, Compass Gallery Glasgow 1976, Piers Art Centre Orkney 1982, New '57 Gallery Edinburgh 1982, Redfern Gallery London 1987 and 1990; group exhibitions incl: Waddington Galleries 1959-62, John Moores Liverpool Exhibition 4 and 5 1963 and 1965, Edinburgh Open 100 1967, Painting in Cornwall 1945-55 (New Art Centre London) 1977, The Women's Art Show 1550-1970 (Castle Museum Nottingham) 1982, Glasgow's Great Britain Art Exhibition (Mclellan Galleries) 1990; collections incl: Tate Gallery, V & A, Nuffield Fndn, Sztuki W Lodzi Museum Poland, Hull City Museum and Art Galleries school collection, Scottish Arts Cncl, Arts Cncl of GB, Graves Collection Sheffield, Sainsbury Centre Norwich; *Recreations* music, reading, dancing, walking; *Style*— Miss Margaret Mellis; Redfern Gallery, 20 Cork St, London W1X 2HL (☎ 071 734 1732, fax 071 494 2908)

MELLISH, Baron (Life Peer 1985), of Bermondsey in Greater London; Robert Joseph Mellish; PC (1967); s of John Mellish, of Deptford, London; *b* 3 March 1913; *Educ* St Joseph's RC Sch Deptford; *m* 1938, Anne Elizabeth, da of George Warner, of Bermondsey; 4 s (Hon Robert, Hon David, Hon Paul, Hon Stephen); *Career* served WWII turn as Lance-Corpl then rose to Maj RE SE Asia; left school at 14, worked as clerk in docks, joined TGWU 1929, organiser of dockers 1938-40, PPS to First Lord of Admlty then to Min for Pensions then to Min of Supply 1950-51, jt Parly sec Miny of Housing 1964-67, min for Public Bldy and Works 1967-69, Parly sec Treasy and govt chief whip 1969-70 and 1974-76 (oppn chief whip 1970-74); MP (Lab 1946-82, Ind Lab 1982) Bermondsey Rotherhithe 1946-50, Bermondsey 1950-74, Southwark Bermondsey 1974-82; Papal Knight Order of St Gregory the Great 1959; *Style*— The Rt Hon Lord Mellish, PC; c/o House of Lords, London SW1

MELLON, Sir James; KCMG (1989, CMG 1979); *b* 25 Jan 1929; *Educ* Univ of Glasgow; *m* 1, 1956, Frances Murray (d 1976); 1 s, 3 da; m 2, 1979, Mrs Philippa Shuttleworth, *née* Hartley; *Career* FO 1963: commercial cnsllr E Berlin 1975-76, head of Trade Rels and Export Dept FCO 1976-78, high cmmr Ghana and ambass to Togo 1978-83, ambass to Denmark 1983-86, consul gen New York 1986-89; chm Scottish Homes 1989-; *Style*— Sir James Mellon, KCMG; Scottish Homes, Rosebery House, Edinburgh EH12 5YA (☎ 031 337 0044)

MELLOR, Clare Ibbetson (Cim); s of Aubrey Rollo Ibbetson Mellor, CBE (d 1977), and Edith Madeline, *née* Anderson; *b* 4 March 1923; *Educ* Shrewsbury, Ch Ch Oxford (MA), Harvard (Henry fell); *m* 12 Oct 1957, Elizabeth Dewar, da of Harry Montgomery Everard; 1 s (Nicholas b 1960), 2 da (Lucy b 1958, Sophie b 1963); *Career* WWII 1942-46, RAFVR Flt Lt; dir: Metal Box plc 1977-83, Business in the Community 1984-86; memb: Collyer Ctee, Mechanical and Electrical Requirements Bd DTI; memb Worshipful Co of Tinplate Workers; FBIM, FRSA; *Recreations* DIY, local community activities, aiding inventors and innovators; *Clubs* Leander, MCC, Huntercombe Golf; *Style*— C I Mellor, Esq; Twilly Springs House, West Hendred, Wantage, Oxon OX12 8RW (☎ 0235 835 035)

MELLOR, David; OBE (1981); s of Colin Mellor (d 1970), and Ivy Mellor (d 1975); *b* 5 Oct 1930; *Educ* Sheffield Coll of Art, Royal Coll of Art (hon fell 1966), Br Sch at Rome; *m* 1966, Fiona, da of Col Gerald Heggart MacCarthy (d 1943); 1 s, 1 da; *Career* designer, manufacturer and retailer; conslt DOE 1963-70, chm Design Cncl Ctee of Inquiry into Standards of Design in Consumer Goods in Britain 1982-84, chm Crafts Cncl 1982-84, tstee V & A Museum 1983-88; *Style*— David Mellor, Esq, OBE; The Round Building, Hathersage, Sheffield S30 1BA (☎ 0433 50220)

MELLOR, Prof David Hugh; s of Sydney David Mellor, and Ethel Naomi, *née* Hughes; *b* 10 July 1938; *Educ* Pembroke Coll Cambridge 1956-60 (BA), Univ of Minnesota (MS), Univ of Cambridge (PhD, ScD); *Career* tech offr ICI Central Instruments Laboratories 1962-63; Univ of Cambridge: asst lectr in philisophy 1965-70, lectr in philosophy 1970-83, reader in metaphysics 1983-86, prof of philosophy 1986-; Philosophy Faculty Univ of Cambridge: librarian 1970-76, chm Bd and Degree Ctee 1976-78 and 1991-93 (sec 1981-85), dir Graduate Studies 1988-90; pres Cambridge Assoc of Univ Teachers 1976-78; Univ of Cambridge: memb Cncl of the Senate 1976-78, memb Library Syndicate 1976-78, memb Bd of Graduate Studies 1989-, chm History and Philosophy of Sci Syndicate 1980-83; official fell Pembroke Coll Cambridge 1966-70 (Draper's res fell 1964-66); dir Studies in Philosophy: Pembroke Coll 1964-83, Downing Coll 1966-83, Trinity Hall 1982-83; Darwin Coll: fell 1971-, organiser Centenery Conf 1980-82, vice-master 1983-87; external examiner in Philosophy: Univ of Khartoum 1978-79, Univ of Warwick 1978-80, Univ Coll of N Wales At Bangor 1982-84; visiting fell in philosophy Aust Nat Univ Inst Advanced Study 1975, Radcliffe Tst Fell in Philosophy 1978-80, visiting prof Philosophy Univ of Auckland 1985, pres Br Soc for Philosophy of Sci 1985-87 (annual conf organiser 1970 and 1986), sec Br Nat Ctee for Logic Methodology and Philosophy of Sci; memb: Cncl Royal Inst of Philosophy 1987-, Exec Ctee Mind Assoc 1982-86; FBA 1983; *Books* The British Journal for The Philosophy of Science (ed, 1968-70), The Matter of Chance (1971), Cambridge Studies in Philosophy (ed, 1978-82), Australasian Journal of Philosophy (memb Editorial Bd, 1977-89), African Philosophical Inquiry (editorial conslt), Science, Belief and Behaviour (ed, 1980), Prospects for Pragmatism (ed, 1980), Real Time (1981), Matters of Metaphysics (1991), Ways of Communicating (ed, 1991); *Style*— Prof David Mellor; 25 Orchard St, Cambridge CB1 1JS (☎ 0223 460332)

MELLOR, His Hon Judge David John; s of John Robert Mellor, of IOM, and Muriel, *née* Field; *b* 12 Oct 1940; *Educ* Plumtree Sch Southern Rhodesia (Zimbabwe), King's Coll London (LLB); *m* 21 May 1966, (Carol) Mary, da of David Morris Clement, CBE, of 19 The Highway, Sutton, Surrey; 2 da (Freya Mary Asquith b 1968, Annabelle Elizabeth Asquith b 1972); *Career* called to the barr Inner Temple 1964, rec Crown Ct 1986-89, circuit judge 1989-; *Clubs* Norfolk; *Style*— His Hon Judge Mellor; The Old Hall, Mulbarton, Norwich (☎ 0508 70241); Norwich Combined Court (☎ 0603 761776)

MELLOR, The Rt Hon David John; PC (1990), QC (1987), MP (C) Putney 1979-; s of Douglas H Mellor; *b* 12 March 1949; *Educ* Swanage GS, Christ's Coll Cambridge; *m* 1974, Judith Mary Hall; 2 s; *Career* chm Univ of Cambridge Assoc 1970; called to the Bar Inner Temple 1972; parly candidate (C) W Bromwich E Oct 1974, PPS to Francis Pym as Ldr of House 1981; parly under sec state: Energy 1981-83, Home Office 1983-86; min of state: Home Office 1986-87, FCO 1987-88, Health 1988-89, Home Office 1989-90, Privy Cncl Office (Min for the Arts) 1990; Chief Sec to the Treasury 1990-; former special tstee Westminster Hosp, hon assoc Br Vet Assoc, vice chm tstees London Philharmonic Orchestra 1989, former memb Cncl Nat Youth Orchestra; FZS; *Style*— David Mellor, Esq, QC, MP; House of Commons, London SW1

MELLOR, Derrick; CBE (1984); s of William Mellor, and Alice, *née* Hirst; *b* 11 Jan 1927; *m* 4 Feb 1954, Kathleen, *née* Hodgson; 2 s (Simon David b 1959, Michael John b 1962), 1 da (Helen Lucy b 1960); *Career* Army 1945-49; BOT 1950-57; Trade Cmmn Serv 1958-64: Kuala Lumpur and Sydney; Dip Serv 1961-: Malaysia, Australia, Denmark, Venezuela; ambass Paraguay 1979-84, ret 1984, re-employed FCO 1984-; occasional lectr SOAS; *Recreations* golf, tennis; *Clubs* Royal Cwlth, Travellers'; *Style*— Derrick Mellor, Esq, CBE; Summerford Farm, Withyham, E Sussex (☎ 089 277 826); FCO, King Charles St, London SW1

MELLOR, Hugh Salusbury; s of Wing Cdr Harry Manners Mellor, MVO (ka 1940), and Diana Marion, *née* Wyld; *b* 16 March 1936; *Educ* Harrow, Christ Church Oxford (MA); *m* 6 Feb 1966, Sally, da of Flt Lt Clive Newton Wawn, DFC, RAF, of 2a Moralla Rd, Kooyang, Victoria, Australia; 2 s (Nicholas Hugh b 29 May 1967, Andrew Harry Clive b 3 Jan 1970), 1 da (Sari b 14 July 1972); *Career* Nat Serv 2 Lt Coldstream Gds 1954-56; asst dir Morgan Grenfell & Co Ltd 1968 (joined 1960), exec Dalgety plc (formerly Dalgety Ltd) 1970 (Bd memb 1968); dir: London Bd Aust Mutual Provident Soc 1979-, Burmah Oil plc 1984, Bank of NZ (London) 1983-, Meghraj Bank Ltd 1987-; FRSPB, fell Br Tst for Ornithology; *Recreations* ornithology, entomology; *Style*— Hugh Mellor, Esq; Blackland Farm, Stewkley, Leighton Buzzard, Beds; Fealar Lodge, Blairgowrie, Perthshire (☎ 0525 240 296); c/o Dalgety plc, 19 Hanover Square, London W1 9AD (☎ 071 499 7712, fax 071 493 0892, telex 23874)

MELLOR, Maj James Thomas Paulton; MC (1946), TD (1948), DL (Argyll 1964); s of Maj James Gerald Guy, MC (d 1950); *b* 15 March 1918; *Educ* Eton; *m* 1946, Eve, da of Lt Col Walter Thomas Forrest Holland, AFC (d 1976); 1 s, 1 da; *Career* served Argyll and Sutherland Highlanders 1939-40, POW 1940-45 (Colditz 1943-45), Maj TA 1946; with Walpamur Co (Darwen) 1946-58; landowner, farmer 1958-; *Recreations* shooting, fishing, curling, ski-bobbing; *Style*— Maj James Mellor, MC, TD, DL; Barndromin Farm, Knipoch, by Oban, Argyll PA34 4QS (☎ 085 26 273)

MELLOR, Ronald William; CBE (1984); s of William Mellor (d 1941), of Highgate, London, and Helen Edna, *née* Thomson (d 1952); *b* 8 Dec 1930; *Educ* Highgate Sch, King's Coll London (BSc); *m* 1 Sept 1956, Jean, da of Albert Sephton, of Rainhill; 1 s (Andrew John b 3 March 1961), 1 da (Ann Margaret b 10 July 1958); *Career* cmmnd 2 Lt Royal Artillery 1950, Capt Royal Artillery TA 1956; Ford Motor Company: mangr of Cortina product planning 1964, mangr of truck product planning 1965, chief res engr 1969, chief engine engr 1970, chief body engr Ford Werke AG W Germany 1974, vice pres of car engrg Ford of Europe Inc 1975, dir Ford Motor Company Ltd 1983-87; Freeman City of London 1991, Liveryman Worshipful Co of Carmen 1991; FIMechE 1980 (memb Cncl 1985-87, chm Automobile Div 1986-87), FEng 1983; *Recreations* yachting; *Style*— Ronald Mellor, Esq, CBE; Institution of Mechanical Engineers, 1 Birdcage Walk, Westminster, London SW1H 9JJ (☎ 071 222 7899, fax 071 222 4557, telex 917944 IMELDN G)

MELLOR, Simon John; s of Raymond Mellor, and Phyllis, *née* Canter; *b* 10 Sept 1954; *Educ* Univ of Bristol (BSc); *m* 3 Feb 1990, (Carolyn) Mary, da of Ewen Langford; 2 step s (Dominic b 18 Nov 1965, Thomas b 23 June 1967); *Career* Saatchi & Saatchi Company plc: asst to Chm 1976-78, corp devpt mangr 1978-84, assoc dir 1984-, dir Main Bd 1985, dep chief exec offr 1988, responsible for co's corp communication 1990; Freeman City of London, memb Worshipful Co of Clockmakers; *Recreations* theatre, cinema, soccer, cricket; *Clubs* RAC; *Style*— Simon Mellor, Esq; Saatchi & Saatchi plc, Berkeley Square, London W1X 5DH (☎ 071 753 5000, fax 071 495 4340)

MELLOWS, Prof Anthony Roger Mellows; TD (1969); s of Laurence Beresford Mellows (d 1984), and Margery Phyllis, *née* Winch; *b* 30 July 1936; *Educ* King's Coll London (LLB, BD, LLM, PhD, LLD); *m* 1973, Elizabeth Angela, da of Ven Benjamin George Burton Fox, MC, TD (d 1978); *Career* admitted slr, with Alexanders 1962-, prof of the law of property London Univ 1974-90 (emeritus prof 1990); dir: Lord Rayleigh's Farms Inc 1980-89, Lord Rayleigh's Dairies Ltd 1987, Strutt and Parker (Farms) Ltd 1985-; KStJ 1988; chllr Order of St John 1991- (registrar 1988-91); *Books* Taxation for Executors and Tstees (1967, 6 edn 1984), Taxation of Land Transactions (1973, 3 edn 1982), The Law of Succession (1970, 4 edn 1983), The Modern Law of Tsts (jt 1966, 5 edn 1983); *Clubs* Athenaeum; *Style*— Prof Anthony Mellows, TD; 22 Devereux Ct, Temple Bar, London WC2R 3JJ; 203 Temple Chambers, Temple Avenue, London EC4Y 0EN (☎ 071 353 6221)

MELLY, (Alan) George Heywood; s of Francis Heywood, and Edith Maud Melly; *b* 17 Aug 1926; *Educ* Stowe; *m* 1, 1955 (m dis 1962), Victoria Vaughan; 1 da; m 2, 1963, Diana Margaret Campion Dawson; 1 s, 1 step-da; *Career* AB RN 1944-47; asst in London Gallery 1948-50; professional jazz singer, music critic and film scriptwriter; with John Chilton's Feetwarmers 1974-; Critic of the Year IPC Nat Press Awards 1970; pres Br Humanist Assoc 1972-74; *Books* incl: I Flook (1962), Owning Up (1965), Revolt into Style (1970), Flook by Trog (1970), Rum Bum and Concertina (1977), The Media Mob (with Barry Fantoni 1980), Tribe of One: Great Naive and Primitive Painters of the British Isles (1981), Mellymobile (1982), Scouse Mouse (1984); *Recreations* trout fishing, singing and listening to 1920s blues, collecting modern painting; *Clubs* Colony Room, Chelsea Arts; *Style*— George Melly, Esq; 33 St Lawrence Terrace, London W10 5SR

MELLY, (Charles) William; s of Flt Lt Charles Patrick Melly, of Flat 3, Cranmere, 35 Station Rd, Budleigh Salterton, Devon, and Daphne Joyce, *née* Ferris; *b* 19 Feb 1947; *Educ* Warwick Sch; *m* 31 May 1980, Gail Elizabeth, da of Lancelot Reginald William Watkins; 3 s (Edward b 1982, William James b 1985, Joseph Patrick b 11 Sept 1990); *Career* Smith Keen Cutler Ltd (now Smith Keen Cutler) 1981-: ptnr 1981-86, dir 1986-87, md 1987-; memb Int Stock Exchange 1970; *Recreations* motor racing, snooker, horse racing; *Clubs* RAC; *Style—* William Melly, Esq; Everglade House, Penn La, Tanworth-in-Arden, Solihull, W Mids B94 5HH; Smith Keen Cutler, Exchange Bldgs, Stephenson Place, Birmingham B2 4NN (☎ 021 643 9977, fax 021 643 0345)

MELROSE, Prof Denis Graham; s of Thomas Robert Gray Melrose (d 1983), of Wells, Somerset, and Floray, *née* Collings (d 1985); *b* 20 June 1921; *Educ* Sedbergh, Univ Coll Oxford (MA, BM, BCh), Univ Coll Hosp London Univ; *m* 18 April 1945, Ann Meredith, *née* Warter; 2 s (Simon Graham Kempthorne b 15 May 1946, Angus John b 27 March 1950); *Career* Surgn Lt RNVR 1946-48; Nuffield travelling fell 1955, Fulbright travelling fell 1956, Heller fell and assoc in surgery Stanford Univ California 1957-58, lectr (later reader) Royal Postgrad Med Sch London 1952-68, prof of surgical science Univ of London 1968- (now emeritus); DHSS: conslt advsr, chief med offr and chief scientific offr; chm Concerted Action for Extracorporeal Respiration EEC, govr Euro and Int Socs of Artificial Organs; contrib numerous articles and chapters in books, particularly on heart surgery, heart/lung machines and med engineering; MRCP, FRCS; memb Cardiac Soc; *Recreations* sailing, skiing; *Clubs* RNSA; *Style—* Prof Denis Melrose; 62 Belvedere Court, Upper Richmond Road, London SW15 6HZ, (☎ 081 788 0116)

MELROSE, Margaret Elstob; *née* Jackson; DL (Cheshire 1987); da of Samuel Chantler Jackson (d 1978), of Prestbury, Cheshire, and Annie Young, *née* Arnot (d 1978); *b* 2 May 1928; *Educ* Howell's Sch, Denbigh, Girton Coll Cambridge (Draper's Co Scholarship); *m* 19 June 1948 (m dis), Kenneth Ramsay Watson, s of late Albert Watson; assumed surname of Melrose by deed poll; 1 da (Joanne b 1953); *Career* vice consul for the Lebanon for N Eng, Scot and NI 1963-67, memb Cheshire CC 1967- (chm 1984-85 and 1986-87); memb: Macclesfield RDC 1968-74, Nether Alderley Parish Cncl (chm) 1968; Cheshire CC Cons Gp: sec 1973-75, dep whip 1975-77, chief whip 1977-83, sec 1983-; Runcorn New Town Devpt Corp 1975-81; chm: NW Regnl Children's Planning Ctee 1977-81, Govrs Crewe and Alsager Coll of Higher Educn, Tatton Park Mgmnt Ctee 1985-; gen cmmr of taxes Salford and N Manchester 1985-; vice pres: Cheshire Agric Soc 1985-, Ploughing and Hedgecutting Soc 1986-; chm Manchester Airport Conslt Ctee 1986-, pres Macclesfield Constituency Cons Assoc 1988-, chm Cheshire Rural Community Cncl 1988-, vice chm Crewe and Alsager Coll of Higher Educn Inc Bd 1988-, memb Miny of Tport Sleep Res Steering Gp 1990-; *Recreations* golf, sailing, horses, bridge, country life; *Clubs* Wilmslow Golf, Cheshire County; *Style—* Mrs Margaret Melrose, DL; The Coach House, Stamford Rd, Alderley Edge, Cheshire SK9 7NS (☎ 0625 585629); County Hall, Chester CH1 1SG (☎ 0244 602424, telex 61347, DX no 19986, fax 0244 603800)

MELSOM, Andrew John; s of Maj John George Melsom, and Anne Sabine Rowbotham, *née* Pasley; *b* 1 Feb 1953; *Educ* Uppingham; *m* 2 Feb 1980, Melanie Clare, da of Maj Derek Hague, MC (d 1965); 2 s (Harry George b 8 Aug 1984, Jack Andrew b 25 Aug 1987, d 1988), 1 da (Edwina Lily b 11 Aug 1989); *Career* with Foote Cone and Belding 1971, dir J Walter Thompson 1982-, founding ptnr BMP Business (Advertising) 1985, author/dir Best of the Fringe Theatrical Revue Duke of Yorks Theatre 1976, memb Cncl of Management The Fndn for the Study of Infant Deaths; *Books* Are you there Moriarty (1979), Play it Again Moriarty (1980); *Recreations* tennis, film; *Style—* Andrew J Melsom, Esq; South House, Ham, Marlborough, Wilts SN8 3RB (☎ 04884 389); BMP Business, 54 Baker St, London W1M 1DJ (☎ 071 486 5566, fax 071 486 0763)

MELVILLE, (Richard) David; s of Col Robert Kenneth Melville, of 12 Cope Place, London, and Joan Emerton, *née* Hawkins; *b* 22 April 1953; *Educ* Wellington, Pembroke Coll Cambridge (MA); *m* 31 Oct 1981, Catharine Mary, da of late Hon William Granville Wingate, QC, of Cox's Mill, Dallington, Heathfield, E Sussex; 1 s (Thomas Wingate b 29 Aug 1985), 1 da (Emma Rose b 21 July 1987); *Career* called to the Bar Inner Temple 1975; *Recreations* sailing; *Clubs* Royal Corinthian Yacht, BAR Yacht; *Style—* David Melville, Esq; 39 Essex St, London WC2R 3AT (☎ 071 353 4741, fax 071 353 3978)

MELVILLE, Sir Harry Work; KCB (1958); s of Thomas Melville (d 1973); *b* 27 April 1908; *Educ* George Heriot's Sch Edinburgh, Univ of Edinburgh (DSc, PhD), Trinity Coll Cambridge (PhD); *m* 1942, Janet Marian Cameron; 2 da; *Career* sci advsr Miny of Supply 1940-43, supt Radar Res Station 1943-45; prof of chemistry: Univ of Aberdeen 1940-48, Univ of Birmingham 1948-56; chief sci advsr for Civil Defence Midlands Regn 1952-56, sec to Privy Cncl for Scientific and Industl Res 1956-65, chm SRC 1965-67, princ Queen Mary Coll London 1967-76, memb Parly and Scientific Ctee 1971-75; FRS; *Style—* Sir Harry Melville, KCB, FRS; Norwood, Dodds Lane, Chalfont St Giles, Bucks (☎ 024 07 2222)

MELVILLE, James; *see*: MARTIN, (Roy) Peter

MELVILLE, Nigel Edward; s of Maj E K L Melville, and P D Melville; *b* 5 June 1945; *Educ* Sedbergh, Trinity Coll Oxford (MA), London Business Sch (MSc); *m* 15 Aug 1970, Maria Hadewij, *née* Van Oosten; 1 s (Christopher Patrick b 8 Dec 1978), 1 da (Sophie Olivia b 15 Dec 1980); *Career* articled clerk Fuller Jenks Beecroft & Co London 1967-70, corp fin exec Samuel Montagu & Co Limited London 1972-74; Baring Brothers & Co Limited: corp fin exec 1974-, corp fin mangr, seconded to ICON Limited (affiliated co in Nigeria) 1975-77, asst dir corp fin 1982-83, dir 1983-87 (seconded to Baring Brothers Asia Limited Hong Kong as md), memb Mgmnt Ctee and dir responsible for int corp fin 1987-; other directorships: Baring Brothers (Espana) SA 1988, Baring Brothers (France) 1988, Baring Brothers (Deutschland) GmbH 1990, Commerce International Merchant Bankers Berhad 1988; FCA; *Recreations* tennis, golf, skiing; *Clubs* Hurlingham, Vanderbilt, Leckford Golf; *Style—* Nigel Melville, Esq; Baring Brothers & Co Ltd, 8 Bishopsgate, London EC2N 4AE (☎ 071 280 1000, 071 280 1104, fax 071 283 3441)

MELVILLE, 9 Viscount (UK 1802); Robert David Ross Dundas; also Baron Duneira (UK 1802); only s of Hon Robert Maldred St John Melville Dundas (ka 1940, yr s of 7 Viscount); suc uncle 1971; the 2 Viscount was First Lord of the Admty (1812-27 and 1828-30) and an enthusiast for Arctic exploration; Melville Sound is named after him; *b* 28 May 1937; *Educ* Cargilfield Sch, Wellington; *m* 23 July 1982, Fiona Margaret, da of late Roger Kirkpatrick Stilgoe, of Derby House, Stogumber, Taunton; 2 s (Robert b 1984, James David Brouncker b 19 Jan 1986); *Heir* s, Hon Robert Henry Kirkpatrick Dundas b 23 April 1984; *Career* served in Scots Gds (Nat Serv), Reserve Capt Scots Gds, Lt Ayrshire Yeo (TA); cncllr and dist cncllr Midlothian; pres Lasswade Civic Soc, tstee Poltonhall Community Assoc; *Recreations* shooting, fishing, golf, chess; *Clubs* Turf, Cavalry and Guards', Midlothian County, House of Lords Motor, Bunnyrigg and Dist Ex-Serviceman's; *Style—* Capt Rt Hon the Viscount Melville; Solomon's Ct, Chalford, nr Stroud, Glos (☎ 0453 883351); 3 Roland Way, London SW7 (☎ 071 370 3553)

MELVILLE, Sir Ronald Henry; KCB (1964, CB 1952); s of Henry Edward Melville (d 1976), of Whitacre, Bengeo, Hertford; *b* 9 March 1912; *Educ* Charterhouse, Magdalene Coll Cambridge; *m* 1940, Enid Dorcas Margaret, da of late Harold Godfrey Kenyon, of Ware, Herts; 2 s, 1 da; *Career* entered Civil Serv 1934, asst under sec of state Air Miny 1946-58, dep under sec of state 1958-60, dep under sec of state War Office 1960-63, second perm under sec of state MOD 1963-66, perm sec Miny of Aviation 1966-71, attached Civil Serv Dept 1971-72, ret; dir Westland Aircraft 1974-82; chm: Nat Rifle Assoc 1972-84, Jt Shooting Ctee for Gt Britain 1985-88; *Clubs* Brooks's; *Style—* Sir Ronald Melville, KCB; The Old Rose and Crown, Braughing, Ware, Herts

MELVILLE-ROSS, Timothy David; s of Lt Cdr Antony Stuart Melville-Ross, RN (ret), of 3 Wallands Crescent, Lewes, Sussex, and Anne Barclay Fane, *née* Gamble; *b* 3 Oct 1944; *Educ* Uppingham, Portsmouth Coll of Technol (Dip); *m* 19 Aug 1967, Camilla Mary Harlackenden, da of Lt-Col Richard Harlackenden Cawardine Probert, of Bevills, Bures, Suffolk; 2 s (Rupert b 1971, James b 1972); 1 da (Emma b 1975); *Career* chief exec Nationwide Anglia Building Society 1987- (chief gen mangr 1985-87); chm Phoenix Initiative, memb Cncl Industl Soc and Policy Studies Inst; *Recreations* reading, bridge, walking, the countryside, family; *Style—* Timothy Melville-Ross, Esq; Little Bevills, Bures, Suffolk (☎ 0787 227424); Nationwide Anglia Building Society, Chesterfield House, London WC1V 6PW

MELVIN, Peter Anthony Paul; s of Charles George Thomas Melvin (d 1959), and Elsie, *née* Paul (d 1983); *b* 19 Sept 1933; *Educ* St Marylebone GS, Poly Sch of Architecture (Dip Arch); *m* 23 April 1960, Muriel, da of Col James Cornelis Adriaan Faure (d 1984); 2 s (Jeremy Paul b 1964, Stephen James b 1967), 1 da (Joanna Claire b 1962); *Career* architect; RIBA: chm Eastern Region 1974-76, memb Cncl 1977-83 and 1985-88, vice pres 1982-83 and 1985-87; visiting fell Natal Sch of Architecture 1983; FRIBA 1971, FRSA; *Recreations* music, walking, sketching, looking; *Clubs* Arts; *Style—* Peter Melvin, Esq; Woodlands, Beechwood Drive, Aldbury, Tring, Hertfordshire HP23 5SB (☎ 044 285 211); Melvin Lansley & Mark, Archway House, 105a High St, Berkhamsted, Hertfordshire HP4 2DG (☎ 0442 862123/4/5)

MELZACK, Harold; s of Lewis Melzack (d 1938), and Celia, *née* Eisenstark (d 1987); *b* 6 Feb 1931; *Educ* Christ's Coll London, Coll of Estate Management; *m* 22 June 1954, June, da of Leonard Lesner, of London NW11; 2 da (Gillian b 1957, Susan b 1960); *Career* chartered surveyor, jt sr ptnr Smith Melzack, former chm Br Numismatic Trade Assoc; Freeman Worshipful Co of Chartered Surveyors; FCIArb; *Recreations* golf, numismatics, historic documents, bridge; *Clubs* Arts, Hartsbourne Golf and Country, Bushey; *Style—* Harold Melzack, Esq; Smith Melzack, 17/18 Old Bond St, London W1X 3DA (☎ 071 493 1613, fax 071 493 5480)

MELZER, Arthur David; s of Albert Cecil Melzer (d 1982), of Brisbane, Australia, and Winifred Le Machond (d 1982); *b* 24 Aug 1932; *Educ* Brisbane Boys GS, Univ of Queensland (BSc, Dip Phys Ed); *m* 1957, Shirley Grace, da of William Tab Rooney, of Brisbane, Australia; 4 s; *Career* geologist; Premier Consolidated Oilfields plc 1982-, md Premier Oil Pacific Ltd 1986; *Recreations* walking, swimming, tennis, squash; *Clubs* Oriental, Tanglin, Broome Park Country; *Style—* David Melzer, Esq; Block 3 No 01-10, Regency Park, Natham Rd, Singapore 1024 (☎ 010 65 7336409); 24 Thorndon Hall, Ingrave, Essex (☎ 0277 812046); Premier Consolidated Oilfields plc, 23 Lower Belgrave St, London SW1W 0HR (☎ 071 730 0752; telex 918121); Premier Oil Pacific Ltd, Representative Office, 541 Orchard Road, No 14-03 Liat Towers, Singapore 0923 (☎ 65 732 6644, telex R S 55017 POPLSE, fax 733 8290)

MENCIK DE MENSTEIN, Ferdinand Adalbert Jan; s of Dr Alexander Vladimir Menčik de Menstein (d 1973), and Eleonora Josefa Dolezal (d 1982); *b* 9 Feb 1916; *Educ* Charles Univ Prague; *m* 20 June 1942, Eva Maria, da of Dr Hugo Forster (d 1973); 2 s (Alexander Frederick b 1951, Richard Hugo b 1957), 2 da (Michaela Maria b 1944, Gabiela Maria b 1945); *Career* exec Bata Shoe Organisation - (multinational) 1946-54, md Batga, NZ Ltd 1954-59, chm and md Fabr de Calzado Peruano Lima 1970-73, dep chm The British Bata Shoe Co Ltd 1965-80; former dir: Bata sa France, Bata BMV Nederland; currently memb Bd of Panels UN Industl Organisation; Cdr of Order of Merit France 1960; Chevalier of Legion d'Honneur France 1975; Kt Soverign Order of Malta 1980; *Recreations* shooting, skiing; *Clubs* Club de la Chasse Paris; *Style—* Ferdinand A J Mencik de Menstein, Esq; 11 Boulevard Delessert, Paris 75016 (☎ 45204114); Mas Pissa Vinaigre, 83680 La Garde Freinet (☎ 94436063); Kinsky, 10 Waldegrave Gdns, Twickenham; Bata sa Europe, 38 Avenue de l'Opera 75083 (☎ 47424171, telex 211854)

MENDEL, Renée; da of Oscar Mendel (d 1940), of Hamburg, Germany, and Sophie Mendel (d 1946); *b* 22 Sept 1908; *Educ* Hamburg Lichtwark Schule; *Career* sculptor; exhibitions and subjects incl: Salon d'Automne Paris 1934, Lord Beaverbrook (Royal Academy) 1942, H E Jean Maisky 1943, Sir Lawrence Olivier, Renee Asherton and Henry V (Sculpture for the Home, exhibited by Heals Department Store), The Beatles (Camden Arts Centre) 1967, Idi Amin (Royal Exchange) 1977, James Joyce (wood carving, Nat Portrait Gallery) 1987, Dr H Winsley-Stolz, GP (bronze portrait head) 1989; *Style—* Miss Renée Mendel; 27 Onslow Gardens, Muswell Hill, London N10 3JT

MENDELOW, (Alexander) David; s of Harry Mendelow, of Johannesburg, and Ruby, *née* Palmer; *b* 19 May 1946; *Educ* Univ of Witwatersrand Nata SA (MB BCh, PhD); *m* 2 s (Trevor Neil b 1971, Robert Kevin b 1974), 1 da (Toni Andrea b 1969); *Career* registrar in neurosurgery Univ of Witwatersrand and Johannesburg Hosp 1970-76, sr registrar Univ of Edinburgh 1977-79, sr lectr Univ of Glasgow 1980-86, reader Univ of Newcastle Upon Tyne 1987-; author of articles in scientific journals and books on head injury and stroke; memb: Soc of Br Neurosurgeons, Surgical Res Soc; FRCSEd 1974; *Books* Fibre Systems of the Brain and Spinal Cord (1981); *Recreations* sailing, squash; *Style—* David Mendelow, Esq; Newcastle General Hospital, Westgate Road, Newcastle upon Tyne NE4 6BE (☎ 091 273 88 11, fax 091 272 26 41)

MENDELSOHN, (Heather) Leigh; da of Maurice Raymond Mendelsohn (d 1989), and Hazel Frances, *née* Keable; *b* 20 Feb 1946; *Educ* Fleetwood GS, Rothwell GS, Pudsey GS; *Career* trainee journalist R Ackrill Ltd Harrogate 1965-69, dep ed Action Desk Western Mail Cardiff 1969-71, dep Women's Page ed Daily Record Glasgow 1971-73, fashion ed Reveille London 1973-74, contract foreign corr The Sun Amsterdam 1975, freelance current affrs res 1976, PR conslt Market-Link PR 1976-78, fndr dir Phoenix PR 1978-; memb: NUJ, PR Conslts Assoc (memb Bd, chm Membership Ctee); *Recreations* tennis, swimming, archery, gardening; *Style—* Ms Leigh Mendelsohn; Phoenix Public Relations, 105-107 Farringdon Rd, London EC1R 3BT (☎ 071 833 8487, fax 071 833 5726)

MENDELSOHN, Martin; s of Arthur Mendelsohn (d 1961), and Rebecca, *née* Caplin (d 1975); *b* 6 Nov 1935; *Educ* Hackney Downs Sch; *m* 20 Sept 1959, Phyllis Linda, da of late Abraham Sobell; 2 s (Paul Arthur b 1962, David Edward b 1964); *Career* admitted slr 1959; Adlers Solicitors: ptnr 1961-90, sr prnt 1984-90, conslt 1990-; ptnr MPM Consultancy 1990-, visiting prof of franchising and dir of the National Westminster Centre for franchise res City Univ Business Sch, legal conslt Br Franchise Assoc; fndr chm Int Franchising Ctee of Section on Business Law Int Bar Assoc, chm Membership Ctee of Int Bar Assoc 1988-, warden Kenton Synagogue 1976-78, supporter of Jewish Welfare Bd, hon slr to various charitable instns; Freeman City of London 1964, Liveryman: Worshipful Co of Solicitors, Worshipful Co of Arbitrators; memb: The Law Soc, Int Bar Assoc, American Bar Assoc; *Books* author: Obtaining A Franchise (for DTI 1977), Comment Negocier une Franchise (jtly, 1983), The Ethics of Franchising (1987), Franchisor's Manual (1987), The Guide to Franchising (1985), How to Evaluate a Franchise (1989), How to Franchise your Business (jtly, 1989), How to Franchise Internationally (1989), International Franchising An Overview (ed 1984), Franchising and Business Development (A Study for the ILO Geneva) (1991), The Journal of

International Franchising and Distribution Law (ed); contrib and lectr to pubns and audiences worldwide; FCIArb, FRSA; *Recreations* cricket, philately; *Clubs* MCC; *Style—* Martin Mendelsohn, Esq; 22-26 Paul St, London, EC2A 4JH, (☎ 071 481 9100, 081 909 170, fax 071 247 4701, car 0836 205353, telex 883831 ADLERS G)

MENDELSON, Prof Maurice Harvey; s of William Maizel Mendelson (d 1959), of London, and Anne, *née* Aaronson; *b* 27 Aug 1943; *Educ* St Marylebone GS, New Coll Oxford (MA, DPhil); *m* 26 Dec 1968, Katherine Julia Olga, da of Bertalan Kertesz, of London; 2 da (Charlotte b 1 Nov 1972, Rachel b 15 Sept 1974); *Career* called to the Bar Lincoln's Inn 1965, in practice 1971-; lectr in law King's Coll London 1968-74, fell and tutor in law St John's Coll Oxford 1975-86, prof of int law UCL 1987-; memb Exec Cncl Br Branch Int Law Assoc; *Recreations* reading, the arts, riding, squash; *Clubs* Athenaeum; *Style—* Prof Maurice Mendelson; Faculty of Laws, University College London, Bentham House, 4 Endleigh Gardens, London WC1H OEG (☎ 071 380 7024, fax 071 387 9597); 2 Hare Court, Temple, London EC4Y 7BH (☎ 071 583 1770, fax 071 583 9269)

MENDES, Samuel Alexander (Sam); s of James Peter Mendes, of London, and Valerie Hélène, *née* Barnett; *b* 1 Aug 1965; *Educ* Magdalen Coll Sch Oxford, Peterhouse Cambridge (scholar, BA); *Career* asst dir Chichester Festival Theatre 1987-88, artistic dir Chichester Festival Theatre Tent 1988-89, artistic dir Minerva Studio Theatre Chichester 1989 (prodns incl Summerfolk and Love's Labour's Lost), freelance dir; prodns incl: London Assurance (Chichester and Haymarket) 1989, The Cherry Orchard (Aldwych) 1989, Troilus and Cressida (RSC, Swan) 1990, Kean (Old Vic and Toronto) 1990; currently dir: Plough and the Stars (Young Vic) 1991, The Alchemist (RSC, Swan) 1991; winner of Hamburg Shakespeare Scholarship 1989, London Critics Circle Most Promising Newcomer award 1989; *Recreations* cricket, music; *Style—* Sam Mendes, Esq

MENDIS, Gehan Dixon; s of Sam Dixon Charles Mendis (d 1986), of Hove, Sussex, and Sonia Marcelle, *née* Labrooy (d 1983); *b* 24 April 1955; *Educ* Brighton Hove & Sussex GS, Bede Coll Durham; partner, Gilly; 1 s (Josh Dixon b 26 Nov 1989), 1 da (Hayley Johana b 11 Dec 1982); *Career* professional cricketer; Sussex CCC 1975-85: awarded county cap 1980, 206 appearances, over 12,000 runs incl 23 centuries; Lancashire CCC 1986-: awarded county cap 1986, 111 appearances, over 7,000 runs incl 13 centuries; Int XI tours: Pakistan 1981-82, W Indies 1982-83; scored over 1,000 runs in a season 11 times; liaison offr Homeowners Financial Services; *Recreations* following motor racing and rugby league; *Style—* Gehan Mendis, Esq; c/o Lancashire County Cricket Club, Old Trafford, Manchester M16 OPX (☎ 061 848 7021)

MENDLESOHN, Paul Francis; s of Harry B Mendlesohn, of 116 Park Road, Prestwich, Manchester M25 8DU, and Clark, *née* Foxler; *b* 21 June 1953; *Educ* Stand GS, Kings Coll Hosp Dental Sch (BDS, LDS), Maharishi Euro Res Univ Switzerland; *Career* practice: Holborn 1976-84, Devonshire Place 1985-, Camden 1989-; memb: BDA 1976, British Homeopathic Dentist Assoc 1990, British Soc for Clinical Dental Nutrition 1985; *Recreations* squash, tennis, skiing, swimming, travel, teaching transcendental meditation; *Clubs* RAC; *Style—* Paul Mendlesohn, Esq; 16 West Hill Court, Millfield Lane, Highgate London N6 655 (☎ 081 341 4955); 28 Devonshire Place, London W1 (☎ 071 935 2217)

MENDONCA, Dennis Raymond; s of Walter Mendonca, and Adelaide, *née* De Jouza; *b* 9 Oct 1939; *Educ* med coll Bombay (MB BS, MS), Univ of London (retrg); *m* 8 Dec 1966, Dr Lorna Maria Mendonca, da of late Joaquim Noguer; 2 s (Neil Dennis b 25 July 1967, Nolan Andrew b 2 Sept 1971), 1 da (Nicola Maria b 3 Dec 1969); *Career* surgn Eng 1967-; sr house surgn Farnborough Kent, registrar Ashford Folkstone and Dover, sr registrar for ENT Sheffield and Leicester, sr registrar Univ of Toronto (sabbatical year), consit ENT surgn Queen Mary's Univ Hosp London 1975-, private practice Harley St; memb: Med Protection Soc, Br Assoc of Otolaryntology, GMC; FRCS 1970, FCPS (India) 1966; *Recreations* playing the piano, accordion, guitar and tennis; *Style—* Dennis Mendonca, Esq; Hollybrush House, 30 Ferncroft Ave, Hampstead, London NW3 7PH (☎ 071 435 2035); 138 Harley St, London W1N 1AH (☎ 071 486 9416); Queen Mary's University Hospital, Roehampton Lane, London SW15 (☎ 081 789 5124)

MENDOZA, June Yvonne; da of John Morton, and Dot, *née* Mendoza; *Educ* Lauriston Girls Sch Melbourne, St Martins Sch of Art; *m* Keith Mackrell; 1 s (Ashley), 3 da (Elliet, Kim, Lee); *Career* portrait painter; work for governments, regiments, med, academia, theatres, literature and sport; exhibited in public and private int collections; portraits incl: HM The Queen, HRH The Prince of Wales, HRH The Princess of Wales, HM Queen Elizabeth The Queen Mother, The Princess Royal, Margaret Thatcher, Corazon Aquino, the Pres of Iceland, the Pres of Fiji, Sir John Gorton; gp portraits incl: House of Commons in Session, Cncl Royal Coll of Surgns, Australian House of Representatives; continuing series of musicians incl: Yehudi Menuhin, Georg Solti, Joan Sutherland, Paul Tortelier; memb: Royal Soc of Portrait Painters, Royal Inst of Oil Painters; Hon DLitt Univ of Bath 1986; Officer of the Order of Australia 1989; *Style—* Miss June Mendoza; 34 Inner Park Rd, London SW19 6DD

MENEVIA, Bishop of (RC) 1987; Rt Rev Daniel Joseph Mullins; s of Timothy Mullins (d 1968), of Kilfinane, Co Limerick, and Mary, *née* Nunan; *b* 10 July 1929; *Educ* Mount Melleray, St Mary's Aberystwyth, Oscott Coll, Univ Coll of S Wales and Monmouth (BA); *Career* ordained priest 1953; curate: Barry 1953-56, Newbridge 1956, Bargoed 1956-57, Maesteg 1957-60; asst chaplain to Univ Coll Cardiff 1964-68, vicar gen Archdiocese of Cardiff 1968, auxiliary bishop 1970-87; chm Ctee for Catechtics, memb Ct Univ Coll Cardiff, pres Catholic Record Soc; fell Univ Coll Cardiff, hon fell St David's Univ Coll Lampeter; *Recreations* golf, walking; *Style—* The Rt Rev the Bishop of Menevia; 79 Walter Road, Swansea, West Glamorgan SA1 4PS (☎ 0792 650534); Curial Offices, Diocese of Menevia, 115 Walter Road, Swansea, West Glamorgan SA1 5RE (☎ 0792 644017)

MENGERS, Johnny Pierre Nicolas; s of Kurt Victor Mengers (d 1977), and Erzsebet, *née* Schlomm (d 1978); *b* 1 April 1933; *Educ* Harrow, Lausanne Univ; *m* 1, 23 July 1958 (m dis), Margaret; m 2, 20 June 1968 (m dis), Joan; 2 s (Jason b 14 April 1970, Jake b 20 June 1972); m 3, 8 April 1980, Christine, da of Karl Sprung, of Vienna, Austria; 1 da (Tiffany b 2 May 1980); *Career* chm DAKS Simpson Group plc 1953- (joined 1983, mangr Ladies Div Export Exec, mktg dir, asst md, jt md, md, dep chm); *Recreations* boxing, judo, sailing, antiques; *Clubs* Annabels, Marks, Harry's Bar, Royal Thames Yacht, Bath & Racquets; *Style—* Johnny Mengers, Esq; 32 Pembroke Gardens Close, London W8 6HR (☎ 071 602 441); 34 Jermyn Street, London SW1Y 6HS (☎ 071 439 8781, fax 01 437 3633, telex 22466 DAKSIM G)

MENHENNET, Dr David; s of Thomas William Menhennet, of Redruth, Cornwall (d 1970), and Everill Waters, *née* Nettle; old Cornish families, both sides; *b* 4 Dec 1928; *Educ* Truro Sch Cornwall, Oriel Coll Oxford (BA), Queen's Coll Oxford (MA, DPhil); *m* 29 Dec 1954, Audrey, da of William Holmes (d 1958), of Accrington, Lancs; 2 s (Mark b 1956, Andrew b 1958); *Career* librarian House of Commons 1976- (dep librarian 1967-76, joined 1954); gen ed House of Commons Library Documents Series 1972-90; chm Bibliographic Servs Advsy Ctee Br Library 1986-; FRSA 1966; visiting fell Goldsmith's Coll Univ of London 1990-; Liveryman Stationers' Co 1990-; *Books* Parliament in Perspective (with J Palmer, 1967), The Journal of the House of Commons: A Bibliographical and Historical Guide (1971), The House of Commons in the Twentieth Century (contrib, 1979), The House of Commons Library: a History (1991); *Recreations* country walking, gardening, writing, visiting old churches; *Clubs* Athenaeum; *Style—* Dr David Menhennet; Librarian, House of Commons, London SW1A 0AA

MENIN, Rt Rev Malcolm James; *see*: Knaresborough, Bishop of

MENKES-SPANIER, Suzy Peta; da of Edouand Gerald Lionel Menkes (d 1943), and Berry Curtis, *née* Lightfoot; *b* 24 Dec 1943; *Educ* Brighton and Hove HS, Newnham Coll Cambridge (BA, MA); *m* 23 June 1969, David Graham Spanier, s of Eric John Spanier (d 1973); 3 s (Gideon Eric Lionel b 26 Sept 1971, Joshua Edouard Graham b 11 Nov 1973, Samson Curtis b 3 Oct 1978), 1 da (Jessica Leonie Salome b 24 May 1977, d 1977); *Career* jr reporter The Times London 1966-69, fashion ed The Evening Standard 1969-77, women's ed Daily Express 1977-80; fashion ed: The Times 1980-87, The Independent 1987-88, International Herald Tribune 1988-; Freeman of Milan 1987; *Books* The Royal Jewels (1985), The Windsor Style (1987), The Knitwear Revolution (1983); *Recreations* family life, opera, theatre; *Style—* Mrs Suzy Menkes-Spanier; International Herald Tribune, 181 Avenue Charles de Gaulle, 92521 Neuilly, France (☎ 010 33 46 37 93 41, fax 010 33 46 37 93 38)

MENNIM, (Alexander) Michael; s of Percy Mennim (d 1965), of York, and Edith Margaret, *née* Allen (d 1985); *b* 2 Nov 1921; *Educ* Pocklington Sch, Leeds Sch of Architecture, Univ of London (Dip TP); *m* 4 Jan 1952, Eleanor Janet, da of James Simms-Wilson (d 1976), of Strensall, York; 1 s (Peter b 1955), 3 da (Elizabeth b 1953, Anne b 1958, Diana b 1960); *Career* Capt Indian Mountain Artillery 1946, served Burma; architect; sr ptnr private practice Ferrey and Mennim, princ works incl: Wolfson Coll Cambridge 1977, conservation of St Magnus Cathedral Kirkwall Orkneys 1984; lectr on conservation of historic buildings Inst of Advanced Architectural Studies Univ of York; conslt conservation architect; ARIBA 1952; hon fell Wolfson Coll Univ of Cambridge; *Recreations* travel associated with the conservation of historic buildings; *Clubs* Yorkshire; *Style—* Michael Mennim, Esq; Croft Cottage, Sutton on the Forest, York Y06 1DP (☎ 0347 810 345)

MENPES, Hon Mrs (Marjorie); 2 da of Baron Cooper of Stockton Heath (Life Peer; d 1988); *b* 1941; *m* 1, 1959 (m dis 1969), Neville Finch; 1 s (Paul Alexander b 1959), 2 da (Kerrie Anika b 1962, Heidi Erica b 1964); m 2, 1974 (m dis 1979), Robert Dennis Menpes; 1 s (Jamie Daniel b 1975); *Career* natural health therapist (kinesiology, aromatherapy, reflexology); work at Thames Television; *Style—* The Hon Mrs Menpes; York Lodge, 56 York Rd, Weybridge, Surrey KT13 9DX

MENSFORTH, Sir Eric; CBE (1945), DL (South Yorks 1971); s of Sir Holberry Mensforth, KCB, CBE (d 1951); *b* 17 May 1906; *Educ* Altrincham HS, Univ Coll Sch, King's Coll Cambridge (MA); *m* 1934, Betty Mensforth, JP, da of late Rev Picton W Francis; 3 da (Elizabeth, Rosemary, Susan); *Career* dir, chm and pres Westland Aircraft Ltd; dir: John Brown and Co Ltd, Boddy Industries Ltd; chm Governing Body Sheffield Poly 1969-75, gen treas Br Assoc for Sci 1971-76; Vice Lord Lt S Yorks 1974-81; Master Worshipful Co of Cutlers in Hallamshire 1965-66; FEng; kt 1962; *Clubs* Alpine, RAC; *Style—* Sir Eric Mensforth, CBE, DL; 42 Oakmead Green, Woodcote Side, Epsom, Surrey KT18 7JS (☎ 03727 42313)

MENSLEY, Michael James; s of John Keith Sayers Mensley, and Lilian May, *née* Pawley; *b* 17 Nov 1951; *Educ* Coalville GS; *m* 9 Dec 1972, Pauline Ann, da of Thomas Turner (d 1953); 2 s (Paul b 1982, Thomas b 1985); *Career* co-fndr and now jt md The Mensley Gp, dir The Leicester and Dist Knitting Indust Assoc Ltd; *Recreations* motor sport; *Style—* Michael Mensley, Esq; 10 Chatsworth Drive, Syston, Leicester (☎ 0533 694037); The Mensley Group, Melton Rd, Syston, Leicester (☎ 0533 605705, telex 341668, fax 0533 607308)

MENTER, Sir James Woodham; s of late Horace Menter, and late Jane Anne, *née* Lackenby; *b* 22 Aug 1921; *Educ* Dover GS, Peterhouse Cambridge (MA, PhD, ScD); *m* 1947, Marjorie Jean, da of late Thomas Stodart Whyte-Smith, WS; 2 s, 1 da; *Career* tres and vice pres Royal Soc 1972-76, princ Queen Mary Coll London Univ 1976-86; dir: Tube Investmts Res Laboratories 1961-68, Tube Investmts 1965-86, Br Petroleum Co 1976-87, Steetley Co 1981-85; FRS; kt 1973; *Style—* Sir James Menter, FRS; Carie, Kinloch Rannoch, by Pitlochry, Perthshire

MENTETH; *see*: Stuart-Menteth

MENTZ, Donald; s of Stanley Mentz (d 1986), of Aust, and Marie Agnes, *née* Bryant (d 1985); *b* 20 Oct 1933; *Educ* Hampton HS Victoria Aust, Dookie Agric Coll (DDA), Univ of Melbourne (BAgSci), Aust Nat Univ (BEcon); *m* 30 May 1959, Mary Josephine, da of Henry Joseph Goldsworthy; 1 s (Peter b 3 April 1969), 2 da (Fiona b 1 Oct 1965, Megan b 19 Aug 1967); *Career* Dept of External Territories Aust 1969-73, Aust devpt asst Bureau of Foreign Affrs 1973-77, dir of ops Asian Development Bank Philippines 1979-81, dep sec Dept of Business and Consumer Affrs Aust 1981-82, dep sec Dept of Territories and Local Govt Aust 1983-84, DG CAB Int UK 1985-; memb: Aust Inst of Agric Sci 1956, Aust Agric Econs Soc 1960; *Clubs* Cwlth (Canberra, Aust), Athenaeum; *Style—* Donald Mentz, Esq; Flat 1, 25 Longridge Road, Earls Court, London SW5 9SB (☎ 071 835 1208); CAB International, Wallingford, Oxon OX10 8DE (☎ 0491 32111, fax 0491 33508, telex 8476964 COMAGG G)

MENUHIN, Hon Mrs (Brigid Gabriel); *née* Forbes-Sempill; da of late Lord Sempill (19 in line) by 2 w, Cecilia, *qv*; half-sis of Lady Sempill, *qv*; *b* 1945; *m* 1983, Jeremy Menuhin, yr s (by 2 m) of Sir Yehudi Menuhin, *qv*; *Style—* The Hon Mrs Menuhin

MENUHIN, Sir Yehudi; OM (1987), KBE (1965); s of Moshe Menuhin; *b* 22 April 1916,NY; *Educ* privately; *m* 1, 1938, Nola Ruby Nicholas, of Australia; 1 s (Krov), 1 da (Zamira Benthall); m 2, 1947, Diana Rosamond Gould; 2 s (Gerard, Jeremy, m Hon Brigid Gabriel, *qv*); *Career* violinist and conductor; début with San Francisco Orch aged 7; gave over 500 concerts during WWII; artistic dir Bath Festival for 10 years and fndr Bath Festival Orch; fndr: Yehudi Menuhin Sch Surrey 1963, Int Menuhin Music Acad Gstaad (venue of summer Festival since 1956), Live Music Now (a charitable orgn); fndr and conductor Asian Youth Orch, princ guest conductor English String Orch; pres: Euro String Teachers' Assoc, Young Musicians' Symphony Orch, Musicians' Int Mutual Aid Fund; former pres (served full term of six years) Int Music Cncl of UNESCO, pres and assoc conductor RPO; sr fell RCA, hon fell and pres Trinity Coll of Music; hon doctorates incl: Oxford (1962), St Andrews (1963), Queen's Belfast (1965), London (1969), Cambridge (1970), Ottawa (1975), Sorbonne (1976); Epée D'Academicien (Academie de Beaux Arts 1988); awards and honours for WWII, humanitarianism and music incl: Croix de Lorraine (Fr), Ordre de la Couronne and Ordre de Léopold (Belgium), Order of Merit (FDR), Nehru Peace Prize (for raising famine funds) India 1968, Buber-Rosenzweig Medaille (Gesellschaften für Christlich-Jüdische Zusammen-Arbeit) Bonn 1990; medals of Cities of Paris New York and Jerusalem, Cobbett medal Worshipful Co of Musicians, Gold and Mozart medals Royal Philharmonic Soc 1962 and 1965, Gold medal Canadian Music Cncl 1975, Albert medal RSA 1981, Una Vita Nella Musica Italy 1983, Brahms medal Hamburg 1987, Brahms Orden Hamburg 1988, Gold medal Univ of Cordoba 1990, Glenn Gould prize Canada 1990; Yehudi Menuhin and Luciano Berio Wolf prize 1991; *Publications* incl: Menuhin Music Guides, Unfinished Journey (autobiography, awarded Peace Prize of German Book Fedn), Music of Man (also CBC TV series), Conversations with Menuhin (with Robin Daniels), The King, the Cat and the Fiddle (for children, with Christopher Hope), Life Class; *Clubs* Athenaeum, Garrick; *Style—* Sir Yehudi Menuhin, OM, KBE;

c/o Anglo Swiss Artists' Management Ltd, 4 Primrose Mews, Sharpleshall Street, London NW1 (☎ 071 586 7711, telex 298787 Yehudi)

MENZIES, (Iain) Alasdair Graham; s of Maj Ian Menzies (1979), of London, and Alice, *née* Stoettinger; *b* 7 Jan 1952; *Educ* Eton, Sorbonne Univ; *m* 1974, Sandra Francoise, da of Cyril Bertram Mills; 3 s (Alexander Graham, Andrew Ian Graham, Johnathan Harwood Graham); *Career* md Merrill Lynch 1984-88 (sales exec 1971-80, dir 1980-84), dir Schroder Securities 1988-; *Recreations* skiing, classic cars; *Clubs* Whites, Annabels; *Style—* Alasdair Menzies, Esq; Schroder Securities Ltd, 120 Cheapside, London EC2V 6DS (☎ 071 382 3205, fax 071 382 3019, car 0836 610397)

MENZIES, Ian Caithness; s of Sir Peter Thomson Menzies *qv*; *b* 11 Feb 1940; *Educ* Uppingham, Univ of Edinburgh (MA), Inst of Chartered Accountants of Scotland; *m* 24 Sept 1966, Elizabeth Ann, da of James Murray, of 19 Thomson Rd, Currie, Edinburgh; 2 s (Rory b 1969, Alexander b 1970), 1 da (Dinah b 1967); *Career* dir: J Henry Schroder Wagg and Co Ltd 1974-85, Head Wrightson Ltd 1974-77, Davy Corporation 1977-80, LCP (Holdings) plc 1980-87, McKay Securities plc 1989-; dir and gen mangr General Accident Fire and Life Assurance Corporation plc 1985-; memb Ind Policy Ctee CBI 1980-85; *Recreations* bridge, tennis, squash, gardening; *Clubs* Caledonian; *Style—* Ian Menzies, Esq; Pitheavlis, Perth, Scotland (☎ 0738 21202, telex 76237, fax 0738 21614 or 071 606 1030)

MENZIES, Ian William; s of Adam Menzies (d 1946), of Muirhead, Glasgow, and Margaret McDermid Stewart, *née* Colvin (d 1961); *b* 30 Dec 1927; *Educ* Coatbridge Sch Strathclyde, Royal Tech Coll Glasgow (BSc), Univ of London (LLB); *m* 1, 3 May 1952, June Alice (d 1978), da of Joseph Mullard (d 1951), of Liverpool; 3 da (Margaret b 1952, Sheena b 1955, Alison b 1957); m 2, 8 Oct 1983, Dr Monica Patricia Hunter, da of Thomas Burrows, of Swansea; 3 step da (Nicola b 1963, Francesca b 1965, Lizette b 1972); *Career* Nat Serv 2 Lt RAEC 1947-49, 2 Lt RE RARO 1949-82; res engr Kuwait 1954-56, ptnr Menzies & Durkin Zambia 1956-59, res engr Ghana 1960-62, ptnr Charles Weiss & Ptnrs 1975-87, dir Charles Weiss Partnership Ltd 1987-; memb: Cncl CIArb (vice pres), Tonbridge Civic Soc; govr W Kent Coll; Freeman City of London, Liveryman Worshipful Co of Arbitrators; FICE, MIStructE, FCIArb, FRSA; *Recreations* armory, genealogy, cosmology; *Style—* Ian Menzies, Esq; Charles Weiss Partnership Ltd, 139/151 Sydenham Rd, London SE26 5HJ (☎ 081 659 9040, fax 081 659 5595, telex 8951165 CTBXXXG)

MENZIES, Dr John Barrie; s of late Henry John Menzies of Sibsey, Boston, Lincs, and Eva Ellen Menzies; *b* 7 Nov 1937; *Educ* Univ of Birmingham (BSc, PhD), City Univ (Dip CU); *m* 2 Sept 1961, Ann, da of late Frank Naylor; 2 s (Ian Anthony b 17 Nov 1963, Robert John b 4 Aug 1965), 1 da (Theresa Margaret b 4 Oct 1962); *Career* dir Geotechnics and Structures Gp Building Res Estab DOE 1982-1990 (joined 1962), ptnr Andrews Kent & Stone Consltg Engrs 1990-; hon prof of engrg Univ of Warwick 1988-; vice chm Construction and Building Standards Ctee BSI 1990-; chm: EC Task GP on Actions 1985-90, Eurocode for Actions Sub Ctee Euro Ctee for Standardisation 1990-; memb Standing Ctee on Structural Safety 1988-, pres Br Masonry Soc 1989, vice chm Br Gp Int Assoc for Bridge and Structural Engrg; IStructE: hon treas 1988-89, hon sec 1989-90; FIStructE 1977, FEng 1989; *Recreations* travel, good food and wine, swimming, walking; *Style—* Dr John Menzies; 42 Sheepcot Lane, Garston, Watford, Hertfordshire WD2 6DT (☎ 0923 675106); Andrews, Kent & Stone, Consulting Engineers, 1 Argyll St, London W1V 2DH (☎ 071 437 6136, fax 071 437 1035)

MENZIES, John Maxwell; s of John Francis Menzies (d 1940), and Cynthia Mary, *née* Graham (d 1988); *b* 13 Oct 1926; *Educ* Eton; *m* 4 June 1953, Patricia Elinor Trevor, yst da of Cdr Sir Hugh Trevor Dawson, 2 Bt, CBE (d 1976); 4 da (Miranda Jane (Mrs Jenkinson) b 1954, Sarah Jane (Mrs Rawlence) b 1955, Cynthia Emma (Mrs Harrison) b 1958, Katherine Patricia b 1960); *Career* Lt Grenadier Gds 1945-48; chm John Menzies plc 1952-; dir: Scottish American Mortgage Co 1959-63, Standard Life Assurance Co 1960-63, Vidal Sassoon Inc 1969-80, Nimslo International Ltd 1970-85, Gordon & Gotch plc 1970-85, Ivory & Sime plc 1980-83; chm: Independent Investment Co plc 1983- (dir 1973-), Atlantic Assets Trust 1983-88 (dir 1973-78), Rocky Mountains Oil & Gas Ltd 1980-85, Personal Assets Trust plc 1981-, Bank of Scotland plc 1984-, Guardian Royal Exchange plc 1984, Guardian Royal Exchange Assurance 1985-, Malcolm Innes & Partners Ltd 1989-; tstee Newsvendors Benevolent Instn (pres 1968-74); memb: Berwickshire CC 1954-57, Royal Co of Archers (Queen's Body Guard for Scotland); landowner (1950 acres); *Recreations* farming, shooting, reading, travel; *Clubs* Turf, Boodle's, New (Edinburgh); *Style—* John Menzies, Esq; Kames, Duns, Berwickshire (☎ 089 084 202); John Menzies plc, 108 Princes St, Edinburgh EH2 3AA (☎ 031 225 8555, fax 031 226 3752)

MENZIES, Sir Peter Thomson; s of John Caithness Menzies (d 1918), and Helen, *née* Aikman; *b* 15 April 1912; *Educ* Musselburgh GS, Univ of Edinburgh (MA); *m* 1938, Mary McPherson Alexander, da of late John Turner Menzies, and Agnes, *née* Anderson; 1 s, 1 da; *Career* dep chm ICI 1967-72 (joined 1939, dir 1956-72); chm Imperial Metal Industs 1964-72 (joined 1962); dir: Commercial Union Assurance Co 1962-1982, Nat West Bank 1968-82; chm: Electricity Cncl 1972-77, London Exec Ctee Scottish Cncl (devpt and indust) 1977-82; gen treas and vice pres Br Assoc for the Advancement of Sci 1981-86; kt 1972; *Clubs* Caledonian; *Style—* Sir Peter Menzies; Kit's Corner, Harmer Green, Welwyn, Herts (☎ 043 871 4386)

MENZIES, (Rowan) Robin; s of Capt George Cunningham Paton Menzies, DSO (d 1968), and Constance Rosabel, *née* Grice Hutchinson; *b* 30 Oct 1952; *Educ* Stowe, Trinity Coll Cambridge (BA); *Career* ptnr Baillie Gifford and Co (investmt mangrs), dir Baillie Gifford Technol plc; *Style—* Robin Menzies, Esq; 3 Glenfinlas St, Edinburgh EH3 6YY (☎ 031 225 2581, fax 031 225 2358, telex 72310 BGCO)

MENZIES-WILSON, Hon Mrs (Christian Victoria Gordon); da (by 1 m) of 2 Baron Catto; *b* 1955; *m* 1983, Charles Menzies-Wilson, er s of W N Menzies-Wilson, of Holland Park, London; 1 s (Richard Napier b 1988), 1 da (Cathryn Lucy b 1986); *Style—* The Hon Mrs Menzies-Wilson; Newport House, Newport Lane, Braishfield, nr Romsey, Hants SO51 OPL

MENZIES-WILSON, William Napier; CBE (1985); s of James Robert Menzies-Wilson (d 1977), of Fotheringhay Lodge, Nassington, nr Peterborough, and Jacobine Joanna Napier, *née* Williamson-Napier (d 1955); *b* 4 Dec 1926; *Educ* Winchester, New Coll Oxford (MA), Northwestern Univ Chicago; *m* 25 July 1953, Mary Elizabeth Darnell, da of Ralph Juckes, MC (d 1982), of Fiddington Manor, nr Tewkesbury, Glos; 2 s (Charles Napier b 1957, James Ralph b 1959), 1 da (Gillian Elizabeth b 1960); *Career* Lt Rifle Bde 1945-47; dir Stewarts & Lloyds Ltd 1964 (joined 1950), dir supplies & tport British Steel Corporation 1968-72; chm: Ocean Transport and Trading plc 1980-87 (dir 1972-80), Edinburgh Tankers plc; dir National Freight Consortium; chm Help The Aged; *Recreations* gardening, shooting, golf; *Clubs* Brooks's, Hon Co of Edinburgh Golfers; *Style—* William Menzies-Wilson, Esq, CBE; Last House, Old, nr Northampton NN6 9RJ (☎ 0604 781 346)

MERCER, Prof Alan; s of Harold Mercer (d 1954), of Stocksbridge, and Alice Ellen, *née* Catterall; *b* 22 Aug 1931; *Educ* Penistone GS, Univ of Cambridge (MA, Dip Math Stat), Univ of London (PhD); *m* 7 Aug 1954, Lillian Iris, da of Charles Frederick Pigott (d 1988), of Penistone; 2 s (Jonathan Andrew Timothy b 1959, Nicholas Anthony Julian b 1961); *Career* NCB 1954-56, UKAEA 1956-62, Armour and Co Ltd 1962-64, Univ of Lancaster 1964-; memb: Central Lancs Devpt Corp 1971-85, NW Econ Planning Cncl 1973-79, Mgmnt and Industl Rels Ctee Social Scis Res Cncl 1980-82; chm: employers side of Whitley Cncl for New Towns Staff 1979-89 (memb 1971-), Indust and Employment Ctee ESRC 1984-87 (vice chm 1982-84), Warrington and Runcorn Devpt Corp 1986-89 (memb 1985-); memb Operation Res Soc 1955; *Books* Operational Distribution Research (jtly, 1978), Implementable Marketing Reseach (1991), European Journal of Operational Research (jt ed); *Recreations* travel, bridge, sport; *Style—* Prof Alan Mercer; 11 The Buoymasters, St George's Quay, Lancaster LA1 1HL (☎ 0524 37244); The Management School, Lancaster University, Bailrigg, Lancaster LA1 4YX (☎ 0524 65201, fax 0524 844885, telex 65111 LANCUL G)

MERCER, Dr David; s of Harold Mercer (d 1983), and Jessie, *née* Emerson (d 1984); *b* 20 April 1930; *Educ* St Albans Sch Herts, Univ of Sheffield; *m* 3 June 1961, Jenifer Anne, da of Stanley James Thompson (d 1984); 1 s (James b 1964), 2 da (Kate b 1962, Nicky b 1968); *Career* Nat Serv RAF 1948-51; conslt physician Plymouth Health Authy 1967-88 (ret); developed modern serv for the elderly in Plymouth Health Dist Hosps; memb: NHS ctees (regnl and local), Age Concern (local and nat), Help Age Int, BMA (former chm Plymouth), Br Geriatrics Soc; *Recreations* sailing (cruising and racing), conservation, gardening, furniture restoration, photography; *Clubs* Royal Western Yacht; *Style—* Dr David Mercer; Cedar Lodge, 95 Fore Street, Plymouth St Maurice, Plymouth PL7 3NB (☎ 0752 337123); Freedom Fields Hospital, Greenbank, Plymouth, Devon

MERCER, Rt Rev Eric Arthur John; s of Ambrose John Mercer (d 1975), of Deal, Kent; *b* 6 Dec 1917; *Educ* Dover GS, Kelham Theol Coll; *m* 1951, Rosemary Wilma, da of John William Denby (d 1963), of Barrow on Humber; 1 s, 1 da; *Career* served WWII, W Desert, Capt and Adj 14 Foresters 1943, Italian campaign 1944 (despatches), dep asst Adj and QMG 66 Inf Bde Palestine 1945, GSO HQ MEF 1945; ordained 1947; rector: St Thomas Stockport 1953-59, St Bridget with St Martin Chester 1959-65; Chester diocesan missioner 1959-65, bishop suffragan of Birkenhead (Dioc of Chester) 1965-73, bishop of Exeter 1973-85; chm C of E Men's Soc 1973-78, dep chm Church Cmmrs' Pastoral Ctee 1976-85, memb bd of govrs Church Cmmrs 1980-85; *Recreations* fly fishing; *Clubs* Army and Navy; *Style—* The Rt Rev Eric Mercer; Frickers House, Chilmark, Salisbury SP3 5AJ

MERCER, Dr (Robert) Giles Graham; s of Leonard Mercer (d 1961), of Langholm, Dumfriesshire, and Florence Elizabeth, *née* Graham; *b* 30 May 1949; *Educ* Austin Friars Sch Carlisle, Churchill Coll Cambridge (MA), St John's Coll Oxford (DPhil); *m* 2 March 1974, Caroline Mary, da of Alfred Harold Brougham (d 1983), of Tackley, Oxfordshire; 1 s (Edward b 1977); *Career* head of history Charterhouse Sch 1974-76, asst princ MOD 1976-78, dir of studies and head of history Sherborne Sch 1979-85, headmaster Stonyhurst Coll 1985-; FRSA 1983; *Books* The Teaching of Gasparino Barzizza (1979); *Recreations* badminton, swimming, art, music, reading; *Clubs* Athenaeum, Public Sch, E India; *Style—* Dr Giles Mercer; St Philip's, Stonyhurst, Lancs BB6 9PT (☎ 025 486 220); Stonyhurst Coll, Stonyhurst, Lancs BB6 9PZ (☎ 025 486 345, fax 025 486 732, telex 635587 STONY G)

MERCER, Ian Dews; s of Eric Baden Royds Mercer (d 1955), of Herongate, Wormbourn, Staffs, and Nellie Irene, *née* Dews; *b* 25 Jan 1933; *Educ* King Edward's Sch Stourbridge, Univ of Birmingham (BA); *m* m 1, 7 July 1957 (m dis 1976), Valerie Jean, da of late Eric Hodgson; 4 s (Jonathan b 1958, Benjamin 1961, Thomas b 1963, Daniel b 1966); m 2, 10 Dec 1976, Pamela Margaret Gillies, da of Maj Thomas Waldy Clarkson; *Career* Nat Serv Sub-Lt RNR 1954-56; warden Slapton Ley Field Centre Kingsbridge Devon 1959-68, lectr St Luke's Coll Exeter 1968-70, co conservation offr Devon CC 1970-73, chief offr Dartmoor Nat Park Authy 1973-90, chief exec Countryside Cncl for Wales 1990-; pres: Field Studies Cncl, Assoc Countryside Rangers, Devonshire Assoc 1983, Devon Wildlife Tst; chm Regnl Advsy Ctee W England Forestry Cmmn 1987-90; memb: England Ctee Nature Conservancy Cncl 1977-87, Gen Advsy Ctee BBC 1981-86, Br Ecological Soc, Assoc Nat Park Offrs; *Books* Nature Guide to South West England, Conservation in Practice (contrib, 1973), Environmental Education (contrib, 1974), National Parks in Britain (contrib, 1987); *Recreations* golf, painting, birdwatching, watching sons play rugby; *Style—* Ian Mercer, Esq; Victoria House, Llanddaniel Y Fab, Anglesey LLGO 6EB; Chief Executive, Countryside Cncl for Wales, Plas Penrhos, Fford Penrhos, Bangor, Gwynedd LL57 2LQ

MERCER, John Charles Kenneth; s of Charles Wilfrid Mercer (d 1975), of Glanyrafan Rd, Tycoch, Swansea, and Cecil Maud, *née* Lowther (d 1949); *b* 17 Sept 1917; *Educ* Ellesmere Coll, Univ of London (LLB); *m* 19 Aug 1944, Barbara Joan, da of Arnold Sydney Whitehead, CB, CBE (d 1966); 1 s (David), 1 da (Susan (Mrs Jones)); *Career* WWII Capt RA; admitted slr 1946; rec 1975-82; memb: Royal Cmmn on Criminal Procedure 1978-81, SW Wales River Authy 1959-84; memb Law Soc; *Recreations* fishing, shooting, golf; *Clubs* Clyne Golf, City & County, Swansea Amateur Anglers; *Style—* John Mercer, Esq; 334 Gower Rd, Killay, Swansea (☎ 0792 202 931); 147 St Helens Rd, Swansea (☎ 0792 650 000, fax 0792 458 212)

MERCER, (Andrew) Philip; s of Maj Laurence Walter Mercer (d 1951), of Huntingtower, Perthshire, and Josephine Madeline, *née* Moran; *b* 24 Aug 1937; *Educ* Stonyhurst, Univ of Edinburgh (BArch); *m* 2 Oct 1965, Alexandra Margaret, da of Capt John Cyril Dawson, of Sussex; 2 da (Claudia Alexandra b 1977, Portia Andrea (twin) b 1977); *Career* CA; princ of architectural practice 1969- (specialising in planning matters in Central London and historic bldgs in Scot); MRIBA; *Recreations* skiing, yachting, tennis, travelling; *Style—* Philip Mercer, Esq; Hillslap Tower, Roxburghshire; 49 Hereford Rd, London W2 5BB (☎ 071 229 6621)

MERCER, Terence; s of Sydney Agnew Mercer (d 1971), of N Yorks, and Molly, *née* Lewis (d 1971); *b* 4 Sept 1931; *Educ* Ermysteds GS Skipton Yorks, Leeds Coll of Commerce; *m* 21 Nov 1959, Frances Karene, da of Col Francis Henry Jordan, DSO, MC (d 1975); 2 s (Nicholas Justin b 1962, Simon Jonathan Jordan de Suakville b 1965); *Career* cmmnd Army, served MELF 1954-56, AER 1956-59; chm Tattersall Advertising Ltd Harrogate 1971; memb Cncl: Ripon Cathedral Tst Appeal, Ripon Diocesan Synod 1970-73, Nat Tst Fountains Abbey Appeal 1984-85; hon publicity advsr: Save the Children Fund, Yorks North Cons Euro Constituency Cncl 1981-83, IAM, ROSPA, Noise Abatement Soc; hon life memb Friends of Harrogate and District Museums 1989; fndr benefactor of The Mercer Gallery Harrogate; FZS, FRSA, MIPA, FInstD; *Recreations* field sports, charity work, sketching, politics; *Style—* Terence Mercer, Esq; Low Bridge House, Markington, Harrogate, North Yorkshire HG3 3PQ (☎ 0765 87393); Tattersall Advertising Ltd, Harrogate, North Yorkshire HG1 5LL (☎ 0423 504676, fax 0423 508092)

MERCER, Dr William Leslie (Les); s of Edward Mercer, of Horwich, Lancs, and Louisa, *née* Meadows; *b* 7 Oct 1932; *Educ* Wigan GS, Univ of Leeds (BSc, PhD); *m* 14 Aug 1954, Barbara Ann, da of Reginald Platt; 2 s (Andrew David b 10 Aug 1955, Geoffrey Ian b 20 June 1959); *Career* res engr GEC/CR Atomic Energy Gp (later UPC, then APC); various posts Gas Cncl (later British Gas plc) 1965-: station dir Engrg Res Station 1978-88 (res mangr then asst dir 1965-78), HQ dir Gas Res 1988-; memb Bd British Pipe Coaters Ltd 1979-; chm Tyne-Wear Metallurgical Soc 1972-74; conslt UKAEA-MAC/IVC 1983-89; visiting prof Dept of Metals and Materials Univ of Newcastle upon Tyne 1985-88; memb: SERC Materials Ctee 1980-83, Cncl SIRA Ltd

1982-, Cncl/Bureau Int Gas Union 1982-88, Cncl Hydraulics Research Ltd 1983-, Cncl Welding Inst 1984-87, Cncl ERA 1985-88, Res Ctee Univ of Newcastle upon Tyne 1987-88, Engrg Cncl Ctee on Professional Instns 1987-, Royal Soc/Fellowship of Engrg Policy Studies Unit 1987-; pres Inst of Gas Engrs 1990- (memb Cncl 1981-88); FIM 1972, FIGasE 1979, FRSA 1984, FEng 1985; *Recreations* the open air, travel, gardening, photography, bridge; *Style—* Dr Les Mercer; British Gas plc, Midlands Research Station, Wharf Lane, Solihull, West Midlands B91 2JW (☎ 021 705 7581, fax 021 711 3470)

MERCER NAIRNE, Lord Robert Harold; s of 8 Marquess of Lansdowne, PC; *b* 1947; *Educ* Gordonstoun, Univ of Kent at Canterbury, Univ of Washington Graduate Sch of Business Admin; *m* 1972, Jane Elizabeth, da of Lt-Col Lord Douglas Gordon; 2 s, 1 da; *Style—* Lord Robert Mercer Nairne; The Old Manse, Kinclave, by Stanley, Perthshire; 10105 SE, 25th Bellevue, Washington 98004, USA

MERCHANT, Piers Rolf Garfield; s of Garfield Frederick Merchant, of Nottingham, by his w Audrey Mary Rolfe-Martin; descended from feudal Barons of Kendal via the Lancaster line; *b* 2 Jan 1951; *Educ* Nottingham HS, Univ of Durham (MA); *m* 1977, Helen Joan, da of James Frederick Albert Burrluck, of Colchester; *Career* MP (C) Newcastle Central 1983-87, prospective Parly candidate (C) Beckenham 1990-; dir of corp publicity Northern Engineering Industries plc1987-90, dir pub affrs The Advertising Assoc 1990-; freelance writer and journalist; *Recreations* DIY, electronics, genealogy; *Clubs* Sr Common Room of Univ Coll Durham; *Style—* Piers Merchant, Esq; 91 St Georges Drive, London SW1 (☎ 071 630 9294)

MERCIER, Sheila Betty; da of Herbert Dobson Rix (d 1966), and Fanny Nicholson; *b* 1 Jan 1919; *Educ* French Convent Hull, Hunmanby Hall E Yorks, Randle Ayrton Coll of Drama Stratford on Avon; *m* 26 March 1951, Peter Edward Alexander Mercier, s of Capt Charles Jerome Andrew Nicholas Mercier, of 247 Plashet Grove, East Ham, London; 1 s (Nigel David b 6 Dec 1954); *Career* WWII LACW WAAF Signals 1941-44, section offr, asst adj and adj 1944-46; post-war toured all over the country with the Repertory Theatre as leading lady, next eleven years spent at the Whitehall Theatre with brother Sir Brian Rix, has spent the last eighteen years playing Annie Sugden in the Yorkshire TV soap opera Emmerdale Farm; memb Cons Assoc; *Style—* Mrs Sheila Mercier; Lyndhurst, 36 Coastal Rd, E Preston, Littlehampton, W Sussex BN16 1SJ (☎ 0903 786032); 56 Denton Ave, Leeds, W Yorkshire LS8 1LE (☎ 0532 666368)

MEREDITH, David John; s of John Meredith (d 1980), of Stansted, and Edith Elizabeth Brown; *b* 30 Nov 1936; *Educ* Bishops Stortford Coll; *m* 10 June 1961, Deirdre Elizabeth, da of Ernest Richard Allen (d 1978), of Garstang; 2 s (Alun John b 1963, Simon David b 1966), 1 da (Bronwen Ann b 1962); *Career* md Crosville Motor Services Ltd 1976-90; *Style—* David Meredith, Esq; Flint Close, Neston, South Wirral, Cheshire (☎ 051 336 2080)

MEREDITH, David Wynn; s of John Ellis Meredith (d 1981), of Aberystwyth, Dyfed, and Elizabeth, *née* Jones; *b* 24 May 1941; *Educ* Ardwyn GS Aberystwyth, Normal Coll Bangor Gwynedd (Univ of Wales Teaching Dip); *m* 23 March 1968, Luned, da of Prof Alun Llywelyn Williams; 3 c (Owain Llywelyn b 11 Feb 1969, Elin Wynn b 6 Jan 1971, Gruffydd Seimon Morgan b 7 Feb 1974); *Career* specialist teacher Welsh Cardiff Educn Authy 1961-65, mid-Wales mangr then advtg and sales exec Wales Tourist Bd 1965-68, head press and PR HTV Cymru/Wales 1968-89, fndr and dir STRATA (PR co) Aberystwyth Dyfed and Cardiff 1989-90, formed own PR co David Meredith PR Cardiff S Wales 1990-; reg contrib to radio and TV in Wales; presenter in Eng and Welsh HTV: Pwy Fase'n Meddwl (quiz series), Gair o Wald y Sais (lit prog), Arlunwyr (art series); fell PR Soc of Wales 1984- (1981-83); memb: Royal Welsh Show Publicity Ctee 1969-, Welsh Ctee ABSA (Business Sponsorship of the Arts) 1988-, Welsh Ctee Live Music Now 1990-; Nat Eisteddfod of Wales Mktg Bd 1990-; *Books* Michelangelo (Life and Work), Rembrandt (Life and Work), (for children) Congrinevo; *Recreations* pottering on the farm; *Style—* David Meredith, Esq; 6 Farleigh Road, Pontcanna, Cardiff, South Glamorgan (☎ 0222 225 947); David Meredith PR (S Wales Office), Penhill House, Penhill, Pontcanna, Cardiff CF1 9PQ (☎ 0222 388332, fax 0222 228452); David Meredith PR (N Wales Office), 8 Victoria Terrace, Bethesda, Gwynedd LL57 3AG (☎ 0248 600578, fax 0248 600587)

MEREDITH, Frederick William Louis; s of William Campbell James Meredith, QC (d 1960), and Marie Berthe Louise Francoise Mills, *née* de Lotbinière Harwood; *b* 24 Nov 1936; *Educ* Bishops Coll Sch Lennoxville Canada, Trinity Coll Cambridge (BA); *m* 11 Sept 1971, Anna Kathleen, da of Sqdn Ldr Ian Grahame Stewart, DFC, AFC (d 1945); 1 s (Mark William Stewart b 1976), 1 da (Samantha Louise Katherine b 1974); *Career* gen mangr Bertram Mills Circus Ltd 1963-65, jt md Fours Ltd 1965-69, dir gen Occupations Study Gp 1983-87, dir Singer GMBH Germany 1985-87, mangr business devpt prog IBM 1989 (joined 1967); pres Br Ice Hockey Assoc 1982; memb: Nat Olympic Ctee, Int Ice Hockey Fedn; *Recreations* tennis, theatre; *Clubs* Phyllis Court; *Style—* Frederick Meredith, Esq; IBM UK Ltd, 389 Chiswick High Rd, London W4 4AL (☎ 081 995 1441, fax 081 995 6855, telex 23295 IBM CHI)

MEREDITH, George Hubbard; s of George Thomas Meredith (d 1959), of Birmingham, and Ivy Lilian, *née* Hubbard (d 1972); *b* 16 Jan 1943; *Educ* Marlborough; *m* 9 April 1983, Wendy, da of Frank David Gardiner, of Exeter, Devon; 1 s (John b 1991), 2 da (Claire b 1984, Jane b 1986); *Career* called to the Bar Gray's Inn 1969; in practice: London 1970-72, Exeter 1972- (head of Chambers 1975-90); hon sec and librarian Exeter Law Library Soc, chm tstees Belmont Chapel; *Recreations* family life, reading, photography, hill walking; *Clubs* Devon and Exeter Inst; *Style—* George Meredith, Esq; 25 Southernhay East, Exeter, Devon (☎ 0392 55777, fax 0392 412021, DX 8353)

MEREDITH, Richard Alban Creed; s of Rev Canon Ralph Creed Meredith (d 1970), Vicar of Windsor, and Sylvia, *née* Aynsley (d 1987); *b* 1 Feb 1935; *Educ* Stowe, Jesus Coll Cambridge; *m* 1968, Hazel Eveline Mercia Parry; 1 s, 1 da; *Career* house master King's Sch Canterbury 1962-70 (asst master 1957-70); headmaster: Giggleswick Sch 1970-78, Monkton Combe Sch 1978-90; area rep Church Missionary Soc 1990-; *Recreations* music, gardening, walking; *Style—* Richard Meredith, Esq; Beacon Knoll, 334 Beacon Rd, Loughborough LE11 2RD (☎ 0509 212008)

MEREDITH HARDY, Simon Patrick; s of Patrick Talbot Meredith Hardy (d 1986), of Bembridge, IOW, and Anne, *née* Johnson; *b* 31 Oct 1943; *Educ* Eton; *m* 26 July 1969, Hon Joanna Mary Meredith Hardy, da of Rt Hon Lord Porritt, GCMG, GCVO, CBE; 2 s (Henry b 1975, George b 1978); *Career* cmmnd LG 1964, ADC to HE The Govr Gen of NZ 1967-68, left army 1969; stockbroker; dir County Natwest Ltd; memb Int Stock Exchange; *Clubs* City of London, Household Division Yacht; *Style—* Simon P Meredith Hardy, Esq; County Natwest, 135 Bishopsgate, London EC2 (☎ 071 375 5000)

MEREDITH-HARDY, Hon Mrs (Joanna Mary); da of Baron Porritt, GCMG, GCVO, CBE (Life Peer and 1 Bt); *b* 19 July 1948; *m* 26 July 1969, Simon Patrick Meredith-Hardy; 2 s; *Style—* The Hon Mrs Meredith-Hardy; 23 Baronsmead Rd, London SW13

MEREDITH-HARDY, Michael Francis; s of late Howard Meredith Hardy; *b* 12 May 1923; *Educ* Eton, Pembroke Coll Cambridge; *m* 1955, Penelope Jane, JP, da of late Hon Bartholomew Pleydell-Bouverie, s of 6 Earl of Radnor and late Lady Doreen Pleydell-Bouverie, da of 6 Earl of Donoughmore; 4 s; *Career* 5 Royal Inniskilling Dragoon Gds 1942, Maj 1947-, Capt City of London Yeo TA, Staff Offr London Armd Div TA 1948-55; barr 1951-76; chm: Nat Insur Appeal Tbnl DHSS 1967-, Nat Insur Appeal Tbnl Dept Employment 1967-, DOE 1969, Appeal Bd Road Traffic Act 1972; Examiner High Ct of Justice 1969-89, immigration appeal adjudicator for Immigration Appeals Authy 1980-, ptnr (W Australia) Plantagenet Wines; High Sheriff Hertford 1980; *Recreations* painting; *Style—* Michael Meredith-Hardy, Esq; Radwell Mill, Baldock, Herts (☎ 0462 730 242)

MEREDITH-HARDY, Richard; s of Maj Michael Francis Meredith Hardy, *qv*, of Radwell Mill, Baldock, Herts, and Penelope Jane, *née* Pleydell-Bouverie; *b* 23 Aug 1957; *Educ* Eton, Birmingham Poly; *m* 5 Dec 1987, Nicola Louise, da of Hugh Morgan Lindsay Smith, of Bank Farm, Brandon Creek, Downham Market, Norfolk; 1 da (Alexandra b 29 Dec 1990); *Career* property developer, farmer, explorer; organiser of safaris to Africa 1980 and 1981, microlight aircraft pilot; achievements: first flight from London to Capetown 1985-86, Steve Hunt Meml Trophy winner 1986 and 1988, Br Nat champion 1987, 1988 and 1990, Gold Colibri winner 1988, Euro Individual and Team champion 1988-89, World Cup champion 1989-90, World champion 1990-; *Recreations* flying; *Clubs* BMAA, Royal Aero; *Style—* Richard Meredith-Hardy, Esq; Radwell Lodge, Baldock, Herts SG7 5ES (☎ 0462 834 776)

MERIVALE-AUSTIN, Hon Mrs (Alison Mary); 3 da of 2 Baron Rankeillour, GCIE, MC (d 1958), and Grizel, *née* Gilmour; *b* 21 Jan 1927; *m* 1, 29 Jan 1945 (m dis 1959), Maj Bruce Gardiner Merivale-Austin, The Black Watch, eldest s of William Merivale-Austin, of Waterford, Barbados; 2 da; *m* 2, 4 June 1960 (m annulled 1963), Maj Cyril Ernest Stearns, OBE, late KRRC (d 1968), 2 s of late Ernest Fuller Stearns, of Teddington, Middx; *Style—* The Hon Mrs Merivale-Austin

MERRETT, Richard James; s of Cecil Ernest Merrett (d 1972), of Seaton, Devon, and Jessie, *née* Lynes (d 1988); *b* 20 Feb 1935; *Educ* Charterhouse, Univ Coll Oxford (MA); *m* 29 May 1965, Rosemary Sarah (Sally), da of Cdr Ian Mike Milsted, RNVR (d 1978), of Bath; 1 s (James b 1973), 2 da (Emma b 1967, Rebecca b 1969); *Career* 2 Lt RA 1953-55, Lt TA 1955-58; called to the Bar Inner Temple 1959, presently head of chambers in Exeter, dep circuit judge/asst rec 1977-82; *Style—* Richard Merrett, Esq; Lark Rise, Kentisbeare, Cullompton, Devon EX15 2AD (☎ 08846 209); Barnfield Chambers, 15 Barnfield Rd, Exeter EX1 1RR (☎ 0392 74898, fax 0392 412368)

MERRIAM, Michael Kennedy; s of Sir Laurence Pierce Brooke Merriam, MC, JP, DL (d 1966), and Lady Marjory, *née* Kennedy (d 1988), da of 3 Marquess of Ailsa; *b* 16 April 1925; *Educ* Eton; *m* 14 June 1947, Anne Teresa, o da of late Lt-Col Philip Moss Elvery, DSO, MC; 1 s (Andrew William Kennedy b 1948), 1 da (Teresa Anne (Mrs Mark Woodhouse) b 1954); *Career* RNVR: ordinary seaman 1943, midshipman and Sub Lt 1944, Lt RNR 1965; dir Bx Plastics Ltd 1963-70 (joined 1946), America Square Assocs Ltd 1971-72, chm and md Bradford & Sons Ltd 1982-90 (md 1972), non-exec dir Blandford & Webb Agriculture Ltd (ret 1990), non-exec dir Somerset Family Health Assoc 1990-; *Recreations* country sports; *Clubs* Naval; *Style—* Michael Merriam, Esq; Stowell House, nr Sherborne, Dorset DT9 4PE; Bradford & Sons Ltd, 98 Hendford, Yeovil, Somerset BA20 2QR (☎ 0935 23 311, fax 0935 32 075)

MERRICK, (Denise) Holly; da of Max Richardson, of London, and Daphne May, *née* Taylor; *b* 6 Feb 1946; *Educ* Hitchin GS for Girls, Univ of Reading, Univ of Sydney; *m* 1967 (m dis 1986), Colin Merrick; 1 s (Simon-Peter b 1968), 2 da (Kate b 1971, Sophy (twin) b 1971); *Career* product mangr General Foods International 1980-81 (asst product mangr 1979-80), consumer mktg mangr Cross Paperware (Bowater) 1981-84, mktg dir Sheaffer Pen Textron 1984-86, divnl gen mangr Thornton (confectioners) 1986-87, managing conslt and head of retail & mktg Binder-Hamlyn/BDO Consulting 1987-88, md Marketing Solutions Ltd 1990- (managing conslt and dir 1988-90); memb Advsy Bd Music in Oxford Ltd; memb: Mktg Soc 1986, IGD 1987; *Style—* Ms Holly Merrick; Marketing Solutions Limited, 70 Salusbury Rd, Queens Park, London NW6 (☎ 071 624 6090, fax 071 328 2499)

MERRICK, Robert David (Bob); s of R T R Merrick (d 1968), and D E Merrick; *b* 23 Aug 1935; *Educ* Shirley Secdy Modern Sch; *m* 28 Sept 1957, Pauline Marjorie; 2 da (Sue (Mrs Handley) b 31 July 1959, Tina b 16 June 1962); *Career* co-fndr own haulage business 1959, acquired H T Hughes & Sons Ltd Portsmouth 1964 (floated 1988); former pres: Nat Fedn of Demolition Contractors (currently hon vice pres), Inst of Demolition Engrs; former chm Nat Demolition Trg Gp, int dir Nat Assoc of Demolition Contractors (chm Health & Safety Ctee); chm and md H T Hughes plc 1987-; memb: Exec Cncl Euro Demolition Assoc (chm Health & Safety Ctee), Nat Econ Devpt Ctee on Nuclear Decommissioning in the UK; *Recreations* shooting, fishing, reading; *Clubs* RAC, Conservative Patrons; *Style—* Bob Merrick, Esq; H T Hughes plc, Dundas Spur, Dundas Lane, Copnor, Portsmouth PO3 5NY (☎ 0705 671674, fax 0705 677524, telex 869294 HUGHES G, car 0839 252255)

MERRICKS, Walter Hugh; s of Dick Merricks, of Icklesham, Rye, E Sussex, and Phoebe, *née* Woffenden (d 1985); *b* 4 June 1945; *Educ* Bradfield Coll Berks, Trinity Coll Oxford (MA); *m* 27 Nov 1982, Olivia, da of late Dr Elio Montuschi; 1 s (William b 1983), 1 da (Susannah b 1986), 1 step s (Daniel b 1971); *Career* slr 1970, Hubbard Travelling Scholar 1971, dir Camden Community Law Centre 1972-76, lectr in law Brunel Univ 1976-81, legal affrs writer New Law Jl 1982-85, asst sec gen Law Soc 1985- (memb 1970-); memb: Royal Cmmn on Criminal Procedure 1978-81, Ctee on Fraud Trials 1984-86; *Style—* Walter Merricks, Esq; The Law Society, 113 Chancery Lane, London WC2A 1PL

MERRIDALE, Philip David; CBE (1988); s of Ernest David Merridale (d 1970), of St Albans, Herts, and Ruby Edith, *née* Paull (d 1965); *b* 2 May 1927; *Educ* St Albans Sch; *m* 10 Sept 1955, (Judith) Anne Bonynge, da of Ernest James Parry (d 1972), of Romsey, Hants; 1 s (David b 1956), 2 da (Catherine b 1959, Alison b 1962); *Career* RA 1945, Intelligence Corps 1946-48; commercial supervisor Marconi Instruments Ltd, antiques and fine arts dealer 1958-88, licenced lay reader Diocese of Winchester 1968-88, memb Hants CC 1973-88; chm: Ramsey and Stockbridge Dist Cncl 1968-67, Hants Educn Authy 1974-88, Nat Cncl of Local Educn Authys 1983, Educn Ctee of Assoc of CCs 1983-85, Teaching as a Career for Sec of State DES 1990-; ldr Employers Panel for Teachers Pay Negotiations 1983-85, govr Portsmouth Poly 1974-88, memb Midlands Industl 1988-; FRSA 1985; *Recreations* walking in the countryside; *Style—* Philip Merridale, Esq, CBE; April Cottage, Pilton, Rutland LE15 9PA (☎ 0780 720092)

MERRIFIELD, Air Cdre Anthony John; s of Rev Sidney Merrifield (d 1980), of Brooke, Norfolk, and Elizabeth Sarah Ann (d 1979); *b* 4 Aug 1926; *Educ* King's Sch Ely Cambs, KCH London (MB BS); *m* 2 Dec 1950, (Gwynedd Frances) Poppy, da of James Parker (d 1967), of Gosport, Hants; 2 s (Charles Matthew b 1952, Robin St Clair b 1954); *Career* RAF Med Branch 1951-87: conslt anaesthetist 1962, dir of anaesthetics 1973, Whittingham prof of aviation med 1985-87, QHP 1985-87; Joseph Clover lectr and Medal 1986, Pask Cert of Hon Assoc of Anaesthetists 1987; memb Bd Govrs King's Sch Ely; numerous contribs to med jls; memb: RSM, BMA, Assoc of Anaesthetics; MRCS 1950, FFARCS 1956, MIBiol 1973; *Recreations* boating, photography, music, reading; *Clubs* RAF; *Style—* Air Cdre Anthony Merrifield; 2 Barton Square, Ely, Cambs CB7 4DF (☎ 0353 664850)

MERRILL, John Nigel; s of Ian N Merrill (d 1989), and Ivy Mabel Phillips (d 1982); *b* 19 Aug 1943; *Educ* Grosvenor House Sch, Wennington Sch; *Career* marathon walker; maj walks incl: Lands End to John O'Groats 1608 miles 1977, the coastline of Britain

6824 miles 1978, The Appalachian Trail USA 2200 miles 1979, The Pacific Crest Trail USA 2700 miles 1980, across Europe walk 2800 miles 1982, coast to coast walk USA 4242 miles 1984, has participated in many charity walks, lectr on walking in GB and USA; *Books* over 100 books published on walking, local history and travel in Britain incl: Turn Right at Lands End, The Limey Way, Short Circular Walks in the Peak District; *Recreations* walking; *Style*— John Merrill, Esq; Yew Cottage, West Bank, Winster, Matlock, Derbyshire DE4 2DQ (☎ 0629 88454); JNM Publications, Winster, Matlock, Derbyshire DE4 2DQ (☎ 0629 88454, fax 0629 88416, car 0860 562193, telex 94016833 JNMP G)

MERRILLS, Austin; OBE (1981); s of Austin Merrills; *b* 15 April 1928; *Educ* King Edward VII Sheffield, Univ of Sheffield; *m* 1953, Daphne Olivia, *née* Coates; 1 s, 2 da; *Career* chm and chief exec Ireland Alloys (Hldgs) Ltd (Scot); *Recreations* skiing, walking, rugby (spectator), travel, paintings, food and wine; *Clubs* Caledonian; *Style*— Austin Merrills, Esq, OBE; Clyde House, Kirkfieldbank, Lanark (☎ 0555 3664, fax 0555 2571; office: 0698 822461, telex 77494, fax 0698 825167)

MERRISON, Lady; Maureen Michèle; *née* Barry; da of John Michael Barry (d 1944), and Winifred Alice, *née* Raymond; *b* 29 Oct 1938; *Educ* Royal Masonic Sch for Girls, Bedford Coll London Univ (BA); *m* 23 May 1970, as his 2 w, Sir Alexander (Alec) Walter Merrison, DL, FRS (d 1989), s of Henry Walter Merrison (d 1965); 1 s (Benedict b 1974), 1 da (Andria b 1972); *Career* lectr in history Univ of Bristol 1964-90; dir: HTV Group plc, Bristol and West Building Society 1990-, Western Provident Assoc 1990-, Greater Bristol Tst; vice pres Bishop Bristol's Urban Fund 1989-, vice chm of Govrs Colston's Girls Sch, memb St John Ambulance Ctee; *Style*— Lady Merrison; The Manor, Hinton Blewett, Bristol BS18 5AN (☎ 0761 52259); The Dept of History, Univ of Bristol BS8 1TB; HTV Group plc, The Television Centre, Culverhouse Cross, Cardiff CF5 6XJ (☎ 0272 303 030/0222 590 590, fax 0222 59613, telex 497703)

MERRITT, Prof John Edward; s of Leonard Merritt (d 1942), and Janet Merritt (d 1960); *b* 13 June 1926; *Educ* Gosforth Modern Sch, Univ of Durham (BA), UCL (DipEd); *m* 12 June 1948, Denise, da of John George Redvers Edmundson (d 1965); 2 s (Austen David, John Quentin); *Career* RAF 1944-45, Green Howards 1945, Sandhurst RMA 1945-46, Lt Border Regt 1946-48; educnl psychologist Lancs LEA 1957-59, sr educnl psychologist Hull LEA 1960-64, lectr Univ of Durham 1964-70, prof of teacher educn Open Univ; chm Fifth World Congress on Reading Vienna 1974, memb Nat Cmmn of Inquiry into Uses of English 1973-75, Int Merit Award Int Reading Assoc 1977, hon res fell Charlotte Mason Coll Ambleside; FRSA 1984-; *Books* Reading and the Curriculum (1971), The Reading Curriculum (1972), Reading: Today and Tomorrow (1972), What Shall We Teach? (1974); *Recreations* fell walking, climbing, running, theatre; *Clubs* Kendal Amateur Athletics; *Style*— Prof John Merritt; Wetherlam, Fisherbeck Park, Ambleside, Cumbria LA22 OAJ (☎ 05394 32259); Charlotte Mason College, Ambleside, Cumbria LA22 OAJ (☎ 05394 33066)

MERRIVALE, 3 Baron (UK 1925); Jack Henry Edmond Duke; s of 2 Baron, OBE (d 1951); *b* 27 Jan 1917; *Educ* Dulwich, Ecole des Sciences Politiques Paris; *m* 1, 30 Sept 1939 (m dis 1974), Colette, da of John Douglas Wise; 1 s, 1 da; m 2, 1975, Betty, widow of Paul Baron; *Heir* s, Hon Derek John Philip Duke; *Career* joined RAF 1940, Flt Lt 1944 (despatches); formerly chm Scotia Investments Ltd, pres Anglo-Malagasy Soc; past pres: Inst of Traffic Admin, Railway Devpt Assoc; chm: Br Ctee for the Furthering of Rels with French-Speaking Africa, Leisure Investments (Gibraltar) Ltd 1990-; Chev Nat Order of Malagasy; fndr memb Club of Dakar 1974; Freeman City of London 1979; FRSA 1964; *Style*— The Rt Hon the Lord Merrivale; 16 Brompton Lodge, 9-11 Cromwell Rd, London SW7 2JA (☎ 071 581 5678)

MERRY, Wing Cdr Robert Thomas George; s of Cyril Arthur Merry (d 1964), and Clara Catherine, *née* Stollmeyer (d 1988); *b* 25 Oct 1937; *Educ* Rossall, Bart's Med Coll (MB BS); *m* 17 Aug 1963, Gillian Irene Kathleen, da of Francis Xavier Perkins (d 1944); 1 s (Charles b 1970), 2 da (Victoria b 1965, Alexandra b 1969); *Career* conslt neurologist, advsr in neurology to the RAF; MRCPsych, FRCP; *Recreations* gardening, rambling, golf; *Clubs* MCC, Royal Soc of Medicine; *Style*— Wing Cdr Robert T G Merry; Myles House, Ashmead, Dursley, Gloucs

MERRYLEES, (Richard) Gavin; s of Richard Krebs Merrylees, and Barbara Joan Merrylees; *b* 12 June 1941; *Educ* Bradford Coll, LSE (LLB); *m* 27 July 1968, Daphne Margaret, da of Lt-Col CCL Pusinelli, RA, OBE, of Chinagarth, Thornton Dale, Pickering, N Yorks; 3 s (Peter Gavin b 15 May 1969, Robert Charles b 30 June 1971, Christopher Michael b 16 Dec 1981), 2 da (Daphne Clare b 18 Oct 1973, Joanna May b 28 Oct 1975); *Career* called to the Bar Gray's Inn 1964; churchwarden St Mary the Virgin Ivinghoe, former parish cncllr Pitstone, subscribes to Gen Cncl of the Bar; *Recreations* walking, gardening, music; *Clubs* Wig & Pen; *Style*— Gavin Merrylees, Esq; Greenacres, Cheddington Rd, Pitstone, nr Leighton Bullard, Beds LU7 9AH (☎ 0296 668046); Francis Taylor Building, Temple, London EC4 7BY (☎ 071 353 9942, fax 071 353 9924)

MERSEY, 4 Viscount (UK 1916); Richard Maurice Clive Bigham; also Master of Nairne (*see below*), and Baron Mersey (UK 1910); s of 3 Viscount Mersey (d 1979), and Lady Katherine Evelyn Constance Petty-Fitzmaurice (since her f's death Lady Nairne in her own right), da of 6 Marquess of Lansdowne; ha to Lordship of Nairne; *b* 8 July 1934; *Educ* Eton, Balliol Coll Oxford; *m* 6 May 1961, Joanna Dorothy Corsica Grey, er da of John Arnaud Robin Grey Murray, CBE; 1 s (and 1 s decd); *Heir* s, Hon Edward John Hallam Bigham b 23 May 1966; *Career* served Irish Gds Germany and Egypt 1952-54, Lt; film dir and prodr (documentary); pres Soc of Industl Emergency Servs Offrs (SIESO) 1987, pres Combined Heat and Power Assoc 1989; *Books* The Hills of Cork and Kerry (1987); *Recreations* mountaineering, music; *Style*— The Rt Hon the Viscount Mersey; 1 Rosmead Rd, London W11 (☎ 071 727 5057)

MERTHYR, Barony of; *see*: Lewis, Trevor

MERTON, John Ralph; MBE (1942); s of Sir Thomas Ralph Merton, KBE (d 1969), and Violet Margery, da of Lt-Col William Harcourt Sawyer; *b* 7 May 1913; *Educ* Eton, Balliol Coll Oxford; *m* 1938, Viola Penelope, da of Adolf von Bernd (d 1975); 3 da (1 decd); *Career* served WWII air photo reconnaissance res, Lt-Col 1944, Legion of Merit USA; painter of portraits and other subjects; works incl: portrait of Jane Dalkeith (now Duchess of Buccleuch), hanging in Drumlanrig Castle (only painting since 1918 to receive a Royal Acad A award), triple portrait of HRH The Princess of Wales, cmmd for The Principality of Wales 1988 and hanging in City Hall Cardiff, portrait drawing of HM The Queen as head of the OM, cmmd by HM The Queen and hanging at Windsor Castle; *Recreations* music, making things, underwater photography; *Clubs* Garrick; *Style*— John Merton, Esq, MBE; Pound House, Oare, Nr Marlborough, Wilts SN8 4JA (☎ 0672 63539)

MERTON, Viscount; Simon John Horatio Nelson; only s, and h, of 9 Earl Nelson; *b* 21 Sept 1971; *Style*— Viscount Merton

MERTON, William Ralph; s of Sir Thomas Ralph Merton, KBE, FRS (d 1969), of Berks, and Violet Marjory Sawyer (d 1976); *b* 25 Nov 1917; *Educ* Eton, Balliol Coll Oxford (MA); *m* 1, 6 July 1950, Anthea Caroline, da of Henry F Lascelles (d 1936); 3 s (Michael b 1951, Rupert b 1953, Jeremy b 1961); m 2, 30 April 1977, Judy, da of Col Alexander John Buckley Rutherford, CVO, CBE (d 1979), of Henley-on-Thames; *Career* WWII served: Operational Res Unit HQ Coastal Cmd RAF 1941-43, sci asst to Lord Cherwell War Cabinet 1943-45; called to the Bar Inner Temple; merchant banker; dir: Fulmer Res Inst 1946-80 (chm 1958-74), Erlangers Ltd 1950-60; chm Alginate Industries Ltd 1952-79, dir Robert Fleming and Co Ltd 1963-80; chm: Robert Fleming Holdings Ltd 1974-80, Technology Investments Trust Ltd, Sterling Trust Ltd US, General Trust Corporation Ltd; *Recreations* gardening, woodworking, tennis; *Style*— William Merton, Esq; Kingsbrook Hse, Headley, Newbury, Berkshire (☎ 0635 268458)

MERTTENS, Peter Mervyn; s of Victor H Merttens, CBE, of Berkhamstead, and Evelyn, *née* Udall (d 1977); *b* 8 April 1930; *Educ* Malvern, St Catharine's Coll Cambridge (MA); *m* 6 July 1957, Mimi Cynthia, da of Stanley A Child, MBE, of Catfield, Norfolk; 2 s (Robin, Brian); *Career* slr; Hamilton Harrison Matthews 1955-57, E African Power & Lighting Co Ltd 1957-62; slr and dir Colmans of Norwich 1962-84 (formerly J J Colman Ltd and Colman Food), slr and ptnr Daynes Hill & Perks 1984- (formerly Daynes Chittock and Back); chm govrs Norwich City Coll of Further and Higher Educn, memb Cncl UEA, pres Norwich S Rotary Club, memb Cncl Norwich & Norfolk C of C; memb Law Soc; *Recreations* decoy duck carving, watercolour painting, golf; *Clubs* Royal Cwlth, Strangers (Norwich), 33 (Norfolk and Norwich), Eaton Golf; *Style*— Peter Merttens, Esq; Chestnuts, Catfield, Norfolk NR29 5DF (☎ 0692 80458); c/o Daynes Hill & Perks, Holland Court, The Close, Norwich NR1 4DX (☎ 0603 611212)

MERZ, Johanna Dalbiac; da of Lt-Col Robert Francis Bridges, RAMC (d 1951), and Charlotte Lucy Chauncy, *née* Luard (d 1972); *b* 1 July 1930; *Educ* Westonbirt Sch, RCM; *m* 6 May 1954, Felix Wolfgang Merz, s of Victor Merz; 2 da (Felicity b 1954, Juliet b 1958); *Career* dir Johanna Merz Photography 1979-86; ed Alpine Journal 1991; *Clubs* Alpine; *Style*— Mrs Johanna D Merz; 14 Whitefield Close, Putney, London SW15 3SS (☎ 081 789 9702)

MESSEL, (Linley) Thomas De Cusance; s of Col Linley Messel, TD (d 1971, er bro of both Oliver Messel, CBE (the portraitist and costume and set designer), and Anne (mother, by 1 husb, of 1 Earl of Snowdon) who later m 6 Earl of Rosse), and his 2 w, Elizabeth Désirée, da of Sir Arthur Downes and formerly w of Bernhart Stehelin; *b* 9 Jan 1951; *Educ* Milton Abbey Sch; *m* 1981, Penelope Jane, da of Timothy Donald Barratt (d 1978), of Hazel Mount, Millom, Cumbria; 1 s (Harold b 1986); *Career* Lt Blues and Royals 1978-82; designer and furniture manufacturer; *Recreations* croquette, archery, dry fly fishing; *Clubs* Brooks's; *Style*— Thomas Messel, Esq; Bradley Court, Wotton-under-Edge, Gloucestershire (☎ 0453 843220, 842980)

MESSER, Cholmeley Joseph; s of Col Arthur Albert Messer, DSO, CBE, FRIBA (d 1934), of Woking, Surrey, and Lilian Hope, *née* Dowling; *b* 20 March 1929; *Educ* Wellington Coll; *m* 1956, Ann Mary, da of Eliot Kingsmill Power (d 1969), of Pirbright, Surrey; 2 da; *Career* 2 Lt, KRRC, ME; slr, ptnr Lawrance Messer and Co slrs 1957-67; dir Save and Prosper Group Ltd 1968-89 (chm 1981-89); chm: Code of Advertising Practice Ctee 1976-78, Unit Tst Assoc 1979-81; chm Bd Br Bobsleigh Assoc, dir Royal London Soc for Blind; memb London Pension Funds Authy; *Recreations* golf, gardening, armchair sport, history; *Clubs* City of London; *Style*— Cholmeley Messer, Esq; The Manor House, Normandy, Guildford, Surrey GU3 2AP (☎ 0483 810910)

MESSERVY, Sir (Roney) Godfrey Collumbell; s of Roney Forshaw Messervy,and Bertha Crosby, *née* Collumbell; *b* 17 Nov 1924; *Educ* Oundle, Cambridge Univ; *m* 1952, Susan Patricia Gertrude, da of Reginald Arthur Nunn, DSO, DSC, RNVR; 1 s, 2 da; *Career* served WWII RE; with Lucas subsid CAV 1949- (dir and gen mangr 1966); dir: Joseph Lucas Ltd 1971-, Joseph Lucas (Industries) 1972-, Costain Group 1978-; chm and chief exec Lucas Industries 1980- (md 1974-80, dep chm 1979-80); memb: C of C Cncl, Soc of Motor Mfrs and Traders Cncl, Engrg Industs Cncl; kt 1986; *Style*— Sir Godfrey Messervy; Lucas Industries Ltd, Great King St, Birmingham B19 2XF (☎ 021 554 5252)

MESSING, Jack Joseph; s of Hyman Messing (d 1963), of Newcastle upon Tyne, and Hylda, *née* Cohen (d 1941); *b* 30 July 1923; *Educ* Royal GS Newcastle upon Tyne, Kings Coll Durham, Sutherland Dental Sch (BDS), RCS (FDS); *m* 30 March 1949, Maureen, da of Prof Ralph Bass (d 1959), of Belfast, NI; 1 s (Allan M b 1955), 1 da (Julie Owen b 1952); *Career* hosp registrar and teacher Newcastle upon Tyne Dental Hosp 1946-52, sr registrar operative Dental Surgery Dept Eastman Dental Hosp London 1952-54; Univ Coll Hosp London: teaching and res at Dental Sch 1954-83, postgrad tutor serving as chm of NW Thames Dental Post Grad Ctee, emeritus reader 1983, conslt in operative dental surgery; visiting teacher Malta Dental Sch (bi-annual); former memb Local Dental Ctee; pres: Br Endodontic Soc 1969-70, Middx and Herts Branch Br Dental Assoc 1976-77; life memb Br Dental Assoc; *Books* Operative Dental Surgery (2 edn with G E Ray, 1982), Endodontics (with C J R Stock, 1988); *Recreations* music, photography, golf, languages; *Style*— Jack Messing, Esq; 28 Dobree Ave, London NW10 2AE (☎ 081 459 1404)

MESTEL, Prof Leon; s of Rabbi Solomon Mestel (d 1966), of London, and Rachel, *née* Brodetsky (d 1974); *b* 5 Aug 1927; *Educ* West Ham Secdy Sch London, Trinity Coll Cambridge (BA, PhD); *m* 15 Nov 1951, Sylvia Louise, da of Lt-Col Stanley James Cole, CMG, OBE (d 1949), of Cambridge; 2 s (Andrew Jonathan b 1957, Benjamin David b 1960), 2 da (Anne Leonora b 1953, Rosemary Judith b 1959); *Career* ICI res fell Univ of Leeds 1951-54, Cwlth fund fell Princeton Univ Observatory 1954-55, fell St John's Coll Cambridge 1957-66, lectr in maths Univ of Cambridge 1958-66 (asst lectr 1955-58), visiting memb Inst of Advanced Studies Princeton 1961-62, JFK fell Weizmann Inst for Sci Israel 1966-67; prof: applied maths Univ of Manchester 1967-73, astronomy Univ of Sussex 1973; FRAS 1952, FRS 1977; *Books* Magnetohydrodynamics (jtly, 1974); *Recreations* reading, music; *Style*— Prof Leon Mestel, FRS; 13 Prince Edward's Rd, Lewes, E Sussex BN7 1BJ (☎ 0273 472731); Division of Physics and Astronomy, University of Sussex, Falmer, Brighton BN1 9QH (☎ 0273 678071, fax 0273 678097, telex 877159, BHVTXS G)

MESTON, Diana, Baroness; Diana Mary Came; o da of late Capt Otto Sigismund Doll, FRIBA, of 16 Upper Cheyne Row, London SW3; *m* 12 July 1947, 2 Baron Meston (d 1984); 2 s; *Style*— The Rt Hon Diana, Lady Meston; Hurst House, Grange Rd, Cookham Rise, Berks

MESTON, 3 Baron (UK 1919); James; s of 2 Baron Meston (d 1984), and Diana, Baroness Meston, *qv*; *b* 10 Feb 1950; *Educ* Wellington, St Catharine's Coll Cambridge; *m* 1974, Jean Rebecca Anne, yr da of John Carder, of Stud Farm House, Chalvington, Sussex; 1 s (Thomas), 2 da (Laura b 1980, Elspeth b 1988); *Heir* s, Hon Thomas James Dougall Meston b 21 Oct 1977; *Career* called to the Bar Middle Temple 1973; *Clubs* Hawks; *Style*— The Rt Hon the Lord Meston; 16 Upper Cheyne Row, London SW3

MESTON, Prof Michael Charles; s of Alexander Morrison Meston (d 1980), of 15 Raeden Ave, Aberdeen, and Isabel Helen, *née* Robertson (d 1968); *b* 13 Dec 1932; *Educ* Robert Gordon's Coll Aberdeen, Univ of Aberdeen (MA, LLB), Univ of Chicago (JD); *m* 5 Sept 1958, Dorothea, da of James Munro (d 1946), of Montrose; 2 s (Donald b 1960, John b 1963); *Career* lectr in private law Univ of Glasgow 1959-64; Univ of Aberdeen: sr lectr 1964-68, prof of jurisprudence 1968-71, prof of scots law 1971, vice princ 1979-82, dean 1988-; hon sheriff Grampian Highlands and Islands 1972-; memb Grampian Health Bd, govr Robert Gordon's Coll, tstee Nat Museum of Antiquities of Scotland 1982-85; memb Law Soc of Scotland 1957; *Books* The

Succession (Scotland) Act 1964 (1964), The Matrimonial Homes (Family Protection) (Scotland) Act 1981 (1981); *Recreations* golf, clock repairing; *Clubs* Royal Northern and Univ, Royal Aberdeen Golf; *Style—* Prof Michael Meston; 4 Hamilton Place, Aberdeen AB2 4BH (☎ 0224 641554); Faculty of Law, University of Aberdeen, Old Aberdeen AB9 2UB (☎ 0224 272440, telex 73458 UNIABN G, fax 0224 487048)

MESTON, Hon William Dougall; yr s of 2 Baron Meston (d 1984), and Diana, Baroness Meston, *qv*; *b* 17 May 1953; *Educ* Wellington; *m* 1982, Elizabeth Mary Anne, yst da of Dr Peter Dawes (d 1990), and Dr Joan Dawes (d 1983); 2 s (Dougall b 1985, Felix b 1987); *Career* dir and fin conslt; *Clubs* Naval and Military; *Style—* The Hon William Meston; 11 The Green, Mistley, Manningtree, Essex CO11 1EU

METCALF, Prof David; s of Geoffrey Metcalf (d 1983), and Dorothy Rosa, *née* Vecchia; *b* 15 May 1942; *Educ* Univ of Manchester (MA), Univ of London (PhD); *m* 20 July 1968, Helen, da of Percival Harnett; 1 s (Thomas b 25 Nov 1980); *Career* special advsr to Min for Social Security 1976-79; prof of: econs Univ of Kent 1977-85, industl rels LSE 1985-; ed Br Jl of Industl Rels 1986-; alderman London Borough of Islington 1971-74; memb: Royal Econ Soc, Br Univs' Industl Rels Assoc; *Books* Minimum Wage Policy in Great Britain (1981), Economics of Vocational Training (1984); *Recreations* watching Tottenham Hotspur FC, horseriding; *Clubs* XYZ; *Style—* Prof David Metcalf; London School of Economics, Houghton St, London WC2 (☎ 071 405 7686, telex 24655 BLPES G, fax 071 242 0392)

METCALF, John; s of John Metcalf (d 1967); *b* 31 Dec 1922; *Educ* Univ Coll Sch, Downing Coll Cambridge; *m* 1954, Shelagh, *née* Branagan; 1 s, 1 da; *Career* chm Dorland Advertising Ltd 1971-84, dep chm and jt md Hobson Bates & Ptnrs Ltd 1955-68; *Recreations* gardening, writing; *Clubs* Garrick, RAF; *Style—* John Metcalf, Esq; Brookland, Wisborough Green, W Sussex (☎ 0403 700325); A13 Albany, Piccadilly, London W1 (☎ 071 439 7600)

METCALF, Dr (David) Michael; s of Rev Thomas Metcalf, and Gladys Metcalf; *b* 8 May 1933; *Educ* St John's Coll Cambridge (MA, DPhil, DLitt); *m* 1958, Dorothy Evelyn, *née* Uren; 2 s, 1 da; *Career* keeper Heberden Coin Room Ashmolean Museum 1984- (asst keeper 1963-84); sec Royal Numismatic Soc 1974-84 (ed Numismatic Chronicle 1974-84); FSA; *Books* Coinage in South-Eastern Europe 820-1396 (1979), Sceattas in England and on the Continent (1984), Coinage in Ninth-century Northumbria (1987); *Style—* Dr Michael Metcalf, FSA; Ashmolean Museum, Oxford OX1 2PH (☎ 0865 278062)

METCALFE, Lady Alexandra Naldera; CBE (1975); da of 1 and last Marquess Curzon of Kedleston (d 1925); *b* 1904; *m* 1925 (m dis 1955), Maj Edward Dudley Metcalfe, MVO, MC, IA (d 1957); 1 s, 2 da; *Career* CStJ, Order of Merit 1 Class of Italy, Order of Merit 4 Class Italian Republic, Cross of Merit 1 Class SMOM Malta; *Style—* Lady Alexandra Metcalfe, CBE; 65 Eaton Place, London SW1X 8DF

METCALFE, Ashley Anthony; s of Tony Metcalfe, of Baildon, W Yorks, and Ann, *née* Barratt; *b* 25 Dec 1963; *Educ* Bradford GS, UCL; *m* Diane Lesley, da of Raymond Illingworth; 1 da (Zoe Natalie b 18 July 1990); *Career* professional cricketer Yorkshire CCC; debut 1983 scoring 122 v Notts, awarded county cap 1986, vice capt 1990-91, 120 Championship appearances; represented: TCCB XI v NZ 1986, MCC v Essex 1987; Benson & Hedges Cup Winner's medal 1987; *Recreations* golf, football, rugby, most other sports; *Style—* Ashley Metcalfe, Esq; c/o Yorkshire County Cricket Club, Headingley, Leeds LS6 3BU

METCALFE, Charles; s of Charles Metcalfe (d 1959), of Belle Bank, Bentham, nr Lancaster, and Agnes, *née* Alderson (d 1973); *b* 27 Feb 1931; *Educ* Cheltenham Coll, Liverpool Coll of Art and Design (NDD); *m* 15 March 1957, Mary Bell, da of Charles Fancourt Harrison; 1 s (Charles Harrison b 17 Nov 1958); *Career* Nat Serv: Intelligence Corps 1951-53; worked in Fabric Dept Dickins and Jones London 1953-55, sales rep Ascher (Fabrics) Ltd London 1955-59; Liverpool Poly (formerly Liverpool Coll of Art): lectr in fashion and textiles 1959-64, sr lectr in charge of fashion 1964-67, head of Dept of Fashion and Textiles 1967-88, dep dir Sch of Art and Design 1988-89; advsy ed Allen & Unwin 1980-84, pub lectr 1982-, dir Polycas Ltd 1983-90; external assessor: Poly of Wales 1977-78, Bradford Coll 1978-79, Bolton Teeh Coll 1979, Manchester Poly 1986-88, N Staffords Poly 1987-90, Bristol Poly 1988-91; Poly Ctee memb: Academic Bd 1970-84 (rep on Poly Govrs Bd 1984), Art and Design Faculty Bd (chm 1971-73), Sci Faculty Bd 1973-75, Humanities and Business Studies Faculty Bd 1985-88; memb: Nat Cncl for Diplomas in Art and Design Fashion and Textile Subject Panel 1972-74, CNAA Fashion and Textile Subject Panel 1978-82, Professional and Educnl Affairs Ctee Textile Inst 1982-84, Product Mktg Gp Textile Inst 1984- (chm 1988-); chm Bluecoat Gallery Liverpool 1988-, memb Bluecoat Soc of Arts 1988 (vice-chm 1989), dir Bluecoat Arts Centre Ltd 1988; *Recreations* watching excellent television, attending European art exhibitions and festivals, opera and ballet; *Clubs* Cheshire and N Wales Orchid Soc; *Style—* Charles Metcalfe, Esq; 5 Mount Olive, Oxton, Birkenhead, Merseyside L43 5TT (☎ 051 652 4898)

METCALFE, David Patrick; s of Maj Edward Dudley Metcalfe, MVO, MC (d 1957), and Lady Alexandra Metcalfe, *qv*; *b* 8 July 1927; *Educ* Eton; *m* 1, 1957 (m dis 1964), Alexandria Irene Boycun, Lady Korda (d 1966); 2 s, 1 da; m 2, 1968 (m dis 1973), Countess Anne Chauvigny de Blot; 1 s; m 3, 1979, Sally Cullen Howe, da of Edward Everett Cullen III, of Pennsylvania, USA; 2 step da; *Career* Lt Irish Gds Germany 1945-48; memb Lloyd's 1952; former dir: Stewart Smith Ltd (Insurance Brokers), Stewart Wrightson Ltd (Insurance Brokers), Wigham Poland Holdings Ltd (Insurance Brokers); currently dir: Sedgwick James Management Services (Insurance Brokers), Triton (Europe) Ltd, Gam International Ltd; *Recreations* skiing, tennis, shooting, golf; *Clubs* White's, Buck's, Travellers' (Paris), The Brook (New York); *Style—* David Metcalfe, Esq; 15 Wilton St, London SW1 (☎ 071 235 1833); Sedgwick House, The Sedgwick Centre, London E1 8DX (☎ 071 377 3838)

METCALFE, George Ralph Anthony; s of Sir Ralph Ismay Metcalfe (d 1977), and Betty Penhorwood, *née* Pelling (d 1976); *b* 18 March 1936; *Educ* Lancing, Univ of Durham (BSc, BSc); *m* 11 Aug 1962, (Anne) Barbara, da of Anthony Watson, of Cumbria; 2 da (Elizabeth Anne (Mrs Smedley), Sarah Rosalind (Mrs Faulkner)); *Career* asst to MD Marine Div Richardsons Westgarth 1954-63, head of planning Polaris Project Vickers Armstrongs Engineers 1963-70, md Initial Services (chm and dir various subsids of BET and Initial Services) 1970-78, md Bath & Portland Group 1978-83, chm and chief exec UMECO Holdings 1983-; memb: S Regnl Cncl CBI, Small Firms Cncl CBI, W of England Branch IOD; vice chm Berks Business Gp; Freeman City of London, Liveryman Worshipful Co of Shipwrights; FRSA; *Recreations* sailing, music, gardening; *Clubs* Travellers; *Style—* George Metcalfe, Esq; 4 Tower St, Cirencester, Glos GL7 IEF (☎ 0285 885303)

METCALFE, Harold Arthur; s of William Metcalfe (d 1930), of Wimbledon, and Marion Joan, *née* Taylor; *b* 2 Jan 1926; *Educ* Prince Henry's GS Yorkshire, Univ of Leeds (Dip Arch), RIBA; *m* 3 Jan 1953, Margaret Doreen, da of William Rawling (d 1965), of Menston, Yorks; *Career* RAFVR 1943-44, Army RA (Field) 1944-48, Lt; architectural works incl: BUPA Hosp Pentwyn Cardiff, Hotels throughout the UK (incl Inn on the Avenue Cardiff), Leisure Complexes (incl Kiln Park Tenby 1987-88), Schls for Dyfed CC (Llandovery Co HS 1986, Whitland GS 1987-88, Ysgol Y Strade 1990), Houses (incl houses for Hammond Innes, and Peter Bowles); Prince of Wales award for Theatre Moridunum, Civic Tst and Civic Soc awards; Hon Testimonial Royal Humane Soc 1963; *Recreations* tennis, golf, swimming; *Style—* Harold A Metcalfe, Esq; The Saltings, Llangain, Carmarthen, Dyfed SA33 5AJ (☎ 026783 428); 32 Spilman St, Carmarthen, Dyfed SA31 1LQ (☎ 0267 237427)

METCALFE, Hugh; s of Clifford Metcalfe, CBE, and late Florence Ellen Metcalfe; *b* 26 June 1928; *Educ* Harrow County GS, Imperial Coll London; *m* 19 April 1952, Pearl Allison; 3 s (Christopher b 1954, Andrew b 1956, Ian b 1960); *Career* air radar mechanic 1946-48; Bristol Aeroplane Company: joined 1951, design depts and project management in guided missiles and space, md Bristol (Naval) Div 1980-81, md Hatfield (Air Weapons) Div until 1982; chief exec Dynamics Gp British Aerospace plc 1982 (main bd dir 1982, dep chief exec 1984-88); dir: Hunting Engineering 1988-, SAC International plc (now Ricardo Group plc) 1989-; memb: CBI Fin & Econ Ctee 184-88, Engineering Industries Trg Bd 1985-88; govr: Hatfield Poly 1988-, St Mary Redcliffe sch 1990-; Hon DSc Hatfield Poly; FRAeS 1968, FEng; *Recreations* Opera London and Opera East (dir), music (London Philharmonic Choir); *Clubs* Athenaeum, Leander, Royal Society of Arts, Savages (Bristol); *Style—* Hugh Metcalfe, Esq, OBE; 28 Druid Stoke Avenue, Stoke Bishop, Bristol BS9 1DD (☎ 0272 684039); Ricardo International plc, Brunswick House, Upper York St, Bristol BS2 8QB (☎ 0272 232162, fax 0272 428349, telex 449107)

METCALFE, Peter; s of Arthur Metcalfe, of 4 Quarlton Drive, Hawkshaw, Tottington, Bury, Lancs, and Marjorie, *née* Smith; *b* 1 Oct 1944; *Educ* Bury GS; *m* 26 July 1969, Patricia Jean, da of Francis Noel Brierley; 1 s (Nicholas Philip b 18 Jan 1975), 1 da (Jane Helen b 11 July 1976); *Career* Peat Marwick Mitchell 1961-70 (Manchester 1961-69, Leeds 1969-70), ptnr J A Crawshaw & Co Bury 1970-87 (merged with Peat Marwick Mitchell 1987, firm became KPMG Peat Marwick McLintock), ptnr KPMG Peat Marwick McLintock 1987-; FCA (1975, ACA 1969); *Recreations* table tennis, soccer, scouts (asst ldr); *Style—* Peter Metcalfe, Esq; KPMG Peat Marwick McLintock Chartered Accountants, 10 St Mary's Place, Bury, Lancs BL9 ODZ (☎ 061 764 7111, fax 061 763 1330, car 0836 586 808)

METCALFE, Stanley Gordon; s of Stanley Hudson Metcalfe, and Jane Metcalfe (d 1975); *b* 20 June 1932; *Educ* Leeds GS, Pembroke Coll Oxford (MA); *m* 1968, Sarah, da of John F A Harter; 2 da; *Career* chm Ranks Hovis McDougall plc 1989- (dep chm 1987-89); *Recreations* golf, cricket; *Clubs* MCC, I Zingari; *Style—* Stanley Metcalfe, Esq; The Oast House, Lower Froyle, Alton, Hants GU34 4LX (☎ 0420 22310); Ranks Hovis McDougall plc, RHM Centre, 67 Alma Rd, PO Box 178, Windsor, Berks SL4 3ST (☎ 0753 857123)

METHERELL, Anthony William; s of William Frederick Metherell (d 1936), and Emily Russell, *née* Brockwell; *b* 28 May 1919; *Educ* Cheltenham, Pembroke Coll Cambridge; *Career* RA (field) 1939-46, cmmnd 2 Lt 1940, served France 1940, Maj personnel selection branch WO 1944-46; underwriting memb Lloyds 1945, farmer 1951; chm: Sanders & Co 1962, James Walker Goldsmith & Silversmith plc 1983; former dir of 20 other cos; memb: BRCS (cert of hon 1973), cncl Feathers Clubs Assoc; tstee Sussex Aids Tst; Freeman: Worshipful Co of Wheelwrights 1946, Worshipful Co of Glovers 1950; *Clubs* Carlton, City Livery; *Style—* Anthony Metherell, Esq; Mullion House, 46 Sussex Sq, Brighton; 34 Falmouth House, Clarendon Place, London W2 2NT; 33 Brook St, London W1 1AJ (☎ 071 629 4752)

METHERELL, Ian Patrick; s of Clarence George Metherell, and Ethel Muriel, *née* Dyer; *b* 19 Sept 1943; *Educ* Bideford GS, Univ of Southampton (BA); *m* 7 April 1968, Louise Whitefield, da of James Edward Westwood (d 1986); 2 s (Andrew b 1977, Nicholas b 1981); *Career* PR conslt; princ Metherell Corporate Consultants; chief exec MPR Leedex Group Ltd 1987-89, treas PR Conslts Assoc 1987-89, non-exec dir Mosaic Management Consulting Group 1984-; FIPR 1988; *Style—* Ian Metherell, Esq; 2 Forge Close, Marsh Gibbon, nr Bicester, Oxfordshire OX6 OHZ (☎ 0869 277 620)

METHERELL, Hon Mrs (Rosamond Ann); raised to the rank of a Baron's da 1980; da of Rt Hon John Emerson Harding Harding-Davies, MBE (who was nominated a Life Peer 16 June 1979, but who d 4 July 1979 before the Peerage was cr), and Baroness Harding-Davies, *qv*; *b* 1946; *m* 1968, Charles Marten Metherell, s of Col Reginald Marten Metherell (d 1954); 2 s, 1 da; *Style—* The Hon Mrs Metherell; 59 Chiddingstone St, London SW6

METHLEY, Peter Charles; s of Charles Harry Methley, of Surrey, and Alice Elizabeth, *née* Stimpson (d 1984); *b* 2 April 1938; *Educ* Kings Coll Sch; *m* 15 July 1961, Marianne, *née* Evans; 1 s (Michael Peter b 1965), 2 da (Lisette b 1963, Annette b 1970); *Career* insur broker Lloyds, dir Lowndes Lambert Group Ltd, chm and chief exec H J Symons Group of Cos, chief exec C E Heath plc 1986; chm: Leslie and Godwin Ltd 1979-85, Stewart and Wrightson International Group 1969-79; played hockey for Guildford and Surrey 1956-70; Freeman City of London; Freeman Worshipful Cos of: Insurers (fndr memb), Paviors; *Recreations* golf, tennis; *Clubs* Sunningdale GC, Royal and Ancient GC of St Andrews; *Style—* Peter Methley, Esq; Longreach, Links Road, Bramley, Surrey GU5 0AL (☎ 0483 893037); Symons House, 22 Alie Street, London E1 8DH (☎ 071 488 2131, fax 071 488 1080, telex 888483)

METHUEN, 6 Baron (UK 1838); Anthony John Methuen; s of 5 Baron Methuen (d 1975, himself s of Field Marshal Lord Methuen who cmd in S Africa during the Boer War and who was in his turn sixth in descent from the yr bro of the Ambass to Portugal who negotiated the treaty with that country which bears his name) and Grace, JP, da of Sir Richard Durning Holt, 1 Bt; *b* 26 Oct 1925; *Educ* Winchester, RAC Cirencester; *Heir* bro, Hon Robert Alexander Holt Methuen; *Career* served Scots Gds and Royal Signals 1943-47; lands offr Air Miny 1951-62; ARICS, QALAS 1954; *Clubs* Lansdowne; *Style—* The Rt Hon the Lord Methuen; Corsham Court, Corsham, Wilts SN13 0BZ (☎ 0249 712214)

METHUEN, Hon Robert Alexander Holt; s of 5 Baron Methuen (d 1975), and hp of bro, 6 Baron; *b* 22 July 1931; *Educ* Shrewsbury, Trinity Coll Cambridge; *m* 1958, Mary Catherine Jane, da of Ven Charles German Hooper, Archdeacon of Ipswich; 2 da; *Style—* The Hon Robert Methuen; Stoneycroft Farm, Kniveton, Ashbourne, Derbys

METLISS, Jonathan Alexander; s of Cyril Metliss, and Anita, *née* Lander; *b* 12 June 1949; *Educ* Haberdashers' Aske's, Univ of Southampton (LLB); *m* 15 Dec 1974, Vivienne Hilary, da of Samuel Woolf; 1 s (Joshua b 25 Nov 1980), 2 da (Miriam b 4 Nov 1983, Elizabeth b 4 July 1988); *Career* slr; asst slr Nabarro Nathanson 1973-76, merchant banker Capel Court Corp Sydney Aust 1976-78, asst slr Berwin Leighton 1978-82, ptnr and dep head Corp Fin Dept SJ Berwin 1982-; vice chm Friends of the Weizmann Inst Fndn, memb Weizmann Inst Fndn; memb: Law Soc, Holborn Law Soc; *Recreations* squash, cricket, travel and work; *Clubs* MCC; *Style—* Jonathan Metliss, Esq; S J Berwin & Co, 236 Gray's Inn Rd, London WC1X 8HB (☎ 071 278 0444, telex 8814928, fax 071 833 2860, car 0836 357574)

METTER, Veronica Ann; da of Louis William Metter, of South Africa, and Valerie Phylis, *née* Harris; *b* 9 Jan 1954; *Educ* Univ of the Witwaterstand (BA), Univ of London (BA); *Career* slr; ptnr Berwin Leighton 1987-; memb Law Soc; *Recreations* theatre, tennis; *Style—* Miss Veronica Metter; Berwin Leighton, Adelaide House, London Bridge, London EC4R 9HA (☎ 071 623 3144, telex 886420, fax 071 623 4416)

MEXBOROUGH, 8 Earl of (I 1766); John Christopher George Savile; also Baron Pollington (I 1753) and Viscount Pollington (I 1766); s of 7 Earl (d 1980; himself gs of the 4 Earl who, as Lord Gaverstock, featured in a minor role in Disraeli's Coningsby, and who, for the last seven and a half months of his life, enjoyed the distinction of being the last living ex-member of the unreformed House of Commons); *b* 16 May 1931; *Educ* Eton, Worcester Coll Oxford; *m* 1, 1958 (m dis 1972), Lady Elisabeth Hariot Grimston, da of 6 Earl of Verulam; 1 s, 1 da; m 2, 1972, Catherine Joyce, da of James Kenneth Hope, CBE, DL, and formerly wife of Maj the Hon Nicholas Crespigny Laurence Vivian; 1 s (Hon James b 1976), 1 da (Lady Lucinda b 1973); *Heir* s, Viscount Pollington; *Career* late 2 Lt Grenadier Gds; *Recreations* travel, motor cars, American music; *Clubs* All England Lawn Tennis, Air Sqdn; *Style—* The Rt Hon the Earl of Mexborough; Arden Hall, Hawnby, York (☎ 043 96 348); 13 Ovington Mews, London SW3 (☎ 071 589 3669)

MEXBOROUGH, Dowager Countess of; Josephine Bertha Emily; da of late Capt Andrew Mansel Talbot Fletcher; *m* 1930, John Raphael Wentworth Savile, 7 Earl of Mexborough (d 1980); 2 s, 1 da (decd); *Style—* The Rt Hon Dowager Countess of Mexborough; The Dower House, Arden Hall, Hawnby, York YO6 5LS (☎ 043 96 213)

MEYER *see also*: de Meyer

MEYER, Sir Anthony John Charles; 3 Bt (UK 1910), of Shortgrove, Newport, Essex; MP (C) Clwyd North West 1983-; s of Sir Frank Meyer, 2 Bt, MP (d 1935), of Ayot House, Ayot St Lawrence, Herts, by his w Georgina (d 1962), *née* Seeley; *b* 27 Oct 1920; *Educ* Eton, New Coll Oxford; *m* 30 Oct 1941, Barbadee Violet, da of A Charles Knight, JP, FSA (d 1958), of Herne Place, Sunningdale; 1 s, 3 da; *Heir* s, (Anthony) Ashley Frank Meyer b 23 Aug 1944; *Career* Lt Scots Gds WWII; Foreign Serv 1947; first sec: Paris 1951-56, Moscow 1956-58; FO 1958-62; PPS to Rt Hon Maurice Macmillan as: chief sec Treasy 1970-72, sec state for Employment 1972-74; chm Franco-Br Parly Rels Ctee; MP (C): Eton and Slough 1964-66, Flint West 1970-1983; fndr and dir of Solon 1969; vice-chm Franco-Brit Cncl; management bd European Movement (Brit Cncl); Offr Légion d'Honneur (France); *Recreations* music, opera, travel, ski-ing, cooking; *Clubs* Beefsteak; *Style—* Sir Anthony Meyer, Bt, MP; 9 Cottage Place, Brompton Square, London SW3 (☎ 071 589 7416); House of Commons, London SW1A 0AA (☎ 071 219 4343)

MEYER, Christopher John Rome; CMG (1988); s of Flt Lt Reginald Henry Rome Meyer (ka 1944), and Evelyn, *née* Campani (now Mrs Sandy Landells); *b* 22 Feb 1944; *Educ* Lancing, Peterhouse Cambridge (MA), Sch of Advanced Int Studies Bologna; *m* 11 Dec 1976, Francoise Elizabeth, da of Air Cdre Sir Archie Winskill, KCVO, CBE, DFC, AE, of Anchors, Coastal Rd, East Preston, West Sussex; 2 s (James b 21 March 1978, William b 20 June 1984), 1 step s (Thomas (Hedges) b 28 Aug 1972); *Career* Dip Serv: third sec West and Central African Dept FO 1966-67, trg Russian language 1967-68, third (later second) sec Br Embassy Moscow 1968-70, second (later first) sec Madrid 1970-73, first sec E Euro and Soviet Dept FCO 1973-76, first sec planning staff 1976-78, first sec UK rep to Euro Community Brussels 1978-82, cnsllr head of chancery Moscow 1982-84, head news dept and chief FCO spokesman 1984-88; visiting fell Centre for Int Affrs Harvard Univ 1988-89; min (commercial) Washington 1989; *Recreations* squash, reading, music; *Style—* Christopher Meyer, Esq, CMG; c/o FCO, King Charles St, London SW1A 2AH

MEYER, Rt Rev Conrad John Eustace; s of late William Eustace Meyer; *b* 2 July 1922; *Educ* Clifton, Pembroke Coll Cambridge, Westcott House; *m* 1960, Mary, da of late Alec John Wiltshire; *Career* Lt (S) RNVR and later chaplain RNVR; vicar Devoran Truro 1954-64; diocesan: youth chaplain 1956-60, sec for educn 1960-69; hon canon of Truro 1960-69, archdeacon of Bodmin 1969-79, examining chaplain to Bishop of Truro 1973-79, area bishop of Dorchester 1979-87, hon asst bishop Truro Dio 1990, provost of Western Div of the Woodard Schs 1970-; vice pres SPCK 1990- (vice chm 1989-90, chm Appeal Ctee until 1990); *Recreations* civil def (fell (HC) Inst of Civil Def), archaeology, swimming, walking; *Clubs* Royal Cwlth Tst; *Style—* The Rt Rev Conrad Meyer; Hawk's Cliff, 38 Praze Rd, Newquay, Cornwall TR7 3AF (☎ 0637 873003)

MEYER, James Henry Paul; s of late Leo Henry Paul Meyer; *b* 5 Nov 1938; *Educ* Hilton Coll SA, Millfield; *m* 1964, Janet, *née* Baker; 3 c; *Career* chm and md Federated Land Ltd 1959-82; *Recreations* squash, showjumping, flying; *Clubs* RAC; *Style—* James Meyer, Esq; Keston Stud, Downs Lane, Leatherhead, Surrey (☎ 0306 5995)

MEYER, Michael Leverson; s of Percy Barrington Meyer (d 1955), of London, and Eleanor Rachel, *née* Benjamin (d 1929); *b* 11 June 1921; *Educ* Wellington, Christ Church Oxford (MA); 1 da (Nora b 1968); *Career* Operational Res Section Bomber Cmd HQ 1942-45; lectr in Eng lit Uppsala Univ Sweden 1947-50; visiting prof of drama: Dartmouth Coll USA 1978 and Univ of Colorado 1986, The Colorado Coll 1988, Hofstra Univ 1989, UCLA 1991; memb: Ed Advsy Bd Good Food Guide 1958-72; author; FRSL 1971, govr LAMDA 1962-; Gold medal of the Swedish Acad (1964), Knight Cdr of the Order of the Polar Star first class Sweden 1977; *Books* Eight Oxford Poets (ed with Sidney Keyes, and contrib 1941), Collected Poems of Sidney Keyes (ed 1945), The Minos of Crete (by Sidney Keyes, ed 1948), The End of the Corridor (1951), The Ortolan (play, 1967), Henrik Ibsen: The Making of a Dramatist (1967), Henrik Ibsen: The Farewell to Poetry (1971), Henrik Ibsen: The Top of a Cold Mountain (1971, Whitbread Biography prize), Lunatic and Lover (play, 1981), Summer Days (ed 1981), Ibsen on File (1985), Strindberg: a biography (1985), File on Strindberg (1986), Not Prince Hamlet (memoirs, 1989; published as Words Through a Windowpane USA); translated: The Long Ships (by Frans G Bengtsson, 1954) Ibsen Brand (1960), The Lady from the Sea (1960), John Gabriel Borkman (1960), When We Dead Awaken (1960), The Master Builder (1960), Little Eyolf (1961), Ghosts (1962), The Wild Duck (1962), Hedda Gabler (1962), Peer Gynt (1963), An Enemy of the People (1960), The Pillars of Society (1963), The Pretenders (1964), A Doll's House (1965), Rosmersholm (1966), Emperor and Galilean (1986), Strindberg: The Father (1964), Miss Julie (1964), Creditors (1964), The Stronger (1964), Playing with Fire (1964), Erik the Fourteenth (1964), Storm (1964), The Ghost Sonata (1964), A Dream Play (1973), To Damascus (1975), Easter (1975), The Dance of Death (1975), The Virgin Bride (1975), Fragments of a Life (by Hedi Fried, 1990), Master Olaf (1991); *Recreations* real tennis, eating, sleeping; *Clubs* Garrick, Savile, MCC; *Style—* Michael Meyer, Esq; 4 Montagu Sq, London W1H 1RA

MEYER, Montague John; s of late John Mount Montague Meyer, CBE; *b* 18 Dec 1944; *Educ* Cranleigh; *m* 1972, Diana Ruth, da of William Edward Curtis Offer; 2 da; *Career* timber merchant; chief and md Montague L Meyer Ltd 1979-82, dep chm and md Meyer Int plc 1982-84, md MacMillan Bloedel Meyer Ltd 1979-84, dir MacMillan Bloedel Ltd Vancouver BC 1980-82; md MBM Forest Products Ltd 1984-; chm Compass Forest Products Ltd 1985-; *Recreations* sports, reading, charity works; *Clubs* MCC; *Style—* Montague Meyer, Esq; 24 Kensington Park Road, London W11 3BU (☎ 081 299 5303)

MEYER, Peter Barrington; s of Percy Barrington Meyer (d 1955) of London, and Eleanor Rachel, *née* Benjamin (d 1929); *b* 26 May 1916; *Educ* Wellington, Trinity Hall Cambridge (MA, LLB, pres Footlights); *m* 9 Sept 1955, Josephine Rees, da of Arthur William Cadbury Butler, wid of Ian Ernest Colquhan; 1 s (Hugh Barrington b 18 June 1956), 1 da (Catherine Eleanor b 25 Aug 1960); *Career* served WWII Bde Maj Royal Berks Regt 1939-45 (despatches); admitted slr 1947; dir Montague L Meyer plc and other cos 1948-84; pres Timber Trade Fedn 1961-63; chm: British Shippers Cncl 1969-72, Contemporary Art Soc 1971-76; translator of: 7 plays by A de Musset, 3 farces and Better Late by G Feydeau, Professor Taranne by A Adamov, Euzydice by J Anouilh and many other French plays for TV stage and radio; *Recreations* looking at pictures; *Clubs* Beefsteak, Garrick; *Style—* Peter Meyer, Esq; 13 Chelsea Square, London SW3 6LF (☎ 071 351 0531); The Mill House, Sandford St Martin, Oxford OX5 4AQ (☎ 060 883 247)

MEYER, Ronald; s of Frederic Charles Meyer (d 1962), and Sarah Anne, *née* Jackson; *b* 17 Sept 1923; *Educ* Lawrence Sherrif GS Rugby, Rugby Tech Coll; *m* 24 Aug 1946, Dorothy, da of Stanley Charles Whiteman (d 1948), of Rugby; 3 s (Malcolm b 1949, Christopher b 1953, Stephen b 1960); *Career* chartered electrical engr; ptnr McAuslan & Partners 1960-88, dir Parkman Group consltg engrs 1988-; chm IEE (Mersey & N Wales Centre) 1980; memb: CEng, FIEE, MCIBSE, MConsE; *Recreations* gardening, model making, walking; *Style—* Ronald Meyer, Esq; Inglefield Cottage, Mill Rd, Higher Bebington, Wirral (☎ 051 608 7981); Parkman Tooth Davies Ltd, 25 Hamilton Square, Birkenhead, Wirral (☎ 051 647 7711, fax 051 666 2203)

MEYER, Shelagh (aka Shelagh Macdonald); da of Frank Brookesmith, of Broadstairs, Kent, and Marjory, *née* Beale; *b* 20 Dec 1937; *Educ* Brockenhurst High Sch Hants, Northfields-Kimbolton Girls' Sch, Blandford GS Dorset; *m* 1, 1968, late Gilbert H Macdonald; m 2, 1984, Philip Meyer, s of late Isaac Meyer; 1 step s (James Meyer b 1955), 1 step da (Margaret (Mrs Bimbane) b 1951); *Career* advertising copywriter 1956-60, head Copy Gp and assoc dir in various agencies 1960-69, creative dir and company ptnr 1976-84, freelance creative conslt 1984-; novels (as Shelagh Macdonald): A Circle of Stones (1973), Five From Me, Five From You (1974), No End To Yesterday (Whitbread Prize,1977); plays (as Shelagh Meyer): A Small Disturbance (1987), Q (1990); memb PEN 1983; *Recreations* arts, theatre, bird & wild-life, books, food, people, learning demotic Greek, walking, swimming; *Style—* Shelagh Meyer; c/o agent, Mark Lucas, of Peter Fraser Dunlop, 5th Floor, The Chambers, Chelsea Harbour, Lots Rd, London SW10 OXF (☎ 071 376 7676, fax 071 352 7356)

MEYJES, Sir Richard Anthony; DL (Surrey 1983); s of late Anthony Charles Dorian Meyjes; *b* 30 June 1918; *Educ* Univ Coll Sch Hampstead; *m* 1939, Margaret Doreen Morris; 3 s; *Career* served WWII; admitted slr 1946; Shell Petroleum Company: London 1946-58 and 1964-70, Manila 1958-64, mktg coordinator dir and personnel coordinator 1972-76; head Business Team Civil Serv 1970-72; dir: Coates Bros plc 1976-84 (chm 1977-84), Foseco 1976-89 (dep chm 1986-89), Portals Holdings 1976-88; chm Cncl Univ of Surrey 1980-85, vice pres Assoc of Optometrists 1988-; High Sheriff Surrey 1984-85; Master Worshipful Co of Spectacle Makers 1985-87; Hon DUniv Surrey 1988; CBIM, FRSA, FIOD; kt 1972; *Style—* Sir Richard Meyjes, DL; Long Hill House, The Sands, nr Farnham, Surrey GU10 1NQ (☎ 025 18 2601)

MEYNELL, Hon Mrs (Alexandra Rachel Mary Catherine Angelica); *née* Lampson; da of 2 Baron Killearn; *b* 1947; *m* 1966, Nicholas Edward Hugo Meynell; 2 s; *Style—* The Hon Mrs Meynell; Ladysmith Farm, Hoar Cross, Burton-on-Trent, Staffs (☎ 028 375 306)

MEYNELL, Dame Alix Hester Marie (Lady Meynell); DBE (1949); da of late Surgn Cmdr L Kilroy, RN, and late Hester Kilroy; *b* 2 Feb 1903; *Educ* Malvern Girls' Coll, Somerville Coll Oxford; *m* 1946, Sir Francis Meynell, RDI (d 1975); *Career* joined Civil Serv Bd of Trade 1925, seconded as sec Monopolies and Restrictive Practices Cmmn 1949-53, under sec Bd of Trade 1946-55, resigned Civil Serv 1955; barr 1956; md Nonesuch Press Ltd 1976-86; memb: SE Gas Board 1956-69, Harlow New Town Corpn 1956-65, ctees of investigation for England, Scotland and GB under Agric Mktg Acts 1956-65, Monopolies Cmmn 1965-68; *Books* Public Servant, Private Woman; *Style—* Dame Alix Meynell, DBE; The Grey House, Lavenham, Sudbury, Suffolk (☎ 0787 247526)

MEYNELL, Hon Mrs (Elizabeth Margaret); *née* Gretton; yr da of 2 Baron Gretton, OBE; *b* 25 July 1945; *Educ* Downham Sch, Switzerland and Italy; *m* 1968, Christopher Mark, s of Canon Mark Meynell; 2 s (Mark John Henrik, Guy Francis); *Style—* The Hon Mrs Meynell; c/o Stapleford Park, Melton Mowbray, Leics (☎ 057 284 229)

MEYNELL, Godfrey; MBE (1963); s of Capt Godfrey Meynell, VC, MC, QVO (ka 1935), and Sophia Patricia, *née* Lowis; Derbyshire landowners since 12th century; *b* 20 July 1934; *Educ* Eton, Magdalene Coll Cambridge (BA); *m* 11 June 1960, Honor Mary, da of Maj J H A Davis (d 1961); 1 s (Godfrey b 1964), 2 da (Diana Violet b 1962, Katharine Jill b 1966); *Career* HM Overseas Civil Serv, asst advsr W Aden Protectorate; Home Civil Serv 1968-, regnl controller (Housing) DOE E Midlands Region; High Sheriff of Derbyshire 1982-83; *Recreations* forestry, conservation; *Style—* Godfrey Meynell, Esq, MBE; Meynell Langley, Derby DE6 4NT (☎ 033 124 207); c/o Dept of Environment, Cranbrook House, Nottingham

MEYNELL, Hugh Bernard; s of Cuthbert Charles Meynell (d 1973), and Irene Mary, *née* Hickman; *b* 7 Jan 1931; *Educ* Ampleforth, Columbia Univ NY; *m* 23 June 1956, Paula Faine, da of Paul Ellis Gibbons (d 1972); 1 s (Edward James b 15 Dec 1959), 1 da (Rosemary Jane (Mrs Macmillan- Douglas) b 11 Oct 1957); *Career* Nat Serv 2 Lt RA 1949-51; chm Meynell Valves Ltd Wolverhampton 1978-88, dir S Staffs Water Co 1982-, chm Dynafluid 1988-; pres Boys Bde Wolverhampton; Freeman: City of London 1985, Worshipful Co of Plumbers 1985; MInstM 1976, memb Inst Sales Mgmnt 1979; *Recreations* shooting, cricket, tennis; *Clubs* MCC; *Style—* Hugh Meynell, Esq; Brockton Court, nr Shifnal, Shropshire TF11 9LZ (☎ 095271 247); Dynafluid Ltd, Hortonwood 33, Telford TF1 4EX (fax 0952 677738)

MEYNELL, Hugo Ivo; s of Lt-Col Hugo Francis Meynell, OBE (d 1974), and Doris Isabel, *née* Morrison; *b* 23 Nov 1931; *Educ* Stowe, RMA Sandhurst; *m* 1, 1961, Sarah Virginia, da of Gen Sir Richard McCreery, GCB, KBE, DSO, MC (d 1967); 2 s (Luke Hugo b 1964, Alexander Michael b 1966), 1 da (Lucia Anna b 1968); m 2, 1985, Audrey Tennant, da of George Henderson (d 1968); *Career* joined 12 Royal Lancers (POW) 1952, Malaya 1952-54, Capt 1955, Suez Landing 1956 (despatches 1957), WO 1960-62; The Economist Newspaper 1963 (dep md 1973, dir 1978), md The Economist Publications 1984-90; memb Cncl Buckingham Univ 1980; *Recreations* country pursuits; *Clubs* Cavalry and Guards; *Style—* Hugo I Meynell, Esq; 38 Halsey St, London SW3 (☎ 071 589 5014); The Old Manor House, Whichford, Shipston on Stour, Warwickshire (☎ 060 884 293); The Economist Newspaper Ltd, 25 St James's St, London SW1A 1HG (☎ 071 839 7000, fax 071 839 2968, telex 24344)

MEYNELL, James Hack Tuke; s of Wilfred A F Meynell, and Marion Meynell (d 1986); *b* 21 April 1940; *Educ* Felsted, Stanford Univ USA (BSc); *m* 1966, Susan Glyn, *née* Prinsep; 2 s (Nicholas b 1969, Lucian b 1971), 1 da (Charlotte b 1976); *Career* conslt: PE Consulting Group 1964-66, The Economist Intelligence Unit 1970-72; prodn mangr Cadbury Schweppes 1966-70, corp fin dir Singer & Friendlander 1973-89; dir: Panmure Gordon Bankers (formerly North Carolina National Bank) 1980-89, Panmure Gordon & Co Ltd 1980-89; currently dir: Third Grosvenor Ltd, Cardiac Controls Inc; non-exec dir Wentworth International Group plc, non-exec chm Southwest Resources plc 1988-; *Recreations* tennis, music, gardening, bridge, book collecting; *Clubs* Queen's; *Style—* James Meynell, Esq; 4 Bolingbroke Grove, London SW11 6ES (☎ 081 673 5606); Wentworth International Group plc, Wentworth Gate, 36 High St, Wimbledon, London SW19 5BY (☎ 081 944 1991)

MEYRIC HUGHES, Henry Andrew Carne; s of Reginald Richard Meyric Hughes (d 1961), and Jean Mary Carne Brooke, *née* Pratt; *b* 1 April 1942; *Educ* Shrewsbury Sch,

Univ of Rennes, Univ of Munich, Univ of Oxford (BA), Univ of Sussex (MA); *m* 3 Aug 1968, Alison Hamilton, da of David Bruce Faulds (d 1976), of Chester; 1 s (Sam b 1975), 1 da (Henrietta b 1971); *Career* Br Cncl: asst regnl dir W Berlin 1968-71, asst rep Lima Peru 1971-73, asst rep Paris France 1973-77, asst dir Fine Arts Dept and curator of the Cncl's Collection 1977-79, dir N Italy Milan 1979-84, dir Visiting Arts Office GB and NI 1984-86, dir Fine Arts Dept (now Visual Arts Dept) 1986-; Br Cmmnr Venice Biennale 1986; author of numerous catalogues and articles on visual arts and cultural policy and translator of related topics from German, French and Italian; observer Arts Panel Arts Cncl of GB and Scottish Arts Cncl 1986-, memb Ct RCA 1986, dir Riverside Tst 1987-, pres Br Branch Int Assoc of Art Critics 1988-; memb: Turner Prize Jury London 1988, Art Advsy Gp South Bank Centre 1988-, Slade Ctee, Advsy Bd Academia Italiana London 1988-, Advsy Bd London Contemporary Art Fair 1988-, Faculty of Fine Art Br Sch at Rome (Academia Britannica) 1988-; senator Academia Italiana Florence Italy 1983-, silver medal Czechoslovakia Soc for Int Cultural Relations 1986; FRSA 1988; *Recreations* music; *Clubs* Groucho, Chelsea Arts; *Style*— Henry Meyric Hughes, Esq; 13 Ashchurch Grove, London W12 (☎ 081 749 5808); Visual Arts Department, The British Council, 11 Portland Place, London W1N 4EJ (☎ 071 930 8466, telex 895 2201 BRICON G, fax 071 493 5035)

MEYRICK; *see*: Tapps-Gervis-Meyrick

MEYRICK, Sir David John Charlton; 4 Bt (UK 1880), of Bush, Pembrokeshire; s of Col Sir Thomas Frederick Meyrick, 3 Bt, TD, DL (d 1983), and his 1 w, Ivy Frances, *née* Pilkington (d 1947); *b* 2 Dec 1926; *Educ* Eton, Trinity Hall Cambridge (MA); *m* 29 Sept 1962, Penelope Anne, da of Cdr John Bertram Aubrey Marsden-Smedley, RN (d 1959); 3 s; *Heir* s, Timothy Thomas Charlton; *Career* chartered surveyor and land agent; *Recreations* riding, sailing; *Style*— Sir David Meyrick, Bt; Bush House, Gumfreston, Tenby, Dyfed SA70 8RA

MEYRICK, Dr Roger Llewellyn; JP(1971-); s of Thidal Francis Meyrick (d 1965), of Swansea, and Helen Viviene, *née* Jones (d 1979); *b* 31 March 1930; *Educ* Dulwich Coll, King's Coll London, King's Coll Hosp Univ of London (MB BS); *m* 6 March 1954, Barbara Treseder, da of Reginald George Coombs (d 1974), of Stroud, Gloucs; 1 s (Huw b 1 Jan 1966), 3 da (Olivia b 1 March 1955, Daryl b 28 April 1956, Clare b 16 Dec 1958); *Career* princ in gen med practice Lewisham London 1954-90, hosp practitioner in dermatology Lewisham Hosp 1972-90, facilitator in gen practice Lewisham and N Southwark 1988-90; RCGP: chm S London Faculty 1969-72, provost S London Faculty 1977-80; pres W Kent Medicochirurgical Soc 1972-73; chm Magistrates Assoc SE London 1987-; Freeman City of London 1970, Liveryman Worshipful Soc of Apothecaries 1970; MRCS, LRCP, FRCGP, FRSM 1967, memb BMA 1954; *Books* Understanding Cancer (ed jtly, 1977), Principles of Practice Management (contrib, 1984), Patient Health Education; *Recreations* local medical history, gardening; *Clubs* Royal Cwlth Soc; *Style*— Dr Roger Meyrick, JP; Boulters Tor, Smeardon Down, Peter Tavy, nr Tavistock, Devon PL19 9NX (☎ 0822 810525)

MEYRICK, Timothy Thomas Charlton; s and h of Sir David Meyrick, 4 Bt; *b* 5 Nov 1963; *Educ* Eton, Bristol Univ; *Style*— Timothy Meyrick, Esq; c/o Bush House, Gumfreston, Tenby, Dyfed

MEYSEY-THOMPSON, Sir (Humphrey) Simon; 4 Bt (UK 1874), of Kirby Hall, Yorkshire; s of Guy Herbert Meysey-Thompson (d 1961), and kinsman of Sir Algar de Clifford Charles Meysey-Thompson, 3 Bt (d 1967); *b* 31 March 1935; *Style*— Sir Simon Meysey-Thompson, Bt; 10 Church St, Woodbridge, Suffolk (☎ 0394 382144)

MIALL, (Rowland) Leonard; OBE (1961); s of Rowland Miall (d 1955), of Lastingham, Yorks, and Sara Grace, *née* Dixon (d 1975); *b* 6 Nov 1914; *Educ* Bootham Sch York, Freiburg Univ, St John's Coll Cambridge; *m* 1, 18 Jan 1941, Lorna Barbara (d 1974), da of George Rackham (d 1974), of Bucks; 3 s (Roger b 1944, Tristram b 1947, St John b 1952), 1 da (Virginia b 1948); m 2, 10 Oct 1975, Sally Greenaway Bicknell, da of Gordon Leith (d 1965), of Johannesburg; *Career* pres Cambridge Union 1936, ed Cambridge Review 1936, lectured in USA 1937, sec Br-American Assoc 1937-39, joined BBC inaugurated talks broadcast to Europe 1939, German talks and features ed 1940-42, memb Br Political Warfare Mission to US 1942-44 (dir of news San Francisco 1943, head NY Office 1944), personal asst to Dep DG Political Warfare Exec 1944, attached to Psychological Warfare Div of SHAEF 1945; BBC: special corr Czechoslovakia 1945, actg dip corr 1945, chief corr in US 1945-53, head of TV Talks 1954, asst controller of Current Affrs and Talks TV 1961, special asst to dir of TV planning start of BBC-2 1962, asst controller of Programme Servs TV 1963-66, rep in USA 1966-71, controller of Overseas and Foreign Rels 1971-74; res historian 1975-84, inaugurated BBC lunchtime lectrs 1962, advsr Ctee on Broadcasting New Delhi 1965, fndr Cwlth Bdcasting Assoc 1975, dir Visnews Ltd 1976-, dep chm BAFTA 1984-85 (overseas dir 1974-), memb Cncl Royal TV Soc 1984-; Fell RTS 1985, FRSA; Certificate of Appreciation NYC 1970; ed Richard Dimbleby Broadcaster 1966; contrib to: DNB, The Independent; *Recreations* travel, gardening; *Clubs* Garrick, Union (Cambridge); *Style*— Leonard Miall, Esq, OBE; Maryfield Cottage, High St, Taplow Village, Maidenhead SL6 0EX (☎ 0628 604195)

MICHAEL, Prof Christopher; s of David Parry Martin Michael, CBE (d 1986), of Newport, and Mary Horner, *née* Hayward; *b* 29 May 1942; *Educ* Jesus Coll Oxford (MA, DPhil); *m* 1964, Marilyn; 2 s (Nicholas b 1964, David b 1967); *Career* staff memb Theory Div CERN Geneva 1969-74, prof of theoretical physics Univ of Liverpool 1974-; FInstP 1976; *Publications* numerous res articles on theoretical high energy physics; *Recreations* underwater hockey, sub aqua diving; *Style*— Prof Christopher Michael; DAMTP, University of Liverpool, Liverpool L69 3BX (☎ 051 794 3771, fax 051 708 6502, telex 627095 UNILPL G)

MICHAEL, Kathryn Jean; da of Charles Godfree Nairn (d 1961), of Harley St, London, and Kaye, *née* Davey; *b* 20 Sept 1941; *Educ* Malvern, Marymount Coll Barcelona Spain; *m* 5 March 1976, Louis Sydney (Bill) Michael, OBE; *Career* Unilever Ltd 1967-69, BBDO Ltd 1969-71, Lint Ltd 1971-78, dir Ogilvy & Mather Ltd 1978-; memb Womens Advtg Club of London (pres 1977-78); MIPA 1976; *Recreations* friends and flowers; *Clubs* RAC; *Style*— Mrs Kathryn Michael; 53 Holland Park, London W11 3RS; Ogilvy & Mather Ltd, Brettenham House, Lancaster Place, London WC2 (☎ 071 836 2466)

MICHAEL, (Elizabeth) Rosemary; da of The Rev Ernest Stanley Rees Mackay Michael (d 1984), and Elizabeth Felicia, *née* Powell; *b* 1 Aug 1939; *Educ* King Alfred Sch; *Career* PA to Dir of Educn Advertising Assoc 1965-68, promotions and events organiser The Sunday Times 1968-74, exec asst to md Thomson Organisation 1974-76, dir of courses and seminars CAM 1976-86 then Advertising Assoc 1986- (CAM courses and seminars transferred to Advertising Assoc 1986); advertising woman of the year (Adwoman Assoc) 1982; *Style*— Miss Rosemary Michael; Advertising Association, Abford House, 15 Wilton Rd, London SW1V 1NJ (☎ 071 828 2771, fax 071 931 0376)

MICHAEL, Simon Laurence; s of Anthony Denis Michael, of London, and Regina, *née* Milstone; *b* 4 Jan 1955; *Educ* Kings Coll London (LLB); *m* 7 Sept 1987, Elaine Laura, da of Cameron Hudson Duncan (d 1983); 1 s (Alastair b 1990), 1 da (Kay b 1988); *Career* called to the Bar Middle Temple 1978; *Books* The Usurper (jtly, 1988), The Cut Throat (1989), The Long Lie (1991); *Style*— Simon Michael, Esq; Francis Taylor Building, Temple, London EC4Y 7BY (☎ 071 353 9942, fax 01 353 9924)

MICHAEL, Dr William Francis; s of Dr Stephen Ernest Michael (d 1971), of Croydon, and Dr Janet Michael, *née* Young; *b* 22 June 1936; *Educ* Winchester, New Coll Oxford (MA, DM); *m* 27 May 1972, Mary Ann, da of Bernard Sadler (d 1982), of Reading; 2 da (Victoria b 1974, Juliet b 1977); *Career* Nat Serv, 2 Lt RA 1955-56; jr med appts: St Thomas's Hosp, National Hosp 1967-70, Bart's 1970-74; conslt neurologist SE Thames Regnl Neurological Unit 1974-; memb: Assoc of Br Neurologists 1974, RSM; FRCP 1981; *Recreations* music, books, gardening, skiing; *Style*— Dr William Michael

MICHAELS, Amanda Louise; da of Leonard Julian Michaels, of Hampstead, and Ruth Gertrude, *née* Sugar; *b* 27 Nov 1955; *Educ* Queen Elizabeth's GS, Univ of Durham (BA), Coll of Europe Bruges (MA); *m* 19 Sept 1986, Dennis Nigel Sharpe, s of Michael Sharpe; *Career* called to the Bar Gray's Inn 1981; *Books* A Practical Guide to Trade Marks (1981); *Recreations* music, travel, food; *Clubs* RAC; *Style*— Miss Amanda Michaels; 5 New Square, Lincoln's Inn, London WC2A 3RJ (☎ 071 404 0404, fax 071 831 6016)

MICHAELS, Prof Leslie; s of Henry Michaels (d 1979), of Nottingham, and Minnie Michaels (d 1982); *b* 24 July 1925; *Educ* Parmiter's Sch London, Westminster Hosp Med Sch Univ of London (MB BS, MD); *m* 21 Sept 1951, Edith, da of Friedrich Waldstein (d 1943); 2 da; *Career* house appts Westminster Hosp 1949-50, trg in pathology Univ of Bristol and Univ of Manchester 1953-57, lectr in pathology St Marys Hosp Med Sch London 1957-59, asst prof Albert Einstein Coll of Med 1959-61, prov pathologist Northern Ontario Canada 1961-69, prof of pathology Inst of Laryngology 1973-90 (sr lectr in pathology 1970-73), prof emeritus Univ of London; FRCPath 1973; *Books* Pathology of the Larynx (1984), Ear, Nose and Throat Histopathology (1987), Atlas of Ear, Nose and Throat Pathology (1990); *Recreations* music, walking; *Style*— Prof Leslie Michaels

MICHAELS, Robert Stewart John; s of Alexander Michaels, of Stanmore, and Evelyn, *née* Susman; *b* 20 Dec 1941; *Educ* Ravensfield Coll Orange Hill, St Martins Sch of Art, Université D'aix En Provence; *m* 19 June 1966, Marilyn, da of Edward Lee; 2 s (Mark John Louis b 4 Oct 1972, Daniel David b 19 Sept 1977); *Career* chm and md Robert Michaels Holdings Ltd 1974-; dir: Mardan Properties Ltd, John Crowther plc 1987, Robert Mark Ltd, Marongate Ltd; tstee Bryanston Tst, underwriting memb Lloyd's, memb Permanent Panel Nat Econ Devpt Office, retailer Garment Mfrs Panel, Cons Cncllr Knightsbridge Ward, dir Westminster Enterprise Agency; Freeman City of London 1979, life memb Guild of Freemen City of London; Liveryman Worshipful Cos: Horners, Farriers, Patternmakers; FInstD 1980; *Recreations* family, reading, tennis, skiing, cricket, racing cars; *Clubs* Annabels, Harry's Bar, Queens, RAC, Ferrari Owners; *Style*— Robert Michaels, Esq; Robert Michaels Holdings Ltd, 12 Great Portland St, London W1N 6JQ (☎ 071 580 1656, fax 071 706 4690)

MICHEL, Keith; s of Capt George Richard Michel, of Thatchdale, Pennymead Drive, E Horsley, Surrey, and Winifred Eve Michel (d 1972); *b* 19 May 1948; *Educ* Bradfield Coll, Fitzwilliam Coll Cambridge (MA, football blue 1968-70, Oxbridge rep team Japan 1969); *m* 16 Dec 1972, Rosemary Suzannah, da of Stanley Joseph Simons, of Southgate, London; 1 s (Edward b 30 April 1980); *Career* slr; articled clerk Coward Chance (now Clifford Chance) 1971-73, asst slr Clyde & Co 1973-75, ptnr Holman Fenwick & Willan 1975- (former asst slr); author of various pubns incl: Lloyd's List, Lloyd's Maritime Commercial Law Quarterly, Law Society's Gazette; memb: Grasshoppers CC, Free Foresters CC, Old Bradfieldion FC, Cncl AFA; tstee Univ of Cambridge FC, clerk to Bd of Govrs Bradfield Coll; memb: Law Soc 1973, City of London Solicitors Co 1990; *Books* Contraband (1988); *Recreations* family life, football, cricket, wind surfing, history, archaeology, wildlife conservation; *Clubs* Hawks; *Style*— Keith Michel, Esq; Marlow House, Lloyds Ave, London EC3N 3AL (☎ 071 488 2300, fax 071 481 0316, telex 8812247 HFW LON)

MICHELL, Keith Joseph; s of Joseph Michell (d 1957), and Alice Maude Alsat (d 1957); *b* 1 Dec 1928; *Educ* Warnertown Sch, Port Pirie HS, SA Sch of Arts and Crafts, Adelaide Teachers Coll, Adelaide Univ, Old Vic Theatre Sch; *m* 1957, Jeannette Laura, da of Frank Sterk (d 1985); 1 s (Paul b 1960), 1 da (Helena b 1961); *Career* artist and actor; memb original Young Vic Theatre Co, first appearance London And so to Bed 1951; leading actor Shakespeare Meml Theatre Co 1952-56: Twelfth Night (Orsino), Macbeth (Macduff), Henry IV (Hotspur), As you like it (Orlando), The Taming of the Shrew (Petruchio), A Midsummer Night's Dream (Theseus); Old Vic (joined 1956): Much Ado about Nothing (Benedick), Anthony & Cleopatra (Anthony), Two Gentlmen of Verona (Proteus); starred in musicals: Irma la Douce (Oscar/Nestor) London and New York 1958-61, Robert and Elizabeth (Robert) London 1964, Man of La Mancha (Don Quixote) London and New York 1968-69, On the 20th Century (Oscar) London 1980, La Cage aux Folles (Georges) San Francisco, New York, Sydney and Melbourne 1985-86; artistic dir Chichester Festival Theatre 1974-; plays incl: The Chances (Don John) Chichester 1962 and London 1966, The Rehearsal New York 1963, King Mare (Henry VIII), Hamlet (Hamlet) London 1972, Abelard and Heloise (Abelard) London and New York 1972, Dear Love (Robert) London 1973, Oedipus Tyrannus (Oedipus), Cyrano de Bergerac (Cyrano), Crucifer of Blood (Sherlock Holmes) London 1979, Othello (Iago and Othello), Twelfth Night (dir and designer), Murder in the Cathedral (Beckett), The Apple Cart (Magnus), Pete McGynty and the Dream Time (Pete McGynty) with Melbourne Theatre Co 1981, On the Rocks (Sir Arthur) Chichester 1982, The Tempest (Prospero) Queensland 1982, Jane Eyre (Rochester) Chichester 1986, Portraits (Augustus John) Malvern and London 1987, Royal Baccarat Scandal (Gordon-Cumming) Chichester 1988 and London 1989; took Chichester Co to Aust with Othello and The Apple Cart 1977; appearances in 8 films, TV and video; many classical prodns: Pygmalion, Mayerling, Wuthering Heights, Ring Round the Moon, An Ideal Husband, Julius Caesar, Anthony and Cleopatra, Six Wives of Henry VIII, Capt Beaky and his Band, Capt Beaky Vol 2, Pirates of Penzance (Maj-Gen), The Gondoliers, Ruddigore (Robin Oakapple), Capt Cook (Cook); records: Ancient and Modern, At the Shows, Words Words Words, Capt Beaky and his Band; one man painting shows: Jamaica 1960, New York 1963, Portugal 1963, Don Quixote 1970, Hamlet 1972, Shakespeare Sonnets (Lithographs) 1975, Capt Beaky 1982; writer and illustrator Practically Macrobiotic Cook Book (1987); Best Musical Actor London Critics 1968, Best Actor Soc of Films and TV Arts 1970, Show Business Personality 1971, Top Actor (SUN) 1971, Special Award Variety Club 1971, Outstanding Actor Performance Emmy Award Nat Acad of TV Arts 1971, Br Film Award 1973, Logie Award 1974; *Recreations* gardening, reading; *Style*— Keith J Michell, Esq; c/o Jean Diamond, London Management Ltd, 235 Regent St, London W1

MICHELL, Prof Robert Hall (Bob); s of Rowland Charles Michell, of 7 Peterson Ct, Worcester Rd, Gt Malvern Worcs WR14 4QW, and Elsie Lorna, *née* Hall; *b* 16 April 1941; *Educ* Crewkerne Sch Somerset, Univ of Birmingham (BSc, PhD, DSc); *m* 13 Jan 1967 (m dis 1971), June Mary; 1 s (Jo b 1974), 1 da (Naomi b 1986); *Career* Harvard Med Sch 1966-68; Univ of Birmingham: res fell 1965-66 and 1968-70, lectr 1970-81, sr lectr 1981-84, reader in biochemistry 1984-86, prof 1986-87, Royal Soc res prof 1987-; memb Ed Bd: Journal of Neurochemistry 1974-78, Cell Calcium 1979-, Biochemical Journal 1982-88 (ed Advsy Panel 1981-82), Current Opinion in Cell

Biology 1988-, Biological Sciences Review 1988-, Proceedings of The Royal Society of London 1989; fndn lectr RC Path, Bertram Lewis Abrahams lectr RCP 1990, Wellcome visiting prof Univ of Vermont; Burlington 1987 memb: Biochemical Soc (CIBA medal 1988), Br Nat Ctee for Pharmacology 1982-87, Br Nat Ctee for biochemistry 1988-89, Physiological Systems and Disorders Res Bd MRC 1985-90, Brain Res Assoc, Br Soc for Cell Biology, Br Assoc for the Advancement of Sci; chm Systems Bd Grants Ctee MRC 1988-90; FRS 1986; *Books* Membranes And Their Cellular Functions (with J B Finean and R Coleman, 1974), New Comprehensive Biochemistry (contrib ed with J B Finean, 1981), Cell Calcium (contrib ed, 1982), Inositol Lipids in Cellular Signalling (ed with J W Putney, 1987), Inositol Lipids and Transmembrane Signalling (ed with M J Berridge, 1988), Inositol Lipids and Cellular Signalling (ed with A H Drummond and C P Downes, 1989); *Style—* Prof Robert Michell; School of Biochemistry, University of Birmingham, PO Box 363, Birmingham B15 2TT (☎ 021 414 5413, fax 021 414 3982)

MICHELL, Roger; s of H D Michell, and J Michell, *née* Green; *b* 5 June 1956; *Educ* Clifton Coll, Queen's Coll Cambridge (exhibitioner, BA); *Career* director; Brighton Actor's Workshop 1977, Thames TV training bursary Royal Ct 1978-80, RSC 1984-90, Drama Director's Course BBC TV 1990; theatre incl: The Catch (Royal Ct), The Key Tag (Royal Ct), Private Dick (Edinburgh Festival, Lyric), Marya (Old Vic); RSC: Temptation, The Dead Monkey, Restoration, Some Americans Abroad, Two Shakespearean Actors, The Constant Couple, Hamlet, Merchant of Venice; Judith E Wilson sr fell Trinity Coll Cambridge 1989; Buzz Goodbody award RSC 1977, Edinburgh Fringe First award 1977, Drama Desk nomination NY 1990; *Style—* Roger Michell, Esq; Royal Shakespeare Company, Barbican, London EC2 (☎ 071 628 3351)

MICHELMORE, Clifford Arthur (Cliff); CBE (1969); s of (Albert) Herbert Michelmore (d 1921), of Cowes, IOW, and Ellen, *née* Alford (d 1947); *b* 11 Dec 1919; *Educ* Cowes HS, RAF Coll, Leicester Coll of Technol; *m* 4 March 1950, Jean, da of Guy Vivian Metcalfe (d 1962), of Reigate, Surrey; 1 s (Guy Alford *qv* b 1957), 1 da (Jenny Gwen b 1959); *Career* RAF 1935-47; Br Forces Network 1947; BBC 1950: Tonight, 24 Hrs, Holiday; Home on Sunday 1984-; md: RMEMI 1970-80, Michelmore Enterprises 1967-, CP Video 1987-; *Books* Businessman's Book of Golf (1981), Holidays in Britain (1986), Two-Way Story (with Jean Metcalfe, 1987); *Recreations* golf, sailing; *Clubs* Garrick, RAF, Walton Heath; *Style—* Cliff Michelmore, Esq, CBE; White House, Upper West St, Reigate RH2 9BU (☎ 0737 245014); Brookfield, Bembridge, IOW PO3 5XW (☎ 09837 2480)

MICHELMORE, Guy Alford; s of Cliff Michelmore, CBE, of Reigate, Surrey, and Jean Metcalfe; *b* 27 Aug 1957; *Educ* St John's Sch Leatherhead, Pembroke Coll Oxford (MA); *m* 12 March 1988, Agnieszka, da of Eugeniusz Piotrowski, of Sopot, Poland; 1 s (Leo Arthur b 26 Dec 1990); *Career* reporter Anglia TV 1981-83, presenter London Plus 1984-85, reporter and presenter BBC Breakfast Time 1985-87 (reporter 1983-84), reporter A Fair Cop (series of police complaints documentaries) 1987-88, presenter Weekend 1988, reporter Friday Report (documentary) 1988-89, main presenter Newsroom South East 1989-; section offr Surrey Special Constabulary 1976-88; *Recreations* writing music, watching birds; *Style—* Guy Michelmore, Esq; BBC Centre, Boreham Wood, Herts WD6 1JF (☎ 081 207 8888, fax 081 207 8765)

MICHELMORE, Col James Franck Godwin; TD (1956, with two clasps), DL (Devon 1973-); s of Sir Godwin Michelmore, KBE, CB, DSO (d 1982) of Exeter, and Margaret Phoebe, *née* Newbolt (d 1965); family in S Devon from 1334 at least, documents from 1570; *b* 15 Feb 1924; *Educ* Rugby, Balliol Coll Oxford (BA, MA); *m* 19 Sept 1953, June Elizabeth, da of Bernard Shaw Harvey (d 1973) of Mylor, Cornwall; 2 s (Robert b 1957, William b 1959), 1 da ((Elizabeth) Kate b 1956); *Career* serv 6 Regt RHA 1943-46 (India 1945-46); Royal Devon Yeo RA (TA) 1947-66, CO 1962-66, Col SW Dist 1967-73, ADC (TA) to HM The Queen 1970-75; chm Devon TAVRA 1974-83; slr 1950, registrar Diocese of Exeter, Consistory Ct and legal sec to Bishops 1963-; played hockey for Devon 1947-57 and W of England 1954; govr St Lukes Coll Exeter 1974-77; chm: Ecclesiastical Law Assoc 1978-81; *Recreations* fishing, walking, gardening; *Clubs* Army and Navy; *Style—* Col James Michelmore, TD; Westhay, Streatham Rise, Exeter EX4 4PE (☎ 0392 73525); 18 Cathedral Yard, Exeter (☎ 0392 436244)

MICHELMORE, Richard Alfred; s of George Walter Michelmore (d 1956), of 16 Garrick Close, Walton on Thames, Surrey, and Mildred, *née* Cooper (d 1977); *b* 24 May 1928; *Educ* Kings Coll Sch Wimbledon, Univ of London; *m* 6 May 1967, Margaret Lilian, da of William Lawrence Horn (d 1983), of 12 St Pauls Way, Finchley, London N3; 1 s (Paul b 1971), 2 da (Ruth b 1968, Jane b 1974); *Career* artist with David Bomberg Messiah Tate Gallery 1953; borough architect Hammersmith 1970-77 (Lyric Theatre), special works architect GLC 1977-85 (restoration of Covent Garden Market, Thames Barrier), fndr Richard Michelmore Artist Architect Town Planner 1986 (designed houses in Dorset and painted pictures on cmmn); methodist preacher; Freeman Worshipful Co of Constructors 1975; RIBA 1958, MRTPI 1970; *Style—* Richard Michelmore, Esq; Studio One, Heathfield, 3 Holden Ave, Woodside Park, London N12 (☎ 081 346 4005)

MICHIE, Alastair John; s of John Michie (d 1965), of Alyth, Pethshire, and Margaret, *née* Heggie; *b* 21 March 1948; *Educ* Blairgowrie HS Pertshire; *m* 28 July 1971, Dawn Elizabeth, da of James Edward Thomson Wittet, of Alyth, Perthshire; 1 s (Graham James b 1980), 1 da (Caroline Jane b 1975); *Career* Clydesdale Bank plc 1964-74; co sec: Lloyds Bank Int Ltd 1981-85 (asst sec 1978-80), Lloyds Bank Plc 1985-; memb AIB (Scotland) 1969, FCIS 1981; *Recreations* golf, squash, swimming; *Style—* Alastair Michie, Esq; 14 Marlyns Close, Burpham, Guildford, Surrey GU4 7LR (☎ 0483 359 75); Lloyds Bank Plc, 71 Lombard St, London EC3P 3BS (☎ 071 626 1500, fax 071 929 2901)

MICHIE, David Alan Redpath; s of James Beattie Michie (d 1959), and Anne Redpath, OBE (d 1965); *b* 30 Nov 1928; *Educ* Hawick HS, Edinburgh Coll of Art (DA); *m* 27 March 1951, Eileen Anderson, James Michie (d 1931); 2 da (Alison b 1953, Lindsey b 1955); *Career* Nat Serv RA 1947-49; lectr in drawing and painting Grays Sch of Art Aberdeen 1957-61; Edinburgh Coll of Art: lectr 1961-74, vice princ 1974-77, head of sch of drawing and painting 1982-90, prof of drawing and painting 1988-; solo exhibitions: Mercury Gallery London 1983 (1966, 1969, 1971, 1974, 1980), Lothian Region Chambers 1977, Scot Gallery Edinburgh 1980, Mercury Gallery Edinburgh 1986; RSA 1972, memb RGI 1986, FRSA 1990; *Recreations* music; *Style—* David Michie, Esq; 17 Gilmour Rd, Edinburgh EH16 5NS (☎ 031 667 2684)

MICHIE, Prof Donald; s of James Kilgour Michie (d 1967), and Marjorie Crain, *née* Pfeiffer (d 1986); *b* 11 Nov 1923; *Educ* Rugby, Balliol Coll Oxford (MA, DPhil, DSc); *m* 1, 1949 (m dis 1951), Zena Margaret, *née* Davies; 1 s (Christopher b 1950); m 2, 1952 (m dis 1958), Anne, *née* McLaren; 1 s (Jonathan), 2 da (Susan, Caroline); m 3, 1971, Jean Elizabeth *née* Crouch; *Career* WWII, FO Bletchley 1942-45; res assoc Univ of London 1952-58, personal chair of machine intelligence Univ of Edinburgh 1967-84 (sr lectr in surgical sci 1958-62, reader 1962-65, dir experimental programming unit 1963-73, head of machine intelligence res unit 1974-84), chief scientist Turing Inst 1986- (dir of res 1984-86); FZS 1953, FRSE 1969, FBCS 1971; *Books* Machine Intelligence and Related Topics (1982), The Creative Computer (with Rory Johnston, 1984), On Machine Intelligence (2 edn, 1986); *Recreations* chess, travel; *Clubs* New (Edinburgh), Athenaeum; *Style—* Prof Donald Michie; 6 Inveralmond Grove, Cramond, Edinburgh EH4 6RA, (☎ 031 336 3826); The Turing Institute, George House, 36 North Hanover St, Glasgow G1 2AD, Scotland, UK, (☎ 041 552 6400, fax 041 552 2985)

MICHIE, Ian Stuart; s of James Kilgour Michie (d 1967), and Marjorie Crain Pfeiffer (d 1986); *b* 4 Jan 1929; *Educ* Marlborough, Harvard Business Sch Advanced Mgmnt Program; *m* 16 June 1966, Maria Teresa, da of Franklin August Reece (d 1968), of Mass; *Career* investmt banker; dir Kleinwort Benson Ltd 1972-74, md Brandts Ltd 1974-75; Liveryman Worshipful Co of Gunmakers; *Recreations* shooting, fishing, stalking, golf, skiing; *Clubs* Cavalry and Guards, Huntercombe Golf, Seniors Golfing Soc, Pilgrims, Green Jackets Golfing Soc; *Style—* Ian S Michie, Esq; 12 Cheyne Gardens, London SW3 5QT (☎ 071 352 9108); Fiduciary Trust (International) SA, 30 Old Burlington Street, London W1X 1LB (☎ 071 439 8946)

MICHIE, Hon Mrs (Janet Ray); *née* Bannerman; MP (Lib) Argyll and Bute 1987-; er da of Baron Bannerman of Kildonan, OBE (Life Peer; d 1969), and Ray, *née* Mundell; *b* 4 Feb 1934; *Educ* Aberdeen HS for Girls, Lansdowne House Sch Edinburgh, Edinburgh Sch of Speech Therapy; *m* 1957, Lt-Col Iain Michie; 3 da; *Career* former area speech therapist Argyll & Clyde Health Bd; MCST; *Style—* The Hon Mrs Michie, MP; House of Commons, London SW1A 0AA

MICHIE, William (Bill); MP (Lab) Sheffield, Heeley 1983-; s of Arthur Michie, and Violet Michie; *b* 24 Nov 1935; *Educ* Secdy Mod Sch; *m* 1987, Judith Ann; 2 s; *Career* shop steward, electrician; *Recreations* darts, soccer; *Clubs* WMC Affiliated; *Style—* Bill Michie, Esq, MP; House of Commons, London SW1

MICKLEM, Prof Henry Spedding; s of Rev Edward Romilly Micklem (d 1960) of Oxford, and Phyllis Winifred, *née* Benham (d 1985); *b* 11 Oct 1933; *Educ* Rugby, Oriel Coll Oxford (MA, DPhil); *m* 21 June 1958, Lisel Ruth (1990), da of William Edgar Wenallt Thomas, MBE (d 1963), of Stroud; 3 s (Thomas b 1963, James b 1965, David b 1967), 1 da (Naomi b 1961); *Career* scientific staff MRC 1957-66; Univ of Edinburgh: lectr 1966-72, reader 1972-88, prof of immunobiology 1988-; visiting fell: Pasteur Inst Paris 1963-64, NY Univ Med Center 1988; visiting prof Stanford Univ 1978-79, author of papers in various scientific jls; memb Scientific Advsy Ctee The Melville Tst 1987-; *Books* Tissue Grafting and Radiation (with JF Loutit, 1966); *Recreations* music; *Style—* Prof Henry Micklem; 1 Dryden Place, Edinburgh EH9 1RP (☎ 031 667 5618); Division of Biological Sciences, University of Edinburgh, Edinburgh EH9 3JT (☎ 031 650 5496, fax 031 667 3210, telex 727442)

MICKLETHWAIT, Richard Miles; o s of Richard Gerald Micklethwait, TD (d 1976), of Ardsley House, Barnsley, Yorks, and Hon Ivy Mary, *née* Stapleton (d 1967), yr da of 10 Baron Beaumont; the Micklethwait family has been seated at Ardsley since the 17 century (*see* Burke's Landed Gentry, 18 edn, vol I, 1965); *b* 21 Nov 1934; *Educ* Ampleforth, ChCh Oxford; *m* 26 Jan 1961, Jane Evelyn, eldest da of William Melville Codrington, CMG, MC (d 1963), of Preston Hall, Oakham, Rutland; 2 s (Richard John b 11 Aug 1962, William James b 13 July 1964); *Career* Capt Grenadier Gds 1954-64; High Sheriff of Rutland 1972; *Clubs* Turf, Pratt's; *Style—* Richard Micklethwait, Esq; Preston Hall, Oakham, Rutland, Leics LE15 9NJ (☎ 057 285 219)

MICKLETHWAIT, Sir Robert Gore; QC (1956); 2 s of St John Gore Micklethwait, KC, JP (d 1951), and Annie Elizabeth, *née* Aldrich-Blake (d 1948); 2 cousin once removed of Richard Miles Micklethwait, *qv*; *b* 7 Nov 1902; *Educ* Clifton, Trinity Coll Oxford (MA); *m* 25 July 1936, Philippa Jennette, 2 da of Sir Ronald Bosanquet, KC (d 1952), of Dingestow Court, Mon; 3 s (Anthony Robert b 1939, Peter Bernard b 1945, Brian Hugh b 1947), 1 da (Daphne Louisa b 1941); *Career* Middle Temple: barrister 1925, bencher 1951, autumn reader 1964, dep treas 1970, treas 1971; rec of Worcester 1946-59, dep chm Staffs QS 1956-59, chief nat insur cmmr 1966-75 (dep cmmr 1959-61, the nat insur cmmr and industl injuries cmmr 1961-66); Hamlyn lectr 1976; Hon LLD Newcastle upon Tyne 1975; hon knight Hon Soc of Knights of the Round Table 1972; kt 1964; *Style—* Sir Robert Micklethwait, QC; 71 Harvest Rd, Englefield Green, Surrey TW20 0QR (☎ 0784 432521)

MICKLEWHITE, Gary; s of Derek Micklewhite, of London, and Mavis Ann, *née* French; *b* 21 March 1961; *Educ* Roan GS; *m* 26 June 1982, Katharine Dawn, da of Michael O'Donnell, of Blackheath, London; 2 da (Samantha b 30 Nov 1983, Mellissa b 11 Sept 1986); *Career* professional footballer; Manchester United 1978-79 (apprentice 1977); Queen's Park Rangers 1979-85: debut 1980, over 100 appearances (incl 1982 FA Cup Final v Tottenham Hotspur), Div 2 Championship 1982-83; Derby County: joined 1985-, over 200 appearances, Div 2 Championship 1986-87; *Recreations* golf, eating out, cars, my family; *Style—* Gary Micklewhite, Esq; Derby County FC, Baseball Ground, Shaftesbury Cres, Derby DE3 8NB (☎ 0332 40105)

MICKLEWRIGHT, Dr (Frederick Henry) Amphlett; s of Frederick William Micklewright (d 1964), and Daisy, *née* Argent (d 1959); *b* 22 April 1908; *Educ* Dulwich, St Peters Hall (now St Peters Coll) Univ of Oxford (BA, MA), UCL (PhD); *m* 9 Aug 1943, Irene Isabel, da of William Burnett (d 1950); 1 da (Jane Clare Bernardette Amphlett (Mrs Rates)); *Career* called to the Bar Middle Temple 1967; numerous antiquarian articles in Notes and Queries 1943-70; contrib legal and historical papers 1975-84: New Land J1, Law Guardian, Criminal Law Reviews, eclesiastical and theological 1935-80, Congregational Quarterly Hibbert J1, Population Studies; FRHistS 1943, FSAScot 1945; *Recreations* reading; *Style—* Amphlett Micklewright, Esq

MIDDLEMAS, Prof (Robert) Keith; s of Robert James Middlemas, of Northumberland, and Eleanor Mary, *née* Crane; *b* 26 May 1935; *Educ* Stowe, Pembroke Coll Cambridge (MA, DPhil, DLitt); *m* 30 Aug 1958, Susan Mary, da of Laurence Edward Paul Tremlett (d 1956); 1 s (Hugo b 1969), 3 da (Sophie b 1961, Lucy b 1964, Annabel b 1965); *Career* Mil Serv Kenya 1953-55; clerk in House of Commons 1958-67, Univ of Sussex 1967-; *Books* The Master Builders (1963), The Clydesiders (1965), Baldwin (with A J L Barnes, 1969), Diplomacy of Illusion (1972), Whitehall Diary by Thomas Jones 3 vols (ed 1969-71), Engineering and Politics in Southern Africa (1975), Politics in Industrial Society (1978), Power and the Party: Changing Faces of Communism in Western Europe (1979), Industry Unions and Government: Twenty-One Years of NEDC (1984), Power Competition and The State: vol I: Britain in Search of Balance 1940-61 (1986), vol II: Threats to The Post-War Settlement 1961-74 (1990); *Recreations* worldwide travel, landscape gardening, sailing; *Clubs* Flyfishers', North London Rifle; *Style—* Prof Keith Middlemas; West Burton House, West Burton, Pulborough, West Sussex (☎ 0798 831516); University of Sussex, Brighton, Sussex (☎ 0273 606755)

MIDDLESBROUGH, Bishop of (RC) 1978-; Rt Rev Augustine Harris; s of Augustine Harris (d 1948), and Louisa Beatrice, *née* Rycroft (d 1951); *b* 27 Oct 1917; *Educ* Upholland Coll, Lancs; *Career* ordained 1942, curate 1942-52, Prison Serv chaplain 1952-65, auxiliary bishop Liverpool 1966-78; *Style—* The Rt Rev the Bishop of Middlesbrough; Bishop's House, 16 Cambridge Rd, Middlesbrough, Cleveland TS5 5NN (☎ 0642 818253); Curial Offices, 49/51 Grange Rd, Middlesbrough, Cleveland TS1 5AU

MIDDLETON, Hon Mrs (Katherine Pulcheria (Katya)); *née* Grenfell; er da (by 2 w) of 2 and last Baron St Just (d 1984); *b* 23 May 1957; *m* 1, 1981 (m dis 1985), Oliver John Gilmour, 2 s of Rt Hon Sir Ian Hedworth John Little Gilmour, 3 Bt, MP, *qv*; 1 da; m 2, 1 Nov 1990, Roger N Middleton; *Style—* The Hon Mrs Middleton; 30

Cambridge Street, London SW1

MIDDLETON, Bernard Chester; MBE (1986); s of Regent Marcus Geoffrey Middleton (d 1985), of Clapham, London, and Doris Hilda, *née* Webster; *b* 29 Oct 1924; *Educ* Central School of Arts and Crafts London; *m* 2 June 1951, Dora Mary, da of Theodore Louis Davies (d 1959), of Kenton, Middx; *Career* craftsman-demonstrator Royal Coll of Art 1949-51, mangr Zaehnsdorf Ltd 1951-53, self-employed book restorer 1953-; chief examiner City and Guilds of London Inst 1957-63; FRSA 1951, fell Designer Bookbinders 1955 (pres 1973-75), memb Art Workers' Guild 1961, FSA 1967; *Books* A History of English Craft Bookbinding Technique (1 edn 1963, 3 edn 1988), The Restoration of Leather Bindings (1 edn 1972, 2 edn 1984); *Recreations* reading about social history, antiques, London; *Style*— Bernard Middleton, Esq, MBE, FSA; 3 Gauden Rd, Clapham, London SW4 6LR (☎ 071 622 5388)

MIDDLETON, Edward Bernard; s of Bernard Middleton (d 1987), and Bettie Mabel, *née* Knight; *b* 5 July 1948; *Educ* Aldenham; *m* 22 May 1971, Rosemary Spence, da of Maj Denis Frederick Spence Brown, TD, of The Close, Dorrington, Lincoln; 3 s (Nicholas b 1976, Simon b 1978, Hugo b 1982); *Career* sr Pannell Fitzpatrick & Co London 1971-73, mangr Pannell Bellhouse Mwangi & Co Nairobi 1973-75, ptnr Pannell Kerr Forster London 1979- (mangr 1975-79); seconded to DTI as dir/under-sec in the Industl Devpt Unit; FCA 1972; *Recreations* sailing, photography, walking; *Clubs* Salcombe Yacht; *Style*— Edward Middleton, Esq; Barrans, Bury Green, Little Hadham, Ware, Herts (☎ 0279 6586 84); Pannell Kerr Forster, New Garden House, 78 Hatton Garden, London EC1N 8JA (☎ 071 831 7383, fax 071 405 6736)

MIDDLETON, (John) Grant; s of Edward Francis Beresford Middleton, MBE, of Low Fell, and Veronica Mary, *née* Seed; *b* 8 March 1934; *Educ* Ushaw Coll Durham, Univ of Durham (LLB); *m* 30 Sept 1961, Pamela, da of Canon David Jones (d 1942); 1 s (James b 1964), 2 da (Catherine b 1966, Jessica b 1974); *Career* Royal Northumberland Fus: 2 Lt 1956-58, Lt 1958-59; Capt Army Legal Serv 1959; admitted slr 1955; sr ptnr Stoneham Langton & Passmore 1986- (ptnr 1961-); memb: Barnes and Sheen CAB, City of Westminster Law Soc (pres 1989-90), Law Soc 1956; *Recreations* Bach choir, chess, bridge, golf, motorcycling; *Clubs* Naval & Military; *Style*— Grant Middleton, Esq; 2 Kitson Rd, Barnes, London SW13 9HJ (☎ 081 748 5773); 8 Bolton St, London W1Y 8AU (☎ 071 499 8000, fax 071 629 4460, telex 21640 INTLAW G)

MIDDLETON, John; s of John Middleton (d 1932), of Newcastle-upon-Tyne, and Martha, *née* Moran; *b* 19 March 1932; *Educ* St Cuthberts GS Newcastle-upon-Tyne; *m* 1971, Lillian, da of Sydney Butcher (d 1973), of Newcastle-upon-Tyne; 1 s (John b 1974); *Career* Nat Serv REME, attached to Highland LI in Egypt; gen sec Tobacco Mechanics Assoc; *Recreations* fishing, camping and rambling, birdwatching; *Style*— John Middleton, Esq; 16 Clifton Terrace, Whitley Bay, Tyne and Wear, NE26 2JD (☎ 091 251 3254)

MIDDLETON, John Skene; s of Col Dr David Skene Middleton, TD (d 1981), of Edinburgh, and Dorothy Urquhart Marr, *née* Dewar (d 1985); *b* 3 June 1935; *Educ* Loretto, Univ of Edinburgh (BSc, NDA), Univ of Durham (NDAgricE); *m* 23 July 1965, Susan, da of Lt-Col Spencer Allen Block, MBE (1979), of Little Gaddesden; 1 s (Ian b 1968), 2 da (Kirsty b 1967, Lindsay b 1970); *Career* mktg mangr: MMG Agrisystems 1978-84, MMG Erosion 1980-84; regnl mangr Miln Masters Gp Ltd 1984-86, mgmnt conslt ICMC 1986-88, chief exec Grand Nat Archery Soc; memb: BOA, CCPR, Sports Cncl; MIAgrE 1969, memb CEI 1973; *Recreations* archery, hill walking, ferroquinology, railway modelling; *Clubs* Coventry Archery; *Style*— John Middleton, Esq; Grand National Archery Society, 7th Street, National Agricultural Centre, Stoneleigh, Kenilworth, Warwickshire CV8 2LG (☎ 0203 696 631)

MIDDLETON, Lance Cyril; s of Cyril Herbert Charles Middleton, and Edna Middleton; *b* 5 June 1938; *Educ* The GS Cambridge, Univ of Lancaster (MA); *m* 23 Oct 1971, Linda Marion, da of Ronald Arthur Bowd; 1 s (Laun b 13 July 1976), 1 da (Ruth b 9 June 1973); *Career* various positions BOC plc 1972-75, md Paines plc St Neots and pres Diastatische Prodn Holland 1977-, pres Lindstrom Canada 1985-; FCA; *Recreations* travel, gardening, golf; *Style*— Lance Middleton, Esq; 9 Long Rd, Cambridge CB2 2PP (☎ 0223 243513)

MIDDLETON, Lawrence Monck; s of late Lt Hugh Jeffery Middleton, RN (3 s of 7 Bt); *b* 23 Oct 1912; *Educ* Eton, Edinburgh Univ (BSc); *Career* h to Baronetcy of bro, Sir Stephen Hugh Middleton, 9 Bt; *Style*— Lawrence Middleton, Esq

MIDDLETON, 12 Baron (GB 1711); Sir (Digby) Michael Godfrey John Willoughby; 13 Bt (E 1677), MC (1945), DL (N Yorks); s of 11 Baron Middleton, KG (d 1970); *b* 1 May 1921; *Educ* Eton, Trinity Coll Cambridge; *m* 14 Oct 1947, Janet, JP (fndr chm Lloyd's External Names Assoc), da of Gen Sir James Handyside Marshall-Cornwall, KCB, CBE, DSO, MC; 3 s; *Heir* s, Hon Michael Charles James Willoughby; *Career* 2 Lt Coldstream Gds 1940, Temp Maj served in NW Europe 1944-45 (despatches and Croix de Guerre); land agent 1951; JP E Riding Yorks 1958; cnclir: E Riding 1964-74, N Yorks 1974-77; memb Yorks and Humberside Econ Planning Cncl 1968-79; pres: Yorks Agric Soc 1976, CLA 1981-83; Hon Col 2 Bn Yorks (TAVR) Volunteers 1976-88; memb: Nature Conservancy Cncl 1986-89, House of Lords select ctee on Euro Community; *Clubs* Boodle's; *Style*— The Rt Hon the Lord Middleton, MC, DL; Birdsall House, Birdsall, Malton, N Yorks YO17 9NR (☎ 094 46 202)

MIDDLETON, Michael Humfrey; CBE (1975); s of Humfrey Middleton (d 1976), and Lilian Irene, *née* Tillard (d 1939); *b* 1 Dec 1917; *Educ* King's Sch Canterbury; *m* 10 April 1954, Julie Margaret, da of Guy James Kay Harrison (d 1980), of Cark Manor, Cark-in-Cartmel, Cumbria; 1 s (Hugo b 1955), 2 da (Kate b 1958, Rose b 1961); *Career* art critic The Spectator 1946-56, asst ed Picture Post 1948-52, ed House and Garden 1955-57, dir Civic Tst 1969-86, sec gen UK Campaign for Euro Architectural Year 1972-76, sec Architectural Heritage Fund 1976-86; Pro Merito Medal of Cncl of Europe 1976; *Books* Group Practice in Design (1967), Man Made the Town (1987), Cities in Transition (1991); *Recreations* travel, the arts; *Style*— Michael Middleton, Esq, CBE; 84 Sirdar Rd, London W11 4EG

MIDDLETON, Michael William; s of Cyril Herbert Charles Middleton, and Edna May, *née* Woods; *b* 3 Sept 1942; *Educ* Chesterton Sch Cambridge; *m* 1966, Elizabeth, da of Albert Allen (d 1942), of Bollington; 1 s (James Spencer b 1969), 1 da (Emma Louise b 1971); *Career* chm Ede & Ravenscroft Group of Cos; dir: Cyril Middleton & Co Group of Cos, Middleton Farms Ltd; *Recreations* shooting; *Clubs* East India; *Style*— Michael Middleton, Esq; 54 Storey's Way, Cambridge CB3 0DX

MIDDLETON, Rear Adm (John) Patrick Windsor; s of Cdr John Henry Dudley Middleton (d 1989), of Wimbledon, and Norna Mary Tessimond, *née* Hitchings; *b* 15 March 1938; *Educ* Cheltenham Coll, RNC Dartmouth, RN Engrg Coll Manadon Plymouth; *m* 31 March 1962, Jane Rodwell, da of Leslie Stephen Gibbs (d 1978), of Letchmore Heath, Radlett, Herts; 1 s (Toby b 1963), 1 da (Isobel b 1965); *Career* RN: entered 1954; serv HMS: Lion 1962, Ambush 1965, Warspite 1969; Cdr 1973, NDC 1976, HMS Blake 1977, Capt 1981; CSO(E): FOSM 1981, Falklands 1983; Capt naval drafting 1984, dir in serv submarines 1987, Rear Adm 1989, CSO(E) Fleet 1989; Liveryman Worshipful Co of Armourers and Brasiers 1971; MIMechE 1965, MiMarE 1965, FBIM 1989; *Style*— Rear Adm Patrick Middleton; HMS Warrior, Eastbury Park, Northwood, Middx (☎ 0923 83 7481)

MIDDLETON, Sir Peter Edward; GCB (1989, KCB 1984); *b* 2 April 1934; *Educ* Sheffield City GS, Univ of Sheffield (BA), Univ of Bristol; *m* 1, Valerie Ann, *née* Lindup (d 1987); m 2, 20 Jan 1990, Constance Jean, *née* Close; 1 s (Tom), 1 da (Emma); *Career* served RAPC 1958-60; HM Treasy: sr info offr 1962, princ 1964, asst dir Centre for Admin Studies 1967-69, private sec to Chllr of the Exchequer 1969-72, press sec 1972-75, head Monetary Policy Div 1975, under sec 1976-, dep sec 1980-83; visiting fell Nuffield Coll Oxford 1981-89, memb Cncl Manchester Business Sch 1985-; govr: London Business Sch 1984-90, Ditchley Fndn 1985; cdre Civil Serv Sailing Assoc; *Clubs* Reform; *Style*— Sir Peter Middleton, GCB; HM Treasury, Parliament St, London SW1

MIDDLETON, Stanley; s of Thomas Middleton (d 1936), of Bulwell, Nottingham, and Elizabeth Ann, *née* Burdett; *b* 1 Aug 1919; *Educ* Bulwell St Mary's, Highbury Sch Bulwell, High Pavement Sch Nottingham, Univ of London (BA), Univ of Nottingham (MEd); *m* 22 Dec 1951, Margaret Shirley Charnley, da of Herbert Welch (d 1971), of Ewell Surrey; 2 da (Penelope b 1956, Sarah b 1958); *Career* WWII RA and RAEC; head of English High Pavement Coll Nottingham 1958-81, Judith E Wilson visiting fell Emmanuel Coll Cambridge 1982-83; jt winner The Booker Prize for fiction (Holiday) 1974; Hon MA Univ of Nottingham 1975; fell PEN; *Books* A Short Answer (1958), Harris's Requiem (1960), A Serious Woman (1961), The Just Exchange (1962), Two's Company (1963), Him They Compelled (1964), Terms of Reference (1966), The Golden Evening (1968), Wages of Virtue (1969), Apple of The Eye (1970), Brazen Prison (1971), Gold Gradations (1972), A Man Made of Smoke (1973), Holiday (1974), Distractions (1975), Still Waters (1976), Ends and Means (1977), Two Brothers (1978), In A Strange Land (1979), The Other Side (1980), Blind Understanding (1982), Entry into Jerusalem (1983), The Daysman (1984), Valley of Decision (1985), An After Dinner's Sleep (1986), After A Fashion (1987), Recovery (1988), Vacant Places (1989), Changes and Chances (1990); *Recreations* music, walking, listening; *Style*— Stanley Middleton, Esq; 42 Caledon Rd, Sherwood, Nottingham NG5 2NG; (☎ 0602 623085)

MIDDLETON, Sir Stephen Hugh; 9 Bt (E 1662), of Belsay Castle, Northumberland; s of Lt Hugh Jeffery Middleton, RN (d 1914, s of 7 Bt); suc unc, Sir Charles Arthur Middleton, 8 Bt, 1942; *b* 20 June 1909; *Educ* Eton, Magdalene Coll Cambridge; *m* 21 May 1962, Mary (d 1972), da of Richard Robinson (d 1933); *Heir* bro, Lawrence Monck Middleton; *Style*— Sir Stephen Middleton, Bt; Belsay Castle, Newcastle-upon-Tyne

MIDDLETON, Tony Charles; s of Peter John Middleton, of Winchester, Hampshire, and Molly Caroline, *née* Carver; *b* 1 Feb 1964; *Educ* Montgomery of Alamein Winchester, Peter Symonds Sixth Form Coll Winchester; *m* 23 Sept 1989, Sherralyn Tessa, da of Phillip Paul Clarke; *Career* professional cricketer; Hampshire CCC 1983-: first class debut 1984, awarded county cap 1990, 36 first class appearances; represented England Schs under 19 1982; off seasons: groundsman for Aust sports club, sales rep for safety wear distributor Hants; *Recreations* squash, badminton, gardening, real ale pubs; *Style*— Tony Middleton, Esq; Hampshire CCC, Northlands Rd, Southampton (☎ 0703 477768)

MIDDLETON, Hon Mrs (Vanessa Rachel); *née* Cornwallis; 2 da of 3 Baron Cornwallis, OBE, DL (by his 2 w); *b* 27 July 1958; *m* 1986, Jeremy Middleton, of Sydney, NSW; *Style*— The Hon Mrs Middleton; 104 Prince Albert Road, Mosman, NSW

MIDDLETON, William; s of Charles Ferdinand Paul Middleton (d 1946), and Linda, *née* De Angelis; *b* 26 Feb 1923; *Educ* Univ of London, Univ Rome; *Career* admitted slr 1954; sr ptnr Middleton Potts London; dir: Pignone Engineering Ltd 1966, Enimont UK Ltd 1968, Snia (UK) Ltd 1970, Italian General Shipping Ltd 1973, BCI Ltd 1974, Zanussi CLV Systems Ltd 1976, Api Services Ltd 1984, Stefanel (UK) Ltd 1984, Euroil Exploration Ltd 1988, Realfim plc 1989; *Recreations* tennis, bridge; *Clubs* Hurlingham, City of London; *Style*— William Middleton, Esq; 68 Albert Hall Mansions, London SW7; Middleton Potts, 3 Cloth Street, London EC1 (☎ 071 600 2333, fax 071 600 0108, telex 928357)

MIDDLETON-SANDFORD, (Millicent) Betty; da of James Middleton Honeychurch (d 1952), and Alice Middleton (d 1954); *b* 13 July 1932; *Educ* Worthing Coll of Art (NDD), Royal Coll of Art (DesRCA); *m* 1, 1955 (m dis 1965) Alan Irvine; 1 s (James Montgomery b 1958); m 2, 21 Aug 1985, John Sutton, s of Gerald John Sutton (d 1958); *Career* textile designer 1954-64: Edinburgh Weavers, Heals, Liberty's; and by specific cmmn: Austin Reeds 1958, London Airport 1958, Industrial Glass Centre and various fashion houses; graphic designer and photographer; illustrations of childrens' books incl: Tales of the Greek Heroes, The Tale of Troy; dir Sandford Gallery 1979-81; *Recreations* drawing on buses and boats in remote countries; *Style*— Mrs Betty Middleton-Sandford; Barclays Bank plc, Fulham Broadway Branch, London SW6 1ER

MIDGLEY, (David) William; JP (North Tyneside); s of Norman Midgley, of Huddersfield, and Margaret, *née* Alderson (d 1986); *b* 1 Feb 1942; *Educ* Huddersfield Coll; *m* 1, 19 Dec 1964, Anne Christine (d 1976), da of Charles Foreman, of Huddersfield; 1 s (Edward William b 1967), 1 da (Rachel Sarah b 1969); m 2, 10 June 1977, Ada Margaret, da of John Banks; 1 da (Louise Isobel b 1980); *Career* md Newcastle Building Soc 1986; chm: Newcastle Estate Agents Ltd 1988, Strachans (Newcastle) Ltd 1989, Adamscastle Ltd; dir NBS (fin servs) Ltd 1987; memb Northern Cncl CBI; memb Ctee: MIND, Newcastle Cncl for the Disabled; govr Feversham Sch Newcastle, non-exec memb N Tyneside Family Health Servs Authy; FCBSI; *Recreations* golf; *Clubs* Northern Constitutional; *Style*— William Midgley, Esq, JP; 17 Beaumont Drive, Whitley Bay, Tyne and Wear NE25 9UT (☎ 091 2511807); Grainger Chambers, Hood St, Newcastle-Upon-Tyne (☎ 091 2326676, fax 091 2610015, car 0860 415847)

MIDLETON, 12 Viscount (I 1717); Alan Henry Brodrick; also Baron Brodrick of Midleton (I 1715) and Baron Brodrick of Peper Harow (GB 1796); the full designation of the Viscountcy is Midleton of Midleton; s of Alan Rupert Brodrick (d 1972), and Alice Elizabeth, *née* Roberts; suc uncle 11 Viscount 1988; *b* 4 Aug 1949; *Educ* St Edmund's Canterbury; *m* 1978, Julia Helen, da of Michael Pitt, of Lias Cottage, Compton Dundon, Somerton, Somerset; 2 s (Hon Ashley Rupert, Hon William Michael b 1982), 1 da (Hon Charlotte Helen b 1983); *Heir* s, Hon Ashley Rupert Brodrick b 25 Nov 1980; *Career* horologist; Keeper of Horology Gershom Parkington Collection Bury St Edmunds 1986-; FBHI; *Recreations* clockmaking, conservation of turret clocks, bicycling; *Style*— The Rt Hon the Viscount Midleton; 2 Burrels Orchard, Westley, Bury St Edmunds, Suffolk IP33 3TH

MIDLETON, Countess of; Irène Lilian; da of late Alfred Edward Creese (d 1943), of Ewell, Surrey, and Emilie, *née* Lees (d 1983); *b* 22 Sept 1917; *Educ* Holy Cross Convent Haywards Heath; *m* 1975, as his 3 w, 2 Earl of Midleton (d 1979 when the Earldom became extinct and the Viscountcy passed to a kinsman); *Career* actress (as Rène Ray), authoress, painter; toured France, Holland, Belgium and Germany in June Mad for ENSA 1945; starred in own play The Tree Surgeon at Bournemouth Palace Court Theatre 1961; 50 films incl The Passing of the Third Floor Back 1935, which made her a star, 35 plays incl An Inspector Calls (NY 1947); 8 TV plays incl The Valiant, Death of a Rat, The Adding Machine, Wuthering Heights, radio plays The Return of the Native (with Michael Redgrave, CBS New York 1947), The Road to Samarkand (with Marlene Dietrich, CBS New York 1947), Conversation Piece (1987);

Inter Arts Guild 1969; Palme d'Or des Beaux Arts Dip, mention speciale du Jury Section Peinture; *Books* Wraxton Marne (1946), Emma Conquest (1950), A Man Named Seraphin (1951), The Garden of Cahmohn (1955), The Strange World of Planet X (1957), The Tree Surgeon (1958), The Christmas Present (1966), Angel Assignment (1988); *Style—* The Rt Hon the Countess of Midleton; Martello Lodge, St Brelade's Bay, Jersey, Channel Islands (☎ 0534 41171)

MIDLETON, Dowager Viscountess; Sheila Campbell; da of late Charles Campbell MacLeod, of Cawthorpe House, Bourne, Lincs; *m* 12 Aug 1940, 11 Viscount Midleton (d 1988); *Style—* The Rt Hon Dowager Viscountess Midleton; Frogmore Cottage, 105 North Road, Bourne, Lincs

MIDWINTER, Dr Eric; *b* 11 Feb 1932; *Educ* St Catharine's Coll Cambridge (BA, MA), Univ of Liverpool (MA), Univ of York (DPhil); *Career* academic appts 1955-68, dir of priority educnl project Liverpool 1968-75, head of Public Affrs Unit Nat Consumer Cncl London 1975-80, dir Centre for Policy on Ageing London 1980-; chm: Advsy Centre for Educn 1976-80, London Regnl Passenger Ctee 1977-, Health and Social Welfare Bd Open Univ 1983-; vice pres Pre-Sch Playgroup Assoc, tstee Nat Community Educn Devpt Centre; Hon Dr Open Univ; *Books* Victorian Social Reform (1968), Social Administration in Lancashire (1969), Old Liverpool (1971), Nineteenth Century Education (1970), Teaching in the Urban Community School (ed, 1972), Education for sale (1977), Make 'em Laugh: Famous Comedians and Their World (1979), W G Grace: His Life and Times (1981), The Wage of Retirement: the Case for a New Pensions Policy (1985), Caring for Cash: the Issue of Private Domiciliary Care (1986), Fair Game: Myth and Reality in Sport (1986), The Lost Seasons: Cricket in Wartime (1987), New Design for Old (1988), Red Roses Crest the Caps (1989), Creating Chances (1990), The Old Order (1990); *Recreations* writing, sport, theatre; *Clubs* MCC, Lancashire CCC, Savage; *Style—* Dr Eric Midwinter; Centre for Policy on Ageing, 25-31 Ironmonger Row, London EC1V 3QP, (☎ 071 253 1787, fax 071 490 4206)

MIDWINTER, Prof John Edwin; OBE (1984); s of Henry Clements Midwinter (d 1970), of Newbury, Berks, and Vera Joyce, *née* Rawlinson; *b* 8 March 1938; *Educ* St Bartholomews GS Newbury, King's Coll London (BSc), External Dept Univ of London (PhD); *m* 15 July 1961, Maureen Ann, da of Charles Richard Holt of Wickham Market, Suffolk; 2 s (Timothy b 15 June 1963, Piers b 23 July 1968), 2 da (Philippa b 16 Sept 1964, Kim b 19 March 1966); *Career* Nat Serv RAF airborne radar instr Yatesbury Wiltshire 1956-58; sr scientific offr MOD RSRE Malvern Worcs 1961-67; sr res physicist: Perkin Elmer Corporation USA 1968-70, Allied Chemical Corporation USA 1970-71; head Optical Communications Div BTRes 1977-84 (head of section 1971-77), Pender Prof and head of Electrical and Engrg Dept UCL 1984-; conslt to: BT, GPT, EEC.RACE, EEC.ESPRIT; conf chm: Euro Conf on Optical Communications 1988, US Topical Meeting on Photonic Switching 1989, Sino Br Conf on Optical Communications 1989; delivered numerous lectures incl: Clifford Patterson Royal Soc, Bruce Preller RSE, Evening Discourse Royal Inst; author of papers in and ed of several engrg jls; cncl memb FEng 1986-89, vice chm Electronic Div IEE 1988- (dep chm elect 1990-); memb: Sci and Engrg Policy Study Unit Royal Soc and FEng 1988-, DTI Optoelectronics Ctee 1989-, Parly and Scientific Ctee Advsy Bd 1989-, numerous other ctees; FInstP 1975, FIEE 1980, FIEEE 1983, FEng 1984, FRS 1985; *Books* Applied Non-Linear Optics (with F Zernike, 1973), Optical Fibres for Transmission (1979), Optical Fibre Communications (contrib, 1979), Fibre and Integrated Optics (contrib, 1979), New Directions in Guided Waves and Coherent Optics (contrib, 1983), Neural Computing Architectures (contrib, 1989), Optical Technology and Wideband Local Networks (ed with others, 1989), Photonic Switching (ed with HS Hinton, 1989); *Style—* Prof John Midwinter, OBE, FRS; Department of Electrical and Electronic Engineering, University College London, Torrington Place, London WC1E 7JE (☎ 071 388 0427, fax 071 388 9307, telex 296273 UCL ENG G)

MIECZKOWSKI, Hon Mrs (Caroline Sarah Aline); da of 2 Baron Grenfell, TD (d 1976), and his 1 w, Elizabeth Sarah Polk, da of Capt Hon Alfred Shaughnessy (ka 1916), 2 s of 1 Baron Shaughnessy (d 1923); *b* 28 July 1933; *m* 1965, Zbyszek Leon Mieczkowski, s of Stefan Mieczkowski de Zagroba (d 1956), of Dzierzanowo, Poland; 1 s (Stefan b 1967), 1 da (Helena b 1970); *Style—* The Hon Mrs Mieczkowski; Rose Cottage, Henley Park, Henley-on-Thames, Oxon RG9 6HY (☎ 0491 572819)

MIECZKOWSKI, Zbyszek Leon; s of late Stefan Mieczkowski de Zagroba (d 1956), of Dzierzanowo Poland; *b* 22 June 1922; *Educ* Zamoyski Gimn, Warsaw, Dlugosz Coll Poland; *m* 1965, Hon Caroline Sarah Aline, *qv*, da of 2 Baron Grenfell, TD (d 1976); *Career* WWII with Polish Forces 1939-45, France and Germany Campaign with Br Liberation Army, 1 Polish Armed Div; Industrialists: chm Polish Library Cncl 1978-81, patron Joseph Conrad Soc (UK); Military Cross of Valour, Cross of Merit; *Recreations* reading, hunting, tennis; *Clubs* Brooks's; *Style—* Zbyszek Mieczkowski, Esq; Rose Cottage, Henley Park, Henley-on-Thames, Oxon RG9 6HY (☎ 0491 572 819)

MIERS, Sir (Henry) David Alastair Capel; KBE (1985), CMG (1979); s of Col R D M C Miers, DSO (d 1974); *b* 10 Jan 1937; *Educ* Winchester, Univ Coll Oxford; *m* 1966, Imelda Maria Emilia, *née* Wouters; 2 s, 1 da; *Career* Dip Serv; head ME Dept FCO 1980-83 (private sec to Min of State FO 1968, Paris 1972, cnsllr Tehran 1977-80), ambass Lebanon 1983-85, asst under sec FCO 1986-88, ambass Greece 1989; *Style—* Sir David Miers, KBE, CMG; c/o Foreign and Cwlth Office, King Charles St, London SW1A 2AH

MIERS, Richenda Francis Capel; da of Rear Adm Peter Douglas Herbert Raymond Pelly, CB, DSO (d 1980), of Alderney, CI, and Gwenllian Violet, *née* Edwardes (d 1987); *b* 27 Jan 1939; *Educ* Ipswich HS, Loreto Convent Gibraltar, Ipswich Tech Coll; *m* 3 April 1959, Col Douglas Alexander Nigel Capel Miers, s of Col Ronald Douglas Martin Capel Miers, DSO (d 1974), of Ross-Shire, Scotland; 1 s (Lucian b 1962), 3 da (Mary b 1961, Victoria b 1964, Henrietta b 1966); *Career* author; *Books* Told From An Island (as Richenda Francis, 1979); as Frances Ramsay: Carve It In Doves (1984), Mine Is The Heart (1984), No Other Desire (1984), Cumbria (1986), Cadogan Guide To Scotland (1987, 1989 and 1991), Cadogan Guide To Thailand, Burma (contrib as Francis Capel, 1988), The Blood Is Strong (as Richenda Francis, 1989); *Recreations* reading, writing, sailing, walking, gardening; *Style—* Mrs Richenda Miers; East Farmhouse, Wylye, Warminster, Wilts BA12 0RQ (☎ 09856 219); Boisdale House, South Lochboisdale, Isle of South Uist, Scotland PA81 5UB

MIKARDO, Ian; s of Morris Mikardo, of Portsmouth; *b* 9 July 1908; *Educ* Portsmouth; *m* 1932, Mary, da of Benjamin Rosetté, of London; 2 da; *Career* MP (Lab): Reading 1945-50, Reading South 1950-55, Reading 1955 1959, Poplar 1964-74, Tower Hamlets Bethnal Green and Bow 1974-83, Bow and Poplar 1983-87; chm Select Ctee on Nationalised Industs 1966-70, pres ASTMS 1968-73, chm Parly Lab Pty March-Nov 1974; vice pres Socialist Int 1978-83 (hon pres 1983-); *Books* Centralised Control of Industry (1944), Frontiers in the Air (1946), Keep Left (jtly, 1947), The Second Five Years (1948), The Problems of Nationalisation (1948), Keeping Left (jtly, 1950), The Labour Case (1950), It's a Mug's Game (1951), Socialism or Slump (1959), Backbencher (1988); *Style—* Ian Mikardo, Esq; 89 Grove Hall Court, London NW8 9NS

MILBANK, Sir Anthony Frederick; 5 Bt (UK 1882), of Well, Co York, and Barningham, Co Durham; s of Sir Mark Vane Milbank, 4 Bt, KCVO, MC (d 1984), and Hon Verena Aileen, da of 11 Baron Farnham; *b* 16 Aug 1939; *Educ* Eton; *m* 1970, Belinda Beatrice, da of Brig Adrian Clements Gore, DSO, of Horton Priory, Sellinge, Ashford, Kent; 2 s (Edward b 1973, Toby b 1977), 1 da (Alexina b 1971); *Heir* s, Edward Mark Somerset Milbank b 9 April 1973; *Career* farmer and landowner; memb: Nature Conservancy Cncl, Ctee for England, CLA Exec Ctee; chm Moorland Assoc; former: dir M & G Securities, govr Royal Marsden Hosp; *Recreations* all sports: field, team, individual and winter; *Style—* Sir Anthony Milbank, Bt; Barningham Park, Richmond, N Yorks DL11 7DW (☎ 0833 21202)

MILBANK, Denis William Powlett; TD (1944); yst s of Sir Frederick Richard Powlett Milbank, 3 Bt (d 1964), and (Harriet Anne) Dorothy, *née* Wilson (d 1970); *b* 6 July 1912; *Educ* Radley; *m* 5 July 1934, Doreen Frances, da of Sir Richard Pierce Butler, OBE (d 1955), of Ballintemple, Carlow, Ireland; 1 s (Mark Richard b 1937), 2 da (Penelope Ann b 1935, Susan Fiona b 1942); *Career* Maj RA (TA) 1938-46, WWII serv Middle E and Italy (despatches); with Walpamun Co 1928-48; farming in Kenya 1948-74, Safari tour ldr 1969-74, dist cmdt Kenya Police Res 1952-59; sec Yorks Regn Br Field Sports Soc 1974-77; *Recreations* shooting, safaris; *Clubs* Muthaiga Country (Nairobi); *Style—* D W P Milbank, Esq, TD; Southbrook, Galphay, Ripon, N Yorks

MILBANK, Hon Lady (Verena Aileen); da of 11 Baron Farnham, DSO (d 1935); *b* 4 Aug 1907; *m* 1, 3 Feb 1934, Charles Lambart Crawley (d 1935); m 2, 12 Feb 1938, as his 2 w, Maj Sir Mark Vane Milbank, 4 Bt, KCVO, MC; *Style—* The Hon Lady Milbank; The Gate House, Barningham, Richmond, N Yorks

MILBORNE-SWINNERTON-PILKINGTON, Richard Arthur; s and h of Sir Thomas Henry Milborne-Swinnerton-Pilkington, 14 Bt; *b* 4 Sept 1964; *Educ* Eton, RAC Cirencester; *Career* insur broker Willis Faber; *Recreations* racing, shooting; *Style—* Richard Milborne-Swinnerton-Pilkington, Esq

MILBORNE-SWINNERTON-PILKINGTON, Sir Thomas Henry; 14 Bt (NS 1635); o s of Sir Arthur William Milborne-Swinnerton-Pilkington, 13 Bt (d 1952), and Elizabeth Mary, er da of late Col John Fenwick Harrison, JP, DL, of King's Walden Bury, Hitchin; *b* 10 March 1934; *Educ* Eton; *m* 1961, Susan, eld da of Norman Stewart Rushton Adamson, of Durban, S Africa; 1 s, 2 da (Sarah b 1962, Joanna b 1967); *Heir* s Richard Arthur Milborne-Swinnerton-Pilkington b 4 Sept 1964); *Career* chm: Charente Steamship Co Ltd 1977-, Thomas & James Harrison Ltd 1980-; *Clubs* White's; *Style—* Sir Thomas Milborne-Swinnerton-Pilkington, Bt; King's Walden Bury, Hitchin, Herts

MILBORROW, Ruan Leslie; s of Robert Leslie Milborrow (d 1986), of Grove Cottage, 31 Nutter Lane, Wanstead, London, and Elizabeth Edith, *née* Cook; *b* 11 July 1958; *Educ* Forest Sch Snaresbrook, RAC Cirencester (MRAC, Dip FM); *Career* sr art dir Yellowhammer Advertising Ltd 1991- (graduate trainee 1984); Freeman City of London 1984; MIPA 1989; *Books* The Riddle of Atrophic Rhinitis (1982), The Official Sloane Ranger Directory (contrib, 1984); *Recreations* music, collecting modern first editions, polo, theatre; *Clubs* RAC, Cirencester Park Polo; *Style—* Ruan Milborrow, Esq; Grove Cottage, 31 Nutter Lane, Wanstead, London E11 2HZ (☎ 081 989 4002); Yellowhammer Advertising, 76 Oxford St, London W1A 1DT (☎ 071 436 5000, fax 071 436 4630, telex 8953837)

MILBURN, Anthony; s of Lawrence Anderson Milburn (d 1958), of Halifax, and Constance, *née* Laskey (d 1985); *Educ* Rastrick GS, Univ of Bradford (BTech), Univ of Birmingham (MSc); *m* 3 June 1983, Julia Margaret, da of Maj Charles Pearson Weeden, of Pangbourne, Berks; 1 s (Richard b 1988), 1 da (Catherine b 1986); *Career* trg mangr National Water Cncl 1972-80, exec dir International Association on Water Pollution Research and Control 1981-; Chilterns Region mangr Charities Aid Fndn, vice-pres Ctee on Water Research International Council of Scientific Unions, govr St Matthews Sch Surbiton, memb Prize Ctee Stockholm Water Prize; Freeman City of London, asst to Court Guild of Water Conservators; MICE 1971, MIWEM 1972; *Books* Water Pollution Research and Control (ed, 1989); *Recreations* sailing, philosophy, modern jazz; *Style—* Anthony Milburn, Esq; International Association on Water Pollution Research and Control (IAWPRc), 1 Queen Annes Gate, London SW1 9BT (☎ 071 222 3848, fax 071 233 1197, telex 918518 WASSOC (IAWPRC))

MILBURN, Sir Anthony Rupert; 5 Bt (UK 1905), of Guyzance, Parish of Acklington, Northumberland; s of Maj Rupert Leonard Eversley Milburn (d 1974, yr s of 3 Bt), and Anne Mary, *née* Scott-Murray; suc unc, Sir John Milburn, 4 Bt (d 1985); *b* 17 April 1947; *Educ* Eton, RAC Cirencester; *m* 1977, Olivia Shirley, yst da of Capt Thomas Noel Catlow, CBE, JP, DL, RN (ret), of Tunstall, Lancs; 2 s (Patrick b 1980, Jake b 1987), 1 da (Lucy b 1982); *Heir* s, Patrick Thomas Milburn b 4 Dec 1980; *Career* landowner; co dir; ARICS, MRAC; *Clubs* New (Ed); *Style—* Sir Anthony Milburn, Bt; Guyzance Hall, Acklington, Morpeth, Northumberland (☎ 0665 711247)

MILBURN, Peter; s of Edward Franklin Milburn, of Bradford, W Yorks, and Joyce, *née* Ostler; *b* 28 Oct 1952; *Educ* Hanson GS Bradford; *m* 9 July 1977 (m dis 1988), Elizabeth Anne, da of David John Terence Cowsill, of Lower Swell, Gloucestershire; 1 s (Benjamin b 1981); *Career* prog controller; Pennine Radio 1979-81, Red Dragon Radio 1987-90; Red Dragon Radio 1990-; memb Radio Acad; *Recreations* travel, reading; *Style—* Peter Milburn, Esq; Red Dragon Radio Ltd, Radio House, West Canal Wharf, Cardiff CF1 5XJ (☎ 0222 384041, fax 0222 384014), 6 Clwyd, North Cliffe, Penarth, S Glamorgan CF4 1DZ (☎ 0222 700931)

MILDRED, Mark; s of John Mildred, of Usk, Gwent, and Eileen Smith (d 1969); *b* 16 Sept 1948; *Educ* Lancing, Clare Coll Cambridge (exhibitioner, BA); *m* 19 Oct 1974, Sarah Ruth, da of Harold Christopher Rackham; 2 s (Joe b 13 July 1976, Tom b 16 May 1979); *Career* articled clerk B M Birnberg & Co 1973-75; ptnr: Messrs Mildred and Beaumont 1978-86, Pannone Blackburn and Pannone Napier 1986-; memb: Law Soc 1975, Soc of Labour Lawyers 1975, Assoc of Personal Injury Lawyers 1990; *Books* 1989 Group Actions - Learning From Opren (Nat Consumer Cncl, 1989), contrib Butterworth's Medical Negligence (chapter on Class Actions, 1990); *Recreations* singing, cooking, childcare, walking, racquet games; *Clubs* Scorpions, Battersea Labour; *Style—* Mark Mildred, Esq; Pannone Blackburn, 20/22 Bedford Row, London WC1R 4EB (☎ 071 430 1987, fax 071 405 6638)

MILES, Adrian Spencer; s of Herbert Beal Miles (d 1952), of London, and Marjorie Phyllis, *née* Harris; *b* 16 Nov 1947; *Educ* Rutlish Sch, QMC London (LLB); *m* 28 June 1975, Hilary, da of William Nelson (d 1980); 1 s (Jonathan Francis b 20 May 1968), 2 da (Julie Clare b 11 Oct 1978, Anna Kirsty b 7 July 1980); *Career* admitted slr 1972, Boodle Hatfield 1972-74, Norton Rose 1974-76, ptnr Wilde Sapte 1976-; memb Law Soc; *Recreations* chess, tennis, music; *Style—* Adrian Miles, Esq; Queensbridge House, 60 Upper Thames St, London EC4V 3BD (☎ 071 236 3050, fax 071 236 9624, telex 887793)

MILES, Anthony John; s of Paul Miles (d 1946), and Mollie, *née* Leitch; *b* 18 July 1930; *Educ* Royal GS High Wycombe; *m* 1 May 1975, Anne Elizabeth, da of William Sidney Bishop, of Turners Oak, New Ash Green, Kent; *Career* Daily Mirror: feature writer 1954-66, asst ed 1967-68, assoc ed 1968-71, ed 1971-74; chm Mirror Group Newspapers 1980-84 (editorial dir 1975-79), dir Reuters Ltd 1978-84, exec publisher Globe Communications Corporation Florida USA 1985-90; memb: Press Cncl 1975-78, Br Exec Ctee Int Press Inst 1976-84; vice pres Newspaper Press Fund; *Recreations* bridge; *Clubs* Reform, Boca Raton Club (Florida); *Style—* Anthony Miles, Esq; 23331 Drayton Drive, Boca Raton, Florida 33433, USA (☎ 407 394 5285); 197 Friern Barnet

Lane, London N20 ONN

MILES, Baron (Life Peer UK 1979), of Blackfriars in the City of London; Bernard James Miles; CBE (1953); s of Edwin James Miles, and Barbara, *née* Fletcher; *b* 27 Sept 1907; *Educ* Uxbridge Co Sch, Pembroke Coll Oxford, City Univ; *m* 1931, Josephine Wilson (d 1990), da of Benjamin Hinchliffe, of Hough End, Bramley, Yorkshire; 1 s, 2 da (1 decd); *Career* actor; fndr with his w of the Mermaid Theatre, Puddle Dock, EC4 1959; author; hon fell Pembroke Coll Oxford 1969, Hon DLitt City Univ 1974; kt 1969; *Books* The British Theatre, God's Brainwave, Favourite Tales from Shakespeare; *Style—* The Rt Hon the Lord Miles, CBE; c/o The House of Lords, London SW1A 0PW

MILES, Brian; RD; s of Terence Clifford Miles (d 1945), and Muriel Irene, *née* Terry; *b* 23 Feb 1937; *Educ* Reeds Sch, HMS Conway Cadet Sch; *m* 10 Oct 1964, (Elizabeth) Anne, *née* Scott; 1 s (Martin b 30 Aug 1966), 2 da (Amanda b 29 May 1968, Sara b 10 April 1970); *Career* P & O Shipping Co: cadet 1954-57, deck offr 1958-64, master mariner (FG) 1964; RNLI: inspr of lifeboats 1964-73, staff appts 1974-81, dep dir 1982-87, dir 1988-; memb Parkstone Rotary Club, chm Dolphin Tst; FNI; Gold Medal Of Spanish Red Cross, Hon Distinguished Serv Medal Japan Lifeboat Inst; *Recreations* country sports, walking, reading, music, theatre; *Style—* Brian Miles, Esq, RD; 8 Longfield Dr, West Parley, Wimborne, Dorset BH22 8TY (☎ 0202 571 739); RNLI West Quay Rd, Poole, Dorset BH15 1HZ (☎ 0202 671 133, telex 41328)

MILES, Hon Mrs (Christine Helena); *née* Weld-Forester; da of 7 Baron Forester (d 1977), and Marie Louise Priscilla, *née* Perrott; *b* 20 March 1932; *Educ* Lawnside Great Malvern; *m* 1, 31 July 1951 (m dis 1981), 7 Baron Bolton; 2 s, 1 da; m 2, 22 July 1985, Philip David Miles, s of Maj Walter Harold Miles (d 1982); *Recreations* hunting, fishing, working gun dogs; *Style—* The Hon Mrs Miles; Hinton Hall, Lea Cross, nr Shrewsbury SY5 8JA (☎ 074 821203)

MILES, Prof Christopher John; s of Capt John Miles, MC (d 1979), and Clarice Baskerville, *née* Remnant (d 1986); *b* 19 April 1939; *Educ* Winchester, Institut des Hautes Études Cinématographies; *m* 10 Nov 1967, Susan Helen Howard, da of John Anderson Armstrong, CB, OBE, TD (d 1990), of Dacre Cottage, Nr Penrith, Cumbria CA11 OHL; 1 da (Sophie b 30 Dec 1970); *Career* offr cadet Intelligence Corps 1959-60; film dir and prodr; bd memb Br Lion Films and Milesian Films 1963; prodns inc: Six Sided Triangle (Hollywood Oscar nomination) 1963, The Virgin and The Gypsy (voted best film in UK and USA by critics) 1969, The Maids (winner Les Yeux Fertiles Cannes Festival) 1974, Alternative Three (nominated TV drama awards) 1976, Priest of Love 1981, Lord Elgin and Some Stones of No Value 1985; work for theatre incl dir Skin of our Teeth Chicago 1973; lectr for Br Cncl during Br Film Year India 1985; *Books* Alternative Three (1977); *Recreations* painting, piano, tennis & cinema; *Clubs* Garrick, Hurlingham; *Style—* Prof Christopher Miles; Royal College of Art, Film Department, Kensington Gore, London SW7 3EU (☎ 071 584 5020, fax 071 225 1487)

MILES, Dillwyn; s of Joshua Miles (d 1932), of Newport, Pembrokeshire, and Anne Mariah, *née* Lewis (d 1946); *b* 25 May 1916; *Educ* Fishguard County Sch, UC of Wales Aberystwyth; *m* 2 Feb 1944, Joyce Eileen (d 1976), da of Lewis Craven Ord (d 1952), of Montreal and London; 1 s (Anthony b 1945), 1 da (Marilyn b 1946); *Career* ME (Army Capt) 1939-45, nat organiser Palestine House London 1945-48; community centres offr Wales 1948-54; dir: Pembrokeshire Community Cncl 1954-75, Dyfed Rural Cncl 1975-81; chm Nat Assoc of Local Cncls 1975-87 (vice pres 1987-); The Herald Bard 1967-; memb: Pembrokeshire CC 1947-63, Cemaes RDC 1947-52, Haverfordwest Borough Cncl 1957-63, Pembrokeshire Coast Nat Park Ctee 1952-75, Prince of Wales Ctee 1971-80, Sports Cncl for Wales 1969-70, Nature Conservancy Cncl for Wales 1966-73, Soc for Promotion of Nature Reserves 1961-73; Mayor of Newport, Pembrokeshire 1950, 1966, 1967 and 1979 (Alderman 1951-); Mayor of Haverfordwest 1961, Sheriff 1963; Burgess of the Ancient Borough of Newport 1935, Burgess of the Borough of Haverfordwest 1974; FRGS 1945; *Books* The Royal National Eisteddfod of Wales (1978), A Pembrokeshire Anthology (1983), Portrait of Pembrokeshire (1984), Pembrokeshire Coast National Park (1987); *Recreations* walking, food, wine; *Clubs* Savile, Wig and Pen; *Style—* Dillwyn Miles, Esq; 9 St Anthony's Way, Haverfordwest, Pembrokeshire, Dyfed SA61 1EL (☎ 0437 5275)

MILES, Hamish Alexander Drummond; OBE (1987); s of James Edward (Hamish) Miles (d 1937), and Sheila Barbara, *née* Robertson (d 1954); *b* 19 Nov 1925; *Educ* Douai Sch, Univ of Edinburgh, Univ of Oxford; *m* 31 Aug 1957, Jean Marie, da of Theodore Richard Smits, of New York; 2 s (Alexander, James), 2 da (Rachel, Helen); *Career* 1944-47: Black Watch, 6 Br Independent Parachute Bde; asst curator Glasgow Art Gallery 1953-54, lectr history of art (formerly asst lectr) Univ of Glasgow 1954-66, visiting lectr Smith Coll Mass 1960-61, prof hist of art Univ of Leicester 1966-70, Barber prof fine arts and dir Barber Inst of Fine Arts 1970-09, dir emeritus Barber Inst of Fine Arts and prof at large Univ of Birmingham 1990-91; tstee: Nat Galleries of Scotland 1967-87, Public Art Cmmns Agency 1987-; memb Museums and Galleries Cmmn 1983-87; *Style—* Hamish Miles, Esq, OBE; 37 Carpenter Rd, Birmingham, West Midlands B15 2JJ; Burnside, Kirkmichael, by Blairgowrie, Perthshire

MILES, Jeremy John; s of Frederick George Miles (d 1976), and Maxine Frances Mary (Blossom), *née* Forbes Robertson (d 1984); *b* 1 Jan 1933; *Educ* Harrow; *m* 1957, Susan (Sue); 1 s (Jonathan b 1959); *Career* 2 Sub Lt RNVR Fleet Air Arm 1951-53 dir: Miles Electronics Ltd 1965-69, Link-Miles Ltd 1969-70, F G Miles Engineering Ltd 1970-75; non-exec dir: Hunting Hivolt Ltd 1976-88, Vanderhoff plc 1976- (chm 1976-85); non exec chm: Persona plc 1986-, Hunting Electronics Ltd 1988-90; *Recreations* sailing, skiing; *Style—* Jeremy Miles, Esq; Sele Priory, Church Lane, Upper Beeding, W Sussex BN4 3HP (☎ 0903 879006, fax 0903 879017, car 0836 226052)

MILES, Prof John Richard; s of Thomas William Miles (d 1988), and Hilda Mary, *née* Davis; *b* 22 June 1944; *m* (m dis); *Career* designer and tutor; colourist designer and conslt Fidelis Furnishing Fabrics (later amalgamated with Tootals) 1969-74, work shown in prototype Exhibition at Design Council 1970; designer of fashion furnishings and household textiles for worldwide market 1969-, clients incl: Courtaulds, Heal's, Liberty's, Christian Dior, Yves Saint Laurant; set up own studio: Calver & Pound Designs 1973-77, Peppermint Prints 1977-81; design dir of home furnishings and apparel fabrics Courtaulds Plc 1986-87 (design dir of home furnishings 1985-86); NEXT Interior: design mangr 1987, design and buying mangr 1987, gen mangr 1987-88; set up own studio Miles Whiston & Wright 1989-; CNAA: chm Fashion and Textile Panel 1984-87 (memb 1978-81), memb Ctee for Art and Design 1984-87 and 1988-, specialist advsr to Ctee for Art and Design 1987; memb: Textile Ctee Design Centre Selection 1985-88 (memb Knitwear Ctee 1984-86), Selection Panel for Youing Designers into Industry RSA 1987-89; sr lectr i/c of textiles St Martin's Sch of Art 1974-75, head of Fashion Dept and Textiles Course leader Brighton Polytechnic 1979-85 prof of textiles and fashion Royal Coll of Art 1989-; pt/t and visiting lectr; memb numerous academic ctees Brighton Polytechnic and Royal Coll of Art; internal and external assessor; memb Assoc of Heads of Degree Courses for Fashion and Textiles 1979-85; *Recreations* gardening, cooking, theatre, films, reading, music; *Style—* Prof John Miles; Royal College of Art, Kensington Gore, London SW7 2EU (☎ 071 584 5020 ext 266)

MILES, John Seeley; s of Thomas Miles (d 1965), and Winifred, *née* Seeley (d 1981); *b* 11 Feb 1931; *Educ* Beckenham GS, Beckenham Art Sch; *m* 1955, Louise Rachel, da of George Rowland Wilson (d 1983); 1 s (Jonathan b 1964), 2 da (Catherine b 1958, Sophia b 1960); *Career* asst to Hans Schmoller Penguin Books 1955-58, formed Banks and Miles with Colin Banks 1958; conslt: Zoological Soc, Regents Park, Whipsnade 1958-62, Expanded Metal Co 1960-83, Consumers Assoc 1964-84, PO 1972-83, Br Cncl 1968-83, Curwen Press 1970-73, E Midlands Arts Assoc 1974-79, Enschede en Zn Netherlands 1980-, BT 1980, Br Airports Authy, Univ of Lancaster 1989 chm arbitration ctee Assoc Typographique Int 1984-, design advsr: Monotype Corpn 1985-; UEA 1990-; typographic advsr HMSO 1985-, Green award for environmental design (with Colin Banks) 1989; govr Central Sch of Arts and Craft 1978-85; memb CGLI 1986; *Books* Design for Desktop Publishing (1987); *Recreations* gardening, painting; *Clubs* Arts, Double Crown; *Style—* John Miles, Esq; 24 Collins St, Blackheath, London SE3 0GU (☎ 071 318 4739); Banks & Miles, 1 Tranquil Vale, Blackheath, London SE3 0BU (☎ 071 318 1131)

MILES, Keith Charles; s of Leslie Maurice Miles, of Reading, Berks, and Doris Ellen Wyard Miles; *b* 28 Nov 1941; *Educ* Owens Sch; *m* 20 Dec 1969, Slava, da of Jože Blenkuš (d 1977); 1 s (Andrew Karel Scott b 1973), 1 da (Jane Helena Louise b 1977); *Career* CA; dir fin and ops Cable Authy 1985-88, dir of fin and admin Inst of Econ Affrs 1988-90, special advsr Putnam Hayes & Barlett 1989-90, co sec and gp fin dir Etam plc 1990-; only English memb Advsy Cncl of the Cabinet of Repub of Slovenia Yugoslavia; Liveryman: Worshipful Co of Glass Sellers, Worshipful Co of CAs; *Recreations* skiing, reading, swimming; *Style—* Keith Miles, Esq; 19 Elmtree Green, Gt Missenden, Bucks HP16 9AF

MILES, Malcolm John; s of John Frederick Miles, MBE, of Kingston-upon-Thames, Surrey, and Phyllis Maud, *née* Umpelby; *b* 5 March 1945; *Educ* London Coll For Distributive Trades (Dip Bus Studies), Univ of Chicago; *m* 22 Nov 1969, Ann Therisa, da of Roy Augustine O'Dwyer, of Dorking, Surrey; 1 s (Alexander Malcolm (Bertie) b 1978); *Career* 225 water sports Binbeca Minorca 1971; assoc dir Ted Bates advertising London 1975-76; McCann Erickson advertising London: account dir 1971-74, assoc dir 1977, Bd dir 1980, dir account mgmnt, dep md 1984, md 1985-; dir McCann Erickson Kenya, chm McCann Network UK; memb: Tobacco Ctee EAAA Brussels 1980-84, Marketing Ctee CBI 1986-88, Cncl CBI 1987, Cncl IPA 1989; MCAM (1973), MAA (1969), FIPA 1990 (MIPA 1980); *Recreations* shooting, gardening, family; *Clubs* RAC, ESU; *Style—* M J Miles, Esq; 36 Howland St, London, W1A 1AT (☎ 071 580 6690, fax 323 2883, car 0836 255 886 and 0860 511084, telex 28231)

MILES, Dame Margaret; DBE (1970); da of Rev E G Miles and Annie, *née* Jones; *b* 11 July 1911; *Educ* Ipswich High Sch, Bedford Coll Univ of London (BA); *Career* history teacher Westcliff High Sch 1935-39, Badminton Sch 193C-44; lectr Dept of Educn Univ of Bristol 1944-46, headmistress Pate's Grammar Sch Cheltenham 1946-52, headmistress Mayfield Sch Putney 1952-73; memb Schools Broadcasting Cncl 1958-68, Educ Advsy Cncl ITA 1962-67, Nat Advsy Cncl on Trg and Supply of Teachers 1962-65, BBC Gen Advsy Cncl 1964-73, Campaign for Comprehensive Educn 1966 (chm 1972, pres 1979-), RSA Cncl 1972-77; chm Central Bureau for Educnl Visits and Exchanges 1978-82, Advsy Ctee on Devpt Educn ODM 1977-79; pres Br Assoc for Counselling 1980-; fell Bedford Coll 1983; Hon DCL Univ of Kent at Canterbury 1973; fell King's Coll Lond 1985; *Books* And Gladly Teach (1965), Comprehensive Schooling, Problems and Perspectives (1968); *Recreations* opera, films, gardening, golf; *Clubs* Univ Women's, Aberdovey Golf; *Style—* Dame Margaret Miles, DBE; Tanycraig, Pennal, Machynlleth, Powys

MILES, (Henry) Michael Pearson; OBE (1989); s of Brig H G P Miles (d 1966), of London, and Margaret, *née* Mounsey (d 1974); *b* 19 April 1936; *Educ* Wellington; *m* 25 Oct 1967, Carol Jane, da of Harold Berg (d 1955); 2 s (Henry James Pearson b 1969, Mark Edward Pearson b 1975), 1 da (Sasha Jane Pearson b 1971); *Career* Nat Serv cmmd Duke of Wellington's Regt 1955-57; md John Swire and Sons (Japan) Ltd 1973-76; dir: Hongkong & Shanghai Banking Corporation 1984-88, John Swire & Sons Ltd 1988- (joined 1958); currently chm: John Swire & Sons (HK) Ltd, Cathay Pacific Airways Ltd, Hong Kong Tourist Assoc; memb Bd: Barings plc, Fraser Insurance Services, Johnson Matthey plc, Portals plc, Thomas Cook Group, Fleming Far Eastern Investmt Tst, Sedgwick Lloyd's Underwriting Agents, Navy Army and Air Force Inst; memb: Int Advsy Bd Creditanstalt Vienna, Anglo-Taiwan Trade Ctee, China-Britain Trade Group; govr Wellington Coll; *Recreations* golf, tennis, shooting; *Clubs* Royal & Ancient Golf, Berkshire Golf, Queen's; *Style—* Michael Miles, Esq, OBE; John Swire & Sons Ltd, Swire House, 59 Buckingham Gate, London SW1E 6AJ (☎ 071 834 7717, fax 071 630 0353, telex 888800)

MILES, Nicholas Charles James; s of Kenneth Norman Miles, of Whitegate Cottage, Crowborough, E Sussex, and Audrey Mary, *née* Rhodes; *b* 23 Oct 1958; *Educ* Tonbridge, CCC Cambridge (BA); *m* 12 May 1990, Suzanne Katharine, *née* Chauvean; *Career* dir: BMP Business Ltd 1985-87, Lowe Bell Financial Ltd 1987-; performed in Death in the Aisles, Nightcap Cambridge Footlights Revues 1979; *Recreations* tennis, golf, revue; *Clubs* Annabel's, RAC, Bachelors; *Style—* Nicholas Miles, Esq; 1 Red Lion Court, London EC4 (☎ 071 353 9203, car 0836 293357)

MILES, (Richard) Oliver; CMG (1984); s of George Cockburn Miles (d 1980), and Olive Catherine, *née* Clapham (d 1973); *b* 6 March 1936; *Educ* Ampleforth, Merton Coll Oxford; *m* 1968, Julia Lyndall, da of Prof Joseph Sidney Weiner (d 1982); 3 s (Joe b 1972, Tom b 1973, Hugh b 1977), 1 da (Lucy b 1979); *Career* ambassador: Libya 1984, Luxembourg 1985; asst under Sec FCO; *Clubs* Travellers; *Style—* Oliver Miles, Esq, CMG; c/o Foreign and Cwlth Office, King Charles St, London SW14 2AH

MILES, Peter Thomas; s of Thomas Harry Miles (d 1968); *b* 1 Aug 1939; *Educ* Bromsgrove Sch; *m* 18 June 1971, Gail, da of Trevor Davies; 2 c (Juliet Elizabeth b 24 Sept 1972, Edward Thomas b 10 Feb 1972); *Career* chartered accountant; ptnr: Russell Durie Kerr Watson & Co 1968, Spicer & Pegler (following merger), Touche Ross & Co 1990- (following merger); ACA; *Recreations* fishing, tennis, gardening; *Style—* Peter T Miles, Esq; Touche Ross & Co, Newater House, 11 Newhall St, Birmingham B3 3NY (☎ 021 200 2211, fax 021 236 1513)

MILES, Sir Peter Tremayne; KCVO (1986); s of Lt-Col E W T Miles, MC (d 1943), of Manor House, Kington Langley, Chippenham, Wilts, and Mary Albinia, *née* Gibbs (d 1979); *b* 26 June 1924; *Educ* Eton, RMA Sandhurst; *m* 1, 25 July 1956, Philippa Helen, da of E M B Jack Tremlett (d 1977), of Noddings Farm, Chiddingfold, Surrey; 2 s (Napier b 1 Sept 1958, Patrick b 1 June 1960), 1 da (Davina b 8 Jan 1964) m 2, 9 Sept 1989, Paul Morgan-Witts, s of Max Morgan Witts; *Career* 1 Royal Dragoons 1944-49; J F Thomasson and Co 1949-59, md Gerrard and Nat Discount Co Ltd 1964-80 (joined 1959); dir: P Murray Jones Ltd 1966-75, Astley and Pearce Hldgs 1975-80 (chm 1978-80), keeper of the privy purse and treas to HM The Queen 1981-87, receiver gen to Duchy of Lancaster 1981-87, memb Prince of Wales' Cncl 1981-87, dir Br and Cwlth Hldgs 1988-90; *Clubs* White's, Pratt's, Cavalry and Guards, Swinley Forest Golf, City of London; *Style—* Sir Peter Miles, KCVO; Mill House, Southrop, Lechlade, Glos (☎ 036 785 287); Flat 4, Kylestrome House, Cundy St, London SW1W 99T (☎ 071 730 5666)

MILES, Philip John; s and h of Sir William Napier Maurice Miles, 6 Bt; *b* 10 Aug 1953; *Style—* Philip Miles Esq

MILES, Roger Tremayne; s of Peter Tremayne Miles (Lt Cdr RN, ret), of

Maidenhead, Berks, and Christine Valerie Walby, *née* Perks; *b* 9 March 1962; *Educ* Tonbridge, Trinity Coll Oxford (exhibitioner, MA); *m* 28 May 1990, Deirdra Mary, da of Patrick Gregory Moynihan, of Sidcup, Kent; *Career* articled clerk Price Waterhouse 1983-85, Charles Barker City Ltd 1985-88 (account exec, account mangr to MD), PR mangr Collett Dickenson Pearce 1988, Charles Barker City Ltd 1988-90 (assoc dir, Bd dir), Bd dir Charles Barker Ltd 1990-; memb: Ctee José Carreras Leukaemia Fndn Gala 1990-91, Civic Trust 1990; ABSA 1987-88, memb PRCA 1989-; *Recreations* music, novels, junk tv, country walks, gadgets, thinking about getting fit; *Style*— Roger Miles, Esq; Charles Barker Ltd, 30 Farringdon St, London EC4A 4EA (☎ 071 634 1000)

MILES, Stephen Antony David; s of Antony Richard Miles, of Chorleywood, Herts, and Marjorie, *née* Allwork; *b* 21 June 1947; *Educ* Marist Brothers Coll Inanda Johannesburg SA, Univ of the Witwatersrand Johannesburg (MB BCh), FRES (Edinburgh); *Career* various trg posts in Johannesburg; sr registrar accident and emergency St Barts and UCH 1979-82, conslt St Barts and Homerton Hosp 1982-; regnl chm Accident and Emergency Advsy Ctee NE Thames RHA, pres elect Accident and Emergency Section RSM; dir London Ambulance Serv 1990, hon sec Br Assoc for Accident and Emergency Med 1990; Freeman City of London 1984; FRCS (Edinburgh) 1975, BMA 1980, RSM 1987; *Recreations* music, ballet, theatre, house renovation; *Style*— Stephen Miles, Esq; Accident And Emergency Department, St Bartholomews Hospital, West Smithfield, London EC1A 7BE (☎ 071 601 7770, fax 071 601 7656)

MILES, (Frank) Stephen; CMG (1964); s of Harry Miles (d 1929), and Mary, *née* Brown (d 1965); *b* 7 Jan 1920; *Educ* John Watson's Sch Edinburgh, Daniel Stewart's Coll Edinburgh, Univ of St Andrews (MA), Harvard Univ (MPA); *m* 1953, Margaret Joy, da of Godfrey Theaker (d 1974); 3 da (Ann, Judith, Susan); *Career* WWII Fleet Air Arm 1942-46, Lt (A) RNVR; Scot Home Dept 1948; Dip Serv 1948-80: NZ 1949-52, E and W Pakistan 1954-57, Ghana 1959-62, Uganda 1962-63, Br dep high cmmr Tanzania 1963-65 (actg high cmmr 1963-64); actg high cmmr Ghana March-April 1966, consul gen St Louis Missouri 1967-70, dep high cmmr Calcutta 1970-74; high cmmr: Zambia 1974-78 and Bangladesh 1978-79; dir of studies overseas servs unit Royal Inst of Public Admin 1980-83, dist cncllr Tandridge DC 1982-90, chm Limpsfield Parish Cncl 1987-89; *Recreations* cricket, tennis, golf; *Clubs* Cwlth Tst, MCC, Tandridge Golf; *Style*— Stephen Miles, Esq, CMG; Maytrees, 71 Park Rd, Limpsfield, Oxted, Surrey RH8 0AN (☎ 0883 713132)

MILES, William Miles; s of William Miles (d 1978), of 30 Highway Rd, Leics, and Gladys Violet, *née* Beaver, *qv*; *b* 26 Sept 1933; *Educ* Wyggeston Sch Leicester, Trinity Hall Cambridge (MA, LLM); *m* 1961, Jillian Anne, da of Robert Walker Wilson (d 1970), of 47 Roehampton Drive, Wigston Fields, Leicester; 3 s (William Robert b 1962, Jonathan Andrew b 1964, David James b 1965); *Career* asst slr Leicester and Doncaster Co Boroughs 1960-65, sr asst slr Exeter 1965-66, asst town clerk Leicester 1966-69, dep town clerk Blackpool 1969-73, city legal advsr Newcastle-upon-Tyne 1973-74, chief exec Gateshead 1974-84, chief exec and clerk, clerk to Lieutenancy West Yorks CC 1984-86, dir Yorkshire Enterprise Ltd 1984-; *Recreations* bridge, athletics, mountain walking; *Style*— William Miles, Esq; 23 Moor Crescent, Gosforth, Newcastle-upon-Tyne NE3 4AP (☎ 091 285 1996)

MILES, Sir William Napier Maurice; 6 Bt (UK 1859), of Leigh Court, Somersetshire; s of Lt-Col Sir Charles William Miles, 5 Bt, OBE (d 1966); *b* 19 Oct 1913; *Educ* Stowe, Jesus Coll Cambridge; *m* 1946, Pamela Dillon; 1 s, 2 da; *Heir* s, Philip John Miles; *Career* chartered architect (ret); ARIBA; *Clubs* Royal Western Yacht; *Style*— Sir William Miles, Bt; Old Rectory House, Walton-in-Gordano, nr Clevedon, Avon (☎ 0272 873365)

MILFORD, John Tillman; QC (1989); s of Roy Douglas Milford (d 1982), of Grianachan, Strathtay, Perthshire, and Essie *née* Rhind (d 1972); *b* 4 Feb 1946; *Educ* Hurstpierpoint, Univ of Exeter (LLB); *m* 1975, Mary Alice, da of Edmund Anthony Spriggs (d 1989), of River House, Wylam, Northumberland; 3 da (Alice b 1977, Sarah b 1979, Emily b 1981); *Career* called to the Bar Inner Temple 1969; practising Newcastle upon Tyne 1970-; rec Crown Court 1985-; *Recreations* fishing, shooting, gardening; *Clubs* Northern Counties, (Newcastle upon Tyne); *Style*— John T Milford, Esq, QC; Hill House, Haydon Bridge, Hexham, Northumberland; 12 Trinity Chare, Quayside, Newcastle-upon-Tyne (☎ 232 1927)

MILFORD, 2 Baron (UK 1939); Sir Wogan Philipps; 2 Bt (UK 1919); s of 1 Baron Milford (d 1962; 6 s of Rev Sir James Philipps, 12 Bt, by Hon Mary Best, sis of 5 Baron Wynford; also yst bro of 1 Viscount St Davids), and Ethel Speke, niece of the African explorer John Speke (discoverer of Lake Victoria and, with Sir Richard Burton, Lake Tanganyika); *b* 25 Feb 1902; *Educ* Eton, Magdalen Coll Oxford; *m* 1, 1928 (m dis 1944), the novelist Rosamond Lehmann; 1 s (and 1 da decd); m 2, 1944, as her 2 husb, Cristina (d 1953), former w of 15 Earl of Huntingdon and da of the Marchese Casati by his w, the Marchesa, subject of the celebrated portrait by Augustus John; m 3, 1954, Tamara, *née* Kravetz, widow of William Rust, sometime ed The Daily Worker; 1 s; *Heir* s, Hon Hugo Philipps; *Career* farmer, painter, trades unionist, former memb Henley and Cirencester RDCs, late Int Brigade; *Style*— The Rt Hon Lord Milford

MILFORD HAVEN, 4 Marquess of (UK 1917); George Ivar Louis Mountbatten; also Earl of Medina and Viscount Alderney (both UK 1917); s of 3 Marquess of Milford Haven, OBE, DSC (d 1970, himself gs of HSH Prince Louis of Battenberg, who relinquished, at the King's request, the style and title of Serene Highness and Prince of Battenberg, instead assuming the surname of Mountbatten by Royal Licence 1917); gn of late Earl Mountbatten of Burma and, through his paternal grandmother (Nada), ggggs of Emperor Nicholas I of Russia; *b* 6 June 1961; *Educ* Gordonstoun; *m* 8 March 1989, Sarah Georgina, er da of George Alfred Walker, *qv*; 1 da (Lady Tatiana Helen Georgia b 16 April 1990); *Heir* bro, Lord Ivar Alexander Michael Mountbatten; *Style*— The Most Hon the Marquess of Milford Haven; Moyns Park, Birdbrook, Essex

MILFORD HAVEN, Janet, Marchioness of; Janet Mercedes Mountbatten; *née* Bryce; JP (Inner London 1979); o da of late Maj Francis Bryce, OBE, KRRC, and Gladys Jean, *née* Mosley; *b* 29 Sept 1937,Bermuda; *Educ* Trafalgar Sch for Girls Montreal Canada; *m* 17 Nov 1960, as his 2 w, 3 Marquess of Milford Haven, OBE, DSC (d 1970); 2 s (George, 4 Marquess of Milford Haven b 1960, Lord Ivar Mountbatten b 1963, *qqv*); *Style*— The Most Hon Janet, Marchioness of Milford Haven, JP; Moyns Park, Birdbrook, Essex

MILHOFER, Anthony Charles; s of Manfred Milhofer (d 1984), of Chislehurst, Kent, and Veronica Catherine, *née* Glover (d 1983); *b* 25 May 1940; *Educ* Cranleigh; *m* 3 Sept 1966, Elizabeth, da of John Ragg (d 1985), of W Byfleet, Surrey; 3 s (Peter John b 1969, Martin Roger b 1972, Ian David b 1979); *Career* Abbey National Building Society: joined 1959, branch mangr Staines 1963-64, asst estab offr 1965-66, dep mangr personnel and trg 1967-70, branch mangr Holborn 1971-73, regnl mangr SE Eng 1974-79, divnl mangr Sales 1979-83, mangr Southern Ops 1984, ret as head of R&D 1988; sales and mktg conslt to fin servs and industry, chm travel agency 1989; Freeman: City of London, Worshipful Co of Horners (1972); FCIS, FBIM 1974; *Style*— Anthony Milhofer, Esq; Grove Farm, Grove, Leighton Buzzard, Bedfordshire LU7 0QU (☎ 0525 372 225)

MILKINA, Nina; da of Jacques Milkine, and Sophie Milkine; *b* 27 Jan 1919; *Educ* privately; *m* 1943, Alastair Robert Masson Sedgwick; 1 s (Alexander Paul b 1958), 1 da (Katrina b 1960); *Career* concert pianist noted for performances of Mozart's piano works; studied: Paris with Leon Conus of Moscow Conservatoire, composition with Sabaniev and Glazunov, in England with Harold Craxton and Tobias Matthay; first public performance with Lamoreux Orchestra in Paris aged 11; BBC cmmn to broadcast all Mozart's piano sonatas, gave Mozart Bicentenary Recital Edinburgh Int Festival; recorded for: Westminster Record Co, Pye, ASV; first composition published aged 11 by Boosey and Hawkes; adjudicator at major music competitions; Hon RAM; *Recreations* chess, swimming; *Style*— Miss Nina Milkina; 20 Paradise Walk, London SW3 4JL (☎ 071 352 2501)

MILL, Ian Alexander; s of Ronald MacLauchlan Mill (d 1984), and Thelma Anita, *née* Boliston; *b* 9 April 1958; *Educ* Epsom Coll, Univ of Cambridge (MA); *m* 13 June 1987, (Mary) Emma, da of Roger Clayden, of Los Gatos, California, USA; *Career* called to the Bar Middle Temple 1981; commercial barr specialising in entertainment law 1982-; *Recreations* cricket, golf, good food and wine, travel; *Clubs* MCC; *Style*— Ian Mill, Esq; 49 Moreton Pl, London SW1V 2NL (☎ 071 834 5804); 2 Hare Ct, Temple, London EC4Y 7BH (☎ 071 583 1770, fax 071 583 9269, telex 27139 LINLAW)

MILLA, Dr Peter John; s of John Milla (d 1961), of 32 Station Ave, Sandown, IOW, and Betty Violet, *née* Barton; *b* 4 Aug 1941; *Educ* Whitgift Sch, St Bartholomew's Hosp Med Coll (MB BS), Chelsea Coll Univ of London (MSc); *m* Sept 1969, (Pamela) Jane, da of John Davis, of 33 Almond Close, Bedhampton, Havant, Hants; 1 s (Richard b 1972), 1 da (Elizabeth b 1974); *Career* sr lectr in child health Inst of Child Health Univ of London 1983- (lectr 1978-83); memb ed bd: Gut, Archives of Disease of Childhood, Journal of Paediatric Gastroenterology and Nutrition, Journal of Gastrointestinal Motility; advsr Wellcome Tst; memb: cncl Euro Soc of Paediatric Gastroenterology and Nutrition, Br Paediatric Assoc, Br Soc of Gastroenterology, Br Soc of Paediatric Gastroenterology and Nutrition; FRCP 1985; *Books* Harries' Paediatric Gastroenterology (ed with D R P Muller, 1988), Disorders of Gastrointestinal Motility (1988); *Recreations* sailing, motoring, gardening, model engineering; *Style*— Dr Peter Milla; Dept of Child Health, Institute of Child Health, University of London, 30 Guildford St, London WC1N 1EH (☎ 071 242 9789)

MILLAIS, Geoffroy Richard Everett; s and h of Sir Ralph Regnault Millais, 5 Bt; *b* 27 Dec 1941; *Educ* Marlborough; *Style*— Geoffroy Millais, Esq

MILLAIS, Sir Ralph Regnault; 5 Bt (UK 1885), of Palace Gate, Kensington, Co Middlesex and of St Ouen, Jersey; s of Sir Geoffroy William Millais, 4 Bt (d 1941); the 1 Bt was Sir John Everett Millais, the artist and pres RA; *b* 4 March 1905; *Educ* Marlborough, Trinity Cambridge; *m* 1, 4 Sept 1939 (m dis 1947), Felicity Caroline Mary Ward, da of Brig-Gen William Ward Warner, CMG (d 1950), and formerly w of Maj John Peyton Robinson, 8 Hussars; 1 s (Geoffroy), 1 da (Caroline); m 2, 22 Oct 1947 (m dis 1971), Irene Jessie (d 1985), er da of late Edward Albert Stone, of St Anne's Mont à l'Abbé, St Helier, Jersey, and formerly w of Stephen Eric Alley; m 3, 1975 Mrs Babette Sefton-Smith, da of Maj-Gen Harold Francis Salt, CB, CMG, DSO (d 1971); *Heir* s, Geoffroy Richard Everett Millais; *Career* joined RAFVR 1939, Sqdn Ldr 1940, Wing Cdr 1941, Belgium, Holland 1944-45, Air Min 1939-46; asst private sec to the Home Secretary 1926-27; business career 1927-39 and 1946-73 (ret 1973); *Recreations* restoration of vintage cars, fishing; *Style*— Sir Ralph Millais, Bt; Gate Cottage, Winchelsea, E Sussex TN36 4HL

MILLAN, Rt Hon Bruce; PC (1975); s of David Millan; *b* 5 Oct 1927; *Educ* Harris Acad Dundee; *m* 1953, Gwendoline May Fairey; 1 s, 1 da; *Career* MP (Lab): Glasgow Craigton 1959-83, Glasgow Govan 1983-88; Parly under-sec: Def (RAF) 1964-66, Scotland 1966-70; min state Scottish Office 1974-76, sec state Scotland 1976-79, oppn front bench spokesman Scotland 1979-83, Euro cmmr 1989-; *Style*— The Rt Hon Bruce Millan; 10 Beech Ave, Glasgow G41 (☎ 041 427 6483)

MILLAR; *see*: Hoyer Millar

MILLAR, Angus George; WS (1955); s of George William Russell Millar (d 1929), of Port Dickson, Malaya, and Audrey Margaret, *née* Watson (d 1954); *b* 1 July 1928; *Educ* Loretto, Jesus Coll Oxford (BA), Univ of Edinburgh (LLB); *m* 25 April 1959, Julia Mary, da of Alan Reginald Cathcart (d 1967), of Kirkcudbright; 3 s (James b 1961, Charles b 1963, Roderick b 1967); *Career* Nat Serv 1950-52 Royal Signals, 2 Lt 1951, Lt 1952; Baillie Gifford and Co Investment Managers Edinburgh: trainee analyst and asst mangr 1955-61, ptnr 1961-89, sr ptnr 1984-89; dir: Investors Capital Trust plc 1970-85, UK Provident Institute 1978-86; dep chm Assoc of Investment Trust Companies 1980-82; memb: Fin Ctee Nat Tst for Scot, Ctee of Friends of Royal Hosp for Sick Children Edinburgh; patron Appeal for Prince's Scot Youth Business Tst; *Recreations* travel, hill walking, visiting art galleries, golf; *Clubs* New (Edinburgh), East India; *Style*— Angus G Millar, Esq, WS; 24 Buckingham Terrace, Edinburgh EH4 3AE (☎ 031 343 1732)

MILLAR, Anthony Bruce (Tony); s of James Desmond Millar (d 1965), and Josephine Georgina, *née* Brice; *b* 5 Oct 1941; *Educ* Haileybury, Imperial Serv Coll; *m* 3 July 1964, Judith Anne, da of Capt John Edward Jester (d 1984), of Drayton, Hants; 2 da (Cassilda Anne b 1966, Katrina Mary b 1967); *Career* asst to gp mgmnt accountant and gp treas Viyella Int Fedn Ltd 1964-67; Utd Tport Overseas Ltd Nairobi 1967-70: chief accountant to subsidiary, gp internal auditor for E Africa, PA to chief agent, dep gp fin controller London 1970-72; conslt Fairfield Property Co 1975-77 (fin dir 1972-75), md Provincial Laundries Ltd 1977-81, dep chm Hawley Group Ltd 1981, exec chm The Albert Fisher Group PLC 1982-; ACA 1964, FCA 1974, CBIM 1986; *Recreations* swimming, walking, bridge; *Clubs* Mark's; *Style*— Tony Millar, Esq; The Albert Fisher Group PLC, Fisher House, 61 Thames St, Windsor, Berks SL4 1QW (☎ 0753 857111, fax 0753 850911)

MILLAR, Dr (Thomas) Cecil; s of Thomas Nicholl Millar (d 1942), of Co Antrim, NI, and Mary Millar, *née* Hollinger (d 1985); *b* 7 Dec 1921; *Educ* Acad Ballymena, Trinity Coll Dublin (BA, MB); *m* 1944, Joan Maureen, da of Tom Fletcher (d 1936); 1 s (Graeme b 1966), 1 da (Jacqueline b 1959); *Career* general practitioner; past pres Rotary Club; pres: Horticultural Assoc, Civic Soc; BCH; BAO; MRCGR; *Recreations* football, rugby, tennis, badminton; *Clubs* Rotary; *Style*— Dr Cecil Millar; Trostan House, Dene Bank Road, Oswaldtwistle, Hyndburn, Lancs (☎ (0254) 32206); 17/19 Rhyddings Street, Oswaldtwistle, Hyndborn, Lancs (☎ (0254) 32206)

MILLAR, David Lindsay; OBE (1976); o s of David McIntyre Millar (d 1942), of Ardler, Perthshire, and Gwendoline Mary Slade, *née* Forbes (d 1990); *b* 21 July 1928; *Educ* Guildford GS, Perth WA; *m* 20 Sept 1957, Jacqueline, da of Col Charles Francis Rivett-Carnac (d 1958), of Oak Farm, Dickleborough, Norfolk; 3 s (Guy, Mark, Nicholas); *Career* chief mangr The Chartered Bank Hong Kong 1971-75; Standard Chartered Bank London: gen mangr 1976-79, sr gen mangr 1980-82, sr exec dir commercial banking ops 1983-87; memb Int Advsy Bd Sing Tao Holdings Limited 1988-, chm Trident Petroleum NL 1989-; chm The Exchange Banks Assoc Hong Kong 1971-73, memb Banking Advsy Ctee to the Hong Kong Govt 1971-75, dir Trade Devpt Cncl Hong Kong 1973-75, chm The Overseas Bankers Club London 1984-86; ACIB 1971 (memb 1947-71), FCIB 1975; *Recreations* tennis, golf, skiing, sailing, fishing; *Style*— David Millar, Esq, OBE; Bepton Lodge, Bepton, Midhurst, W Sussex GU29 0HX (☎ 073081 6130)

MILLAR, David William; s of Brig William Semple Millar, of 104 Park Road,

Camberley, Surrey, and Maureen Heather, *née* Jones; *b* 30 Jan 1951; *Educ* Morrison's Academy, Univ of Edinburgh (BSc); *m* 3 Sept 1977, Daniele Yolande Germaine, da of Maurice Robert Ferreyrol; 1 s (Hamish Robert b 10 June 1983), 1 da (Pascaline Myrto b 10 Aug 1988); *Career* joined J Walter Thompson 1973 (seconded as asst brand mangr RHM Associates 1975), dir J Walter Thompson 1985- (md JW & Direct 1989-); MIPA 1982; *Recreations* golf; *Clubs* Caledonian, Home Park Golf; *Style*— David Millar, Esq; JWT Direct, 40 Berkeley Square, London W1X 6AD (☎ 071 499 4040)

MILLAR, Dr (James) Gavin Burnett; s of Archibald Underwood Millar, MC (d 1953), and Elspeth Margaret, *née* Burnett (d 1954); *b* 13 Nov 1940; *Educ* Epsom Coll, Clare Coll Cambridge, St Mary's Hosp London (BA, MB, BChir, MSc); *m* 1, 3 August 1963 (m dis 1985) Olive *née* Cumming; 2 s (Alan b 6 May 1965, Michael b 31 March 1967); m 2, 8 June 1988, Jill Wendy; *Career* Middx Hosp London: registrar in med 1969-70, registrar in nuclear med 1971-72; sr registrar in med: Central Middx Hosp 1973-74, Middx Hosp 1974-75; sr lectr in med (endocrinology) Univ of Southampton 1975-; St Mary Hosp Portsmouth: hon conslt physician and endocrinologist 1975-, clinical tutor postgraduate med 1977-80; assoc dean Univ of Southampton Med Sch 1981-; govr and med advsr TVS Trust; MRCP 1968, FRCP 1980; *Recreations* music, golf; *Style*— Dr Gavin Millar; Department of Endocrinology, St Marys Hospital, Portsmouth PO3 6AD (☎ 0705 866145)

MILLAR, Graham; s of Maj Francis Robert Millar of Little Holt, Penington Rd, Beaconsfield, Bucks, and Jean, *née* Bullen; *b* 15 Aug 1943; *Educ* Fettes, Pembroke Coll Oxford (MA); *m* 13 May 1972, Priscilla, da of Maj Arthur Stewart Lord, of 42 Moberly Rd, Salisbury, Wilts; 2 s (Neil b 3 Feb 1981, Angus b 20 Jan 1983); *Career* slr Allen Overy 1969-76; stockbroker: Dunkley Marshall Parrish Stockbrokers 1976-88, Raphael Zorn Hemsley Ltd 1988-; chm GRI Gp plc 1984-9; dir: Sempernova plc 1984-, MTS hldgs 1985-90; memb City of London Slrs Co 1970-; memb: Law Soc 1969-, Int Stock Exchange 1978-; *Recreations* golf, walking, bird watching, reading; *Clubs* Carlton, United Oxford and Cambridge, MCC, Royal St George's Golf, Rye Golf, Walton Health Golf, Royal Cinque Port Golf, Moray Golf; *Style*— Graham Millar, Esq; 60 York Mansions, Prince of Wales Drive, London SW11 4BP (☎ 071 622 6844); 10 Throgmorton Ave, London EC2N 2DP (☎ 071 628 4000, telex 885516, fax 071 628 5986)

MILLAR, Sir Oliver Nicholas; GCVO (1988, KCVO 1973, CVO 1963, MVO 1953); s of Gerald Arthur Millar, MC (d 1975); *b* 26 April 1923; *Educ* Rugby, Courtauld Inst of Art; *m* 1954, Delia Mary, da of Lt-Col Cuthbert Dawnay, MC (d 1964); 1 s, (Charles James), 3 da (Cynthia Mary, Lucy Anne, Beatrix Jane); *Career* dir The Royal Collection 1987-88; surveyor emeritus of pictures to HM The Queen 1988- (asst surveyor 1947, dep surveyor 1949-72, surveyor 1972-88); author of books and catalogues relating chiefly to the history of the Royal collection and the arts in Stuart Eng; tstee Nat Portrait Gallery 1972-; memb: Reviewing Ctee on Export of Works of Art 1975-87, Exec Ctee Nat Arts Collection fund 1987-; tstee Nat Heritage Meml Fund 1988-, chm Patrons of Br Art 1990-, memb Cncl of Friends of the Tate Gallery; FBA; *Recreations* drawing, gardening; *Clubs* Brooks's, MCC; *Style*— Sir Oliver Millar, GCVO; The Cottage, Rays Lane, Penn, Bucks (☎ 049 481 2124)

MILLAR, Peter Carmichael; OBE (1978); s of Rev Peter Carmichael Millar (d 1963), and Ailsa Ross Brown, *née* Campbell; *b* 19 Feb 1927; *Educ* Aberdeen GS, Univ of Glasgow, Univ of St Andrews (MA), Univ of Edinburgh (LLB); *m* 1953, Kirsteen Lindsay, da of Col David Carnegie, CB, OBE, TD, DL (d 1961); 2 s (Neil b 1959, Alastair b 1959), 2 da (Anne b 1955, Alison b 1958); *Career* serv RN 1944-47; WS 1954, dep keeper of HM Signet 1983-91; chm: Mental Welfare Cmmn for Scot 1983-, Church of Scot Gen Tstees 1973-85; ptnr: W & T P Manuel WS 1954-63, Aitken Kinnear & Co WS 1963-87, Aitken Nain WS 1987-; *Recreations* golf, hill walking; *Clubs* New (Edinburgh), Hon Co of Edinburgh Golfers, Bruntsfield Links Golfing Soc; *Style*— Peter C Millar, Esq, OBE; 25 Cramond Rd North, Edinburgh EH4 (☎ 031 336 2069); 7 Abercromby Place, Edinburgh EH3 (☎ 031 556 6644, telex 728112, fax 031 556 6509)

MILLAR, Peter John; s of Norman Millar, of Ashby, Lincs, and Maureen Nelson, *née* McMaster; *b* 22 Feb 1955; *Educ* Bangor GS Co Down NI, Magdalen Coll Oxford (MA); *m* 1981, Jacqueline Carol, *née* Freeman; 2 s (Patrick James Arthur b 1984, Oscar Alexander b 1987); *Career* Reuters corr: Brussels 1978-79, E Berlin 1981-83, Moscow 1983-85; journalist Daily Telegraph 1985-86, Euro corr Sunday Telegraph 1986-89, central Euro corr Sunday Times 1989-90, dep ed The European 1990-; Foreign Corr of the Year Granada TV What the Papers Say awards 1989, commended in int reporter category Br press awards 1989-; *Recreations* cooking, skiing, painting; *Clubs* 2 Brydges Place, Vagabonds; *Style*— Peter Millar, Esq; The European, Orbit House, 5 New Fetter Lane, London EC4 (☎ 071 377 4875, fax 071 377 4773)

MILLAR, (John) Richard; s of William Hugh Millar (d 1967), and Eileen Phyllis May Millar; *b* 16 Feb 1940; *Educ* Wellington; *m* 2 Dec 1978, Rosemary Margaret, da of Alfred Thomas Hanson, of 3 Riverside, Gargrave, N Yorks; *Career* admitted slr 1963, sr ptnr Bischoff & Co 1990- (ptnr 1968-); hon slr: Br Uruguayan Soc, West London Ctee for the Protection of Children; memb Law Soc 1963; Freeman: City of London, Worshipful Co of Slrs; *Recreations* sailing, gardening; *Clubs* Offshore Yachts Class Owners Assoc, Little Ship, City of London; *Style*— Richard Millar, Esq; Epworth House, 25 City Rd, London EC1Y 1AA (☎ 071 628 4222, fax 071 638 3345)

MILLAR, Robert Charles; s of William Millar, of Kirkintilloch, Glasgow, and Mary Armstrong Millar (d 1982); *Educ* Shawlands Acad; *m* 5 Dec 1985, Sylvie Berth, da of Albert Transler, of Macey, France; 1 s (Edward b 25 Dec 1988); *Career* Br Amateur Cycle Rd Race champion 1978 and 1979; professional cyclist 1980-; best climber Tour de France 1984 (finished 4 in gen classification), 2 gen classification Tour of Spain 1985 and 1986, 2 gen classification Tour of Italy 1987 (best climber); winner: Tour of Catalogne 1985, Tour of Britain 1989, stage winner Tour de France 1989 (1983, 1984); *Style*— Robert Millar, Esq

MILLAR, Sir Ronald Graeme; s of Ronald Hugh Millar, and Dorothy Ethel Dacre, *née* Hill; *b* 12 Nov 1919; *Educ* Charterhouse, King's Coll Cambridge; *Career* served WWII Sub Lt RNVR; playwright and political writer; speech writer to PM 1975-90; dep chm Haymarket Theatre 1977-; former actor with appearances in Mr Bolfry, The Sacred Flame, Murder on the Nile, Jenny Jones, Zero Hour (own play); screenwriter in London and Hollywood where films worked on incl: The Miniver Story, Scaramouche, Rose Marie, Betrayed, The Unknown Man, Never Let Me Go; plays produced in London incl: Frieda, Waiting for Gillian, The Bride and the Bachelor, The Bride Comes Back, Robert and Elizabeth (book and lyrics), Number 10, Abelard and Heloise; adaptations for the theatre of works by CP Snow incl: The Affair, The New Men, The Masters, The Case in Question, A Coat of Varnish; kt 1980; *Recreations* music; *Clubs* Brooks's, Dramatists'; *Style*— Sir Ronald Millar; 7 Sheffield Terrace, London W8 (☎ 071 727 8361)

MILLARD, Sir Guy Elwin; KCMG (1972, CMG 1957), CVO (1961); s of Col Baldwin Salter Millard, and Phyllis Mary Tetley; *b* 22 Jan 1917; *Educ* Charterhouse, Pembroke Coll Cambridge; *m* 1, 1946 (m dis 1963), Anne, da of Gordon Mackenzie, of Toronto; 1 s, 1 da; m 2, 1964, Mary Judy, da of James Dugdale by his w Pamela (*see* Pamela, Countess of Aylesford); 2 s; *Career* served WW II RN; Foreign Serv 1939-76; min UK Delgn to NATO 1964-67, ambass Hungary 1967-69, min Washington 1970-71; ambass to: Sweden 1971-74, Italy 1974-76; chm Br-Italian Soc 1977-83; *Style*— Sir Guy Millard, KCMG, CVO; Fyfield Manor, Southrop, Glos (☎ 036785 234)

MILLARD, Prof Peter Henry; s of Edward Joseph Millard (d 1968), and Thelma Fanny, *née* Burrows; *b* 18 July 1937; *Educ* (MB BS, MD, MRCP); *m* 27 Jan 1962, Alys Gillian, da of Hubert Morley Thomas, of Swansea, S Wales; 3 s (Paul William b 1963, Stephen b 1964, David b 1969); *Career* consIt in geriatric med St George's Hosp 1968-79, Eleanor Peel prof of geriatric med St George's Hosp Med Sch Univ of London 1979, govr Centre For Policy On Ageing 1983-, hon dir Possums Control UK 1986-; author of numerous articles on ageing dementia and social policy; vice pres Br Assoc Serv To The Elderly; memb: Guild of Catholic Doctors, Br Geriatric Soc, Br Soc Res on Ageing; FRCP 1978, FRIPH 1983; *Books* The Dwarfs And Their King; *Recreations* walking, golf, reading obscure books; *Style*— Prof Peter Millard; Dept of Geriatric Medicine, St George's Hospital Medical Sch, Cranmer Terrace, Tooting, London SW17 OQR (☎ 071 767 5536, telex 945291 SAGEMS G)

MILLBOURN, Lady; Ethel Marjorie; da of late Joseph E Sennett; *m* 1931, Sir (Philip) Eric Millbourn, CMG (d 1982), sometime chm Cncl Administration Malta Dockyard; 1 s, 1 da; *Style*— Lady Millbourn; Conkwell Grange, Limpley Stoke, Bath, Avon BA3 6HD (☎ Limpley Stoke 022 122 3102)

MILLEN, Brig Anthony Tristram Patrick; s of Maj Charles Reginald Millen, MC (d 1959), and Annie Mary, *née* Martin (d 1979); *b* 15 Dec 1928; *Educ* Mount St Mary's Coll, Staff Coll Camberley, Joint Servs Staff Coll; *m* 24 Nov 1954, Mary Alice Featherston, da of Maj Robin Quentin Featherston Johnston (ka 1941); 3 s (Robin b 1956, d 1990, Nicholas b 1958, Patrick b 1964, d 1964), 2 da (Alice b 1961, Philippa b 1966); *Career* 5 Royal Inniskilling Dragoon Gds 1948, CO Royal Hong Kong Regt (The Volunteers) 1969-71, def advsr Br High Cmmn Ottawa 1980-83, ret 1983; chm Army Benevolent Fund (Thirsk area); *Recreations* sailing; *Style*— Brig Anthony Millen; The Manor House, Hutton Sessay, Thirsk, North Yorkshire YO7 3BA (☎ 0845 401 444)

MILLEN, Roger James; s of George James Millen (d 1980), of Hampshire, and Maria Mia, *née* Richards (d 1954); *b* 23 April 1942; *Educ* St Paul's; *m* 30 July 1966, Katharine Mary, da of Edgar Charles Sawkins; 2 s (James Jonathan b 3 Dec 1969, 1 da (Katharine Clare b 14 Sept 1971); *Career* articled clerk Annan Dexter & Co; Dearden Lord Annan Morrish (became Dearden Farrow 1979): mangr 1972-75, ptnr 1975-82, managing ptnr Yorkshire Region 1982-87; pres W Yorkshire Soc of Chartered Accountants 1988-89; FCA 1979 (ACA 1969); *Recreations* golf, walking; *Clubs* Leeds; *Style*— Roger Millen, Esq; BDO Binder Hamlyn, 21 Queen St, Leeds LS1 2TW (☎ 0532 440204, fax 0532 425938)

MILLER, Alain Sydney; s of Roland Miller (d 1974), of Georgetown, Guyana, and Jacqueline Liliane, *née* Delorme; *b* 20 Feb 1961; *Educ* Ernest Bevin Comp Sch London, Thanet Tech Coll, Maidstone Coll of Art, Brighton Poly (BA), Chelsea Sch of Art (MA), Goldsmith's Coll London (MA); *Career* artist; exhibitions incl: Prelude (Kettle's Yard Gallery Cambridge) 1985, Critics Space (Air Gallery) 1986, Whitechapel Open 1987 and 1991, Art History (Hayward Gallery) 1987, The Invisible Man (Goldsmith's Gallery) 1988, Anthony Reynolds group show 1989 and 1990, solo show Anthony Reynolds Gallery 1991; pt/t lectr Bath Coll of Higher Educn 1986-91, artist in residence Hackney Down Secdy Sch, lectr Camberwell Sch of Art 1986-91; *Style*— Alain Miller, Esq; Anthony Reynolds Gallery, 5 Dering St, London W1 (☎ 071 253 5575)

MILLER, Ambrose Michael; s of Ambrose Miller, of Beer, Devon, and Margaret Dorothy, *née* Dennett; *b* 15 April 1950; *Educ* Radley, Magdalene Coll Cambridge, King's Coll London (B Mus); *m* 4 April 1981, Celia Frances Sophia, da of Sir Desmond Arthur Pond (d 1986); *Career* mangr Royal Ballet Orchestra 1974-81, gen mangr Scottish Baroque Ensemble 1981-83, fndr and artistic dir European Community Chamber Orchestra 1983; dir Artslink International Ltd 1986-; Freeman City of London, Liveryman Worshipful Co of Musicians; *Recreations* cooking, reading; *Style*— Ambrose Miller, Esq; Five Bells, Offwell, Honiton, Devon (☎ 0404 83 701); Rougnac, 16320 Villebois Lavalette, France (telex 9312100405 EC G)

MILLER, Prof Andrew; s of William Hamilton Miller (d 1956), and Susan, *née* Anderson (d 1978); *b* 15 Feb 1936; *Educ* Beath HS, Univ of Edinburgh (BSc, PhD), Univ of Oxford (MA); *m* 19 June 1962, Rosemary Singleton Hannah, da of Thomas Carlyle Fyvie (d 1962); 1 s (Stephen Andrew Fyvie b 23 Oct 1968), 1 da (Lisa Rosemary b 7 Aug 1966); *Career* res fell CSIRO Div of Protein Chemistry Melbourne Aust 1962-65, staff MRC Laboratory for Molecular Biology Cambridge 1965-66, lectr in molecular biophysics Univ of Oxford 1966-83, head of Euro Molecular Biology Laboratory Grenoble France 1975-80, prof of biochemistry Univ of Edinburgh 1984- (asst lectr in chemistry 1960-62), dir of res Europe Synchrotron Radiation Facility Grenoble France 1986-; memb: various ctees of Sci and Engrg Res Cncl 1970-86, Univ Grants Cte 1985-88, Biological Sciences Advsy Gp Univ Funding Cncl 1989-; FRSE; *Books* Minerals in Biology (co-ed, 1984); *Recreations* reading, music, walking; *Style*— Prof Andrew Miller; Biochemistry Dept, Medical School, Univ of Edinburgh, European Synchrotron Radiation Facility BP 220, 38043 Grenoble, France (☎ 031 667 1011, 010 33 76 88 20 14, fax 010 33 76 88 21 60)

MILLER, Hon Mrs (Ann Kathleen); da of 12 Baron Aylmer (d 1982), and Althea, Baroness Aylmer, *qv*; *b* 1941; *Educ* Mount Douglas HS, Victoria Coll; *m* 1972, Gregor Byron Miller, s of late John Brown Miller; 1 s, 2 step da; *Recreations* tennis, cycling, music; *Style*— The Hon Mrs Miller; 845 8th Street, West Vancouver BC, V7T 1S1, Canada

MILLER, Barry; s of Maj Howard Alan Miller (d 1988), and Margaret Yvonne, *née* Richardson; *b* 11 May 1942; *Educ* Lancaster Royal GS; *m* 7 Sept 1968, Katrina Elizabeth, da of Maj Bernard Chandler (d 1979); 1 s (Andrew Geoffrey b 1975), 1 da (Caroline Jane b 1974); *Career* exec offr RAE Farnborough 1961-65; asst princ MOD London 1965-69; princ: Def Policy Staff 1969, Naval Personnel Div 1969-72, Equipment Secretariat Army 1972-73, Def Secretariat 1973-75, Civil Serv Dept 1975-77; asst sec: Civilian Mgmnt 1977-80, Def Secretariat 1980-83, Mgmnt Servs Orgn 1985-86; with RCDS 1984, DG Def Quality Assurance 1986-; memb Bd: RN Film Corp 1969-72, BSI 1986-89; hon dep sec First Div Assoc 1969-73, chm Civil Serv Club 1990-; *Recreations* military uniforms; *Style*— Barry Miller, Esq; Ministry of Defence, Royal Arsenal West, Woolwich, London SE18 6ST

MILLER, Sir (Oswald) Bernard; s of Arthur Miller; *b* 25 March 1904; *Educ* Sloane Sch, Jesus Coll Oxford; *m* 1931, Jessica Marie Ffoulkes; 3 s; *Career* John Lewis Partnership: joined 1927, dir 1935, chm 1955-72; former memb: Monopolies Cmmn, Cncl for Industl Design, Econ Devpt Ctee for Distributive Trades (and chm Retail Distributors Assoc 1953); chm South Regnl RSA 1974-80 and memb Cncl RSA 1977-83; Univ of Southampton: chm Cncl 1982-88, treas 1974-82, pro chllr 1983-, Hon LLD 1981; hon fell Jesus Coll Oxford 1968; kt 1967; *Books* Biography of Robert Harley, Earl of Oxford (1927); *Style*— Sir Bernard Miller; 3 Sutton Manor Mews, Sutton Scotney, Winchester, Hants (☎ 0962 760997)

MILLER, Christian Mona; da of Sir Arthur Grant of Monymusk, 10 Bt (d 1931), and Evelyn Alice Lindsay, *née* Wood (d 1976); *b* 3 Dec 1920; *Educ* privately; *m* 1, 14 Nov 1942 (m dis 1951), Michael Fife William Angas (d 1983), s of late Laurence Lee Bazley Angas, of New York; 2 da (Auburn b 1945, Cherill b 1947); m 2, 5 Jan 1953, John Gordon Ogston Miller, s of John Poynter Miller (d 1937); *Career* author; books incl:

The Champagne Sandwich (1969), Daisy, Daisy (1981), A Childhood in Scotland (1981); *Recreations* trying to find some spare time in which to write; *Style—* Mrs John Miller; Old Stables, Newtown, Newbury, Berkshire RG15 9AP (☎ 0635 40945)

MILLER, (James) David Frederick; s of Sir John Wilson Edington Miller KBE, CMG (d 1957), and Jessie Kathleen, *née* Reed (d 1966); *b* 5 Jan 1935; *Educ* Edinburgh Acad, Emmanuel Coll Cambridge (MA), LSE (Dip IPM); *m* 27 Feb 1965, Saffrey Blackett, da of Fred Oxley (d 1963); 3 s (Andrew b 21 Dec 1965, Simon b 13 Sept 1967, Matthew b 10 Aug 1970), 1 da (Katherine b 28 June 1973); *Career* dir: J & P Coats Ltd 1972, Coats Patons plc 1977, The Wolverhampton & Dudley Breweries plc 1984, Scottish Nat Orchestra Soc Ltd 1984, Outward Bound Tst Ltd 1985, The Edinburgh Acad 1985, Coats Viyella plc 1986; govr Scottish Coll of Textiles; memb CBI Employee Involvement Panel; cmmr Queen Victoria School; Freeman: City of London, Worshipful Co of Needlemakers 1983; DUniv of Stirling 1984; FIPM, CBIM; *Recreations* tennis, golf, gardening; *Style—* James Miller, Esq; Coats Viyella plc, 155 St Vincent St, Glasgow G2 5PA (☎ 041 221 8711, fax 041 248 2512, telex 777711)

MILLER, David James; s of James Samuel Miller, of Lymington, Hants, and Beryl Mary, *née* Jones; *b* 28 Feb 1952; *Educ* Stockport GS, Emmanuel Coll Cambridge (MA); *m* 17 Sept 1988, Sophie Kay Voss, da of Flemming Christian Rathsach, of Pindon Manor, Bucks; *Career* called to the Bar Middle Temple, dep chief exec Life Assurance & Unit Tst Regulatory Orgn 1986-89, dep sec Sun Alliance Insurance Group 1989-(legal advsr and unit tst business mangr 1977-86); *Recreations* travel, history of art; *Clubs* United Oxford and Cambridge; *Style—* David Miller, Esq; 37 Granville Square, London WC1X 9PD (☎ 071 833 3963); Sun Alliance, Bartholomew Lane, London, EC2

MILLER, David John; OBE; s of Air Cdre John Douglas Miller, CBE, of Guildford, Surrey, and Sybil Francis, *née* Powell; *b* 7 March 1947; *Educ* Dragon Sch Oxford, St Edwards Sch Oxford, Jesus Coll Cambridge (MA); *m* 24 Jan 1976, Maryrose, da of John Edgar Dulley; 3 s (Fergie b 8 June 1979, Bertie b 26 March 1981, Gregory b 28 Nov 1984); *Career* Joseph Sebag (stockbrokers) 1969-72; Robert Fleming Gp: joined 1972, special advisor to Govt of Abu Dhabi 1975-78, Jardine Fleming Hong Kong 1979-81, Jardine Fleming Tokyo 1981-88, Main Bd dir; *Recreations* golf, tennis, children; *Style—* David Miller, Esq, OBE; Robert Fleming Holdings, 25 Copthall Avenue, London EC2R 7DR (☎ 071 638 5858)

MILLER, Dr David Shaw; s of Bertram Miller (d 1966), and Renée Gertrude Anne, *née* Vieilleville; *b* 11 Aug 1937; *Educ* Beulah Hill, Univ of London (MSc, MB, MRCP); *m* 16 Sept 1967, Margaret Rosamund, da of Alan Hall, of Whitney Oxon; 1 s (William James Shaw b 17 March 1973), 1 da (Katherine Elizabeth Shaw b 10 Oct 1970); *Career* registrar KCH 1965-67, lectr Nottingham Med Sch 1970-75, sr registrar Radcliffe Infirmary Oxford 1978-82, conslt Royal Devon and Exeter Hosp 1982-; pubns in scientific jls based on original res in GB, USA, Africa and India; Hon MA(Oxon) 1980; *Recreations* riding, lawn tennis, walking; *Style—* Dr David Miller; Royal Devon & Exeter Hospital, Exeter, Devon (☎ 0392 405204)

MILLER, Lady Diana Mary; *née* Pelham; da of 5 Earl of Yarborough, MC, DL (d 1948), and Nancye, *née* Brocklehurst, niece of 1 and last Baron Ranksborough; co-heiress (with sis, Lady Wendy Lycett, *qv*) to Baronies of Fauconberg (E ante 24 June 1295) and Conyers (E 1509), through paternal grandmother; *b* 5 July 1920; *m* 1952, Robert Miller, s of Capt Gordon Molineux Miller (d 1952); 2 da (Marcia Anne b 1954, adopted by her aunt, Lady Wendy Lycett, *qv*, whose surname she assumed ; Beatrix Diana b 1955); *Career* SRN; *Style—* The Lady Diana Miller; c/o Zimbank Box 2270, Harare, Zimbabwe

MILLER, Sir Donald John; s of late John Miller, and late Maud, *née* White; *b* 8 Feb 1927; *Educ* Banchory Acad, Univ of Aberdeen (BSc); *m* 1973, Fay Glendinning Herriot; 1 s (Alasdair b 1 March 1979), 2 da (Nicola b 30 June 1974, Jane b 11 May 1976); *Career* engr Metropolitan Vickers 1947-53, Br Electricity Authy 1953-55; engr and mangr Preece Cardew & Rider (consulting engrs) 1955-66, chief engr N of Scotland Hydro-Electric Board 1966-74; S of Scotland Electricity Board: dir Engr 1974-77, dep chm and gen mangr 1977-82, chm 1982-90; chm Scottish Power plc 1990-; Chm Power Div IEE 1977-78; Power Div award and Williams Premium IEE; hon memb BNES, FENG, FIMechE, FIEE, FRSE; kt 1990; *Recreations* sailing, gardening, hill walking; *Clubs* Royal Scottish Automobile; *Style—* Sir Donald Miller; Scottish Power plc, Cathcart House, Spean St, Glasgow G44 4BE (☎ 041 637 7177, ext 2101, fax 041 637 7039)

MILLER, Prof (James) Douglas; s of George McNeil Miller (d 1976), of St Saviour, Jersey, Channel Isles, and Sylvia Heléne, *née* Scriven; *b* 20 July 1937; *Educ* Glasgow Acad, Univ of Glasgow (MB ChB, MD, PhD), Univ of Pa USA; *m* 4 Sept 1964, Margaret (Margot) Scott, da of Samuel Rainey (d 1962), of Melrose, Scotland; 2 s (Derek McNeil b 1966, Kenneth Scott b 1968); *Career* US public health serv fellowship Univ of Pa USA 1970-71, sr lectr in neurosurgery Univ of Glasgow 1971-75, prof of neurosurgery Virginia Cwlth Univ USA 1975-80; Univ of Edinburgh: prof of surgical neurology 1981-, chm Dept of Clinical Neuroscience 1986-90, vice dean faculty of Med 1990-; memb: cncl Euro Assoc Neurosurgery Socs, advsy cncl Soc of Neurological Surgns; FRCPSG 1965, FRCSEd 1978, FACCS 1978, FRCPEd 1982; medal of Swedish Med Soc 1988; *Books* Northfields Surgery of the Central Nervous System (1987), Rehabilitation of the Head Injured Adult and Child (1989); *Recreations* reading, swimming, outdoor pursuits; *Style—* Prof Douglas Miller; Dept of Clinical Neurosciences, University of Edinburgh, Western General Hospital, Edinburgh EH4 2XU (☎ 031 332 2525, telex 727442 UNIVED G, fax 031 332 5150)

MILLER, Sir Douglas Sinclair; KCVO (1972), CBE (1956, OBE 1948); s of Albert Edward Miller (d 1954); *b* 30 July 1906; *Educ* Westminster, Merton Coll Oxford; *m* 1933, Valerie Madeleine Carter; 1 da; *Career* Colonial Serv 1930-61; sec King George's Jubilee Tst 1961-71; devpt advsr Duke of Edinburgh Award Scheme 1971-85; *Style—* Sir Douglas Miller, KCVO, CBE; The Lodge, 70 Grand Ave, Worthing, West Sussex (☎ 0903 501195)

MILLER, Francis Edward; s of Alfred Lewis Miller (d 1971), and Emily Johanna, *née* Lark; *b* 20 Jan 1940; *Educ* Brixton Sch of Building, Central London Poly; *m* 1, 28 Nov 1964 (m dis 1987), Valerie, da of Sydney Victor Read (d 1985); 2 s (Richard Lewis b 7 Nov 1970, John Francis b 24 May 1976); *Career* jr quantity surveyor 1956, later surveyor and mangr of bldg and civil engrg projects, commenced practice 1972 specializing in resolution of disputes in bldg, civil engrg and process industs as conslt, concilator and arbitrator; coopted memb Chartered Inst of Arbitrators' Arbitration Law Reform Working Party; memb arbitration panel: RICS, CIARB; pres offr SE region of Chartered Inst of Arbitrators; memb Worshipful Co of Arbitrators 1981; FRICS, FCIArb 1975, Assoc Inst of Patentees and Inventors 1975, FIOD 1979; *Books* Arbitration - Recommendations & Survey (1988); *Recreations* watercolour painting, writing, walking, talking; *Style—* Francis Miller, Esq; Candida, Harlequin Lane, Crowborough, East Sussex TN6 1HU (☎ 0892 662957)

MILLER, Harry; s of Sir Ernest Henry John Miller, 10 Bt (d 1960); h to Btcy of bro, Sir John Miller, 11 Bt; *b* 1927; *m* 1954, Gwynedd Margaret, da of R P Sherriff, of Paraparaumu, New Zealand; 1 s (Anthony Thomas b 1955), 2 da (Sara Margaret (Mrs Laing) b 1957, Judith Christine b 1960); *Style—* Harry Miller, Esq; 53 Koha Road, Taupo, NZ

MILLER, Sir Hilary Duppa (Hal); MP (C) Bromsgrove 1983-; s of Lt Cdr John Duppa-Miller, GC, of Somerset West, SA, and Hon Barbara (d 1966), yr da of 1 Viscount Buckmaster; *b* 6 March 1929; *Educ* Eton, Merton Coll Oxford, Univ of London; *m* 1, 1956, Fiona McDermid; 2 s, 2 da; m 2, 1976, Jacqueline Roe, yr da of late Thomas Chambers Windsor Roe, of Brighton and Lady Londesborough; 1 s, 1 da; *Career* colonial serv Hong Kong 1955-68; MP (C) Bromsgrove and Redditch 1974-83; PPS to: Sec of State Defence 1979-81, Chllr Duchy of Lancaster 1981 (resigned), Chm of Cons Party 1984; vice chm Cons Party 1984-87; fell of Econ Devpt Inst of World Bank (Washington); kt 1988; *Style—* Sir Hal Miller, MP; Moorcroft Farm, Sinton Green, Worcester WR2 6NW (☎ 0905 640309); House of Commons, London SW1 (☎ 071 219 4531)

MILLER, Hon Mrs (Honor Leslie); *née* Brooke; er da of Baron Brooke of Cumnor, PC, CH (Life Peer, d 1984), and Baroness Brooke of Ystradfellte, DBE (Life Peeress), *qv*; *b* 2 April 1941; *Educ* St Mary's Calne, Univ of Grenoble, St James's Secretarial Coll; *m* 6 Aug 1966, Dr (Thomas) Nigel Miller, er s of Nathaniel Allan Miller, FRCS; 3 s, 2 da; *Career* Nightingale nurse St Thomas's Hosp; *Recreations* music, books, journeys, art, Italy; *Style—* The Hon Mrs Miller; Laurel Hill, Repton, Derby

MILLER, Dr Hugh Craig; s of James Miller, and Helen Elizabeth, *née* Craig; *b* 7 April 1942; *Educ* George Watson's Coll Edinburgh, Univ of Edinburgh (BSc, MB ChB); *m* 14 Sept 1968, Isobel Margaret, da of Robert Paterson; 1 s (James (Jamie) b 1972), 1 da (Catherine Jane b 1976); *Career* Royal Infirmary Edinburgh: house physician and surgn 1966-67, sr house offr 1967-68, registrar of cardiology 1970-72, conslt cardiologist 1975-; MRC res fell 1968-70, sr registrar Brompton Hosp London 1972-75, res fell Duke Univ Durham USA; memb: Br Cardiac Soc, BMA, Assoc of Physicians of GB and Ireland; FRCPE 1979; *Recreations* skiing, squash, sailing; *Style—* Dr Hugh Miller; 12 Dick Place, Edinburgh EH9 2JL (☎ 031 667 4235); Cardiology Dept, Royal Infirmary, Edinburgh (☎ 031 229 2477)

MILLER, Prof Hugh Graham; s of Robert Graham Miller, of Auckland, NZ, and Anne Farmer *née* Fleming (d 1968); *b* 22 Nov 1939; *Educ* Strathallan Sch, Univ of Aberdeen (BSc, PhD, DSc); *m* 4 July 1966 (seperated 1989), Thelma; 1 s (Ewen b 1969), 1 da (Andrea b 1971); *Career* princ scientific offr Macaulay Inst for Soil Res 1976 (scientific offr 1963, sr scientific offr 1970), prof and head of Dept of Forestry Univ of Aberdeen 1984-; memb: Res Advsy Ctee Forestry Cmmn, Forestry Res Coordination Ctee, Scot Forestry Tst, Res Advsy Ctee of Forest Res Inst of Malaysia, FAD Forestry Educn Ctee; FICFor 1979, FRSE 1985, FRSA 1986, FIBiol 1988; *Recreations* the outdoors; *Clubs* Royal Northern and Univ; *Style—* Prof Hugh Miller; 102 Osborne Place, Aberdeen AB2 4DU (☎ 0224 639872); Dept of Forestry, Univ of Aberdeen, Aberdeen AB9 1UD (☎ 0224 272666, telex 73458 UNIABN G, fax 0224 272685)

MILLER, Iain; s of Andrew Barr Miller (d 1960), of Dalry, Ayrshire and Janet Borrows, *née* Boyce; *b* 7 Sept 1944; *Educ* Dalry Sr Secdy, Univ of Glasgow, Univ of Strathclyde (BArch); *m* 25 Oct 1968, Irene Agnes, da of Charles Cunningham Hamilton, of Kilbirnie, Ayrshire; 2 s (A Paul b 1971, Jonathan b 1974); *Career* architect: Glenrothes Devpt Corpn 1968-69, Godstone Rural Dist Cncl 1969-71, Inverclyde Dist Cncl 1971-78, Cumbernauld and Kilsyth Dist Cncl 1978-; pres Assoc of Chief Architects of S Local Authys, cncl memb Royal Incorporation of Architects in S, advsr Convention of S local Authys; FIBA 1968, FRIAS 1988; *Recreations* hill walking, reading, music, photography, bowls; *Clubs* Rostrum; *Style—* Iain Miller, Esq; Liathach, 11 Glen View, Cumbernauld G67 2DA (☎ 0236 722012); Chief Architect, Cumbernauld Kilsyth District Council, Council Offices, Bron Way, Cumbernauld, G67 1DZ (☎ 0236 722131, fax 0236 736258)

MILLER, Jack Michael; s of Col Harry Raymond (Pat) Miller, of 46 St Winifreds Road, Teddington, and Eileen Mary, *née* Whiteing; *b* 10 Jan 1946; *Educ* Cranleigh Sch; *m* 2 June 1972, Elizabeth Alison, da of Lt-Col Ronald Francis Boyd Campbell, of 30 Marine Drive, Torpoint; 1 da (Caroline b 29 Dec 1977); *Career* gunner HAC; slr; articled Rider Heaton Meredith & Mills 1964-70; Midland Bank plc; Legal Dept 1970-, dep sr legal advsr UK Banking 1988-; memb Bedford Parish Soc; Freeman of the City of London, Liveryman of the Worshipful Co of Haberdashers; *Recreations* cricket, sport generally, trivia; *Clubs* MCC, RAC, Tatty Bogle, Cricket Soc; *Style—* Jack Miller, Esq; 41 Fairfax Rd, London W4; 11 Old Jewry, London EC2R 8AA (☎ 071 260 7381, fax 071 260 7393)

MILLER, James; CBE (1986); s of Sir James Miller, GBE (d 1977), of Belmont, Ellersly Rd, Edinburgh, and Ella Jane, *née* Stewart; *b* 1 Sept 1934; *Educ* Edinburgh Acad, Harrow, Balliol Coll Oxford (MA); *m* 1, 27 July 1959, Kathleen (d 1966), da of James Dewar (d 1969), of Edinburgh; 1 s (James b 1962), 2 da (Susan b 1960, Gail b 1962); m 2, 11 Jan 1969, Iris, da of Thomas James Lloyd-Webb (d 1959), of Southampton; 1 da (Heather b 1970); *Career* RE 1956-58, cmmnd 2 Lt 1957; James Miller & Ptnrs (The Miller Gp Ltd 1986): joined 1958, dir 1960, chm and md 1970; chm Fedn of Civil Engrg Contractors 1985 (pres 1990-); pres Edinburgh C of C 1981-83, ct asst Merchant Co of Edinburgh 1982-85 (treas 1990-); chm Ct of Heriot-Watt Univ Edinburgh 1990-; chm: Scottish Section Fedn of Civil Engrs 1981-83, Scottish Branch Chartered Inst of Arbitrators 1985-87; Freeman: City of London 1956, Worshipful Co of Horners 1956; FCIOB 1974, FCIArb 1976, CBIM 1983; *Recreations* shooting; *Clubs* City Livery; *Style—* James Miller, Esq, CBE; Belmont, Ellersly Rd, Edinburgh EH12 6JA (☎ 031 337 6595); The Miller Group Ltd, Miller House, 18 South Groathill Ave, Edinburgh EH4 2LW (☎ 031 332 2585, fax 031 315 2350, telex 727551 MILCON G)

MILLER, James Lawson; s of David Wardrop Miller (d 1966), and Helen Frew, *née* Baxter (d 1952); *b* 26 Jan 1951; *Educ* The John Lyon Sch Harrow, St John's Coll Cambridge (MA); *m* 29 June 1957, Margaret Ann, da of Beverly Robinson (d 1984); 2 s (David b 1958, Jeremy b 1959), 1 da (Jane b 1962); *Career* chartered builder, construction co chief exec; chm and dir: James Lawson Holdings Ltd, J Lawson Building Ltd, J Lawson Timber Products Ltd, Lawson Plant Hire Ltd, J Lawson Property Ltd 1965-; chm R Harding (Cookham) Ltd 1985-; pres The Builders Conference 1985; *Books* Computer Aided Estimating (1977); *Recreations* duplicate bridge, Church of England activities; *Clubs* Leander; *Style—* James L Miller, Esq; Clavering, North Park, Gerrards Cross, Bucks SL9 8JP

MILLER, Jeremy; *b* 26 March 1945; *Educ* Brighton Coll, RMA Sandhurst, St John's Coll Cambridge (MA), Universita per Stranieri Perugia Italy, City Univ London (post grad dip); *m* 1 s, 1 da; *Career* Army 1965-74; cmmnd Royal Corps of Signals 1965, troop cdr Germany 1966, troop cdr with NATO forces Norway 1969, offr on HMA Intrepid in Far East Middle East and Euro waters 1970, instr Sch of Infantry 1972, ret as Capt 1974; head of PR Mermaid Theatre 1975-76; Bd dir and gp account dir Interco Business Consultants 1977-80, Hill and Knowlton (UK) Limited 1980-87, dir Hill & Knowlton 1984 (head Technol Div 1981); Valin Pollen 1987-: joined as account dir and gp head, memb Bd 1987, int dir 1989, asst md 1990; *Recreations* travel, theatre, contemporary cinema, 19 century Euro history, Italian art, cricket, bridge, DIY; *Style—* Jeremy Miller, Esq; 3 Melody Rd, Wandsworth, London SW18 2QW (☎ 081 874 3650, office 071 730 9063, 071 730 3456)

MILLER, Air Cdre John; CBE (1966), DFC (1945), AFC (1953); s of John William

Miller, of Sprotborough, Yorks; *b* 3 Dec 1921; *Educ* Wath upon Dearne GS; *m* 1947, Joan Macgregor (decd); 1 s, 2 da; m 2, 1988, Philippa Anne, da of Maj I S Tailyour; *Career* Air Cdre RAF (ret); dir: UBM Gp Ltd 1970-82, A J Gooding Gp 1982-89, Flying Pictures Ltd, Naturestone Ltd, Brown Shipley Development Capital Ltd; FCA; *Clubs* RAF; *Style—* Air Cdre John Miller, CBE, DFC, AFC; Orchard Close, Pitchcombe, nr Stroud, Glos (☎ 0452 813477)

MILLER, John Albert Peter; s of Albert Ernest Miller (d 1966), and Irene Gertrude Ann, *née* Viellville (d 1989); *b* 30 July 1931; *Educ* St Joseph's Coll Beulah Hill, Croydon Art Sch; *Career* Nat Serv Lt RASC 1949-51; painter; exhibitions incl: London, NY, Vancover; recent cmmns incl: Nat Tst and Lord St Levan 10 historical paintings of St Michael's Mount 1979, Dean and Chapter Truro Cathedral Cornubia-Land of Saints 1980 (unveiled by HRH Prince of Wales); sole agent David Messum Gallery 1981-; public collections: V & A, Cornwall CC, Avon CC; private collections: TRH Prince and Princess of Wales, TRH Prince and Princess Michael of Kent; memb Newlyn Soc of Artists (former chm), art conslt Truro Diocesan Advsy Ctee; FRSA 1964; *Books* Cooking With Vegetables (with late Marika Hanbury Tenison, 1980), Leave Tomorrow Behind (1989); *Recreations* travel, gardens, books; *Style—* John Miller, Esq; Sancreed House, Sancreed, Penzance, Cornwall

MILLER, Prof (Christopher) John; s of Stanley Miller, of Henley on Thames, Oxon, and Joan Beryl Gill; *b* 4 Nov 1941; *Educ* Bishop Veseys GS Sutton Coldfield, Univ of Nottingham (BA, LLM); *m* 4 Sept 1964, Michèle Marie Juliette, da of Raymond Michel Guérault, of Paris; 1 s (Mark), 1 da (Anne Marie); *Career* barr; lectr in law Univ of Durham 1966-70, reader in common law Univ of Leeds (lectr in law 1970-77), prof of law Univ of Warwick 1980-89 (reader 1979), prof of English Law Univ of Birmingham 1989-; pt/t chm social security appeals tbnls; *Books* Product Liability (jtly, 1977), Product Liability and Safety Encyclopaedia (1979-91), Consumer and Trading Law: Cases and Materials (jtly, 1985), Comparative Product Liability (ed, 1986), Contempt of Court (1989); *Recreations* classical music, gardening, walking, sport; *Style—* Prof John Miller; Faculty of Law, Chancellor's Court, University of Birmingham, PO Box 363, Birmingham B15 2TT (☎ 021 414 6294)

MILLER, Sir John Holmes; 11 Bt (E 1705), of Chichester, Sussex; s of Sir Ernest Henry John Miller, 10 Bt (d 1960); *b* 1925; *m* 1950, Jocelyn Edwards; 2 da; *Heir* bro, Harry Holmes Miller; *Style—* Sir John Miller, Bt

MILLER, Air Vice-Marshal John Joseph; CB (1981); s of Frederick George Miller (d 1985), and Freda Ruth, *née* Haskins (d 1985); *b* 27 April 1928; *Educ* Portsmouth GS; *m* 10 Nov 1950, Adele Mary, da of Hubert Colleypriest (d 1957); 1 s (Michael b 1960), 2 da (Penelope b 1953, Robin Jennifer b 1958); *Career* RAF 1946-83; dir Personnel Mgmnt (RAF), MOD 1975-78, asst chief Def Staff (Personnel and Logistics) 1978-81, dir gen Personal Services (RAF) 1982-83; called to the Bar Gray's Inn 1958; dir: Inst of Personnel Mgmnt 1983-89, dir of studies St Georges House Windsor Castle 1989-; *Recreations* theatre, music, book collecting; *Clubs* RAF; *Style—* Air Vice-Marshal John Miller, CB; 35 Huntsmans meadow, Ascot, Berks SL5 7PF (☎ 0344 20413); St Georges House, Windsor Castle, Berkshire SL4 1NJ (☎ 0753 861341)

MILLER, Lt-Col Sir John Mansel; GCVO 1987 (KCVO 1974, CVO 1966), DSO (1944), MC (1944); 3 s of Brig-Gen Alfred Douglas Miller, CBE, DSO, JP, DL (d 1933), and Ella Geraldine, *née* Fletcher (d 1935); *b* 4 Feb 1919; *Educ* Eton, RMA Sandhurst; *Career* 2 Lt Welsh Gds 1939, served WWII, ADC to Field Marshal Lord Wilson Washington DC 1945-47, cmd 1 Bn Welsh Gds 1958-61; Crown Equerry 1961-87; Extra Equerry to HM The Queen 1987-; pres: Coaching Club 1975-82, Hackney Horse Soc 1978-80, Nat Light Horse Breeding Soc 1981-82, Br Driving Soc 1982-, Royal Windsor Horse Show Club 1985-90, Br Show Jumping Assoc 1989-, Wheatley Scouts and RNLI; patron: Side-Saddle Assoc 1982-, Coloured Horse and Pony Soc 1988-; *Recreations* hunting, shooting, polo, driving; *Clubs* Pratt's, White's; *Style—* Lt-Col Sir John Miller, GCVO, DSO, MC; Shotover House, Wheatley, Oxford OX9 1QS (☎ 086 77 2450)

MILLER, John Tennant; TD (1959); s of William Tennant Miller (d 1968), of Ceylon and Sussex, and Dorothy Elizabeth, *née* White (d 1929); *b* 31 Jan 1923; *Educ* Trinity Coll Glenalmond, Univ of Glasgow; *m* 28 Dec 1950, Wendy Moira, da of Rev Douglas Gordon McLean (d 1985), of East Lothian; 1 s (Ian b 1954), 2 da (Jane b 1951, Anne b 1957); *Career* WWII cmmnd RE 1941, 4 Parachute Sqdn RE 1942-45, 300 Parachute Sqdn RE TA 1950-59 (co 1957-59); Ramsay & Primrose (consulting engrs) Glasgow and Edinburgh: jr engr 1951-54, sr engr 1954-63, ptnr 1963-88, ret 1988; vice-chm govrs St Margaret's Sch Newington 1985-87 (memb 1963-87), memb bd of govrs Clifton Hall Sch Newbridge 1985-; fndr memb Woodcutters Cricket Club Edinburgh 1964 (pres 1983-); FIEE 1967, ACE 1969, FRSA 1980; *Recreations* sailing, golf, gardening; *Style—* John T Miller, Esq, TD; Sayorana, Links Rd, Longniddry, E Lothian EH32 ONL (☎ 0875 52170)

MILLER, Dr Jonathan Wolfe; CBE (1983); s of Emanuel Miller, DPM, FRCP; *b* 21 July 1934; *Educ* St Paul's, St John's Coll Cambridge (MB, BCh); *m* 1956, Helen Rachel Collet; 2 s, 1 da; *Career* television, theatre and opera director; former res fell History of Medicine UCL; presenter (BBC series) and author The Body in Question 1978; *Style—* Dr Jonathan Miller, CBE; 63 Gloucester Crescent, London NW1

MILLER, Dr Kenneth Allan Glen; CBE (1988); s of Dr Allan Frederick Miller (d 1967), of Edinburgh, and Margaret Hutchinson, *née* Glen (d 1971); *b* 27 July 1926; *Educ* Upper Canada Coll Toronto, Trinity Hall Cambridge (BA, MA), UCW Aberystwyth (PhD); *m* 24 April 1954, Dorothy Elaine, da of Dr Derek G Brown (d 1967), of W Kilbride; 3 s (Andrew b 1955, Ian b 1957, Allan b 1961); *Career* res asst to Prof of Physics Aberystwyth 1946-49; ICI: various posts on prodn and design Billingham 1949-59, seconded to Br Tport Cmmn 1959-60, asst tech mangr Heavy Organic Chemicals Div 1960-63, engrg mangr 1963-65, engrg dir 1965-71, engrg advsr to main bd 1971-74; md: APV Ltd 1974-77, APV plc 1977-82; dir gen The Engrg Cncl 1982-88; dep chm: ECCTIS 2000 Ltd 1990-, Standing Conf on Schs' Sci and Technol 1990-; memb: Ctee for Indust Technol 1972-76, Univ Grants C 1981-83; chm Steering Ctee for Mfrg Advsy Serv 1977-81, cncl memb Careers Res Advsy Centre 1988-; FIMechE 1965, FEng 1981, CBIM 1985; *Recreations* gardening, photography; *Clubs* Leander; *Style—* Dr Kenneth Miller, CBE; 4 Montrose Gdns, Oxshott, Leatherhead, Surrey KT22 OUU (☎ 0372 842093)

MILLER, Kenneth Harry; s of late Harry Miller, DSM, and late Alice Emily, *née* Cook; *b* 11 April 1936; *m* 2 June 1956, Margaret Mason, da of late George Carson Graham; 1 s (Neil Quenton b 1964), 1 da (Gillian Shelley (Mrs Bateman) b 1962); *Career* admitted slr 1966; slr of Supreme Court, ptnr Markbys (now Cameron Markby Hewitt) 1966, cmmr for oaths 1970; sec Int Carnation Propagators Assoc; memb: Law Soc, The City of London Slr's Co; *Recreations* arts, painting, theatre, walking; *Style—* Kenneth Miller, Esq

MILLER, Lisa; da of Glyn Beynon Davies (d 1979), and Dorothy, *née* Grant; *b* 9 Nov 1939; *Educ* King Edward V1 HS for Girls, Lady Margaret Hall Oxford (MA); *m* 12 Sept 1965, Timothy Peter Francis Miller, s of Col J F Miller, of Camberley; 2 s (Charles b 1977, Alexander b 1983), 2 da (Lucasta b 1966, Cressida b 1968); *Career* child psychotherapist Tavistock Clinic, ed Jl of Child Psychotherapy 1982-85, chm Assoc of Child Psychotherapists 1986-89; tstee Child Psychotherapy Tst; *Books* Closely Oberved Infants (ed jtly, 1989); *Style—* Mrs Lisa Miller; 9 Bartholomew Villas, London NW5 (☎ 071 485 7294; The Tavistock Clinic, Belsize Lane, London NW3 (☎ 071 435 7111)

MILLER, Michael; RD (1966), QC (1974); s of Lt-Cdr John Brian Peter Duppa-Miller, GC, of Somerset West, Cape Province, SA, and The Hon Barbara, *née* Buckmaster (d 1966); *b* 28 June 1933; *Educ* Westminster, ChCh Oxford (BA, MA); *m* 18 Oct 1958, Mary Elizabeth, da of Donald Spiers Monteagle Barlow, of Harpenden, Herts; 2 s (George b 1962, Edward b 1970), 2 da (Charlotte b 1959, Alexandra b 1967); *Career* Ordinary Seaman RNVR 1950, Nat Serv 1955-57, cmmnd Sub-Lt RNVR 1956, Lt-Cdr RNR 1973, qualified Submarines; called to the Bar Lincoln's Inn 1958, practicing at Chancery Bar and Int Bar 1959-, bencher 1984, memb Bar Cncl 1988-, assoc memb Hong Kong Bar Assoc 1976-; memb Lab Pty (Kensington) 1964 (tres 1980-84); *Style—* Michael Miller, Esq, RD, QC; 8 Stone Bldgs, Lincolns Inn, London WC2 (☎ 071 242 5002, fax 071 831 9188, telex 268072)

MILLER, Michael Dawson; s of Cyril Gibson Risch Miller, CBE (d 1976), and Dorothy Alice, *née* North-Lewis; *b* 12 March 1928; *m* 17 July 1954, Gillian Margaret, da of Dr Eric Gordon-Fleming (d 1948); 3 da (Caroline b 1957, Clare b 1961, Jane b 1961); *Career* Parachute Regt Regs 1946-48 (TA 1949), HAC 1957-63; articled clerk 1949, in practice as slr 1954-55, ptnr Thos R Miller & Son 1962-90 (ptnr Bermuda 1969-90, exec 1955-62); dir: AB Indemnitas Stockholm 1983-90, Thos Miller War Risks Services 1985-90; conslt Planning Bd for Ocean Shipping 1970-; Liveryman: Worshipful Co of Shipwrights 1977, Worshipful Co of Solicitors 1986; memb: Law Soc 1954, London Maritime Arbitrators Assoc 1963; Silver medal Hellenic Merchant Marine Greece 1983; *Books* Marine War Risks; *Recreations* offshore racing, cruising, opera, mountain walking, history, reaching remote places, ancient civilisations, targeting intellectuals; *Clubs* Royal Ocean Racing, Royal Bermuda Yacht, City, Hurlingham; *Style—* Michael Miller, Esq; 52 Scarsdale Villas, London W8 6PP (☎ 071 937 9935); Dairy Cottage, Donhead, St Andrews, Wilts; Thos R Miller & Son, International House, 26 Creechurch Lane, London EC3A 5BA (☎ 071 283 4646, fax 071 283 5614, telex 885271)

MILLER, Michael George; s of Robert Miller; *b* 17 June 1925; *Educ* Torquay GS, Wales Univ; *m* 1, 1948, Elizabeth Jane (d 1971); 2 da; m 2, 1972, Sadie Lorna; *Career* chartered engr, dir in charge Racal-Decca Serv Ltd 1981-, dir Decca Radar Ltd 1965-80, serv mangr BAC (GW Div) 1958-63, res offr REME 1944-58; *Recreations* golf; *Clubs* Directors'; *Style—* Michael Miller, Esq; 11 Lyne Place Manor, Bridge Lane, Virginia Water, Surrey (☎ 0932 65532)

MILLER, Michael George; s of George James Miller (d 1977), of Cirencester, and Edith Mary Miller (d 1960); *b* 19 Sept 1927; *Educ* Cirencester GS, RAC; *m* 1957, Elizabeth Mary, JP, da of William Bew Todd (d 1973), of Foston; 2 s, 2 da; *Career* dir Furness Travel Ltd 1973-77, sales mangr Stita Farm Tours 1977-; MRAC; *Recreations* squash, tennis, swimming, walking; *Style—* Michael Miller, Esq; Orchard Cottage, Alstone, Tewkesbury, Glos GL20 8JD; Stita Farm Tours, 1 Bath St, Cheltenham GL50 1YE (tel 0242 515712)

MILLER, Hon Mrs (Patricia); *née* Makins; da of 1 Baron Sherfield, GCB, GCMG; *b* 1946; *m* 1966, Michael Ordway Miller, s of Albert O Miller, of Carmel, California; *Style—* The Hon Mrs Miller; 3 Sunset way, Muir Beach, Calif, USA; 1655, Sequoia, Tahoe City, Calif, USA

MILLER, Dr (John) Paul; s of John Frederick William Miller (d 1961), and Edith Mary Miller; *b* 10 July 1940; *Educ* Repton, Keble Coll Oxford (MA, DPhil, BM BCh), Univ of London (MSc), Guy's; *m* 19 Aug 1978, (Constance) Mary, da of Kenneth Anderson, of Farnham; 1 s (Christopher John Kenneth b 1984), 1 da (Claire b 1981), 1 adopted s (Nicholas Francis Haynes b 1977), 1 adopted da (Jackie Marie Haynes b 1979); *Career* house physician Guy's 1968, house surgn Addenbrooke's Hosp Cambridge 1969, team leader Save the Children Fund Nigerian Civil War, sr house offr and registrar Hammersmith Hosp 1970-72, hon sr registrar St James' Hosp Leeds 1972-75, lectr med Univ of Leeds 1972-75, sr lectr med Univ of Manchester 1975-81, hon conslt physician Univ Hosp of S Manchester 1975-81, visiting prof med Baylor Coll Houston (MRC travelling fell) 1978-79, conslt gastroenterologist Univ Hosp of S Manchester 1981- (clinical sub dean 1982-88), author sci papers and reviews on: respiratory physiology, gastroenterology (especially peptic ulceration), disorders of lipoprotein metabolism; treas Br Hyperlipidaemia Assoc, regnl advsr N W Reg RCP, memb Cases Ctee Med Protection Soc; memb Manchester Literary and Philosophical Soc; memb: Br Soc Gastroenterology, MRS, Assoc Physicians GB and Ireland; fell American Heart Assoc (memb Cncl Arteriosclerosis), FRCP 1982; *Recreations* running, walking, golf; *Style—* Dr. Paul Miller; Department of Medicine, University of Hospital of South Manchester, Manchester M20 8LR (☎ 061 447 3823)

MILLER, Peter Francis Nigel; s of Francis Gerald Miller (d 1969), of Bristol, and Dorothy Emily, *née* Leftwich (d 1973); *b* 8 May 1924; *Educ* King's Sch Canterbury, Sch of Architecture Canterbury; *m* 20 July 1950 (m dis 1984), Sheila Gillian Branthwayt, da of George Frederic Storrs Stratton (d 1937), of Newport, IOW; 1 s (Robert James Stratton b 1962), 2 da (Charlotte Mary Leftwich (Mrs Robert Carter) b 1957, Caroline Elizabeth Bradshaw (Mrs John Davies) b 1959); *Career* Army 1942-47, Lt, served NW Europe, Austria, Italy and India, cmmnd Duke of Cornwall's LI 1943, attached Glasgow Highlanders (HLI) 1944; chartered architect, surveyor and design conslt; asst to: Mrs Gaby Schreiber 1950, Sir Hugh Casson 1952; commenced practice Peter Miller and Sheila Stratton 1954, Miller and Tritton 1956; Purcell Miller and Triton: co-fndr 1965, sr ptnr 1973-88; surveyor to the fabric Ely Cathedral 1974-; conslt 1988-: Norwich, London, Sevenoaks, Winchester, Colchester, Stowmarket; ARIBA 1952, MSIA 1956, FRIBA 1968, FSIA 1968; *Clubs* Norfolk; *Style—* Mr Peter Miller; Thornage Watermill, Holt, Norfolk (☎ 0263 711339); The Chapter House, The College, Ely, Cambridgeshire (☎ 0353 667735)

MILLER, Sir Peter North; s of Cyril Thomas Gibson Risch Miller, CBE (d 1976), and Dorothy Alice North Miller, JP; *b* 28 Sept 1930; *Educ* Rugby, Lincoln Coll Oxford (MA), City Univ (DEc); *m* 1, 3 Sept 1955 (m dis 1979), Katharine Mary, da of Dr Guy Milner (d 1980); 2 s (James b 28 Oct 1956, Andrew b 3 Nov 1958), 1 da (Teresa b 1 April 1966); m 2, 30 Nov 1979 (separated 1989), Leni Tan; *Career* Nat Serv Intelligence Corps 1949-50; joined Lloyd's 1953; barr 1954; Thomas R Miller & Son (Insurance): joined 1953, ptnr 1959, sr ptnr 1971; chm Thomas R Miller & Son (Underwriting Agents) 1969-; Ctee Lloyd's Insur Brokers' Assoc: memb 1973-77, dep chm 1974-75, chm 1976-77; memb: Ctee on Invisible Exports 1975-77, Insurance Brokers' Registration Cncl 1977-81, Ctee of Lloyd's 1977-80, 1982-89; chm: Lloyd's 1984-87, Br Ctee of Bureau Veritas 1980-; memb HM Commission of Lieutenancy for the City of London 1987-; Freeman City of London 1986; Liveryman: Worshipful Co of Insurers 1987, Worshipful Co of Shipwrights 1987; Hon DSc City Univ 1987; FRSA 1986; Commendatore Ordine al Merito della Repubblica Italiana 1989; kt 1988; *Recreations* all sport (except cricket), wine, music, gardening, old churches; *Clubs* City, Brooks's, Vincent's, Thames Hare and Hounds; *Style—* Sir Peter Miller; Dawson House, 5 Jewry St, London EC3N 2EX (☎ 071 488 2345, fax 071 480 6002, telex 888905)

MILLER, Richard Hugh; s of Sir Stephen James Hamilton Miller, KCVO, of London, and Heather Prudence, *née* Motion; *b* 1 Feb 1953; *Educ* Charterhouse, Univ of Sussex

(BSc); *Career* called to the Bar 1976; *Recreations* travel, films; *Style—* Richard Miller, Esq; 6 Pump Court, Temple, London EC4Y 7AR (☎ 071 353 8588, fax 071 353 1516)

MILLER, Richard King; QC (Scot) 1988; s of James Cyril King Miller, WS (d 1979), of Edinburgh, and Ella Elizabeth, *née* Walker; *b* 19 Aug 1949; *Educ* Edinburgh Acad, Magdalene Coll Cambridge (BA), Univ of Edinburgh (LLB, Miller prize in Scots Law); *m* 24 Oct 1975, Lesley Joan, da of Harold Emil Rist, of 170 Morehead Ave, Norman Park, Brisbane 4170, Queensland, Aust; 2 s (Richard Andrew b 6 Oct 1980, John James b 3 March 1983); *Career* called to the Scottish Bar 1975, temp sheriff of all sheriffdoms of Scotland 1988-; memb Faculty of Advocates 1975-; *Recreations* shooting, fishing, tennis, reading; *Style—* Richard Miller, Esq, QC; Leahurst, 16 Gillespie Rd, Colinton, Edinburgh EH13 0LL (☎ 031 441 3737); Advocate's Library, Parliament House, High St, Edinburgh EH1 1RF (☎ 031 226 5071, fax 031 225 3642, telex 727856 FACADV G)

MILLER, Richard M; *Educ* Vanderbilt Univ Nashville (BA), Wharton Sch Univ of Pennsylvania; *m* Betty Ruth, *née* Randolph; 1 s (Richard), 2 da (Ellen, Claire); *Career* 1 Lt US Marine Corps 1953-55; salesman Dominion Insurance Agency 1955-58, fndr and pres Richard M Miller & Company 1958-70 (merged with Synecon corporation 1970), dir, pres and chief exec Synercon Corporation and pres and chief exec Richard M Miller & Company 1970-76 (Synercon Corporation merged with Corroon & Black Corporation 1976); Corroon & Black Corporation: vice pres and chief operating offr 1976-78, pres and chief operating offr 1978-88, chief exec and pres 1988-89, chm and chief exec 1990- (merged with Willis Faber plc 1990); chief exec and dir Willis Corroon plc 1990-; dir: Meridian Insurance Company Bermunda, Consumer Benefit Life Insurance Company, Third National Bank, Third National Corporation; life assoc Vanderbilt University's Owen Graduate Sch of Mgmnt; memb: Nat Assoc of Casualty and Surety Agents Nat Assoc of Insurance Brokers Nat Assoc of Surety Bond Producers; tstee and memb Exec Ctee Insurance Inst of America; *Recreations* golf; *Clubs* The City Midday (NY), Mid Ocean (Bermuda), The Tennessee, Phi Delta Theta Fraternity; *Style—* Richard Miller, Esq; Willis Group, 10 Trinity Square, London EC3P 3AX

MILLER, Robert Beatson (Robin); s of Taverner Barrington Miller, JP (d 1944), of Wadhurst, Sussex, and Catharine Mildred, *née* Beatson (d 1960); *b* 11 Nov 1915; *Educ* Radley, RCM, Royal Sch of Church Music, Hertford Coll Oxford (MA, BMus, ARCO), Yale Univ USA; *m* 1 Aug 1955, Pamela Tregoning, da of Sir Geoffrey Vickers, VC, of Goring-on-Thames; 1 s (Peter Burnell b 1958), 1 da (Anne Tregoning b 1956); *Career* WWII Flt Lt RAFVR 1943-47 (intelligence with Bomber Cmd and and the SE Asia Cmd), organist and choirmaster Philadelphia USA 1938-42, asst music master Tonbridge Sch 1947-48; dir of music: Ardingly Coll Sussex 1948-53, Oundle Sch 1954-72; conductor: Tunbridge Wells Choral Soc 1948-53, Stamford Choral and Orchestral Soc 1954-64; Liveryman Worshipful Co of Grocers 1964; ISM, Music Masters Assoc (pres 1964, hon sec 1974-79); *Recreations* playing the double bass, gardening, making wine; *Style—* Robin Miller, Esq; Orchard House, 39 Benefield Rd, Oundle, Peterborough PE8 4EU

MILLER, Dr Robert Glendinning; s of Lt-Col Sinclair Miller DSO, MC (d 1961), of Harrogate, and Norah Isabel (d 1954), da of Rt Hon Robert Graham Glendinning, PC, MP; *b* 24 Dec 1918; *Educ* King James GS Knaresborough, Trinity Hall Cambridge (BA, MB BChir, MA, MD); *m* 19 April 1954, (Alice) Mary Curzon, da of George Molyneux, of Bolton, Lancs; 1 s (Christopher b 1955), 1 da (Elizabeth b 1957); *Career* cmmnd Lt RAMC (War Emergency cmmn) 1943, promoted to Capt 1944; conslt physician with special interest in geriatrics Bedford Gp of Hosps Beds DHA 1955-83, hon conslt in geriatric med Bedford Gen Hosp 1983-, asst dep coroner Co of Bedford 1982; called to the Bar Gray's Inn 1972; pres Bedford Med Soc 1974-75, dep med dir Bedford Gp of Hosps 1966-68; memb N Beds Cncl for Voluntary Servs 1970-, vice pres Bedford and Dist Branch Burma Star Assoc 1977-82, (pres 1982-); FRCP; *Recreations* gardening, walking, travel, reading; *Style—* Dr Robert Miller; Meadow View, Clapham, Bedford MK41 6EL (☎ 0234 52545)

MILLER, Robert Michael; s of Hugh Begg Miller (d 1979); *b* 4 April 1943; *Educ* Hamilton Acad; *m* 1972, Janis, *née* Fleming; 2 children; *Career* chartered accountant 1968, md The Blackie Publishing Gp 1978-; *Recreations* golf, reading; *Clubs* Caledonian; *Style—* Robert Miller, Esq; 2 Glenburn Rd, Hamilton, Lanarks

MILLER, Robin Anthony; s of William Ernest Alexander Miller, CBE, BEM (d 1970), of Plymouth, Devon, and Winifred Albreta, *née* Tavener; *b* 15 Sept 1937; *Educ* Devonport HS; Wadham Coll Oxford (MA); *m* 25 Aug 1962, Irene Joanna, da of Alistair James Kennedy, MRCVS (d 1977), of Thornhill, Dumfriesshire, Scotland; 2 s (Iain Douglas b 27 Nov 1969, Richard Scott b 23 Nov 1971), 1 da (Helen Lordella b 8 March 1976); *Career* called to the Bar Middle Temple 1960; rec Crown Court 1978-; *Style—* Robin A Miller, Esq; St Michael's Lodge, 192 Devonport Rd, Plymouth PL1 5RD (☎ 0752 564943); 2 King's Bench Walk Temple London EC4Y 7DE

MILLER, (James Adrian) Rodney; s of Walter Miller, of Belfast, and Elizabeth Munnis; *b* 22 Jan 1949; *Educ* Dr Renshaw's Tutorial Coll Belfast, Univ of Ulster Coll of Art & Design (BA); *m* 25 Sept 1975, Patricia Woodburn, da of Frederick Wilmot, of Perth, Western Aust; 1 s (Jonathan Anthony Walter b 1977), 2 da (Victoria Beatrice b 1979, Emma Elizabeth b 1989); *Career* graphic designer: AFA Belfast 1972-73, N Ireland Housing Exec 1973-75; head Design Dept NIHE 1977-79 (sr graphic designer 1975-77), fndr Rodney Miller Associates 1979-; maj design projects: N Ireland Tourist Bd pubns, various public sector design projects; winner Kodak award for Excellence (Br Business Calendar Awards) 1989; MCSD 1977 (chm NW Region CSD 1990); *Recreations* bird watching, fishing, family; *Style—* Rodney Miller, Esq; 16 Circular Road, West, Cultra, Holywood, Co Down BT18 0AT (☎ 02317 5468); Rodney Miller Associates, 21 Ormeau Avenue, Belfast, Northern Ireland BT2 8HD (☎ 0232 240785, fax 0232 232901)

MILLER, Roger Geoffrey; s of Robert Ralph Miller; *b* 5 Aug 1952; *Educ* St Dunstan's Coll London, Trinity Coll Cambridge; *m* 1971, Diana Evelyn, da of late Brig Henry Latham; 3 children; *Career* mgmnt conslt; md RTZ Computer Servs Ltd 1978-; *Recreations* sailing; *Style—* Roger Miller, Esq; 18 Bramcote Rd, London SW15 (☎ 081 788 4309)

MILLER, Roger Simon; s of Rev George Handscomb Miller (d 1966), of Northfield House, Todber, Dorset, and Jean Eileen, *née* Smith (d 1979); *b* 16 Feb 1938; *Educ* Harrow, Trinity Coll Oxford (BA); *m* 1, 16 June 1962 (m dis 1976), Sara Elizabeth Battersby, da of Alfred Perceval Atkins (ka in Malaya 1942), of Kuala Selangor; 2 da (Caroline (Mrs La Costa) b 1964, Anna b 1966); m 2, 27 Oct 1984 (m dis 1988), Roslyn Mary, da of Alfred John Atkinson, of Ryde, IOW; *Career* Nat Serv Lt 3 Greenjackets (The Rifle Bde); Imperial Group Ltd 1966-77, dir Pilgrim Pipe Co 1971-74, proprietor Appleby and McGrath 1977-82, dir International Management Selection 1980-84, schoolmaster Sunningdale Sch 1981-; Parly candidate (Lib): Horncastle Linc 1970 and 1974, Weston-super-Mare 1974; area cmmr St John Ambulance: Avon 1976-79, Wilts 1979-81; Freeman City of London, Liveryman Worshipful Co of Carpenters 1959; *Books* Influential Dates in British History (1988); *Recreations* cricket (formerly with Sussex, later Dorset County Clubs), horses (long distance riding and hunting); *Clubs* Nat Lib; *Style—* Roger Simon Miller, Esq; The Hill, Charters Rd, Sunningdale, Berks (☎ 0990 291116); 23 Netherton Rd, St Margarets, Twickenham, Middlesex (☎ 051 892 0387); Sunningdale Sch, Berks (☎ 0990 20159)

MILLER, Ronald Alan; s of Eric Norman Miller (d 1978), of 20 Evelyn Mansions, Carlisle Place SW1, and Rosemary, *née* Winter; *b* 10 March 1951; *Educ* Westminster, St Bartholomews Hosp (MB BS, MS); *m* 1975, Sarah Jane, da of Richard Griffiths Lumley, of Ross on Wye, Glos; 1 s (Mark Rudolph b 1979), 1 da (Rosalind Margaret Louise b 1982); *Career* Hunterian prof of surgery RCS 1985, Simpson Smith lectr Charing Cross Hosp 1986, currently: dir Dept or Urology Whittington and Royal Northern Hosps, postgrad dean Royal Northern Hosp, hon sr lectr Inst of Urology, 200 papers on urological subjects; Cutler Prize RCS 1984; sec N E Thames Advsy Ctee on Urology, cncl memb Biological Engrg Soc, Instrument Ctee Br Assoc Urological Surgns; memb: BMS, RSM, Br Assoc Urological Surgns, American Urological Assoc, Endo Urology Soc, Minimally Invasive soc; FRCS 1978 (MRCS), LRCP 1974; MS Univ of London 1986; *Books* Percutaneous Renal Surgery (1983), Endoscopic Surgery (1986), Second Generation Lithotripsy (1987); *Recreations* riding, walking, shooting, reading, military history; *Style—* Ronald Miller, Esq; 16 Woodland Gardens, London N10 3UA (☎ 081 444 6475); Wellington Hospital, Wellington Place, London NW8 (☎ 071 586 5959)

MILLER, Ronald Kinsman; CB (1989); s of William Miller (d 1986), of Kelvedon, Essex, and Elsie May, *née* Kinsman (d 1956); *b* 12 Nov 1929; *Educ* Colchester Royal GS; *m* 1952, Doris Alice, da of Patrick Dew (d 1984), of Greenwich; 1 s (Timothy John b 1960), 1 da (Felicity Jane b 1958); *Career* Nat Serv RN 1948-50; called to the Bar Gray's Inn 1953; Inland Revenue: joined Slr's Office 1965, Law Offrs' Dept 1977-79, Solicitor of Inland Revenue 1986-90 (princ asst slr 1981); *Recreations* music, reading, gardening; *Clubs* Athenaeum; *Style—* Ronald Miller, Esq, CB; 4 Liskeard Close, Chislehurst, Kent BR7 6RT (☎ 081 467 8041)

MILLER, Dr Roy Frank; s of Thomas Richard Miller (d 1978), and Margaret Ann, *née* Tattum; *b* 20 Sept 1935; *Educ* Wembley Co GS, Univ of Exeter (BSc), Univ of London (PhD); *m* 18 March 1962, Ruth Naomi, da of William Kenchington (d 1957); 1 s (Stephen b 1965); *Career* Royal Holloway Coll: lectr in physics 1960, sr lectr 1972-73, vice princ 1978, prin 1981-85; vice princ Royal Holloway and Bedford New Coll 1985-; res assoc Case Western Res Univ Cleveland Ohio 1968-; chm: Inst of Classical Studies and Canterbury Hall Univ of London; tstee and govr Strode's Coll Egham; FInstP 1978, FRSA 1983, CPhys 1986; *Recreations* music, climbing; *Clubs* Athenaeum; *Style—* Dr Roy Miller; Celyn, 3 Parsonage Rd, Englefield Green, Egham, Surrey; RHBNC, Egham, Surrey TW20 OEX (☎ 0784 434455, fax 0784 437520)

MILLER, Sidney James; s of Sidney Tomsett Miller (d 1967), of Cambridge, and Mary Ada, *née* Marshall (d 1980); *b* 25 Jan 1943; *Educ* Clifton, Jesus Coll Cambridge (MA); *m* 17 July 1971, Judith Branney, da of Lt-Col Bernard Passingham, OBE, TD; 3 s (Paul b 1973, John b 1976, Mark b 1979), 1 da (Clare b 1984); *Career* Knox fell Harvard 1964-65, VI Form classical master and asst housemaster Clifton 1965-68, head Classical Dept Eton 1971-73 (asst master and classical tutor 1968-73), dep headmaster Bridgewater Hall Comprehensive Sch Milton Keynes 1974-77; headmaster: Kingston GS 1977-86, Bedford Sch 1986-88; professional offr Sch Examinations and Assessment Cncl London 1988-89, higher exec offr DES London 1989-; pres Kingston Rotary Club 1982-83 (memb 1978-86); area chm Int Ctee of Rotary 1983-86 (district chm designate 1986); chm: ISIS London and SE Region Ctee 1981-84 (memb 1978-84), Kingston Boys' Club 1985-86 (vice chm 1984); vice chm Mgmnt Ctee Kingston YMCA 1986 (memb 1984-86); memb: Bedford Rotary Club 1986-88, Bd of Visitors Latchmere House Remand Centre 1979-86 (and Local Review Ctee (Parole)) and Bedford Prison 1987-88, Parochial Church Cncl (Castlethorpe Bucks 1974-77, Claygate Surrey 1979-82), Claygate Men's Fellowship Ctee 1983-86, Headmasters' Conference (HMC) Politics and PR Sub-Ctee 1980-84 and 1987-88, Kinston NAHT Ctee 1982-84, Ctee Jesus Coll Cambridge Soc 1982-85, Cncl ISCO 1984-87; HMC rep on SHA Liaison Ctee 1984-87, tstee Kingston YMCA 1985-86; govr: Denmead Prep Sch Hampton 1979-86, Aldwickbury Sch Harpenden, Beechwood Park Sch Markyate, Kingshott Sch Hitchin and Rushmoor Sch Bedford 1987-88; memb: Kingston GS, Bedford Sch Choral Socs; *Recreations* all sports, especially, athletics and cricket, acting, reading, theatre, cinema, classical music, choral singing; *Clubs* MCC, Achilles; *Style—* Sidney Miller, Esq; 43 Waterloo Rd, Bedford MK40 3PG

MILLER, Sir Stephen James Hamilton; KCVO (1979); s of Stephen Miller; *b* 19 July 1915; *Educ* Arbroath HS, Univ of Aberdeen (MD); *m* 1949, Heather Prudence Motion; 3 s; *Career* ophthalmic surgn: St George's Hosp 1951-80, Nat Hosp Queen Square 1955-78, King Edward VII Hosp for Offrs; surgn Moorfields Eye Hosp 1954-80; surgn oculist to: HM's Household 1965-74, HM The Queen 1974-80; hospitaller St John Ophthalmic Hosp Jerusalem 1980-, chm and tstee The Frost Fndn, vice chm Iris Fund, memb Cncl of the Guide Dogs for the Blind; Freeman City of London, Liveryman Worshipful Soc of Apothecaries; FRCS; KStJ 1978, GCStJ 1988; *Books* Clinical Ophthalmology (1987), Parson's Diseases of the Eye (1989); *Recreations* golf, fishing, music; *Clubs* Caledonian, Muirfield, Woking Golf; *Style—* Sir Stephen Miller, KCVO; Sherma Cottage, Pond Rd, Woking, Surrey GU22 0JT (☎ 0483 762287); 123 Harley St, London W1N 1HE (☎ 071 935 3488)

MILLER, Stewart Crichton; CBE (1990); s of William Young Crichton Miller (d 1964), of Kirkcaldy, Fife, and Grace Margaret, *née* Finlay; *b* 2 July 1934; *Educ* Kirkcaldy HS Univ of Edinburgh (BSc); *m* 25 June 1960, Catherine Proudfoot, da of Alexander McCourtie (d 1957); 2 s (David b 1963, Gordon b 1965), 2 da (Sarah b 1970, Lucy b 1971); *Career* Rolls Royce: joined 1954, held various appts in technology design and devpt, chief engr RB211-535 1977-84, dir advanced engrg 1984-85, bd memb 1985-, dir engrg 1985-90, md Aerospace Gp 1991-; FEng 1987, FRAeS 1986, FIMechE 1987; *Recreations* music, walking; *Style—* Stewart Miller, Esq, CBE; Rolls Royce plc, 65 Buckingham Gate, London SW1E 6AT (☎ 071 222 9020, telex 918 091)

MILLER, Tammy Kelly; da of Peter James miller, of Kampala, Uganda, and Mary Kathleen, *née* McDonnell; *b* 21 June 1967; *Educ* The Red Maids' Sch Bristol, Univ of Exeter (BSc); *Career* hockey player; Clifton Ladies Hockey Club 1985-; England: under 18 and under 21 caps, 34 full caps, debut v Spain 1988, played in World Cup Sydney 1990 (fourth place); trainee actuary Sun Life Assurance Society Bristol; *Recreations* squash, badminton, travel; *Style—* Miss Tammy Miller; c/o All England Women's Hockey Association, 51 High St, Shrewsbury SY1 1ST

MILLER, Timothy Peter Francis; s of Col John Francis Miller, of Camberley, Surrey, and Barbara Mary, *née* Cooke; *b* 9 Nov 1940; *Educ* Douai Sch, Magdalen Coll Oxford (MA); *m* 12 Nov 1965, Lisa, da of Glyn Beynon Davies (d 1979); 2 s (Charles b 1977, Alexander b 1983), 2 da (Lucasta b 1966, Cressida b 1968); *Career* md Framlington Group plc 1983-88 (dir 1979-88); dir: M & G Group plc Lautro; chm: EFIFC Mktg Ctee, Advsy Assoc Fin Advsy Ctee; chm Charter 88 Exec Ctee; Parly candidate (C) Hackney North and Stoke Newington 1979; *Recreations* pictures, books, music, motor sport; *Clubs* Beefsteak, City of London, MCC; *Style—* Timothy Miller, Esq; 9 Bartholomew Villas, London NW5 2LJ (☎ 071 485 7294); M & G Group plc, Three Quays, Tower Hill, London EC3R 6BQ (☎ 071 626 4588)

MILLER, Walter George; s of Bert Miller (d 1968), of Cardiff, and Rosina Miller, *née* Blackmore (d 1978); *b* 2 March 1932; *Educ* Howardian HS Cardiff; *m* Sheila Mary, da of Charles Daw (d 1956), of Cardiff; 1 s (Nicholas Anthony Joseph b 1960), 2 da

(Joanna Veronica (Mrs Kelly) b 1959, Frances Cecilia b 1965); *Career* Nat Serv Gunner RA 1950-52 (active serv Hong Kong and Korea); City Treasurer's Dept: Nairobi Kenya 1955-58, Cardiff 1958-60; chief accountant Caerphilly UDC 1960-63, tech asst Ilford Borough Cncl and London Borough of Redbridge 1963-65; London Borough of Bromley 1965-72 (chief tech asst, asst borough treas and princ asst borough treas); City of Bristol: asst city treas then dep city treas 1972-80, city treas and dep chief 1980-86, acting chief exec 1986-90, chief exec 1990-; chm of govrs St Joseph's RC Primary Sch Portishead; IPFA 1958, FCCA 1960; *Recreations* walking, gardening; *Style—* Walter Miller, Esq; 4 Nore Road, Portishead, Bristol BS20 9HN (☎ 0272 848559); Chief Executive's Office, The Council House, College Green, Bristol BS1 5TR (☎ 0272 222637, 223755, telex 449819 CITBRI G)

MILLER, William; s of Robert Roberts Miller (d 1983), of Stanley, Co Durham, and Elizabeth Ellen, *née* Buck (d 1984); *b* 3 Jan 1931; *Educ* Stanley GS, Univ of Durham (BSc); *m* 23 July 1960, Christine Mary, da of Herbert Frankish (d 1965); 1 s (Steven b 1964), 2 da (Lesley b 1961, Anne b 1967); *Career* chief engr Lighting Div Philips 1960-66, div mangr Heenan International 1969-72; Crompton Lighting Ltd: prodn mangr 1972-75, gen mangr and dir 1976-77, md 1977-90, dep chm 1990-; ret 1990; memb English Golf Union, former memb Doncaster Young Enterprise Bd, life memb Yorkshire Union of Golf Clubs; CEng, MIMechE 1965; *Recreations* golf, photography, carpentry; *Clubs* Doncaster Golf (former capt); *Style—* William Miller, Esq; 24 The Hollows, Bessacarr, Doncaster, S Yorks DN4 7PP

MILLER, Prof William Lockley; s of William Lockley Miller, of Hamilton, and Florence, *née* Ratcliffe (d 1986); *b* 12 Aug 1943; *Educ* Univ of Edinburgh (MA), Univ of Newcastle (PhD); *m* 19 July 1967, Dr Nancy Fiona, da of David Thomson, of Newport-on-Tay, Fife; 2 s (Iain b 3 July 1971, Andrew b 15 June 1977), 1 da (Shona b 9 Nov 1974); *Career* prof of politics Univ of Strathclyde 1985- (lectr 1968-83, sr lectr 1983-85), Edward Caird Prof of politics Univ of Glasgow 1985; *Books* Electoral Dynamics (1977), The End of British Politics? (1981), The Survey Method (1983), Elections and Voters (1987), Irrelevant Elections? (1988), How Voters Change (1990); *Style—* Prof William Miller; Dept of Politics, Adam Smith Building, The Univ, Glasgow G12 8RT (☎ 041 3398855, fax 041 3304071, telex 777070 UNIGLA)

MILLER JONES, Hon Mrs (Betty Ellen); da of 1 and last Baron Askwith, KCB, KC (d 1942), and late Baroness Askwith, CBE, *née* Peel; *b* 26 June 1909; *Educ* Lycée Français London; *m* 1950, Keith Miller Jones (d 1978); *Career* author; FRSL; *Style—* The Hon Mrs Miller Jones; 9/105 Onslow Sq, London SW7 (☎ 071 589 7126)

MILLER MUNDY, Lady Bridget; *née* Elliot-Murray-Kynynmound; da of 5 Earl of Minto (d 1975); *b* 1921; *m* 1, 1944 (m dis 1954), Lt-Col James Averell Clark, Jr, DFC, USAF (d 1990); 1 s; m 2, 1954 (m dis 1963), Maj Henry Lyon Garnett, CBE (d 1990); m 3, 1966 (m dis 1970), Maj (Edward) Peter Godfrey Miller Mundy, MC (d 1981); *Style—* The Lady Bridget Miller Mundy

MILLER OF GLENLEE, Sir (Frederick William) Macdonald; 7 Bt (GB 1788), of Glenlee, Kirkcudbrightshire; s of Sir Alistair George Lionel Joseph Miller of Glenlee, 6 Bt (d 1964), and his 1 w, Kathleen Daisy (d 1978), yr da of Stephen G Howard, CBE, JP, DL, MP Sudbury 1919-22; Sir Macdonald is descended from Sir William Miller of Glenlee, 2 Bt, who as a Lord of Session took the title Lord Glenlee and d 1846; Sir Thomas, 1 Bt (d 1789) was Lord Pres of the Ct of Session, with the courtesy title of Lord Barskimming; *b* 21 March 1920; *Educ* Tonbridge; *m* 2 Sept 1947, (Marion Jane) Audrey, o da of Richard Spencer Pettit (d 1983), of Sudbury, Suffolk; 1 s (b 1953), 1 da (Alison (Mrs Freeman) b 3 Aug 1951); *Heir* s, Dr Stephen William Macdonald Miller of Glenlee, b 20 June 1953; *Career* served 1939-43: Beds and Herts Regt 1940, Black Watch 1941-42, RAC 1943; Cons agent for: Whitehaven Div of Cumberland 1947-50, Wembley North 1950-52, N Norfolk 1952-65, Lowestoft (later renamed Waveney) 1965-83; Suffolk Cons Euro agent 1980-83, political conslt 1983-85; dep Traffic cmmr 1974-85; memb: Eastern Sea Fisheries Jt Ctee 1981-86 (chm 1981-83), Suffolk FPC 1982-90; chm Suffolk CC 1988-89 (vice chm 1986-88, chm educn ctee 1985-88, memb 1977-89); *Recreations* gardening; *Style—* Sir Macdonald Miller of Glenlee, Bt; Ivy Grange Farm, Westhall, Halesworth, Suffolk IP19 8RN (☎ 098 681 265)

MILLER OF GLENLEE, Dr Stephen William Macdonald; s and h of Sir Macdonald Miller of Glenlee, 7 Bt; *b* 20 June 1953; *Educ* Rugby, St Bartholomew's Hosp (MB BS); *m* 1978, Mary Carolyn (d 1989), o da of G B Owens, of Huddersfield; 1 s (James b 1981), 1 da (Katherine b 1983); m 2, 1990, Caroline, da of L A E Chasemore, of Shebbear; *Career* GP Shebbear; FRCS, MRCGP; *Style—* Dr Stephen Miller; The Lawn, Shebbear, Beaworthy, Devon EX21 5RU

MILLES-LADE, Lady Diana; da of Hon Henry Augustus Milles-Lade, JP (d 1937), and sis of 4 Earl Sondes; *b* 1919; *Career* granted 1942, rank, title and precedence as an Earl's da which would have been hers had her father survived to succeed to the title; *Style—* The Lady Diana Milles-Lade; 37 Lennox Gdns, SW1

MILLETT, Anthony Derek; s of Denis Millett (d 1965), of 45 Grosvenor Sq, London W1, and Adele, of 36 Curzon St; *b* 20 April 1936; *Educ* Harrow; *Career* chm and md Millett Stores Ltd; dir: Black & Edgington Ltd, Gaiety Theatre; *Recreations* cricket, theatre, old films, Churchilliana; *Clubs* MCC, Butterflies, Harrow Wanderers, Gentlemen of Leicestershire, Middlesex County Cricket; *Style—* Anthony Millett, Esq; 62c Old Brompton Rd, London SW7 3LQ (☎ 071 584 4978); Black & Edgington Ltd, 53/54 Rathbone Place, London W1

MILLETT, The Hon Mr Justice; Hon Sir Peter Julian Millett; s of Denis Millett (d 1965), of London, and Adele Millett, *née* Weinberg; *b* 23 June 1932; *Educ* Harrow, Trinity Hall Cambridge (MA); *m* 1959, Ann Mireille, da of David Harris (d 1980), of London; 3 s (Richard, Andrew, Robert d 1965); *Career* standing jr counsel to BOT and DTI 1967-73; bencher Lincoln's Inn 1980; memb Insolvency Law Review Ctee 1977-82, High Ct judge Chancery Div (1986), QC (1973), kt (1986); *Style—* The Hon Sir Peter Millett; 18 Portman Close, London W1H 9HJ (☎ 071 935 1152); 38 Kewhurst Ave, Cooden, Sussex (☎ 04243 2970)

MILLETT, Robert David; VRD; s of Douglas Gladstone Millett (d 1980), of 23 St Lucia, West Parade, Bexhill-on-Sea, Sussex, and Mary Ann Elizabeth Coffer, *née* Manclarke; *b* 3 Jan 1930; *Educ* City of London Sch, Peterhouse Cambridge (MA, LLB); *m* 31 Aug 1957, Margaret (Peggy) Pettigrew Brownlie, da of William Smith (d 1970); *Career* Nat Serv RN 1949-50, RNVR then RNR London Div, ret cdr (supply branch) 1976; admitted slr 1956; Lewis and Dick: articled (London) 1953-56, asst slr (Ewell) 1956-59, ptnr (Surrey) 1960-, currently sr ptnr (Surrey and Sussex); immediate past pres Nat Chamber of Trade (Bd memb and chm Legislation and Taxation Ctee until 1987); former: pres Rotary Club of Ewell 1967-68, pres Mid Surrey Law Soc 1983, chm Ewell C of C, chm Surrey Cncl Nat Chamber of Trade, govr Glynn Sch Ewell; Freeman City of London, Liveryman Worshipful Co of Scriveners; memb: HAC, Law Soc; *Recreations* photography, stamp collecting, railways; *Clubs* Royal Automobile, Royal Dart Yacht, Wardroom Mess HMS President; *Style—* Robert Millett, Esq, VRD; Craigmore, 35 Golfside, Cheam Surrey; (☎ 081 643 7761); 12a Wellswood Park, Wellswood, Torquay, South Devon; 443 Kingston Rd, Ewell, Epsom, Surrey (☎ 081 393 0055)

MILLETT, Timothy Patrick; *b* 6 Jan 1951; *Educ* St Benedict's Sch Ealing London, Wadham Coll Oxford (MA); *Career* called to the Bar Gray's Inn 1975; official of Court of Justice of Euro Communities 1976; legal sec to advocate general: Sir Gordon Slynn 1984-88, Francis Jacobs 1988-89; currently princ administrator Court of Justice of Euro Communities; *Books* The Court of First Instance of the European Communities (1990); *Style—* Timothy Millett, Esq; Court of Justice of the European Communities, Luxembourg, L-2925 (☎ 010352 43031, fax 010352 43032600, telex 2771 CJINFO LU)

MILLHAM, David Harry; s of Harry Sidney Millham (d 1982), and Emily Harriet Millham, *née* Edwards; *b* 20 June 1938; *Educ* William Morris Country Tech Coll Walthamstow, IMEDE Lausanne Switzerland; *m* 27 March 1965, Frances, da of Francis William DuBarry; 1 s (Alexander Gareth David b 20 March 1970), 1 da (Lisa Jane b 14 March 1967); *Career* Financial Times 1959-69 (new issues ed, gen fin news writer), The Times 1969-71 (new issues ed, contrib Fin Ed's Column) PR conslt ICFC 1971-74, dir Shandwick PR Company 1974-79; Shandwick Consultants: dep chm 1979-, md Fin PR Div 1990-; Freeman City of London 1988; MIOD; *Recreations* watching football, gardening, reading, music; *Style—* David Millham, Esq; Shandwick Consultants, Dauntsey House, Frederick's Place, Old Jewry, London EC2R 8AB (☎ 071 726 4291, fax 071 600 2249)

MILLIGAN, Dr George William Elliott; s of George Burn Milligan (d 1985), of Tullochard, Kingussie, and Kathleen Dorothea Milligan; *b* 2 April 1945; *Educ* Trinity Coll Glenalmond, Univ Coll Oxford (BA), Univ of Glasgow (MEng), Univ of Cambridge (PhD); *m* 18 July 1968, Baroness Barbara Wanda Borowska, da of Baron Tadeusz Borowski, and Countess Janina, step da of Herbert Charles Story, of Tunbridge Wells; 2 s (Robert George b 1968, Jan Charles b 1970); *Career* chartered civil engnr; lectr Univ of Oxford and tutor and fellow of Magdalen Coll Oxford 1979-, author of tech papers on soil mechanics and co-author of books on basic soil mechanics and reinforced soil; *Recreations* golf, walking, fishing, music; *Style—* Dr George W E Milligan; 9 Lathbury Road, Oxford OX2 7AT (☎ 0865 58558); Dept of Engineering Science, Parks Road, Oxford OX1 3PJ (☎ 0865 273137)

MILLIGAN, Stephen David Wyatt; s of D K Milligan, and R S Milligan, *née* Scutt; *b* 12 May 1948; *Educ* Bradfield, Magdalen Coll Oxford (PPE); *Career* presenter The World Tonight Radio Four 1979-82, ed Foreign Report 1980-81, home ed The Economist 1983 (bureau chief Brussels 1975-80, Euro ed 1981-83), Washington correspondent The Sunday Times 1987-88 (foreign ed 1984-87), Euro correspondent BBC TV 1988-90; selected as (C) prospective parly candidate for Eastleigh July 1990; *Books* The New Barons (1976); *Recreations* golf, skiing, opera, tennis; *Clubs* Royal Mid-Surrey Golf, Ski Club of GB; *Style—* Stephen Milligan, Esq; BBC TV Centre, Wood Lane, London W14 (☎ 081 576 7690)

MILLIGAN, Terence Alan (Spike); s of Capt Leo Alphonso Milligan MSM, RA (d 1969), and Florence Winifred, *née* Kettleband; 4 generations RA Indian Army including Indian Mutiny; *b* 16 April 1918; *Educ* Convent Jesus and Mary Poona, St Paul's Christian Brothers de la Salle Rangoon, SE London Poly; *m* 1, 1952, June Angela, da of Richard Marlowe; 1 s (Séan b 1954), 2 da (Laura b 1952, Silé b 1957); m 2, 1962, Patricia (d 1978), da of Capt William Ridgway; 1 da (Jane b 1966); m 3, 1983, Shelagh, da of Col Gordon Sinclair; *Career* WWII, RA, N Africa, Italy; factory worker, van boy, stockroom asst, asst, stationery salesman, semi-pro musician, radio script writer, solo comic, musical comedy trio; TV script writer, author, poet, illustrator, painter, composer; *Recreations* reading war histories, biographies, dining and wining, squash; *Clubs* Ronnie Scotts (life memb); *Style—* Spike Milligan, Esq; 9 Orme Court, Bayswater, London W2 (☎ 071 727 1544)

MILLIN, Peter Jack; s of Henry Millin (d 1977), of London, and Lily Millin, of USA; *b* 28 Dec 1930; *Educ* Farnham GS, Univ of Liverpool, Sch of Econ Sci, Adleman Soc (Psychology & Hypnotherapy); *m* 1969 (m dis), Nelly; 1 s (David b 1960); *Career* psychologist, counsellor and hypnotherapist 1960-; princ Frendship/Marriage Bureau 1950-60, pres Professional Hypnotherapist Centre, princ Acad of Hynotherapy, lectr various orgns and contrib to various jls; winner of various medals for ballroom dancing; memb Complementary Medicine Soc; *Recreations* philosophy, theatre, classical music, travel; *Clubs* Unique Social (fndr), Kaleidescape; *Style—* Peter Millin, Esq; 28 Lakeside Crescent, East Barnet, Hertfordshire EN4 8QJ (☎ 081 441 9685); Academy of Hypnotherapy, 10 Harley St, London W1 (☎ 081 441 9685)

MILLING, Henry Miles; s of late Henry Robert Milling; *b* 30 Nov 1934; *Educ* Oundle, Imperial Coll London; *m* 1968, Ann Cartledge, née Bradbury; 2 da; *Career* marketing dir Fairey Engrg 1978-, head of sales and marketing NEI Int Combustion 1975-78, proposals mangr GEC Power Station Projects 1970-75; *Recreations* sailing, tennis, golf, skiing; *Style—* Henry Milling, Esq; Beech Tree House, Davenport Lane, Mobberley, Knutsford, Cheshire

MILLING, Peter Francis; s of Frederick William Milling (d 1965), and Audrey Franc Myra, *née* Messervy; *b* 1 April 1916; *Educ* Wimbledon Coll, Stonyhurst, Univ of Cambridge (MA), St Thomas's and Guy's (MB BChir); *m* 9 June 1941, Euphemia Margaret (Peggy), da of Frank Ernest Todd (d 1946); 2 s (Anthony b 1942, Martin b 1945); *Career* Nat Serv Lt RAMC 1941-42 (invalided); jr posts St Thomas's and Guy's Hosp 1940-48; conslt ENT surgeon: Univ Coll Hosp and Harley St 1948, Benenden Chest Hosp 1949, Epsom and Oxted Hosps 1949, Brompton Hosp 1950, ret 1976; memb: Catenian Assoc (past pres Westerham, fndr pres IOM), Spinal Injuries Assoc Visiting Assoc Throat and Ear Surgns of GB (past pres); memb: BMA, Br Assoc Otolaryngologists; FRCS, LRCP; *Recreations* trout fishing; *Style—* Peter Milling, Esq; 3 Homefield Park, Ballasalla, Isle of Man (☎ 0624 823072)

MILLINGTON, Gordon Stopford; s of Percival Richard Millington (d 1981), of Killinchy, and Irene Ellen, *née* Forster; *b* 29 June 1935; *Educ* Campbell Coll Queens Univ of Belfast (BSc); *m* 30 April 1960, Margaret Jean, da of Leslie Pegler (d 1966), of Croydon; 2 s (Mark Stopford b 28 Feb 1962, Gavin Paul b 11 Dec 1965), 1 da (Kathryn Margaret b 26 Feb 1964); *Career* asst engr Sir William Halcrow & Partners 1957-59, ptnr Kirk McClure & Morton 1966-87 (engr 1959-66), sr ptnr Kirk McClure Morton 1988; chm NI Assoc ICE 1979-80, pres Belfast Rotary Club 1980-81; chm: Bd Govrs Grosvenor HS 1983-90, NI Branch IHT 1989-90; vice chm NI 2000 1988-; FICE, FIStructE, FIEI, FIHT, MConsE; *Recreations* yachting; *Clubs* Killyleagh Yacht; *Style—* Gordon Millington, Esq; 27 Greystown Park, Belfast BT9 6UP (☎ 0232 611303); Kirk McClure Morton, 2 Elmwood Ave, Belfast BT9 6BA (☎ 0232 667914, fax 0232 668286)

MILLMAN, Stewart Ian; s of Sidney Woolf Millman (d 1984), of London, and Doris, *née* Gerstein; *b* 21 Nov 1948; *Educ* City of London Sch, New Coll Oxford (BA, MA); *Career* dir Lazard Securities Ltd 1979, ptnr de Zoete & Bevan 1984, dir Barclays de Zoete Wedd Securities Ltd 1986, jt md de Zoete & Bevan Ltd 1988; memb Cncl Soc of Investmt Analysts 1979-89; AMSIA; *Recreations* playing cricket, watching football, travel; *Style—* Stewart Millman, Esq; 31 De Walden St, London W1M 7PJ (☎ 071 486 3029); Ebbgate Hse, 2 Swan Lane, London EC4R 3TS (☎ 071 623 2323, fax 071 626 1879)

MILLN, Hon Mrs (Susan Margaret); *née* Annesley; 2 da of 14 Viscount Valentia, MC, MRCS, LRCP (d 1983; he established his succession 1959 after title had become dormant in 1951 - had not been proved since 1844 when the 9 Viscount died), and Joan, Viscountess Valentia (d 1986); *b* 18 Feb 1931; *Educ* Byculla; *m* 1954, Peter Lindsay Milln, s of Alexander Lindsay Milln (d 1932); 1 s (Jeremy), 3 da (Teresa,

Eleanor, Jesica); *Career* landowner; *Recreations* riding, sailing, (yacht 'Slip-Shod'), gardening; *Style—* The Hon Mrs Milln; Bosinver, St Austell, Cornwall (☎ 0726 72128)

MILLNER, Brian David; s of Edwin Millner (d 1932); *b* 7 Oct 1930; *Educ* Scarborough HS, Cambridge Univ (MA); *m* 1956, Adina Josephine, *née* Tonn; 1 s, 1 da; *Career* sundry Pilkington Gp Appointments 1954-73, marketing mangr Chance Pilkington 1973-79, dir 1979-80; dir: Chance (Optical) Ltd 1976-80, Chance Pilkington KK (Japan) 1977-80; gp public affairs advsr Pilkington plc 1980-; *Recreations* motoring, gardening, reading, travel; *Style—* Brian Millner, Esq; 3 Church Walk, Tarleton, Lancs (☎ 0772 814811); Pilkington plc, Prescot Rd, St Helens, Merseyside WA10 3TT (☎ 0744 692313)

MILLNER, William Frank (Tim); s of William Millner (d 1982), and Una Mary, *née* Wallis; *b* 4 Jan 1932; *Educ* St Paul's, St Thomas's Hosp Med Sch (MB BS); *m* 1, 31 March 1959 (m dis 1984), Patricia Jane Elizabeth, *née* James; 2 s (Russell William James b 1960, Justin Christie James b 1962); m 2, 18 Feb 1984, Margaret-Ann (Maggie), da of James Robin Streather; 1 da (Lucinda Ann Streather b 1984); *Career* Surgn Lt RN 1957-62, MO HMS Resolution Christmas Island Grapple Sqdn (nuclear testing) 1958-59, Families MO HMS Terror Singapore 1959-61; orthopaedic surgn and conslt N Herts Health Authy 1972-; memb NW Thames RHA 1978-86; FRCS, FRCSE; *Recreations* skiing, watching rugby; *Clubs* RSM, Old Pauline; *Style—* Tim Millner, Esq; Radwell Dene, Radwell, Baldock, Herts S97 5ES (☎ 0462 730478); 10 Harley St, London W1 (☎ 071 580 4280)

MILLS, Angela Margaret; da of Dr Ronald Hubert Bonfield Mills (d 1989), and Audrey Vera, *née* Mountjoy; *b* 24 Jan 1948; *Educ* Vaynor and Penderyn Sch, Somerville Coll Oxford (BA, BM BCh, MA); *Career* Nat MO Family Planning Assoc 1983-88, hon lectr joint of Depts of Obstetrics and Gynaecology UCH and Middlesex Hosp 1983-, currently conslt gynaecologist United Elizabeth Garrett Anderson Hosp and Hosp for Women Soho; various pubns in jls; chm London Soc Family Planning Doctors 1985-88, vice chm Nat Assoc of Family Planning Doctors 1989-; memb: Sub Ctee of RCOG on problems assoc with AIDS in relation to obstetrics and gynaecology, Faculty of Community Health, Continuing Educn Sub Ctee of Faculty of Community Health 1990-, American Soc of Fertility and Sterility, Soc of Advancement of Contraception, Br Soc Clinical Colposcopists, BMA; MRCOG; *Recreations* travelling, music, gardening; *Clubs* Network, RSM; *Style—* Miss Angela Mills; The United Elizabeth Garrett Anderson Hospital and Hospital for Women Soho, 144 Euston Rd, London NW1 2AP (☎ 071 387 2501); 115 Harley St, London W1N 1DG (☎ 071 486 5802)

MILLS, Barbara Jean Lyon; QC (1986); da of John Lyon Warnock, and Nora Kitty Warnock; *b* 10 Aug 1940; *Educ* St Helen's Sch Northwood Middx, Lady Margaret Hall Oxford (MA); *m* 1962, John Angus Donald Mills, s of Kenneth McKenzie Mills; 4 children (Sarah b 1963, Caroline b 1965, Lizzie b 1969, Peter b 1971); *Career* called to the Bar Middle Temple 1963, rec 1981-; *Style—* Mrs Barbara J L Mills, QC; The Serious Fraud Office, Elm House, 10-16 Elm St, London WC1X 0BJ (☎ 071 239 7272)

MILLS, Maj Bernard Herbert Gordon; CBE (1989); s of James Gordon Coleman Mills (d 1959), and Ellen, *née* Goodson (d 1974); *b* 21 Feb 1932; *Educ* St John's Sch Leatherhead, RMA Sandhurst, Queens' Coll Cambridge (MA); *Career* enlisted RAC 1950, cmmnd Suffolk Regt 1952; served: Trieste, Germany, Cyprus; 22 SAS Regt 1955-57 Malaya, HQ 4 Div Germany 1959-60, 1 Royal Anglian Regt 1960-62 Berlin and UK, Muscat Regt Sultan of Oman's Armed Forces 1962-64, ret 1964; political advsr: Govt Kingdom of Yemen 1964-67, Govt Kingdom of Saudi Arabia 1967-69; field dir Nigeria Save the Children Fund 1969-70, del (later chief del) Int Union for Child Welfare in Nigeria, E Pakistan and Bangladesh 1970-74, dir Duranton Ltd (Antony Gibbs Gp) 1975-79; UN Relief and Works Agency: offr i/c Central Lebanon Area 1982-83, asst dir i/c operation S Lebanon 1983-85, dep dir Jordan 1985-86, dir ops Gaza and rep Egypt 1986-88; currently dir Bernard Mills Conslts Ltd; *Recreations* walking, conversation; *Clubs* Special Forces; *Style—* Maj Bernard Mills, CBE; 2 The Maltings, Walsham-le-Willows, Bury St Edmunds, Suffolk IP31 3BD (☎ 0359 258830); Flat 7, 71 Charlwood St, London SW1V 4PG (☎ 071 630 7227)

MILLS, Vice Adm Sir Charles Piercy; KCB (1968, CB 1964), CBE (1957), DSC (1953); s of Capt Thomas Piercy Mills (d 1944), of Woking, and Eleanor May Mills (d 1978); *b* 4 Oct 1914; *Educ* RNC Dartmouth; *m* 1944, Anne, da of Cecil Francis Cumberlege (d 1975); 2 da; *Career* joined RN 1928, served WWII (despatches), Korea 1950-52, Capt 1953, Suez Operations 1956, Rear Adm 1963, Vice Adm 1966, Flag Offr 2 i/c Far East Fleet 1966-67, C-in-C Plymouth 1967-69, Lt-Govr and C-in-C Guernsey 1969-74; KStJ 1969; *Recreations* golf, yachting; *Style—* Vice Adm Sir Charles Mills, KCB, CBE, DSC; Park Lodge, Aldeburgh, Suffolk (☎ 0728 452115)

MILLS, Christopher David; s of Fred Mills, of 64 St Anthony Rd, Sheffield, and Grace Amy, *née* Milner (d 1976); *b* 15 April 1949; *Educ* Abbeydale Boys' GS, London Univ (LLB); *m* 24 Oct 1984, (Diane) Elizabeth, da of Eric Skuse; 1 da (Harriet Elisheba Christy); *Career* barr Inner Temple 1972; memb: RSPB, Sorby Nat History Soc; *Recreations* walking, birdwatching, badminton; *Style—* Christopher D Mills, Esq; Little Ranah Farm, Whams Rd, Sheffield, S30 5HJ; 19 Figtree Lane, Sheffield, S1 2DJ (☎ 0742 759 708, 071 738 380)

MILLS, 3 Viscount (UK 1962); Sir Christopher Philip Roger Mills; 3 Bt (UK 1953); also Baron Mills (UK 1957); o s of 2 Viscount Mills (d 1988); *b* 20 May 1956; *m* 29 March 1980, Lesley A, er da of Alan Bailey, of Lichfield, Staffs; *Style—* The Rt Hon Viscount Mills

MILLS, Colin James Edmund; s of James Oliver Mills (d 1986), of Holcot, Northamptonshire, and Ada, *née* Cox; *b* 28 Nov 1937; *Educ* Northampton GS, Leicester Sch of Architecture (Dip Arch); *m* 2 Sept 1961, Eileen Patricia, da of Charles Frederick Swain (d 1986); 1 s (James b 1965), 3 da (Kathryn b 1967, Rosalind b 1969, Clare b 1982); *Career* chartered architect; ptnr Morrison & Partners, dir Morrison Design Partnership 1977-86, princ Colin J E Mills 1986-; *Recreations* painting, ornithology, philately, reading; *Style—* Colin Mills, Esq; Chevindale, 474 Duffield Rd, Allestree, Derby DE3 2DJ (☎ 0332 558805); 28A Ashbourne Road, Derby DE3 3AD (☎ 0332 296414, fax 0332 296309); Road End, Shiskine, Isle of Arran

MILLS, Cdr Denis Woolnough; CBE (1988, OBE 1970), DSC (1943); s of Paymaster Lt Walter Thomas Mills, RNR (d 1955), of Chatham, and Gertrude Ethel, *née* Coomber (d 1978); *b* 31 July 1920; *Educ* Kings Sch Rochester; *m* 1, 1942 (m dis 1948), Deidre Murchie; 2 s (Michael, Nigel); m 2, 1948 (m dis 1960), Lucille Roberta Farnhill; 1 s (Paul), 1 da (Virginia); m 3, 19 Dec 1960, (Eileen) Mary, da of Cecil Surry, of Portsmouth (d 1978); *Career* RN 1937-1970 (Cadet to Cdr); served in HMS: Erebus, Vindictive, Revenge, Ramillies, Birmingham, Dolphin, Maidstone, Ambrose, Forth, Adamant, Theseus, Ausonia; HM Submarines: Cachalot, H43, Clyde, Thunderbolt; Cmd: Seawolf, Sea Devil, Surf, Auriga, Aeneas, Telemachus; Staff Appointments: RN Staff Course, Greenwich, Underwater Detection Estab, Portland, Ops Offr 4 Sub Sqdn, 1 Sub Sqdn/COMSUBMED, Plans (Ops) CINCEASTLANT, Flag Offr Submarines/COMSUBEASTLANT Plans, Intelligence, Polaris Exec, Personnel; Steel Corp 1970-1980: mgmnt training & devpt, IPM Teesside Branch Ctee 1973-81, co-fndr Assoc of Mgmnt Insts on Teesside 1973 (Ctee to 1981), memb Middlesborough Cons Assoc 1983- (hon treas, sec, acting, agent, election agent); FIPM (hon life), MBIM; *Recreations* golf; *Clubs* Naval; *Style—* Cdr Denis Mills, CBE, DSC, RN

MILLS, Edward David William; CBE (1959); s of late Edward Ernest Mills; *b* 19 March 1915; *Educ* Regent St Poly Sch of Architecture; *m* 1939, Elsie May, da of late W Bryant; 1 s, 1 da; *Career* chartered architect and design conslt; sr ptnr Edward D Mills and Ptnrs; patron Soc of Architectural Illustrators 1986-; chm Selection Bd Rome Scholarships in Architecture Br Sch at Rome; author incl books on architecture; Alfred Bossom res fell of RIBA, Churchill fell 1969; FRIBA, FCSD, FRSA; *Recreations* photography, writing, travel; *Style—* Edward Mills, Esq, CBE; The Studio, Gate House Farm, Newchapel, Lingfield, Surrey RH7 6LF (☎ 0342 832 241)

MILLS, Sir Frank; KCVO (1983), CMG (1971); s of Joseph Francis Mills; *b* 1923; *Educ* King Edward VI Sch Nuneaton, Emmanuel Coll Cambridge; *m* 1953, Trilby Foster; 1 s, 2 da; *Career* HM Dip Serv; high cmmr Ghana 1975-78, dir of communications 1978-81, high cmmr Bangladesh 1981-83; chm: Camberwell Health Authy 1984-89, Royal Cwlth Soc for the Blind 1985-; *Style—* Sir Frank Mills, KCVO, CMG; 14 Sherborne Road, Chichester, Sussex PO19 3AA

MILLS, Harold Hernshaw; s of Harold George Mills (d 1988), and Margaret Elliot Mills; *b* 2 March 1938; *Educ* Greenock HS, Univ of Glasgow (BSc, PhD); *m* 1 Aug 1973, Marion Elizabeth, da of John Beattie, of Poulton-Le- Fylde, Lancashire; *Career* cancer res scientist Roswell Park Meml Inst Buffalo NY USA 1962-64; lectr Univ of Glasgow 1964-69; princ Scot Home and Health Dept 1970-76, asst sec Scot Office 1976-81, Privy Cncl Office, 1981-83, under sec Scot Devpt Dept 1984-88 (asst sec 1983-84), princ fin offr Scot Office 1988-; *Style—* Harold Mills, Esq; New St Andrew's House, Scottish Office, St James Centre, Edinburgh (☎ 031 244 4714)

MILLS, Hayley Catherine Rose Vivien; da of Sir John Mills, CBE, *qv*, of Hills House, Denham Village, Buckinghamshire, and Mary Hayley-Bell, JP; *Educ* Elmhurst Ballet Sch, Institute Alpine Videmanette Switzerland; *m* 20 June 1971 (m dis 1977), Roy Alfred Clarence Fitzroy Boulting, *qv*; 2 s (Crispian Boulting Mills, Ace Lawson); *Career* actress; films incl: Tiger Bay 1959, Polyanna 1960, Parent Trap 1961, The Castaways 1962, Summer Magic 1963, The Moonspinners 1964, The Chalk Garden 1964, That Darn Cat 1965, Sky West & Crooked 1965, The Truth About Spring 1965, Whistle Down the Wind 1962, The Family Way 1966, The Trouble with Angels 1966, Pretty Polly 1967, Twisted Nerve 1968, Take A Girl Like You 1970, Endless Night 1972, Mr Forbush and the Penquins 1972, What Changed Charlie Farthing 1975, The Diamond Hunters 1975, Parent Trap II 1986, Parent Trap III 1989, Parent Trap IV 1989, Appointment with Death 1988; theatre incl: Peter Pan 1969, The Wild Duck 1970, Trelawney of the Wells 1972, The Three Sisters 1973, A Touch of Spring 1975, Rebecca 1977, My Fat Friend 1978, Hush of Hide 1979, The Importance of Being Earnest 1979, The Summer Party 1980, Tallys Folly 1982, The Secretary Bird 1983, Dial M for Murder 1984, Toys in the Attic 1986, The Kidnap Game 1991; TV incl: Deadly Strangers 1974, Only a Scream Away 1974, Two Loveboat Specials 1978, The Flame Trees of Thika 1980, Illusion of Life 1981, Amazing Stories 1986, Murder She Wrote 1986, Tales of the Unexpected 1987, Good Morning Miss Bliss 1988, Back Home 1989, Walk of Life 1990; pres St John Ambulance W London Dist; patron: Mountview Theatre Sch, Mobility Tst, Peace Fndn; fndr memb Ark; *Books* My God (1988); *Recreations* reading, travel, walking; *Clubs* St James's, Tramp; *Style—* Miss Hayley Mills; Chatto and Linnit, Prince of Wales Theatre, Coventry St, London W1V 7FE (☎ 071 930 6677)

MILLS, Iain Campbell; MP (C) Meriden 1979-; s of John Steel Mills, and Margaret Leitch; *b* 21 April 1940; *Educ* Prince Edward Sch Salisbury, Rhodesia; *m* 1971, Gaynor Lynne Jeffries; *Career* Dunlop: Rhodesia 1961-64, UK 1964-79; sec to Cons Tport Ctee 1979-81; PPS to: Min State for Indust 1981-82, Sec of State for Employment 1982-85, Sec of State for Trade and Indust 1983-85, Chm Cons Party 1985-87; memb The Employment Select Ctee 1987-; *Clubs* Carlton, House of Commons Yacht; *Style—* Iain Mills, Esq, MP; House of Commons, London SW1

MILLS, Prof Ian Mark; s of John Mills (d 1972), of Streatley, Berks, and Marguerita Alice Gertrude, *née* Gooding (d 1977); *b* 9 June 1930; *Educ* Leighton Park Sch Reading, Univ of Reading, Univ of Oxford; *m* 23 Aug 1957, Margaret Mary, da of Prof Julian Lewis Maynard (d 1954), of Univ of Minnesota, Minneapolis; 1 s (William b 1960), 1 da (Jane b 1962); *Career* res fell: Univ of Minnesota 1954-56, Corpus Christi Coll Cambridge 1956-57; lectr, reader and prof Univ of Reading 1957-; memb Faraday Div Royal Soc of Chem; *Books* Quantities, Units & Symbols in Physical Chemistry (1988); *Recreations* walking, sailing; *Style—* Prof Ian Mills; Department of Chemistry, University of Reading, RG6 2AD (☎ 0734 318456, telex 847813, fax 0734 314404)

MILLS, Ivor; s of John Mills, and Matilda, *née* Breen; *b* 7 Dec 1929; *Educ* Stranmillis Coll, Queen's Univ Belfast; *m* 30 June 1956 (m dis 1987), Muriel, da of Wilson Hay; 1 s (Rory b 1969), 1 da (Claire b 1971); *Career* journalist, prodr, ed and presenter all home networks and World Serv BBC Radio, BBCTV and ITV regions 1959-65, newscaster and corr ITN 1967-78 (reporter 1965-67), head of pub affrs PO 1978-81, dep dir of corp rels and head of pub affrs BT 1981-88; memb Bd Acad of Ancient Music (Christopher Hogwood Conductor); Medaille d'Honneur de L'Etoile Civique L'Academie Francaise 1971; *Recreations* music, theatre, visual arts, food, wine; *Style—* Ivor Mills, Esq; 46B Glenhurst Avenue, Parliament Hill, London NW5 1PS (☎ 071 284 1287, fax 071 485 5961)

MILLS, Joan, Viscountess; Joan Dorothy; da of James Shirreff, of London; *m* 6 Oct 1945, 2 Viscount Mills (d 1988); 1 s (3 Viscount, *qv*), 2 da (Felicity (Hon Mrs Pickford) b 1947, Phillipa (Hon Mrs Arthurton) b 1950); *Style—* The Rt Hon Joan, Viscountess Mills; Whitecroft, 24 Abbey Road, Knaresborough, N Yorks HG5 8HY (☎ 0423 866201)

MILLS, (Laurence) John; CBE (1978); s of Archibald John Mills (d 1963), of Portsmouth, and Annie Ellen *née* Oats (d 1973); *b* 1 Oct 1920; *Educ* Portsmouth GS, Univ of Birmingham (BSc); *m* 9 Dec 1944, Barbara May, da of Albert Edward Warner (d 1928), of Nottingham; 2 s (David John b 1956, Peter Richard b 1958); *Career* Nat Serv Maj RE 1942-46; student mining engr Houghton Main Colliery Yorks 1939-42; NCB: posts in mgmnt at colliery and area level 1947-68, HQ chief mining engr 1968-70, area dir N Yorks area 1970-72, area dir Doncaster Area 1973, memb 1974-82, dep chm 1982-84; chm: Osprey Belt Co Ltd 1986-, Specialist Training and Tech Servs Ltd 1989-; author of numerous engrg papers; Hon FIMinE; hon treas Inst Mining Engrs 1983- (pres 1975-76), chm Int Conf on Coal Res 1983-86; Freeman City of London 1986, Liveryman Worshipful Co of Fullers 1986; CIMEMME, CBIM, FEng; *Recreations* inland waterway cruising; *Style—* John Mills, Esq, CBE; Osprey Belt Co Ltd, Unit 4, Bowers Parade, Harpenden, Herts Al5 2SH (☎ 0582 765385, fax 0582 715796)

MILLS, Sir John Lewis Ernest Watts; CBE (1960); *b* 22 Feb 1908; *Educ* Norwich; *m* 1941, Mary Hayley Bell, playwright; 1 s, 2 da; *Career* actor (won Academy Award Oscar 1971 as best supporting actor, for his part in Ryan's Daughter), prodr, dir; memb Cncl of RADA 1965-, chm of the Stars Organisation for Spastics for 3 yrs, pres Mountview Theatre Sch; kt 1976; *Books* Up in the Clouds, Gentlemen Please (autobiography); *Recreations* golf, painting; *Clubs* Garrick, St James's (chm); *Style—* Sir John Mills, CBE; c/o ICM, 388/396 Oxford St, London W1

MILLS, John Micklethwait; OBE (1989), TD; s of Col Sir John Digby Mills, TD (d

1972), and Carola Marshall, *née* Tuck; *b* 29 Nov 1919; *Educ* Eton, Ch Ch Oxford (MA); *m* 2 Nov 1960, Mrs Prudence Mercy Emmeline Cooper-Key, da of Sir Ronald Wilfred Matthews (d 1959); 1 s (John b 1961); *Career* WWII 2 Lt Hampshire Regt 1939, 7 Commando Bardia and Crete (wounded), Warwicks Yeo ME and Italy, Capt 1943, Maj 1945; chm W Hants Water Co (dir 1948-), appointed by Miny of Agric Avon and Dorset River Bd 1959-63, dep chm Avon & Dorset River Authy 1963-74; Wessex Water Authy: chm Quality Advsy Panel 1974-83, chm Regnl Fishery Ctee 1974-89, Pollution Control Ctee 1988-89; Nat Rivers Authy (Wessex) 1989-90; JP 1948, High Sheriff Hants 1958, DL 1970, Verderer of the New Forest 1960-64, memb Ringwood RDC 1968-74, chm Ringwood bench 1979-84, pres Hampshire Branch CLA 1982-87 (chm 1967-70), fndr memb Timber Growers Orgn 1960 (chm Southern Region 1960-65); ARICS 1948; *Recreations* shooting, fishing; *Clubs* White's, MCC; *Style*— John Mills, Esq, OBE, TD; Bisterne Manor, nr Ringwood, Hampshire BH24 3BN (☎ 0425 474246); 69 Porchester Terr, London W2

MILLS, Leif Anthony; s of Victor William Mills (d 1967), and Bergliot, *née* Strøm-Olsen; *b* 25 March 1936; *Educ* Kingston GS, Balliol Coll Oxford (BA); *m* 2 Aug 1958, Gillian Margaret, da of William Henry Smith (d 1966); 2 s (Adam, Nathanial), 2 da (Susannah, Harriet); *Career* 2 Lt Royal Mil Police 1957-59; Nat Union of Bank Employees (now Banking Insur and Fin Union) 1960-: res offr 1960-62, asst gen sec 1962-68, dep gen sec 1968-72, gen sec 1972-; Parly candidate (Lab) contested: Salisbury gen election 1964, Salisbury by-election 1965; TUC: memb Non Manual Workers Advsy Ctee 1967-72, memb Gen Cncl 1983-, chm Fin Servs Ctee 1983, chm Educn and Trg Ctee 1989-; memb: office of Manpower Econs Advsy Ctee on Equal Pay 1971, Ctee to Review the Functioning of Fin Insts (Wilson Ctee) 1977-80, Civil Serv Pay Res Unit Bd 1978-81, BBC Consultative Gp on Social Effects of TV 1978-80, Armed Forces Pay Review Body 1980-87, Monopolies and Mergers Cmmn 1982-, TUC Ctees and Int Ctees of FIET; *Recreations* rowing, chess; *Clubs* Oxford and Cambridge, Weybridge Rowing; *Style*— Leif Mills, Esq; 31 Station Rd, West Byfleet, Surrey (☎ 09323 42829); Sheffield House, 1b Amity Grove, Raynes Park, London SW20 OLG (☎ 081 946 9151, fax 081 879 3728)

MILLS, Dr (John Owen) Manton; s of Rev Minnis Mills (d 1982), of Belfast, and Gladys Nora, *née* Streeter; *b* 17 May 1940; *Educ* The Methodist Coll Belfast, Queen's Univ Belfast (MB BCH, BAO); *m* 1, 16 Aug 1966 (m dis 1978), Elizabeth, da of Thomas Richardson (d 1965), of Belfast; 3 da (Catherine b 29 Aug 1967, Jennifer b 20 June 1969, Victoria b 28 June 1970); m 2, 5 March 1982, Anna, da of Dennis John McCormack, of London; 2 s (Christopher b 14 June 1983, David b 12 Dec 1985); *Career* conslt radiologist 1974-; dir Dept of Radiological Sciences Royal Brisbane Hosp Australia 1978-79, hon sec Royal Victoria Hosp Med Staff Ctee 1988-90, clinical dir of radiology Royal Gp of Hosps Belfast 1989-; pres Ulster Radiological Soc 1986-87, memb Queensland Med Soc Aust and NI Medico-Legal Soc, hon fell Nova Scotia Assoc of Radiologists 1987; DRCOG 1966, DMRD 1971, FFR 1973, FRCR 1975; *Books* Trauma Care (contrib 1981), Surgery of the Gut and Pancreas (contrib 1985), Textbook of Radiological Diagnosis (contrib 1988); Accident and Emergency Med (advsr and contrib 1989); *Recreations* gardening, reading; *Style*— Dr Manton Mills; Royal Victoria Hospital, Grosvenor Rd, Belfast (☎ 0232 240503)

MILLS, Michael Victor Leighton; s and h of Sir Peter Frederick Leighton Mills, 3 Bt; *b* 30 Aug 1957; *m* 29 Aug 1981, Susan; *Style*— Michael Mills Esq; 15 Paul Place, Paul Ave, Dayan Glen, 1460, Johannesburg, Transvaal, S Africa

MILLS, Neil McLay; s of Leslie Hugh Mills (d 1980), and Gwladys (d 1982); *b* 29 July 1923; *Educ* Epsom Coll, Univ of London; *m* 1950, Rosamund Mary, da of the late Col A C W Kimpton, of Pythouse, Tisbury, Wilts; 2 s, 2 da; *Career* served WWII Lt RNVR (despatches 1944); Lloyd's insur broker; chm: Bland Welch & Co 1965-74, Bland Payne Holdings 1974-79, Sedgwick Forbes Bland Payne 1979-80, Sedgwick Group plc 1980-84; dir: Midland Bank Ltd 1974-79, Wadlowgrosvenor International Ltd 1984-88, Polly Peck International plc 1985-, Thread Needle Publishing Co 1986-; memb Cncl Oak Hill Theological Coll 1958-62, vice pres Insur Inst of London 1971-84, tstee and govr Lord Mayor Treloar Tst 1975-81; *Recreations* mowing; *Style*— Neil McLay Mills, Esq; The Dower House, Upton Grey, nr Basingstoke, Hants (☎ 0256 862 435); 15 Markham Square, London SW3 (☎ 071 584 3995)

MILLS, Sir Peter McLay; *b* 22 Sept 1921; *Educ* Epsom, Wye Coll; *m* 1948, Joan Weatherley; 1 s, 1 da; *Career* farmer 1943-; MP (C): Torrington 1964-74, W Devon 1974-1983, Torridge and W Devon 1983-; Parly sec Miny Ag Fish and Food 1972, Parly under sec NI 1972-74, chm Conservative Agric Ctee 1979-87; memb: Cwlth Parly Assoc Exec Ctee 1979-87 (dep chm UK Branch), Foreign Affrs Select Ctee 1980-82; kt 1982; *Style*— Sir Peter Mills; Priestcombe, Crediton, Devon (☎ 036 34 418)

MILLS, Richard Michael; s of Richard Henry Mills (d 1979), of 11 Adelaide Rd, Surbiton, Surrey, and Catherine, *née* Keeley; *b* 26 June 1931; *m* 1, Feb 1960 (m dis 1967), Lynda, da of Charles Taylor; 1 da (Janey b 1960); m 2, 8 Aug 1983, Sheila Susan, da of James White (d 1986); 2 s (Matthew b 1986, Christopher b 1988); *Career* Nat Serv RAF 1949-51; theatrical producer and mangr; asst stage mangr 1948: worked in every capacity, incl acting and stage mgmnt, in the theatre; Bernard Delfont Ltd 1962-: dir 1967-, dep chm and chief exec 1970-, chm and chief exec 1979; md: Prince of Wales Theatre 1970-, Prince Edward Theatre 1978-; memb: NT Bd 1976 (Finance and Gen Purposes Ctee 1976-), Drama Panel Arts Cncl 1976-77, English Tourist Bd 1982-85; over 100 shows worked on 1948-62 incl: The Iceman Cometh, The Ginger Man, Sammy Davis Jr, Maurice Chevalier, Our Man Crichton, The Night of the Iguana, The Killing of Sister George, Funny Girl, The Odd Couple, Martha Graham, Sweet Charity, Streetcar named Desire, Charley's Aunt, Paul Daniels, over 100 pantomimes and summer seasons; *Recreations* golf, poker; *Clubs* RAC, Wentworth Golf, Royal Mid-Surrey Golf; *Style*— Richard Mills, Esq; Bernard Delfont Ltd, Prince of Wales Theatre, Coventry St, London W1V 8AS (☎ 071 930 9901, fax 071 976 1336)

MILLS, Ronald James; JP (Middlesex); s of Samuel Walter Mills (d 1949), of 1 Warkworth Gardens, Isleworth, Middx, and Ellen Eliza Jane, *née* Urand (d 1967); *b* 8 Feb 1918; *Educ* Sir Walter St John's Sch, Battersea Poly, Inns of Court Sch of Law; *m* 1 Dec 1945, Olive May, da of John King (d 1957), of Wandsworth, London; 2 s (Richard John b 1954, Gordon James b 1957); *Career* RCS: joined 1939, cmmnd 1940, serv E Africa India, Burma 1941-45; transferred to REME 1942, field serv Burma, staff duties HQ SE Asia Cmd, demobbed as Capt 1946; jr engr GPO (Radio Branch) 1937-39; called to the Bar Lincoln's Inn 1954; HM Patent Office: asst examiner 1946-47, examiner 1947-50, sr examiner 1950-79, ret 1979; conslt patent controller Racal-Decca Ltd 1979-86; visiting lectr in law City of London Poly and other colls of higher educn 1970-; memb: Hounslow Health Amenities Assoc, Hounslow Brentford and Isleworth Cons Assoc, Royal Br Legion, Burma Star Assoc, Hounslow Cons Club, Bar Assoc for Commerce Fin and Indust; FIEE 1956, FCIArb 1977; *Recreations* sailing, shooting, photography, motoring, ex serv & fraternal bodies; *Clubs* Civil Serv, Bar Yacht, Civil Serv Sailing, Littleton Sailing (Middx); *Style*— Ronald Mills, Esq, JP; 12 Naseby Close, The Grove, Isleworth, Middx TW7 4JQ (☎ 081 560 7406)

MILLS, Ronald Stephen; s of late Peter Mills, of Nottingham, and Daisy (d 1978); *b* 2 March 1947; *Educ* Glaisdale Sch; *m* 1969, Jean, da of Lenoard Marshall, of Nottingham; 2 da; *Career* CA 1968, dir William Lawrence & Co Ltd; *Recreations* running, church, gardening; *Style*— Ronald Mills Esq; 7 Cedar Tree Rd, Bestwood Lodge, Arnold, Nottingham; William Lawrence & Co Ltd, Colwick, Nottingham (☎ 0602 616484; telex 377973)

MILLS, (William) Stratton; s of John Victor Stratton Mills, CBE (d 1964), of 92 Circular Rd, Belfast, and Margaret Florence, *née* Byford; *b* 1 July 1932; *Educ* Campbell Coll Belfast, Queen's Univ Belfast (LLB); *m* 7 Aug 1959, Merriel Eleanor Ria, da of Robert James Whitla (d 1981), of 4 Knockdarragh Park, Belfast; 3 s (Jeremy Victor b 3 Aug 1966, Rupert James b 5 March 1968, Angus William b 23 Nov 1971); *Career* admitted slr NI 1958, ptnr Mills Selig Solicitors Belfast 1959-; dir various private companies; MP (Unionist & Cons) Belfast North 1959-74 (ret), PPS to Parly Sec Miny of Tport 1961-64, chm Cons Pty Broadleaf Ctee 1970-73; memb: Estimates Ctee 1964-70, Exec Ctee 1922 Ctee of Cons Pty 1967-70 and 1973, One Nation Gp 1972-73; chm Ulster Orchestra Soc Ltd 1980-90; winner Arnold Goodman award (for encouragement of business sponsorship in the Arts) 1990; memb Cncl Winston Churchill Meml Tst 1990; *Recreations* golf, gardening; *Clubs* Carlton, Reform (Belfast); *Style*— Stratton Mills, Esq; 20 Callender St, Belfast (☎ 0232 243 878, fax 0232 231 956)

MILLS, William; s of William Frederick Mills (d 1963), of Blackheath, London, and Ada Maud, *née* East (d 1984); *b* 7 July 1938; *Educ* Sutton Valence; *m* 27 Feb 1965, Pamela Anne, da of Stanley Gilbert Dean; 1 s (James William b 11 July 1974), 2 da (Melissa Jane b 17 May 1970, Kate Emma b 24 Jan 1972); *Career* RE 1957-59; Prudential Assurance: taxation mangr 1977-80, controller 1980-84, chief accountant 1984-85; Prudential Corporation Group 1985-89, md Prudential Mortgage Co 1989-; Freeman: City of London, Worshipful Co of Painters and Stainers; FCCA 1973; *Recreations* opera, gardening; *Style*— William Mills, Esq; Sunbury, Foxhole Lane, Matfield, Tonbridge, Kent (☎ 089 272 3464); Prudential Mortgage Co, Chichester House, 278-282 High Holborn, London WC1V (☎ 071 962 4550)

MILLWARD, Edwina Carole (Mrs David Bicker); da of Eric Millward, and Frances Morris, *née* Norton; *b* 20 Sept 1943; *Educ* Thornes House Sch Wakefield, Ilkley Coll of Housecraft, Univ of London (LLB); *m* 11 Nov 1972, David Charles Bicker, s of Arthur Charles Bicker; *Career* teacher 1965-67; admitted slr 1972; appointed by Lord Chllr to sit as dep registrar in Co Court and Dist Registry High Court 1988, chm and tstee Constitution Advsy Ctee Int Fedn Business and Professional Women 1989-; memb SE Region Electricity Consumers Ctee 1990-, memb Kent Law Soc 1980-, nat pres UK Fedn of Business and Professional Women 1985-87, active memb various ctees, memb Womens Nat Cmmn 1985-87; co sec: Maidstone Hospice Appeal 1987, Maidstone Hospice Trading Ltd 1990; *Recreations* acting, swimming, needlework; *Style*— Miss Edwina Millward; Loanhead, Simmonds Lane, Otham, Maidstone, Kent ME14 8RH; Gill Turner and Tucker, Colman House, King Street, Maidstone, Kent (☎ 0622 59051)

MILLWARD, Dr Neil; s of Haydn Millward (d 1988), of Abergavenny, and Lilian Audrey, *née* Powley; *b* 14 March 1942; *Educ* Queen Elizabeth's Sch Crediton Devon, Univ of Bristol (BSc), Univ of Manchester (PhD); *m* 28 Oct 1972, Pamela Hilary Marion, da of Maj Gilbert Hanley Thorp (d 1984), of Coates, W Sussex; 2 s (Piers b 1975, Christian b 1977); *Career* engr GEC Ltd 1964-66, res fell Univ of Manchester 1966-68, visiting scholar Harvard Business Sch 1968-69, res fell Manchester Business Sch 1969-73, industl rels offr Pay Bd 1973-74, princ res offr Dept of Employment 1974-89, sr fell Policy Studies Inst 1989-; *Books* Workplace Industrial Relations in Britain (with W W Daniel, 1983), British Workplace Industrial Relations 1980-1984 (with M Stevens, 1986); *Recreations* sailing, crafts, music; *Style*— Dr Neil Millward; 53 Cloudesley Rd, London N1 OEL (☎ 071 278 3170); Policy Studies Inst, 100 Park Village East, London NW1 3SR (☎ 071 387 2171)

MILLWARD, Roger; MBE (1982); s of William Millward, of 8 Princess St, Wheldon Rd, Castleford, and Ivy, *née* Lockwood; *b* 16 Sept 1947; *Educ* Castleford Boys Secdy Modern Sch, Castleford GS, Whitwood Mining and Tech Coll; *m* 21 Sept 1968, Carol Ann, da of Charlie Bailey; 1 da (Kay b 27 Nov 1970); *Career* rugby league coach; jr player Castleford under 17 and Yorks under 17; player Castleford 1964-66: 40 appearances, 16 tries, 35 goals; player Hull Kingston Rovers 1966-80: 399 appearances, 207 tries, 597 goals, 10 drop goals; 18 appearances as guest player Cronulla-Sutherland Aust 1976; 12 York caps, 17 England caps (13 as capt), 29 GB caps (10 as capt), World Cup Aust and NZ 3 times, tour Aust and NZ 3 times; coach Hull Kingston Rovers 1977-; most tries in career Hull Kingston Rovers, most points in a Test match v Aust (20 in 1970), record 6 official trips to Aust and NZ; Yorks Cup winners Hull Kingston Rovers (as player) 1966, 1967, 1971, 1974; honours as player-coach Hull Kingston Rovers: BBC Floodlight Competition 1977 (runners up 1978), Championship 1979, Challenge Cup 1980; honours as coach Hull Kingston Rovers: runners up Challenge Cup 1981 and 1986, Premiership 1981 and 1984 (runners up 1985), Championship 1984 and 1985 (runners up 1983), John Player Special Trophy 1985 (runners up 1982); electrical engr Wheldale Colliery 1964-77, lectr in electrical engrg Whitwood Mining and Tech Coll 1980-84; *Recreations* golf; *Style*— Roger Millward, Esq, MBE; c/o R Turner, Esq, Hull K R, Craven Park, Hull, Humberside (☎ 0482 709898)

MILLWATER, Dennis Curtis; s of William Milson Millwater (d 1974), of Rogerstone, Gwent, and Kathleen Irene Millwater (d 1969); *b* 31 March 1934; *Educ* Bassaleg GS Gwent, Univ of Bristol; *m* 5 Aug 1957, Marlene Beatrice, da of Kenneth Collins, of Cliffs End, Ramsgate; 3 s (Christopher b 26 April 1961, Grahame b 28 April 1963, Jonathan b 23 Aug 1967, d 1989), 1 da (Sara b 20 July 1977); *Career* pensions supt Northern Assurance Co Ltd 1957-68, pensions controller Commercial Union Group 1968-69, dir De Falbe Halsey Ltd 1969-71; gp dir: H Clarkson (Insurance Holdings) Ltd 1971-81, Clarkson Puckle Group Ltd 1981-87, Bain Clarkson Ltd 1987; chief exec Bain Clarkson (Fin Services) Ltd; gen cmmr of taxes; FPMI, ACII; *Recreations* golf, music, cycling; *Clubs* Royal St Georges Golf (Sandwich); *Style*— Dennis Millwater, Esq; The Shieling, 32 Harkness Drive, Canterbury, Kent CT2 7RW (☎ 0227 463026); Bain Dawes House, 15 Minories, London EC3 (☎ 071 481 3232, fax 071 481 2324)

MILLWOOD, Yvonne Ann; da of Louis Joseph (d 1958), of Cardiff, and Betty, *née* Cowen (d 1986); *b* 2 Feb 1933; *Educ* Cardiff HS for Girls; *m* 1964; *Career* former advertising specialist IBA; formerly consumer and educn publicist and journalist; *Recreations* fell walking, music, theatre; *Style*— Mrs Yvonne A Millwood; Vine House, off Freeman St, Wells Next The Sea, Norfolk (☎ 0328 711 426)

MILMAN, David Patrick; er s and h of Lt-Col Sir Derek Milman, 9 Bt, MC; *b* 1945; *m* 1969, Christina, da of John William Hunt; 1 s (Thomas Hart b 1976), 1 da (Katharine Jane b 1975); *Style*— David Milman, Esq; 71 Camden Rd, Sevenoaks, Kent

MILMAN, Lt-Col Sir Derek; 9 Bt (GB 1800), of Levaton-in-Woodland, Devonshire; MC; 3 and yst s of Brig-Gen Sir Lionel Charles Patrick Milman, 7 Bt, CMG (d 1962), and Marjorie Aletta, *née* Clark-Kennedy (d 1980); suc his bro, Sir Dermot Lionel Kennedy Milman, 8 Bt (d 1990); *b* 23 June 1918; *Educ* Bedford Sch; *m* 1942, Christine, da of Alfred Whitehouse, of Sutton Coldfield; 2 s (David Patrick b 1945, Terence Martin b 1947); *Heir* s, David Patrick Milman (*qv*); *Career* Lt-Col (ret) 3 E Anglian Regt, formerly Pakistan Army and GSO Lahore Divn, served WWII with 5 Indian Divn in Middle East; *Style*— Lt-Col Sir Derek Milman, Bt, MC; Forge Cottage,

Wilby Rd, Stradbroke, Suffolk IP21 5JN

MILMAN, Muriel, Lady; Muriel; o da of late John Edward Scott Taylor, of King's Lynn, Norfolk; *m* 1941, Sir Dermot Lionel Kennedy Milman, 8 Bt (d 1990); 1 da (Celina Anne b 1945); *Style—* Muriel, Lady Milman; 7 Old Westhall Close, Warlingham, Surrey (☎ 0883 62 4843)

MILMO, John Boyle; QC (1984); s of Dermod Hubert Francis Milmo (d 1973), and Eileen Clare, *née* White; *b* 19 Jan 1943; *Educ* Downside Sch, Dublin Univ (MA, LLB); *Career* called to the Bar Lincoln's Inn 1966, rec Crown Ct 1982-; *Clubs* Utd Services (Nottingham); *Style—* John Milmo, Esq, QC; No 1 High Pavement, Nottingham NG1 1HF (☎ 0602 418218)

MILNE, Alasdair David Gordon; s of Charles Milne, surgeon, by his w Edith; *b* 8 Oct 1930, in Cawnpore; *Educ* Winchester, New Coll Oxford; *m* 1954, Sheila Kirsten Graucob; 2 s, 1 da (Kirsty); *Career* served in Gordon Highlanders; joined BBC as gen trainee 1954, with BBC TV Current Affairs 1955-57, dep ed Tonight 1957-61, ed 1961-62, head Tonight Productions 1963-65; left BBC to become ptnr Jay Baverstock Milne & Co (freelance TV film producers) 1965-67 and ran This Week for Rediffusion TV; controller BBC Scotland 1968-72, dir programmes BBC TV 1973-77, md BBC TV 1977-82, dep dir-gen BBC 1980-82, dir-gen BBC 1982-87; Hon DUniv Stirling 1983, hon fell New Coll Oxford; *Style—* Alasdair Milne, Esq; 30, Holland Park Ave, London, W11 3QU

MILNE, David Alistair; s of Peter Barry Milne, of Edinburgh, and Una Mary, *née* Horton; *b* 29 Aug 1952; *Educ* Malvern, Pembroke Coll Oxford (MA); *m* 30 Aug 1975, Clare Eveline Agatha, da of Maj Peter Howard Crassweller, of Edinburgh; 1 s (Andrew b 11 March 1983), 1 da (Nicola b 26 July 1979); *Career* Nippon Credit Bank 1974-77, dir Guinness Mahon and Co Ltd 1977-87, dir and head of capital markets British and Commonwealth Merchant Bank 1987-; memb Inst of Bankers; *Recreations* tennis, bridge, theatre, ballet; *Clubs* Lansdowne, Riverside, Overseas Bankers; *Style—* David Milne, Esq; 35 York Ave, London SW14 7LQ; British & Commonwealth Merchant Bank, 66 Cannon St, London EC4N 6AE (☎ 071 248 0900, fax 071 248 0906, telex 884040)

MILNE, David Calder; QC (1987); s of Ernest Ferguson Milne, OBE, of Walton Heath, Surrey, and Helena Mary, *née* Harkness; *b* 22 Sept 1945; *Educ* Harrow, Univ of Oxford (MA); *m* 26 May 1978, Rosemary Ann, da of Frederick Bond (d 1979); 1 da (Bryony b 1980); *Career* CA 1969; articled to Whinney Murray & Co (CA) 1966-69, called to the Bar Lincoln's Inn 1970; FCA (1974); *Recreations* natural history, music, golf, rugby football; *Clubs* Garrick, Hurlingham, Gnomes, Walton Heath Golf; *Style—* David Milne, Esq, QC; 14a Castelnau, Barnes, London SW13 9RU (☎ 081 748 6415); 4 Pump Ct, Temple, London EC4Y 7AN (☎ 071 583 9770, fax 071 353 6366, telex 886702 PUMPCO G)

MILNE, Denys Gordon; *Educ* Oxford Univ (MA); *Career* md & ch exec BP Oil Ltd; chm Alexander Duckham & Co; pres Inst of Petroleum; vice pres UK Petroleum Indust Assoc Ltd; dir Dorchester Oil Trading Co Ltd, Scottish Oils Ltd, Shell-Mex and BP Ltd, Silkolene Lubricants 1981-; memb Scottish Econ Cncl; *Style—* Denys Milne Esq; BP Oil Ltd, BP Ho, Victoria St, SW1E 5NJ (☎ 071 821 2000)

MILNE, Hon George Alexander; s and h of 2 Baron Milne; *b* 1 April 1941; *Educ* Winchester; *Style—* The Hon George Milne; 188 Broom Rd, Teddington, Middx (☎ 081 977 9761)

MILNE, 2 Baron (UK 1933); George Douglass Milne; TD; s of Field Marshal 1 Baron Milne, GCB, GCMG, DSO (d 1948); *b* 10 Feb 1909; *Educ* Winchester, New Coll Oxford; *m* 2 April 1940, Cicely, 3 da of Ronald Leslie; 2 s, 1 da; *Heir* s, Hon George Alexander Milne; *Career* Maj (TA) 1940; WWII 1939-45, NWEF, MEF, POW; CA; ptnr Arthur Young McClelland Moores 1947-73, dep chm London & Northern Gp 1973-87; Master Worshipful Co of Grocers 1961-62 (sr memb 1984-90); MICAS; *Style—* The Rt Hon the Lord Milne; 33 Lonsdale Rd, Barnes, London SW13 9JP (☎ 081 748 6421)

MILNE, Gordon Stewart; s of Arthur Milne, OBE (d 1984), of Edinburgh, and Thomasina, *née* Gilroy; *b* 1 Oct 1936; *Educ* Royal HS of Edinburgh, Leith Nautical Coll, Heriot-Watt Coll Edinburgh, Coll of Estate Mgmnt London; *m* 15 Oct 1961, Kathleen Mary; 2 s (Rhoderic Michael Stuart b 12 Feb 1965, Hector Arthur Stuart b 12 July 1966); *Career* md The Scottish Medical Property plc 1986- (dir 1969-73, asst md 1973-79, jt md 1979-86); dir Tourism and Leisure Activities Conf at Aviemore 1968, vice pres Edinburgh Jr C of C 1968-69, DG Euro Conf of Jr C of C 1972; memb: Welcome Ctee Cwlth Games 1970, NEDC Scot Strategy Planning Ctee 1974-76; local dir Guardian Royal Exchange Assurance 1979-, dep chm Sec of State for Scot Valuation Advsy Cncl 1987- (memb 1982-), memb Exec Scot Cncl Devt and Indust, initiator of Retailing in Scotland-2005 res project 1986, memb Clyde Port Authy 1989; FRICS 1964; *Recreations* ornithology, hill walking, swimming, music; *Clubs* Royal Scottish Automobile; *Style—* Gordon Milne, Esq; 5 Woodhall Rd, Colinton, Edinburgh EH13 0DQ (☎ 031 441 2764); Royal Exchange House, 100 Queen St, Glasgow G1 3DL (☎ 041 248 7333, fax 041 221 1196)

MILNE, Hon Iain Charles Luis; s of 2 Baron Milne, and Cicely Abigaile Leslie; *b* 16 Sept 1949; *Educ* Oundle; *m* 15 Aug 1987, Berta (Ita), da of Enrique Urzua Guerrero, of San Felipe, Chile; *Career* FCA 1980 (ACA 1974); Freeman City of London 1971, Liveryman of Worshipful Co of Grocers 1985; *Clubs* Roy Mid Surrey Golf; *Style—* The Hon Iain Milne; c/o BAT Co Ltd, Westminster Ho, 7 Millbank SW1P 3JE

MILNE, Iain Gordon; s of Dr Kenneth Grant Sim Milne, of Edinburgh, and Mary, *née* Gordon (d 1974); *b* 17 June 1956; *Educ* George Heriots Sch Edinburgh, Heriot Watt Univ, Napier Coll Edinburgh; *m* 3 Nov 1989, Marion Margaret, da of George Ian Reid; *Career* Rugby Union tight-head prop Heriot's FP RFC and Scotland (44 caps); Clubs: Heriot's FP RFC 1974-84 (Scottish Champions 1979, capt 1981-83) and 1986- (capt centenary season 1989-90), Harlequins RFC 1984-86, Edinburgh XV 1976-84 and 1986- (capt 1988-89), Anglo Scots XV 1984-86, Middx XV 1984, Barbarians RFC 1979-89, French Barbarians 1987; Scotland: debut v Ireland 1979, Championship and Grand Slam 1984, toured NZ 1981 1990, Aust 1982, USA and Canada 1985, World Cup 1987; British Lions: tour NZ 1983, v World XV 1986; sales mangr; *Style—* Iain Milne, Esq

MILNE, Sir John Drummond; s of Frederick John Milne and Minnie Elizabeth Milne; *b* 13 Aug 1924; *Educ* Stowe, Trinity Coll Cambridge, RMC Sandhurst; *m* 1948, Joan Akroyd; 2 s, 2 da; *Career* chm: Blue Circle Industries plc (cement gp) until 1990, DRG plc (resigned 1989), Royal Insur plc, Avon Rubber plc, Witan Investment Co plc, Solvay & Cie; kt 1986; *Recreations* golf, shooting; *Clubs* Boodles, MCC, Berkshire Golf; *Style—* Sir John Milne; 84 Eccleston Sq, London SW1V 1PX (☎ 071 828 3456, telex 927757 BC LDN G)

MILNE, John Duff; s of Alexander Keen Milne, of Dundee, and Margaret Harrow, *née* Duff; *b* 13 May 1942; *Educ* Harris Acad, Univ of Dundee; *m* 29 March 1967, Jennifer Frances, da of Robert Lewis Brown (d 1989), of Dundee; 2 s (Grigor b 1970, Jonathan b 1973); *Career* newspaper sub ed D C Thomson Dundee 1959-63, newspaper sub ed and feature writer The Scotsman Edinburgh 1963-67, news ed Swiss Broadcasting Corp Bern 1967-71, presenter and reporter BBC Scot 1971-; *Recreations* sport, music; *Style—* John Milne, Esq; BBC Broadcasting House, Queen Margaret Dr, Glasgow G12 8DG (☎ 041 330 2526)

MILNE, John Frederick; s of Alexander Milne, of Essex, and Sheila, *née* Levett; *b* 20 Sept 1952; *Educ* St Joseph's Acad Blackheath, Chelsea Sch of Art, Ravensbourne Coll of Art (BA); *m* 1983, Sarah Letitia Beresford, da of Gp Capt H B Verity, DSO, DFC; 2 s (Alexander b 1983, Hugh b 1985); *Career* novelist; books incl: Styro 1982, London Fields 1983, Out of The Blue 1985, Wet Wickets and Dusty Balls 1986, Dead Balls 1986, Shadow Play 1987, Daddy's Girl 1988; TV scriptwriter contrib to: The Bill, Bergerac, Boon, Perfect Scoundrels, Eastenders; winner John Llewelyn Rhys prize for Out of the Blue 1986; *Recreations* bricolage; *Style—* John Milne, Esq; c/o Charles Walker, A D Peters and Co, The Chambers, Chelsea Harbour, London SW10 0XF (☎ 071 376 7676)

MILNE, Dr Kenneth; OBE (1975); s of Samuel Baxter Milne (d 1978), and Sarah Elizabeth, *née* Birkett (d 1969); *b* 16 Nov 1925; *Educ* Royal GS Newcastle upon Tyne, Rugby Coll Technol & Arts, Univ of London (external, BScEng, PhD); *m* 1949, Audrey Isobel, da of Charles Edward Theodore Nelsey; *Career* BTH Co Ltd Rugby: engrg apprentice 1941-46, engr 1946-50, radar system designer 1950-60; Plessey Radar Ltd Cowes: radar system designer 1960-70, engrg mangr 1970-72, dir res 1972-78; ind electronic systems design consIt 1978-, visiting prof UCL 1978-; memb: MOD Def Sci Advsy Cncl 1967-73 and 1986-88, MOD (PE) Electronics Res Cncl 1963-80, NATO Industl Advsy Gp 1970-73, Ctee IEE 1957-79; organiser various confs IEE; Lord Brabazon Prize (Br IRE, 1965), Oliver Lodge Premium (IEE, 1988); FIEE 1969, FEng 1983; *Books* The Handbook of Antenna Design (jt ed, 1983); *Recreations* music; *Style—* Dr Kenneth Milne, OBE; 53 Bullimore Grove, Kenilworth, Warwickshire CV8 2QF (☎ 0926 512803)

MILNE, Kenneth Stewart; s of Kenneth Grant Sim Milne, of 77 Telford Rd, Edinburgh, and Mary Gordon Milne (d 1974); *b* 1 Dec 1961; *Educ* George Heriots Sch, Stevenson Coll, Edinburgh; *m* 4 July 1987, Eleanor Jane, da of Alan Williamson; 1 s (Stuart Alan Kenneth b 28 Nov 1990); *Career* Rugby Union looker Heriots FP RFC and Scotland (13 caps); clubs: Heriots FP RFC (capt) 1982-, Edinburgh U21, Barbarians RFC; rep: Edinburgh, Scotland B; Scotland: debut v Wales 1989, memb Grand Slam winning team 1990 tour NZ 1990; sales rep Barr Printers Leith; *Recreations* fishing, golf; *Style—* Kenneth Milne, Esq

MILNE, Prof Malcolm Davenport; s of Alexander Milne (d 1951), of Romiley, Cheshire, and Lilian, *née* Gee (d 1962); *b* 22 May 1915; *Educ* Stockport Sch, Univ of Manchester (BSc, MD ChB); *m* 17 June 1941, Mary, da of Matthias Thorpe (d 1935); 1 s (David Malcolm b 1950), 1 da (Janet Mary (Mrs Siegle) b 1946); *Career* WWII RAMC, Lt 1940, Capt 1941; active serv with 8 Army 1941-45: Egypt, Libya, Tripolitania, Tunisia (despatches), Italy, Austria; Actg and Temp Maj 1944-46; lectr in med: Univ of Manchester 1947-52, Univ of London 1952-61; prof of med Westminster Med Sch and Univ of London 1961-80; FRCP 1958, FRS 1978; *Recreations* pure mathematics, haute cuisine; *Clubs* Athenaeum; *Style—* Prof Malcolm Milne; 19 Fieldway, Berkhamsted, Herts HP4 2NX (☎ 0442 864 704)

MILNE, Neil Morrison; s of Brig John Brebner Morrison Milne, OBE, and Marjory, *née* Duncan; *b* 24 June 1951; *Educ* Royal HS Edinburgh, Univ of Edinburgh (MA) Univ of Nottingham (MA); *Career* Butler Till Ltd 1975-78, Standard Life Assurance Co 1978-81, sr mangr Euro Banking Co Ltd, exec dir York Trust Group plc 1984-90, md York Tst Ltd 1990-; *Recreations* tennis, swimming, reading; *Clubs* RAC, Coolhurst Lawn Tennis; *Style—* Neil Milne, Esq; 4 City Rd, London EC1Y 2AA

MILNE, Peter Alexander; s of late Alexander Ogston Milne, and Lilian Winifred, *née* Murray; *b* 23 April 1935; *Educ* Tynemouth Sch, Harwell Reactor Sch, Univ of Durham (BSc), Univ of Newcastle (PhD); *m* 1961, Beatrice Taylor Reid; 2 da; *Career* res asst Univ of Newcastle 1957-60, jr engr Union Castle Steamship 1960-61, tech mangr Wallsend Slipway and Engineering 1961-67 (student apprentice 1951-57), md Swan Hunter Shipbuilders 1974-78 (tech dir 1967-74); British Shipbuilders: md Shipbuilding Ops 1978-81, dir Engrg 1981-84, dir Merchant Shipbuilding and Composite Div 1984-87, dir Ship and Engine Building Div 1987-90, md BMT Cortec Ltd 1990-; former memb: Cncl Inst of Marine Engrs, Advsy Ctee Sch of Marine Technol Univ of Newcastle; vice pres Ctee EEC Shipbuilders Assoc 1987-79 (memb 1984-87), past pres and memb Cncl NE Coast Inst of Engrs and Shipbuilders; memb: Bd Lloyds Register of Shipping 1984-, Northern Regnl Cncl CBI 1985-, Northern Engrg Centre 1990-; tstee and memb Devpt Tst Univ of Newcastle upon Tyne 1981; numerous pubns in learned jls; Liveryman Worshipful Co of Shipwrights 1984; CEng, Eur Ing, FIMarE, FIMechE; *Recreations* squash, cricket; *Style—* Peter Milne, Esq; 104 Holywell Avenue, Whitley Bay, Tyne & Wear (☎ 091 252 2708); BMT Cortec Ltd, Wallsend Research Station, Wallsend, Tyne & Wear NE28 6UY

MILNE ATKINSON, Patricia Wilda (Pat); da of Capt Philip Dennis Fernandes Ferreira (d 1979), and Margaret Cicely, *née* Leman (d 1983); *b* 6 May 1924; *Educ* Overstone Pneu Sch, Midland Agric Coll (Dip Horticulture) now Univ of Nottingham; *m* 29 July 1950, John Harald Milne Atkinson, s of Capt Harald Milne Atkinson (d 1964); 1 s (Charles John b 7 May 1961), 1 da (Annabelle Jane Milne (Mrs Holland) b 17 March 1955); *Career* landscape architect, principal in own private practice 1954-; specialist areas incl: hosp devpts, industl business parks, redesign of estates, sports centres; memb Cncl Landscape Inst 1984-86, fndr memb E Mids Landscape Chapter, memb Cncl Arboricultural Assoc 1983- (memb Mids Gp Ctee); fell Landscape Inst 1958 (assoc 1948), assoc Arboricultural Soc 1982; memb Arboricultural Advsy Bd; *Recreations* vintage cars, fishing, gardening; *Style—* Mrs Pat Milne Atkinson; Hemington House, Hemington, Derby DE7 2RB

MILNE-WATSON, Andrew Michael; s and h of Sir Michael Milne-Watson, 3 Bt, CBE; *b* 10 Nov 1944; *Educ* Eton; *m* 1, 1970, Beverley Jane Gabrielle, er da of late Philip Cotton, of Majorca; 1 s (David b 1971), 1 da (Emma b 1974); m 2, 1983, Mrs Gisella Stafford, da of Hans Tisdall, of Cheyne Walk, London SW10; 1 s (Oliver b 1985); *Career* chm: Lewis Broadbent Advertising 1986-88, Minerva Publications Ltd 1988-90; ptnr GMW Fabrics, marketing dir Aylesford & Co; *Clubs* RAC; *Style—* Andrew Milne-Watson Esq; 22 Musgrave Crescent, London SW6 4QE

MILNE-WATSON, Sir Michael; 3 Bt (UK 1937), of Ashley, Longbredy, Co Dorset, CBE (1953); yr s of Sir David Milne-Watson, 1 Bt, DL, sometime Chief of the Scottish Clans Assoc of London and md and govr of the Gas Light & Coke Co (d 1945); suc bro, Sir Ronald Milne-Watson, 2 Bt, 1982; *b* 16 Feb 1910; *Educ* Eton, Balliol Coll Oxford; *m* 1940, Mary Lisette, da of late Harold Carleton Bagnall, of Auckland, NZ; 1 s; *Heir* s, Andrew Michael Milne-Watson, *qv*; *Career* Sub-Lt RNVR served 1943-45; Gas Light & Coke Co: joined 1933, md 1945, govr 1946-49; chm N Thames Gas Bd 1949-64; Liveryman Grocers' Co 1947; dir Industrial & Commercial Financial Corp Ltd 1963-80, chm Richard Thomas & Baldwins Ltd 1964-67, dep chm Br Steel Corp 1967-69; dir: Northern Assurance Co Ltd 1960-65, Northern & Employers Assurance Co Ltd 1961-68, Commercial Union Assurance Co 1968-81; chm The William Press Group of Cos 1969-74, pres Cncl of Univ of Reading 1975-80, dir Fin Corp for Industry Ltd 1974-80; govr Br Utd Provident Assoc Ltd 1975 (chm 1976-81); pres: Soc of Br Gas Indust 1970-71, Pipeline Indust Guild 1971-72; govr Nuffield Nursing Homes Tst, chm BUPA 1976-81; Kt 1969; *Recreations* fishing, walking; *Clubs* MCC, Leander, Atheneaum; *Style—* Sir Michael Milne-Watson, Bt, CBE; 39 Cadogan Place, London SW1X 9RX; Oakfield, Mortimer, Berks (☎ 0734 832200)

MILNER, Andrew; s of Thomas Milner and Amy, *née* Buckenham; *b* 2 Feb 1951; *Educ* Guthlaxton GS, Hull Coll of Higher Educn; *m* 1978, Linda Catherine, da of David Fullam, of Driffield; 1 s, 2 da; *Career* chm and md Humber Fertilisers Ltd 1980-; chm: Goodlife Holdings Ltd 1988-, Joseph Bentley Ltd 1989-; senator Junior Chamber Int, pres Hull Inc C of C and Shipping 1988; *Recreations* gardening, jogging, Junior Chamber; *Clubs* Farmers'; *Style*— Andrew Milner, Esq; Dale Farm, Dale Road, Brantingham, Brough, North Humberside HU15 1QN (☎ 0482 666875) Winchester Chambers, Stoneferry, Hull (☎ 0482 20458, fax 0482 212825)

MILNER, Lady Charlene Mary Olivia; *née* French; da of 3 Earl of Ypres; *b* 17 May 1946; *m* 1965, Charles Mordaunt Milner, yr s of Sir George E M Milner, 9 Bt; 3 s; *Style*— The Lady Charlene Milner; PO Box 41, Klapmuts 7625, Cape, S Africa

MILNER, George; s of Mieczyslaw Mielczabek (d 1965), of London; *b* 22 July 1931; *Educ* St Edmunds Coll, Univ Coll Dublin (MB BCh, BAO, DPM, FRCPsych); *m* 24 Oct 1959, Sheila Mary, da of Francis Wynne (d 1979), of Worcester; 2 s (Paul b 2 Aug 1961, Andrew b 3 Dec 1963), 2 da (Gabrielle b 22 March 1960, Caroline b 4 Dec 1962); *Career* sr registrar Manchester Regnl Hosp Bd 1962-66, conslt psychiatrist Worcester Health Dist 1966-, hon sr lectr Univ of Birmingham 1988- (clinical tutor 1979-), examiner RCPsych and Univ of Birmingham; pubns: substance misuse, mental health act, Worcester devpt project, general psychiatry; memb: BMA, World Psychiatric Assoc 1988-, Mind, Turningpoint; FRCPsych, Foundation Memb RCPsych 1972; *Recreations* golf, music, arts; *Style*— George Milner, Esq; Acrefield, Norton Close, Worcester WR5 3EY (☎ 0905 353552); Worcester Royal Infirmary, Newtown Branch, Newtown Rd, Worcester (☎ 0905 763333)

MILNER, John; s of James William Milner, of Derby, and Iris May, *née* Young; *b* 11 June 1946; *Educ* Bemrose GS Derby, Courtauld Inst of Art Univ of London (BA, PhD); *m* 1970, Lesley, da of late Denis Hill Marlow; 3 s (Henry George Marlow b 18 Mar 1971, Edward John b 16 July 1975, Michael James Denis b 21 April 1980); *Career* lectr Bournemouth and Poole Coll of Art and Hornsey Coll of Art London 1968-69; Dept of Fine Art Univ of Newcastle upon Tyne; lectr 1969-; sr lectr 1979-, reader 1985-, head of Dept 1985-; dir Hatton Gallery Univ of Newcastle upon Tyne: memb Assoc of Art Historians; *award* Leverhulme fellowship 1985; *Books* Symbolists and Decadents (1971), Russian Revolutionary Art (1979), Vladimir Tatlin and the Russian Avant-Garde (1983), The Studios of Paris, the Captial of Art in the Late Nineteenth Century (1988); *Recreations* painting; *Style*— John Milner, Esq; Dept of Fine Art, University of Newcastle-upon-Tyne NE1 7RU (☎ 091 222 6000 ext 6048)

MILNER, Sir (George Edward) Mordaunt; 9 Bt (GB 1717), of Nun Appleton Hall, Yorkshire; s of Brig-Gen George Francis Milner, CMG, DSO (d 1921), and cousin of 8 Bt (d 1960); *b* 7 Feb 1911; *Educ* Oundle; *m* 1, 1935, Barbara (d 1951), da of H N Belsham, of Hunstanton, Norfolk; 2 s, 1 da; m 2, 1953, Katherine Hoey, of Dunfermline; *Heir* s, Timothy William Lycett Milner; *Career* serv in 1939-45 War with RA (Capt); stipendiary steward of the Jockey Club (SA) 1954-59, exec steward 1977-80, steward Cape Turf Club 1959-76; memb Cncl Thoroughbred Breeders Assoc (SA) 1976-; author; *Books* Inspired Information (1959), Vaulting Ambition (1962), The Last Furlong (1965), Notes on Thoroughbred Breeding, The Godolphin Arabian; *Recreations* writing, racing; *Style*— Sir Mordaunt Milner, Bt; Natte Valleij, Klapmuts, Cape, S Africa (☎ 02211 5171); 40 Avenue Rd, Newlands Capetown, S Africa (☎ 021 66 4146); Mordaunt Milner Stud, Klapmuts (☎ 02211 5573)

MILNER, Hon Richard James; s and h of 2 Baron Milner of Leeds; *b* 16 May 1959; *Educ* Charterhouse, Univ of Surrey (BSc); *m* 25 June 1988, Margaret Christine, yst da of Gerald Francis Voisin, of Jersey, CI; 1 da (Charlotte Emma b 8 May 1990); *Career* assoc fin dir Chelgate Public Relations; Freeman City of London, Liveryman Worshipful Co of Clothworkers 1988; *Style*— The Hon Richard Milner

MILNER, Prof (Arthur John) Robin Gorell; s of Lt-Col John Theodore Milner, OBE (d 1957), of Tisbury, Wilts and Muriel Emily, *née* Barnes-Gorell (d 1971); *b* 13 Jan 1934; *Educ* Eton, King's Coll Cambridge (Major scholar, BA); *m* 16 Nov 1963, Lucy Petronella, da of Frewen Moor (d 1984), of East Meon, Hants; 2 s (Gabriel John b 1965, Barnabas Mark b 1966), 1 da (Chloë June b 1968); *Career* Nat Serv 2 Lt RE 1952-54; mathematics teacher Marylebone GS 1959-60, computer programmer Ferranti Ltd 1960-63, mathematics lectr The City Univ London 1963-68; res assoc: in computing theory Univ Coll Swansea 1968-70, in artificial intelligence Stanford Univ Calif 1970-72; Univ of Edinburgh: lectr in computer science 1973-78, reader 1978-84, prof 1984-; fndr memb Academia Europaea 1988; Hon DSc Chalmers Univ of Technol 1988; FRS, FBCS 1989; *Books* Edinburgh LCF (1978), A Calculus A Communicating Systems (1980), Communication and Concurrency (1989), Definition of Standard ML (1990), Commentary on Standard ML (1990); *Recreations* music, carpentry, walking; *Style*— Prof Robin Milner; 2 Garscube Terrace, Edinburgh EH12 6BQ (☎ 031 337 4823); University of Edinburgh, Computer Science Dept, The King's Buildings, Mayfield Rd, Edinburgh EH9 3JZ (☎ 031 650 5174)

MILNER, Timothy William Lycett; s and h of Sir George Edward Mordaunt Milner, 9 Bt; *b* 11 Oct 1936; *Style*— Timothy Milner Esq

MILNER-BARRY, Sir (Philip) Stuart; KCVO (1975), CB (1962), OBE (1946); s of late Prof E L Milner-Barry; *b* 20 Sept 1906; *Educ* Cheltenham, Trinity Coll Cambridge; *m* 1947, Thelma Tennant, da of Charles Tennant Wells; 1 s, 2 da; *Career* stockbroker L Powell Sons & Co 1929-38, chess correspondent The Times 1938-45, temp civil servant FO 1940-55, princ HM Treasy 1945 (asst sec 1947, under sec 1954), dir Estabs and Orgn Min of Health 1958-60; under sec: HM Treasy 1966, Civil Serv Dept 1968-77; *Clubs* Brooks's; *Style*— Sir Stuart Milner-Barry, KCVO, CB, OBE; 12 Camden Rd, London SE3 (☎ 081 852 5808)

MILNER OF LEEDS, 2 Baron (UK 1951); Arthur James Michael Milner; AE (1952); s of 1 Baron Milner of Leeds, MC, PC (d 1967); *b* 12 Sept 1923; *Educ* Oundle, Trinity Hall Cambridge (MA); *m* 1951, Sheila Margaret, da of late Gerald Hartley, of North Hill Ct, Leeds; 1 s, 2 da; *Heir* s, Hon Richard James Milner; *Career* sits as Labour Peer in House of Lords; joined RAFVR 1942, served 1942-46, cmmnd 1943; served with RAuxAF 609 (W Riding) Sqdn 1947-52, Flight Lt; slr 1951; conslt Gregory, Rowcliffe & Milners; oppn whip House of Lords 1971-74; *Style*— The Rt Hon the Lord Milner of Leeds, AE; 2 The Inner Ct, Old Church St, London SW3 5BY (☎ 071 352 7588); Gregory, Rowcliffe & Milners, 1 Bedford Row, London WC1R 4BZ (☎ 071 242 0631)

MILNER WILLIAMS, Lt-Col Charles William Michael; TD (1984); s of John William Milner Williams, OBE (d 1985), of Wimbledon, and Ernestine Violet (Nan), *née* von Otto (d 1972); *b* 7 Oct 1944; *Educ* Prince of Wales Sch Nairobi Kenya (HMC); *m* 10 Sept 1966, Margaret Joyce, da of Jack Bowerman, of Luton, Beds; 1 da (Victoria b 1971); *Career* Platoon Cdrs Course HAC 1969-70, cmmnd RCT (V) 1974, Capt 1978, Maj OC 285 Movement Control Sqdn 1983, Lt-Col S01 CCCC BRSC Liaison and Movements TA 1986, cmd and staff course TA 1985, Jt Servs Movements Staff Course 1986; Res Dept FCO 1964-68, HM Inland Revenue 1968-; govr: Rutlish Sch London Borough of Merton 1978-89, Ricards Lodge HS 1978 (chm 1986-89), dep chm Wimbledon Cons Assoc 1978-81; ACIS 1983; *Recreations* classical music (early), genealogy and heraldry, walking the dog; *Clubs* Naval and Military; *Style*— Lt-Col Charles Milner Williams, TD; Spur B, Block 6, Government Buildings, Chalfont Drive, Nottingham

MILNER-WILLIAMS, Margaret Joyce; *née* Bowerman; da of Jack Bowerman, of Luton, Beds, and Anne Lilian, *née* James; *b* 28 Dec 1941; *Educ* Burlington Sch London, Goldsmith Coll London (Cert Ed); *m* 10 Sept 1966, Charles William Michael Milner-Williams, s of John William Milner-Williams, OBE (d 1985), of Wimbledon, and Nairobi, Kenya; 1 da (Victoria Margaret Anne b 1971); *Career* asst mistress Hugh Christie Sch Tonbridge 1963-64, organiser Greater London Young Cons Central Off 1964-66, Cons Pty agent West Lewisham constituency 1966-67, princ Hazelhurst Sch Wimbledon 1970 (asst mistress 1967-70), chm Hazelhurst (Wimbledon) Ltd; chm Independent Schs Assoc Inc and memb Jt Cncl 1982-85; memb: Ctee of Independent Schs Info Serv 1985-, ISIS Assoc Ctee 1988-, delegacy Goldsmiths' Coll 1976-82; Page scholar ESU 1988; *Recreations* music, reading, public speaking, travel; *Style*— Mrs Margaret Milner-Williams; 22 Waldemar Rd, Wimbledon, London SW19 7LJ; Parque Santiago, Playa de Las Americas, Tenerife, Canary Islands; Hazelhurst School, 17 The Downs, Wimbledon, London SW20 8HF (☎ 081 946 1704)

MILNES COATES, Prof Sir Anthony Robert; 4 Bt (UK 1911), of Helperby Hall, Helperby, North Riding of Yorkshire; only s of Lt-Col Sir Robert Milnes-Coates, 3 Bt, DSO, JP (d 1982), and Lady Patricia Milnes-Coates, *qv*; *b* 8 Dec 1948; *Educ* Eton, St Thomas's Hosp (BSc, MB BS); *m* 1978, Harriet Ann, yr da of Raymond Burton, of The Old Rectory, Slingsby, York; 2 da (Sara b 1981, Sophie b 1984); *Heir* Thomas b 1986; *Career* MRCP, MD; prof and chm Dept of Medical Microbiology St George's Hosp Med Sch London; *Style*— Prof Sir Anthony Milnes Coates, Bt; Hereford Cottage, 135 Gloucester Rd, London SW7; Helperby Hall, Helperby, York

MILNES-COATES, Lady (Ethel) Patricia; *née* Hare; er da of 4 Earl of Listowel (d 1931); *b* 29 Oct 1912; *m* 1, 1936, Lt-Col Charles Thomas Milnes Gaskell (k in flying accident while on active serv 1943); 3 s (James b 1937, Andrew b 1939, Tom b 1942); m 2, 1945, Lt-Col Sir Robert Edward James Clive Milnes-Coates, 3 Bt, DSO (d 1982); 1 s (Sir Anthony, 4 Bt, *qv*), 1 da (Mrs Peter Brodrick); *Style*— The Lady Patricia Milnes-Coates; Moor Ho Farm, Helperby, York

MILOW, Keith Arnold; s of Geoffrey Keith Milow, of Majorca, Spain, and Joan Ada, *née* Gear (d 1990); *b* 29 Dec 1945; *Educ* Baldock Secdy Modern Sch, Camberwell Sch of Art (DipAD), RCA; *Career* artist; solo exhibitions incl: Nigel Greenwood Inc 1970, 1973, 1974 and 1976, Gregory fellows Exhibition (Leeds City Art Gallery) 1971, J Duffy & Sons NY 1973, Hester Van Royen Gallery London 1975, Kettles Yard Gallery Cambridge 1976, Gallerie Albert Baronian Belgium 1977, Park Square Gallery Leeds 1977, Just Crosses (Roundhouse Gallery) 1978, Galerie Loyse Openheim Geneva 1979, Annina Nosei Gallery NY 1981 and 1982, Nigel Greenwood Gallery 1986, Gouaches (Alexander Wood Gallery, NY) 1987, John Davis Gallery NY 1988, 100 Drawings (Nigel Greenwood Gallery) 1989, 25 Drawings (Gallery 630B New Orleans and Nohra Haime Gallery NY) 1990; over 50 gp exhibitions incl: Young Contemporaries (Tate Gallery, London) 1967, Mostra Mercato d'Arte Contemporan (Florence, Italy) 1968, Six at the Haywood (Haywood Gallery) 1969, Works on Paper (Museum of Modern Art NY) 1970, The Road Show (Sao Paulo Biennale & S American tour) 1971, The New Art (Hayward Gallery) 1972, Homers (The Museum of Modern Art) 1973, Xieme Biennale of Art (Menton, France) 1974, The British Exhibiton (Basel Art Fair) 1975, 25 Years of British Painting (RCA) 1976, Recent British Art (Br Cncl tour) 1977-78, The British Art Show (Sheffield) 1979, British Art Now (Solomon R Guggenheim Museum, NY) 1980, Aspects of British Art Today (Tokyo Metropolitan Museum of Art) 1982, Pintura Britanica Contemporania (Museo Municipal Madrid) 1983, Chill Out (Kenkeleba Gallery NY) 1983, The Show Room (Michael Katz Gallery NY) 1985, Modern British Sculpture (Whitechapel Art Gallery) 1986, Emerging Artists 1978-1988: Selections from the Exxon Series (Solomon R Guggenheim Museum NY) 1987, Modern British Sculpture (The Tate Gallery Liverpool) 1988, Works on Lead (Nohra Haime Gallery NY) 1989, Sixth Sense (Pence Gallery Santa Monica) 1990, Personal Portraits (Annina Nosel Gallery NY) 1991; works in numerous public collections incl: Imperial War Museum, Museum of Modern Art NY, Tate Gallery London, V & A Museum London, Nat Gallery of Australia; awards: Gregory Fellowship Univ of Leeds 1970-72, Harkness Fellowship to USA 1972-74, Calouste Gulbenkian Fndn Visual Arts award 1976, Major award Arts Cncl of GB 1979, first prize Tolly Cobbold/Eastern Arts Second Nat Exhibition 1979, Edward Albee Fndn award 1983-; *Style*— Keith Milow, Esq; 32 W 20th St, New York, NY 1001, USA FOREIGN (☎ 212 929 0124)

MILROY, Rev Dominic Liston; OSB; s of Adam Milroy, by his w Clarita; *b* 18 April 1932; *Educ* Ampleforth, St Benet's Hall Oxford; *Career* prior Int Benedictine Coll of St Anselmo Rome 1974-79, headmaster Ampleforth 1980- (housemaster 1964-74, head modern languages 1963-74); *Style*— The Rev Dominic Milroy, OSB; Ampleforth College, York YO6 4ER (☎ 043 93 224)

MILSOM, Gerald Martin William; OBE (1987); s of Arthur Milsom (d 1983), of Dedham, Essex, and Dorothy Eileen, *née* Chambers (d 1990); *b* 28 Aug 1930; *Educ* Epsom Coll; *m* 1, 28 Sept 1957 (m dis), June Philippa, da of Luther H A Watson (d 1986); 2 s (David b 1 Oct 1958, Paul b 6 Feb 1964), 1 da (Nicola b 9 Dec 1960); m 2, 27 July 1978, Diana Joy, da of Frank Pinhey, of Pond Farm, Gt Bromley, Colchester; *Career* Nat Serv Lt Army Catering Corps 1949-51; hotelier, chm Milsom Hotels Dedham Ltd (incorporating Le Talbooth Restaurant, Maison Talbooth, Dedham Vale Hotel, and the Pier at Harwich); fndr Pride of Britain Consortium of Country House Hotels 1983, chm BHRCA Bd Mgmnt 1989-91 (vice chm 1987-89); memb Essex CC 1963-73 (Alderman 1971), chm East Anglia Tourist Bd 1971-82 (currently vice pres), govr Norwich City Coll; Freeman: City of London 1973, Worshipful Co of Distillers 1973 (memb Ct); FHCIMA 1971, Master Innholder 1979, FInstD 1983; *Recreations* golf, walking; *Style*— Gerald Milsom, Esq, OBE; PO Box 96, Southbroom 4277, Natal, South Africa; Le Talbooth, Dedham, Colchester, Essex CO7 6HP (☎ 0206 323 150, fax 0206 322 752, telex 987083 LETALB G)

MILSOM, (Ernest) James; s of Ernest William Milsom, of Edgware, Middx, and Jane, *née* Somers (d 1979); *b* 2 April 1928; *Educ* St James' RC Secdy Sch Edgware, Middlesex Poly; *m* 23 Feb 1951, Anne Kathleen (Nancy), da of Harry Deadman (d 1945), of Edgware; 2 s (Michael James b 23 April 1955, Séan Francis b 8 Oct 1959), 1 da (Julia Anne b 15 April 1953); *Career* WWII RN 1939-45; conslt engr; ptnr: Henry Goddard & Ptnrs 1963-68, McAuslan & Ptnrs 1968-77; with own practice EJ Milsom & Assocs 1977-; CEng, FIEE, FCIBSE, MConsE, KCSJ 1972, KHS 1990; *Recreations* landscape & portrait painting, music, reading, marquetry; *Style*— E James Milsom, Esq; E J Milsom and Associates, Consltg Engineers - Building Services, 250A Kingsbury Rd, Kingsbury, London NW9 0BS (☎ 081 204 9024)

MILSOM, Prof Stroud Francis Charles (Toby); QC (1985); s of Harry Lincoln Milsom (d 1970), of Rock, Cornwall, and Isobel Vida, *née* Collins (d 1979); *b* 2 May 1923; *Educ* Charterhouse, Trinity Coll Cambridge (BA, MA), Univ of Pennsylvania Law Sch; *m* 11 Aug 1955, Iréne, da of Witold Szereszewski (d 1940), of Wola Krysztoporska, Poland; *Career* Admty 1944-45; lectr and fell Trinity Coll Cambridge 1948-55, fell tutor and dean New Coll Oxford 1956-64, prof of legal history Univ of London 1964-76, Maitland Meml lectr Cambridge 1972, fell St John's Coll Cambridge 1976- (prof of law 1976-90), Ford's lectr in English history Oxford 1985-86; visiting prof: New York Univ Law School 1958-70, Yale Law Sch 1968-, Harvard Law Sch and Dept of History 1973, Colorado Law Sch 1977, Monash Law Sch 1981; pres Selden

Soc 1985-88 (literary dir 1964-80); memb: Royal Cmmn on Historical Manuscripts 1975-, American Philosophical Soc 1984; hon bencher Lincoln's Inn 1970; Hon LLD Glasgow 1981, Hon LLD Chicago 1985; FBA 1967; *Books* Novae Narrationes (intro, translation notes, 1963), Pollock & Maitland History of English Law (intro to reissue 1968), Historical Foundations of the Common Law (1968, 2 edn 1981), The Legal Framework of English Feudalism (1976), Studies in the History of the Common Law (1985), Sources of English Legal History (with JH Baker, 1986); *Clubs* Athenaeum; *Style*— Prof SFC Milsom, QC; 113 Grantchester Meadows, Cambridge CB3 9JN (☎ 0223 354100); St John's Coll, Cambridge CB2 1TP (☎ 0223 338600)

MILSTEIN, Dr César; *b* 8 Oct 1927; *Educ* Colegio Nacional Bahia Blanca, Universidad de Buenos Aires Facultad de Ciencias, Univ of Cambridge (PhD); *m* 1953, Celia Prilleltensky; *Career* Universidad de Buenos Aires 1952-57 (Instituto de Quimica Biologia, Facultad de Ciencias Medicas), Staff of Instituto Nacional de Microbiologia Buenos Aires 1957-58 and 1961-63, Dept of Biochemistry Univ of Cambridge 1958-61, scientific staff Med Res Cncl Laboratory of Molecular Biology Cambridge 1963- (head Protein Chemistry Subdivision 1969-80, memb Governing Bd 1975-79, dep dir 1988-); memb: Euro Molecular Biology Orgn 1974, Deutsche Akademie der Naturforscher Leopolding 1984; hon memb: Scandanavian Immunological Socs 1970, American Inst of Immunologists 1979 (head Molecular Immunobiology Subdiv 1980), la Sociedad de Medicina Interna de Bahia Blanca 1985, British Soc for Immunology 1985, Assoc Argentina de Alergia e Immunologia 1985, Sociedad Cientifica Argentina 1988; foreign hon memb American Acad of Arts and Sciences 1983, founding fell Third World Acad of Sciences 1983; hon fell: Int Soc of Haematology 1986, Nat Acad of Sciences of Argentina 1988; Hon FRCP 1983, Hon FRCPath 1987, FRS 1975, British Cncl Fellowship 1958-60; Royal Soc: Wellcome Fndn Prize 1980, Royal Medal 1982, Copley Medal 1989; Nobel Prize in Physiology of Medicine 1985, RCS Walker Prize 1986; *Publications* author of various papers and review articles on immunoglobulins and phosphoenzimes; *Recreations* cooking, open air activities Sefe (Cambridge); *Style*— Dr Cesar Milstein, FRS; Medical Research Council Centre, Laboratory of Molecular Biology, University Medical School, Hills Rd, Cambridge CB2 2QH (☎ 0223 248011, telex 81532)

MILTON, Alan James; MBE (1983); s of John Phillips Milton (d 1968), and Alice Bowen, *née* Jones (d 1977); *b* 23 June 1935; *Educ* Emanuel Sch London; *m* 25 March 1972, Heather Valerie, da of Douglas Roy Salt, OBE, of 1 The Ridings, Leavenheath, Suffolk; 2 s (Jason James b 1973, Damian John b 1976); *Career* Nat Serv RAF 1953-55; trainee Glyn Mills and Co 1951-53; Standard Chartered Bank Gp: official Bank of Br W Africa Ltd 1955-, mangr Bank of W Africa Ltd 1958-, mangr Standard Bank of W Africa Ltd 1966, mangr Standard Bank Nigeria Ltd 1969-; mangr and asst gen mangr mktg First Bank of Nigeria Ltd 1984, dep regnl mangr The Chartered Bank Bombay 1984 (mangr W India 1986), mangr ops First Bank of Nigeria Ltd London 1988-89 (mangr mktg 1987), currently freelance consit Nigerian affrs; ind distributor of environmental prods for Nat Safety Assocs of America trading as Connaught Enterprises; formerly dir Standard Chartered Insur Brokers Lagos; former tstee: St Saviours Sch Educn Tst Lagos, Corona Schs Lagos, Breach Candy Hosp Tst Bombay; formerly pres UK Citizens Assoc W India; *Recreations* golf, philately, table tennis, walking, reading, boating, classical music; *Clubs* Royal Overseas League, Lagos Yacht, Ikoyi (Lagos), Willingdon (Bombay); *Style*— Alan J Milton, Esq, MBE; 6 Neate House, Lupus St, London SW1V 3EG (☎ 071 821 7992); 24 Kings Walk, Shoreham-by-Sea, West Sussex BN43 5LG (☎ 0273 453931)

MILTON, Prof Anthony Stuart; s of Ernest Thomas Milton (d 1964), of Beckenham, Kent, and Gladys Ethel Milton (d 1989); *b* 15 April 1934; *Educ* Cranleigh Sch, St Catherine's Coll Oxford (BA, MA, DPhil); *m* 16 June 1962, Elizabeth Amaret, da of Russell Freeman, of Richmond, Virginia, USA; 1 s (Nathaniel Gavin Nicolas b 6 Oct 1964), 2 da (Imogen Hillary b 7 Oct 1967, Kirstin Abigail b 8 Dec 1969); *Career* lectr Dartmouth Med Sch New Hampshire USA 1959-60, res fell Stanford Univ California USA 1960-61, res fell and hon lectr Univ of Edinburgh 1961-63, sr lectr Sch of Pharmacy Univ of London 1967-73 (lectr 1966-67), prof of pharmacology Univ of Aberdeen 1973-, md Univ of Aberdeen Trading Co (U-Travel) 1986-; community cncllr 1982-85, tstee Aberdeen Int Youth Festival of Music and Arts 1985-; memb: Physiological Soc, Br Pharmacological Soc; FRSA; *Books* Pyretics and Antipyretics (1982); *Recreations* collecting the stamps of Newfoundland, breeding Border Terriers; *Style*— Prof Anthony Milton; Stone Cottage, Baillieswells Rd, Bieldside, Aberdeen AB1 9BQ (☎ 0224 868651); Division of Pharmacology, University of Aberdeen, Marischal College, Aberdeen AB9 1AS (☎ 0224 273036, fax 0224 645519, telex 73458 UNIABN G)

MILTON, (Robert) Brian; s of Thomas Robert Milton (d 1986), of Howth, Dublin, and Theresa Pauling, *née* Durnan; *b* 17 Sept 1942; *Educ* Salesiar Coll Oxford, Sir William Borlase Sch Marlow, Prince Rupert Sch BAOR, Harrow County GS, RAF Coll Cranwell, City Coll San Francisco; *m* 20 June 1970, Fiona Gale, da of Lt Col Ian Campbell, of Saddell, P O Box 391, Howick 3290, Natal, SA; 1 s (James Ian Campbell Milton b 1 Aug 1975), 1 da (Tracey Kirston Campbell Milton b 15 May 1978); *Career* flight cadet (RAF scholarship) Cranwell; various jobs abroad 1962-70, asst pres offr Liberal Party 1970-71, freelance BBC journalist 1972-82 (incl 2 years editing BBC radio Rush Hour), Industrial and Financial corr, prodr TV-AM 1982-87, independent TV prodr 1987-; cncl memb Br Hang Gliding Assoc 1976-81 (chm Competitions Ctee; fndr Br League, American Cup, Bleriot Cup, 444 Harriet Quimby competition, Superleague); FRGS; *Recreations* hang gliding, microlighting, bridge, reading; *Style*— Brian Milton, Esq; 27 Grove Rd, Coombe Dingle, Bristol BS9 2RJ (☎ 0272 683776)

MILTON, Derek Francis; CMG (1990); s of Francis Henry Milton (d 1970), and Florence Elizabeth Maud, *née* Kirby (d 1950); *b* 11 Nov 1935; *Educ* Preston Manor County GS, Univ of Manchester (BA), Univ of Glasgow (Civil Serv res fellowship); *m* 1, 1960, Helge Kahle; 2 s (Mark Timothy, Robin Kai); m 2, 1977, Catherine Walmsley; *Career* Nat Serv RAF 1954-56; Colonial Office (E African, Int Relations and W Indies Depts) 1959-62, asst private sec to Cwlth and Colonial Sec 1962-64, CRO 1964-67, Cwlth PMs' Meeting Secretariat 1964; FCO: UK Mission to UN (NY) 1967-71, Br Embassy Rome 1972-75, Hong Kong Dept 1975-77, Br Embassy Caracas 1978-79, Dept of Trade 1980-82, Overseas Inspectorate 1982-84, Br Embassy Mexico 1984-87, RCDS 1988, high cmmr Kingston Jamaica 1989-, non-res ambass Haiti 1989-; *Recreations* Poland, travel, music, tennis, Queens Park Rangers FC, reading (incl The Guardian), languages; *Style*— Derek Milton, Esq, CMG; c/o Private Letter Section (Kingston), Foreign & Commonwealth Office, King Charles St, London SW1A 2AH; British High Commission, Trafalgar Rd, Kingston 10, Jamaica (☎ 92 69050)

MILTON, Frank William; s of Capt Cyril Frank, of Worthing, Sussex, and Mabel Laura, *née* Neal; *b* 29 Nov 1949; *Educ* Hove Co GS, Univ Coll Oxford (BA); *m* 29 Sept 1973, Lesley Pamela, da of Capt Dennis Arthur Jack Adams, RE, of Glossop Derbys; 2 s (Andrew Paul Frank, Graham Alexander Neil); *Career* trainee Turner & Newall 1972-73, sales asst Shell Chemicals UK Ltd 1973-75 (sales rep 1975-78), planning mangr Shell International Chemical Co Ltd 1978-80, ptnr Coopers & Lybrand Deloitte Management Consultants 1984 (joined 1980); CDipAF, MInstM; *Recreations* hill walking, windsurfing, running; *Style*— Frank Milton, Esq; Allgin, Norrels Drive, E Horsley, Surrey KT24 5DL (☎ 04865 3832); Hillgate House, 26 Old Bailey, London EC4M 7PL (☎ 071 454 8416, fax 071 236 2367)

MILTON, Stuart Gregory; s of Robert Milton (d 1990), of Leicester, and Dorothy, *née* King (d 1988); *b* 6 Nov 1948; *Educ* Wyggeston GS for Boys Leicester, Leicester Sch of Management, Cranfield Business Sch (MBA); *m* 19 April 1973, Julie Elizabeth, da of Arthur Mills; 2 da (Jemma Louise b 13 Aug 1978, Laura Dee b 6 May 1981); *Career* asst accountant N Corah (St Margaret) Ltd 1967-70, fin supervisor Ford of Europe 1970-75, fin dir: Black & Decker UK Ltd 1976-82, Max Factor Europe 1982-85; gp fin dir Sunbeam International 1985-87, BCMB Group Ltd 1988-; memb CIMA 1970; *Recreations* sport, music, friends; *Clubs* St George's Hill Tennis; *Style*— Stuart Milton, Esq; British & Commonwealth Merchant Banking Group, 62 Cannon St, London EC4N 6AE (☎ 071 248 0900, car 0831 409969)

MILTON-THOMPSON, Surgn Vice Adm Sir Godfrey James; KBE (1988); s of Rev James Milton-Thompson (d 1968), of Pool Hall, Menheniot, Cornwall, and May Le Mare, *née* Hoare (d 1982); *b* 25 April 1930; *Educ* Eastbourne Coll, Queens' Coll Cambridge (MA, MB BChir), St Thomas' Hosp; *m* 1952, Noreen Helena Frances, da of Lieut Col Sir Desmond Fitzmaurice, of Boars Hill Oxford; 3 da (Helena (Mrs Prichard), Richenda (Mrs Dixon), Louisa); *Career* hon physician to HM The Queen 1982-90; Med DG (Naval) 1984-90, surgn gen Def Med Servs 1988-90; Hon Col 211 Wessex Field Hosp RAMC (V) 1990-, chm Cornwall Community Health Tst 1990-; hospitaller OStJ 1991-, KStJ (1990, CStJ 1985), memb Chapter Gen Order of St John 1988-; FRCP, DCH; *Recreations* fishing, literature, collecting English paintings; *Clubs* Naval & Military; *Style*— Surgn Vice Adm Sir Godfrey Milton-Thompson, KBE; c/o Barclays Bank, The Parade, Liskeard, Cornwall PL14 6AR

MILVERTON, 2 Baron (UK 1947); Rev Fraser Arthur Richard Richards; s of 1 Baron Milverton, GCMG (d 1978), and Noelle Benda, da of Charles Basil Whitehead, of Torquay; *b* 21 July 1930; *Educ* Ridley Coll, Ontario, Clifton, Egerton Agricultural Coll Njoro Kenya, Bishop's Coll Cheshunt Herts; *m* 1957, Mary Dorothy, da of Leslie Aubrey Fly (d 1983; a composer of music, teacher and civil servant), of Bath; 2 da (Susan b 1962, Juliet b 1964); *Heir* bro, Hon Michael Hugh Richards; *Career* sits as Cons peer in House of Lords; Royal Signals 1949-50, Kenya Police 1952-53; deacon 1957; curate: St George's Beckenham Kent, St John Baptist Sevenoaks Kent, St Nicholas Great Bookham Surrey; vicar Okewood Hill with Forest Green Surrey, rector Christian Malford with Sutton Benger and Tytherton Kellaways (Wilts) 1967-, chaplain Wilts ACF to 1981; *Recreations* family, current affairs, reading, int rugby, cricket, tennis, swimming; *Style*— The Rev the Rt Hon the Lord Milverton; The Rectory, Christian Malford, Chippenham, Wilts (☎ 0249 720466)

MILWARD, Prof Alan Steele; s of Joseph Thomas Milward (d 1965), and Dorothy, *née* Steele (d 1985); *b* 19 Jan 1935; *Educ* UCL (BA), LSE (PhD); *m* 23 Nov 1963, Claudine Jeanne Amelie, *née* Lemaitre; 1 da (Colette Victoire Zoe b 22 Feb 1977); *Career* lectr: econ history Univ of Edinburgh 1960-65, Sch of Social Studies Univ of East Anglia 1965-68; assoc prof of economics Stanford Univ 1969-71; prof: of Euro studies UMIST 1971-83, of contemporary history Euro Univ Inst 1983-86, of econ history LSE 1986-; visiting prof: Stanford Univ, Univ of Illinois, Ecole des Hautes Etudes en Sciences Sociales, Univ of Oslo; external prof Euro Univ Inst; memb: Econ History Soc, The Econ History Assoc, The Univ Assoc for Contemporary Euro Studies, The German History Soc; Hon MA Manchester 1976; FBA 1987; *Books* The German Economy at War (1965), The New Order and The French Economy (1970), War, Economy and Society, 1939-45 (1979), The Reconstruction of Western Europe, 1945-51 (1984); *Recreations* theatre; *Style*— Prof Alan Milward; Dept of Economic History, London School of Economics, Houghton St, London WC2A 2AE (☎ 071 955 7077, fax 071 955 7730)

MILWARD, Timothy Michael; s of Francis John Milward, and Rosemary Gwendoline, *née* Smedley-Aston; *b* 24 March 1937; *Educ* Rugby, Clare Coll Cambridge (MA, MB BCh); *m* 17 Jan 1970, Susan Isobel, da of Maj Glover Iggulden (d 1983), of Herne Bay, Kent; 4 da (Jessica b 24 Dec 1971, Caroline b 15 June 1973, Eleanor b 21 Aug 1978, Camilla (twin) b 21 Aug 1978); *Career* Nat Serv, midshipman RNR 1955-63, Lt in RNR; med trg St Thomas's Hosp London 1960-63, registrar in plastic surgery Canniesburn Hosp Glasgow 1971-72, sr registrar in plastic surgery QMH London 1972-76, Hand Surgery fell Louisville Kentucky USA 1975; conslt plastic surgn 1976-: Leicester Royal Infirmary, Pilgrim Hosp Boston, Lincoln County Hosp; memb Cncl Br soc for Surgery of the Hand 1982-83, pres Br Assoc of Aesthetic Plastic Surgns 1987-88, memb Cncl Br Assoc of Plastic Surgns 1989-91, county med offr Leicestershire Branch Br Red Cross; FRCS 1966; *Recreations* squash, windsurfing; *Style*— Timothy Milward, Esq; Leicester Royal Infirmary, Leicester LE1 5WW (☎ 0533 585286)

MIMMS, Robert Andrew (Bobby); s of Bernard Mimms, of Doncaster, and Pat, *née* Hall; *b* 12 Oct 1963; *Educ* Easingwold Comp Sch N Yorks; *m* 15 May 1985, Karon, da of Mick Brown; 2 s (Bradleigh b 14 Oct 1986, Josh b 5 Aug 1989); *Career* professional footballer; Halifax Town (no appearances), 89 appearances Rotherham Utd (league debut 1982), 39 appearances Everton, 37 appearances Tottenham Hotspur 1988-90 (joined for a fee of £375,000), Blackburn Rovers 1991-; appearances on loan: 3 Manchester City, 2 Notts County, 4 Sunderland, 7 Blackburn Rovers, 8 Aberdeen; 3 England under 21 caps 1985-86 (v Israel, Eire, Italy); FA Cup Loser's medal Everton v Liverpool 1986; *Recreations* squash, golf, TV; *Style*— Bobby Mimms, Esq; Blackburn Rovers FC, Ewood Park, Blackburn, Lancs (☎ 0254 55432)

MIMPRISS, Peter Hugh Trevor; yr s of Hugh Trevor Baber Mimpriss (d 1990), and Gwyneth Mary, *née* Bartley (d 1982); *b* 22 Aug 1943; *Educ* Sherborne; *m* 18 Sept 1971, Hilary Ann, da of Joseph Leonard Reed, MBE; 2 da (Isobel b 19 Oct 1973, Victoria b 22 Feb 1979); *Career* admitted slr 1967; ptnr Allen and Overy 1972-; dir: Leeds Castle Fndn 1980-, Weston Park Fndn 1986-, Chatham Historic Dockyard Tst 1988-; tstee Edwina Mountbatten Tst; Freeman Worshipful Co of Tallow Chandlers 1989; *Recreations* maritime history, collecting books, pictures; *Clubs* Athenaeum, Garrick; *Style*— Peter Mimpriss, Esq; c/o Allen & Overy, 9 Cheapside, London EC2V 6AD (☎ 071 248 9898, fax 071 236 2192, telex 8812801)

MIMS, Prof Cedric Arthur; s of Arthur Henry Mims (d 1931), and Irene, *née* Davey (d 1931); *b* 9 Dec 1924; *Educ* Mill Hill Sch, UCL (BSc), Middx Hosp Med Sch (MB BS, MD); *m* 7 May 1952, Valerie Iolanthe, da of Frederick Sydney Vickery; 2 s (Simon b 28 Jan 1956, Nicolas b 18 Dec 1958), 2 da (Penelope b 16 Sept 1954, Sarah b 11 Aug 1960); *Career* med res offr Virus Res Inst E Africa High Cmmn Entebbe Uganda 1953-56, professorial fell John Curtin Sch Med Res Aust Nat Univ Canberra Aust 1957-72; res fell: Childrens Hosp Med Centre Boston USA 1963-64, Wistar Inst Philadelphia USA 1968-69; univ prof in microbiology Guys Hosp Med Sch 1972-90; FRCPath 1976; *Books* Viral Pathogenesis and Immunology (1984), Pathogenesis of Infectious Disease (1987); *Style*— Prof Cedric Mims; Sheriff House, Hammingden Lane, Ardingley, West Sussex RH17 6SR (☎ 0444 892243)

MINALE, Marcello; s of Mario Minale (d 1988), of Naples, and Ida, *née* Cardani; *b* 15 Dec 1938; *Educ* Tech Sch Naples, Indust Design Sch Coll of Helsinki; *m* 1, 1965 (m dis 1974), Ebba, *née* Ocjemark; 1 s (Marcello Mario b 15 Feb 1966); m 2, 3 Nov 1975, Roberta, da of George Broadbridge, of Gillingham, Kent; 2 s (Manilo b 3 Nov 1976, Massimo b 15 Nov 1979); *Career* designer; chm Minale Tattersfield and Ptnrs 1978-; pres: Designers and Art Dir Assoc of London 1982, Awards for Outstanding Contrib to Br Design 1987; FCSD 1978; *Books* Design á la Minale Tattersfield (1976), Design:

The World of Minale Tattersfield (1990); *Recreations* rowing; *Clubs* Tideway Sculling Sch; *Style*— Marcello Minale, Esq; Minale, Tattersfield & Partners, The Courtyard, 37 Sheen Rd, Richmond, Surrey (☎ 081 948 7999, fax 081 948 2435)

MINCHIN, Peter David; s of Maj Cecil Redvers Minchin (d 1953), of Ryde, IOW, and Ena Mary, *née* Flux (d 1974); *b* 5 March 1932; *Educ* Ryde Sch IOW, Allhallows Rousdon Devon; *m* 2 April 1960, Angela, da of Maj Henry Hugh Petley (d 1976), of Heathfield House, Old Heathfield, Sussex; 2 s (David b 25 Dec 1963, Jeremy b 3 Sept 1965), 1 da (Alexandra b 2 Aug 1968); *Career* RN 1950-57: Lt (Observer) Fleet Air Arm 1955, ret 1957; ptnr: Kitcat & Aitken 1958-63, Pidgeon de Smitt (and predecessor firms) 1963-81; gen mangr Securities Gp of Kuwait 1982-85, ptnr and dir Scrimgeour Vickers Ltd 1985-86, md Lloyds Bank Stockbrokers Ltd 1986-90 (deputy chm 1990-), dir Lloyds Merchant Bank Ltd 1986-90, chm Chambers & Remington Ltd 1988- (dep chm 1990-), chm Lloyds Investment Managers 1990-; memb: Stock Exchange 1963- (memb Cncl 1976-82 and 1988-), Bd Securities Assoc 1988-; *Recreations* tennis, bridge, reading; *Style*— Peter Minchin, Esq; 83 Defoe House, Barbican, London EC2Y 8DN (☎ 071 588 5748); 48 Chiswell St, London EC1Y 4XX (☎ 071 522 500, fax 071 522 5415)

MINCHINTON, Prof Walter Edward; s of Walter Edward Minchinton (d 1928), of Brixton, London, and Annie Border Clark (d 1982); *b* 29 April 1921; *Educ* Queen Elizabeth's Hosp Bristol, LSE, Univ of London (BSc); *m* 1945, Marjorie, da of Richard Sargood (d 1979); 2 s (Paul Richard b 1949, David Walter b 1958), 2 da (Anne Border b 1952, Susan Clare b 1954); *Career* 1942-45: RAOC, REME, Roy Signals, NW Europe; Univ Coll Swansea: asst lectr 1948-50, lectr 1950-58, sr lectr 1958-64; prof of economic history Univ of Exeter 1964-86 (head of Dept 1964-83), emeritus prof; FRHistS; *Books* incl: The British Tinplate Industry (1957), The Trade of Bristol in the C18th (1957), Politics and the Port of Bristol in C18th (1963), Industrial South Wales 1750-1914 (1969), Mercantilism, System or Expediency (1969), The Growth of English Overseas Trade in the 17th and 18th Centuries (1969), Wage Regulation in Pre-Industrial England (1972), American Material in the House of Lords Record Office (1983), A Guide to Industrial Archaeology Sites in Britain (1984), Devon's Industrial Past: a Guide (1986), Life to the City: an illustrated history of Exeter's water supply from the Romans to the present day (1987), Britain and the Northern Seas: some essays (1988), The Northern Seas: politics, economics and culture (1989); *Recreations* walking, music, industrial archaeology; *Style*— Prof Walter Minchinton; 53 Homefield Rd, Exeter EX1 2QX (☎ 0392 77602)

MINFORD, Prof (Anthony) Patrick Leslie; s of Leslie Mackay Minford (d 1970), and Patricia Mary, *née* Sale; *b* 17 May 1943; *m* 10 Feb 1970, Rosemary Irene, da of Gordon Hedley Allcorn; 2 s (Paul, David), 1 da (Lucy); *Career* econ asst UK Miny of Overseas Devpt 1965-67, econ advsr Malawi Miny of Fin 1967-69, asst on econ matters of fin dir Courtauld Co 1970-71, econ advsr Balance of Payments Div UK Treasy 1971-73 (delgn to Br Embassy Washington 1973-74), Hallsworth res fell Univ of Manchester 1974-75, ed NIESR Econ Review 1975-76, Edward Gonner prof of applied econs Univ of Liverpool 1976; *Books* Substitution Effects, Speculation and Exchange Rate Stability (1978), Unemployment: Cause and Cure (with D H Davies, M J Peel and A Spague, 1983 2 edn 1985), Rational Expectations and the New Macroeconomics (with D A Peel, 1983), The Housing Morass (with M Peel and P Ashton, 1987); *Style*— Prof Patrick Minford; Department of Economics, University of Liverpool, PO Box 147, Liverpool L69 3BX (☎ 051 794 3031/2, fax 051 794 3028, telex 627095 UNILPLG)

MINGAY, Prof Gordon Edmund; s of Lt Cdr William Edmund Mingay (d 1978), and Florence Mabel, *née* Tuckwood (d 1962); *b* 20 June 1923; *Educ* Sir Joseph Williamson's Mathematical Sch Rochester, Univ of Nottingham (BA, PhD); *m* 5 Jan 1945, Mavis, da of Edwin Albert Tippen (d 1983); *Career* Lt RNVR 1942-47; lectr: Thames Poly 1953-56, LSE 1957-65; Univ of Kent: 1983- reader in econ and social history 1965-68, prof agrarian history 1968-83, emeritus prof of agrarian history 1983-; pres Br Agric History Soc 1986-89; memb: Econ History Soc, American Agric History Soc; FRHistS; *Books* English Landed Society in the Eighteenth Century (1963), The Agricultural History Review (ed, 1972-84), The Gentry (1976), Rural Life in Victorian England (1977), The Victorian Countryside (1981), The Transformation of Britian (1986); *Recreations* travel, music; *Style*— Prof Gordon Mingay

MINGAY, (Frederick) Ray; s of Cecil Stanley Mingay (d 1985), and Madge Elizabeth Robinson (d 1976); *b* 7 July 1938; *Educ* Totterham Gs, St Catharine's Coll Cambridge (BA, MA exhibitioner), Univ of London; *m* 7 Aug 1963, Joan Heather, da of Rev David Archibald Ryce-Roberts (d 1976); 3 s (Benjamin b 1965, Rupert b 1966, George b 1976), 1 da (Julia b 1979); *Career* Nat Serv Army 1959-61; Miny of Tport 1962-64, Bd of Trade 1964-68, Rootes and Chrysler Motors 1968-70, consul Milan 1970-73, asst sec Dept of Trade 1973-78, cnsllr Br Embassy Washington 1978-83, under sec DTI 1983-88, consul gen Chicago 1988-; FBIM, FRSA; *Clubs* Chicago, Tavern and Union League; *Style*— Ray Mingay, Esq; HM Consul-General, The British Consulate-General, 33 North Dearborn St, Chicago Illinois 60602, USA (☎ 312 346 1810)

MINNITT, Hon Mrs (Primrose Keighley); *née* Balfour; da of 1 Baron Riverdale, GBE (d 1957); *b* 20 April 1913; *m* 1, 1933, Oliver Grahame Hall (who assumed by deed poll 1945 the christian name of Claude in lieu of Oliver and the surname of Muncaster in lieu of his patronymic who d 1974); 2 s; m 2, 1975, Robert John Minnitt, CMG, *qv*; *Clubs* Lansdowne; *Style*— The Hon Mrs Minnitt; Whitelocks, Sutton, nr Pulborough, Sussex (☎ 079 87 216)

MINNS, (Frederick) John; s of Percival John (d 1915), and Alice Gertrude, *née* Morris (d 1916); *b* 17 June 1910; *Educ* Oxford Municipal Secdy Sch; *m* 1935, Enid Lucy, da of George Ernest Payne (d 1976); 2 s (Michael b 1937, Howard b 1942), 1 da (Carolyn b 1948); *Career* WWII observer Royal Observer Corps 1939-45, offr i/c Oxford Bldg Rescue Squad 1939-45; building contractor; dir and fndr Frederick J Minns & Co Ltd 1934 (chm 1936-69), jt md Swift Training Rifle Co Ltd & STAW 1940-46; chm: Minns Manufacturing Co Ltd 1950-69, Cherwell Land Development Co Ltd 1954-, Oxford Plant Ltd 1955-79, Minox Structures Ltd 1965-85, Minns Oxford Ltd 1956-; cncllr: Oxford City Cncl 1951-57, Abingdon RDC 1938-49; FCIOB; *Recreations* swimming, bridge, snooker, solar energy research and application; *Clubs* Clarendon (Oxford, pres 1956-57), Rotary (Oxford), Isis Probus; *Style*— John Minns, Esq; Solway, Badger Lane, Hinksey Hill, Oxford OX1 5BL (☎ 0865 735245); Minns Oxford Ltd, 7 West Way, Oxford

MINOGUE, Hon Sir John Patrick; s of J P Minogue; *b* 15 Sept 1909; *Educ* St Kevin's Coll Melbourne Univ; *m* 1938, Mary, da of T O'Farrell; *Career* barr 1939, QC Vic 1957, QC NSW 1958, Chief Justice Papua New Guinea 1970-74, Law Reform Cmmr Vic 1977-82 (ret), pres of the Graduate Union of Melbourne Univ 1982-, vice pres of the English Speaking Union (Vic Branch) 1982; kt 1976; *Style*— The Hon Sir John Minogue; Marengo Vale, Seymour, Vic 3660, Australia

MINOGUE, Kenneth Robert; s of Denis Francis Minogue (d 1988), and Eunice Pearl, *née* Porter (d 1949); *b* 11 Sept 1930; *Educ* Sydney Boys' HS, Univ of Sydney (BA), LSE (BSc); *m* 16 June 1954, Valerie Pearson, da of Frederick George Hallett (d 1974); 1 s (Nicholas Robert b 1955), 1 da (Eunice Karen Hallett b 1957); *Career* asst lectr Univ of Exeter 1955-56; LSE: asst lectr 1956, sr lectr 1964, reader 1971, prof 1984; London Sch of Economics and Political Science Univ of London 1984-, dir Govt and Opposition Centre for Policy Studies; *Books* The Liberal Mind (1963), Nationalism (1967), The Concept of a University (1974), Alien Powers: The Pure Theory of Ideology (1984); *Recreations* wine, women and song; *Style*— Prof Kenneth Minogue; 16 Buckland Crescent, London NW3 5DX (☎ 071 722 1474); Dept of Government, London School of Economics and Political Science, Houghton St, London WC2A 2AE (☎ 071 955 7188, fax 071 831 1707, telex 24655 BLPES G)

MINOGUE, Martin Michael; s of Martin Bernard Minogue, of 1 East Park Rd, Harrogate, N Yorks, and Josephine Minogue (d 1985); *b* 23 Dec 1937; *Educ* King James's GS Knaresborough, Gonville & Caius Coll Cambridge (BA, MA); *m* 17 Aug 1968 (m dis 1985), Elizabeth, da of Harold Worthy Wray, of Darley, N Yorks; 2 s (Nicholas b 7 March 1974, Ben b 6 Nov 1975); *Career* Nat Serv RAF 1957-59; second sec HM Diplomatic Serv (formerly third sec) 1962-66, asst princ BOT 1962-66, lectr in social sci Univ of Kent 1966-69; Univ of Manchester: lectr (later sr lectr) 1969-84, dir Int Devpt Centre 1984-; *Books* African Aims and Attitudes (ed with J Molloy 1974), Documents on Contemporary British Government (ed 1977), A Consumers Guide to Local Government (ed 1977 and 1980), Perspectives on Development (ed with P Leeson, 1988); *Recreations* reading, cricket, tennis, golf; *Style*— Martin Minogue, Esq; 8 Bamford Rd, Didsbury, Manchester M20 8GW (☎ 061 445 4669); International Development Centre, University of Manchester, Manchester M9 0FL (☎ 061 275 4794, fax 061 275 4751)

MINOPRIO, (Frank) Charles; 2 s of late (Charles) Anthony Minoprio (whose gf, *née* Franz Carl Anton, was born at Frankfurt but became a naturalised UK citizen 1856, while Franz's gf, Vincenz Alois, was originally a native of Pavia, but adopted Frankfurt citizenship in 1788), of Campden Hill, Kensington; *b* 9 Aug 1939; *Educ* Harrow, Grenoble Univ; *m* Patricia Mary, er da of late Brian W Dixon, of Godstone; 1 s (George b 1969), 2 da (Victoria b 1966, Charlotte b 1972); *Career* served as Lt RA in Germany; wine merchant; Hatch Mansfield & Co, Ltd Haulfryn Est Co Ltd, Master of Wine; chm: Champagne Acad 1986; Master of the Worshipful Co of Distillers 1987; *Recreations* tennis, squash, gardening; *Style*— Charles Minoprio, Esq; The Manor House, Milton Ernest, Bedford (☎ 02302 2237); Hatch Mansfield & Co, Ltd, 19 Ryder St, St James's, London SW1

MINTER, Jonathan Charles; s of John Minter, CBE, of Essex, and Barbara Geraldine MacDonald, *née* Stanford; *b* 22 July 1949; *Educ* Repton, Univ of Birmingham (BA); *m* 9 July 1983, Diana Claire, da of Austin Brown, of Sussex; 1 s (Benjamin b 1986), 1 da (Isabel b 1988); *Career* md: Julius Baer Investment Management Inc, Julius Baer Investments Ltd, dir Julius Baer International Ltd; sr vice pres Bank Julius Baer & Co Ltd; *Recreations* shooting, sailing; *Clubs* Royal Ocean Racing; *Style*— Jonathan C Minter, Esq; Hill Farm House, Langham, nr Colchester, Essex CO4 5NX; Bank Julius Baer & Co Ltd, Bevis Marks House, Bevis Marks, London EC3A 7NE

MINTO, Bruce Watson; s of James Andrew Minto, of Craig-Knowe, of Biggar, and Christina Greenshields, *née* Watson; *b* 30 Oct 1957; *Educ* Biggar HS, Edinburgh Univ (LLB); *m* 27 Aug 1983, Christine Rosemary, da of Dr Richard Thomas Stanley Gunn, of Kingsborough, Glasgow; 2 s (Andrew Richard b 1986, Jonathan Bruce b 1988); *Career* legal asst Dundas & Wilson CS 1981-85 (law apprentice 1979-81), fndr ptnr Dickson Minto WS 1985-; Notary Public; *Recreations* golf, rugby, music; *Style*— Bruce W Minto, Esq; 9 Braid Road, Edinburgh (☎ 031 447 4490); 11 Walker Street, Edinburgh (☎ 031 225 4455, fax 031 225 2712, 22/25 Finsbury Sq, London (☎ 071 628 4455, fax 071 628 1900)

MINTO, 6 Earl of (UK 1813); Gilbert Edward George Lariston Elliot-Murray-Kynynmound; 9 Bt (S 1700), MBE (Mil 1955), OBE (1986), JP (Roxburghshire 1961), DL (Roxburgh, Ettrick and Lauderdale 1983); also Baron Minto (GB 1797) and Viscount Melgund (UK 1813); s of 5 Earl of Minto (d 1975, s of 4 Earl, who was govr gen of Canada 1898-1904 and viceroy of India 1905-10), and Marion, OBE, da of George William Cook, of Montreal; *b* 19 June 1928; *Educ* Eton, RMA Sandhurst; *m* 1, 1952 (m dis 1965), Lady Caroline Child-Villiers, da of 9 Earl of Jersey; 1 s, 1 da; m 2, 1965, Mary Elizabeth (d 1983), da of late Peter Ballantine, of Gladstone, New Jersey, USA; *Heir* s, Viscount Melgund; *Career* 2 Lt Scots Gds 1948, served in Malaya 1949-51; ADC to: C-in-C Far East Land Force 1951, CIGS 1953-55, Govr and C-in-C of Cyprus 1955, RARO 1956, ret Capt; Brig Queen's Bodyguard for Scotland (Royal Co of Archers); chm Scottish Cncl on Alcoholism 1973-87 (pres 1987-), memb Borders Regnl Cncl 1974-80 and 1986-, convener 1990-, dep traffic cmmr Scotland 1975-81; exec vice pres S Scotland C of C 1978-80 (pres 1980-82); dir Noel Penny Turbines Ltd; *Clubs* Puffin's; *Style*— The Rt Hon the Earl of Minto, OBE, JP, DL; Minto, Hawick, Roxburghshire (☎ 045 087 321)

MINTO, Graeme Sutherland; MBE (1984), JP; s of Dr Kenneth Ross Minto (d 1981), and Mona Isobel, *née* Claxon; *b* 18 April 1943; *Educ* Oundle, Christ's Coll Cambridge (MA); *m* 3 Sept 1966, Mary Carolyn, da of John Priest; 1 s (Robert b 1975), 2 da (Lucy b 1968, Catherine b 1969); *Career* former chm Domino Printing Sciences plc (fndr 1978, md 1978-84, chm 1978-88); dir: Elmjet Ltd, Datapaq Ltd, Cantabrian Sports Ltd, The Cambridge Bldg Soc; govr Anglia Higher Educn Coll; DMS, CBIM, MIMechE, MIEE, CEng; *Books* author and lectr on numerous occasions on ink jet printing and growth of high tech businesses; *Recreations* skiing, golf, Rotarian; *Style*— Graeme Minto, Esq, MBE, JP; 10 Chaucer Road, Cambridge CB2 2EB

MINTON, Michael James; s of Christmas Evans Minton (d 1959), of Oxford, and Sarah Ann, *née* Baker (d 1990); *b* 12 Dec 1935; *Educ* City of Oxford Sch, Oriel Coll Oxford (MA, Dip, Crawford Cup, premier prize CIM); *m* Barbara June, da of Eric Walter Walton; 2 da (Deborah Claise b 1960, Penelope Jayne b 1962); *Career* 2 Lt RAEC 1958-59; British Gas SE Region: mgmnt trainee 1960-61, dist mgmnt 1962-68, regnl sales mgmnt 1968-71, regnl mktg mgmnt 1972-75; British Gas S Region: regnl mktg mangr 1975-79, regnl serv mangr 1979-81, regnl dir of serv 1981-90; ops dir British Gas Wales 1990-; devpt: Superwarmth Central Heating Systems 1970-71, Leisure Markets for Gas 1971-73, Servicecare for Gas Service 1981-84; CIM: pres Wessex Branch 1986-91 (chm 1979-81), nat cncllr 1989-91, memb Nat Exec; MCIM, MCAM, professional assoc Inst of Gas Engrs; FCIM; *Recreations* solo and choral singing; *Style*— Michael Minton, Esq; British Gas Wales, Helmont House, Churchill Way, Cardiff CF1 4NB (☎ 0222 239290, fax 0222 239290 ext 3029)

MINTON, Peter Kenneth; s of David James Minton, and Ada, *née* Martin (d 1974); *b* 4 Nov 1935; *Educ* Bromley Co GS; *m* 1, 1956 (m dis 1970) Pamela; 3 da (Lesley Anne b 1957, Jane b 1960, Catherine b 1963); m 2, Christine Jaqueline, *née* Lobb; 2 s (Alexander b 1980, Kenrick b 1982); *Career* electronics engr, technical journalist, industl and financial conslt, investmt analyst; memb: SLD, Henry Doubleday Res Assoc, Bucks and Oxfordshire Naturalists Tst; assoc memb Soc of Investmt Analyts; *Recreations* environmental conservation, long distance walking, organic gardening; *Clubs* National Liberal; *Style*— Peter Minton, Esq; Underwood Hardwick Rd, Whitchurch, Reading (☎ 0734 842516)

MINTON-TAYLOR, Robert; s of Richard Harold Minto-Taylor, MBE, of Pleasant Cottage, The Croft, East Hagbourne, Oxfordshire, and Joan, *née* Bennett; *b* 25 Feb 1948; *Educ* Clayesmore Sch Iwerne Minster Dorset, Wallingford GS Oxfordshire, Bournemouth Poly; *m* 13 Sept 1986, da of late dr Peter Deller, OBE; 1 s (Jasper); *Career* staff journalist Link House Publications Croydon 1967-71, press offr Townsend

Thoresen Car Ferries 1973-75, head of promotions European Ferries Group 1977-79 (sr press and PR exec 1975-77); Burson-Marsteller: account exec 1979-80, sr account exec 1980-81, account dir 1981-84, assoc dir 1984-85, head of travel and tourism 1985-87, main bd dir 1987-, dir leisure travel and tport 1988-89, dir and sr cncllr 1989-90, sr cncllr media servs and dir leisure travel and tport 1990-; PR Week Awards: nominated Best Design for Public Relations (for Atlantic Container Line) 1987, Best International Campaign (for Galileo) 1988, Best Non-Commercial Campaign (for Prince's Youth Business Tst) 1989; winner IPR Sword of Excellence Award for Community Relations 1990; sec Press and PR Div Inst of Journalists 1978-, chm London and SE England Region Inst of Travel and Tourism 1986-90; memb: Travel Indust Mktg Gp Chartered Inst of Mktg 1988-, Hotel Indust Mktg Gp Chartered Inst of Mktg 1990-, Cncl IPR 1990-, vice pres Inst of Journalists 1991-; MIPR 1980; memb: Inst of Journalists 1971, Tourism Soc 1990, Foreign Press Assoc 1991; fell Inst of Travel and Tourism 1986; *Recreations* family, writing, reading, listening to classical and rock music, good food and wine, armchair travelling, European travel particularly France and especially Provence & Brittany, merchant ships; *Clubs* Seahorse (chm); *Style—* Robert Minton-Taylor, Esq; Burson-Marsteller, 24-28 Bloomsbury Way, London WC1A 2PX (☎ 071 831 6262, fax 071 831 0639)

MINTY, Norman; s of Norman Edward Ernest Minty (d 1934), of Oxford, and Gertrude May North (d 1958); *b* 10 Sept 1925; *Educ* Dragon Sch Oxford, St Edwards Sch Oxford, Edinburgh Univ; *m* 15 Sept 1956, Daphne Louise, da of Rev Basil Claude Gadsden (d 1958), of Witney on Wye, Herefordshire; 3 s (Christopher Edward b 1960, Jefery Norman b 1960, Richard Drury b 1962); *Career* Flt Lt 1943-46; snr ptnr Niell & Co Oxford, non-exec dir Minty plc; life memb Oxford Lawn Tennis Club; Freeman City of London; FICA; *Recreations* gardening, tennis; *Clubs* RAF London, Clarendon Oxford, Grewin Oxford; *Style—* Norman Minty Esq; The Old House, Wheatley, Oxford; Cranbrook House, Summertown, Oxford (☎ 0865 52925)

MIQUEL, Raymond Clive; CBE (1981); *b* 28 May 1931; married with children; *Career* Arthur Bell & Sons: joined 1956, md 1968-85, chm 1973-85; chm Wellington Importers Ltd USA 1984-85, Gleneagles Hotels plc 1984-85, chm and chief exec Belhaven plc 1986-88, dir Golf Fund plc 1989-, Douglas Laing and Co Ltd 1989-; visiting prof business devpt Univ of Glasgow, chm Scottish Sports Cncl, govr Sports Aid Fndn; memb: Central Cncl of Physical Recreation, Sports Cncl; CBIM; *Style—* Raymond Miquel, Esq, CBE; Whitedene, Caledonian Crescent, Gleneagles, Perthshire (☎ 076 46 2642)

MIRIC, Robin; s of Milorad Miric, of London, and Sonia Patricia, *née* Forbes; *b* 21 May 1955; *Educ* Highgate Sch London, City of London Poly (LLB); *Career* called to the Bar Gray's Inn 1978; pupil to Michael Hyam and Stephen Hockman, QC, practice in criminal law; admitted and eudem memb Lincoln's Inn 1981, sec Surrey and S London Bar Mess 1990-; *Recreations* opera; *Clubs* National Liberal; *Style—* Robin Miric, Esq; 10 King's Bench Walk, Temple, London EC4Y 7EB (☎ 071 353 2501, fax 071 353 0658)

MIRMAN, Sophie; da of Serge Mirman (d 1980), and Simone, *née* Parmentier; *b* 28 Oct 1956; *Educ* French Lycée London, French Inst London; *m* 19 Oct 1984, Richard Ross, s of Sidney Ross of London; 1 s (William b 25 Feb 1988), 1 da (Natasha b 29 Aug 1986); *Career* mangr Marks and Spencer 1976 (former sec and mangr trainee), md Tie Rack 1981, chm Sock Shop Int plc 1983-90; *Recreations* horseriding, tennis; *Style—* Ms Sophie Mirman; Trotters (Childrenswear and Accessories) Ltd, 34 Kings Rd, London SW3 4UD (☎ 071 259 9620, fax 071 259 9622)

MIRRLEES, Prof James Alexander; s of late Prof George B M Mirrlees; *b* 5 July 1936; *Educ* Trinity Coll Cambridge (BA, PhD), Univ of Edinburgh (MA); *m* 1961, Gillian Marjorie; 2 c; *Career* advsr MIT Center for Int Studies India Project New Delhi 1962-63, asst lectr rising to lectr in economics Univ of Cambridge 1963-68 (fell Trinity Coll Cambridge) advsr Pakistan Inst of Devpt Economics Karachi 1966-68, Edgeworth Prof Univ of Oxford 1968- (fell Nuffield Coll Oxford), visiting prof Dept of Economics MIT 1968, 1970-71, 1976, 1987; Ford visiting prof Dept of Economics Univ of Calif Berkeley 1986, asst editor Review of Econ Studies 1969-74 (memb Bd 1963-); Econometric Soc: fell 1970-, memb Cncl 1970-74, 1976-, vice pres 1980-82, pres 1983-84; memb Treasy Ctee on Policy Optimization 1976-78, co-editor Econometrice 1980-84; foreign hon memb: American Acad of Arts and Scis 1981, American Econ Assoc 1982; memb Cncl Royal Econ Soc 1982-, chm Assoc of Univ Teachers of Economics 1983-87, vice pres Atlantic Econ Soc 1986-, pres Royal Econ Soc 1989-; Hon DLitt Univ of Warwick; fell Br Acad; *Publications* Manual of Industrial Project Analysis in Developing Countries Vol II (with I M D Little, 1969), On Producer Taxation (Review & Economics Studies, 1972), Notes on Welfare Economics, Information and Uncertainty (Essays in Equilibrium Behaviour under Uncertainty 1974, Arguments for Public Expenditure (contemporay Economics Analysis 1979), Social Benefit-Costs Analysis and the Distribution of Income (World Development 1978), The Economic Uses of Utitilariamism (Ultilitarianism and Beyond 1982), Payroll - Tax Financed Soical Insurance with Variable Retirement (The Scandinavian Journal of Economics, with P A Diamond 1986); *Recreations* reading detective stories, mathematics, playing the piano, travelling; *Style—* Prof James Mirrlees; Nuffield College, 11 Field House Drive, Oxford OX2 7NT (☎ 0865 52436)

MIRZOEFF, Edward O; s of late Eliachar Mirzoeff, of Edgware, Middx, and Penina, *née* Asherov; *b* 11 April 1936; *Educ* Hasmonean GS, Queen's Coll Oxford (BA, MA); *m* 4 June 1961, Judith, da of Harry Topper, of Finchley; 3 s (Nicholas b 1962, Daniel b 1965, Sacha b 1969); *Career* market researcher Social Surveys (Gallup Poll) Ltd 1959-60, asst ed Shoppers' Guide Magazine 1962-63; BBC TV 1963-; prodr and dir of many documentaries incl: Metro-land, A Passion for Churches, The Queen's Realm, The Front Garden, The Englishwoman and the Horse, Police - Harrow Road, The Regiment, Target Tirpitz, The Ritz; series prodr: Choice, Bird's-Eye View, Year of the French, In at the Deep End, Just Another Day, The Richard Dimbleby Lecture; exec prodr Documentary Features 1982, ed 40 Minutes 1985-89; awards: BAFTA awards for best documentary 1982, BAFTA award for best factual series 1986 and 1989, BFI TV award 1988, Samuelson award Birmingham Festival 1988; memb BAFTA (memb Cncl 1988-91); *Recreations* opera, theatre, cinema, country walks, books; *Style—* Edward Mirzoeff, Esq; BBC Televison, Kensington House, Richmond Way, London W14 0AX (☎ 081 895 6242, fax 081 895 6773, telex 265781)

MISCAMPBELL, Gillian Margaret Mary; *née* Gibb; OBE (1982); da of Brig Francis William Gibb (d 1969), of Darkfaulds Cottage, Rosemount, Blairgowrie, Perthshire, and Agnes Winifred Gibb; *b* 31 Dec 1935; *Educ* St Leonards Sch; *m* 5 April 1958, Alexander Malcolm Miscampbell, s of Alexander Miscampbell (d 1965), of Carrick Cottage, Stanley Rd, Hoylake, Cheshire; 3 s (Andrew Ian Farquharson b 18 June 1959, Ian Alexander Francis b 27 Feb 1962, Alexander James b 19 Aug 1964); *Career* vice chm Nat Women's Advsy Ctee Cons Pty 1979-80; chm: Aylesbury Cons Assoc 1975-78, Aylesbury Health Authy 1981-, Bucks CC 1989- (memb 1977-, chm Educ Ctee 1985-89), memb: Cncl Univ of Buckingham 1985-, Area Manpower Bd 1985-88, Bd Milton Keynes Devpt Corp 1990-; *Style—* Mrs Alec Miscampbell, OBE; Colonsay, Quainton, Bucks (☎ 0296 75 318); Aylesbury Vale Health Authy, Ardenham Lane, Aylesbury, Bucks (☎ 0296 437 501); Bucks County Council, County Hall, Aylesbury, Bucks (☎ 0296 383126)

MISCAMPBELL, Norman Alexander; MP (C) Blackpool North 1962-; QC 1974; s of Alexander Miscampbell (d 1965); *b* 20 Feb 1925; *Educ* St Edward's Sch, Trinity Coll Oxford; *m* 1961, Margaret, da of Berenger Kendall; 2 s, 2 da; *Career* barr Inner Temple 1952, contested (C) Newton (Lancs) 1955 and 1959, pps to Attorney-Gen 1972-74; *Style—* Norman Miscampbell Esq, MP; 7 Abbey Road, West Kirby, Cheshire

MISCHLER, Norman Martin; s of Martin Mischler (d 1965), of Brondesbury Park, London, and Sarah Martha, *née* Lambert (d 1959); *b* 9 Oct 1920; *Educ* St Paul's, St Catharine's Coll Cambridge (MA); *m* 30 April 1949, Helen Dora, da of Dr Alfred Sinclair (ka 1944); 1 s (Stephen Martin b 1951), 1 da (Kathryn Noel b 1953); *Career* Maj IA served India and Burma; dir: Burts & Harvey Ltd 1954-66, Burt Boulton & Haywood Ltd 1957-66, Baywood Chemicals 1957-66, PR Chemicals 1958-66; vice chm Burt Boulton & Haywood 1963-66; chm: Harlow Chemical Co Ltd 1972-74, Kalle Infotec Ltd 1972-74; dir: Rochas Perfumes Ltd 1975-79, Berger Jenson & Nicholson Ltd 1975- (chm 1975-84); chm: Hoechst UK Ltd 1975-84 (dep md 1966-75), Hoechst Ireland Ltd 1976-84; memb Cncl Chem Industs Assoc 1975-84, vice chm German Chamber of Indust and Commerce 1977-84; Freeman City of London; Officer's Cross of Fed Order of Merit W Germany; *Recreations* golf, opera, fishing; *Clubs* Hawks, Cambridge; *Style—* Norman Mischler, Esq; Scott House, Bungay, Suffolk (☎ 0986 892767)

MISHCON, Hon Peter Arnold; er s of Baron Mishcon (Life Peer), *qv*; *b* 1946; *m* 1967, Penny Green; 1 s (Oliver b 1968), 3 da (Anna b 1972, Kate b 1973, Eliza b 1977); *Style—* The Hon Peter Mishcon

MISHCON, Hon Russell Orde; yr s of Baron Mishcon (Life Peer), *qv*; *b* 9 July 1948; *Educ* City of London Sch; *m* 6 Nov 1975, Marcia Regina Leigh; 1 s (Joel b 1977), 1 da (Portia b 1979); *Career* slr 1971; sr ptnr: Blatchfords 1974-80, Russell Mishcon & Co 1980- 87; ptnr S J Berwin & Co 1987-; *Recreations* polo; *Clubs* Guards' Polo; *Style—* The Hon Russell Mishcon; S J Berwin & Co, 236 Gray's Inn Rd, London WC1X 8HB (☎ 071 278 0444, fax 071 833 2860, telex 8814928, car 0860 282807)

MISHCON, Baron (Life Peer UK 1978), of Lambeth, Greater London; Victor Mishcon; DL (Gtr London); s of Rabbi Arnold Mishcon and Queenie Mishcon; *b* 14 Aug 1915; *Educ* City of London Sch; *m* 1, 2 s, 1 da; m 2, 1976, Joan Estelle, da of Bernard Monty; *Career* sits as Labour Peer in House of Lords; slr 1937, sr ptnr Mishcon De Reya; memb: Royal Nat Theatre Bd 1968-, S Bank Theatre Bd 1977-82; former chm LCC, and chm of various ctees; former memb: GLC (chm Gen Purposes Ctee), ILEA, Lambeth Borough Cncl (chm Fin Ctee); contested (Lab): NW Leeds 1950, Bath 1951, Gravesend 1955 and 1959; chief oppn spokesman: Home Affrs 1983-90, Legal Affairs 1990-; vice chm All Pty Solictors Parly Gp; former memb various governmental ctees; *Style—* The Rt Hon the Lord Mishcon, DL; 125 High Holborn, London WC1V 6QP (☎ 071 405 3711); House of Lords, London SW1A 0AA

MISIEWICZ, Dr George; *b* 28 March 1930; *Educ* Lord Weymouth's GS, Univ of London (BSc, MB BS); *m* Marjorie Alice; *Career* conslt physician and jt dir Dept of Gastroenterology and Nutrition Central Middx Hosp London; memb External Scientific Staff MRC, pres Br Soc of Gastroenterology 1987-88; ed: Gut 1980-87, Euro Jl of Gastroenterology and Hepatology 1989; hon conslt gastroenterologist: BA, RN; FRCP, FRCPE; *Books* Diseases of the Gut and Pancreas (jt ed); *Recreations* friends, music, paintings, reading, theatre, the country; *Style—* Dr J J Misiewicz; 148 Harley St, London W1N 1AH (☎ 071 935 1207, fax 071 224 1528); Department of Gastroenterology and Nutrition, Central Middlesex Hospital, London NW10 7NS (☎ 081 961 4594, fax 081 961 1317)

MISKIN, George William Semark; JP, DL (1982); s of Cdr G S Miskin (d 1972), and Margaret Edith, *née* Facer (d 1974); *Educ* Haileybury & Imperial Serv Coll, Sch of Navigation Southampton; *m* 26 Aug 1959, Mary Hersey, da of William David Murdoch (d 1942); 1 s (Charles b 28 Sept 1960), 2 da (Suzanne b 25 Sept 1962, Jennifer b 19 June 1965); *Career* navigation offr P & OSN Co 1945-60; London Stock Exchange: joined 1960,memb 1962, ptnr 1972-86; non-exec dir: C & W Walker 1972-85, Possum; chm Frensham Fly Fishers; memb: Ct of Univ of Surrey, KGV Fund for Sailors, Dreadnought Seamans Soc; magistrate 1970, High Sheriff 1981-82; Honourable Co of Master Mariners: Liveryman 1968, Warden 1972, Master 1983-84; *Recreations* fishing, skiing, sailing, bibliophile, carpentry; *Clubs* Fly Fishers, Royal Southern; *Style—* George Miskin, Esq, JP, DL; Hankley Edge, Tilford, Surrey GU102DD (☎ 025 125 2122); Parrish Stockbrokers, 4 London Wallbuildings EC2M 5NX (☎ 071 628 9926, fax 071 588 2449, telex 883787)

MISKIN, His Hon Judge Sir James William; QC (1967); s of late Geoffrey Miskin, of Buxted, Sussex; *b* 11 March 1925; *Educ* Haileybury Coll, Brasenose Coll Oxford; *m* 1, 1951, Mollie Joan, da of Eric Milne; 2 s, 2 da; m 2, 1980, Sheila Joan Collett; *Career* Sub Lt RNVR 1943-46; called to the Bar Inner Temple 1951, rec of Crown Ct 1972-75, leader SE Circuit 1974-75, bencher 1976, rec of London 1975-90; memb Bar Cncl 1964-67 and 1970-73, dep chm Herts QS 1968-71; chm Bd of Discipline LSE 1972-75, appeals steward Br Boxing Bd of Control 1972-75, chm Inner London Probation After Care Ctee 1979-88; HM Lt City of London 1976-, magistrate City of London 1976; Liveryman Worshipful Co of Curriers, Hon Liveryman Worshipful Co of Cutlers; kt 1983; *Style—* His Hon Sir James Miskin, QC; Central Criminal Court, City of London, EC4M 7EH

MISKIN, Raymond John; s of Sidney George Miskin (d 1979), and Hilda, *née* Holdsworth (d 1976); *b* 4 July 1928; *Educ* Woking GS for Boys, Southall Technical Coll (HNC Mech); *m* 14 July 1951 (m dis 1981), Betty; 1 s (Gerald d 1971), 1 da (Karen b 1959); *Career* chartered engr, conslt; sec: Inst of Quality Assurance 1969-71, Inst of Production Engrs 1976-87; hon memb: Inst of Industl Engrs, Indian Inst of Production Engrs; memb: Soc of Manufacturing Engineers; FIMechE, FIProdE, MRAeS, FIQA, FRSA; *Recreations* golf; *Clubs* Athenaeum; *Style—* Raymond Miskin, Esq; c/o Lloyds Bank, Addlestone, Surrey GU16 5UU

MISRA, Dr Prem Chandra; JP (Glasgow 1985-); s of Dr Man Mohan Lal Misra (d 1980), of Hardoi India, and Bindeshawri (d 1970); *b* 24 July 1941; *Educ* KK Degree College Lucknow India (BSc), King George's Med Coll Lucknow India (MB BS), Royal Coll of Surgeons and Physicians Glasgow & Edinburgh (DPM); *m* 24 Jan 1970, Sandhya, da of Mr Manohar Lal Khanna, of Bombay, India; 1 s (Vivek b 1985), 2 da (Deepali b 1970, Nisha b 1980); *Career* demonstrator Dept of Human Physiology King George's Med Coll Lucknow India 1967, resident house surgn in gen surgery Royal Infirmary Wigan 1968-69, resident house physician in gen med Whelley Hosp Wigan 1969-70; Bolton Dist Gen Hosp Farnworth: resident sr house offr of gen psychiatry 1970-71, resident registrar of gen psychiatry 1971-73; Hollymoor Hosp Birmingham: sr psychiatric registrar 1973-76, conslt psychiatrist 1976; memb Exec Ctee Strathclyde Community Relations Cncl 1981-87, pres Indian Assoc of Strathclyde, fell American Gerontological Soc, memb affilate Royal Coll of Psychiatrists; fell: Indian Psychiatric Soc 1980-, RSM; memb American Psychiatric Assoc 1974-, pres Br Soc of Med and Dental Hypnosis 1987-89 (hon sec Div of Psychiatry 1980-, memb Ethical Ctee (Eastern Dist Glasgow) 1980-, life memb Scottish Assoc for Mental Health, fndr Glasgow Assoc for Mental Health; memb: Exec Ctee European Soc of Hypnosis, Int Soc of Hypnosis, Int Sci Ctee of Sexuality and Handicap in Paris, Exec Ctee Br Soc of Res on Sex Educn; *Books* Modern Trends in Hypnosis (ed, with Waxman et al, 1985); *Recreations* classical music, walking in Scottish highlands, travelling to various countries in the world; *Style—* Dr Prem Misra; Deputy Physician Superintendent, Garloch Hospital, Gartloch, Glasgow G69 8EJ (☎ 041 771 0771)

MISTRY, Dhruva; s of Pramodray M Mistry, and Kantaben Mistry; *b* 1 Jan 1957; *Educ* MS Univ of Baroda Fine Arts Faculty (MA), RCA London (MA); *Career* artist in residence and fell Churchill Coll Cambridge and Kettles Yard Cambridge 1984-85; own expos at: Arnolfini Bristol, Walker Art Gallery Liverpool 1986, Nigel Greenwood Gallery London 1987 and 1990, Collins Gallery Glasgow 1988, Laing Art Gallery Newcastle upon Tyne; public collections at: Tate Gallery London, Arts Cncl, Br Cncl, Nat Museum of Wales Cardiff, Walker Art Gallery Liverpool, Contemporary Art Soc London, Hakone Open Air Museum Japan; *Recreations* photography, reading, walking; *Style—* Dhruva Mistry, Esq; The Cottage, Dodds Farm, Fryerning, Ingatestone, Essex CM4 0NW; c/o Nigel Greenwood Gallery, 4 New Burlington St, London W1X 1FE

MITCALFE, Capt John Stanley; OBE (1965), VRD (1964); s of (William) Stanley Mitcalfe, MC (d 1962), of Underwood, Riding Mill, Northumberland, and Mary Catherine Louise, *née* Burn (d 1964); *b* 27 Feb 1927; *Educ* Rugby, BNC Oxford (MA); *m* 1, 30 July 1953 (m dis 1974), Ann, da of William Andrew McClelland, of Westering, Silecroft, Cumbria; 4 da (Mary b 6 March 1954, Susan b 30 Oct 1955, Caroline b 28 Sept 1957, Veronica b 19 Feb 1962); m 2, 30 March 1979, Carol Ann, da of late Frederick Bradley, of Carlisle, Cumberland; *Career* joined RNVR 1944, served in Minesweepers in Far Eastern theatre until 1948, HMS Calliope Tyne Div Headquarters, Cdr and exec offr 1962-63, Capt Tyne Div RNR 1966-70, RNR Aide-de-Camp to The Queen 1971, ret 1972; dir various family Cos Northumberland 1952-70; dist cmmnr Boy Scout Assoc (Hexham), co cmmr sea scouts (Northumberland); *Recreations* game fishing, grouse and pheasant shooting; *Style—* Capt J Stanley Mitcalfe, OBE, VRD; Bradley Ings, 5 Aireside Tce, Cononley, N Yorks BD20 8LY (☎ 0535 632414)

MITCHAM, Heather; da of Louis George Pike, and Dorothy Evelyn, *née* Milverton; *b* 19 Dec 1941; *m* 5 Sept 1964, Anthony John Mitcham, s of Francis John Mitcham; 1 s (Jonathan Brooks b 11 Feb 1971), 1 da (Anna Louise b 7 Feb 1973); *Career* examiner Estate Duty Office 1960-67, called to the Bar Gray's Inn 1964, dep chief clerk Inner London Magistrates Serv 1967-74 (dep trg offr 1970-73); Inner London Juvenile Cts: chief clerk 1978-83, sr chief clerk Thames Div 1983-85, sr chief clerk SW Div 1985-86; met stipendiary magistrate 1986-; *Recreations* gardening, riding and horses, racketball; *Clubs* Sutton and Cheam; *Style—* Mrs Heather Mitcham; Camberwell Green Magistrates Court, D'Eynsford Rd, London SE5 7UP (☎ 071 703 0909)

MITCHARD, Anthony Keith; s of Albert Ernest James Mitchard and Florence, *née* West; *b* 26 Dec 1934; *Educ* King Edward's Sch Bath; *m* 31 March 1956, Kathleen Margaret, da of Albert Henry Smith; 2 s (Michael David b 25 Oct 1963, John Robert b 27 June 1967), 3 da (Andrea Marie b 27 Feb 1958, Susan Elizabeth b 16 Aug 1959, Alison Judith b 16 Aug 1971); *Career* dir Avon Rubber Co Ltd 1974; chief exec Avon Rubber plc 1986; dep chm Community Cncl for Wiltshire; tstee Burnbake Tst; FPRI; chm Bureau de Liaison des Industries du Caoutchou (Brussel); *Recreations* golf, cricket, reading; *Style—* Anthony Mitchard, Esq; Avon Rubber plc, Melksham, Wiltshire SN12 8AA (☎ 0225 703101, fax 0225 702130, telex 44142)

MITCHARD, (Gerald Steven) Paul; s of Gerald Albert Michard, of Charlton, nr Malmesbury, Wilts, and Janet Margaret, *née* Gregory; *b* 2 Jan 1952; *Educ* Taunton Sch, Univ of Oxford (MA); *m* 1, 28 June 1980 (m dis 1985), Sherly Anne, *qv*, da of Dennis Robert Wilkins Chappel; m 2, 2 May 1987, Dorothy Neleitha, da of Leslie Grant, of Hornsey, London N8; 2 s (David b 10 Feb 1988, George Henry Steven b 2 Dec 1990); *Career* slr; asst slr Slaughter and May 1977-84, ptnr Simmons & Simmons 1985- (asst slr 1984-85); memb Law Soc 1987; *Recreations* squash, golf; *Style—* Paul Mitchard, Esq; Simmons & Simmons, 14 Dominion St, London EC2M 2RJ (☎ 071 628 2020)

MITCHARD, Shirley Anne; da of Dennis Robert Wilkins Chappell, and Joan Gladys, *née* Woolcott; *b* 15 Feb 1953; *Educ* Weirfield Sch Taunton, Portsmouth Poly (BA); *m* 28 June 1980 (m dis 1985), (Gerald Steven) Paul Mitchard, *qv*; *Career* Peat Marwick McLintock 1975-79 (tax dept 1979-81), Arthur Andersen & Co 1981-84 (sr mangr 1983), ptnr Clark Whitehall 1987 (joined 1985); memb ICAEW 1978, ACA 1978; *Recreations* interior decoration, gardening, psychic studies, tennis, shopping; *Clubs* Network; *Style—* Ms Shirley Mitchard; 151 De Beauvoir Rd, London, N1 4DL (☎ 071 249 4835); Clark Whitehill 25 New Street Sq, London EC4 (☎ 071 353 1577)

MITCHELL, Adrian; *b* 24 Oct 1932; *Career* Nat Serv RAF 1951-52; reporter 1955-63 (Oxford Mail, Evening Standard), freelance journalist Daily Mail, The Sun, Sunday Times; writer; plays for the theatre: Tyger (NT), Man Friday (7:48 Theatre Co), Mind Your Head (Liverpool Everyman), A Seventh Man (Hampstead), White Suit Blues (Nottingham Playhouse), Uppendown Mooney (Welfare State International), The White Deer (Unicorn Theatre for Children), Hoagy Bix and Wolfgang Beethoven Bunkhaus (Tricycle Theatre), Mowgli's Jungle (Contact Theatre), C'mon Everybody (Tricycle Theatre), Satie Day/Night (Lyric Studio Hammersmith), Anna on Anna (Theatre Workshop Edinburgh); stage adaptations NT: Animal Farm (lyrics), The Mayor of Zalamea, Fuente Ove Juna, The Goverment Inspector; stage adaptions with John Barton of RSC: Morat/Sade, Life's a Dream; other stage adaptations: The Great Theatre of the World (Mediaeval Players), Peer Gynt (Oxford Playhouse), Mirandolina (Bristol Old Vic); other stage shows: The Wild Animal Song Contest (Unicorn Theatre), In the Unlikely Event of an Emergency (South West Music Theatre), King Real (Ongar Youth Theatre), The Last Wild Wood in Sector 88 (Derby Music Theatre); tv plays: Daft as a Brush, Silver Giant, Wooden Dwarf, The Fine Art of Bubble Blowing, Something Down There is Crying (BBC), You Must Believe All This, Glad Day (Thames TV); opera Houdini (with Peter Schat); films: Man Friday (1975), King Real and the Hoodlums (1985); novels: If You See Me Comin' (1962), The Bodyguard (1970), Wartime (1973); Poetry: Poems (1964), Out Loud (1968), Ride the Nightmare (1971), The Apeman Cometh (1975), For Beauty Douglas (collected poems 1953-79) (1982), On the Beach at Cambridge (1984), Nothingmas Day (1984), All My Own Stuff (1991); childrens books incl: The Baron Rides Out (1985), The Baron on the Island of Cheese (1986), The Baron all at Sea (1987), Our Mamoth goes to School (1987), Our Mamoth in the Snow (1989); Granada fell in the arts Univ of Lancaster 1967-69; fell centre for the Humanities Wesleyan Univ USA 1972; res writer Sherman Theatre Cardiff 1974-75, Unicorn Theatre 1982-83; visiting fell Billericay Comp Sch 1978-80, Judith E Wilson fellow Univ of Cambridge 1980-81; *Style—* Adrian Mitchell, Esq; c/o Peters, Fraser and Dunlop, 5th Floor, The Chambers, Chelsea Harbour, Lots Rd, London SW10 0XF (☎ 071 376 7676)

MITCHELL, Andrew; MBE (1984); s of Mitchell Andrew (d 1959), of Scotland, and Catherine Mary Macrae (d 1989); *b* 6 Nov 1925; *Educ* Fettes Coll Edinburgh; *m* 1955, Liv Ragnhild, da of Eilert Holst (d 1942), of Norway; 1 s (Andrew b 1969), 1 da (Katrina b 1965); *Career* Capt The Black Watch ME 1944-46; dir: Childrens Film and TV Fndn Ltd, Garrirights Ltd, Contracts Int Ltd; md Goldcrest Elstree Studios; *Style—* Andrew Mitchell, Esq, MBE; 50 Watermint Quay, Craven Walk, off Clapton Common, London N16 6DD (☎ 081 809 7465); Goldcrest Elstree Studios, Borehamwood, Herts WD6 1JG (☎ 081 953 1600, fax 081 207 0860, telex 922436 EFilms G)

MITCHELL, Andrew John Bower; MP (Cons) Gedling 1987; s of Sir David Bower Mitchell, MP, *qv*, and Pamela Elaine, *née* Haward; great-gf Lord Mayor of London and Master of the Vintners Co; *b* 23 March 1956; *Educ* Rugby, Jesus Coll Cambridge (MA); *m* 27 July 1985, Sharon Denise, da of David Benedict Bennett; 2 da (Hannah Katherine b 1987, Rosie Olivia Louise b 1990); *Career* 1 RTR (SSLC) 1975; pres Cambridge Union 1978, chm Cambridge Univ Cons Assoc, chm The Coningsby Club of Cons Graduates 1983-84; contested (C) Sunderland S 1983 general election; PPS FCO to: Hon William Waldergrove MP 1988-90, to Rt Hon John Wakenham, MP, Sec of State for Energy 1990-; chm Lazard Bros & Co Ltd 1979-87; Liveryman Worshipful Co of Vintners; *Recreations* skiing, sailing, reading; *Clubs* Carlton and District Constitutional, Cambridge Union Soc; *Style—* Andrew Mitchell, Esq, MP; 30 Gibson Square, Islington, London N1 (☎ 071 226 5519); Dovecote Farmhouse, Tithby, Nottinghamshire (☎ 09498 39587); House of Commons, London SW1 (☎ 071 219 4494)

MITCHELL, (John) Angus Macbeth; CB (1979), CVO (1961), MC (1946); s of John Fowler Mitchell, CIE (d 1984), of Bath, and Sheila Macbeth Mitchell, MBE; both parents were joint authors of Monumental Inscriptions in 8 Scot counties; *b* 25 Aug 1924; *Educ* Marlborough, Brasenose Coll Oxford (BA); *m* 1948, Ann Katharine, *qv*, da of Herbert Stansfield Williamson (d 1955), of Oxford; 2 s (Jonathan, Andrew), 2 da (Charlotte, Catherine); *Career* served WWII RAC, Capt NW Europe 1943-46; civil servant Scot Off 1949-84, sec Scot Educn Dept 1976-84; chm of Ct Univ of Stirling 1984-, memb Cmmn on Local Authy Accounts in Scotland 1985-89, chm Scot Action on Dementia 1985-, vice-convener Scot Cncl of Voluntary Orgns 1986-, memb Historic Bldgs Cncl for Scot 1988-; Hon LLD Dundee 1983; Kt Order of Orange-Nassau (Netherlands) 1946; *Books* Procedures for the Reorganisation of Schools in England (1987); *Recreations* old Penguins, genealogy, maps; *Clubs* New (Edinburgh); *Style—* Angus Mitchell, Esq, CB, CVO, MC; 20 Regent Terr, Edinburgh EH7 5BS (☎ 031 556 7671)

MITCHELL, Ann Katharine; da of Herbert Stansfield Williamson (d 1955), of Oxford, and Winfred Lilian, *née* Kenyon (d 1990); *b* 19 Nov 1922; *Educ* Headington Sch Oxford, Univ of Oxford (MA), Univ of Edinburgh (MPhil); *m* 13 Dec 1948, (John) Angus Macbeth Mitchell, CB, CVO, MC, *qv*, 2 s (Jonathan b 1951, Andrew b 1958), 2 da (Charlotte b 1953, Catherine b 1956); *Career* Nat Serv GCHQ 1943-45; sociologist with special knowledge of children's experience of divorce; marriage guidance cnsllr and admin 1958-76, res assoc Univ of Edinburgh 1980-84; memb ctees: Scot Cncl for Single Parents, Family Care, Scot Child and Family Alliance, Scot Family Conciliation Serv; *Books* incl: Someone to Turn To: Experiences of Help before Divorce (1981), Children in the Middle: Living through Divorce (1985), When Parents Split Up: Divorce Explained to Young People (1986), Coping with Separation and Divorce (1986), Families (1987), Points of View: Divorce (1990); *Style—* Mrs Angus Mitchell; 20 Regent Terrace, Edinburgh EH7 5BS (☎ 031 5567671)

MITCHELL, Austin Vernon; MP (Lab) Great Grimsby 1983-; s of Richard Mitchell; *b* 19 Sept 1934; *Educ* Woodbottom Cncl Sch, Bingley GS, Manchester Univ, Nuffield Coll Oxford (DPhil); *m* 1 (m dis), Patricia Jackson; 2 da (Kirri, Susan); m 2, Linda McDougall; 1 s (Jonathan), 1 da (Hannah); *Career* MP (Lab) Grimsby 1977-1983, oppn whip; former Univ lectr in history and politics, journalist with Yorks TV 1969-71 and 1973-77, presenter BBC Current Affrs 1972-73; PPS to Mr Fraser Min of State for Prices and Consumer protection 1977-79, opposition whip, Treasy Lab Solidarity, Fell of the Indust and Parly Tst; former opposition front bench spokesman for Trade and Industry; presenter and interviewer Sky Television 1989-; *Books incl* Westminster Man: A Tribal Anthology of the Commons People (1982), The Case for Labour (1983), Whigs in Opposition 1815-30, Politics and People in New Zealand, Half Gallon Quarter Acre Pavlova, Can Labour Win Again, Britain: Beyond the Blue Horizon, Competitive Socialism; *Recreations* photography, comtemplating exercise; *Style—* Austin Mitchell, Esq, MP; House of Commons, SW1 (☎ 071 219 4559); 15 New Cartergate, Grimsby, S Humberside (☎ 0472 42145); 29B Ashley Gardens, Ambrosden Avenue, London SW1 (☎ 071 828 0773)

MITCHELL, Dr Brian Redman; s of Irvin Mitchell (d 1969), of Marsh House, Oxenhope, Yorks, and Dora Eleanor, *née* Redman (d 1981); *b* 20 Sept 1929; *Educ* Sedbergh, Univ of Aberdeen (MA), Peterhouse Cambridge (PhD); *m* 1, 25 Aug 1952, Barbara, da of Douglas Gordon Hay (d 1946); m 2, 11 Sept 1968, Ann Leslie, da of David Leslie Birney (d 1942); 2 s (David b 1969, Peter b 1972); *Career* Flt Lt RAF, ret 1958; Univ of Cambridge: res offr Dept of Applied Econs 1958-67, univ lectr, fell Trinity College 1967-; *Recreations* watching cricket and rugby football, gardening; *Clubs* MCC; *Style—* Dr Brian Mitchell; 20 High Street, Toft, Cambridge CB3 7RL (☎ 0223 262516); Trinity College, Cambridge (☎ 0223 338502)

MITCHELL, (Richard George) Bruce; s of George Fowler Mitchell (d 1953), of Rugby, and Marjorie Alice, *née* Barker (d 1986); *b* 2 Nov 1923; *Educ* Marlborough, Gonville and Caius Coll Cambridge; *m* 10 June 1950, Sheila, da of Francis Moorhouse Dean, MBE (d 1970); 1 s (Ian Moorhouse b 25 Feb 1957); *Career* mktg exec BXL Plastics Ltd 1963-73, mangr Market Devpt British Industrial Plastics Ltd 1973-80, fedn sec Glass and Glazing Fedn 1981-88; memb Parly Advsy Ctee for Tport Safety; Freeman City of London 1977, Liveryman Worshipful Co Horners 1977; fell Plastics and Rubber Inst 1967; *Books* Plastics in the Building Industry (1968), Glass Reinforced Plastics (jtly, 1970), Developments in Plastics Technology (jtly, 1982); *Recreations* freelance journalism, golf; *Style—* Bruce Mitchell, Esq; Danes Way House, 3 Danes Way, Oxshott, Leatherhead, Surrey KT22 OLU (☎ 0372 842851)

MITCHELL, Charles Herbert; DL (Staffordshire); *b* 18 Feb 1932; *Educ* Shrewsbury Sch, London Univ (BSc); *m* 21 Dec 1958, Mary Rose, *née* Shaw; 2 s (Jonathan b 1960, Julian b 1966), 1 da (Annabel b 1962); *Career* Nat Serv RE 1950-52, cmmnd UK and BAOR TA 1952-60, Capt RE; joined William Walker and Sons Ltd 1950; dir: Century Oils Gp plc, AP Oil (UK) Ltd (chm), Century Autoline Inc, Century Lubricating Oils Inc, Century Mayor Ltd (chm), Century Oils Australia Pty Ltd (chm), Century Oils do Brasil Lubrificantes Industriais Limitada (chm), Century Oils BV, Century Oils (Canada) Inc (chm), Century Oils (Deutschland) GmbH, Century Oils France SA, Century Oils Industries NV, Century Oils Group Services Ltd, Century Oils-Hellas ABEE (chm), Century Oils Holdings (Nederland) BV, Century Oils International Ltd (chm), Century Oils Ltd (chm), Century Oils NV, Century Oils Participacoes S/C Limitada (chm), Century Oils SA (Pty) Ltd (chm), Comptoirs Française d'Importation et de Transformation Réunis SA, Eclipsol Oil Ltd (chm), Etablissements Blachier SA, Gavin SA, PHA Smit Doetinchm BV, Snowdrift Lubricants Ltd (chm), Vérine SA, Wood Mitchell & Co Ltd; apptd gen cmmr Taxes 1977, fndr memb and dep chm of Management Ctee of Business Initiative (Enterprise Tst) 1981, cncl memb N Staffordshire Chamber of Commerce Industry 1981; chm: Industrial Ambass Programme, Local Employers Network, UK rep to European Cmmn for Regeneration 1977-80, Staffordshire Trg and Enterprise Cncl, Staffordshire Partnership Steering Ctee, Staffordshire Steering Ctee Industry Year 1986, Staffordshire Forum Industry Matters; pres of UK Delegation to European Union of Independent Lubricant Manufacturers (UEIL) 1982- (European pres of UEIL 1982-83, 1984-85 and re-appted 1986-87); hon fell Staffordshire Poly; *Recreations* golf, tennis, squash, swimming, shooting, fishing, gardening, music; *Style—* Charles Mitchell, Esq, DL; c/o Century

Oils Gp plc, New Century St, Hanley, Stoke-on-Trent ST1 5HU Staffs (☎ 0782 202521)

MITCHELL, Dr Charles James; s of Col P C Mitchell, MC, of Insch, Aberdeenshire, and Josephine Selina, *née* White; *b* 11 Nov 1946; *Educ* Trinity Coll Glenalmond, Univ of Edinburgh (BSc, MB ChB); *m* 21 Oct 1972, Elisabeth Bullen, da of Frank George Meakin, of Manor House, Southfleet, Kent; 1 s (Alexander b 1977), 1 da (Alice b 1975); *Career* house physician Royal Infirmary Edinburgh 1971, SHO and registrar Kings Coll Hosp London 1972-74, registrar Academic Dept of Med Royal Free Hosp London 1974-76, conslt physician Scarborough Health Authy 1981-, hon conslt physician St James Univ Hosp Leeds 1981- (lectr in med 1976-81); memb: Ctee Br Soc of Gastroenterology, Pancreatic Soc of GB and Ireland (memb Ctee 1981-84), Euro Pancreatic Club; FRCPE 1987 (England 1988); *Books* Pancreatic Disease in Clinical Practice (ed jtly and contrib, 1981), Textbook of Gastroenterology (contrib, 1984); *Recreations* field sports, piping, gardening; *Clubs* Royal Scot Pipers Soc; *Style—* Dr Charles Mitchell; The Old Rectory, Ebberston, Scarborough, North Yorkshire; Leafield, Dalton, Dumfriesshire; Department of Gastroenterology, Scarborough Hospital, Scarborough (☎ 0723 368111)

MITCHELL, Christopher Meredyth; s of Francis John Lindley Mitchell (d 1958), of Old Heathfield, Sussex, and Irene Springett, *née* Butt (d 1949); *b* 16 Nov 1925; *Educ* Rossall, Sidney Sussex Coll Cambridge (MA); *m* 13 Sept 1958, Hilary Margaret, da of John Howard Gaunt, of Manchester; 2 s (David b 1960, Steven b 1969), 1 da (Sarah b 1963); *Career* ptnr Kennedy & Donkin 1958, (jt sr pntr 1976-86), dir Kennedy & Donkin Group 1987-90; chm: Assoc of Consulting Engrs 1977-78, Br Conslts Bureau 1988-89; pres Br section Societé Des Ingénieurs et Scientifiques de France 1988-89; pres Woking Mind, chm Godalming-Joigny Friendship Assoc; memb: Woking UDC 1968-74, Woking Borough Cncl 1974-82; mayor of Woking 1974-75; Freeman City of London, Liveryman Worshipful Co of Engrs 1988; FIEE; *Recreations* astronomy, ornithology, music, European languages; *Style—* Christopher Mitchell, Esq; Two Roods, 20 Warren Rd, Guildford, Surrey (☎ 0483 504407); Kennedy & Donkin Gp, Westbrook Mills, Godalming, Surrey (☎ 0483 425900, fax 0483 425136, telex 859373 KDHO G)

MITCHELL, Sir David Bower; MP (C) N W Hampshire 1983-; s of James Mitchell (d 1959), and Mona Elizabeth Blackett, *née* Bower (d 1956); gs of Sir Alfred L Bower and Dorcas M Bower, *née* Blackett (see Blacketts of Wylam-earlier Debretts); *b* 20 June 1928; *Educ* Aldenham; *m* 1954, Pamela Elaine, da of Dr Clifford Haward; 2 s (Andrew, Graham), 1 da (Suki); *Career* former wine shipper and dir El Vino Co Ltd; memb St Pancras Cncl 1956-59, MP (C) Basingstoke 1964-1983, oppn whip 1965-67, PPS to Social Servs Sec 1970-74, chm Cons Smaller Business Ctee 1974-79; Parly under sec of state: Indust 1979-81, NI 1981-83, Tport 1983-; min of state Tport 1986-; kt 1988; *Clubs* Carlton; *Style—* Sir David Mitchell, MP; 1 Hare Peace, London EC4 Y1BT; Berry Horn Cottage Odiham, Hants (☎ 0256 702161)

MITCHELL, David Ronald; s of Sir Frank Herbert Mitchell, KCVO, CBE (d 1951), of Forest House, Crowborough, Sussex, and Grace Penelope, *née* Maffey (d 1959); *b* 26 Sept 1919; *Educ* Eton, Royal Sch of Mines, Imperial Coll (ARSM, BSc); *m* 29 Aug 1953, Joyce Rosamund Amy (Joy), da of Sir Edgar Waterlow, BT (d 1953), of Winscombe House, Crowborough, Sussex; *Career* Opencast mining in Leics, Miny of Fuel and Power 1942-43, Amalgamated Tin Mines of Nigeria (part of London Tin Gp) 1943-45; chm: Anglo Oriental (Malaya) Ltd 1959-67 (joined 1947, dir 1953), London Tin Corp 1972-76 (previously chief exec); dir Chartered Bank and Standard Chartered plc 1974-88; chm Henham Conservation Soc 1978-81; fell Inst of Mining and Metallurgy; *Recreations* music, gardening, previously golf; *Clubs* MCC, City of London; *Style—* David R Mitchell, Esq; Wood End Cottage, Henham, Bishop's Stortford, Herts CM22 6AZ (☎ 0279 850254)

MITCHELL, David William; CBE (1983); s of William Baxter Mitchell (d 1983), and Betty Steel, *née* Allan (d 1959); *b* 4 Jan 1933; *Educ* Merchiston Castle Sch Edinburgh; *m* 1965, Lynda Katherine Marion, da of Herbert John Laurie Guy (d 1975); 1 da (Louisa-Jayne b 1972); *Career* cmmnd (NS) RSF 1950; memb Bd Western Regional Hosp 1965-72, pres Timber Trades Benevolent Soc of UK 1974, Scot Cncl CBI 1979-85, dir Mallinson-Denny (Scotland) 1977-90, Hunter Timber Scotland 1990-; pres: Scot Timber Trade Assoc 1980-82, Scot Cons and Unionist Assoc 1981-83; memb: Scot Cncl (Devpt and Indust) 1984-, bd Cumbernauld New Town 1985 (chm 1987-), treas Scot Cons Pty 1990-; *Recreations* fishing, shooting, golf; *Clubs* Western (Glasgow), Prestwick, Royal and Ancient (St Andrews); *Style—* David Mitchell, Esq, CBE; Dunmullen House, Blanefield, Stirlingshire G63 9AJ; Grangemouth Sawmills, Earls Rd, Grangemouth FK3 8XF (☎ 0324 483294)

MITCHELL, Air Cdre Sir (Arthur) Dennis; KBE (1977), CVO (1961), DFC (1944 and bar 1945), AFC (1943); s of late Col A Mitchell, DSO, RA; gggs of Col Hugh Henry Mitchell (who cmd 4 Bde at Battle of Waterloo and who was only Bde Cdr below the rank of Gen to be mentioned in Duke of Wellington's despatches), and Lady Harriet Somerset, da of 5 Duke of Beaufort; *b* 26 May 1918; *Educ* Nautical Coll Pangbourne, RAF Coll Cranwell; *m* 1949, Mireille Caroline, da of Comte Henri Cornet de Ways Ruart; 1 s (Michael); *Career* joined RAF 1936, served WWII, Dep Capt The Queen's Flight 1956-59, Capt 1962-64; ADC to HM The Queen 1958-62, extra equerry 1962-; md Aero Systems (SA); founder of Brussels Airways (SA), Aero Distributors (SA); *Recreations* golf; *Clubs* Naval and Military, RAF; *Style—* Air Cdre Sir Dennis Mitchell, KBE, CVO, DFC, AFC; 10 Chemin des Chasseurs, 1328 Ohain, Belgium (☎ 02 653 13 01; off: 02 653 00 33)

MITCHELL, Sir Derek Jack; KCB (1974), CB (1967, CVO 1966); s of Sidney Mitchell; *b* 5 March 1922; *Educ* St Paul's, Christ Church Oxford; *m* 1944, Miriam, da of E F Jackson; 1 s, 2 da; *Career* served WWII RAC; sr advsr Shearson Lehman Bros Int 1979-; dir: Bowater Industs plc 1979-, Bowater Incorporated 1984-, Standard Chartered plc 1979-; ind dir The Observer 1981-; memb: Nat Theatre Bd 1977-, Cncl UCL 1978-82, PLA 1979-82; 2 perm sec Treasury 1973-77, econ min, head UK Treasury and Supply Delgn, exec dir IMF and World Bank Washington 1969-72; formerly with Miny Agric and Fish and Dept Econ Affrs; former princ private sec to: chllr Exchequer (Reginald Maudling), and to PMs, Rt Hon Harold Wilson and Rt Hon Sir Alec Douglas-Home; joined Treasury 1947; *Clubs* Garrick; *Style—* Sir Derek Mitchell, KCB, CB, CVO; One Broadgate, London EC2M 7HA (☎ 071 260 2580, telex 899621)

MITCHELL, Duncan; s of John Sangster Mitchell, of Troon, Ayrshire, Scotland, and Agnes Ramsay (d 1987); *b* 10 Dec 1932; *Educ* Kilmarnock Acad, Glasgow Royal Tech Coll, Dundee Inst of Art and Technol (Dip Arch); *m* 14 Oct 1961, Vivian, da of Rubin Ter Petrossian (d 1940), of Baku, USSR; 2 da (Rona b 8 Nov 1962, Sharon b 7 Aug 1969); *Career* architect; O'Connor & Kilham NY 1961-64, res mangr Wilmafar Teheran Iran 1965-69, sr ptnr Wilson Mason & Ptnrs London 1987- (memb 1964-65, ptnr 1969-74, ptnr Middle East 1974-79, ptnr London 1979-89); memb RIBA 1960; *Recreations* sailing, gardening, photography; *Clubs* Caledonian, Rugby London; *Style—* Duncan Mitchell, Esq; Falconwood, Poyle Lane, Burnham, Bucks (☎ 06236 61363); 3 Chandos St, Cavendish Square, London W1M OJU (☎ 071 637 1501, fax 071 631 0325, telex 262597 WILMAP G)

MITCHELL, Geoffrey Bentley; s of Arthur Hale Mitchell (d 1990), and Eunice Bentley, *née* Wood (d 1989); *b* 20 June 1944; *Educ* Univ of Adelaide (BA); *m* 26 Jan 1967, Diedre Maria, *née* McKenna; 2 s (Mark James b 19 Oct 1971, Matthew Paul b 13 Oct 1973), 1 da (Melissa Kate b 22 Sept 1977); *Career* articled clerk Thomas Sara Macklin & Co Adelaide S Aust, Univ of Adelaide 1966-77 (lectr, sr lectr), reader The Flinders Univ S Aust 1977-81, sec gen International Accounting Standards Ctee 1981-85, tech dir ICAEW 1985-90, sr mangr Accounting Policies Chief Accountants Dept Barclays Bank plc 1991-; memb Inst of CA in Aust 1967, FCA 1982; *Books* Principles of Accounting (prentice hall of Aust, 1981); *Recreations* tennis; *Clubs* Naval Military and Air Force; *Style—* Geoffrey Mitchell, Esq; Scriventon Oast, Stockland Green, Speldhurst, Tunbridge Wells TN3 0TU (☎ 0892 86 3223); Barclays Bank plc, Chief Accountants Dept, Barclays House, 1 Wimbourne Rd, Poole, Dorset BH15 2BB (☎ 0202 671212)

MITCHELL, Geoffrey Roger; s of Horace Stanley Mitchell (d 1974), of Fordingbridge, and Madge Amy, *née* Rogers (d 1984); *b* 6 June 1936; *Educ* Exeter Cathedral Choristers' Sch, Brentwood Sch; *Career* Nat Serv leading cadet educnl RN 1954-56; counter tenor lay clerk Ely Cathedral 1957-60; counter tenor vicar choral St Paul's Cathedral 1961-66, gen mangr John Alldis Choir 1966-, prof RAM and conductor chamber choir 1972-, conductor New London Singers 1972-87, dir Geoffrey Mitchell Choir 1975-, choral mangr BBC 1977-; conductor: Trinity Coll Music vocal ensemble 1977-, Camerata Antiqua Curitiba Brazil 1989-; vice chm nat fedn Cathedral Old Chorister Assocs 1987-; hon ARAM 1981; *Recreations* food, collecting antiques and prints, swimming; *Style—* Geoffrey Mitchell, Esq; 49 Chelmsford Rd, Woodford, London E18 2PW (☎ 081 505 4430); BBC, 16 Langham St, London W1A 1AA (☎ 071 927 4370, fax 071 637 3009, telex 265 781 CPLS)

MITCHELL, Dr (Robert) Gordon; s of Robert Stanley Mitchell (d 1948), of Levin, N Is, NZ, and Rina Hinemoa, *née* Bagnall; *b* 28 Oct 1921; *Educ* Loughborough GS, Univ of Manchester (LDS, MB ChB), RCS (FDS); *m* 12 May 1956, Elizabeth Burchell, da of Frank Stanley Edmonds (d 1936); 2 da (Susanne (Mrs Price) b 1957, Juliet (Mrs Burnham) b 1959); *Career* Capt RADC 1945-48; sr registrar oral surgery Eastman Dental Hosp London 1953-56, conslt surgn and dental supt Birmingham Dental Hosp 1957-87, conslt in oral surgery and oral med The Priory Hosp Birmingham Droitwich Private Hosp 1988-; chm: Assoc of Dental Hosps UK 1969-72, Examiner Central Examining Bd for Dental Hygiene 1971-75; memb: Standing Dental Advsy Ctee DOH 1972-81, Dental Advsy Ctee Med Protection Soc 1981-86, Exec Ctee Birmingham Central Health Dist 1969-75; chm Div of Dentistry Univ of Birmingham 1975-81; hon sr lectr Univ of Birmingham; BMA, BDA; FBAOMS, memb Worcs Odontological Soc; *Recreations* cricket, ornithology, gardening; *Style—* Dr Gordon Mitchell; The Hill House, Stoke Rd, Wychbold, Droitwich, Worcs WR9 OBT (☎ 052 786 211); The Priory Hospital, Priory Rd, Edgbaston, Birmingham

MITCHELL, (George) Grant; s of Prof George Archibald Grant Mitchell, OBE, TD, of Fellpark Rd, Northen Moor, Manchester 23, and Mary *née* Cumming (d 1977); *b* 22 Sept 1939; *Educ* William Hulmes GS Manchester, Univ of Manchester Med Sch (MB ChB); *m* 14 July 1982, Sandra Joan; 1 s (Andrew b 1975), 2 da (Caroline b 1963, Victoria b 1965); *Career* house surgn and physician 1962-64: Manchester Royal Infirmary, Oldham Royal Infirmary, St Mary's Hosp; Geigy res fell Manchester Royal Infirmary 1964-65; princ in gen practice Altrincham Cheshire 1965-68; sr house offr and registrar 1968-73: Withington Hosp, St Mary's Hosp, Crumpsall Hosp; sr registrar in obstetrics Withington and Oldham Hosps 1973-76; conslt obstetrician and gynaecologist Salford Royal Hosp and Hope Hosp Salford 1976; hon lectr in obstetrics and gynaecology Univ of Manchester 1976-, dir Assisted Reproduction Unit Hope Hosp Salford, examiner RCOG 1978; memb Manchester Ctee Action Res for the Crippled Child 1979-; memb North of England Obsetrical and Gynaecological Soc 1973, FRCSEd 1974, FRCOG 1984 (MRCOG 1971); *Recreations* travel, music, photography; *Style—* Grant Mitchell, Esq; 16 St John St, Manchester M3 4EA; Hope Hospital, Salford M6 8HD; Salford Royal Hospital, Chapel St, Salford M6 9EP (☎ 061 834 4282/061 787 5259)

MITCHELL, James Bryan; s of Lt Norman Keith Mitchell, of Southampton, and Lt Daphne Jean Mitchell, *née* Howie; *b* 9 April 1951; *Educ* St Joseph's Coll Beulah Hill, Imperial Coll, Univ of London (BSc), LSE (LLB); *m* 19 May 1979, Elaine Louise, da of Herbert Francis Jones (d 1973); 1 s (James Robert Seymour b 26 May 1989), 1 da (Alexandra Frances Diana-Rose b 4 April 1986); *Career* admitted slr 1980; ptnr Barlow Lyde & Gilbert 1984-; memb Law Soc, ARCS 1973, FSS 1974; *Clubs* RAC, Pall Mall; *Style—* James Mitchell, Esq; Rushmere, 62 Pelhams Walk, Esher, Surrey KT10 8QD (☎ 0372 68984), Bariow Lyde & Gilbert Solicitors, Beafort House, 15 St Botoph St, London EC3A 7EE (☎ 071 247 2277, fax 071 782 8500, car 0860 228683)

MITCHELL, Jeremy George Swale Hamilton; s of (George) Oswald Mitchell (d 1969), of Manchester and Bradford, and Josephine Garner (d 1962); *b* 25 May 1929; *Educ* Ampleforth, Brasenose and Nuffield Colls Oxford (MA); *m* 1, 28 July 1956 (m dis 1988), Margaret Mary, *née* Ayres; 3 s ((Paul) Laurence Damian b 1957, d 1986, Dominic Francis John b 1959, Alcuin Richard b 1964), 1 da ((Catherine) Veronica Mary b 1958); m 2, 16 March 1989, Janet Rosemary Powney, *née* Blower; *Career* Mil Serv 2 Lieut RA 1948-49; dep res dir and dir of info Consumers' Assoc 1958-65, asst sec Nat Econ Devpt Office 1965-66, scientific sec then sec Social Sci Res Cncl 1966-74, dir consumer affrs Office of Fair Trading 1974-77, dir Nat Consumer Cncl 1977-86, consumer policy advsr 1986-; vice chm Nat Cncl on Gambling; memb: Ind Ctee for the Supervision of Telephone Info Servs, Direct Mail Servs Standards Bd, Life Assur and Unit Tst Regulatory Orgn Monitoring Ctee, Exec Ctee Voice of the Listener; visiting fell: Euro Inst for the Media Univ of Manchester, Centre for Int Res in Communications and Info Technol Melbourne; FSA; *Books* Social Science Research and Industry (jt ed 1971), Betting (1972), Marketing and the Consumer Movement (ed 1978), Electronic Banking and the Consumer (1988), Money and the Consumer (ed 1988), The Consumer and Financial Services (ed 1990), The Single European Market for Financial Services (1991); *Clubs* Savile; *Style—* Jeremy Mitchell, Esq, FSA; 214 Evering Road, London E5 8AJ (☎ 081 806 5577, fax 081 806 8093); Pantiles, Edgefield Green, Norfolk NR24 2AG (☎ 026 387 4126)

MITCHELL, John Anthony; s of Dennis George Mitchell (d 1978), and Jean Louise, *née* Tinker; *b* 27 Dec 1946; *Educ* King's Coll Taunton, Brasenose Coll Oxford (BA); *m* 24 Feb 1968 (separated), Philippa Lyndsey, da of Harry Richard Minchin, of the Isle of Wight; 2 s (Bendor b 1969, Adam b 1982), 2 da (Samantha Jane b 1968, Jasmin b 1985); *Career* dir Lloyds Merchant Bank Ltd, London, dep chm Lloyds International Ltd Sydney; *Recreations* sailing, golf, reading; *Clubs* Royal Solent Yacht, Royal Sydney Yacht Squadron; *Style—* John Mitchell, Esq; 58 Willeshall Road, London SW4; 40/66 Queen Victoria Street, London EC4 (☎ 071 248 2244)

MITCHELL, John Mackenzie; s of James Lindsay Mitchell (d 1942), and Dorothy Frances, *née* Clinch (d 1989); *b* 2 March 1924; *Educ* Erith GS, Ertih & Dartford Tech Coll, Univ of London (BSc), City & Guilds Coll (DIC); *m* 19 March 1949, Barbara Oqiluie, da of Arthur Paul Miller; 1 s (Paul Lindsay b 25 July 1951), 1 da (Rosemary Christine 7 March 1954); *Career* General Electric Co Ltd Erith Kent: apprentice engr 1940-45, turbine design engr 1946-55, mangr and chief engr Power Plant Division 1963-65 (chief eng 1955-63); dir and chief mechanical engr C A Parsons & Co Ltd Newcastle upon Tyne 1971-74 (chief turbine engr 1965-71), engr devpt dir NEI

Parsons Ltd Newcastle upon Tyne 1984-87 (engrg dir 1974-84); engrg conslt: NEI Parsons Ltd 1987-, Rolls Royce plc Derby 1987-; chm Tech Ctee No5 (Steam Turbines) Int Electrotechnical Cmmn 1976-86, Parsons Memeorial Lecture 1980; FIMechE (MIMechE 1948), FENG 1981; *Books* author of numerous technical papers; *Recreations* travel, industrial archaeology, antiquaxian horology; *Style*— John Mitchell, Esq; 8 Linden Way, Ponteland, Newcastle upon Tyne NE20 9DP (☎ 0661 23824)

MITCHELL, Dr John Matthew; CBE (1975); s of Clifford George Arthur Mitchell (d 1933), and Grace Maud, *née* Jamson (d 1976); *b* 22 March 1925; *Educ* Ilford Co HS, Worcester Coll Oxford, Queens' Coll Cambridge (MA), Vienna Univ (PhD); *m* 5 April 1952, Eva, da of Dr Friedrich V Rupprecht (d 1964); 3 s (Oliver James Clifford b 1952, Gregory Charles Matthew b 1954, Dominic John Frederick b 1965), 1 da (Clarissa Maria b 1956); *Career* WWII Naval Intelligence 1943-46; Br Cncl served: Austria, Egypt, Yugoslavia, E Pakistan, Federal Republic of Germany, Britain (controller educn sci and med div); asst dir gen Br Cncl, ret; currently translator and conslt in int affrs; fell Wolfson Coll Cambridge 1972-73; FIL; *Books* International Cultural Relations (1986); *Recreations* golf, tennis, theatre, chess, bridge; *Clubs* National Liberal, Tandridge GC; *Style*— Dr John Mitchell, CBE; The Cottage, Pains Hill Corner, Limpsfield, Surrey RH8 0RB (☎ 0883 723 354)

MITCHELL, John Wallace; s of George Harold Mitchell (d 1974), of Hove, and Martha Maude, *née* Wallace (d 1984); *b* 31 May 1931; *Educ* Brighton Hove and Sussex GS; *m* 1989, Dheirdre Margaret Jessett, *née* Brown; 1 da (Alison Mairi Wallace b 1990); *Career* telecommunications (radar) engr coast def SE Eng REME 1949-51; CA; Chater Knight & Co 1951-57, Remington Rand Univac Computers 1957-60, Rank Orgn (Mgmnt) Ltd 1960-63, Harold Whitehead & Ptnrs Mgmnt Conslts 1963-67, Thornton Baker Assocs 1967-77, Stoy Horwath Ltd 1977-82, Wallace Mitchell & Co 1982-89; contested local cncl elections 1957; vice chm Ward Ctee 1989; memb: Brighton Hove and Dist Scot Assoc, Sussex Assoc Scot Soc (fndr chm), Aldrington Scot Dance Club, Brighton and Hove Motor Club; treas: United Wards Club of City of London, Livery Music Section, cncl City Livery Club; former: chm Brighton Velo Club, sec Br League Racing Cyclists (Southern Section); chm Livery Motoring Section; Freeman City of London 1977; Liveryman: Worshipful Co of Chartered Accountants 1977, Worshipful Co of Carmen 1986; FCA 1957, FBCS 1958, FInstD 1962, FIMC 1965, FVRS 1972, FMS 1975, WPA 1980, MIAM 1985, FSA (Scotland) 1988, Euro IE 1989; KLJ 1990, KSJ 1990; *Books* Whetherly Books of Scottish Country Dance (Nos 1-23, 1967-90), A Course of Instruction in Scottish Dancing (1984 and 1988); *Recreations* teaching Scottish dancing, motor sport, charitable work; *Clubs* Carlton, RAC, City Livery; *Style*— John Mitchell, Esq; Whetherly House, 52 Shirley Drive, Hove, Sussex BN3 6UF (☎ 0273 553862)

MITCHELL, Jonathan Stuart; s of Rev Ronald Frank Mitchell, and Margery Mabel, *née* Callaghan; *b* 29 Jan 1947; *Educ* Mill Hill Sch, Trinity Coll Dublin (BA, MA); 1 s (Christian Stuart b 21 Nov 1980), 1 da (Emily Katherina b 4 April 1982); *Career* barr Grays Inn, practising SE circuit 1974-; mktg div Couraulds Textiles 1969-72, PR John Laing 1972-73; memb: Exec Ctee SDP Southwark 1981-87, local govt candidate SDP Dulwich 1982, 1984, 1986, SLD 1988-89, Herne Hill Baptist Church; *Recreations* gardening, swimming, rowing; *Style*— Jonathan Mitchell, Esq; 35 Pickwick Rd, Dulwich, London SE21 7JN; 11 South Square, Grays Inn, London WC1R 3EV (☎ 071 831 2311)

MITCHELL, Keith Kirkman; OBE (1979); s of John Stanley Mitchell, and Annie Mitchell; *b* 25 May 1927; *Educ* Loughborough Coll; *m* 1950, Hannah Forrest; 2 s; *Career* teacher physical educn Wisbech GS 1950-52, dir of physical educn Manchester YMCA 1952-55, lectr in physical educn Univ of Leeds 1955-; CCPR: chm Exec Ctee 1981-87 (memb 1971-), chm Games & Sports Div 1976-81, vice pres 1989-; memb: Sports Cncl 1975-87 (Policy & Resources Ctee 1985-87), Nat Olympic Ctee 1987-; Federation Internationale de Basketball: qualified as referee 1956, cmmr 1969-, memb Euro Tech Cmmn 1969-, memb World Tech Cmmn 1969-79, tech delegate to Olympic Games 1972-84, vice pres World Tech Cmmn 1976-84 (ex officio memb 1984-), memb Euro Exec Cmmn 1984-, memb Central Bd 1984-, conf lectr; hon gen sec English Basketball Assoc 1953-84, mangr GB Olympic Team 1960-68; chm: Leeds Amateur Sports Cncl 1965-80, Yorkshire Basketball League 1965-, Sports Devpt Ctee Yorkshire & Humberside Regnl Cncl of Sport & Recreation, British & Irish Basketball Fedn 1973-75, 1979-81 and 1987-, Govrs of Leeds Athletics Inst 1977-80; vice pres: Univs Athletic Union 1960-, English Mini Basketball Assoc; pres: Leeds City Sports Fedn 1976-, Yorkshire & Humberside Sports Fedn 1980- (chm 1968-80), Cwlth Basketball Fedn 1980-, English Basketball Assoc 1985-; *Recreations* fishing, golf, cutting the lawn and sitting on it, food and wine; *Style*— Keith Mitchell, Esq, OBE; 7 Park Crescent, Guiseley, Leeds

MITCHELL, Marilyn Margaret; da of David Glyndwr Walters, of Ottawa, Canada, and Ada Cecelia, *née* Wilson; *b* 11 July 1944; *Educ* St Augustines Convent Ealing, Charing Cross Hosp Med Sch (MB BS, DCH); *m* 1, 1976 (m dis 1979); m 2, 11 Feb 1981, Ian Mitchell, s of Albert Mitchell, of Sheringham, Norfolk; 1 step s (Joel b 1973), 1 s (Janna b 1983), 2 da (Rachel Clare b 1977, Beth b 1985); *Career* house surgn Charing Cross Hosp 1970-71, SHO med and paediatrics Whittington Hosp 1971-72, SHO Barts Hosp and Hackney 1973, registrar psychiatry N Middx Hosp 1974, gp 1975, SHO registrar and sr registrar W Suffolk Hosp and Cambridge 1976, assoc specialist child and family psychiatry Royal Ottawa Hosp 1980; locum conslt: Child and Family Guidence Clinic Esher 1931, adult psychiatry Cornwall 1982-83; Trengweath Hosp 1984-; BMA award for res in mental health 1989; med rep Minds Eye Gp; MRCPsych, memb Med Defence Union; *Recreations* rambling, opera, housecrafts and clinery skills; *Style*— Mrs Marilyn Mitchell; South Point, Beach Road, Carlyon Bay, Cornwall PL25 3PJ (☎ 0726 815624), Trengweath Hospital, Penryn St, Redruth Cornwall TR15 (☎ 0209 219232)

MITCHELL, Sheriff (James Lachlan) Martin; RD (1969); s of Lachlan Martin Victor Mitchell, OBE, MB (d 1956); *b* 13 June 1929; *Educ* Cargilfield, Sedbergh, Univ of Edinburgh (MA, LLB); *Career* Cdr RNR (ret 1974); advocate 1957-74, standing jr counsel in Scotland to Admty Bd 1963-74; Sheriff Lothians and Peebles 1974 Floating Sheriff 1974-78, Sheriff at Edinburgh 1978; *Recreations* fishing, photography, the gramophone; *Clubs* New (Edinburgh), Highland (Inverness); *Style*— Sheriff Martin Mitchell, RD; 3 Great Stuart St, Edinburgh EH3 6AP (☎ 031 225 3384); Sheriff's Chambers, Sheriff Ct, Lawnmarket, Edinburgh EH1 2NS (☎ 031 226 7181)

MITCHELL, Lady; Mary; *née* Pringle; da of late William Pringle, of Whytbank and Yair Selkirkshire; *m* 1947, Col Sir Harold Paton Mitchell, 1 and last Bt (d 1983); 1 da (Mary-Jean b 1951 d 1990, m Peter Brian Green; 2 s); *Career* DStJ; *Recreations* travel, gardening, reading; *Style*— Lady Mitchell; Maison Gornerwald, 3920, Zermatt, Valais, Switzerland; Prospect, Ocho Rios, Jamaica; Marshall's Island, PO Box HM 262, Hamilton HMAX, Bermuda

MITCHELL, Mona Ann; CVO (1985, LVO 1976); da of Maj-Gen Francis Neville Mitchell, CB, CBE, DSO (d 1954), and Ann Christian, *née* Livingstone-Learmonth (d 1988); *b* 20 Feb 1938; *Educ* North Foreland Lodge; *Career* sec: to Mr Fulke Walwyn, CVO, Racehorse Trainer 1958-62, to Mr E Hardy Amies (now Sir Hardy Amies, KCVO) couturier 1963-68; private sec extra lady-in-waiting to HRH Princess Alexandra 1974- (sec and extra lady-in-waiting 1968-74); *Recreations* gardening in Somerset; *Clubs* Army and Navy; *Style*— Miss Mona Mitchell, CVO; Valley Farm, Blackford, Yeovil, Somerset BA22 7EF (☎ 0963 40304)

MITCHELL, Nigel Campbell; s of Lt Cdr Malcolm Alexander Mitchell RN, of Perth, Scot, and Wilhelmina Winifred, *née* Thompson; *b* 10 July 1953; *Educ* St Edwards Sch Oxford, LSE (LLB); *m* 25 June 1988, Prudence Gaynor, da of Clement Rodney Spencer, of Edgbaston, Birmingham; *Career* called to the Bar Lincolns Inn 1978, in practice at 3 Paper Bldgs Temple 1978-; *Recreations* deep sea fishing, scuba diving, golf; *Clubs* RAC; *Style*— Nigel Mitchell, Esq; 3 Paper Buildings, Temple, London EC4Y 7EU (☎ 071 583 8055, car 0836 206 765)

MITCHELL, Norman; s of Walter Arnold Driver (d 1961), of Sheffield, and Elizabeth, *née* Slinn (d 1959); *b* 27 Aug 1918; *Educ* Carter Knowle Cncl Sch Sheffield, Nether Edge GS, Univ of Sheffield, Guildhall Sch of Music & Drama (LGSM); *m* 31 Aug 1946, Pauline Margaret, da of William George Southcombe; 1 s (Christopher b 22 May 1948), 1 da (Jacqueline Margaret b 28 Jan 1955); *Career* serv WWII: Lance Corpl 10 FD Surgical Unit 1939-45 (Western Desert 1940-43, Italy 1943-45), Army Bureau of Current Affrs Play Unit 1945-47; actor; RSC Stratford-upon-Avon and tour of Aust 1948-50, BBC Drama Rep Co 1952 and 53; over 2000 TV transmissions incl: Vanity Fair, All Creatures Great and Small; over 100 films incl: Oliver, St Trinian's series, Carry On series; West End theatre incl: A View from the Bridge and The Visit for Peter Brook, Shadow of Heroes for Sir Peter Hall, The Clandestine Marriage for Sir Anthony Quayle; dir of charities: Royal Gen Theatrical Fund, Entertainments Charities Tst; cncllr Br Actors Equity Assoc 1983-92 (memb exec 1983-85 and 1985-87); memb: Cinema ITV Veterans, Monte Cassino Venerans; Africa Star (8th Army Clasp), Italy Star, VM; *Books* Amos Goes To War (1987); *Recreations* collecting books (fine editions); *Clubs* Savage, Green Room, Folio, BBC; *Style*— Norman Mitchell, Esq; Kingfisher Cottage, 29 Summer Gardens, East Molesey, Surrey KT8 9LT (☎ 081 398 4930); Eric L'Epine Smith & Carney Associaters, 10 Wyndham Place, London W1H 1AS (☎ 071 724 0739)

MITCHELL, Patricia Anne; da of Derek Fairburn (d 1984), and Margaret Crossley, *née* Greenwood (d 1987); *b* 19 Feb 1957; *Educ* Sheffield HS (GPDST), Univ of Durham (BA); *m* 26 June 1982, Andrew Robert Mitchell, s of Malcolm Mitchell, of London; *Career* admitted slr 1981; ptnr Warner Cranston 1988-; memb Action Resource Centre; memb Law Soc; *Style*— Mrs Patricia Mitchell; Laurel House, North Hill, Highgate, London N6 4BS (☎ 071 341 1700); 14 Dominion St, London EC2M 2EJ (☎ 071 628 2020, fax 071 588 4129, telex 888562 SIMMON G)

MITCHELL, The Very Rev Patrick Reynolds; s of Lt-Col Percy Reynolds Mitchell, DSO (d 1954), of Whitestaunton Manor, Chard, Somerset, and Constance Margaret, *née* Kerby (d 1955); *b* 17 March 1930; *Educ* Eton, Merton Coll Oxford (MA), Wells Theological Coll; *m* 1, 1959, Mary Evelyn (d 1986), da of John Savile Phillips (d 1960); 3 s (Andrew Patrick b 1964, Julian Mark b 1968, Nicholas David b 1970), 1 da (Sarah Jane b 1962); m 2, 1988, Mrs Pamela Douglas- Pennant, da of late A G Le Marchant, of Wolford Lodge, Honiton, Devon; *Career* Nat Serv Welsh Gds 1948-49; curate St Mark's Mansfield 1954-57, priest vicar Wells Cathedral, chaplain Wells Theological Coll 1957-61, vicar St James' Milton Portsmouth 1961-67, vicar Frome Selwood Somerset 1967-73, dean of Wells 1973-89, dean of Windsor and register of the Most Noble Order of the Garter 1989-; sr domestic chaplain to HM The Queen 1989-; hon Freeman City of Wells 1986; res fell Merton Coll Oxford 1984; FSA; *Recreations* family, music, gardening; *Style*— The Very Rev Patrick Mitchell; The Deanery, Windsor Castle, Berks SL4 1NJ (☎ 0753 865 561)

MITCHELL, Dr Peter Dennis; s of late Christopher Gibbs Mitchell, OBE, and late Beatrice Dorothy, *née* Taplin; *b* 29 Sept 1920; *Educ* Queens Coll Taunton, Jesus Coll Cambridge (BA, PhD); *m* 4 Nov 1958, Patricia Helen Mary, da of late Col Raymond Patrick Thomas ffrench (Col in Indian Army); 3 s (Jeremy, Jason, Gideon), 1 da (Julia); *Career* Dept of Biochemistry Univ of Cambridge 1943-55 (demonstatorship 1950-55); Univ of Edinburgh: dir of chemistry and biology Dept of Zoology 1955-63, sr lectr 1961-62, reader 1962-63; dir of res Glynn Res Inst 1964-86, chm and hon dir Glynn Res Fndn Ltd 1987-; memb European Molecular Biology Orgn 1973, FRS 1974, memb Econ Res Cncl 1975, hon memb American Soc of Biological Chemists 1975, hon memb American Acad of Arts and Sciences 1975, foreign assoc Nat Acad of Sciences USA 1977, hon fell Royal Soc of Edinburgh 1979, memb Royal Inst of GB 1981, hon memb Soc for Gen Microbiology 1984, hon memb Japanese Biochemical Soc 1984, Associé Étranger de l'Académie des Sciences France 1989, foreign memb Acad of Creators USSR 1989; awards incl: CIBA medal and prize 1973, Warren Triennial prize (jtly with Prof E Racker, Tstees of Mais Gen Hosp USA) 1974, Louis and Bert Freedman Fndn award NY Acad of Sciences 1974, Wilhelm Feldberg Fndn prize 1976, Lewis S Rosenstiel award Brandeis Univ USA 1977, Sir Hans Krebs lectr 1978, medal of European Biochemical socs 1978, Nobel Prize in Chemistry 1978, Fritz Lipman lectr Gesellschaft für Biologische Chemie 1978, Humphry Davy meml lectr Royal Inst of Chemistry and Chilterns and Middx Section The Chem Soc Royal Inst of London 1980, James Rennie Bequest lectr Univ of Edinburgh 1980, Copley medal of Cncl of RS 1981, Gold medal of Hon Athens Municipal Cncl 1982, Croonian Lectr of RS 1987; Hon DUniv Tech Berlin; Hon DSc: Univ of Exeter, Univ of Chicago, Univ of Liverpool, Univ of Bristol, Univ of Edinburgh, Univ of Hull, Univ of Aberdeen; Hon ScD: UEA, Univ of Cambridge; Hon DUniv: York, hon fell UMIST; *Books* Chemiosmotic Coupling in Oxidative and Photosynthetic Phosphorylation (1966), Chemiosmotic Coupling and Energy Transduction (1968); *Recreations* enjoyment of family life, home-building and creation of wealth and amenities, restoration of buildings of architectural and historical interest, music, thinking, understanding, inventing, making; *Clubs* Atheneum; *Style*— Dr Peter Mitchell; The Glynn Research Foundation Ltd, Glynn House, Bodmin, Cornwall PL30 4AU (☎ 020 882 482, fax 020 882 575)

MITCHELL, Peter Stuart; s of William Edmund Chaloner Mitchell (d 1978), and Mabel, *née* Hodson (d 1974); *b* 5 Oct 1935; *Educ* St Andrews Church Sch Preston, King Edward VII Sch Lytham St Anne's; *m* 1, 23 dec 1957 (m dis 1974), Lillah; m 2, 19 July 1974, Barbara, da of James Haynes (d 1974); *Career* apprentice in engrg English Electric Preston Lancs 1952-60, trg in photography John Maltby Hendon 1960-61; photographer: Rolls Royce Spadeadam Cumberland 1961-66, Graphic Group Leeds 1966-69; industl photographer and head of dept Hepworth 4 Grandage (part of AE Group) 1970-78, industl photographer generating own business Foster 4 Skeffington 1979-80; set up own business 1981-; pt/t tutor Herefordshire Coll of Art & Design 1984-; memb Admissions and Qualifications Panel for Industl and Architectural Photography BIPP; Inst of Incorporated Photographers: licentiate 1968, assoc 1972, fell 1976; FBIPP 1976 (memb 1968-), assoc memb Master Photographers' Assoc; *Recreations* photography, reading, classical music; *Style*— Peter Mitchell, Esq; 3 Acacia Close, Hereford HR2 6BP (☎ 0432 270859)

MITCHELL, Raymond; s of John Mitchell, of Helston, Cornwall, and Nora, *née* Polglase; *b* 24 May 1933; *Educ* Probus Sch for Boys, South West Coll of Commerce, Chartered Association of Certified Accountants (Dip in Mgmnt Accounting Business Studies); *m* 15 Feb 1958, Jean Patricia; 3 da (Sandra b 1960, Jennifer (now Mrs Fisher) b 1961, Lorraine b 1962); *Career* auditor Touche Ross & Co 1954-61, mgmnt appts BP 1961-73, gp fin controller BBA Group Ltd 1973-76, dir BBA Automatic Ltd 1976-82, fin dir BBA Group plc 1982-87, chm Mitcor Services Ltd 1988-; corp affairs dir BBA Group plc 1987-88, chm Control Management Services Ltd 1989-, dir J Marslands & Sons Ltd 1989-; JDipMA, memb ACCA Cncl 1979-; *Recreations* golf, badminton; *Clubs* Sand Moor Golf (Leeds, Capt 1990); *Style—* Raymond Mitchell, Esq; 2 Fern Chase, Bracken Pk, Leeds LS14 3JL (☎ 0532 893330)

MITCHELL, Richard Charles (Bob); s of Charles Mitchell (d 1976), and Elizabeth, *née* Ridd (d 1968); *b* 22 Aug 1927; *Educ* Godalming GS, Univ of Southampton; *m* 27 May 1950, Doreen Lilian, da of Albert Gregory (d 1987); 1 s (David Charles b 1965), 1 da (Claire Lesley b 1969); *Career* Queens Royal Regt 1946-48; dep headmaster Bartley Co Secdy Sch 1964-66 (head of Mathematics Dept 1957-64), MP (Lab) Southampton Test 1966-70, PPS to Anthony Crosland Sec of State for Educn, MP Southampton Itchen 1971-83, PPS to Shirley Williams MEP 1975-79, memb Speakers Panel of Ctee Chm 1979-83, joined SDP 1981, lectr in business studies 1984-89, ret 1989; dep leader of Southampton City Cncl 1964-67 (cncllr 1955-67), pres S Hampshire SDP 1985; *Recreations* postal chess; *Style—* Bob Mitchell, Esq; 49 Devonshire Rd, Southampton SO1 2GL (☎ 0703 221781)

MITCHELL, Robert; OBE (1984); s of Robert Mitchell (d 1958), of Woodford, Essex, and Lizzie, *née* Snowdon (d 1958); *b* 14 Dec 1913; *Educ* W Ham Secdy Sch, St John's Coll Cambridge (MA); *m* 31 Jan 1946, Reinholda (Ronnie) Thorretta Louise Clara, da of H R E L Kettlitz (d 1959), of Bilthoven, Holland; 2 s (Robert b 1946, Hugh b 1948), 1 step s (Simon Ritsema van Eck b 1938); *Career* Flt Lt RAF 1939-46, liaison offr Royal Dutch Meteorogical Serv 1945-46; md R Mitchell & Co (Eng) Ltd 1946-81 (chm 1958-81); Parly Candidate (C) W Ham S 1964 and 1966; memb: Wanstead and Woodford Cncl 1958-65 (dep Mayor 1960-61), GLC 1964-86 (chm 1971-72); CBI: memb Ctee State Intervention in Private Indust 1976-78, London and SE Regnl Cncl 1969-79, Smaller Firms Cncl 1977-79; chm Nat Jt Negotiating Ctee Local Authy Fire Bdes 1970-71; memb Ctee Crystal Palace Nat Sports Centre 1965-88, chm Wanstead & Woodford Cons Assoc 1965-68 (vice pres 1968-), govr Chigwell Sch 1966-; chm GLC Ctee for: fire Bde and Ambulance 1967-71, Covent Garden Devpt Ctee 1972-73, Professional and Gen Servs Ctee 1977-79; verderer Epping Forest 1976-; rep: Cambridge Univ Swimming Club 1932-35 (Capt 1935), Eng and GB Waterpolo 1934-48 (incl 1936 & 1948 Olympic Games), Br Univs World Univ Games Swimming and Waterpolo 1933 & 1935, Rest of World v Champions Water Polo Univ Games 1935; Capt Plaistow Utd Swimming Club 1946-49 (pres 1955); Freeman: City of London 1971, Worshipful Co of Gardeners; Grand Offr Order of Orange-Nassau Holland 1972, Order of Rising Sun Japan 1971, Order of Star Afghanistan 1971; *Recreations* looking out of my window watching the seasons change in Epping Forest; *Clubs* Carlton, Hawks (Cambridge); *Style—* Robert Mitchell, Esq, OBE; Hatchwood House, Nursery Rd, Loughton, Essex IG10 4EF (☎ 081 508 9135); Little Brigg, Bessingham, Norwich, Norfolk NR11 7JR

MITCHELL, Robert Henry (Robin); s of Henry Gordon Mitchell, of Emanuel House, Rectory Hill, East Bergholt, Colchester, and Elizabeth Margaret Katherine, *née* Richards; *b* 17 Aug 1955; *Educ* Stowe, Peterhouse Cambridge (MA); *m* 16 June 1979, Helen Miranda, da of John Victor Akerman, of Avenue House, Avenue Rd, Brockenhurst, Hants; 1 s (Jonathan b 1988), 2 da (Philippa 1984, Claire b 1986); *Career* admitted slr 1980, ptnr Norton Rose 1986; *Recreations* hockey, skiing, tennis, swimming; *Style—* Robin Mitchell, Esq; Norton Rose, Kempson House, Camomile Street, London EC3A 7AN (☎ 071 2832434, fax 071 5881181, telex 883652 NOROSE)

MITCHELL, Robin Paul; s of Frederick James Mitchell, of Enfield, Middx, and Maud Patricia, *née* Pawson; *b* 15 Feb 1955; *Educ* Latymer Sch; *m* Maria Ann, da of Sean Joseph Kealy, of Enfield, Middx; 2 s (John Paul b 26 April 1979, David Frederick b 2 Feb 1981), 1 da (Lucy Elizabeth b 9 April 1986); *Career* Charles Stanley & Co: unauthorised clerk 1973-75, authorised clerk 1975-81, sr dealer 1981-85, head dealing 1985-; memb: Int Stock Exchange Securities Assoc; *Recreations* football, cricket; *Clubs* Norseman FC, Old Edmontians; *Style—* Robin Mitchell, Esq; Charles Stanley & Co, Gdn House, 18 Finsbury Circus, London EC2M 7BL

MITCHELL, Terence Croft; s of Arthur Croft Mitchell (d 1956), and Evelyn Violet, *née* Ware (d 1986); *b* 17 June 1929; *Educ* Holderness Sch New Hampshire USA, Bradfield Coll, St Catharine's Coll Cambridge (MA); *Career* craftsman REME 1947-49; asst master St Catherine's Sch Almondsbury 1954-56; resident study Tyndale House Cambridge 1956-58; euro rep Aust Inst of Archaeology 1958-59; Dept of Western Asiatic Antiquities British Museum; asst keeper 1959-74, dep keeper 1974-83, keeper 1983-89; memb: London Diocesan Synod, Kensington Area Synod, Chelsea Deanery Synod (lay chm 1980-84), Diocesan and Area Bishop's Cncl, Cncl Br Sch of Archaeology in Jerusalem; ed Monograph Series Palestine Exploration Fund Ctee, vice chm Br Inst at Amman for Archaeology and History; *Books* Music and Civilsation (Br Museum Yearbook 4 edn 1980), The Bible in the Br Museum Interpreting the Evidence (1988, 1990); *Recreations* music, reading, landscape gardening; *Clubs* Athenaeum; *Style—* Terence Mitchell, Esq

MITCHELL, Terence Leonard; s of Leonard Alfred James Mitchell, and Sarah Anne Mitchell; *b* 19 July 1934; *Educ* Worthing Boys HS, Univ of Auckland NZ (Dip Arch); *m* 1, 1961 (m dis); 1 s, 2 da; m 2, 1989, Antonina Knight, da of late Constantine Popoff; *Career* violinist and music teacher until age 26, played under the batons of Sir Adrian Boult, Sir Malcolm Sargeant and John Hopkins; since qualifying in 1964 practised as architect; now chm Marquis Homes Ltd, dir Venture Inns of Br Ltd; notable works incl: award winning Cathedral Sq (Christchurch NZ) 1974, award winning Norman Kirk Courts (Christchurch NZ) 1978, holiday complex for Sudeley Castle 1985, The Hayes Retirement Village (Prestbury, Glos) 1987, The Allasdon Dene Hotel & Leisure Centre Lydney Glos; now specialising in the restoration of historic buildings; ARIBA, ANZIA; *Recreations* English history and architecture, music, artist; *Style—* Terence Mitchell, Esq; 37 Hailes St, Winchcombe, Glos GL54 5HU (☎ 0242 603910); Marquis Homes Ltd, Marquis House, 2 North St, Wincombe, Glos GL54 5LH (☎ 0242 602243)

MITCHELL, Prof Sir (Edgar) William John; CBE (1976); s of Edgar Mitchell (d 1963), of Kingsbridge, Devon and Caroline Lauretta, *née* Stoneman; *b* 25 Sept 1925; *Educ* Kingsbirdge GS, Univ of Sheffield (BS, MSc), Univ of Bristol (PhD), Univ of Oxford (MA); *m* 1, (m dis 1985); 1 s (Jonathan b 1963); m 2, 25 Jan 1985, Margaret Constance Davies, da of Capt Harry Brown (d 1925), of Kirby, Lonsdale; 1 step s (Martin b 1949), 1 step da (Philippa b 1953); *Career* res physicist Metropolitan Vickers Manchester 1946-51, seconded to Univ of Bristol 1948-50; Univ of Reading: fell 1951-52, lectr 1952, reader 1958, prof 1961, dean 1965-68, dep VL 1976-78; Univ of Oxford: Dr Lees Prof of experimental philosophy 1978-88, fell Wadham Coll 1978-, prof of physics 1988-90; author of numerous scientific papers on condensed matter physics; SERC: memb 1970-74 and 1982-85, chm Physics Ctee 1967-70 (memb 1965-70), chm Neutron Beam Res Ctee 1966-74, memb Nuclear Physics Bd 1980-84, chm 1985-90; acting jt dir Sci Cncl of Inst Laue-Lengerin Grenoble 1973 (memb 1973-), chm SE Region Computing Ctee 1974-76, memb Comité de Direction Solid State Physics Laboratory Ecole Normale and Univ of Paris 1975-79, memb Exec Ctee Univ Cncl for Non-Academic Staff 1979-82, memb Science Planning Gp for Spallation Neutron source 1980-85, memb UGC Physical Sci Ctee 1982-85, memb Cncl Inst of Physics 1982-86, memb Mgmnt Bd Br Nat Space Centre 1986-, memb Scientific Advsy Ctee for Nat Gallery 1988-; Hon DSc: Univ of Reading 1987, Univ of Kent 1988, Univ of Budapest 1988, Univ of Birmingham 1990; FInstP, FRS 1986; *Recreations* opera, food, motoring, walking; *Clubs* Oxford and Cambridge; *Style—* Prof Sir William Mitchell, CBE, FRS; Foxfield, Potkiln Lane, Goring Heath, Oxon RG8 7SR

MITCHELL, Rt Rev Mgr William Joseph; s of William Ernest Mitchell, of Loretto, 4 Stonehill, Hanham, Bristol, and Katherine, *née* O'Donnell; *b* 4 Jan 1936; *Educ* St Brendan's Coll Bristol, Corpus Christi Coll Oxford (MA), Seminaire St Sulpice Paris, Pontifical Gregorian Univ Rome (LCL); *Career* ordained priest 1961, curate Pro-Cathedral Clifton Bristol 1963-64, sec to Bishop of Clifton 1964-75, parish priest St Bernadette Bristol 1975-78, rector Pontifical Beda Coll Rome 1978-87, appointed prelate of honour (monsignor) 1978, vicar gen Clifton and canon Clifton Diocesan Chapter 1987, parish priest St John's Bath 1988-90, parish priest St Antony's Bristol 1990; *Style—* The Rt Rev Mgr William Mitchell; St Antony's Presbytery, Satchfield Crescent, Henbury, Bristol BS10 7BE (☎ 0272 502509)

MITCHELL, William Vernon; s of Peter Mitchell (d 1976), and Ann Mitchell (d 1986); *b* 1 May 1923; *Educ* Dollar Acad, Liverpool Tech Coll; *m* 1944, Muriel Olive, *née* Cooke; 2 c; *Career* tech dir Lever Brothers Ltd to 1983; tech advsr Br Exec Serv Overseas; MRIC; *Recreations* golf, microscopy, philately; *Style—* William Mitchell, Esq; 15 Uplands Way, Sevenoaks, Kent (☎ 0732 456887)

MITCHELL ANDERSON, Hon Mrs (Cecilia Claribel); *née* Cavendish; da of 6 Baron Waterpark by his 1 w Isabel Jay, (Mrs Cavendish); *b* 11 June 1903; *m* 1933, James Mitchell Anderson (d 1963); 2 da (Isabel, Annabel); *Style—* The Hon Mrs Mitchell Anderson; Courtenay Beach, Kingsway, Hove, Sussex BN3 2WF (☎ 0273 733622)

MITCHELL-HEGGS, Dr Nita Ann; da of Maj Lewis Posner (d 1975), and Olive *née* Jones; *b* 6 June 1942; *Educ* N London Collegiate Sch, London Hosp Med Coll (MB BS, MRCP); *m* 26 July 1967, Dr Peter Francis Mitchell-Heggs, of Maj Francis Sansome Mitchell-Heggs (d 1986); 2 da (Emily b 2 July 1974, Sophie b 23 March 1977); *Career* former posts in paediatrics, psychiatry, occupational med, student health, currently dist conslt and occupational physician Wandsworth Health Authy, sr lectr St George's Hosp Med Sch; affiliate RCPsych, memb SOM, DCH, MFOM; *publications* chapters and articles on student mental health anxiety and depression; *Recreations* travel, skiing, theatre, entertaining children's friends!; *Clubs* RAC; *Style—* Dr Nita Mitchell-Heggs; St George's Hospital, Blackshaw Rd, Tooting SW17 (☎ 081 672 1255)

MITCHELL-INNES, Alistair Campbell; s of Peter Campbell Mitchell-Innes (d 1960); *b* 1 March 1934; *Educ* Charterhouse; *m* 1957, Penelope Ann, *née* Hill; 1 s, 2 da; *Career* Lt Queens Own Royal W Kent Parachute Regt 1953-54; dir Macfisheries Ltd 1971-75,vice chm Walls Meat Co Ltd 1975-77, dir Brooke Bond Gp plc 1979-85, chief exec Nabisco Gp Ltd 1985-88, currently dep chm HP Bulmer (Holdings) plc; dir: Next plc, Evans Halshaw plc; *Recreations* golf, walking; *Clubs* Caledonian, MCC, Berks Golf; *Style—* Alistair Mitchell-Innes, Esq; Langton Lodge, Sunningdale, Berks (☎ 0344 24993)

MITCHELL LAMBERT, Ian William; s of Ernest Joseph Lambert (d 1976), of Coventry, and Ivy Muriel, *née* Mitchell; *b* 3 March 1942; *Educ* Slough GS, King Henry VIII Sch Coventry, Univ of Wales Swansea, Univ of Kent; *m* 21 Oct 1978, Mavis Crazencea, da of Agrippa Amado Rogers (d 1980), of SA; 1 s (Derek b 1969); *Career* theologian, author, industl relations conslt; lay pastor Weald Methodist Church; chm and md: CSEC Ltd, Job Generation Ltd; chm Job Generation Training Trust; dir: IPSET, Centre for the Study of Early Christianity (UK office); chm Emeritus Professional Assoc of Teachers; memb: Industrial Tribunals; fell Coll of Preceptors; FBIM; *Clubs* Royal Cwlth; *Style—* Ian Mitchell Lambert, Esq; Tangnefedd, Windmill Road, Weald, Sevenoaks, Kent TN14 6PJ (☎ 0732 463460)

MITCHELL-ROSE, Colin Murray; TD (1987); s of Gordon Mitchell (d 1985), and Margaret Carol, *née* Rose; *b* 11 Feb 1947; *Educ* Fettes, Univ of Edinburgh (BSc); *m* 18 Oct 1975, Fiona Deirdre, da of Lt-Col Richard S Moglove (d 1980); 2 da (Emma b 1978, Poppy b 1980); *Career* Royal Scots Greys 1969-73, Maj Queens Own Yeomanry 1973-88; md Craig & Rose plc 1989 (prodn dir 1984); Asst Co of Merchants Edinburgh 1981-84 (Freeman 1974); *Recreations* skiing; *Style—* Colin Mitchell-Rose, Esq, TD; Craig & Rose plc, 172 Leith Walk, Edinburgh EH6 5EB (☎ 031 5541131, fax 031 5533250)

MITCHENSON, Francis Joseph Blackett (Joe); s of Francis Mitchenson, and Sarah, *née* Roddam; *Educ* privately, Fay Compton Studio of Dramatic Art; *Career* WWII, RHA 1941-43; actor and theatrical historian; first stage appearance Libel! 1934, rep at Cheltenham 1936, joined as stage mangr Portfolio Playhouse 1937 (appearances incl Fenton in Merry Wives of Windsor 1939), season at Gateway Notting Hill Gate 1944, mangr Grand Croydon 1945, dir and actor in Charley's Aunt and The Ghost Train, toured Euro in ENSA 1945-46, Freddy in Pygmalion with ENSA (Germany); other plays incl: Quiet Wedding, George and Margaret; many TV and radio appearances; fndr (with late Raymond Mander) and full time dir Theatre Collection 1939; author, conslt; *Books* Hamlet Through the Ages (1952), Theatrical Companions to: Shaw (1954), Maugham (1955), Coward (1957), A Picture History of British Theatre (1957), The Theatres of London (1961), Musical Comedy (1969), Revue (1971), Pantomime (1973), Victorian and Edwardian Entertainment from Old Photographs (1978), Guide to Somerset Maugham Theatrical Paintings at the National Theatre (1980); *Recreations* collecting anything and everything theatrical, sunbathing; *Style—* Joe Mitchenson, Esq; The Mansion, Beckenham Place Park, Beckenham, Kent BR3 2BP (☎ 081 658 7725)

MITCHESON, (Lavinia) Anne; da of Cyril Howard Moseley (d 1979), of Market Harborough, Leics, and Dorothy, *née* Womersley; *b* 26 Sept 1938; *Educ* Riddlesworth Hall Diss Norfolk, Felixstowe Coll, Northants Inst of Agric; *m* 9 Feb 1971, George Anthony Mitcheson, s of Thomas Broughton Mitcheson (d 1987), of Hadley Wood, Herts; 1 s (Thomas b 6 June 1972); *Career* farmer since 1972; JP Hatfield Bench 1984-, juvenile magistrate Hatfield Bench, memb St Mary's Essendon PCC, memb ctee Herts Co Ladies Golf Assoc; *Recreations* golf, gardening, bridge; *Clubs* Hadley Wood Golf, Royal Thames Yacht, Royal West Norfolk Golf; *Style—* Mrs Anne Mitcheson; Farmleigh, Essendon, Hatfield, Herts AL9 6JS (☎ 0707 58057), School Farm Cottage, Wighton, Wells Next The Sea, Norfolk (☎ 0328 820036)

MITCHISON, Prof Hon (Nicholas) Avrion; s of Baron Mitchison, CBE, QC (Life Peer, d 1970); *b* 5 May 1928; *Educ* Leighton Park Sch, New Coll Oxford; *m* 1957, Lorna Margaret, da of Maj-Gen J S S Martin, CSI; 2 s, 3 da; *Career* prof of zoology and comparative anatomy UCL 1970-; *Style—* Prof the Hon Avrion Mitchison; 14 Belitha Villas, London N1 1PD

MITCHISON, Prof Hon Denis Anthony; CMG (1984); s of Baron Mitchison, CBE (Life Peer, d 1970); *b* 6 Sept 1919; *Educ* Abbotsholme Sch, Trinity Coll Cambridge, Univ Coll Hosp London; *m* 1940, Ruth Sylvia, da of Hubert Gill; 2 s, 2 da; *Career* prof of Bacteriology Royal Postgraduate Med Sch 1971-84, ret; dir Med Res Cncl Unit for Laboratory Studies of Tuberculosis 1956-84, emeritus prof Univ of London; *Style—* Prof Denis Mitchison, CMG; 14 Marlborough Rd, Richmond, Surrey (☎ 081 940 4751, 081 740 3049)

MITCHISON, Prof Hon (John) Murdoch; 2 s of Baron Mitchison, CBE, QC (Life Peer, d 1970), and Naomi Mitchison, *née* Haldane, the writer; *b* 11 June 1922; *Educ* Winchester, Trinity Coll Cambridge; *m* 21 June 1947, Rosalind Mary, da of late

Edward Murray Wrong, of Toronto, Canada; 1 s, 3 da; *Career* prof of zoology Univ of Edinburgh 1963-88; memb Sci Bd SRC 1976-79; memb Royal Cmmn on Environmental Pollution 1974-79; author; FRS; *Style*— Prof the Hon Murdoch Mitchison; Great Yew, Ormiston, E Lothian (☎ 0875 340530, work 031 650 5488)

MITCHISON, Baroness; Naomi Margaret; *née* Haldane; CBE (Civil 1985); da of late John Scott Haldane, CH; *b* 1 Nov 1897; *Educ* Dragon; *m* 1916, Baron Mitchison, CBE, QC (Life Peer, d 1970); 3 s, 2 da; *Career* author; hon fell Wolfson Coll Oxford 1983; Hon DLitt: Strathclyde, Stirling, Dundee, Heriot Watt; *Style*— The Rt Hon the Lady Mitchison, CBE; Carradale House, Carradale, Campbeltown, Scotland

MITFORD, Jessica Lucy (Hon Mrs Treuhaft); da of 2 Baron Redesdale (d 1958); *b* 11 Sept 1917; *m* 1, Esmond Marcus David Romilly (d 1942); 1 da; m 2, 1943, Robert Edward Treuhaft; 1 s; *Career* author; *Books* Hons and Rebels, The American Way of Death, The Trial of Dr Spock, Kind and Usual Punishment, The American Prison Business, A Fine Old Conflict, The Making of a Muckraker, Faces of Philip: A Memoir of Philip Toynbee, Grace Had an English Heart: The Story of Grace Darling, Heroine and Victorian Superstar; *Style*— Miss Jessica Mitford; 6411 Regent St, Oakland, Calif 94618, USA

MITFORD-BARBERTON, Gareth de Bohun; s of Raymond Berners Mitford-Barberton (d 1985), of Bunbury, Western Australia, and Norah Millicent (Peggy), *née* Nisbet (d 1986); *b* 9 Feb 1925; *Educ* Prince of Wales Sch Nairobi Kenya, Stamford Sch, St Edmund Hall Oxford (BM BCh), DTM and H London; *m* 12 Dec 1946, Patricia Mary (d 1989), da of Brian Thorpe (d 1983); 2 s (Philip b 1952, Brian b 1954), 1 da (Helen (Mrs Thomas) b 1949); *Career* Colonial Med Serv Uganda 1951-62, conslt obstetrician and gynaecologist Kettering 1965-90; memb local med and charitable orgns; FRCOG 1975; *Recreations* family archivist; *Style*— Gareth Mitford-Barberton, Esq; 27 Poplars Farm Rd, Barton Seagrave, Kettering, Northants NN15 5AE (☎ 0536 510180); 6 Belvedere, Ghajnsielem, Gozo, Malta

MITFORD-SLADE, Patrick Buxton; changed surname from Mitford to Mitford-Slade by deed poll 1942; s of Col Cecil Townley Mitford-Slade (d 1986), and Phyllis, *née* Buxton (d 1985); *b* 7 Sept 1936; *Educ* Eton, RMA Sandhurst; *m* 1964, Anne Catharine, da of Maj Arthur Holbrow Stanton, MBE; 1 s, 2 da; *Career* Capt Royal Green Jackets 1954-69; asst sec Panel on Takeovers and Mergers 1970-72, ptnr Cazenove & Co 1973-, jt dep chm Cncl Stock Exchange 1982-85 (memb 1976-); chm: City Telecommunications Ctee 1983-, Stock Exchange Projects Ctee 1984-86, Offs Assoc 1985-, Securities Indust Steering Ctee Taurus 1988-90; md Cazenove Money Brokers 1986-; chm Money Brokers Assoc 1989-; memb Stock Exchange 1972; *Recreations* shooting, fishing, gardening, racing; *Clubs* City of London; *Style*— Patrick Mitford-Slade, Esq; Cazenove & Co, 12 Tokenhouse Yard, London EC2 7AN (☎ 071 588 2828)

MITSON, (Sydney) Allen; s of Sydney Mitson, of Snaresbrook and St Margaret's Bay, Kent, and Catherine, *née* Gooding; *b* 24 May 1933; *Educ* Exeter Sch, Forest Sch (BA); *m* 1, 1959 (m dis 1971), Elizabeth Angela, da of R Garner (d 1966), of Buckhurst Hill, Essex; 2 s (Andrew b 1963, Michael b 1966); m 2, 1973, Valerie Angela, da of J Sherratt (d 1988), of Waltham Abbey, Essex; 1 step s (John b 1967); *Career* Nat Serv Royal Signals; sales promotion mangr Rotaflex 1960-65, formed Emess Lighting 1966 (became public co 1980), md Emess Lighting (UK) Ltd 1980-89, chief exec and dep chm Inlite Group 1989-; underwriting memb Lloyds 1977-; Freeman City of London 1983, Liveryman Worshipful Co of Gold and Silver Wyre Drawers 1983; *Recreations* walking, swimming; *Style*— Allen Mitson, Esq; Inlite Group Ltd, 9/10 Grafton St, London W1 (☎ 071 493 0702, fax 071 493 0832)

MITSON, John Dane; s of Capt Leonard Mitson (d 1969), of Nottingham, and Edith, *née* Bradley (d 1973); *b* 28 Feb 1929; *Educ* Oakham Sch, Sidney Sussex Coll Cambridge (MA, LLM); *m* 31 May 1954, Rita (d 1989), da of Neville Thomas Dowen (d 1964), of Leicester; 1 s (Matthew b 30 May 1964), 3 da (Johanna b 21 March 1959, Katharine b 15 May 1960, Emma b 24 Aug 1963); *Career* BQMS RA Singapore 1947-49; admitted slr 1956; legal sec to Bishop and registrar of Diocese of St Edmondsbury and Ipswich 1975-; conslt Birketts Westhorp and Long Ipswich; memb Law Soc; *Recreations* music, theatre, cricket; *Clubs* MCC, Ipswich & Suffolk; *Style*— John Mitson, Esq; Drift Cottage, The Drift, Dedham, Colchester CO7 6AH (☎ 0206 323116); 20-26 Museum St, Ipswich (☎ 0473 232300)

MITTLER, Prof Peter Joseph; CBE (1981); s of Dr Gustav Mittler (d 1962), of Leeds, and Gertrude Mittler (d 1987); *b* 2 April 1930; *Educ* Merchant Taylors', Pembroke Coll Cambridge (BA, MA, PhD); *m* 2 April 1955, Helle, da of Dr Ernest Katscher (d 1980), of Vienna; 3 s (Paul b 1955, Stephen b 1959, Martin b 1964); *Career* Nat Serv Ordnance Corps 1949-50, RAMC 1950- (Capt Res); clinical psychologist 1954-63, lectr in psychology Birkbeck Coll London 1963-68, prof of special educn and dir Hester Adrian Res Centre 1968-82, currently dir Centre for Educnl Guidance and Special Needs and dep dir Sch of Educn Univ of Manchester; former memb: Sch Examination and Assessment Cncl 1988-90, Prince of Wales Advsy Gp on Disability 1984-90; hon fell Manchester Poly 1981; FBPsS 1966, Chartered Psychologist 1989; *Books* Psychological Assessment (1970), Study of Twins (1971), Advances in Mental Handicap Research (2 vols 1981, 1983), Parents, Professionals and Mentally Handicapped People (1983), Staff Training (1987), Training and Special Educational Needs (1988); *Recreations* travel, listening to music; *Style*— Prof Peter Mittler, CBE; 10 Park Road, Cheadle Hulme, Cheshire SK8 7DA (☎ 061 4856491), School of Education, The University, Manchester M13 9PL (☎ 061 2753499, fax 061 2753519, telex 666517 UNIMAN G)

MITTON, Brian Frederick; s of Alfred Mitton (d 1984), and Kate, *née* Jackson; *b* 21 June 1931; *Educ* Carlisle GS, Carlisle Cathedral Choir Sch; *m* 4 Nov 1968, Wendy, da of Inspr John McNeil; 3 s (Bradley John Snowden b 1969, Glenn Frederick Barclay b 1971, Alexander David Clark b 1975); *Career* trainee refrigeration engr 1946-51; with Refrigeration (Mitton) Ltd 1954- (md 1971-); qualified coach in badminton, swimming and squash with Nat Assocns; *Recreations* badminton, squash, running, gardening; *Clubs* Brampton Badminton, Brampton Squash; *Style*— Brian F Mitton, Esq; Quarrybeck House, Brampton, Cumbria CA8 2EY (☎ 06977 2020); Refrigeration (Mitton) Ltd, Polar House, East Norfolk St, Carlisle, Cumbria CA2 5JL (☎ 0228 22481)

MITTWOCH, Prof Ursula; da of Prof Eugen Mittwoch (d 1942), and Dr Anna Hermine, *née* Lipmann (d 1968); *b* 21 March 1924; *Educ* Henrietta Barnett Sch, Univ of London (BSc, PhD, DSc); *m* 21 Dec 1954, Bernard Victor Springer; 1 da (Caroline b 1960); *Career* ext sci staff MRC 1958-62, prof genetics UCL 1985-89 (lectr 1963-80, reader 1980-85), hon visiting prof London Hosp Med Coll 1989-90, visiting prof Queen Mary & Westfield Coll 1990-; FIBiol 1973; *Books* Sex Chromosomes (1967), Genetics of Sex Differentiation (1973); *Recreations* buying books; *Style*— Prof Ursula Mittwoch; 73 Leverton St, London NW5 2NX (☎ 071 267 1560)

MIZRAHI, Jeffrey Isaac Ezzat; s of Jacoub Mizrahi, of Camiore, Provincia Di Lucca, Italy, and Odette Mizrahi; *b* 2 Feb 1940; *Educ* Millfield, Univ of Durham (BA); *m* 1, 1963 (m dis 1978), Joan Rudd; 1 s (James b 1976), 3 da (Jacqueline b 1964, Juliette b 1967, Jeanette b 1972); m 2, 26 Aug 1988, Florence, da of Mathew Kinsella; *Career* econ conslt Economist Intelligence Unit 1965-67, dep chief economist Charter Consolidated 1967-75, chief economist James Capel 1975-78, vice pres Bank of America International 1978-83, dir and chief economist SBCI, Savory Milln 1983-88, dir Swiss Bank Corporation (portfolio mgmnt) 1988-; memb Soc Business Economists, ACII; *Recreations* tennis, bridge, squash; *Style*— Jeffrey Mizrahi, Esq; Swiss Bank Corporation, Norfolk House, 31 St James Square, London SW1 (☎ 071 329 0009, fax 071 321 0370, telex 927 244)

MLINARIC, David; *b* 12 March 1939; *m* 1969, (Katherine) Martha, da of Sir Robert Laycock (d 1968), and Lady Laycock, *qv*; 1 s, 2 da; *Career* interior designer; *Style*— David Mlinaric, Esq; 61 Glebe Place, London SW3 5JB

MO, Timothy Peter; s of Peter Mo Wan Lung, and Barbara Helena, *née* Falkingham; *b* 30 Dec 1950; *Educ* Mill Hill Sch, St John's Coll Oxford (BA); *Career* Novelist: The Monkey King 1978, Sow Sweet 1982, An Insular Profession 1986; *Recreations* diving; *Style*— Timothy Mo, Esq

MOAT, Frank Robert; s of Frank Robert Moat (d 1976), of Tynemouth, and Grace, *née* Hibbert (d 1989); *b* 10 Aug 1948; *Educ* Giggleswick, The Coll of Law (LLB); *Career* called to the Bar Lincoln's Inn 1970; memb Western Circuit, in practice in London and on the Western Circuit, rep on the Bar Cncl Western Circuit 1989 and 1990; memb Wine Ctee of the Western Circuit, fndr memb Ctee Kensington and Chelsea Nat Tst Assoc; *Recreations* theatre, music, antiques, architecture; *Clubs* Garrick; *Style*— Frank Moat, Esq; 5 Prior Bolton St, Canonbury, London N1 2NX (☎ 071 226 8177); 36 Bilberry Ct, Staple Gardens, Winchester, Hants SO23 8SP (☎ 0962 868531); 3 Pump Court, Temple, London EC4Y 7AJ (☎ 071 353 0711, fax 071 353 3319)

MOATE, Roger Denis; MP (C) Faversham 1970-; s of late Harold Stanley Moate, of Chiswick, and Elizabeth Freestone; *b* 12 May 1938; *Educ* Latymer Upper Sch; *m* 1 (m dis), Hazel Joy, da of late F J Skinner, of Somerset; 1 s, 1 da; m 2, Auriol, da of late W B G Cran, of Huddersfield; 1 da; *Career* registered insur broker; underwriting memb Lloyd's, past chm Lloyd's Brokers frank Bradford & Co Ltd, past chm Theatre Prodns plc; dir: Hunter Murray and Co Ltd, Robinco UK Ltd, Euro Mktg Info Ltd; hon sec Br American Parly Gp 1974-81, chm Br Norwegian Parly Gp 1988-, memb Ct of Referees; *Recreations* skiing, tennis; *Style*— Roger Moate Esq, MP; The Old Vicarage, Knatchbull Rd, London SE5

MOBBS, David Martin; s of Alan Herbert Mobbs, of 16 Somerford Rd, Cirencester, Gloucs, and Freda Gladys, *née* Drew; *b* 6 Sept 1941; *Educ* Broad Green Coll; *m* 1 April 1965, Michele, da of (Graciaa) Jean Alexandre Louis (d 1971), of Boissy, St Leger; 1 da (Sophie Anne b 31 Oct 1970); *Career* residential and commercial designer; various positions architects offices culminating in conversion of The Old Hawker Plane Factory into The Kingston Coll of Sci Technol and Art 1967; fndr: The Plan Shop Ltd 1967, Allplans Ltd 1982; involved in 8400 projects incl new housing, flat devpts and industl schemes; worked for: Sutton Cncl 1956, Architects Dept Merton and Morden Cncl until 1959; involved in protecting historical bldgs and amenities Croydon Borough; *Style*— David Mobbs, Esq; The Plan Shop Ltd, 233 Chipstead Valley Rd, Coulsdon, Surrey (☎ 081 668 5534)

MOBBS, Sir (Gerald) Nigel; DL (Bucks 1985); s of Lt-Col Gerald Aubrey Mobbs (d 1976), of Gt Missenden, and Elizabeth, *née* Lanchester; *b* 22 Sept 1937; *Educ* Marlborough, Christ Church Oxford; *m* 14 Sept 1961, Hon (Pamela) Jane Marguerite Berry, *qv*, da of 2 Viscount Kemsley; 1 s (Christopher William b 1965), 2 da (Virginia Elizabeth b 1968, Penelope Helen (twin) b 1968); *Career* Slough Estates plc: joined 1960, dir 1963, md 1971, chm and chief exec 1976-; dir: Barclays Bank plc 1979-, Kingfisher plc 1983-, Cookson Hldgs 1985-, Charterhouse Gp 1974-83 (chm 1977-83), Tishman Hldg Corp (USA) 1989-, Charterhouse Gp Int (USA) 1985-, Howard de Walden Estates 1989-; chm Aims of Indust 1985-, pres Br Property Fedn 1979-81, vice pres Assoc of Br C of C 1976- (chm 1974-76), High Sheriff of Bucks 1982-83, chm Cncl of Univ of Buckingham 1987-, memb Cncl Univ of Reading 1987-90, chm Property Servs Agency Advsy Bd 1980-86, memb Cwlth War Graves Cmmn 1988-, chm Advsy Panel on Deregulation (DTI) 1988-; hon memb RICS 1990; Master Worshipful Co of Spectacle Makers 1989-90; Hon DSc City Univ 1988, hon fell Coll of Estate Mgmnt; OStJ 1987; kt 1986; *Recreations* riding, hunting, skiing, golf; *Clubs* Brooks', Toronto, York; *Style*— Sir Nigel Mobbs, DL; Widmer Lodge, Lacey Green, Aylesbury, Bucks HP17 0RJ (☎ 0494 488 265); Slough Estates plc, 234 Bath Rd, Slough, Bucks SL1 4EE (☎ 0753 37171)

MOBBS, Hon Lady (Pamela Jane Marguerite); *née* Berry; da of 2 Viscount Kemsley; *b* 27 May 1937; *m* 1961, Sir Gerald Nigel Mobbs; 1 s, 2 da; *Style*— The Hon Lady Mobbs; Widmer Lodge, Lacey Green, Aylesbury, Bucks HP17 0RJ (☎ 049 488 8265)

MOBERLY, Sir John Campbell; KBE (1984), CMG (1976); 2 s of Sir Walter Hamilton Moberly, GBE, KCB, DSO (d 1973), and Gwendolen, *née* Gardner (d 1975); *b* 27 May 1925; *Educ* Winchester, Magdalen Coll Oxford (BA); *m* 18 April 1959, Patience, yst da of Sir Richard George Proby, 1 Bt, MC (d 1979), of Elton Hall Peterborough; 2 s (Richard b 1962, Nicholas b 1963), 1 da (Clare b 1967); *Career* serv WWII RN 1943-47 Lt RNVR (despatches); entered HM For (later Dip) Serv 1950; serv: London, Lebanon, Bahrain, Qatar, Greece, USA 1950-73; dir Middle E Centre for Arab Studies 1973-75, ambass to Jordan 1975-79, asst under sec FCO 1979-82, ambass to Iraq 1982-85, ret; *Style*— Sir John Moberly, KBE, CMG; 35 Pymers Mead, Croxted Rd, W Dulwich, London SE21 8NH (☎ 081 670 2680); The Cedars, Temple Sowerby, Penrith, Cumbria CA10 1RZ (☎ 07683 61437)

MOBERLY, Sir Patrick Hamilton; KCMG (1986, CMG 1978); yr s of George Hamilton Moberly, MC (d 1972), and Alice Violet, *née* Cooke-Hurle (d 1954); ggs of George Moberly, headmaster of Winchester and Bishop of Salisbury; *b* 2 Sept 1928; *Educ* Winchester, Trinity Coll Oxford; *m* 5 May 1955, Mary Frances, da of Capt Hugh de L Penfold (d 1979), of Guernsey, CI; 2 s (Andrew b 1960, James b 1962), 1 da (Jennifer b 1958); *Career* HM Dip Serv 1951-87, with postings in Iraq, Czechoslovakia, Senegal, London, Canada and Israel 1953-74, asst under sec of state 1976-81; ambass: Israel 1981-84, S Africa 1984-87; *Recreations* tennis, opera; *Clubs* Utd Oxford & Cambridge Univ; *Style*— Sir Patrick Moberly, KCMG; 38 Lingfield Rd, London SW19 4PZ

MOBERLY, William James Dorward; s of Brig James Vincent Charles Moberly, DSO, OBE (d 1982), and Brida Helen Mary, *née* Espeut (d 1980); *b* 4 Sept 1938; *Educ* Blundell's, Sidney Sussex Coll Cambridge (MA); *m* 17 Oct 1970, Angela, da of Thomas Eric Douglas Mason, of Broomhall, Oxshott, Surrey; 2 s (Nicholas James, Mark Thomas); *Career* CA; articled clerk Ball Baker Deed & Co 1960-63, asst Thomson McLintock & Co 1963-66; ptnr: Ball Baker Deed & Co 1966 (subsequently Ball Baker Carnaby Deed), Pannell Kerr Forster; dir Thousand and One Lamps Ltd; treas Friends of Cobham Cottage Hosp; Liveryman Worshipful Co of Curriers; *Books* Partnership Management; *Recreations* golf, gardening, bridge; *Clubs* St Georges Hill Golf, Rye Golf; *Style*— William Moberly, Esq; 125 Fairmile Lane, Cobham, Surrey; Pannell Kerr Forster, New Garden House, 78 Hatton Garden, London EC1N 8JA (☎ 071 831 7393, fax 071 405 6736, telex 295928)

MODGILL, Vijay Kumar; s of Sansari Lal Modgill, of NZ, and Dwarka, *née* Devi (d 1978); *b* 1 Sept 1942; *Educ* Eastleigh Sch Nairobi, Leeds Univ Med Sch (MB ChB); *m* 14 Sept 1974, (Elizabeth) Margaret, da of John Harrop Lawton, CBE (d 1987), of Wakefield, Yorks; 1 s (Alexander b 1979), 2 da (Victoria b 1977, Elizabeth b 1985);

Career house physician Leeds Univ Med Sch 1967-68, registrar St James's Hosp Leeds 1968-70 (house surgn 1968), sr registrar Leeds and Bradford Hosps 1972, conslt in vascular and gen surgery Halifax Gen Hosp 1975- (clinical tutor 1975-83); chm of Med Staffs Ctee 1986-89, currently chm of Med Ctee of Elland BUPA Hosp; memb Vascular Soc of GB; memb Assoc of Surgns of GB, FRCS 1972, FRCSEd 1972; *Publications* Renal Trasplants; *Recreations* golf, cricket; *Clubs* Lightcliffe Golf (Halifax), Fixby Golf (Huddersfield), member of XL; *Style—* Vijay Modgill, Esq; Linden Lea, Cecil Avenue, Lightcliffe, Halifax, West Yorkshire (☎ 0422 202182); Halifax General Hosp, Salterherbbe, Halifax (☎ 0422 357171); Elland BUPA Hopsital, Elland Lane, Elland, Halifax (☎ 0422 375577)

MODY, Rustomji Hormusji (Russi); s of Sir Homi P Mody (d 1969), of India, and Lady Jerbai Mody (d 1982); *b* 17 Jan 1918; *Educ* Harrow, ChCh Oxford (BA); *Career* Tata Iron & Steel Co Ltd 1939-: dir of Personnel, agent, res dir of Mktg and Raw Materials, res dir Ops, jt md, md 1974, chm 1984; chm: Tata Ltd London, Tata Inc NY, Tata Korf Engrg Services Ltd, Tata Man Ltd, Tata Timkin Ltd; dir: Tata Sons Ltd, Tata Industs Ltd, Tata Unisys Ltd, Tata Engrg & Locomotive Co Ltd, Tata Davy Ltd, Bihar State Industl Devpt Corp, Housing Devpt Fin Corp; former cmmr Port of Calcutta; chosen by BBC as one of 6 top world industrialists for their series Money Makers, hon life memb Indian Nat Inst of Personnel Mgmnt; former pres: Steel Plant Sports Bd, All India Orgn of Employers, Indian C of C; former vice pres Indian Standards Inst; chm: bd of govrs Indian Inst of Technol Kharagpur, Friends of Trees W Bengal, Fin Cmmn Indian Olympic Assoc; memb bd of govrs: Himalayan Mountaineering Inst Darjeeling, India Fndn for PR Educn and Res; memb of numerous nat and local ctees and cncls in India; conferred an award by Indian C of C Calcutta for promotion of the cause of nat integration in India; fell Duke of Edinburgh's Award Scheme; Business India Business Man of the Year 1983, awarded Padma Bushan 1989; *Recreations* cricket, golf, amateur flying, reading, bridge, tennis, music; *Clubs* Royal & Ancient Golf, Royal Calcutta Golf, The Chambers of Bombay, Diners Bombay, Royal Calcutta Turf, Jamshedpur Cocp Flying; *Style—* Russi Mody, Esq; c/o Tata Iron & Steel Co Ltd, Calcutta, India

MOFFAT, Alexander; s of John Moffat (d 1956), of Cowdenbeath, FIFE, and Agnes Hunter, *née* Lawson; *b* 23 March 1943; *Educ* Daniel Stewart's Coll Edinburgh, Edinburgh Coll of Art (Andrew Grant scholar, Dip in Art); *m* 1968 (m dis 1983), Susan Potten; 1 s (Colin b 1969); *Career* artist; photographer Scottish Central Library 1966-74, dir New 57 Gallery Edinburgh 1968-78; visiting lectr: Winchester Sch of Art 1973-74, Croydon Sch of Art 1974-75, RCA 1986-88; sr lectr in painting studios Glasgow Sch of Art 1988- (lectr in painting studios 1979-88); external examiner: Canterbury Coll of Art (Kent Inst) 1988-91, N Staffordshire Poly Stoke 1989-; lectr in new MA Fine Art Course Glasgow Sch of Art 1990-; Scottish Arts Cncl 1982-84 (memb Cncl, memb Art Ctee, chm Awards Panel), memb Bd Fruitmakert Gallery Edinburgh 1986-, chm Bd ALBA magazine 1988-; solo exhibitions incl: A View of the Portrait (Scottish National Portrait Gallery) 1973, Gallery of the Press Club Warsaw 1975, Seven Poets (Third Eye Centre Glasgow and tour) 1981-83, Portrait Drawings (N E of Scotland Library and Museums Service) 1984, Portraits of Painters (Scottish Nat Gallery of Modern Art) 1988, Glasgow Art Gallery & Museum 1990; gp exhibitions incl: Scottish Realism (Scottish Arts Cncl tour) 1971, The Human Clay (Hayward Gallery London and Scottish Nat Gallery of Modern Art) 1976, Three Painters (Midland Gp Gallery, Nottingham) 1978, Narrative Paintings (Arnolfini Bristol and ICA London) 1979, Private Views (Arts Cncl of GB and tour) 1982, In Their Circumstances (Lincoln Usher Gallery) 1985-86, Picturing People: Figurative Painting from Britain 1945-89 (Far East tour) 1989, Scottish Art since 1990 (Scottish Nat Gall of Modern Art) 1989-90, Turning the Century (Raab Gallery London & Berlin) 1990, The Discerning Eye (Mall Galleries London) 1990; work in the public collections of Scottish Nat Portrait Gallery, Scottish Nat Gallery of Modern Art, Arts Cncl of GB, Yale Centre for British Art; writer of numerous catalogue texts; memb Edinburgh Festival Soc; *Clubs* The Glasgow Art; *Style—* Alexander Moffat, Esq; 20 Haddington Place, Edinburgh, Scotland EH7 4AF (☎ 031 556 2731); Glasgow School of Art, 167 Renfrew St, Glasgow G3 6RQ (☎ 041 332 9797)

MOFFAT, Lt-Gen Sir (William) Cameron; KBE (1985, OBE 1975); s of William Weir Moffat (D 1959), and Margaret Robinson, *née* Garrett (d 1973); *b* 8 Sept 1929; *Educ* Kings Park Sch Glasgow, Rothersay Acad, Univ of Glasgow (MB ChB, Rowing blue), RCS (Hallett prize); *m* 29 Sept 1953, Audrey Acquroff, da of Robert Watson (d 1969); 1 s (Christopher John Cameron b 24 March 1961); *Career* RAMC 1954-88: conslt surgn 1964, prof of mil surgery RAMC Coll and RSC 1970-75, CO BMH Rinteln 1978-80, cmd med HQ1 (Br) Corps 1980-83, PMO UKLF 1983-85, surgn gen and DGAMS 1985-88, ret; chief med advsr BRCS 1988-; Hon Freeman Worshipful Co of Barbers; FRCS 1963; CStJ 1985; *Style—* Lt-Gen Sir Cameron Moffat, KBE, OBE; British Red Cross Soc, 9 Grosvenor Crescent, London SW1X 7EJ (☎ 071 235 5454, fax 071 245 6315, telex 918657)

MOFFAT, David A; s of James Graham Moffat, of Broadstairs, Kent, and Myra Constance, *née* Paul; *b* 27 June 1947; *Educ* St Nicholas Sch Northwood, Univ of London (BSc, MB BS); *m* 5 Dec 1970, Jane Elizabeth, da of Flt-Lt David Dougherty Warwick, DFC, of Northwood Middx; 2 s (Simon b 11 May 1976, Mark b 10 Oct 1979), 1 da (Claire b 29 Oct 1974); *Career* sr registrar The London Hosp 1977-79, fell in otoneurosurgery Stanford Univ California 1979-80, conslt ENT surgn Westminster Hosp London 1980, conslt ENT surgn Addenbrookes Hosp Cambridge and associate lectr Univ of Cambridge 1981-, estab E Anglian and Supra Regnl Otoneurosurgical Serv base in Cambridge; author papers and chapters on: otological surgery, otology, otoneurosurgery, audiology, evoked response audiometry, hon sec and memb section of otology RSM; memb: Med Defence Union, Prosper Meniere Soc (fndr memb); MA Univ of Cambridge 1985, LRCP, FRCS, MRCS; *Recreations* theatre, golf; *Clubs* Gog Magog; *Style—* David Moffat, Esq; Dept of Otolaryngology & Otoneurosurgery, Addenbrooke's Hosp, Hills Rd, Cambridge CB2 2QQ (☎ 0223 217579)

MOFFAT, Gwen Mary; *b* 3 July 1924; *Educ* Hove County GS; *Career* author; novels: Lady with a Cool Eye (1973), Deviant Death (1973), The Corpse Road (1974), Miss Pink at the Edge of the World (1975), Over the Sea to Death (1976), A Short Time to Live (1976), Persons Unknown (1978), Die Like a Dog (1982), Last Chance Country (1983), Grizzly Trail (1984), Snare (1987), The Stone Hawk (1989), Rage (1990), The Raptor Zone (1990), Hard Option (1990), The Buckskin Girl (1982); non-fiction: Space Below My Feet (1961), Two Star Red (1964), On My Home Ground (1968), Survival Count (1972), Hard Road West (1981), The Storm Seekers (1989); memb: Soc of Authors, CWA, Mystery Writers of America; *Recreations* mountaineering; *Clubs* Pinnacle, Alpine, Sierra; *Style—* Ms Gwen Moffat; c/o agent, Mark Hamilton, 79 St Martin's Lane, London WC2N 4AA (☎ 071 836 4271)

MOFFAT, Dr Robin John Russell; s of A C Russell Moffat (d 1969), of London, and Gladys Leonora, *née* Taperell; *b* 18 Oct 1927; *Educ* Whitgift Sch Croydon, Guy's Hosp Med Sch, Univ of London (DRCOG); *m* 1, 8 Sept 1949 (m dis 1980), Audrey Heathcote, da of F B H Wride (d 1955), of Winchester; 2 s (Jeremy Guy b 7 Dec 1954, Timothy Julian b 3 Nov 1960), 1 da (Pamela Jane b 25 Aug 1951); m 2, 18 Nov 1980, Beryl Gwendoline Longmoor, *née* Wild; *Career* Nat Serv RN 1946-48, ORA (SBA Branch) RN Hosp Haslar; house surgn Guy's Hosp 1954-55, house physician Croydon Hosp 1957, resident obstetrician Mayday Hosp 1957-58, in gen med practice Croydon 1958-88, met police surgn 1959-88, sr forensic med examiner 1988-; MO Whitgift Fndn 1960-, chief MO TSB Bank 1978-, visiting lectr Dept of Forensic Med Guy's and St George's Hosp London; memb (former pres) Croydon Med Soc, fndr memb Croydon Medico-Legal Soc, chm Met Gp Assoc of Police Surgns; memb: MOs of Schs Assoc (former pres), Br Acad of Forensic Sciences, Cons Med Soc, Int Acad of Legal Med, BMA; Liveryman Worshipful Soc of Apothecaries; FRSM (pres Section of Clinical Forensic Med), LRCP, MRCS, MRCGP; *Recreations* racing, book collection; *Clubs* Carlton, Nat Sporting; *Style—* Dr Robin Moffat; 8 Arundel Terrace, Kemptown, Brighton, E Sussex BN2 1GA (☎ 0273 674 552); 10 Harley St, London WIN 1AA (☎ 071 580 4280, fax 071 637 5227, car phone 0860 228 407)

MOFFAT OF THAT ILK, Maj Francis; MC (1946), JP (Dumfries 1953), DL (Dumfries 1957); Chief of the Name and Arms of Moffat, confirmed by Lord Lyon King of Arms 1983; up to this point the Moffats had been a 'heidless' family for about 420 years; s of Capt William Murdoch Moffat, JP (d 1948), of Craigbeck, Moffat, and Jean Guthrie Troup (d 1918); *b* 21 March 1915; *Educ* Shrewsbury, Trinity Coll Cambridge (BA); *m* 1946, Margaret Eva, da of William Chambers Carrington (d 1945), of Luton; 2 da (Jean b 1947, Margaret b 1950); *Career* serv KOSB 1940-45, NW Europe, Maj; ret landowner and farmer; convener Dumfries CC 1969-75 (vice convener 1961-69); *Recreations* genealogy, reading, photography; *Style—* Maj Francis Moffat of that Ilk, MC, JP, DL; Redacres, Moffat, Dumfriesshire (☎ 0683 20045)

MOFFATT, Clive; s of Harold and Olive Moffatt; *b* 27 Dec 1948; *Educ* Thornes House Sch, LSE (BSc); *m* 1977, Kathleen Elizabeth, da of Robert Maguire; 1 s, 1 da; *Career* res economist to New Zealand Treasury 1972-75; conslt economist and writer Economist Intelligence Unit Ltd London 1975-76, chief sub-ed (fin unit and CEEFAX) BBC 1976-78, business ed Investors Chronicle 1978-79, corporate affrs conslt Guiness Peat Gp plc 1979-81; chief exec Blackrod Ltd (independent TV production subsidiary of Television South plc) 1981-; dir: Blackrod Interactive Servs Ltd, Lifestyle TV Ltd; chm BISFA Video and Television Gp; *Recreations* rugby, cricket, art, music; *Style—* Clive Moffatt, Esq; 53 Lavington Rd, London W13 (☎ 081 567 4716); Blackrod Ltd, Threeways House, 40-44 Clipstone St, London W1P 7EA (☎ 071 637 9376 and 580 6934, telex 269859)

MOFFATT, Prof (Henry) Keith; s of Frederick Henry Moffatt (d 1974), and Emmeline Marchant, *née* Fleming; *b* 12 April 1935; *Educ* George Watson's Coll Edinburgh, Univ of Edinburgh (BSc), Trinity Coll Cambridge (scholar, Ferguson scholar, BA, PhD, ScD, Smith's prize); *m* 17 Dec 1960, Katherine (Linty), da of Rev David Syme Stiven, MC, DD (d 1986); 2 s (Fergus b 1961 d 1987, Peter b 1962), 2 da (Hester b 1966, Penelope b 1967); *Career* Dept of Applied Mathematics and Theoretical Physics Univ of Cambridge: asst lectr 1961-64, lectr 1964-76, head of dept 1983-; Trinity Coll Cambridge: fell lectr and dir Studies in Mathematics 1961-76, tutor 1970-74, sr tutor 1975, professorial fell 1980-; prof of applied mathematics Univ of Bristol 1977-80, prof of mathematical physics Univ of Cambridge 1980-; Royal Society rep on Br Nat Ctee on Theoretical and Applied Mechanics 1976-89, sec IUTAM Congress Ctee 1984- (memb 1980-), memb Gen Assembly of IUTAM 1980-; Docteur h c Inst Nat Poly Grenoble 1987, Hon DSc State Univ of NY 1990; FRS 1986, FRSE 1988; *Books* Magnetic Field Generation in Electrically Conducting Fluids (1978), Topological Fluid Mechanics (ed, 1990); *Recreations* allotmenteering; *Style—* Prof Keith Moffatt, FRS, FRSE; 6 Banhams Close, Cambridge CB4 1HX (☎ 0223 63338); Trinity College, Cambridge; Department of Applied Mathematics and Theoretical Physics, Silver St, Cambridge (☎ 0223 337856, fax 0223 337918)

MOFFATT, Nigel; *b* 22 May 1954; *Career* playwright and poet; founded a writers gp Walsall 1984; writer in residence: Nat Theatre Studio 1985, Haymarket Theatre Leicester 1988; plays: Rhapsody in Black 'n' White (Nat Theatre Studio) 1985, Tony (Nat Theatre Studio 1985, Oval House 1987), Mamma Decemba (Temba Theatre Co and Birmingham Reperatory Co) 1987, Keeping Walsall Boxed In (W Midlands Arts Cncl) 1987, Opportunity (cmmnd by Br Film Inst) 1987, Prime Time (Haymarket Leicester) 1989, Beau Monde (Br Film Inst) 1990; radio plays: Lifetime (BBC) 1988, Lame Ducks (BBC) 1989, Selling Out (BBC) 1989, Wishful Thinking (BBC) 1990; television: When Love Dies (Channel 4) 1989; awards: Samuel Beckett Award for Mamma Decemba 1987, Giles Cooper Award for Lifetime 1987; *Style—* Nigel Moffatt, Esq

MOFFATT, Hon Mrs (Ruth Lesley); *née* Jackson; da of Baron Jackson of Burnley (Life Peer, d 1970); *b* 22 May 1945; *Educ* Sutton HS, Univ of Wales Bangor (BSc), Univ of Aberdeen (MSc); *m* 1970, David John Moffatt; 1 s, 1 da; *Career* Royal Soc Leverhulme scholar 1968-69, lectr Univ of Leeds 1969-70, pt/t tutor for Open Univ 1979-82, parish cncllr; runner-up: Ford Conservation Awards 1987, National Pondwatch Awards 1990; *Recreations* reading, lacemaking, gardening, tennis; *Style—* The Hon Mrs Moffatt; 26 Townsend Lane, Upper Boddington, Daventry, Northamptonshire

MOFFATT, Dr William Henry; OBE (1987), JP (1977); s of John Harry Moffatt, MPSI (d 1967), of Belfast, and Edith Margaret, *née* Reid (d 1961); *b* 11 April 1926; *Educ* Methodist Coll Belfast, Queen's Univ Belfast (MB BCh, BAO); *m* 12 June 1959, Elsie Mary, da of Samuel Bullock, of Enniskillen, Co Fermanagh (decd); 1 s (John Samuel William b 1964), 2 da (Emily Ann b 1961, Christine Mary b 1968); *Career* Nat Serv Capt RAMC Suez Canal Zone 1951-53; conslt physician in Geriatric Medicine Newtownabbey Hosp Gp 1965-, dir NI Hosp Advsy Serv 1984-; memb: tstees Leopardstown Park Hosp Tst, Dublin (disabled Irish ex-servicemen of WWs I&II), and War Pensions Ctee for NI, chm Res Ethical Ctee Univ of Ulster ; FRCPI; *Recreations* gardening, fishing, reading; *Style—* Dr William H Moffatt, OBE, JP; 7 School Lane, Greenisland, Carrickfergus, NI BT38 8RF (☎ 0232 863253)

MOGER, Christopher Richard Derwent; s of Richard Vernon Derwent Moger, of Dartmouth, S Devon, and late Cecile Eva Rosales, *née* Power; *b* 28 July 1949; *Educ* Sherborne, Univ of Bristol (LLB); *m* 27 July 1974, Victoria, da of Arthur George Cecil Trollope, of Overton, Hants; 3 s (Robin b 1979, Sholto b 1981, Dominic b 1985); *Career* called to the Bar Inner Temple 1972; *Recreations* fishing, tennis, chess; *Clubs* Garrick, Hurlingham; *Style—* Christopher Moger, Esq; 4 Pump Court, Temple, London EC4Y 7AN (☎ 071 353 2656, fax 071 583 2036, telex 8813250 Reflex G)

MOGFORD, Stephen George; *b* 20 June 1914; *Educ* Exeter, Univ of London (BA, BSc); *m* 1946; 1 s (Stephen); *Career* int banker; formerly: dep chm Italian International Bank Leadenhall St, vice chm Barclays Bank International, dir Barclays Bank plc; *Recreations* gardening, music; *Clubs* Reform, Overseas Bankers; *Style—* Stephen Mogford, Esq; Warrington Place Farmhouse, Paddock Wood, Kent TN12 6HE

MOGG, Gen Sir John; GCB (1972, KCB 1966, CB 1964), CBE (1960), DSO (1944 and Bar 1944), DL (Oxford 1979); s of Capt H B Mogg, MC, by his w Alice, *née* Ballard; *b* 17 Feb 1913; *Educ* Malvern, RMC Sandhurst (Sword of Honour); *m* 1939, Cecilia Margaret, yr da of Rev John Molesworth (himself 5 in descent from 1 Viscount Molesworth); 3 s (Col Nigel (Royal Green Jackets) b 1940, m Tessa Wright, 2 s; Patrick b 1942; Rev Timothy, who has assumed the name Rawdon-Mogg, b 1945, m Rachel Eastman; 2 s, 1 da); *Career* serv Coldstream Gds 1935-37, Oxf & Bucks LI 1937, serv WWII (despatches), joined Durham LI & serv NW Europe 1944-45; instr

Staff Coll 1948-50, Cdr 10 Para Bn 1950-52, chief instr Warminster Inf Sch 1952-54, GSO 1 IDC 1954-56, Cdr Cwlth Bde Gp Malaya 1958-60, War Office 1961-62, Cmdt RMA Sandhurst 1963-66; Col Cmdt: The Army Air Corps 1964-74, The Royal Green Jackets 1965-75; Cdr 1 Corps 1966-68, GOC-in-C S Cmd 1968, Army Strategic Cmd 1968-70, Adj-Gen 1970-73, Dep Supreme Allied Cdr Europe 1973-76, ADC Gen to HM 1971-74; pres Army Benevolent Fund 1980- (chm 1976); chm Operation Drake for Young Explorers 1978-; dir Lloyds Bank (S Midland Regional Bd) 1976-; Vice Lord-Lt Oxon 1979-; Meritorious Medal (Malaya); *Style*— Gen Sir John Mogg, GCB, CBE, DSO, DL; Church Close, Watlington, Oxon (☎ 049 161 2247)

MOGGACH, Deborah; da of Richard Alexander Hough, and Helen Charlotte, *née* Woodyatt; *b* 28 June 1948; *Educ* Camden Sch for Girls London, Queen's Coll London, Univ of Bristol (BA), Univ of London; *m* 1971 (m dis), Anthony Austin Moggach; 1 s (Alexander b 1 Sept 1975), 1 da (Charlotte Flora b 9 May 1977); *Career* OUP 1970-72, journalist and teacher Pakistan 1972-74, full-time writer (for newspapers, magazines and tv) and novelist 1975-; novels incl: You Must Be Sisters (1978), Close to Home (1979), A Quiet Drink (1980), Hot Water Man (1982), Porky (1983), To Have and To Hold (1986), Smile and Other Stories (1988), Driving in the Dark (1989), Stolen (1990), The Stand-In (1991); short stories in various anthologies incl: Best Short Stories 1986, Best Short Stories 1988, The Best of Fiction Magazine (1986), The Woman's Hour Book of Short Stories (1990); stage play Double-Take (produced 1990), tv series to Have and To Hold and Stolen; *awards* Young Journalist of the Year 1975; *Recreations* riding, gardening, walking through cities at dusk looking into people's windows; *Style*— Mrs Deborah Moggach; Curtis Brown, 162-8 Regent St, London W1R 5TA (☎ 071 872 0331); Rochelle Stevens, 2 Terrett's Place, Upper St, N1 1QZ (☎ 071 359 3900)

MOGGRIDGE, Harry Traherne (Hal); OBE; s of Lt-Col Harry Weston Moggridge, Chevalier de la Legion d'Honneur, CMG (d 1961), of Tonbridge, Kent, and Helen Mary Ferrier Taylor (artist, d 1989); *b* 2 Feb 1936; *Educ* Tonbridge, AA (Leverhulme Scholar); *m* 1 Dec 1963, Catherine (Cass) Greville Herbert; 2 s (Geoffrey b 8 Sept 1967, Lawrence b 19 Feb 1970), 1 da (Harriet b 23 Sept 1965); *Career* Nottinghamshire CC 1960, asst to Sir Geoffrey Jellicoe 1961-63, site architect Sir William Halcrow & Partners Tema Harbour Ghone 1964-65, landscape asst GLC 1966-67, own architectural practice, prof of landscape architecture Univ of Sheffield 1984-86, ptnr Colvin and Maggridge Landscape Consultants 1969- (ptnr with late Brenda Colvin, CBE, continuing today with Christopher Carter); memb Cncl Landscape Inst 1970-83 and 1987- (hon sec vice pres and pres 1979-81, chm Int Ctee and del to Int Fedn of Landscape Architects 1987-); memb: Bd Landscape Res Gp 1983-88, Royal Art Cmmn 1988-, Nat Tst Architectural Panel 1990-; PPLI, FIHort, ARIBA, AAdipl, FRSA; *Publications* author of numerous articles and chapters of books describing works or technical subjects; *Recreations* looking at pictures, gardens, buildings, town, landscapes and people in these places, walking, theatre; *Clubs* Royal Soc of Arts, Farmers; *Style*— Hal Moggridge, Esq, OBE; Colvin and Moggridge, Filkins, Lechlade, Glos GL7 3JQ (☎ 036 786 225, fax 036 786 564)

MOHEKEY, Judith Marie (Judy); da of Gordon William Mohekey, of 1A Webb Street, Palmerston North, NZ, and Dora Lilian, *née* Tietjens; *b* 29 Nov 1954; *Educ* Freyberg HS Palmerston North, Nat Sch of Ballet, Wellington NZ; *m* 8 June 1984, Roger Norman Abbott Spence, s of John Harold Spence; 1 s (Alexander Spence b 9 Nov 1990); *Career* ballerina; NZ Ballet (princ roles in Una Kai's Firebird and Raymonda Act III) 1974, princ Scottish Ballet 1985- (corps de ballet 1975); roles incl: Snow Queen in The Nutcracker 1984, Giulietta in Peter Darrell's Tales of Hoffman 1984, The Woman in Peter Darrell's Five Rückert Songs 1984, title role in Giselle (Theatre Royal Bath) 1986, Sugar Plum in The Nutcracker (Glasgow Theatre Royal) 1986, title role in Darrell's Cinderella 1987, Juliet in Cranko's Romeo & Juliet (His Majesty's Aberdeen) 1988, Wendy and Tinkerbell in Peter Pan 1989, Lea in Darrell's Cheri 1989, The Sylph in La Sylphide (Glasgow Theatre Royal) 1990, leads in Paquita Scotch Symphony and Who Cares (Glasgow Theatre Royal); guest artist tour with Royal New Zealand Ballet (title roles in Serenade and Jack Carter's Melodrama) 1986; winner Gold Duke of Edinburgh award; *Recreations* interior design, dressmaking; *Style*— Ms Judy Mohekey; 21 Glencairn Crescent, Edinburgh EH12 5BT (☎ 031 337 8330)

MOHR, Dr Peter Dean; s of Dean Mohr, of Toledo, Ohio, USA, and Lucy, *née* Smith; *b* 25 Jan 1945; *Educ* St Josephs Coll Blackpool, Univ of Manchester (BSc, MB ChB, MRCP); *m* Julie; 2 s (Neil b 1973, Nicholas b 1975), 1 da (Jaqueline b 1970); *Career* conslt neurologist Salford Royal Hosp and Hope Hosp Salford 1977-; FRCP 1990; *Recreations* history of medicine; *Style*— Dr Peter Mohr; 16 Westminster Rd, Eccles, Salford, Lancs M30 9EB (☎ 061 707 1818); Dept of Neurology, Hope Hospital, Eccles Old Rd, Salford M6 8HD (☎ 061 789 7373)

MOHYEDDIN, Zia; *b* 20 June 1931; *Educ* Punjab Univ (BA), RADA; *m* 1974, Nahid Siddiqui; 3 s; *Career* actor prodr and dir; leading roles in principal theatres: Pakistan 1956-57, UK 1959-71; dir gen Pakistan Nat Performing Ensemble 1971-77, presenter and prodr Here and Now Central TV 1980-; theatre: A Passage to India 1960, The Alchemist 1964, The Merchant of Venice 1966, Volpone 1967, The Guide 1968, On The Rocks 1969, Measure for Measure 1981, Film Film Film 1986; film: Lawrence of Arabia 1961, Sammy Going South 1963, The Sailor from Gibraltar 1965, Khartoum 1965, Ashanti 1982, Assam Garden 1985; TV: The Hidden Truth 1964, Gangsters 1979, The Jewel in the Crown 1983, King of the Ghetto 1986, Mountbatten Last Viceroy 1988, Shalom Salaam 1989; lectr on cultural topics, ctee memb Arts Cncl; *Recreations* reading, bridge; *Clubs* Savile; *Style*— Zia Mohyeddin, Esq; c/o Plunkett Greene Ltd, 4 Ovington Gdns, Knightbridge, London SW13 1LS

MOIR, Christopher Ernest; s and h of Sir Ernest Ian Royds Moir, 3 Bt; *b* 22 May 1955; *Educ* King's Coll Sch Wimbledon; *m* Vanessa; 2 s (Oliver Royds b 1984, Alexander Victor (twin), 1 step da (Nina Louise b 1976); *Heir* Oliver Royds Moir; *Career* CA; *Style*— Christopher Moir Esq; 77 Dora Rd, Wimbledon, London SW19 7JT

MOIR, Sir Ernest Ian Royds; 3 Bt (UK 1916), of Whitehanger, Fernhurst, Co Sussex; s of Sir Arrol Moir, 2 Bt (d 1957); *b* 9 June 1925; *Educ* Rugby, Gonville and Caius Coll Cambridge; *m* 1954, Margaret Hanham, da of George Carter, of Huddersfield, Yorks; 3 s; *Heir* s, Christopher Ernest Moir; *Style*— Sir Ernest Moir, Bt; Three Gates, 174 Coombe Lane West, Kingston upon Thames, Surrey KT2 7DE (☎ 081 942 7394)

MOIR, Lance Stuart; *b* 26 Jan 1957; *Career* account mangr corp banking Grindlays Bank plc 1980-85, treas Br Home Stores plc 1985-86, head corp fin and planning Storehouse plc 1988- (gp tres 1986-88), lectr in training mgmnt Cranford Sch of Mgmnt; memb: Educnl Ctee Assoc Corp Tres, standing Ctee of Convocation Univ of Sheffield; occasional contrib the Treasurer and Banking World; ACIB 1983, FCT 1990; *Books* (editorial panel) Institute of Bankers Textbook on Multinational Corporate Finance; *Recreations* singing, music, opera, theatre, travel; *Style*— Lance Moir, Esq; Storehouse plc, The Heal's Buildings, 196 Tottenham Ct Rd, London W1P 9LD (☎ 071 323 0381, fax 071 323 1450, telex 296475)

MOISEIWITSCH, Prof Benjamin Lawrence; s of Jacob Moiseiwitsch (d 1957), and Chana, *née* Kotlerman (d 1984); *b* 6 Dec 1927; *Educ* Royal Liberty Sch Romford, UCL (BSc, PhD); *m* 20 June 1953, Sheelagh Mary, *née* McKeon; 2 s (Julian b 1962, Nicholas b 1968), 2 da (Tatiana b 1954, Lisa b 1957); *Career* Queen's Univ of Belfast: lectr in applied mathematics 1952-62, reader in applied mathematics 1962-68, prof of applied mathematics 1968-, dean of Faculty of Sci 1972-75, head Dept of Applied Mathematics and Theoretical Physics 1977-89; memb Royal Irish Acad Dublin, fell Former Physical Soc of London; *Books* Variational Methods (1966), Integral Equations (1977); *Recreations* music; *Style*— Prof Benjamin Moiseiwitsch; 21 Knocktern Gardens, Belfast, Northern Ireland BT4 3LZ (☎ 0232 658332); Department of Applied Mathematics And Theoretical Physics, The Queen's University of Belfast, Belfast BT7 1NN (☎ 0232 245133 ext 3158, fax 0232 247895, telex 74487)

MOKE, Johnny; s of James Charles Rowley (d 1974), and Lily May, *née* Skinner; *b* 2 Sept 1945; *Educ* McEntree Techn Sch London; *m* 11 April 1977, Hazel, da of Alberto Gregorio Gomes, of Navelim, Nagmoddem, Salcette Goa, India; 2 da (Sunny Star b 4 Aug 1972, Soraya Sultana b 12 Jan 1988); *Career* shoe designer; collections for fashion shows of: Adeline André Paris 1985-88, Alistair Blair, Anthony Price, Georgina Godley, Vivienne Westwood; exhibitions: Kunst Museum Vienna Austria 1988, Institut Objekt Kultur Glassen Germany 1988, V & A 1990; int coverage in fashion magazines; memb Select Ctee Design Cncl 1987; *Recreations* arts, travel; *Style*— Johnny Moke, Esq; 12 Childs St, London SW5 (☎ 071 370 1859); 396 Kings Rd, London SW10 (☎ 071 351 2232, fax 071 351 2232)

MOLDEN, Nigel Charles; s of Percival Ernest Molden, of 60 York Rd, Headington, Oxford OX3 8NP, and Daisy Mary, *née* Currill; *b* 17 Aug 1948; *Educ* City of Oxford HS, Poly of Central London (BSc), Brunel Univ (MSc); *m* 14 Aug 1971, (Hilary) Julia, da of Frederick Withers Lichfield (d 1969); 3 s (Nicholas Stuart b 1974, Simon Charles b 1977, Alexander Giles b 1983); *Career* md The Magnum Music Group Ltd 1985-; chm Beaconsfield Town Cons Assoc, govr Royal GS High Wycombe, town cncllr Beaconsfield 1989-; Freeman City of London 1990, Liveryman Worshipful Co of Marketers 1989; FCIM 1988, FInstD 1982, FBIM 1987; *Recreations* theatre, rugby football, motor sports; *Clubs* Royal Overseas League; *Style*— Nigel Molden, Esq; Ashcombe House, Deanwood Rd, Jordans, Beaconsfield, Bucks HP9 2UU (☎ 0494 678177); Stone Cottage, Cowl Lane, Winchcombe, Gloucs; Magnum House, High St, Lane End, Bucks HP14 3JG (☎ 0494 882858, fax 0494 882631)

MOLE, Arthur Charles; s of Sir Charles Johns Mole, KBE, MVO (d 1962), of Walton-on-Thames, and his 1 w, Annie, *née* Martin (d 1962); *b* 25 Feb 1926; *Educ* St George's Coll Weybridge, King's Coll London (BSc); *m* 1957, Hon Susan Mary, *qv*, da of Baron Hinton of Bankside, KCB (Life Peer; d 1983); 2 s; *Career* project design engr Atomic Power Constructions Ltd 1957-65, gen mangr Engrg Morganite Carbon Ltd 1965-72, dir Morgan Electrical Carbon Ltd 1968-76, md MBM (Technol) Ltd 1976-86, dir Morganite Refractories 1982-86, dep chm Morgan ROCTEC Ltd 1986-88, ret; *Style*— Arthur Mole, Esq; Polurrian, 2 Second Ave, Worthing, W Sussex BN14 9NX (☎ 0903 209122); 32 Devon Ct, Freshwater East, Pembroke (☎ 0646 672467)

MOLE, David Richard Penton; QC (1990); s of Rev Arthur Penton Mole, of Pershore, Worcs, and Margaret Isobel, *née* Dublin (MA), LSE (LLM); *b* 1 April 1943; *m* 29 March 1969, Anu-Reet, da of Alfred Nigol; 3 s (Matthew David Penton b 20 Nov 1971, Joseph Tobias b 9 April 1974, Thomas Alfred William b 24 Aug 1978), 1 da (Susannah Juliet Martha b 5 July 1984); *Career* lectr City of London Poly 1967-74; called to the Bar Inner Temple 1970 (ad eundem Gray's Inn 1973-), standing jr counsel to the Inland Revenue (Rating and Valuation) 1984-90; *Recreations* sailing, skiing, walking, drawing and painting; *Style*— David Mole, Esq, QC; Ground Floor, 4-5 Gray's Inn Square, Gray's Inn, London WC1R 5AY (☎ 071 404 5252, fax 071 242 7803)

MOLE, Hon Mrs (Susan Mary); da of Baron Hinton of Bankside, KBE, OM (Life Peer, d 1983), and Lillian, *née* Boyer (d 1973); *b* 6 Feb 1932; *Educ* Wentworth Milton Mount; *m* 1957, Arthur Charles Mole, *qv*, s of Sir Charles John Mole, KBE, MVO (d 1962), of Walton-on-Thames; 2 s; *Career* state registered nurse; *Style*— The Hon Mrs Mole; Polurrian, Second Ave, Charmandean, Worthing, W Sussex BN14 9NX (☎ 0903 209122); 32 Devon Ct, Freshwater East, Pembroke (☎ 0646 672467)

MOLES, Andrew James; s of Stuart Norman Francis Moles, of Singapore; *b* 12 Feb 1961; *Educ* Finham Park Comp Sch, Henley Coll of Further Educn, The Butts Coll of Further Educn; *m* 17 Dec 1988, Jacqueline Joy, da of Jurgens Joubert Griessel; 1 s (Daniel Stuart b 9 July 1990); *Career* debut Warwickshire CCC 1985 (co cap 1986, 110 first class appearances), Griqualand W Cricket Union 1986-87 and 1987-88 and 1988-89 seasons (16 appearances), Benson & Hedges night cricket SA Impalas 1987-88 and 1988-89 seasons (5 appearances); world record number of times an opening pair of batsmen in first class cricket have passed 50 runs partnership (with P A Smith); apprentice die sinker and toolmaker, standards room inspr, cricket coach, corp hospitality sales exec; Benson & Hedges Gold award, Natwest Gold award, Natwest winners trophy; *Recreations* golf, all sport; *Style*— Andrew Moles, Esq; Warwickshire County Cricket Club, Edgbaston County Ground, Edgbaston, Birmingham (☎ 021 446 4422)

MOLESWORTH, Allen Henry Neville; s of Col Roger Bevil Molesworth (d 1974); *b* 20 Aug 1931; *Educ* Wellington, Trinity Coll Cambridge; *m* 1970, Gail Cheng Kwai, da of Chan Lum Choon (d 1989), of Singapore; *Career* Lt Queen's Own Hussars; CA; mgmnt conslt 1967-76, fin and admin controller Crown Agents 1976-84, chief accountant BT Properties 1984-90, mgmnt conslt 1990-; *Recreations* skiing, shooting, restoring antiques; *Style*— Allen Molesworth, Esq; c/o Lloyds Bank, 6 Pall Mall, London SW1

MOLESWORTH, 11 Viscount (I 1716); Richard Gosset Molesworth; also Baron Philipstown (I 1716); s of 10 Viscount (d 1961); 3 Viscount (Richard, d 1758), was ADC to Duke of Marlborough, whose life he saved at Battle of Ramillies by giving his horse to the unhorsed Duke (he later became C-in-C of HM Forces in Ireland); *b* 31 Oct 1907; *Educ* Lancing; *m* 1958, Anne Florence (d 1983), da of John Mark Freeman Cohen; 2 s; *Heir* s, Hon Robert Bysse Kelham Molesworth; *Career* serv WWII, RAF (Middle E Forces); former farmer; Freeman City of London 1978; *Style*— The Rt Hon the Viscount Molesworth; Garden Flat, 2 Bishopswood Rd, Highgate, London N6 (☎ 081 348 1366)

MOLESWORTH, Hon Robert Bysse Kelham; s and h of 11 Viscount Molesworth, by his w, Anne, *née* Cohen (d 1983); *b* 4 June 1959; *Educ* Cheltenham, Univ of Sussex (BA); *Style*— The Hon Robert Molesworth; Garden Flat, 2 Bishopswood Rd, Highgate N6 4PR

MOLESWORTH-ST AUBYN, Lt-Col Sir (John) Arscott; 15 Bt (E 1689), MBE (1963), JP (Devon 1971), DL (Cornwall 1971); s of Sir John Molesworth-St Aubyn, 14 Bt, CBE (d 1985), and Celia Marjorie (d 1965), da of Lt-Col Valentine Vivian, CMG, DSO, MVO; *b* 15 Dec 1926; *Educ* Eton; *m* 2 May 1957, Iona Audrey Armatrude, da of Adm Sir Francis Loftus Tottenham, KCB, CBE (d 1966); 2 s, 1 da; *Heir* s, William Molesworth-St Aubyn, b 23 Nov 1958; *Career* serv KRRC and Royal Green Jackets (in Libya, Palestine, Malaya, Brunei, British Guiana and Borneo) 1945-69, Staff Coll 1959, Jt Servs Staff Coll 1964, Lt-Col 1967-69; High Sheriff Cornwall 1975; chm W Local Land Drainage Ctee SW Water Authy and W Local Flood Alleviation Ctee NRA 1974-, memb Exec Cncl Historic Houses Assoc 1978-, vice chm SW Regn Timber Growers UK 1978- (pres Cornwall Branch), memb Nat Cncl CLA; *Recreations* shooting, ornithology; *Clubs* Army and Navy; *Style*— Lt-Col Sir Arscott Molesworth-St Aubyn, Bt, MBE, JP, DL; Pencarrow, Bodmin, Cornwall; Tetcott Manor, Holsworthy, Devon

(☎ 040 927 220)

MOLINEUX, Lt Cdr Peter Ranby; s of Frederick Alfred Molineux (d 1969), of Kent, and Kathleen Margaret, *née* Ranby (d 1975); *b* 28 April 1931; *Educ* RNC: Dartmouth and Greenwich; *m* 30 July 1955, Jane Gwenydd, da of Patrick Erskine Cruttwell (d 1989), of Brompton Ralph, Somerset; 2 s (William b 1959, Patrick b 1966), 2 da (Dr Petronella Horne b 1957, Mrs Lucy Douglas b 1960); *Career* HM Submarines 1952-59, Capt HMS Monkton 1959-61, Lt Cdr 1961, Naval Instr RAF Coll Cranwell 1961-63, HMS Caesar, MHQ Pitreavie, HMS Bulwark, ret 1969; princ DHSS 1969, ret 1991; churchwarden: St John Baptist Wonersh 1976-77, All Saints Witley 1981-88; *Recreations* reading mil and naval history, walking with dogs; *Style—* Lt Cdr Peter Molineux; Vine Cottage, Witley, Surrey (☎ 0428 682298)

MOLL, John Graeme (Francis); s of Frederick Charles Moll, of 62 Silverdale Rd, Sheffield 11, Yorks, and Anita Lilian, *née* Francis; *b* 15 Aug 1947; *Educ* Repton; *Career* sci and med photographer Royal Free Hosp and Sch of Med London 1974- (radiographer 1969-73); chm Braintree and Bocking Civic Soc 1988-, memb Anglian Water Customer Consultative Ctee (S Gp) 1984-89; churchwarden SS Peter and Paul Black Notley 1985-87; Freeman City of London, Liveryman Worshipful Co of Apothecaries (1968); AIMI (1986), ARPS (1986); *Recreations* chess, reading, community affairs, health services research and economics, theatre, music, learning Mandarin, working; *Style—* Francis Moll, Esq; 10 Brook Close, Braintree, Essex (☎ 0376 25974); Dept of Histopathology, Royal Free Hospital School of Medicine, Pond Street, Hampstead, London NW3 2QG (☎ 071 794 0500 ext 3544)

MOLLAN, Prof Raymond Alexander Boyce; s of Alexander Mollan, of Belfast, and Margaret Emma Boyce (d 1984); *b* 10 Aug 1943; *Educ* Belfast Royal Acad, Queens Univ (MB BCh, BAO, HD); *m* 1 Sept 1969, Patricia Ann Fairbanks, da of Alexander Scott (d 1961); 3 s (Ian Alexander b 1972, Andrew John b 1973, David William b 1975), 1 da (Susan Patricia b 1977); *Career* RNR 1968-84; trg grades: med 1964-69, obstetrics 1970-72, surgery 1972-74, orthopaedic surgery 1974-79; conslt orthopaedic surgn Ulster Hosp 1979-80; Queen's Univ Belfast: sr lectr in orthopaedic surgery 1980-84, prof of orthopaedic surgery 1984-; chm educn ctee Cncl Br Orthopaedic Assoc (chm Info Technol Ctee), fndr memb Br Hip Soc, Edinburgh Coll Surgns; memb: BMA, Irish Orthopaedic Assoc; *Recreations* sailing, skiing; *Clubs* The Naval, Royal NI Yacht, Royal Ulster Yacht; *Style—* Prof Raymond Mollan; 167 Bangor Rd, Holywood, Co Down BT18 0ET (☎ 02317 3529); Dept Orthopaedic surgery, Musgrave Park Hosp, Belfast BT18 0ET (☎ 0232 669501, fax 0232 247895, telex 74487)

MOLLISON, Prof Denis; s of Prof Patrick Loudon Mollison, and Margaret Doreen, *née* Peirce; *b* 28 June 1945; *Educ* Westminster, Trinity Coll Cambridge (MA, PhD); *m* 1 June 1978, Jennifer, da of Dr John Hutton; 1 s (Charles b 1986), 3 da (Clare b 1979, Hazel b 1980, Daisy b 1982); *Career* res fell Kings Coll Cambridge 1969-73; Heriot-Watt Univ: lectr 1973-79, reader 1979-86, prof of applied probability 1986-; author of various res papers on epidemics, ecology and wave energy; chm Mountain Bothies Assoc 1978- (sec 1974-78), memb Bernoulli Soc 1980; John Muir Tst: co-fndr 1983, tstee 1986-, chm Property and Res Ctee 1988-; FRSS 1977; *Recreations* hill walking and bothying, photography, music, squash; *Style—* Prof Denis Mollison; The Laigh House, Inveresk, Musselburgh, Scotland EH21 7TD (☎ 031 665 2055); Dept of Actuarial Maths & Statistics, Heriot-Watt University, Riccarton, Edinburgh EH14 4AS (☎ 031 451 3200, fax 031 451 3249)

MOLLOY, Michael John; s of John George Molloy, of Ealing, London, and Margaret Ellen, *née* West; *b* 22 Dec 1940; *Educ* Ealing Sch of Art; *m* 13 June 1964, Sandra June, da of Hubert Edwin Foley (d 1988), of Suffolk; 3 da (Jane b 1965, Catherine b 1966, Alexandra b 1968); *Career* ed: Mirror Magazine 1969-70, Daily Mirror 1975-85; ed in chief Mirror Gp Newspapers 1985-90, dir Mirror Gp Newspapers 1976; *Books* The Black Dwarf (1985), The Kid from Riga (1987), The Harlot of Jericho (1989), The Century (1990); *Recreations* writing; *Clubs* Reform, Savile; *Style—* Michael Molloy, Esq; 62 Culmington Rd, Ealing, London W13 9NH

MOLLOY, Michael William; s of William Molloy (d 1982), of Sydney, Aust, and Alice, *née* McMahon (d 1975); *b* 5 Jan 1940; *Educ* Public Sch Sydney Aust; *m* 10 Nov 1983, Adrienne Esther, da of Charles Dolesch, of Phoenix, Arizona, USA; *Career* camera operator: for Nick Roeg on Performance and Walkabout, for Stanley Kubrick on Clockwork Orange, Barry Lyndon; dir of photography: Mad Dog, Summerfield, The Shout, The Kidnapping of the President, Shock Treatment, Dead Easy, The Return of Captain Invincible, Reflections, The Hit, Bethune, (dir Phillip Borson starred Donald Sutherland on location in China), Scandal (dir Michael Caton-Jones starred John Hurt, Joanne Whalley); memb: Br Soc of Cinematographers; *Recreations* still photography, cooking, fishing; *Style—* Michael Molloy, Esq; 3 Glebe Place, London SW3 5LB;(☎ 071 351 6138); 100 Florence Terrace, Scotland Island, NSW 2105, Australia (☎ 02 997 1282); CCA Personal Management, 4 Court Lodge, 48 Sloane Square, London SW1 8AT

MOLLOY, Baron (Life Peer 1981), of Ealing in Greater London; William John Molloy; s of William John Molloy; *b* 28 Oct 1918; *Educ* Elementary Sch Swansea, Univ of Wales, Univ Coll Swansea; *m* 1, 1946, Eva Lewis (d 1980); 1 da (Hon Marion Ann (Hon Mrs Motl) b 1947); *m* 2, 1981 (m dis 1987), Doris Paines; *Career* serv Field Cos RE 1939-46; memb: TGWU 1936-46, Civil Service Union 1946-52, Co-op and USDAW 1952; Parly advsr COHSE 1974-79, ed Civil Service Review 1947-52, ldr Fulham Borough Cncl 1952-62, MP (Lab) Ealing N 1964-79, former vice chm Parly Lab Pty Gp for Common Market and Euro Affairs, chm PLP Social Services Gp 1974, Parly advsr London Trades Cncl Tport Ctee 1968-79; memb House of Commons Estimates Ctee 1968-70, PPS to PMG and Min of Posts and Telecommunications Assemblies Cncl of Europe and WEU 1969-73; memb: Parly and Scientific Ctee 1982-, EC, CAABU, Ct Univ of Reading 1968, Exec Cncl RGS 1976; Parly and scientific Assoc political conslt: COHSE 1980-, Br Library Assoc 1984-; former advsr to Arab League; pres Metropolitan Area Royal Br Legion 1984, hon pres Univ of London Union and Debating Soc 1983-, pres and tstee Health Visitors Assoc; hon assoc Br Vetinary Assoc; hon fell Univ Wales 1987; fell World Assoc of Arts and Sciences; *Recreations* horse-riding, music, collecting dictionaries; *Style—* The Rt Hon Lord Molloy; 2a Uneeda Drive, Greenford, Middx UB6 8QB; House of Lords, Westminster, London SW1 (☎ 071 219 6710)

MOLONY, (Sir) (Thomas) Desmond; 3 Bt (UK 1925), of the City of Dublin (but does not use title); s of Sir Hugh Francis Molony, 2 Bt (d 1976); *b* 13 March 1937; *Educ* Ampleforth, Trinity Coll Dublin; *m* 1962, Doris, da of late E W Foley, of Cork; 4 da; *Heir* unc, Sir Joseph Thomas Molony, KCVO, QC; *Style—* Desmond Molony Esq

MOLONY, Peter John; s of Sir Joseph Molony, KCVO, QC (d 1977), 2 s of 1 Bt, and Carmen Mary, *née* Dent; gs of Rt Hon Sir Thomas Molony, 1 Bt; hp to Btcy of kinsman Desmond Molony, 3 Bt (*qv*, who does not use title); *b* 17 Aug 1937; *Educ* Downside, Trinity Coll Cambridge (MA); *m* 1964, Elizabeth Mary, da of Henry Clevaux Chaytor, of Cambridge; 4 s (Sebastian b 1965, Benjamin b 1966, Benedict b 1972, Francis b 1975), 1 da (Jane b 1967); *Heir* er s Sebastian; *Career* CA; sr vice pres Sea Containers Inc 1968-73; dir: Post Office 1973-75, Scottish & Newcastle Breweries 1975-79, Rolls Royce plc 1979-86; md Chaytor King Ltd 1986-, memb Exec Ctee Christian Assoc of Business Executives; FCA; *Recreations* music, gardening; *Clubs* Utd Oxford and Cambridge Univ; *Style—* Peter J Molony, Esq; Rock House, Great Elm, nr Frome, Somerset (☎ 0373 812332); 1 Eaton Place, London SW1X 8BN (☎ 071 235 2939)

MOLONY, Sean Charles; s of Patrick Harry Molony, of Ardingly, Sussex, and Rosemary, *née* Ryland Thomas; *b* 31 March 1964; *Educ* Ardingly Coll, Oxford Poly (BSc); *Career* private client portfolio mangr: Quilter Goodison Co (Stockbrokers) 1986-88, ANZ Grindlays Bank (Private bank) 1989-90; institutional fund mangr Cornhill Insurance 1990-; awarded: Securities Industry Dip, Institutional Investment Advice Examination (merit); *Recreations* snooker, squash, running, theatre, music, foreign travel; *Style—* Sean Molony, Esq; 14 Cruikshank Rd, Stratford, London E15 1SN (☎ 081 519 3791); Cornhill Insurance plc, 32 Cornhill, London (☎ 071 626 5410)

MOLSON, Baron (Life Peer UK 1961), of High Peak, Co Derby; (Arthur) Hugh Elsdale Molson; PC (1956); s of late Maj John Elsdale Molson, MD, JP, MP (d 1925), of Goring Hall, Worthing, Sussex, and Mary, *née* Leeson; *b* 29 June 1903; *Educ* Lancing, New Coll Oxford; *m* 1949, Nancy, da of late W H Astington, of Bramhall, Cheshire; *Career* serv 36 Searchlight Regt RA 1939-41; barr; MP (U) W R Yorks (Doncaster Div) 1931-35 and Derbyshire (High Peak Div) 1939-61, Parly sec Min of Works 1951-53, jt Parly sec Min of Tport and Civil Aviation 1953-57, Min of Works 1957-59; memb Monckton Cmmn on Rhodesia & Nyasaland 1960, chm of Cmmn of Privy Cnsllrs on Buganda-Bunyoro Dispute 1962; pres of the Town & Country Planning Assoc 1963-, chm Cncl for the Protection of Rural England 1968-71, pres 1971-80; *Clubs* Athenaeum; *Style—* The Rt Hon the Lord Molson, PC; 20 Marsham Court, Marsham Street, London SW1P 4JY (☎ 071 828 2008)

MOLYNEAUX, Rt Hon James Henry; PC (1983), MP (UU) Lagan Valley 1983-; s of William Molyneaux (d 1953), of Seacash, Killead, Co Antrim; *b* 27 Aug 1920; *Educ* Aldergrove Sch Co Antrim; *Career* RAF 1941-46, memb Antrim CC 1964-1973, vice chm Eastern Special Care Hosp Ctee 1966-73, chm Antrim branch of NI Assoc for Mental Health 1967-1970, MP (UU) Antrim South 1970-1983, vice pres UU Cncl 1974-, ldr UU Pty House of Commons 1974-, UU Pty 1979-; JP Co Antrim 1957-86; *Style—* The Rt Hon James Molyneaux, MP; Aldergrove, Crumlin, Co Antrim, NI (☎ 084 94 22545)

MOLYNEUX, Stephanie; da of Roy Molyneux and Margaret Mary Molyneux (d 1986); *b* 6 Aug 1948; *Educ* Queen Mary Coll London (BSc Econ); *Career* security analyst 1970-74, dep ed Scrip 1974-76, dir Burson-Marstellar 1976-81, mktg mangr Dow Chemical Europe 1986-88 (communications mangr 1981-86), md The Watts Group plc 1989-; pres Jr C of C for London 1980-81; Freeman City of London; *Recreations* backgammon, tennis, travel, original tapestry; *Clubs* Riverside; *Style—* Ms Stephanie Molyneux; The Watts Group plc, 52 St John Street, Smithfield, London EC1M 4DT (☎ 071 490 4747)

MOLYNEUX-CARTER, Brig Kenneth Philip; CBE (1967, OBE 1958), MC (1942); s of Maj-Gen Beresford Cecil Molyneux Carter, CB, CMG (d 1923), and Bertha Isabel Ada, *née* Baines (d 1963); *b* 2 July 1913; *Educ* Reading Sch, RMC Sandhurst, Quetta Staff Coll (psc); *m* 30 Nov 1940, Iris Kathleen, da of Charles Rand Overy, of Kent and Kenya (d 1958); 1 s (Maj Kenneth Beresford), 2 da (Diana Althea (Mrs Garside), Anita Iris (Mrs Leicester)); *Career* cmmnd 2 Lt 20 The Lancashire Fusiliers 1933; served: Palestine, Transjordan, Shanghai, Tientsin, Peking, Quetta; Nigeria Regt RWAFF 1939-41; active serv 3 Nigeria Regt: Kenya, Br Somaliland, Italian Somaliland, Abyssinia (wounded and evacuated to Nigeria); CO 13 Bn Nigeria Regt Lagos 1943, CO 1 Bn The Sierra Leone Regt 1943-45; served: Nigeria, India, Burma (despatches); student Quetta 1945-46, GSO1 W African Liaison Section GHQ Delhi 1946, GSO2 mil advsr on mission to Nepal 1947, GSO2 WO 1947-49, GSO2 Anglo-French Def Talks Kenya and Madagascar 1950, 2 i/c 2/3 Bn KAR Kenya and Mauritius 1951-52, CO E Africa Trg Centre Kenya 1952, 2 i/c 2 Bn 20 The Lancashire Fusiliers Bulford and Trieste 1953, AQMG HQ Trieste 1954-55 (during final evacuation of Br forces), CO 2 Bn The Royal Malay Regt (active serv on anti-terrorist ops) 1955-58, Col GS HQ AFNE Norway (responsible for major NATO exercise) 1959-61, Col WO 1961-64, Brig 1964, def and mil attaché Br Embassy Ankara 1964-68, ret 1968; Johan Mangku Negara Companion in the Most Distinguished Order of Panguan Negara (Malaya); *Recreations* family history, natural history, filming, gardening; *Style—* Brig Kenneth Molyneux-Carter, CBE, MC

MOLYNEUX-CHILD, Lt-Col John Walter; TD (1972); s of Lt-Col Thomas M Child, TD, of Seaforth, Ganghill, Guildford, Surrey, and Agnes Eileen Molyneux (d 1984); *b* 5 Aug 1939; *Educ* Clifton, King's Coll Univ of London (BSc); *m* 14 Sept 1986 (m dis 1978), Sydney Pearl Ann Wilcox; 2 s (Patrick Gordon Osborne b 26 March 1971, Rory William Hugh Allingham b 12 Nov 1975); *Career* cmmnd REME(TA) 1959, Capt and Adj Surrey Yeo 1967-68, Maj 1975, Lt-Col 1984, RARO 1985; dir Surrey Printed Circuits Ltd 1967-, mktg dir Teknis Group Ltd 1968- (gp md 1968-75), gp chm Surrey Group 1978- (gp md 1975-78) pres: Br Electro Static Manufacturers Assoc, The Ripley Soc; Lord of the Manor of Dedswell and Papworth MCIM 1969; *Books* The Evolution of the English Manorial System (1987); *Recreations* golf, countryside conservation, oil painting, local history; *Clubs* Guildford Golf, Send Utd FC (patron); *Style—* Lt-Col John Molyneux-Child, TD; Croxeth Hall, Ripley, Surrey GU23 6EX (☎ 0483 225435); Surrey Group of Companies, Surrey House, London Rd, Staines, Middx TW18 4HN (☎ 0784 461393, fax 0784 461393, telex 894343)

MONAGHAN, Neill Roderick; s of Reginald John Monaghan, of Preston Bowyer, Somerset, and Doreen Margaret, *née* Simpkin; *b* 2 April 1954; *Educ* Maret Sch Washington DC, Royal GS High Wycombe Bucks, Univ of Newcastle upon Tyne (LLB); *m* 11 June 1988, Emma, da of Fred Majdalany, MC (d 1967), Lancashire Fusiliers, of Little Saling, Essex; 1 da (Holly Margaret b 1 Oct 1990); *Career* barr Lincoln's Inn 1979; ward chm Putney (C) Assoc 1984-85; *Recreations* tennis, music, motoring, travel, country pursuits; *Clubs* Chelsea Arts; *Style—* Neill Monaghan, Esq; 3 Temple Gardens, Temple, London EC4Y 9AU (☎ 071 583 1155, fax 071 353 5446)

MONBIOT, Raymond Geoffrey; MBE (1981); s of Maurice Ferdinand Monbiot (d 1976); *b* 1 Sept 1937; *Educ* Westminster, London Business Sch; *m* 1961, Rosalie Vivien Gresham, da of R G Cooke, CBE, MP (d 1970); 3 children; *Career* J Lyons & Co Ltd 1956-78, md Associated Biscuits Ltd 1978-82; chm: Campbell's UK Ltd 1982-88, Campbell's Soups Ltd 1983-88; pres Campbell's Frozen Foods Europe 1987-88; chm and md Rotherfield Mgmnt Ltd 1988-; chm: BIM Westminster branch 1978-82, Upper Thames Euro Constituency 1982-84, Oxon and Bucks Euro Constituency 1984-89, Cons Pty Nat Trade and Indust forum 1988-; pres S Oxfordshire Cons Assoc 1980- (chm 1974-78), cncl memb BIM 1981-84, memb Business Liaison Ctee London Business Sch 1984-88; Duke of Edinburgh award for Industl Projects Northampton then Berks 1976-87, Prince Philip Cert of Recognition 1987; *Books* How to Manage Your Boss (1980); *Recreations* writing, charity work, cooking; *Clubs* IOD, Leander; *Style—* Raymond Monbiot, Esq, MBE; Peppard Hse, Peppard Common, Henley-on-Thames, Oxon (☎ 049 17 424)

MONCADA, Dr Salvador Enrique; s of Salvador Moncada, Tegucigalpa, Honduras, and Jenny Seidner (d 1985); *b* 3 Dec 1944; *Educ* Univ of El Salvador (MD), Univ of London (PhD); *m* 1 April 1966, Dorys, *née* Lemus; 1 s (Salvador Ernesto b 6 May 1972 d 19 May 1982), 1 da (Claudia Regina b 15 Nov 1966); *Career* Gp Social Serv of El Salvador 1969, instr of preventative med Univ of El Salvador 1969-70; The

Wellcome Res Laboratories England: Dept of Pharmacology RCS 1971-73, section leader and sr scientist Prostaglandin Res Gp 1975-77, head of Dept of Prostaglandin Res 1977-85, dir of Theraputic Res Div 1984-86, dir of res 1986-; assoc prof of pharmacology and physiology Dept of Physiological Sciences 1974-75 (instr of physiology and pharmacology 1970-71); editorial work: ed Gen Pharmacology Section Prostaglandins 1975-80, conslt ed Prostaglandins 1980; memb Editorial Bd: British Journal of Pharmacology 1980-85, Atherosclerosis 1980, European Journal of Clinical Investigation 1986, Thrombosis Research 1989, Clinica e Investigacion en Arteriosclerosis 1989; memb Editorial Ctee Archives Venezolanos de Farmacologia y Terapeutica 1980, scientific ed The British Medical Bulletin no 39 Part 3; recipient of numerous int med awards; inventor of various patented pharmaceutical compositions; memb Br Pharmacological Soc 1974, hon memb Colombian Soc of Int Med 1982, hon memb Peruvian Pharmacological Soc 1983; FRS 1988; *Books* Prostacyclin in Pregnancy (ed jtly, 1983), Nitric Oxide from L-arginine: a bioregulatory system (1990); *Recreations* music, theatre, literature; *Style—* Dr Salvador Moncada; 25 Hitherwood Drive, London SE19 1XA; The Wellcome Research Laboratories, Langley Court, Beckenham, Kent BR3 3BS

MONCK, Hon Mrs (Margaret St Clair Sydney); *née* Thesiger; da of 1 Viscount Chelmsford, GCSI, GCMG, GCIE, GBE (d 1933); *b* 1911; *m* 1934, John Monck (who assumed surname of Monck in lieu of Goldman by deed poll), s of Maj Charles Sydney Goldman (d 1958); 2 s; *Style—* The Hon Mrs Monck; Aldern Bridge Hse, Newbury, Berks (☎ 0635 45566)

MONCK, Nicholas Jeremy; CB (1988); s of Bosworth Monck (d 1961), and Stella Mary, *née* Cock; *b* 9 March 1935; *Educ* Eton, King's Coll Cambridge, Univ of Pennsylvania; *m* 1960, Elizabeth Mary Kirwan; 3 s; *Career* asst princ MOP 1959-62, NEDO 1962-65, NBPI 1965-66, sr economist Miny of Agriculture Tanzania 1966-69; HM Treasy 1969: asst sec 1971, princ private sec to Chllr of the Exchequer 1976-77, under sec 1977-84, dep sec 1984-90, second perm sec (public expenditure) 1990-; memb BSC 1978-80; *Style—* Nicholas Monck, Esq, CB; c/o HM Treasury, Parliament St, London SW1P 3AG (☎ 071 270 3000)

MONCK, Hon Mrs ((Isolde) Sheila Tower); *née* Butler; da of 27 Baron Dunboyne (d 1945); *b* 1925; *m* 1949, Cdr Penryn Victor Monck, RNVR; 1 s, 2 da; *Style—* The Hon Mrs Monck; Yaverland Manor, Sandown, I O W

MONCKTON, Alan Stobart; DL (Staffs 1988); s of Maj R F P Monckton, TD, DL (d 1975); *b* 5 Sept 1934; *Educ* Eton; *m* 1961, Joanna Mary, *née* Bird; 2 s (Piers b 1962, Toby b 1970, and 1 s decd), 2 da (Davina b 1964, Sophie b 1967 (twin)); *Career* chartered surveyor, landowner, farmer, forester; dir Halifax Building Soc 1973-90 and various private cos; memb: CLA (chm Staffs branch 1979-81), Timber Growers UK Cncl; High Sheriff of Staffs 1975-76; FRICS; *Recreations* bridge, shooting, philately; *Style—* Alan Monckton, Esq, DL; Stretton Hall, Stafford ST19 9LQ (☎ 0902 850239)

MONCKTON, (Herbert) Anthony; s of Francis Guy Monckton (d 1969), and Jessica Hamilton (d 1979); *b* 13 July 1923; *Educ* Malvern; *m* 1948, Peggy, da of Fred Bunting (d 1978); 2 da; *Career* Lt RM 1942-45; former brewer; historical res author; asst md: Flower & Sons Ltd Stratford upon Avon 1955-68, Whitbread East Pennines Ltd 1968-80; chm and md Publishing and Literary Services Ltd Sheffield 1981-88; memb Inst of Brewing 1949-; *Books* A History of English Ale and Beer, A History of The English Public House, Story of The Brewer's Cooper, Story of British Beer, Story of The British Pub, Story Of The Publican Brewer; *Recreations* walking, bird-watching, historical research; *Style—* Anthony Monckton, Esq; 6 Whirlow Park Rd, Sheffield S11 9NP (☎ 0742 369668)

MONCKTON, Hon Anthony Leopold Colyer; yst s of 2 Viscount Monkton of Brenchley, CB, OBE, MC, DL; *b* 25 Sept 1960; *Educ* Harrow, Magdalene Coll Camb; *m* 1985, Philippa Susan, yr da of late Gervase Christopher Brinsmade Wingfield; 1 s (Edward Gervase Colyer b 1988), 1 da (Camilla Mary b 1989); *Career* cmmnd 9/12 Royal Lancers 1982, Capt 1984; *Clubs* MCC, Cavalry and Guards'; *Style—* Capt The Hon Anthony Monckton; BFPO 33, W Germany

MONCKTON, Hon Christopher Walter; DL; s and h of 2 Viscount Monckton of Brenchley, CB, OBE, MC, DL, by his w Marianna Laetitia, da of Cdr Robert Tatton Bower, RN; *b* 14 Feb 1952; *Educ* Harrow, Churchill Coll Cambridge (MA), Univ Coll Cardiff (Dip Journalism); *m* 19 May 1990, Juliet Mary Anne, da of Jørgen Malherbe Jensen, of Doughty Street, London WC1; *Career* ldr writer Yorks Post 1975-77 (reporter 1974-75), press offr Cons Central Off 1977-78, ed The Universe 1979-81, managing ed Telegraph Sunday Magazine 1981-82, ldr writer The Standard 1982, asst ed Today 1986-; special advsr to PM's Policy Unit (Home Affs) 1982-86; memb: Int MENSA Ltd 1975-, St John Ambulance Bd (Wetherby Div) 1976-77, Hon Soc of the Middle Temple 1979-; sec: Health Study Gp CPS 1981-, Employment Study Gp 1982-; kt SMO Malta 1973, OStJ 1973; *Books* The Laker Story (co-author with Ivan Fallon, 1982); *Recreations* clocks and sundials, computers, cycling, fell walking, inventions, motor-cycling, number theory, politics, public speaking, punting, recreational mathematics, sci fiction, Yorks; *Clubs* Beefsteak, Brooks's, Pratt's; *Style—* The Hon Christopher Monckton, DL; 71 Albert Rd, Richmond, Surrey (☎ 081 940 6528)

MONCKTON, Hon Jonathan Riversdale St Quintin; s (twin) of 2 Viscount Monckton of Brenchley, CB, OBE, MC; *b* 15 Aug 1955; *Educ* Ladycross, Worth; *Career* monk of the Order of St Benedict Worth Abbey; *Style—* The Hon Jonathan Monckton

MONCKTON, Hon (John) Philip; s and h of 12 Viscount Galway and Fiona Margaret Monckton, *née* Taylor; *b* 8 April 1952; *Educ* Univ of W Ontario (MA); *m* 1980, Deborah Kathleen, da of A Bruce Holmes, of Ottawa, Canada; *Career* vice pres Steepe & Co Sales Promotion Agency, memb Canadian Olympic Rowing Team 1974-84, Gold Medal Pan-Am Games 1975, Silver Medal Pan-Am Games 1984, Bronze Medal Olympic Games 1984, BC Premiers Award, Sport Canada Certificate of Excellence, Cara pres Award 1984; *Recreations* rowing, squash; *Clubs* Vancouver Rowing, Burnaby Lake Rowing; *Style—* The Hon J Philip Monckton; 43 Braemar Avenue, Toronto, Ontario, Canada M5P 2L1 (☎ 416 482 3799); Suite 500, 120 Eglinton Avenue East, Toronto, Ontario, Canada M4P 1EZ (☎ 416 488 1999)

MONCKTON, Hon Rosamond Mary; only da of 2 Viscount Monckton, of Brenchley, CB, OBE, MC; *b* 26 Oct 1953; *Educ* Ursuline Convent Tildonk Belgium; *Career* asst md Cartier London 1979, sales and exhibition mangr Tabbah Jewellers (Monte Carlo) 1980, promotions mangr Asprey 1982-85, md Tiffany London 1986-; Freeman Worshipful Co of Goldsmiths 1982; *Recreations* books, dogs, voyages; *Style—* The Hon Rosamond Monckton

MONCKTON, Hon Timothy David Robert; 2 s of 2 Viscount Monckton of Brenchley, CB, OBE, MC; *b* 15 Aug 1955; *Educ* Harrow, RAC Cirencester; *m* 1984, Jennifer, 2 da of Brendan Carmody, of Sydney Australia; 2 s (Dominic b 1985, James Timothy b 1988); *Career* chm Albert Abela & Co Ltd 1985, Knight of honour and devotion Sovereign Order of Malta; *Style—* The Hon Timothy Monckton; Flat 3, 19 Lavender Gdns, London SW11 1DN (☎ 071 350 0190)

MONCKTON, Hon (Rose) Wynsome; da of 11 Viscount Galway (d 1980); *b* 1937; *Career* occupational therapist; *Style—* The Hon Wynsome Monckton

MONCKTON OF BRENCHLEY, 2 Viscount (UK 1957); Maj-Gen Gilbert Walter Riversdale Monckton; CB (1966), OBE (1956), MC (1940), DL (Kent 1970); s of 1 Viscount Monckton of Brenchley, GCVO, KCMG, PC, MC, QC (d 1965), by his w Mary, da of Sir Thomas Colyer-Fergusson, 3rd Bt; *b* 3 Nov 1915; *Educ* Harrow, Trinity Coll Cambridge (MA); *m* 1950, Marianna Laetitia, OStJ, Dame of Honour & Devotion (Sovereign Mil Order Malta), pres St John's Ambulance Kent 1972-80, and High Sheriff Kent 1981-82, 3 da of Cdr Robert Tatton Bower, of Gatto-Murina Palace, Mdina, Malta, by his w Hon Henrietta, *née* Strickland, 4 da of 1 and last Baron Strickland; 4 s, 1 da; *Heir* s, Hon Christopher Walter Monckton; *Career* serv WWII; dep dir Personnel Admin 1962, DPR War Office (Maj-Gen) 1963-65, COS HQ BAOR 1965-67; Liveryman Worshipful Co of Broderers 1962 (Master 1978); pres: Kent Assoc of Boys' Clubs 1965-78, Inst of Heraldic and Genealogical Studies 1965, Kent Archaeological Assoc 1968-75, Medway Productivity Assoc 1968-74, Maidstone and Dist Football League 1968, Br Archaeological Awards; vice-chm Scout Assoc Kent 1968-74; pres Anglo-Belgian Union 1974-80; chm Cncl of the OStJ for Kent 1969-74; Grand Offr Order of Leopold II (Belgium 1978), Cmdr Order of the Crown (Belgium) KStJ; Bailiff Grand Cross Obedience Sov Mil Order Malta, Grand Cross Merit 1980; FSA; *Clubs* Brooks's, MCC, Casino Maltese; *Style—* The Rt Hon the Viscount Monckton of Brenchley, CB, OBE, MC, DL; Runhams Farm, Runham Lane, Harrietsham, Maidstone, Kent (☎ 0627 850 313)

MONCREIFF, Hon Donald Graham Fitz-Herbert; 2 s of 4 Baron Moncreiff (d 1942), and Lucy Vida, *née* Anderson; *b* 1919; *Educ* Dollar Acad; *m* 17 Aug 1955, Catriona Sheila, da of James MacDonald, of Devonshaw House, Dollar, Kinross-shire; 1 s, 3 da; *Career* Lt Argyll and Sutherland Highlanders 1940; *Clubs* New (Edinburgh); *Style—* The Hon Donald Moncreiff; Barrisdale, Comrie, Perthshire

MONCREIFF, 5 Baron (UK 1874); Lt-Col Sir Harry Robert Wellwood Moncreiff; 15 Bt (NS 1626), of Moncreiff and 5 Bt (UK 1871), of Tulliebole; s of 4 Baron (d 1942); *b* 4 Feb 1915; *Educ* Fettes; *m* 1952, Enid Marion Watson (d 1985), da of late Maj H W Locke, of Belmont, Dollar, Clackmannan; 1 s; *Heir* s, Hon Rhoderick Harry Wellwood Moncreiff; *Career* 2 Lt RASC 1939, Maj 1943, ret 1958, Hon Lt-Col; *Style—* The Rt Hon the Lord Moncreiff; Tulliebole Castle, Fossoway, Kinross (☎ Fossoway 236)

MONCREIFF, Hon Rhoderick Harry Wellwood; s and h of 5 Baron Moncreiff; *b* 22 March 1954; *Educ* E of Scotland Coll of Agric (H N D); *m* 1982, Alison Elizabeth Anne, d da of late James Duncan Alastair Ross, of West Mayfield, Dollar, Clackmannanshire: 2 s (Harry James Wellwood b 12 Aug 1986, James Gavin Francis b 29 July 1988); *Heir* (Harry James Wellwood b 1986); *Style—* The Hon Rhoderick Moncreiff

MONCREIFF, Hon Robert Frederick Arthur; s of 4 Baron Moncreiff (d 1942) and Lucy Vida (d 1976), eld da of David Lechmere Anderson; *b* 25 Jan 1924; *Educ* Dollar Acad Scotland; *m* 1951, Aileen Margaret Marr, da of Robert Marr Meldrum (d 1976); 1 s (Richard b 1964), 1 da (Gillian b 1954); *Career* Warrant Offr RAF, Burma; hotelier, ret; *Clubs* Cons (Galashiels); *Style—* The Hon Robert Moncreiff; 26 Croft St, Galashiels, Selkirkshire TD1 3BJ (☎ 0896 2455)

MONCREIFFE OF MONCREIFFE, (Katharine) Elisabeth; 24 Feudal Baroness of Moncreiffe; da of Cdr Sir Guy Moncreiffe of that Ilk, RN, 9 Bt, 22 Feudal Baron and sis of Capt Sir David Moncreiffe of that Ilk, MC, 10 Bt and 23 Feudal Baron; *b* 23 May 1920; *Educ* Private- London, Paris, Munich, Florence; *Heir* Hon Peregrine Moncreiffe, *qv*; *Career* served WWII WRNS, special duties linguist; *Recreations* breeder and int championship judge of German Shepherd dogs; *Clubs* Cavalry and Guards', Kennel; *Style—* Miss Moncreiffe of Moncreiffe; Moncreiffe, Bridge of Earn, Perthshire

MONCREIFFE OF MONCREIFFE, Hon Peregrine David Euan Malcolm; Fiar of the Barony of Moncreiffe and Baron of Easter Moncreiffe (both Scottish territorial baronies); 2 s of late Countess of Erroll (d 1978), and Sir Iain Moncreiffe of that Ilk, 11 Bt (d 1985); *b* 16 Feb 1951; *Educ* Eton, Christ Church Oxford (MA); *m* 27 July 1988, Miranda Mary, da of Capt Mervyn Fox-Pitt, of Grange Scrymgeour, Cupar, Fife; 1 s (b 3 Feb 1991); *Career* Lt Atholl Highlanders; Slains Pursuivant 1970-78; investmt banker; Credit Suisse First Boston 1972-82; Lehman Bros Kuhn Loeb/ Shearson Lehman 1982-86; E F Hutton & Co 1986-88; chm Scottish Ballet; memb Royal Co of Archers (Queen's Body Gd for Scotland); Freeman City of London, memb Worshipful Co of Fishmongers 1987; *Recreations* running, rowing, rustic pursuits, dance; *Clubs* Turf, White's, Pratt's, Beefsteak, Puffin's (Edinburgh), New (Edinburgh), Leander, Royal and Ancient GC (St Andrews), Brook (NY); *Style—* The Hon Peregrine Moncreiffe of Moncreiffe; Easter Moncreiffe, Perthshire PH2 8QA (☎ 0738 812338)

MONCREIFFE OF THAT ILK, Lady; Hermione Patricia; *née* Faulkner; o da of Lt-Col Walter Douglas Faulkner, MC (ka 1940), and Patricia Katharine (now Patricia, Countess of Dundee); *b* 14 Jan 1937; *m* 1 May 1966, Sir Rupert Iain Kay Moncreiffe of that Ilk, 11 Bt (d 1985); 2 step s (Earl of Erroll, Hon Peregrine Moncreiffe of that Ilk, *qqv*), 1 step da (Lady Alexandra Connell, *qv*); *Style—* Lady Moncreiffe of that Ilk; 117 Ashley Gardens, London SW1 (☎ 071 828 8421)

MONCRIEFF *see also*: Scott Moncrieff

MONCRIEFF, Capt Charles St John Graham; s of Lt-Col Douglas Graham Moncrieff, MC (d 1983), of Kinmonth, Rhynd, Perth, and Henrietta Doreen, *née* St John (d 1987); *b* 11 Jan 1931; *Educ* Eton, RMA Sandhurst; *m* 15 June 1957, Joanna Dava, da of Maj Basil Arthur John Peto (d 1954); 1 s (Alexander Charles Graham b 1967), 3 da (Charlotte b 1959, Miranda b 1961, Rosanna b 1965); *Career* Capt Scots Gds 1951 (ret 1960); farmer; memb The Queen's Body Guard for Scotland (Royal Co of Archers); *Recreations* shooting, fishing; *Style—* Capt Charles Moncrieff; Elcho, Rhynd, Perth (☎ 0738 21025)

MONCRIEFF, Lady; Mary Katherine; da of late Ralph Wedmore; *b* 18 May 1908; *m* 1955, as his 2 w, Prof Sir Alan Aird Moncrieff, CBE, MD, FRCP, FRCOG (d 1971, former prof of child health at London Univ); *Style—* Lady Moncrieff; Waterford Cottage, Buckland Rd, Bampton, Oxon 0X8 2AA (☎ 0993 850359)

MOND, Gary Stephen; s of Ferdinand Mond, of London, and Frances, *née* Henry; *b* 11 May 1959; *Educ* Univ Coll Sch Hampstead London NW3, Trinity Coll Cambridge (MA); *Career* CA 1981-84, Guinness Mahon & Co Ltd 1984-86, md Bow Publications Ltd 1987-88, assoc dir Chancery Corporate Services Ltd 1988-89; currently chm of a small public leisure co; chm Gtr London Young Cons 1985-86, asst treas Chelsea Cons Assoc 1986-88, Parly candidate (C) Hamilton Scot 1987, currently prospective Parly candidate (C) Mansfield; competitive butterfly swimmer, Nat Under 14 champion 1972, GB Int and Olympic trialist 1976, Cambridge blue, former World Record holder long distance butterfly (six and a quarter miles) 1980; ACA 1984; *Recreations* swimming, theatre, chess; *Clubs* Coningsby; *Style—* Gary Mond, Esq; 56 Coleherne Ct, Old Brompton Rd, London SW5 0EF (☎ 071 244 7413); 28 Albert St, Mansfield Woodhouse, Notts NG19 8BH (☎ 0623 662667)

MONDAL, Dr Bijoy Krishna; s of Jagneswar Mondal (d 1974), of Pirojpur, Barisal, and Madhu Bala Mondal (d 1983); *b* 28 Sept 1940; *Educ* Dacca Univ (MB BS), Univ of Liverpool (DTM&H); *m* 12 March 1971, Dolly, da of Dr Jagadish Chandra Mandal, of Calcutta; 1 s (Krishnendu b 9 Oct 1981), 2 da (Bipasha b 16 April 1975, Bidisha b 21 April 1980); *Career* house offr in gen surgery Dacca Med Coll Hosp 1964-65, house offr in gen med St Tydfil 1965-66; sr house offr in gen med: Warrington Gen Hosp

1966-67, Ashton Gen Hosp 1967-68; med registrar: in gen med The Grange Hosp Northwich 1968-70, in gen med/chest Ladywell Hosp Salford 1970-74; sr registrar in geriatric med Dudley Rd Hosp Birmingham 1974-75, conslt physician in geriatric med Rotherham Health Authy 1975-, clinical dir Badsley Moor Lane/Wathwood Hosp's Unit 1990- (unit gen mangr 1985-); numerous articles in professional jls on: haematology, endocrinology, rheumatology, neurology; exec memb BMA (chm Rotherham div 1990), past cncl memb Br Geriatric Soc, pres Rotherham Parkinson's Disease Soc, chm Rotherham Stroke Club, memb Overseas Doctors Assoc; FRCPG 1984, FRCPE 1986, FRCP 1987 (MRCP 1973); *Recreations* gardening, photography, travel; *Style—* Dr Bijoy Mondal; Bipasha, 91 Woodfoot Rd, Moorgate, Rotherham, S Yorks S60 3EH (☎ 0709 373985); Rotherham Health Authority, Badsley Moor Lane Hospital, Badsley Moor Lane, Rotherham, S Yorks S65 2QL (☎ 0709 820000)

MONEY, (Israel) Campbell; s of William Campbell Money, of 13 Cairnfield, Ave, Maybole, Ayrshire, and Agnes McColl, *née* Laurie; *b* 31 Aug 1960; *Educ* Carrick Acad Maybole Ayrshire; *m* 11 June 1982, Caroline Ayls, da of Walter Leonard Mc Lachlan; 2 s (Stuart William b 27 Dec 1982, Kenneth Campbell b 14 July 1985); *Career* St Mirren FC: signed 1978, full debut 1978, 250 appearances, won Scot Cup medal beating Dundee United 1-0 1978; capped at youth and under 21 level for Scot, played: Scot B team, Scot against Scot league team in centenary game 1990; formerly worked in creamery, cadet Police Force; now proprietor sports shop Paisley; *Recreations* golf, snooker, looking after my children; *Style—* Campbell Money, Esq; St Mirren Football Club, Love St, Paisley, Renfrewshire, Scotland (☎ 041 889 2558)

MONEY, Ernle David Drummond; s of Lt-Col E F D Money, DSO (d 1970), of Cambridge, and Dorothy Blanche Sidney (d 1984), o da of David Anderson, of Forfar, Scotland; *b* 17 Feb 1931; *Educ* Marlborough, Oriel Coll Oxford (MA); *m* 1960, Susan Barbara, da of Lt-Col Dudley S Lister, MC, The Buffs, of Hurlingham; 1 s (Harry b 1963); 3 da (Sophie b 1961, Julia b 1964, Pandora b 1966); *Career* barr Lincoln's Inn 1958, memb gen Cncl of Bar 1962-66, MP (C) Ipswich 1970-74, oppn shadow min for the Arts 1974, co-opted memb GLC Arts Bd 1973-74, 1975-76; conslt various Art Galleries, Victorian pictures, Fine Arts corr, The Contemporary Review 1968-; pres Ipswich Town FC Supporters 1974-80; ctee memb various heritage organisations; *Books* The Nasmyth Family of Painters (with Peter Johnson 1975), Margaret Thatcher a biography (with Peter Johnson 1976); *Recreations* football, opera, pictures, antiques; *Clubs* Carlton; *Style—* Ernle Money, Esq; 10 St John's Villas, London N19 (☎ 071 272 6815); 1 Gray's Inn Square, Grays Inn, London WC1 (☎ 071 405 8946)

MONEY, John Kyrle; s of Edward Douglas Money (d 1974), and Edith Lillian (d 1984); the Money family have been East India merchants since 1850; *b* 21 March 1927; *Educ* Stowe, Trinity Coll Cambridge; *m* 1, 1957 (m dis), Verena, da of Dr Heinrich Mann, of Frankfurt; 2 da (Patricia b 1958, Joanna b 1961); m 2, 1983, Sally Elizabeth, da of Michael Staples, of Tadworth, Surrey; 1 da (Kate b 1984), 1 s (Oliver b 1986); *Career* East India merchant and co dir 1951-79, chm Rubber Growers Association 1978, dir Peacock Estates Ltd; *Books* A Plantation Family (1979), Planting Tales of Joy and Sorrow (1989); *Clubs* Kandahar, Wentworth; *Style—* John K Money, Esq; 18 Pembroke Gardens Close, London W8 6HR (☎ 071 602 2211)

MONEY, Robert George; s of late Thomas George Money; *b* 18 Feb 1937; *Educ* Poly; *m* 1961, Joan May, 1 c; *Career* md Robert Money Fine Wines Ltd; *Recreations* music; *Clubs* Farmers'; *Style—* Robert Money, Esq; Conifers, Roselands Avenue, Mayfield, Sussex

MONEY-COUTTS, Lt-Col Hon Alexander Burdett; OBE (1946); s of 6 Baron Latymer (d 1949); *b* 1902; *Educ* Eton, New Coll Oxford; *m* 1930, Mary Elspeth (d 1990), da of Sir Reginald Arthur Hobhouse, 5 Bt (d 1947); 1 s, 2 da (adopted); *Career* serv Royal Scots Fus; Lt-Col 1944; Master Worshipful Co of Tobacco Pipe Makers and Tobacco Blenders 1964; *Style—* Lt-Col the Hon Alexander Money-Coutts; Askett House, Askett, nr Aylesbury, HP17 9LT Bucks (☎ 084 44 5498)

MONEY-COUTTS, Hon Mrs ((Penelope) Ann Clare); da of Thomas Addis Emmet (d 1934), and Baroness Emmet of Amberley (Life Peer); *b* 1932; *m* 1951 (m dis 1965), Hon Hugo Nevill Money-Coutts; 2 s, 1 da; *Career* govr Cobham Hall Kent 1962-86; EEC Brussels 1972-73, sec gen Euro Orgn for Res and Treatment of Cancer fndn (EORTC) 1976-; *Style—* The Hon Mrs Money-Coutts; Flat 4, 43 Onslow Sq, London SW7 3LR (☎ 071 581 5191); EORTC Foundation, Kemble House, Kemble St, London WC2B 4AJ (☎ 071 489 4028)

MONEY-COUTTS, Hon Crispin James Alan Nevill; eldest s and h of 8 Baron Latymer, *qv*; *b* 8 March 1955; *Educ* Eton, Keble Coll Oxford; *m* 1978, Hon Lucy Rose Deedes, yst da of Baron Deedes (Life Peer); 1 s (Drummond William Thomas b 11 May 1986), 2 da (Sophia Patience b 1985, Evelyn Rose b 1988); *Style—* The Hon Crispin Money-Coutts; c/o Coutts & Co, 440 Strand, London WC2R 0QS

MONEY-COUTTS, David Burdett; s of Lt-Col the Hon Alexander Burdett Money-Coutts, OBE (2 s of 6 Baron Latymer), and Mary Elspeth (d 1990), er da of Sir Reginald Arthur Hobhouse, 5 Bt; *b* 19 July 1931; *Educ* Eton, New Coll Oxford (MA); *m* 17 May 1958, (Helen) Penelope June Utten, da of Cdr Killingworth Richard Utten Todd, RIN; 1 s (Benjamin b 1961), 2 da (Harriet b 1959, Laura b 1965); *Career* serv 1 Royal Dragoons 1950-51, Royal Glos Hussars (TA) 1951-67; Coutts & Co: joined 1954, dir 1958, md 1970-86, chm 1976-; dir: National Discount Co 1964-69, United States & General Trust Corporation 1964-73, Charities Investment Managers 1964- (chm 1984-), National Westminster Bank 1976-90 (and SE Regn 1969-88, chm 1986-88); chm: S Advsy Bd 1988-, Dun & Bradstreet 1973-87, Phoenix Assurance 1978-85, Sun Alliance and London Insurance 1984-90, M & G Group 1990-, Gerrard & National 1969- (dep chm 1969-89); hon treas Nat Assoc of Almshouses 1960-; govr Middx Hosp 1962-74 and chm Med Sch 1974-88; memb: Cncl UCL 1987-, Health Educn Cncl 1973-76, Kensington Chelsea and Westminster AHA(T) 1974-82 (vice chm 1976-82), Bloomsbury Health Authy 1982-90 (vice chm 1982-88); chm Old Etonian Tst 1976-; tstee: Multiple Sclerosis Soc 1967-, Mansfield Coll Oxford 1988-; *Clubs* Leander; *Style—* David Money-Coutts, Esq; Magpie House, Peppard Common, Henley-on-Thames, Oxon RG9 5JG; 440 Strand, London WC2R OQS

MONIBA, HE Dr Harry Fumba; *Career* Liberian ambass to UK 1981-; *Style—* HE Dr Harry Fumba Moniba; The Liberian Embassy, 21 Princes Gate, London SW7 (☎ 071 589 9405/6/7; home: 081 942 7997)

MONIER-WILLIAMS, His Honour Judge; Evelyn Faithfull; s of Roy Thornton Monier-Williams, OBE (d 1967), and Gladys Maive; *b* 29 April 1920; *Educ* Charterhouse, Univ Coll Oxford (MA); *m* 1948, Maria-Angela (d 1983), da of Rudolf Georg Oswald (d 1939), of Oberhausen, Germany; 1 s (Christopher Roy), 1 da (Vivien Angela, *see* Hon Mrs Mark Piercy); *Career* serv RA Mediterranean and NW Europe as Capt; called to the Bar Inner Temple 1948, circuit judge 1972-, master of the bench Inner Temple, reader 1987, elected tres; *Style—* His Hon Judge Monier-Williams; Inner Temple, London EC4

MONINS, Ian Richard; s of Capt John Eaton Monins, JP (d 1939), of Kent, and Margaret Louise, *née* Carter (d 1982); one of the oldest Kentish families dating back to 11 century; *b* 13 April 1930; *Educ* Groton USA, Eton; *m* 2 April 1954, Patricia Lillian, da of Percival Read (d 1967), of Kent; 2 s (Symond b 1958, Stephen b 1961), 2 da (Gay b 1955, Daryl b 1956); *Career* Nat Serv Lt The Buffs 1950-52; farmer; md Gaychild Ltd 1954-69, chm St Louis Hldgs and subsids 1974-, coinage advsr to Jersey States Treasy 1980-86; vice pres: Societe Jersiase 1981-83, 1985-87 and 1989-90; Jersey Heritage Tst 1986-87; FRNS; *Recreations* tennis, building follies, numismatics; *Style—* Ian R Monins, Esq; Homeland, St John, Jersey (☎ 0534 61618)

MONJACK, Philip; s of Jack Monjack of 53 Beauchamp Court, Marsh Lane, Stanmore, Middlesex and Tilly *née* Levene; *b* 4 Sept 1942; *Educ* The Grocers Co Sch; *m* 5 Sept 1965, Carol Daphne, da of Jack Kohn of 1 Kenlor Ct, Heather Walk, Edgware, Middx; 2 s (Richard b 1967, Jonathan b 1969), 1 da (Suzanne b 1973); *Career* CA 1965; sr ptnr Leonard Curtis & Co; ptnr: Leonard Curtis & Ptnrs, Philip Keith & Co; alternate dir Imry Property Hldgs plc 1983-86; FCA; *Recreations* tennis, soccer; *Clubs* RAC; *Style—* Philip Monjack Esq, FCA; 30 Eastbourne Terrace, London W2 6LF (telex : 22784, fax : 071 723 6059)

MONK, Paul Nicholas; s of George Benbow Monk, of Godalming, Surrey, and Rosina Gwendoline, *née* Ross; *b* 3 Dec 1949; *Educ* Royal GS Guildford, Pembroke Coll Oxford (MA); *m* 14 Feb 1985, Roma Olivia Cannon, da of Hamilton Haigh; 2 da (Georgina, Lucinda); *Career* slr 1974; articled to Durrant Cooper & Hambling 1972-74, Allen & Overy 1975- (ptnr 1979); memb Worshipful Co Slrs; memb: Law Soc 1972, Int Bar Assoc; *Recreations* sailing, cross-country skiing; *Clubs* Hurlingham, Royal Southern Yacht; *Style—* Paul Monk, Esq; 9 Cheapside, London EC2V 6AD (☎ 071 248 9898, fax 071 236 2192, telex 8812801)

MONK, Ronald Frank; s of Wing Cdr Ronald Cecil Howe Monk (d 1972), of Webridge, Surrey, and Madeline, *née* Booth-Haynes (d 1984); *b* 13 Sept 1944; *Educ* Charterhouse; *m* 6 Sept 1969 (m dis 1980), (Felicity) Jane, da of Dr David Arthur (d 1986), of Pyrford, Surrey; 2 s ((Ronald) William Howe b 10 July 1974, Charles David Hambly b 2 Feb 1976); *Career* accountant Finnie Ross Welch & Co 1962-68, merchant banker corporate fin SG Warburg & Co Ltd 1969-72, dir James Finlay plc 1972-79, chm James Finlay Bank Ltd (part of the Finlay Gp), dir and chm Setas Securities Ltd (investmt bankers) 1979-83; fndr chm and chief exec Falcon Resources plc (oil co) 1983-89; FCA 1969; *Recreations* swimming, sailing, foreign travel; *Clubs* Annabels; *Style—* Ronald Monk, Esq; 4 South Park Mews, Woolneigh St, London SW6 3AY (☎ 01 731 6437); 50 Stratton St, London SW1 (☎ 01 731 6437)

MONK, Ronald William (Ron); s of William George Monk (d 1979), of Guildford, Surrey, and Edith May, *née* Barnes (d 1985); *b* 8 Oct 1928; *Educ* Woking Co GS, Coll of Estate Mgmnt; *m* 7 July 1962, Jennifer (Jennie)Leach, da of Capt Warren Leach Smith (d 1977), of Milford, Surrey; 1 s (Alastair b 15 July 1968); *Career* Queen's Westminster's Rifles/Queen's Royal Rifles 1955-62; chartered surveyor, conslt quantity surveyor; RICS: memb Gen Cncl 1973-90, memb Professional Practice Ctee 1973-90, chm Rules of Conduct Ctee 1983-88, chm Surrey Branch 1972-73, memb Official Referees Users Ctee 1982-; construction indust arbitrator 1966-, ind surveyor; chm: Shalford Parish Cncl 1973-83, Surrey Co Assoc of Parish and Town Cncls 1975-78; Freeman: City of London 1979, Worshipful Co of Chartered Surveyors 1979; FRICS 1951, FCIArb 1968; *Recreations* walking, gardening, railways (including model railways); *Style—* R W Monk, Esq; Orchard House, 17 Denton Rd, Meads, Eastbourne, E Sussex BN20 7SS (☎ 0323 26249, fax 0323 649739)

MONK, (William) Roy; s of William Herries Monk (d 1963), and Ethel Jane Monk (d 1965); *b* 4 Aug 1925; *Educ* Bolton GS, Manchester Univ; *m* 25 March 1962, Deirdre Ruth, da of Percival Wilson (d 1983); 2 s (Calvin Anthony b 1964, Gareth Robin b 1965), 1 da (Candida Jane b 1962); *Career* trainee air crew RAF 1943-45; dir: Garnar Booth plc, Garbra Leather Co, Gryfe Tannery Ltd, Derrick Hosegood Gp Ltd, Odell Leather Industs Ltd, Phillips Rubber Co Ltd, Spencer Leather Co, Wilson & Tilt Ltd, Br Leather Confedn; pres E Lancs Sub Aqua Club, life memb Nat Tst; chm fund raising ctee Oakfield Home for Young Mentally Retarded Adults; MIEX 1950; *Recreations* sub aqua, archaeology, walking remote coastlines; *Clubs* RAC; *Style—* W Roy Monk, Esq; Manor Farm House, Easton Maudit, Wellingborough, Northants NN9 7NR; Odell Leather Industries, Odell, Bedford MK43 7BA

MONK, Stephanie; *b* 9 Aug 1943; *m* 25 Oct 1986, Gernot Schwetz; *Career* personnel devpt mangr Tate & Lyle plc 1978-82 (joined 1965), gp personnel and communications dir London International Group plc 1982-90, non-exec gp personnel dir Granada Group plc 1990-; memb CBI Employment Policy Ctee, chm CBI Equal Rights Panel, memb Cncl and Exec Ctee and chm Staffing Sub Ctee Royal Cwlth Soc for The Blind, memb Limelight Ball Ctee (fund raising for Dorton House Sch for the Blind); MInstD; *Style—* Miss Stephanie Monk; Granada Group plc, 36 Golden Square, London W1R 4AH (☎ 071 734 8080, fax 071 494 2768)

MONK BRETTON, 3 Baron (UK 1884); John Charles Dodson; DL (E Sussex 1983); s of 2 Baron, CB, JP, DL (d 1933), by his w Ruth (herself da of Hon Charles Brand and gda of 1 Viscount Hampden and 23 Baron Dacre); *b* 17 July 1924; *Educ* Westminster, New Coll Oxford; *m* 1958, Zoé Diana, da of Ian Douglas Murray Scott (d 1974); 2 s; *Heir* s, Hon Christopher Mark Dodson; *Career* takes Cons whip in House of Lords; farmer; *Clubs* Brooks's; *Style—* The Rt Hon the Lord Monk Bretton, DL; Shelley's Folly, Cooksbridge, nr Lewes, E Sussex (☎ (0273) 231)

MONKOU, Kenneth John; s of late Frank Doornkamp, and Johanna Anastasia Monkou; *b* 29 Nov 1964; *Educ* Mavo, Havo; *Career* professional footballer; Feyenoord Holland 1985-89, transferred for a fee of £100,000 to Chelsea 1989-; 2 Holland caps Olympic team; Zenith Data Systems Cup winners Chelsea 1990; player of the year Chelsea 1989-90; *Recreations* yoga, meditation, business courses; *Style—* Kenneth Monkou, Esq; Chelsea FC, Stamford Bridge, Fulham Rd, London SW6 1HS (☎ 071 385 7495)

MONKS, John; *Educ* Liverpool Polytechnic, RCA (MA); *Career* artist; visiting artist Garner Tullis Workshop Santa Barbara California 1987, British Council artist in residence British Inst Madrid 1990; numerous solo exhibitions incl Evidence 1989 and New Work 1990 (both Paton Gallery London); work in group exhibitions incl: New Contemporaries (ICA London, prizewinner) 1976, Three College Show (RCA) 1979, Alternative Tate (Paton Gallery London) 1982, Artists for the 1990s (Paton Gallery) 1984, Monotypes (Paton Gallery) 1986, Birthday offering (five years of Paton Gallery) 1986, Six Figurative Painters (Paton Gallery) 1987, 20 British Artists (London, Glasgow, NY) 1988, Metropolitan Museum of Art (NY) 1988, Recent Work (Paton Gallery) 1990; work in collections incl: Metropolitan Museum of Art (NY), Contemporary Art Society (London), Gulbenkian Foundation (Lisbon Portugal), Arts Council (GB), British Institute (Madrid), Unilever plc, Ocean Trading and Transport plc; awarded British council grant for working visit to NY 1990; *Style—* John Monks, Esq; Paton Gallery, 2 Langley Court, Long Acre, London WC2

MONKS, John Stephen; s of Charles Edward Monks (d 1970), of Manchester and Bessie Evelyn Monks; *b* 5 Aug 1945; *Educ* Ducie Tech HS Manchester, Univ of Nottingham (BA); *m* 18 July 1970, Francine Jacqueline, da of Franciscus Hendrikus Schenk, of 187 Forest Row, Tunbridge Wells, Kent; 2 s (Matthew b 1973, Daniel b 1975), 1 da (Catherine b 1981); *Career* jr mangr Plessey Radar 1967-69; TUC: asst Orgn Dept 1969-74 (asst sec 1974-77), head Orgn and Industl Rels Dept 1977-87, dep sec gen TUC 1987-; memb Cncl: ACAS 1979, ESRC 1988-; tstee Nat Museum of Labour History 1988-; govr: LSE, Hedgehill Sch; *Recreations* squash, music, swimming; *Clubs* Tulse Hill and Honor Oak Squash; *Style—* John Monks, Esq; Trades Union Congress, Congress House, Great Russell St, London WC1 DLS (☎ 071 636 4030)

MONKSWELL, 5 Baron (UK 1885); Gerard Collier; s of William Adrian Larry Collier, MB (disclaimed Barony of Monkswell for life 1964; d 1984), and his 2 w, Helen, *née* Dunbar; *b* 28 Jan 1947; *Educ* George Heriot's Sch Edinburgh, Portsmouth Poly; *m* 1974, Ann Valerie, da of James Collins, of Liverpool; 2 s (James Adrian b 1977, Robert William Gerard b 1979); 1 da (Laura Jennifer b 1975); *Heir* s Hon James Adrian b 29 March 1977; *Career* Parly conslt; formerly: serv admin mangr MF Industl, product quality engr Massey Ferguson Man Co Ltd; *Recreations* swimming, watching films, reading; *Style—* The Rt Hon the Lord Monkswell; 513 Barlow Moor Rd, Chorlton, Manchester M21 2AQ (☎ 061 881 3887)

MONRO, Sir Hector Seymour Peter; AE (1953), JP (Dumfries 1963), DL (1973), MP (C) Dumfries 1964-; s of late Capt Alastair Monro, Cameron Highlanders (s of Brig Gen Seymour Monro, CB, and Lady Ida, eldest da of 5 Earl of Lisburne), and Marion, child of Lt-Gen Sir John Ewart, KCB, JP; *b* 4 Oct 1922; *Educ* Canford, King's Coll Cambridge; *m* 1949, Elizabeth Anne, da of Maj Harry Welch, of the Sherwood Foresters, formerly of Longstone Hall, Derbyshire; 2 s; *Career* served WWII, Flt-Lt RAF, RAuxAF 1946-53; Scottish Cons whip 1967-70, Lord cmmr Treasy 1970-71, Parly under-sec Scottish Office 1971-74; oppn spokesman: Scottish Affrs 1974-75, Sport 1974-79; Parly under-sec Environment 1979-81 (with special responsibility for sport); chm Dumfriesshire Unionist Assoc 1958-63; memb: Royal Co of Archers (Queen's Bodyguard for Scotland), Dumfries T&AFA 1959-67, NFU Scotland Area Exec Ctee; Hon Air Cdre 2622 (Highlands) RAuxAF Regt Sqdn 1982-, Hon Inspr Gen RAuxAF 1990-; pres: Scottish Rugby Union 1976-77, Auto Cycle Union 1983-90, Nat Small-Bore Rifle Assoc 1987-; memb Nature Conservancy Cncl 1982-; kt 1981; *Recreations* country sports, vintage cars, flying, golf; *Clubs* RAF, RSAC, MCC, R&A; *Style—* Sir Hector Monro, AE, JP, DL, MP; Williamwood, Kirtlebridge, Dumfries (☎ 046 15 213)

MONRO, (Andrew) Hugh; s of Andrew Killey Monro, FRCS, of Rye, Sussex, and Diana Louise, *née* Rhys; *b* 2 March 1950; *Educ* Rugby, Pembroke Coll Cambridge (MA, PGCE); *m* 27 July 1974, Elizabeth Clare, da of Lyndon Rust, of Mayhill, Glos; 1 s (James b 1983), 1 da (Lucy b 1980); *Career* production mangr Metal Box Co 1972-73; teacher Haileybury 1974-79 (Noble & Greenough Boston Mass 1977-78), head of history and housemaster Loretto Sch 1980-86; headmaster: Worksop Coll 1986-90, Clifton College 1990-; govr: Westbourne Sch Sheffield, Terrington Sch Yorks, Glebe Sch Hunstanton; memb Cncl Local Hospice Movement; *Recreations* golf, American politics; *Clubs* Hawks; *Style—* Hugh Monro, Esq; Headmaster's House, Clifton Coll, Clifton, Bristol BS8 2BU

MONRO, James Lawrence; s of John Kirkpatrick Monro, of Marlborough, Wiltshire, and Landon, *née* Reed; *b* 17 Nov 1939; *Educ* Sherborne, The London Hosp Med Coll (MB BS); *m* 29 Sept 1973, Caroline Jane, da of Robert Dunlop, MBE, of Meadow Cottage, Church Lane, Aldingbourne, nr Chichester, W Sussex; 2 s (Charles b 13 Aug 1975, Andrew b 10 Aug 1981), 1 da (Rosanne b 21 Nov 1978); *Career* surgical registrar The London Hosp 1967-69, res surgical offr Brompton Hosp 1969-70; sr registrar Cardio Thoracic Unit: Green Lane Hosp Auckland NZ 1970-72, The London Hosp 1972-73; conslt cardiac surgn Dept Cardiac Surgery Gen Hosp Southampton 1973-; memb BMA 1964, FRCS 1969; memb: Soc of Cardiothoracic Surgeons of GB and I 1974, Euro Assoc for Cardio Thoracic Surgery 1987; *Books* A Colour Atlas of Cardiac Surgery- Acquired Heart Disease (1982), A Colour Atlas of Cardiac Surgery- Congenital Heart Disease (1984); *Recreations* skiing, riding, tennis; *Style—* James Monro, Esq; The Dept of Cardiac Surgery, The General Hospital, Southhampton (☎ 0703 777222 ext 3281)

MONRO, Jean Anne; *b* 31 May 1936; *Educ* St Helen's Sch Northwod Middx, London Hosp Med Coll (MB BS, Dip IBEM); *m* (widowed); 2 s (Alister, Neil); *Career* house offr London Hosp 1960; W Herts Hosp Gp: sr house offr geriatric medicine 1962 (paediatrics 1961), registrar 1963, med asst 1969-79; clinical asst Nat Hosp for Nervous Diseases London 1975-84 (res asst 1974-82), assoc physician Edgware Gen Hosp 1979-82, conslt clinical allergist Humana Hosp Wellington London 1982-84; med dir Depts of Allergy and Environmental Medicine: Nightingale Hosp London 1984-86, Allergy and Environmental Medicine Clinic Hemel Hempstead 1984-88, Lister Hosp London 1986-89, Breakspear Hosp for Allergy and Environmental Medicine Abbots Langley Herts 1988-, Hosp of St John and St Elizabeth London 1989, London Welbeck Hosp; med advsr to: Environmental Medicine Fndn, Sanity, Henry Doubleday Res Assoc, Coeliac Assoc, Foresight Schizophrenia Assoc of GB; author of numerous pubns on allergy and nutrition related topics; formerly med journalist appointed to Hospital Doctor, Doctor and other jls; memb: Br Soc for Allergy and Environmental Medicine, Br Soc of Immunology, Sub Ctee of Central Ctee for Hosp Med Servs; fell American Acad for Environmental Medicine; MRCS, LRCP, FAAEM; *Books* incl: Good Food Gluten Free (ed), Good Food to Fight Migraine (ed), Some Dietary Approaches to Disease Management (1974), Chemical Children (jtly, 1987), Handbook of Food Allergy (contrib, 1987), Immunology of Myalgic Encephalomyelitis (contrib, 1988), Breakspear Guide to Allergies (1991); *Style—* Ms Jean Monro; Breakspear Hospital for Allergy & Environmental Medicine, High St, Abbots Langley, Herts WD5 0PU (☎ 0923 261333, fax 0923 261876)

MONRO, Hon Mrs (Mary Katherine); *née* Lampson; da of 1 Baron Killearn, GCMG, CB, MVO, PC (d 1964), and Rachel Helen Mary (d 1930), yr da of late William Wilton Phipps; *b* 7 Aug 1915; *m* 1952, as his 2 w, Lt-Col Alexander George Falkiner (decd), s of Maj G Nowlan Monro, DL (d 1933); 1 s (adopted); *Career* a lady-in-waiting to HRH the late Princess Royal 1948-51; *Recreations* travelling; *Style—* The Hon Mrs Monro; 10 Derby St, Edinburgh EH6 4SB (☎ 031 552 2472)

MONSELL, 2nd Viscount (UK 1935); Lt-Col Henry Bolton Graham Eyres Monsell; s of 1st Viscount Monsell, GBE, PC (d 1969); *b* 21 Nov 1905; *Educ* Eton; *Heir* none; *Career* served in N Africa with Intelligence Corps (despatches) 1939-45; Medal of Freedom with Bronze Palm (USA); *Clubs* Travellers'; *Style—* The Rt Hon the Viscount Monsell; The Mill House, Dumbleton, Evesham, Worcs WR11 6TR

MONSLOW, Baroness; Jean Baird; da of Rev Angus Macdonald; *m* 1960, as his 2 w, Baron Monslow (d 1966; Life Peer); *Style—* The Rt Hon the Lady Monslow; 4 Kirklea Circus, Glasgow 12

MONSON, Hon Andrew Anthony John; s of 11 Baron Monson; *b* 12 May 1959; *Educ* Eton and Merton Coll, Oxford (BA); *Career* barr, called to the Bar Middle Temple 1983; *Recreations* books, theatre, bridge, boardgames, tennis, skiing; *Clubs* Lincolnshire; *Style—* The Hon Andrew Monson; 7A Melrose Gdns, London W6

MONSON, Maj Hon Jeremy David Alfonso John; 2 s of 10 Baron Monson (d 1958); *b* 29 Sept 1934; *Educ* Eton, RMA Sandhurst; *m* 4 Dec 1958, Patricia Mary, yst da of late Maj George Barker, MFH; 1 s, 1 da; *Career* 2 Lt Grenadier Gds 1954, served in Cyprus Emergency 1956-57, Capt 1959, Maj 1964, mil asst to Def Services Sec 1964-66, ret 1967; memb: CC Berks 1981-; Thames Valley Police Authy 1982-; SBStJ 1971; *Clubs* Cavalry and Guards', White's; *Style—* Major the Hon Jeremy Monson; Keepers Cottage, Scarletts Wood, Hare Hatch, Nr Reading, Berks RG10 9TL

MONSON, 11 Baron (GB 1728); Sir John Monson; 15 Bt (E 1611); s of 10 Baron Monson (d 1958), and Bettie Northrup, da of late Lt-Col E Alexander Powell of Connecticut, USA, (who m 2, 1962, Capt James Arnold Phillips d 1983); *b* 3 May 1932; *Educ* Eton, Trinity Coll Cambridge; *m* 1955, Emma, da of Anthony Devas (d 1958), and Mrs Rupert Shephard; 3 s; *Heir* s, Hon Nicholas John Monson; *Career* sits as Independent in House of Lords; pres Soc for Individual Freedom; *Style—* The Rt Hon the Lord Monson; The Manor House, South Carlton, nr Lincoln (☎ 0522 730263)

MONSON, Sir (William Bonnar) Leslie; KCMG (1965, CMG 1950), CB (1964); s of John William Monson, MBE (d 1929), and Selina Leslie Stewart (d 1958); *b* 28 May 1912; *Educ* Edinburgh Acad, Hertford Coll Oxford (BA); *m* 1948, Helen Isobel, da of Francis Roland Browne (d 1950); *Career* Dominions Office 1935-39, Colonial Office 1939-47, chief sec W African Cncl 1947-51, asst under sec of state Colonial Office 1952-64, high cmmr Zambia 1964-66, dep under sec of state Cwlth Office 1967-68, dep under sec FCO 1968-72, ret; dir overseas relations St John Ambulance HQ 1975-81; KStJ 1975; *Clubs* United Oxford & Cambridge Univ; *Style—* Sir Leslie Monson, KCMG, CB; Golf House, Goffers Rd, Blackheath, London SE3 0UA (☎ 081 852 7257)

MONSON, Hon Nicholas John; s & h of 11 Baron Monson; *b* 19 Oct 1955; *Educ* Eton; *m* 1981, Hilary, only da of Kenneth Martin, of Nairobi; 1 s (Alexander), 1 da (Isabella); *Career* PR and journalist; fndr and ed The Magazine 1982-84; dir Strategic Solutions (PR) 1985-87; md Grenfell Communications Ltd (PR); non-exec dir The Organiser Co (publishing); *Books* The Nouveaux Pauvres (1984); *Recreations* backgammon, chess, tennis; *Clubs* Buck's, The Lincolnshire, Annabel's; *Style—* The Hon Nicholas Monson; 24 Fentiman Rd, London SW8 1LF

MONSON, Hon Stephen Alexander John; s of 11 Baron Monson; *b* 5 Jan 1961; *Career* photographer (commercial, travel, art) and 20th Century Br Fine Art conslt (USA); *Style—* Stephen Monson, Esq; 9 Bray House, Duke of York St, St James's, London SW1Y 6JX (☎ 071 930 5641, 0101 212 832 3630)

MONT, Joan Mary; da of Joseph Francis Stephen Grant (d 1931), of Leeds, and Kathleen, *née* Williamson; *b* 20 March 1930; *Educ* Brighton & Hove HS for Girls, RADA (Dip); *m* 6 Sept 1952, Neville, s of Flt Lt Cyril Mont, of 78 The Drive, Hove, E Sussex; 3 da (Sarah b 1957, Vanessa b 1963, Fiona b 1970); *Career* memb E Sussex CC: Moulsecoomb (Brighton) Div 1975-81, chm Educn Fin and Gen Purposes Sub Ctee 1977-79, chm Sch Sub Ctee 1979-81, chm Educn Ctee 1981-85, Rottingdean (Brighton) Div 1981-, ldr of CC and chm of Policy and Resources Ctee 1985-89, chm 1989-; memb: Ct and Cncl Univ of Sussex 1981, Cncl Brighton Poly 1981-89 (chm Fin and Gen Purposes Ctee 1981-85), Exec Cncl and Educn Ctee ACCs 1985, Cncl Local Educn Authys 1988; govr: Brighton and Hove HS for Girls (GPDST) 1979, Hastings Coll of Art & Technol 1981, Eastbourne Coll of Art & Technol 1981; *Recreations* painting, dressmaking, and reading; *Style—* Mrs Joan Mont; Pelham House, St Andrew's Lane, Lewes, E Sussex (☎ 0273 481401)

MONTACUTE, Mervyn Charles; s of Charles Montacute, of Torquay, Devon, and Myra Annie Mabel, *née* Chinnock; *b* 5 Jan 1946; *Educ* Cheltenham GS, West Seattle HS, King's Coll London (LLB), Plymouth Poly (Dip Mgmnt Studies), Harvard Univ (Master Pub Admin); *m* 22 June 1975, Susan Arleen, da of Sigured Aardal (d 1965), of Seattle, Washington, USA; 2 da (Tamara b 1982, Summer b 1984); *Career* articled clerk Northamptonshire CC 1968-70; ast slr: Glamorgan CC 1970-72, Cornwall CC 1972-75; city slr Wellington City Cncl NZ 1975-79, city mangr Tauranga City Cncl NZ 1981-86, chief exec Dunedin City Cncl NZ 1986-90; memb: Soc of Local Authy Chief Execs, BIM; fell NZ Inst of Mgmnt; *Style—* Mervyn Montacute, Esq; Westminster City Council, Westminster City Hall, 64 Victoria Street, London SW1 (☎ 071 798 2030, fax 071 798 3438)

MONTAGU, Hon Anthony Trevor Samuel; yr s of 3 Baron Swaythling, OBE (d 1990), and his 1 w, Mary Violet, *née* Levy; *b* 3 Aug 1931; *Educ* Eton; *m* 26 June 1962, Deirdre Bridget, yr da of Brig Ronald Henry Senior, DSO, TD, and Hon Norah Marguerite, eldest da of 2 Baron Joicey; 2 s, 1 da; *Career* chm and chief exec Abingworth plc; *Style—* The Hon Anthony Montagu; 78 Chelsea Park Gardens, London SW3 (☎ 071 352 1834)

MONTAGU, John Edward Hollister; does not use courtesy title of Viscount Hinchingbrooke; s and h of Alexander Victor Edward Paulet Montagu (10 Earl of Sandwich, who disclaimed peerages for life 1964), and Rosemary Maud Peto; *b* 11 April 1943; *Educ* Eton, Trinity Coll Cambridge (MA); *m* 1 July 1968, (Susan) Caroline, o da of Canon Perceval Ecroyd Cobham Hayman; 2 s, 1 da; *Career* freelance journalist and ed conslt; info offr Christian Aid 1974-86, ed Save the Children Fund 1987-; *Style—* John Montagu, Esq; 69 Albert Bridge Rd, London SW11 4QE (☎ 071 223 0997)

MONTAGU, Lady Julia Frances; *née* Montagu; has resumed her maiden name; da of Victor Montagu (10 Earl of Sandwich, who disclaimed his peerages for life 1964); *b* 12 April 1947; *Educ* Crantorne Chase; *m* 1, 1972 (m dis 1976), Martin Lee Oakley; m 2, 1976 (m dis 1987), Peter Gerald Edward Body; 1 s (Timothy b 1982); *Style—* The Lady Julia Montagu; The Beck, Wexham Park Lane, Wexham, Slough, Bucks

MONTAGU, Nicholas Lionel John; s of John Eric Montagu (d 1990), and Barbara Joyce Montagu, OBE, *née* Gollin (d 1991); *b* 12 March 1944; *Educ* Rugby, New Coll Oxford (BA); *m* 8 Aug 1974, Jennian, da of Ford Irvine Geddes, MBE; 2 da (Clare Barbara b 1976, Johanna Kythe b 1980); *Career* lectr in philosophy Univ of Reading 1969-74 (asst lectr 1966-69); DHSS (DSS 1989-): princ 1974, seconded to Cabinet Office 1978-79, asst sec 1981, under sec 1986, dep sec 1990; *Publications* Brought to Account (Report of Scrutiny on National Insurance Records) 1981; *Recreations* cooking, wild flowers, fishing; *Style—* Nicholas Montagu, Esq; Department of Social Security, Richmond House, 79 Whitehall, London SW1A 2NS (☎ 071 210 5470, fax 071 210 5480)

MONTAGU, Hon (George Charles) Robert; s of Victor Edward Paulet Montagu (disclaimed Earldom of Sandwich for life 1964); *b* 1949; *Educ* Eton; *m* 1970, Donna Marzia Brigante Colonna, da of Conte Brigante Colonna; 2 s, 2 da; *Style—* The Hon Robert Montagu; The Old Farmhouse, 44 Long St, Cerne Abbas, Dorset (☎ 0300 341 281)

MONTAGU, (Alexander) Victor Edward Paulet; s of 10 Earl of Sandwich; suc f on his death in 1962 and disclaimed peerages for life 1964; 4 Earl sponsored Captain Cook's voyages and gave his name to the Sandwich Islands, as well as to the sandwich; *b* 22 May 1906; *Educ* Eton, Trinity Coll Cambridge; *m* 1, 27 July 1934 (m dis 1958), Rosemary Maud, o da of late Maj Ralph Harding Peto (gs of Sir Morton Peto, 1 Bt); 2 s, 4 da; m 2, 7 June 1962 (m annulled 1965), Lady Anne Cavendish, MBE (d 1981), da of 9 Duke of Devonshire, KG, PC (d 1938), and widow of Christopher Holland-Martin, MP; *Heir* to disclaimed peerages, s, John Edward Hollister Montagu; *Career* joined Northamptonshire Regt (TA) 1926, served in France 1940 and afterwards on gen staff Home Forces; private sec to Rt Hon Stanley Baldwin MP 1932-34; treas Junior Imperial League 1934-35; MP (C, but resigned party whip 1956 in protest at withdrawal from Suez and sat as an Ind C in 1957 only) S Dorset 1941-62; chm Tory Reform Ctee 1943-44, vice chm Cons Foreign Affrs Ctee 1957-58, pres Anti-Common Market League 1962-64, chm Cons Trident Gp 1973-75; contested Lancs (Accrington Div) at gen election 1964; *Style—* Victor Montagu, Esq; Mapperton, Beaminster, Dorset DT8 3NR (☎ 0308 862441)

MONTAGU DOUGLAS SCOTT *see also*: Scott

MONTAGU DOUGLAS SCOTT, Lord George Francis John; s of 7 and 9 Duke of Buccleuch and Queensberry, KT, GCVO (d 1935), and Lady Margaret Bridgeman (da of 4 Earl of Bradford by his w, Lady Ida Lumley, da of 9 Earl of Scarbrough); *b* 8 July 1911; *Educ* Eton, Christ Church Oxford; *m* 1938, Molly (Mary Wina Mannin), da of Lt-Col Harry Bishop, of Harewood, Andover; 1 s, 2 da; *Career* farmer, co dir; Lt-Col TA Reserve ; memb Royal Co of Archers (Queen's Bodyguard for Scotland); *Recreations* racing, gardening; *Clubs* Cavalry and Guards'; *Style—* The Lord George Montagu Douglas Scott; 60 Glebe Place, SW3; The Old Almshouse, Weekley, Kettering, Northants

MONTAGU DOUGLAS SCOTT, Lord (William Henry) John; 2 s of 9 and 11 Duke of Buccleuch and Queensberry, KT, VRD, JP; *b* 6 Aug 1957; *m* 11 Feb 1990, Mrs (Hafize) Berrin Torolsan, o da of Halil Torolsan, of Istanbul, Turkey; *Career* page of honour to HM Queen Elizabeth The Queen Mother; *Style—* The Lord John Montagu Douglas Scott; Valikonagi Caddesi 62, Nisantasi, Istanbul, Turkey

MONTAGU DOUGLAS SCOTT, Hon Mrs ((Marion) Miranda); *née* Phillimore; o da of 4 Baron Phillimore, *qv*; *b* 9 May 1946; *m* 1973 (m dis 1985), Thomas Walter Montagu Douglas Scott, s of Lt-Col Claud Everard Walter Montagu Douglas Scott, MC; 1 da (Alice b 1978); *Style—* The Hon Mrs Montagu Douglas Scott; 65 Cloncurry Street, Bishop's Park, London SW6 6DT

MONTAGU DOUGLAS SCOTT, Lady William; Lady Rachel; *née* Douglas-Home; da of 13 Earl of Home, KT, TD (d 1951), and Lady Lilian Lambton (da of 4 Earl of Durham); is sis of Baron Home of the Hirsel, KT, PC; *b* 10 April 1910; *m* 1937, Lord William Walter Montagu Douglas Scott, MC, MP Roxburgh and Selkirk 1935-50 (d 1958), 2 s of 7 and 9 Duke of Buccleuch and Queensberry, KT, GCVO; 1 s, 4 da; *Style—* The Lady William Montagu Douglas Scott; Beechwood, Melrose, Roxburghshire

MONTAGU DOUGLAS SCOTT, Lady; Valerie Margaret Steriker; *née* Finnis; da of late Cdr Steriker Finnis, RN; *b* 31 Oct 1924; *Educ* Downe House, Waterperry Hort Coll Oxford; *m* 1970, as his 2 w, Sir David John (Montagu Douglas) Scott, KCMG, OBE (d 1986); *Career* horticulture, photography; fndr Merlin Tst; Victoria medal of Honour (Hort) as Valerie Finnis; *Recreations* looking at pictures; *Style—* Lady Montagu Douglas Scott; The Dower House, Boughton House, Kettering, Northants NN14 1BJ (☎ 0536 82279)

MONTAGU DOUGLAS SCOTT, Lady Victoria Doris Rachel; *née* Haig; da of Field Marshal 1 Earl Haig (d 1928); *b* 1908; *m* 1929 (m dis 1951), Brig Andrew Montagu Douglas Scott, DSO, Irish Gds (d 1971); 1 s, 1 da; *Style—* The Lady Victoria Scott; The Pavilion, Park Rd, Isleworth, Middx TW7 6BD

MONTAGU OF BEAULIEU, 3 Baron (UK 1885); Edward John Barrington Douglas-Scott-Montagu; s of 2 Baron, KCIE, CSI, VD, JP, DL, sometime MP New Forest (d 1929, gs of 5 Duke of Buccleuch and Queensberry, KG, KT), by his 2 w, Alice Pearl, *née* Crake (*see* Hon Mrs Edward Pleydell-Bouverie); *b* 20 Oct 1926; *Educ* St Peters Ct Broadstairs, Ridley Coll Ontario, Eton, New Coll Oxford; *m* 1, 1959 (m dis 1974), (Elizabeth) Belinda, o da of Capt Hon John de Bathe Crossley, JP (d 1935, yr bro of 2 Baron Somerleyton); 1 s, 1 da (Hon Mary Rachel b 1964); m 2, 1974, Fiona Margaret, da of R L D Herbert; 1 s (Hon Jonathan Deane b 1975); *Heir* s, Hon Ralph Douglas-Scott-Montagu b 13 March 1961; *Career* sits as Cons peer in House of Lords; proprietor of Beaulieu Abbey (originally a Cistercian fndn of 1204); served with Grenadier Gds 1945-48; fndr opened Montagu Motor Museum 1952 and Motor Cycle Museum 1956, fndr Nat Motor Museum at Beaulieu 1972; fndr and ed Veteran and Vintage Magazine 1956-79; pres: Historic Houses Assoc 1973-78, Union of European Historic Houses 1978-81, Fédération Internationale des Voitures Anciennes 1980-83, Museums Assoc 1982-84; memb: Devpt Cmmn 1980-84, Southern Tourist Bd, Assoc of Br Tport Museums; vice-pres Tport Tst; chm Historic Bldgs and Monuments Cmmn 1983-; pres: Fedn Br Historic Vehicle Clubs 1989-, English Vineyards Assoc; chllr Wine Guild of the UK; author and lectr; *Publications include* The Motoring Montagus (1959), Jaguar (1961), The Gordon Bennett Races (1963), Lost Causes of Motoring: Europe (Vol I and II, 1969 and 1971), Early Days on the Road (1976), Royalty on the Road (1980), Home James (1982), The British Motorist (1987), English Heritage (1987); *Recreations* shooting, water sports, sailing (yacht 'Cygnet of Beaulieu'); *Clubs* House of Lords Yacht (Vice-Cdre), Beaulieu River Sailing (Cdre), Nelson Boat Owners' (Cdre), and many historic vehicle clubs; *Style—* The Rt Hon the Lord Montagu of Beaulieu; Palace House, Beaulieu, Brockenhurst, Hants (☎ 0590 612345); Flat 11, Wyndham House, 24 Bryanston Sq, London W1 (☎ 071 262 2603)

MONTAGU-POLLOCK, Sir Giles Hampden; 5 Bt (UK 1872), of the Khyber Pass; s of Sir George Seymour Montagu-Pollock, 4 Bt (d 1985), and Karen-Sofie, da of Hans Ludvig Dedekam, of Oslo, Norway; *b* 19 Oct 1928; *Educ* Eton, de Havilland Technical Sch; *m* 1963, Caroline Veronica, da of late Richard F Russell, of London; 1 s, 1 da (Sophie b 1969); *Heir* s, Guy b 1966; *Career* with Airspeed Ltd 1949-51, G P Eliot at Lloyd's 1951-52, de Havilland Engine Co Ltd 1952-56; advertising mangr: Bristol Aeroplane Co Ltd 1956-59, Bristol Siddeley Engines Ltd 1959-61; assoc dir J Walter Thompson Co Ltd 1961-69; dir: C Vernon & Sons Ltd 1969-71, Acumen Marketing Group 1971-74, 119 Pall Mall Ltd 1972-78; mgmnt conslt in marketing 1974-, assoc of John Stork & Partners Ltd 1980-88, Korn/Ferry International Ltd 1988-; MCIM; *Recreations* water-skiing, skiing, photography; *Clubs* United Services', Inst of Directors; *Style—* Sir Giles Montagu-Pollock, Bt; The White House, 7 Washington Rd, London SW13 9BG (☎ 081 748 8491)

MONTAGU-POLLOCK, Guy Maximilian; s and h of Sir Giles Hampden Montagu-Pollock, 5 Bt, and Caroline Veronica, da of Richard F Russell; *b* 1966; *Educ* Eton, Hatfield Poly; *Style—* Guy Montagu-Pollock, Esq; c/o The White House, 7 Washington Rd, Barnes, London SW13 9BG

MONTAGU-POLLOCK, Sir William Horace; KCMG (1957, CMG 1946); 3 s of Sir Montagu Montagu-Pollock, 3 Bt, by his w Margaret, *née* Bell, sis of late Countess of Glasgow (w of 8 Earl); Sir William's 1 cous, William Bell, m Belinda, da of Geoffrey Dawson, former ed The Times; *b* 12 July 1903; *Educ* Marlborough, Trinity Cambridge; *m* 1, 1933 (m dis 1945), Frances, da of Sir John Fischer Williams, CBE, KC; 1 s (Hubert), 1 da (Fidelity); m 2, 1948, Barbara, da of late Percy Jowett, CBE, FRCA, RWS (formerly w of Thomas Gaskell, by whom she had a da Josceline, who m David Dimbleby, the TV personality); 1 s (Matthew); *Career* Foreign Service to 1962; ambass to: Damascus 1952-53, Peru 1953-58, Switzerland 1958-60, Denmark 1960-62; *Style—* Sir William Montagu-Pollock, KCMG; 181 Coleherne Court, London SW5 0DU

MONTAGU-SMITH, Gp Capt Arthur; *b* 17 July 1915; *Educ* Whitgift Sch, RAF Staff Coll (psc); *m* 1942, Elizabeth Hood, da of late Thomas Hood Wilson Alexander, JP, FRCSE, of Lhanbryde, Moray (d 1941); 1 s, 1 da; *Career* cmmnd RAF 1935, Adj 99 Sqdn 1938-39; served WW II (NW Europe, N Africa, Med) Fl-Cdr 264 Sqdn 1940 (Battle of Britain rosette), Fl-Cdr 221 Sqdn 1941 (despatches 1942), OC 248 Sqdn 1942-43, dep dir RAF Trg USA (Washington) 1944, OC 104 Wing France 1945; Hon ADC Govr NI 1948-49, Air Advsr New Delhi 1949-50, RAF rep COS Ctee UN New York 1951-53, HM Air Attaché Budapest 1958-60, ret at own request 1961; memb Moray TAFA 1961-68, regnl exec Small Industs Cncl and Scottish Devpt Agency 1962-80; hon county rep Moray and Nairn RAF Benevolent Fund 1964-, dir Elgin and Lossiemouth Harbour Co 1966-90, memb Elgin Dist Cncl 1967-75, former pres Victoria League Moray and Nairn, former chm Moray Assoc of Youth Clubs, chm Elgin and Lossiemouth branch of Scottish Soc for Prevention of Cruelty to Animals 1971-82; DL Morayshire 1970-91; *Clubs* RAF; *Style—* Gp Capt Arthur Montagu-Smith; Woodpark, Elgin, Moray IV30 3LF (☎ 034 384 2220)

MONTAGU-STUART-WORTLEY-MACKENZIE, Lady Rowena; da of 4 Earl of Wharncliffe (d 1987); *b* 14 June 1961; *Style—* The Lady Rowena Montagu-Stuart-Wortley-Mackenzie

MONTAGUE, Adrian Alastair; s of Charles Edward Montague (d 1985), of Godden Green, Sevenoaks, Kent, and Olive, *née* Jones (d 1956); *b* 28 Feb 1948; *Educ* Mill Hill Sch, Trinity Hall Cambridge (MA); *m* 1, May 1970 (m dis 1982), Pamela Joyce; 1 s (Edward b 1977), 2 da (Emma b 1974, Olivia b 1980); m 2, 8 Nov 1986, Penelope Jane Webb; 1 s (William b 1988); *Career* Linklaters & Paines: asst slr 1973-74, asst slr Paris 1974-77, asst slr London 1977-79, ptnr 1979-; non-exec dir: Munichre Investment Holdings 1988-, Munichre Equity Investment Ltd 1988-; Int Bar Assoc section on business law ctee: vice chm 1982-86, chm 1987, sub ctee chm 1988-89; firm rep to Maj Projects Assoc; memb Law Soc; *Books* Joint Ventures (ed with C G E Nightingale, 1989); *Style—* Adrian Montague, Esq; Linklaters & Paines, Barrington House, 59-67 Gresham St, London EC2V 7JA (☎ 071 606 7080, fax 071 606 5113, telex 881334)

MONTAGUE, Michael Jacob; CBE (1970); s of late David Elias Montague and Ethel Montague; *b* 10 March 1932; *Educ* High Wycombe Boys' GS, Magdalen Coll Sch Oxford; *Career* chm: Yale and Valor plc (domestic appliance and security manufacturers) 1965- (md 1963), English Tourist Bd 1979-84; Nat Consumer Cncl 1984-87; *Recreations* walking, rowing; *Clubs* Oriental; *Style—* Michael Montague, Esq, CBE; Yale & Valor plc, Riverside House, Corney Rd, Chiswick, London W4 2SL (☎ 081 995 4104, fax 081 994 9569)

MONTAGUE, Robert Joel; CBE (1991); s of Robert L Montague, of Sevenoaks, Kent, and Freda, *née* Lance; *b* 22 June 1948; *Educ* Bedstone Sch Shropshire, Caius Sch Brighton; *m* 12 Feb 1972 (m dis), Susan Jane; 2 s (Robert Kenneth b 9 June 1975, Benjamin James b 4 Feb 1980), 1 da (Victoria Louise b 11 May 1973); m 2, 23 Sept Sept 1988 (m dis), Jane Laura, m 3, 19 Dec 1990, Silke; *Career* sales and mktg Esso Petroleum Co Ltd 1964-69, dep md Cables Montague Ltd 1971-80 (joined 1969), fndr Tiphook plc 1978-; memb: Cncl Asthma Res Cncl, Cons Pty; Freeman: City of London, Worshipful Co of Carmen; FCIT; *Recreations* shooting, fishing, squash, running; *Style—* Robert J Montague, Esq, CBE; Tiphook plc, 26 St James's Square, London SW1Y 4JH (☎ 071 930 2000, fax 071 839 6096)

MONTAGUE, Air Cdre Ruth Mary Bryceson; da of Griffith John Griffiths, of Buxton, Derbyshire, and Nancy Bryceson Wrigley (d 1987); *b* 1 June 1939; *Educ* Cavendish GS for Girls Buxton, Bedford Coll London (BSc); *m* 12 Feb 1966, Roland Arthur Montague, s of Reginald George Montague (d 1950); *Career* cmmnd RAF 1962, UK and Far E 1962-66, UK 1966-80, HQ Strike Cmd 1980-83, RAF Staff Coll 1983-86, dir Women's RAF 1989- (dep dir 1986-89); ADC to HM The Queen 1989-; *Recreations* cookery, tapestry, gardening, swimming, clay pigeon shooting, world travel; *Clubs* RAF; *Style—* Air Cdre Ruth Montague; Ministry of Defence, Adastral House (Room 326), Theobalds Road, London WC1X 8RU (☎ 071 430 7141)

MONTAGUE BROWNE, Anthony Arthur Duncan; CBE (1965, OBE 1955), DFC (1945); s of Lt-Col A D Montague Browne, DSO, OBE (d 1969), of Ross-on-Wye, and Violet Evelyn, *née* Downes (d 1969); *b* 8 May 1923; *Educ* Stowe, Magdalen Coll Oxford (Scholar), and abroad; *m* 1, 1950 (m dis 1970), Noel Evelyn Arnold-Wallinger; 1 da (Jane Evelyn b 1953); m 2, 1970, Shelagh Margery Macklin, da of late Col Hugh Mulligan, CMG, of Cheshire; *Career* serv WWII as pilot RAF, entered HM Dip Serv 1946, FO 1946-49, Br Embassy Paris 1949-52, private sec to Prime Minister (Sir Winston Churchill) 1952-55, seconded as pte sec to Sir Winston Churchill 1956-65, seconded to Royal Household 1965-67, resigned as cncllr 1967; md Gerrard & National plc 1967-83; dir: Columbia Pictures Prodn (UK) Ltd 1967-72, International Life Insurance Ltd 1967-70; dep chm (and London rep) Guaranty Trust Bank (Bahamas) Ltd 1983-86; chm: Westward Travel Ltd 1984, Land Leisure plc 1987-88; dep chm Highland Participants plc 1987-89, dir Security Pacific Trust (Bahamas) Ltd 1986-89, and other cos; author of various articles in nat press; chm of Cncl and tstee Winston Churchill Memorial Trust, vice pres Univs Fedn for Animal Welfare; Hon DL Westminster Coll Fulton USA (1988); *Recreations* wildlife, reading; *Clubs* Boodles's, Pratts; *Style—* Anthony Montague Browne, Esq, CBE, DFC; Hawkridge Cottages, Bucklebury, nr Reading, Berks RG7 6EG (☎ 0734 712578); 99A Prince of Wales Mansions, Prince of Wales Drive, Battersea, London SW11 (☎ 071 720 4210)

MONTAGUE-JOHNSTONE, Roland Richard; s of Maj Roy Henry Montague-Johnstone, MBE, of 16 Leonard Court, London W8, and Barbara Marjorie, *née* Warre (d 1990); *b* 22 Jan 1941; *Educ* Eton; *m* 24 Feb 1968, Sara Outram Boileau, da of Lt-Col John Garway Outram Whitehead, MC and Bar (d 1983), of 10 Blackfriars St, Canterbury; 2 s (Andrew, William); *Career* KRRC served NI and Berlin 1958-62; admitted slr 1967; ptnr Slaughter and May 1973-91 (articled clerk 1962-67, asst slr 1967-73); memb Law Soc; *Recreations* reading, walking, gardening; *Clubs* Celer Et Audax, Royal Green Jackets, English Speaking Union; *Style—* Roland Montague-Johnstone, Esq; 17 Airedale Ave, Chiswick, London W4 2NW; Poorton Hill, Powerstock, Dorset

MONTEAGLE OF BRANDON, 6 Baron (UK 1839); Gerald Spring Rice; s of 5 Baron (d 1946), and Emilie de Kosenko (d 1981), da of late Mrs Edward Brooks of NY; *b* 5 July 1926; *Educ* Harrow; *m* 1949, Anne, da of Col Guy James Brownlow, DSO, DL (d 1960); 1 s, 3 da; *Heir* s, Hon Charles James Spring Rice; *Career* Capt Irish Gds, ret 1955; memb: London Stock Exchange 1957-76, Lloyd's 1978-, HM Bodyguard of Hon Corps of Gentlemen-at-Arms 1978-; *Clubs* Cavalry and Guards, Pratt's, Kildare St and University (Dublin); *Style—* The Rt Hon the Lord Monteagle of Brandon; 242A Fulham Rd, London SW10 (☎ 071 351 3455)

MONTEFIORE, Rt Rev Hugh William; s of late Charles Sebag-Montefiore, OBE (whose f, Arthur, was paternal gs of Sarah, sis of Sir Moses Montefiore, 1 and last Bt, and a philanthropist); *b* 12 May 1920; *Educ* Rugby, St John's Coll Oxford (MA), Cambridge (BD); *m* 1 Jan 1945, Elisabeth Mary Macdonald, da of late Rev William Paton, DD; 3 da; *Career* ordained priest 1950; former examining chaplain of Bishops of: Newcastle, Worcester, Coventry, Blackburn; dean and fell Gonville and Caius Coll Cambridge 1953-63, canon theologian of Coventry 1959-69, vicar Great St Mary's Cambridge 1963-70, hon canon of Ely Cath 1969-70, bishop suffragan of Kingston-upon-Thames 1970-78, bishop of Birmingham 1978-87; chm C of E Gen Synod's Board of Social Responsibility 1983-87; author; chm Transport 2000 1987-; hon fell St John's Coll Oxford 1981; Hon DD: Aberdeen 1976, Birmingham 1984; *Recreations* walking, water colour painting; *Clubs* Royal Cwlth Soc; *Style—* The Rt Rev Hugh Montefiore; 23 Bellevue Rd, Wandsworth Common, London SW17 7EB (☎ 081 672 669)

MONTEITH, Charles Montgomery; s of James Monteith (d 1965), and Marian Monteith (d 1974); *b* 9 Feb 1921; *Educ* Royal Belfast Academical Inst, Magdalen Coll Oxford (MA, BCL); *Career* served WWII Royal Inniskilling Fusiliers, India and Burma, Maj 1940-45; called to the Bar Gray's Inn 1949; Faber & Faber: joined 1953, dir 1954, vice chm 1974-76, chm 1977-81, sr editorial conslt 1981-; All Souls Coll Oxford: fell 1948-88, sub warden 1967-69, emeritus fell 1989-; Hon DLitt: Univ of Ulster, Univ of Kent; *Clubs* Beefsteak, Garrick; *Style—* Charles Monteith, Esq; c/o Faber & Faber Ltd, 3 Queen Sq, London WC1N 3AR (☎ 071 465 0045)

MONTEITH, Lt-Col (Robert Charles) Michael; OBE (1984), MC (1943), TD (1945), JP (1957), DL (Lanarks 1959); s of Maj Joseph Basil Monteith, CBE, JP, DL (d 1960), and Dorothy, *née* Nicholson (d 1956); *b* 25 May 1914; *Educ* Ampleforth; *m* 19 July 1950, (Mira) Elizabeth, da of John Fanshawe (d 1944); 1 s (Robert b 17 Jan 1952); *Career* joined Lanarkshire Yeo 1933; served WWII: MELF, MEF, BAOR; Lt-Col 1945; qualified as chartered accountant Edinburgh 1939; contested (Unionist) Hamilton Div 1950 and 1951; CC Lanarkshire 1960-64 and 1967, Vice-Lt 1964; landowner (1200 acres); pt/t memb Mental Welfare Cmmn for Scotland 1962-83; memb: Br Assoc SMOM 1956, East Kilbride Devpt Corp 1972-76, chm Clydesdale DC 1974-84; memb Royal Co of Archers (Queen's Body Guard for Scotland); OStJ 1974; *Recreations* field sports, curling; *Clubs* New (Edinburgh), Puffin's (Edinburgh); *Style—* Lt-Col Michael Monteith, OBE, MC, TD, JP, DL; Cranley, Cleghorn, Lanarks (☎ 0555 870 330)

MONTGOMERIE, Lord; Hugh Archibald William Montgomerie; s and h of 18 Earl of Eglinton and Winton; *b* 24 July 1966; *Style—* Lord Montgomerie

MONTGOMERIE, Lorna Burnett (Mrs John Anderson); da of (James) Fraser Montgomerie, of South View, 7A West Lennox Drive, Helensburgh, Dunbartonshire G84 9AB, and Jane Burnett Sangster (Jean), *née* McCulloch; *b* 23 Oct 1953; *Educ* St George's Sch of Montreal Canada, North London Collegiate Sch Edgware, Churchill Coll Cambridge (BA, MA), Coll of Law Lancaster Gate; *m* 8 July 1983, John Venner Anderson, s of Prof John Anderson, of 14 Styles Way, Park Langley, Beckenham, Kent BR3 3AJ; *Career* admitted slr 1978; slr Supreme Ct 1978, asst slr Biddle & Co 1978-80, Annotator Halsbury's Statutes 1981, ed Encyclopaedia of Forms and Precedents (4 edns) 1981-85; Butterworth Law Publishers Ltd: R & D mangr 1985-89, ed systems mangr 1989-; articles written for: Dance 1986-87, The New Law Journal 1987-88; author of Articles in Holborn for Holborn Law Soc 1989; memb: Ctee of Holborn Law Soc 1983-, London Legal Educn Ctee (as representing Holborn Law Soc) 1988-89, Law Soc Panel monitoring articles in Holborn Area 1987-; memb Law Soc 1978-; *Recreations* reading, DIY, house renovation, sailing; *Clubs* Lansdowne; *Style—* Ms Lorna Montgomerie; Butterworth Law Publishers Ltd, 88 Kingsway, London WC2B 6AB (☎ 071 405 6900, fax 071 405 1332)

MONTGOMERIE, Hon Roger Hugh; DFC; s of 16 Earl of Eglinton (d 1945); *b* 1923; *Educ* Eton, New Coll Oxford; *Career* served in RAF 1942-46; *Style—* The Hon Roger Montgomerie, DFC; Lanehead, Dunscore, Dumfries

MONTGOMERY, Dr Alan Everard; s of Philip Napier Montgomery (d 1967), and Honor Violet Coleman, *née* Price; *b* 11 March 1938; *Educ* Royal GS Guildford, County of Stafford Trg Coll (CertEd, colours Rugby), Birkbeck Coll Univ of London (BA, PhD); *m* 16 July 1960, Janet Barton; 1 s (Magnus b 1971), 1 da (Justine b 1976); *Career* Nat Serv Corpl Middlesex Regt 1957-59; teacher: Staffordshire Educn Authy 1961-62, ILEA 1962-65; lectr Univ of Birmingham 1969-72; HM Dip Serv: joined FCO 1972, first sec FCO 1972-75, Dhaka 1975-77, Ottawa 1977-80, FCO 1980-83, cnsllr GATT and UNCTAD UK mission Geneva 1983-87, cnsllr consul gen and head of Chancery Jakarta 1987-89, head Migration and Visa Dept FCO 1989-; *publications* Lloyd George: 12 essays (contrib, 1971), Cambridge Hist Jl (contrib); *Recreations* theatre, jazz, writing pantomimes, gardening; *Style—* Dr Alan Montgomery; c/o Foreign & Commonwealth Office, King Charles Street, London SW1A 2AH

MONTGOMERY, Hon Mrs (Bridget Ann); *née* Fisher; yr da (by 1 m) of 3 Baron Fisher; *b* 24 Dec 1956; *m* 1982, Bruce Stewart Irlam Montgomery, s of Dr S R Montgomery, of Haslemere, Surrey; 1 s (Patrick Christopherson Ross b 1987), 2 da (Caroline b 1984, Katherine b 1985); *Style—* The Hon Mrs Montgomery; c/o Kilverstone Hall, Thetford, Norfolk

MONTGOMERY, (Hugh) Bryan Greville; s of Hugh Roger Greville Montgomery, MC (d 1952), and Molly A Montgomery, OBE, *née* Neele (d 1990); *b* 26 March 1929; *Educ* Repton, Lincoln Coll Oxford (MA); *Career* Nat Serv 1947-49, chm Andry Montgomery Ltd and assoc cos, chm of govrs Building Museum, chm of tstees Br Architectural Library; vice chm Building Conservation Tst, dir Acad of St Martin in the Fields Concert Soc; vice pres Union Des Foires Internationales, cncllr CGLI; memb BOTB 1991-; Freeman City of London; Master Worshipful Co of Tylers and Bricklayers 1980-81; fell Royal Soc for the Advancement of Arts for Indust and Commerce; *Books* Exhibitions: Design & Management (with John Allwood, 1989); *Recreations* contemporary art, wine, travel; *Clubs* United Oxford Cambridge Univ; *Style—* Bryan Montgomery, Esq; Snells Farm, Amersham Common, Bucks; 11 Manchester Square, London W1M 5AB (☎ 071 486 1951, fax 071 486 8770)

MONTGOMERY, Clare Patricia; da of Dr Stephen Ross Montgomery, of Telegraph Cottage, Blackdown, Haslemere, Surrey, and Ann Margaret, *née* Barlow; *b* 29 April 1958; *Educ* Millfield, UCL (LLB); *Career* called to the Bar Gray's Inn 1980; memb Br Ladies Fencing Team 1984-85; *Recreations* fencing; *Style—* Miss Clare Montgomery; 6 Pell St, London W8 7PD; 3 Raymond Buildings, Gray's Inn, London WC1R 5BH (☎ 071 831 3833)

MONTGOMERY, Dr (Robert) Darragh; s of Gp Capt Thomas Montgomery (d 1966), of Belstone, Devon, and Mary, *née* Darragh (d 1979); *b* 10 Aug 1927; *Educ* Campbell Coll Belfast, Gonville and Caius Coll Cambridge (MA, MD, BChir), Middx Hosp London; *m* 30 June 1956, Jean, da of Charles Edward Pratt, of Solihull; 2 s (Charles b 1960, Richard b 1961), 1 da (Joanna b 1958); *Career* Flt Lt RAF, S Rhodesia 1951-54; memb scientific staff MRC 1958-62 (Tropical Metabolism Res Unit Jamaica, Dept of Experimental Med Cambridge), conslt physician W Midlands RHA 1964, sr clinical lectr Dept of Med Univ of Birmingham (hon res fell Dept of Experimental Pathology); author of numerous scientific pubns; former pres W Midlands Physicians Assoc and Midland Gastroenterological Soc; cncllr Royal Soc of Tropical Med & Hygiene; FRSM, FRCP (London and Edinburgh); *Recreations* mountaineering, travel, tennis, golf, writing, poetry; *Style—* Dr R Darragh Montgomery; Greenfields, Burford Lane, Shelfield, nr Alcester, Warwickshire B49 6JH (☎ 0789 488634)

MONTGOMERY, David; CMG (1984), OBE (1972); s of late David Montgomery, and Mary, *née* Walker Cunningham; *b* 29 July 1927; *m* 1955, Margaret Newman; 1 s, 1 da; *Career* RN 1945-48; FO 1949-52, Bucharest 1952-53, FO 1953-55, Bonn 1955-58, Düsseldorf 1958-61, Rangoon 1961-63, Ottawa 1963-64, Regina Saskatchewan 1964-65, FCO 1966-68, Bangkok 1968-72, Zagreb 1973-76, FCO 1976-79, British dep high cmmr to Barbados 1980-84 and (non-resident) to Antigua and Barbuda, Dominica, Grenada, St Kitts and Nevis, St Lucia, St Vincent and the Grenadines; ret 1984; FCO 1987-; *Style—* David Montgomery, Esq, CMG, OBE; 8 Ross Court, Putney Hill, London SW15 3NY

MONTGOMERY, David; *b* 1937,Brooklyn; *Educ* Midwood HS, Juillard Sch of Music; *m* 1 (m dis); 2 da; m 2, 1982, Martine King; 1 s, 1 da; *Career* former musician; apprentice photographer to Lester Bookbinder NY; professional photographer 1964-: for Jocelyn Stevens at Queen Magazine and Mark Boxer at The Sunday Times Magazine; has photographed: HM Queen Elizabeth II, HM Queen Elizabeth The Queen Mother, Lord Home, James Callaghan, Ted Heath, Margaret Thatcher, King Hussein of Jordan, The Duchess of York plus innumerable personalities; winner many int awards; *Style—* David Montgomery, Esq; c/o M & M Management, Studio B, 11 Edith Grove, London SW10 (☎ 071 352 6667, fax 071 351 3714)

MONTGOMERY, Sir (Basil Henry) David; 9 Bt (UK 1801), of Stanhope, Peeblesshire, JP (Kinross-shire 1966), DL (Kinross 1960 and Perth 1975); s of Lt Col Henry Keith Purvis-Russell-Montgomery, OBE (d 1954), and nephew of 8 Bt (d 1964); *b* 20 March 1931; *Educ* Eton; *m* 1956, Delia, da of Adm Sir (John) Peter Lorne Reid, GCB, CVO; 2 s (1 decd), 4 da; *Heir* s, James David Keith Montgomery; *Career* Tayside Regnl Cncl 1974-79, vice-pres Convention of Scottish Local Authorities (COSLA) 1978-79, Nature Conservancy Cncl 1974-79, chm Forestry Commission 1979-89; Hon LLD Dundee 1977; *Style—* Sir David Montgomery, Bt, JP, DL; Kinross House, Kinross

MONTGOMERY, David John; s of William John Montgomery, and Margaret Jean, *née* Flaherty; *b* 6 Nov 1948; *Educ* Bangor GS, Queen's Univ Belfast (BA); *m* 1, 12 April 1971 (m dis 1987), Susan Frances Buchanan, da of James Francis Buchanan Russell, QC; m 2, 6 May 1989, Heidi, da of Dr Edward Kingstone, of McMaster, Ontario; *Career* asst chief sub ed Daily Mirror 1978-80 (sub ed 1973-78), chief sub ed The Sun 1980-82, asst ed Sunday People 1982-84, ed News of the World 1985-87; dir: News Gp Newspapers 1986, Satellite TV plc 1986, News UK 1987-; ed and md Today 1987- (Newspaper of the Year 1988); *Style—* David Montgomery, Esq; News (UK) Ltd, Allen House, 70 Vauxhall Bridge Rd, London SW1V 2RP (☎ 071 630 6951, fax 071 821 0969)

MONTGOMERY, Dr David Pirrie; s of Dr James Montgomery, JP, of 229 Bank St, Irvine, Ayrshire, and Janet Leonora, *née* Nielson; *b* 22 March 1950; *Educ* Edinburgh Acad, Univ of Dundee (MB ChB); *m* 16 July 1977, Hilary, da of John Scotson, of Crescent Ave, Over Hulton, Bolton; 1 s (Robert b 1979), 1 da (Jane b 1982); *Career* sr registrar in radiology Leeds Hosp 1979-81, visiting fell in radiology Mass Gen Hosp Boston USA, conslt radiologist Blackpool 1981-; memb: BMA, Br Soc of Gastroenterology; FRCR 1980, FRCPG 1989; *Recreations* golf, walking, gardening; *Style—* Dr David Montgomery; Fir Tree Farm, Ballam Rd, Lytham, Lancs (☎ 0253 738369); Radiology Dept, Victoria Hospital, Blackpool, Lancs (☎ 0253 303555)

MONTGOMERY, David, né Mackenberg; s of Arthur Montgomery Mackenberg, of Brooklyn, NYC, and Lucille Ruth, *née* Phillips; *b* 8 Feb 1937; *Educ* Midwood HS; *m* 2, 1962, Caroline Blanch Maidlow; 1 s, 3 da; *Career* formerly musician (toured USA); freelance photographer 1960-; work incl HM Queen for Observer Magazine; also contrib to Sunday Times, Vogue and former Queen magazines; jt exhibition ICA 1973; *Recreations* gardening, photography, day dreaming; *Style—* David Montgomery, Esq

MONTGOMERY, Sir (William) Fergus; MP (C) Altrincham and Sale Oct 1974-; s of William and Winifred Montgomery of Hebburn; *b* 25 Nov 1927; *Educ* Jarrow GS, Bede Coll Durham; *m* Joyce, da of George Riddle, of Jarrow; *Career* RN 1946-48; memb Hebburn Cncl 1950-58; Young Cons Orgn: nat vice-chm 1954-57, nat chm 1957-58; contested (C) Consett (Durham) 1955; MP (C): Newcastle upon Tyne E 1959-64, Brierley Hill (Staffs) 1967-Feb 1974, Dudley West Feb 1974; PPS to: Sec of State for Educn and Science 1973-74, Ldr of the Oppn 1975-1976; kt 1985; *Style—* Sir Fergus Montgomery, MP; 181 Ashley Gdns, Emery Hill St, London SW1 (☎ 071 834 7905); 6 Groby Place, Altrincham, Cheshire (☎ 061 928 1983)

MONTGOMERY, Hon Henry David; s of 2 Viscount Montgomery of Alamein, CBE; *b* 2 April 1954; *Educ* Wellington, Seale Hayne Argic Coll; *m* 1980, Caroline J, da of Richard Odey, of Hotham Hall, York; 3 da (Alexa Maud b 30 Aug 1984, Flora Veronica b 4 May 1988, Phoebe Matilda b 4 Feb 1990); *Style—* The Hon Henry Montgomery; Bridge House, Combe, near Presteigne, Powys

MONTGOMERY, James David Keith; s and h of Sir (Basil Henry) David Montgomery, 9 Bt, and Delia, *née* Reid; *b* 13 June 1957; *Educ* Eton, Univ of Exeter; *m* 24 Sept 1983, Elizabeth Lynette, eldest da of Lyndon Evans, of Tyla Morris, Pentyrch, Glamorgan; 1 s (Edward Henry James b 1986), 1 da (Iona Rosanna b 1988); *Career* Capt Black Watch 1976-85; investmt advsr N M Rothschild 1985-89, dir Adam & Co Investment Management 1989-; *Recreations* golf, cricket, sailing, photography; *Style—* James Montgomery, Esq; 70 Hillier Rd, London SW11 6AU (☎ 071 228 5352); Adam & Co, 42 Pall Mall, London SW1Y 5JG (☎ 071 839 4615)

MONTGOMERY, John Duncan; JP (1985); s of Lionel Eric Montgomery (d 1975), of Wimbledon, and Katherine Mary, *née* Ambler (d 1977); *b* 12 Nov 1928; *Educ* King's Coll Sch Wimbledon, LSE (LLB, LLM); *m* 31 March 1956, Pauline Mary, da of Douglas Gordon Sutherland (d 1973), of Croydon; 2 da (Susan (Mrs Thomas) b 1959, Jennifer (Mrs Strudwick) b 1962); *Career* admitted slr 1951; Treasy Slr's Dept 1960-68, legal advsr Beecham Products 1974-75, co sec Shell UK Ltd 1979-88 (head of legal div 1975-88), memb Monopolies and Mergers Cmmn 1989-; former chm Merton Youth Orgns; Freeman City of London 1987, Worshipful Co of Loriners 1988; FRSA 1981; *Recreations* dinghy sailing, photography; *Clubs* MCC, City Livery; *Style—* John Montgomery, Esq, JP; Monopolies and Mergers Commission, New Court, 48 Carey St, London WC2A 2JT (☎ 071 324 1467, fax 071 324 1400)

MONTGOMERY, Richard John; s of Basil Richard Montgomery, of Tonbridge, Kent, and Mary Elizabeth, *née* Goddard; *b* 5 May 1955; *Educ* Tonbridge, Univ of Newcastle upon Tyne (MB BS); *m* 3 July 1982, Angela, da of John Todd, of Newcastle upon Tyne; 1 da (Clare Louise b 1987); *Career* demonstrator in anatomy Univ of Newcastle Med Sch 1979-80; post grad trg Northern Region: surgery 1980-83, orthopaedic surgery 1983-88; orthopaedic res fell Mayo Clinic Rochester Minnesota USA 1986-87, conslt in traumatic and orthopaedic surgery N and S Tees Health Dist 1989-; memb: Br Soc for Childrens Orthopaedic Surgery, Br Orthopaedic Assoc; FRCSEd 1983; *Recreations* aviation (holder of PPL); *Style—* Richard Montgomery, Esq; North Tees General Hospital, Hardwick, Stockton-on-Tees, Cleveland TS21 2BA (☎ 0642 57122 ext 522)

MONTGOMERY, Dr Stephen Ross; s of Sir Frank Percival Montgomery (d 1972), of Belfast, and Joan, *née* Christopherson (d 1990); *b* 15 Jan 1931; *Educ* Trinity Coll Glenalmond, Clare Coll Cambridge (MA), MIT (SM, ScD); *m* 15 June 1955, Ann, da of Stewart Irlam Barlow (d 1942), of Northumberland; 1 s (Bruce b 1956), 3 da (Clare b 1958, Joy b 1961, Jane b 1963); *Career* chartered mechanical engr; dir External Relations UCL, previously lectr and sr lectr in mechanical engineering UCL, mangr London Centre for Marine Technology; *Recreations* converting houses; *Style—* Dr Stephen R Montgomery; Telegraph Cottage, Blackdown, Haslemere, Surrey GU27 3BS (☎ 0428 654297); University College London, Gower St, London WC1E 7JE (☎ 071 380 7202)

MONTGOMERY CAMPBELL, Hon Mrs (Mary); *née* Adderley; da of 6 Baron Norton (d 1961), and Elizabeth, Lady Norton, *née* Birkbeck (d 1952); *b* 8 Sept 1922; *m* 1950, Hugh Montgomery Campbell (d 1980), s of the Rt Rev and Rt Hon Bishop Henry Colville Montgomery Campbell, KCVO, MC, PC, DD (d 1970), sometime Bishop of London); 1 s (Philip), 2 da (Elisabeth, Veronica); *Career* served WW II Third Offr WRNS; *Style—* The Hon Mrs Montgomery Campbell; 16 Ashworth Rd, London W9 (☎ 071 286 5781)

MONTGOMERY CUNINGHAME, Barbara, Lady; Barbara Susanne; MBE (1964); raised to rank of Baronet's widow 1948; 2 da of Lt-Col Hugh Annesley Gray-Cheape, DSO (d 1917), of Forfar, Co Angus, and Carsina Gordon Gray-Cheape (d 1952); *b* 2 March 1911; *m* 1934, Lt-Col Alexander William James Henry Montgomery Cuninghame, DSO, Royal Scots Fusiliers (ka Normandy 1944), eldest s of Col Sir Thomas Andrew Alexander Montgomery Cuninghame, 10 Bt, DSO (d 1945); *Style—* Barbara, Lady Montgomery Cuninghame, MBE; Yalford Kelly, Lifton, Devon PL16

0HQ

MONTGOMERY CUNINGHAME, Sir John Christopher Foggo; 12 Bt (NS 1672), of Corsehill, Ayrshire; s of 10 Bt, DSO, JP (d 1945) and bro of 11 Bt (d 1959); *b* 24 July 1935; *Educ* Fettes, Worcester Coll Oxford; *m* 9 Sept 1964, Laura Violet, 2 da of Sir Godfrey Nicholson, 1 Bt, *qv*; 3 da; *Heir* none; *Career* Nat Serv 2 Lt Rifle Bde; dir: Inertia Dynamics Corporation Arizona, Purolite International Ltd, R A Lee plc; *Style—* Sir John Montgomery Cuninghame, Bt; The Old Rectory, Brightwalton, Newbury, Berks RG16 0BL

MONTGOMERY-MASSINGBERD, Hugh John; s of John Michael Montgomery-Massingberd, Lord of the Manor and Patron of the Living of Gunby, Lincs, and Marsali Winlaw, *née* Seal; *b* 30 Dec 1946; *Educ* Harrow, Law Soc's Coll of Law; *m* 1, 1972 (m dis 1979), Christine Martinoni; 1 s (Luke b 1977), 1 da (Harriet b 1974); m 2, 1983, Caroline, er da of Sir Hugh Ripley, 4 Bt, *qv*; *Career* author, editor, journalist, lecturer and broadcaster; gave up place reading history at Selwyn Coll Cambridge to join editorial staff of Burke's Peerage publications; asst ed 1968-71, ed 1971-83; assoc ed The Field 1984-86; obituaries ed and specialist writer The Daily Telegraph 1986-; former memb Cncl Assoc of Genealogists and Record Agents (AGRA); *Books* The Monarchy (1979), The British Aristocracy (1979), The London Ritz (1980, revised 1989), Royal Palaces, Castles and Homes (1981), Diana - The Princess of Wales (1982), Heritage of Royal Britain (1983), Royal Palaces of Europe (1984), Blenheim Revisited (1985), Her Majesty The Queen (1986), Debrett's Great British Families (1987), Family Seats (1988), Gunby Hall (1990); also edited Burke's Landed Gentry (1972), Burke's Guide to The Royal Family (1973), Burke's Presidential Families of the USA (1975, 2nd edn 1981), Burke's Irish Family Records (1976), Burke's Family Index (1976), Burke's Royal Families of the World (Vol I 1977, Vol II 1980), Burke's Guide to Country Houses (Vol I 1978, Vol II 1980, Vol III 1981), Lord of the Dance: A Moncreiffe Miscellany (1986), and The Daily Telegraph Record of the Second World War (1989); contrib to The Spectator, Literary Review, etc; *Recreations* gluttony, sloth, hanging round stage doors; *Clubs* Travellers' and Academy; *Style—* Hugh Montgomery-Massingberd, Esq; 29 Clanricarde Gardens, London W2 4JL (☎ 071 727 7464, fax 071 229 7056)

MONTGOMERY OF ALAMEIN, 2 Viscount (UK 1946); David Bernard Montgomery; CBE (1975); o s of 1 Viscount Montgomery of Alamein, KG, GCB, DSO (d 1976), and Elizabeth, *née* Hobart (d 1937); *b* 18 Aug 1928; *Educ* Winchester, Trinity Coll Cambridge; *m* 1, 27 Feb 1953 (m dis 1967), Mary Raymond, yr da of Sir Charles Connell (d 1973); 1 s, 1 da; m 2, 30 Jan 1970, Tessa, da of Lt-Gen Sir Frederick A M Browning, GCVO, KBE, CB, DSO (d 1965), and Lady Browning, DBE (Daphne du Maurier, the writer, d 1989), and former w of Maj Peter de Zulueta; *Heir* s, Hon Henry David Montgomery; *Career* sits as Cons peer in House of Lords; dir Yardley International 1963-74, md Terimar Services Ltd (overseas trade consultancy) 1974-; memb Editorial Advsy Bd Vision Interamericana 1974-; cncllr Royal Borough of Kensington and Chelsea 1974-78; chm: Hispanic and Luso Brasilian Cncl Canning House 1978-1980 (pres 1987-), Antofagasta (Chile) and Bolivia Railway Co and subsids 1980-1982, vice pres Brazilian C of C GB 1983- (chm 1980-1982); non-exec dir: Korn/ Ferry Int 1977-, Northern Engrg Industs 1980-87; patron D-Day and Normandy Fellowship 1980-, Eighth Army Veterans Assoc 1984-; pres: Restaurateurs Assoc of GB 1982-90 (patron 1990), Centre for International Briefing Farnham Castle 1983-, Anglo-Argentine Soc 1976-87, Redgrave Theatre Farnham 1978-90; *Clubs* Garrick, Royal Fowey Yacht, Canning; *Style—* The Rt Hon Viscount Montgomery of Alamein, CBE; 54 Cadogan Square, London SW1X 0JW (☎ 071 589 8747)

MONTLAKE, Henry Joseph; s of Alfred Montlake, and Hetty Montlake; *b* 22 Aug 1930; *Educ* Ludlow GS, Univ of London (LLB); *m* 14 Sept 1952, Ruth Rochelle, *née* Allen; 4 s (Jonathan b 18 Oct 1956, Andrew b 2 July 1958, Nicholas b 30 Dec 1959, Charles b 1 Jan 1962); *Career* cmmnd RASC 1954; admitted slr 1952; cmmr for Oaths 1955, sr ptnr H Montlake & Co 1954-, dep registrar of Co Cts 1970-78, dep circuit judge and asst rec 1978-83, rec Crown Ct 1983-; chm Ilford Round Table 1962-63, capt Abridge Golf Club 1965 (chm 1964); pres: W Essex Law Soc 1977-78, Assoc of Jewish Golf Clubs and Socs 1983- (sec 1977-83); memb Law Soc; *Recreations* golf, The Times crossword, people, travel; *Clubs* Wig and Pen, Dyrham Park Golf, Abridge Golf and Country; *Style—* Henry Montlake, Esq; Chelston, 5 St Mary's Ave, Wanstead, London E11 2NR (☎ 081 989 7228); 197 High Rd, Ilford, Essex IG1 1LX (☎ 081 553 1311, fax 081 553 3066)

MONTMORENCY; *see*: de Montmorency

MONTROSE, 7 Duke of (S 1707); Sir James Angus Graham; also Lord Graham (S 1445), Earl of Montrose (S 1505), Marquess of Montrose (S 1644, new charter granted 1706), Marquess of Graham and Buchanan, Earl of Kincardine, Viscount Dundaff, Lord Aberuthven, Mugdock and Fintrie (all S 1707), Earl Graham and Baron Graham (GB 1722); also Hereditary Sheriff of Dunbartonshire; s of 6 Duke, KT, CB, CVO, VD (d 1954), by his w Lady Mary Douglas-Hamilton (da of 12 Duke of Hamilton); collaterally descended from the Hon Sir William Graham, cr 1625 Bt of Braco, Co Perth (a Nova Scotia Btcy); *b* 2 May 1907; *Educ* Eton, Christ Church Oxford; *m* 1, 20 Oct 1930 (m dis 1950), Isobel Veronica (d 1990), da of Lt-Col Thomas Byrne Sellar, CMG, DSO (d 1924); 1 s, 1 da; m 2, 17 April 1952, Susan Mary Jocelyn, widow of Michael Raleigh Gibbs, and da of Dr John Mervyn Semple; 2 s, 2 da; *Heir* s, Marquess of Graham, *qv*; *Career* Lt RNVR 1930, ret, rejoined 1939, Lt-Cdr RNVR; memb Federal Parliament of Rhodesia and Nyasaland 1958; min of agric Lands and natural resources S Rhodesia 1962-64, min of agric Rhodesia 1964-65, Rhodesia min of Defence and External Affairs 1965-68; *Style—* His Grace the Duke of Montrose; Dalgoram, PO Baynesfield, Natal, S Africa 3770 (☎ Thornville Junction 630); Auchmar, Drymen, Glasgow

MONTROSE, Kenneth; s of Harry Montrose (d 1955), of London, and Sophie, *née* Davis (d 1976); *b* 13 Jan 1928; *Educ* Glendale Coll Southend-on-Sea, Westfield Modern Sch Hinckley Leics; *m* 12 March 1949, Mary (d 1984), da of William Joseph Moreton (d 1972), of Hinckley, Leics; 1 s (Michael b 27 Sept 1949), 1 da (Gillian Mary (Mrs Townsend) b 29 Nov 1953); *Career* enlisted boys serv RN 1945, serv air mechanic 1 class Far East, demobbed 1947, seaman (sr position) Merchant Marines 1947-48; tech author Leyland Motors Gp 1950-54 (publicity mangr 1954-63), started own bldg and investmt co 1963, chm Broadgate Printing Group 1963-; contrib to various tech manuals; *Recreations* horse-riding, cars, pubs, walking, swimming; *Clubs* Wellington, Wig & Pen, Chestnuts, Tudor; *Style—* Kenneth Montrose, Esq; Broadgate Printing Group, Crondal Rd, Exhall, Coventry (☎ 0203 361800)

MONYPENNY, Edwin Richard; s of John Henry Gill Monypenny (d 1949), of Sheffield, and Florence Annie, *née* Shepard (d 1977); *b* 25 March 1917; *Educ* King Edward VII Sch Sheffield, Univ of Sheffield (MB ChB); *m* 5 Nov 1945, Isabelle Guthrie, da of John Russell Little (d 1928), of Edinburgh; 1 s (Ian James b 1950), 1 da (Ann Elizabeth b 1947 d 1990); *Career* Capt RAMC India 1944-46; conslt i/c Dept of Radiotherapy and Oncology N Staffs Royal Infirmary 1965-82, jr anatomy lectr Univ of Sheffield 1946-48, surgical registrar appts in Sheffield and London 1948-58, radiotherapy and oncology registrar appointments in Sheffield, Belfast and the Royal Marsden Hosp London 1958-65, memb Faculty Bd for Radiotherapy and Oncology 1976-82, hon conslt WMRHA, memb cncl Royal Coll of Radiologists 1979-82, vice pres RSM 1980-82 (pres Section of Oncology 1980-81, pres Section of Radiology 1981-82); conslt in med educn Cancer Relief Macmillan Educn Unit 1985-88, memb Patient Care Ctee Nat Soc for Cancer Relief 1978-84, chm Cncl of Mgmnt 1982-87; currently pres St Giles Hospice Whittington Lichfield; FRCS, FFR, FRCR; *Recreations* gardening, house improvements, walking; *Clubs* RSM; *Style—* Edwin R Monypenny, Esq; Wilkins Pleck, Whitmore, Newcastle-under-Lyme, Staffordshire ST5 5HN (☎ 0782 680351); Consulting Rooms, 11 King St, Newcastle-under-Lyme, Staffordshire ST5 1EH (☎ 0782 614174)

MOODIE, David Garrioch; s of late Peter Alexander Moodie; *b* 19 May 1926; *m* 1952, Mary Smith Hunter, *née* Williamson; 1 s, 1 da; *Career* CA; md Black & Edgington plc 1973-84, chm Andrew Mitchell Group plc 1984-; MICAS; *Recreations* golf, skiing, sailing; *Clubs* Caledonian; *Style—* David Moodie, Esq; Barnbeth, Bridge of Weir, Renfrewshire (☎ 0505 612201); Andrew Mitchell Group plc, 6 Gareloch Rd, Port Glasgow, Renfrewshire PA14 5XW (☎ 0475 44117)

MOODY, (William) Anthony; s of John Andrews Moody, of Malvern, and Olive Irene, *née* Elliott (d 1988); *b* 14 Aug 1926; *Educ* King's Sch Worcester; *m* 29 Jan 1951, Marjorie June, da of Thomas John Hayward (d 1980); 1 s (Michael b 1955), 1 da (Pamela (Mrs Curtis) b 1953); *Career* dir: Gascoigne Moody Associates Ltd 1984-90, GMA PR 1984-90, GMA Exhibition Servs 1984-90; MIPR; *Recreations* walking, gardening, caravanning; *Clubs* Birmingham Press; *Style—* Anthony Moody, Esq; Yew Tree Cottage, 12 High Park, Stafford, Staffs ST16 1BL (☎ 0785 42004)

MOODY, Rev Aubrey Rowland; s of Capt Rowland Harry Mainwaring (ka 1914), and Sybil Marie Conway Bishop (d 1944); *b* 31 July 1911; *Educ* Eton, RMC Sandhurst; *Career* Coldstream Gds 1931-33, and 1941-46, N Africa and 3 Commando Sicily and Italy, hon attaché HM Embassy Athens 1938-40, personal SO to HM King George of Greece 1942-43; social work in Stepney 1946-47, co cncllr Essex 1949-52, first chm Bd of Visitors Hill Hall Prison Epping 1952; ordained 1955, asst curate Wanstead Parish Church 1955-57, vicar of Feering 1957; *Style—* Rev Aubrey Moody; Feering Vicarage, Colchester, Essex CO5 9NL (☎ 0376 70226)

MOODY, (David) Barry Drury; s of Thomas Drury Moody (d 1988), of Melton Mowbray, and Edna Mary, *née* Jackson; *b* 23 April 1949; *Educ* Uppingham, Univ of Nottingham (LLB); *Career* admitted slr 1973; ptnr Lovell White Durrant formerly Lovell White & King 1978-; Freeman City of London Slrs Co 1974; memb Law Soc 1973; *Recreations* golf, travel, music; *Style—* Barry Moody, Esq; Lovell White Durrant, 65 Holborn Viaduct, London EC1A 2DY (☎ 071 236 0066, fax 071 248 4212, telex 887122 LWD G)

MOODY, Prof (Anthony) David; s of Edward Tabrum Moody, of Lower Hutt, New Zealand, and Nora, *née* Gordon; *b* 21 Jan 1932; *Educ* St Patrick's Coll Wellington NZ, Canterbury Coll Univ of NZ (MA), Univ of Oxford (BA, MA); *Career* Shirtcliffe fell Univ of NZ 1953-55, asst info offr UNHCR Geneva 1957-58, sr lectr Univ of Melbourne 1958-64, Nuffield Fndn travelling fell 1965, memb Dept of English and Related Lit Univ of York 1966-; visiting prof: Br Acad Leverhulme 1988, Univ of Toledo Ohio 1988; *Books* Virginia Woolf (1963), Shakespeare: "The Merchant of Venice" (1964), Thomas Stearns Eliot: Poet (1979), At the Antipodes: Homage to Paul Valèry (1982), News Odes: The El Salvador Sequence (1984); *Recreations* bedlam press, music, hill walking, tennis, travel; *Style—* Prof David Moody; Church Green House, Old Church Lane, Pateley Bridge, W Yorks HG3 5LZ (☎ 0423 711508); Dept of English & Related Literature, Univ of York, York YO1 5DD (☎ 0904 430000)

MOODY, Col (Anthony) Michael Thomas; s of Maj Thomas Allan Moody (d 1959), of Omagh, Co Tyrone, NI, and Margaret Frances, *née* Bell; *b* 30 April 1941; *Educ* Sherborne; *m* 1, 29 Oct 1964, Tatiana Nadezhda (Tanya) (d 1 Jan 1971), da of Charles Edward Pulley, of Cheltenham, Glos; 2 s (Patrick b 17 March 1966, David b 22 Sept 1967); m 2, 27 Nov 1971, Diana Elizabeth, *née* Hazlerigg; 2 da (Victoria b 11 April 1973, Alexandria b 6 July 1976); *Career* cmmd Royal Inniskilling Fus 1961, transfd to Royal Irish Rangers 1968, chief instr RMC Duntroon Aust 1978-81; Royal Irish Rangers: Lt-Col 1981, CO 1 Bn 1981-83; desk offr Central Staffs MOD 1983-86, Dep Cmdt Zimbabwe Staff Coll 1986-89, promoted Col 1987, SM DS Army Jt Serv Def Coll; *Recreations* wildlife conservation, reading, tennis, cricket; *Style—* Col Michael Moody; West Hayes, South St, South Petherton, Somerset TA13 5AD (☎ 0460 40204)

MOODY, Philip Edward; s of Frederick Osborne Moody, and Hilda Laura, *née* Frost; *b* 28 July 1954; *Educ* Bentley GS Calne Wilts; *Career* CA; articled clerk Monahan & Co Chippenham 1972-82, fndr ptnr Solomon Hare Chippenham 1983-88, lead corporate fin ptnr and chief exec Solomon Hare Bristol 1989-; ACA 1980, ATII 1982; *Recreations* walking, photography, theatre, snooker, cricket; *Style—* Philip Moody, Esq; Clevelands, Landsown Hill, Bath, Avon BA1 5TD (☎ 0225 480046); Solomon Hare, Oakfield Ho, Oakfield Grove, Clifton, Bristol BS8 2BN (☎ 0272 238 555/0272 237 000, fax 0272 238 666, car 0836 360084)

MOODY, Ronald; s of Bernard Moody (d 1964), of Hornsey, London N8, and Kate, *née* Ogus (d 1980); *b* 8 Jan 1924; *Educ* LSE (BSc); *m* 14 Dec 1987, Therese, da of Michael John Blackburn, of Penzance, Cornwall; 2 s (Daniel Maximilian, Matthew Alexander), 1 da (Catherine Laura); *Career* Sgt Educn Section RAF 1943-48; actor; stage: For Amusement Only 1955, Candide 1959, Oliver! 1960, Clandestine Marriage, Peter Pan, Richard III, HMS Pinafore, Sherlock Holmes; film: Oliver! 1967, Twelve Chairs 1970, Flight of the Doves, Dogpound Shuffle, Ghost in Monte Carlo; TV: various appearances UK and USA; musicals written: Joey Joey 1966, Saturnalia 1971, Move Along Sideways 1976, The Showman 1977, Nine Lives 1991; awards: Oscar nominee 1969, Golden Globe 1969, Variety Club Film 1969, Moscow Golden Bear 1970, Antoinette Perry nominee 1984, Theatre World 1984; memb: Variety Club of GB, American Acad of Motion Picture Arts and Scis; pres Clowns Int; Freeman City of London 1987; memb: Br Equity (also American and Canadian), Screen Actors Guild; *Books* My LSE (1979), The Devil You Don't (1980), Very Very Slightly Imperfect (1983), Off the Cuff (1987); *Recreations* tennis, oil painting, cartoons, driving; *Style—* Ronald Moody, Esq; c/o Eric Glass Ltd, 28 Berkeley Square, London W1X 6HD (☎ 071 629 7162)

MOODY, Susan Elizabeth; da of Frederick Chesney Horwood (d 1990), and Ursula Margaret (Kym), *née* Wheeler Robinson (d 1989); *Educ* Oxford HS for Girls, Open Univ (BA); *m* 1, 1961, Dr Walter F Bertsch (d 1984), s of Bernard J Bertsch, of San Diego, California; 2 s (Jonathon Andrew Richard b 1962, Timothy David b 1963); m 2, 1972, John Edward James Moody; 1 s (Benedick Adam John b 1973); *Career* author; Penny Black (1984), Penny Dreadful (1984), Penny Post (1985), Penny Royal (1986), Penny Wise (1988), Penny Pinching (1989), Penny Saving (1991), Playing with Fire (1990); memb: Soc of Authors, Crime Writers' Assoc (chm 1989-90), memb Exec Ctee of Int Assoc of Crime Writers', Detection Club 1988; *Style—* Susan Moody; June Hall Literary Agency, 504 The Chambers, Lotts Rd, Chelsea Harbour, London SW10 0XF (☎ 071 352 4233, fax 071 352 7356)

MOOLGAOKER, Arvind Sumant; s of Sumant Moolgaoker (d 1989), of Bombay, India, and Leela, *née* Welingkar; *b* 15 March 1934; *Educ* St Josephs Northpoint Darjeeling India, Cathedral and John Connon Boys HS Bombay, Grant Med Coll Bombay (MB BS, MD); *m* 1, 1964, Jill, *née* Canning (d 1973); 1 s (Anil b 14 Dec 1970), 2 da (Nikki b 9 Sept 1966, Nina b 7 March 1968); m 2, 19 Jan 1975, Jean, da of

David Fielding, of Rossendale Lancs; *Career* lectr and sr registrar Nuffield Dept of Obstetrics and Gynaecology 1966-71, conslt obstetrician and gynaecologist Basingstoke and Dist Hosps 1971-; invented Moolgaokers Obstetric Forceps 1961, former memb Incontinence Branch Disabled Living Fndn, former examiner for PLAB; FRSM 1964, FRCOG 1976; *Recreations* fishing, flydressing, shooting, photography; *Style—* Arvind Moolgaoker, Esq; Kymore, 128 Cliddesden Rd, Basingstoke, Hants RG21 3HH (☎ 0256 55677)

MOOLLAN, Sir Cassam Ismael; QC (Mauritius 1969); s of Ismael Mahomed Moollan (d 1972), and Fatimah, *née* Nazroo (d 1962); *b* 26 Feb 1927; *Educ* Royal Coll Port Louis, LSE, Univ of London (LLB); *m* 1954, Rassool Bibie Adam, da of Adam Sulliman Moollan (d 1964); 1 s (Oomar), 2 da (Aisha, Naseem); *Career* called to the Bar Lincoln's Inn; private practice Mauritius 1951-55, dist magistrate 1955-58, crown counsel 1958-64, sr crown counsel 1964-66, solicitor-gen 1966-70, puisne judge Supreme Court Mauritius 1970-78, sr puisne judge 1978, chief justice Mauritius 1982-88; actg govr-gen on several occasions between 1984-88; legal conslt and dir S E Asia Bank Ltd Mauritius; Chevalier de la Legion d'Honneur France 1986; kt 1982; *Recreations* tennis, bridge, Indian classical and semi-classical music; *Clubs* Port Louis Gymkhana; *Style—* Sir Cassam Moollan, QC; 22 Hitchcock Ave, Quatre Bornes, Mauritius (☎ 4546949); 43 Sir William Newton St, Port Louis, Mauritius (☎ 2120794; 2083881)

MOON; *see*: Graham Moon

MOON, Gertrude, Lady; Mary Gertrude; da of late Herbert E Waggoner, of Bowen, Illinois, USA; *m* 1954, as his 2 w, Sir Richard Moon, 3 Bt (d 1961); *Style—* Gertrude, Lady Moon

MOON, Sir Peter James Scott; KCVO (1979), CMG (1979); *b* 1 April 1928; *m* 1955, Lucile Worms; 3 da; *Career* high commissioner Singapore 1982-84, Tanzania 1978-82, ambass Madagascar 1978- (non-resident), counsellor Cairo 1975-78, also seconded to NATO Brussels, served in New York, Colombo, Cape Town Pretoria (with CRO), formerly with Home Office; *Style—* HE Sir Peter Moon, KCVO, CMG; British Embassy, PO Box Safat 2, Kuwait; c/o Foreign and Commonwealth Office, London SW1

MOON, Richard Henry Quentin Barker; s of Henry John Moon, of 14 Gorway Rd, Walsall, West Midlands, and Audrey Colleen, *née* Barker; *b* 18 May 1962; *Educ* Queen Mary GS Walsall, UWIST (LLB), Magdalene Coll Cambridge (MPhil, Rugby blue); *Career* Rugby Union scrum-half Rosslyn Park RFC and England B (1 cap); clubs: Walsall RFC, Abertillery RFC (capt v Japan 1983), capt UWIST RFC, Cambridge Univ RFC, Nottingham RFC, Harlequins RFC (winner John Player Cup 1988), capt Rosslyn Park RFC, Barbarians RFC; represented: Staffordshire, Midland Division, Welsh Univs, Combined Eng Students, England U23; memb England devpt squad; admitted slr Freshfields; *Recreations* sport, leisure, music; *Style—* Richard Moon, Esq; Freshfields, Whitefriars, 65 Fleet St, London (☎ 071 936 4000); Rosslyn Park RFC, Roehampton, London SW15

MOON, Sir Roger; 6 Bt (UK 1887), of Copsewood Grange, Warwickshire; s of Jasper Moon (d 1975, gs of 1 Bt); suc bro, Sir Edward Moon, 5 Bt, 1988; *b* 17 Nov 1914; *Educ* Sedbergh; *m* 16 Dec 1950, Meg, da of late Col Arthur Mainwaring Maxwell, DSO, MC; 3 da (Sarah Corinna b 1951, Gillian Adèle (Mrs Johnston) b 1954, Patricia Isolda (Mrs Hogg) b 1955); *Heir* bro, Humphrey Moon b 1920; *Recreations* golf, shooting; *Style—* Sir Roger Moon, Bt; Mill House, Ruyton-xi-Towns, Shropshire (☎ 0939 260354)

MOONEY, Bel; s of Edward Mooney, and Gladys, *née* Norbury; *b* 8 Jan 1946; *Educ* Aigburth Vale Girls' HS Liverpool, Trowbridge Girls' HS Wiltshire, UCL (BA); *m* 1968, Jonathan Dimbleby, s of late Richard Dimbleby; 1 s (Daniel Richard b 1974), 1 da (Katherine Rose b 1980); *Career* asst to the ed rising to contributing ed Nova magazine 1971-75, freelance contrib (Guardian, Times, Observer, New Statesman, Sunday Times, Daily Express); columnist: Cosmopolitian 1972-80; Daily Mirror 1972-80, Sunday Times 1980-86, The Listener 1980-86; tv presenter 1980-86, (Mothers By Daughters (C4), Fathers by Sons (C4), Dora Russell (BBC2), Ellen Wilkinson (BBC2)), presenter Radio 4 1985-91 (Women: Equal Sex?, American Authors, Turning Points, A Perspective For Living); non fiction books: The Year of the Child (1979), Differences of Opinion (1984), Bel Mooney's Somerset (1989); novels: The Windsurf Boy (1983), The Anderson Question (1985), The Fourth of July (1988); children's books; Liza's Yellow boat (also illustrated by the author, 1980), I Don't Want To! (1985), The Stove Haunting (1986), I Can't Find It! (1988), It's Not Fair (1989), A Flower Jet (1990), But You Promised! (1990), Why Not? (1990), I Know! (1991), satire Father Kissmass and Mother Claws (with Gerald Scarfe, 1985), anthology From This Day Forward (1989); *Recreations* literature, art, music, friends; *Clubs* The Groucho; *Style—* Miss Bel Mooney; c/o David Higham Associates, 5 Lower John Street, London W1 (☎ 071 437 7888)

MOONEY, Denis; s of Denis Mooney (d 1966), of Greenock, and Catherine McIlroy; *b* 27 Aug 1951; *Educ* St Columbas Sch Greenock, Moray House Edinburgh (DYCS); *m* Sheila, da of Jack Casey (d 1967), of Manchester; 1 s (Jack b 1987), 1 da (Fiona b 1984); *Career* local govt official Lothian Regnl Cncl 1975-80, Sefton Borough Cncl 1980-83, res Granada TV 1983-86, sr prodr Scottish TV 1986-; memb: ACTT, Amnesty Int; *Recreations* golf, watching football; *Clubs* Heraghtys; *Style—* Denis Mooney, Esq; 12a Leslie Rd, Glasgow G41 4PY (☎ 041 423 7862); Scottish Television, Glasgow (☎ 041 332 9999, fax 041 332 6982)

MOONMAN, Prof Eric; s of Bonach Moonman (d 1953), and Leah, *née* Bernstein (d 1959); *b* 29 April 1929; *Educ* Christ Church Southport, Univ of Manchester (MSc), Univ of Liverpool (Dip Social Sci); *m* 9 Sept 1962, Jane, da of Edward Dillon, of Lancs; 2 s (Daniel b 10 July 1966, Joshua b 27 Jan 1972), 1 da (Natasha b 19 April 1968); *Career* Nat Serv Kings Liverpool Regt 1951-53; human rels advsr Br Inst Mgmnt 1956-62, leader of Stepney Cncl 1958-62, memb Tower Hamlets Cncl 1963-67; MP: Basildon 1966-70, Billericay 1974-79; govr Br Film Inst 1978-83, dir Gp Rels Educn Tst 1979-, chm Islington Health Authy 1980-90, memb Bloomsbury and Islington DHA 1990-; HM treas Toynbee Hall 1979-, sr vice pres Bd of Deps of Br Jews, visiting prof of health management City Univ 1990-; FBIM 1959; *Books* The Manager and the Organisation (1961), Communications in an Expanding Organisation (1970), Relevant Partnership (1971), Alternative Environment (1984), Violent society (1987); *Recreations* cinema, theatre, football (watching), tennis (playing); *Style—* Prof Eric Moonman; Natural History Museum, Cromwell Rd, London SW7 (☎ 071 938 8962)

MOOR, Philip Drury; s of Rev David Moor, and Evangeline, *née* White; *b* 15 July 1959; *Educ* Canford, Pembroke Coll Oxford; *m* 18 July 1987, Gillian Elizabeth, *née* Stark; *Career* called to the Bar Inner Temple 1982; memb: Gen Cncl of the Bar 1987-89, Cncl of Legal Educn 1988-, Phillips Ctee on Financing Pupillage 1989; *Books* contrib (with N Mostyn) to Family Law, Family Law Bar Assoc Ctee (1987); *Recreations* cricket, association football; *Style—* Philip Moor, Esq; 1 Mitre Court Buildings, Temple, London EC4Y 7BS (☎ 071 353 0434, fax 071 353 3988)

MOORCOCK, Michael John; s of Arthur Edward Moorcock, of Worthing, W Sussex, and June, *née* Taylor; *b* 18 Dec 1939; *Educ* Michael Hall Sussex, Pitman's Coll Croydon Surrey; *m* 1, 25 Oct 1962 (m dis 1978), Hilary Denham Bailey; 1 s (Max Edward b 24 Feb 1971), 1 da (Sophie Elizabeth b 3 Sept 1963, Katherine Helen b 5 Sept 1964); m 2, 7 May 1978 (m dis 1984), Jill Riches; m 3, 25 Sept 1984, Linda Mullens Steele; *Career* author 1956-; ed: Tarzan Adventures 1957-, Fleetway Publications 1959-, New Worlds 1964-; over 60 novels incl: the Elric Series (14 novels, 1961-85), the Michael Kane series (3 novels, under name Edward P Bradbury, 1963-65), Jerry Cornelius series (9 novels, 1969-1984), Behold The Man (1970), Breakfast in the Ruins (1972), The History of The Runestaff series (4 novels, 1967-69), Books of Corum series (6 novels, 1971-74), The Eternal Champion series (4 novels, 1970-87), Oswald Bastable series (3 novels, 1971-82), The Dancers At The End of Time series (5 novels, 1972-78), Chronicles of Castle Brass series (3 novels, 1973-75), Von Bele Family series (1981-87), Buzantium Endures (1981), The Laughter of Carthage (1984) Casablanca and Other Stories (1989), Mother London (1988), Distant Suns (1989), The Fortress of the Pearl (1989); non-fiction: Epic Pooh (1978), The Retreat from Liberty: the Erosion of Democracy in Today's Britains (1983), Exploring Fantasy Worlds (contrib, 1985), Letters From Hollywood (1986), Wizardry and Wild Romance: A Study of Heroic Fantasy (1987); ed of numerous anthologies, collections and short stories; awards incl: August Declecto award (four times, 1971-75), Nebula award 1968, World Fantasy award 1979, Guardian Fiction prize 1977; memb: Author's Guild, Soc of Authors; *Recreations* camel racing, mountaineering; *Style—* Michael Moorcock, Esq; c/o Anthony Sheil Associates, 43 Doughty St, London WC1N 2LF

MOORE, Alan Edward; CBE (1980); s of Charles Edward Moore (d 1985), of Hemel Hempstead, Herts, and Ethel, *née* Middleton; *b* 5 June 1936; *Educ* Berkhamstead Sch; *m* 2 Sept 1961, Margaret Patricia, *née* Beckley; 1 s (Andrew b 9 May 1968), 1 da (Kathryn Moore b 9 May 1963); *Career* RAF; with Glyn Mills & Co 1953, dep dir Williams & Glyn Bank 1971-, dir gen Bahrain Monetary Agency Bahrain 1974-79, treas Lloyds Bank Int 1981- (dir M East and Africa Div 1980-), dir of treasy Lloyds Bank plc 1985- (dir of corp banking and treasy); AIB 1958, ACIS 1963, FACT 1985; *Recreations* photography, industrial architecture, model railways, steam trains; *Style—* Alan Moore, Esq, CBE; Lloyds Bank Plc, PO Box 545, Faryners House, 25 Monument St, London EC3R 8BQ (☎ 071 283 1000, fax 071 418 3044)

MOORE, Alexander (Alex); s of Alexander Moore, of 14 Crofthead Rd, Stoneyburn, W Lothian, and Mary, *née* Meek; *b* 19 Aug 1963; *Educ* St Kentigern's Acad Blackburn W Lothian, Forestry Indust Centre Inverness; *m* (m dis); 2 s (Gareth b 12 April 1984, Christopher b 4 May 1985); *Career* Rugby Union winger Edinburgh Academical RFC and Scotland (3 caps); clubs: Livingston RFC 1981-84, Gala RFC 1984-87, Edinburgh Academical RFC 1987-; rep: Scotland B debut v Italy (Benevito) 1986; Scotland: debut v All Blacks 1990, Five Nations debut v France (Parc des Princes) 1991; forester Livingston Developement Corporation 1980-86, sales rep Mitchell Timber Edinburgh 1986-; *Recreations* golf, football, music; *Style—* Alex Moore, Esq; Scottish Rugby Union, Murrayfield, Edinburgh

MOORE, Anthony (Tony); s of Percy George Moore, of Leicester and Doris Irene, *née* Mackey; *b* 29 June 1944; *Educ* Mitcham Co GS, St Edmund Hall Oxford (MA); *m* 22 July 1967, Kathryn Muriel (Kate), da of Edward Henry Garfoot, of Leicester; *Career* media mangr Frank Gayton Advertising Ltd 1966-74, dir Meares Langley Moore Ltd 1974-; Bishop Street Methodist Church; MIPA 1971; *Recreations* walking, reading, theatre, squash; *Style—* Tony Moore, Esq; 46 Holmfield Rd, Leicester LE2 ISA (☎ 0533 706 707); Bosworth House, Southgates, Leicester LE1 5RR (☎ 0533 538 611, fax 0533 515 544)

MOORE, Hon Mrs (Astraea Joan Denholm); da of Baron Barnetson (d 1981), and Joan Fairley, *née* Davidson; *b* 24 Sept 1941; *Educ* St Serf's Sch Edinburgh; *m* 1963, John Robert Dawson Moore, s of John Dawson Moore (d 1985); 1 s (Andrew b 1964), 2 da (Jacqueline b 1966, Charlotte b 1972); *Recreations* tennis, swimming, yoga; *Style—* The Hon Mrs Moore; Nether Soonhope House, Peebles, Scotland EH45 8BJ (☎ 0721 20756)

MOORE, Brian; s of James Bernard Moore, and Eileen, *née* McFadden; *b* 25 Aug 1921; *m* Oct 1967, Jean Denney; *Career* novelist; recipient Que Lit Prize 1958, Guggenheim fell 1959, US Nat Arts and Letters award 1961, Canadian Cncl sr fell 1962 and 1976, Fiction Award Gov Gen Canada 1961 and 1975, recipient W H Smith award 1975, James Tait Black Meml award 1975, Scottish Arts Cncl Int fell 1983, Heinemann award Royal Soc Lit 1986, Sunday Express Book of the Year Award 1988; Hon DLitt The Queens University of Belfast 1987; FRCS, FRSL 1968; *Books* The Lonley Passion of Judith Hearne (1955), The Feast of Lupercal (1957), The Luck of Ginger Coffey (1960), An Answer from Limbo (1962), The Emperor of Ice-Cream (1965), I Am Mary Dunne (1968), Fergus (1970), The Revolution Script (1971), Catholics (1972), The Great Victorian Collection (1975), The Doctor's Wife (1976), The Mangan Inheritance (1979), The Temptation of Eileen Hughes (1981), Cold Heaven (1983), Black Robe (1985), The Color of Blood (1987), Lies of Silence (1990); *Style—* Brian Moore, Esq; 33958 Pacific Coast Hwy, Malibu, Ca 90265; c/o Curtis Brown Ltd, 10 Astor Place, New York 10003 (☎ 2124735400)

MOORE, Brian Baden; s of Baden Kimberley Moore (d 1969), of Benenden, Kent, and Elsie Norah, *née* Sharpe (d 1987); *b* 28 Feb 1932; *Educ* Cranbrook Sch Kent; *m* 19 March 1955, Eileen Betty, da of William Cole (d 1973), of Bromley, Kent; 2 s (Christopher b 1958, Simon b 1961); *Career* Nat Serv PO RAF 1950-52; sports reporter and sub ed: World Sports 1955, Exchange Telegraph 1957, The Times 1958; football commentator and presenter BBC Radio 1960-67, football commentator and sports presenter ITV 1967-, presenter of documentary series Brian Moore Meets...; dir Gillingham FC 1978-85; *Style—* Brian Moore, Esq; London Weekend Television, London SE1 (☎ 071 261 3264)

MOORE, Charles Hilary; s of Richard Gillachrist Moore, of Brussels, and Ann Hilary, *née* Miles; *b* 13 Oct 1956; *Educ* Eton, Trinity Coll Cambridge (BA); *m* 1981, Caroline Mary, da of Ralph Lambert Baxter, of Brasted Chart, Kent; 1 s (b 1 April 1990), 1 da ((twin)); *Career* editorial staff Daily Telegraph 1979, ldr writer Daily Telegraph 1981-83, asst ed and political columnist The Spectator 1983-84, ed The Spectator 1984-90, weekly columnist The Daily Express 1987-90, dep ed The Daily Telegraph 1990; *Clubs* Beefsteak; *Style—* Charles Moore, Esq; 16 Thornhill Square, London N1

MOORE, Christopher M; o s of Sir Harry Moore, CBE, *qv*; *b* 1 Dec 1944; *Educ* Winchester, Pembroke Coll Cambridge (MA); *m* 2 Sept 1972, Charlotte C, da of J Glessing, of Montague, Hankham, E Sussex; 3 s (Tercel R, Wiluf M, Frederick C); *Career* banker; merchant dir Jardine Fleming and Co Ltd 1973-76; dir: Robert Fleming and Co Ltd 1977-, Robert Fleming Hldgs 1988-; FCA; *Recreations* hunting, flying, tennis, music, books; *Clubs* White's, Pratt's, Leander; *Style—* Christopher Moore, Esq; Thornborough Grounds, Bourton, Buckingham (☎ 0280 812170); 25 Copthall Avenue, London EC2R 7OR (☎ 071 638 5858, fax 071 638 9110, telex 297451)

MOORE, David John; s of Rev Stanley Moore (d 1977), rector of St Botolphs, Bishopsgate, London, and Gladys Alice Jane, *née* Cory; *b* 8 June 1943; *Educ* Ipswich Sch Suffolk; *Career* articled clerk rising to audit sr Barton Mayhew & Co London 1962-69, audit sr and supervisor Barton Meyhew/Peat Marwick Mitchell Barcelona Spain 1969-72; Grant Thornton (formerly Thornton Baker): mangr London Office 1972-74, gp audit mangr 1974-77, ptnr 1977-, staff ptnr 1981-86, managing ptnr E Anglia 1986-; memb Cncl and chm Iberian Ctee London C of C 1985-88, memb E Region Cncl and chm Suffolk County Ctee CBI 1988-, govr Ipswich Sch 1989-; FCA

(ACA 1968); *Recreations* cricket, travel; *Clubs* MCC, Lord Taverners; *Style—* David Moore, Esq; Grant Thornton, Crown House, Crown St, Ipswich, Suffolk IP1 3HS (☎ 0473 221491, fax 0473 230304)

MOORE, Prof David Moresby; s of Moresby Goerge Moore (d 1979), of 2 Prospect Place, Barnard Castle, Co Durham, and Elizabeth, *née* Grange; *b* 26 July 1933; *Educ* Barnard Castle Sch, Univ Coll Durham (BSc, PhD, DSc); *m* 26 July 1957, Ida ELizabeth, da of Herbert Shaw (d 1956), of 18 Trafalgar St, Carlisle, Cumberland; 2 s (Wayne Peter b July 1961, Lloyd Randal b Sept 1969); *Career* res offr CSIRO Canberra Aust 1957-59, res botanist Univ of California at Los Angeles 1959-61, lectr in botany Univ of Leicester 1961-68, prof of botany Univ of Reading 1976- (reader in plant taxonomy 1968-76); pres Systematics Assoc 1979-82, sec gen Flora Europaea 1985-89, ed Flora de Chile 1987-; memb: Soc Botany Argentina, Botanical Soc of Br; chm Ed Ctee Lichen Flora of GB and I; FLS; Claudio Gay medal Univ Concepción Chile 1987; *Books* Flora Europea (1963-80), Vascular Flora of Falkland Islands (1968), Plant Cytogenetics (1977), Green Planet (1982), Flora of Tierra del Fuego (1983), Flora Europea Checklist and Chromosome Index (1983), Current Concepts in Plant Taxonomy (1984), La Transecta Botanica de Patagonia Austral (1984), Flora of the British Isles (3 edn 1987, revised 1990); *Recreations* walking, reading; *Style—* Prof David Moore; 26 Eric Avenue, Emmer Green, Reading, Berks RG4 8QX (☎ 0734 472132); Dept of Botany, Plant Science Laboratories, University of Reading, Whiteknights, PO Box 221, Readiñg RG6 2AS (☎ 0734 318165, fax 0734 750630, telex 847813 RULIB G)

MOORE, Debbie; 1 da (Lara b 1973); *Career* former fashion model; fndr chm md and fashion designer Pineapple Dance Studios (which joined unlisted securities market 5 Nov 1982) 1979-, 3 Pineapple centres opened in London, licensing of Pineapple name on range of footwear and hosiery; Pineapple Fashion Stores at all centres plus 17 nationwide concessions which sell fashion and dance collections; Business Woman of Year 1984; *Books* Pineapple Dance Book (1983, paperback 1985), When A Woman Means Business (1989); *Style—* Ms Debbie Moore; Pineapple Group Ltd, 60 Paddington St, London W1M 3RR (☎ 071 224 5540)

MOORE, Denis Aubrey; *b* 9 Oct 1924; *Educ* Salesian Coll Farnborough Hants; *m* 14 June 1948, Ellen Craswell Smith; 1 s (Michael John b 31 July 1949), 3 da (Christine Anne b 8 Feb 1952, Susan Margaret b 25 June 1957, Frances Alexandra b 23 July 1967); *Career* Fleet Air Arm 1942-46; fndr Formica Manufacturing Co 1956-58, md Formica Ltd, md Formica Int LTd 1963 (chm 1970); De La Rue Co: joined 1946, dir 1965, memb exec ctee 1970, dir industl ops 1972, dep chief exec 1977-87; FInstD; *Recreations* golf; *Clubs* East India, MCC, St Georges Hill Weybridge; *Style—* Denis Moore, Esq; 10 Weybridge Park, Weybridge, Surrey KT13 8SQ (☎ 0932 842 585); The De La Rue Co plc, 3/5 Burlington Gdns, London W1A 1DL (☎ 071 734 8020)

MOORE, Prof Derek William; s of William McPherson Moore (d 1979), and Elsie Marjorie, *née* Patterson (d 1969); *b* 19 April 1931; *Educ* S Shields Boy's HS, Univ of Cambridge (MA, PhD); *Career* lectr in math Univ of Bristol 1960, sr fell Nat Acad of Sciences 1964, of applied mathematics Imperial Coll 1973 (sr lectr 1967, reader in theoretical fluid mechanics 1968), Sherman Fairchild Distinguished Scholar Cal Inst Tech 1986-87; for hon memb American Acad of Arts and Sciences 1985; FRS 1990; *Recreations* jazz saxophone; *Style—* Prof Derek Moore; Dept of Maths, Imperial College, London (☎ 071 589 5111 ext 5720)

MOORE, Dudley Stuart John; s of John Moore (d 1971), of Dagenham, Essex, and Ada Frances, *née* Hughes (d 1981); *b* 19 April 1935; *Educ* Co HS Dagenham, Guildhall Sch of Music, Magdalen Coll Oxford (BA, BMus); *m* 1, 1966, Suzy Kendall; m 2, 1975 (m dis), Tuesday Weld; 1 s (Patrick b 1976); m 3, 1988, Brogan Lane; *Career* actor and musician; entered TV 1959; appearances incl: Beyond the Fringe, Sunday Night at the London Palladium, Love Story, Royal Command Performance, Wayne and Shuster, Eamonn Andrews Show, Music International, Late Night Line Up, Not Only But Also (2 series), Billy Cotton Band Show, Juke Box Jury, Now, Ready Steady Go, The Whole Scene Going, Prince of Wales Show, Top of the Pops, Bruce Forsyth Show, Dusty Springfield Show, Cilla Black; films incl: The Wrong Box, 30 is a Dangerous Age, Alice in Wonderland, Those Daring Young Men and Their Jaunty Jalopies, Bedazzled, The Bed Sitting Room, Hound of the Baskervilles, Foul Play, 10, Wholly Moses, Arthur (Oscar nomination 1983, Golden Globe Award 1983), Six Weeks, Romantic Comedy, Lovesick, Unfaithfully Yours, Best Defense, Micki and Maude (Golden Globe Award 1985), Santa Claus - the Movie, Like Father Like Son, Arthur II - On the Rocks, Crazy People; winner of 2 Tony and 1 Grammy awards; albums: Beyond The Fringe and All That Jazz, The Other Side of Dudley Moore, Derek and Clive-Live, Derek and Clive-Ad Derek Nauseam, and Clive-Come Again, 30 Is a Dangerous Age Cynthia, Bedazzled, Dudley Moore Trio-Down Under, Dudley Moore and Cleo Laine - Smilin' Through, The Music of Dudley Moore - Double Album; *Clubs* St James's, Annabel's, Harry's Bar, Tramp; *Style—* Dudley Moore Esq; 73 Market St, Venice, California 90291 USA (☎ 213 396 5937)

MOORE, Sir Edward Stanton; 2 Bt (UK 1923), of Colchester, Essex, OBE (1970); s of Maj Edward Cecil Horatio Moore (ka 1917), and Kathleen Mary, *née* Oliver; gs of 1 Bt (d 1923); *b* 28 Dec 1910; *Educ* Mill Hill, Cambridge; *m* 6 Nov 1946, Margaret, er da of late T J Scott-Cotterell; *Career* served in RAF 1940-46, Wing Cdr; vice pres British Chamber of Commerce Belgium and Luxembourg 1963-64, pres British C of C Spain 1969-72, dir European British Cs of C 1970-72; md BEA Spain and Western Mediterranean, 1965-72; dir Gibraltar Airways; *Recreations* walking, gardening, ornithology; *Clubs* Chichester Yacht; *Style—* Sir Edward Moore, Bt, OBE; Church House, Sidlesham, W Sussex PO20 7RE (☎ 024 356 369)

MOORE, Fiona Patricia; da of Maj Samuel James Moore, and Margaret Patricia Moore, *née* Boyd; *b* 18 May 1950; *Educ* Croydon HS for Girls (GPDST), UCL (BSc), UCH Med Sch (MB BS); *m* 12 April 1980, Richard Philip Ward; 2 s (Jonathan b 1982, Patrick b 1988), 2 da (Victoria b 1975, Jennifer b 1985); *Career* registrar in gen surgery St James and St George's Hosps 1980-81, Bayer res fell UCH 1981-83 (registrar in surgery 1978-80), sr registrar in accident and emergency med, Ealing Central Middx and Hammersmith Hosps 1983-85, conslt in accident and emergency med UCH and Middx Hosp 1985-; memb RSM, FRCS, FRCSE; *Recreations* reading, music, walking; *Style—* Miss Fiona Moore; Accident and Emergency Dept, University College Hospital, Gower St, London WC1E 6AU (☎ 071 387 9300 ext 8441, fax 071 380 9728)

MOORE, Gordon Charles; s of Dr John Edward Moore (d 1959), of Westerlea, Keswick, Cumbria, and Jessie Hamilton Moore, *née* Pears (d 1973); *b* 23 July 1928; *Educ* Uppingham, St Catharine's Coll Cambridge (MA, LLM); *m* 1956, Ursula, da of John Rawle (d 1971), of 23 Paganel Rd, Minehead, Somerset; 1 s (Andrew b 1964), 2 da (Davone b 1958, Lindsey b 1961); *Career* slr; town clerk Bradford Co Borough Cncl 1968-73, chief exec Bradford Met Dist Cncl 1973-86; Hon DLitt Bradford; *Recreations* music, railways, walking; *Style—* Gordon C Moore, Esq; 22 Fern Hill Rd, Shipley, W Yorks BD18 4SL (☎ 0274 585606)

MOORE, Rt Rev Harry Wylie; *see*: Cyprus and The Gulf, Bishop of

MOORE, Sir Henry Roderick (Harry); CBE (1971); er s of Roderick Edward Moore (d 1946); *b* 19 Aug 1915; *Educ* Malvern, Pembroke Coll Cambridge; *m* 1944, Beatrice Margaret, da of Maj J W Seigne (d 1955); 1 s, 1 da; *Career* WWII 1939-46, Lt-Col; served: N Africa, Italy, N Europe; chartered accountant 1939, dir Hill Samuel Gp 1949-79; chm: Associated Engineering 1955-75, Staveley Industries 1970-79, Molins plc 1978-85; chm: Bd of Govrs The London Hosp 1960-74, NE Thames RHA 1974-84; High Sheriff Bucks 1966; kt 1978; *Recreations* shooting, racing; *Clubs* White's, Pratt's, Leander, Rand (Johannesburg); *Style—* Sir Harry Moore, CBE; Huntingate Farm, Thornborough, nr Buckingham, Bucks MK18 2DE (☎ 0280 812241); 70 Chesterfield House, Chesterfield Gdns, London W1Y 5TD (☎ 01 491 0666)

MOORE, Prof (William) James; s of William James Reginald Moore (d 1965), and Alice, *née* Lewis (d 1972); *b* 16 Aug 1932; *Educ* King Edwards GS Aston Birmingham, Univ of Birmingham (BSc, BDS, PhD, MB ChB, DSc); *m* 4 Feb 1960, Mary Eileen, da of Edwin Mills (d 1983), of Black Notley, Essex; 1 s (Richard James b 29 Nov 1961), 1 da (Sarah Louise b 3 Oct 1964); *Career* Sqdn Ldr short serv cmmn RAF 1960; lectr in anatomy Univ of Birmingham 1966-68, prof of anatomy Univ of Leeds 1976-88 (sr lectr in anatomy 1970-76); memb: N Yorks Area Health Authy 1982-83, Anatomical Soc GB and Ireland 1966; fell Br Assoc of Clinical Anatomists 1980; *Books* Growth of the Facial Skeleton in the Hominoidea (with Prof C L B Lavelle, 1974), The Mammalian Skull (1981), Anatomy for Dental Students (1983); *Recreations* gardening; *Clubs* RAF; *Style—* Prof James Moore; The Old Post Office, Talaton, Devon EX5 2RL (☎ 0404 822 803)

MOORE, Jane; da of Prof John Moore, of Oxford, and Patricia, *née* Richardson; *b* 17 May 1962; *Educ* Worcester Girls GS, South Glamorgan Inst of Higher Educn Cardiff (Dip); *Career* journalist; trainee reporter Solihull W Midlands 1981-83, news reporter Birmingham Post and Mail 1983-86, freelance reporter The People 1986-, pop columnist The Sun 1986-87, freelance researcher Thames News 1987-88; Today: feature writer 1988, Royal corr 1989, dep news ed 1989, feature ed 1990; *Recreations* canoeing, rock climbing, photography; *Style—* Miss Jane Moore; Today Newspaper, 70 Vauxhall Bridge Rd, London SW1 (☎ 071 630 1300 ext 286, fax 071 630 6839)

MOORE, Hon Mrs (Janie St George); *née* Caulfeild; yr da of 11 Viscount Charlemont (d 1971), and Lydia Clara, *née* Kingston; *b* 9 April 1921; *m* 27 June 1942, David Dominic Moore, BSc, MIE (Aust); 2 da (Colleen, Louise); *Style—* The Hon Mrs Moore; 30 Maxwell St, Turramurra, Sydney, NSW, Australia

MOORE, Maj-Gen Sir (John) Jeremy; KCB (1982, CB 1982), OBE (Mil 1973), MC (1952) and Bar (1962); s of Lt-Col Charles Percival Moore, MC (d 1959), and (Alice Hylda) Mary, *née* Bibby; *b* 5 July 1928; *Educ* Cheltenham; *m* 1966, Veryan Julia Margaret Acworth; 1 s (Andrew b 1971), 2 da (Helen b 1967, Sarah b 1969); *Career* joined RM 1947, CO 42 Commando RM 1972-73, Cmdt RM Sch of Music 1973-75, Royal Coll Defence Studies 1976, Cdr 3 Commando Bde RM 1977-79, Maj-Gen Commando Forces RM 1979-82, Cdr Land Forces Falkland Islands during campaign of 1982, on staff CDS 1982, ret 1983; dir gen Food and Drink Fedn 1984-85, defence consIt 1985-; memb cncl Cheltenham Coll, govr Knighton House Sch; *Recreations* music, painting, sailing, hillwalking; *Style—* Maj-Gen Sir Jeremy Moore, KCB, OBE, MC; c/o Cox's and King's Branch, Lloyds Bank Ltd, 6 Pall Mall, London SW1

MOORE, Joan; da of Duncan Mackay (d 1936), and Martha, *née* Gentle (d 1967); *b* 29 Nov 1918; *Educ* Perse Sch for Girls Cambridge; *m* 7 Jan 1965, Charles James Robotham Moore, s of Charles Moore (d 1938); *Career* ptnr D Mackay Ironmongers & Engrs' Suppliers Cambridge, dir and co sec Donald Mackay Engrg Cambridge Ltd; memb Br Red Cross Soc Cambridge branch, branch ctee memb and organiser Ely Centre; *Recreations* music; *Style—* Mrs Joan Moore; 8 Barton Rd, Ely CB7 4DE (☎ 0353 663 258); 85 East Rd, Cambridge CB1 1BY (☎ 0353 63 132)

MOORE, Brig Jock Arthur Hume; CBE (1966, OBE 1945); s of Herbert Durie Moore, DSO, MBE (d 1964), of Lee-on-Solent, Hants, and Vera *née* Critchley, Salmonson (d 1970); *b* 6 Feb 1913; *Educ* Tonbridge; *m* 23 Aug 1938, Frances (Fan) Robinson, da of Col Thomas Melville Dill, OBE (d 1945), of Bermuda; 2 s (Ian Melville b 22 April 1940, Tom Durie b 21 Dec 1945), 1 da (Joanna Ruth b 7 May 1952); *Career* Lt RAOC 1936, Capt and Adj 5AA Workshop 1938, dep asst dir 6 armd Div (Lt-Col 1942-43), Staff Coll 1944, Dep Cdr REME 7 Base Workship Egypt 1945-46, asst dir REME HQ ME 1946-48, Asst QMG HQ Western Cmd 1954-56, asst dir REME WO 1956-58, Cd and dep dir 1 Br Corps BAOR 1958-60, dir REME Far East Land Forces 1960-62, Inspr Corps of REME 1963-66, dir REME BAOR 1966-68, ret 1968; appeals sec Charity House of St Barnabus 1974-89; FIMechE, CEng; *Recreations* skiing, sailing, travel, reading; *Style—* Brig Jock Moore, CBE; Moorings, 101 Coll Ride, Bagshot, Surrey GU19 5EF (☎ 0276 72472)

MOORE, Col John; OBE (1989), TD (1969), DL (1985); s of Joseph Leslie Moore (d 1982), of Newton Aycliffe, Co Durham, and Kathleen Irene Moore (d 1985); *b* 5 Aug 1932; *Educ* Stockton GS; *m* 23 June 1956, Sheila Margaret, da of Andrew Morton (d 1960), of Newton Aycliffe; 2 da (Margaret b 1958, Alison b 1961); *Career* Nat Serv cmmnd RE 1955; TA 1956-87: Adj Engr Regt 1967-69, OC 120 Field Sqdn 1969-73, CO III Engr Regt 1977-81, Dep Cdr 1982-87; chief asst co surveyor Linsey CC 1969-73, dep dir tech servs Humberside CC 1973-78 (dir 1978-88), dep chief exec Humberside CC 1988-89; chm Humberside Scout Cncl, pres Kilham Branch Royal Br Legion; FICE 1958; *Recreations* golf, caravanning; *Style—* Col John Moore, OBE, TD, DL; The Shieling, West End, Kilham, Driffield, Humberside YO25 0RR (☎ 026 282 254)

MOORE, Hon Sir John Cochrane; s of Ernest W Moore (d 1930); *b* 5 Nov 1915; *Educ* N Sydney Boy's HS, Sydney Univ (BA, LLB); *m* 1946, Julia Fay, o da of Brig Geoffrey Drake-Brockman, MC, of Perth, W Australia; 2 s, 2 da; *Career* AIF 1940, RO Hon Capt 1945; admitted Bar NSW 1940, Dept of External Affairs 1945, second sec Aust Mission to UN 1946-47, barr 1947-59, pres Aust Conciliation and Arbitration Cmmn 1973- (dep pres 1959-72, acting pres 1972-73); kt 1976; *Style—* Hon Sir John Moore; 10 The Grange, McAuley Place, Waitara, NSW 2077, Australia

MOORE, John Edward; s of Sqdn Ldr Joseph Enos Moore, of Marlow, Bucks, and Audrey Sheila, *née* Matthews; *b* 15 Nov 1947; *Educ* Royal GS High Wycombe, Univ of London (LLB); *m* 12 April 1971, Diana, da of John Horend Dixon, MBE, of Ealing; 3 s (James b 1974, Alexander b 1976, Thomas b 1988); *Career* civilian gliding instr RAF(UR)T 1967-77; admitted slr 1973, ptnr Macfarlanes 1979- (head property dept 1986-); lectr and author of articles on agric law, public and private sector ptnrships, commercial property and VAT; memb: Party Sub-Ctee of Agric Law Assoc; Agric Law Assoc; memb City of London Slrs Co; memb Law Soc; *Recreations* flying; *Style—* John Moore, Esq; Messrs Macfarlanes, 10 Norwich St, London EC4A 1BD (☎ 071 831 9222, fax 071 831 9607, telex 296381)

MOORE, Rt Hon John Edward Michael; PC (1986), MP (C) Croydon Centl Feb 1974-; s of Edward O Moore; *b* 26 Nov 1937; *Educ* Licensed Victuallers' Sch Slough, LSE (BSc); *m* 1962, Sheila Sarah Tillotson; 2 s, 1 da; *Career* Nat Serv Royal Sussex Regt Korea 1955-57; chm Cons Assoc 1958-59, pres Students' Union 1959-60, memb Ct of Govrs 1977-; worked in banking and stockbroking and took part in Democratic politics in Chicago 1961-65; chm Dean Witter Int Ltd 1975-79 (dir 1968-79), Lloyd's underwriter 1978-; vice chm Cons Pty 1975-79, parly under sec Energy 1979-83, (min of state) econ sec Treasy June-Oct 1983, fin sec Treasy, responsibilities incl taxation (appointed after promotion of Rt Hon Nicholas Ridley to sec state Tport) 1983-86; sec of state for: Tport 1986-87, Health and Social Servs, Social Security 1988-July 1989; *Recreations* sport; *Clubs* RAC; *Style—* The Rt Hon John Moore, MP; House of

Commons, London SW1

MOORE, Capt Prof John Evelyn; s of Maj William John Moore (d 1958), of Melbourne and Cambridge, and Evelyn Elizabeth, *née* Hooper (d 1935); *b* 1 Nov 1921; *Educ* Sherborne, RN Staff Coll; *m* 8 Jan 1945 (m dis 1967), Joan, da of Capt Frank Pardoe (d 1962), of S Africa; 1 s (Peter b 8 Jan 1958), 2 da (Lavinia b 19 Jan 1947, Fay b 4 Sept 1950); m 2, Barbara, *née* Kerry; *Career* RN: special entry cadet 1939; serv HM Ships (1939-45): Rodney, Impulsive, Nigeria, Challenger; HM Subs: Truant, Rover, Trident, Vigorous, Tradewind 1946-49; in cmd HM Sub Totem 1949-50, RN Staff Coll 1950-51, Staff 2 S/M Sqdn 1951-52, serv HM Ships Dainty and Diamond 1952-54; in cmd: HM Sub Alaric 1954-55, HM Subs Tactician and Telemachus 1955-57; Cdr NATO SO Plans NE Med 1957, Admty (Plans Div) 1960-63, Cdr Sub HMS Dolphin 1963-65, in cmd 7 Sub Sqdn Singapore 1965-67, Capt COS Naval Home Cmd 1967-69, Def Intelligence Staff i/c Soviet Naval Intelligence 1969-72, ret 1972; ed Jane's Fighting Ships 1972-87; prof int rels Univ of St Andrews; FRGS 1942; *Books* Seapower and Politics, The Soviet Navy Today, Submarine Development, Warships of Royal Navy, Warships of Soviet Navy, Submarine Warfare Today and Tomorrow (jtly); *Recreations* gardening, swimming, archaeology; *Clubs* Naval; *Style—* Capt John Moore, RN; Elmhurst, Rickney, Hailsham, E Sussex BN27 1SF (☎ 0323 765862/ 763294)

MOORE, Dr John Michael; JP (Worcester City, 1986); s of Roy Moore, CBE, and Muriel Edith, *née* Shill (d 1959); *b* 12 Dec 1935; *Educ* Rugby, Clare Coll Cambridge (MA); *m* 9 July 1960, Jill Mary, da of Alan Lawson Maycock (d 1967); 1 s (Nicholas b 1962); *Career* asst master: Winchester Coll 1960-64, Radley Coll 1964-83, Headmaster The King's Sch, Worcester 1983-; fell center for Hellenic Studies Washington DC 1970-71, hon fell Inst for Advanced Res in Humanities Univ of Birmingham 1986; *Books* The Manuscript Tradition of Polybius (1965), Res Gestae Divi Augusti (jt ed with P A Brunt, 1967, 2 edn 1973), Variorum (jt ed with J J Evans, 1969), Timecharts (1969), Aristotle and Xenophon on Democracy and Oligarchy (1975, 2 edn 1983), various articles; *Recreations* painting, travel, gardening; *Style—* Dr John Moore, JP; The King's School, Worcester WR1 2LH (☎ 0905 23016)

MOORE, Sir John Michael; KCVO (1983), CB (1974), DSC (1944); s of Algernon William Moore (d 1970), and Amy Elizabeth, *née* Jeffreys (d 1940); *b* 2 April 1921; *Educ* Whitgift Middle Sch Croydon, Selwyn Coll Cambridge; *m* 1, 1947 (m dis 1963), Kathleen, da of Capt C C Pawley (d 1982); 1 s, 1 da; m 2, 1963 (m dis 1985), Margaret, da of J Ward (d 1935); *Career* Lt RNVR 1940-46, with Miny of Transport and DOE 1946-72, dep sec (personnel mgmnt) CSD 1972-78, second Crown Estate cmmr 1978-83; Humane Soc Bronze Medal 1942; *Recreations* sailing, mountain walking; *Style—* Sir John Moore, KCVO, CB, DSC; High Spinney, Old Coach Rd, Wrotham, Kent TN15 7NR (☎ 0732 822340)

MOORE, (Harold) Jonathan; s of Harold Moore, of Cambs, and Edna Rose, *née* Jewson (d 1985); *b* 26 Feb 1947; *Educ* The Leys Sch Cambridge; *m* 1; 3 da (Lucy Anna Elizabeth b 1974, Charlotte Jane b 1976, Susannah Amy b 1980); m 2, 28 April 1990, Jane Rosemary, da of late Dr H Clare, of Canterbury, Kent; *Career* fndr and sr ptnr Moore Young & Co CAs, ret 1987, md Wheelpower Ltd (electro-mechanical and mfrg co); inventor/designer with designs registered in 7 countries; dir Orchard Estates Property Devpt, fin conslt; fndr memb March Port Appreciation Soc; FCA 1972, FCCA 1978, memb IPI; *Recreations* golf, sailing, tennis, skiing; *Clubs* Royal W Norfolk Golf, March and County; *Style—* Jonathan Moore, Esq; Addison House, Addison Rd, Wimblington, Cambs PE15 0QT (☎ 0354 741124); Wheelpower Ltd, West Winch, Kings Lynn, Norfolk (☎ 0553 840261, fax 0354 54846, car ☎ 0836 216032)

MOORE, Dr Kevin Charles; s of Dr Donald Charles Moore (d 1989), and Nellie Partington (d 1985); *b* 25 Jan 1941; *Educ* Giggleswick Sch, Univ of Manchester Med Sch (MB ChB); *m* 23 Feb 1972, Jillian Margaret, da of Frank Bromley (d 1984); 1 da (Alison b 1972); *Career* conslt anaesthetist Oldham 1973-, chm Med Staff Ctee Oldham 1981-85, chm Rochdale Private Surgical Unit 1983-88, treas Br Med Laser Assoc 1987-, vice pres Int Laser Therapy Assoc 1988-, dir Highfield Private Hosp Rochdale 1988-; memb Oldham Health Authy 1987-90, memb Governing Cncl Dr Kershaw's Hospice Oldham 1988-; FFARCS 1972; *Recreations* horse riding, squash, hang gliding; *Style—* Dr Kevin Moore; Hutch Royd Farm, Parrock Nook, Rishworth, Sowerby Bidge, W Yorks HX6 4RF (☎ 0422 823498); Dept of Anaesthesia, The Royal Oldham Hospital, Rochdale Rd, Oldham, Lancs OL1 2JH (☎ 061 624 0420)

MOORE, Lynne Rosamund; da of Roy Rawnsley, of Norland, Yorkshire, and Brenda, *née* Nuttall; *b* 8 Dec 1947; *m* 1, (m dis); 1 s (Julian Mark); m 2, (m dis 1982); 2 da (Joanne Margaret, Caroline Ruth); *Career* painter; work incl: shooting, fishing, Cresta Run, landscapes, gardens, buildings; exhibits regularly in London and works included in private collections worldwide; memb NSPCC, hon memb Game Conservancy; *Recreations* shooting, racing, flying, gardens; *Style—* Ms Lynne Moore; c/o Malcolm Innes Gallery, 172 Walton St, London SW3 (☎ 071 584 0575)

MOORE, (Georgina) Mary; *née* Galbraith; da of Prof Vivian Hunter Galbraith, FBA (d 1976), of Oxford, and Georgina Rosalie, *née* Cole-Baker (d 1982); *b* 8 April 1930; *Educ* The Mount Sch York, Lady Margaret Hall Oxford (MA); *m* 30 Aug 1963, Antony Ross Moore, s of (William) Arthur Moore (d 1962); 1 s (Arthur James b 1967), 2 step da (Rosalind Ingrams b 1943, Julie Hankey b 1947); *Career* entered HM Dip Serv 1951; HM Legation Budapest 1954-56; memb Perm Delgn to UN New York 1956-59; 1 sec 1961; resigned on marriage 1963; princ St Hilda's Coll Oxford 1980-90; JP Bucks 1977-82; tstee: Rhodes Tst 1984-, Br Museum 1982-; memb Cncl for Indust and Higher Educn 1986-90; hon fell: Lady Margaret Hall Oxford 1980, St Hilda's Coll Oxford 1990; *Books* (under the pseudonym Helena Osborne): novels: The Arcadian Affair (1969), Pay Day (1972), White Poppy (1977), The Joker (1979); plays: The Trial of Madame Fahmy (Granada TV 1980), An Early Lunch (BBC Radio 4 1981), An Arranged Marriage (BBC Radio 4 1982), Testimonies (BBC Radio 4 1990); *Clubs* University Women's; *Style—* Mrs A R Moore; Touchbridge, Boarstall, Aylesbury, Bucks HP18 9UJ (☎ 0844 238247)

MOORE, Michael; s of Gerald Edward Moore (d 1975), of Rangoon, Burma, and Shwe Mu Tha Soe; *b* 2 Oct 1955; *Educ* Methodist Eng HS Rangoon, Hackney Downs Sch London, Univ of Leicester (BSc), Univ of Aberdeen (MLitt), Nat Coll for Hypnosis & Psychotherapy, UK Training Centre for Neuro-Linguistic Programming; *Career* pilot RAF VR; memb Contact Counselling Servs: Univ of Aberdeen 1978-79, Univ of Keele 1979-81; res and admin asst Cmmn for Int Justice and Peace 1981-82; psychologist and specialist in human conflict resolution 1982-; memb: Br Psychological Soc 1987, Assoc of Neuro-Linguistic Programming 1987; *Recreations* philosophy, comparative religion, languages, TA, flying; *Style—* Michael Moore, Esq; 130 Harley St, London W1N 1AH (☎ 071 935 6558)

MOORE, Mike; s of Jack Francis Moore, BEM, of Epsom, Surrey and Joan Florence, *née* Walker; *b* 6 Jan 1954; *Educ* Bideford Sch of Art and Design, Reading Sch of Art and Design; *Career* photographer: Thomson Regnl Newspapers 1976-79, London Evening Standard 1980-85, The Today Newspaper 1986-; Midland Bank press awards commendation 1977 and 1978, World Press Photo Fndn Gold medal 1978, Br Press Awards commendation 1981, Ilford Press Awards commendation 1984, Royal Photographer of the Year 1987, Press Photographer of the Year 1987; *Recreations* tennis, watersports; *Clubs* Ferrari Owners; *Style—* Mike Moore, Esq; 3 Evelyn Terrace, Richmond, Surrey, (☎ 081 940 1097); Today Newspaper Picture Desk, 70 Vauxhall Bridge Rd, London SW1 (☎ 071 630 1300, car 0836 242018)

MOORE, Nigel Sandford Johnson; s of Raymond Johnson Moore (d 1977), and Lucy Mary, *née* Kirby; *b* 12 April 1944; *Educ* Radley; *m* 16 Aug 1969, Elizabeth Ann, da of Joseph Henry Bowker (d 1986); 1 s (Peter b 9 Jan 1973), 2 da (Louise b 20 Feb 1974, Rachel b 1 March 1977); *Career* Buckley Hall Devin & Co 1962-68; Ernst and Young: Sydney Aust 1969-71, ptnr (UK) 1973-, human resources 1973-81, mktg dept Dept 1983-86, managing ptnr London Office 1986-88, dir client servs Europe 1988-90, regnl managing ptnr Eastern Europe 1990-; FCA 1977; *Recreations* theatre, golf, tennis; *Clubs* City of London, IOD, The Pilgrims, Wildernesse; *Style—* Nigel Moore, Esq; Vinesgate, Chart Lane, Brasted Chart, Westerham, Kent TN16 1LR (☎ 0959 64510); Becket House, 1 Lambeth Palace Rd, London SE1 7EU (☎ 071 931 3444, fax 071 928 1345, telex 885234)

MOORE, (Sir), Dr Norman Winfrid; 3 Bt (UK 1919), of Hancox, Whatlington, Sussex (but does not use title); s of Sir Alan Hilary Moore, 2 Bt, MB (d 1959); *b* 24 Feb 1923; *Educ* Eton, Trinity Coll Cambridge; *m* 14 July 1950, Janet, o da of Paul Singer; 1 s, 2 da; *Heir* s, Peter Alan Cutlack Moore; *Career* Lt RA, served 1942-45 War; principal scientific offr Nature Conservancy 1958-, sr principal scientific offr 1965-83, ret; visiting prof Wye Coll London Univ 1979-83; *Books* Dragonflies (with Philip S Corbet and Cynthia Lungfield, 1960), Hedges (with E Pollard and M D Hooper, 1974), The Bird of Time: The Science and Politics of Nature Conservation (1987); *Style—* Dr Norman Moore; The Farm House, Swavesey, Cambs

MOORE, Dr Patrick (CALDWELL-); CBE (1989, OBE 1968); s of Capt Charles Caldwell-Moore, MC (d 1947), and Gertrude Lilian, *née* White (d 1981); *b* 4 March 1923; *Educ* private; *Career* served WWII with RAF 1940-45, Flt Lt, navigator with Bomber Cmd; dir Armagh Planetarium 1965-68; author, broadcaster, astronomer; vice-pres Brit Astronomical Assoc (pres 1982-84); Hon DSc: Univ of Lancaster 1979, Hatfield Polytechnic 1989, Univ of Birmingham 1990; FRAS 1945, FRSA 1949; hon memb various foreign scientific socs; *Books* over 120 books, mainly astronomical; *Recreations* cricket, chess, tennis, music (xylophone player); *Clubs* CCC, Lord's Taverners, Sussex; *Style—* Dr Patrick Moore, CBE; Farthings, West St, Selsey, Sussex (☎ 0243 603668)

MOORE, Peter; s of Benjamin Moore (d 1936), of Beverley, N Humberside, and Gladys May, *née* Forrest (d 1960); *b* 29 March 1929; *Educ* Marist Coll Hull, Gordonstoun, HMS Conway (N Wales); *m* Sept 1952, Betty Jean, da of James Stanley (d 1953), of Riversdale Road, Hull; 1 s (Karl b 1954), 1 da (Susan Jane b 1956); *Career* md: Peter Moore (Hull) Ltd 1964-, Harry Oxtoby and Co Ltd 1961; *Recreations* theatre; *Style—* Peter Moore, Esq; The Hill, Woodgates Lane, North Ferrby, N Humberside (☎ 633592); 45 Newland Avenue, Hull (☎ 42366)

MOORE, Very Rev Peter Clement; s of Rev George Guy Moore (d 1967), and Vera Helen, *née* Mylrea (d 1947); *b* 4 June 1924; *Educ* Cheltenham, Ch Ch Oxford (MA, DPhil); *m* 29 June 1965, Mary Claire, da of Malcolm Duror, of Appin Argyll; 1 s (Twysden b 1970), 1 da (Damaris b 1966); *Career* dean St Albans Cathedral 1973-, minor canon Canterbury Cathedral 1947-49, curate Bladon W Woodstock 1949-51, chaplain New Coll Oxford 1949-51, vicar Alfrick with Lulsley 1952-53, Hurd librarian to Bishop of Worcester 1953-62, vicar Pershore with Pinvin and Wick 1963-67, canon residentiary Ely Cathedral 1967-73; memb: Archbishops' Liturgical Cmmn 1968-77, Gen Synod 1978-85 and Governing Body SPCK; former Master Worshipful Company of Glaziers and Painters of Glass; tstee Historical Churches Preservation Tst, select preacher Univ of Oxford 1986-87; OStJ; FSA; *Books* Tomorrow is Too Late (1970), Man Woman and Priesthood (1978), Footholds in the Faith (1980), Crown in Glory (1982), Bishops: but what kind? (1982), In Vitro Veritas (contributor 1985), Synod of Westminster (1986), Sharing the Glory (1990); *Recreations* gardening, bookbinding, fly fishing; *Clubs* United Oxford and Cambridge; *Style—* The Very Rev the Dean of St Albans; The Deanery, St Albans, Herts (☎ 0727 52120); Thruxton House, Thruxton, Hereford (☎ 098121 376)

MOORE, Peter David; s of Frederick Cecil Moore, and Joan Lambert *née* Wickham; *b* 5 June 1945; *Educ* King George V GS Southport Lancs; *m* 28 April 1973, Susan Janet, da of Duncan Ferguson Ure; 1 s (Stephen David b 5 May 1978), 1 da (Philippa Jane b 1 Jan 1976); *Career* CA: Arthur Andersen 1969-71, Money Dealer Bankers Trust Co 1971-72; fin dir Martin Bierbaum Group plc (formerly R P Martin plc) 1979- (co sec 1972-79); FCA 1969; *Recreations* sporting; *Clubs* Richmond RFC, Dorking RFC; *Style—* Peter Moore, Esq; c/o Martin Bierbaum Group plc, 4 Deans Court, London, EC4V 5AA

MOORE, Prof Peter Gerald; TD (1963); s of Leonard Jiggens Moore, of Wimbledon, and Ruby Silvester, *née* Wilburn (d 1978); *b* 5 April 1928; *Educ* King's Coll Sch Wimbledon, UCL (BSc, PhD), Princeton; *m* 27 Sept 1958, Sonja Enevoldson, da of William Ivor Thomas, of Cooden (d 1973); 2 s (Charles b 1967, Richard b 1973), 1 da (Penelope (Mrs Lawrenson) b 1960); *Career* 2 Lt 3 Regt RHA 1949-51, 2 Lt (later Lt then Capt) 290 Field Regt (City of London) RA TA 1951-61, Capt (later Maj) 254 Field Regt RA TA 1961-65; lectr UCL 1951-56, asst econ advsr NCB 1956-59, head statistical servs Reed Paper Group 1959-65; London Business Sch: prof of statistics 1965-, dep princ 1972-84, princ 1984-89; pt/t ptnr Duncan C Fraser 1974-77; pt/t dir: Copeman Paterson Ltd 1984-, Elf Aquitaine UK plc 1989-; fell UCL 1988; memb: Drs and Dentists Renumeration Body 1971-89, Ctee on 1971 Census Security 1971-73, UGC 1978-84 (vice chm 1980-83); conslt Wilson Ctee on Fin Insts 1977-80; memb Cncl: Univ of Sci and Technol Hong Kong 1986-, UCL 1989; Liveryman Worshipful Co of Tallow Chandlers (memb Ct 1987-); Hon DSc Heriot Watt Univ 1985; pres: RSS 1989- (fell 1952), Inst of Actuaries 1984-86 (fell 1956); CBIM 1985; *Books* include: Anatomy of Decisions (1976), Reason By Numbers (1980), The Business of Risk (1983); *Recreations* golf, walking, travelling; *Clubs* Athenaeum, Knole Park Golf; *Style—* Prof Peter Moore, TD; 3 Chartway, The Vine, Sevenoaks, Kent TN13 3RU (☎ 0732 451 936); London Business School, Sussex Place, Regent's Park, London NW1 4SA (☎ 071 262 5050, fax 071 724 7875)

MOORE, Brig Peter Neil Martin; DSO (1942, and bars 1944 and 1952), MC (1941); s of Arthur Montague Moore (d 1966), of 3a Holnest Park House, Sherborne, Dorset, and Amy Dorothy, *née* Peacock (d 1967); *b* 13 July 1911; *Educ* Clifton, RMA Woolwich, Trinity Hall Cambridge (BA); *m* 29 Aug 1953, (Enid) Rosemary, da of Col Herbert Bland Stokes, CBE (d 1962), of South Wraxall Lodge, Bradford on Avon, Wilts; 3 s (Michael b 1955 (decd), Martin b 1960, Robert b 1969), 3 da (Lucinda b 1956, Anne b 1957, Melanie b 1959); *Career* cmmnd 1931, Royal Bombay Sappers and Miners 1935-40; N Africa: Staff Capt 7 Indian Inf Bde 1940, 2 i/c 4 Field Sqdn RE 1941, OC 1 (later 3) Field Sqdn RE 1942; GSO1 instr Middle East Staff Coll 1943, GSO1 Br Liaison Offr with Jugoslav partisans 1943-45, cmd RE 6 Airborne Div Palestine 1946, GSO1 WO 1947, CO 35 Engr Regt 1949, cdr RE 1 Inf Div 1950, cdr 28 Field Engr Regt Cwlth Div Korea 1951, GSO1 instr Jt Servs Staff Coll 1953, cdr 28 Cwlth Inf Bde Malaya 1955, Brig GS weapons WO 1959, Dep Cmdt Sch of Land/Air Warfare 1962, ret 1963; princ MAFF 1963-76, courses res offr Coll of Estate Mgmnt 1976-87; chm local parish cncl; Partisan Gold Star 1970; *Recreations* fly-fishing, military history; *Clubs* Naval and Military, Special Forces, Ocean Racing; *Style—* Brig Peter Moore, DSO, MC; Hastings Hill House, Churchill, Oxford OX7 6NA (☎ 060 871 778)

MOORE, Philip John; s of Cecil Alfred Moore, of Stamford Bridge, York, and

Marjorie Winifred, *née* Brewer; *b* 30 Sept 1943; *Educ* Maidstone GS, RCM; *m* 1, 9 Nov 1968 (m dis 1979); 1 s (Thomas), 2 da (Sophia, Bianca); *Career* asst music master Eton 1965-68, asst organist Canterbury Cathedral 1968-74, organist and master of the choristers Guildford Cathedral 1974-82, organist and master of the music York Minster 1983-; memb: RCM Union 1962, Composers Guild of GB 1987, Performing Rights Soc 1988; Hon BMus Dunelm; FRCO 1962, GRSM, ARCM; *Recreations* motor cars, flying kites; *Style*— Philip Moore, Esq; 1 Minster Court, York YO1 2JJ (☎ 0904 624426)

MOORE, Prof Robert Samuel; s of Douglas Kenneth Moore, of Rhos-on-Sea, and Kathleen Phyllis Moore; *b* 3 June 1936; *Educ* Beckenham and Penge County GS, RNC Dartmouth, Univ of Hull (BA), Univ of Durham (PhD); *m* 16 Aug 1969, Lindy Ruth, da of late Sir Alan Parker, of Shenstone, of Sutton-cum-Beckingham; 1 s (David Kenneth b 1974), 1 da (Heloise Katherine b 1976); *Career* RN 1952-60; sociology lectr Univ of Durham 1965-69, sr lectr in sociology Univ of Aberdeen 1970-75, reader in sociology 1975-77, prof of sociology 1977-89, Eleanor Rathbone prof of sociology Univ of Liverpool 1989-; vice pres Aberdeen City Anti Apartheid, chm Grampian Community Relations Cncl until 1989; memb: Assoc Univ Teachers, Lab Party, CND, Scientists Against Nuclear Arms; Br Sociological Assoc 1964-, Br Assoc 1965-; *Books* Race, Community and Conflict (with John Rex, 1967), Pitmen, Preachers and Politics (1970), Slamming the Door (with Tina Wallace, 1975), Racism and Black Resistance in Britain (1975), The Social Impact of Oil (1982), Women in the North Sea Oil Industry (with Peter Wybrow, 1985); *Recreations* gardening, photography; *Style*— Prof Robert Moore; The University of Liverpool, PO Box 147, Liverpool L69 3BX (☎ 051 794 2985, fax 051 708 6502, telex 627095 UNILPL G)

MOORE, (John) Royston; CBE (1983); s of Henry Roland Moore (d 1944), and Jane Elizabeth, *née* Wood (d 1958); *b* 2 May 1921; *Educ* Manchester Central GS, Univ of Manchester (BSc); *m* 28 March 1947, Dorothy Mackay, da of Charles Roe Hick (d 1960); 2 s (Stephen Charles Royston b 1953, Andrew John Royston b 1957); *Career* princ Bradford Tech Coll (later Bradford Coll of Further and Higher Educn) 1959-80 (ret); cncllr Baildon UDC 1965-70 (leader 1968); W Riding CC 1970-73, W Yorkshire CC 1973-86 (leader 1978-81, opposition leader 1981-86); chm Cons Nat Advsy Ctee on Educn 1967-70; advsr Overseas Dvpt Dept on Further Educn, E Africa 1963-69, San Salvador 1969-73; memb Cncl City and Guilds of London Inst 1978- (chm Ctee for Work Overseas 1973-87); chm Bradford Health Authy 1982-88; memb Cncl Nat Assoc of Health Authorities; dir: Yorkshire Enterprise Ltd (formerly W Yorkshire Enterprise Bd Ltd) 1984-88, White Rose Enterprise Ltd, White Rose Investment Ltd, N Yorkshire Dvpt Ltd, and other cos; Hon MA Bradford, FRCS, C Chem; *Recreations* cricket, bridge; *Style*— Royston Moore, Esq, CBE; Bicknor, 33 Station Road, Baildon, Shipley; W Yorkshire BO17 6HS (☎ 1274 581777)

MOORE, Hon Mrs ((Constance) Sheila); 2 da of 11 Baron Digby, KG (d 1964); *b* 20 Sept 1921; *m* 27 Nov 1945, Charles Arthur Moore (d 1989), eldest s of late Charles Arthur Moore, of Greenwich, Connecticut, USA; *Career* in ATS 1939-40, with British Security Co-ordination 1943-45; *Style*— The Hon Mrs Moore; Bearforest House, Mallow, Co Cork (☎ 022 21568 5310); Chemin de Vie, Atlanta, Georgia 30342 USA (☎ 404 256 9222)

MOORE, Steven Ronald; MBE (1989); s of Douglas Michael Moore (d 1990), of 25 Gainsborough Drive, Beltinge, Kent, and Anson Margaret Christabel, *née* Meade; *b* 3 March 1963; *m* 4 Oct 1986, Hilary Anne, da of Clifford Charles Eaton, of 2 Rutland Gardens, Cliftonville, Kent; 1 s (Andrew Steven b 9 Nov 1990); *Career* waterskier; Br team memb 1981-90, Euro champion 1985-88, Br champion 1985-89, World Cup champion 1986, World champion 1988-89, Euro Cup champion 1989; *Recreations* water skiing, football, squash, most fast sports; *Clubs* Whitstable Water Ski; *Style*— Steven Moore, Esq, MBE; 2 Dane Park Villas, Park Lane, Cliftonville, Kent CT9 1RH (☎ 0843 298205)

MOORE, Terence (Terry); s of Arthur Doncaster Moore, and Dorothy Irene Gladys, *née* Godwin; *b* 24 Dec 1931; *Educ* Strand Sch Univ of London (BScEcon), Harvard Business Sch; *m* 17 Sept 1955, Tessa Catherine, da of Ernest Walter Wynne; 2 s (Simon Jeremy b 1961, Adam Gavin B 1965), 1 da (Anna Louise b 1968); *Career* Nat Serv Army; Shell Int 1948-64 (mktg, fin, econs), economist Locana Corp 1964-65; Conoco Ltd: economist, mangr econs planning, gen mangr and dir 1965-74, dep md mktg ops 1974-79, md supply and trading 1979-86, gp md/chief exec offr 1986-; pres Oil Industs Club 1989-90; ACII, AICS, FRSA; *Recreations* jogging, badminton, reading, music; *Style*— Terry Moore, Esq; 5 Gun Wharf, 130 Wapping High St, Wapping London E1 9NH (☎ 071 481 0853); Conoco Ltd, Conoco House, 230 Blackfriars Rd, London SE1 8NR (☎ 071 408 6759, fax 071 408 6168, telex 887948)

MOORE, Trevor Anthony; s of Ronald Frederick Moore (d 1957), and Jean Daphne, *née* Wallis; *b* 3 Feb 1957; *Educ* Christ's Hosp, St Catharine's Coll Cambridge (MA); *Career* articled clerk Dawson & Co 1979-81, admitted slr 1981, ptnr Freshfields 1987- (joined 1981); memb: Worshipful Co of Slrs, Law Soc; *Recreations* long distance running, squash, French/France; *Style*— Trevor Moore, Esq; 19 Carson Rd, London SE21; Whitefriars, 65 Fleet St, London, EC4Y 1HS (☎ 071 936 4000, fax 071 832 7001)

MOORE, Sir William Roger Clotworthy; 3 Bt (UK 1932), of Moore Lodge, Co Antrim; TD (1963), DL (Co Antrim 1990); s of Sir William Samson Moore, 2 Bt (d 1978), and Ethel Coburn Gordon (d 1973); *b* 17 May 1927; *Educ* Marlborough, RMA Sandhurst; *m* 17 May 1954, Gillian, da of John Brown, of Co Antrim; 1 s, 1 da; *Heir* s, Richard William Moore; *Career* Lt Royal Inniskilling Fusiliers 1945, Maj North Irish Horse 1958; Grand Juror Co Antrim 1952-68, High Sheriff Co Antrim 1964; chm Bd of Visitors HM Prison Castledillon Co Armagh 1971-72; dir numerous cos; BBC broadcaster; *Recreations* shooting, country pursuits, travel; *Clubs* Army and Navy; *Style*— Sir William Moore, Bt, TD, DL; Moore Lodge, Ballymoney, Co Antrim, NI

MOORE-BICK, Martin James; QC (1986); s of John Ninian Moore-Bick, and Kathleen Margaret, *née* Beall; *b* 6 Dec 1946; *Educ* Skinners Sch Tunbridge Wells, Christ's Coll Cambridge (MA); *m* 3 Aug 1974, Tessa Penelope, da of George Michael Gee; 2 s (Christopher b 1980, Matthew b 1983), 2 da (Catherine b 1977, Elizabeth b 1977); *Career* called to the Bar Inner Temple 1969, rec Crown Ct 1990; *Recreations* music, literature, gardening; *Style*— Martin Moore-Bick, Esq, QC; Litle Bines, Witherenden Hill, Burwash, Etchingham, E Sussex (☎ 0435 883 284); 3 Essex Ct, Temple, London EC4 (☎ 071 583 9294, fax 071 583 1341, telex 893468 SXCORT G)

MOORE OF WOLVERCOTE, Baron (Life Peer UK 1986), of Wolvercote in the City of Oxford; Philip Brian Cecil Moore; GCB (1985, KCB 1980, CB 1973), GCVO (1983, KCVO 1976), CMG (1966), QSO (1986), PC (1977); s of Cecil Moore, ICS (d 1950), and Alice Mona, *née* Bath (d 1967); *b* 6 April 1921; *Educ* Dragon Sch Oxford, Cheltenham, BNC Oxford; *m* 28 Aug 1945, Joanna Ursula, da of Capt M E Greenop, DCLI (d 1972); 2 da (Hon Sally Jane (Hon Mrs Leachman) b 9 June 1949, Hon Jill Georgina (Hon Mrs Gabriel) b 2 Dec 1951); *Career* served WW II RAF Bomber Cmd, and POW; PPS to First Lord of the Admty 1957-58 (asst private sec 1950-51), dep high cmmr Singapore 1963-65 (dep UK cmmr 1961-63), chief of PR MOD 1965-66, private sec to HM The Queen and keeper of the Queen's Archives 1977-86 (dep private sec 1972-77, asst private sec 1966-72); hon fell Brasenose Coll Oxford 1981; *Recreations* golf, shooting, fishing; *Clubs* Athenaeum, MCC; *Style*— The Rt Hon Lord Moore of Wolvercote, PC, GCB, GCVO, CMG, QSO; Apartment 64, Hampton Court Palace, Surrey KT8 9AU (☎ 081 943 4695)

MOORE-SMITH, Dr Bryan; s of Dr Cyril Moore-Smith (d 1937), and Kathleen Frances, *née* O'Donoghue (d 1982); *b* 6 Nov 1930; *Educ* Ampleforth, Oriel Coll Oxford (MA, BM BCh), St Thomas's Hosp; *m* 26 May 1962, Elizabeth Jean, da of Leonard George Dale (d 1964); 1 s (James Patrick b 1965), 1 da (Caroline Frances b 1963); *Career* conslt in geriatric med 1968-, clinical dir Directorate of Health Care of Elderly Ipswich Hosp 1990-; memb cncl and treas Br Geriatric Soc 1969-75, memb and sec Geriatrics Ctee RCP 1971-90, dir Ipswich Abbeyfields Soc 1973-, chm Ipswich Hosp Med Staff Ctee Management Team 1976-77, conslt memb Ipswich Dist Mgmnt Team 1977-79, secondments to Health Advsy Serv 1976-, advsr Overseas Div Help the Aged 1983-; Dip in Geriatric Med RCP: fndr memb Examiners Bd 1983-, host examiner 1986-, chm 1990-; memb Occupational Therapist Bd Cncl for Professions Supplementary to Med 1986-, memb Jt Validation Bd Coll of Occupational Therapy CPSM 1989-, conslt memb E Suffolk Health Authy 1987-90; contrib to med pubns 1970-; chm Parents Ctee and Bd of Govrs Convent of Jesus and Mary Ipswich 1973-82, memb Geriatrics Soc 1965; *Recreations* gardening, travel, music, art; *Style*— Dr Bryan Moore-Smith; Wolmers, Stonham Aspal, Stowmarket, Suffolk IP14 6AS (☎ 0449 711261); Dept of Geriatric Medicine, The Ipswich Hospital, Heath Rd, Ipswich, Suffolk IP4 5PD (☎ 0473 704132, fax 0473 270664)

MOOREHEAD, (Hon) Kerena Ann; *née* Mond; does not use style of Hon; er da of 3 Baron Melchett (d 1973); *b* 17 May 1951; *Educ* Univ of E Anglia; *m* 1980, Richard Moorehead; 1 da (Lucy, b 1981); *Style*— Mrs Richard Moorehead; 58 Mallinson Rd, London SW11 1BP

MOORES, Sir John; CBE (1972); s of John William Moores; *b* 25 Jan 1896; *Educ* Higher Elementary Sch; *m* 1923, Ruby Knowles; 2 s (*see* Peter Moores), 2 da (er da Betty m 2 Baron Grantchester, *qv*); *Career* fndr of the Littlewoods Orgn 1924: Littlewoods Pools 1924, Littlewoods Mail Order Services 1932, Littlewoods Stores 1936; kt 1980; *Style*— Sir John Moores, CBE; c/o The Littlewoods Organisation, JM Centre, Old Hall St, Liverpool L70 1AB (☎ 051 235 2222)

MOORES, Peter; s of Bernard Moores, and Winifred Moores; *b* 18 Dec 1962; *Educ* Kings Sch Macclesfield; *m* 28 Sept 1989, Karen Jane, da of Joseph Anthony Mills; *Career* professional cricketer; MCC groundstaff 1982, Worcestershire CCC 1982-85 (debut 1983); Sussex CCC: joined 1985-, debut 1985, awarded county cap 1989, best performance 116 v Somerset 1989; overseas teams: Old Hararians Zimbabwe 1983-84, Rovers SA 1988-89; tours: int ambassadors XI India 1990, MCC Namibia 1991; schoolboys caps: England under 19 1981, MCC under 19 1981; winner's medal Benson & Hedges series SA (Orange Free State v Western Province) 1989; asst res analyst Britannia Building Society Leek 1989-90 and 1990-91 (off seasons); *Recreations* golf, music, photography; *Style*— Peter Moores, Esq; Sussex CCC, Eaton Rd, Hove, Sussex BN3 3AN (☎ 0273 732161)

MOORES, Peter; CBE (1991); s of Sir John Moores, CBE, *qv*, and the late Ruby Moores; *b* 9 April 1932; *Educ* Eton, ChCh Oxford; *m* 1960 (m dis), Luciana, da of Salvatore Pinto, Naples; 2 c; *Career* dir Singer and Friedlander 1972-, chm The Littlewoods Organisation 1977-80 (dir 1965-), Tstee Tate Gallery 1978-85, govr BBC 1981-83; fndr Peter Moores Fndn 1964; hon MA ChCh Oxford, Gold Medal of the Italian Repub 1974; hon memb RNCM; *Recreations* windsurfing, shooting, opera; *Style*— Peter Moores, Esq, CBE; Parbold Hall, Wigan, Lancashire

MOORES, Yvonne; da of Tom Abraham Quick, of Netley Hampshire, and Phyllis, *née* Jeremiah (d 1988); *b* 14 June 1941; *Educ* Itchen GS Southampton, Southampton Sch of Nursing; *m* 1, 1969 (m dis 1973), Bruce Holmes Ramsden; m 2, 8 Nov 1975, Brian Moores, s of Edward Moores (d 1949); *Career* princ nursing offr: North London HMC 1971-72, West Manchester HMC 1973-74; district nursing offr North District Manchester AHA 1974-76, area nursing offr Manchester AHA 1977-81; chief nursing offr: The Welsh Office 1982-88, The Scottish Office Home and Health Dept 1988-; memb: NHS Scotland Management Exec Bd, RCN; fell Royal Soc of Health 1990; *Books* contrib author: NHS Management Perspectives for Doctors, International Administration of Nursing Services; *Recreations* golf, bridge; *Style*— Mrs Yvonne Moores; Grenelefe, Lawhill Road, Law by Carluke, Lanarkshire ML8 5EZ (☎ 0555 72960); The Scottish Office Home and Health Department, St Andrews House, Regent Road, Edinburgh EH1 3DE (☎ 031 244 2314, fax 031 244 2683)

MOORHEAD, Michael Dennis; s of Patrick Moorhead, of Verwood, Ringwood, Hants, and Pamela Eric Beckett, *née* Roper; *b* 13 June 1946; *Educ* Kings Coll Sch, Univ of Manchester (BSc); *m* 10 March 1984, Janette, da of Roger Taylor of Meriden, Coventry; 1 s (Giles b 1984), 2 da (Chloe b 1986, Freya b 1988); *Career* cmmd RAF Engr Branch, Flt-Lt, 1964-78; res fell Univ of Birmingham 1978; dir: Neptune Radar 1983, Neptune Consultants 1986; *Recreations* swimming, skiing, travel; *Clubs* RAF; *Style*— Michael Moorhead, Esq; Neptune Radar Ltd (☎ 0452 730479)

MOORHEAD, Peter Gerard; s of George Aloysius Moorhead (d 1965), and Miriam, *née* Mostyn; *b* 16 Dec 1937; *Educ* Ampleforth, Ch Ch Oxford, Univ of Manchester; *m* 1 Feb 1961, Astrid Josephine, da of John Joseph Muraszkas-Marshall (d 1986); 1 s (Dominic b 27 Nov 1962), 2 da (Julie (Mrs Clouth) b 10 Dec 1961, Susan b 5 April 1965); *Career* Pilot Offr: RAF (Nat Serv) 1956-58, RAFVR 1958-62; md Frank Young & Co Ltd 1965-83; dir: Tonge Dyeing Co Ltd 1965-83, Tonge Dyeing Co (Holdings) Ltd 1968-83; md: Hall Green & Co Ltd 1963-87, Tonge and Young Ltd 1983-; life memb: Oxford Union Soc, Ampleforth Soc, Catholic Union; FInstD, FIOD, memb Textile Inst; *Recreations* watching sport, gardening, photography; *Clubs* Pathfinder; *Style*— Peter Moorhead, Esq; Greystones, 7 Highgate Rd, Altrincham, Cheshire WA14 4QZ, (☎ 061 928 8357); Tonge and Young Ltd, Waterside Works, Blackley New Rd, Manchester M9 3ER, (☎ 061 740 1867 car phone 0860 811344)

MOORHOUSE, Adrian David; MBE (1987); s of Clifford Moorhouse, of Bingley, W Yorks, and Kathleen, *née* Thompson; *b* 24 May 1964; *Educ* Bradford GS; *Career* breaststroke swimmer; Olympic Games 1988 Gold 100m (fourth place 1984); Cwlth Games: 1982 Gold 100m (Silver 4x100m medley relay, Bronze 200m), 1986 Gold 200m (Silver 100m, Silver 4x100m medley relay), 1990 Gold 100m (Silver 4x100m medley relay); Euro Championships: 1983 Gold 200m (Silver 100m), 1985 Gold 100m, 1987 Gold 100m (Bronze 200m),1989 Gold 100m; silver 100m World Championships 1991 holder: world record 100m breaststroke short course, world record 100m breaststroke long course until 1991, Euro and Cwlth record 100m breaststroke long course; min's nominee W Yorks and Humberside Sports Cncl; memb MENSA 1988; *Recreations* music, films, literature; *Style*— Adrian Moorhouse, Esq, MBE; Cottingley Bar, Bingley, West Yorkshire (☎ 0274 562624)

MOORHOUSE, Lady Diana Merial; *née* Coke; da of Hon Arthur George Coke (ka 1915, 2 s of 3 Earl of Leicester) and sis of 6 Earl; raised to the rank of an Earl's da 1977; *b* 7 Nov 1907; *m* 30 July 1930 (m dis 1938), Trevor Moorhouse (d 1975), o s of late Maj S Moorhouse; 1 da (1 s decd); *Style*— The Lady Diana Moorhouse; 1 Stoke Green Cottages, Stoke Poges, Slough, Bucks

MOORHOUSE, Geoffrey; s of William Heald (d 1971), and Gladys, *née* Hoyle; *b* 29 Nov 1931; *Educ* Bury GS; *m* 1, May 1956 (m dis 1974), Janet Marion, da of Alec Murray (d 1978), of Christchurch NZ; 2 s (Andrew b 1961, Michael b 1966), 2 da (Jane b 1960, Brigid b 1965, d 1981); m 2, Sept 1974 (m dis 1978), Barbara Jane, *née* Woodward; m 3, June 1983, Marilyn Isobel, *née* Edwards; *Career* coder RN 1950-52;

journalist 1952-70 (chief features writer Manchester Guardian 1963-70), author; FRGS 1972, FRSL 1982; *Books* The Other England (1964), Against All Reason (1969), Calcutta (1971), The Missionaries (1973), The Fearful Void (1974), The Diplomats (1977), The Boat and The Town (1979), The Best-Loved Game (1979, Cricket Soc award), India Britannica (1983), Lord's (1983), To the Frontier (1984, Thomas Cook award), Imperial City (1988), At the George (1989), Apples in the Snow (1990); *Recreations* listening to music, hill walking, looking at buildings, watching cricket and rugby league; *Clubs* Lancashire CC; *Style—* Geoffrey Moorhouse, Esq; Park Hse, Gayle, nr Hawes, N Yorks DL8 3RT (☎ 0969 667456)

MOORHOUSE, (Cecil) James Olaf; MEP (EDG) London S and Surrey E 1984-, (London S 1979-84); s of late Capt Sidney Moorhouse; *b* 1 Jan 1924; *Educ* St Paul's, King's Coll London (BSc), Imperial Coll London (DIC); *m* 1958, Elizabeth, da of late Dr Charles Huxtable, MC; 1 s (Olaf), 1 da (Phoebe); *Career* project engr BOAC 1948-53, tech advsr Shell Int Petroleum Co and Shell Operating Cos 1953-72; environmental conservation advsr Shell UK Ltd 1972-73, gp environmental affairs advsr RTZ 1973-80 (consIt 1981-84); vice chm and Euro Democratic spokesman on Europe's External Econ Rels, vice chm Ctee EFTA Parliamentarians 1984-86 (Tport spokesman 1987-89); Parly rapporteur: trade and econ rels between Euro Community and Japan, on trade and econ rels between the EC and the countries of the Pacific Basin and on the economic significance of Antarctica; *Clubs* RAC; *Style—* James Moorhouse Esq, MEP; 34 Buckingham Palace Rd, London SW1W 0RE (☎ 071 828 3153)

MOORIN, Raymond Leslie; s of Joseph Wilson Moorin (d 1957), and Edith, *née* Waterston (d 1985); *b* 1 March 1939; *Educ* Emanuel Sch, Wandsworth Tech Coll, Borough Poly; *m* 14 Aug 1965, (Victoria) Wendy, da of Edwin McCleod Miller, of Merseyside; 3 s (Robert b 1966, Patrick b 1969, Matthew b 1971); *Career* bldg servs engr Slough Borough Cncl 1964-70, mechanical and electrical engr Dept Educn & Sci 1970-72, assoc HL Dawson and Assocs 1972-73, sr ptnr Multi Bldg Servs Design Ptnrship 1973-; C Eng, M Inst E 1968, MIMechE 1969, M Inst R 1972, FCIBSE 1975, M Cons E 1976, FRSA 1988; *Recreations* golf, squash, tennis; *Clubs* Burnham Beeches GC; *Style—* Raymond Moorin, Esq; Lyndale, 21 Coates Lane, High Wycombe, Bucks HP13 5EY (☎ 0494 33147); MBS House, 150 West Wycombe Rd, High Wycombe, Bucks HP12 3AE (☎ 0494 441251, fax 0494 441252, car 0836 205514)

MOORMAN, Raymond Anthony Gilbert (Ray); s of Raymond Moorman (d 1980) and Norah Isabel *née* Gilbert; *b* 9 May 1937; *Educ* Blundell's Sch, Univ of Cambridge (MA); *m* 12 Jan 1963, Jane Ethne, da of Stanley Aikman (d 1975); 3 da (Sarah b 14 May 1964, Rebecca b 10 Aug 1966, Lucinda b 5 June 1969); *Career* Nat Serv PO RAF 1955-57; trainee & mangr Union Corp 1960-69; md Capital & Counties plc 1985- (dir 1971, joined 1969); *Recreations* real tennis, golf; *Clubs* St Stephen's Constitutional, Queen's, Royal Tennis Court, Tiverton Golf; *Style—* Ray Moorman, Esq; Capital & Counties plc, 40 Broadway, London SW1

MOORSOM, Christopher Stewart; s of Raisley Stewart Moorsom (d 1981), of Ramsdean End, nr Petersfield, Hants, and Ann, *née* Thomson (d 1987); *b* 26 June 1927; *Educ* Diocesan Coll Capetown, King's Coll Cambridge (MA); *m* 1, 2 May 1956 (m dis 1969), Maria del Pilar, da of Enrique Sanchez del Monte (d 1973), of Havana, Cuba; 3 da (Isabella Maria b 3 Sept 1958, Lucinda Sol (Lady Norreys) b 28 Aug 1960, Consuelo Ileana b 23 Dec 1961); m 2, 23 Jan 1987, Cherry Rosalind, da of late David Long-Price; *Career* fleet air arm RNVR 1945-46; foreign corr and postgrad lectr Madrid 1950-52, econ ed Greek Govt Athens 1952-53; PR consIt in UK, Europe, USA; specialist in working for foreign govts incl Spain and Saudi Arabia; *Clubs* Chelsea Arts; *Style—* Christopher Moorsom, Esq; 28 Draycott Place, London SW3 2SB (☎ 071 589 5850, fax 071 584 3347)

MOORSOM, Patrick William Pierre; s of Frederick William Moorsom (d 1971), of Dinas, Powys, Glamorgan, and Jeanne Juliette, *née* Phelippon; *b* 30 Oct 1942; *Educ* Downside, Jesus Coll Cambridge (BA, Squash blue); *m* 14 Sept 1965, Dominique Ann, da of Andre Leroy; 1 s (Pierre Frederick Andre), 3 da (Natasha Juliet, Sophie Ann, Stephanie Helene); *Career* CA Arthur Andersen & Co 1965-69; dir: Rothschild Intercontinental Bank 1969-78, Barclays Merchant Bank 1978-81; md Cayzer Ltd 1981-87; vice chm: Guinness Mahon & Co Ltd, Guinness and Mahon Ltd (Rep of Ireland); chm: Guinness Mahon Guernsey Ltd, Regent Inns plc; dir Superstores plc; FCA 1971; *Style—* Patrick Moorsom, Esq; 62 Portland Road, London W11 4LQ (☎ 071 727 1455); Guinness Mahon & Co Ltd, 32 St Mary At Hill, London EC3P 3AJ (☎ 071 623 9333)

MOOS, Khursheed Francis; s of Jehangir Dhanjishah Moos (d 1973), and Maria Gerritje, *née* Tulp; *b* 1 Nov 1934; *Educ* Dulwich, Univ of London (BDS, MB BS), Guy's Hosp, Westminster Hosp; *m* 23 June 1962, Katharine, da of George Stewart Addison (d 1952); 2 s (Christopher b 1964, John b 1968), 1 da (Hilary b 1966); *Career* Nat Serv RADC 1959-61, Lt 1959, Capt 1960; registrar in oral surgery Mount Vernon Hosp Middx 1966-67, sr registrar in oral surgery Univ of Wales Cardiff Dental Sch 1967-69; consIt oral surgn: South Warwicks, Coventry, E Birmingham Hosps 1969-74; consIt oral and maxillofacial surgn Plastic and Maxillofacial Unit Canniesburn Hosp Glasgow 1974-, civilian consIt oral surgn to RN 1976-; fellowship examiner: RCSE(d), RCPSGlas; vice pres BAOMS, vice dean Dental Council RCPSGlas, chm Special Advsy Ctee in Oral Surgery and Oral Med 1985-89; memb: BAOMS 1964-, BDA 1958-, BMA 1964-, RSM 1965-, Euro Assoc Cranio Maxillofacial Surgery, Int Assoc Oral Maxillofacial Surgery; *Books* Surgery of the Mouth and Jaws (contrib, 1985), Companion to Dental Studies (contrib, 1986), Plastic Surgery in Infancy and Childhood (contrib, 1988); *Recreations* music, natural history, philately, eastern philosophy, gardening; *Style—* Khursheed Moos, Esq; Dept of Oral and Maxillofacial Surgery, Regional Plastic and Maxillofacial Unit, Canniesburn Hospital, Bearsden, Glasgow G61 1QL (☎ 041 942 2255, fax 041 943 1469)

MOOTHAM, Dolf C; s of Sir Orby Mootham, and Maria Augusta Elisabeth, *née* Niemöller (d 1973); *b* 2 Aug 1933; *Educ* Bryanston Sch, Trinity Coll Cambridge (BA); *Career* dir: TSB Gp plc 1987-, Hill Samuel Bank Ltd 1967-; *Clubs* Brooks's; *Style—* D C Mootham, Esq; 25 Milk St, London EC2V 8LU (☎ 071 606 7070)

MOOTHAM, Sir Orby Howell; ED (1942); s of Delmé George Mootham (d 1954); *b* 17 Feb 1901; *Educ* Leinster House Sch Putney, Univ of London (MSc); *m* 1, 1931, Maria Augusta Elisabeth (d 1973), da of Wilhelm Niemöller, of Cassel, Germany; 1 s, 1 da; m 2, 1977, Beatrix Douglas (d 1990), da of Nigel Douglas Connell, of Taranaki, NZ, and wid of Prof Basil Robert Ward, FRIBA (d 1976); *Career* called to the Bar Inner Temple 1925; chief judicial offr Br Mil Admin Burma 1943-45; judge: Rangoon High Ct 1945-46, Allahabad High Ct 1946-55; chief justice Allahabad India 1955-61, hon bencher 1958; dep chm: Essex QS 1964-71, Surrey QS 1970-71; rec Crown Ct 1972; kt 1962; *Books* Burmese Buddhist Law (1939), The East India Company's Sadar Courts 1801-1834 (1983); *Clubs* Athenaeum; *Style—* Sir Orby Mootham, ED; 25 Claremont Rd, Teddington, Middx TW11 8DH (☎ 081 977 1665)

MORAHAN, Christopher Thomas; s of Thomas Hugo Morahan (d 1969), and Nancy Charlotte, *née* Baker (d 1977); *b* 9 July 1929; *Educ* Highgate, Old Vic Theatre Sch; *m* 1, 1954, Joan, *née* Murray (d 1973); 2 s (Ben, Andrew), 1 da (Lucy d 1990); m 2, 1974, Anna (actress as Anna Carteret), da of Col Peter Wilkinson, of Pulborough, W Sussex; 2 da (Rebecca, Harriet); *Career* Nat Serv RA 1947-49, 2 Lt; TV theatre and film dir; dir Greenpoint films, head plays BBC TV 1972-76; tv prodns incl: Talking to a Stranger 1966, The Gorge 1967, The Jewel in the Crown 1984, In the Secret State 1985, After Pilkington 1987 (Prix Italia 1987), Troubles 1988, The Heat of The Day 1989, Old Flames 1990, Can You Hear Me Thinking? 1990; cinema: Clockwise 1986, Paper Mask 1990; assoc Nat Theatre 1977-88; theatre prodns incl: This Story of Yours, Flint, State of Revolution (NT), Man and Superman (NT), Wild Honey (NT), Melon, Major Barbara; Theatre Awards: Olivier, Plays and Players Drama, London Standard (for Wild Honey), SFTA Best Play Dir 1969, BAFTA Best Series Dir 1985, Desmond Davis Award for Outstanding Creative Achievement in TV 1985, Peabody Award 1985, Broadcasting Press Guild Award 1984, Primetime Emmy Award 1985; *Recreations* photography, birdwatching, Garrick, Chelsea Arts; *Style—* Christopher Morahan, Esq; c/o Michael Whitehall Ltd, 125 Gloucester Rd, London SW7 4TE (☎ 071 244 8466)

MORAN, Graham Dennis; s of Dennis John Moran (d 1986), and Janet Pearl, *née* Challinor; *b* 11 July 1945; *Educ* Donnington Wood Sch, Sir John Hunt Comprehensive Sch; *m* 19 June 1965, Patricia Elizabeth, da of Hugh Thomas Stepney (d 1967), of Westminster; 1 s (Philip b 1967), 1 da (Jacqueline b 1965); *Career* 1 Bn Welsh Gds 1962-87, Colour Sgt, served Germany, Ireland, Cyprus Kenya, Canada, The Falklands; admin (for Nat Tst) Anglesey Abbey 1987-; *Recreations* gardening, game shooting; *Style—* Graham Moran, Esq; The Cottage, Anglesey Abbey, Lode, Cambridge CB5 9EJ (☎ 0223 811 200)

MORAN, Dr John Denton; RD (1977); s of Paul Francis Moran (d 1989), of Marine Gate, Brighton, and Mary, *née* Denton; *b* 3 Nov 1940; *Educ* Downside, Univ of London, St George's Hosp (MB BS), Guy's (LDS, RCS, Cert FPA, Dip Psycho-Sexual Counselling); *m* 16 June 1973, Jane, da of Gen Sir Malcolm Cartwright-Taylor, KCB (d 1969); 1 s (Paul b 29 Jan 1976), 2 da (Iona b 16 Sept 1973, Louise b 18 March 1975); *Career* RNR: Surgn Sub Lt (dental) 1962, Surgn Lt (dental) 1964, Surgn Lt Cdr (dental) 1969, dental offr HMS Centaur RN 1965, med and dental offr White City and Jamaica Rd RMR, resigned 1979; dental house surgn St Bartholomew's Hosp 1964, med house surgn ENT Dept St George's Hosp Tooting 1970, med house physician Christchurch and Boscombe Hosps Bournemouth 1971, GP Brandon Manitoba Canada 1972, private dental practice Harley St 1973-; MO: Margaret Pyke Centre 1974, Marie Stopes 1978-, Menopause Clinic 1979-; Freeman City of London 1979, Liveryman Worshipful Co Barber Surgns 1980; assoc memb Zoological Soc LN, memb BMA, FRSM; *Recreations* golf, shooting, skiing, walking, bridge; *Clubs* RAC, Royal Ashdown, Sloop; *Style—* Dr John Moran, RD; Belvedere Farm, Cinder Hill Lane, Horsted Keynes, W Sussex (☎ 825 790246); 92 Harley St, London W12 (☎ 071 935 2182)

MORAN, 2 Baron (UK 1943); (Richard) John McMoran Wilson; KCMG (1981, CMG 1970); s of 1 Baron, MC (d 1977), formerly Dr (then Sir) Charles McMoran Wilson, and Dorothy, *née* Dufton (d 1983); *b* 22 Sept 1924; *Educ* Eton, King's Coll Cambridge; *m* 29 Dec 1948, Shirley Rowntree, eldest da of late George James Harris, MC, of Bossall Hall, York; 2 s, 1 da; *Heir* s, Hon James Wilson; *Career* served WWII RNVR, HMS Belfast, motor torpedo boats and HM destroyer Oribi; entered Foreign Service 1945, to Portugal 1976-81, ambass Chad 1970-73, Hungary 1973-76, high cmmr Canada 1981-84; sits as cross-bencher in House of Lords; vice-chm: Atlantic Salmon Tst, All-Party Conservation Gp of both Houses of Parliament; pres Welsh Salmon and Trout Anglers Assoc; chm: Regnl Fisheries Advsy Ctee, Welsh Region Nat Rivers Authy; memb cncl RSPB; Grand Cross Order of the Infante Portugal 1978; *Books* CB: A Life of Sir Henry Campbell-Bannerman (Whitbread award for biography 1973), Fairfax (1985); *Recreations* fishing, fly-tying, bird watching; *Clubs* Beefsteak, Flyfishers' (pres 1987-88); *Style—* The Rt Hon Lord Moran, KCMG; c/o House of Lords, Westminster, London SW1

MORAN, Air Vice-Marshal Manus Francis; QHP (1988); s of John Moran (d 1952), of Rathgar, Dublin, and Kathleen, *née* Coyle (d 1965); *b* 18 April 1927; *Educ* Mount St Joseph Abbey Roscrea Ireland, Univ Coll Dublin (MB BCh BAO 1952), MCh 1964, RCP and RCS (DLO 1963), MRAeS (1984); *m* 26 July 1954, Maureen Elizabeth Martin, da of Martin Dilks (d 1950), of Kirby Muxloe, Leicester; 2 s (John b 1956, d 1986, David b 1963), 3 da (Frances b 1955, Anne b 1958, Jane b 1960); *Career* served RAF 1954-, rising to Air Vice-Marshal 1988-; house surgeon and house physician St Vincent's Hosp Dublin 1952, trainee in gen practice Lutterworth nr Rugby 1953, sr house offr 1954 (Marston Green Hosp Birmingham, Hosp for Sick Children Park St Hull); RAF: assigned to Central Med Estab London 1954, trainee ORL Wroughton 1955-57, offr-in-charge ORL Dept: Weeton 1957-59, Akrotiri Cyprus 1959-62, Halton 1964-66; consIt in ORL: Changi Singapore 1965-68, Nocton Hall 1968-79, Wegberg Germany 1979, Princess Alexandra Hosp Wroughton 1979-83; consIt advsr ORL to RAF 1983-88, lectr in otorlaryngology Inst of Aviation Med Farnborough 1983-88, dean of Air Force Med 1988, the sr consIt RAF 1990-; Medical Soc UCD Gold medal, Lady Cade medal RCS for contrib to ORL, fndr memb The Joseph Soc, memb Sections of Laryngology/Otology Royal Soc of Med (pres elect Section of Laryngology 1991-); memb: Cncl of Br Assoc of Otorhinolaryngologists 1980-86, Environmental Noise Advsy Ctee 1980-86, Gen Ctee of 6th Br Academic Conf in ORL 1980-83, ORL Advsy Ctee Wessex Reg NHS, Irish Otological Soc, Portmann Fndn; hon sec Gen Ctee 7th Br Academic Conf in ORL 1984-87; chm: Gen Ctee 8th Br Academic Conf 1989-91, RAF Ethical Sub-Ctee, Marston Meysey Parish Room Ctee (Registered Charity); memb: RCP, RCS, Euro Acad of Facial Plastic Surgery, American Acad of Facial, Plastic & Reconstructive Surgery; Freeman City of London; CStJ 1990; *Publications* Upper Respiratory Problems in the Yellow Nail Syndrome (jtly); contribs to jls on ORL; *Recreations* walking, poetry, theology; *Clubs* RAF; *Style—* Air Vice-Marshal Manus Moran, QHP

MORAN, Peter Myles; s of Myles Moran (d 1957); *b* 3 Aug 1936; *Educ* St Edward's Coll, Univ of Liverpool (LLB); *m* 1963, Miriam Rosemary, *née* Macey; 2 da; *Career* sr ptnr Chattertons; pt/t chm Social Security Appeal Tbnls; treas Soc of Cons Lawyers, memb Lincolnshire County Ctee CLA, chm E Lindsay Cons Assoc; *Recreations* tennis, golf; *Clubs* Carlton; *Style—* Peter Moran, Esq; Langton House, Horncastle, Lincs (☎ 065 82 2296); office: Chattertons, Solicitors, 5 South Street, Horncastle, Lincs LN9 6DS (☎ 065 82 2456/7011, fax 065 822445)

MORAY, Countess of; Barbara; da of John Archibald Murray, of Fifth Av, NY; *b* 1903; *m* 21 June 1924, 18 Earl of Moray (d 1943); 3 da; *Style—* The Rt Hon Barbara, Countess of Moray; 174 Ebury St, London SW1

MORAY, 20 Earl of (S 1562); Douglas John Moray Stuart; JP (Perthshire 1968); also Lord Abernethy and Strathearn (S 1562), Lord Doune (S 1581), Lord St Colme (S 1611), and Baron Stuart of Castle Stuart (GB 1796); s of 19 Earl of Moray (d 1974; himself 11 in descent from 1 Earl, an illegitimate s of James V of Scotland, Regent of Scotland from 1567 until his murder in 1570 by Hamilton of Bothwellhaugh), and Mabel Helen Maud (May) (d 1968), only child of late Benjamin 'Matabele' Wilson, of Battlefields, S Rhodesia; *b* 13 Feb 1928; *Educ* Trinity Coll Cambridge (BA), Hilton Coll Natal; *m* 27 Jan 1964, Lady Malvina Dorothea Murray, er da of 7 Earl of Mansfield (d 1971); 1 s, 1 da (Louisa); *Heir* s, Lord Doune; *Career* FRICS; *Clubs* New (Edinburgh); *Style—* The Rt Hon the Earl of Moray, JP; Darnaway Castle, Forres,

Moray (Forres 0309 72101); Doune Park, Doune, Perthshire (☎ 0786 841333)

MORAY ROSS AND CAITHNESS, Bishop of 1970-, Rt Rev George Minshull Sessford; s of Charles Walter Sessford (d 1951), of Aintree, Lancs, and Eliza Annie, *née* Minshull; *b* 7 Nov 1928; *Educ* Oulton HS, Liverpool Collegiate Sch, Univ of St Andrews (MA); *m* 1, 25 June 1952, Norah (d 1984), da of David Hughes (d 1951), of Aintree; 3 da (Christine Mary (Mrs Parker) b 23 Oct 1953, Aileen Margaret (Mrs McHardy) b 14 Nov 1956, Clare Louise (Mrs Coutts) b 3 Nov 1958); m 2, 8 Aug 1987, Joan Gwendoline Myra, wid of Rev Charles Wilfred Black; *Career* Nat serv RASC, 8 Br Inf Bde 1947-49; curate St Mary's Cathedral Glasgow 1953-58, chaplain Anglican Students Univ of Glasgow 1955-58, parish priest Holy Name Cumbernauld 1958-66, rector Forres 1966-70; *Recreations* sailing; *Style*— The Rt Rev the Bishop of Moray Ross and Caithness; Spynie House, 96 Fairfield Rd, Inverness IV3 5LL (☎ 0463 231059)

MORCOS, Dr Sameh Kamel; *b* 19 April 1949; *Educ* Maronite Sch Cairo Egypt, Univ of Cairo (MB BCh); *Career* radiologist; pre-regisration house jobs Cairo Univ Teaching Hosps 1971-72, resident in gen surgery and orthopaedics Benha Gen Hosp Egypt 1972-73; sr house offr: in orthopaedics and casualty Bedford Gen Hosp England 1973, in casualty Noble's Hosp IOM 1973-74, in orthopaedics Queen Mary's Hosp for Children Carshalton Surrey 1974-75, in orthopaedics Rowley Bristow Orthopaedic Hosp Pyrford Surrey and St Peter's Hosp Chertsey Surrey 1975-76, in surgical rotation Taunton and Somerset Hosps 1976-78; sr registrar in radiodiagnosis Sheffield Teaching Hosps 1981-83 (registrar 1978-81), conslt radiologist Northern Gen Hosp and Lodge Moor Hosp Sheffield UK 1983-; winner of Graham-Hodgson scholarship RCR 1987; ECF MG (USA) 1974, FRCS (Glasgow) 1978, DMRD (London) 1981, fell Faculty of Radiologists RCS (Dublin) 1982, FRCR (London) 1982, memb Chest Radiologists' Assoc, FRCPS; memb: BRS, BMA (Sheffield Div: vice chm 1990-91, chm 1991-92); hon fell Overseas Doctor's Assoc 1988 (memb Nat Exec Ctee 1982-); *publications:* numerous publications in learned jls; *Style*— Dr Sameh Morcos; Northern General Hospital, Herries Rd, Sheffield S5 7AU (☎ 0742 434343 ext 4339); Lodge Moor Hospital, Redmires Rd, Sheffield S10 4LH (☎ 0742 630222 ext 6367)

MORDANT, Sally Rachel; da of Capt Henry Collins (d 1948), and Eileen Marjorie Rachel, *née* Davis (d 1971); *m* 12 April 1957, Richard Alfred Colman Mordant, s of the late Philip Mordant; 2 s (Simon b 1959, Jonathan b 1961); *Career* freelance journalist and PR conslt; md SRM Consultancy Services Ltd; MIPR 1979; *Recreations* entertaining, theatre, literature; *Style*— Mrs Sally Mordant; Apartment 11, 23 Hyde Park Square, London W2 2NN (☎ 071 262 6208)

MORDAUNT, Gerald Charles; s of Eustace John Mordaunt (d 1988), and Anne Francis, *née* Gilmour (d 1976); *b* 16 July 1939; *Educ* Wellington Coll; *m* Sept 1965 (m dis 1981), Carol, da of Brig R M Villiers, DSO (d 1973), of Scotland; 2 s (James b 1967, Christopher b 1969), 2 da (Tanya b 1974, Harriet b 1980); *Career* chm Laing and Cruickshank 1987- (joined Laing and Cruickshank 1959, head of equities 1986); memb Stock Exchange; *Recreations* tennis, shooting, wine; *Style*— Gerald C Mordaunt, Esq; Hovells Farm, Coggeshall, Colchester, Essex (☎ 03765 61700); Laing and Cruickshank, Broadwalk House, 5 Appold St, London, EC2A 2DA (☎ 071 588 4000, fax 071 588 0290)

MORDAUNT, Sir Richard Nigel Charles; 14 Bt (E 1611), of Massingham, Parva, Norfolk; s of Lt-Col Sir Nigel John Mordaunt, 13 Bt, MBE (d 1979); *b* 12 May 1940; *Educ* Wellington; *m* 1964, Myriam Atchia; 1 s, 1 da (Michele b 1965); *Heir* s, Kim John Mordaunt b 1966; *Style*— Sir Richard Mordaunt, Bt; 12 Ebor Rd, Palm Beach, New South Wales, Australia

MORDUE, Richard Eric; s of Ralph Yielder Mordue (d 1979), of Hexham, and Helen Mary, *née* Downie; *b* 14 June 1941; *Educ* Royal GS Newcastle upon Tyne, King's Coll Durham (BSc), Michigan State Univ (MS); *m* 30 June 1979, Christine, da of Dr Jack Phillips; 1 s (John b 13 May 1980), 1 da (Heather b 15 March 1982); *Career* dir Econs and Statistics MAFF 1989- (economist 1964-82, head of Horticulture Div 1982-88); *Recreations* golf, bridge; *Clubs* Civil Service; *Style*— Richard Mordue, Esq; Ministry of Agriculture, Fisheries and Food, Whitehall Place (West), London SW1A 2HH (☎ 071 270 8539)

MORE-MOLYNEUX, Maj James Robert; OBE (1983); s of Brig-Gen Francis More-Molyneux Longbourne, CMG, DSO, and Gwendoline, da of Rear Adm Sir Robert More-Molyneux, GCB; *b* 17 June 1920; *Educ* Eton, Univ of Cambridge; *m* 1948, Susan, da of Capt Frederick Bellinger; 1 s (Michael George); *Career* Nat Serv WWII, Italy; landowner; chm: Loseley Park Farms, and fndr Loseley Dairy Products Ltd, Guildway Ltd; Vice Lord-Lt Surrey 1982- (former DL); *Clubs* Farmers'; *Style*— Maj James More-Molyneux, OBE; Loseley Park, Guildford, Surrey GU3 1HS (☎ 0483 66090); estate office (☎ 304440)

MORE NISBETT, Patrea Evelyn; da of David Agar MacDonald (d 1967), of Dorset, and Elisabeth May, *née* Ferguson; *b* 2 March 1944; *Educ* Cranborne Chase, Sorbonne, House of Citizenship Bucks; *m* 2 March 1968, George Alan More Nisbett, s of Surgn Cdr John Graham More Nisbett, of East Lothian; 3 s (William David Hamilton b 1979, Alexander Talbot John b 1982, Charles Neilson George b 1984); *Career* Scottish ed Harpers and Queen Magazine, contrib Sloane Ranger Handbook, occasional writer Observer and Scotsman, Scottish correspondent The Good Schools Guide, advsr to travel indust; *Style*— Mrs Patrea Evelyn More Nisbett; 43 Godfrey St, London SW3 (☎ 071 352 3259, car 0836 703412); The Drum, Gilmerton, Edinburgh EH17 8RX (☎ 031 664 7215)

MOREAU, David Merlin; s of Capt Reginald Ernest Moreau (d 1970), of Curlews, Sutton St Nicholas, Herts, and Winifred Mary Moreau (d 1982); *b* 9 Oct 1927; *Educ* King's Sch Canterbury, Jesus Coll Cambridge (BA, MA); *m* 22 Dec 1956, Elizabeth Mary, da of John Walter Rees; 1 s (Alexander Piers Merlin b 5 Aug 1966), 1 da (Sally P J b 20 Nov 1964 d 1988); *Career* Nat Serv radar specialist and head Educn Centre RAF Gibraltar 1946-48; export mangr John Wyeth & Brothers 1956-64, euro market controller Beecham Overseas 1956-64, fndr and md Syntex Pharmaceuticals Maidenhead 1965-70, chm Weddel Pharmaceuticals 1970-80, md Elga Products Ltd Lane End Bucks 1972-80, dir Dewplan Group 1980-84, md Chiltern Water Treatment 1980-83, dir DNAX California; author of numerous articles incl: Sunday Times, New Scientist, Financial Times, Chemical Engineer, Defence Journal, Guardian, Director, Chief Executive; own series BBC Radio 4 1984-; memb: Ctee Local Cons Pty, Cncl Assoc of Br Pharmacological Indust, Cncl SIMA, Soc of Authors 1963; Freeman City of London 1989, Liveryman Worshipful Co of Air Pilots and Navigators 1989; FZS 1968, FRSM 1972, CBIM 1979; *Books* The Simple Life (1963), That Built-In Urge (1965), Summers End (1966), Look Behind You (1973), More Wrestling than Dancing (1990); *Recreations* piloting own plane, radio broadcasting, languages, skiing, collecting Ferraris, guitar, photography; *Clubs* RSM; *Style*— David Moreau, Esq; Rowley Cottage, Langley Park, Slough, Bucks SL3 6DT (☎ 0753 663201); c/o Dewplan Ltd, Beechwood Hall, Kingsmead Rd, High Wycombe, Bucks HP11 1LA (☎ 0494 35671, fax 0494 465489, telex 837139)

MOREL, Jean-Yves; s of Joseph Morel (d 1975), of Pont-de-Beauvoisin, France, and Paulette, *née* Reynaud (d 1987); *b* 26 June 1948; *Educ* Lycee Technique of Pont-de-Beauvoisin; *m* May 1982, Mary-Anne, da of John Brewer; *Career* Chef and restaurant proprietor; trained as a charcutier in France, worked for the Roux brothers at le Gavroche, and in various London restaurants; opened Morels (a french restaurant in Haslemere Surrey) 1980; featured in all major food guides incl: Good Food Guide, Egon Ronay Guide, AA Guide and Michelin Guide; Morels was named Egon Ronay Guide's Restaurant of the Year 1988; *Recreations* snooker, chess; *Clubs* Ritz; *Style*— Jean-Yves Morel; Morels, 25-27 Lower St, Haslemere, Surrey GU27 2NY (☎ 0428 651462)

MORELAND, Robert John; s of Samuel John Moreland, MC, TD, of 3 The Firs, Heathville Rd, Gloucester, and Norah Molly, *née* Haines (d 1980); *b* 21 Aug 1941; *Educ* Glasgow Acad, Dean Close Sch Cheltenham, Univ of Nottingham (BA), Univ of Warwick; *Career* civil servant Canada 1966-72, mgmnt conslt Touche Ross & Co 1974-, MEP (EDG) Staffs 1979-84, chm Section on Regnl Policy and Town Planning 1990-, cncllr Knightsbridge Ward Westminster City Cncl 1990-; memb Econ and Social Ctee of Euro Community 1986-; *Books* Transport for Europe (jtly 1983); *Recreations* swimming, skiing, golf, watching cricket; *Clubs* Carlton, RAC; *Style*— Robert Moreland, Esq; 3 The Firs, Heathville Rd, Gloucester GL1 3EW (☎ 0452 22612); 7 Vauxhall Walk, London SE11 5JT (☎ 071 582 2613); Economic and Social Committee, rue Ravenstein 2, B-1000 Brussels, Belgium (☎ 010 322 519 9011, fax 010 322 513 4893); Strategy Network International, 10 Storeys Gate, London SW1 3AY (☎ 071 222 2933, fax 071 222 1252)

MORETON, Anthony John; s of William Herbert Moreton (d 1969), of Cardiff, and Margaret Clara, *née* Jenkins (d 1978); *b* 8 July 1930; *Educ* Penarth County Sch, Cardiff Tech Coll, Ruskin Coll Oxford, Exeter Coll Oxford (MA); *m* 27 May 1967, Ena, da of Thomas Kendall (d 1955), of Merthyr Tydfil; *Career* Nat Serv cmmnd Flying Offr RAF 1954-56; ldr writer and sub ed Western Mail 1956-58, features sub ed New Chronicle 1958-60, Daily Telegraph 1960-63 Financial Times 1963, welsh corr 1987-, regnl affrs ed 1977-87; cncllr: London Borough Wandsworth 1962-65 (chm Libraries Ctee), London Borough Lambeth 1965-68 (chm Fin and Gen Purposes Ctee); treas Holy Trinity Clapham 1962-74, chm Lambeth Arts and Recreations Assoc 1966-72, church warden St Gwynno's Vaynor Merthyr Tydfil 1985-89; Freeman Worshipful Co Glovers 1985; *Recreations* golf, gardening, walking; *Clubs* Cardiff and County, Aberdare Golf; *Style*— Anthony Moreton, Esq; Pandy Farm, Merthyr Tydfil CF47 8PA (☎ 0685 723003)

MORETON, Lord; David Leslie Moreton; s and h of 6 Earl of Ducie; *b* 20 Sept 1951; *Educ* Cheltenham, Wye Coll London (B Sc Agric); *m* 1975, Helen, da of M L Duchesne, of Brussels; 1 s (James b 1981), 1 da (Claire b 1984); *Style*— Lord Moreton; Talbots End Farm, Cromhall, Glos

MORETON, Sir John Oscar ; KCMG (1977, CMG 1966), KCVO (1976), MC (1944); s of Rev Charles Oscar Moreton, of Chipping Norton, Oxon; *b* 28 Dec 1917; *Educ* St Edward's Sch Oxford, Trinity Coll Oxford; *m* 1945, Margaret Katherine, da of Sir John Claud Fortescue Fryer, KBE, FRS (d 1948); 3 da; *Career* served WWII RA, Maj 1945; asst master Uppingham 1946-48; Colonial Office 1948-: Kenya 1953-55, private sec to Sec of State 1955-59, CRO 1960, Nigeria 1961-64, IDC 1965, asst under sec Cwlth Office 1965-69, ambass Vietnam 1969-71, high cmmr Malta 1972-74, dep perm rep (status of ambass) UK Mission to UN 1974-75, min Br Embassy Washington 1975-77; dir Wates Fndn 1978-87; Gentleman Usher of the Blue Rod Order of St Michael and St George 1979-; *Clubs* Army and Navy; *Style*— Sir John Moreton, KCMG, KCVO, MC; Woodside House, Woodside Rd, Cobham, Surrey KT11 2QR

MORETON, (Cecil) Peter; s of Cecil Roland Moreton, of 27 Castle St, Wellingborough, Northants, and Jessie Maud Moreton, of Northants; *b* 25 July 1927; *Educ* Wellingborough Sch, Univ of London, Coll of Estate Mgmnt; *m* 6 April 1953, Eileen, da of Walter Harry Frost (d 1962), of 71 Polwell Lane, Barton Seagrave, Kettering, Northants; 1 s (Nicolas b 1961), 1 da (Penny b 1958); *Career* articled clerk W & H Peacock Bedford 1944-52, asst H P Barnsley Hereford 1952-53, asst Stimpson Lock & Vince Watford 1953-59, regnl surveyor Northampton Town & Co Building Soc 1959-70, chief surveyor Anglia Building Soc 1977-87 (dep chief surveyor 1970-77), regular appearances on nat & local TV and radio as spokesman on housing & valuation matters, regular writer in UK & Int magazines, ed Surveyors Insurance News Serv, exec ed The Surveyors Handbook, free-lance weekly broadcaster for BBC 1982-, conslt surveyor to RICS Insur Servs London, regular lectr on surveying matters; pres Round Table Watford and Northampton (past chm, sec, pres), past chm RICS branches Beds, Herts, Leics, Northants (sec), past pres Nene Valley Rotary Club (sec), dist govr nominee Rotary Dist 107 1991-92, past appeals organiser OPWA; past chm: ARC Ctee, Deaf Appeal, Northants 47 Surveyors, CBSI Branch, 41 Club; chm Happy Feet Appeal, past memb Surveyors Panel to the BSA 1977-87; memb: RICS Residential Valuation & Survey Ctee, Derngate Soc, The Charter Soc; FRICS 1965, FCBSI 1985, FSVA 1988, Paul Harris Fell Rotary Int 1985; *Recreations* sport, golf, cricket, gardening, music; *Clubs* Rotary; *Style*— Peter Moreton, Esq; 86 Church Way, Weston Favell, Northampton NN3 3BY (☎ 0604 406 371); RICS Insur Servs Ltd, Plantation House, 31-35 Fenchurch St, London (☎ 071 481 1445)

MORETON, Hon Robert Matthew; s of 6 Earl Ducie; *b* 8 March 1964; *m* 9 July 1988, Heather, da of Colin Lynton-Jenkins, of Alveston, Avon; 1 da (Olivia Alexandra Rose b 5 Jan 1991); *Style*— The Hon Robert Moreton

MOREY, Anthony Bernard Nicholas (Tony); s of Bernard Rowland Morey (d 1976), of Christchurch, Dorset, and Madeleine Mary Rose, *née* Dowling; *b* 6 Dec 1936; *Educ* Wimbledon Coll; *m* 3 Feb 1961, Agni Campbell, da of William Lavery Kerr, of Epsom, Surrey; 2 s (Paul David b 1965, John Michael Anthony b 1970), 1 da (Nicola Anne b 1962); *Career* memb of HM Dip Serv 1957-; postings incl: Kuwait, Madras, Tehran, Kabul, Washington, Zagreb, Lagos; consul gen Moscow 1985-88, dep High Cmmr Madras 1989-; *Recreations* gardening, music, viticulture, golf, cats; *Clubs* Royal Cwlth; *Style*— Tony Morey, Esq; The Coach House, Nutcombe Lane, Hindhead, Surrey; c/o Foreign and Commonwealth Office, London SW1

MORGAN; *see*: Hughes-Morgan

MORGAN, Alan William; s of Alfred Charles Morgan, ISO, of Stoke Bishop, Bristol, and Eliza Dora, *née* Sproul-Cran; *b* 4 Oct 1951; *Educ* Clifton, Trinity Coll Oxford (MA), Harvard Business Sch (MBA); *m* 17 Oct 1981, Janet Cullis, da of Rainier Campbell Connolly, of London; 2 s (Campbell b 1983, Edward b 1986), 1 da (Georgina b 1988); *Career* called to the Bar 1974, joined Brandts 1974-76, Harvard Business Sch 1976-78, McKinsey & Co 1978 (ptnr 1984); *Recreations* horse racing, theatre, books, walking; *Clubs* RAC, United Oxford and Cambridge; *Style*— Alan Morgan, Esq; 74 St James's St, London SW1 (☎ 071 839 8040)

MORGAN, Andrew Vladimir Rhydwen; s of His Hon Judge Peter Hopkin Morgan, of Chippenham, Wilts, and Josephine Mouncey, *née* Travers; *b* 20 Oct 1942; *Educ* Abermâd Sch Aberystwyth, Harrow, RADA; *m* 21 Jan 1967, Jacqueline, da of Dennis Webb, of Knaresborough, Yorks; 1 s (Nicholas Simon Hopkin b 9 June 1968), 1 da (Zöe Olivia Lucy b 28 Dec 1972); *Career* freelance film and TV dir; work incl: Swallows and Amazons for Ever, Knights of God, Hard Cases, Dr Who, Casualty, Little Sir Nicholas; Freeman City of London 1965, Liveryman Worshipful Co Fishmongers 1965; *Recreations* inland waterways; *Style*— Andrew Morgan, Esq; 28 Wyndham St, London W1H 1DD (☎ 071 723 4507)

MORGAN, Arthur William Crawford (Tony); s of late Arthur James Morgan, and late Violet Morgan; *b* 24 Aug 1931; *Educ* Hereford HS, Westcliff HS, Inst of Business

Mgmnt; *m* 18 June 1955, Valerie Anne, da of late Arthur J Williams; 3 s (Simon Anthony Crawford b 31 July 1957, Christopher James Crawford b 25 Oct 1958, Timothy John Crawford b 24 April 1961); *Career* Nat Serv RAF Mountbatten; Silver medallist sailing Flying Dutchman Tokyo Olympics 1964, chm and chief exec Purle Bros 1964-71, dir Redland 1971-73, govr of The BBC 1971-76, fndr and ptnr Morgan Hemmingway Investment Bank 1973-77, dep chm Wimpey Waste Management 1978-81, chm Wistech plc 1984-90; fndr and chm Nat Assoc Waste Disposal Contractors 1968-73; fndr: Campaign for Social Democracy 1973, Nat Ctee for Electoral Reform; jt Yachtsman of the Year 1965; memb: Br Olympic Yachting Appeal 1970, Cncl Royal Yachting Assoc 1968-72; chm The Hunger Project Tst 1984-89; FRSA; *Publications* author of various technical papers; *Recreations* running, skiing, squash, windsurfing, sailing (yacht 'More Opposition' in Admiral's Cup); *Clubs* Royal Thames; *Style—* Tony Morgan, Esq; Bovingdon, Marlow Common, Buckinghamshire SL7 2QR

MORGAN, Bruce; s of Flying Offr Francis William Morgan, DFC, of Stourbridge, Worcestershire, and Phyllis Marie Morgan (d 1979); *b* 30 March 1945; *Educ* Oswestry Sch; *m* 30 July 1988, Sandra Joy, da of Robert Beresford, of Sillhoth, Cumbria; 2 da (Polly Nimali Beresford b 1990, Sophie Chamilla Prothero b 1990 (twin)); *Career* asst slr Prothero and Prothero 1964-73, ptnr Lickfolds Wiley and Fowles 1973-87; stipendiary magistrate: Met 1987-89, Birmingham 1989-; chm Greenwich Round Table; memb Birmingham Magistrates Cts Ctee 1990; memb: Br Acad of Forensic Sciences 1970, Lego Medico Soc 1970, London Criminal Cts Slrs Assoc 1969; *Recreations* butterfly and bird watching, attending auctions, entertaining at home; *Style—* Bruce Morgan, Esq; Birmingham Magistrates' Court, Victoria Law Courts, Corporation Street, Birmingham, West Midlands B6 (☎ 021 235 4704)

MORGAN, Ven Chandos Clifford Hastings Mansel; CB (1974); s of Arden Henry William Llewelyn Morgan (d 1940), of Anglesey, and Elinor Clifford, *née* Hughes (d 1948); direct descendants of the Morgans of Biddlesden Park, Bucks, and Hughes of Kinmel Hall, nr St Asaph, N Wales; *b* 12 Aug 1920; *Educ* Stowe, Jesus Coll Cambridge (MA); *m* 1946, Dorothy Mary, da of John Latham Oliver (d 1963), of Fordcombe, Tunbridge Wells; 1 s (Arden); *Career* clerk in Holy Orders, ordained Holy Trinity Tunbridge Wells 1944; chaplain RN 1951-75, chaplain of the fleet and archdeacon of RN 1972-75; chaplain Dean Close Sch Cheltenham 1976-83, rector St Margarets Lothbury 1983-89, chaplain to the Lord Mayor of London 1988-89; *Recreations* riding, gardening; *Clubs* National; *Style—* The Ven Chandos Morgan, CB; Westwood Farmhouse, Lydford-on-Fosse, Somerton, Somerset (☎ 096 324 301)

MORGAN, Christopher; s of Geoffrey Morgan, of Ashtead, Surrey, and Bertha Florence, *née* Jaffe (d 1948); *b* 6 Oct 1937; *Educ* Oundle, St John's Coll Cambridge (MA), Heidelberg Univ; *m* 18 Sept 1971, Pamela Rosamund, da of John Kellock Laurence, of Ham Common, Richmond, Surrey; 1 s (James Edward b 1977), 2 da (Juliette Rachel b 1973, Claudia Lucy b 1974); *Career* articled Deloitte Haskins & Sells: articled 1959, ptnr 1973-; ACA 1962, FCA 1972; *Books* A Brief Guide to the Sandilands Report (1975), The Securities Association's Capital Adequacy Requirements (1988), Auditing Investment Businesses (1989); *Recreations* music, mountain walking, astronomy, tropical marine fish and corals; *Clubs* Riverside; *Style—* Christopher Morgan, Esq; Barnes, London SW13; Coopers & Lybrand Deloitte, PO Box 207, 128 Queen Victoria St, London EC4P 4JX

MORGAN, Prof Colyn Grey; s of Edwin John Morgan (d 1972), and Margaret, *née* Williams (d 1963); *b* 29 March 1925; *Educ* Amman Valley GS, Univ Coll Swansea (BSc, MSc, PhD); *m* Menna, da of David Hopkin (d 1959); 1 s (Timothy Grey b 1960); *Career* princ scientific offr UKAEA 1957-60, conslt CERN 1965-70, head of physics dept Univ of Wales Swansea 1987 (prof of physics 1971); govr of HOST (Br Cncl, FCO, Victoria League); memb various Br Cncl Ctees and Sci and Engrg Res Cncl Ctees; CEng, CPhys, FIEE, FInstP; *Books* Fundamentals of Electric Discharges in Gases (1965); *Recreations* yachting; *Clubs* Royal Over-Seas League; *Style—* Prof Colyn Grey Morgan; 6 Westport Ave, Ridgewood Park, Swansea SA35 5EA (☎ 0792 403033); Department of Physics, University of Wales - Swansea, Singleton Park, Swansea SA2 8PP (☎ 0792 295372, fax 0792 295324, telex 48358 ULSWAN G)

MORGAN, David George; RD; s of Frederick David Morgan (d 1981), and Betty Suzanne, *née* Henderson; *b* 21 Sept 1946; *Educ* Forres Acad, Univ of St Andrews (BSc); *m* 1, 17 May 1969, Helen, *née* Campell; 1 s (Hamish Robert David b 1 Feb 1971), 1 da (Fiona Helen Ruby b 22 Oct 1974); m 2, 21 July 1989, Ruth Mary Morgan, JP, da of John Culpan, of Harrogate; *Career* Lt Cdr RNR 1975-89; Cooperative Insurance Society 1968-71, Royal Liver Friendly Society 1974-78, asst gen mangr Ideal Insurance Company Ltd 1978-84, pensions mangr AE Pensions 1984-85, pensions mangr Rowntree Pensions 1985-; pres Birmingham Actuarial Soc 1982-83, treas Yorkshire Rural Community Cncl 1988-, memb Cncl Nat Assoc of Pension Funds 1990-, chm Yorkshire Gp Nat Assoc of Pension Funds 1991-, FIA 1970; *Recreations* reading, walking; *Style—* David Morgan, Esq, RD; Chantlers, Linton Lane, Linton, Wetherby, West Yorkshire LS22 4HL (☎ 0937 586019); Rowntree Pensions, York YO1 1XY (☎ 0904 653 071, fax 0904 612 477)

MORGAN, David Gethin; s of Edgar Morgan (d 1979), of Pontlliw, Swansea, and Ethel Morgan Jones (d 1984); *b* 30 June 1929; *Educ* Cheltenham GS, Jesus Coll Oxford (MA); *m* 13 Aug 1955, Marion, *née* Brook; *Career* Royal Hampshire Regt Army Educational Corps Sgt Instructor 1947-49; graduate accountant Staffordshire Co Cncl 1952-58, mgmnt servs offr Cheshire Co Cncl 1958-62, co mgmnt servs offr Durham Co Cncl 1962-65, dep co treas Leicestershire Co Cncl 1968-73 (asst co treas 1965-68), co treasurer Avon Co Cncl 1973-; vice chm Local Govt Ctee of Chartered Inst of Public Finance and Accountancy 1986-; hon treas Soc of Co Treasurers in England and Wales 1990; Freeman City of London 1989; FInstAM, CIPFA, AMBIM; *Recreations* tai chi, local history, architecture; *Clubs* Victory Services; *Style—* David Morgan, Esq; Avon House, Haymarket, Bristol BS99 7RT (☎ 0272 293050)

MORGAN, David Graham; s of Edward Aneurin Morgan (d 1985), and Ceridwen Isabel, *née* Davies; *b* 18 May 1943; *Educ* Sexey's Sch Bruton Somerset, Univ of Wales (BSc); *m* 1 Jan 1966, Gloria Patricia, da of John Simon Cartlidge, of Swansea; 1 s (Stephen James b 1972), 1 da (Anna Louise b 1976); *Career* planning asst Kent CC 1966-69, sr planner Glamorgan CC 1969-71, princ planner Cardiff City Cncl 1971-73, dir W S Atkins Conslts 1984- (princ planner 1973-79, assoc planner 1979-84); memb Land Use Panel CBI, treas Assoc of Conslt Planners, memb Royal Town Planning Inst; MRTPI 1970; *Recreations* athletics, tennis, gardening; *Style—* David Morgan, Esq; Glendale, Deepdene Park Rd, Dorking, Surrey RM5 4AW (☎ 0306 883105); W S Atkins Planning Consultants, Woodcote Grove, Ashley Rd, Epsom, Surrey KT18 5BW (☎ 0372 726140, fax 0372 743006, telex 266701)

MORGAN, David Llewellyn; s of David Bernard Morgan, JP (d 1955), of Cardiff, and Eleanor Mary, *née* Walker; *b* 5 Oct 1932; *Educ* Charterhouse, Trinity Coll Cambridge (MA); *Career* admitted slr 1959; asst slr: Richards Butler 1959-63 (ptnr 1965-), Herbert Smith 1963-65; non-exec dir Deymel Investmts Ltd 1966- (chm 1977-); Liveryman: Worshipful Co of Clockmakers 1963, City of London Slrs Co; memb: Law Soc 1959, City of London Law Soc (Co Law Sub Ctee); *Recreations* DIY in house and garden; *Clubs* United Oxford and Cambridge Univs, Travellers', Cardiff and Co; *Style—* D Ll Morgan, Esq; Flat 15, 52 Pont St, London SW1X 0AE (☎ 071 589 3538); 15 St Botolph St, London EC3A 7EE (☎ 071 247 6555, fax 071 247 5091, telex 949494 RBLAW G)

MORGAN, David Reginald; s of late Reginald Morgan; *b* 28 Jan 1945; *Educ* Monkton Combe Sch; *m* 1968, Annabella, da of late Dr Thomas Owen Mason; 2 children; *Career* dir Avon Tin Printers Ltd 1974-83, md 1983-; Avon Tin Inc (USA) 1979-, chm ATP Management Ltd; hon tres Metal Packaging Mfrs Assoc of GB 1985 (cncl memb); Liveryman Tinplate alias Wire Workers Co; *Recreations* shooting, photography, reading; *Style—* David Morgan, Esq; Rock Cottage, Quarry Rd, Frenchay, Bristol (☎ 0272 566853)

MORGAN, David Rhys; s of Emrys John Morgan, of 11 Pinch Hill, Marhamchurch, Bude, Cornwall, and Effie Corinna Margaret, *née* Robinson; *b* 15 June 1949; *Educ* Bude GS, Bournemouth Tech Coll (HND), Watford Tech Coll (Dip in Advtg and Mktg); *Career* progress controller J Walter Thompson London 1971-72, account exec Ogilvy Benson & Mather 1973-76, mktg services mangr Interlink Advertising 1979 (account mangr 1976-78), account dir Geers Gross Advertising 1986 (account mangr 1980-86); (In The) Marketplace London Ltd: account dir 1987, Bd dir 1988, dir Marketplace Communications (subsid) 1990-; *Recreations* skiing, motor sport, squash, travel; *Style—* David Morgan, Esq; Marketplace Communications, 7 Holyrood St, London SE1 2EL (☎ 071 403 8993, fax 071 403 8996/7)

MORGAN, Prof David Rhys; s of Philip Haydn Percival Morgan (d 1974), and Annie Irene, *née* Rees (d 1981); *b* 22 May 1937; *Educ* Queen Elizabeth GS Carmarthen, Jesus Coll Oxford (MA), Emmanuel Coll Cambridge (PhD); *m* 27 July 1963, Sally Lewis, da of Colton Theodore Lewis (d 1984), of Binghamton, NY, USA; 2 s (Christopher b 18 July 1968, Timothy b 18 Sept 1970), 1 da (Siân b 28 June 1973); *Career* Nat Serv RAF 1955-57; Univ of Liverpool: lectr 1965, sr lectr 1973, reader 1987, prof 1989; visiting prof: State Univ of NY Albany USA 1974-75, George Washington Univ Washington DC 1981-82, Rhodes Coll Memphis Tennessee USA 1986; guest scholar Brookings Inst Washington DC 1978 and 1979; memb: Cncl of American Political Sci Assoc 1986-88, Exec Ctee Political Studies Assoc UK 1988-; FRHistSoc 1981; *Books* Suffragists and Democrats (1972), Suffragists and Liberals (1975), City Politics and the Press (with Harvey Cox, 1973), The Capitol Press Corps (1978), The Flacks of Washington (1986); *Recreations* walking, travel; *Style—* Prof David Morgan; The Dean, Faculty of Social and Environmental Studies, The University, PO Box 147, Liverpool L69 3BX (☎ 051 794 2426, fax 051 708 6502, telex 627095 UNILPI G)

MORGAN, Col David Richard; OBE (1971), TD (1963), DL (Merseyside 1976); s of Samuel Morgan (d 1966), and Elizabeth, *née* Roberts (d 1956); *b* 27 Aug 1921; *Educ* Neath, St Luke's Coll Univ of Exeter (Dip Physical Educn); *m* 1955, Sarah Gaynor, da of David Charles Roberts (d 1968), of Liverpool; 2 s (Huw, John), 1 da (Siân); *Career* served Palestine and Cyprus, Lt-Col, CO Univ of Liverpool OTC 1963-72, Hon Col Merseyside ACF; chm: ACF Sports & PA Ctee NW England 1983-90, Army Benevolent Fund Merseyside Appeal; schoolmaster (ret); memb: Cncl The King's Regt, Mil Educn Ctee Univ of Liverpool; High Sheriff of Merseyside 1989-90; *Recreations* rugger, music, tree husbandry; *Clubs* Waterloo, Artists; *Style—* Col David Morgan, OBE, TD, DL; 28 Hastings Rd, Birkdale, Southport, Merseyside PR3 2LW (☎ 0704 64298)

MORGAN, David Treharne; TD (1983); s of Maj Hugh Treharne Morgan, OBE, TD, of Alchornes, Lordswell Lane, Crowborough, Sussex, and Betty Gladys Boys, *née* Schreiber; *b* 21 Oct 1941; *Educ* Dragon Sch, Winchester, Innsbruck Univ; *m* 7 July 1973, Heather, da of William Thomson (d 1953), of Steilston House, Dumfries; 1 da (Claire b 2 Aug 1979); *Career* TA; joined HAC 1964, cmmnd 2 Lt 1975, transferred RCT 1977, Lt mvmnt control offr 1977, Capt 2 i/c 282 MC Sqdn 1979, Maj Cmdg 281 MC Sqdn 1984, Lt Col Liaison offr to MOD (Netherlands) 1988; admitted slr 1970, ptnr R A Roberts 1973-83, Wright Son & Pepper 1987-; chm: N Norfolk Railway plc 1973-, Tport Tst, Assoc of Railway Preservation Socs Ltd, The S Yorkshire Railway Ltd; dir: West Somerset Railway plc 1982-, The Assoc of Ind Railways Ltd, The Solent Steam Packet Ltd; treas Int Trauma Fndn; Freeman City of London 1982, Liveryman Worshipful Co of Glaziers; memb Law Soc 1970, FInstD; *Recreations* skiing, preserved railways; *Clubs* Norfolk; *Style—* David Morgan, Esq, TD; 7 Cheyne Place, London SW3 4HH (☎ 071 352 6077); Wright Son & Pepper, 9 Grays Inn Square, London WC1R 5JF (☎ 071 242 5473, fax 071 831 7454)

MORGAN, David William; s of Capt William Thomas Morgan, of 11 The Cloisters, Parkway, Welwyn Garden City, and Amy Elizabeth, *née* Hurren; *b* 21 Oct 1943; *Educ* Enfield GS, St Catharine's Coll Cambridge (MA); *m* 14 July 1984, Janis Irene, da of Richard Tyler, of Stevenage, Herts; 2 s (Christopher William, James David), 1 step da (Tara Jane Lawrence); *Career* gp dir Hunting Gate Group Ltd 1971-88, Willmott Dixon Holdings Ltd 1989-, slr in private practice Morgans; govr Hitchin Girls Sch, dir Hitchin Town FC, vice chm N Herts Cons Assoc; memb Law Soc, RICS; *Recreations* tennis, travel, skiing, soccer; *Style—* David Morgan, Esq; Beech House, London Road, St Ippollitts, nr Hitchin, Herts (☎ 0462 454608)

MORGAN, Derek William Charles; s of Thomas Brinley Morgan (d 1978), of Neath, and Brenda Vanessa, *née* Megraw; *b* 28 Nov 1934; *Educ* Neath GS, Univ of Nottingham (BA); *m* 17 Aug 1963, Anne Yvette, da of Evan Morgan Davies (d 1977), of Bridgend; 2 da (Siân, Louise); *Career* Nat Serv RE 1956-58; mangr Littlewoods Ltd 1958-61, plant mangr Ilford Ltd 1961-67, dir PA Consltg Gp 1967-90; non-exec dir: Morganite Electrical Carbon Ltd 1982-, Corgi Toys Ltd 1987-89; High Sheriff of Mid Glamorgan 1988-89; Neath Devpt Partnership 1981-88, memb Welsh Health Common Servs Authy 1982-, govr Univ Coll Swansea 1982-, exec Second Mgmnt Ltd 1984-90; memb: Manpower Steering Gp 1986-, Mid Glamorgan Health Authy 1987-, Wales Regnl Cncl CBI 1987-, Birmingham Chamber of Indust and Commerce 1987-90; dir Business Action Team (Birmingham) Ltd 1988-90; chm Ogwr Partnership Tst 1988-, Artificial Limb and Appliance Serv Ctee for Wales 1988-, Mid Glamorgan Educn Business Partnership 1989-, Welsh Wildlife Appeal 1989-; pres Cardiff C of C and Industry 1990-91, chm St David's Hall Trust 1990-; Freeman City of London 1986, Liveryman Worshipful Co of Tin plate (wire) Workers 1986; FIMC 1976, FBIM 1979; *Recreations* walking, wine, reading, cricket; *Clubs* Cardiff and Co (Cardiff); *Style—* Derek Morgan, Esq; Erw Graig, Merthyr Mawr, Bridgend, Mid Glamorgan CF32 0NU

MORGAN, Domini Margaret; da of The Hon Alfred Clive Lawrence, CBE (d 1926), of Middleton House, Middleton Cheney, Banbury, Oxon, and Mildred Margaret Dew (d 1964); *b* 8 May 1925; *Educ* St Giles Sch Blandford; *m* 14 June 1979, Arnold Frank Morgan, s of Frank Augusts Morgan (d 1982); *Career* professional horsewoman, judge, breeder and coach; formerly translator and sec FO; show jumping winner Area Int Trials; dressage competitions: Pris St George's Rotterdam 1967, England and Int Grand Prix successes on San Fernando (11 place Olympics Mexico 1968), Dressage Horse of the Year 1969-73, winner Hamburg Dressage Derby 1971 (3 place 1970); breeder of nat champion showjumpers; awarded Churchill Fellowship for Dressage 1973; Br Dressage Ctee 1970-; memb, memb trg ctee 1970-, selector 1975, memb Young Rider Ctee 1981-, list 1 judge 1980 (candidate 1978), official int judge 1989; initiated Talent Spotting Scheme; coached winning W Aust Pony Club team 1981-88; *Recreations* skiing, travelling, European languages, clay modelling of horses and dogs, husband's farm; *Style—* Mrs Domini Morgan; Tedders, Filching, Jevington, Tolegate, E Sussex BN26 5QA (☎ 03212 4816)

MORGAN, Douglas; s of Douglas Morgan (d 1940), of Nottingham, and Margaret Gardner Morgan; *b* 5 June 1936; *Educ* High Pavement GS Nottingham; *m* 19 Aug 1960, Julia Morgan, da of Frederick Bywater (d 1975), of Llanelli; 2 s (Alistair Craig b 1963, Jonathan Shaun b 1965); *Career* Nat Serv RAF 1954-56; asst to treas W Suffolk CC 1967-70, asst then dep co treas Lindsey CC 1970-73, co treas Lancs CC 1985- (dep co treas 1973-85); hon treas: Lancs Playing Fields Assoc, NW Region Library Systems, NW Sound Archive; former pres and chm CIPFA regnl orgns, treas Lancs Ctee Royal Jubilee and Prince's Tsts, memb Exec Ctee Soc of County Treasurers; memb IPFA, FRSA; *publications* author of various articles for public finance and accountancy and other professional journals; *Recreations* golf and collecting golf courses, playing gypsy in motor caravan, listening to jazz; *Clubs* Fairhaven Golf; *Style*— Douglas Morgan, Esq; 8 Croyde Rd, St Annes-on-Sea, Lancashire FY8 1EX (☎ 0253 725808); County Treasurer, Lancashire County Council, County Hall, Preston, Lancashire PR1 0LD (☎ 0772 264701, fax 0772 264999)

MORGAN, Douglas Charles; s of Herbert Morgan (d 1918), and Elsie Morgan (d 1969); *b* 22 Sept 1918; *m* 11 May 1941, Jean Eileen, da of William Marjoram (d 1974); 2 s (Michael David Charles b 1949, Gerald Dennis b 1950); *Career* TA 1938, Br and Indian Army 1939-46; builders' merchant, memb Lloyds; memb Cncl: City of London Livery Club, United Wards Club of the City of London; memb: Guild of Freemen, Freeman of England, Lime St Coleman St Ward Clubs, Cncl Soc of St George; memb Ctee: Farringdon Ward Clubs, IOD City of London Branch; Liveryman: Worshipful Co of Builders' Merchants 1979, Worshipful Co of Loriners 1985; FInstBM 1969, FInstD 1973, FInstOR 1980; *Style*— Douglas Morgan, Esq; Alde Cottage, Baker St, Orsett, Essex (☎ 0375 891 498); Kentford, Leiston Rd, Aldeburgh, Suffolk; D C Morgan Co Ltd, 36 Lodge Lane, Grays, Essex (☎ 0375 373 815, fax 0375 390 280)

MORGAN, Lady; Ena Muriel; *née* Evans; late Edward Franklin Evans; *m* 1930, Sir Clifford Naunton Morgan (d 1986); *Style*— Lady Morgan; Rolfe's Farm, Inkpen, Berks

MORGAN, Fay (Mrs Roger Oates); da of Philip Hugh Morgan, of Goodwick, Dyfed, and Iris Friend, *née* John; *b* 18 Dec 1946; *Educ* Bishopswood Secdy Sch, Hornsey Coll of Art (DipAD), RCA (MDes); *m* 31 July 1976, Roger Kendrew Oates, *qv*, s of William Oates; 1 s (Daniel Morgan Oates b 25 Jan 1979); *Career* textile designer; set up own studio London 1970-75, dir Weavers Workshop Edinburgh 1973-75, pt/t lectr Goldsmith's Coll London 1975-79; Morgan Oates Partnership at the House in the Yard Ledbury 1975- 86; Morgan & Oates Ltd 1986-, designing for own label and clients incl: Ralph Lauren, Christian Dior, Sonia Rykiel, Donna Karan, Laura Asley; sr ptnr Roger Oates Design Associates partnership 1987-; work in exhibitions incl: The Craftsman's Art (V & A Museum) 1973, The House in the Yard Textiles from the Workshop of Fay Morgan and Roger Oates (Welsh Arts Cncl Cardiff and tour) 1978, Tufted Rugs (Environment London) 1980, Texstyles (Crafts Cncl London and Tour) 1984-85, Design Awards (Lloyds Building London) 1988; awarded: USA ROSCOE award 1984, British Design awards 1988, Duke of Edinburgh's Certificate for Services to Design; contibs to TV prodns; *Books* Clothes Without Patterns (1977); *Style*— Ms Fay Morgan; Roger Oates Design Associates, Church Lane, Ledbury, Herefordshire HR8 1DW (☎ and fax 0531 2718)

MORGAN, Fidelis; da of Peter N Horswill, of Colchester, and Fidelis, *née* Morgan; *b* 8 Aug 1952; *Educ* Farnborough Hill Convent, Upper Chine Sch, Univ of Birmingham (BA); *Career* actress and writer; *theatre roles* Clara Hibbert in The Vortex (Garrick and Glasgow Citizens), Angustias in The House of Bernarda Alba (Nottingham Playhouse), Arturo Ui in Arturo Ui (Liverpool Everyman), Ruth Fischer in Berlin Days/Hollywood Nights (The Place and tour); Glasgow Citizens Theatre: Queen Elizabeth in Mary Stuart, Ruth in Blithe Spirit, Anna in Anna Karenina, The Mother in The Mother, Kath in Entertaining Mr Sloane, Andree in A Waste of Time, Putana in 'Tis a Pity She's a Whore, Duchess of Berwick in Lady Windemere's Fan, Metella in French Knickers, Hippolyta in The Custom of the Country Lucrezia in the Impressario of Smyrna, Mrs Peachum in Threepenny Opera, Brigida in Country Life; *TV appearances* Jeeves and Wooster, Mr Majeika, The Bill, Lizzies Pictures; *books* The Females Wits (1981), A Woman of No Character (1986), Bluff Your Way in Theatre (1986), The Well Known Trouble-maker (1988), A Misogynist's Source Book (1989), The Female Tatler (1991); *plays* Pamela (with Giles Havergal, 1985), Hangover Square (1990); nominated Most Promising Playwright in Plays & Players 1986; *Recreations* music, stained glass, cooking, reading; *Clubs* Curry, Golden Nugget; *Style*— Ms Fidelis Morgan; c/o Ken McReddie, 91 Regent St, London W1R 7TB (☎ 071 439 1456)

MORGAN, Hon Mrs (Fionn Frances Bride); *née* O'Neill; da of 3 Baron O'Neill (d 1944); *b* 9 March 1936; *Educ* Heathfield, St Anne's Coll Oxford; *m* 26 July 1961 (m dis 1976), John Albert Leigh Morgan, CMG (now Sir John Morgan), *qv*; 1 s, 2 da; *Style*— The Hon Mrs Morgan; 182 Ebury St, London SW1W 8VP (☎ 071 730 1140)

MORGAN, Geoffrey Thomas; CB (1991); s of Thomas Evan Morgan (d 1979), of Wargrave, Berkshire, and Nora, *née* Flynn (d 1984); *b* 12 April 1931; *Educ* Roundhay Sch Leeds; *m* 2 Apr 1960, Heather Maureen, da of Capt William Henry Trick (d 1984), of Neath, Glamorgan; 2 da (Siân b 1964, Emma b 1967); *Career* Nat Serv RCS 1950-52; civil servant; Ministries of Supply and Aviation 1952-65, HM Treasy 1965-68 and 1981-83, CSD 1968-81, seconded to Arthur Guinness Son & Co 1970-72, Cabinet Office 1983- (under sec 1985), dir Public Appointments Unit 1985; advsr: World Bank (Washington) 1977-78, UN (NY) 1987-88, People's Republic of China (Beijing) 1988-, Republic of Hungary (Budapest) 1990-; chm Public Admin Ctee Western European Union 1990-; *Recreations* keeping lists of the Great and the Good; *Clubs* Civil Service; *Style*— Geoffrey Morgan, Esq, CB; Cabinet Office, Office of the Minister for the Civil Service (OMCS), Horseguards Rd, London SW1P 3AL (☎ 071 270 6220)

MORGAN, (William) Geraint Oliver; QC (1971); s of Morgan Morgan (d 1950), of Woad Farm, Newport Pagnell, Bucks, and Elizabeth, *née* Oliver (d 1980); *b* 2 Nov 1920; *Educ* Aberystwyth, Cambridge (BA), London Univ (LLB); *m* 7 Sept 1957, Jill Sheila McGlashan, da of John Archibald Maxwell (d 1952), of 8 Westcliffe Rd, Southport, Merseyside; 2 s (Owen b 11 June 1964, Llewelyn b 25 June 1968), 2 da (Frances (Mrs Parry) b 2 July 1959, Bronwen (Mrs Campbell) b 8 Nov 1962); *Career* WWII RM, demob with hon rank of Maj 1946; called to the Bar Gray's Inn 1947, rec Crown Ct 1972, memb Payne Ctee on Recovery of Judgement Debts 1965-59; Parly cand (Cons) Merioneth 1951 and Huyton 1955; MP (Cons) Denbigh: 1959, 1964, 1966, 1974, 1979; resigned Cons Pty 1983 and now generally supports Welsh Nat Pty (Plaid Cymru), chm Welsh Parly Pty 1966-67; memb: Investiture Ctee of HRH The Prince of Wales 1968-69, Gorsedd of Royal Nat Eisteddfod of Wales 1969; formerly FCIArb; *Recreations* reading; *Style*— Geraint Morgan, Esq, QC; 13 Owen Road, Prescot, Merseyside L35 0PJ (☎ 051 426 4133)

MORGAN, (John) Gwynfryn; s of Arthur Glyndwr Morgan (d 1964), Mary, *née* Walters (d 1963); *b* 16 Feb 1934; *Educ* Aberdare GS, UCW Aberystwyth (BA, MA, Dip Ed); *m* 1, 27 Aug 1960 (m dis 1975), (Joan) Margaret, *née* Taylor; 1 da (Sian b 2 Jan 1964); m 2, 6 April 1979 (m dis 1989) Colette Ann, *née* Rumball; 2 s (Gregory b 24 Dec 1974, Eliot b 22 Sept 1979), 1 da (Joanna b 23 Aug 1977); m 3, 9 Feb 1990, Margery Sue, *née* Greenfeld; *Career* pres NUS 1960-62, sec gen Int Student Conferences 1962-65, dep gen sec Br Lab Pry 1968-72 (int sec 1965-68), chef de cabinet Rt Hon George Thomson EC Cmmn 1973-75, head EC office Wales 1975-79, head press and info EC degn Canada 1979-83, head EC representation Turkey 1983-87, head EC degn Israel 1987-; author of numerous articles in political jls; assoc prof Univ of Guelph Canada, vice pres London Welsh Rugby Club, fell Royal Cwlth Soc; commandeur d'honneur Chaine des Rotisseurs; *Recreations* rugby, cricket, crosswords, wine tasting; *Clubs* Reform, Cardiff and Co, MCC; *Style*— Gwynfryn Morgan, Esq; 79 Hazorea St, Kfar Shmaryahu, 46910 Tel Aviv, Israel (☎ 010 972 3 52583995); EC Delegation, The Tower, 3 Daniel Frisch St, 64731 Tel Aviv, Israel (☎ 010 972 3 264166)

MORGAN, Howard James; s of Thomas James Morgan, of Sutton Coldfield, and Olive Victoria, *née* Oldnall; *b* 21 April 1949; *Educ* Fairfax HS Sutton Coldfield, Univ of Newcastle Upon Tyne (MA); *m* 27 Aug 1977, Susan Ann, da of Alexander Sandilands; 1 s (Alexander James b 26 May 1985), 1 da (Romilly Grace Victoria b 27 March 1989); *Career* artist; numerous royal and private cmmns incl for: HM The Queen, HM The Queen of the Netherlands (Unilever Tricentennial celebrations), HRH Prince Michael of Kent (for Mark Masons), TRH The Prince and Princess of Hanover; permanent display of work Nat Portrait Gallery; exhibitions incl: Anthony Mould 1983, Richmond Gallery 1986-87, 1988, 1989, 1990 (incl: 'Difficult Red', 'Le Soirée du Comte Frédérique de la Chasseur', 'Dinner Party- Tiananmen Square', 'Exhibition'), Cadogan Contemporary Watercolours 1988, 1989, 1990, 1991, Claridges 1989; memb RSPP 1986; *Recreations* riding, 1938 Citroën, books; *Clubs* Chelsea Arts; *Style*— Howard Morgan, Esq; 12 Rectory Grove, Clapham Old Town, London SW4 (☎ 071 720 7460); studio 401, 1-2 Wandsworth Rd, Battersea, London SW8 (☎ 017 720 1181)

MORGAN, Hugh Marsden; s of Hugh Thomas Morgan (d 1986), of Cycnoed, Cardiff, and Irene, *née* Rees (d 1969); *b* 17 March 1940; *Educ* Cardiff HS, Magdalen Coll Oxford (open scholar, BCL, MA); *m* 18 March 1967, Amanda Jane, da of John Hubert Morton Tapley (d 1987), of Temple Cloud, Bath, Somerset; 2 s (Richard b 1972, Charles b 1978), 1 da (Zoë b 1975); *Career* called to the Bar Grays Inn 1964; in practice on SE Circuit, rec Crown Court 1987-; memb Lord Chllr's Matrimonial Causes Rule Ctee 1989-; memb: Fees and Legal Aid Ctee Senate and Bar Cncl 1976-82, Ctee of Family Law Bar Assoc 1976-89, Wine Ctee SE Circuit 1986-88; *Recreations* gardening, reading, listening to people; *Style*— Hugh Morgan, Esq; 1 King's Bench Walk, Temple, London EC4 (☎ 071 583 6266, fax 071 583 2068)

MORGAN, James Rees; s of Dr Richard Glyn Morgan MC, (d 1972), of Newport Gwent, and Nancy, *née* Griffiths (d 1984); *b* 14 Aug 1936; *Educ* Mill Hill Sch, Magdalene Coll Cambridge (MA), Univ of Birmingham (MSc); *m* 5 Nov 1960, Jane, da of David Murray MacFarlane (d 1988), of Newport, Gwent; 1 s (Charles James Glyn b 1962), 1 da (Amelia Kate b 1963); *Career* Nat Serv RAF 1954-56, pilot 1955 (qualified 1956), PO Royal AAF, 614 Sqdn 1956; Massey Ferguson 1959-62, gp planning engr Automotive Products 1963-64, mgmnt conslt Arthur Young & Co 1964-66, operational res scientist Inst for Operational Res 1966-73; Arthur Young: mgmnt conslt 1973-90, dir 1978, ptnr 1981; fndr James Morgan Associates 1990; memb: Stratford upon Avon RDC 1969-74, Stratford DC 1973-76; business efficiency advsr to HM's Chief Inspr of Constabulary 1990, chm Home Office Working Group on Partnership in Crime Prevention 1990; CENG, MIProdE 1967; *Recreations* gardening, skiing, watching rugby football, theatre; *Clubs* RAF (Birmingham); *Style*— James Morgan, Esq; Kineton, Warwicks (☎ 0926 640459)

MORGAN, Dr Janet P; da of Frank Morgan, and Sheila, *née* Sadler; *b* 5 Dec 1945; *Educ* Newbury Co Girls GS, St Hugh's Coll Oxford (MA), Nuffield Coll Oxford (DPhil), Univ of Sussex (MA), Kennedy Meml Scholar Harvard Univ; *Career* res fell Wolfson Coll Oxford and res offr Univ of Essex 1971-72, res fell Nuffield Coll Oxford 1972-74, lectr in politics Exeter Coll Oxford 1974-76, dir of Studies St Hugh's Coll Oxford 1975-76 and lectr in politics 1976-78; memb: CPRS Cabinet Office 1978-81, visiting fell All Souls Coll Oxford 1983; dir Satellite Television plc 1981-83, special advsr to DG BBC 1983-86, advsr to Bd Granada Group 1986-89, vice pres Videotext Indust Assoc 1985-; dir Hulton Deutsch Collection 1988-89; non-exec dir: Cable & Wireless plc 1988-, WH Smith Group plc 1989-, Midlands Electricity Ltd 1990-; tstee: American Sch in London 1985-88, Fairground Heritage Tst 1987-, Cyclotron Tst 1988-89; memb: Lord Chllr's Advsy Cncl on Public Records 1982-86, Editorial Bd Political Quarterly, Bd Br Cncl 1989-, Ancient Monuments Bd for Scotland 1990-; *Books* The House of Lords and the Labour Government 1964-70 (1975), Reinforcing Parliament (1976), The Diaries of a Cabinet Minister 1964-70 by Richard Crossman 3 Vols (ed, 1975, 1976, 1977), Backbench Diaries 1951-63 by Richard Crossman (ed, 1980), The Future of Broadcasting (ed with Richard Hoggart, 1982), Agatha Christie: A Biography (1984), Edwina Mountbatten: A Life of her Own (1991); *Recreations* music of Handel, sea-bathing, gardens; *Style*— Dr Janet Morgan; Cable & Wireless plc, Mercury House, Theobalds Rd, London WC1X 8RX (☎ 071 315 4000, fax 071 315 5000, telex 920000)

MORGAN, John (David) Howard; s of John Herbert Morgan, of Johannesburg, S Africa, and Enid Joan, *née* Coke-Smith (d 1979); *b* 4 Oct 1938; *Educ* Frensham Heights Sch, King's Coll Cambridge (MA), Roy Sch of Mines Imp Coll (MSc, DIC); *m* 24 Oct 1967, Barbara Mary, da of Alan Hanna (d 1947), of Durban S Africa; 3 s (Matthew b 1970, Oliver b 1973, Jasper b 1973); *Career* mech engr 1960-75, stockbroker/mining analyst; dir Shearson Lehman Hutton Securities 1988-; Freedom of the State of Montana USA (1987) MIMM 1977, CEng, Stock Exchange London 1978; *Recreations* tennis, gardening, skiing; *Clubs* Hurlingham; *Style*— David Morgan, Esq; 1 Campden Grove, London W8 4JG (☎ 071 937 2050); 1 Broadgate London EC2M 7HA (☎ 071 260 2716)

MORGAN, Sir John Albert Leigh; KCMG (1989, CMG 1982); s of John Edward Rowland Morgan and Ivy Ann Ashton; *b* 21 June 1929; *Educ* LSE (BSc), Univ of Korea (Hon DSc); *m* 1, 1961 (m dis 1975), Hon Fionn Frances Bride, *qv*, da of 3 Baron O'Neill (d 1944); 1 s, 2 da; m 2, 1976, Angela Mary Eleanor, da of Patrick Warre Rathbone; 1 s, 1 da; *Career* served Army 1947-49, cmmnd 1948; entered Foreign Service 1951, served in Moscow (twice), Peking and Rio de Janeiro, head Far Eastern Dept FCO 1970-72, head Cultural Relations Dept FCO 1972-80; ambass: Korea 1980-83, Poland 1983-86, Mexico 1986-89, (ret) hon fell LSE; Hon LLD Mexican Inst of Int Law, Hon DSc Univ of Korea; FRAS; *Clubs* Travellers'; *Style*— Sir John Morgan, KCMG; 41 High Street, London SW1V 1QV

MORGAN, John Christopher; s of Ieuan Gwyn Jones Morgan, of Winchester, and Gwen, *née* Littlechild; *b* 31 Dec 1955; *Educ* Peter Symonds Winchester, Univ of Reading (BSc); *m* 1 Sept 1984, Rosalind Jane, da of John Kendrew; 2 s (James b 1986, Charles b 1988); *Career* chm: Morgan Lovell plc 1977-, Overbury & Sons Ltd 1985-; ISVA; *Recreations* sailing, reading; *Clubs* RAC; *Style*— John Morgan, Esq; 52 Poland St, London W1 (☎ 071 434 4192)

MORGAN, (Ivor) John; s of Capt Alfred Morgan (d 1961), of London, and Dorothy, *née* Barnet; *b* 25 April 1931; *Educ* Taunton Sch Somerset; *m* 9 June 1956, Shirley, da of Henry Morison Bullen (d 1987), of Staindrop, Co Durham; 2 da (Penelope b 1957, Jane b 1960); *Career* Lt RA 1953-56; Higgs & Hill plc 1948-60; md: Builders Amalgamated Ltd 1960-66, Higgs & Hill Property Holdings 1966-74; pres dir gen Golf St Cyprien SA 1975-79, md British Urban Development 1989-, sr ptnr John Morgan Association 1979-; fndr memb Mary Rose Tst; vice chm govrs Wispers Sch Haslemere 1970-75, hon librarian to Fly Fishers' Club; Diplome de Prestige De Tourisme France 1977; Freeman City of London 1955, Liveryman Worshipful Co of Paviors 1974;

FCIOB, MCInstM; *Recreations* fly-fishing, sailing, vintage sports cars; *Clubs* Fly-Fishers' Piscatorial Soc, Royal Artillery Yacht, Vintage Sports Car; *Style*— John Morgan, Esq; George House, Petworth, Sussex (☎ 0798 42312); Le PetitMas, Golf St Cyprien, St Cyprien, France; 22 Queen Anne's Gate, London SW1

MORGAN, John Mansel; s of Jestyn Mansel Morgan, of Los Angeles, USA, and Sally (d 1979); *b* 18 May 1939; *Educ* Dynevor GS, Univ Coll Swansea, Univ of Wales (BSc); *m* 24 Aug 1963, Janice Dennis, da of Daniel Jones (d 1975); 2 da (Justine Fay b 19 Sept 1969, Julia Sian b 21 Nov 1971); *Career* Laporte Titanium Ltd 1961-65, Porvair Ltd 1965-71, Flotex Ltd 1971-76, Orr & Boss & Partners 1976-79, chm and chief exec Porvair plc 1979-; chm Roydon Parish cncl, dir Norfolk & Waveney trg and enterprise cncl: CEng, MIMChemE; *Recreations* cricket, skiing, golf; *Style*— John Morgan, Esq; Porvair plc, Estuary Rd, Kings Lynn (☎ 0553 761111)

MORGAN, John William Harold (Bill); s of John Henry Morgan (d 1973), and Florence Ada, *née* Dorricott (d 1989); *b* 13 Dec 1927; *Educ* Wednesbury Boys HS, Univ of Birmingham (BSc); *m* 1952, Barbara, da of Wilfred Harrison; 2 da (Elaine, Jane); *Career* Nat Serv Flying Offr RAF 1949-51; various sr mgmnt roles in English Electric Co 1951-69, md English Electric-AEI Machines Gp (following merger with GEC) 1969-73; asst md and mainboard dir: GEC plc 1973-83, Hill Samuel & Co 1983-89, Simon Engineering plc 1983-88; dep chm Petbow Holdings plc 1983-86; chm: AMEC plc 1984-88 (dir 1983), Staffs Cable Ltd 1989-, Trafford Park Development corporation 1990-; dir AMEC plc 1988-, Pitney Bowes plc 1989-, Tekdata Ltd 1989, UMIST Ventures Ltd 1989; Winner of Royal Soc SG Brown award and medal 1968 for outstanding contrib to the promotion and devpt of mechanical inventions; memb Cncl Fellowship of Engrg 1987-90; FEng, FIMechE, MIEE, FRSA; *Style*— J W H Morgan, Esq; Mullion, Whitmore Heath, Newcastle-under-Lyme, Staffs (☎ 0782 680462); Trafford Wharf Rd, Trafford Park, Manchester (☎ 0618 488000)

MORGAN, Keith John; s of Conway Frederick John Morgan (d 1940), and Winifred, *née* Allen; *b* 14 Dec 1929; *Educ* Manchester GS, Brasenose Coll Oxford (Brackenbury scholar, jr and sr Hulme scholar, BA, BSc, MA, DPhil); *m* 23 March 1957, Hilary Adeline, da of Irby Chapman; 1 da (Susan Jane b 18 March 1963); *Career* sr res fell Miny of Supply 1955-57, res fell ICI 1957-58, lectr Univ of Birmingham 1958-64, AEC fell Purdue Univ USA 1960-61; Dept of Chemistry Univ of Lancaster: lectr 1964-65, sr lectr 1965-68, prof 1968-86; sr pro-vice chllr Univ of Lancaster 1978-86 (pro-vice chllr 1973-78), vice chllr Univ of Newcastle NSW Australia 1987-; chm: ISCOL Ltd 1978-86, LANCORD Ltd 1978-86, Uldeco Ltd 1978-86; dir TUNRA Ltd 1987-; dep chm Hunter Technol Devpt Centre 1987-, dir Newcastle C of C 1988-, memb Hunter Econ Devpt Cncl 1989-; chm: Australian Inst of Management (NSW) 1989-, Inst for Industl Econs 1990-, AVCC Copyright Ctee 1990-; memb NSW Environmental Res Tst 1990-; Lancashire County Council: vice-chm Dist Liaison Ctee for Educn 1983-86 (memb 1977-86), memb Storey Inst Management Ctee 1982-86, memb Adult Educn Co-ordinating Ctee 1983-86; memb Cncl Lancashire Polytechnic 1985-87, chm Bentham GS 1982-86 (govr 1974-86); author of numerous contribs to learned jls; FRSC, FRACI, FAIM; *Recreations* cricket, mountains, Mozart; *Clubs* Royal Cwlth Soc, Newcastle NSW; *Style*— Keith Morgan, Esq; 48 Ridgeway Rd, New Lambton, NSW 2305, Australia; The University of Newcastle, NSW 2308, Australia

MORGAN, Kenneth; OBE (1978); s of Albert Edward Morgan (d 1975), of Downend, Bristol, and Lily Maud, *née* Stafford; *b* 3 Nov 1928; *Educ* Stockport GS; *m* 1950, Margaret Cynthia, da of Roland Ellis Wilson (d 1981), of Stockport; 3 da (Helen, Sarah, Jane); *Career* Lt RAOC 1946-49 (Egypt and Palestine); journalist: Stockport Express, Kemsley Newspapers 1944-, Exchange Telegraph Co 1956-62; Central London sec NUJ 1962-66; nat organiser NUJ 1966-70; gen sec NUJ 1970-77; memb exec ctee Nat Fedn of Professional Workers 1970-77; Press Cncl: consultative memb 1970-77, jt sec 1977-78, dep dir and conciliator 1978-79, dir 1980-; memb Jt Standing Ctee Nat Newspaper Indust 1976-77; Assoc Int Press Inst 1980; tstee Reuters 1984; dir: Journalists in Europe Ltd, Reuters Founders Share Co; FRSA; *Recreations* theatre, history, inland waterways; *Style*— Kenneth Morgan Esq, OBE; 151 Overhill Rd, Dulwich, London SE22 (☎ 081 693 6585); 1 Salisbury Square, London EC4 (☎ 071 353 1248)

MORGAN, Kenneth; s of Edward John Morgan (d 1981), of 19 Long Drive, East Acton, London, and Kate, *née* Reed; *b* 8 July 1946; *Educ* St Clement Danes GS; *m* 28 June 1969, Jean Margaret, da of Edward Albert Woods, of 36 Singleton Rd, Dagenham, Essex; 4 da (Sarah b and d 1972, Alexandra Jane b 1973, Joanna Louise b 1976, d 1978, Elizabeth Susan b 1979); *Career* CA 1968; sr ptnr Summers Morgan & Co 1977- (jr ptnr 1970); FCA; *Recreations* ldr of St Andrew's Church Chorleywood Youth Gp; *Style*— Kenneth Morgan, Esq; Old Berkeley, Homefield Rd, Chorleywood, Herts WD3 5QJ (☎ 0923 284459); Summers Morgan & Co, 1st Floor, Sheraton House, Lower Rd, Chorleywood, Herts WD3 5LH (☎ 0923 284212, telex 925753 SMCO G, fax 0923 284056)

MORGAN, Prof Kenneth Owen; s of David James Morgan (d 1978), of Aberystwyth, and Margaret, *née* Owen; *b* 16 May 1934; *Educ* Univ Coll Sch, Oriel Coll Oxford (BA, MA, DPhil, DLitt); *m* 4 Jan 1973, Jane, da of Gunther Keeler (d 1949), of W Germany; 1 s (David b 4 July 1974), 1 da (Katherine Louise b 22 Sept 1978); *Career* lectr history Univ Coll Swansea 1958-66 (sr lectr 1965-66), visiting fell American Cncl of Learned Socs Univ of Columbia NY 1962-63, fell and praelector modern history and politics The Queen's Coll Oxford 1966-89, lectr Univ of Oxford 1967-89, princ and pro vice chllr Univ Coll of Wales Aberystwyth 1989-; BBC political commentator, radio and tv 1964-79; ed Welsh History Review 1965-; memb: Bd Celtic Studies 1972-, Welsh Political Archive 1985-, Cncl Nat Library of Wales 1989-; trustee St Deiniol's Library; hon fell Univ Coll of Swansea 1985; FRHistS 1964, FBA 1983; *Books* contrib: David Lloyd George: Welsh Radical as World Statesman (2 edn 1964), Freedom or Sacrilege? (1966), Keir Hardie (1967), Lloyd George: Family Letters 1885-1936 (1973), Lloyd George (1974), Keir Hardie: Radical and Socialist (1975), Consensus and Disunity: the Lloyd George Coalition Government 1918-1922 (1979), Wales in British Politics 1868-1922 (3 edn, 1980), Portrait of a Progressive: the Political Career of Christopher, Viscount Addison (1980), Rebirth of a Nation: Wales 1880-1980 (1981), David Lloyd George 1863-1945 (1981), The Age of Lloyd George (3 edn, 1983), Welsh Society and Nationhood: Historical Essays (1984), The Oxford Illustrated History of Britain (1984), Labour People: Leaders and Lieutenants - Hardie to Kinnock (1987), The Oxford History of Britain (1988), The Red Dragon and the Red Flag: The Cases of James Griffiths and Aneurin Bevan (1989), The People's Peace: British History 1945-1989 (1990); official biographer Lord Callaghan of Cardiff; *Recreations* sport, music, travel (especially France and Italy), architecture; *Clubs* Athenaeum; *Style*— Prof Kenneth Morgan; Plas Penglais, Aberystwyth, Dyfed SY23 3DF (☎ 0970 623 583); Univ Coll of Wales, Old College, King Street, Aberystwyth, Dyfed SY23 2AX (☎ 0970 617 192, fax 0970 611 446)

MORGAN, Kenneth S; s of Edward Henry Morgan, and Florence May, *née* Wheeler; *b* 6 Aug 1925; *Educ* Battersea, Dartford GS; *m* 1 Nov 1952, Patricia Eva, da of Joseph Hunt, of Kingsway, Derby; 1 s (Richard b 1962), 1 da (Lindsay b 1956); *Career* ed Official Report (Hansard) House of Commons 1979-89; pres Cwlth Hansard Eds Assoc; *Books* The Falklands Campaign (digest of Parly debates); *Recreations* military history; *Style*— Kenneth S Morgan, Esq; 3 Highfield Rd, Bexleyheath, Kent (☎ 0322 525333); House of Commons (☎ 071 219 3388)

MORGAN, (Frank) Leslie; CBE (1988, MBE 1973); s of Edward Arthur Morgan (d 1959), of Llanfair-Caereinion, Powys, and Beatrice, *née* Jones (d 1930); *b* 7 Nov 1926; *Educ* Llanfair GS, Univ Coll of Wales (BA); *m* 16 June 1962, Victoria Stoker, da of Harold Jeffery (d 1972), of Wollaston, Worcs; 1 s (Christopher b 1969), 2 da (Amanda b 1964, Penelope b 1966); *Career* Capt RAOC 1945-48 (res 1950-59); chm: Morgan Bros (Mid Wales) Ltd 1959-, Mid Wales Devpt 1981-89; memb: Welsh Cncl 1970-79, Welsh Devpt Agency 1981-89, Welsh Tourist Bd 1982-89, Br Tourist Authy Devpt Ctee 1982-89; dir: Abbey Nat Bldg Soc 1981-90, Devpt Corp Wales 1981-83; chm and pres Montgomeryshire Cons Assoc 1964-81; pres: Montgomeryshire Agric Soc 1986, Montgomeryshire Cons Assoc 1989-; *Recreations* reading, travel, jogging, swimming, cycling; *Style*— Leslie Morgan, Esq, CBE; Wentworth House, Llangyniew, Welshpool, Powys, UK (☎ 0938 810462)

MORGAN, Marilynne Ann; da of J Emlyn Williams (d 1984), and Roma Elizabeth, *née* Ellis; *b* 22 June 1946; *Educ* Gads Hill Place Sch, Bedford Coll (BA); *m* 26 Sept 1970, Nicholas Alan Morgan, s of Rear Adm Sir Patrick Morgan, KCVO, CB, DSC (d 1989); *Career* called to the Bar Middle Temple 1972, princ asst slr Grade 3 DHSS 1985 (legal asst 1973, sr legal asst 1978, asst slr 1982), DSS 1988, contrib of articles to learned jls; chm Legal Section First Div Assoc 1984-86 (vice-chm 1983-84); memb Gen Cncl of the Bar 1986-; *Books* Halsbury's Laws of England (contrib, 4 edn); *Recreations* homely pursuits; *Clubs* Univ Women's; *Style*— Mrs Marilynne A Morgan; New Court, 48 Carey St, London WC2A 2LS

MORGAN, Michael Albert Joseph; *b* 22 April 1943; *Educ* Dyffryn GS, Univ Coll of Wales Aberystwyth (BSc); *m* 26 July 1969, Beryl, da of Henry Culpan (d 1972); 1 s (Owen b 1972), 1 da (Katie b 1975); *Career* conslt English Electric Leo Marconi Computers 1965, personnel dir Northern Dairies 1978 (personnel offr 1967), personnel dir Northern Foods; memb Hull DHA; MIPM; *Recreations* Hull Football Club; *Style*— Michael Morgan, Esq; Northern Foods plc, Beverley House, St Stephen's Square, Hull HU1 3XG (☎ 0482 25432, fax 0482 226136, telex 597149 NFOODS G)

MORGAN, His Hon Peter Trevor Hopkin; QC (1972); o s of Cyril Richard Morgan (d 1979), of 12 Windmill Close, Llantwit Major, Glamorgan, and Muriel Arceta, *née* Hole (d 1970); *b* 5 Feb 1919; *Educ* Bryntirion Bridgend Glamorgan, Mill Hill Sch London, Magdalen Coll Oxford (BA); *m* 1942, Josephine Mouncey, da of Ben Travers, CBE, AFC; 1 s (Andrew b 20 Oct 1942), 3 da (Caroline b 9 Nov 1946, Josephine b 25 March 1954, Rebecca b 16 Sept 1955); *Career* called to the Bar Middle Temple 1949 (in practice Wales and Chester Circuit); lectr in law Univ of Wales (Cardiff and Swansea) 1950-55, circuit judge 1972-87, dep judge 1987-; liaison judge to Gwent Magistrates and JP 1973-87, a judge of the Provincial Ct Church in Wales 1987-; Liveryman Worshipful Co of Fishmongers; *Recreations* reading, wine making, gardening; *Clubs* Garrick; *Style*— His Hon Peter Morgan, QC; 26 Westmead Lane, Chippenham, Wilts SN15 3HZ (☎ 0249 658633)

MORGAN, Richard Francis; s of David Francis Morgan, OBE (d 1961), of Latches, Oxshott, Surrey, and Helen Joyce, *née* Stallard (d 1971); *b* 29 Aug 1929; *Educ* Charterhouse, Kings Coll Cambrige (MA), Univ of London (LLB); *m* 3 Sept 1966, Sarah Pereerine, da of Cdr Edward Owen (d 1943), of Petersfield Hants; 2 s (Jonathan b 1967, Daniel b 1968); *Career* 2 Lt RASC 1948-50; fin dir: Central Wagon 1969-72, RHP Group plc 1972-81, Laporte plc 1981-84, BICC plc 1985-90; non-exec dir: Manweb plc, Scholes Group plc, fell Scottish CA's 1953-; *Recreations* mountaineering; *Style*— Richard Morgan, Esq; 11 Malbrook Rd, London SW15 (☎ 081 788 6251)

MORGAN, Richard Martin; s of His Hon Judge H Trevor Morgan, QC, DL (d 1976), of Swansea, W Glamorgan, and Leslie Martin, *née* Phillips (d 1982); *b* 25 June 1940; *Educ* Sherborne, Univ of Cambridge (MA, Dip, Ed), Univ of York; *m* 20 July 1968, Margaret Kathryn, step da of The Rt Rev Bishop Launcelot Fleming, KCVO (d 1990); 3 da (Pippa b 1969, Victoria b 1971, Rachel b 1975); *Career* housemaster Radley Coll 1969 (asst master 1963), headmaster Cheltenham Coll 1978-90, warden Radley Coll 1991-; *Recreations* watercolours, walking, rackets; *Clubs* Free Foresters, Jesters; *Style*— Richard Morgan, Esq; Radley College, Abingdon, Oxon OX14 2HR (☎ 0235 520294)

MORGAN, Robert; s of James Morgan, of 13 Windmill Close, Llantwit Major, S Glamorgan, and Edith, *née* Templeman; *b* 27 March 1967; *Educ* Llaniltud Fawr Comp Sch; *Career* international diver; clubs: Cardiff 1979-82, Highgate 1982-89 and 1990-, Barnet Copthal 1989-90; achievements incl: Amateur Swimming Assoc under 14 springboard champion 1980, Br highboard champion 1984-, Br springboard champion 1985, 1989, 1990, Gold medal Wales highboard Cwlth Games 1990 (Bronze 1986); also competed: Olympic Games 1984 and 1988, World Cup 1989, Goodwill Games 1990, World Championships 1991 (sixth place higboard); records: Br highboard 1989, Cwlth Games highboard 1990; *Recreations* sport, golf; *Style*— Robert Morgan, Esq; 13 Windmill Close, Llantwit Major, South Glamorgan CF6 9SW (☎ 0446 794203)

MORGAN, Robin Richard; s of Raymond Morgan, and Jean Edith, *née* Bennett; *b* 16 Sept 1953; *Educ* King Edward VI GS; *m* 31 July 1977, Ruth Winefride Mary; 2 s, 1 da; *Career* Evening Echo Hemel Hempstead 1976-78; Sunday Times 1979-89: reporter 1979-83, dep news ed 1983-85, ed Insight 1985-87, features ed 1987-89; ed Sunday Express 1989-; *Books* The Falklands War (co-author, 1982), Rainbow Warrior (co-author, 1986), Bullion (co-author, 1988), Manpower (ed, 1988), Ambush (co-author, 1989); *Recreations* riding, reading, travel; *Style*— Robin Morgan, Esq; Sunday Express, Ludgate House, 245 Blackfriars Rd, London SE1 9UX (☎ 071 922 7335, fax 071 620 1656, telex 21841)

MORGAN, Roger Hugh Vaughan Charles; CBE (1991); o s of Charles Langbridge Morgan, FRSL, membre de l'Institut de France (d 1958), and Hilda Campbell Vaughan, FRSL (d 1985); bro of Marchioness of Anglesey, DBE, *qv*; *b* 8 July 1926; *Educ* Phillips Acad Andover Mass, Eton, BNC Oxford (MA); *m* 1, 15 Sept 1951 (m dis 1965), (Catherine Lucie) Harriet, da of Gordon Waterfield, of Hythe Kent; 1 s (James b 1955), 1 da (Lucie b 1959), and 1 s decd (Piers b 1952); m 2, 26 Feb 1965, Susan, da of Hugo Vogel (d 1966), of Milwaukee, USA; 1 s (Tobias b 1968); *Career* Gren Guards 1944-47 (Capt); House of Commons Library 1951-63, House of Lords Library 1963- (librarian 1977-); FRSA; *Recreations* photography, painting; *Clubs* Garrick, Beefsteak; *Style*— Roger Morgan, Esq, CBE; 30 St Peter's Square, London W6 9UH; Cliff Cottage, Laugharne, Dyfed

MORGAN, Dr Thomas Clifford Naunton; s of Sir Clifford Naunton Morgan (d 1986), of Rolfe's Farm Inkpen, Berks, and Ena Muriel, *née* Evans; *b* 3 March 1948; *Educ* Harrow, Univ of London St Bartholomew's Hosp (MRCS, LRCP, MB BS); *m* 16 June 1974, Dr Rosemary Naunton Morgan, da of Maj Arthur William Hayward Broadstreet (d 1987), of Potters Green, Buxted, Sussex; 3 da (Nicole Anne b 3 Dec 1977, Katherine Lucy b 24 Aug 1981, Louise Polly b 8 Oct 1985); *Career* house surgn 1974; conslt radiologist: West Middlesex Univ Hosp 1988-, Royal Masonic Hosp 1988-; hon conslt radiologist Charing Cross Hosp 1988-; Liveryman Worshipful Co Barbers 1974, Freeman City of London 1974; memb: BMA, MDU; FRCS 1978, FRCR 1987; *Recreations* shooting, tennis, windsurfing; *Clubs* Roehampton; *Style*— Dr Thomas Naunton Morgan; 3 Campion Rd, Putney, London SW15 6NN (☎ 081 789 5211); West Middlesex Hosp, Isleworth TW7 6AF (☎ 081 867 5865/6/7); Royalmasonic Hosp, Ravenscourt Park W6 0TN (☎ 081 748 4611); Charing Cross Hosp, Fulham

Palace Rd W6 8RF (☎ 081 846 1234)

MORGAN, Vernon Alick; s of Lionel Haydn Morgan, of Dorchester, Dorset, and Anne, *née* Coombe; *b* 15 June 1960; *Educ* Dorchester Secdy Modern, Bournemouth Coll of Art, Salisbury Coll of Art (scholarship, professional qualifying exam); *m* 4 May 1985, Nicola Anne, da of Thomas Francis (Tom) Sutton; 1 s (Charlie Thomas Dorset b 24 May 1988), 1 da (Jessie Anne b 14 Aug 1985); *Career* pt/t apprentice G Woollat 1972-74, photographer 1979-80, photographer Roles & Parker Advertising 1979-80, studio mangr and photographer Charles Barker and Rapier Arts 1980-82, freelance work for Charles Barker 1982-83, proprietor Vernon Morgan Studios 1983- (studio specialises in photographing food for editorial and advtg clients), opened props and wardrobe hire business 1991; inclusion AFEAF awards 1986-87, Deloitte Bookseller award for best jacket 1988; memb Assoc of Photographers 1981-91 (treas 1983-85); *Recreations* travel in Europe especially France, eating, fine wines, ornothology; *Style—* Vernon Morgan, Esq; 6 Wyneham Rd, London SE24 9NT (☎ 071 326 0210); Vernon Morgan Studios, 16A Crane Grove, Highbury, London N7 8LE (☎ 071 601 5837, 071 607 5803, fax 071 607 0640)

MORGAN, Prof (David) Vernon; s of David Vernon Grenville Morgan (d 1941), and Isobel Lovinia, *née* Emanuell; *b* 13 July 1941; *Educ* Llanelli Boys GS, Univ of Wales Aberystwyth (BSc), Gonville and Caius Coll Cambridge (PhD), Univ of Leeds (DSc); *m* 31 July 1985, Jean, da of Francis Anderson (d 1979); 1 s (Dyfrig b 3 Sept 1973), 1 da (Suzanne b 22 Jan 1969); *Career* Cavendish Laboratory Cambridge: Univ of Wales fell 1966-68, Harwell fell 1968-70; Univ of Leeds: lectr 1970-77, sr lectr 1977-80, reader 1980-85; visiting prof Cornell Univ 1978-, prof of microelectronics Univ of Wales Cardiff 1985-; IEE: Divnl Bd on Electronics, Accreditation Ctee; MOD Electronic Materials and Devices Ctee; FIEE, FInstP, sr memb IEEE of USA; *Books* Introduction to Semiconductor Microtechnology (1983), Gallium Arsenide for Device and Integrated Circuits (1986); *Recreations* golf, hill walking; *Style—* Prof Vernon Morgan; Electrical Electronic Systems Engrg, PO Box 904, Bute Building, Univ of Wales, Cardiff, Wales (☎ 0222 874424, fax 0222 974192)

MORGAN, Prof Walter Thomas James; CBE (1959); s of Walter Morgan (d 1917), and Annie Morgan (d 1961); *b* 5 Oct 1900; *Educ* Raines Fndn, Univ of London (PhD, DSc), ETH Zurich Switzerland (Dr Sc tech); *Career* Beit Memorial Med res fell 1927-28, first asst and biochemist serum Dept Lister Inst 1928-37, Rockfeller res fell ETH Zurich 1936; Lister Inst: reader 1938-57, prof of biochemistry 1951-68 (now prof emeritus), dep dir 1952-68, dir 1972-75; memb Sci Advsy Cncl 1956; hon memb: Biochemical Soc 1968, Br and Int Soc of Blood Transfusion 1980, Int Endoloxin Soc 1988; Croonian Lecture Royal Society 1959; winner: Conway Evans prize 1964, Karl Landsteiner award USA 1967, Royal medal Royal Soc 1968, Paul Ehrlich prize Germany 1968, Philip Levine award in Clinical Pathology USA 1990; Hon MD Univ of Basle 1964, Hon DSc Univ of Michigan USA 1969; FRS 1949 (vice pres 1961-63), Hon FRCP 1982; *Clubs* Athenaeum; *Style—* Prof Walter Morgan, CBE, FRS; 57 Woodbury Drive, Sutton, Surrey SM2 5RA (☎ 081 642 2319)

MORGAN, Prof William Basil; s of William George Morgan (d 1962), and Eunice Mary Boston, *née* Heys; *b* 22 Jan 1927; *Educ* King Edward's Sch Birminhgam, Univ of Oxford (MA), Univ of Glasgow (PhD); *m* 24 July 1954, Joyce Alice, da of Mark Gardner (d 1981); 1 s (Richard William b 18 March 1961), 1 da (Joanna Edith b 14 Oct 1958); *Career* lectr in geography: Univ of Glasgow 1948-53, Ibadan Univ Nigeria 1953-59, Univ of Birmingham 1959-67; King's Coll London: lectr in geography 1967-71, prof 1971-, head of Dept of Geography 1982-87, emeritus prof 1987-; advsr UN Univ Tokyo 1977-84; FRGS 1948; *Publications* incl: Agriculture in the Third World (1978), 60 papers in sci jls, main res and recent pubns on rural devpt in Poland; *Style—* Prof William Morgan; Geography Department, King's College London, Strand, London WC2R 2LS (☎ 071 873 2622)

MORGAN-GILES, Rear Adm Sir Morgan Charles; DSO (1944), OBE (1943, MBE 1942), GM (1942), DL (Hants 1983); s of F C Morgan-Giles, OBE (Naval Architect, d 1964), of Teignmouth, Devon, and Ivy Carus-Wilson (d 1936); *b* 19 June 1914; *Educ* Clifton; *m* 1, 11 May 1946, Pamela (d 1966), da of Philip Bushell, of Sydney, Australia; 2 s (Philip b 1949, Rodney (m Sarah, da of Sir Hereward Wake, Bt, *qv*) b 1955), 4 da (Penelope (Mrs Cartwright) b 1947, Melita (m Victor Lampson, s of late Lord Killearn) b 1951, Camilla (m John, er s of Sir Eric Drake, CBE, DL, *qv*) b 1953 d 1988, Alexandra (m Maj Edward Bolitho) b 1958); *Career* Cadet RN 1932, China Station 1933-35, HMS Echo 1936, torpedo specialist 1938; WWII: Atlantic convoys, Norway, Med, West Desert and Tobruk Garrison 1941, attached RAF 1942, sr naval offr Vis (Dalmatia) and liaison with Commandos and Marshal Tito's Partisan Forces 1943-44, RN Staff Coll 1945, Force West Indies Bangkok and Far East, HMS Norfolk 1946; Trieste 1948-49, i/c HMS Chieftain 1950-51, Admty 1953-54, Capt Chief of Intelligence staff Far East 1953-54, Capt (D) Dartmouth Trg Sqdn 1957-58, Capt HMS Vernon 1959-60, i/c HMS Belfast Far East Station 1961-62, Rear Adm Pres RN Coll Greenwich 1962, ret 1964; vice chm Cons Def Ctee 1965-75, chm HMS Belfast Tst 1971-78, life vice pres RNLI 1989- (memb Mgmnt Ctee 1971-); MP (C) Winchester 1964-79; Prime Warden Worshipful Co of Shipwrights 1987-88 (Freeman 1965-); Partisan Star Yugoslavia 1953; kt 1985; *Recreations* sailing (yacht 'Melita'), country pursuits; *Clubs* Royal Yacht Sqdn; *Style—* Rear Adm Sir Morgan Morgan-Giles, DSO, OBE, GM, DL; Frenchmoor Farm, West Tytherley, Salisbury SP5 1NU (☎ 0794 41045)

MORGAN-GRENVILLE, Gerard Wyndham; s of Maj Hon Robert William Morgan-Grenville, qv, and Elizabeth Hope, *née* Bine Renshaw (d 1968); *b* 26 March 1931; *Educ* Eton; *m* 1, 27 April 1955 (m dis 1981), Virginia Anne, da of Major Peto, MP; 2 s (Hugo b 5 Aug 1958, George b 4 June 1964), 1 da (Laura b 1 Jan 1961); m 2, 1984 (m dis 1986), Fern, *née* Roberts; m 3, Margaret, *née* Doyle; *Career* Nat Serv Rifle Bde 1951-53, ADC to Gen Festing (Chief of Staff SHAPE) 1952-53; dir: Dexam Int Ltd (fndr), Dexam Int Hldgs Ltd, Industrial Agencies Ltd, Goodwood Metalcraft Ltd, Charterbarge Ltd, Charterbarge Sarl (France), Quarry Trading Co, Great Scottish and Western Railway Ltd; chm Soc for Environmental Improvement, vice pres Abercombie and Kent Inc, chm and fndr Nat Centre for Alternative Technol; cmmr Countryside Cmmn 1983-85, memb Countryside Cmmn for Wales 1983-84; *Books* Cruising the Sahara, Barging into France, Barging into Burgundy, Barging into Southern France, Nuclear Power - What it means to you; *Recreations* hill walking, exploring, sand-yachting; *Clubs* St James'; *Style—* Gerard Morgan-Grenville, Esq; Le Manoir De L'Eglise, Sully 14400 Bayeux, France (☎ 010 3331 2147 12, fax 010 333 121 5734)

MORGAN-GRENVILLE, John Richard Bine; s of The Hon Robert William Morgan-Grenville (d 1988), and Elizabeth Hope Bine, *née* Renshaw (d 1969); *b* 10 July 1927; *m* 7 July 1955, Joan Margaret, da of Air Chief Marshal Sir Wilfrid Freeman, Bt, GCB, DSO, MC; 1 s (Roger Temple b 18 Dec 1959), 1 da (Joanna Jane b 26 Sept 1957); *Career* Capt KRRC, TA; md Dexam Int Hldgs Ltd gp of cos; chm Exec Ctee King Edward VII Hosp Midhurst W Sussex, parish cnclir, DL W Sussex 1986, High Sheriff W Sussex 1989; FCA 1952; *Recreations* shooting, gardening, skiing; *Style—* John Morgan-Grenville, Esq; Upperton House, Upperton, nr Petworth, West Sussex (☎ 0798 42512); Dexam Int (Hldgs) Ltd, Linchmere Rd, Haslemere, Surrey (☎ 0428 4172, telex 858397, fax 0428 56378)

MORGAN-JONES, Digby; s of Stanley Alfred Morgan Jones (d 1984), of Beach Lodge, Lane End, Bembridge, IOW, and Eileen Mary Morgan-Jones (d 1973); *b* 14 April 1931; *Educ* Merchant Taylors'; *m* 27 June 1959, Jean, da of Charles Paterson (d 1969), of Hove, Sussex; 2 s (Kevin b 8 Nov 1961, Paul b 2 May 1967), 1 da (Fiona b 30 Dec 1964); *Career* Nat Serv RAF 1955-57; CA 1954-, FCA in Practice Crane & Ptnrs (ptnr 1962-); former pres Soc of Assoc of Executives; previously dir: Samuel Royston Devpts Ltd, Travel Ideas Ltd; dir: Clean Air Soc, The Fedn of Piling Specialists; chm Assoc of Industl Filter and Separator Manufactors; exec sec Nat Assoc of Title Distributers; sec Fedn of Drum Reconditioners; FCA; *Recreations* sport, youth work (Crusaders and Scouts); *Clubs* Canning; *Style—* Digby Morgan-Jones, Esq; Meadowsteep, Berry Lane, Chorleywood, Herts WD3 5EY (☎ 0923 28 2123); 20/21 Tooks Court, London EC4A 1LB (☎ 071 831 7581)

MORGAN-OWEN, John Gethin; CB (1984), MBE (1945), QC (1981); s of Maj-Gen Llewellyn Isaac Gethin Morgan-Owen, CB, CBE, DSO (d 1960), of Alton, Hants, and Ethel Berry, *née* Walford (d 1950); family descends from Sir John Owen, Royalist Sgt-Maj-Gen in N Wales during Civil War; *b* 22 Aug 1914; *Educ* Shrewsbury, Trinity Coll Oxford (BA); *m* 1950, Mary, da of Capt Frederick James Rimington, MBE, (d 1941); 2 s (Gethin, Huw), 1 da (Margaret); *Career* served WWII, 2 Lt Supplementary Res S Wales Borderers 1939, 2 Bn S Wales Borderers 1939-44, N Norway 1940, D Day landing 1944, DAA & QMG 146 Inf Bde 1944-45; called to the Bar Inner Temple, Wales and Chester Circuit, practised at Cardiff, dep judge advocate 1952, asst judge advocate gen 1966, dep judge advocate gen Germany 1970-72, vice judge advocate gen 1972-79, judge advocate gen of the Forces 1979-84, jt chm Disciplinary Appeals Ctee ICAEW 1985-87; *Recreations* beagling, inland waterways, travel; *Clubs* Army and Navy; *Style—* John Morgan-Owen, Esq, CB, MBE, QC; St Nicholas House, Kingsley Bordon, Hants GU35 9NW

MORGAN-OWEN, John Maddox; DL (Derby 1986); s of Lt-Col Morgan Maddox Morgan-Owen, DSO, TD, JP (d 1950), of Willington Hall, Derbys, and Doris Marjorie, *née* Turner (d 1957); *b* 26 June 1931; *Educ* Shrewsbury; *m* 4 Oct 1958, Elsa Courtenay (Jill), da of Cdr Ronald Arthur Orlando Bridgeman, RD, RNR (d 1962), of Rockliffe Hall, Flintshire; 1 s (Timothy Maddox b 1961); *Career* Derbyshire Yeo 1949-52, 24 Regt of Foot S Wales Borderers 1952-55; insurance conslt; gen cmmr of Income Tax 1972-, chm E Mids Museum Serv 1988-; memb: Derbyshire CC 1967- (dep ldr Cons Gp 1977-), S Derbyshire Dist Cncl 1973-79, COSIRA Derbyshire Ctee 1972-88; vice chm Derbyshire Historic Bldgs Tst 1984-; *Recreations* shooting, music; *Clubs* MCC; *Style—* John Morgan-Owen, Esq, DL; Pennfield House, Melbourne, Derby DE1 1EQ (☎ 0332 862774)

MORGAN-WITTS, Maxwell; s of George Frederick Vincent Lionel Morgan-Witts (d 1944); *b* 27 Sept 1931; *Educ* Mount Royal Coll Calgary, Acad of TV and Film Arts Toronto; *m* 1958, Pauline Ann Lynette, da of Alan Lawson (d 1982); 1 s, 1 da; *Career* CBC TV actor/presenter 1952; radio prodr/writer India, Ceylon, Aust and Canada 1953-55; Granada TV exec prodr 1956-64; BBC TV documentary film series exec ed 1964-72; author, independent prodr of films and corporate videos 1972-; chm: AZUR Productions Ltd, Max Morgan-Witts Productions Ltd; *Books* (written with a co-author) incl: The San Francisco Earthquake, Voyage of the Damned, The Day Guernica Died, Ruin From The Air, The Day The Bubble Burst, Pontiff, The Year of Armageddon; *Recreations* sailing, swimming, skiing, theatre, travel; *Clubs* Hurlingham Racquet; *Style—* Maxwell Morgan-Witts, Esq; 3 Place du Lac, Le Village, Les Hauts de Vaugrenier, 06270 Villeneuve-Loubet, France; 26 Woodsford Sq, London W14 8DP

MORGANS, Ronald Leslie; s of Oliver Leslie Morgans, of Maidstone, and Dorothy, *née* Dean; *b* 21 Nov 1942; *Educ* Samuel Pepys Sch; *m* 18 Sept 1967 (m dis 1988), Janet Lillian, da of Sydney Cutbill (d 1972); 2 da (Samantha b 11 Nov 1969, Catherine b 1 Nov 1972); *Career* journalist; Sunday Express 1959-63, Daily Herald and Sun 1963-67, picture ed Daily Express 1969-72, picture exec Daily Mail 1976-79, exec picture ed Sun 1980-82, assoc picture ed Daily Mirror 1982-85, launch picture ed Today 1985-89 (asst ed 1989-); dep chm Picture Eds Ctee Newspaper Proprietors Assoc; friend: Royal Acad, Fedn of Br Artists; *Books* Great Pictures of the Year (1969); *Recreations* clay shooting, collecting contemporary art and sculpture; *Clubs* Windsor Yacht; *Style—* Ronald Morgans, Esq; Today Newspaper, Allen House, 70 Vauxhall Bridge Rd, Pimlico, London SW1 (☎ 071 630 1300, fax 071 630 6839, car 0836 212868)

MORGENSTERN, Philip Louis; s of Maurice Joseph Morgenstern (d 1966), and Celia, *née* Hausmann; *b* 15 Jan 1932; *Educ* St Paul's, Univ of London (BA); *m* 1961, Estelle Pamela, da of Jakoba Erenberg; 2 s (Neil Hardy Iain b 31 March 1965, Matthew Joseph b 6 Jan 1968), 2 da (Ava Miriam b 18 Oct 1963, Deborah Sarah b 15 April 1972); *Career* Nicholson Graham & Jones: articled clerk 1954, ptnr 1962, sr ptnr 1981; sec GB-Sasakawa Foundation 1986; tstee: Inst Jewish Studies 1989, Jewish Law Publication Fund; Freeman City of London; memb: Law Soc, Worshipful Co of Slrs; *Recreations* hermeneutic and rhetorical exegesis of ancient texts, music, art history; *Style—* Philip Morgenstern, Esq; Nicholson Graham & Jones (Slrs), 25-31 Moorgate, London EC2R 6AR (☎ 071 628 9151, fax 071 638 3102)

MORIARTY, Gerald Evelyn; QC (1974); s of Lt Col Gerald Rwash Moriarty (d 1981), and Eileen, *née* Maloney (d 1978); *b* 23 Aug 1928; *Educ* Downside, St John's Coll Oxford (MA); *m* 17 June 1961, Judith Mary, da of Hon William Robert Atkin (d 1984); 4 s (Michael b 25 Aug 1962, Matthew b 12 Aug 1963, Thomas b 20 Jan 1966, John b 12 Jan 1973); *Career* called to the Bar Lincoln's Inn 1951, rec 1976, chm exam in public Bedfordshire Structure Plan 1978, bencher 1983, memb Gen Cncl of the Bar 1986-90; *Recreations* golf, reading; *Clubs* Reform; *Style—* Gerald Moriarty, Esq, QC; 3 Stone Buildings, Lincoln's Inn, London WC2A 3XL (☎ 071 430 2318); 2 Mitre Court Buildings, Temple, London EC4Y 7BX (☎ 071 583 1380)

MORIARTY, Michael John; CB (1988); s of Edward William Patrick Moriarty, OBE, and Mary Lilian, *née* Bostock (d 1987); *b* 3 July 1930; *Educ* Reading Sch, St John's Coll Oxford (Sir Thomas White scholar, MA); *m* 1960, Rachel Milward, da of John Thomspon; 1 s (Patrick b 1966), 2 da (Joanna b 1961, Clare b 1963); *Career* Home Office: asst princ 1954, private sec to Parly Under Secs of State 1957-59, princ 1959, Civil Serv Selection Bd 1962-63, Cabinet Office 1965-67, asst sec 1967, private sec to Home Sec 1968, asst under sec of state 1975-84, head Criminal Policy Dept 1975-79, seconded to NI office 1979-81, head Bdcasting Dept 1981-84, deputy under sec of state and princ estab offr 1984-90; chm Cncl of Euro Ctee on Crime Problems 1978-79 (UK rep 1976-79), memb Radio Authy 1991-; *Style—* Michael Moriarty, Esq, CB; 22 Westgate, Chichester, West Sussex PO19 3EU (☎ 0243 789985)

MORIARTY, Michael John Patrick; s of Alexander Hugo Moriarty; *b* 22 Nov 1942; *Educ* St Stephen's, Welling, Kent; *m* 1965, Pearl Joy; l s, 2 da; *Career* memb Stock Exchange 1977; dir: Shaw & Marvin Ltd 1978-80, Zootopia 1979-83; *Recreations* gardening; *Style—* Michael Moriarty Esq; Woodside, Foxendown Lane, Meopham, Kent (☎ 0474 812232)

MORIARTY, Richard Daniel; s of Gordon John Moriarty, of 30 Seventh Ave, Clase, Morriston, Swansea, and Margaret Lillian, *née* Richards; *b* 1 May 1957; *Educ* Bishop Vaughan Sch Morriston Swansea; *m* 5 Aug 1989, Claire Andrea, da of Stanley Evan Simcock; 1 s (Scott Richard b 9 July 1990); *Career* Rugby Union no8 and lock forward Swansea RFC and Wales (24 caps); Swansea RFC 1977- (over 400 appearances); Wales: debut v Aust 1981, capt South Seas tour 1986, capt World Cup team 1987, captained Wales 8 times; self employed dir; *Style*— Richard Moriarty, Esq; The Lodge, off Bryntawe Rd, Ynystawe, Swansea

MORICE, Prof Peter Beaumont; s of Charles Henry Morice, of 12 Abbotts Way, Southampton, and Mabel Stephanie, *née* Horspool (d 1978); *b* 15 May 1926; *Educ* Farnham GS, Univ of Bristol (BSc), Univ of London (PhD, DSc); *m* 1, 23 May 1952 (m dis 1986), Margaret, *née* Ransom; 1 s (Simon b 1953), 2 da (Verity (Mrs Laing) b 1955, Katherine (Mrs Daley) b 1961); m 2, 15 Oct 1986, Rita Corless, *née* Dunk; *Career* asst engr Surrey CC 1947-48, res engr and head of structures res Cement and Concrete Assoc 1948-57, prof of civil engrg Univ of Southampton 1958-, visiting prof Ecole Nationale des Ponts et Chaussées 1986-; memb: Engrg Cncl, Engrg Profs Conference, Soc for Nautical Res, Local Art Soc; FEng, FICE, FIStructE; Order of Sultan Qaboos Oman 1986; *Books* Prestressed Concrete (1956), Linear Structural Analysis; *Recreations* painting, pottery, sailing, gardening; *Clubs* Island Sailing; *Style*— Prof Peter Morice; 12 Abbotts Way, Highfield, Southampton SO2 1QT (☎ 0703 557641); 47 Sun Hill, Cowes, IOW; Le Bourg, Valliquerville, 76190 Yvetot, France; Department of Civil Engineering, The University, Southampton SO9 5NH (☎ 0703 592860, telex 47661 SOTONU G, fax 0703 593017)

MORISON, Hugh; s of Archibald Ian Morison, of 19 Old Rectory Gardens, Felpham, Sussex, and Enid Rose, *née* Mawer; *b* 22 Nov 1943; *Educ* Chichester HS for Boys, St Catherine's Coll Oxford (MA); *m* 1971, Marion, da of Fred Aubrey Smithers, of 84 Yarborough Crescent, Lincoln; 2 da (Emma b 1972, Lucy b 1975); *Career* Civil Serv SO 1966-: under sec Scottish Home and Health Dept 1984-88, Indust Dept for Scotland 1988-; *Recreations* hill walking, cycling, literature, archaeology; *Clubs* Royal Commonwealth Soc; *Style*— Hugh Morison, Esq; Industry Department for Scotland, Alhambra House, 45 Waterloo St, Glasgow G2 6AT (☎ 041 242 5466)

MORISON, John Lowson; s of John Miller Morison (d 1982), of Mavisbank, Guildtown, Perth, and Janet Muriel, *née* Jackson; *b* 6 May 1945; *Educ* Cargilfield, Edinburgh, Rugby, Univ of Edinburgh; *m* 22 May 1970, Gillian Anne, da of (John) Kirke Craig (d 1984), of Rock Cottage, Clachan Seil, by Oban, Argyll; 3 s ((John) Courtenay b 1971, Barclay Jackson b 1972, Barnaby Lowson b 1977), 1 da (Nicola Helen b 1976); *Career* farmer Australia and NZ 1965-67, former dist cncllr, dir Royal Highland and Agric Soc Scotland, memb exec bd Nat Sheep Assoc; *Recreations* shooting, skiing, tennis, sailing; *Clubs* Royal Perth Golfing Soc, Clyde Corinthian Sailing; *Style*— John Morison, Esq; Newmiln, Guildtown, Perth PH2 6AE (☎ 0738 51132)

MORISON, The Honourable Lord; (Alastair) Malcolm Morison; QC (1965); s of Sir Ronald Peter Morison, QC (d 1976), of Iden, Sussex, and Frances Isabelle, *née* Salvesen; *b* 12 Feb 1931; *Educ* Winchester, Edinburgh Univ (MA, LLB); *m* 1, 1957 (m dis 1975), Lindsay Oatts; 1 s (Simon), 1 da (Joanna); m 2, 2 Feb 1980, Birgitte, da of Axel Hendil, of Copenhagen, Denmark; *Career* senator Coll of Justice in Scotland 1985; *Recreations* fishing; *Clubs* New (Edinburgh); *Style*— The Honourable Lord Morison, QC; 6 Carlton Terr, Edinburgh (☎ 031 556 6766); Parliament House, Edinburgh

MORISON, Thomas Richard Atkin; QC (1979); s of late Harold Thomas Brash Morison, of Ensor Mews, London, and Hon Nancy Morison, *née* Atkin (d 1978); gs of Lord Atkin (Baron Atkin of Aberdovey) and Lord Morison; *b* 15 Jan 1939; *Educ* Winchester, Univ of Oxford; *m* 1963, Judith Rachel Walton, da of Rev R J W Morris, OBE, of Shaftesbury; 1 s (Ben b 1969), 1 da (Lucy b 1967); *Recreations* sailing; *Clubs* Oriental; *Style*— Thomas Morison, Esq, QC; Fountain Ct, Temple, London EC4 9DH (☎ 071 583 3335, telex 8813408 FONLEG G)

MORLAND, Brig Anthony Douglas; MBE (1974); s of Philip Maynard Morland (d 1967), of Borth, and Kathleen, *née* Douglas (d 1986); *b* 27 Jan 1935; *Educ* Allhallows, Staff Coll, NDC; *m* 30 June 1962, Jenefer, da of Lt-Col R A Sawers (d 1978), of Rustington; 2 s (Giles Philip Maxwell b 1964, Charles Peregrine b 1967), 1 da (Jane b 1963); *Career* cmmnd RA RMA Sandhurst 1953, Battery Cdr G Para Battery RHA 1972-75, CO 49 Field Regt 1977-80, dep Cdr Artillery Div 1980-83, dep nat rep SHAPE 1983-86, def and mil attaché Madrid 1986-89; chief exec Anthony Nolan Res Centre 1989; Economienda de Orden Civil Spain 1988; *Recreations* golf, gardening, antiques, St Bernard dogs, philately; *Style*— Brig Anthony Morland, MBE; Anthony Nolan Research Centre, Royal Free Hospital, Pond St, London NW3 2QG (☎ 071 431 5306, fax 071 431 5267)

MORLAND, Charles F H; s of Sir Oscar Morland, GBE, KCMG (d 1980), and Alice, *née* Lindley; *b* 4 Sept 1939; *Educ* Ampleforth, Kings Coll Cambridge (MA); *m* 19 Sept 1964, Victoria, da of Lt-Col R B Longe, of Suffolk; 2 s (Nicholas b 1967, Henry b 1969); *Career* md Riggs AP Bank Ltd; *Recreations* opera, travel; *Style*— Charles F H Morland, Esq; Marston Hill Farm, Greatworth, Banbury, Oxfordshire (☎ 029576 639)

MORLAND, Martin Robert; CMG (1985); s of Sir Oscar Morland, GBE, KCMG (d 1980), and Alice, da of Rt Hon Sir F O Lindley, GCMG, PC; *b* 23 Sept 1933; *m* 1964, Jennifer Avril Mary Hanbury-Tracy; 2 s, 1 da; *Career* Nat Serv Grenadier Gds 1954-56; HM Dip Serv: Br Embassy Rangoon 1957-60, News Dept FO 1961, UK Delgn Geneva 1965-67, private sec to Lord Chalfont 1967-68, Euro Integration Dept FCO 1965-73, cnsllr Rome 1973-77, seconded to Cabinet Off as head of EEC Referendum Unit 1975, head of Maritime Aviation and Enviroment Dept FCO 1977-79, cnsllr and head of Chancery Washington 1979-82, seconded to Hardcastle & Co Ltd 1982-84, under-sec Cabinet Off 1984-86, ambass to Burma 1986-; *Clubs* Garrick; *Style*— Martin R Morland, Esq, CMG; c/o FCO, London SW1

MORLAND, Miles Quintin; s of Cdr Henry Morland, RN, and Vivienne Yzabel Suzanne Nicholson Walters, *née* Hogg; *b* 18 Dec 1943; *Educ* Radley, Lincoln Coll Oxford; *m* 10 March 1972, Guislaine, da of Guy Vincent Chastenet de la Maisoneuve; 2 da (Catherine Natasha b 29 Aug 1973, Georgia Susanna b 18 Dec 1976); *Career* md The First Boston Corpn 1983-; *Recreations* foreign weekends; *Clubs* Travellers (Paris); *Style*— Miles Morland, Esq; 6 Hereford Sq, London SW7; United Kingdom House, 2A Great Titchfield St, London W1

MORLEY, Alastair Robert; s of Charles Geoffrey Morley, of Chigwell, Essex, and Elizabeth Jay Mackison; *b* 21 Nov 1950; *Educ* Felsted Sch, Pembroke Coll Oxford (MA); *m* 6 Aug 1977, Pamela Margaret, da of Ralph Lusty; 1 s (William b 8 Mar 1984), 2 da (Susannah b 23 Oct 1979, Emma b 21 May 1981); *Career* admitted slr 1977; ptnr Herbert Smith 1986 (joined 1975); memb Law Soc, memb Int Bar Assoc, ACIArb; *Style*— Alastair Morley, Esq; Herbert Smith, Watling House, 35 Cannon St, London EC4M 5SD (☎ 071 836 8000, telex 886633, fax 071 236 5733)

MORLEY, Dr Colin John; s of Cedric Morley, of Cambridge, and Hilda Catherine; *b* 19 April 1943; *Educ* Eltham Coll, Univ of Cambridge (MA, MB BChir, DCH); *m* Ruth, da of Henry Doling, of Cambridge; 2 s (Malcolm b 1970, Simon b 1972); *Career* hon conslt paediatrician Addenbrookes Hosp 1979-, lectr Univ of Cambridge 1979-; BPA, FRCP; *Style*— Dr Colin Morley; 23 High Street, Great Shelford, Cambridge CB2 5EH (☎ 0223 842985); Dept of Paediatrics, Addenbrookes Hospital, Cambridge CB2 2QQ (☎ 0223 336886)

MORLEY, David Howard; s of Glyn Morley, of Bromsgrove, Worcs, and Yvonne, *née* Auvache; *b* 21 Sept 1956; *Educ* Queens Park HS Chester, St Johns Coll Cambridge; *m* 4 Sept 1982, Susan Diana, da of Denis C Radcliffe, of Huxley, nr Chester, Cheshire; 2 s (William b 27 Jan 1987, Thomas b 13 April 1989), 1 da (Emma b 20 May 1985); *Career* admitted slr 1982, ptnr 1988; memb Law Soc; *Style*— David Morley, Esq; Allen & Overy, 9 Cheapside, London EC2V 6AD (☎ 071 248 9898, fax 071 236 2192, telex 8812801)

MORLEY, Elliot Anthony; s of Anthony Morley, of Ormskirk, and Margaret, *née* Walsh (d 1985); *b* 6 July 1952; *Educ* St Margaret's HS Liverpool, Hull Coll of Educn (CertEd, BEd); *m* 20 Oct 1975, Patricia Winnifrid Broderick, da of Chief Supt Matthew Hunt, QPM, of Yarm; 1 s (Jonathan b 1985), 1 da (Kathryn b 1981); *Career* teacher 1975-87, head of special needs Greatfield Senior HS, cncllr Hull City 1979-86, chm Hull City Tport Ctee 1981-85, opposition spokesman on food agric and rural affairs with responsibility for fisheries 1989-; vice pres Wildlife Link; memb Cncl: RSPB, Br Tst for Ornithology; *Recreations* ornithology, travel, conservation; *Clubs* Kinsley Labour; *Style*— Elliot Morley, Esq, MP; House of Commons, Westminster, London (☎ 0724 842000)

MORLEY, Eric Douglas; s of William Joseph Morley (d 1921), of London, and Bertha Louise, *née* Menzies (d 1929); *b* 26 Sept 1918; *Educ* St Martins in the Fields, Whitstable GS, Army Sch of Educn; *m* 13 Aug 1960, Julia Evelyn, da of William Pritchard; 4 s (Julian b 1958, Michael b 1961, Stephen b 1963, John b 1964), 1 da (Kathryn b 1968 d 1985); *Career* band boy Royal Fusiliers 1934, Sgt Inf 1939, cmmnd Lt 1943, later Capt RASC, demobilised 1946; Mecca Dancing: publicity sales mangr, dir 1951, asst md 1953, jt md 1959, md 1964; dir Grand Metropolitan Ltd 1969, chm Mecca Ltd 1971; presenter BBC TV's Come Dancing world's longest running TV series, introduced first Miss World competition 1951; resigned: Mecca Ltd 1979, Grand Metropolitan Ltd 1979; jt chm Belhaven Brewery 1979; chm: Miss World when floated on USM 1983, Trans World Communications; former pres Variety Clubs Int, pres Outward Bound Tst, Parly candidate Dulwich 1979, pres Dulwich Cons Assc, tstee KCH; Liveryman Worshipful Co of Marketors 1984 (Freeman 1980); French Dunkirk medal; *Books* Miss World Story (1967); *Recreations* music, the French horn, all sports incl marathon; *Clubs* MCC; *Style*— Eric Morley; 21 Golden Square, London W1R 3PA (☎ 071 734 9211, telex 27654, fax 071 439 1218)

MORLEY, John; s of William John Morley, of Beckenham, and Annie Daisy, *née* Miller; *b* 12 Sept 1942; *Educ* Ravensbourne Coll of Art, Royal Acad Schools; *m* 22 Dec 1972, Diana Rosemary Morley; 1 da (Tess b 12 June 1973); *Career* artist; one-man expos: Charleston Festival Sussex 1974, Royal Acad of Art London 1975, Festival Gallery Bath 1977, Piccadilly Gallery 1987 (1982, 1985); gp expos incl: Royal Acad Summer Expos 1962-89, Eggs Langton Gallery London 1977, Nat Arts Collections Fund Toubridge 1980, The Garden Expo Ellingham Mill Art Soc 1982, The Glory of the Garden Sotheby & Co in conjunction with Royal Horticultural Soc 1987, The Garden Show Gainsborough's Home Sudbury; the BBC TV film A Week in the Country 1982, The Long Perspective (Nat Tst Properties, cmmnd by Nat Tst's Fndn of Art) 1987, Artists in National Parks (V&A, Stafford Art Gallery, Berwick Borough Museum, Hexham Abbey, York City Art Gallery, Birmingham Museum and Art Gallery) 1988, Kings Lynn Festival Contemporary Paintings a Personal Choice by Brinsley Ford (Fermoy Gallery) 1988; awarded Herbert Baker scholarship by pres of RA 1985; *Books* illustrated: Nine Poems (Even Machin, 1987), The Secret Garden (1989), Great Tew (Simon Rae, 1989), Laelia Anceps (Orchid) The Plantsman Vol II (1989); *Recreations* gardening, music; *Style*— John Morley, Esq; North Green Only, Stoven, Beccles, Suffolk

MORLEY, John Austin; s of Austin Morley, of Hunters' Moon, Little Aston Park, Staffordshire, and Patricia Martha, *née* De Bray; *b* 13 Dec 1924; *Educ* Uppingham, St John's Coll Cambridge; *Career* cmmnd Coldstream Gds 1943 (3H Bn 1943-46); wrote and performed in two college revues, a pantomime and Cambridge Footlights Revue; Private View (Fortune Theatre) 1948, Music at Midnight (Her Majesty's) 1950, Fancy Free (Prince of Wales Theatre) 1951-53, Call Me Madam Tour 1953-54, Noel Coward's After the Ball (Globe Theatre) 1954, Jubilee Girl (Victoria Palace) 1956, The Crystal Heart (Saville Theatre) 1958, Marigold (Savoy Theatre) 1959, Follow that Girl (Vaudeville Theatre) 1960, Performer and writer under cabaret contract to the Café de Paris 1955-60, Puss in Boots (London Palladium) 1963, Houdini Man of Magic (Piccadilly Theatre) 1966, The Littlest Clown (Round House Theatre) 1972, Big Night Out (Thames TV series including Beatles Night Out, Blackpool Night Out, Boxing Night Out 1963-66); BBC TV pantomimes: Babes in the Wood 1972, The Basil Brush Pantomime 1980, Aladdin and the Forty Thieves 1983; Basil Brush Series 1979-81; theatre pantomime writer 1963-; *Books* The Magic of Houdini (1978), The Performing Arts (1980); *Recreations* riding, swimming, period architecture and furniture, travel, Wagnerian opera, history of pantomime, British folklore, The Industrial Revolution; *Style*— John Morley, Esq; 4 Stafford Terrace, London W8 7BH (☎ 071 937 5575)

MORLEY, John Harwood; s of George Frederick Morley (d 1990), and Doris, *née* Simpson Rushton (d 1987); *b* 5 Dec 1933; *Educ* Henry Mellish GS, Exeter Coll Oxford (MA); *m* 2 Jan 1960, Jacqueline, da of Kenneth Edward Morgan (d 1988); 3 da (Harriet b 2 Oct 1960, Emily b 12 Nov 1963, Alice b 24 May 1966); *Career* archivist Ipswich Corporation 1958-59, art asst Herbert Art Gallery Coventry 1959-61, keeper of art Leicester Museums 1961-65; dir: Bradford City Museums 1965-68, Royal Pavillion Arts Gallery & Museums Brighton 1968-85; keeper Dept of Furniture and Interior Design V & A museum 1985-89; sec and fndr memb Friends of the Royal Pavilion 1972-85, chm and fndr memb The Brighton Soc 1973-75, chm Decorative Arts Soc 1975-85 (pres 1986), patron The Thirties Soc 1985; memb Cncl: Nat Tst 1985-89, Attingham Summer Sch Tst 1983-88; tstee: The Edward James Fndn 1976-82, The Geffrye Museum 1990-; FMA 1967; *Books* Death, Heaven and the Victorians (1971), Designs and Drawings: The Making of the Royal Pavilion (1984); *Recreations* music, gardening, reading, museums & houses; *Style*— John Morley, Esq; 11 Vine Place, Brighton, East Sussex

MORLEY, 6 Earl of (UK 1815); Lt-Col John St Aubyn (Parker); JP (Plymouth 1972); Viscount Boringdon (UK 1815), Baron Boringdon (GB 1784); s of Hon John Holford Parker (d 1955); suc unc, 5 Earl, 1962; *b* 29 May 1923; *Educ* Eton; *m* 1955, Johanna Katherine, da of Sir John Molesworth-St Aubyn, 14 Bt, CBE; 1 s, 1 da; *Heir* s, Viscount Boringdon; *Career* 2 Lt KRRC 1942, transferred to Royal Fus 1947; served: NW Europe 1944-45, Palestine and Egypt 1945-48, Korea 1952-53, ME 1953-55 and 1956; Staff Coll Camberley 1957, cmd 1 Bn Royal Fus 1965-67, Lt-Col, ret 1970; pres: Plymouth Inc Chamber of Trade and Commerce 1970-, W Country Tourist Bd 1971-89, Fedn of C of C and Traders Assocs of Co of Cornwall 1972-79; chm Farm Indust Ltd Truro 1970-86; regnl dir Devon and Cornwall Regnl Bd Lloyds Bank 1971; dir: Lloyds Bank Ltd 1974-78, Lloyds Bank UK Management Ltd 1978-85; chm Plymouth Sound Ltd 1974-; govr: Seale-Hayne Agric Coll 1973, Plymouth Poly 1975-82 (chm 1977-82); memb Devon and Cornwall Regnl Ctee Nat Tst 1969-84; Devon: DL 1973, Vice Lord-Lt 1978-82, Lord-Lt 1982-; KStJ; pres: Cncl of Order of St John for Devon 1979, Devon Co FA 1979-87; Hon Col: Devon ACF 1978-87, 4 Bn Devonshire and Dorset Regt 1987-; *Style*— The Rt Hon the Earl of Morley, JP; Pound House, Buckland Monachorum, Yelverton, S Devon PL20 7LJ (☎ 0822 853162)

MORLEY, Michael Bates; Henry Gordon Morley (d 1979), and Violet Phyllis, *née* Sales; *b* 18 Nov 1935; *Educ* Eastbourne Coll; *m* 1957, Ingrid Hannah, *née* Hellmann; 1 s , 2 da; *Career* cmmnd RA 1954-56; Harris & Hunter Ltd 1960-67 (joined 1960, elected to the Bd 1961); Daniel J Edelman Inc: joined as ptnr 1967, opened German office 1969, pres Edelman International Corporation 1980-, responsible for relocating int headquarters in NY; *Style—* Michael Morley, Esq; Daniel J Edelman Inc, 1500 Broadway, 25th Floor, New York, NY 10036 USA (☎ 0101 212 704 8138, fax 0101 212 704 0176)

MORLEY, Michael Harlow Fenton; s of Very Rev Dean Fenton Morley, of Bath, and Marjorie Rosa, *née* Robinson; *b* 18 June 1940; *Educ* Radley, Univ of Cambridge (MA), Univ of Harvard (MBA); *m* 1963, Delia Elizabeth, da of Charles J Robertson, of Combe Hay Manor, Bath (d 1983); 1 s (Oliver b 1971), 2 da (Candida b 1965, Octavia b 1968); *Career* Samuel Montagu & Co 1968-72, chm London & Western Tst Ltd 1972-74, chief exec C Tennant Sons & Co Ltd 1974-81, md Charterhouse Gp plc 1981-84, chm Paragon Gp Ltd 1984-88, chief exec and dep chm Portals Holdings plc 1988-; Monteverdi Tst 1985-; non-exec dir: Close Brothers Gp plc 1985-, Globe Investment Trust plc 1989-; *Recreations* tennis, shooting, skiing, piano; *Clubs* Brooks's, Leander; *Style—* Michael Morley, Esq; The Manor House, Priston, Bath BA2 9EH; 12 Kensington Place, London W8 7PT

MORLEY, Dr (William) Neil; RD (1969, clasp 1979); s of Eric Morley, JP (d 1964), of 22 North Park Rd, Bradford, West Yorks, and Barbara, *née* Mitchell (d 1986); *b* 16 Feb 1930; *Educ* Merchiston Castle Sch Edinburgh, Univ of Edinburgh (MB ChB); *m* 13 March 1958, Patricia, da of Walter McDonald; 3 s (David b 1963, Alistair b 1964, Christopher b 1966), 1 da (Carolyn b 1961); *Career* Surgn Lt HMS Falcon 1955-57, served Malta, Surgn Lt Cdr RNR 1959-84; conslt dermatologist Gtr Glasgow Health Bd 1963-, civil conslt to RN in Scotland 1979-; memb Med Appeal Tbnl DHSS 1979; FRCP Edinburgh 1970, FRCP Glasgow 1977, memb Incorporation of Barbers of Glasgow 1987, FRSM; *Books* Colour Atlas of Paediatric Dermatology; *Recreations* golf, fishing; *Clubs* Glasgow GC; *Style—* Dr Neil Morley, RD; Parkhall, Balfron, Glasgow G63 OLQ (☎ 0360 40124)

MORLEY, Peter John; s of Edward Joseph Morley, and Edith Ella, *née* Westerside; *b* 9 Aug 1955; *Educ* Thorpe House, Hutton; *m* 29 June 1985, Amanda Julie Jane, da of Edward Ashton St John Salt; 1 s (Edward James Peter b 21 Nov 1988); *Career* account exec Eagle Alexander 1977-81, account dir Travel Press Serv 1981-83, dir SGL Communications plc Gp 1983-, md SGL Property Ltd 1983-; MIPR, PRCA; *Recreations* shooting, most sport, boys' trips; *Clubs* RAC, Annabels, Scribes; *Style—* Peter Morley, Esq; SGL, Kingsgate House, 536 Kings Rd, London SW10 0UH (☎ 071 351 2377)

MORLEY, Sheridan Robert; s of Robert Morley and Joan, *née* Buckmaster; *b* 5 Dec 1941; *Educ* Sizewell Hall Suffolk, Merton Coll Oxford (MA); *m* 1965, Margaret Gudejko; 1 s, 2 da; *Career* newscaster, reporter and scriptwriter ITN 1964-67, interviewer Late Night Line Up BBC 2 1967-71, presenter Film Night BBC 2 1972, dep features ed The Times 1973-75, drama critic and arts ed Punch 1975-89, London Drama Critic Int Herald Tribune 1979-; arts journalist of the year (BP Awards 1990); author of Noel and Gertie (Comedy Theatre London 1990); regular presenter: Kaleidoscope BBC Radio 4, Meridian BBC World Service, Radio 2 Arts Programme 1990-; frequent radio and tv broadcasts on the performing arts; memb Drama Panel Br Cncl 1982-, narrator: Side by Side by Sondheim 1981-82, Noël and Gertie (Coward anthology) 1983-86; *Books* A Talent to Amuse: the life of Noël Coward (1969), Review Copies (1975), Oscar Wilde (1976), Sybil Thorndike (1977), Marlene Dietrich (1977), Gladys Cooper (1979), Noël Coward and his Friends (1979), The Stephen Sondheim Songbook (1979), Gertrude Lawrence (1981), The Noël Coward Diaries (1982), Tales from the Hollywood Raj (1983), Shooting Stars (1983), The Theatregoers' Quiz Book (1983), Katherine Hepburn (1984), editor of theatre annuals and film and theatre studies including Punch at the Theatre (1980), The Other Side of The Moon (the biography of David Niven) and Spread A Little Happiness (1987), Elizabeth Taylor (1988), Out in the Midday Sun (1988), Odd Man Out: The Life of James Mason (1989), Our Theatres in the 80s (1990); contributions to The Times, Evening Standard, Radio Times, Mail on Sunday, Sunday Telegraph, Playbill (NY), High Life and The Australian; *Recreations* talking, swimming, eating, narrating *Side by Side by Sondheim* and *Noël and Gertie*; *Clubs* Garrick; *Style—* Sheridan Morley, Esq; 19 Carlyle Court, Chelsea Harbour, London SW10 0UQ

MORLEY-JOEL, Lionel; s of Samuel Joel (d 1970), of Finchley, and Hannah, *née* Parker (d 1979); great nephew of Solly Joel the colourful character who became a diamond magnate in S Africa; *b* 2 Jan 1922; *Educ* Finchley HS, business studies at an Acad in Brussels; *m* 1, 25 Feb 1943, Joyce Margaret, da of Frederick Charles Grierson (d 1961); 1 da (Wendy b 1947); m 2, 30 Aug 1986, Maria Christina, da of Charles Lett Lynch (d 1986), 1 step s (Gerald b 1964); *Career* fndr Newbourne Pubns Gp 1946 (md and chm 1946-84), md Classic Publications 1954-84, dir Recorder Press 1952-84, md City and Rural Properties 1985-87, dir Magnet Advertising, currently conslt in advertising and mktg to Newbourne Gp; *Recreations* golf, amateur radio, horology; *Style—* Lionel Morley-Joel, Esq; Whitespar, Queen Hoo Lane, Tewin, Herts AL6 0LT (☎ 043 879 201, business 0235 510344)

MORNINGTON, Earl of; Arthur Gerald Wellesley; s and h of Marquess of Douro, and HRH Princess Antonia von Preussen; gs of 8 Duke of Wellington; *b* 31 Jan 1978; *Style—* Earl of Mornington

MORO, Hon Mrs (Anne Margaret Theodosia); da of 5 Baron Huntingfield, KCMG (d 1969); *b* 1918; *m* 1940 (m dis 1984), Peter Moro; 3 da; *Style—* The Hon Mrs Moro

MORPETH, Sir Douglas Spottiswoode; TD; s of Robert Spottiswoode Morpeth (d 1979), and Louisa Rankine, *née* Dobson (d 1989); *b* 6 June 1924; *Educ* George Watson's Coll Edinburgh, Univ of Edinburgh (BCom); *m* 1951, Anne Rutherford, da of Ian Cardean Bell, OBE, MC (d 1966); 2 s, 2 da; *Career* Lt-Col cmdg 1 Regt HAC (RHA) 1964-66, former sr ptnr Touche Ross & Co, chm Clerical Med & Gen Life Assur Soc, first chm Tstees Br Telecom Staff Superannuation Scheme 1982-, dep chm Brixton Estate plc, chm Br Borneo Petroleum Syndicate, dir Allied Irish Bank, dep chm Leslie Langton Hldgs Ltd; vice-pres HAC 1986-88, Master Worshipful Co of CAs 1977, hon treas RCM 1984-; FCA, FRCM; kt 1981; *Recreations* golf, tennis, gardening; *Clubs* Athenaeum, RAC, City Livery; *Style—* Sir Douglas Morpeth, TD; Summerden House, Shamley Green, nr Guildford, Surrey GU5 0UD (☎ 0483 892689); Clerical Medical Investment Gp, 15 St James's Sq, London SW1Y 4LQ (☎ 071 930 5474, fax 071 321 1846)

MORPETH, Viscount; George William Beaumont Howard; Master of Ruthven; s and h of 12 Earl of Carlisle, MC; *b* 15 Feb 1949; *Educ* Eton, Balliol Coll Oxford; *Heir* Master of Ruthven; *Career* joined 9/12 Royal Lancers 1967, Lt 1970, Capt 1974, Maj (Prince of Wales, Royal Armoured Corps) 1981-87, Parly candidate (Lib) Easington Co Durham 1987; *Clubs* Beefsteak; *Style—* Maj Viscount Morpeth; 8 Mill Terrace, Easington Village, County Durham (☎ 0915 272946)

MORPETH, Iain Cardean Spottiswoode; s of Sir Douglas Spottiswoode Morpeth, TD, KT, of Summerden House, Shamley Green, Guildford, Surrey, and Anne Rutherford, *née* Bell; *b* 28 Dec 1953; *Educ* Fettes, Univ of Bristol (LLB); *m* 30 June 1979, Angela Susan, da of Sir Thomas Gordon Devitt, Bt, of 49 Lexden Rd, Colchester, Essex; 2 s (Richard Douglas Gordon b 18 Nov 1985, Duncan Hugh Sinclair b 1 Dec 1987), 1 da (Catherine Louise Nicholl b 10 Feb 1990); *Career* HAC TA 1976-, Maj 1990-; admitted slr 1978, ptnr Clifford Chance 1988; Freeman Worshipful Co of Slrs 1978; memb Law Soc; *Recreations* fishing, hill walking, TA; *Clubs* Honourable Artillery Company; *Style—* Iain Morpeth, Esq; 9 Polworth Road, London SW16 2ET (☎ 081 677 3280), Clifford Chance, Blackfriars House, 19 New Bridge Street, London EC4V 6BY (☎ 071 353 0211, fax 071 489 0046, telex 887847 LEGIS G)

MORPHET, David Ian; s of Albert Morphet (d 1960), and Sarah Elizabeth, *née* Marsden; *b* 24 Jan 1940; *Educ* St John's Coll, Cambridge; *m* 2 Marsh 1968, Sarah Gillian, da of Maj Michael Francis Sedgwick; 2 s (William b 1971, Matthew b 1973), 1 da (Jessica b 1970); *Career* HM Dip Serv 1961-74; asst private sec to Foreign Sec 1966-68, first sec Br Embassy Madrid 1969-72; Dept of Energy 1975-78; Midlands Electicity Bd: dep chm 1978-79, under sec Electricity Energy Policy and Atomic Energy Divs 1980-89; dir: BICC Cables Ltd 1981-89, planning and devpt Balfour Beatty Ltd 1989-; FRSA 1987; *Clubs* Athenaeum; *Style—* David Morphet, Esq; Balfour Beatty Ltd, Thornton Heath, Sussex CR4 7XA (☎ 081 683 6040)

MORPHET, Richard Edward; s of Horace Morphet (d 1987), and Eleanor, *née* Shaw; *b* 2 Oct 1938; *Educ* Bootham Sch York, LSE (BA); *m* 1965, Sally, *née* Richmond; 2 da (Selina b 1967, Thea b 1969); *Career* Fine Arts Dept British Council 1963-66; Tate Gallery: asst keeper 1966-73, dep keeper of the Modern Collection 1973-86 (keeper 1986-); author of various exhibition catalogues and magazine articles; *Style—* Richard Morphet; Tate Gallery, Millbank, London SW1P 4RG (☎ 071 821 1313, fax 071 931 7512)

MORPURGO, Jack Eric; s of Mark Morpurgo (d 1953), of Islington, London, and Nancy, *née* Cook (d 1934); *b* 26 April 1918; *Educ* Christ's Hosp, Univ of New Brunswick Canada, Coll of William and Mary in Virginia (BA), Univ of Durham, Univ of London; *m* 16 July 1947, Catherine Noel Kippe, da of Prof Emile Cammaerts, CBE (Ordre de Léopold, d 1955), of Radlett, Herts; 3 s (Pieter b 1941, Michael b 1943, Mark b 1948), 1 da (Katherine b 1953); *Career* RA: enlisted 1939, cmmnd 1940, served in India, Eritrea, Middle East, Greece and Italy, Capt 1942, Maj 1944, sr ops SO Allied Forces Piraeus 1944, Lt-Col 1945, GSO I PR WO 1945, demobilised 1946; Penguin Books Ltd: PR offr 1945-46, ed and hist advsr 1946-69; asst dir Nuffield Fndn 1951-54; Nat Book League: DG 1955-70, dep chm 1961-71, vice pres 1971-85; conslt to UNESCO; dir of Asian seminars or reading: Rangoon 1957, Madras 1959; prof: American Studies Univ of Geneva 1968-70, American Lit Univ of Leeds 1970-83; visiting professorships have included Rockefeller Res Center; dir: Sexton Agency & Press Ltd 1983-, P & M Youngman Carter Ltd 1984-; chm Nuffield Working Party on Medical and Nursing Libraries, govr Abbotsholme Sch 1953-56; Christ's Hosp: donations govr 1968, almoner 1972, dep chm 1984-85; chm Pestalozzi Village 1969-74, govr Br and Foreign Schs Soc 1970-75, reg broadcaster on radio and TV; hon fell: Coll of William and Mary, Australian Nat Univ; Hon DLitt Univ of Maine 1961, Hon LitD Almina 1965, Hon DHL Whilliam and Mary 1971, Hon DHum Idaho 1983; Phi Beta Kappa 1947; *Books* American Excursion (1949), Charles Lamb and Elia (1949), Poems of John Keats (ed, 1953), History of the United States (with Russel B Nye, 1955), The Road to Athens (1963), Venice (with Martin Hurlimann, 1964), Cooper The Spy (ed, 1968), Barnes Wallis (1972), Treason at West Point (1975), Their Majesties' Royal College (1976), Allen Lane: King Penguin (1979), Verses Humorous and Post-humorous (1981), Cobbett in America (ed, 1984), Christ's Hospital (with G A T Allan, 1984), Master of None: An Autobiography (1990); *Recreations* watching rugby football, listening to music; *Clubs* Army and Navy, Christ's Hospital Pilgrims; *Style—* Prof Jack Morpurgo; 12 Laurence Mews, Askew Road, London W12 9AT (☎ 081 740 0122); Sexton Agency and Press Ltd, 12 Laurence Mews, Askew Rd, London W12 9AT (☎ 081 743 5676)

MORPURGO DAVIES, Prof Anna Elbina Laura Margherita; da of Augusto Morpurgo (d 1939), and Maria, *née* Castelnuovo, of Rome; *b* 21 June 1937; *Educ* Liceo-Ginnasio Giulio Cesare Rome, Univ of Rome (MA); *m* 8 Sept 1962 (m dis 1978), John Kenyon Davies, s of Harold Davies; *Career* assistente in classical philology Univ of Rome 1959-61, jr fell Center for Hellenic Studies Washington DC 1961-62, lectr in classical philology Univ of Oxford 1964-71, fell St Hilda's Coll Oxford 1966-71, prof of comparative philology Univ of Oxford 1971-, fell Somerville Coll Oxford 1971-; visiting prof: Univ of Pennsylvania 1971, Yale Univ 1977; Collitz prof Linguistic Soc of America 1975, Semple lectr Univ of Cincinnati 1983, TBL Webster prof Stanford Univ 1988, Jackson lectr Harvard Univ 1990; hon fell St Hilda's Coll Oxford 1972; Hon DLitt Univ of St Andrews 1981; FBA 1985, FSA 1974, foreign hon memb American Acad of Arts & Sciences 1986, corresponding memb Oesterreichische Akademie der Wissenschaften (Wien) 1988, memb Academia Europaea 1989; *Books* Mycenaeae Graecitatis Lexicon (1963), Linear B/A 1984 Survey (ed with Y Duhoux, 1985); numerous articles in Br and foreign periodicals; *Style—* Prof Anna Morpurgo Davies; Somerville College, Oxford OX2 6HD (☎ 0865 270 600)

MORRELL, Anthony (Tony); s of Matthew Morrell, of Hartlepool, and Patricia Ann, *née* Hoggart; *b* 3 May 1962; *Educ* Brinkburn Comp Sch; *m* 4 Sept 1982, Lesley, da of Brian Clark; 1 s (Richard Anthony b 2 Aug 1987); *Career* middle distance runner; memb: Wolverhampton and Bilston Athletic Club, Br Milers Club, Int Athletic CLub; AAA indoor champion 1987 and 1988 (Silver award for best indoor champion 1987); runner up AAA Outdoor Championships: 800m 1987, 1500m 1989; full sr athlete 1985-; rep GB: in 800 metres at World Championships 1987, Cwlth Games 1990; memb GB winning team Europa Cup 1989; ran the second fastest 800 metres indoors in history 1988 (1.45.72), holder UK Allcomers Record over 1000 metres indoors, Bronze medallist Euro Championships Indoors 1990; apprentice heating and ventilating engr 1978-82 (qualified 1982 and worked as such until 1987), sports motivator Leisure Dept Local Authy 1988-89; *Style—* Tony Morrell, Esq

MORRELL, Frances Maine; da of Frank Gallaway, and Beatrice Galleway; *b* 28 Dec 1937; *Educ* Queen Anne Sch York; *m* 1964, Brian Morrell; 1 da; *Career* leader ILEA 1983-87, memb GLC Islington S and Finsbury 1981-86; former policy advsr to: Sec of State for Indust, Sec of State for Energy 1974-79; sec Speaker's Cmmn on Citizenship 1988-; memb Sadler's Wells bd of dirs; *Books* From the Elect of Bristol: a study of consultants' grievances, A Ten Year Industrial Strategy for Britain (with Benn and Cripps), A Planned Energy Policy for Britain (with Benn and Cripps), Manifesto: A radical strategy for Britain's future (jtly), Children of the Future: The Battle For Britain's Schools (1989); *Style—* Mrs Frances Morrell; 91 Hemingford Rd, London N1

MORRELL, John; s of John Morrell (d 1938), of Sunderland, and Dorothy Ann, *née* Thompson; *Educ* Beds Collegiate Sunderland; *m* 27 Dec 1947, Nora, da of John Edward Bates (d 1960), of Ripley, Derbys; 1 s (Nicholas John b 9 July 1952), 1 da (Patricia Margaret b 23 July 1957); *Career* WWII RAF 1940-46, radar mechanic Lancaster Sqdn, radar teacher Cranwell; CA; ptnr W J James & Co Brecon S Wales 1952-; former pres Brecon Chamber of Trade, treas Brecon Rotary Club, fndr and former Capt Penoyre GC; FCA 1951; *Recreations* golf, sports; *Clubs* Cradoc GC; *Style—* John Morrell, Esq; Brendon, 1 Sunnybank, Brecon, Powys LD3 7RW (☎ 0874 2576); Bishop House, 10 Wheat St, Brecon, Powys LD3 7DG (☎ 0874 2381, fax 0874 2427)

MORRELL, Leslie James; OBE (1986), JP (1962); s of James Morrell, DL, and Eileen, *née* Browne; *b* 26 Dec 1931; *Educ* Portora Royal Sch Enniskillen, Queen's Univ Belfast (BAgric); *m* 1958, Anne, da of Robert W Wallace, OBE (d 1973), of Belfast; 2 s (Richard, Jonathan), 1 da (Clare); *Career* Londonderry CC 1968-73, NI Assembly 1973-75, Miny of Agric NI Exec 1973-74, fndr chm James Butcher Housing

Association Ltd 1976-82 (sec 1982-); chm: Virus Tested Seed Potato Growers' Assoc 1978-88, NI Water Cncl 1982-, NI Agric Advsy Ctee of BBC 1986-90, Gen Advsy Ctee of BBC 1980-86; fndr memb: NI Fedn Housing Assoc (chm 1978-80), NI Inst of Agric Science 1960-; memb: Coleraine Borough Cncl 1973-77, Royal Ulster Agric Soc; *Style*— Leslie J Morrell, Esq, OBE, JP; Dunboe House, Castlerock, Coleraine, BT51 4UB (☎ 0265 848352)

MORRELL, Peter Richard; s of Frank Richard Morrell (d 1974), of Whitehill House, Dane End, Hertfordshire, and Florence Ethel, *née* Gleave; *b* 25 May 1944; *Educ* Westminster, Univ Coll Oxford (MA); *m* 6 June 1970, (Helen) Mary Vint, da of Capt William Norman Collins, of Peterborough; 2 da (Helen b 1971, Harriet b 1976); *Career* admitted slr 1970; called to the Bar Gray's Inn 1974; rec Crown Ct 1990-; chm Nassington and Yarwell Cons Assoc, pres Nassington and Yarwell Garden Soc, govr Harrogate Ladies' Coll, Parly candidate Ilkeston Derbys 1974; *Recreations* shooting, fishing, stalking, photography; *Style*— Peter Morrell, Esq; 2 Crown Office Row, Temple, London EC4Y 7HJ (☎ 071 353 1365, fax 071 353 4591)

MORRICE, Philip; s of William Hunter Morrice (d 1967), of Aberdeen, and Catherie Jane, *née* Cowie (d 1988); *b* 31 Dec 1943; *Educ* Robert Gordon's Coll Aberdeen; *m* 1 April 1989, (Margaret) Clare, da of Dr John Bower, of 3 Boxhall Grove, Guildford, Surrey; 1 s (Nicholas), 1 da (Rachael); *Career* Dip Serv: FCO 1967-69, Br High Cmmn Kuala Lumpur 1964-67, Br Embassy Caracas 1969-72, memb UK delegation to OECD Paris 1973-75, UK permanent rep to EC Brussels 1975-78, FCO 1978-81, Br Embassy Rome 1981-85, economic and commercial cnsllr Br High Cmmn Lagos 1986-88, minister-cnsllr, consul gen and dir of trade promotion Br Embassy Brasilia 1988-; *Books* The Schweppes Guide to Scotch (1983), The Whisky Distilleries of Scotland and Ireland (1987); *Recreations* tennis, golf, travel, writing; *Clubs* RAC, Royal Overseas League; *Style*— Philip Morrice, Esq; c/o Foreign & Commonwealth Office (Brasilia), King Charles St, London SW1A 2AH; British Embassy, Brasilia (☎ 010 55 61 225 2710)

MORRIS *see also*: Temple-Morris

MORRIS, Air Marshal Sir Alec; KBE (1981), CB (1979); s of Harry Morris; *b* 11 March 1926; *Educ* King Edward VI Sch E Retford, King's Coll London, Southampton Univ; *m* 1946, Moyna Patricia, da of Norman Boyle; 1 s (Piers), 1 da (Susan (twin)); *Career* RAF 1945, RCDS 1974, dir Signals 1975-76, dir gen Strategic Electronic Systems MOD 1976-79, AO Engrg HQ Strike Cmd 1979, chief engr RAF 1981-83, ret; exec Br Aerospace 1984-; pres Soc Electronic and Radio Technicians 1975-80; *Style*— Air Marshal Sir Alec Morris, KBE, CB; 6 Liverpool Rd, Kingston upon Thames, Surrey

MORRIS, Sir (Arnold) Alec; KBE (1981), CB (1979); s of Harry Morris (d 1973), and Ivy, *née* Marshal (d 1987); *b* 11 March 1926; *Educ* King Edward Sch East Retford, Kings Coll London, Univ of Southampton; *m* 8 June 1946, Moyna Patricia, da of Norman Boyle (d 1950); 1 s (Piers Hamilton b 1954), 1 da (Susan Catriona (twin) b 20 Oct 1954); *Career* cmmnd RAF 1945, SASO HQ No 90 Gp 1972, RCDS 1974, dir signals 1975-76, dir gen strategic electronic systems MOD 1976-79, AO i/c engrg HQ Strike Cmd 1979-81, Chief Engr RAF 1981-83, ret as Air Marshall; exec Br Aerospace 1984-; tstee Young Electronic Designer Awards 1987-; pres: Herts Sci and Technol Regnl Orgn 1984-, Soc of Electronic and Radio Technicians 1975-89; FEng 1989, FIEE 1971, FRAeS 1973; *Recreations* tennis, gardens; *Clubs* RAF; *Style*— Sir Alec Morris, KBE, CB; 6 Liverpool Road, Kingston-upon-Thames, Surrey; British Aerospace (Dynamics) Ltd, Stevenage, Herts SG1 2DA (☎ 0438 755192, telex 825125)

MORRIS, Rt Hon Alfred; PC (1979), QSO (1989), MP (Lab & Co-op) Manchester Wythenshawe 1964-; s of George Henry Morris, and Jessie, *née* Murphy; *b* 23 March 1928; *Educ* Ruskin Coll Oxford, St Catherine's Coll Oxford; *m* 1950, Irene Jones; 2 s, 2 da; *Career* former schoolmaster; contested (Lab & Co-op) Liverpool Garston 1951; PPS to: MAFF 1964-67, lord pres of Cncl and ldr of House of Commons 1968-70; memb Gen Advsy Cncl BBC 1968-74 and 1983-; chm PLP Food and Agric Gp 1971-74 (vice chm 1970-71), Britain's first min for the disabled 1974-79; chm World Planning Gp appointed to draft Charter for the 1980s for disabled people world wide 1979-80; oppn front bench spokesman: social servs 1979-81 (and 1970-74), for the disabled 1981-; chm: Co-op Parly Gp 1982-, Anzac Gp of MPs and Peers 1982-; jt treas Br-American Parly Gp 1983-; piloted Chronically Sick and Disabled Persons Act 1970 through Parly as a private memb, also the Food and Drugs (Milk) Act 1970 and the Police Act 1972; first recipient of Field Marshal Lord Harding award for distinguished serv to the disabled 1971; Louis Braille Meml award for outstanding servs to the blind 1972; Tstee of Crisis at Christmas and Earl Snowdon's Fund for Handicapped Students; chm Managing Tstees of Parly Contributory Pension Scheme and of House of Commons Members' Fund; chm Parly and Sci Ctee 1989-; hon fell Manchester Poly 1990; hon assoc BVA 1982; *Books* Human Relations in Industry (1960), VAT: A Tax on the Consumer (1970), Parliamentary Scrutiny by Committee (1971); author of numerous publications on the problems and needs of disabled people; *Recreations* gardening, tennis, snooker and chess; *Style*— The Rt Hon Alfred Morris, QSO, MP; House of Commons, London SW1A 0AA; 20 Hitherwood Drive, London SE19 1XB

MORRIS, Alfred Cosier; s of Stanley Bernard Morris (d 1970), of Anlaby, E Yorks, and Jennie, *née* Fletcher; *b* 12 Nov 1941; *Educ* Hymers Coll Hull, Univ of Lancaster (MA); *m* 26 Sept 1970, Annette, da of Eamonn Donovan, of Cork, Ireland; 1 da (Jessica b 24 April 1980); *Career* articled clerk Oliver Mackrill 1958-63, co sec fin controller and dir various cos 1963-71, sr Leverhulme res fell in univ planning and orgn Univ of Sussex 1971-74, visiting lectr in fin mgmnt Univ of Warwick 1973; gp mgmnt accountant Arthur Guiness Ltd 1974-76, mgmnt conslt Deloitte Haskins & Sells 1976-77, fin advsr subsids of Arthur Guiness 1977-80; acting dir South Bank Poly 1985-86 (dep dir 1980-85); advsr House of Commons Select Ctee on Educn Sci and Arts 1980-83, dir Bristol Poly 1986-; fell Humberside Coll; tstee Bristol Cathedral; FCA 1963, FSS, FRSA; *Books* Resources and Higher Education (jt ed and contrib, 1982); *Recreations* windsurfing, sailing; *Clubs* Athenaeum; *Style*— Alfred Morris, Esq; Park Court, Sodbury Common, Old Sodbury, Avon BS17 6PX (☎ 0454 319900); Bristol Polytechnic, Coldharbour Lane, Frenchay, Bristol BS16 1QY (☎ 0272 656 261, fax 0272 583 758)

MORRIS, Prof Alun Owen; s of Arthur Morris (d 1969), of Ruthin, and Jennie, *née* Owen; *b* 17 Aug 1935; *Educ* Brynhyfryd Sch Ruthin, Univ Coll of North Wales Bangor (BSc, PhD); *m* 16 April 1960, Margaret Erina (d 1987), da of Rev William Jones, of Caernafon; 1 s (Iwan b 1964), 2 da (Lowri b 1962, Angharad b 1971); *Career* vice princ UCW Aberystwyth 1986- (asst lectr 1959-61, lectr 1961-66, sr lectr 1966-69, prof 1969-); memb Cncl London Mathematical Soc 1974-78 (ed jt 1983-88), Mathematics Ctee UGC 1986-89, advsr to Univ Funding Cncl 1989-; memb: London Mathematical Soc 1960, American Mathematical Soc 1962; *Books* Linear Algebra - An Introduction (1978, 2 edn 1982); *Style*— Prof Alun Morris; Hiraethog, Cae Melyn, Aberystwyth, Dyfed SY23 2HA (☎ 0970 62364), Dept of Mathematics, The University College of Wales, Aberystwyth, Dyfed SY23 3BZ (☎ 0907 622752)

MORRIS, Andrew John; s of Robert John Morris, and Dorothy, *née* Prangle; *b* 30 Nov 1961; *m* July 1987 (m dis 1989), Susan, *née* Cheeseborough; *Career* gymnast; Br gymnastics champion 1983-84 and 1986-87, 7 times Welsh champion, 5 times Champions Cup winner, top Western Euro Gymnast 1983, memb Olympic team LA and Seoul 1984; life memb of Wales Gymnastic Assoc; *Style*— Andrew Morris, Esq; Sport and Recreation Section, Leisure Services Department, The Guidhall, Swansea, West Glam, Wales (☎ 0792 467432)

MORRIS, Dr Anthony Isaac; s of Moshe Morris, of Manchester, and Betty, *née* Harris (d 1977); *b* 18 Aug 1946; *Educ* Salford GS, Univ of Manchester (BSc, MSc, MB ChB, MD); *m* 16 Sept 1972, (Joan) Sheila, da of Eric Broadhurst, (d 1970); 2 s (Daniel b 19 Feb 1976, David b 2 Aug 1978); *Career* sr house offr Manchester Royal Infirmary 1971-72 (house offr 1970-71), med registrar Whittington and UCH London 1972-74, lectr in med Univ of Manchester 1974-79, res fell in hepatology Univ of Pittsburgh USA 1978-79, sr lectr in med Univ of Liverpool 1979-85, conslt physician and gastroenterologist 1985-; chm: Henry Cohen House, Merseyside and Lancs Cncl on Alcoholism; memb Educn and Sci Ctee Br Soc of Gastroenterology (educn offr Endoscopy Ctee); FRCP 1985 (MRCP 1972); *Books* ECG'S for Examinations (1975); *Recreations* sailing, music; *Style*— Dr Anthony Morris; 7 Cromptons Lane, Calderstones, Liverpool L18 3EU; 52 Link Unit, Royal Liverpool Hospital, Prescott St, Liverpool L7 8XP (☎ 051 706 3554)

MORRIS, Lady (Victoria) Audrey Beatrice; da of late Charles John Alton Chetwynd, Viscount Ingestre, MVO (d 1915) and sis of 21 Earl of Shrewsbury and Waterford (d 1980); raised to the rank of an Earl's da 1921; *b* 1910; *m* 1, 1932 (m dis 1936), 6 Baron Sheffield (d 1972); m 2, 1945, His Honour Judge Gwyn Morris, QC; *Style*— Lady Audrey Morris; Penylan Hall, Llechryd, Cardiganshire

MORRIS, (Albert) Bert; *b* 21 Oct 1934; *Educ* Skerrys Coll Liverpool, MIT; *m* 14 Dec 1987, Patricia, *née* Lane; 1 s (Jonathan), 1 da (Ailsa); *Career* Nat West Bank plc: head of money transmission 1979-83, gen mangr Mgmnt Servs (former dep gen mangr 1983-85) 1985-88, chief exec Support Servs 1989; dir: Nat West Bank plc 1989, Westments Ltd 1985, Eftpos UK Ltd 1987, APACS (admin) Ltd; chm: BACS Ltd, Off Banking Ombudsman Bd 1985-87; FCIB; *Recreations* golf, politics; *Style*— Bert Morris, Esq; 41 Lothbury, London EC2P 2BP (☎ 071 726 1717, fax 071 726 1743)

MORRIS, Brian Robert; s of Robert Oliver Morris (d 1981), of Ventor IOW, and Phyllis Marian, *née* Larkin (d 1985); *b* 11 June 1941; *Educ* Haberdashers' Aske's, University of Aston (MSc); *m* 16 August 1968, Jane Anne, da of George Frederick Green; 2 s (Christopher Edward, Julian Alexander); *Career* gp personnel advsr Guest Keen and Nettlefolds Limited 1972-73, Cabinet Office HM Treasy 1974-82, dep head PM's Efficiency Unit 10 Downing St 1982-84, NZ State Servs Cmmn 1984-85, head of Superannuation Div HM Treasy 1985-86, dep chm Willis Consulting Limited 1989- (md 1987-); *Books* The European Community - A Guide for Business and Government (3 edn 1990, Best Business Reference Book of The Year 1982); *Style*— Brian Morris, Esq; Willis Consulting Ltd, Ten Trinity Square, London EC3P 3AX (☎ 071 860 9101, 071 860 9138)

MORRIS, Hon Mrs (Carolie Madge Warrand); *née* de Montmorency; da of 7 Viscount Mountmorres (d 1951), and Katherine Sofia Clay, *née* Warrand (d 1971); *b* 29 Aug 1920; *Educ* Brentwood Sch Southport, Chelsea Coll of Physical Educn (DipPhysEd), W London Sch of Physiotherapy (MCSP); *m* 1947, Douglas Osmond Morris, s of Walter Osmond Morris (d 1944); 1 s (Andrew ka Falkland Islands 1982), 1 da (Diana); *Career* served 1940-45, WAAF Section Offr; physiotherapist; superintendent Poole Gen Hosp 1965-81, now in private practice; *Style*— The Hon Mrs Morris; Danebury Hill, 15 Greenwood Ave, Lilliput, Poole, Dorset (☎ 0202 707688)

MORRIS, Charles Evan Henry (Harry); CBE (1990); s of Thomas Silvan Morris (d 1981), of Swansea, West Glamorgan, and Mary Isobel, *née* Williamson; *b* 7 May 1926; *Educ* Rugby, Clare Coll Cambridge (BA); *m* 1955, Mansil, da of Iorri Owen Martin; 2 s (Martyn b 1956, Stephen b 1959); *Career* RN 1947-49; The Steel Company of Wales: trainee and shift foreman 1949-52, asst to chief engr 1952-54, works engr 1954-56, chief devpt engr 1956-59, dep chief engr Steel Div 1959-62, gen mangr Iron and Steel Div 1964-66 (asst gen mangr 1962-64), dir ops 1966-67; tech md British Steel Corporation 1970-77 (dir-in-charge SCW Div 1967-70), pres and exec Ferrco Engineering Ltd (subsid of Co-Steel International) 1977-83, tech vice pres Co-Steel International Ltd 1983-85, dir Sheerness Steel Company plc 1991- (chief exec 1985-91); chm Ctee on Technol IISI 1975-77; memb: Cncl Nat Acad Awards, Gen Advsy Cncl BBC, Cncl IMechE, Cncl CBI; former pres: The Inst of Metals 1988-89, Br Ind Steel Prodrs Assoc 1988; memb Cncl and vice pres: Iron and Steel Inst (unitl 1974), Metals Soc (until 1977); chm SE Region CBI, dep chm Kent TEC Limited; Liveryman Worshipful Co of Engrs 1990, Freeman City of London; FIM 1984, FEng 1988, FIMechE; *Recreations* golf, bridge, photography; *Clubs* Royal Over-Seas League; *Style*— Harry Morris, Esq, CBE; Old Forge House, Boughton Aluph, Ashford, Kent TN25 4JB (☎ 0233 643301); Sheerness Steel Company plc, Sheerness, Kent ME12 1TH (☎ 0795 663333, fax 0795 580671)

MORRIS, Rt Hon Charles Richard; PC (1978), MP (Lab) Manchester Openshaw Dec 1963-; s of George Morris; *b* 14 Dec 1926; *Educ* Brookdale Park Sch Manchester; *m* 1950, Pauline, da of Albert Dunn, of Manchester; 2 da; *Career* served RE 1945-48; oppn front bench spokesman and shadow dep leader of the House 1981-; min of state: CSD 1974-79, Environment March-Oct 1974; PPS to Harold Wilson when Leader Oppn 1970-74, dep chief whip 1969-70, vice-chamberlain HM Household 1967-69, asst govt whip 1966-67, PPS to Postmaster Gen 1964; fought Cheadle 1959, pres Clayton Labour Party 1950-52, sec NW Gp Labour MPs 1979-; memb Manchester Corpn 1954-64 (chm Tport Ctee 1959-62, dep chm Establishment Ctee 1963-64), memb Post Office Workers Union (on NEC 1959-63), chm Aedham and Rochdale Groundwork Trust 1983-, dep chm Ponti's Group Ltd 1987-; DL Greater Manchester 1984; *Style*— The Rt Hon Charles Morris, MP; 24 Buxton Rd West, Disley, Stockport, Cheshire (☎ 066 376 2450)

MORRIS, Christopher Barry (Chris); s of Peter George Morris, of 2 Glamis Road, Newquay, Cornwall, and Evelyn Josephine, *née* Nolan; *b* 24 Dec 1963; *Educ* Newquay Tretherras Secdy Sch; *m* 3 Jan 1988, Helen Elanie, da of David Batty; 1 s (Christopher Liam b 24 July 1990), 1 da (Rebecca Anne b 19 Sept 1988); *Career* professional footballer; 78 appearances Sheffield Wednesday 1982-87 (debut 1983); transferred for a fee of £125,000 to Celtic 1987-, over 150 appearances; 3 England schoolboys under 18 caps; Republic of Ireland: 27 full caps, played in Euro Championships Germany 1988, played in World Cup Italy 1990; *Recreations* golf, piano playing; *Style*— Chris Morris, Esq; Celtic FC, 95 Kerrydale St, Glasgow (☎ 041 556 2611)

MORRIS, Hon (Charles) Christopher; s of Baron Morris of Grasmere, KCMG (Life Peer); *b* 24 May 1929; *Educ* Keswick Sch, Balliol Coll Oxford; *m* 1951, Cynthia Prudence, da of Sir Alan Parsons, KCIE (d 1964); 2 s, 2 da; *Career* asst youth employment offr Newcastle upon Tyne 1952-54, teacher Wilsthorpe County Secdy and Melton Mowbray Modern Boys' Schs 1955-63, asst then head of Liberal Studies Mid Herts Coll of Further Educn 1963-67, vice-princ Sutton Coldfield Coll 1967-89; *Style*— The Hon Christopher Morris; 3 Conchar Close, Sutton Coldfield, W Midlands B72 1LN (☎ 021 354 7821)

MORRIS, Prof Colin; s of Henry Morris (d 1940), and Catherine Victoria, *née* Metham (d 1990); *b* 16 Sept 1928; *Educ* Hymers Coll Hull, Queen's Coll Oxford (BA,

BA); *m* 26 Dec 1956, Brenda, da of Herbert Gale (d 1972); 2 s (Christopher b 1957, Michael b 1962), 1 da (Gillian b 1959); *Career* supernumerary fell Pembroke Coll Oxford 1969- (chaplain fell 1953-69), prof of medieval history Univ of Southampton 1969-; FRHistS 1972; *Books* The Discovery of the Individual 1050-1200 (1972), The Papal Monarchy, Oxford History of the Christian Church (1989); *Style—* Prof Colin Morris; Department of History, The University, Southampton SO9 5WH (☎ 0703 592236)

MORRIS, David Edward Alban; s of Clifford Morris (d 1981), and Florence Irene, *née* Thomas; *b* 24 Aug 1935; *Educ* Shrewsbury, Univ Coll Oxford (MA); *m* 23 Sept 1972, Moira Louise, da of Dr Alfred William Callaghan; 2 s (William b 11 Sept 1974, Richard b 16 June 1977); *Career* CA, ptnr KPMG Peat Marwick McLintock 1974-; memb Cncl: Br Consits Bureau, Templeton Coll Oxford; former pres Mgmnt Consit Assoc; FCA; *Clubs* Hurlingham; *Style—* David Morris, Esq; 3 Spencer Hill, London SW19 4PA; KPMG Peat Marwick McLintock, 1 Puddle Dock, Blackfriars, London EC4V 3PD (☎ 071 236 8000)

MORRIS, (Edwin) David; s of Edwin Morris (d 1958), and Evelyn Amanda, *née* Griffiths (d 1976); *b* 31 July 1928; *Educ* Neath GS, Bridgend GS, Welsh Nat Sch of Medicine (MB BCh, MD, Hepburn medal, Maclean medal); *m* 21 Aug 1954, Barbara May, da of Rowland Henry Evans; 1 s (Peter David b 10 Aug 1960), 1 da (30 July 1956); *Career* Mill Serv Capt RAMC 1951-53; Cardiff: house surgn Professorial Surgical Unit 1950, house surgn O and G Unit 1951, lectr in anatomy 1953-55; sr house offr St Davids and Lansdowne Cardiff 1955-56, casualty offr and surgical registrar Dulwich 1956-58, registrar O and G Cardiff Royal Infirmary 1958-60, sr lectr Charing Cross 1960-62, res obstetrician Queen Charlotte's 1962-66, consit obstetrician Swansea 1966-67, consit Guys Hosp and Queen Charlotte's Hosp 1967-; author of various papers and contrib to books; visiting professorial exchange Johns Hopkins Hosp Baltimore 1967, regnl obstetric advsr Confidential Reports on Maternal Mortality in SE Region 1976-; consit civilian advsr to the Army 1983-; memb: Cncl RCOG 1962-85, Blair Bell Res Soc, Chelsea Clinical Soc, W London Medico-Chirurgical Soc, Br Soc for Colposcopy, Welsh Obstetrical and Gynaecological Soc, Gynaecological Visiting Soc; examiner: Univ of London, Central Midwives Bd, RCOG, Royal Coll of Surgns; pres Obstetrical and Gynaecological Section RSM; memb: BMA, Br Soc Colposcopy; DObs RCOG 1951, FRCS 1958, FRSM 1962, FRCOG 1972 (MRCOG 1960); *Recreations* glass blowing, music, walking, DIY; *Style—* David Morris, Esq; 22 Sheen Common Drive, Richmond, Surrey TW10 5BN; Guys Hospital, St Thomas St, SE1 (☎ 071 955 5000); Queen Charlottes & Chelsea Hospitals, Goldhawk Rd, London W6 (☎ 081 748 4666)

MORRIS, David Elwyn; s of Rev S M Morris (d 1958), and K W Morris, *née* Irish (d 1952); *b* 22 May 1920; *Educ* Mill Hill Sch, Brasenose Coll Oxford (MA); *m* 1, 1947, Joyce Hellyer (d 1977); 1 s (Barry b 1951), 1 da (Ann b 1949); m 2, Gwendolen Wood (d 1988), wid of Dr J K Pearce; m 3, 29 June 1990, Clova Margaret Tudor, *née* Pryor; *Career* Capt Br Army India 1944-46; Friends Ambulance Unit in China 1942-44; in practice as barr 1949-54, slr 1955-76, registrar of princ Registry of Family Div of High Ct Justice 1976-; *Publications* China Changed My Mind (1948), The End of Marriage (1971), Pilgrim Through This Barren Land (1974); *Recreations* reading; *Style—* David E Morris, Esq; Beech Grove, Grove Hill, Mawnan Smith, Falmouth, Cornwall TR11 5ER (☎ 0326 250 463)

MORRIS, David Glyndwr; s of Owen Glyndwr Morris, and Doreen Iris Morris; *b* 12 Aug 1941; *Educ* King Henry VIII Sch Coventry, Lanchester Coll Coventry; *m* 1966, Susan Joan, da of Edwin Taylor (d 1972); 2 da (Shelley b 1969, Justine b 1972); *Career* chm and md: Criterion Insur Co Ltd, Criterion Life Assur Ltd, Criterion Fin Servs Ltd 1984-; ind md Criterion Hldgs Ltd; *Recreations* golf, shooting, travel; *Clubs* IOD, Bramshaw GC; *Style—* David G Morris, Esq; Criterion Assurance Gp, Swan Court, Swan Street, Petersfield, Hants (☎ 0730 63281)

MORRIS, David Griffiths; s of Capt Thomas Griffiths Morris, and Margaret Eileen, *née* Osborne; *b* 10 March 1940; *Educ* Abingdon Sch, Kings Coll London (LLB); *m* May 1971, Carolyn Mary, *née* Miller; 1 s (Owen Thomas b January 1977), 1 da (Hannah Bethan b April 1975); *Career* called to the Bar Lincoln's Inn 1965, asst rec 1979-84, head chambers Cardiff 1984- (local jr 1981-87, rec 1984-); fndr memb: Llanmaes Community Cncl 1982-84, Llantwit Major Round Table, Llantwit Major 41 Club, Llantwit Major Rotary Club (pres 1984-85); *Recreations* rugby union football, cricket, swimming, theatre, reading, gardening; *Clubs* Cardiff and County, United Services Mess Cardiff; *Style—* David Morris, Esq; Bryn Hafren, Newport Rd, Castleton, Nr Cardiff, S Glamorgan CF3 8UN; 30 Park Place, Cardiff, S Glam CF1 3BA (☎ 0222 398421, fax 0222 3987245)

MORRIS, Prof David Lawson; s of John Lawson Morris, of Herefordshire, and Mary J E, *née* Lewis; *b* 28 May 1952; *Educ* Univ of Birmingham (MB ChB, MD), Univ of Nottingham (PhD); *m* 11 May 1974, Milja Katrina, da of Osmo Taito Vuori (d 1985), of Mantsala Finland; 1 s (Christopher Lawson b 1979), 2 da (Maija Bronwen b 1975, Katherine Saija b 1976); *Career* res fell to prof M R B Keighly The Gen Hosp Birmingham 1980-83, reader in surgery Univ Hosp Nottingham 1989 (lectr 1983-86, sr lectr 1986-89), pubns on upper gastro-intestinal bleeding, chemotherapy of hydatid disease and hormonal control of gastro-intestinal cancer; memb Br Soc Gastroenterology, fell Surgical Res Soc, FRSTM&H; *Style—* Prof David Morris; Dept of Surgery, St George Hospital, Kogarah, Sydney, New South Wales 2217, Australia

MORRIS, David Scott; s of John Hilary Morris, of Bow Brickhill, Bucks, and Frances Deans, *née* Cooper; *b* 20 Dec 1940; *Educ* Westmont Sch IOW, Royal Liberty GS Essex; *m* 23 Oct 1965, Jennifer Lois, da of Alan George Skinner (d 1986), of Pymble, Sydney, Australia; 1 da (Catriona Lucy Scott b 1967); *Career* admitted slr 1965; HM coroner for Huntingdon 1987, dep coroner for Bedfordshire 1990; pres: Milton Keynes and Dist Law Soc 1985-86, Beds Law Soc 1987-88; dir of several private cos; legal memb Mental Health Review Tbnl 1989; memb: Law Soc, IOD; *Recreations* travel, gardening, cycling, walking; *Clubs* Carlton; *Style—* David S Morris, Esq; The Old Vicarage, Granborough, Bucks (☎ 029667 217); 64-70 St Loyes, Bedford (☎ 0234 350444, telex 825263, fax 0234 219635)

MORRIS, Dr Desmond John; s of Capt Harry Howe Morris (d 1942), and Dorothy Marjorie Fuller, *née* Hunt; *b* 24 Jan 1928; *Educ* Dauntsey's Sch Wiltshire, Univ of Birmingham (BSc), Univ of Oxford (DPhil); *m* 1952, Ramona Joy, da of Windsor Baulch, of Marlborough Wiltshire; 1 s (Jason b 1968); *Career* zoological res worker Univ of Oxford 1954-56, head of Granada TV and Film Unit at Zoological Soc of London 1956-59, curator of mammals at Zoological Soc of London 1959-67, dir Inst of Contemporary Arts 1967-68, res fell Wolfson Coll Oxford 1973-81; tv series: Zootime (weekly, 1956-67), Life (fortnightly, 1965-67), The Human Race (1982), The Animals Roadshow (1987-89), The Animal Contract (1989); one man (paintings) shows: London Gallery 1950, Ashmolean Museum Oxford 1952, Stooshnoff Fine Art London 1974, Quadrangle Gallery Oxford 1976, Lasson Gallery London 1976, Public Art Gallery Swindon 1977, Galerie d'Eendt Amsterdam 1978, Mayor Gallery London 1987, Shippee Gallery New York 1988, Keats Gallery Knokke 1988, Mayor Gallery London 1989; *Books* The Reproductive Behaviour of the Ten-spined Stickleback (1958), The Story of Congo (1958), Curious Creatures (1961), The Biology of Art (1962), Apes and Monkeys (1964), The Big Cats (1965), The Mammals, a Guide to the Living Species (1965), Men and Snakes (with Ramona Morris, 1965), Men and Apes (with Ramona Morris, 1966), Men and Pandas (with Ramona Morris, 1966), Zootime (1966), Primate Ethology (ed, 1967), The Naked Ape (1967), The Human Zoo (1969), Patterns of Reproductive Behaviour (1970), Intimate Behaviour (1971), Manwatching, a Field-guide to Human Behaviour (1977), Gestures, their Origins and Distribution (jtly, 1979), Animal Days (autobiography, 1979), The Soccer Tribe (1981), Inrock (fiction, 1983), The Book of Ages (1983), The Art of Ancient Cyprus (1985), Bodywatching, a Field-guide to the Human Species (1985), The Illustrated Naked Ape (1986), Catwatching (1986), Dogwatching (1986), The Secret Surrealist (1987), Catlore (1987), The Animals Roadshow (1988), Horsewatching (1988), The Animal Contract (1990), Animalwatching (1990); *Recreations* painting, archaeology; *Style—* Dr Desmond Morris; c/o Jonathan Cape, 25 Vauxhall Bridge Rd, London SW1V 2SA

MORRIS, Hon Edward Patrick; yr twin s of 2 Baron Morris (d 1975), and Jean Beatrice, *née* Maitland-Makgill-Crichton (d 1989, having m 2, Baron Salmon (Life Peer), *qv*); gs of 1 Baron Morris (d 1935, last PM of Newfoundland 1909-18 and memb of War Cabinet 1916-18); *b* 9 Dec 1937; *Educ* Downside; *m* 1963, Mary Beryl, da of Lt-Col D H G Thrush, of Canterbury; 1 s (Edward Patrick b 1965), 1 da (Elizabeth Mary b 1968); *Career* co dir (Export) Barrow Hepburn 1973-75, export mangr Portex Ltd Hythe Kent 1976-83, sales dir Concord Laboratories Ltd Folkestone 1983-84; *Recreations* golf, veteran car (1930 Rolls-Royce); *Style—* The Hon Edward Morris; Dormer Cottage, Petham, Canterbury, Kent (☎ 0227 70 329)

MORRIS, Hon Mrs (Elizabeth); *née* Hill; 2 da of Baron Hill of Luton, PC, MD (Life Peer; d Aug 1989), and Marion Spencer, *née* Wallace (d Nov 1989); *b* 21 March 1935; *m* 6 June 1964, David Maxwell Morris, eld s of Maxwell Morris, of 12 Cleveland Row, St James's, London SW1; 2 s, 1 da; *Style—* The Hon Mrs Morris; 9 St Leonards Rd, Exeter

MORRIS, Ernest John (Johnny); OBE (1984); s of Ernest Edward Morris (d 1951), and Fanny Collorick (d 1933); *b* 20 June 1916; *m* 1951, Sybil Eileen (d 1989), da of Charles Minett (d 1951); *Career* broadcaster; radio: Johnny's Jaunts, Around the World in 25 Years; TV: The Hot Chestnut Man, Animal Magic (ran for 21 yrs); concert performances incl several one-man operas (words by Johnny Morris, music by David Haslam, Douglas Coombes and Sidney Sager); *Recreations* singing, gardening, watching wildlife; *Style—* Johnny Morris, Esq, OBE; Hopgrass Barn, Bath Road, Hungerford, Berks RG17 0SL

MORRIS, Gareth Charles Walter; s of Walter Henry Morris (d 1938), and Enid, *née* Payne (d 1981); *b* 13 May 1920; *Educ* Bristol Cathedral Sch, Royal Acad of Music; *m* 1, 1954 (m dis 1974); 1 da (Emily b 14 June 1955); m 2, 18 Dec 1975, Patricia Mary, da of Neil Murray, of Romsey, Hampshire, and Sheila Murray; 1 s (Thomas Neil Gareth b 12 Oct 1976), 2 da (Mary Eleanor b 24 July 1978, Catharine Margaret b 13 Oct 1981); *Career* RAF 1939-45; prof RAM 1945-85; flautist and soloist; princ flautist Philharmonia Orch 1948-72, adjudicator GB and abroad, played at Coronation Westminster Abbey 1953; first performances of many compositions; memb Cncl and chm Music Ctee RSA; govr RSM, tstee Loan Fund for Musical Instruments; memb RSM, FRAM 1950 (ARAM 1945), FRSA 1967; *Recreations* antiquarian horology, books; *Clubs* Royal Overseas League; *Style—* Gareth Morris, Esq; 4 West Mall, Clifton, Bristol BS8 4BH (☎ 0272 734966)

MORRIS, Ingrid Mary; da of R W Morris and Mrs Morris, *née* Bundy; *b* 10 Oct 1945; *Educ* Nat Cathedral Sch for Girls Washington DC, Herts and Essex HS Bishop's Stortford, Architectural Assoc Sch of Architecture (AA Dip, RIBA, SADG); *m* 1 s (Vasiles b 1981); *Career* architect; estab Bone and Morris private practice with Jeanne Bone 1976 (formerly with McNab and Jamieson 1968-69, Piano and Rogers 1972-74); former memb Co of Women in Architecture 1974-76; visiting lectr: Royal Univ of Malta 1974-77, Univ of Queensland 1982; hon librarian and memb of cncl Architectural Assoc Sch of Architecture 1985-91, RIBA rep on ARCUK Educn Ctee 1987, RIBA assessor RIBA Housing Awards Northern Region 1988; *Recreations* swimming, skiing, painting; *Clubs* Arts; *Style—* Miss Ingrid Morris; 37 Mossop St, London SW3 (☎ 071 589 8535); Bone and Morris, 81 Cromwell Rd, London SW7 3BW (☎ 071 835 1172, fax 071 244 8722)

MORRIS, Jack Anthony; s of Samuel Cyril Morris, of London, and Golda, *née* Berkovitch, of London; *b* 23 June 1956; *Educ* Christ's Coll GS; *m* 1 Nov 1983, Susan Anne, da of Harry Lee, of London; 1 s (Robert Edward b 27 May 1987), 1 da (Emily Kate b 14 May 1985); *Career* dep chm City Industry Ltd 1980-, The Business Design Centre London 1985-; FID 1988; *Recreations* running, 1930s & 1940s popular music, cinema history, music hall, vaudeville, variety; *Style—* Jack Morris, Esq; Business Design Centre, Upper St, Islington Green, London N1 OQH (☎ 071 359 3535, fax 071 226 0590, telex 264488-Aggie)

MORRIS, James Nathaniel; s of Arthur Russel Morris (d 1977), and Mildred Maud Langley, *née* Rogers; *b* 6 Nov 1942; *Educ* Wycliffe Coll Glos, Univ of Birmingham (BSc); *m* 1965, Barbara, da of Henry Herbert Goldstaub; 2 s, 2 da; *Career* md Electrothermal Engrg Ltd 1976-; CEng, MIChemE; *Recreations* squash, music; *Style—* James Morris, Esq; 18 Snakes Lane, Woodford Green, Essex IG8 0BS (☎ 081 504 2365); Electrothermal Engineering Ltd, 419 Sutton Rd, Southend-on-Sea, Essex SS2 5PH (☎ 0702 612211, telex 995387)

MORRIS, James Peter; s of Frank Morris, MBE, JP (d 1978), of Kexbrough, Yorks, and Ann Mary Collindridge (d 1968); *b* 17 Sept 1926; *Educ* Holgate GS Barnsley, Univ of Manchester (BA, Teaching Dip); Later Dip CAM; *m* 1, 1953 (m dis), Peggy; m 2, 1974, Margaret, da of Alan Law (d 1987), of Paisley; *Career* serv RAF UK 1945-48; Res Dept Lab Pty 1952-59; Govt Info Servs: HM Treasury and other depts 1960-73 (chief info offr 1968-73); dir info GLC 1973-77; sec-gen Nat Cold Storage Fedn 1978-90; FIPR 1990; *Recreations* cricket, painting, politics, theatre, voluntary activity in community; *Clubs* MCC, Reform; *Style—* J Peter Morris, Esq; 88 Ridgmount Gardens, London WC1E 7AY (☎ 071 637 2141)

MORRIS, James Richard Samuel; CBE (1986); s of James John Morris (d 1976), and Kathleen Mary, *née* McNaughton (d 1976); *b* 20 Nov 1925; *Educ* Ardingly Coll, Univ of Birmingham (BSc Chem Eng); *m* 1958, Marion Reid, da of Dr James Sinclair; 2 s (Simon b 1960, Andrew b 1962), 2 da (Jane b 1963, Katherine b 1965); *Career* mil serv 1944-48, Capt Welsh Gds; Courtaulds Ltd 1950-80, dir BNFL 1971-85, visiting prof of chem engrg Univ of Strathclyde 1979-87, chm and md Brown and Root (UK) Ltd 1980-, chm UK Nirex Ltd 1989-; chm of cncl and pro-chllr Univ of Loughborough 1982-, industl advsr Barclays Bank 1980-85; *Recreations* gardening, farming, shooting; *Clubs* Athenaeum; *Style—* James Morris, Esq, CBE; Breadsall Manor, Breadsall Village, Derby (☎ 0332 83168); Brown & Root (UK) Ltd, 150 The Broadway, Wimbledon, London SW19 (☎ 081 534 0172)

MORRIS, James Shepherd; s of Thomas Shepherd Morris (d 1985), and Johanna Sime, *née* Malcolm (d 1985); *b* 22 Aug 1931; *Educ* Daniel Stewarts Coll Edinburgh, Edinburgh Sch of Architecture (Dip Arch), Univ of Pennsylvania (MLA); *m* 27 June 1959, Eleanor Kenner, da of Lawrence Meredith Clemson Smith, OBE; 2 s (Malcolm b 2 Aug 1962, Houston b 7 March 1966), 1 da (Alexandra b 28 Aug 1969); *Career* Nat Serv 2 Lt RE 1957-59; ptnr Morris and Steedman Architects Edinburgh; works incl: Univ of Edinburgh, Univ of Strathclyde, Princess Margaret Rose Hosp, Countryside Cmmn for Scotland; water colour artist (exhibited RSA); chm Fellowship Ctee RIAS

1985-87; memb Cncl: RIAS, Edinburgh AA 1969-71, Royal Scot Academy 1990; memb Br Arts Cncl London 1973-80, tstee Nat Museum of Antiquities 1980-86, vice chm Scottish Arts Cncl 1970-80 (chm Art Ctee 1976-80); RSA 1989, ARSA 1975, FRIAS, ALI, ARIBA; British Steel award 1971, RIBA award 1974, Euro Architectural Heritage award 1975, Euro Heritage Business and Indust award 1975, 9 Civic Tst awards 1962-90; *publications* author of various articles in RIBA Jls; *Recreations* golf, tennis, skiing, painting, hillwalking; *Clubs* New (Edinburgh), Philadelphia Cricket (Philadelphia), Valderrama (Spain); *Style—* James Morris, Esq; 38 Young Street Lane North, Edinburgh, Scotland EH2 4JU (☎ 031 226 6563, fax 031 220 0224)

MORRIS, (Catharine) Jan; *b* 2 Oct 1926; *Educ* Univ of Oxford (MA); *Career* author; *Books* Venice (1960), Spain (1964), Oxford (1965), The Pax Britannica Trilogy (1973-78), Conundrum (1974), The Matter of Wales (1984), Last Letters from Hav (1985), Among the Cities (1985), Manhattan '45 (1987), Hong Kong (1988), Pleasures of a Tangled Life (1989), The Oxford Book of Oxford (ed, 1978); 5 books of collected travel essays; *Style—* Ms Jan Morris; Trefan Morys, Llanystumdwy, Gwynedd, Cymru (☎ 0766 522222)

MORRIS, Jean Daveena Ogilvy; CBE (1989, MBE 1973); da of the Rev David Porter Howie (d 1973), of Kilmarnock, and Veena, *née* Christie (d 1955); *b* 28 Jan 1929; *Educ* Kilmarnock Acad, Univ of St Andrews (MA, MEd); *m* 3 Sept 1952, William James, s of William John Morris (d 1958), of Cardiff; 1 s (David b 1960); *Career* clinical psychologist: Royal Hosp for Sick Children Edinburgh 1950-52, St David's Hosp Cardiff 1952-53; conslt clinical psychologist Quarrier's Homes Bridge of Weir Renfrewshire 1971-87; cncllr and bailie Peterhead Town Cncl 1959-67, cncllr Aberdeen CC 1962-67; memb Abbeyfield Society Scotland Ltd 1967-89, chm BBC and ITV Appeals Ctee for Scot 1967-73, chm Parole Bd for Scot 1980- (memb 1974-80), vice chm TSB Scot Fndn 1986-, chm Scotia House Development Co Glasgow 1986-, memb Scot Advsy Bd Abbey National plc 1986-; OStJ (1989); *Recreations* swimming; *Clubs* New (Edinburgh), Royal Scottish Automobile (Glasgow); *Style—* Mrs Jean Morris, CBE; 94 St Andrews Drive, Glasgow G41 4RX (☎ 041 427 2757); Scotia House Ltd, 15a Woodside Crescent, Glasgow G3 7UL (☎ 041 332 5792)

MORRIS, Rt Hon John; PC (1970), QC (1973), MP (Lab) Aberavon 1959-; s of D W Morris, of Talybont, Cardiganshire; *b* 1931; *Educ* Ardwyn Aberystwyth, Univ Coll of Wales Aberystwyth, Gonville and Caius Cambridge, Acad of Int Law The Hague; *m* 1959, Margaret, da of Edward Lewis, OBE, JP, of Llandysul; 3 da; *Career* served Royal Welch Fusiliers and Welch Regt; oppn spokesman Legal Affrs 1979-81, sec state Wales 1974-79, Min Defence (Equipment) 1968-70, jt parly sec Tport 1966-68, parly sec Miny Power 1964-66; memb UK Delgn Consultative Assembly Cncl of Europe and WEU 1963-64, N Atlantic Assembly 1970-74; barr Gray's Inn 1954, legal advsr Farmers' Union of Wales, rec SE circuit 1982-, opposition spokesman legal affrs and shadow attorney gen 1983-; Hon LLD Wales 1983; *Style—* The Rt Hon John Morris, QC, MP; House of Commons, SW1

MORRIS, John Edward; s of George Edward Morris, and Jean, *née* Pennance; *b* 1 April 1964; *Educ* Shavington Comp Sch Cheshire, Dane Bank Coll of Further Education; *m* 30 Sept 1990, Sally Ann, da of Patrick Walter Fish; *Career* professional cricketer; debut Derbyshire CCC 1982-, awarded county cap 1986; Griqualand West SA off-season 1988-89; England: Test match debut v India Lord's 1990, played in all 3 Tests v India 1990, memb tour Aust and NZ 1990-91, played eight one day internationals; Refuge Assurance League winners Derbyshire 1990; youngest player ever to score 100 in the history of Sunday League Cricket; *Recreations* fly fishing, golf, avid sports watcher; *Style—* John Morris, Esq; c/o Derbyshire County Cricket Club, County Cricket Ground, Nottingham Road, Derby DE2 6DA (☎ 0332 383211)

MORRIS, John Llewelyn; s of John Noel Morris, of Tonyrefail, and Myfanwy Jones, *née* Moss Davies; *b* 19 Sept 1943; *Educ* Tywyn Secdy Sch, Univ of Leicester (BSc), Univ of St Andrews (PhD); *m* 11 Sept 1965, Sylvia Eileen, da of William Lloyd Williams (d 1961); 2 s (Jamie b 15 June 1966, Jules b 13 Nov 1970), 1 da (Rachel b 28 March 1969); *Career* Univ of Dundee: NCR post-doctoral fell 1967-69, lectr in computer sci 1969-75, prof 1986-; Waterloo Univ: visiting assoc prof 1973-74, assoc prof 1975-83, prof 1983-86; FIMA 1972; *Books* Computers and Computing (with J R Rushforth, 1973), Computational Methods in Elementary Numerical Analysis (1983); *Recreations* squash, hill walking, music, reading; *Style—* Prof John Morris; 11 Whinfield Place, Newport-on-Tay, Fife, Scotland DD6 8EF (☎ 0382 541770); Mathematics & Computer Science Department, University of Dundee, Dundee, Scotland (☎ 0382 23181, fax 0382 201604, telex 76293)

MORRIS, Hon John Martin; s (twin) of 3 Baron Killanin, MBE, TD; *b* 4 April 1951; *Educ* Ampleforth, St Conleth's Coll Dublin; *m* 1972, Thelma, da of Mrs Mansfield, of Monkstown, Co Dublin; 2 s (Roderic, Michael); *Career* photographer; *Recreations* falconry, fishing; *Style—* The Hon John Morris; 5 Rus-in-Urbe, Lower Glenageary Rd, Dun Laoghaire, Co Dublin

MORRIS, John Michael Douglas; s of Charles Edward Douglas Morris (d 1988), of Northampton, and Mary Kathleen, *née* Murphy; *b* 10 Aug 1935; *Educ* Dulwich, John Fisher Sch; *m* 5 June 1958, Jill Margaret, da of Wilfred John Walker (d 1962), of Northampton; 2 s (Matthew b 1964, Robert b 1968), 2 da (Nicola (Mrs Kilpin) b 1959, Joanne (Mrs Gooding) b 1961); *Career* Nat Serv discharged due to injury 1957; reporter Northampton Chronicle and Echo 1953-60; sports sub ed Evening Standard 1960-67, gp sports ed Utd Newpapers 1967-77, freelance writer and publican 1977-79, run sports freelance agency Northampton 1979-86, gen sec Br Boxing Bd of Control 1986-; former chm and hon sec Br Boxing Writers Club, admin steward Br Boxing Bd of Control 1981-86; *Books* Sports biographies: Come in No 3 (1977), Box On (1984); Play Better Tennis; *Recreations* amateur acting, reading; *Style—* John Morris, Esq; 55 Heath Cottages, Mill Place, Chislehurst, Kent BR7 5ND (☎ 081 467 9541); British Boxing Board of Control, 70 Vauxhall Bridge Rd, London SW1V 3RP (☎ 071 828 2133, fax 071 931 0989)

MORRIS, John Stanley; s of Sydney Morris, of Sonning-on-Thames, Berks, and Betty Joan, *née* Talbot; *b* 14 April 1939; *Educ* Uppingham; *m* 6 Oct 1962, Diane Mary Druce, da of Leonard William Chopping, of Henley-on-Thames, Oxon; 3 s (William b 27 Nov 1963, Simon b 8 May 1966, Ashley b 11 Jan 1969); *Career* qualified CA 1962; ptnr: Fryer Sutton Morris & Co 1962-69, Fryer Whitehill & Co 1969-77; fin dir Lubrication Engineering Group 1977-81 (conslt 1982-); fndr treas Reading Valley Round Table; memb Worshipful Co of Feltmakers; FCA 1969; *Recreations* golf; *Clubs* Calcot Park Golf (Capt 1974), Phyllis Court (Henley); *Style—* John Morris, Esq; Rowan House, New Lane Hill, Reading RG3 4JJ (☎ 0734 427578, fax 0734 451113)

MORRIS, Hon Jonathan David; s and h of 2 Baron Morris of Kenwood; *b* 5 Aug 1968; *Style—* The Hon Jonathan Morris

MORRIS, Capt Jonathan Jeremy Creighton; s of John William Creighton Morris (d 1967), of Gorstage Hall, Cuddington, Cheshire, and Cynthia Dorothy, *née* Leake; *b* 12 March 1942; *Educ* Ampleforth Coll York; *Career* Offr Cadet Mons Offr Cadet Sch 1960-61; Scots Guards 1961-70: 1 Bn Gravesend 1961, Lt Jr Guardsman's Co Pirbright 1961-65, 2 Bn Caterham 1965, 1 Bn Malaya Borneo 1965-67, 2 Bn Malaya Borneo 1965-67, 2 Bn Scots Guards BAOR-Iserlohn, Munster 1967-70; stockbroker L Messel and Co 1970-72, ptnr Fielding Newson-Smith and Co 1972-86, dir County Securities 1986-88, dir Kitcat and Aitken 1988-; Freeman City of London 1989; General Service Medal Borneo clasp 1966; *Recreations* polo, skiing, shooting, ballet; *Clubs* Turf, Guards Polo; *Style—* Capt Jonathan Morris; 32 Henning St, Battersea, London SW11 3DR (☎ 071 223 5258); Carr Kitcat and Aitken, Stockbrokers, London EC1 TJ (☎ 071 378 7050)

MORRIS, Judith Anne; da of Harold Morris (d 1986), of London, and Eve, *née* Sutton; *b* 23 Aug 1948; *Educ* Buckingham Gate Sch, Camden HS for Girls, City Univ London (BSc, MSc); *Career* sr sessional optometrist Contact Lens Dept Moorfields Eye Hosp London 1971-, sr lectr Inst of Optometry London 1983-; pres Br Contact Lens Assoc 1983-84 (ed jl of Br Contact Lens Assoc 1984-89), memb Lambeth Southwark and Lewisham FPC 1988-90, pres Br Coll of Optometrists 1989-90 (cncl memb and examiner 1980-) ; Freeman City of London 1972, Liveryman Worshipful Co of Spectacle Makers 1971; fell Br Coll of Optometrists 1971; *Recreations* theatre, ballet, bridge; *Style—* Miss Judith Morris; 9 Cosway St, London NW1 5NR (☎ 071 724 1176); The Institute of Optometry, 56 Newington Causeway SE1 (☎ 071 407 4183)

MORRIS, Keith Norton; s of Capt Alfred Lawrence Morris (d 1984), and Marywyn, *née* Norton; *b* 3 July 1950; *Educ* Bishop Veseys GS; *m* 6 Sept 1972, Valerie, *née* Coombes; 1 s (Timothy), 2 da (Charlotte, Abigail); *Career* articled clerk Binder Hamlyn 1968-74, gp accountant Deblen Finance Ltd 1974-75, fin dir Forthminster Holdings Ltd 1975-84, md W H Wilkins Ltd 1984-, fin controller Aqua Gp 1987; FCA, FIOD, MBIM; *Recreations* gardening, DIY, travel; *Style—* Keith Morris, Esq; Wood Mill Farm, Ellerdine, Telford, Shropshire TF6 6RT (☎ 095 283 759, 021 541 1601 (work), fax 021 552 0386)

MORRIS, Mali; *b* 5 Feb 1945; *Educ* Sir Hugh Owen GS Caernarfon, John Bright GS Llandudno, Univ of Newcastle upon Tyne (Hatton scholarship in painting, BA), Univ of Reading (MFA); *Career* artist; pt/t lectr Dept of Fine Art Univ of Reading, visiting artist Royal Coll of Art and Chelsea Sch of Art; twelve solo shows since 1979; gp exhibitions incl: Summer Show 3 1977, Whitechapel Open 1983, 1985, 1986, 1988, On A Plate (Serpentine Gallery) 1987, Athena Awards (Barbican) 1988, Tree of Life (South Bank Centre and touring) 1989, John Moores (Walker Art Gallery Liverpool) 1980 and 1989, Colour in Modern Painting (Stoke-on-Trent) 1990; int shows: France, Netherlands, Cyprus, USA, Eastern Europe, Canada, Brazil, Botswana; pub collections incl: Arts Cncl of GB, Br Cncl, Contemporary Art Soc, Northern Arts, Welsh Arts Cncl, Lloyds of London, Nat Museum Gaborone; *Awards*: Arts Cncl award 1976, GLAA Major award 1979, Elephant Tst award, Univ of Reading res award 1983; *Style—* Mali Morris; Francis Graham-Dixon Gallery, 17-18 Great Sutton St, London EC1V ODN (☎ 071 250 1962, fax 071 490 1069)

MORRIS, Mary, Baroness; Mary; da of late Rev Alexander Reginald Langhorne; *m* 2 Baron Morris (d 1975); *Style—* The Rt Hon Mary, Lady Morris; The Old Farmhouse, Lower Denford, Hungerford, Berks RG17 0UN

MORRIS, Max; *b* 15 Aug 1913; *Educ* Hutcheson's Glasgow, Kilburn GS London, UCL (BA), Inst of Educn London, LSE; *m* 1961, Margaret; *Career* Capt RASC 1944; headmaster Willesden HS 1967-78, pres NUT 1973-74, cnsllr Harringay Borough Cncl 1984-86; *Books* The People's Schools (1939), From Cobbett to the Chartists (1948), Your Children's Future (1955), An A-Z of Trade Unionism & Industrial Relations (with Jack Jones, 1982 and 1986), co ed Thirteen Wasted Years (1987); *Recreations* walking, swimming; *Style—* Max Morris, Esq; 44 Coolhurst Rd, London N8 8EU

MORRIS, 3 Baron (UK 1918); Michael David Morris; er twin s of 2 Baron Morris (d 1975), and Jean Beatrice, *née* Maitland-Makgill-Crichton (d 1989, having m 2, Baron Salmon (Life Peer), *qv*); *b* 9 Dec 1937; *Educ* Downside; *m* 1, 1959 (m dis 1962), Denise Eleanor, da of Morley Richards; m 2, 1962 (m dis 1969), Jennifer, da of Tristram Gilbert; 2 da; m 3, 1980, Juliet Susan, twin da of Anthony Buckingham; 2 s, 1 da (Hon Lucy Juliet b 18 June 1981); *Heir* s, Hon Thomas Morris; *Career* sits as Conservative in House of Lords; FICA; *Style—* The Rt Hon Lord Morris; 8 Carlos Place, London W1 (☎ 071 499 2807)

MORRIS, Hon Michael Francis Leo (Mouse); known as 'Mouse'; s (twin with John) of 3 Baron Killanin, MBE, TD; *b* 4 April 1951; *Educ* Ampleforth, St Conleth's Coll Dublin; *m* Shanney (Shanny) Clark; 2 s (James, Christopher); *Career* former steeple chase jockey, race horse trainer; *Recreations* fox hunting; *Clubs* Turf; *Style—* The Hon Michael Morris; Everards Grange, Fethard, Co Tipperary, Ireland (☎ 052 31474)

MORRIS, Michael Wolfgang Laurence; MP (C) Northampton 1974-; s of Cyril Laurence Morris; *b* 25 Nov 1936; *Educ* Bedford Sch, St Catharine's Coll Cambridge (MA); *m* 1960, Ann Phyllis, da of Percy Appleby (d 1973); 2 s (Julian b 1961, Jocelyn b 1972), 1 da (Susannah b 1965); *Career* served Nat Serv, pilot offr RAF and NATO Wings; dir Benton & Bowles (advertising agency) 1971-81, fndr AM Int Public Affrs Conslts 1976-; Parly candidate (C) Islington N 1966, PPS to NI Min of State 1979-81, memb of Pub Accounts Ctee 1979-; chm: Br-Sri Lanka Parly Gp, Br Singapore Parly Gp, Br Malaysia Gp, Br Burma Gp; vice chm Br-Indonsia Gp; treas: Br-Thailand Gp, Br Asian Gp; memb Cncl of Europe and Western Euro Union 1983-; Mr Speaker's Panel 1984-; chm Bedford Sch 1989- (govr 1982-); *Recreations* field sports, cricket, golf (capt Parly Golf Soc), shooting, tennis, heritage, forestry, budgerigars; *Clubs* Carlton, George Row (Northampton), John O'Gaunt Golf; *Style—* Michael Morris, Esq, MP; Caesar's Camp, Sandy, Beds (☎ 0767 80388)

MORRIS, Nicholas Guy Ussher; s of Cdr Guy Philip Ussher Morris, DSC (d 1941), and Sybil Ernestine, *née* Lee; *b* 15 April 1940; *Educ* Charterhouse, Christ Church Oxford (MA); *m* 27 July 1963, (Charlotte) Susan Margaret, da of T L Wilkinson; 1 s (Richard b 1968), 2 da (Elizabeth b 1966, Katherine b 1971); *Career* Vickers da Costa 1962-65, Beecham Gp Ltd 1965-69, group sec H P Bulmer (Hldgs) Ltd 1969-78, corp sec Br Shipbuilders 1978-82, gp sec Unigate plc 1982-; memb cncl Malvern Coll; *Recreations* family; *Style—* Nicholas Morris, Esq; Woodfield House, Oxford Road, Clifton Hampden, Oxon OX14 3EW (☎ 0867 307149); Unigate plc, Unigate House, Western Avenue, London W3 0SH (☎ 081 992 3400, fax 081 993 3945, telex 927592)

MORRIS, Prof Norman Frederick; s of Frederick William Morris (d 1974), of Luton, Beds, and Evelyn, *née* Biggs (d 1971); *b* 26 Feb 1920; *Educ* Dunstable Sch, St Mary's Hosp Med Sch Univ of London (MB BS); *m* 2 June 1944, Lucia Xenia (Lucy), da of Dr Benjamin Rivlin (d 1964), of Stratford, London; 2 s (David, Nicholas), 2 da (Jacqueline, Vanessa); *Career* Sqdn Ldr RAFVR (Med Section) 1946-48; res surgical offr East Ham Meml Hosp 1945-46 (dep res 1944-45), sr registrar Dept of Obstetrics & gynaecology Royal Postgrad Med Sch 1950-53 (departmental reader 1956-58), prof of obstetrics and gynaecology Charing Cross Hosp Med Sch 1958-85, med dir IVF Unit Cromwell Hosp 1986-; dean Faculty of Med Univ of London 1971-76 (dep vice chllr 1974-80), dep chm NW Thames Health Authy 1976-80; fndr and pres Int Soc of Psychosomatic Obstetrics and Gynaecology 1972-; chm Br Soc of Psychosomatic Obstetrics and Gynaecology and Andrology 1988-, Advsy Ctee to Cwlth Secretariat Health Devpt Programme 1990-; hon memb: Societas Gynaecologa et Obstetrica Italica 1979, Aust Soc of Psychosomatic Obstetrics and Gynaecology 1981; fell RSM (pres Section of Obstetrics and Gynaecology 1979), FRCOG; *Books* The Baby Book (1953), Sterilisation of Men and Women (1976); *Recreations* travelling, music, reading; *Clubs* Athenaeum; *Style—* Prof Norman Morris; 16 Provost Rd, London NW3 4ST; Cromwell Hosp, Cromwell Rd, SW5 (☎ 01 722 4244)

MORRIS, Lady; Olive Irene; da of William Davies, of Swansea; *m* 4 June 1938, Sir

Herbert Edward Morris, 7 Bt (d 1947); 29 Belle Vue Rd, West Cross, Swansea

MORRIS, Patrick Lindsay; s of Christopher Lindsay Morris, of Newcastle upon Tyne, and Elspeth Jane, *née* Gerstenberg; *b* 3 July 1961; *Educ* Whickham Comp Sch, Univ of Bristol (BA); *Career* graduate trainee Bank of America NT and SA London 1983-84, dir KHP Group London 1985-86, chm MMI plc (USM quoted fin mktg gp) 1986-; Outstanding Young Achiever PR Week Awards; author of the Financial On-Line Information Report FMI (1985); *Recreations* reading, gardening, contemporary art; *Style*— Patrick Morris, Esq; MMI plc, 67 Hatton Garden, London EC1N 8JY (☎ 071 242 0171, fax 071 831 1519)

MORRIS, Paul Christopher Early; s of Christopher John Morris, of Kensington, London W8, and Alice Ruth, *née* Early; *b* 21 Sept 1950; *Educ* Westminster Abbey Choir Sch, Westminster, UCNW Bangor (BA); *Career* organist and choirmaster Christ Church Llanfairfechan N Wales 1970-73; admitted slr 1978, ptnr Winckworth & Pemberton 1981- (asst slr 1978-81); jt registrar Diocese of Southwark, hon sec Avenues Youth Project N Westminster; Freeman City of London 1984, Liveryman Worshipful Co of Wheelwrights 1984, Freeman Worshipful Co of Weavers 1988; *Recreations* music; *Clubs* Oriental; *Style*— Paul Morris, Esq; 35 Great Peter St, Westminster SW1P 3LR (☎ 071 222 7811, fax 071 222 1614)

MORRIS, Paul William; s of William Henry Morris (d 1987), of Bexhill-on-Sea, and late Norah, *née* Abbott; *b* 20 May 1942; *Educ* Downsmeade Sch Eastbourne; *m* 30 Jan 1965, Carole, da of William Joseph Cornelius Owden, of Tunbridge Wells; 2 s (Nicholas b 1967, Dominic b 1972), 2 da (Karen b 1969, Elizabeth b 1979); *Career* articled clerk HS Humphrey and Co Eastbourne 1966, sr tax ptnr BDO Binder Hamlyn 1988- (joined 1972); Freeman City of London, Liveryman Worshipful Co of Painter Stainers; FCA 1966; *Recreations* cricket, tennis, walking, painting, art, theatre; *Style*— Paul Morris, Esq; BDO Binder Hamlyn, 20 Old Bailey, London EC4M 7BH (☎ 071 489 9000, fax 071 489 6060, telex 8812282)

MORRIS, Peter Christopher West; s of Christopher Thomas Richard Morris, of Westbrook, Rottingdean, Sussex, and Lillian Beatrice, *née* Briggs; *b* 24 Dec 1937; *Educ* Seaford Coll, Christ's Cambridge (MA, LLB); *m* 1, 20 June 1959 (m dis), Joy Florence; 2 s (Mark b 1962, James b 1964), 1 da (Amanda b 1960); m 2, 1987, Terese Lindsay; 1 step s (Maxim b 1974), 2 step da (Phillippa b 1972, Victoria b 1976); *Career* Nat Serv 76 Co Lt RASC 1956-58 (cmmnd 2 Lt 1957); admitted slr 1965; ptnr Wild Hewitson and Shaw of Cambridge 1965, called to the Bar Middle temple 1982; rec of the Crown Court 1980-84, voluntary removal from roll of slrs 1982, resigned recordership 1984; hockey player for Wales 1982-85; co dir 1985-; *Recreations* hockey, tennis, golf; *Clubs* Hawks; *Style*— Peter Morris, Esq

MORRIS, Prof Peter Edwin; s of Stewart Silvester Morris, and Doris Maud, *née* Wilson; *b* 13 Nov 1947; *Educ* Weston-super-Mare GS, Univ of Exeter (BA, PhD); *m* 17 Sept 1976, Priscilla Jane, da of Ronald Kelley, of Costa Di Vaghia, 20122 Quenza, Corse Du Sud, France; 2 da (Lucy b 1979, Susan b 1988); *Career* lectr in psychology Open Univ 1972-74, prof of psychology and personal chair Univ of Lancaster 1989- (lectr 1974-84, sr lectr 1984-89, head of Psychology Dept 1987); memb Exec Ctee Save Br Sci 1986-88; Br Psychological Soc: hon gen sec 1983-86, chm Scientific Affrs Bd 1988-89, pres elect 1989-90, pres 1990-91; memb Experimental Psychology Soc, FBPsS, CPsychol; *Books* Visual Imagery and Consciousness (jtly, 1983), Cognition in Action (1987); ed: Aspects of Memory (1978), Practical Aspects of Memory (1978), Applied Problems in Memory (1979), Everyday Memory, Actions and Absentmindedness (1984), Modelling Cognition (1987), Practical Aspects of Memory: Current Research and Issues (2 vols, 1988); *Recreations* fell walking, local history, bird watching, gardening; *Style*— Prof Peter Morris; Psychology Dept, Lancaster University, Lancaster LA1 4YF (☎ 0524 65201 ext 3576, telex 65111 Lancuf G, fax 0524 841710)

MORRIS, Hon (George) Redmond Fitzpatrick; s and h of 3 Baron Killanin, MBE, TD; *b* 24 Jan 1947; *Educ* Gonzaga Coll Dublin, Ampleforth, Trinity Coll Dublin; *m* 1972, Pauline, da of Geoffrey Horton, of The Lawns, Cabinteely, Co Dublin; 1 s (Luke), 1 da (Olivia); *Career* film prodr; *Style*— The Hon Redmond Morris; 4 The Vineyard, Richmond, Surrey

MORRIS, (Thomas) Richard; s of Capt Thomas Griffiths Morris, and Margaret Eillen, *née* Osborne; *b* 29 Oct 1945; *Educ* Abingdon Sch, Univ of Birmingham (LLB); *m* 18 Oct 1975, Vanessa Jane; 1 s (Nicholas b 30 April 1979), 1 da (Miriam b 12 Feb 1978); *Career* Lt 6 QEO Gurkha Rifles 1969-71, served Malaysia, Hong Kong, Nepal, India, Capt 6 Queens Regt (Vol) 1971-75; articled clerk Norton Rose Botterell & Roche London 1971-73, admitted slr 1974, ptnr D J Freeman & Co London 1987-; occasional contribs Estates Times Magazine, Architects Journal; ward clerk Ward of Bishopsgate London 1986; Freeman City of London 1981, Liveryman Worshipful Co of Slrs 1981; memb Law Soc; *Recreations* hockey, swimming, gardening; *Clubs* City Livery; *Style*— Richard Morris, Esq; D J Freeman & CO, 1 Fetter Lane, London EC4A 1BR (☎ 071 583 5555, fax 071 583 3232, telex 913434)

MORRIS, Sir Robert Byng; 10 Bt (UK 1806), of Clasemont, Glamorganshire; s of late Percy Byng Morris, himself gs of Sir John Morris, 2 Bt (whose wife was Hon Lucy Juliana Byng, 7 and yst da of 5 Viscount Torrington); suc second cousin, Sir Cedric Morris, 9 Bt, 1982; *b* 25 Feb 1913; *m* 1947, Christine Kathleen, da of Archibald Field, of Toddington, Glos; 1 s (Allan Lindsay), 3 da (Geraldine b 1948, Gillian b 1950, Roberta b 1965); *Heir* s, Allan Lindsay Morris, b 27 Nov 1961, m 1986, Cheronne, eld da of Dale Whitford, of Par, Cornwall; *Style*— Sir Robert Morris, Bt; RR2 Norton Creek Rd, St Chrysostome, Québec, Canada

MORRIS, Robert Leslie; s of Lt-Col John Douglas Leslie Morris, OBE, of 1 Grove Rd, Melton Constable, Norfolk, and Doris Mabel, *née* Young; *b* 16 Sept 1939; *Educ* Felsted; *m* 10 Aug 1963, Maureen Iris, da of Edward Day; 1 s (David Leslie b 1967), 1 da (Lynda Leslie b 1965); *Career* CA 1963, articled clerk Grant Thornton (formerly Thornton Baker), asst accountant Williams Harvey Ltd 1965-67, chief accountant A King & Sons Ltd 1967-70, Glaciator Ltd 1970-74, co sec Cresswell & Williamson Ltd 1974-83, self-employed CA 1983-88, ptnr Harris Kafton 1988-; FCA 1963, ATII 1963; *Recreations* sea and freshwater angling, backstage local operatic soc; *Clubs* Fakenham Angling, Fakenham Operatic; *Style*— Robert Morris, Esq; Old White Horse, Briningham, Melton Constable, Norfolk NR24 2PY (☎ 0263 860 514); 1 Royal Oak Chambers, Fakenham, Norfolk NR21 9DY (☎ 0328 851306)

MORRIS, Robert Lyle; s of Robert Neil Morris, of Flagler Beach, Fla, and Lyal, *née* Bish; *b* 9 July 1942; *Educ* Crafton HS, Univ of Pittsburgh (BS), Duke Univ (PhD); *m* Joanna, da of John Du Barry (d 1984); 2 da (Lila b 1977, Vanessa b 1977); *Career* postdoctoral fell Center for the Study of Ageing and Human Devpt Duke Univ 1969-71, res co-ordinator Psychical Res Fndn 1971-74, lectr sch of social sciences Univ of Carlifornia Irvine 1978-80 (lectr tutorial prog Santa Barbara 1974-80), sr res scientist Sch of Computer and Info Sci Syracuse Univ 1980-85, Koestler prof of parapsychology Dept of Psychology Univ of Edinburgh 1985-; memb: Parapsychological Assoc 1967-, Soc for Scientific Exploration 1982-, Bd of Tstees Soc for Psychical Res 1985-; *Books* Foundations of Parapsychology (jtly, 1986); *Style*— Prof Robert Morris; Psychology Dept, University of Edinburgh, 7 George Square, Edinburgh EH8 9JZ (☎ 031 667 1011 ext 4473, fax 667 7938)

MORRIS, Robert Vernon; s of Harold Vernon Morris (d 1986), of 82 Lichfield Ave, Hereford, and Dorothy Agnes, *née* Foulkes; *b* 27 May 1932; *Educ* St Mary's Coll Bitterne Park Southampton, LSE (LLB); *m* 19 Sept 1959, Patricia Margaret, da of Thomas Norman Trevor (d 1968), of 66 Laynes Rd, Glos; 3 s (Nicholas b 1960, Timothy b 1963, James b 1965), 1 da (Sally b 1970); *Career* Nat Serv 1956-58 Intelligence Corps GCHQ Cheltenham; sr Supreme Ct 1957, sr ptnr Rowberry Morris Glos (offices at Bristol, Hereford, and six assoc offrs); chm: Glos Legal Assoc 1985-88, Glos Social Security Appeal Tbnl 1984; pres Glos Rotary Club 1981-82, chm Glos Civic Tst 1983-, sec Glos Historic Bldgs 1980-; cdr St John Ambulance Glos 1988-; memb Law Soc 1957; OStJ 1986; MRCVS; *Recreations* jogging, Inner city conservation; *Clubs* St John House, LSE; *Style*— Robert Morris, Esq; The Hill House, Hartpury, Glos GL19 3DB (☎ 0452 70 235); Morroway House, Station Rd, Glos GL1 1DW (☎ 0452 301 903, fax 0452 411 115)

MORRIS, Roger John Bowring; s of Timothy George Bowring Morris, of Shrewsbury, and Mabel, *née* Baxter; *b* 13 June 1946; *Educ* Liverpool Coll, Peterhouse Cambridge (MA, LLM); *m* 6 July 1985, Ann, da of George Morris Whittle, of Brentwood, Essex; 1 s (Edward b 1986); *Career* slr 1970, articled clerk and asst St Helens CBC 1968-72, asst town clerk 1973, (assoc town clerk 1973-74, dir of admin Great Grimsby Borough Council 1974-81; town clerk and chief exec: City of Durham 1981-86, Northampton BC 1986-; pres Assoc of Dist Secs 1979-80, hon slr Soc Local Authy Chief Exec 1984-; Freeman (joiner) City of Durham 1986; memb Law Soc 1970; *Books* Parliament and The Public Libraries (1977), Solicitors and Local Authorities (1982, Supplement 1986), Local Government Ground Rules (1990); *Recreations* family, writing, tennis, hill walking, skiing; *Clubs* Northampton Rotary; *Style*— Roger Morris, Esq; Highway House, 95 High Street, Weston Favell, Northampton NN3 3JX (☎ 0604 405922); Northampton Borough Council, 61 Derngate, Northampton NN1 1UW (☎ 0604 29033)

MORRIS, Rear Adm Roger Oliver; CB (1990); s of Dr Oliver Nixon Morris (d 1983), of Plymouth, and Sybil Helga (Mollie), *née* Hudson (d 1973); *b* 1 Sept 1932; *Educ* Mount House Sch Tavistock, RNC Dartmouth; *Career* Cmd HM Ships: Medusa 1964-65, Beagle 1968-70, Fawn 1972, Hecla 1975-78, Hydra 1970-71 and 1979-80; RCDS 1978; dir of hydrographic Plans and Surveys in Hydrographic Dept Taunton 1980-82 (asst hydrographer 1982-84), hydrographer of the Navy 1985-90; chm Cncl Soc for Nautical Res 1989; FRGS, FRIN; *Recreations* heraldry, opera, ornithology; *Clubs* Royal Cwlth Soc; *Style*— Rear Adm R O Morris, CB; c/o Lloyds Bank plc, 52 Devonport Rd, Plymouth PL3 4DG

MORRIS, Rosalind Anita; da of Dennis Bernard Robin (d 1987), and Susan, *née* Kaye; *b* 20 Jan 1950; *Educ* St Paul's Girls' Sch; *m* 23 March 1972 (m dis 1978), Ronald Michael; *Career* sr buyer Marks and Spencer Fashion Gp; former chm: Women in Business, Joint Israel Appeal (JIA); memb Network; *Recreations* theatre, art, interior design, tennis, needlework; *Style*— Mrs Rosalind Morris; Marks and Spencer plc, Michael House, 57 Baker Street, London, WI (☎ 071 935 4422)

MORRIS, Simon James; s of Kenneth Stapleton Morris, of Cape Town, and Grace, *née* Skitmore; *b* 24 Jan 1958; *Educ* Whitgift Sch, Gonville and Caius Coll Cambridge (MA); *Career* admitted slr 1982; ptnr Cameron Markby Hewitt 1988-; chm Cambridge Univ Cons Assoc 1979, memb Cncl London Topographical Soc 1983-; *Books* Financial Services: Regulating Investment Business (1989); *Recreations* Victorian maps of London; *Style*— Simon Morris, Esq; 40 Tower Hill, London EC3N 4BB (☎ 071 702 2345, fax 071 702 2302)

MORRIS, Stewart John Southan; s of William Southan Morris (d 1979), of 19 Viceroy Court, Prince Albert Rd, London, and Gwendoline Florence, *née* Morris; *b* 30 March 1930; *Educ* Winchester; *m* 1, June 1954 (m dis 1959), Brenda, *née* Peel; m 2, Sept 1960 (m dis 1971), Sylvia Leah, *née* Koffman; 1 s (Southan b 13 Jan 1965), 3 da (Samantha b 28 Dec 1962, Shelly b 18 April 1972, Suzanne (twin)); m 3, July (m dis 1982), Karen Joy, *née* Knight; *Career* exec prodr BBC TV 1958-; over 1000 network prodns incl: 7 Royal TV Performances, 5 Eurovision Song Contests, opening ceremony 1986 Cwlth Games Edinburgh; winner numerous awards worldwide; *Recreations* photography, cinematography, powerboating, clay-pigeon shooting; *Style*— Stewart Morris, Esq; Copperfield House, Petersham, Surrey TW10 4AU (☎ 081 940 2522, fax 081 948 3682); BBC Television, London W12 7RJ (☎ 081 576 1913, 081 743 2457, fax 071 743 2457, car 0860 322 228)

MORRIS, Timothy Denis; DL (W Midlands 1975); s of Denis Edward Morris, OBE, of 123 Clare Park, Crondall, nr Farnham, Surrey, and Angela Mary Skey, *née* Moore; *b* 14 Feb 1935; *Educ* Tonbridge, Pembroke Coll Cambridge (MA); *m* 12 Sept 1959, Caroline, da of Edward Victor Wynn (d 1983), of Chipping Campden, Glos; 1 s (Andrew b 23 April 1962), 1 da (Juliet b 30 July 1964); *Career* Nat Serv Sub Lt RNVR 1953-55; newspaper exec; dir: The Birmingham Post and Mail Ltd 1967-90 (chm 1982-90), Cambridge Newspapers Ltd 1970, Press Assoc Ltd 1980-87 (chm 1985-86), Burton Daily Mail Ltd 1983-, South Hams Newspapers Ltd 1985- (chm 1985-86), Yattendon Investment Trust Ltd 1985-, Reuters Founder Share Co Ltd 1987-; chm Packet Newspapers Ltd 1986-; co cmmr Warwickshire Scouts 1974-77, pres W Midlands Newspaper Soc 1975-76, chm Birmingham Civic Soc 1979-83, dir Birmingham Hippodrome Theatre Tst 1980- (chm 1989-); pres Newspaper Soc 1984-85; *Recreations* golf, philately; *Clubs* Naval; *Style*— Timothy Morris, Esq, DL; Yattendon Investment Trust Ltd, PO Box 18, 28 Colmore Circus, Queensway, Birmingham B4 6AX (☎ 021 236 3366, fax 021 233 1175, car 0860 632485)

MORRIS, Tony Richard; *b* 7 July 1946; *Educ* Queen Mary's GS Basingstoke; *Career* fin accountant Roberts Construction Co 1974-76, audit mangr Deloitte Haskins & Sells 1976-79, dep inspr Int Stock Exchange 1979-85, gp compliance dir Midland Gp 1985-; memb CIPFA 1973, FCCA 1981; *Recreations* gardening, golf; *Style*— Tony Morris, Esq; Midland Bank plc, Compliance Gp, Poultry, London EC2P 2BX (☎ 071 260 8640)

MORRIS, Prof Trevor Raymond; s of Ivor Raymond Morris, CBE (d 1970), and Dorothy May, *née* Parker (d 1975); *b* 11 April 1930; *Educ* Rendcomb Coll, Univ of Reading (BSc, PhD, DSc); *m* 17 April 1954, (Elisabeth) Jean; 3 s (Stephen b 1956, Jonathan b 1959, Andrew b 1962), 2 da (Wendy b 1957, Virginia b 1964); *Career* Nat Serv RASC 1954-56; prof Univ of Reading 1981- (lectr 1957-69, reader 1969-81); FIBiol 1974; *Style*— Prof Trevor Morris; Middle Nesley, 36 Shinfield Road, Reading RG2 7BW (☎ 0734 872529); University of Reading, Whiteknights, Reading RG6 2AT (☎ 0734 318470)

MORRIS, Rev William James; JP (Glasgow 1971); o s of William John Morris, and Eliza Cecilia Cameron Johnson; *b* 22 Aug 1925; *Educ* Cardiff HS, Univ of Wales (BA, BD), Univ of Edinburgh (PhD); *m* 1952, Jean Daveena Ogilvy, CBE, o da of Rev David Porter Howie, of Kilmarnock, Ayrshire; 1 s; *Career* ordained 1951; minister: St David's Buckhaven 1953-57, Peterhead Old Parish 1957-67; chaplain HM Prison Peterhead 1963-67; memb Convocation of Univ of Strathclyde, chm Cncl Soc of Friends of Glasgow Cathedral, minister of Glasgow Cathedral 1967-; chaplain to: HM The Queen in Scotland 1969-, the Lord High Cmmr to Gen Assembly of Church of Scotland 1975-76; memb: IBA Scotland 1979-84, Bd of Govrs Jordanhill Coll of Educn 1983-; hon pres City of Glasgow Soc of Social Serv; hon memb: Rotary Clubs of Dennistoun and Glasgow, Royal Scottish Automobile Club, RNVR Club; chaplain Strathclyde Police; Sub-ChStJ; Hon LLD Strathclyde 1974, Hon DD Glasgow 1979,

Hon FRCPS Glasgow; *Books* A Walk Through Glasgow Cathedral (1986); *Recreations* being a paternalistic do-gooder, gardening, sunbathing in SW France; *Clubs* New (Edinburgh); *Style*— Rev William Morris, JP; 94 St Andrews Drive, Glasgow (☎ 041 427 2757)

MORRIS JONES, Hon Mrs (Jane Elizabeth Stirling); *née* Howard; da (by 1 m) of 4 Baron Strathcona and Mount Royal; *b* 23 Jan 1955; *Educ* Sherborne Sch for Girls, Somerville Coll Oxford; *m* 17 Oct 1987, Nigel Morris Jones, o s of M H Morris Jones, of Tarvin, Cheshire; *Style*— The Hon Mrs Morris Jones; 143 Portland Rd, London W11 4LR (☎ 071 243 8252)

MORRIS-MARSHAM, Jack Richard; s of Richard Henry Anstruther Morris-Marsham (d 1975), of Spilfeathers, Ingatestone, Essex, and Iris Rose Sophia Blackburn, *née* Larking (refer Peerage and Baronetage, E of Romney); *b* 27 Nov 1936; *Educ* Eton; *m* 1, 7 Sept 1963 (m dis 1978), Agnes Margaret (Molly), da of Maj-Gen Walter Rutherfoord Goodman, CB, DSO, MC (d 1976), of Little Bealings Holt, Woodbridge, Suffolk; 2 s (James Jonathan b 1964, Dominic Rutherfoord b 1967), 1 da (Tiffany Jane b 1969); m 2, 30 June 1978, Ann Christine (d 1980), da of Howard Sarjent Backhouse (d 1990), of Storrington, Sussex; m 3, 28 May 1983, Serena Sybil, da of Gp Capt Geoffrey K Fairtlough, of Ashfield Ct, Ballybriffas, Co Leix; *Career* Lt Cdr RNR 1954-73; mktg dir BMW Concessionaries 1970-74; The Colt Car Co Ltd: mktg dir 1974-81, md 1981-82, vice chm 1982-; *Recreations* bridge, shooting, snorkelling, gardening; *Clubs* Naval; *Style*— Jack Morris-Marsham, Esq; Brookside, Ewen, Cirencester, Glos GL7 6BU (☎ 0285 770 555); The Colt Car Co Ltd, Watermoor, Cirencester, Glos GL7 1EF (☎ 0285 65 5777, telex 43452, fax 658026, car 083 174363)

MORRIS OF BALGONIE AND EDDERGOLL, Yr; Stuart Gordon Cathal Morris; s of Raymond Stanley Morris of Balgonie and Eddergoll, and Margaret Newton Morris, *née* Stuart; *b* 17 April 1965; *Educ* Bell-Baxter HS, Elmwood Coll, Univ of Birmingham; *Career* historian, armorist, author; fndr memb of Heraldry Soc of Scotland; Liveryman Worshipful Co of Meadmakers 1982; FSA (Scot) 1983, FRSA 1990 (assoc 1986); Cdr Order of Polonia Restituta 1990; *Recreations* archery, heraldry, genealogy, mead making, historical researching; *Style*— The Younger of Balgonie and Eddergoll; Balgonie Castle, by Markinch, Fife KY7 6HQ (☎ 0592 750119)

MORRIS OF CASTLE MORRIS, Baron (Life Peer UK 1990), of St Dogmaels in the County of Dyfed; Brian Robert Morris; s of Capt William Robert Morris, RN (d 1964), of Cardiff, and Ellen Elizabeth, *née* Shelley (d 1977); *b* 4 Dec 1930; *Educ* Cardiff HS, Worcester Coll Oxford (MA, DPhil); *m* 18 Aug 1955, Sandra Mary, da of Percival Samuel James (d 1967); 1 s (Hon Christopher Justin Robert b 1959), 1 da (Hon Lindsay Alison Mary (Hon Mrs Boxall) b 1957); *Career* Nat Serv with 1 Bn Welch Regt 1949-51, 4 Bn Welch Regt (TA) 1951-56; fell Shakespeare Inst Univ of Birmingham 1956-58; lectr Univ of Reading 1960-65 (asst lectr 1958-60), sr lectr Univ of York 1967-71 (lectr 1965-67), prof of Eng lit Univ of Sheffield (becoming dep dean and public orator) 1971-80; princ St David's Univ Coll Lampeter 1980-; chm: Lit Panel Yorks Arts Assoc 1973-77, UGC/NAB Working Pty on Librarianship and Info Sci 1986-87, Museums and Galleries Cmmn 1985- (memb 1975-); vice-pres: Cncl for Nat Parks 1985-, Museums Assoc 1985-, Welsh Advsy Ctee Br Cncl 1983-, Anthony Panizzi Fndn 1987-; memb: Archbishops' Cncl on Evangelism 1971-75, Cncl Poetry Soc 1980-, Nat Library of Wales 1981-, Br Library Bd 1980-, Welsh Arts Cncl 1983-86 (memb lit ctee 1978-86); tstee: Nat Portrait Gallery 1977-, Nat Heritage Meml Fund 1980; gen ed: New Mermaid Dramatists 1964-, New Arden Shakespeare 1974-82; *Books* The Poems of John Cleveland (with Eleanor Withington, 1967), John Cleveland: a Bibliography of his Poems (1967), New Mermaid Critical Commentaries 1 to 3 (1969-72), Mary Quant's London (1973), Ritual Murder (ed, 1980); edited plays: Ford's The Broken Heart (1965), 'Tis Pity She's A Whore (1968), Tourneur's The Atheist's Tragedy (with Roma Gill, 1976), Shakespeare's The Taming of the Shrew (1981): poetry: Tide Race (1976), Stones in the Brook (1978), Dear Tokens (1987); *Recreations* music, mountains, museums; *Clubs* Athenaeum, Beefsteak; *Style*— The Rt Hon Lord Morris of Castle Morris; Bryn, North Rd, Lampeter, Dyfed SA48 7HZ (☎ 0570 422335); The Old Hall, Foolow, Eyam, Derbyshire S30 1QR; St David's University College, Lampeter, Dyfed SA48 7ED (☎ 0570 422351, fax 0570 423423)

MORRIS OF KENWOOD, 2 Baron (UK 1950); Philip Geoffrey Morris; JP (Inner London 1967); s of 1 Baron (d 1954); *b* 18 June 1928; *Educ* Loughborough Coll Sch, Loughborough Coll; *m* 1958, Hon Ruth Joan Gertrude Rahle, da of Baron Janner (Life Peer); 1 s, 3 da; *Heir* s, Hon Jonathan David Morris; *Career* served 1946-49 with RAF, rejoined 1951-55, flying offr 1953; *Style*— The Rt Hon the Lord Morris of Kenwood, JP; Lawn Cottage, Orchard Rise, Kingston, Surrey KT2 7EY (☎ 081 942 6321)

MORRIS OF KENWOOD, Baroness; Hon Ruth Joan Gertrude Rahle; da of Baron Janner (Life Peer); *b* 1932; *m* 1958, 2 Baron Morris of Kenwood; *Career* slr 1956; former memb GAC of IBA, exec memb Steering and Management Ctee WOYL; govr Broadwood Hall Sch, patron New Working Woman; tstee: Rowan Educn Tst, Jewish Youth Fund; vice-chm Ivy Lake Water Ski Club; *Style*— The Rt Hon the Lady Morris of Kenwood; Lawn Cottage, Orchard Rise, Kingston upon Thames, Surrey

MORRISH, Mr John Edwin (Jack); s of Henry Edwin Morrish, of London and Shanklin, IOW, and Ada Minnie, *née* Tapping; *b* 23 Sept 1915; *Educ* Univ Coll Sch Hampstead, Northampton Poly, Univ of Leicester (MA); *m* 1 Oct 1937 (m dis 1943), Norah, *née* Lake; 1 da (Anna b 1938); m 2, 12 Aug 1944 (m dis 1977), Violet, da of Daniel Saunders; 1 s (Victor b 1947), 1 da (Elizabeth b 1952); m 3, 17 July 1984, Betty Lupton, da of John Wear, of Heckmondwicke, W Yorks (d 1990); *Career* PO engr 1932-43 and 1945-54; coalminer 1943-45, asst sec CS Union 1954 -72, gen sec Customs & Excise Gp 1972-76, asst gen sec Soc CS 1974- 76, with various vol orgns 1977-81, census offr 1981 and 1991, dep ldr and co cnllr Northants 1981-85 (chm Educn Ctee); memb: Assoc of CCs and Educn Ctee 1981-85, Advsy Ctee for Supply and Educn of Teachers 1981-84, Burnham Ctee 1981-86; chm govrs Nene Coll 1981-85, borough cncllr Hounslow (vice chm Educn Ctee) 1986-90, bd memb Nat Fedn for Educn Res 1986-90, memb Assoc for Met Authorities and Educn Ctee 1986-90, educn conslt 1990-; *Books* The Future of Forestry (1971); *Recreations* thinking, pursuit of justice, education studies, music, theatre; *Clubs* Civil Serv; *Style*— Jack Morrish, Esq; The Old Bakehouse, 1 Church St, Broughton, Kettering, Northants NN14 1LU (☎ 0536 790 914)

MORRISH, John Sutherland Cavers; s of Capt Leo Grafton Morrish; *b* 4 Nov 1946; *Educ* George Watson's Coll, Edinburgh Univ; *m* 1977, Elspeth Joan, da of Robert Leslie Findlay; 2 c; *Career* fin dir GEC Medical Equipment Ltd 1976-81, fin and investment mangr, small business div of Scottish Devpt Agency 1981-; *Recreations* golf; *Style*— John Morrish, Esq; c/o Scottish Development Agency, 17 Cockspur Street, London SW1

MORRISH, Peter Sydney; s of Sydney Victor Morrish (d 1969), of Hove, Sussex, and Elizabeth McLaren, *née* Dewar (d 1969); *b* 30 Dec 1924; *Educ* Sutton Valence, Emmanuel Coll Cambridge (MA); *m* 18 Sept 1954, June Seymour, da of Lancelot Stephen Richard Monckton (d 1979), of Bearsted, Kent; 1 s (Lancelot Peter b 19 Oct 1956), 1 da (Annabel June b 24 Feb 1959); *Career* Sub Lt RNVR 1942-46, Channel, Far East Coastal Forces and attached Fleet Air Arm; land agent and chartered surveyor; ptnr Burrows Clements Winch & Sons 1952-55; chm: Castlemaine Farms Ltd 1955-90, Wealden Hops Ltd 1986-90; memb Friends of Kent Churches; Freeman City of London 1964; memb: Worshipful Co of Broderers 1964, Worshipful Co of Fruiterers 1975; ARICS 1946; *Recreations* skiing, golf, environment; *Clubs* Farmers', Royal St George's Golf, Rye Golf; *Style*— Peter S Morrish, Esq; Castlemaine, Horsmonden, Tonbridge, Kent (☎ 089 272 2780)

MORRISH, Hon Mrs (Rosalind Beatrice); *née* Wade; yr da of Baron Wade, DL (Life Peer, d 1988); *b* 11 Dec 1937; *m* 21 Oct 1961, Richard David Morrish, s of late Eric John Morrish, of Leeds; 2 s (Jonathan b 1964, Thomas b 1966), 1 da (Judith b 1969); *Style*— The Hon Mrs Morrish; 34 St Margaret's Rd, Horsforth, Leeds

MORRISON, Hon Alasdair Andrew Orr; s of 1 Viscount Dunrossil, GCMG, MC, PC, QC (d 1961); *b* 25 March 1929; *Educ* Fettes, Balliol Coll Oxford, Chicago Univ; *m* 1958, Frances Mary, da of late Wilfrid Rippon Snow, of Adelaide, S Australia; 1 s, 2 da; *Career* chm Orchid Ctee RHS; *Style*— The Hon Alasdair Morrison; Maisemore Lodge, nr Gloucester, Glos (☎ 0452 21747); work: Shell International Petroleum Co Ltd (☎ 071 934 2286)

MORRISON, Hon Alasdair Godfrey; s of 2 Viscount Dunrossil; *b* 4 April 1962; *m* 19 Sept 1987, Tania, o da of J A Redman, of Minehead, Somerset; *Style*— The Hon Alasdair Morrison; 90 St Stephen's Ave, London W12

MORRISON, Alastair McLeod; MC (1944); s of Brig Hugh McLeod Morrison, MC (d 1984); *b* 2 March 1924; *Educ* Imperial Serv Coll; *m* 1957, Diana Elizabeth, da of late Col Forester Metcalfe Griffith-Griffin, MC; 1 s, 2 da; *Career* served 4/7 Royal Dragoon Gds, NW Europe and Palestine, Capt, ret 1952; dir Howard Machinery Ltd 1970-84 (overseas md France 1953-57, USA 1957-60), chm J Mann & Son Ltd 1973 (md 1970-73), dir AO Smith Harvestore Inc USA 1979-84; patron Tree Cncl; *Recreations* field sports; *Clubs* Cavalry and Guards; *Style*— Alastair Morrison, Esq, MC; Leigh Hill, Savernake, nr Marlborough, Wilts SN8 3BH (☎ 0672 810230)

MORRISON, His Hon Judge Alexander John Henderson; s of Dr Alexander Morrison (d 1980), and Jean Walker Murdoch (d 1961); *b* 16 Nov 1927; *Educ* Derby Sch, Emmanuel Coll Cambridge (MA, LLB); *m* 1978, Hon Philippa Ann *qv*, da of 1 Baron Hives (d 1965); *Career* called to the Bar Gray's Inn 1951, dep chm Derbyshire QS 1964-71, Crown Ct rec 1971-80, regnl chm of Industl Tbnls 1971-80; pres Mental Health Review Tribunals 1983; circuit judge 1980-; *Recreations* golf (pres Derbyshire Union of Golf Clubs 1979-81); *Style*— His Hon Judge Morrison; Derby Combined Court Centre, Morledge, Derby

MORRISON, Alistair Neil; s of Jamie Ian Morrison, of Bermuda, and Aileen Rose, *née* Wingate; *b* 4 Nov 1956; *Educ* Ardingly, Harrow Coll (BA); *m* 25 July 1980, Janis Anne, da of James Cecil Edwards, OBE, JP (d 1964); 1 s (Nicholas James b 14 Nov 1981), 1 da (Olivia Rose b 24 Dec 1985); *Career* freelance photographer 1982; clients incl: Observer Magazine, Sunday Times Magazine, Sunday Telegraph Magazine, You Magazine Illustrated London News, The Field, Country Homes and Interiors, Riva, Mirabella, Harpers and Queen, Amica, Interview; selected exhibitions: NT 1982, Faces of Our Time (NT) 1985, Stars of the British Screen (Nat Portrait Gallery) 1985-86, Twenty For Today (Nat Portrait Gallery) 1986, Oliver 80th Birthday Tribute (Nat Portrait Gallery and Hamiltons Gallery) 1989; works in the collection of Nat Portrait Gallery; *Recreations* swimming, travelling; *Style*— Alistair Morrison, Esq; 9 Highfield Crescent, Northwood HA6 1EZ (☎ 09274 25491, fax 0923 836135)

MORRISON, Hon Sir Charles Andrew; MP (C) Wilts (Devizes Div) 1964-; 2 s of 1 Baron Margadale, TD, JP, *qv*; bro of The Hon James, The Hon Peter (MP) and of Hon Dame Mary Anne Morrison *qqv*; gs of 2 Viscount Hambleden; *b* 25 June 1932; *Educ* Eton; *m* 1, 28 Oct 1954, Hon (Antoinette) Sara Frances Sibell, da of 2 Viscount Long; 1 s, 1 da; m 2, 1984, Rosalind Elizabeth, da of late Hon Richard Edward Lygon (d 1970), and formerly w of Gerald John Ward; *Career* 2 Lt Life Gds 1951-52, Capt Royal Wilts Yeo 1952-66; chm: The Game Conservancy 1987-, Br Tst for Conservation Volunteers 1972-78 (pres 1978-82); pres Nat Anglers Cncl; prime warden Fishmongers Co 1986-87; memb Cncl Salmon & Trout Assoc; vice chm 1922 Ctee 1974-83 chm Nat Ctee for Electoral Reform 1985-; kt 1988; *Recreations* shooting, gardening, fishing; *Clubs* White's, Pratt's; *Style*— The Hon Sir Charles Morrison, MP; House of Commons, London SW1 (☎ 071 219 5012/4008); Brook House, Luckington, nr Chippenham, Wilts (☎ 0666 840371)

MORRISON, Hon Mrs (Charlotte Anne); *née* Monckton; o da of 9 Viscount Galway (d 1971), and Lady Teresa Agnew, *née* Fox-Stangways (d 1989), da of 7 Earl of Ilchester; *b* 16 April 1955; *m* 24 Sept 1983 (m dis 1987), Guy Martin James Morrison, s of Martin James Faber Morrison; 1 s (Simon b 1984); *Style*— The Hon Mrs Morrison; Melbury House, Dorchester, Dorset DT2 0LF (☎ 0935 83231); Bishopfield House, Bawtry, Doncaster, Yorks (☎ 0777 818224); 83 Onslow Gardens, London SW7

MORRISON, David Du Bois; s of John Macfarlane Morrison (d 1978), and Eleanor Buell, *née* Morris; *b* 3 April 1952; *Educ* George Watson's Coll Edinburgh, St Andrews Univ (BSc); *Career* ptnr Wood Mackenzie and Co 1983 (joined 1976), dir Co Natwest Wood Mackenzie and Co Ltd; memb: Stock Exchange, Institute of Petroleum, Soc of Investment Analysts; *Recreations* music, painting, photography, running, squash; *Clubs* New (Edinburgh); *Style*— David Morrison, Esq; Beehive Cottage, Aston, Herts; County Natwest Wood Mackenzie & Co, 135 Bishopsgate, London (☎ 071 375 5000)

MORRISON, 2 Baron (UK 1945); Dennis Glossop Morrison; s of 1 Baron, PC (d 1953); *b* 21 June 1914; *Educ* Tottenham County Sch; *m* 1, 1940 (m dis 1958), Florence, da of Augustus Hennes, of Tottenham; m 2, 1959, (m dis 1975), Joan, da of Willam Meech, of Acton; *Heir* none; *Career* formerly with Metal Box Co; Lord-Lt's rep for Tottenham 1955-, vice pres Acton C of C until 1987; *Style*— The Rt Hon the Lord Morrison; 7 Ullswater Avenue, Felixstowe, Suffolk (☎ 039 42 77405)

MORRISON, Dennis John; s of Leonard Tait Morrison, of Sale, Cheshire, and Alice, *née* Hutson; *b* 20 May 1942; *Educ* Ashton upon Mersey Boys Sch, Lymm GS, Univ of Manchester (BA, Dip Town and Country Planning); *m* 18 March 1967, Frances Joan (Polly), da of Frank Pollard, of Roundhay, Leeds; 1 s (Duncan John b 1971), 1 da (Rosalyn Jane b 1973); *Career* planning offr Lancashire CC 1966-70, sr planning offr Welsh Office Cardiff 1970-75; DOE Manchester: reg superintending planner 1975-81, head NW Enterprise Unit 1981-84, regnl controller Mersey Task Force Liverpool 1984-89, regnl dir E Midlands Region DOE and Tport Nottingham 1989-; memb: Consultative Ctee Liverpool Tate Gallery, Exec Ctee Liverpool Anglican Cathedral; Freeman Burgess of the Altrincham Court LEET; MRTPI, FRGS; *Recreations* antiquarian horologist, collector of antiquarian books, gardening, hill walking; *Clubs* Altrincham 41; *Style*— Dennis Morrison, Esq; Departments of Environment and Transport, East Midlands Region, Cranbrook House, Cranbrook St, Nottingham NG1 1EY (☎ 0602 476121, telex 377681, fax 0602 476121)

MORRISON, Derrick John Richard; JP; s of John Cyril (d 1972), and Violet Constance Osborne (d 1988); *b* 4 Aug 1922; *Educ* Eastcote Boys' Sch, Trent Park Coll of Educn, London Univ (LCP, Dip Ed); *m* 18 Aug 1951, Patricia Margaret, da of Claude Tilly (d 1966); *Career* RAF Med Branch 1941-47; headmaster West Hill Sch Leatherhead 1960-87, chm Woking Juvenile Ct 1970-87, memb Surrey Magistrates Soc; *Recreations* sailing, golf, gardening; *Clubs* Rotary Int; *Style*— Derrick J R Morrison, Esq, JP; Cherrywood, Brentmoor Rd, West End, Woking, Surrey GU24

9NF

MORRISON, Cdr Edwin Allen; OBE (1982), DL (Hampshire 1977); s of John Wheatley Morrison (d 1945), of Snows Green House, Shotley Bridge, Co Durham, and Kathleen, *née* King (d 1953); *b* 13 May 1905; *Educ* Royal Naval Coll: Osborne, Dartmouth; *m* 16 Dec 1931, Valerie Patricia Anne, da of Col Harold Charles Wortham, CMG, DSO; 1 s (Euan b 1941), 3 da (Elspeth b 1936, Fenella b 1943, Malvina b 1946); *Career* served HMS: Thunderer 1922-23, RNEC Keyham 1923-27, Iron Duke 1927, Effingham 1927-29, Fisgard 1930-32, Curacoa 1932-33, RNEC 1933-35, Hero 1936-37, Nelson 1937-40, Daedalus 1940-41, Charybdis 1941-42, Spartan 1942-44, Landrail 1944-45, Merganser 1945-46, President 1946-48, Condor 1948-49, Resource 1949, ret as Cdr RN 1950; mangr family shipping and property interests; memb Chapter Gen OStJ; formerly: cdr St Johns Ambulance, memb Hosp Mgmnt, chm Diocesan Finance; Citizen and Pattenmaker of London 1950; KStJ 1944; *Recreations* sailing; *Clubs* Army & Navy, Royal Yacht Sqdn Royal Ocean Racing, Royal Lymington YC; *Style*— Cdr Edwin Morrison, OBE, DL; The Bury House, Odiham, nr Basingstoke, Hampshire RG25 1LZ (☎ 0256 702 103)

MORRISON, Frances Margaret (Fran); da of Lt-Cdr William Morrison, RNVR, of Cove, Scotland, and Hilary Mary, *née* Wootton; *Educ* Queen's Park Sch Glasgow, St Andrews Univ (MA); *m* 22 Sept 1984 (m dis), Trevor Deaves, s of Alan Deaves, of Cranleigh, Surrey; 2 s (Adam b 1984, Dominic b 1986); *Career* broadcaster and media conslt, news and current affrs reporter/presenter BBC Radio and TV, sole female memb presenting team of BBC TV's Newsnight at its launch 1979; reporter/presenter BBC TV: Nationwide 1981-83, 60 Minutes 1983-84; reporter BBC TV Watchdog 1984-85, reporter various documentary progs BBC TV 1978-86, presenter various arts and music progs BBC TV 1978-; reporter/presenter Thames TV, Channel 4, Sky TV and BBC Radio Womans Hour 1986-90; media conslt 1986-, freelance journalist 1978-; *Recreations* travel, theatre, visual arts; *Clubs* Network; *Style*— Ms Fran Morrison; c/o Jon Roseman Assocs, 103 Charing Cross Rd, London WC2H ODT (☎ 071 439 8245)

MORRISON, Prof George Chalmers; s of Donald Crerar Morrison (d 1965), of Bearsden, Glasgow, and Annie Sibbald, *née* Johnston (d 1984); *b* 14 May 1930; *Educ* Bearsden Acad, Univ of Glasgow (BSc, PhD); *m* 7 Oct 1961, Prudence, da of Albert Donald Valentine Knowers (d 1975), of Lymington, Hants; 3 da (Leslie b 25 Aug 1962, Vanessa b 10 Jan 1965, Nicola b 24 Dec 1965); *Career* res assoc Univ of Chicago USA 1957-60, princ scientific offr Aere Harwell 1961-65 (res fell 1954-57), scientist Argonne Nat Laboratory Illinois USA 1965-73; Univ of Birmingham: prof 1973- (chair of nuclear structure), dep dean Faculty of Sci 1985-88, dean Faculty of Sci 1988-, head Sch of Physics and Space Res 1990-; author of numerous papers in int scientific jls and contributor to scientific pubns; SERC: memb Nuclear Structure Ctee 1982-86 (1974-78), memb Nuclear Physics Bd 1984-87, memb Physics Ctee 1984-87; memb Working Gp on Physics Euro Sci Fndn 1981-84, memb Bd of Nuclear Physics Div Euro Physical Soc 1984-; FIOP, FAPS; *Recreations* golf, walking, philately; *Clubs* Harborne Golf; *Style*— Prof George Morrison; 184 Lordswood Rd, Harborne, Birmingham, West Midlands B17 8QH (☎ 021 427 3248); School of Physics and Space Research, The University of Birmingham, Edgbaston, Birmingham B15 2TT (☎ 021 414 4653, fax 021 414 6709, telex 333762 UOBHAM G)

MORRISON, Hon Mrs (Helena Geneva); *née* Garner; o da of Baron Garner, GCMG (d 1983; Life Peer); *b* 28 Jan 1947; *Educ* Bishop Strachan Sch, Toronto, Canada; Tortington Park; *m* 1981, Iain Morrison; *Style*— The Hon Mrs Morrison; 33 North Street, Marcham, Abingdon, Oxon

MORRISON, Maj Hon James Ian; TD (1963), DL (Wilts 1977); s and h of 1 Baron Margadale, *qv*; eld bro of The Hon Sir Charles and The Hon Sir Peter Morrison (MPs), and of The Hon Dame Mary Anne Morrison, *qqv*, and Margaret Ester Lucy, *née* Smith, da of 3 Viscount Hambleden (d 1980), ggs of James Morrison who purchased much of the property at present owned; *b* 17 July 1930; *Educ* Eton, RAC Cirencester; *m* 1952, Clare, da of Anthony Lister Barclay, of Broad Oak End, Hertford; 2 s (Alastair, Hugh), 1 da (Fiona) (*see* Viscount Hon Hugh Trenchard); *Career* 2 Lt Life Gds 1949-50, Maj Royal Wilts Yeo; farmer, landowner and co dir; Wilts C Cncllr 1955 and 1973-77, alderman 1969, High Sheriff Wilts 1971; pres W Wilts (Westbury) Cons Assoc 1972-84 (chm 1967-71); chm: Tattersall's Ctee 1969-80, Wilts CLA 1978-81; Hon Col: A (Royal Wilts Yeo) Sqdn Royal Yeo RAC TA 1982-89, (Royal Wilts Yeo) Sqdn Royal Wessex Yeo 1982-89, Royal Wessex Yeo RAC TA 1984-89; memb: Queen's Body Guard for Scotland, Royal Company of Archers; *Recreations* racing, field sports; *Clubs* White's, Jockey; *Style*— Maj The Hon James Morrison, TD, DL; Hawking Down, Hindon, Salisbury, Wilts (☎ 074 789 234); Estate Office, Fonthill Bishop, Salisbury, SP3 5SH (☎ 074 789 246); Islay Estate Office, Bridgend, Islay, Argyll PA44 7PB (☎ 049 681 221)

MORRISON, James Stewart; s of Stewart Kirkwood Morrison (d 1933), of Chelsea, and Felice, *née* Showell (d 1989); *b* 12 Oct 1926; *Educ* Merchant Taylors', Wadham Coll Oxford (MA); *m* 27 Sept 1958, Dr Jane Bomford, da of Dr Edgar Davey; 1 s (Charles b 1964), 1 da (Catherine b 1972); *Career* dir Clarnico Ltd 1953-70, dep chm Associated Deliveries Ltd 1986 (md 1970-85), dep appeals dir Assoc for Spina Bifida and Hydrocephalus (ASBAH) 1986-89; pres Jr C of C London 1966-67, memb Cncl London C of C and Indust 1969-80; Confectioners Benevolent Fund: pres 1982, chm 1987-88, tstee 1988-; Freeman City of London 1967; MBIM 1951, memb Lloyds 1985; *Recreations* travel, reading, gardening; *Clubs* London Rowing; *Style*— James Morrison, Esq; Washwell House, Painswick, nr Stroud, Glos GL6 6SJ (☎ 0452 813556; 26 Ormonde Gate, Chelsea, London SW3 4EX (☎ 071 352 7152)

MORRISON, John; s of Thomas Patrick Morrison, and Marie, *née* Boylan; *b* 6 March 1949; *Educ* St Edward's Coll Liverpool, St Catherine's Coll Oxford (BA); *m* 29 Feb 1980, Judith, da of Ronald Lee, of Bury, Lancashire; 1 s (Nicholas b 1981), 1 da (Joanna b 1984); *Career* news trainee BBC 1971, scriptwriter ITN 1973, prog ed Channel 4 News 1982, features ed The Independent 1986, ed Newsnight BBC 1987, ed Assignment BBC 1990; *Style*— John Morrison, Esq; BBC, Lime Grove, London W12 (☎ 081 576 7236)

MORRISON, Ven John Anthony; s of Maj Leslie Claude Morrison (d 1967), of Hastings, Sussex, and Mary Sharland, da of Sir Frank Newson-Smith, 1 Bt (d 1971); *b* 11 March 1938; *Educ* Haileybury, Jesus Coll Cambridge (BA, MA), Lincoln Coll Oxford (MA), Chichester Theol Coll; *m* 20 July 1968, Angela, da of Maj Jonathan Eric Bush (d 1978), of Leatherhead; 2 s (Dominic b 19 June 1970, Nicholas b 11 May 1974), 1 da (Philippa b 26 March 1972); *Career* ordained deacon 1964; curate: St Peter Birmingham 1964-68, St Michael-at-the-North Gate Oxford 1968-74; priest Birmingham 1965, chaplain Lincoln Coll Oxford 1968-74, examining chaplain to Bishop of Oxford 1973-, vicar Basildon Berks 1974-82, rural dean Bradfield 1978-82, vicar Aylesbury Bucks 1982-90, rural dean Aylesbury 1985-89, archdeacon Buckingham 1990-; memb Gen Synod 1980-90; Freeman City of London 1961, Liveryman Worshipful Co of Spectaclemakers 1962; *Recreations* rowing, gardening; *Clubs* Leander, Vincent's; *Style*— The Ven the Archedeacon of Buckingham; 60 Wendover Rd, Aylesbury, Bucks HP21 9LW (☎ 0296 23269)

MORRISON, Hon Mrs (Louisa Mary Constance); da of 14 Baron Napier and (5) Ettrick; *b* 5 Feb 1961; *m* 25 July 1987, Capt Alexander F Morrison, er son of Peter Morrison; 1 s (Oliver Charles Francis b 19 Aug 1989); *Style*— The Hon Mrs Morrison; Forest Lodge, Great Park, Windsor

MORRISON, Margaret Jane; BEM (1972); da of William Campbell (d 1987), and May, *née* Christie; *b* 20 March 1924; *Educ* Royal Jubilee Jrs Newcastle, Sandyford Secdy Modern Newcastle; *m* June 1943, Thomas Turnbull Morrison, s of Thomas Morrison; 1 da (May Campbell b 16 Dec 1944); *Career* Civil Serv Union Nat Exec Ctee 1968-78, pres CSU 1980-87 (vice pres 1978-79), dep pres Nat Union of Civil & Public Servants (NUCPS) 1987-89; vice chm Northern Regnl TUC 1980-, chm Womens Advsy Gp Northern Regnl TUC 1980-, memb Women's Ctee TUC 1979-89; dir: Northern Development Co 1984-89, Entrust 1984-; memb Euro Women's TUC and Steering Ctee 1982-; exec ctee memb Women's Nat Cmmn 1987- (memb 1981-, co chm 1989-91); hon life memb NUCPS, hon life pres Northern Region TUC; awarded: TUC Gold Badge for Women Trade Unionist of the Year 1973, Harry Cowan Meml Award for Outstanding Serv to TUC; *Publications* co produced the report Homelessness Amongst Women (1983); *Recreations* music, reading, swimming, conversation; *Clubs* Victory (London); *Style*— Mrs Margaret Morrison, BEM; Women's National Commission, Government Offices, Horseguards Rd, London SW1P 3AL (☎ 071 270 5903, fax 071 270 5828)

MORRISON, Hon (Dame) Mary Anne; DCVO (1982, CVO 1970); does not use style of Dame; da of 1 Baron Margadale, sis of the Hon James, the Hon Sir Charles and the Rt Hon Sir Peter Morrison, *qv*; *b* 17 May 1937; *Educ* Heathfield Sch Ascot, abroad; *Career* woman of the bedchamber to HM The Queen 1960-; *Style*— The Hon Mary Morrison, DCVO; c/o Islay Estate Office, Bridgend, Islay, Argyll (☎ 049 681 221); Fonthill House, Tisbury, Wilts SP3 5SA (☎ 0747 870202)

MORRISON, Michael John; s of John Percy Morrison, JP, and Kathleen Morrison; *b* 31 March 1939; *Educ* Fettes, St Catharine's Coll Cambridge (MA, LLB); *m* 11 Sept 1965, June; 1 s (Nicholas James b 21 Dec 1967), 1 da (Louise Charlotte b 23 June 1971); *Career* admitted slr 1965; ptnr Parker Garrett 1969-82; sr ptnr: Taylor Garrett 1988 (ptnr 1982-88), Taylor Joynson Garrett 1989-; dir: Yuills Ltd 1975-, Leif Hoegh UK Ltd 1978-, Norwegian American Cruises UK Ltd 1980-87; memb Law Soc; *Recreations* golf, squash; *Clubs* RAC, Moor Park Golf; *Style*— Michael Morrison, Esq; Lansdowne, Bedford Rd, Moor Park, Northwood, Middx (☎ 09274 21436); Taylor Joynson Garrett, 180 Fleet St, London EC4 (☎ 071 430 1122, fax 071 528 7145, car 0831 414 621)

MORRISON, Rev Hon Nial Ranald; s of 1 Viscount Dunrossil, GCMG, MC, PC, QC (d 1961), and Catharine Allison, *née* Swan (d 1983); *b* 27 July 1932; *Educ* Fettes Coll, Jesus Coll Oxford (MA); *m* 1959, Sheila Mary, da of late Alexander Forbes, of Gloucester; 3 s, 2 da; *Career* ordained 1956, asst curate St Catharine's Gloucester 1956-58, Stroud Parish Church 1959-62, vicar Randwick Stroud 1962-, minor canon Gloucester Cathedral 1979-86, C of E chaplain Standish Hosp 1982-; *Recreations* music, cycling, botany; *Style*— The Rev the Hon Nial Morrison; The Vicarage, Randwick, Stroud, Glos (☎ 0453 764727)

MORRISON, Nigel Murray Paton; QC; s of David Paton Morrison (d 1968), of Edinburgh, and Dilys Trenholm Pritchard (or Morrison); *b* 18 March 1948; *Educ* Rannoch Sch; *Career* called to the Bar Inner Temple 1972, admitted to Scot Bar 1975; asst ed Session Cases 1976-82, asst clerk to Rules Cncl 1978-84, clerk of faculty Faculty of Advocates 1979-86, standing jr counsel to Scot Devpt Dept (planning) 1982-86, temp sheriff 1982-, chm Social Security Appeal Tbnl 1982-, counsel to Sec of State under the Private Legislation Procedure (Scot) Act (1936) 1986-, first counsel to Lord Pres of Ct of Session 1989- (jr and second counsel 1984-89); contrib to Stair Memorial Encyclopaedia of the Laws of Scotland; tstee Nat Library of Scot 1989-; memb Faculty of Advocates; *Recreations* music, riding, Scottish country dancing, walking; *Clubs* New (Edinburgh); *Style*— Nigel Morrison, Esq, QC; 9 India St, Edinburgh EH3 6HA (☎ 031 225 2807); Advocates' Library, Parliament House, Edinburgh EH1 1RF (☎ 031 226 2881, fax 031 225 3642, telex 727856)

MORRISON, Rt Hon Sir Peter Hugh; MP (C) Chester 1974-; 3 s of 1 Baron Margadale, *qv*; bro of Hon James, Hon Sir Charles (MP), and Hon Dame Mary Anne Morrison, *qqv*; *b* 2 June 1944; *Educ* Eton, Keble Oxford; *Career* formerly PA to Peter Walker; investment mangr, ind businessman; oppn whip 1976-79; Lord Cmmr Treasy 1979-81, under sec of state Employment 1981-83; min of state: Employment 1983-85, Trade and Indust 1985-1986; dep chm Conservative Party 1986-89, Min of State Energy 1987-90; pps to PM 1990; chm One Nation Forum 1987-89 and Cons Collegiate Forum 1986-89; hon fell Keble Coll Oxford; FRSA; kt 1990; *Clubs* White's, Pratt's; *Style*— The Rt Hon Sir Peter Morrison, MP; 81 Cambridge St, London SW1; Eallabus, Bridgend, Islay, Argyll; Stable House, Puddington, Wirral, Cheshire

MORRISON, Hon Mrs (Philippa Ann); *née* Hives; da of 1 Baron Hives, CH, MBE (d 1965); *b* 1928; *m* 1980, His Hon Judge Morrison, *qv*; *Style*— The Hon Mrs Morrison; 17 Eastwood Drive, Littleover, Derby (☎ 0332 45376)

MORRISON, Hon Ranald John; s of 2 Viscount Dunrossil, Govr of Bermuda, and Mavis Viscountess Dunrossil, *née* Dawn Spencer-Payne; *b* 19 Dec 1956; *Educ* Summerfields, Westminster, Univ Coll London (BSc); *m* 1979, Henrietta Frances, da of late J H Wilson, of Addison Road, London (d 1969); 1 s (Richard b 1983), 2 da (Allison b 1984, Rebecca b 1987); *Career* proprietor Garage Door Co estab 1982; *Recreations* cricket; *Clubs* Withington CC, Old Westminster CC; *Style*— The Hon Ranald Morrison; 37 Brigstocke Rd, St Pauls, Bristol; 5 Glenfrome Road, St Werburghs, Bristol, Avon (☎ 0272 554594)

MORRISON, Prof Ronald; s of David Morrison, of Airdrie, and Catherine, *née* Turner (d 1958); *b* 15 April 1946; *Educ* Eastbank Acad, Univ of Strathclyde (BSc), Univ of Glasgow (MSc), Univ of St Andrews (PhD); *m* 17 Oct 1975, Ann Margaret, da of Alistair MacDonald, of Edinburgh; 1 s (David b 1979), 1 da (Catriona b 1981); *Career* prof of software engrg Univ of St Andrews 1985- (sr res fell 1971-72, lectr 1972-84, reader 1984-85); pres Scottish Cross Country Union 1986-87; Davie & Morrison Recursive Descent Compiling (jtly, 1981), Cole & Morrison Introduction to S-Algol Programming (jtly, 1982), Sommerville & Morrison Software Development with Ada (jtly, 1987), Atkinson, Burneman & Morrison Data Types and Persistence (1988), Hull, Morrison, Stemple Database Programming Languages (1989); *Recreations* golf, athletics, cross-country running; *Clubs* St Andrews Golf, Fife Athletic; *Style*— Prof Ronald Morrison; 8 Trinity Place, St Andrews, Fife KY16 8SG (☎ 0334 75649); Department of Mathematical and Computational Science, University of St Andrews, North Haugh, St Andrews, Fife KY16 9SS (☎ 0334 76161, fax 0334 74487)

MORRISON, Hon Mrs ((Antoinette) Sara Frances Sibell); *née* Long; da of 2 Viscount Long (ka 1944), and (Frances) Laura, *née* Charteris (d 1990); *b* 9 Aug 1934; *Educ* England, France; *m* 1954 (m dis 1985), Hon Charles Andrew Morrison; 1 s, 1 da; *Career* dir Gen Electric Co 1975-; non-exec dir: Abbey National Building Society 1979-, The Fourth Channel Television Co 1980-85, Imperial Group 1982-86; chm Nat Cncl for Voluntary Organisations 1977-81 (vice chm 1970-77); memb: Cncl of Imperial Coll 1986-, Cncl of Policy Studies Inst 1983-; former memb: Nat Consumer Cncl, The Volunteer Centre, Wilts CC (until 1970); dir Nat Radiological Protection Bd 1989-; *Style*— The Hon Mrs Morrison; 16 Groom Place, London SW1X 7BA; Wyndham's Farm, Wedhampton, Devizes, Wilts SN10 3QE

MORRISON, Lady Sophia Louise Sydney; *née* Cavendish; yst da of 11 Duke of Devonshire, MC, PC, *qv*; *b* 18 March 1957; *m* 1, 1979 (m dis 1987), Anthony William

Lindsay Murphy, er s of Christopher Murphy, of 17 Napier Ave, SW6; m 2, 19 July 1988, Alastair Morrison, eld s of the Hon James Morrison, *qv*; *Books* The Duchess of Devonshire's Ball (1984), The Mitford Family Album (1985); *Recreations* racing; *Style*— The Lady Sophia Morrison; The Quadrangle, Tisbury, Wilts SP3 5SD (☎ 0747 870709)

MORRISON, William Garth; DL (1984); s of Walter Courtenay Morrison, of Dale Court, Gullane, East Lothian, and Audrey Elizabeth, *née* Gilbert; *b* 4 Aug 1943; *Educ* Pangbourne Coll (Queen's Gold medal), RNC Dartmouth (Queen's Telescope), RNEC Manadon (Queen's Sword), RNC Greenwich; *m* 25 July 1970, Gillian, da of Stanley Cheetham, of Oldham, Lancs; 2 s (Alastair b 22 Nov 1972, Christopher b 15 May 1974), 1 da (Clare (twin) b 15 May 1974); *Career* served RN 1961-73 (ret Lt); farmer in family partnership 1973-, dir Top Hat Holdings (formerly Scotfresh Ltd) 1975; The Scout Assoc: area cmmr E Lothian 1973-81, chief cmmr Scotland 1981-88, chief scout UK and dependent territories 1988-; memb: Lothian and Borders Ctee of Royal Jubilee and Prince's Tsts 1979-86, Scot Community Educn Cncl 1988-; tstee Lamp of Lothian Collegiate Tst 1978-; MIEE 1973; *Books* chapter in The Scottish Juvenile Justice System (ed Martin and Murray, 1982); *Recreations* golf, sailing, scouting; *Clubs* Naval; *Style*— W Garth Morrison, Esq, DL; West Fenton, North Berwick, East Lothian EH39 5AL (☎ 0620 842154); W Courtenay Morrison & Co, West Fenton, North Berwick, East Lothian EH39 5AL (☎ 0620 842154, fax 0620 842052)

MORRISON, Eur Ing William McKenzie Meek; s of William Morrison (d 1968), and Helen McGregor McKenzie (d 1977); *b* 6 Sept 1925; *Educ* Charles Adams GS Wem Salop, Birmingham Tech Coll; *m* 1, 1950, Margaret Millicent Hinton (d 1978); 2 s; m 2, 1980, Irmgard Anne Adelheid, da of late William Karl Köhrner of W Germany; 1 step s; *Career* dir: Turner MFG Co Ltd 1955-79, Hydraulics & Pneumatics Ltd 1957-78; tech dir Spicer Drivetrain Gp-Dana Ltd 1979-83; former chm Midlands Branch Inst of Marine Engrs; awarded Crompton-Lanchester Medal (IMechE) 1974; CEng, FIMarE, FIProdE, FIMechE, memb Soc of Automotive Engrs (USA); *Recreations* oil painting, motoring; *Style*— Eur Ing W M Morrison; 57 Seagar St, Sandwell, W Bromwich, W Midlands (☎ 021 525 1142); W M Morrison & Associates, Consulting Engineers, Bridge House, 57 Seagar St, Sandwell, W Bromwich, W Midlands (☎ 021 525 1142)

MORRISON-BELL, Sir William Hollin Dayrell; 4 Bt (UK 1905); s of Capt Sir Charles Reginald Francis Morrison-Bell, 3 Bt (d 1967), and Prudence Caroline, *née* Davies; *b* 21 June 1956; *Educ* Eton, St Edmund Hall Oxford; *m* 6 Oct 1984, Cynthia Hélène Marie, yr da of Teddy White, of 41 Iverna Gardens, London, W8; 1 s; *Heir* s, Thomas Charles Edward Morrison-Bell b 13 Feb 1985; *Style*— Sir William Morrison-Bell, Bt; 106 Bishops Rd, London SW6 7AR (☎ 071 736 4940)

MORRISON-LOW, Sir James Richard; 3 Bt (UK 1908), of Kilmaron, Co Fife, DL (Fife 1978); s of Sir Walter John Morrison-Low, 2 Bt, JP (d 1955; assumed by deed poll the additional surname of Morrison 1924), and Dorothy Ruth, *née* de Quincey (d 1946); Sir James Low, 1 Bt, was Lord Provost of Dundee 1893-96; *b* 3 Aug 1925; *Educ* Harrow, Merchiston, Faraday House (Dip); *m* 1953, Ann Rawson, da of Air Cdre Robert Gordon, CB, CMG, DSO (d 1954); 1 s, 3 da (Alison, Jean, Susan); *Heir* s, Richard Walter Morrison-Low, *qv*; *Career* serv 1943-47, Royal Corps of Signals, Capt; CEng, MIEE, FInstD 1982; electrical engineer Osborne & Hunter Ltd Glasgow 1952, dir 1956-89; ptnr Kilmaron Electrical Co 1982-; trustee TSB: Cupar 1958-78, Fife Area Bd TSB 1978-82; chm Scottish Traction Engine Soc 1961-63; dir Nat Inspection Cncl for Electrical Installation Contracting 1982-88, pres Electrical Contractors Assoc of Scotland 1982-84; memb: Technical Ctee Assoc Internationale des Entreprises d'Equipment Electrique 1981-, Wiring Regulations Ctee Inst of Electrical Engrs 1982-; chm Fife Area Scout Cncl 1966-84; Hon Pipe Maj of Royal Scottish Pipers' Soc 1981-83; landowner (320 acres); *Recreations* piping, shooting, fishing, steam rollers & traction engines; *Clubs* New (Edinburgh); *Style*— Sir James Morrison-Low, Bt, DL; Kilmaron Castle, nr Cupar, Fife KY15 4NE (☎ 0334 52248)

MORRISON-LOW, Richard Walter; s and h of Sir James Richard Morrison-Low, 3 Bt; *b* 4 Aug 1959; *Style*— Richard Walter Morrison-Low, Esq

MORRISON-LOW, Dowager Lady; (Henrietta) Wilhelmina Mary; da of Maj Robert Walter Purvis (d 1956) and Henrietta Walton, *née* Gilmour (d 1962), of Gilmerton House, nr St Andrews, Fife; *b* 25 March 1914; *Educ* Queens Gate Sch London; *m* 1948, as his 2 w, Sir Walter John Morrison-Low, 2 Bt (d 1955); *Style*— Dowager Lady Morrison-Low; Kingsbarns House, 6 The Square, Kingsbarns, nr St Andrews, Fife KY16 8SS (☎ 033 488 245)

MORRISON-SCOTT, Sir Terence Charles Stuart; DSC (1944), DL (W Sussex 1982); o s of Robert Charles Stuart Morrison Morrison-Scott, DSO (d 1940); *b* 24 Oct 1908; *Educ* Eton, Ch Ch Oxford, Royal Coll of Sci; *m* 1935, Rita, 4 da of late E J Layton; *Career* served WWII, RN; dir: Br Museum (Natural History) 1960-68 (scientific staff 1936-), Sci Museum 1956-60; memb Properties Ctee Nat Tst 1968-83, chm Nature Conservation Panel 1970-81, Architectural Panel 1973-82; kt 1965; *Clubs* Athenaeum, Brooks's; *Style*— Sir Terence Morrison-Scott, DSC, DL; Upperfold House, Fernhurst, Haslemere, Surrey GU27 3JH (☎ 0428 653046)

MORRISS, Nicholas Anson; s of Kenneth Cherry Morriss, MBE, of Haslemere, Surrey, and Diana Mary, *née* Gunning; *b* 17 Sept 1950; *Educ* Radley, Univ of York (BA); *m* 29 June 1974, Suzette Anne, da of Richard Tilney, of Orford, Suffolk; 1 s (Alexander b 11 Feb 1984), 1 da (Fenella b 27 June 1987); *Career* CA; Price Waterhouse: London 1972-76, Cape Town 1976-78, mangr London 1978-79; asst dir Barclays de Zoete Wedd (formerly Barclays Merchant Bank) 1979-86, ptnr corp fin Coopers & Lybrand Deloitte (formerly Deloitte Haskins & Sells) 1986-, dir Deloitte Corporate Finance 1986-; FCA 1975; *Recreations* squash, golf, skiing, tennis; *Style*— Nicholas Morriss, Esq; 3 Akehurst St, Roehampton, London SW15 5DR (☎ 071 788 8590); Coopers & Lybrand Deloitte, Athene House, 66-73 Shoe Lane, London EC4A 3BJ (☎ 071 822 8536, fax 071 822 8500)

MORRISS, Peter Warren; s of George Edward Morriss, of Low Lorton, Cumbria, and Esther Christina Frances, *née* Moodie; *b* 14 Feb 1942; *Educ* Bancroft's Sch; *m* 1968, Heather Eva Morton; 2 s (Christopher Warren b 1974, Stephen James b 1980); *Career* Thomson McLintock & Co (now KPMG Peat Marwick McLintock): apprentice, qualified ICAS 1968, ptnr 1977-; conslt lectr City Univ Business Sch 1974-; memb: EDP Ctee ICAS 1977-80, IT Gp ICAEW; FCA (ACA 1977), FBCS 1981 (MBCS 1975), assoc memb Inst of Internal Auditors; *Recreations* golf, music, sailing; *Clubs* Scribes, Chigwell Golf; *Style*— Peter W Morriss, Esq; KPMG Peat Marwick McLintock, 1 Puddle Dock, Blackfriars, London EC4V 3PD (☎ 071 236 8000)

MORRISSEY, Lady Joanna Agnes; *née* Townshend; da of 7 Marquess Townshend; *b* 1943; *m* 1, 1962 (m dis 1968), Jeremy George Courtenay Bradford; 1 s; m 2, 1978, James Barry Morrissey; *Style*— The Lady Joanna Morrissey

MORRISSEY, Michael Peter; s of Peter Anthony Morrissey, of Langshott Wood, Surrey, and Sheila Margaret, *née* Berrett (d 1984); *b* 15 Aug 1959; *Educ* Worth Sch Sussex; *m* 30 May 1987, Sally-Anne, da of Derek Harris, of Weybridge, Surrey; 1 da (Rosie b 16 Aug 1990); *Career* enlisted 1977, RMA Sandhurst 1978; Irish Guards: cmmnd 2 Lt 1978, Lt 1980, Capt 1983, Maj 1988, Company Command 1IG; serv: Cyprus, Kenya, NI, Belize, Canada, Germany; Thornton Management Ltd London 1989-; *Recreations* shooting, riding, rugby, cricket; *Clubs* Cavalry and Guards; *Style*— Michael Morrissey, Esq; 38 Tonsley Hill, London SW18 1BB

MORROCCO, Alberto; s of Domenico Antonio Morrocco (d 1935), and Celesta, *née* Crolla (d 1956); *b* 14 Dec 1917; *Educ* Sunnybank Sch Aberdeen, Gray's Sch of Art Aberdeen (DA), Carnegie Travelling scholar; *m* 15 Jan 1941, Vera Cockburn, da of Laurence Mercer, MM (d 1963); 2 s (Leon Francesco b 1942, Laurence John Nicholas b 1947), 1 da (Annalisa Celesta Camilla Madhuri Simonetta); *Career* RAMC 1941-46; head Sch of Painting Duncan of Jordanstone Coll of Art 1950-82; memb: Scot Fine Arts Cncl, Saltire Soc Arts Panel; Guthrie award Gray's Sch of Art; Hon LLD Univ of Dundee, Hon DUniv Stirling; RSA 1962 (ARSA 1951), memb RSW 1965, RP 1975, memb RGI 1977; *Clubs* Scottish Arts; *Style*— Alberto Morrocco, Esq; Binrock House, 456 Perth Road, Dundee, Scotland (☎ 0382 69319)

MORROW, Anne Margaret; da of Reginald Andrew Morrow (d 1960), and Winifred Maude Biddulph Townsend; *Educ* Cheshunt County GS, Hornsey Coll of Art (NDD), Royal Coll of Art; *m* (m dis 1970), John Michael Edwards, s of Benjamin Edwards (d 1946); 1 da (Astrid); *Career* illustrator; advertising 1973-85: Habitat, Birds Eye Foods, Yorkshire Bank, The Post Office; media 1973-89: Sunday Times, The Observer, The Independent, in house illustrator Financial Times 1985-88, The Guardian 1988-; publishing 1975-85: BBC Pubns, Penguin Books, Oxford University Press Educn Div, Marshall Cavendish, Octopus Books; television 1976-85: TVS (Land of Green Ginger), BBC TV (Jackanory, Mata Hari), Thames TV (Rainbow, Miss World 1985); exhibitions: RCA, Assoc Illustrators 1980, European Illustration 1981, 1983, Henry Moore Gallery RCA 1988; fndr memb and hon treas RCA Soc 1981-83, memb Assoc Illustrators Gallery Ctee 1982-83; appointed ex student to RCA Coll Court 1982-86 and 1988-; ARCA; *Recreations* painting, theatre, music, travel, exploration; *Style*— Miss Anne Morrow; 15 The Terrace, Barnes, London SW13 0NP (☎ 081 876 5599); The Guardian, 119 Farringdon Rd, London EC1 (☎ 071 239 3939)

MORROW, Sir Ian Thomas; s of Thomas George Morrow (d 1973), and Jamesina, *née* Hunter (d 1919); ggs of Tom Morris who was Open Golf Champion and gn of Young Tom Morris who was also Open Golf Champion; *b* 8 June 1912; *Educ* Dollar Acad; *m* 1, 1940 (m dis 1967), Elizabeth Mary Thackeray (decd); 1 s, 1 da; m 2, 1967, Sylvia Jane, da of Arthur Taylor; 1 da; *Career* jt sr ptnr Robson Morrow & Co 1942-51, md Brush Group 1953-58, dep chm and md UK Optical & Industrial Holdings 1958-86 (chm 1979-86); chm: Kenwood Manufacturing Co 1961-68, Associated Fire Alarms 1965-72, MAI plc 1974-, Laird Group 1975-87 (dep chm 1973-75, dir 1975-), Strong and Fisher (Holdings) plc 1981-90, Additional Underwriting Agencies (No 3) Ltd 1985-, International Harvester Co of GB Ltd 1974-85; dep chm: Rolls Royce Ltd 1970-71, Siebe Gorman Holdings 1970-82, Rolls Royce (1971) Ltd 1971-73, CMD 1971-72; dir Hambro's plc 1972-90; chm: Walbrook Insurance Co Ltd 1990-, Efamol Holdings plc 1986-; memb Press Cncl 1974-80; CA, FCMA, JDipMA, FBIM; kt 1973; *Recreations* reading, music, golf, skiing; *Clubs* Nat Lib, RAC, Royal and Ancient (St Andrews); *Style*— Sir Ian Morrow; 2 Albert Terrace Mews, London NW1 7TA (☎ 071 722 7110); 41 Tower Hill, London EC3N 4HA (☎ 071 702 3524)

MORROW, (Herbert) Stanley; s of Rev John William Morrow (d 1974), and Isabel, *née* Davison (d 1964); *b* 21 Feb 1915; *Educ* Houghton-Le-Spring GS, Univ of Durham (BCom); *m* 10 July 1942, Marjorie, da of Robert William Davison (d 1981); *Career* dir YMCA: Cambridge 1947-56, Swansea 1960-65, Swansea 1960-65, Stockwell 1965-69; head of appeals & PR Nat Cncl of YMCAs of Eng, Ireland & Wales 1969-80, ind PR conslt 1980-; vice pres and chm Fin Ctee Durham Univ Soc, govr Rotary Int 1987-88, chm RIBI PR 1988-90, vice pres Methodist sacramental fellowship; MIPR 1970; *Recreations* gardening, reading, travel; *Clubs* Wig & Pen; *Style*— Stanley Morrow, Esq; Dunelm, Maes Y Cnwce, Newport, Dyfed SA42 0RS (☎ 0239 820875)

MORSE, Christopher George John (Robin); s of John Morse, of Swansea, and Margaret, *née* Maliphant; *b* 28 June 1947; *Educ* Malvern, Wadham Coll Oxford (MA, BCL); *m* 26 March 1983, Louise Angela, da of Ronald Slott (d 1974), of Mirfield, W Yorks; 1 s (Richard b 24 May 1985); *Career* called to the Bar 1971; visiting prof: John Marshall Law Sch Chicago 1979-80, Leuven Univ Belgium 1982; reader in law King's Coll London 1988- (lectr 1971-88); *Books* Benjamins Sale of books (ed 3 edn, 1971), Torts in Private International Law (1978), The Conflicts of Laws (ed 11 edn, 1987), Transnational Relationships (1991); *Recreations* travel, Swansea City AFC; *Style*— Robin Morse, Esq; School of Law, King's College, London WC2R 2LS (☎ 071 836 5454, fax 071 836 1799)

MORSE, Capt David Henry; CBE (Mil), RN; s of Rear Adm Harold Edward Morse, DSO, of Dorset (d 1975), and Helen Aileen, *née* Currie (d 1970); *b* 28 Jan 1932; *Educ* RNC Dartmouth; *m* 27 July 1957, Jill Salwey, da of Gerald William Leigh Holland (d 1971), of Switzerland; *Career* RN 1945-84; served: in Korean War, Suez 1956, Kuwait 1961, Hong Kong riots 1967, withdrawal from Aden 1967; CO HMS Crofton 1961-63, promoted Cdr 1967, CO HMS Lowestoft 1970-71, Staff Offr Ops to Flag Offr 1 Flotilla 1974-75, promoted Capt 1975, operational requirements staff Central Staff MOD 1976-79, Capt HMS Intrepid 1979-80, Capt RN Presentation Team 1980-81, Dir RN Staff Coll 1981-82, Cdre Clyde and Capt HMS Neptune 1982-84, ret from active list RN 1985; farmer and charity conslt 1985-; *Recreations* golf; *Style*— Capt David H Morse, CBE, RN; Kings House, Powerstock, Dorset DT6 3TG (☎ 030 885 361)

MORSE, David Thomas; s of Thomas Walter Morse (d 1984), of London, and Emily Annie, *née* Garrett; *b* 10 Nov 1943; *Educ* Royal Ballet School, White Lodge; *m* 9 Oct 1971, Marion, da of Charles Arnold Browell Tait, OBE; *Career* ballet dancer; with the Royal Ballet 1961-65; princ character artist Sadler's Wells Royal Ballet 1989-; roles with co incl: the rake in The Rake's Progress, Jaspar in Pineapple Poll, Hilarion in Giselle, Polichinelle in Meadow of Proverbs, Punch in Punch and the Street Party, Popular Song in Facade, Bootface in The Lady and the Fool, Carabosse in The Sleeping Beauty, Henry Hobson in Hobson's Choice; choreography incl the works Pandora and Birdscape for Sadler's Wells; awarded Polish ballet's bicentenial medal of honour; *Recreations* photography, reading, music; *Style*— David Morse, Esq; Birmingham Royal Ballet, Birmingham Hippodrome Theatre, Thorp St, Birmingham B5 4AU (☎ 021 622 2555)

MORSE, Hon Mrs (Jennifer); yr da of Baron Delfont (Life Peer), *qv*; *b* 1949; *m* 1974, Andrew Morse; 2 s; *Style*— The Hon Mrs Morse; c/o Rt Hon Lord Delfont, c/o 7 Soho St, Soho Sq, London W1V 5FA

MORSE, Sir (Christopher) Jeremy; KCMG (1975); s of late Francis John Morse, and Kinbarra, *née* Armfield-Marrow; *b* 10 Dec 1928; *Educ* Winchester, New Coll Oxford; *m* 1955, Belinda Marianne, da of Lt-Col R B Y Mills; 3 s, 1 da; *Career* Nat Serv Lt KRRC 1948-49; exec dir Bank of Eng 1965-72, chm Lloyds Bank 1977- (dep chm 1975-77), non exec dir ICI 1981-; chm: Ctee of London Clearing Bankers 1980-82, Deputies Ctee of Twenty IMF 1972-74; pres: Br Bankers Assoc 1984-, Euro Banking Fedn 1988-; memb: Cncl of Lloyds 1987-, NEDC 1977-81; former chm City Arts Tst, FIDE judge for Chess Compositions 1975-; Warden Winchester 1987-; chllr Univ of Bristol 1988-; *Recreations* poetry, problems and puzzles, coarse gardening, golf; *Clubs* Athenaeum; *Style*— Sir Jeremy Morse, KCMG; 102a Drayton Gdns, London SW10 9RJ (☎ 071 370 2265)

MORSE, Rodney John; s of James Morse (d 1986), and Elsie, *née* Cripps; *b* 26 Jan 1944; *m* 25 May 1968, (Maureen) Ann, da of John Kenny Woodward (d 1990), of Leighton Buzzard, Beds; 1 da (Carrie Alisa b 25 Aug 1971); *Career* underwriter Lloyds

1986-; dir: Wellington Underwriting Agencies Ltd 1986-, Lloyds Aviation Claims Centre Ltd; ACII; *Style—* Rodney Morse, Esq; Linwood, Sevenoaks Rd, Ightham, Sevenoaks, Kent (☎ 0732 882537); 120 Fenchurch St, London EC3M 5BA (☎ 071 929 2811, fax 071 220 7234, telex 268892 WELTN G)

MORSON, Dr Basil Clifford; CBE (1987), VRD (1970); s of Albert Clifford Morson, OBE (d 1975), of London, and Adela Frances Maud Phené (d 1982); *b* 13 Nov 1921; *Educ* Beaumont Coll, Wadham Coll Oxford, Middx Hosp Med Sch; *m* 1, (m annulled 1982), Pamela, *née* Gilbert; m 2, 9 Feb 1983, Sylvia Morson, MBE, da of Hugh Frederick Dutton (d 1972), of Yorks; 1 s (Christopher Alan), 2 da (Caroline Mary, Clare Elizabeth (Mrs Morris)); *Career* ordinary seaman RN 1942, Sub Lt RNVR 1943, Surgn Lt 1953, ret as Surgn Cdr RNR 1971; conslt pathologist: St Marks Hosp London 1956-86, RN (emeritius civilian conslt in pathology); treas RCPath 1983-88 (vice pres 1978-81); memb Worshipful Co of Barbers; FRCS, FRCP, FRCPath; Hon FRACS 1990; *Books* Textbook of Gastrointestinal Pathology (1972, 1979, 1990), Pathology of the Alimentary Tract (1987), Atlas of Gastrointestinal Pathology (1988); *Recreations* gardening, ornithology; *Style—* Dr Basil Morson, CBE, VRD; 14 Crossways Park, West Chiltington, West Sussex RH20 2Q2 (☎ 07983 3528)

MORTENSEN, Henrik Evegod; s of Erik Evegod Mortensen, of Denmark, and Lene, *née* Hermansen; *b* 12 Feb 1968; *Partner* Pernille Whitt; *Career* professional footballer; 108 appearances Aarhus Denmark 1984-85 and 1988-90 (32 goals), 15 appearances Anderlecht Belgium 1985-88 (3 goals), Norwich City 1990-; Denmark caps: 16 under 16, 8 under 18, 4 under 21; Young Player of the Year Denmark 1984, Politikens Sportsperson of the Year 1984; *Recreations* books, tennis, good films; *Style—* Henrik Mortensen, Esq; Norwich City FC, Carrow Rd, Norwich, Norfolk

MORTENSEN, Juliet Lilias; da of Rear Adm RSW Sherbrooke VC, CB, DSO (d 1972), of Oxton, Notts, and Rosemary Neville, *née* Buckley; *b* 27 Feb 1931; *Educ* Hatherop Castle; *m* 15 Oct 1955, Cdr Axel Mortensen, DL, RN (d 1983), s of Andreas Mortensen, of Yorks; 3 da (Andrea (Mrs O'Donnell) b 1957, Olivia b 1960, Emily (Mrs Eadie) b 1963); *Career* chm Notts Branch of CLA; *Style—* Mrs Juliet Mortensen

MORTENSEN, Neil James McCready; s of Peter John McCready Mortensen, of Laleham, Middx, and Rhoda, *née* Bamber; *b* 16 Oct 1949; *Educ* Hampton Sch, Univ of Birmingham (MB ChB), Univ of Bristol (MD); *m* 16 June 1973, Jane Alison, da of Lt-Col Paul Baker, of Shortlands, Kent; 1 s (James b 1979), 2 da (Gemma b 1977, Chloe b 1981); *Career* conslt sr lectr Univ of Bristol and Dept of Surgery Bristol Royal Infirmary 1983-86, conslt surgn John Radcliffe Hosp Oxford 1986-, hon lectr in surgery Univ of Oxford 1986-; memb ctee Surgical Section Br Soc Gastroenterology 1987, memb Green Coll Oxford 1987, hon treas Surgical Res Soc 1988; FRCS 1980; *Books* Int Jl Colo Rectal Disease (co ed, 1985-), Colo Rectal Cancer (1989); *Recreations* tennis, farming; *Style—* Neil Mortensen, Esq; 18 Cranham Terrace, Oxford OX2 6DG (☎ 0865 52549); Spring Farm, Regil, nr Chew Magna, Bristol, Avon; Dept of Surgery, John Radcliffe Hospital, Oxford OX3 9DU (☎ 0865 220926); Felstead House, 23 Banbury Rd, Oxford

MORTIMER, Dr Ann Margaret; da of Harry Mortimer, of Gomersal, W Yorks, and Muriel, *née* Wood; *b* 11 May 1957; *Educ* Heckmondwike GS, Univ of Leicester (BSc), Univ of Leeds (MB ChB, MMedSc); *m* 5 Jan 1985, (Edward) John Turner; *Career* sr house offr in psychiatry York Hosps 1982-84, registrar in psychiatry Leeds Hosps 1984-86, lectr in psychiatry Univ of Leeds 1986-88, conslt psychiatrist in adult mental illness St Luke's Hosp Huddersfield 1988, conslt psychiatrist to Huddersfield Poly; memb Health Advsy Serv, chm Yorkshire Secure Provision Gp, guest lectr Huddersfield Poly and Univ of Leeds; MRCPsych 1985; *Books* 10 pubns on schizophrenia; *Recreations* mountain sports (especially skiing), music (especially playing piano), the garden; *Clubs* The Vibram Mountaineering; *Style—* Dr Ann Mortimer; St Luke's Hospital, Huddersfield HD4 5RQ (☎ 0484 654711)

MORTIMER, David John; s of Eric Richardson Mortimer (d 1976), and Doris Mabel, *née* Somes; *b* 3 May 1938; *Educ* King's Sch Canterbury, St John's Coll Oxford (MA); *m* 1965, Sheila Gail, *née* Ross; 2 s (Mark, Gavin); *Career* publisher; dir: Longman Gp Ltd 1972-85, Int Language Centres Ltd 1983-85, Macmillan Educn Ltd 1985-88; chief exec offr Business Trg; chief exec Macmillan Intek Ltd 1989-91 (chm 1985-88), chief exec Intek Europe plc 1991-, pres Intek Systems de Capacitacion (Spain) 1989-; *Recreations* music, sport, hill walking, literature; *Clubs* MCC; *Style—* David Mortimer, Esq; Calidcote, High St, Lindfield, W Sussex (☎ 04447 3115)

MORTIMER, Edward James; s of Robert Cecil Mortimer, DD, Bishop of Exeter 1949-73 (d 1976), and Mary Hope Walker; *b* 22 Dec 1943; *Educ* Summer Fields Oxford, Eton, Balliol Coll Oxford; *m* 1968, Elizabeth Anne, da of John Zanettii; 2 s (Horatio b 1970, Matthew b 1973), 2 da (Frances b 1978, Phoebe b 1980); *Career* asst d'Anglais Lycée Faidherbe St Louis-du-Sénégal 1962, fell All Souls Coll Oxford 1965-72 and 1984-86, foreign specialist and leader writer The Times 1973-85 (asst Paris corr 1967-70), sr assoc Carnegie Endowment (NY) 1980-81, series conslt Roosevelt Children (Channel 4) 1985-87, asst foreign ed and foreign affairs columnist Financial Times 1987-, res assoc IISS 1990-91; winner first David Watt Meml prize 1988; *Books* France and the Africans (1969), Eurocommunism, Myth or Reality (1979), Faith and Power, The Politics of Islam (1982), Rise of the French Communist Party (1984), Roosevelt's Children (1987); *Recreations* conversation, travel, family life; *Clubs* Beefsteak, Groucho; *Style—* Edward Mortimer, Esq; Financial Times, 1 Southwark Bridge, London SE1 9HL (☎ 071 873 4855, fax 071 873 3193)

MORTIMER, John Clifford; CBE (1986), QC (1966); s of Clifford Mortimer, and Kathleen May, *née* Smith; *b* 21 April 1923; *Educ* Harrow, Brasenose Coll Oxford; *m* 1, 1949, Penelope Ruth, *née* Fletcher; 1 s, 1 da; m 2, Penelope, *née* Gollop; 2 da; *Career* barr, playright and author; called to the Bar 1948, master of the bench Inner Temple 1975; plays incl: The Dock Brief (1958), What Shall We Tell Caroline (1958), The Wrong Side of the Park (1960), Two Stars for Comfort (1962), The Judge (1967), Voyage Round My Father (1970, filmed 1982), I Claudius (1972, adapted from Robert Graves), Collaborations (1973), The Bells of Hell (1977); film script John Mary (1970); television scripts incl: Brideshead Revisited (1981), Edwin (1984); works of fiction incl: Charade (1947), Three Winters (1956), Will Shakespeare and Entertainment (1977), Rumpole of the Bailey (1978, BAFTA Writer of the Year Award), The Trials of Rumpole (1979), Rumpole's Return (1980, televised), Regina vs Rumpole (1981), Rumpole for the Defence (1982), Rumpole and the Golden Thread (1983, televised), Paradise Postponed (1985, televised 1986), Rumpole's Last Case (1987), Summers Lease (1988, televised 1989), Rumpole and the Age of Miracles (1989), Titmuss Regained (1990), Rumpole À La Carte (1990); trans incl: A Flea in Her Ear (1965), The Lady From Maxim's (1977), A Little Hotel on the Side (for Nat Theatre) 1984, Die Fledermaus (for Covent Gdn Opera) 1988; interviews incl: In Character (1983), Character Parts (1986); autobiog Clinging to the Wreckage (1982); pres Berks Bucks & Oxon Naturalists Tst 1984-90, memb Nat Theatre Bd 1968-89; chm: RSL 1989-, Royal Ct Theatre 1990; Hon DLitt Susquehanna Univ 1985, Hon LLD Exeter (1986), Hon DLitt St Andrews 1987, Hon DLitt Nottingham 1988, HonD Brunel Univ 1990; Italia Prize 1958; FRSL (chm 1989-); *Recreations* working, gardening, opera; *Clubs* Garrick; *Style—* John Mortimer, Esq, CBE, QC

MORTIMER, Katharine Mary Hope; da of Robert Cecil Mortimer, DD, Bishop of Exeter 1949-73 (d 1976), and Mary Hope, *née* Walker; *b* 28 May 1946; *Educ* St Mary and St Anne Abbots Bromley, Somerville Coll Oxford (BA, BPhil); *m* 7 July 1973 (m dis 1986), John Noel Nicholson, s of Rev John Malcolm Nicholson (d 1982); 1 s (Andrew Robert b 1982); m 2, 19 May 1990, Robert Michael Dean, s of Daniel Dean; *Career* dir: N M Rothschild & Sons Ltd 1985-1989 (non-exec 1988-89), N M Rothschild Asset Mgmnt (Holdings) 1987-89 (non-exec 1988-89); policy dir Securities and Investments Bd, dir 1985-87, Nat Bus Co 1979-, chief exec Walker Books Ltd 1988-89, ind conslt 1989-; govr Imperial Coll of Sci and Technol June 1987-, memb Cncl ESRC July 1984-86, memb governing body Inst of Devpt Studies Sussex June 1983-, non-exec dir Centre for Econ Policy Res June 1986-; memb: BBC General Advsy Cncl October 1987-, Royal Cmmn for the Exhibition of 1851 (1987-), tstee Inst for Policy Res 1989-; *Style—* Miss Katharine Mortimer; Lower Corscombe, Okehampton, Devon EX20 1SD (☎ 0837 840431)

MORTIMER, Penelope Ruth; da of Rev Arthur Forbes Gerard Fletcher (d 1959), and Caroline Amy, *née* Maggs (d 1973); *b* 19 Sept 1918; *Educ* Croydon HS, New Sch Streatham, Blencathra Rhyl, Garden Sch Lane End, St Elphin's Sch for Daughters of the Clergy, Univ Coll London; *m* 1, 1937 (m dis 1949), Charles Francis Dimont; 4 da (Madelon, Caroline, Julia, Deborah); m 2, 1949 (m dis 1972), John Clifford Mortimer, QC; 1 s (Jeremy), 1 da (Sally); *Career* writer; *Books* Johanna (as Penelope Dimont, 1947), A Villa in Summer (1954), The Bright Prison (1956), With Love & Lizards (with John Mortimer, 1957), Daddy's Gone A-Hunting (1958), Saturday Lunch with The Brownings (1960), The Pumpkin Eater (1962), My Friend Says It's Bulletproof (1967), The Home (1971), Long Distance (1974), About Time (autobiog, 1979), The Handyman (1983), Queen Elizabeth: A Life of the Queen Mother (1986); *Style—* Penelope Mortimer; The Old Post Office, Chastleton, Moreton-in-Marsh, Glos GL56 0AS (☎ 060 874 242)

MORTIMORE, Prof Peter John; s of Claude Mortimore (d 1982), of Richmond, Surrey, and Rose, *née* Townsend; *b* 17 Jan 1942; *Educ* Chiswick GS, Univ of London (BSc, MSc, PhD); *m* 19 April 1965, Jo Marie, da of Michael Hargaden (d 1986), of Monmouth, Gwent; 3 da (Joanna b 1966, Rebecca b 1967, Claudia b 1968); *Career* teacher secdy sch 1965-73; res offr Inst of Psychiatry 1975-78, memb HMI 1978, asst educn offr (sec) ILEA 1985-88 (dir of res and statistics 1979-85), prof and dir Sch of Educn Lancaster Univ 1988-, prof of educn London Univ and dep dir Inst of Educn (London Univ) 1990-; memb: Br Psychological Soc, Assoc for Child Psychology and Psychiatry, Br Educnl Res Assoc, American Educnl Res Assoc; FBPsS 1988, FRSA 1990; *Books* Fifteen Thousand Hours (co-author, 1979), Behaviour Problems in Schools (1984), Helpful Servant not Dominating Master (1986), School Matters (1988); *Recreations* music, theatre, tennis, walking; *Style—* Prof Peter Mortimore; Institute of Education, University of London, 20 Bedford Way, London WC1H 0AL (☎ 071 636 1500, fax 071 436 2186)

MORTON, Alan James; s of Walter Morton (d 1974), and Agnes, *née* Watson; *b* 7 May 1944; *Educ* Roundhay GS; *m* 8 Aug 1970, Celia Joan, da of Dixon Charles Merry-Howe, 2 s (Iain James b 10 Feb 1974, Andrew Charles b 19 Feb 1977); *Career* CA 1969; ptnr i/c Leeds office Armitage & Norton 1985-87 (articled clerk, ptnr 1974, memb Nat Exec 1985-87); KPMG Peat Marwick McLintock: ptnr 1987-, regnl business servs co-ordinator NE Region 1987-, memb Nat Business Servs Ctee 1987-, office managing ptnr Huddersfield 1990-; *Recreations* golf, badminton, watching rugby union; *Clubs* Moortown Golf, Roundhegians; *Style—* Alan Morton, Esq; 9 Gateland Drive, Shadwell, Leeds LS17 8HU (☎ 0532 737292); KPMG Peat Marwick McLintock, Station St Buildings, Huddersfield HD1 1LZ (☎ 0484 421433, fax 0484 518447, car 0860 670624)

MORTON, Hon Mrs (Alicia Dorothy); *née* Maffey; yr da of 2 Baron Rugby (d 1990), and Margaret, *née* Bindley; *b* 14 Jan 1960; *m* 1981, Richard M Morton, 2 s of John Morton, of Draycote, Rugby; 2 s (Samuel Richard b 1986, John Alan Kynaston b 1990), 1 da (Eleanor Margaret b 1984); *Style—* The Hon Mrs Morton; The Flat, Manor Farm, Draycote, Rugby, Warwicks

MORTON, Hon Alistair Charles Ralph; eldest s of Baron Morton of Shuna, QC (Life Peer); *b* 1958; *Educ* Royal High Sch Edinburgh, Glasgow Univ (MA); *m* 1983, Jacqueline Anne, da of William Brown, of Edinburgh; *Style—* The Hon Alistair Morton

MORTON, (John) Andrew; s of John Douglas Morton (d 1975), of Nutfield, Surrey, and Anne Marjorie, *née* Gray; *b* 5 July 1943; *Educ* Charterhouse, Merton College Oxford (BA); *m* 6 Dec 1975, Angela Fern Gage, da of Lt Cdr Leonard Gage Wheeler, RN, of Alresford, Hants; 1 da (Fiona Anne b 1978); *Career* Univ of Oxford Air Sqdn RAFVR 1963-65; admitted slr 1968; ptnr Allen & Overy 1973- (asst slr 1968-73); dir: Canadian Pacific Newsprint Ltd, Canadian Pacific Forest Services Ltd; dir Slrs Benevolent Assoc; *Recreations* sailing, golf, skiing; *Clubs* Royal Harwich Yacht, Royal Wimbledon Golf; *Style—* Andrew Morton, Esq; Allen & Overy, 9 Cheapside, London EC2V 6AD (☎ 071 248 9898, fax 071 236 2192, telex 8812801)

MORTON, Adm Sir Anthony Storrs; GBE (1982), KCB (1978), DL (1989); s of Dr Harold Morton, of Bridlington; *b* 6 Nov 1923; *Educ* St Anselm's Bakewell, Loretto; *Career* joined RN 1941, Cdr 1956, Capt 1964, Sr Naval Offr NI 1968-70, Rear Adm 1971, naval memb Sr DSD RCDS 1971-72, ACDS (Policy) 1973, Vice Adm 1975, flag offr First Flotilla 1975-77, Vice CDS 1977-78, vice chief Naval Staff 1978-80, UK mil rep NATO 1980-83, ret RN 1984; King of Arms of Order of British Empire 1983-, Vice Adm of UK 1990-; OStJ (1990); *Recreations* sailing, fishing, shooting; *Clubs* RYS, RCC, ICC; *Style—* Adm Sir Anthony Morton, GBE, KCB; c/o Barclays Bank Plc, 50 Jewry St, Winchester SO23 8RG

MORTON, Sir Brian; s of Alfred Oscar Morton (d 1954); *b* 24 Jan 1912; *Educ* Campbell Coll Belfast, Coll of Estate Mgmnt London; *m* 1937, Hilda Evelyn Elsie, da of John Hillis (d 1950); 1 s (and 1 s decd); *Career* chartered surveyor and estate agent 1936-64, memb Craigavon Devpt Cmmn 1967-69; chm: Londonderry Devpt Cmmn 1969-73, Harland & Wolff (shipbuilders) 1975-80; Hon DSc Univ of Ulster; FRICS; kt 1973; *Recreations* golf, gardening, sailing, landscape painting; *Clubs* Royal Co Down Golf, Malone Golf; *Style—* Sir Brian Morton; Rolly Island, Comber, Co Down, NI BT23 6EL

MORTON, (William) Douglas; s of William Douglas (d 1973), of Doncaster, and Emma Elizabeth *née* Jowitt; *b* 11 June 1924; *Educ* Doncaster GS, St John's Coll Cambridge; *m* 16 April 1949, Beryl, da of Alfred George Tucker (d 1969), of Doncaster; 2 s (Nicholas Michael b 1954, Christopher David b 1957); *Career* md: GEC AEI Engrg Ltd Manchester 1967-68, GEC Power Engrg Ltd 1968-70, GEC Telecommunications Ltd Coventry 1970-82; dir: Telephone Mfrs of SA (Pty) Ltd 1970-82, Gen Electric Co plc London 1973-83; gp md Aurora plc Sheffield 1983-89, dir Telfos plc 1990-; pres Tema Telecommunications Engrg and Mfrg Assoc 1979-80; *Recreations* gardening, contract bridge; *Style—* Douglas Morton, Esq; Woodside, Nesfield, Off Hackney Lane, Barlow, Sheffield S18 5TB (☎ 0742 890531)

MORTON, George Martin; s of Rev Thomas Ralph Morton (d 1977), and Janet Maclay MacGregor, *née* Baird (d 1986); *b* 11 Feb 1940; *Educ* Fettes Coll Edinburgh, Edinburgh Coll of Art (Dip Arch), Univ of Glasgow (Dip in Town & Regnl Planning); *Career* architect and planner Hugh Wilson and Lewis Womersley 1968-76, sr planner Trafford Borough Cncl 1976-78 and 1986-, sec Tameside & Glossop Community Health Cncl 1984-86; memb: Manchester Corp 1971-74, Greater Manchester Cncl

1973-77; MP (Lab) Manchester Mosside 1978-83; ARIBA 1969; *Style*— George Morton, Esq; 4 St Annes Rd, Manchester M21 2TG (☎ 061 881 8195); Planning Department, Trafford Borough Council, Town Hall, Talbot Rd, Stretford, Manchester M21 2TG (☎ 061 872 2101 ext 4814)

MORTON, 21 Earl of (S 1458); John Charles Sholto Douglas; DL (West Lothian 1982); also Lord Aberdour (no actual cr, but designation of the eld s & h, incorporated with the Earldom in a charter of 1638, where the Earls of Morton are described as *domini Abirdour*); s of Hon Charles William Sholto Douglas (d 1960, 2 s of 19 Earl of Morton); suc cous, 20 Earl 1976; *b* 19 March 1927; *m* 1949, Mary Sheila, da of late Rev Canon John Stanley Gibbs, MC, of Didmarton House, Badminton, Glos; 2 s, 1 da; *Heir* s, Lord Aberdour, *qv*; *Career* md Dalmahoy Country Club, Scottish dir Bristol & W Building Soc, ptnr Dalmahoy Farms, chm Edinburgh Polo Club; *Clubs* Edinburgh Polo, Dalmahoy Country; *Style*— The Rt Hon the Earl of Morton, DL; Dalmahoy, Kirknewton, Midlothian

MORTON, Hon Kenneth John; 2 s of Baron Morton of Shuna, QC (Life Baron); *b* 1960; *Educ* Broughton HS Edinburgh, Edinburgh Univ (BSc); *m* 1984, Isobel Ann, da of John McLean Cowan, of Greenock; *Career* chartered engr; MIEE; *Style*— The Hon Kenneth Morton

MORTON, Dr Paul Greville; s of John Morton (d 1974), of Springfield Rd, Wolverhampton, and Ethel Harvey (d 1974); *b* 7 Aug 1922; *Educ* Wolverhampton Secdy Sch, Univ of London (BSc, DSc); *m* 18 April 1943, Florence Beatrice, da of Benjamin Hughes; 2 s (Raymond Paul b 23 July 1944, John Graham b 15 Aug 1949), 1 da (Maxine Susan b 31 March 1959); *Career* Boulton Paul Aircraft Wolverhampton: aircraft apprentice 1938-43, aircraft designer 1944-50, project engr 1951-59; supt Nelson Engineering Laboratories English Electric Company 1960-72, head Mechanical Div Stafford Laboratory GEC 1973-77, mangr Mechanical Laboratory GEC Research Ltd 1978-87; visiting prof: Univ of Strathclyde 1982-88, Univ of Bath 1989-; *Award* Nelson Gold medal awarded by GEC 1985; FIMechE 1967, FEng 1985, FRSA 1987; *Recreations* music; *Style*— Dr Paul Morton; 15 Firsway, Wolverhampton WV6 8BJ (☎ 0902 762770)

MORTON, Reginald John (Reg); s of Maj John Henry Morton (d 1987), of Manchester, and Alice Blanche Gladys, *née* Chappelier (d 1990); *b* 17 Sept 1951; *Educ* Manchester GS, Univ of Birmingham (LLB); *m* 6 Oct 1979, Jennifer Mary, da of Reginald Carr, of Small Dole, W Sussex; 2 s (Jonathan b 1985, Thomas b 1988); *Career* slr Clifford Chance (formerly Clifford-Turner) 1975-85, ptnr Titmuss Sainer & Webb 1987- (joined 1985) memb: Law Soc 1975; *Recreations* snooker, golf; *Style*— Reg Morton, Esq; 2 Serjeants Inn, London EC4 (☎ 071 583 5353, fax 071 353 3683, car 08367 45939, telex 23823 ADVICE G)

MORTON, Dr Richard Emile; s of Donald Morton, and Mary, *née* Wilkinson; *b* 10 Nov 1949; *Educ* Bexley GS, St Johns Coll Oxford (BA, BM BCh), UCH; *m* 1 May 1976, April Joy Georgina, da of William Milne (d 1979); 1 s (Robert William), 2 da (Alice Elizabeth, Lucy Jenniffer); *Career* registrar in paediatrics Hosp for Sick Children Gt Ormond St, sr registrar in paediatrics London Hosp and Queen Elizabeth Hosp for Children Hackney, conslt paediatrician Derbyshire Childrens Hosp; chm Umbrella, vice chm Derbyshire Disabled Childrens Fund; MRCP; *Recreations* family, music, running; *Style*— Dr Richard Morton; Derbyshire Childrens Hospital, North St, Derby (☎ 0332 47141)

MORTON, Robert Edward; s of Charles Morton, and Yvonne, *née* Galea; *b* 20 May 1956; *Educ* Canford Sch Wimborne Dorset, Oriel Coll Oxford (MA); *m* 12 Dec 1981; 2 da (Caroline b 13 Aug 1983, Georgina b 21 Jan 1985); *Career* res analyst: Simon & Coates 1978-83, de Zoete & Bevan 1983-86 (ptnr 1986-); dir Barclays de Zoete Wedd 1986 - (head conglomerates and overseas traders res teams); memb Stock Exchange; *Recreations* squash, gardening, music; *Clubs* Gresham, Royal Thames Yacht, RAC; *Style*— Robert Morton, Esq; 28 Cambridge St, Pimlico, London SW1V 4QH (☎ 071 828 7955)

MORTON JACK, His Hon Judge David; s of Col William Andrew Morton Jack, OBE (d 1950), of Lemonfield Co, Galway, and Margery Elizabeth Happell (d 1978); o heir of the O'Flaherties of Lemonfield where he still owns what remains of the O'Flahertie estate; *b* 5 Nov 1936; *Educ* Stowe, Trinity Coll Oxford (MA); *m* 1972, Elvira Rosemary, da of Francis Gallo Rentoul, of 1 Chara Place, W4; 4 s (Edward b 1975, Richard b 1977, Henry b 1979, George b 1981); *Career* 2 Lt Royal Irish Fusiliers 1955-57 (LT AER 1957-60); called to the Bar Lincoln's Inn; barr SE Circuit 1962-86; rec Crown Ct 1979-86; circuit judge 1986-; *Recreations* fishing, shooting, reading, music; *Style*— His Hon Judge David Morton Jack; 1 Harcourt Buildings, Temple EC4Y 9DA (☎ 086 733 223)

MORTON LEE, Cdr John; OBE (1973); s of Lt Cdr Henry Morton Lee (d 1983), of Chichester, W Sussex, and Gladys Mildred, *née* Smith; *b* 18 Jan 1930; *Educ* RN Coll Dartmouth; *m* 23 April 1957, Patricia Lee, da of late George Garnet Pendray, of Lourenco Marques; 2 s (Michael b 30 Nov 1958, Peter b 13 Jan 1964); *Career* Midshipman HMS Anson and HMS Vengeance 1948-49, Sub Lt Greenwich 1949, HMS Sluys 1950, HMS Unicorn 1951, Lt i/c HMSDML 3514 1951-53, language trg 1954, HMS Undaunted 1954-55, i/c HMS Chelsham 1956, i/c HMS Upton 1957-58, HMS Ganges 1958-60, Lt Cdr HMS Leopard 1961-62, RN Staff Coll Greenwich 1963, i/c HMS Pellew 1964-65, Cdr SO Ops to FO2 Far East Fleet 1965-66, i/c HMS St George 1967-68, i/c HMS Eskimo 1969-70, Staff Planning Offr to Comnavsouth 1970-73, Naval Asst to Dir PR 1973-75, Naval Attaché Spain 1976-79, memb Admty Interview Bd 1979-81, Project Offr NATO Frigate for 90's 1981-84, ret 1984; fine art dealer 1984-; exhibitor at antique fairs across the country; memb SE Hants C of C; memb: CGA, London and Provincial Antique Dealers Assoc, Br Maritime League, Nat Tst, Trout and Salmon Fishing Assoc; *Recreations* golf, fishing; *Clubs* Naval, Royal Navy Club of 1765 and 1785, Hayling GC; *Style*— Cdr John Morton Lee, OBE; Cedar House, Bacon Lane, Hayling Island, Hants PO11 0DN (☎ 0705 464 444)

MORTON OF SHUNA, Baron (Life Peer UK 1985), of Stockbridge in the District of the City of Edinburgh; Hugh Drennan Baird; QC; s of Rev Thomas Ralph Morton, DD (d 1977), and Janet Maclay MacGregor, da of Hugh Baird, of Glasgow; *b* 10 April 1930; *Educ* Glasgow Acad, Glasgow Univ (BL); *m* 1956, Muriel, da of Charles Miller, of Edinburgh; 3 s (Hon Alistair Charles Ralph b 1958, Hon Kenneth John b 1960, Hon Douglas William b 1963); *Career* admitted Faculty of Advocates 1965, advocate depute 1967-71 and 1974-79; memb Criminal Injuries Compensation Bd 1979-88; Senator of the Coll of Justice in Scotland 1988; *Style*— The Rt Hon Lord Morton of Shuna; 25 Royal Circus, Edinburgh EH3 6TL

MOSCOW, Dr David; s of Emanuel Moscow (d 1981), and Rachel, *née* Davidovitch; *b* 3 May 1937; *Educ* Parmiter's GS London, Univ of London (BSc), Univ of Leicester, Univ of Leeds (PhD); *m* 1, 1960 (m dis 1972), Jennifer Dianne, da of William Thomas Redgate (d 1986); 4 da (Sarah b 1964, Susan b 1967, Emma b 1968, Linda b 1969); m 2, 1975, Patricia Ann, da of Frank Edward Gostling, OBE, of Oxshott, Surrey; *Career* personnel offr BAC 1960-63, lectr Univ of Leeds 1963-67, res assoc Netherlands Inst for Preventive Med 1967-70, jt md Sheppard Moscow and Assoc Ltd 1984-86 (chm 1970-84); conslt to: ICI, Shell, nat orgns NHS, Bank of England; FID 1977; FBIM 1983, FIMC 1986; *Recreations* golf, sculpture; *Style*— Dr David Moscow; Cross Keys House, Cross Keys, Sevenoaks, Kent (☎ 0732 457411)

MOSDELL, (Lionel) Patrick; s of William George Mosdell (d 1938), of Mortimer, Berks, and Sarah Ellen, *née* Gardiner (d 1963); *b* 29 Aug 1912; *Educ* Abingdon Sch, St Edmund Hall Oxford (BA, MA); *m* 3 Aug 1945, (Muriel) Jean, da of John Oscar Sillem (d 1958), of Hove, East Sussex; 1 s (John b 15 Aug 1949), 1 da (Susan b 27 May 1946); *Career* WWII Gunner Sussex Yeo RA 1939, cmmnd RB 1941, serv Libyan Arab Force, Force 133 Capt, No 1 Special Force; serv: Egypt, Cyrenaica, Eritrea, Abyssinia, Italy; demob 1945; admitted slr 1938; called to the Bar Gray's Inn 1952, sr resident magistrate Northern Rhodesia 1956 (registrar Lands and Deeds 1946, resident magistrate 1950); High Ct judge: Tanganyika 1960-64, Kenya 1966-72; asst slr Law Soc 1964-66; pt/t chm: Surrey and Sussex Rent Assessment Panel 1972-82, S London Regnl Nat Insur Local Tbnl 1974-84, Immigration Appeal Tbnl 1975-84, Pensions Appeal Tbnls 1976-86; SSAFA (V) 1988; Distintivo d'Onore Instituto Per i Patrioti Voluntari della Libertà (Italy) 1945; *Recreations* cycling; *Clubs* Special Forces, Royal Cwlth Soc; *Style*— Patrick Mosdell, Esq; 10 Orpen Rd, Hove, East Sussex BN3 6NJ

MOSELEY, Sir George Walker; KCB (1982, CB 1978); s of William Moseley, MBE, and Bella Moseley; *b* 7 Feb 1925; *Educ* Glasgow HS, St Bees Sch Cumberland, Wadham Coll Oxford (MA); *m* 1, 1950, Anne Mercer (d 1989), m 2, 1990, Madge James; 1 s, 1 da; *Career* serv RAF and RAF Levies Iraq 1943-48; Miny Housing and Local Govt: asst private sec to Min 1951-52, private sec to Parly Sec 1952-54, princ private sec to Min 1963-65, asst sec 1965-70, under sec 1970-76; dep sec DOE 1976-78, dep sec CSD 1978-80, second perm sec DOE 1980-81, perm sec DOE 1981-85; cmmr Historic Bldgs and Monuments Cmmn 1986-; chm: Br Cement Assoc 1987-, Civic Tst 1990-; memb Advsy Cncl on Public Records 1989-; *Style*— Sir George Moseley, KCB; Windy Ridge, Cornells Lane, Widdington, Saffron Walden, Essex CB11 3SP

MOSELEY, His Hon Judge (Thomas) Hywel; QC (1985); s of Rev Luther Moseley, of Porthceiro, Llanbadarn Fawr, Aberystwyth, and Megan Eiluned, *née* Howells (d 1977); *b* 27 Sept 1936; *Educ* Caterham Sch Surrey, Queens' Coll Cambridge (MA, LLM); *m* 25 June 1960, Monique Germaine Thérèse, da of Edmond Gaston Drufin (d 1977); 3 da (Catrin b 1961, Eirian (twin) b 1961, Gwenda b 1969); *Career* called to the Bar Gray's Inn 1964, in practice Wales and Chester Circuit 1964, rec 1981, circuit judge 1989; prof of law Univ Coll of Wales Aberystwyth 1970-83; *Recreations* beekeeping; *Style*— His Hon Judge Hywel Moseley, QC; Nantceiro, Llanbadarn Fawr, Aberystwyth, Dyfed SY23 3HW (☎ 0970 62 3532)

MOSELEY, Dr Ivan Frederick; s of Frederick Clarence Moseley, of Torrevieja, Spain, and Edith Sophia, *née* Smith (d 1987); *b* 29 May 1940; *Educ* Latymer Upper Sch, Univ of London (BSc, MD, MB BS); *m* 22 April 1967, Mary Cheyne Thomson, da of George Malcolm, of Royston, Cambs; 1 s (James b 1978), 1 da (Hannah b 1968); *Career* conslt radiologist: Nat Hosp 1975-, Moorfields Eye Hosp 1984-; conslt Neuroradiologist: Wellington Hosp London 1975-87, hon Royal Surrey Co Hosp 1986-; sec: Jt Neurosciences Ctee 1986-90, Br Soc of Neuroradiologist 1986-90; memb Br Inst of Radiology; pres Club Taurino of London; FRCR 1972, FRCP 1986, FRSM 1980; *Books* Computer Tomographie des Kopfes (contrib 1978), Computed Tomography in Neuro-Ophthalmology (contrib, 1982), Diagnostic Imaging in Neurological Disease (1986), Magnetic Resonance Imaging in Diseases of the Nervous System (1988); *Recreations* music, wine, bullfighting; *Clubs* Arts; *Style*— Dr Ivan Moseley; 65 St Mary's Grove, London W4 3LW (☎ 081 995 5668); National Hospital for Neurology & Diseases, Queen Square, London WC1N 3BG (☎ 071 837 3611)

MOSELEY, Kevin; s of Victor and Christine Moseley, of Tedustan House, Pontllanfraith, Gwent; *b* 2 July 1963; *Educ* Oakdale Comprehensive Sch, Brunel Tech Coll; *m* 29 May 1987, Carol da of Colin Williams; 1 da (Cara Lea b 21 July 1987); *Career* Rugby Union lock forward Newport RFC and Wales; clubs: Blackwood RFC (50 appearances) 1981-82, Pontypool RFC (260 appearances) 1982-91, Newport RFC 1991-, Bay of Plenty NZ; Wales: debut v NZ Aukland 1988, Five Nations debut v Scotland Murrayfield 1989, tour NZ 1988; *Recreations* training, family, music; *Style*— Kevin Moseley, Esq; Newport Rugby Club, Rodney Parade, Newport, Gwent

MOSER, Sir Claus Adolf; KCB (1973), CBE (1965); s of Dr Ernest Moser and Lotte Moser; *b* 24 Nov 1922; *Educ* Frensham Heights Sch, LSE; *m* 1949, Mary Oxlin; 1 s, 2 da; *Career* LSE: asst lectr 1946-49, lectr 1949-55, reader 1955-61, prof of social statistics 1961-70, visiting prof 1970-75; statistical advsr Ctee Higher Educn 1961-64, dir Central Statistical Office and head of Govt Statistical Serv 1967-78, visiting fell Nuffield Coll Oxford 1972-80, pres Royal Statistical Soc 1978-80; memb: Governing Body RAM 1967-79, BBC Music Advsy Ctee 1971-; chm Bd of Dirs Royal Opera House Covent Garden 1974-87, vice chm N M Rothschild & Sons 1978-84 (dir 1984-90); dir: Economist Intelligence Unit 1979-83, The Economist 1979-, Equity and Law Life Assurance Society 1980-87, Octopus Publishing Group 1982-88, chm Harold Holt Ltd 1990-; warden Wadham Coll Oxford 1984-; tstee Pilgrims Tst 1982-, tstee Br Museum 1988-, London Philharmonic Orch 1988-; pres Br Assoc for the Advancement of Sci 1989-90; FBA 1969; Hon FRAM, hon fell LSE; Hon DSc: Southampton, Leeds, City Univ, Sussex, Wales; Hon DUniv: Keele, Surrey, York; Hon DTech Brunel; Cdr de l'Ordre National du Mérite (France); *Style*— Sir Claus Moser, KCB, CBE; 3 Regent's Park Terrace, London NW1 7EE (☎ 071 458 1619)

MOSER, Robin Allan Shedden; s of Allan Hugh Shedden Moser (d 1970), of Betchworth, Surrey, and Mary Dorothy Chatfeild-Clarke, *née* Shanks; *b* 3 June 1947; *Educ* Radley; *m* 17 Feb 1973, Sally, da of Walter Douglas Knowles (d 1985), of Beckenham, Kent; 3 s (Robert David b 1975, Patrick Allan b 1978, Edward Alexander b 1983); *Career* CA and banker; dir Credit Lyonnais Capital Markets plc 1986, md and chief exec Alexanders Discount plc 1984, chm Alexanders Discount Futures Ltd 1983; FCA; *Recreations* golf, sailing; *Clubs* Saffron Wadlden Golf; *Style*— Robin Moser, Esq; Mill End, Clavering, Saffron Walden, Essex (☎ 0799 550 360); Alexanders Discount plc, Broadwalk House, 5 Appold St, London EC2A 2DA (☎ 071 588 1234)

MOSES, Geoffrey Haydn; s of Canon Haydn Moses (d 1983), of Llanelu Vicarage, Dyfed, and Beryl Mary, *née* Lloyd); *b* 24 Sept 1952; *Educ* Ystalyfera GS, Emmanuel Coll Cambridge (BA), King's Coll London (PGCE); *m* 24 July 1981, Anne Elizabeth, da of Harry Mason; *Career* opera singer; debuts: WNO Barber of Seville (princ singer 1978-82), Royal Opera House Covent Garden Tales of Hoffman 1981, Glyndebourne Touring Opera Don Giovanni 1982, Kent Opera Don Giovanni 1983, Opera North Madam Butterfly 1983, Glynebourne Festival Opera Arabella 1983 Scottish Opera Barber of Seville 1984, Belgian Opera Simon Boccanegra 1983, Hamburg State Opera Barber of Seville 1984, Netherlands Opera Salomé 1988; concerts and recitals at : Gothenberg, Frankfurt Alte Oper, Royal Festival Hall, Royal Albert Hall; *Recreations* walking, swimming, reading, wine; *Style*— Geoffrey Moses, Esq; 12 Ferrers Rd, Lewes, E Sussex (☎ 0273 473 088); Harrison/Parrot Ltd, 16 Penzance Pl, London W11 4PA (☎ 071 229 9166, fax 071 221 5042, telex 892 791 Birds G)

MOSES, Very Rev Dr John Henry; s of Henry William Moses (d 1975), of London, and Ada Elizabeth Moses; *b* 12 Jan 1938; *Educ* Ealing GS, Univ of Nottingham, Trinity Hall and Dept of Educn Cambridge, Lincoln Theol Coll (BA, PhD, Gladstone Meml prize); *m* 25 July 1964, Susan Elizabeth, da of James Wainwright (d 1980), of London; 1 s (Richard), 2 da (Rachel, Catherine); *Career* asst curate St Andrew's Bedford 1964-70, rector Coventry East Team Minstry 1970-77, examining chaplain to Bishop of

Coventry 1972-77, rural dean Coventry East 1973-77, archdeacon of Southend 1977-82, provost of Chelmsford 1982-; chm Chelmsford Cathedral Festival of Music 1984-; memb Gen Synod 1985-, chm Cncl of Centre for Study of Theology Univ of Essex 1987-, church cmmr 1988-; visiting fell Wolfson Coll Cambridge 1987-; *Clubs* Athenaeum; *Style*— The Very Rev the Provost of Chelmsford; The Provost's House, 3 Harlings Grove, Waterloo Lane, Chelmsford, Essex CM1 1YQ (☎ 0245 354 318); The Cathedral Office, Guy Harlings, New St, Chelmsford, Essex CM1 1NG (☎ 0245 263 660)

MOSES, Dr Kenneth (Ken); CBE (1988); s of Thomas Moses, of Adelaide, S Aust, and Mary, *née* Holland; *b* 29 Nov 1931; *Educ* Cowley GS St Helens Lancs, Wigan and Dist Mining Coll (HND); *m* 1949, Mary, da of William Price (d 1958), of St Helens, Lancs; 1 s (Philip b 1952), 2 da (Linda b 1949, Carol b 1962); *Career* mining engr; area dir North Derbyshire Br Coal 1981-85, tech dir Br Coal 1985; memb Corpn Br Coal 1986; Univ of Nottingham MPhil 1988, PhD 1990; FIMinE, FEng, Fell Inst of Mining Mech and Mining Electrical Engrs, hon fell IMinE 1990, FRSA, companion BIM; *Recreations* reading, gardening, walking; *Style*— Dr Ken Moses, CBE; Oaktrees, 6 Heath Ave, Mansfield NG18 3EU (☎ 0623 653843); British Coal, Eastwood Hall, Eastwood, Notts (☎ 0773 531313)

MOSESSON, John Gunnar; s of Torsten Johannes Mosesson (d 1974); *b* 9 July 1938; *Educ* Frensham Heights Sch, Univ of Keele (BA), Royal Coll of Music (ARCM); *m* 1, 1968 (m dis 1980), Jennifer Wendy; 2 s (Dargan Torsten Oliver b 1972, Truan Inigo Axel b 1976), 1 da (Gaël Kerstin Clare b 1970); m 2, 1985 (m dis 1990), Jennifer Ruth Trevelyan; m 3, 1990, Baroness Anna Cecilia Maria; 1 da (Cecilia Astrid Brita b 1991); *Career* staff memb: John Laing Res and Devpt 1959-61, Univ of Keele 1961-65; chm T F Sampson Ltd 1974 (md 1966), chm TF Sampson Ltd 1974, md Stramit Ltd 1974, md Stramit Int 1980-; chm Historic Houses Assoc E Anglia, vice pres Friends Aldeburgh Fndn, memb Cncl E Anglian Tourist Bd; *Recreations* music, tennis, golf, heritage issues, conservation; *Clubs* Arts; *Style*— John Mosesson, Esq; Otley Hall, Otley, Suffolk IP6 9PA (☎ 0473 890264, fax 0473 890803)

MOSHINSKY, Elijah; s of Abraham Moshinsky, and Eva, *née* Krasavitsky; *b* 8 Jan 1946; *Educ* Camberwell, Melbourne Univ (BA), Oxford Univ (D Phil); *m* 5 June 1970, Ruth, da of Oscar Dyttman, of Melbourne, Aust; 2 s (Benjamin b 6 Dec 1980, Jonathan b 5 May 1983); *Career* assoc prodr Royal Opera House 1988- (princ guest prodr 1975-88); prodns at Royal Opera House: Peter Grimes 1974, Lohengrin 1979, The Rakes Progress 1980, Macbeth 1981, Samson and Delilah 1981, Handel's Samson 1985 Otello 1986, Die Entführung aus dem Serail 1987, Attila 1990; for ENO: Le Grand Macabre 1980, The Mastersingers of Nuremberg 1984; for BBC TV: All's Well that Ends Well 1980, A Midsummer Nights Dream 1981, Cymbeline 1982, Coriolanus 1983, Love's Labours Lost 1984, Ghosts 1986; for West End: Three Sisters 1987, Light Up the Sky 1987, Another Time (Ronald Harwood) 1990, Shadowlands 1990; film: The Green Man (Kingsley Amis) 1990; *Recreations* reading, music; *Clubs* Garrick; *Style*— Elijah Moshinsky, Esq; 28 Kidbrooke Grove, London SE3 0LG (☎ 081 858 4179)

MOSIMANN, Anton; s of Otto Albert Mosimann, and Olga, *née* Von Burg (d 1966); *b* 23 Feb 1947; *m* 13 April 1973, Kathrin, da of Jakob Roth; 2 s (Philipp Anton b 1975, Mark Andreas b 1977); *Career* apprentice Hotel Baeren Twann Switzerland 1962-64, commis entremetier Palace Hotel Villars 1964-65, chef tournant and sous- chef Queen Elizabeth Hotel Montreal 1966-69, 1 chef tournant Palace Hotel St Moritz 1969-70, exec chef Swiss Pavilion Expo 70 Osaka Japan 1970, sous chef Kulm Hotel St Moritz winter seasons 1972-73 and 1973-74 (chef restaurateur 1971-72), commis pâtissier Palace Hotel Gstaad 1974-75, dir of cuisine Dorchester London 1986-88 (maître chef des cuisines 1975), chef patron Mosimann's London 1988-; frequent TV and radio appearances; winner of numerous Gold medals and awards worldwide; Hon Dr Culinary Arts Johnson and Wales Univ South Carolina; La Croix de Chevalier du Mérite Agricole; *Books* Cuisine à la Carte (1981), The Great Seafood Book (1985), Cuisine Naturelle (1985), Anton Mosimann's Fish Cuisine (1988), The Art of Anton Mosimann (1989), Cooking with Mosimann (1989); *Recreations* jogging, squash, vintage cars, collecting antique cookery books; *Style*— Anton Mosimann, Esq; 46 Abingdon Villas, Kensington W8 6XD (☎ 071 937 4383); Mosimann's, 11B West Halkin St, Belgrave Square, London SW1X 8JL (☎ 071 235 9625, fax 071 245 6354)

MOSKEY, Stamatis; s of Moskos Stamatis Moskey (d 1979), and Irene, *née* Foscolo (d 1967); *b* 17 July 1939; *Educ* Georgetown Univ Washington DC, Univ of Cincinnati (BA), Sch of Law Western Reserve Cleveland Ohio (JD); *m* 4 Oct 1969, Mary Katherine, da of John Love; 1 s (Matthew Love b 16 June 1976), 1 da (Marina Louise b 9 Sept 1973); *Career* tanker broker: Jones & Thompson NY 1965-73, Clarkson Broudo Piraeus 1973-82, H CLarkson & Co Ltd London 1973-82; Order of St Andrew Greek Ecumenical Patriarchate; patron: Greek Patriarchate Jerusalem (Evergetis), Petra municipality Lesbos Greece; patron of New Art Tate Gallery London; *Clubs* Piping Rock (Locust Valley Long Island NY), Yacht Club of Greece (Piraeus); *Style*— Stamatis Moskey, Esq; Avington Park House, Avington, Hampshire SO21 1DD (☎ 096 278 424); 10 Rossetti Garden Mansions, Flood St, London SW3 5QY (☎ 071 351 5608)

MOSLEY, Prof Derek John; s of Frederick Mosley (d 1981), of Potters Bar, and Louise Ellen, *née* Wallis; *b* 11 Nov 1934; *Educ* Watford Boys GS, Univ of Durham (BA), Univ of Cambridge (MA, PhD); *m* 29 Dec 1962, Margot, da of Harry Firth (d 1946), of Lytham St Annes; 2 da (Karen Angela b 9 June 1967, Nicole Andrea b 22 June 1969); *Career* Univ of Sheffield: asst lectr in classics and ancient history 1959-62, lectr 1962-68, sr lectr 1968-75, reader 1975, prof of ancient history and classical archaeology 1975-88, dean of arts 1987-88; prof of classics and ancient history Univ of Warwick 1988-; visiting lectr in history Univ of Michigan 1965-66; memb AUT (pres Sheffield Local Assoc 1982-84); *Books* Envoys and Diplomacy in Ancient Greece (1973), Ancient Greek Diplomacy (with FE Addock, 1975), Antike Diplomatie (jtly, 1980); *Recreations* music, walking, philately; *Clubs* Concordia Theatre; *Style*— Prof Derek Mosley; School of Classics and Ancient History, Universtiy of Warwick, Coventry CV4 7AL (☎ 0203 523523 ext 2369)

MOSLEY, Hon Lady (Diana); *née* Freeman-Mitford; da of 2 Baron Redesdale, JP (d 1958); one of the Mitford sisters; *b* 17 June 1910; *m* 1, 1929 (m dis 1934), Hon Bryan Walter Guinness (afterwards 2 Baron Moyne, *qv*); 2 s (Jonathan, Desmond Guinness, *qqv*); m 2, 1936, as his 2 w, Sir Oswald Ernald Mosley, 6 Bt (d 1980); 2 s (Alexander, Max); *Publications* A Life of Contrasts (memoirs), The Duchess of Windsor, Loved Ones (memoirs), The Writings of Rebecca West; *Style*— The Hon Lady Mosley; 1 rue des Lacs, 91400 Orsay, France (☎ 010 331 60104211)

MOSLEY, Hon Ivo Adam Rex; 2 s of 3 Baron Ravensdale, MC, by his 1 w; *Educ* Bryanston Sch, New Coll Oxford; *m* 1977, Xanthe Jennifer Grenville, da of Sir Michael Bernard Grenville Oppenheimer, 3 Bt; 3 s (Nathaniel b 1982, Felix b 1985, Scipio b 1988); *Style*— The Hon Ivo Mosley; Courtyard, Neopardy, Crediton, Devon

MOSLEY, Max Rufus; 4 s (but only 2 by his 2 w, Diana, *see* Hon Lady Mosley) of Sir Oswald Mosley, 6 Bt; half bro of Hon Jonathan Guinness, *qv*; *b* 13 April 1940; *Educ* Ch Ch Oxford; *m* 1960, Jean Marjorie, er da of James Taylor; 2 s (Alexander b 1970, Patrick b 1972); *Career* sec Oxford Union Soc 1960, called to Bar Gray's Inn 1964, fndr dir March Cars Ltd, legal advsr to Formula One Constructors Assoc; pres of the Mfrs Cmmn of the Fedn Internationale du Sport Automobile; *Recreations* wine, skiing, walking; *Style*— Max Mosley, Esq; 3 Egerton Gardens Mews, London SW3 2EH

MOSLEY, Hon Michael; granted 1967 the title rank and precedence of a Baroness's son, which would have been his had his mother survived to succeed to Barony of Ravensdale; s of Sir Oswald Ernald Mosley, 6 Bt (d 1980), by his 1 w Lady Cynthia Curzon (da of 1 and last Marquess Curzon of Kedleston); n of Baroness Ravensdale (d 1966); *b* 1932; *Educ* Eton, LSE; *Style*— The Hon Michael Mosley; Durham Cottage, Christchurch St, Chelsea, London SW3 (☎ 071 352 5409)

MOSLEY, Nicholas; *see*: 3 Baron Ravensdale

MOSLEY, Hon Robert; 3 s of 3 Baron Ravensdale, MC, by his 1 w; *b* 1955; *Educ* Bedales; *m* 1980, Victoria McBain; 1 s (Gregory b 1981), 1 da (Vija b 1984); *Style*— The Hon Robert Mosley; Ballagawne Farm, Kirkmichael, IOM

MOSLEY, Hon Shaun Nicholas; s and h of 3 Baron Ravensdale, MC; *b* 5 Aug 1949; *Educ* Bryanston Sch, Hertford Coll Oxford; *m* 1978, Theresa Clifford; 1 s (Daniel b 1982); *Style*— The Hon Shaun Mosley

MOSLEY, Simon James; yr s of John Arthur Noel Mosley (3 s of Sir Oswald Mosley, 5 Bt, and his 1 w, Katharine, da of Capt Justinian Edwards-Heathcote), and his 1 w, Caroline Edith Sutton, *née* Timmis; *b* 8 April 1927; *Educ* Eton, Christ Church Oxford; *m* 15 Dec 1957, Maria, o da of Iraklis Zeris (d 1980); 1 s (George b 1959), 1 da (Claire b 1964); *Career* slr 1956-, pres Holborn Law Soc 1967-68, memb Cncl Law Soc 1969-81; govr The Coll of Law 1973-; chm: Trinity International Holdings plc Group 1985-, Octavian Group Ltd 1984-; *Clubs* Cavalry and Guard's; *Style*— Simon Mosley, Esq; 23 Little Boltons, London SW10 9LJ

MOSS, Anthony David; s of David Samuel Moss (d 1970), of Eltham Coll, London, and Phyllis Holland, *née* Newton (d 1973); *b* 24 Jan 1932; *Educ* Cranbrook, Jesus Coll Cambridge (MA); *m* 25 Aug 1956, Jennifer Ann, JP, da of Prof William Hume-Rothery, OBE, FRS (d 1968), of Oxford; 1 s (Nicholas Hume), 2 da (Philippa Jane (Dr Madgwick), Charlotte Katharine (Mrs Nobbs)); *Career* Nat Serv cmmnd Libya 1951-52; Metal Box Co Ltd 1956-64; admitted slr 1968; ptnr Hyde Mahon Bridges (formerly Hyde Mahon & Pascall) 1969-; memb Ct of Common Cncl Corp of London 1989-, memb the Georgian Gp, govr Christs Hosp, tstee Geffrye Museum; Freeman City of London 1964, Liveryman and memb Ct Worshipful Co of Ironmongers (Master 1987-88); *Recreations* historic buildings, walking; *Clubs* City Livery; *Style*— Anthony Moss, Esq; 5 John Trundle Court, Barbican, London EC2Y 8DJ (☎ 071 256 6018); The Bury Farm, Chesham, Bucks HP5 2JU (☎ 0494 775878); Hyde Mahon Bridges (Solicitors), 52 Bedford Row, London WC1R 4UH (☎ 071 405 9455, fax 071 831 6649, telex 25210)

MOSS, Anthony David (Tony); s of Frank Richard Moss, of Middx, and Daphne Olive, *née* Brown; *b* 29 Jan 1956; *Educ* St Clement Danes GS, Univ of Sussex (BA); *m* Susan Courtault; 1 s (Daniel b 15 Jan 1985), 1 da (Natalie b 11 Nov 1988); *Career* full time offr NUS 1980, prodr and dir current affairs dept LWT 1986, ed special programmes 1987-; *Books* In Search of Christianity (1987); *Recreations* piano, jazz; *Clubs* Ronnie Scott's; *Style*— Tony Moss, Esq; LWT, Upper Ground, London SE1 9LT (☎ 071 261 3434, fax 071 928 5948)

MOSS, David Anscombe; s of Edwin John Moss, and Catherine Moss; *b* 27 Dec 1927; *m* 14 July 1951, Joan (d 1969), da of David Lee; 1 s (Vincent-David b 1958), 1 da (Carolyn Fleur b 1960); *Career* ret political agent W Herts Constituency Lab Pty (formerly Hemel Hempstead); former: book keeper, asst to civil engr, tport mangr; memb: Hemel Hempstead Rural Dist Cncl 1962-67, Kings Langley Parish Cncl 1962-67, Herts Co Cncl 1973-77, 1981-; govr: Dacroum Coll of Further Educn, John F Kennedy School; *Recreations* reading, walking; *Style*— David Moss, Esq; 19 Priory Gardens, Berkhamsted (☎ 0442 873 512)

MOSS, David John; s of John Henry Moss, and Doris Fenna; *b* 23 May 1947; *Educ* Sevenoaks Sch, St Johns Coll Cambridge (MA), Central London Poly (DMS); *m* 24 May 1975, Susan Elizabeth, da of Reginald Victor Runnalls (d 1982); 3 s (Oliver Richard b 21 April 1976, Benjamin Roland (twin), Jonathan Edward b 1 Dec 1980); *Career* mgmnt accountant Philips 1970-73 (mgmnt trainee 1968-70), asst fin offr St Thomas Hosp 1973-74; dist fin offr: Enfield 1974-79, East Dorset 1979-85; unit gen mangr: Poole Gen Hosp 1985-88, Southampton Gen Hosp 1988-90; gen mangr Southampton Univ Hosps 1990-; memb CIPFA 1979, FCMA 1981, FBIM 1984, memb Inst of Health Servs Mgmnt 1979; *Books* Managing Nursing (co-author, 1984); *Recreations* history, golf, badminton, opera, tennis, cricket; *Style*— David Moss, Esq; Southampton University Hospitals, Southampton General Hospital, Tremona Rd, Southampton, Hants (☎ 0703 876172)

MOSS, David Joseph; CMG (1989); s of Herbert Joseph Moss (d 1961), and Irene Gertrude Moss; *b* 6 Nov 1938; *Educ* Hampton GS; *m* 3 June 1961, Joan Lillian, da of Alfred Herbert Tyler (d 1987); 1 s (James b 1970), 1 da (Catherine b 1971); *Career* Nat Serv RAF 1957-59; FO 1966-69 (1957 and 1959-62), FCO 1970-73, Br Embassy first sec and head of chancery The Hague 1974-77 (third, later second sec Bangkok 1962-65, first sec La Paz 1969-70), UK Mission cnsllr and dep permanent rep in Geneva 1983-87, FCO asst under sec of state 1987-90 (head of dept 1978-83), Br High Cmmr NZ and Govr (non-resident) Pitcairn, Henderson, Dulcie and Oeno Islands 1990-; *Recreations* reading, walking; *Style*— David Moss, Esq, CMG; British High Commission, Wellington, NZ

MOSS, Dr Edward; s of George Moss (d 1962), of Shipley, W Yorks, and Elizabeth Mary, *née* Dunn; *b* 10 Sept 1948; *Educ* Bradford GS, Univ of Edinburgh (MB ChB, MD); *m* 10 July 1972, Elizabeth Marie, da of the late William Arthur Tonkin, of Douglas, IOM; 2 s (Nicholas William George, Christopher Edward Stuart); *Career* house offr in gen surgery Bradford Royal Infirmary 1973 (house offr in med 1972), sr house offr in anaesthetics United Leeds Hosps 1973, resgistrar anaesthetics The Gen Infirmary at Leeds 1974, lectr in anaesthesia Univ of Leeds 1976, sr registrar in anaesthetics Yorks RHA 1977, conslt anaesthetist Leeds Western Health Authy 1979, sr clinical lectr Univ of Leeds 1989 (clinical lectr in anaesthesia 1979); memb: Yorks Soc of Anaesthetists, The Neuroanaesthetists Travelling Club; memb BMA, Assoc of Anaesthetists of GB and Ireland; FCAnaes; *Books* Aspects of Recovery from Anaesthesia (ed with I Hindmarch, J G Jones, 1987); *Recreations* golf; *Style*— Dr Edward Moss; 10 Dunstarn Lane, Adel, Leeds LS16 8EL (☎ 0532 679635); Dept of Anaesthetics, The General Infirmary at Leeds, Great George St, Leeds, W Yorkshire LS1 3EX (☎ 0532 437172)

MOSS, Dr Edward Herbert St George; s of Sir George Sinclair Moss, KBE, of N Devon (d 1959), and Lady Gladys Lucy Moss, *née* Moore (d 1971); *b* 18 May 1918; *Educ* Marlborough, Pembroke Coll Cambridge (BA, MA), Univ of Surrey (PhD); *m* 2 June 1948, Shirley Evelyn, da of Alfred Seymour Baskett (d 1960), of Bournemouth; 2 s (Anthony b 1949, Andrew b 1955), 1 da (Nicola b 1951); *Career* served W Desert (Army), Intelligence Offr 50 Div, Lt-Col and instr Mil Govt Staff Centre; diplomat, civil servant, writer; entered Foreign (Dip) Serv 1945 (served in: Tokyo, Belgrade (first sec, head of Chancery 1951), Detroit, London); asst sec (head of DS3 DS8) MOD 1960, Dept of Educn and Sci; under sec Univ Grants Ctee 1971; ret 1978; *Books* Fire from a Flint - Daily Readings with William Law (ed, 1986), Seeing Man Whole - A New Model for Psychology (1989); *Recreations* gardening, writing; *Style*— Dr Edward Moss; Prospect, 29 Guildown Ave, Guildford, Surrey GU2 5HA; (☎ 0483 66984)

MOSS, John Ringer; CB (1972); 2 s of late James Moss, of Fressingfield, Suffolk, and Louisa, *née* Ringer; *b* 15 Feb 1920; *Educ* Manchester GS, BNC Oxford (MA); *m* 1946, Edith Bland, da of George Wheeler, of Liverpool; 2 s (Michael, Martin), 1 da (Charlotte); *Career* Army 1940-46, Capt RE serv India, Burma, Malaya; Civil Serv: dep sec Miny of Agric 1970-80 (joined 1947, princ private sec 1959-60); advsr to cos in Assoc Br Foods Gp 1980-; chm Cncl Royal Veterinary Coll 1983-89; *Style—* John Moss, Esq, CB; 16 Upper Hollis, Great Missenden, Bucks

MOSS, Lewis David; CBE (1985), DL (Berks 1984); s of Samuel Algernon Montague Moss (d 1948), and Lily, *née* Goodman (d 1959); *b* 15 Feb 1922; *Educ* Univ Coll Sch, City of London Coll; *m* 1, 17 April 1947, Elizabeth Joy (d 1982), da of Sydney Flatau (d 1953); 2 s (Roger b 1950, Stephen b 1952), 1 da (Mrs Virginia Campus b 1956); m 2, 24 Oct 1987, Vivien Lowenstein, *née* Lissauer; *Career* Capt RA 1941-46, served N Africa, Italy, Greece, Austria; sr ptnr Moss & Ptnrs; chm: Grosvenor Securities Gp of Companies, Terminus Securities Ltd, Michael Druitt Wines; London Dockland Devpt Corpn: memb Bd 1981-, memb Exec Ctee 1985-, chm Skillnet 1988-, memb Bd Docklands Light Railway 1988-, chm Docklands Enterprise Centre 1989; memb: London City Airport Consultative Ctee 1988-, Tower Hamlets Health Authy 1989-; ACC: memb Exec Cncl 1977-89, ldr and chm Policy Ctee 1983-86 (vice chm 1985-86), memb Liaison Body with Audit Cmmn 1983-86, memb Local Authys Conditions of Service Advsy Bd 1983-86, memb Consultative Cncl on Local Govt Fin 1983-89, memb Cmmn for Local Admin in England 1983-89, memb Standing Conf of Local and Regnl Authys of Europe 1983-89; co cncllr Wokingham 1971-89; Berks CC: chm Policy Ctee and ldr 1977-79, vice chm 1979-80, chm 1980-82; memb Thames Valley Police Authy 1977-89, tstee Wokingham Cons Assoc 1978-, chm Co Cons Gp 1983-86; memb: Exec Ctee Nat Union Cons and Unionist Assocs 1983-89, Nat Local Govt Advsy Ctee 1983-89; chm Property Advsy Ctee (South regn) 1989-, tstee Wokingham and Dist Assoc for Elderly, memb Cncl Order of St John Berks, patron Coll Estate Mgmnt Univ of Reading, memb Corpn Univ Coll Sch; Freeman City of London, memb Worshipful Co Glovers 1965; FSVA (nat pres 1969-70), memb Int Real Estate Fedn; High Sheriff Berkshire 1991-92; *Recreations* travel, skiing, boating, art collection; *Clubs* Carlton, United & Cecil, Guards Polo, Royal Automobile; *Style—* Lewis Moss, Esq, CBE, DL; Tilney House, 5 Tilney St, London W1X 6JI (☎ 071 629 9933)

MOSS, Malcolm Douglas; MP (C) Cambs NE 1987; s of Norman Moss (d 1976), and Annie, *née* Gay; *b* 6 March 1943; *Educ* Audenshaw GS, St John's Coll Cambridge (MA, Cert Ed); *m* 28 Dec 1965, Vivien Lorraine, da of Albert Peake (d 1964); 2 da (Alison Claire b 1969, Sarah Nicole b 1972); *Career* asst master Blundell's Tiverton Devon 1966-68 (head dept 1968-70), insur conslt Barwick Assocs 1971-72 (gen mangr 1972-74), co-fndr and dir Mandrake (Insur and Fin Brokers) Ltd 1974- (chm 1986-, changed name to Mandrake Assocs Ltd 1988); dir : Mandrake (Insur Servs) Ltd 1976-81 (resigned), Mandrake Collinge Ltd 1977-86 (resigned), Mandrake (Insur Advsy Serv) Ltd 1978, Mandrake (Fin Mgmnt) Ltd 1985-87 (resigned); chm Mandrake Gp plc 1986-88 (resigned); dir Fens Business Enterprises Tst Ltd 1983-, chm Fens Business Enterprise Tst Ltd 1983-87 (resigned); *Recreations* amateur dramatics, tennis, skiing; *Clubs* Oxford and Cambridge, Lords and Commons Tennis and Ski; *Style—* Malcolm Moss, Esq, MP; Boston House, South Brink, Wisbech, Cambs PE14 0RT (☎ 0945 65997); 88 St George's Square, London SW1 (☎ 071 821 0269); House of Commons (☎ 071 219 6933, secretary 071 219 4037); Business address: 6 North Brink, Wisbech, Cambs PE13 1JR (☎ 0945 65177)

MOSS, Martin Grenville; CBE (1975); s of Horace Grenville Moss (d 1975), and Gladys Ethel, *née* Wootton (d 1981); *b* 17 July 1923; *Educ* Lancing; *m* 2 Feb 1953, Jane Hope, *née* Bown; 2 s (Matthew b 4 June 1955, Hugo b 24 Feb 1962), 1 da (Louisa b 25 Oct 1958); *Career* WWII: RAF 1942-46, pilot, Sqdn Ldr; sr welfare offr Iraq and Persia 1945-46; md: Woollands Knightsbridge 1953-66, Debenham and Freebody 1964-66, Simpson Piccadilly 1966-73 and 1980-85; chm and chief exec offr May Department Stores International USA 1974-80, dir Nat Tst Enterprises 1985-88; dep chm Design Cncl 1971-75 (memb 1964-75); chm Cncl RSA 1983-85 (memb cncl 1977-); memb: Cncl RCA 1953-58, Royal Fine Art Commn 1982-84; Order of the Lion of Finland 1970; *Recreations* gardening, painting, classic cars; *Clubs* RAF; *Style—* Martin Moss, Esq, CBE; Parsonage Farm, Bentworth, Alton, Hants GU34 5RB

MOSS, Montague George; s of Harry Neville Moss (d 1982), and Ida Sophia, *née* Woolf (d 1971); *b* 21 April 1924; *Educ* Harrow, New Coll Oxford; *m* 28 Sept 1955, Jane, da of David Levi, of 23 Ranulf Rd, London; 2 s (Andrew b 7 Feb 1958, David b 15 Sept 1959), 1 da (Joanna b 15 Aug 1956); *Career* served Army 1943-47, cmmnd KRRC 1944, demob as Capt; Moss Bros Ltd: dir 1953-87, chm 1981-87, pres 1987-; pres: Fedn of Merchant Tailors of GB 1965-66 and 1985-86, Tailor's Benevolent Inst 1980-; Freeman: City of London 1948, Worshipful Co of Carmen 1949; FRSA; *Recreations* public speaking, music; *Clubs* Jesters, MCC, Old Harrovian Eton Fives; *Style—* Montague Moss, Esq; 4 Melina Place, London NW8 9SA (☎ 071 286 0114); Moss Bros, 131 New Bond St, London W1 (☎ 071 629 4723)

MOSS, (Victor) Peter Cannings; s of Frederick James Reynolds Moss (d 1979), of Marlborough, Wilts, and Olive May Moss *née* Cannings (d 1987); *b* 12 March 1921; *Educ* Marlborough GS, Worcester Trg Coll; *m* Jan 1949, Joan, da of Samuel Holland (d 1978), of Kidderminster, Worcs; 1 da (Melanie b 1950), 1 s (Peter b 1963); *Career* author; teaching various schools and colls 1950-70; full time writer, broadcaster, lectr 1970-; broadcasts: mainly world serv, numerous radio and TV programmes mainly literary; memb Soc of Authors (memb Ctee Educational Writers Gp); *Publications* over 50 on History, English, Sociology, Commerce, Statistics, series of 9 for Chinese Schools in Hong Kong; other pub: Encounters with the past (hypnotic regression pub UK, USA, France, Holland, Australia), Ghosts over Britain (Pub UK and Hungary); *Recreations* opera, travel, wine, work; *Style—* Peter Moss, Esq; Brook Cottage, Ripe, Lewes, Sussex BN8 6AR (☎ 032 183 216)

MOSS, Peter Jonathan; s of Capt John Cottam Moss, of Sutton Green, Nr Guildford, and Joyce Alison, *née* Blunn (d 1977); *b* 29 March 1951; *Educ* Charterhouse; *m* Rosanne Marilyn, da of Alexander James Houston, of Compton, Nr Chichester; 3 s (Alexander b 28 Oct 1981, Benjamin b 14 Nov 1983, Patrick b 22 April 1987); *Career* called to the Bar Lincoln's Inn 1976; memb of Lloyds 1986; Freeman City of London 1985, Liveryman Worshipful Co of Clockmakers 1987; *Recreations* golf, windsurfing, skiing, cricket, filling in questionnaires; *Clubs* New Zealand Golf, MCC; *Style—* Peter Moss, Esq; 3 Temple Gdns, Temple, London EC4 (☎ 071 353 3102, fax 071 353 0960)

MOSS, Stirling; OBE (1957); s of Alfred Moss, and Aileen Moss; *b* 17 Sept 1929; *Educ* Haileybury, Imperial Service Coll; *m* 1, 1957 (m dis 1960), Kathleen, da of F Stuart Molson, of Canada; m 2, 1964 (m dis 1968), Elaine, da of A Barbarino, of New York; 1 da; m 3, 1980, Susan, da of Stuart Paine of London; 1 s; *Career* racing driver 1947-62; learnt to drive aged 6, built own Cooper-Alta 1953, Br Nat Champion 1950-52, 1954-59 and 1961; winner: Tourist Trophy 1950-51, 1955 and 1958-61, Coupe des Alpes 1952-54, Alpine Gold Cup 1954, Italian Mille Miglia 1955 (only Englishman to win); competed in 494 races, rallies, sprints, land speed records and endurance runs, completed 366 and won 222; Grand Prix & successes incl: Targa Florio 1955, Br 1955 and 1957, Italian 1956-57 and 1959, NZ 1956 and 1959, Monaco 1956 and 1960-61, Leguna Secq 1960-61, US 1959-60, Aust 1956, Bari 1956, Pesara 1957, Swedish 1957, Dutch 1958, Argentine 1958, Morocco 1958, Buenos Aires 1958, Melbourne 1958, Villareal 1958, Caen 1958, Portuguese 1959, S Africa 1960, Cuba 1960, Austrian 1960, Cape Town 1960, Watkins Glen 1960, German 1961, Modena 1961; Driver of the Year 1954 and 1961, holder of 1500cc World speed record driving MG EX181 at 240mph; md Stirling Moss Ltd; dir: Designs Unlimited Ltd, SM Design & Interior Decorating Co, Hankoe Stove Enamelling Ltd, former dir of racing Johnson's Wax; judge: Miss World (4 times), Miss Universe 1974; former demonstrator Dunlop Rubber Co (travelled across India and Malaysia); conslt incl work for: Ferodo Opel Germany and Chrysler Aust; has given numerous lecture tours across US and in UK, NZ, Aust and Hong Kong; *Books* Stirling Moss's Book of Motor Sport (1955), In the Track of Speed (1957), Stirling Moss's Second Book of Motor Sport (1958), Le Mans (1959), My Favourite Car Stories (1960), A Turn at the Wheel (1961), All But My Life (1963), Design and Behaviour of the Racing Car (1964), How to Watch Motor Racing (1975), Motor Racing and All That (1980), My Cars, My Career (1987); *Recreations* snow skiing, water skiing, dancing, spear-fishing, model making, theatre, designing; *Clubs* Br Racing Driver's, Br Automobile Racing, Br Racing and Sports Car, Road Racing Drivers of America, 200mph, Lord's Taverners, RAC, International des Anciens Pilotes des Grand Prix; chm or pres of 36 motoring clubs; *Style—* Stirling Moss, Esq, OBE; 46 Shepherd St, London W1Y 8JN (☎ 071 499 7967, 071 499 3727, fax 071 499 4104)

MOSS, Stuart; s of Morris Moss (d 1976), of London, and Bertha Moss; *b* 31 Dec 1944; *Educ* Grocers Co Sch (Dip Arch); *m* 24 June 1973 (m dis 1978), Layn Sandra, da of Ronald Feldman, of London; 2 s (Lucas Ryan b 1974, Daniel Miles b 1979), 1 da (Zoë Anastasis b 1982); *Career* qualified as chartered architect 1972; assoc with Robert Turner Architects 1973-75, formed partnership with John Bennett 1975-84, formed Moss & Co Architects 1985-; author of various articles written for architectural magazines; memb RIBA, ARCUK; *Recreations* films and the visual arts, reading, travel, swimming; *Style—* Stuart Moss, Esq; Moss & Co Architects, 165 Brecknock Rd, London N19 5AD (☎ 071 485 0770, fax 071 485 1005)

MOSS, Hon Mrs (Susannah Elizabeth); *née* Yerburgh; o da of 2 Baron Alvingham, CBE, *qv*; *b* 1953; *m* 1979, Edward I J G Moss; 2 da (Alice Elinor b 1983e, Victoria Elizabeth b 1986); *Style—* The Hon Mrs Moss; 24 Rusham Rd, London SW12 8TH

MOSS, Timothy Campbell; s of William Denniss Moss, and Phyllis May *née* Charnock (d 1971); *b* 31 Jan 1937; *Educ* Wintringham GS; *m* 13 Sept 1969, Sheila Elizabeth, da of Samuel Dunwoody (d 1983); 2 da (Claire b 1971, Rachel b 1973); *Career* Nat Serv RAEC 1959-61, sgt; articled clerk Forrester Boyd & Co 1953-58, Coopers & Lybrand 1961- (ptnr 1974-); memb ICAEW, FCA 1959; *Recreations* golf, bridge; *Clubs* Croham Hurst Golf; *Style—* Timothy C Moss, Esq; Coopers & Lybrand Deloitte, Plumtree Court, London EC4A 4HT (☎ 071 822 8507, fax 071 822 8500)

MOSS, Dr Trevor Simpson; s of William Moss (d 1937), of Highfield, Willslock, Uttoxeter, and Florence Elizabeth, *née* Simpson (d 1954); *b* 28 Jan 1921; *Educ* Alleyne's GS Uttoxeter, Downing Coll Cambridge (BA, MA, PhD, ScD); *m* 6 March 1948, Audrey, da of Ernest Nelson (d 1948), of Holly St, Durham City; *Career* WWII various hon cmmns as Flt Lt RAF 1943-45: N Africa 1943, invasion of Normandy and S France 1944, Denmark 1945; res scientist: TRE 1941-53, RAE 1953-68; head Radio and Navigation Dept RAE 1968-78, dep dir RSRE 1978-81; exec ed: Infrared Physics 1961-, Progress in Quantum Electronics 1978-; Max Born prize Br and German Physical Socs 1975, Dennis Gabor award Int Soc of Optical Engrs 1988; AMIEE 1949, FInstP 1968, CPhys 1987; *Books* Photoconductivity (1952), Optical Properties of Semiconductors (1959), Semiconductor Optoelectronics (1973), Handbook on Semiconductors (4 vols 1980-82), over 100 papers published in int jls; *Style—* Dr Trevor Moss; Acathon, Shelsley Meadow, Colwall, Malvern, Worcs (☎ 0684 40079)

MOSSÉ, Peter Sylvain; s of Leon Mossé (d 1980), of Monaco, and Leonie, *née* King; *b* 25 Jan 1925; *Educ* Shrewsbury, RMA Sandhurst; *m* 6 Sept 1967, (Evelyn) Sheila, da of Carl Moritz Dunsford Belton; 2 da (Jennifer (Mrs Pettman), Carol (Mrs Grant)); *Career* Capt 14/20 King's Hussars 1943-54; dir C T Bowring & Muir Beddal Lloyds Brokers 1964, chm P S Mossé & Ptnrs Ltd 1968-90 (hon life pres 1990-); govr Sandroyd Prep Sch; memb LIBA; *Recreations* golf, skiing, woodwork; *Clubs* Cavalry and Guard's; *Style—* Peter Mossé, Esq; P S Mossé & Ptnrs Ltd, 4-5 Queen Victoria Terrace, Sovereign Close, London EC1 9HA (☎ : 071 488 4303)

MOSSE, Richard Hugh; s of Rev Charles Herbert Mosse (d 1970), and Beatrice Elizabeth, *née* Watson (d 1981); *b* 30 May 1924; *Educ* Radley; *m* 29 May 1954, Barbara Mary, da of Lt-Col Harold Montague Towlson (d 1970); 3 da (Kate b 1961, Caroline (Mrs Matthews) b 1965, Elizabeth b 1966); *Career* Capt Welsh Guards; France and Germany 1944-45, Palestine 1946-48; admitted slr 1957, NP 1976; pres Chichester and Dist Law Soc 1978-79, clerk to gen cmmr of taxes Chichester and Bognor Regis 1988-90, former sr ptnr Rapers Slrs, author articles on capital taxation; sec to Bd of Chichester Festival Theatre 1966-, pres Aldwick Branch Royal Br Legion 1971, life govr Imperial Cancer Res Fund 1987, chm Fishbourne PC 1987-89; memb Law Soc 1957; *Books* Capital Transfer Tax (1975); *Recreations* golf, fell walking; *Clubs* RAC; *Style—* Richard Mosse, Esq; 3 The Old Stables, Grassmere Close, Felpham Village, Bognor Regis, W Sussex (☎ 0243 860553)

MOSSELMANS, Carel Maurits; TD; s of Adriaan Willem Mosselmans (d 1956), of The Hague, Holland, and Nancy Henriette van der Wyck (d 1963); *b* 9 March 1929; *Educ* Stowe, Trinity Coll Cambridge (MA); *m* 4 Jan 1962, Hon Prudence Fiona, da of Baron McCorquodale of Newton, KCO, PC (d 1971); 2 s (Michael b 1962, Julian b 1964); *Career* dir Sedgwick Collins and Co Ltd 1963 (joined 1952), md Sedgwick Collins (Underwriting) Ltd 1972 (dir 1971), dir Sedgwick Forbes Holdings Ltd 1978; chm: Sedgwick Forbes Underwriting Agencies 1974-89, Sedgwick Forbes Marine Ltd 1974-78, Sedgwick Forbes Services Ltd 1978-81, Sedgwick Ltd 1981-84, Sedgwick Group Plc 1984-89 (dep chm 1982-84), The Sumitomo Marine & Fire Insurance Co (Europe) Ltd 1981-90 (dir 1975-90); non-exec dir Coutts & Co 1981-; chm: N M Rothschild Asset Management Ltd 1989-, N M Rothschild International Asset Management Ltd 1989-, N M Rothschild Fund Management Ltd 1990-; dir Rothschilds Continuation Ltd 1990-; *Recreations* shooting, music, fishing, golf; *Clubs* White's, Cavalry & Guard's; *Style—* Carel M Mosselmans, Esq, TD; 15 Chelsea Sq, London SW3 6LF (☎ 071 352 0621); N M Rothschild Asset Management Limited, Five Arrows House, St Swithin's Lane, London EC4N 8NR (☎ 071 634 2804)

MOSSELMANS, Hon Mrs (Prudence Fiona); da of 1 and last Baron McCorquodale of Newton (d 1971), and Winifred Sophia Doris Clark (d 1960); *b* 27 June 1936; *m* 1962, Carel Maurits Mosselmans, TD, *qv*; 2 s; *Style—* The Hon Mrs Mosselmans; Seameads, Sandwich Bay, Kent (☎ 030 461 3558); 15 Chelsea Square, London SW3 (☎ 071 352 0621)

MOSSMAN, Frances Anne; da of Francis Joseph McGarry, of Southampton, Hants, and Kathleen, *née* Gralton; *b* 6 Jan 1949; *Educ* La Sante Union Convent HS Southampton, Winchester Sch of Art, Trent Poly (Dip Fashion and Textiles); *m* 7 July 1978, Andrew Vernon Mossman, s of John Vernon Mossman, of Putney, London, and Diss, Norfolk; 1 s (Tomás b 28 April 1988); *Career* design dir Sabre Int Textiles 1978-84; Next plc: merchandise dir (menswear) 1985-86, product dir (all clothing) 1986-87, ed dir Next Directory 1987; assessor: RCA, CNAA Kingston Poly; *Recreations* reading, walking in the country; *Style—* Mrs Frances Mossman; 79A

Warrington Crescent, London W9 1EH (☎ 071 289 2337); Home Farm, Little Everdon, Northants (☎ 032 736 233); Next plc Desford Rd, Enderby, Leicester (☎ 0533 866 411)

MOSTYN, Lady; Cristina Beatrice Maria; o da of Marchese Pier-Paolo Vladimiro Orengo, of Casa Orengo, La Mortola, Italy; *m* 23 June 1963, Sir Jeremy John Anthony Mostyn, 14 Bt (d 1988); 1 s (Sir William, 15 Bt, *qv*), 2 da (Casimira Anita Maria b 3 Dec 1964, Rachel Joanna Maria b 26 Aug 1967); *Style*— Lady Mostyn; The Coach House, Lower Heyford, Oxon

MOSTYN, Gen Sir (Joseph) David Frederick; KCB (1984), CBE (1974, MBE 1962); s of J P Mostyn (d 1929), and M C Keenan, *née* Moss; *b* 28 Nov 1928; *Educ* Downside, RMA Sandhurst; *m* 1952, Diana Patricia, da of Col Sheridan, MC (d 1950), 4 s (Philip, Mark, Rupert, Matthew), 2 da (Celia, Kate); *Career* cmmnd Oxford and Bucks LI 1948, Canadian Staff Coll 1958, instr Staff Coll Camberley 1963-66, MOD 1967-68, cmd 2 Royal Green Jackets 1969-71, Cmdt Tactics Wing Sch of Infantry 1971-72, cmd 8 Inf Bde 1972-74, dep dir Army Trg 1974-75, RCDS 1976, BGS Rhine Army 1977, dir Personal Servs 1978-80, GOC Berlin 1980-83, mil sec 1983-86, Adj-Gen 1986-88; Col Cmdt: Light Div 1983-86, Army Legal Corps 1983-88, ADC (Gen) 1986-89; landowner (200 acres); *Recreations* all field sports; *Clubs* Army and Navy; *Style*— Gen Sir David Mostyn, KCB, CBE; c/o Lloyds Bank, 54 Broad St, Lyme Regis, Dorset

MOSTYN, Hon Llewellyn Roger Lloyd; s and h of 5 Baron Mostyn, MC, by his 1 w Yvonne (*see* Maj Sir William Wrixon-Becher, Bt, MC); *b* 26 Sept 1948; *Educ* Eton, The Inns of Ct Sch of Law; *m* 1974, Denise Suzanne, da of Roger Duvanel, an artist, of France; 1 s (Gregory Philip Roger Lloyd b 1984), 1 da (Alexandra Stephanie b 1975); *Career* late Capt Army Legal Servs; called to the Bar Middle Temple 1973 (practising Criminal Bar), pt/t teacher at Bromley Coll of Technol; *Recreations* literature, history, classical music, tennis, sport, rugger; *Clubs* White's; *Style*— The Hon Llewellyn Mostyn; 9 Anderson Street, London SW3 (☎ 071 584 3059); 185 Temple Chambers, Temple Avenue, London EC4 (☎ 071 353 3507/8)

MOSTYN, 5 Baron (UK 1831); Capt Sir Roger Edward Lloyd Lloyd-Mostyn; 6 Bt (GB 1778), MC (1942); s of 4 Baron (d 1965); *b* 17 April 1920; *Educ* Eton, RMC Sandhurst; *m* 1, 1943, Yvonne Margaret, da of A Stuart Johnson, of Henshall Hall, Congleton, Cheshire; 1 s, 1 da; m 2, Mrs Sheila Edmondson Shaw, DL (Clwyd 1982), da of Maj Reginald Fairweather; *Heir* s, Hon Llewellyn Roger Lloyd Lloyd-Mostyn; *Career* 2 Lt 9 Lancers 1939 (despatches 1940), temp Maj 1945; *Style*— The Rt Hon the Lord Mostyn, MC; Mostyn Hall, Mostyn, Clwyd, N Wales (☎ 0745 222)

MOSTYN, (Sir) William Basil John; *de jure* 15 Bt (E 1670), of Talacre, Flintshire, but claim has not yet been submitted for entry on the Official Roll of the Baronetage; o s of Sir Jeremy John Anthony Mostyn, 14 Bt (d 1988), and Cristina Beatrice Maria, o da of Marchese Pier-Paolo Vladimiro Orengo; snr male rep of Tudor Trevor, Lord of Hereford (10 cent); *b* 15 Oct 1975; *Heir* unc, Trevor Alexander Richard Mostyn b 23 May 1946; *Style*— William Mostyn, Esq; The Coach House, Lower Heyford, Oxon

MOSTYN-OWEN, Elizabeth; da of Lt-Col Roger Arthur Mostyn-Owen, DSO (d 1947), of Oswestry, Shropshire, and Margaret Eva, *née* Dewhurst (d 1976); *b* 10 July 1926; *Educ* St Mary's Sch Wantage, Univ of London (BA); *m* 9 July 1947 (m dis 1960), Harold Warren Freeman-Attwood, s of Maj-Gen H A Freeman-Attwood, DSO, OBE, MC (d 1963); 1 s (Julian David Warren Freeman-Attwood b 1953), 1 da (Rosamond Margaret Freeman-Atwood b 1951); *Career* freelance art historian, lectr, journalist; memb Exec Ctee Int Assoc of Art Critics, London correspondent for Il Giornale dell'Arte; *Style*— Mrs Elizabeth Mostyn-Owen; 38 Ladbroke Square, London W11 3ND (☎ 071 727 3491)

MOSTYN-WILLIAMS, Stephen Robert Pyers; s of Pyers Mostyn Williams, of Dorset, and Mary, *née* Ormesby; *b* 25 Feb 1956; *Educ* St Peter's Sch Bournemouth, Univ of Bristol (LLB); *m* 31 March 1979, Felicity Vosper, da of Raymond Kenneth Hilton, of Dorset; 1 s (Finbar David Ormesby), 2 da (Anna, Arabella Lorna Isabelle); *Career* slr; ptnr Barlow Lyde and Gilbert; *Recreations* opera, horses, sailing; *Style*— Stephen Mostyn-Williams, Esq; 17 Aubert Park, Highbury, London N5 1TL (☎ 071 359 6705); Beaufort House, 15 St Botolph St, London EC3A 7NJ (☎ 071 247 2277, telex 913287, fax 071 782 8504)

MOTHERWELL, Bishop of (RC) 1983-; Rt Rev Joseph Devine; s of Joseph Devine, of Nazareth House, Glasgow, and Christina, *née* Murphy (d 1981); *b* 7 Aug 1937; *Educ* Blairs Coll Aberdeen, St Peter's Coll Dumbarton, Pontificial Scots Coll Rome, Gregorian Univ Rome (PLD); *Career* personal sec to Archbishop of Glasgow 1964-66, lectr in philosophy St Peter's Coll Dumbarton 1966-74, chaplain Glasgow Univ 1974-77, auxiliary bishop Glasgow 1977-83; Papal Bene Merenti 1962; *Recreations* reading, music, soccer; *Style*— The Rt Rev the Bishop of Motherwell; Bishop's House, 17 Viewpark Rd, Motherwell ML1 3ER (☎ 0698 63715); Diocesan Centre, Coursington Rd, Motherwell (☎ 0698 69114/5)

MOTION, Andrew; s of Lt-Col A R Motion, of Braintree, Essex, and C G Motion (d 1982); *b* 26 Oct 1952; *Educ* Radley, Univ Coll Oxford; *m* 1985, Jan, da of C M Dalley, of Maldon, Essex; 2 s (Andrew Jesse b 26 July 1986, Lucas Edward b 19 May 1988), 1 da (Sidonie Gillian Elizabeth (twin) b 19 May 1988); *Career* ed Faber and Faber; prizes incl: Avon Observer prize 1982, John Llewelyn Rhys prize 1984, Somerset Maugham award 1987, Dylan Thomas prize 1988; *Books* Dangerous Play, The Lamberts, Natural Causes, The Pale Companion, Love in a Life, Famous for the Creatures; *Style*— Andrew Motion, Esq; Faber & Faber, 3 Queen Square, London WC1

MOTION, Hon Mrs (Penelope Mary); da of 2 Viscount Harcourt, KCMG, OBE (d 1979); *b* 1933; *m* 1954, Capt Anthony David Motion; 1 s; *Style*— The Hon Mrs Motion; Buckland, Irishtown, via Northam, Western Australia (☎ 096 221130)

MOTL, Hon Mrs (Marion Ann); *née* Molloy; da of Baron Molloy (Life Peer), by his 1 w, Eva Mary (d 1980); *b* 3 June 1947; *Educ* Holland Park Comprehensive Sch, Charing Cross Hosp Sch of Nursing (SRN, SCM); *m* 1974, Laurence George Motl, s of Charles Leopold Motl; 2 da (Julia, Ann); *Career* staff nurse Charing Cross Hosp 1970, staff mid-wife and sister Central Middx Hosp 1973; *Style*— The Hon Mrs Motl; 6225 Idylwood Lane, Edina, Minneapolis 55436, USA

MOTT, Dr David Hugh; s and h of Sir John Harmar Mott, 3 Bt; *b* 1 May 1952; *Educ* Shrewsbury, Univ of Sussex (BSc), Birkbeck Coll London (MSc), QMC London (PhD); *m* 1980, Amanda Jane, da of Lt Cdr D W P Fryer, RN, of Fleet, Hants; 2 s (Matthew b 1982, Jonathan b 1984); *Career* princ conslt Thorn EMI Software; memb BCS; CEng; *Style*— Dr David Mott

MOTT, John Charles Spencer; *b* 18 Dec 1926; *Educ* Brixton Sch of Building, Battersea Poly, Rutherford Coll of Technol Newcastle upon Tyne; *m* 1953, Patricia Mary; 2 s; *Career* serv Lt RM 1943-46; chm and chief exec French Kier Holdings plc 1974-86 (dir 1963-); chm: May Gurney Holdings Ltd (construction gp) 1986-89, William Sindall plc (construction group) 1990-; FEng, FICE, FIStructE, CBIM; *Recreations* golf; *Clubs* Danish; *Style*— John Mott, Esq; 91 Long Rd, Cambridge (☎ 0223 841320)

MOTT, Sir John Harmar; 3 Bt (UK 1930), of Ditchling, Co Sussex; s of Sir Adrian Spear Mott, 2 Bt (d 1964), and Mary Katherine, *née* Stanton (d 1972); *b* 21 July 1922; *Educ* Dragon, Radley, New Coll Oxford (MA, BM, BCh), Middx Hosp; *m* 1950, Elizabeth, da of Hugh Carson (d 1981); 1 s (David), 2 da (Jennifer, Alison); *Heir* s, David Hugh Mott; *Career* served 1939-45 RAF, Flying Offr 1943-46, Far East; qualified med practitioner 1951; regnl med offr DHSS 1969-84, ret; pt/t med referee; vice chm Kingsley Branch Eddisbury Cons Assoc 1988, memb Mid-Cheshire Pitt Club 1988; MRCGP; *Recreations* photography, classical archaeology and history; *Style*— Sir John Mott, Bt; Staniford, Brookside, Kingsley, Cheshire WA6 8BG (☎ 0928 88123)

MOTT, His Hon Judge Michael Duncan; s of Francis John Mott (d 1979), and Gwendolen, *née* Mayhew; *b* 8 Dec 1940; *Educ* Rugby, Gonville and Caius Coll Cambridge (MA); *m* 19 Dec 1970, Phyllis Ann, da of V James Gavin, of Dubuque, Iowa, USA; 2 s (Timothy b 1972, Jonathan b 1975); *Career* called to the Bar Inner Temple 1963, chambers Birmingham 1964-69, res magistrate Kenya 1969-71, Midland and Oxford circuit 1972-85, dep circuit judge 1976-80, rec 1980-85, circuit judge 1985-; parish cnclr 1982-86, parish organist 1984-; memb Hon Soc of Inner Temple; *Recreations* music, travel, skiing, tennis; *Clubs* Cambridge Union, Union and County (Worcs); *Style*— His Hon Judge Mott; c/o Circuit Administrator, Midland & Oxford Circuit, 2 Newton St, Birmingham B4 7LU

MOTT, Sir Nevill Francis; s of Charles Francis Mott (d 1967); *b* 30 Sept 1905; *Educ* Clifton, St John's Coll Cambridge (MA); *m* 1930, Ruth Eleanor, da of Gerald Horder (d 1939); 2 da; *Career* Henry Overton prof Univ of Bristol 1948-53 (Melville Wills prof of theoretical physics 1933-48), Cavendish prof of physics Univ of Cambridge 1953-71; Nobel Prize for Physics 1977; FRS 1936; kt 1962; *Clubs* Athenaeum; *Style*— Sir Nevill Mott, FRS; 63 Mount Pleasant, Aspley Guise, Milton Keynes MK17 8JX (☎ 0908 583257); The Cavendish Laboratory, Madingley Rd, Cambridge CB3 0HE

MOTT, Philip Charles; s of Charles Kynaston Mott (d 1981), of Taunton, Somerset, and Elsa, *née* Smith; *b* 20 April 1948; *Educ* King's Coll Taunton, Worcester Coll Oxford (BA, MA); *m* 19 Nov 1977, Penelope Ann, da of Edward Caffery; 2 da (Sarah b 1981, Catherine b 1983); *Career* called to Bar Inner Temple 1970, practising Western Circuit 1970-, rec of the Crown Ct 1987-; *Recreations* the countryside, sailing; *Clubs* Bar Yacht, Hampshire (Winchester), Exeter and County (Exeter); *Style*— Philip C Mott, Esq; Lamb Building, Temple, London EC4Y 7AS (☎ 071 353 6381, fax 071 583 1786)

MOTT-RADCLYFFE, Sir Charles Edward; DL (Norfolk 1976); assumed additional surname of Mott 1927; s of Lt-Col Charles Edward Radclyffe, DSO, of Little Park, Wickham, Hants, and Theresa Caroline, only child of John Stanley Mott, of Barningham Hall, Norfolk; *b* 25 Dec 1911; *Educ* Eton, Balliol Coll Oxford; *m* 1, 1940, Diana (d 1955), da of Lt-Col William Gibbs, CVO, JP (d 1963); 3 da; m 2, 1956, Stella Constance, da of Lionel GS Harrisson (d 1953), of Caynham Cottage, Ludlow; *Career* serv Capt Rifle Bde in Greece, Syria, and Italy (RARO); hon attaché HM Diplomatic Corps Athens 1936, Rome 1936-38; MP (C) Windsor Berks 1942-70; chm Cons Pty Foreign Affrs Ctee 1951-59; memb: Historic Buildings Cncl for Eng 1962-70, Plowden Ctee on Overseas Representational Servs 1962-63; pres CLA Norfolk Branch 1973-87; High Sheriff Norfolk 1974-75; pres Norfolk CCC 1973-74 (chm 1975-89); Cdr of Order of Phoenix (Greece); kt 1957; *Recreations* cricket, shooting; *Clubs* Bucks, Turf, MCC; *Style*— Sir Charles Mott-Radclyffe, DL; Barningham Hall, Matlaske, Norfolk (☎ 026 377 250)

MOTTERSHEAD, Derek Stuart; s of Alan Mottershead (d 1954), of Domicile, Blackpool, and Irene, *née* Huyton; *b* 2 Sept 1947; *Educ* Royal Masonic Sch Bushey Herts, Univ of Manchester (BSc); *m* 1 Sept 1969 (m dis 1988), Jean, da of James Arthur Wright, of Domicile, Nelson, Lancs; 2 da (Sarah b 11 April 1972, Lucy b 17 Feb 1982), 1 adopted da (Gillian b 30 May 1964); *Career* mktg dir Pretty Polly Ltd (winner Br Mktg awards 3 consecutive years) 1976-80, Euro mktg dir Lee Apparel UK Ltd (subsid Vanity Fair Corpn America) 1980-82, mktg dir Lee Cooper Ltd 1982-84, md All-time Sportswear UK Ltd 1984-87, gp md Prontaprint plc 1987- (chm Prontaprint Communications Ltd, md Prontaprint International Ltd, dir Continuous Stationery plc); vice chm Br Franchise Assoc; memb: Br Inst of Mktg, IOD; *Recreations* private aviation, shooting; *Clubs* Teeside Flying; *Style*— Derek Mottershead, Esq; Prontaprint plc, Coniscliffe House, Coniscliffe Rd, Darlington DL3 7EX (☎ 0325 483333, fax 0325 488665, car 0860 222225, telex 587835 P PRNTG)

MOTTISTONE, 4 Baron (UK 1933); David Peter Seely; CBE (1984); 4 s of 1 Baron Mottistone, CB, CMG, DSO, TD, PC (d 1947; himself 4 s of Sir Charles Seely, 1 Bt), by his 2 w, Hon Evelyn Izmé Murray, JP, da of 10 Lord and 1 Viscount Elibank and widow of George Nicholson (s of Sir Charles Nicholson, 1 Bt) - by whom she was mother of Sir John Nicholson, 2 Bt ; Lord Mottistone succeeded his half-bro, 3 Baron, 1966; *b* 16 Dec 1920, (HRH The Duke of Windsor stood sponsor); *Educ* RN Coll Dartmouth; *m* 1944, Anthea Christine, da of Victor McMullan, of Co Down; 2 s, 3 da (1 decd); *Heir* s, Hon Peter John Philip Seely; *Career* sits as Cons in House of Lords; Cdr RN 1955, Capt RN 1960 (D) 24 Escort Sqdn 1963-65; ret at own request 1967; dir personnel trg Radio Rentals Ltd 1967-69, dir Distributive Indust Trg Bd 1969-75; dir Cake & Biscuit Alliance 1975-81, parly advsr Biscuit, Cake, Chocolate & Confectionary Alliance 1981- (export sec 1981-83); dep Lt IOW 1981; Lord Lt IOW 1986-; KStJ 1989; pres East Wessex TAVRA 1990-; FIEE, FIPM, FBIM; *Clubs* Royal Yacht Sqdn, Royal Cruising, Royal Naval Sailing Assoc, Island Sailing, Royal Cwlth Soc; *Style*— The Rt Hon the Lord Mottistone, CBE; Old Parsonage, Mottistone, IOW PO30 4EE (☎ 0983 740264)

MOTTLEY, Peter Henry; s of Edward George Mottley (d 1969), and Elizabeth Louisa, *née* Watt; *b* 29 Jan 1987; *Educ* Edmonton Co GS, Univ of Sheffield (BA); *m* 1964 (m dis 1982), Diana Margaret, da of Leslie Fisher Griffiths (d 1970); 1 da (Jocelyn b 1967); *Career* creative conslt/writer; professional actor 1960-62, creative dir Nicklin Advertising 1978-81; plays: Liz (1980), The Last Will and Testament of Popsy Petal (1984), After Agincourt (1986); *Books* The Sex Bar (1972); *Recreations* theatre, supporting West Ham Utd, music, cooking; *Style*— Peter Mottley, Esq; 9 Aston Close, Pangbourne, Berks (☎ 0734 842826)

MOTTRAM, Maj-Gen John Frederick; CB (1982), MVO (1976), OBE (1969); s of F W Mottram (d 1972), and Margaret Mottram (d 1984); *b* 9 June 1930; *m* 1956, Jennifer, da of M J Thomas (d 1971); 1 s, 1 da; *Career* RM 1948, jt warfare attaché Br Embassy Washington 1974-77, Col Gen Staff Dept of Cmdt Gen RM and ADC to HM The Queen 1978-80, Maj-Gen Trg and Res Forces RM 1980-83; dir gen Fertiliser Mfrs Assoc 1983-86; chief exec Gen Cncl of Bar 1987-; *Recreations* fishing; *Clubs* Army and Navy; *Style*— Maj-Gen John Mottram, CB, MVO, OBE; c/o Army and Navy Club, Pall Mall, London SW1

MOTTRAM, Richard Clive; s of John Mottram, of Chislehurst, Kent, and Florence Bertha, *née* Yates; *b* 23 April 1946; *Educ* King Edward VI Camp Hill Sch Birmingham, Univ of Keele (BA); *m* 24 July 1971, Dr Fiona Margaret, da of Keith David Erskine (d 1974); 3 s (Keith b 1974, David b 1981, Thomas b 1985), 1 da (Ruth b 1977); *Career* Home CS, assigned MOD 1968, Cabinet Office 1975-77, private sec to Perm Under Sec of State 1979-81, private sec to Sec of State for Def 1982-86, asst under sec MOD 1986-89, dep under sec (policy) MOD 1989-; *Recreations* theatre, cinema, tennis; *Style*— Richard Mottram, Esq; c/o MOD, Whitehall, London SW1 (☎ 071 218 9000)

MOTYER, Rev John Alexander (Alec); s of Robert Shankey Motyer (d 1959), of Dublin, and Elizabeth Maud, *née* Nelson (d 1969); *b* 30 Aug 1924; *Educ* The High

School Dublin, Univ of Dublin (MA, BD), Wycliffe Hall Oxford; *m* 30 Aug 1948, Beryl Grace, da of William George Mays (d 1975), of Dublin; 2 s (Stephen b 1950, Mark b 1952), 1 da (Catherine b 1968); *Career* curate: Penn Fields Wolverhampton 1947-50, Holy Trinity Old Market Bristol 1950-54; tutor Tyndale Hall Bristol 1952-54, vice princ Clifton Theological Coll Bristol 1954-65 (tutor 1950-54), vicar St Luke Hampstead 1965-70, dep princ Tyndale Hall Bristol 1970-71, princ and dean Trinity Coll Bristol 1971-81, vicar Christ Church Westbourne Bournemouth 1981-89, ret 1989; *Books* The Message of Amos (1973), The Message of Philippians (1984), The Message of James (1985); *Recreations* reading, DIY; *Style—* The Rev Alec Motyer; 10 Littlefield, Bishopsteignton, Devon TQ14 9SG (☎ 0626 770986)

MOUBRAY-JANKOWSKI, Anthony; s of Josef Orzel-Jankowski, VM (d 1967), of Aberdour, Fife, and Barbara, *née* Moubray (d 1964); *b* 2 Oct 1946; *Educ* King's Sch Canterbury; *m* 13 Oct 1969, Danielle Marian, da of Leslie Green; 1 s (Arran b 1970), 2 da (Selena b 1972, Barbara b 1979); *Career* CA; sr ptnr Lee Evans Ptnrship; RIBA: former chm Canterbury Chapter, sec Architects in Agriculture and the Countryside; conslt: King's Sch Canterbury, Strutt and Parker; ARIBA; *Recreations* music, theatre, skiing, swimming, social work; *Style—* Anthony Moubray-Jankowski, Esq; Kenfield House, Petham, Canterbury (☎ 022 770 721); 9 Lower Grosvenor Place, London SW1 (☎ 071 630 7981, fax 071 630 6152)

MOUGHTIN, Dr (James) Clifford; s of Moughtin James Henry (d 1979), and Mary Eleonor, *née* Brown (d 1984); *b* 14 May 1932; *Educ* Mold Alun GS, Bootle GS, Univ of Liverpool (BArch, MCD, MA), Queens Univ of Belfast (PhD); *m* 1, 1956 (m dis 1980), Maureen Philomena; 3 s (Mark James b 1957, Nicholas Paul b 1959, Timothy John b 1964); m 2, 21 Sept 1981, Catherine, da of John McMahon (d 1971); *Career* architect; Singapore Improvement Tst 1957-60, Univ of Kwame Nkrumah Ghana 1960-61, Univ of Ahmadu Bello Nigeria 1961-63, Univ of Liverpool 1963-64, lectr and prof Queens Univ of Belfast 1964-74, prof Univ of Nottingham 1974-; memb RIBA, RTPI, RAI; *Books* Hausa Architecture (1985), Nigerian Traditional Architecture (1987), Who Needs Development (1990); *Recreations* water colour painting and travel; *Style—* Dr Clifford Moughtin; 1 Yeomans Court, The Park, Nottingham (☎ 0602 472933); Casa McMahon-Moughtin, Valley of Indolence, Eira Da Palma, Tavira, Portugal; Dept of Architecture and Planning, Institute of Planning Studies, Paton House, University of Nottingham, Nottingham (☎ 0602 484848)

MOUGHTON, Barry John; s of Victor John Moughton (d 1940), and Doris Emma, *née* Bosworth; *b* 28 May 1932; *Educ* Merchant Taylor's, Brasenose Coll Oxford (MA), McGill Univ Montreal (MCL); *m* 13 Sept 1958, Elizabeth Anne, da of Harold Edwin Parr, of Ferring, Worthing, Sussex; 1 s (Jonathan), 2 da (Katharine (Mrs Nisbet), Julia (Mrs Palejowska)); *Career* Nat Serv 2 Lt RA 1950-51; admitted slr 1958, ptnr Turner Kenneth Brown 1963- (formerly Turner Peacock, prev EF Turner and Sons); chm: Churches of Dorking Housing Assoc 1965-, Surrey Fedn Housing Assoc 1974-81; vice chm Leith Hill Music Festival 1979-85, pres Rotary Club London 1984-85, fndr chm Rotary Dist 113 1977-78, chm Dorking Urban Dist Cncl 1967-68 (cncllr 1962-68), JP 1967-70; Freeman City of London 1984, memb Worshipful Co of Solicitors 1985; memb Law Soc 1959; *Recreations* choral singing; *Style—* Barry Moughton, Esq; 100 Fetter Lane, London EC4A 1DD (☎ 071 242 6006, fax 071 242 3003)

MOULAND, Mark Gary; s of Sidney Mouland, of Kenilworth Golf Club, Crew Lane, Kenilworth, Warickshire, and Shirley Anne Easby; *b* 23 April 1961; *Educ* Westbourne House Penarth, Millfield; *m* 4 Dec 1985, Marianne, da of Richard Essam; 2 da (Stephanie Louise b 24 Oct 1987, Kimberley Jane b 11 March 1989); *Career* golfer; amateur: Br Boy champion 1976, BBC Wales Jr Sportsman of the Year 1976, Welsh Boy Int 1976-78 (capt 1978), Br Boy Int (v Continent of Europe) 1977 and 1978, Welsh Int 1978 and 1979; professional 1981-: winner Care Plan Int 1986, winner KLM Dutch Open 1986, participant Dunhill Cup 1986, 1988, 1989, 1990, World Cup 1988, 1989, and 1990, Kirin Cup 1988; *Recreations* snooker, travel, tv, shooting; *Style—* Mark Mouland, Esq; c/o Kenilworth Golf Club, Crew Lane, Kenilworth, Warwicks CV8 2LA (☎ 0926 512732)

MOULD, Christopher Peter; s of Peter Sidney Mould, of Pembrokeshire, and Phyllida Charlotte Elaine, *née* Ormond; *b* 30 Nov 1958; *Educ* Royal GS High Wycombe, Magdalen Coll Oxford (BA), LSE (MSc); *m* 18 Aug 1979, Angela Geraldine, da of Roger Ellis Druce; 3 da (Hannah Elizabeth b 26 Dec 1984, Verity Ruth b 20 June 1986, Alicia Ellen Joy b 27 April 1990); *Career* fund raiser LEPRA 1982, planning asst NE Thames RHA 1982-83, planning mangr Southend Health Authy 1983-86, hosp mangr Southend Hosp 1986-88; gen mangr Community and Mental Health Servs S Beds Health Authy 1989- (gen mangr Mental Health 1988-89); appraisal fellowship Nuffield Prov Hosps Tst, 4th prize RIPA/May Award for Managerial Innovation 1989; elder Ampthill Christian Fellowship; AHSM; *Recreations* jazz guitar, squash, hockey; *Style—* Christopher Mould, Esq; General Manager, Community and Mental Health Services, Fairfield Hospital, Nr Stotfold, Hitchin (☎ 0462 730123)

MOULE, Brian; s of Richard Moule (d 1952), and Amy, *née* Westwood; *b* 7 April 1932; *Educ* Coventry St Sch, St George's and Sladen; *m* 1956, Phyllis Ruth; 1 s (Steven b 1969), 1 da (Wendy b 1968); *Career* memb Wyre Forest DC 1980-, Mayor of Kidderminster 1982 and 1986; govr: St Mary's C of E Sch, St Oswald's C of E Sch; gen sec Power Loom Carpet Weavers' & Textile Workers' Union 1982-90, gen sec Nat Affiliation of Carpet Trade Unions; memb: NEDO, TUC jt Textile Ctee, Health and Safety Exec, Br Standards Inst for Wool Textile; *Style—* Brian Moule, Esq; 17 Batham Rd, Kidderminster (☎ 0562 824608)

MOULTON; *see*: Fletcher-Moulton

MOULTON, Dr Alexander Eric; CBE (1976); s of John Coney Moulton, and Beryl Latimer, *née* Greene; *b* 9 April 1920; *Educ* Marlborough, Kings Coll Cambridge (MA); *Career* innovating engr, inventor of the Moulton Bicycle, and Hydrolastic and Hydragas Car suspension and Moulton Coach etc; fndr: Moulton Development Ltd 1957, Moulton Bicycles 1962; chm Ctee on Engrg Design Educn Design Cncl 1975-76 (Moulton Report); Awards incl: Design Centre Award 1964, Gold Medal Triennale Milan 1964, Bid Lake Memb Plaque for Encouragement to Cycling 1964, Queens Award to Indust 1967, Design Medal Soc of Industl Artists and Designers 1976, James Clayton Prize, Crompton-Lanchester Medal, Thomas Hawksley Gold Medal; Royal Designer for Indust (Master of Faculty 1981-83); Hon Dr Royal Coll of Art 1967, Hon DSc Univ of Bath 1971; MIMechE 1979, FEng 1980 (vice pres 1988); *Publications* numerous on engrg and educn; *Recreations* cycling, canoeing, shooting; *Clubs* Brook's; *Style—* Dr Alexander Moulton, CBE; The Hall, Bradford-on-Avon, Wilts BA15 1AH (☎ 02216 5895, fax 02216 4742, telex 44356 MOULTN G)

MOULTON, Jonathan Paul (Jon); s of Douglas Cecil Moulton, of Stoke-on-Trent, and Elsie Turner Moulton (d 1984); *b* 15 Oct 1950; *Educ* Hanley HS, Univ of Lancaster (BA); *m* 13 Aug 1973, Pauline Marie, da of Stanley Dunn, of Stoke-on-Trent; 1 s (Spencer Jonathan b 1980), 1 da (Rebecca Clare b 1978); *Career* mangr Coopers & Lybrand 1972-80; Citicorp Venture Capital: dir NY 1980-81, gen mangr London 1981-85, managing ptnr Schroder Ventures 1985-; non-exec dir: Hornby Hobbies plc 1981-, Halls Homes & Gardens plc 1982-, Parker Pen Ltd 1986-, Haden MacLellan Holdings plc 1987-, Interconnection Systems Ltd 1987-, Technology Holdings plc 1989-, Appledore Holdings Ltd 1990-; FCA 1983, FBIM; *Recreations* chess, fishing; *Style—* Jon Moulton, Esq; 57 Kippington Rd, Sevenoaks, Kent TN13 2LL (☎ 0732 450025); Schroder Ventures, 20 Southampton St, London WC2E 7QG (☎ 071 632 1000, fax 071 240 5072)

MOULTRIE, John Farbon (Jack); CBE (1980); s of John Felix Hawksford Moultrie (d 1961), and Elsie May, *née* Wass; *b* 26 June 1914; *Educ* Loxford Secdy Modern Ilford, Coll of Estate Mgmnt; *m* 2 Sept 1939, Irene Hazel (d 1982), da of Thomas James Cast (d 1945); 3 da (Margaret b 1942, Vivian b 1944, Katherine b 1946); *Career* Capt HG 1940-44; chartered surveyor; articled 1930, sr ptnr 1956-86; cncllr Dagenham Borough Cncl 1950-60, Hornchurch UDC 1960-65; London Borough Cncl of Havering 1965-86: cncllr 1965-86, ldr 1968-71, 1974-77, 1979-82 and 1982-84, ldr of oppn 1971-74, Mayor 1977-78; chm: Rush Green Hosp League of Friends (fndr and pres), Oldchurch Hosp Scanner Appeal, Gen Cmmr of Taxes (Barking), LAMIT; pres: Upminster Cons Assoc, Rotary Club Dagenham 1962-63; served on LBA and AMA; JP 1954-86 (chm Barking Bench NE London); Liveryman Worshipful Co of Bakers 1964; Freeman: City of London 1964, London Borough of Havering 1986; FRICS; *Recreations* bowls, gardening, local politics; *Clubs* Carlton; *Style—* Jack Moultrie, Esq, CBE; 11 The Woodfines, Hornchurch, Essex RM11 3HR (☎ 04024 42244); 1 High Road, Chadwell Heath, Romford, Essex RM6 6PX (☎ 081 590 1219)

MOUND, Dr Laurence Alfred; s of John Henry Mound, and Laura May, *née* Cape; *b* 22 April 1934; *Educ* Warwick Sch, Univ of London (BSc, DSc); *m* 1, 27 Aug 1958 (m dis 1985), Jean Agnes, da of Andrew Solari, of Lincoln; 1 s (Nicholas b 1960), 2 da (Sarah Anne b 1965, Helen Catherine b 1967); m 2, 22 June 1987, Sheila Helen, da of Maurice Frank Halsey, of Hythe; *Career* entomologist; Federal Dept of Agric Res Nigeria 1959-61, Empire Cotton Growing Corpn Sudan 1961-64, keeper of entomolgy Br Museum Natural History 1981-(sci offr 1964-75, dep keeper of entomology 1975-81), conslt dir Cwlth Inst of Entomology 1980-; hon prof Dept of Pure and Applied Biology Univ of Wales; FLS, FRES; *Recreations* looking at insects; *Style—* Dr Laurence Mound; British Museum (Natural History), Cromwell Rd, London SW7 5BD (☎ 071 938 9474)

MOUNFIELD, Dr Peter Reginald; s of Reginald Howard Mounfield (d 1969), of Brynteg, Maes Llydan, Benllech, Anglesey, Gwynedd, and Irene, *née* Williams; *b* 15 Feb 1935; *Educ* Canon Slade GS Bolton, Univ of Nottingham (BA, PhD); *m* 12 Sept 1959, Patricia, da of Ernest John Jarrett, 2 Holmleigh Gardens, Thurnby, Leics; 1 s (John, David); *Career* asst lectr then lectr Dept of Geography and Anthropology Univ Coll of Wales Aberystwyth 1958-68, visiting assoc prof Dept of Geography and Regnl Planning Univ of Cincinnati Ohio USA 1966-67, sr Fulbright scholar 1966-67, sr visiting res fell Jesus Coll Cambridge 1988, head Dept of Geography Univ of Leicester 1989- (lectr then sr lectr 1968-); *Books* World Nuclear Power (1990); *Recreations* playing tennis, walking, watching cricket; *Clubs* RGS; *Style—* Dr Peter Mounfield; Department of Geography, University of Leicester, University Rd, Leicester LE1 7RH (☎ 0533 523840, fax 0533 522200, telex 347250 LEICUN G)

MOUNSEY, Joseph Backhouse; s of Colin Anthony Mounsey, of Clover House, Kingston Hill, Surrey, and Helen, *née* Roake; *b* 27 March 1949; *Educ* Leighton Park Sch Reading, New Coll Oxford (MA); *m* 18 Nov 1978, Elizabeth Anne, da of Peter William Burton (d 1970); 1 da (Elizabeth Helen b 1979); *Career* The Manufacturers Life Insurance Co: vice pres int investmts 1980-86, gen mangr 1986-, sr vice pres 1988, exec vice pres insur operations 1988; chm: The Manulife Gp plc, Western Tst & Savings Ltd, Western Trust & Savings Hldgs Ltd; dir: Manulife Mgmnt Ltd, Manulife Int Investment Mgmnt Ltd, The Manufacturers Life Insurance Co (UK) Ltd, The Manufacturers Life Insurance Co (USA), Manulife (Int) Ltd, The Regional Trust Company; *Clubs* Reform; *Style—* Joseph Mounsey, Esq; 48 Gordon Rd, North York, Ontario M2P IEI, Canada (☎ 010 1 416 250 0399); Manulife House, St George's Way, Stevenage, Herts SG1 1HP (☎ 0438 356101)

MOUNSEY, Simon Charles Finch; s of Charles Francis Ewart Mounsey (d 1964), and Mrs Audrey Trollope; *b* 25 Aug 1937; *Educ* Stowe; *m* 1963, Susan, da of Lt-Col George Edwin Noel Everett; 3 da; *Career* served 2 Lt Cyprus 1956-57; md Hays Business Services Ltd 1982-; *Recreations* golf; *Clubs* Piltdown Golf; *Style—* Simon Mounsey, Esq; Barnes House, Piltdown, Uckfield, East Sussex TN22 3XN (☎ 082 572 2144); Hays Business Services Ltd, Quadrant House, 15 Stockwell Green London SW9 9JJ (☎ 071 733 0099)

MOUNSEY-HEYSHAM, Giles Gubbins; s of Maj Richard Herchard Gubbins Mounsey-Heysham (d 1960), of Castletown, Rockcliffe, Carlisle, and Mrs Isobel Margaret Rowcliffe; *b* 15 Aug 1948; *Educ* Gordonstoun, Royal Agric Coll Cirencester; *m* 24 April 1982, Penelope Auriol, da of William Anthony Twiston-Davies (see Debrett's Peerage and Baronetage, Archdale, Bt); 3 s (Toby b 23 Jan 1984, Benjamin b 3 March 1986, Rory b 2 Feb 1989); *Career* chartered surveyor; Smiths Gore 1970-72, Cluttons 1973-(ptnr 1976); FRICS 1982 (memb 1972); *Recreations* music, skiing, walking, travelling, shooting; *Clubs* Boodles (dep chm); *Style—* Giles Mounsey-Heysham, Esq; Castletown, Rockcliffe, Carlisle CA6 4BN (☎ 0228 74 792); Cluttons, Castletown, Rockcliffe, Carlisle (☎ 0228 74 792, fax 0228 74 464)

MOUNT, (William Robert) Ferdinand; s of late Robert Francis Mount (2 s of Sir William Mount, 1 Bt, CBE) and Lady Julia Pakenham, da of 6 Earl of Longford; hp of unc, Sir William Mount, 2 Bt; *b* 2 July 1939; *Educ* Eton, Vienna Univ, Ch Ch Oxford; *m* 1968, Julia Margaret, twin da of Archibald Julian Lucas; 2 s (and 1 s decd), 1 da; *Career* former CRD desk offr (home affrs and health and social security); former chief ldr writer Daily Mail, columnist The Standard 1980-82, political correspondent The Spectator to 1982; head PM's Policy Unit 1982-83, literary ed The Spectator 1984-85, columnist Daily Telegraph 1985-90, ed Times Literary Supplement 1991-; *Books* The Theatre of Politics (1972), The Man Who Rode Ampersand (1975), The Clique (1978), The Subversive Family (1982), The Selkirk Strip (1987); *Style—* Ferdinand Mount, Esq; 17 Ripplevale Grove, London N1 1HS (☎ 071 607 5398)

MOUNT, Paul Morrow; s of Ernest Edward Mount, and Elsie Gertrude, *née* Morrow; *b* 8 June 1922; *Educ* Newton Abbot GS, Paignton Sch of Art, RCA; *m* 1, 1947 (m dis), Jeanne Rosemary Martin; 1 s (Martin b 1950), 1 da (Margaret b 1956); m 2, 11 Oct 1978, June Sylvia, da of Lt Col William George Hilary Miles, RM; *Career* served WWII with Friends' Ambulance Unit, attached to 13 EME Bn Med, 2 EME Div Blindee (Free French); initiated and ran Art Dept Yaba Nigeria 1955-61, freelance sculptor 1962; cmmns incl: Br Steel Corpn, Fibreglass Ltd St Helens, York House Bristol, CRS and Leo supermarkets, Swiss Embassy Tafawa Balewa Sq, Chase Manhattan Bank Lagos, Bauchi Meml Nigeria, cabinet offices Accra; ARCA (1948), RWA, memb Penwith Soc; *Recreations* music; *Style—* Paul Mount, Esq; Nancherrow Studio, St Just, Penzance, Cornwall TR19 7LA (☎ 0736 788 552)

MOUNT, Lt-Col Sir William Malcolm; 2 Bt (UK 1921), of Wasing Place, Reading, Berks, ED (1942), DL (Berks 1946); s of Sir William Arthur Mount, 1 Bt, CBE, MP, JP, DL (d 1930); *b* 28 Dec 1904; *Educ* Eton, New Coll Oxford; *m* 1929, Elizabeth Nance, JP, da of Owen John Llewellyn; 3 da; *Heir* n, (William Robert) Ferdinand Mount; *Career* Lt 99 Bucks and Berks Yeo, Field Bde RA (TA) 1926, Capt 1937, Maj 1938, transfd Reconnaissance Corps 1941, Lt-Col; jt master S Berks Foxhounds 1935-39; memb Berks CC 1938 (vice-chm 1960); High Sheriff 1947, Vice-Lt 1960-75; *Clubs* Farmers'; *Style—* Lt-Col Sir William Mount, Bt, ED, DL; Wasing Place, Aldermaston, Berks RG7 4NG (☎ 0734 713398)

MOUNT CHARLES, Earl of; Henry Vivian Pierpoint Conyngham; s and h of 7th Marquess Conyngham by his 1 w, Eileen; *b* 23 May 1951; *Educ* Harrow, Harvard Univ; *m* 1, 1971 (m dis 1985), Juliet Ann, da of Robert R B Kitson, of Churchtown, Morval, Cornwall; 1 s, 1 da (Lady Henrietta Tamara Juliet b 1976); m 2, 1985, Lady Iona Charlotte Grimston, yr da of late 6 Earl of Verulam; *Heir* s, Viscount Slane; *Career* Irish Rep Sothebys 1976-78; consultant Sothebys 1978-84; chm: Slane Castle Ltd, Slane Castle Productions; tstee Irish Youth Foundation; dir Grapevine Arts Centre, Dublin; landowner (1450 acres); *Clubs* Kildare St & Univ, Dublin (Dublin); *Style*— Earl of Mount Charles; Beauparc House, Beauparc, Navan, Co Meath

MOUNT CHARLES, Countess of; Iona Charlotte; da of 6 Earl of Verulam (d 1973), of Gorhambury, St Albans, Herts, and Marjorie Ray, *née* Duncan; *b* 25 Oct 1953; *m* 1985, Henry Vivian Pierpoint, s of Marquess Conyngham; *Style*— Countess of Mount Charles; Beauparc House, Beauparc, Navan, Co Meath

MOUNT EDGCUMBE, 8 Earl of (GB 1789); Robert Charles Edgcumbe; also Viscount Mount Edgcumbe and Valletort (GB 1781) and Baron Edgcumbe of Mount Edgcumbe (GB 1742); yr s of George Aubrey Valletort Edgcumbe (d 1977, bro of 7 Earl, who d 1982) and his 1 w, Meta, da of late Charles Robert Lhoyer, of Nancy, France; descended from Sir Richard Edgcombe (d 1489), a supporter of Henry Tudor, Earl of Richmond (later Henry VII), who was knighted on the field of Bosworth, and later became a PC and comptroller of the Household; *b* 1 June 1939; *m* 1960, Joan, da of Ernest Wall, of Otorohanga; 5 da; *Heir* half-bro, Piers Edgcumbe, *qv*; *Career* farmer; ex mangr Lands and Survey Dept NZ; landowner (2200 acres); *Style*— The Rt Hon The Earl of Mount Edgcumbe; Empacombe House, Mount Edgcumbe, Cornwall PL1 0HZ

MOUNTAIN, Sir Denis Mortimer; 3 Bt (UK 1922), of Oare Manor, Co Somerset, and Brendon, Co Devon; s of Lt-Col Sir Brian Edward Stanley Mountain, 2 Bt (d 1977), and Doris Elsie, Lady Mountain, *qv*; *b* 2 June 1929; *Educ* Eton; *m* 18 Feb 1958, (Hélène) Fleur Mary, da of John William Kirwan-Taylor, of Switzerland; 2 s (Edward, William), 1 da (Georgina); *Heir* s, Edward Brian Stanford Mountain; *Career* Lt Royal Horse Guards; chm and md Eagle Star Insur Co Ltd 1974-85 (dir 1959), pres Eagle Star Hldgs plc 1985-; dir: Philip Hill Investmt Tst plc 1967-86, Rank Orgn plc 1968-, Bank of Nova Scotia (Canada) 1978-, Allied London Properties plc 1986-; *Recreations* fishing, shooting; *Clubs* Nat Sporting, Blues and Royals; *Style*— Sir Denis Mountain, Bt; 12 Queens Elm Square, Old Church St, London SW3 6ED (☎ 071 352 4331); The manor, Morestead, nr Winchester, Hants SO21 1LZ (☎ 0962 74237); Eagle Star Holdings plc, 60 St Mary Axe, London EC3A 8BA (☎ 071 929 1111)

MOUNTAIN, Doris, Lady; Doris Elsie; eld da of late Eric Charles Edward Lamb; *m* 8 June 1926, Sir Brian Edward Stanley Mountain, 2 Bt (d 1977); 2 s, 1 da; *Style*— Doris, Lady Mountain; 75 Eaton Square, London SW1W 9AW

MOUNTAIN, Edward Brian Stanford; s and h of Sir Denis Mortimer Mountain, 3 Bt; *b* 19 March 1961; *m* 24 Oct 1987, Charlotte Sarah Jesson, da of His Honour Judge Henry Pownall, QC, of 57 Ringmer Ave, London SW6; 1 s (Thomas Denis Edward b 14 Aug 1989); *Career* Army Officer, Adjt The Blues and Royals; *Recreations* shooting, fishing, skiing; *Clubs* Cavalry and Guards'; *Style*— Edward Mountain, Esq

MOUNTAIN, John Letten; s of Lt-Col Harold Mountain (d 1946), of Nunsfield, Grimsby, and Dorothy Somerville, *née* Letten (d 1987); *b* 31 Dec 1913; *Educ* Malvern, Univ of Cambridge (MA); *m* 10 Nov 1942, Dawn, da of Chauncy Robert Dashwood Strettell (d 1948), of Claygate, Surrey; 1 s (Charles b 1948), 2 da (Vanessa (Mrs Walduck) b 1947, Juliet (Mrs Donald) b 1952); *Career* Lt 5 Lincolns TA RE 1938, Capt AA RA until 1946; slr and NP 1938, sr ptnr Bates and Mountain 1946-90, ret; clerk to Co Justices (pt/t) 1946-64, clerk to Cmmrs of Inland Revenue 1946-88; Lloyd Underwriter 1971-; former: chm Grimsby & Cleethorpes Church Extension Soc, govr St James Choir Sch; memb Law Soc; *Recreations* travel, shooting, tennis; *Style*— John Mountain, Esq; Little Grimsby Hall, Louth, Lincolnshire LN11 0UU (☎ 0507 602 757); Casa de Arriba, La Novia, Mijas, Malaga (☎ 010 3452 485 385); 37 Bethlehem St, Grimsby, S Humberside DN31 1JJ (☎ 0472 357 291, fax 0472 241 118)

MOUNTAIN, Nicholas Brian Edward; yr s of Sir Brian Edward Stanley Mountain, 2 Bt (d 1977), and Doris Elsie, *née* Lamb; *b* 15 Feb 1936; *Educ* Eton, St Catharine's Coll Cambridge (BA); *m* 30 July 1965, Penelope, yr da of late Maurice Holberton Shearme, of Brompton Square, London SW3; 1 s (Henry b 1967), 1 da (Nathalie b 1970); *Career* Lt RHG 1954-56; joined Eagle Star Insurance Co Ltd 1959: gen mangr UK business 1974, exec dir UK business 1984, exec dir investment and property 1987, ret 1989; *Recreations* shooting, fishing, skiing; *Style*— Nicholas Mountain, Esq; 17 Hollywood Rd, London SW10 9HT (☎ 071 352 6634); Lower Lanham, Old Alresford, Hants (☎ 096273 2531)

MOUNTBATTEN, Lord Ivar Alexander Michael; s of 3 Marquess of Milford Haven, OBE, DSC (d 1970); hp of bro, 4 Marquess; *b* 9 March 1963; *Educ* Gordonstoun Sch Scotland, Middlebury Coll Vermont USA; *Style*— The Lord Ivar Mountbatten; Moyns Park, Birdbrook, Essex

MOUNTBATTEN OF BURMA, Countess (UK 1947); Patricia Edwina Victoria Knatchbull; CD (1976), JP (Kent 1971), DL (Kent 1973); also Viscountess Mountbatten of Burma (UK 1946), Baroness Romsey (UK 1947); da of Adm of the Fleet 1 Earl Mountbatten of Burma, KG, GCB, OM, GCSI, GCIE, GCVO, DSO, PC, FRS (assas 1979) and Hon Edwina Ashley, CI, GBE, DCVO (d 1960, da of 1 and last Baron Mount Temple, himself gs of 7 Earl of Shaftesbury, the philanthropist); Edwina's mother was Maud, da of Sir Ernest Cassel, the banker and friend of Edward VII; sister of Lady Pamela Hicks, *qv*; *b* 14 Feb 1924; *Educ* Malta, England, NYC; *m* 26 Oct 1946, 7 Baron Brabourne, *qv*; 4 s (and 1 s k 1979, with his gf), 2 da; *Heir* s, Lord Romsey, *qv*; *Career* served 1943-46 WRNS; Col-in-Chief Princess Patricia's Canadian Light Inf 1974; vice Lord Lieut Kent 1984; vice-pres: BRCS, Kent Rural Community cncl, SSAFA, FPA, Nat Childbirth Tst, Royal Life Saving Soc, Shaftesbury Soc, Royal Coll of Nursing, Nat Soc for Cancer Relief, Royal Nat Coll for the Blind; vice patron Burma Star Assoc; patron: Commando Assoc, VAD (RN) Assoc, Nurses' Welfare Service, Compassionate Fields, HMS Kelly Reunion Assoc, East Kent Hospice, Kent Cncl on Drug Addiction, Kent Chest Heart and Stroke Assoc, Mote House, Cheshire House, Kent Handicapped Orphans' Caring Assoc, Kent Childrens' Houses Society, Chatham Dockyard Hist Soc, Ashford Samaritans, Ashford Umbrella Club, T S Churchill Sea Cadets Ashford; dep vice chm NSPCC; chm: Sir Ernest Cassel Educn Tst, Edwina Mountbatten Tst; pres: SOS Children's Villages, Shaftesbury Homes and Arethusa, Kent Branch Save the Children Fund, Kent Branch Relate, Friends of William Harvey Hosp; govr Ashford Sch, memb Cncl Caldecott Community Kent, tstee The Kent Community Housing Tst; DStJ 1981; *Style*— The Rt Hon the Countess Mountbatten of Burma, CD, JP, DL; Newhouse, Mersham, Ashford, Kent TN25 6NQ (☎ 0233 623466); 39 Montpelier Walk, London SW7 1JH (☎ 071 589 8829)

MOUNTEVANS, 3 Baron (UK 1945); (Edward Patrick) Broke Andvord Evans; s of 2 Baron Mountevans (d 1974); *b* 1 Feb 1943; *Educ* Rugby, Trinity Coll Oxford; *m* 1974, Johanna, da of Antonius Keyzer, of The Hague; *Heir* bro, Hon Jeffrey de Corban Richard Evans; *Career* Lt ret 74 MC regt RCT, AER 1966; joined management of Consolidated Gold Fields Ltd 1966; joined British Tourist Authority 1972, mangr Sweden and Finland 1973, mangr Promotion Services 1976, asst marketing mangr 1982-; *Recreations* reading, travel; *Style*— The Rt Hon the Lord Mountevans; c/o The House of Lords, London SW1

MOUNTEVANS, Deirdre, Baroness; Deirdre Grace; da of John O'Connell, of Buxton House, Co Cork; *m* 1940, 2 Baron Mountevans (d 1974); *Career* memb Governing Body Age Concern, hon pres Kensington and Chelsea Age Concern, hon vice pres Elderly Accomodation Council, house chm DGHH Vicarage Nursing Home; *Style*— The Rt Hon Deirdre, Lady Mountevans; 2 Durwood House, Kensington Court, London W8

MOUNTFIELD, Peter; s of Alexander Stuart Mountfield (d 1984), of Lanthwaite, Hightown, Liverpool, and Agnes Elizabeth, *née* Gurney (d 1987); *b* 2 April 1935; *Educ* Merchant Taylor's Crosby, Trinity Coll Cambridge (BA), Harvard Univ; *m* 1958, Evelyn Margaret, da of Walter Frederick Smithies (d 1963), of Liverpool; 3 s (Andrew b 1962, Benjamin b 1964, Christopher b 1968); *Career* civil serv HM Treasy 1958- (under sec 1977-); *Recreations* walking, reading, looking at buildings; *Style*— Peter Mountfield, Esq; HM Treasury, Parliament St, London SW1A 2RG

MOUNTFORD, Margaret Rose; *née* Gamble; da of James Ross Gamble, of Bangor, NI, and Kathleen Margaret, *née* Stevenson; *b* 24 Nov 1951; *Educ* Strathearn Sch Belfast, Girton Coll Cambridge (MA); *Career* admitted slr 1976, ptnr Herbert Smith 1983-; Liveryman Worshipful Co of Solicitors; memb Law Soc; *Recreations* travel, opera, wine; *Clubs* Cwil; *Style*— Ms Margaret Mountford; Exchange House, Primrose St, London EC2 (☎ 071 374 8000, fax 071 496 0043)

MOUNTFORD, Roger Philip; s of Stanley W A Mountford, of Leatherhead, Surrey (d 1984), and Evelyn Mary Richardson (d 1979); *b* 5 June 1948; *Educ* Kingston GS, LSE (BSc), Stanford Graduate Sch of Business (Sloan fell, MS); *m* 24 July 1981, Jane Rosemary, da of The Rev Canon Eric Edwin Stanton, hon Canon of Canterbury (d 1984); 3 da (Laura Jane b 1983, Annabel Louise b 1985, Nicola Mary b 1989); *Career* PA to Rt Hon Edward Heath 1969-70 and during 1974 gen elections, nat chm Fedn of Cons Students 1970-71, memb Carlton Club Political Ctee 1990-; merchant banker; md Hambro Pacific Ltd Hong Kong 1983-89, Hambros Bank Ltd 1971- (dir 1984-); *Recreations* riding, opera; *Clubs* Carlton, Hong Kong, Royal Hong Kong Jockey; *Style*— Roger Mountford, Esq; 25 Abbotsbury Rd, London W14 8EJ (☎ 071 602 8237); Hambros Bank Ltd, 41 Tower Hill, London EC3N 4HA (☎ 071 480 5000)

MOUNTFORD, (John) Toby; s of John Dennis Mountford, of Mead House, 3 Station Rd, Thames Ditton, Surrey, and Wendy, *née* Gowlland; *b* 4 Nov 1954; *Educ* Wellington, Univ of Durham (BSc Econ); *Career* articled clerk then accountant Price Waterhouse London 1976-80, mgmnt accountant Int Div Beecham Pharmaceuticals 1980-81, fin PR dir Steets Financial Ltd 1981-87, dir Citigate Communications Ltd 1987-; tstee The Holy Trinity Malshanger Tst; ACA 1990; *Books* Practice Development - A Guide to Marketing Techniques for Accountants (1985); *Recreations* skiing, walking, swimming, theatre; *Clubs* Cottons, London Bridge PCC, Holy Trinity Church Brompton; *Style*— Toby Mountford, Esq; Citigate Communications Limited, 7 Birchin Lane, London EC3V 9BY (☎ 071 623 2737, fax 071 623 9050)

MOUNTGARRET, 17 Viscount (I 1550); Richard Henry Piers Butler; also Baron Mountgarret (UK 1911, which sits as in House of Lords); s of 16 Viscount Mountgarret (d 1966); hp to Earldoms of Ossory and Ormonde, also to Chief Butlership of Ireland; *b* 8 Nov 1936; *Educ* Eton, Sandhurst; *m* 1, 1960 (m dis 1969), Gillian, da of Cyril Buckley, of Chelsea; 2 s, 1 da; m 2, 1970, Mrs Jennifer Fattorini, da of Capt D Wills, of Wrington, Somerset; m 3, 1983, Mrs Angela Ruth Waddington, da of Thomas Porter, of Tadcaster; *Heir* s, Hon Piers James Richard Butler; *Career* formerly Capt Irish Gds; pres Yorkshire County Cricket Club 1984-90; *Recreations* shooting, stalking, cricket; *Clubs* White's, Pratt's; *Style*— The Rt Hon the Viscount Mountgarret; Stainley House, South Stainley, Harrogate, Yorks (☎ 0423 770087); 15 Queensgate Place, London SW7 (☎ 071 584 6998)

MOURBY, Adrian Roy Bradshaw; s of Roy Mourby, of Welshpool, Montgomeryshire, and Peggy, *née* Bradshaw; *Educ* King Edward VI Camp Hill Sch Birmingham, Univ of Wales (BA), Univ of Bristol Film Sch; *m* 19 July 1980, Katharine Mary, da of John Richard Trevena Nicholas (d 1971), of West Penwith, Cornwall; 1 da (Miranda Jane b 1987), 1 s (John James b 1990); *Career* BBC floor mangr 1979-83, radio drama prodr Wales 1983-88, ed The Archers 1988, series prodr Wales Playhouse BBC TV 1989, assoc prodr Mr Wakefield's Crusade BBC 1 1990, prodr The Old Devils BBC 2 1991; Smith-Kline award for medical journalism 1982, Commendation Sony Radio awards 1984; regular contrib to The Listener; plays incl: The Corsaint (1985), Inside Me (1990), Other Men Do (1990), Landlocked (1991); *Recreations* interior and exterior design (passive), fine wine, the films of Woody Allen; *Style*— Adrian Mourby, Esq; BBC Wales, Broadcasting House, Llandaf, Cardiff, Wales CF5 2YO (☎ 0222 572888, fax 0222 552973)

MOURGUE, Harold George; s of Alfred George Mourgue (d 1972), and Maria May, *née* Hunter (d 1969); *b* 7 Sept 1927; *Educ* Colfes GS, Ilfracombe GS; *m* 3 April 1949, Joan Elsa Stella, da of John William Simms (d 1974); 1 s (Anthony John b 1950), 1 da (Jacqueline Susan b 1953); *Career* RN 1945-47; Harker Holloway & Co CAs 1948-53, CA 1953; mgmnt accountant and mangr Unilever 1953-60, fin controller, dir and gen mangr Ultra Radio & TV Ltd 1961-63, chief accountant Thorn Electrical Industries 1962-68; Thorn EMI plc: co sec 1967-72, fin dir 1970-85, vice chm 1985-87; non-exec dir: Turner & Newall plc 1983-, Rolls Royce plc 1985-, Thames Television plc, N M Rothschild Asset Management Ltd, Nuswift plc 1989-; chm: Kenwood Ltd 1989-, Thorn EMI Pension Fund, Rolls Royce Pension Fund, T & N Pension Fund; tstee Laporte plc Pension Fund; memb Industrial Devpt Advsy Bd 1985-; FCA, CBIM; *Recreations* music, theatre, gardening, literature; *Style*— Harold Mourgue, Esq; Myton, 8 Baslow Rd, Eastbourne, E Sussex BN20 7UJ (fax 0323 639547); N M Rothschild Asset Management Ltd, Five Arrows House, St Swithins Lane, London EC4 8NR (☎ 071 280 5000, fax 071 929 1643)

MOUSSA, Pierre Louis; *b* 5 March 1922; *Educ* Lycée Ampère and Lycée du Parc Lyon France, École Normale Supérieure (Lettres) Paris, Agrege des Lettres 1943; *m* 14 August 1957, Anne-Marie, *née* Trousseau; *Career* various assignments with French Admin 1949-62: tech advsr to the Sec for Fin and Econ Affrs 1949-51, dir of Cabinet Min for French Overseas Territories 1954, under-sec for econ affrs and planification for French overseas territories 1954-59, dir of civil aviation 1959-62; dir Dept of Ops Africa World Bank 1962-64, chm Fedn of French Insur Co 1965-69; Paribas Group 1969-81: sr exec vice pres, dep chm, chm and chief exec offr; fndr Finance and Development Inc 1982 (chm 1982-87), fndr and chm Pallas Holdings Luxembourg 1984, fndr Pallas Invest Luxembourg 1989 (chm 1989-); chm: Pallas Ltd UK, FRANDEV (France), Cresvale Partners (Luxembourg), Pallas Monaco; dir: Banque Pallas France, Pallas Finance France, PARINDEV-PME (France), Banque Pallas (Suisse), Broad Inc (USA), Kaufman and Broad Home Corporation (USA), CERUS (France), Sedgwick Group plc (UK); former prof: Inst for Political Studies Paris, Nat Sch of Administration Paris; Officier de la Légion d'Honneur (France 1976), Officier de l'Ordre National du Mérite (France 1966), Medaille Aéronautique (France 1962), Commandeur de l'Ordre National Mauritanien (1965), Commandeur de l'Ordre National de l'Etoile Equatoriale (Gabon 1972), Commandeur de l'Ordre National du Lion (Senegal 1975), Officier de l'Ordre National de Boyaca (Colombia 1954), Officier du Ouissam Alaouite, Officier de l'Ordre de la République Tunisienne (1972), Officier du nicham el Anouar, Chevalier de l'Etoile Noire du Bénin; Les Chances Économiques de la Communauté Franco-Africaine (1957), Les Nations Prolétaires (1959), L'Économie de la Zone France (1960), Les Etats-Unis et Les Nations Prolétaires (1965), La Roue de la Fortune, Souvenirs d'un Financier (1989); *Clubs* RAC, Automobile Club de France (Paris); *Style—* Pierre Moussa, Esq; Pallas Ltd, Berkeley Square House, Berkeley Square, London W1X 5LA (☎ 071 408 2123, telex 268276, fax 071 408 1420); Banque Pallas France, 61 Rue de Monceau, 75008 Paris, France (☎ 1 40 74 2000, fax 1 40 74 2148)

MOUTAFIAN, Princess Helena; MBE (1976); da of Prince Alexei Gagarin (d 1938), and Countess Ana Phillipovitz (d 1944); *b* 2 May 1930; *m* 14 Jan 1955, Artin Moutafian, s of Nikogos Moutafian (d Armenia 1914); 2 s (Nicholas b 6 Nov 1958, Mark b 21 Dec 1960); *Career* dir Moutafian Commodities Ltd; vice pres Help the Aged (pres Ladies Ctee), pres Save the Russian Children Fund, vice pres Ladies Ctee European Atlantic Gp, memb Br Assoc of Women Entrepreneurs, hon vice pres Women's Cncl, life patron NSPCC; patron: Nat Assoc for Health, SOS (Sleeping on Streets), Br Cncl Univ for Peace; involved in projects for uniting world religions; DStJ 1990; Croix de Chavalier Ordre de la Coutoisie Française 1976, Etoile Civique, Grande Medaille de Vermeil de la Ville de Paris 1977; Freedom City of Paris 1977; awarded silver medal of Grollo d'Ordre for paintings in Venice; *Recreations* painting, writing; *Clubs* English Speaking Union; *Style—* Princess Helena Moutafian, MBE; 12 Greenaway Gardens, Hampstead, London NW3 7DH

MOVERLEY, Rt Rev Gerald; *see*: Hallam, Bishop of

MOWAT, Prof Alexander Parker; s of William Mowat (d 1986), and Isabella Parker, *née* Mair (d 1973); *b* 5 April 1935; *Educ* Fordyce Acad, Univ of Aberdeen (MB ChB); *m* 23 Sept 1961, (Mary) Ann Shanks, da of Samuel Hannah; 2 s (Neil, Adrian); *Career* Nat Serv Lt and Capt RAMC Hong Kong 1959-61; house offr: Aberdeen Teaching Hosp 1958-61, Gt Ormond St Hosp for Sick Children 1962-64; registrar Hosp for Sick Children Aberdeen 1964-68, res assoc Albert Einstein Coll of Med and Rowett Res Inst 1968-70, conslt paediatrician KCH 1970-, prof of paediatric hepatology King's Coll Sch of Med and Dentistry; memb: Br Paediatrics Assoc (chm Working Pty on Liver Transplantation), Children's Liver Disease Fndn; *Recreations* golf, sailing, wind-surfing; *Style—* Prof Alex Mowat; 11 Cator Rd, London SE26 5DI (☎ 081 659 5033); Department of Child Health, King's College Hospital, Denmark Hill, London SE5 9RS (☎ 071 326 3214)

MOWAT, Catherine Mary; da of John Alastair Stevenson Mowat, of 17 Culland View, Crich, Derbyshire, and Pamela Frances, *née* Hunt; *b* 20 Sept 1952; *Educ* Queen Mary Sch Lytham Lancs, Westfield Coll Univ of London (BA); *Career* cricketer; memb: Middx Women's Cricket Team 1974-, England Women's Cricket Team 1977-84; sec Middx Women's Cricket Assoc 1978-, chm Women's Cricket Assoc 1986-; *Recreations* cricket (playing), rugby (watching), newspapers (reading); *Style—* Miss Catherine Mowat; Flat C, 28 Greyhound Rd, London W6 8NX (☎ 071 381 5710); Eurotunnel plc, Victoria Plaza, 111 Buckingham Palace Rd, London SW1W OST (☎ 071 834 7575)

MOWAT, David McIvor; JP (Edinburgh 1968); s of Ian McIvor Mowat (d 1985), and Mary Isabelle Simpson, *née* Steel; *b* 12 March 1939; *Educ* Edinburgh Acad, Univ of Edinburgh (MA), Open Univ (BA); *m* 20 June 1964, (Elinor) Anne, da of Eric Edward Birtwistle (d 1974); 3 da (Sarah Jane b 4 Sept 1965, Anna Katherine (Kate) b 25 April 1967, Julia Claire b 9 Jan 1969); *Career* journalist, broadcaster, conslt; chief exec: Edinburgh Chamber of Commerce and Manufactures 1968-90, Chamber Developments Ltd 1974, Edinburghs Capital Ltd, Who's Who in Business In Scotland Ltd; dir Contact 1991 Ltd; former pres Br Chamber of Commerce Execs 1987-89; FRSA 1986; *Style—* David Mowat, Esq, JP; 37 Orchard Rd South, Edinburgh EH4 3JA (☎ 031 332 6865)

MOWAT, Magnus Charles; s of John F M Mowat, MBE (d 1988), of Lake House, Ellesmere, Shropshire and Elizabeth Rebecca, *née* Murray (d 1977); *b* 5 April 1940; *Educ* Haileybury; *m* 27 April 1968, Mary Lynette St Lo, da of Alan D Stoddart, of Crowcombe, Taunton, Somerset; 3 s (Charles b 15 April 1969, Alexander b 27 June 1970, Hugh b 7 June 1973); *Career* CA; Peat Marwick Mitchell & Co 1959-67, Hill Samuel & Co Ltd 1968-70, ptnr Illingworth & Henriques Stockbrokers 1970-84, dir Barclays de Zoete Wedd Ltd 1984-90; chm: Manchester YMCA, Booths Charities Manchester; memb govrs Packwood Haugh Sch Shrewsbury; FCA 1964; *Recreations* shooting, gardening, music; *Clubs* St James' (Manchester); *Style—* Magnus Mowat, Esq; New Park House, Whitegate, Northwich, Cheshire (☎ 0606 882 084); Caprons Cottage, Triscombe, Taunton, Somerset; Barclays de Zoete Wedd Ltd, 50 Fountain St, Manchester (☎ 061 832 7222, fax 061 833 9374, car 0836 519 329)

MOWBRAY, Sir John Robert; 6 Bt (UK 1880), of Warennes Wood, Berkshire; JP (W Suffolk 1972); s of Sir George Robert Mowbray, 5 Bt, KBE (d 1969); *b* 1 March 1932; *Educ* Eton, New Coll Oxford; *m* 1957, Lavinia Mary, da of Lt-Col Francis Edgar Hugonin, OBE; 3 da; *Heir* none; *Style—* Sir John Mowbray, Bt, JP; Hill Farm, Duffs Hill, Glemsford, Suffolk CO10 7PP (☎ 0787 281930)

MOWBRAY, SEGRAVE AND STOURTON, 26, 27 and 23 Baron (E 1283, 1295 and 1448 respectively); Charles Edward Stourton; CBE (1982); s of 25 Baron Mowbray, (26) Segrave and (22) Stourton, MC, JP (d 1965; himself gs of 23, 24 and 20 Baron, who had inherited the Barony of Stourton from his f, and had abeyance of Baronies of Mowbray and Segrave terminated in his favour 1878) and of Sheila, da of Hon Edward W K Gully, CB (d 1931; 2 s of 1 Viscount Selby); *b* 11 March 1923; *Educ* Ampleforth, Ch Ch Oxford; *m* 1952, Hon Jane Faith de Yarburgh-Bateson, da of 5 Baron Deramore (d 1964), by his w Nina Macpherson-Grant; 2 s; *Heir* s, Hon Edward William Stephen Stourton; *Career* sits as Conservative in House of Lords; Lt Grenadier Gds 1943; memb of Lloyd's 1952; dir Securicor (Southern) Ltd 1965-66, Securicor (Scotland) 1966-70; Cons whip in House of Lords and front bench spokesman 1967-70 and 1974-78; lord in waiting 1970-74 and 1979-80; dep chief oppn whip House of Lords 1978-79; chllr of the Primrose League 1974-79; hon pres Safety Glazing Assoc 1975-78; Kt of Honour and Devotion SMO Malta; *Style—* The Rt Hon the Lord Mowbray, Segrave and Stourton, CBE; Marcus, by Forfar, Angus (☎ 030 785 219); 23 Warwick Sq, London SW1

MOWBRAY, SEGRAVE AND STOURTON, Baroness; Hon Jane Faith; *née* de Yarburgh-Bateson; da of late 5 Baron Deramore; *b* 1933; *m* 1952, 26 Baron Mowbray, Segrave and Stourton, *qv*; *Style—* The Rt Hon the Lady Mowbray, Segrave and Stourton; 23 Warwick Sq, London SW1; Marcus, By Forfar, Angus

MOWER, Brian Leonard; s of Samuel William Mower (d 1975), and Nellie Elizabeth Rachel Mower (d 1976); *b* 24 Aug 1934; *Educ* Hemel Hempstead GS; *m* 1 Oct 1960, Margaret Ann, da of Cecil Roland Wildman; 1 s (John b 1964), 1 da (Kerry b 1961); *Career* RAF 1954-56; exec Service Advertising Co 1956-66; Civil Serv: sr info offr HM Treasy 1966-69, princ info offr CSO 1969-78, dep head of info HM Treasy 1978-80, head of info Dept of Employment 1980-82, dep press sec PM 1982, dir of info Home Office 1982, head of News Dept FCO 1990-; *Recreations* bridge, walking, reading; *Clubs* Reform; *Style—* Brian Mower, Esq; 34 Wrensfield, Hemel Hempstead, Herts HP1 1RP (☎ 0442 252277); Foreign and Commonwealth Office, London SW1A 2AH (☎ 071 270 3098)

MOWER, Roger Leonard; s of Maj Leonard Charles Mower (d 1983), of Manchester, and Beatrice, *née* Monahan; *b* 19 April 1951; *Educ* Bolton Sch Lancs; *m* 25 March 1972, Pauline Carole, da of Geoffrey Holland Barlow, of Audlem, Cheshire; 2 s (James b 1979, Paul b 1981); *Career* dir Clarke Construction Ltd 1979-84, md Mears Contractors Ltd 1985-86, chief exec Multi (UK) Ltd 1987-; *Style—* Roger Mower, Esq; Pitt Cottage, The Mount, Highclere, Newbury, Berks; Multi (UK) Ltd, 15 Berkeley St, Mayfair, London W1X 5AE (☎ 071 493 1404)

MOWLAM, Dr Marjorie; MP (Lab) Redcar 1987-; da of Frank William Mowlam (d 1980), and Bettina Mary, *née* Rogers; *b* 18 Sept 1949; *Educ* Coundon Court Comp Sch, Univ of Durham (BA), Univ of Iowa (AMA, PhD); *Career* res asst to: Tony Benn MP 1971-72, Alvis Toffler 1972-73; lectr: Univ of Wisconsin 1976-77, Florida State Univ 1977-78, Univ of Newcastle upon Tyne 1979-83; sr admin Northern Coll Barnsley 1984-87; Lab Pty: joined 1969, chm and sec at constituency level, exec memb at constituency and dist level Yorkshire and Tyneside, del to Regnl and Nat Pty Confs, memb Nat Lab Pty NEC Sub Ctee on Energy, oppn frontbench spokesperson on NI 1988, pty spokesperson for City and Corp Affrs in Trade and Industry Team; memb TGWU, sponsored by COHSE; *Books* Debate on Disarmament (jt ed, 1982); *Recreations* walking, jigsaws, swimming; *Style—* Dr Marjorie Mowlam, MP; House of Commons, Westminster, London SW1A 0AA (☎ 071 219 5066, fax 071 219 6693)

MOWLL, Christopher Martyn; s of Christopher Kilvinton Mowll (d 1940), and Doris Ellen, *née* Hutchinson (d 1986); *b* 14 Aug 1932; *Educ* Epsom Coll, Gonville and Caius Coll Cambridge (MA); *m* 4 Oct 1958, Margaret Francis, da of John Maclelland Laird (d 1988); 4 s (Gordon Howard Martyn b 1959, Ian Robert b 1961, David Christopher b 1961, Richard Laird b 1965); *Career* admitted slr 1956; slr and clerk to Worshipful Co of Clothworkers and sec to Clothworker's Fndn 1978-; memb: Cncl Nat Library for the Blind 1964-79, Cncl Metropolitan Soc for the Blind 1964- (treas 1965-79, vice chm 1971-79, chm 1979-), Exec Cncl RNIB 1982-, Br-Australia Bicentennial Ctee 1984-88; Freeman City of London 1979, Liveryman Worshipful Co of Clothworkers 1979; memb Law Soc 1956-; *Style—* Christopher Mowll, Esq; Clothworkers' Hall, Dunster Court, Mincing Lane, London EC3R 7AH (☎ 071 623 7041)

MOXHAM, Dr John; s of Wilson Moxham (d 1949), and Marie, *née* Blande; *b* 9 Dec 1944; *Educ* Prince Henry's GS Evesham, LSE (BSc), UCH (MB BS, MD); *m* 4 June 1978, Nicola Dawn, da of (Alec William) Larry Seaman; 3 da (Jessica Hannah b 4 May 1980, Madeleine Emily b 15 Dec 1985, Rose Harriet b 20 Dec 1985); *Career* Kings Coll Hosp: conslt physician 1982-, sr lectr in med at sch of med and dentistry 1989; hon sr lectr Nat Heart and Lung Inst London 1987; author of numerous papers, chapters and reviews on respiratory physiology; memb Assoc of Physicians, sec Br Thoracic Soc 1988- (memb 1980); FRCP 1987 (MRCP 1975); *Recreations* my wonderful daughters; *Clubs* The Lord Lyndhurst; *Style—* Dr John Moxham; 96 Lyndhurst Grove, London SE15 5AH (☎ 071 703 4396); Dept of Thoracic Medicine, Kings College Hospital, Denmark Hill, London SE5 9PJ (☎ 071 326 3165)

MOXLEY, Raymond James (Ray); s of Rev Henry Roberts Moxley (d 1953), of Oxford, and Ruby Alice, *née* Gems (d 1972); *b* 28 July 1923; *Educ* Caterham, Oxford Sch of Architecture; *m* 12 Oct 1949 (m dis 1972), Jacqueline Marjorie, da of Orlando Beater (d 1954), of Standlake, Oxon; 1 s (Mike Moxley b 1950), 2 da (Caroline b 1956, Alison b 1959); *Career* trooper RHG 1942, RE: joined 1943, cmmnd 1944, Capt 1945, demobbed 1946; architect; Public Sector Depts of Architects 1949-53, fndr own practice 1953-65, fndr dir and chm Moxley Jenner & Ptnrs (London) Ltd 1986 (fndr ptnr 1965); visiting lectr 1953-: Univ of Bristol Sch of Architecture, Univ of Reading, Univ of Manchester; RIBA: assessor regnl awards 1968, rep Ct of Univ of Bath 1968-69, Cncl memb 1972-78, first hon librarian 1975-77, vice pres 1973-75; DOE Housing Awards: assessor E Midlands regn 1977, chm SE regn 1979, chm London regn 1980; chm: Bristol Bldg and Design Centre 1965-70, Assoc of Conslt Architects 1974-77, Soc for Alternative Methods of Mgmnt 1978, London Assoc of Conslt Architects 1984-86; Design and Industs Assoc 1989; pres: Wessex Assoc of Architects in Private Practice 1974- (chm 1969-74), Bristol and Somerset Soc of Architects 1968-69; W of Eng Coll of Art 1965-69, Bristol Poly 1969-71; hon fell Bristol Poly 1989; Freeman City of London 1975, Liveryman Worshipful Co of Basketmakers: FRIBA, FRSA; *Books* Building Construction Vol 1 (23 edn); ed: Build International (1973-74), ACA Illustrated Directory of Architects (1983 and 1984), The Architects Guide to Fee Negotiation (1983), Architects Eye; *Recreations* sailing, flying; *Clubs* Royal Western Yacht, RAC, Kingair; *Style—* Ray Moxley, Esq; Moxley Jenner & Partners (London) Ltd, 1 Hobhouse Court, Suffolk St, St James's, London SW1Y 4HH (☎ 071 930 2721, fax 071 930 2980, car 0836 299375)

MOXOM, John Matthew Cameron; s of Reginald John Moxom (d 1988), of 97 Queens Rd, Hertford, Herts, and Jeannie Bryce, *née* Mitchell (d 1986); *b* 6 April 1945; *Educ* Pilgrims' Sch Winchester, Winchester, Queens' Coll Cambridge (BA, MA); *Career* called to the Bar 1968, pupillage 1968-69, in practice 1969-88; litigation dept Steed and Steed Slrs 1988-90; chm St Christophers Fellowship 1982- (vice chm 1979-82, memb 1970-); memb Belchamp St Paul Parish Cncl 1988-; Freedom City of London, Liveryman Worshipful Co of Goldsmiths; *Books* Kemp and Kemp on the Quantum of Damages (asst ed 1975-); *Recreations* walking, gardening, cinema, theatre; *Style—* John Moxom, Esq; Pannells, Belchamp St Paul, nr Sudbury, Suffolk CO10 7BS (☎ 0787 277410)

MOXON, (Roland) James; OBE (1958); s of Thomas Allen Moxon (d 1943), and Evelyn Goodwin, *née* Stroyan (d 1990); *b* 7 Jan 1920; *Educ* Denstone Coll Uttoxeter Staffs, St John's Coll Cambridge (MA); *Career* gunner signaller trainee 1940, Capt Accra Koforidua Home Guard 1941-44; Colonial Admin Serv (Gold Coast) 1941-57: dist cmmnr Koforidua, Kpandu, Akuse, Accra 1941-48, dir info servs 1948-57; Ghana Civil Serv 1957-67: dir info servs 1957-60, advsr to PM info servs 1960-67, dir PR Volta River Authy 1963-67; publisher and author 1967-; chm: Aburi Agric Show 1944, Odumase Agric Show 1946, Ghana Troops Comforts Fund (Congo) 1960; Mayor Accra 1947-48; elected and gazetted as chief in Ghana; memb Int PEN 1967-; *Books* Volta-Man's Greatest Lake (1969, 1984), The Baden Powell Ashanti Diaries (1991), Autobiography (1991); *Recreations* rugby football, athletics; *Clubs* Utd Oxford and Cambridge Univ; *Style—* James Moxon, Esq, OBE; The Butts, Ashford Carbonel, Ludlow, Shropshire SY8 4DF (☎ 058 474 259); Nana Kofi Obonyaa, Odikro of Onyaase and Ankobea of Aburi; PO Box M160, Accra, Ghana; Onyaase, Kitasi, Aburi, Ghana

MOXON, Martyn Douglas; s of Derek Moxon (d 1984), of Barnsley, South Yorks, and Audrey, *née* Scarborough; *b* 4 May 1960; *Educ* Holgate GS Barnsley; *m* Susan, da of late (Edgar) Duncan Slack; 1 da (Charlotte Louise b 13 March 1990); *Career* professional cricketer; capt N of England under 15 and under 19 teams; Yorkshire CCC: scored 116 on debut v Essex 1981, awarded county cap 1984, Capt 1990-; England: 10 Test matches (debut v NZ Lords 1986), 8 one day Ints (debut v India Nagpur 1985), tours to India/Australia 1984-85 and NZ/Aust 1988, B tour to Sri Lanka 1986; trainee Barclays Bank 1978-80; *Recreations* supporting Barnsley FC and Everton FC; *Style—* Martyn Moxon, Esq; Yorkshire CCC, Headingley Cricket Ground, Leeds LS6 3BU (☎ 0532 787394, fax 0532 784099)

MOXON, Rev Canon Michael Anthony; s of Rev Canon Charles Moxon (Canon Residentiary and Precentor of Salisbury Cathedral, d 1985), of Hungerford Chantry, The Close, Salisbury, Wilts, and Phyllis Mary, *née* Carter; *b* 23 Jan 1942; *Educ* Merchant Taylor's, Univ of Durham, Univ of London (BD), Salisbury Theol Coll; *m* 9 Jan 1969, Sarah Jane, da of Francis Kynaston Needham Cresswell (d 1982), of

Littlehampton; 2 s (twins, Nicholas and Benjamin b 21 Nov 1969), 1 da (Emma-Jane b 1 Aug 1971); *Career* ordained: deacon 1970, priest 1971; asst priest Lowestoft Gp Ministry 1970-74, minor canon St Paul's Cathedral 1974-81 (jr cardinal 1974-78, sr cardinal 1978-79), warden Coll of Minor Canons 1979-81, sacrist St Paul's Cathedral 1977-81, vicar Tewkesbury with Walton Cardiff 1981-90, canon of Windsor and chaplain in the Great Park 1990-; proctor in convocation (memb Gen Synod) 1985-90, chaplain to HM The Queen 1986-; memb Cncl for the Care of Churches; *Recreations* reading, music, cricket; *Style*— The Rev Canon Michael Moxon; The Chaplain's Lodge, The Great Park, Windsor, Berks SL4 2HP (☎ 0784 432434)

MOXON, Prof (Edward) Richard; s of Gerald Richard Moxon, CBE (d 1980), and Margaret, *née* Forster Mohun; *b* 16 July 1941; *Educ* Shrewsbury Sch, St Johns Coll Cambridge (BA, MA, BChir); *m* 20 Oct 1973, Marianne, da of Prof George Graham; 2 s (Christopher Alan b 1978, Timothy Stewart b 1987), 1 da (Sarah Graham b 1981); *Career* sr house offr Hosp for Sick Children 1969, res fell Childrens Hosp Med Centre Boston USA 1971-74 (asst resident paediatric 1970), asst prof paediatrics John Hopkins Hosp Baltimore USA 1974-78 (assoc prof and Eudowood chief of paediatric infectious diseases 1978-84), prof of paediatrics Univ of Oxford 1984-; *Recreations* sport, music, literature; *Style*— Prof Richard Moxon; 17 Moreton Rd, Oxford OX2 7AX; Dept of Paediatrics, John Radcliffe Hospital, Headington OX3 9DU

MOXON-BROWNE, Robert William; QC (1990); s of Kendall Edward Moxon-Browne, and Sheila Heron, *née* Weatherbe; *b* 26 June 1946; *Educ* Gordonstoun, Univ Coll Oxford (BA); *m* 26 June 1968, Kerstin Elizabet, da of Oscar Warne; 1 s (James Weatherbe b 7 April 1978), 1 da (Emily Kendall b 20 Oct 1973); *Career* called to Bar Gray's Inn 1969; *Recreations* skiing, sailing, squash; *Style*— Robert Moxon-Browne, Esq, QC; 37 Mowbray Road, London NW6 7QS

MOY, Peter Charles Duffield; s of Eric Thomas Moy (d 1980), and Andrea Katherine Stillingfleet, *née* Duffield (d 1966); *b* 18 July 1927; *Educ* Charterhouse; *m* 12 March 1967, Judith Webb, da of Dr Eric Arthur Cashmore (d 1972), of Sandiway, Cheshire; 1 da (Lucy Andrea b 1969); *Career* HM Grenadier Gds and Essex Regt 1945-48; mechanical and solar engrg design and devpt; grantee of several Br and foreign letters patent; *Recreations* gardening, golf; *Style*— Peter C D Moy, Esq; Highfield Lodge, North Creake, Fakenham, Norfolk (☎ 0328 738108)

MOYA, (John) Hidalgo; CBE (1966); s of Hidalgo Moya (d 1926), of Pasadena, Calif, USA, and Lilian, *née* Chattaway (d 1965); *b* 5 May 1920; *Educ* Oundle, Royal West of England Coll of Art, Architectural Assoc Sch of Architecture (Dip); *m* 1, 1947 (m dis 1985), Janniffer Innes Mary Hall; 1 s (Timothy James Hidalgo b 1950), 2 da (Susan Georgia b 1948, Joanna b 1955); m 2, 1988, Jean Conder; *Career* architect in private practice; ptnr Powell and Moya (later Powell Moya & Partners) 1946-; buildings incl: Churchill Gardens Flats Westminster 1948-62, Skylon (for Festival of Britain) 1951, Mayfield Sch Putney 1955, Chichester Festival Theatre 1962, British National Pavilion Expo 1970 Osaka Japan, undergraduate rooms Brasenose Coll Oxford 1961, picture gallery Christ Church Oxford 1967 undergraduate rooms St John's Coll 1967 and Queens' Coll Cambridge 1978, general hosps at Swindon Slough High Wycombe Wythenshawe Woolwich and Maidstone, Sch for Advanced Urban Studies Univ of Bristol extensions 1980, Queens's Building RHBNC Egham 1986; Royal Gold medal for architecture RIBA 1974; MRIBA 1956; *Recreations* painting, drawing, early american jazz music; *Style*— Hidlago Moya, Esq, CBE; Point Hill South, Rye, East Sussex TN31 7NP (☎ 0797 224413); 21 Upper Cheyne Row, London SW3 5JW (☎ 071 351 3882, fax 071 351 6307)

MOYES, James Christopher (Jim); *b* 29 April 1943; *Educ* Maidstone Coll of Art, Univ of Kent (BA); *m* 1, 1969 (m dis 1981), Elizabeth McKee; 1 da (Sara Jo b 1969); m 2, 1987, Joanna Margaret, da of Col David E G Price; 2 da (Beatrice Oliphant b 1987, Clementine b 1990); *Career* laboratory asst and quality control technician Watneys Laboratories 1959-64, merchant marine 1964-66, artist and gallery asst 1971-, fndr Momart plc (int fine art serv co), lectr art handling techniques; estab Momart fellowship (artist in residence Tate Gallery Liverpool), vice chm SPACE 1990-; memb: Museums Training Inst, Assoc of American Museums Registrars Ctee, Museums Assoc; *Recreations* art exhibitions and other arts related activities; *Style*— Jim Moyes, Esq; Momart plc, 199-205 Richmond Rd, London E8 3NJ (☎ 081 986 8624, 081 985 5387, fax 081 533 0122)

MOYLAN, His Honour Judge (John) David FitzGerald; s of Sir John FitzGerald Moylan, CB, CBE (d 1967), of Haywards Heath and Bury, W Sussex, and Ysolda Mary Nesta Moylan, *née* FitzGerald (d 1966); *b* 8 Oct 1915; *Educ* Charterhouse (sr scholar), Ch Ch Oxford (Holford exhibitioner); *m* 1946, Jean Mary Valerie, da of Frederick Cormack Marno-Edwards (d 1981), of Clare, Suffolk; 1 s (Andrew), 2 da (Susan, Anne); *Career* served WWII 1939-46 in RM, Maj; formerly judge of County Ct 1967-72, circuit judge 1972-90; *Style*— His Honour David Moylan; Ufford Hall, Fressingfield, Diss, Norfolk

MOYLE, Rt Hon Roland Dunstan; PC (1978); s of Baron Moyle, CBE, JP, sometime MP Stourbridge & PPS to Clement Attlee (Life Peer d 1974), and his 1 w, Elizabeth; *b* 12 March 1928; *Educ* Bexleyheath and Llanidloes County Sch Powys, Univ Coll of Wales (Aberystwyth), Trinity Hall Cambridge; *m* 1956, Shelagh Patricia Hogan; 1 s, 1 da; *Career* served Royal Welch Fusiliers 1949-51; called to the Bar Gray's Inn; served various industrial relations posts in Wales Gas Bd, Gas Cncl, Electricity Cncl; MP (Lab): Lewisham N 1966-74, Lewisham East 1974-83; PPS to: chief sec Treasury 1966-69, Home Sec 1969-70; oppn spokesman: Army 1971, Higher Education and Science 1972-74; parly sec Miny Agric Fisheries and Food 1974; min: NI 1974-76, State Health 1976-79; front bench oppn spokesman: Health 1979-81, Foreign and Cwlth Affrs 1981-83, Defence and Disarmament 1983-; dep chm Police Complaints Authy 1985-; former memb Race Relations and Immigration Select Ctee, vice-chm PLP Def Gp, sec and exec cncl memb British American Parly Gp 1968-83; *Style*— The Rt Hon Roland Moyle; 19 Montpelier Row, Blackheath, London SE3 0RL

MOYNE, 2 Baron (UK 1932); Bryan Walter Guinness; s of Rt Hon 1 Baron Moyne, DSO, TD, PC (assass Cairo 1944, as min resident in M East; né Hon Walter Guinness, 3 s of 1 Earl of Iveagh, KP, GCVO), and Lady Evelyn Erskine (d 1939; da of 14 Earl of Buchan); *b* 27 Oct 1905; *Educ* Eton, Christ Church Oxford; *m* 1, 1929 (m dis 1934), Hon Diana Freeman Mitford, da of 2 Baron Redesdale; 2 s; m 2, 1936, Elisabeth, da of Thomas Nelson (ka 1917), of Edinburgh and Achnacloich; 3 s (and 1 s decd), 5 da; *Heir* s, Hon Jonathan Guinness; *Career* late Maj M East, France; called to the Bar 1930; vice-chm Arthur Guinness Son & Co 1949-79; tstee Iveagh and Guinness Housing Charitable Tsts; poet, novelist, playwright; FRSL; memb Irish Acad of Letters; *Books* writes as Bryan Guinness; *novels include* Singing Out of Tune (1933), Landscape with Figures (1934), A Week by the Sea (1936), A Fugue of Cinderellas (1956), The Giant's Eye (1964), The Girl with the Flower (1966), Helenic Flirtation (1978); memoirs: Dairy (sic) not kept (1975); Potpourri from the Thirties (1982); Personal Patchwork (1987); *poetry*: 23 Poems (1931), Under the Eyelid (1935), Reflexions (1947), Collected Poems (1956), The Clock (1973); *plays*: The Fragrant Concubine (1938), A Riverside Charade (1954); *Recreations* hurdle rod splitting, travel, gardening; *Clubs* Athenaeum, Carlton, University and Kildare Street (Dublin); *Style*— The Lord Moyne (alternatively Bryan Guinness); Knockmaroon House, Castleknock, Co Dublin, Ireland; Biddesden House, Andover, Hants (☎ 0264 790237)

MOYNIHAN, 3 Baron (UK 1929); Sir Antony Patrick Andrew Cairnes Berkeley Moynihan; 3 Bt (UK 1922); s of 2 Baron Moynihan, sometime Chm Exec Ctee Liberal Pty (d 1965), by his 1 w Ierne; *b* 2 Feb 1936; *Educ* Stowe; *m* 1, 1955 (m dis 1958), Ann, da of Reginald Herbert; m 2, 1958 (m dis 1967), Shirin Berry; 1 da; m 3, 1968 (m dis 1979), Luthgarda Maria, da of Alfonzo Fernandez; 3 da (Hon Antonita Maria Carmen b 31 March 1969, Hon Aurora Luzon Maria Dolores b 1971, Hon Kathleen Maynila Helen Imogen Juliet b 1974); m 4, 1981 (m dis 1990), Editha Eduarda, da of late Maj-Gen Eduardo Ruben, Philippine Army; 1 s (Hon Andrew Berkeley b 1989 d 1990); m 5, 1990, Jinna, *née* Sabiaga; 1 s (Hon Daniel Antony Patrick Berkeley b 1991); *Heir* s, Hon Daniel Antony Patrick Berkeley Moynihan b 12 Jan 1991; *Career* Lt Coldstream Guards; dog breeder; engaged in experimental vegetable farming in the Philippines 1970-, food columnist on local newspaper; *Style*— The Rt Hon the Lord Moynihan

MOYNIHAN, Hon Colin Berkeley; MP (C) Lewisham East 1983-; s of 2 Baron Moynihan, OBE, TD (d 1965), and June Elizabeth, *née* Hopkins; *b* 13 Sept 1955; *Educ* Monmouth Sch, Univ Coll Oxford (MA, Boxing and Rowing double blue); *Career* pres Oxford Union Soc 1976; personal asst to chm Tate & Lyle Ltd 1978-80, mangr Tate & Lyle Agribusiness 1980-82; chief exec Ridgways Tea and Coffee Merchants 1980-83; political asst to Foreign Sec 1983, PPS to Rt Hon Kenneth Clarke as Min of Health and PMG 1986-87, Parly under-sec of state: DOE and min for Sport 1987-90, Dept of Energy 1990-; memb: Bow Gp 1978 (chm Bow Gp Industry Ctee 1985-87), Paddington Cons Mgmnt Ctee 1980-81; sec: Foreign and Cwlth Affairs Ctee 1985, Major Spectator Sports Ctee CCPR 1979-87, CCPR Enquiry into Sponsorship of Sport 1982-83; memb Sports Cncl 1982-85, steward British Boxing Bd of Control 1979-87; tstee: Oxford Univ Boat Club 1980-83, Sports Aid Tst 1983-87; govr Sports Aid Fndn (London and SE) 1980-82, chm All Party Gp on Afghanistan 1984, vice chm Cons Backbenchers Sports Ctee; Freeman City of London 1978, Liveryman Worshipful Co of Haberdashers; Olympic Silver medal Rowing 1980; Int Rowing Fedn: World Gold medal Lightweight Rowing 1978, World Silver medal Rowing 1981; *Recreations* collecting Nonsuch books, music, sport; *Clubs* Brooks's, Royal Commonwealth Soc, Vincent's (Oxford); *Style*— The Hon Colin Moynihan, MP; House of Commons, London SW1A 0AA

MOYNIHAN, Ierne, Baroness; Ierne Helen; *née* Candy; da of Cairnes Candy (d 1949), of Mt Barker, W Australia; *b* 1910; *Educ* Private; *m* 1931 (m dis 1952), 2 Baron Moynihan (d 1965); 1 s, 2 da; *Clubs* Hurlingham, Queen's, Zoological Soc (life fell); *Style*— Ierne, Lady Moynihan; 56 Holland Park Av, London W11 3QY (☎ 071 727 7986)

MOYNIHAN, Sir Noël Henry; s of Dr Edward B Moynihan (d 1956); *b* 24 Dec 1916; *Educ* Ratcliffe, Downing Coll Cambridge (MA, MB BChir); *m* 1941, Margaret Mary (d 1989), da of William Lovelace (d 1938), barr at law, and sometime sec of Brooks's Club and Turf Club; 2 s, 2 da; *Career* served WWII Pilot RAF (despatches 2); family doctor 1954-; co-fndr Medical Cncl on Alcoholism 1963 (memb Cncl 1963-87, vice pres 1972-87); pres: Harveian Soc of London 1967 (memb of Cncl 1963-68 and 1978-81, hon life memb 1984), pres Chelsea Clinic Soc 1978 (memb of Cncl 1969-78, memb 1985); Hon life sec Medical Soc of London 1981-82 (memb Cncl 1980-85), memb Bd Royal Med Benevolent Fund 1973-77; pres Downing Coll Cambridge Assoc 1985-86, chm Save the Children Fund 1977-82 (vice-chm 1972-77); Freeman City of London 1959; Kt SMOM 1958 (Offr of Merit 1964, Cdr of Merit 1979), Kt St Gregory 1966; CStJ; assoc fell Downing Coll Cambridge; MRCS, LRCP, FRCGP; kt 1979; *Books* The Light in the West (1956), Rock Art of the Sahara (1979); *Recreations* Save the Children Fund, studying rock art of the Sahara; *Clubs* Carlton, MCC, Hawks (Cambridge), Achilles; *Style*— Sir Noël Moynihan; Herstmonceux Place, Flowers Green, East Sussex (☎ 032383 2017)

MOYOLA, Baron (Life Peer UK 1971), of Castledawson, Co Londonderry; James Dawson Chichester-Clark; PC (NI 1966), DL (Co Derry 1954); s of Capt James L C Chichester-Clark, DSO and bar (d 1933), and Mrs C E Brackenbury, of Moyola Park, Castle Dawson, Co Derry, N Ireland; bro of Sir Robin Chichester-Clark, *qv*; *b* 12 Feb 1923; *Educ* Eton; *m* 1959, Moyra Maud, da of Brig Arthur de Burgh Morris, CBE, DSO, and wid of Capt T G Haughton; 1 step s, 2 da (Hon Fiona b 1960, Hon Tara Olivia (Hon Mrs Whitley) b 1962); *Career* sits as Cons Peer in House of Lords; memb N Ireland Parliament 1960-71: chief whip 1963-67, ldr of the House and chief whip 1966-67, min of Agric 1967-69; prime minister 1969-71; *Recreations* shooting, fishing, gardening; *Style*— The Rt Hon the Lord Moyola, PC, DL; Moyola Park, Castledawson, Co Derry, N Ireland

MUCKLOW, Dr Edward Stuart; s of Dr Stuart Leslie Mucklow (d 1976), and Dr Alexandra Winifred, *née* Groves (d 1981); *b* 24 Jan 1932; *Educ* Radley, Exeter Coll Oxford (BA, MA, BM BCh), UCH Med Sch London (DObst, DCH), Univ of Edinburgh; *m* 2 April 1966, Dr Mary Lynn Cashel, da of Maurice Cashel; 2 s (Stuart b 1968, Gordon b 1975), 2 da (Clare b 1970, Celia b 1972); *Career* Nat Serv Capt RAMC 1960-62; ships surgn Messrs Submarine Cables Ltd Brazil 1959, house offr obstetrics Royal Postgrad Med Sch London 1959, sr house offr Hosp for Sick Children Gt Ormond St 1962-63, jr lectr in paediatrics UCH Med Sch 1963-64 (house physician and surgn 1958-59), lectr in child health Univ of Oxford 1966-68, seconded as chief of paediatrics Abdulla Fouad Hosp Dammam Saudi Arbia 1979-80, conslt paediatrician IOW and Portsmouth Health Dist 1968-, hon clinical lectr in child health Univ of Southampton Med Sch 1973-; author of various articles on: the newborn, tuberculosis, diabetes, genetics, pancreatitis in children rheumatic fever incl leader article in The Lancet 1985; former pres and chm IOW Hockey Club, life memb Ryeworth CC, memb Oxford Univ Occasionals Hockey Club, participant in Veteran World Hockey Cup 1986; memb: Editorial Bd Practical Diabetes (dep ed 1984-89), BPA, BMA Neonatal Soc; FRSM 1963 (memb Cncl paediatric section 1983-86), FRCPEd 1986 (memb 1966), FRCP 1989; *Recreations* learning arabic and modern greek, hockey, cricket, gardening, islamic art and arab history; *Style*— Dr Edward Mucklow; Keep Cottage, 5 Castle Lane, Carisbrooke, Isle of Wight PO30 1PH (☎ 0983 522096); Paediatric Dept, St Mary's Hospital, Newport, Isle of Wight PO30 5TG (☎ 0983 524081, ext 4280, fax 0983 822569, telex 869466 Taravs G)

MUDDIMAN, (Colin) Trevor; s of Arthur Edgar Lanwer Muddiman (d 1961); *b* 4 June 1929; *Educ* Wellington; *m* 1962, Stella Kathleen; *Career* farmer; memb Eastern Electricity Bd 1973-78 and 1980-89; chm: Eastern Electricity Consultative Cncl 1973-78, Farmers' Club Charitable Tst; memb Lloyds; Freeman Worshipful Co of Farmers 1960 (Memb Ct 1975, Master 1985); *Clubs* Farmers' (chm and pres 1981), Royal London Yacht; *Style*— C Trevor Muddiman, Esq; Gade House, Little Gaddesden, Berkhamsted, Herts HP4 1QT

MUDGE, Hon Mrs (Maureen Ann); da of Baron Wigg, PC (Life Peer); *b* 1934; *m* 1964, Alfred John Mudge; *Style*— The Hon Mrs Mudge; 1580 Mississauga Valley Blvd, Mississauga, Ont, Canada

MUELLER, Dame Anne Elisabeth; DCB (1988, CB 1980); da of Herbert Constantin Mueller (d 1952), and Phoebe Ann, *née* Beevers (d 1973); *b* 15 Oct 1930; *Educ* Wakefield Girls HS, Somerville Coll Oxford (MA); *m* 1958 (m dis 1978), James Hugh Robertson, s of Sir James Robertson, GCMG, GCVO (d 1983); *Career* dep sec Dept of Trade and Indust 1977-84, dir European Investment Bank 1978-84; second perm sec: Cabinet Office (head of Mgmnt and Personnel (Office) 1984-87, HM Treasy 1987-90; *Clubs* United Oxford & Cambridge University; *Style*— Dame Anne Mueller, DCB; 46 Kensington Heights, Campden Hill Rd, London W8 7BD

MUFF, Hon Peter Raymond; s of 2 Baron Calverley (d 1971); *b* 12 Aug 1953; *Educ* Grange Boys' Sch Bradford; *Career* asst engineer control and instrumentation and info technol Nat Power; IEng, MIElecIE; *Recreations* squash, fell walking, clay pigeon shooting, electronics, domestic cat shows; *Clubs* Harrogate Hockey & Squash, Abyssinian Cat; *Style*— The Hon Peter Muff; Oakhurst Farm, 377 Shadwell Lane, Leeds LS17 8AH

MUGURIAN, Gordon Haig; s of Murgadich Mugurian (d 1942), of 19 Worsley Rd, Hampstead, London, and Hilda Louise, *née* Hammond (d 1957); *b* 29 Dec 1926; *Educ* Eaglehurst Coll Northampton, Northampton Polytechnic London; *m* 9 Oct 1965, Jan Olive, da of Hugh Caley Parker, of 77 Yarmouth Rd, Thorpe St Andrew, Norwich, Norfolk; 1 s (Robert b 1968), 1 da (Helen b 1971); *Career* three year articled pupillage to County Engr and Surveyor Middlesex 1944-47, site engr agent and construction mangr John Mowlen and Co 1947-56, agent and construction mangr Tarmac Civil Engineering Ltd 1969-73, ET Leach and Ptnrs Whitchurch 1973-77, fndr G H Mugurian and Ptnrs 1977, commenced sitting as arbitrator 1988; memb Mgmnt Cncl: Inst of Civil Engrg Surveyors 1977- (chm Cncl 1979-85), Chartered Inst of Arbitrators 1990 (memb NW Branch Ctee 1985); memb Soc of Construction Law 1983; Freeman City of London 1982, Liveryman Worshipful Co of Arbitrators 1984 (Freeman 1981); FInstCES 1972, life vice-pres Inst CES 1986, ACIArb 1980, FCIArb 1984, AMAPM 1989; *Recreations* sail cruising, gardening, painting; *Clubs* Royal Welsh Yacht; *Style*— Gordon H Mugurian, Esq; G H Mugurian and Partners, Brookdale House, Tattenhall, Chester CH3 9PX (☎ 0829 70740, fax 0829 71075)

MUIR, Andrew Peter; s of Leslie Malcolm Muir, of Weaverham, Cheshire, and Audrey Britland, *née* Hill; *b* 25 Dec 1955; *Educ* Bromsgrove, Lanchester Poly (HND); *m* 6 May 1978, Bernie Ann, da of Charles George Overton, of Bromsgrove, Worcs; 2 s (Christopher Stuart b 1985, Gordon James b 1986); *Career* dir: Nationwide Refrigeration Supplies Ltd 1984-87, Cory Coffee Ltd 1986-87, (group systems) Suter plc Distribution Group 1985-87; md Imrex Systems Ltd 1987-89, dep chm Compass Software Ltd 1987-89, ptnr Lloyd MacKenzie Mgmnt Conslts 1989-90; dir and chief exec Logistics Solutions Ltd 1990-, AMBCS 1985; *Recreations* swimming, shooting, motorcycling; *Style*— Andrew Muir, Esq; Chisbury Lane House, Chisbury, Marlborough, Wilts SN8 3JA (☎ 0672 870187); La Jouverie, Coulouvray Boisbenatre, 50670 St Pois, Normande, France; Logistics Solutions Ltd, 3704 Windsor House, 311 Gloucester Road, Causeway Bay, Hong Kong (☎ 010 852 576 0122, fax 010 852 576 1520)

MUIR, Elizabeth Jean; da of Capt Kenneth Edward Muir, MBE, of Bridgend, S Wales, and Elsie, *née* Harris; *b* 20 Aug 1947; *Educ* Cowbridge Girls HS, Homerton Coll Cambridge, Cardiff Coll of Educn (Dip Ed); *Career* mktg conslt, freelance writer and guest speaker; maths and physics teacher Cardiff Secdy Sch 1967-73, creative exec Parke-Davis Pharmaceuticals 1973-76, prod gp mangr Warner Lambert Animal Health, sales and mktg controller Memory Lane Cakes (Dalgety Spillers Co) 1978-82, fndr and md The Alternative Mkgt Dept Ltd 1982-; specialist mktg in Europe particularly Greece (veterinary prods, professional and govt servs); first woman memb Welsh Regnl Cncl CBI 1985-; memb: Syllabus Advsy Gps BTEC courses and Nursing Dip, Br Hellenic C of C, Women and Trg; bd memb: Welsh Water Authy 1986-89, Health Promotion Authy for Wales 1987-, Secdy Housing Assoc for Wales 1988-, S Glam Family Health Serv Authy 1990-; MCInstM, MInstSM; *Recreations* pt/t study for Msc (Econ) in women's studies, dinner parties with friends, travel in Greece; *Style*— Miss Elizabeth Muir; Sunningdale House, 13 Tydraw Rd, Roath Pk, Cardiff CF2 5HA (☎ 0222 499214, fax 0222 398209)

MUIR, Frank; CBE (1980); s of Charles James Muir, and Margaret, *née* Harding; *b* 5 Feb 1920; *Educ* Chatham House Ramsgate, Leyton County HS; *m* 16 July 1949, Polly, *née* McIrvine; 1 s (Jamie), 1 da (Sally); *Career* served RAF 1940-46; writer and broadcaster with Denis Norden 1947-64, collaborated for 17 yrs writing comedy scripts, resident in TV and radio panel games, asst head of BBC Light Entertainment Gp 1964-67, head of entertainment London Weekend TV 1968-69, resumed TV Series Call My Bluff 1970; Lord Rector St Andrew's Univ 1977-79; Hon LLD Univ of St Andrews 1978, Hon DLitt Univ of Kent 1982; *Books Incl:* The Frank Muir Book: An Irreverent Companion to Social History, A Book at Bathtime, What-a-Mess children's stories, The Oxford Book of Humorous Prose; *Recreations* working; *Clubs* Garrick; *Style*— Frank Muir, Esq, CBE; Anners, Thorpe, Egham, Surrey (☎ 0932 562759); A Torra, Monticello, Corsica

MUIR, Dr (Isabella) Helen Mary; CBE (1981); da of George Basil Fairlie Muir, ICS (d 1959), and Gwladys Helen Muir (d 1969); *b* 20 Aug 1920; *Educ* Downe House, Somerville Coll Oxford (MA, DPhil, DSc); *Career* res fell Sir William Dunn Sch of Pathology Oxford Univ 1947-48, scientific staff Nat Inst for Medical Research Biochemistry Div (London) 1948-54; Empire Rheumatism res fell St Mary's Hosp Medical Unit 1954-58, Pearl res fell and hon lectr St Mary's Hosp Med Sch 1959-66, head Biochemistry Div Kennedy Inst of Rheumatology 1966-86 (dir 1977-90); tstee Wellcome Tst 1982-90; hon prof Charing Cross Hospital Medical Sch 1979-; Hon DSc: Edinburgh 1982, Strathclyde 1983, Brunel 1990; Heberden orator London 1976, Feldberg Fndn award 1977, Bunim medal of American Arthritis Assoc 1978, Neil Hamilton Fairley medal of the Royal College of Physicians for an outstanding contribution to medicine 1981, Ciba medal of the Biochemical Society 1981, Steindler award Orthopaedic Soc of USA, hon memb American Soc of Biological Chemists; foreign memb Royal Swedish Acad of Sci 1989, FRS 1977; *Recreations* gardening, equestrian sports, natural history; *Style*— Dr Helen Muir, CBE, FRS; Department of Biochemistry, Charing Cross - Westminster Medical School, Fulham Palace Road, London W6 8RF (☎ 081 846 7053)

MUIR, Jean Elizabeth (Mrs Leuckert); CBE (1984); da of Cyril Muir, and Phyllis, *née* Coy; *Educ* Dame Harper Sch Bedford; *m* 1955, Harry Leuckert; *Career* fashion designer; Dress of the Year Award Br Fashion Writers Gp 1964, fndr Jean Muir Ltd 1966; Jean Muir Exhibitions: Lotherton Hall Leeds, Birmingham, Belfast, Bath, Stoke on Trent; memb Bd for Design BTEC 1977-78; Awards: Ambass Award for Achievement 1965, Maison Blanche Rex Int Fashion Award New Orleans (1967, 1968, 1974), Hommage de la Mode Award Fedn Francaise du Prêt á Porter Feminin, Br Fashion Cncl Award for Servs to Indust 1985, Chartered Soc of Designers Medal for Outstanding Achievement 1987, Textile Inst Medal 1987, Aust Govt Bicentennial Award presented by T R H Prince and Princess of Wales at Sydney Opera House 1988; tstee V&A 1983, memb Design Cncl 1983-88; Hon Citizen of New Orleans, Hon Doctor RCA 1981, Hon DLitt Newcastle 1985, Hon DLitt Ulster 1987; FRSA, RDI, FCSD; *Style*— Miss Jean Muir, CBE; 59-61 Farringdon Rd, London EC1M 3HP (☎ 071 831 0691, fax 071 831 0826, telex 25883 JEMUIR G)

MUIR, Sir John (Harling); 3 Bt (UK 1892), of Deanston, Perthshire, TD, DL (Perthshire 1966); s of James Finlay Muir (d 1948), and nephew of 2 Bt (d 1951); *b* 7 Nov 1910; *Educ* Stowe; *m* 1936, Elizabeth Mary, da of late Frederick James Dundas; 5 s, 2 da; *Heir* s, Richard James Kay Muir; *Career* served WWII 1939-45; dir: James Finlay & Co Ltd Glasgow 1946-80, Grindlay's Holdings Ltd, Royal Insurance Co Ltd, Scottish United Investors Ltd; memb Queen's Body Gd for Scotland (Royal Co of Archers); *Recreations* shooting, fishing, gardening; *Clubs* Oriental; *Style*— Sir John Muir, Bt, TD; Bankhead, Blair Drummond, Perthshire (☎ 0786 841207)

MUIR, Lady Linda Mary; *née* Cole; da of 6 Earl of Enniskillen, MBE; *b* 1944; *m* 1975, as his 2 w, Richard James Kay Muir, *qv*; 2 da; *Style*— The Lady Linda Muir; Park House, Blair Drummond, by Stirling, Perthshire

MUIR, Dr Richard Ernest; s of Kenneth Richard Muir, of Station Rd, Birstwith, Harrogate, and Edna Violet, *née* Huggall; *b* 18 June 1943; *Educ* Univ of Aberdeen (MA, PhD); *m* 13 Oct 1978, Nina Bina-Kumari, da of Indrajit Rajpal; *Career* lectr in geography Trinity Coll Univ of Dublin 1970-71, lectr and sr lectr in geography Cambridge Coll of Art and Technol 1971-80, freelance author and photographer 1981-; ed: Nat Tst Histories, Countryside Cmmn Nat Parks; Yorks Arts Literary Award 1982-83; various articles in Observer, Sunday Times, Geographical Magazine, NY Times; memb: FOE, Green Alliance, Yorks Wildlife Tst, Yorks Dales Soc; *Books* Modern Political Geography (1975), Geography Politics and Behaviour (1980), The English Village (1980), Riddles in The British Landscape (1981), The Shell Guide to Reading The Landscape (1981), The Lost Villages of Britain (1982), History From The Air (1983), Visions of The Past (with C Taylor, 1983), The National Trust Guide to Prehistoric and Roman Britain (with H Welfare, 1983), A Traveller's History of Britain and Ireland (1984), The Shell Countryside Book (with E Duffey, 1984), The National Trust Guide to Dark Age and Medieval Britain 1985, The National Trust Guide to Rivers of Britain (with N Muir, 1986), Landscape and Nature Photography (1986), Old Yorkshire (1987), Hedgerows (N Muir, 1988), The Countryside Encyclopaedia (1988), Fields (with N Muir, 1989), Portraits of the Past (1989); *Recreations* historical and environmental issues relating to British landscape; *Style*— Dr Richard Muir; Waterfall Close, Station Rd, Birstwith, Harrogate HG3 3AG (☎ 0423 771644)

MUIR, Richard James Kay; s and h of Sir John Muir, 3 Bt, TD; *b* 25 May 1939; *m* 1, 1965 (m dis 1974), Susan Elizabeth Gardner; 2 da; m 2, 1975, Lady Linda Mary Cole, da of 6 Earl of Enniskillen; 2 da; *Style*— Richard Muir, Esq; Park House, Blair Drummond, by Stirling, Perthshire

MUIR, Robert Wallace; s of Capt William Wallace Muir, RN (d 1964), and Mary *née* Claris; *b* 7 Sept 1954; *Educ* Christ's Hosp Horsham, Univ Coll London UCL (LLB); *m* 26 Sept 1987, Carole Ann, da of John Hobbs, of Doncaster; 1 da (Olivia Jane b 14 Dec 1990); *Career* slr; Titmuss Sainer and Webb 1977-82, Herbert Oppenheimer Nathan and Vandyk 1982-83, Knapp Fishers 1983-86, McKenna & Co 1987-; memb Law Soc; *Clubs* RAC, Old Blues RFC; *Style*— R W Muir, Esq; McKenna & Co, Mitre House, 160 Aldersgate St, London EC1A 4DD (☎ 071 606 9000, fax 071 606 9100)

MUIR, Lady Rosemary Mildred; *née* Spencer-Churchill; da of 10 Duke of Marlborough (d 1972), and Hon Alexandra Mary Cadogan (d 1961); *b* 24 July 1929; *m* 1953, Charles Robert Muir (d 1972), s of Roland Huntly Muir (d 1975); 2 s (Alexander, Simon), 1 da (Mary); *Career* a train bearer to HM The Queen at the Coronation 1953; *Clubs* Sunningdale Golf, Berkshire Golf; *Style*— The Lady Rosemary Muir; Orange Hill House, Binfield, Berks (☎ 0344 483485)

MUIR MACKENZIE, Sir Alexander Alwyne Brinton; 7 Bt (UK 1805), of Delvine, Perthshire; s of Sir Robert Henry Muir Mackenzie, 6 Bt (d 1970), and Charmian Cecil de Vere, *née* Brinton (d 1962); *b* 8 Dec 1955; *Educ* Eton, Trinity Coll Cambridge; *m* 1984, Susan Carolyn, da of John David Henzel Hayter; 1 s (Archie b 17 Feb 1989), 1 da (Georgina Mary b 1987); *Heir* s, Archie Robert David Muir Mackenzie b 17 Feb 1989; *Style*— Sir Alexander Muir Mackenzie, Bt; Buckshaw House, Holwell, nr Sherborne, Dorset DT9 5LD

MUIR MACKENZIE, Mary, Lady; Mary Teresa; er da of late Dr James Mathews and wid of John Geoffrey Turner, of Farnham, Surrey; *m* 25 July 1963, as his 2 w, Capt Sir Robert Henry Muir Mackenzie, 6 Bt (d 1970); *Style*— Mary, Lady Muir Mackenzie; Flat A, 62 Pont St, London SW1

MUIR-SIMPSON, Richard Mannington; s of Denzil Lorimer Muir-Simpson, TD (d 1976), and Bridget Katherine Grant, *née* Sayers; *b* 24 April 1946; *Educ* Loretto Sch, Univ of Sheffield (LLB), ICAS; *m* 8 Oct 1976, Patricia Guthrie, da of Guthrie Baxter Wilson, of Angus; 2 s (Andrew b 1978, Simon b 1980); *Career* investmt mangr Ivory & Sime plc; dir of cos incl: Lyle Fin Int Ltd 1976-81, Log Servs Ltd 1978-81, Fenton Barns (Scotland) Ltd 1981-82, Wavebreaker Marine Ltd 1981-82, Gaeltec Ltd 1981-83, Omega Electric Ltd 1983-85, Stepp Electronics Ltd 1983-87; deacon The Incorporation of Wrights in Glasgow 1981-82, pres The Grand Antiquity Soc of Glasgow 1983-84, memb The Trades House of Glasgow 1981-84; *Recreations* tennis, skiing, gardening, politics, music; *Clubs* RSAC, Edinburgh Sports; *Style*— Richard Muir-Simpson, Esq; Redmarley, Kippen, Stirlingshire FK8 3HS (☎ 0786 87351); Ivory & Sime plc, 1 Charlotte Square, Edinburgh EH2 4DZ (☎ 031 225 1357, telex 727242, fax 031 225 2375)

MUIR WOOD, Sir Alan Marshall; s of Edward Wood; *b* 8 Aug 1921; *Educ* Abbotsholme Sch, Peterhouse Cambridge; *m* 1943, Dr Winifred Lanagan Wood; 3 s; *Career* served WWII, engr offr RN; former asst engr BR (Southern Region) and res asst Docks and Inland Waterways Exec; sr ptnr Sir William Halcrow & Partners 1979-84 (ptnr 1964-84, formerly asst then sr engr, now conslt); dir: Halcrow Fox & Associates 1977-84, Orange Fish Consultants; first (and hon life) pres Int Tunnelling Assoc; studies for Channel Tunnel (intermittently 1958-); fell Imperial Coll 1981; hon fell: Peterhouse 1982, Portsmouth Poly 1984; Hon LLD Dundee 1985; Hon DSc: City Univ 1978, Univ of Southampton 1986; recipient of Telford medal 1976, James Alfred Ewing medal 1984; FEng, FICE (pres 1977-78), FRS; kt 1981; *Books* Coastal Hydraulics (1969, 2 ed with C A Fleming 1981); *Clubs* Athenaeum; *Style*— Sir Alan Muir Wood, FEng, FRS; Franklands, Pangbourne, Berks RG8 8JY (☎ 0734 842833)

MUIRHEAD, Capt (James) Alan; MBE (1971), JP (1968); s of Brig James Ingram Muirhead, CIE, MC (d 1964), of Moffat, Dumfriesshire, and Dorothy Alaine Denholm, *née* Fraser (d 1978); *b* 18 Nov 1924; *Educ* Sherborne, Bishop Cotton Sch's Bangalore and Simla; *m* 24 July 1948, Mary, da of Lt-Col Joseph Charles Annear, TD (d 1958), of Falmouth; 1 s (James David Charles b 1949), 1 da (Julia Anne b 1953); *Career* Capt RE; served India, Malaya, Java 1942-49; perm cmmn 1946, ret 1949; dir: J C Annear & Co Ltd 1953-73, J H Bennetts Ltd 1978-88 (chm 1983-88); Co Cncllr Cornwall 1988-; *Recreations* sailing, gardening; *Clubs* Royal Cornwall Yacht; *Style*— Capt Alan Muirhead, MBE, JP; Sparnon, Budock, Falmouth, Cornwall TR11 5DJ (☎ 0325 72560)

MUIRHEAD, Alastair William (Sandy); s of William Calliope Muirhead, OBE (d 1983), and Joan Andrade, *née* Sutherland; *b* 12 Sept 1953; *Educ* Tonbridge, St John's Coll Oxford (BA); *m* 19 April 1980, Linda Anne, da of Robert Johnson, of Wakefield; 3 da (Joanna b 19 Feb 1983, Nicola b 12 March 1985, Catriona b 16 Aug 1989); *Career* Price Waterhouse 1976-80, Saudi International Bank 1980-84, md Charterhouse Bank Ltd 1989- (joined 1984); Hon MA Oxon; ACA; *Recreations* fly-fishing, gardening, hill walking; *Style*— Sandy Muirhead, Esq; Charterhouse Bank Ltd, 1 Paternoster Row, St Pauls, London EC4M 7DH (☎ 071 248 4000, fax 071 248 6522)

MUIRHEAD, Sir David Francis; KCMG (1976, CMG 1964), CVO (1957); s of late David Muirhead; *b* 30 Dec 1918; *Educ* Cranbrook Sch; *m* 1942, Hon Elspeth, *née* Hope-Morley (d 1989); 2 s, 1 da; *Career* served WWII; FO: joined 1947, cnsllr 1960-65, under sec 1966-67; ambass: Peru 1967-70, Portugal 1970-74, Belgium 1974-78; Grand Cross Mil Order of Christ (Portugal) 1973, Grand Cross Order of Distinguished

Serv (Peru) 1985; *Clubs* Travellers'; *Style—* Sir David Muirhead, KCMG, CVO; 16 Pitt St, London W8 4NY (☎ 071 937 2443)

MUIRHEAD, William Mortimer; s of Denis Butler Muirhead; *b* 11 July 1947; *Educ* The Armidale Sch NSW, St Dunstans Coll SE6; *m* Jeanne Elizabeth, nee Meins; 2 s; *Career* dir: Saatchi & Saatchi Garland-Compton, Saatchi & Saatchi 1980-; *Recreations* rugby, tennis, squash, skiing; *Clubs* RAC, Zanzibar, Mortons; *Style—* William Muirhead Esq; 'Ightham', Merlewood Drive, Chislehurst, Kent; 'Tramontana', Encounter Bay, Victor Harbour, S Australia

MUIRHEAD-ALLWOOD, William Forster Gillespie; s of Maj W R Muirhead (d 1946), and Joyce, *née* Forster; *b* 4 Jan 1947; *Educ* Wellington, St Thomas Hosp Med Sch (BSc, MB BS, MRCS, LRCP); *m* 1983, Jane Elizabeth, da of Mervyn Miles; 2 s (William Ritchie b 12 Sept 1984, James Miles b 3 July 1986); *Career* St Thomas' Hosp: house surgn 1971-72, sr house offr 1972-73, anatomy demonstrator 1973; sr house offr Stoke Mandeville Hosp 1973-74; registrar: UCH 1974-77, Charing Cross Hosp 1977-78; sr registrar 1978-84 (Queen Mary's Hospital Roehampton, Westminster Hosp, Royal Nat Orthopaedic Hosp, UCH), conslt orthopaedic surgn Whittington Hosp 1984, hon sr clinical lectr UCL 1984, hon conslt St Lukes Hosp for the Clergy 1984; memb: Br Orthopaedic Assoc 1980, BMA 1983, Br Hip Soc 1989; FRCS; *Books* contrib: Joint Replacement - State of the Art (1990), Recent Advances in Orthopaedic Surgery (1991); *Recreations* golf, sailing; *Clubs* Highgate Golf; *Style—* Mr William Muirhead-Allwood; 19 Wimpole St, London W1M 7AD (☎ 071 935 8488, fax 071 636 5758)

MUIRSHIEL, Viscount (UK 1964); John Scott Maclay; KT (1973), CH (1962), CMG (1944), PC (1952), JP (Renfrewshire 1968), DL (Renfrewshire 1981); 5 s of 1 Baron Maclay (d 1951); *b* 26 Oct 1905; *Educ* Winchester, Trinity Coll Cambridge; *m* 1930, Betty L'Estrange (d 1974), da of Maj Delaval Astley, CB, JP, DL (d 1951, g nephew of 16 Baron Hastings); *Heir* none; *Career* Capt 57 Searchlight Regt RA TA, seconded to Min of War Tport 1940; memb British Shipping Mission to USA 1941, head of mission 1944; MP (Lib Nat) Montrose Dist of Burghs 1940-50, MP (Nat Lib & C) Renfrewshire (Western Div) 1950-64; parly sec to Min of Production 1945, min Transport and Civil Aviation 1951-52, min of state Colonial Affairs 1956-57, sec of state Scotland 1957-62; chm: Jt Exchequer Bd for N Ireland 1965-73; former dir: Maclay & Macintyre Ltd, Clydesdale Bank, National Provincial Bank, P & O Steamship Co Ltd; tstee National Galleries of Scotland 1966-76; chm: Scottish Civic Trust 1967-89, Tstees Burrell Collection; Lord-Lt of Renfrewshire 1967-80; Hon LLD: Edinburgh 1963, Strathclyde 1966, Glasgow 1970; *Clubs* Boodle's, Western (Glasgow), Royal Yacht Sqdn; *Style—* The Rt Hon the Viscount Muirshiel, KT, CH, CMG, PC, JP, DL; Knapps Wood, Kilmacolm, Renfrewshire PA13 4NQ (☎ 050 587 2770)

MUKHAMEDOV, Irek; s of Djardat Rasulievich Mukhamedov, of Kazan, USSR, and Rashida Nizamorna, *née* Fatkulina; *b* 8 March 1960; *Educ* Moscow Ballet School; *m* 23 March 1990, Maria, da of Leonid Kovbas; 1 da (Alexandra Cholpon b 22 Aug 1990); *Career* soloist Moscow Classical Ballet 1978-81, former princ dancer The Bolshoi Ballet (performances incl: Spartakus, Don Quixote, Ivan the Terrible, Golden Age, Romeo and Juliette, Raymonda, Giselle, Nutcracker, Swan Lake); other performances incl: Roland Petit's Cyrano de Bergerac, Nureyev's Sleeping Beauty (Grand Opera Paris and Vienna Opera Vienna), Nureyev's Don Quixote (Flanders Ballet), Balanchine (Apollo Vienna); currently princ dancer Royal Ballet (performances incl: Bayadere, Manon (2 roles), Nutcracker, Raymonde, Winter Dreams); winner: Grand Prix Moscow IV competion, Gandersen Best Dancer in World, Laurence Olivier Best Acting prize; *Recreations* dedication to art of ballet, family; *Style—* Irek Mukhamedov, Esq; Royal Opera House, Covent Garden, London WC1

MUKHERJEE, Tara Kumar; s of Sushil Chandra Mukherjee (d 1976), of Calcutta, India, and Sova Moyee, *née* Banerjee; *b* 20 Dec 1923; *Educ* Scottish Church Collegiate Sch Calcutta India, Univ of Calcutta; *m* 15 May 1951, Betty Patricia, da of David Derby (d 1982), of Leicester; 1 s (Karl b 1956), 1 da (Jasmin b 1952); *Career* shop mangr Bata Shoe Co Ltd India 1941-44, buyer Brevitt Shoes Leicester 1951-56, sundries buyer British Shoe Corporation 1956-66, prodn admin Priestley Footwear Ltd Gt Harwood 1966-68, head store mangr British Shoe Corporation 1968-70, branch mangr Save and Prosper Group 1978-84 (dist mangr 1970-78), area mangr Guardian Royal Exchange 1985-88, md Owl Financial Services Ltd 1988; pres: Confedn of Indian Orgns UK 1975-, Indian Film Soc Leicester; memb: Br Euro Movement, Cncl of Mgmnt Coronary Prevention Gp 1985-; tstee: Haymarket Theatre Leicester, Asian Community Resources Tst London; current chm Charter 90 for Asians; played for Bihar Ranji Cricket trophy 1941; FLIA; *Recreations* first class cricket; *Clubs* Leicestershire CC, Indian Nat (Leicester); *Style—* Tara Mukherjee, Esq; Tallah, 1 Park Ave, Hutton, Brentwood, Essex CM13 2QL (☎ 0277 215438); 1 Britannia Rd, Brentwood, Essex CM14 2QL (☎ 0277 263207, 0277 226127)

MULCAHY, Geoffrey John; s of late Maurice Frederick Mulcahy; *b* 7 Feb 1942; *Educ* King's Sch Worcester, Univ of Manchester, Harvard Univ; *m* 1964, Valerie Elizabeth, *née* Ison; 1 s, 1 da; *Career* fin dir British Sugar Corporation Ltd 1977-82, gp chief exec Kingfisher plc; *Recreations* squash, sailing; *Clubs* Lansdowne; *Style—* Geoffrey Mulcahy, Esq

MULCAHY, Russell Ian; s of Edward Joseph Mulcahy (d 1988), and Joan, *née* Sydney; *b* 23 June 1953; *Educ* Corrimal HS NSW Aust; *Career* film ed Channel 7 Sydney Aust, winner Sydney Film Fest with 2 short films 1976 and 1977, moved to England 1978; filmed numerous pop videos and video albums 1980- incl: Derek and Clive Get the Horn (for Peter Cook and Dudley Moore), Duran Duran The Video Album, The Tubes Completion Backwards Principle, Elton John The Fox; feature films incl: Razorback 1984, Arena An Absurd Notion (with Duran Duran) 1985, Highlander (with Christopher Lambert and Sean Connery) 1986, Highlander II 1990, Ricochet (with Denzil Washington and John Lithgow) 1991; awards incl: BAFTA Special Craft Award 1982, American Videos Award best dir 1982, Int Film and TV Festival silver and bronze awards 1983, two Grammy Awards best long and short videos 1983, D & AD Awards best dir and best music video 1983, Br Phonographic Indust Award video of the year 1984, three American video Awards 1984, Golden Rose of Montreux best story-line (music section) 1986, (USA) Clio Award for best corporate TV commercial 1989 BP The Mission; memb Directors Guild of America; *Recreations* scuba diving, writing, cinema, theatre; *Clubs* Brown's; *Style—* Russell Mulcahy, Esq; c/o Limelight, 1724 Nth Whitley Ave, Hollywood, Los Angeles, CAL 90028, USA (☎ 213 464 5808, fax 213 464 3109); Limelight (UK), 3 Bromley Place, London W1 (☎ 071 255 3939, fax 071 255 3999, 081 464 4334)

MULCHINOCK, Michael Cyril George; s of Cyril Edward Mulchinock (d 1977), and Alethea Mary, *née* Bone (d 1988); gs of William Pembroke Mulchinock, the poet who wrote 'The Rose of Tralee'; *b* 5 June 1929; *Educ* Monkton Combe, Royal W of England Acad Sch of Architecture; *m* 5 Feb 1955 (m dis 1987), (Doreen) Elizabeth, da of Gordon Bunce (d 1967); 1 s (Simon b 9 March 1963), 2 da (Sarah b 5 April 1959, Emily b 23 May 1967); *Career* asst staff architect Gallaher Ltd 1958-63; princ in private practice 1963-65; ptnr Elsworth Sykes Ptnrship 1965-86 (dir 1986-); dir: Elsworth Sykes Property Servs 1986-, Elsworth Sykes Northern 1988-, ESP Planning 1988-, Folio Personnel 1988-; memb Architects Benevolent Soc Exec 1985- (memb cncl and chm Winter Charity Ball ctee 1981-85); chm: Knockholt (Kent) Amenity Soc 1970-77, Judd Street Ress Assoc (London WC1) 1985-86; FRIBA, memb SPAB; *Recreations* writing, community interests; *Clubs* Reform; *Style—* Michael Mulchinock, Esq; 2 Sandwich St, London WC1H 9PL (☎ 071 388 3558); Elsworth Sykes Partnership, 27 Queen Anne St, London W1M 9FB (☎ 071 580 5886, fax 071 872 9547, telex ESPLON G)

MULDOON, Rt Hon Sir Robert David; GCMG (1983), CH (1977), PC (1976), MP Tamaki 1960-; s of James Henry Muldoon, and Mamie R Muldoon; *b* 25 Sept 1921; *Educ* Mt Albert GS; *m* 1951, Thea Dale, *née* Flyger; 1 s, 2 da; *Career* CA; pres NZ Inst of Cost Accountants 1956; Parly under-sec to Min of Fin 1963-66, min of Tourism 1967, min of Finance 1967-72, dep PM 1972, dep ldr Nat Pty and dep ldr of the oppn 1972-74, ldr of the oppn 1974-75; chm Bd of Govrs IMF and World Bank 1979-80, chm Ministerial Cncl OECD 1982, Prime Minister New Zealand and min of Fin 1975-84; FCANZ, CMANZ, FCIS, FCMA; *Books* The Rise and Fall of a Young Turk (1974), Muldoon (1977), My Way (1981), The New Zealand Economy, A Personal View (1985), No 38 (1986); *Clubs* Professional (NZ); *Style—* The Rt Hon Sir Robert Muldoon, GCMG, CH, MP; 7 Homewood Place, Birkenhead, Auckland 10, New Zealand

MULGRAVE, Earl of; Constantine Edmund Walter Phipps; s and h of 4 Marquess of Normanby, KG, CBE; *b* 24 Feb 1954; *Educ* Eton, Worcester Coll Oxford; *m* 1990, Nicola, da of Milton Shulman; *Career* writer, co dir; *Publications* (as Constantine Phipps) Careful with the Sharks (1985), Among the Thin Ghosts (1989); *Clubs* Travellers; *Style—* Earl of Mulgrave; Mulgrave Castle, Whitby, N Yorks

MULHOLLAND, Brian Henry; only s and h of Sir Michael Henry Mulholland, 2 Bt, by his 2 w, Elizabeth, *née* Hyde (d 1989); *b* 25 Sept 1950; *Educ* Eton; *m* 1976, Mary Joana, yst da of Maj Robert J F Whistler, of Achaeon, Camberley, Surrey; 2 s (Andrew b 1981, William b 1986), 1 da (Tara b 1980); *Career* co dir; brands mangr Matthew Clark Gp plc. with responsibility for Irish Distillers 1982-85; dir Lanyon Devpts Ltd 1985-; *Recreations* fishing, gardening; *Clubs* MCC; *Style—* Brian Mulholland, Esq; The House by the Green, Worplesdon Hill, nr Woking, Surrey GU22 0QY (☎ 04867 2481)

MULHOLLAND, (Hugh) Connor; s of William Hugh Mulholland (d 1987), of Belfast, and Agnes, *née* Connor; *b* 10 Sept 1938; *Educ* Campbell Coll Belfast, Queens Univ Belfast (BSc, MB BCh, BAO); *m* 18 Dec 1968, (Hannah Eileen) Sandra, da of Frederick William Hedgecock (d 1984), of Belfast; 2 s (Michael b 1969, Gareth b 1975), 1 da (Shona 1972); *Career* asst prof Dept of Med Christian Med Coll Univ of Punjab 1969-71; res fellowship: NI Hosp Authy 1972-74, Ontario Heart Fndn 1974-76; conslt paediatric cardiologist Royal Belfast Hosp for Sick Children 1976-, co chm regnl med cardiology centre Royal Group of Hosps 1983-, clinical dir cardiology and cardiothoracic surgn Royal Gp of Hosps 1990-; memb: Br Cardiac Soc, Irish Cardiac Soc, Assoc of Euro Paediatric Cardiologists, Ulster Paediatric Assoc (pres elect), BMA, Belfast City YMCA (vice chm); FRCPE 1979; *Recreations* hill walking, reading, photography; *Style—* Dr Connor Mulholland; Regional Medical Cardiology Centre, Royal Victoria Hospital, Belfast 12 (☎ 0232 240503)

MULHOLLAND, John Peter Patrick; s of John Llewellyn Mulholland (d 1989), and Helen, *née* Moss; *b* 2 Sept 1929; *Educ* Berkhamsted Sch, Sch of Slavonic Studies London (BA), Trinity Coll Dublin (BL), Royal Agric Coll (Dip Advanced Farm Mgmnt); *m* 15 Dec 1973, Rosemary Kathleen Vaughan, da of Charles Hawkins, of Cirencester; 2 s (John Charles b 1975, James Patrick b 1977); *Career* freelance journalist 1955-: latin american corr News Chronicle 1959-61, prog organiser BBC External Serv 1963-69, numerous articles on fin and tax; called to the Bar: Middle Temple 1969, King's Inn Dublin 1975; in practice: Southampton and London 1969-, Repub of Ireland 1975-; sr lectr in law Royal Agric Coll 1980-88; memb Lincoln's Inn 1971, MRAC 1980, memb Agric Law Assoc 1989; *Books* Practical Puppetry (1961), Brazil 1968 (1968), Ploughing of Rights of Way (jtly, 1988); *Recreations* archery, shooting, sailing, walking; *Clubs* Newport Sailing; *Style—* John Mulholland, Esq; Chesterfield, Somerford Rd, Cirencester, Glos GL7 1TX (☎ 0285 653170); 17 Carlton Crescent, Southampton SO9 5AL (☎ 0703 636036, fax 0703 223877); 17 Old Buildings, Lincoln's Inn, London WC2A 3UP

MULHOLLAND, Martin Edward Harcourt; s of Hon John Mulholland, MC (d 1948, yst s of 2 Baron Dunleath), and Hon Olivia Vernon, DCVO, *née* Harcourt (d 1984), 2 da of 1 Viscount Harcourt; *b* 23 Feb 1927; *Educ* Eton; *m* 24 Feb 1953, (Lilian) Diana Tindall, da of Maj John Lucas, MC (d 1968); 3 s (John b 1953, Simon b 1955, Giles b 1959); *Career* Lt Irish Gds 1945-48, Palestine 1947-48; High Sheriff of Co Antrim 1961; Liveryman Pipemakers' and Tobacco Blenders' Co 1986; with Gallaher Ltd 1948-86 (gen mangr Public Affairs 1979-86), chm and md Public Affairs Advice Ltd 1986-; *Recreations* shooting, fishing, politics; *Style—* Martin Mulholland, Esq; North Hall, E Chiltington, Lewes, Sussex BN7 3QS (☎ 0273 890251); Public Affairs Advice Ltd, North Hall, E Chiltington, Lewes, Sussex BN7 3QS (☎ 0273 890821)

MULHOLLAND, Maj Sir Michael Henry; 2 Bt (UK 1945), of Ballyscullion Park, Co Derry; s of Rt Hon Sir Henry Mulholland, 1 Bt (d 1971), of Ballyscullion Park, Bellaghy, NI; hp to Barony of Dunleath; *b* 15 Oct 1915; *Educ* Eton, Pembroke Coll Cambridge; *m* 1, 1942 (m dis 1949), Rosemary, da of late Maj David Ker, OBE; m 2, 1949, Elizabeth (d 1989), da of Laurence Hyde; 1 s; *Heir* s, Brian Henry Mulholland; *Career* 2 Lt Oxford and Bucks LI 1936, served WWII 1939-45, Maj 1946; joined Yorks & Flax Spinning Co Ltd Belfast as buyer in Belgium 1950, ret 1959; *Style—* Maj Sir Michael Mulholland, Bt; Storbrooke, Massey Ave, Belfast (☎ 0232 63394)

MULHOLLAND, Robert Charles; s of Philip Mulholland (d 1965), and Eileen, *née* Dwyer; *b* 4 Dec 1934; *Educ* Prior Park Coll Bath, London Hosp Med Sch; *m* 5 June 1965, Elizabeth, da of George Kennedy (d 1960); 2 s (Andrew b 19 Dec 1967, Seamus b 9 April 1969), 1 da (Sarah (twin) b 9 April 1969); *Career* Aust Navy 1959-61; sr house offr Royal Nat Orthopaedic Hosp 1965, registrar Bart's 1965-67, registrar and sr registrar Robert Jones and Agnes Hunt Orthopaedic Hosp 1967-72, instr and on faculty Univ of Washington Seattle 1969-71, conslt orthopaedic surgn Harlow Wood Orthopaedic Hosp and Nottingham Univ Hosp 1972-; pres: Soc of Back Pain Res 1981-84, Int Soc for Study of the Lumbar Spine 1989-90; author pubns on aspects of low back pain and problems of the lumbar spine; memb: RSM, Br Orthopaedic Assoc; FRCS; *Books* Back Pain Methods of Clinical Investigation and Assessment (ed with D Hukins, 1986); *Recreations* sailing; *Style—* Robert Mulholland, Esq; 39 Private Rd, Sherwood, Nottingham NG5 4DD (☎ 0602 609389); 34 Regent St, Nottingham (☎ 0602 609389)

MULJI, Hon Mrs (Rosaleen Elisabeth); *née* Guinness; da of 2 Baron Moyne; *b* 1937; *Educ* St Anne's Coll Oxford (MA); *m* 1965, Sudhir Mulji; 2 s, 2 da; *Style—* The Hon Mrs Mulji; 150 Malcha Marg, New Delhi, 110021

MULKERN, John; CBE (1987), JP (Surrey 1988); s of Thomas Mulkern (d 1973), of Stretford, Manchester, and Annie Proctor, *née* Tennant (d 1984); *b* 15 Jan 1931; *Educ* Stretford GS, Harvard Business Sch; *m* 5 June 1954, May Egerton, da of Arthur Peters (d 1987), of Leatherhead, Surrey; 1 s (Neil b 1959), 3 da (Susan b 1957, Gaynor b 1962, Rosalind b 1967); *Career* Minys of Supply and Aviation (final post princ) 1949-65; Br Airports Authy 1965-87: head of fin, dep dir admin and personnel, dep gen mangr Heathrow, dir Gatwick, md and Bd memb 1977-87, chm Br Airports

International Ltd 1978-82; int aviation conslt 1987-, chm Manchester Handling Ltd 1988-; pres: Western Euro Airports Assoc 1981-83, Int Civil Airports Assoc (Europe) 1986-87; chm Airports Assocs Coordinating Cncl 1982, memb Bd Airport Operators Cncl Int 1978-81; Ordre Du Zaire 1975 (Chevalier Zaire Nouveau Civil), Malaysian Distinguished Order of Chivalry Class Five 1974, Cavalheiro Order of Rio Branco Class Five Brazil 1976, Chevalier de L'Ordre National Du Mérite France 1976; FCIT 1973 (memb Cncl 1979-82), CBIM 1981, FInstD 1982; *Recreations* travel, music, theatre; *Style—* John Mulkern, Esq, CBE, JP; Dorwyn, 23 St Mary's Rd, Leatherhead, Surrey KT22 8HB (☎ 0372 372 378)

MULLALY, Terence Frederick Stanley; s of Col Brian Reginald Mullaly (d 1965), and Eileen Dorothy Stanley (d 1973); gf Maj Gen Sir Herbert Mullaly, KCMG, CB, CSI, Cdr East Coast Defences during 1914-18 War; *b* 14 Nov 1927; *Educ* in India, England, Japan and Canada, Downing Coll Cambridge (BA, MA); *m* 1949, Elizabeth Helen, da of Frank Burkitt, of Bournemouth; *Career* art historian and art critic The Daily Telegraph 1958-86; visiting prof Finch Coll NY 1967-72; pres Br Section Int Assoc of Art Critics 1967-73, vice-chm Br Art Medal Soc 1982-87 (pres 1988-); memb: Advsy Ctee of the Cracow Art Festival 1974, Palermo Art Festival 1976, Cncl of the Attingham Summer Sch Tst 1985-, Cncl of the Derby Porcelain Int Soc 1985-88; artistic advsr of Grand Tours 1975-89, dir of Special Tours 1986, UK del to the Conference on Security and Co-op in Europe (CSCE) Cultural Forum Budapest 1985, Premio Pietro Torta per il Restauro di Venezia 1983; FSA, FRNS, FRSA; Commendat£re Ordine Al Merito della Repubblica Italiana 1974, l'Ordre du Mérite Culturel Poland 1974, OM Poland (Silver medal) 1977, SM Ordine Constantiniano di S Giorgio 1982; *Books* Ruskin a Verona (1966), catalogue of the exhibition Disegni veronesi del Cinquecento (1971), Cinquant' Anni di Pittura veronese 1580-1630 (contrib, 1974), catalogue of the exhibition Modern Hungarian Medals (ed and contrib, 1984), Caterina Cornaro, Queen of Cyprus (1989), author of articles in numerous learned jls and magazines; *Style—* Terence Mullaly, Esq; Waterside House, Lower St, Pulborough, W Sussex RH20 2BH (☎ 07982 2104)

MULLAN, Lt Cdr Charles Heron; CBE (1979), VRD (1949), DL (Co Down 1974); s of Frederick Heron Mullan, DL (d 1972), of Cairn Hill, Newry, and Minnie, *née* Broackes (d 1948); *b* 17 Feb 1912; *Educ* Castle Park Dalkey, Rossall, Clare Coll Cambridge (BA, MA); *m* 6 Sept 1940, Marcella Elizabeth Sharpe, da of James Alexander McCullagh (d 1954), of Ballycastle, Co Antrim; 1 s (Christopher Desmond Heron b 5 Sept 1947); *Career* joined RNVR 1936, Lt 1940, Lt Cdr 1948; served 1939-45 with RN: Channel, N Sea, N Atlantic; slr 1948; MP (UU) Imperial Parliament Co Down 1946-50; memb Ulster Unionist Cncl 1946-60; resident magistrate N Ireland 1960-82, stipendiary magistrate Belfast 1964-79; King Haakon VII War Decoration (Norway) 1944; *Recreations* ornithology, walking; *Style—* Lt Cdr Charles Mullan, CBE, VRD, DL; Casanbarra, Carrickmore Road, Ballycastle, Co Antrim BT54 6QS, Northern Ireland (☎ 02657 62323)

MULLARD, Paul Vivian; s of Frederick William Mullard (d 1974), and Barbara Norma, *née* Deeks; *b* 5 Sept 1952; *Educ* Bishop Vesey's GS Sutton Coldfield, Univ of Manchester (LLB); *m* 5 Jan 1980, Teresa Laurie, da of Roy Alfred Fielder (d 1976); 2 s (James b 7 Jan 1981, William b 15 Jan 1983); *Career* admitted slr 1977, ptnr Edge & Ellison 1981-; memb: Law Soc, Birmingham Law Soc (and Revenue Law Ctee); *Style—* Paul Mullard, Esq; Edge & Ellison, Rutland House, 148 Edmund St, Birmingham B3 2JR (☎ 021 200 2001, fax 021 200 1991)

MULLARKEY, David Charles; s of Daniel Francis Mullarkey, of Finchley, London, and Alice Cecelia, *née* Dillon; *b* 4 Feb 1956; *Educ* Finchley Catholic GS, Univ of Nottingham (LLB); *m* Aug 1984, Beverley Ann, da of Anthony George Carter, of Beckenham, Kent; 1 s (Daniel Nicholas b 14 Aug 1989), 1 da (Lura Ann b 10 June 1987); *Career* admitted slr 1982; Linklaters & Paines: Tax Dept 1982-84, Hong Kong Office 1984-86, ptnr 1988; memb Tax Ctee Unit Assoc; memb: Law Soc, Int Bar Assoc; *Style—* David Mullarkey, Esq

MULLEN, Dr Richard; s of Dr Richard W Mullen, of 300 McBride Ave, Paterson, NJ, USA, and Eleanor Wild Mullen; *b* 25 May 1945; *Educ* Seton Hall Univ (BA), Fordham Univ (MA), St Edmund Hall Oxford (DPhil); *Career* tutor in history and politics Univ of Oxford and London 1969-78, literary ed Christian World 1978-79, historical advsr CBS TV 1981, author numerous historical and literary features for BBC Radio 1981-, ed Contemporary Review 1991; edited: The Pamphleteer 1813-28 (29 vols, 1978), Frances Trollope Domestic Manners of the Americans (1984), Malachi's Cove and Other Stories and Essays by Anthony Trollope (1985); books: Victoria: Portrait of a Queen (with James Munson, 1987), Anthony Trollope: A Victorian in His World (1990), The Sayings of Anthony Trollope (1991); BBC documentaries and features incl progs on Queen Victoria, Anthony Trollope, Charles Lamb, John Galsworthy, William Pitt, Lord Palmerston, Scott Fitzgerald, Edward Fitzgerald; Weaver fellowship 1972; *Recreations* music, walking, reading; *Style—* Dr Richard Mullen; 27 Middle Way, Oxford OX2 7LG (☎ 0865 57831)

MULLEN, Jr, Larry; s of Larry Mullen, of Dublin, and Maureen Mullen; *b* 31 Oct 1961; *Educ* Mount Temple Sch; partner, Ann Acheson; *Career* drummer and fndr memb U2 1978-; U2 formed in Dublin with Bono, *qv* (vocals, guitar), The Edge, *qv* (guitars, piano, vocals), Adam Clayton, *qv* (bass); U2 played first London dates and released U23 (EP 1979, CBS Ireland) 1979, band signed to Island Records and released Boy (LP 1980) and three singles 1980, toured UK, US, Belguim and Holland 1980, released October (LP 1981, Silver disc) which entered UK charts at No 11 and three singles Fire, Gloria and A Celebration giving the band their first UK charts entries 1981-82, band toured extensively in UK, US, Ireland and Europe 1981-83, New Year's Day (single 1983) gave band their first UK Top Ten hit, War (LP 1983, US Gold disc) entered UK charts at No 1 and US Top Ten, band toured US and UK 1983, Under A Blood Red Sky (live album 1983, UK Platinum disc) entered UK charts at No 2, voted Band of the Year Rolling Stone Writers Poll 1984, Pride (In the Name of Love) single produced by Brian Eno and Daniel Lanois reached No 3 in UK charts gaining Silver disc 1984, band toured Aust, NZ and Europe, The Unforgettable Fire (LP 1984) entered UK charts at No 1, Unforgettable Fire (single 1985) entered UK charts at No 8; played: Madison Square Garden NY, Longest Day Festival Milton Keynes Bowl, Croke Park Dublin, Live Aid Wembley (Best Live Aid Performance Rolling Stone Readers Poll 1986) 1985; voted Best Band Rolling Stone Readers Poll 1986 (joint No 1 Critics Poll); played: Self Aid Dublin, A Conspiracy of Hope (Amnesty Int Tour) 1986; The Joshua Tree (LP 1987, Grammy award Album of the Year, 12 million worldwide sales) entered UK charts at No 1 as fastest selling album in Br music history and reached No 1 in US charts; With Or Without You (single 1987), I Still Haven't Found What I'm Looking For (single 1987), Where The Streets Have No Name (single 1987) released and entered UK charts; first three singles from The Joshua Tree reached No 1 in US charts; world tour opens Arizona 1987; 100 shows in US and Europe incl: Wembley Stadium, Madison Square Gardens NY, Sun Devil Stadium Arizona and Croke Park Dublin (winners Grammy award Best Rock Performance 1987-88); Desire (single 1988) gives U2 their first No 1 single, Rattle & Hum (LP 1988) entered UK charts at No 1, U2 play Smile Jamaica (Dominion Theatre) in aid of hurricane disaster relief 1988, world premiere U2 Rattle & Hum (film 1988) Dublin, Angel of Harlem (single 1988) entered UK charts at No 10; Grammy awards: Best Rock Performance (Desire) 1989, Best Video (Where The Streets Have No Name) 1989; When Love Comes to Town (single 1989), All I Want Is You (single 1989) released, band toured Aust 1989, New Year's Eve 1989 concert at Point Depot Dublin (broadcast live to Europe and USSR, 500 million estimated audience), recorded Night & Day for Aids benefit LP (Red, Hot & Blue) 1990; *Style—* Larry Mullen, Jr; c/o Principle Management, 30-32 Sir John Rogersons Quay, Dublin 2, Ireland (☎ 01 777 330, fax 777 276)

MULLENS, Lt-Gen Sir Anthony Richard Guy; KCB (1989), OBE (1978, MBE 1974); s of Brig Guy John de Wette Mullens, OBE (d 1981), and Gwendoline Joan, *née* Maclean; *b* 10 May 1936; *Educ* Eton, RMA Sandhurst; *m* 31 Oct 1964, Dawn Elizabeth Hermione, da of Lt-Col John Walter Pease (d 1983); *Career* cmmnd 4/7 Royal Dragoon Gds 1956, ADC to Comd 1 Br Corps 1958-60, Adj 1963, Staff Coll Camberley 1967-68, MOD 1968-70, regtl duty 1970-72, Bde Maj 1972, dir of staff Staff Coll 1973-76, CO 4/7 Royal Dragoon Gds 1976-78, HQ BAOR 1978-80, Comd Cdr 7 Armd Brigade 1980-82, MOD 1982-85, GOC 1 Armd Div 1985, MOD 1987; Dep Chief of Def Staff (Systems) 1989-; Liveryman: Worshipful Co of Armourers and Brasiers 1974, Worshipful Co of Coachmakers & Coach Harness Makers 1977; Niedersachsen Verdienst Kreuz (Am Bande 1982, First Class 1987); *Recreations* travel, riding, skiing; *Clubs* Cavalry and Guards, Hurlingham; *Style—* Lt-Gen Sir Anthony Mullens, KCB, OBE; c/o Lloyds Bank, Guards & Cavalry Section, 6 Pall Mall, London SW1

MULLENS, Peter Arthur Glanville; OBE (1985); s of George Glanville Mullens (d 1969), and Mabel Lavinia; *b* 16 March 1925; *Educ* Llandovery Coll, Sidney Sussex Coll Cambridge; *m* 5 April 1952, Edwina Mary, da of Dr Rufus John Isaac (d 1978); 1 s (William b 1953), 2 da (Fiona b 1956, Lynette b 1961); *Career* RAF 1943-47, Accountant Offr 1945-47, served Hong Kong, Shanghai, Fl-Lt; CA; ptnr Mullen & Robinson 1953-90, ret; conslt Mullens & Robinson 1990-; memb: Port Talbot Incorporated C-of-C, Ct and Cncl Univ of Wales; vice pres Univ Coll of Swansea; FCA 1951; *Recreations* reading, walking, riding; *Style—* Peter Mullens, Esq, OBE; Archways, 2 Stratford Drive, Porthcawl, Mid Glamorgan CF36 3LG (☎ 0656 771 639); Mullens & Robinson, 18 Station Rd, West Glamorgan SA13 1B4 (☎ 0639 885 203)

MULLER, Franz Joseph; QC (1978); s of Wilhelm Muller (d 1982), and Anne Maria Muller, *née* Ravens; *b* 19 Nov 1938; *Educ* Mount St Mary's Coll, Univ of Sheffield (LLB); *m* 1985, Helena, da of Mieczyslaw Bartosz; 1 s (Julian b 1986); *Career* graduate apprentice Utd Steel Cos 1960-61, commercial assoc Workington Iron & Steel Co Ltd 1961-63; barr 1964, recorder Crown Ct 1977; non exec dir: Richards of Sheffield Hldgs plc 1969-77, Satinsteel Ltd 1970-77, Rodgers Wostenholm Ltd 1975-77; memb SRC Univ Coll Durham 1981, govr Mount St Mary's Coll 1984-86; *Recreations* fell walking, listening to music, skiing; *Style—* Franz Muller, Esq, QC; Sheffield (☎ 0742 669187); Witherslack, Cumbria (☎ 044 852 492); 11 Kings Bench Walk, Temple, London EC4 (☎ 071 353 3337)

MULLETT, (Aidan) Anthony; QPM (1982); s of Bartholomew Joseph Mullett (d 1976), and Mary Kate, *née* Sheehan (d 1980); *b* 24 May 1933; *Educ* Moat Boys Sch Leicester; *m* 7 Sept 1957, Monica Elizabeth, da of Paul Gerald Coney (d 1968); 1 s (Philip b 1963), 1 da (Beverley b 1958); *Career* RAF 1950-56; Leicester City Police 1957, Leicestershire and Rutland Constabulary 1966, asst Chief Constable West Mercia Constabulary 1975, dep Chief Constable Dyfed Powys Police 1982, Chief Constable West Mercia Constabulary 1985; chm: Assoc of Chief Police Offrs Crime Ctee, Hereford and Worcester Outward Bound Assoc; pres Shropshire Outward Bound Assoc; memb Hereford Worcester and Shropshire St John Ambulance Cncl, vice pres Hereford and Worcester Co Scout Cncl; *Recreations* golf; *Clubs* Weston-super-Mare Golf, Evesham GC; *Style—* Anthony Mullett, Esq, QPM; West Mercia Constabulary, Police Headquarters, Hindlip Hall, Worcester WR3 8SP (☎ 0905 723 000, fax 0905 54 226)

MULLEY, Hon Corinne; *née* Stevens; da of Baron Mulley (Life Baron); continues to be known by maiden name; *b* 1953; *m* 1983, Nicholas Stevens, of Stafford; *Style—* The Hon Corinne Mulley

MULLEY, Baron (Life Peer UK 1984), of Manor Park in the City of Sheffield; Frederick William Mulley; PC (1964); eldest s of late William Mulley, of Leamington Spa; *b* 3 July 1918; *Educ* Bath Place C of E Sch, Warwick Sch, ChCh Oxford; *m* 1948, Joan Doreen, da of Alexander Morris Phillips, of London; 2 da (Hon Deirdre b 1951, Hon Corinne b 1953); *Career* served WWII, Worcs Regt (POW Germany 1940-45); fell St Catharine's Coll Cambridge 1948-50, called to the Bar Inner Temple 1954; MP (Lab) Sheffield Park 1950-83, PPS to Min of Works 1951, dep sec of state for def and min of def for army 1964-65, min of aviation 1965-67, jt min state Foreign and Cwlth Office 1967-69, min of disarmament 1967-69, min of tport 1969-70 and 1974-75, sec of state for educn and sci 1975-76, sec of state for def 1976-79, pres Assembly of WEU 1980-83; memb Nat Exec Ctee Lab Pty 1957-58, 1960-64 and 1965-80, chm Lab Pty 1974-75, a vice pres Peace Through NATO 1985-; dep chm Sheffield Development 1988-; *Style—* The Rt Hon the Lord Mulley, PC; 3 Denny Crescent, London SE11 4UY

MULLIGAN, Andrew Armstrong; s of Col Hugh Waddell Mulligan, CMG, MD, DSc (d 1982), and Beatrix Aimee Armstrong; Mulligans settled in Co Down Ulster in 1610, prominent landowners, in professions and Presbyterian Church; *b* 4 Feb 1936; *Educ* Gresham Sch Norfolk, Magdalene Coll Cambridge (rugby blue, MA); *m* 1964, Pia Ursula, da of Eiler Theodore Schiuler; 4 da (Fionn, Maia, Joachim, Kate); *Career* pres: Mulligan Communications Inc, Service de Television Mitgrational; former dir (min and cnsllr) Delgn of Cmmn of Euro Communities Washington DC, sec gen EEC Cmmn Brussels, former prodr and reporter BBC Panorama and ITN, foreign corr Observer Paris, memb Irish Wanderers Ulster, capt Irish Rugby Team 1960; memb: Br Lions Aust and NZ 1959, Barbarians Canada 1957 and SA 1958; *Recreations* tennis, skiing, landscape painting, yacht ('Wildgoose'); *Clubs* Kildare Univ (Dublin), Hawks (Cambridge); *Style—* Andrew Mulligan, Esq; 1855 Shepherd St, Washington DC 20011, USA

MULLIGAN, Reginald Graham; s of Frederick George Mulligan, of Marbella, Spain, and Gladys Mulligan; *b* 4 Dec 1944; *Educ* Ottershaw Sch, Coll of Air Trg Hamble; *m* 10 Nov 1974, Linda Mary, da of Lenord Wood; 2 s (Maxwell Thomas b 6 Dec 1976, Daniel Graham b 24 April 1979); *Career* pilot: BEA 1965-66, BOAC 1966-78; chm Fairflight 1978-; *Recreations* golf; *Clubs* Royal MD Surrey Golf; *Style—* Reginald Mulligan, Esq; Fairflight Ltd, Biggin Hill Airport, nr Westerham, Kent TN16 3B (☎ 0959 74651, fax 0959 71929)

MULLIGAN, Dr Rosemary Anne; da of Lawrence Alfred Mulligan, of Selsey, Chichester, Sussex, and Mary, *née* Munro; *Educ* Roseberry GS Epsom Surrey, Royal Free Hosp Sch of Med Univ of London (BSc, MB BS, MD); *m* Alan James King, s of Alan George King (d 1976), of Northampton; 1 s (Alistair Lawrence b 18 June 1967), 1 da (Katharine Jane b 19 Oct 1965); *Career* res fell Dept of Med Royal Free Hosp 1965-67, registrar and sr registrar Royal Free and Brompton Hosps 1967-73, conslt physician with an interest in chest disease Queen Elizabeth Hosp King's Lynn 1973-; E Anglian regnl post grad dean Faculty of Med Univ of Cambridge 1986-; memb: Br Thoracic Soc, Nat Tst; friend and sponsor Kings Lynn Centre for the Arts, Kings

Lynn Festival of Music at the Arts; FRCP 1978 (MRCP 1965); *Recreations* skiing, tennis, music, reading, gardening, Italy; *Style—* Dr Rosemary Mulligan; Queen Elizabeth Hospital, Gayton Rd, King's Lynn, Norfolk PE30 4ET (☎ 0553 766266)

MULLIN, Christopher John (Chris); MP (Lab) Sunderland South 1987-; s of Leslie Mullin, and Theresa, *née* Foley; *b* 12 Dec 1947; *Educ* St Joseph's (De La Salle) Birkfield, Univ of Hull (LLB); *m* 1987 Nguyen Thi Ngoc, da of Nguyen Tang Minh, of Kontum, Vietnam; 1 da (Sarah b 2 Nov 1989); *Career* trainee scheme Mirror Group Newspapers 1969-71, Parly candidate (Lab) North Devon 1970, freelance journalist 1972-74, Parly Candidate (Lab) Kingston upon Thames 1974, BBC World Service 1974-78, Freelance Journalist 1978-82, ed Tribune 1982-84, author 1984-87; *Publications* The Tibetans (1981), How to Select or Reselect your MP (1981), A Very British Coup (1982), The Last Man Out of Saigon (1986), Error of Judgement The Truth about the Birmingham Pub Bombings (1986), The Year of the Fire Monkey (1991); *Recreations* walking, talking, travelling; *Style—* Chris Mullin, Esq, MP

MULLIN, Geoffrey Kenneth; s of Kenneth Mullin (d 1986), of Garstang, Lancs, and Lily, *née* Butcher (d 1976); *b* 11 Sept 1942; *Educ* Burnage GS for Boys Manchester, Royal Victoria Coll of Music (Dip); *m* 5 Dec 1970 (m dis 1989), Caroline Moira, da of William Frederick Irving Stephenson (d 1988), of Henley, Oxon; 1 da (Crystal b 1973); *Career* schoolteacher 1960-61, civil servant 1962-64, professional musician, singer, songwriter with recordings for DECCA and CBS 1964-68; advertising mangr and journalist 1968-70: Record Mirror, Music Week, Billboard; freelance prodr with BBC 1970-73, record prodr for various artists incl Marmalade and the Troggs 1970-73; prodr BBC Radio Two 1973-: Simon Bates 1973-74, Jack Jackson, Terry Wogan 1975-79, David Hamilton 1979-80, Kenny Everett 1980-82, Sounds of the Sixties (Keith Fordyce) 1983-84, Ken Bruce 1985-86, Your Hundred Best Tunes (Michael Aspel and Alan Keith) 1987, Anne Robinson, Michael Aspel, The Earl Spencer, Wally Whyton 1988-90, Jimmy Young 1991; *Recreations* squash, skiing, reading, travel, music, films, theatre; *Style—* Geoffrey Mullin, Esq; 36 Brooklands Court, Hatfield Rd, St Albans, Herts AL1 3NS (☎ 0727 48222); Western House, 99 Great Portland St, London W1A 1AA (☎ 071 927 4573, fax 071 436 5247)

MULLIN, Prof John William; s of Frederick Mullin (d 1972), of Queen's Ferry, Chester, and Kathleen Nellie, *née* Oppy (d 1988); *b* 22 Aug 1925; *Educ* Hawarden Co Sch, Univ Coll Cardiff (BSc, DSc), UCL (PhD); *m* 22 Aug 1952, Averil Margaret, da of William Davies (d 1971), of Cwmgwili, Camarthen; 1 s (Jonathan b 1957), 1 da (Susan b 1960); *Career* RAF 1945-48; UCL: lectr chemical engrg 1956-61, reader 1961-69, prof 1969-85, Ramsay meml prof and head of dept 1985-90, dean of engrg 1975-77, vice provost 1980-86; dean of engrg Univ of London 1980-85; memb Ct of Govrs Univ Coll Cardiff 1982-, vice chm Cncl Sch of Pharmacy 1988 (memb 1983-); winner of Moulton medal Inst of Chem Engrs 1970; Dr (hon causa) Institut National Polytechnique de Toulouse 1989; Freeman City of London 1984, memb Worshipful Co of Engrs 1984; fell: Univ Coll Cardiff 1981, UCL 1981; FRSC (1958), FIChemE 1959, FEng 1983; *Books* Crystallization (2 edn, 1972), Industrial Crystallization (ed, 1976); *Recreations* gardening; *Clubs* Athenaeum; *Style—* Prof John Mullin; 4 Milton Rd, Ickenham, Uxbridge, Middx UB10 8NQ; Department of Chemical Engineering, UCL, Torrington Place, London WC1E 7JE (☎ 071 387 7050)

MULLINER, Stephen Nigel; s of Dr Gerald Norman Mulliner, of Osmington, Weymouth, Dorset, and Kathleen Wilma, *née* Ritchie; *b* 4 Sept 1953; *Educ* Downside, Emmanuel Coll Cambridge (MA, LLB), Inns of Court Sch of Law; *m* 18 Aug 1979, Sarah Lucinda, da of Lt-Col John Arthur Speirs, of Coombe Bissett, Salisbury, Wilts; 2 s (Andrew b 1983, Jonathan b 1985), 2 da (Lucy b 1983, Charlotte b 1989); *Career* called to the Bar 1978; assoc dir SBCI Swiss Bank Corporation Investment Banking Ltd 1987-89, gen mangr Tokai International Ltd 1989-, non exec chm James Smith Estates plc 1989- (non exec dir 1988 and 1990); Br Open Croquet Champion 1988, President's Cup Winner 1981, 1983, 1986 and 1987, Men's Champion 1985 and 1986, World Invitation Singles Champion 1986 1987 and 1988, Br Open Doubles Champion 1980 1981 1984 1986 and 1988; chm The Croquet Assoc 1990-; *Books* The World of Croquet (1987), Play The Game - Croquet (1989); *Recreations* croquet, golf, bell ringing, running, computing; *Clubs* Roehampton; *Style—* Stephen Mulliner, Esq; Witherden, Weydown Rd, Haslemere, Surrey GU27 1DT; Tokai International Ltd, Mercury Hse, Triton Ct, 14 Finsbury Sq, London EC2 (☎ 071 638 6030)

MULLINS, Alan; s of Philip Mullins, of Herts, and Betty Mullins (d 1981); *b* 29 July 1987; *Educ* Christ's Coll Finchley, LSE; *m* 15 Feb 1974, Elizabeth Anne, da of Eric Victor Aylott, of Herts; 2 da (Elizabeth Anne b 1954, Geraldine b 1957); *Career* dir: Baco Aluminium Supply Co Ltd 1963-69, Skymetals Ltd 1979-; *Recreations* 3 day eventing, squash, skiing; *Style—* Alan Mullins, Esq; Beech House, Benington, Herts; Skymetals Ltd, Enterprise Way, Four Ashes, Staffs (☎ 0902 791919, fax 0902 791950)

MULLINS, Anthony Roy (Tony); s of Royston George Mullins (d 1985), and Evelyn Hilda Mullins; *b* 20 Sept 1939; *Educ* Loughton Sch, SW Sussex Tech Coll, London Sch of Printing; *m* 1964, Patricia Janet, da of Leslie John Stone (d 1973); 2 s (John b 1969, Benjamin b 1973), 1 da (Nichola b 1971); *Career* art asst: BDMW Design Group 1960-61, Sunday Times Magazine 1962-64; art ed: The Observer Magazine 1967-76 (art asst 1964-67), The Observer Newspaper 1976-; winner of various D&AD awards for magazine work and newspaper design awards (jtly); *Recreations* few; *Style—* Tony Mullins, Esq; 19 Longdene Road, Haslemere, Surrey GU27 2PG (☎ 0428 652535); The Observer, Chelsea Bridge House, Queenstown Rd, London SW8 4NN (☎ 071 627 0700, fax 071 627 5570)

MULLINS, Edwin Brandt; s of Claud William Mullins (d 1968), and Elizabeth Gwendolen, *née* Brandt; *b* 14 Sept 1933; *Educ* Midhurst GS, Merton Coll Oxford (BA, MA); *m* 1, 1960, Gillian (d 1982); 1 s (Jason), 2 da (Frances, Selina); m 2, 1984, Anne; *Career* author, tv and radio scriptwriter; TV series incl: 100 Great Paintings, The Great Art Collection, A Love Affair with Nature, Masterworks, Paradise on Earth, Montparnasse Revisited; *Books* Alfred Wallis (1967), Braque (1968), The Pilgrimage to Santiago (1974), Sirens (1983), The Painted Witch (1985), The Golden Bird (1987), The Lands of the Sea (1988); *Recreations* art galleries, reading, walking, natural history, watching cricket; *Style—* Edwin Mullins, Esq; 7 Lower Common South, London SW15 1BP

MULLINS, Brig Keith Alexander; s of Reginald Mullins (d 1983), of Yeovil, Somerset, and Mabel Phylis, *née* Rochester (d 1989); *b* 9 March 1937; *Educ* Porchester Sch Bournemouth, Univ of Exeter (BA, CBiol); *m* 1, 16 Dec 1961 (m dis 1985), Janet; 1 s (Stephen John b 16 Oct 1964), 1 da (Vanessa Louise b 22 June 1967); m 2, 8 Jan 1986, Carolyn Margaret, da of George William Charlton Thompson, of Newcastle-upon-Tyne; *Career* RAF (Suez Campaign 1956) 1955-58, Army 1963- (Lt 1963); schoolmaster 1961-63, Nat Def Coll 1979 (NDC), CO 1 Ord Bn 1981-83 (Lt Col) 1 Armd Div, DCOS Falklands 1983-84 (Col) HQ BFI, DA Jakarta 1985-87 (Col) British Embassy, ACOS Cyprus 1987-89 (Col) HQ BF Cyprus, dir DSCS 1989- (Brig) Bicester; memb Nat Computing Centre (NCC), FBIM 1985, MIBiol 1984; *Recreations* reading, farming, tennis, war games; *Clubs* The Naval Club; *Style—* Brig Keith Mullins; Rochester House, Lower Easthams, nr Crewkerne, Somerset TA18 7NU; Director of Supply Computer Services, Ministry of Defence, Arncott, Bicester, Oxon OX6 OLP (☎ 0869 253311)

MULLINS, Hon Mrs (Sarah Virginia); *née* Samuel; o da of 4 Viscount Bearsted, MC, TD, *qv*; *b* 1947; *m* 1, 1969 (m dis), Duncan John Lloyd Fitzwilliams, yr s of late Charles Collinsplatt Fitzwilliams, TD, JP, DL, of Cilgwyn, Newcastle Emlyn, S Wales; m 2, 1980, Brian Mullins; *Style—* The Hon Mrs Mullins; c/o The Rt Hon Viscount Bearsted, MC, TD, Farley Hall, Farley Hill, nr Reading, Berks RG7 1UL

MULLOCK, David; s of Denis Wilson Mullock, of Southwold, Suffolk, and Peggy, *née* Westray (d 1983); *b* 20 Dec 1935; *Educ* Uppingham, Emmanuel Coll Cambridge (BA); *m* 17 Oct 1964, Hilary Jean, da of Henry Samuel Wills (d 1944); 1 s (James b 15 April 1969), 1 da (Charlotte b 10 Dec 1971); *Career* 2 Lt 1 Bn Suffolk Regt 1954-56; Shell International Petroleum Co Ltd 1959-60, Lustre Fibres 1960-61; admitted slr 1964; Coward Chance 1961-67, ptnr Norton Rose 1969- (joined 1967, managing ptnr 1982-87); Freeman City of London 1973; memb Law Soc 1967; *Recreations* music, literature, wine; *Clubs* Oriental, City Univ; *Style—* David Mullock, Esq; Norton Rose, Kempson House, Camomile St, London EC3A 7AN (☎ 071 283 2434, fax 071 588 1181)

MUMFORD, Lady Mary Katharine; *née* Fitzalan Howard; CVO (1982, LVO 1974); da of 16 Duke of Norfolk, KG, GCVO, GBE, TD, PC (d 1975); hp to Lordship of Herries of Terregles; *b* 14 Aug 1940; *m* 1986, Gp Capt Anthony Mumford, CVO, OBE; *Career* lady-in-waiting to HRH Princess Alexandra, the Hon Lady Ogilvy, GCVO 1964-; *Style—* The Lady Mary Mumford, CVO; North Stoke Cottage, North Stoke, Arundel, W Sussex; Lantonside, Glencaple, Dumfries

MUMFORD, William Frederick; CB (1989); s of Frederick Charles Mumford (d 1968), and Hester Leonora, *née* Hunter (d 1973); *b* 1930; *Educ* St Albans Sch, Lincoln Coll Oxford (MA); *m* 1958, Elizabeth Marion, da of Nowell Hall (d 1977); 3 s (Richard b 1963, Timothy b 1965, Simon b 1968), 1 da (Lucy b 1970); *Career* Nat Serv RA 1949-50 (Lt); Home Civil Serv (Air Miny) 1953-: asst princ 1953-58, princ 1958-60, 1 sec UK Delgn to NATO (Paris) 1960-65, princ 1965-67, asst sec 1967-73, def secretarial MOD, dep head UK Delgn to MBFR Exploratory Talks (Vienna) 1973, princ private sec to Sec of State for Def 1973-75, under sec Machinery of Govt Div, CS Dept 1975-76; asst sec-gen for Def Planning and Policy, NATO (Brussels) 1976-80, asst under-sec of state MOD 1980-89, acting dep under-sec of state 1989, memb Chm's Panel Civil Serv Selection Bd 1989-; *Recreations* book collecting, music; *Style—* William Mumford, Esq, CB; c/o Ministry of Defence, London SW1

MUMMERY *see also*: Lockhart-Mummery

MUMMERY, Sir John Frank; s of Frank Stanley Mummery, of Bridge, Kent, and Ruth, *née* Coleman; *b* 5 Sept 1938; *Educ* Oakleigh House, Dover Co GS, Pembroke Coll Oxford (MA, BCL); *m* 11 March 1967, Elizabeth Anne Lamond, da of Dr Glyn Lackie (d 1985), of Edinburgh; 1 s (David b 1974), 1 da (Joanna b 1968); *Career* Nat Serv Border Regt RAEC 1957-59; called to the Bar Gray's Inn 1964, bencher 1985, rec 1989, High Ct judge Chancery Div 1989-; counsel attorney gen in charity matters 1977-81, jr treasy counsel Chancery 1981-89; memb Legal Advsy Cmmn of Gen Synod of C of E 1988-; hon fell Pembroke Coll Oxford 1989; jt ed Copinger and Skone on Copyright (13 edn, 1991); kt 1989; *Recreations* long walks with family, friends and alone; *Style—* Sir John Mummery; Royal Courts of Justice, Strand, London WC2A 2LL

MUNASINGHE, (Leelananda) Sepala; s of Lairis Appu Munasinghe, of Kurunegala, Sri Lanka, and Joslyn, *née* Samarasinghe (d 1990); *b* 2 Jan 1937; *Educ* Trinity Coll Kandy Sri Lanka; *m* 21 May 1964, Dorothea Brunhildis, da of Wilhelm Karger (d 1968), of Ostbevern, Germany; 2 da (Karin b 1965, Gitanjali b 1968); *Career* called to the Bar Lincoln's Inn 1963; advocate Surpreme Court of Ceylon 1964, attorney at law Supreme Court of Sri Lanka 1972, chm Social Security Appeals Tribunal UK 1986; govr Waldegrave Sch for Girls 1980-83, memb Birmingham City Cncl Public Inquiry into Handsworth Riots 1986; *Recreations* cooking, reading, travelling; *Clubs* Capri (Colombo); *Style—* Sepala Munasinghe, Esq; 235 London Rd, Twickenham, Middx TW1 1ES (☎ 081 892 5947); 5 Essex Court, Temple, London EC4Y 9AH (☎ 071 353 4363, fax 071 583 1491)

MUNDAM, Eric Alec; s of John Munday (d 1978), of London E17, and Katherine Munday, *née* Jessup (d 1982); *b* 7 Oct 1927; *Educ* Sir George Monoux GS (FCA); *m* 17 Dec 1950, Margaret Elizabeth, da of Ernest Wilson, of London E17; 2 s (Jonathan b 1959, Jeremy b 1962); *Career* war service; HO Naval Air Mechanic 1946-48; CA; Plessey Co 1957-83, Rosenthal China Ltd 1955-57; cncllr Heath Park Ward London Branch (chm Planning Ctee); Dep Mayor 1984, Mayor 1985; *Recreations* bringing up grandson; *Clubs* Romford Conservative; *Style—* Eric A Mundam, Esq; 25 Pettits Lane, Romford, Essex (☎ 0708 20575)

MUNDAY, Norman Sidney; s of Sidney Ernest Munday, of Chingford, E4, and Phyllis May, *née* Morris (d 1979); *b* 8 July 1935; *Educ* Sir George Monoux GS (AIWSc); *m* 22 Nov 1958, Pauline Lily Elizabeth, da of George Charles Butler (d 1973), of Walthamstow E17; 1 s (Adam b 1963), 1 da (Amanda b 1959); *Career* chm Tower Timber Group Ltd 1975-91, hon chm Timber Res & Devpt Assoc 1986-88; chm and md Clanwood Ltd, chm Indo Turm Ltd; memb: GLC 1967-73, Ct of Assts Guild of Freemen City of London, Inst of Directors, AIWSc; *Recreations* golf, travel; *Clubs* West Essex Golf (capt 1984), City Livery; *Style—* Norman Munday, Esq; Birkdale, Hornbeam Lane, Sewardstone Bury, London E4 7QJ; Indo Turm Ltd, 77-79 Station Road, Chingford, London E4 7BU (☎ 081 524 5285, telex 896 864)

MUNDAY, Peter James; s of Frederick Lewis James Munday (d 1987), of Esher, Surrey, and Lily Charlotte Rebecca, *née* Fowler; *b* 31 Oct 1938; *m* 1 (m dis 1984), Inger Kristina Fageresjo; 1 da (Lisa Kristina b 1975); m 2, 22 Dec 1984, Linda Ann (Lin), da of Leslie Breckon, of 102 Wenalt Rd, Cardiff; 2 da (Emma Sophie b 1986, Zara Jane b 1989); *Career* Nat Serv RCS 1957-59; admitted slr 1968, sr ptnr Mundays 1976- (ptnr 1968-); NP 1975; chm & tstee The Princess Alice Hospice Esher; tstee: Esher War Meml Property Fund, the Friends of St Georges Church Esher, The Hospice Education Centre Trust; Freeman City of London, Liveryman Worshipful Co of Bakers; memb: Law Soc 1968, Notaries Soc 1975; *Recreations* hockey, squash, cricket; *Clubs* MCC; *Style—* Peter Munday, Esq; Pinewood Lodge, Warren Lane, Oxshott, Surrey (☎ 0372 467272); Crown House, Church Road, Claygate, Esher, Surrey (☎ 0372 467272, fax 0372 463782)

MUNDAY, Eur Ing Raymond Geoffrey Todd; s of John Dale Munday (d 1925), of Lancs, and Florence Adelaide, *née* Worthington (d 1980); *b* 15 March 1922; *Educ* King George V Sch Southport (BSc), RCS London; *m* 14 Sept 1946, Angela Catherine, da of Horace Clive Burdett (d 1964); 1 s (David b 1947), 2 da (Catherine b 1954, Rosemary b 1958); *Career* aerospace engr Bristol Aeroplane Co 1949, chartered engr 1968; Br Aerospace: dir of electronic and space systems (Bristol) 1978, dir and gen mangr Space and Communications Div Stevenage 1981, ret 1984; chm UK Industl Space Ctee 1982-84, Eur Ing 1988, currently conslt and UK rep Arianespace; ARCS, FRAeS; *Clubs* Naval; *Style—* Eur Ing Raymond G T Munday; 53 High St, Ashwell, Herts SG7 5NP (☎ 0462 742760)

MUNDEN, Michael Ronald; s of Alfred Gilburt Munden, of bridport, Dorset, and Sheila Munden; *b* 8 Jan 1946; *Educ* Hardyes Sch, Univ of Aix Marseille, Univ of Southampton (LLB); *m* 30 Oct 1971, Sally Léontine, step da of Dr Peter McGregor; 2 s (Thomas b 27 May 1978, Marc b 19 June 1980); *Career* ptnr Herbert Smith (joined 1970); Freeman City of London Slrs' Co; memb Law Soc 1970; *Recreations* riding, tennis, amateur farming; *Clubs* RAC; *Style—* Michael Munden, Esq; Bricky Farm,

Toller Porcorum, Dorset (☎ 0300 20868); Herbert Smith, Exchange House, Primrose St, London EC2

MUNDY, Anthony Richard; s of Peter Gordon Mundy, of Bedford Ave, London, and Betty, *née* Hall; *b* 25 April 1948; *Educ* Mill Hill Sch, Univ of London (MB BS, MS); *m* 20 Sept 1975, Marilyn June, da of Edward Ashton, of South Ockendon, Essex; 1 s (Harry b 1986), 1 da (Emily b 1977); *Career* CO and conslt surgn Muscat Oman 1977-78, conslt urological surgn Lewisham Hosp 1981-86, sr lectr in urology UMDS 1981-, conslt urological surgn Guy's Hosp 1981-, sr lectr in urology and conslt urological surgn Inst of Urology 1986-; ctee memb Br Assoc Urological Surgns; MRCP 1974, FRCS 1975; *Books* Urodynamics: Principles Practice and Application (1984), Scientific Basis of Urology (1986), Current Operative Surgery-Urology (1988); *Style—* Anthony Mundy, Esq

MUNDY, Lady Bridget; *née* Elliot-Murray-Kynynmound; da of 5 Earl of Minto (d 1975); *b* 1921; *m* 1, 1944, Lt-Col James Averell Clark, Jr, DFC, USAF; 1 s (Christopher); m 2, 1954 (m dis 1963), Maj Henry Claude Lyon Garnett, CBE; m 3, 1966 (m dis 1970), Maj (Edward) Peter Godfrey Miller Mundy, MC; *Style—* The Lady Bridget Mundy

MUNFORD, Dr William Arthur; MBE (1946); s of Ernest Charles Munford (d 1948), of London, and Florence Margaret, *née* Dinneen (d 1959); *b* 27 April 1911; *Educ* Hornsey Co Sch, LSE (BSc, PhD); *m* 25 Aug 1934, Hazel Despard, da of Frank Arthur Wilmer (d 1956), of London; 2 s ((Arthur) Michael b 1935, Jeremy b 1940), 1 da ((Linda) Alison Cynthia b 1945); *Career* borough librarian Dover 1934-45, food exec offr and emergency feeding organiser Dover 1939-45, city librarian Cambridge 1945-53, dir gen and librarian Nat Library for the Blind 1954-82 (librarian emeritus 1982-); tstee Ulverscroft Fndn, memb Soc of Bookmen; FLA 1933, Hon FLA 1977-; *Books* Books for Basic Stock (1939), Penny Rate (1951), William Ewart MP (1960), Edward Edwards (1963), Louis Stanley Jast (with W G Fry, 1966), James Duff Brown (1968), A History of the Library Association 1877-1977 (1976), The Incomparable Mac: Sir J Y W Macalister (with S Godbolt, 1983), Who Was Who in British Librarianship 1800-1985 (1987); *Recreations* reading, writing, rough gardening, wood sawing, cycling, serendipity; *Clubs* National Liberal; *Style—* Dr William Munford, MBE; 11 Manor Court, Pinehurst, Grange Rd, Cambridge CB3 9BE (☎ 0223 62962)

MUNIR, (Ashley) Edward; s of The Hon Sir Mehmed Munir, CBE (d 1957), and Vessime, *née* Ziai (d 1979); *b* 14 Feb 1934; *Educ* Brentwood, St John's Coll Cambridge MA, King's Coll London (MPhil); *m* 6 June 1960, Sureyya, da of Shukri Dormen, of Istanbul, Turkey; 1 s (Simon b 24 Oct 1964); *Career* called to the Bar Gray's Inn 1956, crown counsel 1960-64, legal asst Govt Legal Serv 1964, under sec MAFF 1982 (asst slr 1975); *Books* Perinatal Rights (1983); *Recreations* walking, playing the double-bass, listening to music; *Clubs* United Oxford and Cambridge Univ; *Style—* Edward Munir, Esq; 55 White Hall, London SW1 (☎ 071 270 8369)

MUNKENBECK, Alfred Hedges III; s of Alfred Hedges Munkenbeck Jr, of Old Greenwich, Connecticut, USA, and Adelaide Celina, *née* Rickert; *b* 26 March 1947; *Educ* Le Rosey Rolle Switzerland, The Canterbury Sch USA, Dartmouth Coll USA (BA), Harvard (MArch); *Career* architect; worked with James Stirling Architects on Stuttgart Contemporary Art Museum 1977-80, conslt for new towns and palaces Saudi Arabia 1980-85; sr ptnr Munkenbeck & Marshall 1985-; projects incl: Raymond Review Bar, Yohji Yamamoto shop Sloane St, Health Club Point W apartments Kensington, office buildings at Jessica Sq Wandsworth and 87 Lancaster Rd, Notting Hill, golf resort Bahrain, private houses for Charles Saatchi and Norman Parkinson London; lectr in architectural design: Univ of Cambridge, Kingston Poly, The AA; author of articles on Munkenbeck & Marshall in relevant pubns; memb RIBA 1980; *Recreations* skiing, sailing; *Clubs* Groucho, The Architecture Club; *Style—* Alfred Munkenbeck, Esq; Munkenbeck & Marshall, 113-117 Farringdon Rd, London EC1 R3BT

MUNN, Geoffrey Thomas; s of Leslie Morris Munn (d 1967), of Carshalton Beeches, Surrey, and Dorothy Isabel Blanche *née* Thomas (d 1983); *b* 1 Nov 1933; *Educ* Wallington Co G S; *m* 18 July 1959, Ann Rebbeca, da of Vincent Wood (d 1961), of Fetcham, Surrey; 1 s (Nigel b 1965), 1 da (Nicola (Mrs Selby) b 1964); *Career* Midland Bank 1950-68, Morgan Grenfell & Co Ltd 1968-: dir 1976-, head treasy 1986-, gp dir treasy 1989-; chm London Forex Assoc 1978-80; Assoc Cambiste Internationale: sec-gen 1980-83, pres 1983-86, hon pres 1986-; *Recreations* soccer, golf, horticulture; *Style—* Geoffrey Munn, Esq; Cornerways, Meadow Way, W Horsley, Surrey (☎ 04865 2692); Morgan Grenfell & Co Ltd, 23 Great Winchester St, London EC2P 2AX (☎ 071 826 7793, fax 071 588 5598, telex 8951841)

MUNN, Sir James; OBE (1976); s of Douglas Herbert Hamilton Munn (d 1973), and Margaret Graham, *née* Dunn (d 1965); *b* 27 July 1920; *Educ* Stirling HS, Univ of Glasgow (MA); *m* 1946, Muriel Jean Millar, da of Norman MacLeod Moles (d 1964); 1 da (Elizabeth); *Career* Indian Civil Serv 1941-48, dep sec Supply Dept Govt of Bihar; teacher 1948-83; rector: Rutherglen Acad 1966-70, Cathkin HS 1970-83; chm: Consultative Ctee on the Curriculum 1980-87, Manpower Servs Ctee for Scotland 1984-88, Manpower Servs Cmmn 1987-88, Univ cmmr 1988-; Officier d' Académie (1967); *Style—* Sir James Munn, OBE; 4 Kincath Avenue, Rutherglen, Glasgow G73 4RP (☎ 041 634 4654)

MUNN, Prof Robert William; s of William Anderson Munn (d 1989), and Kathleen Maud, *née* Bishop (d 1981); *b* 16 Jan 1945; *Educ* Huish's GS Taunton, Univ of Bristol (BSc, PhD), Univ of Manchester (DSc); *m* 24 June 1967, Patricia Lorna, da of Robert William Moyle (d 1965); 1 s (Nicholas b 1971), 1 da (Philippa b 1974); *Career* postdoctorate fell Nat Res Cncl of Canada 1968-70, ICI Postdoctoral fell Univ of Edinburgh 1970-71, visiting fell Aust Nat Univ 1982, vice princ UMIST 1987-90 (lectr 1971-80, reader 1980-84, prof of chemical physics 1984-); coordinating ed Jl of Molecular Electronics 1985-, numerous pubns in scientific jls; FRSC, CChem 1987, FInstP, CPhys 1987; *Books* Molecular Electromagnetism (with A Hinchliffe); *Recreations* guitar, linguistics; *Style—* Prof Robert Munn; Dept of Chemistry, UMIST, PO Box 88, Manchester M60 1QD (☎ 061 200 4534, fax 061 200 4484, telex 666094 UMIST G)

MUNRO; *see*: Gun-Munroe

MUNRO, HE Sir Alan Gordon; KCMG (1990, CMG 1984); s of Sir Gordon Munro, KCMG, MC (d 1967), and Lilian Muriel, *née* Beit (d 1976); *b* 17 Aug 1935; *Educ* Wellington, Clare Coll Cambridge (MA); *m* 1962, Rosemary Grania, da of Cdr N A Bacon; 2 s (twins), 2 da; *Career* HM Dip Serv; consul gen Rio de Janerio 1974-77, FCO head of East African Dept 1977-78, head of Middle East Dept 1979, head of Personnel Operations Dept 1979-81, dir of Def Sales MoD, ME 1981-83, HM ambass Algiers 1984-87, dep under sec of state FCO 1987-89, HM ambass Riyadh 1989-; *Recreations* conservation, history; *Clubs* Travellers; *Style—* HE Sir Alan Munro, KCMG; c/o Foreign and Commonwealth Office, King Charles St, London SW1 2AH

MUNRO, Alan Keith; s of Angus Alexanda Munro, of Scotland, and Brenda Margaret Martin; *b* 14 Jan 1967; *Educ* Barnwell Sch Stevenage; *Career* professional jockey March 1990-; apprentice to: B Hills Esq 1983-86, M Brittain Esq 1986-89; retained by W O'Gorman Esq as first jockey 1990-, second retainer Mrs L Ramsdon 1990-, full jockey March 1990-; first ride Newbury 1984 (Papperetto), first win Yarmouth 1985 (Sentimental Roses), rode in Italy close season 1986, rode in USA close season 1987, 1988, 1989; major wins: Spanish Derby 1990 (Akalarre), Spanish Grand Prix 1990 (Akalarre), Heinz 57 Group 1 1990 (Mac's Imp); rode Timeless Times to record-equalling 16 wins for a two-year old in one season 1990, rode five winners in a day Aug 23 1990, placed eighth in Flat Jockeys' Table 1990; *Style—* Alan Munro, Esq

MUNRO, Alexander; s of William Munro (d 1985), and Jane Munro; *b* 5 June 1943; *Educ* Acad Fortrose, Univ of Aberdeen (MB ChB, ChM); *m* 17 July 1970, Maureen; 2 s (Niall b 1971, Calum b 1982), 1 da (Kirsty b 1973); *Career* sr surgical registrar Aberdeen Royal Infirmary 1975-78, res surgical offr St Mark's Hosp 1977, conslt gen surgn Raigmore Hosp 1978-, hon sr lectr Univ of Aberdeen 1978; author of various scientific papers, prodr video films on surgical procedures; current res interest use of simulators in surgical trg; pres Highland Div Ileostomy Assoc GB, memb Educ Ctee Assoc of Surgeons GB and I; FRSM, FRCSEd 1972; *Recreations* gardening, church activities, outdoor sports; *Style—* Alexander Munro, Esq; 23 Eriskay Rd, Inverness IV2 3LX (☎ 0463 223804); Dept of Surgery, Raigmore Hospital, Inverness IV2 3UJ

MUNRO, Dame Alison; DBE (1985, CBE 1964); da of John Donald (d 1927), of Paisley, and Helen Barrow Wilson (d 1927); *b* 12 Feb 1914; *Educ* Girls HS Wynberg SA, St Paul's Girls Sch London, St Hilda's Coll Oxford (MA); *m* 3 Sept 1939, Alan Lamont Munro (da 1941), s of Prof J W Munro, CBE (d 1968), of Sunningdale, Berks; 1 s (Alan b 1941); *Career* Miny of Aircraft Prodn 1942-45, princ Miny of Civil Aviation 1945, asst sec Miny of Tport and Civil Aviation 1949, under sec Miny of Aviation 1958, high mistress St Paul's Girls Sch 1964-74; chm: Merton Sutton and Wandsworth AHA 1974-82, Chichester Health Authy 1982-88; memb: Bd Br Euro Airways 1966-73, Br Library 1973-79, Br Tourist Authy 1973-81; chm: Central Tport Consultative Ctee 1980-85, DHSS Maternity Servs Advsy Ctee 1980-85, Code Monitoring Ctee on Baby Milk 1985-89; *Recreations* tennis, Scottish country dancing, sailing; *Clubs* Royal Cwlth Soc; *Style—* Dame Alison Munro, DBE; Harbour Way, Ellanore Lane, W Wittering, W Sussex PO20 8AN (☎ 0243 513274)

MUNRO, Alison Lorne; da of Neil Munro (d 1986), of Hordle, near Lymington, Hants, and Anne Monteith, *née* Blyth (d 1989); *b* 19 April 1943; *Educ* Fernhill Manor Sch for Girls, New Milton, Hampshire; *m* 30 July 1966, Peter James Hamilton, s of Keith Hamilton Wadley; 1 s (James Rufus Hamilton b 22 June 1973), 1 da (Katie Amber b 26 March 1971); *Career* asst feature writer Woman magazine 1964-65 (fashion asst 1962-64), jr fashion ed Sunday Times 1965-66, proprietor children's clothes shop Cambridge 1966-67, Lesley Lake Public Relations 1967-71 (account exec, account mangr, dir); md: Munro Deighton Public Relations Limited 1971-84, Munro & Forster Public Relations Limited 1985-; PRCA; *Recreations* work, family, skiing, cooking; *Style—* Miss Alison Munro; Munro & Forster Public Relations Ltd, 37 Soho Square, London W1V 5DG (☎ 071 439 7177, fax 071 437 0553)

MUNRO, Christopher Iain Craddock; s of W H Munro (d 1970), and Mary Roll, *née* Craddock; *b* 5 March 1949; *Educ* Trinity Coll Glenalmond, Univ of Edinburgh (LLB); *m* 1973, Hon Diana Mary Munro, *née* Colville, da of The Rt Hon the Lord Clydesmuir, *qv*; 1 s (Andrew James William b 26 Dec 1979), 1 da (Fiona Mary b 11 June 1976); *Career* articled clerk Watson Galbraith & Co 1972-75; Robert Fleming & Co: joined 1976, dir Jardine Fleming Holdings and Jardine Fleming Securities HK 1984-86, dir Robert Fleming Securities 1986, dir Robert Fleming Holdings 1988-; ACA 1975; *Recreations* shooting, golf, skiing, tennis; *Clubs* R & A, Hon Co of Edinburgh Golfers (Muirfield); *Style—* Christopher Munro, Esq; Robert Fleming & Co, 25 Copthall Ave, London EC2R 7DR (☎ 071 638 5858)

MUNRO, Colin Andrew; s of Capt Frederick Bertram Munro (d 1963), and Jane Eliza, *née* Taylor; *b* 24 Oct 1946; *Educ* George Watson's Coll Edinburgh, Univ of Edinburgh (MA); *m* 1967, Ehrengard Maria, da of Rudolf Heinrich (d 1981); 2 s (Peter b 25 Dec 1967, Richard b 27 Jan 1978); *Career* asst princ Bd of Inland Revenue 1968-69, third sec FCO 1969-71, third then second sec Bonn 1971-73, second then first sec Kuala Lumpur 1973-77, FCO 1977, private sec to Min of State 1979-80, head of chancery Bucharest 1981-82, FCO 1983, dep head Western Euro Dept 1985, dep head of mission E Berlin 1987-90, HM consul-gen Frankfurt 1990; *Recreations* sports especially hockey, cricket, skiing; *Clubs* Royal Selangor Kuala Lumpur, Rotary, Frankfurter Gesellschat für Handel, Industrie Und Wissenschaft; *Style—* Colin Munro, Esq

MUNRO, Hon Mrs (Diana Mary); *née* Colville; da of 2 Baron Clydesmuir, KT, CB, MBE, TD; *b* 1947; *m* 1973, Christopher I C Munro; 1 s, 1 da; *Career* temp lady in waiting to HRH The Duchess of Gloucester 1980-; *Style—* The Hon Mrs Munro; 26 Pembroke Square, London W8 6PB

MUNRO, Dr Dowling Donald; s of John Munro (d 1980), of Gt Missenden, Bucks, and Etta Mansfield, *née* Cottrell; *b* 29 May 1931; *Educ* Merchant Taylor's Sch Crosby, Univ of London, Royal Free Hosp Sch of Med; *m* 1, 7 Sept 1962, Pamela Grace (d 1977); 2 da (Fiona b 1964, Janet b 1966); m 2, 22 March 1980, Isabella Sinclair, da of Alexander Baillie Macdonald (d 1954), of Lanarkshire, Scot; 2 step da (Jane Turnbull b 1964, Helen Turnbull b 1967); *Career* Capt RAMC Cyprus; US public health res fell in dermatology Western Reserve Univ of Cleveland Ohio 1964; conslt dermatologist: St Bartholomews Hosp London and Harley Street 1968; civilian conslt dermatologist RN 1981; pubns in med jls incl British Journal of Dermatology; MD; *Books* Steroids and the Skin (ed, 1976); *Recreations* apiculture, horticulture, ornithology; *Clubs* RSM; *Style—* Dr Dowling D Munro; Old Ley, Burtons Lane, Chalfont St Giles, Bucks HP8 4BQ (☎ 0494 762189); 99 Harley St, London W1N 1DF; St Bartholomews Hospital, London EC1

MUNRO, Hon Mrs (Elizabeth Mary); *née* Bannerman; yr da of Baron Bannerman of Kildonan, OBE (Life Peer, who d 1969); *b* 8 Sept 1938; *m* 1, 1960 (m dis 1971), Daniel Shade Munro; m 2, 1972 (m dis 1980), Ian Buchanan Anderson; m 3, 1990, John Daniel Scott; *Style—* The Hon Mrs Munro; The Braes, Uplawmoor, Renfrewshire, Scotland

MUNRO, Hugh Murray; s of Hugh Munro, of Aberdeen, and Alice Wilson, *née* Murray (d 1985); *b* 30 Dec 1946; *Educ* Aberdeen GS, Univ of Strathclyde (BA), Univ of Glasgow (MEng); *m* 9 Aug 1974, Valerie Morag, da of Stuart Ingram (d 1984), of Glasgow; 1 s (Craig), 1 da (Lorna); *Career* ptnr Arthur Andersen and Co Glasgow 1981-87 (joined 1968); managing ptnr: Arthur Young Aberdeen 1987-89, Ernst & Young Aberdeen 1989-; MICAS; *Recreations* skiing, gardening; *Clubs* Aberdeen Petroleum, FP, Aberdeen Rotary; *Style—* Hugh Munro, Esq; Ernst & Young, 50 Huntly St, Aberdeen (☎ 0224 640033, fax 0224 630753, telex 739458)

MUNRO, Dr Ian Arthur Hoyle; s of Gordon Alexander Munro (d 1934), of Bradford, Yorks, and Muriel Rebecca, *née* Hoyle (d 1938); *b* 5 Nov 1923; *Educ* Huddersfield Coll, Royal Lancaster GS, Paston Sch North Walsham, Royal Liberty Sch Romford, Univ of London Guy's Hosp Med Sch (MB BS); *m* 4 Aug 1948, Dr Olive Isabel, da of Ernest John Jackson (d 1946); 3 s (Andrew b 1950, Robert b 1960, John b 1965), 2 da (Jane b 1952, Deborah b 1956); *Career* RAMC 1947-50, radiologist Br Mil Hosp Klagenfurt BTA; editorial staff The Lancet 1951- (ed 1976-88); FRCP 1984; *Recreations* cricket, crosswords; *Clubs* Athenaeum, Yorks CCC; *Style—* Dr Ian Munro; Oakwood, Bayley's Hill, Sevenoaks, Kent TN14 6HS (☎ 0732 454993)

MUNRO, Sir Ian Talbot; 15 Bt (NS 1634), of Foulis-Obsdale, Ross-shire; s of Robert Hector Munro and first cousin once removed of Sir Arthur Herman Munro, 14 Bt (d 1972); *b* 18 Dec 1929; *Educ* Bradfield Sch Berks; *Heir* unc, Malcolm Munro; *Career*

marine consultant; *Style—* Sir Ian Munro, Bt

MUNRO, Malcolm; s of Charles Munro, FAA, FLAA (d 1959); h to Btcy of n Sir Ian Talbot Munro, 15 Bt; *b* 24 Feb 1901; *m* 1931, Constance, da of late William Carter; 1 da; *Style—* Malcolm Munro, Esq; Whitegates, Rock, Wadebridge, Cornwall (☎ 020 886 3360)

MUNRO, (David) Michael; s of Charles Rowcliffe Munro, of 17 Succoth Place, Edinburgh, and Moira Rennie, *née* Ainslie; *b* 3 Nov 1944; *Educ* Trinity Coll Glenalmond; *m* 22 Sept 1973, Jeanine (Tina) Beverley, da of Lt-Col James Lindsay-Stewart, of Cuesta de Reina, Jesus Pobre, Prov Alicante, Spain; 3 da (Alexandra b 22 Dec 1977, Antonia b 22 May 1982, Annabel b 31 Jan 1987); *Career* CA 1968; investment analyst Kleinwort Benson 1968-70, ptnr Chiene & Tait CA 1970-83, jt md Quayle Munro Ltd 1983; dir: Shanks & McEwan Gp plc, The Life Assoc of Scotland Ltd; *Recreations* fishing, shooting; *Clubs* New (Edinburgh); *Style—* Michael Munro, Esq; Cockairnie House, Aberdour, Fife KY3 0RZ (☎ 0383 860363); 42 Charlotte Sq, Edinburgh EH2 4HQ (☎ 031 226 4421, fax 031 225 3391, telex 72244)

MUNRO, Robert Malcolm; s of late Malcolm William Munro, of Chelmsford, and Sheila Mary, *née* Lamont (d Jan 1975); *b* 16 May 1937; *Educ* Trinity, Mid-Essex Tech Coll, Manchester Business Sch; *m* 25 March 1961, Irene Mavis, da of William David Percy, of Chelmsford; 2 s (Nigel Robert b 1964, Philip Spencer b 1966); *Career* dir Nordic Bank Ltd 1980-83, md Williams & Glyns Leasing Co Ltd, 1972-80, exec dir The Union Discount Co of London plc 1984-90, leasing conslt Robert Munro Associates 1990-; *Recreations* tennis, golf, music, theatre; *Style—* Robert Munro, Esq; 115 Queens Quay, Upper Thames St, London EC4V 3EH

MUNRO-FERGUSON OF RAITH AND NOVAR, Arthur Brocklehurst Luttrell; assumed name Munro-Ferguson and recognised by the Lord Lyon in the designation 'Munro-Ferguson of Raith and Novar' 1951; s of Ralph Paganel Luttrell (d 1978), and Alice, *née* Brocklehurst (d 1958); his father's mother was sis of 1 and last Viscount Novar of Raith (d 1934); *b* 10 Nov 1921; *Educ* Stowe, Trinity Coll Cambridge (BA), Univ of Edinburgh, Univ of Aberdeen (BSc); *m* 1, 1952 (m dis 1980), Jane Euphemia Beatrice, da of Lewis Reynolds (d 1940), of Natal; 2 s, 2 da; m 2, Mary Griselda, da of William Robertson (d 1935), and formerly w of John Chubb; *Career* served WWII in Far East, Royal Corps of Signals, Capt; chm Scottish Woodland Owners and Timber Growers 1977-80; *Clubs* Army and Navy, New (Edinburgh); *Style—* Arthur Munro-Ferguson of Raith and Novar; Novar, Evanton, Ross-shire IV16 9XL (☎ 0349 830284); Novar Estates Office, Evanton IV16 9XL (☎ 0349 830208)

MUNRO OF FOULIS, Capt Patrick; TD; assumed by decree of Lyon Court 1937 the surname and arms of Munro of Foulis and recognised as Chief of Clan Munro, in succession to his gf, Sir Hector Munro of Foulis, 11 Bt (d 1935); s of Lt-Col Cecil Hugh Orby Gascoigne, DSO (d 1929), and Eva Marion Munro (d 1976), eldest da of Sir Hector Munro of Foulis, 11 Bt; *b* 1912; *Educ* Imperial Serv Coll, RMC; *m* 1946, Eleanor Mary, da of Capt the Hon William French (3 s of 4 Lord De Freyne (d 1974)), and Victoria Louise, *née* Bellasis, *qv*; 3 s, 1 da; *Heir* Hector Munro, Younger of Foulis; *Career* serv WWII: (POW), Capt Seaforth Highlanders; DL Ross and Cromarty (Vice-Lt 1969), Hon Sheriff 1973; *Clubs* Puffin's (Edinburgh), MCC; *Style—* Capt Patrick Munro of Foulis, TD; Foulis Castle, Evanton, Ross-shire

MUNRO OF LINDERTIS, Sir Alasdair Thomas Ian; 6 Bt (UK 1825), of Lindertis, Angus; s of Sir (Thomas) Torquil Alphonso Munro of Lindertis, 5 Bt, JP (d 1985) and his 1 w, Beatrice Maude (d 1974), da of Robert Sanderson Whitaker, of Villa Sofia, Palermo; *b* 6 July 1927; *Educ* Landon Sch USA, Georgetown Univ Washington, Pennsylvania Univ, IMEDE Lausanne Switzerland; *m* 1954, Marguerite Lillian, da of late Franklin R Loy, of Dayton, Ohio, USA; 1 s, 1 da (Karen Fiona b 1956); m 2, 1980, Robert David MacMichael, Jr; *Heir* s, Keith Gordon Munro b 1959; *Style—* Sir Alasdair Munro of Lindertis, Bt; River Ridge, Box 34E, Waitsfield, Vermont 05673, USA; Ruthven Mill, Meigle, Perthshire

MUNROW, Roger Davis; s of William Davis Munrow, CBE (d 1986), former chief inspector of Audit Ministry of Housing and Local Government, and Constance Caroline, *née* Moorcroft (d 1977); *b* 20 March 1929; *Educ* Bryanston, Oriel Coll Oxford (MA); *m* 5 Oct 1957, Marie Jane, da of Jack Edward Beresford (d 1982); 3 da (Julia b 1958, Virginia b 1962, Kate b 1965); *Career* admitted slr 1956; entered Treasy Slrs Dept 1959 (under sec (legal)) 1981-85, chief master The Supreme Court (Chancery Div 1986, master 1985-86); *Recreations* swimming; *Style—* Roger Munrow, Esq; Royal Courts of Justice, Strand WC2

MUNSON, Alma Russell; s of Russell Oliver Munson, of Emdon, Straight Rd, Boxted, Colchester, Essex, and Gladys Mary, *née* Clarke; *b* 15 May 1934; *Educ* NE Essex Tech Coll, Colchester (ACA); *Career* Nat Serv 1952; CA: articled clerk Evans Peirson and Co 1956-62, accountant in charge and audit mangr Deloitte Haskins and Sells 1962-71, compliance offr Guardian Royal Exchange 1985-88 (internal audit mangr 1971-85), chief accountant Guardian Assurance plc 1988-; memb Fin Gp Inst of Chartered Accountants; memb South London Bd Princes Youth Business Tst; Freeman City of London 1980, Liveryman Worshipful Co of Chartered Accountants 1980; FCA 1962, FIIA 1986; *Recreations* opera, music, theatre; *Style—* Alma Munson, Esq; 8 Devonshire Mews West, London W1; 98 Mile End Rd, Colchester, Essex (☎ 071 486 7023); Guardian Royal Exchange, Royal Exchange, London EC3V 3LS (☎ 071 283 7101, telex 883232)

MUNSTER, Countess of; (Dorothy) Alexa; da of Lt-Col E B Maxwell, OBE, MC (d 1973); *b* 22 Dec 1924; *Educ* St Leonard's Sch, Univ of Edinburgh (MusBac); *m* 1979, as his 3 w, Viscount Fitz-Clarence, now 7 Earl of Munster, *qv*; *Career* pianist, harpsichordist and organist; coach and repetiteur for BBC Radio and TV, ITV and LWT 1952-78; korrepetitorin Zürich Opera House 1965-66; lectr in harpsichord, piano and Baroque workshop RSAMD 1978-84; lectr and coach at Inst of Adult Educn and freelance pianist, organist and harpsichordist 1984-; LRAM, ARCO; *Recreations* fishing, gardening; *Style—* The Rt Hon the Countess of Munster; Mulberry Cottage, Park Farm, Haxted Rd, Lingfield, Surrey RH7 6DE

MUNSTER, 7 Earl of (UK 1831); Anthony Charles Fitz-Clarence; also Viscount FitzClarence and Baron Tewkesbury (both UK 1831); s of 6 Earl of Munster (d 1983), and his 1 w, Monica Sheila Grayson, da of Lt-Col Sir Mulleneux Grayson, KBE, 1 Bt (she d 1958, having obtained a divorce 1930); gggs of King William IV and Mrs Jordan, the actress, by whom he had ten children; *b* 21 March 1926; *Educ* St Edward's Sch Oxford; *m* 1, 1949 (m dis 1966), Louise Marguerite Diana, da of Louis Delvigne, of Liège, Belgium; 2 da; m 2, 1966 (m dis 1979), Mrs Pamela Margaret Hyde, da of Arthur Spooner; 1 da; m 3, 1979, Alexa, *qv*; *Heir* none; *Career* served RN 1942-47; graphic designer 1950-57, Daily Mirror Newspapers 1957-66, IPC Newspaper Div (SUN) 1966-69, freelance 1971-79, stained glass conservator for the Burrell Museum 1979-83, conservator with the Chapel (stained glass) Studio 1983-89; FRSA 1987; *Style—* The Rt Hon the Earl of Munster; Mulberry Cottage, Park Farm, Haxted Rd, Lingfield, Surrey RH7 6DE

MUNSTER, Vivian, Countess of; Vivian; *née* Schofield; da of late Benjamin Schofield, JP, of Greenroyde, Rochdale, Lancs, step da of late Judge A J Chotzuer (MP Upton); *Educ* Roedean and Paris; *m* 1939, as his 2 w, 6 Earl of Munster (d 1983); *Heir* Antony Charles, 7 Earl of Munster (b 1926); *Recreations* swimming, walking, bridge; *Clubs* Hurlingham; *Style—* The Rt Hon Vivian, Countess of Munster; 1 Arundel Court, Jubilee Place, London SW3 3TJ

MUNTON, Timothy Alan (Tim); s of Alan Munton, of Chadwell, Melton Mowbray, Leicestershire, and Brenda Mary, *née* Cox; *b* 30 July 1965; *Educ* King Edward VIII Upper Sch Melton Mowbray Leics; *m* 20 Sept 1986, Helen Lesley, da of Paul Phillip Jones; 1 da (Camilla Dallas b 13 Aug 1988); *Career* cricketer; played for: Leicestershire 2nd XI 1982-84, Nat Cricket Assoc Tour to Holland 1983, England Schools v Young Australia 1983; Warwickshire CCC: joined 1985, County Championship debut 1986, memb Natwest trophy winning side 1989, county cup 1989, Warwickshire Player of the Year 1990; memb England A Tour to Pakistan 1991; brewery salesman Bass Mitchells and Butlers Sales for Winters 1988-89, 1989-90, 1990-91; *Style—* Tim Munton, Esq; Warwickshire County Cricket Club, The County Ground, Edgbaston, Birmingham B5 (☎ 021 446 4422)

MURAKAMI, Takashi; *b* 28 March 1937; *Educ* Keio Univ Tokyo (BA), Univ of California Berkeley (MBA); *m* 26 June 1965, Masako; 1 s (Gen b 1971), 2 da (Junko b 1966, Akiko b 1968); *Career* Nikko Securities Co Ltd 1960-86, md Nikko Capital Management UK Ltd 1987-; *Recreations* golf, baseball; *Style—* Takashi Murakami, Esq; Nikko Capital Management (UK) Ltd, 17 Godliman St, London EC4V 5BD (☎ 071 248 0592, fax 071 236 1531, telex 885879 NICAM G)

MURANKA, Tony; s of Albert Muranka, of 62 Oakleigh Avenue, Clayton, Bradford, West Yorkshire, and Freda Joyce, *née* Fieldhouse; *b* 21 May 1952; *Educ* Grange GS, Bradford Coll of Art (DA); *Career* art dir; Designers and Art Directors Assoc Silver award: 1978, 1984, 1987; Campaign Press Silver award 1986, Campaign Poster Silver award 1981; Creative Circle Honours Gold awards: 1984, 1985 (twice), 1986 (twice), 1987, 1988 (twice), 1989; Br TV Silver award 1985; *Recreations* Enduro competitor, sleeping; *Style—* Tony Muranka, Esq; 23 Clarence Rd, Kew, Richmond, Surrey TW9 3NL (☎ 081 948 7443)

MURCELL, (Arthur) George; s of Chesley Gordon Murcell (d 1975), and Lucy Victoria, *née* Bougeia; *b* 30 Oct 1925; *Educ* Bungay GS, Surrey Poly, RADA; *m* 1, 25 Jan 1950 (m dis 1958), Josephine Vivian, da of Maj Roger John Tweedy (d 1971); 1 da (Jennifer Margaret); m 2, 1960, Elvi Patricia Pugh-Morgan; 1 s (James Michael); *Career* WWII, pilot trg 1943, demob WO Air Gunner 1947; actor; theatre performances incl: Tamberlaine (Old Vic), The Lark, The Threepenny Opera, Platanov, The Dark is Light Enough, The Cherry Orchard (RSC), A Patriot for Me (Chichester, London, USA); appearances in maj films and TV programmes; fndr St Georges Theatre recreation of Elizabethan Playhouse in London (artistic dir 1976-89); *Recreations* playing traditional jazz, fishing; *Style—* George Murcell, Esq; St Georges Theatre, Tufnell Park Rd, London N7 (☎ 071 607 7978)

MURCHISON, Prof Duncan George; s of John Kenneth Murchison (d 1934), and Maude Gertrude Mitchell Murchison, *née* Tordoff (d 1964); *b* 13 Jan 1928; *Educ* Glasgow HS, Morrisons Acad Crieff, Univ of Durham (BSc, PhD); *m* 23 July 1953 (m dis 1981), Dorothy Jean, da of Edward Charlton (d 1961); 2 s (Roderick b 28 June 1957, Torquil b 22 Sept 1959), 2 da (Kate b 10 March 1962, Rona b 10 March 1962 (d 1962)); m 2, 27 July 1982, Gail Adrienne, da of Robert Hermon (d 1960); 1 s (Peter b 23 Feb 1984), 2 da (Hanna b 28 Oct 1981, Rosie b 26 July 1988); *Career* lectr Univ of Durham 1960-64, pro vice-chllr Univ of Newcastle 1986- (lectr 1964-68, sr lectr 1968-71, reader in geochemistry 1971-76, dean of Faculty of Sci 1980-83, head of Dept of Geology 1982-86); author of numerous publications in fields of reflected light microscopy, organic petrology and geochemistry; pres Royal Microscopial Soc 1976-78, pres Int Cmmn on Coal Petrology 1979-83; hon FRMS, FGS, FRSE; *Recreations* fishing, philately; *Style—* Prof Duncan Murchison, FRSE; 42 Sanderson Rd, Jesmond, Newcastle-upon-Tyne NE2 2DS ; Pro-Vice-Chancellor's Office, University of Newcastle upon Tyne, 6 Kensington Terrace, Newcastle upon Tyne NE1 7RU (☎ 091 222 6000, telex 53654, fax 091 261 1182)

MURCHISON, Lilian Elizabeth; da of John Alexander Murchison (d 1958), of Alness, Ross and Cromarty, Scotland, and Mary Nicholson, *née* MacIver; *b* 29 April 1936; *Educ* Invergordon Acad, Univ of Edinburgh (MB ChB), Univ of Glasgow (PhD); *Career* memb sci staff MRC Atheroma Res Unit Glasgow 1963-68, sr tutor Royal Victoria Hosp Belfast 1969-71, lectr Dept of Theraputics and Clinical Pharmacology Univ of Aberdeen 1971-76, conslt physician and hon clinical sr lectr Aberdeen Royal Infirmary 1976-; regnl sec Grampian and Highlands and Islands Christian Medical Fellowship, fell RSPB, fndr Friends of Scottish Monuments, memb Nat Tst (Scotland); MRCP(UK) 1970, FRCP Edinburgh 1981, FRCP London 1987; *Recreations* overseas travel, hill walking; *Style—* Miss Lilian Murchison; 9 Highgate Gardens, Aberdeen, Scotland AB1 2TZ (☎ 0224 588532); Wards 27/28, Aberdeen Royal Infirmary, Foresterhill, Aberdeen AB9 2ZB (☎ 0224 681818 ext 52258)

MURDEN, Michael John; s of Jack Murden (d 1985) and Leslie *née* Price; *b* 2 Dec 1943; *Educ* Bolton Sch, Univ of Newcastle Upon Tyne (BSc); *m* 25 July 1973, Mary Angela, da of Felix Sullivan (d 1984) of Jarrow; 3 s (Philip Daniel b 22 Aug 1975, Christopher James b 10 Feb 1978, Simon Charles b 12 Nov 1979); *Career* prodn mangr: Vickers Ltd 1967-69 (student apprentice 1962-66), Swan Hunter Shipbuilders Ltd 1969-72; md Cammell Laird Shipbldg Ltd 1984-88 (devpt mangr 1973-74, shipbldg gen mangr 1974-76, prodn dir 1976-82, dep md 1982-84); md Northumbrian Water 1989-, non exec dir Vickers Shipbldg & Engrg 1985; dir: Merseyside C of C, (dep chm) Wirral C of C, Cavendish Enterprises Ltd, In Business Ltd; memb NW cncl CBI, govr Wirral Met Coll, chm Wirral Phoenix Initiative; C Eng, MRINA; *Recreations* music, sailing, swimming; *Style—* Michael Murden, Esq; 23 West Ave, Gosforth, Newcastle upon Tyne NE3 4ES (☎ 091 284 3283); Northumbrian Water, Northumbrian House, Regent Centre, Gosforth, Newcastle Upon Tyne NE3 3PX (☎ 091 284 3151)

MURDIN, Dr Paul Geoffrey; OBE (1988); s of Robert Samuel Frederick Rodham Murdin, and Ethel, *née* Chubb; *b* 5 Jan 1942; *Educ* Trinity Sch of John Whitgift, Wadham Coll Oxford (BA), Univ of Rochester NY (PhD); *m* 8 Aug 1964, Lesley Carol, da of Frederick Milburn; 2 s (Benedict Neil b 1966, Alexander Nicholas b 1970), 1 da (Louisa Jane b 1974); *Career* princ scientific offr Royal Greenwich Observatory 1974-75 (sr res fell 1971-74), princ res scientist Anglo-Australian Observatory 1975-78; Royal Greenwich Observatory: princ scientific offr 1978-81, sr princ scientific offr and head La Palma Ops Dept 1981-87, head Astronomy Dept 1987-91, dep dir 1990-91; dir Royal Observatory Edinburgh 1991-; memb: Bd of Tstees Nat Maritime Museum, Mgmnt Bd Armagh Observatory; sec Int Scientific Ctee Canary Islands Observatories; memb Int Astronomical Union, FRAS; *Books* Astronomers Telescope (1962), Radio Waves From Space (1964), New Astronomy (1978), Catalogue of the Universe (1979), Colours of the Stars (1984), End in Fire (1990); *Style—* Dr Paul Murdin, OBE; Royal Observatory, Blackford Hill, Edinburgh EH9 (☎ 031 668 8261)

MURDOCH, Andrew James; s of James Clive Leonard Murdoch (d 1981), and Adela Marjorie, *née* Gepp; *b* 16 Nov 1949; *Educ* Charterhouse, Pembroke Coll Cambridge (MA); *m* 1972, Lynn Hilary, da of Vernon Cecil Thompson; 1 s (Simon Scott b 16 April 1976), 1 da (Hilary Caroline Noel b 17 Dec 1979); *Career* architect; HKPA 1973-78, Eric Lyons Cunningham Partnership 1978-79, Cambridge Design 1979-80, John S Bonnington Partnership 1980-84, The Fitzroy Robinson Partnership 1984-; memb RIBA; *Recreations* painting, golf; *Clubs* Royal Ashdown Forest Golf; *Style—* Andrew Murdoch, Esq; 16 Maids Causeway, Cambridge CB5 8DA (☎ 0223 65845);

DEBRETT'S PERSONALITIES OF TODAY

PHOTOGRAPH: ISABELLE BLONDIAU

John Keane

Nico Ladenis

Cherie Lunghi

DEBRETT'S PERSONALITIES OF TODAY

The Rt Hon John Major

Paul McCartney

Sir Ian McKellen

The Fitzroy Robinson Partnership, 77 Portland Place, London W1N 4EP (☎ 071 636 8033, fax 0223 460285, car 0860 548726)

MURDOCH, Dame Elisabeth Joy; DBE (1963), CBE (1961), AC (1989); da of Rupert Greene and Marie, *née* de Lancey Forth; *b* 1909; *m* 1928, Sir Keith Arthur Murdoch (d 1952, chm and md The Herald and Weekly Times, dir and fndr Aust Newsprint Mills Pty Ltd, dir-gen of Information for Cwlth of Australia); 1 s, 3 da; *Career* pres Royal Children's Hosp Melbourne 1954-65, tstee Nat Gallery Vic 1968-76; chm: Ctee of Mgmnt Victorian Tapestry Workshops 1986-88, tstess McClelland Gallery; Hon LLD Melbourne 1982; *Style*— Dame Elisabeth Murdoch, DBE, AC; Cruden Farm, Langwarrin, Vic 3910, Australia

MURDOCH, Gordon Stuart; s of Ian William Murdoch (d 1978), and Margaret Henderson McLaren, *née* Scott (d 1974); *b* 7 June 1947; *Educ* Falkirk HS, Sidney Sussex Coll Cambridge (MA, LLB); *m* 27 Dec 1976, Sally Kay, da of Henry Cummings, of Ludlow, Shropshire; 2 s (Thomas b 1979, Alexander b 1982); *Career* called to the Bar Inner Temple 1970; *Style*— Gordon Murdoch, Esq; 4 Paper Buildings, Temple, London EC4Y 7EX (☎ 071 583 0816, fax 071 353 4979)

MURDOCH, Dame Iris; DBE (1987, CBE 1976); da of Wills John Hughes Murdoch, and Irene Alice Richardson; *b* 1919; *Educ* Froebel Educnl Inst London, Badminton Sch Bristol, Somerville Coll Oxford (hon fell 1977); *m* 1956, Prof John Oliver Bayley, Warton prof of English Lit and fell St Catherine's Coll Oxford; *Career* asst princ HM Treasury 1942-45, admin offr UNRRA 1945-46, Studentship Newnham Coll Cambridge 1947-48, fell and tutor St Anne's Coll Oxford 1948-63 (hon fell 1963-), lectr Royal Coll of Art 1964-67, Hon DLitt Oxon 1987; philosopher; author; *Books* Sartre, Romantic Rationalist (1953), Under the Net (1954), The Flight from the Enchanter (1955), The Sandcastle (1957), The Bell (1958), A Severed Head (1961, play 1963), An Unofficial Rose (1962), The Unicorn (1963), The Italian Girl (1964, play 1967), The Red and the Green (1965), The Time of the Angels (1966), The Nice and The Good (1968), Bruno's Dream (1969), A Fairly Honourable Defeat (1970), The Sovereignty of Good (1970), An Accidental Man (1971), The Black Prince (1973, James Tait Black Memorial Prize), A Word Child (1975), Henry and Cato (1976), The Fire and the Sun (1977), The Sea, the Sea (1978, Booker Prize 1978), Nuns and Soldiers (1980); *Plays* The Servants and the Snow (1970), The Three Arrows (1972), Art and Eros (1980); *Poems* A Year of Birds (1978), The Philospher's Pupil (1983), The Good Apprentice (1985), Acastos (1985), The Book and the Brotherhood (1987), The Message to the Planet (1989); *Style*— Dame Iris Murdoch, DBE

MURDOCH, Dr Peter Stevenson; s of John Duncan Murdoch, TD (d 1988), and Zoe Mann, *née* Hannay (d 1987); *b* 16 Oct 1950; *Educ* Haileybury, Guy's Hosp Med Sch (MB BS); *m* 28 Dec 1974, Sarah, da of Tor Ingemar Lundegard; 2 s (Neil b 1976, John b 1979); *Career* med supt Presbyterian Jt Hosp Uburu Nigeria 1975-81, sr registrar in geriatric med Royal Victoria Hosp Edinburgh 1981-82, conslt physician in geriatric med Falkirk and Dist Royal Infirmary 1983-; chm: Liaison Ctee RCPsych, Br Geriatrics Soc; memb Cncl Br Geriatrics Soc, tstee and vice chm Dementia Servs Devpt Tst; FRCPE 1988; *Style*— Dr Peter Murdoch; 4 Abercromby Place, Stirling, Falkirk FK8 2QD (☎ 0786 73087); Falkirk and District Royal Infirmary, Falkirk FK1 5QE (☎ 0324 24000)

MURDOCH, Robert Clive; s of Lt-Col Clive Murdoch, DSO (d 1944), and Janet Homewood, *née* Motion (d 1963); *b* 7 March 1922; *Educ* Wellington; *m* 1, 1951 (m dis 1976), Mary Anne, da of late Capt A K MacEwan; 3 da (Miranda Jane b 1954, Serena Janet b 1957, Camilla Anne b 1958); m 2, Susan Mary, da of late Eric Graham Mattingley; *Career* WWII Capt Grenadier Gds, served N Africa, Italy 1942-46; farmer 1947-; dir Hops Mktg Bd 1955-82, Checkers and Checkers Growers Ltd 1957-88; *Recreations* farming, all country pursuits; *Clubs* Farmers; *Style*— Robert C Murdoch, Esq; Wester Hill, Linton, Maidstone, Kent ME17 4BT (☎ 0622 7452277); Murdoch & Allfrey Ltd, Clockhouse, Linton, Maidstone, Kent (☎ 0622 743173)

MURDOCH, Robert Henry; MBE (1944); s of George Murdoch (d 1969), of Denburn, Newport on Tay, Fife, and Emma Elizabeth, *née* Shewring (d 1984); *b* 3 July 1914; *Educ* Univ Coll Sch; *m* 28 June 1940, Jill, da of James Malcolm Kinkaid (d 1954), of Monkseaton, Northumberland; 1 s (David b 1942), 2 da (Janet b 1944, Susan b 1948); *Career* 2 Lt RE (SR) 1938, Capt RE BEF 1939-40, Maj HQ Southern Cmd 1941, Lt-Col AQMG (M) 21 Army Gp HQ 1944; traffic apprentice LNER 1932; NCB: tport mangr Scottish Div 1947, mktg mangr Lothians area 1960, commercial mangr Scottish Region 1967, mktg dir Scotland 1973-78; memb: Tport Users Consultative Ctee Scotland 1948-54, Clean Air Cncl Scotland 1973-78; chm: Branch Area Ctee Scotland BIM 1972-74 (chm Edinburgh and Borders Branch 1969-72), Mgmnt Assoc SE Scotland 1976; pres Rotary Club Edinburgh 1978-79, govr dist 102 Rotary Int 1985-86; FBIM; *Recreations* golf, gardening; *Style*— Robert Murdoch, Esq, MBE; 3 Westerdunes Court, North Berwick, East Lothian (☎ 0620 3331)

MURDOCH, (Keith) Rupert; AC (1984); only s of Sir Keith Murdoch, sometime chm & md The Herald & Weekly Times Ltd, Melbourne Herald, Sun-News Pictorial, Weekly Times (d 1952), by his w Dame Elisabeth Murdoch, DBE (herself da of Rupert Greene by his w Marie, *née* de Lancey Forth), president of the Royal Children's Hospital Melbourne; *b* 11 March 1931; *Educ* Geelong GS, Worcester Coll Oxford (MA); *m* 1, 1956 (m dis); 1 da (Pru); m 2, 1967, Anna Maria, da of J Torv, of Scotland; 2 s (Lachlan, James), 1 da (Elisabeth); *Career* hon fellow Worcester Coll Oxford 1982-; publisher; gp chief exec News Ltd Australia, chief exec The News Corporation Ltd, chm and pres News America Publishing Inc, jt chm Ansett Transport Industries 1982- (jt ch exec and md 1979-82); dir: William Collins 1981-, United Telecasters Sydney, News International (UK); UK newspapers owned incl The Sun and The Times; *Style*— Rupert Murdoch Esq, AC; 2 Holt St, Sydney, NSW 2000, Australia; c/o News America Inc, 1211 Avenue of the Americas, New York 10036, USA; 1 Virginia St, London E1

MURDOCK, Christopher; s of Dr Charles Rutherford Murdock (d 1968), and Eirene Nolan, *née* Baird; *b* 15 Aug 1946; *Educ* Brackenber House Belfast, Portora Royal Sch Enniskillen; *m* 31 Jan 1970, Dorothy Rosemary Richardson; 2 s (Chrisopher Jeremy b 1973, Antony John b 1975), 1 da (Rosemary Sarah Alexandra b 1980); *Career* joined NHS 1965, asst dist admin offr Armagh and Dungannon Dist 1974-75, dist personnel offr S Belfast Dist 1975-76, asst dist admin offr E Belfast and Castlereagh Dist 1976-84; gp admin Purdysburn Unit of Mgmnt 1984- (currently on secondment as NHS reforms/restructuring co-ordinator to Eastern Health and Social Services Bd HQ); hon treas E Down Foxhounds; *Recreations* photography, supporting children's equestrian interests; *Style*— Christopher Murdock, Esq; c/o Eastern Health and Social Services Board, 12-22 Linenhall St, Belfast BT2 8BS (☎ 0232 321313)

MURDOCK, John; s of James Duncan Murdoch, OBE (d 1979), and Elsie Elisabeth, *née* Hardman (d 1989); *b* 1 April 1945; *Educ* Shrewsbury, Magdalen Coll Oxford (BA), King's Coll London (MPhil); *m* 9 Sept 1967 (m dis 1986), Prudence Helen, da of Brig WR Smith-Windham, CBE, DSO, of Pitney, Somerset; 1 s (Thomas Duncan b 1970), 2 da (Clarissa Helen b 1972, Rosamond Elsie b 1977); *Career* asst keeper Dept of Art City Museum and Art Gallery Birmingham 1969-73; V&A: dep keeper Dept of Paintings 1977-85 (asst keeper 1973-77), keeper dept of prints drawings photographs and paintings 1986-89, asst dir in charge of collections 1989-; tstee: Wordsworth Library and Museum Dove Cottage, The William Morris Gallery Walthamstow; exec ctee memb: Assoc of Art Historians, Walpole Soc; *Books* David Cox (1970), Byron (1974), Forty-Two English Watercolours (1977), The English Miniature (1981), Discovery of the Lake District (1984), Painters and The Derby China Works (1987); *Style*— John Murdock, Esq; Brickhill, Burghclere, nr Newbury, Berks (☎ 063 527295), Victoria and Albert Museum, London SW7 (☎ 071 938 8602)

MURE, Kenneth Nisbet; QC; s of late Robert Mure, and Katherine Mure; *b* 11 April 1947; *Educ* Glasgow HS, Univ of Glasgow (MA, LLB); *Career* admitted to the Scots Bar 1975, called to the Bar Grays Inn 1990; lectr Law Faculty Univ of Glasgow 1971-83; temp sheriff Scotland 1982-; FTII 1971; *Style*— Kenneth Mure, Esq, QC; Advocates' Library, Edinburgh EH1 1RF (☎ 031 226 5071)

MURERWA, HE Dr Herbert Muchemwa; s of Amon Gamanya Murerwa, of Chinyika Sch, Goromonzi, Zimbabwe; *b* 31 May 1941; *Educ* Mutare Teachers' Coll, George Williams Coll Illinois USA (BA), Harvard Univ (Ed M, Ed D); *m* 23 Sept 1969, Ruth Chipo, da of Rev Elijah Dhliwayo; 1 s (Simbarashe b 9 Aug 1982), 4 da (Mudiwa b 23 Sept 1969, Gamu b 25 May 1971, Tapiwa b 23 May 1975, Danai b 16 Aug 1980); *Career* programme dir Zimbabwe YMCA 1964-69; coll lectr Salem Coll Mass USA 1973-75; econ affrs offr UN 1978-80; permanent sec: Min of Manpower Planning and Devpt Zimbabwe Govt 1980-82, Min of Labour and Social Welfare 1982-84; Zimbabwe high cmmr to UK and ambass to Ireland 1984-; *Recreations* reading, tennis, jogging; *Clubs* Travellers'; *Style*— HE Dr Herbert Murerwa; 26 Denewood Rd, London N6 4AJ (☎ 071 836 7755); Zimbabwe House, 429 Strand, London WC2R 0SA (☎ 071 836 7755)

MURFITT, Catriona Anne Campbell; da of Dr Alfred Ian Campbell Murfitt (d 1983), and Anne, *née* Ritchie; *b* 16 Jan 1958; *Educ* St Mary's Convent Sch Ascot, Leicester Poly Sch of Law (BA); *Career* called to the Bar Gray's Inn 1981; in practice S Eastern circuit 1982-; memb Family Law Bar Assoc; *Recreations* skiing, gardening, art, sacred choral music; *Style*— Miss Catriona Murfitt; 1 Mitre Court Buildings, Temple, London EC4 (☎ 071 353 0434, fax 071 353 3988)

MURIE, John Andrew; s of John Andrew Murie, of 6 Rosemount Court, Airdrie, and Jessie, *née* Sutherland; *b* 7 Aug 1949; *Educ* Univ of GLasgow (BSc, MB ChB, MD), Univ of Minnesota Minneapolis USA, Univ of Oxford (MA); *m* 7 Sept 1977, Edythe, da of James Munn, of 36 Bradfield Ave, Glasgow; 1 da (Emma Jane b 1986); *Career* clinical reader in surgery Univ of Oxford 1984-89, conslt surgn John Radcliffe Hosp Oxford 1984-89, fell Green Coll Oxford 1984-89, conslt surgn The Royal Infirmary of Edinburgh 1989-, hon sr lectr in surgery Univ of Edinburgh 1989-, assoc ed The British Journal of Surgery 1989-; FRCPS 1979; *Recreations* golf, swimming, food and wine; *Style*— John Murie, Esq; 105 Caiyside, Edinburgh EH10 7HR (☎ 031 445 3334); Dept of Surgery, The Royal Infirmary, 1 Lauriston Place, Edinburgh EH3 9YW (☎ 031 229 2477 ext 2271); Murrayfield Hospital, 122 Corstorphine Rd, Edinburgh EH12 6UD (☎ 031 334 0363, fax 031 334 7338, telex 727442 UNIVED G)

MURISON, Robert Fraser; OBE (1978), QPM (1971), DL (Fife 1975); s of William Murison (d 1937); *b* 15 Feb 1919; *Educ* Dunfermline HS, Univ of Glasgow; *m* 1948, Isobel Stirrat, *née* Tennent; 2 da; *Career* serv WWII Black Watch and 8 Gurkha Rifles 1942-46, Capt India and Sumatra; police offr Lanarkshire Constabulary 1937-42 and 1946-63, dep cmdt Scottish Police Coll 1963-65, chief constable Fife 1965-84, N Zone Home Def Police Cdr Designate 1974-84; *Recreations* gardening, amateur radio; *Style*— Robert F Murison, Esq, OBE, QPM, DL; 2 Abbots Walk, Kirkcaldy, Fife KY2 5NL (☎ 0592 262436)

MURLEY, Sir Reginald Sydney; KBE (1979), TD (1948); s of Sydney Herbert Murley (d 1968), of New York, and Beatrice Maud, *née* Baylis (d 1951); *b* 2 Aug 1916; *Educ* Dulwich, St Bartholomew's Hosp Univ of London (MB BS, MS); *m* 1 Feb 1947, Daphne, da of Ralph Eddowes Garrod (d 1964); 3 s (David Peter b 1949, Gavin Michael b 1951, Anthony Jonathan b 1957), 3 da (Susan Elizabeth Butler (step da) b 1942, Jennifer Jane b 1948, Hilary Daphne b 1953); *Career* RAMC, WWII, Field Units, Surgn to No 1 and 2 Maxillofacial Surgical Units; No 53 Field Surgical Unit, Maj 1939-45, TA Middle E, E Africa, Italy, NW Europe; anatomy demonstrator 1946, surgical chief asst St Bartholomews 1946-54; conslt surgeon: St Albans Hosp 1947-80, Royal Northern Hosp 1952-80; hon conslt surgn St Bart's Hosp; Mackenzie Mackinnon res fell RCP and RCS, Cattlin res fell 1950-51; pres: RCS 1977-80, Hunterian Soc 1970, Med Soc London 1982, Harveian Soc 1983, John Charnley Tst 1983-; Hunterian Soc orator 1978; hon fell: RACS, RCS in Ireland 1980-, Coll of Surgeons SA; hon memb: Italian Surgical Soc 1979, RCS Eng 1981, Polish Surgical Soc 1983, Br Assoc of Plastic Surgns 1983-, Br Assoc of Clinical Anatomists 1983-, Reading Pathological Soc 1985-; Hon FDS; vice-pres Int Soc of Surgery 1985-86; RCS: Hunterian prof 1950, orator 1981, Bradshaw lectr 1981; Syme orator RACS 1979, pres Fellowship for Freedom in Med 1972-86, memb Cncl Freedom Assoc 1982-, patron Jagiellonian Tst, memb Cncl Health and Welfare Unit of Inst Economic Affairs, memb Cncl Social Affairs Unit; patron of Youth and Family Concern 1984; *Publications*: author of various med and surgical papers on thyroid, breast, vascular, and salivary diseases; contribs to: surgical textbooks, papers on medical economics and surgery; MRCS 1939, LRCP 1939, FRCS 1946, MS 1948; *Recreations* reading, history & economics, gardening, music; *Clubs* Royal Automobile; *Style*— Sir Reginald Murley, KBE, TD; Cobden Hill House, 63 Cobden Hill, Radlett, Herts WD7 7JN; Consulting Suite, Wellington Hospital, Wellington Place NW8 9LE

MURPHY, Alexander James; s of James Murphy, and Sarah Alice, *née* Smith; *b* 22 April 1939; *m* 4 June 1960, Alice, da of John Mellan; 1 da (Ann (Mrs Neal)); *Career* Nat Serv RAF 1960-62; signed as professional rugby player 1955; played for St Helens 1955-66 (Wembley winners 1961, capt 1966), total twenty seven appearances 1958-71; memb: World Cup Squad 1960, GB tour Aust 1966 (1958); rugby coach; Leigh: 1966-71 (Wembley winners 1971, league leaders 1980-82 and 1985); Warrington 1971-78: Capt Morgan Trophy, Floodlit Trophy, Lancs Cup, Players No 6 Trophy, Challenge Cup; World Cup Squad Aust 1975, Salford 1978-80, Wigan 1982-84 (Wembley runners up 1983); St Helens 1985-90 (won John Player Trophy 1987 and 1989, Wembley runners up 1987 and 1989); *Books* Saints Hit Double Top (1967), Murphy's Law (1988); *Style*— Alexander Murphy, Esq

MURPHY, Sheriff Andrew John; s of Robert James Murphy, of Glasgow, and Robina, *née* Scott; *b* 16 Jan 1946; *Educ* Allan Glen's Sch Glasgow, Univ of Edinburgh (MA, LLB); *m* 20 Nov 1980, Susan Margaret, da of Dr Peter Dewar Thomson, OBE, of Dingwall; 2 s (Patrick Andrew Sean b 1983, Simon Peter Scott b 1987), 2 da (Lucy Jane Robina b 1978, Sarah Belle Margaret b 1979); *Career* 2 Lt RA (TA) 1971-73, Flt-Lt RAF 1973-75; admitted Faculty of Advocates 1970; called to the Bar Scotland 1970, Middle Temple 1970; Crown counsel Hong Kong 1975-79, standing jr counsel to Registrar Gen for Scotland 1982-85, temp Sheriff 1983-85, appointed Sheriff of Grampian Highlands and Islands at Peterhead and Banff; *Clubs* Caledonian, Edinburgh, Royal Northern and University (Aberdeen); *Style*— Sheriff Andrew Murphy; Sheriff's Chambers, Sheriff Court House, Queen St, Peterhead (☎ 0779 76676)

MURPHY, Anthony; s of Eric Murphy, of Wirral, Merseyside, and Ethel, *née* Dailey; *b* 23 Sept 1945; *Educ* Queen's Univ Belfast (BA), Univ of Sussex (MA Educnl Psychology); *Career* chartered psychologist; educnl psychologist Essex CC 1976-81, sr educnl psychologist E Sussex CC 1981-85, princ educnl psychologist London Borough of Hounslow 1985-89, fndr Complete Psychological Services (an ind consultancy)

1989-; assoc FBPsS, assoc memb Assoc of Educnl Psychologists; *Recreations* jazz; *Style—* Anthony Murphy, Esq; 15 Warfield Rd, Hampton, Middx TW12 2AY (☎ 081 783 1250); Complete Psychological Services, 136 Harley St, London W1N 1AH (☎ 071 224 6129)

MURPHY, Prof Brian; s of James Murphy (d 1987), of Huddersfield, and Winifred Helen, *née* Ellis (d 1990); *b* 20 May 1940; *Educ* Rotherham GS, Univ of Lancaster (MSc), Open Univ (BA); *m* 18 Dec 1982, Vivienne; *Career* rating and auditing asst Rotherham County Borough 1956-61, accountancy and auditing asst Castleford Borough Council 1961-63, head of Accountancy Section West Riding County Council 1963-64, sr accountant Oxford County Borough Council 1964-66, lectr in management accountancy Worcester Tech Coll 1966-69; Huddersfield Poly: sr lectr in management accountancy 1969-70, princ lectr 1970-71, head of Accountancy Div 1971-72, head of Dept of Accountancy and Fin 1972-87, prof (for life) 1987; md The Yorkshire Unit Trust Managers Limited 1988-; dir and co sec: Clifton Language Services Ltd, PSI-Soft Ltd; former dir and co sec: Double M Construction Ltd, Daleside Developments Ltd; memb: Inst of Public Finance and Accountancy 1963, Chartered Inst of Cost and Management Accountants 1971; fell Assoc of Certified Accountants 1982; FRSA 1987; *Books* Management Accounting (3 edn, 1986); *Recreations* golf, cycling; *Style—* Prof Brian Murphy

MURPHY, Brian Arthur; s of Arthur Albert Murphy (d 1982), and Constance Margaret, *née* Young; *b* 3 May 1951; *Educ* Emanuel Sch London, Keble Coll Oxford (BA); *m* 30 April 1977, Jane, da of John Champion Stevenson, of Atherstone, Warks; 1 s (Giles b 10 March 1980), 1 da (Leila b 14 June 1982); *Career* slr, dep head legal servs Allied Lyons plc 1982, sr assoc Ashurst Morris Crisp 1989; chm Danesborough Branch of Milton Keynes Cons Assoc; Freeman City of London, Liveryman Worshipful Co of Founders; memb Law Soc 1976; *Clubs* Ski Club of GB; *Style—* Brian Murphy, Esq; The Old Rectory, Little Brickhill, Bucks MK17 9NA (☎ 071 638 1111, fax 071 972 7990)

MURPHY, Brian Gerald; s of Norman George Murphy (d 1957), of Newport on Tay, Fife, and Agnes, *née* O'Grady; *b* 30 Aug 1943; *Educ* Abbey Sch Fort Augustus; *m* Christine, *née* Dench; 1 s (Simon Richard b 18 Nov 1985), 1 da (Louise Victoria b 30 Sept 1972); *Career* trainee surveyor Bell Ingram 1963-69, surveyor D M Hall 1969; Bell Ingram: surveyor Ayrshire Office 1970-73, ptnr Aberdeen Office 1973-82, ptnr Glasgow 1982-87; dir Royal life Estates (chief exec Northern Region) 1987-; FRICS; *Recreations* farming, fishing; *Style—* Brian Murphy, Esq; Walston Farm, Grassyards Road, Kilmarnock, Ayrshire (☎ 056 07 278); Royal Life Estates, Park House, Park Circus Place, Glasgow (☎ 041 332 1909, fax 041 332 3482)

MURPHY, Brian Gordon; s of Albert Gordon Murphy, and Doris Edna Murphy; *b* 18 Oct 1940; *Educ* Mill Hill Sch; *m* 3 Nov 1973, Judith Ann, da of Frederick Robert Parkinson; *Career* admitted slr 1966, ptnr Knapp Fishers Westminster 1968, ptnr Farrer and Co Lincoln's Inn Fields London 1987; memb Cncl Law Soc 1982-, pres City of Westminster Law Soc 1983-84, chm Employment Law Ctee Law Soc 1987-90; *Recreations* sailing, theatre, photography, travel; *Style—* Brian Murphy, Esq; Farrer & Co, 66 Lincoln's Inn Fields, London WC2A 3LH (☎ 071 242 2022, fax 071 831 9748, telex 24318)

MURPHY, Hon Christopher Philip Yorke; s of Philip John Murphy, and Dorothy Betty Murphy; *b* 20 April 1947; *Educ* Devonport HS, Queen's Coll Oxford (MA); *m* 1969, Sandra Gillian, da of William John Ashton; *Career* former assoc dir D'Arcy MacManus & Masius; pres Oxford Univ Cons Assoc 1967; held number of Cons Party Offices 1968-72; parish cncllr Windlesham Surrey 1972-76; Parly candidate (C) Bethnal Green and Bow Feb and Oct 1974, MP (C) Welwyn Hatfield 1979-87, memb Select Ctee on Statutory Instruments 1980-87 (and its representative on Cwlth Delegated Legislation Ctee 1980-87); vice chm: Cons Parly Urban and New Town Affairs Ctee 1980-87, Cons Parly Arts and Heritage Ctee 1981-86; UK delegate to Cncl of Europe/WEU 1983-87; memb Chief Pleas of Sark 1989-90; vice pres: C of E Artistic Heritage Cmmn 1984-87, C of E Youth and Drugs Cmmn 1986-87, Int Ctee of Chief Pleas 1989-90; memb: Nat Ctee for 900 Anniversary of Domesday Book 1986, Cncl La Sociètè Guernesiaise 1988-90, Arts Cncl of Bailiwick of Guernsey 1988-90; life memb Cwlth Parly Assoc; Freeman City of London; hon Citizen of Cork; writer, lectr and conslt; Hon Sec La Sociètè Serequioise 1988-90; FRSA; *Recreations* arts, heritage, travel, conservation, politics, walking, horticulture; *Clubs* Oxford Union; *Style—* Hon Christopher Murphy; Cooil Voorath, The Cronk, Ballaugh, Isle of Man

MURPHY, Gerald James; JP; s of James Murphy (d 1956), and Agnes Murphy, *née* Youles; *b* 28 June 1989; *Educ* Finchley GS, The Architectural Association Sch of Architecture (AADipl); *Career* fndr ptnr architectural practice Gerald Murphy & Ptnrs 1962; after amalgamation sr ptnr Gerald Murphy Burles Newton & Ptnrs; works of note inc: Brentwood Cathedral, New Docklands Church, conversion Wembley Stadium for Pope's visit; vice chm Borough of Haringey Dist Health Authy 1981-; Cons Pty candidate 1973-78, chm London N Euro Constituency Cncl 1978-84, former int pres Serra Int, vice chm Issues Ctee Catholic Union of GB; Freeman City of London; KCSG, kt Cdr with Star of the Religious Order of the Holy Sepulchre of Jerusalem; ARIBA, ACIArb; *Recreations* filming, painting; *Style—* Gerald J Murphy, JP; 8 Highgate High St, London N6 5JL (☎ 081 341 1277); 4 Highgate High St, London N6 5JL (☎ 081 341 1307, fax 081 341 0851)

MURPHY, Harry Maughan; s of Harry Murphy (d 1961), of Grimsby, Lincolnshire, and Mary Ellen, *née* Donald (d 1959); *b* 7 June 1924; *Educ* Humberstone Fndn Sch Clee Lincs, Univ of Durham, Cambridge Univ, Univ of London (BSc); *m* 1, 20 Jan 1947 (m dis), Margaret Jean, da of James Edward Simpson (d 1949), of Middleton, Lancs; m 2, Minnie, *née* Fisher; 1 s (Harry Edward b 1962), 1 da (Charlotte Emma b 1964); *Career* RAF 1942-47, Pilot 1943, Russian interpreter 1946; with The APV Co (Eastern Euro Sales) 1950-56; Colonial Serv: lab offr employment and trg offr Dept of Lab and Mines N Rhodesia Govt 1956-66; lectr Grimsby Coll of Technol 1966-68, cmmr of lab Gilbert and Ellice Islands 1968-73, dep dir of lab industl relations offr Gibraltar Govt 1973-83, industl relations conslt; chm Gibraltar Clay Pigeon Shooting Assoc, cncllr Crawley Sussex 1955, memb Legislative Assembley and Exec Cncl Gilbert and Ellice Islands Colony; *Recreations* shooting; *Clubs* Grimsby Cons, Gibraltar Clay Pigeon Shooting, Casino Calpe Gibraltar; *Style—* Harry Murphy, Esq; 4A Rulanda, Vineyards, Gibraltar (☎ Gibraltar 71812); P O Box 726, Gibraltar

MURPHY, Ian Patrick; s of Patrick Murphy, of Cardiff, and Irene Grace, *née* Hooper; *b* 1 July 1949; *Educ* St Illtyd's Coll Cardiff, LSE (LLB); *m* 31 Aug 1974, Penelope Gay, da of Gerald Hugh-Smith (d 1965), of Hove, Sussex; 2 da (Anna b 1982, Charlotte b 1984); *Career* chartering clerk Baltic Exchange 1970-71, called to the Bar 1972, rec 1990 (asst rec 1986-90); *Recreations* golf, skiing, rugby and cricket; *Clubs* Royal Porthcawl GC, Cardiff County; *Style—* Ian Murphy, Esq, 3 Llandaff Chase, Llandaff, Cardiff CF5 2NA (☎ 0222 553741)

MURPHY, Rev Canon John Gervase Maurice Walker (Gerry); LVO (1987); s of Capt William Stafford Murphy, MC (d 1951), of Bangor NI, and Yvonne Iris, *née* Wilson (d 1971); *b* 20 Aug 1926; *Educ* Methodist Coll Belfast, Dublin Univ (BA, MA); *m* 1957, Joy Hilda Miriam, da of Canon T L Livermore, MA, of Heacham; 5 da (Maryan, Desiree, Nicola, Geraldine, Felicity); *Career* Royal Army Chaplains Dept 1955-77; sr chaplain: Br Cwlth Bde 1964-67, RMA Sandhurst 1971-73; asst chaplain gen Germany: BAOR 1973-75, SEAT Dist 1975-77; bishop's chaplain to Holiday Makers Norfolk Broads; rural dean: Blofield 1978-79, Heacham and Rising 1985-; rector of Sandringham Gp of Parishes and domestic chaplain to HM The Queen 1979-; hon canon Norwich 1987- (canon emeritus 1987), chaplain to HM The Queen 1987-; *Recreations* sports (played int rugby for Ireland 1952/54/58, Barbarians 1957); *Clubs* London Irish RFC, Public Sch Wanderers RFC; *Style—* The Rev Canon John Murphy, LVO; Rectory, Sandringham, Norfolk PE35 6EH

MURPHY, John Terence; s of Francis Joseph Murphy, of Blandford St Mary, Dorset, and Barbara Pauline, *née* Daft; *b* 16 Jan 1948; *Educ* Downside, Magdalen Coll Oxford (MA); *m* 11 Sept 1981, Jocelyn, da of Joseph Wang (d 1986), of Honiara, Guadalcanal, Solomon Islands; 1 da (Georgia Elizabeth b 1988); *Career* admitted slr 1971; ptnr Crawley & de Reya 1976-78, Bartletts de Reya 1978-88, Theodore Goddard 1988-; memb: Law Soc Working Pty on USSR and E Europe, Int Cncl for New Initiatives in East/West Cooperation, DTI Soviet Working Pty on Consortia Jt Ventures, Int C of C Ctee on E Euro Rels; sec: Br-Polish Legal Assoc, Br-Hungarian Legal Assoc; vice chm Br Advsy Bd to Know How Funds; *Books* Joint Ventures in Poland (1987), Joint Ventures in the Soviet Union (1988), Joint Ventures in Poland: The New Legislation (1990), Joint Ventures in Hungary (1990); *Recreations* sailing, swimming, music, reading; *Clubs* RNVR Yacht, Law Soc Yacht, E Europe Business; *Style—* John Murphy, Esq; 94 Bromfelde Rd, London SW4 6PS (☎ 071 622 0229); 150 Aldersgate St, London EC1A 4EJ (☎ 071 606 8855, fax 071 606 4390, telex 884678)

MURPHY, Kenneth John (Kenny); s of Noel Arthur Murphy, of Cork, and Noelle Catherine, *née* Vaughan; *b* 31 July 1966; *Career* Rugby Union full back Cork Constitution FC and Ireland (7 caps); Irish Schs V NZ 1985; clubs: Cork Constitution FC 1986-, Barbarians RFC (Easter tour 1990, v Eng 1990, v Northants 1990), Wolfhounds RFC 1990; rep: Munster U20 1986-87, Munster 1987- (v All Blacks 1989, Ireland B (v Scotland) 1989; Ireland: debut v England 1990, v France 1991, v Wales (Rep) 1991; self employed in family business; *Recreations* horse racing, hurling, gaelic football; *Style—* Kenneth Murphy, Esq; 17 Halldene Villas, Bishopstown, Cork, Ireland (☎ 021 541877); Cork Constitution FC, Temple Hill, Blackrock, Cork

MURPHY, Sir Leslie Frederick; s of Frederick Charles Murphy; *b* 17 Nov 1915; *Educ* Southall GS, Birkbeck Coll London; *m* 1940, Marjorie Iris Cowell; 1 s, 1 da; *Career* chm: NEB 1977-79 (dep chm 1975-77); dir: Petroleum Economics 1980-88 (and chm), Unigate 1968-75, Schroders 1979-89 (dep chm 1973-75), Simon Engrg 1980-85; memb NEDC 1977-79; memb Bd Church Army 1964-, chm Church Army Housing 1973-82; kt 1978; *Recreations* golf, music; *Clubs* Oriental; *Style—* Sir Leslie Murphy; Hedgerley, Barton Common Rd, Barton-on-Sea, Hants; Petroleum Economics Ltd, 17-19 Barter St, London WC1A 2AQ (☎ 071 404 0221, telex 22573 PETECS G)

MURPHY, Michael; s of Francis Murphy, and Dorothy Byrne Kenny; *b* 12 Feb 1954; *Educ* Lourdes Secdy Sch Glasgow, Napier Coll Edinburgh; *m* 29 May 1982, Carolynne Dawn, da of Derrick Thomas Evans; 1 s (Michael Stuart b 1984), 1 da (Kimberly Jane b 1987); *Career* md PR Consultants Scotland Ltd, chm Quorom Graphic Design Consultants Ltd; *Recreations* curling, reading; *Style—* Michael Murphy, Esq; Erroldene, Bridge of Weir Rd, Kilmacolm, Renfrewshire PA13 4NX; 9 Lynedoch Crescent, Glasgow G3 6EQ (☎ 041 333 0557, fax 041 332 7990, car 0836 700984)

MURPHY, Dr Michael Furber; s of Arthur Furber Murphy (d 1989), and Dr Jean Marjorie Frazer; *b* 2 May 1951; *Educ* Malvern, St Bartholomew's Hosp (MB BS); *m* 1 Sept 1984, Dr (Elizabeth) Sarah Green, da of Prof L L Green, of Seafield Cottage, De Grouchy St, W Kirby, Wirral, Merseyside; *Career* St Bartholomew's Hosp: house physician 1974, registrar in haematology 1978-79, sr registrar 1979-83, sr lectr and hon conslt 1983-; sr house offr in med: St Leonard's Hosp, Brompton Hosp and Nat Heart Hosp 1975-78; MRCP 1976, MRCPath 1982, MD 1988; *Recreations* theatre, golf, wine tasting; *Style—* Dr Michael Murphy; 69 Cholmeley Crescent, Highgate, London N6 5EX (☎ 081 340 5814); Dept of Haematology, St Bartholomew's Hospital, London EC1A 7BE (☎ 071 601 8888)

MURPHY, Michael Joseph; s of Joseph Murphy (d 1972), and Delia Hurst (d 1964); *b* 10 Dec 1919; *Educ* Christian Brothers Coll Dun Laoghaire; *m* 1941, Joan (d 1980), da of William Stanley Huggard (d 1952); 2 s, 4 da; *Career* co dir; pres Golfing Union of Ireland 1963-65, chm Council of Nat Golf Unions 1969; dir Ulster Bank Ltd 1969; *Recreations* reading, golf administration; *Clubs* United Servs, Dublin, Royal & Ancient GC; *Style—* Michael Murphy, Esq; Hilltop, Ballina, Co Mayo, Eire (☎ 096 21754); work: Lord Edward St, Ballina, Co Mayo, Eire (☎ 096 21344)

MURPHY, (Cornelius McCaffrey) Neil; MBE (1982); s of Edward Murphy (d 1973), and Annie Murphy; *b* 31 May 1936; *Educ* Holyrood Sch, Univ of Glasgow (MA); *m* 1963, Joan Anne, da of William Tytler; 2 da (Emma Jane, Samantha Anne); *Career* ed in chief Building Magazine 1983-87 (ed 1974-83); md: Building (Publishers) Ltd 1981-, Builder Group plc 1990- (joined 1962, dir 1979-); chm PTT Ltd (Periodical Trg Cncl) 1986-90; Freeman Worshipful Co of Tylers and Bricklayers; *Recreations* reading, racing, golf; *Clubs* RAC; *Style—* Neil Murphy, Esq, MBE; Builder House, 1 Millharbour, Isle of Dogs, London E14 9RA

MURPHY, Patrick James; CMG (1985); s of Dr James Vincent Murphy (d 1946), and Cicely Mary, *née* Crowley; *b* 11 March 1931; *Educ* Cranbrook Kent, Gonville and Caius Coll Cambridge (BA); *m* 1, 10 Oct 1959, Barbara; 2 s (Michael b 1962, John b 1964); m 2, 26 June 1974, Jutta; 1 s (Nicholas b 1977); *Career* RAF 1950-52, Pilot Offr Fighter Control Branch Royal Aux AF 1952, Flt Lt on reserve 1952-55; memb Oxford & Cambridge Far Eastern Expedition 1955-56; asst prodr BBC general overseas serv 1956-57; entered FO (later FCO) 1957: serv FO 1957, Frankfurt 1958, Berlin 1959, FO 1962, second sec (commercial) Warsaw 1962-65, FCO 1965-66, first sec (commercial) and consul Phnom Penh 1966-69, consul Dusseldorf 1969-71, consul Hamburg 1971-74, FCO 1974-77, first sec Vienna 1977-81, cnslr FCO 1981-87, ret HM Dip Serv 1987; sr advsr Sultanate of Oman 1987- 90; *Recreations* travel, history, boating, skiing; *Clubs* RAF; *Style—* Patrick Murphy, CMG; c/o R 3 Section, Lloyds Bank, 6 Pall Mall, London SW1

MURPHY, Paul Peter; MP (Lab) Torfaen 1987-; s of Ronald Murphy, and Marjorie Murphy (d 1984); *b* 25 Nov 1948; *Educ* St Francis RC Sch Abersychan, W Monmouth Sch Pontypool, Oriel Coll Oxford (MA); *Career* oppn front bench spokesman Welsh Affrs 1988-; memb Torfaen Borough 1973-87; lectr in history and politics Ebbw Vale Coll of Further Educn 1971-87; *Recreations* music; *Style—* Paul Murphy, Esq, MP; House of Commons, Westminster, London SW1A 0AA

MURPHY, Penelope Gay; da of Gerald Hugh-Smith (d 1965), of Hove, Sussex, and Pamela Daphne, *née* Miller; *b* 28 Oct 1949; *Educ* Brighton & Hove HS, LSE (LLB); *m* 31 Aug 1974, Ian Patrick, s of Patrick Murphy, of Cardiff, South Glamorgan; 2 da (Anna b 1982, Charlotte b 1984); *Career* ct clerk Dir of Pub Prosecutions Old Bailey 1971-73, admitted slr 1976, ptnr Edwards Geldard of Cardiff 1978-; treas S Wales Branch Assoc of Women Slrs 1984-; memb Law Soc 1976-; *Recreations* family life, swimming, skiing, tennis; *Style—* Mrs Penelope Murphy; 3 Llandaff Chase, Llandaff, Cardiff, South Glamorgan CF5 2NA (☎ 0222 238239); Edwards Geldard, 16 St Andrews Crescent, Cardiff CF1 3RD (☎ 0222 238239, fax 0222 237268)

MURPHY, Stuart John; s of John William Murphy, OBE (d 1978), of 25 Fowler's Hill, Salisbury, Wilts, and Kathleen Beryl, *née* Lait; *b* 7 Feb 1933; *Educ* City of London Sch, Poly of Central London (DipArch, Dip Town Planning); *m* 1 Dec 1966, Jane

Elizabeth, da of George Tinkler (d 1963), of London; 1 s (Giles b 1969), 1 da (Sara b 1972); *Career* London Div RNVR 1950-63, Nat Serv 1958-59, Sub Lt RNR 1959, serv 1 Lt Vernon Sqdn; ret 1963; architect; Architects Dept London CC 1956-63, sr architect Llewellyn Davies & Weeks 1963-65, gp architect City of Westminster Dept Architecture and Planning 1965-68, controller of architecture (borough architect) London Borough of Harrow 1971-76 (dep borough architect and planner 1968-71), city architect and planning offr Corp of City of London 1979-86 (dep city architect and planning offr 1976-79), conslt architect town-planner and urban design conslt to govt depts and private clients 1987-; vice pres RIBA, former pres Cities of London and Westminster Soc Architects 1984-86; chm: Pub Sector Gp 1987-89 (Disciplinary Ctee 1989-); sr vice pres Soc of Chief Architects of Local Authys, memb various socs involved with civic amenity and urban design, parish clerk St Lawrence Jewry Next Guildhall Church 1978-; Freeman City of London 1954, Liveryman Worshipful Co Merchant Taylors 1968, memb Worshipful Co Parish Clerks 1978, fndr memb Worshipful Co Chartered Architects (chm Organising Ctee 1984-85, Renter warden); FRIBA 1970, FRTPI 1973, FRSA 1977, FBIM 1978, MBAE 1988; *Books* Debrett's Great Cities of the World (contrib, 1987), Scala Yearbook (ed, 1987-90); *Recreations* theatre and music hall history, gardening; *Clubs* Players Theatre; *Style—* Stuart Murphy, Esq; Hillier House, 509 Upper Richmond Rd, London SW14 7EE (☎ 081 878 3227, fax 081 878 7153, telex 9413819 HILHOUG)

MURPHY-O'CONNOR, Rt Rev Cormac; *see*: Arundel and Brighton, Bishop of

MURRAY, Alan Adams; s of William Murray (d 1973), and Christina Margaret, *née* Adam; *b* 16 Dec 1948; *Educ* Perth Acad, Heriot-Watt Univ Edinburgh (Dip in Banking and Fin Studies); *m* 1970, Margaret Lucretia, *née* McBeth; 1 s (Steven Alan b 1975), 1 da (Lynne Louise b 1977); *Career* Bank of Scotland 1965-75; British Linen Bank Ltd: asst loans controller 1975-77, loans controller 1977-79, exec asst 1979, asst mangr 1980-82, mangr 1982-83, asst dir 1983-84, divnl dir 1984-87, dir 1987-, head of banking 1989-; AIB (Scot) 1972; *Recreations* tennis, badminton, golf; *Style—* Alan Murray, Esq; The British Linen Bank Ltd, PO Box 49, 4 Melville St, Edinburgh EH3 7NZ (☎ 031 243 8341, fax 031 243 8393)

MURRAY, Hon Mrs (Amanda Muriel Mary); *née* Neville; eldest da of 10 Baron Braybrooke, DL, and his 1 w, Robin Helen, *née* Brockhoff; *b* 8 April 1962; *m* 1989, Stephen Christopher Jerningham Murray, o s of Christopher Mark Henry Murray, of La Glinette, St Aubin, Jersey, CI; *Style—* The Hon Mrs Murray

MURRAY, Sir (John) Antony Jerningham; CBE (1980); s of Capt John Challenger Murray (d 1939), of Oaksey Manor, Malmesbury, Wilts, and Cecilia Annette, *née* Jerningham; *b* 21 Jan 1921; *Educ* Eton, New Coll Oxford; *m* 23 July 1943, Hon Winifred Mary Hardinge, da of 2 Baron Hardinge of Penshurst, GCB, GCVO, MC, PC (d 1960); 1 s ((George) Alexander John b 8 Dec 1947); *Career* 2 Lt Grenadier Guards 1941, Capt 1945, Maj 1946, ret; dir Christmas Island Phosphate Co Ltd 1947-51; dep chm W India Ctee 1961-63 (chm 1963-65, vice-pres 1966-); hon advsr to govt of Barbados in UK 1961-; pres N Cerney Cricket Club; tstee Sir Frank Worrell UK Meml Fund; kt 1987; *Recreations* salmon fishing; *Clubs* Boodle's, White's, RAC; *Style—* Sir Antony Murray, CBE; Woodmancote Manor Cottage, Cirencester, Glos GL7 7ED (☎ 028583 226); c/o Barbados High Commission, 1 Great Russell Street, London WC1 (☎ 071 631 3391)

MURRAY, Athol Hollins; s of Richard Hollins Murray, (d 1957; invented reflective road studs (Cats' Eyes)), of Dinmore Manor, Herefordshire, and Elsie Gwendoline, *née* Knee (d 1959); *b* 27 Jan 1922; *Educ* Shrewsbury; *m* 16 Aug 1947, Sheila, da of Herman Edward Hulme, MBE (d 1964), of Bowdon, Cheshire and Beaumaris, Anglesey; 2 s (Andrew b 1954, Charles b 1958), 2 da (Katherine b 1962, Elizabeth b 1965); *Career* RAF 1941-46, Air Sea Rescue and Marine Craft Serv; inc valuer; ptnr Stuart Murray & Co Manchester and Branches 1949-78, md The Hollins Murray Gp Ltd 1978-; chm: Northern Realty Co Ltd, Barrowmore Village Settlement nr Chester 1979-; FSVA 1968 (pres 1972-73), ASA 1974; *Recreations* golf, philately; *Clubs* Hale and Ringway Golf, Royal Philatelic Soc (London and Cape Town); *Style—* Athol Murray, Esq; Erlesdene Garden Cottage, Green Walk, Bowdon, Altrincham, Cheshire WA14 2SL (☎ 061 941 6006); The Hollins Murray Group Ltd, Hollins House, Cottesmore Gardens, Hale Barns, Altrincham, Cheshire WA15 8TS (☎ 061 904 9412)

MURRAY, Dr Athol Laverick; s of George Murray (d 1949), of Tynemouth, Northumberland, and Margery, *née* Laverick (d 1974); *Educ* Lancaster Royal GS, Jesus Coll Cambridge (BA, MA), Univ of Edinburgh (LLB, PhD); *m* 11 Oct 1958, (Irene) Joyce, da of George Kilpatrick Cairns (d 1953), of Edinburgh; 1 s (Ewan George b 1968), 1 da (Helen Cairns b 1966); *Career* res asst FO 1954; Scottish Record Off: asst keeper 1954-83, dep keeper 1983-84, keeper 1985-90; author of articles on Scottish history in various jls; chm of cncl Scottish Record Soc 1981-90, chm Conf of Medieval Scottish Historical Res 1986-89; FRHistS 1971, FSA Scot 1982 (vice pres 1989-); *Books* The Royal Grammar School Lancaster (1951), Sebright School Wolverley (1953), The Lag Charters (1957); *Recreations* bowls, reading; *Clubs* Cwlth House; *Style—* Dr Athol Murray; 33 Inverleith Gardens, Edinburgh EH3 5PR (☎ 031 552 4465)

MURRAY, Maj Charles Graham; MBE (1945), JP (1962), DL (1975) S Yorks; s of Charles Graham Murray (d 1946); *b* 28 Jan 1920; *Educ* St Cyprian's Sch Eastbourne, Stowe; *m* 1949, Susan Madeleine, da of William Raymond Stephenson Bennet Grange Sheffield; 3 da; *Career* Capt RA 1940-46, Maj RA (TA) 1947-52; md Tempered Spring Co Sheffield 1948-82; Master Cutler 1974-75; *Recreations* walking, gardening; *Clubs* Sheffield; *Style—* Maj Graham Murray, MBE, JP, DL; 3 Belgrave Drive, Sheffield S10 3LQ (☎ 0742 30 2123)

MURRAY, Colin Keith; s of Brig George Murray, CBE, DSO, MC (d 1983), and Elizabeth Agnes, *née* Wheeler (d 1982); *b* 18 June 1932; *Educ* Wellington; *m* 1 Feb 1964, Precelly Elizabeth Caroline, da of Col David Gwyn Davies-Scourfield MC, of Eversley Cross House, Eversley Cross, Hants; 1 s (William b 1970), 2 da (Sophia b 1965, Harriet b 1966); *Career* Seaforth Highlanders 1950, 2 Lt seconded 1 Bn Kings African Rifles 1951, Capt 11 Bn Seaforth Highlanders (TA) 1952-64; reinsurance broker CT Bowring & Co Ltd 1953-63; R J Kiln & Co Ltd: dep underwriter and dir 1963-74, active underwriter non marine syndicates 1974-84, chm 1985; Lloyds: memb Cncl 1989- (1983-86), dep chm 1989-90; Freeman Worshipful Co of Insurers; *Recreations* music, bridge, gardening, country sports; *Clubs* The City; *Style—* Colin Murray, Esq; The Long House, Hurstbourne Priors, nr Whitchurch, Hampshire (☎ 0256 892 606); R J Kiln & Co Ltd, 117 Fenchurch St, London EC3M 5AL (☎ 071 481 9601, fax 071 488 1848, telex 8955661)

MURRAY, David Edward; s of David Ian Murray (d 1975), and Roma Murray; *b* 14 Oct 1951; *Educ* Fettes, Broughton HS; *m* 22 July 1972, Louise Violet; 2 s (David Douglas b 1973, Keith Andrew b 1975); *Career* fndr and chm Murray International Holdings and subsidiaries 1976-, chm Rangers Football Club plc 1988-; chm UK 2000 Scotland 1987-88, govr Clifton Hall Sch 1987-89; Hon Dr of Business Heriot Watt Univ 1986; *Recreations* collecting wine, watching sport; *Style—* David Murray, Esq; Murray House, 4 Redhevghs Rigg, South Gyle, Edinburgh EH12 9OQ (☎ 031 317 7000, fax 031 317 7111, telex 727821)

MURRAY, Hon David Paul; s of Baron Murray of Epping Forest (Life Peer), and Lady Murray, *née* Heather Woolf; *b* 8 April 1960; *Educ* Buckhurst Hill Co HS; *m* 1984, Moria Denise, da of Patrick Joseph Roche of Milltown, Dublin; 1 da (Elizabeth b 1985), 1 s (Joseph b 1987); *Career* govt serv; *Clubs* RAF; *Style—* Sqdn Ldr the Hon David Murray; MOD RAF PMC Innsworth, Gloucester GL3 1EZ (☎ 0452 712612)

MURRAY, Hon Mrs (Diana Lucy); da of Baron Home of the Hirsel, KT, PC, (Life Peer); *b* 1940; *m* 1963 (m dis 1976), James Archibald Wolfe Murray; *Style—* The Hon Mrs Murray

MURRAY, Dr the Hon Dinah (Dinah Karen Crawshay); yr da of Baron Greenwood of Rossendale, PC (Life Peer, d 1982); *b* 1946; *Educ* PhD; *m* 1970, David Murray; 3 s (Bruno b 1974, Leo b 1976, Fergus b 1978); *Style—* Dr the Hon Dinah Murray; 42 Cheverton Road, London N19

MURRAY, The Hon Mr Justice; Sir Donald Bruce; s of Charles Benjamin Murray (d 1977), and Agnes Mary, *née* Patterson (d 1955); *b* 24 Jan 1923; *Educ* Belfast Royal Acad, Queen's Univ Belfast (LLB), Trinity Coll Dublin (BA); *m* 21 Aug 1953, Rhoda Margaret, da of Thomas Parke (d 1973); 2 s (Adrian Timothy Lawrence b 30 Oct 1954, Paul Ralph Stephen b 27 April 1961), 1 da (Rosalind Louise b 9 May 1958); *Career* called to the Bar Grays Inn 1945, asst party draftsman to NI Govt 1945-51, asst lectr faculty of law Queen's Univ Belfast 1951-53, called to the Bar NI 1953, QC NI 1964, high ct Judge Chancery divn NI 1975; govr Belfast Royal Acad, memb bd Cathedral of St Anne Belfast, chm bd SLS Legal Publns NI; memb Hon Soc of Inn of Ct NI (Bencher 1971), memb Hon soc of Grays Inn (Hon Bencher 1987); *Recreations* playing the piano, dx-ing, snooker; *Clubs* Royal Belfast GC; *Style—* The Hon Mr Justice Murray; Royal Courts Of Justice, Chichester St, Belfast, N Ireland (☎ 0232 235 111)

MURRAY, Sir Donald Frederick; KCVO (1983), CMG (1973); s of Archibald Thomas Murray (d 1960), and Freda May, *née* Byfield (d 1964); *b* 14 June 1924; *Educ* Colfes GS, Kings Sch Canterbury, Worcester Coll Oxford; *m* 17 Dec 1949, Marjorie, da of Charles Culverwell (d 1977); 3 s (Ian b 1951, Neil b 1958, Alexander b 1960), 1 da (Gillian b 1953); *Career* RM (41 Commando) 1943-46; Foreign Serv: entered FO 1948, third sec Warsaw 1948, FO 1951, second sec Vienna 1953, first sec political office ME Forces 1956, FO 1957, first sec commerce Stockholm 1958, first sec and head of chancery Saigon 1962, FO 1964, cnsllr 1965, head of SE Asia Dept 1966, cnsllr Tehran 1969, RCDS 1973, HM ambass Tripoli 1974, asst undersec of state FCO 1977, HM ambass Stockholm 1980, ret 1984; assessor chm Civil Serv Selection Bd 1984-86, dir Goodlass Wall & Co Ltd 1985-; chm Kent Co SSAFA 1985-90, tstee World Resource Fndn 1986-, complaints cmmr Channel Tunnel 1987-; Grand Cross Order of North Star Sweden 1983; *Style—* Sir Donald Murray, KCVO, CMG; Oxney House, Wittersham, Kent TN30 7ED

MURRAY, Douglas James; s of James Charles Murray (d 1938), of Croydon, Surrey, and Emily Agnes, *née* Ludgate (d 1957); *b* 26 Feb 1914; *Educ* Whitgift Sch; *m* 4 Nov 1939, Joan Margaret, da of James Frederick Lintott (d 1962), of Croydon, Surrey; 2 da (Elizabeth Ann b 1942, Susan Margaret b 1949); *Career* banker; joined TA 1932, serv WWII India and Burma (Maj); chm Barclays Bank London Mangrs Club 1965; AIB; *Recreations* golf, photography; *Clubs* Royal Eastbourne Golf; *Style—* Douglas Murray, Esq; 7 Wells Close, Eastbourne BN20 7TX (☎ 0323 639237)

MURRAY, Ewan Skinner; OBE (1984); s of Alexander Murray (d 1959), of Glasgow, and Sophia, *née* Smith (d 1984); *b* 18 Sept 1931; *Educ* Hyndland Sr Secdy Sch Glasgow; *Career* Nat Serv RAF Tenga, Singapore 1950-51; insur official Iron Trades Insurance Group 1960-; memb Garscube Harriers 1947- (hon sec 1952-62), Ctee memb Scottish Cross Country Union 1956- (hon gen sec 1963-71, pres 1972, life vice pres 1979-), ctee memb Scottish Amateur Athletic Assoc 1960- (hon treas 1970-71, hon gen sec 1971-83, life vice pres 1981-); Br Olympic Assoc: athletics admin offr Moscow 1980, cncl memb 1984-89, dir 1987-; Cwlth Games Cncl for Scotland: cncl memb 1973-83, athletics team mangr Brisbane 1982, vice chm 1983-87, chm 1987-; Br Amateur Athletic Bd: cncl memb 1972-84, selection ctee memb 1972-84, team admin offr 1978-80, chm 1984-89, hon life vice pres 1987-; cncl memb Euro Athletic Assoc 1987-; OStJ 1987, FSA Scotland; *Recreations* athletics; *Clubs* Western (Glasgow); *Style—* Ewan Murray, Esq, OBE; 25 Bearsden Rd, Glasgow G13 1YL (☎ 041 959 4436); Iron Trades Insurance Group, 105 West George St, Glasgow G2 1QN (☎ 041 204 0441, fax 041 221 8928)

MURRAY, Hon Geoffrey Charles; 2 s of 11 Earl of Dunmore; *b* 1949; *m* 1974, Margaret Irene, da of H Bulloch, of Blackwall, Tasmania; *Style—* The Hon Geoffrey Murray; 73 Pomona Rd, Riverside, Tasmania

MURRAY, Gordon; s of James Murray (d 1965), of Aberdeen, and Annie Hardie Center (d 1970); *b* 25 Aug 1935; *Educ* Kirkcaldy HS, Univ of Edinburgh (BSc, PhD); *m* 28 March 1964, Janet, da of George Yerrington (d 1961), of Wolverhampton; 2 s (Andrew, Peter), 1 da (Helen); *Career* res fell: Atomic Energy of Canada 1960-62, UKEAE Harwell 1962-65; lectr Univ of Manchester 1965-69, princ Scottish Home and Health Dept 1970-77, asst sec Scot Educn Dept 1977-79, Central Servs Scot Office 1979-86, dir Scot Cts Admin 1986-; *Recreations* reading, hill walking, gardening; *Style—* Gordon Murray, Esq; 26-27 Royal Terrace, Edinburgh EH7 5AH (☎ 031 556 0755 ext 238, fax 031 556 3604)

MURRAY, Harry Henry; s of Harry Murray (d 1975), of Worsley, Greater Manchester, and Frances Caroline Murray (d 1990); *b* 31 Dec 1939; *Educ* Walkden Secdy Mod, Worsley Tech Coll, Royal Tech Coll Salford (OND); *m* 26 Aug 1967, Susan Catherine, da of Charles Davies; 3 s (Jason H b 9 Sept 1968, James CC b 13 Aug 1972, Neil A b 6 Feb 1975); *Career* trainee mangr: Midland Hotel Manchester 1957-61, George V Paris 1961-62, Westminster Hotel 1962, Paris Plage 1962, Glendower Hotel St Annes 1962-63; dep gen mangr Grand Hotel Manchester 1964-67 (asst food and beverage mangr 1963-64); gen mangr: N Stafford Hotel Stoke-on-Trent 1967-69, Majestic Hotel Harrogate 1969-70, Parkview Hotel Durban 1970-72, President Hotel Johannesburg 1972-73, Landdrost Hotel Johannesburg 1973-76, Imperial Hotel Torquay 1976-81 (exec dir 1982-); govr and chm Advsy Ctee Hotel and Catering Dept 5 Devon Tech Coll, dir Main Bd Trg & Enterprise Cncl Devon and Cornwall, chm Master Innholders 1985-86, memb Reunion des Gastronomes; *Awards* Hotelier of the Year (UK) 1986, Cheu Bretvin, offr Maitre de Table Restauranteur de la Chaine des Rotisseurs; Freeman City of London; FBIM, FHCIMA, FCFA; *Recreations* reading, running (participated: Comrades Marathon 1972, Torbay Marathon 1982); *Style—* Harry Murray, Esq; The Imperial Hotel, Parkhill Rd, Torquay, Devon TQ1 2DG (☎ 0803 294301, fax 0803 298293)

MURRAY, (James) Iain; s of James Ian Murray (d 1977), and Jean Parker, *née* McLeod Baxter (d 1984); *b* 12 Nov 1932; *Educ* Rugby, Corpus Christi Coll Cambridge (BA, MA); *m* 21 March 1969, Ursula Jane, da of Eric Sayle, MD (d 1985); 1 s (Alexander b 9 Nov 1972), 2 da (Katharine b 13 July 1970, Fiona b 10 Aug 1979); *Career* Nat Serv 1951, Sgt RCS; articled clerk Freshfields 1956-59, admitted slr 1959, Robert Fleming & Co Ltd 1960-62 (seconded for 9 months on Wall St to G H Walker Investmt Bankers), slr Linklaters & Paines 1963- (ptnr 1967); Co Law Ctee: City of London Slrs Co 1967-77, Law Soc 1968-78, CBI Co Ctee 1987-; memb of the Incorporation of Maltmen in Glasgow 1954, Liveryman City of London Slrs Co, memb Law Soc 1959; *Recreations* walking; *Clubs* The City of London, Travellers, New (Edinburgh); *Style—* Iain Murray, Esq; Linklaters and Paines, Barrington House, 59-67 Gresham St, London EC2V 7JA (☎ 071 606 7080, fax 071 606 513, telex 884349/

888167)

MURRAY, Sir James; KCMG (1978, CMG 1966); s of James Hamilton Murray (d 1938), of King's Cross, Isle of Arran, by his w Hester Macneill Buie; *b* 3 Aug 1919; *Educ* Bellahouston Acad, Univ of Glasgow; *m* 1982, Mrs Jill Charmian Chapuisat, *née* Gordon-Hall; 2 step da; *Career* serv WWII RA India, Burma, Malaya, Scotland rising to GSO 2 WO; with FO (later FCO) 1947-79: ambass to Rwanda and Burundi 1962-63, dep head UK Delegn to EEC 1963-65, cnsllr Djakarta 1967, head Far East Dept FO 1967-70, consul-gen San Francisco 1970-73, asst under-sec FCO 1973-74, dep perm rep in NY 1974-78 with rank of ambass 1976-, ambass and perm rep to UN at Geneva 1978-79; Hanson Industs NY 1983; *Clubs* Brook (NY), Brooks's, Beefsteak, Pratt's; *Style—* Sir James Murray, KCMG; 220 Columbia Heights, Brooklyn Heights, New York, NY 11201, USA

MURRAY, Prof James Dickson; s of Peter Murray, and Sarah Murray; *b* 2 Jan 1931; *Educ* Dumfries Acad, Univ of St Andrews (BSc, PhD), Univ of Oxford (MA, DSc); *m* 1959, Sheila Todd Murray; 1 s, 1 da; *Career* lectr: Univ of Durham 1955-56, Harvard (Gordon MacKay lectr and res fell) 1956-59, UCL 1959-61; fell and maths tutor Hertford Coll Oxford 1961-63, res assoc Harvard 1963-64, prof engrg mechanics Univ of Michigan 1964-67, visiting fell St Catherines Coll Oxford 1967, prof of maths Univ of NY 1967-70, Guggenheim Fell Pasteur Inst Paris 1968; fell Corpus Christi Coll 1970-; Univ of Oxford: reader 1972-86, dir Centre for Mathematical Biology 1983-, sr res fell Corpus Christi 1985-86 (fell and tutor 1970-85), prof mathematical biology 1986-, professorial fell Corpus Christi 1986-; visiting prof: Nat Tsing Hua Univ 1975, Univ of Florence 1976, MIT 1979, Univ of Iowa 1979, Univ of Utah 1979 and 1985, Univ of Guelph 1980, Univ of Heidelberg 1980, CIT 1983, Southern Methodist Univ Dallas 1984, Univ of Calif 1985; Univ of Washington 1988-: Robert F Philip prof, prof of applied maths, adjunct prof of zoology; memb ed bd: Jl Theoretical Biol, Jl Mathematical Biol, Jl Maths Applied in Med and Biol, Lecture Notes in Biomaths, Biomaths series; author of numerous articles in learned jls; FRSE 1979; *Books* Asymptotic Analysis (1974, 2 edn 1984), Nonlinear Differential Equation Models in Biology (1977), Theories of Biological Pattern Formation (co-ed S Brenner, L Wolpert 1981), Modelling Patterns of Space and Time (co-ed W Jäger 1984), Mathematical Biology (1989); *Style—* Prof James Murray, FRS; Robert F Philip Professor; Department of Applied Mathematics FS-20, University of Washington, Seattle, WA 98195, USA (☎ 0101 206 685 9298, secretary 0101 206 685 2841, fax 0101 206 685 1440)

MURRAY, Jennifer Susan (Jenni); da of Alvin Bailey, of Barnsley, Yorks, and Winifred, *née* Jones; *b* 12 May 1950; *Educ* Barnsley Girls HS, Univ of Hull (BA); *m* 1 (m dis), Brian Murray; 2 s (Edward Louis b 1983, Charles Edgar b 1987); *Career* prodr and presenter BBC Radio Bristol 1973-76, presenter reporter BBC TV South 1977-82; presenter: Newsnight BBC TV Lime Grove 1983-85, Today BBC Radio 4 1986-87, Womans Hour BBC Radio 4 1987-; documentary films for TV incl: The Duchy of Cornwall, Everyman, Stand by Your Man, Breaking the Chain; *Recreations* horses, books, swimming, the children; *Style—* Ms Jenni Murray; Womans Hour, BBC, Broadcasting House, London (☎ 071 580 4468)

MURRAY, John A R Grey; CBE (1975, MBE 1945); s of Thomas Robinson Grey, and Dorothy, da of Sir John Murray, KCVO, JP, DL, himself ggs of John Murray, the friend and publisher of Byron; added the surname Murray by Deed Poll 1930; *b* 25 June 1941; *Educ* Eton, Magdalen Coll Oxford; *m* 1939, Diana, da of Col Bernard James and Hon Angela Kay-Shuttleworth, da of 1 Baron Shuttleworth; 2 s (John b 1941, m Virginia Lascelles; Hallam b 1950), 2 da (Joanna b 1940, m 4 Viscount Mersey, *qv*; Mrs Nigel (Freydis Marianne) Campbell); *Career* late Maj RA, serv WWII; publisher; sr dir John Murray (Publishers) 1968-, asst ed Quarterly Review, co-ed Cornhill Magazine; *Recreations* Byron, archives, music; *Clubs* Brooks's, Pratt's, Beefsteak; *Style—* John Murray, Esq, CBE; 50 Albemarle Street, London W1

MURRAY, John Joseph; s of Kevin Thomas Murray, of Bridge of Weir, Renfrewshire, and Mary, *née* Leahy (d 1973); *b* 10 May 1953; *Educ* Fort Augustus Abbey Sch, Univ of Leeds (LLB); *Career* admitted slr 1979; articled clerk Smallpeice & Merriman 1977-79, ptnr Nabarro Nathanson 1986- (asst slr 1979); *Recreations* reading, travel, music, cinema, sport; *Style—* John Murray, Esq; 144 Broadhurst Gardens, West Hampstead, London NW6 3BH (☎ 071 328 8834); Nabarro Nathanson, 50 Stratton Street, London W1X 5FL (☎ 071 493 9933, fax 071 629 7900, telex 8813144 NABAROG)

MURRAY, Prof John Joseph; s of John Gerald Murray (d 1980), of Bradford, W Yorks, and Margaret Sheila, *née* Parle (d 1979); *b* 28 Dec 1941; *Educ* St Bedes GS Bradford, Univ of Leeds (PhD, MChD, BChd); *m* 28 March 1967, Valerie, da of Harry Allen (d 1969), of Heanor, Derbys; 2 s (Mark b 14 March 1975, Christoper b 3 Nov 1976); *Career* res fell in childrens dentistry Univ of Leeds 1966-70, reader inst of dental surgery Univ of London 1975-77 (sr lectr in childrens dentistry 1970-75), prof of child dental health Univ of Newcastle upon Tyne 1977- (dental postgrad sub dean 1982-); asst scientific ed British Dental Journal, pres Br Paedodontic Soc 1985 (conslt advsr to chief med offr); Dept of Health: memb Standing Dental Advsy Ctee 1980-, memb Ctee on Continuing Educn Trg 1985-; memb BDA, FDS RCS 1973; *Books* The Acid Etch Technique in Paedodontics and Orthodontics (jtly), Fluorides in Cavities Prevention (jtly, 1976), Prevention of Dental Disease (ed, 1983); *Recreations* golf, bridge, photography; *Clubs* Ponteland Golf; *Style—* Prof John Murray; Department of Child Dental Health, Dental School, Framlington Place, University of Newcastle upo Tyne, Newcastle upon Tyne NE2 4BW (☎ 091 222 6000)

MURRAY, Jonathan Aidan Muir; s of Maj George Muir Murray (d 1967), and Esyllt, *née* Roberts; *b* 16 Aug 1951; *Educ* Daniel Stewart's Coll Edinburgh, Univ of Edinburgh (BSc, MB ChB, MD); *m* ; 2 s (Craig Muir b 1976, Grant Aidan b 1979), 2 da (Nicola Hamilton b 1978, Louise Aitken b 1980); *Career* conslt otolaryngologist: NZ 1982-83, Lothian Health Authy Board 1983-, Borders Health Authy 1983-; pt/t sr lectr Univ of Edinburgh 1983-; govr Donaldson's Sch for the Deaf Edinburgh ; FRCSEd 1979, FRACS 1983; *Recreations* swimming, fishing, golf; *Style—* Jonathan Murray, Esq; Beechwood House, Murrayfield Hospital, 122 Corstorphine Rd, Edinburgh EH12 6UD (☎ 031 334 0363)

MURRAY, Kenneth Alexander George; CB (1977); s of late George Dickie, and Isobella Murray; *b* 17 June 1916; *Educ* Skene St and Central Schs Aberdeen, Univ of Aberdeen (MA, BEd); *m* 1942, Elizabeth Ward, da of late Arthur Simpson; 1 da (Alison); *Career* dir Civil Serv Selection Bd and Civil Serv cmmr 1964-77; special advsr to the Home Off on: Police Serv, Prison Serv, Fire Serv Selection 1977-; dir Home Off Unit 1977-80; selection advsr to Church of Scotland and C of E; formerly selection advsr: Govt of Nigeria, Govt of Pakistan, Govt of India; fell Br Psychological Soc; *Recreations* reading, theatre, bridge, cricket; *Clubs* MCC, Royal Cwlth Soc; *Style—* Kenneth Murray, Esq, CB; 15 Melvinshaw, Leatherhead, Surrey (☎ 0372 372995)

MURRAY, Martin Charles; s of Brian Murray, Crosby, and Muriel Gertrude, *née* Spense; *b* 13 April 1955; *Educ* Merchant Taylors', Emmanuel Coll Cambridge (MA, LLB), Harvard Univ (LLM); *Career* admitted slr 1981, Clifford-Turner 1979-83, S&W Berisford plc 1983-86, Hanson plc 1986-; memb Law Soc; *Recreations* hedonism; *Style—* Martin Murray, Esq; 45 Mexfield Rd, Putney, London SW15 2RG (☎ 01 874 5063); Hanson plc, 1 Grosvenor Place, London SW1X 7JH (☎ 071 245 1245, fax 071 245 9939)

MURRAY, Prof Maxwell; s of Maxwell Murray (d 1981), and Martha Letham, *née* Davidson; *b* 3 May 1939; *Educ* Shawlands Acad, Univ of Glasgow (BVMS, PhD, DVM); *m* 8 Sept 1976, Christine Madelaine, da of Maj Ronald Lewis Allen, of 117 Titwood Rd, Glasgow; 1 s (Maxwell b 1979), 2 da (Katie b 1978, Kirsty b 1983); *Career* lectr in vet pathology Univ of Nairobi 1963-65, sr scientist Int Laboratory for Res on Animal Diseases Nairobi 1975-85, prof of vet med Univ of Glasgow 1985- (sr lectr in vet pathology 1974-75, lectr 1965-74); FRCPath 1984, FRSE 1984; *Books* Current Trends in Immunology and Genetics and their Implications for Parasitic Diseases (1978), Livestock Productivity and Trypanotolerance: Network Training Manual (1983); *Recreations* family football, philosophy; *Clubs* Savage; *Style—* Prof Maxwell Murray; 21 Ledcameroch Rd, Bearsden, Glasgow G61 4AE (☎ 041 942 6476); Dept of Veterinary Medicine, University of Glasgow Veterinary School, Bearsden Rd, Bearsden, Glasgow G61 1QH (☎ 041 339 8855, fax 041 942 7215, telex 777070 UNIGLA)

MURRAY, Michael Charles; s of Michael Murray, of Leigh, Lancashire, and Margaret, *née* Garrigan; *b* 24 Sept 1946; *Educ* Leigh GS, St John Rigby GS, Open University (BA), London Business Sch (MSc, Economist prize); *m* 19 Dec 1970; Penelope Doris, da of Harry Eatock; 1 s (Neil Michael b 14 July 1976), 1 da (Kerry Martine b 21 March 1984); *Career* mgmnt trainee Samuel Courtauld & Co Ltd 1964-67; work study engr: Small & Parkes Ltd 1967-69, Warrington Borough Council 1971-74 (asst 1969-71); mgmnt services and personnel offr South Ribble Borough Council 1974-79, sector administrator North Manchester Health Authority 1984-86 (district personnel offr 1979-84, unit gen mangr Mid Staffordshire Health Authority 1986-90; chief exec: Mental Health Foundation of Mid Staffordshire NHS Trust 1990-; Caring Together Foundation 1989-90; Allan Brooking Travelling fell 1986, Kings Fund fell 1988; MIMS 1972, MIPM 1974, MIAM (Dip) 1974; *Recreations* speaker for Survive-Miva; *Style—* Michael Murray, Esq; 5 Castle Way, Stafford ST16 1BS (☎ 0785 46668); St George's Hospital, Corporation St, Stafford ST16 3AG (☎ 0785 57888 ext 5500, fax 0785 58969)

MURRAY, Cdr (Douglas) Neil (Toler); s of Thomas Prain Douglas Murray, MBE (d 1986), of Angus, and Sybil Enid Murray, MBE, *née* Toler; *b* 4 July 1932; *Educ* Stowe; *m* 4 April 1959, Avril Jocelyn, da of John Wardrop-Moore (d 1977), of London SW1; 1 s (Samuel Patrick b 1975), 1 da (Cicely Catherine b 1970); *Career* RN 1950-75, Lt 1954, cmd HMS Brinkley 1960-61, Lt Cdr 1962, cmd HMS Exmouth 1965-66, HMS Tenby 1970-72, ret 1975; marine conslt Offshore Oil Indust 1980-; memb Royal Co of Archers (Queen's Bodyguard for Scotland); *Clubs* Royal Northern, Univ of Aberdeen; *Style—* Cdr Neil Murray, RN; Cleish Hills, Kinross (☎ 05775 205)

MURRAY, Neil Alastair Charles; s of Alastair Richardson Murray, of Hong Kong, and Patricia Stella Ray, *née* Jones; *b* 25 Feb 1954; *Educ* King George V Sch Hong Kong, Univ of Southampton (LLB), City Univ (MA); *m* 1 Sept 1984, Patricia Susan, da of John Herbert Mulholland, of Connecticut, USA; 1 s (James b 4 July 1987), 1 da (Stephanie b 18 June 1989); *Career* admitted slr 1980; Boodle Hatfield & Co London 1978-80, Legal Dept ICI 1980, Norton Rose 1980-85, ptnr Travers Smith Braithwaite 1987- (joined 1985); Freeman Worshipful Co of Slrs; memb Law Soc; *Recreations* music, golf, skiing, fitness; *Clubs* Wig and Pen; *Style—* Neil Murray, Esq

MURRAY, Nicholas Julyan Edward; s of Sir (Francis) Ralph Hay Murray, KCMG, CB (d 1986), of Whaddon Hall Mews, Whaddon, Bucks, and Mauricette, *née* Countess Kuenburg; *b* 7 March 1939; *Educ* Bedford Sch, English Sch Cairo, Univ of St Andrews (MA); *m* 14 July 1973, Caroline Anne, da of Capt A McClintock, of Glenbower, Coolbawn, Nenagh, Co Tipperary, Ireland; 1 da (Anstice Aileen Thérèse b 22 Jan 1981); *Career* SH Benson Ltd 1962-71 (dir 1968); dir: Ogilvy Benson & Mather Ltd 1971-72, md Murray Parry & Ptnrs 1972-81, dir Woodyer Hutson Chapman 1981-86; md Conzept Int Mgmnt Business Devpt Conslts 1986-; memb and professional advsr Bd of Trade (missions Tokyo 1968, San Francisco 1969); chm Friends of the Vale of Aylesbury 1987 (memb ctee 1975-, vice-chm 1985); FInstD; *Books* Chronicle of the Villages of the Vale of Aylesbury (1986); *Recreations* sailing; *Clubs* Sussex Yacht, Lough Derg Yacht; *Style—* Nicholas Murray, Esq; The Old Vicarage, Aston Abbotts, Aylesbury, Bucks HP22 4NB (☎ 0296 681 617); 38 Perrers Rd, London W6; Conzept Int, Riverview House, Beavor Lane, London W6 (☎ 081 748 7874)

MURRAY, Noreen Elizabeth; da of John and Lillian Grace Parker; *b* 26 Feb 1935; *Educ* King's Coll London (BSc), Univ of Birmingham (PhD); *m* 1958, Kenneth Murray; *Career* res assoc: Stanford Univ 1960-64, Univ of Cambridge 1964-67, Molecular Genetics Unit MRC Edinburgh 1968-74; Dept of Molecular Biology Univ of Edinburgh: lectr 1974, then sr lectr, then reader 1978-88; scientist Euro Molecular Biology Laboratory Heidelberg 1980-82; memb: EMBO, Genetics Soc USA; pres Genetical Soc 1987-90; author of original res papers and reviews of genetics and molecular biology; FRS 1982, FRSE 1989; *Recreations* gardening; *Style—* Prof Noreen Murray, FRS, FRSE; Department of Molecular Biology, University of Edinburgh, Mayfield Road, Edinburgh EH9 3JR (☎ 031 667 1081)

MURRAY, Norman Loch; s of Thomas Loch Murray, of Norward, 6 Auchinleck Rd, Cumnock, Ayrshire, and May Fox, *née* Davidson; *b* 17 March 1948; *Educ* George Watson's Coll Edinburgh, Heriot Watt Univ Edinburgh (BA), Harvard Grad Sch of Business Admin Cambridge Mass USA (PMD); *m* 17 March 1972, Pamela Anne, da of George Low; 2 s (Niall, Andrew); *Career* Scottish and Newcastle Breweries plc Edinburgh 1971-73, Arthur Young & Co Edinburgh 1973-77, Peat Marwick Mitchell & Co Hong Kong 1977-80, The Royal Bank of Scotland plc Edinburgh 1980-85; dir: Charterhouse Development Capital Ltd Edinburgh 1985-89, Morgan Grenfell & Co Ltd 1989- (dep chief exec Morgan Grenfell Devpt Capital Ltd); memb Res Ctee and Educn Working Pty Inst CAs Scotland, memb Co of Merchants of City of Edinburgh; MICAS, FRSA; *Books* Making Corporate Reports Valuable (jtly, 1988); *Recreations* squash, golf, hillwalking; *Clubs* Royal Scottish Automobile, Watsonian, Harvard Business School, Royal Hong Kong Yacht; *Style—* Norman Murray, Esq; Morgan Grenfell Development Capital Ltd, 35 St Andrew Square, Edinburgh EH2 2AD (☎ 031 557 8600, fax 031 557 8306, telex 727273 MG SEDI G)

MURRAY, Norman Wood; s of Peter Wood Murray (d 1982), of Thorpe Underwood House, Northamptonshire, and Annie, *née* McCracken (d 1983); *b* 7 May 1930; *Educ* Chigwell Sch Essex; *m* May 1954, Hazel Margaret, da of Leslie Tucker; 2 s (Stuart Wood b 13 Nov 1957, Bruce Wood b 25 April 1961), 1 da (Fiona (Dr Underhill) b 29 Jan 1959); *Career* CA; Lord Foster & Co: articled clerk 1947-52, qualified sr 1952-54, ptnr 1954-87 (various mergers 1954-87, culminating in Dearden Farrow), nat managing ptnr Dearden Farrow 1980-86, ptnr BDO Binder Hamlyn 1987-; memb ICAEW 1953-; *Recreations* church activities, reading, walking; *Style—* Norman Murray, Esq; BDO Binder Hamlyn, 20 Old Bailey, London EC4M 7BH (☎ 071 489 9000, fax 071 489 6060)

MURRAY, Pete; OBE; s of Harry James (d 1937), of IOW, and Violet Caroline, *née* Reece; *b* 19 Sept 1925; *Educ* St Pauls Hammersmith, RADA; *m* 1, 23 Feb 1952 (m dis 1963), Germaine Graff; m 2, 22 May 1973, Patricia Alice, da of Harry Victor Crabb, of 9 Deepdale, London; 1 s (Michael Murray b 1981); *Career* WWII RAF 1943-45; Arts Repertory Theatre Cambridge, played Cliff in Power Without Glory Booth Theatre NY 1948, Last Glory TV and nominated Actor of Year 1956, Six Five

Special rock and jazz show BBC TV 1957, Open House BBC Radio Two 1969-80, LBC Radio 1984-89, currently disc-jockey Pete Murray London Talkback Radio; memb: Stars Orgn of Spastics, Lord Taverners, Grand Order of Water Rats; *Books* One Day I'll Forget My Trousers (1975); *Recreations* tennis, golf, theatre; *Clubs* Roehampton; *Style*— Pete Murray, Esq, OBE; LBC Radio, PO Box 261, London EC4P 4LP (☎ 071 955 0055, fax 071 353 4478)

MURRAY, Roger Garth; s of John Sefton (d 1961) of London, and Irene Constance, *née* Leatherdale; *b* 24 April 1930; *Educ* St Martins Sch of Art London; *m* 1, 24 Oct 1955 (m dis), Ann, da of Norman Garrett; 1 da (Lyndsy b 1957); m 2 (m dis), Jean Margaret, *née* Ayre; 1 da (Ailsa b 1965); m 3 (m dis), Margaret, *née* Bayes; 1 da (Claire b 1971); *Career* Nat Serv Army 1948; chm: Stowe Bowden Wilson Ltd 1985, McCann Erickson Ltd 1985-; memb Bd of Govrs: Ocean Youth Club, Br Sail Trg Orgn; *Recreations* sailing, hot air ballooning, painting; *Style*— Roger Murray, Esq; McCann Erickson Ltd, Bonis Hall, Prestbury, Cheshire, (☎ 0625 828274)

MURRAY, Rt Hon Lord; Ronald King; PC (1974); s of James King Murray; *b* 15 June 1922; *Educ* George Watson's Coll Edinburgh, Univ of Edinburgh, Jesus Coll Oxford; *m* 1950, Sheila Winifred Gamlin; 1 s, 1 da; *Career* serv WWII REME India and SEAC; called to Scottish Bar 1953, standing jr counsel to BOT in Scotland 1961-64, QC Scotland 1967, sr advocate dep 1967-70 (advocate-depute 1964-67), Lord Advocate 1974-79, Lord of Session 1979-; MP (Lab) Leith 1970-79; *Recreations* sailing; *Style*— The Rt Hon Lord Murray; 31 Boswall Rd, Edinburgh EH5 3RP (☎ 031 552 5602)

MURRAY, Dr Ronald Ormiston; MBE (1945); s of John Murray (d 1921), of Glasgow, and Elizabeth Ormiston, *née* MacGibbon (d 1922); *b* 14 Nov 1912; *Educ* Glasgow Acad, Loretto, St John Coll Cambridge, St Thomas's Hosp London (MB, BChir, MA, MD); *m* 1, 20 July 1940, Catherine Joan Suzette (d 1980), da of Sir Henry John Gauvain (d 1945); 1 s (Nigel b 1944), 2 da (Clare b 1948, Virginia b 1950); m 2, 1981, Jane, *née* Tierney, wid of Dr J G Mathewson; *Career* WWII cmmnd Lt RAMC TA 1939, attached 2 Bn London Scottish, Maj OC 3 Field Dressing Station 1943-45, Lt-Col CO 130 Field Ambulance 1945-46; assoc prof of radiology American Univ Hosp Beirut Lebanon 1954-56, conslt radiologist Royal Nat Orthopaedic Hosp and Inst of Orthopaedics London 1956-77; Robert Jones lecture RCS 1973, Baker travelling prof Australasia 1974, Caldwell lectr American Roengten Ray Soc 1975, Skinner lectr RCR 1979; memb: Cambridge Univ Swimming Team 1933-34, Br Univs Swimming Team 1934; played rugby for: Cambridge Univ XV 1933-34, Scotland XV 1935; Hon FACR 1968, FRACR 1979, FFR RCSI 1981, FRCPEd, FRCR; *Books* Radiology of Skeletal Disorders (with H G Jacobson and D J Stoker, 3 edn 1989), Orthopaedic Diagnosis (with H A Sissons and H B S Kemp, 1984), contrib to Sutton's Textbook of Radiology and Imaging (4 edn 1987); *Recreations* golf, bridge; *Clubs* Utd Oxford and Cambridge Univ, Berks Golf, Rye Golf, Hawks (Cambridge); *Style*— Dr Ronald Murray, MBE; Little Court, The Bury, Odiham, Hants RG25 1LY (☎ 0256 702 982)

MURRAY, Dame (Alice) Rosemary; DBE (1977), JP (Cambridge 1953), DL (Cambs 1982); da of Adm Arthur John Layard Murray, CB, DSO, OBE (d 1959), and Ellen Maxwell, *née* Spooner; *b* 28 July 1913; *Educ* Lady Margaret Hall Oxford (MA, DPhil, hon fell); *Career* serv WRNS WWII; memb: Wages Cncl 1968-, Cncl GPSDT 1969-, Armed Forces Pay Review Body 1973-83; dir Midland Bank 1978-84; ind dir The Observer 1981-; former lectr in chemistry: Girton Coll Cambridge Univ of Sheffield' Royal Holloway Coll London; past pres: Nat Assoc Adult Educn, New Hall Cambridge; former vice chllr Univ of Cambridge; hon fell: New Hall, Girton Coll and Robinson Coll Univ of Cambridge Lady Margaret Hall Univ of Oxford; Hon DSc: New Univ Ulster, Univ of Leeds, Univ of Pa, Wellesley; Hon DCL Univ of Oxford; Hon DL Univ of S California; Hon LLD: Univ of Sheffield, Univ of Cambridge; *Style*— Dame Rosemary Murray, DBE, JP, DL; 9 Grange Court, Cambridge CB3 9BD

MURRAY, Rowland William; s and h of Sir Rowland William Patrick Murray, 14 Bt; *b* 22 Sept 1947; *m* 1970, Nancy Diane, da of George C Newberry, of Orlando, Fla; 2 s (Ryan b 1974, Rowland b 1979); *Style*— Rowland Murray, Esq

MURRAY, Sir Rowland William Patrick; 14 Bt (NS 1630), of Dunerne, Fifeshire; s of Rowland William Murray (d 1946), and nephew of 13 Bt, DSO (d 1958); *b* 26 Oct 1910; *Educ* Univ of Georgia; *m* 1944, Josephine Margaret, da of Edward D Murphy; 4 s, 2 da; *Heir* s, Rowland William Murray; *Career* enlisted US Army 1942, 2 Lt 1943, serv with 84 Div 335 Inf Regt, ret Capt 1946; *Style*— Sir Rowland Murray, Bt; 2820 Peachtree Road NE, Atlanta, Georgia 30305, USA

MURRAY, Ruby, Lady; Ruby; da of S Hearn, of Helmdon, Northants; *m* 1938, as his 2 w, Lt-Col Sir Edward Robert Murray, 13 Bt, DSO (d 1958); *Style*— Ruby, Lady Murray

MURRAY, Hon Mrs (Sally Ann Hale); *née* Willis; da of Baron Willis (Life Peer); *b* 8 Jan 1951; *Educ* Chislehurst & Sidcup Girls' GS, Crownwoods Sch; *m* 1974, Robin James Murray, s of James Patrick Murray, of Charing; 1 s (James Edward b 24 Sept 1980), 2 da (Alice Louise b 14 July 1982, Helen Jane b (twin) 14 July 1982); *Career* Civil Serv 1974-77, advice worker Citizens Advice Bureau 1977-80, legal cashier 1988-; *Recreations* cooking, embroidery, needlework; *Style*— The Hon Mrs Murray; Inglenook Cottage, 12 Pump Close, Leybourne, W Malling, Kent ME19 5HH (☎ 0732 870917)

MURRAY, Hon Mrs (Virginia); da of Baron Bowden (Life Peer, d 1989); *b* 3 April 1943; *Educ* E Anglian Girls' Sch, Univ of Reading, Univ of Manchester; *m* 1967, David Ian Murray; *Career* sch teacher; *Style*— The Hon Mrs Murray; 61 Woburn Drive, Hale, Cheshire

MURRAY, Hon Lady (Winifred Mary); *née* Hardinge; da of 2 Baron Hardinge of Penshurst, GCB, GCVO, MC, PC (d 1960), and Helen Mary, *née* Cecil (d 1979); f Private Sec to HMS King George V, Edward VIII and George VI, gf Viceroy of India; *b* 2 May 1923; *Educ* private; *m* 23 July 1943, Maj Sir (John) Antony Jerningham Murray, CBE, *qv*; 1 s; *Career* artist; exhibited: Artist Int, Grosvenor Gallery, Upper St Gallery, Clarendon Gallery; *Style*— The Hon Lady Murray; Woodmancote Manor Cottage, Cirencester, Glos GL7 7ED (☎ 028583 226)

MURRAY, Yvonne Carole Grace; MBE (1991); *b* 4 Oct 1964; *Career* athlete; memb Edinburgh Athletics Club, jr UK int 1981-82, full UK int 1983-; achievements at 3000m: Scot champion 1982, WAAA champion 1988, UK champion 1985 and 1987, Bronze medal Euro Championships 1986, Bronze medal Cwlth Games 1986, Silver medal Euro Cup 1987 and 1989, Gold medal Euro Indoor Championships 1987 (Bronze 1984, Silver 1985), Bronze medal Olympic Games 1988, Gold medal World Cup 1989, Silver medal Cwlth Games 1990, Euro champion 1990; UK 5000m champion 1983, Scot 800m champion 1983, winner Gaymers' road race series 1985; holder various Scot and UK records; female athlete of the year Br Athlectics Writers' Assoc 1989 and 1990; *Style*— Miss Yvonne Murray, MBE; Amateur Athletic Association, Edgbaston House, 3 Duchess Place, off Hagley Road, Edgbaston, Birmingham B16 8NM (☎ 021 456 4050)

MURRAY-AYNSLEY, Lady; Annemaria Eleanor; da of late Judge Emil Curth (d 1940), of Trebnitz, Silesia, and Gertrude Curth (d 1942); *b* 24 Feb 1904; *Educ* Real Gymnasium Hirschberg, Vienna Univ, Munich Univ, Heidelberg Univ (MD), Pisa Univ (MD); *m* 1, Dr Erich Goldberg (d 1942); m 2, 1952 as his 2 w, Sir Charles Murray Murray-Aynsley (d 1967); *Career* MD Heidelberg and Pisa, specialist in children's diseases; registered MD Gen Med Cncl London March 1939; former dist surgeon St John Ambulance Bde Singapore, hon conslt Singapore Anti-TB Assoc; prisoner Sumatra 1942-45; memb; BMA, Ordine dei Medici di Firenze, German Paediatric Assoc; *Recreations* music, reading; *Clubs* Utd Oxford and Cambridge Univ, Women's Corona; *Style*— Lady Murray-Aynsley; 5 Piazza Conti, Florence 50132, Italy (☎ 010 39 55 582404)

MURRAY-LEACH, Roger; s of Robert Murray-Leach, of Newport, Shropshire (d 1949), and Mary Barbara, *née* Caisley (d 1986); *b* 25 June 1943; *Educ* Aldenham, Architectural Assoc Sch; *m* 1 June 1968 (m dis), Sandra Elizabeth, da of John Tallent, of Herefordshire; 1 s (Robert b 17 Feb 1978), 1 da (Tamsin b 13 April 1972), 1 s adopted (Jon James (JJ) b 20 April 1974); *Career* prodn designer; films incl: Local Hero 1983, Defence of the Realm 1986, A Fish Called Wanda 1988; Freeman: Worshipful Co of Haberdashers 1970, City of London 1969; *Recreations* riding, skiing; *Style*— Roger Murray-Leach, Esq; 108 Kings Rd, Windsor, Berks SL4 2AP

MURRAY-LESLIE, Dr Christian Francis Victor; s of Francis Murray-Leslie, of Boxnoor, Herts, and Nancy Joan, *née* Brenthall (d 1947); *b* 12 July 1944; *Educ* Hemel Hempstead GS, Middlesex Hosp Med Sch (MB BS); *m* 7 June 1972, Margaret Ann, da of Arthur Charles Harmer, of Hartshorne, Derbyshire; 2 s (Nicholas John b 1972, Robin Charles b 1974), 1 da (Catherine Arbella b 1980); *Career* registrar in med 1971-72, registrar in med and cardiology 1972-73, lectr and res asst 1973-74, sr registrar in rheumatology and rehabilitation Univ of Leeds 1974-77, conslt in rheumatology and rehabilitation med Derbyshire Royal Infirmary 1977, conslt i/c Nat Demonstration Centre in Rehabilitation Derby 1980, dir Orthotics and Disability Res Centre Derby 1980, visiting prof Univ of Loughborough 1988; dir Derby Disabled Driving Centre, chm Assoc of Driver Educn of People With Disabilities; memb: BMA, Br Soc Rehabilitation Med, Soc for Res in Rehabilitation; *Books* Recent Advances in Rheumatology (contrib); *Recreations* walking, birdwatching, gardening, music; *Style*— Dr Christian Murray-Leslie; Westmead, Derby Rd, Melbourne, Derbyshire DE7 1FL (☎ 0332 862921); Derbyshire Royal Infirmary, London Rd, Derby DE1 2QY (☎ 0332 47141)

MURRAY-LYON, Dr Iain Malcolm; s of Ranald Malcolm Murray-Lyon (d 1970), of Edinburgh, and Jennipher, *née* Dryburgh; *b* 28 Aug 1940; *Educ* Loretto, Univ of Edinburgh (BSc, MB ChB, MD); *m* 7 Nov 1981, Teresa Elvira, da of Antonio Gonzalez Montero, of Buenos Aires; 1 s (Andrew Malcolm b 1984), 1 da (Caroline Claire b 1982); *Career* hon sr lectr Liver Unit KCH 1972-74, conslt physician and gastroenterologist Charing Cross Hosp 1974-; hon conslt physician Hosp of St John & St Elizabeth 1976-, King Edward VII Hosp for Offrs 1990-; author of over 150 pubns in the areas of liver disease and gastroenterology; chm Liver Section Br Soc of Gastroenterology, former sec Br Assoc for Study of the Liver (memb); Liveryman Worshipful Soc of Apothecaries; FRCP 1980, FRCPE 1980; *Recreations* golf, skiing, tennis; *Clubs* Brooks's, Hurlingham; *Style*— Dr Iain Murray-Lyon; 12 St James's Gardens, London W11 (☎ 071 602 1806), 6 Devonshire Place, London W1N 1HH (☎ 071 935 6747/935 7017), Charing Cross Hosp, London W6 8RF

MURRAY OF BLACKBARONY, Lady; Diane Margaret; da of Robert Campbell Bray, of Buenos Aires Argentina, and Enriqueta Carolina, *née* Edye; *b* 3 April 1949; *m* 1980, Sir Nigel Andrew Digby Murray of Blackbarony, 15 Bt, *qv*; *Recreations* tennis, rowing, painting (oils), piano, music; *Clubs* Venado Tuerto Polo and Athletic, Tigre Boat; *Style*— Lady Murray of Blackbarony; CC 115, (2624) Arias, Provincia de Cordoba, Argentina

MURRAY OF BLACKBARONY, Sir Nigel Andrew Digby; 15 Bt (NS 1628), of Blackbarony, Peeblesshire; s of Sir Alan John Digby Murray of Blackbarony, 14 Bt (d 1978), and Mabel Elisabeth, *née* Schiele; *b* 15 Aug 1944; *Educ* St Paul's Sch Argentina, Salesian Agric Tech Sch, RAC Cirencester; *m* 1980, Diana Margaret, da of Robert Campbell Bray; 1 s (Alexander b 1981), 2 da (Rachel Elizabeth Vanda Digby b 1982, Evelyn Caroline Digby b 1987); *Heir* s, Alexander Nigel Robert Murray; *Career* farms own land (crops, dairy, bees); private pilot's licence from Midland Sch of Flying at Castle Donnington; landowner (1180 acres); *Recreations* tennis, golf, rowing, camping, mountain walking, fishing, skiing; *Clubs* Venado Tuerto Polo and Athletic, Tigre Boat; *Style*— Sir Nigel Murray of Blackbarony, Bt; Establecimiento Tinamú, CC 115, 2624 Arias, Provincia de Córdoba, Argentina (☎ 010 54 0462 60031)

MURRAY OF EPPING FOREST, Baron (Life Peer UK 1985), of Telford, Co Shropshire; Lionel (Len) Murray; OBE (1966), PC (1976); *b* 2 Aug 1922; *Educ* Wellington GS Salop, London Univ, NCLC, New Coll Oxford; *m* 1945, Heather Woolf; 2 s (Hon Stephen William b 1959, Hon David Paul b 1960), 2 da (Hon Nicola Ruth b 1954, Hon Sarah Isobel b 1959); *Career* gen sec TUC 1973-84 (joined 1947, head econ dept 1954-69, asst gen sec 1969-73); memb NEDC 1973-; memb Anglo-German Fndn for Study of Industl Soc Bd Tstees 1977-; hon fell: Sheffield City Poly, New Coll Oxford; Hon DSc: Aston, Salford; Hon LLD St Andrews; *Style*— The Rt Hon the Lord Murray of Epping Forest, OBE, PC; 29 The Crescent, Laughton, Essex

MURRAY OF GRAVESEND, Baroness; Margaret Anne; *née* Wakeford; JP (1971); da of Frederick Charles Wakeford, of Crayford; *b* 6 Dec 1928; *m* 1960, Baron Murray of Gravesend (Life Peer) (d 1980); 1 s, 1 da; *Career* mangr Gravesend Churches Housing Assoc; memb: Lambeth Cncl 1958-65, Dartford and Gravesend Dist Health Authy 1982-89, Co-Operative Party, Fabians Soc, Soroptimists, Labour Party; pres: N Kent Sunday Football League 1980-, Gravesend Branch Nat Assoc of Widows 1981-, Gravesend Branch NSPCC 1985-; vice pres Gravesend Cncl for Racial Equality, chm Wrotham CP School Gravesend; govr: Holy Trinity C of E Sch, St John's RC Sch; clerk to Knights Almshouse Tst Northfleet; *Style*— The Rt Hon Lady Murray of Gravesend, JP; 13 Parrock Rd, Gravesend, Kent (☎ 0474 365958); Gravesend Churches Housing Association, 28 Harmer St, Gravesend (☎ 0474 357361)

MURRAY OF NEWHAVEN, Baron (Life Peer UK 1964), of Newhaven, Co and City of Edinburgh; Sir Keith Anderson Hope Murray; KCB (1963); s of Lord Murray, CMG, PC, a Scottish Lord of Session (d 1936), and Annie Florence, *née* Nicolson (d 1968); *b* 28 July 1903; *Educ* Edinburgh Acad, Edinburgh Univ (BSc), Cornell Univ NY (PhD), Oriel Coll Oxford (BLitt, MA); *Career* serv WWII, Fl-Lt RAF 1941-42; Agric Econ Res Inst 1929-39, Miny of Food 1939-40; seconded from RAF as dir of food and agric Middle E Supply Centre 1942-45; late JP Oxford; formerly dir Bristol Aircraft and Metal Box Co; res offr Oxford Univ 1932-39, fell Lincoln Coll Oxford 1937 (bursar 1937-53, rector 1944-53); chm Univ Grants Ctee 1953-63; dir Leverhulme Tst 1964-72; chllr Southampton Univ 1964-74; visitor Loughborough Univ 1968-78; hon fell: Oriel and Lincoln Colls Oxford, Downing Coll Cambridge, Birkbeck Coll London; Hon LLD: W Aust, Bristol, Cambridge, Hull, Edinburgh, Southampton, Liverpool, Leicester, California, London, Strathclyde; Hon DCL Oxford; Hon DLitt Keele; Hon DUniv: Stirling, Essex; kt 1955; *Clubs* United Oxford and Cambridge University; *Style*— The Rt Hon the Lord Murray of Newhaven, KCB; 224 Ashley Gardens, London SW1P 1PA (☎ 071 828 4113)

MURRAY OF OCHTERTYRE, Sir Patrick Ian Keith; 12 Bt (NS 1673), of Ochtertyre, Perthshire; s of Sir William Patrick Keith Murray of Ochtertyre, 11 Bt (d 1977) and Susan Elizabeth Hudson, *née* Jones; *b* 25 March 1965; *Educ* Christ Coll Brecon Powys, London Acad of Music & Dramatic Art; *Heir* kinsman, Maj Peter Keith-Murray; *Style*— Sir Patrick Murray of Ochtertyre, Bt; Sheep House, Hay-On-

Wye, Hereford

MURRAY-SMITH, (Sheila) Joanne; da of Victor Leo Sargent (d 1976), of Newbury, and Sheila Sargent (d 1966); *b* 22 April 1952; *Educ* Queen's Sch, Windsor Girls Sch Germany, Shaw House Newbury; *m* 7 Dec 1979, David John George Murray-Smith, s of Maj George William Murray-Smith; 2 da (Natasha, Jessica); *Career* ptnr racehorse trg business; horses have won: Irish Grand National, Fairy House, Ireland Riz Club Handicap Chase, Cheltenham; *Recreations* reading, swimming; *Style*— Mrs Joanne Murray-Smith; Frenchman's House, Upper Lambourn, Nr Newbury, Berkshire (☎ 0488 71041, fax 0488 71065, car 0836 525212)

MURRELL, David Brian; s of William Percy John Murrell (d 1988), of Minehead, Somerset, and Muriel Mary Elizabeth, *née* Stevens (d 1988); *b* 7 Feb 1946; *Educ* Taunton Sch; *m* 29 Nov 1969, Sheila Mary, da of Lt Alured Francis Fairlie-Clarke (d 1984), of Norton Fitzwarren, Somerset; 1 s (Alan b 1970), 2 da (Deborah b 1972, Julia b 1974); *Career* qualified as CA with Amherst and Shapland of Minehead 1967; KPMG Peat Marwick McLintock 1968-: ptnr 1981, head of media and entertainment indust practice: 1984- (reporting accountant on offer for sale prospectuses issued by Chrysalis 1985 and Virgin 1986, delisting of Virgin 1988); accounting tax and consulting servs provided to: The Observer, Virgin, Poly Gram, LWT, Cable Authy, Saatchi and Saatchi, Rank Orgn, RCA/Columbia, Working Title Films, Radio Acad, Mechanical Copyright Protection Soc, IPPA, Cinema and TV Benevolent Fund, Pink Floyd, Amnesty and Rolling Stones pop tours, Campaign for Quality Television; Joint sponsor: Br Cinema Advertising Awards, Br TV Advertising Awards, Campaign Press Awards, Ind Radio Advertising Awards, IPA Effectiveness Awards and Jazz FM Film Review of Week; fin advsr Comic Relief, fin tutor Nat Film and TV Sch, barker Variety Club; memb: BAFTA, Producers' Assoc; ACA 1968, FCA 1978; *Books* author of numerous articles on fin and tax in leading media & entertainment indust trade magazines; *Recreations* golf, photography; *Clubs* West Hill Golf, Old Tauntonians London Golfing Soc (former capt); *Style*— David Murrell, Esq, KPMG; Peat Marwick McLintock, 1 Puddle Dock, Blackfriars, London EC4V 3PD, (☎ 071 236 8000, fax 071 248 6552)

MURRELL, Geoffrey David George; OBE (1987); s of Stanley Hector Murrell (d 1976), and Kathleen Margaret, *née* Martin (d 1980); *b* 19 Dec 1934; *Educ* Minchenden GS Southgate, Lincoln Coll Oxford (BA); *m* 26 Nov 1962, Kathleen Ruth, *née* Berton; 1 s (Timothy John b 1967), 3 da (Sarah Louise b 1964, Kate Elizabeth b 1970, Alice Margaret b 1978); *Career* Br Embassy Moscow: third sec 1961-64, second sec 1968-70; princ res offr FCO 1970-75, first sec Belgrade 1975-78, reg dir Res Dept FCO 1978-83, cnsllr Moscow 1983-87, res cnsllr for Soviet Affairs FCO 1988-; *Recreations* tennis, guitar; *Clubs* United Oxford and Cambridge Univ; *Style*— Geoffrey Murrell, Esq, OBE; c/o Foreign & Commonwealth Office, King Charles St, London SW1A 2AH (☎ 071 210 6255)

MURRIE, Sir William Stuart; GCB (1963, CB 1946), KBE (1951); s of Thomas Murrie (d 1907); *b* 19 Dec 1903; *Educ* Harris Acad Dundee, Univ of Edinburgh, Balliol Coll Oxford; *m* 1932, Eleanor Boswell (d 1966); *Career* sec Scot Educn Dept 1952-57, sec Scot Home Dept 1957-59, perm under sec state Scot Office 1959-64; *Clubs* New (Edinburgh); *Style*— Sir William Murrie, GCB, KBE; 7 Cumin Place, Edinburgh, Scotland EH9 2JX (☎ 031 667 2612)

MURRISH, Peter; s of John James Murrish (d 1962), of Cornwall, and Rita Alice, *née* Mennear (d 1989); *b* 20 April 1929; *Educ* Penzance Co GS; *m* 19 Feb 1951, Margaret Ethel, da of Maj Wilson James Stedman (d 1957), of Cornwall; 1 s (Stephen Peter b 1955), 2 da (Deborah Roxanne b 1953, Suzanne Jacqueline b 1961); *Career* charity admin, PR and fund-raising conslt; PR and devpt offr Northern Arts Assoc 1968-69, dir Parsons Lewis Davis & Ptnrs Ltd 1970-72, capital appeals The Spastics Soc 1971-76, dir John F Rich Co Ltd 1976-79, md Franks Murrish (Appeals) Ltd 1979-82, chm Cornwall Animal Welfare Tst 1984-, dir Isles of Scilly Environmental Tst 1985-, chm Cinnamon Tst 1986-89; memb Hertfords CC 1964-67; *Recreations* walking, reading, socialising; *Clubs* Scillonian; *Style*— Peter Murrish, Esq; Hugh House, St Mary's, Isles of Scilly TR21 0LS (☎ 0720 22156); Wingletang, Academy Terrace, St Ives, Cornwall TR26 1HJ (☎ 0736 796515); Hamewith, The Parade, St Mary's, Isles of Scilly TR21 0LP (☎ 0720 22153)

MURSELL, Sir Peter; MBE (1941), DL (W Sussex 1962); s of T A Mursell, of Kettering; *b* 20 Jan 1913; *Educ* Bedales Sch, Downing Coll Cambridge; *m* 1938, Cicely, da of M F North, of Weybridge; 2 s, 2 da; *Career* Serv WWII as Sr Cdr ATA; former memb: Ctee Mgmt in Local Govt, Royal Cmmn on Local Govt in England, Water Space Amenity Cmmn, Inland Waterways Amenity Advsy Cncl; chm W Sussex CC 1962-67 and 1969-74 (memb 1947-74), vice Lord Lt W Sussex 1974-90; kt 1969; *Clubs* Farmers'; *Style*— Sir Peter Mursell, MBE, DL; Taints Orchard, The Street, Washington, W Sussex RH20 4AS (☎ 0903 893 062)

MURTA, Prof Kenneth Hall; s of John Henry Murta (d 1976), of Sunderland, Co Durham, and Florence, *née* Hall (d 1977); *b* 24 Sept 1929; *Educ* Bede GS, Univ of Durham (Dip Arch, BArch); *m* 1 April 1955, Joan, da of Joseph Wilson; 2 s (Andrew John b 1956, Eden Wilson b 1966), 2 da (Catherine Anne b 1958, Patricia Zaria b 1960); *Career* Nat Serv RAF 1947-49; Newcastle City architect, SW Milburn & Ptnrs (Sunderland) 1954-56 (princ architect 1956-59); sr lectr Amahdu Bello Univ (Zaria Nigeria) 1959-62; Univ of Sheffield: lectr, sr lectr 1962-74, prof 1975, dean Faculty Of Architectural Studies 1974-77 and 1984-88; significant designs incl: Anglican Cathedral Kaduna Northern Nigeria, All Saints Dewsbury, St Laurence Heanor, Christ Church Pitsmoor Sheffield; memb Fabric Advsy Ctee Sheffield Cathedral; memb Bd and vice chm Arch Ed, ARCUK, chm Yorks regn RIBA 1985; ARIBA 1954, FRIBA 1968, FRSA 1981; *Recreations* cricket, soccer, travel, church visiting, walking in cities on Sundays; *Style*— Prof Kenneth Murta; Underedge, Back Lane, Hathersage, Derbyshire

MURTON, Hon (Henry) Peter John Connell; s of Baron Murton of Lindisfarne (Life Peer); *b* 1941; *m* 1962 (m dis 1972), Louisa, da of late Maj Percy Montague Nevile, of Skelbrooke Park, Yorks; *Style*— The Hon Peter Murton; 49 Carlisle Mansions, Carlise Place, London SW1P 1HY

MURTON OF LINDISFARNE, Baron (Life Peer UK 1979), of Hexham, Co Northumberland; (Henry) Oscar Murton; OBE (1946), TD (1947, clasp 1951), PC (1976), JP (Poole 1963); o s of late Henry Edgar Crossley Murton, of Hexham, Northumberland; *b* 8 May 1914; *Educ* Uppingham; *m* 1, 1939, Constance (d 1977), da of Fergus O'Loughlin Connell, of Low Fell, Co Durham; 1 s (Hon (Henry) Peter John Connell b 1941), 1 da (Hon Melanie Frances Isobel Connell (Hon Mrs Vickery) b 1946 d 1986); m 2, 1979, Pauline Teresa, yst da of late Thomas Keenan, of Johannesburg; *Career* serv Royal Northumberland Fus (TA) 1934-39, Staff Coll Camberley 1939, Lt-Col Gen Staff 1942-46; md Dept Stores NE England 1949-57; MP (C) Poole 1964-79, asst govt whip 1971-72, lord cmmr Treasy 1972-73, dep chm Ways and Means 1973-76 (chm and dep speaker 1976-79), dep chm of Ctees House of Lords 1981-, dep speaker 1983-; *Recreations* sailing, painting, reading history; *Style*— The Rt Hon the Lord Murton of Lindisfarne, OBE, TD, PC; 49 Carlisle Mansions, Carlisle Place, London SW1P 1HY (☎ 071 834 8226)

MUSCHAMP, John Victor; s of Victor Muschamp (d 1971), of Lytham St Annes, and Mary Edith, *née* Partington; *b* 19 Dec 1941; *Educ* Berkhamsted Sch; *m* 27 May 1965, Vivienne Gwendoline Anne, da of late Michael Farr; 1 s (Mark John b 8 Aug 1971), 2 da (Emma b 28 March 1966, Lisa b 26 Oct 1961); *Career* sales mangr M E Motors Ltd Berkhamsted 1958-61, dir Coachwork Conversions Ltd Leighton Buzzard 1962-71, chm and md Coachwork Walker Ltd Colne 1971-, md Truckman Ltd 1990; memb Cncl Soc of Motor Manufacturers and Traders, memb Bd and former chm Vechicle Builders and Repairers Assoc; MIMI; *Recreations* vintage cars, squash; *Clubs* RAC, Pall Mall; *Style*— John Muschamp, Esq; Truckman Ltd, Unit C6, Baker Street, Gloucester GL1 5RL (☎ 0452 332233, fax 0452 332040)

MUSGRAVE, Christopher John Shane; s and h of Sir Richard James Musgrave, 7 Bt; *b* 23 Oct 1959; *Style*— Christopher Musgrave Esq

MUSGRAVE, Sir Christopher Patrick Charles; 15 Bt (E 1611), of Hartley Castle, Westmorland; s of Sir Charles Musgrave, 14 Bt (d 1970); *b* 14 April 1949; *m* 1978, Megan, da of Walter Inman: 2 da (Helena b 1981, Antonia b 1987); *Heir* bro, Julian Nigel Chardin Musgrave; *Recreations* sailing; *Style*— Sir Christopher Musgrave, Bt; c/o Royal Bank of Scotland plc, Silver St, Kingston upon Hull, E Yorks HU16 5PJ

MUSGRAVE, Julian Nigel Chardin; s of Sir Charles Musgrave, 14 Bt (d 1970); h to Btcy of bro, Sir Christopher Patrick Charles Musgrave, 15 Bt; *b* 8 Dec 1951; *Educ* S Wymondham Coll, QMC London (BSc); *m* 1975, Gulshanbanu Buddrudin; 2 da (Anar b 1980, Ruth b 1983); *Career* md Games World Ltd; dir Orkfest Ltd; mktg conslt; MInstM; *Recreations* creative bookkeeping; *Style*— Julian Musgrave, Esq

MUSGRAVE, Mark Jonathan; s of Sir (Frank) Cyril Musgrave, KCB (d 1986), of Needles Eye, Drinkstone Green, Bury St Edmunds, Suffolk, and Lady Jean Elsie, *née* Soulsby; *b* 5 Oct 1952; *Educ* Haileybury; *m* 1 Sept 1979, Belinda Joan, da of John Hugh Clerk (d 1976), of Kingston, Jamaica; 2 s (William b 1984, George b 1988), 1 da (Chloe b 1987); *Career* admitted slr 1977; Speechly Bircham: dep managing ptnr 1989-90, personnel ptnr 1988-, ptnr 1981-; memb Justinians 1989; memb Law Soc 1977; *Recreations* tennis, gardening, travel; *Style*— Mark Musgrave, Esq; Parsonage Farmhouse, Messing, Colchester, Essex CO5 9TA (☎ 0376 71596); Bouverie House, 154 Fleet St, London EC4A 2HX (☎ 071 353 3290)

MUSGRAVE, Sir Richard James; 7 Bt (I 1782), of Tourin, Waterford; s of Sir Christopher Norman Musgrave, 6 Bt, OBE (d 1956); *b* 10 Feb 1922; *Educ* Stowe; *m* 1958, Maria, da of late Col M Cambanis, of Athens; 2 s, 4 da; *Heir* s, Christopher John Shane Musgrave; *Career* 2 Lt 1940, serv 1940-45 India, Middle E, Capt Poona Horse, 17 Queen Victoria's Own Cavalry; *Recreations* shooting, bridge; *Clubs* Kildare Street (Dublin); *Style*— Sir Richard Musgrave, Bt; Knightsbrook, Trim, Co Meath, Republic of Ireland (☎ 046 31372); Komito, Syros, Greece (fax 0281 23508)

MUSGRAVE, Hon Mrs (Rosemary Jane); *née* Watkinson; da of 1 Viscount Watkinson, CH, PC; *b* 1947; *m* 1976, Barrie Musgrave, 1 s; *Style*— The Hon Mrs Musgrave

MUSGRAVE, Thea (Mrs Peter Mark); da of James P Musgrave (d 1971), of Edinburgh, and Joan, *née* Hacking; *b* 27 May 1928; *Educ* Moreton Hall Oswestry, Univ of Edinburgh (MusB), private study in Paris with Nadia Boulanger; *m* 2 Oct 1971, Peter Mark, s of Irving Mark (d 1987), of Sarasota, Florida; *Career* composer; orchestral works incl: Concerto for Clarinet and Orchestra (cmmnd Royal Philharmonic Soc) 1968, Horn Concerto 1971, Viola Concerto (cmmnd BBC) 1973, Peripeteia (cmmnd RPO) 1981, The Seasons (cmmnd Acad of St Martin's in the Fields) 1988; chamber and instrumental works incl: Chamber Concerto No 1 1962, Chamber Concerto No 2 1966, Chamber Concerto No 3 1966, Space Play (cmmnd Serge Koussevitsky Music Fndn) 1974, Pierrot 1985; vocal and choral music incl: Rorate Coeli 1974, An Occurrence at Owl Creek Bridge (cmmnd BBC) 1981, For the Time Being Advent 1986; operas incl: The Voice of Ariadne (cmmnd Royal Opera House) 1973, Mary Queen of Scots (cmmnd Scot Opera) 1977, A Christmas Carol (cmmnd Virginia Opera Assoc) 1979, Harriet, The Woman Called Moses (cmmnd jtly Royal Opera House and Virginia Opera Assoc) 1984; Beauty and the Beast (ballet) 1968; increasingly active as conductor of own work; performances at festivals: Edinburgh, Warsaw, Aldeburgh, Cheltenham, Zagreb, Florence Maggio Musicale, Venice Biennale; numerous broadcastings and recordings; distinguished prof Queen's Coll City Univ NY; memb: Central Music Advsy Panel BBC, Music Panel Arts Cncl GB, Exec Ctee Composers' Guild GB, Ctee Award for Cwlth Fund of NY; hon fell New Hall Cambridge 1973; Hon Doctorates: Cncl Nat Academic Awards 1976, Smith Coll USA 1979, Old Dominion Univ Norfolk Virginia 1980; *Style*— Miss Thea Musgrave; c/o Novello & Co Ltd, 8 Lower James St, London WIR 3PL

MUSGROVE, Harold John; s of Harold John Musgrove (d 1984), and Francis, *née* Clements (d 1983); *b* 19 Nov 1930; *Educ* King Edward GS Birmingham, Birmingham Tech Coll; *m* 1959, Jacquelin; 2 s (Michael b 1963, James b 1972), 2 da (Sarah b 1969, Laura b 1970); *Career* cmmnd RAF 1945, navigator; chm and chief exec Austin Rover Gp Ltd 1982- (apprentice 1945, sr mgmnt positions within Truck and Bus Gp 1963, chm and md Austin Morris Ltd 1980-, chm Light Medium Cars Gp 1981-); vice-pres Motor Mfrs and Traders 1986-; Midlander of the Year award 1980, Instn of Prodn Engrs Int award 1981, The Soc of Engrs Churchill Medal 1982; *Style*— Harold Musgrove Esq; Austin Rover Gp Ltd, Fletchamstead Highway, Canley, Coventry CV7 9GS (☎ (0203) 75511, telex 31567)

MUSGROVE, Kevin; *b* 4 March 1949; *Career* fin dir and co sec: Cocker Bros Ltd 1976-79, Springline Spares Ltd 1979-81; chief accountant Spencer & Halstead Ltd 1981-82; currently: dir and co sec William Cook plc, non-exec dir SCRATA; Freeman Worshipful Co of Cutlers 1990; FCMA 1988; *Style*— Kevin Musgrove, Esq; William Cook plc, Parkway Avenue, Sheffield S9 4WA (☎ 0742 700 895, fax 0742 724 553)

MUSHIN, Alan Spencer; s of Dr Louis Mushin (d 1984); *b* 31 Jan 1938; *Educ* Haberdashers' Aske's, London Hosp Med Coll (MB BS); *m* 27 Feb 1972, Joan Carolyn, da of Dr Simon Behrman, of Harley St, London; 1 s (James b 1976), 1 da (Rosalind b 1974); *Career* conslt: ophthalmic surgn Moorfield Eye Hosp London, Royal London Hosp, Queen Elizabeth Hosp for children; memb Br Paediatric Assoc; fell Coll of Ophthalmologists of UK; BMA, FRSM, FRCS; *Books* papers on paediatric ophthalmology; *Recreations* photography, philately, gardening; *Clubs* Savage; *Style*— Alan S Mushin, Esq; 935 Finchley Rd, London NW11 7PE (☎ 081 455 7212); 82 Harley Street, London W1N 1AE (☎ 071 580 3116); The Dower House, Oxney, St Margarets-at-Cliffe, Kent

MUSKER, Sir John; s of Capt Harold Taylor Musker, JP (d 1946), of Snarehill Hall, Thetford, and Margaret Gray, *née* McMonies (d 1952); *b* 25 Jan 1906; *Educ* privately, St John's Coll Cambridge; *m* 1, 6 June 1932 (m dis 1955), late Elizabeth Susan Eva, yr da of Capt Henrik Loeffler, of 51 Grosvenor Sq, London W1; 2 da; m 2, 14 Sept 1955, Rosemary Honor (d 1980), da of Maj-Gen Merton Beckwith-Smith, DSO, MC, and formerly w of John Llewellyn Pugh; m 3, 1982, Hon Audrey Elizabeth, *née* Paget (d 1990), da of 1 and last Baron Queenborough (d 1949); *Career* serv WWII, Lt RNVR; banker; chm: Cater Brightwen & Co (bankers) 1938-, Cater Ryder & Co 1960-71 (dir 1960-79); hon treas London Municipal Soc 1936-46; memb LCC City of London 1944-49; kt 1952; *Clubs* White's; *Style*— Sir John Musker; 4 Cliveden Place, London SW1; Shadwell Park, Thetford, Norfolk (☎ 0842 753257)

MUSKER, Lady Rose Diana; *née* Lambton; da of Anthony Lambton (6 Earl of Durham, peerages disclaimed 1970); *b* 1952; *m* 1979, Herbert Oliver Fitzroy Musker; *Style*— The Lady Rose Musker

MUSSELL, Hon Mrs (Margaret Jean); *née* Shaw; da of 2 Baron Craigmyle (d 1944);

b 20 Feb 1915; *m* 1949, (Laurence) Shirl Mussell (d 1956); 3 da (1 adopted); *Style*— The Hon Mrs Mussell; Dyke Croft, Ravenglass, Cumbria CA18 1RN

MUSSELWHITE, Nigel; QFSM (1984); s of Reginald Musselwhite (d 1964), and Lilian Kate, *née* Thornbury (d 1976); *b* 29 Nov 1939; *Educ* Bromley County GS; *m* 19 Sept 1971, Mary Gwendoline, da of Eric Shipton (d 1964); 1 s (Bryn Edward b 1972), 1 da (Anna-Marie b 1975); *Career* fireman; divnl offr London 1959-74; City of London Police 1960-61, London Fire Brig 1961-76 (1959-60), divnl offr and sr instr Fire Servs Coll 1974-76; Somerset Fire Brig: dep chief offr 1976-78, chief fire offr 1978-89; Her Majesty's Inspr of Fire Servs 1989; awarded fire serv medal for long serv and good conduct 1981; OStJ; memb GIFireE, MISM; Merité Fédéral France 1981; *Recreations* motor racing, golf, sailing, model making; *Clubs* St Johns; *Style*— Nigel Musselwhite, Esq, QFSM; Rhodes House, Thuloxton, Taunton, Somerset TA2 8RH (☎ 0823 412127); 29 Hawksbury Close, Redditch, Worcs; Le Canard Pompette, Belle Fontaine, Perrou, Normandy, France; Fire Service Inspectorate, Ladywood House, 6th Floor, Stephenson St, Birmingham B2 4DT (☎ 021 631 3014, fax 021 643 7944)

MUSSON, Hon Lady (Elspeth Lorraine); *née* Bailey; granted title rank and precedence of a Baron's da which would have been hers had her f survived to succeed to the title of Baron Glanusk 1948; da of Hon Herbert Crawshay Bailey, JP (d 1936; 4 s of 1 Baron Glanusk), and Hon Mrs Bailey (d 1948); sis of 4 Baron; *b* 1915; *m* 1939, Gen Sir Geoffrey Randolph Dixon Musson, GCB, CBE, DSO, *qv*; 1 s, 1 da (decd); *Style*— The Hon Lady Musson; Barn Cottage, Hurstbourne Tarrant, Andover, Hants SP11 0BD (☎ 026 476 354)

MUSSON, Gen Sir Geoffrey Randolph Dixon; GCB (1970), CBE (1945), DSO (1944); s of Robert Dixon Musson (d 1957); *b* 9 June 1910; *Educ* Shrewsbury, Trinity Hall Cambridge; *m* 1939, Hon Elspeth Lorraine, *qv*; 1 s, 1 da (decd); *Career* 2 Lt KSLI 1930, Brig 1944, cmd Cwlth Forces in Korea 1954-55, Maj-Gen 1958, Maj-Gen cmd 7 Armd Div 1958 and 5 Div 1958-59, COS MELF 1959-62, Col KSLI 1963-68, Lt-Gen GOC Northern Cmd 1964-67, Adj Gen MOD 1967-70, Gen 1968, Col KSLI 1963-68, Col LI 1968-72; vice chm Nat Savings Ctee, chm HM Forces Savings Ctee 1970-78, vice pres Royal Patriotic Fund Corpn 1974-83, pres Victory (Servs) Club 1970-80; *Clubs* Army and Navy; *Style*— Gen Sir Geoffrey Musson, GCB,CBE, DSO; Barn Cottage, Hurstbourne Tarrant, Andover, Hants SP11 0BD (☎ 026 476 354)

MUSSON, John Nicholas Whitaker; s of Dr J P T Musson, OBE (d 1968), and Gwendoline, *née* Whitaker (d 1981); *b* 2 Oct 1927; *Educ* Clifton, BNC Oxford (MA); *m* 12 Sept 1953, Ann, da of A S Priest (d 1983), of Santa Barbara, California; 1 s (Richard b 1965), 3 da (Caroline (Mrs McIntosh) b 1955, Clare (Mrs Bourne) b 1960, Kate b 1962); *Career* guardsman and Lt, The Lancs Fusiliers in Austria 1945-48; dist offr Northern Nigeria HM Colonial Admin Serv 1951-59, staff dept BP London 1959-61, asst master and housemaster Canford Sch Dorset 1961-72, warden Glenalmond Coll (formerly Trinity Coll Glenalmond) 1972-87; chm Scottish div HMC 1981-83, currently Scottish sec Independent Schs Careers Orgn, govr and memb cncl Clifton Coll, govr George Watson's Coll Edinburgh; *Clubs* New (Edinburgh); *Style*— John Musson, Esq; 47 Spylaw Rd, Edinburgh EH10 5BP (☎ 031 337 0089)

MUSSON, Peter John; s of Eric Thomas Musson, of W Yorks, and Mary Veronica, *née* Daly (d 1987); *b* 29 March 1947; *Educ* Heath GS; *m* 20 Dec 1975, Anne Marie, da of Bruce Hamilton Woods (d 1961); 2 s (Michael b 1982, George b 1988), 1 da (Katharine b 1977); *Career* mgmnt conslt (corporate) 1974; dir: Manchester C of C & Indust 1981-82, Cardiokinetics Ltd 1983, Dial-a-Phone plc 1990; FCA 1968; *Style*— Peter J Musson, Esq; Sunnybank, 85 North Road, Glossop, Derbyshire SK13 9DX (☎ 04578 67022)

MUSTILL, Hon Mr Justice; Hon Sir Michael John; s of Clement William Mustill; *b* 10 May 1931; *Educ* Oundle, St John's Coll Cambridge; *m* 1960 (m dis 1983), Beryl Reid Davies; *Career* barr Gray's Inn 1955, QC 1968, rec Crown Ct 1972-78, judge High Ct of Justice (Queen's Bench Div) 1978-; chm Civil Serv Appeal Tbnl 1971-78; kt 1978; *Style*— The Hon Mr Justice Mustill; 8 Prior Bolton St, London N1

MUSTO, (Franklyn) Keith; s of Frank Lawson Musto, and May Musto (d 1945); *b* 12 Jan 1936; *m* 31 Oct 1959, Gillian, Reginald Walter Marrison, of Essex; 1 s (Nigel b 1965), 1 da (Joanne b 1969); *Career* dir Musto Ltd 1966-; won: Heron Nat Championship 1955, Albercore Nat Championship 1960, Hornet Nat Championship 1961, FD Br Nat Championship 1962, 1963 and 1964; second in the FD Worlds 1963; won silver medal at Tokyo Olympics and Euro FD Championship 1964; formed Co Musto & Hyde Sails 1965; won Tempest Euro Championship 1967; formed Musto & Hyde Accessories 1971; nat sailing coach to Japanese Olympic Squad 1973; co began devpt of three-layer clothing system 1980; Dutch Yacht "Flyer" won the Whitbread Round The World Race (crew wearing Musto inner, middle and outler layer clothing) 1982; co won Silk Cut Design Award 1985; co expanded into second factory and doubled the size of its production facility 1986; co winner Br Design Award 1987; *Recreations* sailing; *Clubs* Thorpe Bay Yacht, Royal Yachting Assoc; *Style*— Keith Musto, Esq; Hunts Farm, Heath Rd, Ramsden Heath, Billericay, Essex; Musto Ltd, 1 Armstrong Rd, Benfleet, Essex (☎ 0268 759466, fax 0268 795541, telex 995466)

MUSTOE, Anne; *née* Revill; *b* 24 May 1933; *Educ* Girton Coll Cambridge (MA); *m* 1960, Nelson Edwin, QC (d 1976); *Career* admin asst Guest Keen & Nettlefolds Ltd 1956-60, head of economics and classics and careers advsr Francis Holland Sch London 1965-69, ind tour operator 1969-72, dep headmistress Cobham Hall Kent 1975-78, headmistress St Felix Sch Southwold 1978-87; mgmnt conslt CORAT (Christian Orgns Res and Advsy Tst) 1988-; pres Girls' Schs Assoc 1984-85, chm ISIS 1986-87; JP (Suffolk) 1981-85; *Recreations* cycling, music; *Style*— Mrs Anne Mustoe; c/o PCA Finance, 90 Gloucester Mews, West London W2 6DY (☎ 071 402 9082)

MUSTOW, Stuart Norman; s of Norman Eric Mustow (d 1976), of 50 Glyn Farm Rd, Birmingham, and Mabel Florence, *née* Purcell (d 1972); *b* 26 Nov 1928; *Educ* King Edward VI GS Birmingham, Coll of Advanced Tech Birmingham (now Univ of Aston) (BSc); *m* 8 Aug 1964, Sigrid Hertha, da of Georg Wendt, of Germany; 2 s (Stephen Eric b 16 March 1966, Paul Stuart b 19 Sept 1969), 1 da (Ruth Eleanor b 11 Oct 1967); *Career* trg Borough of Oldbury 1949-52, various appointments in local govt, dep borough engr and surveyor Wolverhampton 1966-69, city engr and surveyor Stoke-on-Trent 1969-74, county surveyor West Midlands CC 1974-86, private conslt 1986-; dir WS Atkins (Midlands) 1986-, chm Streetworks Advsy Ctee to Sec of State for Tport 1987-, chm Birmingham Standing Conf for the Single Homeless 1988-; pres Inst Municipal Engineers 1980, vice pres ICE 1990, Viva award Worshipful Co of Carmen (joint with West Mids CC) 1984, Parkman medal ICE (with P B Ronan) 1989; FICE 1969, FIHT 1970, FEng 1982, FRSA; *Recreations* mountain walking, skiing, church, social work; *Style*— Stuart Mustow, Esq; c/o Insitution of Civil Engineers, 1-7 Gt George St, London SW1P 3AA

MYATT, Alan Arthur; s of Capt Percy Edward Myatt, MC (d 1950), of 104 Blakesley Rd, Stechford, Birmingham, and Alice Maud, *née* Brown (d 1968); *b* 9 March 1923; *Educ* Solihull Sch; *m* 6 Nov 1947, Marjorie, da of Arthur John Barker (d 1953), of Noctorum Highwood, Uttoxeter; 1 s (Richard b 2 Nov 1952), 1 da (Diana (Mrs Tait) b 4 June 1949); *Career* RA 1942-45, 153 Field Regt Leicestershire Yeo; AHS Waters & Partners 1945-49, Tarmac Ltd 1949-51; ptnr: Willcox Raikes & Marshall 1969-73 (joined 1963), Mander Raikes & Marshall 1973-88, ret; memb: Wellington UDC 1951-58, Chelmsford Borough and Rural Dist Joint Sewerage Ctee; FICE 1949-, MConsE 1969, FIWEM; *Recreations* golf, bridge, travel; *Clubs* Fulford Heath Golf, Sutton Coldfield Golf; *Style*— Alan Myatt, Esq; 9 Forest Lawns, 124 Streetly Lane, Sutton Coldfield, W Midlands (☎ 021 353 0532)

MYDDELTON, Prof David Roderic; s of Dr Geoffrey Cheadle Myddelton, of Glutieres-sur-Ollon, Switzerland, and Jacqueline Esther, *née* Nathan; *b* 11 April 1940; *Educ* Eton, Harvard Business Sch (MBA); *m* 28 April 1986, Hatherly Angela D'Abo; 1 step s (Charles b 1975), 1 step da (Louise b 1974); *Career* CA 1961; lectr fin and accounting Cranfield 1965-69, lectr accounting London Business Sch 1969-72; Cranfield: prof fin and accounting 1972-, acting head sch mgmnt 1985-86; ACIS 1966, FCA 1971; *Books* The Power to Destroy (1969), On A Cloth Untrue (1984), The Economy And Business Decisions (1984), Essential Management Accounting (1987), The Meaning of Company Accounts (1988), Accounting and Financial Decisions (1991); *Recreations* crossword puzzles, jigsaw puzzles; *Style*— Prof D R Myddelton; 112 Randolph Ave, London W9 1PQ (☎ 071 286 0880); Cranfield Sch of Mgmnt, Cranfield, Bedford MK43 OAL (☎ 0234 751 122)

MYDDELTON, Lady (Mary) Margaret Elizabeth; *née* Mercer Nairne; da of late Maj Lord Charles George Francis Mercer-Nairne, MVO (2 s of 5 Marquess of Landsdowne), and sis of 8 Marquess; *b* 1910; *Educ* privately; *m* 1931, Lt-Col Ririd Myddelton, LVO, JP, DL (d 1988); 2 s, 1 da; *Recreations* painting, breeding Welsh ponies, fishing, gardening; *Style*— The Lady Margaret Myddelton; Chirk Castle, Chirk, Clwyd LL14 5AF

MYDDELTON, Hon Mrs (Sarah Cecily); *née* Allsopp; da of 5 Baron Hindlip; *b* 1944; *m* 1967, Hugh Robert Myddleton, s of Lt-Col Ririd Myddleton, LVO, JP, DL (d 1988), and Lady Mary Myddleton (sis of 8 Marquess of Lansdowne, PC); *Style*— The Hon Mrs Myddelton; 139 Holland Park Ave, WII

MYERS, Bernard Ian; s of Edward Nathan Myers (d 1986), and Isabel Violet, *née* Viner; *b* 2 April 1944; *Educ* Hendon Co GS, LSE (BSc Econ); *m* 17 Sept 1967, Sandra Hannah, da of Samuel Barc (d 1980); 1 s (Andrew b 1972), 2 da (Lara b 1969, Lyndsey b 1974); *Career* accountant 1962-72, merchant banker 1972-; dir many cos incl: Shield Tst Ltd 1976-, Spiremore Ltd 1986-, N M R Int NV 1983, Rothschild Inc 1984-, Smith New Ct plc 1985-, Arrow Capital Ltd 1987-, md (gp fin and overseas) N M Rothschild & Sons Ltd 1988-, (dir 1976); FCA; *Recreations* opera, tennis, theatre; *Style*— Bernard I Myers, Esq; N M Rothschild & Sons Ltd, New Ct, St Swithin's Lane, London EC4P 4DU (☎ 071 280 5000, fax 071 929 1643)

MYERS, Brig Edmund Charles Wolf (Eddie); CBE (1944), DSO (1943); s of Dr C S Myers, CBE (d 1946), of Winsford, nr Minehead, Somerset, and Edith, *née* Seligman (d 1965); *b* 12 Oct 1906; *Educ* Haileybury, RMA Woolwich, Univ of Cambridge (BA), Sch of Mil Engrg; *m* 12 Oct 1943, Louisa Mary Hay (Lutie), da of Aldred Bickham Sweet-Escott (d 1945), of W Somerset; 1 da (Thalia b 1945); *Career* cmmnd RE 1926, Subaltern Field Co Aldershot 1929-35, Capt (later Maj) Egypt 1935-40, ME Staff Coll Haifa 1940, OC Field Sqdn W Desert N Africa 1940-41, Lt-Col instr ME Staff Coll 1941 and combined Trg Centre Egypt 1942, Col (later Brig) cmd SOE mil mission to Greek Resistance 1942-43, liaison offr SOE HQ London and SHAEF 1944, cmd 1 Airborne Div RE (incl Arnhem and Norway) 1944-45, Col asst dir intelligence HQ SACSEA 1945-46, sr mil rep Jt Intelligence Bureau MOD 1946-49, Lt-Col cmd 32 Assault Engr Regt UK 1949-50, Col GS TA Directorate WO 1950-51, Cdr 1 Br Cwlth Div RE Korea 1951-52, dir staff RAF Staff Coll 1952-54, Brig chief engr Br troops in Egypt 1955-56, dep dir personnel admin WO 1956-59, ret 1959; chief civil engr Cleveland Bridge & Engrg Co 1959-65, construction mangr Power Gas Corporation Davy International 1965-68; regnl sec BFSS 1968-70, chm local Royal Br Legion Benevolent Ctee 1973-83; MICE 1960, memb Inst RE 1926; Dutch Bronze Lion 1944, USA Order of Merit 1952, Norwegian Liberty Medal 1945; *Books* Greek Entanglement (1955, 2 edn 1985); *Recreations* gardening, formerly riding and flying; *Clubs* Army and Navy, Special Forces; *Style*— Brig Eddie Myers, CBE, DSO; Wheatsheaf House, Broadwell, Moreton-in-Marsh, Glos GL56 OTY (☎ 0451 30183)

MYERS, Dr Edward David; s of Barnet Myers (d 1965), of Harare, Zimbabwe, and Annie Hilda, *née* Rubinstein (d 1978); *b* 15 July 1925; *Educ* Prince Edward Sch Harare Zimbabwe, Capetown Univ (MB ChB, DTM&H, DPM); *m* 14 Jan 1966, Sybil Brearley, da of John Chatfield (d 1981), of Audley, Stoke-on-Trent, Staffs; 2 s (Benjamin John b 19 March 1967, David Edward b 4 Jan 1969); *Career* res med offr Gen Hosp Salisbury S Rhodesia 1949; house physician: High Wycombe War Meml Hosp Bucks, St Andrews Hosp London, Whittington Hosp London, Neuro-surgical Unit Oldchurch Hosp Romford Essex 1950-52; med registrar Royal Infirmary Preston 1952-54, psychiatric registrar Banstead, Surrey and Charing Cross Hosps 1956-59, conslt psychiatrist in private practice and sessional conslt in psychiatry Harare Central Hosp Slaisbury S Rhodesia 1960-62, sr psychiatric registrar St Edwards Hosp Cheddleton and City Gen Hosp Stoke-on-Trent 1963-66, conslt psychiatrist N Staffs Health Dist 1966-, sr res fell in psychiatry Dept of Postgrad Med Univ of Keele 1980-90; author of several papers on compliance with treatment, attempted suicide and psychoendocrinology; memb: Br Assoc of Psychopharmacology, Hosp Conslts and Specialists Assoc; FRCP(Ed), FRCPsych; *Recreations* fly-fishing, bowls, theatre-going; *Style*— Dr Edward Myers; St Davids, 96 Lancaster Rd, Newcastle-under-Lyme, Staffordshire ST5 1DS; City General Hospital, Newcastle Rd, Stoke-on-Trent ST4 6QG (☎ 0782 621133 ext 2312)

MYERS, (Harry) Eric; QC (1967); s of Harry Moss Myers, and Alice Muriel, *née* Serjeant; *b* 10 Jan 1914; *Educ* Bedford Sch; *m* 1951, Lorna Babette Kitson, *née* Blackburn; *Career* joined HAC City of London 1931; admitted slr 1936, called to the Bar Middle Temple 1945, prosecuting counsel to Bd of Inland Revenue 1965; QC Gibraltar 1977; *Style*— Eric Myers, Esq, QC; 10 Kings Bench Walk Temple, London EC4Y 7EB

MYERS, Gordon Elliot; CMG (1979); s of William Lionel Myers (d 1984), and Yvonne, *née* Alexander (d 1938); *b* 4 July 1929; *Educ* Kilburn GS, Univ Coll Oxford (MA); *m* 23 April 1963, Wendy Jane, da of Charles Thomas Lambert (d 1971), of London; 2 s (Andrew James b 1964, Malcolm John b 1965), 1 da (Lucinda Joy Lambert b 1968); *Career* formerly under sec of Arable Crops, Pigs & Poultry MAFF; min of Agric Office of UK Permanent Representative to Euro Communities 1975-79, ret 1989; *Recreations* music, theatre, gardening, tennis; *Clubs* Utd Oxford and Cambridge; *Style*— Gordon Myers, Esq, CMG; Woodlands, Nugents Park, Hatch End, Middx HA5 4RA; Ministry of Agriculture Fisheries & Food, 10 Whitehall Place, London SW1A 2AA

MYERS, Ian David; s of Stuart Charles Myers, of Teddington, Middx, and Enid, *née* Alexander; *b* 3 Aug 1954; *Educ* Latymer Upper Sch London, Pembroke Coll Oxford (MA); *m* 1976, Helen Rosemary, *née* Bennett; 2 s (Nikolai James Elliot b 23 April 1982, Anatoly Cornelius Constantine Wreyland b 18 Dec 1987), 1 da (Anastasia Tiffany b 2 July 1979); *Career* White Weld & Co London 1977 (NY office 1976-77), chm PaineWebber Int (UK) Ltd 1990- (joined 1978, dir 1987), dir PaineWebber Inc 1989-; *Style*— Ian Myers, Esq; PaineWebber International (UK) Ltd, 1 Finsbury Ave, London EC2M 2PA (☎ 071 377 0055, fax 071 247 5373, car 0860 411 539)

MYERS, John David; s of Frank Myers (d 1949), and Monica, *née* Paden (d 1973); *b* 30 Oct 1937; *Educ* Marist Coll Hull, St Marys Coll Strawberry Hill Middx, Loughborough Coll of Physical Educn, Univ of Hull; *m* 17 April 1974, Anne

McGeough, wid, da of Michael Purcell (d 1985); 1 s (Ian James b 1972); *Career* sch master 1958-64, called to the Bar Gray's Inn 1968, Hull practice 1969-82, chm Industl Tbnls 1982-; *Recreations* music, wine, golf, bridge, cooking; *Clubs* Hull Golf; *Style*— John Myers, Esq; Strand House, 75 Beverley Rd, Hull

MYERS, Prof Norman; s of John Myers (d 1963), of Higher Lees Farm, Whitehall, nr Slaidburn, Yorks, and Gladys, *née* Haworth; *b* 24 Aug 1934; *Educ* Clitheroe Royal GS, Keble Coll Oxford (MA), Univ of California, Berkeley (PhD); *m* 11 Dec 1965, Dorothy Mary, da of Frank Halliman (d 1966), of Nairobi, Kenya; 2 da (Malindi b 3 Oct 1970, Mara b 13 Aug 1973); *Career* Nat Serv RA 1952-53 (invalided out); Dist Offr Overseas Admin Kenya 1958-60, teacher Delamere Boys Sch Nairobi 1961-64, professional wildlife photographer and TV film-maker E Africa 1965-68, conslt in environment and devpt 1972-; res and projects in over 80 countries incl assignments for: The World Bank, UN agencies, Nat Acads of US, OECD, EEC, World Cmmn Environment and Devpt; chm and visiting prof of int environment Univ of Utrecht Netherlands, Regents lectr Univ of California, adjunct prof Univ of Michigan, res assoc Oxford Forestry Inst and Int Devpt Centre Oxford Univ; sr fell World Wildlife Fund US, visiting fell East-West Center Honolulu; Gold medal and Order of Golden Ark World Wildlife Fund International, Gold medal of New York Zoological Soc, Global 500 Roll of Honour UN Environment Programme, Special Achievement award International Environment Protection Sierra Club US, Distinguished Achievement award Soc for Conservation Biology; fell: World Acad Arts and Sci 1988, American Assoc for the Advancement of Science 1990; memb Int Platform Assoc; Gold medal San Diego Zoological Soc; *Books* The Long African Day (1972), The Sinking Ark (1979), Conversion of Tropical Moist Forests (1980), A Wealth of Wild Species (1983), The Primary Source: Tropical Forests and Our Future (1984), The Gaia Atlas of Planet Management (1986), Future Worlds (1990); *Recreations* marathon running, photography, mountaineering; *Clubs* Achilles; *Style*— Prof Norman Myers; Upper Meadow, Old Road, Headington, Oxford OX3 8SZ (☎ 0865 750387, fax 0865 741538, telex 83147 VIAOR G attn Myers)

MYERS, Sir Philip Alan; OBE (1977), QPM (1972), DL (Clwyd 1983); *b* 7 Feb 1931; *m* 1951, Hazel; 2 s; *Career* Shrops Constabulary 1950-67, W Mercia Police 1967-68, dep chief constable Gwynedd Constabulary 1968-70, chief constable N Wales Police 1970-81, one of HM's Insprs of Constabulary 1982-; kt 1985; *Style*— Sir Philip Myers, OBE, QPM, DL

MYERS, Rosemary Sylvia Dagmar; da of Dr George Norman Myers (d 1981), of Harrogate, and Florence Karen, *née* Danielsen (d 1979); *b* 31 May 1938; *Educ* Perse Girls Sch Cambridge, Harrogate Sch of Art, Cambridge Sch of Art (NDD); *m* 21 May 1962 (m dis 1968), Peter Goodliffe; 1 s (Jonathan Michael b 14 Feb 1963), 1 da (Judith Tamzin b 19 June 1965); *Career* artist; freelance illustrator 1962-73 for: The Times, The Economist, Wine Magazine; transferred to print-making 1973, acquired own press 1977 (well known for unusual use of lino and wood in printing); works exhibited in: Open Br Print Bristol, New English Art Club Mall Gallery, Soc of Wood Engravers, Royal W of Eng Acad, Royal Soc of Painters, Etchers and Engravers; print prize awards 1978-79; pres Cambridge Drawing Soc 1989-; *publications* has written and illustrated numerous articles on dolls' houses, currently featured in Int Dolls' House News; Cat Cuts (contrib, 1989); *Style*— Ms Rosemary Myers; 2 Babraham Rd, Cambridge (☎ 0223 247370)

MYERS, Stephen David; s of Leon Daniel Myers, of London, and Matilda, *née* Cohen (d 1968); *b* 15 Sept 1942; *Educ* Quintin Sch, Univ of Durham (BSc); *m* 28 Jan 1965, Marion Elaine, da of Geoffrey Michael Myers, of London; 1 s (Joel b 1970), 1 da (Nicola b 1966, d 1985); *Career* consit civil engr; assoc J D & D M Watson 1972-79 (Milan and Athens) ptnr Watson Hawksley Gp 1979-; invitation lectr Water Pollution Control and Enviromental Mgmnt: City of Beijing PRC, Univ of Turin, Univ of Harloin, Univ of Newcastle; conslt Asian Devpt Bank Manila 1985, gp mission ldr to Turkey Br Water Inds 1987; FICE 1968, FIWEM 1970, FHKIE 1981; *Recreations* photography, trekking, bridge; *Clubs* Royal Hong Kong

MYERSCOUGH-JONES, (Arthur) David; s of Frederick Cecil Sidney Jones, of 2 Lansdown Mansions, Lansdown Rd, Bath, and Lilian Dorothy Jones; *b* 15 Sept 1934; *Educ* Bickertn House Sch Southport, Southport Sch of Art, Central Sch of Art (DA); *m* 23 Feb 1963, (Ursula Theodora Joy) Pelo, da of Charles Graham Cumpston (d 1968), of Barton Hall, Pooley Bridge, Cumbria; 1 s (Richard b 23 June 1969), 3 da (Frances b 21 Feb 1966, Ellen b 21 July 1971, Madeleine b 15 Sep 1974); *Career* theatre designer; Citizens Theatre Glasgow 1958-60, res designer Mermaid Theatre London 1961-65; tv designer Owen Wingrace B Britten (world premiere) 1971, The Flying Dutchman (Royal TV Soc Award) 1976, Therese Raquin (BAFTA Design Award, D & AD Gold Silver Award) 1983, Cosi Fan Tutte and The Theban Plays (ACE Nomination for Art Direction Los Angeles) 1988 and 1989; recent prodns for BBC TV incl: Virtuoso, Metamorphosis, Bomber Harris, adapted Trevor Nunn's RSC prodn of Othello for television 1989, freelance prodn designer 1990-; FCSD 1985; *Recreations* music, opera and painting; *Style*— David Myerscough-Jones, Esq; 6 The Vineyards, Bath, Avon BA1 5NA (☎ 0225 319 479)

MYERSON, His Hon Judge Arthur Levey; QC (1974); s of Barnett Myerson, of Leeds, and Eda Jane, *née* Lewene; *b* 25 July 1928; *Educ* Blackpool GS, Queens' Coll Cambridge (BA, LLB), Open Univ (BA); *m* 1960, Elaine Shirley, da of Sam Harris, of Leeds; 2 s (Simon, Nicholas); *Career* RAF 1946-48 AC1; called to the Bar 1952, circuit judge 1978, pres Cncl of Circuit Judges 1991- (memb Ctee 1985-); *Recreations* reading, walking, sailing; *Clubs* Royal Cwlth, Moor Allerton Golf; *Style*— His Hon Judge Arthur Myerson, QC

MYERSON, Jonathan Scott; s of Aubrey Selwyn Myerson, QC (d 1986), and Helen Margaret, *née* Lavis; *b* 12 Jan 1960; *Educ* Westminster, Lincoln Coll Oxford (MA, ed Isis, vice pres OUDS); ptnr Julie Susan Pike; 1 s (Jacob Aubrey b 31 Jan 1989), 1 da (Chloë Emilia b 1 Jan 1991); *Career* dir and playwright; awarded Regional Theatre Trainee Directors Bursary 1983, resident dir Harrogate Theatre 1983-85; prodns (1983-85) incl: Wait Until Dark, Abigails Party, How The Other Half Loves, Loot, Steaming, Ubu (writer-dir), Jane Eyre and The Woman In White (writer); staff dir Nat Theatre 1986-87; dir: Sung and Unsung, Wiener Schnitzler and Diary of a Somebody (writer-dir), freelance dir: This King's Happy Breed (Drama Centre London) 1987, Diary of a Somebody (King's Head) 1987, Happy Birthday Sir Larry (NT, Olivier) 1987, Every Good Boy Deserves Favour (RPO at Queen Elizabeth Hall) 1987, Sheep Go Bare (Footlights Revue) 1988, The Idiot (Guildhall) 1989, Tartuffe Today (Lyric Theater Belfast) 1989, Beyond Therapy (Café Theater Frankfurt) 1989, Two Planks and a Passion (Guildhall) 1990; writer: Tantalus (Edinburgh) 1983, Making a Difference (Oxford Playhouse Co) 1981, Candide (Oxford Playhouse) 1981, Wiener Schnitzler (NT Lyttleton) 1987; radio plays incl: One of Our Aircraft Is Missing (BBC Radio 4) 1987, God's Scapegoat (BBC Radio 3) 1987, In Spite or Because (BBC Radio 4) 1990, episodes of Citizens (BBC Radio 4) 1989; TV: episodes of The Bill, episodes of Jupiter Moon; film: Simon and Zoe; memb Cncl Directors Guild of GB 1986 and 1988-89 (vice chm 1990); *Recreations* cricket (playing but preferably watching), buying books; *Style*— Jonathan Myerson, Esq; c/o Valerie Hoskins, Noel Gay Artists, 24 Denmark St, London WC2H 8NJ (☎ 071 836 3941)

MYHILL, Stephen Richard; s of Frederick James Myhill, and Sybil Eileen Myhill (d 1976); *b* 17 June 1945; *Educ* Hatfield Sch; *m* 1, 24 Sept 1966 (m dis 1980), Anne Beatrice, da of Eric William Hyatt (d 1990), of Birch Green, Hertford; 2 s (Carl b 23 July 1968, Douglas b 12 Nov 1970); m 2, 26 Jan 1985, Susan Ann, da of Peter Cresswell, of Kensington; 1 s (Edward b 16 May 1990), 2 da (Kirsty b 29 Oct 1985, Sophie b 18 Aug 1987); *Career* securities offr Midland Bank 1962-71, business devpt exec Access Credit Card 1972-79, gen mangr Diners Club Saudi Arabia 1979-80, dir of mktg Citibank (UK) 1981-87, dir personal banking Girobank 1987-; ACIB 1967, memb Mktg Soc 1988; *Recreations* golf, tennis, travel; *Style*— Stephen Myhill, Esq; 10 Milk St, London EC2 (☎ 071 600 6020)

MYLAND, (Howard) David; CB (1988); s of John Tarrant Myland (d 1957), and Frances Grace, *née* Hopgood (d 1978); *b* 23 June 1929; *Educ* Queen Mary's Basingstoke; *m* 18 Aug 1951, Barbara Pearl, da of Sydney Walter Mills (d 1982); 2 s (Richard b 1955, Anthony b 1960), 1 da (Sarah b 1957); *Career* Intelligence Corps 1948-50; Exchequer and Audit Dept (became Nat Audit Office 1984) 1948-89: dep dir 1972, dir 1977, dep sec 1979, asst auditor gen 1982, dep comptroller and auditor gen 1984-89; memb Inst of Public Fin and Accountancy 1981; *Recreations* travel, contract bridge; *Style*— David Myland, Esq, CB

MYLES, David Fairlie; CBE (1988); s of Robert Cownie Myles (d 1973), of Dalbog, Edzell, Brechin, Scotland, and Mary Ann Sidey, *née* Fairlie (d 1963); *b* 30 May 1925; *Educ* Brechin HS; *m* 7 Feb 1951, Janet Isabella, da of David Gall, of Glenskenno, Montrose; 2 s (Robert Gall, Peter David), 2 da (Catherine MacDonald (now Mrs Booth), Lorna Isobel (now Mrs Sinclair)); *Career* RM 1943-46; tenant hill farmer 1958-; dir Kincardineshire Auction Mart Ltd 1963-81; memb: Tport Users Consultative Ctee Scotland 1973-79, Meat Promotion Exec MLC 1975-79, N of Scotland Hydro-Electric Bd 1985-89, Dairy Produce Quota Tbnl for Scotland 1985-; govt appointee Potato Mktg Bd 1988-; MP (Cons) Banff 1979-83, Cons candidate Orkney and Shetland election 1983, dist cncllr Angus 1984-; NFU Scotland: exec chm Angus area, memb Cncl 1970-79, convenor Orgn and Publicity Ctee 1976-79; pres N Angus and Mearns Cons Pty 1974-78 (chm 1971-74), memb Angus Tourist Bd 1984-; *Recreations* curling, traditional Scots fiddle music; *Clubs* Brechin Rotary, London Farmers; *Style*— David Myles, Esq, CBE; The Gorse, Dunlappie Rd, Ezell, Angus DD9 7UB (☎ 035 64 207); Dalbog, Edzell, Brechin, Angus DD9 7UU (☎ 035 64 265)

MYLNE, Nigel James; QC (1984); s of Maj Harold James Mylne, 10 Royal Hussars (d 1942), and Dorothy Evelyn Hogg, *née* Safford (d 1985); *b* 11 June 1939; *Educ* Eton; *m* 1, 4 April 1967 (m dis 1978), Julie Felicity Selena, da of Cdr Christopher Phillpotts, RN (d 1982); 2 s (Jonathan b 1970, Dominic b 1972), 1 da (Jessica b 1969); m 2, 18 Jan 1980, Mrs Judy Camilla Wilson, da of Maj Francis Gawain Hamilton Monteith (d 1975); 1 s (James b 1981); *Career* Nat Serv 2 Lt 10 Royal Hussars; called to the Bar Middle Temple 1963; rec Crown Ct 1983-; Liveryman Worshipful Co of Haberdashers; *Recreations* beekeeping; *Clubs* White's, Garrick, Pratt's; *Style*— Nigel Mylne, Esq, QC; 67 Thurleigh Road, London SW12 8TZ (☎ 081 673 2200); 2 Harcourt Bldgs, Temple, London EC4 (☎ 071 353 2112)

MYLNE, Vivienne Gower; da of Rev Clement Noble Mylne (d 1970), and Winifred Nellie, *née* Gower (d 1951); *b* 19 Oct 1922; *Educ* Southend-on-Sea HS, Jersey Girls' Coll, Lady Margaret Hall Oxford (BA), UCL (PhD); *Career* asst lectr then lectr Swansea Univ Coll 1955-65; Univ of Kent at Canterbury: lectr then sr lectr then reader then prof 1965-82, personal chair 1977, currently emeritus prof; hon fell UCL; worker for Oxfam, pres Br Soc of Eighteenth-Century Studies 1977-79; Chevalier des Palmes Académiques France 1964; *Books* The Eighteenth-Century French Novel (1965), Prévost: Manon Lescaut (1972), Bibliographie du genre romanesque français 1751-1800 (with A Martin and R L Frautschi, 1977), Diderot: La Religieuse (1981); *Recreations* music, television, book-binding; *Style*— Miss Vivienne Mylne; 348 Banbury Rd, Oxford, Oxfordshire 0X2 7PP (☎ 0865 58419)

MYLVAHAN, Dr Natarajan; s of Nurani Natarajan, and Saraswathy; *b* 20 June 1948; *Educ* Sri Lanka (MB BS, MD, DCH); *m* 4 July 1976, Kalpana, da of K Ranganathan; 1 s (Kailash Natarajan Mylvahan); *Career* registrar in med Mansfield Dist and Gen Hosp Notts 1979-80, sr registrar in geriatrics St Mary's Gp Paddington London 1980-82, conslt physician for elderley Derbyshire Royal Infirmary 1982-; *Style*— Dr Natarajan Mylvahan; Hawksworth, 54 Ford Lane, Allestree, Derby DE3 2EW (☎ 0332 553370); Derbyshire Royal Infirmary, London Rd, Derby (☎ 0332 47141)

MYNORS, David Rickards Baskerville; OBE (1985); s of Rev Aubrey Baskerville Mynors (d 1937), Rector of Langley Burrell, Wilts, and Margery Musgrave, *née* Harvey (d 1974), sis of Sir Ernest Harvey, 1 Bt; yr bro of Sir Humphrey Mynors, 1 Bt (d 1989) and Sir Roger Mynors (d 1989); *b* 16 Sept 1915; *Educ* Eton, New Coll Oxford (MA, Rowing blue); *m* 6 July 1938, Mary Laurence, da of Charles Leslie Garton (d 1940), of Oxon; 5 s (Robert b 1939, Peter b 1941, Edward b 1947, James b 1949, Charles b 1952), 1 da (Eleanor b 1950); *Career* Maj Scots Gds serv ME and Italy 1939-45, (despatches, US Bronze Star); Courtaulds 1937-67 (dir 1955); dir: Nat Provident Inst 1957-87 (dep chm 1968-87), Imperial Tobacco 1967-71, RFD Group 1972-86 (chm 1974-83), Berisfords Group 1976-87 (chm 1980-87), HP Bulmer 1974-83; memb: Oxfordshire Health Authy 1974-85 (vice-chm 1979-85), Ct of Assts Worshipful Co of Weavers 1955- (upper bailiff 1968-69); *Clubs* Cavalry and Guards', Leander; *Style*— David Mynors, Esq, OBE; Quarry House, Shellingford, Faringdon, Oxon SN7 7QA (☎ 0367 710508)

MYNORS, Lydia, Lady; (Lydia) Marian; o da of Prof Sir Ellis Hovell Minns (d 1953), and Violet, *née* Nalder (d 1949); *m* 14 Oct 1939, Sir Humphrey Charles Baskerville Mynors, 1 Bt (d 1989); 2 s (1 decd), 4 da; *Style*— Marian, Lady Mynors; 3 Mount Way, St Weonards, Hereford HR2 8NN

MYNORS, Sir Richard Baskerville; 2 Bt (UK 1964), of Treago, Co Hereford; s of Sir Humphrey Charles Baskerville Mynors, 1 Bt (d 1989); *b* 5 May 1947; *Educ* Marlborough, Corpus Christi Coll Cambridge; *m* 1970, Fiona Bridget, da of Rt Rev George Edmund Reindorp; 3 da (Alexandra b 1975, Frances b 1978, Victoria b 1983); *Heir* none; *Career* schoolmaster and asst dir of music King's Sch Macclesfield 1970-73; dir of music: Wolverhampton G S 1973-81, Merchant Taylors' Sch Crosby 1981-88, Belmont Abbey Sch Hereford 1988-90; landowner and freelance musician 1990-; *Recreations* gardening, DIY, organ building; *Style*— Sir Richard Mynors, Bt; Treago, St Weonards, Hereford HR2 8QB (☎ 09818 208)

MYRDDIN-EVANS, George Watkin; s of Sir Guildhaume Myrddin-Evans, KCMG, CB (d 1964), formerly of Chester Place, Regents Park; *b* 26 March 1924; *Educ* Rugby, ChCh Oxford (MA in law); *m* 1966, Anna Katharine, 2 da of John Fowell Buxton, TD, of Morley Hall, Ware, sometime High Sheriff of Herts (ggn of Sir Edward Buxton, 2nd Bt), by his w Katharine (yst da of Sir Nicholas Bacon, 13 Bt); 1 s (David Guildhaume, b 14 April 1967); *Career* serv in France 1944, Capt Coldstream Gds 1945; memb Lloyd's 1951-, chm Gardner Mountain & Capel-Cure Agencies 1973-84, Oxford Rugby Football and Athletics versus Cambridge; Cons memb St Pancras Borough Cncl 1953-56 & 1959-62, dep mayor 1961, memb Tst for Sick Children in Wales; *Recreations* shooting, fishing, real tennis; *Clubs* White's, Pratt's, City of London, Cardiff & Co; *Style*— George Myrddin-Evans, Esq; Church House, Llandefalle, Brecon, Powys (☎ 087 485 210); 10 Campana Rd SW6 4AU (☎ 071 731 3281)

MYRES, Rear Adm John Antony Lovell; s of Dr (John) Nowell Linton Myres, CBE, FSA (d 1989), of The Manor House, Kennington, Oxford, and Joan Mary Lovell, *née*

Stevens; *b* 11 April 1936; *Educ* Winchester; *m* 21 Aug 1965, Alison Anne, da of Lt David Lawrence Carr, RN (ka 1941); 3 s (David Miles b 1966, Peter John Lukis b 1967, Charles Christopher Linton b 1969); *Career* RN; joined 1954, specialized hydrographic surveyor 1959; commands: HMS Woodlark 1969-71, HMS Fox 1972-73, HMS Hecla 1974 (also 1977-78 and 1981-82); Hydrographer Royal Australian Navy 1982-85; RN: Dir Hydrographic Plans and Surveys 1986-87, Capt Hydrographic Surveying Flotilla 1988-89, Hydrographer of the Navy 1990-, Chief Exec Hydrographic Office Defence Support Agency 1990-; Freeman City of London, Liveryman Worshipful Co of Chartered Surveyors, Younger Brother of Trinity House, Guild Burgess of Preston 1952; FRICS 1974, FBIM 1987, MRIN 1989, memb Hydrographic Soc 1985; *Recreations* naval history, medallic history; *Style*— Rear Adm John Myres; Hydrographer of the Navy, Lacon House, Ministry of Defence, Theobalds Rd, Holborn, London (☎ 071 430 6356)

MYRTLE, Brig Andrew Dewe; CB (1988), CBE (1979, MBE 1967); s of Lt-Col J Y E Myrtle, DSO (ka N Africa 1941), and Doreen Mary, *née* Lake; *b* 17 Dec 1932; *Educ* Winchester, RMA Sandhurst; *m* 19 Oct 1973, Mary-Rose, da of Neville Montague Ford, of North Close Cottage, North Close Rd, Bembridge, IOW; 2 da (Lucy Jane b 10 June 1975, Emma Mary b 30 March 1977); *Career* 1 KOSB: NI 1953-55, Malaysia and Singapore 1956-58, Berlin 1959-60; Sch of Inf 1960-62, Army Staff Coll 1962; 1 KOSB Radfan 1963, Bde Maj 24 Inf Bde Aden 1964-66; 1 KOSB: BAOR 1967-69, CO BAOR and Belfast 1969-71; mil asst to Adj Gen 1971-74, cmdt jr div Staff Coll 1974-77, Bde Cdr NI 1977-79, RCDS 1979, DDMO MOD 1980-83, asst cmdt RMAS 1983-85, cdr Land Forces Cyprus 1986-88; ADC to HM the Queen 1985-88; chief exec and sec Tennis and Rackets Assoc 1989-; FBIM 1985; *Recreations* golf, tennis, rackets, real tennis, fly fishing; *Clubs* Army and Navy, MCC, Queens, Huntercombe; *Style*— Brig Andrew Myrtle, CB, CBE; c/o The Queen's Club, Palliser Rd, West Kensington, London W14 9EQ (☎ 071 381 4746)

N

NAAS, Lord; Charles Diarmuidh John Bourke; s and h of 10 Earl of Mayo; *b* 11 June 1953; *Educ* St Aubyn's Rottingdean, Portora Royal Sch Enniskillen, Queen's Univ Belfast, Bolton St Coll of Technol Dublin; *m* 1, 1975 (m dis 1979), Marie Antoinette Cronnelly; 1 da (Hon Corinne Mary Jane b 1975); m 2, 1985, Marie Veronica Mannion; 2 s (Richard Thomas b 1985, Eoin Patrick b 1989); *Style*— Lord Naas; Derryinver, Beach Rd, Clifden, Co Galway, Eire

NABARRO, David Joseph Nunes; s of Eric John Nunes Nabarro, JP, of 11 The Marlowes, London, and Cecily, *née* Ornstein; *b* 5 July 1948; *Educ* Clifton Coll Bristol, Univ of Newcastle upon Tyne; *m* 26 March 1976 (m dis 1985), Victoria Marsland, da of John Lloyd Owen (d 1966), of Cheadle, Cheshire; 2 s (Leo b 4 Feb 1980, Alexei b 19 Oct 1982); *Career* trainee Joseph Sebag and Co 1969-72, ptnr Laurie Mibank and Co 1972-85, exec dir Prudential Bache Capital Funding (Equities) Ltd 1986-90; dir: MAID Systems Ltd 1986, Savoy & Strand Group, Penguin Group Hotel plc; Freeman City of London; memb Int Stock Exchange, AMSIA; *Recreations* skiing, garden design; *Clubs* City of London; *Style*— David J N Nabarro, Esq; (☎ car 0860 511125)

NABARRO, Eric John Nunes; JP (1972); s of Joseph Nunes Nabarro (d 1948), and Rosetta Nabarro (d 1972); *b* 5 April 1917; *Educ* Clifton; *m* 1947, Cecily, da of Henry Orenstein (d 1937); 1 s, 1 da; *Career* Capt RA, Iceland, N Africa, Italy; sr ptnr Eric Nabarro & Co Chartered Accountants 1960-82; treas Bd of Deputies of Br Jews 1973-79, pres Spanish and Portuguese Jewish Congregation 1984-88 (vice pres 1982-84), tstee Ravenswood Fndn 1985-, vice pres Victoria Community Centre 1963-; FCA; *Recreations* travel, golf, jogging; *Clubs* MCC, RAC; *Style*— Eric Nabarro Esq, JP; 11 The Marlowes, London NW8 6NB (☎ 071 586 1240)

NABARRO, Sir John David Nunes; s of Dr David Nunes Nabarro (d 1958); *b* 21 Dec 1915; *Educ* Oundle, UCL (MD); *m* 1948, Joan Margaret, da of William Gladstone Cockrell (d 1946); 2 s, 2 da; *Career* actg Lt-Col RAMC TA; physician; emeritus conslt physician Middx Hosp, hon conslt physician Royal Prince Alfred Hosp Sydney; dir: Cobbold Laboratories, Middx Hosp Med Sch; fell UCL, chm Jt Conslts Ctee 1979-84; kt 1982; *Recreations* gardening; *Style*— Sir John Nabarro; 33 Woodside Ave, London N12 8AT (☎ 081 445 7925)

NACPHERSON, Hon Mary Stewart; yr da of 1 and last Baron Drumalbyn, KBE, PC (d 1987); *b* 1942; *m* 1967 (m dis 1991), Philip D Wilson; *Style*— The Hon Mary Macpherson; 46 Chiddingstone Street, London SW6 3TG

NAERGER, Maurice John; s of Robert Henry Naerger (d 1982), and Beatrice, *née* Lewis (d 1968); *b* 4 March 1931; *Educ* Weymouth GS; *m* 7 April 1956, Brenda Mary, da of Edward Cross (d 1966); 1 s (Harry b 4 June 1961), 1 da (Melanie (Mrs McPherson) b 4 Dec 1958); *Career* dir WH Smith (Hldgs) plc 1975-81, conslt BR Stations Devpt 1982-83; chm 1982-: Helping Hand Charity Shops Ltd, CJC Appeals Ltd; chm: Valuation and Community Charge Tbnl; MBIM 1971, FIPM 1972; *Recreations* sailing, bowling, music, current affairs; *Style*— Maurice Naerger; 7 Burywick, West Common, Harpenden, Herts AL5 2AD (☎ 0582 760636); Helping Hand Charity Shops Ltd, Trenton House, 16 Eversley Rd, Bexhill on Sea, E Sussex TN40 1HE (☎ 0424 211693, fax 0424 222787)

NAESMYTH OF POSSO, Maj (Richard) William; s of Rev George Cresswell Naesmyth Naesmyth of Posso (d 1983), and Christobel Sara, *née* Slatter; 16th Naesmyth of Posso (Peeblesshire) since Charter in 1554; Sir James Naesmyth of Posso (d 1720) was cr a Baronet of Nova Scotia 1706 (ext 1928); *b* 19 Dec 1938; *Educ* Haileybury; *m* 22 March 1980, Xenia Angela Mary, da of Very Rev Rudolph Henderson-Howat (d 1957), Dean of Brechin; 1 s (Alexander Cresswell Benedict b 3 April 1983), 1 da (Georgina Charlotte Xenia b 30 April 1981); *Career* cmmnd RA 1959, served in Germany thrice during 1960s, attached Zambia Artillery 1965-67, Trucial Oman Scouts/Union Def Force 1970-74; *Recreations* genealogy, heraldry; *Style*— Major William Naesmyth of Posso, RA; Royal School of Artillery, Larkhill, Wilts SP4 8QT

NAGDA, Kanti; s of Vershi Bhoja Nagda of India; *b* 1 May 1946; *Educ* City HS Kampala Uganda, Coll of Further Educn Chippenham, E African Univ Uganda; *m* 1972, Bhagwati, *née* Desai; 2 children; *Career* accountant Hollander Hyams Ltd 1972-82; pres Anglo-Indian Circle 1973-, sec gen Confedn of Indian Orgns (UK) 1975-, hon ed conslt Int Asian Guide and Who's Who 1975-, asst ed Oshwah News 1975-83, mangr Community Centre 1982-, pres Greenfords Lions Club 1988-89; *Recreations* cricket, photography; *Style*— Kanti Nagda, Esq; 170 Tolcarne Drive, Pinner, Middx HA5 2DR (☎ 081 863 9089)

NAGGAR, Guy Anthony; s of Albert Naggar, of Italy, and Marjorie, *née* Smouha; *b* 14 Oct 1940; *Educ* Ecole Centrale des Arts et Manufactures Paris; *m* 6 Dec 1964, Hon Marion, da of Baron Samuel of Wych Cross (Life Baron, d 1987); 2 s (Albert b 15 July 1967, Jonathan b 24 Jan 1971), 1 da (Diane b 11 May 1969); *Career* dir: Banque Financière de la Cité Geneva 1970-88, Charterhouse Group Ltd 1980-81; chm Dawnay Day & Co Ltd 1981-; *Style*— Guy Naggar, Esq; 15 Grosvenor Gardens, London SW1W 0BD (☎ 071 834 8060)

NAGGAR, Hon Mrs (Marion); *née* Samuel; da of Baron Samuel of Wych Cross (Life Peer); *b* 1944; *m* 1964, Guy Antony Naggar; 2 s, 1 da; *Style*— The Hon Mrs Naggar; 61 Avenue Rd, London NW8

NAHUM, Peter John; s of Denis Ephraim Nahum, of Columbia, and Allison Faith, *née* Cooke; *b* 19 Jan 1947; *Educ* Sherborne; *m* 29 Aug 1987, Renate Angelika, da of Herr Ewald Meiser, of Germany; *Career* dir Peter Wilson's Sotheby's 1966-84; regular contrib as painting expert Antiques Roadshow 1980- (discover lost Richard Dadd painting 1986, subsequently sold to Br Museum); *Books* Prices of Victorian Painting Drawings and Watercolours (1976), Monograms of Victorian and Edwardian Artists (1976); *Recreations* gardening, sailing, photography, theatre, travel, walking; *Clubs* Reform; *Style*— Peter Nahum, Esq; 12 Islington Park St, London N1 1PU (☎ 071 607 3232); 5 Ryder St, London SW1Y 6PY (☎ 071 930 6059)

NAILOR, Prof Peter; s of Leslie Nailor (d 1960), of Wokingham, Berks, and Lily Matilda, *née* Jones (d 1961); *b* 16 Dec 1928; *Educ* Mercers' Sch, Wadham Coll Oxford (BA, MA); *Career* Home Civil Serv: Admty 1952, MOD 1964, asst sec 1967; prof of politics Univ of Lancaster 1969-76, visiting prof Carleton Univ Ottawa 1976-77, visiting res fell ANU Canberra 1977, prof of history RNC Greenwich 1977 (dean and academic princ 1982-84 1986-88) visiting lectr City Univ 1977-88, visiting prof Univ of Poona 1983, provost Gresham Coll 1988; external examiner 1970-88: King's Coll London, LSE, Univ of Aberdeen, Univ of Lancaster, Univ of Manchester, Univ of Reading, Univ of Salford, Univ of Southampton, Stafford Poly; univ res thesis examiner: Aberdeen, Dundee, E Anglia, Edinburgh, Exeter, Keele, Lancaster, London, Manchester, Oxford, Salford, Southampton, Wales, York, ANU; chm Br Int Studies Assoc 1984-86, cncl memb Royal Inst of Int Affairs 1984-90 (chm Res Ctee 1986-90); author of numerous books and articles on def topics; memb: FCO Advsy Panel on Arms Control and Disarmament 1975-88, Postgraduate Trg Bd Social Sci Res Cncl 1979-81, MOD Advsy Panel on Historical Records 1979-88, ed bd The Journal of Arms Control and Disarmament 1980; chm Political Sci and Int Rels Ctee of Social Sci Res Cncl 1979-81; Liveryman Worshipful Co of Mercers 1972; *Books* The Nassau Connection (1988); *Recreations* gardening, cooking; *Style*— Prof Peter Nailor; c/o Gresham College, Mercers' Hall, Ironmonger Lane, London EC2V 8HE

NAINBY-LUXMOORE, Dr (Bertie) Richard Chave; s of Maj Chave Nainy-Luxmooore (d 1984), of Bembridge, IOW, and Irene Dora Violet, *née* Scott (d 1945); *b* 20 Jan 1926; *Educ* Eton, Univ of Cambridge (BA, MA, MB BChir, LRCP); *m* 20 July 1957 (m dis 1977), Dr Ruth Morlock, da of Herbert Victor Morlock, MC (d 1975), of Court Lodge, West Farleigh, Kent; 2 s (Jonathan b 1958, James b 1959), 1 da (Mary b 1962); m 2, 1989, Queenie Jill, da of John Sanger, of Bury, W Sussex; *Career* WWII serv Scots Gds 1944-46 (invalid out); asst anaesthetist Med Coll Virginia 1957, res asst Nuffield Dept Anaesthetics, conslt Portsmouth 1965-89, ret 1990; published prize winning papers in Anaesthesia; memb: Br Med Soc, Portsmouth Med Soc, Assoc of Anaesthetists; FFARCS 1961; *Recreations* skiing, sailing, shooting; *Style*— Dr Richard Nainby-Luxmoore; The Old Vicarage, Southwick Village, Nr Fareham, Hants PO17 6DY (☎ 0705 327792); 12 Harbour Strand, Bembridge, Isle of Wight, PO35 5NP (☎ 0983 873176)

NAIPAUL, Sir Vidiadhar Surajprasad (Vidia); *b* 1932; *Educ* Univ Coll Oxford (BA); *m* 1955, Patricia Ann Hale; *Career* author; Hon DLitt Cambridge 1983, Hon DLitt London 1988; kt 1990; *Books* The Mystic Masseur (winner of John Llewelyn Rhys Memorial prize, 1958), A House for Mr Biswas (1961), In A Free State (winner of Booker prize, 1971), A Bend in the River (1979), The Return of Eva Peron (1980), Among the Believers (1981), The Enigma of Arrival (1987), A Turn in the South (1989), India: A Million Mutinies Now (1990); *Style*— Sir Vidia Naipaul; c/o Aitken & Stone, Literary Agents, 29 Fernshaw Rd, London SW10 0TG

NAIRAC, Lady Jane Fortune Margaret; *née* Ogilvy; da of 13 Earl of Airlie, DL; *b* 24 June 1955; *m* 1980, François Nairac, son of Paul Nairac, of Vacoas, Mauritius; 2 da (Jessica Doune b 1985, Annabel Lydia b 1988); *Style*— The Lady Jane Nairac; 57 Westover Road, London SW18 2RF

NAIRN, Andrew; s of Capt Andrew Nairn, MC (d 1971), of Glasgow, and Margaret Cornfoot, *née* Turner (d 1972); *b* 31 July 1944; *Educ* Strathallan Sch; *m* 1, 25 April 1970 (m dis 1983), Susan Anne, da of Richard Alphonse Napier; 1 s (Jonathan Richard b 1981), 1 da (Penelope Margaret b 1976); m 2, 1983, Glynis Vivienne, *née* Sweet; 1 step s (Barnaby Craggs b 1971), 1 step da (Charlotte Craggs b 1974); *Career* trainee CA Thomson Jackson Gourlay and Taylor 1962-67; Kidsons Impey (formerly Hodgson Impey): joined 1967, ptnr 1970-, London region managing ptnr 1990-; dep chm Dulwich Cons Assoc 1978; MICAS; *Recreations* fly fishing, golf; *Clubs* Vagabonds, Savile; *Style*— Andrew Nairn, Esq; 52 Redhill Wood, New Ash Green, Kent DA3 8QP (☎ 0474 873 724); Kidsons Impey, 20-26 Cursitor St, London EC4A 1HY (☎ 071 405 2088, fax 071 831 2206)

NAIRN, Sir Michael; 4 Bt (UK 1904), of Rankeilour, Collessie, and Dysart House, Dysart, Fifeshire; s of Sir (Michael) George Nairn, 3 Bt, TD (d 1984), and Helen Louise, *née* Bruce; *b* 1 July 1938; *Educ* Eton, INSEAD; *m* 1, 1972, Diana Gordon (d 1982), eldest da of F Leonard Bligh, of Pejar Park, Woodhouselee, NSW, Australia; 2 s (Michael Andrew b 1973, Alexander Gordon b 1975), 1 da (Emma Helen Beatrice b 1980); m 2, 1986, Sally Jane Hastings; *Heir* s, Michael Andrew b 1973; *Style*— Sir Michael Nairn, Bt; PO Box 55, Dundee DD1 9JJ

NAIRNE, Alexander Robert (Sandy); s of Rt Hon Sir Patrick Dalmahoy Nairne, KCB, MC, *qv*, of Yew Tree, Chilson, nr Charlbury, Oxon, and Penelope Chauncy, *née* Bridges; *b* 8 June 1953; *Educ* Radley, Univ Coll Oxford (BA, memb Isis Boat Crew); partner, Sylvia Elizabeth Tickner (Lisa); 1 s (Kit b 1984), 1 da (Eleanor b 1987); *Career* asst dir: Museum of Modern Art Oxford 1974-76, Modern Collection Tate Gallery London 1976-79; dir of exhibitions ICA London 1980-84, freelance curator and writer 1984-87, dir visual arts Arts Cncl of GB London 1987-; memb: Exec Ctee Art Galleries Assoc 1976-81, Exec Ctee Gtr London Arts 1983-86, Art and Architecture Advsy Panel RSA 1990-; advsr Works of Art Ctee Br Library 1990-; *Books* British Sculpture in the Twentieth Century (jt ed, 1981), Picturing the System (jt ed, 1981), State of the Art (1987); *Recreations* punting; *Clubs* Chelsea Arts; *Style*— Sandy Nairne, Esq; 43 Lady Somerset Road, London NW5 1TY (☎ 071 485 7992); Arts Council of Great Britain, 14 Great Peter St, London SW1 (☎ 071 333 0100)

NAIRNE, Lady (12 holder of S Lordship cr 1681); Lady Katherine Evelyn Constance Bigham; *née* Petty-Fitzmaurice; da of 6 Marquess of Lansdowne, DSO, MVO (d 1936), and Elizabeth, da of Sir Edward Hope, KCB (ggs of 2 Earl of Hopetoun); suc bro, 7 Marquess (ka 1944), in the Lordship of Nairne; *b* 22 June 1912; *m* 1933, 3 Viscount Mersey (d 1979); 3 s (incl 4 Viscount); *Heir* s, 4 Viscount Mersey; *Style*— The Rt Hon the Dowager Viscountess Mersey; Bignor Park, Pulborough, Sussex

NAIRNE, Rt Hon Sir Patrick Dalmahoy; GCB (1981, KCB 1975, CB 1971), MC (1943), PC (1982); s of Lt-Col Charles Silvester Nairne (d 1966), of Plover Hill, Compton, Winchester, and Edith Dalmahoy, *née* Kemp (d 1975); *b* 15 Aug 1921; *Educ* Radley, Univ of Oxford (MA); *m* 1948, Penelope Chauncy, er da of Lt-Col Robert Francis Bridges, RAMC, by his w Charlotte, da of Edward Luard (seventh in descent from Abraham Luard, who settled in England 1685 as a result of the Revocation of the Edict of Nantes); 3 s (Alexander b 1953, James b 1960, Andrew (twin) b 1960), 3 da (Katharine b 1949, Fiona b 1951, Margaret b 1961); *Career* formerly with Admty (joined 1947); perm sec DHSS 1975-81, second perm sec Cabinet Office 1973-75, dep under sec MOD 1970-73 (asst under sec logistics 1967-70, private sec to Def Sec 1965-67); master St Catherine's Coll Oxford 1981-88 (hon fell 1988), chllr Univ of Essex 1983-; tstee: Nat Maritime Museum 1981, Joseph Rowntree Fndn, Nat Aids

Tst; vice pres Soc of Italic Handwriting 1987, chm W Midlands Bd Central Ind TV, Advsy Bd Oxford Museum of Modern Art; pres Seamen's Hosp Soc; FRSA; Hon LLD: Univ of Leicester 1980, Univ of St Andrew's 1984; Hon DUniv Essex 1983; *Recreations* water colour painting; *Clubs* United Oxford and Cambridge Universities; *Style*— The Rt Hon Sir Patrick Nairne, GCB, MC; Yew Tree, Chilson, nr Charlbury, Oxford OX7 3HU

NAISH, John Alexander; s of William Henry Naish (d 1987), and Elizabeth Lyon, *née* Pirie; *b* 12 April 1948; *Educ* Queen Elizabeth's Hosp Bristol, Dr Challoner's GS Amersham, City of London Coll (BA); *m* 18 Sept 1982, Bonnie Kam Pik, da of Pham Tak, of Hong Kong; 2 s (William b 3 April 1987, Henry b Aug 1989); *Career* dir Hill Samuel Bank Ltd 1985; FCIB 1983; *Recreations* golf, astronomy; *Style*— John Naish, Esq; 405 Homat Sharon, 9-3 Minami Azabu 4-Chome, Minato Ku, Tokyo (☎ 010 813 3446 8264); Hill Samuel Bank Ltd, 6th Floor Shoyu Kaikan Bldg 3-3-1 Kasumigaseki, Tokyo (☎ 010 813 3501 6491, fax 010 813 3597 0471, telex 0222304)

NAISMITH, Robert James; s of Robert James Sinclair Naismith (d 1967), and Ann, *née* Smith (d 1970); *b* 4 March 1916; *Educ* Heriot-Watt Coll, Edinburgh Coll of Art (Dip Art in Architecutre, Dip TP); *Career* architect; engaged in post-war plans for Greenock after blitz and future plans coalfields in Lothians, jt sr ptnr Sir Frank Mears and Ptnrs 1952-85 (ptnr 1950); borough architect: Penicuik 1945-75, Dalkeith 1950-75; planning conslt Perth 1950-75; conslt at various periods to: Edinburgh, Inverness, Lanark, Hawick, Tranent, Inverkeithing; Civic Tst Award for rebuilding in town centre Selkirk, Civic Tst Commendation for Conservation in High St Dalkeith; dir survey of bldgs in Scot countryside 1983-85; restoration work: Darnley House, Glennarry Lodge, Spittals House; exhibited architectural Watercolours in: Royal Acad, Royal Scot Acad, RHA, Glasgow; various pubns in jls; memb: Nat Ctee Scot Heritage Soc, RIAS Cncl, Ctee RIBA, Ctee ARCUK; vice chm Edinburgh Architectural Assoc; FRIBA, FSA Scot, FRIAS, FRTPI; *Books* Buildings of the Scottish Countryside (1985), The Story of Scotland's Towns (1989); *Recreations* travel, painting and drawing, photography; *Clubs* Scottish Arts; *Style*— Robert Naismith, Esq; 14 Ramsay Garden, Royal Mile, Edinburgh EH1 2NA (☎ 031 225 2273)

NAKHLA, Nassef Latif; s of Latif Nakhla (d 1941), and Lily Elias (d 1977); *b* 12 July 1930; *Educ* English Sch Cairo, Battersea Poly (BSc Eng); *m* 6 Nov 1953, Joan, da of Anthony Sidonio (d 1944); 1 s (Karim b 1959), 1 da (Dina b 1957); *Career* dir: Lennard Devpts Ltd 1966-71 (chm and md 1971-90), Poly-Lina Ltd; *Recreations* squash, swimming, music, socialising; *Clubs* RAC; *Style*— Nassef L Nakhla, Esq; Poly-Lina Ltd, Millmarsh Lane, Brimsdown, Enfield, Middx EN3 7PU (☎ 081 804 8141, telex 266032, fax 081 805 0059)

NALDER, Hon Sir Crawford David; s of H A Nalder; *b* 14 Feb 1910; *Educ* State Sch Wagin, Wesley Coll Perth; *m* 1, 1934, Olive M (d 1973); 1 s, 2 da; m 2, 1974, Brenda Wade (d 1988); *Career* MLA WA (Country Pty): for Wagin 1947-50, for Katanning 1950-74; min: for War Serv Land Settlement 1959-66, for Agric 1959-71, for Electricity 1962-71; ldr Country Pty 1962-73, dep premier WA 1962-71; farmer; kt 1974; *Style*— The Hon Sir Crawford Nalder; Unit 4, 7 Dale Place, Booragoon, W Aust 6154

NALL, Sir Michael Joseph; 2 Bt (UK 1954), of Hoveringham, Co Nottingham, DL (Notts 1970); s of Col Sir Joseph Nall, 1 Bt, DSO, TD, DL (d 1958); *b* 6 Oct 1921; *Educ* Wellington; *m* 1951, Angela Loveday Hanbury, da of Air Chief Marshal Sir Alex Coryton, KCB, KBE, MVO, DFC; 2 s; *Heir* s, Edward William Joseph Nall; *Career* joined RN 1939, serv 1939-45, qualified in gunnery 1946-47, 1949 psc(m), Lt Cdr 1950, ret 1961; gen mangr Guide Dogs for the Blind Assoc 1961-64, High Sheriff Notts 1971, Vice Lord Lt of Notts 1989-91; pres Nottingham Chamber of Commerce & Industry 1972-74; banker, ret; chm: Southwell Diocesan Pastoral Ctee 1968-86, Nottinghamshire Scout Assoc 1968-88, Robin Hood Charity Tst 1974-88; *Recreations* field sports; *Clubs* Army & Navy, United Service, Nottingham; *Style*— Sir Michael Nall, Bt, DL; Hoveringham Hall, Nottingham NG14 7JR (☎ 0602 663634)

NALL-CAIN, Hon David Lawrence Robert; JP (Cheshire 1964); 2 s of 2 Baron Brocket (d 1967), and Angela Beatrix, *née* Pennyman, of Ormsby Hall, N Yorks; *b* 1 Sept 1930; *Educ* Eton, Magdalene Coll Cambridge (MA); *m* 1958, Lady Katherine Elizabeth Palmer, yr da of Maj Viscount Wolmer (ka 1942; eldest s of 3rd Earl of Selborne, whom he predeceased); granted the rank of an Earl's da 1985; 1 s (James b 1961), 2 da (Caroline b 1959, Annabel b 1963); *Career* cmmnd 12 Royal Lancers 1949, also Derbys Yeo; chartered surveyor, dir Tetley Walker 1960-65; chm Hertfords Soc 1967-69, govr St Patricks Hosp Dublin 1973-77; FRICS; *Recreations* fishing, shooting, stalking; *Clubs* Cavalry and Guards'; *Style*— The Hon David Nall-Cain, JP; Ballacleator, St Judes, IOM (☎ 0624 880 753)

NALL-CAIN, Hon David Michael Anthony; s of Hon Ronald Charles Manus Nall-Cain (d 1961), and gs of 2 Baron Brocket (d 1967); raised to the rank of a Baron's son 1969; *b* 1955; *Educ* Harrow; *Style*— The Hon David Nall-Cain

NALL-CAIN, Lady Katherine Elizabeth; *née* Palmer; da of Viscount Wolmer (ka 1942; s of 3 Earl of Selborne), and Priscilla (*see Baron Newton*); granted the rank of an Earl's da 1985; *b* 24 July 1938; *m* 1958, Hon David Lawrence Robert Nall-Cain, *qv*; 1 s, 2 da; *Style*— The Lady Katherine Nall-Cain; Ballacleator, St Judes, IOM

NALL-CAIN, Hon Richard Christopher Philip; s of Hon Ronald Charles Manus Nall-Cain (d 1961), and Elizabeth Mary Trotter, *née* Stallard; gs of 2 Baron Brocket (d 1967); raised to the rank of a Baron's s 1969; *b* 5 April 1953; *Educ* Eton; *m* 9 Dec 1978, Juliet Paula Vivian, da of J E V Forester, of Villa Mont Gras d'Eau, St Brelade, Jersey, CI; 1 s (Sam Richard Christopher b 8 June 1987 d 1987), 2 da (Rebecca Elizabeth Emily b 11 July 1981, Claire Antonia Louise b 1 Nov 1982); *Career* RMAS 1971, Lt Royal Green Jackets 1972-78; served: Belize, Gibraltar, Cyprus, UK; Hawker Siddeley Dynamics Engrg Ltd 1979-84: successively asst mktg mangr, admin mangr, engrg admin mangr; dir Edeco Hldgs Ltd 1984 (gp planning dir 1985, chief exec 1986-89); business conslt 1989-; FBIM 1988, FInstD 1979, MInstP 1984, AFA 1988; *Recreations* photography, shooting, cricket, DIY; *Clubs* MCC, Henley Royal Regatta, National Rifle Assoc; *Style*— The Hon Richard Nall-Cain; Potters Hall, Dane End, Ware, Herts SG12 OTU (☎ 0920 438298); office (☎ 0920 438719, fax 0920 438808)

NANCE, His Hon Francis James; JP (Lancs 1963); s of Herbert James Nance, of SA (d 1922); *b* 5 Sept 1915; *Educ* St Francis Xavier's Coll Liverpool, Univ of Liverpool; *m* 1943, Margaret Gertrude, *née* Roe (d 1988); 2 s; m 2, 1988, Theodora Wilhelmina Maria McGinty, *née* Marchand; *Career* Capt Royal Signals NW Europe (despatches 1945) 1940-45; barr 1936, dep chm Lancs QS 1963-66, cmmr Liverpool and Manchester Crown Cts 1966-71, county ct judge 1966-71, circuit judge 1972-90, ret 1990; *Recreations* chess, travel; *Clubs* Athenaeum (Liverpool); *Style*— His Hon F J Nance; c/o Queen Elizabeth II Law Courts, Liverpool, Merseyside

NANDI, Kalpana; da of S P Dhar, of 150 Becharam Chatterjee Rd, Calcutta-61, India, and Pratima, *née* Sarkar; *b* 26 April 1947; *Educ* TN HS Durgapur W Bangal, Univ of Calcutta (MB BS, DA), Univ of London (DA); *m* 1 June 1969, Dr Debal Kumar Nandi, s of Saroj Nandi; 1 s (Kunal b 1980), 1 da (Mahua b 1974); *Career* conslt anaesthetist 1980; memb: Coll of Anaesthetists, Midland Soc of Anaestheitists, Midland Soc of Anaesthetists, BMA, Assoc of Anaesthetists of GB and Ireland; FFARCS; *Recreations* music; *Style*— Dr Kalpana Nandi; New Cross Hosp, Wedensfield Rd, Wolverhampton WV10 0QP (☎ 0902 732255)

NANDY, Hon Mrs (Ann Luise); *née* Byers; da of Baron Byers, OBE, PC, DL (Life Baron, d 1984), and Baroness Byers, *qv*; *b* 30 April 1946; *Educ* Sherborne, Univ of York (BA), Univ of Bradford (MA); *m* 1972, Dipak Nandy; 2 da (Francesca b 1977, Lisa b 1979); *Career* library clerk House of Commons Library 1968-71, asst ed Where magazine 1971-73, head family servs dept London Cncl of Social Serv 1973-77, res student Univ of Bradford 1977-82, res with Granada TV 1982-84, prodr with Granada TV 1984-; *Style*— The Hon Mrs Nandy; c/o Hunters Hill, Blindley Heath, Lingfield, Surrey

NANKIVELL, Owen; s of John Hamilton Nankivell (d 1967), and Sarah Ann, *née* Mares (d 1975); *b* 6 April 1927; *Educ* Torquay GS, Univ of Manchester (BA, MA); *m* 1956, Mary Burman, da of Hubert Earnshaw (d 1966); *Career* statistician; Colonial Office 1952-56, Central Statistical Office 1956-65, chief statistician Dept of Econ Affrs 1965-68, under sec HM Treasy 1968-72, asst dir Central Statistical Office Cabinet Office 1972-79, chief economist Lucas Industries plc 1979-82, econ conslt and dir The Hinksey Centre 1982-; *Books* All Good Gifts, A Christian View of Affluence (1979); *Recreations* singing, travel, practising Christian; *Style*— Owen Nankivell, Esq; 18 Ash Hill Road, Torquay, Devon TQ1 3HZ (☎ 0803 297719)

NAPIER, Hon Mrs Neville; (Helen) Catherine; *née* Sanderson; *m* 1967, as his 2 wife, Cdr the Hon Neville Archibald John Watson Ettrick Napier, RN (d 1970); *Style*— The Hon Mrs Neville Napier; Kippilaw, St Boswells, Roxburghshire (☎ 0835 22742)

NAPIER, Christopher Lennox; s of Capt Lennox William Napier, DSO, DSC, RN, and Elizabeth Eve, *née* Lindsay; *b* 5 Dec 1944; *Educ* Sherborne, Britannia RNC Dartmouth; *m* 18 Dec 1971, Susan Margaret, da of Iain MacLauchlan (d 1985); 1 s (James b 1972), 1 da (Georgina b 1976); *Career* joined BRNC Dartmouth 1962, qualified submarines 1966, ret as Lt Cdr 1976; Clifford Turner: articled clerk 1976-78, admitted slr 1979, slr 1979-83, ptnr 1983-; ptnr Clifford Chance (formerly Clifford Turner) 1983-; pres Petersfield Soc, conslt CPRE (Sussex); Freeman City of London 1987; memb: Law Soc 1979, Nautical Inst; MRIN 1975; *Recreations* walking, reading, skiing, sailing; *Style*— Christopher Napier, Esq; Clifford Chance, Blackfriars House, 19 New Bridge St, London EC4 (☎ 071 353 0211, fax 071 489 0046, telex 887847 LEGIS G)

NAPIER, Master of; Hon Francis David Charles Napier; s and h of 14 Lord Napier and (5) Ettrick; *b* 3 Nov 1962; *Educ* Stanbridge Earls Sch; *Career* Lloyd's Agency; *Style*— The Master of Napier; Forest Lodge, Great Park, Windsor, Berks SL4 2BU

NAPIER, Isabel, Lady; Isabel Muriel; *née* Surtees; da of Maj Henry Siward Balliol Surtees, JP, DL (d 1955), of Redworth Hall, Co Durham; *m* 1931, Sir Joseph William Lennox Napier, 4 Bt, OBE (d 1986); 2 s (Robert, John); *Style*— Isabel, Lady Napier; 17 Cheyne Gdns, Chelsea, London SW3 5QT (☎ 071 352 4968)

NAPIER, Hon Mrs Greville; Juliet Elizabeth Hargreaves; *née* Durie; o da of Sir Alexander Charles Durie, CBE, *qv*; *b* 1942; *m* 1968, Hon (John) Greville Napier (d 1988), s of 13 Lord Napier and (4 Baron) Ettrick; 2 da (Lucilla Fleur Scott b 1969, Araminta Elizabeth Muir b 1972); *Style*— The Hon Mrs Greville Napier; Underhill, Treyford, Midhurst, Sussex

NAPIER, Maj-Gen Lennox Alexander Hawkins; CB (1983), OBE (1970), MC (1957), DL (1984); s of Maj Charles McNaughton Napier; *b* 28 June 1928; *Educ* Radley, RMA Sandhurst; *m* 1959, Jennifer Wilson; 1 s, 2 da; *Career* cmmnd S Wales Borderers 1948, cmd 1 Bn S Wales Borderers and 1 Bn Royal Regt of Wales 1967-70, instr Jt Staff Services Coll 1970-72, MOD 1972-74, Bde Cdr Berlin Inf Bde 1974-76, Div Brig Prince of Wales's Div 1976-80, GOC Wales 1980-83, ret; Col Cmdt Prince of Wales's Div 1980-83, Col Royal Regt of Wales (24/41 Foot) 1983-89; inspr Public Inquiries 1983-, chm Central Tport Consultative Ctee 1985-; OStJ 1969; *Books* Armed Services Careers Year Book 1987-88; *Recreations* riding, shooting; *Clubs* Landsdowne; *Style*— Maj-Gen Lennox Napier, CB, OBE, MC, DL; c/o Barclays Bank, 17/18 Agincourt Sq, Monmouth, Gwent

NAPIER, Hon (Hugh) Lenox; 4 s of 13 Baron Napier and (4) Ettrick, TD (d 1954), and (Violet) Muir, er da of Sir Percy Wilson Newson, 1 and last Bt (d 1950); *b* 18 July 1943; *Educ* privately; *Style*— The Hon Lenox Napier

NAPIER, Hon (Charles) Malcolm; s of 13 Baron Napier and 4 Ettrick, TD (d 1954); *b* 1933; *Educ* Canford; *m* 1969, Lady Mariota Cecilia Murray, *qv*; 3 da (Eloise, Maryel, Cecilia); *Career* formerly Lt 1 Royal Dragoons, served 1952-53; fndr-memb cncl Anglo-Rhodesian Soc, memb of Queen's Body Gd for Scotland (Royal Co of Archers); *Clubs* Cavalry and Guards', Pratt's, Turf, City and Civil Service (Cape Town); *Style*— The Hon Malcolm Napier; Bardmony House, Alyth, Perthshire (☎ 082 83 2645); 1 Newton Spicer Drive, Highlands, Harare, Zimbabwe

NAPIER, Lady Mariota (Cecilia); *née* Murray; da of 7 Earl of Mansfield and Mansfield (d 1971); *b* 1945; *m* 1969, Hon (Charles) Malcolm Napier, *qv*; *Style*— Lady Mariota Napier; Bardmony House, Alyth, Perthshire (☎ 082 83 2645); Hanover Place, 314 Rhodes Ave, Salisbury, Zimbabwe

NAPIER, Hon Michael Elibank; s of Brig Lord Robert John Napier (d 1987), 5 Baron Napier of Magdala, OBE, of 8 Mortonhall Rd, Edinburgh, and Lady Elizabeth Marian Napier, *née* Hunt; *b* 25 April 1953; *Educ* Trinity Coll Glenalmond, St Johns Coll Cambridge (MA), Univ of Newcastle (PhD); *Career* univ lectr, Univ of Nottingham 1984-90, conslt 1990-; *Recreations* real tennis, orienteering, music; *Style*— The Hon Michael Napier; 3 Elswick Drive, Beeston, Nottingham NG9 1NQ (☎ 0602 252095)

NAPIER, (Thomas) Michael; s of Montague Keith Napier (d 1975), and Mary, *née* Mather (d 1953); *b* 11 June 1946; *Educ* Loughborough GS, Hulme Hall Univ of Manchester (Open Exhibition, First XV Rugby); *m* 27 Dec 1969, Denise Christine; 1 s (Frederick John b 31 Oct 1980), 2 da (Holly Danielle b 26 June 1973, Amy Abigail b 9 June 1975); *Career* articled clerk Malcolm H Moss Moss Toone & Deane Loughborough 1968-70, asst slr W H Thompson Manchester 1970-72, sr ptnr Irwin Mitchell Sheffield and Birmingham 1983 (ptnr Sheffield 1973), jt fndr Pannone Napier 1985-; ed conslt: Personal & Medical Injuries Law Letter, Journal of Forensic Psychiatry; Mental Health Act Cmmn: joined 1983, jt vice chm 1985-88, chm NE region 1985-89; former pres S Yorks Medico-Legal Soc, memb Governing Bd Assoc of Trial Lawyers of America, sec Assoc of Personal Injury Lawyers; memb Law Soc 1970; *Recreations* sport generally, relaxing on N Norfolk coast; *Style*— Michael Napier, Esq; The Bridge House, Ford, Ridgeway, Sheffield S12 3YD (☎ 0246 433 221); The Manor House, Great Walsingham, Norfolk (☎ 0328 820 213); Irwin Mitchell, St Peter's House, Hartshead, Sheffield S1 2EL (☎ 0742 767 777, fax 0742 753 306); Pannone Napier, St Peter's House, Hartshead, Sheffield S1 2EL (☎ 0742 755 899, fax 0742 753 306, car 0860 268 553)

NAPIER, (Trevylyan) Miles Wentworth; s of Cdr Trevylyan Michael Napier, DSC, RN (d 1940), of Stokehill Wood, Buckland Monachorum, S Devon, and Priscilla, *née* Hayter (da of Sir William Goodenough Hayter, KBE, KCMG); *b* 12 Oct 1934; *Educ* Wellington, Millfield; *m* 20 April 1971, Mary Philomena Ann, da of Edward Bourke, of Rathfarnham, Co Dublin; 1 s (Lennox b 20 May 1975); *Career* Rifle Bde and 60 Rifles 1952-54, offr cadet Leics and Derbys Yeo 1967-68; handicapper to Jockey Club and Nat Hunt Ctee 1964-67, conslt to Bloodstock and Racing Data (Prestel) 1981-; memb: Racing Press 1973-, Br Sporting Art Tst, Friends of Pavilion Opera; author; *Books*

Thoroughbred Pedigrees Simplified (1973), Breeding a Racehorse (1975), Blood Will Tell (1978), The Racing Men of TV (1979), Keylocks Dams or Winners of all Flat races in Great Britain and Ireland (co-compiler 1967-68 and 1979-84), Treasures of the Bloodstock Breeders Review (compiled with Leon Rasmussen); *Recreations* riding, sporting art, history, opera; *Style—* Miles Napier, Esq; Banbury House, Gt Easton, Market Harborough, Leicestershire (☎ 0536 770 449)

NAPIER, Sir Oliver John; s of James Joseph Napier (d 1975), of Belfast, and Sarah Frances Napier, *née* Bready; *b* 11 July 1935; *Educ* St Malachys Coll Belfast, Queens Univ Belfast (LLB); *m* 1961, Kathleen Brigid, of Belfast; 3 s (James, John, Kevin), 5 da (Brigid, Veronica, Nuala, Emma, Mary-Jo); *Career* slr, memb Bd of Examiners Law Soc of NI 1964-68, min of Law Reform NI Exec 1973-74; memb: Belfast City Cncl 1977-89, NI Assembly 1973-74 and 1982-86, NI Constitutional Convention 1975-76; ldr Alliance Pty of N Ireland 1973-84, chm Standing Advsy Cmmn on Human Rights 1988-; kt 1985; *Recreations* gardening; *Clubs* Northern Law; *Style—* Sir Oliver Napier; Glenlyon, Victoria Rd, Holywood, Co Down, NI (☎ 02317 5986); Napier & Sons Solicitors, 1/9 Castle Arcade, High St, Belfast (☎ 0232 244602)

NAPIER, Robert Stewart; s of Andrew Napier (d 1967), and Lilian V, *née* Ritchie; *b* 21 July 1947; *Educ* Sedbergh, Sidney Sussex Coll Cambridge (BA, MA), Harvard Business Sch (AMP); *m* 17 Dec 1977, Patricia Gray Stewart; 1 da (Catriona Rose Stewart b 1984); *Career* Rio Tinto Zinc Corp 1969-73, Brandts Ltd 1973-75, Fisons Ltd 1975-81; Redland: fin dir 1981-87, gp md 1988-90, chief exec 1991-; *Style—* Robert Napier, Esq; Redland PLC, Redland House, Reigate, Surrey RH2 0SJ (☎ 0737 242488, fax 0737 221938, telex 28626)

NAPIER, Sir Robin Surtees; 5 Bt (UK 1867), of Merrion Square, Dublin; assumed forenames of Robin Surtees in lieu of those of Robert Aubone Siward; s of Sir Joseph William Lennox Napier, 4 Bt, OBE (d 1986), by his w, Isabel Muriel, *née* Surtees; *b* 5 March 1932; *Educ* Eton; *m* 1971, Jennifer Beryl, da of late Herbert Warwick Daw, of Flint Walls, Henley-on-Thames; 1 s; *Heir* s, Charles Joseph b 1973; *Career* 2 Lt Coldstream Gds 1950-51; dir Charterhouse Japhet plc (Merchant Bankers) 1967-83, chm Standard Fireworks plc 1980-86; dir: Brickhouse Dudley plc 1981-86, Marlar International 1983-89, Dane & Company Ltd 1987-, Test and Itchen Fishing Assoc 1981-88; UK rep for Rothschild Bank AG 1983-; *Recreations* shooting, fishing, gardening; *Clubs* MCC, City of London, Flyfishers', Union (Sydney); *Style—* Sir Robin Napier, Bt; Upper Chilland House, Martyr Worthy, Winchester, Hants SO21 1EB (☎ 096278 307); New Court, St Swithin's Lane, London EC4P 4DU (☎ 071 280 5000)

NAPIER AND ETTRICK, 14 Lord (Napier S 1627) and 5 Baron (Ettrick UK 1872); Sir Francis Nigel Napier; 11 Bt (Nova Scotia 1666), of Thirlestane, CVO (1985, LVO 1980), DL (Selkirk 1974, Ettrick and Lauderdale 1975); eld s of 13 Lord Napier and Ettrick, TD, JP, DL (d 1954, eleventh in descent from first Lord, himself s of John Napier of Merchistoun, the inventor of logarithms); the Napiers of Merchistoun are co-heirs general of the ancient Celtic Earls of Lennox; *b* 5 Dec 1930; *Educ* Eton, RMA Sandhurst; *m* 1958, Delia Mary, da of Archibald D B Pearson; 2 s (Master of Napier b 1962, Hon Nicholas b 1971, *qv*), 2 da (Hon Louisa (Hon Mrs Morrison) b 1961, Hon Georgina b 1969); *Heir* s, Master of Napier; *Career* Maj Scots Gds (R of O), Malaya 1950-51 (invalided); Adjt 1 Bn Scots Gds 1955-57; equerry to HRH the late Duke of Gloucester 1958-60 (ret 1960), sits as Ind Peer in House in Lords, in the City 1960-62, dep ceremonial and protocol sec Cwlth Rels Off 1962-68; Cons Whip House of Lords 1970-71, comptroller and equerry to HRH The Princess Margaret, Countess of Snowdon 1973- (private sec, comptroller and equerry 1974); pres St John Ambulance Assoc and Bde London 1975-83; memb Royal Co of Archers (Queen's Body Gd for Scotland 1953-), on behalf of The Queen handed over the Instruments of Independence t Tuvalu (Ellice Islands) 1979; CStJ 1988 (OStJ 1982); Liveryman Worshipful Co of Grocers 1963; *Clubs* White's, Pratt's, Royal Caledonian Hunt; *Style—* Major the Lord Napier and Ettrick, CVO, DL; Forest Lodge, The Great Park, Windsor; Thirlestane, Ettrick, Selkirkshire; Nottingham Cottage, Kensington Palace, London W8 4PU

NAPIER AND ETTRICK, Dowager Baroness; (Violet) Muir; da of Sir Percy Wilson Newson, 1 and last Bt (d 1950), and Helena (d 1967), da of late Col Denham Franklin, RAMC; *b* 26 Aug 1909; *Educ* Heathfield Ascot; *m* 1928, 13 Baron Napier and (4) Ettrick, TD (d 1954); 4 s (1 decd); *Career* nat pres YWCA of Scotland 1961-82; *Style—* The Rt Hon Dowager the Lady Napier and Ettrick; Bardmony, Alpeth, Blairclowne, Perthshire PA11 8NY

NAPIER OF MAGDALA, 6 Baron (UK 1868), in Abyssinia and of Caryngton, Co Chester; Robert Alan Napier; eld s of 5 Baron Napier of Magdala, OBE (d 1987), and Elizabeth Marian, *née* Hunt; *b* 6 Sept 1940; *Educ* Winchester, St John's Coll Cambridge (MA); *m* 4 Jan 1964, Frances Clare, er da of late Alan Frank Skinner, OBE, of Monks Close, Woolpit, Suffolk; 1 s (Hon James Robert b 29 Jan 1966), 1 da (Hon Frances Catherine b 2 July 1964); *Heir* s, Hon James Robert Napier; *Recreations* sailing, music; *Clubs* Leander; *Style—* The Rt Hon Lord Napier of Magdala; Fingerbread House, Woolpit, Suffolk IP30 9QP (☎ 0359 40235)

NAPIER OF MERCHISTOUN, Sir John Archibald Lennox; 14 Bt (NS 1627), of Merchistoun; s of Sir William Archibald Napier, of Merchistoun, 13 Bt (d 1990), and Kathleen Mabel, *née* Greaves; descended from John Napier, inventor of logarithms; *b* 6 Dec 1946; *Educ* St Stithians, Univ of Witwatersrand Johannesburg (MSc, PhD); *m* 9 Dec 1969, Erica Susan, da of late Kurt Kingsfield, of Johannesburg; 1 s (Hugh Robert Lennox b 1977), 1 da (Natalie Ann b 1973); *Heir* s, Hugh Robert Lennox Napier b 1 Aug 1977; *Career* res engr; *Clubs* Johannesburg Country; *Style—* Sir John Napier of Merchistoun, Bt; Merchistoun, PO Box 65177, Benmore 2010, Transvaal, S Africa (☎ 010 27 011 783 2611)

NAPLEY, Sir David; s of Joseph Napley; *b* 25 July 1915; *Educ* Burlington Coll; *m* 1940, Leah Rose, da of Thomas Saturley; 2 da; *Career* served WWII Queen's Royal (W Surrey) Regt and Indian Army; Parly Candidate (C) Rowley Regis and Tipton 1951, Gloucester 1955; admitted slr 1939; sr ptnr Kingsley Napley; pres Law Soc 1976-77 (memb Cncl 1962-86, vice pres 1975-76); memb: Ed Bd Criminal Law Review 1967-, Home Office Law Revision Ctee 1971-; dir Br Academy of Forensic Sciences 1974- (chm 1960-74, pres Exec Cncl 1967), chm Examining Bd ISVA 1981-84, pres West Ham Boys' Club 1981- (tstee 1979-), chm Cncl Imperial Soc Kts Bachelor 1981-; kt 1977; *Books* incl: Not Without Prejudice (1982), Rasputin in Hollywood (1990); *Style—* Sir David Napley; 107-115, Long Acre, London WC2E 9PT (☎ 071 240 2411, telex 28756)

NAPPER, John Pelham; s of John Mortimer Napper (artist, d 1951), and Dorothy Charlotte, *née* Hill (Dorothy Ilma, actress and singer, d 1976); *b* 17 Sept 1916; *Educ* Frensham Heights, private tutors, Royal Acad Schs of Art; *m* 1, 8 June 1935 (m dis 1945), Hedwig Sophie Armour; m 2, 20 Nov 1945, Pauline, da of Col Paul Victor Davidson, DSO, Royal Warwicks Regt (d 1946); *Career* served WWII, cmmnd RA 1941, War Artist to Ceylon Cmd 1943, seconded to RNVR 1944, demobbed 1946; painter; teacher life painting St Martin's Sch of Art 1949-57, lived and worked in France 1957-68, visiting prof Fine Arts Univ of Southern Illinois Carbondale USA 1968-69; one man exhibitions: The Leicester Galleries London 1949, 1961 and 1962,The Adams Gallery London 1957 and 1959, The Walker Art Gallery Liverpool (Retrospective) 1959, La Maison de la Pensée Francaise Paris 1960, Galerie Lahumière Paris 1963 and 1965, Galerie Hervé Paris 1965, Larcada Gallery NY 1967, 1970, 1972, 1975 and 1977, Browse & Darby Ltd London 1978 and 1980, Oldham Art Gallery (Retrospective) 1984, Thos Agnew and Sons Ltd London 1986, Albemarle Gallery London 1988 and 1990; Prizes: Medaille d'Argent Salon des Artistes Françaises (Paris) 1947, Int Exhibition of Fine Arts (Moscow) 1957, The Critics Prize (awarded by the Int Assoc of Art Critics) 1961; AAUP 1968; *Books* Life Drawing (with Nicholas Mosley, 1954); *Recreations* cookery, gardening, book collecting; *Style—* John Napper, Esq; c/o The Albemarle Gallery, 18 Albemarle St, London W1X 3HA (☎ 071 355 1880, fax 071 493 9272)

NAQVI, (Syed Zakir Husain) Haider; s of Syed Ather Husain Naqvi (d 1954), and Saghir Fatima, *née* Rizvi; *b* 14 Oct 1949; *Educ* Karachi Univ (BCom, MA); *m* Marja-Liisa, da of Paavo Ilmari Nyssönen, of Sorsakoski, Finland; 2 da (Chantal Samreen b 1980, Sabrina Yasmeen b 1986); *Career* CA; internal auditor Philip Industs (UK) Ltd 1975-77, gp fin controller London Export Corp (Hldgs) Ltd 1977-78, ptnr Haider Naqvi & Co CAs 1978-; FCA 1973, assoc Inst of Chartered Secs and Admins 1974; *Recreations* squash, keeping fit, snooker, chess; *Style—* Haider Naqvi, Esq; 225 Hale Lane, Edgware, Middx HA8 9QF (☎ 081 958 8015, fax 081 958 8535, telex GECOMS-G 8951182)

NARAYAN, Rudy; s of Sase Narayan (d 1947), and Taijberiti; *b* 11 May 1938; *m* 1, (m dis 1974), Dr Naseem Akbar; 2 da (Sharmeen, Yasmeen); m 2, 26 March 1988, Saeeda Begum, *née* Shah; 2 da (Sahira, Aerem); *Career* HM Forces BAOR 1958-60, HM Forces HQ MELF 1960-1963, HQ RAOC 1963-65; called to the Bar Lincoln's Inn 1968; fndr and first sec Soc of Black Lawyers 1973, fndr and first chm Black Rights UK 1982, currently dir Civil Rights UK, memb Soc of Authors; *Books* Black England (1977), Barrister for the Defence (1985); *Recreations* cricket, theatre, debating; *Clubs* Wig and Pen; *Style—* Rudy Narayan, Esq; 23 Woodbourne Ave, London SW16 1LP (☎ 081 769 5776); Justice House, 402 Brixton Rd, London SW9 7AW (☎ 071 978 8545, fax 071 978 8873, car 0836 223925)

NARES, Anthony James; s of John George Alastair MacKintyre Nares, RN (ka 1942), of Villa Pavillon, Monte Carlo, Monaco, and Marguerite Emily Louise Buchanan-Dunlop, *née* McFarlane; *b* 17 Feb 1942; *Educ* Charterhouse; *m* 19 July 1975, Thomasin Sarah, da of (Alfred) Ronald Dashwood Gilbey, CBE (d 1978), of Dorset; 1 s (George b 10 Aug 1982); *Career* Royal Horse Gds (The Blues) 1964-68; md: Lippincott & Margulies 1969-78, Centaur Communications 1978-; launched: Marketing Week 1978, Creative Review 1981, Money Marketing 1984, Design Week 1985, New Accountant 1988; *Recreations* skiing, shooting; *Clubs* Turf; *Style—* Anthony Nares, Esq; 8 Bloomfield Terr, London SW1W 8PG (☎ 071 439 4222); Ellingham Farm, Ringwood, Hants; 50 Poland St, London W1 (☎ 071 494 0300, car 0836 226298)

NASH, David Harwood; s of Victor Nash, of Welwyn, Herts, and Anne, *née* Richardson; *Educ* St Albans Sch, Radley; *m* 20 June 1963, Susan Margaret, da of John Charlesworth Haldane; 1 s (James Harwood), 2 da (Charlotte Louise Harwood, Annabel Haldane); *Career* ptnr: Binder Hamlyn 1966-76, Pannell Kerr Forster (and predecessor firms) 1977-91; dir Midstates plc, Pelham Investment Property plc 1984-, memb Lloyds; memb Brompton Soc; FCA; *Recreations* skiing, sailing, tennis; *Clubs* MCC; *Style—* David Nash, Esq; 10 Pelham St, London SW7 2NG (☎ 071 225 0702); 78 Hatton Garden, London EC1 (☎ 071 831 7393)

NASH, (Denis Frederic) Ellison; OBE (1982), AE (1944); s of late Frederic Arthur Nash; *b* 10 Feb 1913; *Educ* Dulwich, St Bartholomew's Hosp Med Coll London; *m* 1938, Joan Mary, *née* Andrew; 2 s, 2 da; *Career* consulting surgn St Bartholomew's Hosp, formerly dean of Medical Coll Univ of London; interest in special educn with contribs recognised by naming of schs (Nash House at W Wickham and Dulwich Coll Prep Sch); FRCS; *Recreations* gardening, photography, work with disabled; *Clubs* Guild of Freemen, City of London; *Style—* D F Ellison Nash, Esq, OBE, AE; 28 Hawthorne Rd, Bickley, Kent (☎ 081 467 1142)

NASH, Eric Charles; s of Charles Nash (d 1984), and Ellen, *née* Fowkes (d 1981); *b* 6 March 1927; *Educ* Carshalton Sch; *m* 15 March 1952, Jean, da of James Murray Miller (d 1963); 2 s (Ian b 18 March 1953, Andrew b 24 Dec 1955); *Career* Army 1944-48; Distillers Co Ltd 1948-58, non marine mangr W E Found & Co Ltd 1958-76; account exec: Alexander Howden & Co Ltd 1976-87, How F Devitt & Sons Ltd 1987-89; pres Southern Co Athletic Assoc, vice pres AAA, pres Cambridge Harriers; Freeman: City of London, Worshipful Co of Bakers 1982; MBIM, MIEX; *Recreations* athletics; *Clubs* City Livery; *Style—* Eric Nash, Esq; 12 Margaret Rd, Bexley, Kent DA5 1DU (☎ 081 303 4573)

NASH, Eric Stanley; s of Stanley Noah Nash (d 1975), of Paulton, Somerset, and Ina Louisa Nash (d 1978); *b* 17 May 1944; *Educ* Midsomer Norton GS, Univ of Bristol (BDS), Univ of Wales (MSc); *m* 14 June 1969, Enid Dorothy, da of Walter Perry, of Farrington Gurney, Avon; 2 s (Richard John b 10 Oct 1981, Michael James b 8 June 1983); *Career* jr posts: Bristol Hosps 1967-68, United Cardiff Hosps 1968-72; lectr Univ of Wales Coll of Med 1973-79; conslt oral and maxillofacial surgn: Mid Glamorgan Health Authy; articles in Br Jl Oral Surgery, lectr; Central Ctee Hosp Dental Servs, Welsh Dental Ctee, Welsh Med and Scientific Ctee, Welsh post grad advsr Royal Coll; FDS, RCS, Fell Assoc of Oral and Maxillofacial Surgery 1979; *Recreations* church organisation, organist, music; *Style—* Eric Nash, Esq; Mendip House, 43 Penwyne Road, Whitchurch, Cardiff, South Glamorgan CF4 2AB (☎ 0222 627548); Oral Surgery Department, Princess of Wales Hospital, Bridgend, Mid Glamorgan

NASH, Howard Douglas; s of Gordon Douglas Nash (d 1977), of Harpenden, and Enid, *née* Robertson; *b* 29 July 1944; *Educ* Queen Elizabeth's GS Barnet, Univ of Newcastle upon Tyne (BA, BArch); *m* 21 April 1965 (m dis 1974), (Margaret Ruth) Jennifer (d 1986), da of Ian Fenwick; 3 s (William b 1966, Steven b 1971, Thomas b 1972); *Career* London Borough of Islington 1970-71, Nash Parker Architects 1971-; ctee memb Franco-Br Union of Architects; memb RIBA; *Recreations* sailing; *Style—* Howard Nash, Esq; 50 Westbourne Park Road, London W2 5PH (☎ 071 221 5238); Nash Parker Architects, 1 Prince of Wales Passage, 117 Hampstead Rd, London NW1 3EF (☎ 071 387 4427, fax 071 387 9624)

NASH, James Gardiner; MBE; s of Col William Nash, CBE, TD (d 1981), and Eileen, *née* Kirkcaldie (d 1985); *b* 30 July 1934; *Educ* Stowe; *m* 15 Aug 1965 (m dis 1984), Sally Anne Randall; 2 s (Thomas b 1967, Matthew b 1969); *Career* Nat Serv 1953-55, 2 Lt 12 Royal Lancers in Malaya, Leics and Derby Yeo 1955-59; political offr Aden Protectorate 1959-65 (Colonial Office), FO London and Bahrain 1965-67; chartered surveyor: City of London 1969-88, Egypt 1974-77; walked Venice to Addis Ababa 1956-57, rode a horse Istanbul to Jerusalem 1988; govr Alexandria Schs Tst, sec Ward of Cheap Club 1984-88; Freeman: City of London 1982, Worshipful Co of Broderers Co 1982; FRICS 1977-89; CStJ 1989, OStJ 1978; *Recreations* cooking, gardening, Middle East, writing poor verse; *Clubs* Cavalry & Guards; *Style—* James Gardiner Nash, Esq, MBE; 72 Buttesland St, London N1 6BY (☎ 071 253 0638)

NASH, John Alfred Stoddard; s of Lewis John Alfred Maurice Nash, of New Cottage, High Rd, Chipstead, Surrey, and Josephine Karen, *née* Stoddard (d 1962); *b* 22 March 1949; *Educ* Milton Abbey Sch, CCC Oxford (MA); *m* 6 Aug 1983, Caroline Jennifer, da of Geoffrey Hamilton Paul (d 1985), of Kirton Lodge, Ipswich, Suffolk; 1 s (Charles b 1985), 1 da (Josephine b 1984); *Career* asst dir Lazard Brother and Co Ltd 1975-83, md Advent Ltd 1986 (joined 1983), chm British Venture Capital Association 1988-89, chm Nash, Sells & Partners Ltd 1989-; *Recreations* golf, tennis, skiing; *Clubs* Turf; *Style—* John Nash, Esq; Nash, Sells & Partners Ltd, 25 Buckingham Gate, London SW1E 6LD (☎ 071 828 6944)

NASH, John Edward; s of Joseph Ronald Nash (d 1977); *b* 25 June 1925; *Educ* Univ of Sydney (BEcon), Balliol Coll Oxford (BPhil); *m* 1947, Ralda Everard Tyndall, *née* Herring; 2 s (Antony James, Jeremy Robert), 2 da (Regina Jane, Camilla Kate); *Career* dir: Samuel Montagu & Co Ltd 1956-73, monetary affrs EEC Cmmn 1973-77, Reckitt & Colman Ltd 1977-87 (1966-73), SG Warburg & Co Ltd London 1977-87; chm: Mercury Money Mkt Tst 1978-86, memb advsy bd SG Warburg Bank AG Zurich 1987- (chm 1977-87); hon treas and memb bd of tstees World Wide Fund for Nature 1985-; *Recreations* golf, skiing, horse racing, music; *Clubs* Turf, Buck's, MCC; *Style—* John Nash, Esq; Chalet Gstelli, CH-3781 Gsteig-bei-Gstaad, Switzerland (☎ 010 41 30 51162)

NASH, Norman Charles Russell; s of Robert Russell Nash (d 1966), of Ballymoney, NI, and Eva Alice Nash, *née* Phillips (d 1976); *b* 15 Sept 1928; *Educ* Uppingham; *m* 2 April 1956, Mary Elizabeth, da of Lt-Col J R H Greeves, TD, JP (d 1988), of Altona, Strandtown, Belfast, NI; 1 s (Patrick b 1958), 2 da (Cressida b 1960, Polly b 1963); *Career* CA; articled to Macnair Mason Evans & Co London 1947, qualified 1951, ptnr Burke Covington & Nash London 1952, fndr and sr ptnr Nash Broad Wesson 1973-90, chm GMN Int 1990- (fndr and int sec 1977-90), fndr and dir Unity Security Balloting Services Ltd 1987-; vice pres Rosslyn Park FC 1959- (hon treas 1957-59), chm Fin Ctee Hurlingham Club 1970-75 (memb Ctee 1960-76), hon treas Assoc of Hon Stewards Wimbledon Lawn Tennis Championships churchwarden St Margarets Church Putney 1982-86 (memb Cncl 1960-86), chm Calibre Cassette Library of Recorded Books Ltd 1983-, treas London Soc of Chamber Music 1990 (memb Ctee 1984-), memb Cncl and memb Gen Purposes Ctee Royal Sch of Church Music 1985- ACA 1952, FCA 1957; *Recreations* skiing, gliding, music, canal boats; *Clubs* MCC, City of London; *Style—* Norman Nash, Esq; Flat 5J, Portman Mansions, Chiltern St, London W1H 1PU (☎ 071 935 5570); The Red House, Burdrop, Sibford Gower, Banbury, Oxon OX15 5RQ (☎ 029 578 275); Nash Broad Wesson Chartered Accountants, 42 Upper Berkeley St, London W1H 8AB (☎ 071 723 7293, fax 071 724 3488, telex 23722)

NASH, Paul Frank Anthony; s of Frank Nash, of 25 Romberg Rd, Tooting, London, and Hilda, *née* Chorley (d 1969); *b* 18 Nov 1946; *Educ* Salesian Coll Battersea; *m* 27 Feb 1971, Jill Antonia, da of Jack Mallett, of 24 Burnt Wood Grove, Wandsworth Common, London; 1 s (Henry b 1980), 2 da (Victoria b 1973, Charlotte b 1974); *Career* md RP Martin plc 1987 (dir 1977); chm For Exchange and Currency Deposit Brokers Assoc 1987; *Recreations* golf, cricket, gardening; *Clubs* MCC; *Style—* Paul Nash, Esq; RP Martin plc, 4 Deans Ct, London EC4V 5RA (☎ 071 600 8691, fax 071 236 3537)

NASH, Philip; *b* 23 Jan 1942; *Educ* Hipperholme GS Yorkshire, Univ of Sheffield; *m* ; 3 c; *Career* city inspr Legal & General Assurance Soc 1961-67, asst pensions mangr Fairey Company Hounslow 1967-68, dep pensions mangr CIBA-GEIGY 1968-70, divnl dir Leslie and Godwin Limited 1970-74, head of pension fund Bowater Corporation 1974-80, dir Wyatt Company (UK) Limited 1980-82, md Sedgwick 1982-87, jt md Fidelity Pensions Management Limited 1987-; author of articles in newspapers and trade jls, int lectr on pensions, investmt and related matters; former memb Cncl Pensions Mgmnt Inst; FPMI, FCII; *Recreations* current affairs, art, music, running, mountain walking, maritial arts, most sports; *Style—* Philip Nash, Esq; Brackenhill, 3 Birch Crescent, Aylesford, Kent ENT0 7QE (☎ 0622 718274); Fidelity Pensions Management Limited, 25-26 Lovat Lane, Londòn EC3R 8LL (☎ 071 283 9911)

NASH, Philip; s of John Hollett Nash (d 1975), of Bushey, Herts, and Edith Grace, *née* Knee (d 1987); *b* 14 March 1930; *Educ* Watford GS; *m* 27 June 1953, Barbara Elizabeth, da of George Bangs, of Bushey, Herts; 1 s (Simon John b 1959); *Career* Nat Serv RAF 1949-50; HM Customs and Excise 1950-90: on loan Civil Serv Coll 1970-75, asst sec and head mgmnt servs 1978-81, asst sec customs directorate 1981-86, cmmr and dir customs 1986-90; *Style—* Philip Nash, Esq; 149 Merryhill Rd, Bushey, Watford WD2 1DF (☎ 081 950 1048)

NASH, Raymond Cecil; MBE (1945); s of George Percy Nash (d 1950), of 4 Holmes Grove, Henleaze, Bristol, and Rosina Louise, *née* Wilkins (d 1916); *b* 13 Jan 1914; *Educ* St Brendans Coll Clifton Bristol; *m* 24 June 1939, Betty Denise, da of Gilbert Frank Bulphin (d 1953), of 50 Harcourt Rd, Redland, Bristol; 1 s (Michael b 1943), 1 da (Hazel b 1941); *Career* Princess Louise's Kensington Regt TA 1939, WWII, cmmnd Glos Regt 1940, 2 Bn the Glos Regt 1940 (ADI 1942) (served Normandy D Day Landings); IDC 1937; WH Grigg & Perkins CAs of Bristol (later Grigg Nash & Co Accountants of Minehead): joined 1948, sr ptnr 1963-, ret 1988; sec Minehead and Dist Chamber of Trade 1947-72, formerly chm Minehead Publicity Assoc, cdre Minehead Sailing Club; former memb Ctee: Taunton and Dist Youth Employment Ctee, SW Dist Soc of CAs; Worshipful Master Exmoor Lodge of Freemasons, dep prov then grand master prov Grand Lodge of Mark Master Masons of Somerset 1986-89; FCA 1937; *Recreations* sailing, golf, freemasons; *Style—* Raymond Nash, Esq, MBE; Carmel, 4 Warden Rd, Minehead, Somerset TA24 5DS (☎ 0643 702869)

NASH, Brig (Llewellyn James) Richard; s of Brig Llewellyn Charles Montgomery Nash, OBE, DL (d 1979), and Janet Catherine, *née* Adam (d 1988); *b* 1 Nov 1940; *Educ* Wellington, RMA Sandhurst, Staff Coll Camberley; *m* 8 May 1971, Rosamond Diana, da of Montague George de Courcy-Ireland (d 1987); 3 da (Emma b 1974, Louise b 1976, Juliet b 1981); *Career* cmmnd 12 Lancers 1960, 9/12 Lancers 1960, helicopter pilot, instr Aust Staff Coll 1980-81, Cmd 9/12 Royal Lancers (Prince of Wales) 1982-84, chief of personal staff to Dep Cdr in Chief AFHQ Central Europe 1985 Cdr 143 Inf Bde 1988-; *Recreations* hunting, fishing, skiing, tennis; *Clubs* Cavalry & Guards; *Style—* Brig Richard Nash; c/o Bank of Scotland, 141 Princes St, Edinburgh EH2 4BT (☎ 0743 262242, car 0860 748103)

NASH, Terence John (Terry); OBE (1979), AFC (1978); *b* 21 May 1937; *Educ* Latymer GS, Enfield Tech Coll; *m* 2 s; *Career* Mil Serv RAF 1957-83 (ret as Gp Capt Gen Duties Offr); mangr of advanced aerospace project 1978-80, chief exec Govt tech and operational complex 1980-82, asst dir MOD Procurement Exec 1982-83, chief exec Leeds Utd FC 1983-85, md Relcom Communications Ltd 1986, chief exec Bristol C of C 1987-89, dir gen Chartered Inst of Mktg 1990-; *award* Queen's Commendation for Valuable Services; DipM, MCIM, FBIM, MRAeS; *Recreations* property renovation, golf, squash, tennis, bridge; *Style—* Terry Nash, Esq, OBE, AFC; c/o Mrs Jackie Stead, The Chartered Institute of Marketing, Moor Hall Cookham, Maidenhead Berkshire SL6 9QH (☎ 0628 524922, fax 0628 531382, car 0860 282793)

NASH, Dr Timothy Paul (Tim); s of Flt Lt Laurence Nash (d 1970), and Margaret Ellen, *née* Davis (d 1985); *b* 13 Aug 1946; *Educ* Changi GS, Andover GS, Univ Coll Hosp Med Sch London Univ (MB BS); *m* 18 Oct 1969, Bridget Eleanor, da of William Albert Harrison, of Tonbridge; 1 s (Matthew b 2 Dec 1981), 3 da (Deborah b 23 Feb 1972, Rebecca b 24 April 1974, Juliette b 3 April 1980); *Career* conslt anaesthetics and pain relief Basingstoke and N Hants Health Authy 1976-, ed Frontiers of Pain 1988-, asst ed The Pain Clinic 1989-; memb Cncl The Pain Soc (fndr ed IPS Forum 1982-85, sec 1985-88); FFARCS 1974; *Books* contrib to: Pain (1985, 1986), Chronic Non-Cancer Pain (1987), The Pain Clinic (1987 and 1990), British Medical Journal (1988), British Journal of Hospital Medicine (1991), Medicine International (1991); *Recreations* music, reading, hiking; *Style—* Dr Tim Nash; Basingstoke Dist Hosp, Park Prewett, Basingstoke, Hants (☎ 0256 473202)

NASH, Ven Trevor Gifford; s of Frederick Walter Gifford Nash (d 1963), of Bedford, and Elsie Violet Louise Nash, JP, *née* Martin (d 1984); *b* 3 May 1930; *Educ* Haileybury, Clare Coll Cambridge (MA), Cuddesdon Coll Oxford; *m* 28 Oct 1957, Wanda Elizabeth, da of Sir Leslie Brian Freeston, KCMG, OBE (d 1958), of Kent; 4 da (Lois b 1958, Penelope b 1960, Phoebe b 1964, Joanna b 1968); *Career* Nat Serv Greece 1948-50; ordained 1955, chaplain TA 1956-61; curate: Cheshunt, Kingston upon Thames 1955-61; priest-in-charge Stevenage 1961-63, vicar of Leagrave Luton 1963-67, sr chaplain St George's Hosp London 1967-73, vicar St Lawrence and St Swithin Winchester 1973-82, Bishop's advsr for Miny of Healing 1973-, priest-in-charge Holy Trinity Winchester 1977-82, rural dean of Winchester 1977-82, archdeacon of Basingstoke 1982-90, memb Gen Synod 1983-90; exec co-ordinator Acorn Tst for Bishop's Advsrs for Miny of Health and Healing York and Canterbury, pres Guild of Health 1990-; dir of Luton Samaritans 1966-67; *Recreations* music, sport, reading, clay modelling; *Style—* The Ven the Archdeacon of Basingstoke; The Corner Stone, 50b Hyde Street, Winchester, Hants SO23 7DY (☎ 0962 861759)

NASH, Prof William Frederick; CBE (1987); s of William Henry Nash (d 1960), and Doris, *née* Jenkins; *b* 28 Jan 1925; *Educ* Amman Valley GS, Univ Coll of Wales Swansea (BSc, MSc), Univ of Manchester (PhD); *m* 18 Aug 1951, (Gladys) Christabel, da of Stephen Williams (d 1942); 1 s (Dylan Llywellyn b 16 April 1962), 1 da (Siân Christabel (Mrs Crosby) b 16 May 1959); *Career* res physicist Metropolitan Vickers Manchester 1945-48, head dept of physics Univ of Nottingham 1981-84 (asst lectr, lectr, sr lectr 1950-64, reader in physics 1964-74, prof of physics 1974-, pro vice chllr 1974-80), over 100 articles on cosmic rays and astro physics; chm Home Defence Scientific Advsy Ctee, chief regnl advsr number 3 regn Home Defence, chm E Midlands Univs Military Educn Ctee 1973-90, memb Astronomy and Space Res Bd SERC 1980-84; Jubilee medal 1977; CPhys, FInstP, FRAS, FRSA; *Recreations* rugby (played when young), operatic singing, walking, travel; *Style—* Prof William Nash, CBE; 6 Spean Drive, Aspley Hall, Nottingham NG8 3NQ (☎ 0602 296607); Department of Physics, The University, Nottingham NG7 2RD (☎ 0602 484848 ext 2809, fax 0602 229792, telex 37346 UNINOTG)

NASON, Col Ian Geoffrey; s of Lt Col C F Nason, OBE (d 1988), of Guernsey, and Eleanor Ethel May, *née* Carey; *b* 11 Nov 1936; *Educ* Wellington; *m* 31 Dec 1960, Anne Mary, da of Lt-Col J W McKergow (d 1961), of NZ; 2 s (Andrew John Fortescue b 18 Oct 1965, James Henry Fortescue b 18 Nov 1970), 2 da (Julia Anne b 24 Aug 1962, Sara Anne Catherine b 24 July 1964); *Career* cmmnd Seaforth Highlanders 1956, Staff Coll Canada 1967, Nat Def Coll 1977, cmd 1 Bn Queen's Own Highlanders 1977-79, instr Nigerian Staff Coll 1979-81, COS HQ Br Forces Falkland Islands 1983, Col Cdr RMA Sandhurst 1984-86, DA Br High Cmmn 1987-91; Chief Aku-Tubo of Bakana Rivers State Nigeria; *Books* Enjoy Nigeria (1991); *Recreations* bird photography, golf, travel; *Clubs* Ikoyi (Lagos); *Style—* Col Ian Nason; c/o Midland Bank plc, PO Box 31, Guernsey, Channel Islands

NASTA, Krishna (Kris); s of Kanayalal Nasta (d 1967), and Winifred Mary, *née* Milnthorpe; *b* 28 Aug 1943; *Educ* Eltham Coll, Univ of Salford (BSc); *m* 5 July 1969, Ann Beatrice, da of William Frederick Clifton; 1 s (Matthew b 27 Sep 1975), 1 da (Alison b 17 June 1972); *Career* GEC 1967-69, Reyrolle-Parsons 1969-70, ITT Business Systems 1970-71, home sales exec Plessey Office Systems 1976-79 (mktg exec 1971-75), gen mangr European Telecommunications Teradyne Ltd 1980-89, vice pres Teradyne Inc 1989; *Recreations* bridge, music, reading, raquet sports; *Style—* Kris Nasta, Esq; 7 Hilgay Close, Guildford, Surrey (☎ 0483 66569); Teradyne Ltd, The Western Centre, Bracknell, Berks (☎ 0344 426899, fax 0344 481355, telex 049713)

NATHAN, Clemens Neumann; s of Kurt Arthur Nathan (d 1958), of London, and Dr Else Nathan, *née* Kanin; *b* 24 Aug 1933; *Educ* Berkhampsted Sch, Scot Coll of Textiles, Univ of Leeds; *m* 4 June 1963, (Barbara) Rachel, da of Geoffrey H Whitehill (d 1971), of London; 1 s (Richard Abraham b 15 Oct 1965), 2 da (Jennifer Ruth b 13 May 1964, Elizabeth Rebecca b 18 Oct 1970); *Career* chm Cunart Co Ltd 1958-, conslt textile technologist on bd of various textile orgns, govt advsr; vice pres Anglo Jewish Assoc (pres 1983-89), jt chm CCJO (UN NGO); presidential advsr Alliance Israelite Universelle; former vice pres Textile Inst, memb Int Cncl; author of books on mktg and textiles; Textile Inst Medal (for servs to textile indust and Inst) 1987; Freeman City of London, memb Worshipful Co of Glovers; CTex, FTI, FRAI; Cavaliere Al Merito Della Republica Italiana, Israel Econ Cncl Medal; *Recreations* swimming, mountaineering, art, history, music; *Clubs* Athenaeum; *Style—* Clemens Nathan, Esq; 2 Ellerdale Close, London NW3; 231 Oxford St, London W1 (☎ 071 437 1355, fax 071 439 6721, telex 25362)

NATHAN, Derek Maurice; s of Joseph Albert (d 1973), and Grace Julia, *née* Abrahams; ggf fndr of Glaxo, gggf fndr of Shell; *b* 24 Sept 1929; *Educ* Oundle, Univ of London; *m* 15 Dec 1954, Mary Catherine, da of Louis Lavine (d 1940); 1 s (Timothy b 1957), 1 da (Sara b 1956); *Career* md: Dual Devpts Ltd Printbrokers 1967-89, Douglas A Lyons & Assocs Ltd Sound Reproduction Factors 1973-89; *Recreations* philately, golf; *Clubs* Royal Philatelic Soc London, British West Indies Study Circle, Wimbledon Park Golf, Ramblers Golfing Soc (convenor); *Style—* Derek M Nathan, Esq; 7 Cromford Way, New Malden, Surrey KT3 3BB (☎ 081 942 3881)

NATHAN, Michael Ronald; e s of Maj Cyril H Nathan (d 1977), of Prestwick, Chiddingfold, Surrey, and Violet, *née* Simon (d 1974); *b* 20 July 1927; *Educ* St Cyprian's Sch, Charterhouse; *m* 21 Oct 1984, Jennifer Madelin, da of Mr Eric Abrahams; *Career* articled clerk Whinney Smith & Whinney 1948-51, conslt Baker Tilley (and predecessor firms) 1990- (ptnr 1953-90); pres Stepney Jewish (B'nai B'rith) Clubs & Settlement 1978- (hon treas 1954-), memb Cncl Guild of Glass Engravers 1981- (chm 1982-85), hon treas Assoc for Jewish Youth 1954-, hon treas Jewish Welfare Bd 1959-69, memb Advsy Cncl Jewish Youth Fund 1955-, chm United Charities Fund Liberal Jewish Synagogue 1962-; Master Worshipful Co of Glass Sellers 1973-74 (tstee Charity Fund 1974-); FCA 1958 (ACA 1951); *Recreations* art, glass (especially modern glass engraving), music, reading, gardening, cricket, entertaining family and friends; *Clubs* The Samuel Pepys; *Style—* Michael Nathan, Esq; Baker Tilly, 2 Bloomsbury St, London WC1B 3ST (☎ 071 413 5100)

NATHAN, Peter Geoffrey; s of Maj Cyril H Nathan (d 1977), of Prestwick, Chiddingfold, Surrey, and Violet, *née* Simon (d 1974); *b* 27 July 1929; *Educ* Charterhouse, Oriel Coll Oxford (MA), Univ of Paris (Dip in Etudes de Civilisation Française); *m* 14 May 1970, Caroline Monica, da of Lt Cdr Anthony C Mullen, RINVR; 2 s (Hugo b 1975, Anthony b 1981), 2 da (Arabella b 1972, Venetia b 1973); *Career* writer RN 1948-49; admitted slr 1958; Herbert Oppenheimer Nathan & Vandyk 1954-88 (ptnr 1959-88), conslt Boodle Hatfield 1988-; chm London Playing Fields Soc 1984-, memb Ct City Univ, memb Cncl Anglo-Swiss Soc, memb Cncl of the Br Heart Fndn, tstee Oriel Coll Devpt Tst, chm Butterflies CC, hon memb Geographical Assoc, fndr memb Post Office Users Area Cncl for EC1 to EC4; chm Chiddingfold Branch of Farnham Cons Assoc 1965-70, memb Community Health Cncl for Kensington, Chelsea and Westminster representing Royal Borough of Kensington and Chelsea 1974-78;

Master Worshipful Co of Gold and Silver Wyre Drawers 1989; *Recreations* cricket, tennis, riding, reading, opera; *Clubs* MCC, Vincent's, Oriental, City Livery, City Univ; *Style*— Peter Nathan, Esq; 59 Rowan Rd, London W6 7DT; 43 Brook St, London W1Y 2BL (☎ 071 629 7411, fax 071 629 2621, telex 261414)

NATHAN, Philip Charles; s of Denis William Nathan, of S Woodham Ferrers, Essex, and Grace Pauline, *née* Brennan; *b* 11 May 1951; *Educ* Alexandra Park Sch; *Career* stockbroker; head of dealing Charles Stanley & Co Ltd; dist offr Lions International E Anglia (former pres: Rayleigh, S Woodham Ferrers Essex); memb: Int Stock Exchange, Securities Assoc; *Style*— Philip Nathan, Esq; Charles Stanley & Co Ltd, 25 Luke St, London EC2A 4AR (☎ 071 739 8200, fax 071 739 7798, telex 8952218, car 0836 251559)

NATHAN, 2 Baron (UK 1940); Capt Roger Carol Michael Nathan; s of 1 Baron, PC (d 1963); bro of Hon Lady Waley-Cohen; *b* 5 Dec 1922; *Educ* Stowe, New Coll Oxford; *m* 1950, Philippa, da of Maj Joseph Bernard Solomon, MC, of Sutton End, Pulborough, Sussex; 1 s, 2 da; *Heir* s, Hon Rupert Harry Bernard Nathan; *Career* served WWII, Capt 17/21 Lancers (despatches, wounded twice); slr; sr ptnr Herbert Oppenheimer Nathan & Vandyk until 1986, conslt Denton Hall Burgin and Warrens, assoc memb Bar Assoc of City of New York and New York County Lawyers Assoc; pres Jewish Welfare Bd 1967-71, hon pres Central Br Fund for Jewish Relief and Rehabilitation 1977 (chm 1971-77), vice pres RSA 1977 (chm 1975-77); vice chm Cancer Res Campaign 1987- (chm Exec Ctee 1970-75, treas 1979-87); memb: Royal Cmmn on Environmental Pollution 1979-89, House of Lords Select Ctee on Euro Communities 1983-88 and 1990-; chm: House of Lords Select Ctee on Murder and Life Imprisonment 1988-89, Animal Procedures Ctee 1990-, Environment Sub Ctee 1983-87 and 1990-; pres: UK Environmental Law Assoc 1987-, Nat Soc for Clean Air 1987-89; chm: Inst of Environment Assessment 1990-, Ct of Discipline of Univ of Cambridge; Master Worshipful Co of Gardeners 1963; Hon LLD Sussex; FSA, FRSA, FRGS; *Clubs* Athenaeum, Cavalry and Guards; *Style*— The Rt Hon the Lord Nathan, FSA; 5 Chancery Lane, London WC2 (☎ 071 242 1212); Collyers Farm, Lickfold, Petworth, W Sussex (☎ 079 85 284)

NATHAN, Hon Rupert Harry Bernard; s and h of 2 Baron Nathan; *b* 26 May 1957; *Educ* Univ of Durham (BA); *m* 17 Oct 1987, Ann, da of A S Hewitt, of Aldingbourne, Chichester, Sussex; *Career* exporter; *Recreations* motorcycles, travel, house renovation, boxing (to watch *not* participate!); *Style*— The Hon Rupert Nathan; St George's Home Farm Court, Shillinglee, Chiddingfold, Surrey

NATHANSON, Hon Mrs (Victoria Elizabeth Anne); *née* Thorneycroft; da of Baron Thorneycroft, CH, PC, by his 2 w, Carla, da of Conte Malagola-Cappi, of Ravenna, and formerly w of Conte Giorgio Roberti; *b* 25 June 1951; *Educ* St Mary's Convent Ascot; *m* 1975, Richard H Nathanson; 2 s (Daniel b 1978, Alexander b 1980), 1 da (Susannah b 1985); *Style*— The Hon Mrs Nathanson; 25 Enmore Rd, London SW15 (☎ 081 788 2718)

NAUGHTON, Philip Anthony; QC (1988); s of Francis Naughton, of Littlehampton, Sussex, and Madeleine, *née* Wales; *b* 18 May 1943; *Educ* Wimbledon Coll, Univ of Nottingham (LLB); *m* 6 July 1968, Barbara Jane, da of Prof F E Bruce, of Esher, Surrey; 2 s (Sebastian b 18 March 1974, Felix b 24 April 1978), 1 da (Charlotte b 8 Sept 1972); *Career* in indust 1964-71, called to the Bar Gray's Inn 1970; *Recreations* walking, fishing, sailing, theatre, music; *Style*— Philip Naughton, Esq, QC; 3 Serjeants' Inn, London EC4Y 1BQ (☎ 071 353 5537, fax 071 353 0425, telex 264093 SERJIN G)

NAWRAT, Christopher John (Chris); s of Stanislaw Jerzy Nawrat (d 1976), of London, and Margaret Jane Patricia, *née* Maguire; *b* 6 Feb 1949; *Educ* Salesian Coll London, Univ of Edinburgh, Univ of Essex (BA); *m* 26 July 1975, Christine Patricia, da of Daniel Patrick Boyle; *Career* sports journalist Morning Star 1979-81, ed National Student 1981-83; The Sunday Times: columnist (Inside Track) 1983-85, dep sports ed 1986-88, sports ed 1988-; Pools Forecaster of the Year 1979-80, Sports Reporter of the Year (special joint award with Nick Pitt) 1984-85, Sports Pages Design award Nat Sunday Newspapers 1987 and 1988; memb: NUJ, Sports Writers Assoc; *Recreations* reading, cinema, theatre, cooking, television, Spain; *Clubs* Reform; *Style*— Chris Nawrat, Esq; Sports Department, The Sunday Times, 1 Pennington St, London E1 9XW (☎ 071 782 5714/8/9, fax 071 782 5658)

NAYLER, Georgina Ruth; da of Dennis Victor Nayler, of Chitterne, Wiltshire, and Yvonne Dorothy, *née* Loader; *b* 16 March 1959; *Educ* Brentwood Co HS, Univ of Warwick (BA); *Career* Nat Heritage Memorial Fund: joined 1982, asst dir 1986, dep dir 1988, dir 1989-; memb Historic Buildings Cncl for Scotland 1990-; *Recreations* gardening, interior decoration, collecting china; *Style*— Miss Georgina Nayler; National Heritage Meml Fund, 10 St James's St, London SW1A 1EF (☎ 071 930 0963, fax 071 930 0968)

NAYLOR, Albert Edward (Eddy); s of Albert Victor Naylor (d 1989), and Mary, *née* Roberts (d 1987); *b* 12 Oct 1925; *Educ* Alsop HS Liverpool, Univ of Liverpool (BEng, MEEng, Dip Tp); *m* 10 Sept 1949, Mildred, da of Archibald Milton Gillies; 1 s (Mervyn Edward b 4 July 1956), 3 da (Susan Mildred (Mrs Wood) b 20 Dec 1951, Janet Averil (Mrs Relfe) b 10 Sept 1953, Fiona Mary (Mrs Ollier) b 6 May 1962); *Career* graduate under agreement to Sir James Drake Co Surveyor of Lancashire 1946, civil engr to City of Liverpool 1949, sr engr to Co Borough of Birkenhead 1952, asst borough engr to Co Borough of Bootle 1956, dep borough engr to Co Borough of Luton 1964, city engr to city of Leeds and engr to Leeds and Bradford Airport 1970, exec dir of transportation and traffic W Yorks Met Co and engr to Leeds and Bradford Airpot 1974, co engr to Gtr Manchester Met Co 1979-86, engr to Manchester Int Airport 1979-86; md: Waste Treatment Ltd 1979-86, md Man-Oil Ltd 1983-88; ret local govt 1986; consulting engr and transportation advsr 1986-; advsr to Dept of Tport, chm Assoc of Municipal Engrs, vice pres ICE, FIHT 1964, FICE 1976, FEng 1982, FRSA 1982; *Recreations* reading, family historical society; *Clubs* Rotary; *Style*— Eddy Naylor, Esq; 'Greenhill', Greenhill Common, Lower Whitley, Warrington, Cheshire WA4 4JD (☎ 0925 73396)

NAYLOR, (Richard) Christopher; s of Thomas Humphrey Naylor (d 1966), and Dorohty Isabel Durning, *née* Holt (d 1986); *b* 30 Jan 1936; *Educ* Eton; *m* 27 Jan 1966, Penelope Mary Albina, da of John Fowell Buxton (d 1970); 1 s (Thomas b 1967), 1 da (Harriet b 1970); *Career* 2 Lt Scots Guards 1955, TA Cheshire Yeomanry: Lt 1960, Capt & Adj 1965; P & O Containers Ltd: joined 1968, gen mangr 1978, dir subsidiary cos 1980-89; garden designer 1990-; *Recreations* shooting, racing, gardening; *Style*— Christopher Naylor, Esq; Birch Lane House, Flaunden, Hemel Hempstead HP3 0PT (☎ 0442 833335); 21 Hurlingham Square, London SW6 3DZ (☎ 071 371 5785); Rynettin, Nethy Bridge, Inverness-shire PH25 3EF

NAYLOR, David Malcolm Broadley; s of Frank Broadley Naylor (d 1968), of Guiseley, nr Leeds, and Joyce, *née* Clarke (d 1990); *b* 2 July 1944; *Educ* Rossall Sch Fleetwood Blackpool Lancs; *m* (m dis); 2 s (James b 7 June 1971, Robert b 28 April 1973); *Career* articled clerk Smithson Blackburn & Co Leeds 1961-66, qualified chartered accountant 1966; Grant Thornton (formerly Thornton Baker): joined 1966, ptnr 1976-, managing ptnr Leeds office 1981-90, memb Policy Bd 1987-90, managing ptnr NE Region 1990-; memb Cncl Leeds C of C 1978-90; FCA (ACA 1966); *Recreations* collection and restoration of vintage MG sports cars, model railways, DIY; *Clubs* Leeds, MG Car; *Style*— David Naylor, Esq; Catton House, 29 Breary Lane, Bramhope, Leeds LS16 9AD (☎ 0532 679802); Grant Thornton, St Johns Centre, 110 Albion St, Leeds LS2 8LA (☎ 0532 455514)

NAYLOR, Lt-Col Donald Russell; MBE (1945); s of John Alfred Naylor (d 1937), of Glenshee Lodge, Trinity Rd, Wandsworth Common, London SW18, and Ellen Louise, *née* Russell (k by enemy action 1940, at The Thatch, Petersham, Richmond); *b* 22 Feb 1916; *Educ* Emanuel Sch, ICL (BSc); *m* 19 Aug 1939, Olive Lucy, da of Charles William Johns (d 1965); 2 s (John b 1943, Philip b 1953), 1 da (Judith b 1940); *Career* Sapper RE 1939, cmmnd 2 Lt RAOC (Mech Eng) 1941, Capt OME RAOC 1 Army 1942, Capt EME 16 Base W/Shops REME N Africa 1943, Maj DADME AFHQ Italy 1944-45, Lt-Col ADME AFHQ 1946 (hospitalised with poliomielitis contracted in Italy), Lt-Col 1948; chm Rosser & Russell Ltd 1976-78 (dir 1948-78); chm and dir: H & V Welfare Ltd 1973-86, CCH Ltd & Welfare Hldgs Ltd 1973-86, TES Ltd 1978-81; pres Heating & Ventilating Contractors Assoc UK 1972-73, chm Coombe Roads Assoc Ltd 1980-86; Freeman City of London, Liveryman Worshipful Co of Fanmakers 1976; CEng, MIMechE, ACGI, FCIBSE, FInstD, FRSA; *Recreations* boat building, motor cruising, shooting, bric-a-brac; *Style*— Lt-Col Donald Naylor, MBE; 15 Kingsdown, 115A Ridgway, Wimbledon, London SW19 4RL (☎ 081 947 6385)

NAYLOR, Edward Michael; s of Frederick Naylor (d 1988), and Margaret Mary, *née* Corfield (d 1984); *b* 27 Aug 1936; *Educ* St Marys Coll Crosby, Univ of Liverpool (LLB); *m* 6 Aug 1964, Anne Veronica, da of Alan Yates; 2 s (Gregory Michael b 11 Jan 1967, Matthew John b 28 May 1973), 3 da (Sarah Jane b 29 May 1965, Lucy Marguerite b 17 April 1970, Emily Marcella b 29 Aug 1974); *Career* slr; Herbert Green & Co: articled 1956-60, asst slr 1961-63, ptnr 1963-68 (merged Rutherfords 1986); ptnr: Rutherfords 1986-88 (merger 1988), Weightman Rutherfords 1988-; govr of four schs, life govr Imperial Cancer Res Fund, memb Liverpool Law Soc 1961-; memb Law Soc 1961; *Recreations* squash, tennis, sailing; *Clubs* Racquet (Liverpool), Aughton Law Tennis; *Style*— Edward Naylor, Esq; Plumtree House, Prescot Rd, Aughton, Lancs L39 6TA (☎ 0695 422301); Weightman Rutherfords, Richmond House, 1 Rumford Place, Liverpool L3 9QW (☎ 051 227 2601, fax 051 227 3223)

NAYLOR, Prof Ernest; s of Joseph Naylor (d 1961), and Evelyn Keeton (d 1981); *b* 19 May 1931; *Educ* Swanwick Hall, Univ of Sheffield (BSc), Univ of Liverpool (PhD, DSc); *m* 7 Sept 1956, (Carol) Gillian, da of Harold Denovan Bruce (d 1970); 2 da (Elizabeth, Helen); *Career* cmmnd RAF Educn Branch 1954-56; reader in zoology Univ Coll Swansea 1968 (asst lectr 1956, lectr 1959, lectr 1963), prof of marine biology Univ of Liverpool 1971-82, dir Port Erin Marine Laboratory IOM 1971-82; Univ Coll of N Wales: Lloyd Roberts prof of zoology 1982-88, head of Sch of Animal Biology 1983-88, Lloyd Roberts prof of marine zoology Sch of Ocean Sci 1988-; cncl memb NERC 1976-82, specialist advsr to House of Lords Select Ctee on Marine Sci and Tec 1985, memb Coordinating Ctee on Marine Sci and Technol 1988; FIBiol 1972; *Books* British Marine Isopods (1972), Cyclical Phenomena in Marine Plants and Animals (jt ed with R G Hart 1979); *Recreations* gardening; *Style*— Prof Ernest Naylor; School of Ocean Sciences, University College of North Wales, Marine Science Laboratories, Menai Bridge, Anglesey, Gwynedd (☎ 0248 351151, fax 0248 716367)

NAYLOR, (Charles) John; s of Arthur Edgar Naylor, MBE, and Elizabeth Mary Naylor; *b* 17 Aug 1943; *Educ* Royal GS Newcastle upon Tyne, Haberdashers' Aske's, Clare Coll Cambridge (MA); *m* 1968, Margery; 2 s; *Career* jr and sr exec posts in indust 1965-75, dir YMCA Nat Centre Lakeside Cumbria 1975-80, dep nat sec Nat Cncl of YMCA's 1980-82, nat sec Nat Cncl of YMCA's 1982-, vice-chm Nat Cncl for Vol Youth Servs 1985-88, memb Nat Advsy Cncl for the Youth Serv 1985-88; *Recreations* running, the outdoors particularly mountains, theatre, church, golf, growing family; *Style*— C John Naylor, Esq; National Council of YMCA's, 640 Forest Rd, London E17 3DZ (☎ 081 520 5599)

NAYLOR, Prof Malcolm Neville; RD (1967); s of Roland B Naylor, MBE (d 1969), of Walsall, Staffs, and Mabel Louisa, *née* Neville (d 1976); *b* 30 Jan 1926; *Educ* Queen Mary's Sch Walsall, Univ of Glasgow, Univ of Birmingham (BSc, BDS), Univ of London (PhD); *m* 10 Jan 1956, (Doreen) Mary, da of Horace E Jackson, CBE (d 1966), of Gerrard Cross, Bucks; 1 s (Andrew b 1960); *Career* RNVR and RNR 1943-77: Seaman Offr 1943-47, served HMS Suffolk, dental offr 1954-77, ret as Surgn Capt (D) and sr dental surgn RNR; civil conslt dental surgn RN 1969-, jr hosp appts Birmingham and Dundee 1954-59; Guys Hosp and Univ of London: res fell dental sch 1959-62, sr lectr in preventive dentistry dental sch 1962-66, reader 1966-70, hon conslt 1966-, prof of preventive dentistry 1970-, head of Dept of Periodontology and Preventive Dentistry 1980-; Univ of London: chm Sea Cadet Sport Cncl 1975-, chm Cncl Mil Educn Ctees of Univs of UK 1982-89, chm Bd of Studies in Dentistry 1990- (dep chm 1986-89); memb Sea Cadet Assoc Cncl 1976, vice chm Bacons Sch 1978-90, chm of govrs St Saviours and St Olaves Sch 1987-; govr: Whitelands Coll Roehampton Inst for Higher Educn; lay reader C of E 1974-; Queen's hon dental surgn 1976; Hon Col Univ of London OTC 1979-; Hon Liveryman Worshipful Co of Bakers 1981, Freeman City of London 1981; BDA 1955, IADR Br Div 1959 (treas Br Div 1974-90, pres 1990-), RSM 1959 (pres Odontology Section 1984-85); *Recreations* sailing (cruising off-shore), home and family; *Clubs* Royal Yacht Assoc, RN Sailing Assoc; *Style*— Prof Malcolm N Naylor, RD; Carrick Lodge, Roehampton, London SW15 5BN (☎ 081 788 5045); Guy's Hospital, London SE1 SRT (☎ 071 955 5000 ext 4032, fax 071 407 6736)

NAYLOR, Martin James; s of James Naylor (d 1989), of Morley Yorks, and Lilian Farrar (d 1990); *b* 11 Oct 1944; *Educ* Dewsbury and Batley Tech and Art Sch, Leeds Art Coll, RCA; *Career* sculptor and artist; solo exhibitions incl: Lane Gallery Bradford 1966, Serpentine Gallery London 1972, Arnolfini Gallery Bristol 1973, Rowan Gallery London 1974, 1975, 1977 and 1980, Sculpture and Drawings 1973-76 (Sunderland Arts Centre and MOMA Oxford) 1976, XIV Saô Paulo Biennal 1977, A View Beyond the City (Rowan Gallery London) 1978, Installation Corroboree Gallery (Univ of Iowa) 1979, Works on Paper - Paris 1982 (Juda Rowan Gallery) 1983, Newcastle Poly Art Gallery 1983, Between Discipline and Desire (Galerie Artem Quimper France) 1985, Galeria Principal (Altos de Chavon La Romana Dominican Repub) 1985, La Galeria Santo Domingo 1986, Serpentine Gallery London 1986, Walker Art Gallery Liverpool 1987, Galerie Leger Malmö Sweden 1988, Between Discipline and Desire (Centro Cuiindad de Buenos Aires Argentina, Museu Nacional de Artes Plasticas Uruguay, Museu de Arte Moderna Rio de Janeiro Brazil) 1990; gp exhibitions incl: Young Contemporaries (FBA Galleries London) 1969, Three Sculptors from the RCA (Eton) 1970, Drawings (MOMA Oxford) 1972, Art into Landscape (Serpentine Gallery) 1974, Contemporary British Drawings (XIII Bienal de San Paolo) 1975, Gallery Artists (Rowan Gallery) 1976, Royal Acad Summer Exhibition 1977, 1978 and 1985, Artists Market (Covent Garden) 1978, Sculptors Drawings (Minories Gallery Colchester) 1979, Growing Up with Art (Leicestershire collection Whitechapel Gallery) 1980, Hayward Annual 1982: British Drawing (Hayward Gallery London and Fruitmarket Gallery Edinburgh) 1982, John Moores Liverpool Exhibition 15 (Walker Art Gallery Liverpool) 1987, Athena award (Barbican Centre London) 1987, Homage to the Square (Flaxman Gallery London) 1988, Group Show - Selected Works by Gallery Artists and Summer Exhibition (Mayor Rowan Gallery London) 1990; work in numerous pub collections; various teaching appts; art advsr Psychology Dept Univ of Leeds 1966-67; lectr: Lancaster Poly 1970-71, RCA 1972-78, Hornsey Coll of Art 1972-73, Wimbledon

Art Sch 1972-73; visiting prof: Ecole Nationale des Arts Decoratifs Nice 1972-73, Ecole Nationale des Beaux Arts Bourges 1976; tutor RCA 1974-75 and 1977-84, assoc visiting lectr Chelsea Sch of Art 1974-75, head Sculpture Dept Hornsey Coll of Art 1977-84 (resigned pt/t lectr 1974-75), artist in residence Cife Internationale des Arts Paris 1982, artist in residence Altos de Chavon La Romana Dominican Repub 1985; *awards* Peter Stuyvesant Fndn prize 1969, Arts Cncl award 1971, Gregory fell in sculpture Univ of Leeds 1973, jt first prize Art into Landscape Serpentine Gallery 1974, Gulbenkian Fndn Visual Arts award 1975, prizewinner John Moores Liverpool Exhibition II 1978, Arts Cncl of GB award 1979, Lorne bequest Univ of London 1984, purchase grant Elephant Tst 1984, Henry Moore Fndn award 1985; artist in residence sr visiting fell Br Sch at Rome 1987; FRSA 1989; *Recreations* horseriding; *Clubs* Chelsea Art; *Style—* Martin Naylor, Esq; Studio, 1 Cahill St, London EC1Y 8PH

NAYLOR, Maj-Gen (David) Murray; MBE (1972); s of Thomas Humphrey Naylor (d 1966), of The Grange, Ashton, Chester, and Dorothy Isobel Durning, *née* Holt (d 1986); *b* 5 March 1938; *Educ* Eton; *m* 31 July 1965, Rosemary Gillian, da of Major WW Hicks Beach, TD, DL (d 1974), of Witcombe Park, Gloucester; 3 s (Nicholas John b 13 March 1967, Duncan Hugh b 17 Oct 1968, Christopher William b 29 May 1972); *Career* Nat Serv enlisted 1956, cmmnd 1957, 2 Bn Scots Gds UK Strategic Res 1957-61, Northern Frontier Regt of Sultan of Oman's Armed Forces 1961-62, Adj 2 Bn Scots Gds Kenya 1963-65, GSO 3 Ops at HQ 4 Gds Bde Iserlohn 1965-67, 1 Bn Scots Gds UK 1967-68, Def Servs Staff Coll Wellington S India 1970, GSO 2 Ops SD Training at HQ 3 Div Bulford 1971-72, 2 Bn Scots Gds UK and NI 1973-74, Bde Maj 11 Armoured Bde Minden 1975, 2 Bn Scots Gds Munster and Londonderry 1976-79, GSO 1 Dir Staff at Staff Coll Camberley 1979-80, asst dir Def Policy Staff MOD 1980-81, Cdr 22 Armoured Bde Hohne W Germany 1982-84, RCDS course 1984, dep mil sec MOD 1985-87, Cdr NE Dist 1987-89 (also Cdr 2 Infantry Div), dir TA and Orgn in army dept MOD 1989-; *Recreations* tennis, shooting, stalking, walking, travel; *Clubs* Cavalry and Guards; *Style—* Maj-Gen Murray Naylor, MBE; c/o MOD (Main Building), Whitehall, London SW1A 2HS

NAYLOR, (Thomas) Peter; DL (Cumbria 1981); s of Thomas Humphrey Naylor (d 1966), of Ashton, Chester, and Quenelda Anne, *née* Williamson (d 1942); *b* 5 Dec 1923; *Educ* Eton; *m* 22 June 1946, Patricia Elisabeth, da of Maurice Illingworth (d 1965), of Far Sawrey; 1 s (Adam b 1954); *Career* Pilot, RAFVR 1942-46, served Coastal Cmd 1944-45; chm Demerara Co (Holdings) Ltd Liverpool 1968-69 (dir 1954-59, md 1960-69), non-exec dir Provident Group plc 1970- (formerly Provident Insurance Co Ltd); memb: N Lonsdale Rural DC 1970-74, Cumbria CC 1974-85 (chm 1976-80); chm: Cncl Inc Liverpool Sch Tropical Med 1969-73, tstees Lake Dist Art Gallery and Museum Tst 1983-; jt hon rep Nat Art-Collections Fund Cumbria 1984-88; High Sheriff Cumbria 1990-91; ACA 1950, FCA 1955; *Recreations* field sports; *Clubs* Boodle's, RAF; *Style—* Peter Naylor, Esq, DL; The Clock House, Far Sawrey, Ambleside, Cumbria LA22 0LJ (☎ 09662 3528)

NAYLOR, Robert Antony; s of Francis Thomas Naylor, of Reading, and Kathleen Mary, *née* Donellan; *b* 13 Nov 1949; *Educ* Salesian Coll Oxford, Presentation Coll Reading, Univ of London (BSc); *m* 9 Nov 1974, Jane Karen, da of Charles Evans; 1 s (James Richard), 1 da (Victoria Jane); *Career* graduate mgmnt trainee NW Thames RHA 1972-74, hosp sec Nat Hosp for Nervous Diseases London 1974-77, sector admin Kent AHA 1977-79 (dist admin 1979-84), gen mangr East Birmingham Hosp 1986-90; ASHM; *Recreations* golf, squash; *Style—* Robert Naylor, Esq; Langland, Broad Lane, Tanworth-in-Arden, Warwickshire B94 5HP; East Birmingham Hospital, 45 Bordesley Green East, Birmingham B9 5ST (☎ 021 766 6611)

NAYLOR-LEYLAND, Lady Isabella; da of Antony Lambton (formerly 6 Earl of Durham); *b* 17 May 1958; *m* 1980, Sir Philip Vyvian Naylor-Leyland, 4 Bt, *qv*; 2 s, 1 da; *Style—* The Lady Isabella Naylor-Leyland

NAYLOR-LEYLAND, Jameina, Lady; Jameina Flora; *née* Reid; da of James Freeman Reid; *m* 1980, as his 3 w, Sir Vivyan Edward Naylor-Leyland, 3 Bt, who d 1987; 2 da (Virginia b 16 April 1983, Jessica Pamela b 27 March 1987); *Style—* Jameina, Lady Naylor-Leyland; Le Neuf Chemin, St Saviour's, Guernsey, Channel Islands; Domaine de Montmoreau, 24300 La Chapelle Montmoreau, France

NAYLOR-LEYLAND, Sir Philip Vyvian; 4 Bt (UK 1895), of Hyde Park House, Albert Gate, London; s of the late Sir Vivyan Edward Naylor-Leyland, 3 Bt (d 1987), and Elisabeth-Anne Marie Gabrielle, da of late Viscount Fitzalan of Derwent; *b* 9 Aug 1953; *Educ* Eton, Sandhurst, Univ of New York, RAC Cirencester; *m* 1980, Lady Isabella, 5 and yst da of Antony C F Lambton, *qv* (6 Earl of Durham, who disclaimed his peerage 1970); 2 s (Thomas Philip b 1982, a son b 1989), 1 da (Violet Mary b 1983); *Heir* Thomas Philip; *Career* Lt, LG (ret); *Recreations* hunting, coursing, shooting; *Clubs* Whites; *Style—* Sir Philip Naylor-Leyland, Bt; Nantclwyd Hall, Ruthin, N Wales; The Ferry House, Milton Park, Peterborough, Cambs

NAYLOR-SMITH, Ruth Elizabeth; da of Wilfred Naylor of Retford, Notts, and Phyllis Mary, *née* Hague; *b* 15 June 1951; *Educ* Chislehurst and Sidcup Girls GS, Poly of Central London (Dip for Sec Linguists), Univ of Barcelona (Dip Ed); *Career* teacher La Casa Inglesa Madrid 1972-74, organised and ran holiday courses for foreign students Regent School of English London 1974-77, Linguaphone Institute Ltd 1977-81 (sales exec, sales mangr), md Mardev Ltd (now pt of Reed Business Publishing) 1986-, memb Sr Mgmnt Gp Reed Business Publishing; vice chm Br List Brokers Assoc 1987-89, memb Advertising Assoc Data Protection Ctee 1987-89, chm Br Direct Marketing Assoc 1989-; memb: Bd Direct Mail Servs Standards Bd 1990, Int Advsy Bd American Direct Marketing Assoc 1990-; *Publications* BDMA Direct Marketing Handbook (contrib, 1991); *Recreations* golf, reading, swimming, embroidery; *Style—* Ms Ruth Naylor-Smith; Mardev Ltd, 88-98 College Rd, Harrow, Middlesex HA1 1AX (☎ 081 427 8880, fax 081 427 9009)

NAZIR-ALI, Rt Rev Dr Michael; *b* 19 Aug 1949; *Educ* Univ of Karachi (BA), Fitzwilliam Coll and Ridley Hall Cambridge, St Edmund Hall Oxford (Blitt, Oxford Soc Graduate Award), Univ of Cambridge (Burney and Langham student, MLitt), Univ of NSW and Centre for World Religions Harvard (PhD); *m* 1972, Valerie Cree; 2 s (Shamaoun b 1975, Ross b 1979); *Career* asst: Christ Church Cambridge 1970-72, St Ebbe's Church Oxford 1972-74, Holy Sepulchre Cambridge 1974-76; tutorial supervisor in theology Divinity Faculty Univ of Cambridge 1974-76; recalled to Karachi by Church of Pakistan: tutor then sr tutor Karachi Theol Coll 1976-81, assoc presbyter Holy Trinity Cathedral Karachi 1976-79, priest-in-charge St Andrew's Akhtar Colony 1979-81, provost Lahore Cathedral 1981-84, bishop of Raiwind 1984-86; asst to Archbishop of Canterbury and co-ordinator of studies 1986-89 (also ed Lambeth Conference), based St Margaret's Church Oxford 1986-90, dir Oxford Centre for Mission Studies 1986-, currently asst bishop Diocese of Southwark, gen sec Church Missionary Society 1989-; Charles Sadleir Lectr Wycliffe and Trinity Colls Toronto 1987, lectr on church and state rels Univ of Cambridge 1988, Church of Ireland lectr Queen's Univ Belfast 1989, Henry Martyn lectr Univ of Cambridge 1990, visiting lectr Selly Oak Colls Birmingham; former memb Standing Ctee CMS; memb: Inter-Faith Consultative Ctee BMU, Conf for World Mission, Partnership for World Mission, Oxford Diocesan Advsy Gp on mission; dir Christian Aid, tstee Traidcraft, sec to Archbishop of Canterbury's Cmmn on Communion and Women in the Episcopate 1988-; *Books* Islam - A Christian Perspective (1982), Frontiers in Christian-Muslim Encounter (1987), From Everywhere to Everywhere (1990), Martyrs and Magistrates: Toleration and Trial in Islam (1989), The Roots of Islamic Tolerance: Origin and Development (1990); author of numerous articles; ed various papers and reports; *Recreations* cricket, hockey, table tennis, reading fiction, listening to music, watching tv; *Style—* Rt Rev Dr Michael Nazir-Ali; Church Missionary Society, 157 Waterloo Road, London SE1 8UU (☎ 071 928 8681)

NEAGLE, Hon Mrs (Lena Margaret); *née* Hall; eldest da of 2 Viscount Hall (d 1984); *b* 31 Oct 1950; *Educ* Godstowe Sch, Wycombe Abbey, Univ of St Andrew's; *m* 1985, Frederick Neagle, eldest s of late William Neagle; *Style—* The Hon Mrs Neagle; Belgrave Cottage, Upper Belgrave St, London SW1

NEAGU, Paul; s of Tudor Neagu, and Rozalia, *née* Florian (d 1988); *b* 1938, Bucharest; *Educ* Lyceum Simion Barnutiu Timisoara, Inst of Beaux Arts N Grigorescu Bucharest Romania; *Career* moved to UK 1969; fine art lectr: Hornsey Sch Art 1972-79, Royal College of Art 1976-78, Chelsea Sch of Art 1976-80, Slade Sch of Art 1985-90; external assessor CNNA, artist sculptor and painter; Palpable and Tactile Object (early combinations of materials) 1968-72, Human Figure (drawing for rites) 1972-74, Anthropocosmos (organicity and cosmos) 1969-81, Performance (four rituals) 1970-77, Generative Art Gp (amalgamated works by five fictional artists), 1974-76, Hyphen (first analogical abstract sculpture) 1975-89, Modern Energy Painting (oils on plywood, canvas) 1977-91, Architecture (visionary sketches (visionary sketches) 1977-90, Drawings on Photographs (projected context) 1975-79, Nine Catalytic Stations (polyphonic gp) 1975-87, Public Monuments (real site) 1969-90, Visual Hermeneutics (collges, charts, drawings) 1981-88, Unnamed (infinity, zero-form, environmental installations), 1983-88, Poems (working poems) 1969-89; *Recreations* swimming, cycling, reading; *Style—* Paul Neagu, Esq; c/o Generative Arts, 31c Jackson Road, London N7 6ES (☎ 071 607 7858)

NEAL, Prof Alan Christopher; s of Harold Joseph Neal, of Bath, and Gladys May, *neæe* Lovelock; *b* 9 Jan 1950; *Educ* City of Bath Boys' Sch, Univ of Warwick (LLB), LSE (LLM), Univ of Stockholm Sweden (DGLS); *m* 30 July 1981, Alessandra, da of Dr Alessandro Tadini (d 1974), of Lucca Italy; 1 s (James Alexander b 1984), 1 da (Francesca Jane b 1986); *Career* called to the Bar 1975; ed in chief The International Journal of Comparative Labour Law and Industrial Relations 1984-, prof of law Univ of Leicester 1988- (lectr 1976-86, sr lectr 1986-88); *Books* A Perspective on Labour Law (1982), Law and the Weaker Party (ed, 5 vols 1981-90), Colletive Agreements and Collective Bargaining (1984); *Recreations* hockey (formerly Somerset and Warwickshire), skiing, squash, music; *Style—* Prof Alan Neal; High Trees House, Hall Wood, Hallaton, Leicestershire LE16 8UH (☎ 085 889 465); Faculty of Law, The University, Leicester LE1 7RH (☎ 0533 522362/3/8, telex 347250 LEICUN G, fax 0533 522200, car 0860 567749)

NEAL, Sir Eric James; s of James Charles Neal (d 1971), and May Neal (d 1981); *b* 3 June 1924; *Educ* Adelaide Sch of Mines; *m* 1950, Thelma Joan, da of Richard Edwin Bowden; 2 s; *Career* dir: Boral Ltd 1972- (chief exec 1973-, md 1982), Wormald Int Ltd 1978-, The Aust Inst of Petroleum Oil Co of Aust 1982; memb Def Review Ctee 1981-82; kt 1982; *Style—* Sir Eric Neal; 93 Pentecost Ave, St Ives, NSW 2075, Australia

NEAL, Frederick Albert; CMG (1990); s of Frederick William George Neal (d 1971), and Fanny Elizabeth Neal (d 1979); *b* 22 Dec 1932; *Educ* Univ of Cambridge, Univ of London (BA); *m* 1958, Gloria Maria, da of Alfred Moirano, of London; *Career* Govt Serv, econ cnsllr Br High Cmmn Ottawa 1975-80, Dept of Trade 1980-83, UK permanent rep to Int Civil Aviation Orgn 1983-; *Recreations* golf; *Clubs* Naval & Military, Royal Overseas League, South Herts Golf, Royal Montreal Golf; *Style—* Frederick Neal, Esq, CMG; Suite 928, 1000 Sherbrooke St West, Montreal, Canada H3A 3G4

NEAL, Harry Morton; s of Godfrey French Neal (d 1985), and Janet Bryce Morton (d 1960); *b* 21 Nov 1931; *Educ* Uppingham, Univ of London (BSc), City and Guilds Coll (FCGI); *m* 1954, Cecilia Elizabeth, da of Col Mervyn Crawford, DSO (d 1977); 1 s (Michael b 1956), 3 da (Camilla b 1960, Janet b 1961, Alexandra b 1967); *Career* Flying Offr RAF 1953; md Harry Neal Ltd (bldg and civil engrg contractors) 1963-86 (chm 1985); chm: City and Guilds of London Inst 1979-, Connaught Hotel Ltd 1980-; dir Savoy Hotel 1982-; memb: Lloyd's, Technician Educn Cncl 1982-83, Business and Technician Educn Cncl 1983-, Ct of City Univ 1982-, Mgmnt Ctee Courtauld Inst of Art 1983-; memb Bd of Govrs: Willesden Tech Coll 1983-86, Imperial Coll Univ of London 1988-, Francis Holland Sch 1988-; pres Gtr London NW Co Scout Cncl 1983-; Liveryman Worshipful Co of Carpenters; Chev de Tastevin 1981; FIC, FCIOB, FRSA; *Recreations* gardening, shooting; *Style—* Harry Neal, Esq; Great Sarratt Hall, Sarratt, nr Rickmansworth, Herts WD3 4PD

NEAL, Capt John Harry; s of Harry Neal (d 1983), and Gladys Eva, *née* Gasser (d 1987); *b* 22 Oct 1928; *Educ* Latymer Upper Sch, King Edward VII Nautical Sch, Sir John Cass Coll; *m* 6 June 1954, (Ruby Lily) Jane, da of Richard Henry Craswell (d 1971); 1 s (Andrew b 29 April 1959), 2 da (Sarah b 23 June 1962, Rebecca b 30 July 1964); *Career* Navigating Offr: Anglo Saxon Petroleum Co (formerly Cadet) 1946-52, Royal Fleet Aux Serv 1952-57, Cable and Wireless plc (later Capt and mangr marine and survey) 1957, Assoc Submarine Cable Conslts Ltd 1984-; steward and guide Romsey Abbey; memb: Ctee Romsey Horse and Cattle Show, Ctee Southampton Master Mariners Club; memb: RIN 1952, RINA 1956; Liveryman Worshipful Co of Master Mariners 1974 (memb 1968), Freeman City of London 1974; *Recreations* fishing and gardening; *Clubs* Southampton Master Mariners; *Style—* Capt John Neal; 32 The Harrage, Romsey, Hants

NEAL, Sir Leonard Francis; CBE (1971); s of Arthur Henry Neal (d 1939), and Emma Mary Neal (d 1947); *b* 27 Aug 1913; *Educ* LSE, Trinity Coll Cambridge (MA); *m* 1939, Mary Lillian Puttock; 1 s (Geoffrey), 1 da (Susan); *Career* industl rels consIt; memb Br Railways Bd 1967-71; chm: Cmmn on Industl Rels 1971-74, MAT Tport Int Gp 1974-83; non exec dir Pilkington Bros 1976-83; chm: Employment Conditions Abroad Ltd 1976-84, Trade Union Reform Ctee, Centre for Policy Studies 1978-86; sometimes visiting prof of industl rels Univ of Manchester, broadcaster and lectr; kt 1974; *Books* Managers Guide to Industrial Relations; *Recreations* gardening, reading; *Style—* Sir Leonard Neal, CBE; Towcester, Northants

NEAL, Michael Harry Walker; s of Harry Morton Neal, of Herts, and Cecilia Elizabeth, *née* Crawford; *b* 9 July 1956; *Educ* Eton, Univ of St Andrews (MA), Bartlett Sch of Architecture (UCL, MSc); *m* 4 July 1987, Sophia Mary, da of Sir Geoffrey Christopher John Palmer, Bt; 1 s (Harry Neal b 1988); *Career* md Harry Neal (City) Ltd 1987, memb Lloyds 1984; govr Willesden Tech Coll 1990; Freeman City of London 1977; Liveryman: Worshipful Co of Carpenters 1977, Worshipful Co of Loriners 1989; *Recreations* fishing; *Clubs* The Royal Perth Golfing Soc; *Style—* Michael Neal, Esq; c/o Harry Neal City Ltd, 117 Baker Street, London W1M 2EE

NEAL, Richard Clive; s of Philip Neal, of Hong Kong, and Dorothy Alice, *née* Watson (d 1967); *b* 19 March 1939; *Educ* Wellesbourne House Sch; *m* 9 May 1964, Barbara Maureen, da of David Price (d 1983), of Dudley; *Career* md: Supra Chemicals and Paints Ltd 1965 (chm 1972), Supra Group plc 1972 (chm 1983); dir Evode Group plc 1987, chm Rimstock Ltd 1984; *Recreations* golf; *Clubs* Stourbridge Golf, Ferrari Owners; *Style—* Richard Neal, Esq; Green Ridges, Ounty John Lane, Pedmore,

Stourbridge, W Midlands DY8 2RG; Rimstock Ltd, Church Lane, West Bromwich, W Midlands (☎ 021 525 2525, fax 021 553 1083, telex 339488)

NEALE, Sir Alan Derrett; KCB (1972, CB 1968), MBE (1945); s of W A Neale (d 1941); *b* 24 Oct 1918; *Educ* Highgate, St John's Coll Oxford; *m* 1956, Joan Frost; 1 s; *Career* WWII served with Intelligence Corps; Bd of Trade: entered 1946, asst sec 1958, under-sec 1963, second sec 1967-68; third sec HM Treasy 1968-71, second perm sec 1971, perm sec MAFF 1973-78; memb Monopolies and Mergers Cmmn 1981-86 (dep chm 1982-86), dep chm Assoc of Futures Brokers and Dealers 1987-91; *Clubs* Reform; *Style—* Sir Alan Neale, KCB, MBE; 95 Swains Lane, Highgate Village, London N6 6PJ (☎ 081 340 5236)

NEALE, Frank Leslie George; s of Hugh Neale, and Mona, *née* Clarkson; *b* 25 Aug 1950; *Educ* King Henry VIII Sch Coventry, St John's Coll Cambridge (MA), Manchester Business Sch (MBA); *m* 16 June 1976, Helen, da of Ronald Carter; 3 s (Michael James b 29 May 1979, Jeremy John Simon b 20 Jan 1985, Rory William b 1 Jan 1989); *Career* econ intelligence unit 1973-77, PA Mgmnt Conslts 1977-83, Citicorp Venture Capital 1983-88, ptnr Phildrew Ventures; cncl memb Br Venture Capital Assoc; MIMC; *Recreations* ballet, swimming, reading, memb Watford FC Supporters Club; *Style—* Frank Neale, Esq; Triton Court, 14 Finsbury Square, London EC2 1PD (☎ 071 628 6366, fax 071 638 6217)

NEALE, Sir Gerrard Anthony; MP (C) North Cornwall 1979-; s of Charles Woodhouse Neale (d 1985), of Painswick, Glos, and Phyllis Muriel, *née* Harrison; *b* 25 June 1941; *Educ* Bedford Sch; *m* 29 Dec 1965, Deirdre Elizabeth, da of late Charles Howard McCann (Lt Cdr RN), of Cornwall; 1 s (Alexander Charles b 7 June 1973), 2 da (Belinda Clare b 23 July 1967, Tania Katharine b 7 Jan 1970); *Career* admitted slr 1966; ptnr Heald Nickinson Solicitors; Parly candidate (C) N Cornwall 1974; kt 1990; *Recreations* sailing; *Style—* Sir Gerrard Neale, MP; House of Commons, Westminster, London SW1A 0AA (☎ 071 219 3610)

NEALE, Prof Guy Richard Irvine; s of Lt Cdr Arundel Richard York Neale, DSC (d 1977), and Barbara Marie, *née* Liardet (d 1979); *b* 27 Dec 1941; *Educ* Kings Sch Worcester, Univ of London (BA, PhD); *m* 6 Dec 1986, Martine Gabriele Theres, da of Clacide Herlant, of Wolnwe St Pierre, Belgium; 2 s (Joel b 3 Aug 1988, Magali (twin)); *Career* lectr history Wales 1967-69, res fell Univ of Edinburgh 1969-75, prof history Amsterdam Netherlands 1978-80, directeur de recherche Paris 1981-85 (maitre de recherche 1975-78), prof histroy London 1986-; memb Soc Res in Higher Educn; FRSA 1987; *Books* How They Fared (1975), An Improper Sixth Year (jtly, 1976), Modéles D'Egaline (1976), The EEC And Education (1985), La Communidad European Y La Education (1987); *Recreations* jogging, bricolage; *Clubs* Anglo-Belgian; *Style—* Prof Guy Neale; 27 Ridley Rd, London SW19 1ET; 26 Ave De La Guillemotte, F78112 Foureueux, France; Int Assoc of Univs, 1 rue Miollis, F75732 Paris Cedex 15, France (☎ 33 145 68 2545, fax 33 147 34 70 05)

NEALE, Prof John William; s of John William Neale (d 1975), of Bewdley, Worcs, and Elsie Mabel, *née* Preston (d 1982); *b* 19 Nov 1926; *Educ* King Charles I Sch Kidderminster, Univ of Manchester (BSc, DSc), Univ of Hull (PhD); *m* 30 July 1952, Patti Myrena, da of Frank Cyril Hullah (d 1973), of Derby; 2 s (John Anthony George b 1957, William Lawrence b 1966), 1 da (Elizabeth Myrena b 1955); *Career* RNVR, demobbed 1947; visiting prof: Univ of Kansas USA 1964-65, Univ of Rio Grande Do Sol Brazil 1971, Univ of Waterloo Canada 1975; prof of micropalaeontology Univ of Hull 1979- (asst lectr 1949, lectr, sr lectr, reader), visiting prof Univ of Shizuoka Japan 1985; author of over 100 scientific pubns, world authority on ostracod crustacea, ed Stero-Atlas of Ostracod Shells 1975-88; field work worldwide incl: Aust, China, Russian Caucasus, Tibet; has 4 species and 12 genera named after him, awarded John Philips medal for contrib to palaeontology and stratigraphy in the N of E 1986; pres: Br Micropalaeontological Soc 1978-80, Yorks Geological Soc 1980-82; currently memb Int Geological Cmmn Working Gp on Jurassic Cretaceous boundary and non marine Cretaceous correlation; fndr memb Br Micropalaeontological Soc, memb Yorkshire Geological Soc 1949, hon life memb Hull Geological Soc; *Books* Grundzüge der Zoologichen Micropaläeontologië (ed and part trans 2 vols 1963 and 1965), The Taxonomy, Morphology and Ecology of Recent Ostracoda (1969), The Ostracod Fauna from the Santonian Chalk of Gingin W Aust (1975); *Recreations* gardening, music, singing in local operatic societies, travel; *Style—* Prof John Neale; Etherington House, 640 Beverley High Rd, Hull HU6 7JH (☎ 0482 445873); Dept of Geology, University of Hull, Cottingham Rd, Hull HU6 7RX (☎ 0482 465425)

NEALE, Michael Cooper; CB (1987); s of Frank Neale (d 1966), of Findon, Sussex and Nottingham, and Edith Kathleen, *née* Penney; *b* 2 Dec 1929; *Educ* W Bridgford GS Nottingham, QMC London (BSc, MSc); *m* 13 Oct 1956, Thelma, da of Charles Weare (d 1971), of Worthing, Sussex; 1 s (Nicholas b 1961), 2 da (Judith b 1959, Elizabeth b 1962); *Career* engr offr RAF 1953-56, served Aden; Scientific Civil Serv 1956-87, dep dir (R&D) Nat Gas Turbine Estab 1973-80, dir gen engines MOD 1980-87; currently industl conslt and non-exec co dir; sec Royal Cmmn for the Exhibition 1851; Royal Aeronautical Soc Silver Medallist 1987; *Recreations* following cricket, railway history; *Style—* Michael Neale, Esq, CB; 108 Wargrave Rd, Twyford, Reading, Berks RG10 9PJ (☎ 0734 341759); Royal Commission for the Exhibition of 1851, Sherfield Building, Imperial College of Science Technol and Medicine, London SW7 2AZ

NEALE, Michael John; OBE (1984); s of Harold Arthur Neale (d 1940), of Surbiton, and Patricia Kathleen, *née* MacMahon (d 1985); *b* 14 Dec 1926; *Educ* St Edwards Oxford, Imperial Coll London (Whitworth scholar, BSc, DIC); *Career* apprentice Rolls Royce Engrg 1944-49, res assoc Imperial Coll London 1950-55, mangr design and technol Glacier Metal Co Ltd 1958-62 (engrg res mangr 1956-58), ind consltg engr 1962-75, chm Michael Neale and Assoc Ltd 1975- (md 1975-90); FEng 1981, FIMechE 1965 (pres 1990-91); *Books* The Tribology Handbook (1973); *Recreations* restoring antique furniture, buildings and machinery; *Clubs* Athenaeum; *Style—* Michael Neale, Esq, OBE; Chalkdell, Herriard, Hants RG25 2PR (☎ 025683 380); Michael Neale & Associates Ltd, 43 Downing St, Farnham, Surrey GU9 7PH (☎ 0252 722255, fax 0252 737106)

NEALE, Phillip Anthony (Phil); s of Geoffrey Baker Neale, and Elsie May, *née* Waby; *b* 5 June 1954; *Educ* Frederick Gough GS Scunthorpe, John Leggot Sixth Form Coll Scunthorpe, Univ of Leeds (BA); *m* 26 Sept 1976, Christine Mary Barton; 1 s (Craig Andrew b 11 Feb 1982), 1 da (Kelly Joanne b 9 Nov 1979); *Career* professional cricketer; Worcestershire CCC: debut 1975, awarded county cap 1978, capt 1982-, benefit 1988; represented England B 1982; honours as capt Worcestershire CCC: (County Championship 1988 and 1989, Refuge Assurance League 1987 and 1988 (runners up 1989)); record for ten seasons as capt Worcestershire 1991, player of the year Britannic Assurance Championship 1989; professional footballer Lincoln City off-seasons 1974-85 (over 350 appearances), teacher Royal GS Worcester 1986-89, currently mktg mangr PE International Management Consultancy; *Books* A Double Life (autobiography, 1990); *Recreations* reading, golf, spending time with my family; *Style—* Phil Neale, Esq; Worcestershire CCC, County Ground, New Rd, Worcester WR2 4QQ (☎ 0905 748474)

NEALE, Timothy Peter Graham; s of Maj Archibald Graham Neale, TD, of St Anthonys, Burwash, E Sussex, and Ann Urling (d 1989), *née* Clark; *b* 15 Dec 1939; *Educ* Radley; *m* 18 April 1970, Elizabeth Francis, da of William Frank George Harvey (d 1988); 2 da (Elizabeth b 1972, Jennifer b 1974); *Career* CA; ptnr: Hope Agar 1967-88, Kidsons Impey 1988-90; bursar Croham Hurst Sch South Croydon 1990-; treas Sidlow Bridge PCC 1967-87 and 1989, govr Micklefield Sch Reigate 1980-, capt Reigate Hockey Club 1972-76, chm Reigate Redhill and Dist Railway Users Assoc 1987-; ACA 1963, FCA 1972; *Recreations* gardening, watching sport; *Clubs* RAC, MCC; *Style—* Timothy Neale, Esq; 20 Raglan Rd, Reigate, Surrey RH2 0DP (☎ 0737 243588); Croham Hurst Sch, 79 Croham Rd, South Croydon, Surrey CR2 7YN (☎ 081 688 3863)

NEAMAN, Prof Yfrah; OBE (1983); *b* 13 Feb 1923; *Educ* Birkbeck Coll London, Premier Prix Conservatoire National Supérieur de Musique Paris, studies with Carl Flesch, Jacques Thibaud and Max Rostal; *m* 16 March 1953, Gillian Mary, da of Maurice E Shaw (d 1977), of London; 1 s (Samuel Lister b 1964), 1 da (Rachel Cecilia b 1965); *Career* GSM: prof of violin, head of Strings Dept 1962-78, head of Dept of Advanced Solo Studies 1974-; recitals, concerts with orchestras, radio and TV appearances, public master classes in Europe, N and S America, China, Japan, Korea, Africa and Asia; artistic conslt London Int String Quartet Competition, artistic advsr Wells Cathedral Sch England; recordings made for: Argo, Lyrita, and Yugoton records; ed several works by various composers; Freeman City of London Liveryman Worshipful Co of Musicians; FGSM; *Style—* Prof Yfrah Neaman, OBE; 11 Chadwell St, London EC1R 1XD (☎ 071 837 4455); Guildhall Sch of Music & Drama, Barbican, London EC2Y 8DT (☎ 071 628 2571)

NEAME, Basil Desmond; CBE (1970); s of Sir Thomas Neame (d 1972), of Preston Lea, Faversham, Kent, and Gwendolyn Mary, *née* Thompson, CBE (d 1972); *b* 14 Oct 1921; *Educ* Cheltenham; *m* 3 April 1948, Stella (d 1991), da of Lt-Col William Edward Roe (d 1956), of Valence Dene, Godmersham, nr Canterbury, Kent; 2 s (Andrew b 1951, Charles b 1957), 2 da (Patricia (Mrs Cuomo) b 1949, Bridget (Mrs Schillereff) b 1954); *Career* Signalman Royal Signals 1941, cmmnd 2 Lt Cadet RE 1942, Field Co attached Madras Sappers & Miners 1942, Lt 405 Ind Field Co, Capt 1944, Maj 1945, demob 1946, despatches 1946; farmer Kent; chm E Kent Packers Ltd 1973-80 (dir 1970-), local dir Royal Insur Co 1955-87; Nat Farmers Union: chm Kent 1956-58, memb Nat Cncl 1960-66, memb Agric Apprenticeship Ctee Kent (chm 1953-61, chm Nat Cncl 1960-67); chm Agric Trg Bd 1966-70; govr: Wye Coll 1971-87, E Malling Res Station 1960-87 (tstee 1985); memb Apple & Pear Res Cncl 1989; *Recreations* bird watching; *Clubs* Farmers; *Style—* Basil Neame, Esq, CBE; Macknade Manor, Faversham, Kent ME13 8XE (☎ 0795 532 070); Macknade, Faversham, Kent ME13 8XF (☎ 0795 532 216)

NEAME, Christopher Elwin; s of Ronald Neame, and Beryl Yolanda Heanly; *b* 24 Dec 1942; *Educ* Kings Sch Canterbury; *m* April 1966 (m dis 1972), Heather Marilyn, da of Dick Wade (d 1972); 1 s (Gareth Elwin b 8 March 1967), 2 da (Shuna b 16 July 1968, Emma b 28 May 1970); *Career* prodr tv series The Flame Trees of Thika 1980, wrote stage play of Monsignor Quixote 1988 (produced and wrote screenplay which won Christopher Award, NY 1987); memb: BAFTA, The Writers Guild of GB, Producers Guild of America, Dirs Guild of GB; *Recreations* photography; *Style—* Christopher Neame, Esq; Corbett's Wharf, Cherry Garden Pier, London SE16 4TU (☎ 071 232 0559, fax 071 231 5443, mobile 0836 26 2345)

NEAME, Robert Harry Beale; s of Jasper Beale Neame (d 1961), and Violet Evelyn, *née* Cobb (d 1976); The Neame family have been resident in E Kent and can be traced back 500 years; *b* 25 Feb 1934; *Educ* Harrow; *m* 1, 1961, Sally Elizabeth, *née* Corben; 1 s (Jonathan), 2 da (Charlotte, Sarah); m 2, 1974, Yvonne Mary, *née* Mackenzie; 1 da (Moray); *Career* cmmnd 17/21 Lancers 1953-55 (army Racquets champion 1954); chm Shepherd Neame Ltd 1971- (joined 1956, dir 1957, mktg dir 1961), former dir and chm Faversham Laundry Co, regnl dir Nat Westminster Bank plc 1982-; dir: Kent Econ Devpt Bd 1984-, Folkestone Racecourse 1984-; local dir Royal Insurance (UK) Ltd 1971-; memb Faversham CC 1965-89, ldr Kent CC 1982-84; chm: SE Eng Tourist Bd 1979-90, Int Union of Local Authys 1986-89; memb Assoc of Brewing; *Recreations* shooting, riding, cricket, golf, squash, racquets; *Clubs* MCC, I Zingari, Butterflies, Escorts, Jesters, Band of Brothers, Press, Roy St George's, Free Forresters; *Style—* Robert Neame, Esq; Dane Court Farmhouse, Kits Hill, Selling, Faversham, Kent (☎ 030381 284); c/o Shepherd Neame Ltd, 17 Court St, Faversham, Kent (☎ 079 5822206)

NEARN, Graham Bradshaw; s of Henry John Nearn (d 1986), and Eva Charlotte, *née* Sayers; *b* 29 Sept 1933; *Educ* Purley County GS, City of London Coll; *m* 5 March 1966, (Margaret) Jane, da of Dr John Stewart Norwell (d 1984); 2 s (Robert Bradshaw b 24 April 1967, Simon John 27 March 1969), 2 da (Eliza Alexandra Jane b 2 Nov 1972, Janina Charlotte 5 May 1977); *Career* md Caterham Cars Ltd (mfr Caterham super 7 Sports car, formerly Lotus Super 7) 1970- (dir 1959-70), dir District Finance Ltd 1970, chm London Property Conversions Ltd 1972-; chm Specialist Car Mfrs Gp Soc of Motor Mfrs and Traders; *Books* The Caterham & Lotus Sevens (1986); *Recreations* golf, sailing, motor sport; *Clubs* Edenbridge Golf, Whitstable Yacht, Aston Martin Owners, Lotus 7; *Style—* Graham Nearn, Esq; Winburne, Ashurst, Kent TN3 9TB (☎ 0892 740341); 34 Island Wall, Whitstable, Kent; Caterham Cars Ltd, Seven House, Townend, Caterham, Surrey CR3 5UG (☎ 0883 346666, fax 0883 349086, car 0836 340683)

NEARS, Colin Gray; s of William Charles Nears (d 1974), of Ipswich, and Winifred Mildred, *née* Gray (d 1983); *b* 19 March 1933; *Educ* Ipswich Sch, King's Coll Cambridge (MA); *Career* freelance tv dir; prodr music and arts BBC TV 1967-87, author and dir of progs (on lit, the Visual Arts, music and dance); ed Review 1971-72; memb Cncl and chm Advsy Panel on Dance Arts Cncl of GB 1982-90, memb Ballet Bd Royal Opera House 1990-; BAFTA Award for Best Specialised Programme 1973, Prix Italia Music Prize 1982; *Recreations* reading, gardening, painting, swimming; *Style—* Colin Nears, Esq; 16 Ashchurch Terrace, London W12 9SL (☎ 081 749 3615)

NEARY, Jack Edward; s of Albert Edward Neary (d 1963), and Grace, *née* Lewin (d 1974); *b* 1 April 1922; *Educ* Sir Anthony Brown's Sch Brentwood Essex, Coll Estate Mgmnt (Dip RICS); *m* 6 Aug 1949, (Margaret) Katherine Ferguson, da of Ferrers Augustus Collyer Munns (d 1975); 1 s (Robert b 1950), 1 da (Sara b 1954); *Career* cmmnd RA, served 25 Indian Mountain Regt and 7 Indian Div Burma Campaign Kohim Rangoon; chartered quantity surveyor; sr ptnr Banks Wood & Ptnrs; RICS: memb Ctee Central London Branch 1964-72 (hon sec 1964-69, chm 1971-72), memb Continental Gp Ctee 1971-75 and 1980, memb Int Ctee 1971-77 and 1980-84, memb Gen Cncl 1972-73 and 1982-84; rep on Br Standards Inst 1981-84; Quantity Surveyors' Div: memb Div Cncl 1968-77, memb Div Exec Ctee 1972-77, chm Int Affrs Ctee 1972-77, memb Branch Ctee 1970-72, rep Gen Practice Div Cncl 1971-73, rep Bldg Surveyors' Div Cncl 1973-74; Queen's Sheriff City of London 1985-86; former pres: Bishopsgate Ward Club, City Livery Club, Aldgate Ward Club, United Wards Club; Past Master Tower Ward Club; hon treas Save the Children Fund Brentwood; OStJ 1986; Freeman City of London 1952; Liveryman Worshipful Co of: Shipwrights 1955 (Freeman 1947, Prime Warden 1984-85), Chartered Surveyors 1977; Master Worshipful Co of constructors 1988-89, Renter Warden Guild of Freemen City of London; FRICS (1956, ARICS 1951); *Recreations* motor sport; *Clubs* City Livery, IOD, Wings (NY); *Style—* Jack Neary, Esq; Honeywood, Glanthams Close, Shenfield,

Essex CM15 8DD (☎ 0277 223598); Flat 1, 8 York Bldgs, London WC2N 6JN (☎ 071 930 4869); Banks Wood & Partners, 6 Kinghorn St, London EC1A 7BP (☎ 071 600 0260, fax 071 606 3350, car 0836 603 65)

NEARY, Martin Gerard James; s of Leonard Walter Neary, of 25 Manor House, Marylebone Rd, London, and Jeanne Marguerite, *née* Thébault; *b* 28 March 1940; *Educ* City of London Sch, Chapel Royal Choir, Gonville and Caius Coll Cambridge (organ scholar, MA); *m* 22 April 1967, Penelope Jane, da of Sir Brian Warren, of London, and Dame Josephine Barnes, DBE, *qv*; 1 s (Thomas b 1974), 2 da (Nicola b 1969, Alice b 1972); *Career* prof of organ Trinity Coll London 1963-72, organist and master of music St Margaret's Westminster 1965-71; conductor: Twickenham Musical Soc 1966-72, St Margaret's Westminster Singers 1967-71, Waynflete Singers 1972-87; organist and master of the music Winchester Cathedral 1972-87, organist and master of the choristers Westminster Abbey 1988-; guest conductor: Academy of Ancient Music, English Chamber Orchestra, London Symphony Orchestra, Winchester Baroque Ensemble 1982-87, Westminster Baroque Ensemble 1988; 12 foreign tours with Winchester Cathedral Choir 1978-87, toured America, France, Hungary, Switzerland, with Westminster Abbey Choir 1988-90; dir Southern Cathedrals Festival 1972, 1975, 1978, 1981, 1984 and 1987; many organ recitals and broadcasts in UK, Europe and America, has conducted premières of music by many Br composers, numerous recordings incl Lloyd Webber Requiem (golden disc); pres: Cathedral Organists' Assoc 1985-88, Royal Coll Organists 1988-90, organists' Benevolent League 1988-; hon citizen Texas 1971; Hon FTCL 1969, Hon RAM 1988; FRCO; *Books* Early French Organ Music (ed 2 vols 1975); *Recreations* watching cricket; *Clubs* Athenaeum, Middx CCC; *Style—* Martin Neary, Esq; 2 Little Cloister, Westminster Abbey, London SW1P 3PL (☎ 071 222 6923); Chapter Office, 20 Deans Yard, London SW1P 3PA (☎ 071 222 5152)

NEATE, Francis Webb; s of Francis Webb Neate (d 1982), of 1 Holmesdale Road, Kew, Richmond, Surrey, and Fiona L M, *née* O'Brien; *b* 13 May 1940; *Educ* St Wilfrid's Sch Seaford Sussex, St Paul's, Brasenose Coll Oxford (BA), Univ of Chicago Law Sch (JD); *m* 25 Aug 1962, Patricia Ann, da of Anthony Vincent Hugh Mulligan (d 1984), of 6 Daylesford Ave, Putney, London; 2 s (Vincent b 1968, Patrick b 1970), 2 da (Polly b 1966, Emily b 1973); *Career* admitted slr 1966; Slaughter and May: articled clerk 1964-66, asst slr 1966-71, ptnr 1972-; memb: Law Soc, City of London Slrs Co, Int Bar Assoc; *Recreations* cricket, reading, family; *Clubs* MCC, Berkshire CCC, Richmond CC, Falkland CC; *Style—* Francis Neate, Esq; 2 Daylesford Ave, Putney, London SW15 5QR; Slaughter and May, 35 Basinghall St, London EC2V 5DB (☎ 071 600 1200)

NEAVE, Maj Sir Arundell Thomas Clifton; 6 Bt (GB 1795), of Dagnam Park, Essex, JP (Anglesey 1950); s of Sir Thomas Lewis Hughes Neave, 5 Bt (d 1940); *b* 31 May 1916; *Educ* Eton; *m* 1946, Richenda Alice Ione, da of Sir Robert Joshua Paul, 5 Bt (d 1955); 2 s, 2 da; *Heir* s, Paul Arundell Neave; *Career* served 1939-45 (Dunkirk), Maj Welsh Gds 1945, ret 1947; *Clubs* Carlton, Pratt's; *Style—* Maj Sir Arundell Neave, Bt, JP; Greatham Moor, Liss, Hants

NEAVE, Julius Arthur Sheffield; CBE (1978, MBE 1944), JP (Brentwood), DL (Essex 1983); s of late Col Richard Neave, and Helen Mary Elizabeth, *née* Miller; *b* 17 July 1919; *Educ* Sherborne; *m* 1951, Helen Margery, da of the late Col P M Acton-Adams, DSO; 3 da; *Career* served in 13/18 Royal Hussars; gen mangr Mercantile & General Reinsurance Company Ltd 1966- (joined 1938, md 1980-82), dir Prudential Corporation plc; first chm Reinsurance Offices Assoc, received Founders Award Gold medal of Int Seminars 1977; pres: Insurance Inst London 1976-77, Geneva Assoc 1983-86, Chartered Insurance Inst 1983-84; Master Worshipful Co of Insurers' 1984; High Sheriff of Essex 1987-88; *Recreations* golf, shooting, fishing, tennis, needlework; *Clubs* Cavalry & Guards; *Style—* Julius Neave, Esq, CBE, JP, DL; Mill Green Park, Ingatestone, Essex CM4 0JB (☎ 0277 353 036)

NEAVE, Hon (Richard) Patrick Sheffield; s of Airey Middleton Sheffield Neave, DSO, OBE, MC, TD, MP (assass 1979), and Baroness Airey of Abingdon (Life Peeress), *qv*; *b* 12 Nov 1947; *Educ* Eton, City of London Poly; *m* 1980, Elizabeth Mary Catherine, da of Cuthbert Edward Riddell, of Hermeston Hall, Worksop, Notts; 2 s (James Riddell Airey b 1983, Thomas Edward Riddell Airey b 1985); *Career* business devpt The London Futures and Options Exchange; *Style—* The Hon Patrick Neave; 16 Maze Rd, Kew, Richmond, Surrey

NEAVE, Paul Arundell; s and h of Sir Arundell Thomas Clifton Neave, 6 Bt; *b* 13 Dec 1948; *Educ* Eton; *m* 1976, Coralie Jane Louise, da of Sir Robert George Caldwell Kinahan, ERD; 2 s; *Career* stockbroker; *Recreations* photography; *Style—* Paul Neave Esq; 7 Franconia Rd, London SW4 (☎ 071 622 0491)

NEAVE, Hon William Robert Sheffield; yr s of Baroness Airey of Abingdon (Life Peeress), *qv*, and Airey Middleton Sheffield Neave, DSO, OBE, MC, TD, MP (assass 1979); *b* 13 Aug 1953; *Educ* Eton; *m* 17 May 1986, Joanna Mary Stuart, 2 da of James Stuart Paton, of The Old Vicarage, Gt Hockham, Norfolk; 2 s (Richard Digby Stuart b 21 May 1987, Sebastian Airey Stuart b 11 May 1989); *Career* dep underwriter: H R Dumas Syndicate, Wellington Underwriting Agencies Ltd; *Recreations* photography, books; *Style—* The Hon William Neave; 20 Kirkstall Rd, London SW2 4HF

NEAVES, David O; *Educ* St Paul's, Twickenham Coll of Art and Technol; *Career* Mil Serv RE 1955-56; advertising exec Roles & Parker Ltd 1957-60, asst advertising mangr Bentalls Ltd 1960-64, sr advertising mangr Ilford Ltd 1964-68, PR and publicity offr for Basildon New Town 1968-70, int publicity mangr Moore Business Forms Group 1970-78; dir Primary Contact (specialist agency in O&M/WPP Group) 1984- ; chm Assoc of Business Advertising Agencies; Freeman City of London 1989, Liveryman Worshipful Co of Woolmen 1989; *Recreations* music, historical model engrg with special interest in the narrow gauge railways of N Wales; *Style—* David Neaves, Esq; Primary Contact Ltd, 33 St John St, London EC1M 4AA

NEBHRAJANI, Vir Tirathdas; s of Tirathdas Totaldas Nebhrajani (d 1975), and Dharmi, *née* Sirwani; *b* 9 Aug 1930; *Educ* Premier HS Karachi, Univ of Bombay, Assam Med Coll (Indian Central Govt scholar), Gauhati Univ Assam (MB BS), RCS (DLO); *m* 1 Sept 1961, Jayantee, da of Arun Kumar Chanda; 2 da (Sharmila b 30 March 1966, Malini b 22 Jan 1969); *Career* res offr ENT and gen surgery Assam Medical Coll 1958-60, various appts 1960-72 (Dudley Road Hosp Birmingham, Whipps Cross Hosp London, Western Infirmary Glasgow); present appts: conslt otologist John Scott Audiology Clinic City and Hackney Family Health Servs Authy, conslt ENT surgn Manor House Hosp London and BUPA Roding Hosp Redbridge; exec and fndr memb Doctors Assoc for Medical Aid (working primarily in India); memb: Rotary Club Redbridge Essex, Sindhi Assoc UK; chm Anandam UK, patron Bengali Cultural Assoc UK; memb BMA 1960, FRCS, FRCSEd 1969; *Recreations* cultural activites, fund raising for charities, photography and reading; *Style—* Vir Nebhrajani, Esq; 22 Harley St, Suite 5, London W1N 1AA (☎ 071 637 0491)

NEC, Bronislaw; OBE (1978); s of Emil Netz (d 1958), and Helena, *née* Kaminska; *b* 4 Nov 1924; *Educ* early educn in Germany and Poland, Glasgow (CDA), Newton Abbot (Dipfm); *m* 30 April 1949, Jessie Anderson Banks, da of Archibald Small (d 1971); 1 s (Anthony b 1957), 1 da (Helena b 1949); *Career* agronomist; HMOCS served Malawi: livestock offr 1955-68, princ animal husbandry offr 1969-71, chief agric offr 1971-75, dir of planning Miny of Agric 1975-78; agric advsr to EEC delgn in Tanzania and Ghana 1978-87; *Recreations* golf, game shooting, game fishing; *Clubs* Country Gentlemen's Assoc; *Style—* Bronislaw Nec, Esq, OBE; Summerfield, E Boldre, nr Brockenhurst, Hants SO42 7WU (☎ 059 065 618)

NEEDHAM, Hon Christopher David; s of 5 Earl of Kilmorey (d 1977); *b* 30 July 1948; *Educ* Milton Abbey; *m* 1974, Marina, eld da of Rodi Malvezzi, of Milan, Italy; 1 s (Francis b 22 June 1982), 1 da (Armyne b 31 Oct 1978); *Career* mktg dir Young and Rubicam Milan; *Recreations* fishing, skiing, swimming, photography; *Style—* The Hon Christopher Needham; 63 Foro Buonaparte, Milan, Italy (☎ 02 879029)

NEEDHAM, David Arthur (Dan); s of Arthur Needham (ka 1941), and Kathleen Elizabeth, *née* Mathews; *b* 27 Sept 1941; *Educ* King Edward VI GS East Retford Notts, RAF Coll Cranwell, Open Univ (BA); *m* 1 Aug 1964, Margaret, da of Albert Clayton (d 1963); 2 s (Paul b 23 July 1970, James b 16 May 1973), 1 da (Marianne b 11 Dec 1979); *Career* cmmnd RAF 1963, 101 Sqdn 1964-68, 12 Sqdn 1971-73, Sqdn Ldr 1971, Wing Cdr 1981, Gp Capt 1990; *Recreations* family, tennis, skiing; *Clubs* RAF; *Style—* Gp Capt D A Needham; Station Commander, RAF Turnerhouse, Edingburgh EH10 0AQ (☎ 031 339 5393)

NEEDHAM, Hon Mrs Peter; Janet Beatrice Winifred; da of late Capt George Taylor Ramsden, MP; *m* 1951, Hon (Arthur Edward) Peter Needham (d 1979, raised to the rank of an Earl's s 1962), s of late Maj Hon Francis Edward Needham, MVO (2 s of 3 Earl of Kilmorey); 2 s, 1 da; *Style—* The Hon Mrs Peter Needham; The Old Manor House, Helmsley, York

NEEDHAM, Hon (Patrick) Jonathan; s of 5 Earl of Kilmorey; *b* 20 March 1951; *m* 1979, Jane, da of Geoffrey Hinbest, of Bristol; *Career* chef; *Style—* The Hon Jonathan Needham; Flat 1, 26 Marlborough Buildings, Bath, Avon

NEEDHAM, Peter Southwood; s of William Needham, of Hobart, Tasmania; *b* 9 Jan 1924; *Educ* Hobart HS; *m* 1, 1945, Anne Louise; 2 da (Elizabeth Anne (Mrs McCormick), Rosemary Jane (Mrs Semke)); m 2, 1971, Susan Augusta, da of Philip H Band, of Westhampton Beach, NY; 3 step children; *Career* business conslt, dir GHN Limited; *Clubs* Hurlingham, RAF; *Style—* Peter Needham, Esq; c/o GHN, 16 Hanover Sq, London W1R 9AJ

NEEDHAM, Phillip; s of Ephraim Needham, of Dunstable, and Mabel Jessie, *née* Foskett; *b* 21 April 1940; *Educ* Ashton GS Dunstable, Univ of Birmingham (BSc), Imperial Coll London (MSc); *m* 24 March 1962, Patricia Ann, da of Henry Farr, of Leighton Buzzard; 2 s (Paul b 1963, David b 1964), 2 da (Jennifer b 1967, Claire b 1974); *Career* agric devpt and advsy servs MAFF: head of soil sci 1982-85, sr agric scientist 1985-87, dep dir R & D 1987-88, dir farm and countryside serv and commercial dir 1988; *Style—* Phillip Needham, Esq; MAFF, Nobel House, 17 Smith Square, London SW1P 3HX (☎ 071 238 5776)

NEEDHAM, Richard Francis; MP (C) N Wilts 1983-; 6 Earl of Kilmorey (I 1822), also Hereditary Abbot of the Exempt Jurisdiction of Newry and Mourne, Viscount Kilmorey (I 1625) and Viscount Newry and Morne (I 1822), but does not use titles; s of 5 Earl of Kilmorey (d 1977), and Helen, da of Sir Lionel Faudel-Phillips, 3 and last Bt; *b* 29 Jan 1942; *Educ* Eton; *m* 1965, Sigrid Juliane, da of late Ernst Thiessen, and Mrs John Gairdner; 2 s (Viscount Newry and Morne b 1966, Hon Andrew b 1969), 1 da (Lady Christina b 1977); *Heir* s, Viscount Newry and Morne; *Career* memb of Lloyds; formerly: cncllr Somerset, chm RGM Print Holdings Ltd 1970-85; govr Br Inst of Florence 1983-85, fndr memb Anglo-Japanese 2000 Gp; personal asst to Rt Hon James Prior, MP, oppn spokesman on Employment 1974-79, MP (C) Chippenham 1979-1983, sec Cons Employment Ctee 1979-81 (vice-chm 1981-83), memb Public Accounts Ctee 1982-83, PPS to Rt Hon James Prior Sec of State for NI 1983-84, PPS to Rt Hon Patrick Jenkins Sec of State for Environment 1984-85; min of Health and min of Environment for NI 1985-; min for the Economy for NI 1989-; *Publications* The Honourable Member (1983); *Clubs* Pratts; *Style—* Richard Needham, Esq, MP; House of Commons, London SW1

NEEDHAM, Richard Joseph; s of Douglas Martyn William Needham, of Timber Edge, Heath End, Wigginton, nr Tring, Herts, and Vera Gwenllian, *née* Bowen; *b* 2 July 1946; *Educ* Berkhamsted Sch Herts, Poly of North London (BSc, DipArch); *m* 11 Dec 1976, Rosalyn Jill, da of Leslie James Attryde, of Crestwood, Hill Green Lane, Wigginton, Herts; 2 s (Robert b 29 Nov 1981, Edward b 16 Nov 1985); *Career* John Penton Chartered Architect St Albans specialising design for disabled 1974-77, ptnr Melvin Lansley & Mark Chartered Architects 1988-90 (joined 1977, assoc 1981), conslt Hurd Rolland Partnership (incorporating Melvin Lansley & Mark) 1990- (specialising in construction technol, bldg litigation); concervation and failure investigation; memb Cons pty; ARCUK 1975, MRIBA 1981, MBAE 1989; *Recreations* photography, walking, cycling, reading, gardening; *Style—* Richard Needham, Esq; Hurd Rolland Partnership

NEEDHAM, Sheila June; da of Steven Ellis Needham (d 1981), and Grace Kathleen, *née* Tarrant (d 1987); *b* 22 June 1937; *Educ* Sutton HS; *Career* held several secretarial positions in London and USA 1955-71; dir Scribe-Ex Ltd 1965-74, fndr and md Needham Printers Ltd 1974-; tstee: Haberdashers' Aske's Hatchem, City Technol Coll; pres: NE Dist London Printing Assoc 1981, Farringdon Ward Club 1984-85; memb: Inst of Printing 1985, Br Assoc of Women Entrepreneurs; fell Royal Soc for the Encouragement of Arts Mfrs and Commerce; Freeman City of London, Liveryman Worshipful Co of Stationers and Newspaper Makers; FBIM; *Recreations* travel, theatre, walking, gardening, sunshine; *Clubs* City Livery, IOD, City Women's Network, Forum UK; *Style—* Miss Sheila J Needham; Needham Printers Ltd, Titchfield House, 69-85 Tabernacle St, London EC2A 4BA (☎ 071 250 3338)

NEESON, David Ivor; s of (Horace) Ivor Charles Neeson, of Belchamp, St Paul, Essex, and Jean Gibson, *née* Wade; *b* 19 Oct 1946; *Educ* Beal GS Ilford Essex; *m* 28 Dec 1972, Christine Pearl, da of Frank Hunt (d 1980), of Romford, Essex; 1 s (Rory), 1 da (Eloisa); *Career* investmt asst corpn of Lloyds 1965-67, stock (jobber) and ptnr Bisgood Bishop and Co 1967-76, vice pres Merrill Lynch Int 1976-82; Morgan Stanley Int: joined 1982, vice pres 1984, exec dir 1985, md 1986-; memb Int Stock Exchange; *Recreations* golf, tennis, shooting, hiking; *Clubs* Wentworth, Wildernesse Golf (Seal); *Style—* David Neeson, Esq; Morgan Stanley International, Kingsley House, 1A Wimpole St, London W1 (☎ 071 709 3898)

NEGRETTI, Antony Simon Timothy; s of Paul Antony Negretti, *qv*; *b* 2 Dec 1945; *Educ* Eton; *Career* bill broker and banker; dir: Page & Gwyther Holdings Ltd, Page & Gwyther Ltd, Page & Gwyther Investments Ltd; *Recreations* tennis, golf, skiing, shooting; *Clubs* Boodle's; *Style—* Antony Negretti Esq; 15 Roland Way, London SW7 (☎ 071 370 1887)

NEGUS, Her Hon Judge; Norma Florence (Mrs David Turner-Samuels); *née* Miss Norma Shellabear; da of George David Shellabear and Kate Laura, *née* Calvert; *b* 31 July 1932; *Educ* Malvern Girls Coll; *m* 1, 1956 (m dis 1960), Richard Negus; m 2, 1976, David Jessel Turner-Samuels, QC; *Career* fashion promotion in UK Canada and USA 1950-61, merchandise ed Harper's Bazaar 1962-63, asst promotion mangr Vogue and House and Garden 1963-65, unit mangr Trends merchandising and fashion promotion unit 1965-67, export mktg mangr Glenoit UK 1967-68; called to the Bar Gray's Inn 1970; Met stipendiary magistrate 1984-90, asst rec 1985-89, rec 1989-90, circuit judge South Eastern Circuit 1990-; *Recreations* writing, swimming, travel; *Style—* Her Hon Judge Negus; New Court, Temple, London EC4Y 9BE (☎ 071 353

7613)

NEGUS, Richard Charles; s of Bertie Arthur Charles Negus (d 1967), of Quendon, Essex, and Kate, *née* Brassington (d 1947); *b* 29 Aug 1927; *Educ* Battersea GS, Camberwell Sch of Arts & Crafts; *m* 20 Sept 1949, Pamela Denise; 2 s (Dominic Charles b 1952, Toby Wheatcroft b 1953), 1 da (Kate Georgina b 1955); *Career* conslt designer; staff Fest of Br 1948-51; fndr ptnr: Negus Sharland 1951, Negus & Negus 1970-87; private practice 1987-; conslt to: Cotton Bd 1960-67, BNEC 1969-75, Lloyds Bank 1972-75, City of Westminster 1973-75, Pakistan Airlines 1975-90, Rank Organisation 1979-82, Vickers plc & Rolls Royce plc 1980-82, SDP 1981-87, N Dairies 1985-87, Royal Armouries 1984-, Nat Maritime Museum 1984-86, Science Museum 1987-89, John Lewis 1987-89, English Heritage 1983-, Royal Parks & Palace DOE; memb: Designers & Art Dirs Assoc, Post Office Stamps Advsy Ctee; FRSA, memb Design Cncl; assessor schs of Art: Birmingham, Bradford, Norwich; memb Ct of RCA; former govr schs of Art: Camberwell, Chelsea; lectr various Colls of Art; memb: CNAA, BTEC; memb Tylers & Bricklayers Co; FCSD (former pres), FSTD, FRSA; *Books* Designing for Export, Airline Liveries; contrib to: The Designer, Design Magazine, Graphics, Gebrauchgraphick, Architectural Review, Architect's Journal, Rolls Royce Magazine; *Recreations* the countryside, yachting; *Style—* Richard Negus, Esq; 44 Canonbury Park South, London N1 (☎ 071 226 2381); Little Gravenhurst, Stairbridge Lane, Bolney, W Sussex (☎ 071 226 2381)

NEIDPATH, Lord; James Donald Charteris; full title Lord Douglas of Neidpath, Lyne and Munard; s and h of 12 Earl of Wemyss and (8 of) March, KT, JP, *qv*; *b* 22 June 1948; *Educ* Eton, Univ Coll Oxford, St Antony's Oxford, RAC Cirencester (BA, DPhil, Dip Rural Estate Mgmnt); *m* 1983 (m dis 1988), Catherine Ingrid, da of Hon Jonathan Bryan Guinness, *qv*, of Osbaston Hall, Nuneaton, Warwicks; 1 s, 1 da (b 1987); *Heir* s, Hon Francis Richard Charteris, b 15 Sept 1984; *Career* page of honour to HM Queen Elizabeth The Queen Mother 1962-64, memb Royal Co of Archers (Queen's Body Guard for Scotland); land agent, ARICS; *Books* The Singapore Naval Base and the Defence of Britain's Eastern Empire 1919-41 (1981); historial reviews in The Spectator, Literary Review and Field; *Recreations* history; *Clubs* Brooks's, Pratt's, Puffin's, Ognisko Polskie; *Style—* Lord Neidpath; Stanway, Cheltenham, Glos (☎ 038673 469)

NEIL, Andrew Ferguson; s of Maj James Neil (d 1987), and Mary, *née* Ferguson; *b* 21 May 1949; *Educ* Paisley GS, Univ of Glasgow (MA); *Career* political advsr to Sec of State Environment (Rt Hon Peter Walker) 19 UK ed The Economist 1982-83 (joined staff 1973), ed The Sunday Times 1983-, exec chm Sky TV 1988-90; *Books* The Cable Revolution (1982); *Recreations* skiing, dining out in London, New York and Aspen, Colorado; *Clubs* RAC, Tramp; *Style—* Andrew Neil, Esq; The Sunday Times, 1 Pennington St, London E1 9XY (☎ 081 782 5000, fax 081 782 5658)

NEIL, Arthur; s of James McDavid Neil (d 1987), of Falkirk, Stirlingshire, and Catherine, *née* Dunn (1978); *b* 2 Nov 1929; *Educ* Falkirk HS, Scottish Hotel Sch; *m* 3 March 1958, Rosemary Georgina, da of George Paterson Gibson; 1 s (James Gibson b 8 Dec 1958), 2 da (Jennifer Marguerite b 8 June 1960, Victoria Catherine b 4 Sept 1962); *Career* apprentice cook Glasgow Central Hotel 1946-47, messing offr Acc 1949-51, asst mangr Goring Hotel London 1951-52, stagiaire Bellevue Palace Hotel Berne 1952-53, mangr rising to dir Open Arms Hotel 1954-, md Grange Inn St Andrews 1965-75, dir Shieldness Produce Ltd 1950-86, md Howard Hotel Edinburgh 1970-89; scot mangr Hotel and Catering Industry Tbnl Bd 1967-70, govr Queen Margaret Coll Edinburgh 1974-80, chm Innholder 1982 (master 1978), memb Bd Scotvec 1986-88; Freeman City of London 1979, FHCIMA; *Recreations* golf, shooting, travel, reading; *Clubs* East India, New (Edinburgh), Hon Coy of Edinburgh Golfers (Muirfield); *Style—* Arthur Neil, Esq; 1 Marly Knowe, Windygates Rd, North Berwick, East Lothian, Scotland EH39 4QP (☎ 0620 3515); Open Arms Hotel, Dirleton, East Lothian EH39 5BG (☎ 0620 85241, fax 0620 85570)

NEIL, John Knox; s of William Neil, and Anna, *née* Holland; *b* 23 April 1922; *m* 10 April 1972, Jeanie Elizabeth, da of John Dunlop; 1 s (Robert Bruce Dunlop b 11 Nov 1973), 1 adopted s (Philip John b 8 Feb 1969), 1 adopted da (Susan Margaret b 16 Feb 1965); *Career* md and co sec Doorfit Products Ltd 1980- (jt md 1958-80); *Recreations* squash; *Clubs* Stourbridge; *Style—* John Neil, Esq; Doorfit Products Ltd, Icknield House, Heaton St, Birmingham B18 5BA (☎ 021 554 9291, fax 021 554 3859)

NEILD, Dr Paul Graham; s of Edward Neild, of Blackpool, Lancs, and Mona Neild; *b* 18 Feb 1946; *Educ* Merchant Taylors', Liverpool Univ (BA), Manchester Univ (MA), Wellington Univ New Zealand (PhD); *m* 10 Feb 1968, Shian Helena, da of Llewelyn Thomas (d 1983), of Liverpool; 3 s (Simon b 1975, Adrian b 1975, Mark b 1978); *Career* Phillips and Drew 1971 (jr ptnr 1975, managing ptnr 1977, dir 1985-88), business conslt 1988; special econ advsr: House of Commons select ctee on the Treasy and Civil Serv 1979-85, Domestic Equity Markets ctee Stock Exchange 1987-88; memb Stock Exchange; *Recreations* horse racing; *Style—* Dr Paul Neild; The Hermitage, Rideaway, Hemingford Abbots, Cambs

NEILL, Alistair; s of Alexander Neill, MBE (d 1969), of Edinburgh; *b* 18 Nov 1932; *Educ* George Watson's Coll, Edinburgh Univ (MA), Wisconsin Univ (MS); *m* Mary Margaret; 1 s, 2 da; *Career* Instr Lt RN 1968-70; actuary; gen mangr Scot Widows Fund; vice pres Faculty of Actuaries; FFA, FIA; *Books* Life Contingencies; *Recreations* golf, curling, squash rackets; *Style—* Alistair Neill, Esq; Scottish Widows Fund & Life Assurance Society, PO Box 902, 15 Dalkeith Road, Edinburgh, EH16 5BU

NEILL, Rt Hon Lord Justice; Rt Hon Sir Brian Thomas; PC (1985); s of Sir Thomas Neill, JP (d 1937); bro of (Francis) Patrick Neill, *qv*; *b* 2 Aug 1923; *Educ* Highgate, CCC Oxford (MA); *m* 1956, Sally Margaret Backus; 3 s; *Career* served WWII Rifle Bde; called to the Bar Inner Temple 1949, QC 1968, rec of the Crown Ct 1972-78, judge of the High Ct (Queen's Bench Div) 1978-84, lord justice of appeal 1985-; chm ctee on Rhodesia Travel Restrictions 1973-78; Master Worshipful Co of Turners 1980-81; kt 1978; *Style—* The Rt Hon Lord Justice Neill, PC; c/o Royal Courts of Justice, Strand, London WC2

NEILL, George Edwin; s of Capt Edwin Meakin Neill, MC (d 1977), of Deganwy, and Violet Gertrude, *née* Schunck (d 1986); *b* 9 Jan 1929; *Educ* Shrewsbury; *m* 17 March 1951, (Kathleen) June, da of James Arthur Dawes (d 1968), of Bowdon, Cheshire; 2 s (Christopher Edwin b 23 July 1953, Peter Mark b 18 Nov 1954); *Career* 2 Lt 4/7 Royal Dragoon Gds 1947, served in Tripoli 1948-49; ret; *Recreations* sailing, hunting, tennis, skiing; *Clubs* Cruising Assoc; *Style—* George E Neill, Esq; Paradise Farm, Lower Withington, Macclesfield, Cheshire (☎ 0477 71240)

NEILL, Sheriff Gordon Webster McCash; DSO; *b* 1919; *Educ* Edinburgh Acad; *m* 1950, Margaret Mary, *née* Lamb; 1 s (John Victor), 1 da (Fiona Margaret); *Career* WWII RAF 1939-46; legal apprentice 1937-39, ptnr Neill & Gibb 1947, amalgamated business to form Neill & Mackintosh SSC 1967 (princ), amalgamated with Thornton Oliver WS (conslt 1989-); Notary Public 1947, Hon Sheriff; former chm Dundee Area Bd Br Law Insur Co Ltd, former chm Scottish Gliding Assoc; chm Arbroath C of C 1980-83; memb: Soc of Slrs and Procurators in Angus (pres 1977-80), Soc of Slrs in Supreme Cts of Scotland, Law Soc of Scotland, Scottish Law Agents' Soc; FIOD 1958; *Clubs* Rotary (Arbroath, former pres); *Style—* Sheriff Gordon Neill, DSO; 29 Duncan Ave, Arbroath, Angus, Scotland DD11 2DA

NEILL, Rt Hon Sir Ivan; PC (NI 1950); *b* 1 July 1906; *Educ* Ravenscroft Nat Sch, Shaftesbury House Tutorial Coll Belfast, Queen's Univ Belfast (BSc); *m* 1928, Margaret Helena Allen; *Career* WWII Maj RE; memb NI Parliament 1949-73; min of: Lab and Nat Insur 1950-62, Home Affrs 1952, Educn 1962-64, Fin and ldr of House of Commons 1964; resigned from govt 1965, min of Devpt 1968-69, speaker House of Commons 1969-73; FRGS; kt 1973; *Style—* The Rt Hon Sir Ivan Neill; Greenlaw, Ballywilliam, Donaghadee, Co Down, N Ireland

NEILL, Very Rev Ivan Delacherois; CB (1963), OBE (1958); s of Robert Richard Neill (d 1951), and Bessie Montrose, *née* Purdon (d 1950); *b* 10 July 1912; *Educ* St Dunstans Coll, Jesus Coll Cambridge (MA); *m* 1938, Enid Eyre Godson, da of Roderick George Bartholomew (d 1969), of The Orchards, Outwood, Surrey; 1 s (Robert), 1 da (Patricia); *Career* ordained 1936, Chaplain's Dept Reg Army 1939-66, BEF 1939-40, Orkneys 1941-42, Sandhurst 1942, sr chaplain N Aldershot 1943, sr chaplain 43 Wessex Div BLA/BWEF 1943-45 (despatches), dep asst chaplain gen 1 Br Corps 1945-46, sr chaplain Gds Depot 1946-50, DACG Canal N Egypt 1950-53, DACG Catterick 1953-54, warden Chaplain's Depot Bagshot 1954-57; SCF SHAPE Paris 1958, ACG ME 1958-60; chaplain gen 1960-66; QHC 1962; chaplain to HM Queen 1962-66; chm of govrs Monkton Combe Sch 1971-82 (govr 1964-82), emeritus provost of Sheffield 1974- (provost 1966-74), pres C of E Fndn at St Paul and St Mary Cheltenham 1978-88; Knight Offr Order of Orange Nassau with swords 1946; *Recreations* continuing Christian ministry, off-shore boating; *Clubs* National; *Style—* The Very Rev Ivan Neill, CB, OBE; Greathed Manor, Lingfield, Surrey RH7 6PA (☎ 0342 833992)

NEILL, Lt-Col James Hugh; CBE (1969), TD (1950), JP (S Yorks 1985); s of Col Sir Frederick Neill, CBE, DSO, TD (d 1967); *b* 29 March 1921; *Educ* Rugby; *m* 1, 1943, Jane Margaret (d 1980), *née* Shuttleworth; 2 da (and 1 decd); m 2, 1982, Catherine Anne Maria, *née* O'Leary; 1 s; *Career* WWII Lt-Col served: Norway, India, Burma, Germany; chm James Neill Holdings Ltd 1963-89; pres Sheffield C of C 1984-85; Master Cutler Hallamshire 1958-59, High Sheriff Hallamshire 1971-72, Lord Lt S Yorks 1985- (DL 1974); *Recreations* golf, racing, horse trials, shooting; *Clubs* R & A, Hon Co of Edinburgh Golfers, Lindrick Golf (Sheffield), E India, Sports; *Style—* Lt-Col Hugh Neill, CBE, TD; Barn Cottage, Lindrick Common, nr Worksop, Notts S81 8BA (☎ 0909 562806)

NEILL, John Mitchell; s of Justin Bernard Neill, and Johanna Elisabeth, *née* Bastiaans; *b* 21 July 1947; *Educ* George Heriott Sch Edinburgh, Univ of Strathclyde (BA, MBA, DBA); *m* 24 May 1975, Jacqueline Anne, da of Phillip Brown (d 1985); 2 s (Richard John b 19 July 1979, Alexander James b 4 Nov 1982); *Career* mktg mangr Europe AC Delco 1972-73 (planning mangr 1969-71), sales and mktg dir Br Leyland Parts & KD Div 1976 (merchandising mangr 1974-75); md: Leyland Car Parts Div 1977-78, BL Components 1979-80, Unipart Gp 1981-82, gp md Unipart Gp Ltd 1983-86, gp chief exec Unipart Gp of Cos 1987-, non-exec dir Midlands Electricity Bd; memb: Pres Ctee Business in the Community, Bd HOE TEC; FInstM; *Recreations* tennis, skiing; *Style—* John M Neill, Esq; UGC Ltd, Unipart House, Cowley, Oxford OX4 2PG (☎ 0865 778966, fax 0865 713790, telex 83331)

NEILL, John Whitley; s of Lt-Col Frederick Henry Neill (d 1985), of Farnham, Surrey, and Elizabeth, *née* Whitley (d 1986); *b* 15 May 1934; *Educ* Rugby; *m* 6 Nov 1971, Cecilia Anne, da of late Air Vice-Marshal Neill Charles Ogilvie-Forbes, OBE, of Marlow, Bucks; 1 s (John James Whitley b 16 July 1972); *Career* Nat Serv 1958-60, sr under offr OCS, 2 Lt RA 22 Field Regt; articled CA Whinney Smith and Whinney 1952-57, mgmnt trainee Greenall Whitley and Co (Brewers) 1960-65; dir: Greenall Whitley and Co Warrington 1965-70, Mackie and Co Ltd (newspaper propietors) 1962-75; accountant Artgate Ltd 1975-86 (dir 1979-86); dir: Joca Properties Ltd (investmt property co) 1970-, Tyerheath Ltd (property devpt co) 1987-; hockey player for GB at Olympic Games in 1960, 1964 and 1968 (capt), hockey selector for England 1986-90; sec Local Property Holders Assoc; former tax cmmr Warrington and Exeter; FCA; *Recreations* hockey, tennis, squash, gardening; *Clubs* Naval; *Style—* John Neill, Esq; 5 Baring Cres, Exeter EX1 1TL

NEILL, Sir (Francis) Patrick; QC (1966); s of Sir Thomas Neill, JP (d 1937); bro of Rt Hon Sir Brian (Thomas) Neill, *qv*; *b* 8 Aug 1926; *Educ* Highgate Sch, Magdalen Coll Oxford; *m* 1954, Caroline Susan, da of Sir Piers Debenham, 2 Bt (d 1964); 4 s, 2 da; *Career* served Rifle Bde 1944-47; fell All Souls Oxford 1950-77 (warden 1977-); Grays Inn: called to the Bar 1951, bencher 1971, treas 1990; rec of Crown Ct 1975-78, judge of Cts of Appeal of Jersey and Guernsey 1977-; chm Press Cncl 1978-83, first chm Cncl for Securities Industry 1978-85, chm DTI Ctee of Inquiry into Regulatory arrangements at Lloyds; vice chllr Univ of Oxford 1985-89; kt 1983; *Style—* Sir Patrick Neill, QC; All Souls College, Oxford

NEILL, Robert James MacGillivray; s of John MacGillivray Neill, of Ilford, Essex, and Elsie May, *née* Chaston; *b* 24 June 1952; *Educ* Abbs Cross Sch Hornchurch Essex, LSE (LLB); *Career* called to the Bar Middle Temple 1975; dir: NE Thames Business Advsy Centre 1984-, Energy Concern Ltd 1986-; memb: Havering London Borough Cncl 1974- (chief whip), GLC for Romford (C) 1985-86; first ldr London Fire & Civil Defence Authy 1985-87, oppn spokesman Fire and Public Protection Ctee Assoc of Met Authorities; Parly candidate (C) Dagenham 1983 and 1987; chm Greater London Conservative Political Centre 1990-; memb Conservative Political Centre Nat Advsy Ctee 1989-; *Books* author of various articles and pamphlets on civil defence, legal affairs, small businesses, etc; *Recreations* sailing, travel, opera; *Clubs* Athenaeum, Carlton, St Stephen's Constitutional, Bar Yacht; *Style—* Robert Neill, Esq; 3 Hare Ct, Temple, London, EC4Y 7BJ (☎ 071 353 7561, fax 071 353 7741)

NEILL, Rose Mary Margaret; da of Roger Henry James Neill (d 1979), and Doreen Elizabeth, *née* Morrice; *b* 29 Nov 1958; *Educ* Mount Sch York, City and E London Coll; *m* 22 Feb 1985, (Robert) John Magill, s of Thomas Steward Magill (d 1987); 2 s (Roger Thomas b 23 June 1986, Henry Harley Peter b 11 Sept 1988); *Career* newscaster, sports presenter and gen prog presenter; Ulster TV Ltd 1978-86; BBC Belfast 1986-: co presenter main evening news prog, newscaster and writer for other daily bulletins, regular broadcaster Pick of the Week radio prog, writer and presenter various TV documentaries; involved in annual Children in Need TV presentation; memb ctee NI Mother and Baby appeal, supporter Ulster Cancer Res Campaign; *Recreations* hunting, skiing (water and snow), sailing, travelling; *Clubs* Royal Ulster Yacht, Strangford Lough Yacht, E Down Fox Hounds; *Style—* Miss Rose Neill; BBC, Ormeau Ave, Belfast BT2 8HQ (☎ 0232 244400, fax 0232 240246)

NEILL, (James) Ruary Drummond; s of Thomas Neill (d 1969), and Elsie Margaret Wilson, *née* Sharp; *b* 9 Jan 1959; *Educ* Glebe House Sch Norfolk, Greshams Sch Norfolk, Univ of London (BA); *m* 5 Sept 1987, Hilary Jane Vipen, da of Peter Harvery Bourne; 1 da (Georgina Kim Jane b 13 Feb 1990); *Career* Chartered Bank Abu Dhabi UAE 1981-83, Chartered Bank Hong Kong 1983-85, Roue & Pitman then Warburg Securities London 1985-88; Schroder Securities Ltd: joined 1988, dir 1990-, md (Hong Kong Ltd) 1990-; *Recreations* shooting, farming, reading; *Clubs* American (Hong Kong); *Style—* Ruary Neill, Esq; Hirdling House, Tilney, St Lawrence, King's Lynn, Norfolk (☎ 0553 849 6046); House N, Orient Crest, 76 Peak Rd, The Peak, Hong Kong; Schroder Securities Hong Kong Ltd, 26th Floor, 2 Exchange Square, 8 Connaught Rd, Central, Hong Kong (☎ 5 211660)

NEILLY, Gordon Joseph; *b* 2 July 1960; *Educ* Univ of Edinburgh (BComm); *m*

(Elizabeth) Ruth Neilly; *Career* CA; Peat Marwick McLintock 1981-84, fin dir Ivory & Sime PLC 1990- (accountants 1984-90); *Recreations* football, rugby, water skiing, driving; *Style*— Gordon Neilly, Esq; Ivory & Sime PLC, One Charlotte Square, Edinburgh, Scotland EH2 4DZ (☎ 031 225 1357, fax 031 225 2375)

NEILSON, Lt-Col Ian Godfrey; DFC (1944), TD (1951); s of James Wilson Neilson (d 1927), of Glasgow, and Marion Beatrice, *née* Saunders (d 1976); *b* 4 Dec 1918; *Educ* Glasgow Acad, Univ of Glasgow (BL); *m* 2 June 1945 (Dorothy) Alison St Clair, da of Robert Alexander Aytoun (d 1920), of Birmingham; 1 s (Hamish Rollo Aytoun Beattie-Smith b 1949), 1 da (Catherine Alison St Clair Kellett b 1951); *Career* RA: cmmnd 2 Lt TA 1939, Field Artillery 1940, flying trg No 8 EFTS RAF 1940, Capt (RA) 651 Air Observation Post Sqdn RAF 1941, later 652 Sqdn, serv Normandy 1944; GSO2 (Maj): RA branch HQ 21 Army Gp 1944, Royal Signals branch HQ BAOR 1945; cmd War Crimes Investigation Unit 1945 as Lt-Col, demobilised 1946; formed and cmd 666 (Scottish) Air Observation Post Sqdn RAuxAF as Maj RA (TA) 1948 (relinquished cmd 1953); legal apprentice Wright Johnson & Mackenzie 1936, admitted slr 1946; RICS: scottish sec 1946, asst sec London 1953, undersec HQ 1961; bde sec Boys' Bde 1966, clerk to govrs Cripplegate Fndn 1974, ret 1981; BIM City of London branch: hon sec 1976-79, chm 1979-81, vice pres 1981-87; sr instr RYA 1977-87, pres London branch Glasgow Academical Club 1977-79; chm: Epsom Choral Soc 1977-81, tstees St George's Chapel 1983-, Queenhithe Ward Club Lonodn 1977-78; dir and jt sec Utd Reformed Church Tst 1982- (church elder Cheam 1972-), vice pres Air Observation Post Offrs Assoc 1978-, hon vice pres Boys' Bde 1972-, cncl memb Christ Church Marlborough 1984-90; tstee: St Peters 1985-, Douglas Haig Meml Homes Assoc 1979-; Freeman: City of London 1975, Liveryman Guild of Air Pilots and Air Navigators 1978- (Freeman 1976-78); FBIM 1980; *Books* Tower and Town (hon ed 1984-); *Recreations* golf, music, gardening, sailing; *Clubs* Athenaeum, Marlborough Golf, Chartered Surveyors' Golfing, St Mawes Sailing; *Style*— Lt-Col Ian Neilson, DFC, TD; The Paddock, Kingsbury St, Marlborough, Wiltshire SN8 1HZ (☎ 0672 515114); The United Reformed Church Trust, Church House, 86 Tavistock Place, London WC1H 9RT (☎ 071 837 7661)

NEILSON, Maj Nigel Fraser; MC; s of Lt-Col William Neilson, DSO (d 1960), of Hawkes Bay, NZ, and Maud Frances Alice, *née* Anson (d 1967); *b* 12 Dec 1919; *Educ* Wellington House Westgate-on-Sea, Hereworth NZ, Christ's Coll NZ, RADA; *m* 22 Oct 1949, Pamela Catherine Georgina, da of Capt Samuel Marshal Philpot Sheppard (d 1945), of Well Cottage, Coulsden, Surrey; 1 s (Peter Nigel b 1958), 1 da (Susan Catherine Hiraani b 1952); *Career* Staffs Yeo, served 1 Cavalry Div Palestine, transferred to Trans-Jordanian Frontier Force Cavalry Regt (took par the last cavalry charge in history against French Spahis), returned Staffs Yeo (tanks) El Alamein Western Desert, GSO3 7 Armd Div, Anzio landing Italy, Allied force HQ Algiers, psc, joined SAS HQ, transferred 2 Liaison French SAS served Holland and France, served COS Bergen Norway; returned to theatre 1946, played and sang in many shows and concerts in London and USA, had own BBC programme Beginners Please, 2 i/c PR dept J Walter Thomson, left to become personal conslt to A S Onassis (introduced by Sir Win Churchill), opened own int PR Co representing major int cos: London, NZ, Malaysia, Singapore, US, Australia; helped produce HRH Prince Charles's first int Broadcast, represented Queen's Silver Jubilee Appeal, memb Cncl of Drake Fellowship, former pres and memb Ctee NZ Soc, currently independent int PR conslt; Legion D'Honneur, Croix de Guerre Avec Palme; *Recreations* shooting; *Clubs* Buck's, Annabel's, Wig and Pen, Special Forces; *Style*— Maj Nigel Neilson, MC; c/o Coutts & Co, 1 Old Park Lane, London W1Y 4BS; Neilson Associates, 12A Gledhow Gardens, London SW5 0AY

NEILSON, Richard Alvin; CMG (1987), LVO (1968); s of Robert Neilson (d 1974), and Ethel, *née* Duke; *b* 9 July 1937; *Educ* Burnley GS, Univ of Leeds (BA, MA), Univ of Wisconsin; *m* 21 Aug 1961, Olive, da of Herbert Stanley Tyler, of 13 Digby Rd, Leighton, Buzzard, Beds; 1 s (Paul b 8 Jan 1963); *Career* asst lectr Univ of Edinburgh 1960-61; joined FO 1961; second sec Leopoldville (Kinshasa) 1963-65 (third sec), treasy Centre for Admin Studies 1965, first sec Santiago 1966-69 (second sec), first sec Canberra 1969-73, FCO 1973-77, cnsllr 1977, seconded to NI office head of political affrs Belfast 1977-79, dep high cmmr Lusaka 1979-80, chargé 1979-80, dep govr and political advsr Gibraltar 1981-84, head SED FCO 1984-86; HM ambassador: Bogota 1987-90, Santiago 1990-; FRGS 1964, FBIM 1982; *Recreations* chess, golf, sailing; *Clubs* Royal Cwlth, Prince of Wales Country (Santiago); *Style*— Richard Neilson, Esq, CMG, LVO; Foreign & Commonwealth Office, King Charles St, London SW1A 2AH; British Embassy Santiago, La Concepcion 177, Apartado Areo Casi Ua 72-D, Chile

NEIVENS, Peter; OBE (1982), QPM (1974); s of Charles Neivens (d 1953), and Matilda Rose Neivens, *née* Costello (d 1977); *b* 4 June 1922; *Educ* Sir John Cass Tech Sch Aldgate; *m* 1948, Margaret Dorothy; 1 s; *Career* 9 years Merchant Navy, 2 offr British Tankers 1938-47; 24 years Metropolitan Police (rank of dep asst cmmr, dir of information); dir Trident (special responsibility for compliance) 1981-; 1939-45 Star, Atlantic Star, Burma Star, Victory Medal 1939, Police Long Service Medal and Good Conduct Medal 1969; *Recreations* cricket, birdwatching, walking; *Clubs* Clermont; *Style*— Peter Neivens, Esq, OBE, QPM; 25 Third Ave, Walton-on-the-Naze, Essex (☎ 0255 3521); Trident House, 29 Farm St, London W1X 8AA

NELDER, Prof John Ashworth; s of Reginald Charles Nelder (d 1979), and Edith May Ashworth Briggs (d 1954); *b* 8 Oct 1924; *Educ* Blundell's, Sidney Sussex Coll Cambridge, Univ of Birmingham (DSc); *m* 13 Jan 1954, Mary, da of Reginald Hawkes (d 1969); 1 s (Jan b 1956), 1 da (Rosalind b 1958); *Career* WWII RAF 1943-46; head Statistics Dept: Nat Vegetable Res Station 1950-68, Rothamsted Experimental Station 1968-84; visiting prof Imperial Coll London 1972-; pres: Int Biometric Soc 1978-79, Royal Statistical Soc 1985-86; Hon DSc Université Paul Sabatier Toulouse 1981; FRS 1981, Fell Int Statistical Inst; *Books* Generalized Linear Models (with P McCullagh); *Recreations* music (especially piano playing), natural history; *Style*— Prof John Nelder, FRS; Cumberland Cottage, Crown St, Redbourn, St Albans AL3 7JX (☎ 058 279 2907); Imperial College, Mathematics Dept, 180 Queen's Gate, London SW7 2BZ (☎ 071 589 5111 ext 5839)

NELIGAN, His Hon Judge Michael Hugh Desmond; s of Desmond West Edmund Neligan, of Storrington, W Sussex, and Penelope Anne, *née* Mason; *b* 2 Dec 1936; *Educ* Bradfield, Jesus Coll Cambridge; *m* 4 Sept 1965, Lynn, da of late Keith Taylor Maidment; 3 da (Sophie Leonara b 27 Feb 1967, Francesca Beth b 8 Feb 1969, Alexandra Louise b 30 Aug 1975); *Career* Nat Serv cmmnd 2 Lt Royal Sussex Regt, 1955-57 (seconded to Kings African Rifles serving with 23, 2/3 and 4 Bns Kenya and Uganda); called to the Bar Middle Temple 1962, prosecuting counsel to The Crown Central Criminal Court 1972-87 (to Inland Revenue 1970-72), stipendiary magistrate 1987-90, circuit judge 1990-; *Style*— His Hon Judge Neligan; The Crown Court, Barker Rd, Maidstone, Kent (☎ 0622 754 966)

NELIGAN, Timothy Patrick Moore; s of Moore Dermot Neligan (d 1977), of Worthing, and Margaret Joan, *née* Cockell (d 1975); *b* 16 June 1934; *Educ* Tonbridge; *m* 30 Nov 1957, Felicity Caroline, da of Norman Rycroft, of Thornton Hough, Cheshire; 2 s (Patrick b 1963, Timothy b 1963), 2 da (Henrietta b 1958, Kate b 1959); *Career* pupil Capt H Ryan Price racehorse trainer 1953-55, exec Agric Div ICI 1955-57, brewer and mangr Arthur Guinness (Park Royal) Ltd 1957-73, dir Goodwood Racecourse Ltd 1973-77, md United Racecourses Ltd 1977-; pres no 621 cadet div St John Ambulance, vice chm Epsom and Walton Downs Conservators, memb SE Eng Tourist Bd; Freeman City of London 1980, Liveryman Worshipful Co Farriers (Master 1990-91); MInstM 1977, MCIM 1989; OStJ 1990; *Books* The Epsom Derby (with Roger Mortimer, 1984); *Recreations* fishing, travel; *Style*— Timothy Neligan, Esq; Toll House, Sandown Park, Esher, Surrey KT10 9AJ (☎ 0372 467839); Sandown Park Racecourse, Esher, Surrey KT10 9AJ (☎ 0372 464348, fax 0372 465205)

NELLIST, David John; MP (Lab) Coventry South-East 1983-; *b* 1952,July; *Style*— David Nellist Esq, MP; House of Commons, London SW1A 0AA

NELLIST, Robert Henry Harger (Bob); s of John Harger Nellist (d 1966), of Rickmansworth, Herts, and Mary Ellen, *née* Eyles; *b* 25 Aug 1937; *Educ* St Edward's Sch Oxford, Trinity Coll Oxford (MA); *m* 31 Aug 1963, Audrey May, da of Harry John (Bill) Aubon (d 1982), of Harrow, Middx; 2 s (Andrew John b 29 July 1964, James Harry b 5 Feb 1969), 2 da (Annabel Kate b 28 June 1966, Louisa Mary (twin) b 5 Feb 1969); *Career* Nat Serv RM 1956-58, cmmnd Temp 2 Lt, troop offr 45 Commando Cyprus and Malta; CA; mangr Binder Hamlyn 1961-66, mgmnt conslt McKinsey & Co Inc 1966-69, divnl md (later gp fin dir) Hestair plc 1971-77, dir accounting Rolls-Royce plc 1977-79, dep fin dir The Plessey Co plc 1979-84, gp fin dir Thorn EMI plc 1984-89, chm Young Samuel Chambers Ltd; memb fraternity of friends St Albans Abbey, hon guide St Albans Cathedral; FCA 1964, MIMC 1970, JDipMA 1981, CBIM 1985; *Recreations* reading, hi-fi, music, trying to be fit not fat, personal computing; *Clubs* Vincents; *Style*— Bob Nellist, Esq; Spooner's, 28 Park Lane, St Albans, Herts AL2 2JB (☎ 0727 72319); Young Samuel Chambers (YSC) Ltd, 22 Grosvenor Square, Mayfair, London W1X 9LF (☎ 071 495 1806)

NELSON, Alan David; s of W S A Neslon, of West Moors, Dorset, and Olive Violet, *née* Hillman; *b* 6 June 1954; *Educ* Sir Bernard Lovell Boys Sch, Prince of Wales Coll Dover Kent; *m* 13 Sept 1985, Margaret Pauline, da of William Kennefick, of Cloyne, Co Cork, Ireland; *Career* art dealer Lane Fine Art 1974-; memb: BADA, LAPADA; *Recreations* yachting, golf; *Clubs* East Cork Golf; *Style*— Alan Nelson, Esq; 13 Halkin Mews, Belgravia, London SW1; Loughane, County Cork, Rep of Ireland; 123 New Bond St, London W1 (☎ 071 499 5020, fax 071 495 2496)

NELSON, Lt-Col Andrew Sclanders; TD, JP (Kirkcudbrightshire 1966), DL (Wigtown 1982); s of R F W R Nelson, of Bothwell, Lanarks; *b* 1915; *Educ* Glenalmond; *m* 1940, Diana Dorothy Nicholson, of Eyamdale House, Eyamdale, Derbys; 1 s, 2 da; *Career* WWII (despatches twice), ret as Lt-Col; JP Lanarks 1952, DL Lanarks 1960; AMIMechE; *Style*— Lt-Col Andrew Nelson, TD, JP, DL; Auchinleck Lodge, Minnigaff, Newton Stewart, Wigtownshire DG8 7AA (☎ 0671 2851)

NELSON, (Richard) Anthony; MP (C) Chichester Oct 1974-; s of Gp Capt R Gordon Nelson; *b* 11 June 1948; *Educ* Harrow, Christ's Coll Cambridge (MA); *m* 1974, Caroline Victoria, da of B A Butler; 1 s (Carlton b 1981), 1 da (Charlotte-Anne b 1979); *Career* contested (C) E Leeds Feb 1974; memb Select Ctees: Sci and Technol 1975-79, Televising Proceedings of the House 1988-; PPS: Min for Housing and Construction 1979-83, Min for Armed Forces 1983-; dir Chichester Festival Theatre 1962-; FRSA; *Recreations* music, rugby; *Style*— Anthony Nelson, Esq, MP; House of Commons, London SW1

NELSON, Cathleen, Lady; (Annie) Cathleen Elizabeth; da of Lt-Col Loftus Bryan, DL; *m* 1923, as his 2 w, Sir James Hope Nelson, 2 Bt (d 1960); *Style*— Cathleen, Lady Nelson

NELSON, David George Hargraves; OBE (1984); s of Sir Amos Nelson (d 1947), of Gledstone Hall, Skipton-in-Craven, Yorks, and Harriet, *née* Hargraves; *b* 13 June 1933; *Educ* Harrow, Ch Ch Oxford (MA); *m* 27 Feb 1965, Armorel Brandreth, da of Brig Basil Hildebrand Ryves-Hopkins (d 1959); 1 s (James b 1971), 2 da (Lucinda b 1966, Victoria b 1968); *Career* Nat Serv Kings Dragoon Gds 1951-53; dir: Amos Nelson 1958-, James Nelson 1959-63, David Nelson 1968-, Skipton Building Soc 1970-74; chm: Skipton Cons Assoc 1970-77, Skipton and Ripon Cons Assoc 1983-88; chm cncl Order of St John N Yorks; *Recreations* shooting; *Clubs* Lansdowne; *Style*— David Nelson, Esq, OBE; Old Gledstone, Nr Skipton, N Yorks BD23 3JR; Les Vouguets, 26160 Pont-de-Barret, France

NELSON, Edward Holgate; s of James Nelson (d 1957), and Elsie, *née* Holgate (d 1960); *b* 26 Jan 1934; *Educ* Stowe; *m* 30 April 1957, Jean Elizabeth, da of Leonard Brown, of Heights House, Salterforth, Lancashire; 3 s (Mark b 1959, Simon b 1963, Matthew b 1968), 1 da (Sarah b 1966); *Career* Nat Serv RASC 1952-54; dir: Hartley Nelson and Co Ltd 1978-, E Gomme Ltd 1978-86, Clover Mill Ltd 1978-89, G Plan Ltd 1978-89, Gomme Holdings Ltd 1986-89, Silas Poker Ltd 1987-89, Polytex Holdings Ltd 1987-; pres N Lancs Furniture Manufacturers 1978-81; Freeman City of London 1987, Liveryman Worshipful Co of Furniture Makers 1987; *Recreations* travel in France, French wines; *Clubs* Sloane; *Style*— Edward Nelson, Esq; Wynstone, Colne, Lancashire BB8 9QW (☎ 0282 863423); La Chassagne, Blanzay, 86400, Civray, France (☎ 010 33 4987 0734)

NELSON, Edward Spencer; s of Amos Christopher Nelson (d 1974), and Mary, *née* Spencer; *b* 10 Sept 1907; *Educ* Canford; *m* 21 Nov 1969, Sanda Elizabeth, da of John H Powell, of Corner Cottage, Coates, nr Cirencester, Glos; 1 s (Amos John b 10 April 1978), 1 da (Daisy Sophia Elizabeth b 13 June 1980); *Career* cmmnd 2 Lt 12 Royal Lancers 1953, Lt Yorks Hussars 1955, Capt Duke of Lancaster's Own Yeo 1956, resigned cmmn 1966; mangr in family firm James Nelson Textiles 1955-62, mgmnt Coutaulds 1962-64, professional racing driver 1964-68 (Springbok Champion 1967-68), sr mgmnt Mirror Group Newspapers 1968-79, dir Fleet Deliveries Ltd 1979-87, exec Pergamon Holdings 1987-; dir Br Racing Drivers Club 1972-; bobsleighed for GB World Championships 1965 and 1966; Freeman City of London 1982, Liveryman Worshipful Co of Weavers 1982; memb Bruderschaft St Christoph Austria; *Recreations* motor racing, shooting, skiing, motorcycling; *Clubs* Cavalry and Guards, City Livery; *Style*— Edward S Nelson, Esq; 104 Tachbrook Street, Pimlico, London SW1; Pergamon Holdings Ltd, 33 Holborn Circus, London EC1 (☎ 071 822 2216)

NELSON, Hon Lady (Elizabeth Ann Bevil); *née* Cary; da of 14 Viscount Falkland; *b* 1927; *m* 1945, Sir William Vernon Hope Nelson, 3 Bt, OBE; *Style*— The Hon Lady Nelson; c/o Barclays Bank, Market St, Crewkerne, Somerset

NELSON, Dr Elizabeth Hawkins; da of Harry Dadmun Nelson (d 1965), of Summit, New Jersey, and Gretchen, *née* Hawkins (d 1984); *b* 27 Jan 1931; *Educ* Hanover HS Hanover New Hampshire USA, Middlebury Coll Vermont USA (BA), Inst of Psychiatry Univ of London (PhD); *m* 1, 1960 (m dis 1972), Ivan Piercy; 2 s (Christopher b 5 March 1963, Nicholas b 3 Aug 1965), 1 da (Catherine b 15 Sept 1961); m 2, 26 July 1975, Claude Jacob Esterson, s of Elias Esterson; *Career* res psychologist Mars Ltd 1953-55, dir and md Res Unit Benton and Bowles Ltd 1957-64 (market res exec 1955-57), fndr dir and chm Taylor Nelson Gp 1965-; chm Addison Consultancy Group plc 1989-, non-exec dir The Royal Bank of Scotland plc 1987-; pres World Assoc of Public Opinion Res, memb Family Practitioners Ctee Open Univ 1986-; Freeman Worshipful Co of Marketors; fell and memb Cncl Royal Soc of Arts, Assoc Memb BPsS (chartered psychologist); *Recreations* bridge, choral singing, opera; *Style*— Dr Elizabeth Nelson; 57 Home Park Rd, Wimbledon, London SW19 (☎ 081

946 2317); Taylor Nelson Group Ltd, Taylor Nelson House, 44-46 Upper High St, Epsom, Surrey KT17 4QS (☎ 03727 29688, fax 03727 44100, car 0860 223690)

NELSON, Hon Henry Roy George; s and h of 2 Baron Nelson of Stafford; *b* 26 Oct 1943; *Educ* Ampleforth, King's Coll Cambridge (MA); *m* 8 June 1968, Dorothy, yr da of Leslie Caley, of Tibthorpe Manor, Driffield, E Yorks; 1 s (Alistair b 1973), 1 da (Sarah Jane b 1981); *Career* joined RHP Bearings 1970; gen mangr: transmission bearings 1973-78, automotive bearings 1978-81: mfrg dir industl bearings 1981-83; md: Hopkinsons Ltd 1983-85, industl and distribution divs Pegler-Hattersley plc 1985-86; gp md GSPK Ltd 1986-; memb Govt Ctee of Enquiry into Engrg Profession 1978-80; FIMechE, MIEE, CEng; *Style—* The Hon Henry Nelson; Ackworth Grove, Pontefract Rd, High Ackworth, nr Pontefract, Yorks WF7 7EE (☎ 0977 704742)

NELSON, Ian Digby; s of Theodore Nelson Nelson (d 1959), of Cleevelands, Cheltenham, Glos, and Hannah Willis (d 1966); *b* 9 June 1926; *Educ* Edward VI GS Morpeth, Univ of London, Univ of Loughborough (BSc, DLC); *m* 12 Aug 1949, Eileen Nellie, da of Frederick James Caldwell (d 1965), of Outwoods Drive, Loughborough; 3 s (Richard b 1950, John b 1953, Andrew b 1955); *Career* Lt Royal Engrs 1945-48; dir: Engrg Rolls-Royce Motors (dir Resources and Special Projects 1 gen works mangr 1971-76, Personnel and Admin 1967-71), Plan Investment Group plc 1984, Nelson Hind Catering Management 1990; pres Engrg Employers Assoc Cheshire Merseyside N Wales and S Lancs 1978-79; dep chm NW Liaison Ctee of Understanding Br Indust Project 1977-82; MIMechE, CEng; *Recreations* gardening, caravanning; *Style—* Ian Nelson, Esq; 128 Main Rd, Wybunbury, Nantwich, Cheshire CW5 7LR (☎ 0270 841200)

NELSON, Hon James Jonathan; s of 2 Baron Nelson of Stafford; *b* 17 June 1947; *Educ* Ampleforth, McGill Univ Canada (BCom); *m* 18 Nov 1977, Lucilla Mary, da of Roger Gopsill Brown, of Albrighton, Shropshire; 3 da (Camilla Amy b 1982, Lara Kitty b 1986, Eloise Violet b 1988); *Career* commercial banking offr Morgan Guaranty Tst Co of New York 1969-73, dir Foreign & Colonial Management Ltd 1974-, md Foreign & Colonial Ventures Ltd 1985-; Freeman of City of London 1986, Liveryman Worshipful Co of Goldsmiths 1989; *Recreations* golf, tennis, skiing, shooting, fishing; *Clubs* Queen's, Hurlingham, New Zealand; *Style—* The Hon James Nelson; 61 Fentiman Rd, London SW8; 8 Floor, Exchange House, Primrose St, London EC2A 2NY (☎ 071 782 9829, fax 071 782 9834)

NELSON, Jamie Charles Vernon Hope; s and h of Sir William Vernon Hope Nelson, 3 Bt, OBE; *b* 23 Oct 1949; *m* 25 June 1983, Maralyn Pyatt Hedge; 1 s (Liam Chester b 1982); *Career* forester, teacher; *Style—* Jamie Nelson, Esq; 39 Montacute Road, Tintinhull, Yeovil, Somerset BA22 8QD

NELSON, Lady (Margaret) Jane; *née* FitzRoy; er da of William Henry Alfred FitzRoy, Viscount Ipswich (ka 1918), and sis of 9 Duke of Grafton (d 1936); raised to rank and precedence of a Duke's da 1931; *b* 1916; *m* 1936, Maj-Gen Sir (Eustace) John Blois Nelson, KCVO, CB, DSO, OBE, MC, *qv*; 2 da; *Style—* The Lady Jane Nelson; Tigh Bhaan, Appin, Argyll, Scotland (☎ 063 173)

NELSON, Hon Mrs (Joanna); *née* Quinton; da of Baron Quinton (Life Peer), and Marcelle, *née* Wegier; *b* 1955; *m* 1, 1974 (m dis 1981), Francis Joseph Fitzherbert-Brockholes; m 2, 1981, Jonathan Nelson, of New York, NY, USA; issue; *Style—* The Hon Mrs Nelson

NELSON, Maj-Gen Sir (Eustace) John Blois; KCVO (1965, MVO 1953), CB (1964), DSO (1944), OBE (1948), MC (1943); s of Roland Hugh Nelson (d 1940), and Hylda Blois, da of Sir John Blois, Bt (d 1955); *b* 15 June 1912; *Educ* Eton, Trinity Coll Cambridge (MA); *m* 1936, Lady (Margaret) Jane, *qv*; 2 da (yr da Juliet m 1960 Sir Montague Cholmeley, Bt, *qv*); *Career* cmmnd Grenadier Gds 1933, WWII served in France, N Africa, Italy (wounded 3 times, despatches) cmd 3 Bn Grenadier Gds 1944-45 served Italy, 1 Gds Parachute Bn 1946-48 served Palastine, 1 Bn Grenadier Gds 1951-53 served N Africa, IDC 1958, Brig cmdg 4 Gds Bde Gp 1959-61, GOC London Dist and Maj-Gen cmdg Household Bde 1962-65, GOC Berlin (Br Sector) 1966-68, ret; chm Christian Youth Challenge Tst; pres Trident Project; Silver Star (USA) 1944; *Recreations* sailing, fishing; *Style—* Maj-Gen Sir John Nelson, KCVO, CB, DSO, OBE, MC; Tigh Bhaan, Appin, Argyll, Scotland (☎ 063 173252)

NELSON, John Graeme; s of Charles Nelson (d 1985), and Jean, *née* Blackstock; *b* 19 June 1947; *Educ* Aylesbury GS, Slough GS, Univ of Manchester (BA); *m* 19 June 1971, Pauline Viola, da of Stanley Arthur Dickinson, of Hayes, Bromley, Kent; 2 s (Andrew b 1973, Ian b 1976), 1 da (Clare b 1979); *Career* BR: management trainee Western Region 1968-71, asst station mangr Liverpool St 1971-73, area passenger mangr Shenfield 1973-77, passenger sales offr Leeds 1977-79, passenger mangr Sheffield Div 1979-81, PA to Chief Exec BRB 1981-82, parcels mangr Southern Region 1982-84, nat business mangr Red Star Parcels 1984-87, gen mangr Eastern Region 1987-; memb Yorkshire & Humberside CBI Regnl Cncl; *Recreations* piano, football, badminton, rugby league; *Clubs* Yorkshire; *Style—* John Nelson, Esq; British Railways, Eastern Region, Main Headquarters, York YO1 1HT (☎ 653022 ext 2200, fax 653022, 3392)

NELSON, Hon Mrs John; Kathleen Mary; *née* Burr; *m* 1941, Capt Hon John Marie Joseph Horatio Nelson (d 1970); 2 s, 1 da; *Style—* The Hon Mrs John Nelson; 306 Chartleigh House, Beach Rd, Sea Point, Cape Town 8001, SA

NELSON, Michael Edward; s of Thomas Alfred Nelson (d 1977); *b* 30 April 1929; *Educ* Latymer Upper Sch, Magdalen Coll Oxford; *m* 1960, Helga Johanna, da of Pieter Den Ouden (d 1942); 2 s (Patrick, Paul), 1 da (Shivaun); *Career* journalist; jt mangr Reuters Economic Services 1960-62 (mangr 1962-75), dep md and gen mangr Reuters Ltd 1981-89 (asst gen mangr 1967-73, jt dep md and gen mangr 1976-81); chm Visnews Ltd 1985-89; chm tstees Reuters Fndn 1984-90; *Clubs* Garrick; *Style—* Michael Nelson, Esq; 44 Phillimore Gardens, London W8 7QG (☎ 071 937 1626)

NELSON, Paul Maurice; s of Aubrey Nelson, of Putney, London, and Myrtle, *née* Herman; *b* 22 Aug 1956; *Educ* Latymer Upper Sch, CCC Cambridge (BA, MA); *m* 1 May 1983, Dora Jennifer, da of Max Lawson; *Career* ptnr Linklaters & Paines 1987 (articled clerk 1979-81, asst slr 1981-87; memb Law Soc 1981; *Recreations* reading, TV, law, cinema; *Style—* Paul Nelson, Esq; Barrington House, 59-67 Gresham St, London EVC2 (☎ 071 606 7080)

NELSON, Dr Peter Gerald; s of Maurice Gerald Nelson, of Rosefield, Ballylesson, Nr Belfast, and Gladys Hazel, *née* Abraham; *b* 28 Feb 1943; *Educ* Royal Belfast Academical Instn, Queen's Univ Belfast (MB BCh, BAO); *m* 6 July 1962, Valerie Frances Deirdre, da of Colin Alan Gleadhill; 1 da (Juliet b 23 Oct 1962); *Career* res fell in diabetes mellitus Kings Coll Hosp 1973-75, conslt in accident and emergency med Royal Victoria Hosp Belfast 1975-; memb: Casualty Surgns Assoc, Br Diabetic Assoc; FRCP 1984; *Books* Accident and Emergency Medicine (jtly, 1989); *Recreations* sailing, golf, travel; *Clubs* Royal Belfast Golf, Strangford Lough Yacht; *Style—* Dr Peter Nelson; Royal Victoria Hospital, Accident and Emergency Dept, Grosvenor Rd, Belfast BT12 6BA (☎ 0232 240503 ext 2090)

NELSON, 9 Earl (UK 1805); Peter John Horatio Nelson; also Baron Nelson of the Nile and of Hilborough (UK 1801) and Viscount Merton of Trafalgar and of Merton (UK 1805); s of Capt Hon John Nelson, RA (5 s of 5 Earl and yr bro of 6, 7 and 8 Earls); Lord Nelson (suc uncle, 8 Earl, Sept 1981) is fifth in descent from the 2 Earl; The 2 Earl's mother Susannah was sister to the 1 Earl and his yr bro, the celebrated naval hero; Horatio Nelson's Barony of Nelson (GB) and Viscountcy of Nelson (UK) were extinguished with him, but his Barony of Nelson of the Nile & of Hilborough have descended to the present Peer along with his er bro's Earldom and Viscountcy (the two last titles being created, like the aforesaid Barony, with special remainder to ensure the survival of dignities honouring one of Britain's greatest sons); The Admiral's Dukedom of Brontë, however, passed, through the marriage of the 1 Earl's da Charlotte with the 2 Baron Bridport, to the Viscounts Bridport, *qv*; *b* 9 Oct 1941; *Educ* St Joseph's Coll Ipswich, Nat Inst of Agric Lincs; *m* 1969, Maureen Diana, da of Edward Patrick Quinn, of Kilkenny; 1 s (and 1 s, Peter Francis Horatio, b and d 1970), 1 da (Lady Deborah b 1974); *Heir* s, Viscount Merton, *qv*; *Career* pres: Royal Naval Commando Assoc, Nelson Soc; vice-pres Jubilee Sailing Tst; hon life memb: Royal Naval Assoc, Royal Naval Museum; pres Int Fingerprint Soc; chm Retainacar Ltd; non-exec dir: British Navy Pursers Rum Ltd, Reinhold Estates Ltd; *Clubs* St James's; *Style—* The Rt Hon the Earl Nelson; House of Lords, London SW1A 0PW

NELSON, Air Marshal Sir (Sidney) Richard Carlyle; KCB (1963, CB 1962), OBE (1949); s of M O Nelson, of Smithville, Ontario, Canada, and Jane Amelia, *née* Cartwright (d 1970); *b* 14 Nov 1907; *Educ* Univ of Alberta Canada (MD), Graduate RAF Staff Coll; *m* 1939, Christina Elizabeth, da of W S Powell, of London; 2 s (Richard, Peter); *Career* joined RAF 1935, served WWII, Gp Capt 1953, Air Cdre 1957, PMO Tech Trg Cmd 1957-59, Air Vice-Marshal 1959, PMO Bomber Cmd 1959-62, QHP 1961-67, Air Marshal 1962, dir-gen RAF Med Servs 1962-67, ret; dir of res and med servs Aspro-Nicholas 1967-72; *Recreations* fishing, golf; *Clubs* Royal Lymington Yacht, RAF; *Style—* Air Marshal Sir Richard Nelson, KCB, OBE; Caffyn's Copse, Shappen Hill Lane, Burley, Ringwood, Hants BH24 4EP

NELSON, Richard William; s of Cyril Aubrey Nelson (d 1971), and Gillian Mary, *née* Nelson; *b* 14 June 1950; *Educ* Nottingham HS, Univ of Bristol (LLB); *m* 29 April 1978, Elizabeth Mary, da of Percy Graham Cope, of Burton Joyce, Nottingham; 1 s (William Henry b 1987), 1 da (Charlotte Louis b 11 March 1990); *Career* slr; J & A Bright Richards & Flewitt 1977-80, ptnr Freeth Cartwright & Sketchley 1980-83, sr ptnr Nelson Johnson & Hastings 1983-; chm: Stanmarsh Ltd, Homeland Videos Ltd; dir: Denmoors Ltd, Media Music Productions Ltd; vice chm and cncl memb Nottingham Hospice, memb Ctee: Old Nottinghamians Soc, Nottingham Law Soc Criminal Ctee, former capt Old Notts CC; *Recreations* sport, rugby union, cricket, fishing, cinema, comedy; *Style—* Richard Nelson, Esq; 165 Harrow Rd, Wollaton Park, Nottingham (☎ 0602 287 140); Pennine House, 8 Stanford Street, Nottingham NG1 7BQ (☎ 0602 586262, fax 0602 584702)

NELSON, Robert Franklyn; QC (1985); s of Clarence William Nelson, of North Rigton, Harrogate, Yorks, and Lucie Margaret, *née* Kirkby; *b* 19 Sept 1942; *Educ* Repton, St Johns Coll Cambridge (BA, MA); *m* 14 Sept 1968, Anne-Marie Sabina, da of Francis William George Hall, of Bellingham House, Hook Green, Wilmington, Kent; 2 s (Joshua b 1970, Bartholomew b 1973); *Career* called to the Bar Middle Temple 1965, rec 1986-; *Recreations* opera, cricket, golf; *Style—* Robert Nelson, Esq, QC; Fairseat Manor, Fairseat, nr Wrotham, Kent; 1 Paper Buildings, Temple, London EC4

NELSON, Vincent Leonard; s of Simeon Augustus Nelson, of Mandeville, Jamaica, and Leah Rebecca, *née* Wright; *b* 12 Jan 1958; *Educ* Fairfax Sch Yorks, Univ of Birmingham (LLB); *m* 17 Sept 1988, Ina Frances Nelson, da of John Frances Easton, of The Old Hall, Barley, Herts; *Career* called to the Bar Inner Temple 1980, legal advsr Thames TV International 1982-83, Channel 4 1983-84, head of business affrs HTV 1984-89, chm HEL Ltd 1989-; memb Hon Soc Inner Temple; *Recreations* collector of modern British paintings 1900-58; *Style—* Vincent Nelson, Esq; 6 Fawnbrake Ave, London SE24 OBY (☎ 071 274 3424); 262A Fulham Rd, London SW10 9EL

NELSON, Maj Sir William Vernon Hope; 3 Bt (UK 1912), of Acton Park, Acton, of Denbigh, OBE (Mil 1952); s of William Hope Nelson (d 1953), and nephew of 2 Bt (d 1960); *b* 25 May 1914; *Educ* Beaumont, RMA Sandhurst; *m* 21 Nov 1945, Hon Elizabeth Ann Bevil Cary, da of 14 Viscount Falkland (d 1984); 3 s, 3 da; *Heir* s, Jamie Charles Vernon Hope Nelson; *Career* 2 Lt 8 Hussars 1934, Palestine 1936-39 (despatches, medal with clasp), Korea 1950-51; *Style—* Maj Sir William Nelson, Bt, OBE; c/o National Westminster Bank, Market St, Crewkerne, Somerset

NELSON, Winifred, Countess; Winifred Mary; da of G Bevan, of Swansea; *m* 1945, 8 Earl Nelson (d 1981); 1 da (Lady Sarah Roberts, *qv*); *Style—* The Rt Hon Winifred, Countess Nelson; 9 Pwlldu Rd, Bishopston, Swansea SA3 3HA (☎ 044 128 2682)

NELSON-JONES, John Austen; s of Dr Archibald Nelson-Jones, of Putney, and Constance Vera, *née* Riley; *b* 26 July 1934; *Educ* Repton, Trinity Coll Oxford; *m* 31 Aug 1963, Helene, da of John George William Wood (d 1976); 2 s (Michael, Martin); *Career* Nat Serv 2 Lt 1 Regt RHA 1954-55; admitted slr 1963, ptnr Field Fisher and Martineau 1968-89, currently business devpt ptnr Field Fisher Waterhouse; memb Cncl: Nat Consumer Cncl 1987- (chm Legal Advsy Panel), City Technol Tst 1987-; memb Bd Job Ownership Ltd 1986-, res sec Bow Group 1968 and 1969, taxation ed Law Soc Gazette 1972-80; memb: Law Soc 1963, Int Bar Assoc 1982 (chm Travel and Tourism Law Ctee 1987-); *Books* Nelson-Jones Practical Tax Saving (3 edn, 1976), Package Holiday Law and Contracts (2 edn, 1989), Employee Ownership (1987), contrib numerous articles to professional jls; *Recreations* tennis, music, reading; *Clubs* Hurlingham; *Style—* John Nelson-Jones, Esq; Field Fisher Waterhouse, 41 Vine St, London EC3N 2AA (☎ 071 481 4841, fax 071 488 0084, telex 262613 ADIDEM G)

NELSON-JONES, Rodney Michael; s of Dr Archibald Nelson-Jones, of Putney, London, and Constance Vera, *née* Riley; *b* 11 Feb 1947; *Educ* Repton, Hertford Coll Oxford (MA); *m* 21 Sept 1988, Kusum, da of Babulal Keshavji, of Derby; *Career* admitted slr 1975; Prothero & Prothero 1973-77, L Bingham & Co 1977-83, ptnr Field Fisher Waterhouse (formerly Martineau) 1983-; *Books* Product Liability: The New Law Under The Consumer Protection Act 198 (1987), Nelson-Jones and Nuttall's Tax and Interest Tables (1988/89/90), Medical Negligence Case Law (1990); *Recreations* cinema, music, tennis, travel; *Clubs* Campden Hill LTC, RAC; *Style—* Rodney Nelson-Jones, Esq; 69 Warrington Crescent, London W9 1EH (☎ 071 289 2243); Field Fisher Waterhouse, 41 Vine St, London EC3N 2AA (☎ 071 481 4841)

NELSON OF STAFFORD, 2 Baron (UK 1960); Sir Henry George Nelson; 2 Bt (UK 1955); s of 1 Baron Nelson of Stafford (d 1962), sometime chm English Electric Co; *b* 2 Jan 1917; *Educ* Oundle, King's Coll Cambridge (MA); *m* 1940, Pamela Roy, da of Ernest Roy Bird, MP (d 1933); 2 s, 2 da; *Heir* s, Hon Henry Roy George Nelson; *Career* chllr Aston Univ Birmingham 1966-79, lord high steward Borough of Stafford 1966-71, dir English Electric Co Ltd 1943 (dep md 1949, md 1956, chm 1962-66) chm The Gen Electric Co plc 1966-83 (dir until 1987); jt dep chm Br Aircraft Corporation 1960-77, chm Royal Worcester plc 1978-83; dir: Bank of England 1961-87, International Nickel Co of Canada 1964-88, Enserch Corporation USA 1984-89, London Bd of Advice Nat Bank of Australasia 1950-81; pres: Soc of Br Aircraft Constructors 1961-62, Beama 1966-67, Orgalime 1968-80, Inst of Electrical Engrs 1970-71; chm: Def Industries Cncl 1971-77, Br Nat Ctee World Energy Conf 1971-74; pres Sino-Br Trade Cncl 1973-83; memb House of Lords Select Ctee on Science and Technol; Freeman City of London, Prime Warden Worshipful Co of Goldsmiths 1983-84; Benjamin Franklin medal RSA 1959; FEng, FICE, Hon FIMechE, Hon FIEE, FRAeS;

Clubs Carlton; *Style—* The Rt Hon the Lord Nelson of Stafford; Wincote Farm, Eccleshall, Stafford; 244 Cranmer Court, Whiteheads Grove, London SW3

NELSON-ROBERTS, Lady Sarah Josephine Mary; *née* Nelson; da of 8 Earl Nelson (d 1981); *b* 7 Jan 1947; *m* 1978, Dr John Clive Roberts; *Style—* The Lady Sarah Nelson-Roberts; Oak End, Chalfont Park, Gerrards Cross, Bucks (☎ 0753 882880)

NELSON-SMITH, David Austin; s of Adrian Nelson-Smith (d 1978); *b* 6 April 1936; *Educ* Brighton Coll, CCC Cambridge; *m* 1965, Joyce Yvonne, *née* Naef; 1 s (Mark b 1966), 1 da (Nicola b 1968); *Career* chm and md Tradax England Ltd 1978-83, dir Cargill UK Ltd 1983-; pres Grain and Feedstuffs Trade Assoc 1985-86; pres Comité du Commerce des Cereales et des Aliments du Béta la CEE 1987-88; *Style—* David Nelson-Smith, Esq; Cargill UK Ltd, 3 Shortlands, London W6 8RT

NELTHORPE, Lt-Col Roger Sutton; MBE (1945), TD (1949, and 3 clasps), JP (1947), DL (1950); s of late Col Oliver Sutton Nelthorpe; *b* 5 March 1918; *Educ* Eton, RAC Cirencester; *Career* Lt-Col TA 1959; landowner and farmer; *Recreations* shooting, forestry, agric; *Style—* Lt-Col Roger Nelthorpe, MBE, TD, JP, DL; Scawby Hall, Scawby Brigg, S Humberside, DN20 9LX (☎ 0652 54205); Estate Office, Scawby, Brigg, S Humberside DN20 9AE (☎ 0652 54272)

NEOPTOLEMOS, John Phitoyiannis; *b* 30 June 1951; *Educ* Owen's GS N London, Churchill Coll Cambridge, Guy's Hosp London (MA, MB BChir), Univ of Leicester (MD); *m* 2 Feb 1974, Linda Joan, da of Richard Blaylock, of Kenton, Newcastle-upon-Tyne; 1 s (Ptolemy b 11 Aug 1978), 1 da (Eleni b 12 May 1981); *Career* Guys Hosp London 1976-77, Leicester Royal Infirmary 1978-84 and 1986-87, UCSD San Diego California 1984-85, reader Univ Dept of Surgery and conslt surgn Dudley Rd Hosp 1987-, Hunterian prof of surgery RCS 1987-88; Rodney Smith prize 1987, Moynihan travelling fell Assoc of Surgns of GB and I 1988, RSM travelling prof 1989; significant scientific contribs to aetiology, diagnosis and treatment of gastrointestinal disease especially relating to the pancreas, bilary tree and colorectum; memb Ctee: Pancreatic Soc of GB and I 1987-, Pancreatic Section Br Soc of Gastroenterology 1988-; memb Working Party: on Liver Metastases UK Coordinating Ctee on Cancer Res 1990, on Colorectol Cancer MRC 1990-; FRCS; *Recreations* squash; *Clubs* Edgbaston Priory (Birmingham); *Style—* John Neoptolemos, Esq; 68 Sir Harry's Rd, Edgbaston, Birmingham B15 2UX (☎ 021 440 2530); University Department of Surgery, Dudley Rd Hospital, Birmingham B18 7QH (☎ 021 554 3801 ext 4594, fax 021 472 1230)

NEPEAN, Lt-Col Sir Evan Yorke; 6 Bt (UK 1802), of Bothenhampton, Dorsetshire; s of Maj Sir Charles Evan Molyneux Yorke Nepean, 5 Bt (d 1953); *b* 23 Nov 1909; *Educ* Winchester, Downing Coll Cambridge (MA); *m* 1940, (Georgiana) Cicely, da of late Maj N E G Willoughby; 3 da; *Heir* none; *Career* served 1932-57 with Royal Corps of Signals, UK, India, Middle East and BAOR, Lt-Col 1943, ret 1957; MIEE, CEng; *Recreations* bell ringing, amateur radio; *Style—* Lt-Col Sir Evan Nepean, Bt; Goldens, Teffont, Salisbury, Wilts SP3 5RP (☎ 0722 716275)

NERINA, Nadia (*née* Nadine Judd); da of Frank Lawrence Judd (d 1958), of Capetown, SA, and Joan Nerine, *née* Goss (d 1944); *b* 21 Oct 1927; *m* 11 Oct 1955, Charles Gordon, s of Sholom Gordon (d 1965); *Career* prima ballerina; joined Sadler's Wells Theatre Ballet Co 1946 (after 2 months at Sadler's Wells Ballet Sch); roles: Polka in Facade, The Girl in Spectre de la Rose, Les Sylphides, Sugar Plum Fairy in Casse Noisette, Khadra, The Girl in Vagabonds; creation: Circus Dancer in Mardi Gres; transferred to Sadler's Well Ballet Royal Opera House (now royal Ballet): ballerina 1951-67, soloist 1967-69; roles: Princess Avrora in Sleeping Beauty, Ondine, Odette-Odile in Swan Lake, Swanhilda in Coppelia, Syliva, Giselle, Cinderella, Firebird, Can Can Dancer in La Boutique, Ballerina in Petrushka, Columbins in Carnaval, Mazurka, Little Waltz, Prelude in Les Sylphides, Mam'zelle Angot, Ballet Imperial, Scene de Ballet, Flower Festival of Genzano, Les Rendevous, The Bride in A Wedding Bouquet; creations: Fairy Spring in Cinderella, Queen of the Earth in Homage to the Queen, Faded Beauty in Noctambules, Variation on a Theme, Birthday Offering, Lise in la Fille Mal Gardee, Electra, The Girl in Home, Clorinda in Tancredi; appeared with Royal Ballet (Europe, SA, USA, Canada, USSR, Bulgaria, Romania); recital tours with Alexis Rassine: SA 1952-55, England 1956 and 1957; concert performances: Royal Albert Hall, Royal Festival Hall (1958 and 1960); guest appearances incl: Turkish Nat Ballet 1957, Bolshoi Ballet 1960, Kirov Ballet 1960, Munich Ballet 1963, Nat Finnish Ballet 1964, Royal Danish Ballet 1964, Stuttgart Ballet 1965, Ballet Theatre Chicago 1967, Royal Command Variety Performances 1963-66; mounted and produced: charity gala performances for RSPCA (London Palladium 1969, 1971, 1972), Anton Dolin Int Gala (Royal Opera House 1984); conslt on ballet Ohio Univ 1967-69, Br Jury Memb 3rd Int Ballet Competition (Moscow 1977), fell Cecchetti Soc 1959 (patron 1964), memb Cncl RSPCA 1969-74; *Books* contrib La Fille Mal Gardée (1960), Ballet and Modern Dance (1974); *Style—* Ms Nadia Nerina; c/o Royal Opera House, Covent Garden, London WC2

NERURKAR, Richard David; s of David Janardan Nerurkar, and Iris Elizabeth, *née* Griffiths; *b* 6 Jan 1964; *Educ* Bradford GS, University Coll Oxford (BA), Harvard Univ (Harkness fell, MA); *Career* teacher Marlborough Coll 1989-; int athlete 1989-: 18th place World Cross-Country Championships 1990 (49th place 1989), 5th place (10,000m) European Athletic Championships 1990; *Style—* Richard Nerurkar, Esq; Marlborough College, Wiltshire SN8 1PA (☎ 0672 515568)

NESBITT, Garry; s of Harry Nesbitt (d 1968), and May Nesbitt; *b* 6 Dec 1942; *Educ* Aida Foster Stage Sch; *m* 28 Aug 1971, Penny, da of E S A Baker; 2 s (Tristan b 1974, Julian b 1989), 2 da (Tania b 1978, Carola b 1981); *Career* fndr Our Price Music Retail Chain 1971, business floated publicly 1984 and acquired by WH Smith 1986; chm: Crockfords Casino, Ragdale Hall Health Hydro Leics; *Recreations* keeping fit, tennis, water skiing, fine wine collecting; *Style—* Garry Nesbitt, Esq

NESBITT, John Sheridan; s of Leslie Haughton Nesbitt (d 1954), and Charlotte Sims (d 1984); *b* 8 Nov 1929; *Educ* William Hulme's GS Manchester, Manchester Univ (LLB); *m* 15 Nov 1958, Elizabeth Anne, da of Arthur Cecil Harker; 3 s (Colin b 1959, Michael b 1961, David b 1963); *Career* called to the Bar Grays Inn 1954; publisher Schofield & Sims Ltd Educnl Publishers (dir 1955, md 1974-81, chm 1981-); *Recreations* angling (flyfishing); *Clubs* Kilnsey Angling; *Style—* John S Nesbitt, Esq; The Old School House, Elslack, Skipton, North Yorkshire (☎ 0282 842476); Schofield & Sims Ltd, Dogley Mill, Fenay Bridge, Huddersfield, W Yorkshire

NESBITT, Hon Mrs (Patricia Catherine); da of 2 Baron Bethell (d 1965); *b* 20 May 1933; *Educ* St Mary's Convent Ascot; *m* 1956, Michael William Nesbitt, DFC, s of Philip Nesbitt (d 1955); 1 s, 2 da; *Style—* The Hon Mrs Nesbitt; Rotherwood, Fittleworth, Pulborough, Sussex

NESBITT, Prof Robert William; s of Thomas Dodgson Nesbitt (d 1977), of Blyth, Northumberland, and Mary Florence Nesbitt (d 1983); *b* 26 Sept 1936; *Educ* Blyth GS, Univ of Durham (BSc, PhD); *m* 24 Oct 1959, Catherine, da of Peter Robertson (d 1976), of Blyth, Northumberland; 3 da (Carolyn Anne b 1960, Joanne Louise b 1964, Jacqueline Clare b 1969); *Career* geologist Greenland Geological Survey 1958-59; Univ of Adelaide Aust: lectr 1962-68, sr lectr 1968-72, reader 1972-80; visiting res fell Univ of Yale 1968, visiting prof Universite de Rennes 1979, dean of sci Univ of Southampton 1987- (prof of geology 1980-); subject advr Univ Funding Cncl; FGSA 1976, FGS 1980; *Recreations* golf, scuba diving; *Style—* Prof Robert Nesbitt; Dept of Geology, University of Southampton, Southampton, Hants SO9 5NH (☎ 0703 592037)

NESS, Lady Brigid Katharine Rachel; *née* Guinness; da of 2 Earl of Iveagh, KG, CB, CMG (d 1967), and Gwendoline, *née* Onslow (d 1966); *b* 20 July 1920; *m* 1, 1945, HRH Prince Frederick von Preussen (d 1966); 3 s, 2 da; m 2, 1967, Maj Anthony Patrick Ness, s of Capt Gordon Stuart Ness, of Braco Castle, Perthshire (ka 1914); *Career* farmer; *Style—* The Lady Brigid Ness; Patmore Hall, Albury, Ware, Herts SG11 2JU

NESS, Air Marshal Sir Charles Ernest; KCB (1980, CB 1978), CBE (1967, OBE 1959); s of Charles Wright Ness (d 1934); *b* 4 April 1924; *Educ* George Heriot's Sch, Univ of Edinburgh; *m* 1951, Audrey Parker; 1 s; *Career* joined RAF 1943, flying and staff appts with Bomber Cmd and USAF; Station Cdr Steamer Pt Aden 1965-67, Air Cdr Gibralter 1971-73, dir orgn and admin plans RAF 1974-75, Cdr S Maritime Air Region 1975-76, dir gen personnel mgmnt (RAF) MOD 1976-80, air memb for personnel 1980-83; Govt relations advsr to ICL 1983-, mil advsr to DESC 1990-, chm Air League 1987-90 (vice pres 1990-); chm: govrs Duke of Kent Sch, RAF Benevolent Fund Educnl Tst 1987-; *Style—* Air Marshal Sir Charles Ness, KCB, CBE; Perseverance Cottage, Wentworth, Nr Ely, Cambs

NESTOR, Capt Martin John Ralph; OBE (1985); s of John Martin Nestor (d 1985), of Huddersfield, Yorks, and Gladys, *née* Earnshaw (d 1985); *b* 29 Jan 1940; *Educ* Royds Hall GS Huddersfield; *m* 28 Dec 1963, Jacqueline, da of Frederick James Collier, of Golcar, Yorks; 3 da (Clare b 19 Aug 1966, Julia b 30 March 1968, Sarah b 27 Feb 1974); *Career* joined RN 1967: nuclear trg and submarine serv 1967-70, HMS Norfolk 1971-73, RN air station Yeovilton 1973-75, exchange offr USN 1976-78, HMS Hermes 1978-80, RN Staff Coll 1980, Cdr 1980, HMS Collingwood 1980-81, special appt MOD London (Falklands' War) 1982, HMS Invincible 1982-84, MOD London 1984-88, Capt 1986, NATO Def Coll Rome 1988-89; NCB 1958-59, ICI 1963-67; memb (later treas) North Curry PCC 1985-88; ARIC 1965; *Recreations* tennis, gardening; *Clubs* Army and Navy; *Style—* Capt Martin Nestor, OBE, RN; International Military Staff, NATO NQ, 1110 Brussels, Belgium (☎ 010 322 728 5505, fax 010 322 728 4117)

NETHERTHORPE, Belinda, Baroness; Belinda; o da of late Frederick Hedley Nicholson, of Friars Gate, Firbeck, Worksop, Notts; *m* 1960, 2 Baron Netherthorpe (d 1982); 2 s, 2 da; *Style—* The Rt Hon Belinda, Lady Netherthorpe; Boothby Hall, Boothby Pagnell, Grantham, Lincs (☎ 047685 374)

NETHERTHORPE, 3 Baron (UK 1959); James Frederick Turner; s of 2 Baron Netherthorpe (d 1982); *b* 7 Jan 1964; *Educ* Harrow; *m* 10 Dec 1989, Elizabeth Curran, da of Edward William Fahan, of Redding, Connecticut, USA; *Heir* yr bro, Hon Patrick Andrew Turner b 4 June 1971; *Style—* The Rt Hon the Lord Netherthorpe; Boothby Hall, Boothby Pagnell, Grantham, Lincs (☎ 047685 374)

NETHERTHORPE, Margaret, Baroness; Margaret Lucy; *née* Mattock; da of James Arthur Mattock, of Sheffield; *b* 13 July 1916; *Educ* Hunmanby Hall, Scarborough; *m* 3 Oct 1935, 1 Baron Netherthorpe (d 1980); 4 s; *Recreations* gardening, travel; *Style—* The Rt Hon Margaret, Lady Netherthorpe; The Garden House, Monken Hadley, Hertfordshire EN5 5QF

NETHERTON, Derek Nigel Donald; s of John Gordon Netherton, of London, and Beryl Agnes, *née* Freeman; *b* 4 Jan 1945; *Educ* Charterhouse, Kings Coll Cambridge (MA); *m* 8 May 1976, Pamela Jane, da of Col W Rollo Corkill, of Banstead, Surrey; 4 s (Charles b 1981, George b 1984, Patrick b 1987, David (twin) b 1987); *Career* dir Schroder Wagg 1981-; FIA; *Style—* Derek Netherton, Esq; c/o J Henry Schroder Wagg & Co Ltd, 120 Cheapside, London EC2V 6DS (☎ 071 382 6000)

NETHERWOOD, John; s of Willie Netherwood, of Huddersfield, and Florence, *née* Girling; *b* 5 Nov 1944; *Educ* Rawthorpe Sch Huddersfield; *m* 19 Feb 1967, Anita Margaret, da of Raymond Jessop (d 1987); 2 da (Jane Alison b 1969, Joanne Helen b 1970); *Career* chm: United Forktrucks Ltd 1975-, B V (UK) Ltd 1972-; exec dir Allied Partnership Gp plc 1985-; *Recreations* flying, sailing; *Style—* John Netherwood, Esq; Briarwood, Parker Lane, Mirfield, West Yorkshire (☎ 0924 496094); United Forktrucks Limited, Huddersfield Road, Mirfield (☎ 0924 496831, telex 556676, fax 0924 497912

NETTLE, David Richard; s of Gerald Nettle, of Redruth, and Viola, *née* Tregenza; *b* 10 June 1956; *Educ* Redruth GS, RCM London; *Career* concert pianist; worldwide appearances with Richard Markham as Nettle-Markham Piano Duo: North American debut 1979, London debut (Wigmore Hall) 1982, Far East tour 1983, Middle East tours 1983 and 1985, frequent performances at princ Euro festivals incl BBC Proms; recordings incl: The Rite of Spring and Petrushka by Stravinsky (1984), The Planets by Holst (1985), The Blacksmiths by Dyson (1987), Delius and Grainger Folksongs (1988), Scenes from West Side Story by Bernstein (arranged by Nettle and Markham), Fantasy on Porgy and Bess by Gershwin (arranged by Grainger), Four Piece Suite by Bennett (1988), Petite Messe Solennelle by Rossini (1990), Carnival of the Animals by Saint-Saens (1991); awarded: Norris prize 1977, Music Retailers' Assoc award for best chamber music record 1985; *Recreations* tennis, chess, photography, languages, writing, naturism; *Style—* David Nettle, Esq; The Old Power House, Atherton St, London SW11 2JE (☎ 071 738 9427)

NEUBERG, Roger Wolfe; s of Klaus Neuberg, of London, and Herta, *née* Hausler (d 1986); *b* 24 May 1941; *Educ* Hendon Co GS, Middx Hosp Med Sch (MB BS); *m* 16 Aug 1964, Ruth Denise, da of Manning Ephron (d 1984), of Bournemouth; 2 s (Guy b 1966, Kim b 1967); *Career* conslt obstetrician and gynaecologist; registrar Middlesex Hosp and Hosp for Women; sr registrar: John Radcliffe Hosp, Oxford and Royal Berkshire Hosp; conslt and dir of infertility servs Leicester Royal Infirmary; memb LRCP 1965; MRCS 1965, FRCOG 1983; *Books* So you want to have a Baby (1985); *Recreations* aikido, old time music hall, gardening; *Style—* Roger Neuberg, Esq; 9 Barrington Rd, Stoneygate, Leicester LE2 2RA (☎ 0533 553933); Maternity Dept, Leicester Royal Infirmary, Leicester (☎ 0533 541414)

NEUBERGER, Prof Albert; CBE; s of Max Neuberger (d 1931), of Hassfurt, Bavaria, and Bertha, *née* Hiller (d 1973); *b* 15 April 1908; *Educ* Gymnasium Würzburg, Univ of Würzburg (MD), Univ of London (PhD); *m* 1943, Lilian Ida, da of Edmond Dreyfus; 4 s (David Edmond b 19 Jan 1948, James Max b 4 Nov 1949, Anthony John b 30 Nov 1951, Michael Samuel b 2 Nov 1953), 1 da (Janet b 27 Aug 1957, d 1985); *Career* advsr (Brig) med directorate GHQ Delhi 1945; Beit Meml res fell 1936-40, researcher Biochemistry Dept Cambridge 1939-42, memb scientific staff MRC 1943, head Biochemistry Dept Nat Inst for Med Res 1950-55, chair of chemical pathology St Mary's Hosp Med Sch 1955-73, princ Wright Fleming Inst of Microbiology 1958-62; chm: Jt ARC/MRC Ctee on Food and Nutrition Res 1971-73, Governing Body Lister Inst of Preventive Med 1971-88, Inter-Res Cncl Ctee on Pollution Res 1975-78; hon pres Br Nutrition Fndn 1982-86; memb: MRC 1962-66, Cncl of Scientific Policy 1968-69, ARC 1969-79, Ind Ctee on Smoking and Health 1973-83, Scientific Advsy Ctee Rank Prize Funds 1982-86; Hon LLD Aberdeen 1967, Hon PhD Jerusalem 1968, Hon DSc Hull 1981; FRS 1951, FRIC 1957, FRCP 1966, for hon memb American Acad of Arts and Scis 1972; Kaplun Prize Israel 1973; *Clubs* Athenaeum; *Style—* Prof Albert Neuberger, CBE, FRS; 37 Eton Court, Eton Ave, London NW3 3HJ (☎ 071 586 5470); Department of Biochemistry, Charing Cross and Westminster Medical School, St Dunstan's Rd, London W6 8RP (☎ 081 741 4032, 071 846 7031)

NEUBERGER, David Edmond; QC (1987); s of Prof Albert Nevberger, CBE, FRS, and Lillian, *née* Dreyfus; *b* 10 Jan 1948; *Educ* Westminster, Christ Church Oxford; *m* Angela, Brig Peter Holdsworth; 2 s (Nicholas b 1979, Max b 1981), 1 da (Jessica b 1977); *Career* N M Rothschild & Sons 1970-73, called to the Bar Lincoln's Inn 1974, recorder 1990; *Style—* David Neuburger, Esq, QC; Falcon Chambers, Falcon Court, London EC4Y 1AA (☎ 071 353 2484, fax 071 353 1261)

NEUBERGER, Dr James Max; s of Prof Albert Neuberger, CBE, of London, and Lilian Ida, *née* Dreyfus; *b* 4 Nov 1949; *Educ* Westminster, ChCh Oxford (MA, BM, BCh, DM); *m* 14 Sept 1979, Belinda Patricia, da of Patrick Joseph Keogh, of Manchester; 2 s (Oliver b 1980, Edmund b 1984), 2 da (Francesca b 1982, Octavia b 1988); *Career* sr lectr in med King's Coll Hosp London 1980-86, conslt physician 1986-; MRCP 1977; *Books* Liver Annual (1988); *Recreations* fishing, gardening, reading; *Style—* Dr James Neuberger; The Moat House, Radford Rd, Alvechurch, Worcs B48 7ST (☎ 021 445 1773); Queen Elizabeth Hosp, Edgbaston, Birmingham B15 2TH (☎ 021 472 1311)

NEUBERGER, Rabbi Julia Babette Sarah; da of Walter Manfred Schwab, of 61 Antrim Mansions, Antrim Rd, London NW3, and Alice, *née* Rosenthal; *b* 27 Feb 1950; *Educ* S Hampstead HS for Girls, Newnham Coll Cambridge, Leo Baeck Coll London; *m* 17 Sept 1973, Anthony John Neuberger, s of Prof Albert Neuberger, CBE, of 37 Eton Court, Eton Ave, London NW3; 1 s (Matthew b 2 July 1981), 1 da (Harriet b 16 June 1979); *Career* rabbi S London Liberal Synagogue 1977-89, visiting fell King's Fund Inst 1989-; tstee Citizenship Fndn; memb Cncl: St George's House Windsor, St George's Hosp Med Sch, N London Hospice Gp; chair Patients Assoc, govr Br Inst Human rights; *Books* The Story of Judaism (for children) (1986), Caring for Dying People of Different Faiths (1987), Days of Decision (ed, 1987); *Clubs* Groucho; *Style—* Rabbi Julia Neuberger; King's Fund Institute, 126 Albert St, London NW1 (☎ 071 485 9589)

NEUBERT, Sir Michael Jon; MP (C) Romford 1983-; s of Frederick Neubert; *b* 3 Sept 1933; *Educ* Queen Elizabeth's Sch Barnet, Bromley GS, RCM, Downing Coll Cambridge; *m* 1959, Sally Felicity Bilger; 1 s; *Career* industl and travel conslt; Parly candidate (C): Hammersmith N 1966, Romford 1970; ldr Bromley Cncl 1967-70, Mayor 1972-73; chm Bromley Cons Assoc 1968-69, MP (C) Romford Havering Feb 1974-83; PPS to: Min Social Security and Disabled 1980, Mins of State NI Office 1981, Min State Employment 1981-82, Lord Cockfield as Trade Sec 1982-83; asst govt whip 1983-86, govt whip and Lord Cmmr of the Treasy 1986-88; vice-chamberlain of the Royal Household 1988; under-sec of state: for the Armed Forces 1988-89, for Def Procurement 1989-90; kt 1990; *Books* Running your own Society (1967); *Recreations* music, theatre, cinema, literature, script, writing, countryside; *Clubs* Romford Cons and Constitutional; *Style—* Sir Michael Neubert, MP; House of Commons, London SW1A 0AA

NEUFELD, Charles Walter; s of Carl Neufeld, of Graz, Styria; *b* 7 July 1924; *Educ* Austrian Gymnasium, Newbury GS, Univ of Reading; *m* 1947, Dolores René, da of Luke Marcus François (d 1964), of Durban; 4 children; *Career* chm Newfeld Gp: Newfeld Ltd, C W Neufeld Ltd, Bendy Toys Ltd, Conallcrete Products, Ovation Ltd, Guthrie Bendy Ltd, Bendy Int; *Recreations* sport, music; *Style—* Charles Neufeld, Esq; 54 Hans Place, London SW1; Upper Ribsden, Windlesham, Surrey

NEUMANN, Jan; CBE (1984); s of Frantisek Neumann (d 1940); *b* 26 June 1924; *Educ* Friends' Sch Gt Ayton, Univ of London (BSc); *m* 1947, Barbara Joyce, da of Ernest Gove (d 1938); 2 s; *Career* Flt Sgt RAF, Flt Engr Coastal Cmd; CEng; dir: Yard Ltd 1969-1988, Yarrow & Co Ltd 1978-87, Scottish Nuclear Ltd 1989- (non-exec); memb Bd S of Scotland Electricity Bd 1986-88; FEng; *Recreations* swimming, bowling; *Style—* Jan Neumann, Esq, CBE; 38 Norwood Park, Bearsden, Glasgow (☎ 041 942 5371); Scottish Nuclear Ltd, Minto Building, 6 Inverlair Ave, Glasgow G44 4AD (☎ 041 633 1166)

NEVILE, Christopher William Kenneth; s of Kenneth Nevile (d 1960), of Swinderby, Lincoln, and Elizabeth Mary, *née* Brown; *b* 27 April 1957; *Educ* St Hugh's Wood Hall SPA, Rugby, Exeter Univ (LLB); *Career* stockbroker; assoc dir Scrimgeour Vickers until 1987, dir Adams & Nevile Ltd 1987-; *Recreations* shooting, fishing, golf, cricket, squash; *Clubs* Cannons; *Style—* Christopher W K Nevile, Esq; 53 Hambalt Road, London SW4 (☎ 081 675 2628); Adams & Nevile Ltd, Warnford Court, Throgmorton Street, London EC2N 2BD (☎ 071 638 0321)

NEVILL, Amanda Elizabeth; da of John Henry Howard King, of Bardsey, Yorkshire, and Jill, *née* Livett; *b* 21 March 1957; *Educ* Bar Covent York, British Inst France; *m* 3 May 1980 (m dis 1986), Dominic John Nevill, s of John Nevill, of Folkstone, Kent; 2 da (Abigail b 15 July 1982, Cordelia b 19 Oct 1984); *Career* Rowan Gallery London 1978-79, Francis Kyle Gallery London 1979-80, Bath Int Festival Contemporary Art Fair 1980, admin and co fndr The Royal Photographic Soc Bath 1985 (sec 1990-), admin Nat Centre of Photography 1985-90; *Recreations* art, literature, music; *Style—* Mrs Amanda Nevill; The Royal Photographic Society, Milson St, Bath, BA1 1DN (☎ 0225 462841, fax 0225 448688)

NEVILL, Lady Beatrix Mary; da of Lord Lambton; *b* 1949; *m* 1, 7 June 1971, George William Bowdrey, s of Henry George Bowdrey; 1 da (Rose Violet b 17 Nov 1973); m 2, 1982, Guy Rupert Gerard Nevill, er s of Lord Rupert Nevill, CVO, JP, DL (d 1982); *Style—* The Lady Beatrix Nevill; The Garden House, Eridge Park, Tunbridge Wells, Kent; 25 Musgrave Rd, New King's Rd, London SW6

NEVILL, Prof Bernard Richard; s of R G Nevill (d 1941); *b* 24 Sept 1934; *Educ* St Martin's Sch of Art, RCA; *Career* lectr: Shoreditch Coll 1954-56, Central Sch Art and Design 1957-60, St Martin's Sch of Art and RCA 1959-74; freelance illustrator 1956-60 (incl Good Housekeeping, Womans' Journal, Vogue, Harpers Bazaar), freelance journalist 1956-60 (incl Vogue, Sketch), designer then design dir Liberty Prints 1961-71, advsy panel Nat Dip Design 1964-66, art critic Vogue 1965-66, govr Croydon Coll Art 1966-67, designer and design dir Ten Cate Holland 1969-71, design conslt Cantoni Italy 1971-84, prof textile design RCA 1984-89 (fell 1985); commissions and collections incl: Cotton Board Manchester 1950, For Liberty 1961-71, Verve 1960, Cravate, Islamic 1963, Jazz 1964, Tango 1966, Renaissance 1967, Chameleon 1969, Cantoni Casa 1977, Int Wool Secretariat 1975-77, English Country House Collection for Sekers Int 1981-82, Romanex de Boussac France 1982-87; designed costumes for: films (Genevieve 1953, Next to No Time 1955, The Admirable Crichton 1957), musicals (Marigold 1958), opera (Cosi fan tutte Glyndebourne 1960); redesigned Long Gallery, British Embassy Washington 1982; presently restoring interiors of Eastnor Castle, Herefordshire and Fonthill Abbey and Grounds; memb: Victorian Soc, Chelsea Soc; FRSA 1966-77, FSIA 1970-87, FCSD 1987; *Recreations* admiring well-built walls and buildings, passionate conservationist and environmentalist, tree worshipper; *Style—* Prof Bernard Neville; West House, Glebe Place, London SW3 5JP; Fonthill Abbey, nr Salisbury, Wiltshire

NEVILL, Lady Rupert; Lady (Anne) Camilla Eveline; *née* Wallop; da of 9 Earl of Portsmouth (d 1984); *b* 12 July 1925; *Educ* Longstowe Hall; *m* 1944, Lord Rupert Nevill, CVO, JP, DL (d 1982), yr s of 4 Marquess of Abergavenny, sometime private sec to HRH The Duke of Edinburgh ; 2 s (Guy b 1945, page of honour to HM 1958-61; Christopher b 1955), 2 da (Angela b 1948, Henrietta b 1964); *Career* served with WREN in London; pres: Regnl Arts Assoc for Kent Surrey and Sussex (chm 1972-89), E Sussex and W Kent branch of NSPCC; dir Southern Television, former tstee Charities Aid Fndn, memb Reviewing Ctee on Export of Works of Art 1982-86, tstee Glyndebourne Arts Tst, chm Regnl Ctee Kent and E Sussex Nat Tst, vice pres Brighton Festival, tstee Royal Pavilion Brighton; *Style—* The Lady Rupert Nevill; 35 Upper Addison Gardens, London W14 (☎ 071 603 4919/603 4957); Old House Farm, Glynde, Lewes, Sussex (☎ 0273 813706)

NEVILL, Guy Rupert Gerard; er s of Lord Rupert Nevill, CVO, JP, DL (d 1982), by his w Lady Anne, *née* Wallop, da of 9 Earl of Portsmouth; hp to unc, 5 Marquess of Abergavenny; *b* 29 March 1945; *Educ* Eton; *m* 1982, Lady Beatrix Lambton, da of Lord Lambton; *Career* page of honour to HM 1958-61; *Style—* Guy Nevill, Esq; The Garden House, Eridge Park, Tunbridge Wells, Kent; 10c Bramerton St, London SW3; 25 Musgrave Rd, New King's Rd, London SW6

NEVILL, John Robert Ralph Austin; s of Frederick Reginald Nevill (d 1949), of Rosecroft, Newbury, Berks, and Jeanne, *née* Fageol (d 1975); *b* 15 Feb 1928; *Educ* Ampleforth; *m* 30 July 1955, Ann Margaret Mary, da of Archibald Corble (d 1944), of Cookham, Berks; 4 s (Dominic b 1957, Ralph b 1959, Christopher b 1962, Anthony b 1966), 2 da (Cecilia b 1956, Caroline b 1960); *Career* Lt DCLI 1947-48; dir: Nevill Developments 1956-, The Nevill Gallery; formerly: dir Family Housing Assoc Folkestone Area, chm and vice pres Canterbury and E Kent Branch English Speaking Unio chm and pres SE Region English Speaking Union, memb Ctee SE Arts Assoc; memb Ctee Canterbury Arts Cncl; Freeman City of London, Liveryman Worshipful Co of Gardeners; memb Hon Soc of Gray's Inn 1951; Knight of Honour and Devotion Br Assoc Sovereign Mil Order of Malta; *Recreations* travelling, fishing, photography, painting; *Clubs* Carlton, The English Speaking Union; *Style—* John Nevill, Esq; 5 Tite St, London SW3 4JU; 8 Radnor Cliff, Folkestone, Kent CT20 2JN (☎ 071 352 7368/ 0303 48403); Nevill Gallery, 43 St Peter's St, Canterbury, Kent CT1 2BG (☎ 0227 65291)

NEVILL, Capt (Cosmas Guy) Richard; s of Maj-Gen C A R Nevill, CB, CBE, DSO, *qv*, of Holt, Boxford, Colchester, Essex, and Grania, *née* Goodliffe; *b* 12 July 1937; *Educ* Summer Fields Sch Oxford, Harrow, RMA Sandhurst; *m* 8 April 1961, Caroline Jane, da of Adm Sir Guy Grantham, GCB, CBE, DSO, *qv*, of Tandem House, Nayland, Colchester, Essex; 2 s (Giles b 12 Oct 1963, Alexander b 11 Nov 1965), 1 da (Serena b 30 Oct 1967); *Career* cmmnd 1 Bn Royal Fus (City of London Regt) 1957; served 1957-64: Bahrain, Kenya, Malta, N Africa, Germany; Capt 1962, ret 1964; investmt mangr Nevill Hldgs: Dublin 1964-69, Jersey 1969-; chm Birdstown Estate Co Donegal 1964-80; dir: Londonderry Properties 1974-89, Tandem Tweeds Colchester 1974-88; investmt mangr Joyce Ltd Kenya 1979-88, asst mangr Cavendish Furniture Co Ltd Suffolk 1986-87; *Recreations* sport, travel, fishing, shooting, philately, music; *Clubs* Army & Navy, MCC, I Zingari, Free Foresters, Tennis & Rackets Assoc, Hampton Court Royal Tennis; *Style—* Capt Richard Nevill; Woodlands, Great Horkesley, Colchester, Essex (☎ 0206 271 226)

NEVILLE, Dr Adam Matthew; TD (1963); *b* 5 Feb 1923; *Educ* QMC (BSc), Univ of London (MSc, PhD, DSc), Univ of Leeds (DSc); *m* 29 March 1952, Mary Hallam, *née* Cousins; 1 s (Adam Andrew b 11 May 1953), 1 da (Elizabeth Louise b 5 Feb 1955); *Career* War Serv Middle East and Italy, Maj RETA; practising and academic engr 1950-, prof of civil engrg Univ of Leeds 1968-78, princ and vice chllr Univ of Dundee 1978-87; pres Concrete Soc 1974-75, chm Ctee of Princs of Scottish Univs 1984-86, pres Cncl of Europe Ctee on Univs 1984-86; Freeman City of London 1977; memb: Worshipful Co of Fan Makers 1978, Bonnetmaker Craft of Dundee 1979; Hon LLD St Andrews 1987, hon memb American Concrete Inst 1986; OStJ 1983; FICE, FIStructE, FCIArb, FRSE, FEng; *Books* Properties of Concrete (1963), Basic Statistical Methods (with J B Kennedy, 1964), Creep of Concrete: plain, reinforced and prestressed (1970), Structural Analysis: a unified classical and matrix approach (with A Ghali, 1977), Hardened Concrete: physical and mechanical aspects (1971), High Alumina Cement Concrete (1975), Creep of Plain and Structural Concrete (with W H Dilger and J J Brooks, 1983), Concrete Technology (with J J Brooks, 1987); *Recreations* skiing, travel; *Clubs* Athenaeum, New (Edinburgh), Travelers' Century (Los Angeles); *Style—* Adam Neville, Esq, TD, FRSE; 24 Gun Wharf, 130 Wapping High St, London E1 9NH (☎ 071 265 1087)

NEVILLE, Donald George; s of Lionel George Neville (d 1963), of Bexhill, and Letitia Helen, *née* Puddicombe (d 1987); *b* 31 Dec 1929; *Educ* Merchant Taylors', Univ of London (LLB), Sch of Law; *m* 18 April 1953, Daphne Elizabeth, da of Ernest Hall (d 1967), of Pinner, Middx; 2 s (Richard b 1955, Stuart b 1957), 2 da (Virginia b 1962, Miranda b 1964); *Career* Nat Serv 1952-54, 2 Lt RAPC (later Capt/Paymaster) 5 Queen's Royal Regt TA 1957-63; sr ptnr Cardales McLeish (slrs London and Surrey) 1974-86; dir various cos; dep chm Dominion International Group plc 1975-88; chm SE Region Historic Houses Assoc 1979-81; owner various historic houses open to public incl: Detillens, Limpsfield, Castle Mill Dorking, and Haxted Mill Edenbridge; *Publications* Medal Ribbons and Orders of Imperial Germany and Austria (1974), Medal Ribbons of the World (1977), History of the Early Orders of Knighthood and Chivalry (1979); *Recreations* gardening, antiques, study and collection of orders of chivalry; *Clubs* IOD, Thames Rowing; *Style—* Donald Neville, Esq; Castle Mill, Reigate Road, Dorking, Surrey (☎ 0306 887979)

NEVILLE, His Hon Judge (Eric) Graham; *b* 12 Nov 1933; *Educ* Kelly Coll Tavistock, Sidney Sussex Coll Cambridge; *m* 20 August 1966, Jacqueline Catherine; *Career* RAF Gen Duty Flying Offr 1952-54; rec Crown Ct 1975, circuit judge 1980-; *Recreations* yachting; *Clubs* Royal Western Yacht, Royal Fowey Yacht; *Style—* His Hon Judge Graham Neville; Exeter Crown Court, The Castle, Exeter

NEVILLE, Prof (Alexander) Munro; s of Alexander Munro Neville (d 1983), of 48 Cailes Rd, Troon, Ayrshire, and Georgina Stewart, *née* Gerrard (d 1989); *b* 24 March 1935; *Educ* Univ of Glasgow (MB ChB, PhD, MD), Harvard Univ Boston, Univ of London (DSc), RCPath; *m* 5 Sept 1961, Anne Margaret Stroyan, da of Dr Hugh Black (d 1975), of 2 Alton Rd, Paisley; 1 s (Munro b 26 Nov 1964), 1 da (Judeth b 25 Nov 1963); *Career* sr lectr pathology Univ of Glasgow 1967-70, res fell Inst of Cancer Res MRC London 1970-73, prof pathology Univ of London 1973-85, dir Ludwig Inst for Cancer Res Zurich 1985- (dir London 1975-85); MRCPath 1969, FRCPath 1979; *Recreations* golf, gardening, history; *Clubs* Athenaeum, Banstead Downs; *Style—* Prof Munro Neville; 42 Eagle St, London WC1R 4AP (☎ 071 405 9005); Feldblumenstr 125, 8134 Adliswil, Switzerland (☎ 010 41 1710 9409); Ludwig Institute for Cancer Research, Stadelhoferstr 22, 8001 Zurich Switzerland (☎ 010 41 1251 5377), fax 010 41 1251 5438)

NEVILLE, Sir Richard Lionel John Baines; 3 Bt (UK, 1927), of Sloley, Norfolk; s of Sir Reginald James Neville, 1 Bt (d 1950); suc half-bro, Sir (James) Edmund Henderson Neville, 2 Bt, MC, 1982; *b* 15 July 1921; *Educ* Eton, Trinity Coll Cambridge; *Heir* none; *Career* served Burma 1943-45 as Capt Oxford and Bucks and W African Frontier Force; *Style—* Sir Richard Neville, Bt; Sloley Hall, Norwich

NEVILLE, Thomas; *b* 28 June 1931; *Educ* Glasgow HS; *m* Wendy Elizabeth, *née* Gee; 1 s, 1 da; *Career* fin dir: Rolls Royce Motors Ltd 1971-80, Vickers plc 1980-87; non-exec dir: BASF plc 1985-, Murray Vernon Holdings Ltd 1987-, Simon Engineering plc 1987-, EIP Group plc 1989-, Pendragon plc 1989-; non-exec chm Eurocamp Group Ltd 1990-; FCA (Scot); *Recreations* golf, shooting; *Clubs* Royal and Ancient, Caledonia, Delamere Forest, Royal Liverpool, Woodhall Spa; *Style—* Thomas Neville, Esq;

Eurocamp Group Ltd, Beech Tree House, Woore Rd, Audlem, Crewe, Cheshire CW3 0BP (☎ 0270 811606, fax 0270 812097)

NEVILLE-JONES, (Lilian) Pauline; CMG (1987); da of Roland Neville-Jones, RAMC (ka 1941), and Cecilia Emily Millicent Winn, *née* Rath; step f Dr John Michael Winn; *b* 2 Nov 1939; *Educ* Leeds Girls' HS; Lady Margaret Hall Oxford (BA); *Career* Dip Serv; joined FCO 1963, third sec Salisbury Rhodesia 1964-65, third sec (later second sec) Singapore 1965-68, FCO 1968-71 (dealing with Med), first sec Washington 1971-75, dep chef de cabinet (later chef de cabinet) to Christopher Tugendhat, Cmmn of Euro Communities Brussels 1977-82, sabbatical Royal Inst of Int Affrs London and Institut Francais des Relations Internationales Paris 1982-83, head policy planning staff FCO 1983-87, min (econ) Bonn Embassy 1987- (min 1988-); *Recreations* cooking, gardening, antiques; *Style—* Miss Pauline Neville-Jones, CMG; c/o Royal Bank of Scotland, Westminster Branch, 21-23 Victoria St, London SW1A 0HA; British Embassy, Friedrich Ebert Allee 77, 5300 Bonn I, W Germany

NEVILLE-ROLFE, Marianne Teresa (Mrs D W Blake); da of Edmund Neville-Rolfe, of Ark Farm, Tisbury, Wiltshire, and Margaret Elizabeth, *née* Evans; *b* 9 Oct 1944; *Educ* St Mary's Convent Shaftesbury, Lady Margaret Hall Oxford (BA); *m* 16 Sept 1972, David William John Blake; *Career* with CBI 1965-73 (head Brussels Office 1971-72); DTI: princ 1973, asst sec 1982, grade 3 under sec 1987; chief exec and princ Civil Service Coll 1990-; *Style—* Ms Marianne Neville-Rolfe; Sunningdale Park, Ascot, Berks SL5 0QE (☎ 0344 23444, fax 0344 842491)

NEVIN, Eric; s of William Albert Nevin, and Mabel, *née* Griffiths (d 1974); *b* 12 July 1931; *Educ* St Mary's Coll Crosby, HMS Conway Sch, Liverpool Tech Coll, Sch of Navigation, Liverpool Coll of Commerce, City of London Coll; *m* 1958, Jean (d 1984), da of late John Gardner, of Liverpool; 1 s (Michael), 1 da (Cheryl); *Career* served at sea with Alfred Holt & Co 1948-58, gained Master's Foreign-going Certificate 1957, asst dist sec MNAOA Liverpool 1959 (nat sec 1961, asst gen sec 1971, gen sec 1974-); dir: Merchant Navy Offrs Pension Fund Tstees Ltd, Merchant Navy Offrs Pensions Investmts Ltd, Ensign Tst plc, Merchant Navy Investmts Mgmnt Ltd, Oceanair Servs Ltd, Conway Cadet Sch Tst Ltd, Merchant Navy Welfare Bd Ltd; memb: Thames Water Authy, Jt Ctee for Nat Awards in Nautical Science, Cncl for Nat Acad Awards Marine Studies Subject Bd, Ship and Marine Technol Requirements Bd (and its successor Marine Technol Ctee), Nat Econ Depts Ctee for the Movement of Exports, King George's Fund for Sailors, Merchant Seamen's War Meml Soc, Marine Soc, Conway Tst, Nat Maritime Bd, Merchant Navy Welfare Bd, Merchant Navy Officers' Pension Fund; govr: HM Conway Merchant Navy Sch, London Nautical Sch, Merchant Navy Coll (vice-chm), City of London Poly; *Style—* Eric Nevin, Esq; Oceanair House, 750 High Road, Leytonstone, London E11 3BB (☎ 01 989 6677, telex 892648 NUMAST G)

NEVIN, His Hon Judge; Thomas Richard Nevin; TD (1949 and Bar), JP (1965); s of late Thomas Nevin, JP, of Mirfield, Yorks; *b* 9 Dec 1916; *Educ* Bilton Grange, Shrewsbury Sch, Leeds Univ (LLB); *m* 1955, Brenda Micaela, da of of Dr B C Andrade-Thompson, MC; 1 s (and 1 decd); *Career* Lt-Col RA, London Bombardment, India and Burma; barr NE Circuit for 19 years, asst rec of Leeds 1961-64, rec of Doncaster 1964-67, dep chm Yorks W Riding QS 1965-71 (E Riding 1968-71), chm Northern Agric Land Tbnl 1963-67 (dep chm 1961-63), a circuit judge and crown ct liaison judge (formerly judge of County Cts) 1967-84, a dep high court judge 1974-84; Freeman City of London; *Recreations* numismatics and our past; *Style—* His Hon Judge Nevin, TD, JP; c/o 11 King's Bench Walk, Temple, EC4 (☎ 071 236 3337)

NEW, Anthony Sherwood Brooks; s of Valentine Gill New (d 1963), and Grace Fanny, *née* Baines (d 1981); *b* 14 Aug 1924; *Educ* Highgate Sch, Northern Poly Sch of Architecture (Dip Arch); *m* 11 April 1970, (Ann) Elizabeth, da of Bernard Harding Pegge (d 1972), of Elsted, Sussex; 1 s (Nicholas b 1976), 1 da (Susannah b 1972); *Career* Nat Serv leading radio mechanic RN 1945-47; architect; private practice, Derby Cathedral 1970-, numerous churches in London; OStJ; Freeman City of London 1976; FRIBA 1952, MIStructE 1954, FSA 1971; *Books* Observer's Book of Postage Stamps (1967), Observer's Book of Cathedrals (1972), A Guide to the Cathedrals of Britain (1980), P S A Guide to Historic Buildings (London) (1983), A Guide to the Abbeys of England & Wales (1985), New Observer's Book of Stamp Collecting (1986), A Guide to the Abbeys of Scotland (1988); *Recreations* travel, photography, drawing; *Style—* Anthony New, Esq, FSA; Architect's Office, Priory Church of St Bartholomew The Great, W Smithfield, London EC1A 7JQ (☎ 071 600 8512)

NEW, Dudley Holt; s of Joseph New (d 1937), of Worthing, and Bessie, *née* Holt (d 1953); *b* 17 Nov 1907; *Educ* Dauntseys Sch, Imperial Coll London (BSc Eng, DIC); *m* 9 April 1936, Doris Edith, da of Frederick George Berry (d 1955), of Bideford; 2 s (David b 1937, Kenneth b 1940); *Career* joined RE supplementary reserve 1932, garrison engr Sheerness 1939-41, CO 39 (Fortress) CO RE Freetown 1941-42, DCRE Freetown 1942-43, transferred to army reserve 1942, garrison engr Truro 1943, Adj and ACRE 102 CRE 1943-44, CO 207 Works Section RE Antwerp 1944-45, Engr and Tport Staff Corps RE TA 1962, Lt-Col RE TA; apprentice fitter GWR Works Swindon 1923-28, designer The Trussed Concrete Steel Co Ltd 1935-39; chief engr: Holland & Hannen and Cubitts Ltd 1945-52, Nuclear Civil Constructors 1952-62; ptnr G Maunsell and Ptnrs 1962-73 (conslt 1973-), author of various papers on engrg matters; cncllr London Borough of Lewisham 1947-54, former chm of govrs SE London Coll; former govr: Sedgehill Comprehensive Sch, Malory Comprehensive Sch; Liveryman Worshipful Co of Engrs; FICE 1934, FIMechE 1947, FIStructE 1938, MConsE 1963, FCIArb 1975, CEng, FCGI; *Recreations* reading, gardening; *Clubs* RAC; *Style—* Dudley New, Esq; Ennerdale, 54A Allerford Rd, Catford, London SE6 3DF (☎ 081 697 2728); G Maunsell and Ptnrs, Yeoman House, 63 Croydon Rd, London SE20 7TP (☎ 081 778 6060, telex 946171)

NEW, Maj-Gen Sir Laurence Anthony Wallis; CB (1986), CBE (1980); s of Lt-Col Stanley William New, MBE (d 1956), of Grayshott House, Grayshott, Hants, and Constance Mary, *née* Marshall (d 1970); *b* 25 Feb 1932; *Educ* King William's Coll Isle of Man, RMA Sandhurst; *m* 11 Aug 1956, Anna Doreen, da of Gp Capt Conrad Edward Howe Verity, OBE (d 1984), of Farthings, Earleydene, Ascot, Berks; 2 s (Richard b 1961, Robert b 1969), 2 da (Amanda b 1958, Deborah Ann b 1966); *Career* cmmnd RTR 1952; served in Hong Kong, Germany, Malaya and Borneo, CO 4 RTR 1971-73, Bde Maj 20 Armd Bde 1971, Def and Mil attaché Tel Aviv 1974-77, Col GS MOD 1977-79, Brig GS MOD 1980-82, ACGS (Op Reqs) 1983-84, ACDS (Land Systems) MOD 1984-85; Lt Govr of the Isle of Man and pres of Tynnald 1985-90; col Cmdt RTR 1986-, vice pres TA & VRA 1985-90, county pres St John Ambulance 1985-90, chm Princes Tst IOM 1985-90, church warden St Peter upon Cornhill London 1987-, pres Soldiers' and Airmens' Scripture Readers Assoc 1986-, vice pres Offrs Christian Union 1989-; gen sec offrs Pensions Soc Ltd 1991-, dir OPS Investment Co Ltd, pres Assoc of mil Christian Fellowships 1991; Freeman City of London, Liveryman Worshipful Co of Glass Sellers 1985; FBIM 1979, CBIM 1986; KStJ 1985; kt 1990; *Recreations* water colour painting, cello, walking; *Clubs* Army and Navy; *Style—* Maj-Gen Sir Laurence New, CB, CBE; 15 Buckingham Gate, London SW1

NEWALL, Alexander Severin; *b* 15 Nov 1913; *Career* chm and md Alexander Newall Group of Co's; co-fndr and pres Br Aerophilatelic Fedn; *Style—* Alexander Newall, Esq; 81 Redington Rd, Hampstead NW3 7RR (☎ 071 794 2644); 338 City Rd, London EC1V 2PX (☎ 071 837 0192, fax 071 837 9642, telex 263672

NEWALL, Christopher Stirling; s of Peter Stirling Newall, Callaley, Northumberland, and Rosemary, *née* Marriage; *b* 8 April 1951; *Educ* The Downs Sch, Abbotsholme Sch, Courtauld Inst of Art Univ of London (BA); *m* 10 Oct 1985, Jenifer Hylda, da of the late Sir Derek Ryan, 3 Bt; 2 s (Alfred Stirling b 8 Feb 1987, George Stirling b 20 Jan 1990); *Career* writer and art historian; *Books* Victorian Watercolours (1987), George Price Boyce (catalogue Tate Gallery exhibition, 1987), The Engravings after Burne-Jones (intro to catalogue, 1987), The Art of Lord Leighton (1990); *Style—* Christopher Newall, Esq; 17 Londale Square, London N1 1EN (☎ 071 607 4360)

NEWALL, Hon David William Norton; s of 2 Baron Newall; *b* 2 July 1963; *Educ* Eton, Sandhurst; *Career* estate agent; co dir; *Clubs* Winchester House, RAC; *Style—* The Hon David Newall; The Power House, Cromwell Grove, London W6 7RQ

NEWALL, 2 Baron (UK 1946); Francis Storer Eaton Newall; s of Marshal of the RAF 1 Baron Newall, GCB, OM, GCMG, CBE, AM (d 1963, Chief of Air Staff during Battle of Britain); *b* 23 June 1930; *Educ* Eton, Sandhurst; *m* 1956, Pamela, da of Hugh Rowcliffe, TD, of Pinkney Park, Malmesbury (d 1978), by his 1 w, Margaret (da of Sir Henry Farrington, 6 Bt); 2 s, 1 da; *Heir* s, Hon Richard Newall; *Career* takes Cons whip in Lords; Capt 11 Hussars, served Germany, Malaya, Singapore, NI; adj Royal Glos Hussars; conslt and company dir; Cons whip and oppn front bench spokesman Lords 1976-79, fndr memb House of Lords All Pty Def Study Gp, del W Euro Union and Cncl of Europe 1983-, responsible for Farriers Registration Acts and Betting and Gaming amendment (Greyhound Racing) Acts; led Parly visits to Cyprus, Oman, Bahrain, Qatar, Morocco; chm Br Greyhound Racing Bd; friend of Romania; *Recreations* shooting, tennis, travel; *Clubs* Cavalry and Guards'; *Style—* The Rt Hon the Lord Newall; Wotton Underwood, Aylesbury, Bucks (☎ 0844 238376); 18 Lennox Gdns, London SW1 (☎ 071 589 9370)

NEWALL, Paul Henry; TD (1967), DL (Greater London 1977); s of Leopold Newall (d 1956), and Frances Evelyn, *née* Bean (d 1981); *b* 17 Sept 1934; *Educ* Harrow, Magdalene Coll Cambridge (MA); *m* 1 March 1969, Penelope Moyra, da of Sir Julian Ridsdale, CBE, MP, *qv*; 2 s (Rupert b 1971, James b 1973); *Career* Nat Serv 1953-55: cmmnd Royal Fusiliers, served Egypt and Sudan; TA 1955-70: Maj 1961, cmd City of London Co 5 Bn RRF 1967-70; chm City of London TA & VRA 1986-, vice chm TAVRA for Gtr London 1989-, ptnr Loeb Rhoades & Co 1971-77; overseas dir: Shearson Loeb Rhoades (UK) 1979-81, Shearson American Express (UK) 1981-84; dir Shearson Lehman Int Ltd 1985-; exec dir: Shearson Lehman Hutton Securities 1988-90, Lehman Bros Securities 1990-; vice pres City of London sector Br Red Cross, govr Mencap City Fndn, patron Samaritans Nat Appeal, churchwarden St Stephen's Walbrook; JP City of London, hon visiting magistrate HM Tower of London, one of HM's Lts for the City of London 1975-; elected Ct of Common Cncl 1980, Alderman (Walbrook Ward) City of London 1981-, Sheriff of the City of London 1989-90; master Worshipful Co of Bakers 1990-91, memb Ct Guild of Freeman of City of London; Liveryman Worshipful Co of Gold and Silver Wyre Drawers; OStJ; *Recreations* fencing, fly fishing, water skiing, tennis, trees; *Clubs* City Livery, Walbrook Ward (pres), United Wards, MCC; *Style—* Paul Newall, Esq, TD, DL; One Broadgate, London EC2

NEWALL, Hon Richard Hugh Eaton; s and h of 2 Baron Newall; *b* 19 Feb 1961; *Style—* The Hon Richard Newall

NEWBERRY, Raymond Scudamore (Ray); OBE (1989); s of James Henry Newberry, of Westbury-on-Trym, Bristol, and Doris Ada, *née* Scudamore (d 1989); *b* 8 Feb 1935; *Educ* Bristol GS, Selwyn Coll Cambridge (BA), Univ of Leeds (DipTefl), Univ of Bristol (DipEd); *m* 26 Aug 1967, Angelina, da of Odell Nance (d 1948), of South Carolina, USA; 1 s (Conrad b 1972), 1 da (Clare b 1969); *Career* Nat Serv Intelligence Corps 1953-55; lectr in English Univ of Baghdad 1959-62; Br Cncl 1962-: lectr Tehran 1963-64, educn offr Eastern India 1964-66, head Dept of English Advanced Teacher Trg Coll Winneba Ghana 1966-70, advsr Miny of Educn Singapore 1970-74, rep Colombia 1975-80, dir North and Latin America Dept 1980-82, dir America and Pacific Dept 1982-84, rep Australia 1984-89, dir Brazil 1990-; *Books* Between You and Me (with Alan Maley 1970); *Recreations* bookbinding, golf; *Style—* Ray Newberry, Esq, OBE; The British Council, Caixa Postal 6104, 70740 Brasilia DF, Brazil

NEWBIGGING, David Kennedy; OBE (1982); s of David Locke Newbigging, CBE, MC (d 1948), and Lucy Margaret Newbigging (d 1970); *b* 19 Jan 1934; *Educ* Oundle; *m* 1968, Carolyn Susan, da of Geoffrey Band (d 1974); 1 s, 2 da; *Career* 2 Lt Nat Serv KOSB; Jardine Matheson & Co Ltd: joined 1954, dir 1967, md 1970, chm and sr md 1975-83; chm and md Hong Kong Land 1975-83; chm: Hongkong & Kowloon Wharf & Godown Co Ltd 1970-80, Hongkong Electric Holdings Ltd 1982-83 (dir 1975-83), Jardine Fleming Holdings Ltd 1975-83, Hong Kong Tourist Assoc 1977-82, Hong Kong General Chamber of Commerce 1980-82, Rentokil Group PLC 1987- (dir 1986), Redfearn PLC 1988, NM UK LImited 1990-; dep chm: Ivory Sime PLC 1990- (dir 1987-), Provincial Group PLC 1985-91 (dir 1984-91); dir: Hongkong & Shanghai Banking Corp 1975-83, Hongkong Telephone Co Ltd 1975-83, Rennies Consolidated Holdings Ltd 1975-83, Provincial Insurance PLC 1984-86, Provincial Life Assurance Co Ltd 1984-86, The British Coal Corporation (formerly the National Coal Bd) 1984-87, CIN Management Ltd 1985-87, United Meridian Corporation (USA) 1987-, Faupel Trading Group PLC 1989-; memb: Int Cncl Morgan Guaranty Tst Co of NY 1977-85, Hongkong Legislative Cncl 1978-82, Hongkong Exec Cncl 1980-84; *Recreations* most outdoor sports; *Clubs* Boodle's, Hurlingham, Turf, The Royal Hongkong Jockey; *Style—* D K Newbigging Esq, OBE; 26 Little Chester Street, London SW1X 7AP (☎ 071 823 2545)

NEWBOLD, Sir Charles Demorée; KBE (1970), CMG (1957), QC (Jamaica 1947); s of Charles Elches Newbold (d 1962), of Port-of-Spain, Trinidad, and Laura May Newbold (d 1962); *b* 11 June 1909; *Educ* Lodge Sch Barbados, Keble Coll Oxford (BA); *m* 1936, Ruth, da of Arthur Louis Vaughan (d 1960), of Port-of-Spain; 2 da; *Career* called to the Bar Gray's Inn 1931; joined Colonial Legal Servs: magistrate Trinidad 1937, legal draftsman Jamaica 1941-43, slr gen Jamaica 1943-48, legal sec E Africa High Cmmn 1948-61; memb E Africa Central Legislative Assembly 1948-61; E Africa Ct of Appeal: justice of appeal 1961-65, vice pres 1965-66, pres 1966-70; jt ed Trinidad Law Reports 1923-33, ed E African Tax Laws Report 1948-61; chm Ctee of Supply 1948-61, cmmr for Revision of E Africa High Cmmn Laws 1951; Grand Cordon Star of Africa (Liberia); kt 1966; *Recreations* cricket, tennis; *Style—* Sir Charles Newbold, KBE, CMG, QC; 7 St Mary's Garden, Chichester, West Sussex (☎ 0243 532431)

NEWBOLD, Yvette Monica (Yve); da of Thomas Peter Radcliffe (d 1963), and Anne Gertrude, *née* Flynn; *b* 6 July 1940; *Educ* Sacred Heart Convent Hove Sussex, Kings Coll Univ of London (LLB), Coll of Law; *m* 1958, Anthony Newbold; 3 s (Timothy b 1960, Jonathan b 1964, Toby b 1965), 1 da (Lorraine b 1959); *Career* slr (1970), staff lawyer IBM (UK) 1968-71, chief staff counsel Rank Xerox 1972-79, int counsel Xerox Corporation USA 1979-82, euro counsel Walt Disney Production Ltd 1982-86, co sec Hanson plc 1986-; govr London Business Sch 1990; memb: Adsvy Bd Crime Concern 1990, Final Selection Bd Civil Serv 1990; memb Law Soc; *Style—* Mrs Yve Newbold; Hanson plc, 1 Grosvenor Place, London SW1X 7JH (☎ 071 245 1245, fax 071 235

3455)

NEWBON, Gary; s of Jack Newbon (d 1982), and Preeva, *née* Cooklin; *b* 15 March 1945; *Educ* Culford Sch Bury-St-Edmunds Suffolk; *m* 26 Oct 1973, Katharine Janet, da of Bernard While (d 1982), of Birmingham; 2 s (Laurence Jon b 16 Aug 1977, Neil Christie (twin) b 16 Aug 1977), 1 da (Claire Rosalie b 5 June 1975); *Career* Fournalist Jeacock's News Agency Cambridge 1964-67; sports writer: Hayter's Sports Agency, Westward TV Plymouth 1970-71 (sports presenter 1968-70), ATV Network Ltd 1977-81 (sports presenter 1971-74, sports presenter and ed 1974-77); controller sport Central Ind TV 1987- (head sport 1982-87), dep head ITV Sport; ITV reporter: Olympic Games (1972, 1980, 1988), World Cup Soccer (1974, 1982, 1986, 1990); memb: Lord's Taverners, Variety Club, SOS; *Books* Over the Sticks and Under Starters Orders (with late Michael Ayres, 1970 and 1971); *Recreations* jazz, drinking champagne; *Style*— Gary Newbon, Esq; Central Independent TV plc, Broad St, Birmingham B1 2JP (☎ 021 643 9898, fax 021 616 1699, telex 338966)

NEWBOROUGH, 7 Baron (I 1776); Lord Robert Charles Michael Vaughan Wynn; 9 Bt (GB 1742), DSC (1942); s of 6 Baron Newborough, OBE, JP, DL (d 1965); *b* 24 April 1917; *Educ* Oundle; *m* 1, 1945 (m dis 1971), Rosamund, da of Maj Robert Barbour, of Bolesworth Castle, Tattenhall, Cheshire; 1 s, 2 da; m 2, 1971, Jennifer, yst da of late Capt Cecil Allen, RN, and Lady (Eirene) Morgan, *qv*; *Heir* s, Hon Robert Wynn; *Career* served 2 Lt 9 Lancers, 5 Inniskilling Dragoon Gds and Lt 16/5 Lancers 1935-39, invalided 1940, took part in Dunkirk evacuation as civilian, RNVR Cmmn, cmd MTB 74 St Nazaire raid 1942 (despatches and DSC) wounded, (POW Colditz, escaped); farmer; High Sheriff Merioneth 1963; *Recreations* fishing, yachting; *Clubs* Naval & Military, Goat and Bembridge Sailing; *Style*— The Rt Hon the Lord Newborough, DSC; Rûg, Corwen, Clwyd, N Wales (☎ 0490 2510; Estate Office: 2153)

NEWBOUND, Maurice Ernest; s of Ernest Henry Newbound (d 1959), and Violet Lily, *née* Roberts (d 1969); *b* 13 April 1925; *m* 1, 22 March 1945 (m dis 1973), Ivy Christine, da of Charles Young; 1 s (David b 1952); m 2, 12 April 1975, Shirley Jean Nena, da of Arthur Ratcliffe; *Career* RAF 1943-45; md and chm: Westbourne Int Hldgs Ltd 1957-83, Westbourne Gp Pty Ltd 1969-73, G S Estates Ltd 1974-; chm Swan House Special Events Ltd 1988-, md Painting & Decorating Promotions Ltd 1988-; launched: Britain's first shopfitting magazine 1954, several pubns and exhibitions at home and abroad, still a conslt on several; pres: Advsy Cncl of IDD 1965-, Natural Health Network 1982-; chm: Somerset Centre IOD 1979-81, Holistic Health Contact Gp 1984-, Advsy Cncl for UK Natural Health Week 1988; memb: Parly Gp for Alternative and Complementary Med, Br Export GP 1958-64, Ctee Somerset Rural Devpt Cmmn 1981-; vice pres Nat Consultative Cncl 1991-; FInstM 1977; *Recreations* swimming, gardening; *Clubs* Victory; *Style*— Maurice Newbound, Esq; Chardstock House, Chard, Somerset TA20 2TL (☎ 04606 3229, fax 04606 3809)

NEWBURGH, 12 Earl of (S 1660); Filippo Giambattista Camillo Francesco Aldo Maria Rospigliosi; also Viscount Kynnaird and Lord Levingston (S 1660), Prince Rospigliosi (HRE 1668 by Emperor Leopold I and Papal 1854 by Pope Pius IX), 14 Prince of Castiglione (by the Sicilian cr of 1602, and a further cr of the kingdom of Italy 1897), 11 Duke of Zagarolo (Papal 1668), Marquis of Giuliana (Sicily 1543, It 1897), Count of Chiusa (Sic 1535, It 1897), Baron di Valcorrente e della Miraglia (Sic 1780, It 1897), Lord (Signore) of Aidone, Burgio, Contessa, and Trappeto (1854), conscribed Roman Noble (1854), and Patrician of Venice (1667), Genoa (1786) and Pistoia; s of 11 Earl of Newburgh (d 1986), and Donna Giulia, da of Don Guido Carlo de Duchi Visconti di Modrone, Count of Lonate Pozzolo; *b* 4 July 1942; *m* 1972, Baronessa Donna Luisa, da of Count Annibale Caccia Dominoni; 1 da (Princess Benedetta Francesca Maria b 1974); *Heir* da, Mistress of Newburgh, b 4 June 1974; *Style*— Prince Rospigliosi; Piazza St Ambrogio 16, 20123 Milan, Italy

NEWBURY, Anthony Charles; s of Charles Renton Newbury (d 1986), of Aust, and Isabella Dawson, *née* Davie; *b* 19 Jan 1940; *Educ* Melbourne C of E GS, Univ of Melbourne (BDSc, LDS, MDSc, John Tomes medal in oral surgery, prize in orthodontics); *m* 1, 16 May 1964, Delia Kate Frances, da of Frank Kelynge Miles; 1 s (Andrew Charles b 9 May 1967), 1 da (Kim Frances b 9 Dec 1965); m 2, 4 Oct 1986, Brigitte, da of Hans Eigenberger (d 1990); *Career* pt/t sr lectr Dept of Anatomy and sr clinical demonstrator Dept of Restorative Dentistry Univ of Melbourne 1964-69, gen dental practice Melbourne 1963-64, specialist orthodontic practice Melbourne 1965-70, private practice Harley St London 1972-; fndr memb: The Oral Hygiene Centre 1977, Dental Diners Study Club 1968, Euro Dental Soc 1983, Br Dental Soc for Clinical Nutrition 1985; memb: Fedn Dentaire Internationale 1964-, Myofunctional Therapy Assoc of America, Soc of Orthobionomy, Br Soc for the Study of Orthodontics 1971-, Euro Orthodontic Soc 1970-; fndr tstee Oral Hygiene Fndn Charity 1978, fell Int Coll of Dentists 1980, invited memb Pierre Fauchard Acad 1987, assoc memb American Dental Assoc; Aust Dental Assoc: sec Dental Health Ctee 1966-69, memb Organising Ctee Nat Congress 1968; Br Dental Assoc: memb organising Ctee (World Congress 1974, Centenary Congress 1978), pres Metropolitan Branch 1982-83 (hon sec 1976-82); memb Cncl Odontological Section of Royal Soc of Medicine, past cncllr Br Dental Fndn, past memb Chicago Dental Soc; *Books* contrib to Mercury and Other Toxic Metals in Humans (1989); *Recreations* tennis, golf, reading, art; *Clubs* Royal Soc of Med, Lansdowne, Hurlingham, Queens, Peninsula Country Golf, Cwlth Golf; *Style*— Anthony Newbury, Esq; 72 Harley St, London W1N 1AE (☎ 071 580 3168, fax 071 436 0959)

NEWBURY, Hon Mrs (Julia Elizabeth Heather); *née* Hamilton; da of 13 Lord Belhaven and Stenton; *b* 1956; *m* 1, 1975 (m dis) Richard Newbury; m 2, 1979, Stephen Hobbs; *Style*— The Hon Mrs Hobbs

NEWBURY, (George) Malcolm; JP (1979); s of George Theodore Newbury, of Droitwich, Worcs, and Kathleen Mary, *née* Partridge; *b* 14 Feb 1936; *Educ* King Edwards Sch Birmingham, St John's Coll Cambridge (MA); *m* 29 July 1960, Lone, da of Arne Petersen-Hinrichsen, of Copenhagen, Denmark; 1 s (Nicholas George Arne b 1972), 2 da (Pollyanna b 1962, Amanda b 1965); *Career* farmer; chm Lincs Ctee The Prince's Trust 1985; *Recreations* gardening, tree planting, hare coursing, sport, travel; *Style*— Malcolm Newbury, Esq, JP; Birthorpe Manor, Sleaford, Lincolnshire NG34 0EX

NEWBY, Hon Mrs (Ailsa Ballantyne); da of Baron Thomson of Monifieth (Life Peer); *b* 1956; *m* 1978, Richard Newby; 1 s (Mark b 1985); *Style*— The Hon Mrs Newby

NEWBY, (George) Eric; s of George Arthur Newby, and Hilda, *née* Pomroy; *b* 6 Dec 1919; *Educ* St Paul's; *m* 1946, Wanda, da of Viktor Skof; 1 s, 1 da; *Career* served WWII with the Black Watch and Special Boat Section 1939-45 (POW 1942-45); Dorland Advertising 1936-38; apprentice and ordinary seaman 4 masted Finnish barque Moshulu 1938-39; Women's Fashion Business 1946-56 (with Worth Paquin 1955-56), Secker & Warburg 1956-59, central buyer model dresses John Lewis Partnership 1959-63, travel ed The Observer and gen ed Time Off Books 1964-73; travels and explorations: explored in Nuristan and made an unsuccessful attempt to climb Mir Samir in Afghan Hindu Kush 1956, descended Ganges with wife 1963; *publications*: The Last Grain Race (1956), A Short Walk in the Hindu Kush (1958), Something Wholesale 1962, Slowly Down the Ganges (1966), Time Off in Southern Italy (1966), Grain Race: Pictures of Life Before the Mast in a Windjammer 1968, The Wonders of Britain (jt author, 1968), The Wonders of Ireland (jt author, 1969), Love and War in the Apennines (1971), The World of Evelyn Waugh (jt author, 1973), Ganga (with photographs by Raghubir Singh, 1973), World Atlas of Exploration (1975), Great Ascents (1977), The Big Red Train Ride (1978), A Traveller's Life (1982), On the Shores of the Mediterranean (1984), A Book of Travellers' Tales (1985), Round Ireland in Low Gear (1987), What the Traveller Saw (1989); memb Assoc of Cape Horners; *Recreations* walking, running, cycling, gardening; *Clubs* Garrick; *Style*— Eric Newby, MC, Esq; West Bucknowle House, Bucknowle, Wareham, Dorset BH20 5PQ (☎ 0929 480374)

NEWBY, Dr Frank; OBE (1986), JP (Horsham); s of Alexander Gilbert Leslie (d 1963), of Harrogate, and Dorothy, *née* Broadbank (d 1984); *b* 29 May 1927; *Educ* Wallington Co Sch, Harrogate GS, Univ of Loughborough (DLC), Univ of Manchester (MEd), Univ of Southampton (PhD); *m* 10 Sept 1949, Margaret Jean, da of Frank Thomsett (d 1966), of Croydon; 2 da (Lindsey Margaret Davies b 1953, Amanda Ruth Distin b 1959); *Career* Sgt RAFVR 1944-48; head lower sch Hazlewick Sch 1955-61; headmaster: Eastwood Sch Keighley 1962-67, Forest Community Sch Horsham 1967-90; co pres W Sussex teachers assoc NUT 1978-79 and 1988-90; dep chm Horsham bench (chm domestic panel); memb St Marys Parish Church, former pres Horsham Rotary Club, chm Horsham Temp Accommodation Charitable Tst; Freeman: City of London 1979, Worshipful Co of Musicians 1984; FCollP 1983, FBIM 1986; *Recreations* music, reading, sailing; *Style*— Dr Frank Newby, OBE, JP; 44 Heron Way, Horsham, West Sussex RH13 6DL (☎ 0403 62920)

NEWBY, Prof Howard Joseph; s of Alfred Joseph Newby, and Constance Annie, *née* Potts; *b* 10 Dec 1947; *Educ* John Port GS Etwall Derbyshire, Atlantic Coll Glamorgan, Univ of Essex (BA, PhD); *m* 4 July 1970, Janet Elizabeth; 2 s (Stephen b 1980, Jake b 1983); *Career* Univ of Essex: lectr in sociology 1972-75, sr lectr 1975-79, reader 1979-83, prof of sociology 1983-88; dir ESRC Data Archive 1983-88, prof of sociology and rural sociology Univ of Wisconsin Madison USA 1980-83; visiting appts: Univ of NSW Sydney 1976, Univ of Newcastle upon Tyne 1983-84; chm ESRC 1988-; *Books* incl: The Deferential Worker (1977), Green and Pleasant Land? (2 edn, 1985), Country Life (1987), The Countryside in Question (1988); jtly: Community Studies (1971), Property Paternalism and Power (1978), The Problem of Sociology (1983), Social Class in Modern Britain (1988); *Recreations* family life, gardening, Derby county, railways; *Clubs* Athenaeum; *Style*— Prof Howard Newby; The Old Mill, Mill Lane, Corston, Malmesbury, Wilts SN16 0HH (☎ 0793 513838); Economic & Social Research Council, Cherry Orchard East, Kembrey Park, Swindon SN2 6UQ (☎ 0793 513838, fax 0793 487916)

NEWBY, (Percy) Howard; CBE (1972); s of Percy Newby (d 1961), of Wendover, Bucks, and Isobel Clutsam, *née* Bryant (d 1980); *b* 25 June 1918; *Educ* Hanley Castle GS Worcester, St Paul's Coll Cheltenham; *m* 12 July 1945, Joan, da of Harry Charles Thompson (d 1965), of Wendover, Bucks; 2 da (Sarah (Mrs Schenk) b 1947, Katharine b 1963); *Career* RAMC 1939-42; lectr Cairo Univ 1942-46; BBC Radio 3 (formerly the Third Programme) 1958-78: controller 1958-, dir of programmes 1971-75, md 1975-78; chm English Stage Company 1978-85; Atlantic Award for Literature 1946, Somerset Maugham Prize 1948, Yorkshire Post Fiction Award 1968, Booker Prize 1969; memb Soc of Authors 1947; *Books* A Journey to the Interior (1945), The Picnic of Sakkara (1955), Something to Answer For (1968), Saladin in his Time (1983), Coming In With The Tide (1991); *Style*— Howard Newby, Esq, CBE; Garsington House, Garsington, Oxford OX9 9AB (☎ 086 736 420)

NEWBY, John; s of Harry Newby, of Garforth, Leeds, and Ann Newby; *b* 17 Dec 1939; *Educ* St Annes Sch Leeds, City HS Leeds; *m* 28 Sept 1963, Margaret Ann, da of Andy Wilson, of Scarborough; 2 da (Helen b 31 Aug 1966, Carmel b 28 July 1968); *Career* dir: Wiggins Plant Ltd 1983, Wiggin Gee Homes Ltd 1988-; Wiggin Gee Property Ltd 1988-, md: Wiggins Contruction Ltd 1985- (dir 1982), Gee Walker & Slater Ltd 1986, Headcrown Construction 1986-; gp md Wiggins Gee Gp 1988-; *Recreations* golf, philately, gardening; *Clubs* London Rugby, Chelsea, Ballard Golf; *Style*— John Newby, Esq; 57 Hart Rd, Thundersley, S Benfleet, Essex (☎ 0268 792 591)

NEWCASTLE, 10 Bishop of (1882) 1981-; Rt Rev Andrew Alexander Kenny Graham; patron of the Archdeaconries of Northumberland and Lindisfarne, four residentiary Canonries, the Hon Canonries, and seventy-five livings; the see of Newcastle was founded in May 1882; s of Andrew Harrison Graham (d 1954), and Magdalene Graham (d 1955); *b* 7 Aug 1929; *Educ* Tonbridge, St John's Coll Oxford; *Career* warden Lincoln Theol Coll 1970-77, bishop suffragan of Bedford 1977-81; chm: Advsy Cncl for Church's Ministry 1983-87, Doctrine Cmmn 1987-; *Recreations* hill walking; *Clubs* Utd Oxford and Cambridge; *Style*— The Rt Rev the Lord Bishop of Newcastle; Bishop's House, 29 Moor Road South, Gosforth, Newcastle upon Tyne NE3 1PA (☎ 091 2852220)

NEWCASTLE, Diana, Duchess of; Lady Diana; *née* Montagu Stuart Wortley; da of 3 Earl of Wharncliffe, of Wortley Hall, Sheffield (d 1953), and Elfrida Wentworth Fitzwilliam (d 1980); *b* 2 June 1920; *m* 1946 (m dis 1959), 9 Duke of Newcastle, OBE (d 1988); 2 da; *Career* served WWII Mechanised Tport Corps; *Recreations* living; *Style*— Diana, Duchess of Newcastle; Cortington Manor, Warminster, Wilts

NEWCASTLE, Duchess of; Sally Anne Wemyss Hope; er da of Brig John Henry Anstice, DSO, of Kyrenia, Cyprus, and Sydney, *née* Williamson; *m* 1 (m dis), Fikret Jemal; m 2, 23 Oct 1959, as his 3 w, 9 Duke of Newcastle, OBE (d 1988); *Style*— Her Grace the Duchess of Newcastle; 5 Quay Hill, Lymington, Hants

NEWCOMB, Mary; da of Charles Slatford, and Mabel May, *née* Lupton; *b* 25 Jan 1922; *Educ* Univ of Reading (BSc); *m* Aug 1950, Godfrey, s of Lt Col Clive Newcomb; 2 da (Hannah, Tessa); *Career* painter; regular one man shows Crane Kalman Gallery London 1970-; exhibitions: Italy, Holland, Sweden, Germany, Paris, NY; work in pub and private collections; *Style*— Mrs Mary Newcomb; Rushmeadow, Flordon Rd, Newton Flotman, Norwich, Norfolk NR15 1QX (☎ 0508 470371)

NEWCOMBE, John Fernley; s of Arthur Fernley Newcombe (d 1978), of Worksop, Notts, and Norah Kathleen Newcombe; *b* 12 May 1928; *Educ* King Edward VI Sch Retford, Trinity Coll Cambridge (MA), Bart's London (MB MChir); *m* 4 July 1953, Barbara Joan, da of Charles Arnold Brittain (d 1979), of 110 Furniss Avenue, Dore, Sheffield; 1 s (Guy Charles Fernley b 1962), 1 da (Alyson Clare b 1960); *Career* conslt surgn Central Middx Hosp London 1965-, sub dean Middx Hosp Med Sch 1970-76; pres Med Soc of London 1986-87; FRCS (memb Ct of Examiners); *Recreations* golf, sailing, painting; *Style*— John Newcombe, Esq; 36 Sandy Lodge Rd, Rickmansworth, Herts WD3 1LJ (☎ 09274 22370)

NEWCOMBE, Timothy Richard; TD (1985); s of Dr John Newcombe (d 1990), of Tockwith, York, and Elizabeth Edith Esme, *née* Thornley-Taylor; *b* 28 Nov 1947; *Educ* Pocklington Sch East Yorks; *m* 31 July 1988, Margaret, da of Eamonn Callaghan, of Leeds; *Career* Royal Green Jackets 1961-62; Yorkshire Volunteers: 1 Bn 1972-83, 3 Bn 1983-87; Res List 1987-; called to the Bar Inner Temple 1972; *Recreations* fishing, shooting; *Clubs* Sloane; *Style*— Timothy Newcombe, Esq, TD; St Pauls House, 23 Park Square South, Leeds LS1 2ND (☎ 0532 455 866, fax 0536 455 807)

NEWCOMBE, William Francis Lister; CBE (1976, OBE 1955, MBE 1946), TD

(1950); s of William Arthur Newcombe (d 1930), of Sussex, and Marjorie Beatrice, *née* Greaves (d 1977); *b* 8 Dec 1912; *Educ* Haileybury; *m* 15 Sept 1934, Eileen Marjorie, da of Percy Joseph Hood (d 1937), of IOW; 2 da (Josephine b 1935, Veronica b 1936); *Career* 2 Lt RA (TA) 1938, Capt 1940, ADGB 1939-42, WO 1942-45; gen sec Army Cadet Force Assoc 1946-77, sec CCF Assoc 1952-77; hon sec Haileybury Soc 1957-80 (pres 1981-82), life govr Haileybury and ISC 1958- (Cncl memb 1961-81); ed Haileybury Register 1984; *Recreations* reading, gardening; *Clubs* East India, Devonshire, Sports, Public Schs, MCC; *Style—* William F L Newcombe, Esq, CBE, TD; Trout End, Wendens Ambo, Saffron Walden, Essex CB11 4JY (☎ 0799 40267)

NEWELL, Prof Alan Francis; *b* 1 March 1941; *Educ* St Philip's GS, Univ of Birmingham; *m* 31 July 1965, Margaret Eleanor, *née* Morgan; 1 s (David b 1976), 2 da (Anna b 1968, Catherine b 1969); *Career* res engr Standard Telecommunication Laboratories 1965-69, lectr in electronics Univ of Southampton 1969-80; Univ of Dundee 1980-: NCR prof of electronics and microcomputer systems, dir microcomputer centre; tstee Int Soc for Augmentative and Alternative Communication, sci advsr Scottish Cncl for Spastics, memb Advsy Bd Coll of Occupational Therapy; FIEE, MBCS; *Recreations* family life, sailing; *Clubs* Wormit Boating; *Style—* Prof Alan Newell; Microcomputer Centre, Department of Mathematics & Computer Science, The University, Dundee DD1 4HN, Scotland (☎ 0382 23181, fax 0382 23435, telex 76293)

NEWELL, Frances (Mrs John Sorrell); *m* John Sorrell, *qv*; 3 c; *Career* former illustrator, fndr and co chm Newell and Sorrell Ltd (corporate identity consits) 1976-; clients incl: BAA, The Berol Corporation, The Body Shop International, Boots Company plc, British Rail, Charbonnel et Walker, InterCity; awards: D&AD Silver for Most Outstanding Graphics (for Safety at Sea Stamps) 1986, Conservation Papers/ Design Week (for Body Shop USA mail order catalogue) 1989, Design Week, Design Effectiveness, Clio; judge: BBC Design awards, D&AD awards; memb Colour gp; FCSD; *Style—* Frances Newell; Newell & Sorrell Ltd, 4 Utopia Village, Chalcot Road, London NW1 8LH (☎ 071 722 1113, fax 071 722 0259)

NEWELL, Michael; s of (Michael) Barry Newell, of Nottingham, and (Elizabeth) Janet Newell; *b* 25 Feb 1965; *Educ* West Bridgford Sch; *m* 23 Sept 1989, Jayne, da of Malcolm Shaw; *Career* professional cricketer; Nottinghamshire CCC 1984-: first class debut 1986, awarded county cap 1987, highest score 203 not out v Derbyshire 1987; youngest player to make a double hundred Nottinghamshire; honours: County Championship 1987, NatWest Trophy 1987; *Style—* Michael Newell, Esq; Nottinghamshire CCC, Trent Bridge, Nottingham NG2 6AG (☎ 0602 821525, fax 0602 455730)

NEWENS, Peter Gordon; s of John Newens, and Mabel Gordon Newens; *b* 8 March 1902; *Educ* Richmond Co Sch; *m* 8 Oct 1946, Edith Joan, da of Harold Shotton, of Shrewsbury; 1 s (Peter John b 31 July 1948); *Career* WWII serv: E Surrey Regt, transferred Army Physical Trg Corps Argyle Southern Highlanders Regt; proprieter The Maids of Honour Shop Kew (family business 1853); *Recreations* horse driving, riding, flying; *Clubs* Hackney Driving, Fairoaks Flying, Veteran Car; *Style—* Peter Newens, Esq

NEWENS, (Arthur) Stanley; MEP (London Central) 1984-; s of Arthur Ernest Newens (d 1977), of Loughton, Essex, and Celia Jenny, *née* Furssedonn (d 1966); *b* 4 Feb 1930; *Educ* Buckhurst Hill Co HS, UCL (BA); *m* 1, 1954, Ann (d 1962), da of John Barlow Sherratt (d 1966), of Stoke-on-Trent; 2 da; m 2, 1966, Sandra Christina, da of John Arthur McMullen Frith, of Chingford; 1 s, 2 da; *Career* miner (coalface worker) 1952-56, teacher 1956-64 and 1970-74; MP: Epping (Lab) 1964-70, Harlow (Lab and Co-op) 1974-83; chm Liberation (formerly Movement for Colonial Freedom) 1967-; former memb Central Exec Ctee Co-op Union and Exec Ctee Co-op Pty, pres London Co-op Soc 1977-81 (dir 1971-77); chm: PLP Foreign Affrs Ctee 1982-83, Tribune Gp of Lab MPs 1982-83; organising sec Harlow Cncl for Vol Servs 1983-84; chm Br Labour Gp in EP 1985-87; author of several books, pamphlets on politics and local history; *Recreations* family, reading, historical research, gardening; *Style—* Stanley Newens, Esq, MEP; The Leys, 18 Park Hill, Harlow, Essex (☎ 0279 420108)

NEWEY, Hon Judge John Henry Richard; QC (1970-); s of Lt-Col Thomas Henry Newey, ED (d 1983), and Irene Kathleen Mary Newey (d 1989); *b* 20 Oct 1923; *Educ* Ellesmere Coll Shropshire, Queens' Coll Cambridge (foundation scholar, MA, LLM); *m* 31 July 1953, Mollie Patricia, JP, da of Herbert Chalk (d 1982); 3 s (Robert b 1956, Guy b 1959, Michael b 1963), 2 da (Jane b 1962, Annabel b 1966); *Career* served Capt, Central India Horse, Indian Army 1942-47 in India, ME, Italy and Greece; called to the Bar Middle Temple 1948; bencher Middle Temple 1977, prosecuting counsel to PO SE Circuit 1963-64, standing counsel to PO at Common Law 1964-70, personal injuries jr to Treasy 1968-70, dep chm Kent Quarter Sessions 1970-71, commissary gen of City and Dio of Canterbury 1971-, recorder 1972-80, Judge of Official Referees Ct in London 1980-, Parly boundary cmmr for Eng 1980-88; chm: Sevenoaks Soc 1962-65, Sevenoaks Div Cons Assoc 1965-68; alternate chm Burnham and Other Teachers Remuneration Ctees 1969-80, memb Judicial Ctee Acad of Experts 1979-, FCIArb 1979; US Bronze Star 1944; *Publications* Official Referees Courts (1988), Construction Disputes (jtly, 1989); *Recreations* excursions, history; *Style—* His Hon Judge Newey, QC; St David's, 68 The Drive, Sevenoaks, Kent TN13 3AF (☎ 0732 454597); Offical Referees' Court, St Dunstan's House, 133-137, Fetter Lane, London EC4A 1HD

NEWEY, Sidney Brian; s of Sydney Frank Newey, of Burton upon Trent, and Edith Mary, *née* Moore; *b* 8 Jan 1937; *Educ* Burton upon Trent GS, Worcester Coll Oxford (MA); *m* 16 Dec 1967, Margaret Mary, da of Rev Canon David Stevens, of Belton in Rutland, Leics; 1 s (Edmund); *Career* BR: joined as mgmnt trainee 1960, stationmaster Southall 1965-70, freight planning mangr W Region 1970-78, div mangr Birmingham 1978- 80, dep gen mangr London Midland Region 1980-85, gen mangr W Region 1985-87, dir prov BR HQ 1987; MCIT; *Recreations* fell walking, reading, music, carpentry, village and church affairs; *Style—* Sidney Newey, Esq; Chestnut Cottage, The Green South, Warborough, Oxon OX9 8DN (☎ 086 732 8322); British Rail Headquarters, 24 Eversholt St, London NW1 1DZ (☎ 071 922 4123)

NEWHOUSE, Archie Henry; s of George Newhouse (d 1982), of Walthamstow London, and Mildred Louise, *née* Goltenboth (d 1988); *b* 4 March 1933; *Educ* Leyton County HS; *m* 11 Nov 1953, Vera May, da of William Blow (d 1944), of Tottenham, London; 3 s (Colin b 1946 (by adoption), Douglas b 1955, David b 1956), 1 da (Vivienne b 1947 (by adoption)); *Career* sports editor: West Herts Post 1953-55; Greyhound Express: chief sub ed 1956-60, ed 1960-65; greyhound ed Sporting Life 1965-84; Nat Greyhound Racing Club: dep sec to sec 1985-87, chief exec 1987-; chief exec British Greyhound Racing Bd 1987-, sec gen World Greyhound Racing Fedn 1990-, sec to tstees Retired Greyhound Tst 1987-; *Recreations* travel, photography, opera, sport; *Clubs* Naval and Military, Wig and Pen; *Style—* Archie Newhouse, Esq; 24-28 Oval Road, London NW1 7DA (☎ 071 267 9256, fax 071 482 1023)

NEWHOUSE, Ernest George; s of Herbert Henry Newhouse (d 1970), and Ilse Therese, *née* Frank; *b* 16 Dec 1937; *Educ* Merchant Taylors', Northwood, St John's Coll Oxford (scholar, MA, MSc); *m* 26 July 1969, Jean, da of Graham William Gready (d 1984); 1 s (Richard b 1970), 1 da (Caroline b 1973); *Career* Unilever 1961-68, fin analyst W R Grace Ltd 1969-73, fin mangr Wallington Weston & Co (Marley Tile Gp) 1973-78, head of fin BBC Bristol 1978-82, chief accountant BBC World Serv 1982-; *Recreations* travel, piano, astronomy; *Clubs* Amersham and Wells Lions; *Style—* Ernest Newhouse, Esq; Capesthorne, 80 Bois Lane, Chesham Bois, Amersham, Bucks HP6 6BZ (☎ 0494 726915); Bush House, Strand, London WC2B 4PH (☎ 071 257 2646, fax 071 379 5510)

NEWILL, Dr Robert George Douglass; s of Robert Daniel Newill (d 1955), of Wellington, Shropshire, and Gladys Victoria, *née* Beckett (d 1978); *b* 5 Dec 1921; *Educ* Shrewsbury, St Bart's Hosp and Univ of London (MD); *m* 25 March 1950, Patricia Margaret, da of Humphrey Charles Bradshaw-Bowles (d 1958), of Baslow, Derbyshire; 2 da (Heather b 1956, Angela b 1958); *Career* Capt RAC 1941-46; reproductive endocrinologist UCH London (ret 1985); *Books* Infertile Marriage and author of res papers on infertility subjects; *Recreations* yachting, ornithology, choral singing; *Clubs* Aldeburgh Yacht, Little Ship; *Style—* Dr Robert Newill; Fern Court, Park Road, Aldeburgh, Suffolk IP15 5ET (☎ 0728 453109)

NEWINGTON, Michael John; CMG (1982); s of John Tompsett Newington, of Spalding, Lines, and Grace, *née* Lumley (d 1990); *b* 10 July 1932; *Educ* Stamford Sch, St John's Coll Oxford (MA, Swimming half blue); *m* 29 Dec 1956, Nina, da of Richard Gordon-Jones (d 1940); 1 s (Nicholas Gordon Tompsett b 1962), 1 da (Nina Michelle b 1958); *Career* Nat Serv Pilot Offr RAF 1951-52; HM Dip Serv: joined 1955, Economic Survey Section Hong Kong 1957-58; resigned 1959; Metals Div ICI 1959-60; HM Dip Serv: rejoined 1960, second later first sec (economic) British Embassy Bonn 1961-65, first sec British High Cmmn Lagos 1965-68, asst head Sci & Technol Dept FCO 1968-72, cnsllr (sci & technol) Bonn 1972-75, cnsllr and consul gen Tel Aviv 1975-78, head Rep of Ireland Dept FCO 1978-81, HM consul gen Düseldorf 1981-85, hon ambassador Caracas and Sancho Domingo 1985-87, hon ambassador Brazilia 1987-; *Recreations* golf, gardening; *Style—* Michael Newington, Esq, CMG; British Embassy, PO Box, Brasilia DF, Brazil (☎ 225 2710, fax 225 1777)

NEWIS, Kenneth; CB (1967), CVO (1970, MVO 1958); s of Herbert Thomas Newis (d 1943), of Manchester, and Gladys, *née* Lindop (d 1961); *b* 9 Nov 1916; *Educ* St John's Coll Cambridge (MA); *m* 1943, Kathleen, da of John Barrow (d 1977), of Davenport, Cheshire; 2 da (Gillian, Margaret); *Career* civil servant, sec Scot Devpt Dept Scot Office 1973-76, ret 1976; chm Queen's Hall (Edinburgh) Ltd; vice chm: MHA Housing Association Ltd, Cockburn Assoc (Civic Tst Edinburgh); *Recreations* music; *Clubs* New (Edinburgh); *Style—* Kenneth Newis, Esq, CB, CVO; 11 Abbotsford Park, Edinburgh EH10 5DZ (☎ 031 447 4138)

NEWLAND, Prof David Edward; s of Robert William Newland (d 1979), of Knebworth, Herts, and Marion Amelia, *née* Dearman; *b* 8 May 1936; *Educ* Alleyne's Sch Stevenage, Selwyn Coll Cambridge (BA, MA, ScD), MIT (ScD); *m* 18 July 1959, Patricia Frances, da of Philip Mayne, of Marton, N Yorkshire; 2 s (Andrew David William b 1961, Richard David Philip b 1963); *Career* English Electric Co London 1957-61, instr and asst prof MIT 1961-64, lectr (later sr lectr) Imperial Coll London 1964-67, prof of mechanical engrg Univ of Sheffield 1967-76, prof of engrg (1875) Univ of Cambridge 1976-, fell Selwyn Coll Cambridge 1976; memb Royal Cmmn on Environmental Pollution 1984-89, visitor Tport and Road Res Laboratory 1990-, cncl memb Fellowship of Engrg 1985-88, govr St Paul's Schs 1978-, churchwarden Ickleton 1979-87; FEng, FIMechE, FIEE; *Books* An Introduction to Random Vibrations and Spectral Analysis (2 edn, 1984), Mechanical Vibration Analysis and Computation (1989); *Clubs* Athenaeum; *Style—* Prof David Newland; Cambridge University Engineering Department, Trumpington St, Cambridge CB2 1PZ (☎ 0223 332670, fax 0223 359153, telex 81239)

NEWLAND, Peter John; s of Alec John Newland, of Stratford-upon-Avon, and Mary Monica, *née* Leahy; *b* 30 March 1943; *Educ* Douai Sch; *m* 29 June 1969, Philippa Ernestine Marshall, da of Philip Marshall Healey; 3 da (Isabel Louise b 12 June 1971, Joanna Lucy b 20 July 1974, Susannah Elizabeth b 29 March 1981); *Career* articled clerk Clement Keys & Son Birmingham 1960-66, qualified chartered accountant 1966, Peat Marwick Mitchell & Co Birmingham 1966-68, fin planner Unbrako Limited Coventry 1968-70, mangr Arthur Young McClelland Moores & Co Birmingham 1970-75; ptnr: Arthur Young Bristol 1975, Ernst & Young (following merger); govr Prior Park Coll Bath; FCA (ACA 1966); *Recreations* golf, gardening, theatre; *Clubs* Bristol Commercial Rooms; *Style—* Peter Newland, Esq; The Cottage, Northfields, Lansdown, Bath, Avon BA1 5TN (☎ 0225 315143); Ernst & Young, One Bridewell St, Bristol BS1 2AA (☎ 0272 290808, fax 0272 260162)

NEWLANDS, Rev Prof George McLeod; s of George Newlands (d 1973), of Perth, and Mary Newlands; *b* 12 July 1941; *Educ* Perth Acad, Univ of Edinburgh (MA, BD, PhD), Univ of Heidelberg, Churchill Coll Cambridge (MA); *m* 1 Sept 1967, (Mary) Elizabeth, da of Rev Prof Ronald S Wallace, of Edinburgh; 3 s (Stewart b 1971, Murray b 1974, Craig b 1977); *Career* minister Church of Scotland, priest C of E; lectr in divinity Univ of Glasgow 1969-73, univ lectr in divinity Univ of Cambridge 1973-86, fell Wolfson Coll Cambridge 1975-82, fell and dean Trinity Hall Cambridge 1982-86, prof of divinity Univ of Glasgow 1986- (dean faculty of divinity 1988-); *Books* Hilary of Poitiers (1978), Theology of the Love of God (1980), The Church of God (1984), Making Christian Decisions (1985); *Recreations* walking, golf; *Style—* The Rev Prof George Newlands; 8 Hills Avenue, Cambridge CB1 4XA (☎ 0223 248631); 14 Great George Street, Glasgow G12 8NA (☎ 041 334 4712); Faculty of Divinity, The University, Glasgow G12 8QQ (☎ 041 339 8855)

NEWLANDS OF LAURISTON, William Alexander; s of Frank Newlands (d 1971), of Balnamuir, Ballinluig, Perthshire, and Annie Shand-Henderson (d 1986); the family is descended from Jasper Newlands of that Ilk (in record 1469) of the barony of Newlands in the Sheriffdom of Kincardine; Laird of Lauriston (Castle founded 1243), St Cyrus, Kincardineshire; granted the sole arms of Newlands by Warrant of the Lord Lyon, King of Arms, 1987; *b* 5 Nov 1934; *Educ* Dollar Acad, Robert Gordon's Coll Aberdeen; *m* 1, 1960, Kathleen Cook (m dis 1976); 1 s (Hamish Newlands of Lauriston Ygr b 1965); 2 da (Fiona b 1960, Riona b 1962); m 2, 1985, Dorothy Straton, da of late John Walker, of Montrose, and 20th in direct descent from Sir Alexander Straton of Lauriston, who fell at the battle of Harlaw (1411); *Career* Far East Air Force 1953-55, Game Conservancy, Int Union for Conservation of Nature (Morges, Switzerland); (as Willy Newlands) travel ed Daily Mail 1982-; (Travel Writer of the Year 1983-84 and 1987-88); *Clubs* Caledonian; *Style—* William Newlands of Lauriston; Lauriston Castle, St Cyrus, Kincardineshire (☎ 0674 854 88)

NEWLING, John Bevan; s of Bevan Newling (d 1966), and Dorothy, *née* James; *b* 22 Nov 1952; *Educ* North Staffs Poly (BA), Chelsea Sch of Art (MA), Wolverhampton Poly (MPhil); *m* Ann, da of Anthony Taylor; 1 s (Jack Stanley b 27 July 1983); *Career* artist; as Fulbright fell worked and installed pieces in Los Angeles, San Francisco, Washington DC and NY, sr lectr Nottingham Poly; solo exhibitions: Seven Trestles (Midland Gp Nottingham) 1980, Birmingham Arts Lab 1980, Sculpture (Stoke-on-Trent Sch of Art) 1981, IKON Gallery 1982, Ian Berksted Gallery London 1982, The Mineta Move Gallery Brussels 1983, New Works (Ian Berksted Gallery) 1983, State and Church (Midland Gp) 1984, Jolenbeck Gallery Cologne Germany 1987, Edward Totah Gallery London 1987, Sculpture (Dean Clough Arts Fndn) 1987, Krefeld Kanstverine (Krefeld Germany) 1988, Orchard Gallery Derry NI 1989, Art Site Gallery 1990, Edward Totah Gallery 1990, Henry Moore Trust Exhibition Halifax 1990, The

Minnories Colchester 1990; gp exhibitions incl: Peter Moore Exhibition (The Walker Art Gallery, Liverpool) 1981, Sculptors (Chelsea Sch of Art) 1981, New Sculpture (Gallery Jölenbeck, Cologne) 1984, Inside/Outside (Castle Museum, Nottingham) 1988, Edward Totah Gallery 1988, Cologne Art Fair Germany 1989, Tyne International Newcastle 1990; *Awards* The Wolverhampton fellowship 1975-78, Sainsbury award for Fine Art 1975; Arts Cncl award West Midlands Arts 1979 and E Midlands Arts 1981 1984 and 1986, Br Cncl award 1984 and 1986, Henry Moore Tst Residency Dean Clough 1990; *Style—* John Newling, Esq; 130 Hucknall Rd, Carrington, Nottingham NG5 1AD (☎ 0602 621574, 0602 418418 ext 3106); Edward Totah, The Edward Totah Gallery, 13 Old Burlington Street, London (☎ 071 734 0343)

NEWMAN, Hon Lady (Ann Rosemary Hope); raised to the rank of a Baron's da; da of Capt Hon Claude Hope Hope-Morley (d 1968), and sis of 3 Baron Hollenden; *b* 10 Aug 1916; *m* 1946, Sir Ralph Alured Newman, 5 Bt (d 1968); *Style—* The Hon Lady Newman; Blackpool House, Dartmouth, S Devon

NEWMAN, Archibald Richard (Archie); s of Arthur Percy Newman (d 1948), of London, and Ada Ethel Toms (d 1977); *b* 10 April 1931; *Educ* Latymer's GS, Univ of London; *m* 5 July 1958, Rita Margaret, da of Eugene William Beushaw (d 1986), of London; 1 s (Nigel Richard Ellery b 1970), 1 da (Josephine Margaret b 1967); *Career* Nat Serv 1949-51, No 2 Higher Educn Centre Aldershot; Press and Pubns Dept London Transport Exec 1952-57, res asst British Transport Advertising 1957-59, dep head of press and PR (Eastern Regn) BR 1959-61; press offr: Associated TV 1961-63, The Electricity Council 1963-65; press and info offr GLC 1965-66, dir of public offrs and sponsorship RPO 1966-85; proprietor: Archie Newman Communications, Musical Safaris 1985-; chm: Edmonton Youth Cncl 1946-48, St Bartholomew-the-Great 850th Anniversary Festival 1974, UN Year of Shelter for the Homeless, Dance and Music Galas 1987; memb Govt Arts and Heritage Advsy Ctee 1986-, hon life memb RPO 1985; memb NUJ, MRIPA 1955-65, MIPR 1958-70, MRSM 1987, FRPS; *Books* Beecham Stories (with Harold Atkins, 1978); *Recreations* visual and performing arts, walking, gardening, photography, travel; *Clubs* Royal Overseas', Wig and Pen; *Style—* Archie Newman, Esq; 57 Quebec Court, 21 Seymour St, Marble Arch, London W1H 5AD (☎ 071 262 3951, fax 071 706 2184); Falmer Corner, 11 Ashurst Drive, Goring-by-Sea, Worthing, West Sussex BN12 4SN (☎ 0903 44625)

NEWMAN, Hon (Corinne Deborah); da of Baron Lloyd of Hampstead (Life Peer); *b* 23 July 1951; *Educ* City of London Sch for Girls, Camberwell Sch for Arts & Crafts; *Style—* The Hon Mrs Newman; 12, 600 Military Road, Mosman, Sydney, NSW 2088, Australia

NEWMAN, His Hon Judge Cyril Wilfred Francis; QC (1982); s of Wilfred James Newman (d 1970), and Cecilia Beatrice Lily Newman (d 1977); *b* 2 July 1937; *Educ* Sacred Heart Coll Droitwich, Lewes Co GS, Merton Coll Oxford (MA); *m* 1966, Winifred, da of Theodore de Kok, of Zürich, Switzerland; 2 s, 1 da; *Career* barr 1960; asst cmmr Parly Boundary Cmmr for Eng 1976, rec SE circuit 1982-, memb Criminal Injuries Compensation Bd 1985-86, circuit judge SE circuit 1986-; pres Oxford Univ Law Soc 1959, memb OU Middle Temple Soc 1959; *Recreations* sailing, country sports, skiing, swimming, opera and church music; *Clubs* Bar Yacht (hon treas 1973-88, rear cdre 1985); *Style—* His Hon Judge Cyril Newman, QC; Orlestone Grange, Orlestone, nr Ashford, Kent TN26 2EB (☎ 023 373 2306)

NEWMAN, Derek Anthony; s of Maurice John Newman, of Ashtead, Surrey and Christine Newman, *née* Grieve; *b* 7 April 1944; *Educ* Chorlton GS Manchester, City Univ (MBA); *m* 1968, Patricia Ann Wynne; 3 c (Michelle b 15 March 1972, David b 14 Jan 1975, Lisa b 3 Nov 1977); *Career* audit mangr Touche Ross 1968-73 (articled clerk 1965-68), fin controller First National Finance Ltd 1973-75; Chemical Bank: fin controller 1975-76, vice pres fin 1976-78, vice pres and head of corp fin NY 1978-81, vice pres fin insts 1981-85; Canadian Imperial Bank of Commerce: gen mangr UK and Ireland 1985-86, sr vice pres Europe, Africa and ME 1987-90 (vice pres 1986-87), head of Europe 1990-, chief executive CIC/Wood Gundy Group Europe 1990-; FCA; *Recreations* windsurfing, golf, swimming; *Clubs* RAC; *Style—* Derek Newman, Esq; Canadian Imperial Bank of Commerce, Cottons Centre, Cottons Lane, London SE1 2QL (☎ 071 234 6559, fax 071 407 6456)

NEWMAN, Sir Francis Hugh Cecil; 4 Bt (UK 1912), of Cecil Lodge, Newmarket, Cambridge; s of Sir Gerard Robert Henry Sigismund Newman, 3 Bt (d 1987); *b* 12 June 1963; *Educ* Eton, Univ of Pennsylvania USA; *m* 18 Dec 1990, Katharine M, yr da of (Cecil Ralph) Timothy Edwards, of Grendon Court, Upton Bishop, Ross-on-Wye, Herefordshire; *Career* N M Rothschild Asset Mgmnt Ltd, Harry Neal Ltd; *Recreations* shooting, rowing; *Clubs* Eton Vikings; *Style—* Sir Francis Newman, Bt; Burloes, Royston, Herts (☎ 0763 242150); 40 Cadogan Place, London SW1 (☎ 071 235 3331)

NEWMAN, Sir Geoffrey Robert; 6 Bt (UK 1836), of Mamhead, Devonshire; s of Sir Ralph Alured Newman, 5 Bt (d 1968), and Hon Ann Rosemary Hope Newman, *née* Hope-Morley; *b* 2 June 1947; *Educ* Heatherdown Sch, Kelly Coll; *m* 1980, Mary Elizabeth, da of Col Martin St John Valentine Gibbs, CB, DSO, TD; 1 s (Robert b 1985), 3 da (Frances b 1983, Elsie b 1987, Louisa b 1990); *Heir* s, b 4 Oct 1985; *Career* 1 Bn Grenadier Gds 1967-70, Lt T&AVR until 1979; memb Transglobe Expedition 1977-79; in corporate film and video prodn 1980-; *Style—* Sir Geoffrey Newman, Bt; Blackpool House, Dartmouth, S Devon

NEWMAN, George Michael; QC (1981); s of Wilfred James Newman (d 1970), of Seaford, Sussex, and Celia Beatrice Lily, *née* Browne (d 1977); *b* 4 July 1941; *Educ* Lewes Co GS, St Catharine's Coll Cambridge; *m* 1966, Hilary Alice Gibbs, da of late Robert Gibbs Chandler, of Battle, Sussex; 2 s (Benedict b 1968, Matthew b 1970), 1 da (Clarissa b 1971); *Career* called to the Bar, rec 1985, bencher Middle Temple 1989; *Recreations* tennis, skiing, walking; *Style—* George Newman, Esq, QC; 1 Crown Office Row, Temple, London EC4 (☎ 071 583 9292, telex 8953152)

NEWMAN, Graham Reginald; s of A H G Newman (d 1948), and Ethel, *née* Wadey (d 1979); *b* 26 July 1924; *Educ* Canford, Hertford Coll Oxford; *m* 26 July 1952, Joycelyn Helen; *Career* RCS India and Far East 1941-46, ret Capt; chm: Tatham Bromage gp of cos 1953-; elected to Baltic Exchange 1947, chm Baltic 1977-79, pres Baltic Charitable Soc 1982-84; memb Ctee of Mgmnt (and sub ctees) RNLI; Past Prime Warden Worshipful Co of Shipwrights; FICS; *Recreations* sailing; *Style—* Graham Newman, Esq; 2 Makepeace Ave, Highgate, London N6 6EJ (☎ 081 340 6452)

NEWMAN, James Bernard Havard; s of Maj Herbert Gwynne Newman, TD (d 1970), and Jean Fergusson, *née* Arnott (d 1989); *b* 21 April 1932; *Educ* Dalhousie Castle Sch, Rossall Sch, Univ of Edinburgh; 31 Jan 1976, Fiona Grant Murray, da of George Hunter Keith (d 1989); 1 s (Keith Newman b 1980), 1 da (Mary Newman b 1977); *Career* CA; apprentice Carter Greig & Co Edinburgh 1952-58, qualified CA 1958, Allan Charlesworth & Co London 1958-60, Cooper Bros & Co 1960-61, Lindsay Jameson & Haldane Edinburgh 1962-64, Graham Smart & Annan Edinburgh 1964-69, G H Kerr & Co 1969-71, Murray Beith & Murray WS Edinburgh 1971-75, Dickson Middleton & Co Stirling 1975-76, Telfer Craig & Co Glasgow 1976-77, Whyte Stevenson & Roberts Glasgow 1977-81, self employed J B H Newman CA 1981-; Christ Church St James Church Edinburgh: hon treas 1967-79, auditor 1979-; Stirling & Country Club: hon sec 1983-85, auditor 1986-; hon treas Central Scotland branch of BIM 1983-; MICAS 1958, ABIM 1982; *Recreations* family, episcopal church, philately, classical music; *Clubs* Stirling and Country Club; *Style—* James Newman, Esq; 4 Pullar Court, Bridge of Allan, Stirling FK9 4SS (☎ 0786 833760); J B H Newman CA, 4 Pullar Court, Bridge of Allan, Stirling FK9 4SS (☎ 0786 833760)

NEWMAN, Hon Mrs; Hon Jean Sybil; *née* Loch; da of 2 Baron Loch, CB, CMG, MVO, DSO (d 1942); *b* 1908; *m* 1930, Guy Arthur Newman, s of late Sir Sigmund Neumann, 1 Bt; 3 da; *Style—* The Hon Mrs Newman; Stanners Hill Manor, Chobham, Surrey

NEWMAN, John Arthur; s of C Gordon Newman, of West Clandon, and Ruth, *née* Seabrook; *b* 12 Dec 1946; *Educ* St Albans Sch Herts, St John's Coll Cambridge; *m* (m dis); 2 s (Alexander John b 18 May 1971, Michael Christopher b 22 Dec 1973); *Career* articled clerk Cooper Bros and Co 1967, mangr Tax Dept Arthur Andersen 1971, sr internal tax mangr Touche Ross & Co 1973, estab own practice 1976, merged with Chantrey Vellacott 1986; memb LSCA 1979-87; memb Cncl: ICAEW 1987-, Assoc of Accounting Technicians 1989-; FCA; UK/US Double Tax Agreement (1980), Controlled Foreign Corporations (1985); *Recreations* hellendophile; *Clubs* Lesbian - Plomarion Mitilene; *Style—* John A Newman, Esq; 132 Culford Rd, London N1 4HU 071 923 2030); Chantrey Vellacott, Russell Sq House, 10-12 Russell Square, London WC1B 5LF (☎ 071 436 3666, fax 071 436 8884)

NEWMAN, John Francis; s of Sir Cecil Gustavus Newman, 2 Bt (d 1955), and Joan, CBE (d 1969), da of Canon Hon Robert Grimston (s of 2 Earl of Verulam); *b* 25 Jan 1930; *Educ* Eton, Sandhurst; *m* 1963, Caroline, da of Lt-Col Angus Rose, of Perthshire (d 1981); 1 s, 2 da; *Career* formerly Lt RHG; chm Rom River Co, Hoogovens UK Ltd, dir Blick plc and other cos; *Recreations* shooting, farming, golf; *Clubs* White's, Pratt's, MCC; *Style—* John Newman Esq; 28 St Luke's St, SW3 3RP (☎ 071 352 7808); Compton Park, Compton Chamberlayne, Salisbury, Wilts (☎ 072 270 294)

NEWMAN, Dr John Howard; s of Edward Howard Newman (d 1975), of Sevenoaks, Kent, and Mary Newman; *b* 14 June 1943; *Educ* Clare Coll Cambridge (MA), Guys Hosp (MB BChir); *m* 31 July 1971, (Elizabeth) Anne, da of David Reynolds Cox, of Torquay; 2 s (Bruce b 1973, Ian b 1979), 1 da (Rachel b 1975); *Career* conslt orthopaedic surgn Bristol Royal Infirmary 1978-; memb: Specialist Advsy Ctee in Orthopaedics, BMA; memb doctors trg ctee: RCS, BOA 1971, BASK 1984; FRCS 1971; *Recreations* rackets, watersports; *Clubs* Boasters; *Style—* Dr John Newman; 2 Clifton Park, Bristol, Avon (☎ 0272 734262)

NEWMAN, John Victor; s of Jack Newman (d 1980), and Florence Celia, *née* de Fraine; *b* 23 Jan 1943; *Educ* Whitgift Sch; *m* 19 April 1969, Pamela Jane, da of Lionel Charles Thomas Box (d 1981), of Coulsdon; 5 s (James Alexander b 26 April 1972, Robin Anthony Mark b 25 April 1974 d 1974, Jeremy Edward b 6 Aug 1975, Christopher Jon b 15 July 1978, Anthony Jonathan b 15 Dec 1986); *Career* CA 1968; ptnr Spain Bros Newman & Co CAs 1971-74, dir Co of Veteran Motorists Ltd 1971; Guild of Experienced Motorists: chief exec 1984, chm 1987; treas: PCC 1980-86, Parish Centre 1987-; registered insur broker 1979; FCA 1978, FInstIC 1979; *Clubs* Gravetye Manor Country, Sloane; *Style—* John Newman, Esq; Woodside, Bonfire Lane, Horsted Keynes, Haywards Heath, W Sussex RH17 7AG (☎ 0825 790582); Gem Station Rd, Forest Row, E Sussex RH18 5EN (☎ 0342 825676, car 0860 321987)

NEWMAN, John Watson; s of Frederick John Newman, of Cobham, and Joan G Newman; *b* 24 Nov 1945; *Educ* Woodbridge Sch; *m* 11 Oct 1969, Lesley Jean, da of Jack Barber, of 5 Lincoln Ct, Weybridge, Surrey; 1 s (Richard b 1979), 2 da (Amanda b 1974, Sarah b 1975); *Career* CA/industrialist; acquisition mangr Hanson Tst plc 1969-77; dir: T T Group plc, Newship Group; *Recreations* tennis; *Style—* John Newman, Esq; Longridge, South Rd, St George's Hill, Weybridge, Surrey; Fernside Place, 1979 Queen's Rd, Weybridge, Surrey

NEWMAN, Karl Max; CB (1979); s of Dr Karl Neumann (d 1978), and Alice *née* Gruenebaum (d 1958); *b* 26 March 1919; *Educ* Ottershaw Coll, Ch Ch Oxford (MA); *m* 1952, Annette Muriel, da of Ronald Cross Sheen (d 1973); 1 s, 1 da; *Career* Army 1940-42; called to the Bar Gray's Inn 1946, barr 1946-49; under sec Lord Chllr's Office 1972-82 (legal asst 1949-56, sr legal asst 1956-62), legal advsr Euro Unit Cabinet Office 1972-82, counsel to Chm of Ctees House of Lords 1982-87, bencher Gray's Inn 1987; *Recreations* travelling, philately, visiting picture galleries; *Clubs* Utd Oxford and Cambridge Univ; *Style—* Karl Newman, Esq, CB; 17 Marryat Rd, Wimbledon, London SW19 5BB (☎ 081 946 3430)

NEWMAN, Sir Kenneth Leslie; GBE (1987), QPM (1982); s of John William Newman and Florence Newman; *b* 1926,Aug; *Educ* Univ of London (LLB); *m* 1949, Eileen Lilian; 1 s, 1 da; *Career* WWII RAF; Palestine Police 1946-48, Met Police 1948-73, Cdr New Scotland Yard 1972, Chief Constable RUC 1976-79 (Sr Dep Chief Constable 1973), Cmdt Bramshill Police Coll and HM inspr Constabulary 1980-82, Met Police cmmr 1982-87; vice pres Def Manufacturers Assoc, tstee Police Fndn, non-exec dir various cos; visiting prof of law Univ of Bristol 1987-88; Grand Offr of the Order of Orange-Nassau (Netherlands) 1982, Commandeur de l'Ordre National de la Legion d'Honneur (France) 1984, Ecornierda de Numero del Order del Merito Coivil (Spain) 1986, Knight Commander of the Order of Merit (W Germany) 1986, Grand offr of the Order of the Lion of Malawi (Malawi) 1985, Nat Order of the Aztec Eagle (Class II, Mexico) 1985, Medal of Merit (Class I, Quatar) 1985, Order of King Abdul Aziz (Class I, Saudi Arabia) 1987, Grand Officer du Wissam Alouite (Morocco) 1987, Order of Bahrein (Class II, Bahrein) 1984; CBIM, KStJ; kt 1978; *Style—* Sir Kenneth Newman, GBE, QPM; c/o New Scotland Yard, Broadway, London SW1

NEWMAN, Michael Francis; s of Oliver Frank Newman, of Winchmore Hill, London N21, and Beatrice Elizabeth, *née* Watts; *b* 20 Oct 1946; *Educ* St Ignatius Coll, UCW Aberystwyth (BSC), Hatfield Poly (MSC); *m* Maura, da of James Slattery; 1 s (Matthew Paul Francis b 27 Jan 1981), 2 da (Jennifer Elizabeth b 22 Nov 1978, Angela Marie b 18 Oct 1980); *Career* programmer GEC 1968, communications programmer IPC 1970 (worked on Munich Olympics Scoreboard System 1972), sr programmer ITT 1973; joined Stock Exchange: sr programmer 1975, mangr special systems gp 1981, head info tech 1983, project mangr SEAQ 1984, dir mktg technol 1987, dir servs mktg 1988; occasional memb Stock Exchange Chess Third Team; MBCS 1975; *Recreations* golf, soccer, chess; *Clubs* Bishop Stortford Golf; *Style—* Michael Newman, Esq; The International Stock Exchange, London EC2 (☎ 071 588 2355 ext 28148)

NEWMAN, Michael Henry; s of Henry Ernest Newman, of E Croydon, Surrey, and Rhoda May, *née* Symonds (d 1986); *b* 19 Oct 1945; *Educ* Whitgift Sch; *m* 15 Jan 1977, Jennifer Mary, da of Matthew McCargo Roger (d 1977), of Glasgow; *Career* CA 1968; chief exec Britannia Arrow Holdings plc 1979-86 (dir from 1977), dep chm Nat Employers Life Assurance Co Ltd 1983-86, dir Singer & Friedlanders 1984-86, chief exec Prudential Corporation Asia Ltd 1989-90, sr mgmnt Prudential Corporation plc 1990-; *Recreations* travel, gardening; *Clubs* Singapore Town; *Style—* Michael Newman, Esq; 37 Wool Rd, Wimbledon, London SW20 0HN (☎ 081 947 9756); 1 Stephen St, London W1P 2AP (☎ 071 548 3519, fax 071 548 3699)

NEWMAN, Nanette (Mrs Bryan Forbes); da of Sidney Newman, and Ruby Newman; *b* 29 May 1939; *Educ* Sternhold Coll London, Italia Conti Stage Sch, RADA; *m* 1958, Bryan Forbes, *qv* ; 2 da (one of whom Sarah, m Sir John Leon, 4 Bt, *qv*); *Career* actress, writer; films incl: The L-Shaped Room 1962, The Wrong Arm of the Law

1962, Seance on a Wet Afternoon 1963, The Wrong Box 1965, The Whisperers 1966, Deadfall 1967, The Madwoman of Chaillot 1968, The Raging Moon 1971 (Variety Club best film actress award), The Stepford Wives 1974, International Velvet 1978 (Evening News best film actress award); tv appearances incl: Call my Bluff, What's My Line, The Fun Food Factory (Series), London Scene, Stay with me till Morning, Jessie (title-role), Let There be Love, Late Expectations, The Endless Game; books incl: God Bless Love (1972), Lots of Love (1973), Vote for Love (1976), The Root Children (1978), The Pig Who Never Was (1979), The Dog Lovers Coffee Table Book (1982), The Cat Lovers Coffee Table Book (1983), My Granny was a Frightful Bore (1983), A Cat and Mouse Love Story (1984), Christmas Cookbook (1984), Pigalev (1985), Archie (1986), Summer Cookbook (1986), Small Beginnings (1987), Entertaining with Nanette Newman (1988), Bad Baby (1988), Charlie the Noisy Caterpillar (1989), Sharing (1989), ABC (1990); *Recreations* needlepoint; *Style—* Miss Nanette Newman; Chatto & Linnit Ltd, Prince of Wales Theatre, Coventry St, London W1

NEWMAN, Peter John; s of Peter Laurence Newman; *b* 5 July 1938; *Educ* St John's Johannesburg, St John's Coll Cambridge; *m* 1963, Patricia Anne, *née* Wright; 3 s; *Career* Davy Corpn cos 1960-: gen mangr Loewy Robertson Engrg Co 1979- (Queen's award for Export 1980), md Davy McKee (Sheffield) 1984-87, chief exec Metals Div 1988-90, main bd dir Human Resources Davy Corporation 1990; pres Dorset C of C 1983, chm Bd of Govrs Sheffield City Poly, memb of bd Sheffield Devpt Corpn; memb: Co of Cutlers in Hallamshire, Cncl CBI; *Recreations* sailing, gardening; *Style—* Peter Newman, Esq; White Edge, Froggatt Edge, Calver, nr Sheffield (☎ 0433 30314)

NEWMAN, Philip Harker; CBE (1976), DSO (1940), MC (1942); s of John Harker Newman (d 1942), of Ingatestone, Essex, and Violet Grace, *née* Williams (d 1960); *b* 22 June 1911; *Educ* Cranleigh Sch, Middx Hosp Med Sch Univ of London; *m* 7 Oct 1943, (Elizabeth) Anne, *née* Basset; 2 s (Richard b 1944, Anthony (Tony) b 1946), 1 da (Penelope (Penny) b 1948); *Career* RAMC 1939-45; Lt 1939, Maj 1939, Lt-Col 1945; conslt orthopaedic surgn Middx Hosp and King Edward VII Hosp for Offrs 1946-76, conslt surgn Royal Nat Orthopaedic Hosp and Inst of Orthopaedics 1946-76; former pres Br Orthopaedic Assoc, chm Med Bd St John Ambulance 1977-82; memb: Cncl of Mgmnt Jl of Bone and Joint Surgery; memb: BMA, RSM; hon fell SA Coll of Surgns; FRCS; *Books* Safer Than A Known Way - An Escape Story of World War II (1983); *Recreations* golf; *Clubs* Aldeburgh Golf (Capt 1986); *Style—* Philip Newman, Esq; Foxearth, Saxmundham Rd, Aldeburgh, Suffolk (☎ 072 885 3373)

NEWMAN, Richard Claude; s of Sir Ralph Alured Newman, 5 Bt (d 1968); *b* 2 May 1951; *Style—* Richard Newman, Esq; Blackpool House, Dartmouth, S Devon

NEWMAN, Prof Ronald Charles; s of Charles Henry Newman (d 1983), and Margaret Victoria May, *née* Cooper (d 1985); *b* 10 Dec 1931; *Educ* Tottenham GS, Imperial Coll London (BSc, DIC, PhD); *m* 7 April 1956, Jill Laura, da of Robert Charles Weeks (d 1949); 2 da (Susan Laura (Mrs Lee) b 1959, Vivienne Heather (Mrs Cadman) b 1962); *Career* res scientist AE1 Central Res Laboratory Aldermaston Court Aldermaston Berks 1955-63, sr res scientist AE1 Res Laboratory Rugby Warwickshire 1964, visiting prof Univ of Reading 1989 (lectr J J Thomson Physical Laboratory 1964-69, reader 1969-75, prof 1975-88), prof and assoc dir IRC semi-conductor materials Imperial Coll 1989-; memb: SERC ctees on physics semiconductors and neutron beam, SERC DTI Semiconductor Ctee, Br Assoc for Crystal Growth, Material Res Soc USA; ARCS, FInstP; *Books* Infrared Studies of Crystal Defects (1973); *Recreations* music, photography, foreign travel; *Style—* Prof Ronald Newman; Maiden Oak, 23 Betchworth Ave, Earley, Reading, Berks RG6 2RH (☎ 0734 663816); Interdisciplinery Research Centre for Semiconductor Materials, The Blackett Laboratory, Imperial College of Science Technology and Medicine, Prince Consort Rd, London SW7 2BZ (☎ 071 589 5111 ext 6991, fax 071 225 8901, telex 929484)

NEWMAN, Lady Selina Mary; *née* Abney-Hastings; da of Countess of Loudoun; *b* 1946; *m* 1967, William E Newman; 1 s (Christopher James Loudoun b 1972), 1 da (Selina Anne b 1968); *Style—* The Lady Selina Newman

NEWMAN, Sydney; QC (1981); *b* 1 April 1917; *Educ* Central Sch Toronto; *m* 1981, Margaret Elizabeth, *née* McRae (d 1981); 3 da (Deirdie, Jennifer, Gillian); *Career* painter (stage and industl), interior designer, still and cinema photographer; splicer boy Nat Film Bd of Canada 1941, ed and dir Armed Forces trg films and war info shorts 1942, prodr Canada Carries On 1945-52, exec prodr i/c of all films for cinema incl: short films, newsreels, films for children and travel films 1947-52; prodr of over 300 documentaries incl: UN Suffer Little Children It's Fun to Sing (Venice award), Ski Skill, After Prison, What? (Canada award), assigned to NBC NY to report on TV techniques for Nat Film Bd of Canada 1949-50; CBS: TV dir of features and outside broadcasts supervisor of drama and prodr of (General Motors Theatre, On Camera, Ford Theatre, Graphic 1954); prodr of first plays by Authur Hailey, supervisor of drama and prodr Armchair Theatre ABC TV Eng 1958 (cmmnd first on-air plays of Alun Owen, Harold Pinter, Angus Wilson, Robert Muller, Hugh Leonard and Peter Luke), head of Drama Gp BBC TV 1963-68 (cr Dr Who and The Avengers), exec prodr of feature films Associated Picture Corp 1969; awards from: Soc of Film and TV Arts Writers Guild of GB; special recognition award from Soc of Motion Pictures and TV Engrs (US) 1975; dir: progs CRTC Ottawa 1970, Canadian Film Devpt Corp 1970-75, CBC 1972-75; tstee Nat Arts Centre 1970-75, govt film cmmnr and chief exec Nat Film Bd of Canada 1970-75, special advsr on film to Sec of State 1975-77, govr Canadian Conf to the Arts 1978-82; memb: New Western Film and TV Fedn 1978-84, BAFTA; RTS, Kt of Mark Twain (US), hon life memb Dirs Guild of Canada, fell Royal Soc of Film and TV Arts (UK), FRSA (UK) 1967, FRTS 1990; *Recreations* sculpture, painting; *Style—* Sydney Newman, Esq, QC; 3 Nesbitt Drive, Toronto, Ontario M4W 2GS, Canada

NEWMAN, Tony William; s of William Newman (d 1973), of London, and Annie Newman; *b* 3 Sept 1947; *Educ* St Bernards Sch; *Career* BBC TV: floor asst 1971-72, asst floor mangr 1972-77, prodn mangr 1977-82; dir: shows including Top of the Pops, Blankety Blank, Bobs Full House, Jim'll Fix It, Every Second Counts, Roland Rat Show, Guiness Hall of Fame, I've Got a Secret, Keith Harris Series, Wogan; *Recreations* golf, antiques, tae kwon do; *Style—* Tony Newman, Esq; 32 Honor Oak Rise, Honor Oak, Forest Hill, London SE23 (☎ 081 291 3365); Light Entertainment Department, BBC TV, Wood Lane, London W12 (☎ 081 743 8000 ext 2775)

NEWMAN, Warren J; *b* 20 July 1947; *Educ* LCP (DipCAM (PR), MAIE(Dip)); *m* Avril; 1 s, 1 da; *Career* asst to Gen Ed John Lewis Partnership 1963-68, gp ed South Londoner Newspapers 1968-72, sr info offr London Borough of Newham 1972-74, chief public relation offr London Borough of Hounslow 1974-78, head of public relations London Borough of Southwark 1978-84, dir of public relations NFU 1984-89, dir of communications AEA Technology (UK Atomic Energy Authority) 1989-; lectr at several business schs and conferences; FIPR; memb: Int PR Assoc, IPR Govt Affairs Gp; *Books* The Practice of PR (contrib); *Style—* Warren Newman, Esq; 8 Thalia Close, Greenwich, London SE10 9NA (☎ 081 858 4918); AEA Technology, 11 Charles St, London SW1Y 4QP (☎ 071 389 6565, fax 071 389 6904, car 0831 316795)

NEWMAN, William Frederick; s of Lt William Daniel Newman, of 1 Hanover Ct, Highbury St, Old Portsmouth, and Peggy Annie Georgina, *née* Hill; *b* 9 May 1943; *Educ* Arts Educnl Tst; *m* 1, 4 Sept 1966 (m dis), Margaret Rosica, da of Basil Clark Fred Vinter, of London; 2 s (William Alexander b 1981, Matthew Lawrence b 1985), 2 da (Caron Tracy b 1967, Amanda Jane b 1970); m 2, Sally Elizabeth, da of Samuel George Packham; *Career* architectural conslt; Eric Cumine (Hong Kong) 1961-64, Ian Fraser Turner Lansdown Holt Architects 1964-74, currently princ of Architects and Bldg Surveyors; *Style—* William Newman, Esq; 6 Holmesdale Rd, Teddington, Middx (☎ 081 977 1196); 19 Bloomsbury Square, London WC1A 2NS (☎ 071 637 3688, fax 071 637 3680, car 0860 382462)

NEWMARCH, Michael George (Mick); s of George Langdon Newmarch, and Phyllis Georgina, *née* Crandon; *b* 19 May 1938; *Educ* Tottenham Co GS, Univ of London (BSc external); *m* 10 Oct 1959, Audrey Ann, da of Cecil Clark; 1 s (Timothy b 1963), 2 da (Kate b 1966, Joanne b 1971); *Career* The Prudential Corporation: joined Economic Intelligence Dept Prudential Assurance Co Ltd 1955, sr asst investmt mangr 1976-78, dep investmt mangr 1979-80, investmt mangr and chief exec offr Prudential Portfolio Managers Ltd 1981-89, chief exec Prudential Corporation 1990-, chm Prudential Assurance Company 1990-, chm Prudential Portfolio Managers 1990-; AMSIA; *Style—* Mick Newmarch, Esq; Prudential Corporation, 1 Stephen St, London W1P 2AP (☎ 071 548 3143, fax 071 548 3465)

NEWNES, William Anthony Paul; s of Henry Newnes; *b* 6 Dec 1959; *Educ* Saint Francis Xaviours Sch; *m* Gudrun, da of Kurt Lepa (racehorse trainer in Germany); *Career* racehorse jockey; apprentice to Henry Candy 1976-82, first ride 1978, first winner 1979 (on pledge at Ascot), champion apprentice 1982, European Champion 1982, winner Epsom Oaks 1982; Golden Spurs award, Lester Piggot award; *Recreations* football, boxing, squash; *Style—* William Newnes, Esq; 1 Collett Way, Grove, Wantage, Oxfordshire OX12 ONT (☎ 02357 68168; agent: 027 188 3813 or 0831 235 560)

NEWNS, Sir (Alfred) Foley (Francis Polden); KCMG (1963, CMG 1957), CVO (1961); s of Rev Alfred Newns (d 1930); *b* 30 Jan 1909; *Educ* Christs' Hosp, St Catharine's Coll Cambridge; *m* 1, 1936, Emma Jean (d 1984), da of Ambrose Bateman (d 1950); 1 s, 1 da; m 2, 9 April 1988, Mrs Beryl Wattles; *Career* colonial admin serv Nigeria 1932, sec to Cncl of Ministers 1951-54, sec to Govr Gen and Cncl of Ministers 1955-59, dep govr Sierra Leone 1960, actg govr 1960, advsr to Govt 1961-63, sec to Cabinet Govt of Bahamas 1964-71; FRSA; *Recreations* nature study, music, art, African affairs; *Style—* Sir Foley Newns, KCMG, CVO; 47 Barrow Rd, Cambridge CB2 2AR (☎ 0223 356903)

NEWNS, George Henry; s of George Newns (d 1916); *b* 27 July 1908; *Educ* Whitgift Sch, King's Coll London, KCH Med Sch (MD); *m* 1936, Eileen Deirdre, da of late Lawrence Kenny; 1 s, 1 da; *Career* chm Leukaemia Res Fund 1962-, civilian paediatric conslt to Admty 1962-74, hon conslt in Paediatrics to the Army 1966-74, dean Inst of Child Health London Univ 1949-73 (dean emeritus 1974-), conslt paediatrician-physician Hosp for Sick Children Gt Ormond St 1946-73, hon consulting physician 1974-; FRCP; *Recreations* walking, reading, music; *Style—* George Newns Esq; 12 Milborne Grove, London SW10 (☎ 071 373 2011)

NEWPORT, Helen Mary; da of George Alan Newport (d 1984), and Jeanne Mary, *née* Cross; *b* 29 Feb 1944; *Educ* Bicester GS, Oxford Coll of Technol; 1 da (Emma b 1986); *Career* ski teacher Verbier Ski Sch; restaurant proprietor 1974-79; md Helen Newport & Co Ltd (representing Allied Dunbar plc), leading lady in UK insurance business, speeches on fin planning nationally and internationally; wrote regularly as 'Our Girl in the Alps' for Ski Magazine; *Recreations* travel, skiing, racing, eventing; *Clubs* Vine and Craven Hunt, Sloane, Ski of GB, LIA (Achievement Forum), Millon Dollar Round Table, Network; *Style—* Miss Helen Newport; Choctaw Cottage, 5 Stroud Green, Newbury RG14 7JA (☎ 0635 41649); Helen Newport & Co Ltd, c/o Allied Dunbar plc, Allied Dunbar House, 65 London Rd, Newbury, Berks (☎ 0635 36660, fax 0635 521402)

NEWRY AND MORNE, Viscount; Robert Francis John; s and h of Richard Needham, 6 Earl of Kilmorey (who does not use the title); *b* 30 May 1966; *Educ* Eton, Lady Margaret Hall Oxford; *Career* sales mangr Lewmar Marine Ltd; *Style—* Viscount Newry and Morne; Flat 2, 69 Victoria Road, North Southsea, Hampshire PO5 1PP

NEWSAM, John Ernest; s of John Bower Newsam (d 1945), of Liverpool, and Elizabeth Abbie, *née* Havloran (d 1945); *b* 24 Sept 1926; *Educ* Liverpool Inst, Univ of Edinburgh; *m* 1, 16 June 1951 (m dis 1972), Virginia, da of John Cape, of Ontario, Canada; 3 s (John Michael b 1954, Christopher Paul b 1958, Mark b 1963), 2 da (Nicola b 1952, Virginia b 1956); m 2, 1972, Avril Gladys, *née* McCowan; *Career* RAMC 1951-53; conslt urological surgn 1966, hon sr lectr Univ of Edinburgh 1966; asst ed Br Jl of Urology 1978, chm Ed Bd Jl of RCSE 1989; memb: RCSE, Br Assoc of Urological Surgeons 1966; *Books* Urology and Renel Medicine (1981); *Recreations* golf, reading; *Style—* John Newsam, Esq; 14 Comely Bank, Edinburgh EH4 1AN

NEWSAM, Peter Anthony; s of William Oswald Newsam (d 1974), of Maidenhead; *b* 2 Nov 1928; *Educ* Clifton, Queens' Coll Oxford; *m* 1953 (m dis), Elizabeth Joy Greg; 4 s, 1 da; m 2, 1988, Sue Addinell; 1 da; *Career* former civil servant BOT (asst princ); schoolmaster 1956-63, asst educn offr Yorks N Riding 1963-66, asst dir of educn Cumberland 1966-70, dep educn offr Yorks W Riding 1970-72, educn offr ILEA 1977-82 (dep educn offr 1974-76), chm Cmmn for Racial Equality 1982-87, sec Assoc of CCs 1987-89, dir Inst of Educn Univ of London 1989-; kt 1987; *Style—* Sir Peter Newsam; The Institute of Education, University of London, 20 Bedford Way, London WC1 (☎ 071 636 1500)

NEWSOM, George Harold; QC (1956); s of Rev George Ernest Newsom (d 1934), and Alethea Mary, *née* Awdry (d 1961); *b* 29 Dec 1909; *Educ* Marlborough, Merton Coll Oxford (MA); *m* 11 May 1939, Margaret Amy, da of Lucien Arthur Allen, OBE, of London; 2 s (George Lucien b 10 June 1948, William Arthur Charles b 24 Sept 1951), 1 da (Elizabeth Margaret Alethea (Mrs Thompson) b 6 Feb 1942); *Career* served WWII as princ in Trading with Enemy Dept Treasy and Bd of Trade; called to the Bar Lincoln's Inn 1934 (bencher 1962, treas 1980); dep chm Wiltshire QS 1964-71; chllr: Diocese of St Albans 1958-, Bath and Wells 1971-, London 1971-; memb Ctee of Management International Exhibition Cooperative Wine So 1963-67; *Books* The Faculty Jurisdiction of the Church of England (with late C H S Preston, 1988); Restrictive Covenants affecting Freehold Land and Limitation of Actions (with late CHS Preston); *Recreations* walking, wine; *Clubs* Athenaeum; *Style—* George Newsom, Esq, QC; The Old Vicarage, Bishop's Cannings, Devizes, Wilts SN10 2LA (☎ 0380 86 660)

NEWSOME, Dr David Hay; s of Capt Charles Todd Newsome, OBE (d 1970), of Gannaway Farm, Norton Lindsey, Warwickshire, and Elsie Mary, *née* Hay (d 1960); *b* 15 June 1929; *Educ* Rossall, Emmanuel Coll Cambridge (MA, LittD); *m* 12 April 1955, Joan Florence, da of Lt-Col Leslie Hamilton Trist, DSO, MC (d 1979), of Coldwaltham, Sussex; 4 da (Clare Elizabeth b 25 May 1956, Janet Mary b 22 Sept 1958, (Anne) Louise b 25 Jan 1960, Cordelia Jane b 22 Jan 1961); *Career* Nat Serv 1948-50, Capt RAEC (substantive Lt); asst master Wellington Coll 1954-59; fell Emmanuel Coll Cambridge 1959-70 (sr tutor 1965-70), univ lectr in ecclesiastical history Cambridge 1961-70, headmaster Christ's Hospital Horsham 1970-79, master of Wellington Coll 1980-89; memb Governing Bodies: Westcott House Cambridge 1960-65, Ardingly Coll 1965-69, Eastbourne Coll 1965-69, Epsom Coll 1965-69; FRHistS

1970, FRSL 1980; *Books* A History of Wellington College 1859-1959 (1959), Godliness and Good Learning (1961), The Parting of Friends (1966), Two Classes of Men (1974), On the Edge of Paradise: A C Benson the Diarist (1980, Whitbread prize for biography of the year), Edwardian Excursions (1981); *Recreations* music, opera, fell-walking; *Clubs* East India, Devonshire, Sports and Public Schools; *Style*— Dr David Newsome; The Retreat, Thornthwaite, Keswick, Cumbria (☎ 059 682 372)

NEWSOME, Victor George; s of George Newsome, of Leeds, and Margaret Westmoreland (d 1968); *b* 16 June 1935; *Educ* Leeds Coll of Art, Rome (scholar in painting); *m* thrice; 1 s (Joseph), 1 da (Susanna); *Career* Nat Serv 1955-57; artist and sculptor; teaching appts at: Leicester Sch of Art 1962-63, Nottingham Sch of Art 1963-64, Hull Coll of Art 1964-70; teaching appts between 1970-77: Camberwell Sch of Art and Crafts, Goldsmith's Coll Univ of London, Faculty of Art and Design Brighton Poly, Canterbury Coll of Art, Wimbledon Sch of Art and Chelsea Sch of Art; solo exhibitions: Grabowski Gallery London 1966, Anthony d'Offay Gallery London 1976, Hester van Royen Gallery London 1979, Ikon Gallery Birmingham 1979, Anne Berthoud Gallery London 1981, Marlborough Fine Art London 1987; gp exhibitions incl: The Visual Adventure (Drian Gallery London) 1962, London Group (Camden Art Centre London) 1963, The Inner Image (Grabowski Gallery London) 1964, The New Generation (Whitechapel Gallery London) 1966, Edinburgh Open 100 (Univ of Edinburgh) 1967, Interim (Whitechapel Gallery London) 1968, Six at the Hayward Gallery 1969, Play Orbit (ICA Gallery London) 1969, British Painting '74 (Hayward Gallery London) 1974, Artists' Market (Warehouse Gallery London) 1973, 1976 and 1978, The British Art Show (Arts Cncl touring exhibition) 1979-80, Peter Moores Show (Walker Art Gallery Liverpool) 1981, Recent Work by Gallery Artists (Marlborough Fine Art London) 1983, 1984, 1988, 1989, and 1990, British Artists in Italy 1920-80 (Canterbury Coll of Art touring exhibition) 1985, The Foundation Veranneman invites Marlborough (Kruishoutern Belgium) 1986-87; work in several private and public collections incl Arts Cncl of GB and V & A Museum; *Awards* prix de Rome 1960, Peter Stuyvesant travel bursary to America 1966, prizewinner Structure '66, jt first prizewinner Edinburgh Open 100 1967; *Recreations* being sociable; *Style*— Victor Newsome, Esq; Marlborough Fine Art (London) Ltd, 6 Albemarle St, London W1X 4BY (☎ 071 629 5161, fax 071 629 6338, telex 266 259)

NEWSON-SMITH, Sir John Kenneth; 2 Bt (UK 1944), of Totteridge, Co Hertford, DL (City of London); s of Sir Frank Newson-Smith, 1 Bt (d 1971); *b* 9 Jan 1911; *Educ* Dover Coll, Jesus Coll Cambridge; *m* 1, 1945, Vera Margaret (m dis 1971), da of late Dr Wilfred Greenhouse Allt, CVO, CBE; 1 s, 2 da; m 2, 1972, Anne, da of Harold Burns (d 1987); m 3, 1988, Sarah Lucretia Wimberley Ramsay; *Heir* s, Peter Frank Graham Newson-Smith; *Career* joined HAC 1933, RN 1939, Lt RNVR 1941; memb: Ct of Common Cncl 1945 (dep 1961-), HM Cmmn of Lieutenancy for City of London (HM Lt 1947); chm London United Investmts Ltd 1968-71 (dep chm 1971-); *Clubs* City Livery and Naval; *Style*— Sir John Newson-Smith, Bt, DL; 39 Godfrey St, London SW3 (☎ 071 352 0722)

NEWSON-SMITH, Peter Frank Graham; s and h of Sir John Kenneth Newson-Smith, and Vera Margaret Greenhouse Allt; gf Lord Mayor of London (paternal), gf Dr Greenhouse Allt, CVO, CBE, princ of Trinity Coll of Music London (maternal); *b* 8 May 1947; *Educ* Dover Coll, Trinity Coll of Music; *m* 1974, Mary-Ann, da of Cyril C Collins and w of Anthony Owens; 1 s (Oliver), 1 da (Emma); *Heir* Oliver Nicholas Peter Newson-Smith; *Career* dir of music Clayesmore Preparatory Sch; Freeman City of London 1969, Liveryman Worshipful Co of Musicians 1971; *Recreations* gardening, sailing; *Style*— Peter Newson-Smith, Esq; Lovells Court, Burton Street, Marnhull, Sturminster Newton, Dorset DT10 1JJ; Clayesmore Preparatory School, Iwerne Minster, Blandford Forum, Dorset DT11 8PH

NEWTON, Alice, Lady; Alice Mary; da of late Henry Barber, of Surbiton and widow of Glyn Rosser; *m* 1968, as his 2 w, Sir Edgar Henry Newton, 2 Bt (d 1971); *Style*— Alice, Lady Newton; 14 Castle Hill View, Sidford, Sidmouth, Devon

NEWTON, Rt Hon Antony Harold; PC (1988), OBE (1972), MP (C) Braintree Feb 1974-; s of Harold Newton, of Dovercourt, Harwich; *b* 29 Aug 1937; *Educ* Friends' Sch Saffron Walden, Trinity Coll Oxford; *m* 1, 1962 (m dis 1986), Janet Dianne, er da of Phillip Huxley, of Sidcup; 2 da; m 2, 1986, Mrs Patricia Gilthorpe; *Career* former sec and res sec Bow Gp, asst dir CRD 1970-74 (head Econ Section 1965-70), govt whip 1981-82 (asst govt whip 1979-81); DHSS: parly under sec 1982, min for the Disabled 1983-84, min for Social Security and the Disabled 1984-86, min for Health 1986-88; chllr Duchy of Lancaster 1988-89, sec of state for Social Security DSS 1989-; parly candidate (C) Sheffield Brightside 1970; vice chm Fedn of Univ Cons and Unionist Assocs; economist; *Clubs* St Stephen's; *Style*— The Rt Hon Antony Newton, OBE, MP; House of Commons, SW1

NEWTON, Air Vice-Marshal Barry Hamilton; CB (1988), OBE (1975); s of Bernard Hamilton Newton (d 1932), of Southgate, Middx, and Dorothy Mary Newton, *née* Thomas (d 1979); *b* 1 April 1932; *Educ* Highgate, RAF Coll Cranwell; *m* 1959, Lavinia, da of Col John James Aitken, CMG, DSO, OBE (d 1947), of Taunton, Somerset; 1 s (Charles), 1 da (Melanie); *Career* cmmnd RAF 1953, Personal Staff Offr to Cdr Second Allied Tactical Air Force and CINC RAF Germany 1967, OC Ops Wing RAF Cottesmore 1969, asst dir Def Policy 1978, Cabinet Office 1979-81, Air Cdre Flying Trg HQ RAF Support Cmd 1982, sr dir Staff (Air) RCDS 1984, Cmdt Jt Serv Def Coll Greenwich 1986, ADC to HM The Queen 1983; a gentleman usher to HM The Queen 1989-, memb Cncl TA&VR Assoc 1989-; *Recreations* shooting, music, reading; *Clubs* RAF; *Style*— Air Vice-Marshal Barry Newton, CB, OBE; c/o Nat Westminster Bank plc, 48 Blue Boar Row, Salisbury, Wilts SP1 1DF

NEWTON, Dr Charmian Rosemary; da of Frederick Cleland Newton, of Weybridge, Surrey, and Mildred Edith, *née* Owen; *b* 3 April 1943; *Educ* St Maur's Convent Weybridge, King's Coll London, Westminster Med Sch (MB BS, DObstRCOG); *m* 30 Jan 1971, Timothy Richard Hornsby, s of Harker William Hornsby (d 1974); 1 s (Adrian b 1977), 1 da (Gabrielle b 1975); *Career* house offr Westminster Hosp and Queen Mary's Hosp Roehampton 1965-66, sr house offr in med Whittington Hosp 1967-68, med registrar St Mary's Hosp Paddington 1968-69, res registrar St Mark's Hosp London 1969-72, med registrar St George's Hosp London 1972-73; sr med registrar: Central Middx Hosp 1973-75, Middx Hosp 1975-77; conslt physician: S London Hosp for Women 1978-84, St James's Hosp 1978-88, St George's Hosp 1988-; memb: BSG 1973, BMA 1965; MRCP 1967 (collegiate memb 1979), FRSM 1970, memb BDA 1981; *Recreations* opera, ballet, skiing; *Clubs* RSM, SCGB; *Style*— Dr Charmian Newton; Norman Tanner Unit, St George's Hospital, Blackshaw Rd, London SW17 0QT (☎ 081 672 1255 ext 53032)

NEWTON, Christopher David; TD (1971), JP (Inner London 1974); s of James George Newton (d 1979), and Ethel Jane, *née* Davies (d 1987); *b* 2 Jan 1938; *Educ* John Fisher Sch Surrey; *m* 12 Sept 1970, Jennifer Mary, da of Maj David Turville Constable Maxwell, TD (d 1985), of Bosworth Hall, Husbands Bosworth, Leics; 1 s (James Nicholas Turville b 1971), 1 da (Lucinda Rosalinde Mary b 1975); *Career* served Welsh Guards 1955-58, Westminster Dragoons (TA) 1959-72, Capt, ret; dir and chm: John Newton & Co Ltd, John Newton (Devpts) Ltd, Newtonite Ltd, Mktg Servs (London) Ltd 1978-; Freeman City of London 1985-, Livery memb Ctee Fanmakers Co 1986-, underwriting memb of Lloyds 1988-; Liveryman Worshipful Co of Fanmakers; *Recreations* hunting, cross-country skiing; *Clubs* Cavalry and Guards, Lansdowne; *Style*— Christopher Newton, Esq, TD, JP; Rumsey House, Calne, Wilts SN11 9LT (☎ 0249 816283); 160 Piccadilly, London W1V 0BX (☎ 071 409 0414, fax 071 629 2279)

NEWTON, Christopher John; s of Henry Newton (d 1975), of Leicester and London, and Florence Alice, *née* Wilton (d 1978); *b* 24 June 1936; *Educ* Market Bosworth GS, Royal Ballet Sch Sadler's Wells; *Career* joined Royal Ballet Co Corps de Ballet 1954-1970 (soloist 1958-70), joined Faculty of US Int Univ San Diego California to teach dance notation and repertoire 1970-73; Royal Ballet: re-joined as dance notator and repetiteur 1973-80, ballet master 1980-88, artistic co-ordinator 1988; has re-produced ballets of Frederick Ashton, Antony Tudor, Rudolph Nureyev and Roland Petit 1970-88 for American Ballet Theatre, Joffrey Ballet, SF Ballet, Paris Opera Ballet and Deutsch Oper Ballet of Berlin, also staged own production of Swan Lake - Act III for Pennsylvania Ballet; re-produced and staged Frederick Ashton's 3 act ballet Ondine from incomplete film records 1988, (created in 1958 and last performed in 1966); MRAD, AIChor; *Recreations* textile crafts; *Style*— Christopher Newton, Esq; Royal Ballet Company, Royal Opera House, Covent Garden, London WC2E 7QA (☎ 071 240 1200, telex 27988)

NEWTON, Derek Henry; s of Sidney Wellington Newton (d 1976), of Worthing, Sussex, and Sylvia May, *née* West (d 1959); *b* 14 March 1933; *Educ* Emanuel Sch; *m* 18 May 1957, Judith Ann, da of Rowland Hart (d 1973); 2 da (Katherine Jane (Mrs Smith) b 3 Sept 1960, Amanda Jean b 4 Nov 1962); *Career* Nat Serv Lt RA 1952-54; insur broker; chm C E Heath plc 1983-87 (ret); dir: Glaxo Insur (Bermuda) Ltd 1980-, Glaxo Tstees Ltd 1980-, Glaxo Pharmaceuticals Tstees Ltd 1980-, Forecast Trading Ltd 1984-, Farley Health Products Pensions Ltd 1985-, Glaxo Animal Health Pensions Ltd 1985-, Clarges Pharmaceuticals Tstees Ltd 1985-; govr BUPA Med Res & Devpt Ltd 1981-; chm Surrey Co Cricket Club 1980-; FCII 1957; *Recreations* cricket, golf; *Clubs* Surrey Co Cricket (chm 1980-), MCC; *Style*— Derek Newton, Esq; Pantiles, Meadway, Oxshott, Surrey KT22 OLZ (☎ 0372 842273); Surrey County Cricket Club, The Oval, Kennington, London SE11 5SS (☎ 071 582 6660)

NEWTON, George Peter Howgill; s and h of Sir Harry Michael Rex Newton, 3 Bt; *b* 26 March 1962; *Educ* Sherborne, Pembroke Coll Cambs (MA); *m* 30 Jan 1988, Jane L, twin da of John Rymer; 1 da (Sarah Rebecca b 4 Jan 1991); *Career* parish assist; memb Girdlers' Livery Co; *Style*— George Newton, Esq

NEWTON, Sir (Leslie) Gordon; s of John Newton; *b* 1907; *Educ* Blundell's, Sidney Sussex Coll Cambridge; *m* 1935, Peggy Ellen Warren; 1 s (decd); *Career* ed The Financial Times 1950-72 (dir 1967-72); chm LBC 1974-77; dir: Trust House Forte 1973-80, Mills & Allen (International); kt 1966; *Style*— Sir Gordon Newton; 51 Thames House, Phyllis Court Drive, Henley-on-Thames, Oxon RG9 2NA

NEWTON, Ian Stenhouse; s of Peter Stenhouse Newton (d 1982), of Cardiff, and Esme, *née* Jones; *b* 6 Sept 1951; *Educ* Cardiff Hs, New Coll Oxford (MA); *m* 20 Aug 1973, (Elizabeth) Vanessa, da of Capt William Alan Wilson; 2 da (Kate b 1979, Ailsa b 1983); *Career* articled clerk and slr Biddle & Co 1974-77; Percy Ptnrship: legal advsr 1978-81, admin and fin ptnr 1982-; dir and sec Insight Computer Systems Ltd 1981-, ptnr and sec PTP Landscape 1985-, dir Wren Insurance Association Ltd 1987-, ptnr and sec PTP Design Group 1990-; past memb Ptnrship Secs Panel ICSA 1985-89, past chm Cardiff and SE Wales Branch ICSA 1986, hon sec Chartered Secs Golf Soc 1989-; ACIArb 1978, FCIS 1981, FBIM 1985; *Recreations* golf, eastern philosophy; *Clubs* Cardiff and County, Royal Porthcawl Golf, Llanishen Golf, Wig and Pen; *Style*— Ian Newton, Esq; 10 Cathedral Rd, Cardiff, South Glamorgan CF1 9YF (☎ 0222 224334, fax 0222 342839, car 0836 689451)

NEWTON, Joanna Dawson (Mrs Richard Oulton); *née* Newton; da of Guy Geoffrey Frederick Newton (d 1969), and Rosemary Enid, *née* Stowers; *b* 28 May 1921; *Educ* Headington Sch Oxford, Banbury Art Sch, Bryam Shaw Sch of Art; *m* 14 Sept 1985, Richard Arthur Courtenay Oulton, s of Harry Charles Neil Maxwell Oulton, MC (d 1981); *Career* painter; exhibitions incl: Whitechapel Gallery 1982, Nat Portrait Gallery (Imperial Tobacco Portrait Award) 1983, Vanessa Devereux Gallery 1984, Royal Acad (summer exhibition) 1985, The Mall Galleries (Nat Art exhibition) 1986, National Portrait Gallery (Imperial Tobacco Portrait award) 1986, Royal Acad (summer exhibition 1988 and 1989, Whitechapel Open 1989); *Recreations* tennis, films, art galleries; *Clubs* Chelsea Arts; *Style*— Ms Joanna Newton; 14 Chesilton Rd, London SW6 (☎ 071 731 5581)

NEWTON, Rev Dr John Anthony; s of Charles Victor Newton (d 1963), and Kathleen, *née* Marchant; *b* 28 Sept 1930; *Educ* Boston GS, Univ Coll Hull (BA), Inst of Historical Res Univ of London (PhD), Fitzwilliam Coll Cambridge (MA); *m* 28 Dec 1963, Rachel, da of Maurice Horne Giddings (d 1968), of Louth, Lincs; 4 s (Mark b 5 Nov 1964, Christopher b 27 Sept 1966, David b 31 Dec 1970, William b 24 March 1976); *Career* chaplain Kent Coll Canterbury 1955, asst tutor Richmond Coll 1958, min Louth Lincs 1961; tutor in church history: Didsbury Coll Bristol 1965, St Paul's Coll Limuru Kenya 1972; princ Wesley Coll Bristol 1973, supt W London Mission, pres Methodist Conf 1981-82, chm Liverpool Dist of Methodist Church 1986, Free Church moderator for Merseyside and jt pres Merseyside Churches Ecumenical Assembly 1987, hon canon Lincoln Cathedral 1988; chm Merseyside Cncl of Voluntary Serv, tstee Liverpool Industl Mission Ecumenical Ctee, hon memb Merseyside C of C and Indust; Hon DLitt Hull 1982; *Books* Susanna Wesley and the Puritan Tradition in Methodism (1969), The Palestine Problem (1971), Search for a Saint: Edward King (1977), Marcus Ward (1984); *Recreations* walking, gardening, reading, book collecting; *Clubs* Athenaeum (Liverpool), Penn; *Style*— Rev Dr John Newton; 49 Queen's Drive, Mossley Hill, Liverpool L18 2DT (☎ 051 722 1219)

NEWTON, John Garnar; s and h of Sir Kenneth Garnar Newton, 3 Bt, OBE, TD; *b* 10 July 1945; *Educ* Reed's Sch Cobham; *m* 27 May 1972, Jacynth Anne Kay, *née* Miller; 3 s (Timothy Garnar b 1973, Alistair Blair (twin) b 1973, Andrew Robert b 1975); *Style*— John Newton Esq

NEWTON, Dr John Henry; s of Dr JE Newton (d 1979), and Jessie Elizabeth, *née* Sherwood (d 1985); *b* 8 Oct 1939; *Educ* Blundell's, Charing Cross Hosp and Univ of London (MB BS, DMRD); *m* 24 Aug 1968, Valerie Faith, da of Frederick Arthur Mullineux (d 1977); 1 s (Simon James b 1970), 2 da (Antoinette Sophie b 1969, Lucinda Helen b 1972); *Career* registrar Bristol United Hospital 1967-69, sr registrar Charing Cross Hospital 1970-72, conslt radiologist Bedford General Hospital 1972-, chm Radiodiagnostic Sub-ctee NW Thames RHA 1989-; FFR 1971, FRCR 1975; *Recreations* travel, opera, photography; *Style*— Dr John Newton; 8 Days Lane, Biddenham, Bedford MK40 4AD (☎ 0234 363828); Bedford General Hospital, Kempston Rd, Bedford MK42 9DJ (☎ 0234 355122)

NEWTON, Prof John Richard; s of Geoffrey Tayler Newton, of Woking, Surrey, and Nora, *née* Waddington (d 1986); *b* 14 April 1938; *Educ* Uppingham, Bart's Hosp Med Sch (MB BS, MD); *m* 1 July 1967, Mary Patricia, da of Henry Percy Burdis (d 1986); 1 s (Geoffrey Waddington b 4 July 1969 d 1975), 2 da (Rebecca Sophie Patersson b 26 Sept 1971, Shelley Marianne b 19 May 1975); *Career* postgrad med trg: Bart's, Queen Charlotte's Hosp for Women, Royal Sussex County Hosp, KCH, London, Univ Hosp Uppsala Sweden, Health Sci Centre San Antonio Texas USA; sr lectr and hon conslt KCH 1972-79, Lawson Tait Prof of obstetrics and gynaecology

Univ of Birmingham 1979-; author of numerous pubns on human reproduction and contraception; chm: FPA Med Advsy Ctee 1980-, WHO task force on long acting methods of contraception 1987-; hon sec Br Fertility Soc (fndr memb); memb: Exec Ctee Int Fedn of Fertility Socs, Uphill Ski Club (for mentally and physically handicapped), Birmingham and Midland Obstetrics and Gynaecology Soc, Blair Bell Res Soc, Soc for the Advancement of Contraception, Med Laser Soc; MRCOG 1987, FRCOG 1982; *Books* Pocket Obscetrics & Gynaecology (edns 9, 10, 11, 12, 13); *Recreations* sailing, skiing; *Style—* Prof John Newton; Dept of Obstetrics and Gynaecology, Birmingham University Medical School, Queen Elizabeth Medical Centre, Edgbaston, Birmingham B15 2TG (☎ 021 4721377, fax 021 41415756 portable tel 0836 678063)

NEWTON, Sir Kenneth Garnar; 3 Bt (UK 1924), of Beckenham, Kent; OBE (1969, MBE 1944), TD; s of Sir Edgar Henry Newton, 2 Bt (d 1971); *b* 4 June 1918; *Educ* Wellington; *m* 1, 1944, Margaret Isabel (d 1979), da of Rev Dr George Blair, of Dundee; 2 s; m 2, 1980, Pamela, wid of F T K Wilson; *Heir* s, John Garnar Newton; *Career* served WWII, Lt-Col 1944; gen cmmr for Income Tax 1961-; md Garnar Booth plc 1961-83 (chm 1972-87); pres: Br Leather Fedn 1968-69, Int Cncl of Tanners 1972-78; Master: Worshipful Co of Leathersellers 1977-78, Worshipful Co of Feltmakers 1983-84; chm Govrs Colfe's Sch 1982-; *Style—* Sir Kenneth Newton, Bt, OBE, TD; Wildways, High Broom Lane, Crowborough, E Sussex TN6 3SP

NEWTON, Mark Robert; s of Robert William Banner Newton (d 1982), and Cicely Kathleen, *née* Radmall (d 1989); *b* 2 June 1954; *Educ* Eton, RAC Cirencester; *m* 12 May 1979, Diana Sarah, da of Maj Sir Robert David Black, BT, of Elvendon Priory, Goring-on-Thames, Oxon; 1 s (William David Rupert b 7 Dec 1989); *Career* chartered surveyor; ptnr Fisher Hoggarth 1985-; memb: Game Conservancy, Royal Forestry Soc; FRICS 1986; *Recreations* fishing, shooting; *Style—* Mark Newton, Esq; The Old Rectory, Church Langton, Leics (☎ 0858 84 600); Fisher Hoggarth, 40 High St, Market Harborough, Leics (☎ 0858 410200, fax 0858 410207, car 0860 514474)

NEWTON, Sir (Harry) Michael Rex; 3 Bt (UK 1900), of The Wood, Sydenham Hill, Lewisham, Kent and Kottingham House, Burton-on-Trent, Co Stafford; s of Sir Harry Kottingham Newton, 2 Bt, OBE (d 1951); *b* 7 Feb 1923; *Educ* Eastbourne Coll; *m* 1958, Pauline Jane, da of Richard John Frederick Howgill, CBE, of Branscombe, Sullington Warren, Storrington, Sussex; 1 s, 3 (adopted) da; *Heir* s, George Peter Howgill Newton; *Career* served 1941-46 with KRRC; dir Thomas Parsons & Sons Ltd; memb Girdlers' Co; Freeman City of London; *Clubs* Bath, Roy Ocean Racing; *Style—* Sir Michael Newton, Bt; Weycroft Hall, nr Axminster, Devon (☎ 0297 3232)

NEWTON, 4 Baron (UK 1892); Peter Richard Legh; JP (Hants 1951); s of 3 Baron (d 1960); *b* 6 April 1915; *Educ* Eton, Ch Ch Oxford; *m* 1948, Priscilla (who had m, 1936, Capt Viscount Wolmer, s and h of 3 Earl of Selborne and who was k accidentally while on active serv 1942; 2 s, 1 da), da of Capt John Egerton-Warburton (d 1915) and Hon Mrs Waters (d 1968, herself da of 2 Baron Newton); 2 s; *Heir* s, Hon Richard Thomas Legh; *Career* 2 Lt Grenadier Gds 1937, Capt 1941, Maj 1945; MP (C) Hampshire (Petersfield) 1951-60; asst govt whip 1953-55, a lord cmmr of the Treasy 1955-57, vice-chamberlain HM Household 1957-59 (treas 1959-60); jt Parly sec Min of Health 1962-64, min of state Dept of Educn and Science 1964; CC Hants 1949-52 and 1954-55; *Style—* The Rt Hon the Lord Newton; Vernon Hill House, Bishop's Waltham, Hants (☎ 048 93 2301)

NEWTON, Rodney Stephen; s of Amos Bernard Newton (d 1981), of Birmingham, and Winifred Nellie, *née* York; *b* 31 July 1945; *Educ* Kings Heath HS Birmingham, Lordwood Boys' Sch Birmingham, Birmingham Sch of Music; *m* 19 Sept 1970, Jennifer Kathleen, da of Denis Williams, of Halesowen, Worcs; 2 s (Matthew b 15 Sept 1977, Christopher b 24 April 1980); *Career* orchestral timpanist percussionist and composer 1967-; BBC trg orchestra 1967-70, ENO orchestra 1974-85, promotion mangr United Music Publishers 1979-82, music conslt London Int Film Sch 1988-; compositions in: 9 symphonies, 5 string quartets, flute concerto, chamber and vocal works; film and TV scores incl: The Pyrates, The Watch house (BBC TV), Theatre of Paint BEU prodns, Change at Clapham Junction (Thames TV); memb Knights of St Columbia; memb Composers Guild of GB, Assoc of Professional Composers (exec ctee memb); *Recreations* reading, cinema, eating out; *Style—* Rodney Newton, Esq; c/o London International Film School, 24 Shelton St, London WC2H 9HP (☎ 071 240 0168)

NEWTON, (John) Simon; s of John David Newton, and Mary, *née* Bevan; *b* 22 Aug 1945; *Educ* The Birkenhead Sch, UCL (LLB); *m* 4 July 1970, Katharine Margaret Headlay, da of Sir Terence Garvey (d 1986); 1 s (Thomas b 1975), 1 da (Alexander b 1973); *Career* called to the Bar Middle Temple 1970; chm Salmon & Trout Assoc (Liverpool and Merseyside branch); *Recreations* golf, fishing; *Clubs* Royal Liverpool Golf; *Style—* Simon Newton, Esq; Refuge Assurance House, Derby Square, Liverpool L2 1TS (☎ 051 709 4222)

NEWTON, Hon Mrs (Ursula Helen Rank); da of 1 and last Baron Rank (d 1972); *b* 1919; *m* 1952, Robert Lancelot Newton (d 1969); 1 s, 2 da; *Style—* The Hon Mrs Newton; Church Farm, Saltby, Melton, Mowbray, Leics

NEWTON DUNN, William Francis (Bill); MEP (Cons) 1979- Lincolnshire and Gibraltar; s of Lt-Col Owen F Newton Dunn, OBE, and Barbara Mary, *née* Brooke; *b* 3 Oct 1941; *Educ* Marlborough, Gonville and Caius Cambridge (MA), Insead Business Sch Fontainebleau (MBA); *m* 17 Oct 1970, Anna Terez, da of Michel Arki; 1 s (Thomas b 1973), 1 da (Daisy b 1976); *Career* formerly with Fisons Fertilisers; *Books* Greater in Europe (1986); *Style—* Bill Newton Dunn, Esq, MEP; 10 Church Lane, Navenby, Lincoln LN5 0EG (☎ 0522 810812)

NEY, Kevin Philip; s of John Martin Ney (d 1938), of Crosby, and Frances Sheils (d 1977); *b* 31 March 1922; *Educ* St Mary's Coll Crosby; *Career* served RNVR 1941-46, Lt 1944 (despatches 1944) in N Atlantic, Sicily, Salerno, Normandy and Pacific Fleet; CA 1946; ptnr: Robert J Ward & Co 1948-71, Tansley Witt & Co 1971-79, Arthur Andersen & Co 1979-81; dir: Burns Oates & Washbourne 1955-71, John Wainwright & Co 1962-, Brasseys Publishers 1977-79, Britannia Arrow Hldgs plc 1977-; chm Nat Employers Life Assur Co 1983-90; hon treas The Catholic Union of GB 1973-; FCA; *Recreations* gardening, chess, photography, graphology; *Clubs* Naval and Military, Bath and County; *Style—* Kevin P Ney, Esq; 150 Cliffords Inn, Fetter Lane, London EC4; Coley House, East Harptree, Bristol BS18 6AW

NG, Dr Weng Cheong; s of Kam Sooi Ng, and Ng-Sung Ngan-Lui; *b* 18 Sept 1943; *Educ* Methodist Boy's Sch Penang, Univ of Singapore (MB BS), Royal Coll of Physicians and Surgeons (DPath), Univ of London (DCP), Univ of Mahidol (DTM&H); *m* 25 Sept 1971, Chew Pek Choo, da of Chew Poh Leang; 1 s (Paul b 4 Jan 1979); *Career* MO: Rural Health Trg Sch Jitra Malaysia 1970-71, Inst of Med Res Kuala Lumpur Malaysia 1971-75; registrar Gen Infirmary Salisbury 1978; sr registrar Southampton and Poole Gen Hosps 1978-80, pathology dept Singapore 1981-83; conslt histopathologist Princess Margaret Hosp Swindon 1983-; memb: Assoc of Clinical Pathologists, Br Soc of Clinical Cytology, BMA; MRCPath 1979, FCAP 1982, FRCPath 1991; *Recreations* chess, music, swimming; *Style—* Dr Weng Cheong Ng; Pathology Department, Princess Margaret Hospital, Okus Rd, Swindon, Wiltshire SN1 4JU (☎ 0793 536231 ext 3336)

NIAS, Prof Anthony Hugh Wade; s of Major Alfred Wade Nias, MC, TC (d 1959), and Emily Mary, *née* Dixon (d 1990); *b* 3 Aug 1926; *Educ* Peter Symonds Sch Winchester, Oxford Univ (MA, DM, BCh); *m* 26 July 1952, Birgitta Cecilia, da of Dr Ernst Mikael Valdemar Akerblom (d 1965), of Sweden; 1 s (Peter b 1953), 1 da (Kristina b 1956); *Career* RN 1944-48; registrar in radiotherapy Churchill Hosp Oxford 1957-59, MRC clinical res fell Oxford Univ 1959-62, princ res offr Christie Hosp Manchester 1962-72, conslt med radiation biologist Glasgow Inst of Radiotherapeutics 1972-78, Richard Dimbleby prof of cancer res St Thomas Hosp Univ of London 1978-; FRCR, MRCPath 1986; *Books* Clinical Radiobiology (2 edn, 1988), An Introduction to Radiobiology (1990); *Recreations* gardening, golf, music listening; *Clubs* Royal Society of Medicine; *Style—* Prof Anthony Nias; 98 Ditton Road, Surbiton, Surrey KT6 6RH (☎ 071 399 3620); Richard Dimbleby Department of Cancer Research, St Thomas' Hospital, London SE1 7EH (☎ 071 928 9292 ext 2242, fax 071 928 4599, telex 27913 STH LDN G)

NIBLOCK, Henry (Pat); OBE (1972); s of Joseph Niblock (d 1932), of Belfast, and Isabel, *née* Bradford (d 1928); *b* 25 Nov 1911; *Educ* Elementary and Business Trg Sch Belfast; *m* 14 May 1940, Barbara Mary, da of Capt Wilshire Davies, OBE (d 1948), of Reading; 2 s (Michael b 21 Feb 41, Timothy b 13 Oct 1942); *Career* Dip Serv; vice consul: Bremen 1947-50, Bordeaux 1950; commercial attaché Copenhagen 1951-52; consul: Frankfurt am Main 1953-57, (chargé d'affaires) Monrovia 1957-58, Houston 1959-62; chargé d'affaires Port au Prince 1962-63, first sec and consul Brussels 1964, consul (commercial) Cape Town 1965-68, consul-gen Strasbourg 1968-72; memb Past Rotarians Club Eastbourne; *Recreations* bowls, walking; *Clubs* Civil Serv; *Style—* Pat Niblock, Esq; 10 Clifton House, 2 Park Ave, Eastbourne, E Sussex BN22 9QN (☎ 0323 505 695)

NICE, Geoffrey; s of William Charles Nice, and Mahala Anne, *née* Tarryer (d 1982); *b* 21 Oct 1945; *Educ* St Dunstans Coll Catford, Keble Coll Oxford; *m* 1974, Philippa, da of Kemlo Abbot Cronin Gross, OBE, ERD; 3 da (Amelia b 1975, Taffa b 1976, Mahalah b 1980); *Career* barr, rec Crown Court 1987-, QC 1990; Parly candidate (SDP/Lib Alliance) Dover 1983 and 1987; *Style—* Geoffrey Nice, Esq; Farrars Building, Temple, London EC4 (☎ 071 583 9241)

NICHOL, David Brett; s of Philip George Nichol (d 1974), of Gullane, E Lothian, and Kathleen, *née* Brett; *b* 20 April 1945; *Educ* Sedbergh; *m* 22 July 1977, Judith Mary, da of Godfrey Arthur Parker (d 1966), of Godalming, Surrey; 4 da (Alexandra b 1979, Tessa b 1981, Leonie b 1982, Flora b 1986); *Career* CA; Deloitte & Co 1962-68, County Bank London 1968-70, Martin Corpn Australia 1970-71, W I Carr Hong Kong 1971-72, dir Ivory & Sime plc 1972-, md Ivory & Sime Asia Ltd 1989-; tstee Royal Botanic Gdns Edinburgh 1986-89; FCA; *Recreations* shooting, skiing, golf; *Clubs* New, R & A, Hon Co of Edinburgh Golfers, Shek-o (Hong Kong); *Style—* David B Nichol, Esq; Rossie, Forgandenny, Perthshire PH2 9EH; Ivory & Sime plc, One Charlotte Square, Edinburgh, EH2 4DZ (☎ 031 225 1357, fax 031 225 2375, telex 727242 IVORYS G

NICHOL, Duncan Kirkbride; CBE (1988); s of James Nichol (d 1989), and Mabel Nichol (d 1984); *b* 30 May 1941; *Educ* Bradford GS, Univ of St Andrews (MA); *m* 18 March 1972, Elizabeth Elliott Mitchell, da of Herbert Wilkinson (d 1967), of Blackpool; 1 s (Andrew b 1973), 1 da (Rachael b 1977); *Career* hosp sec Manchester Royal Infirmary 1969-73, dep gp sec and acting gp sec Univ Hosp Mgmnt Ctee of S Manchester 1973-74, dist admin S Manchester Dist 1974-77, area admin Salford DHA 1977-81, regnl gen mangr Mersey RHA 1984-89 (regnl admin 1981-84), chief exec offr NHS Mgmnt Exec 1989-; memb Central Health Servs Cncl 1980-81, pres IMSM 1984-85 (memb Cncl 1976-), chm Kings Fund Educn Ctee 1987-; CBIM 1988; FHA 1990; *Recreations* golf, walking; *Style—* Duncan Nichol, Esq, CBE; 1 Pipers Close, Heswell, Wirral, Merseyside L60 9LJ (☎ 051 342 2699); Richmond House, 79 Whitehall, London SW1 2NS (☎ 071 210 5160, fax 071 210 5409)

NICHOL, Scott Alan; s of Ronald Nichol, of Selkirk, and Joyce Coutts, *née* Reid; *b* 18 June 1970; *Educ* Selkirk HS; *Career* Rubgy Union fly half Selkirk RFC; Selkirk RFC 1988-; rep: Scottish Schs 1987-88 (tour NZ 1988), Scotland U19 1989, Scotland U21 1990, Scotland B 1990 (debut v Ireland B); postman 1989-90, fireman 1990-; U15 Border Tennis Champion; *Recreations* golf; *Style—* Scott Nichol, Esq; Montras, 22 Victoria Crescent, Selkirk TD7 5DE (☎ 0750 21763); Selkirk Rugby Club, Philipaugh, Selkirk (☎ 0750 20403)

NICHOL, Dr William Dorrien; s of John Buchanan Nichol (d 1947), of Dunedin, New Zealand, and Annie Elizabeth, *née* Cavanagh (d 1939); *b* 12 Dec 1914; *Educ* Otago Boys' HS, Otago Univ Med Sch NZ (MB ChB); *m* 24 May 1952, Joan Pauline, da of Ralph Palmer Taylor (d 1962), of Edinburgh; 2 s (Robert Moray b 1956, John Alastair b 1957), 1 da (Helen Catriona b 1953); *Career* NZ Med Corps 1943-6 CMF Capt; asst in radiology Harvard Coll and clinical fell Massachusetts Gen Hosp 1952-53; conslt radiologist: PPP Med Centre London, St Bartholomews Hosp London 1951-80, dir X-ray dept St Bartholomew's Hosp 1971-80; FFR, FRCR; *Recreations* golf, electronics, woodwork; *Style—* Dr William Nichol; Chasewood House, Chasewood Avenue, Enfield, Middlesex (☎ 071 363 9444); 121 Harley St, London W1 (☎ 071 935 2235)

NICHOLAS, Alison Margaret; da of Dr Alfred David Gwynne Nicholas, of 16 Barker Hades Rd, Letwell, nr Worksop, and Cynthia, *née* Neary; *b* 6 March 1962; *Educ* Sch of St Mary's and St Annes, Abbots Bromley, Staffs; *Career* golfer; amateur record: N of Eng Girl's Champion 1982-83, Br Strokeplay Champion 1983, Yorks Champion 1984; professional tournament victories: Weetabix Ladies Open 1987, Laing NSPCC Charity Ladies Classic 1987, Br Olivetti Tournament 1988, Variety Club Celebrity Classic 1988, James Capel Guernsey Open 1988, Qualitair La Manga Classic 1988, 89, Lufthansa German Open 1989, Gislaved Swedish Open 1989; Women's Professional Golfers Euro Tour 1984-90, Ladies Professional Golf Assoc America 1990; memb Professional Golf Assoc 1984-; *Style—* Alison Nicholas

NICHOLAS, (John) Barry Moylan; s of Archibald John Nicholas (d 1978), and Rose Elizabeth, *née* Moylan (d 1947); *b* 6 July 1919; *Educ* Downside, Brasenose Coll Oxford (MA); *m* 9 July 1948, Hildegart Elizabeth, da of Prof Hans Cloos (d 1953), of Bonn; 1 s (Peter b 1955), 1 da (Frances b 1950); *Career* RCS 1939-45, Maj 1943; called to the Bar Inner Temple 1950; Univ of Oxford: fell Brasenose Coll 1947-78, tutor 1947-72, All Souls reader in Roman law 1949-71, prof of comparative law 1971-78, memb Hebdomadal Cncl 1975-83, princ Brasenose Coll 1978-89; hon: bencher Inner Temple 1984, Dr Paris V 1987; FBA 1990; *Books* Introduction to Roman Law (1962), Jolowicz and Nicholas Historical Introduction to Roman Law (3 edn 19 French Law of Contract (1982); *Style—* Barry Nicholas, Esq; 18A Charlbury Rd, Oxford OX2 6UU (☎ 0865 58512)

NICHOLAS, Sir David; CBE (1982); *b* 25 Jan 1930; *Educ* Neath GS, Univ Coll of Wales Aberystwyth (BA); *m* 1952, Juliet Powell Davies; 1 s (James), 1 da (Helen); *Career* Nat Serv Army 1951-53; journalist: Wakefield Express, Yorkshire Post, Daily Telegraph, Observer; ITN: joined 1960, dep ed 1963, ed and chief exec 1977-89, chm and chief exec 1989-; dir Worldwide TV News (WTN); fell UCW Aberystwyth; Hon LLD Univ of Wales; FRTS; kt 1989; *Recreations* sailing, walking, riding; *Clubs* Reform; *Style—* Sir David Nicholas, CBE; c/o Independent Television News, 200 Gray's Inn Rd, London WC1X 8X2

NICHOLAS, Prof Herbert George; s of Rev William Daniel Nicholas, of Treharris, and Mary Elizabeth Nicholas; *b* 8 June 1911; *Educ* Mill Hill, New Coll Oxford (BA, MA), Univ of Yale; *Career* American Div MOI 1941-45, first sec Br Embassy

Washington 1945-46, fell and tutor Exeter Coll Oxford 1944-51 (lectr 1938-44); lectr modern history and politics Univ of Oxford 1948-56, faculty fell Nuffield Coll Oxford 1948-57, fell New Coll Oxford 1951-78 (hon fell 1980-), Nuffield reader in comparative study of insts 1956-69, Rhodes prof of American history and instns 1969-78; dir New Coll Devpt Fund 1989-; chm Br Assoc for American Studies 1960-62; Hon DUniv of Pittsburgh 1968; FBA 1969 (vice pres 1975-76); *Books* The American Union (1948), The British General Election of 1950 (1951), To the Hustings (1956), The United Nations as a Political Institution (1952, 5 edn 1975), Britain and the United States (1963), The Nature of American Politics (1980), Washington Despatches 1941-45 (ed, 1981); *Recreations* gardening, listening to music; *Clubs* Athenaeum; *Style—* Prof HG Nicholas; New Coll, Oxford OX1 3BN (☎ 0865 279 533)

NICHOLAS, Sir Herbert Richard (Harry); OBE (1949); s of Richard Henry Nicholas; *b* 13 March 1905; *Educ* Elementary Sch Bristol, evening classes, correspondence courses; *m* 1932, Rosina Grace Brown; *Career* asst-gen sec Tport and Gen Workers' Union 1956-68 (actg gen sec 1964-66); TUC Gen Cncl 1964-67, memb Nat Exec Ctee Labour Party 1956-64 and 1967-68, treas Labour Party 1960-64, gen sec Labour Party 1968-72; kt 1970; *Style—* Sir Harry Nicholas, OBE; 33 Madeira Rd, Streatham, London SW16 2DG (☎ 081 769 7989)

NICHOLAS, James Donald; s of Capt Donald Louis Nicholas (d 1973), and Evadne Chavasse; one of mother's father's twin brothers, Noel Godfrey Chavasse won VC and Bar 1914-18 War; *b* 1 April 1951; *Educ* Bradfield, Royal Agric Coll Cirencester; *m* 20 May 1975, Rachael Jane, da of Cecil Gifford, of Cheltenham, Gloucs; 1 step s (Rupert b 1969), 2 step da (Katherine b 1965, Abigail b 1973); *Career* dir District Estates and assoc cos 1985; ptnr S Wales Fishery Michaelchurch-on-Arrow 1978-; memb Salmon and Trout Assoc; *Recreations* fly fishing for trout and salmon, stalking, shooting, travel, gastronomy; *Clubs* Boodles, Flyfishers; *Style—* James Nicholas, Esq; Welsh Court, Yatton, Ross-on-Wye, Herfordshire (☎ 053 184 294)

NICHOLAS, (Angela) Jane Udale; OBE (1990); da of Bernard Alexander Royle Shore, CBE (d 1985), and Olive Livett, *née* Udale (d 1981); father a leading viola player, teacher and writer; *b* 14 June 1929; *Educ* Ballet Rambert Sch, Arts Educn Tst, Sadler's Wells Sch; *m* 1964, William Alan Nicholas, s of Percy Edgar Nicholas (d 1960); *Career* ballet dancer, fndr memb Sadler's Wells Theatre Ballet 1946-50, memb Sadler's Wells Ballet at Covent Garden 1950-52; freelance dancer, singer, actress 1952-60; drama offr Br Cncl 1961-70, music offr and dance offr Arts Cncl 1970, dir Dance and Mime 1979-89 (asst dir 1975-79); memb Bd of Dirs: Creative Dance Artists Tst (1990), The Riverside Tst (1991); memb Exec Ctee Dance UK (1991); FRSA 1990; *Recreations* collecting antique china; *Style—* Mrs Jane Nicholas, OBE; 21 Stamford Brook Rd, London W6 0XJ (☎ 081 741 3035)

NICHOLAS, Mark Charles Jefford; s of Peter Jefford Nicholas (d 1968), and Anne Evelyn (stage name Loxley, now Mrs Brian Widlake); *b* 29 Sept 1959; *Educ* Bradfield; *Career* professional cricketer Hampshire CCC 1977-: debut 1978, awarded county cap 1982, capt 1984-; capt: 4 unofficial Test matches v Sri Lanka 1986, 3 unofficial Test matches v Zimbabwe 1990, 10 unofficial one day Ints, England under 25 v NZ 1986, England Counties tour Zimbabwe 1985, MCC v Aust 1985 (scored 115 not out); winner Benson & Hedges Cup 1988; Advtg Dept The Observer 1980, PR conslt Hill & Knowlton (UK) Ltd 1987-88, publisher various cricket magazines, author of foreword in Benson & Hedges Yearbook, TV and radio commentator; *Recreations* music, theatre, golf, politics; *Style—* Mark Nicholas, Esq; Hampshire CCC, Northlands Rd, Southampton SO9 2TY (☎ 0703 333788)

NICHOLAS, Trevor Ian; s of Harold Lionel Nicholas (d 1990), of 15 Riverview Gardens, Twickenham, Middx, and Gwendoline Doris, *née* Blyth; *b* 14 Sept 1936; *Educ* Hampton GS, Harvard Business Sch; *m* 17 Oct 1959, Ruth, da of Gottlieb Joswig (d 1954); 2 da (Kim b 1 April 1961, Katja b 12 Sept 1963); *Career* Barclays Bank plc 1974-: mangr business advsy serv 1974-75, gen mangr asst 1977, asst gen mangr software devpt 1978-79, div gen mangr Barclaycard 1980-82, div gen mangr mgmnt servs 1982-84, gen mangr resources 1985-87, dir info systems and resources 1988-89, chief info offr 1989-90, ind info technol advsr; pres Barclays Bank Hort Soc; memb: Nat Tst, RSPB, Woodland Tst, Ramblers Assoc RHS, English Heritage, RVC Animal Care Tst, Wildfowl Tst, Historic Houses Assoc, Royal Forestry Soc; FCIB; *Recreations* music, reading, photography, natural history, eisteddfod, conservation; *Style—* Trevor Nicholas, Esq; 16 Oakwood, Berkhamsted HP4 3NQ (☎ 0442 866 921)

NICHOLL, His Hon Judge Anthony John David; s of Brig David William Dillwyn Nicholl (d 1972), and Mrs D W D Nicholl (d 1975); *b* 3 May 1935; *Educ* Eton, Pembroke Coll Oxford; *m* 1961, Hermione Mary, da of William Harcourt Palmer Landon (d 1978); 1 s (William b 19 May 1962), 2 da (Charlotte b 30 Oct 1963, Lucy b 4 June 1967); *Career* called to the Bar Lincoln's Inn 1958, in practice London 1958-61 and Birmingham 1961-88, head of Chambers 1976-87, rec Crown Ct 1978-88, chm Fountain Ct Chambers Birmingham 1984-88, circuit judge MO Circuit 1988-; memb Birmingham Medico-Legal Soc; *Recreations* history, walking, gardening, riding; *Style—* His Hon Judge Anthony Nicholl; 2 Fountain Court, Steelhouse Lane, Birmingham B4 6DR (021 236 3882)

NICHOLL, Christopher John (Chris); s of Jack Nicholl, and Lillian Merle, *née* Rowland; *b* 12 Oct 1946; *Educ* Wimslow GS; *m* 3 Nov 1969, Jane Lynne, da of Charles Edward Wain (d 1977), of Manchester; 1 s (Paul b 1972), 1 da (Cathy b 1974); *Career* football player: Halifax Town 1968, Luton Town 1972, Aston Villa 1978, Southampton 1984, Grimsby Town; promotion to higher division: Halifax, Luton, Aston Villa (twice), Southampton; 53 int appearances for NI incl World Cup final Spain 1982, two League Cup wins Aston Villa, mangr Southampton FC 1985-; *Recreations* golf, tennis, chess, computers; *Style—* Chris Nicholl, Esq; Southampton FC, The Dell, Southampton (☎ 0703 220505)

NICHOLL, Lt-Col Henry Rice; s of Maj Basil Rice Nicholl (ka 1916); *b* 28 April 1909; *Educ* Winchester, RMC Sandhurst; *m* 1936, Marjorie Joicey, da of Robert Dickinson (d 1927), of Styford Hall, Stocksfield; 2 s (Charles, Edward), 1 da (*see* St John, Edmund Oliver); *Career* served in WWII in N Africa and Italy; cmmnd Rifle Bde 1929, cmd 7 Bn Rifle Bde 1946, ret 1948; High Sheriff Northumberland 1969, MFH Haydon 1959-67; *Style—* Lt-Col Henry Nicholl; High Lipwood, Haydon Bridge, Hexham, Northumberland NE47 6EB (☎ 043 484 205)

NICHOLLS; *see*: Harmar-Nicholls

NICHOLLS, Brian; s of Ralph Nicholls, of Crieff, Scotland, and Kathleen, *née* Bulled (d 1966); *b* 21 Sept 1928; *Educ* Haberdashers Aske's, Regent St Poly (BSc), Harvard Business Sch; *m* 1961, Mary Elizabeth, da of Alexander Harley, of Milnathort, Scotland; 1 s (Simon b 1964), 2 da (Jane b 1966, Anne b 1968); *Career* dir: CJB Projects Ltd 1972-75, CJB Pipelines Ltd 1974-75, CJB - Mohandessi Iran (dep chm) 1975; John Brown Engrg 1978-, JBE Inc (USA) 1982-90; vice pres: John Brown Power Ltd 1987-90, Rugby Power co 1989-; industl advsr Dept of Trade 1975-78; memb Cncl: Br Chemical Engrg Contractors Assoc 1973-75, Br Overseas Trade Bd 1978; memb Exec Ctee Scottish Cncl Devpt and Indust 1984-; *Recreations* hill walking, sailing, music, writing; *Clubs* Royal Northern and Clyde Yacht; *Style—* Brian Nicholls, Esq; Croy, Shandon, by Helensburgh, Dunbartonshire Scotland G84 8NN

NICHOLLS, Dr Christine Stephanie; da of Christopher James Metcalfe (d 1986), of Mombasa, Kenya, and Olive, *née* Kennedy (d 1982); *b* 23 Jan 1943; *Educ* Kenya HS, Lady Margaret Hall Oxford (BA, MA), St Antony's Coll Oxford (DPhil); *m* 12 March 1966, Anthony James Nicholls, s of Ernest Alfred Nicholls (d 1981), of Carshalton, Surrey; 1 s (Alexander b 1970), 2 da (Caroline b 1972, Isabel b 1974); *Career* Henry Charles Chapman res fell Inst of Cwlth Studies Univ of London 1968-69, freelance writer BBC 1970-74; *Books* The Swahili Coast (1971), Cataract (with Philip Awdry, 1985), Dictionary of National Biography (jt ed, 1971 and ed, 1989), Power, a Political History of the Twentieth Century (1990); *Recreations* reading novels; *Style—* Dr Christine Nicholls; 27 Davenant Rd, Oxford OX2 8BU (☎ 0865 511320); Dictionary of National Biography, Clarendon Building, Bodleian Library, Broad St, Oxford OX1 3BG (☎ 0865 277232/277236)

NICHOLLS, Clive Victor; QC (1982); s of Alfred Charles Victor Nicholls, and Lilian Mary, *née* May; *b* 29 Aug 1932; *Educ* Brighton Coll, Trinity Coll Dublin (MA, LLB), Sidney Sussex Coll Cambridge (BA, LLM); *m* 23 July 1960, Alison Virginia, da of late Leonard Arthur Oliver; 3 s (Jeremy Oliver b 1962, James Colin Oliver b 1967, John Patrick Oliver b 1969), 3 da (Jacqueline Alison b 1963, Judie Victoria b 1965, Jill Caroline b 1965); *Career* called to the Bar Gray's Inn 1957, rec of Crown Court 1984-, master of the Bench 1989; chm tstees of Bob Champion Cancer Tst; patron Multiple Birth Assoc; *Recreations* sailing, fly-fishing; *Style—* Clive Nicholls, Esq, QC; 3 Raymond Buildings, Gray's Inn, London WC1R 5BH (☎ 071 831 3833, fax 071 831 4989)

NICHOLLS, Colin Alfred Arthur; QC (1981); s of Alfred Charles Victor Nicholls (d 1987), and Lilian Mary, *née* May; *b* 29 Aug 1932; *Educ* Brighton Coll, Univ of Dublin (MA, LLB); *m* 23 Oct 1976, Clarissa Allison Spenlove, da of Clive Dixon (d 1976); 2 s (Benjamin Clive b 30 Aug 1977, Jonathan Charles b 6 Jan 1979); *Career* called to the Bar Gray's Inn 1957, rec of Crown Ct 1983-, bencher Gray's Inn 1989; vice pres Cwlth Lawyers' Assoc, patron Multiple Births Fndn; *Recreations* painting (exhibitor RHA); *Clubs* Garrick; *Style—* Colin Nicholls, Esq, QC; 3 Raymond Buildings, Gray's Inn, London WC2 1RR (☎ 071 831 3833, fax 071 242 4221, car 0836 717 941)

NICHOLLS, David Alan; CB (1989), CMG (1984); s of Thomas Edward Nicholls (d 1971), and Beatrice Winifred Nicholls; *Educ* Cheshunt GS, St John's Coll Cambridge (MA); *m* 1955, Margaret; 2 da (Amanda, Camilla); *Career* entered Home Civil Serv 1954; asst sec MOD 1969-75, Cabinet Office 1975-77, under sec MOD 1977-80, asst sec-gen NATO 1980-84, dep under sec MOD 1984-90; visiting fell Magdalene Coll Cambridge 1989-90; assoc fell RIIA 1990-91; def conslt; chm Soc for Italic Handwriting; *Recreations* sketching, printmaking; *Clubs* Nat Lib; *Style—* David Nicholls, Esq, CB, CMG; c/o Midland Bank, Church St, Stretton, Shropshire

NICHOLLS, Lady; Dominie; da of Peter Vlasto (d 1941), of The Woodlands, Fulwood Park, Liverpool, and Aziza Pallis; the Vlasto family settled in the (then) Genoese Island of Chios after the fall of Constantinople in 1453 and fled to England and France after the massacres there in 1823; *b* 30 Dec 1911; *Educ* Priors Field; *m* 1935, Sir John Walter Nicholls, GCMG, OBE (d 1970), s of William Nicholls, of Kenwood, Radlett, Herts; 1 s (John Peter Benedict), 2 da (Julia Anne, Caroline Dominie); *Career* the w of a British diplomat for thirty-five years, minister's w in Moscow (1949-51), ambassador's w in Israel, Yugoslavia, Belgium and S Africa; *Recreations* gardening, walking; *Style—* Lady Nicholls; The Burgh House, London Rd, Saffron Walden, Essex CB11 4ED (☎ 0799 513541)

NICHOLLS, Rt Hon Lord Justice; Sir Donald James Nicholls; PC (1986); *b* 1933; *Career* barr 1958, QC 1974, High Court judge; lord justice of appeal; kt 1983; *Style—* The Rt Hon Lord Justice Nicholls; Royal Courts of Justice, Strand, London WC2A 2LL

NICHOLLS, Dr Graham William; s of Leslie Nicholls (d 1986), of Manchester, and Evelyn Joyce, *née* Baker; *b* 27 March 1947; *Educ* Blackpool GS, Univ Coll Swansea (BA), St David's Univ Coll Lampeter (PhD); *m* 26 Aug 1972, June, da of John Richards of Horwich, Lancs; 1 da (Lucy Olivia b 1983); *Career* Una Ellis Fermor Postgraduate Scholar Bedford Coll 1972-73, curator Johnson Birthplace Museum Lichfield 1973-, literary sec Johnson Soc 1974-89, ed Transaction of the Johnson Soc 1974-89, chm Vale of Trent Tourism Assoc 1986-90; memb Arts Cncl Literature Panel 1981-82; FRSA 1988; *Books* Johnson in the Midlands (1984), Measure For Measure: Text and Performance (1986); *Recreations* reading, music, theatre; *Style—* Dr Graham Nicholls; 40 Walsall Rd, Lichfield, Staffs WS13 8AF (☎ 0543 254562); Samuel Johnson Birthplace Museum, Breadmarket St, Lichfield, Staffs WS13 6LG (☎ 0543 264972)

NICHOLLS, Prof John Graham; s of Dr Nicolai Nicholls, and Charlotte, *née* Kaphan; *b* 19 Dec 1929; *Educ* Berkhamsted Sch, King's Coll London (BSc), UCL (PhD), Charing Cross Hosp (MB BS); *m* 22 Oct 1988, Nancy Venable; 2 s (Julian b 11 May 1964, Stephen b 7 June 1966); *Career* house offr Casualty and Radiotherapy Charing Cross Hosp 1956-57, Beit meml fell UCL 1957-60, departmental demonstrator Dept of Physiology Oxford 1960-62, assoc prof of physiology Yale Med Sch 1965-68, assoc prof of neurobiology Harvard Med Sch 1968-73 (res assoc 1962-65), prof of neurobiology Stanford Med Sch 1973-83, prof of pharmacology Biocenter 1983-; FRS 1988; *Books* From Neuron to Brain (2 edn with S W Kuffler and A R Martin, 1984), The Search for Connexions (1987); *Recreations* music, literature, S American history; *Clubs* Athenaeum; *Style—* Prof John Nicholls, FRS; Turkheimerstrasse 73, Basel 4055, Switzerland (☎ 010 41 61 44 96 54); Dept of Pharmacology, Biocenter, Klingelbergstrasse 70, Basel 4056, Switzerland (☎ 010 41 61 25 38 80, fax 010 41 61 25 67 60)

NICHOLLS, Mandy; da of Derek Langridge, of Barkham Berks, and Gloria, *née* Harrison; *b* 28 Feb 1968; *Educ* Whitton Secdy Sch Middlesex; *m* 1 Sept 1990, James Nicholls, s of Dr John Nicholls; *Career* hockey player; over 100 appearances Ealing Ladies Club 1987-; England: under 18 1985-86, under 21 1988-89, full debut v Holland 1989, Wembley debut v Holland 1990, total caps 17; memb GB training squad 1990-91 and Olympic training squad 1991; honours with Ealing: nat indoor champions 1986, nat outdoor champions 1987-89, represented English Clubs in Euro Clubs Championships 1988-90; nat honours: Silver medal under 21 Euro Cup Paris 1988, winner and player of under 21 Home Counties Tournament Nottingham 1989, fourth place World Cup Sydney 1990; other sporting achivements: runner up Middlesex Squash Tournament under 16, borough cross country champion 1983, winner 1500m Borough Schs Athletics Championship 5 times; most promising young hockey player of the year (Sports Aid Fndn award) 1989; employment: Barclays Bank Twickenham 1984, currently Barclays Bank Sports Club Ealing; *Recreations* training, running, cycling, music, cats, reading, films, food, travelling; *Style—* Mrs Mandy Nicholls; Ealing Ladies Hockey Club, c/o Ealing Cricket Club, Corfton Rd, Ealing, London W5 (☎ 081 997 1858)

NICHOLLS, Nigel Hamilton; CBE (1982); s of Bernard Cecil Hamilton Nicholls, of Dorking, Surrey (d 1969), and Enid Kathleen Nicholls, *née* Gwynne; *b* 19 Feb 1938; *Educ* King's Sch Canterbury, St John's Oxford (BA, MA); *m* 14 Oct 1967, Isobel Judith, da of Rev Canon Maurice Dean, of Verwood, Dorset; 2 s (Jonathan b 1969, Christopher b 1972); *Career* asst princ Admty 1962, MOD 1964, asst private sec Min for RN 1965-66 (princ 1966), directing staff RCDS 1971-73, asst private sec to Sec of State for Def 1973-74 (asst sec 1974), def cnsllr UK Delgn to MBFR Talks Vienna 1977-80 (dep head of delgn 1978-80), asst under sec of state 1984-, Cabinet Office 1986-89; *Recreations* choral singing, genealogy, mountain walking; *Clubs* United Oxford and Cambridge Univ; *Style—* Nigel Nicholls, Esq, CBE; Ministry of Defence,

Whitehall, London SW1A 2HB

NICHOLLS, Patrick Charles Martyn; MP (C) Teignbridge 1983-; s of Douglas Charles Martyn Nicholls (d 1950), and Margaret Josephine Nicholls (d 1982); *b* 14 Nov 1948; *Educ* St Peter's Harefield, Redrice Coll; *m* 1976, Bridget Elizabeth Fergus, da of Edward Alan Owens, of Otterton, Devon; 1 s, 2 da; *Career* slr 1974; jt sec Legal Ctee 1983-, co-opted memb Soc of Cons Lawyers 1983-; vice chm Exec Ctee Soc of Cons Lawyers; memb: Standing Ctee on Police and Criminal Evidence Bill, Standing Ctee on Video Recordings Bill; PPS to Rt Hon J S Gummer, min of state MAFF July 1986-May 87; Parly under sec of state: Dept of Employment 1987-90, DOE July-Oct 1990; steward Br Boxing Bd 1985-87; *Recreations* skiing, opera, theatre and historical research; *Style—* Patrick Nicholls, Esq, MP; c/o House of Commons, London SW1A 0AA (☎ 071 219 4095)

NICHOLLS, Dr (David) Paul; s of Albert Edward Nicholls, of 13 Barnfield, Much Hoole, Preston, Lancs, and Alice, *née* Thomson (d 1967); *b* 10 Sept 1946; *Educ* Hutton GS Preston, Univ of Manchester (MB ChB, MD); *m* 1, Mary Nash (d 1977); m 2, 18 July 1981, Esme Mary, da of Norman Whitehead, of 4 Killowen Crescent, Lisburn; 1 s (Stephen b 1989), 2 da (Riona b 1985, Ciara b 1986); *Career* tutor in med Hope Hosp Salford, sr registrar in med Belfast City Hosp, currently conslt physician Royal Victoria Hosp Belfast; MRCP 1974, FECS 1989; *Recreations* music, sailing, golf, photography, old cars; *Clubs* Royal Portrush Golf, Carrickfergus Sailing; *Style—* Dr Paul Nicholls; 3 Ballymacash Road, Lisburn, Co Antrim BT28 3DX (☎ 0846 672044); Royal Victoria Hospital, Belfast BT12 6BA (☎ 0232 240503)

NICHOLLS, Robert Michael (Bob); s of Herbert Edgar Nicholls (d 1977), and Bennetta L'Estrange, *née* Burges; *b* 28 July 1939; *Educ* Hampton Sch, UCW (BA, treas Students' Union, dep ldr expedition to Kurdistan), Univ of Manchester (DSA); *m* 9 Dec 1961, Dr Deirin Deirdre, da of Dr Frank O'Sullivan (d 1955); 4 s (Kevin Paul b 1965, Clive Ranulf John b 1967, Liam Dougal b 1969, Alec Eoin b 1971); *Career* house govr St Stephens Hosp Chelsea 1966-68, asst clerk of the govrs St Thomas' Hosp 1968-72, dep gp sec Southampton Univ Hosp Mgmnt Ctee 1972-74, dist admin Southampton and S West Hampshire Health Dist 1974-77, area admin Newcastle Area Health Authy 1977-81, regnl admin S Western Regnl Health Authy 1981-85, dist gen mangr Southmead Health Dist 1985-88, regnl gen mangr Oxford Regnl Health Authy 1988-; memb: Inst of Health Serv Mangrs (former memb Cncl, nat pres 1983-84), King's Fund Educn Ctee 1974-79, Health Educn Cncl 1984-87, Regnl Health Authy Chm's Pay and Personnel Gp 1989-; assoc memb Green Coll Oxford; AHSM 1965; *Books* Resources in Medicine (contrib, 1970), Working with People (contrib, 1983); *Recreations* cricket, golf, walking, birdwatching, opera, jazz; *Clubs* Lensbury, Ronnie Scotts; *Style—* Bob Nicholls, Esq; Oxford Regional Health Authority, Old Rd, Headington, Oxford OX3 7LF (☎ 0865 226753, fax 0865 741907)

NICHOLLS, Sue; *see*: Harmar-Nicholls, Hon Susan

NICHOLLS, Rt Rev Vernon Sampson; s of Ernest C Nicholls (d 1957), of Truro, Cornwall, and Ellen Nicholls (d 1970); *b* 3 Sept 1917; *Educ* Truro Sch, Univ of Durham, Clifton Theol Coll Bristol; *m* 1943, Phyllis, da of Edwin Potter (d 1965), of Stratford upon Avon; 1 s, 1 da; *Career* chaplain to the Forces 1944-46, vicar of Meopham 1946-56, rural dean of Cobham 1954-56, vicar and rural dean of Walsall 1956-67, archdeacon of Birmingham 1967-74, bishop of Sodor and Man and dean of St German's Cathedral 1974-83; memb The Tynwald 1974-83; hon asst Bishop of Coventry 1983-; JP (IOM) 1974-83; *Recreations* gardening, meeting people; *Clubs* Royal Cwlth Soc; *Style—* The Rt Rev Vernon Nicholls; Thie My Chree, 4 Winston Close, Hathaway Park, Shottery, Stratford upon Avon CV37 9ER (☎ 0789 294478)

NICHOLLS, Hon Mrs (Virginia Jean Furse Maud); da of Baron Redcliffe-Maud, GCB, CBE (Life Peer; d 1982); *b* 1943; *m* 1970, Roger Frank Nicholls; *Style—* The Hon Mrs Nicholls; Ennore, Kenwyn Rd, Truro, Cornwall

NICHOLS, Andrew Charles; s of Dudley Nichols (d 1965), of Kent, and Winifred Gertrude, *née* Burrows (d 1982); *b* 23 April 1949; *Educ* Cranbrook Sch, Univ of Bristol (BA, BArch), Univ of Pennsylvania (MLA); *m* 15 Sept 1978, Evelyn Margaret, da of Stewart Gould; 1 s (Christopher b 1984), 1 da (Louisa Madeleine b 1988); *Career* architect and landscape planner in practice as Hutton Nichols Partnership 1979-, lectr Univ of Bristol 1977-79, dir Hawthorn Farm 1984-87; RIBA 1974, ALI 1978; *Style—* Andrew C Nichols, Esq; Pond House, Northend, Henley-on-Thames, Oxon RG9 6LG (☎ 0491 63354, fax 0491 63 228)

NICHOLS, Rev Canon Barry Edward; s of Albert Owen Nichols (d 1986), and Gwendoline Cicely, *née* Rumbold (d 1981); *b* 23 Jan 1940; *Educ* Epsom Coll, Southwark Ordination Course; *m* 28 Feb 1970, Anne, da of Frederick Albert Hastings, BEM, of 19 Dulverton Court, Adelaide Rd, Surbiton, Surrey; 1 s (Stephen b 1977), 2 da (Sarah b 1972, Rebecca b 1977); *Career* joined Arthur Young 1957 (ptnr 1970-1989, firm managing ptnr 1983-85), ptnr Ernst and Young 1989-; ordained priest C of E 1970, hon curate St Andrews and St Marks Surbiton Surrey 1969-, hon canon Southwark Cathedral 1990-; dean for Ministers in Secular Employment Kingston Episcopal Area 1990-; FCA; *Recreations* gardening, reading, swimming; *Style—* The Rev Canon Barry Nichols; 32 Corkran Rd, Surbiton, Surrey KT6 6PN (☎ 081 390 3032); Ernst & Young, Beckett House, 1 Lambeth Palace Road, London SE1 7EU (☎ 071 928 2000, fax 071 928 1345, direct line 071 931 3644)

NICHOLS, Prof David; s of Capt Arnold William Nichols (d 1972), of Broadmayne, Dorset, an Kathleen Jessie, *née* Harries (d 1975); *b* 21 June 1930; *Educ* Hardye's Sch Dorchester, Univ of Oxford (BA, MA, DPhil); *m* 6 Aug 1955, Anne, da of Frank Dutton Rowland (d 1983), of Weymouth, Dorset; 1 s (John b 17 April 1964), 3 da (Jocelyn b 8 June 1958, Jennifer b 4 Sept 1959, Jane b 26 Dec 1962); *Career* Nat Serv RAF 1949-51, Flying Offr 1951; lectr in zoology Univ of Oxford 1957-69, fell of St Peter's Coll Oxford 1964-69, dean of sci Univ of Exeter 1984-87 (dep vice chllr 1987-, prof of biological sci 1969-); memb: Cncl of The Marine Biological Assoc of UK 1970-73, 1977-80 and 1983-86, Ctee NERC 1980-83, Advsy Ctee on Sci for The Nature Conservancy Cncl 1982-85; FIBiol; *Books* Echinoderms (4 edn, 1969), The Oxford Book of Invertebrates (1971); *Recreations* walking, photography; *Style—* Prof David Nichols; Department of Biological Sciences, Hatherly Laboratories, Prince of Wales Rd, Exeter, Devon EX4 4PS (☎ 0392 263700, fax 0392 263108, telex 42894 EXUNIV G)

NICHOLS, Sir Edward Henry; TD; s of Henry James Nichols; *b* 27 Sept 1911; *Educ* Queen Elizabeth GS Mansfield, Selwyn Coll Cambridge (BA, LLB); *m* 1941, Gwendoline Hetty Elgar; 1 s; *Career* served WWII RA (TA), Hon Lt-Col; slr 1936, town clerk and clerk of peace Derby 1949-53, town clerk of London 1953-74; Hon DLitt City Univ; kt 1972; *Clubs* City Livery; *Style—* Sir Edward Nichols, TD; 4 Victoria Place, Esher Park Avenue, Esher, Surrey KT10 2GX (☎ 0372 65102)

NICHOLS, Jeremy Gareth Lane; *b* 20 May 1943; *Educ* Lancing, Fitzwilliam Coll Cambridge (MA, Athletics half blue), Univ of Perugia (Dip of Teaching); *m* ; 1 s (Rupert), 3 da (Lucy, Victoria, Emma); *Career* house tutor Rugby Sch 1966-67; Eton Coll: asst Eng master 1967-89, house master 1980-89, master i/c of soccer and first XI coach 1969-79, second cricket XI coach and master 1974-79, Exchange Scheme Gilman Sch Baltimore Maryland 1979-80 (elected to Cum Laude Soc); headmaster Stowe Sch 1990; Villiers Park Educnl Tst 1969-76; govr: Aysgarth Sch Yorks, Beachborough Sch Northants, Davenies Berks, Lockers Park Herts, Papplewick Berks, Swanbourne House Bucks, Wellesley House Kent; memb Ctee Friends of Lancing Chapel; *Style—* Jeremy Nichols, Esq; Kinloss, Stowe, Bucks MK18 5EH (☎ 0280 813164, fax 0280 822769)

NICHOLS, (Peter) John; s of Peter Nichols, of 3 Newington Ct, Bowdon, Cheshire, and Edith Nan, *née* Rhodes; *b* 24 Dec 1949; *Educ* Shrewsbury, Univ of Leicester (BSc); *m* 15 Sep 1973, Elaine Mary, da of William H W Chadwick, of 38 Hillington Rd, Sale, Cheshire; 2 s (James b 1979, Matthew b 1982), 1 da (Katharine b 1986); *Career* J N Nichols (Vimto) plc: joined 1970-, dir 1978-86, md 1986-; *Recreations* golf, sailing, skiing; *Clubs* Ringway Golf; *Style—* John Nichols, Esq; Southwood, Hargate Drive, Hale, Cheshire; J N Nichols (Vimto) plc, Ledson Road, Wythenshawe, Manchester M23 9NL (☎ 061 998 8801, fax 061 998 9446, telex 667482, car 0836 744326)

NICHOLS, Kenneth Gordon; s of Harry Archibald Nichols (d 1976), and Christina McKenzie Young (d 1973); *b* 4 Jan 1925; *Educ* Uppingham, Downing Coll Cambridge; *m* 18 Dec 1946, Dorothy Karalena, da of Robert Simpson Friends (d 1932), 2 s (Stephen b 1951 d 1970), Harry b 1953), 1 da (Caroline b 1956); *Career* served WWII Flt Lt RAF, fighter pilot Middle East 1943-46; former chm Belfast Linen Gp; dir: Restwell Belfast Linen Warehouse Co Ltd, Wholesale Textile Co Cambridge Ltd, DM & KG Nichols Ltd; pres City of London Linen Trades Assoc 1977; *Recreations* golf; *Clubs* RAF (London), Gog Magog Golf, Cambridge, Woburn Golf and Country, Cannes Golf (France); *Style—* Kenneth Nichols, Esq; Trinity House Hills Rd, Cambridge CB2 2BE (☎ 0223 247784); Belfast Linen Group, Coldhams Rd, Cambridge (☎ 0223 411311)

NICHOLS, Peter Richard; s of Richard George (d 1965), of Bristol, and Violet Annie Ladysmith Poole; *b* 31 July 1927; *Educ* Bristol GS, Bristol Old Vic Theatre Sch; *m* 1960, Thelma, da of George Reginald Reed, of Bristol; 1 s (Daniel), 3 da (Abigail d 1971, Louise, Catherine); *Career* author and playwright; screen and stage plays: The Gorge (TV), A Day in the Death of Joe Egg (stage), Forget-me-not Lane (stage), Privates on Parade (stage and screen), Passion Play (stage), Poppy (stage musical); FRSL; *Books* Feeling You're Behind (autobiography, 1984); *Recreations* planning to overthrow the existing political structure, playing the vibraphone; *Style—* Peter Nichols, Esq; Old Rectory, Hopesay, Nr Craven Arms, Shropshire; Agent: Margaret Ramsay Ltd, 14 Goodwin's Ct, London WC2 (☎ 071 240 0691)

NICHOLS, Robin Anthony; s of Thomas George Nichols (d 1981), of Eastcote, Middx, and Irene Joan Buck; gs of Thomas George Nichols, OBE (despatches thrice, 1935); *b* 28 April 1944; *Educ* Pinner Co GS, City of London Coll for Chartered Bldg Soc Exams; *m* 5 March 1967, Paula Theresa, da of Joseph Severin Spiegelhalter (d 1984), of Wembley, Middx; 1 s (Grant Anthony b 1970), 1 da (Sarah Kate b 1973); *Career* md Greenwich Building Society 1981-, dir Building Society Ombudsman Co Ltd 1987; cncl memb Bldg Soc Assoc 1983, Bldg Soc Ombudsman 1987; govr Blackheath HS 1987-; FCBSI; *Recreations* sport, music, theatre, MENSA; *Style—* Robin Nichols, Esq; 15 Highfield Drive, Shortlands, Bromley, Kent BR2 0RX (☎ 081 460 3369); 279 Greenwich High Rd, London SE10 8NL (☎ 081 858 8212)

NICHOLS, Prof Roy Woodward; s of late Ernest Nichols, of Rawson, Yorkshire, and late Sarah Jane, *née* Woodward; *b* 9 June 1923; *Educ* Loughborough Coll, Univ of Sheffield (BMet, DMet, Mappin Nesthill and Ledbury medals and prizes); *m* 30 Aug 1948, Jacqueline, da of late Velentine Woods, of Barrow-on-Soar; 2 s (Mark Andrew, Paul Stewart), 1 da (Clare Angele); *Career* Lt AEA RNVR 1942-46; design apprentice Kirkstall Forge Ltd 1939-42, scientific and sr scientific offr Miny of Supply Woolwich Armament Res & Devpt Estab 1949-56, princ scientific offr and res mangr Materials Res Laboratory UK AEA Culcheth 1956-71, head Engrg and Materials Laboratories UK AEA Risley 1976-85 (dep head 1971-76); visiting prof: Paisley Coll Scot 1980-, Imperial Coll London 1985-; private conslt 1985-, chm Management Bd Prog for Inspection of Steel Components OECD/CEC 1980-; pres Int Cncl on Pressure Vessel Technol, chm UK Govt Enquiry on Pressure Vessels 1969; former pres: Inst of Metallurgists, Int Congress on Fracture; former chm The Welding Inst Cncl; FIM 1950, FEng; hon fell: The Welding Inst 1960, BINDT, Int Congress on Fracture, Canadian Fracture Fndn; FIMechE; *Books* International Journal of Pressure Vessels and Piping (ed, 1971-), Pressure Vessel Engineering Technology (ed, 1971), Developments in PV Engineering Technology (Vol 1 1979, Vol 5 1987), Non-Destructive Testing (1989); *Recreations* music, gardening, bridge, walking; *Style—* Prof Roy Nichols; Nichols Consultancies, 'Squirrels', 35 Cockney Hill, Tilehurst, Reading RG3 4HF (☎ 0734 417892)

NICHOLS, Rt Rev Mgr Vincent Gerard; s of Henry Joseph Nichols, and Mary Nichols, *née* Russell; *b* 8 Nov 1945; *Educ* St Mary's Coll Crosby, Gregorian Univ Rome (STL, PhL), Univ of Manchester (MA), Loyola Univ Chicago (MEd); *Career* chaplain St John Rigby VI Form Coll Wigan 1972-77, priest in the inner city of Liverpool 1978-81, dir of Upholland Northern Inst Lancs (with responsibility for the in-service training of clergy and for adult Christian educn 1981-84); advsr Cardinal Hume and Archbishop Worlock at the Int Synods of Bishops 1980, 1983 and 1987, gen sec Bishops' Conf of England and Wales 1984-; *Style—* Rt Rev Mgr Vincent Nichols; Bishops' Conference Secretariat, 39 Eccleston Sq, London SW1V 1PD (☎ 071 630 8220)

NICHOLSON, Andrew Broadfoot; s of John Nicholson, of Kidsdale, Whithorn, Newton-Stewart, and Helen, *née* Macfie; *b* 20 June 1933; *Educ* Sedbergh, Univ of Aberdeen (BSc); *m* 11 April 1973, Joanna Mary, da of Noel Bechely-Crundall (d 1968), of Membury House, Ramsbury, Wilts; 2 s (Rupert, Charles); *Career* Nat Serv 1956-57, cmmnd KOSB; dep chm (following takeover by TSB) Bell Lawrie White Ltd 1989- (chm 1986-89); memb Stock Exchange 1962-; *Recreations* shooting, fishing, skiing; *Clubs* Caledonian; *Style—* Andrew Nicholson, Esq; The Old Manse, Bedrule, Denholm, Hawick; 7 Drumsheugh Gardens, Edinburgh EH3 7QH (☎ 031 225 2566)

NICHOLSON, Hon Mrs (Ariadne Maria); *née* Balfour; da of 4 Baron Kinross, OBE, TD; *b* 31 Jan 1939; *m* 1961 (m dis 1990), Richard, s of late Robert Nicholson, and Mrs Kenneth Seth-Smith (stepmother of Viscountess Buckmaster); 3 s, 1 da; *Style—* The Hon Mrs Nicholson; 2 Halesden Road, Heaton Chapel, Stockport SK4 5ER

NICHOLSON, Sir Bryan Hubert; s of Reginald Hubert Nicholson (d 1977); *b* 6 June 1932; *Educ* Palmers Sch Grays, Oriel Coll Oxford; *m* 1956, Mary Elizabeth, da of Albert Cyril Harrison; 2 children; *Career* Nat Serv Lt; chm Rank Xerox (UK) Ltd 1980-84 (dir 1972-80); dir: Rank Xerox Ltd 1977-87, Sperry Rand Ltd 1969-72, Sperry Rand (Aust) Party Ltd 1966-69, Evode Group plc 1981-84, Baker Perkings Holdings plc 1982-84; chm: Manpower Servs Cmmn 1984-87, PO 1987-, CNAA 1988-91, Nationalised Industs Chms Gp 1988-90, Nat Cncl for Vocational Qualifications 1990-, CBI Educn and Trg Affrs Ctee 1990-, Industl Soc 1990-; memb NEDC 1985; kt 1987; *Recreations* tennis, bridge; *Clubs* United Oxford and Cambridge University; *Style—* Sir Bryan Nicholson; Point Piper, Lilley Drive, Kingswood, Surrey KT20 6JA

NICHOLSON, Charles Christian; s and h of Sir John Norris Nicholson, 2 Bt, KBE, CIE; *b* 15 Dec 1941; *Educ* Ampleforth, Magdalen Coll Oxford; *m* 1975, Martha Rodman, da of Stuart Warren Don, and wid of Niall Hamilton Anstruther-Gough-Calthorpe; *Style—* Charles Nicholson, Esq; Turners Green Farm, Elvetham, Hants

NICHOLSON, Clive Anthony Holme; s of Dennis Thomas Holme Nicholson, MBE, of Barnet, Herts, and Eileen Blanche, *née* Fitkin; *b* 24 Feb 1947; *Educ* Merchant Taylors'; *m* 12 Dec 1970, Patricia Mary, da of Ernest Johnson (d 1979), of Lancaster;

3 da (Amanda b 5 Dec 1972, Zoe b 27 May 1975, Gemma b 8 Aug 1981); *Career* CA; Deloitte & Co Lusaka Zambia 1970-72; Saffery Champness (formerly Safferys) 1972- (ptnr 1975-, managing ptnr 1990-); Liveryman Worshipful Co of Merchant Taylors 1974; FCA 1979, FHKSA 1985; *Style*— Clive A H Nicholson, Esq; Squirrel Lodge, Longworth House Estate, Longworth, Abingdon OX13 5HH (☎ 0865 820276); Fairfax House, Fulwood Place, Gray's Inn, London WC1V 6UB (☎ 071 405 2828, fax 071 405 7887, telex 889108 RYSAF G)

NICHOLSON, David; s of Herbert Charles Denton (Frenchie) Nicholson (d 1987), of Prestbury, Cheltenham, Glos, and Diana, *née* Holman; *b* 19 March 1939; *Educ* Haileybury, ISC; *m* 31 May 1962, Dinah Caroline, da of John Geoffrey Pugh; 2 s (Philip b 1963, John Charles b 1965); *Career* racehorse trainer 1968-, jockey 1951-74; first winner at 16 in first ride over hurdles, third place in Nat Hunt table with 63 winners 1960-61; major wins incl: Imperial Cup on Farmer's Boy 1960, 3 successive Welsh Grand Nationals on Limonali (twice) and Clover Bud 1959-61, Schweppes Gold Trophy on Elan 1965, Whitbread Gold Cup on Hill House 1967, County Hurdle Cheltenham 1973; ret after a winning ride on What A Buck at Hereford 1974 bringing his career total to 594; took out trainer's licence 1968; big race wins incl: SGB Chase Ascot with What A Buck 1974, Grand Military Gold Cup Sandown (twice) with Burnt Oak 1985 and 1987, Mackeson Gold Cup Cheltenham Embassy Chase Final Ascot and Black & White Gold Cup Chase Leopardstown with Very Promising 1985, Daily Express Triumph Hurdle Cheltenham with Solar Cloud 1986, Tote Gold Cup Cheltenham with Charter Party 1988, Arkle Trophy Cheltenham 1989 and Castleford Chase Wetherby 1990 with Waterloo Boy, Arlington Chase Final Cheltenham with Al Hashimi 1990; ran Nat Hunt Cricket XI for 20 years; *Recreations* cricket, spectator all sports; *Style*— David Nicholson, Esq; Cotswold House, Condicote, Stow-on-the-Wold, Gloucs GL54 1ES (☎ 0451 30417, fax 0451 32271)

NICHOLSON, Hon Sir David Eric; s of J A Nicholson; *b* 26 May 1904; *m* 1934, Cecile (d 1987), da of M E Smith; 2 s, 2 da; *Career* dir; MLA Qld 1950-72, speaker of Legislative Assembly 1960-72; kt 1972; *Style*— The Hon Sir David Nicholson; Villa 37, Peninsula Gdns, 56 Miller St, Kipper Ring, Qld 4021, Aust

NICHOLSON, David John; MP (C) Taunton 1987-; s of John Francis Nicholson, and Lucy, *née* Warburton Battr; *b* 17 Aug 1944; *Educ* Queen Elizabeth GS Blackburn, Christ Church Oxford (MA); *m* 23 May 1981, Frances Mary, da of Brig T E H Helby (d 1984), of Aveton Gifford, nr Kingsbridge, S Devon; 2 s (Julian b 1984, Alexand b 1990), 1 da (Eleanor b 1986); *Career* head of Political Section Cons Res Dept 1974-82, dir Home Affairs Assoc of Br C of C 1982-86 (dep dir gen 1986-87), sec Cons Backbench Social Security Ctee 1988-90, PPS to Rt Hon Lynda Chalker min for Overseas Devpt 1990-, sec All-Party Parly Gp on Population and Development 1990-, vice chm Cons South West Membs Ctee 1990-; *Books* The Leo Amery Diaries (Vol I 1980), The Empire at Bay (Vol II 1988); *Recreations* travel, gardening, music, the country; *Clubs* Taunton Cons, Wellington Cons; *Style*— David J Nicholson, Esq, MP; Allshire, nr Brushford, Somerset EX16 9JG; House of Commons, London (☎ 071 219 3000)

NICHOLSON, Dennis Thomas Holme; MBE (1946); s of Thomas Holme Nicholson, OBE (d 1954), and Ethel Lilian, *née* Turner (d 1956); *b* 6 May 1921; *Educ* Merchant Taylors'; *m* 22 Sept 1945, Eileen Blanche, da of S A Fitkin; 2 s (Clive Anthony Holme b 1947, Paul Thomas Holme b 1957), 1 da (Wendy Barbara Holme b 1950); *Career* served WWII in HAC and Border Regt; CA 1949-, ptnr Saffery Champness 1950-81, ret 1986; dir: Berry Star Quest plc, GT Japan Investment Trust plc; Liveryman City of London, Master Worshipful Co of Merchant Taylors 1983; Cross of Knight of the Royal Order of the Phoenix (with swords) 1946; FCA; *Recreations* sport, gardening, charitable activities; *Clubs* MCC, Totteridge Cricket, Special Forces, Barnet RFC; *Style*— Dennis Nicholson, Esq, MBE; Gilts, 62 Hadley Highstone, Barnet, Herts EN5 4PU (☎ 081 449 9664)

NICHOLSON, Hon Mrs (Diana Mary); *née* Seely; da of 4 Baron Mottistone, and Anthea Christine, da of Victor McMullan of NI; *b* 30 July 1954; *Educ* The Queens Sch Chester; *m* 1977, Edward Anthony Spours Nicholson, s of Anthony John Nicholson; 1 s (Alexander James Edward b 8 Oct 1988) 1 da (Zoë Mary Louisa b 18 Dec 1990); *Career* Fodor Guidebooks NY 1978-79, Simon & Shuster Inc NY 1979-80, ed Marmac Publishing Co Atlanta USA 1980-83, mangr Dark Blues Management Ltd 1983-86, freelance writer 1986-; *Recreations* sailing, skiing; *Clubs* Island Sailing; *Style*— The Hon Mrs Nicholson; Calle del Valle de Laciana 66, 28034 Madrid, Spain

NICHOLSON, Emma Harriet; MP (C) Torridge and W Devon 1987-; da of Sir Godfrey Nicholson, 1 Bt, *qv*; *b* 16 Oct 1941; *Educ* Portsdown Lodge Sch Sussex, St Mary's Sch Wantage, RAM; *m* 9 May 1987, Sir Michael Harris Caine, *qv*, s of Sir Sydney Caine, KCMG; *Career* computer programmer, programming instr and systems analyst ICL 1963-66, computer conslt John Tyzack & Ptnrs 1967-69, gen mgmnt and computer conslt McLintock Mann and Whinney Murray 1969-73; dir of fundraising The Save the Children Fund 1977-85 (joined 1974), fndr and bd memb Stichtung Redt de Kinderen Netherlands 1982-88, fndr and memb Comite d'Honneur Sauvez Les Enfants France 1983; conslt 1985-87: World Assoc of Girl Guides and Girl Scouts, The Duke of Edinburgh's Award Scheme, Foster Parents Plan UK; parly candidate Blythe Valley 1979, vice chm Cons Party (with special responsibility for women) 1983-87, memb Select Ctee on Employment 1990-, sec Cons Back Bench Environment Ctee 1990-; memb: Euro Union of Women 1983-, Cncl for Br-Arab Understanding 1985-90, Br-Turkish Parly Gp 1987-, Franco-Br Parly Gp 1987-, Steering Ctee the Cons Cncl of E Europe 1987-, Cons Friends of Israel 1987-, Br Argentinian Parly Gp 1990-, All Party Parly Gp on Aids 1990-, Parly Panel Royal Coll of Nursing 1990-, Cncl The Hansard Soc 1990-, Tory Green Initiative 1990-; treas Br Caribbean All Party Gp 1987-, cncl memb PITCOM (Parly Info Technol Ctee) 1988-, fell Indust & Parly Tst (IBM) 1990-; patron: CRUSAID 1986-, The Devon Care Tst 1987-, The Suzy Lamplugh Tst 1987- (tstee 1989-), Br Deaf Accord 1988-, Women into Info Technol Fndn 1989-, Devon/HIV Aids Tst 1990-, Nat Assoc of Deafened People 1990-, Nat Deaf-Blind and Rubella Assoc 1990-; pres: Br Tinnitus Fndn 1990-, MENCAP (Tavistock Branch) 1991-; memb: RAM Appeal Ctee 1986-, Cncl the Howard League 1989-, Advsy Bd Cosmopolitan Women of Tomorrow Awards 1989, Exec Ctee Cons Disability Gp 1990-, Advsy Bd Cosmopolitan Achievement Awards 1990, Royal Assoc in Aid of Deaf People 150 Anniversary Appeal Ctee 1990-, The Prince of Wales Advsy Tst on Disability 1991-; dep chm: The Duke of Edinburgh's 30 Anniversary Tribute Project 1986, The Duke of Edinburgh's Award Int Project 87 1987; tstee: The Ross McWhirter Fndn 1989-, Covent Garden Cancer Res Tst 1990-, The Little Fndn 1990-, Motor Neurone Disease Assoc 1990-; chm: Friends of the Duke of Edinburgh's Award 1988-89, ADAPT (Access for Disabled People to Arts Premises Today) 1989-; dir Cities in Schs 1988-, fndr & jt chm Parly Appeal for Romanian Children 1990-, friend Societe des Amies d'Enfance Poland 1990-, govr Mary Hare GS Berkshire 1990-, vice patron The Child Psychotherapy Tst 1990-, vice pres The Small Farmers Assoc 1990-; memb: Forum UK, Centre for Policy Studies, Royal Inst for Int Affrs, Royal Horticultural Soc; LRAM, ARCM; *Recreations* music, walking; *Clubs* Reform; *Style*— Emma Nicholson MP; c/o The House of Commons, London SW1A 0AA

NICHOLSON, Rev Dr Ernest Wilson; s of Ernest Tedford Nicholson (d 1977), Veronica Muriel, *née* Wilson (d 1963); *b* 26 Sept 1938; *Educ* Portadown Coll, Trinity Coll Dublin (BA, MA), Univ of Glasgow (PhD), Univ of Cambridge (BD, DD), Univ of Oxford (DD by incorporation); *m* 5 April 1962, Hazel, da of Samuel John Jackson; 1 s (Peter), 3 da (Rosalind, Kathryn, Jane); *Career* lectr in Hebrew and Semitic languages Trinity Coll Dublin 1962-72, univ lectr in divinity Univ of Cambridge 1967-79, fell Wolfson Coll 1967-69, fell and chaplain Pembroke Coll 1969-79, dean 1973-79, Oriel prof of the interpretation of Holy Scripture Univ of Oxford 1979-90 (fell), provost Oriel Coll 1990-; *Recreations* music, walking; *Style*— The Rev Dr Ernest Nicholson; Provost's Lodgings, Oriel College, Oxford OX1 4EW (☎ 0865 276533)

NICHOLSON, George Howard Joseph; er s of Roydon Joseph Nicholson, of Amberley, W Sussex, and Evelyn Sophia Carlton, *née* Reader; *b* 4 April 1936; *Educ* Wellington; *m* 13 Aug 1974, Adèle Janet, er da of late Richard Barbour, of Bolesworth Castle, Tattenhall, Chester; 2 s (Joseph William b 1975, Oliver Christian b 1977); *Career* Nat Serv King's Dragoon Gds, Lt Inns of Ct Regt (TA); cub reporter Vancouver Sun 1956, advertising and fundraising exec; appeal sec: Br Olympic Assoc 1978-, Commonwealth Games Cncl for England 1978-90; memb Ctee Incorporated Church Bldg Soc 1966-78, former gp chm Westminster Christian Cncl, former chm Human Rights Soc, govr Bacon Sch Bermondsey 1965-75; former borough cncllr RBK and C, Parly candidate (C) Bermondsey and Rotherhithe 1970; Liveryman Worshipful Co of Leathersellers (Warden 1986-87); *Recreations* visiting historic churches; *Clubs* Brooks's; *Style*— George Nicholson, Esq; 16 Chelsea Embankment, London SW3 4LA (☎ 071 352 9202); Coomb Dale Lodge, Bickerton, Malpas Cheshire; British Olympic Association, 1 Wandsworth Plain, London SW18 1EH (☎ 081 874 8978, fax 081 871 9104)

NICHOLSON, Sir Godfrey; 1 Bt (UK 1958), of Winterbourne, Royal Co of Berks; s of Richard Francis Nicholson (d 1940), of Woodcott, Hants, and Helen Violet Portal (d 1927); *b* 9 Dec 1901; *Educ* Winchester, Ch Ch Oxford; *m* 1936, Lady Katharine Constance, *née* Lindsay (d 1972), da of 27 Earl of Crawford and 10 Balcarres (d 1940); 4 da (*see* Richard Luce, Sir John Montgomery Cunninghame, Michael Caine); *Heir* none; *Career* served with Royal Fus and Commandos 1939-42; MP (C): Morpeth 1931-35, Farnham Div Surrey 1937-66; distiller; FSA; *Clubs* Pratt's, Athenaeum; *Style*— Sir Godfrey Nicholson, Bt, FSA; Bussock Hill House, Newbury, Berks (☎ 0635 248260)

NICHOLSON, (Charles) Gordon Brown; QC (1982), Sheriff Princ (Lothian and Borders 1990); s of William Addison Nicholson, OBE, of Edinburgh (d 1987), and Jean Brown (d 1967); *b* 11 Sept 1935; *Educ* George Watson's Coll Edinburgh, Univ of Edinburgh (MA, LLB); *m* 1963, Hazel Mary, da of Robert Riddle Nixon (d 1976); 2 s (David, Robin); *Career* called to the Bar Scotland 1961, advocate depute 1968-70; sheriff of Dumfries and Galloway at Dumfries 1970-76, sheriff Lothian and Borders 1976-82; cmmr Scot Law Cmmn 1982-89; *Books* The Law and Practice of Sentencing in Scotland 1981 (supplement, 1985); *Recreations* music; *Clubs* New (Edinburgh); *Style*— Sheriff Principal Gordon Nicholson, QC; 1A Abbotsford Park, Edinburgh EH10 5DX (☎ 031 447 4300); Sheriff Court Hse, Lawnmarket, Edinburgh (☎ 031 226 7181)

NICHOLSON, Graham Beattie; s of John Arthur Nicholson (d 1975), and Ena Patricia Nicholson; *b* 22 Feb 1949; *Educ* Bloxham Sch, Trinity Hall Cambridge; *m* 30 Oct 1982, Pamela Soei Luang, *née* Tan; 1 da (Vanessa b 1978); *Career* slr; Freshfields: NY office 1979-80, ptnr 1980, Singapore office 1980-83, manging ptnr Co Dept 1986-90, managing ptnr 1990-; memb City of London Slrs Co 1983; memb Law Soc; *Recreations* music, sailing, racquet sports; *Style*— Graham Nicholson, Esq; Whitefirars, 65 Fleet St, London EC4Y 1HS (☎ 071 936 4000)

NICHOLSON, James Frederick (Jim); s of Thomas Richard Nicholson, of Ballyards, Armagh (d 1987), and Matilda, *née* Morrow (d 1984); *b* 29 Jan 1945; *m* 30 Nov 1968, Elizabeth, *née* Gibson; 6 s, 1 da; *Career* elected: Armagh Dist Cncl 1975-, NI Assembly 1982-86; MP 1983-85; farmer; *Recreations* walking, football; *Style*— Jim Nicholson, Esq, MEP; 3 Glengall St, Belfast

NICHOLSON, Lady; Jean; da of late Alexander Landles; *m* 1927, Sir Harold Stanley Nicholson, 14 Bt (d 1961 when the title became dormant); *Style*— Lady Nicholson; Brough Lodge, Fetlar, Shetland, Grimista, Shetland

NICHOLSON, Jeremy Dawson; s of Major Rodney Scholfield Nicholson, of Birdham, and Leta E, *née* Dawson; *b* 14 March 1945; *Educ* Wellington; *m* 15 June 1968, Sarah Helen, da of Michael Richards; 2 s (Anthony Charles b 31 May 1969, Michael Dawson b 21 May 1973), 1 da (Charlotte Helen b 23 March 1971); *Career* Josolyne Layton-Bennett (formerly Layton-Bennett Billingham & Co): articled clerk 1964-68, mangr 1971-75, ptnr 1975-81; ptnr: Arthur Young 1981-89, Ernst & Young 1989-; FCA 1979 (ACA 1968); *Recreations* golf, theatre, music; *Clubs* MCC, Caledonian Club; *Style*— Jeremy Nicholson, Esq; Ernst & Young, Apex Plaza, Forbury Rd, Reading, Berkshire RG1 1YE (☎ 0734 500611)

NICHOLSON, John Clifford; CBE (1986); s of John William Nicholson (d 1976), and Susan May, *née* Allsop; *b* 8 Aug 1933; *Educ* King James I GS, Bishop Auckland; *m* 2 July 1955, Beryl, da of Henry Alfred Davies Wells; 1 s (Philip John b 18 June 1965), 1 da (Catherine Susan b 14 May 1963); *Career* Nat Serv 1949-51; Dist Audit Serv 1953-77, London dist advsr 1977-79, dep chief inspr audit 1979-82, dep controller and dir ops Audit Cmmn 1983-; vice pres CIPFA, FCCA; *Clubs* Royal Overseas League; *Style*— John Nicholson, Esq, CBE; The Audit Commission For Local Authorities In England & Wales, 1 Vincent Square, London SW1P 2PN (☎ 071 828 1212, fax 071 976 6187)

NICHOLSON, Sir John Norris; 2 Bt (UK 1912), of Harrington Gdns, Royal Borough of Kensington, KBE (1971), CIE (1946); s of Capt George Crosfield Norris Nicholson (ka 1916), s of 1 Bt, and Hon Evelyn Izme, JP (who m 2 1917, as his 2 w, 1 Baron Mottistone, CB, CMG, DSO), da of 10 Baron and 1 Viscount Elibank and gs of Sir Charles Norris Nicholson, 1 Bt (d 1918); *b* 19 Feb 1911; *Educ* Winchester, Trinity Coll Cambridge; *m* 1938, (Vittoria) Vivien, da of Percy Trewhella, of Villa St Andrea, Taormina, Sicily; 2 s, 2 da; *Heir* s, Charles Christian Nicholson; *Career* Lt 4 Bn Cheshire Regt 1939, Capt 1940, min of Shipping 1941, rep of min of War Tport in Delhi; formerly chm: Ocean Steamship Co Ltd, Martin's Bank Ltd; dir: Barclays Bank, Royal Insurance Co; pres Chamber of Shipping 1970; JP and Vice Ld-Lt Isle of Wight 1974-80; Keeper of the Rolls Isle of Wight 1974-86; Ld-Lt 1980-86; *Clubs* Royal Yacht Sqdn (Cdre 1980-86); *Style*— Sir John Nicholson, Bt, KBE, CIE; Mottistone Manor, Isle of Wight (☎ 0983 740322)

NICHOLSON, John Rugeley; JP (Armagh 1989); s of George Henry Nicholson, DSO, DFC (d 1976), and Edith Evelyn, *née* Davidson; *b* 11 April 1945; *Educ* Royal Sch Dungannon; *m* 23 Nov 1974, Jane Rockley, da of Geoffrey Mason; 4 da (Katie b 18 April 1977, Emma b 29 March 1979, Susan and Sarah b 7 June 1981 (twins)); *Career* head Agriculture BBC NI 1987, managing prodr BBC TV NI 1989, currently acting head television BBC NI; Young Farmers Clubs Ulster, first winner W D Morrow award 1985 (journalist scholarship studying food and dietary considerations in N America); Assoc FRAgS; *Style*— John Nicholson, Esq; Crannagael House, Cranagill, Portadown, Co Armagh, N Ireland (☎ 0762 851359); BBC Broadcasting House, Ormeau Ave, Belfast, N Ireland (☎ 0762 851359)

NICHOLSON, (John) Leonard; s of Percy Merwyn Nicholson (clan McLeod of McLeod, d 1938), and (Jane) Winifred, *née* Morris (d 1965); b 18 Feb 1916; *Educ* Stowe, Inst Actuaries, LSE (BSc, MSc); *Career* Inst Statistics Univ of Oxford 1940-

DEBRETT'S PERSONALITIES OF TODAY

Sir Michael Richardson

Peter Scudamore

PHOTOGRAPH: ROGER PARKER

Yuko Shiraishi

DEBRETT'S PERSONALITIES OF TODAY

John Simpson

Vivienne Westwood

Jeanette Winterson

47, Miny of Home Security 1943-44, chief statistician Central Statistical Office 1952-68 (statistician 1947-52), Simon Res Fell Univ of Manchester 1962-63, chief econ advsr DHSS 1968-76, prof quantitative econs Brunel Univ 1972-74, sr fell Policy Studies Inst 1976-81, fell Rockefeller Fndn 1984, fell Royal Statistical Soc 1940-; memb: Int Assoc Res Income and Wealth 1952-, Int Inst Public Finance 1969-; *Books* Variations in Working Class Family Expenditure (1949), The Interim Index of Industrial Production (1949), Redistribution of Income in the UK (1965), Poverty Inequality and Class Structure (contrib, 1974), The Personal Distribution of Incomes (contrib 1976), Public Economics and Human Resources (with V Halberstadt and A J Culyer, 1977), Human Resources Employment and Development vol 2: Concepts, Measurement and Long-run Perspective (1983), Social Security Research (DHSS, 1977), Definition and Measurement of Poverty (DHSS, 1979); author of articles in economic and statistical jls; *Recreations* enjoyment of music, painting, real tennis; *Clubs* MCC, Saville, Queen's, Arts Theatre; *Style—* Leonard Nicholson, Esq; 53 Frognal, London NW3 6YA (☎ 071 435 8015)

NICHOLSON, Malcolm G C; *b* 4 March 1949; *Educ* Haileybury, Univ of Cambridge (BA, LLB), Brussels (Dip en Droit Européen); *m* Diana Fay Nicholson, 4 da (Claire, Laura, Briany, Emily); *Career* ptnr Slaughter and May 1981 (specialising in European, Regulatory and Commercial Law); *Books* Common Market Law of Competition (contrib); *Style—* Malcolm Nicholson, Esq

NICHOLSON, Mavis; da of Richard John Mainwaring, and Olive Irene Mainwaring; *b* 19 Oct 1930; *Educ* Neath Co Sch for Girls, Univ of Swansea; *m* 16 Aug 1952, Geoffrey George Nicholson, s of George Llewelyn Nicholson; 3 s (Steve b 24 July 1958, Lewis b 13 May 1960, Harry b 10 Feb 1963); *Career* advertising copywriter; Hulton scholarship Mather and Crowther; employed by: LPE, Greenleys, Clifford Bloxhams; freelance writer, home ed Nova; writer: Observer, Sunday Times, Evening Standard, personal column Family Circle; TV presenter 1971-, progs incl: Good Afternoon, Afternoon, Afternoon Plus, A+, Mavis Meets, Mavis Wanting to Know, BBC Open Air, Mavis of 4, Mavis Catches up With, BBC Garden Party, Relative Values; hon fell Univ of Swansea; memb Amnesty Int; *Books* Help Yourself (1974); *Recreations* table tennis, photography, reading, gardening; *Style—* Mrs Mavis Nicholson; c/o Jon Thurley (Agent), 213 Linen Hall, 156 Regent St, London W1R 5TA (☎ 071 437 9545)

NICHOLSON, (Edward) Max; CB (1948), CVO (1971); s of Edward Prichard Nicholson (d 1945), of Hangersley, Ringwood, Hants, and Constance Caroline, *née* Oldmeadow (d 1945); *b* 12 July 1904; *Educ* Sedbergh, Hertford Coll Oxford; *m* 1, 6 Aug 1932 (m dis 1964), Eleanor Mary Lloyd, da of George Edward Crawford, of Putney, London; 2 s (Piers b 1934, Thomas Gavin b 1938); m 2, 1965, Marie Antoinette Mauerhofer; 1 s (David Ian b 1965); *Career* asst ed The Week-End Review London 1930-33, gen sec PEP 1933-39, controller of lit Miny of Info 1939, head Econ and Int Allied Branch Miny of Shipping (became Miny of War Tport 1940), head Allocation of Tonnage Div and Miny rep on Anglo-US Combined Shipping Adjustment Bd Miny of War Tport 1941-45, chm Anglo-Soviet Shipping Ctee (attended Quebec, Yalta and Potsdam Confs) 1941-45, head office of Lord Pres of the Cncl 1945-52, DG Nature Conservancy 1952-65, chm Land Use Consilts 1965-89 (currently princ in gp practice); chm: Br Tst for Ornithology 1947-49 (first hon sec 1933-39), Official Ctee Festival of Br 1951, London Looks Forward Conf 1977, Environmental Ctee of London Celebrations for the Queen's Jubilee 1977; tstee Earthwatch Europe (chm 1989-90); memb: Advsy Cncl on Scientific Policy 1948-64, Cwlth Scientific Ctee, Special Ctee of Int Cncl of Scientific Unions for Int Biological Programmes (convener conservation section) 1963-74; tstee The Observer 1952-65, pres RSPB 1980-85; hon memb: Br Ecological Soc, Royal Town Planning Inst; corresponding fell American Ornithologists' Union, Scientific Fell Zoological Soc, Hon Fell RIBA; Europa Preis für Landespflege 1972, Commandeur Order of the Golden Ark Netherlands 1973; MBOU, FRSA, FRGS; *Books* incl: Birds in England (1926), How Birds Live (1927), Birds and Men (1951), Oxford Birds of the Western Palearctic (ed 7 vols, 1977-), The System (1967), The Environmental Revolution (1970), The New Environmental Age (1987); *Clubs* Athenaeum; *Style—* Max Nicholson, Esq, CB, CVO; 13 Upper Cheyne Row, London SW3 5JW; Land Use Consultants, 43 Chalton St, London NW1 (☎ 071 383 5784, fax 071 383 4798)

NICHOLSON, His Hon Mr Justice; Sir (James) Michael Anthony; s of Cyril Anthony de Lacy Nicholson, QC, DL (d 1963), of Beech Hill, Ardmore, Co Londonderry, and Eleanor Gerad, *née* Caffrey (d 1972); *b* 4 Feb 1933; *Educ* Downside, Trinity Coll Cambridge (MA); *m* 7 July 1973, Augusta Mary Ada, da of Thomas F Doyle (d 1979), of Ardmanagh, Passage West, Co Cork; 1 s (Thomas b 7 May 1977), 2 da (Emma b 10 Jan 1975, Tessa b 26 July 1978); *Career* called to the Bar: NI 1956, Gray's Inn 1962, Ireland 1975; QC 1971, bencher Inn of Ct of NI 1978- (treas 1990-); sr crown counsel: Co Fermanagh 1971-73, Co Tyrone 1973-77, Co Londonderry 1977-81, Judge High Ct of Justice NI 1986-; chm Mental Health Review Tbnl 1973-76; memb Standing Advsy Cmmn on Human Rights in NI 1976-78; High Sheriff Co Londonderry 1972; *Recreations* cricket, chess; *Clubs* MCC; *Style—* His Hon Mr Justice Sir Michael Nicholson; Royal Courts of Justice, Chichester St, Belfast, Northern Ireland BT1 3JF (☎ 0232 235111)

NICHOLSON, Michael Thomas; Alan Alfred Nicholson (d 1956), of Romford, and Doris Alice, *née* Reid (d 1963); *b* 9 Jan 1937; *Educ* Prince Rupert Wilhemshaven Germany, Univ of Leicester (BA); *m* Diana; 2 s (Tom b 19 Jan 1972, Will b 17 May 1973); *Career* served RAF 1955-57; political writer DC Thompson 1962-63; ITN: foreign corr 1963-82 and 1985-, bureau corr Southern Africa 1976-81, newscaster 1982-85, currently sr corr; anchorman The World This Week (Channel 4); wars covered incl: Nigeria/Biafra 1968-69, Ulster 1968-75, Vietnam 1969-75, Cambodia (incl invasion of Laos) 1972-75, Jordan (incl Dawson's Field and Black September) 1970, Indo-Pakistan War 1971, Yom Kippur War 1973, Rhodesian War 1973-80, invasion of Cyprus 1974, Beirut Lebanon 1975, Angolan Civil War 1975-78, Falklands War (Falklands medal awarded) 1982, Gulf War 1991; *Awards* American Emmy nomination 1969, British Broadcasting Guild award 1974, RTS award 1974, Silver Nymph award (for Vietnam report) Monte Carlo Film Festival 1975, RTS Reporter of the Year (for Angola 1979, for Falklands 1983), BAFTA Richard Dimbleby award 1983, VALA award 1983; FRGS 1983, memb Royal Cwlth Soc 1983; *Books* Partridge Kite (1978), Red Joker (1979), December Ultimatum (1981), Across The Limpope (1985), Pilgrims Rest (1987), A Measure of Danger (1991); *Recreations* tennis, sailing, skiing; *Clubs* Groucho, Reform; *Style—* Michael Nicholson, Esq; Independent Television News, 200 Gray's Inn Rd, London WC1 (☎ 071 833 3000)

NICHOLSON, Pamela Mary Reina; *née* de Pommard; da of Boris Nicoloff de Pommard (d 1980), of Paris, and Aime, *née* Salomon; *b* 11 Sept 1937; *Educ* Northlands Buenos Aires Argentina, Roedean, La Chatelainie St Blaise Neuchatel Switzerland; *m* 10 May 1958, William John Nicholson, s of William Douglas Marshall Nicholson, JP (d 1986); 2 s ((William) Guy Marshall b 8 Jan 1961, Tom Marshall b 8 June 1985), 1 da (Deborah Mae Marshall (Mrs Bigley) b 15 May 1962); *Career* mktg and sales dir William Nicholson & Son Ltd Leeds 1970-85 (dir 1962-85), ptnr Art Study Tours 1978-, dir Country Travels Ltd 1987-; memb: Nat Bee Keepers Assoc, regnl Br Heart Fndn 1968-73, regnl Royal Br Legion 1968-, Women's Inst; Nat Assoc Decorative and Fine Art Socs: hon sec and chm Harrogate gp, memb Nat Exec Cncl, fndr chm and vice pres Nidd Valley branch; *Recreations* photography, skiing, apiculture, painting, writing; *Style—* Mrs William Nicholson; South Hill, Whixley, York YO5 8AR (☎ 0423 330533)

NICHOLSON, Paul Douglas; DL (Co Durham 1980); eld s of Frank Douglas Nicholson, TD, DL (d 1984), and Pauline, yr da of Maj Sir Thomas Lawson-Tancred, 9 Bt; *b* 7 March 1938; *Educ* Harrow, Clare Coll Cambridge; *m* 1970, Sarah, 4 and yst da of Sir Edmund Bacon, 13 and 14 Bt, KG, KBE, TD (d 1982), of Raveningham Hall, Norfolk; 1 da; *Career* Lt Coldstream Guards; chm Vaux Gp plc 1976-; chm: northern region CBI 1977-79, northern bd Nat Enterprise Bd 1979-84, Northern Investors Ltd 1984-89, Tyne & Wear Urban Devpt Corp 1987-; High Sheriff of Co Durham 1980-81; *Recreations* shooting, deerstalking, flying; *Clubs* Boodle's, Northern Counties; *Style—* Paul Nicholson, Esq, DL; Quarry Hill, Brancepeth, Durham, DH7 8DW (☎ 091 3780275); Vaux Group plc, The Brewery, Sunderland, Tyne and Wear SR1 3AN (☎ 091 5676277)

NICHOLSON, Richard Arthur; *b* 14 May 1935; *Educ* Stowe, Guys Hosp (LRCP); *m* 18 Jan 1964, Diana Mary, da of Lt-Col Arthur Robinson (d 1985), of Magdalen Farm, Hedon, nr Hull; 2 s (Mark b 1 March 1965, Philip b 31 July 1968), 1 da (Sally b 30 Sept 1966); *Career* Nat Serv Lt (former sub Lt) RNVR 1953-55; conslt orthopaedic and accident surgn: Pontefract Gen Infirmary, Methley Park Private Hosp; dep chm (former chm) Caldaire Independent Hospital plc; memb: BMA, Br Orthopaedic Assoc; MRCS, FRCS Glasgow; *Books* papers: Blunt Abdominal Trauma in Head Injuries (1966), Peptic Ulceration in Myocardial Infarction (1967), 20 Years of Bone and Joint Tuberculosis (1975); *Recreations* hunting, shooting, listening to music, silversmith with own mark registered at Goldsmith Hall; *Style—* Richard Nicholson, Esq; Thorpe Grange Farm, Thorpe Audlin, nr Pontefract, W Yorkshire WF8 3HG (☎ 0977 620629); The Orthopaedic Department, Pontefract General Infirmary, Southgate, Pontefract (☎ 0977 600600); Methley Park Private Hospital, Metley Lane, Methley, nr Leeds (☎ 0977 518518)

NICHOLSON, Sir Robin Buchanan; s of Carroll and Nancy Nicholson; *b* 12 Aug 1934; *Educ* Oundle, St Catharine's Coll Cambridge (PhD); *m* 1958, Elizabeth Mary (d 1988), da of Sir Sydney Caffyn; 1 s, 2 da; *Career* md Inco Europe 1976-81 (dir 1975-81), chief sci advsr Cabinet Office 1981-85; metallurgist; prof metallurgy Univ of Manchester 1966; dir Pilkington plc 1986-; non exec dir: Rolls Royce plc 1986-, BP plc 1987-; memb SRC 1978-81; FEng, FRS, FIM, MInstP; kt 1985; *Clubs* MCC; *Style—* Sir Robin Nicholson; Whittington House, 8 Fisherwick Rd, Whittington, nr Lichfield, Staffs WS14 9LH (☎ 0543 432081)

NICHOLSON, (Edward) Rupert; s of Alfred Edward Nicholson (d 1950), and Elise, *née* Dobson (d 1949); *b* 17 Sept 1909; *Educ* Whitgift Sch; *m* 18 June 1935, Mary (Peggy) (d 1983), da of Richard Elley (d 1936); 1 s (Anthony Richard b 1939), 1 da (Brenda Mary (Mrs Wright) b 1943); *Career* ptnr Peat Marwick (Mitchell) McLintock 1949 (joined 1933), liquidator Davies Investmts Ltd Wimbledon 1967, receiver Rolls Royce Ltd 1971, liquidator Court Line Ltd 1974; chm: Tech Advsy Ctee Inst of CA in England and Wales 1969-70, Whitgift Fndn 1978- (govr 1976-) Croydon Business Venture Ltd 1983-89; memb PO Review Ctee 1976; Master Worshipful Co of Horners 1984 (Liveryman 1964); FCA 1932; *Recreations* golf, gardening; *Clubs* Caledonian, Walton Heath; *Style—* Rupert Nicholson, Esq; Grey Wings, The Warren, Ashtead, Surrey KT21 2SL (☎ 0372 272655)

NICKELL, Prof Stephen John; s of John Edward Hilary Nickell (d 1962) and Phyllis, *née* Vicary (d 1975); *b* 25 April 1944; *Educ* Merchant Taylors', Pembroke Coll Cambridge (scholarship, BA), LSE (MSc, Ely Devons prize); *m* 25 June 1976, Susan Elizabeth, da of Peter Nicholas Pegden, of Bridlington, Yorks; 1 da (Katherine Jane b 30 Sept 1979), 1 s (William Thomas b 16 Oct 1981); *Career* mathematics teacher Hendon Co Sch 1965-68; prof of economics: LSE 1979-84 (lectr 1970-77, reader 1977-79), (and dir) Inst of Economics and Statistics Univ of Oxford 1984-; professorial fell Nuffield Coll Oxford 1984-; chm Research Grants Bd ESRC 1990- (also memb); memb Cncl Royal Economic Soc 1984-, fell Econometric Soc 1980 (memb Cncl 1987-); *Books* The Investment Decisions of Firms (1978), The Rise in Umemployment (ed, 1987), Unemployment (1991); *Recreations* reading, riding; *Style—* Prof Stephen Nickell; Church Wing, Old Rectory, Somerton, Oxford OX5 4NB (☎ 0869 346770); Institute of Economics and Statistics, St Cross Building, Manor Rd, Oxford OX1 3UL (☎ 0865 271087, fax 0865 271094)

NICKLESS, Christopher John; yr s of Rev Canon Victor George Nickless, of Ford Place, Ford Lane, Wrotham Heath, Kent, and Grace Kathleen, *née* Hepburn- Whyte; *b* 17 Sept 1947; *Educ* The King's Sch Rochester, Univ of Birmingham (BA); *m* 11 April 1987, Mairi, da of Lt-Col Robert Andrew Garden, of Naini, 164 St George's Rd, Sandwich, Kent; *Career* asst master The King's Sch Rochester 1968-82; Jr Sch King's Sch Rochester: dep master 1982-87, dep headmaster 1987-90; headmaster pre prep and prep sch King's Sch Rochester 1988-90; ind memb St Margaret's Ward Rochester City Cncl 1972; elected: Medway DC 1973, Medway Borough Cncl 1976, 1979, Rochester upon Medway City Cncl 1983 and 1987; steward Cathedral Church of Christ and the Blessed Virgin Mary Rochester, govr RNLI, pres Borstal CC, memb Kent Archaeological Soc; *Recreations* cricket, music, gardening, walking; *Style—* Christopher Nickless, Esq; The Hawthorns, 121 Maidstone Road, Chatham, Kent ME4 6JA (☎ 0634 841037); The Preparatory School, King Edward Rd, Rochester, Kent ME1 1UB (☎ 0634 843657)

NICKLIN, Keith Richard; s of James Edward Nicklin (d 1979), of London, and May Marjorie; *b* 12 Dec 1935; *m* 12 Aug 1983, Judith Louise, da of Leslie Eric Whiting (d 1983); 2 da (Amy b 1983, Sophie b 1986); *Career* chm and chief exec Nicklin Group Holdings Ltd; chm: Nicklin Advertising Ltd, John Bowler Associates Ltd; *Recreations* horse racing, fishing; *Clubs* Les Ambassadeurs; *Style—* Keith Nicklin, Esq; Benifold, Headley Down, Hampshire; Northway House, Bracknell, Berks (☎ 0344 51061, fax : 0344 55131, car ☎ 0836 240859)

NICKLIN, Stephen Richard; s of Richard Patrick Nicklin (d 1982), of Rugby, Warwicks, and Elsie Joan, *née* Crisp; *b* 20 April 1952; *Educ* Sloane GS; *m* 3 March 1979, (Mary) Theresa, da of Vincent O'Shea, of Collooney, Co Sligo, Eire; 3 s (Edward b 1981, Anthony b 1988, Luke (twin) b 1988), 1 da (Emily b 1985); *Career* BBC 1970; unit mangr: Newsnight BBC 1984-87, American Elections BBC 1984, Election 87 BBC 1985-87, Channel 4 News ITN 1987-89; ed mangr ITN 1989-; memb: RTS, BAFTA; *Style—* Stephen Nicklin, Esq; 200 Gray's Inn Rd, London WC1X 8XZ (☎ 071 833 3000)

NICKOLL, Eric William (Bill); s of Albert William Nickoll (d 1980), of Poole, Dorset, and Winifred Elizabeth, *née* Phillpot; *b* 25 April 1939; *Educ* Orange Hill GS; *m* 1, 1964 (m dis 1980), Dorothy Margaret, da of John Walley Holme, of Chorley, Lancs; 1 da (Rebecca b 1971); m 2, 1982, Margaret Rita, da of Phillip Reginald Dodge, of Hanwell, London; 1 s (Matthew b 1983); *Career* serv mangr NCR 1962-72; md: Gen Comp Sys Ltd 1972-84, Bell Tech Servs Ltd 1984-86; chm Intersect Ltd 1986-, md Kalamazoo plc 1987-89, pres Kalamazoo Inc 1988-; FBIM 1981, FIOD 1984; *Recreations* gardening, horology, woodworking, business; *Style—* Bill Nickoll, Esq; Manor Lodge, 12 Golden Manor, London W7 (☎ 081 567 7459); Kalamazoo plc, Northfield, Birmingham B31 2RW (☎ 021 411 2345, fax 021 475 7566, car 0836 660 633, telex

336700)

NICKOLLS, Malcolm Charles; s of Capt Charles Nickolls (d 1985), and Lillian Rose, *née* Taylor; *b* 20 March 1944; *Educ* Rickmansworth GS, Brighton Coll of Art (Dip Arch), Thames Poly (Dip Landscape Arch); *m* 26 Aug 1967, Mary Delia Margaret, da of Ronald Edward Groves, CBE; 2 da (Joanna Helen b 1973, Deborah Sally b 1976); *Career* architect and landscape architect; private practice under style of NKD Architects 1975-; chm Professional Purposes 1982-, hon offr ARCUK 1982-; princ building J Paul Getty Jr Conservation Centre; publishing Electronic Art Studio, Photography and Computer Graphics; MRIBA 1970-(memb Cncl), memb Landscape Inst 1977, MCIA 1976, ARCUK (memb Cncl), FRSA 1989; *Recreations* cycling, computers, technology, science, invention; *Clubs* MENSA; *Style—* Malcolm Nickolls, Esq; Bishops Meadow, Weedon, Buckinghamshire (☎ 0296 641666); Friars House, Rickfords Hill, Aylesbury, Buckinghamshire (☎ 0296 88122, fax 0296 436330, telecom gold 81:TWH129)

NICKSON, Sir David Wigley; KBE (1987, CBE 1981), DL (Stirling and Falkirk 1982); s of Geoffrey Wigley Nickson (d 1983), and Janet Mary, *née* Dobie; *b* 27 Nov 1929; *Educ* Eton, RMA Sandhurst; *m* 18 Oct 1952, (Helen) Louise, da of late Lt-Col Louis Latrobe Cockcraft, DSO, MVO; 3 da (Felicity (Mrs James Lewis) b 3 Nov 1955, Lucy (Mrs Melfort Campbell) b 8 July 1959, Rosemary b 11 Feb 1963); *Career* reg cmmn Coldstream 1949-54; William Collins plc: joined 1954, dir 1959, vice chm and gp md 1976-83; pres of the CBI 1986-88, chm CBI for Scot 1979-81, dir Radio Clyde Ltd 1981-85; chm: Scot & Newcastle Breweries 1983-89 (dep chm 1982), Countryside Cmmn for Scot 1983-85, Top Salary Review Body 1989, Scot Devpt Agency 1989-91, Scot Enterprise 1990-; dir: Gen Accident Fire & Life Assurance Corp plc, Clydesdale Bank plc (dep chm 1990), Edinburgh Investment Trust plc, Hambros plc, Scottish and Newcastle Breweries plc; memb: Queen's Bodyguard for Scot (Royal Co of Archers), Scot Ind Devpt Advsy Bd 1974-79, Scot Econ Cncl 1979-, NEDC 1985-88; chm Atlantic Salmon Tst 1988-; Dr: Univ of Stirling, Napier Coll; fell Royal Soc of Edinburgh; *Recreations* fishing, shooting, stalking, birdwatching, countryside; *Clubs* Boodle's, Flyfishers', MCC, Western (Glasgow); *Style—* Sir David Nickson, KBE, DL; Renagour House, Aberfoyle, Stirling FK8 3TF (☎ 08772 275); Scottish Enterprise, 120 Bothwell Street, Glasgow

NICKSON, Edward Anthony (Tony); DL (Lancashire 1982); s of Sydney Nickson (d 1945), and Elizabeth, *née* Bailey (d 1972); *b* 14 Dec 1918; *Educ* Shrewsbury; *m* 27 April 1946, da of Alexander Gammie (d 1970), of Aberdeen; 2 da (Avril b 1949, Gill b 1952); *Career* CA 1949; author; Royal Lytham St Annes Golf Club: hon treas 1963-86, Capt 1968 and Centenary Year 1986, life memb 1989; pres Lancashire Union of Golf Clubs 1983-84, chm English Golf Union Northern Gp of Counties 1986-89; High Sheriff Lancs 1980-81; FCA; *Books* The Lytham Century (ed, 1985); *Recreations* golf; *Clubs* Royal Lytham & St Annes Golf, R & A, Merion (USA); *Style—* Tony Nickson, Esq, DL; 12 Regent Avenue, Lytham-St-Annes, Lancs FY8 4AB

NICKSON, Jack; s of Clifford Nickson (d 1985), of London W1, and Violet Lily, *née* Keen (d 1970); *b* 31 Jan 1926; *Educ* Malden Coll, Univ of London (MB BS); *m* 1, 1954 (m dis), Betty Helena, da of William Kift (d 1941); 1 s (Martin Christopher b 1959), 1 da (Jacqueline b 1963); m 2, 14 July 1979, Elly Ingegärd, da of Ivar Jansson (d 1979), of Sweden; 1 s (Steven Erik b 1982), 1 da (Annika Christine b 1980); *Career* physician, princ in gen practice 1958-86 (ret), currently orthopaedic physician conslt; dir Jaywood Properties Ltd 1964-87; *Recreations* ornithology, gardening, travel, pastel painting, inventing; *Style—* Dr Jack Nickson; Warren Down, Peasemore, Newbury, Berks (☎ 0635 248331); The Surgery, High St, Chieveley, Newbury (☎ 0635 248251)

NICOL, Alexander David (Sandy); *b* 11 July 1938; *Career* md NEI Peebles 1976-83, appt dep chief exec Br Linen Bank Ltd 1989 (dir 1983-); *Style—* Sandy Nicol, Esq; 35 Ravelston Dykes, Edinburgh EH12 6HG (☎ 031 337 3442); The British Linen Bank Ltd, 4 Melville St, Edinburgh EH3 7NS (☎ 031 243 8304, telex 727221, fax 031 243 8393)

NICOL, Angus Sebastian Torquil Eyers; s of Henry James Nicol (d 1977), and Phyllis Mary, *née* Eyers; *b* 11 April 1933; *Educ* RNC Dartmouth; *m* 20 April 1968, Eleanor Denise, da of Lt Cdr William Lefevre Brodrick (ka 1943); 2 da (Catharine Sophia b 1968, Augusta Devorgilla Margaret b 1972); *Career* RN (ret as Sub-Lt 1956), served HMS Euryalus, HM MMS 1630, HMS Brocklesby, and HMS Coquette; literary ed Cassell & Co 1956-61; called to the Bar Middle Temple 1963, rec 1982-; author of poems and short stories in Gaelic; fndr memb and first vice chm The Monday Club 1961, dir The Highland Soc of London 1981- (sec 1982-), sr steward The Argyllshire Gathering 1983, lectr in Gaelic Central London Adult Educn Inst 1983-, conductor London Gaelic Choir 1985-90, tstee of Urras Clann Mhic Neacail 1987-; chm: Disciplinary Ctee Potato Mktg Bd 1988-, VAT Tribunal 1988-; cmmr Clan Macnicol for all the Territories of GB S of the River Twee for Europe, memb Gaelic Soc of Inverness; FSAS; *Recreations* shooting, fishing, sailing, music, gastronomy, Gaelic literature; *Clubs* Flyfishers', Royal Highland Yacht; *Style—* Angus Nicol, Esq; 5 Paper Buildings, Temple, London EC4Y 7HB (☎ 071 353 8494)

NICOL, Dr Davidson Sylvester Hector; CMG (1964); s of Jonathan Josibiah Nicol (d 1952), and Winifred Clarissa Willoughby (d 1978); *b* 14 Sept 1924; *Educ* CMS Sch, Kaduna & Port Harcourt Nigeria, Prince of Wales Sch Sierra Leone, Cambridge Univ, London Univ; *m* 1950, Marjorie (m dis), da of Arthur Johnston (d 1958); 3 s (Charles, Olu, Syl), 2 da (Aina, Ayo); *Career* fell and supervisor in Nat Sciences and Medicine Christ's Coll Cambridge 1957-59 (hon fell 1972), princ Fourah Bay Coll Sierra Leone 1960-68, first vice chllr Univ of Sierra Leone 1966-68, permanent rep and ambass for Sierra Leone to UN 1969-71 (memb Security Cncl 1970-71, pres 1970, chm Ctee of 24-Decolonisation, memb Econ and Social Cncl 1969-70), high cmmr for Sierra Leone in London 1971-72, ambass to Norway, Sweden and Denmark 1971-72; dir: Central Bank of Sierra Leone, Consolidated African Selection Tst Ltd (London), Davesme Corpn; memb Cwlth PM's Conf London 1965 and 1969, Singapore 1971; pres World Fedn of UN Assoc 1983-88 (hon pres 1988-), under sec gen of the UN, exec dir UN Inst for Trg and Res (UNITAR) 1972-82, hon sr fell UNITAR 1983, vice pres Royal African Soc; Hon DSc: Newcastle upon Tyne, Kalamazoo Michigan, Laurentian Ontario, Univ of Sierra Leone; Hon DLitt Davis and Elkins Coll; Hon LLD Leeds: Tuskegee Alabama, Univ of West Indies; Hon LHD Barat Illinois, Independence medal Sierra Leone 1961; Grand Cdr: Order of Rokel Sierra Leone 1974, Star of Africa Liberia 1974; International Peace Gold Medal (Indian Fedn UNAs) 1986; memb Royal Cwlth Soc; *Publications* Africa, A Subjective View (1964); contributions to: Malnutrition in African Mothers and Children (1954), HRH the Duke of Edinburgh's Study Conference (vol 2, 1958), The Mechanism of Action of Insulin (1960), The Structure of Human Insulin (1960), New and Modern Roles for Commonwealth and Empire (1976); editor: Paths to Peace, Essays on the UN Security Council and its Presidency (1981), Regionalism and the New International Economic Order (1981), The United Nations Security Council: towards greater effectiveness (1981), Creative Women (1982); also contributed to: Journal of Tropical Medicine, Biochemistry Journal, Nature, Journal of Royal African Soc, The Times, Guardian, New Statesman, Encounter, West Africa, Journal of Modern African Studies; *Recreations* rowing, travel, creative writing; *Clubs* United Oxford & Cambridge Univ, Royal Cwlth Soc; *Style—* Dr Davidson Nicol, CMG; 140 Thornton Rd, Cambridge CB3 0ND Cambs; Christ's Coll, Cambridge CB2 3BU

NICOL, Prof Donald MacGillivray; s of Rev George Manson Nicol (d 1957), and Mary Patterson, *née* MacGillivray; *b* 4 Feb 1923; *Educ* King Edward VII Sch Sheffield, St Paul's London, Pembroke Coll Cambridge (MA, PhD), Br Sch of Archaeology Athens; *m* 15 July 1950, Joan Mary, da of Lt-Col Sir Walter Campbell, KCIE (d 1974); 3 s (Christopher, Stephen, Theodore); *Career* Friends' Ambulance Unit 1942-46; lectr in classics Univ Coll Dublin 1952-64, visiting fell Dumbarton Oaks Washington DC 1964-65, visiting prof Byzantine history Univ of Indiana 1965-66, sr lectr and reader in Byzantine history Univ of Edinburgh 1966-70; King's Coll London: Koraes prof of modern Greek and Byzantine history language and literature 1970-88, asst princ and vice princ 1977-81; prof emeritus Univ of London 1988-; dir The Gennadius Library Athens 1989-; FBA, MRIA, FRHistS, FKC; *Books* The Despotate of Epiros 1204-1267 (1957), The Byzantine Family of Kantakouzenos (1968), The Last Centuries of Byzantium 1261-1453 (1972), Byzantium - Its Ecclesiastical History and Relations with the Wester (1972), Meteora - The Rock Monasteries of Thessaly (2 edn, 1975), Church and Society in the Last Centuries of Byzantium (1979), The End of the Byzantine Empire (1979), The Despotate of Epiros 1267-1479 - A Contribution to the History of the Middle Ages (1984), Studies in Late Byzantine History and Prosopography (1986), Byzantium and Venice - A Study in Diplomatic and Cultural Relations; *Recreations* book-binding; *Clubs* Athenaeum; *Style—* Prof Donald Nicol; 16 Courtyards, Little Shelford, Cambridge CB2 5ER (☎ 0223 843 406); The Gennadius Library, American School of Classical Studies, Souedias 54, Athens, Greece

NICOL, Michael John; s of John Chalfont Nicol, of Barnet, Herts, and Jean Etta, *née* Crawley; *b* 8 May 1940; *Educ* Queen Elizabeth's Barnet, Univ of London (LLB); *m* (m dis 1985), Carol Ann, *née* Howie; 3 da (Kate b 1969, Amanda b 1971, Lucy b 1975); *Career* admitted slr 1963; currently ptnr Wedlake Bell; memb Law Soc 1963; *Recreations* bridge, badminton, croquet; *Clubs* MCC, Savage, British Sportman's; *Style—* Michael Nicol, Esq; 16 Wedlake Bell, Bedford Street, Covent Garden, London WC2 (☎ 071 379 7266, fax 071 836 6117, telex 25256/28899)

NICOL, Stephen (Steve); s of James Caldwell Nicol (d 1986), of Troon, Ayshire, and Helen, *née* Murchie; *b* 11 Dec 1961; *Educ* Marr Coll; *m* 9 June 1982, Eleanor, da of James McMath; 1 s (Michael Stephen b 1984), 1 da (Katy Caldwell b 1986); *Career* professional footballer; Ayr Utd 1979-81 (89 appearances); Liverpool 1981-: joined for a fee of £300,000, full debut Aug 1982, over 200 appearances; Scotland: 13 under 21 cups (a record), 23 full cups, appeared in World Cup 1986 in Mexico; represented Ayshire at rugby and athletics; 4 League Championship medals, 2 FA Cup Winners medals (and 1 Loser's), 1 Milk Cup Winner's medal, 1 European Cup Winner's medal (and 1 Loser's); Football Writer's Assoc player of the year 1989; *Recreations* pool, golf, tennis, squash, snooker, playing with the kids; *Style—* Steve Nicol, Esq; Liverpool Football Club, Anfield Road, Anfield, Liverpool L4 0TH (☎ 051 263 2361)

NICOL, Baroness (Life Peer UK 1982), of Newnham, Co Cambridge; (Olive Mary) Wendy Nicol; JP (1972); da of James Rowe-Hunter (d 1962), and Harriet Hannah (d 1932); *b* 21 March 1923; *Educ* Cahir Sch Ireland; *m* 1947, Dr Alexander Douglas Ian Nicol, CBE, s of Alexander Nicol (d 1962); 2 s (Hon Adrian Timothy b 1949, Hon Colin Douglas b 1950), 1 da (Hon Jane Lesley (Hon Mrs John) b 1954); *Career* Civil Serv 1943-48; memb: Cambs City Cncl 1972-82, Supplementary Benefits Tbnl 1976-78, Careers Serv Consultative Panel 1978-81; oppn dep chief whip 1987-89; spokesman on natural environment; public serv in many and varied areas; *Recreations* reading, walking; *Style—* The Rt Hon the Lady Nicol, JP; 39 Grantchester Rd, Newnham, Cambridge CB3 9ED (☎ 0223 323 733)

NICOLL, (Walter Lyon) Gordon; s of Walter Nicoll (d 1964), of Killichassie, Perthshire, and Ethel, *née* Brown (d 1967); *b* 25 March 1925; *Educ* Trinity Coll Glenalmond, Leys Cambridge; *m* 2 Aug 1951, Willa Ellen Mary, da of Richard Clay (d 1980), of Kingscliffe, Northants; 1 s (Andrew Gordon b 1952), 3 da (Fiona Mary b 1954, Willow Anne Alison b 1956, Rowena Heather Annys b 1958); *Career* Home Guard 1940-42, RAF Europe and India 1942-48 (39-45 star, France/Germany star, Defence medal, War medal); fndr Harford Opio Pumps 1959, conslt Ionian Bank 1962, sales dir and gen mangr the Rotherham Group of Coventry Precision Engineering 1962, fndr Scarab Engineering 1964, md The Humber Group 1967, gp md Nocorrode Group 1972; FInstPI, FIDHE, FInstD, MIRI, MPI; *Books* Centenary of OLFC (1978); *Recreations* travel, motoring, inventing; *Clubs* Hurlingham, OLFC (Centenary pres), OLU (London pres); *Style—* Gordon Nicoll, Esq; 57 Hurlingham Court, London SW6 3UP (☎ 071 736 1434)

NICOLL, William; CMG (1974); s of Ralph Nicoll (d 1947), of Dundee, and Christina Mowbray, *née* Melville (d 1959); *b* 28 June 1927; *Educ* Morgan Acad Dundee, Univ of St Andrews (MA), Univ of Dundee (LLD); *m* 1954, Helen Morison, da of William Morison Martin, MM (d 1970), of Pitlochry; 2 da (Sheila, Barbara); *Career* dep UK perm rep to the EEC 1977-82, dir gen Cncl of Euro Communities 1982-; *Books* Government and Industry (contrib, 1986), Understanding the European Communities (with Prof T C Salmon, 1990); *Clubs* Royal Cwlth Soc; *Style—* William Nicoll Esq, CMG; 170 Rue de la Loi, Brussells 1048 (☎ 02 234 6246)

NICOLLE, Geoffrey Reginald; s of Reginald Francis Nicolle (d 1961), of Caerleon, Gwent, and Hilda Alice, *née* Shepherd (d 1965); *b* 5 June 1934; *Educ* Caerleon Endowed Sch, W Monmouth GS, UCL Aberystwyth (BA); *m* 28 March 1959, Sonia Aileen, da of Harry Joseph Bain (d 1960), of Hockley, Essex; 1 s (Philip David b 1963), 1 da (Mary Olwen (Mrs McSparron) b 1962); *Career* headmaster Rosemarket Voluntary Sch (Pembrokeshire) 1965-89; holder of the nat collection of primula (garden and border auriculas) for Nat Cncl for the Conservation of Plants and Gardens, pres Dyfed Co Div NUT 1988-89; *Books* Rosemarket: A Village Beyond Wales (1982); *Recreations* gardening, plant breeding, garden plant conservation, local history; *Style—* Geoffrey Nicolle, Esq; Rising Sun Cottage, Nolton Haven, Haverfordwest, Pembs, Dyfed (☎ 0437 710 542)

NICOLLE, Robert Arthur Bethune (Bobby); s of Arthur Villeneuve Nicolle (d 1970), of St Peter's House, Jersey, and Alice Margarite, *née* Cobbold (d 1980); *b* 24 Sept 1934; *Educ* Eton, Trinity Coll Cambridge (MA); *m* 21 Jan 1963, Anne Carolyn, da of Sir Anthony Kershaw, MC, MP, of West Barn, Didmarton, Badminton, Glos; 2 s (Darcy b 1965, Harry b 1971), 1 da (Fiona b 1967); *Career* Lt Grenadier Gds active serv Cyrpus 1957-58; joined Kleinwort Sons & Co merchant bankers 1958; formerly dir Kleinwort Benson Ltd, currently dir Matheson Investment Mgmnt Ltd; treas IRIS Fund 1973, dir Colonial Mutual Life Insur of Aust 1987-, special tstee St Thomas' Hosp 1981, advsr Worldwide Fund for Nature in Switzerland (formerly World Wildlife Fund) 1988-; *Recreations* skiing, shooting, fox hunting; *Clubs* Buck's; *Style—* Bobby Nicolle, Esq; 45 Gloucester St, London SW1; The Tithe Barn, Didmarton, Badminton GL9 1DT; Jardine House, 6 Crutched Friars, London EC3N 2HT (☎ 071 528 4000)

NICOLSON, Allan Thomas McLean; s of John Nicolson (d 1969), and Elizabeth Helen Allan, *née* Thomson; *b* 25 April 1949; *Educ* Hamilton Acad, Univ of Glasgow (LLB); *m* 10 Aug 1974, Allison Stoddard, da of Douglas Lawson Fullarton (d 1986); 2 s (John Douglas b 1979, Richard Thomas b 1985), 1 da (Claire Elizabeth b 1977); *Career* ptnr McGrigor Donald 1975-, called to the Scottish Bar 1982, dir Legal Resources Ltd 1989-; hon sec to St Mungo prize 1979-; memb Law Soc of Scotland;

Recreations rugby, cricket, opera, family life; *Clubs* Western Glasgow; *Style*— Allan Nicolson, Esq; McGrigor Donald, Pacific House, 70 Wellington St, Glasgow G2 6SB (☎ 041 248 6677, fax 041 204 1351, telex 778744 M)

NICOLSON, Sir David Lancaster; s of Murdoch Charles Tupper Nicolson (d 1940), of Amherst, Nova Scotia; *b* 20 Sept 1922; *Educ* Haileybury, St Paul's, Imperial Coll London (BSc); *m* 1945, Joan Eileen, da of Maj W H Griffiths, RA (d 1973); 1 s, 2 da; *Career* WWII served Royal Corps Naval Constructors at sea and Europe (despatches Normandy 1944); prodn mangr Bucynes Erie Co Milwankee 1950-52, mangr (later dir) Prodn Engr Ltd 1953-62; chm: PE Consulting Group 1963-68, BTR plc 1969-84, BA 1971-75, Rothmans Int 1975-84, Bulk Transport 1984-87, Euro Movement 1985-89, VSEL 1986-87, Lazard Leisure Fun 1986, DRG plc 1989; dir: Todd Shipyards Corp 1976-, Ciba-Geigy plc (UK) 1978-89, Confederation Life Insurance Co 1981-88, Farmer Stedall plc 1982-87, LASMO plc 1983-, Northern Telecom plc 1987-88, Britannia Arrow Holdings plc 1987 (now Invesco MIM plc), STC plc 1987, Union Group plc 1987, GKN plc 1984-89, Northern Telecom Ltd (Can) 1987, Dawnay Day International Ltd 1988-, Leisure International 1989-; Euro advsr NY Stock Exchange 1985; pro chllr Univ of Surrey 1987; MEP London Central 1979-84; memb: Br Shipbuilding Mission to India 1957, City and Guilds London Inst 1968-76, SRC Engrg Bd 1969-71, Cncl CBI 1972, Cncl Templeton Coll 1982-; pres Assoc for Br C of C Commerce 1983-86; chm: Mgmnt Conslts Assoc 1964, America Euro Community Assoc 1981-; govr Imperial Coll Univ of London 1966-77 (hon fell 1971), govr Cranleigh Sch 1979-89; lectr and broadcaster on mgmnt subjects USA and UK; FEng 1977; Fell Imperial Coll 1971; memb: BIM 1964-69, IProdE 1966-88, IOD 1971-76; FIBM, FRSA; kt 1975; *Books* contribs to tech jls; *Recreations* sailing, collecting antiques; *Clubs* Brook's, Royal Thames Yacht; *Style*— Sir David Nicolson; Howicks, Dunsfold, Surrey (☎ 048 649 296)

NICOLSON, Hon Mrs (Katharine Ingrid Mary Isabel); *née* Ramsay of Mar; da and heiress of Lady Saltoun, *qv*, by her husb Capt Alexander Ramsay of Mar, Grenadier Gds; assumed surname and arms of Fraser by Warrant of Lord Lyon Kings of Arms 1973; through her f's mother (late Lady Patricia Ramsay, da of HRH The Duke of Connaught, 3 s of Queen Victoria), Mrs Nicolson is 3 cous of HM The Queen; *b* 11 Oct 1957; *m* 3 May 1980, Capt Mark Malise Nicolson, Irish Gds, o s of Malise Nicolson, MC, *qv*, of Frog Hall, Tilston, Malpas, Cheshire; 1 s (Alexander William Malise Fraser b 5 July 1990), 2 da (Louise Alexandra Patricia b 2 Sept 1984, Juliet Victoria Katharine b 3 March 1988); *Style*— The Hon Mrs Nicolson; 41 Napier Ave, London SW6 3PS

NICOLSON, Nigel; MBE (1945); s of Hon Sir Harold Nicolson, KCVO, CMG, sometime MP Leics W (d 1968, the biographer, critic and broadcaster, 3 s of 1 Baron Carnock), and Hon 'Vita' (Victoria) Sackville-West, CH, JP (also a writer, author of The Edwardians), only child of 3 Baron Sackville; bro of late Benedict Nicolson, the art historian; hp to 1 cousin, 4 Baron Carnock; *b* 19 Jan 1917; *Educ* Eton, Balliol Coll Oxford; *m* 1, 1953, Philippa, da of Sir Eustace Tennyson d'Eyncourt, 2 Bt; 1 s (Adam b 1957, m 1982 Olivia Fane), 2 da (Juliet b 9 June 1954, m 1977 James Macmillan Scott (2 da, Clementina b 1981, Flora b 1985); Rebecca b 1963); *Career* dir Weidenfeld and Nicolson 1946-; MP (C) Bournemouth and Christchurch 1952-59; FRSL; author; *Books Incl:* Lord of the Isles (1969), Great Houses of Britain (1965), Harold Nicolson; Diaries and Letters 1930-39 (1966), 1939-45 (1967), 1945-62 (ed of 3 vols, 1968), Portrait of a Marriage (1973), Alex (Field Marshal Alexander of Tunis) (1973), Letters of Virginia Woolf (editor 6 vols, 1975-1980), Mary Curzon (1977, Whitbread Prize), Kent (1988), Jane Austen's Houses (1991); *Recreations* archaeology; *Clubs* Beefsteak; *Style*— Nigel Nicolson, Esq, MBE; Sissinghurst Castle, Cranbrook, Kent (☎ 0580 714239)

NICOLSON, Sanders Nairn; s of William Holmes Nicolson (d 1966), of Glasgow, and Eleanor Mary, *née* Dunlop; *b* 23 July 1944; *Educ* Glasgow HS for Boys, Gordonstoun (Duke of Edinburgh's Gold Award), Regent St Poly London; *Partner* Maureen Angela Gray; 1 s (Jamie Nairn Nicolson-Gray b 3 May 1986), 1 da (Rosanna Cailin Nicolson-Gray b 14 Dec 1988); *Career* starving artist, gardener and dish washer 1966-68, self-taught fashion photographer Foto Partners 1968-71, freelance photographer 1971-; solo exhibitions: Waves (Pentax Gallery London 1979), Maske (The Association Gallery London 1989); *Awards* AFAEP awards: Gold 1984, Silver 1986, Silver merit 1989; *Recreations* fly-fishing, gardening, music, food and wine, painting, photography; *Style*— Sanders Nicolson, Esq; Sanders Nicolson & Associates Ltd, Resolution House, 19 Perseverance Works, 38 Kingsland Rd, London E2 8DD (☎ 071 739 6987, fax 071 729 4056)

NICOLSON OF TARANSAY, (Aeofric Lachlan) Bryan; s of Seymour Nicolson (d 1985), and Margaret Isabella, *née* Baillie; *b* 27 Aug 1945; *Educ* New Silksworth HS, Ruskin Coll, Coll of Piping Glasgow, Dr Kenneth MacKay's Sch of Piping Laggan Newtonmore; *Career* writer, historian, armorist; fndr and Armiger Principal The Most Hon Co of Armigers; genealogist and compiler of histories of the Clan Nicolson and its heraldry; memb: The White Lion Soc, The Heraldry Soc of Scotland, The Surtees Soc, The Br Falconers Club, The Heraldry Soc London, Heraldisch-Genealogische Gesellschaft ADLER Vienna, The Augustan Soc USA; *Recreations* fishing, golf, music, gardening, falconry, restoration of castellated and crenellated buildings, heraldry, literature, Piobaireachd, yacht design; *Clubs* Naval; *Style*— A L B Nicolson of Taransay; 49 Avebury Drive, Washington Village, District 9, Tyne-Wear NE38 7BY (☎ 416 4429)

NIDDRIE, Robert Charles (Bob); s of Robert Hutchin Niddrie (d 1975), of Morestead, Winchester, and Gladys Ellen, *née* Vaudin; *b* 29 Jan 1935; *Educ* Brockenhurst GS; *m* 11 Sept 1965, Maureen Joy, da of Leonard Willis (d 1976), of Morestead, Winchester; 1 s (Alastair b 13 Sept 1967), 2 da (Alison b 15 Dec 1969, Rachel b 30 Dec 1971); *Career* RMR 1957-59 (MNE) and 1962-72 (Capt), Nat Serv RM and 2 Lt Queen's Own Nigeria Regt 1959-61; Whittaker Bailey & Co 1952-75 (ptnr 1963-75, amalgamated with Price Waterhouse 1975), ptnr Price Waterhouse 1975- (sr ptnr i/c Southampton Office); Round Table: chm Southampton No 4 1971-72, chm Area 1 1973-74, pres 1978-79; fndr chm IOD Hants Branch 1980-86 (memb Ctee 1980-89, memb Cncl 1980-86); memb: Rotary Club Southampton, 41 Club Southampton, Bd of Mgmnt Western Orchestral Soc; tstee TVS Telethon Tst, govr King Edward VI Sch Southampton; FCA 1958, ATII 1964; Independence medal (Nigeria) 1960, Congo medal (UN) 1961; *Recreations* gardening, books, travel, music, theatre, fine food, wine; *Clubs* Royal Southern Yacht, Royal Southampton Yacht; *Style*— Bob Niddrie, Esq; Morestead House, Morestead, Winchester, Hants SO21 1LZ (☎ 0962 777 397); Price Waterhouse, The Quay, 30 Channel Way, Ocean Village, Southampton SO1 1XF (☎ 0703 330 077, fax 0703 223 473)

NIEHAUS, Robert Henry; s of Robert Frederick Niehaus, of Charlottesville, Virginia, and Joanne Cecil, *née* Fath; *b* 18 Aug 1955; *Educ* Princeton (BA), Harvard (MBA); *m* 19 June 1982, Kate, da of George Howard Southworth, of Corning, NY; 2 s (John b 1986, Peter b 1988), 1 da (Ann b 1990); *Career* vice pres American Computer Sales & Leasing 1978-80; Morgan Stanley: assoc Mergers and Acquisitions 1982-86, vice pres Merchant Banking 1987, principal Merchant Banking 1988-89; non-exec dir: Fort Howard Corporation 1988-, Silgan Corporation 1987-, Sweetheart Cup Company 1989-, Waterford Wedgwood plc 1990-; md Morgan Stanley & Co 1990-; tstee Class of 1977 Princeton Univ; memb: Student Sponsor Partnership NY, Republican Pty, Cooperation Ireland; *Recreations* tennis, squash, skiing; *Clubs* Abpawamis, Cottage; *Style*— Robert Niehaus, Esq; Morgan Stanley & Co, 1251 Avenue of the Americas, New York, NY 10580 (☎ 212 703 8724)

NIELD, Sir Basil Edward; CBE (1956, MBE (Mil) 1943), DL (Ches 1962); s of Charles Edwin Nield, of Upton Grange, Upton-by-Chester (d 1941), and F E L Nield, *née* Whalley (d 1931); *b* 7 May 1903; *Educ* Harrow, Magdalen Coll Oxford (MA); *Career* Lt-Col, serv ME and Western Europe (despatches); called to the Bar 1925, KC 1945; MP (C) Chester 1940-56; rec Salford 1948-56, chllr Dio of Liverpool 1948-56, rec Manchester 1956-60, judge of the High Ct 1960-78; only judge to have presided at all 61 towns in England and Wales; kt 1957; *Books* Farewell to the Assizes (1972); *Recreations* travel, photography; *Clubs* Carlton; *Style*— Sir Basil Nield, CBE, DL; Osborne House, Isle of Wight PO32 6JY (☎ 0983 200 056)

NIELD, Sir William Alan; GCMG (1972), KCB (1968, CB 1966); s of William Herbert Nield, of Stockport; *b* 21 Sept 1913; *Educ* Stockport GS, St Edmund Hall Oxford; *m* 1937, Gwyneth Marion, *née* Davies; 2 s, 2 da; *Career* RAF and RCAF WWII, Wing Cdr (despatches); joined Civil Serv 1946, under sec MAFF 1959-64, dep sec of the Cabinet 1966-68, perm under sec of state Dept of Economic Affrs 1968-69 (dep under sec of state 1965-66), perm sec Cabinet Office 1969-72, perm sec NI Office 1972-73, dep chm Rolls Royce Ltd 1973-76; pres St Edmund Hall Assoc 1981-83, hon fell St Edmund 1990; *Clubs* Farmers; *Style*— Sir William Nield, GCMG, KCB; South Nevay, Stubbs Wood, Chesham Bois, Bucks (☎ 020 43 3869)

NIGHTINGALE, Sir Charles Manners Gamaliel; 17 Bt (E 1628), of Newport Pond, Essex; s of Sir Charles Athelstan Nightingale, 16 Bt (d 1977); *b* 21 Feb 1947; *Educ* St Paul's, Open Univ; *Heir* 2 cous, Edward Lacy George Nightingale; *Career* sr exec offr Dept of Health 1989-; *Style*— Sir Charles Nightingale, Bt; 14 Frensham Court, 27 Highbury New Park, London N5 2ES

NIGHTINGALE, Edward Lacy George; s of late Manners Percy Nightingale, MRCS, LRCP; hp of 2 cous Sir Charles Manners Gamaliel Nightingale, 17 Bt; *b* 11 May 1938; *Educ* Exeter Sch; *Career* Master Mariner 1966, left Merchant Navy 1974; sub-postmaster Lynmouth; memb Devon CC 1981-85; vice chm Exmoor Nat Park Ctee 1982-85; memb N Devon DC 1987-; *Recreations* all types of sport; *Style*— Edward Nightingale, Esq; Kneesworth, Lynton, N Devon EX35 6HQ (☎ 0598 52204)

NIGHTINGALE, Hon Mrs (Evelyn Florence Margaret Winifred); *née* Gardner; da of Baron Burghclere (d 1921); *b* 1903; *m* 1, 1928 (m dis 1930), Evelyn Arthur St John Waugh; m 2, 1930 (m dis 1936), John Edward Nourse Heygate (later 4 Bt and who d 1976); m 3, 1937 Ronald Nightingale (d 1977); 1 s (Benedict), 1 da (Virginia); *Style*— The Hon Mrs Nightingale; 12 Church St, Ticehurst, Sussex TN5 7AH

NIGHTINGALE, Sir John Cyprian; CBE (1970), BEM (1941), QPM (1965), DL (Essex 1975); s of Herbert Paul Nightingale (d 1965), of Sydenham, London; *b* 16 Sept 1913; *Educ* Cardinal Vaughan Sch, UCL; *m* 1947, Patricia Mary, da of Dr Norman Maclaren, of West Kilbride, Ayrshire; *Career* serv RNVR 1943-45; joined Metropolitan Police 1935; chief constable Essex 1962 and 1975-78 (asst chief constable 1958-62), chief constable of Essex and Southend on Sea 1969-75, chm Police Cncl 1976-78, memb Parole Bd 1978-82; kt 1975; *Style*— Sir John Nightingale, CBE, BEM, QPM, DL; Great Whitman's Farm, Purleigh, Essex

NIGHTINGALE, Lady; Nadine; da of late (Charles) Arthur Diggens; *m* 1932, Sir Charles Athelstan Nightingale, 16 Bt (d 1977); 1 s, 2 da; *Style*— Lady Nightingale; 12 Jacob's Pool, Okehampton, Devon

NIGHTINGALE, Richard Mervyn; s of Edward Humphrey Nightingale, CMG, of Nunjoro Farm, Naivasha, Kenya, E Africa, and Evelyn Mary, *née* Ray; *b* 9 July 1954; *Educ* Rugby, Emmanuel Coll Cambridge (MA, DipArch); *Career* architect; with practices in Nairobi, London and Hong Kong 1977-81, Colin St John Wilson and Partners 1981-85, estab partnership with Hugh Cullum as Hugh Cullum and Richard Nightingale Architects 1985; articles published in: Architects Journal, Building Design, International Architect, Interni, Baumeister; work exhibited at: Royal Acad, RIBA, Fitzwilliam Museum Cambridge, Building Centre London, Br Cncl Nairobi; memb RIBA; *Publications* House in Hampstead (1988), New British High Commission Nairobi (1989); *Recreations* travel, tennis, polo; *Style*— Richard Nightingale, Esq; 30A Parkhill Rd, London NW3 (☎ 071 482 1213); 61 Judd St, London WC1H 9QT (☎ 071 383 4466, fax 071 383 4465)

NIGHTINGALE, Robert Daniel (Danny); s of Dr George McDonald Nighingale, Pilton Somerset, and Joan Margaret Nightingale; *b* 21 May 1954; *Educ* Wells Cathedral Sch Somerset, Univ of Loughborough (BSc, CertEd); *m* 28 Aug 1976, Elizabeth Jane, da of John Duglas Smith; 4 s (James Daniel b 8 Aug 1978, Toby Alexanda b 7 April 1982, Jack Ainsley b 31 Aug 1984, Frederick Charles b 2 Dec 1986); *Career* athlete; *Awards and Achievements* ASA Prelim Teachers award, BAAB Club Coach award, Silver Duke of Edinburgh award, memb County athletic and cross country team 1970-72, sixth All Eng Schs 2000m steeplechase 1972, thirty-second class B Karimor Mountain Marathon 1979, seventh Int Iron Man 1982, finalist BBC Superstars 1979 and 1982, sixth Br Epee Championships 1984; modern pentathlon: Pony Club Nat Tetrathlon Champion 1972, Br Jr Modern Pentathlon champion 1974 and 1975, Br Sr Modern Pentathlon champion 1976-78, tenth individual and team Gold medal Olympic Games Montreal 1976, winner Sportakiad Moscow 1979 (only Westerner ever to win), fifteenth individual and team capt GB Olympic Games Moscow 1980, first reserv Olympic Games LA 1984; memb BBC Sports Team of the Year 1976; rep Br Olympic Assoc, Modern Pentathlon Assoc of GB, Union of Int Modern Pentathlon and Biathlon at XI Int Olympic Congress 1981, rep Modern Pentathlon Assoc of GB Int Congress 1986, coach Ladies World Championship 1985 and 1986, coach Olympic Team Seoul 1988, memb Union of Int Modern Pentathlon and Biathlon Congress Seoul 1988, coach Jr Men World Championships 1990, chm Devpt and Coaching Ctee of Modern Pentathlon Assoc of GB (memb Exec Ctee), memb Nat Pony Club Tetrathlon Ctee; other activities: asst sports mangr Ashton Ct Country Club Failand Bristol 1976-78, lectr in physical Educn Cleveland Tech Coll (pt/t lectr 1986-89), nat devpt offr Modern Pentathlon Assoc of GB, lectr Plymouth Coll of Further Educn 1990; teacher of physical educn: Bassleton Sch Thornaby 1990, Keldholme Sch Middlesbrough 1991-; *Style*— Danny Nightingale, Esq

NIGHTINGALE OF CROMARTY, Michael David; OBE (1960); Baron of Cromarty (feudal); s of Victor Russell John Nightingale (d 1951), of Wormshill, Kent, and Bathsheba, *née* Buhay (d 1942); *b* 6 Dec 1927; *Educ* Winchester, Wye Coll London (BSc), Magdalen Coll Oxford (B Litt); *m* 28 April 1956, Hilary Marion Olwen, da of John Eric Jones (d 1933), of Swansea; 2 s (John b 1960, Alexander b 1964), 3 da (Emma b 1957, Rebecca b 1958, Rachel b 1966); *Career* asst to investmt mangr Anglo-Iranian Oil 1951-53, investmt advsr Univ of London 1954-66, dir Charterhouse Japhet Ltd 1965-70; chm: Anglo-Indonesian Corporation plc 1971-, The Chillington Corporation plc 1986-89, Anglo-Eastern Plantations plc 1985-90; memb Bd Cwlth Devpt Corp 1985; sec: Museums Assoc and ed Museums Journal 1954-60, Museum Ctee Carnegie UK Tst 1954-60; memb: Advsy Cncl for Export of Works of Art 1954-60, Br Ctee Int Cncl of Museums 1956-60, Canterbury Diocesan Advsy Ctee 1964-79, Kent CC 1973-77, Maidstone Borough Cncl 1973- (chm Planning Ctee 1973-77, ldr 1976-77), Mayor 1984-85, Exec Ctee SE Arts Assoc 1974-77, Area Archaeological

Advsy Ctee SE England 1974-79, Panel of Chairmen Gen Synod C of E 1984-85 (joined 1979); chm: Churches Ctee of Kent Archaeological Soc 1973-, North Downs Soc 1983-; Esquire Bedell Univ of London 1953-, dep Steward Royal Manor of Wye 1954-, Mayor of Maidstone 1984-85, warden Rochester Bridge 1989- (memb 1985-), pres Cobham New Coll 1989-, Lord of the Level of Romney Marsh, Lord of the Manor of Wormshill and a Lord of the Level of Romney Marsh; Freeman City of London; FSA (1956); *Recreations* antiquarian, musical; *Clubs* Athenaeum; *Style—* Michael Nightingale of Cromarty, OBE, FSA; Cromarty House, Ross and Cromarty (☎ 038 17 265); Wormshill Ct, Sittingbourne, Kent (☎ 062 784 235)

NIGHTINGALE OF CROMARTY, Yr, John Bartholomew Wakelyn; er s and h of Michael David Nightingale of Cromarty, OBE, *qv*; *b* 7 Sept 1960; *Educ* Winchester, Magdalen Coll Oxford (MA, DPhil); *Career* Harmsworth sr res scholar Merton Coll Oxford 1984-86; fell Magdalen Coll Oxford 1986-; tstee: Cromarty Harbour, Cromarty Arts Tst; author of articles on medieval history; *Recreations* woodland management, restoration of old buildings; *Style—* John Nightingale of Cromarty, Yr; Cromarty House, Ross and Cromarty IVII 8XS (☎ 03817 265); 21 Dartmouth Row, Greenwich, London SE10 8AW

NIMMO, Derek Robert; s of Harry Nimmo (d 1959), and Marjorie Sudbury, *née* Hardy (d 1988); *b* 19 Sept 1932; *Educ* Quarry Sch Liverpool; *m* 9 April 1955, Patricia Sybil Anne, da of Alfred John Brown (d 1955), of Santiago, Chile; 2 s (Timothy St John b 1956, Piers James Alexander b 1967), 1 da (Amanda Kate Victoria b 1959, m 1983 Hon Nicholas Howard, *qv*); *Career* actor, author, producer; first appearance Bolton Hippodrome as Ensign Blades in Quality St; stage appearances incl: Waltz of The Toreadors Criterion 1957, Duel of Angels Apollo 1958, The Amorous Prawn Savill 1959, See How They Run Vaudeville 1964, Charlie Girl Adelphi 1965-71 and overseas 1975, Why Not Stay for Breakfast? Apollo 1973 (and overseas 1975), See How They Run, A Friend Indeed Shaftesbury 1984; television series incl: All Gas and Gaiters, Oh Brother, Oh Father, Sorry I'm Single, The Bed Sit Girl, My Honourable Mrs, The World of Wooster, Blandings Castle, Life Begins at Forty, Third Time Lucky, Hell's Bells, If It's Saturday it must be Nimmo, Just a Nimmo; films incl: Casino Royale, The Amorous Prawn, The Bargee, Joey Boy, A Talent for Loving, The Liquidator, Tamahine, One of our Dinosaurs is Missing; radio Just a Minute 1967-91, produced and appeared in numerous prodns which toured world-wide for Intercontinental Entertainment; *Books* Derek Nimmo's Drinking Companion (1979), Shaken & Stirred (1984), Oh Come On All Ye Faithful! (1986), Not In Front Of The Servants (1987), Up Mount Everest Without A Paddle (1988), As the Actress Said to the Bishop (1989), Wonderful Window Boxes (1990), Derek Nimmo's Table Talk (1990); *Recreations* travel, collecting 17th and 18th century English walnut furniture, horse racing; *Clubs* Garrick, Athenaeum (Liverpool), Lord's Taveners; *Style—* Derek Nimmo, Esq; c/o Barry Burnett, Suite 42, Grafton House, 2 Golden Square, London W1

NIMMO, Ian Alister; *b* 14 Oct 1934; *Educ* Royal Sch of Dunkeld, Breadalbane Acad; *m* 11 July 1959, Grace Boyd; 2 s (Alastair b 1962, Struan b 1973), 1 da (Wendy b 1960); *Career* Nat Serv 2 Lt RSF 1955-57; ed: The Weekly Scotsman 1963-66, Teesside Evening Gazette 1970-76, Edinburgh Evening News 1976-89; vice pres Newspaper Press Fund, chm Target Work Campaign, memb Ctee Tenovus, memb Teesside Advsy Security Cncl; *Books* Robert Burns (1965), Portrait of Edinburgh (1968), The Bold Adventure (1969), Scotland at War (1989), The Commonwealth Games (1989); *Recreations* the outdoors, fly fishing, painting, writing; *Clubs* Edinburgh Arts; *Style—* Ian Nimmo, Esq; The Yett, Lamancha, by West Linton, Peebleshire, Scotland (☎ 0968 75457)

NIMMO SMITH, William Austin; QC (1982); s of Dr Robert Herman Nimmo Smith, and Ann Nimmo Smith, *née* Wood; *b* 6 Nov 1942; *Educ* Eton; Balliol Coll Oxford (BA), Univ of Edinburgh (LLB); *m* 1968, Dr Jennifer, da of Rev David Main; 1 da (Harriet b 1972), 1 s (Alexander b 1974); *Career* advocate admitted to Faculty of Advocates 1969, standing jr counsel to Dept of Employment 1977-82, advocate dep 1983-86, chm Med Appeal Tbnls 1986-; pt/t memb Scot Law Cmmn 1988-; *Recreations* hill walking, music; *Clubs* New (Edinburgh); *Style—* William A Nimmo Smith, Esq, QC; 29 Ann St, Edinburgh EH4 1PL (☎ 031 332 0204); Advocates Library, Parliament House, Edinburgh EH1 1RF (☎ 031 226 5071)

NIND, Philip Frederick; OBE (1979), TD (1946); s of William Walker Nind, CIE (d 1964), of Oxford, and Lilian Marie Feodore, *née* Scott (d 1968); *b* 2 Jan 1918; *Educ* Blundell's, Balliol Coll Oxford (MA); *m* 8 Aug 1944, Fay Allardice, da of Capt John Roland Forbes Errington (d 1945); 2 da (Nicola b 1945, Charlotte b 1949); *Career* WWII 1939-46 Royal Fusiliers, SOE Greece and Albania 1943-44, Mil Govt Berlin 1945-46, ret Maj; Shell Gp of Cos 1939-68: Venezuela, Cyprus, Lebanon, Jordon, London; dir Fndn for Mgmnt Educn 1968-83, sec Cncl of Indust for Mgmnt Educn 1969-83; vice-pres Euro Fndn for Mgmnt Devpt Brussels 1978-83; served on various ctees of: CBI, CNAA, UGC, NEDO; memb Exec Ctee Royal Acad of Dancing 1970-88, chm Abinger Common Cons Assoc 1977-79; hon fell London Business Sch; CBIM 1968-83, FRSA 1983; Chevalier Order of Cedars of Lebanon 1959, Grand Cross Orders of St Mark and Holy Sepulchre Greek Orthodox Church 1959; *Books* A Firm Foundation (1985); *Clubs* Special Forces; *Style—* Philip Nind, Esq, OBE, TD

NINIS, Ven Richard Betts; s of Capt George Woodward Ninis, and Mary Gertrude, *née* Betts; *b* 25 Oct 1931; *Educ* Sherborne, Lincoln Coll Oxford (MA), Bishop's Hostel Lincoln Theological Coll; *m* 29 May 1967, (Penelope) Jane, da of Sir Edmund George Harwood, CB, KBE (d 1964), of Alfriston, Sussex; 2 s (Robert George, James Andrew Meredith), 1 da (Rachel Hilary); *Career* curate Poplar All Saints London 1955-62, vicar Hereford St Martin 1962-71, diocesan missioner 1969-74, prebendary of Hereford Cathedral 1970-74, Telford planning offr 1970-74, canon residentiary and treas Lichfield Cathedral 1974-; archdeacon: of Stafford 1974-80, of Lichfield 1980-; chm United Soc for Propagation of the Gospel 1988-91, govr Derbyshire Coll of Higher Educn; *Recreations* gardening; *Style—* The Ven The Archdeacon of Lichfield; 24 The Close, Lichfield, Staffordshire WS13 7LD (☎ 0543 258813)

NISBET, Prof Hugh Barr; s of Thomas Nisbet (d 1977), of Edinburgh, and Lucy Mary, *née* Hainsworth; *b* 24 Aug 1940; *Educ* Dollar Acad, Univ of Edinburgh (MA, PhD); *m* 26 Dec 1962 (m dis 1981), Monika Luise Ingeborg, da of Wilhelm Otto Uecker, of Guben, Germany; 2 s (Arnold b 1966, Marcus b 1968); *Career* reader Univ of Bristol 1972-73 (asst lectr 1965-67, lectr 1967-72), prof German Univ of St Andrews 1974-81, prof modern languages (German) and fell Sidney Sussex Coll Cambridge; memb: Ctee Modern Humanities Res Assoc 1972-84, Gen Teaching Cncl Scotland 1978-81, Bd Govrs Dollar Acad 1978-81, Cncl English Goethe Soc 1978-, Nat Cncl for Modern Languages 1983-; pres Br Soc Eighteenth Century Studies 1986-88 (vice pres 1984-86), tstee Kurt Hahn Tst 1988-; *Books* Herder and the Philosophy and History of Science (1970), Goethe and the Scientific Tradition (1972); *Recreations* music, art history, cycling; *Style—* Prof H B Nisbet; Sidney Sussex Coll, Cambridge CB2 3HU (☎ 0223 338877)

NISBET, Prof Robin George Murdoch; s of Robert George Nisbet (d 1955), of Glasgow, and Agnes Thomson, *née* Husband (d 1973); *b* 21 May 1925; *Educ* Glasgow Acad, Univ of Glasgow (MA), Balliol Coll Oxford (MA); *m* 16 April 1969, (Evelyn Pamela) Anne, da of Dr John Alfred Wood (d 1953); *Career* tutor in classics CCC Oxford 1952-70, prof of Latin Univ of Oxford 1970; hon fell Balliol Coll Oxford 1989; FBA 1967; *Books* commentary on Cicero in Pisonem (1961); commentary on Horace: Odes I (1970), Odes II (1978); *Style—* Prof Robin Nisbet; 80 Abingdon Rd, Cumnor, Oxford OX2 9QW (☎ 0865 862 482); Corpus Christi College, Oxford (☎ 0865 276 757)

NISBET, Scott; s of David Nisbet, and Tracy, *née* Bogie; *b* 30 Jan 1968; *Educ* Ainslie Park Edinburgh; *m* June 1990, Anna Devine-Nisbet, da of Brian Devine; *Career* professional footballer; Salveson Boys Club Edinburgh, turned professional Glasgow Rangers 1985-; Scotland caps: 3 boys, 30 youth, 7 under 21; played in Youth World Cup Chile 1988, centre-half player of the tournament award; *Recreations* snooker, golf; *Style—* Scott Nisbet, Esq; Glasgow Rangers FC, Ibrox Stadium, Edmiston Drive, Glasgow G51 (☎ 041 427 8500)

NISBET, William Maltman (Kit); s of James Maltman Wilson Nisbet (d 1979), of London, and Victoria Agnes Nisbet (d 1990); *b* 1 Aug 1934; *Educ* St Paul's; *m* 1963, Valerie Joan; 2 da (Katharine Fiona b 1966, Gemma Claire b 1970); *Career* advertising exec; trainee then exec Colman Prentis & Varley 1956-61, account exec Notley Advertising 1961-63; account mangr: Crossley Lennon & Newell 1963-65, Pritchard Wood & Partners 1965-69; dir and memb Exec Bd Wasey Campbell Ewald 1969-76, fndr Kit Nisbet & Associates 1976-86, ptnr and dir client services Wood Brigdale, Nisbet & Robinson 1986-; rowed for GB in European Championships 1959; Freeman: Worshipful Co of Drapers 1978, City of London 1978; *Recreations* rowing, theatre, music, rural interests and activities; *Clubs* Garrick, Leander Boat, Lansdowne; *Style—* Kit Nisbet, Esq; Wood Brigdale, Nisbet & Robinson Ltd, Kent House, Market Place, London W1N 7AJ (☎ 071 636 3152, fax 071 631 4654)

NISBET-SMITH, Dugal; s of David Nisbet-Smith, and Margaret Nisbet-Smith, of Invercargill, NZ; *b* 6 March 1935; *Educ* Southland Boys' HS NZ; *m* 1959, Dr Ann Patricia Nisbet-Smith, da of John Taylor, of Gt Harwood, Lancs; 1 s, 2 da; *Career* Scottish Daily Record and Sunday Mail: devpt mangr 1969-71, prodn dir 1971-73, md 1974-78; dir Mirror Group Newspapers 1976-78, dir and gen mangr Times Newspapers Ltd 1978-80, md Times Newspapers 1980-81, int publishing advsr to HH The Aga Khan 1981-83; dir The Newspaper Soc 1983-; *Recreations* travel, sculpture, painting; *Clubs* RAC; *Style—* Dugal Nisbet-Smith, Esq; 19 Highgate Close, Hampstead Lane, London N6

NISH, Prof Ian Hill; CBE (1990); s of David C Nish (d 1961), of Edinburgh, and Marion, *née* Hill; *b* 3 June 1926; *Educ* George Watson's Coll Edinburgh, Univ of Edinburgh (MA), Univ of London (MA, PhD); *m* 29 Dec 1965, Rona Margaret, da of Harold Thomas Speirs, CBE (d 1982), of Hampton Ct, Middx; 2 da (Fiona Rosalind b 1967, Alison Margaret b 1969); *Career* Army 1944-48, demobbed Capt; Univ of Sydney NSW 1957-62, prof int history LSE 1980- (joined 1962-), dean faculty econs and political sci Univ of London 1986-90; pres: Br Assoc Japanese Studies 1979-80, Euro Assoc Japanese Studies 1985-88; chm Japan Fndn Endowment Ctee 1981-90; *Books* Anglo-Japanese Alliance (1964), Story of Japan (1968), Alliance in Decline (1972), Anglo-Japanese Alienation (1978), Origins of Russo-Japanese War (1984), European Studies on Japan (1987); *Recreations* golf, music, tennis; *Style—* Prof Ian Nish, CBE; Oakdene, Charlwood Drive, Oxshott, Surrey KT22 0HB (☎ 037 284 2975); LSE, Houghton St, Aldwych, London WC2A 2AE (☎ 071 405 7686, fax 071 242 0392, telex 24655 BLPES G)

NISSEN, David Edgar Joseph; s of Tunnnock Edgar Nissen, of Hove, and Elsie, *née* Thorne; *b* 27 Nov 1942; *Educ* King's Sch Chester, UCL (LLB); *m* 1 Nov 1969, Pauline Jennifer, da of Harry George Spencer Meaden, of Bexhill-on-Sea; 2 da (Rachel Jane b 1973, Sarah Elizabeth b 1976); *Career* prosecuting slr Sussex Police Authy 1970-73; HM Customs and Excise: joined 1973, asst slr 1983-87, princ asst slr 1987-90; legal advsr to Dept of Energy Treasy Slr's Office 1990-; memb Law Soc 1969; *Recreations* photography, opera, walking; *Style—* David Nissen, Esq; Department of Energy, 1 Palace St, London SW1E 5HE

NISSEN, George Maitland; CBE (1987); s of Col Peter Norman Nissen (d 1930), and Lauretta, *née* Maitland (d 1954); *b* 29 March 1930; *Educ* Eton, Trinity Coll Cambridge; *m* 1956, Jane Edmunds, *née* Bird; 2 s, 2 da; *Career* KRRC 2/Lt, Royal Greenjackets TA Capt; memb Cncl of Int Stock Exchange 1973-, dep chm of the Stock Exchange 1978-81, sr ptnr Pember & Boyle 1982-86, dir Morgan Grenfell Gp 1985-87, chm Investmt Mgmnt Regulatory Orgn 1989-; memb Stock Exchange 1956-; *Recreations* music, railways, walking; *Style—* George Nissen, Esq, CBE; Swan House, Chiswick Mall, London W4 (☎ 081 994 8203); Morgan Grenfell Group plc, 23 Great Winchester St, London EC2P 2AX (☎ 081 588 4545, telex 8953511)

NISSEN, Karl Iversen; s of Christian Nissen, of Milton NZ (d 1939), and Caroline, *née* Hollick (d 1932); *b* 4 April 1906; *Educ* Otago Boys HS Dunedin NZ, Otago Univ (BSc, MB ChB, MD); *m* 15 June 1935, (Mary Margaret) Honor, da of Charles Henry Schofield, (d 1970), of Bridlington, Yorks; 1 s (John Christian Doughty b 1941), 1 da (Margreta b 1938); *Career* WWII Surgn Lt Cdr RNVR 1943-45; surgn Royal Nat Orthopaedic Hosp London 1946-71; orthopaedic surgn: Harrow Hosp 1946-71, Peace Meml Hosp Watford 1948-71; chm Friends of Holwell Village Sch; FRCS 1937; *Recreations* foreign travel; *Clubs* Naval; *Style—* Karl Nissen, Esq; Prospect House, The Ave, Sherborne, Dorset DT9 3AJ (☎ 0935 81 35 39)

NIVELLES, Patrick Lawrence; s of Louis Henri Nivelles, of France, and Katherine Mary, *née* McLaughlin (d 1958); *b* 1 April 1946; *Educ* Worth Abbey Sussex, UEA (BA), Univ of Warwick (MSc); *m* 25 Jan 1969, Marie-Andree, da of John Cyril Smith, of Warwickshire; 1 s (Guy b 1974), 1 da (Faye b 1976); *Career* merchant banker; previously with: First Nat Bank of Boston, GKN plc; currently gen mangr Bank Hispano Ltd; *Recreations* shooting, travel; *Clubs* East India, Cowdray Park Polo; *Style—* Patrick L Nivelles, Esq; Brookhurst Grange, Holmbury Hill, Ewhurst, Surrey; 15 Austin Friars, London EC2N 2DJ (☎ 071 628 4499)

NIVEN, Dr Alastair Neil Robertson; s of Harold Robertson Niven, and Elizabeth Isobel Robertson, *née* Mair; *b* 25 Feb 1944; *Educ* Dulwich, Univ of Cambridge (MA), Univ of Ghana (MA), Univ of Leeds (PhD); *m* 22 Aug 1970, Helen Margaret, da of Claude William Trow (d 1983); 1 s (Alexander b 1985), 1 da (Isabella b 1981); *Career* lectr: Univ of Ghana 1968-69, Univ of Leeds 1969-70, Univ of Stirling 1970-78; dir gen Africa Centre London 1978-84, Chapman fell Inst of Cwlth Studies Univ of London 1984-85, special asst to Sec Gen Assoc of Cwlth Univs 1985-87, dir Literature Arts Cncl GB 1987-; chm: Public Schs Debating Assoc England and Wales 1961-62, UK Cncl for Overseas Student Affrs 1987-, Literature Panel Gtr London Arts Assoc 1981-84; *Books* D H Lawrence: The Novels (1978), The Yoke of Pity: The Fictional Writings of Mulk Raj Anand (1978), D H Lawrence (1980), The Commonwealth of Univs (with Sir Hugh W Springer, 1987), Under Another Sky: The Commonwealth Poetry Prize Anthology (ed, 1987); *Recreations* theatre, travel; *Clubs* Royal Cwlth Soc; *Style—* Dr Alastair Niven; Eden House, 28 Weathercock Lane, Woburn Sands, Bucks MK17 8NT (☎ 0908 582310); Arts Council, 14 Gt Peter St, London SW1P 3NQ (☎ 071 333 0100)

NIVEN, Dr Colin Harold Robertson; s of Harold Robertson Niven, of 52 Lock Chase, Blackheath SE3, and Elizabeth Isobel Robertson, *née* Mair; *b* 29 Sept 1941; *Educ* Dulwich, Gonville and Caius Coll Cambridge (MA, BNC), Univ of Oxford (dip educn), Nancy (LésL), Lille (Dr de l'Université); *Career* teacher and housemaster Fettes 1965-73, head of modern languages Sherborne 1973-83, princ Island Sch Hong

Kong 1983-87, princ St George's English Sch Rome Italy 1987-; FRSA; *Books* studies of: Voltaire's Candide (1980), Thomas Mann's Tonio Kröger (1982); critical edn of Vailland's Un Jeune Homme Seul (1983); *Recreations* travel, opera, sport; *Clubs* Royal Overseas League, Royal Cwlth Soc; *Style—* Dr Colin Niven; 121 Lenthay Rd, Sherborne, Dorset; St Georges English School, Via Cassia KM16, Rome, Italy (☎ 06 3790141, fax 06 3792490)

NIVEN, Sir (Cecil) Rex; CMG (1954), MC (1918); s of late Rev Dr George Cecil Niven, and Jeanne Niven, of Torquay, Devon; *b* 20 Nov 1898; *Educ* Blundell's Sch Tiverton, Balliol Coll Oxford (MA); *m* 1, 1925, Dorothy Marshall (d 1977), da of David Marshall Mason, formerly MP Coventry and E Edinburgh (d 1956); 1 da (and 1 da decd); m 2, 1980, Pamela Mary Catterall, da of George Catterall Leach (d 1937), of Sibton Park Kent; *Career* 2 Lt RFA 1918-19, Corpl Lagos Def Force 1939-42; admin offr and finally sr resident Nigeria 1921-54, speaker N Nigeria Assembly 1953-60, special cmmr N Nigeria 1960-62; dep sec Southwark Diocesan Office 1962-70; memb: Cncl RSA, Paddington Hospital's Mgmnt Ctee 1962-72, Cncl Imperial Soc of Knights Bachelor 1966-, Gen Synod of C of E 1975-80; patron Deal Protection Soc, fndr pres NE Kent Br Oxford Soc 1986-; FRGS 1919, life memb BRCS 1963, memb AA 1985; kt 1960; *Books* author of 13 books on Africa incl A Nigerian Kaleidoscope (1983); *Clubs* Royal Over Seas League; *Style—* Sir Rex Niven, CMG, MC; 12 Archery Sq, Walmer, Kent CT14 7HP (☎ 0304 361863)

NIX, Prof John Sydney; s of John William Nix (d 1968), of SE London, and Eleanor Elizabeth, *née* Stears (d 1978); *b* 27 July 1927; *Educ* Brockley Co Sch, Univ Coll of the South-West (BSc Econ), Cambridge (MA); *m* 7 Oct 1950, Mavis Marian, da of George Cooper, of Teignmouth; 1 s (Robert David John b 10 Jan 1955), 2 da (Alison Mary b 23 July 1952, Jennifer Ann b 7 May 1959); *Career* Instr Lt RN 1948-51; sr res offr Farm Econs Branch Univ of Cambridge 1957-61 (1951-61); Wye Coll London: farm mgmnt liaison offr and lectr 1961-70, sr tutor 1970-72, sr lectr 1972-75, head Farm Business Unit 1974-89, reader 1975-82, prof of farm business mgmnt (personal chair) 1982-89, emeritus prof 1989-; fndr memb Farm Mgmnt Assoc 1965, prog advsr Southern TV 1966-81; chm: Educn Ctee of Farm Management (CMA) 1971-, Bd of Farm Mgmnt (BIM) 1979-81; Nat Award for Outstanding Contrib to Advancement of Mgmnt in Agric I BIM 1982, author of numerous articles for jls, memb various nat study gps and advsy ctees; CBIM 1983, FRSA 1984, FRAgS 1985; *Books* Farm Planning and Control (with C S Barnard, 2 edn, 1979), Farm Mechanisation For Profit (with W Butterworth, 1983), Land and Estate Management (2 edn 1989), Farm Management Pocketbook (21 edn 1990); *Recreations* theatre, cinema, travel, rugby, cricket; *Clubs* Farmers; *Style—* Prof John Nix; Wye Coll, Wye, Ashford, Kent TN25 5AH (☎ 0233 812 401, fax 0233 813 320, telex 96118)

NIXON, Anthony Michael; s of (Hector) Michael Nixon, of Eng, and Joan Dorothy, *née* Whitaker; *b* 24 June 1957; *Educ* Canford Sch Wimborne Dorset, Trinity Coll Cambridge (MA); *m* Sheila Frances Richardson, da of Hugh Richardson, of Eng; *Career* barr 1979, asst legal advsr Overseas Containers Ltd 1983-85, commercial lawyer Amersham Int plc 1985-87, dir of legal res S J Berwin & Co 1987-88, conslt Hewitt Assocs 1988-, co sec The Monotype Corporation plc 1990-; reader and writer St Albans Talking Newspaper; Freeman City of London; hon guide Cathedral and Abbey Church of St Alban; ACIArb 1982, BACFI 1982; *Recreations* music, walking, painting, birdwatching; *Style—* Anthony Nixon, Esq; Hewitt Associates, Romeland House, Romeland Hill, St Albans, Herts AL3 4EZ (☎ 0727 866233, fax 0727 830122)

NIXON, Maj Cecil Dominic Henry Joseph; MC; s of late Maj Sir Christopher William Nixon, DSO, 2 Bt, and hp of bro Rev Sir Kenneth Michael John Basil Nixon, SJ, 4 Bt; *b* 5 Feb 1920; *Educ* Beaumont Coll; *m* 1953, Brenda, da of late Samuel Lycett Lewis and wid of Maj M F McWhor; 3 s, 2 da; *Heir* Simon Michael Christopher; *Career* Maj, Royal Ulster Rifles, bursar The Med Coll; chm: The Devon Sheltered Homes Tst of St Bartholomew's Hospital; *Recreations* ornithology, rugby, cricket, gardening; *Style—* Maj Cecil Nixon, MC; 9 Larpent Ave, SW15

NIXON, Sir Edwin Ronald; CBE (1974), DL (Hampshire 1986); s of William Archdale Nixon, and Ethel, *née* Corrigan; *b* 21 June 1925; *Educ* Alderman Newton's Sch Leicester, Selwyn Coll Cambridge (MA); *m* 1952, Joan Lilian, *née* Hill; 1 s, 1 da; *Career* IBM UK Hldgs Ltd: chief exec 1965-85, chm and chief exec 1979-85, chm 1979-90; dep chm Nat West Bank plc 1987- (dir 1974-), chm Amersham Int plc 1988- (dir 1987-), dir Royal Insur plc 1980-; kt 1984; *Recreations* music, golf; *Clubs* Athenaeum; *Style—* Sir Edwin Nixon, CBE, DL; Starkes Heath, Rogate, nr Petersfield, Hants GU31 5EJ (☎ 0730 821504); National Westminster Bank plc, 41 Lothbury, London EC2P 2BP (☎ 071 726 1000)

NIXON, (Philip) Graham; s of Horace Stanley Nixon of Greenacre, Rugby Road, Burbage, Leicestershire, and Dorothy Mary, *née* Collidge; *b* 12 June 1942; *Educ* Hinckley GS, Leicester Coll of Art; *m* 3 July 1965, Maureen, da of Edward Wilford, of Sunways, Doctors Fields, Earl Shilton, Leics; 2 s (Mark b 1967 (decd), Paul b 1969); *Career* chm: Ferry Pickering Group plc; dir: Ferry Pickering Sales Ltd, Ferry Pickering Boxes Ltd, Ferry Pickering Publishing Ltd, Ferry Pickering Plastics Ltd, Ferry Pickering Mouldings Ltd, Ferry Pickering Toolmakers Ltd; *Recreations* shooting and sports in general; *Style—* Graham Nixon, Esq; The Old Rectory, Rectory Lane, Nailstone, Nuneaton CU13 0QQ; Ferry Pickering Group plc, PO Box 6, Coventry Road, Hinckley, Leicestershire (☎ 0455 38171)

NIXON, James Robert; s of Dr Robert Samuel Nixon, of Bangor, Co Down, and Veda, *née* McKee; *b* 2 Sept 1943; *Educ* Bangor GS Co Down, Trinity Coll Dublin (MB BCh, BAO, MA), Univ of Liverpool (MChOrth); *m* 23 June 1967, Katherine, da of Ronald Stoddart Nesbitt, of Dublin; 1 s (Alexander b 1972), 1 da (Holly b 1968); *Career* conslt orthopaedic surgn Belfast City and Musgrave Park Hosps, clinical lectr in orthopaedics Queens Univ Belfast, examiner RCS Ireland; sec Irish Orthopaedic Assoc, chm RYA NI 1983-86; FRCS Ireland 1971, FRCS England 1972; *Recreations* yachting, fishing; *Clubs* Royal North of Ireland Yachting, Royal Ulster Yacht, Irish Cruising; *Style—* James Nixon, Esq; Farm Hill, Cultra, Co Down BT18 OAD NI (☎ 0232 428196); Withers Orthopaedic Centre, Musgrave Park Hosp, Belfast 9, NI (☎ 0232 669501)

NIXON, Lady; Joan Lucille Mary; da of Robert Felix Mervyn Brown, of Rangoon, Burma; *m* 1949, Maj Sir Christopher John Louis Joseph Nixon, 3 Bt, MC (d 1978); 3 da (Anne (Dr A L Miller) b 1954, Mary (Mme Nixon-Léchaire) b 1957, Sally (Mrs A K Robson) b 1961; *Style—* Lady Nixon; c/o Lloyds Bank, St George's Road, Wimbledon, London SW19

NIXON, John Edwin; s of Edwin Nixon, of Durham, and Dorothy, *née* Hall; *b* 5 Dec 1948; *Educ* Univ of Edinburgh Med Sch (MB ChB, ChM), Univ of Oxford (MA); *m* Bridget Anne, da of Dr S John Coulson, of Stratton-on-the-Fosse Nr Bath, Somerset; 1 s (David John b 1976), 2 da (Susannah Jane b 1980, Natasha Elizabeth b 1985); *Career* clinical reader in orthopaedic surgery Univ of Oxford, conslt orthopaedic surgn Kings Coll Hosp, examiner Univ of London; pubns on hip replacement; memb BMA; fell Girdlestone Orthopaedic Soc, FRCS, FRSM; fell: Br Orthopaedic Assoc, Chelsea Clinical Society; *Books* ed int reference work on Spinal Stenosis; *Recreations* family, travel; *Clubs* memb sr common room Oriel Coll Oxford; *Style—* John Nixon, Esq; 148 Harley St, London W1 (☎ 071 935 1207); Kings College Hospital, Denmark Hill, London SE5 (☎ 071 326 3070, car 0860 267861)

NIXON, Prof John Forster; s of Edward Forster Nixon, MBE (d 1989), and Mary, *née* Lytton; *b* 27 Jan 1937; *Educ* Whitehaven GS, Univ of Manchester (BSc, PhD, DSc), Univ of Cambridge, Univ of Southern California USA; *m* 19 Nov 1960, Dorothy Joan (Kim), da of John Thomas Smith (d 1987); 1 s (Jonathan Forster b 23 March 1966), 1 da ((Susan) Joanna Forster b 16 July 1964); *Career* ICI res fell Cambridge 1962-64, lectr in chemistry Univ of St Andrews 1964-66, dean Sch of Chemistry Univ of Sussex 1989- (lectr in chemistry 1966, reader 1975, prof 1986); visiting prof: Victoria Univ Canada 1971, Simon Fraser Univ Canada 1976; titular memb Inorganic Nomenclature Cmmn IUPAC 1986-88, memb: Inorganic Chemistry Panel SERC 1986-89, editorial bd Phosphorus, Sulphur, Silicon Jl 1989-; *Publications* contribs to a variety of chemistry jls; *Recreations* playing tennis, squash, walking, theatre, watching cricket; *Style—* Prof John Nixon; School of Chemistry and Molecular Sciences, University of Sussex, Brighton, Sussex BN1 9QJ

NIXON, Rev Sir Kenneth Michael John Basil; 4 Bt (UK 1906), of Roebuck Grove, Milltown, Co Dublin and Merrion Sq, City of Dublin, SJ; s of late Sir Christopher William Nixon, 2 Bt, DSO, and bro of 3 Bt (d 1978); *b* 22 Feb 1919; *Educ* Beaumont Coll, Heythrop Coll Oxon; *Heir* bro, Maj Cecil Dominic Henry Joseph Nixon, MC; *Career* RC priest; ordained 1952; teaching memb of the Jesuit Community at St George's Coll Salisbury 1954-; *Style—* Rev Sir Kenneth Nixon, Bt, SJ; St George's Coll, PB 7727, Causeway, Zimbabwe (☎ 0722 24650)

NIXON, Neville John; JP (1980); s of John Henry Nixon (d 1980), of Cheadle Hulme, Cheshire, and Catherine Ada, *née* Birchall (d 1991); *b* 26 July 1934; *Educ* Stockport GS; *m* 16 Sept 1961, (Alice) Margaret (d 1990), da of James Ernest Lugton, FRPS (d 1956), of Cheadle Hulme; 1 da (Shirley Margaret (Mrs Palk) b 1964); *Career* RAF 1956-58; ptnr John H Nixon & Co (CAs) 1958-; dir: Blackfriars Vintners Ltd 1978-80, Gaythorn Fin Co Ltd 1983-, Nixon & Ptnrs Ltd 1988-; life govr Imperial Cancer Res Fund; CA 1956, ATII 1963; *Recreations* genealogy, walking, gardening; *Style—* Neville J Nixon, Esq, JP; John H Nixon & Co, Chartered Accountants, Athena House, 35 Greek Street, Stockport, Cheshire SK3 8BA (☎ 061 477 8787)

NIXON, Patrick Michael; CMG (1989), OBE (1984); s of John Moylett Gerard Nixon, of Chilmark, Wilts, and late Hilary Mary, *née* Paterson (d 1956); *b* 1 Aug 1944; *Educ* Downside, Magdalene Coll Cambridge (MA); *m* 26 Oct 1968, Elizabeth Rose, da of Edward Carlton, of Southampton; 4 s (Simon b 1970, Paul b 1971, Christopher b 1975, Damian b 1978); *Career* Dip Serv 1965, MECAS Lebanon 1966-68, 3 sec (later sec) Br Embassy Cairo 1968-70, 2 sec (commercial) Br Embassy Lima 1970-73, 1 sec FCO 1973-77, 1 sec and head of Chancery Br Embassy Tripoli 1977-80, dir Br Info Servs NY 1980-83, asst (later head) NE and N Africa dept FCO 1983-87, HM Ambass to State of Qatar at Doha 1987-90, cnsllr FCO 1990-; Offr Brazil Order of the Southern Cross 1976; *Style—* Patrick Nixon, Esq, CMG, OBE; c/o FCO, King Charles St, London SW1

NIXON, Dr William Charles; s of Charles Marlborough Nixon (d 1951), and Winifred Westcott (d 1975); *b* 28 Nov 1926; *Educ* Humberside Collegiate Inst, Toronto, Queen's Univ Kingston Ontario (BA, MA, skiing champion and capt of ski team 1946-47) Univ of Cambridge (PhD, ScD); *m* 1, 3 June 1948, Joyce (d 1986), da of Arthur Angus Fraser; 1 s (Douglas Fraser b 12 June 1960), 1 da (Andrea Carol b 14 June 1958); m 2, 22 July 1989, Glenys Baker, da of Wilfred Hutchinson; *Career* Air Arm Pilot Cadet Royal Navy Fleet 1944-45; industl res asst General Electric Company USA 1952-53, nat sci fndn fell Stanford and Redlands Univs Calif 1956; Univ of Cambridge: academic researcher (physics) 1953-55, assoc electrical industs fell in physics 1956-59, asst dir of res Engrg Dept 1959-62, lectr Engrg Dept 1962-89, fell of Peterhouse 1962-, proctor Univ of Cambridge 1991-; fndr ed and ed in chief Microelectronic Engineering Journal 1981-; shared award Electrochemical Soc of America 1982; chm: Electron Microscopy Gp Inst of Physics 1970-72 (former memb Ctee), Cambridge Area Ctee IEE 1985-86, E Anglian Centre Ctee 1990-91; memb: Professional Gp E5 IEE 1976-82, Mgmnt and Design M1 Ctee IEE 1984-87, Sci Educn and Technol Divnl Bd IEE 1987-93, Centres Bd IEE 1989-92, Cncl IEE 1989-92, Royal Inst; vice pres and memb Cncl Soc for the Application Res Cambridge, FInstP 1969, CPhys, FIEE 1981, CEng 1981, FEng 1986; *Books* X-Ray Microscopy (with VE Cosslett, 1960), Electron Microscopy and Analysis (ed, 1971), Scanning Electron Microscopy: Systems and Applications (ed, 1973), Microcircuit Engineering (ed with H Ahmed, 1980); *Recreations* travel; *Style—* Dr William Nixon; Peterhouse, University of Cambridge, Cambridge CB2 1RD (☎ 0223 338200, fax 0223 337578)

NOAD, Mark John; s of john William Noad, 13 Bridge Rd, Epsom, and Barbara, *née* Maher; *b* 22 Nov 1965; *Educ* Glyn Sch Epsom, Epsom Sch of Art and Design, Norwich Sch of Art (BA); partner, Alice Louise Chalk; *Career* graphic designer Pentagram Design 1988-; major projects incl: sign system and poster design Tate Gallery London, design and art direction Bloomsbury Books; *Recreations* photography, hiking, cycling; *Style—* Mark Noad, Esq; Pentagram Design, 11 Needham Road, London W11 2RP (☎ 071 229 3477, fax 071 727 9932)

NOAKES, George; *see*: Wales, Archbishop of

NOAKES, Michael; s of Basil Henry Noakes (d 1969), of Horley and then Reigate, Surrey, and Mary Josephine, *née* Gerard (d 1989); *b* 28 Oct 1933; *Educ* Downside, Reigate Sch of Art, Royal Academy Schools London; *m* 9 July 1960, Vivien Noakes (writer), da of late Marcus Langley, of Reigate, Surrey; 2 s (Jonathan b 1963, Benedict b 1965), 1 da (Anya b 1961); *Career* Nat Serv 1954-56, Subaltern; portrait and landscape painter; exhibited: RA, ROI, RBA, RSMA, RP, Nat Soc, Young Contemporaries, Contemporary Portrait Soc, Grosvenor and Upper Grosvenor Galleries, Grafton Galleries (also New Grafton, Upper Grafton), Woodstock Galleries, RGI; represented in collections of: Prince of Wales, Br Museum, Nat Portrait Gallery Perm Collection, numerous univs, House of Commons, Frank Sinatra, Guildhall London; portraits incl: The Queen (cmmnd for centenary of Manchester Town Hall in the Queen's Silver Jubliee Year), The Queen (as Col-in-Chief, the Queen's Lancs Regt), Queen Elizabeth The Queen Mother (as Chllr of Univ of London), Queen Elizabeth The Queen Mother (as Patron Royal Assoc for Disability and Rehabilitation), The Princess Royal (for Saddlers' Co), The Princess Royal (as Col-in-Chief Royal Signals), The Prince of Wales (as Col-in-Chief 2 KEO Gurkhas), The Duke and Duchess of York (for City of York), The Duchess of Kent (for Clothworkers' Co), The Prime Minister, Margaret Thatcher (for Grocers' Co), Princess Ashraf of Iran, Sir Timothy Bevan (as chm Barclays), Lord Denning (as Master of the Rolls), Sir Alec Guinness, Cardinal Hume, Robert Hardy, Sir Andrew Huxley (as pres Royal Soc), Lord Justice of Appeal Sir Donald Nicholls, Airey Neave, JB Priestley, Sir Ralph Richardson, Archbishop Runcie of Canterbury, Lord Selwyn-Lloyd (as speaker House of Commons), Lord Wolfenden (as dir Br Museum); gp portraits incl: Queen Elizabeth The Queen Mother opening Overlord Embroidery to public view (with The Duke of Norfolk, Princess Alice Countess of Athlone, Earl Mountbatten, and others), The Princess Royal being admitted to Livery of Worshipful Co of Woolmen, The Five Lords of Appeal in Ordinary for the Middle Temple (Lord Cross, Lord Diplock, Lord Salmon, Lord Wilberforce, Lord Simon), a commission for the Corporation of London to mark the Royal Silver Wedding featuring many senior members of the Royal Family; numerous TV and radio appearances on art subjects; subject: Portrait BBC 2 (with Eric Morley, 1977), Changing Places BBC1 (with Jak, 1989); art corr Town & Around

BBC 1964-68; ROI: elected memb 1964, vice pres 1968-72, pres 1972-78, hon cncl memb 1978-; RP: elected memb 1967, memb cncl 1969-72 (also 1972-74, 1978-80); dir Fedn Br Artists 1981-83 (govr 1972-81), hon memb: Nat Soc, United Soc; former chm Contemporary Portrait Soc, former FRSA; platinum disc award (for record sleeve Portrait of Sinatra, 1977); *Books* A Professional Approach to Oil Painting (1968), contrib to various journals and books on art subjects; *Recreations* idling; *Clubs* Garrick; *Style—* Michael Noakes, Esq; 146 Hamilton Terrace, St John's Wood, London NW8 9UX (☎ 071 328 6754)

NOAKES, Vivien; da of Marcus Langley (d 1977), and Helen, *née* Oldfield Box (d 1983); *b* 16 Feb 1937; *m* 9 July 1960, Michael, s of Basil Noakes (d 1969); 1 da (Anya b 19 June 1961), 2 s (Jonathan b 15 May 1963, Benedict b 9 Feb 1965); *Career* writer; guest curator of the Maj Exhibition, Edward Lear at the Royal Acad of Arts and Nat Academy of Design NY 1985; Philip and Frances Hofer Lectr Harvard Univ 1988; *Books* Edward Lear: The Life of a Wanderer (1968, 2 edn 1979, 3 edn 1985), For Lovers of Edward Lear (1978), Scenes from Victorian Life (1979), Edward Lear 1812-1888 (1985), Selected Letters of Edward Lear (1988), The Painter Edward Lear (1991); *Recreations* friends, reading, cooking; *Clubs* Arts; *Style—* Ms Vivien Noakes; 146 Hamilton Terrace, London NW8 9UX (☎ 071 328 6754)

NOBES, Prof Christopher William; s of Harold Alfred Nobes, and Beryl Muriel, *née* Ramsay; *b* 20 March 1950; *Educ* Portsmouth GS, Univ of Exeter (BA, PhD); *m* 27 March 1982 (m dis 1988); *Career* head internal audit Hambro Life Assur 1973-75, lectr Univ of Exeter 1975-82; prof: Univ of Strathclyde 1982-86, Univ of Reading 1987-; memb Accounting Standards Ctee UK and Ireland, UK rep consolidation ctee Fédération Des Experts Comptables Européens; FCCA 1973; *Books* incl: Comparative International Accounting (1981, 1985), Accountants Liability in the 1980's (with E P Minnis 1985), Pocket Accountant (1986), Issues in Multinational Accounting (with R H Parker 1988), Interpreting US Financial Statements (1988); contribs incl: Some Topics in International Accounting (1978), The Fourth Directive and the United Kingdom (1984), Imputation Systems of Corporation Tax within the EEC (1984, 1985); *Style—* Prof Christopher Nobes; Univ of Reading, Dept of Econs, Reading, Berks RG6 2AA (☎ 0734 318228, fax 0735 750236)

NOBLE, Adrian Keith; s of William John Noble (d 1987), of Chichester Sussex, and Violet Ena, *née* Wells; *b* 19 July 1950; *Educ* Chichester HS, Univ of Bristol (BA), Drama Centre London; *Career* assoc dir: Bristol Old Vic Co 1976-80, RSC Co 1981-89 (appointed artistic dir elect 1990, artistic dir 1991-); guest dir Manchester Royal Exchange Theatre Co; *Style—* Adrian Noble, Esq; c/o Barbican Theatre, London EC2Y 8BQ (☎ 071 628 3351)

NOBLE, Andrew Stephen; s of Sir Peter Scott Noble, and Mary, *née* Stephen; *b* 14 Feb 1934; *Educ* Aberdeen GS, Univ of St Andrews (MA), St John's Coll Cambridge (MA), Univ of Aberdeen (LLD); *m* 7 Aug 1959, Margaret Birrell, *née* Rayne; 2 s (Michael James b 28 May 1963, Peter Stephen b 12 Sept 1966), 1 da (Alison Mary b 29 March 1961); *Career* ICI plc: asst mangr admin servs Billingham Agric Div 1963-65 (tech offr 1959-63), gp operational mangr Gp Mgmnt Servs Dept 1965-69, tech sec to Main Bd Policy Gp Head Office 1969-73; Debenhams plc (Head Office): corp planning mangr 1973-76, main Bd dir of devpt and planning 1976-79, md Admin Servs and Devpt 1979-81, md Store Ops and Servs 1981-86; chm: Assoc of Retail Distributors 1981-82, Oxford St Assoc 1984-85, Specialeyes plc 1986-, G & F Retail Ltd 1988-; vice pres Br Retailers Assoc 1988- (chm 1984-86); non-exec dir: Bentalls plc 1987-, G & F Retail Ltd 1988-; dep chm Retail Consortium 1988-; memb Cncl: ESRC 1984-90, Manchester Business Sch 1985-; memb Ealing Health Authy 1990-; FCMA, FIMA, FBIM, JP; *Recreations* golf, theatre, opera, reading; *Clubs* Oriental, Royal Scottish Automobile, The Wimbledon, Wimbledon Park Golf, Royal Wimbledon Golf; *Style—* Andrew S Noble, Esq; Bentalls plc, Anstee House, Wood St, Kingston upon Thames, Surrey KT1 1TS (☎ 081 546 2002)

NOBLE, Barrie Paul; s of Major Frederic Arthur Noble (d 1978), of Witney, Oxon, and Henrietta, *née* Evans; *b* 17 Oct 1938; *Educ* Hele's Sch Exeter, New Coll Oxford (BA), Univ of Dakar Senegal; *m* 17 July 1965, Alexandra (Sandra) Helene, da of Robert Frederick Truman Giddings (d 1989), of Cap Del Prat Gran, Encamp, Andorra; 1 s (Timothy b 1966); *Career* HM Dip Serv; FO 1962, third later second sec Br Embassy Leopoldville (Kinshasa) 1965, second sec (commercial) Br Dep High Cmmr Kaduna 1967, first sec FCO 1969, Br Embassy Warsaw 1972, FCO 1975, cnsllr UK Mission to the UN Geneva 1980, cnsllr FCO 1984-89, cnsllr Br Embassy Paris 1989-; *Recreations* skiing, bridge, ancient cars, grass cutting; *Clubs* RAF, Ski of GB, Rolls Royce Enthusiasts; *Style—* Barrie Noble, Esq; c/o Foreign & Commonwealth Office, Paris

NOBLE, Sheriff David; JP (1970); s of Donald Noble (d 1942), of Inverness, and Helen Kirk Lynn, *née* Melville (d 1971); *b* 11 Feb 1923; *Educ* Inverness Royal Acad, Univ of Edinburgh (MA, LLB, summa cum laude); *m* 1947, Marjorie Scott, da of James Scott Smith (d 1971), of Bramhall Cheshire; 2 s (Andrew, David), 1 da (Jill); *Career* served RAF Bomber Cmd Europe 1942-46, Flt Lt; slr; WS Edinburgh 1949-83; sheriff at Oban, Campbeltown and Fort William 1983-; *Recreations* sailing (Jennie G); *Style—* Sheriff David Noble, JP; Woodhouselee, North Connel, Oban, Argyll PA37 1QZ (☎ 063 171 678)

NOBLE, Sir David Brunel; 6 Bt (UK 1902), of Ardmore and Ardardan Noble, Cardross, Co Dumbarton; er s of Sir Marc Brunel Noble, 5 Bt, CBE (d 1991), and Jennifer Lorna (Jane), *née* Austin; *b* 25 Dec 1961; *m* 26 Sept 1987, Virginia Ann, yr da of late Roderick Lancaster Wetherall, MBE, of Platt Oast, St Mary's Platt, Kent; 2 s (Roderick Lancaster Brunel b 8 Dec 1988, Alexander David b 28 Feb 1990); *Heir* s, Roderick Lancaster Brunel Noble b 8 Dec 1988; *Style—* Sir David Noble, Bt

NOBLE, Prof Denis; s of George Noble (Flt Lt RFC, d 1957), and Ethel, *née* Rutherford; *b* 16 Nov 1936; *Educ* Emanuel Sch London, UCL (BSc, PhD); *m* Jan 1965, Susan Jennifer, da of Flt Lt Leslie H Barfield; 1 da (Penelope Jean b 27 Aug 1967), 1 adopted s (Julian Aidan b 29 Aug 1970); *Career* asst lectr physiology UCL 1961-64, tutorial fell Balliol Coll Oxford 1963-84, praefectus of Holywell Manor 1971-89, Burdon Sanderson prof in cardiovascular physiology Univ of Oxford 1984, fndr dir Oxsoft Ltd 1984-; has made numerous appearances on radio and TV, and writer of various articles published in nat press; fell UCL 1986, foreign sec The Physiological Soc 1986- (hon sec 1974-80), memb founding gp Save Br Sci; hon MRCP 1988; FRS 1979; correspondant etranger de l'Académie Royale de Medecine de Belgique; *Books* The Initiation of the Heart Beat (1975), Electric Current Flow in Excitable Cells (1975), Goals, No Goals and Own Goals (1989), Sodium-Calcium Exchange (1989); *Recreations* foreign languages, guitar; *Style—* Prof Denis Noble; University Laboratory of Physiology, Parks Road, Oxford OX1 3PT (☎ 0865 272528, fax 0865 272 469)

NOBLE, Sir (Thomas Alexander) Fraser; MBE (1947); s of Simon Noble, of Cromdale, Morayshire (d 1926); *b* 29 April 1918; *Educ* Nairn Acad, Univ of Aberdeen; *m* 1945, Barbara Anne Mabel, da of John Sinclair, of Nairn; 1 s, 1 da; *Career* mil serv 1939-40; entered ICS 1940, serv NWFP 1941-47; lectr in political economy Univ of Aberdeen 1948-57, sec Carnegie Tst for Scottish Univs 1957-62, vice chllr Univ of Leicester 1962-76, memb and chm various govt advsy ctees; chm: Advsy Cncl on Probation and After Care 1965-70, UK Ctee of Vice Chllrs and Princs 1970-72; vice chllr and princ Univ of Aberdeen 1976-81; Hon LLD: Aberdeen 1968, Leicester 1976, Glasgow 1981, Washington Coll Maryland USA 1981; kt 1971; *Recreations* golf; *Clubs* Royal Northern and Univ (Aberdeen); *Style—* Sir Fraser Noble, MBE; Hedgerley, Victoria St, Nairn (☎ 53151)

NOBLE, (Charles Henry Scott) Harry; s of Charles Scott Noble (d 1983), and Betty Balfour Noble, *née* Corsar; *b* 5 Jan 1947; *Educ* Fettes Coll, Edinburgh U (LLB); *Career* chartered accountant; Thomson McLintock and Co 1968-74; asst dir Kleinwort Benson Ltd 1982- (joined 1974); *Recreations* skiing; *Style—* Harry Noble, Esq; 7 Amner Road, London SW11 (☎ 071 223 5755); c/o Kleinwort Benson Ltd, 20 Fenchurch St, EC3 (☎ 071 623 8000)

NOBLE, Sir Iain Andrew; 3 Bt (UK 1923), OBE, of Ardkinglas and Eilean Iarmain; er s of Sir Andrew Napier Noble, 2 Bt, KCMG (d 1987), and Sigrid, *née* Michelet; *b* 8 Sept 1935; *Educ* Eton, Univ Coll Oxford (MA); *m* 27 Oct 1990, Lucilla Charlotte James, da of Col Hector Andrew Courtney Mackenzie (d 1988), of The House of Rosskeen, Invergordon, Ross-shire; *Heir* bro, Timothy Peter Noble, *qv*; *Career* Nat Serv 1954-56, 2 Lt Intelligence Corps 1956-59, 2 Lt Argyll and Sutherland Highlanders (TA); jt fndr and md Noble Grossart Ltd (Merchant Bankers) Edinburgh 1969-72, co fndr and chm Seaforth Maritime Ltd Aberdeen (offshore oil servs) 1972-77, fndr and chm Lennox Oil Co plc Edinburgh 1980-84; currently dir: Adam & Co plc 1983-, Darnaway Venture Capital plc 1984-, New Scotland Insur Gp plc 1986-; exec Scottish Cncl (Devpt and Indust) Edinburgh 1964-69, proprietor Fearann Eilean Iairmain estate in Skye 1972-, dep chm Traversee Theatre Co 1966-69, memb Ct Univ of Edinburgh (issuing House) 1980-; tstee: Nat Museums of Scotland 1985-, Sabhal Mor Ostaig (Gaelic Business Coll, co fndr) 1973-85; memb The Securities Assoc 1988, chm Scottish-Australian Bicentenial Cairn Ctee 1987-88; Scotsman of the Year (Knights Templer Award) 1982; *Clubs* New (Edinburgh); *Style—* Sir Iain Noble of Eilean Iarmain, OBE; An Lamraig, Eilean Iarmain, An t-Eilean Sgitheanach IV43 8QR; offices: An Oifig, Eilean Iarmain, Isle of Skye IV43 8QR (☎ 047 13 266, telex 75252 IARMAIN G, fax 047 13 260); 5 Darnaway St, Edinburgh EH3 6DW (☎ 031 225 9677, fax 031 225 5479)

NOBLE, James (Douglas Campbell); s of Capt Frederick Burnaby Noble, RN (d 1946), and Elsie Mackintosh, *née* Mackintosh (d 1962); *b* 20 April 1921; *Educ* Bradfield Coll, Canford; *m* 1, 25 Aug 1956, Patricia Jean, da of Harold Strange Taylor-Young, FRCS; 1 s (Robert b 1955), 3 da (Sarah b 1957, Charlotte b 1960, Diana b 1961); m 2, 15 April 1978, Teresa Jane, da of Lt-Col Douglas Forster, DSO (d 1983) 11th Hussars (Prince Albert's Own); *Career* Mil Service; The Royal Sussex Regt 1940, cmmnd The Argyll & Sutherland Highlanders 1940, 2 Battalion A & S H Singapore 1941, POW Thailand 1942-45, ret 1946; Investmt Dept Kleinwort Sons & Co 1946-52, memb The Stock Exchange London 1953-82, ptnr Fielding Newson & Smith & Co 1953-62, finance dir H M Tennent Ltd 1958-73, investment advsr to King George V's Pension Fund for Actors and Actresses (1911) 1960-82, ptnr Colegrave & Co The Stock Exchange London 1962-73, chm H M Tennent Ltd 1973-77, ptnr Kitcat & Aitken the Stock Exchange London 1973-81; memb: Bd of Visitors and Local Review Ctee HM Prison Chelmsford 1972-87, Investmt Ctee Peterhouse Cambridge 1983-85; tstee: Royal Ballet Benevolent Fund 1978-84, Cambridge Health Authy Tst Fndn 1986-88; appointed: official speaker for The Far East POWs Assoc (E Anglia) 1984-, lectr to 22 Special Air Services Regt Courses Stirling Lines Hereford 1985-, official speaker for the Burma Star Herts Cambs and Essex Borders Branch, fndr memb A Company of Speakers 1989; *Recreations* walking, reading, writing, correspondence, conversation, travel, preaching, lecturing; *Clubs* The City of London, The Free Foresters, The Arabs CC; *Style—* James Noble, Esq; 25 Portugal Place, Cambridge (☎ 0223 312277)

NOBLE, Hon Mrs (Mary Myfanwy); da of 1 Baron Davies (d 1944); *b* 1923; *m* 1958 (m dis 1979), Hugh McAskill Noble; 3 s; *Career* formerly in Women's Royal Canadian Naval Serv; CStJ; *Style—* The Hon Mrs Noble; 17 Dick Place, Edinburgh

NOBLE, Peter Saxton Fitzjames; CBE (1977); 2 s of Sir Humphrey Noble, 4 Bt, MBE, MC (d 1968), of Walwick Hall, Humshaugh, Hexham, Northumberland, former High Sheriff of Northumberland (d 1968), and Celia Stewart Weigall (d 1982); bro of Sir Marc Noble, 5 Bt (d 1991), and descendant of Sir Andrew Noble, 1 Bt, famous physicist and expert on explosives; *b* 22 May 1929; *Educ* Eton, Magdalene Coll Cambridge; *m* 1, 1954 (m dis 1966), Elizabeth Emmeline, da of Launcelot William Gregory Eccles, CMG, MC; 1 s (Simon Peter Saxton Fanshaw b 1958); m 2, 1966 (m dis 1980), Helena Margaret, da of Thomas Essery Rose-Richards and formerly w of David Anthony Harries; 1 s (James Essery Brunel b 1968); m 3, 1980, Penelope Margaret, da of late Leslie Landeau; *Career* int wine conslt; former chm: UK Wine and Spirit Assoc, Wine Devpt Bd; président d'honneur EEC Wine and Spirit Gp; dir: Int Wine & Spirit Competition Ltd, The Grape Connection Ltd; *Style—* Peter Noble, Esq, CBE; Flax Cottage, 17 Ham Common, Richmond, Surrey TW10 7JB (☎ 081 940 7576)

NOBLE, Robert Milne; s of John Noble (ka 1940), and Mary Bella *née* Milne; a fishing family from a remote NE Scotland village; *b* 2 Dec 1931; *Educ* Macduff High Sch Scotland; *m* 11 Sept 1954, 1 s (Robert b 1963), 2 da (Janet b 1957, Helen b 1961); *Career* chm: Noble Barker Bruce Partnership Ltd, Maison Lheraud Ltd, Denebase Ltd; ACCA, ACIS; *Recreations* golf, walking; *Clubs* RAC, Leander, Huntercombe Golf; *Style—* Robert Noble, Esq; Hart House, Sonning on Thames, Berkshire

NOBLE, Lady; Sigrid; *née* Michelet; 2 da of Johan Michelet, Norwegian Diplomatic Service; *m* 16 Oct 1934, Sir Andrew Napier Noble, 2 Bt, KCMG (d 1987); 2 s, 1 da; *Style—* Sigrid, Lady Noble; 11 Cedar House, Marloes Rd, London W8 5LA (☎ 071 937 7952)

NOBLE, Timothy Peter; yr s of Sir Andrew Napier Noble, 2 Bt, KCMG (d 1987); hp of bro Sir Iain Andrew Noble, 3 Bt; *b* 21 Dec 1943; *Educ* Eton, Univ Coll Oxford (MA), INSEAD Fontainebleau (MBA); *m* 1976, Elizabeth Mary, da of late Alexander Wallace Aitken; 2 s (Lorne Andrew Wallace b 1980, Andrew Iain Brunel b 1984), 1 da (Sasha Heidi Elizabeth b 1978); *Career* called to the Bar Gray's Inn 1969; exec dir: Lyle Shipping plc Glasgow 1976-84, Noble & Co Ltd Edinburgh 1984-; chm Business Archives Cncl of Scot; *Clubs* New (Edinburgh); *Style—* Timothy Noble, Esq; Ardnahane, Barnton Ave, Edinburgh 4

NOEL, Col Archibald Charles William; MC (1940); s of Col the Hon Charles Hubert Francis Noel, OBE (d 1947), and Jane Francis Regina Mary, *née* Douglas Dick (d 1964); *b* 5 Jan 1914; *Educ* The Oratory Sch, RMC Sandhurst; *m* 30 Aug 1945, Bridget Mary (d 1976), da of Brig WA Fetherstonhaugh, CB, CBE, DSO (d 1947); 2 s (Charles b 1948, Edward b 1956); m 2, 22 Dec 1977, Andrée Marie, da of Pierre Duchen, of Bayonne, France; *Career* Welsh Guards 1934, served France 1939-40, (POW), Staff Coll 1946, cmd 1 Bn Welsh Guards 1952-56, mil sec HQ Eastern Cmd 1957-58, SHAPE 1960-62, mil attaché SA 1962-66; *Clubs* Cavalry and Guards; *Style—* Col A C W Noel, MC

NOEL, Hon Edward Andrew; The Honourable; s of 5 Earl of Gainsborough and Mary, da of Hon John Joseph Stourton, TD; *b* 22 Oct 1960; *Educ* Farleigh House Sch Basingstoke, Ampleforth, L'Institut Brittanique (Paris); *m* 5 July 1990, Lavinia J, o da of Cdr George Bingham, RN, of Droxford, Hants; *Career* businessman; underwriting memb of Lloyd's 1984-; *Recreations* travelling, scuba-diving, shooting, music; *Clubs* Boodle's, St James's, Bembridge Sailing; *Style—* The Hon Edward Noel; Flat 4, 14

Edith Grove, London SW10 0NW (☎ 071 352 0023/4); Cuckoo Farm, Exton, Oakham, Leics (☎ 078 086 534)

NOEL, Hon Gerard Edward Joseph; s of 5 Earl of Gainsborough; *b* 23 Jan 1955; *Educ* Ampleforth, London Univ; *m* 1985, Charlotte, yr (twin) da of Sir William Stratford Dugdale, 2 Bt, CBE, MC; *Style*— The Hon Gerard Noel; The Manor House, Withington, nr Cheltenham, Glos

NOEL, Hon Gerard Eyre Wriothesley; s of 4 Earl of Gainsborough, OBE (d 1927); *b* 1926; *Educ* Georgetown USA, Exeter Coll Oxford; *m* 1958, Adele Julie Patricia, da of late Maj Vivian Nicholas Bonville Were; 2 s, 1 da; *Career* barr Inner Temple 1952; author (works incl books on Harold Wilson, Barry Goldwater and Princess Alice, Queen Victoria's Forgotten Daughter); publisher & journalist, former dir Herder Book Co, dir Search Press 1972-; asst ed Catholic Herald 1968-71 (ed 1971-76, editorial dir 1976-81, ed-in-chief 1981-); contested (L) Argyll 1959; memb Exec Ctee Cncl of Christians and Jews 1974-; Liveryman Worshipful Co of Stationers and Newspapermakers; Freeman City of London; *Books* Paul VI, The Path from Rome, Goldwater, Harold Wilson, Princess Alice, The Great Lock-Out of 1926, Ena, Spain's English Queen; *Clubs* Garrick, Beefsteak; *Style*— The Hon Gerard Noel; Chipping Campden, Glos

NOEL, Capt Gerard John Hamlyn; s of Maj Edward Francis Hamlyn Noel, MRCVS (d 1953), and Doris Marie, *née* Verrieres (d 1983); *b* 8 Dec 1930; *Educ* Wellington; Mil Coll of Sci; *m* 7 Sept 1963, Gillian Ralphia, da of Walter Terence Barrand Head (d 1983); 1 s (Richard b 1965), 1 da (Victoria b 1969); *Career* Royal Engrs, serv BAOR 1951-52, Far E 1958-61, attached Army Air Corps as Pilot, BAOR 1961-67, ret 1967; fruit farming; *Recreations* shooting, skiing, tennis; *Style*— Capt Gerard J H Noel; Squirrels Hall, Stratford St Mary, by Colchester, Essex (☎ 0206 298276)

NOEL, Hon Thomas; s of 5 Earl of Gainsborough; *b* 9 March 1958; *Educ* Ampleforth, RAC Cirencester (MRAC 1980); *Career* joined Savills 1981, Humberts 1983, Bride Hall plc 1984; dir: Bride Hall plc 1987-, Barnsdale Lodge Ltd 1989-, Drones Restaurant Ltd 1988-; chm and chief exec Metropolitan Realty Tst (UK) Ltd 1984-; conslt Humberts; memb: CLA, Royal Forestry Soc; FRICS 1982; *Recreations* shooting, skiing, flying fixed and rotary aircraft (vintage and modern); *Clubs* Boodle's, Pratt's, The Air Squadron; *Style*— The Hon Thomas Noel; 24 Lennox gardens, London SW1 (☎ 071 589 1841); Bride Hall plc, 19 Queen Street, London W1 (☎ 071 493 3996, fax 071 499 4388, car 0836 261 647)

NOEL-BAKER, Hon Francis Edward; s of late Baron Noel-Baker, PC (Life Peer UK 1977, d 1982), and Irene (d 1956); *b* 7 Jan 1920; *Educ* Westminster, Gordonstoun, King's Coll Cambridge; *m* 1957, Barbara Christina, yr da of late Engineer Josef Sonander (d 1936), of Norrköping, Sweden; 4 s (1 decd), 1 da; *Career* joined Royal Tank Regt 1940, transferred Intelligence Corps 1941 (despatches), Capt 1942; MP (Lab): Brentford and Chiswick 1945-50, Swindon 1955-69, resigned from Lab Pty 1969 and joined SDP 1981, left and joined Cons Pty 1984; chm: Br Greek Parly Gp 1958-69, PLP Overseas Devpt Ctee 1964-68, UN Parly Ctee 1966-69; pres Euro Cncl for the Village and Small Town (ECOVAST), hon pres Union of Forest Owners of Greece 1968-, govr Campion Sch Athens 1974-78; dir: North Euboean Enterprises Ltd 1973-, Fini Fisheries Cyprus 1976-; memb Ecology Party 1978-, Soil Assoc 1979-; *Books* Greece the Whole Story (1945), Spanish Summary (1946), The Spy Web (1954), The Land & People of Greece (1957), Looking at Greece (1968), My Cyprus File (1986), Book Eight (1987), Three Saints and Poseidon (1988); *Recreations* gardening, writing; *Clubs* Special Forces (London), Athens Club, Travellers (London); *Style*— The Hon Francis Noel-Baker; Greece (☎ 0227 41204, fax 30 227 41204); office: 27 Bryanston Square, London W1 (☎ 071 723 9405, fax 071 935 3199)

NOEL-BUXTON, 3 Baron (UK 1930); Martin Connal Noel-Buxton; s of 2 Baron Noel-Buxton (d 1980), by his 1 w, Nancy, *née* Connal; *b* 8 Dec 1940; *Educ* Bryanston, Balliol Coll Oxford; *m* 1, 1964 (m dis 1968), Miranda Mary, da of H A Chisenhale-Marsh, of Gaynes Park, Epping, Essex; m 2, 1972 (m dis 1982), Sarah Margaret Surridge (she m, 1982, Peter E W Adam), da of Neil Charles Wolseley Barrett TD, of Twickenham Rd, Teddington; 1 s, 1 da (Hon Lucy Margaret b 1977); m 3, 18 Dec 1986, Mrs Abigail Marie Granger, da of Eric Philip Richard Clent; 1 da (Hon Antonia Helen Flora b 11 Dec 1989); *Heir* s, Hon Charles Connal Noel-Buxton b 17 April 1975; *Career* slr 1966; *Style*— The Rt Hon the Lord Noel-Buxton; House of Lords, London SW1A 0PW

NOEL-BUXTON, Hon Michael Barnett Noel; s of 1 Baron Noel-Buxton, PC (d 1948); *b* 1920; *Educ* Harrow, Balliol Coll Oxford; *Career* serv RA 1940-46, with Colonial Civil Serv (Gold Coast) 1947-59; *Clubs* Flyfishers'; *Style*— The Hon Michael Noel-Buxton; Stretchney, Diptford, Totnes, Devon (☎ 054 882 342)

NOEL-PATON, Hon (Frederick) Ranald; o s of Baron Ferrier, ED, DL (Life Peer), *qv*; *b* 7 Nov 1938; *Educ* Rugby, Haverford Coll Pennsylvania, McGill Univ Montreal (BA); *m* 1973, Patricia, da of late Gen Sir William Gurdon Stirling, GCB, CBE, DSO; 4 da; *Career* Br Utd Airways Ltd 1965-70, Br Caledonian Airways Ltd 1970-86; gen mangr: W Africa 1975-79, Far E 1980-86; dir Caledonian Far E Airways 1984-86; gp md John Menzies plc; dir: Pacific Assets Tst plc, Gen Accident plc, The Royal Bank of Scotland plc, Macallan-Glenlivet plc; *Recreations* gardening, golf, fishing, ornithology, the arts; *Clubs* New (Edinburgh), Hong Kong, Shek O Country; *Style*— The Hon Ranald Noel-Paton; Easter Dunbarnie, Bridge of Earn, Perth PH2 9ED (☎ 073881 2395)

NOEST, Peter J; *b* 12 June 1948; *Educ* St George's Coll, Weybridge, The RAC Cirencester; *m* Lisabeth Penelope Moody; 1 s (Timothy Peter b 1974), 1 da (Lisa Jane b 1976); *Career* chartered surveyor (land agency and general practice); Knight Frank & Rutley: ptnr Amsterdam 1972-77, ptnr London 1977-81, full equity ptnr 1981, resigned 1983; Hampton & Sons: conslt, sr commercial ptnr 1984; dir of devpt Lambert Smith Hampton Group Ltd; FRICS; *Books* contributor to Office Development, Estates Gazette (1985); *Recreations* hunting, tennis, farming, conservation, forestry, travel, wine; *Clubs* Turf, Oriental, Landsdowne; *Style*— Peter Noest, Esq; Little Park, Wootton Bassett, Wilts SN4 7QW (☎ 0793 852348)

NOKES, Barbara Ann; da of Harry Smith, of Exeter, Devon, and Beatrice Maud, *née* Kirk; *b* 29 April 1942; *Educ* Clapham Co Sch, Friern Rd Secdy Sch; *m* 1, 29 Feb 1962 (m dis 1970), Stewart Chartens; m 2, 28 June 1974, Roger Nokes, s of Charles Nokes, of Woodford, Essex; 1 s (Luke Charles Edward b 6 July 1984), 1 da (Daisy Lysistrata b 27 Oct 1978); *Career* various secretarial positions until 1962; copywriter: various agencies incl Royda of London Advertising Agency until 1968, Doyle Dane Bernbach Ltd 1969-75 and 1976-80, CDP 1975-76, Boase Massimi Pollitt 1981-82; fndr ptnr and currently dep creative dir and memb Bd Bartle Bogle Hegarty Ltd 1982-; winner of numerous Gold and Silver awards D & AD, Campaigning Press and Poster, Cannes TV and BTAA Awards for work in clients incl: Volkswagen, Robertson's, Levi's, Audi; memb: D & ADA, Creative Circle; MIPA; *Recreations* horse riding, restoring antiques, reading; *Clubs* Groucho's; *Style*— Ms Barbara Nokes; Bartle Bogle Hegarty Ltd, 24-27 Great Pulteney St, London W1A (☎ 071 734 1677, fax 071 437 3666)

NOKES, David Leonard; s of Anthony John Nokes, and Ethel Murray, *née* Smith; *b* 11 March 1948; *Educ* King's Coll Sch Wimbledon, Christ's Coll Cambridge (open scholar, BA, PhD); *Career* Adelaide Stoll res scholar Christ's Coll Cambridge 1969, reader in Eng lit King's Coll London 1988- (lectr Eng 1973-); *Books*: Jonathan Swift, A Hypocrite Reversed (1985, James Tait Black prize for biography), Raillery and Rage, A Study of 18th Century Satire (1987), Joseph Andrews, A Master Study (1987); television: No Country for Old Men: The Long Exile of Jonathan Swift (BBC Omnibus film) 1981, The Count of Solar (BBC Screen Two) 1991; regular reviewer for TLS, The Spectator and BBC Radio; memb Br Soc for Eighteenth-Century Studies (treas 1982-83); *Recreations* reading, writing; *Clubs* The Johnson; *Style*— David Nokes, Esq; Department of English, King's College, University of London, Strand, London WC2R 2LS (☎ 071 836 5454)

NOLAN, Bernard; s of Edward Nolan, MBE (d 1974), of Balerno, Midlothian, and Mary, *née* Howarth (d 1981); *b* 17 Aug 1926; *Educ* St Joseph's Coll Blackpool, Univ of Edinburgh (MB ChB, ChM); *m* 23 Sept 1958, Dr Margaret Winifred Coleman, da of Francis Coleman (d 1952), of Kilwinning, Ayrshire; 2 s (Geoffrey b 1961, John b 1963); *Career* Nat Serv RAMC Egypt and Cyrenaica 1951-53, Maj, sr specialist in surgery Suez Emergency 1956; res fell Harvard Med Sch 1962, conslt surgn Royal Infirmary Edinburgh 1962-89, conslt surgn Nuffield Transplant Surgery Unit Edinburgh 1968-78, sr lectr in surgery Univ of Edinburgh 1962-89 (lectr 1959-62), ret 1989; FRCSEd 1955, FRCS 1957; *Recreations* hill walking, photography; *Clubs* Edinburgh Univ; *Style*— Bernard Nolan, Esq; 7 East Castle Rd, Edinburgh EH10 5AP (☎ 031 229 3054)

NOLAN, Dr Daniel Joseph; s of Peter Nolan (d 1972), of 1 Seacrest, Vevay Rd, Bray, Co Wicklow, Ireland, and Norah Josephine, *née* Hegarty; *b* 17 Aug 1937; *Educ* Presentation Coll Bray Co Wicklow, Univ Coll Dublin (MD); *m* 29 March 1967, (Brighid) Rosarie, da of Martin Commins (d 1969); 2 s (Donald b 1970, Edward b 1973), 1 da (Winifred b 1968); *Career* house physician Master Misericordiae Hosp Dublin 1965-66; house offr: Rotunda Hosp Dublin 1966-67, Chase Farm Hosp Enfield 1967-68; registrar and sr registrar radiology Utd Bristol Hosps 1968-74, conslt radiologist Oxfordshire Health Authy 1974-, clinical lectr Univ of Oxford 1974-; MRCP, FRCR; *Books* Radiological Atlas of Biliary and Pancreatic Disease (jtly 1978), The Double Contrast Barium Meal - A Radiological Atlas (1980), Radiological Atlas of Gastrointestinal Disease (1983); *Clubs* sailing, cycling; *Style*— Dr Daniel Nolan; 10 Apsley Rd, Oxford OX2 7QY (☎ 0865 58195); Department of Radiology, John Radcliffe Hospital, Oxford OX3 9DU (☎ 0865 817238)

NOLAN, David John; s of late David Nolan, of Liverpool, and Constance Cordelia, *née* O'Donaghue; *b* 8 May 1949; *Educ* St Edwards Coll Liverpool, Royal Manchester Coll of Music; *m* 7 Jan 1977, Lynn Marie, da of Henry Steven Broughton, of Vermont, USA; 1 s (Jonathan David b 1978); *Career* princ violin LSO 1974-76, ldr London Philharmonic Orchestra 1976-, frequent soloist with Br's maj orchs and conductors, and a large concerto repertoire ranging from Bach to Berg; ARMCM; *Recreations* jogging, curries; *Style*— David Nolan, Esq; Blythewood, West Rd, St Georges Hill, Weybridge, Surrey KT13 0LY (☎ 0932 844449)

NOLAN, Deidre Patricia (Dee); (Mrs Reginald Southgate); da of Raphael Harvey Nolan, of Naracoorte, S Aust, and Zita Anne, *née* McVeigh; *b* 2 April 1953; *Educ* Loreto Convent Adelaide S Aust, St Catherine's Ontario Canada; *m* 1, 1976 (m dis) Michael Gough, s of Roy Gough; m 2, 1988, John Reginald Southgate, s of Reginald Samuel Southgate; *Career* journalist; staff reporter The Herald Melbourne Aust 1971-76, The Australian Women's Weekly 1976-79 (feature writer, dep bureau chief), dep features ed Women's Own 1980-81, Women 1981-84 (features ed, asst ed), Daily Express 1984-85 (dep women's ed, dep features ed), features ed Daily Mirror 1985-86; ed: Sunday Express Magazine 1986-89, Metropolitan Home 1989-; chm Br Soc of Magazine Eds; *Recreations* golf, food and wine, opera; *Style*— Ms Dee Nolan; 49 Studdridge St, London SW6 3SL (☎ 071 731 0450); Harmsworth Meredith Magazines, 141-143 Drury Lane, London WC2B 5TB (☎ 071 497 1199, fax 071 497 1919)

NOLAN, Michael Alfred Anthony; s of Sir Michael Patrick Nolan, and Margaret, *née* Noyes; *b* 17 June 1955; *Educ* Ampleforth, St Benet's Hall Oxford (BA), City Univ (Dip Law); *m* 26 May 1984, Adeline Mei Choo, da of Henry S H Oh, of Singapore; 1 s (Hugh b 1986), 1 da (Sophia b 1989); *Career* called to the Bar Middle Temple 1981; contrib to Atkins Court Forms (Arbitration, Carriers, Commercial Court); memb: Commercial Bar Assoc, London Common Law and Commercial Bar Assoc; *Recreations* swimming, tennis, skiing, books, plays, films, opera; *Clubs* Oxford Union, RAC, Millenium; *Style*— Michael Nolan, Esq; 2 Essex Court, Temple EC4 9AP (☎ 071 583 8381, fax 071 353 0998)

NOLAN, Rt Hon Lord Justice; Rt Hon Sir Michael Patrick Nolan; PC (1991); yr s of James Thomas, Nolan and Jane, *née* Walsh; *b* 10 Sept 1928; *Educ* Ampleforth, Wadham Coll Oxford; *m* 1953, Margaret, yr da of Alfred Noyes, CBE, the poet, by his w Mary, da of Capt Jasper Graham Mayne, CBE, of Gidleigh Park, Chagford, Devon, by his w Cecily; 1 s, 4 da; *Career* served RA 1947-49 and TA 1949-55; High Court Judge (Queen's Bench) 1982-91; Lord Justice of the Court of Appeal 1991-; presiding judge Western Circuit 1985-88; rec Crown Ct 1975-82, QC 1968, QC (NI) 1974, called to the Bar NI 1974, called to the Bar Middle Temple 1953, memb Bar Cncl 1973-74, memb Senate Inns of Ct and Bar 1974-81, treas 1977-79, Lord Justice of Appeal 1991; memb: Sandilands Ctee on Inflation Accounting 1973-75, memb Governing Body Convent of Sacred Heart Woldingham 1973-82, govr Combe Bank Sch 1974-82; kt 1982; *Style*— The Rt Hon Lord Justice Nolan; Royal Courts of Justice, Strand, London WC2A 2LL

NOLAN, Sir Sidney Robert; OM (1983), CBE (1963); s of late S Nolan; *b* 22 April 1917; *Educ* Melbourne State & Tech Schs; *m* 1948, Cynthia Hansen (d 1976); 1 da; *Career* artist; winner of numerous art awards; represented in: Tate Gallery London, Museum of Modern Art NY, all state national art galleries in Australia; exhibited in Brussels, London, New Delhi, New York, Pittsburgh, Venice; Hon LLD ANU, Hon DLitt (hon causa) Sydney, hon fell York Univ; kt 1981; *Style*— Sir Sidney Nolan, OM, CBE; c/o Marlborough Fine Art Ltd, 6 Albermarle Street, London W1

NOON, Anthony John; s of John Michael Noon (d 1967), of Lane End, Rose Hill Park West, Sutton, Surrey, and Amelia Lucy, *née* Newman (d 1958); *b* 20 Dec 1932; *Educ* Boys HS Sutton, Epsom Coll (LLB); *m* 30 March 1964, Cecilia Mary, da of William Cecil Graham, of Epsom, Surrey; 2 da (Jennifer Caroline b 1965, Jacqueline Anne b 1975); *Career* RAF Pilot Officer 1956; slr 1955, asst slr Wanstead and Woodford Borough Cncl 1958-60, slr Babcock & Wilcox Ltd 1963-71, dir legal and contract Servs The Plessey Co plc 1976- (dep legal advsr 1963-71, legal advsr 1971-76); memb Law Soc 1955; *Recreations* reading, walking, windsurfing; *Style*— Anthony Noon, Esq; 15 Aldeburgh Place, Woodford Gn, Essex I68 0PT (☎ 081 504 2047); The Plessey Company plc, Vicarage Lane, Ilford, Essex IG1 4AQ (☎ 081 553 8055, fax 081 553 8372, telex 897971)

NOONE, Dr Paul; s of Michael John Noone, OBE (d 1982), of Darlington, and Florence Miriam, *née* Knox (d 1988); *b* 4 March 1939; *Educ* Christ Church Oxford (BA), Oxford Univ and Middx Hosp Med Sch (BM, CLB, MA); *m* 1, 1962 (m dis 1981), (Pamela) Ahilya Nehaul, da of Dr Balbir Balgreen Nehaul, OBE, of Leeds; 2 s (Michael b 7 Sept 1963, Thomas b 8 Jan 1971); m 2, 29 July 1982, Mailia Rudrani Tambimultu, da of Dr James Tambinulta, of Sri Lanka; 1 step s (Amrik b 23 Jan 1973), 3 step da (Kamani b 28 Sept 1969, Amirthi b 29 Aug 1970, Dheemati b 8 Nov 1976); *Career* sr registrar in microbiology 1969-70, lectr in bateriology sch of pathology Middx

Hosp Med Sch 1971-72, conslt med microbiologist 1972-; chm NHS Conslts Assoc 1978-88, memb ASTHS delgn to TUC Annual Congress 1971-72; lectured extensively throughout the world on various aspects of antibiotics and infection; contrib over 90 articles to med jls; MRCPath 1971, FRCPath 1983; *Books* A Clinician Guide to Antimicrobial Therapy (second edn 1980); *Recreations* spending time with family & friends; *Style—* Dr Paul Noone; 39 Wykeham Hill, Wembley, Middx HA9 9RY (☎ 081 908 3392); Royal Free Hosp, Pond St, Hampstead, London NW3 2QG (☎ 071 794 0500)

NORBURN, Prof David; s of Rev Canon Richard Greville Norburn (d 1978), and Constance Elizabeth, *née* Flint; *b* 18 Feb 1941; *Educ* Bolton Sch, LSE (BEcon), City Univ (PhD); *m* 1, 1962 (m dis 1975), Veronica, *née* Ellis; 1 s (Joel b 5 Nov 1969), 1 da (Sophie b 15 April 1967); m 2, 6 June 1975, Prof Sue Birley; *Career* sr res fell in business policy City Univ London 1970-72, sr lectr in business policy London Business Sch 1972-82, Franklin D Schurz prof in strategic mgmnt (inaugural chair), Univ of Notre Dame USA 1982-85, chair of strategic mgmnt Cranfield Sch of Mgmnt 1986-87, inaugural chair of mgmnt Univ of London 1987-; dir: The Mgmnt Sch Imperial Coll of Sci Technol and Med 1987, Main Bd Newchurch & Co 1985; ed Euro Business Jl 1987, fndr memb Strategic Mgmnt Soc, exec memb Br Acad of Mgmnt; numerous articles in scholastic jls; FRSA 1988, CBIM 1989; *Books* British Business Policy (with D Channon and J Stopford, 1975); *Recreations* antiquarian horology, competitive tennis, carpentry; *Clubs* Athenaeum; *Style—* Prof David Norburn; The Management School, Imperial College of Science, Technology & Medicine, 53 Prince's Gate, Exhibition Rd, London SW7 2PG (☎ 071 589 5111, fax 071 823 7685, telex 261503)

NORBURY, John Karel; s of Frederick Thomas Henry Norbury (d 1985), of Morville, Shropshire, and Magdalena, *née* Potmesilova; *b* 16 May 1940; *Educ* Latymer's Sch, Univ Coll of Wales Aberystwyth (BSc); *m* 1964, Rachel Elizabeth, da of Dr John Richard Timmis Turner; 2 s (Nicholas John b 4 Sept 1968, Giles Richard b 2 April 1970); *Career* CF Middleton & Co 1963-67 (articled clerk, asst), co accountant Sun Valley Poultry Ltd 1967-69, audit mangr Russell Durie-Kerr Watson & Co Birmingham 1969-74, ptnr Spicer and Pegler (later Spicer and Oppenheim) Birmingham 1974-90 (memb Nat Partnership Bd 1988), ptnr Touche Ross & Co Birmingham (following merger) 1990-; pres: Birmingham & West Midlands Soc of CAs 1987-88, Birmingham Book Club 1989-; FCA (ACA 1968); *Recreations* flyfishing, shooting, walking; *Clubs* The Fly-fishers', The Birmingham; *Style—* John Norbury, Esq; Morville Hall, nr Bridgnorth, Shropshire WV16 5NB (☎ 074 631224); 18 Arundel Gardens, London W11; Touche Ross & Co, Kensington House, 136 Suffolk St, Queensway, Birmingham B1 1LL (☎ 021 631 2288)

NORBURY, 6 Earl of (I 1827); Noel Terence Graham-Toler; also Baron Norwood (I 1797), Baron Norbury (I 1800), and Viscount Glandine (I 1827); s of 5 Earl (d 1955); *b* 1 Jan 1939; *m* 1965, Anne, da of late Francis Mathew; 1 s, 1 da (Lady Patricia Margaret b 1970); *Heir* s, Viscount Glandine; *Clubs* RAC; *Style—* The Rt Hon the Earl of Norbury

NORBURY, Lt-Col Peter; s of Robert Norbury (d 1963), of Jersey, and Edith Fortuna Victoria, *née* Lansell (d 1981); *b* 21 Feb 1924; *Educ* Melbourne GS Victoria, St Lawrence Coll Ramsgate, Oundle, Truro Cathedral Sch; *m* 2 Jan 1948, Barbara Joy, da of Griffith Bowen Morgan (d 1955), of Maidstone; 2 s (Mark b 1949, David b 1953), 1 da (Sally b 1950); *Career* enlisted 1942, cmmnd RE 1943, OC 4 Dog Platoon NW Europe 1944-45; chief trainer War Dogs Trg Sch 1946-47, IOI CRE (Lts) 1948-49, Singapore Plant Sqn 1950-52, GHQ Far E Land Forces 1953-54, Staff Coll Camberley 1955, Field Sqn BAOR 1960-62, Jt Servs Staff Coll 1962, HQ 1 (BR) Corps BAOR 1963-65, staff of exercise LOGTRAIN Thailand (SEATO) 1965, 2 i/c Div Engrs 1965-66, Cmdg Depot Regt RE 1967-69, Br Advsr Sudanese Staff Sch Omdurman 1969-70, staff of C-in-C's Ctee 1970-73, ret 1973; housing & planning inspr Planning Inspectorate DOE 1973-89 (sr inspr 1976-89), ret; currently conslt inspr; Liveryman Worshipful Co of Arbitrators 1988, Freeman City of London; ACIArb, MBIM; *Recreations* model engrg, general workshop practice; *Clubs* Naval; *Style—* Lt-Col Peter Norbury; Apple Tree House, Gussage All Saints, Wimborne, Dorset BH21 5ET (☎ 0258 840552)

NORCLIFFE, (Thomas) Anthony Firth; s of Thomas Stainthorpe Norcliffe, of The Ave, Liphook, Hants, and Doris Margaret, *née* Firth; *b* 21 Jan 1939; *Educ* Felsted, Royal Free Hosp Med Sch, Royal Dental Hosp, Univ of the Pacific Dental Sch (BDS, LDS, RCS); *m* 1 April 1966, Susan Howard, da of Michael Howard Rawlings (d 1943); 1 s (Thomas b 1977), 2 da (Sarah b 1967, Belinda b 1970); *Career* dental surgn Harley St London 1963-, sr ptnr Norcliffe Invest Jacobs & Ward; fell: Int Coll of Dentists 1984, Piere Fauchard Acad 1987; Freeman City of London 1978, Liveryman Worshipful Co of Curriers 1978; memb: BDA, FDI; *Recreations* English watercolours, music, golf, fishing, tennis; *Clubs* RSM; *Style—* Anthony Norcliffe, Esq; 6 Green St, London W1 (☎ 071 629 0043); Verneys, Swanthorpe, Bentley, Hants; 90 Harley St, London W1 (☎ 071 935 2240/2249)

NORCROSS, Eric; s of William Edwards Norcross (d 1959), and Ruth, *née* Haworth (d 1957); *b* 17 Aug 1932; *Educ* Queen Elizabeth's GS Blackburn, Univ of Manchester, (BSc); *m* 23 July 1958, Megan Veronica, da of John North (d 1963), of Middlestown, Yorks; 1 da (Fiona Heather b 1959); *Career* works mgmnt Mullard Ltd 1954-69, asst sec Dept of Employment 1969-76, dir ACAS 1976-; FIPM; *Recreations* home life; *Clubs* Civil Serv; *Style—* Eric Norcross, Esq; Ponderosa, Barncroft Rd, Berkhamsted, Herts HP4 3NL (☎ 044 286 2408); ACAS, 27 Wilton St, London SW1 (☎ 071 210 3720)

NORCROSS, Lawrence John Charles; OBE (1986); s of Frederick Marshall Norcross (d 1934), and Florence Kate, *née* Hedges (d 1979); *b* 14 April 1927; *Educ* Moor Lane Sch Chessington Surrey, Ruskin Coll Oxford, Univ of Leeds (BA); *m* 17 Aug 1958, (Janet) Margaret, da of John William Wallace; 3 s (Matthew b 25 May 1959, Alastair b 22 Sept 1960, Daniel b 14 April 1969), 1 da (Joanna b 27 Aug 1962); *Career* serv RN 1942-49 (E Indies Fleet 1944-45, HMS Nigeria); asst master: Singlegate Sch 1957-61, Abbey Wood Sch 1961-63; housemaster Battersea Co Sch 1963-74, headmaster Highbury Grove Sch 1975-87 (dep head 1974-75); memb Exec Ctee Nat Cncl for Educnl Standards 1977- (tstee 1982-); memb: Educn Study Gp Centre for Policy Studies 1980-, Univ Entrance and Schools Examination Cncl Univ of London 1979-84; tstee: Grant Maintained Schools Tst, Ind Primary and Secdy Educn Tst (IPSET), Educn Res Tst 1985-; memb: Hillgate Gp, Headmasters' Conf 1985-87; *Books* The ILEA, A Case for Reform (with F Naylor, 1981), The ILEA after the Abolition of the GLC (with F Naylor and J McIntos 1985), The Wayward Curriculum (contrib, 1986), GCSE: The Egalitarian Fallacy (1990); *Recreations* watching cricket, wining and dining, listening to music, solving crosswords; *Clubs* Surrey CCC; *Style—* Lawrence Norcross, Esq, OBE; 3 St Nicholas Mansions, 6-8 Trinity Crescent, London SW17 7AF (☎ 081 767 4299); Crockwell Cottage, Crockwell Street, Long Compton, Shipston-on-Stour, Warwickshire

NORDEN, Denis; CBE (1980); s of George Norden (d 1977), and Jenny Norden (d 1979); *b* 6 Feb 1922; *Educ* City of London Sch; *m* 1943, Avril Rosen; 1 s (Nicolas), 1 da (Maggie); *Career* writer and bdcaster, co-author (with Frank Muir) radio series Take it From Here and tv series Whacko, has appeared for 2 decades in radio series My Word!, radio and tv series My Music; written and appeared in tv series Looks Familiar 1973-, also various outbreaks of It'll be Alright on the Night; *Books* My Word (series with Frank Muir), Coming To You Live (with Sybil Harper and Norma Gilbert); *Recreations* loitering; *Clubs* Odeon Saturday Morning; *Style—* Denis Norden, Esq, CBE; c/o April Young, The Clockhouse, 6 St Catherine's Mews, Milner St, London SW3 2PU (☎ 071 584 1274)

NORDEN, Desmond Spencer; s of Percy Spencer Norden (d 1977), and Letitia, *née* Elliott (d 1977); *b* 10 April 1925; *Educ* SE Essex Tech Coll; *m* 14 June 1947, Sheila Mary, da of William Alfred Shrubb (d 1974); 1 s (Robert Spencer b 1948), 1 da (Linda Margaret b 1950); *Career* enlisted RE 1945, transfd E Surrey Regt, cmmnd 1946, demob Lt 1947; works accountant Mackay Industrial Equipment Ltd 1958, co sec Mechanical Handling Equipment Co Ltd, accountant Mackay Industrial Equipment Ltd 1962-65, chm and md Fry Pollard Ltd 1984 (accountant 1966, md 1970); life vice pres Worcester Park Athletic Club (joined 1951, treas 1963 chm 1978-84); Freeman: City of London 1983, Worshipful Co of Builders Merchants 1984; *Recreations* golf, cricket; *Clubs* Surbiton Golf, Worcester Park Athletic; *Style—* Desmond Norden, Esq; 15 Gilhams Ave, Banstead, Surrey SM7 1QL (☎ 081 393 5139); Fry & Pollard Ltd, 30 Engate St, London SE13 7HA (☎ 081 852 1092, fax 081 318 0236)

NORELL, Dr Jacob Solomon (Jack); s of Henry Norell (d 1981), and Moulouk, *née* Nehorai (d 1988); *b* 3 March 1927; *Educ* Guy's Hosp Med Sch (MB BS, MRCS, LRCP, LMSSA); *m* Aug 1948 (m dis 1971), Brenda; 3 s (Paul b 1952, David b 1953, Michael b 1954); *Career* princ GP 1956-90; memb and ldr Balint Gps 1957-; postgrad and med trainer 1966-89, dean of studies RCGP 1974-81, exec offr JCPTGP 1976-81; ed The Practitioner 1982-83; pres: Balint Soc UK 1984-87, RSM Section of General Practice 1989-90, Int Balint Fedn 1989-93; memb: Med Soc of London, Hunterian Soc, Balint Soc, RSM, RAM; FRCGP 1972; *Books* Six Minutes for the Patient (1973), Training for General Practice (1981), What Sort of Doctor? (1985), What Balint Means to Me (1989); *Style—* Dr Jack Norell; 50 Nottingham Terrace, York Gate, Regent's Park, London NW1 4QD (☎ 071 486 2979)

NORFOLK, Jeremy Paul; s of David Ernest Norfolk, and Olive, *née* Bellerby; *b* 7 March 1948; *Educ* Kingswood Sch Bath, The King's Sch Canterbury, Univ of Aberdeen (MA); *m* 20 July 1972, Rosemary Frances, da of George Austen Raffan (d 1980); 1 s (Guy b 15 July 1974), 1 da (Claire b 3 Nov 1976); *Career* Citibank NA 1975-83; md Adam & Co plc 1988- (joined 1983); *Recreations* golf, tennis, gardening; *Style—* Jeremy Norfolk, Esq; 8 Henderland Rd, Edinburgh (☎ 031 337 2640); Adam & Co plc, 22 Charlotte Square, Edinburgh (☎ 031 225 8484, fax 031 225 5136, telex 72182)

NORFOLK, Lavinia, Duchess of; Hon Lavinia Mary; *née* Strutt; LG (1990), CBE (1971); da of 3 Baron Belper (d 1956), and Eva, Countess of Rosebery, DBE, *qv*; *b* 22 March 1916; *m* 1937, 16 Duke of Norfolk, KG, GCVO, GBE, TD, PC (d 1975); 4 da (Lady Herries, Lady Mary Mumford, Lady Sarah Clutton, Countess of Ancram, *qqv*); *Career* a bearer of the Queen's Canopy at Coronation of King George VI; Lord Lt of W Sussex 1975-90; first non-royal lady to receive the Order of the Garter; *Style—* Her Grace Lavinia, Duchess of Norfolk; Arundel Park, Sussex (☎ 0903 882104)

NORFOLK, Leslie William; CBE (1973, OBE 1944), TD (1946); s of Robert Norfolk (d 1954), of Nottingham, and Edith Florence, *née* Preston (d 1948); *b* 8 April 1911; *Educ* Southwell Minster GS, Univ Coll Nottingham (BSc); *m* 21 July 1944, Anne Isabel Etta Waller (Nancy), da of Sir Hugh Wesley Allen Watson (d 1952), of London; 2 s (Wiliam b 13 April 1945, James b 22 March 1947), 1 da (Jane b 5 Jan 1949); *Career* serv WWII: cmmnd 2 Lt 5 Bn The Sherwood Foresters (TA) 1931, 1 War Staff Course Staff Coll Camberley 1939, transferred to RE, BEF 1940, Lt-Col Staff Offr RE Gilraltar 1941, Staff Offr RE HQ Northern Cmd 1944, Col 1 CE Works Z Res 1951; asst and subsequently ptnr E G Phillips Son & Norfolk (Conslt Engrs) Nottingham 1933; ICI: construction mangr dyestuffs div 1945, resident engr Kingston Onario Canada 1954, asst chief engr metals div 1955, engrg mangr Severnside Works 1957, engrg dir Duperial SAIC Buenos Aires 1959, personnel & servs dir HOC div 1964; chief-exec Royal Dockyards MOD (Navy) 1969, engrg conslt Bath 1972; memb ctee: mgmt Bath Indust Heritage Centre 1974, Bath & Co Club 1969 (pres); MIEE 1938, MIMechE 1949, MICE 1943; *Recreations* home workshop, indust archaeology, gardening; *Style—* Leslie Norfolk, Esq, CBE, TD; Beechwoods, Beechwood Rd, Combe Down, Bath BA2 5JS (☎ 0225 832104)

NORFOLK, 17 Duke of (Premier E Dukedom 1483 with precedence 1397); Miles Francis Fitzalan Howard; KG (1983), GCVO (1986), CB (1966), CBE (1960), MC (1944), DL (W Sussex 1977); also Earl of Arundel (E 1139 if the claim by tenure, which was admitted by the Crown in 1433, is recognised; otherwise 1292; either way, the Premier E Earldom), Baron Beaumont (E 1309), Baron Maltravers (E 1330), Earl of Surrey (E 1483), Baron FitzAlan, Baron Clun, Baron Oswaldestre (all E 1627), Earl of Norfolk (E 1644), and Baron Howard of Glossop (UK 1869); Earl Marshal and Hereditary Marshal of England (1672) and Chief Butler of England; s of 3 Baron Howard of Glossop, MBE (d 1972) and Baroness Beaumont, OBE (d 1971); suc 2 cous once removed (16 Duke) 1975; *b* 21 July 1915; *Educ* Ampleforth, Ch Ch Oxford (MA, hon student 1983); *m* 1949, Anne Mary Teresa jt chm Help The Hospices, da of Wing Cdr Gerald Constable-Maxwell, MC, DFC, AFC, through whom she enjoys the same degree of kinship with the 16 Duke as her husb; 2 s, 3 da; *Heir* s, Earl of Arundel; *Career* sits as Cons in House of Lords; serv WWII France, N Africa, Sicily, Italy (despatches, MC) and NW Europe; head of Br Mil Mission to Russian Forces in Germany 1957-59, cmd 70 Bde KAR 1961-63, GOC 1 Div 1963-65; dir: Mgmnt and Support Intelligence MOD 1965-66, Serv Intelligence MOD 1966-67, ret Maj-Gen Grenadier Gds; chm Arundel Castle Tstees Ltd, pres Building Socs Assoc 1982-86; hon fell St Edmund's House Cambridge 1983; kt SMO Malta; hon Bencher Inner Temple 1984-; *Style—* Maj-Gen His Grace The Duke of Norfolk, KG, GCVO,CB,CBE,MC,DL; Carlton Towers, Goole, Humberside DN14 9LZ (☎ 0405 860 243); Bacres House, Hambleden, Henley-on-Thames, Oxon RG9 6RY (☎ 0491 571 350); Arundel Castle, Sussex (☎ 0903 882173); 61 Clabon Mews, London SW1X OEQ (☎ 071 584 3430)

NORLAND, Christopher Charles; s of Richard Felix Norland (d 1962), and Mary Wanklyn, *née* Black (d 1980); *b* 26 May 1937; *Educ* Leighton Park Sch; *m* 15 Dec 1962, Patricia Ann Noel, da of Richard Noel Jones, of Burwash, East Sussex; 1 s (David Richard Christopher b 26 March 1966), 2 da (Annelies b 2 May 1964, Gabrielle Clare b 24 Aug 1973); *Career* Nat Serv RAF 1955-57; CA; articled clerk rising to sr ptnr elect Finnie & Co Chartered Accountants and predecessor firms 1958-82, md IFICO plc 1982-89; non-exec dir: Reliance Security Group plc 1980-, Trumpf Ltd 1984-, Castle Communications Ltd 1986-, Exmoor Dual Investment Trust plc 1988-, FISCL Capital Partners Ltd 1990-, Zeon Ltd 1990-; non-exec chm: Frank Usher Holdings plc 1986-, Silk Industries Ltd 1989-; dir corp fin Rea Brothers Ltd 1990-; Freeman City of London; FCA 1972 (ACA 1963); *Recreations* tennis, skiing, walking, opera; *Clubs* Lansdowne; *Style—* Christopher Norland, Esq; Rea Brothers Ltd, Alderman's House, Alderman's Walk, London EC2M 3XR (☎ 071 623 1155, fax 071 623 2694, telex 886503)

NORLAND, Otto Realf; s of Realph I O Norland (d 1963), and Aasta, *née* Saether (d 1968); *b* 24 Feb 1930; *Educ* Norwegian Univ Coll of Econ and Business Admin Bergen Norway, Inst of Bankers London; *m* 1955, Gerd Ellen, da of Alfred Andenaes (d

1971); 1 s (Realph), 2 da (Karen, Eva); *Career* dir: Alcoa of Great Britain 1968-84 (chm 1978-84), Aluminium Fedn 1979-84 (vice pres 1981, pres 1982); London rep Deutsche Schiffsbank AG 1984-, Hambros Bank Ltd 1953-84 (md 1964-79), chm Otto Norland Ltd, FCIB; *Recreations* salmon fishing, skiing, polar exploration; *Clubs* Norwegian, London, Norske Selskab Oslo; *Style—* Otto R Norland, Esq; Grocers' Hall, Princes St, London EC2R 8AQ (☎ 071 726 8726, telex 889205)

NORMAN, Andrew; s of Russell Norman, of 12 Halifax Rd, Ipswich, and Nora Norman; *b* 21 Sept 1943; *Educ* Tower Ramparts Secdy Sch Ipswich; *m* (m dis); 1 s (Steven b 9 Oct 1970), 1 da (Kirsti b 24 Sept 1972); *Career* sports admin; promotions offr BAAB 1987-; IAAF: memb Mktg Cmmn, memb Grand Prix Cmmn, memb Advtg Gp; memb Working Pty on Amateurism in Sport CCPR 1988; *Recreations* sport, theatre; *Style—* Andrew Norman, Esq; BAAB, Edgbaston House, 3 Duchess Place, Hagley Rd, Birmingham B16 8NM (☎ 021 456 4050, fax 021 456 4061)

NORMAN, Anthony Joseph (Tony); s of William Arthur Norman, of Shotton, Clwyd, and Eileen, *née* Cartwright; *b* 24 Feb 1958; *Educ* St Richard Gwyn HS Flint; *m* 15 Dec 1980, Shirley Anne, da of Brian Palmer; 2 s (Philip Anthony b 26 June 1981, Peter John b 1 July 1983), 1 da (Elizabeth Helen b 27 Oct 1989); *Career* professional footballer; Burnley 1976-80 (no first team appearances), 442 appearances Hull City 1980-88, over 80 appearances Sunderland 1988-; 5 full Wales caps 1986-88; schoolboy player: Deeside Primary Schs, Flintshire Co under 16, GB Catholic Schoolboys, 2 caps Welsh Schoolboys; *Recreations* golf, fishing, gardening; *Style—* Tony Norman, Esq; Sunderland FC, Roker Park, Grantham Road, Sunderland, Tyne & Wear SR6 9SW (☎ 091 514 0332)

NORMAN, Rear Adm Anthony Mansfeldt; CB (1989); s of Cecil Mansfeldt Norman (d 1963), and Jean Seymour, *née* Vale (d 1963); *b* 16 Dec 1934; *Educ* RNC Dartmouth; *m* 26 March 1962, Judith, da of Raymond Pye (d 1984); 1 s (Christopher b 31 Oct 1964), 1 da (Caroline Louise b 26 Dec 1962); *Career* RN; various appts at sea and ashore 1948-65, exchange with USN San Diego California 1965-67, staff ops offr 2 Frigate Sqdn 1967-69, staff ops offr Flag Offr Aircraft Carriers 1969-72, Admty Underwater Estab 1972-73, Nat Def Coll 1974, CO HMS Mohawk 1975, CO HMS Argonaut 1976, Fleet anti-submarine warfare offr 1976-78, CO HMS Broadsword 1978-81, dep dir Naval Plans 1981-83, Capt 2 Frigate Sqdn and CO HMS Broadsword 1983-85, Capt Sch of Maritime Ops 1983-85, DG Naval Personnel Servs 1986-89; bursar St Catharines Coll Cambridge 1989; FIPM; *Recreations* tennis, squash, hill walking, bridge, music appreciation; *Clubs* Army and Navy, Anchorites, Veterans of Great Britain LTC; *Style—* Rear Adm Anthony Norman, CB; c/o National Provincial Bank, 208 Piccadilly, London W1A 2DG

NORMAN, Archie; *Career* worked for Citibank NA, former ptnr McKinsey & Co Ltd (joined 1979), fin dir Kingfisher plc 1989-, currently fin dir and chm Chartwell Land plc, currently non-exec dir Geest plc; *Style—* Archie Norman, Esq; Kingfisher plc, North West House, 119 Marylebone Rd, London NW1 5PX (☎ 071 724 7749, fax 071 724 1160)

NORMAN, Hon Mrs Barbara Jacqueline; *née* Boot; JP; da of 2 and last Baron Trent, KBE (d 1956), and Margaret Joyce Pyman (1975); *b* 26 Sept 1915; *m* 1934 (m dis 1973), Maj Willoughby Rollo Norman, 2 s of Maj Rt Hon Sir Henry Norman, 1 Bt (d 1939); 1 s, 2 da; *Style—* The Hon Mrs Barbara Norman, JP; Wilton Lodge, Lovell Rd, Winkfield, Berks

NORMAN, Barry Leslie; s of Leslie Norman (film prod (Mandy, The Cruel Sea) and dir (Dunkirk, The Long and the Short and the Tall)), and Elizabeth *née* Crafford; *b* 21 Aug 1933; *Educ* Highgate; *m* 1957, Mary Diana, da of late Arthur Narracott; 2 da (Samantha, Alexandra); *Career* author and broadcaster; dir Film Fin Corp 1980-85; writer and presenter BBC TV: Film 1987-91, Talking Pictures 1988; presenter BBC Radio 4: To-day, Going Places, Breakaway, The Chip Shop; winner: Richard Dimbleby award BAFTA 1980, Publishing Magazine award for Columnist of the Year Radio Times 1990; *Books* Fiction: The Matter of Mandrake, The Hounds of Sparta, End Product, To Nick A Good Body, A Series of Defeats, Have A Nice Day, Sticky Wicket; Non-fiction: Tales of the Redundance Kid, The Hollywood Greats, Film Greats, The Movie Greats, Talking Pictures; *Recreations* cricket; *Clubs* Groucho, BAFTA, Lords Taverners; *Style—* Barry Norman, Esq; c/o Curtis Brown, 162-168 Regent St, London W1

NORMAN, David Mark; s of Lt-Col Mark Richard Norman, CBE, of Garden House, Moor Place, Much Hadham, Herts, and Helen, *née* Bryan; *b* 30 Jan 1941; *Educ* Eton, McGill Univ (BA), Harvard Business Sch (MBA); *m* 9 July 1966, Diana Anne, da of John Vincent Sheffield, CBE, of New Barn House, Laverstoke, Whitchurch, Hampshire; 1 s (Jonathan b 1972), 3 da (Anna b 1967, Isabella b 1971, Davina b 1981); *Career* Norcros Ltd 1967-77 (dir of ops and main bd dir 1975-77), chief exec Norcros Printing & Packaging 1971-75, md Russell Reynolds Associates Inc 1978-82 (exec dir 1977-78); chm: Norman Resources Ltd 1982-83, Norman Broadbent International Ltd 1983-, BNB Resources plc 1987-; govr Royal Ballet Sch, chm Tennis and Rackets Assoc, memb Royal Opera House Ballet Bd; *Recreations* golf, tennis, rackets, classical music, opera, ballet; *Clubs* Boodle's, All England Lawn Tennis and Croquet, Queen's, RAC; *Style—* David Norman, Esq; Burkham House, Alton, Hants GU34 5RS (☎ 025 683 211); BNB Resources plc, 30 Farringdon Street, London EC4A 4EA (☎ 071 634 1075, fax 071 489 9330, telex 883588)

NORMAN, Hon Mrs (Doreen Albinia de Burgh); *née* Gibbs; da of 1 Baron Wraxhall (d 1931); *b* 1913; *m* 1937, Charles Bathurst Norman; 1 s, 1 da; *Style—* The Hon Mrs Norman; Villa Villetri, Vallée des Vaux, Jersey

NORMAN, (Aleida) Elisabeth Mabel May; da of Willem Roosegaarde Bisschop (d 1944), of 35 York Terrace, London, and May *née* Cowan (d 1964); *b* 25 Sept 1921; *Educ* Queen's Coll London, Somerville Coll Oxford (MA, BM BCh); *m* 11 March 1950, Archibald Percy Norman, s of George Percy Norman (d 1940), of Eastbourne; 5 s; *Career* jr hosp appts: Radcliffe Infirmary Oxford 1946, Queen Elizabeth Hosp for Children London 1947, Hosp for Sick Children Great Ormond St 1947-48; chm: Friends of Royal Earlswood 1967-82, Bd of Govrs Royal Earlswood and Tadworth Ct Hosp Schs 1976-81; memb: E Surrey Community Health Cncl 1975-79, Mid Surrey Dist Health Authy 1982-90; vice chm Mid Surrey Community Health Cncl 1979-82, memb and vice chm Surrey MENCAP 1975-83 (memb Nat Cncl 1981-87), vice chm MENCAP 1987- (chm Med Advsy Panel 1991-); *Style—* Mrs Elisabeth Norman; White Lodge, Heather Close, Kingswood, Surrey KT20 6NY (☎ 0737 832626)

NORMAN, Geoffrey; JP (Inner London 1982); s of William Frederick Trafalgar Norman (d 1972), and Vera May Norman (d 1988), *née* Goodfellow; *b* 25 March 1935; *Educ* Harrow Co Sch, Brasenose Coll Oxford (MA); *m* 1958, Dorothy Frances (d 1978), da of Donald Thomas Henry King of Devon (d 1989); 2 s (Neil, Mark), 2 da (Helen, Clare); *Career* admitted slr 1959, clerk to the Justices N Hertfordshire 1966-77, sec Magistrates' Assoc 1978-86, memb Magistrates' Courts Rules Ctee 1989-; memb Legal Aid Duty Slr Ctee 1983-85, dep sec of Cmmns 1986-; Freeman: City of London, Worshipful Co of Curriers; *Recreations* painting, badminton; *Style—* Geoffrey Norman, Esq, JP; Easter Cottage, Gosmore, Hitchin, Herts

NORMAN, Vice Adm Sir (Horace) Geoffrey; KCVO (1963), CB (1949), CBE (1942); s of W H Norman (d 1945); *b* 25 May 1896; *Educ* Trent Coll, RNC Keyham, Univ of Cambridge; *m* 1923, Norah Frances, da of late Brig-Gen S Geoghegan, CB, of Bournemouth; 1 s, 1 da; *Career* joined RN 1914, served HMS Queen Elizabeth 1914-16, which he commanded in 1943; Capt 1938, Rear Adm 1947, Chief of Staff to C-in-C Mediterranean Station 1948-50, Admty 1950, Vice-Adm 1951 (ret); sec Nat Playing Fields Assoc 1953-63; *Style—* Vice Adm Sir Geoffrey Norman, KCVO, CB, CBE; Chantry Cottage, Wickham, Fareham, Hants (☎ 0329 832248)

NORMAN, Geraldine Lucia; da of Harold Hugh Keen (d 1974), and Catherine Eleanor Lyle, *née* Cummins; *b* 13 May 1940; *Educ* St Marys Sch Calne Wilts, St Annes Coll Oxford (MA); *m* 16 July 1971, (John) Frank Norman; *Career* sale room corr The Times 1969-87, art market corr The Independent 1987-; News Reporter of the Year 1977; bd memb Cooperative Devpt Agency 1978-81; *Books* The Sale of Works of Art (as Geraldine Keen, 1971), Nineteenth Century Painters and Painting: A Dictionary (1977), The Fake's Progress (jtly, 1977), Mrs Harper's Niece (as Florence Place, 1982), Biedermeier Painting (1987); *Recreations* transcendental meditation, patchwork; *Style—* Mrs Geraldine Norman; 5 Seaford Court, 22 Great Portland St, London W1 (☎ 071 387 6067); The Independent, 40 City Rd, London EC1 (☎ 071 253 1222, fax 071 956 1558)

NORMAN, Jeremy Gordon; yr s of Roland Frank Holdway Norman (d 1958), of London, and Muriel (Peggy) Harvard, *née* Johnson (now Mrs Sim); *b* 18 May 1947; *Educ* St Andrew's Eastbourne, Harrow, Univ of Cambridge (MA); ptnr (since 1978), Derek Norton Frost, *qv*; *Career* chm and md Burke's Peerage Ltd 1974-83; started and owned night clubs: Embassy 1978-80, Heaven 1979-83; dir: Derek Frost Design Ltd, Blakenhall & Co Ltd (property); formerly dir: Pasta Pasta, La Reserve Wines, Power Station Health Club; fndr tstee Nat Aids Tst (resigned 1989), fndr chm CRUSAID (resigned 1987); *Recreations* boats, archaeology, weight training, natural history; *Clubs* Mark's; *Style—* Jeremy Norman, Esq; Moreton Yard, London SW1V 2NT; 2 Needsore, Warren Lane, Beaulieu, Hants; Firm 4 Ltd, The Furniture Cave, 533 King's Rd, London SW10 0TZ (☎ 071 828 6270, fax 071 976 5059)

NORMAN, Jessye; da of Silas Norman, and Janie King; *b* 15 Sept 1945; *Educ* Howard Univ Washington DC (BM), Peabody Conservatory Univ of Michigan (MMus); *Career* operatic debut Deutsche Opera Berlin 1969, La Scala Milan 1972, Royal Opera House Covent Garden 1972, NY Metropolitan Opera 1982; American debut Hollywood Bowl 1972, Lincoln Centre NYC 1973; tours incl: N and S America, Europe, Middle E, Australia, Israel; many int festivals incl: Aix-en-Provence, Aldeburgh, Berlin, Edinburgh, Flanders, Helsinki, Lucerne, Salzburg, Tangle wood, Spoleto, Hollywood, Ravinia; Hon DMus: Howard 1982, Univ of the Sewanee 1984, Boston Conservatory 1984; Musician of the Year Musical America 1982; prizes include: Grand Prix du Disque (Acad du Disque Francais) 1975, 1976, 1977, 1982, 1984; Grand Prix de Disque (Acad Charles Cros) 1983; Deutscher Schallplatteboreus 1975, 1982; Cigale d'Or Aix-en-Provence Festival 1977, IRCAM record award 1982, commandeur de l'Ordre des Arts et des Lettres France 1984; DMus Univ of Michigan 1987; Grammy Award 1984; *Style—* Miss Jessye Norman; c/o Shaw Concerts Incorporated, 1995 Broadway, New York, NY 100023 USA

NORMAN, Prof John; s of Sydney Norman (d 1973), of Knaresborough, Yorkshire, and Annie, *née* Wilkinson; *b* 22 Feb 1935; *Educ* King James' GS Knaresborough, Univ of Leeds (MB ChB, PhD); *m* 10 Jan 1962, Rowena Mary, da of William Walker Lister, of Otley, Yorkshire; 2 s (Andrew, Alistair); *Career* sr lectr anaesthetics Royal Postgrad Med Sch and hon conslt anaesthetist Hammersmith Hosp London 1967-75, fndn prof anaesthetics Univ of Southampton 1975-; memb Cncl Coll Anaesthetists; FCAnaes, FFARACS; *Recreations* music, aviation, walking; *Style—* Prof John Norman; 2 Russell Place, Highfield, Southampton, Hants SO2 1NU (☎ 0703 555177); Shackleton Department of Anaesthetics, Southampton General Hospital, Tremona Rd, Southampton SO9 4XY (☎ 0703 777222)

NORMAN, (Herbert) John La French; s of Herbert La French Norman, of 26 Park Farm Close, London, and Hilda Caroline, *née* West; *b* 15 Jan 1932; *Educ* King Edward VI Sch Norwich, Imperial Coll London (BSc); *m* 11 Aug 1956, Jill Frances, da of Bernard Thomas Sharp (d 1953); 1 s (Bernard b 1965), 2 da (Elizabeth b 1961, Sarah b 1962); *Career* Wm Hill & Son and Norman & Beard Ltd (organ builders by appt to HM The Queen): dir 1960-70, md 1970-74; responsible for work on organs in cathedrals incl: Gloucester, Norwich, Lichfield, Chelmsford, Brisbane; other work incl organs in: Bath Abbey, Southwell Minster, concert hall of Royal Coll of Organists; organ conslt 1974- at: Lancing Coll, Harrow Sch, Mill Hill Sch, Sherborne Abbey, Pershore Abbey; memb: Organs Advsy Ctee Cncl for Care of Churches 1987-, Organs Sub Ctee London Diocesan Advsy Ctee 1975-, Musical Instruments Consultative Ctee, City of London Polytechnic; churchwarden Holy Trinity Lyonsdown New Barnet 1986-, memb Synod Diocese of St Albans 1980-86; Freeman City of London, Liveryman Worshipful Co of Musicians 1972; ARCS, FIMIT, fell Inc Soc of Organ Builders; *Books* The Organ Today (1966, revised edn 1980), The Organs of Britain (1984), ed Musical Instument Technology 1969-, ed The Organbuilder 1983-; *Recreations* writing about organs, listening to music; *Style—* John Norman, Esq; 15 Baxendale, London N20 0EG (☎ 081 445 0801)

NORMAN, Keith John; s of Wilson Norman (d 1974), of Wigston Magna, Leicestershire, and Ivy May Langham (d 1985); *b* 8 July 1931; *Educ* Kibworth GS; *m* 25 March 1954, Barbara Lucy, da of Oswald Tomlin Johnson (d 1968), of Wigston Magna, Leicestershire; 1 s (Christopher Keith b 1959), 1 da (Claire Lucy b 1955); *Career* RAF, LAC 1949-51; fin dir: William Cotton Ltd, John Jones Loughborough Ltd, George Woodcock & Sons Ltd Scotland 1969-74; chm and chief exec Ladies Pride Gp of Cos 1987- (gp fin dir and sec 1974-84, dep chm and jt md 1984-87); chm and jt md Leslie Wise Gp plc 1987-; *Recreations* Rotary International, sailing; *Style—* Keith J Norman, Esq; The Farm, Newgate End, Wigston Magna, Leicestershire; 346 St Saviours Road, Leicester (☎ Leics 730071)

NORMAN, Sir Mark Annesley; 3 Bt (UK 1915), of Honeyhanger, Parish of Shottermill, Co Surrey; s of Sir Nigel Norman, 2 Bt, CBE (d 1943), and Lady Perkins, (d 1986); *b* 8 Feb 1927; *Educ* Winchester, RMC; *m* 1953, Joanna, da of Lt-Col Ian Kilgour and Aura (ggda of Gen Sir George Walker, 1 Bt, GCB, KCTS); 2 s (Nigel James b 5 Feb 1956, Antony Rory b 9 Sept 1963), 1 da (Lucinda Fay b 7 Dec 1965); *Heir* s, Nigel Norman; *Career* late Lt Coldstream Gds and Flying Offr 601 (Co of London) Sqdn RAuxA dir aviation and shipping companies 1948-88; High Sheriff Oxfordshire 1983/84, Air Cdre RAuxAF 1983, Hon Air Cdre 4624 (Co of Oxford) Movements Sqdn RAuxAF 1984-; dep Lt Oxfordshire 1985-; chm St Luke's Oxford 1986-88; patron and churchwarden St Peter's Church Wilcote; *Recreations* gardening, workshop, offshore motor cruising; *Clubs* White's, Pratt's, RAF, RSN Yacht, MCC; *Style—* Sir Mark Norman, Bt; Wilcote Manor, Charlbury, Oxon (☎ 099 386 8357)

NORMAN, Nigel James; s and h of Sir Mark Norman, 3 Bt; *b* 5 Feb 1956; *m* 1985 (m dis 1989), Joanna, *née* Naylor-Leyland; *Career* 13/18 Royal Hussars (QMO), Sultan of Oman's Armoured Regt, ret as Maj 1983; Morgan Grenfell Asset Management Ltd, dir Morgan Grenfell International Funds Management Ltd 1990-; *Clubs* White's, Annabel's; *Style—* Nigel Norman, Esq; Wilcote Manor, Charlbury, Oxon

NORMAN, Peter Alfred; s of Capt Lionel Norman, MC (ka 1916 Scots Gds), of London, and Violet May, *née* Bevan (d 1956); *b* 15 Nov 1907; *Educ* Eton, King's Coll Cambridge (MA); *m* 6 April 1939, Patricia Mary, da of Maj William Edward Wilders (d 1940), of Duffcarrick, Ardmore, Co Waterford, Ireland; 2 s (Kerry Lionel Patrick b 3

Jan 1941, d 28 Aug 1962, Shane Henry b 12 Sept 1946); *Career* RASC: gazetted 2 Lt 1940, landed Aandalsnes Norway 1940 (despatches), returned to UK 1940, Capt seconded to W African Frontier Force, served Sierra Leone, Nigeria, India, Burmah; demobbed 1946; trainee Barclays Bank (DC & O) Ltd 1929-31, trainee and export sales Ford Motor Co Ltd (Trafford Park and Dagenham) 1931-40, sales mangr Henry Ford & Son Ltd Cork Ireland, devpt mangr Mercantile Credit Co of Ireland Ltd 1959-63, ptnr O'Donnell & Fitzgerald (stockbrokers) 1964, firm merged to become Bloxham Toole O'Donnell 1981; dir Standard Chartered Bank (Ireland) Ltd; chm Aldbourne Civic Soc; *Recreations* shooting; *Clubs* Kildare St and Univ Club, Dublin; *Style*— Peter A Norman, Esq; Barn Cottage, South St, Aldbourne, Wilts SN8 2DW (☎ 0672 40357)

NORMAN, Baroness; Priscilla; CBE (1963), JP (Co of London 1944); da of late Maj Robert Reyntiens by his w Lady Alice Bertie (da of 7 Earl of Abingdon); *b* 1899; *m* 1, 1921 (m dis 1929), Col Alexander Koch de Gooreynd (who assumed surname of Worsthorne by deed poll 1923); 2 s (*see* Simon Towneley and Peregrine Worsthorne); m 2, 1933, 1 and last Baron Norman, DSO, PC (d 1950); *Career* vice-pres RCN; vice-chm Women's Voluntary Serv for Civil Def 1938-41; author; *Books* In the Way of Understanding (1982); *Style*— The Rt Hon the Lady Norman, CBE, JP; 67 Holland Park, London W11 3SG (☎ 071 229 6483)

NORMAN, Dr Remington Harvard; s of Wing Cdr Roland Frank Holdway (d 1957), of London, and Prof Muriel Harvard Sim, *née* Johnson; *b* 3 Dec 1944; *Educ* Harrow, Hertford Coll Oxford (MA, DPhil), Inst of Masters of Wine (MW); *m* 1 (m dis 1980), Camilla, *née* Cordwell; 1 s (James Fortesque b 1980), 1 da (Glenda Camilla b 1979); m 2, 23 Sept 1984, Geraldine Marie Claire Norman; *Career* chm Holding Group of Companies 1972-88; *Books* The Great Domaines of Burgundy; *Recreations* qualified ski instr, opera (esp Wagner), organ music; *Clubs* Garrick, MCC; *Style*— Dr Remington Norman

NORMAN, Sir Richard Oswald Chandler; KBE (1987); s of Oswald George Norman (d 1941), of London, and Violet Maud, *née* Chandler (d 1981); *b* 27 April 1932; *Educ* St Paul's, Balliol Coll Oxford; *m* 30 Dec 1982, Jennifer Margaret, da of William James Tope, of London; *Career* fell and tutor Merton Coll Oxford and univ lectr in chemistry 1958-65; prof of chemistry Univ of York 1965-83; chief scientific advsr: MOD 1983-88, Dept of Energy 1988-; rector Exeter Coll Oxford 1987-; *Books* Principles of Organic Synthesis (1968), Modern Organic Chemistry (1972); *Recreations* gardening, music, watching cricket; *Clubs* Utd Oxford and Cambridge Univ; *Style*— Sir Richard Norman, KBE; The Rector's Lodging, Exeter College, Oxford OX1 3DP (☎ 0865 279 644)

NORMAN, Ronald; OBE (1986); s of Leonard William Norman (d 1970), of Hendon, London, and Elsie Louise, *née* Cooke (d 1978); *b* 29 April 1937; *Educ* Dulwich, King's Coll London (BSc); *m* 1, 15 July 1961 (m dis 1973), Jennifer Mary, da of Edward Lionel Mansfield (d 1984), of Troutbeck, Cumbria; 2 s (Guy b 1962, Richard b 1964), 1 da (Sally-Ann b 1968); m 2, Joyce, da of George William Lyon (d 1971), of Hartlepool; *Career* 2 Lt RE; md CM Yuill Hartlepool Developers 1966-76 (chm and md 1976-85), chm R Norman Durham Developers 1985-; memb Bd English Industl Estates 1983-, chm Teeside Devpt Corpn 1987-; MICE; *Recreations* walking, photography, book-collecting; *Style*— Ronald Norman, Esq, OBE; Hart-on-the-Hill, Dalton Piercy, Hartlepool, Cleveland TS27 3HY; 3E Mountjoy Research Centre, Durham DH1 3UR (☎ 091 3846120, fax 091 384 2962)

NORMAN, Prof (Kenneth) Roy; s of Clement Norman (d 1978), and Peggy, *née* Nichols (d 1980); *b* 21 July 1925; *Educ* Taunton Sch Somerset, Downing Coll Cambridge (BA, MA); *m* 12 Aug 1953, Pamela Norman, da of George Raymont; 1 s (Timothy), 1 da (Felicity); *Career* WWII Lt RA serv Br and Indian Armies; fell and tutor Downing Coll Cambridge 1952-64, prof of Indian studies Univ of Cambridge 1990- (lectr 1955-78, reader 1978-90); foreign memb Royal Danish Acad 1983; FBA 1985; *Books* Elders Verses I (1969), Elders Verses II (1971), Pali Literature (1983), The Group of Discourses (1984); *Recreations* walking and reading; *Style*— Prof K R Norman; 6 Huttles Green, Shepreth, Royston, Herts SG8 6PR (☎ 0763 260541); Faculty of Oriental Studies, University of Cambridge, Sidgwick Ave, Cambridge CB3 9DA (☎ 0223 335133)

NORMAN, Shane Henry; s of Peter Alfred Norman, of Barn Cottage, South St, Aldbourne, Wilts, and Patricia Mary, *née* Wilders; *b* 12 Sept 1946; *Educ* Ampleforth, Lincoln Coll Oxford (MA); *m* 29 Aug 1981, Claudia Maria Leonor, da of Dr Jorge Antonio Villabona Abril, of Bucaramanga, Colombia; 1 s (Alexander b 22 July 1985); *Career* account exec James Capel & Co London 1968-78, assoc dir James Capel (Far East) Ltd Hong Kong 1978-80, int investment mangr Nat Employers Mutual Gen Insurance Assoc London 1980-82, investment dir NM Rothschild & Sons (Hong Kong) Ltd 1982-88, md and gen mangr Pierson Heldring and Pierson NV Hong Kong 1988; memb: Ctee on Unit Tsts of Securities and Futures Cmmn Hong Kong, Hong Kong Soc of Security Analysts; *Recreations* sailing, motoring, music, photography; *Clubs* Aberdeen Marina (HK), Overseas Bankers' (HK); *Style*— Shane Norman, Esq; Pierson Heldring & Pierson NV 3301 Gloucester Tower, The Landmark, Central, Hong Kong (☎ 010 852 522 5191, telex 61173 PHPHK HX, fax 010 852 8681487)

NORMAN, Dr the Hon Stella Maria; da of Baron Zuckerman, OM, KCB (Life Peer), and Baroness Zuckerman (Lady Joan Rufus Isaacs, da of 2 Marquess of Reading); *b* 1947; *Educ* Cranborne Chase Sch, Univ of E Anglia, Univ of London; *m* 1977, Dr Andrew R Norman; 1 s, 1 da; *Style*— Dr the Hon Stella Norman; Waterfield Sudbourne, Woodbridge, Suffolk

NORMAN, Rev Canon William Beadon; er s of Maj-Gen Charles Wake Norman, CBE, DL (d 1974), of West Farleigh Hall, Maidstone, Kent, and Nora, *née* Beadon; descended from James Norman (d 1787), of Bromley Common, Kent (*see* Burke's Landed Gentry, 18 edn, vol I, 1965); *b* 14 Feb 1926; *Educ* Eton, Trinity Coll Cambridge (BA, MA), Ridley Hall Cambridge; *m* 8 Oct 1952, Beryl, er da of John George Embleton Welch (d 1963), of Wolverhampton, Staffs, and later of Harrisburg, Pennsylvania, USA; 3 s (Stephen b 1954, James b 1959, Paul b 1961), 4 da (Henrietta b 1956, Julia (Mrs Dickens) b 1956 (twin), Sarah (Mrs Whitehouse) b 1961 (twin), Charity b 1964); *Career* serv RAC 1944-46, cmmnd 9 Lancers 1946, (war substantive) Lt 1946-47; called to the Bar Lincoln's Inn 1950; ordained: deacon 1952, priest 1953; curate of St John Beckenham 1952-54; CMS Missionary tutor and actg princ Buwalasi Theological Coll Uganda 1955-65, vicar of Alne with Aldwark Diocese of York 1965-74, vicar of Blackheath Diocese of Birmingham 1974-79, team rector Kings Norton diocese of Birmingham 1979-91; rural dean: of Warley 1974-79, of Kings Norton 1982-87; Hon Canon: of Mbale Uganda 1963-65, of Birmingham 1978-; warden of Diocesan Readers' Bd 1984-91; *Recreations* reading, walking; *Style*— The Rev Canon William Norman; The Rectory, Kings Norton, Birmingham B30 3EX (☎ 021 458 7522)

NORMAN-BUTLER, Belinda Margaret Thackeray; da of William Thackeray Denis Ritchie (d 1964), and Margaret Paulinà, *née* Booth (d 1979); *b* 10 Dec 1908; *Educ* RCM; *m* 24 Nov 1931, Col Edward Norman-Butler, TD (d 1963), s of Arthur Francis Norman-Butler, OBE; 1 s, 2 da; *Career* tstee Campden Charities 1958-; chm Nightingale Cncl 1963-84, cncl memb Arts Educn Tst 1963, ctee memb Kensington Housing Tst 1963-; govr Purcell Sch of Music 1975-87, pres Cncl Chelsea Red Cross Concert Ctee (former chm), chm Branches and Cultural Affrs Ctee ESU, ARCM, memb RSL 1981, FSA 1989; *Books* Victorian Aspirations (1967); *Recreations* music, gardening, reading, travelling, conversation; *Clubs* ESU; *Style*— Mrs Belinda Norman-Butler, FSA

NORMAN-NOTT, Dr Maud; da of William David Edmund Richard Connoly (d 1967), of Rotterdam, Holland, and Hendrina Maria Petronella, *née* Van Veen; *b* 6 Oct 1938; *Educ* Rotterdam GS, Univ of Leiden Medical Sch Holland (DRS, ARTS); *m* 16 Nov 1968, Dr Peter N Nott, s of Sidney Norman-Nott (d 1989), of Cardiff; 2 s (Nicholas William b 14 July 1974, Jeremy Carradoe b 8 Aug 1979), 2 da (Philippa Sonia b 25 April 1970, Arabella Sabriella b 12 Oct 1972); *Career* specialist training sr registrar Leiden and Oxford 1968-75; conslt psychiatrist and psychotherapist: Southampton 1975-80, Winchester and Basingstoke 1980-; in private practice 1975- (specialist in Psychosexual Therapy, Family Therapy and Marital Therapy); memb: Exec Ctee of Royal Coll of Psychiatrists, Local Ethical Res Ctee, Special Professional Panel Basingstoke Dist Hosp, BMA Winchester, Inst of Family Therapy, Gp Analytical Soc; conslt: Marriage Guidance Cncl (conslt to Psychosexual Clinic 1975-80), Pastoral Counselling Serv 1984-90; FRCPsych, DPM; *Recreations* skiing, swimming, photography, gardening, travelling, windsurfing; *Clubs* Anglo Netherlands Soc, Nederlandia; *Style*— Dr Maud Norman-Nott; The Limberlost, St Giles Hill, Winchester, Hampshire SO21 8HH (☎ 0962 69674)

NORMANBY, Marchioness of; Hon Grania Maeve Rosaura; *née* Guinness; o da of 1 Baron Moyne, DSO, TD, PC (assas in Cairo 1944), and Lady Evelyn Erskine (d 1939), da of 14 Earl of Buchan; *b* 14 April 1920; *m* 10 Feb 1951, 4 Marquess of Normanby; 2 s, 5 da; *Career* formerly Section Offr, WAAF; pro chllr Univ of Dublin 1985; JP North Yorks 1971-83; Hon LLD Dublin; *Style*— The Most Hon the Marchioness of Normanby; Lythe Hall, nr Whitby, N Yorks (☎ 0947 83269); Argyll House, 211 King's Rd, London SW3

NORMANBY, 4 Marquess of (UK 1838); Oswald Constantine John Phipps; KG (1985), CBE (1974), JP (NR Yorks 1971), DL (1960); Baron Mulgrave (I 1767), Baron Mulgrave (GB 1794), Earl of Mulgrave and Viscount Normanby (UK 1812); s of Rev 3 Marquess of Normanby (d 1932); *b* 29 July 1912; *Educ* Eton, ChCh Oxford; *m* 10 Feb 1951, Hon Grania Maeve Rosaura Guinness, JP, da of 1 Baron Moyne, DSO, PC (assas 1944); 2 s, 5 da; *Heir* s, Earl of Mulgrave; *Career* serv WWII, Lt 5 Bn The Green Howards (wounded, prisoner, repatriated); PPS: to Sec of State for Dominion Affrs 1944-45, to Lord Pres of the Cncl 1945; a lord in waiting to HM The King 1945; Cncl of St John for North Yorks (formerly NR of Yorks): chm 1948-77, pres 1977-87; chm King's Coll Hosp 1948-74; Lord-Lt: NR Yorks 1965-74, N Yorks 1974-87; pres: TA&VR Assoc for N England 1971-74, TA&VRA N Yorks and Humberside 1980-83; Hon Col Cmdt Green Howards 1970-82, Dep Hon Col 2 Bn Yorks Volunteers 1971-72; vice pres RNLI 1984- (memb Ctee of Mgmnt 1972-84); pres Nat Library for the Blind 1977-88 (chm 1946-77); vice pres: St Dunstan's 1980- (cncl memb 1944-80), chm Nat Art Collections Fund 1981-86; High Steward York Minster 1980-88; KStJ; Hon DCL Durham 1963, Hon DCL York 1985; fell King's Coll Hosp Med Sch; *Style*— The Most Hon the Marquess of Normanby, KG, CBE, JP, DL; Lythe Hall, nr Whitby, N Yorks (☎ 0947 83269); Argyll House, 211 King's Rd, London SW3 (☎ 071 352 5154)

NORMAND, Hon Mrs William; Ann Elizabeth; da of James Cumming (d 1974), of Biggar, Lanarkshire; *b* 12 Jan 1923; *Educ* Downe House; *m* 1945, Hon William Normand (d 1967, s of Baron Normand, Life Peer and Lord of Appeal who d 1962); 1 s, 1 da (*see* Macdonald Lockhart, Angus H); *Style*— The Hon Mrs William Normand; 15 Ravelston Heights, Edinburgh EH4 3LX (☎ 031 332 2308)

NORMAND, Prof (Ian) Colin Stuart; s of Sir Charles William Blyth Normand, CIE (d 1982), of Winchester, and Alison, *née* Maclennan (d 1953); *b* 18 Feb 1928; *Educ* Winchester Coll, Balliol Coll Oxford (MA, DM), St Marys Hosp Med Sch; *m* 30 June 1961, Dr Jean McIldowie, da of Dr John McIldowie Hope Smellie (d 1960), of Liverpool; 1 s (Capt Christopher Normand b 1963), 2 da (Alison b 1962, Caroline b 1966); *Career* Capt RAMC 1954-58, service in UK and Malaya; resident posts and military serv 1953-59; sr paediatric registrar UCH 1960-64, res fell Johns Hopkins Hosp 1964-65, sr lectr paediatrics UCH Med Sch 1966-71, dean Faculty of Med Univ of Southampton 1990- (prof of child health 1971-); *Recreations* golf, skiing, gardening; *Style*— Prof Colin Normand; 23 St Thomas Street, Winchester, Hants S023 9HJ (☎ 0962 852550); Faculty of Medicine, Level C, South Block, Southampton General Hospital, Tremona Rd, Southampton, Hants SO9 4XY (☎ 0703 796581)

NORMANTON, 6 Earl of (I 1806); Shaun James Christian Wellbore Ellis Agar; also Baron Mendip (GB 1794), Baron Somerton (I 1795 & UK 1873, which sits as), and Viscount Somerton (I 1800); s of 5 Earl of Normanton (d 1967), and his 2 w, Lady Fiona Pratt, da of 4 Marquess Camden; *b* 21 Aug 1945; *Educ* Eton; *m* 29 April 1970, Victoria Susan, da of Jack Beard (d 1989), of Ringwood, Hants; 1 s, 2 da (Lady Portia b 1976, Lady Marisa b 1979); *Heir* s, Viscount Somerton b 1982; *Career* Capt Blues & Royals until 1972; farmer (owns 7,000 acres in Hants); *Recreations* shooting, skiing; *Clubs* White's, Royal Yacht Sqdn; *Style*— The Rt Hon the Earl of Normanton; Somerley, Ringwood, Hants (☎ 0425 473253; office: 0425 473621)

NORMANTON, Sir Tom; TD; s of late Tom O Normanton; *b* 12 March 1917; *Educ* Manchester GS, Univ of Manchester (BA); *m* 1942, Annabel Bettine, da of late Dr Fred Yates; 2 s, 1 da; *Career* WWII 1939-46 (Europe and N Africa despatches), Maj; Parly candidate (C) Rochdale 1959 and 1964, MP (C) Cheadle 1970-87, UK memb Euro Parl Strasbourg 1973-79, oppn energy spokesman 1975-79, MEP (EDG) Cheshire E 1979-89; vice chm Manchester Branch IOD 1969-71, pres Br Textile Employers Assoc 1970-71; dir: Manchester C of C 1970-89, Industrial Training Services Ltd 1972-, N Regnl Bd Commercial Union Assurance Ltd 1974-86; pres Int Fedn of Cotton and Allied Textiles Industs 1976-78, chm Euro All Pty Gp of Friends with Israel 1979-89; memb: Supervisory Bd Euro Inst for Security 1986-, Bd Paneuropean Union 1989-; kt 1987; *Clubs* Beefsteak, RYS, St James's (Manchester); *Style*— Sir Tom Normanton, TD; Nelson House, Nelson Place, Lymington, Hants (☎ 0590 675095)

NORREYS, Lord; Henry Mark Willoughby Bertie; er s and h of 14 Earl of Lindsey and (9 of) Abingdon; *b* 6 June 1958; *Educ* Eton, Univ of Edinburgh; *m* 8 Dec 1989, Lucinda S, da of Christopher Moorsom, of Chelsea, and Mrs Bayard Osborn, of Andalusia, Spain; *Heir* bro, Hon Alexander Michael Richard Bertie; *Clubs* Puffin's (Edinburgh); *Style*— Lord Norreys; Gilmilnscroft, Sorn, Mauchline, Ayrshire KA5 6ND

NORRIE, 2 Baron (UK 1957); George Willoughby Moke; s of 1 Baron Norrie, GCMG, GCVO, CB, DSO, MC (d 1977), and Jocelyn Helen (d 1938), da of Richard Henry Gosling, of Hawthorn Hill; *b* 27 April 1936; *Educ* Eton, RMA Sandhurst; *m* 1964, Celia Marguerite, JP, da of Major John Pelham Mann, MC, of New York, USA; 1 s, 2 da (Hon Clare b 1966, Hon Julia b 1968); *Heir* s, Mark Willoughby John Norrie b 31 March 1972; *Career* cmmnd 11 Hussars (PAO) 1956, ADC to C in C M East Cmd 1960-61, GSO3 (int) 4 Gds Bde 1967-69, ret 1970; dir: Fairfield Nurseries (Hermitage) Ltd 1976-89, Int Garden Centre (Br Gp) Ltd 1984-86, Hilliers (Fairfield) Ltd 1989; memb Tree Cncl 1991; pres Br Tst for Conservation Volunteers 1989-; dir Conservation Practice Ltd 1988; House of Lords Euro Communities Ctee (Environment) 1988; *Clubs* MCC, Cavalry; *Style*— The Rt Hon the Lord Norrie; East Gate House, Craven Hill, Hamstead Marshall, Newbury, Berks RG15 0JD (☎ 0488 57026)

NORRIE, Hon Guy Bainbridge; s of 1 Baron Norrie, GCMG, GCVO, CB, DSO, MC (d 1977), and his 2 w, Patricia Merryweather, da of late Emerson Muschamp

Bainbridge, MP; *b* 3 May 1940; *Educ* Eton; *m* 1968, Sarah Georgina, o da of Maj George Rudolph Hanbury Fielding, DSO, of Val d'Ogoz, Château d'Oex, Vaud, Switzerland; 2 s (Andre 1970, James b 1973); *Career* Lt-Col (ret) Royal Hussars; GSO3 HQ 1 Br Corps 1966-67, RN Staff Coll 1972, GSO2 MOD Directorate of Army Trg 1973-74, GSO1 Directing Staff, Staff Coll Camberley 1977-78; appointed one of HM Body Guard of the Hon Corps of Gentlemen at Arms 1990; Lloyd's underwriting agent; dir: Willis Faber & Dumas (Agencies) Ltd 1980-83, Beaumont Underwriting Agencies Ltd 1981-85, Wellington Underwriting Agencies Ltd 1986-, Wellington Members Agency Ltd 1990-; *Recreations* fishing, shooting, skiing; *Clubs* City of London, Cavalry and Guards'; *Style—* The Hon Guy Norrie; Old Church Farm, Broughton, nr Stockbridge, Hants SO20 8AA; Wellington Underwriting Agencies Ltd, 120 Fenchurch St, London EC3M 5BA (☎ 071 929 2811)

NORRIE, Patricia, Baroness; Patricia Merryweather; *née* Bainbridge; DStJ; da of Emerson Bainbridge, MP (d 1911), of Auchnashellach, Ross-shire, by his 2 wife Norah Mossom, *née* Merryweather; *b* 8 Dec 1906; *Educ* St James West Malvern; *m* 1938, as his 2 w, 1 Baron Norrie, GCMG, GCVO, CB, DSO (d 1977); 1 s, 2 da; *Style—* The Rt Hon Patricia, Lady Norrie; The Old Vicarage, Leckhampstead, Newbury, Berks (☎ 048 82 282)

NORRINGTON, Humphrey Thomas; s of late Sir Arthur Norrington, and late Edith Joyce, *née* Carver; *b* 8 May 1936; *Educ* Dragon Sch Oxford, Winchester, Worcester Coll Oxford; *m* 14 Sept 1963, Frances Guenn, da of Charles John Percy Bateson; 2 s, 2 da; *Career* dir Barclays Bank plc 1985- (joined 1960); trustee: Historic Arts Trust, Springhead Trust; dir City Arts Trust, chm South Cathedral Development Trust, memb Resources Ctee Nat Assoc of Boy's Clubs; Freeman City of London, memb Worshipful Co of Skinners; FCIB; *Recreations* music, countryside; *Clubs* Utd Oxford & Cambridge Univ; *Style—* Humphrey Norrington, Esq; Barclays Bank plc, Johnson Smirke Building, 2 Royal Mint Court, London EC3N 4HJ (☎ 071 626 1567, fax 071 626 4252, telex 886111 answerback BARGTS G)

NORRINGTON, Ian Arthur; s of Charles Arthur Norrington, of Peterborough, Victoria, Aust, and Georgina Marina, *née* Beardmore (d 1974); *b* 1 Oct 1936; *Educ* Downside; *m* 21 Sept 1968, Brigitte Maria, *née* Albrecht; 1 s (Christopher Charles b 1972), 1 da (Antonia Jane b 1974); *Career* Midshipman RNVR served Home and Med Fleets 1955-57, Lt RNR 1958-64 (Sub Lt 1957); De Beers Consolidated Mines Ltd (The Diamond Trading Co Ltd) 1957-71: mangr Govt Diamond Office Kenema Sierra Leone W Africa 1964-67, mangr Br Congo Diamond Distributors Ltd Kinshasa Zaire 1967-70; ptnr W I Carr Sons and Co 1971-79, dir Ian Norrington Ltd, ptnr Grieveson Grant and Co 1979-86, dir Kleinwort Benson Securities Ltd 1986-90, conslt Fiduciary Trust International Ltd 1991; Liveryman Worshipful Co of Goldsmiths; memb Int Stock Exchange 1974; *Recreations* shooting, fishing, tennis, fine jewellery design and manufacture; *Clubs* Naval and Military; *Style—* Ian Norrington, Esq; Burrows Close, Burrows Cross, Shere, Surrey

NORRINGTON, Roger Arthur Carver; CBE (1990, OBE 1980); s of late Sir Arthur Norrington, and late Edith Joyce, *née* Carver; *b* 16 March 1934; *Educ* Dragon Sch Oxford, Westminster, Clare Coll Cambridge (BA); *m* 1, 1964 (m dis 1982), Susan Elizabeth McLean, *née* May, 1 s, 1 da; m 2, 1986, Karalyn Mary, *née* Lawrence; *Career* conductor music dir Shütz Choir of London 1962-, freelance singer RCM 1962-72, princ conductor Kent Opera 1966-84; débuts: Br 1962, BBC radio 1964, TV 1967, Germany Austria Denmark and Finland 1966, Portugal 1970, Italy 1971, France and Belgium 1972, USA 1974, Holland 1975, Switzerland 1976; musical dir: London Classical players 1978-, Orchestra of St Lukes NY 1990-; co-dir Early Opera Project 1984-, princ conductor Bournemouth Sinfonietta 1985-89, chief guest conductor Jerusalem Symphony Orch 1986-88, co-dir Historic Arts 1986; guest conductor for many Br and Foreign Orchs appearing at: Covent Garden, The Coliseum, The Proms, NY, Boston, San Francisco, Paris, Vienna and elsewhere; regular broadcasts at home and abroad, numerous recordings, occasional contrib to various musical jls; Cavaliere Order al Merita della Repubilica Italiana 1981; *Style—* Roger Norrington, Esq, CBE

NORRIS; *see*: Foxley-Norris

NORRIS, Alan John; s of Jesse Oliver Norris (d 1980), of Newport, Gwent, and Queenie Iris Norris; *b* 7 June 1942; *Educ* St Julians Newport Gwent, Newport and Monmouthshire Coll of Advanced Technol (HNC, Dip); *m* 1, 31 July 1965 (m dis 1969), Jane Margot Inkin, da of Vernon Dixon; m 2, 14 June 1975, Penelope Catherine, da of Lt-Col (William) Edwin Daniel (d 1974), of Leigh, Surrey; 1 s (Oliver William Edwin b 28 June 1982); *Career* graduate trainee to o & m offr Alcan 1960-66, princ o & m offr Osram (GEC) 1966-67, latterly systems and programming mangr United Glass (formerly sr systems analyst, computer ops mangr) 1967-76, London branch mangr Computer People 1976-79, chm and chief exec Gatton Consltg Gp (formerly Computastaff Gp) 1979-; chm Fecon Ltd; dir Ashby (Blackfriars) Ltd; chm Computing Sec FRES; MInstM 1968; *Recreations* skiing, swimming, golf, travel, wine, meteorology; *Clubs* RAC; *Style—* Alan Norris, Esq; Lovelands Mead, Lovelands Lane, Kingswood, Tadworth, Surrey KT20 6XG (☎ 0737 248151); Gatton Place, St Matthews Rd, Redhill, Surrey RH1 1TA (☎ 0737 774100, fax 0737 772949)

NORRIS, Prof Christopher Charles; s of Charles Frederick Norris (d 1979), of Leigh-on-Sea, Essex, and Edith Eliza, *née* Ward; *b* 6 Nov 1947; *Educ* East Ham GS, Univ of London (BA, PhD); *m* 17 April 1971, Alison, da of Thomas W Newton, of Fakenham, Norfolk; 2 da (Clare Tamasin b 1978, Jennifer Mary b 1983); *Career* lectr Univ of Duisburg W Germany 1974-76, asst ed Books and Bookmen 1976-77; Univ of Wales: lectr 1978-85, reader 1985-87, personal chair 1987; *Books* incl: William Empson and the Philosophy of Literary Criticism (1978) Deconstruction: theory and practice (1982), The Deconstructive Turn: essays in the rhetoric of philosophy (1983) The Contest of Faculties: philosophy and theory after deconstruction (1985), Derrida (1987), Paul de Man: deconstruction and the critique of aesthetic ideology (1988), Deconstruction and the Interests of Theory (1989); *Recreations* music (memb Côr Cochion, Cardiff), travel, recent fiction; *Style—* Prof Christopher Norris; 14 Belle Vue Terrace, Penarth, South Glamorgan, Wales CF6 1DB (☎ 0222 708165); Dept of English, Univ of Wales, PO Box 94, Cardiff CF1 3XE (☎ 0222 874822, telex 498635, fax 0222 371921)

NORRIS, David Owen; s of Albert Norris, of Long Buckby, Northants, and Margaret Amy, *née* Owen; *b* 16 June 1953; *Educ* Daventry GS, Royal Acad of Music, Keble Coll Oxford (BA, MA); *m* 23 Oct 1985, Fiona, da of Alan Clarke, of Aldringham, Suffolk; 2 s (Barnaby William b 1987, Josiah George b 1989); *Career* pianist; prof RAM 1978-, dir Petworth Festival 1986-, radio presenter (incl "The Works" series); staff union sec RAM 1984-87; govr Herbert Shiner Sch Petworth, memb Ctee Park Lane Group 1985-, memb SE Arts Music Panel; FRAM; *Recreations* naval and detective fiction; *Style—* David Owen Norris, Esq; Magog Lodge, Brinksole, Petworth, W Sussex (☎ 0798 426 02); 60 Old Oak Lane, London NW10 6UB (☎ 081 961 4830)

NORRIS, Derrick Strickland; s of James Norris (d 1973), of Liverpool, and Maud, *née* Briggs (d 1981); *b* 17 March 1940; *Educ* Liverpool Inst Boys HS, Univ of Liverpool (BSc); *m* 3 April 1965, Pamela Anne, da of Robert Geoffrey Mottram (d 1967), of Romiley, Cheshire; 1 s (Robert b 1971), 1 da (Susan b 1976); *Career* statistician and programmer Assoc Octel 1963-67, sr asst Cheshire CC 1967-69, sr systems analyst Lancashire CC 1969-74, dep computer mangr Devon CC 1974-78, asst county treas Northants CC 1978-79, dir of info technol Glasgow City Cncl 1979-; memb Bridge of Weir Community Cncl (chm 1986-88), nat chm Assoc of Bull Computer Users 1987-88; FBCS 1988 (MBCS 1963), CEng 1990; *Recreations* walking, swimming, stock market; *Style—* Derrick Norris, Esq; 29 St Andrews Drive, Bridge of Weir, Renfrewshire PA11 3HT (☎ 0505 612772); 112 Ingram St, Glasgow G1 1ET (☎ 041 227 4067, fax 041 227 5599)

NORRIS, Sir Eric George; KCMG (1969, CMG 1963); s of Henry Frederick Norris, of Bengeo, Hertford (d 1944); *b* 14 March 1918; *Educ* Hertford GS, St Catharine's Coll Cambridge; *m* 1941, Pamela, da of Cyril Crane, of Southsea, Hants; 3 da; *Career* Nat Serv Maj RCS 1940-46; joined Dominions Office 1946, Br Embassy Dublin 1948-50, UK High Cmmn Pakistan 1952-55, UK High Cmmn Delhi 1956-57, dep high cmmr Bombay 1957-60, IDC 1961, dep Br high cmmr Calcutta 1962-65, Cwlth Office 1965-68, Br high cmmr Kenya 1968-72, dep under sec of State FCO 1972-73, Br high cmmr Malaysia 1974-77 (ret); dir: Gray Mackenzie Ltd 1978-88, London Sumatra Plantations Ltd 1978-88; chm Royal Cwlth Soc 1980-84, dep chm Inchcape and Co 1981-86 (dir 1977-88); *Clubs* E India; *Style—* Sir Eric Norris, KCMG; Homestead, Great Amwell, Herts (☎ 0902 870739)

NORRIS, John; s of Arthur Henry Norris (d 1986), of Bishopthorpe, York, and Elsie Eleanor, *née* Robinson (d 1958); *b* 12 Sept 1929; *Educ* Marlborough, Gonville and Caius Coll Cambridge (BA); *m* 7 July 1956, Elizabeth Ann, da of Col Francis Edward Buller Girling, OBE, MC (d 1949), of Fleet, Hants; 1 s (Peter John b 1961), 2 da (Jane Elizabeth b 1960, Rachel Mary b 1964); *Career* Nat Serv; ptnr Thomson McLintock & Co 1966-87, ptnr Peat Marwick McLintock 1987-89; chm Teeside Soc of CAs 1970-71, memb Review Body to Consider the Govt and Admin of Univ of Durham 1981-83, memb Cncl St John's Coll Durham; FCA 1960; *Recreations* fell walking, reading, DIY, gardening; *Clubs* Northern Counties; *Style—* John Norris, Esq; 47 Moor Crescent, Gosforth, Newcastle upon Tyne NE3 4AQ (☎ 091 285 3591)

NORRIS, Malcolm Watson; s of Ernest Delamare Norris (d 1964), and Dora Venel, *née* Watson (d 1944); *b* 25 May 1931; *Educ* Merchant Taylors', St Johns Coll Oxford (BA), Univ of Birmingham (MSc, PhD); *m* 5 Aug 1961, Lauriston (Laurie) Betteridge, da of Bernard Charles Newman, Chev Legion d'Honneur (d 1969); 3 s (Robert b 23 July 1963, Rufus b 16 Jan 1965, Duncan b 25 Oct 1967), 3 da (Vivien b 25 June 1966, Hilary b 20 Jan 1971, Meriel b 1 Aug 1972); *Career* Nat Serv, LAC RAF 1949-51; admin offr HM Overseas Civil Serv 1956-61, prov local govt offr Tanzanian Govt 1961-64, assoc dir Inst of Local Govt Studies Univ of Birmingham 1983- (res assoc 1965-66, seconded lectr Ahmadu Bello Univ Nigeria 1966-68, seconded lectr Haile Selassie Univ Ethiopia 1969-71, seconded lectr Univ Malaya Malaysia 1972-77 (sr letcr 1977), dir devpt admin Univ of Birmingham; vice-pres Monumental Brass Soc; FSA; *Books* Brass Rubbing (1965), Local Government in Peninsular Malaysia, Monumental Brasses - The Craft (1977), The Memorials (1977); *Recreations* church monuments, chess; *Style—* Malcolm Norris, Esq, FSA; Development Administration Group, The University of Birmingham B15 2TT (☎ 021 414 5012, fax 021 414 4989, telex 333762 UOBHAM)

NORRIS, Steven John; MP (C) Epping Forest 1988-; s of John Francis Birkett Norris, of Nottingham, and Eileen Winifred, *née* Walsh; *b* 24 May 1945; *Educ* Liverpool Inst HS, Worcester Coll Oxford (MA); *m* 23 Aug 1969, Peta Veronica, da of Rear Adm Peter Cecil-Gibson, CB; 2 s (Anthony Hugh b 4 Sept 1974, Edward George Steven b 26 Dec 1985); *Career* MP (C) Oxford E 1983-87; chm: Motor Distribution Co, The Crime Concern Tst Ltd; vice-chm W Berks DHA 1982-85 and 1977-85; memb Berks CC 1977-85, govr Mary Hare GS for the Deaf, memb Select Ctee on Social Servs 1985; Freeman City of London, Liveryman Worshipful Co of Coachmakers' and Coach Harness Makers; *Recreations* reading; *Clubs* Carlton; *Style—* Steven Norris, Esq, MP; House of Commons, London SW1A OAA

NORRIS, Sydney George; s of George Samuel Norris (d 1980), of Liverpool, and Agnes Rosa, *née* George; *b* 22 Aug 1937; *Educ* Liverpool Inst HS for Boys, Univ Coll Oxford (MA), Univ of Cambridge (Dip in Criminology), Univ of California (MCrim); *m* 1965, Brigid Molyneux, da of Geoffrey Molyneux FitzGibbon (d 1990), of Wotton under Edge; 2 s (Simon b 1969, Daniel b 1971), 1 da (Sarah b 1967); *Career* 2 Lt Intelligence Corps 1956-58; Harkness fell 1968-70, princ Home Office 1967-74 (asst princ 1963-67), sec Advsy Cncl on Penal System 1970-73, princ private sec Home Office 1973-74; asst sec: Prison Dept 1974-79, Treasy 1979-81, Home Office Estab Dept 1981-82; princ estab and fin offr NI Office 1982-85; dir Operational Policy Prison Serv 1985-88, asst under sec Police Home Office 1988-90, princ fin offr Home Office 1990-; *Recreations* running, fell walking, gardening, piano; *Style—* Sydney G Norris, Esq; Home Office, London SW1

NORRIS, Thomas Eric; s of Eric Tobias Norris (d 1979), of Hunstanton, and Calah Mary, *née* Bullard; *b* 16 Sept 1930; *Educ* Manchester GS, Univ of Manchester (BSc); *m* 21 Sept 1957, Patricia Cecilia, da of Bernard Winters (d 1968), of London and Buenos Aires; 3 s (Michael b 1958, Peter b 1961, Phillip b 1961); *Career* Nat Serv Lt RNVR 1953-55; ptnr Merz and McLellan 1976-89 (engr 1955-76), incl engrg 1989-; memb: Latin America Trade Advsy Gp 1985-88, Cncl of ACE 1986-89, ind Consulting Engineer 1989; FIEE, FIMechE, MConsE, CEng; *Books* Hydro-Electric Engineering Practice (contrib, 1972), Electrical Engineers Reference Book (contrib, 1983); *Recreations* running, antiques, clocks, mid-Northumberland chorus; *Style—* Thomas Norris, Esq; 17 Rectory Park, Morpeth, Northumberland NE61 2SZ (☎ 0670 514943, fax 0670 518084)

NORRIS, Prof (William) Tobias; s of Eric Tobias Norris (d 1979), and Calah Mary, *née* Bullard; *b* 18 April 1937; *Educ* Manchester GS, Pembroke Coll Cambridge (MA), MIT (ScD); *m* 26 Aug 1978, Joan, da of Clifford Robert Rivers (d 1984); 1 s (Robert b 1982), 2 da (Calah b 1979, Emily b 1985); *Career* res offr Central Electricity Res Laboratories 1962, res mangr CEGB NW 1971, head Electrical Engrg Div CERL Leatherhead 1973, Nat Grid prof of power engrg Univ of Aston 1985; chm Br Orienteering Fedn 1979-82; FIEE, FIMechE, FCSD; *Recreations* orienteering, watercolouring; *Style—* Prof Tobias Norris; Dept of Electrical Engineering, University of Aston, Birmingham B4 7ET (☎ 021 359 3611, fax 021 359 6470, telex 336997 UNIAST G)

NORRIS, William John; s of John Phillips Norris, QGM, of Salisbury, Wilts, and Joan Hattersley, *née* Barnes; *b* 3 Oct 1951; *Educ* Sherborne, New Coll Oxford (MA); *m* 3 Oct 1987, Lesley Jacqueline, da of Douglas Osborne of Hythe, Kent; 1 da (Charlotte Louise b 15 Oct 1988); *Career* called to the Bar Middle Temple 1974; amateur jockey; *Books* The Collected Letters of C W Catte (ed); *Recreations* racing, sailing, cricket; *Clubs* Royal Cruising, Lobsters; *Style—* William Norris, Esq; Lobster Cottage, Lower Daggons, Fordingbridge, Hants (☎ 07254 375); Farrars Building, Temple, London EC4 (☎ 071 583 9241)

NORRIS, William Vernon Wentworth; s of William Henry Norris, of 9 Dunnally Park, Shepperton-on-Thames, Middx, and Eileen Louise, *née* Willmott; *b* 11 May 1937; *Educ* Bedford Sch; *m* 1, 10 Oct 1960 (m dis 1982), Penelope Anne, da of Herbert James Dimmock (d 1987), of Brookwood, Surrey; 1 s (Richard b 1965), 1 da (Sally b 1962); m 2, 5 May 1982, Catherine, da of Bernard James Knowles; 1 da (Katie b 1982); *Career* admitted slr 1959; lectr Gibson & Weldon 1959-61, Allen & Overy 1961- (ptnr 1964); past chm Law Soc Revenue Law Ctee, govr Christs Hosp, memb Addington Soc; memb Law Soc 1959; *Recreations* poetry; *Style—* William Norris, Esq; 9 Cheapside, London, EC2V 6AD (☎ 071 248 9898, fax 071 236 2192, telex 8812801)

NORSTER, Robert Leonard; s of Leonard George Norster, of Blaina, Gwent, and Evelyn Marian, *née* King; *b* 23 June 1957; *Educ* Hafod-y-Ddol GS, Nantyglo Comp, Gwent Coll of HE, S Glamorgan Coll of HE (BA); *m* 10 Sept 1986, Catherine Halina, da of Ronald Delwyn James Price; *Career* Rugby Union lock forward Cardiff RFC and Wales (34 caps); Abertillery RFC 1975-76, Cardiff RFC 1977- (capt 1987, 1988); Wales: debut v Romania 1979, Five Nations debut v Scotland 1982, most capped Welsh lock forward; British Lions: tour NZ (2 test appearances) 1983, tour Australia (1 test appearance) 1989; memb World XV v S Africa 1989, many appearances for Barbarians; Rank Xerox (UK) Ltd 1982-89, mktg mangr Standard Chartered Group 1990-; Rugby Writers Player of the Year 1986; *Recreations* golf, country life; *Style—* Robert Norster, Esq; c/o Welsh Rugby Union, PO Box 22, Cardiff (☎ 0222 390111)

NORTH, Barony of (E 1554);; abeyant 1941; *see* Hon Mrs Bowlby and Hon Mrs North-Beauchamp

NORTH, Hon Mrs (Carolyn); da of 2 Baron Banbury of Southam; *b* 1947; *m* 1977, Christopher (Kim) J A North (d 1988); *Style—* The Hon Mrs North

NORTH, Hon Charles Evelyn; s of 8 Earl of Guilford (d 1949); *b* 1918; *Educ* Eton, Univ of London (BSc); *m* 1, 1942 (m dis 1957), Maureen O'Callaghan, da of Maj F C B Baldwin; 1 s, 1 da; m 2, 1959, Joan Aston, da of Maj F B Booker (d 1954), of Edenmore House Raheny, Co Dublin; *Career* PO RAFVR 1940, Flt Lt 1942, on staff Air Miny and MAP; dir J M W North and Co Ltd London, professional engr DOE, ret 1983; memb Inst of Advanced Motorists, MIMechE; *Recreations* rural life, riding, steam engines; *Style—* The Hon Charles E North; Park End House, Eythorne, Dover, Kent (☎ 0304 830368)

NORTH, Christopher; *b* 4 Nov 1954; *Educ* Wellington, Trinity Coll Oxford; *m* ; 2 c; *Career* J Walter Thompson 1972-73, The Direct Mail Centre 1976-77, PR account exec Press Release and Distribution Services Ltd 1977-78, prodn mangr Saudi Advertising International 1978-79; The VPI Group and Subsids London 1980-91: prodn mangr Valin Pollen 1980, assoc dir Creative and Prodn Serv Valin Pollen 1982, dir Bd Valin Pollen Ltd and Falcon Designs Ltd 1984, dir Bd APT Photoset 1986, exec asst to VPI Group chm and chief exec Reg Valin 1987; chm and chief exec: APT Photoset, APT Holdings and Falcon Designs 1989; dir: Bd Valin Pollen International plc 1989-, Fishburn Hedges Boys Williams 1991-; *Style—* Christopher North, Esq

NORTH, Geoffrey; MBE (1976), JP (1978); s of William Henry North (d 1971), and Florence, *née* Parr (d 1930); *b* 26 July 1924; *Educ* Hillhouse Central Sch Huddersfield; *m* 21 Dec 1946, Yvonne Elizabeth, da of John Richard Barrett (d 1971); 1 s (Antony b 3 Nov 1947), 2 da (Laraine b 26 May 1951, Julie b 31 Jan 1956); *Career* cmmnd PO 1945 and Flying Offr 1946, RAF 1943-46; md Avon Rubber Co Ltd Bridgend 1974-82, chm and md Avonride Ltd 1982-90; memb: Rotary Club Bridgend (former pres), Mid Glam Probation Ctee; former chm Bridgend YMCA; FIIM; *Recreations* rugby, union football; *Style—* Geoffrey North, Esq, MBE, JP; 12 Fitzhamon Rd, Porthcawl, Mid-Glam CF36 3JA (☎ 0656 716 194); Avonride Ltd, Spelter, Site, Caerau Maesteg, Mid Glam (☎ 0656 739 111, fax 0656 737 677, car 0836 765 399, telex 498660)

NORTH, Maj Geoffrey Edward Ford; MC (1943), JP (South Molton 1970), DL (Devon 1982); s of S T Ford North (d 1963), of Comeragh Ct, Hook Heath, Surrey, and Margaret Wilmot, *née* Booth (d 1978); *b* 21 Jan 1917; *Educ* Winchester, New Coll Oxford; *m* 9 March 1950, Hon Margaret Isolda de Grey, 2 da of Lt-Col 8 Baron Walsingham, DSO, OBE, DL (d 1965), of Merton Hall, Thetford, Norfolk; 1 s (David John Ford b 1959), 3 da (Amanda Ford (Lady Weldon) b 1951, Joanna (Hon Mrs K I M Fraser) b 1953, Belinda Jane b 1955); *Career* WWII serv 10 Royal Hussars, Adj 1942, Sqdn Ldr GSO I (Equitation) Eighth Army HQ 1945, 2 i/c 10 Royal Hussars 1945 (despatches twice, C in C Commendation for Gallantry 1942); called to the Bar 1939; chm: City Offices Co Ltd 1978-83 (dir 1951-78), Greycoat Group 1981-83; British rep World Hereford Conf 1976 and 1980, chm South Molton Bench 1981-87; memb: Devon Co Ctee CLA 1958-88, Cncl Devon Co Agric Assoc 1962-88 (pres 1978); pres: Hereford Cattle Breeders 1978, Devon Co Show 1978; High Sheriff Devon 1990-91; *Recreations* fishing, shooting, skiing, bicycling; *Style—* Maj Geoffrey North, MC, JP, DL; Holmingham, Bampton, Devon (☎ 0398 31259); La Farigoulette, Le Rey d'Agneou, 83550 Vidauban, Var, France (☎ 94 73 03 42)

NORTH, Jeremy William Francis; s and h of Sir (William) Jonathan Frederick North, 2 Bt; *b* 5 May 1960; *Educ* Marlborough; *Style—* Jeremy North Esq; Frogmore, Weston-under-Penyard, Herefordshire

NORTH, Prof John David; s of John Ernest North (d 1988), of Cheltenham, Glos, and Gertrude Anne North (d 1989); *b* 19 May 1934; *Educ* Batley GS, Merton Coll Oxford (MA, DPhil), London (BSc); *m* 6 April 1957, Marion Jean Pizzey, da of J H Pizzey of Eastbourne; 1 s (Richard b 1961), 2 da (Julian b 1962, Rachel b 1965); *Career* Univ of Oxford: Nuffield res fell in history and philosophy of science 1963-68, Museum of History of Science 1968-77; prof of history of philosophy and the exact sciences Univ of Groningen The Netherlands 1977-; memb and assessor Royal Dutch Acad, foreign memb Royal Danish Acad; Acad Int d'Hist des Sciences: secrétaire perpétuel, Médaille Alexandre Koyré 1989; *Books* The Measure of the Universe (1965, 1967), Richard of Wallingford (1976), Horoscopes and History (1986), Chaucer's Universe (1988), The Universal Frame (1989), Stars, Minds and Fate (1989); *Style—* Prof John North; 28 Chalfont Rd, Oxford OX2 6TH (☎ 0865 58458); Kamperfoelieweg 25, 9765HJ Paterswolde, The Netherlands (☎ 05907 1846 (NL)); Filosofisch Instituut, Westersingel 19, 9718 CA Groningen, The Netherlands (☎ 050 63 61 53 (NL), fax 050 63160 (NL))

NORTH, John Joseph; s of Lt-Col Frederick James North, MC (d 1948), of Halifax, Nova Scotia, Canada, and Annie Elizabeth, *née* Matthews (d 1977); *b* 7 Nov 1926; *Educ* Rendcomb Coll, Univ of Reading (BSc), Univ of California (MS); *m* 3 May 1958, Sheila Barbara, da of Frederick George Mercer (d 1959), of Walton on the Hill, Stafford; 2 s (Christopher Frederick John b 29 Oct 1960, David Charles b 16 May 1964); *Career* RN 1945-48; agric offr Nat Agric Advsy Serv 1951-54, Kellog fellowship Univ of California 1954-56; MAFF: regnl agronomist 1956-71, regnl agric offr 1971-73, sr agric offr 1973-79, chief agric offr 1979-85; sr visiting res assoc Univ of Cambridge 1987- (sr visiting fell 1985), memb Cncl Royal Agric Soc England, chm Br Crop Protection Cncl; FBiol 1974-; *Recreations* golf, gardening; *Style—* John North, Esq; Summerfield, 28 Hauxton Road, Little Shelford, Cambridge CB2 5HJ (☎ 0223 843369); University of Cambridge, Department of Land Economy, 19 Silver St, Cambridge (☎ 0223 337127)

NORTH, Sir (William) Jonathan Frederick; 2 Bt (UK 1920), of Southwell, Co Nottingham; s of late Hon John Montagu William North (s of 8 Earl of Guilford), and his late 1 w, Muriel Norton Hicking; suc (under special remainder) his maternal gf, Sir William Norton Hicking, 1 Bt, 1947; *b* 6 Feb 1931; *Educ* Marlborough; *m* 1956, Sara Virginia, da of late Air Chief Marshal Sir Donald Hardman, GBE, KCB, DFC (*see* Hardman, Lady); 1 s, 2 da; *Heir* s, Jeremy William Francis North; *Style—* Sir Jonathan North, Bt; Frogmore, Weston-under-Penyard, Herefordshire HR9 5TQ

NORTH, Hon Mrs (Margaret Isolda); *née* de Grey; 2 da of 8 Baron Walsingham, DSO, OBE (d 1965); *b* 14 Aug 1926; *m* 9 March 1950, Maj Geoffrey Edward Ford North, MC, s of Stephen Thomas Ford North, of Ashdale, Woking, Surrey; 1 s, 3 da; *Career* serv WWII WRNS 1943-46; *Recreations* bicycling; *Style—* The Hon Mrs North; Holmingham Farm, Bampton, Tiverton, Devon

NORTH, Michael Robert Thomas; s of Robert Baden North, of Burton-on-Stather, Humberside, and Vera, *née* Evans; *b* 8 Jan 1950; *Educ* Frederick Gough GS Lincolnshire, Imperial Coll London (BSc); *m* 7 Aug 1971, Carolyn Margaret, da of Geoffrey Harold Vickers; 2 s (Richard b 10 June 1976, John b 13 April 1978); *Career* actuarial trainee: Legal and General Assurance Society 1971-72, Yorkshire-General Life Assurance Co Ltd 1972-75 (valuation planning actuary 1975-77), vice pres and actuary Jamaica Mutual Life Assurance Society 1977-81, dep mangr UK Life Mktg Victory Insurance Co Ltd 1981-83, dir and actuary Skandia Reassurance UK Ltd 1983-87, pensions mangr Provident Mutual Life Assurance Association 1989- (asst actuary 1987-89); FIA 1975, ASA (USA) 1977, MBIM 1978; *Style—* Michael North, Esq; Provident Mutual Life Assurance Association, Wedgwood Way, Stevenage, Hertfordshire SG1 4PU (☎ 0438 739000, fax 0438 739375)

NORTH, Dr Peter Machin; CBE; s of Geoffrey Machin North (d 1974), and Freda Brunt, *née* Smith; *b* 30 Aug 1936; *Educ* Oakham Sch, Keble Coll Oxford; *m* 1960, Stephanie Mary, eld da of Thomas L Chadwick (d 1963); 2 s (Nicholas Machin b 1964, James William Thomas b 1971), 1 da (Jane Amanda b 1962); *Career* Lt Royal Leics Regt Cyprus 1955-56; teaching asst Northwestern Univ Sch of Law Chicago 1960-61; lectr: Univ Coll of Wales Aberystwyth 1961-63, Univ of Nottingham 1963-65; tutor in law Keble Coll Oxford 1965-76 (fell 1965-84), law cmmr for Eng and Wales 1976-84, princ Jesus Coll Oxford 1984-; chm Road Traffic Law Review 1985-88; hon fell: Keble Coll Oxford 1984, Univ Coll of N Wales; hon bencher Inner Temple; FBA; *Recreations* locking; *Clubs* Utd Oxford and Cambridge Univs; *Style—* Dr Peter North, CBE; Jesus College, Oxford OX1 3DW (☎ 0865 279701)

NORTH, Lord; Piers Edward Brownlow; s and h of 9 Earl of Guilford, DL; *b* 9 March 1971; *Style—* Lord North; Waldershare Park, Dover, Kent

NORTH, Roger Dudley; s of Adm Sir Dudley North, GCVO, CSI (d 1961), and Eilean Flora, *née* Graham (d 1989); *b* 1 Aug 1926; *Educ* Harrow, Univ Coll Oxford, Royal Acad of Music (LRAM); *m* 3 April 1965, Rosamund, da of Herbert Leonard Shreeves (d 1979); 2 da (Sarah b 1967, Jessie b 1969); *Career* RM 1944-47, cmmnd 1946, Lt 1946; teaching appts and conductorships of amateur choir and string orch and accompanist to modern dance classes Morley Coll 1951-60, 100 bdcast talks and discussions on music BBC 1960-71, tutor Morley Coll 1965-, composer; works incl: orchestral, choral, chamber works, film scores, songs, electro acoustic works; examples incl: Clarinet Sonata premiere 1955, The Jubilee one act opera premiere 1968, Ludes for String Trio premiere 1969; memb Composers Guild of GB 1965; *Books* The ABC of Music Book I of The Musical Companion (1977), ENO Guide - The Rhinegold (1985); *Style—* Roger North, Esq; 24 Strand-on-the-Green, Chiswick, London W4 3PH (☎ 081 995 9174)

NORTH, Hon Mrs (Rosemary Victoria); *née* Orde-Powlett; da of 7 Baron Bolton and his 1 w, Hon Christine Helena, *née* Weld Forester (*see* Hon Mrs Miles); *b* 1952; *m* 1974, John Richard Bentley North; 1 s, 1 da; *Style—* The Hon Mrs North; RMB 590, Boddington, W Australia 6390

NORTH-BEAUCHAMP, Hon Mrs (Susan Silence); *née* North; da of late Hon Dudley William John North, MC, and sis of 13 Baron North (d 1941); *b* 19 Jan 1920; *m* 1944, Frederick Guy Beauchamp, MD, MRCS; 3 da; co-heiress to Barony; *Career* assumed by deed poll 1943 the additional surname of Beauchamp; *Style—* The Hon Mrs North-Beauchamp; 19 Beaumont St, London WI

NORTHAMPTON, 7 Marquess of (UK 1812); Spencer Douglas David Compton; DL (Northants 1979); also Earl of Northampton (UK 1618), Earl Compton, and Baron Wilmington (both UK 1812); patron of 9 livings; s of 6 Marquess of Northampton, DSO (d 1978), and his 2 w, Virginia, yst da of David Rimington Heaton, DSO, of Brookfield, Crownhill, S Devon; *b* 2 April 1946; *Educ* Eton; *m* 1, 13 June 1967 (m dis 1973), Henriette Luisa Maria, o da of late Baron Adolph William Carel Bentinck, sometime Netherlands ambass to France; 1 s, 1 da; m 2, 1974 (m dis 1977), Annette Marie, da of Charles Anthony Russell Smallwood; m 3, 1977 (m dis 1983), Rosemary Ashley Morritt, o da of P G M Hancock, of Truro, and formerly w of Hon Charles Dawson-Damer (bro of 7 Earl of Portarlington); 1 da; m 4, 1985 (m dis 1989), Hannelore Ellen (Fritzi), da of late Hermann Erhardt of Landsberg-am-Lech, and formerly w of Hon Michael Pearson, *qv*; 1 da; m 5, 10 Dec 1990, Mrs Pamela Kypriol; *Heir* s, Earl Compton; *Career* landowner and proprietor of Castle Ashby (constructed 1574, with an Inigo Jones frontage of 1635) and Compton Wynyates (built 1480-1520); *Clubs* Turf; *Style—* The Most Hon the Marquess of Northampton, DL; Compton Wynyates, Tysoe, Warwick (☎ 029 588 229); Castle Ashby, Northampton (☎ 060 129 234)

NORTHARD, John Henry; CBE (1987, OBE 1979); s of William Henry Northard (d 1979), and Nellie, *née* Ingham (d 1989); *b* 23 Dec 1926; *Educ* St Bede's GS Bradford Yorks, Barnsley Mining and Tech Coll; *m* 11 Oct 1952, Marian Josephine, da of George Frederick Lay (d 1938); 2 s (Richard b 1953, Martin b 1955), 2 da (Barbara b 1957, Victoria b 1970); *Career* colliery mangr Yorks 1955-57, gp mangr Leics Collieries 1963-65 (colliery mangr 1957-63), dep chief mining engr Staffs Collieries 1965-70; NCB: area dir N Derby area 1973-81 (area dep dir (mining) 1970-73), area dir Western Area 1981-85, dir corp ops 1985; dep chm British Coal Corporation 1988 (memb Bd 1986); pres Inst of Mining Engrs 1982, vice pres Coal Trades Benevolent Assoc (nat chm 1986), first vice chm Organising Ctee World Mining Congress; SBStJ 1981; CEng, FEng, Hon FIMinE, CBIM, FRSA; *Style—* John Northard, Esq, CBE; British Coal Corporation, Eastwood Hall, Eastwood, Nottingham NG16 3EB (☎ 0773 531313, fax 0773 531313 ext 32576)

NORTHBOURNE, 5 Baron (UK 1884); Sir Christopher George Walter James; 6 Bt (GB 1791); only s of 4 Baron Northbourne (d 1982), of Northbourne Court, Kent, and Katharine Louise (d 1980), yr da of late George Nickerson, of Boston, Mass, and his w Ellen (d 1950), who m as her 2 husb Rear Adm Hon Sir Horace Hood, KCB, MVO, DSO (ka Jutland 1916), and was by him mother of 6 and 7 Viscounts Hood; *b* 18 Feb 1926; *Educ* Eton, Magdalen Coll Oxford (MA); *m* 29 July 1959, Marie-Sygne, da of Henri Louis Claudel and gda of Paul Claudel, poet and diplomat; 3 s (Hon Charles Walter Henri b 14 June 1960, Hon Anthony Christopher Walter Paul b 14 Jan 1963, Hon Sebastian Richard Edward Cuthbert b 7 March 1966), 1 da (Hon Ophelia Mary Katherine Christine Aliki b 23 Aug 1969); *Heir* eldest s, Hon Charles b 14 June 1960; *Career* farmer; co dir; sits as Ind in House of Lords; FRICS; *Clubs* Brooks's, Farmers', Royal Yacht Squadron; *Style—* The Rt Hon the Lord Northbourne; Coldharbour, Northbourne, Kent (☎ 0304 611277); 11 Eaton Place, London SW1 (☎ 071 235 6790); Evistones, Otterburn, Northumberland; office: Betteshanger Farms Ltd, Betteshanger, Deal, Kent (☎ 0304 611281)

NORTHBOURNE, Baroness; Marie-Sygne; da of Henri Louis Claudel, of France, and Christine, *née* Diplarakos; *b* 13 Feb 1937; *Educ* Lycée Francais de Bruxelles Sorbonne; *m* 29 July 1959, 5 Baron Northbourne, *qv*; 3 s, 1 da; *Career* dir Invicta Radio 1984-; chm of govrs Northbourne Park Sch 1979, memb Cncl Univ of Kent at Canterbury 1984, tstee Kent Fndn 1987, chm Kent Community Housing Tst 1990; *Style—* The Rt Hon Lady Northbourne; Coldharbour, Northbourne, Deal, Kent (☎

0304 611 277); 11 Eaton Place, London SW1 (☎ 071 235 6790); Invicta Radio, Invicta Sound plc, 15 Station Rd East, Canterbury, Kent (☎ 0227 767 661, car tel 0860 464 127)

NORTHBROOK, 6 Baron (UK 1866), of Stratton, Co Hants; Sir Francis Thomas Baring; 8 Bt (GB 1793); o s of 5 Baron Northbrook (d 1990), and Rowena Margaret, da of Brig- Gen Sir William Henry Manning, GCMG, KBE, CB (d 1932); *b* 21 Feb 1954; *Educ* Winchester, Bristol Univ; *m* 27 June 1987, Amelia Sarah Elizabeth, er da of Dr Reginald David Taylor, of Hursley, Hants; 1 da (Hon Arabella Constance Elizabeth b 1989); *Heir* (to Baronetcy only) kinsman, Peter Baring b 1939; *Style—* The Rt Hon Lord Northbrook; c/o House of Lords, London SW1

NORTHCOTE, Lady Catherine Cecilia Mary; da of 3 Earl of Iddesleigh (d 1970); *b* 1931; *Educ* Univ Coll London; *Career* lectr, sr lectr and head of history Maria Assumpta Coll of Educn 1964-79; later EFL teacher Hishôten Coll Osaka Japan; *Books* People of the Past Series (OUP), Nurse in the Crimea (1966), A 12th Century Benedictine Nun (1967), A Docker goes on Strike (1968), Radio Script (BBC School History); *Style—* The Lady Catherine Northcote; c/o Pynes, Exeter, Devon EX5 5EF

NORTHCOTE, Donald Henry; s of Frederick Northcote (d 1983); *b* 27 Dec 1921; *Educ* George Monoux GS, Univ of London, Univ of Cambridge (BSc, MA, PhD, ScD); *m* 1948, Eva Marjorie, nee Mayo; 2 da; *Career* prof plant biochemistry Univ of Cambridge 1972-89 (Master Sidney Sussex Coll 1976-); FRS; *Recreations* sailing (yacht 'Sprite'); *Clubs* United Oxford and Cambridge; *Style—* Donald Northcote, Esq, FRS; The Masters Lodge, Sidney Sussex Coll, Cambridge (☎ 0223 355860)

NORTHCOTE, Hon Edward Frederic; TD (1975); s of 3 Earl of Iddesleigh (d 1970); *b* 29 July 1934; *Educ* Downside, Trinity Coll Oxford (MA); *m* 1963 (m dis 1980), Vivien Sheena, da of Col Robert John Augustine Hornby, OBE, of Banbury, Oxon; 2 s, 1 da; *Career* serv Oxford Univ OTC 1953-55; Maj Intelligence Corps, serv Cyprus 1957; chartered cost and mgmnt accountant; princ offr HM Treasy 1969-71; *Style—* The Hon Edward Northcote, TD; c/o Lloyds Bank, 16 St James's St, London SW1

NORTHCOTE, His Hon Judge; Peter Colston; s of William George Northcote (d 1936), and Edith Mary, *née* Watkins (d 1943); *b* 23 Oct 1920; *Educ* Ellesmere Coll, Univ of Bristol; *m* 1947, Patricia Elizabeth, da of James Roger Bickley (d 1983); 2 s (Robin, Michael); *Career* WWII Maj Rajput Regt Far E 1939-46; called to the Bar Inner Temple 1948, circuit judge 1973-89; chm: Nat Inst Tbnl, W Midland Rent Tbnl, AG Land Tbnl; *Recreations* travel, music, winter sports; *Clubs* Army and Navy; *Style—* His Hon Judge Northcote; Wroxeter Grange, Shrewsbury, Salop (☎ 074 375 279)

NORTHCOTE, (Cecil Henry) Stafford; OBE (1982); 2 s of Capt (Hon Maj) Cecil Stafford Northcote (Rifle Brigade) (d 1912), and Ida, o da of Capt Joseph Boulderson; Cecil was gs of the Rev Stafford Northcote, the latter being 3 s of Sir Stafford Northcote, 7th Bt, and yr bro of 1st Earl of Iddesleigh; *b* 8 June 1912, (posthumously); *Educ* Douai Sch, Queen's Coll Oxford (MA); *m* 28 Dec 1936, Winifreda Iola Marguerite (Freda), da of Frederick Williams (d 1913); 2 s (Amyas Henry b 25 Nov 1937, Hugh b 22 Nov 1938), 1 da (Julia b 17 July 1941); *Career* RAEC 1941-42; headmaster St Bedes Bishton Hall Prep Sch 1936-78; memb: Euro Cncl Stafford and Salop Div, Colwich Parish Cncl 1949- (chm 1955-58), Staffordshire CC 1958-81; former memb Stafford RDC, Mid-Staffordshire Cons Assoc rep on Staffordshire E Euro Constituency Cncl; fndr govr Newman Coll Birmingham 1970-; chm: Colwich & Little Haywood Branch Cons Assoc 1948-88, chm Stafford and Stone Cons Assoc 1972-81 (pres 1982-85); pres Mid-Staffordshire Cons & Unionist Assoc 1985-88; former govr various local educn estabs; memb Ct Univ of Keele; High Sheriff of Staffordshire 1981-82; OStJ 1984; Knight of the Sovereign and Mil Order of Malta (Honour and Devotion) 1957, KSG 1977; *Recreations* walking, gardening (assisting), cricket (watching); *Clubs* Staffordshire County; *Style—* C Stafford Northcote, Esq, OBE; Bishton Hall, Wolseley Bridge, Staffs (☎ 0889 881277)

NORTHCOTT, Montague Walter Desmond; s of Cdr W C Northcott, JP, DL, RNR (d 1965), of 9 Ranulf Rd, London NW2, and Irene Violet, *née* Lay (d 1972); *b* 25 April 1931; *Educ* Harrow; *m* 24 Aug 1966, Annie Margaret; 1 s (Richard Walter Montague b 1967), 1 da (Joanna Rosemary Marion b 1969); *Career* Royal Navy 1949-52; Cunard Steamship Co 1952-67, Hogg Robinson Travel 1968-; underwriting member of Lloyds, tstee Northcott Fndn; govr: Haberdashers' Aske's Schs 1972-82, Jones GS Fndn 1985-88; chm St Andrews Church Restoration Appeal; Master: Worshipful Co of Haberdashers' 1985, Worshipful Co of Painter-Stainers' 1989; Liveryman Worshipful Co of Loriners'; FRSA; *Recreations* tennis, golf, swimming, gardening; *Clubs* RAC, City Livery; *Style—* Montague Northcott, Esq; The Old Rectory, Little Berkhamsted, Hertfordshire SG13 8LP

NORTHCOTT, Simon John; s of Maj Guy Denis Stanley Northcott, of Basingstoke, Hants, and Sylvia Mary Rait Kerr; *b* 22 June 1954; *Educ* Wellington Coll, Nottingham Univ (BSc), Cranfield Sch of Management (MBA); *m* 18 Aug 1979, Susan Caroline Elizabeth, da of Neville Poyser, of Rio de Janeiro, Brazil; *Career* md Petrocon Drilling Tools plc 1984-86; dir and gen mangr Victaulic Industl Polymers 1987-; *Recreations* skiing, golf, shooting, sailing; *Style—* Simon J Northcott, Esq; 8 Barnwell, nr Oundle, Northants PE8 5PM (☎ 0832 73145); St Peters Road, Huntingdon, Cambs PE18 7DJ (☎ 0480 52121, telex 32221, fax 0480 50430)

NORTHESK, Betty, Countess of; Elizabeth; da of late Anthony A Vlasto; *m* 1929, 11 Earl of Northesk (d 1963); 1 da (adopted); *Style—* The Rt Hon Betty, Countess of Northesk; Glenley Farmhouse, Glenogil, by Forfar, Angus, Scotland DD8 3SY (☎ 035 65 216)

NORTHESK, 13 Earl of (S 1647); Robert Andrew Carnegie; also Lord Rosehill and Inglismaldie (S precedence 1639); s of 12 Earl of Northesk (d 1975), and Dorothy, da of Col Sir William Campion, KCMG, DSO, DL, s of Col William Campion, CB, VD, JP, DL, and Hon Gertrude Brand, da of 1 Viscount Hampden and 23 Baron Dacre, GCB, PC; the 1 Earl of Northesk was yr bro of 1 Earl of Southesk; *b* 24 June 1926; *Educ* Pangbourne, Tabor Naval Acad Mass USA; *m* 1949, Jean (d 1989), yr da of Capt John MacRae, of Argyll, and Lady Phyllis Hervey, da of 4 Marquess of Bristol; 1 s (David b 1954), 2 da (Karen b 1951, Mary b 1953) (and 1 s decd); m 2, 29 Dec 1989, Brownie Elizabeth, *née* Scott Grimason, widow of Carl L Heimann; *Heir* s, Lord Rosehill; *Career* serv RN 1942-45; landowner and farmer; memb Br Racing Drivers Club 1957-; dir Int Fedn Charolais Cattle, Cncl Br Charolais Cattle Soc 1972-; chm Midhurst RDC 1972-74; dir: Chandler Hargreaves Whittall (IOM) 1979-, IOM Bank 1980-, Buchan Sch (IOM) 1980-, NEL Britannia International Assurance 1984-89, Royal Skandia Life Assurance Ltd 1989-; *Recreations* gardening, shooting, motor racing, silversmithing; *Style—* The Rt Hon the Earl of Northesk; Springwaters, Ballamodha, IOM (☎ 0624 823291)

NORTHFIELD, Baron (Life Peer UK 1975), of Telford, Co Shropshire; (William) Donald Chapman; s of William Henry Chapman, of Barnsley, Yorks; *b* 25 Nov 1923; *Educ* Barnsley GS, Emmanuel Coll Cambridge (MA); *Career* sits as Lab peer in House of Lords; formerly memb Cambridge Borough Cncl, gen sec Fabian Soc 1949-53, MP (Lab) Birmingham (Northfield) 1951-70; res fell Nuffield Coll Oxford 1971-73, visiting fell Centre for Contemporary European Studies Univ of Sussex 1973; chm: HM Devpt Cmmrs 1974-80, Telford New Town Devpt Corpn 1975-87, Consortium Devpts Ltd 1985; co dir; economist, writer; *Style—* The Rt Hon the Lord Northfield; House of Lords, London SW1

NORTHLAND, Viscount; Edward John Knox; er s and h of 7 Earl of Ranfurly, *qv*; *b* 21 May 1957; *m* 1980 (m dis 1984), Rachel S, da of Frank Hilton Lee; *Style—* Viscount Northland; 48 Marville Rd, London SW6

NORTHMORE-BALL, Martin Dacre; s of Dr Godfrey Dacre Jennings Ball, of Warminster, Wilts, and Judith Marion, *née* Northmore (d 1979); *b* 14 Feb 1943; *Educ* Clifton, King's Coll Cambridge (MA), St Thomas' Hospital Med Sch (MB BChir); *m* 26 July 1969, Averina Constance Frances, da of Prof Sir Francis Gerald William Knowles, 6 Bt (d 1974), of Avebury Manor, Wilts; 2 s (Dacre b 1970 d 1975, Lawrence b 1986), 1 da (Laetitia b 1976); *Career* registrar Charing Cross and King's Coll Hosps 1973-76, sr registrar Addenbrooke's Hosp Cambridge 1979-81 (registrar 1975-78), clinical fell Univ of Toronto 1978-79; currently: conslt orthopaedic surgn and dir Unit for Jt Reconstruction Robert Jones and Agnes Hunt Orthopaedic Hosp Oswestry, conslt orthopaedic surgn Leighton Hosp Crewe; memb BMA, fndr memb Br Hip Soc, fell Br Orthopaedic Assoc, FRCS 1973, CIMechE; *Recreations* study of antiquities, books, travel; *Style—* Martin Northmore-Ball, Esq; Higher Grange, Ellesmere, Shropshire SY12 9DH (☎ 0691 623737); The Robert Jones and Agnes Hunt Orthopaedic Hospital, Oswestry, Shropshire SY10 7AG (☎ 0691 655311)

NORTHUMBERLAND, Archdeacon of; *see*: Thomas, Ven William Jordison

NORTHUMBERLAND, Duchess of; Elizabeth Diana; er da of 8 Duke of Buccleuch, KT, GCVO, TD, PC; *b* 20 Jan 1922; *m* 12 June 1946, 10 Duke of Northumberland, KG, GCVO, TD, PC, JP (d 1988); 3 s, 3 da (and 1 da decd); *Career* served WW II 1942-46 in the WRNS; *Style—* Her Grace the Duchess of Northumberland; Alnwick Castle, Northumberland NE66 1NG; Syon House, Brentford, Middlesex TW8 8JF; Clive Lodge, Albury, Surrey GU5 9AF

NORTHUMBERLAND, 11 Duke of (GB 1776); Henry Alan Walter Richard Percy; 14 Bt (E 1660); also Baron Percy (GB 1723), Earl of Northumberland and Baron Warkworth (GB 1749), Earl Percy (GB 1776), Earl of Beverly (GB 1790), and Lord Lovaine, Baron of Alnwick (GB 1784); eldest s of 10 Duke of Northumberland, KG, GCVO, TD, PC, JP (d 1988); *b* 1 July 1953; *Educ* Eton, ChCh Oxford; *Heir* br, Lord Ralph Percy, *qv*; *Career* landowner; pres: Alnwick and Dist Ctee for the Disabled 1981-, Northumbria Club, Alnwick Working Men's Club and Inst, Royal Northumberland Yacht Club, Northumbrian Anglers' Fedn, The Natural History Soc of Northumbria, Northumberland Assoc of Boys' Clubs, Tyne Mariners Benevolent Inst, Craster Branch RNLI; patron: The Berwick-upon-Tweed Preservation Tst, Assoc of Northumberland Local History Assocs, Int Centre for Child Studies (ICCS), N E Branch The Mental Health Fndn, Northumberland Bldgs Preservation Tst, Hounslow and Twickenham Branch of Arthritis Care; Jt Master Percy Hunt; pres N of England Cancer Research Campaign; vice pres Ancient Monuments Soc; pres Surrey Farming and Wildlife Advsy Gp; patron: Northern Counties Sch for the Deaf, Theatre West 4; FRSA; *Recreations* tennis, shooting, National Film Institute; *Clubs* Turf, Queen's; *Style—* His Grace the Duke of Northumberland; Alnwick Castle, Alnwick, Northumberland NE66 1NG (☎ 0665 2456); Syon House, Brentford, Middlesex TW8 8JF (☎ 081 560 2353); Clive Lodge, Albury Park, Guildford, Surrey GU5 9AF (☎ 048 641 2695)

NORTON, Hon Adam Gregory; yr s of 2 Baron Rathcreedan, TD; *b* 2 April 1952; *Educ* Wellington Coll, Lincoln Coll Oxford; *m* 1980, Hilary Shelton, da of Edmond Ryan, of Anchorage, Kentucky, USA; 2 da (Emily Beatrice Norton b 25 July 1984, Georgina Christine Ryan b 4 June 1988); *Clubs* Savile; *Style—* The Hon Adam Norton; 60 Marmora Rd, East Dulwich, London SE22 ORY

NORTON, Cyril Arthur John; CBE (1980); yr s of John Henry Norton (d 1939), of Hayes, Kent, and Louisa Alice, *née* Block (d 1970); *b* 13 Oct 1916; *Educ* Haberdashers' Aske's, Hatcham Sch; *m* 8 Dec 1945, Jacqueline Yvonne Monica, da of Frank Richmond-Coggan (d 1958), of Hayes, Kent; 1 s (Anthony b 1951 d 1980), 1 step s (Peter (Thompson) b 1944 d 1968); *Career* Nat Serv WWII cmmnd Queen's Royal Regt 1940, Maj 1943, serv NW Europe 1944-45; Cons agent: E Woolwich 1948-50, Battersea 1950-56; Cons Central Office Agent Northern Counties 1956-61, sec Gtr London Planning Ctee 1961-63, chief Central Office Agent Gtr London Area 1963-73; dir The Russell Partnership Ltd (public and Parly affrs advsrs) 1974-; chm Political Ctee Junior Carlton Club 1975-77 (vice chm 1973-75); Freeman: City of London 1937, Worshipful Co of Shipwrights 1937; Polonia Restituta (offr), awarded by Polish Govt in exile 1971; *Recreations* theatre, travel, watching cricket; *Clubs* Carlton, Army and Navy, MCC; *Style—* Cyril Norton, Esq, CBE; Flat 2, 7 Third Ave, Hove, Sussex BN3 2PB (☎ 0273 739823); The Russell Partnership Ltd, 16 Great College St, London SW1P 3RX (☎ 071 222 2096, fax 071 222 8550)

NORTON, Hon Elizabeth Ann; da of 2 Baron Rathcreedan; *b* 1954; *Educ* Benenden; *m* 3 Sept 1988, Alastair Scott, s of Prof James Scott, of Knaresborough; *Career* dir Supertravel Ltd 1989; *Recreations* skiing, food and drink; *Style—* The Hon Elizabeth Ann Norton; 35 Lancaster Road, London W11 1QJ

NORTON, Col (Ian) Geoffrey; TD (1963), JP (1973), DL (S Yorks 1979-); s of Cyril Needham Norton, MBE (d 1979), of 18 Slayleigh Lane, Sheffield, and Winifred Mary, *née* Creswick (d 1973); *b* 8 June 1931; *Educ* Stowe; *m* 4 April 1961, Eileen, da of Ernest Hughes, of 5 Normancroft Court, Sheffield; *Career* Nat Serv 1949-51, cmmnd RASC 1950, TA 1951-76, Hallamshire Bn York and Lancaster Regt 1951-67, Yorks Volunteers 1967-72, cmd 1 Bn Yorks Volunteers 1970-72, Dep Cdr (TAVR) NE Dist 1973-76, Regtl Col Yorkshire Volunteers, ADC to HM The Queen 1973-78; Hon Col: 1 Bn Yorkshire Vols 1989-, Univ of Sheffield OTC 1990-; chm: John Norton and Son (Sheffield) Ltd 1976- (md 1965-76), Chartan-Aldred Ltd (formerly Shirley Aldred and Co Ltd) 1976- (dir 1959-76); chm: Yorks and Humberside TAVR Assoc 1985-91, Friends of Sheffield Childrens Hosp 1979-85, St Georges Chapel Sheffield Cathedral 1982-; FInstD; *Recreations* pottering in the garden, music, reading; *Clubs* Army and Navy; *Style—* Col Geoffrey Norton, TD, JP, DL; 22 Cortworth Rd, Sheffield S11 9LP (☎ 0742 366304); Chartan-Aldred Ltd, Retford Rd, Worksop, Notts S80 2PS (☎ 0909 476861, fax 0909 500632)

NORTON, Hilary Sharon Braverman (known professionally as Hilary Blume); da of Henry Braveman (d 1986), of London, and Muriel, *née* Millin; *b* 9 Jan 1945; *Educ* LSE, Univ of Sussex; *m* 1, 5 Sept 1965 (m dis 1977), Prof Stuart Blume; 2 s (Toby b 22 Aug 1972, Joby b 12 July 1975); m 2, 25 July 1977, Michael Aslan Norton, s of Richard Michael Norton (d 1985); 1 da (Poppy b 15 June 1978); *Career* dir Charities Advsy Tst 1982-; tstee Finnart House Tst; *Books* Fund-raising: A Comprehensive Handbook, The Charity Trading Handbook, The Museum Trading Handbook, Charity Christmas Cards; *Style—* Mrs Michael Norton; Charities Advisory Trust, Radius Works, Back Lane, London NW3 1HL (☎ 071 7949835)

NORTON, James Henry Llewelyn; s of Adam Henry Williams Petre Norton, and Margaret Vera Vittery, *née* Stephens; *b* 16 Feb 1948; *Educ* Eton; *Career* Morgan Grenfell Gp plc; chm Morgan Grenfell CI Ltd, dir Morgan Grenfell and Co Ltd; *Recreations* architecture, skiing; *Clubs* Turf, Annabels; *Style—* James Norton, Esq; Colerne Manor, Chippenham, Wilts SN14 8AY; c/o Morgan Grenfell & Co Ltd, 23 Gt Winchester St, London EC2 (fax 071 588 5598, telex 8953511 MGLDN G)

NORTON, 7 Baron (UK 1878) John Arden Adderley; OBE (1964); s of 6 Baron (d 1961); *b* 24 Nov 1915; *Educ* Radley, Magdalen Coll Oxford; *m* 1946, Betty Margaret,

JP, da of late James McKee Hannah, of Domaine de Fontvieille, Aix-en-Provence; 2 s; *Heir* s, Hon James Nigel Arden Adderley; *Career* Lt RE 1940, served 1940-45, Maj 1944; Oxford Univ Greenland Expedition 1938, asst master Oundle Sch 1938-39; *Style—* The Rt Hon the Lord Norton, OBE; Fillongley Hall, Coventry, W Midlands (☎ 0676 40303)

NORTON, John Charles; *b* 22 April 1937; *Educ* Dulwich Coll, Univ Coll Oxford (MA); *m* 1962, Dianne, *née* Lloyd; 2 s (James b 1963, Adam b 1968), 1 da (Emma b 1966); *Career* ptnr Arthur Anderson & Co 1971- (joined 1961); ACA 1964, FCA 1974, FInstPet 1975; *Recreations* opera, rugby, travel; *Clubs* Brooks's, Vincent's; *Style—* John Norton, Esq; Arthur Andersen & Co, 1 Surrey Street, London WC2R 2PS

NORTON, John Lindsey; s of Frederick Raymond Norton (d 1981), of Burma, Woodcote Ave, Wallington, Surrey, and Doris Ann, *née* Jobson (d 1988); *b* 21 May 1935; *Educ* Winchester, Univ of Cambridge (MA); *m* 10 Oct 1959, Judith Ann, da of Arthur Bird; 3 da (Bridget Ann b 6 Dec 1960, Claire Elizabeth b 25 May 1963, Sophie b 6 April 1965); *Career* articled clerk Blackburn Robson Coates & Co 1959-63; BDO Binder Hamlyn: joined 1963, ptnr (specialist in taxation, fin advice, mergers, acquisitions and audit) 1966, nat managing ptnr 1981, chm Nat Partnership Ctee 1987-, chm BDO Binder (int firm) 1987; memb: Central Exec Ctee NSPCC 1989, Disciplinary Appeals Ctee ICAEW 1989; hon treas NSPCC 1991; ACA, FCA; *Recreations* tennis, gardening, walking; *Style—* John Norton, Esq; BDO Binder Hamlyn, 20 Old Bailey, London EC4M 7BH (☎ 071 489 9000, fax 071 489 6267)

NORTON, Mary (Mrs A L Bonsey); da of Reginald Spencer Pearson, and Minnie Savile, *née* Hughes; *b* 10 Dec 1903; *Educ* St Katherine's Convent East Grinstead Sussex; *m* 1, 4 Sept 1926 (m dis 1970), Robert Charles Norton, s of George Norton, of Quinta Das Aguas Livres, Bellas, Portugal; 2 s (Robert George b 24 May 1929, Guy b 21 Nov 1931), 2 da (Ann-Mary b 17 Sept 1927, Caroline b 22 Jan 1937); m 2, 24 April 1970, A L Bonsey (d 1989); *Career* WW II serv RN naval intelligence; children's writer; *Books* Bed Knobs and Broomsticks (1950), The Borrowers (1952, Carnegie Award, Hans Christian Honours Award), The Borrowers Afield (1955), The Borrowers Aloft (1961), The Borrowers Afloat (1975), The Borrowers Avenged (1982); *Recreations* theatre, show jumping, swimming, gardening; *Clubs* Lansdowne, Sloane; *Style—* Mrs Mary Norton; Town's End, West St, Hartland, N Devon EX39 6BQ (☎ 0237 441617); Aitken & Stone, 29 Fernshaw Rd, London SW10 0TG (☎ 071 351 7561)

NORTON, Hon Michael Adrian; s of 1 Baron Rathcreedan (d 1930); *b* 6 Aug 1907; *Educ* Wellington, Trinity Coll Cambridge (BA); *Recreations* foreign travel; *Clubs* Reform; *Style—* The Hon Michael Norton; 6 Carisbrooke Ct, 63/69 Weymouth St, London W1N 3LD (☎ 071 386 4756)

NORTON, Lady (Olive Penelope); MBE (1968); da of Col Arthur Mordaunt Murray, CB, MVO (gggs of 3 Duke of Atholl; d 1920) and his 2 w, Mabel, *née* Nicholson (d 1964); *b* 28 Jan 1908; *Educ* Royal School for Officers' Daughters Bath; *m* 1, 1928 (m dis 1942), Charles Russell Wood; 1 s (Peter b 1930); m 2, 1948, Sir (Walter) Charles Norton, MBE, MC (d 1974); *Career* many charity commitments; *Clubs* Hurlingham; *Style—* Lady Norton, MBE; 23 Hans Place, London SW1

NORTON, Prof Philip; s of George Ernest Norton (d 1987), and Ena Dawson, *née* Ingham; *b* 5 March 1951; *Educ* Univ of Sheffield (BA, PhD), Univ of Pennsylvania (MA); *Career* Univ of Hull: lectr in politics 1977-82, sr lectr in politics 1982-84, reader in politics 1984-86, prof of govt 1986- (youngest prof of politics in UK); memb Exec Ctee: Study of Parl Gp 1981-, Br Politics Gp in USA 1983- (pres 1988-90), Political Studies Assoc of UK 1983-89; assoc ed Political Studies 1987-; *Books* incl: The Commons in Perspective (1981), Conservatives and Conservatism (jtly, 1981), The Constitution in Flux (1982), The British Polity (1984, 2 edn 1990), Parliament in Perspective (1987), Legislatures (ed, 1990), Parliaments in Western Europe (ed, 1990); *Recreations* table-tennis, walking; *Clubs* Royal Cwlth Soc; *Style—* Prof Philip Norton; 30 Mizzen Road, Hull, North Humberside HU6 7AG (☎ 0482 807538); Department of Politics, Univ of Hull, Hull HU6 7RX (☎ 0482 465863, fax 0482 466366)

NORTON, Richard Glover; s of Ven Hugh Ross Norton (d 1969; chaplain Bde of Gds 1938-44, asst chaplain gen 1944-45, archdeacon of Sudbury 1945-58), and Jessie Muriel, *née* Glover (d 1965); *b* 1 Nov 1925; *Educ* Denstone Coll; *m* 1953, Philippa Margaret, da of Capt William Laurence Thompson Fisher (d 1968), of Billockby Hall, Norfolk; 2 s (Richard b 1959, George b 1962); *Career* Grenadier Gds 1943-47 Capt (Germany 1945-47); slr; ptnr Slaughter & May 1957-86, dir The Law Debenture Corp plc 1986-90; *Clubs* Cavalry and Guards, MCC; *Style—* Richard Norton, Esq; Burnham Wood, Welwyn, Hertfordshire AL6 0ES (☎ 043 879 254)

NORTON, Hon Richard William Brinsley; s of 7 Baron Grantley, MC, and Lady Deirdre Elisabeth Freda Hare, da of 5 Earl of Listowel; *b* 30 Jan 1956; *Educ* Ampleforth, New Coll Oxford (MA, pres Union); *Career* merchant banker; Conservative Research Dept 1977-81, cllr Royal Borough of Kensington and Chelsea 1982-86, Conservative candidate for Wentworth in 1983 general election; Kt SMO Malta, OStJ; *Recreations* Bridge; *Clubs* White's, Pratt's; *Style—* The Hon Richard Norton; 8 Halsey St, London SW3

NORTON, Robert; s of Ernest Robert Norton (d 1981), and Elsie Margaret, *née* Nix (d 1981); *b* 6 Jan 1941; *Educ* Downing Coll Cambridge, St Thomas's Hosp Med Sch (MA, MB BChir); *m* 29 July 1967, Ann Venetta Anderson, da of Romeo Alfredo Pazzi (d 1967); 2 s (Andrew b 20 Nov 1968, Christopher b 26 July 1970), 1 da (Colette b 23 Nov 1973); *Career* sr registrar in cardiothoracic surgery Edinburgh Royal Infirmary and City Hosps 1976-80; conslt cardiothoracic surgn West Midlands Regnl Health Authy 1980-; memb: Soc of Cardiothoracic Surgns, Br Cardiac Soc; FRCS 1972; *Style—* Robert Norton, Esq; Northfield, 6 Amherst Rd, Kenilworth, Warwickshire CV8 1AH (☎ 0926 57870); Walsgrave Hospital, Coventry CV2 2DX (☎ 0203 602020); Priory Hospital, Edgbaston, Birmingham B5 7UG (☎ 021 440 2323)

NORTON, Tom; TD (1966), JP (1961), DL (1962); s of Tom Norton, JP (d 1955), of Llandrindod Wells; *b* 15 April 1920; *Educ* Hanley Castle, Univ of Birmingham; *m* 1948, Pauline Fane, da of late A L F Evans, DIG Indian Police; 3 s, 1 da; *Career* joined TA (RA) 1939, served in WWII (despatches 1946), demobilised as Hon Capt 1946, cmmnd TA (REME) 1947; chm The Automobile Palace (Holdings) Ltd (dir 1947-); High Sheriff Radnorshire 1966; Queen's Silver Jubilee medal 1977; *Recreations* gardening, old cycles; *Style—* Tom Norton, Esq, TD, JP, DL; Sargodha, Brookfields, Cefnllys Lane, Llandrindod Wells, Powys (☎ 0597 822079)

NORTON, Prof Trevor Alan; s of Alan Norton, and Agnes, *née* Walsh; *b* 28 July 1940; *Educ* Blyth GS, Univ of Liverpool (BSc, PhD); *m* 26 July 1968, Win Marian; 1 s (Paul Martin b 1974), 1 da (Rachel Jane b 1971); *Career* Regius prof of marine biology Bergen Norway 1981, titular prof of botany Univ of Glasgow 1982-83, prof of marine biology Univ of Liverpool 1983-, dir of Port Erin Marine Laboratory 1983-; author of 150 res pubns; pres Br Phycological Soc, chm Aquatic Life Sciences Natural Enviromental Res Cncl; cncl memb: Marine Biological Assoc UK, Int Phycological; FRSE 1985, FIBiol 1987; *Books* The Zonation of Rocky Shores, in the Ecology of Rocky Coasts (1985), An Atlas of the Seaweeds of Britain and Ireland (1986), Marine Ecology in Biology of the Red Algae (1990), The Exploitable Living Resources of the Irish Sea (1990); *Recreations* writing, gardening, watching movies; *Style—* Prof Trevor Norton, FRSE; Whindyke, Bradda West, Port Erin, Isle of Man (☎ 0624 832027, fax 0624 835788)

NORTON-GRIFFITHS, Sir John; 3 Bt (UK 1922), of Wonham, Betchworth, Co Surrey; s of Sir Peter Norton-Griffiths, 2 Bt (d 1983), and Kathryn, *née* Schrafft (d 1980); *b* 4 Oct 1938; *Educ* Eton; *m* 1964, Marilyn Margaret, da of Norman Grimley of Liverpool; *Heir* bro, Dr Michael Norton-Griffiths; *Career* Sub-Lt RN; chartered accountant, pres Main Street Computers Inc 1980-; FCA; *Style—* Sir John Norton-Griffiths, 3 Bt; 17 Royal Drive, Bricktown, NJ 08723, USA

NORTON-GRIFFITHS, Dr Michael; yr s of Sir Peter Norton-Griffiths, 2 Bt (d 1983); hp of bro, Sir John Norton-Griffiths, 3 Bt; *b* 11 Jan 1941; *Educ* Eton, Keble Coll Oxford (BA, DPhil); *m* 9 Jan 1965, Ann, o da of late Gp Capt Blair Alexander Fraser, RAF, of Bath (whose mother was Joan, da of Blair Cochrane, OBE, JP, ggs of 9 Earl of Dundonald); 1 s (Alastair b 1976); *Career* dir Serengeti Ecological Monitoring Programme Tanzania 1969-73; ind environmental conslt Kenya 1974-76; md EcoSystems Ltd environmental conslts Kenya 1977-87; Sahel programme coordinator, International Union for the Conservation of Nature and Natural Resources (IUCN), East African regnl office Kenya 1987-88, coordinator Pan African environment monitoring network UN Environment Prog (UNEP) Nairobi 1989-90, coordinator UNEP/UNITAR (UN Inst for Trg and Res) African Programme Nairobi 1990-; *Books* Counting Animals (2nd edn, 1978), Serengeti: Dynamics of an Ecosystem (1979), The IUCN Sahel Studies 1989 (1989); *Recreations* flying, ballooning, deep sea fishing, snakes; *Clubs* Muthaiga Country; *Style—* Dr Michael Norton-Griffiths; Box 21791, Nairobi, Kenya

NORTON-SEALEY, John Evan; s of Clarence Norton-Sealey (d 1980), of Clevedon, Avon, and Amy Gwendoline, *née* Hodges (d 1965); *b* 19 Sept 1939; *Educ* St Nicholas Public Sch Clevedon Avon, St Davids Sch (now Millfield) Congresbury Somerset; *Career* sales mangr G E Taylor & Sons Bristol 1956, dir Rexmore (Taylor) Bristol 1984, divnl dir West England Rexmore Wholesale Ltd 1986, dir Covefold Ltd 1987; involved with Crimewatch for many years under Chief Constable Donald Smith of Avon and Somerset; life memb NATD, aux memb Nat Assoc Teachers of Movement and Dancing GB; hon memb Nat Geographic Soc Washington DC 1975; *Recreations* travelling extensively USA, USSR, Poland and Central America; *Clubs* Cadbury Ct Country (Yatton Bristol); *Style—* John Norton-Sealey, Esq; 37 Cecil Avenue, Bristol, Avon BS5 7SE; G E Taylor & Sons (RSW) Ltd, Wapping Wharf, Cumberland Rd, Bristol BS1 6UP (☎ 0272 291 616, fax 0272 250 616)

NORTON-TAYLOR, Richard Seymour; *b* 6 June 1944; *Educ* King's Sch Canterbury, Hertford Coll Oxford (BA), Coll of Europe Bruges; *Career* freelance journalist; positions 1969-73 incl: EEC corr Washington Post, writer The Economist, writer Financial Times, broadcaster BBC Brussels; The Guardian: corr Brussels 1973-75, corr Whitehall 1975-85, security and intelligence corr 1985-; contrib to various radio and TV progs on the intelligence services; Freedom of Information Campaign Journalist of the Year 1986; *Books* Whose Land Is It Anyway (1981), The Ponting Affair (1985), Blacklist (1988), In Defence Of The Realm? (1990); *Style—* Richard Norton-Taylor, Esq; The Guardian, 119 Farringdon Rd, London EC1R 3ER (☎ 071 278 2332, fax 071 239 9787)

NORWICH, Dean of; *see*: Burbridge, Very Rev (John) Paul

NORWICH, 2 Viscount (UK 1952); John Julius Cooper; s of 1 Viscount Norwich, GCMG, DSO, PC (Duff Cooper), sec of State for War 1935-37, First Lord of Admiralty 1937-38, min of Info 1940-41, and ambass to France 1944-47, and Lady Diana Cooper, *née* Manners (d 1986); *b* 15 Sept 1929; *Educ* Upper Canada Coll Toronto, Eton, Univ of Strasbourg, New Coll Oxford; *m* 1, 1952 (m dis 1985), Anne Frances May, da of Hon Sir Bede Clifford, GCMG, CB, MVO (yst s of 10 Baron Clifford of Chudleigh), and Alice, *née* Gundry, of Cleveland Ohio; 1 s, 1 da; m 2, 1989, Mary Mollie, da of 1 Baron Sherfield, GCB, GCMG, and former w of Hon Hugo John Laurence Philipps; *Heir* s, Hon Jason Cooper; *Career* author, broadcaster (as 'John Julius Norwich'); with FO 1952-64; chm Venice in Peril Fund, memb Exec Ctee Nat Tst 1969-; maker of some thirty programmes (historical or art-historical) for television; FRSL, FRGS; Ordine al Merito della Republica Italiana; *Books* two-volume history of Norman Sicily: The Normans in the South, The Kingdom in the Sun; two-volume history of Venice: The Rise to Empire, The Greatness and the Fall; Mount Athos, Sahara, The Architecture of Southern England, Christmas Crackers, Fifty Years of Glyndebourne, Byzantium: The Early Centuries, More Christmas Crackers; *Recreations* Venice, commonplace books; *Clubs* Garrick, Beefsteak; *Style—* The Rt Hon the Viscount Norwich; 24 Blomfield Rd, London W9 1AD (☎ 071 286 5050)

NORWICH, 70 Bishop of (cr 1091), 1985-; Rt Rev Peter John Nott; s of Cecil Frederick Wilder Nott (d 1956), and Rosina Mabel, *née* Bailey; *b* 30 Dec 1933; *Educ* Bristol GS, Dulwich Coll, RMA Sandhurst, Fitzwilliam Coll Cambridge (MA), Westcott House Cambridge; *m* 1961, Elizabeth May, da of Herman Philip Maingot (d 1942); 1 s (Andrew), 3 da (Joanna, Victoria, Lucy); *Career* Regular Army 1951-55, Lt RA; deacon 1961, priest 1962; curate of Harpenden 1961-64, chaplain and fell Fitzwilliam Coll Cambridge 1964-69, chaplain New Hall Cambridge 1966-69, rector of Beaconsfield 1969-77, bishop of Taunton 1977-85; *Recreations* gardening, sketching, fishing; *Clubs* Royal Cwlth Soc, Norfolk (Norwich); *Style—* The Rt Rev the Bishop of Norwich; Bishop's House, Norwich NR3 1SB (☎ 0603 629001)

NOSS, John Bramble; s of John Noss (d 1956), of Portsmouth, and Vera Ethel, *née* Mattingly; *b* 20 Dec 1935; *Educ* Portsmouth GS; *m* 6 July 1957, Shirley May, da of Harry Cyril Andrews (d 1986), of Portsmouth; 2 s (Steven John b 1961, Robin Philip b 1966), 1 da (Kim Caroline Graham b 1959); *Career* RAF 1955-57; Dip Serv: Br Embassy Beirut 1957-59, Br Embassy Copenhagen 1960-63, FO 1964, Russian language trg 1964-65, third (later second) commercial sec Br Embassy Moscow 1965-68, second commercial sec Br Embassy Santiago 1968-70, FCO 1970-73, first sec econ Br Embassy Pretoria 1974-77, first sec commercial Br Embassy Moscow 1977-78, FCO 1978-81, consul inward investmt Br Consulate Gen NY 1981-85, Br high cmmr honiara Solomon Islands 1986-88, dep head of Mission, cnsllr commercial and econ Br Embassy Helsinki 1988-; *Recreations* reading, photography, jogging, golf; *Style—* John Noss, Esq; c/o Foreign and Cwlth Office, King Charles St, London SW1A 2AH; Itäinen Puistotie 17, 00140 Helsinki, Finland (☎ 010 358 0 661293, fax 010 358 0 661342, telex 121122 A/B UKHKI SF)

NOSSITER, Prof Thomas Johnson; s of Alfred Nossiter (d 1989), of 28 Bransdale Ave, Guiseley, Leeds, and Margaret, *née* Hume; *b* 26 Dec 1937; *Educ* Stockton GS, Exeter Coll Oxford (BA), Nuffield Coll Oxford (DPhil); *m* Jean Mary, da of Irvin Clay of Marsden, W Yorks; 2 s (Thomas b 1976, William b 1978); *Career* Nat Serv Royal Signals 1956-58; LSE Univ of London: lectr 1973, sr lectr 1977, chm Bd of Examiners BSc external 1980-, reader 1983, chm of the working party on revision of BSc external 1983, chm Bd of Studies in Economics 1984-85, dean of Graduate Sch 1986-89, academic govr 1988- professorship in govt 1989-; state guest Kerala India 1977, visiting prof of politics Kerala India 1973 1977 and 1983, state guest W Bengal 1983, visiting res fell and acting dir of centre for TV res Univ of Leeds (lectr in social studies 1964); dir Sangam Books London, co-fndr Newlay Conservation Soc Leeds bdcasting, cmmnd evidence to Peacock Ctee 1986; memb Political Studies Assoc RIIA; *Books* ed: Imagination and Precision in the Social Sciences (1971), Influence, Opinion and Political

Idioms in Reformed England (1975), Communism in Kerala (1982), Research on Range and Quality of Broadcasting Services (1986), Marxist State Goverments in India (1988), Broadcasting Finance in Transition (with J G Blumler, 1991); *Recreations* gardening and walking; *Style*— Prof Thomas Nossiter; London School of Economics, Houghton St, London WC2A 2AE (☎ 071 405 7686, fax 071 242 0392, telex 24655 BLPES G)

NOTT, Brig Donald Harley; DSO (1941), OBE (1954), MC (1939 and bar 1942), DL (Worcs 1963); s of late John Harley Nott; *b* 27 April 1908; *Educ* Marlborough, Sandhurst; *m* 1, 1933 (m dis), Eve, *née* Harben; 1 da; m 2, 1947, Elfriede Eugenie, da of Maj Eugen August von Kahler, Imperial Austrian Army; 1 s, 1 da; *Career* serv 1939-45 Palestine, ME, Ethiopia; psc Canada, NATO Defence Coll Paris; asst Civil Defence offr Worcs 1959-69; Col The Worcestershire Regt 1961-67; Haile Selassie Mil Medal; OStJ; *Recreations* archery, fishing, shooting, painting; *Style*— Brig Donald Nott, DSO, OBE, MC, DL; Four Seasons, Battenhall Ave, Worcester (☎ 0905 354402)

NOTT, Rt Hon Sir John William Frederic; KCB (1983), PC (1979); s of Richard W K Nott, and Phyllis, *née* Francis; *b* 1 Feb 1932; *Educ* Bradfield, Trinity Coll Cambridge; *m* 1959, Miloska Sekol; 2 s, 1 da; *Career* served 2 Gurkha Rifles 1952-56, barr 1959, gen mangr S G Warburg 1960-66; MP (C) Cornwall St Ives 1966-83, min of state Treasy 1972-74; oppn spokesman: Trade 1976-79, Treasy and Econ Affrs 1975-76; trade sec 1979-81, def sec 1981-83; chm Lazard Bros 1985-90 (exec dir 1983-), dir Royal Insurance plc 1986-; *Style*— The Rt Hon Sir John Nott, KCB; 21 Moorfields, London EC2 (☎ 071 588 2721)

NOTT, Kathleen Cecilia; da of Philip A Nott (d 1932), and Ellen Cecilia Nott (d 1972); *Educ* Mary Datchelor Sch, Somerville Coll Oxford (BA), King's Coll London; *m* 1929 (m dis), Christopher Gervase Bailey; *Career* WWII ARP; poet, novelist, critic, philosopher; vice pres PEN English Centre (pres 1974-75), pres Progressive League 1960-62; poetry: Landscapes and Departures (1947), Poems from the North (1956), Creatures and Emblems (1960), Elegies and Other Poems (1981); novels: Mile End (1938), The Dry Deluge (1947), Private Fires (1960), An Elderly Retired Man (1963); philosophy and criticism: The Emperor's Clothes (1953), Philosophy and Human Nature (1982), A Soul in the Quad (1969), The Good Want Power (1977); general: A Clean Well-Lighted Place - A Private View of Sweden (1961); FRSL; *Recreations* playing the piano, gardening; *Clubs* University Women's, Society of Authors, PEN; *Style*— Ms Kathleen Nott; 17 Roman Crescent, Old Town, Swindon, Wilts (☎ 0793 52197)

NOTT, Rt Rev Peter John; *see* Norwich, Bishop of

NOTTAGE, Raymond Frederick Tritton; CMG (1964); s of Frederick Nottage, and Frances Nottage; *b* 1 Aug 1916; *Educ* Hackney Downs Secdy Sch; *m* 1941, Joyce Evelyn, da of Sidney Philpot; 3 da; *Career* dir gen Royal Inst of Public Admin 1949-78, memb Ctee on Trg in Public Admin for Overseas Countries 1961-63, vice-pres Int Inst of Admin Scis 1962-68, memb body of govrs Inst of Devpt Studies Univ of Sussex 1966-76, dep chm assoc of Lloyd's Members 1985-, chm The Bobath Centre 1987-; *Books* Sources of Local Revenue (with S H H Hildersley, 1968), Financing Public Sector Pensions (1975), Pensions - a Plan for the Future (with Gerald Rhodes, 1986); *Style*— Raymond Nottage, Esq, CMG; 36E Arkwright Rd, London NW3 6BH (☎ 071 794 7129)

NOTTINGHAM, Bishop of (RC) 1974-; Rt Rev James Joseph McGuinness; s of Michael McGuinness, and Margaret, *née* McClean; *b* 7 Oct 1925; *Educ* St Colum's Coll Derry, St Patrick's Coll Carlow, Oscott Coll Birmingham; *Career* ordained 1950, curate St Mary's Derby 1950-53, sec to Bishop Ellis 1953-56, parish priest Corpus Christi Parish Clifton Nottingham 1956-72, vicar gen Nottingham Diocese 1969, coadjutor Bishop of Nottingham and titular Bishop of St German 1972-; *Recreations* gardening; *Style*— The Rt Rev the Bishop of Nottingham; Bishop's House, 27 Cavendish Rd East, The Park, Nottingham NG7 1BB (☎ 0602 474 786, fax 0602 475 235)

NOULTON, John David; s of John Noulton, of 44 Littleton St, London SW18, and Kathleen, *née* Sheehan; *b* 5 Jan 1939; *Educ* Clapham Coll; *m* 7 Oct 1961, Anne Elizabeth, da of Edward Byrne (d 1985); 3 s (Mark John b 1963, Stephen Anthony b 1965, Simon Anthony b 1966), 1 da (Jane Antonina b 1968); *Career* asst princ Dept of Tport 1970-72, princ DOE 1972-76, private sec to Min of State Rt Hon Denis Howell, MP 1976-78, sec Property Servs Agency 1976-81, under sec Dept of Tport 1985-89 (asst sec 1981-85); dir Br Channel Tunnel Co plc 1982-89, chm Channel Tunnel Intergovernmental Cmmn 1989, dir Marine and Ports 1989, admin dir Transmanche Link 1989-, Friend of Richmond Park, memb Kingston Soc; MCIT 1986; *Recreations* walking, riding, boating, writing, music; *Style*— John Noulton, Esq; 12 Ladderstile Ride, Kingston Hill, Coombe, Surrey KT2 7LP (☎ 081 541 0734); Transmanche Link, Shearway House, Shearway Road, Folkestone CT19 4QU (☎ 0303 278978)

NOURSE, Christopher Stuart; s of Rev John Nourse, of Devon, and Helen Jane Macdonald, *née* Allison; *b* 13 Aug 1946; *Educ* Hurstpierpoint Coll Sussex, Univ of Edinburgh (LLB); *Career* legal exec Life Offices Assoc 1970-72; various managerial positions: Royal Opera House, English Opera Gp, Royal Ballet New Group 1972-76; gen mangr and admin Sadler's Wells Royal Ballet 1976-90, mgmnt Royal Opera House 1988-, admin dir The Birmingham Royal Ballet 1990; memb Hon Soc of Middle Temple; *Recreations* the performing and visual arts, the Orient, the countryside; *Style*— Christopher Nourse, Esq; Royal Opera House, Covent Garden, London WC2E 9DD (☎ 071 240 1200); Birmingham Hippodrome, Thorp St, Birmingham B5 4AU (☎ 021 622 2555)

NOURSE, Rt Hon Lord Justice; Rt Hon Sir Martin Charles; PC (1985); s of late Henry Edward Nourse, MD, MRCP, of Cambridge, and Ethel Millicent, da of Rt Hon Sir Charles Henry Sargent, Lord Justice of Appeal (*see* Sir Edmund Sargent); *b* 3 April 1932; *Educ* Winchester, Corpus Christi Coll Cambridge; *m* 1972, Lavinia, da of Cdr David Malim; 1 s, 1 da; *Career* 2 Lt (Nat Service) Rifle Bde 1951-52, London Rifle Bde Rangers (TA) 1952-55, Lt 1953; barr Lincoln's Inn 1956, memb Gen Cncl of the Bar 1964-68, jr counsel to Bd of Trade in Chancery Matters 1967-70, QC 1970, attorney-gen Duchy of Lancaster 1976-80, judge of the Courts of Appeal of Jersey and Guernsey 1977-80, judge of the High Court of Justice Chancery Division 1980-85, Lord Justice of Appeal 1985- ; kt 1980; *Style*— The Rt Hon Lord Justice Nourse; Royal Courts of Justice, Strand, London WC2

NOWAK, Krysia Danuta Michna; da of Sqdn Ldr Wladyslaw Jan Nowak (d 1982), and Henrietta Nowak; *b* 18 March 1948; *Educ* Notre Dame GS Sheffield, Henry Hartland GS Workshop, Ealing Coll London (BA), Garnett Coll Univ of London (PGCE); *Career* pt/t positions held at: The Drian Galleries London 1973, The Grabowski Gallery London 1973, Inst of Contemporary Art London 1973, 359 Gallery Nottingham 1974 (asst), Sheffield City Art Galleries 1975-87 (art educn offr); one woman expos: Drian Galleries, Waterloo Gallery, Stoke on Trent, Nottingham Playhouse, Crucible Theatre Sheffield, Philip Francis Gallery Sheffield, Worksop Library, Univ of Sheffield; public subway mural Hollywood Parade Sheffield; paintings in public and private collections; Br Cncl lectr Poznan Univ Poland 1977 and 1978; lectr American Inst of Foreign Study in Paris, Florence, Rome, Amsterdam and Munich 1979-82; voluntary work: League of Friends N Gen Hosp 1979-82, sec Polish Med Aid Appeal Sheffield 1981, organiser charity fashion show for Ethiopia Graves Art Gallery Sheffield 1985, organiser designer fashion show Wentworth House 1987; pres Worksop Soc of Artists 1976; Sheffield City Cncl: memb Cleansing Dept Keep Br Tidy 1985-87, dept of Land and Planning A City Centre for People 1985-87, arts designer and advsr Arundel Gate Scheme 1985-87; tstee York Arts Space Assoc 1986-87, fndr memb Anglo-Polish Soc Sheffield 1986-87, memb Open Learning Ctee BBC Radio Sheffield 1986-87; *Books* Poland (contrib), The Planet of the Towers (illustrator, 1982); *Recreations* painting, cooking, travelling, design (interior design and graphics), mural painting; *Style*— Miss Krysia Nowak; 4 Sycamore Close, Worksop, Notts S80 1XA

NOWELL, Peter Jack; s of Roger Nowell (d 1991), of Reading, and Suzanne Elisabeth Nowell; *b* 13 Oct 1948; *Educ* Reading Sch, LSE (MSc); *m* 1 May 1976, Wendy Margaret, da of Raymond Bonfield (d 1986); 2 da (Lucy b 1977, Emma b 1980); *Career* equity fund mangr Prudential Assur Co Ltd 1971-81, fixed income dir Prudential Portfolio Mangrs 1982-87, chief exec Prudential Corp Pensions 1988-90 (gp chief actuary 1991-); FIA 1974; *Recreations* skiing, squash; *Style*— Peter Nowell, Esq; Prudential Corporation, 1 Stephen St, London, W1P 2AP (☎ 071 548 3152, fax 071 548 3422)

NUGEE, Edward George; TD (1964), QC; s of Brig George Travers Nugee, CBE, DSO, MC (d 1977), and Violet Mary Brooks, *née* Richards, of Jacaranda Cottage, Binfield Heath, Henley-on-Thames, Oxon; *b* 9 Aug 1928; *Educ* Radley, Worcester Coll Oxford (BA, MA), Eldon Law Scholarship 1953; *m* 1 Dec 1955, Rachel Elizabeth Nugee, JP, *qv*, da of Lt-Col John Moritz Makower, MBE, MC (d 1989), of Hampstead Farmhouse, Binfield Heath, Henley-on-Thames, Oxon; 4 s (John b 1956, Christopher b 1959, Andrew b 1961, Richard b 1963); *Career* Nat Serv RA 1947-49 (office of COS Far East Land Forces, Singapore 1948-49), TA serv Intelligence Corps 100 APIU 1950-64, ret Capt 1964; called to the Bar Inner Temple 1955 (bencher 1976) ad eundem Lincoln's Inn 1968, poor man's lawyer Lewisham CAB 1954-72; memb: Bar Cncl 1961-65, CAB Advsy Ctee Family Welfare Assoc 1969-72, Ctee Gtr London CAB 1972-74, Mgmnt Ctee Forest Hill Advice Centre 1972-76, Cncl Legal Educn 1967- (chm bd of studies 1976-82), Common Professional Examination Bd 1976-89 (chm 1981-87), Advsy Ctee on Legal Educn 1971-90, Inst of Conveyancers 1971 (pres 1986-87); jr counsel to Land Cmmn 1967-71, counsel for litigation under Commons' Registration Act (1965) 1968-77; conveyancing counsel 1972-77 to: Treasy, WO, MAFF, Forestry Cmmn, MOD, DOE; Lord Chllrs Law Reform Ctee 1973-; conveyancing cncl of the Ct 1976-77, chm Ctee of Inquiry into Mgmnt of Privately Owned Blocks of Flats 1984-85; chm govrs Brambletye Sch 1972-77, memb Cncl Radley Coll 1975-, churchwarden Hampstead Parish Church 1979-83, Church Cmmr 1990-; *Books* Nathan on the Charities Act 1960 (jtly, 1962), Halsbury's Laws of England (3rd Edn Landlord and Tenant, jt ed 1958; Real Property, jt ed 1960; 4th edn Real Property, jt ed 1982); *Recreations* travel, history, church and family life; *Style*— Edward Nugee, Esq, TD, QC; 10 Heath Hurst Rd, Hampstead, London NW3 2RX (☎ 071 435 9204); Wilberforce Chambers, 3 New Sq, Lincoln's Inn, London WC2A 3RS (☎ 071 405 5296, fax 071 831 6803)

NUGEE, Rachel Elizabeth; JP (Inner London Thames 1971, dep chm 1985-); da of Lt-Col John Moritz Makower, MBE, MC (d 1989), and Adelaide Gertrude Leonaura, *née* Franklin (d 1984); *b* 15 Aug 1926; *Educ* Roedean, Lady Margaret Hall, Oxford (MA), Univ of Reading (Dip Social Studies); *m* 1 Dec 1955, Edward George Nugee, s of Brig George Travers Nugee, CBE, DSO, MC (d 1977); 4 s (John b 9 Nov 1956, Christopher b 23 Jan 1959, Andrew b 1 Oct 1961, Richard b 3 June 1963); *Career* Mothers' Union (voluntary serv): vice chm Central Pubns Ctee 1970-74, pres London Dio 1974-76, central (int) pres 1977-82, vice chm Central Social Concern Ctee 1983-85, rep Womens Nat Cmmn 1983-88, chm Bookshop Advsy Gp 1989-91; memb: House Ctee and Patients' Servs Ctee Royal Free Hosp 1961-72, London Diocesan Bd for Social Responsibility 1984-85 and 1987-90, Lord Chllr's Advsy Ctee on Conscientious Objectors 1986-, Inner London Family Panel of Magistrates 1991-; chm Edmonton area SR Policy Ctee 1987-90, tstee Marriage Res Fund 1984-; *Recreations* active support of church and family life; reading (especially history), visiting friends; *Style*— Mrs Rachel Nugee, JP; 10 Heath Hurst Rd, Hampstead, London NW3 2RX (☎ 071 435 9204)

NUGENT, Christopher George Ridley; s and h of Sir Robin George Colborne Nugent, 5 Bt; *b* 5 Oct 1949; *Educ* Eton, Univ of E Anglia; *m* 1985, Jacqueline, *née* Vagba; 2 s; *Style*— Christopher Nugent, Esq

NUGENT, Lady Elizabeth Maria; *née* Guinness; JP (Berks 1981); da of Maj Arthur Onslow Edward Guinness, Viscount Elveden and sis of 3 Earl of Iveagh; raised to the rank of an Earl's da 1969; *b* 31 Oct 1939; *Educ* Priorsfield Godalming Surrey; *m* 1960, David Hugh Lavallin Nugent, s of Sir Hugh Nugent, 6 Bt; 3 s, 1 da; *Recreations* racing; *Style*— The Lady Elizabeth Nugent, JP; Chaddleworth House, Chaddleworth, Newbury

NUGENT, Sir John Edwin Lavallin; 7 Bt (I 1795), of Ballinlough, Westmeath; JP (Berks 1962); a Count of the Holy Roman Empire; er s of Sir Hugh Charles Nugent, 6 Bt (d 1983), and Margaret, Lady Nugent, *qv*; *b* 16 March 1933; *Educ* Eton; *m* 1959, Penelope Anne, er da of Brig Richard Nigel Hanbury, CBE, TD, DL (d 1972); 1 s, 1 da (Grania Clare b 1969); *Heir* s, Nicholas Myles John b 17 Feb 1967; *Career* Lt Irish Gds; md Lambourn Holdings Ltd; High Sheriff Berkshire 1981; *Recreations* gardening, shooting, fishing; *Clubs* Kildare and University (Dublin); *Style*— Sir John Nugent, Bt, JP; Ballinlough Castle, Clonmellon, Navan, Co Meath, Ireland (☎ 010 353 46 33135)

NUGENT, John Michael; s of James Patrick Nugent, of 16 Sandford Rd, Sale, Cheshire, and Beatrice May, *née* Peart; *b* 26 Jan 1942; *Educ* Stretford GS, Univ of Manchester (BA (Econ)); *m* 1967, Kay, da of Thomas Thompson, of Barton Moss, Manchester; *Career* WCB Containers Ltd: sales dir 1971-72, md 1972-79, chm 1979-82; dir White Child & Beney Ltd 1973-80, chm White Child & Beney Group Ltd 1980-82; chm 1982-: The Stamford Group Ltd, Opto International Ltd, Opto International Inc, Mailbox International Ltd, Mailbox Mouldings Ltd, Micropol Ltd, Stamford Profiles Ltd, Topline Leisure Ltd; *Recreations* golf, cricket, supporting Manchester United, travel; *Clubs* Mellor and Townscliffe Golf; *Style*— John M Nugent, Esq; 38 Fernwood, Marple Bridge, Cheshire SX6 5BE (☎ 061 449 8567); Bayley St, Staly Bridge, Cheshire (☎ 061 330 6511)

NUGENT, Maisie, Lady; Maisie Esther; da of late Jesse Arthur Bigsby; *m* 1921, Capt Sir (George) Guy Bulwer Nugent, 4 Bt (d 1970); *Style*— Maisie, Lady Nugent; Bannerdown House, Batheaston, Bath

NUGENT, Margaret, Lady; Margaret Mary Lavallin; da of late Rev Herbert Lavallin Puxley, of The White House, Chaddleworth, Newbury, Berks; *b* 22 Jan 1911; *Educ* The Vyne Hants; *m* 28 Sept 1931, Sir Hugh Charles Nugent, 6 Bt (d 1983); 2 s; *Style*— Margaret, Lady Nugent; Cronk Ghennie House, Bowring Rd, Ramsey, Isle of Man (☎ 0624 812887)

NUGENT, Wing-Cdr Neil Algernon David; s of Maj Lionel Hugh Nugent (d 1970), and Coral Valentine, *née* Goudie; *b* 6 Nov 1926; *Educ* (DMS); *m* 27 April 1957, Diana Clare, da of Wing-Cdr Reginald George Burnett, MBE, of Emsworth, Hants; 2 s (Christopher, David), 3 da (Clare, Gail, Lindsay); *Career* RAF navigator RCAF Winnipeg 1954, 52 Sqdn Changi 1955, exchange duties 426 and 437 Sqdns RCAF Trenton 1960, Specialist Navigation RAF Coll of Air Warfare Manby 1964, Flight Cdr 511 Sqdn 1967, Sqdn-Cdr 53 Sqdn 1970; SO to: inspr of air transport servs 1973, C in

C's Ctee (home) 1973; co emergency planning offr Surrey 1983- (dep offr 1979-83); played hockey for Kent and S Eng 1950 and 1951, represented GB at the Olympic Games 1952 (Bronze medal), capt Hindhead GC 1988; *Recreations* golf, gardening, caravanning; *Style*— Wing-Cdr Neil Nugent; Cherry Tree, Linkside South, Hindhead, Surrey GU26 6NX (☎ 0428 604230); County Hall, 6 Penrhyn Rd, Kingston-upon-Thames (☎ 081 541 9160, fax 081 541 9005)

NUGENT, Hon Patrick Mark Leonard; 2 s of 13 Earl of Westmeath; *b* 6 April 1966; *Educ* Douai; *Style*— The Hon Patrick Nugent

NUGENT, Sir Peter Walter James; 5 Bt (UK 1831), of Donore, Westmeath; s of Sir Walter Richard Nugent, 4 Bt (d 1955); *b* 26 July 1920; *Educ* Downside; *m* 1947, Anne Judith, da of Maj Robert Smyth, of Gaybrook, Mullingar, Co Westmeath; 2 s, 2 da; *Heir* s, Walter Richard Middleton Nugent; *Career* 2 Lt Hampshire Regt 1941, and with 10 Baluch Regt in India, Maj 1945; Tattersalls Irish agent 1973-83; dir Tattersalls Newmarket and Tattersalls (Ireland) ret 1989; *Style*— Sir Peter Nugent, Bt; Blackhall Stud, Clane, Co Kildare (☎ 045 68263)

NUGENT, (Walter) Richard Middleton; s and heir of Sir Peter Walter James Nugent, 5 Bt; *b* 15 Nov 1947; *Educ* Downside; *m* Okabe Kayoko; *Career* fin dir (Keiri Torishimariyaku) IMS Japan Kabushiki Kaisha; FCA 1970; *Recreations* gardening, piano; *Style*— Richard Nugent, Esq; 61-66 Yaguchi-dai, Naka-ku, Yokohama, 231, Japan

NUGENT, Sir Robin George Colborne; 5 Bt (UK 1806), of Waddesdon, Berkshire; s of Sir George Guy Bulwer Nugent, 4 Bt (d 1970), of Bannerdown House, Bath; *b* 11 July 1925; *Educ* Eton, RWA Sch of Architecture; *m* 1, 1947 (m dis), Ursula Mary, da of Lt-Gen Sir Herbert Cooke, KCB, KBE, CSI, DSO (d 1936); 2 s, 1 da; m 2, 1967, Victoria Anna Irmgard, da of Dr Peter Cartellier; *Heir* s, Christopher George Ridley Nugent; *Career* Lt Grenadier Gds 1944-48; ARIBA; *Style*— Sir Robin Nugent, Bt; Bannerdown House, Bannerdown Road, Bath, Avon BA1 7LA (☎ 0225 858481)

NUGENT, Baroness; Rosalie; da of late Brig-Gen Hon Charles Strathavon Heathcote-Drummond-Willoughby, CB, CMG, 2 s of 1 Earl of Ancaster by his w, Lady Evelyn Gordon (2 da of 10 Marquess of Huntly); Brig-Gen Hon Charles Heathcote-Drummond-Willoughby m Lady Muriel Erskine, da of 14 Earl of Buchan; *m* 1935, 1 and last Baron Nugent (d 1973); *Career* is in remainder to Barony of Willoughby de Eresby; *Style*— The Rt Hon Lady Nugent; 40 Bramerton St, London SW3 (☎ 071 352 8861)

NUGENT, Sean Charles Weston; does not use title of Lord Delvin; s and h of 13 Earl of Westmeath; *b* 16 Feb 1965; *Educ* Ampleforth; *Career* computer programmer; *Style*— The Hon Sean Nugent

NUGENT OF GUILDFORD, Baron (Life Peer UK 1966), of Dunsfold, Co Surrey; Sir (George) Richard Hodges Nugent; 1 Bt (UK 1960), PC (1962), JP (Surrey 1941); yr s of Col George Roubiliac Hodges Nugent, OBE, RA (d 1935), of Churt, Surrey, and Violet Stella, *née* Sheppard (d 1966); *b* 6 June 1907; *Educ* Imperial Service Coll, RMA Woolwich; *m* 29 July 1937, Ruth, da of late Hugh Granville Stafford, of Tilford, Surrey; *Career* CC 1942, county alderman Surrey 1951-52; MP (C) Guildford 1950-66; Parly sec: Miny of Agric Fisheries and Food 1951-57, Miny of Transport 1957-59; sits as Cons in Lords, dep speaker House of Lords; chm: Thames Conservancy 1960-74, Select Ctee for Nationalised Industries 1961-64, Standing Conference on London and SE Regional Planning 1962-81, Nat Water Cncl 1973-78; past pres Assoc of River Authorities 1965-74; memb Diocesan Synod 1970-; pres Royal Soc for Prevention of Accidents 1985-88; chm Mount Alvernia Hosp Guildford 1987-; Hon Freeman Borough of Guildford 1985; DUniv Surrey; FRSA, Hon FIPHE; pres Univ of Surrey Soc; *Clubs* RAC; *Style*— The Rt Hon the Lord Nugent of Guildford, PC, JP; Blacknest Cottage, Dunsfold, nr Godalming, Surrey GU8 4PE (☎ 048 649 210)

NUNAN, Manus; QC (1962); s of Manus Timothy Nunan, (d 1979); *b* 26 March 1926; *Educ* St Mary's Coll Dublin, Trinity Coll Dublin; *m* 1, 1960 (m dis), Anne Monique, da of Jean Fradin (d 1978); 1 s (Manus b 1972), m 2, 1971 (m dis), Anne, *née* Harrison; 1 da (Nathalie b 1961); m 3, 1987, Valerie, *née* Robinson; *Career* called to the Bar King's Inns 1950, ad eundem Gray's Inn 1956; Colonial Legal Servs 1953-64: crown counsel Nigeria 1953-62, slr gen Northern Nigeria 1962-64, min of Govt and memb Exec Cncl of Northern Nigeria 1962; rec Crown Ct 1978-84; lectr 1986- on: Life and Trials of Oscar Wilde, Dr Samuel Johnson and his circle, Talleyrand; Evelyn Wrench lectr English Speaking Union of US 1988, visiting lectr Broward Community Coll Florida US 1989; lectr: American Irish Historical Soc NY 1990, Nat Portrait Gallery 1991; *Clubs* Kildare St and Univ (Dublin); *Style*— Manus Nunan, Esq, QC; La Calmeraie, Route de l'Aude, 09110 Ax les Thermes, France (☎ 61 64 24 93)

NUNBURNHOLME, 4 Baron (UK 1906); Ben Charles Wilson; s of 3 Baron Nunburnholme (d 1974), and Lady Mary Thynne (da of 5 Marquess of Bath); *b* 16 July 1928; *Educ* Eton; *m* 1958 (m dis), Ines Dolores, da of Gerard Walravens; 4 da; *Heir* bro, Hon Charles Thomas Wilson; *Career* Capt RHG 1953, Maj 1962, resigned 1969; *Style*— The Rt Hon the Lord Nunburnholme

NUNDY, Julian William; s of George William Nundy, of Fairlight, East Sussex, and Lilian, *née* Eckersley; *b* 3 March 1947; *Educ* Archbishop Tenison's GS, Univ of Nottingham (BA), Kiev Univ USSR; *m* 26 Nov 1976, Fabienne Sylvie Marie Christine, da of Joseph Moullot (d 1983), 1 da (Sophie Marie Chloë b 23 May 1985); *Career* Reuters: joined 1970, corr Moscow 1971-74, corr Paris 1975-80, chief corr Brussels 1980-81; bureau chief Cairo Newsweek 1981-83 (Beirut 1981), International Herald Tribune 1983-89 (news ed, copy ed, corr), asst foreign ed Independent on Sunday 1989-; winner Mary Hemingway award The Overseas Press Club of America for the best magazine coverage from abroad (Israeli invasion of Lebanon); *Style*— Julian Nundy, Esq; The Independent on Sunday, 40 City Rd, London EC1Y 2DB (☎ 071 415 1330, fax 071 415 1333)

NUNN, Antony Stuart; s of C Stuart Nunn (d 1974); *b* 24 May 1927; *Educ* Haileybury; *m* 1956, Pamela May, da of late William Hall, MBE; 2 da; *Career* marine underwriter, chm (dep chm 1980-81) Inst of London Underwriters 1982, dir Malvern Insurance Co Ltd 1978-, dir Kyoei Marine & Fire Insurance Co (UK) Ltd 1971-, dir Sirius Insurance Co (UK) Ltd 1978-, dep underwriter Lloyd's Syndicate, memb Lloyds 1970-71; *Recreations* golf, cricket, hockey; *Clubs* MCC, Sloane; *Style*— Antony Nunn, Esq; Shirlands, 158 Old Woking Rd, Pyrford, Surrey

NUNN, Dr Christopher Miles Hasler; s of Maj William Hasler Nunn, of Leics, and Eleanor Jean, *née* Spencer; *b* 8 Aug 1940; *Educ* Sedbergh, St Thomas' Hosp Univ of London (MB BS, MD); *m* 1 Jan 1964, Davina Beryl; 3 s (Mark b 1965, Miles b 1969, Charles b 1971), 1 da (Amanda b 1964); *Career* psychiatrist Repub of Zambia 1967-70, sr res assoc Univ of Newcastle upon Tyne 1970-72 (formerly psychiatric registrar), psychiatric advsr Dominica 1972, conslt psychiatrist Royal S Hants Hosp Southampton 1973-; MRCPsych 1972, FRCPsych 1986; *Recreations* sailing, medieval history; *Style*— Dr Christopher Nunn; 75 Northlands Road, Banister Park, Southampton SO1 2LP (☎ 0703 224635), Dept of Psychiatry, Royal South Hants Hosp, Southampton (☎ 0703 634288)

NUNN, Dr John Francis; s of Francis Nunn (d 1929), of Colwyn Bay, and Lilian, *née* Davies (d 1980); *b* 7 Nov 1925; *Educ* Wrekin Coll, Univ of Birmingham (MB ChB, PhD, MD); *m* 24 Sept 1949, Sheila Ernestine, da of Ernest Carl Doubleday (d 1952); 1 s (Geoffrey Francis b 1951), 2 da (Carolyn b 1954, Shelley (twin) b 1954); *Career* Nat Serv Colonial Med Serv Malaya 1949-53; Leverhulme res fell RCS 1957-64, prof of anaesthesia Univ of Leeds 1964-68, head of Div of Anaesthesia Clinical Res Centre MRC 1968-, dean Faculty of Anaesthetists RCS 1979-82, pres Section of Anaesthetists RSM 1984-85; hon fell: FARACS, FARCSI; FFARCS 1955, FRCS 1983, memb RSM; *Books* Applied Respiratory Physiology (3 edn, 1987), General Anaesthesia, (ed, fifth edn, 1989); *Recreations* Egyptology, geology, skiing, model engineering; *Style*— Dr John Nunn; 3 Russell Rd, Moor Park, Northwood, Middx HA6 2LJ; 17 Queen's Rd, Swanage, Dorset; Division of Anaesthesia, Clinical Research Centre, Harrow, Middx HA1 3UJ (☎ 081 864 5311)

NUNN, Rear Adm John Richard Danford; CB (1980); s of Surgn Capt Gerald Nunn, OBE, (d 1967), and Edith Florence, *née* Brown; *b* 12 April 1925; *Educ* Epsom Coll, RN Engrg Coll (BSc), RN Coll Greenwich (MSc), Downing Coll Cambridge (MPhil); *m* 1951, Katharine Mary, da of Leonard Paris (d 1970); 3 da; *Career* RN, served: Home Fleet and British Pacific Fleet 1945 (HMS Devonshire, HMS Vengeance 1947), Korean and Malaysian Emergency 1950 (HMS Amethyst), Mediterranean 1957 (HMS Tiger), Home Fleet and Far East 1967 (HMS Glamorgan); chief engr Sea Dart 1968-70, Cabinet Office 1970-73, NATO Defence Coll 1974-75, SACLANT 1975-78, Port Admiral Rosyth 1978-80, fell commoner Downing Coll Cambridge 1980, ed The Naval Review 1980-83; bursar and official fell Exeter Coll Oxford 1981-88; *Recreations* sailing (yacht 'Solenteer'), tennis, gliding, travel; *Clubs* Naval, Royal Naval Sailing Assoc; *Style*— Rear Adm John Nunn, CB; Warner's Cottage, Keepers Hill, Corhampton, Southampton, Hants SO3 1LL (☎ 0489 877287); 2 Sadler Walk, St Ebbe's, Oxford OX1 1DP (☎ 0865 244681)

NUNN, Peter George; s of Ernest Nunn (d 1983), of Ferndown, Dorset, and Greta, *née* Houlton; *b* 21 April 1946; *Educ* The County GS Wath-upon-Dearne S Yorks; *m* 10 Sept 1977, Joan Margearet, da of Lawrence Smith (d 1961), of Pinner, Middx; *Career* called to the Bar Lincoln's Inn; dir: Ingham Int (insur brokers) Ltd, Ingham Int (investmts) Ltd, Ingham Int (fin planning) Ltd, Paul Davies Hair Studios Ltd; FPMI; *Recreations* golf, horse racing, good food and wine, English 18th century porcelain, English Setters, flying; *Clubs* Alderney Flying, Alderney Golf; *Style*— Peter Nunn, Esq; Melbury, 8 Longis Road, Alderney, Channel Islands

NUNN, Trevor Robert; CBE (1978); s of Robert Alexander Nunn, and Dorothy May, *née* Piper; *b* 14 Jan 1940; *Educ* Northgate GS Ipswich, Downing Coll Cambridge (BA), Univ of Newcastle upon Tyne (MA); *m* 1, 1969 (m dis 1986), Janet Suzman; 1 s (Joshua b 1980); m 2, 1986 Sharon Lee, *née* Hill; 2 da (Laurie b 1986, Amy b 1989); *Career* prodr Belgrade Theatre Coventry, assoc dir Royal Shakespeare Co (chief exec and artistic dir 1968-78, chief exec and jt artistic dir 1978-86); dir: Cats (worldwide) 1981, Starlight Express (London and NY) 1984, Lady Jane (film) 1984, Les Miserables (London and worldwide, with John Caird) 1985, Chess (London and NY) 1986, Aspects of Love (London and NY) 1989; *Style*— Trevor Nunn, Esq, CBE; Homevale Ltd, Third Floor, 140A Gloucester Mansions, Cambridge Circus, London WC2H 8HD (☎ 071 240 5435, fax 071 240 1945)

NUNNELEY, Charles Kenneth Roylance; s of Robin Michael Charles Nunneley, of Edgefield, Norfolk, and Patricia Mary, *née* Roylance, of Pluckley, Kent; *b* 3 April 1936; *Educ* Eton; *m* 1961, Catherine Elizabeth Armstrong, da of Sir Denys Burton Buckley, of 105 Onslow Square, London SW7; 1 s (Luke b 1963), 3 da (Alice b 1964, Clare b 1967, Frances b 1969); *Career* 2 Lt Scots Gds, served chiefly BAOR; chartered accountant (qualified 1961); merchant banker; dep chm Robert Fleming Hldgs 1986- (dir 1968), chm Save & Prosper Group 1989-; chm or dir of various other Fleming Gp cos; memb Court of Assts Worshipful Co of Grocers 1975- (master 1982-83), dep chm Clerical Medical and Gen Life Assurance Soc 1978- (dir 1974) dir: Monks Investmt Tst 1977-, Macmillan Ltd 1982-, Investmt Mgmnt Regulatory Orgn 1986-; chm Institutional Fund Mangrs Assoc 1989-; govr Oundle Schs 1975-; *Recreations* shooting, photography, tennis; *Clubs* Hurlingham; *Style*— C K R Nunneley, Esq; 19 Rosaville Rd, London SW6 7BN (☎ 071 381 6683); Fyfield House, Pewsey, Wilts SN9 5JS (☎ 0672 62588); office: 25 Copthall Ave, London EC2R 7DR (☎ 071 638 5858)

NUREYEV, Rudolf; s of Hamet Nureev and Farida Nureeva; *b* 17 March 1938; *Educ* UFA, Vaganova Sch attached to Kirov Ballet Leningrad; *Career* ballet dancer, choreographer, leading dancer Kirov Ballet 1958-61, defected at Le Bourget airport 1961, joined de Cuevas Grand Ballet 1961, debut in London in gala organized by Fonteyn 1961, debut with Royal Ballet London in Giselle 1962, since has appeared regularly with all leading ballet companies of the world, his repertoire ranging from classic to modern ballets; choreographic prodns include: La Bayadere (1963), Swan Lake, Raymouda (1964), Tancredi, Sleeping Beauty, Don Quixote (1966), Nutcracker (1967), Romeo and Juliet (1977), Manfred (1979), The Tempest (1982), Washington Square (1985); films: An Evening with the Royal Ballet (1963), Romeo and Juliet, Swan Lake, Le Jeune Homme et la Mort (1966), I am a Dancer (1982), Exposed (1983); artistic dir Paris Opera Ballet 1983-; *Recreations* music; *Style*— Rudolf Nureyev, Esq; c/o S A Gorlinsky Ltd, 33 Dover Street, London W1X 4NJ

NURNBERG, Walter; OBE (1974); *b* 18 April 1907; *Educ* GS in Berlin, Reiman Sch of Art Berlin; *m* Rita, *née* Kern; 1 s (Andrew b 16 Oct 1947), 1 da (Monica b 24 July 1942); *Career* photographer; banking and business admin 1925-31; advertising photographer London 1934-40; serv WWII in HM Forces 1940-44; freelance photographer (specialising in industl photography as a means of communication in the field of mktg and industl rels) 1945-; clients incl: Alcan (UK), Booker Bros, British Gypsum, English Electric Co, GEC, ICI, Mullard, Philips (Holland), Turner & Newall, Thomas W Ward, Wiggins Teape; exhibitions incl: Fotokina Cologne 1960, Science Museum London 1979, Staatsbibliothek Berlin 1984, Industrie Haus Essen 1985; architectural photography: The Enchantment of Architecture Kodak Museum London, RPS, RGS, Woburn Abbey, Lincoln Cathedral; became a naturalised Br subject 1947; teacher: PCL, Harrow Coll for Higher Educn; conslt Wolverhampton Coll, head Guildford Sch of Photography at W Surrey Coll of Art and Design 1968-74 (dir communication studies 1971), contributing ed Br Jl of Photography 1975-90; Hon FBIPP, Hon FRPS (Hood medallist); *Books* The Science and Technique of Advertising Photography (1938), Lighting for Photography (1940, 18 impressions), Baby the Camera and You (1946), Lighting for Portraiture (1948, 9 impressions), Pocket Wisdom of Photography (1950); *Recreations* music and travel; *Clubs* Reform; *Style*— Walter Nurnberg, Esq, OBE

NURSAW, James; CB (1983), QC (1988); s of William George Nursaw, and Lilian May, *née* Howell; *b* 18 Oct 1932; *Educ* Bancroft's Sch, Christ's Coll Cambridge (MA, LLB); *m* 29 Aug 1959, Eira, da of E W Caryl-Thomas (d 1968); 2 da (Margaret (Mrs Hallybone), Catherine); *Career* Nat Serv Flying Offr RAF; called to the Bar Middle Temple 1955; sr res offr Univ of Cambridge Dept of Criminal Sci 1958, joined HO 1959, legal sec Law Offices Dept 1980-83, legal advsr HO and NI Office 1983-88, HM procurator gen and treasy slr 1988-, bencher Middle Temple 1989; Liveryman Worshipful Co of Loriners; *Clubs* United Oxford and Cambridge Univ, MCC; *Style*— James Nursaw, Esq, CB, QC; Queen Anne's Chambers, Broadway, London SW1H 9JS

NURSE, Bramwell William Henry; s of Brig William Henry Nurse (d 1976), and Minnie Florence, *née* Whitmill (d 1983); *b* 19 May 1921; *Educ* St Dunstan's Coll Catford London; *m* 9 July 1949, Beatrice Annie, da of Brig William Frederick Curl (d

1973); 1 s (Gordon Bramwell b 1950), 1 da (Joy Beatrice (Mrs Humphries) b 1953); *Career* CA, gp md Howes Gp, hon treas Motor Agents Assoc 1981-86, former chm Peugeot/Talbot Dealer Assoc; chm: Morlwy Nurseries Ltd (Wicklewood), Plaxtol Bakery Ltd, SA Wood (confectioners) Ltd; FCA, FIOD; *Recreations* music, yachting; *Style—* Bramwell Nurse, Esq; 2 Yare Valley Drive, Cringleford, Norwich NR4 7SD (☎ 0603 52159)

NURSE, Prof Paul Maxime; *b* 25 Jan 1949; *Educ* Harrow County GS, Univ of Birmingham (BSc, John Humphreys meml prize), UEA (PhD); *m* ; 2 da; *Career* res asst Microbiology Dept Twyford Laboratories 1967, Royal Soc res fell Inst of Microbiology Univ of Bern Switzerland 1973, SERC res fell Dept of Zoology Univ of Edinburgh 1974-78 (advanced res fell 1978-80), MRC sr res fell Sch of Biology Univ of Sussex 1980-84, visiting prof Univ of Copenhagen 1981, memb Advsy Editorial Bd Jl of Theoretical Biology 1981, head of Cell Cycle Control Laboratory Imperial Cancer Res Fund London 1984-87, Fleming lectr Soc of Gen Microbiology 1985, Iveagh prof of microbiology Univ of Oxford 1987-, Florey lectr Royal Soc 1990, Marjory Stephenson lectr Soc of Gen Microbiology; author of almost 100 pubns in learned jls; speaker at over 200 seminars in res insts worldwide; speaker chm and organiser at over 30 int meetings and confs dealing with yeast molecular biology and genetics and cell cycle and growth control; memb: EMBO 1987, Ctee UK Genetical Soc 1987 (pres 1990-), EMBL Scientific Advsy Ctee 1989; FRS 1989; *Awards* CIBA medal UK Biochemical Soc 1990; *Style—* Prof Paul Nurse, FRS; Dept of Microbiology, Univ of Oxford, South Parks Rd, Oxford OX1 3QU

NURTON, Brig (John) Michael Anthony; OBE, MC; s of Francis John Nurton (d 1989), and Rhoda Winifred, *née* Morgan (d 1983); *b* 22 Jan 1940; *Educ* Wellington Coll, Trinity Coll Cambridge (MA); *m* 28 Oct 1972, (Elisabeth Ann) Annabel, da of J R Catchpole; 1 s (George b 22 Mar 1976), 1 da (Katherine b 9 June 1974); *Career* cmmnd Scots Gds 1961, 1 Bn Scots Gds in Far East and UK 1961-69, Staff Coll Camberley 1973, Cdr 9 Bn UDR 1981-83, MA to Dep Chief of Def Staff 1983-86, Cdr 56 London Bde 1988-91, dir IT strategy MOD 1991-; *Recreations* sailing, real tennis, skiing; *Clubs* Royal Yacht Squadron, Cavarly and Guards; *Style—* Brig Michael Nurton, OBE, MC; c/o Lloyds Bank, 6 Pall Mall, London SW1

NUSSEY, Dr Ian David; OBE (1988); s of Dr Adolf Marcus Nussey, and Susannah Rayner Nussey (d 1981); *b* 4 April 1936; *Educ* Bromsgrove Sch, Downing Coll Cambridge (MA, Engrg Assoc prize), Univ of Birmingham (PhD); *m* 1976, Gillian Patricia, da of Dr Thomas Russell Stevens; 1 da (Jessica Clare b 1977), 1 step da (Emma Frances Wiltshire b 1966); *Career* Lucas Industries 1958-62, IBM United Kingdom Ltd 1963-; contrib to various jls associated with mktg and info technol; various public service appts; visiting prof: Univ of Newcastle, Univ of Salford, Univ of Wales; vice pres Inst of Mfrg Engrs 1990; winner Sargent award Soc of Mfrg Engrs USA 1988; Freeman City of London, memb Worshipful Co of Engrs 1983; FEng 1985, FIMechE, FIMfgE, FBCS; *Recreations* gardening, theatre going, canal restoration, skiing, golf; *Clubs* Athenaeum; *Style—* Dr Ian Nussey, OBE; Cidermill Farm House, Ardens Grafton, nr Alcester, Warwickshire B49 6DS (☎ 0789 773356); IBM United Kingdom Ltd, PO Box 31, Warwick CV34 5JL (☎ 0926 332525, fax 0926 311345)

NUTLEY, Ronald Frank; s of Walter Francis Nutley (d 1987), of Tonbridge, Kent, and Lucy, *née* Sabin (d 1962); *b* 17 April 1932; *Educ* Sussex Road Sch, Tonbridge, London Coll of Printing; *m* 22 June 1957, Patricia, da of Charles James Percy Waghorn (d 1988), of 2 Priory St, Tonbridge, Kent; 1 da (Jennifer Jane b 1963); *Career* signaller 1 Bn Queen's Own Royal West Kent served Malaya 1950-52; BR engr, works and Personnel dir Brown Knight & Truscott Ltd 1972-80 (gen mgmnt 1955-80), md David Evans & Co, dir Sekers International plc 1982, chief exec Sekers Silks Ltd 1986, dir Richard Allan Scarves, ret with consultancies for the food and Agric Orgn UN and the UK Silk Indust; MIOP, FBIM, FInstD; *Recreations* reading, art and design, jogging, swimming, tennis, golf, community service; *Clubs* Tonbridge Lions, IOD, RAC; *Style—* Ronald Nutley, Esq; Aalsmeer, 13 Higham Lane, Tonbridge, Kent TN10 4JB (☎ 0732 351 017)

NUTT, John Allister; s of Henry Nutt (d 1976), and Frances Plowright; *b* 13 July 1933; *Educ* Worksop Coll; *m* 2, 1976, Jean Rosemary, da of Sir Arnold Hodson, KCMG (d 1942); 2 da, 2 step da; *Career* chm: SPP plc 1972-, Braithwaite Gp plc 1987-, Booker McConnell Engineering 1981-, dir Booker McConnell plc 1983-84; chm British Pumps Manufacturers Assoc 1978-81; memb Nat Econ Dvpt Office Pumps and Valves Sector Working Party 1976-81; FCA; *Clubs* Royal Commonwealth; *Style—* John Nutt, Esq; Filbert House, East Ilsley, Newbury, Berks RG16 0LG; office: Theale Cross, Reading, RG3 1JD (☎ 0734 425555, telex 848189)

NUTTALL, Beris Muriel; DL (Stafford 1974); da of Fred Nuttall (d 1975), of Holme View, 50 Delph Lane, Netherton, Huddersfield, and Dorothy, *née* France (d 1980); *b* 8 July 1924; *Educ* Holme Valley GS Huddersfield, Avery Hill Coll London (teachers certificate of Univ of London with distinction); *Career* school teacher, dep head Longton HS Stoke on Trent 1968-84, memb mgmnt Leonard Cheshire Home Sandbach 1970-; chm Staffs Branch Animal Health Tst 1982-; MCCEd 1958, FRSA 1960; *Recreations* philately, collecting commemorative ware, owner 1911 Swift Car 2 seater tourer; *Clubs* Veteran Car of GB, Swift (Owners), Lady Memb Yorkshire CCC, Shepley Croquet (Yorks); *Style—* Miss Beris M Nuttall, DL; 14 Little-Field, Trent Vale, Stoke on Trent ST4 5LR (☎ 0782 46162); Holme View, 50 Delph Lane, Netherton, Huddersfield (☎ 0484 665301)

NUTTALL, Christopher Guy; s of Derek Reginald Nuttall, of Northwich, Cheshire, and Doris Joan Bentley, *née* Johnson; *b* 16 Aug 1957; *Educ* Sir John Deane's GS Northwich Cheshire, UCL (BA); *Career* journalist; with: Warrington Guardian Series newspapers 1978-81, BBC Radio 1982-, foreign corr BBC World Serv 1988; appointed Sri Lankan corr for: BBC, The Guardian, The Economist 1988-; *Recreations* tennis, horse racing, travel; *Style—* Christopher Nuttall, Esq; 61 Chardmore Rd, London N16 6JA (☎ 081 806 3022); c/o BBC World Service News, Bush House, Strand, London WC2B 4PH (☎ 071 240 3456, telex 265781, fax 071 580 7725); Suite 901, Colombo Hilton, PO Box 1000, Colombo 1, Sri Lanka

NUTTALL, Rev Derek; MBE (1990); s of Charles William Nuttall (d 1956), of Codnor Park, Derbyshire, and Doris (d 1976); *b* 23 Sept 1937; *Educ* Somercotes Secdy Sch Derbyshire, Overdale Theol Coll Selly Oak Birmingham; *m* 24 July 1965, Margaret Hathaway, da of Rev Principal Arthur Lawson Brown (d 1984); 2 s (David b 2 May 1969, Andrew b 12 May 1971), 1 da (Alison b 30 March 1967); *Career* semi skilled industl work 1953-60, office clerk 1960-61, Theol Coll 1961-65, Ministry Falkirk 1965-67, ordained 1967, vice chm Central Scotland Branch The Samaritans, miny and community work Aberfan 1967-74, dir CRUSE Bereavement Care 1978-90 (nat organiser 1974-78), minister Windsor United Reformed Church 1990-; gen sec: Community Care Assoc, Church and Community Ctees; memb Exec of Int Fedn of Widow/Widower Organisations 1980-89, sec Working Pty on Social and Psychological Aspects of Disasters 1989-; FRSM; *Recreations* golf, reading, music; *Style—* The Rev Derek Nuttall, MBE; 10 Clifton Rise, Windsor, Berkshire (☎ 0753 854558); Christ Church United Reformed Church, William St, Windsor, Berkshire

NUTTALL, Harry; s and h of Sir Nicholas Keith Lillington Nuttall, 3 Bt; *b* 2 Jan 1963; *Style—* Harry Nuttall Esq

NUTTALL, (Margaret) Jean; da of James Nabb Rushton, of Anderton, Bolton, Lancs, and Anne, *née* Barritt (d 1978); *b* 24 Jan 1944; *Educ* Stand GS for Girls; *m* 11 Jan 1963, Peter Nuttall, s of Richard Nutall (d 1976); 1 s (Peter b 1963); *Career* dir and co sec Rushton & Barlow Ltd 1972-, dir JPN Engineering Co Ltd 1980-; gen sec Rossendale Ski Club 1978-80 (membership sec 1975-77), chm NW Ski Fedn 1984-87 (sec 1978-83), pres Eng Ski Cncl 1988-90 (vice pres 1984-87); *Recreations* skiing, gardening; *Style—* Mrs Jean Nuttall; 252 Turton Rd, Tottington, nr Bury, Lancs BL8 4AJ; Rushton & Barlow Ltd, Albion St, Elton, Bury, Lancs BOL8 2AD (☎ 061 7641108, fax 061 7640967)

NUTTALL, Sir Nicholas Keith Lillington; 3 Bt (UK 1922), of Chasefield, Parish of Bowdon, Co Chester; s of Lt-Col Sir (Edmund) Keith Nuttall, 2 Bt (d on active service 1941); *b* 21 Sept 1933; *Educ* Eton, RMA Sandhurst; *m* 1, 1960 (m dis 1971), Rosemary Caroline, da of Christopher York, DL, sometime MP for Ripon (whose mother was Violet, er da of Rt Hon Sir Frederick Milner, 7 Bt, and whose paternal ggf's mother was Lady Mary Lascelles, yst da of 1 Earl of Harewood), of Long Marston Manor, Long Marston; 1 s, 1 da; m 2, 1971, Julia Jill, da of Thomas Williamson; m 3, 1975 (m dis 1983), Miranda Elizabeth Louise, former w of late Peter Sellers, CBE, the actor, and da of Richard Quarry by his former w Diana, who m, 1951, 2 Baron Mancroft; 3 da (Gytha Miranda b 1975, Amber Louise b 1976, Olympia Jubilee b 1977); m 4, 1983, Eugenie Marie Alicia, eldest da of William Thomas McWeeney; 1 s (Alexander b 1985); *Heir* s, Harry Nuttall; *Career* Maj RHG, ret 1968; *Clubs* White's; *Style—* Sir Nicholas Nuttall, Bt; PO Box N7776, Nassau, Bahamas (☎ 809 32 67938)

NUTTALL, Peter Scott; s of Dr John Ramsbottom Nuttall (d 1986), of Pool-in-Wharfedale, Yorks, and Alice, *née* Bradford; *b* 25 June 1934; *Educ* Oakham Sch, Worcester Coll Oxford (MA); *m* 1, 1959, Sylvia, da of Harold Barker, of Bilbrough, York; 1 s (Mark b 1962), 1 da (Katie b 1961); m 2, 1983, Sheila Mary, da of Edwin Wilson, of Grimsby, Lancs; *Career* md Kitcat & Aitken 1986-88 (sr ptnr 1982-86), chm RBC Kitcat Ltd 1986-90, vice chm Carr Kitcat & Aitken Ltd 1990-, vice chm RBC Dominion Securities International Ltd 1988-90; *Recreations* walking, cricket; *Style—* Peter Nuttall, Esq; Old Beams, Whitchurch, Aylesbury, Bucks (☎ 0296 641167); No 1 London Bridge, London SE1 9TJ (☎ 071 528 0100, telex 8956121, fax 071 403 0755)

NUTTALL, Richard Wardleworth; s of Henry Clarence Wardleworth Nuttall (d 1972); *b* 20 Oct 1927; *Educ* Marlborough, St John's Coll Cambridge (MA); *m* 1953, Veryll Bambury, da of William Sever (d 1972); 1 s (David), 3 da (Fiona, Veronica, Heather); *Career* fin conslt, former dir: RTZ Sales Ltd, RTZ Servs Ltd, Alreco Ltd, RTZ Metals Ltd (dep md), RTZ Metals Stockholding Ltd (md), Devon Boats Ltd (chm and md), Haven Assocs Ltd; *Recreations* gardening, athletics; *Style—* Richard Nuttall, Esq; Stoke Vale Cottage, Stoke Canon, Exeter EX5 4EE (☎ 0392 841610)

NUTTALL, (Benjamin William) Stuart; MBE (1990), JP (Chesterfield); s of William Nuttall (d 1972), and Eleanor, *née* Broomhead; *b* 14 Jan 1933; *Educ* Lady Manners GS Bakewell, Leicester Coll of Advanced Technol, Chesterfield Coll of Technol; *m* 19 Feb 1955, Eileen Margaret, da of Francis Joseph Eady (d 1977); 2 da (Jacqueline (Mrs Thornhill) b 24 April 1958, Caroline (Mrs Ludlam) b 8 Oct 1959); *Career* Nat Serv RAF 1951-53; mgmnt trainee to prodn mangr heavy tube div Tube Investmts Ltd 1953-66, prodn mangr Cable Div Aerialite Ltd 1966-68, plant mangr Corby Tube Works 1968-70, dep md USI Engrg 1970-72, md The Clay Cross Co 1972-; currently: chm and chief exec Biwater Industries Ltd, corporate dir Biwater Ltd; dir: Chesterfield and N Derbys C of C, Br Cast Iron Res Assoc; nat chm Br Foundry Assoc, vice-pres Chesterfield and Dist Bowls Assoc; pres: Clay Cross div St John's Ambulance Bde, Biwater Pipes and Casting sports clubs; memb Worshipful Co of Founders, Freedom City of London 1988; CEng 1977, FIProdE 1960, FIBF 1977, FIQ 1982, FIIM 1979, FInstD 1985; *Recreations* motor sport, horse breeding, various sporting activities; *Clubs* Aston Martin Owners, RAC; *Style—* Stuart Nuttall, Esq, MBE, JP; The Spinney, Ashover Rd, Woolley Moor, Derbys DE5 6FF (☎ 0246 590266); Biwater Industries Ltd, Clay Cross, Chesterfield, Derbys S45 9NG (☎ 0246 250740, fax 0246 250741, telex 547903, car 0860 622329)

NUTTER, Thomas Albert; s of Christopher Nutter (d 1983), and Dorothy Lucy, *née* Banister; *b* 17 April 1943; *Educ* Camrose Sch Edgware, Willesden Tech Coll; *Career* clothes designer, made-to-measure tailor, menswear retailer; opened own shop in Savile Row 1969, clients included: the Beatles (three of whom wore his suits in the Road album cover), Mick and Bianca Jagger, Eric Clapton; designer Lincroft Kilgour Gp 1977, launched first major ready-to-wear collection for Austin Reed shops designer for Daido Worsted Mills (and the Milliontex Corpn) 1980, went solo again with shop in Savile Row 1982, customers today (apart from those already named) incl: Lord Montagu Beaulieu, Elton John, Peter Bowles, Sir Roy Strong, John Schlesinger; most recently tailored the Joker costumes for Jack Nicholson in the Batman 1989; memb: Fedn of Master Tailors, Master Craftsman Assoc; *Style—* Thomas Nutter, Esq; Flat 3, 26-27 Conduit St, London W1R 9TA; 19 Savile Row, London W1X 2EB (☎ 071 734 0831)

NUTTGENS, Patrick John; CBE (1982); s of Joseph Edward Nuttgens (d 1982), and Kathleen Mary, *née* Clarke (d 1937); *b* 2 March 1930; *Educ* Ratcliffe Coll Leicester, Univ of Edinburgh (MA, PhD), Edinburgh Coll of Art (DipArch); *m* 21 Aug 1954, Bridget Ann, da of Dr Alexander Guthrie Badenoch (d 1964), of Edinburgh; 5 s (Nicholas, James, Giles, Alexander, Tom) 3 da (Lucy, Susan, Peggy); *Career* lectr Univ of Edinburgh 1957-62, prof Univ of York 1968-70 (reader 1962-68), dir Leeds Poly 1970-86; chm York Georgian Soc 1970- (sec 1962-70); Royal Cmmn on Historical Monuments for Scotland, Royal Fine Art Cmmn 1983-90; DUniv: York 1985, Open Univ 1985; DLitt: Univ of Sheffield 1985, Heriot Watt Univ 1990; ARIBA, FRSA, ARIAS; *Books* Landscape of Ideas (1972), York the Continuing City (1974), Leeds (1979), Mitchell Beazley Pocket Guide to Architecture (1980), Story of Architecture (1983), Understanding Modern Architecture (1988), What Should We Teach And How Should We Teach It? (1988), The Home Front (1989); *Recreations* reading, writing, drawing, broadcasting; *Clubs* Yorkshire; *Style—* Patrick Nuttgens, Esq, CBE; Roselea Cottage, Terrington, York, YO6 4PP (☎ 065 384 408); University of York, The Kings Manor, York

NUTTING, Rt Hon Sir (Harold) Anthony; 3 Bt (UK 1902), of St Helens, Booterstown, Co Dublin, PC (1954); s of Lt-Col Sir Harold Stansmore Nutting, 2 Bt (d 1972); *b* 11 Jan 1920; *Educ* Eton, Trinity Coll Cambridge; *m* 1, 1941 (m dis 1959), Gillian Leonora, da of Edward Joliffe Strutt (3 s of Hon Edward Strutt, CH, 5 s of 2 Baron Rayleigh); 2 s (John, *qv*, David b 1944), 1 da (Zara Nina, b 1947, m 1966 Martin Stephenson); m 2, 1961, Anne Gunning (d 1990), da of Arnold Barthrop Parker, of Cuckfield, Sussex; *Heir* s, John Grenfell Nutting; *Career* served in Leicestershire Yeo 1939-40, served in HM Foreign Service in France, Spain and Italy 1940-45; MP (C) Leics 1945-56, jt Parly under sec state for Foreign Affairs 1951-54, min state 1954-56, ldr UK Delegation to UN Assembly and to UN Disarmament Cmmn 1954-56; resigned 1956; chm: Young Conservative Movement 1946, Cons Nat Union 1950, Cons NEC 1951; special writer New York Herald Tribune 1957-59; author; *Books* Lawrence of Arabia (1961), The Arabs (1964), Gordon of Khartoum (1966), No End of a Lesson (1967), Scramble for Africa (1968), Nasser (1972); *Style—* The Rt Hon Sir Anthony Nutting, Bt; Achentoul, Kinbrace, Sutherland

NUTTING, David Anthony; DL (Essex 1988); yr s of Rt Hon Sir (Harold) Anthony

Nutting, 3 Bt, *qv*; *b* 13 Sept 1944; *Educ* Eton, Trinity Coll Cambridge (MA); *m* 25 April 1974, Tessa Anne, o da of Sir Nigel John Mordaunt, 13 Bt, MBE (d 1979); 3 da (Belinda b 18 Aug 1975, Serena b 24 Nov 1977, Alexandra b 27 Dec 1978); *Career* chm: Strutt & Parker (Farms) Ltd 1987-, Select Sires Ltd 1982-89; dir: Lord Rayleigh's Dairies Ltd 1970, Bridge Farm Dairies Ltd 1987-; chm: Essex Agric Soc, Br Cattle Breeders Club 1978-79; memb Advsy Bd Inst of Animal Physiology 1983-86; pres Holstein Friesian Soc 1990; memb Freeman Worshipful Co of Farmers 1975; *Recreations* fishing, shooting, racing; *Style—* David Nutting, Esq, DL; Whitelands, Hatfield Peverel, Chelmsford, Essex CM3 2AG (☎ 0245 380372)

NUTTING, Prof Jack; s of Edgar Nutting (d 1973), of Mirfield, W Yorkshire, and Ethel, *née* France (d 1985); *b* 8 June 1924; *Educ* Univ of Leeds (BSc, PhD), Univ of Cambridge (MA, ScD); *m* 4 Sept 1950, Thelma, da of Thomas Kippax (d 1967), of Morecambe; 1 s (Peter Robert b 1961), 2 da (Alison Rosemary (Mrs Murray) b 1953, Jean Ruth (Mrs Tyson) b 1957); *Career* lectr Dept of Metallurgy Univ of Cambridge 1954-60 (demonstrator 1949-54); Univ of Leeds: prof of metallurgy and head of dept 1960-89, emeritus prof 1989; former pres: Inst of Metallurgists, The Metals Soc, Hist Metallurgy Soc; pres Richard Thorpe Soc Mirfield His; Awards: Beilby Medal and Prize 1964, Hatfield Medal and Prize 1967, Platinum Medal 1988; Hon SDc Acad Mining and Metallurgy Krakow Poland 1969, Hon DSc Univ of Moratuwa Sri Lanka; FIM 1960, FEng 1981; *Books* The Microstructure of Metals (1965); *Recreations* walking, photography, cooking, gardening; *Style—* Prof Jack Nutting; 57 Weetwood Lane, Leeds LS16 5NP, West Yorkshire (☎ 0532 751400); School of Materials, Division of Metallurgy, University of Leeds, Leeds LS2 9JT, West Yorkshire (☎ 0532 332349, fax 0532 422531, telex UNILDSG 556473)

NUTTING, John Grenfell; s and h of Rt Hon Sir (Harold) Anthony Nutting, 3 Bt, *qv*; *b* 28 Aug 1942; *Educ* Eton, McGill Univ Canada (BA); *m* 1973, Diane, da of Capt Duncan Kirk, and widow of 2 Earl Beatty; 1 s, 1 da, 1 step s, 1 step da; *Career* barr Middle Temple 1968; sr treasy counsel 1988- (jr treasy counsel 1981, first jr treasy counsel 1987-88), rec of the Crown Court 1986-; memb Bar Cncl 1976-80 and 1986-87, chm Young Bar 1978-79; *Clubs* White's; *Style—* John Nutting, Esq; 3 Raymond Buildings, Gray's Inn, London WC2; Chicheley Hall, Newport Pagnell, Bucks MK16 9JJ; K3, Albany, Piccadilly, London

NUTTING, Peter Robert; JP (Inner London 1978); s of Capt Arthur Ronald Stansmore Nutting, OBE, MC (d 1964), of N Breache Manor, Ewhurst, and Patricia Elizabeth, *née* Jameson; *b* 22 Oct 1935; *Educ* Cheam, Eton; *m* 1965, Cecilia Hester Marie-Louise, da of Cosmo Rea Russell, of Parapet House, Lenham, Kent; 2 s, 1 da; *Career* Lt Irish Gds, Suez Canal 1955-56; stockbroker; ptnr W I Carr & Sons Co 1963-67, last chm E & J Burke Ltd 1965-68 (gf, Sir John Nutting, 1 Bt, was fi chm); chm Travel and General Insurance Co plc; dir of other public and private cos; memb Cncl Lloyd's; landowner (350 acres); *Recreations* shooting, fishing, tennis, golf, sailing; *Clubs* Royal Yacht Squadron, Boodle's, Pratt's; *Style—* Peter Nutting, Esq, JP; North Breache Manor, Ewhurst, Surrey (☎ 0483 277328); 103 More Close, St Pauls Court, London W14 (☎ 081 846 9734)

NYE, Prof John Frederick; s of Hadyn Percival Nye, MC (d 1977), of Hove and Old Marston, and Jessie Mary, *née* Hague (d 1950); *b* 26 Feb 1923; *Educ* Stowe, King's Coll Cambridge (MA, PhD); *m* 28 Dec 1953, Georgiana, da of Walter Ernest Wiebenson, of Bellingham, Washington, USA; 1 s (Stephen b 1960), 2 da (Hilary b 1957, Carolyn b 1963); *Career* univ demonstrator Dept of Mineralogy Univ of Cambridge 1949-51, memb Tech Staff Bell Telephone Labs N Jersey USA 1952-53; Univ of Bristol: lectr 1953-65, reader 1965-69, prof 1969-85, Melville Wills prof of physics 1985-88, emeritus prof 1988-; pres: Int Glaciological Soc 1966-69, Int Cmmn of Snow and Ice 1971-75; Antarctic Serv medal USA 1974; FRS, 1976, foreign memb Royal Swedish Acad of Sci; *Books* Physical Properties of Crystals (2 edn, 1985); *Recreations* gardening; *Style—* Prof John Nye, FRS; 45 Canynge Rd, Bristol BS8 3LH (☎ 0272 733769); H H Wills Physics Laboratory, Tyndall Ave, Bristol BS8 1TL (☎ 0272 303030)

NYE, Robert Thomas; s of Oswald William Nye (d 1990), of Southend-on-Sea, Essex, and Frances Dorothy, *née* Weller; *b* 15 March 1939; *Educ* Southend HS; *m* 1, 1959 (m dis 1967), Judith Pratt; 3 s (Jack, Taliesin, Malory); m 2, 1968, Aileen, da of Robert Campbell (d 1972), of Whang House, Beith, Ayrshire; 1 da (Rebecca), 1 step s (Owen), 1 step da (Sharon); *Career* poet, novelist and critic; reviewer of new fiction The Guardian 1966-, poetry ed The Scotsman 1967-, poetry critic The Times 1971-; Eric Gregory award 1963, Guardian Fiction prize 1976, Hawthornden prize 1977; *Publications* poems: Juvenilia 1 (1961), Juvenilia 2 (1963), Darker Ends (1969), Divisions on a Ground (1976), A Collection of Poems 1955-88 (1989); novels: Doubtfire (1967), Falstaff (1976), Merlin (1978), Faust (1980), The Voyage of the Destiny (1982), The Memoirs of Lord Byron (1989), The Life and Death of My Lord Gilles de Rais (1990); short stories: Tales I Told My Mother (1969), The Facts of Life and Other Fictions (1983); editions: A Choice of Sir Walter Raleigh's Verse (1972), William Barnes of Dorset; A Selection of his Poems (1973), A Choice of Swinburne's Verse (1973), The Faber Book of Sonnets (1976), The English Sermon 1750-1850 (1976), PEN New Poetry (1986); *Recreations* gambling; *Style—* Robert Nye, Esq; Anthony Sheil Assocs, 43 Doughty St, London WC1N 2LF

NYMAN, Dr Cyril Richard; s of James Nyman (d 1955), and Rose Caroline, *née* James; *b* 19 May 1943; *Educ* The GS Malmesbury Wilstshire, Univ of London (MB BS, LRCP, MRCS); *m* 6 June 1970, Jill Elizabeth, da of Robert Charles Ricketts; 1 da (Sarah b 1976); *Career* HS professorial surgical unit St Mary's Hosp London 1968, registrar gen and thoracic med St Thomas's Hosp London 1971-78, sr registrar cardiorespiratory med St Mary's Hops 1975-709, conslt physician in cardiorespiratory med pilgrim Hosp Lincs 1979-; chm: Pilgrim Scanner Appeal, Pilgrim Heart and Lung Fund; pre Boston Branch Br Hearth Fndn, memb: Br Lung Fndn, Br Cardiac Soc, Br Thoracic Soc; DRCOG 1970, MRCP 1971, FRCP 1987; *Books* Some Common Medical Disorders (1988), Heart and Lung Disease (1989); *Recreations* swimming, jogging, shooting, archery, music; *Clubs* London Rd Runners, Br Marathaon, Boston Swimming; *Style—* Dr Cyril Nyman; Stoke Lodge, 116 Tower Road, Boston, Lincolnshire PE21 9AU (☎ 0205 317148), Pilgrim Hosp, Sibsey Rd, Boston Lincs PE21 9QS (☎ 0205 364801)

O

O'BOYLE, Patrick John; s of James O'Boyle, of Glasgow, Scotland, and Elizabeth, *née* Dunlop (d 1980); *b* 12 April 1941; *Educ* St Aloysius Coll Glasgow, Univ of Glasgow (MB ChB); *m* 4 Sept 1967, Emilia Maria, *née* Galli; 1 s (Stephen James b 26 1973), 1 da (Marie-Claire b 16 Aug 1971); *Career* lectr Univ of Leeds 1972-74, sr urological registrar Liverpool 1974-79, conslt urologist Somerset 1979-, numerous pubns on devpts in technol applicable to surgery; FRCSEd; *Recreations* golf, skiing, sailing; *Clubs* Taunton and Pickeridge; *Style—* Patrick O'Boyle, Esq; Wild Oak Cottage, Wild Oak Lane, Trull, Taunton (☎ 0823 278057); Musgrove Park Hospital, Taunton, Somerset (☎ 0823 333444 Ext 2103

O'BRIEN, Barry John; s of John O'Brien, and Patricia, *née* Barry; *b* 27 Oct 1952; *Educ* St Illtyd's Coll Cardiff, UCL (LLB); *m* 29 Sept 1984, Susan Margaret; 1 s (William James), 1 da (Joanna Elizabeth); *Career* slr Slaughter and May 1978-83 (articled clerk 1976-78), ptnr Freshfields 1986- (slr 1983-86); Liveryman Worshipful Co Slrs; memb Law Soc; *Recreations* sport; *Style—* Barry J O'Brien, Esq; 9 Highbury Terrace, London N5 (☎ 071 359 2354); Whitefriars, 65 Fleet St, London EC4 (☎ 071 936 4000)

O'BRIEN, Prof Denis Patrick; s of Patrick Kevin O'Brien (d 1944), of Oaklands, Welwyn, Herts, and Dorothy Elizabeth, *née* Crisp (d 1985); *b* 24 May 1939; *Educ* Douai Sch, UCL (BSc), Queen's Univ Belfast (PhD); *m* 5 Aug 1961, Eileen Patricia (d 1985), da of Martin O'Brien (d 1987), of Bognor Regis; 1 s (Martin Michael), 2 da (Ann Elizabeth, Alison Mary); *Career* reader in econs Queen's Univ Belfast 1970-72 (asst lectr 1963-65, lectr 1965-70), prof of econs Univ of Durham 1972-; memb Cncl Royal Econ Soc 1978-83; FBA; *Books* J R McCulloch (1970), The Correspondence of Lord Overstone (3 vol, 1971), Competition in British Industry (jntly, 1974), The Classical Economists (1975), Competition Policy, Profitability and Growth (jtly, 1979), Pioneers of Modern Economics in Britain (jtly, 1981), Authorship Puzzles in The History of Economics: A Statistical Approach (jtly, 1982), Lionel Robbins (1988); *Recreations* the violin; *Style—* Prof Denis O'Brien; Dept of Economics, University of Durham, 23-26 Old Elvet, Durham DH1 3HY (☎ 091 374 2274)

O'BRIEN, Dermod Patrick; QC (1983); s of Lt Dermod Donatus O'Brien (d 1939), and Helen Doreen Lesley, *née* Scott O'Connor (d 1971); for family history see History of the O'Briens by Hon Donough O'Brien 1949, O'Brien of Thomond by Ivar O'Brien 1986; *b* 23 Nov 1939; *Educ* Ampleforth, St Catherine's Coll Oxford (MA); *m* 1974, Zoë Susan, da of Roderick Edward Norris, of Sussex; 2 s (Edward b 1977, Timothy b 1980); *Career* called to the Bar Inner Temple 1962; rec of the Crown Ct (Western Circuit) 1978; landowner; *Recreations* fishing, shooting, skiing; *Style—* Dermod P O'Brien, Esq, QC; Little Daux Farm, Billingshurst, West Sussex RH14 9DB (☎ 0403 784800); 2 Temple Gardens, Temple, London EC4Y 9AY (☎ 071 583 6041)

O'BRIEN, Sir Frederick William Fitzgerald; QC (1960); s of Dr Charles Henry Fitzgerald O'Brien, of 7 Brandon Street, Edinburgh (d 1968), and Helen Jane MacDonald (d 1962); *b* 19 July 1917; *Educ* Royal HS, Univ of Edinburgh (MA, LLB); *m* 1950, Audrey Muriel, da of Joseph Lloyd Owen, of 2131 Niagara Street, Windsor, Ontario; 2 s (David b 1954, Neil b 1957), 1 da (Susan b 1952); *Career* admitted Faculty of Advocates 1947, cmmr Mental Welfare Cmmn of Scot 1962-65, home advocate depute 1964-65; sheriff princ: Caithness Sutherland Orkney and Shetland 1965-75, (interim) Aberdeen Kincardine and Banff 1969-71, N Strathclyde 1975-78, Lothian and Borders 1978-89; sheriff of Chancery in Scot 1978-89, interim sheriff princ of S Strathclyde 1981; chm: Sheriff Ct Rules Cncl 1975-81, Northern Lighhouse Bd 1983-84 and 1985-87, Med Appeal Tbnls 1990-, Edinburgh Sir Walter Scott Club 1989-; *Recreations* music, golf; *Clubs* New (Edinburgh), Scot Arts, Bruntsfield Golf; *Style—* Sir Frederick O'Brien, QC; 22 Arboretum Road, Edinburgh EH3 5PN (☎ 031 552 1923)

O'BRIEN, Hon Mrs Henry - Edith Lawrie; widow of T M Steele; *m* 1964, as his 2 w, Capt the Hon Henry Barnaby O'Brien (d 1969); *Style—* The Hon Mrs Henry O'Brien; 3 Ibris Place, N Berwick, E Lothian

O'BRIEN, James Patrick Arland; yr s of late John David O'Brien; hp of bro, Sir Timothy O'Brien, 7 Bt, *qv*; *b* 22 Dec 1964; *Style—* James O'Brien, Esq

O'BRIEN, Hon Mrs Fionn; Josephine Reine; da of Joseph Eugene Bembaron (d 1953), of The Old House, Westcott, Surrey; *m* 1939, Hon Fionn Myles Maryons O'Brien (d 1977), s of 15 Baron Inchiquin; 1 s (18 Baron), 1 da; *Recreations* portrait painting; *Style—* The Hon Mrs Fionn O'Brien; Bow House, 24 Bolingbroke Grove, London SW11 6EN

O'BRIEN, Most Rev Keith Michael Patrick; *see*: St Andrews and Edinburgh, Archbishop of (RC)

O'BRIEN, Michael Anthony; s of Dr Donal O'Brien, and Patricia Mary, *née* Dowdall (d 1990); *b* 7 Sept 1950; *Educ* The Oratory Sch Reading, Trinity Coll Dublin (BA, BAI); *m* 7 Sept 1971, Robin Patricia Antonia, da of Roger Greene (d 1954), of Wellington Quay, Dublin; 4 da (Louise b 1974, Pippa b 1976, Tara b 1977, Alice b 1987); *Career* CA; asst dir C T Bowring & Co (Lloyd's Insurance Brokers) 1975-78, gp fin controller Mining Investment Corporation Ltd 1978-79, chief exec Anglo International Mining Corporation Ltd 1979-82; chm and chief exec: Bannertill Ltd, KDM Leasing Ltd, Leisure Projects Int Ltd, Loupiptar plc, Mineral and Energy Resources Corp Ltd, Mineral and Energy (UK) Ltd; FCA; *Recreations* horses, ponies, swimming, tennis; *Clubs* Br Show Pony Soc, S of England Agric Soc; *Style—* Michael O'Brien, Esq; 57 High St, Tunbridge Wells, Kent TN1 1XU (☎ 0892 511866, fax 0892 548440); Rylands, Plumpton, East Sussex BN7 3AB

O'BRIEN, (Charles) Michael; s of Richard Alfred O'Brien, CBE (d 1970), of Beckenham, Kent, later of Queensland, Aust, and Nora, *née* McKay (1956); *b* 17 Jan 1919; *Educ* Westminster, Ch Ch Oxford (MA); *m* 4 Nov 1950, Joyce, da of Rupert Henry Prebble (d 1956), of Beckenham, Kent; 2 s (Philip b 1952, Christopher b 1954); *Career* WWII, cmmnd 2 Lt RA 1940, Capt RA Burma (despatches), demobbed 1946; actuary; asst actuary Equitable Life Assurance Society 1952, gen mangr and actuary Royal National Pension Fund for Nurses 1955-84, dir M & G Assurance Group Ltd 1984-; govr Westminster Sch 1972-, memb Limpsfield Common Mgmnt Ctee NT, chm Federated Pension Servs 1983-89; FIA 1949 (hon sec 1961-63, pres 1976-78), FPMI; *Recreations* shooting, training and working gundogs; *Style—* Michael O'Brien, Esq; The Boundary, Goodley Stock, Crockham Hill, Edenbridge, Kent TN8 6TA (☎ 0732 866349)

O'BRIEN, Hon Michael John; o s of Baron O'Brien of Lothbury, GBE, PC (Life Peer); *b* 1933; *Educ* Marlborough; *m* 1964, Marion Sarah, da of late Walter Graham Blackie; 2 s (James Leslie Graham b 1967, Charles John b 1972), 1 da (Sarah Christina b 1969); *Career* memb of London Stock Exchange; *Recreations* fishing, shooting, stalking; *Clubs* Boodles; *Style—* The Hon Michael O'Brien; The Lodge, Thursley, nr Godalming, Surrey GU8 6QF (☎ 0252 702235)

O'BRIEN, Oswald; MP (Lab) for Darlington 1983-; s of Thomas O'Brien, and Elizabeth O'Brien; *b* 6 April 1928; *Educ* St Mary's GS Darlington, Fircroft Coll Birmingham, Univ of Durham (BA); *m* 1950, Freda Rosina Pascoe; 1 s; *Career* RN 1945-48; Tutor WEA 1963-64, staff tutor Univ of Durham 1964-78, sr industl rels offr Cmmn on Industl Rels 1970-1972 (secondment), dir of studies and vice princ Co-Op Coll 1978-83; Dept of Employment second ACAS arbitrator in shipbuilding 1968-78, chm Soc of Industl Tutors 1978-82, former pres, sec and treas Darlington Lab Pty (and sec), former memb Darlington County Borough and Dist Cncls, co-opted memb Durham Co Educn Ctee; FBIM; *Books* Going Comprehensive (jtly 1970); *Recreations* singing, dancing, reading, conversation; *Style—* Oswald O'Brien, Esq, MP; House of Commons, London SW1

O'BRIEN, Prof Patrick Karl; s of William Patrick O'Brien, of Coggeshall, Essex, and Elizabeth, *née* Stockhausen; *b* 12 Aug 1932; *m* 15 April 1959, Cassy, da of Charles Cobham; 1 s (Stephen b 23 March 1972), 2 da (Karen b 18 Nov 1964, Helen b 18 Nov 1966); *Career* Univ of London: res fell 1960-63, lectr 1963-70, reader in economics and econ history 1967-70, univ reader in econ history and professorial fell St Anthony's Coll Oxford 1984-90 (univ lectr in econ history and faculty fell 1970-84); FRHistS, memb Econ History Soc; *Books* The Revolution in Egypt's Economic System (1966), The New Economic History of the Railways (1977), Productivitiy in the Economics of Europe in the 19th and 20th Centuries (ed jtly 1983), Railways and the Economic Development of Western Europe 1930-1914 (ed 1983), International Productivity Comparisons 1750-1939 (ed 1986), The Economic Effects of the Civil War (1988), contrib numerous learned jls; *Recreations* tennis, squash, art history, walking; *Style—* Prof Patrick O'Brien; 33 Tavistock Square, London WC1; Institute of Historical Research, Senate House, London University, London WC1E 7HU (☎ 071 636 0272, fax 071 436 2183)

O'BRIEN, Richard; s of Alec James Morley-Smith, of 50 Kings Ave, Tauranga, New Zealand, and Doreen Mary, *née* O'Brien; *m* 1, 1971 (m dis 1979), Kimi Wong; 1 s (Linus b 1 May 1972); m 2, 1982, Jane Elizabeth Moss; 1 s (Joshua b 22 June 1983), 1 da (Jane b 9 Jan 1989); *Career* actor/writer 1967-; early theatre work incl: Robert and Elizabeth, Gullivers Travels, Hair, Jesus Christ Superstar; 4 prodns at Royal Court Theatre (writer of 2 incl The Rocky Horror Show), actor and writer for film and theatre, writer A Hymn for Jim (BBC TV); *Awards* (for Rocky Horror Show) Evening Standard award for Best Musical of 1973, Plays and Players award for Best Musical of 1973, Golden Scroll award from The Academy of Science Fiction, Fantasy and Horror Films; dir Druidcrest Music Publishing; memb: British Actors Equity, Publishing Rights Soc; *Recreations* work; *Clubs* The Chelsea Arts, The Gothic Soc; *Style—* Richard O'Brien, Esq; c/o Chatto and Linnit, Prince of Wales Theatre, Coventry St, London W1 (☎ 071 930 6677, 071 930 0091)

O'BRIEN, Sir Richard; DSO (1944), MC (and bar 1942, 1944); s of Dr Charles O'Brien and Marjorie Maude O'Brien; *b* 15 Feb 1920; *Educ* Oundle, Clare Coll Cambridge; *m* 1951, Elizabeth M D Craig; 2 s, 3 da; *Career* served WWII N Africa, ME, Italy and Greece with Sherwood Foresters and Leicester Regt, PA to C-in-C 21 Army Gp 1945-46; Richard Sutcliffe Ltd (rose to position of prodn dir 1948, left 1958); dir and gen mangr Head Wrightson Mineral Engr 1958-61, dir indust rels BMC 1961-66, indust manpower advsr DEA 1966-68; memb: Cncl Indust Soc 1962-85, Policy Studies Inst 1978- (chm Cncl 1984-91); dir manpower and exec dir Delta Metal 1972-76 (joined 1968), chm Manpower Services Cmmn 1976-82, memb NEDC 1977-82, former chm CBI Employment Policy Ctee, chm Crown Appts Cmmn 1979-, chm Engr Indust Trg Bd 1982-85; JP Wakefield 1955-61; Hon DSc Aston, Hon DLitt Warwick 1983; Hon LLD: Bath 1981, Liverpool 1981, Birmingham 1982; Hon DCL (Lambeth) 1987, Hon DL (CNAA) 1988, hon fell Sheffield Poly, memb Cncl Univ of Birmingham; kt 1980; *Style—* Sir Richard O'Brien, DSO, MC; 24 Argyll Rd, London W8 (☎ 071 937 8944)

O'BRIEN, Prof (Patrick Michael) Shaughn; s of Patrick Michael O'Brien (d 1978), of Treforest, Glamorgan, and Joan, *née* Edelston; *b* 1 April 1948; *Educ* Pontypridd Boys' GS, Univ of Wales, Welsh Nat Sch of Med (MB BCh, MD); *m* 10 Aug 1985, Sandra Louise, da of Edward Arthur Norman (d 1979), of Henley-on-Thames; 1 s (James b 1986), 1 da (Louise b 1988); *Career* lectr and hon sr registrar Univ of Nottingham 1979-84, sr lectr and hon conslt in obstetrics and gynaecology Royal Free Hosp Sch of Med London 1984-89, fndn prof of Obstetrics and Gynaecology Univ of Keele 1989-, conslt obstetrician and gynaecologist North Staffordshire Hosps 1989-; MRCOG, memb RSM; *Books* Premenstrual Syndrome (1987); *Recreations* classical music, jazz, clarinet/saxophone, skiing, tennis; *Style—* Prof Shaughn O'Brien; Upper Farm House, Field Aston, Newport, Shropshire TF10 9LE (☎ 0952 811510); University of Keele, Academic Department of Obstetrics & Gynaecology, School of Postgraduate-Medicine & Biological Sciences, Thornburrow Drive, Hartshill, Stoke-on-Trent, Staffordshire ST4 7QB (☎ 0782 49144 ext 4047)

O'BRIEN, (Robert) Stephen; CBE (1987); s of Robert Henry O'Brien (d 1969), and Clare Winifred, *née* Edwards (d 1975); *b* 14 Aug 1936; *Educ* Sherborne; *m* 1, 1958, (m dis 1989), Zoe O'Brien; 2 s (Dermot b 1962, Paul b 1969), 2 da (Rachel b 1965, Louise b 1966), m 2, 30 June 1989, Meriel, *née* Barclay; *Career* Charles Fulton and Co Ltd: joined 1956, dir 1964, chm 1970-82; chm Foreign Exchange & Currency Deposit Assoc 1968-72, chief exec Business in the Community 1983-; chm: Christian Action 1976-88, Fullemploy Gp 1973-, UK 2000 1988-; fell and cncl memb RSA; *Recreations* gardening, tennis; *Style—* Stephen O'Brien, Esq, CBE; CBE; Business in the Community, 227A City Rd, London EC1V 12X (☎ 071 253 3716, fax 071 253 2309)

O'BRIEN, Timothy Brian; s of Brian Palliser Tighe O'Brien (d 1966), and Elinor Laura, *née* Mackenzie; *b* 8 March 1929; *Educ* Wellington, Corpus Christi Coll Cambridge (MA), Yale; *Career* designer: BBC Design Dept 1954, Assoc Rediffusion

1955-56; head of design ABC TV 1956-66, theatrical designer and chm Soc of Br Theatre Designers in partnership with Tazeena Firth (estab 1961), most recent prodn Love's Labours Lost RSC 1990; Gold Metal for set design Prague Quadriemale 1975; *Recreations* sailing (co owner 'Bathsheba Everdene'); *Style*— Timothy O'Brien, Esq; 33 Lansdowne Gdns, London SW8 2EQ (☎ 071 622 5384)

O'BRIEN, (Michael) Vincent; s of Daniel Patrick O'Brien (d 1943); *b* 9 April 1917; *Educ* Mungret Jesuit Coll Limerick; *m* 1951, Jacqueline, *née* Wittenoom; 2 s (David, Charles), 3 da (Elizabeth McClory, Susan Magnier, Jane Myerscough); *Career* racehorse trainer; began training Co Cork 1944, moved to Co Tipperary 1951, won all major English and Irish steeplechases (3 consecutive Grand Nationals, Champion Hurdles and 4 Gold Cups); since 1959 has concentrated on flat racing; trained winners of: 16 English classics (incl 6 Derbys) and 27 Irish classics (incl 6 Irish Derbys), French Derby, 3 Prix de l'Arc de Triomphe, Washington Int; trainer of Nijinsky (first triple crown winner since 1935); Hon LLD Nat Univ 1983; *Recreations* golf, fishing; *Style*— Vincent O'Brien, Esq; Ballydoyle House, Cashel, Co Tipperary, Ireland (☎ 062 61222, telex 70714, fax 062 61677)

O'BRIEN, William; JP (Wakefield 1979), MP (Lab) Normanton 1983-; *Educ* Univ of Leeds; *m* Jean; 3 da; *Career* oppn front bench memb for Environment Covering Housing, Local govt fin, Local govt); memb: Fin and Gen Purposes Ctee 1973-83 (former dep ldr and chm), Pub Accounts Ctee 1983, Energy Select Ctee 1986; memb: Yorks Water Authy 1974-83, NUM 1945- (local branch official 1956-83); *Recreations* reading; *Style*— William O'Brien, Esq, JP, MP; House of Commons, London SW1

O'BRIEN, Adm Sir William Donough; KCB (1969, CB 1966), DSC (1942); s of Maj William Donough O'Brien (d 1916); *b* 13 Nov 1916; *Educ* RNC Dartmouth; *m* 1943, Rita, da of Lt-Col Albert Micallef, ISO, of Malta; 1 s, 2 da; *Career* joined RN 1930, served WWII, Flag Offr Aircraft Carriers 1966-67, Cdr Far East Fleet 1967-69, Adm 1969, C-in-C Western Fleet 1970-71, ret; chm: King George's Fund for Sailors 1974-86, Kennet and Avon Canal Tst 1974-; pres Assoc of RN Offrs 1974-88 (Rear-Adm UK 1979-84, Vice Adm UK 1984-86); *Clubs* Army and Navy; *Style*— Adm Sir William O'Brien, KCB, DSC; The Black Barn, Steeple Ashton, Trowbridge, Wilts BA14 6EU (☎ 0380 870496)

O'BRIEN OF LOTHBURY, Baron (Life Peer UK 1973), of City of London; Leslie Kenneth O'Brien; GBE (1967), PC (1970), FRCM (1979); eldest s of late Charles John Grimes O'Brien; *b* 8 Feb 1908; *Educ* Wandsworth Sch; *m* 1, 1932, Isabelle Gertrude (d 1987), da of Francis John Pickett, MBE; 1 s (Hon Michael John b 1933); m 2, 6 Jan 1989, Mrs Marjorie Violet Taylor, da of Albert Cecil Ball; *Career* sits as ind peer in House of Lords; Private Artists Rifles 1928-32; Bank of England 1927-73: chief cashier 1955-62, govr 1966-73; pres Br Bankers Assoc 1973-80, vice chm Banque Belge 1981-88, dir Belgian & Gen Investmts 1981-88; advsr: J P Morgan & Co 1973-79, Morgan Grenfell 1974-87; *Recreations* music, theatre, tennis; *Clubs* Athenaeum, Boodle's, Garrick, Grillions, MCC, AELTC; *Style*— The Rt Hon the Lord O'Brien of Lothbury; 3 Peter Ave, Oxted, Surrey (☎ 0883 712535)

O'BROIN, Breandan; s of Michael O'Broin (d 1962), of Dublin, and Kathleen O'Broin (d 1975); *b* 21 Jan 1946; *Educ* Colaiste Mhuire Dublin, Coll of Commerce Dublin; *m* 3 April 1970, Miriam Frances, da of Frank Murray (d 1985), of Edinburgh; 2 s (Hugh b 1972, Timothy b 1976), 2 da (Kate b 1971, Judith b 1974); *Career* copywriter: Arks 1964-68, Young Advertising 1968-70; creative dir CDP Assocs 1970-; ICAD 1966, MIAPI 1968; *Recreations* cricket, badminton, walking; *Clubs* Merrion CC; *Style*— Breandan O'Broin, Esq; 2 Sandycove Ave West, Sandycove, Co Dublin (☎ 0001 808267); CDP Associates, 46 Wellington Rd, Dublin 4 (☎ 0001 689627, fax 0001 681341, telex 30334)

O'CATHAIN, Detta; OBE (1983); da of Caoimhghin O'Cathain (d 1986), of Dublin, and Margaret, *née* Prior (d 1977); *b* 3 Feb 1938; *Educ* Laurel Hill Limerick Ireland, Univ Coll Dublin (BA); *m* 4 June 1968, William Ernest John Bishop, s of William Bishop, of Bristol (d 1968); *Career* former md milk marketing Milk Marketing Board; dir: Midland Bank plc 1984, Tesco plc 1985, Sears plc 1987; md Barbican Centre 1990-; memb Cncl Industl Soc; *Recreations* reading, walking, swimming, theatre, music; *Style*— Miss Detta O'Cathain, OBE; Eglantine, Tower House Gardens, Arundel, W Sussex (☎ 0903 883775); 121 Shakespeare Tower, Barbican, London EC2Y 8DR; Barbican Centre, Barbican, London EC2Y 8DS (☎ 071 638 4141, car 0836 360151)

O'CONNELL, Bernard John; s of William O'Connell, and Dorothy, *née* Veale; *b* 22 Nov 1942; *Educ* St Brendan's Coll, Univ of Sheffield; *m* 12 Feb 1966, Mary Jacqueline, da of Capt Norman Clark (d 1959); 1 s (James b 1967), 1 da (Anna b 1971); *Career* consumer res mangr Cadburys 1967-69, mktg mangr Imperial Tobacco 1969-72, chm and md Market Solutions 1973-78, md Noble Whelan O'Connell 1978-84, chm The O'Connell Partnership 1984-; mktg awards: Silver 1975, Gold 1975 and 1977, Grand Prix 1977; *Recreations* golf, skiing, guitar; *Clubs* Chartridge Grange Golf, Launceston Golf; *Style*— Bernard O'Connell, Esq; Woodland Ct, Long Park, Chesham Bois, Amersham, Bucks (☎ 02403 3338)); 10 Wrights Lane, London W8 6TA (☎ 071 937 2575, fax 071 937 7534)

O'CONNELL, David Henry Anthony; s of David Andrew O'Connell, and Ellen Mary, *née* Paul; *b* 26 Feb 1955; *Educ* Presentation Brothers Coll Cork Ireland, Univ Coll Cork Ireland (MB BCh, BAO), Univ of London (DRCOG, MICGP); *Career* house physician and house surgn Royal Hosp Wolverhampton 1978-79, trainee GP St Bartholomew's and Hackney Hosp VTS 1979-82, chm and dist jr exec City and Hackney Health Dis 1980-81, med advsr and memb Mgmnt Ctee St Wilfrid's Residential Home Chelsea, jr ptnr Sir Noel Moynihan and O'Connell 1984-86 (sr ptnr 1986-), co-fndr and ptnr Corporate Medical Services Ltd 1989; memb Exec Ctee and sec Audit Sub Ctee and chm Insur Sub Ctee Ind Doctors' Forum 1991; Yeoman Worshipful Soc of Apothecaries 1985; memb BMA 1978, FRSM 1982; fell: Med Soc of London 1985, Chelsea Clinical Soc 1985, FRSA 1989; Cross of Merit, Sovereign Mil Order of Malta 1987; *Books* author various contribs to popular med press; *Recreations* wine, travel; *Clubs* RAC; *Style*— Dr David O'Connell; 92 Beaufort Mansions, Beaufort Street, London SW3 (☎ 071 351 0764); 25 Sloane Court West, London, SW3 4TD; Corporate Medical Services, 137 Harley St, London W1N 1AA (☎ 071 730 1828, fax 071 730 2362, 0831 381 702)

O'CONNELL, Prof James Michael; s of James Patrick O'Connell (d 1942), and Agnes, *née* Harrington (d 1935); *b* 22 Oct 1925; *Educ* Nat Univ of Ireland (BA, MA), Univ of Louvain (PhD); *m* 21 March 1975, Rosemary, da of Albert Victor Harris, of 25 Ashford Ave, Bangor, Co Down; 1 s (Patrick b 7 Oct 1980), 2 da (Sheila b 29 May 1976, Deirdre b 10 May 1978), 1 step da (Sanjida b 30 June 1970); *Career* lectr UCL 1958-67, prof of govt Ahmadu Bello Univ Nigeria 1967-75, dean of arts NI Poly 1976-78, prof of peace studies Univ of Bradford 1978- (prov vice chllr 1982-86); assoc Inst of Devpt Studies Univ of Sussex, chm Advsy Ctee CSISV Univ of Leicester, memb Race and Community Rels Ctee Bd for Social Responsibility C of E; *Books* Education and Nation Building in Africa (1965), Nigeria 1965: crisis and criticism (1966), Education and Power in Nigeria (1977), The Meaning of Irish Place Names (1980), The Meaning of English Place Names (1984), Peace With Work To Do (1985), Notes Towards a Theology of Peace (1989), Making The Future: thinking and acting about peace in Britain (1989); *Recreations* study of the meaning of place names, reading novels; *Style*— Prof James O'Connell; 9 Wheatley Ave, Ben Rhydding, Ilkley, West Yorkshire (☎ 0943 608 378); Dept of Peace Studies, University of Bradford, Richmond Rd, Bradford, West Yorkshire BD7 1DP (☎ 0274 733466, telex 51309 UNIBFD, fax 0274 305340)

O'CONNELL, Judith Anne; *née* Shennan; da of (Robert) Gordon Shennan (d 1982), and Gladys, *née* Coomber (d 1989); *b* 11 June 1944; *Educ* Gardeners Rd Sydney Australia; *m* 1, 1962 (m dis 1971), Maurice Charles O'Connell; m 2, 1972 (m dis 1976), Alasdair Sutherland; *Career* advertising copywriter Sydney Aust 1958-62, photographic fashion model Sydney, Paris and London 1962-73, modelled spring collections Pierre Cardin Paris 1967, PR Janice Wainwright London 1974-75, set up London office and shops Mulberry (Design) Ltd 1976-83, fndr O'Connell Trievnor Agencies (Br and Euro fashion and mktg 1983-), freelance columnist trade and consumer magazines; *Recreations* writing, reading, photography, cats, rock and roll, tennis; *Clubs* Groucho; *Style*— Ms Judith O'Connell; 686B Fulham Road, London SW6 5SA

O'CONNELL, Sir Maurice James Donagh MacCarthy; 7 Bt (UK 1869), of Lakeview, and of Ballybeggan; er s of Sir Morgan Donal Conail O'Connell, 6 Bt (d 1989); *b* 10 June 1958; *Heir* bro, John O'Connell b 1960; *Style*— Sir Maurice O'Connell, Bt; 41 Lowndes St, London SW1; Lakeview House, Killarney, Co Kerry, Ireland

O'CONNOR, Bryan Connor; s of Dr Gerard Vincent O'Connor (d 1975), of Sheffield, and Margaret, *née* Russell; *b* 5 March 1934; *Educ* Mount St Mary's Coll; *m* 24 April, 1965, Anne, da of Stuart Birks Davidson, TD; 2 s (Mark b 28 Feb 1966, Robert b 5 May 1969); *Career* Nat Serv cmmn W Yorkshire Regt in NI Suez Cyprus 1955-57, Maj TA 1957-69; engrg apprenticeship 1951-55, prodn mangr English Steel Corpn 1957-60, tech sales Norton Abrasives 1960-67, md Joseph Gillot Ltd 1967-76, dir Glynwed Steels Ltd 1967-76, chm md Ruscon Steels/Ruscon Plastics Ltd 1976-, conslt United Engrg Steels 1988; memb Worshipful Co of Cutlers in Hallamshire; *Recreations* skiing, golf; *Clubs* Naval and Military; *Style*— Bryan O'Connor, Esq; Ruscon Steels Ltd, Ruscon Works, Rotherham Rd, Parkgate, Rotherham S62 6EZ (☎ 0709 527751, fax 0709 523298, telex 547791, car 0860 298180)

O'CONNOR, Des; *Career* entertainer and chat-show host; former Butlin's Red Coat; theatre: professional debut Palace Theatre Newcastle 1953, compere Sunday Night at the London Palladium (completed 1,000th performance at Palladium 1972), cabaret artist Talk of the Town London, one-man show UK and Aust 1980-, pantomine London Palladium (Cinderella) 1985 and Theatre Royal Plymouth 1990, numerous Royal Show appearances and summer seasons; Canada & USA headlined 3 seasons London Palladium Show Toronto and Ottawa, seasons at Royal York Hotel and Royal Alexandra Theatre, 2 all star galas MGM Grand Hotel Las Vegas; Aust: theatre and cabaret performances 1971-, broke all box-office records St George's League Club Sydney 1975, appeared at Sydney Opera House, various tours; TV host: Spot the Tune 1958, own series 1963, two series screened US then worldwide 1975, Des O'Connor Tonight (ITV) 1977-, Des O'Connor Now 1985, TV Times Awards ceremony 1989/90 and 1990/91; recording artist: first record Careless Hands reached number one in charts and sold over one million copies 1967, numerous singles and albums released since, album Des O'Connor sold over 250,000 copies 1984, released Sky Boat Song with Roger Whittaker 1986; *Style*— Des O'Connor, Esq; c/o Clifford Elson (Publicity) Ltd, 1 Richmond Mews, off Dean St, London W1V 5AG (☎ 071 437 4822, fax 071 287 6314)

O'CONNOR, Maureen Christina; da of Michael Joseph O'Connor (d 1977), and Bridget, *née* McMahon; *b* 20 Feb 1956; *Educ* Palmers GS for Girls Grays Essex, Grays Tech Coll; *Career* account liaison administrator Marketing Improvements Ltd 1975-80, ops mangr Grecian Holdings 1980-86, dir Maxwell Clarke Ltd 1988- (joined as account mangr 1986, promoted to account dir); sits on panel of judges for The Annual Br Recruitment Awards; memb: Manchester Publicity Assoc 1986-, Manchester C of C 1988-; *Recreations* squash, keep fit/aerobics, swimming, reading gardening; *Style*— Miss Maureen O'Connor; 122 Goodshaw Avenue North, Loveclough, Rossendale, Lancs BB4 8RW (☎ 0706 218809); Maxwell Clarke Ltd, Television House, Mount St, Manchester M2 5WS (☎ 061 833 0042, fax 061 832 9972, car 0831 123146)

O'CONNOR, Air Vice-Marshal Patrick Joseph Gerard; CB (1975), OBE (1943); s of Charles Edward O'Connor (d 1942), of Boston House, Straffan, Co Kildare, Ireland, and Mary Josephine, *née* Doyle (d 1966); *b* 21 Aug 1914; *Educ* Mount St Joseph Coll Roscrea Co Tipperary, Nat Univ of Ireland; *m* 16 July 1946, Elsie Elizabeth, da of David Craven (d 1945), of Leeds, Yorks; 1 s (Charles b 1951), 3 da (Mary b 1947 d 1977, Anna b 1948, Geraldine b 1950); *Career* RAF med branch 1940-77, Air Vice-Marshal, conslt advsr neurology and psychiatry RAF, hon physician to HM The Queen; conslt neurology and psychiatry: CAA 1977-, BA 1977, Harley St 1977-; memb: RSM 1950, Int Acad Aviation Med, ABN; FRCPsych, FRCP; *Books* International Civil Aviation Organization Manual, Standards for Neurology and Psychiatry (1970); *Recreations* gardening; *Clubs* RAF; *Style*— Air Vice-Marshal Patrick O'Connor, CB, OBE; St Benedicts, Bacombe Lane, Wendover, Bucks HP22 6EQ (☎ 0296 623 329); 10 Harley St, London W1N 1AA (☎ 071 636 6504, fax 071 637 5227)

O'CONNOR, Rt Hon Sir Patrick McCarthy; PC (1980), QC (1960); s of William Patrick O'Connor; *b* 28 Dec 1914; *Educ* Downside, Merton Coll Oxford (hon fell 1987); *m* 1938, Mary Garland (d 1984), da of William Griffin, KC, of Vancouver; 2 s, 2 da; *Career* called to the Bar Inner Temple 1940; jr counsel to PO 1954-60, rec Southend 1961-66 (Kings Lynn 1959-61), high ct judge (Queen's Bench) 1966-80, lord justice of Appeal 1980-89, ret from Bench 1989; govr Guy's Hosp 1956-60, dep chm IOW QS 1957-71, vice chm Parole Bd 1974-75; kt 1966; *Style*— The Rt Hon Sir Patrick O'Connor, QC; 210 Rivermead Court, London SW6 3SG (☎ 071 731 3563)

O'CONNOR, Hon Mr Justice; Rory; s of James Edward O'Connor (d 1956); *b* 26 Nov 1925; *Educ* Blackrock Coll, Univ Coll Dublin; *m* 1963, Elizabeth, *née* Dew; 1 s (Rory Brendan b 1967), 2 da (Fiona b 1964, Siobhan b 1981); *Career* called to the Bar King's Inns 1949, resident magistrate Kenya 1956, magistrate Hong Kong 1962, dist judge 1970, Supreme Ct judge Hong Kong 1977-; memb of The Judicial Servs Cmmn 1987; *Recreations* travel, reading; *Clubs* Utd Servs Recreation (Hong Kong); *Style*— The Hon Mr Justice O'Connor; Flat 7E, Barnton Court, 9 Canton Rd, Kowloon, Hong Kong (☎ 3 7227315)

O'CONOR CAMERON, Desmond Roderic; s and h of Denis Armar O'Conor, The O'Conor Don, and Elizabeth, *née* Marris (now Mrs James Cameron); *b* 22 Sept 1938; *Educ* Sherborne; *m* 23 May 1964, Virginia Anne, da of late Sir Michael Sanigear Williams, KCMG; 1 s (Philip Hugh b 17 Feb 1967), 2 da (Emma Joy (Mrs Mark Leveson-Gower) b 17 April 1965, Denise Sarah b 8 Dec 1970); *Career* Bank of London and Montreal Ltd Guatemala and Honduras 1960-64, J Henry Schroder Wagg & Co Ltd London 1964-79, dir Schroders Int Ltd Rio de Janeiro 1977-78; dir: Kleinwort Benson España SA Madrid, Kleinwort Benson Iberfomento Fusiones y Adquisiciones SA Madrid; dir Latin American Trade Advisory Gp (LATAG) 1986-89 (Bd of Trade sponsored organisation), chm Soldiers and Sailors Home Eastbourne; *Recreations* tennis, skiing, sailing; *Style*— Desmond O'Conor Cameron, Esq; Kleinwort Benson Ltd, 20 Fenchurch St, London EC3 (☎ 071 623 8000); Horsegrove House, Rotherfield, Sussex

O'CONOR DON, The; Denis Armar O'Conor; O Conchubhair Dun; s of Charles O'Conor Don (27 in descent from Conor, Concovar or Conchobhar, King of Connaught in tenth century and from whom the family name derives), and Evelyn, yst da of Adm the Hon Armar Lowry-Corry, himself 2 s of 3 Earl of Belmore; the present O'Conor Don's forbear 23 generations back was Turlough Mor O'Conor (d 1163), High King over all Ireland; suc his 2 cous (a Jesuit priest) Nov 1981; *b* 1912; *Educ* Downside; *m* 1, 1937 (m dis 1943), Elizabeth, da of Rev Stanley Punshon Marris; 1 s; m 2, 1943, Rosemary June, da of Capt James Piers O'Connell-Hewett; 2 s (Kieran Denis b 1958, Rory Dominic b 1963); *Heir* s, Desmond Roderic Cameron O'Conor (b 1938, m 1964 Virginia, eldest da of Sir Michael Williams, KCMG, *qv*; 1 s Philip b 1967, 2 da Emma b 1965, Denise b 1971); *Career* former Lt Lincolnshire Regt; KCLJ, KMLJ; *Recreations* hound breeding and showing, beagling; *Style*— The O'Conor Don; Ashbourne, Corrig Rd, Dun Laoghaire, Co Dublin, Eire (☎ 0001 80 24 22)

O'DELL, Denis Herbert; s of Edmund James O'Dell (d 1973), of 123 Coventry Rd, Bedford, and Gertrude Emma, *née* Witney; *b* 18 Dec 1919; *Educ* Bedford Modern Sch; *m* 22 April 1950, Elizabeth Mary, da of Stanley Richard Evans (d 1960), of 12 Biddenham Turn, Bedford; 1 s (William Richard b 1951), 1 da (Judith Mary b 1952); *Career* RAF 1940-46, flying offr, served Malta 1941-43, trg cmd S Rhodesia, flying instr 1943-45; proprietor O'Dell's Garage 1946-52, md O'Dells Garage Ltd 1952-73, chm Sheerwater Motors Ltd 1990- (dir 1973-74, md 1974-90), dir Ben Housing Assoc Ltd 1982-87; pres Rotary Club of Woking Dist 1981, dir Ben Motor and Allied Trades Benevolent Fund 1987-89, chm Ben Welfare Ctee 1986-89; TEng, FIMI; *Recreations* natural history, walking, Lynwood Ben Club, trade politics; *Clubs* RAF, RSPB, Nat Trust, FMI, WWF, Woodland Tst, CGA, Rotary (sec Bude Branch); *Style*— Denis O'Dell, Esq; End Cottage, Elmscott, Hartland, Devon EX39 6EX (☎ 0237 441620); Sheerwater Motors Ltd, Sheerwater, Woking, Surrey GU21 5JZ (☎ 0483 761517)

O'DELL, June Patricia; da of Lt Leonard Frederick Vickery (d 1940), and Myra Sarah *née* Soden (d 1972); *b* 9 June 1929; *Educ* Edgehill Girls' Coll Bideford N Devon, Plymouth Tech Coll; *m* 9 Feb 1951 (m dis 1963), Ronald Desmond O'Dell; 1 s (Richard Patrick b 27 Feb 1952), 2 da (Caroline b 16 Nov 1955, Alison Julia b 27 July 1957); *Career* princ Chesneys Estate Agents 1965-88, dep chair Equal Opportunities Cmmn 1986-90; nat pres UK Fedn of Business and Professional Women 1983-85, chair Int Fedn of Business and Professional Women Employment Ctee 1983-87, memb Euro Advsy Ctee for Equal Treatment Between Women and Men 1986-90, dir Eachdale Devpts 1988-; memb: Womens' Fin Panel Nat and Provincial Bldg Soc 1988, RSA Womens' Advsy Gp 1985-; FRSA 1987; *Recreations* opera, music, reading, theatre, the countryside, watching equestrian events; *Clubs* University Womens; *Style*— Mrs June O'Dell; Vale Farm, Kimblewick, Aylesbury, Bucks HP17 8SX (☎ 0296 614030); Equal Opportunities Commission, Overseas House, Quay St, Manchester M3 3HN (☎ 061 833 9244)

O'DONNELL, Hugh; s of John O'Donnell of Ireland, and Jean O'Donnell; *Educ* Camberwell Coll of Art, Falmouth Coll of Art (BA), Birmingham Coll of Art (HDip AD, prize Sir Whitworth Wallace Tst), RCA; *m* Tina Eden; 1 da (Kirstie b 1983); *Career* artist; selected one man exhibitions: Works on Paper (Nishimura Gallery Tokyo) 1976, Air Gallery London 1977, Paintings and Drawings (Ikon Gallery Birmingham) 1979, Rahr-West Museum Wisconsin 1983, Marlborough Gallery (London 1985, NY 1986 and 1987)), Works on Paper and Monoprints (Marlborough Gallery NY) 1984, Works on Paper (Marlborough Graphics London) 1984, Paintings (Marlborough Gallery NY) 1987, Paintings (Eva Cohen Gallery Chicago) 1990, Hokin Gallery Palm Beach Florida 1989), Paintings and Works on Paper Eva Cohen 1990, Paintings (Marlborough Gallery NY) 1991; selected gp exhibitions (first exhibition 1972): Br Art Now (Guggenheim Museum NY) 1980, Decorative Arts Award 1988 (designs for jewels - collaboration with Ros Conway, Sotheby's London Museum of Modern Art), Kyoto Japan, Arte & Alchimia (XLII Venice Biennale) 1986, The Question of Drawing (South Campus Gallery Miami, travelled) 1989; Works on paper: Amenoff, Barth, O'Donnell (Tomoko Liguori Gallery NY) 1990, Marlborough en Pelaires (Centre Cultural Contemporani Pelaires Palma de Mallorca) 1990; selected pub collections: Br Cncl UK, Solomon R Guggenheim Museum NY, London Contempory Arts Soc, Met Museum of Modern Art NY, Museum of Modern Art NY, V & A; Purchase award Arts Cncl of GB 1978 (Arts Cncl award 1978); set and costume designs for: Red Steps (London Contemporary Dance Theatre), Drawn Breath (Siobhan Davies Dance Company, 1989 Digit Dance award); *Style*— Hugh O'Donnell, Esq; Marlborough Gallery Inc, 40 West 57th Street, New York, NY 1009, USA (☎ 212 541 4900, fax 212 541 4948)

O'DONNELL, Dr Michael; s of Dr James Michael O'Donnell (d 1957), and Nora, *née* O'Sullivan (d 1976); *b* 20 Oct 1928; *Educ* Stonyhurst, Trinity Hall Cambridge, St Thomas's Hosp; *m* 1952, Catherine, da of Frank Dorrington Ward (d 1972); 1 s (James), 2 da (Frances, Lucy); *Career* family doctor 1953-64; ed World Medicine 1966-81, contrib to Stop the Week BBC 1977-, chm My Word BBC 1983-; written and presented TV documentaries in USA and UK incl: Inside Medicine BBC 1973, A Part of Life YTV 1977, Is Your Brain Really Necessary? YTV 1978, Medical Express BBC 1983, Plague of Hearts BBC 1983, O'Donnell Investigates BBC 1985, 1986 and 1988, Health, Wealth, and Happiness BBC 1989, writer and presenter Relative Values 1987-; memb GMC 1971-; FRCGP; *Books* The Devil's Prison (1982), An Insider's Guide to the Games Doctors Play (1986), The Long Walk Home (1988), How to Suceed in Business without Sacrificing Your Health (1988); contrib: The Times, The Guardian, Daily Mail, International Management, British Medical Journal; *Recreations* walking, golf, music; *Clubs* Garrick; *Style*— Dr Michael O'Donnell; Handon Cottage, Markwick Lane, Loxhill Godalming, Surrey GU8 4BD (☎ 048 632 295)

O'DONNELL, Ron; s of James Brogan O'Donnell (d 1989), and Susan McKee, *née* McCartney; *b* 28 Oct 1952; *Educ* Jacqueline, da of William John McDonald; 2 s (Robert b 12 March 1977, Ross b 14 Aug 1979), 1 da (Kim b 21 Feb 1974); *Career* trainee photographer Stirling Univ 1970-76; solo exhibtion The Vigorous Imagination (Scottish Nat Gallery of Modern Art) 1987; gp exhibitions incl: Cross References (Walker Art Centre, Minneapolis), 1987, The Rampant Scots (Art Space, San Francisco) 1988, Masters of Photography (V & A Museum) 1986, Mysterious Coincidences (Photographers Gallery, London) 1987, Sanders Gallery New York 1987, British Cncl Barcelona 1988, Scottish Art since 1900 (Nat Gall of Modern Art) 1989, Through the Looking Glass (Barbican) 1989, Raab Gallery Berlin 1989, The New North (Tate Gallery Liverpool and tour), Betzalel Hebrew Univ Jerusalem 1989, L'Invention d'un Art (Centre Georges Pompidou) 1989, California State Univ Los Angeles 1990; awards: Scottish Arts Cncl award for Photography 1979, Foix Talbot award for Photography 1987; *Style*— Ron O'Donnell, Esq

O'DONOGHUE, Daniel; s of Daniel O'Donoghue, of Knockroe, Castlerea, Roscommon, Eire, and Sabina, *née* Carey (d 1975); *b* 27 March 1947; *Educ* St Bede's Coll Manchester, Univ of Sheffield (BA); *m* 1 April 1972, Suzanne Lynne Andromeda, da of Harold Hamer Holman; 3 s (Timothy Peter Joseph b 4 Dec 1977, James Edward Michael b 27 Aug 1980, Alexander Daniel Hogarth b 13 Sept 1982), 1 da (Johanna Morgan Driella b 12 Jan 1985); *Career* advtg exec; trainee GUS 1968-69; market res mangr Europe Rowntree 1973-76 (market res offr 1969-73), marketing offr Shepherd Building 1976-77, account planner Ogilvy Benson Mather 1977-79; planning dir: CDP/Aspect 1979-82, McCormicks 1982-87, Publicis (formerly McCormicks) 1987-88; dep chm Publicis-FCB Group 1989-, jt chief exec Publicis 1991- (vice chm 1988-91); chm Bibliography Ctee IPA 1989-90, memb Cncl IPA 1989-; memb MRS 1973; *Recreations* fine art collecting, football and rugby; *Style*— Daniel O'Donoghue, Esq; Woodcroft Castle, Marholm, Peterborough, Cambridgeshire PE6 7HW Publicis Ltd, 67 Brompton Road, London SW3 1EF (☎ 071 823 9000, fax 071 823 8389)

O'DONOGHUE, Hughie Eugene; s of Daniel O'Donoghue, of Knockroe, Castelrea, Co Roscommon Rep of Ireland, and Sheila Carey (d 1976); *b* 5 July 1953; *Educ* St Augustines RC GS Manchester, Trinity and All Saints Colls Leeds, Goldsmiths Coll Univ of London (MA, CertEd); *m* 18 May 1974, Clare, da of Thomas Patrick Reynolds (d 1987); 2 s (Matthew Thomas b 12 Nov 1974, Vincent John Domhnall b 26 July 1987), 1 da (Kathryn Sabina b 20 July 1985); *Career* artist; solo exhibitions incl: Air Gallery London 1984, Nat Gallery London 1985, Fabian Carlsson Gallery London 1986 and 1989, Galleria Carini Florence Italy 1987, Art Now Gallery Gothenburg Sweden 1987; gp exhibitions incl: Whitechapel Open (Whitechapel Art Gallery London) 1982, 1983, 1986, 1988, 10 Years at Air (Air Gallery London) 1984, Works on Paper (Anthony Reynolds Gallery London and Galleria Carini Florance Italy) 1986, New Year New Work (Fabian Carlsson Gallery London) 1987, Nuovi Territori dell Arte: Europa/America (francavilla al Mare Italy) 1987, The Romantic Tradition in Contemporary British Painting (Sala de Exposiciones Murcia, Circulo de Bellas Artes Madrid, Ikon Gallery Birmingham) 1988, Landscape and Beyond (Cleveland Gallery Middlesborough) 1989, Ways of Telling (Oriel Mostyn Llandudno Wales) 1989, Drawing '89 Cleveland (UK) 9th Int Drawing Biennale (prizewinner) School of London 1989, Works on Paper (Odette Gilbert Gallery London) 1989, Roads to Abstraction (Whitworth Art Gallery Manchester) 1990, The Forces of Nature - Landscape as Metaphor (Manchester City Art Galleries) 1990; work in several pub collections; *Awards* Artist's awards Lincolnshire and Humberside Arts Assoc 1977, 1978, 1979, Artist in Industry fellowship Yorkshire Arts Assoc 1983, artist in residence Nat Gallery London (Nat Gallery and Arts Cncl of GB) 1984; pubns incl: Hughie O'Donoghue Paintings and Drawings 1983-86 (1986), Hughie O'Donoghue Opera 1986-87 (1987), Crow Paintings Hughie O'Donoghue (1989), Fires (1989); *Style*— Hughie O'Donoghue, Esq; 24 Hammelton Rd, Bromley, Kent BR1 3PY (☎ 081 464 1946); Ravenscroft Studios, 49 Columbia Rd, London E2 (☎ 071 739 9785)

O'DONOGHUE, His Hon Judge Michael; s of Dr James O'Donoghue, MB (d 1948), of Boundary St, Liverpool, and Vera Maude, *née* Cox (d 1981); *b* 10 June 1929; *Educ* Rhyl County Sch, Univ of Liverpool (LLB); *Career* served RAF 1951-53, Flying Offr; HM circuit judge; *Recreations* music, sailing (yacht Equity III), photography, painting; *Clubs* Athenaeum (Liverpool), Royal Welsh Yacht; *Style*— His Hon Judge Michael O'Donoghue

O'DONOGHUE OF THE GLENS, The; Geoffrey Vincent Paul O'Donoghue; *b* 1937; *m* Frances Kelly; *Heir* s, Conor, b 1964; *Style*— The O'Donoghue of the Glens; Glas Choill, Screggan, Tullamore, Co Offaly; The Glens, Flesk, Co Kerry

O'DONOVAN, Prof Katherine; da of Prof John O'Donovan, TD (d 1982), of Dublin, and Kathleen, *née* Mahon; *b* 7 Feb 1942; *Educ* Nat Univ of Ireland (BCL), Univ of Strasbourg (Diplôme De Droit Comparé), Harvard Law Sch (LLM), Univ of Kent (PhD); *m* 5 June 1971, Julian Davey, s of F V Davey, of Fernhurst, Sussex; 1 da (Julia b 4 Nov 1979); *Career* lectr in law: Queen's Univ Belfast 1965-69, Haile Sellassie I Univ Ethiopia 1969-72, Univ of Sussex 1972-73, Univ of Kent 1973-79, Univ of Malaya 1979-81, Univ of Kent 1981-85, Univ of Hong Kong 1985-88, Univ of Kent 1988-; visiting prof Univ of Paris; memb: Specialist Panel on Law CNAA, Cwlth Soc, Int Soc on Family Law, Cncl Soc of Pub Teachers of Law, Nat Tst, RSPB; govr Canterbury Sch; *Books* Sexual Divisions in Law (1985), Equality and Sex Discrimination Law (1988); *Clubs* Hong Kong, Cwlth Tst; *Style*— Prof Katherine O'Donovan; Rutherford College, The University, Canterbury, Kent CT2 7NX (☎ 0227 764000)

O'DONOVAN, The; Morgan Gerald (Daniel) O'Donovan; s of Brig The O'Donovan, MC (Morgan (John) Winthrop, d 1969), of Hollybrook House, Skibbereen, Co Cork, and Cornelia, *née* Bagnell (d 1974); officially recognised Chief of the Name of one of the most ancient families of Ireland, traceable from Gaelic times; *b* 4 May 1931; *Educ* Stowe, Trinity Coll Cambridge (MA); *m* 19 Sept 1959, Frances Jane, da of Field Marshal Sir Gerald Walter Robert Templer, KG, GCB, GCMG, KBE, DSO (d 1979); 1 s (Morgan (Teige) Gerald b 1961), 2 da (Katharine Jane b 1962, Cecilia (Mary) Cornelia b 1966); *Heir* s, Morgan (Teige) Gerald O'Donovan; *Career* farmer; J & P Coats Ltd Glasgow 1954-63, mgmnt appts in Cuba, Colombia, Singapore, Australia, Revertex Ltd London 1963-70, md Wates & Co Ltd Dublin 1972-77 (joined 1970); memb Gen Synod of Church of Ireland, govr Middleton Coll Co Cork; *Recreations* fishing, bird watching, vintage cars; *Clubs* Kildare Street and University Dublin; *Style*— The O'Donovan; Hollybrook House, Skibbereen, Co Cork Ireland (☎ 028 21245)

O'DONOVAN, Prof Oliver Michael Timothy; *b* 28 June 1945; *Career* ordained priest 1973 (deacon 1972), tutor Wycliffe Hall Oxford 1972-77, hon asst curate St Helen's Abingdon 1972-76, prof of systematic theology Wycliffe Coll Toronto Sch of Theology 1972-82 (asst 1977-81, assoc 1981-82), memb Church of England Bd for Social Responsibility 1976-77 & 1982-85, examining chaplain to Bishop of Toronto and memb Candidates Ctee of Diocese of Toronto 1978-82, regius prof of moral and pastoral theology Univ of Oxford and canon of Ch Ch Oxford 1982-; memb: Canadian Anglican-Roman Catholic Dialogue 1979-82, Jt Orthodox-Anglican Doctrinal Discussions 1982-85, Archbishop of Canterbury's Gp on the Law of Affinity 1982-84, Working Pty on Human Fertilization and Embryology of the Church of England Bd for Social Responsibility 1982-85, Mgmnt Ctee Ian Ramsey centre St Cross Coll Oxford 1983-89 (memb Cncl 1989-), Anglican Roman Catholic Int Cmmn 1985-, Cncl Wycliffe Hall Oxford 1985-; Chevasse Lectr Wycliffe Hall Oxford 1985, Church of Ireland Theological lectr Queen's Univ Belfast 1986, pastoral theology lectr Univ of Durham 1987, select preacher Univ of Oxford 1982, 1987, 1988, Assize preacher Birmingham Cathedral 1988, Hulsean preacher Univ of Cambridge 1989, visiting lectr St Patrick's Coll Maynooth Ireland 1989, Payton lectr Fuller Theological Seminary Passadena Calif 1989, Paddock lectr Gen Theological Seminary NY 1990-, chm Bd of Faculty of Theology Univ of Oxford 1990-; *Books* The Problem of Self-Love in Saint Augustine (1980), Begotten or Made? (1984), Resurrection and Moral Order (1986), On the Thirty Nine Articles: a Conversation with Tudor Christianity (1986), Peace and Certainty; a theological essay on deterence (1989); *Style*— Prof Oliver O'Donovan; Christ Church, Oxford OX1 1DP (☎ 0865 276219)

O'DONOVAN, Timothy Charles Melville (Tim); s of John Conan Marshall Thornton O'Donovan (d 1964), of London, and Enid Muriel Liddell (d 1958); *b* 10 Feb 1932; *Educ* Marlborough; *m* 19 Sept 1958, Veronica Alacoque, da of Leslie White (d 1981), of Hawkley, Hants; 2 s (Michael b 1962, Richard b 1966); *Career* Nat Serv with Life Gds 1950-52; dir: Common Cause Ltd 1964-, pub affrs Bain Clarkson 1987; chm Eckersley Hicks & Co Ltd Lloyd's Brokers 1979-84; tstee Br Monarchy Museum Tst 1979-; chm: A Princess for Wales Exhibition 1981, Pollution Abatement Technol Award Scheme 1983-87, Better Environment Awards for Industry 1987-; dep vice capt St George's Chapel Windsor Castle 1983-(steward 1978), tstee The Environment Fndn 1985-; memb The Queen's Birthday Ctee 1986; exhibitions organised: EIIR A Celebration 1986, Sixty Years a Queen 1987 Windsor Castle, Ninety Memorable Years to Celebrate The Queen Mother's 90th birthday; author of annual survey of Royal Family duties since 1979 in The Times and Illustrated London News; FRSA 1984; *Books* Above The Law?; *Recreations* watching cricket, collecting royal memorabilia, reading the Court Circular; *Clubs* MCC; *Style—* Tim O'Donovan, Esq; Mariners, The Avenue, Datchet, nr Windsor, Berks SL3 9DH; 15 Minories, London EC3N 1NJ (☎ 071 481 3232, fax 071 480 6137, telex 8813411)

O'DOWD, Chief Constable David Joseph; QPM (1988); s of Michael Joseph O'Dowd (d 1972), of Oadby, Leicestershire, and Helen, *née* Merrin; *b* 20 Feb 1942; *Educ* Gartree HS Oadby Leicester, Univ of Leicester (Dip Social Studies), Open Univ (BA), Univ of Aston (MSc), FBI Nat Acad USA; *m* 7 Sept 1963, Carole Ann, da of Charles Albert Watson of Leicester; 1 s (Andrew David b 29 Jan 1967), 1 da (Sharon Marie b 3 Dec 1964); *Career* Sgt, Inspr and Chief Inspr CID Leicester City Police 1961, Supt W Midlands Police Coventry and Birmingham 1977; head of traffic policing, dir of complaints and discipline Investigation Bureau and head of strategic planning and policy Analysis Unit Metropolitan Police New Scotland Yard 1984; Chief Constable Northamptonshire Police 1986- (Asst Chief Constable head of operations 1982); rep Br Chief Constables Nat Exec Inst FBI Acad Washington 1988, nat co dir Acelerated Promotion Services Command Extended Interview Scheme; visiting teaching fell Mgmnt Centre Univ of Aston Birmingham; memb: Regnl Bd BIM, St John Cncl, NAYC Cncl; pres Northamptonshire Royal Life Saving Assoc; CBIM 1988; *Recreations* squash, golf, gardening, decorating; *Style—* Chief Constable David J O'Dowd, QPM; Police HQ, Wootton Hall, Northampton NN4 0JQ (☎ 0604 700700, fax 0604 703028, telex 312141)

O'DRISCOLL, John P; s of Prof M Kieran O'Driscoll, of Dublin, Ireland, and Robina, *née* Hanley; *b* 24 June 1950; *Educ* Clongowes Wood Coll, Trinity Coll Dublin (BA), Wharton Univ of Penn (MBA); *m* 23 June 1977, Catherine Elizabeth, da of Henri Pierre Fortier (d 1977); 2 s (Shane Brice b 20 May 1982, Finnian Xavier b 17 June 1989), 1 da (Ciara Violaine b 9 Sept 1979); *Career* md Mellon Securities Ltd 1988-, gen mangr Mellon Bank (London branch) 1989- (area head Europe, ME, Africa); *Recreations* riding, squash; *Style—* John O'Driscoll, Esq; 6 Devonshire Sq, London EC2M 4LB (☎ 071 626 9828)

O'DRISCOLL, Michael; s of Michael James O'Driscoll, of The Bungalow, Finkle St, Hemingbrough, N Yorks, and Esther O'Driscoll; *b* 6 Aug 1939; *Educ* Archbishop Holgate's GS York, Univ of Leeds (MB, ChB), Univ of Bristol (MCh); *m* 28 Nov 1966, Susan Leah, da of Sam Lewis (d 1982), of Leeds; 2 s (Daniel b 1 July 1968, Gavin b 9 Aug 1969), 1 da (Philippa b 11 May 1972); *Career* offr's trg corps parachute section Univ of Leeds 1957-62; lectr orthopaedics Univ of Bristol 1969-77, visiting orthopaedic surgn Hebden Green Special Sch Winsford, currently conslt orthopaedic surgn Robert Jones and Agnes Hunt Orthopaedic Hosp Shropshire and Leighton Hosp Cheshire; memb: Fortress Study Gp, Back Pain Soc; patron Darren Kennerley Tst; FRCS 1967, memb SICOT 1983; *Recreations* fell walking, travelling, study of fortification, architecture, tanks and aircraft; *Clubs* Old Oswestrians; *Style—* Michael O'Driscoll; Leighton Hosp, Crewe, Cheshire; Robert Jones and Agnes Hunt Orthopaedic Hosp, Oswestry, Shropshire (☎ 0270 255141)

O'DRISCOLL, Suzanne Elizabeth; da of William George O'Driscoll, of Ash Barn House, Blackthorn, Bicester, Oxon, and Cynthia Anne, *née* Wright; *b* 7 June 1955; *Educ* St Josephs Convent Reading, Berkshire Coll of Art, Central Sch of Art and Design London (BA), Slade Sch of Fine Art UCL (MND, Boise travelling scholarship to Mexico and Guatemala); *Career* artist; solo exhibitions incl: Air Gallery 1984, Anderson O'Day Gallery London 1987, 1989, South Hill Park Art Centre Bracknell Berkshire 1987; gp exhibitions incl: Three Decades of Artists from Inner London Art Schs 1953-83 (Royal Acad London) 1983, St Johns Smith Sq 1985, Space Artists (B P London) 1985, Air Gallery Picture Fair (London) 1986, Anderson O'Day Gallery 1986, Open Studio Show (Berry St London) 1987, Heads (Anderson O'Day) 1987, Contemporary Arts Soc Market (London) 1987, 1988, 1989 and 1990, Oxford Gallery (Oxford) 1988, Drawing Show (Thumb Gallery London) 1988, Fish Exhibition (South Hill Park, Bracknell) 1988, Int Contemporary Art Fair London 1989 and 1990, Bath Contemporary Arts Fair 1989, Painting of the Week (Channel 4 TV) 1989, Works on Paper (Thumb Gallery London) 1990; cmmns for: Southampton Gen Hosp 1985, Harold Wood Gen Hosp Essex 1986, Radcliffe Infirmary Hosp Oxford 1986; work in various collections; artist in residence: Bracknell Sch Bershire 1987, Rhos y Gwalian Wales 1987, Maidenhead Teachers Centre 1988; featured in Assessment and Evalution in the Arts 1987; *Style—* Ms Suzanne O'Driscoll; Flat 4, 29 Adolphus Rd, London N4 2AT (☎ 081 800 9274); Space Studios, 142D Leabridge Rd, London E5 (☎ 081 533 7454); Anderson O'Day Gallery, 225 Portobello Rd, London W11 1LR (☎ 071 221 7592)

O'DWYER, Thomas Rankin (Thom); s of Bryan Keating O'Dwyer (d 1982), and Patricia Rang O'Dwyer; *b* 30 April 1954; *Educ* George Washington HS Alexandria Virginia USA, Parson's Sch of Design NY USA (BA), St Martins Sch of Art; *Career* fashion conslt Nigel French Enterprises Ltd 1971-79; fashion ed: Men's Wear Magazine 1980-86, Fashion Weekly 1986-88, Sunday Mirror and Magazine 1988-90, ed-in-chief He Lines 1990-; freelance work incl: Marie Claire, The Guardian (men's fashion corr 1984-88), DR - The Fashion Business, Living, Daily Express, DX Magazine, Daily Mirror, Clothes Show Magazine, Underlines, Unique, Ritz, Blitz, Evening Standard, Chat, Take a Break, Ms London, Vada, Wales on Sunday, Daily Star, Clothes Show Magazine; TV appearances incl: Night Network, South of Watford, Six O'Clock Show, Calendar Yorkshire TV (won documentary of the year award/ BAFTA), After the News; radio appearances incl: Loose Ends, (first all male) Woman's Hour, Radio One; chm seminar on men's fashion at ICA; judge: Woman Magazine Designer of the Year competition, Courtelle Design Awards; memb NUJ; *Recreations* eclectic and catholic, incl touring picturesque East End pubs, 18th Century art, rap music, kite flying; *Style—* Thom O'Dwyer, Esq; 38 The Cloisters, 145 Commercial St, London E1 6BU (☎ 071 377 6201); John Ward Publicity, 11 Bolt Court, Fleet St, London EC4 (☎ 071 936 2127, 071 353 7887, fax 071 585 2800)

O'FAOLAIN, (Anna) Julia; da of Sean O'Faolain, of Aclare House, 4/5 Tivoli Terrace South, Dun Laoghaire, Co Dublin, Ireland, and Eileen, *née* Gould (d 1989); *b* 6 June 1932; *Educ* Convent of The Sacred Heart Monkstown, Univ Coll Dublin (BA, MA), Università di Roma, Sorbonne Paris; *m* 1957, Lauro René, *née* Martines; 1 s (Lucien Christopher b 1959); *Career* writer; worked as translator and teacher; fiction: We Might See Sights! and other stories (1968), Godded and Codded (1970, published as Three Lovers 1971), Man in the Cellar (1974), Women in the Wall (1975), No Country for Young Men (1980), Daughters of Passion (1982), The Obedient Wife (1982), The Irish Signorina (1984); Not in God's Image: Women in History from the Greeks to the Victorians (co-ed, 1973); translator: Two Memoirs of Renaissance Florence: The Diaries of Buonaccorso Pitti and Gregorio Dati (1967), A Man of Parts (1968); memb Soc of Authors; *Recreations* karate, gardening; *Style—* Ms Julia O'Faolain; Rogers, Coleridge & White Ltd, 20 Powis Mews, London W11 1JN (☎ 071 221 3717, 071 229 9084)

O'FERRALL, Lady Elizabeth (Cecilia); *née* Hare; da of 4 Earl of Listowel (d 1931); *b* 1914; *m* 1, 1936, Maj Viscount Elveden, RA (TA) (d 1945), s of 2 Earl of Iveagh; m 2, 1947, Edward Rory More O'Ferrall; *Style—* Lady Elizabeth O'Ferrall; The Old Rectory, Elveden, Suffolk; Gloucester Lodge, Regent's Park, London NW1

O'GORMAN, Dr Margaret Elizabeth Nelson; da of William James O'Gorman (d 1957), and Mary Ethel O'Gorman; *b* 20 July 1938; *Educ* Ipswich HS, Univ of Glasgow (MB ChB, DipPsychMed); *Career* former sr registrar Royal Hosp Sick Children Glasgow, conslt Child and Adolescent Psychiatry Forth Valley Health Bd Stirling Royal Infirmary 1971-, currently hon visiting lectr Dept Sociology Univ of Stirling; MRCPsych 1971; *Recreations* gardening, windsurfing, quilting; *Style—* Dr Margaret O'Gorman; Dept of Child & Adolescent Psychiatry, The Royal Infirmary, Stirling FK8 2AU (☎ 0786 73151)

O'GRADY, Prof Francis William; CBE (1984), TD (1970); s of Francis Joseph O'Grady (d 1961), and Lilian Maud Hitchock (d 1977); *b* 7 Nov 1925; *Educ* St Ignatius Coll, Archbishop Tenison's GS, Univ of London (MSc, MD); *m* 17 May 1951, Madeleine Marie-Therese, da of Julien Becquart (d 1950); 3 da (Siobhan b 1952, Catherine b 1955, Michele b 1959); *Career* Nat Serv sr specialist in pathology 1954-56, T and AVR 1956-73; asst pathologist Middx Hosp: 1952-54, 1956-58, 1961-62; asst prof of med John Hopkins Univ 1959-60, reader and prof of bacteriology St Bartholomew's Hosp 1962-74, fndn prof of microbiology Univ of Nottingham 1974-88, chief scientist DHSS 1986-90; Ctee on Safety of Med 1971-75, Ctee on Review of Meds 1975-79; memb: Public Health Laboratory Serv Bd 1980-86, MRC 1980-84 and 1986, Nat Biological Standards Bd 1983-86; FRCPath 1972, FRCP 1976; *Books* Antibiotic and Chemotherapy (6 ed, 1991), Microbial Perturbation of Host Responses (1981); *Style—* Prof Francis O'Grady, CBE, TD; Department of Physiology and Pharmacology, Medical School, Queen's Medical Centre, Nottingham NG7 2UH (☎ 0602 709464)

O'GRADY, The; Lt-Col Gerald Vigors de Courcy O'Grady; MC (1945); s of late Lt-Col Standish de Courcy O'Grady, CMG, DSO; *b* 5 Sept 1912; *Educ* Arnold House, Wellington, RMA; *m* 1, 1941 (m dis 1961), Pamela Violet, da of Lt-Col T A Thornton, CVO, DL, of Brockhall, Northampton; 1 s, 1 da; m 2, 1961, Mollie, da of Robert Mclean, of Gibson Island, Maryland, USA; 2 da; *Career* joined RA 1932, Lt 1935, ADC to C-in-C India 1939, Maj 1940, instr RMA Sandhurst 1947, ret 1947; chm Limerick Show Soc 1975-78; chm: Irish Friesian Breeders Club, Irish Grassland Assoc, Limerick Hunt 1974-82; *Style—* The O'Grady of Kilballyowen, MC; Kilballyowen, Bruff, Co Limerick, Ireland (☎ 061 82213)

O'GRADY, Hon Mrs (Joan Eleanor); *née* Ramsbotham; da of late 1 Viscount Soulbury, GCMG, GCVO, OBE, MC; *b* 1917; *m* 1950, Maj Robert Hardress Standish O'Grady, MC, Irish Gds; 1 s, 2 da; *Style—* The Hon Mrs O'Grady; Midford Place, Midford, Bath, Avon

O'HAGAN, Antony Richard (Tony); TD (1976, 1 Clasp 1982, 2 Clasp 1988); s of Capt Desmond O'Hagan, CMG, of Kianjibbi, Kiambu, Kenya, and Pamela Jane, *née* Symes-Thompson; *b* 3 Oct 1942; *Educ* Wellington; *m* 6 Dec 1975, Caroline Jessica, da of Walter Herbert Franklin (d 1987), of Clements Farm, Gt Rissington, Glos; 1 s (Richard Franklin b 19 Oct 1979), 1 da (Clare Pamela b 6 Sept 1976); *Career* HAC: non-cmmnd serv 1962-67, 2 Lt 1967, Capt 1975, Maj 1982; TA watch keeper 3 Armd Div HQRA 1984-90; mangr Coopers & Lybrand 1972-73, gp accountant Hays Wharf Group 1973-76, fin accountant Freemans Mail Order 1977-82, fin dir St Martins Property Corporation Ltd 1986- (chief accountant 1982-85); memb Fin and Mgmnt Ctees Hightown Housing Assoc Ltd, vice pres HAC 1990- (treas 1987-90); Freeman City of London 1979, Liveryman Worshipful Co of Fanmakers 1980 (chm Livery Ctee 1989); FCA (1978); *Recreations* tennis, swimming, skiing, fishing, gardening; *Clubs* Army and Navy; *Style—* Antony R O'Hagan, Esq, TD; 8 Anglefield Rd, Berkhamsted, Herts HP43JA (☎ 0442 875 682); St Martins Property Corporation Ltd, Adelaide House, London Bridge EC4R 9DT (☎ 071 626 3411)

O'HAGAN, 4 Baron (UK 1870); Charles Towneley Strachey; MEP (EDG) Devon 1979-; s of Hon Anthony Strachey (d 1955), who assumed surname Strachey *vice* Towneley-O'Hagan 1938 and added forename Towneley; he was s of 3 Baron O'Hagan (d 1961) by his 1 w, Hon Frances Strachey (da of 1 Baron Strachie); *b* 6 Sept 1945; *Educ* Eton, New Coll Oxford; *m* 1, 1967 (m dis 1984), HSH Princess Tamara, former w of Lt Cdr Thomas Smith-Dorrien-Smith, of Tresco Abbey, Isles of Scilly, and er da of HSH Prince Michael Imeretinsky (of the Princely family of Bagration, sometime rulers of an independent Georgia), RAFVR, of Menton; 1 da (Hon Nino b 1968); m 2, 1985, Mrs Mary Claire Parsons, only da of Rev Leslie Roose-Francis, of Trencoth, Blisland, Bodmin, Cornwall; 1 da (Hon Antonia b 1986); *Heir* bro, Hon Richard Strachey; *Career* page of honour to HM 1959-62; ind memb Euro Parl 1973-75, jr oppn whip Lds 1977-79, sits as Cons in House of Lords; *Clubs* Pratt's, Turf; *Style—* The Rt Hon the Lord O'Hagan, MEP; Rashleigh Barton, Wembworthy, Chulmleigh, N Devon

O'HAGAN, Simon Timothy Byard; s of Alan Bernard O'Hagan, of Langley Heath, Kent, and Heather Mary Byard, *née* White; *b* 25 Sept 1957; *Educ* King's Sch Rochester, Univ of Birmingham (BA); *m* 6 May 1989, Lindsay Carol, da of Laurence Frederick John Bray; 1 da (Isabel Clare b 23 Dec 1990); *Career* reporter and sports writer Kent Messenger Newspaper 1978-81, dep sports ed The Times 1988-89 (sports sub-ed 1982-86, dep chief sports sub-ed 1986-88), sports ed The Independent on Sunday 1990- (former dep sports ed); ed Talk (the magazine of the National Deaf Children's Soc) 1983-85; *Recreations* cricket, golf; *Style—* Simon O'Hagan, Esq; The Independent On Sunday, 40 City Road, London EC1 (☎ 071 415 1315, fax 071 415 1333)

O'HALLORAN, Sir Charles Ernest; s of Charles O'Halloran; *b* 26 May 1924; *Educ* Conway St Central Sch Birkenhead; *m* 1943, Annie Rowan; 1 s, 2 da; *Career* served WWII RN; provost Ayr 1964-67 (memb Ayr Cncl 1953, Freeman of Burgh 1975), Parly candidate (Lab) Ayr Burghs 1966, convener Strathclyde Regnl Cncl 1978-82, chm Irvine New Town Development Corporation 1982-85, memb Local Authys Accounts Cmmn for Scotland 1983-85, chm Citizens Advice Scotland 1988-90; kt 1981; *Style—* Sir Charles O'Halloran; 40 Savoy Park, Ayr

O'HALLORAN, Michael Joseph; s of Martin O'Halloran (d 1968); *b* 20 Aug 1928; *Educ* Clohanes Nat Sch (Ireland); *m* 1956, Stella Beatrice, da of James McDonald (d 1934); 1 s decd, 3 da (Diane b 1961, Bernadette d 1963, Mary b 1966); *Career* MP (Lab, NUR sponsored until 1981, SDP until 1983, Lab Ind 1983) Islington N 1969-83; former railway worker and building works mangr, returned to building indust 1983; *Recreations* rugby football, soccer football; *Clubs* Challoner; *Style—* Michael O'Halloran, Esq; 149 Cheam Rd, Cheam, Surrey SM1 4BR

O'HARA, James Patrick; s of William O'Hara (d 1978), and Breeda O'Hara (d 1990); *b* 8 March 1935; *Educ* Christian Bros Sch Ballinroe Mayo, Harvard; *m* 21 April 1965, Patricia Marion, da of John Whyte (d 1985); 2 s (Patrick b 12 Feb 1966, Connor b 23 Feb 1971); *Career* Bank of Ireland: joined 1952, mangr Cork area office 1969, sr rep N America 1971, asst gen mangr Cork, gen mangr ops Dublin 1983, gen mangr branch banking London 1988, exec dir Bank of Ireland Group Holdings Britain Ltd, non exec dir Home Mortages Ltd; non exec dir Br Credit Tst; memb Inst of Bankers in Ireland; *Recreations* golf, tennis, fishing; *Clubs* Burhill Golf, Foxhills Golf; *Style—* James O'Hara, Esq; Bank of Ireland, 36 Queen St, London EC4A 1BN (☎ 071 329 4500, fax 071 489 1313, telex 8812635)

O'HARE, Kevin Patrick; s of Michael J O'Hare, and Anne Veronica, *née* O'Callaghan;

Educ White Lodge (Royal Ballet Lower Sch), The Royal Ballet Upper Sch, Royal Danish Ballet; *Career* ballet dancer; performances with Sadlers Wells Royal Ballet (now Birmingham Royal Ballet): Swan Lake (Prince Sigfried), Giselle (Albrecht), Les Syphides (The Poet), Lazaris (Jesus); principle roles: Choros, Hobsons Choice, Theme and Variations, Sleeping Beauty, Flowers of the Forest; created roles in: The Snow Queen, Those Unheard; promoted to: first soloist 1989, principal dancer 1990; currently dances all classical and created roles in ballets by David Bintley, Graham Lustig and William Tukett; *Style—* Kevin O'Hare, Esq; Birmingham Royal Ballet, Thorpe Street, Birmingham

O'HARE, Michael James; s of Michael Joseph O'Hare, and Anne Veronica, *née* O'Callaghan; *b* 7 Dec 1960; *Educ* Marist Coll Hull, The Royal Ballet Sch; *Career* ballet dancer; Sadlers Wells Royal Ballet (became The Birmingham Royal Ballet 1990): joined 1980, soloist 1984, princ 1987-; performed a wide range of princ roles within repertoire (character, demi-character and classical) in ballets by: Ashton, Macmillan, Balachine, De Valois, Cranko and others; the only dancer to perform all three male roles (Alain, Colas and Widow Simone) in Ashton's La Fille Mal Gardee; has danced numerous seasons at Sadlers Wells and the Royal Opera House Covent Garden and toured extensively worldwide; has worked with numerous younger choreographers; created role of Will Mossop in Hobson's Choice with choreographer David Bintley (first performance Royal Opera House 1989 and shown on BBC 2 1990); *Style—* Michael O'Hare, Esq; The Birmingham Royal Ballet, Birmingham Hippodrome, Thorp St, Birmingham B5 4AU (☎ 021 622 2555)

O'HIGGINS, Prof Paul; s of Richard Leo O'Higgins, MC (d 1973), of Rochester House, Uxbridge, Middx, and Elizabeth, *née* Deane (d 1984); *b* 5 Oct 1927; *Educ* St Columba's Coll Rathfarnham Co Dublin, Trinity Coll Dublin (MA, LLD), Clare Coll Cambridge (MA, PhD, LLD); *m* May 1951, Rachel Elizabeth, da of Prof Alan Dudley Bush, of Radlett, Herts; 1 s (Niall b 29 May 1961), 3 da (Maeve b 16 Feb 1953, Siobhan b 21 Sept 1956, Niav b 23 April 1964); *Career* Univ of Cambridge: fell Christ's Coll 1959-, univ lectr 1965-79, reader in labour law 1979-84; lectr in labour law Cncl of Legal Educn and Inns of Ct Sch of Law 1976-84, regius prof of laws Trinity Coll Dublin 1984-87, prof of law King's Coll London 1987-; author; Joseph L Andrews Bibliographical award of the American Assoc of Law Libraries 1987; memb Office of Manpower Economics Advsy Ctee on Equal Pay 1970-72; chm Cambridge branch: Nat Cncl for Civil Liberties 1970-78, Assoc of Univ Teachers 1971-75; memb: Bureau Euro Inst of Social Security 1970-, Staff Side Panel Civil Serv Arbitration Tbnl 1972-84; tstee Cambridge Union Soc 1973-84; vice pres: Inst of Safety and Public Protection 1973-, Haldane Soc 1981-, Inst Employment Rights 1989-; govr Br Inst of Human Rights 1988-; MRIA 1986; *Books* Bibliography of Periodical Literature relating to Irish Law (1966, supplements 1975 and 1983), Public Employee Trade Unionism in the UK: The Legal Framework (with Ann Arbor, 1971), Censorship in Britain (1972), A Bibliography of British & Irish Labour Law (1975), Workers' Rights (1976), Employment Law (4 edn 1981), Labour Law in Great Britain and Ireland to 1978 (1981), Discrimination in Employment in Northern Ireland (1984), A Bibliography of Irish Trials and other Legal Proceedings (1986), A Bibliography of the Literature on British & Irish Social Security Law (1986), A Biography of British and Irish Labour Law 1979-88 (1991); *Recreations* travel, talk, wine; *Clubs* Royal Dublin Soc; *Style—* Prof Paul O'Higgins; Christ's Coll Cambridge CB2 3BU (☎ 0223 334900)

O'KEEFFE, (Peter) Laurence; CMG (1983), CVO (1974); s of Richard O'Keeffe (d 1982), and Alice Gertrude Chase; *b* 9 July 1931; *Educ* De la Salle Coll Toronto Canada, St Francis Xavier's Coll Liverpool, Univ of Oxford (BA); *m* 1954, Suzanne Marie, da of Francis Jousse, of Versailles France; 3 da (Catherine, Isabel, Juliet); *Career* HM ambass Dakar Senegal (also accredited to Mali, Mauretania, Guinea, Guinea-Bissau, Cape Verde Islands); resident chm Civil Serv Selection Bd (Dip Serv) 1986, ambass/head of delgn to the Vienna CSCE conf 1986-89, HM Ambass to Czechoslovakia 1989-; *Books* as Laurence Halley: Simultaneous Equations (1975), Abiding City (1986), Ancient Affections (1985); *Recreations* photography; *Clubs* Utd Oxford and Cambridge Univ, Dutch Treat (NY); *Style—* Laurence O'Keeffe, Esq, CMG, CVO; HM Ambassador at Prague, British Embassy, Thunovska 14, Prague 1, Czechoslovakia (☎ 010 42 2 533340)

O'KEEFFE, Ronald Dixon; s of Harvey Dixon O'Keeffe, of Dublin, and May Rose, *née* Burn (d 1985); *b* 20 Nov 1938; *Educ* Wesley Coll Dublin; *m* 1963, Gillian Ruth, da of Cyril John Chasmar; 1 s (Andrew Dixon b 5 Oct 1966), 1 da (Sonya Clare b 12 Dec 1967); *Career* Nat Serv 1960-61; trainee accountant 1958-60, sales training mangr Nestle 1965-67 (joined 1962), regnl sales mangr Standard Brands 1970-74 (account mangr 1968-70); The Jenks Gp: nat account mangr 1974-78, nat account controller 1978-87, divnl dir 1984-, sales dir 1987-; *Recreations* golf; *Clubs* Hartley Wintney Golf; *Style—* Ronald O'Keeffe, Esq; The Jenks Group, Castle House, 71-75 Desborough Rd, High Wycombe, Bucks (☎ 0494 33456, fax 0494 463245)

O'KELLY, Elizabeth; MBE (1959); da of Alfred Percival O'Kelly, (d 1940), and Nina Marguerite, *née* Stevens (d 1947); *b* 19 May 1915; *Educ* Withington Girls Sch, Royal Manchester Coll of Music (ARMCM); *Career* 2 Offr WRNS 1941-46; princ community devpt offr Cameroons 1950-62, advsr Govt of Sarawak on Woman's Insts 1962-65, actg dir Asian Christian Serv Vietnam 1967-69, gen sec Assoc Country Women of the World 1969-72; contrib numerous articles and conference papers on Third World Problems; memb ACWW, Int Womans Trib Centre NY, E Sussex Fedn of WI, Pestalozzi Int Children's Village Tst, Intermediate Tech Devpt GP; Order of the Star of Sarawak 1964; *Books* Aid and Self Help (1973), Rural Woman, their Integration in Development Programmes (1978), Water and Sanitation for All (1982), Simple Technologies for Rural Woman in Bangladesh (1977), Processing and Storage of Food Grains for Rural Families (1979); *Recreations* music, gardening, walking; *Style—* Miss Elizabeth O'Kelly, MBE; Flat 2, Downash House, Rosemary Lane, Flimwell, E Sussex TN5 7PS (☎ 058 587 569)

O'KELLY, Hon Mrs (Mary Gail); *née* Mitchell-Thomson; da of 3 Baron Selsdon; *b* 1939; *m* 1963, Patrick John O'Kelly, MB, BCH; 3 s; *Style—* The Hon Mrs O'Kelly

O'LEARY, Catherine Elizabeth (Mrs Martyn Bennett); da of late Cornelius Raphael O'Leary, and late Hannah Elizabeth Dennehy, *née* Neville; *b* 14 Aug 1957; *Educ* Hollies Convent GS, Univ of Liverpool (LLB); *m* 6 Sept 1980, (John) Martyn Bennett, s of Dr John Garner Bennett, JP, of Crosby, Liverpool; 2 s (Henry b 1985, Edwin b 1987); *Career* called to the Bar Grays Inn 1979; pupil Lincolns Inn 1979-80, practising on Wales and Chester circuit 1980-; memb: Family Law Bar Assoc, Wales and Chester Fees and Legal Aid Ctee; *Recreations* drama, cooking, riding; *Style—* Miss Catherine O' Leary; Stanthorne House, Burton Lane, Duddon, nr Tarporley, Cheshire CW6 0EP (☎ 082 924 303); 40 King St, Chester (☎ 0244 323 886)

O'LEARY, Maj (John) Charles; s of Francis Aloysious O'Leary (d 1970), and Helen Mary Agnes O'Leary (d 1938); *b* 23 Aug 1927; *Educ* Laxton; *m* 18 Oct 1952, Barbara, da of Dr Sydney Wray (d 1958); 2 s (Simon b 1954, Anthony b 1957), 1 da (Catherine (Mrs Walsh) b 1953); *Career* enlisted Army 1945, RMA Sandhurst 1947-48, cmmnd RA 1948, Regtl Serv 1948-58, Staff Coll 1959, Staff Regtl Serv 1960-77, ret Maj 1977; memb Ctee W Surrey Hydon Hill Cheshire Home 1977-; Liveryman: Worshipful Co of Barbers 1981, Worshipful Soc of Apothecaries 1987 (clerk 1977); MBIM 1977; *Recreations* walking, gardening, birdwatching; *Clubs* HAC; *Style—* Maj Charles O'Leary; Brackens Edge, 21 Kingswood Firs, Grayshott, nr Hindhead, Surrey GU26 6ET; Society of Apothecaries, Apothecaries Hall, Black Friars Lane, London EC4V 6EJ (☎ 071 236 1180)

O'LEARY, Prof Cornelius; s of Michael Joseph O'Leary (d 1950), of Foynes Co Limerick and Mary, *née* Donworth (d 1980); *b* 15 Aug 1927; *Educ* Clongowes Wood Coll, Univ Coll Cork (BA, MA, DLitt), Nuffield Coll Oxford (D Phil); *Career* prof Queen's Univ Belfast 1979- (lectr political sci 1960-66, reader 1966-79); vice pres Irish Ctee Historical Scis 1975-76 (sec 1969-72), pres Political Studies Assoc of Ireland 1988-90 (vice pres 1987-88); memb Royal Irish Acad 1983; *Books* The Irish Republic and its Experiment with Proportional Respresentation (1961), The Elimination of Corrupt Practices in British Elections 1868-1911 (1962), Belfast: Approach to Crisis: A Study of Belfast Politics 1613-1970 (with Ian Budge, 1973), Irish Elections 1918-1977 (1979), The Northern Ireland Assembly 1982-1986: A Study in Constitutional Development (jtly, 1988); *Recreations* swimming; *Clubs* Ulster Arts; *Style—* Prof Cornelius O'Leary; Department of Political Science, Queen's University of Belfast, Belfast BT7 1NN (☎ 0232 245133, telex 74487, fax 0232 247895)

O'LEARY, (Edmund) Eamon; s of James O'Leary (d 1961), and Margaret Mary, *née* Cullinane; *b* 14 Aug 1933; *Educ* St Kieran's Coll Kilkenny, Univ Coll Cork (BE); *m* 9 June 1958, Denise, da of Dennis Coffey (d 1955); 2 da (Michele Ann b 26 Nov 1960, Clodagh Denise b 10 March 1964); *Career* res engr Waterford CC 1954-58, asst engr Rendel Palmer Tritton 1958-59, ptnr Veryard & Walsh and Partners 1959-61, sr ptnr Veryard & Ptnrs 1971- (ptnr 1961-71); chm: S Wales Branch ICE 1978, S Wales Inst of Engrs 1988, Concrete Soc Wales 1970 and 1976 (pres 1989); memb Exec Ctee Tenovus; hon res fell Univ of Wales Cardiff; FICE, FIEI, FInstrucE, MIHT, FRSA, MConsE; *Recreations* golf; *Clubs* Royal Porthcawl Golf, Radyr Golf (Capt 1977); *Style—* Eamon O'Leary, Esq; 39 Heol Don, Whitchurch, Cardiff CF4 2AS (☎ 0222 626516); Veryard & Partners, Crwys House, Crwys Rd, Cardiff CF2 4NB (☎ 0222 222664, fax 0222 384520)

O'LEARY, Terence Daniel; CMG (1982); s of Daniel O'Leary (d 1948), and Mary, *née* Duggan (d 1979); *b* 18 Aug 1928; *Educ* Dulwich Coll, St John's Coll Cambridge (MA); *m* 1960, Janet Douglas, da of Dr Hugh Berney (d 1978), of Masterton, NZ; 2 s (John, Daniel (twins)), 1 da (Helen); *Career* served Queen's Royal Regt, Capt RARO; HM Dip Serv 1953-88; serv ed: NZ, India, Tanganyika, Australia, Cabinet Off, S Africa, NZ; sr civil dir Nat Def Coll 1978-81; Br high cmmr: Sierra Leone 1981-84, NZ, Western Samoa; govr of Pitcairn 1984-87, chm Petworth Preservation 1989-; *Clubs* Travellers', Wellington (NZ); *Style—* T D O'Leary, Esq, CMG; The Old Rectory, Petworth, W Sussex

O'LOGHLEN, Sir Colman Michael; 6 Bt (UK 1838), of Drumconora, Ennis; s of Henry Ross O'Loghlen (d 1944), and n of 5 Bt (d 1951); *b* 6 April 1916; *Educ* Xavier Coll Melbourne, Melbourne Univ (LLB); *m* 1939, Margaret, da of Francis O'Halloran, of Melbourne; 6 s, 2 da; *Heir* s, Michael O'Loghlen; *Career* served 1942-45 with AIF New Guinea, Capt 1945; stipendiary magistrate Lae New Guinea, former actg judge of Supreme Ct of Territory of Papua and New Guinea; *Style—* Sir Colman O'Loghlen, Bt; 98 Williamsons Rd, Doncaster, Vic 3108, Australia

O'LOGHLEN, Michael; s and h of Sir Colman O'Loghlen, 6 Bt, LLB; *b* 21 May 1925; *Style—* Michael O'Loghlen Esq

O'MAHONY, Jeremiah Francis; s of Philip Joseph O'Mahony (d 1979), and Maria, *née* Kavanagh; *b* 23 Dec 1946; *Educ* Challoner Sch Finchley, Finchley GS; *m* 27 Jan 1973, Mary Josephine, da of Christopher James Blaney (d 1975); 4 s (Oliver James b 1976, Ronan b 1977, Ruadhri b 1980, Theodore b 1983), 1 da (Cressida b 1987); *Career* vice chm and gp fin dir Ladbroke Group plc 1990-; FCA; *Recreations* running, swimming, tennis, reading, family; *Style—* Jeremiah O'Mahony, Esq; Ladbroke Gp plc, 10 Cavendish Place, London W1M 9DJ

O'MALLEY, Donald Albert; s of Peter O'Malley, and Florence Rose O'Malley, *née* Evans; *b* 3 Feb 1931; *Educ* St Mary's Harry Cheshire; *m* 1954, Brenda Eileen, da of Jesse Wall (d 1984); 1 s (Simon), 1 da (Kim); *Career* carpet weaver; pres Power Loom Carpet Weavers' & Textile Workers' Union; *Style—* Donald O'Malley, Esq; 46 Castle Rd, Cookley, nr Kidderminster, Worcs (☎ 0562 850637); Gilt Edge Carpets, Mill St, Kidderminster, Worcs (☎ 0562 3434)

O'MALLEY, His Honour Judge Stephen Keppel; *b* 21 July 1940; *Educ* Ampleforth, Waltham Coll Oxford; *m* 1963, Frances Mary, da of James Ryan; 4 s, 2 da; *Career* barr Inner Temple 1962, rec 1978-89, circuit judge (Western Circuit) 1989-; wine treas of the Western circuit 1986-; co-fndr Bar European Gp 1977; *Books* The Manual of European Practice (1988), O'Malley & Layton Manual of European Practice (with Alexander Layton); *Style—* His Honour Judge O'Malley

O'MORCHOE, The; David Nial Creagh O'Morchoe; CB (1979), MBE (1966); formerly of Oulartleigh and Monamolin; s of Col Nial Creagh O'Morchoe (The O'Morchoe), d 1970, when suc by his s David as Chieftain; *b* 17 May 1928; *Educ* St Columba's Coll Dublin, RMA Sandhurst; *m* 1955, Margaret (*Style* Madam O'Morchoe), da of Frank Brewitt, of Cork; 2 s (Dermot b 1956, Kevin b 1958), 1 da (Maureen b 1964); *Career* served Royal Irish Fus from 1948 in M East, Med, NW Europe, Kenya, Oman; late Cdr of Sultan of Oman's Land Forces; *Recreations* sailing, sheep farming; *Clubs* Friendly Brothers, Irish Cruising; *Style—* The O'Morchoe, CB, MBE; c/o Ulster Bank, Cork, Eire

O'NEIL, (James) Roger; s of James William O'Neil (d 1980), and Claire Williams O'Neil (d 1981); *b* 22 Feb 1938; *Educ* Laurel Hill Acad USA, Univ of Notre Dame (BSc), Cornell Univ (MBA); *m* 30 Oct 1976, Joan, da of Mark Mathewson, of California, USA; 1 s (Mark Daniel b 1983), 1 da (Claire Kathyrn b 1980); *Career* Mobil Oil Corpn 1961-; former chm: Mobil Oil Cyprus Ltd, Mobil SE Asia, Mobil Oil Italiana SPA; chm and chief exec Mobil Oil Co Ltd 1987-; vice pres: UK Petroleum Indust Assoc, Inst of Petroleum; memb: President's Cncl Asia Soc NY, Advsy Bd Cornell Univ Johnson Sch of Business NY; FRSA 1988, FInstPet 1988; *Recreations* tennis, skiing, music, archaelogy; *Clubs* RAC, Hurlingham; *Style—* Roger O'Neil, Esq; 6 Kingston Hse North, Princes Gate, London SW7; Mobil Oil Co Ltd, 54-60 Victoria St, London SW1E 6QB (☎ 071 828 9777, fax 071 828 9777 ext 2432, telex 8812411 MOBIL G)

O'NEILL, David John; s of John Richard O'Neill, of St Helens, Merseyside, and Josephine Elizabeth, *née* Morris; *b* 1 May 1954; *Educ* West Park GS St Helens, Open Univ (BA), Inst of Health Servs (Mangr's Dip); *m* 8 Aug 1981, Patricia, da of Patrick Walsh; 2 s (Luke David b 1 Feb 1985, Thomas Francis b 19 Sept 1988); *Career* in trg Mersey Regnl Health Authy 1974-78, hosp admin Stockport Health Authy 1978-84, unit admin SE Staffs Health Authy 1984-86, dep gen mangr South Tees Health Authy 1984-89 gen mangr Trafford Health Unit 1989-; memb Inst of Health Servs Management 1974-; *Recreations* swimming, music, reading, travel; *Style—* David O'Neill, Esq; Trafford General Hospital, Moorside Rd, Davyhulme, Manchester M31 3SL (☎ 061 748 4022, ext 555, fax 061 746 8556)

O'NEILL, Denis Basil; s of Gilbert Joseph Lane O'Neill (d 1961), of Putney, London, and Winifred Mary, *née* Erskine-White (d 1980); *b* 23 July 1922; *Educ* Douai Sch, Imperial Coll London (BSc, ACGI); *m* 27 Feb 1954, Jacqueline Mary, da of Guy Holman Tatum (d 1968), of Kensington, London; 2 s (Duncan b 1957, Robin b 1960), 1 da (Susan (Mrs Paul Austen) b 1955); *Career* WWII Maj RE DAQMG HQ Central

Cmd India 1942-47; consltg engr (vibration and noise) 1949-, chm Hawkes & Co Savile Row 1969-71, dir Civil Engrg Dynamics Ltd 1989-; memb: Drafting Ctee British Standard Code of Practice 2012, Ctee Soc for Earthquake and Civil Engrg Dynamics 1972-77, Steering Ctee CIRIA Piling Vibration Res Project 1982-; author First TRRL Report on Traffic Vibration and Heritage Bldgs 1988; MICE 1963; *Recreations* music, theatre, travel, video photography, grandchildren; *Style*— Denis O'Neill, Esq; 2 Halsey St, London SW3

O'NEILL, Dennis James; s of Dr William Patrick O'Neill (d 1986), of Adelaide House, Pontardulais, S Wales, and Eva Ann, *née* Rees; *b* 25 Feb 1948; *Educ* Gowerton GS, studied singing privately with Frederick Cox in London and Campogalliani (Mantova) Ricci in Rome; *m* 1, 4 April 1970 (m dis 1987), Margaret Ruth da of Rev Edward Collins, of Old Harlow, Essex; 1 s (Sean b 22 Dec 1979), 1 da (Clare b 21 July 1977); m 2, 11 Jan 1988, Ellen, da of Hans Einar Folkestad, of Tybakken, Norway; *Career* tenor and broadcaster; operatic debut: Royal Opera House Covent Garden 1979 (thereafter annually), Metropolitan Opera NYC 1986 (thereafter annually), Vienna State Opera 1981, Hamburg State Opera 1981, San Francisco 1984, Chicago Lyric 1985, Paris Opera 1986; many recordings; presenter Dennis O'Neill BBC 2; pres Friends of WNO, fndr Dennis O'Neill Bursary; *Recreations* cookery, photography; *Style*— Dennis O'Neill, Esq; c/o Ingpen & Williams, 14 Kensington Ct, London W8 (☎ 071 937 5158/9, fax 0222 340660)

O'NEILL, Derham Charles; s of Charles Daniel O'Neill (d 1984), and Phyllis, *née* Derham (d 1983); *b* 4 July 1943; *Educ* St Mary's Coll Crosby, Univ of Manchester (LLB), Manchester Business Sch (MBA); *m* 5 Aug 1967, Patricia, da of William Kay (d 1963); 1 s (Derham Aidan b 1977), 1 da (Katharine Alexandra b 1975); *Career* admitted slr 1968; md Brown Shipley Fund Mgmnt Ltd 1979-81, corp fin ptnr Clifford Turner (now Clifford Chance) 1981-; Freeman Worshipful Co of Slrs; memb Law Soc; *Books* Management Buyouts (contrib 1988); *Recreations* windsurfing, skiing, swimming, moral philosophy; *Style*— Derham O'Neill, Esq; Royex House, Aldermanbury Square, London EC2V 7LD (☎ 071 600 0808, fax 071 726 8561, telex 8959991)

O'NEILL, Hon Hugh Torrens; o s and h of 2 Baron Rathcavan (by his 1 w); *b* 14 June 1939; *Educ* Eton; *m* 1983, Sylvie Marie-Thérèse, da of Georges Wichard, of Provence, France; 1 s (François b 1984); *Career* Capt Irish Gds; journalist: Irish Times, Observer, Financial Times; dir: Lamont Holdings plc, Ulster Financial Ltd, The Old Bushmills Distillery Co Ltd, St Quentin Ltd, Savoy Management Ltd; chm: NI Airports Ltd, NI Tourist Bd, FRX International Ltd; *Recreations* food, travel; *Clubs* Beefsteak, Garrick; *Style*— The Hon Hugh O'Neill; 14 Thurloe Place, London SW7 2RZ (☎ 071 581 3511); Cleggan Lodge, Broughshane, Ballymena, Co Antrim BT43 7JW (☎ 0266 84209)

O'NEILL, Rev Prof John Cochrane; s of John Archibald O'Neill (d 1982), of Melbourne, Australia, and Beni Alberta, *née* Cochrane; *b* 8 Dec 1930; *Educ* Melbourne C of E GS, Univ of Melbourne (BA), Ormond Coll Theol Hall (BD), Univ of Cambridge (PhD); *m* 17 April 1954, Judith Beatrice, da of John Ramsden Lyall (d 1980), of Melbourne, 3 da (Rachel b 1957, Catherine b 1959, Philippa b 1961); *Career* Dunn prof of New Testament language, lit and theol Westminster Coll Cambridge 1964-85, prof of New Testament language, lit and theol Univ of Edinburgh 1985; *Books* The Theology of Acts in its Historical Setting (2 edn, 1970), The Puzzle of 1 John (1966), The Recovery of Paul's Letter to the Galatians (1972), Paul's Letter to the Roman's (1975), Messiah: Six Lectures on the Ministry of Jesus (2 edn, 1984), The Bible's Authority: A Portrait Gallery of Thinkers from Lessing to Bultmann (1991); *Recreations* swimming, gardening in the allotment, walking; *Style*— The Rev Prof John O'Neill; 9 Lonsdale Terrace, Edinburgh EH3 9HN (☎ 031 229 6070); New College, The Mound, Edinburgh EH1 2LX (☎ 031 225 8400, fax 031 220 0952)

O'NEILL, Martin John; MP (Lab) Clackmannan 1983-; s of John O'Neill; *b* 6 Jan 1945; *Educ* Trinity Acad Edinburgh, Heriot Watt Univ, Moray House Educn Coll Edinburgh; *m* 1973, Elaine Samuel; 2 s; *Career* former insur clerk, asst examiner Scottish Estate Duty Office, secondary schoolteacher, tutor Open Univ; MP (Lab) Stirlingshire E and Clackmannan 1979-1983, memb Select Ctee Scottish Affrs 1979-80, oppn front bench spokesman on: Scottish Affrs 1980-84, Def and Disarmament 1984-88; princ spokesman June 1988-; *Style*— Martin O'Neill, Esq, MP; House of Commons, London SW1A 0AA (☎ 071 219 4548); constituency office: 19 Mar St, Alloa FK10 1HR (☎ 0259 721536)

O'NEILL, Hon Patrick Arthur Ingham; o s of Baron O'Neill of the Maine (Life Peer, d 1990); *b* 18 Jan 1945; *Educ* Eton; *m* 1, 1975 (m dis 1984), Anne, da of Douglas Lillecrapp, of Adelaide, S Australia; 2 da (Sophie b 1976, Elizabeth Mary b 1981); m 2, 1984, Stella Mary, da of Sir Alexander Downer, KBE (d 1981), of Martinsell, Williamstown, S Australia; *Career* Lt QRI Hussars; reporter ABC TV, prodr Channel 10 Current Affairs; cllr: Nat Tst of S Australia 1982-84, Nat Tst of Australia NSW 1976-77; *Recreations* travel, conversation, music; *Style*— The Hon Patrick O'Neill

O'NEILL, 4 Baron (UK 1868); Raymond Arthur Clanaboy O'Neill; TD (1970), DL (Co Antrim 1967); s of 3 Baron O'Neill (ka Italy 1944); the O'Neills stem from the oldest traceable family in Europe; *b* 1 Sept 1933; *Educ* Eton, RAC Cirencester; *m* 1963, Georgina Mary, da of Lord George Montagu Douglas Scott (3 s of 7 Duke of Buccleuch), of The Alms House, Weekley, Kettering, Northants; 3 s (Hon Shane b 1965, Hon Tyrone b 1966, Hon Rory b 1968); *Heir* s, Hon Shane O'Neill; *Career* Lt-Col RARO, served with 11 Hussars Prince Albert's Own, also NI Horse (TA); dir: Shanes Developments Ltd, Shanes Castle Estates Co, Romney Hythe & Dymchurch Railway plc; chm: Ulster Countryside Ctee 1972-76, Royal Ulster Agric Soc Fin Ctee 1975-83 (pres 1984-86), NI Museums Advsy Ctee 1989-; memb: NI Tourist Bd 1973-80 (chm 1975-80), NI Nat Tst Ctee 1980- (chm 1981-); tstee Ulster Folk and Tport Museum 1969-90 (vice chm 1987-90); memb Museums and Galleries Cmmn 1987-; pres The Railway Preservation Soc of Ireland; Hon Col NI Horse (TA) 1986-; *Recreations* railways, vintage motoring, gardening, boats, shooting; *Clubs* Turf, Ulster Reform; *Style*— The Rt Hon the Lord O'Neill, TD, DL; Shanes Castle, Antrim, NI BT41 4NE (☎ 08494 63264); Conigre House, Calne, Wilts (☎ 0249 812354)

O'NEILL, Richard; s of Ashworth Richard O'Neill (d 1984), of Blucher, Newcastle upon Tyne, and Mabel Annie, *née* Page (d 1972); *b* 11 May 1926; *Educ* Lemington GS; *m* 18 March 1950, Eileen, da of Frederick Hudson Forster (d 1975), of Scotswood, Newcastle upon Tyne; 3 s (Terence Carey b 1951, Richard Carey b 1952, Shaun Carey b 1959); *Career* MN 1944-46; accountant NCB 1947-65, chief accountant Reed Int 1966-72, dir and gen mangr Reedpack Ltd (Newcastle) 1972-; ACMA 1959, FBIM 1972; *Recreations* gardening, golf; *Style*— Richard O'Neill, Esq; 40 Chapel House Rd, West Denton, Newcastle upon Tyne (☎ 091 2677564); Field Packaging, Station Rd, Killingworth, Newcastle upon Tyne NE12 0RH (☎ 091 216 0303, telex 53404 NFIELD G)

O'NEILL, Robert James (Robin); CMG (1978); s of Robert Francis O'Neill (d 1978), of Chelmsford, Essex, and Dorothy May, *née* Golding (d 1983); *b* 17 June 1932; *Educ* King Edward VI Sch Chelmsford, Trinity Coll Cambridge (MA); *m* 1958, Helen Mary, da of Horace Wells Juniper; 1 s (Mark), 2 da (Celia, Miranda); *Career* HM Dip Serv (formerly HM For Serv) 1955, served Ankara 1957-60, Dakar 1961-63, Bonn 1968-72, dep govr Gibraltar 1978-81, under-sec Cabinet Off 1981-84, asst under-sec of State For and Cwlth Off 1984-86, ambass to Austria and concurrently head of UK delgn to negotiations on mutual reduction of forces and armaments and associated measures in Centl Europe 1986-89, ambass to Belgium 1989-; *Recreations* hill walking; *Clubs* Travellers'; *Style*— Robin O'Neill, Esq, CMG; c/o FCO, King Charles St, London SW1A 2AH

O'NEILL, Prof Robert John; AO (1988); s of Joseph Henry O'Neill (d 1982), of Melbourne Australia, and Janet Gibbon, *née* Grant; *b* 5 Nov 1936; *Educ* Scotch Coll Melbourne, Royal Mil Coll of Aust, Univ of Melbourne (BE Rankine prize in Mgmnt), BNC Oxford (Rhodes scholar, MA, DPhil); *m* 23 Oct 1965, Sally Margaret, da of Donald Frank Burnard, of Adelaide Aust; 2 da (Katherine Melinda b 1968, Jennifer Louisa b 1971); *Career* Aust Army 1955-68: staff cadet 1955-58, Lieut 1958-62, Capt 1962-67 (active serv Vietnam 1966-67, despatches 1967), Maj 1967-68; lectr: mil history Royal Mil Coll of Aust, sr fell Dept of Int Relations Res Sch of Pacific Studies Aust Nat Univ 1969, head Aust Nat Univ Stategic and Defence Studies Centre 1971-82 (professional fell 1977), conslt Aust Govt and expert witness before various Parly Ctee enquirees 1969-82, dir IISS London 1982-87, Chichele prof of the History of War Univ of Oxford (fell All Souls Coll, hon fell BNC Oxford); chm: Int Studies Task Force, Campaign for Oxford, Round Table Moot, Editorial Bd of The Round Table The Cwlth Journal of Int Affairs, Mgmnt Ctee Sir Robert Menzies Centre for Aust Studies Univ of London, Bd Centre for Defence Studies King's Coll London, Int Nuclear History Prog; memb: US Social Sci Res Cncl Ctee on Peace and Int Security Studies, Bd Int Peace Acad New York, Advsy Bd Investmt Corp of America LA, Cwlth Sec Gen's Advsy Gp on Security of Small States 1984-85; govr Ditchley Fndn, tstee Imperial War Museum, armed servs ed Australian Dictionary of Biography; fell Acad of Social Sciences in Australia (1978), FRHS 1989, FIE (Aust) (1981); *Books* The German Army and the Nazi Party 1933-39 (1966), Vietnam Task (1968), General Giap: Politician and Strategist (1969), Australia in the Korean War 1950-53 (Vol 1 1981, Vol 2 1985), The Strategic Nuclear Balance (1975), Insecurity: the Spread of Weapons in the Indian and Pacific Oceans (ed 1978), Security in East Asia (ed 1978), The Conduct of East-West Relations in the 1980s (ed 1985), Doctrine, the Alliance and Arms Control (ed 1986), New Technology and Western Security Policy (ed 1985), East Asia, The West and International Security (ed 1987), Prospects for Security in the Mediterranean (ed 1988), New Directions in Strategic Thinking (ed with David Horner, 1981), The West and the Third World (ed with John Vincent, 1990); *Recreations* walking, local history; *Style*— Prof Robert O'Neill; All Souls College, Oxford OX1 4AL

O'NEILL, Hon Shane Sebastian Clanaboy; s and h of 4 Baron O'Neill, TD, DL; *b* 25 July 1965; *Educ* Eton, RAC Cirencester; *Style*— The Hon Shane O'Neill

O'NEILL, Shirley; da of Patrick O'Neill, of Atherstone, Warwicks, and Betty, *née* Ford; *b* 21 Aug 1947; *Educ* Nuneaton Sch of Art, Walthamstow Coll of Art, The Royal Academy Sch; *Career* artist; gp exhibitions: as a memb of The Wapping Studio Collective of Artists 1975-84, summer show at Serpentine Gallery 1982, Francis Graham Gallery 1988; first solo exhibition Francis Graham-Dixon Gallery 1989; *Recreations* travelling for the stimulus it provides my painting and photography; *Style*— Miss Shirley O'Neill; Studio 3, 98-100 Tottenham Road, London N1 4DP (☎ 071 249 7292); Francis Graham- Dixon Gallery, 17-18 Great Sutton St, London EC1V ODN (☎ 071 250 1962, fax 071 490 1069)

O'NEILL, Terence Patrick (Terry); s of Leonard Victor O'Neill (d 1980), of Cork, Ireland, and Josephine Mary, *née* Gallagher (d 1978); *b* 30 July 1938; *Educ* Gunnersbury GS; *m* 1, Vera Day; 1 s (Keegan Alexander), 1 da (Sarah Jane); m 2, Faye Dunaway; 1 s (Liam Walker); *Career* professional jazz drummer since 1952 in leading London clubs incl The Flamingo, The Florida and The Mapleton; Nat Serv PT instr; professional photographer: took first published pictures of The Beatles and The Rolling Stones, photographic biographer of emerging 60s personalities incl Jean Shrimpton, Terence Stamp and Michael Caine, became int celebrity photographer to politicians, royalty and rock and pop stars, work published in 52 countries (average 500 front covers per annum); *Books* Legends; *Recreations* music, reading, cooking, all sport; *Style*— Terry O'Neill, Esq

O'NEILL, Hon Mrs Nial; Virginia Lois; *née* Legge; da of John Douglas Legge, MC, former Capt Coldstream Gds (s of Lt-Col Hon Edward Legge, sometime asst serjeant-at-arms House of Commons and 3 s of 4 Earl of Dartmouth); *b* 5 May 1922; *m* 21 June 1966, Hon Nial O'Neill (d 1980), 3 and yst s of 1 Baron Rathcavan, PC; *Style*— The Hon Mrs Nial O'Neill; Crowfield House, Crowfield, Ipswich, Suffolk IP6 9TP

O'NEILL OF THE MAINE, Baroness; Katharine Jean O'Neill; *née* Whitaker; yst da of William Ingham Whitaker, JP, DL (d 1936), of Pylewell Park, Lymington, Hants, and Hon Hilda Guilhermina Dundas (d 1971), yr da of 6 Viscount Melville, ISO; *b* 16 Jan 1915; *m* 4 Feb 1944, Baron O'Neill of the Maine, PC, DL (Life Peer; d 1990); 1 s (Hon Patrick Arthur Ingham, *qv*), 1 da (Hon Penelope Anne (Hon Mrs Crutchley) b 1947); *Style*— The Rt Hon Lady O'Neill of the Maine; Lisle Court, Lymington, Hants

O'NIANS, Henry Melmoth (Hal); s of Percy Henry O'Nians (d 1957), of Tonbridge, Kent, and Agnes Aithnah, *née* Scott (d 1973); *b* 8 May 1923; *Educ* Tonbridge, Trinity Coll Oxford (BA); *m* 5 Oct 1951, Esmé Winifred, da of Arthur Cecil Howells (d 1978), of Abersychan, Mon; 3 da (Rachel (Mrs Hahn) b 1953, Judith (Mrs Stewart) b 1955, Helen b 1958); *Career* WWII RAC 1942-47; 2 Lt 141 RAC (The Buffs) 1944, Lt 1944, liaison offr HQ 31 Tank Bde 1944 (Normandy, France and Germany), 1 RTR 1945, Staff Lt Royal Mil Police Germany 1945-47; Bute St Gallery 1956-60, 6 Ryder Street Gallery 1960-84, King St Galleries St James's 1985-; Freeman City of London 1988, Liveryman Worshipful Co of Poulters; *Recreations* swimming, art exhibitions; *Clubs* Army and Navy; *Style*— H M O'Nians, Esq; 66 Upper Berkeley St, London W1 (☎ 071 724 3799); King Street Galleries, 17 King St, St James's, London SW1Y 6QU (☎ 071 930 9392/3993)

O'REGAN, (Bartholomew) Martin; s of Timothy O'Regan, RN (d 1965), of Stanmore, Middx, and Ellen, *née* Murphy (d 1981); *b* 2 Oct 1933; *Educ* Salvatorian Coll Harrow Weald, Univ of London (BSc); *m* 1, 1961 (m dis 1982), Romaulde Sabine, da of Richard Schulz; 1 s (Marc b 1962); m 2, 1984 (m dis 1990), Ann Patricia Lovell, da of James William Gamble Jones (d 1983), of Dublin; *Career* Nat Serv 1959-61, cmmnd 1960, on staff 2 Div BAOR winter warfare ski trg camp 1960-61, TA HAC 1955-59 and 1961-63, Lt (R) 1963; CA; Coopers & Lybrand 1955-63, Anglo-American Corp Africa 1963-66, dir Davies & Newman Holdings Ltd and Dan-Air Services Ltd 1966-78, fndr dir and chief exec Air Europe Ltd 1978-82; int aviation conslt (based Monaco) 1982-; chm: CA Students Soc of London 1958-59, SE London Accountants Gp 1980-81; memb Cncl Br Civil Aviation Standing Conf 1980-82; Freeman City of London 1977, Liveryman Worshipful Co of CAs 1977; ICA 1959, ICIA 1983, CIMA 1966; *Recreations* golf, swimming, aviation and travel; *Clubs* RAC and HAC; *Style*— Martin O'Regan, Esq; c/o Coutts & Co, 440 Strand, London WC2

O'REILLY, Francis Joseph; s of Lt-Col Charles Joseph O'Reilly, DSO, MC (d 1952), of Naas, Co Kildare, and Dorothy Mary Martin (d 1978); *b* 15 Nov 1922; *Educ* Ampleforth, Trinity Coll Dublin (BA, BAI, LLD); *m* 1950, Teresa Mary, da of Capt John Williams, MC (d 1965), of Co Offaly, Ireland; 3 s (Charles, Peter, Paul), 7 da (Mary, Jane, Olivia, Margaret, Rose, Louise, Julie); *Career* Lt RE 1943-46, 7 Indian Divnl Engrs SE Asia Cmd 1945-46; chm: John Power & Son Ltd 1955-66, Player and

Willis (Ireland) Ltd 1964-81, Irish Distillers Group plc 1966-83, TI Irish Raleigh 1971-80, Ulster Bank Ltd 1982-90; dir: Ulster Bank Ltd 1961-74 (dep chm 1974-82), National Westminster Bank plc 1982-90, Irish Distillers Group plc 1983-88; pres: Royal Dublin Soc 1986-89 (chm Exec Ctee 1980-86), Equestrian Fedn of Ireland 1964-79, Mktg Inst of Ireland 1983-85, Inst of Bankers in Ireland 1985-86; chllr Trinity Coll Univ of Dublin 1985- (pro-chllr 1983-85); Irish rep Fedn Equestre Internationale 1964-79; memb and tstee: Turf Club 1967-, Irish Nat Hunt Steeplechase Ctee 1967-; chm Kildare Hunt Club 1968-; *Recreations* foxhunting, racing, gardening, reading; *Clubs* Kildare Street and Univ (Dublin), Turf (Ireland); *Style*— Francis O'Reilly, Esq; The Glebe, Rathmore, Naas, Co Kildare, Ireland (☎ 045 62136)

O'REILLY, Gary Miles; s of Gerrard Desmond O'Reilly, of 62 Radburn Close, Harlow, Essex, and Mary Rita, *née* Clements; *b* 21 March 1961; *Educ* Latton Bush Comp Sch Harlow, Middlesex Poly; *m* 20 June 1987, Susan, da of John Ferguson Wood; *Career* professional footballer; schoolboy player: Essex Schs 1974-79, England under 18 1977-79, Eire youth 1978-79; Tottenham Hotspur 1979-84: signed professional Sept 1979 (former youth player), debut v Southampton Dec 1980, 56 appearances; 92 appearances Brighton & Hove Albion 1984-87, over 80 appearances Crystal Palace 1987-, 12 appearances on-loan IF Elfsberg Sweden 1988; achievements with Tottenham Hotspur: squad memb FA Cup finals 1981 and 1982, Wembley debut Charity Shield v Liverpool 1982, squad player UEFA Cup 1983-84; honours with Crystal Palace: promotion to Div 1 1989, runners up FA Cup 1990; javelin: Essex youth champion 1977-78, England Schs finalist 1978, AAA jrs finalist 1976 (fourth place 1977); currently studying for diploma in wine; *Recreations* wine, all sports; *Style*— Gary O'Reilly, Esq; Crystal Palace FC, Selhurst Park, London SE25 (☎ 081 653 4462)

O'REILLY, Dr John Francis; s of Denis Patrick O'Reilly, of Kuntsford Cheshire, and Mary, *née* Ward; *b* 2 May 1952; *Educ* St Ambrose Coll Halebarns Cheshire, Trinity Coll Cambridge (MA, MB BChir); *m* 16 July 1977, Carol Linda, da of Harold Hanson (d 1984), of Tunbridge Wells, Kent; 1 s (David b 1981), 1 da (Sarah b 1979); *Career* conslt physician in gen and thoracic med Victoria and Fylde Coast Hosps Blackpool; MRCP 1978; *Recreations* sailing; *Style*— Dr John F O'Reilly; Fairways, Laburnum Ave, Lytham St Annes, Lancs; Victoria and Fylde Coast Hospitals, Blackpool, Lancs (☎ 0253 303477)

O'REILLY, Prof John James; s of Patrick William O'Reilly (d 1969), of Bromsgrove, Worcs, and Dorothy Anne Lewis (d 1968); *b* 1 Dec 1946; *Educ* Sacred Heart Coll Droitwich, Brunel Univ (BTech), Univ of Essex (PhD); *m* 18 July 1968, Margaret, da of Lewis Brooke (d 1983), of Coven, Staffs; 1 s (Edward James b 1986), 1 da (Jenny Ann b 1978); *Career* Ultra Electonics Ltd 1969-72, sr lectr Univ of Essex 1972-85, researcher PO Res Centre 1978-79, prof and head of Sch Univ of Wales at Bangor 1985-, chief exec IDB Ltd 1985-; govr Gwynedd Tech Coll, memb SERC/DTI Communications and Distributed Systems Ctee; CEng, MIEE 1983, FIEE 1988, CPhys, FInstP; *Books* Telecommunication Principles (1984, 2 edn 1989), Optimisation Methods in Electronics and Communications (1984), Problems of Randomness in Communications Engineering (1984); *Recreations* family, music, theatre; *Style*— Prof John O'Reilly; School of Electronic Engineering Science, University of Wales at Bangor, Dean St, Bangor, Gwynedd LL57 1UT (☎ 0248 351151, telex 61100, fax 0248 361429)

O'RIORDAN, Brian Colman; s of Patrick Joseph O'Riordan (d 1974), and Bridget, *née* Madigan; *b* 25 Oct 1935; *Educ* Blackrock Coll Dublin, Univ Coll Cork (BDSI); *m* 17 Aug 1963, Valerie Ann, da of Rev Richard Rogers; 2 s (Sean Peter b 12 March 1968, Kieran Paul b 5 Oct 1970), 2 da (Rebecca Jane b 3 July 1969, Susannah Niamh b 24 Oct 1971); *Career* conslt oral surgn: Mount Vernon Hosp 1970, St Albans City Hosp 1970, Royal Nat Orthopaedic Hosp 1970; conslt dental radiologist King's Coll Sch of Med and Dentistry London; pres Br Soc of Dental and Maxillo-Facial Radiology 1981-82, rep Bd of Br Dental Assoc 1984-, treas Br Soc of Oral and Maxillo-Facial Surgery 1986-89 (memb Cncl 1983-86); chm: Cncl of Middx and Herts Branch BDA 1986-89, Steering Ctee to set up Euro Assoc for Dental and Maxillo-Facial Radiology, Regnl Dental Ctee NW Thames RHA, Regnl Ctee for Hosp Dental Services, Regnl Postgrad Ctee Br Postgrad Med Feb; memb: Exec Central Ctee for Hosp Dental Services, Examining Bd RCR; Hon Diploma in Dental Radiology 1984; memb: BDA, BAOMS, BSDMFR, IADMFR; FDI; FDSRCS (Eng); *Books* Forensic Dentistry (contrib 1974); *Recreations* photography, singing, archaeology, taking a sideways look; *Style*— Brian O'Riordan, Esq; Dept of Oral and Maxillo-Facial Surgery, Mount Vernon Hospital, Rickmansworth Rd, Northwood, Middx HA6 2RN (☎ 0895 78436)

O'RIORDAN, Prof Jeffrey Lima Hayes; s of Dr Michael Joseph O'Riordan (d 1975), of Newport, Monmouthshire, and Mary Lima, *née* Jones (d 1969); *b* 27 March 1931; *Educ* Newport HS for Boys, Pembroke Coll Oxford, Middx Hosp; *m* 6 July 1963, Sara Julia, da of Lt-Col Robert Leslie Berridge, MC (d 1986), of Owenmore, Currabiny, Co Cork, Ireland; 3 s (Dermot b 1964, Mark b 1965 d 1982, Dominic b 1968), 3 da (Shelagh b 1966, Kathleen b 1973, Philippa b 1978); *Career* Nat Serv 1959-61; current posts held at Middx Hosp London: prof in Metabolic Med, dep dir Professional Med Unit, hon conslt physician (former registrar); former visiting assoc Nat Inst of Arthritis and Metabolic Disorders Bethesda, former examiner Med Conjoint Bd; author of numerous papers on immuno-assay of peptide hormones, hyperparathyroidism, metabolic bone disease, thyrocalcitonin and vitamin D deficiency; memb: Assoc of Physicians, American Endocrine Soc; FRCP 1971 (memb 1959); *Books* Essentials of Endocrinology; *Recreations* sailing; *Clubs* Royal Cruising; *Style*— Prof Jeffrey O'Riordan; Endocrine and Metabolic Unit, The Middlesex Hospital, Mortimer St, London W1 (☎ 071 380 9373, fax 071 636 3151)

O'RIORDAN, Rear Adm John Patrick Bruce (Paddy); CBE (1982); s of Surgn Capt Timothy Joseph O'Riordan, RN (d 1966), of White Willows, Bergh Apton, Norwich, and Bertha Carson, *née* Young (d 1983); *b* 15 Jan 1936; *Educ* Kelly Coll; *m* 15 Aug 1959, Jane, da of John Alexander Mitchell, of Kirkcudbright, Scotland; 1 s (Tim b 1965), 2 da (Susie (Mrs Graham) b 1960, Katherine (Mrs Beattie) b 1966); *Career* Nat Serv, midshipman RNVR 1954, transferred RN, Capt cmd HMS Porpoise 1968-69 and HMS Dreadnought 1972-74; cmd: Submarine Sub Trg Orgn 1976-78, RCDS 1979, guided missile destroyer HMS Glasgow 1980-81 (disaster relief ops St Lucia after Hurricane Allen 1980); asst COS policy to Supreme Allied Cdr Atlantic Virginia USA 1982-84, dir naval warfare MOD 1984-86 (ADC to HM Queen 1985), Rear Adm mil dep cmdt NATO Def Coll Rome 1986-89; chief exec St Andrew's Hosp Northampton 1990-; FBIM 1985, assoc Inst Nuclear Engrs 1985; *Recreations* sailing, sketching, rugby football, travel; *Clubs* The Royal Navy of 1765 and 1785, Army and Navy, Royal Yacht Sqdn, RNSA; *Style*— Rear Adm Paddy O'Riordan, CBE; The Manor House, Islip, Kettering, Northamptonshire NN14 3JL; 903A Fulham Park Studios, Fulham Park Rd, London SW6 5HU (☎ 08012 2325, 081 384 2669)

O'RIORDAN, Prof Timothy; s of Kevin Denis O'Riordan, and Norah Joyce, *née* Lucas; *b* 21 Feb 1942; *Educ* Heriot's Sch Edinburgh, Univ of Edinburgh (MA), Cornell Univ (MS), Univ of Cambridge (PhD); *m* 18 May 1968, Ann Morison, da of Elmsley Philip; 2 da (Katharine Louise b 24 Jan 1977, Alice Janet b 31 May 1979); *Career* asst prof Dept of Geography Simon Fraser Univ Burnaby BC 1967-70 (assoc prof 1970-74), reader Sch of Environmental Scis UEA 1974-80 (prof 1980-); memb: Broads Authy (chm Environment Ctee), Econ and Social Res Cncl (chm Environment Working Gp), England Ctee Nature Conservancy Cncl; *Books* Progress in Resource Management (1971), Environmentalism (1976, 1981), Sizewell B: An Anatomy of the Inquiry (1988); *Recreations* classical music (double bass playing); *Style*— Prof Timothy O'Riordan; Wheatlands, Hethersett Lane, Colney, Norwich NR4 7TT (☎ 0603 810534); School of Environmental Sciences, University of East Anglia, Norwich NR4 7TJ (☎ 0603 592840, fax 0603 507719)

O'RORKE, Timothy Mawdesley; s of Michael Sylvester O'Rorke, CBE; *b* 10 July 1929; *Educ* Haileybury, Queens' Coll Cambridge; *m* 1964, Anne Patricia, da of Brig Theodore Edward Dudley Kelly, CBE; 1 s (Nicholas b 1968), 2 da (Kelly b 1966, Patricia b 1969); *Career* CA; Imperial Continental Gas Assoc: joined 1956, sec 1969, fin dir 1972, md 1979-85); chm St Marylebone Housing Assoc 1986-; *Recreations* tennis, golf, gardening, skiing; *Style*— Timothy O'Rorke, Esq; Denstone, Wadhurst, Sussex (☎ 0892 782282)

O'ROURKE, His Excellency Andrew; *b* 7 May 1931; *Educ* Trinity Coll Dublin (BA, BComm, DPA); *m* 1962, Hanne Stephensen; 1 s, 2 da; *Career* dep perm rep European Community 1974-78, sec gen Dept of Foreign Affairs Dublin 1978-81, perm rep of Ireland to EC 1981-86, Irish ambass to France 1986-87, ambass to Ct of St James's 1987-; *Clubs* Garrick, RAC; *Style*— His Excellency the Irish Ambassador; Irish Embassy, 17 Grosvenor Place, London SW1X 7HR (☎ 071 235 2171)

O'SHAUGHNESSY, Hon Mrs (Maud Elizabeth); *née* Grosvenor; da of late 4 Baron Ebury, DSO, MC; *b* 1909; *m* 1, 1931 (m dis 1942), 2 Viscount Harcourt (d 1978); 3 da; m 2, 1942, late Lt-Col Edward O'Shaughnessy; 2 da (twins); *Style*— The Hon Mrs O'Shaughnessy; The Cottage, Buckland, Irishtown, via Northam 6401, W Aust

O'SULLEVAN, Peter John; OBE (1977); s of late Col John Joseph O'Sullevan, DSO; *b* 3 March 1918; *Educ* Hawtreys, Charterhouse, Coll Alpin Switzerland; *m* 1951, Patricia, da of late Frank Duckworth of Manitoba Canada; *Career* racing commentator BBC TV 1946- incl: Australia, S Africa, Italy, USA; racing corr Daily Express 1950-86; *Books* Calling The Horses (autiobiog, 1989); *Recreations* racehorses, travel, reading, art, food and wine; *Style*— Peter O'Sullevan, Esq, OBE; 37 Cranmer Court, Sloane Ave, London SW3 (☎ 071 584 2781)

O'SULLIVAN, Bernard Anthony; s of Michael Brendan O'Sullivan (d 1966), and Monica, *née* Thompson; *b* 23 Nov 1948; *Educ* St Benedict's Ealing, St Catharine's Coll Cambridge (MA); *Career* called to the Bar Inner Temple 1971; *Recreations* travel; *Style*— Bernard O'Sullivan, Esq; 27 Bonnington Square, London SW8 1TF (☎ 071 820 0208); 2 Harcourt Buildings, Temple, London EC4Y 9DB (☎ 071 583 9020)

O'SULLIVAN, Rt Rev Mgr James; CBE (1973); s of Richard O'Sullivan (d 1957), and Ellen, *née* Ahern (d 1959); *b* 2 Aug 1917; *Educ* St Finnbarr's Coll Cork, All Hallows' Coll Dublin; *Career* cmmnd Royal Army Chaplains Dept 1942, chaplain 49 Div Normandy 1944, sr chaplain (RC) Malaya 1952-54, chaplain Irish Gds 1954-56, princ chaplain MOD 1968-73, officiating chaplain to RAMC and QA Trg Centres 1973-; *Style*— The Rt Rev Mgr James O'Sullivan, CBE; Osgil, Vicarage Lane, Ropley, Alresford, Hants

O'SULLIVAN, John Conor; s of James Vincent O'Sullivan (d 1976), of Harley St, London, and Maura O'Connor; *b* 25 Sept 1932; *Educ* Ampleforth, Oriel Coll Oxford (MA), Westminster Hosp Med Sch (BM, BCh); *m* 26 April 1958, Maureen, da of Douglas Charles Mitchell (d 1977), of Wembley; 1 s (Hugh b 1966), 3 da (Marika b 1959, Claire b 1960, Catherine b 1962); *Career* Nat Serv RAMC 1960-62, dep asst dir Med Serv HQ London dist, T/Maj 1961; conslt obstetrician and gynaecologist Central Middx Hosp 1974-86, conslt in gynaecological oncology Hammersmith Hosp 1976-84, sr lectr Royal Postgrad Sch Inst Obstetrics and Gynaecology 1984-; Freeman City of London 1955, Liveryman Worshipful Soc of Apothecaries; FRCS 1967, FRCOG 1983; *Recreations* golf, skiing; *Clubs* Royal Wimbledon Golf; *Style*— John O'Sullivan, Esq; 96 Arthur Rd, Wimbledon, London SW19 7DT (☎ 081 946 6242); 115 Harley St, London W1 (☎ 071 580 6966/370 4233)

O'SULLIVAN, Hon Mrs (Lesley Priscilla); *née* Ross; er da of Baron Ross of Newport (Life Peer), *qv*; *b* 2 Nov 1950; *m* Finian O'Sullivan; *Style*— The Hon Mrs O'Sullivan; 44 Station Road, Netley, Southampton

O'SULLIVAN, Sally Angela; da of Albert James Lorraine, of Jersey, Channel Islands, and Joan, *née* Crawley (d 1969); *b* 26 July 1949; *Educ* Ancaster House Sch Bexhill-on-Sea, Trinity Coll Dublin; *m* 2 Oct 1980, Charles Martin Wilson; 1 s (Luke b 18 Dec 1981), 1 da (Lily b 21 Aug 1985), 1 step da (Emma b 18 July 1970); *Career* freelance writer 1971-77, dep ed Womens World 1977-78, freelance writer NY 1978-80; womens ed: Daily Record 1980-81, Sunday Standard 1981-82; ed Options, launch ed and originator of Country Homes and Interiors 1986; ed: She 1989, Harpers & Queen 1989-; Magazine Ed of the Year 1986; *Books* Things My Mother Never Told Me, Looking Good; *Recreations* spending time with my family, riding; *Style*— Sally O'Sullivan; Harpers & Queen, National Magazine House, 72 Broadwick St, London W1V 2BP

O'TOOLE, Peter; s of Patrick Joseph O'Toole; *b* 1932; *Educ* RADA; *m* (m dis) Sian Phillips; 2 da; *Career* actor; with Bristol Old Vic Co 1955-58; artistic dir Royal Alexander Theatre Co 1978; *Clubs* Garrick; *Style*— Peter O'Toole Esq; c/o Veerline Ltd, 54 Baker St, London W1M 1DJ (☎ 071 486 5888)

OAKELEY, Anne-Marie, Lady; Anne-Marie; *née* Dennis; da of Etienne Pierre Felix Dennis (d 1922), a cotton merchant of Le Havre, Seine Maritime, France, and Annabella Agnes Wilson; *m* 1, late Terence McKenna; 1 da (Virginia McKenna, actress *qv*, m Bill Travers); m 2, Jack Drummond Rudd (m dis); m 3, 1957, as his 3 w, Sir Charles Richard Andrew Oakeley, 6 Bt (d 1959); *Career* professional pianist; composes music under the name of Anne de Nys; *Style*— Anne-Marie, Lady Oakeley; Winiscombe, Furze Hill, Kingswood, Surrey KT20 6EP

OAKELEY, Dr Henry Francis; s of Rowland Henry Oakeley, of Gower Bank, Littleworth, Chipping Campden, Glos, and Diana Margaret, *née* Hayward; *b* 22 July 1941; *Educ* Clifton, St Thomas's Hosp Med Sch, Univ of London (MB BS); *m* 20 Jan 1968 (m dis 1988), Penelope Susan, da of Dr Wilfred Barlow; 2 s (Matthew Thomas b 15 Dec 1968, Edward James b 29 March 1970), 1 da (Rachel Mary b 15 Jan 1973); *Career* house offr and sr house offr 1965-69: St Thomas's Hosp, Nat Hosp Queen Square, Frenchay Hosp; registrar 1970-72: St Thomas's Hosp, Maudsley Hosp, St George's Hosp; sr registrar Maudsley Hosp 1972-73, conslt psychiatrist St Thomas's Hosp 1973-; awarded AM/RHS for: Lycaste Locusta (Penny) 1978 and Lycaste Ciliata (St Thomas's) 1989, RMS Gold medal Chelsea 1990; former sec Historical Section RSM, former chm Lambeth Caring Houses Tst, memb Orchid Soc of GB; Freeman: Worshipful Soc of Apothecaries 1974, City of London 1980; MRCPsych 1972, FRCP 1989 (MRCP 1969); *Books* Psychiatric Emergencies in Metabolic Diseases (contrib, 1980), Richard Oakeley: Royalist and Country Gentleman 1580-1653 (1989); *Publications* various articles in American Orchid Society Bulletin (1990) and Orchid Review (1989) incl: Culture of Lycastes and Anguloas, Xanthanthae Lycastes, Fimbriatae Lycastes and their hybrids; *Recreations* orchids, gardening, history of medicine, genealogy; *Style*— Dr Henry Oakeley; St Thomas's Hosp, London SE1 7EH (☎ 071 928 9292)

OAKELEY, Sir John Digby Atholl; 8 Bt (GB 1790), of Shrewsbury; s of Sir Atholl Oakeley, 7 Bt (d 1987); *b* 27 Nov 1932; *Educ* by private tutor; *m* 1958, Maureen

Frances, da of John Cox (d 1965), of Hamble, Hants; 1 s (Robert John Atholl b 13 Aug 1963), 1 da (Marina Anne b 1961); *Heir* s, Robert John Atholl Oakeley b 13 Aug 1963; *Career* md Dehler Yachts UK; competed in Nat, Euro and World Championships in numerous sailing craft incl 12 metre, rep GB in Olympics (sailing); author; *Books* Winning, Downwind Sailing, Sailing Manual; *Recreations* sailing (yacht 'Daylight'); *Clubs* Warsash Sailing; *Style—* Sir John Oakeley, Bt; 10 Bursledon Heights, Long Lane, Bursledon, Hants (☎ 042 121 5894); Dehler Yachts UK, Hamble Point, Hamble, Hants (☎ 0703 456595)

OAKES, Sir Christopher; 3 Bt (UK 1939), of Nassau, Bahama Islands; s of Sir Sydney Oakes, 2 Bt (d 1966); *b* 10 July 1949; *Educ* Bredon Tewkesbury, Georgia Military Acad USA; *m* 1978, Julie Dawn, da of Donovan Cowan, of Canada; 1 s, 1 da; *Heir* s, Victor Oakes b 7 March 1983; *Style—* Sir Christopher Oakes, Bt; PO Box SS 5529, Nassau, Bahamas

OAKES, Christopher John; s of William Oakes (d 1970) and Kathleen Self; *b* 13 Aug 1955; *Educ* Butley Modern Sch Suffolk, Ipswich Civic Coll Suffolk, Colchester Tech Coll Essex; *m* 16 June 1984, Caroline, da of Nowell Dyrek Scott; *Career* apprentice (under Mr Malcolm Long) Seckford Hall Hotel Woodbridge Suffolk 1971-73, apprentice and commis Le Talbooth Restaurant Dedham Essex 1973-74, chef tournant Post Hotel Davos Switzerland 1974-75, sr chef de partie and sous chef (under Mr Sam Chalmers) Le Talbooth Restaurant Dedham Essex 1975-77, Gleneagles Hotel Scotland 1977, understudy to Mr Colin Cooper-English Plough Restaurant Clanfield Oxon 1977-78, sous chef (under Mr Chris Oakley) Pier at Harwich Essex 1978-80, head chef The Castle Hotel Taunton 1983-86 (sous chef under Mr John Hornsby 1980-83), opened Oakes Restaurant 1986; *awards* nominated in 10 Star Chefs of Tomorrow AA Guide 1984, rosette AA Guide 1984-86 and 1988-91, star in Michelin Guide 1984-87 and 1989-91, star in Egon Ronay Guide 1984-86 and 1988-91, entry in Good Food Guide 1985-86, 1988-91, entry Good Hotel Guide 1984-1985, entry Ackerman Guide 1987-88 and received White 4-leaf Clover award 1989-90 and 1990-91; master chef of GB 1986- (assoc memb Inst of Master Chefs of GB 1983-); grand officier du Cordon Bleu Culinaire, epicurien prix d'excellence gastronomique of Circle Epicurien Mondial; *Recreations* reading and collecting cookery books, walking; *Style—* Christopher Oakes, Esq; Oakes Restaurant, 169 Slad Road, Stroud, Gloucestershire GL5 1RG (☎ 0453 759950)

OAKES, Rt Hon Gordon James; PC (1979), MP (Lab) Halton 1983-; s of James Oakes (d 1957), of Widnes, and Florence, *née* Hewitt (d 1949); *b* 22 June 1931; *Educ* Wade Deacon Sch Widnes, Univ of Liverpool (BA); *m* 11 Sept 1952, Esther, da of Joseph O'Neill (d 1976), of Widnes; 3 s (Howard b 1956, Timothy b 1960, Julian b 1963); *Career* slr 1956; Mayor Widnes 1964-65 (memb borough cncl 1952-), chm Widnes Lab Pty 1953-58; contested (Lab): Bebington 1959, Moss Side Manchester (by-election) 1961; MP (Lab): Bolton W 1964-70, Widnes 1971-1983; parly under-sec: Environment 1974-76, Energy 1976; oppn front bench spokesman Environment 1970-74 (incl local govt) and 1979-, Min State DES 1976-79; memb: Br delgn NATO Parliamentarians 1967-70, Race Rels Select Ctee 1969-70, NW Regnl Exec Lab Pty, Cwlth Parly Assoc Exec Ctee 1979-; vice-pres: Inst of Public Health Insprs ACC 1983-, Bldg Soc Assoc 1984-; *Recreations* caravanning, travel; *Style—* The Rt Hon Gordon Oakes, MP; House of Commons, London SW1A 0AA (☎ 071 219 4139)

OAKES, Harry Philip; s of late Sir Harry Oakes, 1 Bt; *b* 30 Aug 1932; *m* 1958, Christiane, da of Rudolf Botsch, of Hamburg, Germany; 3 s, 1 da; *Style—* Harry Oakes, Esq; P O Box N222, Nassau, Bahamas

OAKES, James Scudamore; s of George Clifton Oakes (d 1933), of Njoro River Farm, Njoro, Kenya, and May Elizabeth, *née* Scudamore (d 1970); descendent of Lt-Col O H Oakes of Nowton Court, Bury St Edmunds; see Burke's Landed Gentry 18 Edn Vol II; *b* 13 July 1927,Nakuru, Kenya; *Educ* Wellington, Trinity Coll Oxford (MA); *m* 17 March 1956, Gillian Walsham, da of Lt-Col Henry Richard Hopking, Suffolk Regt (d 1965), of Monks Vineyard, Nowton, Bury St Edmunds, Suffolk; 1 s (Christopher b 1957), 2 da (Victoria b 1960, Caroline b 1961); *Career* Nat Serv Fleet Air Arm RN 1945-48, Col Engr and Tport Staff Corps RE (TA) 1985-; joined asst engr Kennedy and Donkin 1952-57, gp and res engr Hunterston Nuclear Power Station Ayreshire 1957-64, Cockenzie Power Station: res engr 1964-68, ptnr 1965-86, gp conslt 1987-; FIMechE, FIEE, MACE; *Recreations* shooting, fishing, tennis; *Style—* James Oakes, Esq; Hoppery Hill, Headley, Hants GU35 8TB (☎ 0428 712583); Westbrook Mills, Godalming, Surrey (☎ 04868 25900, telex 859373 KDHOG, fax 04868 25136)

OAKES, Judith Miriam; MBE (1987); da of Geoffrey Redford Oakes, of 37 Copse Avenue, West Wickham, Kent, and Marjorie Olive Oakes; *b* 14 Feb 1958; *Educ* Bullers Wood Secdy Sch; *Career* athlete; memb Croydon Harriers 1971-, jr UK int 1974-76, 58 sr UK caps 1976-90; achievements at shotput: Gold medal Cwlth Games 1982 (Silver 1986 and 1990, Bronze 1978), Bronze medal Euro Indoor Championships 1979, fourth place Olympic Games 1984, winner 30 Br titles; achievements at powerlifting: world champion 1981, 1982, 1988 (runner up 1983 and 1990), Euro champion 1983-90, Br champion 10 times; achievements at weightlifting: Bronze medal clean and jerk World Championships 1988, Bronze medal snatch and overall World Championships 1989, Gold medal snatch and overall Euro Championships 1989 (Silver clean and jerk), Gold medal clean and jerk and overall Euro Championships 1990 (Silver Snatch), first all sections EEC Championships 1990; records: UK shotput, various UK powerlifting and weightlifting, most Br titles; bank clerk 1976-82, self-employed fitness coach Wimbledon FC 1982-85, currently mangr and instructor ICAS Fitness Centre Wimbledon, lectr in fitness Raworth Centre Coll; athletes' rep BAAB 1983-84, life memb Br Amateur Weightlifting Assoc; *Recreations* cooking Chinese food, science fiction books and films, memb WWF, conscious of environmental issues; *Style—* Miss Judith Oakes, MBE; ICAS Fitness Centre, Belgrave Hall, Denmark Rd, Wimbledon, London SW19 4PG (☎ 081 944 6603)

OAKES, William Lyness; OBE (1987); s of William Lyness Oakes (d 1964), and Hilda Mary, *née* Hardy (d 1970); *b* 20 Feb 1919; *Educ* Bedford Sch, Guy's Hosp (LDS, RCS); *m* 1, 1 Oct 1942, Joan Anne (d 1972), da of late Maj T L Squires, OBE; 1 s (Robert b 1948), 2 da (Wendy b 1944, Susan b 1950); m 2, 2 Feb 1974, Helen Patricia, da of Howard Green, of Bussage, Stroud, Glos; *Career* dental surgn RN 1942-46; in private practice 1946-81; hon dental surgn: Gloucester Infirmary 1947-48, Horton Rd Hosp 1947-48; chm Glos Local Dental Ctee 1968-80, former memb SW Region Dental Advsy Ctee, chm Glos Family Practitioner Ctee 1977-90 (memb 1974-90), memb Glos CC 1981-89, chm Glos Tourist Jt Ctee 1986-89, vice pres Heart of Eng Tourist Bd 1989- (exec memb 1981-89, chm Devpt Ctee 1986-89); *Recreations* gardening, music, meeting people; *Style—* William Oakes, Esq, OBE; Birds Frith Farm, Far Oakridge, Stroud, Glos, GL6 7PB (☎ 028576 482); Oakes House, 53-59 London Rd, Gloucester GL1 3HE

OAKESHOTT, Matthew Alan; s of Keith Robertson Oakeshott, CMG, of Horsham, Sussex (d 1974), and Jill Oakeshott, *née* Clutterbuck; *b* 10 Jan 1947; *Educ* Charterhouse, Univ Coll and Nuffield Coll Oxford (scholar, MA); *m* 1976, Dr Philippa Poulton, da of Dr Christopher Poulton; 2 s (Joseph Andrew b 1979, Luke Christopher b 1985), 1 da (Rachel Jill b 1982); *Career* economist Kenya Miny of Fin and Econ Planning 1968-70, special advsr to Rt Hon Roy Jenkins, MP 1972-76, investmt mangr then dir Warburg Investment Management Ltd (now Mercury Asst Management) 1976-81, investmt mangr Courtaulds Pension Fund 1981-85, chm Aubrey Investments Ltd 1985-, fndr and jt md Olim Ltd 1986-; jt investmt dir: Value & Income Trust plc 1986-, Olim Convertible Trust plc 1989-; city cncllr Oxford 1972-76; parly candidate: (Lab) Horsham and Crawley Oct 1974, (SDP/Lib Alliance) Cambridge 1983; *Books* By-Elections in British Politics (contrib, 1974); *Recreations* music, football, elections; *Style—* Matthew Oakeshott, Esq; Olim Limited, Pollen House, 10-12 Cork St, London W1X 1PD (☎ 071 439 4400)

OAKFORD, Colin Richard; s of Percy D Oakford (d 1963), and Constance Mary, *née* Newman; paternal connections with construction of GWR tunnel at Box, Wiltshire; *b* 9 Aug 1944; *Educ* Hardyes Sch Dorchester, Birmingham Sch of Arch (Dip Arch); *Career* sr architect Stockbuild Ltd 1967-71, in private practice 1971; dir design bldg co 1986; ARIBA; *Recreations* watching rugby, squash, walking, architecture; *Clubs* Old Hardyeans, Dorchester; *Style—* Colin Oakford, Esq; 34 Maiden St, Weymouth; Le Vaujoint, Chielle 37190 Azay Le Rideau

OAKLEY, Andrew; s of Donald William Oakley, of Birmingham, and Minnie Andrews; *b* 4 March 1940; *Educ* King Edward VI GS Birmingham, Univ of Birmingham (B Comm); *m* 24 Nov 1978, Patricia May, da of Thomas O'Connell; *Career* Ernst and Young (formerly Ernst and Whinney): joined Birmingham 1965, London 1970-, ptnr 1971-, ptnr with nat responsibility for high tech 1985-88, practice devpt ptnr 1988-; ICEAW: memb Auditing Practices Ctee 1983-86, memb of cncl 1986-, chm of info tech gp 1986-; ACA (1965), BCS (1968), FCA (1970), FBCS (1970); *Recreations* travel, gastronomy, occasional golf and chess; *Style—* Andrew Oakley, Esq; Ernst & Young, Becket House, 1 Lambeth Palace Rd, London SE1 7EU (☎ 071 928 2000 ext 3372, fax 071 928 1345, telex 885234)

OAKLEY, Christopher John; s of Ronald Oakley (d 1965), of Tunbridge Wells, Kent, and Joyce Barbara, *née* Tolhurst; *b* 11 Nov 1941; *Educ* The Skinners, Sch Tunbridge Wells Kent; *m* 8 Oct 1962 (m dis 1986), Linda Margaret, da of William John Edward Viney, of Tunbridge Wells, Kent; 1 s, 2 da; *Career* ed: Liverpool Echo 1983-, Lancashire Evening Post 1981-83; dep ed Yorkshire Post 1976-81; dir: Lancashire Evening Post Ltd 1982-83, Liverpool Daily Post and Echo Ltd 1983-89; ed in chief/ dep md Birmingham Post and Mail Ltd 1989-; memb: Guild of British Newspaper Editors, Assoc of British Editors; *Style—* Christopher Oakley, Esq; Birmingham Post and Mail Ltd, PO Box 18, 28 Colmore Circus, Queensway, Birmingham B4 6AX (☎ 021 236 3366, fax 021 233 0173)

OAKLEY, (George) David Gastineau; s of Douglas Edward Oakley, and Barbara Mary, *née* Earle; *b* 26 April 1948; *Educ* Rugby, Cambridge Univ (MB BChir, MA), Westminster Med Sch; *m* 29 Sept 1979, Clare Elizabeth, da of Christopher Brent-Smith; 1 s (Sam b 1982), 1 da (Charlotte b 1988); *Career* former sr house offr and registrar City General Hosp Stoke-on-Trent, registrar cardiology Hammersmith Hosp 1977-79; Northern Gen Hosp Sheffield: sr registrar 1979-84, currently conslt cardiologist N Trent Regnl Health Authy (hon appt Univ of Sheffield); articles: ischaemic heart disease, pregnancy and heart disease, athletes hearts; memb: Br Cardiac Soc, ctee Br Heart Fndn; FRCP 1988 (MRCP 1975); *Recreations* music, skiing; *Style—* David Oakley, Esq; Cardiothoracic Unit, Northern Gen Hosp, Sheffield S5 7AU (☎ 0742 434343 ext 4953)

OAKLEY, Geoffrey Michael Whittall; s of Harold Whittall Oakley, of St Martins, Guernsey, and Hazel Louise, *née* Peters; *b* 22 April 1953; *Educ* Oundle; *m* 3 April 1987, Joanna Helen, da of Fred Morgan Hodges, of Harborne, Birmingham; 1 s (Nicholas Frederick James b 1989), 2 da (Georgina Louise b 1987, Olivia Sarah Helen b 1990); *Career* ptnr Margetts & Addenbrooke 1977-86; non-exec dir: Aero Needles Group plc 1976-84, Margetts Financial Services Ltd 1985; dir: National Investment Group plc 1986-90, Capel-Cure Myers Capital Management 1990-; memb: Stock Exchange 1976, Int Stock Exchange 1976; *Recreations* theatre, local history, antiques; *Style—* Geoffrey Oakley, Esq; St Mary's Close, 10 St Mary's Rd, Harborne, Birmingham B17 OHA (☎ 021 427 7150); Capel-Cure Myers Capital Management, York House, 38 Great Charles St, Birmingham B3 3JU (☎ 021 200 2002)

OAKLEY, John Davidson; CBE (1980), DFC (1944); s of Richard Oakley and Nancy Mary Oakley; *b* 15 June 1921; *m* 1943, Georgina Mary, da of George Curzon Hare; 2 s; *Career* Sqdn Ldr RAF; formerly with Ford Motor Co, then Standard Triumph (Liverpool) Ltd; md: Copeland & Jenkins Ltd 1963-71, R Woolf & Co Ltd 1964-67; gp md L Sterne & Co 1967-69; chm: General Electric & Mechanical Systems Ltd 1970-73, Berwick Timpo Ltd 1970-82, Edgar Allen Balfour Ltd 1974-79, Australian Br Trade Assoc 1977-81; former dir: Blairs Ltd, Eagle & Globe Steel Ltd NSW, Nexos Office Systems Ltd; chm Grosvenor Devpt Capital Ltd 1981-, chm Berwick Timpo Toys to May 1982, chm Robert Jenkins Holdings Ltd 1983-, dep chm Gardners Transformers Ltd 1983-; dir: Beau Brummel Ltd 1972-84, Isis Industl Servs plc 1982-, Ionian Securities 1978-; memb Br Overseas Trade Advsy Cncl 1977-; chm Grosvenor Technol Fund 1985; memb Essex Cnty Cncl 1982-85; FRSA, FBIM, MIBCAM, FInstPS; *Recreations* golf, walking, tennis, bridge, politics; *Clubs* Reform, RAF, Bishop's Stortford Golf; *Style—* John Oakley Esq, CBE, DFC; 25 Manor Links, Bishop's Stortford, Herts CM23 5RA (☎ 0275 507552)

OAKLEY, Margaret Mary; da of Roger Dickinson (d 1951), and Hilda, *née* Smart (d 1951); *b* 3 Sept 1928; *Educ* Notre Dame Leeds, Mount Pleasant Training Coll Liverpool; *m* Aug 1950, Kenneth Oakley; 2 s (Martin b Nov 1952, Christopher b Oct 1954); *Career* athletics administrator; involved in schools athletics 1948-, involved in club and county athletics admin 1954-, team official England and GB athletic teams 1965-86 (incl Olympic Games 1976 and 1980, Cwlth Games 1978, 1982, 1986); chm Womens Amateur Athletic Assoc 1983- (hon sec Northern Counties WAAA 1965-), memb Br Amateur Athletics Bd 1980-; primary sch teacher 1948-89 (headteacher for 16 years); *Style—* Mrs Margaret Oakley; 10 Byemoor Close, Great Ayton, North Yorks TS9 6LY (☎ 0642 723182)

OAKLEY, Michael Dudley; s of Lt Cdr George Eric Oakley, RN, of Clifton on Teme, Worcester, and Dr Margaret Dudley, *née* Brown; *b* 5 Nov 1944; *Educ* Oundle, Coll of Law; *m* 7 Oct 1967, Jennifer Catherine, da of Richard Percy Lazenby (d 1987), of Oak Cottage, Bulmer, York; 1 s (William b 3 Oct 1973), 2 da (Catherine b 2 Nov 1969, Victoria b 6 Nov 1971); *Career* slr; ptnr Denison Till; HM coroner N Yorks 1979-, NP 1985-; lay memb Gen Synod C of E representing diocese of York 1980-; memb: Cncl of Archbishop of York, Working Party on Ordination of Women to the Priesthood, Cathedral Statutes Cmmn, various legislative revision ctees, panel of chm of Gen Synod; non-exec memb York Health Authy 1990-, vice pres Yorkshire Law Soc 1990-91; *Recreations* tennis, swimming, fishing, shooting; *Clubs* Yorkshire, East India; *Style—* Michael Oakley, Esq; Rose Cottage, Oswaldkirk, York YO6 5XT (☎ 0439 3339); 4 Old Malton Gate, Malton, N Yorks YO17 0EQ (☎ 0653 600070, fax 0653 600049, car 0860 789957)

OAKLEY, Dr Nigel Wingate; s of Dr Wilfrid George Oakley, of London, and Hermione Violet Oakley; *b* 6 Dec 1933; *Educ* Rugby, King's Coll Cambridge (MA, MD); *m* 20 Oct 1962, Nicole Paule, da of Albert Mertz (d 1975); 1 da (Francesca b 1963); *Career* conslt physician, St George's Hosp London, hon sr lectr St George's Hosp Med Sch, conslt physician St Luke's Hosp for the Clergy; previously dep dir Metabolic Unit St Mary's Hosp London and Nuffield fell in med Univ of Pittsburgh; 1 reserve Br Olympic Rifle Team 1956, world individual Small-Bore Rifle Champion

(50m), world Rifle Championships Moscow 1958, memb Br Int Small Bore Rifle Teams 1952-58; *Recreations* music, rifle shooting, DIY; *Clubs* RSM; *Style—* Dr Nigel W Oakley; The Homestead, London SW13 9HL (☎ 081 741 3311); 84 Harley Street, London W1N 1AE (☎ 071 580 9771)

OAKLEY, Robin Francis Leigh; s of Joseph Henry Oakley, of East Molesey, Surrey, and Alice Barbara Oakley; *b* 20 Aug 1941; *Educ* Wellington, BNC Oxford (MA); *m* 4 June 1966, Carolyn Susan Germaine, da of late Leonard Rumball; 1 s (Alexander Guy Leigh b 12 Aug 1973), 1 da (Annabel Louise Germaine b 19 July 1971); *Career* political corr Liverpool Daily Post 1967-70 (feature writer then sub ed 1964-67), crossbencher columnist then asst ed Sunday Express 1970-79, political ed and asst ed Now! magazine 1979-81, asst ed Daily Mail 1981-86, political ed The Times 1986-; currently: reg presenter Week in Westminster BBC Radio Four, contrib to various radio and TV progs; presenter The Power of Patronage BBC Radio series Jan 1991; author of school books on current affairs issues; *Books* The Political Year 1970 (with Peter Rose), The Political Year 1971 (with Peter Rose); *Recreations* theatre, horse racing, swimming, bird watching; *Clubs* RAC; *Style—* Robin Oakley, Esq; The Times, Press Gallery, House of Commons, Westminster, London SW1A 0AA (☎ 071 219 5241, fax 071 782 5239)

OAKLEY, (Horace) Roy; CBE (1977); s of Horace William Oakley (d 1977), of Luton, and Beatrice Ann, *née* Parker (d 1973); *b* 26 Dec 1920; *Educ* Ashton GS Dunstable, UCL (BSc, MSc); *m* 1 Sept 1949, Evelyn Elsie, da of Joseph Albert Mariner, JP (d 1970); 1 s (Richard b 1956), 3 da (Elizabeth b 1953, Susan b 1957, Katharine b 1961); *Career* WWII cmmnd RE and served NW Europe (despatches) 1943-46; TAVR served Engr and Tport Staff Corps Maj 1970, Col 1981, ret 1985; lectr UCL 1948-52, sr ptnr JD DM Watson (now Watson Hawksley) 1969-85 (ptnr 1952-); memb Cncl: ICE 1969-75, UCL 1977-87; memb Bd Br Standards Inst 1982-88, vice pres Construction Indust Res & Inf Assoc 1986-89 (chm 1982-86), pres Inst of Water Pollution Control 1983-84; FICE 1960, FIWEM 1970, FEng 1983 (memb cncl 1987-89); *Recreations* sport, walking, gardening, painting; *Style—* Roy Oakley, Esq, CBE; 53 The Park, St Albans, Herts AL1 4RX (☎ 0727 55 928); Terriers House, Amersham Rd, High Wycombe, Bucks (☎ 0494 26 240)

OAKLEY, Stephen Edward; s of Stanley Edward Oakley, of 246 Willow Rd, Enfield, Middlesex, and Maureen Rose, *née* Carr; *b* 19 June 1952; *Educ* Ambrose Fleming Tech GS, Enfield, Middlesex; *m* 1975, Patricia Anne, da of Francis John Hyde, of 4 Saxon Rd, Wheathampstead, Hertfordshire; 1 s (Marc Stephen Edward b 1986), 1 da (Laura Jane b 1981); *Career* Price Waterhouse Co 1969-79, chief and fin offr Mitsubishi Electric (UK) Ltd 1979-84, dir United Merchants plc 1984-88, gp fin dir Macarthy plc 1988-; FCA, ATII; *Recreations* soccer; *Style—* Stephen E Oakley, Esq; 31 Earlings Rd, Harpenden, Hertfordshire AL5 2AW (☎ 0582 761 200); Macarthy plc, Delta House, 33 Hockcliffe St, Leighton Buzzard Bedfordshire (☎ 0525 850 470, fax 0525 382 381, car 0836 535 066)

OAKS, Agnes; da of Juhan Oaks, of Estonia, and Valentina, *née* Troffimova; *b* 29 May 1970; *Educ* Tallin Ballet Sch, Vaganova Inst Moscow; *m* 1990, Thomas Edur, s of Enn Edur; *Career* Estonia Ballet Theatre: Coppelia 1987, Paquita 1988, Sleeping Beauty 1989, Swan Lake 1990, Romeo & Juliet 1990; English National Ballet: Coppelia 1990, Nutcracker 1990, Les Sylphide 1990, 3 Preludes 1990, Our Waltzes 1990, Sanguine Fan 1990; best couple in Jackson Competition Mississippi; *Recreations* walking, travel; *Style—* Ms Agnes Oaks

OAKSEY, 2 Baron (UK 1947), and 4 Baron Trevethin (UK 1921); John Geoffrey Tristram Lawrence; OBE, JP; known as Lord Oaksey; s of 3 and 1 Baron Trevethin and Oaksey, DSO, TD (d 1971); *see* also Gp Capt Hugh S L Dundas; *b* 21 March 1929; *Educ* Eton, New Coll Oxford, Yale Law Sch; *m* 1, 1959 (m dis 1987), Victoria Mary, da of Maj John Dennistoun, MBE (d 1980); 1 s (Hon Patrick), 1 da (Hon Sara Victoria b 1961); m 2, 7 March 1988, Mrs Rachel Crocker; *Heir* s, Hon Patrick John Tristram Lawrence b 29 June 1960; *Career* P/O RAFVR and Lt 9 Lancers; racing corr to: Daily Telegraph (as 'Marlborough') 1957-, Sunday Telegraph 1961-88, Horse and Hound (as 'Audax') 1959-88; columnist Racing Post 1988-90; commentator for ITV on Racing (World of Sport) 1969-, Channel Four; pres: Amateur Boxing Assoc, York Univ Turf Club; dir HTV; *Recreations* riding, skiing; *Clubs* Brooks's; *Style—* The Rt Hon the Lord Oaksey, OBE, JP; Hill Farm, Oaksey, Malmesbury, Wilts (☎ 066 67 303)

OAKSHOTT, Hon Sir Anthony Hendrie; 2 Bt (UK 1959), of Bebington, Co Palatine of Chester; s of Baron Oakshott, MBE (Life Peer and 1 Bt, d 1975); *b* 10 Oct 1929; *Educ* Rugby; *m* 1965 (m dis 1981), Valerie, formerly w of (1) Donald Ross and (2) Michael de Pret-Roose, and da of Jack Vlasto, of Hurst, Berks; *Heir* bro, Hon Michael Oakshott; *Clubs* White's; *Style—* The Hon Sir Anthony Oakshott, Bt; Beckley House, Bledington, Oxfordshire (☎ 06087 527)

OAKSHOTT, Hon Michael Arthur John; s of Baron Oakshott, MBE (Life Peer and 1 Bt, d 1975); hp to Baronetcy of bro, Hon Sir Anthony Oakshott, 2 Bt; *b* 12 April 1932; *Educ* Rugby; *m* 1, 27 April 1957, Christina Rose Methuen (d 1985), da of late Thomas Banks, of Solai, Kenya; 3 s (Thomas Hendrie b 1959, Charles Michael b 1961, Angus Withington b 1965); m 2, 8 April 1988, Helen Clare Jones, da of late Edward Ravell, of Woodhall Spa, Lincs; *Style—* The Hon Michael Oakshott; Isle Tower, Holywood, Dumfries DG2 0RW (☎ 0387 720596, fax 0387 721234)

OATES, Geoffrey Donald; s of Thomas Oates (d 1970), of Bryn Hafod, Branksome Park, Poole, Dorset, and Dorothy Verne, *née* Jones (d 1967); *b* 16 May 1929; *Educ* Wolsingham GS Co Durham, Univ of Birmingham (BSc, MB ChB), Univ of Illinois Chicago USA (MS); *m* 1, 23 June 1954, Molly Parfitt (d 1973), da of Thomas Edwards (d 1977), of Abercynon, Glamorgam; 1 s (John b 1955), 1 da (Susan b 1957); m 2, Elizabeth Anne, da of Archibald Ronal Wife (d 1975), of Toftwood, E Dereham, Norfolk; *Career* Capt RAMC 1955-57; Fulbright Travel scholarship 1963-64, res fell and instr in surgery Univ of Illinois 1963-64, conslt surgn United Birmingham Hosps and sr clinical lectr Univ of Birmingham 1967-; memb: Colo-Rectal Sub-Ctee UK Co-ordinating Ctee for Cancer Res, Br Assoc of Endocrine Surgery, Int Assoc of Endocrine Surgns, Br Assoc of Surgical Oncology, Societé Internationale de Chirurgie; RSM: pres Section of Oncology 1980-81, pres Section of Colo-proctology 1989-90; pres: Assoc of Colo-proctology of GB and Ireland 1990-, W Midlands surgical Soc 1991-92; scientific sec Working Pty on Rectal Cancer MRC; hon memb Société Nationale Française de Colo-Proctologie 1990; fell Assoc of Surgns of GB and Ireland, FRCS 1959, FRSM 1967; *Books* contrib: The Pathological Basis of Medicine (1972), Clinical Trials (1977); *Recreations* salmon fishing, golf, skiing, photography; *Clubs* Army and Navy; *Style—* Geoffrey Oates, Esq; 14 Hintlesham Avenue, Edgbaston, Birmingham, West Midlands B15 2PH (☎ 021 454 3257); The General Hospital, Steelhouse Lane, Birmingham B4 6NH (☎ 021 236 8611 ext 5475, fax 021 233 9189); Consulting Rooms, 81 Harborne Rd, Edgbaston, Birmingham B15 3HG (☎ 021 455 9496)

OATES, Rev Canon John; s of John Oates (d 1964), of Yorkshire, and Ethel, *née* McCann (d 1959); *b* 14 May 1930; *Educ* Queen Elizabeth Sch Wakefield, Soc of the Sacred Mission Kelham; *m* 16 Jan 1962, Sylvia Mary, da of Herbert Charles Harris (d 1977), of Rickmansworth, Herts; 3 s (Jeremy b 20 Aug 1963, Alistair b 19 May 1968, Jonathan b 28 Dec 1969), 1 da (Rebecca b 6 Feb 1966); *Career* curate Eton Coll Mission Hackney Wick 1957-60, devpt offr C of E Youth Cncl and memb staff Bd of Educn 1960-64, devpt sec C of E Cncl for Cwlth Settlement 1964-65 (gen sec 1965-70), sec C of E Ctee on Migration and Int Affairs 1969-71; vicar Richmond Surrey 1970-84, rural dean Richmond and Barnes 1979-84, rector St Bride's Fleet St 1984-; commissary: to Archbishop of Perth W Aust and Bishop of N W Aust 1968-75, to Archibishop of Jerusalem 1969-75, to Bishop of Bunbury 1969-; hon canon Bunbury 1969-; chaplain: Press Club, Inst of Journalists, Inst of PR, Publicity Club of London; pres Richmond and Barnes Mental Health Assoc 1972-74; Freeman City of London; chaplain: Worshipful Co of Marketers, Worshipful Co of Stationers and Newspaper Makers; *Recreations* walking, travel, squash, broadcasting; *Clubs* Athenaeum, London Press, Wig and Pen; *Style—* The Rev Canon John Oates; St Bride's Rectory, Fleet St, London EC4Y 8AU (☎ 071 583 0239, 071 353 1301)

OATES, (John) Keith; s of John Alfred Oates (d 1983), of Bispham, Blackpool, Lancs, and Katherine Mary, *née* Hole; *b* 3 July 1942; *Educ* King's Sch Chester, Arnold Sch Blackpool, LSE (BSc), UMIST (Dip Tech), Univ of Bristol (MSc); *m* 25 May 1968, Helen Mary, da of Donald Charles Matthew Blake (d 1985), of Sale, Cheshire; 1 s (Jake b 1976), 3 da (Cathee b 1970, Kristen b 1971, Felicity b 1982); *Career* work study trainee Reed Paper Gp 1965-66, budgets and planning mangr IBM Uk Ltd 1966-73, gp fin controller Rolls Royce Ltd 1973-74, controller Black & Decker Europe 1974-78, vice pres fin Thyssen Bornermisza 1978-74, fin dir Marks & Spencer Plc 1984-, non exec dir John Laing Plc 1987-89; memb Cncl CBI 1988; BBC govr 1988-; memb 100 Gp of CAs 1985; FCT 1982; *Recreations* sepctator sports, association football, boxing & cricket, skiing, tennis; *Clubs* Supporter de L'Association Sportive de Monaco, Tennis Club de Monaco; *Style—* Keith Oates, Esq; Marks & Spencer plc, Michael House, Baker St, London W1A IDN (☎ 071 268 6427, fax 071 935 3571, telex 267141)

OATES, Roger Kendrew; s of William Oates (d 1987), and Mary Dorothy, *née* Mayne (d 1957); *b* 25 June 1946; *Educ* Thirsk Sch, York Sch of Art, Farnham Sch of Art (DipAD), Kidderminster Coll; *m* 31 July 1976, Fay Morgan, *qv*, da of Philip Hugh Morgan; 1 s (Daniel Morgan Oates b 25 Jan 1979); *Career* textile designer; set up own Studio Ledbury Herefordshire 1971-75, dir and chm Craftsman's Mark Ltd 1971-75, lectr at numerous colls of art England and Aust 1971-75; Morgan: Oates partnership at The House in the Yard Ledbury 1975-86; Morgan & Oates Ltd 1986-, designing for own label and clients incl: Ralph Lauren, Christian Dior, Sonia Rykiel Donna Karan, Laura Ashley; sr ptnr Roger Oates Design Associates partnership 1987-; work in exhibitions incl: The Craftsman's Art (V & A Museum) 1973, The House in the Yard - Textiles from the Workshop of Fay Morgan & Roger Oates (Welsh Arts Council Cardiff and tour) 1978, Tufted Rugs (Environment London) 1980, Texstyles (Crafts Council London and tour) 1984-85, Design Awards (Lloyds Building London) 1988; awarded: USA ROSCOE award 1984, British Design awards 1988, Duke of Edinburgh's Certificate for services to design; contribs to tv prodns; *Style—* Roger Oates, Esq; Roger Oates Design Associates, Church Lane, Ledbury, Herefordshire HR8 1DW (☎ and fax 0531 2718)

OATES, Sir Thomas; CMG (1962), OBE (1958, MBE 1946); er s of Thomas Oates, of Wadebridge, Cornwall; *b* 5 Nov 1917; *Educ* Callington GS Cornwall, Trinity Coll Cambridge (MA); *Career* Admty Scientific Staff 1940-46, temp Lt RNVR; entered Colonial Admin Serv 1948, seconded to HM Treasy 1953, fin sec Br Honduras 1955, Aden 1959-63, dep high cmmr Aden and Protectorate of South Arabia 1963-67, perm sec Gibraltar 1968-69, dep govr Gibraltar 1969-71, govr and C-in-C St Helena 1971-76; kt 1972; *Recreations* photography; *Clubs* East India, Royal Cwlth Soc; *Style—* Sir Thomas Oates, CMG, OBE; Tristan, Trevone, Padstow, Cornwall PL28 8QX

OATLEY, Sir Charles William; OBE (1956); s of William Oatley (d 1944); *b* 14 Feb 1904; *Educ* Bedford Modern Sch, St John's Coll Cambridge (MA); *m* 1930, (Dorothy) Enid, *née* , West; 2 s; *Career* lectr and reader Engrg Dept Univ of Cambridge 1945-60 (prof of electrical engrg 1960-71, emeritus prof 1971-), fell Trinity Coll Cambridge 1945-; FRS (Royal Medal 1969, Mullard award 1973), FEng, FIEE, FIEEE; Foreign Assoc, Nat Acad of Engrg USA 1979; kt 1974; *Clubs* Athenaeum; *Style—* Sir Charles Oatley, OBE, FRS; 16 Porson Rd, Cambridge CB2 2EU (☎ 0223 356194)

OATLEY, Clive; s of James William Oatley, OBE, of Burcote, Inglewood Park, St Lawrence, Isle of Wight, and Christina Margaret, *née* Webb; *b* 3 April 1938; *Educ* St Paul's, St Catharine's Coll Cambridge (MA); *m* 1, 1963; 1 s (Maxwell James); m 2, 1980, Brooke Randolph, da of Hon Joseph Simpson Farland, former US ambass to Panama, Pakistan and Iran, of Virginia USA; 1 s (Maxwell b 1976), 1 da (Virginia b 1977); *Career* Lt 5 Royal Inniskilling Dragoon Gds 1956-58; chm: Bridge Oil Gp of Cos; *Recreations* golf, tennis; *Clubs* Hawks, Royal Wimbledon Golf, RAC, Monaco Yacht; *Style—* Clive Oatley, Esq; Offices: Bridge Oil Ltd, 140 Brompton Rd, London SW3

OBOLENSKY, Prof Sir Dimitri; s of Prince Dimitri Obolensky (d 1964), of Antibes, France, and Mary, *née* Countess Shuvalov; descended from Rurik, the Scandinavian fndr of the Russian state ca 862, whose dynasty ruled Russia until 1598; *b* 1 April 1918; *Educ* Lycée Pasteur Paris, Trinity Coll Cambridge (MA, PhD), Univ of Oxford (DLitt); *m* 1947 (m dis 1989), Elisabeth Lopukhin; *Career* lectr in Slavonic studies Univ of Cambridge 1946-48, prof of Russian and Balkan history Univ of Oxford 1961-85 (reader in Russian and Balkan medieval history 1949-61, student (fell) Ch Ch 1950-85); visiting prof in many foreign univs; fell Trinity Coll Cambridge 1942-48, vice-pres Br Acad 1983-85; Hon Dr: Sorbonne 1980, Sofia Univ of Bulgaria 1989; Hon DLitt Univ of Birmingham; FBA, FSA, FRHistSoc; kt 1984; *Clubs* Athenaeum; *Style—* Prof Sir Dimitri Obolensky; 29 Belsyre Court, Woodstock Road, Oxford OX2 6HU (☎ 0865 56496)

OBOLENSKY, Prince Nikolai; s of Prince Michael Obolensky, of Madrid, Spain, and Anne, *née* Helbronner (d 1980); descends from Rurik who conquered Russia in 870s; *b* 7 June 1956; *Educ* Harrow, RMA Sandhurst,Univ of Durham (BA), IMEDE Lausanne (MBA); *m* 1987, Charlotte Isabella, *née* Sharpe; 1 s (Alexei b 24 Nov 1990); *Career* Maj 17/21 Lancers 1986- (cmmnd 1976, Lt 1978, Capt 1981), ret 1988; Ernst & Young: conslt 1989, sr conslt 1990, managing conslt 1991-; FRGS; *Recreations* mountaineering, flying, athletics; *Clubs* Cavalry and Guards', Lansdowne; *Style—* Prince Nikolai Obolensky; 28 Cameron Rd, Chesham, Bucks HP5 3BS (☎ 0494 773155)

OBORNE, Brig John Douglas; OBE (1989); s of Lt-Col T D Oborne, DSO (d 1985), and Elsie Cottrill, *née* Booth; *b* 28 Feb 1928; *Educ* Wellington, RMA Sandhurst; *m* 9 Oct 1954, Margaret Elizabeth, da of Cdr A R P Brown (d 1973); 3 s (Peter Alan b 1957, Nicholas David b 1961, James Richard b 1963); *Career* Br Army cmmnd into 4/7 Royal Dragoon Gds 1948; Staff Coll Camberley 1961, Jt Servs Staff Coll 1968, Br Liason Offr US Army Armor Centre Fort Knox 1969-71, chief instr Junior Div Staff Coll 1971-73, cdr Br Army Trg Team in Sudan 1973-75, def advsr Br High Cmmn India 1977-80, vice pres Regular Cmmns Bd 1980-82; ADC to HM The Queen 1980-82; Def Attaché Br Embassy Dublin 1984-89, Br sec British-Irish Inter-Parly Body 1990-; *Recreations* golf, travel; *Clubs* Cavalry and Guards'; *Style—* Brig John Oborne, OBE

OCEAN, Humphrey; s of Capt Maurice Erdeswick Butler-Bowdon, OBE (1984), and Anne, *née* Darlington; *b* 22 June 1951; *Educ* Ampleforth, Canterbury Coll of Art (BA);

m 3 March 1982, Miranda, da of Dr Michael Argyle, of Oxford; 2 da (Ruby b 1982, Beatrice b 1986); *Career* artist; winner of 1982 John Player Portrait Award; one man exhibitions: Nat Portrait Gallery 1984, touring exhibition organised by Ferens Art Gallery Hull 1986-87; portrait commissions incl: Philip Larkin, Paul McCartney, A J Ayer, Graham Greene, Lord Callaghan; work in collections of: Imperial War Museum, Scot Nat Portrait Gallery, Ferens Art Gallery, RAF Museum, National Portrait Gallery London, Fishmongers Co, QMC London, Hertford Coll Oxford, Royal Library Windsor, Royal Soc of Chemistry, Royal Opera House (Covent Garden); *Books* The Ocean View (1982), Big Mouth: The Amazon Speaks (1990); *Recreations* motorcycling; *Style*— Humphrey Ocean, Esq; 22 Marmora Rd, London SE22 0RX (☎ 081 693 8387)

OCKENDEN, Brig Robert Vaughan (Rob); CBE (1982, OBE 1977); s of William Ockenden (d 1983), of Chigwell, Essex, and Norah Vaughan, *née* Paterson (d 1981); *b* 14 April 1933; *Educ* Chigwell Sch, RMA; *m* 13 April 1963, Patricia Alice Walker Taylor, da of Robert Cauwood (d 1987), of Wheal Vor, Cornwall; 1 s (Paul b 1967), 1 da (Jessica b 1969); *Career* cmmnd 2 RTR 1953, Col Staff Offr to QMG 1979-82, Col Staff Offr to SACEUR 1983-85, dir Def Operational Requirements 1985-88; chief exec NRA 1988-; FBIM 1988; *Recreations* the countryside, bird watching, gardening, motoring; *Clubs* Army and Navy; *Style*— Brig Rob Ockenden, CBE; Glovers Cottage, Faversham Rd, Lenham, Kent; National Rifle Assoc, Bisley Camp, Brookwood, Woking, Surrey (☎ 0483 797777, fax 0483 797 285)

OCKRENT, Mike Robert; s of Charles Ockrent (d 1980), of London and Eve, *née* Edels; *b* 18 June 1946; *Educ* Highgate Sch, Univ of Edinburgh (BSc); *m* 1975, Susan, da of William Carpenter; 2 c (Natasha Mary b 1978, Ben Charles b 1981); *Career* trainee dir (ITV scholar) Perth Theatre 1969-73 (later assoc dir to Joan Knight), artistic dir Traverse Theatre Edinburgh 1973-76, freelance dir 1976-; prodns incl: Union Jack and Bonzo (Hampstead), The Plumber's Progress (Prince of Wales), The Admirable Crichton (Greenwich) Once a Catholic (Royal Court and Wyndham, Helen Hayes Theatre), A Respectable Wedding (Open Space), And A Nightingale Song (Queen's), Ducking Out (Duke of York), Short List (Hampstead), The Nerd (Aldwych), Who Plays Wins (Vaudeville), Look No Hans (Strand), Educating Rita (Piccadilly, Best Comedy award West End Mangrs), Passion Play (Wyndham, Best Play Evening Standard award), Me And My Girl (Adelphi, Oliver, Ivor Novello, Drama Magazine awards for best musical; Marquis Theatre NY, Drama Desk award best dir, nominated for 13 Tony awards, Follies (Shaftesbury, Laurence Oliver, Evening Standard, Plays & Players and Drama Magazine awards for best musical), Look! Look! (Aldwych), Just So (Tricycle), Atkinson at the Atkinson; NT prodns: Watch on the Rhine, Inner Voices, Laurence Oliver's 80th Birthday Celebrations, Int Workshops Santa Fe, New Mexico; film Dancin' Thru The Dark (BBC, Formost Pictures, British Screen; Popular Choice Venice Film Festival, Confederation International des Cinema d'Art et Essai award La Baule Festival) 1990; memb: Equity, Dirs Guild of UK, SSDC (USA); *Recreations* tennis, swimming; *Style*— Mike Ockrent, Esq; Saraband, 265 Liverpool Rd, London N1 1LX (☎ 071 609 5313, fax 071 609 2370)

ODAM, George Neville; s of George Odam (d 1979), of Beccles, Suffolk, and Muriel, *née* Tawell (d 1964); *b* 30 Sept 1938; *Educ* Sir John Leman Sch, Univ of Manchester (BA Mus), Univ of London (Music Teachers Cert), Univ of Southampton (BMus, MPhil); *m* 15 April 1963, Penelope Anne Lloyd, da of Oliver Lloyd Smith (d 1979), Beccles, Suffolk; 1 s (Timothy b 1964), 1 da (Joanna b 1966); *Career* Totton GS Hants 1961-65, Bath Coll of Higher Educn 1966, Peredur-Opera 1979, Concerto for piano and timpani 1980; compositions: Cantata for Christmas 1967, Angry Arrow 1969, St George and the Dragon 1970, Tutankhamun 1971, Inca 1975, Robin Hood 1978, Baba Yaga 1984; fndr and conductor Nat Scouts and Guides Symphony Orchestra, chm UK Cncl for Music Educn and Trg 1988-, vice chm SEAC Music Ctee; memb ISM (warden of MES 1986-87), chm SW Arts Educn Steering Gp Ctee 1988-, chm Selection Ctee UK for ISME Conf Helsinki 1990; *Books* Silver Burdett and Ginn Music Books 1-4 (1989); *Recreations* drawing and painting, computer graphics and DTP, poetry, travel; *Clubs* Cannons; *Style*— George Odam, Esq; 55 Newbridge Hill, Bath, Avon BA1 3PR (☎ 0225 423216); Bath College of Higher Education, Newton Park, Newton St. Loe, Bath BA2 9BN (☎ 0225 873701 ext 340)

ODAM, Joseph; JP (1969), DL (Cambs 1989-); s of Frank Moore Odam (d 1953), and Edna Jessie Maud Miller (d 1967); *b* 8 Dec 1925; *Educ* King's Sch Peterborough, Bedford Sch, Worcester Coll Oxford (Short Mil Course); *m* 21 April 1956, Jane Margaret, da of Harold Howarth (d 1956), of Curwen Woods, Burton in Kendal, Westmoreland; 2 da (Stella Jane b 1957, Josephine Ann Lucinda b 1963); *Career* Reg Army Capt 1 Royal Tank Regt 1944-51; dir: Sydney C Banks plc 1966-, Peterborough Evening Telegraph 1967-, Howsan Ltd 1975-, Banks Odam Dennick Ltd 1990-; memb Lloyd's 1977; dep pres E of Eng Agric Soc 1980- (chm 1969-72, hon life vice pres 1976-), memb Exec Ctee NFU Peterborough; JP 1969 (chm Peterborough bench 1985-); Liveryman of the City of London, memb Worshipful Co of Farmers 1980; Jubilee Medal (1977); Shrieve of the Co of Cambridgeshire 1989-; *Recreations* tennis; *Clubs* Farmers; *Style*— Joseph Odam, Esq, JP, DL; Haynes Farm, Thorney Rd, Eye, Peterborough, Cambs PE6 7UA (☎ 0733 222456)

ODDIE, Christopher Peter; s of Alfred Birtwistle Oddie, of N Lancs, and Elsie Mary, *née* Bateman; *b* 26 Sept 1948; *Educ* King Edward VII Sch Lytham Lancs; *m* 12 June 1971, Gail, da of Maj Horace George Ablett; 2 s (Simon Christopher b 19 Sept 1975, Matthew David b 1 July 1979); *Career* CA 1978; articled clerk T & H P Bee Preston 1967-72; ptnr: Tyson Westall CAs Lancs 1973-76, Grant Thornton CAs (formerly Thornton Baker) 1976-86; sr ptnr Lonsdale and Partners CAs Lancaster and branches 1986-; treas Lancaster Cons Assoc, Lancaster Loyne Rotary Club; FICA; *Recreations* sailing; *Clubs* Royal Windermere Yacht; *Style*— Christopher Oddie, Esq; 10 Forgewood Drive, Halton, Lancaster, Lancs (☎ 0524 811 486); Lonsdale & Partners, Priory Close, St Marys Gate, Lancaster LA1 1XB (☎ 0524 628 01, fax 0524 377 64)

ODDIE, Elaine Anne; s of Brian John Cory of Hartley, Kent, and Molly, *née* Williams; *b* 11 Feb 1955; *Educ* Gravesend Girls Sch Kings Coll Cambridge (MA); *m* 3 July 1976, Alan James Oddie, s of William Green Oddie; *Career* articled clerk Brebner Allen & Trapp 1976-79, fin accountant Yardley International Ltd 1979-82; ptnr: Mason Charlesworth & Co 1982-89, Morison Stoneham 1989-; memb N Thames Gas Consumers Cncl 1981-84, pres S Essex Soc of Chartered Accountants 1990-91; FCA 1989 (ACA 1979); *Recreations* squash, gardening, walking; *Clubs* Network; *Style*— Mrs Elaine Oddie; Morison Stoneham, Moriston House, 75 Springfield Rd, Chelmsford, Essex CM2 6JB (☎ 0245 492920, fax 0245 490841, car phone 0860 268777)

ODDY, (William) Andrew; s of William Tingle Oddy (d 1985), and Hilda Florence, *née* Dalby; *b* 6 Jan 1942; *Educ* Bradford GS, New Coll Oxford (BA, BSc, MA); *m* 4 Aug 1965, Patricia Anne, da of Albert Edward Whitaker, of Upton upon Severn, Worcs; 1 s (Guy b 1968), 1 da (Frances b 1970); *Career* Br Museum: scientific offr 1966-69, sr scientific offr 1969-75, princ scientific offr 1975-81, head of Conservation 1981-85, keeper of Conservation 1985-; author over 150 papers, articles, notes and reviews in learned jls, ed and jt ed of the proceedings of 8 conferences; memb several learned socs and numerous ctees connected with the conservation of museum objects; Freeman: Worshipful Co of Goldsmiths 1986, City of London 1986; FSA 1973; *Books* Romanesque Metalwork: Copper Alloys and their Decoration (with Susan La Niece and Neil Startford, 1986); *Recreations* travel; *Style*— Andrew Oddy, Esq, FSA; 6 Ashlyns Rd, Berkhamsted, Hertfordshire HP4 3BN; Dept of Conservation, The British Museum, London WC1B 3DG (☎ 071 323 8223, fax 071 323 8480, telex 94013362 BMUS G)

ODDY, Christine; MEP (Lab) Midlands Central 1989-; da of Eric Lawson Oddy, and Audrey Mary, *née* Latham; *b* 20 Sept 1955; *Educ* UCL (LLB), Institute d'Études Européenes Brussels (licenciée speciale en droit européen, Belgian Govt Scholar, Walter Page Hine Travel Scholar, Cncl of Europe Travel Scholar), Birkbeck Coll London (MSc Econ); *Career* Stagiaire at European Commission Brussels 1979-80, articled clerk 1980-82, admitted slr 1982, practiced slr 1982-84, law lectr City of London Poly 1984-89; memb: Bentham Soc, Haldine Soc, Industl Law Soc, Law Soc; *Recreations* arts, cinema, theatre and wine; *Clubs* English Speaking Union; *Style*— Ms Christine Oddy, MEP; 3 Copthall House, Station Square, Coventry CV1 2FZ (☎ 0203 552328, fax 0203 551424)

ODELL, Prof Dr Peter Randon; s of Frank James Odell (d 1978), of Coalville, Leicester, and Grace Edna, *née* Randon (d 1954); *b* 1 July 1930; *Educ* King Edward VII GS Coalville Leicester, Univ of Birmingham (BA, PhD, WA Cadbury prize, Univ Graduate Scholarship), Fletcher Sch of Law and Diplomacy, Tufts Univ Boston USA (AM); *m* 17 Aug 1957, Jean Mary, da of Ewan John McKintosh, of Isle of Man; 2 s (Nigel Peter b 1958, Mark John b 1965), 2 da (Deborah Grace b 1960, Susannah Mary b 1967); *Career* RAF educn offr 1954-57, flying offr 1954-56, Flt Lt 1956-57; economist Shell International Petroleum Company Ltd 1958-61, sr lectr in econ geography LSE 1966-68 (lectr 1961-66); prof of econ geography: Netherlands Sch of Economics 1968-73, Erasmus Univ Rotterdam 1973-81; prof of Int energy studies Erasmus Univ Rotterdam 1981-; visiting prof: Coll of Europe Bruges 1984-90, LSE 1985-; Killam visiting fell Univ of Calgary Canada 1989; Euro Parly candidate (SLD) Suffolk and S E Cambridgeshire 1989; memb: The Euro Movement, Royal Cwlth Tst, Chatham House, RIIA; FInstPet, FRSA; *Books* An Economic Geography of Oil (1963), Natural Gas in Western Europe: A Case Study in the Economic Geography of Energy Resources (1969), Oil and World Power: A Geographical Interpretation (1970, 8 edn 1986), Economies and Societies in Latin America: A Geographical Interpretation (with D A Preston, 1973, 1978), The West European Energy Economy: The case for Self-Sufficiency (1976), The Pressures of Oil: A Strategy for Economic Revival (with L Vallenilla, 1978), The Future of Oil (with K E Rosing, 1980, 1983); *Recreations* mountain walking, local history, gardening; *Style*— Prof Dr Peter Odell; De Lairesselaan 191, 3062 PH Rotterdam, The Netherlands (☎ 010 31 10 4525341); 7 Constitution Hill, Ipswich, Suffolk IP1 3RG (☎ 0473 253376); Erasmus Univ, Postbus 1738, 3000 DR Rotterdam, Netherlands (☎ 010 31 10 408 1461, fax 010 31 10 452 7009)

ODELL, Sir Stanley John; s of George Frederick Odell (d 1990), and Florence May, *née* Roberts, (d 1972); *b* 20 Nov 1929; *Educ* Bedford Modern Sch; *m* 4 Dec 1952, (Eileen) Grace, da of Reginald Edward Percival Stuart; 4 da (Sally (Mrs Strong) b 1954, Carol (Mrs Parry) b 1956, Julie (Mrs Warner) b 1958, Susan (Mrs Dann) b 1961); *Career* former chm Mid Bedfordshire Cons Assoc and Cons E Provincial Area, chm Nat Union of Cons and Unionist Assocs, chm Anglo-American Ctee RAF Chicksands, chm Restoration Ctee All Saints Church Campton; kt 1986; *Recreations* politics, shooting; *Clubs* Farmers'; *Style*— Sir Stanley Odell; Woodhall Farm, Campton, Shefford, Beds SG17 5PB (☎ 0462 813 230)

ODGERS, Graeme David William; s of William Arthur Odgers (d 1950), and Elizabeth Minty, *née* Rennie (d 1987); *b* 10 March 1934; *Educ* St John's Coll Johannesburg, Gonville and Caius Coll Cambridge, Harvard Business Sch (MBA); *m* 1957, Diana Patricia, *née* Berge; 1 s (John), 2 da (Mary, Juliet) and 1 da decd; *Career* dir Keith Shipton & Co Ltd 1965-72, chm Odgers & Co (mgmnt conslts) 1970-74, C T Bowring (Insurance) Holdings Ltd 1972-74, dir Indust Devpt Unit DOI 1974-77, assoc dir (fin) GEC 1977-78, gp md Tarmac plc 1983-86 (gp fin dir 1979-83); BT: pt/t memb Bd 1983-86, UK govt dir 1984-86, dep chm and chief fin offr 1986-87, gp md 1987-90; non exec dir: Dalgety 1987-, National and Provincial Building Society; chief exec Alfred McAlpine plc 1990-; *Recreations* golf; *Clubs* City of London, Reform, Wilderness; *Style*— Graeme Odgers, Esq; Brome House, High St, W Malling, Kent ME19 6NE

ODGERS, Paul Randell; CB (1970), MBE (1945), TD (1949); s of late Dr Paul Norman Blake Odgers, of Oxford, and Mabel Annie, *née* Higgins; *b* 31 July 1915; *Educ* Rugby, New Coll Oxford (MA); *m* 21 April 1944, Diana, da of Rupert Edward Francis Fawkes, CBE (d 1967), of Lechlade, Gloucestershire; 1 s (Robin (Dr Odgers) b 1948), 1 da (Caroline (Mrs Compston) b 1946); *Career* 2 Lt Oxford & Bucks LI 1939-40, Staff Capt 184 Inf Bde 1940-41, Staff Coll Camberley 1941, Staff Capt and Bde Maj Centl Inf Bde Malta 1941-42, DAAG HQ Malta Cmd 1942-43, GS02 HQ 8 Army 1943-44, GS02 Tactical HQ 21 Army Gp 1944-45; entered Bd of Educn 1937; Miny of Educn: princ 1945-48, asst sec 1948-56; asst sec Cabinet Office 1956-58, under sec Miny of Educn 1958-67, office of first sec of state 1967-68, office of sec of state for Soc Servs 1968-70, Cabinet Office 1970-71, dep sec DES 1971-75; memb: Cncl Girl's Public Day Sch Tst 1976-90, Exec Ctee GBGSA 1978-86; govr St Marys C of E First Sch Haddenham, vice pres Soc for Promotion of Roman Studies, memb Ctee Haddenham Village Soc; *Clubs* United Oxford and Cambridge Univ; *Style*— Paul Odgers, Esq, CB, MBE, TD; Stone Walls, Aston Rd, Haddenham, Bucks HP17 8AF (☎ 0844 291 830)

ODGERS, Richard Michael Douglas; DFC (1944); s of Dr Paul Norman Blake Odgers (d 1962), and Mabel Annie, *née* Higgins; *b* 11 Jan 1920; *Educ* Rugby, New Coll Oxford (MA); *m* 16 July 1949, Miriam Cholerton, da of Horace Charles Sydney Tyler (d 1946); 1 s (James b 1954), 2 da (Charlotte b 1951, Clare b 1953); *Career* Capt RA 1940-46, served Italy 651 Air OP Sqdn RAF; APV Co Ltd 1947-57, overseas film distribution Rank Orgn 1957-64, Curtis Brown Ltd (literary agents) 1964-84 (chm 1980); *Recreations* sailing, skiing, music; *Clubs* Garrick; *Style*— Richard Odgers, Esq, DFC; The Coach House, Leeson, Langton Matravers, Swanage, Dorset BH19 3EU (☎ 0929 422636)

ODLING, Christopher Arthur; s of Harold Robert Odling (d 1975), of Esher, Surrey, and Myrtle Agnes, *née* Huband (d 1976); *b* 1 Dec 1929; *Educ* Radley, St Mary's Hosp London, Exeter Coll Oxford; *m* 6 Dec 1963, Patricia Blayney, da of Lt-Col B G B Mitchell, DSC, DL, RM (d 1983), of Wiston; 1 s (Richard b 1970), 2 da (Philippa b 1964, Claire b 1966); *Career* Nat Serv Royal Warwicks Regt 1949-50; banker Hongkong and Shanghai Corp 1952, admin Br Bank of The Middle East Oman 1981, fin mangr Gabbitas Thring Educn Tst 1982-83, admin mangr Centre for Int Briefing 1984-85; govr Sir Thomas Picton Sch Haverfordwest, dist cmmr Pembroke Scout Assoc (memb 1955); memb Governing Body of Church in Wales; MBIM 1977; Medal of Merit, Hong Kong Medal for Good Servs; *Recreations* scouting, walking; *Clubs* Royal Hong Kong Jockey; *Style*— Christopher A Odling, Esq; Manor House, Wiston, Haverfordwest, Dyfed SA62 4PN (☎ 0437 731258)

ODLING-SMEE, John Charles; s of Rev Charles William Odling-Smee (d 1990), of Brearton, N Yorks, and Katharine Hamilton, *née* Aitchison; *b* 13 April 1943; *Educ* Durham Sch, St John's Coll Cambridge (BA); *Career* res offr Inst of Econs and Statistics Univ of Oxford 1968-71 and 1972-73 (asst res offr 1965-66, fell in econs Oriel Coll 1966-70), econ res offr Govt of Ghana 1971-72, sr res offr Centre for Urban

Econs LSE 1973-75, econ advsr Central Policy Review Staff 1975-77, sr econ advsr HM Treasy 1977-80, sr economist IMF 1981-82, dep chief econ advsr HM Treasy 1989-90 (under-sec in econs 1982-89), sr advsr IMF 1990-; author of articles in learned jls; *Books* British Economic Growth 1855-1973 (with RCO Matthews and CH Feinstein, 1982); *Style*— John Odling-Smee, Esq; 2210 R Street NW, Washington DC 20008, USA (☎ 202 234 7059)

ODLING-SMEE, Peter Guy; s of Lt-Col Alfred John Odling-Smee, OBE (d 1987), of Newton Ferrers, nr Plymouth, Devon, and Dorothy Nancy, *née* Bowles (d 1982); *b* 30 June 1938; *Educ* Charterhouse, Britannia RNC Dartmouth; *m* 12 July 1968, Marianne, da of Grosser Helge Fischer (d 1972), of Korsor, Denmark; 2 s (Christopher b 19 Oct 1970, Michael Kristian b 22 Nov 1973); *Career* RN; Sub Lt 1959, trg HMS Victorious and minesweepers, joined RN Surveying Serv 1960, specialised in hydrographic surveying worldwide, i/c RN Antarctic Survey Pty 1967-68, offr responsible for initiating Radio Navigational Warnings 1970, sr instr RN Sch of Hydrographic Surveying HMS Drake Plymouth, ret Lt Cdr 1976; sr surveyor Kelvin Hughes Ltd (worked Saudi Arabia, Indonesia, Libya) 1976-79, princ Odling-Smee Oberman Assoc 1979-, sr lectr in marine sci Polytechnic South West 1982-89; UK rep Advsy Bd on Standards of Competence for Hydrographic Surveyors, memb Training and Education Ctee RICS; FRICS; *Recreations* horse riding, foxhunting, skiing, sailing; *Clubs* Royal Western Yacht; *Style*— Peter Odling-Smee, Esq; Hanger Farm, Cornwood, nr Ivybridge, Devon PL21 9HP (☎ 075 537 370, fax 075 537 815)

ODLING-SMEE, (George) William; s of Rev Charles William Odling-Smee (d 1990), of Brearton, nr Harrogate, Yorkshire, and Katharine Hamilton, *née* Aitchison; *b* 21 April 1935; *Educ* Durham Sch, Kings' Coll Newcastle upon Tyne, Univ of Durham; *m* 30 July 1959, Anne Marie, da of Walter Louis Thacker (ka 1944); 3 s (Patrick William b 1963, James Louis b 1965, Hugh Hamilton b 1973), 3 da (Margaret Emma b 1960, Katherine Anne b 1962, Elizabeth Mary b 1971, d 1974); *Career* med supt St Raphael's Hosp Giddalur South India 1961-64, dir Child Med Care Unit Enugu Nigeria 1969, sr tutor in surgery Queen's Univ of Belfast 1970-73, sr lectr in surgery and consIt surgn Royal Victoria Hosp Belfast 1973-; FRCS (England) 1968 (memb Ct), FRCS (Ireland) 1987- (memb Ct); *Books* Trauma Care (1981), Breast Cancer (1989); *Recreations* theology; *Style*— William Odling-Smee, Esq; 10 Deramore Park South, Belfast BT9 5JY, Nortern Ireland; Royal Victoria Hospital, Grosvenor Rd, Belfast BT12 8BA (☎ 240503 ext 2658)

ODONI, Prof Robert Winston Keith; s of Anthony Vincent (Walter) Odoni, of London, and Lois Marie, *née* Conner (d 1984); *b* 14 July 1947; *Educ* Queen Elizabeth's GS, Univ of Exeter (BSc), Downing Coll Cambridge (PhD); *m* 1 July 1972, Josephine Anne, da of Joseph Ding, of Cambridge; 2 s (Martin b 1975, Russell b 1984), 1 da (Theresa b 1973); *Career* temp lectr pure maths Liverpool Univ 1971-72, res fell pure maths Glasgow Univ 1972-73; Exeter Univ: lectr pure maths 1973-79, reader number theory 1979-85, prof number theory 1985-89; prof mathematics Glasgow Univ 1989-; memb: London Mathematical Soc 1973 (memb editorial bd 1987-), Cambridge Philosophical Soc 1973, American Mathematical Soc 1976, Société Mathématique de France 1981; *Books* author of numerous res articles in major mathematical jls; *Recreations* music, foreign languages, country walks, swimming, cricket; *Style*— Prof Robert Odoni; Dept of Mathematics, Univ of Glasgow, Glasgow G12 8QW (☎ 041 339 8855)

ODY, Jonathan Wilmot; s of Robert Henry Morton Ody (d 1978), and Joan Elizabeth, *née* Hunter; *b* 24 Dec 1941; *Educ* Malvern; *m* 13 Sept 1967 (m dis 1973), Evelyn, *née* Bruce; 2 s (Andrew, Ian); m 2, 28 Feb 1981, Noelle Maria Anne, *née* Bolton; 1 s (Robin), 1 step s (Ben); *Career* admitted slr 1965; ptnr: Pattinson & Brewer 1968-69, Norton Rose 1973-; Liveryman Worshipful Co of Slrs 1973; memb Law Soc 1964; *Recreations* food and wine, France; *Clubs* MCC, Le Cercle de la Fraternité; *Style*— Jonathan Ody, Esq; Kempson House, PO Box 570, Camomile St, London EC3A 7AN (☎ 071 283 2434, fax 071 588 1181)

OEHLERS, Maj-Gen Gordon Richard; CB (1987); s of Dr Roderick Clarke Oehlers (d 1950), and Hazel Ethne Oehlers; *b* 19 April 1933; *Educ* St Andrew's Sch, Singapore; *m* 27 Oct 1956, Rosie; 1 s (Michael b 1963), 1 da (Elizabeth b 1966); *Career* cmmnd RCS 1958, UK and ME 1958-64, Adj 4 Div Signals Regt 1964-66, CO 7 Signal Regt 1973-76, cdr 1 Br Corps RCS 1977-79, dir Ops Requirements 4 Army 1979-84; asst CDS (cmd, control, communications and info system) 1984-87, Col Cmdt RCS 1987; dir of Security and Investigation Br Telecom 1987-; chm Royal Signals Inst 1990; Hon Col 31 Signal Regt (Volunteers) 1988-; FIEE, CEng; *Recreations* lawn tennis, golf, bridge; *Style*— Maj-Gen Gordon Oehlers, CB; c/o Nat Westminster Bank plc, Petersfield, Hants

OESER, Francis Oscar Drury; s of Prof Oscar Oeser (d 1983), of Aust, and Dr Mary Drury Clarke (d 1976); *b* 19 May 1936; *Educ* Scotch Coll Melbourne, Univ of Melbourne (BA Arch, Dip TRP); *m* 1 Feb 1963, Ann Charina, da of Keith Forge (d 1982), of Aust; 2 s (Marc Drury b 1969, Kim Francis b 1973), 1 da (Mia Elisabeth b 1971); *Career* architect and planner, photographer, flautist, teacher, writer, performer; private practice: Sydney 1963-66, London 1976-; pt/t tutor: Univ of NSW (1964-66), NE London Poly (1976-80); author of report 'Persian Tiling Practice' (1967); judge Britain in Bloom Competition 1976-; memb RIBA, MRTPI, FRAIA; *Books* Black Notes (1983), Seasons End (1984), Africa Sung (1987), Baybreak (1991); Exhibition: The Way to Santiago (1988); *Recreations* skiing, sailing, cycling, history & lit, music, theatre; *Style*— Francis Oeser, Esq; 21 Dartmouth Park Ave, London NW5 1JL (☎ 071 267 6344); 122 Dartmouth Park Hill, London N19 5HT (☎ 071 263 9317)

OESTREICHER, Christine Marguerite Nunes; da of Bryan Harold Nunes Carvalho, and Margaret Elizabeth, *née* Guthrie; *b* 29 Oct 1940; *Educ* St Paul's Girls Sch; *m* 1, 1958, Andrew Hall Montagu Best; 2 da (Francesca Jane b 1959, Katherine Elizabeth b 1961); m 2, 1963, Milton Daniel Oestreicher; 1 da (Lily Josephine b 1964); *Career* film prodr; set up Flamingo Pictures (with James Scott) 1981; films incl Chance History Art (co-produced with James Scott 1979, Silver prize Melbourne Film Festival 1981), Couples and Robbers 1981, A Shocking Accident 1982 (Oscar winner 1983), Samson and Delilah 1983, Every Picture Tells A Story 1984, Loser Takes All 1989; memb: Prodrs Assoc, ACTT, Acad of Motion Picture Arts and Sciences; *Style*— Christine Oestreicher

OF MAR; *see*: Mar

OFFEN, James Frank; s of Frank George Offen (d 1985), of Oxford, and Edna May, *née* Smith (d 1986); *b* 19 July 1935; *Educ* Sir William Borlase Sch, Marlow Coll of Estate Management; *m* 1, 14 Dec 1957, Dorinne Ellen Gardner; 3 s (Nicholas John b 19 June 1959, Simon Brian b 18 Oct 1962, Christopher James b 12 Nov 1967); m 2, 6 Sept 1982, Susan Mary, *née* Burton; *Career* surveyor; articled pupil Herbert Dulake & Co chartered surveyors Oxford 1952-55; professional asst: Jackson Stops & Staff land agents & surveyors Northants 1955-56, Howard Son & Gooch estate agents Amersham 1956-57, Kemp & Kemp rating & town planning surveyors Oxford 1957-58; regnl organiser Oxfam Berks, Bucks and Oxon 1958-60, estates surveyor Lagos Exec Devpt Bd Nigeria 1960-62; Buckell & Ballard chartered surveyors Oxford: sr asst 1962-65, ptnr 1965-82, chm Bd of Mgmnt (following sale of Buckell & Ballard to Black Horse Agencies) 1982-85; sr ptnr James Offen & Partners chartered surveyors and estate agents; hon treas RICS 1990- (memb Gen Cncl 1973-90, memb Educn and Membership Ctee 1978-84), chm Bd Coll of Estate Mgmnt 1985-90; Freeman City of London 1977, Liveryman Worshipful Co of Chartered Surveyors 1977; FRICS 1965; *Recreations* reading, travel, playing tennis, skiing, watching cricket; *Clubs* Athenaeum, MCC; *Style*— James Offen, Esq; Linden Cottage, Union Street, Woodstock, Oxford OX7 1JF (☎ 0993 813194, fax 0993 813242); James Offen & Partners, 25 Beaumont St, Oxford OX1 2NP (☎ 0865 512394, fax 0865 310237)

OFFIELD, Norman Lionel; s of Lionel Norman Offield, of 45 Warburton Rd, Twickenham, Middx, and Kathleen Daisy, *née* Kempson; *b* 12 Dec 1938; *Educ* Twickenham Tech Coll of Engrg; *m* 1 Feb 1960, Wendy Doris, da of Charles Leonard Britten (d 1959), of Stamford, Lincolnshire; 1 s (Adrian b 30 April 1974), 3 da (Deborah b 1 June 1962, Sharon b 26 Nov 1963, Michelle b 8 April 1967); *Career* RAF 1957-69, RS TA 1974-76; computer conslt int co specialising in bonded warehousing, haulage and distribution, fndr and dir NL Offield Data Ltd 1970-; asst co dir Saint John Ambulance Assoc W Sussex; memb: Royal Soc of St George, English Speaking Union, City of London Historical Soc, Peterborough Medieval Jousting Soc, Monarchist League, The Historical Soc; co fndr and knight princ Londinium Chapter of the Order of The Knights and Ladies of the Round Table; Champion to the MacMhuirrich Baron Currie of Balilone, Knight Champion to Laird of Balgonie Castle; Freeman: City of London 1989, Co of Information Technologists 1990; memb Guild of Freemen 1989; FSAS 1990, FRSA 1990; memb Inst Data Processing Mgmnt; *Recreations* mediaeval jousting, armoury, history; *Clubs* The English Speaking Union; *Style*— Norman Offield, Esq; 14 Mina Close, Stanground, Peterborough PE2 8TG (☎ 0733 342374)

OFFORD, Prof Robin Ewart; s of Frank Etchelles Offord, of Wissett, Suffolk, and Eileen Elisabeth, *née* Plunkett; *b* 28 June 1940; *Educ* Owen's Sch, Peterhouse Cambridge (MA, PhD); *m* 3 July 1963, Valerie Edna, da of Ronald Wheatley (d 1971); 1 s (Alan b 1964), 2 da (Jane b 1967, Alice b 1973); *Career* fell Univ Coll Oxford 1968-73 (Univ lectr in molecular biophysics 1972-80), fell and tutor in biochemistry Christ Church Oxford 1973-80, prof and dir Département de Biochimie Médicale Université de Genéve 1980-, ed Biochemical Journal 1972-79; memb: local ctees of Christian Aid 1970-80, editorial bds of various scientific jls 1972-, various ctees and bds of the UK Med Res Cncl and UK Miny of Health, Comité Scientifique de la Fondation Jeantet de Médecine 1985-88; *Books* A Guidebook to Biochemistry (with MD Yudkin, 1971), Comprehensible Biochemistry (with MD Yudkin, 1973), Biochemistry (1975, Spanish translation 1976), Semisynthetic Peptides and Proteins (with C di Bello, 1977), Simple Macromolecules (1979), Macromolecular Complexes (1979), Semisynthetic Proteins (1980); *Recreations* comparative linguistics, scuba diving, windsurfing, cross-country skiing; *Style*— Prof Robin Offord; Collex-Bossy, Switzerland; Church Hanborough, Oxon; Département de Biochimie Médicale, Centre Médical Universitaire, 1211 Genéve 4 Suisse (☎ Geneva 22 90 15, fax Geneva 47 33 34, telex 421330 CMU CH)

OGBORN, Anthony Douglas Ronald (Tony); s of Dr Ronald Sherrington Ogborn, of Sutton Coldfield, and Margery Mary, *née* Norris; *b* 22 Dec 1938; *Educ* King Edward's Sch Birmingham, Univ Coll Oxford (BA, MA, BM BCh); *m* 5 Aug 1967, Monica, da of Oswald Faithfull Shipton; 1 s (Ian b 1969); *Career* sr registrar in obstetrics and gynaecology Northampton and Hammersmith Hosps 1973-77, sr conslt obstetrician and gynaecologist NW Thames Region at Bedford Gen Hosp 1977-; treas NW Thames Regnl Ctee Hosp Med Servs 1980-86; memb: N Beds Health Authy 1982-86, NW Thames Region Perinatal Working Pty 1982-89, N Beds Dist Advsy Bd 1988-90; MRCOG 1969, FRCOG 1982; *Recreations* gardening, photography, windsurfing; *Clubs* Priory Sailing (Bedford); *Style*— Tony Ogborn, Esq; Bedford General Hospital, Kempston Rd, Bedford (☎ 0234 355122 ext 3346)

OGDEN, Alan; s of Graeme Ogden (d 1985), and Mary, *née* Howes; *b* 5 July 1948; *Educ* Eton, RMA Sandhurst; *m* Josephine, da of Sir Ian Hunter; 1 s (Richard b 1980); *Career* Capt Grenadier Gds 1966-78; mangr Financial Times Ltd 1978-82, devpt dir St James Corporate Communications 1982-83, devpt dir and dep chief exec offr Charles Barker City 1983-88, md Hill and Knowlton 1988-; MIPR, FBIM; *Recreations* travelling; *Style*— Alan Ogden, Esq; Hill and Knowlton, 5-11 Theobalds Rd, London WC1X 8SH (☎ 071 413 3000, fax 071 413 3114)

OGDEN, Eric; MP (elected as Labour but resigned from party 1981 after failure to be reselected as constituency candidate, and joined SDP Oct 1981) Liverpool West Derby 1964-; s of Robert Ogden (d 1959); *b* 23 Aug 1923; *Educ* Queen Elizabeth's GS Middleton, Wigan Tech Coll; *m* 1; 1 s (David Norman); m 2, 1964, Marjorie, *née* Smith; 2 s (Mark Robert b 1966, Martin Branston b 1967), 2 step da (Christine Davies, Deborah Birtwes); *Career* Br Dutch and US Mercantile Marines 1942-46, coal miner, memb and sponsored by NUM; *Recreations* gardening, motoring, surviving; *Clubs* Europe House, Gillmoss & Dovecot; *Style*— Eric Ogden, Esq, MP; House of Commons, Westminster, London SW1 (☎ 071 219 5201)

OGDEN, Sir (Edward) Michael; QC (1968); s of Edward Cannon Ogden (d 1933), of Hove, Sussex, and Daisy, *née* Paris; *b* 9 April 1926; *Educ* Downside, Jesus Coll Cambridge (MA); *m* 21 Dec 1951, Joan Kathleen, da of Pius Charles Brodrick, of Bolton; 2 s (Edward, Henry), 2 da (Celia (Comtesse de Borchgrave d'Altena), Lucy); *Career* Royal Gloucs Hussars, Capt 16/5 Queen's Royal Lancers 1944-47, Capt Inns of Ct Regt TA 1950-56; called to the Bar Lincoln's Inn 1950-, rec Hastings 1971, rec Crown Ct 1972-, treas Bar Cncl 1972-75, ldr SE Circuit 1975-78, bencher 1977; memb cncl: Union Internationale Des Avocats 1962-83, Legal Educn 1969-74, Int Bar Assoc 1983-87; chm Criminal Injuries Compensation Bd 1975-89 (memb 1968-89), assessor of compensation for persons wrongly imprisoned or charged 1977-89; kt 1989; *Style*— Sir Michael Ogden, QC; 2 Crown Office Row, Temple, London EC4Y 7HJ (☎ 071 353 9337, fax 071 583 0589, telex 8954005 TWOCOR G)

OGDEN, Dr Peter James; s of James Platt Ogden, and Frances Ogden; *b* 26 May 1947; *Educ* Univ of Durham (BSc,PhD), Harvard Business Sch (MBA); *m* 22 Aug 1970, Catherine Rose, da of Harold Blincoe; 2 s (Cameron b 9 Oct 1977, Edward b 18 Aug 1981), 1 da (Tiffany b 1 Oct 1975); *Career* exec dir Merrill Lynch International Bank Ltd 1976-81; md: Merrill Lynch White Weld Capital Markets Group 1976-81, Morgan Stanley & Co 1981-87 (advsy dir 1987-); chm Computacenter Ltd 1987-; *Style*— Dr Peter Ogden; Computacenter Ltd, 93-101 Blackfriars Rd, London SE1 8HW

OGILVIE, Sir Alec Drummond; s of Sir George Drummond Ogilvie, KCIE, CSI (d 1966); *b* 17 May 1913; *Educ* Cheltenham Coll; *m* 1945, Lesley Constance Woollan; 2 s; *Career* served WWII Gurkha Rifles IA (POW); chm Andrew Yule & Co Calcutta 1962-65 (md 1956); pres Associated Chambers of Commerce and Industry India 1964-65; chm Powell Duffryn 1969-78 (dep chm 1967-69); dir: Westinghouse Brake & Signal Co Ltd 1966-79, Lindustries 1973-79, J Lyons & Co 1977-78; memb Cncl: King Edward VII's Hosp for Offrs 1967- (vice pres 1979-), Cheltenham Coll 1973-85 (dep pres 1983-85); kt 1965; *Recreations* gardening, walking; *Clubs* Oriental, MCC; *Style*— Sir Alec Ogilvie; Townlands, High St, Lindfield, West Sussex RH16 2HT (☎ 044 41 48 3953)

OGILVIE, Philip John; s of Maj Jasper John Ogilvie, MBE (d 1974), of Cricket St Thomas, Somerset, and Rosemary Margaret De Courcy Hughes, *née* Thurlow; *b* 12 Nov 1948; *Educ* Farleigh House, Ampleforth; *m* 9 Oct 1981, Loreto, da of Col Eduardo Vega de Seoane y Barroso, of Madrid; 3 s (Ian Alexander b 14 May 1985,

William Jasper Charles b 1 April 1988, James Edward George b 23 April 1990); *Career* CA, articled Binder Hamlyn & Co 1966-70, ptnr Binder Dijker Otte & Co Madrid 1974-82, Barclays Bank Madrid & UK 1982-89, currently finance dir Promotora Playas Espanolas SA Madrid and Marbella; pres Br C of C Spain 1985-86, hon sec Cncl Br C of C in Europe 1986-, memb Somerset and W Dorset Euro-Cncl (Cons pty) 1986-88; FCA 1971; Knight of the Order of Malta; *Recreations* fishing, skiing; *Clubs* Army and Navy; *Style—* Philip Ogilvie, Esq; The Old Rectory, Hinton St George, Crewkerne, Somerset TA17 8SP (☎ 0460 73131); Apartmentos Tenis 23, 4, Sotogrande, 11310 Cadiz, Spain (☎ 010 3456 792209)

OGILVIE-LAING OF KINKELL, Gerald; *b* 11 Feb 1936; *Educ* Berkhamsted Sch, RMA Sandhurst, St Martin's Sch of Art; *m* 1, 1962 (m dis 1967), Jennifer Anne Redway; 1 da (Yseult (Mrs Hughes) b 8 April 1962); m 2, 1969 (m dis 1985), Galina Vasilievna Golikova; 2 s (Farquhar Piotr b 12 March 1970, Alexander Gerald Vasili b 2 Feb 1972); m 3, 1988, Adaline Havemeyer, *née* Frelinghuysen; *Career* cmmnd 5 Fus (Royal Northumberland Fus) 1955-60; artist; artist in residence Aspen Inst for Humanistic Studies Colorado 1966; visiting prof: Univ of New Mexico 1976-77, Univ of Columbia NY 1986-87; work in collections of: Tate Gallery, V & A Museum, Nat Portrait Gall, Museum of Modern Art NY, Whitney Museum, Museum of Modern Art NY, Whitney Museum NY; maj cmmns incl: Callanish Univ of Strathclyde, Wise and Foolish Virgins Edinburgh, Fountain of Sabrina Bristol, Conan Doyle Meml Edinburgh, Axis Mundi Edinburgh; Civic Tst award 1971; memb: Ctee Scot Arts Cncl 1978-80, Royal Fine Art Cmmn for Scot 1987-, Royal Soc of Br Sculptors; *Books* Kinkell: The Reconstruction of a Scottish Castle (1974, 2 edn 1984); *Clubs* Chelsea Arts; *Style—* Gerald Ogilvie-Laing of Kinkell; Kinkell Castle, Ross-shire, Scotland IV7 8AT (☎ 0349 61485); 139 East 66th St, New York, NY 10021, USA (☎ 0101 212 628 5693)

OGILVIE THOMPSON, Julian; s of Hon N Ogilvie Thompson (chief justice SA to 1974), of Cape Province; *b* 27 Jan 1934; *Educ* Diocesan Coll Rondebosch Cape, Worcester Coll Oxford (Rhodes Scholar); *m* 1956, Hon Tessa Brand (*see* Hon Mrs O T); 2 s (Christopher William b 1958, Anthony Thomas b 1964), 2 da (Rachel Amanda (Mrs R M Keene) b 1960, Leila Katharine (Mrs H K Barnett) b 1965), all four of whom are in remainder to the Barony of Dacre; *Career* chm: Anglo American Corpn SA, De Beers Consolidated Mines, Minorco SA, DeBeers Centenary; dir First National Bank of SA; *Recreations* shooting, fishing, golf; *Clubs* White's, Rand (Johannesburg), Kimberley, Brook (NY); *Style—* Julian Ogilvie Thompson, Esq; Froome, Froome St, Athol Ext 3, Johannesburg, S Africa (☎ 011 884 3925, office 011 638 2157)

OGILVIE THOMPSON, Hon Mrs (Tessa Mary); *née* Brand; da of late 4 Viscount Hampden and sis of Baroness Dacre, *qv*; *b* 21 April 1934; *m* 24 July 1956, Julian Ogilvie Thompson, *qv*; 2 s, 2 da; *Style—* The Hon Mrs Ogilvie Thompson; Froome, Froome St, Athol Extension, Johannesburg, S Africa (☎ 010 27 11 884 3925)

OGILVY, Hon Sir Angus James Bruce; KCVO (1989); s of 12 (de facto 9) Earl of Airlie, KT, GCVO, MC (d 1968); *b* 14 Sept 1928; *Educ* Eton, Trinity Coll Oxford (MA); *m* 1963, HRH Princess Alexandra of Kent (*see* Royal Family section); 1 s (James Robert Bruce, *qv*), 1 da (Marina Victoria Alexandra b 31 July 1966); *Career* Scots Gds 1946-48; memb HM Body Guard for Scotland (The Royal Co of Archers); pres: The Imperial Cancer Res Fund 1964-, Youth Clubs UK (formerly Nat Assoc of Youth Clubs) 1969-89 (chm 1964-69), The Carr-Gomm Soc 1983-; chm Cncl of the Prince's Youth Business Tst 1986-; patron Arthritis Care (formerly The Br Rheumatism and Arthritis Soc) 1978- (chm 1963-69, pres 1969-78); patron The Scottish Wildlife Tst 1974- (pres 1969-74); vice-pres The Friends of the Elderly & Gentlefolk's Help 1969- (chm 1963-69, treas 1952-63); vice patron The Nat Children's Homes 1986-; tstee: The Leeds Castle Fndn 1975-, The Great Britain-Sasakawa Fndn 1985-; memb: Governing Cncl of Business in the Community 1984-, Governing Cncl of SPCK 1984-; dir various public cos; *Recreations* architecture, reading, music; *Clubs* White's; *Style—* The Hon Sir Angus Ogilvy, KCVO; Thatched House Lodge, Richmond Park, Surrey (☎ 081 546 8833)

OGILVY, Lady Caroline; *née* Child-Villiers; da of 9 Earl of Jersey; *b* 1934; *m* 1, 1952 (m dis 1965), Viscount Melgund, MBE (now 6 Earl of Minto); 1 s, 1 da; m 2, 1969 (m dis 1972), the Hon John Douglas Stuart, s of 1 Viscount Stuart of Findhorn, CH, MVO, MC (d 1971); m 3, 1980, Hon James Donald Diarmid Ogilvy, s of 12 Earl of Airlie; *Style—* The Lady Caroline Ogilvy; Sedgebrook Manor, nr Grantham, Lincs

OGILVY, Lord; David John Ogilvy; s and h of 13 Earl of Airlie; *b* 9 March 1958; *m* 1981 (m dis 1990), Hon Geraldine Theodora Mary Gabriel Harmsworth, da of 3 Viscount Rothermere; 1 da (Hon Augusta b 1981); *Career* page of honour to HM The Queen 1971; md Richard L Feigen (UK) Ltd; musician; *Style—* Lord Ogilvy; Airlie Castle, Kirriemuir, Angus

OGILVY, Sir David John Wilfrid; 13 Bt (NS 1626), of Inverquharity, Forfarshire, JP (E Lothian 1957), DL (1971); s of Gilbert Francis Molyneux Ogilvy, JP (4 s of Sir Reginald Ogilvy, 10 Bt, JP, DL, and Hon Olivia, da of 9 Lord Kinnaird, KT), and Marjory Katharine (d 1961), da of Charles Clive and Lady Katharine Feilding, da of 7 Earl of Denbigh; suc unc, Sir Herbert Ogilvy, 12 Bt, 1956; *b* 3 Feb 1914; *Educ* Eton, Trinity Coll Oxford (MA); *m* 31 Dec 1966, Penelope Mary Ursula, o da of Arthur Lafone Frank Hills, of White Court, Tonbridge, and Moira Emelina, eldest da of Henry Seymour Guinness, of the extensive brewing and banking family; 1 s; *Heir* s, Francis Gilbert Arthur Ogilvy b 22 April 1969; *Career* served WWII RNVR, unexploded bomb disposal and miscellaneous weapon devpt in Britain and Sri Lanka; farmer and landowner; *Recreations* forestry; *Style—* Sir David Ogilvy, Bt, JP, DL; Winton Cottage, Pencaitland, East Lothian EH34 5AT (☎ 0875 340222)

OGILVY, Hon James Donald Diarmid; s of 12 Earl of Airlie, KT, GCVO, MC, and Lady Alexandra Coke, da of 3 Earl of Leicester; *b* 28 June 1934; *Educ* Eton; *m* 1, 1959, (Magda) June, da of Robert Ducas, of New York, by his 1 w, Magdalen, da of Maj Herbert Stourton, OBE (gs of 19 Baron Stourton, DL), and Hon Frances, only da of 4 Viscount Southwell; 2 s (Shamus Diarmid Ducas b 1966, Diarmid James Ducas b 1970), 2 da (Laura Jane b 1960, Emma Louise b 1962); m 2, 1980, Lady Caroline, *née* Child-Villiers, da of 9 Earl of Jersey and former w of (1) Viscount Melgund, MBE (now 6 Earl of Minto), and (2) Hon John Stuart (s of 1 Viscount Stuart of Findhorn); *Career* Lt Scots Gds 1952-54; page of honour to King George VI 1947-51; ptnr Rowe & Pitman 1962-86, chm Rowan Investment Managers 1972-86, chm Mercury Rowan Mullens 1986-88, vice chm Mercury Asset Management 1986-88, chief exec Foreign and Colonial Management Ltd 1988-; govr Queen Charlotte's and Chelsea Hosps 1966-76; chm Inst of Obstetrics and Gynaecology 1983-86; memb Royal Co of Archers (Queen's Bodyguard for Scotland); *Clubs* White's; *Style—* The Hon James Ogilvy; Sedgebrook Manor, Sedgebrook, Grantham, Lincs (☎ 0949 42337); 51 Eaton Sq, London SW1 (☎ 071 235 7595); Foreign & Colonial Management Ltd, Exchange House, Primrose Street, London EC2A 2NY (☎ 071 628 8000)

OGILVY, James Robert Bruce; o son of Hon Sir Angus Ogilvy, KCVO, and HRH Princess Alexandra, GCVO, o da of HRH 1 Duke of Kent; *b* 29 Feb 1964; *Educ* Eton; *m* 30 July 1988, Julia Caroline (b 28 Oct 1964), eldest da of Charles Frederick Melville Rawlinson, *qv*; *Style—* James Ogilvy, Esq

OGILVY-WEDDERBURN, Maj Sir Andrew John Alexander; 7 Bt (UK 1803), of Balindean, Perthshire; descended from Sir Alexander Wedderburn, 4 Bt (S 1704), of Blackness, who served as a volunteer at the Battle of Culloden (1746) where he was taken prisoner and executed, and his estate forfeited. His descendants continued to assume the title until Sir David (7 Bt, but for the attainder) was cr Bt in the present UK creation, with special remainder to the heirs male of the 4 Bt of the original creation; s of Cdr Sir (John) Peter Ogilvy-Wedderburn, 6 Bt (d 1977), and Elizabeth Katharine, *née* Cox; *b* 4 Aug 1952; *Educ* Gordonstoun; *m* 1984, Gillian Meade, da of Richard Boyle Adderley, MBE, of Shepherds Hill, Pickering, N Yorks; 3 s (Peter Robert Alexander, Geordie Richard Andrew (twins) b 1987, Sam b 1990), 1 da (Katherine b 1985); *Heir* s, Peter Robert Alexander Ogilvy-Wedderburn; *Career* Maj Black Watch (Royal Highland Regt); memb Br Bobsleigh Team 1974-80, British Olympic Team (Bobsleigh) 1976 Innsbruck (1980 Lake Placid), Br 2 Man Bobsleigh champion 1976-77 and 1978-79; *Recreations* bobsleighing, skiing, shooting; *Style—* Maj Sir Andrew Ogilvy-Wedderburn, Bt; Silvie, Alyth, Perthshire (☎ 082 83 2362)

OGLESBY, Peter Rogerson; CB (1982); s of Leonard William Oglesby (d 1978), and Jessie, *née* Rogerson (d 1980); *b* 15 July 1922; *Educ* Woodhouse Grove Sch Yorks; *m* 1947, Doreen Hilda, da of Douglas James Hudson (d 1963); 3 da (Susan b 1952, Jane b 1955, Mary b 1957); *Career* civil servant; princ private sec to: Douglas Houghton 1964-66, Michael Stewart 1966-68, Richard Crosman 1968; Cabinet Office 1968-70: sec of Occupational Pension Bd 1973-74, under sec and head of Social Security Fin Div 1975-79, dep sec of Social Security Policy 1979-82; *Recreations* gardening; *Style—* Peter Oglesby, Esq, CB; 41 Draycot Rd, Wanstead, London E11 2NX

OGMORE, Constance, Baroness; (Alice Alexandra) Constance; JP (Croydon); da of late Alderman Walter Robert Wills, Lord Mayor of Cardiff 1945-46, and Ada Mary, *née* Johns; *m* 1930, 1 Baron Ogmore, TD, PC (d 1976); 2 s, 1 da; *Style—* The Rt Hon Constance, Lady Ogmore, JP; 48 Cheyne Court, Royal Hospital Rd, London SW3 (☎ 071 352 6131)

OGMORE, 2 Baron (UK 1950); Gwilym Rees Rees-Williams; s of 1 Baron Ogmore (d 1976), and Constance, *née* Wills; *b* 5 May 1931; *Educ* Mill Hill; *m* 1967, Gillian, da of Maurice Slack, of Hindley, Lancs; 2 da (Christine b 1968, Jennet b 1970); *Heir* bro, Hon Morgan Rees-Williams; *Recreations* reading, driving, walking; *Style—* The Rt Hon Lord Ogmore; c/o House of Lords, London SW1

OGNALL, Hon Mr Justice; Sir Harry Henry; QC (1973); s of Leo Ognall, and Cecilia Ognall; *b* 9 Jan 1934; *Educ* Leeds GS, Lincoln Coll Oxford (MA), Univ of Virginia (LLM); *m* 1; 2 s, 1 da; m 2, 1977, Elizabeth Young; 2 step s; *Career* called to Bar Gray's Inn 1958, bencher 1983, joined NE Circuit, rec 1972-86; judge of the High Ct 1986-, memb Criminal Injuries Compensation Bd 1976, arbitrator Motor Insurers' Bureau Agreement 1979-85, memb Senate of Inns of Ct 1980-83 (memb Planning Ctee and Professional Conduct Ctee), chm Criminal Ctee Judicial Studies Bd 1986-89, memb Parole Bd England & Wales 1989- (vice chm 1990-); kt 1986; *Recreations* golf, travel, music; *Style—* The Hon Mr Justice Ognall; Royal Courts of Justice, Strand, London WC2A 2LL

OGORKIEWICZ, Prof Richard Marian; s of Col Marian Anthony Ogorkiewicz (d 1962), of Poland, and Waldyna, *née* Pryfer (d 1986); *b* 2 May 1926; *Educ* SRW Sch Warsaw, Lycée de C Norwid Paris, George Heriot's Sch Edinburgh, Imperial Coll London (BSc, MSc); *Career* devpt engr: Ford Motor Co 1952-55, Humber Ltd 1955-57; lectr in mech engrg Imperial Coll London 1957-85, conslt to various cos involved with armoured fighting vehicles 1972-; consulting ed Int Defense Review 1988-; visiting prof RMCS; memb: various sci advsy ctees 1964-, Miny of Aviation 1964-70, Miny of Technol 1967-71, MOD 1972-; pres Soc of Friends of the Tank Museum Dorset 1987-; FIMechE 1970; *Books* Armour (1960), Design and Development of Fighting Vehicles (1968), Armoured Forces (1970); *Recreations* gardening, walking; *Style—* Prof Richard Ogorkiewicz; 18 Temple Sheen, East Sheen, London SW14 7RP (☎ 081 876 5149)

OGSTON, Prof Derek; s of Frederick John Ogston (d 1981), of Aberdeen, and Ellen Mary, *née* Duncan; *b* 31 May 1932; *Educ* King's Coll Sch Wimbledon, Univ of Aberdeen (MA, MB ChB, PhD, MD, DSc); *m* 19 July 1963, (Cecilia) Marie, da of William Charles Clark (d 1975), of Aberdeen; 1 s (Keith b 1969), 2 da (Catriona b 1971, Nicola b 1973); *Career* Univ of Aberdeen: regius prof 1977-83, prof of med 1983-, dean Faculty of Med 1984-87, vice princ 1987-; FRCPE 1973, FRCP 1977, FRSE 1982, FIBiol 1987; *Books* Physiology of Hemostasis (1983), Antifibrinolytic Drugs (1984), Venous Thrombosis: Causation and Prediction (1987); *Recreations* travel; *Style—* Prof Derek Ogston, FRSE; 64 Rubislaw Den South, Aberdeen, Grampian (☎ 0224 316 587); Dept of Medicine, Polwarth Building, Foresterhill, Aberdeen, Grampian (☎ 0224 681 818, ext 53016)

OGUS, Prof Anthony Ian; s of Samuel Joseph Ogus (d 1981), of Blackheath, and Sadie Phyllis, *née* Green; *b* 30 Aug 1945; *Educ* St Dunstan's Coll, Magdalen Coll Oxford (BA, BCL, MA); *m* 26 July 1980, Catherine, da of Marc Klein (d 1975), of Strasbourg; *Career* asst lectr Univ of Leicester 1967-69, tutorial fell Mansfield Coll Oxford 1969-75, sr res fell Centre for Socio-Legal Studies Oxford; prof: Univ of Newcastle upon Tyne 1978-87, Univ of Manchester 1987-; *Books* Law of Damages (1973), Law of Social Security (with E M Barendt, 1978, 2 edn, 1982, 3 edn, 1988), Policing Pollution (with G M Richardson and P Burrows, 1983), Readings in the Economics of Law and Regulation (with C Veljanouski, 1984), Report to the Lord Chancellor on the Costs and Effectiveness of Conciliation in England and Wales (with M Jones-Lee, J Walker and others, 1989); *Recreations* theatre, music, reading, walking; *Style—* Prof Anthony Ogus; Faculty of Law, University of Manchester, Oxford Road, (☎ 061 275 3572, fax 061 275 3579) Manchester M13 9PL

OGUS, Hugh Joseph; s of Louis Ogus (d 1951), of London, and Anne, *née* Goldstein (d 1986); *b* 23 Jan 1934; *Educ* Central Fndn Sch London, Queen Mary Coll London (BA); *m* 14 Aug 1960, Mavis, da of Michael Mendel (d 1971), of London; 1 s (Simon b 1964), 1 da (Deborah b 1967); *Career* various jr mgmnt posts Philips Electrical Ltd 1957-67, commercial dir Salamandre Metalworks Ltd 1968-73, chm and md Poselco Ltd 1984-(md 1973-84); cncl memb Light Indust Fedn 1977-(pres 1982-83), chm of fin Mary Hare GS for the Deaf 1980-(vice chm of govrs 1984-), vice chm of govrs London Sch of Foreign Trade 1982-87, cncl memb Chartered Inst of Building Servs Engrs 1986-89, chm of govrs Mill Hill Oral Sch for Deaf Children 1987-89 (treas 1977-87); hon vice pres (former chm) 4 Hendon Scouts and Guides, pres Hendon North Liberal Assoc 1984-87 (chm 1981-84); Freeman City of London 1983, Liveryman Worshipful Co of Lightmongers (Ct asst), Assoc CIBSE 1977, FInstD 1983; *Recreations* music, travel, swimming, horology; *Style—* Hugh J Ogus, Esq; 2 Haslemere Ave, London NW4 2PX (☎ 081 202 7092); Poselco Ltd, Walmgate Rd, Perivale, Middx UB6 7LX (☎ 081 998 1431, fax 081 997 3350, telex 917972 POLITE G)

OHLENSCHLAGER, Brig Richard Norman; MBE (1963), JP; s of Cdr Norman Albert Gustav Ohlenschlager, DSO, RN (d 1937), of Fareham, Hants, and Ima Millicent Jones; *b* 22 April 1925; *Educ* Radley; *m* 15 April 1948, Ann Felicity Mary, da of Lt-Col Arthur Cyril Whitcombe, MBE, RA (d 1979), of Seaview, IOW; 1 s (Guy b 1952), 2 da (Carol b 1950, Susan b 1954); *Career* Army Offr 1943-78; cmdt Royal Sch of Artillery Larkhill Wilts 1976-78; chm Ohlenschlager Bros Ltd 1969-81; civil servant; *Recreations* sailing, skiing, gardening; *Clubs* Royal Yacht Sqdn, Seaview Yacht, Army and Navy; *Style—* Brig Richard N Ohlenschlager, MBE, JP; Goodworth Cottage, Goodworth Clatford, Andover, Hampshire SP11 7QX (☎ 0264 352511)

OHLSON, Sir Brian Eric Christopher; 3 Bt (UK 1920), of Scarborough, North Riding of Co of Yorkshire; s of Sir Eric (James) Ohlson, 2 Bt (d 1983) and Lady Ohlson, *qv*; *b* 27 July 1936; *Educ* Harrow, RMA Sandhurst; *Heir* bro, Peter Michael Ohlson; *Career* cmmnd Coldstream Gds 1956, Capt, ret 1961; money broker; *Recreations* racing, cricket, theatre, bridge; *Clubs* Naval and Military, Hurlingham, MCC, Cavalry and Guards'; *Style—* Sir Brian Ohlson, Bt; 1 Courtfield Gdns, London SW5

OHLSON, Lady; Marjorie Joan; 2 da of late Charles Henry Roosmale-Cocq, of Dorking, Surrey; *m* 8 May 1935, Sir Eric James Ohlson, 2 Bt (d 1983); 2 s (*see* Sir Brian Ohlson, 3 Bt), 1 da; *Style—* Lady Ohlson

OHLSON, Peter Michael; s of Sir Eric Ohlson, 2 Bt (d 1983); hp of bro Sir Brian Ohlson, 3 Bt; *b* 18 May 1939; *Educ* Harrow, Trinity Coll Cambridge (BA); *m* 18 Oct 1968, Sarah, o da of Maj-Gen Thomas Brodie, CB, CBE, DSO; 2 da; *Career* ptnr Tyzack & Partners; *Style—* Peter Ohlson, Esq; 33 The Avenue, Kew, Surrey

OKEOVER; *see*: Walker-Okeover

OKUBADEJO, Dr Olumade Adetola; s of Chief Adedeji Okubadejo (d 1978), and Chief Olabisi, *née* Jibowu (d 1982); *b* 27 Sept 1928; *Educ* Christ Church Cathedral Sch Lagos Nigeria, Igbobi Coll Yaba Nigeria, Kings Coll Hosp London (MB BS), Univ of London postgrad Med Sch (MD, DCP); *m* 26 June 1958, (Rosemary) Fay, da of Dick Reginald Richards (d 1978); 1 s (Adeyoola b 10 Feb 1963), 2 da (Tinuade b 14 April 1960, Lynette b 1 July 1964); *Career* house surgn St Giles Hosp London 1958-59, house physician Univ Coll Hosp Ibadan Nigeria 1959-63, bacteriol registrar Royal Postgrad Med Sch Hammersmith Hosp 1963-66, sr lectr Univ of Ibadan Nigeria 1968-71, microbiology conslt Portsmouth and IOW Health Authy 1972-, memb panel Diagnosis of Smallpox Hants 1972-, dir Pub Health Laboratory Portsmouth 1983-; hon clinical sr lectr Univ of Southampton, hon civilian conslt in microbiology RN Haslar; memb: bd visitors HM Prison Kingston, Portsmouth Diocesan Cncl for Social Responsibility; FRCPath 1982; *Recreations* classical music, ceramics, antique collection and study; *Style—* Dr Olumade Okubadejo; Pub Health Laboratory, St Mary's Hospital, Portsmouth PO3 6AQ (☎ 0705 822331/3201, fax 0705 824652)

OLDENBURG, HH Duke Friedrich August Nikolaus Udo Peter Philipp of; elder s of HH Duke Peter of Oldenburg (2 s of HRH Nikolaus, Hereditary Grand Duke of Oldenburg, descended from Egilmar I, Count of Aldenburg, who was living in 1108. Hereditary Grand Duke Nikolaus m HSH Princess Helene of Waldeck and Pyrmont, whose paternal grandmother was HSH Princess Helene of Nassau. Princess Helene of Nassau's paternal gf's mother was Princess Caroline of Orange, whose mother was Princess Anne (Princess Royal), eldest da of King George II of Great Britain), by his w HSH Princess Gertrud, 2 da of HSH Udo, 6 Prince zu Löwenstein-Wertheim-Freudenberg; *b* 26 Sept 1952; *m* 1982, Belinda, da of Maj (Alison) Digby Tatham Warter, DSO, of Nanyuki, Kenya, and Jane, *née* Boyd (whose mother was Lady Mary Egerton, o da of 5 Earl of Wilton); 2 da (Anastasia b 10 Oct 1982, Alice b 15 April 1986); *Career* farmer; *Style—* His Highness Duke Friedrich August of Oldenburg; Anstey Hall, Anstey, Buntingford, Herts SG9 0BY

OLDFIELD, Hon Mrs (Alexandra Frances Margaret); *née* Davidson; el da of 2 Viscount Davidson; *b* 13 April 1957; *m* 1982, Richard John (b 1955), s of late Christopher Charles Bayley Oldfield (himself eighteenth in descent from Sir Alanus de Aldefeld, fndr and endower of the chapel at Aldefeld, who d 1281), and Mrs B R P Brooks, of London W6; 1 s (Christopher b 1986), 1 da (Leonora b 1985); *Style—* The Hon Mrs Oldfield

OLDFIELD, Bruce; OBE (1990); *b* 14 July 1950; *Educ* Spennymoor GS Durham, Ripon GS, Sheffield Poly (DipEd), Ravensbourne Coll of Art, St Martin's Coll of Art; *Career* fashion designer; designed for Henri Bendel NY and other stores 1973-74, freelance cmmns incl film wardrobe for Charlotte Rampling 1974-75, first collection 1975, estab couture div 1978, opened London shop and redeveloped ready-to-wear collection with couture collection 1984-, Br rep Aust Bicentennial Wool Collection Fashion Show Sydney Opera House 1988; memb Panel Whitbread Literary Awards 1987, organised Bruce Oldfield for Barnardos Gala evenings attended by HRH The Princess of Wales 1985 and 1988; Northern Personality of the Year Variety Club 1985, subject of TV documentary A Journey into Fashion (Tyne Tees TV) 1990; hon fell: Sheffield City Poly 1987, Royal Coll of Art 1990; *Books* Bruce Oldfield's Season (contrib 1987); *Recreations* reading, music, films, driving; *Style—* Bruce Oldfield, Esq, OBE; c/o Rosalind Woolfson, Shandwick Communications Ltd, 50 Upper Brook St, London W1Y 1PG (☎ 071 491 4568, fax 071 629 0425)

OLDFIELD, Lady (Mary) Elisabeth; *née* Murray; yr da of late 8 Earl of Dunmore, VC, DSO, MVO; *b* 28 Nov 1913; *m* 29 April 1937, Major Peter Carlton Oldfield, OBE, Warwicks Yeo, yst s of Carlton Olfield, of Moor Hill, Harwood, Yorkshire; 1 da; *Style—* The Lady Elisabeth Oldfield; Ham Cottage, Sydmonton, Newbury, Berks

OLDFIELD, Brig John Briton; OBE (1980), DL (Hants 1973); s of William Aitken Oldfield, JP (d 1966), of Sandsend, N Yorks, and Violet Ethelind, *née* Rickell (d 1951); *b* 28 April 1918; *Educ* Repton, RMC Sandhurst; *m* 25 March 1949, Pamela Carrol, da of Maj Robert Geoffrey Ward (d 1971), of Southampton; 1 s, 1 da; *Career* cmmnd The Green Howards 1938, served Palestine 1938-39, France and Western Desert (despatches 1945), Malaya 1951-52 (despatches 1953), dep sec Int Standing Gp NATO Washington DC 1957-59, CO 1 Bn The Green Howards 1960-62, staff NATO Defence Coll Paris (Col) 1962-64, Cdr TA Bde 1965-67, Dep Cdr Aldershot Dist 1967-69, ret 1969, Col The Green Howards 1975-82, Hon Col 2 Bn The Wessex Regt 1980-83, sec E Wessex TAVR Assoc 1970-82; *Books* The Green Howards in Malaya (1953); *Recreations* field sports, painting, memb Soc of Equestrian Artists; *Clubs* Army and Navy; *Style—* Brig John Oldfield, OBE, DL; Paddock Cottage, Bramshaw, Lyndhurst, Hants SO43 7JN (☎ 0794 390 233)

OLDFIELD, Lady Kathleen Constance Blanche; *née* Balfour; yst da of 2 Earl of Balfour (d 1945); *b* 1912; *Educ* Newnham Coll Cambridge (MA); *m* 23 Aug 1933, Richard Charles Oldfield (d 1972), s of Sir Francis du Pre Oldfield; 2 da; *Recreations* gardening; *Clubs* Salisbury Centre, Edinburgh; *Style—* The Lady Kathleen Oldfield; Woodhall Cottage, Pencaitland, East Lothian

OLDHAM, Alan John; s of John Albert Oldham (d 1952), of Hyde, Cheshire, and Hilda Pennington Oldham, *née* Beech (d 1981); *b* 6 March 1926; *Educ* Wrekin Coll, Clare Coll Cambridge (MA); *m* 29 June 1963, Jane Louise England, da of Norman Percival Fish (d 1972) of Somerset; 2 s (John b 1964, Paul b 1968), 1 da (Melanie b 1966); *Career* actuary; asst gen mangr Equity & Law Life Assur Soc plc 1973-86, consltg actuary, gen cmmr Income Tax High Wycombe Dist 1979-, chm High Wycombe Div S Bucks & E Berks C of C 1984-85; memb Cncl and hon treas Croquet Assoc; FIA; *Recreations* croquet, philately; *Style—* Alan J Oldham, Esq; Terriers Green, Terriers, High Wycombe, Bucks HP13 5AJ (☎ 0494 26527)

OLDHAM, Christopher David Fitzjohn; s of Cdr Frederick William Fitzjohn Oldham, OBE (d 1984), of Gosfield Hall, Halstead, Essex, and Thereza Jessie, *née* Hawes; *b* 22 May 1934; *Educ* Harrow; *m* 21 Aug 1975, Susan Hilary, da of Hugh Arthur Heneage Fitzgerald Finch (d 1975), of 10 Broadwater Down, Tunbridge Wells, Kent; 1 s (William b 1976); *Career* Nat Serv RN 1952-54; admitted slr 1960, sr ptnr Vizards London; churchwarden, former dep chm Lansdowne Club, stewardship advsr Southwark Diocese; memb Law Soc; *Recreations* gardening, stalking, railway modelling, historical reading; *Clubs* Lansdowne; *Style—* Christopher Oldham, Esq; 6 Parkfields, Putney, London SW15 6NH (☎ 081 789 5765); Vizards, 42/43 Bedford Row, London WC1R 4LL (☎ 071 405 6302, fax 071 405 6248, telex 261045)

OLDHAM, Gavin David Redvers; s of David George Redvers Oldham, of Buckinghamshire, and Penelope Barbara, *née* Royle; *b* 5 May 1949; *Educ* Eton, Trinity Coll Cambridge (MA); *m* 17 May 1975, Virginia Russell, da of Rodney Fryer Russell, of Dorset; *Career* CSE Aircraft Servs Ltd 1971-76, ptnr Wedd Durlacher Mordaunt & Co 1984-86 (joined 1976, head Dept of Gilt Settlement and Money 1979-83, head of Futures Clearing Co Ltd 1982-84), secretariat Barclays de Zoete Wedd 1984-86, chm Barclayshare Ltd 1989-90 (chief exec 1986-89); chief exec The Share Centre Ltd 1990-; memb: Cncl Wider Share Ownership 1977-, Cncl Economic Res 1989-, The Stock Exchange; MInstD; *Clubs* Leander; *Style—* Gavin Oldham, Esq; PO Box 1000, Tring, Herts HP23 6PY (fax 024 029 790)

OLDHAM, Sheila Dorothy; JP (1970); da of John Cunliffe Jackson (d 1965), of E Beach, Lytham St Annes, Lancs, and Dorothy May, *née* Fenton (d 1979); paternal gf William Jackson ARCS, fndr Ceramic Soc, jt inventor of Thermoscope; *b* 25 May 1928; *Educ* Howell's Denbigh, Liverpool Sch of Architecture; *m* 3 Aug 1948, Frederick Howard (d 1979), s of Harold Oldham (d 1976), of Rawtenstall, Lancs; 3 s (David Howard b 1949, Michael Jonathan b 1951, Charles Nicholas b 1957); *Career* cncllr (C): Haslingden Borough 1968, Rossendale (C) 1974; magistrate Rossendale Bench 1970, mayor Rossendale 1979-80; fndr chm: Friends of Rossendale Hosp 1971-78, Rossendale Br Heart Fndn 1980-; tstee Richard Whitaker Charitable Tst; memb NW Regnl Health Authy 1982-86; chm Ctee for Employment of Disabled People E Lancs 1983-; memb: Lancashire Area Manpower Bd 1986-89, DHSS Appeals Tbnl 1979-; pres: Helmshore Old People's Welfare; Rossendale Amateur Operative Soc, Rossendale Ladies' Choir; *Recreations* gardening; *Style—* Sheila Oldham, JP; Stable House, Helmshore, Rossendale, Lancs (☎ 0706 220819)

OLDMAN, Paul Anthony; s of Dennis Russell Oldman, (d 1977), and Dorothy Pamela, *née* Bradnum; *b* 22 Dec 1952; *Educ* Great Yarmouth GS, Univ of Manchester (LLB); *Career* ptnr Lovell White Durrant slrs (formerly Lovell White & King) 1987- (joined 1980), memb Law Soc; Freeman Worshipful Co of Slrs; *Recreations* reading novels, swimming, theatre, travel; *Style—* Paul Oldman, Esq; 19 Petherton Rd, London N5; 65 Holborn Viaduct, London EC1A 2DY (☎ 071 236 0066, fax 071 236 0084)

OLDRIDGE, John Norman Leslie; *b* 26 Jan 1947; *Educ* Oundle, Oxford Sch of Architecture (Dip Arch); *Career* ptnr Chapman Taylor Partners 1987- (joined 1973, assoc 1977); MRIBA 1977, memb Ordre des Architectes 1990; *Recreations* offshore sailing, skiing; *Clubs* Royal Lymington Yacht; *Style—* John Oldridge, Esq; Chapman Taylor Partners, 96 Kensington High St, London W8 (☎ 071 938 3333)

OLDROYD, James Colin; JP (1974); s of Joseph Chamberlain Oldroyd (d 1975), of Dewsbury, Yorks, and Lydia Helen, *née* , Lyons (d 1984); *b* 28 May 1935; *Educ* St Peter's Sch York, King's Coll Cambridge (MA); *m* 4 March 1961, Susan Norah, da of Edward Denville Hill (d 1988), of Cheadle; 2 s (Paul b 1961, Graham b 1961); *Career* 2 Lt RA 1957, Capt RA (TA) 1963; md Graham Motor Group plc 1984-88, dir Swan National Motors Ltd 1988-90, dir Quicks Group plc 1990-; CBIM 1986; *Style—* James Oldroyd, Esq; Roxburgh, Legh Rd, Knutsford, Cheshire WA16 8NR (☎ 0565 633027)

OLDWORTH, Richard Anthony; s of Anthony Gilbert Frederick Oldworth, of Blackdown, Sussex, and Patricia, *née* Thompson; *b* 5 June 1957; *Educ* Radley, City of London Poly; *Career* CA; Peat Marwick Mitchell 1976-80, corporate finance exec County Bank 1980-83, head of corporate finance Bisgood Bishop & Co 1983-84, md Buchanan Communications 1984-; ACA 1980; *Recreations* flying, motorsport; *Clubs* City of London, Royal Solent Yacht; *Style—* Richard Oldworth, Esq; 22 Abercrombie St, London SW11; 36 St Andrew's Hill, London EC4 (☎ 071 489 1441, fax 071 489 1436)

OLINS, Wallace (Wally); s of Alfred Olins (d 1970), and Rachel, *née* Muscovitch (d 1961); *b* 19 Dec 1930; *Educ* Highgate Sch, St Peter's Coll Oxford (MA); *m* 1, 1957 (m dis 1989), Renate Maria Olga Laura, da of Heinz Steinert (d 1987); 2 s (Rufus Laurence b 1961, Benjamin Toby b 1967), 1 da ((Sarah) Edwina b 1959); m 2, 1990, Dornie; 1 da (Harriet Rachel Hildegard); *Career* Nat Serv 1950-51; SH Bensons (now part of Ogilvy & Mather): joined 1954, in India latterly as md Bombay 1957-62; md Caps Design London 1962-64, jt fndr Greers Gross Olins 1964, chm Wolff Olins (jt fndr with Michael Wolff 1965); visiting lectr in design mgmnt London Business Sch 1984-, visiting prof Mgmnt Sch Imperial Coll 1987; vice pres SIAD 1982-85, chm Design Dimension Educnl Tst 1987; tstee Design Museum 1988, memb Cncl RSA 1989; FCSD; *Books* The Corporate Personality (1978), The Wolff Olins Guide to Corporate Identity (1983), The Wolff Olins Guide to Design Management (1985), Corporate Identity (1989); *Recreations* looking at buildings, shopping for books, theatre, old cars; *Clubs* Groucho; *Style—* Wally Olins; The Wolff Olins Business Limited, 22 Dukes Rd, London WC1H 9AB (☎ 071 387 0891, fax 071 388 6639, telex 261438, car 0836 742879)

OLIPHANT, Capt (Laurence) Hugh; CBE (1977), DSC (1945); s of Rear Adm L R Oliphant, CBE (d 1951), of Miller's Hill, Thornton Le Dale, Yorks, and Hon Daphne Adelaide, *née* Willoughby; *b* 4 April 1922; *Educ* Nautical Coll Pangbourne; *m* 7 Feb 1953, Meriel, da of Arthur Hudson Fynn (d 1962), of The Barn, Helston, Cornwall; 2 da (Annabel b 1955, d 1980, Virginia (twin)); *Career* cadet RN 1940, volunteered for submarines 1942, 1 Cmnd HMS Tiptoe 1949, Cdr 1959, dir of staff Staff Coll 1965, Capt 1968, cmnd 1 Submarine Sqdn 1973, ret 1977; fundraising to establish Submarine Museum Gosport 1978-79, actg asst gen sec Missions to Seaman 1986-87 (dir Southern regn 1980-86); sec Lynchmere PCC 1987; *Recreations* travel, gardening; *Style—* Capt Hugh Oliphant, CBE, DSC, RN; Forest Mead, Lynchmere, Haslemere, Surrey GU27 3NE (☎ 0428 727 021)

OLIPHANT OF CONDIE, Lt Cdr Ralph Henry Hood Laurence; s of Capt Henry Gerard Laurence Oliphant, DSO, MVO (d 1955), of Condie and Newton, and Ruth Barry (d 1967); *b* 3 Aug 1915; *Educ* Radley; *m* 1, 13 Sept 1941, Barbara Mary (d 1979), da of Rev Preb Herbert Mackworth Drake; 3 da (Susannah Mary b 1943, Charlotte b 1946, Barbara Louise b 1952, d 1969); m 2, 27 Nov 1980, Mary Diana Ryde, da of Denis George Mackail (d 1971); *Career* PO RAF 1935, RN 1938; served WWII 1939-45 Fleet Air Arm Salerno & Normandy; cmd 886 Sqdn served in: HMS Orion, HMS Eagle, HMS Illustrious, HMS Formidable, HMS Attacker; Croix de Guerre (despatches), ret 1957; *Recreations* fishing, cricket; *Clubs* Naval and Military, MCC; *Style—* Lt Cdr Ralph Oliphant of Condie; National Westminster Bank, 352 Kings Rd, London SW3 5UX

OLIVER, Hon David Keightley Rideal; QC (1986); o s of Baron Oliver of Aylmerton, PC (Life Peer), *qv*, and his 1 w, Mary Chichester, *née* Rideal (d 1985); *b* 4 June 1949; *Educ* Westminster, Trinity Hall Cambridge (BA), Université Libre de Bruxelles (Lic Special en Droit Européen); *m* 1, 5 April 1972 (m dis 1987), Maria Luisa, da of Juan Mirasierras, of Avenida Reina Vitoria, Madrid, Spain; 2 s (Daniel b 1974, Thomas b 1976); m 2, 20 Feb 1988, Judith Britannia Caroline, da of David Henry John Griffiths Powell; 1 s (Rhodri b 1990); *Career* barr Lincoln's Inn 1972; standing counsel to dir gen of Fair Trading 1980-86; *Recreations* gardening, bird watching, rough shooting, tennis; *Style—* The Hon David Oliver, QC; 13 Old Square, Lincoln's Inn, London WC2A 3UA (☎ 071 404 4800, fax 071 405 4267)

OLIVER, Dawn; da of Ernest Gordon Borrett Taylor (d 1989), and Ann Zoë Mieke Taylor (d 1961); *b* 7 June 1942; *Educ* Notting Hill and Ealing HS, Newnham Coll Cambridge (BA, MA); *m* 6 Jan 1967, Stephen J L Oliver, s of Capt P D Oliver, RN (d 1979); 1 s (Adam b 1970), 2 da (Rebecca b 1969, Rosemary b 1972); *Career* called to the Bar Middle Temple 1965; in practice 1965-69, conslt Legal Action Gp 1973-76; sec: Social and Lib Democratic Lawyers' Assoc 1988-89, Newnham Coll Associates 1988-; *Books* The Changing Constitution (ed with J L Jowell, 1985, 2 edn 1989), Cohabitation: The Legal Implications (1987), New Directions in Judicial Review (ed with J L Jowell, 1988), Economical with the Truth: The Law and the Media in a Democracy (ed with D Kingsford Smith, 1989); *Style—* Ms Dawn Oliver; Univ Coll London, Law Faculty, Bentham Hse, Endsleigh Gdns, London WC1H 0EG (☎ 071 387 7050)

OLIVER, Dr Dennis Stanley; KSG (1980), CBE (1981); s of James Thomas (d 1961), and Lilian Mabel, *née* Bunn (d 1976); *b* 19 Sept 1926; *Educ* Deacon's Sch Peterborough, Univ of Birmingham (Bsc, MSc, PhD); *m* 1, 1952 (m dis 1984), Enid Jessie; m 2, 1987, Elizabeth; *Career* res fell Dept of Physics Univ of Bristol 1949-52, UKAEA head of Metallurgy Dounreay 1952-63, chief R&D offr Richard Thomas & Baldwin Ltd 1963-68, gp dir R & D Pilkingtons plc 1968-77 (exec dir 1977-86), admin L'Ecole Superieure du Verre, Charleroi, govr Euro Ind Res Man Assoc 1975-82 (pres 1977-81), pres Sci and Tech Ed Merseyside 1978-81 (patron 1981-), memb Ct and Cncl Cranfield Inst of Technol 1976-88 (visiting prof 1984-88); govr: Liverpool Inst of Higher Educn 1977-85, Christ's & Notre Dame Coll Liverpool 1977-87, Royal Nat Coll for Blind 1981-85; founding dir and dep chm cmmn of St Helens Tst 1978-86; dir: Anglo American Venture Fund Ltd 1980-84, National Research and Development Corporation 1981-, Nat Enterprise Bd 1981-; founding dir and chm: Industl Experience Projects Ltd 1981-86, Monotype Corp Ltd 1985-90; visiting prof MIT 1986-; founding tstee Anfield Tst 1983-88, memb Advsy Cncl on Sci and Technol 1986-89; Liveryman: Worshipful Co of Spectaclemakers 1983- (asst 1985-88), Worshipful Co of Engrs 1985; FEng 1981, FIM, FInstP, FBIM; *Recreations* music, poetry, cooking; *Clubs* City Livery; *Style—* Dr Dennis Oliver, KSG, CBE; Castell Bach, Bodfari, Denbigh, Clwyd LL16 4HT (☎ 074575 354)

OLIVER, Edward Morgan; s of Raife Morgan Oliver (d 1963), of Little Hall, Liston, Long Melford, Suffolk, and Nancy Evelyn, *née* Cutler (d 1985); *b* 22 April 1942; *Educ* Felsted; *m* 7 Aug 1965, (Carol) Louise, da of Edgar Cecil Watts (d 1975), of The Grove, Ditchingham, Bungay, Suffolk; 1 s (Raife Morgan b 1967), 1 da (Lynn Bridget b 1970); *Career* CA; ptnr: Peters Elworthy & Moore 1967-70, Shipley Blackburn 1970-; sec King George's Pension Fund for Actors and Actresses 1971-; memb Herts CC 1972-80 (chm Highways Ctee 1977-80), Cons candidate NE Derbys 1979; Freeman City of London, Liveryman Worshipful Co of Vintners 1966; FCA 1965; *Recreations* field sports, amateur dramatics, gardening; *Style—* Edward Oliver, Esq; Maple Cottage, Arkesden Rd, Clavering, nr Saffron Waldon, Essex; 14-16 Regent St, London SW1Y 4PS (☎ 071 839 4311)

OLIVER, Sir (Frederick) Ernest; CBE (1955), TD (1942), DL (Leicester 1950); s of Sir Frederick Oliver (d 1939); *b* 31 Oct 1900; *Educ* Rugby; *m* 1928, Mary Margaret (d 1978), da of Herbert Simpson (d 1931); 1 s (decd), 2 da; *Career* served WW II RA (UK and Burma); memb Leicester Cncl 1933-74, lord mayor Leicester 1950-51, chm George Oliver (Footwear) 1950-73; pres: Leicester Cons Assoc 1952-66, Multiple Shoe Retailers' Assoc 1964-65; hon Freeman City of Leicester 1971; kt 1962; *Style—* Sir Ernest Oliver, CBE, TD, DL

OLIVER, Greig Hunter; s of (Robert) Lawrie Oliver, and Marlene, *née* Borthnick; *b* 12 Sept 1964; *Educ* Hawick HS, Napier Coll Edinburgh; *Career* Rugby Union scrum-half Hawick RFC and Hawick PSA RFC, Hawick Trades RFC, Hawick RFC 1982-; rep: Scotland U21 (capt), Scotland B (2 caps); Scotland: debut v Zimbabwe 1987, memb World Cup squad 1987, tour Zimbabwe 1988, Japan 1989, NZ 1990 (replacement in second test, came on for second cap); computer operator; *Recreations* golf, tennis; *Style—* Greig Oliver, Esq; 4 Bourtree Bank, Hawick, Scotland (☎ 0450 78442)

OLIVER, Ian David; s of Col Claude Danolds Oliver, OBE, TD, DL (d 1987), and Vera Scott, *née* Grieve (d 1987); ggf George Oliver founded Footwear Retail Company now The Oliver Gp plc with 500 branches throughout UK; *b* 16 Nov 1934; *Educ* Uppingham; *m* 10 Nov 1973, Janet, da of Royden Swinfen (d 1984); 2 s (Louis b 1962, Edward b 1981), 1 da (Katie b 1976); *Career* chm: G Oliver Footware plc; pres: Multiple Shoe Retailers Assoc 1984-86 (chm 1981-84), Footwear Disstributors Fedn 1985-87; *Recreations* family, gardening; *Style—* Ian Oliver, Esq; Haddon Dale, West End, West Haddon, Northants (☎ 078 887 214); The Oliver Gp plc, Grove Way, Narborough, Leicester (☎ 0533 630444, telex 341270 OLIVER G, fax 0533 892921)

OLIVER, Keith David; s of David Oliver, of Holwell, Sherborne, Dorset, and Dora Mabel, *née* King; *b* 9 March 1953; *Educ* Foster's GS for Boys Sherborne Dorset; *m* 11 March 1978, Lynn, da of Sidney Arthur Bolton, of London; 2 s (Richard Keith b 25 July 1981, Philip Keith b 5 Feb 1987); *Career* mangr Lanz Hotels 1972-78, sales exec Lanier Business Products 1979-81, major account mangr Rank Xerox 1982-84, dealer mangr Herman Miller 1984-86, dir Interdec Design Gp 1986-; *Recreations* swimming, caravaning, fitness training; *Clubs* Caravan, Livingwell; *Style—* Keith Oliver, Esq; 32 Cartmel Close, Bletchley, Milton Keynes MK3 5LT (☎ 0908 371496); Interdec Design Group, Hunters Mill, Deaneshanger, Milton Keynes (☎ 0908 562928)

OLIVER, Michael Edgar; s of Alan Oliver, and Marguerite, *née* Moore (d 1986); *b* 20 July 1937; *Educ* St Clement Danes GS; *Career* presenter: Music Weekly BBC Radio 3 1975-90, Kaleidoscope BBC Radio 4 1975-87, Soundings BBC Radio 3 1990-; reviewer Gramophone 1973-; memb: Critics' Circle, An Comunn Gaidhealach (The Highlands Assoc), Sabhal Mor Ostaig (Gaelic Coll), Nat Tst for Scotland; former chm English Song Award; formerly active in anti-nuclear movement; contributor to: British Music Now (ed Foreman, 1975), End Games (ed Stewart, 1989), Song on Record (ed Blyth, 1988), Choral Music on Record (ed Blyth, 1991); *Recreations* travel, visual arts, food; *Style—* Michael Oliver, Esq

OLIVER, Prof Michael Francis; CBE (1985); s of Capt Wilfrid Francis Lenn Oliver, MC (d 1940); *b* 3 July 1925; *Educ* Marlborough, Univ of Edinburgh (MD); *m* 1, 1948 (m dis 1979), Margaret Yool, da of Maj James Yool Abbey, DSO, MC (d 1932); 2 s (and 1 s decd), 1 da; m 2, 1985, Helen Louise, da of Cyril Cockrell; *Career* Duke of Edinburgh Prof of Cardiology Univ of Edinburgh 1979-89, dir Wynn Inst for Metabolic Res London, hon prof Univ of London at Nat Heart and Lung Inst, emeritus prof Univ of Edinburgh; UK rep Advsy Panel for Cardiovascular Diseases WHO 1972-; chm: BBC Med Advsy Gp Scotland 1975-80, personal prof of cardiology 1976-79, DOT Advsy Panel on Cardiovascular Diseases 1983-90; pres: Br Cardiac Soc 1981-85, RCPEd 1985-88; examiner Cambridge and Edinburgh; Hon MD Karolinska 1980, Hon MD Bologna 1985; FRCP, FRCPE, FFCM, Hon FACC, FRSE 1987; *Books* 5 books and 300 papers on metabolic, clinical and epidemologic aspects of heart disease; *Recreations* all things Italian; *Clubs* Athenaeum, New (Edinburgh); *Style—* Prof Michael Oliver, CBE; Barley Mill Hse, Pencaitland, East Lothian (☎ 0875 340433); 28 Chalcot Rd, London NW1

OLIVER, (James) Michael Yorrick; JP (1987); s of Sqdn Ldr George Leonard Jack Oliver (d 1984), of Ca'n Brotat, Pollensa, Mallorca, Balearics, Spain, and Patricia Rosamund, *née* Douglas; *b* 13 July 1940; *Educ* Wellington Coll; *m* 22 June 1963, Sally Elizabeth Honor, da of George Gerhard Exner (d 1965), of 77 Harley Street, London W1; 2 da (Sophia Tugela Rosamund b 14 Oct 1969, Justine Umthandi Electra b 29 Dec 1971); *Career* Rediffusion Ltd 1959-63, mangr Helios Ltd 1965-70, ptnr Kitcat & Aitken 1977-86 (joined 1970); dir: Kitcat & Aitken & Co 1986-90, Carr Kitcat & Aitken Ltd 1990-; Br Museum backed expdn to Alamut Valley Iran 1960; govr: Bishopsgate Fndn Christ's Hosp Sch; memb: Fin Devpt Bd Order of St John, Museum of London Devpt Cncl, City of London Court of Common Cncl 1980-87, Alderman Ward of Bishopsgate 1987-; Freeman City of London 1962, Sr Warden Worshipful Co of Ironmongers 1990 (Liveryman and memb Ct); FRGS 1962, memb Stock Exchange 1975, AMSIA 1978, OStJ 1979; *Recreations* archaeology, travel, fives, windsurfing; *Clubs* City Livery; *Style—* Michael Oliver, Esq; Carr Kitcat & Aitken, 1 London Bridge, London SE1 9TJ (☎ 071 528 0100, fax 071 403 0755); Paradise House, Paradise Island, off Grantchester St, Cambridge CB3 9HY

OLIVER, Dr Ronald Martin; CB (1989), RD; s of Cuthbert Hanson Oliver (d 1972), of Strawberry Hill, and Cecilia *née* O'Dockery (d 1981); *b* 28 May 1929; *Educ* King's Coll Sch Wimbledon, King's Coll London, St George's Hospital London (MB BS, MRCS, LRCP, MD, MRCP, MFPHM, MFOM, DCH DIH, DPH); *m* 2 March 1957, Susanna (Sue) Treves, da of Dr Alfred Delatour Blackwell, of Taunton; 3 s (Richard b 1958, James b 1960, Philip b 1966), 1 da (Sarah b 1971); *Career* Surgn Lt RNVR 1953-55, Surgn Lt Cdr 1959; jr hosp appts St George's Hosp 1952-56, trainee asst GP 1956-57, asst county MO Surrey CC 1957-59; MO: London Tport Exec 1959-62, Treasy Med Serv 1962-64; physician Br Embassy Moscow 1964-66, MO later sr MO CS Med Advsy Serv 1966-74, SMO later sr princ MO DHSS, dep CMO Dept of Health 1974-89; memb BMA, FRSM; *Recreations* golf, gardening, sailing; *Style—* Dr Ronald Oliver, CB, RD; Greenhill House, Beech Ave, Effingham, Surrey KT24 5PH (☎ 0372 452887)

OLIVER, Hon Mrs; Sarah Chichester; o da of Baron Oliver of Aylmerton (Life Peer), *qv*; has resumed her maiden name; *m* 1974 (m dis 1983), James Robert Goldsack; 2 da (Katy Louise b 1980, Rebecca b 1983); *Style—* Hon Mrs Sarah OLiver

OLIVER, Stephen John Lindsay; QC; s of Phillip Daniel Oliver (Capt RN, d 1979),of Carlton, and Audrey Mary Taylor; *b* 14 Nov 1938; *Educ* Rugby Sch 1952-56, Oriel Coll Oxford 1959-62 (MA) Jurisprudence; *m* 1967, Ann Dawn, da of Gordon Taylor, of Gerrards Cross; 1 s (Adam b 1970), 2 da (Rebecca b 1969, Rosemary b 1972); *Career* RNVR (submariner) 1958-59; barr; asst parly cmmr, rec; chm Blackheath Concert Halls 1986; *Recreations* music, sailing; *Clubs* Groucho; *Style—* Stephen J L Oliver, Esq, QC; 4 Pump Court, Temple, London EC4Y 7AN (☎ 071 583 9770)

OLIVER, Vaughan William; s of Ernest Oliver, and Doreen, *née* Tindale; *b* 12 Sept 1957; *Educ* Ferryhill GS, Newcastle upon Tyne Poly (BA Hons); *Career* graphic designer, artist; packaging designer: Benchmark 1980, Michael Peters Gp 1981; record cover designer (under name 23 Envelope, with Nigel Grierson), 4AD (record co) 1983-88, freelance 1988-; record covers for gps incl: Clan of Xymox, Cocteau Twins, Colourbox, Dead Can Dance, Dif Juz, Lush, Modern English, Pale Saints, Pixies, Spireax, This Mortal Coil, Throwing Muses, Ultra Vivid Scene, Wolfgang Press, Xmal Deutschland; 23 Envelope exhibitions incl: UK-OK (Tokyo) 1985, 23 Envelope/4AD (solo, Tokyo) 1986, Pop-Eyes (Paper Point London) 1986, Disc Cover (City Art Gallery Edinburgh) 1986-87, Sleeves By (solo, Rotterdam ABK) 1988, Design in Print (The Design Council London) 1988, Around Sound (Boston Photographic Resource Centre) 1988-89; gp exhibitions incl: Artificial Light (Poly Gallery Newcastle) 1979, Young Blood (Barbican Gallery London) 1983, British Design, New Traditions (Boymans Museum Rotterdam) 1989, Pictures of Rock (Denmark) 1990, British Design 1790-1990 (Calif) 1990, The Art of Selling Songs 1690-1990 (V&A) 1991; solo exhibitions: Exhibition/Exposition (Nantes, St Brieuc) 1990, Exhibition/Exposition (Parco Gallery Tokyo), Grande Hall de la Villette Paris) 1991; other design work includes: book jackets (Serpents Tale, Picador), book design (Shinro Ohtake), freelance projects (Virgin, RCA), conf publicitiy (Kingston Poly, V&A Museum), fashion catalogues (John Galliano); *Style—* Vaughan Oliver, Esq; 15 Alma Road, London SW18 1AA (☎ 081 870 9724, fax 081 874 6600)

OLIVER-BELLASIS, Hugh Richard; s of Lt-Col John Oliver-Bellasis, DSO, JP, DL (d 1979), and Anne Mary, *née* Bates; *b* 11 April 1945; *Educ* Winchester, RMA Sandhurst; *m* 7 Aug 1971, Daphne Phoebe, da of Arthur Christopher Parsons, of Hatchwood House, Odiham; 2 da (Joanna b 8 April 1975, Nicola b 12 June 1978); *Career* 2 Lt Royal Fusiliers City of London Regt 1964, Welsh Gds 1970, Maj 1977 (ret); dir Manydown Co 1964, farmer 1980-, chm Hants Farm Devpts 1985-; vice chm Parish Cncl 1980-; memb: Rural Devpt Strategy Steering Gp 1987-, SE Regnl Panel Miny of Agric 1988; Hants Co rep Cncl NFU 1990 (memb Exec 1989); chm: Basingstoke Branch NFU 1991-, Farmland Ecology Unit Game Conservancy 1990, Br Deer Soc 1986-; memb: Grasshoppers Assoc 1989-, Cncl RASE, Game Conservancy Tst, Ctee FACE (UK); Freeman City of London 1967, Liveryman Worshipful Co of Merchant Taylors 1971, Worshipful Co of Gunmakers 1990; assoc RAS 1990; *Recreations* field sports, wine, food, motor racing; *Clubs* Army and Navy, Boodle's, Farmer's, MCC; *Style—* Hugh Oliver-Bellasis, Esq; Wootton House, Wootton St Lawrence, Basingstoke, Hants RG23 8PE; The Manydown Co, Worting Wood Farm, Basingstoke, Hants RG23 8PA (☎ 0256 464292, fax 0256 782270)

OLIVER OF AYLMERTON, Baron (Life Peer UK 1986), of Aylmerton, Co Norfolk; Peter Raymond Oliver; PC (1980); s of David Thomas Oliver (d 1947), and Alice Maud, da of George Kirby; *b* 7 March 1921; *Educ* The Leys Sch Cambridge, Trinity Hall Cambridge (hon fellow 1980); *m* 1, 1945, Mary Chichester (d 1985), da of Sir Eric Keightley Rideal, MBE, FRS; 1 s (Hon David Keightley Rideal b 1949), 1 da (Hon Sarah Chichester b 1951); m 2, 1987, Wendy Anne, widow of Ivon Lloyd Lewis Jones; *Career* barr Lincoln's Inn 1948; QC 1965; High Court Judge (Chancery) 1974-80; Lord Justice of Appeal 1980-86; memb Restrictive Practices Ct 1976-80; chm Review Body on High Ct Chancery Div 1979-81; memb Supreme Court Rule Ctee 1982-85; Lord of Appeal in Ordinary 1986; kt 1974; *Style—* The Rt Hon Lord Oliver of Aylmerton; The Canadas, Aylmerton, Norfolk

OLIVEY, Alan Keith; s of Hugh Norman Olivey (d 1980), of Upper Norwood, London, and Kathleen, *née* Mills; *b* 14 Oct 1947; *Educ* Heath Clark GS Croydon; *m* 11 Sept 1971, Janet Mary, da of Raymond Edgar Crewes Hutton, of Beckenham, Kent; 1 s (Richard b 1981), 1 da (Louise b 1977); *Career* CA; Sydenham Snowden Nicholson & Co 1964-71, ptnr Ernst & Young 1980- (joined 1971); FCA 1970, ATII 1970; *Recreations* badminton, gardening, philately, photography; *Style—* Alan Olivey, Esq; 75 Elwill Way, Beckenham, Kent BR3 2RY (☎ 081 658 1519); Becket House, 1 Lambeth Palace Rd, London SE1 7EU (☎ 071 931 3293, fax 071 928 1345, telex 885234 ERNSLO G)

OLIVIER, Hon Julie-Kate; da of Baron Olivier (Life Peer, d 1989), and his 3 w, Joan Plowright, *qv*; *b* 1966; *Educ* Bedales; *Career* actress; *Style—* The Hon Julie-Kate Olivier; 3rd Floor Flat, 37 Colville Terrace, London W11 2BU

OLIVIER, Hon Richard; s of Baron Olivier (Life Peer, d 1989), and his 3 w, Joan Plowright, *qv*; *b* 1961; *Educ* UCLA; *m* 28 June 1987, Shelley Marie, *née* Herrich; 1 s (Troylus b 1988), 1 da (Natalie Alexandre b 1990), and 1 step da (Kaya Rose); *Career* theatre and film dir; *Style—* The Hon Richard Olivier

OLIVIER, Hon Tamsin; da of Baron Olivier (Life Peer, d 1989), and his 3 w, Joan Plowright, (*qv*); *b* 1963; *Educ* Bedales; *Style*— The Hon Tamsin Olivier

OLIVIER, Hon (Simon) Tarquin; s of Baron Olivier (Life Peer, d 1989), and his 1 w, Jill Esmond (d 1990); *b* 1936; *m* 1965, Riddelle, da of Patrick Boyce Riddell Gibson; 1 da; *Clubs* Garrick; *Style*— The Hon Tarquin Olivier

OLIZAR, Michael George; s of Bohdan Olizar (d 1985), Lt Polish Forces, and Isabella, *née* Will; Col Adam Olizar served in King Jan Sobieski's army at relief of Vienna 1683; *b* 20 Jan 1947; *Educ* Salesian Coll Battersea, Central London Poly (MSc); *m* 23 Sept 1978, Sarah Jane, da of Alistair Sawrey-Cookson (d 1973); 1 s (Douglas b 1985), 3 da (Helena b 1979, Isabel b 1981, Clare b 1983); *Career* transportation planner; memb Cncl and Exec Ctee of the Polish Inst and Sikorski Museum London, pres Serpentine Swimming Club 1989-; AMIEE, MCIT; *Recreations* swimming, hill-walking; *Clubs* Serpentine Swimming (pres), Hurlingham, Long Distance Walkers' Assoc; *Style*— Michael Olizar, Esq; 18 Hazlewell Rd, London SW15 6LH (☎ 081 788 3115)

OLLARD, John Deacon; s of Alfred Ernest Ollard, and Violet Grace, *née* Taylor; *b* 1 Jan 1947; *Educ* Strand Sch London, LSE (BSc); *m* 20 March 1971 (m dis 1988), Pauline Jenniffer, da of Ernest John Simmonds (d 1985); 1 s (Mark Deacon b 17 June 1974); *Career* CA; Touche Ross & Co 1969-73, gp chief accountant Engelhard industries Ltd 1973-77, gen mangr and chief exec engineered materials div Engelhard Corp; fndr memb Local Employers Network Surrey; memb MENSA, FCA (1972), JDipMA (1979); *Recreations* sport of all kinds, particularly cricket; *Style*— John Ollard, Esq; 69 Pine Walk, Carshalton Beeches, Surrey SM5 4HA (☎ 081 642 2209); Engelhard Ltd, Davis Rd, Chessington, Surrey (☎ 081 397 5292)

OLLENNU, Ashitey Kwame Nii-Amaa; s of The Hon Mr Justice Nii-Amaa Ollennu (d 1987), of Accra, and Emily Adjo, *née* Jiagge; *b* 3 June 1950; *Educ* Lancing, Ealing Coll (BA); *m* 24 Jan 1976, Sylviana, da of Werner Kussmaul, of Öschelbronn, W Germany; 2 da (Amerley-Amanda b June 1984, Harriett b Feb 1988); *Career* called to the Bar Lincoln's Inn 1981, ad eundem Middle Temple 1982, in practice since 1983, Donald Gordon's Chambers 1983-90, Geoffrey Hawker's Chambers 1991-; churchwarden Golders Green Parish Church 1988-; memb: Golders Green Cncl of Churches, Barnet Deanery Synod, Edmonton Area Synod, Exec Ctee Anglo Ghanaian Soc; chairperson Barnet Race Equality Cncl 1990-; *Recreations* cricket and singing; *Style*— Ashitey Ollennu, Esq; 5th Floor, 199 The Strand, London WC2R 1DR (☎ 071 497 9757, fax 071 497 9710); 144 Westgate Chambers, Lewes, E Sussex BN7 1XT (☎ 0273 480510)

OLLERENSHAW, Dame Kathleen Mary; DBE (1971), DL (1987); da of Charles Timpson, JP (d 1967), and Mary Elizabeth, *née* Stops (d 1954); *b* 1 Oct 1912,Manchester; *Educ* Ladybarn House Sch Manchester, St Leonards Sch St Andrews, Somerville Coll Oxford (MA, DPhil); *m* 1939, Col Robert Ollerenshaw, ERD, TD, JP, DL (d 1986): 1 s, 1 da (decd); *Career* chm: Assoc of Governing Bodies of Girls Public Schs 1963-69, Manchester Educn Ctee 1967-70, Manchester Poly 1968-72, Ct of RNCM 1968-86 (companion 1978), educn ctee assoc Municipal Corp 1968-71; author of numerous res papers in mathematical jls; Manchester CC 1956-80: alderman 1970-74, Lord Mayor 1875-76, dep Lord Mayor 1976-77, ldr Cons oppostition 1977-79, Hon Alderman 1980; vice pres Br Assoc for Commercial and Industl Educn (memb delgn to USSR 1963) memb: central advsy cncl on Educn in England 1960-63, CNNA 1964-74, SSRC 1971-75, Layfield Ctee of Enquiry into Local Govt Fin 1974-76; pres: St Leonards Sch St Andrews 1976-, Manchester Technol Assoc 1981 (hon memb 1976-), Manchester Statistical Soc 1983-85; hon fell: City and Guilds London Inst 1980 (memb educn ctee 1960-73), Inst of Mathematics and its Applications 1986-(fell 1964, memb cncl 1972-), UMI 1987 (vice pres 1977-86); hon memb: Manchester Literary and Philosophical Soc 1981; dep pro chllr Univ of Lancaster 1978-, pro chllr Univ of Salford 1983-89; dir Manchester Ind Radio Ltd 1972-83; hon Col Manchester and Salford Univ OTC 1977-81; DStJ 1983 (CStJ 1978, chm Cncl OStJ Greater Manchester 1974-89, memb Chapter General OStJ 1978-); Mancunian of the year Jr C of C 1977; Hon Fell Somerville Coll Oxford 1978; Freeman City of Manchester 1984; Hon DSc Salford 1975, Hon LLD Manchester 1976, Hon DSc CNAA 1976; Hon FIMA 1988, FCP FCGI; *Books* Education of Girls (1958), The Girls' School (1967), Returning to Teaching (1974), The Lord Mayor's Party (1976), First Citizen (1977); *Clubs* English-Speaking Union; *Style*— Dame Kathleen Ollerenshaw, DBE, DL; 2 Pine Rd, Didsbury, Manchester M20 0UY (☎ 061 445 2948)

OLLEY, Martin Burgess; s of Robert William Olley (d 1969), of Sheringham, Norfolk, and Dorothy Lillian Alexander, *née* Burgess (d 1941); *b* 11 Aug 1932; *Educ* Gresham's Sch Holt Norfolk, Coll of Estate Mgmnt London; *m* 1 (m dis 1971), Averil Rosemary Phyllis, *née* Cann; 2 s (Clive Matthew Burgess b 1961, Edward Martin Burgess b 1967), 1 da (Lucy Ann Burgess b 1963); m 2, 14 June 1980, Moira Bernadette, da of Joseph Kelly (d 1968); *Career* RAF 1950-52; Norwich Union: London Estates mangr 1973-80, Norwich estates mangr 1980-82, chief estates mangr 1983-; memb gen cncl Br Property Fedn, former pres Norwich Wanderers CC; Freeman City of London 1974, Liveryman Worshipful Co of Woolmen's 1978; FRICS; *Recreations* golf, boating, squash, tennis, walking; *Clubs* RAC, Pall Mall, Norfolk Broads Yacht; *Style*— Martin Olley, Esq; 1 Marston Lane, Eaton, Norwich, Norfolk NR4 6LZ (☎ 0603 56495); 55 Netheravon Rd, Chiswick, London W1 (☎ 081 994 5985); Norwich Union Real Estate Managers Ltd, Sentinel House, 37 Surrey St, Norwich NR1 3PW (☎ 0603 682256, fax 0603 683950, telex 97388)

OLNEY, Robert C; s of Herbert M Olney, of USA; *b* 19 Aug 1926; *Educ* Cornell (BA); *m* 1948, Wanda, *née* Gasch (d 1988); 3 c; *Career* vice pres and gen mangr Nat Adv Co Chicago 1976- (div dir 1973, mktg dir 1969, gen sales mangr 1959) non-exec chm and md 3M UK plc 1979-88; dir Yale and Valor plc; chm: Jersey Overseas Investment Management Ltd, St Helier CI; pres Tuon Holdings Inc; Companion BIM, MInstD; vice-pres Sports Aid Fndn; *Recreations* golf, skiing; *Clubs* Burhill Golf, Hinsdale Golf, RAC; *Style*— Robert C Olney, Esq; Tudor Hall, 10 Farmleigh Grove, Burwood Park, Walton on Thames, Surrey KT12 5BU

OLSEN, Gary Kenneth (formerly Grant); s of Kenneth George Grant (d 1968), and Patricia, *née* Haste (d 1966); *b* 3 Nov 1957; *Educ* Archbishop Tenison GS; *Career* actor; plays incl: Metamorphosis 1986, Up On The Roof 1987, Serious Money 1987-88; TV incl: The Bill 1984, Prospects 1985, Come Home Charlie and Face Them 1990; *Recreations* golf, snooker; *Clubs* Addington Court Golf, Kings Cross Snooker, Fred's; *Style*— Gary Olsen, Esq; c/o Lou Coulson, 37 Berwick St, London W11 (☎ 071 734 9633)

OLSEN, Richard Frank; RD (1983); s of Frank Maurice Lyche Olsen, of Bellings Barn, Eastbourne, Midhurst, W Sussex, and Dora Winifred, *née* Wyatt; *b* 15 June 1943; *Educ* Mill Hill, Worcester Coll Oxford (MA); *m* 23 Sept 1978, Jeraine Dickin, da of John Kenneth Dickin Roberts; 2 s (Jamie b 16 Oct 1982, Andrew b 13 Aug 1984); *Career* RNR 1967-87; admitted slr 1969; Constant & Constant 1970-72, Scandinavian Inst Maritime Law, Oslo Univ 1972-73; ptnr: William A Crump & Son 1977-86 (joined 1974), Stephenson Harwood 1986-; Freeman Worshipful Co of Slrs; memb Law Soc 1966; *Publications* The Value of a Salved Ship (1974), various articles on shipping law in maritime and legal jls; *Recreations* photography, offshore sailing, skiing, enjoying good wine and good books; *Clubs* Royal Ocean Racing, United Oxford & Cambridge Univ; *Style*— Richard Olsen, Esq, RD; 23 St Paul's Place, Canonbury, London N1 2QF (☎ 071 354 2000); Stephenson Harwood, 1 St Paul's Churchyard, London EC4M 8SH (☎ 071 329 4422, fax 071 606 0822, telex 886789)

OLSEN, Roy; s of John Sigmund Olsen (d 1971), and Florence Mary, *née* Ashworth; *b* 20 April 1945; *Educ* Margaret's Anfield Liverpool, Art HS Liverpool, Coll of Bldg Liverpool; *m* 22 July 1972, Francesca Carey, da of Capt William Sidney Hall, MC, of Wales; 2 s (Luke Joen b 1975, Alexander Hall b 1976); *Career* architect; princ private practice Olsen Assocs; dir: Bontddu Properties Ltd, Link Property Servs Ltd; architectural awards Snowdonia Nat Park; memb: Stone Fedn, RIBA; *Recreations* golf; *Clubs* Royal St David's Golf; *Style*— Roy Olsen, Esq; Trem Yr Eglwys, Dolgellau, Gwynedd, Wales (☎ 0341 423071); Arran Buildings, Dolgellau, Gwynedd, Wales (☎ 0341 422932, fax 0341 422044)

OLSEN, (James) Wilfred; s of August Mauritz Olsen (d 1957), of East Sheen, London, and Ellen, *née* Lyche (d 1959); *b* 6 Feb 1920; *Educ* Kings Coll Sch Wimbledon; *m* 28 Feb 1953, Georgina Frances; 2 s (Roger, Jeremy); *Career* Lt (Special Branch) RNVR 1940-46, Naval Intelligence Div Admty 1940-45, SO (Intelligence) Kristiansand S Norway 1945; sec: D & W Gibbs Ltd (Unilever) 1948-51, Hudson & Knight Ltd (Unilever) 1951-55; former chief accountant Associated Newspapers Ltd; chm PO Advsy Ctee Bromley, former chm Bromley and Dist Consumers Gp, local referee CAs Benevolent Assoc; Worshipful Co of CAs 1980; FCA 1947, ACIS 1948; Christian X Freedom Medal (Denmark) 1945; *Recreations* bridge, consumerism, caravanning; *Clubs* Royal Over-Seas League; *Style*— Wilfred Olsen, Esq; Correnden, 4 Waldegrave Rd, Bromley, Kent BR1 2JP (☎ 081 467 5218)

OLSZOWSKI, Stefan; s of Tadeusz Olszowski (d 1988), of Sevenoaks, Kent, and Zofia, *née* Zembrzuska; *b* 25 Jan 1936; *Educ* The Oratory; *m* 17 Sept 1960, Patricia Margaret, da of John B Coates (d 1987); 2 s (Mark b 1962, Gregory b 1968), 2 da (Catharine b 1961, Susan b 1963); *Career* chm Bracefine Holdings Ltd 1976, dep chm Coates Bros plc 1980, dir JS Hamilton Holdings Ltd 1986; *Recreations* sailing, shooting, travel; *Clubs* Itchenor Sailing; *Style*— Stefan Olszowski, Esq; East Hoe Manor, Hambledon, nr Portsmouth, Hants PO7 6SZ; Meon House, Petersfield, Hants GU32 3JN (☎ 0730 64674)

OLVER, Sir Stephen John Linley; KBE (1975), MBE (1947, CMG 1965); s of late Rev S E L Olver; *b* 16 June 1916; *Educ* Stowe; *m* 1953, Maria, da of Gino Morena, of Gubbio, Italy; 1 s; *Career* served Indian Political Service 1944-47, Br Diplomatic Service Karachi 1947-50, FO 1950-53, Berlin 1953-56, Bangkok 1956-58, FO 1958-61, cnsllr Washington 1961-64, FO 1965-66, The Hague 1967-69; high cmmr: Sierra Leone 1969-72, Cyprus 1973-75; *Clubs* MCC; *Style*— Sir Stephen Olver, KBE, MBE, CMG; 7 Seymour Sq, Brighton BN2 1DP

OLYMPITIS, Emmanuel John; s of John Emmanuel Olympitis, and Argyro, *née* Theodorou; *b* 19 Dec 1948; *Educ* King's Sch Canterbury, Univ Coll London (LLB); *m* 26 Oct 1979 (m dis 1983), Jan Cushing, da of Arnold Golding (d 1946), of NY, USA; 1 s (John Emmanuel b 1981); *Career* dir Bankers Trust International Ltd 1976-80, vice pres Bankers Trust Co NY 1976- 80, pres Centaur Resources Inc NY 1980-84, ptnr America Acquisitions Co NY 1981-85; md: Aitken Hume Group 1986-88, Whittington International plc (part of Aitken Hume Group) 1986-89; chief exec and dir Aitken Hume International plc 1988-89; dir: Aitken Hume Bank plc 1988-89, Sentinel Life plc 1988-89, National Securities & Resorces Corporation NY 1988-89; *Books* By Victories Undone (1988); *Recreations* writing, tennis, sailing; *Clubs* Turf, Newport Reading Room Rhode Island USA; *Style*— Emmanuel Olympitis, Esq; 45 Eaton Square, London SW1 (☎ 071 235 9005); Kalymnos, Dodecanese Islands, Greece

OMAN, Dr Julia Trevelyan; CBE (1986); da of Charles Chichele Oman (d 1982), and Joan, *née* Trevelyan; *b* 11 July 1930; *Educ* RCA; *m* 1971, Sir Roy Colin Strong, *qv*; *Career* designer; BBC TV 1955-67 (incl Alice in Wonderland 1966); theatre: Brief Lives 1967 and 1974, Country Dance 1967, Forty Years On 1968, The Merchant of Venice 1970, Othello 1971, The Importance of Being Earnest (Vienna) 1976, Hay Fever and the Wild Duck (London) 1980, The Shoemaker's Holiday (National Theatre) 1981, Mr and Mrs Nobody (Garrick) 1986, A Man for All Seasons (Chichester and Savoy) 1987, The Best of Friends (Apollo) 1988; ballet: Enigma Variations (Royal Ballet) 1968, A Month in the Country Royal Ballet 1976, Le Papillon (Ashton Pas-de-Deux) 1977, Voices of Spring (Ashton Pas-de-Deux, Royal Ballet 1977, Het Nationale Ballet Amsterdam 1989), Sospiri (Ashton Pas-de-Deux) 1980, Swan Lake (Boston Ballet) 1981, Nutcracker (Royal Ballet) 1984; opera: Eugene Onegin (Covent Garden) 1971, Un Ballo in Maschera (Hamburg) 1973, La Boheme (Covent Garden 1974), Die Fledermaus (Covent Garden) 1977, Die Csardasfürstin (Kassel) 1982, Otello (Stockholm) 1983, Arabella (Glyndebourne) 1984, The Consul (Connecticut Grand Opera) 1985; TV: Hay Fever (Denmark) 1978, Separate Tables (HTV and HBO) 1982; films incl: The Charge of the Light Brigade (art dir) 1967, Julius Caesar (prodn designer) 1969, Straw Dogs (design conslt) 1971; exhibitions: Samuel Pepys (Nat Portrait Gallery) 1970, Mme Tussaud's Hall of Historical Tableaux; Designer of the Year 1967, NCTA Best Art Dir award 1983; photographic contrib Architectural Review and Vogue; Hon DLitt Univ of Bristol 1987; FCSD, RDI 1977; *Books* Street Children (photographs (text by B S Johnson), 1964), Elizabeth R (with Roy Strong, 1971), Mary Queen of English Year (1982); *Style*— Dr Julia Trevelyan Oman, CBE; Oman Productions Ltd, The Laskett, Much Birch, Hereford HR2 8HZ

OMAND, David Bruce; s of James Bruce Omand (d 1980), and Esther, *née* Dewar; *b* 15 April 1947; *Educ* Glasgow Acad, Corpus Christi Coll Cambridge (fndn scholar, BA); *m* Feb 1971, Elizabeth Marjorie, da of Geoffrey Wales (d 1990); 1 s (Duncan b 1978), 1 da (Helen b 1975); *Career* asst princ 1970, private sec to Chief Procurement Exec 1973, asst private sec to Sec of State for Def 1973-75 and 1979-80, princ 1975, asst sec 1981, private sec to Sec of State for Def 1981-82, seconded as def cnsllr to FCO Delgn to Nato Brussels 1985-88, under sec grade 3 1988, Mgmnt Strategy 1988-; *Recreations* hillwalking, opera; *Clubs* Reform; *Style*— David Omand, Esq; Ministry of Defence, Whitehall, London SW1 (☎ 071 218 2727)

ONG, Benny; Anglo-Chinese Sch Singapore, St Martin's Sch of Art; *b* 7 March 1956; *Career* designer; Benny Ong Designer Collection 1975-, Benny Ong Diffusion Labels ONG 1989-, represented GB in Young Designer Show sponsored by Snia Viscosa Italy Milas 1979, examiner in fashion St Martin's Sch of Art 1986, selected designer GUS Mail Order 1987-89; maj projects incl: BAA corporate uniform 1987-89, BT corporate uniform 1989, uniform for Raffles Hotel Preservation Project 1991, Sch of Meditation London; *Recreations* swimming, tennis, philosophy; *Style*— Benny Ong, Esq; 3 Bentick Mews, London W1 (☎ 071 487 5954, fax 071 224 4771)

ONIANS, Richard Anderson; s of Frank Arnold Onians (d 1986), of Thetford, Norfolk, and Marie Elise, *née* Anderson (d 1957); *b* 21 April 1940; *Educ* Thetford GS, Stanford Exec Program; *m* 29 July 1961, Marianne Dorothy, da of Archibald Laidlaw (d 1978); 1 s (Henry b 1965), 1 da (Sarah b 1963); *Career* various positions in USA and Europe (latterly vice pres electronics and venture capital) Monsanto Co 1959-84, chief exec Baring Bros Hambrecht and Quist Ltd 1984-; dir: Baring Bros & Co Ltd, British Rail Anglia Region, Design Marketing Ltd, York Ltd, ARCA Merchant Milan, Banco Bilbao Viszcaya Gestiones Madrid; fndr chm Euro Venture Capital Assoc 1985-86; FRSA 1986; *Recreations* books, history, visual arts; *Clubs* Savile, Fifty Four; *Style*—

Richard Onians, Esq; 140 Park Lane, London W1Y 3AA (☎ 071 408 0555, fax 071 493 5153)

ONIONS, Ronald Edward Derek; OBE (1984); s of Benjamin Edward Onions (d 1970), and Elizabeth Amelia, *née* Lewin (d 1973); *b* 27 Aug 1929; *Educ* Edmonton County GS; *m* 1951, Doris Margaret, da of Reginald Monro Moody (d 1987); 2 da (Sarah, Louise); *Career* journalist; newspaper journalist 1950-58; Southern TV news ed 1958-60, reporter prod and newscaster BBC News and Current Affrs 1960-67, BBC news prodr NY and co-ordinator for EBU 1967-72, head of news Capital Radio 1973-74, ed IRN 1974-77, ed dir LBC/IRN 1977-83, managing ed Special Projects Visnews 1983-89, station dir Jazz FM 1989-; *Recreations* skiing, bird watching; *Style—* Ronald Onions, Esq, OBE; 53 Portsmouth Road, Surbiton, Surrey (☎ 081 390 0654); 41 Oaklands Avenue, Saltdean, Sussex (☎ 0273 304077); London Jazz Radio, 26/27 Castlereagh St, London W1H 5YR (☎ 071 706 4100)

ONSLOW, Rt Hon Cranley Gordon Douglas; PC (1988), MP (C) Woking 1964-; s of Francis Robert Douglas Onslow (d 1938); *b* 8 June 1926; *Educ* Harrow, Oriel Coll Oxford, Univ of Geneva; *m* 1955, Lady June Ann, *qv*; 1 s, 3 da; *Career* serv RAC 1944-48 and Co of London Yeo (TA) 1948-52; FO 1951-60 (serv Burma); memb Exec 1922 Ctee: exec memb 1968-72, 1981-82 and 1983-, chm 1984-; chm Cons Aviation Ctee 1970-72 and 1979-82, Parly under sec (Aerospace and Shipping) DTI 1972-74; oppn spokesman: Health and Social Security 1974-75, Def 1975-76; memb UK Delegation Cncl Europe and WEU 1977-81, chm Select Ctee on Def 1981-82, min of state FCO 1982-83; dir Argyll Gp plc, chm Redifon Ltd; has represented the House of Commons at cricket, bridge, fishing and rifle shooting; *Style—* The Rt Hon Cranley Onslow, MP; Highbuilding, Fernhurst, Haslemere, Surrey

ONSLOW, Sir John Roger Wilmot; 8 Bt (GB 1797), of Althain, Lancashire; s of Sir Richard Wilmot Onslow, 7 Bt, TD (d 1963); *b* 21 July 1932; *Educ* Cheltenham; *m* 1, 1955 (m dis 1973), Catherine Zoia, da of Henry Atherton Greenway, of The Manor, Compton Abdale, nr Cheltenham; 1 s, 1 da; m 2, 1976, Susan Fay, da of E M Hughes, of Frankson, Vic, Aust; *Heir* s, Richard Onslow; *Style—* Sir John Onslow, Bt; c/o Barclays Bank Ltd, Fowey, Cornwall

ONSLOW, Lady June Ann; *née* Hay; da of 14 Earl of Kinnoull (d 1938), by his 2 w, Mary; *b* 1932; *m* 1955, Cranley Gordon Douglas Onslow, MP; 1 s, 3 da; *Career* tstee: Leonard Cheshire Fndn 1974-85, Guide Dogs for the Blind 1984-88, Bristol Cancer Help Centre 1989-; govr King Edward's Sch Witley Surrey 1986-; *Style—* The Lady June Onslow; Highbuilding, Fernhurst, Sussex

ONSLOW, 7 Earl of (UK 1801); Sir Michael William Coplestone Dillon Onslow; 11 Bt (E 1674, of 2 cr, with precedency 1660); also Baron Onslow (GB 1716), Baron Cranley (GB 1776), and Viscount Cranley (UK 1801); high steward of Guildford; s of 6 Earl, KBE, MC, TD (d 1971), and Pamela, Countess of Onslow, *qv*; bro-in-law of Auberon Waugh, *qv*; *b* 28 Feb 1938; *Educ* Eton, Sorbonne; *m* 1964, Robin, o da of Maj Robert Lee Bullard III, of Atlanta, Ga (Lady Onslow's mother subsequently m Lord Aberconway as his 2 w); 1 s, 2 da (Lady Arabella b 1970, Lady Charlotte b 1977); *Heir* s, Viscount Cranley, *qv*; *Career* sits as Conservative in House of Lords; Lloyd's underwriter, dir of various insur cos; farmer (800 acres in Surrey), dir of garden centre at Clandon 1982-; served Life Gds M East; sometime govr Univ Coll Buckingham, govr Royal GS Guildford; *Style—* The Rt Hon the Earl of Onslow; Temple Court, Clandon Park, Guildford, Surrey (☎ 0483 222754)

ONSLOW, Jo, Countess of - (Nina); MBE (1953); da of Thomas Sturdee; *m* 1962, 6 Earl of Onslow, KBE, MC, TD (d 1971); *Style—* The Rt Hon Jo, Countess of Onslow, MBE; Sturdee's, Freeland, Oxford

ONSLOW, Pamela, Countess of - Hon Pamela Louisa Ellinor; JP (Guildford 1952); da of 19 Viscount Dillon, CMG, DSO (d 1946); *b* 1915; *m* 1936 (m dis 1962), 6 Earl of Onslow, KBE, MC (d 1971); 1 s, 1 da; *Style—* Pamela, Countess of Onslow, JP; 12 Callcott St, W8

ONSLOW, Richard; s of Rt Hon Cranley Onslow, PC, MP, of Highbuilding, Fernhurst, W Sussex, and Lady June Hay; *b* 27 June 1956; *Educ* Harrow, Oxford Univ (MA), City Univ (DPL); *m* 27 July 1985, Phyllida, da of Michael Moore, OBE, of Folly Farm, Lindsey, Ipswich, Suffolk; 1 da (Isabella); *Career* called to the Bar Inner Temple 1982; *Recreations* shooting, fishing, real tennis, cricket; *Clubs* MCC, Stragglers of Asia Cricket, Lords and Commons Cricket; *Style—* Richard Onslow, Esq; 2 Harcourt Bldgs, Temple, London EC4 (☎ 071 353 2112, fax 071 353 8339)

ONSLOW, Richard Paul Atherton; s and h of Sir John Roger Wilmot Onslow, 8 Bt; *b* 16 Sept 1958; *Style—* Richard Onslow Esq

ONZIA, Koenraad Roger Mathilde (Koen); s of Hubert Onzia, and Paula, *née* Dils; *b* 3 March 1961; *Educ* Ballet Sch of Antwerp; *Career* princ ballet dancer; began performing career with Royal Ballet of Flanders; London Festival Ballet: joined 1982, soloist 1984 (rejoined Royal Ballet of Flanders until 1986), princ dancer 1986; princ dancer: Houston Ballet 1989, English National Ballet 1990-; guest artist performances with Paris Opera, the Deutch Opera Berlin, Brussels Cirque Royale, Nat Ballet of Caracas in Madrid and Caracas, Inoue Ballet Fndn Tokyo; partners incl: Galina Panova, Trinidad Sevillano, Lynn Charles; repertoire incl: Don Quixote Pas de deux and Le Corsaire, George Balanchine's Allegro Brilliante and Apollo, Romeo in Rudolf Nureyev's Romeo and Juliet, the jester in Ben Stevenson's Cinderella, Ronald Hynd's The Seasons, Natalia Makarova's La Bayadère and the prince in Swan Lake, Romeo in Valery Panov's Romeo and Juliet, the prince in Cinderella, Prince Myshkin in The Idiot, Michael Jackson in Moves, the prince in Peter Schaufuss's The Nutcracker, Albrecht in Alicia Alonso's Giselle, Lenski in John Cranko's Onegin, Chopin in Vincente Nebrada's George Sand, the young man in Masao Sugi's Snow Princess, Harold Lander's Etudes, the leading man in Maurice Bejart's Bolero, Frantz in Ronald Hynd's Coppelia, Siobban Davies' Dancing Ledge; *Awards* Bronze medallist Varna Int Ballet competition, Gold medallist Lausanne and Jackson Mississippi, nominee SWET award for Outstanding Individual Performance of the Year (Ronald Hynd's The Seasons) 1983, nominee Lawrence Olivier awards (for Christopher Bruce's Cruel Garden and Swansong) 1988; *Style—* Koen Onzia, Esq; English National Ballet, Markova House, 39 Jay Mews, London SW7 2ES

OPENSHAW, Hon Mrs (Julia); da of Baron Cross of Chelsea, PC (Life Peer, d 1989); *b* 1953; *m* 1, 1973 (m dis) , Barney Walker; 1 s (Woolf b 1976), 1 da (Joanna b 1978); m 2, 1987, David Openshaw; *Style—* The Hon Mrs Openshaw; c/o Rt Hon Lord Cross of Chelsea, PC, The Bridge House, Leintwardine, Craven Arms, Shropshire

OPENSHAW, (Charles) Peter Lawford; s of His Hon Judge William Harrison Openshaw (d 1981), of Park House, Broughton, Preston, Lancs, and Elisabeth Joyce Emily, *née* Lawford; *b* 21 Dec 1947; *Educ* Harrow, St Catharine's Coll Cambridge (MA); *m* 15 Dec 1979, Caroline Jane, da of Vincent Seymour Swift, of Brookhouse, Lancs; 1 s (Henry b 1986), 1 da (Alexandra b 1984); *Career* called to the Bar 1970, practised on Northern circuit, junior 1973, asst recorder 1984, recorder 1988; *Recreations* general country pursuits; *Clubs* United Oxford and Cambridge; *Style—* Peter Openshaw, Esq; 2 Old Bank St, Manchester (☎ 061 832 3791)

OPIE, Alan John; s of Jack Opie (d 1985), and Doris Winifred, *née* Bennetts; *b* 22 March 1945; *Educ* Truro Sch, Guildhall Sch of Music and Drama (AGSM), London Opera Centre (Cinzano scholar); *m* 18 April 1970, Kathleen Ann, da of Ernest Smales; 1 s (James Alexander b 1976), 1 da (Helen Louise b 1979); *Career* princ baritone ENO 1973-; performed with: Royal Opera, Glyndebourne Festival Opera, Scottish Opera, Eng Opera Gp, Chicago Lyric Opera, Bayreuth Festival, Paris Opera, Netherlands Opera, Brussels Opera, Hong Kong Festival, Buxton Festival, Stadtsoper Berlin, Wexford Festival; concerts in: UK, Europe, USA; recordings with: CBS, EMI, Decca, Hyperion; *Recreations* golf; *Clubs* Leatherhead Golf; *Style—* Alan Opie, Esq

OPIE, Iona Margaret Balfour; da of Sir Robert George Archibald, CMG, DSO (d 1953), and Olive Chapman, *née* Cant (d 1982); *b* 13 Oct 1923; *Educ* Sandecotes Sch; *m* 2 Sept 1943, Peter Mason Opie (d 1982); 2 s (James b 13 Oct 1944, Robert b 5 April 1947), 1 da (Letitia b 25 Oct 1949); *Career* author; pubns with Peter Opie incl: The Oxford Dictionary of Nursery Rhymes (1951), The Lore and Language of Schoolchildren (1959), Children's Games in Street and Playground (1969), The Oxford Book of Children's Verse (1973), The Classic Fairy Tales (1974), The Singing Game (1985); Hon MA: Univ of Oxford 1962, Open Univ 1987; Hon D Litt Univ of Southampton 1987; *Recreations* eating picnics on hillsides; *Style—* Mrs Iona Opie; Westerfield House, West Liss, Hants GU33 6JQ (☎ 0730 893309)

OPIE, Lisa Jane; da of Rex Opie, of St Martin's, Guernsey, CI, and Robina Mary, *née* Waller; *b* 15 Aug 1963; *Educ* Blanchelande Convent Sch (Guernsey); *Career* squash player; world jr champion Canada 1981; winner: Br Nat Championship 1981, 83, 86, 87, Aust Open 1986, 87, Singapore Open 1988, 89, Malaysian Open 1988, Irish Open 1986, 88; runner up: Br Open 1981, 83, 85, 86, World Open 1985, 87; memb England team 1981-, winner World Teams Event 1985, 87 (capt); memb Women's Int Squash Players Assoc; *Recreations* christianity, listening to music, pop concerts, art, cooking; *Clubs* The Park Squash (Nottingham), Kings Squash (Guernsey); *Style—* Miss Lisa Opie; Nottingham Squash Club, Tattershall Drive, The Park, Nottingham (☎ 0602 417022)

OPIE, Roger Gilbert; CBE (1976); s of Frank Gilbert Opie (d 1969), of Adelaide, S Aust, and Fanny Irene Grace Opie (d 1969); *b* 23 Feb 1927; *Educ* Prince Alfred Coll S Aust, Univ of Adelaide (BA, MA, South Australian Rhodes scholar), Univ of Oxford (BA, BPhil, jr then sr G W Medley scholar); *m* 10 Sept 1955, Norma Mary, da of Norman Canter (d 1979), of Highgate, N London; 2 s (Christopher Francis b 1956, Julian Gilbert b 1958), 1 da (Mary Jane Tregoning b 1962); *Career* asst lectr in econs and statistics Univ of Adelaide 1949-51, asst lectr and lectr in econs LSE 1954-61, econ advsr HM Treasy 1958-60, fell New Coll Oxford 1961-; asst dir: HM Treasy Centre for Admin Studies 1964, planning div Dept of Economic Affrs 1964-66; econ advsr to chm NBPI 1967-70; memb: Monopolies and Mergers Cmmn 1968-81, Price Cmmn 1977-80; city cncllr Oxford 1972-74, dist cncllr Oxford 1974-76; *Recreations* sailing; *Style—* Roger Opie, Esq, CBE; New College, Oxford OX1 3BN (☎ 0865 270000)

OPPEN, Richard John Stuart; s of Arthur Harrie Oppen (d 1976), and Muriel Evelyn, *née* Dent (d 1984); *b* 29 Jan 1937; *Educ* Dulwich, City of London Sch; *m* 1 June 1963, Wendy, da of Leslie William Day Suffield (d 1979); 1 s (James b 11 July 1969), 1 da (Lucy b 27 Jan 1972); *Career* Nat Serv 3 Carabiniers (3DG) 1955-57; dir Galbraiths Ltd 1984-88, md Berge of CIA (UK) Ltd 1989-; Freeman City of London 1980, Liveryman Worshipful Co of Shipwrights 1982; *Recreations* country pursuits; *Clubs* Naval & Military; *Style—* Richard Oppen, Esq; 1 Clarendon Way, Chislehurst, Kent (☎ 0689 25253); 47 Albermarle St, London W1 (☎ 071 499 3186, fax 071 495 4808, telex 261675)

OPPENHEIM, (Tan Sri) Sir Alexander; OBE (1955); s of Rev Harris Jacob Oppenheim (d 1944); *b* 4 Feb 1903; *Educ* Manchester GS, Balliol Coll Oxford; *m* 1930 (m dis 1977), Beatrice Templer *née* Nesbit; 2 s, 1 da; *Career* tutor in mathematics Univ of Oxford 1924-27, lectr in mathematics Univ of Edinburgh 1930-31, prof of mathematics Raffles Coll 1931-48; Univ of Malaya: prof of mathematics 1949-57, dean of Faculty of Arts 1949-51 and 1954, acting vice chllr 1955, vice chllr 1957-65; ret 1965; visiting prof: Univ of Reading 1965-68, Univ of Ghana 1968-73, Univ of Benin Nigeria 1973-77; kt 1961; *Style—* Sir Alexander Oppenheim, OBE; Matson House, Remenham, Henley-on-Thames, Oxon RG9 3HB (☎ 0491 572049)

OPPENHEIM, Lady Bridget Sarah; *née* Sinclair; da (by 2 m) of late 19 Earl of Caithness; *b* 1947; *Educ* Butterstone House Perthshire, Runton Hill Norfolk; *m* 1976, Nicholas Anthony Oppenheim, s of Sir Duncan Oppenheim; 1 s, 2 da; *Style—* Lady Bridget Oppenheim; 61 Park Rd, Chiswick, London W4

OPPENHEIM, Sir Duncan Morris; s of late Watkin Oppenheim, TD, of St Helens, Lancs; *b* 6 Aug 1904; *Educ* Repton; *m* 1, 1932, Joyce Mary Mitcheson (d 1933); m 2, 1936, Susan May (d 1964), da of Brig-Gen Ernest Macnaghten, CMG, DSO (d 1948); 1 s, 1 da; *Career* admitted slr 1929; asst slr with Linklaters & Paines 1929-34; Br American Tobacco Co: slr 1934, dir 1943, chm 1953-66, pres 1966-72, advsr 1972-74; dir: Lloyds Bank 1956-74, Equity & Law Life Assurance Society 1966-75; chm: RCA 1956-72, Design Cncl (formerly Cncl of Industl Design) 1960-72, Br Nat Ctee of Int C of C 1963-64, Court of Govrs Admin Staff Coll Henley 1963-71, Royal Inst of Int Affrs 1966-71, Tobacco Securities Tst 1969-74, Overseas Devpt Ctee of CBI 1970-74, V&A Associates 1976-81 (memb Advsy Cncl V&A 1967-80); dep chm Cwlth Devpt Fin Co 1968-74; dep chm Crafts Cncl (formerly Crafts Advsy Ctee) 1971-83; govr Repton Sch 1959-79; Hon FCSD 1972; Hon Dr and hon fell RCA; Bicentenary medal RSA 1969; kt 1960; *Clubs* Athenaeum, Royal Yacht Sqdn; *Style—* Sir Duncan Oppenheim; 43 Edwardes Square, Kensington, London W8 (☎ 071 603 7431)

OPPENHEIM, Martin John Marcus; s of Henry John Oppenheim of Maidenhead and Beryl *née* Harpham; *b* 25 May 1950; *Educ* Cheadle Hulme Sch, King Edward VII Lytham; *m* 1, 2 Nov 1971, Dawn, da of Stanley Wells of Maidenhead; 3 s (Marcus b 1976, Karl b 1979, Maximillian b 1981), 1 da (Alexis b 1981); m 2, 6 Sept 1986, Krystyna, da of Stanislaw Banasiak of Southend on Sea; *Career* chartered accountant 1973; *Recreations* yachting, bridge; *Style—* Martin Oppenheim, Esq; 6 Porter St, London W1M 1HZ (☎ 071 935 2372, fax 071 486 0640, car 0836 213174)

OPPENHEIM, (James) Nicholas; *b* 15 June 1947; *Educ* Edinburgh Acad, Univ of Columbia; *Career* dir: Kellock Trust plc 1976-86, Sterling Credit Group plc 1980-82, Argyle Trust plc 1982-, The Smaller Companies International Trust plc 1982-89, Sterling Trust plc 1983-, Courtwell Group plc 1986-90, Whitegate Leisure 1987-, Tranwood plc 1988; *Style—* Nicholas Oppenheim, Esq; Whitegate Leisure plc, 39 King St, London EC2V 2DQ (☎ 071 623 9021, fax 071 606 3025)

OPPENHEIM, Hon Phillip Anthony Charles Lawrence; MP (C) Amber Valley 1983-; o s of Henry M Oppenheim (d 1980), and Baroness Oppenheim-Barnes, PC (Life Peer), *qv*; *b* 20 March 1956; *Educ* Harrow, Oriel Coll Oxford (MA); *Career* former dir What to Buy plc (own co founded 1978, sold to Reed International 1989); publishing offices in London and New York; PPS to Sec of State for Educn and Sci 1990-; rugby player for Amber Valley RUFC; landowner (270 acres); *Publications* One New Masters (1991) and 3 books on new technology; *Recreations* rugby, chess, travel, reading, tennis, skiing; *Clubs* Leabrooks Miners Welfare, Annabels; *Style—* The Hon Phillip Oppenheim, MP

OPPENHEIM-BARNES, Baroness (Life Peer UK 1989), of Gloucester in the Co of Gloucester; Sally Oppenheim-Barnes; PC (1979); da of late Mark and Jeanette Viner, of Sheffield; *b* 26 July 1930; *Educ* Sheffield HS, Lowther Coll N Wales; *m* 1, 1949, Henry M Oppenheim (d 1980); 1 s (Hon Philip Anthony Charles Lawrence, *qv*), 2 da (Hon Caroline Selman, Hon Roseane Oppenheim); m 2, 1984, John Barnes; *Career* MP (Cons) Gloucester 1970-87 (when her s Philip, *qv*, was elected MP 1983, it was the first time that both a mother and son sat in the same Parl); formerly social worker with ILEA; chm Cons Parly Prices and Consumer Protection Ctee 1973-74 (vice-chm 1971-73), front bench oppn spokesman (seat in Shadow Cabinet) Prices and Consumer Protection 1974-79, min state (consumer affrs) Dept of Trade 1979-82, chm Ctee of Enquiry into Pedestrian Safety at Public Road Level Crossings 1982-; non-exec dir: Boots Co Main Bd 1982-, Fleming High Income Investment Tst 1989-, HFC Bank plc 1990-; memb House of Commons Ctee of Privileges, pres Br Red Cross Soc Glos Dist; chm Nat Consumer Cncl 1987-89; Nat Waterway Museum Tst; *Recreations* tennis, bridge; *Clubs* Glos Cons Assoc, Vanderbilt Racquet; *Style—* The Baroness Oppenheim-Barnes, PC; Quietways, The Highlands, Painswick, Gloucestershire

OPPENHEIMER, Brent; s of Klaus Oppenheimer of Fidaz Switzerland, and Jetty, *née* Knecht; *b* 5 Oct 1962; *Educ* Hyde Park HS Johnannesburg S Africa, Technican Witwatersrand (HND, Gold award Int Letraset Student Design Competition 1984); *Career* Nat Serv S African Def Force Bombardier 14 Field Artillery; freelance art dir Collet Dickenson Pearce & Ptnrs and G M H Advertising (Johannesburg S Africa) 1984-85; art dir Publicis FCB Lausanne Switzerland 1985-89, assoc dir graphic design Addison Design Consultants London 1989-; nat advtg campaigns incl: Stellenbosch Farmers Winery (SA) 1984, Nesquik (Switzerland) 1988, Union Swiss Banks (Switzerland) 1988, Heineken Beer (Switzerland) 1989, Nespresso (Europe) 1989; nat and int design progs incl: Nestlé (Switzerland) 1985-89, corporate identify prog Telefonie (Switzerland 1987, AVE (Alta Velocidad Español) Spain 1990-91; *Recreations* squash, skiing, travel; *Style—* Brent Oppenheimer, Esq; Addison Design Consultants, 60 Britton St, London EC1M 5NA (☎ 071 250 1887, fax 071 251 3712)

OPPENHEIMER, Lady (Laetitia) Helen; da of Sir Hugh Munro-Lucas-Tooth, 1 Bt (d 1985), of Burgate Court, Fordingbridge, Hants, and Lady Munro-Lucas-Tooth, OBE, *née* Laetitia Florence Findlay (d 1978); *b* 30 Dec 1926; *Educ* Cheltenham Ladies' Coll, Lady Margaret Hall Oxford (BPhil, MA); *m* 12 July 1947, Sir Michael Bernard Grenville Oppenheimer, Bt, qv, s of Sir Michael Oppenheimer, Bt, (d 1933), of Johannesburg S Africa; 3 da (Henrietta (Mrs Adam Scott) b 1954, Matilda (Mrs Neil King) b 1956, Xanthe (Hon Mrs Ivo Mosley) b 1958); *Career* lectr in ethics Cuddesdon Theological Coll 1964-69; served on: Archbishop of Canterbury's Gp on the law of divorce (report, Putting Asunder 1966), C of E Marriage Cmmn (report, Marriage Divorce and the Church 1971), Working Party Advsy Cncl for the Church's Miny Report (Teaching Christian Ethics 1974), C of E Working Party on Educn in Personal Relationships (chm), The Inter-Anglican Theological and Doctrinal Cmmn (report For the Sake of the Kingdom 1986), Gen Synod Working Party on the Law of Marriage (report An Honourable Estate 1988); pres Soc for the Study of Christian Ethics 1989; *Books* Law and Love (1962), The Character of Christian Morality (1965, 2 ed 1974), Incarnation and Immanence (1973), The Marriage Bond (1976), The Hope of Happiness (1983), Looking before and after: The Archbishop of Canterbury's Lent Book for 1988, Marriage (In series Ethics: our choices 1990); *Style—* Lady Oppenheimer; L'Aiguillon, Grouville, Jersey, Channel Islands JE3 9AP (☎ 0534 54466)

OPPENHEIMER, Michael Anthony; s of Felix Oppenheimer (d 1962), of Highgate, and Ingeborg Hanna Oppenheimer; *b* 22 Sept 1946; *Educ* Westminster, LSE (LLB); *m* 14 April 1973, Nicola Anne, da of Basil Vincent Brotherton (d 1961), of Pinner; 1 s (James b 1980), 1 da (Rebecca b 1978); *Career* called to the Bar Middle Temple 1970 (Blackstone exhibitioner); memb SE Circuit, asst rec 1985, rec 1989; memb: Common Law and Commercial Bar Assoc, Family Law Bar Assoc; *Recreations* cinema, theatre, books, performing and listening to music; *Clubs* Athenaeum; *Style—* Michael Oppenheimer, Esq; 58 Airedale Avenue, London W4 2NN (☎ 081 994 5090); 5 Raymond Buildings, Gray's Inn, London WC1R 5BP (☎ 071 831 0720, fax 071 831 0626)

OPPENHEIMER, Sir Michael Bernard Grenville; 3rd Bt (UK 1921), of Stoke Poges, Co Bucks; s of Sir Michael Oppenheimer, 2nd Bt (d 1933 after a flying accident), and Caroline da of Sir Robert Harvey, 2, last Bt, and sis of Diana, Lady Balfour of Inchrye (divorced w of 1 Baron); *b* 27 May 1924; *Educ* Charterhouse, ChCh Oxford (BLitt, MA); *m* 1947, (Laetitia) Helen, er da of Sir Hugh Munro-Lucas-Tooth, 1 Bt; 3 da (Henrietta (Mrs Adam Scott) b 1954, Matilda (Mrs Neil King) b 1956, Xanthe (Hon Mrs Ivo Mosley) b 1958); *Heir* none; *Career* served WWII, Middle East and Italy, SA Artillery, Lt; university lecturer in politics: Lincoln Coll Oxford 1955-68, Magdalen Coll Oxford 1966-68; *Clubs* Kimberley (S Africa), Victoria (Jersey); *Style—* Sir Michael Oppenheimer, Bt; L'Aiguillon, Grouville, Jersey, CI

OPPENHEIMER, Peter Morris; s of Friedrich Rudolf Openheimer, of London, and Charlotte Oppenheimer; *b* 16 April 1938; *Educ* Haberdashers' Aske's, The Queen's Coll Oxford (BA); *m* 30 July 1964, Catherine Violet Rosalie Pasternak, da of Eliot Trevor Oakeshott Slater, CBE, MD (d 1983); 2 s (Daniel b 1967, Joseph b 1971), 1 da (Tamara b 1973); *Career* Nat Serv RN 1956-58, ret Lt Cdr RNR 1978; Bank for International Settlements 1961-64, res fell and actg investmt bursar Nuffield Coll Oxford 1964-67, fell econs Ch Ch Oxford 1967-, visiting prof int fin London Graduate Sch of Business Studies 1977-78, chief economist Shell Int Petroleum Co 1985-86; Freeman Worshipful Co of Haberdashers 1987; *Recreations* swimming, skiing, theatre, opera, music; *Style—* Peter Oppenheimer, Esq; 8 Lathbury Rd, Oxford OX2 7AU (☎ 0865 58226); Christ Church, Oxford OX1 1DP (☎ 0865 276220, fax 0865 276276, car 0831 114616)

OPPENHEIMER, Sir Philip Jack; s of Otto Oppenheimer, and Beatrice, *née* Rose; *b* 29 Oct 1911; *Educ* Harrow, Jesus Coll Cambridge (BA); *m* 1935, Pamela Fenn, da of Carl Ludwig Stirling, CBE, QC; 1 s, 1 da; *Career* served WW II RA, cmmnd Berkshire Yeomanry 1940, combined ops Special Service 1942, Lt-Col Italy and M East; chm The Diamond Trading Co (Pty) Ltd, dep chm Charter Consolidated to 1982; dir: De Beers Consolidated Mines, Anglo American Corporation of South Africa Ltd; Bronze Cross of Holland 1943, Cdr Ordre de Leopold 1977; kt 1970; *Recreations* horse racing and breeding, golf; *Clubs* Jockey, White's, Portland; *Style—* Sir Philip Oppenheimer

OPPERMAN, Hon Sir Hubert Ferdinand; OBE (1952); s of late A Opperman; *b* 29 May 1904; *Educ* Armadale State Sch; *m* 1928, Mavys Paterson, da of Harold Craig; 1 s, 1 da (decd); *Career* former champion cyclist, holder of numerous world cycling records; MHR for Corio Vic 1949-67, chief govt whip 1955-60; min for: Shipping and Transport 1960-63, Immigration 1963-67; Aust high cmmr in Malta 1967-72; Medals of City of Paris 1971, Brest 1971, Verona 1972, Médaille Mérite French Cycling Fedn 1978; OStJ 1974; kt 1968; *see Debrett's Handbook of Australia and New Zealand for further details*; *Style—* The Hon Sir Hubert Opperman, OBE; 6A-12 Marine Parade, St Kilda, Vic 3182, Australia

ORAM, Baron (Life Peer UK 1975), of Brighton, in the Co of E Sussex; Albert Edward Oram; s of Henry Oram (d 1963), and Ada Edith Oram; *b* 13 Aug 1913; *Educ* Burgess Hill Elementary Sch, Brighton GS, LSE; *m* 1956, (Frances) Joan, da of Arthur Charles Barber, of Lewes, Sussex; 2 s (Hon Mark b 1967, Hon Robin b 1968); *Career* served WWII 1942-45; sits as Labour peer in House of Lords; research offr Co-operative Party 1946-55; MP (Lab and Co-op) East Ham (South) 1955-74; Parly sec Miny Overseas Devpt 1964-69; a lord-in-waiting to HM The Queen (govt whip) 1976-78, Lords rep on Shadow Cabinet 1983-87; chm Co-Operative Development Agency 1978-81; *Books* Changes in China (with Nora Stettner); *Style—* The Rt Hon the Lord Oram; 19 Ridgeside Ave, Patcham, Brighton, E Sussex BN1 8WD (☎ 0273 505333)

ORAM, Daphne Blake; da of James Oram, MBE, JP (d 1964), of Devizes, Wiltshire, and Ida Murton Talbot (d 1972); *b* 31 Dec 1925; *Educ* Sherborne; *Career* music balancer BBC 1943-57, co-fndr and dir BBC Radiophonic Workshop 1958; dir: Oramics Studio 1959-, Essconic Ltd 1959-75; visiting lectr: Morley Coll London 1959, Christ Church Coll Canterbury 1982-89; Gulbenkian Fndn Awards 1962 and 1965, Arts Cncl bursary 1986, RVW Tst 3 year grant 1986-89; lectures and concerts: Edinburgh Festival, Mermaid Theatre, Inst of Physics, various univs and schs; inventor Oramics (graphic sound); various compositions for film, TV, radio, ballet; memb: Music Ctee Arts Cncl 1968-78, Mgmnt Ctee Performing Right Soc London (Members Fund); *Books* An Individual Note of Music, Sound and Electronics; *Recreations* megalithic archaeology, reading, animals; *Style—* Daphne Oram; Tower Folly, Fairseat, Wrotham, Sevenoaks, Kent TN15 7JR

ORAM, Douglas Richard; s of Alfred Richard Oram (d 1980), of London, and Gladys, *née* Lungley (d 1955); *b* 29 March 1942; *Educ* Licensed Victuallers' Sch, Southgate Co GS, Hendon Tech Coll; *m* 24 Sept 1966, Jannet Adyne, da of Ascensio Joseph Echevarria (d 1988), and Obdulia Ines, *née* Irureta, of Villajoyosa, Alicante, Spain; 2 s (Somerset b 17 March 1981, Sebastian b 12 Nov 1982); *Career* purchasing mangr then dir Centre Hotels (Cranston) Ltd 1965-75, purchasing mangr The Dorchester 1975-78, purchasing dir Comfort Hotels Int 1978-85, Metropole Hotels 1985-; former memb POUNC; former chm: Membership Servs Ctee BHRCA, Champagne Acad; memb: English Advsy Ctee on Telecommunications, Telecommunications Numbering and Addressing Bd, Ctee of Mgmnt Hotel and Catering Benevolent Assoc, Old Metronians Assoc; vice chm Child Growth Fndn; co-ordinator Boue Dysplasia Gp; FHCIMA 1984, MInstPS 1988; *Style—* Douglas Oram, Esq; Metropole Hotels (Holdings) Limited, PO Box 335, National Exhibition Centre, Birmingham B40 1PT (☎ 021 780 4266, telex 94011994, fax 021 780 2116)

ORAM, Rt Rev Kenneth Cyril; s of Alfred Charles Oram (d 1962), of London, and Sophie Oram (d 1944); *b* 3 March 1919; *Educ* Selhurst GS, King's Coll London (BA, AKC), Lincoln Theol Coll; *m* 4 Sept 1943, Kathleen Mary, da of William Gregory Malcolm (d 1949); 3 s (Andrew b 1945, Stephen b 1949, Vincent b 1955), 1 da (Ruth b 1947); *Career* ordained: deacon 1942, priest 1943; asst curate: Cranbrook Kent 1942-45, St Mildred Addiscombe Croydon 1945-46, Upington and Prieska SA 1946-48; rector: Prieska 1949-51, Mafeking 1952-59, archdeacon of Bechuanaland and diocesan dir of Educn 1953-59; dean: Kimberley 1960-64, Grahamstown 1964-74; bishop Grahamstown SA 1974-87 (dean of province 1983-87), asst bishop Lichfield 1987; *Recreations* music, walking; *Style—* The Rt Rev Kenneth Oram; 10 Sandringham Road, Stafford ST17 OAA (☎ 0785 53974)

ORAM, Dr Samuel; s of Samuel Henry Nathan Oram (d 1956), and Ada, *née* Dennis (d 1966); *b* 11 July 1913; *Educ* King's Coll London, King's Coll Hosp London (MD, LRCP, MRCP); *m* 20 Jan 1940, Ivy Rose, da of Raffaele Amato (d 1961); 2 da (Helen Ivy (Mrs Bellringer) b 1942, Christine Rose (Mrs Oram-Rayson) b 1947); *Career* WWII Lt-Col RAMC: serv Europe, W Africa, India, Andaman Islands; conslt physician in private practice 1947-; King's Coll Hosp: conslt physician 1947-78, dir Cardiac Dept 1959-78, sr physician 1969-78; conslt cardiologist Croydon Gp of Hosps 1948-69, chief med offr Sun Life of Canada Life Assurance Co 1952-83, med advsr Rio Tinto Zinc Corpn Ltd 1970-85; examiner in medicine: Univ of London, RCP, Soc of Apothecaries; assessor of MD Theses Univ of Cambridge, censor RCP 1972-74, conslt cardiologist King's Health Dist (teaching) 1980, emeritus lectr in med King's Coll Med Sch 1980; hon sec and treas Br Cardiac Soc 1951-56, pres Soc of Cardiological Technicians 1969-72; author of over 100 published papers; MRCS, FRCP; *Books* Clinical Heart Disease (2 edn, 1981); *Recreations* golf, French; *Style—* Dr Samuel Oram; 133 Cedar Drive, Parklands, Chichester, W Sussex PO19 3EL (☎ 0243 785521); 73 Harley St, oondon W1N 1DE (☎ 071 935 9942)

ORANGE, Brian Peter Harvey; s of Richard Brian Orange (d 1963), and Mary Alice Kekewich, *née* Harvey (d 1979); *b* 4 March 1946; *Educ* Winchester, Univ of Birmingham (BSc); *m* 23 May 1970, Anne Denise, da of Hon Denis Gomer Berry (d 1983), of Brockenhurst Park; 3 s (Michael b 1973, Simon b 1974, Jonathan b 1976); *Career* md Orange Chemicals Ltd Winchester 1976-; cdr St John Ambulance Bde Hampshire 1985-; CStJ 1987; *Recreations* sailing, shooting, skiing and collecting bookmatches; *Clubs* Hampshire, Bembridge Sailing; *Style—* Brian P H Orange, Esq; Fromans House, Kings Somborne, Hants (☎ 0794 388 235); Orange Chemicals Ltd, 34 St Thomas Street, Winchester, Hampshire (☎ 0962 842525)

ORANGE, Charles William; s of Richard Brian Orange (d 1963), of Oxshott, Surrey, and Mary Alice Kekewich, *née* Harvey (d 1979); *b* 23 June 1942; *Educ* Winchester; *m* 14 July 1973, Jane (d 1990), da of (George) Peter Humphreys-Davies, CBE (d 1986), of Bucks Green, Sussex; 3 s (Richard b 1975, Hugh b 1978, George b 1980); *Career* asst mangr Peat Marwick Mitchell & Co 1968-71, gp fin controller UBM Gp plc 1973-82; fin dir: AAH Hldgs plc 1982-84, Assoc Br Ports 1985-, Assoc Br Ports Hldgs plc 1987-; former: ctee memb West of Eng Soc of CAs, chm sch PTA; FCA; *Recreations* tennis, opera, sheep; *Style—* Charles Orange, Esq; Hascombe, Godalming, Surrey GU8 4JA; Associated British Ports Holdings plc, 150 Holborn, London EC1N 2LR (☎ 071 430 1177, fax 071 430 1384, telex 23913)

ORANMORE AND BROWNE, 4 Baron (I 1836); Dominick Geoffrey Edward Browne; also (sits as) 2 Baron Mereworth (UK 1926); s of 3 Baron, KP, PC (d 1927), and Lady Olwen Ponsonby, da of 8 Earl of Bessborough, KP; *b* 21 Oct 1901; *Educ* Eton, Ch Ch Oxford; *m* 1, 1925, Mildred Helen (m dis 1936 and who d 1980 having m as her 2 husb Hon Hew Dalrymple, 2 s of 12 Earl of Stair), da of Hon Thomas Egerton (d 1953, 3 s of 3 Earl of Ellesmere and unc of 6 Duke of Sutherland) and Lady Bertha, *née* Anson, da of 3 Earl of Lichfield; 2 s, 1 da (and 2 da decd); m 2, 1936 (m dis 1950) Oonagh, da of Hon Arthur Ernest Guinness (d 1949), gda of 1 Earl of Iveagh and sis of Maureen Marchioness of Dufferin and Ava; 1 s (and 2 s decd); m 3, 1950, Constance Vera (the actress Sally Gray), da of Charles Stevens; *Heir* s, Hon Dominick Geoffrey Thomas Browne; *Style—* The Rt Hon the Lord Oranmore and Browne; 52 Eaton Place, London SW1

ORBIT, William (real name William Wainwright); s of William Mark Wainwright, of London, and Doreen Christina, *née* Ferrari; *Educ* Minchenden Comprehensive Sch; *m* 1980 (m dis 1985), Linda Mary Vizor; 1 da (Emily Evelyn b 12 April 1980); *Career* prodr, remixer and memb Bass-O-Matic and Torchsong, film maker, DJ recordings incl: Exhibit A (LP 1987, IRS Records) Torchsong, Strange Cargo (solo LP 1990, IRS Records); Bass-O-Matic recordings: In The Realm of the Senses (single 1990), Fascinating Rhythm (single 1990), Ease On By (single 1990); produced and remixed: Belinda (LP 1986, IRS Records, Platinum disc) Belinda Carlise, Star (12 inch 1990, Mute Records) Erasure, Batdance (12 inch 1990, Worner Bros) Prince, The Future (12 inch 1990, Warner Bros) Prince, Hey Music Lover and Mantra For A State of Hind (12 inch 1989, Rhythm King Records) S-Express, Deep In Vogue (12 inch 1989, CBS Records) Malcolm McLaren, Englishman in New York (12 inch 1990, Rough Trade) Sting, Justify My Love (12 inch, Sire Records) Madonna, Krazy (12 inch, ZTT

Records) Seal, In Between Days (single 1990, Fiction Records) The Cure, She's A Woman (12 inch 1990, Virgin) Scritti Politti; *Recreations* sculpture; *Style*— William Orbit, Esq; c/o O'Dell Artists Management, 10 Sutherland Ave, London W9 2HQ (☎ 071 286 5487, fax 071 266 3283)

ORCHARD, John Charles Johnson; s of Ronald Stark Orchard, of London and Nancy Margaret, *née* Heywood (d 1986); *b* 9 March 1939; *Educ* Harrow Emmanuel Coll Cambridge (MA, LLB); *m* 12 Aug 1967, Cynthia Diana, da of Cdr Clifford Maddocks (d 1974); 1 s (Alaister b 1971), 1 da (Alexandra b 1969); *Career* Nat Serv Sub Lt RNR 1958-60; admitted slr 1967; Syndey Morse & Co London 1963-68, managing ptnr Pinsent & Co Birmingham (joined 1968); *Recreations* Chinese porcelain, shooting, flyfishing, prawning, gardening, English period furniture, pre-Columbian pottery; *Style*— John Orchard, Esq; Pinsent & Co, Post & Mail House, 26 Colmore Circus, Birmingham B4 6BH (☎ 021 200 1050, fax 021 200 1040, telex 335101 PINCO G)

ORCHARD, Jurat John James Morel; s of James William Orchard (d 1960), and Dorothy, *née* Harwood; *b* 4 June 1924; *Educ* UK and Ireland; *m* 24 Dec 1949, Maureen; 3 s (Martin b 1952, Nicholas b 1957, Jeremy b 1963); *Career* served Air Crew RAF 1942-47; with Midland Bank Ltd 1940-82; dir: Bank of Ireland (Jersey) Ltd 1983-, Aberdeen Mortgage Placement Co (CI) Ltd 1984-, Planet Financial and Legal Services Ltd 1984-; chm Bank of Ireland Tst Co (Jersey) Ltd 1984- (dir 1983); Jurat of The Royal Ct 1986-; AIB; *Recreations* sailing; *Clubs* Royal Channel Islands Yacht (Cdre); United; *Style*— Jurat John Orchard; La Vieille Maison, St Peter, Jersey, CI

ORCHARD, Hon Mrs (Modwena Louise); da of 6 Baron Hatherton (d 1973), by his 2 w, Mary, Baroness Hatherton, *qv*; *b* 1947; *Educ* St Catherine's (Bude), Châtelard (Switzerland), Lonsdale (Norwich); *m* 1, 1968 (m dis 1974), Edward Willison; 2 da (Trecia b 1969, Rachel b 1971); m 2, 1978, Peter Fleming Orchard, s of Capt Frederick Henry Orchard (d 1958); 1 child; *Style*— The Hon Mrs Orchard; Copper Beeches, 9A Hartland Rd, Epping, Essex (☎ 0378 75601)

ORCHARD, Peter Francis; CBE (1982); s of Edward Henslowe Orchard (d 1958); *b* 25 March 1927; *Educ* Downside, Magdalene Coll Cambridge; *m* 1955, Helen, da of Sir Joseph Sheridan (d 1964); 2 s (Rupert b 1957, Timothy b 1963), 2 da (Marianne b 1959, Josephine b 1964); *Career* Capt 60 Rifles 1944-48; The De La Rue Co plc 1950- (chief exec 1977-87, chm 1987-), md Thomas De La Rue Int 1962-70, dir Delta plc 1981-; memb: Ct of Assts Worshipful Co Drapers' (Master 1982); Hon Col 71 Yeo Signal Regt 1984-88; *Recreations* gardening, swimming, building, cricket; *Clubs* Travellers', MCC; *Style*— Peter Orchard, Esq, CBE; Willow Cottage, Little Hallingbury, Bishop's Stortford, Herts (☎ 0279 654101); The De La Rue Company plc, 5 Burlington Gardens, London W1A 1DL (☎ 071 734 8020)

ORCHARD, Dr Robin Theodore; s of George William Orchard, of Bexley Heath, Kent, and Christobel Edith Orchard; *b* 4 Oct 1940; *Educ* Chislehurst and Sidcup GS, Charing Cross Hosp Med Sch Univ of London (MB BS); *m* 5 June 1965, Ann Seymour, da of Dr Thomas Seymour Jones (d 1986), of Wimborne, Dorset; 2 s (Timothy, Christopher), 2 da (Kathryn, Elizabeth); *Career* sr registrar Charing Cross Hosp WC2 and W6 1970-74, sr lectr in med Royal Dental Hosp 1976-82, post grad clinical tutor St Helier Hosp 1978-86; conslt physician 1974-: St Helier Hosp Carshalton, Sutton Hosp, St Anthony's Hosp N Cheam; hon sr lectr St George's Hosp Med Sch 1982-, Univ of London examiner in medicine and dental surgery 1982-; churchwarden St John's Selsdon, Sy 1982-; Univ memb Croydon D H A 1987-90, med advsr St Helier Hosp Tst 1991; FRCP 1982, MRCS; *Recreations* cricket; *Style*— Dr Robin Orchard; Bowlers End, 67 Croham Rd, S Croydon, Surrey CR2 7HF (☎ 081 680 0253); St Helier Hosp, Wrythe Lane, Carshalton (☎ 081 644 4343)

ORCHARD-LISLE, Geoffrey; s of Edwin Orchard-Lisle (d 1934), and Lucy Ellen Orchard-Lisle, *née* Lock; *b* 11 June 1910; *Educ* W Buckland Sch, Devon; *m* 16 Oct 1944, Rhona, da of George Comrie Nickels (d 1953); 2 s (John David b 1945, Simon Comrie b 1949); *Career* WWII Maj RA (anti-aircraft) England; jt md J Avery & Co (Est 1834) and subsid cos (md 1953-70); pres Nat Assoc of Window Blind Manufacturers; *Recreations* cricket, golf; *Clubs* East Hert Golf, MCC, Southgate (represented CC Conference 1934, captained West End CC Business Assoc 1933); *Style*— Geoffrey Orchard-Lisle, Esq; Old Gaylors, Westmill, Buntingford, Herts SG9 9LB (☎ 0763 71530)

ORCHARD-LISLE, Mervyn Christopher; s of Ulric Lock Orchard-Lisle (d 1955), and Thelma Julie Spelman, *née* Burdett; *b* 6 June 1946; *Educ* Marlborough, Univ of Newcastle upon Tyne (BA, BArch); *m* 24 March 1979, Angela Jane, da of Edmund Louis Saunders, of Henham, Essex; 1 s (Alexander b 1985), 1 da (Lucy b 1983); *Career* chartered architect in private practice 1973-, sr ptnr Gotelee Orchard-Lisle; RIBA 1973; *Recreations* watercolours, books, motor cars, family life; *Style*— Mervyn Orchard-Lisle, Esq; Shepherd's Cottage, Heath End, East Woodhay, Newbury, Berks (☎ 0635 254282); c/o Gotelee Orchard-Lisle, 6 Cromwell Place, Northbrook St, Newbury, Berks (☎ 0635 36600, fax 0635 31421)

ORCHARD-LISLE, Mervyn George; MBE (1946); s of late Edwin Orchard-Lisle, of Wembley, Middx, and late Lucy Ellen, *née* Lock; *b* 10 Oct 1912; *Educ* West Buckland Sch Devon, Coll of Estate Mgmnt; *m* 1, 5 June 1937, Phyllis Eileen Yvonne (d 1976), da of David Jones, of Wembley, Middx; 1 s (Paul David b 3 Aug 1938); m 2, 9 Dec 1977, Judith Ann, *née* Harrington; *Career* Maj RM Served RM Div, Combined Ops Landing Craft, 4 Commando Bde 1940-45, Admiralty 1945-46; Healey & Baker: joined 1930, ptnr 1947-76, sr ptnr 1974-76, ret 1976; pres: Herts Golf Union 1964-67, Herts Co Professional Golf Union 1959-63, the Golf Club Stewards Assoc of GB 1955-65; memb: bd of govrs St Paul's, St Phillip's and St Peter's Hosps 1957-64, Ctee Mgmnt Inst of Urobgy 1959-66; FRICS; *Recreations* cricket, golf, travel, racing; *Clubs* Carlton, Turf, MCC; *Style*— Mervyn Orchard-Lisle, Esq, MBE; Les Vergers, Route De Fuont De Purgue, Tourrettes-sur-loup, 06140, Vence, France (☎ 01033 93 59 34 92, fax 01033 93 59 38 39)

ORCHARD-LISLE, Paul David; CBE (1988), TD (1971), DL (1986); s of Mervyn George Orchard-Lisle, MBE, of Les Vergers, Tourrettes sur Loup, Vence, France, and Phyllis Yvonne, *née* Jones (d 1975); *b* 3 Aug 1938; *Educ* Marlborough, Trinity Hall Cambridge (MA); *Career* chartered surveyor, sr ptnr Healey & Baker 1988; pres RICS 1985-6; Brig (TA) UKLF 1985; govr: Harrow Sch 1987, West Buckland Sch 1985; memb Cncl of Univ of Reading; FRICS, FRSA; *Recreations* golf, squash; *Clubs* Athenaeum; *Style*— Paul Orchard-Lisle, Esq, CBE, TD, DL; Bedford House, Bidwell, Bedfordshire LU5 6JP (☎ 0582 867317); Healey & Baker, 29 St George St, Hanover Square, London W1A 3BG (☎ 071 629 9292)

ORD, Richard John; s of Richard Ord, of 42 Truro Ave, Murton, Seaham, Co Durham, and Enid, *née* Walton; *b* 3 March 1970; *Educ* Easington Secdy Sch; partner, Nicola Jane Stevens; *Career* professional footballer; Sunderland 1987-, won 7-0 on debut v Southend Utd, 80 appearances; 3 league appearances on-loan York City 1990; 1 England under 21 cap v Wales; *Recreations* cricket, golf; *Style*— Richard Ord, Esq; 32 Windslonnen, Murton Seaham, Co Durham (☎ 091 5269326); Sunderland FC, Roker Park, Sunderland, Tyne & Wear (☎ 091 5140332)

ORD, Robert Andrew; s of Robert Ord, of 116 Heath Park Ave, Heath ,Cardiff, and Joan Margaret, *née* Watson; *b* 14 Jan 1948; *Educ* King's Coll Hosp London (BDS), Univ Hosp Wales Cardiff (MB BCh); *m* 30 Dec 1970, Philippa Ruth, *née* Matthew; 3 s (Robert Matthew, James Rhodri, Joel Anthony); *Career* registrar of maxillofacial surgery Canniesburn Hosp Glasgow 1978-80; sr registrar 1980-84: King's Coll London, Queen Victoria Hosp E Grinstead; conslt oral and maxillofacial surgery 1985-: Sunderland, Durham, Shotley Bridge, South Shields Hosps; memb: BAOMFS, EAMFS, IAOMFS, EAFPS, AHNOGN; LDSRCS, FDSRCPS, FRCS(Ed); *Books* Medical Wall Blowouts (1981), Retro-Bulbar Haemorrhage (1981), Cancrum Oris (1983), Parotid Disease in Nigeria (1984), Osteomyelitis of the Mandible in Children (1987), Carcinoma of the Lip (1987), Metastatic Melanoma of the Parotid (1989); contrib: Oral Cancer and Jaw Tumours (1988), Dental Patient Vol 1 (1988), Mouth and Perioral Tissues Vol 2 (1989), Clinical Dentistry in Health and Disease (1989), Year Book of Dentistry (1989); *Recreations* flyfishing, watercolour painting; *Style*— Robert Ord, Esq; 116 Heath Park Ave, Heath, Cardiff; 10356 Tuscany Rd, Ellicott City, Maryland 20143, USA; Dept of Oral and Maxillo-Facial Surgery, Sunderland District General Hospital, Kayll Rd, Sunderland, Tyne and Wear SR2 7TW (☎ 0222 751939)

ORD-HUME, Arthur W J G; s of Arthur W Ord-Hume (d 1957), and Rosina May, *née* Tickner (d 1955); *b* 20 May 1932; *Educ* Wellington, Harrow, Univ of London (BSc); *m* 1, 4 April 1952 (m dis 1967), June Brenda, da of Brig-Gen Jack Castles (d 1965); m 2, 1968, Judith Rose, *née* Resnick; 2 s (James Edward b 1953, John Geoffrey b 1971), 1 da (Elizabeth Ann b 1973); *Career* Serv RAF 1949-55; historian, restorer of musical instruments; chief of design Agricultural Aviation Co, mangr Southern Aircraft Co, dir Britten-Norman Ltd, md Phoenix Aircraft Ltd, prof of history of instruments of music, their technology and restoration, ed Music and Automata (jl); fndr and curator The Ord-Hume Library of Mechanical Music and Horology, fndr and former pres Musical Box Soc of UK, memb numerous socs and musical assocs; *Books* incl: Collecting Musical Boxes and How to Repair Them (1967), Clockwork Music - An Illustrated History (1973), Perpetual Motion (1975), Restoring Musical Boxes (1980), Pianola - The History and Development of the Self-Playing Piano (1984), Harmonium - the History and Development of the Free Reed Organ (1986); *Recreations* music, flying; *Style*— Arthur W J G Ord-Hume, Esq; Plestor House, Farnham Rd, West Liss, Hampshire GU33 6JQ (☎ 0730 894059, fax 0730 895298)

ORDE; *see*: Campbell-Orde

ORDE, David John; JP (Northumberland 1965-87); s of Charles William Orde, KCMG (d 1980), and Frances Fortune, *née* Davidson (d 1949); *b* 25 Aug 1917; *Educ* Eton, ChCh Oxford (BA, MA); *m* 1, 14 April 1942 (m dis 1947), Olivia Frances, da of late Richard Evelyn Beauchamp Meade-King; m 2, 10 June 1950, Audrey Elizabeth, da of Alfred Douglas Boot (d 1936); 1 s (Michael b 1957), 3 da (Lucinda (Mrs DWV Bennett) b 1951, Rosemary (Mrs HD Oliphant) b 1953, Daphne (Mrs DIM Farquharson) b 1956); *Career* WWII Capt RA 1939-46; chartered surveyor and land agent; High Sheriff Northumberland 1970; FLAS 1954, FRICS; *Recreations* walking; *Style*— David Orde, Esq, JP; 14 Thorp Ave, Morpeth, Northumberland NE61 1JS (☎ 0670 514435)

ORDE, His Hon Judge Denis Alan; s of John Orde, CBE, of Littlehoughton Hall, Northumberland, and Charlotte Lilian Orde (d 1975); *b* 28 Aug 1932; *Educ* Univ of Oxford (MA); *m* 1961, Jennifer Jane, da of Dr John Longworth (d 1982), of Mill Hill, Masham, Yorks; 2 da (Georgina Jane, Phillipa Denise); *Career* served Army 1950-52, cmmnd 2 Lt 1951; RA (TA) 1952-64; barr Inner Temple 1956, recorder 1972-79, circuit judge 1979-, liaison judge to Magistrates 1983-, res judge of a Crown Court 1986-; Chollerton PCC 1980-, vice pres Lawn Tennis Assoc 1982-, memb Lord Chllr's Co Advsy Ctee 1986-; *Recreations* cricket, listening to music, biography, oil paintings of 19th Century, travel in France; *Clubs* Northern Counties; *Style*— His Hon Judge Orde; Chollerton Grange, Chollerton, nr Hexham, Northumberland; 11 King's Bench Walk, Temple, London EC4

ORDE-POWLETT, Hon (Patrick) Christopher; s of late 6 Baron Bolton; *b* 1931; *Educ* Eton, Jesus Coll Cambridge (MA); *m* 1962, Elizabeth Jane, da of A S Kent, of Worlington, Bury St Edmunds; 2 da; *Career* forestry adviser; fin mgmnt conslt Allied Dunbar; ARICS; *Style*— The Hon Christopher Orde-Powlett; Little Bordeaux, Little Chesterford, Saffron Walden, Essex CB10 1UA (☎ : 0799 30410); (office ☎ 0223 323811)

ORDE-POWLETT, Hon Harry Algar Nigel; s and h of 7 Baron Bolton and his 1 w, Hon Christine Weld-Forester (now Hon Mrs Miles), da of 7 Baron Forester; *b* 14 Feb 1954; *Educ* Eton; *m* 1977, Philippa, da of Maj Peter Tapply; 3 s (Thomas Peter Algar b 16 July 1979, William Benjamin b 1981, Nicholas Mark b 1985); *Style*— The Hon Harry Orde-Powlett; The Corner House, Wensley, Leyburn, N Yorks

ORDE-POWLETT, Hon Michael Brooke; yr s of 7 Baron Bolton and his 1 w, Hon Christine Helena, *née* Weld-Forester (now Hon Mrs Miles), da of 7 Baron Forester; *b* 21 April 1959; *Educ* Gordonstoun; *m* 17 Jan 1985, Kate Mary, da of George William Laing, of Newsham, N Yorks; 1 s (James Michael b 21 May 1987), 1 da (Emma Katherine b 29 Nov 1988); *Career* farmer, landowner (420 acres); *Recreations* water skiing, skiing, motor cycling; *Style*— The Hon Michael Orde-Powlett; Howe Hills Farm, Leyburn, N Yorks (☎ 0969 23746)

ORFORD, Dr Philip; s of Basil Henry Orford (d 1984), of Hampton in Arden, and Jacqueline Mary, *née* Hesketh; *b* 27 Oct 1953; *Educ* Wellesbourne Sch, Greenmore Coll, Queen's Coll, Karlsruhe Univ, Kensington Univ, California State Univ (MSc, PhD); *m* 6 April 1985, Carole Anne; 1 s (Alexander Graham b 6 Oct 1988), 1 da (Heidi Louise b 24 Oct 1990); *Career* Greenmore Coll Offr Trg Unit 1967-72; chm Wang Communications User Gp, reviewer Univ of California Riverside, ctee memb Unix Interest Gp (Computing), Esprit-It specialist Brussels, systems devpt conslt incl implementation of large scale computer aided design systems; govr: Royal Agric Soc of England, Three Counties Agric Soc; memb Assoc of Agric; FPWI, MIEEE, MIDPM; memb BCS; *Books* Analogue Design Concepts (1978), Design & Development of a 16 Channel Multi-Plexer (1982), Robotics & Artificial Intelligence (1985); *Recreations* farming, electronics, country pursuits; *Clubs* Fentham, Sheraton Int, Carlton; *Style*— Dr Philip Orford; Railway Technical Centre, London Rd, Derby DE2 8UP (☎ 0332 42442, fax 0332 290585, car 00 1042)

ORFORD, Richard Christopher Lewis; s of Christopher Wilson Orford (d 1978), late of Seer Green, Bucks, and Elizabeth Alice, *née* Sharpe, f in law was an eminent E N T surgeon at St Bartholomew's Hosp; *b* 13 Jan 1940; *Educ* Uppingham, Nat Inst of Dry Cleaning Silver Spring America; *m* 5 July 1969, Joan Emilia, da of Frederick Cecil Wray Capps (d 1970), of 16 Kent Terr, London NW1; 1 s (William b 1970), 1 da (Emily b 1972); *Career* launderer and dry cleaner; chm and md: Blue Dragon Hillingdon Ltd, Blue Dragon Beacon's Field Ltd, Blue Dragon Dry Cleaners Ltd; dir: Assoc of Br Launderers & Cleaners Ltd 1979, Assoc of Br Laundry Cleaning and Rental Servs Ltd 1984-88; Liveryman Worshipful Co of Launderers; *Recreations* sailing, skiing; *Clubs* Royal Southampton Yacht, Down Hill Only (skiing), Beaconsfield RFC (vice pres); *Style*— Richard Orford, Esq; Hutchins End, Knotty Green, Beaconsfield, Bucks HP9 1XL (☎ 0494 674642); Blue Dragon Hillingdon Ltd, Whiteleys Parade, Wybridge Rd, Hillingdon, Middx UB10 0NZ (☎ 0895 36571)

ORGA (D'ARCY-ORGA), (Hüsnü) Ateş; s of Capt Irfan Orga (d 1970), of Wadhurst, E Sussex, and Margaret Veronica, *née* D'Arcy-Wright (d 1974); *b* 6 Nov 1944; *Educ* Univ of Durham (B Mus), Trinity Coll of Music (FTCL); *m* 23 Nov 1974 (sep 1989), Josephine, da of Walter Richard Sidney Prior, of Ticehurst, E Sussex; 1 s (Alexander b 1983), 1 da (Chloë b 1980); *Career* prog annotator London Sinfonietta 1968-73, music info and presentation asst BBC Music Div London 1971-74, record prodr 1972-, lectr in music and concert dir Univ of Surrey 1975-90, artistic dir Inst of Armenian Music London 1976-80 (dir Music Armenia 78 London 1978), princ prog annotator London Symphony Orch 1976-81; examiner: Univ of Cambridge Local Examinations 1978-85, Associated Bd of the Royal Schools of Music 1981-; artistic conslt Sutton Place Heritage Tst Guildford 1983-86, artistic advsr Acad of the London Mozarteum 1988-, record prodr and conslt Collins Classics 1988-90, music dir V & A Museum Club 1988, special projects conslt The Entertainment Corp 1990, artistic dir Guildford 91 Int Music Festival 1991; mmeb Jury Royal Philharmonic Soc/Charles Heidsiech Champagne Music Awards 1990; contrib: The Listener, The Literary Review, Music and Musicians International, The Musical Times, Records and Recording, Hi Fi News; music panel chm S E Arts regnl arts assoc 1985-88 (vice chm 1984); *Books* The Proms (1974), Chopin: His Life and Times (1976), Beethoven: His Life and Times (1978), Records and Recording Classical Guides (1977-78), Portrait of a Turkish Family (1988); *Recreations* music occidental and oriental, food, watching people, matters Eastern European; *Style—* Ateş Orga, Esq; 102 Glisson Road, Cambridge CB1 2HQ (☎ 0223 65795, fax 0223 67627)

ORGAN, (Harold) Bryan; s of Harold Victor and Helen Dorothy Organ; *b* 31 Aug 1935; *Educ* Loughborough Coll of Art, Royal Academy Schs London; *m* Sandra Mary Mills; *Career* artist; lectr in drawing and painting Loughborough 1959-65; one-man exhibitions: Leicester, London, New York, Baukunst Cologne, Turin; represented: Kunsthalle, Darmstadt, Mostra Mercatao d'Arte Contemporanea Florence, 3rd Int Exhibitions of Drawing Germany, Sao Paulo Museum of Art Brazil; works in private and public collections in England, France, Germany, Italy, Switzerland, USA, Canada, Brazil; portraits include: Sir Michael Tippett, David Hicks, Mary Quant, Princess Margaret, Elton John, Harold Macmillan, The Prince of Wales, The Princess of Wales, Lord Denning, James Callaghan, The Duke of Edinburgh 1983; Hon MA Loughborough, Hon DLitt Univ of Leicester; *Style—* Bryan Organ, Esq; The Stables, Marston Trussell, nr Market Harborough, Leics; c/o Redfern Gallery, 20 Cork St, London W1

ORIEL, Susan Margaret Julie; da of David Keith Oriel, of Faversham, Kent, and Joan Julie, *née* Chapman (d 1985); *b* 15 June 1958; *Educ* James Allen's Girls' Sch Dulwich, Trinity Hall Cambridge (exhibitioner, BA), City of London Poly; ; 1 s (James Alexander b 19 Sept 1987); *Career* world travel 1981-83 (incl one year market res project Angus & Coote Pty Ltd Sydney), media trainee John Ayling & Associates 1983-84, media exec WCRS plc 1984-85, media dir FCO Ltd 1990- (joined as media mangr 1985); *Recreations* making cushions, removing lego from video machines, opera; *Style—* Ms Susan Oriel; FCO Limited, Eldon House, 1 Dorset St, London W1H 4BD (☎ 071 935 0334)

ORKNEY, 8 Earl of (S 1696); Cecil O'Bryen Fitz-Maurice; also Viscount Kirkwall and Lord Dechmont (both S 1696); s of late Douglas Frederick Harold Fitz-Maurice (himself gs of Cdr Hon Frederick Fitz-Maurice, who was in turn 3 s of 5 Earl); suc kinsman, 7 Earl, 1951; *b* 3 July 1919; *m* 1953, Rose Katherine Durk, da of late J W D Silley; *Heir* kinsman, Oliver Peter St John; *Career* sits as Conservative peer in House of Lords; joined RASC 1939, served 1939-45 (N Africa, Italy, France, Germany and Holland) and 1950-51 (Korea); *Style—* The Rt Hon Earl of Orkney; 4 Summerland, Princes Rd, Ferndown, Dorset (☎ 0202 893178)

ORLEBAR, Capt Christopher John Dugmore; s of Col John H R Orlebar, (d 1989), OBE, of St Helens, IOW, and Louise, *née* Crowe; *b* 4 Feb 1945; *Educ* Rugby, Univ of Southampton, Coll of Air Trg Hamble; *m* 5 Feb 1972, Nicola Dorothy Mary, da of Dr Leslie Ford (d 1987), of Sheringham, Norfolk; 1 s (Edward b 1977), 1 da (Caroline b 1979); *Career* Cadet Pilot Southampton Univ Air Sqdn 1964-66, trainee pilot Coll of Air Trg Hamble 1967-69, First Offr and Navigator VC10 (awarded basic Instrs Trg Course), CAA course Stansted for examiner/instr 1973, Sr First Offr Concorde 1976-86, appointed examiner/instr to Concorde Fleet, chartered 2 Concordes for celebration of 50 anniversary of Schneider Trophy 1981; organised BBC documentary on Concorde in QED series 1983, writer and presenter BBC TV series Jet Trail 1984, initiater and conslt Faster than a Speeding Bullet (C4 Equinox) 1989; Capt Boeing 737 with BA 1986-; Freeman City of London 1975, Liveryman Guild of Air Pilots and Air Navigators; memb Royal Aeronautical Soc, MRAeS 1984; *Books* The Concorde Story (with BA and Air France, 1986), Seventh Impression (1990); *Recreations* family, photography, music, sailing, canoeing, tennis, gardening; *Clubs* Air League; *Style—* Capt Christopher Orlebar; Holt Cottage, Fairoak Lane, Oxshott, Surrey KT22 0TW (☎ 0372 842100); British Airways, London (Gatwick) Airport

ORLEBAR, Richard Michael; s of Capt Richard Astry Bourne Orlebar (d 1980), of Hinwick House, Northants, and Barbara, da of Capt Frederick Charles Pilcher (d 1953); *b* 25 Oct 1938; *Educ* Stowe; *m* 1963, Barbara Anne, yst da of Francis Edward Gardner (d 1975), of Glebe Farm, Cranford, Kettering; 1 s (Richard Charles Edward b 1965); *Career* Royal Norfolk Regt 1957-60; dir of various private cos; landowner and proprietor of Hinwick House; *Recreations* shooting, skiing, swimming; *Style—* Richard Orlebar, Esq; Hinwick House, nr Wellingborough, Northants (☎ 0933 53624)

ORLIK, Simon George; s of Herbert Orlik (d 1980), of Coombe, Granville Rd, St George's Hill, Weybridge, Surrey, and Joan Primrose, *née* Gliksten; *b* 24 July 1946; *Educ* Charterhouse; *m* 24 July 1971, Jeanette Ann, da of Michael Lynch-Watson, of Worcester Park, Surrey; 1 s (Elliott b 1974); *Career* dir: L Orlik Ltd 1972-, Roy Tallent Ltd 1972, Mansells Ltd 1972-89, Chapman Graham Mills Ltd 1981-87; memb cncl Tobacco Trade Benevolent Assoc, treas Brentwood Veterans Hockey Club; Liveryman (memb ct) Worshipful Co of Tobacco Pipe Makers and Tobacco Blenders 1972; MInstD, FICAEW 1969; *Recreations* hockey, squash, tennis, music, travel, golf; *Style—* Simon Orlik, Esq; Orchard Cottage, Birch Lane, Stock Ingatestone, Essex CM4 9NA

ORMAN, Dr Stanley; s of Jack Orman (d 1974), and Ettie, *née* Steiner (d 1984); *b* 6 Feb 1935; *Educ* Hackney Downs GS, King's Coll London (BSc, PhD); *m* 1960, Helen, da of Joseph Hourman (d 1982); 1 s (David b 1961), 2 da (Ann b 1963, Lynn b 1969); *Career* Fullbright scholar, post doctoral res Brandeis Univ Waltham Mass USA, res in materials sci 1961-74, chief weapon system engr Chevaline 1981-82, min and cncllr Br Embassy Washington 1982-84, under sec MOD 1984-, dir gen Strategic Def Initiative Participation Off 1986- (dep dir Awre Aldermaston 1984-86); chief exec GTS Inc Washington 1990-; Jelf Medalist Kings Coll 1957; published over 40 original papers in scientific jls; *Recreations* sport, reading, designing bow ties; *Style—* Dr Stanley Orman; 311 The Meadway, Reading, Berks RG3 4NS (☎ 0734 424880); MOD, Northumberland House, Northumberland Ave, WC2N 5BP; 17825 Stoneridge Drive, G Sithersburg, Maryland, 20878, USA

ORME, Prof Michael Christopher L'Estrange; s of Christopher Robert L'Estrange Orme, TD (d 1979), of Poole, Dorset, and Muriel Evelyn Janet, *née* Thomson; *b* 13 June 1940; *Educ* Sherborne, Univ of Cambridge (MA, MB BChir, MD); *m* 15 April 1967, (Joan) Patricia, da of Stanley Abbott, OBE, of Coulsdon, Surrey; 1 s (Robert Martin b 10 July 1969); *Career* Univ of Liverpool: sr lectr clinical pharmacology 1975-81, reader 1981-84, prof pharmacology and therapeutics 1984-, dean of Faculty of Medicine 1991-; hon conslt physician Liverpool Health Authy; sec: clinical pharmacology section Br Pharmacological Soc 1982-88, clinical section Int Union Pharmacology 1987-; FRCP 1980; *Books* medicines - The Self Help Guide (1988), Human Lactation (1989); *Recreations* sailing, astronomy; *Clubs* Dee Sailing; *Style—* Prof Michael Orme; Wychwood, 80 Brimstage Rd, Heswall, Wirral, Merseyside L60 1XQ (☎ 051 342 3269); Dept of Pharmacology and Therapeutics, New Med Sch Ashton St, Liverpool L69 3BX (☎ 051 794 5544, fax 051 794 5540)

ORME, Prof Nicholas; s of Edward Howell Orme, and Kathleen, *née* Plowright (d 1971); *Educ* Bristol Cathedral Sch, Magdalen Coll Oxford (BA, MA, DPhil, DLitt); *m* 4 July 1981, Rona, da of James S Monro; 1 da (Verity b 1984); *Career* Univ of Exeter: lectr 1964-81, reader in history 1981-88, prof of history 1988-; chm Exeter Cathedral Fabric Ctee, pres Exeter Hist Assoc, ed Devon and Cornwall Record Soc; FSA 1985; FRHistS 1979; *Books* English Schools in the Middle Ages (1973), Education in the West of England (1976), The Minor Clergy of Exeter Cathedral (1980), Early British Swimming (1983), From Childhood to Chivalry (1984), Exeter Cathedral As It Was (1986), Education and Society in Medieval and Renaissance England (1989), John Lydgate, Table Manners for Children (ed, 1989), Unity and Variety: A History of the Church in Devon and Cornwall (ed, 1991); *Clubs* Devon & Exeter Inst; *Style—* Prof Nicholas Orme; Dept of History and Archaeology, University of Exeter, Exeter EX4 4QH (☎ 0392 264340)

ORME, Rt Hon Stanley (Stan); PC (1974), MP (Lab) Salford E 1983-; s of Sherwood Orme; *b* 5 April 1923; *Educ* pt/t tech sch, Nat Cncl Labour Colls & WEA; *m* 1951, Irene Mary, da of Vernon Fletcher Harris; *Career* served RAF as Warrant Offr Air-Bomber Navigator (Bomber Cmd) 1942-47 in Europe & M East; fought (Lab) Stockport S 1959, MP (Lab) Salford W 1964-1983; min state: NI 1974-76, DHSS 1976, Social Security 1976-77; min of social security (with seat in Cabinet) 1977-79; chief oppn spokesman and memb shadow cabinet: Indust Dec 1980-Nov 1983, Energy Nov 1983-87; chm Parly Lab Party 1987-; memb AUEW; Hon DSc Univ of Salford 1985; *Recreations* walking, reading American literature, music (jazz & opera), supporting Manchester United; *Clubs* Lancs County Cricket; *Style—* The Rt Hon Stan Orme, MP; 8 Northwood Grove, Sale, Cheshire M33 3AW (☎ 061 973 5341)

ORME-SMITH, Hon Mrs (Teresa Caroline); *née* Shaw; da of Baron Kilbrandon, PC (Life Peer; d 1989); *b* 1940; *m* 1969, Christopher Orme-Smith; 1 s (Andrew b 1974), 2 da (Philippa b 1969, Nicola b 1971); *Style—* The Hon Mrs Orme-Smith; PO Rongai, Kenya

ORMEROD, Alec William; s of William Ormerod (d 1958), and Susan Ormerod (d 1972); *b* 19 July 1932; *Educ* Nelson, Christ's Coll Cambridge (MA, LLM); *m* 23 Oct 1976, Patricia Mary, da of George Frederick Large, of Alsager, Cheshire; *Career* Nat Serv Army 1956-58; admitted slr 1956, local govt 1958-63, sr ptnr Boyle & Ormerod Aylesbury 1963-88, met magistrate 1988-; cncllr Aylesbury Borough Cncl; Freeman City of London 1973; *Recreations* fine art, travel; *Clubs* Naval and Military; *Style—* Alec Ormerod, Esq; Camberwell Green Court, London SE5 (☎ 071 703 0909)

ORMEROD, Brig Denis Leonard; CBE (1976, MBE 1950); s of Harold Eric Ormerod, CBE (d 1959), and Kathleen Mary, *née* Bourke (d 1957); *b* 17 Feb 1922; *Educ* Downside; *m* 7 Oct 1950, Frances Mary Shewell, da of Brig Charles Edward Francis Turner, CBE, DSO, of Wadhurst, E Sussex; 2 s (Giles b 1957, Jonathan b 1962), 6 da (Jennifer (Mrs P Tolhurst) b 1951, Julia (Mrs A Wells) b 1953, Teresa (Mrs M Bromley Gardner) b 1959, Jessica b 1960, Clare (Mrs A Torrance) b 1964, Katherine b 1968); *Career* cmmnd 1941 2 KEO Goorkhas (IA) served in India, Italy, Greece 1941-47, transferred to RIrF 1947, served in Palestine, Egypt 1947-48, Malaya 1948-50 (seconded to 1/2 Goorkhas), (despatches 1949), Regt Serv RIF N Ireland, BAOR, Berlin, Tripoli 1950-60, RN Staff Coll 1960-61, Staff Sch of Inf 1961-63, CO 1 Bn RIF 1965-67 (BAOR, UK, Swaziland, Bechuanaland, Aden), asst Mil Sec Southern Cmd, Army Strategic Cmd 1967-69, Col GS MOD 1969-71, Cmd Ulster Def Regt (11 Bns) 1971-73 (despatches 1973), Brig Inf 1 (BR) Corps 1973-76, sec NW England and IOM TA and VR Assoc 1976-87; DL Merseyside 1983-87; *Recreations* country pursuits, horses, music, gardening; *Clubs* Rhinefield Polo; *Style—* Brig Denis Ormerod, CBE; Kirkbank House, High Halden, Kent TN26 2JD (☎ 023 3850 249)

ORMEROD, Dr Walter Edward; s of Prof Henry Arderne Ormerod, MC (d 1964), and Mildred Robina, *née* Caton (d 1984); *b* 22 Feb 1920; *Educ* Winchester, Queens Coll Oxford (MA, DSc, DM); *m* 7 Jan 1950, Elizabeth Noel, da of Thomas Henry Gilborn Stamper, MC (d 1980); 3 s (Henry b 1951 d 1987, William b 1952, Thomas b 1961), 5 da (Anne b 1953 d 1978, Sarah b 1954, Eleanor b 1955 d 1971, Philippa b 1958, Edith Mary b 1959); *Career* staff memb Nat Inst for Med Res 1949-51, lectr applied pharmacology St Mary's Hosp Med Sch 1951-54, sr lectr (reader and emeritus reader) London Sch of Hygiene & Tropical Medicine 1954-85 (sr res fell 1988-); *Publications* On the Pathology and Treatment of African Sleeping Sickness; on economic development and "aid" as major causes of ecological degradation and poverty in the tropics; *Style—* Dr Walter Ormerod; The Old Rectory, Padworth, Reading RG7 4JD; Dept of Medical Parasitology, London School of Hygiene & Tropical Medicine, Keppel St, London WC1E 7HT (☎ 071 636 8636)

ORMISTON, James Alexander; MBE (1986), TD (1970), DL (Gtr Manchester 1990); s of Sydney Alexander Ormiston (d 1972), of Wetheral, Cumberland, and Ada Joan, *née* Johnston (d 1988); *b* 26 Sept 1928; *Educ* Carlisle GS; *m* 7 June 1952, Maureen Daphne, da of William Christopher Strong (d 1951); 2 da (Melanie Daphne b 1955, Victoria Marguerite b 1958); *Career* cmmnd Loyal Regt 1947, RWAFF 1947-49, S Lancs and Parachute Regts 1949-51, Bde Adj Lancs Bde 1951-53, Adj Army Sch of Physical Trg 1953-56; Border Regt TA 1956-74, unposted list MOD 1975-88 (Actg Lt-Col 1983-84); Grainger & Percy Building Society 1960, exec Midleton Building Society 1969, asst gen mangr Colne Bldg Soc 1978, asst regnl mangr Britannia Building Society 1983-; chief cmdt Gtr Manchester Police Special Constabulary, vice pres Coldstream Gds Assoc Manchester, asst co dir St John's Ambulance Assoc Lancs 1980-83, chm NW Gp Bldg Socs Inst 1983-85, asst orgn sec Modern Pentathlon Assoc of GB 1953-56; memb Ctee: SSAFA Cumberland 1962-69, Army Benevolent Fund Manchester 1971-78; tstee regtl chapel Carlisle Cathedral; CBSI 1970, MBIM 1976; *Recreations* inland waterways, reading, fishing, home and family; *Clubs* Army, Police; *Style—* James A Ormiston, Esq, MBE, TD, DL; c/o Britannia Building Society, Newton House, Leek, Staffs (☎ 0538 399 399)

ORMOND, Leonée; *née* Jasper; *b* 27 Aug 1940; *Educ* Ware GS for Girls, St Anne's Coll Oxford (BA), Univ of Birmingham (MA); *m* 11 May 1963, Richard Louis Ormond, s of Conrad Ormond (d 1979); 2 s (Augustus b 1972, Marcus b 1974); *Career* King's Coll London: asst lectr 1965-68, lectr 1968-85, sr lectr 1985-89, reader in English 1989-; tstee GF Watts Gallery Compton Surrey, memb Mgmnt Ctee Linley Sambourne Museum Kensington; *Books* George Du Maurier (1969), Lord Leighton (with Richard Ormond 1975), J M Barrie (1987); *Clubs* Univ Women's; *Style—* Mrs Richard Ormond; English Department, King's College, Strand, London WC2R 2LS

ORMOND, Richard Louis; s of Conrad Eric Ormond (d 1979), of Old Rectory, Cleggan, Co Galway, and Dorothea Charlotte (d 1987), da of Sir Alexander Gibbons, 7 Bt; *b* 16 Jan 1939; *Educ* Marlborough, Brown Univ USA, Ch Ch Oxford (MA); *m* 10 May 1963, Leonée Jasper; 2 s (Augustus b 1972, Marcus b 1974); *Career* asst keeper Nat Portrait Gallery 1965-75, dep dir 1975-83, head of Picture Dept Nat Maritime Museum 1983-86, dir Nat Maritime Museum 1986-; chm: Tstees Watts Gallery Compton, Friends of Leighton House; memb Cncl Cutty Sark Maritime Tst; *Books* J S

Sargent (1970), Early Victorian Portraits in the National Portrait Gallery (1973), Lord Leighton (1975), Sir Edwin Landseer (1982), The Great Age of Sail (1986), F X Winterhalter and the Courts of Europe (1987); *Recreations* cycling, opera, theatre; *Clubs* Garrick; *Style—* Richard Ormond, Esq; National Maritime Museum, Greenwich, London SE10 9NF (☎ 081 312 6611)

ORMONDE, 7 Marquess of (I 1825); James Hubert Theobald Charles Butler; MBE (1921); also Earl of Ormonde (I 1328), Earl of Ossory (I 1527), Viscount Thurles (I 1536), Baron Ormonde (UK 1821), and 31 Hereditary Chief Butler of Ireland (1177); s of Rev Lord James Butler (d 1929, 4 s of 2 Marquess, KP) and Annabella (d 1943), o da Rev Cosmo Reid Gordon; 12 Earl cr Duke of Ormonde 1661 as reward for fidelity to the crown, 2 Duke was attainted 1715 for supporting the Stuarts; suc 1 cous, 6 Marquess, 1971; *b* 19 April 1899; *Educ* Haileybury, Sandhurst; *m* 1, 1935, Nan (d 1973), da of Garth Gilpin, of USA; 2 da (Lady Ann Soukup b 1940, Lady Cynthia Robb b 1946); m 2, 1976, Elizabeth (d 1980), da of Charles Rarden, of USA; *Heir* to Marquessate, Viscountcy and Barony none, to Earldoms of Ormonde and Ossory and Hereditary Chief Butlership: 17 Viscount Mountgarret (descends from 8 Earl of Ormonde); *Career* served WWI, late Lt KRRC; US businessman, ret; *Clubs* Naval and Military; *Style—* The Most Hon the Marquess of Ormonde, MBE; 6101 S County Line, Buzz Ridge, Illinois, USA 60521

ORMROD, Hon Mrs (Barbara Helen); *née* FitzRoy; 4 da of Capt 2 Viscount Daventry, RN (d 1986); descent from Henry FitzRoy, 1 Duke of Grafton 2 illegitimate s of King Charles II and Barbara Villiers, Duchess of Cleveland; *b* 19 Dec 1928; *m* 18 April 1952, Col Peter Charles Ormrod, MC, JP, DL *qv*; 2 da (Mrs Julian Holloway b 1958, Alice b 1964); *Recreations* sailing, gun dog trg; *Style—* The Hon Mrs Ormrod; Pen-y-Lan, Ruabon, Wrexham, Clwyd (☎ 0978 823336)

ORMROD, Col Peter Charles; MC, JP (1958), DL (Clwyd 1972); s of Maj James Ormrod (d 1945), of Pen-y-lan, Ruabon, Wrexham, and Winifred Selina, *née* Bulkeley (d 1974); *b* 31 Aug 1922; *Educ* Harrow, RMC Sandhurst; *m* April 1952, Barbara Helen, da of Capt 2 Viscount Daventry, RN; 2 da (Emma Jane Caroline (Mrs Holloway) b Jan 1969, Alice Amelia b Dec 1974); *Career* Capt 3 Bn Scots Gds 1941-47, NW Europe 1944-45, Maj 8 KR Irish Hussars 1947-55, Korea 1950-51, 4 Bn Royal Welsh Fusiliers TA 1957-64, Hon Col 3 Bn Royal Welsh Fusiliers 1984-89; dir: John Hughes (contractors) Ltd 1956-60, Flintshire Woodlands Ltd 1960-74; ind forestry conslt 1974-; dir: Abbey National Building Society, Wrexham and Denbighshire Water Co; High Sheriff of Clwyd 1962; memb: Home Grown Timber Advsy Ctee, Regnl Advsy Ctee Forestry Cmmn, NRA, Welsh Fisheries Advisory Ctee; AMICE, MICFor; *Recreations* shooting, sailing, photography; *Style—* Col Peter Ormrod, MC, JP, DL; Pen-y-Lan, Ruabon, Wrexham, Clwyd LL14 6HS (☎ 0978 823336)

ORMROD, Rt Hon Sir Roger Fray Greenwood; PC (1974); s of Oliver Ormrod; *b* 20 Oct 1911; *Educ* Shrewsbury, Queen's Coll Oxford; *m* 1938, Anne Lush; *Career* serv RAMC WWII; pres Res Def Soc 1982-; QC 1958; Ld Justice Appeal 1974-82, when ret, High Ct judge (Family Div) 1961-74, barr Inner Temple 1936; hon fell Queen's Coll Oxford 1966, BM, BCh (Oxon), hon fell Manchester Poly, Hon FRCPsych, Hon LLD Leicester; chm: London Marriage Guidance Cncl, Notting Hill Housing Tst, Ctee Mgmnt Inst of Psdychiatry; Br Med Postgrad Fedn; visitor Royal Postgrad Med Sch 1975-, former hon prof Legal Ethics Birmingham Univ; FRCP; kt 1961; *Style—* The Rt Hon Sir Roger Ormrod; 4 Aubrey Rd, W8 (☎ 071 727 7876)

ORMSBY GORE, Hon Alice Magdalen Sarah; da of 5 Baron Harlech, PC, KCMG (d 1985), and his 1 w Sylvia (d 1967), da of Hugh Lloyd Thomas CMG, CVO; *b* 22 April 1952; *Style—* The Hon Alice Ormsby Gore; Paris, France; c/o Rainey Race Course Road, Oswestry, Salop

ORMSBY GORE, Hon John Julian; s of 2 survg s of 4 Baron Harlech, KG, GCMG, PC (d 1964), and Lady Beatrice DCVO, el da 4 Marquess of Salisbury; *b* 12 April 1925; *Educ* Eton, New Coll Oxford; *Career* Capt Coldstream Gds 1944; *Style—* The Hon John Ormsby Gore; 14 Ladbroke Rd, London W11

ORNSBY, John Sidney; s of Leslie Sidney Ornsby, of 28 The Lawns, Manadon, Plymouth, Devon, and Evelyn, *née* Buckland (d 1978); *b* 3 Oct 1936; *Educ* Bancroft's Sch Woodford Green Essex, QMC London (BSc); *m* 18 July 1959, Heather Doreen, da of Eric Stephen Padmore, of 21 Meryln, Devonshire Place, Eastbourne, E Sussex; 1 da (Suzanne Doreen b 1963); *Career* graduate engr Mobil Oil Co 1958-60; Ready Mixed Concrete Gp: joined 1960, dir UK Ltd and subsidary cos 1971-; dir Hall Ham River Ltd 1968-71, vice-pres Inst of Quarrying 1981- (chm 1979-81), chm Sand & Gravel Assoc of GB Ltd 1988-90, appt to Verney Ctee on Aggregates 1973-77; FIQ 1978, CEng 1983, MIMechE 1983, FRICS 1989; *Recreations* bridge, gardening; *Clubs* St George's Hill, Claremont Park Golf; *Style—* John Ornsby, Esq; Northfield House, Northfield Place, Weybridge, Surrey KT13 0RF (☎ 0932 847856); RMC House, 53/55 High St, Feltham, Middx (☎ 0932 568833, fax 0932 568933, telex 918150)

ORPEN-SMELLIE, Lt-Col Herbert John (Larry); OBE (1980); s of Maj William Archibald Smellie (ka 1940), and Elizabeth Staples, *née* Irwin, MBE; *b* 18 Jan 1930; *Educ* Wellington, RMA Sandhurst, Staff Coll Quetta; *m* 6 March 1954, Jean Rackley, da of Abram Rackley Watson, MBE (d 1987); 1 s (Giles b 1959), 1 da (Jane b 1963); *Career* cmmnd Essex Regt 1949 (joined 1948), Lt 1951, Temp Capt and instr Small Arms Wing Sch of Inf 1952-54, Capt 1955, Parachute Regt 1958 (Temp Maj 1958-59 and 1960-62), Adj 1 Para 1958-59, Staff Coll 1961, Maj 1962, GSO 2 instr Fed of Malaya Armed Forces 1962-64, GSO 2 Ops HQ ME 1967, GSO 2 Coord DG Weapons MOD 1968-70, 2 i/c 3 Para 1970-72, GSO 2 Staff Duties HQ NE Dist 1973-74, DAAG Mobilisation MOD 1974-76, chief instr Small Arms Wing Sch of Inf 1977-80, Lt-Col 1977, Special List 1980, ret 1984; RO III regtl sec 3 Royal Anglian Regt 1984-85, RO II G3 Trg HQ E Dist 1985-, Lt HSF 1985, Maj OC 5 (HSF) Coy 10 Para 1985-90; various GB Teams rifle shooting 1952-88 (Capt Canada 1975, Bisley 1980, NZ and Aust 1984), Capt Army Eight 1968-82; prizes: Queen's Silver medal Bisley 1965 (Prince of Wales Prize 1988), Grand Aggregate Silver Cross 1990, Govr's shield Hong Kong 1955 and 1956, Nova Scotia Grand Aggregate Canada 1960 (Ontario 1975, Govr Gen first stage 1956, 1960 and 1975); memb Cncl Nat Rifle Assoc 1974-; pres: Essex County Rifle Assoc, SE Essex Branch Parachute Regt Assoc; memb RBL, govr local sch; MBIM 1973-86, MInstAM 1976-86; *Recreations* rifle shooting; *Style—* Lt-Col Larry Orpen-Smellie, OBE

ORR, Rt Hon Sir Alan Stewart; OBE (Mil 1944), PC (1971); s of William Orr (d 1948), and Doris, *née* Kemsley (d 1913); *b* 21 Feb 1911; *Educ* Fettes, Univ of Edinburgh (MA), Balliol Coll Oxford (LLB); *m* 1933, Mariana Frances Lilian (d 1986), da of Capt J C Lang, KOSB (ka Gallipoli 1915); 4 s; *Career* served WWII RAF, Wing Cdr (despatches); called to the Bar Middle Temple 1936; pt/t law lectr UCL 1948-50, jr cnsl to Cmmrs Inland Revenue 1957-63, rec Windsor 1958-65, QC 1963, dep chm Oxford QS 1964-71, rec Oxford 1965, High Court judge (Probate Divorce and Admty) 1965-71, presiding judge NE circuit 1970-71, Lord Justice of Appeal 1971-80; kt 1965; *Recreations* golf; *Clubs* United Oxford and Cambridge Univ; *Style—* The Rt Hon Sir Alan Orr, OBE; The Steps, Ratley, Banbury, Oxon OX15 6DT (☎ 029587 364)

ORR, Arthur Sidney Porter; VRD (1964, and bar 1974), DL (Co Down 1988); s of Sidney Orr (d 1980), of Old Holywood Rd, Belfast, and Winifred Margurite, *née* McCurry (d 1974); *b* 18 Nov 1928; *Educ* Brackenber House Sch Belfast, St Columba's Coll Rathfarnham Co Dublin; *m* 17 March 1956, Evelyn Jane Ferguson, da of Derrick Harris (d 1932), of Malone Park, Belfast; 1 s (Timothy b 30 Sept 1962), 2 da (Dilys b 16 Sept 1957, Judith b 27 April 1959); *Career* Ordinary Seaman RNVR 1948, Midshipman 1949, Sub Lt 1950, Lt 1952, transferred RNR 1956, Lt Cdr 1960, CO HMS Kilmorey 1960-61, Cdr 1966, Capt 1968, CO HMS Caroline (Ulster Div RNR) 1969-72; ADC to HE The Govr of NI The Lord Wakehurst 1958-60, ADC to HM The Queen 1972; chm and md: McCaw Stevenson & Orr Ltd 1972 (works dir 1956), McCaw Stevenson & Orr (Printers) Ltd 1980, McCaw Stevenson & Orr plc 1984, OBH Plastics Ltd; chm Bd of Govrs NI War Meml Building, ctee memb Belfast C of C and Shipping, hon treas Eldon LOL VII; memb: Belfast Master Mariners Assoc, Lighthouse Advsy Ctee St Mary Axe; memb Royal Inst of Navigation; *Recreations* sailing, gardening; *Clubs* Royal North of Ireland Yacht, Irish Cruising, Cruising Assoc; *Style—* Arthur Orr, Esq, VRD, DL; Evergreen, Old Holywood Rd, Belfast BT4 2HJ (☎ 0232 63601); McCaw Stevenson & Orr plc, 162 Castlereagh Rd, Belfast BT5 5FW (☎ 0232 452 428, fax 0232 731 827)

ORR, Craig Smith; *b* 4 Sept 1945; *Educ* Univ of Aberdeen (MA); *Career* asst ed Evening News until 1975, night ed and scot exec ed Daily Express 1975-85, asst ed You Magazine 1985-86, managing ed Evening Standard 1986-; *Recreations* working, sailing, films, talking to women; *Style—* Craig Orr, Esq; Evening Standard, Northcliffe House, 2 Derry St, Kensington, London W8 5EE (☎ 071 938 7503, fax 071 937 2849)

ORR, Sir David Alexander; MC (and Bar 1945); s of Canon Adrian William Fielder Orr (1964), of Dublin, and Grace, *née* Robinson (d 1967); *b* 10 May 1922; *Educ* Dublin HS, Trinity Coll Dublin (BA, LLB); *m* 1949, Phoebe Rosaleen, da of Harold Percival Davis (d 1980, late Indian Forest Service), of Dublin; 3 da (Catherine, Bridget, Paula); *Career* served WWII RE; chm Unilever 1974-82 (joined 1948, dir 1967-82), vice chm Unilever NV 1974-82; chm: Leverhulme Trust, Armed Forces Pay Review Bd 1982-84; exec chm Inchcape 1983-86 (dep chm 1986-); non exec dir: Rio Tinto Zinc, Shell Tport, CIBA-Geigy UK 1982-90, Bank of Ireland (memb Ct 1982-90); pres Liverpool Sch of Tropical Medicine 1981-89 (vice pres 1989-), chm Br Cncl 1985-, pres The Children's Med Charity 1991-; memb The Shakespeare Globe Tst 1985-; Hon LLD: Univ of Dublin, Univ of Liverpool; Hon DUniv Surrey; Cdr Order of Orange Nassau 1979; FRSA; kt 1977; *Recreations* travel, golf, theatre; *Style—* Sir David Orr, MC; Home Farm House, Shackleford, Godalming, Surrey GU8 6AH (☎ 0483 810350); 81 Lyall Mews West, London SW1 (☎ 071 235 7970); Inchcape plc, St James's House, 23 King St, London SW1Y 6QY

ORR, Sir John Henry; OBE (1972), QPM (1977); *b* 13 June 1918; *Educ* George Heriot's Sch Edinburgh; *m* 1942, Isobel, *née* Campbell; 1 s, 1 da; *Career* WWII flying RAF; chief constable: Dundee 1960-68, Lothian and Peebles 1968-75, Lothian and Borders 1975-83; OStJ; FBIM; Jubilee Medal; kt 1979; *Style—* Sir John Orr, OBE, QPM; 12 Lanark Rd West, Currie, Midlothian EH14 5ET

ORR, Dr Robin Gooch; s of Daniel Orr (d 1959), of St Leonards-on-Sea, E Sussex, and Elizabeth, *née* Gooch (d 1933); *b* 23 Jan 1924; *Educ* Caterham Sch Surrey, Guy's Hosp Med Sch London Univ, London Sch of Hygiene and Tropical Med London Univ (MB BS); *m* 11 Sept 1951, (Muriel) Joy Morley, da of Capt William Harvey Stones (d 1940), of Harrogate, Yorks; 1 s (Jeremy b 1963, d 1975); *Career* Capt REME 1945-47; house appts Guys Hosp London 1953-55, asst indust med offr Boots Pure Drug Co 1956-59; indust med offr: AERE Harwell 1959-71, Beecham Pharmaceuticals 1971-74 (chief occupational med offr 1974-89); memb St Paul's Church Dorking; Freeman: City of London 1978, Worshipful Co of Apothecaries 1978; memb Soc of Occupational Med 1986, MFOM (RCP) 1979; *Recreations* golf, bridge, tennis; *Style—* Dr Robin Orr; 9 Pointers Hill, Westcott, Dorking, Surrey RH4 3PF (☎ 0306 888 596)

ORR, Prof Robin Robert Kemsley; CBE (1972); s of Robert Workman Orr (d 1942), and Florence Mary, *née* Kemsley (d 1943); *b* 2 June 1909; *Educ* Loretto Sch, RCM, Pembroke Coll Cambridge (MA, MusD); *m* 1, 1937 (m dis 1979), Margaret Ellen, da of late A C Mace; 1 s, 2 da; m 2, 1979, Doris Ruth, da of late Leo Meyer-Bechtler of Zürich; *Career* Nat Serv RAFVR 1941-45, Flt Lt; composer; organist St John's Cambridge 1938-51, lectr Cambridge 1947-56; prof RCM 1950-56; prof of music: Univ of Glasgow 1956-65, Univ of Cambridge 1965-76 (emeritus 1976-); chm Scot Opera 1962-76, dir Welsh Nat Opera 1977-83; fell St John's Coll Cambridge 1948-56 and 1965-76 (hon fell 1987-), hon fell Pembroke Coll Cambridge 1988-; Hon DMus Univ of Glasgow, Hon LLD Univ of Dundee; FRCM, FRSAMD, Hon RAM; *Compositions incl* Oedipus at Colonus (Cambridge 1950), Rhapsody for string orch (English Chamber Orch 1967), Symphony in One Movement (Edinburgh Festival 1965), Symphony No 2 (Edinburgh Festival 1975), Symphony No 3 (Llandaff Festival 1978); *Operas* Full Circle (1 act - 30 performances on TV and radio 1968-69), Hermiston (3 acts - Edinburgh Festival 1975), On The Razzle (3 acts - RSAMD commn and premiere Glasgow 1988); *Recreations* gardening, mountain walks; *Style—* Prof Robin Orr, CBE; 16 Cranmer Rd, Cambridge CB3 9BL (☎ 0223 352858)

ORR EWING, Archibald Donald; s and h of Sir Ronald Orr Ewing, 5 Bt; *b* 20 Dec 1938; *Educ* Gordonstoun, Trinity Coll Dublin (BA); *m* 1, 1965 (m dis 1972), Venetia, da of Maj Richard Turner; m 2, 1972, Nicola, da of Reginald Black, of Brook House, Fovant, nr Salisbury, Wiltshire, and (Eloise) Jean Horatia, *née* Innes-Ker, niece of 8 Duke of Roxburghe; 1 s (Alastair b 1982); *Career* landowner; memb Royal Co of Archers (Queen's Body Guard for Scotland); *Recreations* shooting, fishing, stalking, opera, theatre; *Clubs* New (Edinburgh), Pratt's; *Style—* Archibald Orr Ewing, Esq; 13 Warriston Cres, Edinburgh EH3 5LA (☎ 031 556 9319)

ORR EWING, Maj Edward Stuart; DL (Wigtownshire 1970); s of Capt David Orr Ewing, DSO, DL (d 1964, s of Charles Orr Ewing, MP Ayr, 5 s of Sir Archibald Orr Ewing, 1 Bt), and Mary, da of late Benjamin Noaks, of Nylstroom, SA; *b* 28 Sept 1931; *Educ* Sherborne; *m* 1958 (m dis 1981), Fiona Anne Bowman, da of Anthony Hobart Farquhar, of Hastingwood House (*see* Burke's Landed Gentry 1965); 1 s (Alastair b 1964) 2 da (Jane b 1961, Victoria b 1962); m 2, 1981, Diana Mary, da of William Smith Waters, OBE, of Greenfoot, Dalston, Cumbria; *Career* serv The Black Watch 1950-69, Maj; landowner and farmer 1969-; Lord Lt Dumfries and Galloway Dist of Wigtown 1989-; *Recreations* country pursuits; *Clubs* New (Edinburgh); *Style—* Maj Edward Orr Ewing, DL; Dunskey, Portpatrick, Wigtownshire (☎ 077 681 211)

ORR EWING, Maj Sir Ronald Archibald; 5 Bt (UK 1886), JP (Perth 1956), DL (1963); s of Brig-Gen Sir Norman Archibald Orr Ewing, 4 Bt, CB, DSO (d 1960), and Laura Louisa, *née* Robarts (d 1968); *b* 14 May 1912; *Educ* Eton, RMC Sandhurst; *m* 6 April 1938, Marion Hester, da of late Col Sir Donald Walter Cameron of Lochiel, KT, CMG, and Lady Hermione Graham, da of 5 Duke of Montrose, KT; 2 s (Archibald *qv*, Jamie b 9 Jan 1948), 2 da (Janet (Mrs John Wallace) b 9 Nov 1940, Fiona (Mrs Adrian Drewe) b 3 March 1946); *Heir* s Archibald Donald Orr Ewing; *Career* Scots Guards 1932-53, ret as Maj; serv WWII, Middle E (POW 1942-45); memb Queen's Body Guard for Scotland (Royal Co of Archers); Grand Master Mason of Scotland 1965-69; *Recreations* travel, forestry; *Clubs* New (Edinburgh); *Style—* Maj Sir Ronald Orr Ewing, Bt, JP, DL; Cardross, Kippen, Stirling FK8 3JY (☎ 08775 220)

ORR-EWING, Hon (Ian) Colin; 2 s of Baron Orr-Ewing, OBE (Life Peer); *b* 1942; *Educ* Harrow, Trinity Coll Oxford (BA); *m* 1, 1973 (m dis 1980), Deirdre, eldest da of Lance Japhet, of Sandhurst, Johannesburg; 1 s (Francis Ian Lance b 1975), 1 da (Bridget Joanna b 1977); m 2, 1986, Fleur P M, yr da of late Dr Gavin Knight, of

Blackwood, Gwent; 2 da (Cordelia b 1988, Daisy Caroline b 1990); *Career* dir: Kells Minerals plc, Simcol Investmts; ACCA; *Style*— The Hon Colin Orr-Ewing; Yew Tree House, Hungerford Newtown, Berks

ORR-EWING, Hamish; s of Capt Hugh Eric Douglas Orr-Ewing (gs of James Ewing, yr bro of Sir Archibald Orr Ewing, 1 Bt, JP, DL, MP) and his 2 w Esme, sis Sir Kenneth Stewart, 1 Bt; Hamish is 3 cous of Baron Orr-Ewing, *qv*; *b* 17 Aug 1924; *Educ* Heatherdown, Eton; *m* 1 1948 (m dis 1954), Morar Margaret, sis of the TV journalist Ludovic Kennedy, *qv*, and da of late Capt Edward Kennedy, RN (ggs of Hon Robert Kennedy, 3 s of 11 Earl of Cassillis); 1 s (Roderick b 1951), and 1 da decd; m 2 1954, Ann Mary Teresa, da of late Frederick Terry; *Career* Capt Black Watch 1942-47; chm Rank Xerox Ltd 1980-; dir Tricentrol Ltd 1975-; *Recreations* mechanics, country life, the Roman Empire; *Style*— Hamish Orr-Ewing Esq; 51 Clifton Hill, NW8 (☎ 01 624 5702); Fox Mill, Purton, Nr Swindon, Wilts (☎ 0793 770496)

ORR-EWING, Baron (Life Peer UK 1971), of Little Berkhamsted, Co Hertford; Sir (Charles) Ian Orr-Ewing; 1 Bt (UK 1963), OBE (Mil 1945); s of Archibald Ian Orr-Ewing (d 1942), and Gertrude Bertha, *née* Runge; *b* 10 Feb 1912; *Educ* Harrow, Trinity Coll Oxford (MA); *m* 1939, Joan Helen Veronica, da of William Gordon McMinnies (d 1982), of Stoke Orchard, nr Cheltenham; 4 s (Hon Simon *qv*, Hon Colin *qv*, Hon Malcolm *qv*, Hon Robert *qv*); *Heir* to Btcy only, s, Hon (Alistair) Simon Orr-Ewing; *Career* sits as (C) peer in House of Lords; serv WWII RAF, Wing Cdr 1941, Radar Branch, served N Africa and Italy 1943, chief radar offr Gen Eisenhower's Staff 1945; graduate apprentice EMI 1934-37, employed BBC (TV) 1937-39, (dir Outside Bdcasts 1946-49); MP (C) Hendon N 1950-70; PPS to Min of Lab 1951-55, Parly under sec Air Miny 1957-59, Parly and fin sec to Admty 1959, civil lord of the Admty 1959-63; a vice chm Cons 1922 Ctee 1966-70, vice chm Assoc of Cons Peers 1978-86; chm: Ultra Electric Holdings 1965-79, Clayton Dewandre Ltd; dir: Carl Byoir plc 1977-86, Hill & Knowlton 1986-88, MK Holdings 1977-83, Dowty 1978-82; chm Metrication Bd 1972-77; pres: Harrow Wanderers 1983-, Harrow Assoc 1986-87; vice pres Lords and Commons Cricket 1988-, fndr and pres Lords and Commons Ski Club; *Books* A Celebration of Lords and Commons Cricket 1850-1988 (1989); *Recreations* tennis, cricket, skiing; *Clubs* Boodle's, MCC, Vincent's (Oxford), All England LTC (Wimbledon); *Style*— The Rt Hon Lord Orr-Ewing, OBE; 9 Cheyne Gardens, London SW3 5QU

ORR-EWING, Hon Malcolm Archie; 3 s of Baron Orr-Ewing, OBE (Life Peer) *qv*; *b* 1946; *Educ* Harrow, Munich; *m* 1973, Clare Mary, da of Brig George Robert Flood, MC, of Cheverell Mill, Little Cheverell, Devizes, Wilts; 1 s (Edward Archie b 25 April 1990), 2 da (Harriet Kate b 1975, Charlotte Rose b 1978); *Style*— The Hon Malcolm Orr-Ewing; The Priory, Syresham, nr Brackley, Northants NN13 5HH

ORR-EWING, Hon Robert James; 4 and yst s of Baron Orr-Ewing, OBE (Life Peer) *qv*; *b* 1953; *Educ* Harrow; *m* 1982, Susannah, da of Mark Bodley Scott, of Uppfield, Sonning-on-Thames, Berks; 2 s (William Robert b 1985, Jack Alexander Bodley b 1987); *Career* barr Inner Temple 1976; proprietor Property Letting Co 1982-; *Style*— The Hon Robert Orr-Ewing; 2 Billing St, London SW10; 110-112 King's Rd, London SW3 (☎ 071 581 8025)

ORR-EWING, Hon (Alistair) Simon; eldest s of Baron Orr-Ewing, OBE (Life Peer and 1 Bt), *qv*; ha to baronetcy; *b* 10 June 1940; *Educ* Harrow, Trinity Coll Oxford (MA); *m* 1968, Victoria, da of Keith Cameron (d 1981), of Fifield House, Oxon; 2 s (Archie Cameron b 1969, James Alexander b 1971), 1 da (Georgina Victoria b 1974); *Career* chartered surveyor; cncllr Royal Borough of Kensington and Chelsea 1982-, chm Town Planning Ctee 1986-88; Lloyd's Underwriter 1986-; FRICS; *Recreations* skiing, tennis, shooting; *Clubs* MCC, Boodle's, IOD; *Style*— The Hon Simon Orr-Ewing; 29 St James Gardens, London W11 4RF (☎ 01 602 4513); office: Simcol Investments Ltd, 46 St James's Place, London SW1 (☎ 071 493 9586)

ORSON, Rasin Ward; CBE (1985); s of Rasin Nelson Orson, and Blanche, *née* Hyre; *b* 16 April 1927; *Educ* Stratford GS, LSE (BSc); *m* 1, 1950, Marie Goodenough; 2 s; m 2, 1979, Lesley Jean Vallance; *Career* memb The Electricity Cncl 1976-88; dir Chloride Silent Power Ltd 1974-88; COMPIEE; *Style*— Rasin Orson, Esq, CBE; The Old Garden, Dunorlan Park, Tunbridge Wells TN2 3QA (☎ 0892 24027)

ORTON, David Wallace; s of Wallace Orton (d 1970), and Elsie, *née* Woods (d 1960); *b* 16 March 1923; *Educ* Lindisfarne Coll; *m* 1950, Marguerite Bremner; *Career* film prodr; dir D Orton Films Ltd; pres Guild of Film Prodn Execs 1985-86 (vice-pres 1987-90); memb various ctees of the Br Film and TV Producers' Assoc; *Recreations* reading, gardening, country interests; *Clubs* St James's; *Style*— David Orton, Esq; The Red House, 3 King St, Potton, Beds SG19 2QT (☎ 0767 260272); Pinewood Studios, Iver, Bucks (☎ 0753 651 700)

ORTON, Michael Francis; s of Harry Orton (d 1957), and Mary Elizabeth, *née* Turner (d 1982); *b* 3 Oct 1931; *Educ* Co Tech Coll Wednesbury Staffs; *m* 23 July 1955, Angela Diane, da of Herbert Brown (d 1956); 2 da (Diana Mary, Tina Elizabeth); *Career* Nat Serv RMP 1952-54; sr ptnr LG Mouchel & Ptnrs (consulting engrs), dir Mouchel Assocs Ltd, ptnr LG Mouchel & Ptnrs Asia, dir Mouchel Asia Ltd; FIStructE, MIMechE, FRSA, memb Inst of Engrs; *Recreations* sailing; *Clubs* Papercourt SC; *Style*— Michael Orton, Esq; 18 Vincent Rd, Stoke D'Abernon, Cobham, Surrey (☎ 09326 3640); L G Mouchel & Partner, Consulting Engineers, West Hall, Parvis Rd, W Byfleet, Weybridge, Surrey (☎ 09323 41155, fax 09323 40673, telex 261309 MOUCHL G)

OSBALDESTON, Geoffrey; *b* 15 July 1940; *Career* admitted slr 1963; lectr Coll of Law 1963-67, private practice 1967-74; Abbey National Building Society: asst chief slr 1974-78, chief slr 1978-81, asst gen mangr Housing Div 1981-86, asst gen mangr Field Operations Div 1986-88, gen mangr Abbey National Estate Agency Ltd 1988-; examiner in building soc law and practice 1978-86; memb: Legal Advsy Panel Building Societies Assoc 1978-86, Lord Chancellor's Standing Ctee on conveyancing 1985-87; dir Ombudsman for Corp Estate Agents Ltd 1990-; *Style*— Geoffrey Osbaldeston, Esq; Abbey National plc, Abbey House, Baker Street, London NW1 6XL (☎ 071 486 5555)

OSBORN, Fuller Mansfield; CBE (1972), DL (1975); s of Fuller Mansfield Osborn; *b* 1915; *Educ* Grocers' Co Sch Hackney Downs; *m* 1949, Mary Armstrong, da of William James Auld; *Career* WWII Maj RA SEAC; chm Northern Rock Building Soc 1982-87 (md 1949-78); chm: Cncl of Bldg Socs Assoc 1969-71, Northern Region Advsy Ctee of Land Cmmn, NE Regn and Newcastle/Tyne, Abbeyfield Soc 1959-78, Northern Rock Housing Tst; pres: Euro Fedn of Bldg Socs 1979-82, Chartered Bldg Socs Inst 1984-85; memb Northern Econ Planning Cncl 1969-78, dep chm Washington New Town Corp 1973-88, memb Ct and Cncl Univ of Newcastle upon Tyne; High Sheriff Tyne and Wear 1974-75; *Recreations* golf, beagling, cricket; *Clubs* Northern Counties (Newcastle upon Tyne); *Style*— Fuller Osborn Esq, CBE, DL; Arundel, 9 Furzefield Rd, Gosforth, Newcastle upon Tyne NE3 4EA (☎ 091 285 7703; office: 091 285 7191)

OSBORN, Sir John Holbrook; MP (Nat Lib and U) Sheffield, Hallam Div 1959-64, (C) 1964-87; s of Samuel Eric Osborn and Aileen Decima, da of Col Sir Arthur Holbrook, KBE, MP; *b* 14 Dec 1922; *Educ* Rugby, Trinity Hall Cambridge (MA), Nat Foundry Coll; *m* 1, 1952 (m dis), Molly Suzanne, *née* Marten; 2 da (Sallie, Rachel); m 2, 1976, Joan Mary MacDermot, *née* Wilkinson (d 1989); m 3, 1989, Patricia Felicity, *née* Read; *Career* RCS 1943-47, served Capt W Africa; RA TA 1948-1955, Maj; joined Samuel Osborn & Co Ltd 1947 (co founded by ggf Samuel Osborn): asst works mangr, prodn controller, cost controller in foundry and engrg subsid, dir Samuel Osborn and subsids 1951-79, gen mangr new precision casting foundry 1954-59; MP (Nat Lib and U) Sheffield, Hallam Div 1959-64, (C) 1964-87; PPS to Sec of State for Cwlth Relations and Colonies (Duncan-Sandys) 1963-64, MEP 1975-79, hon assoc and former memb Assembly Cncl Europe and Western Euro Union 1973-75 and 1980-87, life memb Sheffield C of C; former memb: Assoc of Br C of C, CBI (Yorks and Humberside); memb: IOD (jt hon sec 1922, Ctee 1968-87), Exec Nat Union Cons Pty 1970-87; vice chm Cons Energy Ctee 1979-81, chm Cons Tport Ctee and All-Pty Road Study Gp 1970-74, life memb (former offr and pres); Parly and Scientific Ctee 1960-87, memb Select Ctee on Sci and Technol 1970-73, sr (C) memb Select Ctee for Educn Sci and the Arts; memb Cncl Br Branch Inter-Parly Union 1968-75; former chm Anglo-Swiss Parly Gp and Br Soviet Parly Gp; chm: All Pty Channel Tunnel Gp 1984-87, Friends of Progress 1990-, Business In Devpt Ctee UK Chapter Soc of Int Devpt 1990-; life memb and former chm Parly Gp for Energy Studies 1985-87, memb Interim (formerly Voluntary) Licensing Authy 1987-, hon life memb Industl Soc (memb Cncl 1963-79); Freeman (former Searcher) Cutlers' Co Hallamshire; FIM, FRSA; kt 1983; *Publications* Change or Decay; *Recreations* golf, tennis, photography, gardening, skiing; *Style*— Sir John Osborn; Flat 13, 102 Rochester Row, London SW1 (☎ office 071 219 4189)

OSBORN, Neil Frank; s of George James Osborn, of Hemel Hempstead, and Georgina Rose, *née* Nash; *b* 24 Oct 1949; *Educ* St Albans Sch, Worcester Coll Oxford (MA); *m* 15 April 1975, Holly Louise, da of Lt-Col George Francis Smith, of McLean, Virginia, USA; *Career* reporter The Daily Progress Charlottesville Va USA 1972-74, freelance reporter Lloyds List and Liverpool Daily Post 1975-77, sr ed Instituion Investor NY 1978-83, US ed Euromoney NY 1983-85, ed Euromoney London 1985-90, publisher Euromoney 1990-; dir: Euromoney Inc 1985-, Euromoney Publication 1988-; *Style*— Neil Osborn, Esq; Flat 4, 16 Wetherby Gdns, London SW5 OJP; Euromoney Publications plc, Nestor House, Playhouse Yard, London EC4V 5EX (☎ 071 779 8888, fax 071 779 8653, telex 2907003 EUROMO G)

OSBORN, Sir Richard Henry Danvers; 9 Bt (E 1662), of Chicksands, Bedfordshire; s of Sir Danvers Lionel Rouse Osborn, 8 Bt (d 1983), and Constance Violette, *née* Rooke (d 1988); *b* 12 Aug 1958; *Educ* Eton; *Heir* kinsman, William Danvers Osborn, *qv*; *Career* Christie's 1978-83, ind fine paintings conslt; *Recreations* real tennis, shooting, racing; *Clubs* Turf, MCC, Quuen's; *Style*— Sir Richard Osborn, Bt; The Dower House, Moor Park, Farnham, Surrey GV10 1QX; 25 Queens Gardens, London W2 3BD

OSBORN, William Danvers; s of late Danvers Osborn and late Inez, da of Henry Smith, of Victoria BC; hp of kinsman Sir Richard Osborn, 9 Bt; assumed name William Danvers in lieu of Christian names George Schomberg 1936; 1 Bt received Baronetcy in recognition of all the family had suffered in the cause of Charles I 1662, 3 Bt altered spelling of family name from Osborne to avoid confusion with the family of the Duke of Leeds, He was govr of NY and d there 1753; *b* 1909; *m* 1939, Jean Burns, da of R B Hutchinson, of Vancouver, BC; 1 da (Cheryl Elizabeth b 1945); *Style*— William Osborn, Esq; 2676 Seaview Rd, Victoria, BC, Canada

OSBORNE, Alan; s of Maurice Rowell Osborne (d 1985), of Melbourn, Cambridge, and Muriel Gwendoline, *née* Artis (d 1990); *b* 29 Feb 1928; *Educ* Warwick Sch, Univ of Birmingham (BA); *m* 9 May 1953, Judith Patricia Margaret, da of Charles John Powell (d 1977), of Warham Farm, Breinton, Hereford; 1 s (Robert Charles b 25 Feb 1961), 2 da (Elizabeth Jane b 10 May 1956, Katherine Mary b 30 July 1958); *Career* md Tarmac Construction 1947-88, exec dir Tarmac plc 1975-90; chm: Tarmac Construction Ltd 1988-, Birmingham Business Action Team Ltd 1988-, Construction Industry Standing Conference 1990-; chief exec Birmingham Heartlands Ltd 1988-, non-exec dir Tarmac plc 1990-, dir Wolverhampton TEC 1990-, also currently dir Schal International Ltd; various conferences: Private Finance for Motorways (All Party Study Group of MP's), Construction of Trywym Dam (ABG International Conference Germany), Construction of Public Health Works (Congress Seminar of Inst of Public Health Engrs), Thames Barrier (Major Project Association), Birmingham Heartlands Ltd (Public Works Congress 1989), Financing of Motorways (ICE Conference Harrogate); *Recreations* sailing, shooting, skiing, photography, painting; *Style*— Alan Osborne, Esq; Tarmac Construction Limited, Birch St, Wolverhampton WV1 4HY

OSBORNE, Anthony Robert; s of Robert Bertram Osborne, of Dorset, and Olive May, *née* Russell; *b* 20 Oct 1944; *Educ* Univ of Bristol (LLB); *m* 8 May 1971, Anna, da of Kenneth Charles Smith, of Dorset; 2 s (James b 1975, Thomas b 1980), 1 da (Kate b 1974); *Career* slr Clarke Willmott & Clarke; *Recreations* field sports; *Style*— Anthony Osborne, Esq; Tilworth House, Tilworth, Axminster, Devon (☎ 02977 200); 50-54 Fore St, Chard, Somerset (☎ 0460 62777, telex 46269, fax 0460 677450)

OSBORNE, Charles Thomas; s of Vincent Lloyd Osborne; *b* 24 Nov 1927; *Educ* Brisbane State HS; *m* 1970 (m dis 1975), Marie Korbelarova; *Career* author; lit dir Arts Cncl of GB 1971-86, chief theatre critic Daily Telegraph 1987-; *Books* The Complete Operas of Verdi (1969), W H Auden: the life of a poet (1979), Dictionary of the Opera (1983), Giving It Away: memoirs (1986), The Complete Operas of Richard Strauss (1988), The Complete Operas by Richard Wagner (1990); *Recreations* travel; *Style*— Charles Osborne, Esq; 125 St George's Road, London SE1 6HY (☎ 071 928 1534)

OSBORNE, David Francis; s of William Henry Osborne (d 1969), of Surrey, and Beatrice Irene, *née* Hinge; *b* 24 Oct 1937; *Educ* Dulwich, Jesus Coll Oxford (MA); *m* 25 March 1964 (m dis 1977), Sheila, *née* Atkins; 1 s (Martin b 1965), 2 da (Katharine b 1967, Juliet b 1968); *Career* Unilever Ltd 1960-66, PA International Management Consultants 1966-82, Hill Samuel & Co Ltd 1982-87, dir Electra Investmt Tst PLC 1987-; MBIM, MICMA, MIMC; *Recreations* cricket, golf, ballet, reading, languages, bridge; *Clubs* MCC; *Style*— David Osborne, Esq; White Rose Cottage, 95 High St, Wargrave, Reading, Berks RG10 8DD (☎ 0734 40 4176); Electra Investment Trust plc, 65 Kingsway, London WC2B 6QT (☎ 071 831 6464, fax 071 242 1806, telex 265525 ELECG G)

OSBORNE, HE Dr Denis Gordon; CMG (1990); s of Alfred Gordon Osborne, of Woodburn Common, Bucks, and Frances Agnes Osborne; *b* 17 Sept 1932; *Educ* Dr Challoner's GS Amersham Bucks, Univ of Durham (BSc, PhD); *m* 16 May 1970, Christine Susannah, da of Percy Rae Shepherd (d 1987); 2 da (Ruth b 1971, Sally b 1973); *Career* lectr in physics: Univ of Durham 1957, Fourah Bay Coll Freetown SA 1958, Univ of Ghana 1958-64; dean of sci Univ of Dar Es Salaam 1968-70 (reader in physics 1964-66, prof of physics 1966-71), conslt World Bank Malaysia 1971 and Ethiopia 1972, res fell in physics UCL 1971-72; ODA London: princ UN 1972-75, princ ME 1975-77, sci and technol 1977-80, asst sec natural resources 1980-84, asst sec Eastern and Western Africa 1984-87; High Cmmr in Malawi 1987-; reader: St Barnabas Church Dulwich, St Peter's Church Lilongwe; author of papers on geophysics, technol, educn and devpt; govr Dulwich Coll Prep Sch; CPhys, FInstP 1966; *Books* Way Out: Some Parables of Science and Faith (1977); *Recreations* reading, writing, attempts at windsurfing; *Clubs* Athenaeum, Royal Cwlth Soc; *Style*— HE Dr Denis Osborne, CMG; c/o FCO, King Charles St, London SW1A 2AH

OSBORNE, Hugh Daniel; OBE (1989); s of Francis Mardon Osborne (d 1964), of

Chagford, Devon, and Winifred Mary, *née* Bartlet; *b* 12 Aug 1927; *Educ* Harrow; *m* 12 July 1954, Geraldine Mary, da of Richard George Spring (d 1957), of Wexford, Ireland; 2 s (Charles Hugh b 13 June 1957, Henry Richard b 5 Feb 1961), 1 da (Clare Madeline b 13 April 1959); *Career* RM 1945-47; The Law Debenture Corpn plc: tst mangr 1963, dir 1967, md 1976-88, non exec dir 1988-; chm debenture and loan stock ctee Assoc of Corp Tstees 1979-82; *Recreations* walking, fishing; *Clubs* City of London; *Style—* Hugh Osborne, Esq, OBE; 27 Montserrat Rd, Putney, London SW15 2LD; Ivy Cove, Chivelstone, Devon, (☎ 01 789 9498); The Law Debenture Corporation, Princes House, 85 Gresham St, EC2V 7LY, (☎ 071 606 5451, fax 071 606 0643, telex 888347)

OSBORNE, Prof John; s of Leonard Osborne (d 1948), and Gladys Ellen, *née* Ward; *b* 31 Dec 1938; *Educ* Royal Masonic Sch, Univ Coll Swansea (BA), Univ of Göttingen, Univ of Cambridge (PhD); *m* 7 Sept 1962, Janet Elizabeth, da of Alan George Hart, of Hove, Sussex; 1 s (Luke b 1979), 3 da (Helen b 1966, Josephine b 1968, Mary b 1975); *Career* lectr in German Univ of Southampton 1965-68, lectr and reader in German Univ of Sussex 1968-79, Alexander von Humboldt res fell Univ of Göttingen 1972-73 and 1976-77, prof of German Univ of Warwick 1979-, visiting prof Univ of Metz 1985-86; memb Cncl Eng Goethe Soc; *Books* The Naturalist Drama in Germany (1971), J M R Lenz: The Renunciation of Heriosm (1975), Die Meininger: Texte zur Rezeption (1980), Meyer or Fontane? (1983), The Meiningen Court Theatre (1988); *Recreations* listening to music, travel, swimming; *Style—* Prof John Osborne; 30 Waverley Rd, Kenilworth, Warwickshire CV8 1JN (☎ 0926 512126); Department of German Studies, University of Warwick, Coventry CV4 7AL (☎ 0203 523523)

OSBORNE, John James; s of Thomas Godfrey Osborne and Nellie Beatrice, *née* Grove; *b* 12 Dec 1929; *Educ* Belmont Coll Devon; *m* 1, 1951 (m dis 1957), Pamela Elizabeth Lane; m 2, 1957 (m dis 1963), Mary Ure (d 1975); m 3, 1963 (m dis 1968), Penelope Gilliatt; m 4, 1968 (m dis 1977), Jill Bennett (d 1990); m 5, 1978, Helen Dawson; *Career* dramatist and actor, first stage appearance, No Room at the Inn (Sheffield 1948); plays filmed: Look Back in Anger 1958, The Entertainer 1959 and 1975, Inadmissible Evidence 1965, Luther 1971; Films: Tom Jones (Oscar for Best Screenplay 1964); dir of Woodfall Films; *Books* Plays incl: Look Back in Anger 1957, The Entertainer 1957, Epitaph for George Dillon (with A Creighton), The World of Paul Slickey 1959, Luther 1960, A Subject of Scandal and Concern 1960, Plays for England 1963, A Bond Honoured 1966 (adapted), The Hotel in Amsterdam 1967, Hedda Gabler (adapted) 1970, West of Suez 1971, A Place Calling Itself Rome 1972, A Better Class of Person 1981; Hon Dr RCA 1970; *Clubs* Garrick; *Style—* John Osborne, Esq; c/o Fraser & Dunlop, The Chambers, Lots Road, London SW10 0XF

OSBORNE, Col John Lander; CBE (1969, MBE 1943), TD (1947), DL (W Midlands 1975); s of Frank John Osborne, MC (d 1959), of Solihull, W Midlands, and Ida Marie, *née* Lander (d 1972); *b* 30 June 1917; *Educ* Solihull Sch, Villiars (Switzerland), Birmingham Sch of Architecture; *m* 1, 1942, Kate Honour (d 1980), da of Col Duncan Cameron, of Glasgow and Rawalpindi (d 1929); 1 da; m 2, 1981, Phyllis Mary Tipper, da of Harold Dyas James, of Little Aston, W Midlands (d 1964); *Career* WWII Lt-Col BEF Belgium and France 1939-40; serv 1942-46: N Africa, Middle E, Sicily, Italy; rejoined TA 1947, Regt Cdr RE 1950-57, chief engr W Mids Dist 1958-66, Hon Col 48 Div Engrs 1957-66, ADC to HM The Queen 1968-72; ptnr The John Osborne Partnership Chartered Architects 1947-82, conslt 1982-87; pres Birmingham and Five Counties Architectural Assoc 1962-64; chm W Midlands Regn RIBA 1970-72; *Recreations* sailing (yacht 'Wetherley'), skiing, golf, horticulture; *Clubs* Army and Navy, Royal Thames Yacht, Birmingham, Little Aston Golf; *Style—* Col John Osborne, CBE, TD, DL; Maidenwell, Broad Campden, Chipping Campden, Glos GL55 6UR (☎ 0386 840772)

OSBORNE, John Leslie; s of Frederick James Osborne, of Lampeter, Wales, and May Doris, *née* Brown; *b* 20 March 1942; *Educ* The London Hosp Med Coll Univ of London (MB BS); *m* 4 Jan 1969, (Ann Doreen) Jillian, da of Samuel Greer Telford (d 1980), of Durban, SA; 2 s (Andrew b 1972, James b 1979), 2 da (Clare b 1969, Julia b 1981); *Career* lectr in obstetrics and gynaecology Inst of Obstetrics and Gynaecology 1974-79, conslt obstetrician and gynaecologist Queen Charlotte's and Chelsea Hosp for Women and combined Univ Coll and Middx Hosp 1979-; hon sr lectr: Inst of Urology, Inst of Obstetrics and Gynaecology; Freeman Worshipful Soc Apothecaries; FRCOG 1985 (MRCOG 1973), memb RSM; *Recreations* music, photography, old cars (Bentley); *Clubs* Bentley Drivers; *Style—* John Osborne, Esq; 61 Harley House, Marylebone Rd, London NW1 5HL (☎ 071 935 1682)

OSBORNE, The Honourable Lord Kenneth Hilton; QC (Scot) 1976; s of Kenneth Osborne and Evelyn Alice, *née* Hilton; *b* 9 July 1937; *Educ* Larchfield Sch Helensburgh, Merchiston Castle Sch Edinburgh, Univ of Edinburgh; *m* 1964, Clare Ann Louise Lewis; 1 s, 1 da; *Career* admitted to Faculty of Advocates in Scotland 1962; chm: disciplinary ctee Potato Mktg Bd 1975-90, legal aid ctee Supreme Ct 1979-81; advocate-depute 1982-84; pt/t legal memb Lands Tbnl for Scot 1985-87, sen Coll of Justice in Scotland 1990-; *Clubs* New (Edinburgh); *Style—* The Honourable Lord Osborne, QC; 42 India St, Edinburgh EH3 6HB (☎ 031 225 3094) Primrose Cottage, Bridgend of Lintrathen, by Kirriemuir, Angus DD8 5JH (Lintrathen 057 56 316)

OSBORNE, Sir Peter George; 17 Bt (I 1629); s of Lt-Col Sir George Francis Osborne, 16 Bt, MC (d 1960), and Mary, *née* Horn (d 1987); Richard Osborne cr 1 Bt of Ireland 1629, and supported Parl against the crown; 2, 7, 8, 9 and 11 Bt's were MPs (8 Bt, PC); *b* 29 June 1943; *Educ* Wellington, Ch Ch Oxford; *m* 1968, Felicity, da of late Grantley Loxton-Peacock; 4 s (George b 1971, Benedict b 1973, Adam b 1976, Theo b 1985); *Heir* s, George Oliver Osborne b 23 May 1971; *Career* chm Osborne & Little plc; *Style—* Sir Peter Osborne, Bt; 36 Porchester Terrace, London W2; Vinnicks, Highclere, nr Newbury, Berks

OSBORNE, Richard Ellerker; s of William Harold Osborne (d 1984), and Georgina Mary, *née* Farrow; *b* 22 Feb 1943; *Educ* Worksop Coll, Univ of Bristol (BA, MLitt); *m* 18 Jan 1986, Hailz-Emily, da of Michael Ewart Wrigley, of Streetly, W Midlands; *Career* head of English Bradfield Coll Berks 1982-88 (teacher 1967-88, head 6 form gen studies 1979-88); contrib: Records and Recording 1967-73, Gramophone 1974-, Opera, Times Literary Supplement, The Independent; presenter BBC Radio 3 Saturday Review 1988-; chm music section Critics' Circle 1984-87; *Books* Rossini (1986), Conversations with Karajan (1989); *Recreations* cooking, fell walking; *Style—* Richard Osborne, Esq; Old Rectory, Bradfield, Berks RG7 6AY (☎ 0734 744395)

OSBORNE, Hon Mrs (Rosemary Alys Audrey); *née* Graves; da of 6 Baron Graves (d 1937), and Mary Isabel Ada, *née* Parker (d 1962); *b* 10 June 1910; *m* 1938, Maj Herbert Edward Osborne, MC (d 1951); *Recreations* riding; *Style—* The Hon Mrs Osborne; 30A Rose Bush Court, 35/41 Parkhill Rd, London NW3 2PE (☎ 071 586 2248)

OSBORNE, Trevor; s of Alfred Osborne, of Teddington, Middx, and Annie, *née* Edmonson (d 1986); *b* 7 July 1943; *Educ* Sunbury GS; *m* 26 July 1969, Pamela Ann, da of William Stephenson; 1 s (John b 1977), 1 da (Sarah b 1972); *Career* fndr and chm Speyhawk plc 1977-, non-exec dir Redland plc, vice pres Br Property Fedn, memb Cncl Assoc of City Property Owners, memb Royal Opera House Devpt Bd, ldr Wokingham Dist Cncl 1980-82, pres Windsor Community Arts Centre; Freeman Worshipful Co of Chartered Surveyors; FRSA, FRICS; *Recreations* travel, theatre, tennis; *Clubs* Arts, Carlton; *Style—* Trevor Osborne, Esq; Pinewood House, Nine Mile Ride, Wokingham, Berks; Flat 3, 113 Mount St, London W1; Speyhawk plc, Osprey House, Lower Square, Old Isleworth, Middlesex TW7 6BN (☎ 081 560 2161, fax 081 568 7603)

OSERS, Ewald; s of Paul Osers, (d 1923), of Prague, and Fini, *née* Anders (d 1942); *b* 13 May 1917; *Educ* Schs in Prague Czechoslovakia, Prague Univ, Univ of London (BA); *m* 3 June 1941, Mary, da of Arthur Harman (d 1959); 1 s (Richard b 1951), 1 da (Ann Margaret b 1947); *Career* translator/writer; BBC 1939-77, chm Translators' Assoc 1971, 1980-81, 1983-84; chm Translators' Guild 1975-79; vice-pres Int Fedn of Translators 1977-81, 1984-87; Schlegel-Tieck Prize 1971, CB Nathhorst Prize 1977, Josef Dobrovsky Medal 1980, Gold Pin of Honour of the German Translators' Assoc, Silver Pegasus of the Bulgarian Writers Union 1983, Dilia Medal Czechoslovakia 1986, European Poetry Translation Prize 1987, Vitezslav Nezval Medal of the Czech Literary Fndn 1987, P-F Caillé Medal 1987, Golden Pen of the Macedonian Translators Union 1988, Austrian Translation Prize 1989; FRSL 1984; translated over 100 books, 28 of them poetry; *Books* Wish You Were Here (poems, 1976); *Recreations* music, skiing; *Style—* Ewald Osers, Esq; 33 Reades Lane, Sonning Common, Reading RG4 9LL (☎ 0734 723196)

OSLEAR, Donald Osmund (Don); s of John Osmund Oslear, of Cleethorpes, S Humberside, and Violet Maude, *née* Shepheard; *b* 3 March 1929; *Educ* Elliston St Secdy Sch Cleethorpes, Colwyn Bay Coll N Wales; *m* 1965 (m dis 1986), Doreen, *née* Mulhall; 1 da (Sara Elizabeth b 25 Feb 1970); *Career* cricket umpire; minor counties and second team level 1972-74, first class Panel of Umpires 1975-, Test Match Panel 1980-, World Cup Panel 1983; chm Panel of First Class Umpires TCCB 1990-, memb Assoc of Cricket Umpires; conducted numerous cricket lectures in UK and over 500 overseas incl: NZ, W Indies, Sri Lanka, Zinbabwe, Israel; first Test umpire not to have played professional cricket; sporting achievements incl: footballer Grimsby Town 1951-52 (amateur player 1945), various ice hockey teams incl Grimsby Redwings 1952-58, semi-professional footballer Denaby Utd 1958-63, local football 1963-69, memb Cleethorpes Cricket Club 1942- (player then tour organiser); only net minder to secure a shut-out for Grimsby Redwings v Streatham Royals 1953; chm Grimsby and Dist Umpires Assoc 1976-80; *Publications* author of numerous articles for county club handbooks; *Recreations* studying the laws of cricket; *Style—* Don Oslear, Esq; 425 Louth Rd, New Waltham, Grimsby, S Humberside DN36 4PP (☎ 0472 822903)

OSLER, John Murray; s of Peter Alfred George Osler (d 1990), and Estelle Cordiner, *née* Murray (d 1981); *b* 1 March 1937; *Educ* Charterhouse, Gonville and Caius Coll Cambridge (MA); *m* 26 Oct 1963, Pamela Hilary, da of Robert Oliver Scott; 3 s (Jeremy Joseph Scott b 17 Sept 1971, Charles Samuel Scott b 27 July 1981, William Daniel Scott (twin) b 27 July 1981), 1 da (Rosemary Beatrice Scott b 10 Sept 1974); *Career* articled clerk Ryland Martineau & Co Birmingham 1960-63; asst slr: Frere Cholmeley London 1963-67, Stephenson Harwood London 1967-71; ptnr: Herbert Oppenheimer Nathan Vandyk 1972-88 (asst slr 1971), S J Berwin & Co London 1988-; memb: Worshipful Co of Slrs, Law Soc 1963-; *Recreations* music, theatre, skiing; *Style—* John Osler, Esq; S J Berwin & Co, 236 Gray's Inn Rd, London WC1X 8HB (☎ 071 278 0444, fax 071 833 2860)

OSMAN, David Antony; s of Colin Alfred Earnest Osman, of 14 Fairgreen, Cockfosters, Barnet, Herts, and Grace Florence, *née* White; *b* 13 April 1953; *Educ* Minchenden GS, Univ of Nottingham (BA); *m* 4 Sept 1986, Helen, da of Randall Jones-Pugh, of St Brides View, Roch, Dyfed; 2 da (Caroline b 15 Nov 1984, Nicola b 23 Jan 1987); *Career* dir: RP Publishing Co Ltd 1975-78 (non-exec dir 1978-), RP Typesetters Co Ltd 1980-; UK economist Joseph/Carr Sebag & Co 1978-82, UK and int economist Laing & Cruickshank 1982-84, int economist James Capel & Co 1984-; fndr memb Enfield SDP 1981-87, SDP/Lib Alliance Pty candidate for Upminster 1983, vice chm (fndr memb and sec) City SDP 1984-88, fndr and memb Enfield Lib Democrats 1988-; sec City Democratic Forum 1988-89; memb City Lib Democrats 1990-, memb Soc of Business Economists; *Recreations* chess, cycling, football, golf, snooker; *Clubs* Old Minchendenians Football; *Style—* David Osman, Esq; 10 Old Park Ridings, Winchmore Hill, London N21 2EU (☎ 081 360 4343); James Capel & Co, 6 Bevis Marks, London EC3A 7JQ (☎ 071 621 0011, fax 071 621 0496, telex 888866)

OSMOND, Sir Douglas; OBE (1958), QPM (1962), CBE (1968); *b* 27 June 1914; *Educ* Univ of London (BSc); *Career* chief constable: Shropshire 1946-62, Hampshire 1962-77; memb Royal Cmmn on Criminal Procedure 1978-81; pres Assoc of Chief Police Offrs 1967-69, chm Police Cncl for UK 1972 and 1974; memb: Bd of Govrs Police Coll 1968-72, Inter Departmental Ctee on Death Certification and Coroners 1964-71; OStJ 1971; kt 1971; *Style—* Sir Douglas Osmond, CBE, QPM, DL; Woodbine Cottage, Ovington, Alresford, Hants SO24 0RF (☎ 096 273 3729)

OSMOND, Lady; Olivia Sybil; *née* Wells; JP (1971); da of Ernest Edward Wells, JP, (d 1948), of Kegworth, Leics, and Olivia Maud, *née* Orton (d 1956); *Educ* St Elphins Sch Darley Dale, Newnham Coll Cambridge (MA, MSc); *m* 5 Feb 1942, Sir Paul Osmond, CB, *qv*, 2 s (Oliver b 1944, Andrew b 1949); *Career* economist and statistician Nat Inst of Econ and Social Res 1938-39, Miny of Econ Warfare 1939-41, FO 1942-44, Int Fedn of Agric Prodrs 1951-60, econ advsr Miny of Health 1967; memb: Br Section Exec European Union of Women 1961-86, Bd of Govrs Bethlem Royal and Maudsley Hosp 1968-82 (vice chm 1980-82), Cncl Cambridge Soc 1980- (chm Exec Ctee 1988-), Cncl Independant Schs Careers Orgn 1986-; govr St Elphins Sch 1967-, assoc Newnham Coll 1977-90; *Recreations* gardening, travel, theatre; *Clubs* Utd Oxford and Cambridge Univ; *Style—* Lady Osmond, JP; 20 Beckenham Grove, Shortlands, Bromley, Kent BR2 0JU (☎ 081 460 2026)

OSMOND, Sir (Stanley) Paul; CB (1966); s of late Stanley C Osmond (d 1966), of Bristol; *b* 13 May 1917; *Educ* Bristol GS, Jesus Coll Oxford; *m* 1942, Olivia Sybil, JP, *qv*, da of late Ernest E Wells, JP; 2 s; *Career* The Buffs, WWII Glos Regt and staff 1940-46; Home Civil Serv 1939-75; sec to the Church Commrs 1975-80, chm Nat Marriage Guidance Cncl 1982-88, pres Bromley Marriage Guidance Cncl 1982-90; kt 1980; *Clubs* Athenaeum; *Style—* Sir Paul Osmond, CB; 20 Beckenham Grove, Bromley, Kent BR2 0JU (☎ 081 460 2026)

OSMOTHERLY, Edward Benjamin Crofton; s of Crofton Robert Osmotherly, of London, and Elsie May, *née* Sargent (d 1967); *b* 1 Aug 1942; *Educ* East Ham GS, Fitzwilliam Coll Cambridge (MA); *m* 6 June 1970, Valerie Ann, da of L R Mustill, CBE, (d 1984); 1 s (John Nicholas b 1975), 1 da (Clare b 1972); *Career* asst princ Miny Housing and Local Govt 1963-68 (private sec to parly sec and Min of State 1966-68), princ DOE 1968-76, asst sec DOE and Tport 1976-82, dep sec Dept of Tport 1989- (under sec 1982-88); Harkness fell Brookings Instn USA and exec fell Univ of California (Berkeley) 1972-73, sec Ctee on Railway Fin 1982; *Recreations* squash, reading; *Style—* Edward Osmotherly, Esq; Dept of Transport, 2 Marsham St, London SW1

OSSELTON, Prof Noel Edward; s of Charles Turney Osselton (d 1964), and Evelyn Maude, *née* Scupham (d 1975); *b* 14 April 1927; *Educ* Staines GS Middx, King's Coll Univ of London (MA), Univ of Groningen The Netherlands; *m* 17 Aug 1955, Catharina Johanna, da of Jacob Bleeker (d 1961); 3 da (Johanna, Elizabeth, Catharine); *Career* RAF 1945-48, served Belgium and Holland (missing res and enquiry); lectr in English

Univ of Southampton 1954-69; prof of English: Univ of Leiden Holland 1969-83 (chm English language), Univ of Newcastle 1984; memb Euro Assoc For Lexicography (pres 1985-88); *Books* Branded Words in English Dictionaries (1958), The Dumb Linguists (1973); *Style—* Prof Noel Osselton; University of Newcastle, Dept of English Language, Newcastle upon Tyne (☎ 091 222 6000)

OSTROM, Neil Ian Eric; s of Erik Hugo Magnus Ostrom (d 1981), and Florence Louise, *née* Mees (d 1971); *b* 26 July 1923; *Educ* Bedford Sch, Univ of Cambridge, Univ of London (BA); *m* 23 May 1953, Fay, da of William Henry Ceney (d 1982); 2 s (Mark, Toby), 1 da (Tessa); *Career* RAFVR 1942-47: trg as Air Observer 1942-43, Bomber Cmd 1944, Pathfinder Force Navigator 1944, (POW 1944-45); dir: E V Hawtin Ltd 1958-68, Glynn Manson Organisation Ltd 1973; chm: Stewart Nairn Group plc 1974-82, Central London Branch BIM 1989-; Freeman Guild of Air Pilots and Air Navigators 1991; FInstD 1984, FBIM 1984; *Recreations* languages, travel, writing, water sports, astronomy, music, investments; *Style—* Neil Ostrom, Esq; Priestfield, Watts Lane, Chislehurst, Kent BR7 5PJ (☎ 081 467 1989)

OSWALD, Lady Angela Mary Rose; *née* Cecil; 3 da of 6 Marquess of Exeter, KCMG (d 1981), and yst da by his 1 w, Lady Mary, *née* Montagu Douglas Scott da of 7 Duke of Buccleuch; *b* 21 May 1938; *m* 1958, (William Richard) Michael Oswald, CVO, *qv*; 1 s (William Alexander Michael b 1962), 1 da (Mrs Alexander Fergus Matheson *qv*); *Career* Woman of the Bedchamber to HM Queen Elizabeth, The Queen Mother 1983- (Extra Woman of the Bedchamber 1981-83); *Style—* The Lady Angela Oswald; Flitcham Hall, King's Lynn, Norfolk PE31 6BY (☎ 0485 600319); Apt 8a, Hampton Court Palace, E Molesey, Surrey (☎ 081 977 5673)

OSWALD, Eduard; *b* 21 July 1951; *Educ* Univ of Economics Vienna (BSc Econ); *m* 8 Dec 1990, Elena, *née* Mondelli; *Career* Girozentrale Vienna: fin analyst 1976-78, asst to chm 1979-82, departmental dir new issues sales and research 1983-87; md Girozentrale Gilbert Eliott 1988-; *Style—* Eduard Oswald, Esq; Girozentrale Gilbert Eliott, Salisbury House, London Wall, London EC2M 5SB (☎ 071 628 6782, fax 071 628 3500)

OSWALD, Adm Sir (John) Julian Robertson; GCB (1989, KCB 1987); s of Capt George Hamilton Oswald, RN (d 1971), of Newmore, Invergordon, and Margaret Elliot, *née* Robertson (d 1947); *b* 11 Aug 1933; *Educ* Beaudesert Park Sch, Britannia RNC Dartmouth, RCDS; *m* 25 Jan 1958, Veronica Therese Dorette, da of Eric James Thompson, OBE (d 1975); 2 s (Timothy b 1958, Christopher b 1960), 3 da (Elisabeth b 1963, Victoria b 1967, Samantha b 1970); *Career* Cadet RN 1947-51, Midshipman 1952-53 (HM Ships Vanguard and Verulam), Sub Lt 1953-55 (HMS Theseus), Lt 1955-63 (HM Ships Newfoundland, Jewel, Excellent (gunnery specialist course), Victorious and Yarnton), Lt Cdr 1963-68 (HM Ships Excellent, Naiad, MOD (Naval Plans)), Cdr 1969-73 (HMS Bacchante, MOD (Def Policy Staff)), Capt 1974-82 MOD (asst dir Def Policy), RCDS, HMS Newcastle, RN Presentation Team BRNC Dartmouth, Rear Adm 1982-86, Asst Chief of Def Staff (Programmes), Asst Chief of Defence Staff (Policy and Nuclear), Vice Adm 1986-87 (Flag Offr Third Flotilla and Cdr ASW Striking Force), Adm 1987- (C-in-C Fleet, Allied C-in-C Channel, C-in-C Eastern Atlantic), First Sea Lord and Ch of Naval Staff 1989-; memb Cncl RSWI 1989; First and Princ ADC to HM The Queen 1989-; *Recreations* gliding, tennis, fishing, family, stamps; *Clubs* Mensa; *Style—* Admiral Sir Julian Oswald, GCB, ADC; c/o Naval Secretary, Old Admiralty Building, Whitehall, London SW1 (☎ 071 218 9000)

OSWALD, (William Richard) Michael; CVO (1988, LVO 1979); s of Lt-Col William Alexander Hugh Oswald, ERD (d 1974), of Little Orchard, St George's Hill, Weybridge, Surrey, and Rosie-Marie, *née* Leahy (d 1985); *b* 21 April 1934; *Educ* Eton, King's Coll Cambridge (MA); *m* 21 April 1958, Lady Angela Mary Rose Cecil, *qv*, da of 6 Marquess of Exeter, KCMG (d 1981); 1 s (Capt William Alexander Michael b 1962), 1 da (Katharine Davina Mary (Mrs Alexander Matheson) b 1959); *Career* 2 Lt 1 Bn King's Own Royal Regt 1953, BAOR and Korea, Lt 8 Bn Royal Fusiliers (TA) 1955, Capt 1958-61; memb Cncl of The Thoroughbred Breeders Assoc 1964-, chm Bloodstock Indust Ctee Animal Health Tst; mangr: Lordship and Egerton Studs Newmarket 1962-69, The Royal Studs 1970-; *Recreations* shooting, painting; *Clubs* White's; *Style—* Michael Oswald, Esq, CVO; Flitcham Hall, King's Lynn, Norfolk PE31 6BY (☎ 0485 600319); Apt 8A Hampton Court Palace, E Molesey, Surrey (☎ 081 977 5673); The Royal Studs, Sandringham, Norfolk (☎ 0485 540588, fax 04 855 43 272)

OTTAWAY, Richard Geoffrey James; s of Prof Christopher Wyndham Ottaway (d 1977), and Grace; *b* 24 May 1945; *Educ* Backwell Secdy Mod Sch, Univ of Bristol (LLB); *m* 1982, Nicola Evelyn, da of John Kisch, CMG; *Career* Lt RN, Lt Cdr RNR; PPS to Baroness Young and Tim Renton, MP Min of State FCO; slr; head of legal servs Europe and Far E Coastal Corpn 1988; MP (Cons) Nottingham N 1983-87, prospective Parly candidate (Cons) Croydon South; *Books* Road to Reform, Thoughts for a Third Term (jtly, 1987); *Recreations* yachting; *Clubs* Carlton, Island Sailing; *Style—* Richard Ottaway, Esq; The Studio, 20 Church St, London W4 2PH

OTTER, Robert George (Robin); s of Francis Lewis Otter, MC (d 1946), of Ottershaw, Surrey, and Helen, *née* Stephens (d 1988); *b* 25 Feb 1926; *Educ* Marlborough, Univ Coll Oxford (BA, MA); *m* 16 Dec 1958, Elisabeth Ann, da of Eric Reginald St Aubrey Davies, MBE (d 1986); 2 s (Robert b 1960, David b 1966), 1 da (Lisette b 1968); *Career* Nat Serv RNVR 1944-47, cmmnd 1945, serv Far E 1945-46; dist offr/ cmmr Kenya Colony Colonial Admin Serv 1951-62 (despatches 1957), slr and ptnr Moore, Brown & Dixon Tewkesbury 1963-; Parly liaison offr of Law Soc; lay chm Tewkesbury Deanery Synod, memb Gloucester Diocesan Synod and Bishops Cncl, govr Alderman Knight and Abbey Schs Tewkesbury, govr Three Counties Agric Soc, parly candidate 1966, 1970 and 1974, Euro parly candidate 1979; memb: Law Soc, Glos & Wilts Law Soc; *Books* contrib to Law, A Modern Introduction (ed Paul Denham, 1989); *Recreations* breeder of Gloucester cattle; *Clubs* Royal Cwlth Soc, Mombasa Club (Kenya), Oxford Union; *Style—* Robin Otter, Esq; Kemerton Grange, Tewkesbury, Glos GL20 7JE (☎ 0684 292341, fax 0684 295147)

OTTEWILL, Prof Ronald Harry; OBE (1989); s of Harry Archibald Ottewill (d 1976), of Bristol, and Violet Dorien, *née* Bucklee (d 1989); *b* 8 Feb 1927; *Educ* Southall Co Sch Middx, Queen Mary Coll London (BSc, PhD), Fitzwilliam Coll Cambridge (MA, PhD); *m* 31 Aug 1952, Ingrid Geraldine, da of Henry Roe (d 1963), of Frinton-on-Sea, Essex; 1 s (Adrian Christopher b 1958), 1 da (Geraldine Astrid b 1956); *Career* asst dir of res Univ of Cambridge 1958-63 (sr asst in res 1955-58), Leverhulme prof of physical chemistry 1982- (lectr in physical chemistry 1964-66, reader in colloid sci 1966-70, prof of colloid sci 1971-81, head of Dept of Physical Chemistry 1973-), dean Faculty of Sci 1988-); memb various ctees SERC 1969-85, chm Neutron Beam Res Ctee 1982-86; pres Faraday Div Royal Soc of Chem 1989-; FRS 1982; *Books* Surface Area Determination (1970), Science and Technology of Polymer Colloids (1983), Adsorption from Solution (1983), An Introduction to Polymer Colloids (1990), Scientific Methods for the Study of Polymer Colloids and their Applications (1990); *Recreations* gardening, music; *Style—* Prof Ronald Ottewill, OBE, FRS; School of Chemistry, University of Bristol, Cantocks Close, Bristol BS8 1TS (☎ 0272 303680)

OTTLEY, David Charles; s of Walter Jeremiah Ottley, and Jean Edna, *née* Jarman; *b* 5 Aug 1955; *Educ* Gable Hall Sch, Borough Road Coll; *Career* rep GB 36 occasions javelin; main achievements: 6 times AAAs Champion, World Student Games Silver Medal 1977, UK Closed Champion 1978-82, Olympic Silver Medal 1984, memb of Euro select team at Canberra World Cup 1985, Cwlth Gold Medal 1986; pres Telford Gateway Club (for the mentally handicapped), sec Telford Track Appeal; ILAM 1988; *Clubs* Telford Athletic; *Style—* David Ottley, Esq; Marlo, 8 Station Rd, Admaston, Telford, Shropshire, TF5 0AL (☎ 0952 57885); Wrekin District Council, Malinslee House, Telford, Shropshire (☎ 0952 202 100)

OTTLEY, Robert Jeremy Mark Linn; *Career* dir Greenwell Montagu Stockbrokers 1967-; *Style—* Robert Ottley, Esq; Greenwell Montagu Stockbrokers, 114 Old Broad Street, London EC2P 2HY

OTTO-JONES, John Alcwyn; s of Col Thomas Otto-Jones, CBE, TD, DL (d 1953), of Bredwardine, Hereford, and Kathleen Mary, *née* Hale (d 1979); *b* 7 Feb 1930; *Educ* Christ Coll Brecon, Univ of Cardiff (BA), Wadham Coll Oxford (MA); *m* 1 Oct 1960, Bridget Mary, da of Ernest Jackson, Mansfield, Nottinghamshire; 1 s (Justin b 1963), 1 da (Candida b 1966); *Career* cmmnd RAEC 1950; admitted slr 1957, NP; Under Sheriff of Glamorgan 1985; *Recreations* vintage cars, reading; *Clubs* RAC, Cardiff and County; *Style—* John Otto-Jones, Esq; The Court, St Nicholas, South Glamorgan (☎ 0446 760255); 29 Park Place, Cardiff (☎ 0222 225591)

OTTON, Sir Geoffrey (John); KCB (1980, CB 1978); s of late John Alfred Otton; *b* 10 June 1927; *Educ* Christ's Hosp, St John's Coll, Cambridge (MA); *m* 1952, Hazel Lomas, *née* White; 1 s, 1 da; *Career* second permanent sec DHSS 1979- (under sec 1971-75, dep sec 1975-79); chief advr to Supplementary Benefits Cmmn 1976-; *Style—* Sir Geoffrey Otton, KCB; 72 Cumberland Rd, Bromley, Kent (☎ 081 460 9610)

OTTON, Hon Mr Justice; Hon Sir Philip (Howard); s of late H A Otton; *b* 28 May 1933; *Educ* Bablake Sch Coventry, Birmingham Univ (LLB); *m* 1965, Helen Margaret, da of late P W Bates; 2 s, 1 da; *Career* called to the Bar Gray's Inn 1955, dep chm Beds QS 1970-72, jr counsel to the Treasy (Personal Injuries) 1970-75, rec Crown Ct 1972-83, QC 1975, govr Nat Heart and Chest Hosps 1979-84, master Bench Gray's Inn 1983-, High Ct judge 1983-; presiding judge Midland and Oxford circuit 1986-88; chm: Royal Brompton & Nat Heart & Lung Hosps SHA 1991-, Nat Heart & Lung Inst 1991-; presiding judge Official Referees 1991-; kt 1983; *Recreations* theatre, opera, travel; *Clubs* Garrick, Pilgrims, Roehampton; *Style—* The Hon Sir Philip Otton; Royal Courts of Justice, Strand, London WC2A 2LL

OTWAY, Mark McRae; s of Henry Arthur McRae Otway, of Surrey, and Ann, *née* Ingman; *b* 4 Oct 1948; *Educ* Dulwich, Churchill Coll Cambridge (MA); *m* 10 July 1973, Amanda Mary, da of Roland Stafford; 2 s (Miles Daniel b 1983, Paul David b 1985); *Career* ptnr (now head of business operations mgmnt) Andersen Consulting 1982- (mangr 1975, joined 1970); *Recreations* sailing, music, theatre; *Clubs* United Oxford and Cambridge University; *Style—* Mark Otway, Esq; 22 Albany Park Road, Kingston-on-Thames, Surrey KT2 5SW (☎ 081 546 8116); 2 Arundel Street, London WC2R 3LT (☎ 071 438 3835, car 0860 200743)

OUGH, Dr Richard Norman; s of Rev Conrad Jocelyn Ough (d 1977), and Alice Louisa, *née* Crofts; *b* 25 Jan 1946; *Educ* Stamford Sch, St Mary's Hosp Med Sch Univ of London (MB BS), City Univ London (MA, Dip Law); *m* 1, 1976 (m dis 1982), Shelley Jean Henshaw; 1 s (Geoffrey b 1977), 1 da (Elizabeth b 1978); m 2, 1984 (m dis 1988), Rona Mary Louise Hallam; *Career* med practioner Canada 1974-83; barr 1985, MRCS, LRCP, fell RSM; memb Hon Soc of Inner Temple, memb Hon Soc of Gray's Inn; *Books* The Mareva Injunction and Anton Piller Order (1987); *Recreations* music, theatre; *Style—* Dr Richard Ough; 4 Paper Bldgs, Temple EC4Y 7EX (☎ 071 583 3366, fax 071 353 5778)

OUGHTRED, Peter B; JP; s of Col John Alwyn Oughtred MC, (d 1958), and Phyllis Brown, *née* Jackson (d 1981); *b* 6 April 1921; *Educ* Leys Sch; *m* 1950, Lorna Agnes, da of John McLaren (d 1955); 3 s (Christopher, Angus, Nicholas), 1 da (Louise); *Career* WWII Capt E Yorks Regt UK and overseas 1940-47; chm and jt md Wm Jackson and Son plc, chm Crystal Hull Ltd, dir Beverley Race Co Ltd; farmer & landowner; High Sheriff of Humberside 1987-88; FBIM, FID, FIGD; *Recreations* shooting, fishing, racing; *Clubs* Flyfishers'; *Style—* Peter B Oughtred, Esq, JP; Raby Lodge, 26 Cave Rd, Brough, N Humberside HU15 1HL (☎ 0482 667381); Wodencroft Lodge, Cotherstone, Barnard Castle, Co Durham (☎ 083350 239); William Jackson & Son plc, 40 Derringham St, Hull HU3 1EW (☎ 0482 224131)

OULTON, Sir (Antony) Derek Maxwell; GCB (KCB 1984, CB 1979), QC (1985); s of late Charles Cameron Courtenay Oulton; *b* 14 Oct 1927; *Educ* St Edward's Sch Oxford, King's Coll Cambridge (MA, PhD); *m* 1955, Margaret Geraldine, JP (d 1989), da of late Lt-Col G S Oxley, MC; 1 s, 3 da; *Career* called to the Bar Gray's Inn 1952; dep sec Lord Chancellor's Off 1976-82, perm sec 1982-89; dep clerk of the Crown in Chancery 1977-82, clerk of the Crown in Chancery 1982-89; fell Magdalene Coll Cambridge 1990-, visiting prof in law Univ of Bristol 1990-91; tstee Nat Gallery 1989-; *Style—* Sir Derek Oulton, GCB, QC; Magdalene College, Cambridge CB3 0AG

OULTON, Therese; da of Robert Oulton, of Fir Tree Place, Radborough Common, Stroud, Glos, and Matilda, *née* Glover; *b* 20 April 1953; *Educ* St Martin's Sch of Art London, RCA London; *Career* artist; solo exhibitions: Fool's Gold: New Paintings (Gimpel Fils London) 1984, Recent Painting (MOMA Oxford) 1985, Letters to Rose (Galerie Krinzinger Vienna) 1986, Skin Deep (Galerie Thomas Munich, Galerie am Moritzplatz Berlin) 1986, Monoprints (Marlborough Graphics London) 1987, Lachrimae (Marlborough Fine Arts London) 1988, Hirschl & Adler NY 1989, Therese Oulton - Works on Paper (Marlborough Graphics London) 1989, Marlborough Fine Art London 1990, Paintings and Works on Paper (LA Louwer, LA California) 1991; gp exhibitions incl: John Moores (Walker Art Gallery Liverpool) 1982, 1985, Landscape Memory and Desire (Serpentine Gallery) 1984, The Image as Catalyst (Ashmolean Museum Oxford) 1984, New Painters (Squire's Gallery Newcastle) 1985, How Much Beauty Can I Stand: Contemporary Landscape Painting (Aust Centre for Contemporary Art, S Yarra, Victoria) 1986, British Art and Design (Künstlerhaus Vienna) 1986, American/ European: Painting and Sculpture (LA Louver Gallery Calif) 1986, Kunst aus des achtziger Jahren (Sammlung Thomas All Art Forum Munich) 1987, Oulton Prengenberg Snyder (Hirsch & Alder NY) 1987, Turner Prize Display (Tate Gallery London) 1987, The Romantic Tradition in Contemporary British Painting (Sola de Exposiciones de Palacio de San Estelson Murcia and Circulo de San Estelson Madrid) 1988, 100 Years of Art in Britain (Leeds City Art Gallery) 1988, The British Picture (LA Louver Gallery Calif) 1988, Blasphemies Ecstacies Cries (Serpentine Gallery London and tour) 1989, The New British Painting (Contemporary Arts Center Cincinnati and tour) 1989, 3 Ways (Br Cncl/RCA touring exhibitions) 1990, Venice Bienale (Aperto) 1990, The Forces of Nature (Manchester City Art Galleries and Harris Museum and Art Gallery) 1990-91; work in pub collections: Arts Cncl of GB London, Br Cncl London, Harris Museum and Art Gallery Preston, Metropolitan Museum of Art NY, John Moores Liverpool, Tate Gallery; *Style—* Ms Therese Oulton; 38 St Stephen's Gardens, London W2 5NS

OUTHWAITE, Richard Henry Moffitt; s of Richard Moffitt Outhwaite (d 1971), and Barbara, *née* Hainsselin; *b* 1 Nov 1905; *Educ* Ashville Coll Harrogate; *m* 1, 3 May 1958 (m dis 1979), Lilian Irma, da of Paul Walter Heinemann (d 1977); 2 s (Paul, Alan), 2 da (Fiona, Susan); m 2, 2 Sep 1983, Ann Margaret, da of Donald Walter Mellor, CBE, of The Red House, West Hanningfield, Essex; 2 da (Katherine, Sophie); *Career* dir: R J Merrett Syndicates Ltd 1969-74, RHM Outhwaite Syndicates 1974-;

Freeman: Worshipful Co of Shipwrights, Worshipful Co of Insurs; *Recreations* music, golf, field sports; *Style*— Richard Outhwaite, Esq; 85 Gracechurch St, London EC3 (☎ 071 623 1481)

OUTRAM, Sir Alan James; 5 Bt (UK 1858); s of late James Ian Outram (gs of 2 Bt), and Evelyn Mary, *née* Littlehales; suc gt uncl, Sir Francis Davidson Outram, 4 Bt, OBE, 1945; Lt-Gen Sir James Outram, GCB, KBE, received Baronetcy 1858 for service in Persia and India; *b* 15 May 1937; *Educ* Marlborough, St Edmund Hall Oxford; *m* 1976, Victoria Jean, da of late George Dickson Paton; 1 s, 1 da (Alison b 1977); *Heir* s, Douglas Benjamin James Outram b 15 March 1979; *Career* Hon Lt-Col TA & VR; housemaster Druries Harrow Sch 1979- (formerly asst master); *Recreations* bridge, golf, tennis, cycling; *Style*— Sir Alan Outram, Bt; Harrow School, Harrow-on-the-Hill, Middlesex

OUTRIM, Hon Mrs (Olive Fenna); *née* Brockway; da of Baron Brockway (Life Peer), and his 1 w, Lilla, *née* Harvey-Smith; *b* 1924; *m* 1944 (m dis 1986), Cecil Outrim; children; *Style*— The Hon Mrs Outrim

OUTTEN, Alan Gilbert; s of Mark (Bertie) Outten (d 1986), and Mabel Letitia, *née* Griffiths; *b* 12 Jan 1933; *Educ* Drayton Manor GS, Univ of London (LLB); *m* 28 May 1960, Margaret Therese, da of R James Joseph Hearty, of Newry, Co Down (d 1955); 4 s (Andrew b 1961, Brian b 1963, Alan b 1966, Christopher b 1973), 2 da (Catherine b 1965, Gemma b 1979); *Career* actuary; dir Forward Trust Group Ltd and subsidiary cos, dep chm Motability Fin Ltd, former chm Equipment Leasing Assoc; *Recreations* tennis, theatre, music; *Style*— Alan Outten, Esq; 16 Cleveland Rd, West Ealing, London W13 (☎ 081 997 6517); The Barn, Alfriston, East Sussex (☎ 0323 87000)

OVENDEN, Graham Stuart; s of Henry Ovenden (d 1986), of Winchester, and Gwendoline Dorothy, *née* Hill (d 1988); *b* 11 Feb 1943; *Educ* Itchen GS, Southampton Coll of Art, Royal Coll of Music (ARCM), Royal Coll of Art (ARCA, MA); *m* 1 March 1969, Ann Dinah, da of George Walter Gilmore (d 1963), of Upper Winchendon, Bucks; 1 s (Edmund Dante b 1972), 1 da (Emily Alice b 1976); *Career* painter, poet, art historian; numerous exhibitions incl the Tate Gallery and Royal Acad, one man shows in most major western countries; fndr memb The Brotherhood of Ruralists 1976; *Books* Illustrators of Alice (1971), Victorian Children (with Robert Melville, 1972), Pre-Raphaelite Photography (1972), Hill and Adamson Photographs (1973), Alphonse Mucha Photographs (1973), Clementina Lady Hawarden (1973), Victorian Erotic Photography (1973), Aspects of Lolita (1975), A Victorian Family Album (with Lord David Cecil, 1976), Satirical Poems and Others (1983), The Marble Mirror (poetry, 1984), Lewis Carroll Photographer (1984); *Recreations* music, architecture; *Style*— Graham Ovenden, Esq; Barley Splatt, Panters Bridge, Mount, Cornwall (☎ 020 882 336)

OVENSTONE, Dr Irene Margaret Kinnear; da of David Ovenstone (d 1951), and Edith Margaret Ovenstone (d 1984); *b* 25 Oct 1989; *Educ* Harris Acad Dundee Scotland, Univ of St Andrews (MB ChB, PPH), Univ of Leeds (DPM), Univ of Dundee (MD); *Career* asst registrar MCH Huddersfield 1957-61, sr registrar psychiatry Westminster Hosp London 1964-68, memb Scientific Staff and hon lecturer MRC Unit Epidemiological Studies Psychiatry Edinburgh 1969-72, conslt psychiatrist specialising in psychiatry old age and clinical teacher Univ of Nottingham 1973-, sec and chm Nottingham Area Psychiatric Div 1974-79; memb Working Pty: Psychiatric Nurse Education 1974, Drug Custody and Admin 1977, Home for Elderly Project Notts Social Services Dept 1981; chm Notts Health Care Planning Team for Elderly 1981-82; memb: Mental Health Tbnls 1981-, Mental Health Cmmn 1983-86, Health Advsy Service 1989-; author of papers on suicidal behaviour, mental neurosis, admissions to old peoples homes in Nottingham; MRCPsych 1973, FRCPsych 1978; *Recreations* ballet, music, theatre, archeology, art, wildlife; *Style*— Dr Irene Ovenstone; 10 Moor Park, Calverton, Nottingham NG14 6FW (☎ 0602 653309); St Francis Unit, City Hospital, Hucknall Rd, Nottingham NG5 1PB (☎ 0602 691169, car 0836 532823)

OVER, Chief Constable John Edwin; CPM (1980), QPM (1983); s of Herbert George Over, and Winifred Ellen, *née* Barnett; *b* 14 Dec 1930; *Educ* Woking GS; *m* 16 Jan 1953, June Rose, da of Robert George Tickner; 1 da (Dawn (Dr)); *Career* joined Met Police 1951; Surrey 1957, Hong Kong 1970, Asst Chief Constable Surrey 1974-76, Dep Chief Constable Dorset 1976-78, Sr Asst Cmmr Royal Hong Kong Police 1978-80, Chief Constable Gwent 1980-; chm Traffic Ctee Assoc Chief Police Offrs 1984-90 (sec); *Recreations* gardening; *Style*— John Over, Esq, CPM, QPM; Police HQ, Croesyceiliog, Gwent (☎ 0633 838111)

OVEREND, Prof (William) George; s of Harold George Overend (d 1986), of Shrewsbury, and Hilda, *née* Parry (d 1974); *b* 16 Nov 1921; *Educ* Priory Sch Shrewsbury, Univ of Birmingham (BSc, PhD, DSc); *m* 12 July 1949, Gina Olava, da of Horace Bertie Cadman (d 1980), of Birmingham, Warwicks; 2 s (George Edmund (Ted) b 1958, Desmond Anthony b 1963), 1 da (Sheila Hilda b 1961); *Career* assoc prof Pennsylvania State Coll 1951-52; Univ of London: reader in organic chemistry 1955-57, prof of chemistry 1957-87, emeritus prof 1987-, Leverhulme emeritus fell 1987-89; Birkbeck Coll London: head Dept of Chemistry 1957-79, vice master 1974-78, master 1979-87; senator Univ of London 1978-87; memb: Br Pharmacopoeia Cmmn 1962-80, Home Office Poisons Bd 1966-, vice pres Perkin Div Royal Soc of Chemistry 1976-78, chm Cncl of Govrs S Bank Poly 1980-89 (memb Bd of Govrs 1989-); memb Cncl Royal Soc of Chemistry 1972-78; Lampitt Medallist Soc of Chemical Indust 1965; Hon FCP 1986; hon fell: Birkbeck Coll 1987, S Bank Poly 1989; Hon DUniv Open Univ 1988; CChem, FRSC, FBIM, FRSA; *Books* The Use of Tracer Elements in Biology (1951), Programmes in Organic Chemistry I-VIII (ed, 1966-73); *Recreations* gardening; *Clubs* Athenaeum, RAC; *Style*— Prof George Overend; The Retreat, Nightingales Lane, Chalfont St Giles, Bucks HP8 4SR (☎ 0494 763996); Department of Chemistry, Birkbeck College (University of London), Gordon House, Gordon Street, London WC1E 7HX (☎ 071 380 7479)

OVERTON, Sir Hugh Thomas Arnold; KCMG (1983, CMG 1975); s of late Sir Arnold Overton, KCB, KCMG, MC, and Bronwen Cecilie Vincent; *b* 2 April 1923; *Educ* Dragon Sch Oxford, Winchester, Clare Coll Cambridge; *m* 1948, Claire-Marie, da of Jean Binet (d 1961); 1 s, 2 da; *Career* served RCS (France and Germany) 1943-45; Dip Serv 1947; served in Eastern Europe, Near East, Germany, N America; head of N America dept FCO 1971-74, consul gen Düsseldorf 1974-75, min (econ) Bonn 1975-80, consul gen NY and dir gen Br Trade Devpt USA 1980-83, ret; memb exec and fin ctee Barnardo's 1988 (memb Cncl 1985); tstee Bell Educnl Tst, Taverner Concerts Tst; *Clubs* RAC, Royal Inst of Int Affairs; *Style*— Sir Hugh Overton, KCMG; 30 North End House, Fitzjames Ave, London W14 0RS (☎ 071 603 6795)

OVERY, Paul Vivian; s of Arthur Frederick Overy, of Hampstead, London, and Joan Vivien, *née* Major (d 1987); *b* 14 Feb 1940; *Educ* UCS London, King's Coll Cambridge (BA, MA); *Career* art critic: The Listener 1966-68 and 1978-82, Financial Times 1968-71; book reviews ed New Society 1970-71, chief art critic The Times 1973-75, tutor in cultural history RCA London 1975-87, art critic The International Herald Tribune 1980-82, freelance art critic 1982-, contributing ed The Journal of Art 1990-; currently teacher of art architecture and design history: Univ of London, The London Inst, Middlesex Poly; guest lectr Slade Sch of Fine Art; exhibitions incl: 18 Artists from Hungary (Third Eye Centre Glasgow) 1987, Rietveld Furniture & the Schröder House (Warwick Univ Arts Centre) 1990, Whitworth Gallery Manchester, Collins Gallery Glasgow, City Art Gallery Southampton, Nat Museum of Modern Art Dublin 1991, Royal Festival Hall London 1991; Italian Govt scholar to Italy 1970, Leverhulme Res fell Paris 1984-85; memb: Assoc Internationale des Critiques d'Art 1987, NUJ 1970, Assoc of Art Historians 1987; *Books* Kandinsky: The Language of the Eye (1969), De Stijl (d 1969), Concepts of Modern Art (contrib, 1974), The New Art History (contrib, 1986), The Rietveld Schröder House (1988); *Recreations* reading, walking; *Style*— Paul Overy, Esq; 13 Christchurch Square, London E9 7HU (☎ 081 986 7556); c/o Andrew Hewson, John Johnson (Author's Agents Ltd), Clerkenwell House, 47 Clerkenwell Green, London EC1R 0HT (☎ 071 251 0125, fax 071 251 2172)

OVEY, Richard; o s of Richard Henry Ovey, JP (d 1947), of Hernes, and Elizabeth Henderson, *née* Danforth (d 1974); descended from Thomas Ovey (d 1635), of Watlington, Oxfordshire; gs of Lt-Col Richard Lockhart Ovey, DSO, TD, JP, DL (d 1946), who acquired Hernes (*see* Burke's Landed Gentry, 18 edn, vol II, 1969); *b* 26 July 1939; *Educ* Eton, North of Scotland Coll of Agric; *m* 17 July 1965, Gillian Mary, o da of Cecil James Smith (d 1984), of Church Cottage, Rotherfield Greys, nr Henley-on-Thames, Oxon; 2 s (Richard (Dick) b 1967, Andrew b 1971), 1 da (Clare b 1969); *Career* landowner; chm Rotherfield Greys Parish Cncl; past pres and memb Ctee H & DAA; past vice-chm SOCUA; *Recreations* shooting, fishing, sailing; *Style*— Richard Ovey, Esq; Hernes, Henley-on-Thames, Oxon (☎ 0491 573245)

OWEN, (Albert) Alan; s of Thomas Emrys Owen (d 1989), and Zenta, *née* Jerums; *b* 14 May 1948; *Educ* Oriel Sch Zimbabwe, RAM; *m* 1 (m dis 1974); 1 s (Hywel b 11 Sept 1969); m 2, 8 Sept 1978, Katherine, da of John Richard Sweeney, of 12 Moor Lane, Liverpool 23 4TW; 2 da (Cari b 26 Nov 1982, Alys b 9 Sept 1986); *Career* prof RAM 1976-89, tutor Working Men's Coll 1979-; composer; music performed widely incl: South Bank, Wigmore Hall, Edinburgh Fringe, Halley's Comet Royal Gala Concert 1986; composer numerous TV themes; memb cncl and mgmnt ctee Working Men's Coll 1984-; memb: Musicians Union 1974, Composers Guild 1974, Performing Rights Soc 1982; *Recreations* motoring, walking, camping, snooker; *Clubs* Working Mens College, RAM; *Style*— Alan Owen, Esq; 59 Biffel Rd, London NW2 4PG (☎ 081 450 5394)

OWEN, Alan Charles; s of Thomas Charles Owen, and Florence Edith, *née* Blake; *b* 7 March 1939; *Educ* Elliot Central Sch Southfields London; *m* 11 Oct 1974, Janet Ann, da of William David Butcher; 1 s (Ian Charles), 1 da (Larraine Carol); *Career* mangr Gilbert Eliott & Co Stockbrokers 1970 (ptnr 1977), memb Stock Exchange 1976, div dir Girozentrale Gilbert Eliott 1987-; memb Int Stock Exchange; *Recreations* squash; *Style*— Alan Owen, Esq; Girozentrale Gilbert Eliott, 381 Salisbury House, London Wall, London EC2M 5SB (☎ 071 628 6782, fax 071 628 3500, telex 888886)

OWEN, Alun Davies; s of Sidney Owen (d 1977), of Liverpool, and Ruth, *née* Davies (d 1950); *b* 24 Nov 1925; *Educ* Oulton HS Liverpool, Cardigan Co Sch Dyfed Wales; *m* 12 Dec 1942, (Theodora) Mary, da of Dr Stephen O'Keefe (d 1942), of Dublin; 2 s (Teifion, Gareth Robert); *Career* coal miner(Bevin Boy) 1943; playwright and actor; author of plays for stage and TV incl: The Rough and Ready Lot 1961, Progress to the Park 1962, The Rose Affair 1962, A Hard Days Night 1964, Dare to be a Daniel 1965, George's Room 1971, Norma 1971; awards incl: Screenwriters and Prodrs Guild script of the year 1960, Screenwriters Guild award best play 1961, Daily Mirror award best play 1961, Golden Star award best playwright 1967, Oscar nomination A Hard Day's Night 1964, Emmy award The Male of the Species 1969, BAMFFE award Canada best play 1985; memb Writers Guild of GB; *Recreations* reading, swimming; *Clubs* Chelsea Arts; *Style*— Alun Owen, Esq; c/o Julienn Friedmann, Blake Friedmann Literary Agency, 37-41 Gower St, London WC1E 6HH (☎ 071 631 4331)

OWEN, Hon Mrs (Ardyne Mary); da of 2 Viscount Knollys, GCMG, MBE, DFC (d 1966); *b* 1929; *m* 1958, Ronald James Owen; *Style*— The Hon Mrs Owen; Paradise Wood, Upper Hartfield, Sussex

OWEN, His Hon Judge Aron; *b* 16 Feb 1919; *Educ* Tredegar Co GS, Univ of Wales (BA, PhD); *m* 1946, Rose, JP, da of Solomon Alexander Fishman, Freeman City of London (d 1936); 1 s, 2 da; *Career* called to the Bar Inner Temple 1948; circuit judge 1980-; Freeman City of London; *Recreations* travel, gardening; *Style*— His Hon Judge Aron Owen; 44 Brampton Grove, Hendon, London NW4 4AQ (☎ 081 202 8151)

OWEN, Bill John; MBE; s of William George Davenport Rowbotham, and Louise Matthews; *b* 14 March 1914; *m* 1, 14 Feb 1946 (m dis 1964), Edith, da of Thomas Stevenson; 1 s (Thomas William Stevenson b 8 April 1949); m 2, 3 March 1977, Kathleen O'Donoghue; *Career* Nat Serv 2 Lt RPC 1940-42; actor, dir and writer; roles incl: Touchstone in As You Like It (NY) 1949-50, Mack the Knife in The Threepenny Opera 1956, Ko-Ko in The Mikado (Sadler's Wells Opera) 1963, Tommy Pasmore in March on Russia 1989, Jubilee (NT) 1990; writer of book and lyrics for Matchgirls (Globe Theatre) 1966; involved in numerous film and TV credits incl Last of the Summer Wine; vice pres London Fedn of Boys' Clubs (arts adviser); chm: Unity Theatre Tst, Arts for Labour; vice chm Yorks Soc London; *Style*— Bill Owen, Esq, MBE; Bill Owens Ltd, 2a Priory Gardens, London N6

OWEN, (Alfred) David; s of Sir Alfred George Beech Owen, CBE (d 1975), and Eileen Kathleen Genevieve, *née* McMullan; *b* 26 Sept 1936; *Educ* Brocksford Hall, Oundle, Emmanuel Coll Cambridge; *m* 1966, Ethne Margaret, da of Frank H Sowman, of Solihull; 2 s, 1 da; *Career* Nat Serv Lt RASC; chm Rubery Owen Gp, tstee Community Projects Fndn 1978-, memb Br Overseas Trade Bd 1979-83, pres Birmingham C of C 1980-81; vice pres SMMT 1987-90; Hon DSc Univ of Aston 1988; pres Comité de Liaison de la Construction d'Equipments et de Pièces d'Automobiles 1988-90 (CLEPA); *Recreations* industrial archaeology, ornithology, walking, photography, music; *Clubs* National, RAC; *Style*— A David Owen, Esq; Mill Dam House, Mill Lane, Aldridge, Walsall, WS9 0NB (☎ 021 353 1221); Rubery Owen Holdings Ltd, PO Box 10, Darlaston, Wednesbury, W Midlands

OWEN, Rt Hon David Anthony Llewellyn; PC (1976), MP (Lab to 1981, SDP thereafter) Plymouth Devonport 1974-; s of Dr John William Morris Owen; *b* 2 July 1938; *Educ* Bradfield Coll, Sidney Sussex Coll Cambridge (hon fell 1977), St Thomas's Hosp (BA, MB BChir, MA); *m* 1968, Deborah Schabert (Deborah Owen, literary agent); 2 s, 1 da; *Career* St Thomas's Hosp: house appts 1962-64, neurological and psychiatric registrar 1964-66, res fell med unit 1966-68; contested (Lab) Torrington 1964; pps to MOD (Admin) 1967, parly under-sec of state for Def for RN 1968-70, resigned over EEC 1972; MP (Lab) Plymouth Sutton 1966-74; parly under-sec of state DHSS 1974, min of state DHSS 1974-76 & FCO 1976-77, sec of state for Foreign and Cwlth Affairs 1977-79; oppn spokesman on energy 1979-81; fndr memb SDP 1981, chm SDP Parly Ctee 1981-82, dep leader SDP MPs Oct 1982-87, elected SDP Leader following resignation of Rt Hon Roy Jenkins after election June 1983-, resigned over merger with Liberals 1987, re-elected SDP leader 1988; *Style*— The Rt Hon David Owen, MP; 78 Narrow St, Limehouse, E14 (☎ 071 987 5441); The Old Rectory, Buttermere, nr Marlborough, Wilts (☎ 04884 258); House of Commons, SW1 (☎ 071 219 4203)

OWEN, Prof David Gareth; s of Oscar Vivian Owen (d 1988), and Mary Gwladys, *née* Davies (d 1961); *b* 6 Nov 1940; *Educ* Christ Coll Brecon, Downing Coll Cambridge (MA, PhD), Univ of London (BA); *m* 2 July 1966, Ann Valerie, da of Stanley Wilfred

Owen Wright (d 1988); 2 da (Ceridwen b 1969, Rachel b 1971); *Career* graduate engr John Laing & Son 1966-67, sr engr Marconi Space and Defence Systems Portsmouth 1970-72, visiting assoc prof Univ of New Hampshire USA 1976, prof of offshore engrg Heriot-Watt Univ 1986- (lectr Dept of Civil Engrg 1972-75, sr lectr Dept of Offshore Engrg 1977, head of dept 1981-); vice pres Edinburgh and Leith Petroleum Club 1990-91; FICE, CEng; *Recreations* music, travel, languages; *Style*— Prof David Owen; 7 Oak Lane, Edinburgh EH12 6XH (☎ 031 339 1740); Department of Offshore Engineering, Heriot-Watt University, Riccarton, Edinburgh EH14 4AS (☎ 031 451 3150)

OWEN, (Francis) David Lloyd; TD (1967); s of Robert Charles Lloyd Owen, of Glanmorfa, Dolgellau, Meirionnydd, and Jane Ellen, *née* Francis; *b* 24 Oct 1933; *Educ* Wrekin Coll; *m* 28 Oct 1965, Jennifer Nan, da of Richard Eric Knowles Rowlands, of The Grange, Mickle Trafford, Chester; 2 da (Charis Jane b 7 May 1971, Anna Clare b 2 June 1974); *Career* Nat Serv 1952-54, cmmnd 22 Cheshire Regt 1953, TA 1954-67, Maj 1963; admitted slr 1961; practising slr 1961-66, called to the Bar Gray's Inn 1967; practising Northern Circuit, actg stipendiary magistrate 1981, dep circuit judge and asst rec 1977-88, rec 1988; *Recreations* country pursuits, sailing, genealogy; *Clubs* Grosvenor (Chester); *Style*— David Owen, Esq, TD; The Pool House, Tarvin, Chester (☎ 0829 40300); Refuge Assurance House, Derby Square, Liverpool (☎ 051 709 4222, fax 051 708 6311); Goldsmith Building, Temple, London EC4 (☎ 071 353 7881, fax 071 353 5319)

OWEN, Hon Mrs (Eiddwen Sara); *née* Philipps; yst da (by 1 m) of 2 Viscount St Davids, *qv*; *b* 28 June 1948; *m* 1986, Clive Geoffrey Owen; issue; *Style*— The Hon Mrs Owen; 4 Quarry Road, Kenilworth, Warwickshire CV8 1AE

OWEN, Dr Gareth; CBE (1988); s of John Richard Owen (d 1942), and Bronwen May, Davies (d 1975); *b* 4 Oct 1922; *Educ* Pontypridd Boys' GS, Univ of Wales (BSc), Univ of Glasgow (DSc); *m* 28 March 1953, Beti, da of Rev Giraldus Jones (d 1978); 1 s (Geraint b 1958), 2 da (Shân b 1954, Gwyneth b 1956); *Career* Nat Serv pilot RAF 1942-47; lectr in zoology Univ of Glasgow 1950-64, pro vice chllr Queen's Univ Belfast 1974-79 (prof of zoology and head of dept 1964-79), princ UCW Aberystwyth 1979-89, vice chllr Univ of Wales 1985-87; memb: Royal Irish Acad 1976, Nature Conservancy Cncl 1984- (chm Welsh ctee 1985-); pres Welsh Centre for Int Affrs 1989-; hon memb of the Gorsedd; Hon DSc Queen's Univ Belfast 1982, Hon LLD Univ of Wales 1989; FIBiol 1964; *Recreations* reading, photography; *Style*— Dr Gareth Owen, CBE; 6a St Margaret's Place, Whitchurch, Cardiff CF4 7AD (☎ 0222 6921990)

OWEN, Lt-Col Garth Henry; TD; s of Henry Owen (d 1964); *b* 4 May 1924; *Educ* Rugeley GS; *m* 1948, Madeleine, *née* Day; *Career* served WWII RN 1941-46, RAFVR 1948-53, 639th Heavy Field Regt RA (TA) 1953-57, 125th (Staffordshire) Engr Regt (TA) 1957-67, Hon Col 125th (Staffordshire) Field Support Sqdn, RE (V) and The 143rd Plant Sqdn RE (V) T & AVR; DL (1967) Staffs; *Style*— Lt-Col Garth Owen, TD, DL; Carioca Cottage, Brackenridge, Fair Oak, Slitting Mill, Rugeley Staffs (☎ 088 94 2875)

OWEN, Gerald Victor; QC (1969); s of Samuel Owen (d 1972), and Ziporah Owen (d 1974); *b* 29 Nov 1922; *Educ* Kilburn GS, St Catharine's Coll Cambridge (MA), Queen Mary Coll London (sci scholarship), Univ of London (LLB); *m* 21 March 1946, Phyllis; 1 s (Michael b 15 Oct 1948), 1 da (Juliet b 26 Dec 1952); *Career* called to the Bar Gray's Inn 1949, ad eundem Inner Temple 1969; QC 1969; dep circuit judge 1971; rec of Crown Ct 1979-; chm: Dairy Produce Quota Tribunal 1984-85, Med Appeal Tribunal 1984-; FRStatS; *Recreations* music; *Style*— Gerald Owen, Esq, QC; 3 Paper Buildings, Temple, London, EC4Y 7EU (☎ 071 583 1183)

OWEN, Gordon Michael William; CBE (1991); s of Christopher Knowles Owen, and Margaret Joyce Milward, *née* Spencer (d 1986); *b* 9 Dec 1937; *Educ* Cranbrook Sch; *m* 2 Nov 1963, Jennifer Pearl, da of Basil John Bradford; 1 s (Timothy Derek b 14 Feb 1969), 1 da (Alison Carole b 29 Jan 1966); *Career* dep chief exec Cable & Wireless 1988- (joined 1954, md subsid co Mercury Communications Ltd 1984, dir 1986, jt md 1987, dep chief exec 1988), chm Mercury 1990; CBIM; *Recreations* golf (poor!), sailing, bee-keeping; *Style*— Gordon Owen, Esq, CBE; Braye House, Egypt Lane, Farnham Common, Bucks SL2 3LF; Cable & Wireless plc, Mercury House, Theobalds Rd, London WC1X 8RX (☎ 071 315 4000)

OWEN, (John) Graham; s of (John) Hugh Owen, of Bridgend, and Mair Eluned, *née* Evans; *b* 30 Aug 1952; *Educ* Epsom Coll, Guy's Hosp (BDS, LDS); *m* Belle Steadman, da of Harry Mooney (d 1985), of Hounslow; 3 s (Robert b 28 Dec 1981, Jonathan b 27 June 1984, Martin b 17 Oct 1986), 1 da (Annabelle b 7 Feb 1983); *Career* Guy's Hosp: house offr 1977, sr house offr 1978, pt/t lectr Maxillo facial and oral surgy 1980-82-; hon sec Dental Soc of London 1990; *Recreations* rugby, cricket, athletics; *Style*— Graham Owen, Esq; High View, 339 Main Road, Westerham Hill, Kent TN16 2HP (☎ 0959 73180); 84 Harley St, London W1 (☎ 071 935 8084)

OWEN, Sir Hugh (Bernard Pilkington); 5 Bt (UK 1813); s of Sir John Arthur Owen, 4 Bt (d 1973), and Lucy, *née* Pilkington (d 1985); *b* 28 March 1915; *Educ* Chillon Coll Switzerland; *Heir* bro, John William Owen; *Style*— Sir Hugh Owen, Bt; 63 Dudsbury Rd, Ferndown, Dorset

OWEN, Ivor Henry; s of Thomas Owen, and Anne Owen; *b* 14 Nov 1930; *Educ* Liverpool Coll of Technol, UMIST; *m* 1954, Jane Frances Graves; 2 s , 1 da; *Career* apprentice engr Wingrove & Rogers Ltd 1946-51, sr design engr Crave Bros (Manchester) Ltd 1951-57; English Electric Co Ltd: mfrg devpt engr Steam Turbine Div Rugby 1957-62, mangr Netherton Works Bootle 1962-66, mangr English Electric Computers Ltd Winsford 1966-69; mfrg mangr ICL Midlands 1969-70, md RHP Bearings Ransome Hoffman Pollard Ltd 1970-81; Thorn EMI: chief exec Gen Engrg Dir 1981-83, chm Appliances and Lighting Gp 1984-87, dir 1984-87; dir gen The Design Council 1988-; CBIM, FRSA, FIMechE, fell Royal Inst, CEng; *Recreations* theatre, reading, running, gardening; *Clubs* Carlton; *Style*— Ivor Owen, Esq; 9 Cheyne Court, Flood Street, London SW3 (☎ 071 351 6008); The Design Council, 28 Haymarket, London SW1Y 4SU (☎ 071 839 8000)

OWEN, The Hon and Rt Worshipful Sir John Arthur Dalziel; QC (1970); s of Robert John Owen (d 1940), and Olive Barlow, *née* Hall-Wright; *b* 22 Nov 1925; *Educ* Solihull Sch, BNC Oxford (MA, BCL); *m* 26 July 1952, Valerie, da of William Ethell (d 1988), of Solihull; 1 s (James Alexander Dalziel b 1 June 1966), 1 da (Melissa Clare (Hon Mrs Michael-John Knatchbull) b 12 Nov 1960); *Career* cmmnd 2 King Edward's Own Gurkha Rifles 1944; barr Gray's Inn 1951, dep chm Warwickshire QS 1967-71, rec of Crown Ct 1972-84, memb Senate of Inns of Ct and Bar 1977-80, dep ldr Midland and Oxford Circuit 1979-84, Dean of the Arches and Auditor of Chancery Ct York 1980-, circuit judge at Old Bailey 1984-86, judge High Court 1986-; chm W Midlands Area Mental Health Review Tribunal 1972-80; kt 1986; *Clubs* Garrick; *Style*— The Hon and Rt Worshipful Mr Justice John Owen; Royal Courts of Justice, Strand, London WC2A 2LL; 1 Verulam Buildings, Gray's Inn, London WC1R 5LQ (☎ 071 242 7722)

OWEN, John Aubrey; s of Douglas Aubrey Owen (d 1964), and Patricia Joan, *née* Griggs (d 1968); *b* 1 Aug 1945; *Educ* City of London Sch, St Catharine's Coll Cambridge (MA); *m* 8 May 1971, Julia Margaret, da of Thomas Gordon Jones, of Shrewsbury; 1 s (Charles Aubrey b 1972), 1 da (Lucy Margaret b 1975); *Career* joined Miny of Tport 1969, asst private sec to Min for Tport Industs 1972, DOE 1972-75, Dept of Tport 1972-78, seconded to Cambs CC 1978-80, DOE 1980-, regnl dir Northern Regnl Office DOE and Dept of Tport 1987-; *Recreations* gardening, opera; *Style*— John Owen, Esq; 1 Darvall Close, Beaumont Park, Whitley Bay, Tyne and Wear NE25 9UJ (☎ 091 251 3741); Departments of the Environment and Transport, Northern Regional Office, Wellbar House, Gallowgate, Newcastle upon Tyne (☎ 091 232 7575)

OWEN, Prof John Bryn; s of Owen William Owen (d 1960), of Hafan, Llanddeusant, Anglesey, Gwynedd, and Jane Owen (d 1953); *b* 23 May 1931; *Educ* Ffestiniog GS, Univ of Wales Bangor (BSc, PhD), Univ of Cambridge (MA); *m* 10 Aug 1955, Margaret Helen, da of Hugh James Hughes, MBE (d 1979), of Arfon, 4 Norton Close, Bath Rd, Worc; 2 s (Gareth b 1956, David b 1958), 1 da (Helen b 1964); *Career* farms mangr Huttons Ambo Estate Yorks 1956-58, lectr in agric UCW Aberystwyth 1958-82, lectr and dir of studies in agric Emmanuel Coll Cambridge 1962-72, prof of animal prodn and health Univ of Aberdeen 1972-78, prof of agriculture Univ of Wales Bangor 1978-, dean faculty of sci Bangor 1987-89, head Sch of Agric and Forest Sciences 1989-; FIBiol 1970, FRSA 1975, FRAgS 1980; *Books* incl: Performance Recording in Sheep (1971), Detection and Control of Breeding Activity in Farm Animals (1975), Sheep Production (1976), Complete Diets for Cattle and Sheep (1979), Cattle Feeding (1983), Sheep (Defaid) (1984), New Techniques in Sheep Production (1987); *Recreations* choral singing; *Clubs* Farmers' (London); *Style*— Prof John Owen; School of Agricultural and Forest Sciences, University of Wales, Deiniol Rd, Bangor, Gwynedd (☎ 0248 351151)

OWEN, John Halliwell; OBE (1975); s of Arthur Llewellyn Owen, OBE (d 1976), of Bebington, Wirral, and Doris Spencer, *née* Halliwell; *b* 16 June 1935; *Educ* Sedbergh, Queen's College Oxford (MA); *m* 1, 14 Dec 1963 (m dis 1971), Jacqueline Simone, da of James Ambrose (d 1989) of Coín, Spain; 1 s (Adrian b 1967), 1 da (Carina b 1964); m 2, 15 Jan 1972, Dianne Elizabeth, da William George Lowry (d 1974), of St Stephens, Canterbury; 1 da (Catherine b 1972); *Career* Nat Serv 2 Lt RA 1954-56; Overseas Civil Serv Tanganyika Govt 1960-65: dist offr prov admin 1960-62, dist cmmr 1962-63, dist magistrate regnl local cts offr 1963-65; FO 1966-: second sec Dar-Es-Salaam 1968-70, FCO 1970-73, first sec Dhaka 1973-75, FCO 1975-76, first sec Accra 1976-80, FCO 1980-82, cnsllr Pretoria 1982-86, cnsllr FCO 1986-90, ret 1990; *Recreations* wildlife, travel, gardening; *Clubs* Dar-Es-Salaam Yacht; *Style*— John H Owen, Esq, OBE; Foreign & Commonwealth Office, London SW1

OWEN, Maj-Gen John Ivor Headon; OBE (1963); s of Maj William Headon Owen, MC (d 1954), and Norita Alexandrina, *née* Morgan (d 1970); *b* 22 Oct 1922; *Educ* St Edmund's Sch Canterbury; *m* 1948, Margaret Jean, da of Edwin Hayes (d 1931); 3 da; *Career* RM commando 1942, Far East 1943-46, Constable Met Police 1946-47, rejoined RM, regtl serv to 1955, Staff Coll Camberley 1956, Bde Maj, MOD (Admty) 1962-64, jssc 1966-67; CO 45 Commando 1967-69; RCDS 1971, Maj-Gen Commando Forces RM Plymouth 1972-73, Maj-Gen 1972; UK partnership sec to KMG Thomson McLintock 1974-87, Rep Col Cmdt RM 1985-86; dir Opus Resource Management Ltd; treas Clergy Orphan Corp, memb Ctee of Sons of Clergy Corp; chm: Ctee Bowles Outdoor Centre, Tstees RM Museum; *Books* Brassey's Infantry Weapons of the World, and others; ed Current Military Literature; *Recreations* woodworking, gardening; *Clubs* Army and Navy; *Style*— Maj-Gen John Owen, OBE; c/o Midland Bank plc, 89 Queen Victoria Street, London EC4V 4AQ

OWEN, John Wyn; s of Idwal Wyn Owen (d 1984), of Bangor, and Myfi, *née* Hughes; *b* 15 May 1942; *Educ* Friars Sch Bangor, St John's Coll Cambridge (BA, MA), Kings Fund Hosp Admin Staff Coll; *m* 1 April 1967, Elizabeth Ann, da of William MacFarlane (d 1980), of Bangor; 1 s (Dafydd b 1974), 1 da (Sian b 1971); *Career* hosp sec Glantawe HMC Swansea 1967-70, staff trg offr Welsh Hosp Bd Cardiff 1968-70, divnl admin Univ Hosp of Wales HMC Cardiff 1970-72, asst clerk St Thomas' Hosp London 1972-74, admin St Thomas' Health Dist 1974-79; exec dir United Medical Enterprises London 1979-85; dir: Allied Medical Group London 1979-85, Br Nursing Cooperations London 1979-85, Allied Med Gp Healthcare Canada 1982-85, Allied Shanning London 1983-85; chm Welsh Health Common Servs Authy 1985-, dir Welsh NHS 1985-; tstee: Florence Nightingale Museum Tst 1983-90, Mgmnt Advsy Serv 1986-90; organist Utd Free Church Cowbridge 1985; AHSM; *Recreations* organ playing, opera, travel; *Clubs* Athenaeum; *Style*— John Wyn Owen, Esq; Welsh Office, Cathays Park, Cardiff CF1 3NR (☎ 0222 823695)

OWEN, John Wynne; MBE (1979); s of Thomas David Owen (d 1977), of Pontardulais, S Wales, and Mair Eluned, *née* Richards (d 1988); *b* 25 April 1939; *Educ* Gowerton GS; *m* 1, 14 July 1962, Thelma Margaret (d 1987), da of Arthur James Gunton (d 1984), of Yarmouth, Isle of Wight; 1 s (David b 1970), 2 da (Sandra b 1963, Karen b 1969), 1 step da (Fiona Roberts b 1977); m 2, 19 March 1988, Carol, da of John Edmunds, of Wootton, IOW; *Career* HM Foreign Serv 1956-58, Nat Serv RS 1958-60, cmmnd 2 Lt 1959; HM Foreign Serv (later Dip Serv): Indonesia 1960-61, Vietnam 1961-62, Paris 1962-63, El Salvador 1963-67, resigned between 1967 and 1970, returned to FO 1970-73, 3 later 2 sec Br Embassy Tehran 1973-77, vice consul and later consul (commercial) Br Consulate Gen Sao Paulo Brazil 1978-80, 1 sec and consul Br Embassy Peking 1980-82, 1 sec FO 1983-85, special unpaid leave 1985-89, cnsllr FO 1990; chm Gunham Plastics Ltd 1985 (dir since 1967), chm Channel Distribution Ltd 1986-90, chm and md Gunham Distribution Ltd 1986-90, Gunham Holdings Ltd 1987-90, chm Br Laminated Plastics Fabricators Assoc 1987; dir: HS Bassett Ltd 1988-90; Freeman City of London, Liveryman Worshipful Co of Loriners; FInstD 1980, FBIM 1985; *Recreations* swimming, tennis, walking; *Clubs* RAC, City Livery; *Style*— John Owen, Esq, MBE

OWEN, Prof Joslyn Grey; CBE (1979); s of William Owen, MBE (d 1973), and Nell, *née* Evans (d 1960); *b* 23 Aug 1928; *Educ* Cardiff HS, Worcester Coll Oxford (MA); *m* 24 June 1961, Mary Patricia, da of William Brooks (d 1969), of Rustington; 3 s (Mark William b 1963, Stephen Grey b 1966, Matthew James b 1968); *Career* RAF 1946-48; classics master and housemaster King's Sch Canterbury 1953-58; asst educn offr: Croydon 1958-62, Somerset 1962-66; chief educn offr Devon 1972-89 (dep chief educn offr 1968-72), Rolle chair of educn Poly of the SW 1989-; sec The Schs Cncl for Curriculum & Examinations 1966-68; memb: Cncl Exeter Univ, Mgmnt Ctee Atlantic Coll, St Luke's Fndn Tstees, Open Sch Tstees, Govrs Dartington Coll of the Arts; hon fell Plymouth Poly 1978; FRSA 1972, FCP 1974; *Books* Management of Curriculum Development (1973); *Recreations* reading, music; *Clubs* Reform; *Style*— Prof Joslyn Owen, CBE; 4 The Quadrant, Exeter, Devon EX2 4LE (☎ 0392 743 26); Rolle Faculty of Education, Exmouth, Devon EX8 2AT

OWEN, Brig Michael Charles; s of John Joseph Owen (d 1948), and Mary May, *née* McSweeney (d 1973); *b* 27 Nov 1936; *Educ* Aberdare GS, RMA Sandhurst; *m* 29 Dec 1960, Patricia Mary, da of George Tennant (d 1958); *Career* SOI (DS) Staff Coll 1975, CRAOC 1 Armoured Div 1976, AA and QMG AQ Ops and Plans 1979, Col Ord 1 1980, DACOS LOG HQ AFCENT 1983, Cdr RAOC Trg Centre 1988, Cmd Supply BAOR 1989; Anglican lay reader licenced 1978, selector C of E's advsy cncl for the Churches Ministry; MBIM 1971, FInstPS 1988; *Recreations* walking, ornithology, sports (as a spectator); *Style*— Brig Michael Owen; Commander Supply, Supply Directorate, HQ BAOR, BFPO 140 (☎ 02151 47 2002)

OWEN, (John) Michael Holland; s of Col Robert Leslie Owen, OBE, TD (d 1973), of

Austwick, nr Settle, N Yorks, and Kathleen, *née* Steen (d 1989); *b* 4 March 1932; *Educ* St Edward's Sch Oxford; *m* 28 Jan 1968, (Patricia) Anne, da of Col JB Gartside, DSO, MC, TD, JP, DL (d 1964), of Crimble Cottage, Rochdale; 2 s (Robert b 15 Dec 1968, William b 11 March 1970), 1 da (Jennifer b 1 March 1972); *Career* Nat Serv 1950-52, appointed 2 Lt 1 Bn 22 (Cheshire) Regt, Capt 7 Bn 22 (Cheshire) Regt TA 1952-66; Whitecroft plc (formerly Bleachers Assoc Ltd) 1953-72; gen mangr: Ashworth & Smith Ltd 1960-63, River Etherow Bleaching Co Ltd 1963-64; md Chorley Bleaching Co Ltd and dir Inver Bleaching Co and Bulwell Dyeing Co Ltd 1964-71, dir Shiloh plc 1972-, non-exec dir WM Supplies UK Ltd 1974-, md Amberguard Ltd 1977-; memb Ward Ctee Cons Pty 1975-85; *Style*— Michael Owen, Esq, TD; Amberguard Ltd, Elk Mill, Broadway, Chadderton, Oldham OL2 5HS (☎ 061 620 4328)

OWEN, Peter Francis; CB (1990); s of Arthur Owen (d 1988), and Violet, Winifred, *née* Morris; *b* 4 Sept 1940; *Educ* Liverpool Inst, Univ of Liverpool (BA); *m* 27 July 1963, Ann, da of William Henry Preece (d 1974); 1 s (David b 8 April 1969), 1 da (Poppy b 13 Sept 1973); *Career* joined Miny of Public Bldgs of Works (now part of DOE) 1964, Cabinet Office and private sec to successive Ministries of Housing and Construction 1971-74, asst sec housing policy review DOE 1974-77, asst sec local govt fin DOE 1977-80, regnl dir Northern Yorks and Humberside Regns DOE and Dept of Tport 1980-82, dir rural affrs DOE 1982-83, under sec local govt fin policy DOE 1983-86, dep sec housing and construction DOE 1986-90, dep sec Cabinet Office 1990-; *Recreations* gardening, french language and lit; *Style*— Peter Owen, Esq, CB; Cabinet Office, Whitehall, London SW1

OWEN, Peter Lothar; s of Arthur Owen, and Winifred, *née* Friedmann; *b* 24 Feb 1927; *Educ* King's Sch Harrow on Hill; *m* 1, 1953, Wendy, da of Henry Demoulins; 1 s (Benedict David), 2 da (Antonia Beatrice Demoulins, Georgina Alexis (Mrs Trythall); m 2, 2 Jan 1986, Jan Kenny Treacy; *Career* RAF; publisher; md and fndr own co Peter Owen 1951; *Books* Springtime 2 and Springtime 3 (ed, 1950), Publishing the Future (ed, 1988), The Peter Owen Anthology (1991); *Recreations* swimming, literature, collecting; *Style*— Peter Owen, Esq; 73 Kenway Rd, London SW5 (☎ 071 373 5628, fax 071 373 6760)

OWEN, Philip Anthony; s of Alec Owen (d 1959), of Hornsea, East Yorks, and Katherine Mary, *née* Pink; *b* 25 Aug 1944; *Educ* Pitman's Coll Hull, Queens' Coll Cambridge; *m* 5 Sept 1984, Deborah Anne, da of Arthur Harry Lewin, of Auckland, NZ; 1 s (Simon b 1988), 1 da (Julia b 1987); *Career* admitted slr 1968; ptnr Allen & Overy 1982-(joined 1973); Liveryman Worshipful Co Slrs; memb Law Soc 1968; *Recreations* ocean racing, golf, skiing; *Clubs* Royal Ocean Racing, Royal Yorkshire Yacht, Royal Wimbledon Golf; *Style*— Philip Owen, Esq; 9 Cheapside, London EC2V 6AD (☎ 071 248 9898, fax 071 236 2192, telex 8812801)

OWEN, Philip Loscombe Wintringham; TD (1950), QC (1963); s of Rt Hon Sir Wintringham Stable, MC (d 1977), of Plas Llwyn Owen, Llanbrynmair, Powys, and Lucy Haden Stable (d 1976); assumed surname of Owen by deed poll 1942; *b* 10 Jan 1920; *Educ* Winchester, Ch Ch Oxford (MA); *m* 1949, Elizabeth Jane, da of Lewis Trelawny Widdicombe (d 1953); 3 s, 2 da; *Career* served WWII Royal Welch Fus, Maj TARO; received into RC Church 1943; called to the Bar Middle Temple 1949, memb Gen Cncl of Bar of Eng and Wales 1971-77; dep chm of QS: Montgomeryshire 1959-71, Cheshire 1961-71; bencher 1969; rec: Merthyr Tydfil 1971, Crown Court 1972-85; ldr Wales and Chester circuit 1975-77; legal assessor to: Gen Med Cncl 1970-, Gen Dental Cncl 1970-, RICS 1970-; Parly candidate (C) Montgomeryshire 1945; JP: Montgomeryshire 1959, Cheshire 1961; dir Swansea City AFC Ltd 1975-86; vice pres Montgomeryshire Cons and Unionist Assoc, former pres Montgomeryshire Soc; *Recreations* shooting, fishing, forestry, music, association football; *Style*— Philip Owen, Esq, TD, QC; Plas Llwyn Owen, Llanbrynmair, Powys SY19 7BE (☎ 06503 542); Brick Court Chambers, 15-19 Devereux Court, Strand, London WC2R 3JJ (☎ 071 583 0777)

OWEN, Dr Richard Charles; s of Alfred Roy Warren Owen (d 1978), of Rottingdean, Sussex, and Florence Mary, *née* Walker; *b* 14 July 1947; *Educ* Varndean GS, Univ of Nottingham (BA), LSE (MSc), Stanford Univ (PhD) Univ of Calif (Harkness scholarship); *m* 1 May 1982, Julia Anne, da of Clive Raymond Crosse; 1 s (Laurence b 22 Aug 1988), 2 da (Eleanor Owen b 2 May 1983, Isabel Owen b 2 May 1983); *Career* script writer and prodr BBC External Servs 1973-79, asst prodr BBC TV Current Affrs 1979-80; The Times 1980-; ldr writer 1980-82, Moscow corr 1982-85, Brussels corr 1985-88, Jerusalem corr 1988-91, dep foreign ed 1991-; *Books* Letters from Moscow (1985), Crisis in the Kremlin (1986), The Times Guide to 1992, Britain in a Europe without Frontiers (1990); *Style*— Dr Richard Owen; The Times, 1 Pennington St, London E1 9BD (☎ 071 782 5234)

OWEN, Robert Michael; QC (1988); s of Gwynne Llewellyn Owen (d 1986), of Fowey, Cornwall and Phoebe Constance Owen; *b* 19 Sept 1944; *Educ* Durham Sch Exeter Univ (LLB); *m* 9 Aug 1969, Sara Josephine, da of Sir Algernon Rumbold, KCMG, of Shortwoods, West Clandon, Surrey; 2 s (Thomas b 10 Nov 1973, Huw b 4 Jan 1976); *Career* called to the Bar 1968, rec 1987-; *Clubs* MCC, Royal Fowey Yacht; *Style*— Robert Owen, Esq, QC; 1 Crown Office Row, Temple, London EC4 (☎ 071 353 1801)

OWEN, Prof (David) Roger Jones; s of Evan William Owen (d 1962), of Llanelli, and Margaret, *née* Jones (d 1990); *b* 27 May 1942; *Educ* Llanelli Boys' GS, Univ Coll Swansea (BSc, MSc), Northwestern Univ USA (PhD), Univ of Wales (DSc); *m* 12 Feb 1964, Janet Mary, da of William James Pugh (d 1983), of Llanelli; 2 da (Kathryn b 1967, Lisa b 1970); *Career* prof Univ of Wales 1982, dir Inst for Numerical Methods in Engrg Univ Coll Swansea 1987, md Rockfield Software Ltd, dir Pineridge Press Ltd; author of numerous pubns: memb Cncl Nat Assoc On Finite Element Methods and Standards, memb SERC ctees FICE 1983; *Books* with E Hinton: Finite Element Programming (1977), An Introduction to Finite Element Computations (1979), Finite Elements in Plasticity (1980), A Simple Guide to Finite Elements (1980), Engineering Fracture Mechanics: Numerical Methods and Applications (1983); *Recreations* flying, golf, tennis; *Clubs* Langland Bay Golf, Swansea; *Style*— Prof Roger Owen; Dept of Civil Engineering, University College Swansea, Singleton Park, Swansea SA 2 9PP (☎ 0792 295252, fax 0792 295676, telex 48149 UICS G)

OWEN, Roy Howard; s of Ernest Henry Owen (d 1944), of Selwyn, Queens Drive, Liverpool, and Gladys Owen, *née* Edwards (d 1966); *b* 22 June 1926; *Educ* Liverpool Inst, HS Univ of Liverpool (BArch, MCD); *m* 18 June 1968, Frances Maire, da of Joseph Patrick McNamara (d 1945), of Westcroft, Town Row, Liverpool; 1 s (David b 1976), 1 da (Sarah b 1972); *Career* chartered architect and town planning conslt; pres Liverpool Architectural Soc 1988-89; chm: W Derby Wastelands Charity 1980-, Liverpool Regnl Jt Cons Ctee for Bldg 1978-79; memb RIBA; MRTPI; *Recreations* opera, golf, assoc football, cricket; *Clubs* Liverpool Sportsmans Assoc, West Derby Golf, English Golf Union; *Style*— Roy Owen, Esq; Studley, Vyner Road South, Oxton, Birkenhead L43 7PN (☎ 051 652 2898); 619/621 India Buildings, Water St, Liverpool L2 0RA (☎ 051 236 0353)

OWEN, Sally Ann; da of Robert James Owen, of Plas Llysyn, Carno, Powys, and Rhoda, *née* Betteridge; *b* 11 May 1952; *Educ* Hengrove Comp Sch Bristol, Bristol Sch of Dancing, Rambert Sch of Ballet London; *Career* dancer, actress and choreographer; soloist Ballet Rembert 1971-81; Second Stride 1983-91; works incl: The Brilliant and the Dark Java Jive, Minor Characters, Cosi Fan Tutti, New Tactics, Further and Further Into Night, Bösendorfer Walses, Weighing the Heart, Heavan Ablaze in his Breast, Lives of the Great Poisoners; Direct Current 1985-88; works incl: A Personal Appearance, Mary Mary, The Super Hero Project; involved with: Secret Gardens (ICA and Micary Theatre Amsterdam) 1983, IQ of 4 (ICA) 1984, Lindsay Kemp (Italy, Sadlers Wells Theatre, Theatre Royal Brighton) 1985, Michael Matou (Barcelona 1985, Gateway to Freedom (The Place London) 1987-91, Fugue (Channel 4 TV) 1988; choreographic works incl: Paper Sunday (Ballet Rambert) 1980, Unsuitable Case (Ballet Rambert) 1981, Mascaritas (Emma Dance Co) 1982, Giraffes and Jellyfish and Things (Extemposary Dance Theatre) 1982, We Shall Fight Them on the Beaches (English Dance Theatre) 1983, The Dead Moon (Junior Co of Nederlands Dance Theatre) 1984, Did eat the Bait and Fisherman beguile (Transitions Dance Co) 1987, The Tailor of Gloucester (National Youth Music Theatre) 1989, Midday Sun (ICA); *Style*— Ms Sally Owen; c/o Sadler's Wells Theatre, Rosebery Ave, London EC1R 4TN (☎ 071 278 2917, fax 071 278 5927)

OWEN, Sheila Yorke; da of Capt William Owen (d 1950) (S African Mounted Rifles), of Hassocks, Sussex, and Ethel Lucy Yorke, *née* Weedon (d 1974); *b* 13 March 1912; *Educ* Berkhamsted GS for girls, Queen Anne's Sch Caversham, Freiburg im Breisgau, Lycée Française, Univ of Geneva; *Career* sec/translator Unilever Ltd London and Paris 1932-68; sec to: Mr V Cavendish-Bentinck (Duke of Portland) 1947-68, Ctee of Br Industl Interests in Germany 1950-68; hon sec Cons Assoc Branch: Hernhill Kent 1968-70, Dolgellau 1985-87, Meironnydd Nant Conwy 1986-87; FIL (languages Dutch, Norwegian, Polish, Welsh, French, German); *Recreations* mountain walking, gardening; *Clubs* Royal Over Seas League, Monday; *Style*— Miss Sheila Owen; Clawdd Dewi, Aberarth, Aberaeron, Dyfed SA46 0JX (☎ 0545 571 008)

OWEN, Thomas Arfon; s of Hywel Peris Owen, of Tumble; *b* 7 June 1933; *Educ* Ystalyfera GS, Magdalen Coll Oxford (MA); *m* 1955, Mary Joyce, da of Tom Ellis Phillips, of Ystalyfera (d 1972); 3 s, 1 da; *Career* dir Welsh Arts Cncl 1984-; registrar Univ Coll of Wales Aberystwyth 1967-84; memb Consumer Ctee for GB 1975-90; High Sheriff of Dyfed 1976-77; memb: Health Authy S Glam 1984-87 (vice chm 1986-87), Cncl UWIST 1987-88, Cncl Univ of Wales Coll at Cardiff 1988-, cncl Nat Library of Wales 1987-; FRSA; *Recreations* reading, crosswords, public service; *Style*— Thomas Owen, Esq; 35 Caswell House, The Crescent, Llandaf, Cardiff CF5 2DL (☎ 0222 567695)

OWEN, Trevor Bryan; CBE (1987); s of Leonard Owen, CIE (d 1965), of Gerrards Cross, and Dilys, *née* Davies Bryan; *b* 3 April 1928; *Educ* Rugby, Trinity Coll Oxford (MA); *m* 1955, Gaie, da of Cyril Dashwood Houston (d 1975), of Newark, Notts; 1 s (Jonathan b 1958), 1 da (Jane b 1956); *Career* dir paints, agric and plastics divns ICI 1955-78; md Remploy Ltd 1978-88; chm: Bethlem and Maudsley Special Health Authy 1988-, Inst of Psychiatry 1990-, PHAB 1988-91; memb: govt of N Ireland Higher Educn Review Gp 1979-81, Nat Advsy cncl on the Employment of Disabled People 1978-88, CNAA 1973-79, Cncl CBI 1982-88, Cncl Ind Soc 1967-88, Cncl Inst of Manpower Studies 1975-87; chm Bd of Govrs, Nat Inst for Social Work 1985-91; *Books* Making Organisations Work (1978), The Manager and Industrial Relations (1979); *Style*— Trevor B Owen, CBE; 8 Rochester Terrace, London NW1 9JN (☎ 071 485 9265)

OWEN, Tudor Wyn; s of Abel Rhys Owen (d 1974), of Aberdare, Glamorgan, and Mair, *née* Jenkins; *b* 16 May 1951; *Educ* Aberdare GS, King's Coll London (LLB Hons); *Career* called to the Bar Gray's Inn 1974, in practice South Eastern Circuit, inspr DTI 1989, asst recorder of the Crown Court 1990; memb: Ctee Criminal Bar Assoc 1987-, Gen Cncl of the Bar 1988-, Bar Professional Conduct Ctee 1989-91, Bar Ctee 1990- (vice chm 1991-), Bar Public Affairs Ctee 1990-91, Legal Servs Ctee 1991-; *Recreations* shooting, flying WWII fighter aircraft, skiing, riding the Cresta Run, music, theatre; *Clubs* Carlton, Royal Aero; *Style*— Tudor Owen, Esq; 25 Dancer Rd, Parson's Green, London SW6 4DU (☎ 071 731 7940); Chambers, 4 Paper Bldgs, Temple, London EC4Y 7EX (☎ 071 583 7765, fax 071 353 4674)

OWEN-JONES, David Roderic; s of John Eryl Owen-Jones, CBE, JP, DL, *qv*, and Mabel Clara, *née* McIlvride; *b* 16 March 1949; *Educ* Llandovery Coll Dyfed, UCL (LLB, LLM); *Career* called to the Bar Inner Temple 1972; in practice S Eastern Circuit; Parly candidate: (Lib) Carmarthen Div Feb and Oct 1974, (Lib Alliance) Rugby and Kenilworth 1983 and 1987; govr Int Students Tst 1981-84 (tstee 1981-), vice chm Assoc of Lib Lawyers 1986-88, memb Lord Chancellor's Advsy Ctee on the Appointments of JPs for Inner London; FRSA 1984; *Books* The Prosecutional Process in England and Wales (jtly); *Recreations* theatre, historical biography; *Clubs* Nat Lib (chm 1988-), Reform; *Style*— David Owen-Jones, Esq; 17 Albert Bridge Rd, London SW11 (☎ 071 622 1280); 3 Temple Gdns, Temple, London EC4Y 9AU (☎ 071 583 1155)

OWEN-JONES, (John) Eryl; CBE (1969), JP (1974), DL (Caerns 1971, Gwynedd 1974); s of John Owen-Jones (d 1962), of Colwyn Bay; *b* 19 Jan 1912; *Educ* Portmadoc GS, UCW Aberystwyth (LLB), Gonville and Caius Coll Cambridge (MA); *m* 1944, Mabel Clara, da of Grant McIlvride of Bombay (d 1920); 1 s (David ,*qv*), 1 da (Ann (Mrs Davies)); *Career* Sqdn Ldr RAFVR 1945; admitted slr 1938, asst slr Chester Corpn 1939, legal staff offr Judge Advocate General's Dept Med, dep clerk Caernarvonshire CC 1946; clerk: Caerns CC 1956-74, of the Peace 1956-72, N Wales Combined Probation Ctee, Gwynedd Police Authy 1956-67; dep clerk Snowdonia Park Jt Advsy Ctee, Clerk of Lieutenancy, memb Gorsedd Devidic Order Royal Nat Eisteddfod of Wales 1990; memb: Central Cncl Magistrates' Courts Ctees 1981, Bd Civic Tst for Wales 1982-, Bd Gwynedd Archaeological Tst Ltd 1982-; hon sec Caernarvonshire Historical Soc 1956-74, chm Caernarvon Civic Soc 1979-89; FRSA 1987; *Recreations* music, photography, gardening; *Style*— Eryl Owen-Jones Esq, CBE, JP, DL; Rhiw Dafnau, Caernarfon, Gwynedd LL55 1LF (☎ 0286 67 3370)

OWEN-JONES, Peter Charles; s of Dr Alan Owen-Jones (d 1962), of Edenbridge, Kent, and Daphne May Lewis-Turner; *b* 23 Dec 1957; *Educ* Epsom Coll; *m* Jacqueline, da of Bernard Herbert Hood; 1 da (India Ruth b 11 July 1990); *Career* messenger boy Wright Collins Rutherford Scott 1980, creative dir Toys in the Attic Ltd 1990; *Recreations* fishing, walking, the Doors; *Style*— Peter Owen-Jones, Esq; Toys In The Attic, 10-11 Moor Street, London W1 (☎ 071 287 1165, fax 071 437 1739)

OWEN-SMITH, Dr Brian David; s of Cyril Robert Smith, OBE, and Margaret Jane, *née* Hughes; *b* 29 May 1938; *Educ* Dulwich, Queens' Coll Cambridge (MA, MB BChir, RCP), Guy's Hosp London (DPhys, Med); *m* 24 Sept 1966, Rose Magdalen, da of Lord Ponsonby of Shulbrede (d 1976); 1 s (Timothy Clive b 25 April 1968), 1 da (Emma Elizabeth Jane b 22 Aug 1971); *Career* Lilly Fell in clinical pharmacology Indiana Univ USA 1970, sr registrar rheumatic diseases Royal Nat Hosp Bath 1972; currently: conslt in rheumatics and rehabilitation St Richard's Hosp Chichester W Sussex, med dir Younger Disabled Unit Donald Wilson House, conslt sports injuries BUPA Hosp Havant; memb Chichester Soc; Freeman: City of London, Worshipful Co of Apothecaries; LRCP, FRCP, MRCS; *Recreations* squash, tennis, sailing; *Clubs* RSM, IOD; *Style*— Dr Brian Owen-Smith; 48 Westgate, Chichester PO19 3EU (☎ 0243 786 688)

OWENS, Bernard Charles; s of Charles Albert Owens, and Sheila, *née* O'Higgins (d 1985); *b* 20 March 1928; *Educ* Solihull Sch, LSE; *m* 1954, Barbara Madeline, da of Thomas Murphy (d 1971); 2 s (Michael b 1955, Peter b 1960); 4 da (Jacqueline b 1955, Jennifer b 1957, Teresa b 1961, Susan b 1963); *Career* chm: Unochrome Int Ltd (now Unochrome Ind plc) 1964-79 Van der Horst worldwide incl 70 other assoc cos; dir: Hobbs Savill & Bradford Ltd 1957-62, Trinidad Sugar Estates Ltd 1965-67, Cornish Brewery Co Ltd 1987-, Br Jewellery and Giftware Fedn Ltd 1987- (vice pres); md: Stanley Bros Ltd 1961-67, Coronet Insustl Securities Ltd 1965-67; memb: Monopolies and Mergers Cmmn 1981-, Cncl Zoological Soc of London 1987-90 (fell 1980-); memb: Order of Malta 1979, Lloyd's 1978, HAC 1984; life govr RNLI 1984, Parly candidate (Cons) Small Heath Birmingham 1959 and 1961; cncllr Solihull UDC and Borough Cncl 1954-64 (chm finance 1957-64); Lord of the Manor of Southwood; Freeman City of London 1981, Liveryman Worshipful Co of Gardeners 1982; FLS, FRSA, FRGS; *Clubs* Carlton, City Livery, MCC, Wig and Pen, City Livery Yacht (hon sec), Stroud RFC; *Style—* Bernard Owens, Esq; The Vatch House, Stroud, Gloucestershire GL6 7JY (☎ 045376 3402)

OWENS, Charles Arthur; LVO (1976); s of William Henry Owens (d 1969), of Birmingham, and Doris Owens, *née* Chew (d 1972); *b* 18 Feb 1922; *Educ* Holly Lodge HS; *m* 19 May 1947, Betty Goddard, da of Walter Wigglesworth (d 1966), of Doncaster; 1 s (Robert Charles b 26 March 1952), 1 da (Susan Elizabeth (Mrs Connelly) b 20 May 1949); *Career* RAF Halton 1938-40, Flt Lt Pilot 1942-46; DNL (Norwegian Airlines) 1946, BEA 1949, mangr Comet Flight 1958 (later flt ops dir), Bd of Mgmnt BEA/BA 1977, aviation conslt 1977; Guild of Air Pilots and Air Navigators 1946, Freeman City of London (Master 1975), Liveryman City of London; FCIT 1970, FRAeS 1976, FBIM 1980; *Books* Flight Operations (1982); *Recreations* travelling, swimming; *Clubs* RAF; *Style—* Charles Owens, Esq, LVO; 1 Chetwynd, 170 Canford Cliffs Rd, Poole, Dorset BH13 7ES (☎ 0202 700 997)

OWENS, Prof David Howard; s of Maurice Owens, of Derby, and Joan, *née* Browes; *b* 23 April 1948; *Educ* Dronfield Henry Fanshawe, Imperial Coll London (BSc, Phd); *m* 18 July 1969, Rosemary, da of John Cecil Frost, of Sheffield; 1 s (Benjamin David b 1976), 1 da (Penelope Rosemary Jane b 1979); *Career* scientific offr UK AEA Atomic Energy Estab Winfrith 1969-73, reader in control engrg Univ of Sheffield 1982 (lectr 1973, sr lectr 1981), prof of dynamics and control Univ of Strathclyde 1988-90 (prof of engrg mathematics 1985), prof of systems and control engrg Univ of Exeter 1990-; ctee work and conference orgn: Inst of Electrical Engrs, IMechE, Inst of Mathematics and its Applications; FIMA 1976, MIEE 1979, MIEEE 1990; *Books* Feedback and Multivariable Systems (1978), Multivariable and Optimal Systems (1981), Analysis and Control of Multipass Processes (with J B Edwards, 1982); *Recreations* sketching, cycling, reading, guitar; *Style—* Prof David Owens; School of Engineering, University of Exeter, North Park Rd, Exeter EX4 4QF (☎ 0392 263689, fax 0392 217965, telex 42894)

OWENS, John Ridland; s of Dr Ridland Owens (d 1968), of Lymington, and Elsie, *née* Smith (d 1990); *b* 21 May 1932; *Educ* Merchant Taylors', St John's Coll Oxford (MA); *m* 1, 1958 (m dis 1981), Susan Lilian, da of Cdr G R Pilcher, RN, of Yelverton; 2 s (David Ridland b 23 Feb 1962, James Graham b 27 Sept 1966), 1 da (Elizabeth Clare b 1 July 1960); m 2, 27 Sept 1985, Cynthia Rose, da of Sir Archibald Forbes, GBE, of Portman Sq, London W1; 1 s (Thomas Alasdair Ridland); *Career* Nat Serv 2 Lt RA served Germany 1951-52, Lt TA 1952-57, Gunner HAC 1957-61; section mangr ICI Ltd 1955-67, md Cape Asbestos Fibres Ltd 1967-72, dir gen Dairy Trade Fedn 1973-83 (vice pres Assocn Industrie Laitière du Marché Commun, dir Nat Dairy Cncl, memb Food and Drink Indust Cncl), dep dir gen CBI 1983-90, dir gen Building Employers Confedn 1990-, bd memb UK Skills; memb: Exec Ctee PRONED 1983-90, Indust Ctee RSA 1984-87, Assoc of Business Sponsorship of the Arts Cncl, Advsy Bd RA City and Guilds Inst Cncl 1988-90, City Univ Ct, Cncl Franco-Br Cncl 1989-90; Freeman City of London, Liveryman Merchant Taylors' Co (member ct); FRSA; *Recreations* painting, music, walking; *Clubs* Reform; *Style—* John Owens, Esq; 40 Blenheim Terrace, London NW8 0EG; Building Employers Confederation, 82 New Cavendish St, London W1M 8AD (☎ 071 580 5588)

OWENS, (John) Robin; s of Col Theobald David Cogswell Owens, MC (d 1984), of Chichester, Hampshire and Irene, *née* Hamilton (d 1949); *b* 26 May 1939; *Educ* Wellington, Welbeck Coll, RMA Sandhurst, Emmanuel Coll Cambridge (MA); *m* 1963, Margaret Ann, da of Harry Arthur Overton (d 1979), of Norfolk; 1 s (Nicholas b 1966), 1 da (Philippa b 1969); *Career* Second in cmd of the Hong Kong Fortress Sqdn 1964-67, Projects Offr of the 1 Bn Royal Engrs 1966-68, ret with rank of Capt, 1968; chm Airlease Int Fin 1977-78; dir: Midland Montagu Leasing Ltd 1978-80, Forward Tst Gp 1980-84, GATX Lease Fin Ltd 1984-85; md: Park Place Fin 1985-86, Medens Tst 1986-89; dir Brown Simply & Co Ltd 1989-; FCA 1972; *Recreations* tennis, sailing; *Clubs* The Utd Oxford and Cambridge Univ, Royal Temple Yacht; *Style—* Robin Owens, Esq; Park Cottage, Teston, Maidstone, Kent (☎ 0622 812208); Founders Court, Lothbury, London EC2 (☎ 071 606 9833)

OWERS, Gary; s of Maurice Mathew Joseph Owers, of Gateshead, and Jennifer Anne, *née* Billclough (d 1990); *b* 3 Oct 1968; *Educ* Lord Lawson Comp Sch; *Career* professional footballer; Sunderland: apprentice 1985-87, professional 1987-, debut v Brentford 1988, over 150 appearances; Div 3 Championship 1988, promotion to Div 1 1990; represented Tyne & Wear: football, basketball, rugby; high jump champion Tyneside Sr Schs; *Recreations* listening to music, relaxing; *Style—* Gary Owers, Esq; Sunderland FC, Roker Park, Grantham Road, Sunderland, Tyne & Wear (☎ 091 514 0332)

OWTRAM, Col (Henry) Cary; OBE (1970), TD (1946), DL (Lancs 1967); s of Lt-Col Herbert Hawkesworth Owtram, OBE, JP (d 1952), of Newland Hall, nr Lancaster, and Ethel, *née* Fair (d 1921); *b* 8 Sept 1899; *Educ* Shrewsbury; *m* 2 Aug 1922, Dorothy, da of Lt-Col Charles James Daniel, CBE, DSO; 1 s (Charles Robert Cary Owtram, MBE b 4 Oct 1930), 2 da (Ethel Patricia b 19 June 1923, Dorothy Jean b 7 Nov 1925); *Career* WWI 2 Lt RM Artillery France 1918, Capt 88 Fd RA 1920-30; WWII: Maj 137 FD RA 1939, Lt-Col Malaya (despatches twice) 1942 (POW 1942-45); Lt-Col 337 HAA RA 1947-50, hon Col 288 AA RA 1960-68; dir cotton spinning companies 1930-72, chm Lunesdale Farmers Ltd 1953-74, pres Preston Farmers Ltd 1974-84; JP Lancashire 1953-73, High Sheriff Lancashire 1965; ; Royal Lancs Agric Soc: memb Cncl 1958-74, chm 1974-80, pres 1981-82, hon life vice pres 1987-; *Recreations* shooting, fishing, gardening; *Clubs* St James's (Manchester); *Style—* Col Cary Owtram, OBE, TD, DL; Newland Hall, nr Lancaster, Lancs (☎ 0524 751 207)

OXFORD, Sir Kenneth Gordon; CBE (1981), QPM (1976), DL (Co of Merseyside 1988-); s of Ernest George Oxford, and late Gladys Violet, *née* Seaman; *b* 25 June 1924; *Educ* Caldecot Sch, Lambeth; *m* 1954, Muriel, *née* Panton; *Career* RAFVR 1942-47, Bomber Cmd, SEAC; served Met Police 1947-69 (constable to detective chief supt), asst chief constable (crime) Northumbria Constabulary 1969-74, chief constable Merseyside Police 1976-89 (dep chief constable 1974-76, ret 1989), regnl dir Lloyds Bank plc 1988-; Hon Col 156 (Merseyside and Gtr Manchester), Tport Regt RCT(V) 1989-, conslt dir Securicor Gp plc 1989-90; memb Forensic Sci Soc 1970; Medico-Legal Soc 1975; chm: Crime Ctee Assoc of Chief Police Offrs of Eng, Wales and NI 1977-89, Jt Standing Ctee on Police use of Firearms 1979-89, Assoc of Chief Police Offrs Sub-Ctee on Terrorism and Allied Matters 1982-89; rep ICPO (Interpol) 1983; pres: NW Police Benevolent Fund 1978-89, Assoc Chief Police Offrs of England, Wales and NI 1982-83; chm Merseyside Rgnl Ctee of Princes Tst 1978-82; pres Merseyside Branch BIM 1983- (chm 1978-82); dep pres Merseyside branch St John Ambulance Assoc 1985- (vice pres 1988-89, co dir 1976-84); Freeman City of London 1983; CBIM, FRSA; OStJ 1977; kt 1988; *Publications* author of various articles and papers on crime and kindred matters; *Recreations* shooting, cricket, music, books, roses; *Clubs* Royal Cwlth Soc, Special Forces, Surrey Co Cricket, Lancs Co Cricket, Liverpool St Helens Rugby Football; *Style—* Sir Kenneth Oxford, CBE, QPM, DL; c/o Chief Constable's Office, PO Box 59, Liverpool L69 1JD (☎ 051 709 6010)

OXFORD, 41 Bishop of (1542) 1987-; Rt Rev Richard Douglas Harries; patron of over 116 livings and the Archdeaconries of Oxford, Buckingham and Berks; the Bishopric was originally endowed with lands of dissolved monasteries by Henry VIII, but in Elizabeth I's reign many of these were removed from it; s of Brig William Douglas Jameson Harries, CBE, and Greta Miriam, da of A Bathurst Brown, MB, LRCP; *b* 2 June 1936; *Educ* Wellington, RMA Sandhurst, Selwyn Coll Cambridge (MA), Cuddesdon Coll Oxford; *m* 1963, Josephine Bottomley, MA, MB BChir, DCH; 1 s, 1 da; *Career* Lt RCS 1955-58; curate Hampstead Parish Church 1963-69, chaplain Westfield Coll 1966-69, lectr Wells Theological Coll 1969-72, warden Wells, Salisbury and Wells Theological Coll 1971-72, vicar All Saints' Fulham 1972-81, dean King's Coll London 1981-87, conslt to Archbishop on Jewish Christian Relations, chm The Johnson Soc 1988; The Sir Sigmund Sternking award 1987; FKC; *Books* Prayers of Hope (1975), Turning to Prayer (1978), Prayers of Grief and Glory (1979), Being a Christian (1981), Should Christians Support Guerrillas? (1982), The Authority of Divine Love (1983), Praying Round the Clock (1983), Seasons of the Spirit (1984), Prayer and the Pursuit of Happiness (1985), Morning has Broken (1985), Christianity and War in a Nuclear Age (1986), CS Lewis: The Man and his God (1987), The One Genius (1987), Christ has Risen (1988); contributor: What Hope in an Armed World (and ed, 1982), Reinhold Niebuhr and the issues of our Time (and ed, 1986), Stewards and the Mysteries of God (1975), Unholy Warfare (1983), The Cross and the Bomb (1985), Julian, Woman of our Time (1985), The Reality of God (1986); *Recreations* theatre, literature, sport; *Style—* The Rt Rev the Bishop of Oxford; Diocesan Church House, North Hinksey, Oxford OX2 0NB (☎ 0865 244566)

OXFORD AND ASQUITH, 2 Earl of (UK 1925); Julian Edward George; KCMG (1964, CMG 1961); also Viscount Asquith (UK 1925); s of Raymond Asquith (ka the Somme 1916; s of the Lib PM, Rt Hon Sir Herbert Henry Asquith, KG, later 1 Earl (d 1928)), and Katharine Frances (d 1976), da of Sir John Horner, KCVO (d 1927); *b* 22 April 1916; *Educ* Ampleforth, Balliol Coll Oxford (MA); *m* 28 Aug 1947, Anne Mary Celestine, CStJ, da of late Sir Michael Palairet, KCMG; 2 s, 3 da; *Heir* s, Viscount Asquith, *qv*; *Career* 2 Lt RE 1940; sits as Independent in House of Lords; asst dist cmmr Palestine Admin 1942-48, dep chief sec Br Admin Tripolitania 1949, dir of the Interior Tripolitanian Govt 1951, advsr to PM of Libya 1952, admin sec Zanzibar 1955, admin St Lucia 1958-61, govr and C-in-C Seychelles 1962-67, and cmmr Br Indian Ocean Territory 1965-67, constitutional cmmr Cayman Islands 1971, constitutional cmmr Turks and Caicos Islands 1973-74; KStJ; *Style—* The Rt Hon the Earl of Oxford and Asquith, KCMG; The Manor House, Mells, Frome, Somerset (☎ 0373 812324)

OXFUIRD, 13 Viscount of (S 1651); Sir George Hubbard Makgill; 13 Bt (NS 1627); also Lord Makgill of Cousland (S 1697); claim to Viscountcy admitted by Ctee for Privileges, House of Lords 1977; s of Sqdn Ldr Richard James Robert Haldane Makgill (d 1948, yr s of 11 Bt) and Elizabeth Lyman, *née* Hubbard (d 1981); s uncle 1986; *b* 7 Jan 1934; *Educ* Wanganui Collegiate Sch NZ; *m* 1, 1967 (m dis 1977), Alison Campbell, da of late Neils Max Jensen, of Randers, Denmark; 3 s (Master of Oxfuird b 1969, Hon Robert Edward George b (twin) 1969, Hon Hamish Max Alistair b 1972); m 2, 1980, Venetia Cunitia Mary, da of Major Charles Anthony Steward, of The Platt, Crondall, nr Farnham, Surrey; 1 s (Hon Edward Anthony Donald b 1983); *Heir* s, Hon Ian Arthur Alexander Makgill, Master of Oxfuird b 14 Oct 1969; *Career* external affrs mangr Lansing Linde Ltd 1979-; dep chm House of Lords; *Recreations* shooting, gardening, cricket, fishing; *Clubs* Caledonian; *Style—* The Rt Hon the Viscount of Oxfuird; c/o House of Lords, London SW1

OXFUIRD, Maureen, Viscountess of; Maureen; *née* Magan; yr da of Lt-Col Arthur Tilson Shaen Magan, CMG (d 1965), and Kathleen Jane, *née* Biddulph (d 1969); *b* 11 Nov 1914; *m* 1, 9 Sept 1939 (m dis 1949), Lt-Col John Herbert Gillington, OBE, MC (d 1970); 1 s; m 2, 6 Oct 1955, as his 2 wife 12 Viscount of Oxfuird (d 1986); *Style—* The Rt Hon Maureen, Viscountess of Oxfuird; 2 Hillside, Heath Rd, Newmarket, Suffolk CB8 8AY (☎ 0638 666726)

OXLADE, Roy; s of William Oxlade (d 1955), of Bexley Heath, Kent, and Emily, *née* Fenn; *b* 13 Jan 1929; *Educ* Bromley Coll of Art, RCA (PhD); *m* 10 Aug 1957, Rose, da of Alexander Forrest Wylie, OBE (d 1964), of Hythe, Kent; 1 s (Luke-John b 7 Aug 1958), 2 da (Elizabeth b 11 April 1960, Henrietta b 18 July 1966); *Career* painter; gp exhibitions: Young Contempories 1952, 1953 and 1954, Borough Bottega 1954 and 1955, Winnipeg Biennale 1960, John Moores 1964, Hayward Annual 1982, Odette Gilbert Gallery 1984 and 1985-90, Royal Acad Summer Exhibition 1984, 1985, 1989 and 1990, Rocks and Flesh 1985, Olympia Art Fair 1986, Chicago Art Fair 1987, Los Angeles Art Fair 1987, Waddington Schiel Toronto 1987, Jan Turner Los Angles 1988, Cleveland Int Drawing Biennale 1989; solo exhibitions: Vancouver Art Gallery 1963, Midland Gp Gallery 1975, New Metropole Gallery Folkestone 1983, Air Gallery 1983, Odette Gilbert Gallery 1985, 1987 and 1988; *Publications* David Bomberg - RCA Papers III (1981), The Visual Arts in Adult Education and The Arts (contrib, 1981), Modern Painters Magazine (contrib); *Style—* Roy Oxlade, Esq; Odette Gilbert Gallery, 5 Cork St, London W1 (☎ 071 437 3175)

OXLADE, Zena Elsie; CBE (1984); da of James Oxlade (d 1983), and Beatrice May, *née* Oliver (d 1962); *b* 26 April 1929; *Educ* Latymer GS, Univ of London; *Career* SRN and registered nurse tutor; chm Gen Nursing Cncl for England and Wales 1977-83 (memb 1975-83); area nursing offr Suffolk 1978-, regnl nursing offr East Anglia 1981-89, ret 1989; memb UK Cncl for Nurses Midwives and Health Visitors 1983-88; *Recreations* motoring, reading, handicrafts; *Clubs* Soroptomist Int; *Style—* Miss Zena Oxlade, CBE; 5 Morgan Court, Claydon, Ipswich, Suffolk IP6 0AN (☎ 0473 831895); East Anglian Regional Health Authority, Union Lane, Chesterton, Cambs CB4 1RF (☎ 0223 61212)

OXLEY; *see*: Rice-Oxley

OXLEY, David; OBE (1989); s of Robert Lacey Oxley (d 1980), of Hull, and Reena, *née* Stokes; *b* 5 Jan 1938; *Educ* Hymers Coll Hull, Worcester Coll Oxford (BA, MA, DipEd); *m* 1, 1961 (m dis 1975), Elizabeth Mary Joan, *née* Walford; 1 s (Mark b 10 Jan 1968), 1 da (Alyson b 29 Aug 1965); m 2, 1977, Bridget Anne, da of Stanley Wisdom; 1 da (Lucy b 12 Sept 1979), 1 adopted s (Simon b 14 April 1966); *Career* chief exec Rugby Football League 1987- (sec-gen 1974-87); teacher: Merchant Taylors Sch Northwood 1962-66, St Edwards Sch Oxford 1966-69; head of Eng Dept St Peters Sch York 1969-72, dep headmaster Duke of York's Royal Military Sch Dover 1972-76; vice chm Yorks and Humberside Cncl for Sport & Recreation 1986-, chm Br Assoc of Nat Sports Admins 1984-87 (memb Exec 1980-), memb Exec CCPR 1988, govr Sports Aid Fndn (Yorks & Humberside); hon fell Humberside Poly 1990; *Style—* David Oxley,

Esq, OBE; Rugby Football League, 180 Chapeltown Rd, Leeds LS7 4HT (☎ 0532 624637, fax 0532 623386)

OXLEY, Peter John Reginald; s of Lt-Col Richard George Reginald Oxley (d 1969), and Jean Elspeth, *née* Anderson; *b* 2 March 1934; *Educ* Cheam, Eton, Magdalene Coll Cambridge (BA); *m* 3 Feb 1959, Vanla Joy, da of Capt Clive Denison Arbuthnot, RN (d 1965); 2 s (Stephen b 1959, Timothy b 1962), 1 da (Rachel b 1966); *Career* dir: Skye Ceramics Ltd 1967-88, Witham Vale Contractors Ltd 1968-, Surdaw Press Ltd 1983-; treas Somerton & Frome Constituency Cons Assoc 1986-90; *Recreations* fishing, shooting, golf; *Style*— Peter Oxley, Esq; Queen Camel House, nr Yeovil, Somerset (☎ 0935 850269)

OXMANTOWN, Lord; (Laurence) Patrick Parsons; s and h of 7 Earl of Rosse; *b* 31 March 1969; *Educ* Aiglon Coll Switzerland; *Style*— Lord Oxmantown; Birr Castle, Birr, Co Offaly, Republic of Ireland; 41 rue Madame, 75006 Paris, France; 94 rue de Faubourg Saint-Honoré, 75008 Paris, France (☎ 42 68 11 11)

OXTOBY, David Jowett Greaves; s of John Henry Oxtoby (d 1972), of Horsforth, Yorks, and Ann Jowett, *née* Greaves (d 1978); *b* 23 Jan 1938; *Educ* Horsforth Cncl Sch, Bradford Coll of Art, RA Sch Piccadilly; *Career* artist, best known for visual interpretations of pop music, 44 one man shows, numerous exhibits in gp exhibitions; works in public collections incl: Br Museum, LA County Museum, Museum of Modern Art NY, Minneapolis Inst of Art, Tate Gallery, Victoria & Albert Museum; lectr numerous colls incl RA, visiting prof painting Mineapolis Inst of Art 1964-65, ret teaching 1972; *Books* painting reprod in: Oxtoby's Rockers (D Dandison 1978), V & A Museum Calendar (1985), Once Upon a Christmas (D Sandison 1986); *Recreations* cycling; *Style*— David Oxtoby, Esq; c/o David Sandison, 96 Brunswick, Park Rd, London N11 1JJ (☎ 081 368 3683)

ÖZBEK, (Ibrahim Mehmet) Rifat; s of Abdulazim Mehmet Ismet Özbet, of Istanbul, and Melike, *née* Pekis; *b* 8 Nov 1953; *Educ* Isik Lisesi Istanbul, St Martin's Sch of Art (BA); *Career* fashion designer Waiter Albini for Trell Milan 1977-79, Monsoon Co 1979-84, presented first collection 1984; Br Fashion Cncl Designer of the Year 1988; *Style*— Rifat Özbek, Esq; 18 Haunch of Venison Yard, London W1Y 1AF (☎ 071 491 7033, fax 071 629 1586)

P

PACE, Franco Giustino; s of Edmondo Pace (d 1959); *b* 28 Sept 1927; *Educ* Bologna Univ (doctorate in industl engrg), Milan Univ (post grad specialisation in chemistry); *m* 1955, Maria Vittoria, da of Dr Ing Salvatore Picchetti, of Italy; 1 s (Valerio); *Career* dir: Montedison UK Ltd 1973-89, Polyamide Intermediates Ltd 1974-83, Farmitalia Carlo Erba Ltd 1978-88, Himont UK Ltd 1987-, Himont Holdings UK Ltd 1987-, Accademia Italiana 1989-; chm: Montefibre UK Ltd 1974-89, Acna UK Ltd 1976-88, Cedar Service UK Ltd 1982-88, Internike Ltd 1984-88, Selm International Ltd 1986-88, Rubber and Chemicals Ltd 1989-, Euroil Exploration Ltd 1989-; vice pres Italian Chamber of Commerce for Great Britain 1981-88, sec gen Italian C of C for GB 1988-; Commendatore al merito della Repubblica Italiana (1987); *Clubs* Hurlingham; *Style—* Franco G Pace, Esq; 10 Kensington Court Gardens, London W8 5QE (☎ 071 937 7143); Italian Chamber of Commerce for Great Britain, 296 Regent St, London W1R 6AE (☎ 071 637 3062, fax 071 436 6037)

PACEY, Albert Howard; QPM; s of William Albert Pacey, of Lincoln, and Gwendoline Annie, *née* Quibell (d 1987); *b* 18 Dec 1938; *Educ* City Sch Lincoln, NDC Latimer, Police Staff Coll; *m* 20 Aug 1960, Ann Elizabeth, da of Alfred Hedley Wood (1985); 2 s (Mark b 1961, Simon b 1963), 1 da (Helen (Mrs Parker) b 1967); *Career* constable to chief superintendant Lincs Constabulary 1958-76 (police cadet 1955), staff offr to HM Inspr of Constabulary 1976, asst chief constable Humberside Police 1977-83, dep chief constable Lancs Constabulary 1983-87, chief constable Glos Constabulary 1987-; advsr on police trg to Nigeria Govt, memb of St John's Cncl for Glos, rep of Countryside Sports Cncl for Assoc of Chief Police Offrs; memb Assoc of Chief Police Offrs; *Recreations* golf, fell walking, gardening, reading; *Clubs* Cormorant; *Style—* Albert Pacey, Esq, QPM; Chief Constable, Gloucestershire Constabulary, Holland House, Lansdown Rd, Cheltenham, Glos GL51 6QH (☎ 0242 521321, fax 0242 224089)

PACKARD, Lt-Gen Sir (Charles) Douglas; KBE (1957, CBE 1945, OBE 1942), CB (1949), DSO (1943); s of Capt C Packard, MC, of Copdock, Suffolk; *b* 17 May 1903; *Educ* Winchester, RMA Woolwich; *m* 1937, Marion Cargill Thomson (d 1981), da of Dr James Lochhead, of Edinburgh; 1 s, 2 da; m 2, 1982, Mrs Patricia Miles-Sharp; *Career* 2 Lt RA 1923, WWII ME and Italy, dep chief Staff 15 Army Gp 1944-45, temp Maj-Gen and chief Staff Allied Cmmn Austria 1945-46; dir Mil Intelligence War Office 1948-49, cmd Br Mil Mission to Greece 1949-51 chief of Staff GHQ MELF 1951-53, VQMG War Office 1953-56, mil advsr to W African Govts 1956-58, Lt-Gen 1957, GOC-in-C NI 1958-61; *Recreations* gardening and travel; *Style—* Lt-Gen Sir Douglas Packard, KBE, CB, DSO; Park Side, Lower Ufford, Woodbridge, Suffolk IP13 6DL (☎ 0394 460418)

PACKARD, Gilian Elizabeth; da of John Laurence Packard (d 1981), and Rachel Alice, *née* Kaye (d 1981); *b* 16 March 1938; *Educ* Claremont Sch Esher, Kingston Sch of Art, Central Sch of Arts and Crafts, RCA (DesRCA); *m* 6 March 1965 (m dis 1972), Dennis Nigel Johns Parris; *Career* jeweller: head Dept of Silversmithing and Jewellery Glasgow Sch of Art 1979-83, asst dir of design Worshipful Co of Goldsmiths 1983-88, project dir City of London Poly and Br Jewellers Assoc 1989-; exhibitor of designs worldwide; winner Diamonds Int awards 1963 and 1964, first prize and commended De Beers Competition for the diamond engagement ring 1964; work in collections V & A Goldsmiths Co, De Beers; chm and Br rep World Crafts Cncl 1968-72; memb: Crafts Advsy Ctee 1971-74, Scot Crafts Consultative Ctee 1979-83; Freeman: City of London, Worshipful Co of Goldsmiths 1971; RSA, FCSD, FSD-C; *Style—* Ms Gilian Packard; 8:2 Stirling Court, 3 Marshall St, London W1V 1LQ (☎ 071 437 5902); 195 High St, Aldeburgh, Suffolk IP15 5AL

PACKARD, Brig (Joseph) John; s of Maj Joseph Thomas Packard, OBE (d 1955), and Rachel, *née* Powell (d 1944); *b* 14 May 1910; *Educ* Leiston GS, RMC Sandhurst; *m* 8 June 1942, (Mary) Faith, da of Capt Gerard Harrison; 4 s (Peter John b 9 April 1943, Mark Anthony Clive b 21 March 1947, Timothy Paul b 18 Jan 1952, Simon David b 27 June 1955), 1 da (Mary Anne Faith (Mrs Gray) b 16 March 1949); *Career* cmmnd E Yorks Regt 1932, serv 1932-36 (Lucknow, Dinapore, NW Frontier), Adj depot E Yorks Regt Beverley 1937-38, WO Intelligence 1938-39, GSO 3 (Intelligence) GHQ BEF in France 1939-40, Staff Coll Camberley 1940, cmdt Tactical Sch Iceland 1940-42, CO Hallamshire Bn York and Lancaster Regt 1942-43, serv Assam and Burma 1943-45, GSO1 (Inf) Delhi 1945-46, regtl and staff appts Austria and Germany 1947-51, memb Temple Ctee for army reorganisation 1951, 1 Bn Welch Regt Korea 1951-52, head mission to French forces in Germany 1952-56, mil attaché Vienna 1956-60, head mission to Soviet forces in Germany 1960-61; head info servs Fisons Ltd 1961-64; chm: Cripplegate Fndn 1985-86, Welch House Homes for the Elderly 1976-87, St Margaret's House Bethnal Green 1980-85; tstee City Parochial Fndn 1983-89, memb Blyth RDC 1964-71, chm Port and City of London Health and Social Servs 1978-80, Common Councilman City of London; Freeman City of London 1972, Liveryman Worshipful Co of Wax Chandlers 1974; *Books* The Fields and Field Names of Easton Suffolk (1971), Church and Churchyard Inscriptions of All Saints Easton Suffolk (1972), The Packards (1987); *Recreations* local history, genealogy; *Clubs* Guildhall; *Style—* Brig John Packard; 143 Thomas More House, Barbican, London EC2Y 8BU (☎ 071 628 6904)

PACKARD, Richard Bruce Selig; s of John Jacob Packard, of Delray Beach, Florida, USA, and (Priscilla) Lilian, *née* Joseph; *b* 20 Feb 1947; *Educ* Harrow, Middlesex Hosp Med Sch (MD, DO); *m* 1, 21 March 1974 (m dis 1986), Veronica Susan, da of Michael Bird, CBE, of Esher, Surrey; 2 s (Rupert Alexander b 1978, Hugo Philip b 1980), 1 da (Elvira Rose b 1984); m 2, 24 April 1986, Fiona Catherine, da of Walter F Kinnear, of Kilspindie, Perthshire; 1 s (Ian Charles b 1990); *Career* specialist trg in ophthalmology; house surgn in ophthalmology Middx Hosp 1970; held various jr med appointments 1971-75, res surgery offr Moorfields Eye Hosp 1975-78, sr registrar in ophthalmology Charing Cross Hosps Fulham 1978-82, conslt ophthalmic surgn Prince Charles Eye Unit King Edward VII Hosp Windsor 1982-; tstee Cyclotron Tst for Cancer Treatment; chm Oxford RHA Ophthalmology Sub-Ctee; FRCS 1976, FCOphth 1991, memb American Acad of Ophthalmology; *Books* Cataract and Lens Implant Surgery (jtly, 1985), Emergency Surgery (jtly, 1986), Manual of Cataract and Lens Implant Surgery (jtly, 1991); *Recreations* fly-fishing, wine, music; *Clubs* Garrick, MCC; *Style—* Richard Packard, Esq; 96 Harley Street, London W1 (☎ 071 935 9555, fax 0734 343059)

PACKARD, Simon Henry; s of Henry Nesbitt Packard, of Sunderland, and Freda Murial, *née* Rain; *Educ* Broadway Sch, Bede Sch, Sunderland Poly, Brighton Poly (BA), RCA (MA, Henry Moore bursary); *Career* artist; fell in printmaking Gloucestershire Coll of Art 1987-88; visiting tutor (Brighton Poly, Byham Shaw Sch of Art, Bristol Poly), artist-in-residence in schs for Gloucestershire Educn Authy; most important works: Japanese Erang woodcut 1987, Hound-Dog on Holiday 1989; Lloyds Bank Young Printmaker of 1986; represented GB at: BP Int Print Biennale Bradford (Invitation only), 13 Artists form EEC Countries Le Havre 1990, L'air du temp, Graphic Arts Jubljana Yugoslavia 1991; played cricket for Sussex CCC XI 1982-85; *Recreations* sport, walking my dogs; *Style—* Simon Packard, Esq; 4 Kitesnest Lane, Lightpill Stroud, Glos (☎ 0453 860150, 0453 755429); The Studio, The Green, Uley, nr Dursley, Glos

PACKER, Kerry Francis Bullmore; AC (1983); s of late Sir Douglas Frank Hewson Packer, KBE (d 1974), and Gretel Joyce, *née* Bullmore (d 1960); *b* 17 Dec 1937; *Educ* Cranbrook Sch Sydney NSW, Geelong C of E GS Vic; *m* 1963, Roslyn Redman, da of late Dr F H Weedon; 1 s, 1 da; *Career* exec Aust Consolidated Press Ltd 1955, chm Consolidated Press Hldgs Ltd and gp of cos 1974-; *Recreations* polo, golf, tennis, cricket; *Clubs* Royal Sydney Golf, Australian Golf, Elanora County, Tattersall's, Athenaeum (Melbourne); *Style—* Kerry F B Packer, Esq, AC; 54 Park St, Sydney, NSW 2000, Australia (☎ 02 282 8000, fax 02 267 2150, telex AA120514)

PACKER, Linda Frances Jean; da of Frank Harold Packer (d 1973), and Jean Grace, *née* Row; *b* 18 June 1959; *Educ* Associated Arts Sch Wimbledon, Arts Educnl Sch London (Markova award for Ballet); *Career* princ dancer Scottish Ballet 1983- (joined 1978; princ roles incl: Sugar Plum Fairy in The Nutcracker, the Girl in John Gilpen's revival of Le Spectre de la Rose; title roles in: Giselle, Carmen, Cinderella, Juliet in John Cranko's Romeo & Juliet; *Recreations* astrology, alternative medicine; *Style—* Ms Linda Packer; Scottish Ballet, 261 West Princes St, Glasgow G4 9EE (☎ 041 331 2931)

PACKER, Dr Paul Frederick; *b* 30 Dec 1941; *Educ* Salford GS, Univ of Durham, Univ of Newcastle upon Tyne (MB BS); *m* 16 July 1966, Marie Anita, *née* Malcolm; 1 s (Jago Christopher b 1969), 1 da (Victoria Michelle b 1973); *Career* house surgn and med registrar Wanganui Hosp NZ 1966-68; conslt and clinical lectr in radiology: Univ of Newcastle upon Tyne, Freeman and Gen Hosps Newcastle 1972-82; conslt radiologist: St Elizabeth Hosp Arnhem Holland 1974-79, Riyadh Forces Hosp KSA 1982-86, Grimsby Dist Gen Hosp 1986; memb DMRD (RCP and RCSEng) 1970; FFR 1972, FRCR 1975; *Style—* Dr Paul Packer; Church Farm, Church Lane, Brigsley, South Humberside DN37 0RH (☎ 0472 822440); Grimsby Dist Gen Hospital, Grimsby, South Humberside (☎ 0472 74111 ext 7277)

PACKER, Richard John; s of George Charles Packer (d 1979), and Dorothy May Packer; *b* 18 Aug 1944; *Educ* City of London Sch, Univ of Manchester (BSc, MSc); *m* 1, Alison Mary, *née* Sellwood; 2 s (James b 1969, George b 1971), 1 da (Rachel b 1973); m 2, Lucy Jeanne, da of Edmund Neville-Rolfe, of Tisbury, Wilts; 3 s (Thomas b 1981, William b 1984, Harry b 1988); *Career* MAFF: joined 1967, asst princ, 1 sec Office of UK Representative to EC 1973-76, princ private sec Minister 1976-78, asst sec 1979, under sec 1985, dep sec MAFF 1989; dir ABM Chemicals 1985-86; *Recreations* many sporting and intellectual interests; *Style—* Richard J Packer, Esq; Room 117, Whitehall Place East, London SW1A 2HH (☎ 071 270 8109)

PACKER, Robin John; s of Eswin James Packer, and Alma, *née* Lodge; *b* 6 May 1948; *Educ* Catford Sch; *m* 1 Aug 1970, Diane Irana, da of Kenneth Derek Jones; 2 da (Melanie b 28 Dec 1973, Natalie b 1 Aug 1977); *Career* dir Zoete & Gordon 1964-66, Goveti Sons 1966-74, Cazenove 1974-76; Wood MacKenzie & Co: joined 1976, ptnr 1984-87, dir 1986-87; currently depty md UK equites UBS Phillips & Drew (joined 1987); memb local Cons Assoc; memb Stock Exchange; *Recreations* golf, game fishing; *Style—* Robin Packer, Esq; Southfields, Telegraph Hill, Higham by Rochester, Kent ME3 7NW (☎ 0634 721420); UBS Phillips & Drew, 100 Liverpool St, London EC2 (☎ 071 901 1386)

PACKER, William John; s of Harold George Edward Rex Packer (d 1967), and Evelyn Mary Packer, *née* Wornham (d 1983); *b* 19 Aug 1940; *Educ* Windsor GS, Wimbledon and Brighton Colls of Art; *m* 1965, Ursula Mary Clare, da of Thomas Winn (d 1990); 3 da (Charlotte b 1968, Claudia b 1973, Katherine b 1976); *Career* painter and critic; art critic Financial Times 1974-; selector of several exhibitions including Arts Cncl's first Br Art Show 1979-80; served on juries of many open exhibitions incl: John Moore's Liverpool Exhibition 1982, John Player Portrait award 1983-87; teacher 1964-67, part-time 1967-77, external examiner 1979-87; memb: Fine Art Bd of Cncl for Nat Academic Awards 1976-83, Advsy Ctee to Govt Art Collection 1977-84, Crafts Cncl 1980-87; hon fell RCA 1988; *Books* The Art of Vogue Covers (1980), Fashion Drawing in Vogue (1983), Henry Moore, A Pictorial Biography (1985), René Bouët-Willaumez (1989), Carl Erickson (1989); *Recreations* hockey, cricket, bookshops, riding; *Clubs* Brooks's, Chelsea Arts; *Style—* William Packer, Esq; 39 Elms Rd, Clapham, London SW4 9EP (☎ 071 622 1108)

PACKETT, Charles Michael; s of Sydney Duncan Packett, of Bradford, and Margaret Kathleen, *née* Smith; *b* 19 Aug 1955; *Educ* Ashville Coll Harrogate N Yorks; *m* 15 Aug 1981, Jayne Louise, da of Alan Childerstone Benson, of Baildon, Shipley; 2 da (Claire Louise b 21 Dec 1983, Sara Jayne b 2 Aug 1986); *Career* dir Sydney Packett & Sons Ltd (joined 1973, later assoc dir); memb Insur Advsy Panel Bradford C of C; ACII, ABIBA; *Recreations* fishing, shooting, golfing, walking, gardening, reading; *Clubs* Shipley GC, Shipley Cons, Fly Fishers (Hawksworth), Scotton Angling; *Style—* Charles Packett, Esq; 9 Firbeck, Harden, Bingley, W Yorks (☎ 0535 275 232); Sydney Packett & Sons Ltd, Lloyds Bank Chambers, Hustlergate, Bradford BD1 1PA (☎ 0274 308 755)

PACKETT, (Charles) Neville; MBE (1974), JP (1964); s of Sydney Packett, JP (d 1980), and Alice Maude Packett (d 1972); *b* 25 Feb 1922; *Educ* Bradford GS, Queen Elizabeth GS Kirkby Lonsdale Cumbria, Ashville Coll Harrogate Yorks; *m* 1969, Audrey Winifred, da of Frank Vincent Clough (d 1975); *Career* WWII RAOC Middle E and N Africa; md Sydney Packett & Sons 1975-87 (dir 1942-75); pres Insurance Inst of Bradford 1959-60, hon vice pres The Utd Commercial Travellers' Assoc 1976- (nat pres 1975-76), chm house ctee Ashville Coll Harrogate 1977- (govr 1970-), co cmdr S and W Yorks St John Ambulance Bde 1984-90, pres The Bradford Club 1985-86; Master: Worshipful Co of Woolmen 1979-80 (Liveryman 1959-), Worshipful Co of Tin Plate Workers (Liveryman 1957-); Hon Adm Texas Navy USA 1978; FRSA, FRGS, ACII; awarded title The Chartered Insurance Practitioner (1989); Grand Cross Order of St Agatha Repub of San Marino 1980, Tonga Royal Medal of Merit in silver 1976; KStJ 1985; *Books* The County Lieutenancy in the UK, Republic of San Marino, Tongatapu Island (Kingdom of Tonga), The Republic of Nauru, The Firm of Sydney Packett & Sons Ltd, The Texas Navy - A Brief History (1983); *Recreations* travel, amateur cine, heraldry, writing; *Clubs* City Livery (London), Nat Lib, Bradford; *Style*— Neville Packett, Esq, MBE, JP; Flat 20, Wells Court, Wells Promenade, Ilkley, W Yorks LS29 9LG (☎ 0943 601398); Lloyds Bank Chambers, Hustlergate, Bradford, W Yorks BD1 1PA (☎ 0274 308755)

PACKHAM, Jenny; da of Colin Packham, of 10 Cleveland Road, Midanbury, Southampton, and Marion Rita, *née* Smith; *b* 11 March 1965; *Educ* Bitterne Park Sch Southampton, Southampton Art Coll (DA TEC) St Martin Sch of Art London (BA, RSA bursary award and fellowship); ptnr, Mathew John Anderson; *Career* started fashio design business with Mathew Anderson (received at Br Designer Show for four seasons selling to many int stores; joined London Designer Collection 1990 (evening wear); clients incl: Bergdoff Goodman Saks (NY), Joyce (Hong Kong), Yvette (Knightsbridge), Toyah Wilcox, Paula Yeates, Kylie Minogue, Catherine Bailey; FRSA; *Recreations* workaholic!; *Style*— Ms Jenny Packham; Packham Anderson Ltd, Studio 26, Acklam Workshop, 10 Acklam Rd, London W10 5QZ (☎ 081 969 6585)

PACKMAN, Martin John; s of Ivan Desmond Packman, of Addington, Surrey, and Joan Emily, *née* Cook (d 1982); *b* 29 April 1949; *Educ* Simon Langton GS Canterbury, Welwyn Garden City GS, Univ of Lancaster (MA); *m* 17 Dec 1978, Lyn, da of James Green, of Holt, Norfolk; 1 s (Myles b 1980), 1 da (Charlotte b 1984); *Career* chartered accountant; dir Baring Bros & Co Ltd 1987- (banking & capital mkts); FCA 1973; *Books* UK Companies Operating Overseas - Tax and Financing Strategies (jtly, 1981); *Recreations* riding, tennis, skiing; *Style*— Martin Packman, Esq; Port Hill House, Bengeo, Hertford, Herts (☎ 0992 500950); Baring Bros & Co Ltd, 8 Bishopsgate, London EC2 (☎ 071 280 1000, fax 071 283 4235, telex 883622)

PACKSHAW, Charles Max; s of Savile Packshaw (d 1969), and Muriel, *née* Newton; *b* 30 Jan 1952; *Educ* Westminster, Bristol Univ (BSc), London Business Sch (MSc); *m* 9 July 1983, Helena Mary, da of Peter Youngman; 2 s (Harry b 1984, Edward b 1987); *Career* with Costain 1973-78, sr conslt Cresap 1980-84, exec dir Lazard Bros Co Ltd (joined 1984); CEng, MICE 1978; *Style*— Charles Packshaw, Esq; c/o Lazard Brothers Co Ltd, 21 Moorfields, London EC2P 2HT (☎ 071 588 2721)

PACKSHAW, Robin David; s of Savile Packshaw (d 1969), and Doris Mary (Fay), *née* Francis (d 1948); *b* 20 March 1933; *Educ* Eaton House, Bradfield Coll Berkshire; *m* 1, (m dis 1967), Elizabeth Anne Warrack; 3 s ((Andrew) Giles David b 1957, Julian Robert b 1961, Justin James b 1966), 1 da (Amanda Jane (Mrs Cassar Toregiani) b 1956); m 2 (m dis 1975), Mairi Phoebe Elizabeth MacRae; m 3, 10 May 1980, Susan Granville Louise, da of Francis Neville Osborne (d 1969); 2 step da (Amanda Louise Pezzack (Mrs Pike) b 1960, Victoria Anne Granville Farmer b 1962); *Career* Nat Serv Special Boat Service Royal Marines UK and Br Rhine Squadron 1951-53, Lt Special Boat Service Royal Marines Reserve 1953-58; Iraq Petroleum Company Ltd 1953-62, O and M 1953-58 (Personnel and Industl Rels 1958-63); dir: Long Till Colvin Ltd (local authy brokers) 1962-67, Guy Butler Company Ltd (sterling money brokers) 1967-69; founding md Packshaw and Associates (local authy brokers) 1969-73, dir Charles Fulton & Co Ltd (int FX and currency brokers) 1973-82; chm: Fulton Packshaw (sterling money brokers) 1973-82, Charles Fulton Group 1982-85, International City Holdings plc 1985-89, conslt Business in the Community 1990-; memb: Bank of England, Jt Standing Ctee for Princs and Brokers in the Sterling Markets, Steering Gp LIFFE 1981-82, Membership and Rules Ctee LIFFE 1983-89, Governing Cncl Business in the Community 1983-89, Fin Ctee Radionics Assoc 1984, church warden All Saints Stour Row 1984, chm Stours Branch N Dorset Cons Assoc; Freeman City of London 1983, memb Guild of Freeman of the City of London 1983; *Recreations* farm in Dorset, travel, people, Church of England; *Clubs* RAC; *Style*— Robin Packshaw, Esq; Baskerville Farm, Stour Road, Shaftesbury, Dorset (☎ 0747 85483); 25 Lennox Gardens, London SW1X 0DE (☎ 071 584 3969)

PADFIELD, Michael George Braddock; s of Stephen Padfield (d 1978), of Lambourne Hall, Abridge, Essex, and Brenda, *née* Sewell (d 1979); *b* 30 Dec 1922; *Educ* Loughton Sch for Boys; *m* 1, (m dis); 1 s (Matthew b 1958), 3 da (Clare b 1956, Charlotte b 1960, Abigail b 1963); m 2, Jane, *née* Dilks; *Career* farmer on own account: Stondon Hall Ongar Essex 1944-45, Wimbish Hall, Saffron Walden, Essex 1945-; memb Cambs NFU exec ctee 1962-, chm Saffron Walden NFU 1965 and 1987-88; Freeman City of London, Liveryman Worshipful Co of Farmers; *Recreations* shooting, hunting, skiing, tennis; *Clubs* Farmers, Whitehall Ct, Wig & Pen; *Style*— Michael Padfield, Esq; Wimbish Hall, Saffron Walden, Essex (☎ 079 987 202)

PADGETT, Robert Alan; s of William Thomas Padgett (d 1985), of Radlett, Herts, and Winifred Emily, *née* Duncan; *b* 27 May 1943; *Educ* Haileybury, Wadham Coll Oxford (MA), Univ of Pennsylvania (MBA); *m* 6 June 1975 (m dis 1988), Gillian Diana, da of Stanley Arthur Herbert Hunn, of Rustington, Sussex; 1 s (Christopher b 1977); *Career* corp fin exec N M Rothschild and Sons Ltd 1970-73, dir Cripps Warburg Ltd 1973-75, mangr Brown Harriman and International Banks Ltd 1975-77; fin dir: PO Staff Superannuation Fund 1977-83, Postel Investment Management Ltd 1983-; non-exec dir Gateway Building Society 1985-88, The Beckenham Group plc 1987-; chm Working Gp drafting accounting standard on segmental reporting ICAEW; tstee: Shipwrecked Mariners Soc, The Hunger Project; FCA; *Books* Financial Reporting 1987-88 (contrib, 1988); *Recreations* ending world hunger, improving environment; *Style*— Robert Padgett, Esq; 2 Queen's Gate, London SW7 5EH (☎ 071 589 2985); Postel Investment Management Ltd, Standon Hse, 21 Mansell St, London E1 8AA (☎ 071 702 0888, fax 071 702 9452, telex 8956577)

PADGHAM, Hugh Charles; s of Charles Arthur Padgham, of Aylesbury, Bucks, and Ursula Mary, *née* Samuelson; *b* 15 Feb 1955; *Educ* The Beacon Sch Chesham Bois, St Edwards Sch Oxford; *Career* asst Advision Studios 1974-75, engr/asst Lansdowne Studios 1975-77, engr Townhouse Studios 1977-80, freelance prodr and engr 1980-; produced and engineered: Conflicting Emotions (A&M 1980) Split Enz, Time and Tide (A&M 1982) Split Enz, Brucseology (Polydor 1982) The Waitresses, Something's Going On (single with Phil Collins, EPIC 1987) Frida, No One Is To Blame (single with Phil Colins, WEA 1986) Howard Jones, Hysteria (Virgin 1984 & 1987, Gold disc) Human League, English Settlement (Virgin 1983, Silver disc) XTC, Remembrance Days (WEA 1987) The Dream Academy, React (MCA 1987) The Fixx, Between Two Fires (CBS 1986, Platinum disc) Paul Young, Press To Play (Parlaphone 1988, Gold disc) Paul McCartney, Tonight (EMI 1985, Gold disc) David Bowie, Ghost in The Machine (A&M 1981, Platinum disc) The Police, Synchronicity (A&M 1983, Platinum disc, Grammy award 1983) The Police, Every Breath You Take (A&M 1986, 3 Platinum discs) The Police, Face Value (Virgin 1983, 6 Platinum discs) Phil Collins, No Jacket Required (Virgin 1985, Platinum disc, Grammy award 1985) Phil Collins, Hello I Must Be Going (Virgin 1988, Platinum disc) Phil Collins, Genesis (Virgin 1983, 2 Platinum discs, Grammy award 1984) Genesis, But Seriously (Virgin 1989, 8 Platinum discs) Phil Collins, Invisible Touch (Virgin 1986, 4 Platinum discs) Genesis, tracks from Porcelain (CIRCA 1989, Silver disc) and Julia Fordham (CIRCA 1988, Gold disc) Julia Fordham, The Soul Cages (A&M 1991) Sting; engineered; Drums and Wires (Virgin 1979 & 1985) XTC, Black Sea (Virgin 1980 & 1984) XTC, The Third (Virgin 1986, Gold disc) Peter Gabriel, Abacab (Virgin 1983, Gold disc) Genesis; mixed numous tracks incl: H2O (RCA 1982, Platinum disc) Hall & Oates, Nothing Like The Sun (A&M 1987, Platinum disc) Sting, In The Air Tonight (Virgin 1988 remix, Gold disc) Phil Collins, Brian Wilson (Warner Bros 1989), Days of Open Hand (A&M 1990, Gold disc) Suzanne Vega, Love & Affection (A&M 1991 remix) Joan Armatrading; Best British Producer Music Week award 1985, Producer of the Year Grammy award 1985, Best Producer nomination BPI awards 1985 and 1986, Producer of the Year nomination (with Phil Collins) Grammy award 1990; *Recreations* motor racing (part owner Int Gp C sports car team), windsurfing, skiing; *Style*— Hugh Padgham, Esq; Dennis Muirhead Management, 202 Fulham Rd, London SW10 9JP (☎ 071 351 5167, fax 071 352 1514)

PADMORE, Elaine Marguirite; da of Alfred Padmore (d 1971), and Florence, *née* Stockman; *b* 3 Feb 1947; *Educ* Newland HS Hull, Arnold Girls Sch Blackpool, Univ of Birmingham (MA, BMus), Guildhall Sch of Music London; *Career* musician, singer, writer and broadcaster; ed music dept OUP 1970-71, lectr in opera RAM 1972-85, radio prodr music dept BBC 1971-76, chief prodr opera BBC Radio 1976-82, announcer BBC Radio 3 1982-90; artistic dir: Wexford Festival Opera (Ireland) 1982-, Dublin Grand Opera Soc 1989-90, Classical Productions (UK) Ltd; Sunday Independent Award for servs to music in Ireland 1987; Hon ARAM 1984; *Books* Wagner (Great Composers series), New Grove Dictionary of Music and Musicians (contrib); *Recreations* gardening, cats; *Style*— Miss Elaine Padmore; 11 Lancaster Ave, Hadley Wood, Herts EN4 0EP (☎ 081 449 5369)

PADMORE, Sir Thomas; GCB (1965, KCB 1953, CB 1947); s of Thomas William Padmore; *b* 23 April 1909; *Educ* Central Sch Sheffield, Queens' Coll Cambridge (MA); *m* 1, 1934, Alice (d 1963), da of Robert Alcock; 2 da (1 s decd); m 2, 1964, Rosalind, LVO (1938), OBE (1949), yst da of late F W S Culhane, of Hastings, Sussex; *Career* PPS to Chllr of Exchequer 1943-45, second sec HM Treasury 1952-62, perm sec Miny of Tport 1962-68; dir Metropolitan Cammell Ltd 1969-80, Laird Group Ltd 1970-79; chm Handel Opera Soc 1963-86, hon treas Inst of Cancer Res 1973-82; FCIT; *Clubs* Reform; *Style*— Sir Thomas Padmore, GCB; 39 Cholmeley Crescent, Highgate, London N6 (☎ 081 340 6587)

PADOVAN, John Mario Faskally; s of Dr Umberto Mario Padovan (d 1966); *b* 7 May 1938; *Educ* St George's Coll Weybridge, King's Coll London (LLB), Keble Coll Oxford (BCL); *m* 1963, Sally Kay; 3 s; *Career* CA 1963; County Bank Ltd: chief exec 1976-83, dep chm 1982, chm 1984; exec dep chm Hambros Bank Ltd 1984-86; dir: Tesco plc 1982-, MS Instruments plc 1985-; dir and head of corporate fin Barclays de Zoete Wedd Hldgs Ltd 1986-, dir Mabey Holdings Ltd 1989-; *Style*— John Padovan, Esq; 61 Cleaver Square, London SE11 4EA

PAGAN, Dr Francis Stephen; s of Francis Edmund Pagan, of L5 Albany, Piccadilly, London W1, and Margaret Jocelyn Neel (d 1971); *b* 22 July 1941; *Educ* Westminster, Univ of Cambridge (MA, MB BChir); *m* 12 Sept 1970, Nina Dilys, da of John Noël Mason Ashplant Nicholls, OBE, KPM (d 1977), of Stewards Hse, Pulham St Mary, Norfolk; 2 da (Isabel b 1975, Rosemary b 1978); *Career* house offr: surgery Royal Portsmouth Hosp 1968, med Medway Hosp Gillingham Kent 1968-69; sr house offr pathology Gen Hosp Nottingham 1969-70, registrar pathology Gen Hosp Southampton 1970-72, sr registrar microbiology Edgware Gen Hosp 1972-74, lectr bacteriology Middx Hosp London 1974-77, conslt microbiologist Meml Hosp Darlington 1977-; memb BMA, FRCPath 1986; memb: Assoc Clinical Pathologists, Br Soc of Antimicrobial Chemotherapy, Assoc of Med Microbiologists; *Recreations* running, swimming, foreign travel, family life, herbs; *Style*— Dr Francis Pagan, Elly Hill Hse, Barmpton, Darlington, Co Durham DL1 3JF (☎ 0325 464682); Dept of Microbiology, Meml Hosp Darlington, Co Durham DL3 6HX (☎ 0325 380100)

PAGAN, Jill Catling; da of Robert William Charles Catling (d 1967), of Manchester, and Edna Catling (d 1978); *Educ* Loreburn Coll, Inns of Court Sch of Law; *m* 15 Feb 1974, Hugh Edmund, s of Francis Edmund Pagan, of Albany, London; 2 s (Robert b 27 Dec 1974, Thomas b 17 Jan 1978); *Career* called to the Bar Inner Temple 1972; int tax conslt: Tansley Witt & Co 1975-79, Thomson McLintock KMG 1980-82; practised at Revenue Bar 1982-89, int tax conslt J F Chown & Co Ltd 1989-; dir Hugh Pagan Ltd 1987-; contrib ed International Tax Report 1982-, founding ed Inner Temple Yearbook; author numerous articles on int fin, int and UK taxation; memb Bar Liaison ctee Inner Temple 1985-90, ctee memb UK Branch Int Fiscal Assoc; *Books* Taxation Aspects of Currency Fluctuations (1 edn 1983, 2 edn 1991); *Recreations* family and travel; *Style*— Mrs Jill Pagan; c/o J F Chown & Co Ltd, 51 Lafone St, London SE1 2LX (☎ 071 403 0787, fax 071 403 6693)

PAGE, Prof Alan Chisholm; s of Samuel Chisholm Page, of Broughty Ferry, and Betsy Johnston, *née* Melville; *b* 7 April 1952; *Educ* Grove Acad Broughty Ferry, Univ of Edinburgh (LLB), City Univ (PhD); *m* 16 Aug 1975, Sheila Duffus, da of Ian Dunlop Melville, of Glasgow; 1 s (Michael b 1983), 1 da (Rebecca b 1986); *Career* lectr in law Univ of Cardiff 1975-80, dean Faculty of Law University of Dundee 1986-89 (sr lectr in law 1980-85, prof of pub law 1985-); *Books* Legislation (2 edn, 1990); *Recreations* mountaineering; *Style*— Prof Alan Page; Westlands, Westfield Rd, Cupar, Fife (☎ 0334 55576); Dept of Law, Univ of Dundee, Dundee DD1 4HN (☎ 0382 23181 ext 4633)

PAGE, Sir Alexander Warren (Alex); MBE (1943); s of Sydney E Page; *b* 1 July 1914; *Educ* Tonbridge, Clare Coll Cambridge; *m* 1 1940 (m dis), Anne Lewis Hickman; 2 s, 1 da; m 2, 1981, Mrs Andrea Mary Wharton; *Career* serv WWII REME rising to rank of Lt-Col; chief exec Metal Box Ltd 1970-77 (joined 1936, md 1966, chm 1970-79); chm: Paine & Co 1981-87, Electrolux 1978-82, GT Pension Services Ltd 1982-85; dir: J Lyons Co Ltd 1977-78, C Shippam 1979-85; memb Food Sci and Technol Bd 1973-, pres British Food Mfrg Industs Res Assoc 1978-84; chm PFC Int Portfolio Fund; govr Colfe's Sch Lewisham 1977-90; former memb IBA; FIMechE, CBIM; kt 1977; *Style*— Sir Alex Page, MBE; Beldhamland Farm, Skiff Lane, Wisborough Green, West Sussex RH14 0AJ (☎ 0403 752567/753105)

PAGE, Annette; da of James Lees Page (d 1979), and Margaret, *née* Johnson (d 1991); *b* 18 Dec 1932; *Educ* Altrincham GS, Sadlers Wells Ballet Sch; *m* June 1957, Ronald Hynd, s of WJ Hens; 1 da (Louise b 20 April 1968); *Career* ballerina; Sadlers Wells Theatre Ballet 1950-55 (solo roles in: Khadra, Les Rendevous, Les Sylphides, Beauty and the Beast, Lady and the Fool, Coppelia), Major Sadlers Wells Ballet (later Royal Ballet) 1955-67; major roles in: Symphonic Variations, Scenes de Ballet; title roles in: The Firebird, Sleeping Beauty, Swan Lake, Giselle, Fille Mal Gardee, Romeo and Juliet, Cinderella; after ret from stage: teacher Royal Acad of Dancing and London Contemporary Dance, choreographic asst to Ronald Hynd; asst dir of Bayerischestaats Ballet Munich 1984-86; memb of Arts Cncl of GB (memb of dance and music panels) 1967-84; *Recreations* singing, languages, travel, music, pottering around in Suffolk; *Style*— Ms Annette Page

PAGE, Surgn-Col (John Patrick) Anthony; s of Dr Alfred Patrick Menzies Page, JP (d 1979), and Olive Frances Page (d 1964); *b* 9 June 1937; *Educ* Bedford Sch, Gonville and Caius Coll Cambridge (MA, MB BChir); *m* 1, 4 Oct 1963 (m dis 1981), Carolyn Jane, da of Joseph Clement Deeks, MBE, of Sunningdale, Berks; 2 s (Timothy b 1963, Alexander b 1965), 2 da (Joanna b 1968, Louise b 1972); m 2, 16 Dec 1981, Alison Leila da of Maj Denis Thomas Keiller Don (d 1983); 2 s (Edward b 1986, James b 1989), 1 da (Victoria b 1983); *Career* cmmnd RAMC 1963, transferred to Household Cavalry RHG 1967, serv as Regtl MO to RHG Blues and Royals (on formation 1969), and to Household Cavalry Regt (Mounted), resigned 1974; GP Odiham Hamps 1974-78, rejoined as Regtl MO Blues and Royals Household Cavalry Regt and LG 1978-90, cmd Med HQ 1990, London District Med Offr Guards Polo Club Windsor 1990-, memb Ctee Med Equestrian Assoc 1990-; UN Medal (Cyprus) 1965; *Recreations* hunting, fishing, gardening, family matters; *Clubs* The Cavalry and Guards, MCC; *Style*— Surgn-Col Anthony Page

PAGE, Ashley John, né Laverty; s of John Henry Laverty, of Gillingham, Kent, and Sheila Rachael, *née* Medhurst; *b* 9 Aug 1956; *Educ* St Andrews Rochester Kent, Royal Ballet Lower and Upper Sch; partner, Nicola Roberts; *Career* Royal Ballet: joined 1976 (after trg with Educnl Unit Ballet for All 1975), soloist 1980, principal dancer 1984; roles incl many created specially by resident & visiting choreographers plus a wide variety within Royal Ballet's repertoire incl: Romeo and Benvolio, Afternoon of a Faun, the Poet in Les Illuminatious, The Prodigal Son, the Tutor in A Month in the Country, the Boy with Matted Hair in Shadowplay, Ferdinand in The Tempest, Lescaut in Manon, King of the South in Prince of the Pagodas, Tirreneo in Ondine, the brother in My Brother My Sisters, Mars in the Planets, Troyte in Enigma Variations, the tango dancer in Isadora, the Angel of Light in Orpheus, Bruno in Valley of Shadows, Drum Major in Different Drummer, Solo Boy in Agon, Midsummer, Lysander in The Dream, Friday Night in Elite Syncopations, La Fin du Jour, an angel in Dances of Albion, pas de trois in Voluntaries, Rag Mazurka in Les Birches, Les Noces, the zebra in Still Life at the Penguin Cafe, 4 song in Song of the Earth, lead boy in Gloria, 6 song in Requiem, Paul in Wedding Bouquet, lead boy in Rhapsody, Apollo in Young Apollo, 3 song in Dark Elegies, Green and White Monotones, Saturday's child in Jazz Calender; choreographer 1984-; work for Royal Ballet at Royal Opera House incl: A Broken Set of Rules 1984, Pursuit 1987, Piano 1989, Bloodlines 1990; work for Rambert Dance Company (under Richard Alston): Carmen Arcadiae 1986, Soldat 1988, Currulao 1990; choreographer: Savage Water dance film Channel 4 1989, numerous works for Dance Umbrella (incl collaborative work with Gaby Agis) 1983-87; winner first Frederick Ashton Choreographic award 1982, first Frederick Ashton Meml Cmmn (which produced Currulao) 1990; *Style*— Ashley Page, Esq; Royal Ballet, Royal Opera House, Covent Garden, London WC2E (☎ 071 240 1200)

PAGE, Bruce; s of Roger Page and Amy Beatrice Page; *b* 1 Dec 1936; *Educ* Melbourne HS, Melbourne Univ; *m* 1, 1964 (m dis 1969), Anne Gillison; m 2, 1969, Anne Louise, da of Frank G Darnborough; 1 s, 1 da; *Career* journalist: The Herald Melbourne 1956-60, Evening Standard 1960-62, Daily Herald 1962-64, Sunday Times 1964-76, Daily Express 1977; tech dir The New Statesman 1982- (ed 1978-82); software developer; md Executive Producers Ltd 1983-, Paul Rose Pagesystems; *Style*— Bruce Page, Esq; 35 Duncan Terrace, N1 8AL (☎ 071 359 1000); Paul Rose Pagesystems, 11-13 Macklin St, London WC2B 5NH (☎ 071 831 0961)

PAGE, Lady Cecilia Norah; *née* Stopford; da of 7 Earl of Courtown, OBE (d 1956), and Cicely Mary, OBE, JP (d 1973), yr da of late John Arden Birch; *b* 1917; *m* 1947, Cdr Thomas Philip Frederick Urquhart Page, RN, s of Sir Leo Francis Page; 1 s, 2 da; *Career* junior commander ATS 1939-45; *Style*— The Lady Cecilia Page; Toller House, Toller Porcorum, Dorchester, Dorset

PAGE, Maj-Gen Charles Edward; CB (1974), MBE (1944), DL (1986); s of late Sir (Charles) Max Page, KBE, CB, DSO; *b* 23 Aug 1920; *Educ* Marlborough, Trinity Coll Cambridge, Univ of London (BSc); *m* 1948, Elizabeth Marion, da of late Sir William Smith Crawford, KBE; 2 s, 1 da; *Career* Cdr Corps RS 1 (BR) Corps 1966-68, sec NATO Mil Ctee Brussels 1968-70, Dir Combat Devpt (A) 1971-74, ret 1974; Col Cmdt Royal Corps of Signals 1974-80; Hon Col Women's Tport Serv (FANY); *Recreations* shooting, fishing, golf; *Clubs* Army & Navy, Royal and Ancient (St Andrews); *Style*— Maj-Gen Charles Page, CB, MBE, DL; Church Farm House, Old Bosham, Chichester, W Sussex PO18 8HL (☎ 0243 573191)

PAGE, (Christopher John) Chris; s of Albert Harold Page (d 1987), and Doris May, *née* Clarke; *b* 28 May 1947; *Educ* Eton House Sch, South Bank Poly (Dip Arch); *m* 7 July 1979, Janice Anne, da of Andrew John Sharman, of Wickford, Essex; 1 s (Richard b 1981), 1 da (Jacqueline b 1984); *Career* architect/program mangr; md: Atlanta Program Mngmnt Ltd 1986-, Atlanta Interiors 1987-; ptnr Chris Page Assocs, chm Atlanta Recruitment Ltd; *Recreations* sailing, sketching, pre-history in UK; *Clubs* Eton House Old Boys; *Style*— Chris Page, Esq; 35 Challacombe, Thorpe Bay, Essex SS1 3TY (☎ 0702 585710); 10a Lant St, London SE1 1QR (☎ 071 407 3307)

PAGE, Dr Christopher Howard; s of Ewert Lacey Page, and Marie Victoria, *née* Graham; *b* 8 April 1952; *Educ* Sir George Monoux Sch, Univ of Oxford (BA, MA), Univ of York (DPhil); *m* 15 Sept 1975, Régine, *née* Fourcade; *Career* currently lectr in middle eng Univ of Cambridge; fell Sidney Sussex Coll Cambridge (formerly fell Jesus Coll Oxford); ldr of the ensemble Gothic Voices and prodr of acclaimed records; Gramophone Early Music Records of the Year: Hildegard of Bingen 1983 (also Guardian Choral Record of the Year), The Service of Venus and Mars 1988, A Song for Francesca (1989); chm Nat Early Music Assoc, artistic dir of Early Music Centre Festival, fell Fellowship of Makers and Restorers of Historical Instruments; *Books* Voices and Instruments of the Middle Ages (1987), Sequences of Hildegard of Bingen (1986), The Owl and the Nightingale (1989); *Recreations* research and performance; *Style*— Dr Christopher Page; Sidney Sussex College, Cambridge (☎ 0223 338800, fax 0223 338884)

PAGE, David Norman; s of Bernard Page, of Edinburgh, and Catherine Page, *née* Adam; *b* 4 Sept 1957; *Educ* Bearsden Acad Strathclyde, Univ of Strathclyde (BSc, BArch); *m* 14 Dec 1982, Fiona Sinclair, da of Archibald Sinclair, of Helensburgh; *Career* architect in private practice 1981-, lectr dept of arch and building sci Univ of Strathclyde 1982-; *Style*— David N Page, Esq; Roseangle, 49A William St, Helensburgh (☎ 0436 76781); 20A Royal Crescent, Glasgow (☎ 041 333 0686)

PAGE, Hon Mrs (Emma Rachel); *née* Lubbock; da of 3 Baron Avebury; *b* 16 April 1952; *Educ* Univ of Oxford (MA); *m* 1977, Michael Charles Page, s of Maj-Gen Charles E Page, CB, MBE, DL; 2 da (Sophie b 1982, Natasha b 1984); *Career* ptnr Price Waterhouse; FCA, ATII; *Style*— The Hon Mrs Page; Lepe House, Exbury, Southampton, Hants

PAGE, Ewan Stafford; s of late Joseph William Page; *b* 17 Aug 1928; *Educ* Wyggeston GS Leicester, Christ's Coll Cambridge (MA, PhD, Raleigh Prize 1952), London Univ (BSc); *m* 1955, Sheila Margaret Smith; 3 s, 1 da; *Career* instr RAF Tech Coll 1949-51, lectr in statistics Durham Colls 1954-57, dir Durham Univ Computing Lab 1957-63, Newcastle Univ Computing Lab 1963-78, visiting prof Univ of N Carolina 1962-63, prof of computing and data processing Univ of Newcastle upon Tyne 1965-78 (pro vice chllr 1972-78, acting vice chllr 1976-77); vice chllr Univ of Reading 1979-; memb: West Berks Districts Health Authy 1981-, Gen Optical Cncl 1984- (dep chm 1990-); chm: Review of Veterinary Manpower and Educn MAFF/DES 1989-90, Food Advsy Ctee MAFF 1989-; CEng, CBIM, fell Royal Statistical Soc (hon treas 1983-89); hon fell: Newcastle upon Tyne Poly, American Statistical Assoc; Chevalier dans l'Ordre des Palmes Académiques 1991; *Publications* approximately 50 papers in: Computer Jls, Jls of the Royal Statistical Soc, Biometrika, Technometrics, Applied Statistics; Information Representation and Manipulation in a Computer (with L B Wilson), Information Representation and Manipulation using Pascal (with L B Wilson); *Style*— Dr E S Page; University of Reading, Whiteknights, Reading, Berks (☎ 0734 875123)

PAGE, Sir Frederick William; CBE (1961); s of late Richard Page, and Ellen Sarah Page; *b* 20 Feb 1917; *Educ* Rutlish Sch Merton, St Catharine's Coll Cambridge (MA); *m* 1940, Kathleen Edith de Courcy; 3 s, 1 da; *Career* chief engr English Electric Aviation 1950, chief exec (Aircraft) 1959; dir Panavia Aircraft GmbH Germany 1969-83 (chm 1977-79), chm BAC Ltd 1977; jt chm Sepecat (France) 1966-73, chm and chief exec Aircraft Gp of Br Aerospace 1977-83; British Gold Medal Aeronautics 1962, RAeS Gold Medal 1974; Hon FRAeS 1980, FRS, FEng; hon fell UMIST 1970, Hon DSc Cranfield 1979; kt 1979; *Clubs* United Oxford and Cambridge Univ; *Style*— Sir Frederick Page, CBE, FRS; Renvyle, 60 Waverley Lane, Farnham, Surrey GU9 8BN (☎ Farnham 714999)

PAGE, Graham Guy; s of Sgt George Henry Page, and Edna, *née* Guy (d 1947); *b* 27 June 1946; *Educ* Riland Bedford HS Sutton Coldfield, Univ of Aston; *m* 2 July 1966, Ann Maureen, da of late Tom Daniel, of Northallerton, Yorks; 3 da (Sharon Louise b 10 Feb 1970, Jayne Diane (twin) b 10 Feb 1970, Joanne Rachel b 13 Dec 1971); *Career* mktg dir: Ansells Brewery Ltd (trading co of Allied Lyon plc) 1978-86, Ansells Ltd (retailers, hoteliers, wholesalers, restauranteurs) 1985-86; dir: Ansells Brewery Co Ltd 1981-86, Ansells Cambrian Brewery Ltd 1981-86, Solden Oaks Inns Ltd 1981-86; sales dir: Ansells Ltd 1986-88, Ansells Sales Ltd 1988; md Holt Plant and Deakin Ltd (brewers and retailers) 1988-89; memb Variety Club of GB; MIPA 1966, assoc memb Inst of Marketing 1976, memb Marketing Soc 1978; *Recreations* tennis, badminton, squash, golf, jogging, video photography; *Style*— Graham Page, Esq; 7 Lowercroft Way, Sutton Coldfield, W Midlands B74 4XF (☎ 021 352 0195); Holt Plant & Deakin Ltd, Dudley Rd, Wolverhampton, W Midlands (☎ 0902 50504)

PAGE, (John) Graham; s of George Ronald Page (d 1966), and Lilian Alice, *née* Kay (d 1982); *b* 16 Feb 1943; *Educ* Robert Gordon's Coll Aberdeen (MB ChB); *m* 30 Aug 1989, Sandra; 1 s (Andrew b 11 Jan 1972), 2 da (Caroline b 12 April 1974, Alison b 21 March 1977); *Career* conslt accident and emergency surgn Aberdeen Royal Infirmary 1981- (house physician and surgn 1968-69, surgical registrar 1970-78), hon sr lectr in surgery Univ of Aberdeen 1981- (terminable lectr in pathology 1969-70), res fell Harvard Univ Boston USA 1974-75, hon conslt Br Antarctic Survey Med Unit 1983-; memb: BMA, Edinburgh Royal Coll Surgns, Euro Undersea Biomedical Assoc; FRCS, ChM 1977; *Books* with KLG Mills and R Morton: A Colour Atlas of Accidents and Emergencies (1984), A Colour Atlas of Cardiopulmonary Resuscitation (1986), A Colour Atlas of Plaster Techniques (1986); *Recreations* skiing, sailing; *Style*— Graham Page, Esq; 16 Kingswood Ave, Kingswells, Aberdeen AB1 8AE (☎ 0224 742945); Aberdeen Royal Infirmary, Accident and Emergency Dept, Aberdeen, AB9 2ZB (☎ 0224 681818 ext 53306, fax 0224 662856)

PAGE, (Charles) James; CBE (1978), QPM (1971); s of Charles Page; *b* 31 May 1925; *Educ* Sloane GS, Chelsea; *m* 1, 1947, Margaret Dobson; 2 s; m 2, 1971, Shirley Marina Woodward; *Career* HM Inspector of Constabulary, 1977-; vice-pres Police Athletic Assoc 1977; FBIM; CStJ 1974; Officer of Legion d'Honneur 1976; *Clubs* City Livery; *Style*— James Page, Esq, CBE, QPM; Government Buildings, Ovangle Rd, Lancaster

PAGE, Sir (Arthur) John; s of Sir Arthur Page, QC, K-i-H (d 1958), late Chief Justice of Burma, and Margaret, *née* Symes Thompson; *b* 16 Sept 1919; *Educ* Harrow, Magdalene Coll Cambridge; *m* 9 Dec 1950, Anne Gertrude, da of Charles Micklem, DSO, JP, DL (d 1957); 4 s (Hugo b 1951, Nathaniel b 1953, Henry b (twin) 1953, Rupert b 1963); *Career* served WWII, gunner RA 1939, Maj Norfolk Yeo 1945, served Middle East (wounded), France and Germany; contested (C) Eton and Slough, Gen Election 1959, MP (C) Harrow 1960-87, sec Cons Parly Labour Affairs Ctee 1960-61 (vice-chm 1964-69, chm 1970-74), memb Br Delegn to Cncl of Europe and WEU 1972-87; dir Long & Hambly Ltd 1960-81; chm Frederick Clarke (Furnishings) Ltd 1955-88; dir: Colne Valley Water Co 1984-89 (chm 1987-), N Surrey Water Co 1988-; chm Three Valleys Water Services Plc 1989-; pres: Independent Schools Assoc 1971-83, Water Companies Assoc 1986-89; vice-pres British Insurance Brokers Assoc 1980-; chm Cncl for Ind Educn 1974-80, elected substitute pres (Int) Inter-Parly Union 1983; Freeman of the City of London, Liveryman of Worshipful Co of Grocers 1970; kt 1984; *Recreations* painting, politics; *Clubs* Brooks's, MCC; *Style*— Sir John Page; Hitcham Lodge, Taplow, Maidenhead, Berks (☎ 0628 605056); Three Valleys Water Services Plc, Hatfield, Herts (☎ 0707 268111)

PAGE, John Brangwyn; s of late Sidney John Page, CB, MC; *b* 23 Aug 1923; *Educ* Highgate (Foundation Scholar), King's Coll Cambridge; *m* 1948, Gloria Vail; 1 s, 1 da; *Career* RAF 1942-46; Cambridge 1946-48; chief cashier Bank of England 1970-80, exec dir 1980-82; chm Agricultural Mortgage Corp 1982-85; dir: Standard Chartered plc 1982-89, Nationwide Anglia Building Society 1982-; FIB, CBIM; *Style*— John Page, Esq; National Anglia Building Society, Chesterfield House, Bloomsbury Way, London WC1V 6PW

PAGE, Maj-Gen John Humphrey; CB (1977), OBE (1967), MC (1952); s of Capt W J Page, JP (d 1961), of Devizes, and Alice Mary Page (d 1981); *b* 5 March 1923; *Educ* Stonyhurst; *m* 1956, Angela Mary, da of Bernard Bunting (d 1962); 3 s, 1 da; *Career* cmmnd RE 1942; Asst Cmdt RMA Sandhurst 1971-74, dir of Personal Servs (Army) Miny of Def 1974-78, ret; dir London Law Tst 1979-88, vice chm Soldiers' Sailors' and Airmen's Families' Assoc 1983-87; chm Bd of Govrs St Mary's Sch Shaftesbury; govr Stonyhurst Coll 1980-90; chm and tstee Home Start Consultancy 1981-90; *Style*— Maj-Gen John Page, CB, OBE, MC; c/o Lloyds Bank, Somerton, Somerset

PAGE, Sir John Joseph Joffre; OBE (1959); s of William Joseph Page (d 1935), and Frances Page (d 1977); *b* 7 Jan 1915; *Educ* Emanuel Sch; *m* 1939, Cynthia Maynard, da of Lionel Maynard Swan, CBE (d 1969); 2 s; *Career* RAF 1933-38 and 1939-46 (despatches 1943), Gp Capt; Iraq Petroleum Gp of Cos: 1938-39 and 1946-70, gen mangr 1955-58, chief rep 1961-70; Mersey Docks and Harbour Co: chm 1972-77 and 1980-84, chief exec 1975-77; dep chm Br Ports Assoc 1974-77; chm: Nat Ports Cncl 1977-80, Chester Health Authy 1981-82, NW RHA 1982-88, Christie Hosp NHS Trust 1991-; kt 1979; *Recreations* music, fishing; *Clubs* Oriental, RAF, MCC; *Style*— Sir John Page, OBE; The Cottage, Hockenhull Lane, Tarvim, Chester CH3 8LB

PAGE, John Leslie; s of Leslie John Page, of 3 Lime Close, Clacton on Sea, Essex, and Florence Evelyn, *née* Lochhead; *b* 21 June 1940; *Educ* Halbutt St Secdy Mod Sch, SE Essex Tech Coll; *m* 1, 1 Oct 1960 (m dis 1972), Jean Mary, *née* Cleary; 1 s (John Darrel b 9 Nov 1963), 3 da (Wendy Sue b 12 July 1962, Karen Jane b 1 Feb 1965, Dawn Yvette b 6 Sept 1967); m 2, June 1975 (m dis 1978), Lynne Joyce, *née* Delville; m 3, 25 June 1982, Kathleen Linda, da of Terance Henry Tyler, of Newhaven, Dunton Rd, Little Burstead, Essex; *Career* fndr chm and dir Page Int Ltd specialist engrg and designers worldwide 1962-; memb IOD 1968, MIED 1975, FFA 1978, MBIM 1981, MECI 1981, memb Inst of Engrs 1989; *Recreations* shooting, photography, reading, gardening, DIY; *Style*— John Page, Esq; Kirmond Hall, Kirmond Le Mire, Lincolnshire

LN3 6HZ (☎ 067 383 509); Kirmond Business Centre, PO Box 3, Binbrook, Lincolnshire (☎ 0673 844200, fax 0673 844593, telex 56289 (PAGE G), car 0860 457524, mobile tel 0860 457525)

PAGE, Lady Katharine Rose Celestine; *née* Asquith; da of 2 Earl of Oxford and Asquith, KCMG; *b* 16 Oct 1949; *Educ* Mayfield Convent Sussex, King's Coll London; *m* 1, 1970 (m annulled 1984), Adam Nicholas Ridley (now Sir Adam Ridley) *qv*; m 2, 1985, (John) Nathaniel Micklem Page, 2 s of Sir (Arthur) John Page; *Career* art dealer; *Style—* The Lady Katharine Page; Foreign and Commonwealth Office, King Charles Street, London SW1

PAGE, Michael Brian; s of James Gourlay Page, of Chester-le-Street, Co Durham, and Mary Jane, *née* McTeague; *b* 14 April 1937; *Educ* Chester-le-Street GS Co Durham, Univ of Aston Birmingham (BSc Eng); *m* 1961, Jennifer Grace Elizabeth, da of Joseph Victor Wetton (d 1966); 3 da (Joanna b 1966, Kathryn b 1968, Sally b 1971); *Career* sales dir Brush Electrical Machines Ltd 1977-84; chm Hawker Siddeley Power Engrg Inc (USA) 1984, dir Hawker Siddeley Electric Ltd 1986-, md Hawker Siddeley Power Engrg Ltd & assoc companies 1984-; CEng, FIEE, FIMechE, FBIM, FInstD; *Recreations* golf, chess; *Clubs* Rothley Park Golf; *Style—* Michael Page, Esq; Blue Haze, 90 Station Rd, Cropston, Leicestershire LE7 7HE (☎ 0533 362527); Cliff Works, Burton on the Wolds, Loughborough LE12 5TT (☎ 0509 880541, fax 0509 881210, telex 341068)

PAGE, Nicola Caroline; da of Rodney Hale-Sutton, of Hillside, Waterford Common, Waterford, nr Hertford, Herts, and Pauline Audrey Knowles, *née* Burbidge; *b* 25 Jan 1960; *Educ* Stheredes Comp Sch, Univ of Manchester (BA, BArch); *m* 5 Sept 1987, Robert Stephen Page, s of John William Alfred Page, of Barnes, London; *Career* architect; Frederick Gibbard Coombes and Partners 1981-82, assoc of Hale-Sutton Thomas partnership 1986 (joined 1984), ptnr Hale-Sutton Thomas Page 1988; fund raising chm Ladies Circle, memb Cncl and asst church warden Stapleford Parochial Church; MRIBA 1966, memb ARCUK 1985; *Recreations* golf, skiing, squash; *Clubs* Hertfordshire Country; *Style—* Mrs Robert Page; Hale-Sutton Thomas Page; 49-53 Fore St, Hertford, Herts SG13 1AL (☎ 0992 552191, fax 0992 554253)

PAGE, Richard Lewis; MP (C) Hertfordshire South West 1979-; s of Victor Charles Page (d 1968), and Kathleen Page; *b* 22 Feb 1941; *Educ* Hurstpierpoint Coll, Luton Tech Coll; *m* 3 Oct 1964, Madeleine Ann, da of Geoffrey Ronald Brown; 1 s (Mark Lewis b 29 March 1968), 1 da (Tracey Louise b 25 April 1970); *Career* dir of family co 1964-; cncllr Banstead UDC 1969-72; MP (C) Workington 1976-79; PPS to: Sec of State for Trade, Ldr of the House 1982-87; nat treas Leukemia Research Fund 1988-; Freeman City of London, Liveryman Worshipful Co of Pattenmakers 1979; *Recreations* riding, shooting; *Style—* Richard Page, Esq, MP; House of Commons, London SW1

PAGE, Simon Richard; s of Eric Rowland Page (d 1985), and Vera, *née* Fenton; *b* 7 March 1934; *Educ* Lancing, LSE (LLB external); *m* 1, 1963 (m dis 1977); 3 s, 1 da; m 2, 1984; *Career* 2 Lt RA 1958-59; slr 1959-75, pres W Surrey Law Soc 1972-73; dist registrar High Court of Justice, registrar Guildford, Epsom and Reigate Co Courts, recorder Crown Court from 1980, pres Assoc of County Court and District Registrars 1983-84; *Recreations* squash, lawn tennis, cricket, bridge; *Style—* Simon R Page, Esq; c/o The Law Courts, Guildford

PAGE, Prof Trevor Francis; s of Cyril Francis Page (d 1980), of Lichfield, Staffs, and Gladys Mary, *née* Boston; *b* 6 Jan 1946; *Educ* King Edward VI GS Lichfield Staffs, Jesus Coll Cambridge (MA, PhD); *m* 7 Aug 1971, Andrea Gail, da of Cyril James Jones, of Cambridge; 1 s (Mathew Nicholas James b 1976), 1 da (Victoria Sophie Louise b 1979); *Career* Univ of Cambridge: SERC res fell 1971-72, demonstrator in metallurgy and materials sci 1972-76, lectr 1976-86, fndn fell Robinson Coll 1976-86; Cookson Gp prof of engrg materials Univ of Newcastle 1987-; author of numerous scientific papers, reviews and encyclopaedia articles on applications of microscopy and the devpt of ceramic materials; SERC: memb Materials Cmmn Equipment Ctee, memb Ceramics and Inorganic Materials Ctee 1985-90; chm Tyne and Wear Metallurgical Soc 1988-90; fell Royal Microscopical Soc 1971; memb: American Ceramic Soc 1976, Inst of Metals 1984; fell Inst of Ceramics 1987; *Recreations* family, gardening, classical music, opera, theatre, cinema, food and wine, photography, riding, badminton; *Style—* Prof Trevor Page; Materials Division, Dept Techanical Materials & Manufacturing Engineering, Herschel Building, The University, Newcastle upon Tyne NE1 7RU (☎ 091 222 7201, fax 091 261 1182)

PAGE CROFT, Hugo Douglas; s of Maj Richard Arthur Fitzroy Page Croft, of The Round House, Ware, Herts, and Mrs A Page Croft, *née* McClymont; *b* 23 May 1944; *Educ* Shrewsbury; *m* 13 Dec 1969, Dawn, da of William Pryde (d 1980); 3 s (Richard, Edward, James), 1 da (Arabella); *Career* brewer; Harrington Page & Co maltsters 1962, mangr and barley buyer R & W Paul Ltd maltsters 1964; md: Moray Firth Maltings 1980-86 (fndr 1967-86), William Younger & Co Ltd 1986-88; gp dir Scottish & Newcastle Breweries plc 1988; chm: Scottish Brewers Ltd, Matthew Brown plc; memb: Scottish Cncl Devpt and Indust, CBI Scottish Cncl, Incorp of Maltmen, Inst of Brewing; Freeman Worshipful Co of Brewers'; *Recreations* shooting; *Clubs* Pilgrim; *Style—* Hugo Page Croft, Esq; Scottish & Newcastle Breweries plc, 111 Holyrood Rd, Edinburgh EH8 8YS (☎ 031 556 2592, fax 031 556 4665, telex 72356, car 0836 722530)

PAGE-TURNER, Noel Frederick Augustus; DL (Devon 1989); yr s of Frederick Ambrose Wilford Page-Turner (d 1936); ggs of Rev Dr Frederick Henry Marvell Blaydes, noted classical scholar; direct descendant of Andrew Marvell the Puritan poet and gggs of Sir Edward George Thomas Page-Turner, 5 Bt, of Ambrosden, Oxfordshire; *b* 6 May 1934; *Educ* privately, RAC Cirencester; *m* 1960, Christine Mary, yst da of late R F Tetley, one of the brewing family of Boston Spa Yorkshire; 2 s (Edward b 1961, Gregory b 1964), 1 da (Cassandra b 1966); *Career* cmd Royal Devon Yeomanry Sqdn, Maj 1974-78, second in cmd Royal Wessex Yeomanry 1978-83; gen cmmr Income Tax (Axminster div) 1984; landowner and farmer; *Recreations* shooting, heraldry, genealogy, the arts; *Style—* Noel Page-Turner, Esq, DL; Woodhayes, Honiton, Devon EX14 0TP (☎ 0404 42011)

PAGE WOOD, Lady; Evelyn Hazel Rosemary; da of late Capt George Ernest Bellville; assumed by deed poll 1956 the additional surname of Page; *m* 1947, Sir David John Hatherley Page Wood, 7 Bt (d 1955); *Style—* Lady Page Wood; The Old Cottage, Wolverton, Basingstoke, Hants

PAGE WOOD, Matthew Page; s of Sir John Stuart Page Wood, 6 Bt (d 1955), and hp of nephew, Sir Anthony Page Wood, 8 Bt; assumed by deed poll 1955 the additional surname of Page before his patronymic; *b* 13 Aug 1924; *Educ* Radley Coll; *m* 1947, Betsann, da of Lt-Col Francis Christesson Darby Tothill; 2 da (Belinda Jane b 1952 (m 1, Richard John Crowder; m 2, Charles Hoste; 1 s), Miranda Elizabeth b 1962); *Career* Capt Coldstream Gds, ret 1948; New York Stock Exchange; memb: London Stock Exchange 1949-60, CDN Investmt Banker 1960-79; chm Hammersmith Cons Assoc 1963-74 (pres 1974-83); *Recreations* golf, fishing; *Clubs* Brooks's, City of London, MCC; *Style—* Matthew Page Wood, Esq; 31 Halsey St, London SW3 (☎ 071 584 6008)

PAGE-WOOD, Sir Anthony John; 8 Bt (UK 1837), of Hatherley House, Gloucestershire; s of Sir David John Hatherley Page Wood, 7 Bt (d 1955); *b* 6 Feb 1951; *Educ* Harrow; *Heir* unc, Matthew Page b 13 Aug 1924; *Career* dir Société Générale Strauss Turnbull (London) 1982-; *Style—* Sir Anthony Page-Wood, Bt; 77 Dovehouse St, London SW3

PAGEL, Prof Bernard Ephraim Julius; s of Traugott Ulrich Walter Pagel (d 1983), and Maria Magdalene Emilie Koll (d 1980); *b* 4 Jan 1930; *Educ* Merchant Taylors', Sidney Sussex Coll Cambridge (BA, PhD), Cambridge Observatories and Univ of Michigan; *m* Annabel Ruth, da of Edmond Scialom Tuby, of 160 Fordwych Rd, London NW2; 2 s (David Benjamin b 1961, Jonathan Francis b 1966), 1 da (Celia Ann b 1959); *Career* res fell Sidney Sussex Coll Cambridge 1953-56, Radcliffe student Pretoria S Africa 1955, astrophysicist Sacramento Peak Observatory 1960; Royal Greenwich Observatory: princ scientific offr 1956-61, sr princ scientific offr 1961-71, dep chief scientific offr 1971-90; Univ of Sussex: visiting reader in astronomy 1966-70, visiting prof of astronomy 1970-; prof of astrophysics Nordita Copenhagen-; RAS: memb 1955, jt ed Monthly Notices 1970-84, vice pres and foreign corr 1973-75, Gold medal 1990; served on ctees and panels of RAS and SERC concerned with grants and telescope time allocations, Kelvin lectr Br Assoc 1962; memb Int Astronomical Union 1958; *Books* Théorie des Atmosphéres Stellaires (1971), Evolutionary Phenomena in Galaxies (1989); *Recreations* music, cycling, skiing; *Style—* Prof Bernard Pagel; Groombridge, Lewes Road, Ringmer, East Sussex BN8 5ER (☎ 0273 812729); Nordita, Blegdamsvej 17, DK-2100 Copenhagen, Denmark (☎ 010 45 31 38 99 54, fax 010 45 31 38 91 57, telex 15216 NBI DK)

PAGET, David Christopher John; s of Henry Paget, of Johannesburg, SA, and Dorothy, *née* Colenutt; *b* 3 Feb 1942; *Educ* St John' s Coll Johannesburg; *m* 21 March 1968, Dallas Wendy, da of Brian Thomas Hill; 2 da (Henrietta b 1975, Alexandra b 1987); *Career* called to the Bar Inner Temple 1967, fifth sr prosecuting counsel to the Crown Central Criminal Ct (jr prosecuting counsel 1982, first jr 1988), rec of Crown Ct 1986; *Recreations* walking, bird watching, listening to music; *Style—* David Paget, Esq; Queen Elizabeth Buildings, Temple, London EC4Y 9BS (☎ 071 583 5766, fax 071 353 0339)

PAGET, Hon Mrs (Enid Louise); da of 1 and last Baron Queenborough (d 1949); *b* 1923; *m* 1947 (m dis) Count (Roland) de la Poype; 1 da; resumed the surname Paget; *Style—* The Hon Mrs Paget

PAGET, Henry James; s and h of Sir Julian Tolver Paget, 4 Bt; *b* 2 Feb 1959; *Educ* Radley Coll; *Career* Coldstream Guards; md Aachen Holdings Ltd; *Recreations* fishing, shooting and property renovation; *Clubs* RAC, Norfolk; *Style—* Henry Paget, Esq; 3, Bell Road, Norwich, Norfolk NR3 4PA (☎ Norwich 403087)

PAGET, Sir John Starr; 3 Bt (UK 1886), of Cranmore Hall, Co Somerset; s of Sir Richard Arthur Surtees Paget, 2 Bt (d 1955), and Lady Muriel Evelyn Vernon Finch-Hatton, CBE (d 1938); *b* 24 Nov 1914; *Educ* Oundle, Chateau D'Oex, Trinity Coll Cambridge (MA); *m* 1944, Nancy Mary Parish, JP, da of late Lt-Col Francis Woodbine Parish, DSO, MC, 60 Rifles; 2 s, 5 da; *Heir* s, Richard Herbert Paget, b 2 Feb 1957; *Career* dir: Napier & Sons 1959-61, Glacier Metal Group 1963-65, Thermal Syndicate Ltd Wallsend 1939-83 (chm 1973-80), Hilger & Watts 1965-68, Rank Precision Industries Ltd 1968-70, Somerset Fruit Machinery Ltd 1986-; sr ptnr Haygrass Cider Orchards; Silver medal IProdE 1950; Hon DTech Brunel; CEng, FIMechE; *Recreations* cooking, music; *Clubs* Athenaeum; *Style—* Sir John Paget, Bt; Haygrass House, Taunton, Somerset TA3 7B (☎ 0823 331779)

PAGET, Lt-Col Sir Julian Tolver; 4 Bt (UK 1871), of Harewood Place, Middlesex, CVO (1984); s of Gen Sir Bernard Paget, GCB, DSO, MC (d 1961), and n of Sir James Francis Paget, 3 Bt (d 1972); *b* 11 July 1921; *Educ* Radley, ChCh Oxford; *m* 1954, Diana Frances, da of late F S H Farmer; 1 s, 1 da; *Heir* s, Henry James Paget; *Career* joined Coldstream Gds 1940, served NW Europe 1944-45, ret as Lt-Col 1968; gentleman usher to HM The Queen 1971-; author; *Books* Counter-Insurgency Campaigning (1967), Last Past Aden 1964-67 (1969), The Story of the Guards (1976), The Pageantry of Britain (1979), The Yeomen of the Guard (1985), Wellington's Peninsular War (1990); *Clubs* Cavalry and Guards', Pratt's, Flyfishers'; *Style—* Lt-Col Sir Julian Paget, Bt, CVO; 4 Trevor St, London SW7 1DU (☎ 071 584 3524)

PAGET, Richard Herbert; s and h of Sir John Starr Paget, 3 Bt; *b* 17 Feb 1957; *Educ* Eton; *m* 1985, Richenda Rachel, da of Rev Preb John Collins; 2 da (Emma Rachel b 17 June 1986, Richenda Elizabeth b 29 Dec 1988); *Career* computer sales and marketing, currently at SAS Inst; *Recreations* tennis, cricket, parachuting, carriage driving; *Clubs* Naval and Military; *Style—* Richard Paget, Esq; Burridge Heath Farm, Little Bedwyn, Marlborough, Wilts; 20 Marloes Rd, London W8 (☎ 071 373 9760)

PAGET, Lord Rupert Edward Llewelyn; 2 s of 7 Marquess of Anglesey, DL; *b* 21 July 1957; *Educ* Dragon Sch, Westminster, Oxford Air Training Sch (Commercial Pilot's Licence); *m* 21 Aug 1982, Louise Victoria, da of Peter Hugh Youngman, of Charsfield Hall, Woodbridge, Suffolk; 1 s (Jack William Kyffin b 9 May 1989); *Career* farmer; *Recreations* yachting; *Clubs* Royal Anglesey Yacht; *Style—* The Lord Rupert Paget; Plas Llanedwen, Llanfair PG, Anglesey LL61 6DQ (☎ 0248 715525); Llwynonn Farm, Llanfair PG, Gwynedd LL61 6DQ

PAGET OF NORTHAMPTON, Baroness; Sybil Helen; *née* Gibbons; da of late Sills Clifford Gibbons, of Scaynes Hill, Sussex; *m* 1, 16 July 1918, Sir John Bridger Shiffner, 6 Bt (ka Sept 1918); m 2, 22 Sept 1922 (m dis 1931), Victor Basil John Seely, later Sir Victor Seely, 4 Bt (d 1980); 1 s (Sir Nigel Edward Seely, 5 Bt, *qv*); m 3, 21 Sept 1931, Baron Paget of Northampton, QC (Life Peer, d 1990); 2 adopted s, 2 adopted da; *Style—* The Rt Hon the Lady Paget of Northampton; 9 Grosvenor Cottages, London SW1 (☎ 071 730 4034)

PAGET-TOMLINSON, Edward William; s of Edward Edmondson Paget-Tomlinson (d 1953), of Ulverston, Cumbria, and Alison, *née* Wordie (d 1958); *b* 17 March 1932; *Educ* Sherborne, Trinity Hall Cambridge (MA); *m* 20 March 1968, Pamela Lesley, da of Leslie Stuart Williams (d 1978), of Ulverston, Cumbria; 1 s (John Edward b 1976), 1 da (Lucy Elizabeth b 1980); *Career* keeper of shipping Liverpool Museum 1956-69, sr keeper and conslt Hull Town Docks (Maritime) Museum 1975-78; *Books* Complete Book of Canal and River Navigations (1978), Montreux Oberland Bernois Railway (1985), The Railway Carriers (1990); *Recreations* drawing, walking; *Style—* Edward William Paget-Tomlinson, Esq; Easton House, Easton, nr Wells, Somerset BA5 1EF (☎ 0749 870227)

PAGETT, Nicola Mary; da of H W F Scott, of High Malden, Kent, and Barbara, *née* Black (d 1985); *b* 15 June 1945; *Educ* Convent Yokohama, The Beehive Bexhill on Sea, Ashford Secretarial Coll, RADA; *m* 9 July 1977, Graham Swannell, s of Maj William Swannell, MC (d 1982); 1 da (Eve Barbara Louise b 16 April 1979); *Career* theatre and TV actress; plays incl: School for Scandal Duke of York, Ophelia Regina and Masha Greenwich, Helen of Troy and Suzannah in The Marriage of Figaro NT, Voyage Round My Father West End, Old Times in London and Los Angeles West End, The Light of Day Lyric Theatre 1987, numerous plays in repertory and several more in the West End; films incl: Oliver's Story, Privates on Parade; TV series incl: Upstairs Downstairs, Anna Karenina, A Bit of a Do; *Recreations* gardening, cooking; *Style—* Ms Nicola Pagett; c/o James Sharkey, 15 Golden Square, London W1 (☎ 071 434 3801)

PAGLIERO, (Keith) Michael; s of Sqdn Ldr Leonard Pagliero, OBE, of Ruislip, Middx, and Winifred Edith, *née* Berry; *b* 29 June 1938; *Educ* Merchant Taylors', Guys Hosp Med Sch (MB BS); *m* 9 July 1966, (Margaret) Anne, da of Flt-Lt Edgar Francis

Saunders, of Looe, Cornwall; 3 s (David b 6 Feb 1970, George b 26 Sept 1972, Henry b 15 March 1974), 1 da (Helen b 22 Aug 1971); *Career* conslt thoracic surgn Devon Area Health Authy 1976, clinical tutor Univ of Bristol 1978, res fell surgical oncology Univ of Exeter 1988; chm National Assoc of Clinical Tutors; LRCP 1962, MRCS 1962, FRCS 1967; *Recreations* golf, squash; *Clubs* East Devon Golf, Cranford (Exmouth); *Style*— Michael Pagliero, Esq; 20 Copp Hill Lane, Budleigh Salterton, Devon EX9 6DU (☎ 03954 2620); Royal Devon and Exeter Hosp, Barrack Rd, Wonford, Exeter Devon (☎ 0392 402670)

PAGNAMENTA, Peter John; s of Charles Francis Pagnamenta, of Pershore, Worcs, and Daphne Isabel, *née* Kay (d 1990); *b* 12 April 1941; *Educ* Shrewsbury, Trinity Hall Cambridge; *m* 13 April 1966, Sybil, da of Frances Howard Healy of New York, USA; 1 s (Robin b 1973), 1 da (Zoe b 1969); *Career* BBC: joined 1964, asst prodr Tonight 1965, prodr 24 Hours 1966, prodr New York office 1968, ed 24 Hours 1971, ed Midweek 1972, ed Panorama 1975; dir news and current affairs Thames Television 1977; BBC: exec prodr Documentary Dept 1980 and 1988, prodr All Our Working Lives 1984, ed Real Lives series 1984, head of Current Affairs Group 1985, prodr Nippon 1990; *Books* All Our Working Lives (with Richard Overy, 1984); *Style*— Peter Pagnamenta; BBC Television, Kensington House, Richmond Way, London W12 (☎ 081 743 1272)

PAGNI, Patrick Robert Marie; s of Robert Pagni, of 1 Rue de Marnes, 92410 Ville D'Array, France, and Elaine, *née* Sanouller; *b* 15 July 1949; *Educ* Ecole St Louis de Gonzague Paris, Universite Paris IX Dauphine (Master in Management), Harvard Univ (MBA); *m* 2 Oct 1978, Viviane, da of Andre Guyot; *Career* Societe Generale: joined 1970, asst mangr Paris 1974, dep branch mangr Paris 1976, vice pres NY Branch 1979, regnl mangr Western US 1981, gen mangr Hong Kong Branch 1984; Societe Generale Strauss Turnbull Securities: exec dir 1988, chief exec 1990; *Recreations* photography; *Clubs* Royal Hong Kong Jockey; *Style*— Patrick Pagni, Esq; 12 Elystaqn St, London SW3 3PR (☎ 071 584 9863); Societe Generale Strauss Turnbull Securities Ltd, Exchange House, Primrose St, London EC2A 2DD (☎ 071 522 1001, fax 071 374 8407)

PAICE, Dr Elisabeth Willemien; da of Ervin Ross Marlin, of Berkhamsted, and Hilda van Stockum, HRHA; *b* 23 April 1945; *Educ* Int Sch Geneva, Trinity Coll Dublin, Westminster Med Sch (BA, MB BCh, BAO); *m* 6 July 1968, Clifford Charles Dudley, s of Owen Paice (d 1973); 1 s (Matthew b 1972), 2 da (Katharine b 1973, Joanna b 1977); *Career* sr registrar: Stoke Mandeville Hosp 1977-78, High Wycombe Hosp 1978-79, UCH 1980-82; conslt rheumatologist Whittington Hosp 1982-; memb Br Soc of Rhematology; FRCP 1989; *Style*— Dr Elisabeth Paice; Dept of Rheumatology, Whittington Hospital, Highgate Hill, London N19 (☎ 071 272 3070)

PAICE, James Edward Thornton; MP (C) SE Cambridgeshire 1987-; s of Edward Percival Paice, of Trust Farm, Dennington, Suffolk, and Winifred Mary Paice, *née* Thornton; *b* 24 April 1949; *Educ* Framlingham Coll Suffolk, Writtle Agric Coll (NDA); *m* 6 Jan 1973, Ava Barbara, da of late Robert Stewart Patterson, of Church Farm, Earl Soham, Suffolk; 2 s (Gordon b 1976, James b 1977); *Career* gen mangr/exec dir Framlingham Mgmnt and Training Services Ltd 1985-87 (non-exec dir 1987-89), non-exec dir United Framlingham Farmers Ltd 1989-; memb Select Ctee on Employment 1987-89; PPS: to Min of State of Agric 1989-90, to Min of Agric Fisheries and Food 1990-; *Recreations* windsurfing, shooting; *Style*— James Paice, Esq, MP; House of Commons, London SW1 (☎ 071 219 4101)

PAICE, Peter John; s of Lt-Col John L Paice, DSO, ISO, MBE, and Mary Gwendoline, *née* Whitby; *b* 22 Dec 1943; *Educ* Gordonstoun, Univ of Oxford (BA), INSEAD (MBA), Harvard Univ (PhD); *m* 28 Sept 1974 (m dis 1986), Jackie, *née* Elliot; 2 s (David b 4 June 1978, Walter b 19 Sept 1981); *Career* planning offr Plessey Company Ltd 1967-68, export area mangr American Cyanamid Corp 1968-71, mangr Export Div Kimberly Clarke Ltd 1971-74, dep md International Chemical Co Ltd 1974-76, vice pres (Philippines) Jardine Davies Inc 1976-80; chief exec: (Hong Kong) Zung Fu Co Ltd 1980-84, Spinneys (1948) Ltd 1984-85; dep chief exec Steel Brothers Holdings plc 1985-87, chm (Netherlands) Euryza Holdings BV 1987-88, dir Reliance Property Holdings Ltd 1988-, gp md Reliance Security Group plc 1988-, md Reliance Security Services Ltd 1988-; non-exec dir: UK Security Services (Holdings) Ltd 1989-, Grant and Taylor Security Systems Ltd 1990-, UK Security Services (N East) Ltd 1989-, Dunville Security Systems Ltd 1989-, Dominion Security Systems Ltd 1990-, Cathcart Public Relations Ltd 1974-, Salmander BV (Netherlands) 1986-, Herweg GmbH 1985-, Decorative Services Ltd 1976-; chm: Reliance Security Services (Scotland) Ltd 1988-, Reliance Security Systems (Scotland) Ltd 1988-, Reliance Electronics Ltd 1990-; MInstD 1981; *Recreations* tennis, squash, photography, wine; *Clubs* Hurlingham, Naval and Military, Roehampton; *Style*— Peter Paice, Esq; Surety House, 81 Chester Square, London SW1W 9DR (☎ 071 730 9716, fax 071 823 5625, car 0860 613329)

PAICE, Robert Tasker; s of Charles Tasker Paice (d 1960), of Hythe, Kent, and Joan Kathleen, *née* Commin (d 1981); *b* 2 July 1921; *Educ* Marlborough, Magdalene Coll Cambridge (MA), Grenoble France; *m* 8 Oct 1955, Rosemary Alison, da of Richard Arthur Denys Foster (d 1987), of St Martins, Guernsey, CI; 2 s (William b 1959, Edward b 1962), 1 da (Catherine (Mrs Finney) b 1957); *Career* cmmnd RNVR 1941, serv HMS Liverpool, HMS Newfoundland, HMS Vengeance and HMS Indefatigable, demobbed Lt Cdr 1946; Union Bank of Scotland 1947-49, md Ryders Discount Co Ltd 1960-81, dep chm Cater Allen Holdings plc (ret 1985); involved with Royal Br Legion; FCIB; *Recreations* tennis, sailing, walking, painting; *Clubs* Royal Thames Yacht, City of London, Royal Ocean Racing, Naval; *Style*— Robert Paice, Esq; Andredsbourne, Mayfield, E Sussex TN20 6UN (☎ 0435 873119); c/o Cater Allen Ltd, 20 Birchin Lane, London EC3V 9DJ (☎ 071 623 2070)

PAIGE, Elaine; da of Eric Bickerstaff, of London; *Career* actress 1968-; films: Oliver, Whatever Happened to What's His Name; tv: Love Story, The Lady Killers, Phyllis Dixey, View of Harry Clark, Unexplained Laughter; created role of Eva Peron in Evita London stage 1978, Show Business Personality of the Year Variety Club of GB Award 1978, Best Actress in a Musical SWET Award 1978, created role of Grizabella in Cats 1981, created role of Florence in Chess 1986, Reno Sweeney in Anything Goes 1989 (nominated for 1989 Olivier Awards for the outstanding performance of the year by an actress in a musical; albums: Stages (triple platinum) 1983, Cinema (gold) 1984, Chess album 1985, I Know Him So Well (duet with Barbara Dickson, No 1 Hit Single) 1985, Love Hurts (platinum) 1985, Christmas 1986, Recording Artiste of the Year Variety Club of GB Award 1986, Memories compilation album (platinum) 1987, The Queen Album 1988 (8th consecutive gold album); UK concert tours 1985 and 1987, Head of the Year Award! 1987; *Recreations* skiing, antiques; *Style*— Miss Elaine Paige; EP Records Ltd, 196 Shaftesbury Ave, London WC2H 8JL (☎ 071 240 5617)

PAIGE, Victor Grellier; CBE (1978); s of Victor Paige; *b* 5 June 1925; *Educ* East Ham GS, Univ of Nottingham; *m* 1948, Kathleen Winifred, da of Arthur Harris; 1 s, 1 da; *Career* dep chm National Freight Corporation 1977-82, chm Iveco (UK) Ltd 1984-85; memb MSC 1974-80; chm: Port of London Authy 1980-85, Mgmnt Bd NHS; second perm sec DHSS 1985-86; Freeman City of London, Cdr Order of Orange Nassau The Netherlands; CIPM, FCIT, FBIM; *Style*— Victor Paige, Esq, CBE; Queen's Wood, Frithsden, Berkhamsted, Herts

PAIN, Barry Newton; CBE (1979), QPM (1976); s of Godfrey William Pain; *b* 25 Feb 1931; *Educ* Waverley GS Birmingham; *m* 1952, Marguerite Agnes King; 1 s, 1 da; *Career* constable Birmingham City Police 1951, dir Home Off Detective Training Sch 1965-67; supt 1967, dep divnl cdr Birmingham 1967, Staff offr HM Inspr of Constabulary Birmingham 1967, asst chief constable Staffs Constabulary (in charge of Crime and Public Order, Traffic and Communications, and Administration and Training), chief constable of Kent 1974-82, vice-pres Assoc of Chief Police Offrs 1980-81, pres 1981-82, Cmdt Police Staff Coll and HM Insprs of Constabulary for England and Wales 1982-87, attached to Turkish Police Force to advise on reorganization and training (ret); *Style*— Barry Pain, Esq, CBE, QPM

PAIN, Hon Mr Justice; Hon Sir Peter (Richard); QC (1965); s of Arthur Richard Pain; *b* 6 Sept 1913; *Educ* Westminster, Christ Church Oxford; *m* 1941, Barbara Florence Maude Riggs; 2 s; *Career* called to the Bar Lincoln's Inn 1936, bencher 1972, a judge of the High Court of Justice Queen's Bench Div 1975-88; chm Race Relations Bd Conciliation Ctee for Greater London 1968-71, South Metropolitan Conciliation Ctee 1971-73, memb Parole Bd 1978-80, pres Holiday Fellowship 1977-83; kt 1975; *Style*— The Hon Sir Peter Pain; Loen, St Catherine's Rd, Frimley, Surrey

PAIN, Richard; s of Sir Peter Richard Pain, of Loen, St Catherines Rd, Frimley, Surrey, and Lady Barbara Florence Maud Pain, *née* Riggs; *b* 23 Sept 1942; *Educ* Westminster; *m* 6 Oct 1973, Adrienne Joyce, da of Myles Joseph Esmonde, of 18 Russell Sq, Longfield, Kent; 1 s (Peter b 1977), 1 da (Catherine b 1975); *Career* ptnr Hyman Isaacs Lewis and Mills 1967-74, ptnr Beachcroft Hyman Isaacs 1974-88, ptnr Beachcroft Stanleys 1988-; memb City of London Law Soc; *Recreations* cricket; *Style*— Richard Pain, Esq; Beachcroft Stanleys, 20 Furnival St, London EC4A 1BN (☎ 071 242 1011, fax 071 831 6630, telex 264607 BEALAW G)

PAIN, Richard Henry; s of Henry Francis Pain (d 1973), of Halfway House Farm, South Weald, Brentwood, Essex, and Hannah May, *née* Guttridge (d 1986); *b* 7 Sept 1929; *Educ* Brentwood Sch, Felsted; *m* 3 Oct 1959, Ruth Constance, da of William Frederick Murrell (d 1969), of Brentwood, Essex; 2 s (Matthew Henry b 1960, Cosmo William b 1965), 1 da (Charlotte Mary (Mrs Taylor) b 1962); *Career* actuary Atlas Assurance Co 1948-52; stockbroker: Rowe Swann & Co 1952-54, Grieveson Grant & Co 1954-62, Capel Cure Myers 1962-85 (ptnr until 1985), ANZ Merchant Bank 1985-89; chm Walthamstow Building Society 1989-90 (dir 1978, dep chm 1986); chm Ctee: FT Actuaries All Share Index 1972-, FT Actuaries World Index 1985-; seconded to Talisman Ctee Stock Exchange 1970-71; FT Stock Exchange Ctee, Eurotrack Index Ctee; govr St Felix Sch Southwold 1985, chm Anglo Euro Comp Sch Ingatestone 1988 (govr 1973-); contrib to various investmt and fin pubns and to jl Soc of Investmt Analysts; Freeman City of London 1984, Liveryman Worshipful Co of Actuaries 1984; memb Soc of Investmt Analysts, FIA; *Recreations* walking, collecting modern Br paintings; *Style*— Richard Pain, Esq; c/o Cheltenham & Gloucester Building Society, 869 Forest Rd, Walthamstow, London E17 4BB (☎ 081 531 3231)

PAIN, Lt-Gen Sir (Horace) Rollo Squarey; KCB (1975, CB 1974), MC (1945); s of late Horace Davy Pain; *b* 11 May 1921; *m* 1950, Denys Sophia, *née* Chaine-Nickson; 1 s, 2 da; *Career* late 4/7 Royal Dragoon Gds; head Br Def Staff Washington 1975-78, ret; Col Cmdt Mil Provost Staff Corps 1974-83, Col 4/7 Royal Dragoon Gds 1979-83, ret; *Recreations* repairing the village church; *Clubs* Cavalry and Guards'; *Style*— Lt-Gen Sir Rollo Pain, KCB, MC; Eddlethorpe Hall, Malton, N Yorks (☎ 065 385 218)

PAINE, Dr Christopher Hammon; s of Maj John Hammon Paine (d 1987), of Chapel House, Gt Coxwell, Faringdon, Oxon, and the Hon Mrs J Shedden, MBE, *née* Vestey; *b* 28 Aug 1935; *Educ* Eton, Merton Coll Oxford (MA, MSc, DM); *m* 3 Nov 1959, Susan, da of D Martin, of Bridgwater; 2 s (Edward b 1960 ,Simon b 1964), 2 da (Lucy b 1962, Alice b 1968); *Career* conslt in radiotherapy and oncology 1974-; dir clinical studies Univ of Oxford 1980-84, gen mangr Oxfordshire Health Authy 1984-88, chm Oxfordshire Health Authy Med Staff Cncl 1991-, dean Faculty of Clinical Oncology RCR 1990-; FRCP, FRCR; *Recreations* smallholding, country pursuits; *Clubs* Farmers; *Style*— Dr Christopher Paine; Dame Alice Farm, Watlington, Oxfordshire OX9 5EP (☎ 049161 2255); Dept of Radiotherapy, Churchill Hospital, Headington, Oxford OX3 7LJ (☎ 0865 225659, fax 0865 225660)

PAINE, Graham Ernest Harley; s of Harley Joseph Paine, of Greywood, Coombe Hill Rd, Kingston on Thames, Surrey, and Ninette, *née* Sutch; *b* 2 Sept 1954; *Educ* Dulwich Coll, Univ of Bristol (LLB); *Career* admitted slr 1980; ptnr Wilde Sapte 1984- (articled clerk 1978-80, asst slr 1980-84); memb London Young Slrs Gp; memb Law Soc; *Recreations* golf, skiing, theatre, tennis; *Style*— Graham Paine, Esq; Wilde Sapte, Queensbridge House, 60 Upper Thames St, London EC4 (☎ 071 236 3050, fax 071 236 9624, telex 887793)

PAINE, Jonathan; s of Cecil Finch Paine, and Freda Helen, *née* Weedon; *b* 3 Oct 1952; *Educ* Rugby, Merton Coll Oxford (BA); *m* 30 June 1979, Julie, da of Ronald Jork Barnes; *Career* J Henry Schroder Wagg & Co Ltd 1975-82; dir: Enskilda Securities 1982-87, exec dir corporate fin Swiss Bank Corpn Investment Banking 1988-; *Style*— Jonathan Paine, Esq; 1 High Timber St, London EC4 (☎ 071 329 0329)

PAINE, Peter Stanley; CBE (1980), DFC (1944); s of Arthur Bertram Paine; *b* 19 June 1921; *Educ* King's Sch Canterbury; *m* 1942, Sheila Mary, da of late Frederick Wigglesworth; 2 s, 2 da; *Career* served 1940-46, Flt-Lt 2 Gp RAF; Punch Publishing Office 1946-48, sales promotion manager Newnes Pearson 1948-52, Odhams Press 1952; sales dir and dir: Tyne Tees Television 1958-67, Yorks Television 1967; md Tyne Tees Television, dir Trident Television, chm Oracle Teletext Ltd; memb Cncl ITV Assoc; *Style*— Peter Paine, Esq, CBE, DFC; Briarfield, Ashwood Rd, Woking, Surrey GU22 7JW (☎ 0483 773183)

PAINES, Anthony John Cooper; s of Henry Wilfred Paines, KHS (d 1973), of Northwood, Middx, and Mary Agnes, *née* Cooper (d 1989); *b* 17 Nov 1925; *Educ* Mount St Mary's Coll, Lincoln Coll Oxford (MA); *m* 26 April 1952, Anne, da of Charles Philip Billot (d 1981), of St Martin, Jersey, CI; 2 s (Nicholas b 1955, Justin b 1963), 2 da (Caroline b 1957, Cathryn b 1959); *Career* RN 1944-47; admitted slr 1952, ptnr Allen & Overy 1958-88; memb Slrs Disciplinary Tbnl 1974-, cmmr of Tax Appeals (Jersey) 1988-; JP 1967-77; *Recreations* travel, boating, fishing, reading; *Clubs* Victoria, St Helier Yacht; *Style*— Anthony J C Paines, Esq; La Chaumière, St Martin, Jersey, CI (☎ 0534 62441, fax 0534 65156); 28 Battersea Bridge Rd, London SW11 (☎ 071 585 1375)

PAINES, Nicholas Paul Billot; s of Anthony John Cooper Paines, and Anne, *née* Billot; *b* 29 June 1955; *Educ* Downside, Univ of Oxford (MA), Université Libre de Bruxelles (Licence Spéiale en Droit Européen); *m* 11 May 1985, Alison Jane, da of Eric Sargent Roberts (d 1969); 1 s (Rupert b 1986), 1 da (Emily b 1989); *Career* called to the Bar Gray's Inn 1978, practising barr 1980-; memb Bar Cncl 1991-; memb Cncl St Christopher's Fellowship 1984-; *Books* Halsbury's Laws of England (contrib), Vaughan, Law of the European Communities (contrib, 1991), Bellamy's and Child, Common Market Law of Competition (contrib, 1991); *Recreations* family life, voluntary work; *Style*— Nicholas Paines, Esq; 4 Raymond Buildings, Gray's Inn, London WC1R 5BP (☎ 071 405 7211, fax 071 405 2084); Rue de Toulouse 28, 1040 Brussels

PAINTER, Brig John Lannoy Arnaud; s of Brig Gordon Whistler Arnaud Painter, DSO (d 1960), and Kathleen Hay Lannoy, *née* Tweedie (d 1986); *b* 3 Jan 1925; *Educ* Lancing, Staff Coll Camberley, RNC Greenwich; *m* 4 Feb 1956, (Janet) Lois, da of

Arnold Stanley Munro (d 1986); 2 s (Anthony Munro Arnaud b 24 Sept 1957, Angus Robin Arnaud b 29 May 1966), 1 da (Lindsay Caroline b 3 Sept 1959); *Career* served KRRC and RA 1943-76: WWII serv NW Europe 8RB (wounded), Korea, Malaya (with SAS), Palestine, Cyprus, W Africa (with RWAFF) Brig CRA 2 Div 1970-71, DDRA 1972-75; sr master Cundall Manor Sch 1976-88; *Recreations* walking, skiing, riding; *Style*— Brig John L A Painter; Abbayville, Upper Dunsforth, Great Ouseburn, Yorkshire YO5 9RU (☎ 0423 322842)

PAINTER, Dr Michael John; s of James Frederick Painter, of Bredbury, Cheshire, and Lettice Gillian, *née* Payne; *b* 24 Oct 1948; *Educ* Strode's Sch Egham Surrey, St Mary's Hosp Med Sch Univ of London (MB BS), Univ of Manchester (MSc); *m* 26 May 1973, Gillian Elizabeth, da of David Alexander Burgess (d 1973); *Career* conslt public health med, med offr environmental health Manchester City Cncl, port med offr Manchester Airport, memb Bd Public Health Lab Serv 1986-, jt author papers on haemophilia and meningitis; Freeman City of London 1982, Liveryman Worshipful Co of Coopers 1982; memb: BMA 1973, Faculty Community Medicine 1985; *Recreations* photography, model railways, cycling; *Style*— Dr Michael Painter; 108 Wythenshawe Rd, Northenden, Manchester M23 OPA (☎ 061 998 9688); PO Box 362, Town Hall, Manchester M60 2JB (☎ 061 234 4867, fax 061 234 4872)

PAINTER, Michael William; s of William Bentley Painter (d 1984), of Coventry, and Maria, *née* Eggleton (d 1982); *b* 2 March 1938; *Educ* Bablake Sch Coventry; *m* 1, 23 Sept 1963, Jillian Margeret (d 1985), da of Harold Lane (d 1976); 1 s (Steven Michael b 1966), 2 da (Sarah b 1968, Rebecca b 1973), m 2, 26 Sept 1987, Susan Anne, da of Frederick Morley, of Swindon; 2 step da (Michelle b 1981, Rosanne b 1983); *Career* Nat Serv RAF 1958-60; dir Hogg Robinson UK Ltd 1973-85, dir Bowring UK Ltd 1985-, chief exec Bowring London Ltd 1985-; FCII, FBIIBA, FBIM; *Recreations* walking; *Clubs* RAC; *Style*— Michael Painter, Esq; Bowring London Ltd, The Bowring Building, Tower Place, London EC3 (☎ 071 283 3100, fax 071 929 2705, telex 882191)

PAINTER, Terence James; CB (1990); s of Edward Lawrence Painter (d 1971), and Ethel Violet Painter (d 1969); *b* 28 Nov 1935; *Educ* City of Norwich Sch, Downing Coll Cambridge (BA); *m* 12 Dec 1959, Margaret Janet, *née* Blackburn; 2 s (James b 30 May 1964, Ian b 17 Feb 1966), 2 da (Susan (Mrs Wallace) b 14 March 1963, Alison b 29 Oct 1968); *Career* dep chm Bd Inland Revenue 1986- (asst princ 1959, princ 1962, seconded civil service selection bd 1967-68, asst sec 1969, seconded HM Treasy 1973-75, under sec 1975-86; *Recreations* reading, hill walking, music, gardening; *Style*— Terence Painter, Esq, CB; Board of Inland Revenue, Somerset House, London WC2

PAINTING, Norman George; OBE (1976); s of Harry George Painting, and Maud Painting; *b* 23 April 1924; *Educ* Leamington Coll, King Edward VI Sch Nuneaton, Univ of Birmingham (BA), Ch Ch Oxford; *Career* anglo-saxon tutor Exeter Coll Oxford 1946-48, writer and dir BBC 1949-50; freelance writer dir and performer 1950-; radio performances incl: longest serving actor in a daily radio serial as Philip Archer in The Archers 1950-; written work incl: 1198 episodes of The Archers (as Bruno Milna), many TV films, radio scripts, plays, articles; TV appearances incl: chm of TV Quiz The Garden Game 1977-82, Wogan, Stop the Week, Quote Unquote, On the Air; team capt Gardening Quiz R4; patron Tree Cncl, tstee Warwicks and Coventry Historic Churches Tst (chm 1979-82); vice pres: Friends of Birmingham Cathedral, Friends of St Mary's Warwick, hon life govr RASE 1976, hon memb High Table Ch Ch Oxford 1985-, life fell RHS, life memb CPRE, memb Nat Tst Hon MA ChCh Oxford 1989; *Books* Stories of the Saints (with M Day, 1956), More Stories of the Saints (with M Day, 1957), St Antony: The Man Who Found Himself (with M Day, 1958), Forever Ambridge (1975), Reluctant Archer (Autobiography, 1982); *Recreations* music, poetry, swimming, gardens, things Italian, being quiet, high table dining; *Style*— Norman Painting, Esq, OBE; c/o BBC Broadcasting House, London W1A 1AA

PAIRMAN, (Lynda) Annette; *née* Miles; da of William John Edward Miles, of Edinburgh, and Sarah, *née* Carr; *b* 11 Feb 1958; *Educ* The Mary Erskine Sch Edinburgh, Univ of Edinburgh (LLB); *m* 20 Aug 1977, Gordon Alexander Pairman, s of Alexander George Pairman, of Glasgow; *Career* W & J Burness WS 1978-83 (ptnr 1984-), Herbert Smith & Co 1983-84; memb: Law Soc of Scot, Soc of Writers to HM Signet; *Clubs* Royal Scottish Automobile, Caledonian; *Style*— Mrs Annette Pairman; 238 West George Street, Glasgow (☎ 041 248 4933, fax 041 204 1601, car 0836 782129)

PAISH, Geoffrey Lane; MBE (1974); s of Arthur Paish (d 1957), and FLorence Mary, *née* Lane (d 1957); *b* 2 Jan 1922; *Educ* Whitgift Middle Sch; *m* 18 Nov 1944, Sylvia Joan, da of John Frederick Carr (d 1972); 1 s (John b 1948), 1 da (Deborah (Mrs Miller) b 1955); *Career* Civil Serv Inland Revenue 1939-82; tennis player: memb Br Davis Cup team 1947-55, Br Covered courts men's singles champion 1951, S of Eng champion 1951-55; Lawn Tennis Assoc: memb Cncl 1970-79 chm 1979, vice pres 1980-; memb Ctee of Mgmnt The Championships Wimbledon 1979-90, pres Surrey Co Lawn Tennis Assoc 1983-; *Recreations* tennis; *Clubs* All England LTC, Int LTC of GB; *Style*— Geoffrey Paish, Esq, MBE

PAISLEY, Rev Ian Richard Kyle; MP (DUP) North Antrim 1974-, MEP (Democratic Unionist Pty) NI 1979-; s of late Rev J Kyle Paisley; *b* 6 April 1926; *Educ* Ballymena Model Sch, Ballymena Tech HS, S Wales Bible Coll, Reformed Presbyterian Theol Coll Belfast; *m* 1956, Eileen Emily Cassells; 2 s, 3 da; *Career* ordained 1946; MP (Prot U) N Antrim 1970-74; minister Martyrs Memorial Free Presbyterian Church Belfast 1946-; memb: Int Cultural Soc of Korea; FRGS; *Books* History of 59 Revival, Christian Foundations (1960, 2 edn 1985), Exposition of Epistle to Romans (1968, 2 edn 1985), Massacre of St Bartholomew (1972), Ulster the Facts (1981), No Pope Here (1982), Paisley's Pocket Preacher (1987), Be Sure - 7 rules for public speaking (1987); *Style*— The Rev Ian Paisley, MP, MEP; House of Commons, London SW1; The Parsonage, 17 Cyprus Ave, Belfast BT5 5NT

PAISLEY, Rt Rev the Bishop John Aloysius Mone; s of Arthur Mone (d 1964), and Elizabeth, *née* Dunn (d 1979); *b* 22 June 1929; *Educ* Holyrood Secdy Sch, Sulpician Seminaries in France of Issy-les-Moulineaux and Paris, Institut Catholique Paris; *Career* ordained priest Glasgow 1952, St Ninian's Glasgow 1952-75, Our Lady and St George 1975-79, St Joseph's Tollcross 1979-84, bishop of Abercorn and bishop auxiliary 1984-88; Scottish nat Chaplain Girl Guides 1971; chm Scottish Catholic Ind Aid Fund 1974 (pres 1985-), Scottish Marriage Advsy Cncl 1982-84; pres Justice and Peace Cmmn 1987-; *Recreations* golf, piano playing; *Clubs* Hamilton Golf; *Style*— The Rt Rev the Bishop of Paisley; Diocesan Centre, 13 Newark St, Greenock, Renfrewshire PA16 7UH (☎ 0475 25161/2); Diocessan Office, 8 East Buchanan St, Paisley PA1 1HS

PAJARES, Ramon; s of Juan Antonio Pajares Garcia (d 1954), of Jaen Spain, and Rosario Salazar (d 1964); *b* 6 July 1935; *Educ* sr sch Jaen Spain, Madrid Inst of Hotel and Tourism Studies; *m* 13 July 1963, Jean Kathleen, 1 s (Roberto Javier b 17 March 1971), 2 da (Sofia Ramona b 14 June 1967, Maria del Rosario b 25 Aug 1969); *Career* Spanish Nat Serv Spanish Navy 1955-57; Hotel Ritz Barcelona 1954-55, Hotel San Jorge Playa de Aro 1957, Hotel Parque Llavaneras 1957-59, Mansion Hotel Eastbourne 1959-61, Kleiner Reisen Koblenz Germany 1961, Hotel Feldbergerhof Feldberg Germany 1961-62, Le Vieux Manoir Morat Switzerland 1962, Hotel Reina Isabel Las Palmas Canary Is 1965-69, food and beverage dir Inn on The Park 1969-71, gen mangr San Antonio Lanzarate Canary Is 1972-74, gen mangr Inn On The Park London W1 1975-; *awards* medal of Merito Civil awarded by HM King of Spain 1984, Hotelier of the Year award of Br Hotel and Catering Industry 1984, Personalité de l'Année for The Hotel Indust 1986, medal of Oficial de la Orden de Isabel la Catolica awarded by HM King of Spain 1989; Freeman City of London 1988; memb: Association Culinaire Française 1971-, Bd of Fells Skål 1972, Cookery and Food Assoc 1973, Confrerie de la Chaîne des Rotisseurs 1978-, Confrerie des Chevaliers du Sacavin 1979-, Euro Hotel Mangr Assoc 1982-, Caballeros del Vino 1987; officier de L'Ordre des Coteaux de Champagne, chev du Tastevin 1982, FHCIMA 1982, Master Innholder 1988; *Clubs* Les Ambassadeurs, Annabels; *Style*— Ramon Pajares, Esq; Four Seasons Inn On The Park, Hamilton Place, Park Lane, London W1A 1AZ (☎ 071 499 0888)

PAKENHAM, Hon Kevin John Toussaint; s of Lord Longford, and Elizabeth, *née* Harman; *b* 1 Nov 1947; *Educ* New Coll Oxford (scholar, MA), St Antony's Coll Oxford (MPhil); *m* 1, Ruth, *née* Jackson; 1 s (Thomas John Chamberlain), 1 da (Catherine Ruth); m 2, Clare, *née* Hoare; 2 s (Benjamin John, Dominic Balthazas), 1 da (Hermione); *Career* sr economist Rothschild Intercontinental Bank 1972-75, md of investmt management in London American Express Bank 1978-83 (chief economist 1975-78), md Foreign and Colonial Management 1983-88, chief exec John Govett and Co Ltd 1988-; editorial advsr Amex Bank Review; treas Ireland Fund of GB (registered Charity); *Recreations* sailing, chess, golf; *Clubs* MCC, City of London, Hurlingham, Rye, Sailing; *Style*— The Hon Kevin Pakenham; John Govett & Co, Shackleton House, 4 Battle Bridge Lane, London SE1 (☎ 071 378 7979)

PAKENHAM, Hon Michael Aidan; 3 s of 7 Earl of Longford, KG, PC; *b* 3 Nov 1943; *Educ* Ampleforth, Trinity Coll Cambridge, Rice Univ Texas; *m* 1980, Meta (Mimi) Landreth, da of William Conway Doak, of Maryland, USA; 2 da (Alexandra b 1981, Clio b 1985); *Career* HM Dip Serv: cnsllr (External Affairs) UK Representation to European Communities, Brussels; *Recreations* tennis, golf, reading, bridge; *Clubs* MCC; *Style*— The Hon Michael Pakenham; FCO, King Charles St, London SW1A 2AH

PAKENHAM, Hon Patrick; s of 7 Earl of Longford, KG, PC; *b* 1937; *Educ* Ampleforth, Magdalen Coll Oxford; *m* 1968 (m dis), Mary Elizabeth, da of Maj H A J Plummer, of Winchester; 3 s; *Career* barr Inner Temple 1962; *Style*— The Hon Patrick Pakenham; 24 Chesil Ct, Chelsea Manor St, London SW3

PAKENHAM, Hon Mrs (Susan Elizabeth Moon); *née* Lever; da of 3 Viscount Leverhulme, TD; *b* 1938; *m* 1957 (m dis 1973) (Hercules) Michael Roland Pakenham; 1 s, 1 da (both adopted); *Style*— The Hon Mrs Pakenhamn; Oaklands, Lr Common Rd, W Wellow, Romsey, Hants

PAKENHAM, Thomas Frank Dermot; s and h of 7 Earl of Longford, KG, PC, but does not use courtesy title; *b* 14 Aug 1933; *Educ* Ampleforth, Magdalen Coll Oxford; *m* 1964, Valerie Susan, da of Maj Ronald Guthrie McNair Scott; 2 s, 2 da; *Style*— Thomas Pakenham Esq; Tullynally, Castelpollard, Co Westmeath (☎ 044 61159)

PAKENHAM-WALSH, John; CB (1986); s of Rev Wilfrid Pakenham-Walsh (d 1974), and Guendolen Maud, *née* Elliott (d 1990); *b* 7 Aug 1928; *Educ* Bradfield Coll, Univ Coll Oxford (MA); *m* 29 Sept 1951, Deryn Margaret, da of Gp Capt Reginald Edgar Gilbert Fulljames, MC (d 1985); 1 s (John b 25 Nov 1961), 4 da (Carolyn 23 May 1953, Elizabeth b 19 Jan 1956, Sarah b 25 May 1965, Andrea b 7 Sept 1968); *Career* called to the Bar Lincoln's Inn 1951, Crown Counsel Hong Kong 1953-57, Parly counsel Fedn of Nigeria 1958-61, joined Legal Advsrs Branch Home Office 1961, under sec (legal) Home Office 1980-88, standing counsel to Gen Synod of the Church of England 1988-; *Clubs* Athenaeum; *Style*— John Pakenham-Walsh, Esq, CB; Crinken House, Pathfields Close, Haslemere, Surrey, GU27 2BL (☎ 0428 642033); 36 Whitehall, London, SW1 (☎ 071 210 6791)

PAKENHAM-WALSH, Mabel; da of Dr Robert Pakenham-Walsh (d 1969), of Well House, Lancaster, Lancs, and Joyce, Braithwaite, *née* Savory; *b* 2 Sept 1937; *Educ* Lancaster and Wimbledon Colls of Art; *Career* woodcarver; Pinewood and Shepperton film studios 1960-61, painted wood carving in the Craftsmans Art V & A 1973; exhibitions: The Crafts Cncl London 1973-91, The Mappin Gallery Sheffield 1980, Nat Museum of Wales Cardiff, Int Exhibition of Applied Arts Bratislava, Aberystwyth Univ Art Centre, Sotheby's first decorative arts exhibition 1988, touring exhibitions and workshops in carving at Drumcroom Wigan and Centre for Alternative Technology (memb); carvings permanently exhibited at: Grizedale Park Cumbria, Ulster Museum Belfast; memb: Contemporary Applied Arts Covent Garden, Spinal Injuries Assoc, Mind, Survival International, The Woodland Tst; *Recreations* swimming, Peter, bird-wrecking & Colour, planting trees; *Clubs* Contemporary Applied Arts, Crafts Cncl; *Style*— Miss Mabel Pakenham-Walsh; Archnoa, Tanyfynwent, Llanbadarn, Fawr, Aberystwyth SY23 3RA (☎ 0970 625276)

PAKINGTON, Hon John Humphrey Arnott; s and h of 6 Baron Hampton; *b* 24 Dec 1964; *Educ* Dyson Perrins C of E HS, Shrewsbury, Exeter Coll of Art and Design (BA); *Career* freelance photographer in London; *Style*— The Hon John Pakington

PALACHE, Robert; s of Ralph Palache of London, and Rosalind, *née* Simons; *b* 11 Nov 1957; *Educ* JFS Sch, Magdalene Coll Cambridge (MA); *m* 28 July 1979, Johanne Helen, da of Michael George Barrett, MBE; 2 da (Abigail b 22 Aug 1984, Dora b 24 May 1987); *Career* slr Coward Chance 1982-87, ptnr Clifford Chance 1988- (slr 1987); *Recreations* reading, swimming; *Style*— Robert Palache, Esq

PALEY, Maureen; da of Alfred Paley, of Oceanport New Jersey, and Silvia, *née* Tiffel; *Educ* Sarah Lawrence Coll Bronxville NY, Brown Univ Providence Rhode Island (BA), RCA (MA); *Career* worked in photography and film 1980-84, freelance curator 1980-84; opened art gallery Interim Art 1984, W End branch opened 1990; memb: GLA Visual Arts Advsy Panel 1989-91, Visual Arts Project Ctee Arts Cncl 1989-91, Advsy Panel on Visual Arts Arts Cncl 1991-; *Style*— Miss Maureen Paley; 21 Beck Rd, London E8 4RE; Maureen Paley Interim ARt, 20 Dering St, London W1R 9AA (☎ 071 495 4580, fax 071 495 3552)

PALIA, Dr Satnam Singh; s of Daljit Singh Palia, of Punjab, India, and Pritam Kaur, *née* Harar; *b* 5 Oct 1952; *Educ* Govt Med Coll Amritsar India (MB BS, DPM), Univ of Wales (MSc); *m* 4 July 1976, Valwinder Kaur, da of Jaswant Karir of Southampton; 3 da (Satwinder Kaur b 4 Nov 1977, Navjinder (Dimple) b 12 Aug 1980, Rajinder (Rosie) b 13 Oct 1981); *Career* registrar in psychiatry St Annes Hosp Poole Dorset 1981-83, sr registrar in psychiatry Univ of Wales Heath Hosp Cardiff 1983-85, conslt psychiatrist Glanrhyd and Penyfai Hosps and hon postgrad organiser and clinical teacher Coll of Med Univ of Wales 1986-; author of papers on water intoxication in psychiatric patients and mood disorders in epileptic patients; clinical tutor and course organiser RCPsych 1986-; former chm Sikh Assoc of S Wales; MRCPsych 1981, FRSH 1987; *Recreations* music, reading, badminton; *Style*— Dr Satnam Palia; 35 Herbert March Close, Radyr Vale, Danescourt, Cardiff CF5 2TD (☎ 0222 555503); Glanrhyd and Penyfai Hospitals, Tondu Rd, Bridgend, Mid Glamorgan CF34 LN (☎ 0656 766100)

PALIN, Maj Hugh Mair; MBE (1943), TD (1960); s of Vero Calveley Palin (d 1937), and Margaret Janet, *née* Mair (d 1952); *b* 31 May 1912; *Educ* Brighton Coll; *m* 1, 10 Sept 1938 (m dis 1960), Enid Margery Maud, da of late Capt Thomas Free, MN; 1 s

(Michael John b 1944), 1 da (Rosemary Grace b 1950); m 2, 28 Jan 1962, Peggy Ailsa Thelma, *née* Bailey; 1 s (Jonathan Hugh b 1963); *Career* Westminster Dragoons TA 1938-39, cmmnd 2 Lt RTR 1940, Capt 1941, Staff Coll Camberley 1942, Major N Africa 1942-43, served with 33 Armd Bde Normandy and NW Europe 1944-45, demob 1945; Warwicks Yeo TA 1948-53; dir Br Cycle and Motorcycle Mfrs Union 1953-67, dir Norton Villiers Triumph Ltd 1967, purchasing dir Skoda (GB) Ltd 1976-80; non exec dir: RAC 1979-88 (chm Motorcycle Ctee 1972-88), Auto Cycle Union 1979-; pres: Br Motorcyclists Fedn 1976, Bureau Permanent International des Constructeurs de Motorcycles 1977, Motor Cycle Assoc of GB; advsr to Bd Norton Group plc 1987-88, chm of Cncl Nat Motor Museum Beaulieu; Freeman Stratford-on-Avon (as CO Stratford Sqdn Warwicks Yeo); Fell Motor Indust; *Clubs* RAC, Cavalry and Guards; *Style—* Maj Hugh Palin, MBE, TD; Bay View, Freshwater East, Pembroke, Dyfed (☎ 0646 672 629)

PALING, Her Hon Judge Helen Elizabeth (Mrs W J S Kershaw); da of A Dale Paling; *b* 25 April 1933; *Educ* Prince Henry's GS Otley, LSE (LLB); *m* 1961, William John Stanley Kershaw, PhD; 1 s, 3 da; *Career* called to the Bar Lincoln's Inn 1955, recorder of the Crown Court 1972-85, circuit judge 1985-; *Style—* Her Hon Judge Paling

PALING, Robert Roy; s of Reginald Roy Paling (d 1978), and Margery Emily, *née* Lyford; *b* 10 June 1940; *Educ* Shrivenham Sch, Faringdon Sch, The Coll Swindon; *m* 20 Feb 1965, Judith Dow, da of Reginald Albert Sheppard (d 1985); 1 da (Portia Dow b 1968); *Career* sr conveyancing exec Lemon & Co Slrs Swindon 1980, conslt Dow Sheppard Relocation 1981, compiled Mortgage Guide for CBI Employee Relocation Cncl 1988; Sr Jt Master Shrivenham Beagles, memb Old Berks Hunt, Assoc of Masters of Harriers and Beagles 1970; memb Soc Licensed Conveyancers 1987, assoc Inst of Legal Execs 1965; *Recreations* hunting, cross country riding, shooting; *Clubs* RMCS Shrivenham; *Style—* Robert Paling, Esq; Orchard House, High St, Shrivenham, Swindon SN6 8AW (☎ 0793 782214); Lemon & Co, 34 Regent Circus, Swindon SN1 1PY (☎ 0793 27141, fax 0793 782328, car 0860 221 808)

PALLANT, Jean; da of Victor Robinson Hodge (d 1968), of Surrey, and Ellen Rose, *née* Bragg; *b* 10 March 1944; *Educ* Kingston Coll of Art (BA); *m* 1964, Martin Pallant, gv; *Career* fashion designer; cruisewear designer Jaeger 1965-66, lectr Kingston Coll of Art 1966-69; estab Jean & Martin Pallant Partnership (ladies designer fashion) 1969; jt md: Jean & Martin Pallant Ltd 1973-, Pallant (London) Ltd 1988-; consistently voted one of top ten UK fashion designers; *Style—* Mrs Jean Pallant; Jean & Martin Pallant Limited, Ferry Works, Summer Rd, Thames Ditton, Surrey KT7 0QJ (☎ 081 398 8853, fax 081 398 8058); Pallant (London) Ltd, The Pantechnicon, Motcomb St, London SW1W 8LB (☎ 071 259 6046)

PALLANT, John; s of Dennis Pallant, of 58 Parkstone Avenue, Southsea, Hants, and Doreen, *née* Hirst; *b* 10 Aug 1955; *Educ* St John's Coll Southsea, Univ of Reading (BA); *Career* copywriter: Griffin & George Ltd 1977, Acroyd Westwood Associates 1977, Boase Massimi Pollitt 1978, Collett Dickenson Pearce 1980, Gold Greenless Trott 1982; copy writer and gp head Boase Massimi Pollitt 1983, copywriter Saatchi & Saatchi Advertising 1988; *awards* D & ADA awards (for TV, press, public service and poster campaings): Gold 1985, Silver 1981 (two), 1985 (three) and 1989; Br TV Awards Silver 1981; Cannes Int Advertising Awards: Silver 1981, Bronze 1988; Campaign Press Awards: Gold 1985, Silver 1985 (two), 1989 and 1990; Campaign Poster Awards: Gold 1985, Silver 1983, 1985 (two), 1990 (two); Independent Radio Awards Silver 1990; *Style—* John Pallant, Esq; Saatchi & Saatchi Advertising, 80 Charlotte St, London W1A 1AQ (☎ 071 636 5060 ext 3501, fax 071 637 8489)

PALLANT, Martin; s of Frank Wilfred Pallant (d 1989), of Kent, and Irene Mary Claris, *née* Smyth; *b* 16 Feb 1943; *Educ* Kingston GS, Kingston Coll of Art (BA), RCA; *m* 1964, Jean Pallant, *qv*, *née* Hodge; *Career* fashion designer; freelance designer 1965-69, estab Jean & Martin Pallant Partnership (ladies designer fashion) 1969; jt md: Jean & Martin Pallant Ltd 1973-, Pallant (London) Ltd 1988-; consistently voted one of top ten UK fashion designers; *Style—* Martin Pallant, Esq; Ferry Works, Summer Road, Thames Ditton, Surrey KT7 0QJ (☎ 081 398 8865, fax 081 398 8058); Pallant (London) Ltd, The Pantechnicon, Motcomb St, London SW1W 8LB (☎ 071 259 6046)

PALLETT, Norman Ivor; s of Walter Albert Stanley Pallett (d 1949), of Hastings, and Helen Rebecca, *née* Shearman (d 1977); *b* 22 April 1929; *Educ* Alleyns Sch Dulwich; *m* 20 Sep 1952, Margaret Evelyn, da of Marcus Edward Turk, of Hastings; 1 s (Robert Nigel b 1954); *Career* CH Dobbie conslt engrs: joined 1951, ptnr 1970-84, managing ptnr 1984-90; md Babtie Dobbie Ltd consulting engrs 1990-; work incl: coastal engrg, public health, highways, railways; FICE, MIHT, MConsSE, FBIM; *Recreations* archaeology, railways, the Arab world; *Clubs* St Stephen's Constitutional; *Style—* Norman Pallett, Esq; Babtie Dobbie Ltd, Consulting Structural and Civil Engineers, 17 Lansdowne Rd, Croydon CR9 3UN (☎ 081 686 8212, fax 081 681 2499, telex 917220)

PALLEY, Dr Claire Dorothea Taylor; da of Arthur Aubrey Swait, Durban; *b* 17 Feb 1931; *m* 1952 (m dis 1985), Ahrn Palley; 5 s; *Career* princ St Anne's Coll Oxford 1984-; memb UN Sub Cmmn on Prevention of Discrimination and Protection of Minorities 1988-; *Books* The Constitutional History and Law of S Rhodesia (1966), contrib numerous articles in learned jls; *Style—* Dr Claire Palley; St Anne's College, Oxford

PALLEY, Eall Marcon (Marc); s of Dr Ahrn Palley, of Zimbabwe, and Dr Claire Dorothea Taylor, *née* Swait, qv; *b* 2 May 1954; *Educ* Clifton, St John's Coll Oxford (BA); *m* 28 July 1979, Sabina Mary, da of Maj-Gen F W E Fursdon, qv; 3 s (Charles b 9 Dec 1982, Frederick b 6 June 1985, Harry b 15 May 1988); *Career* admitted slr 1978; Allen & Overy 1978-85, ptnr Berwin Leighton 1985-; *Style—* Marc Palley, Esq

PALLI, Lady Hermione; *see*: della Grazia, Duchessa

PALLISER, Prof David Michael; s of Herbert Leslie Palliser (d 1973), and Doris Violet, *née* Brown (d 1969); *b* 10 Sept 1939; *Educ* Bootham Sch York, Worcester Coll Oxford (BA, MA, DPhil); *Career* asst princ Home Civil Serv 1961-64, res fell Univ of Keele 1967-73, lectr then sr lectr then reader in economic history Univ of Birmingham 1974-85, GF Grant prof of history Univ of Hull 1985-; chm Urban Res Ctee Cncl for Br Archaeology 1978-84; memb Cncl York Archaeological Tst 1980-, Royal Historical Soc 1986-90; FRHistS 1974, FSA 1977; *Books* The Staffordshire Landscape (1976), Tudor York (1979), York as They Saw It (with B M Palliser, 1979), York (with J H Hutchinson, 1980), The Age of Elizabeth (1983); *Style—* Prof David Palliser; Dept of History, Univ of Hull, Hull, E Yorks HU6 7RX (☎ 0482 465607)

PALLISER, Rt Hon Sir (Arthur) Michael; GCMG (1977, KCMG 1973, CMG 1966), PC (1983); s of Adm Sir Arthur Palliser, KCB, DSC, of South Kensington (d 1956), and Margaret Eva, Lady Palliser; *b* 9 April 1922; *Educ* Wellington, Merton Coll Oxford (MA, hon fell 1986); *m* 1948, Marie Marguerite, da of Paul-Henri Spaak (d 1972), sometime PM of Belgium and sec gen NATO; 3 s; *Career* late Capt Coldstream Gds; entered FO 1947, private sec to PM 1966, min Paris 1969, ambass and head to UK Delegn to EEC Brussels 1971, ambass and UK perm rep to EEC 1973-75, perm under sec and head of Dip Serv FCO 1975-82; appointed PM's special advsr during Falklands Crisis 1982, assoc fell Harvard Univ Center for Int Affrs 1982; dep chm Midland Bank plc 1987-; non-exec dir: Samuel Montagu & Co Ltd 1983- (chm 1984-), Booker McConnell 1983- (now Booker plc), Ibec Inc (now Arbor Acres Farm Inc, agribusiness assoc of Booker plc based in Connecticut) 1983-, BAT Industries 1983-, Eagle Star Holdings 1983-, Shell Transport and Trading 1983-, United Biscuits (Holdings) 1983-89; chm Cncl Int Inst for Strategic Studies 1983-90; memb Cncl Royal Inst of Int Affairs 1982-89, pres Br section Int Social Servs 1982-, memb Security Cmmn 1983-; Chev Order of Orange Nasssau 1944, Chev Légion d'Honneur 1957; *Recreations* travel, theatre; *Clubs* Buck's; *Style—* Rt Hon Sir Michael Palliser, GCMG; c/o Midland Bank plc, Poultry, London EC2P 2BX (☎ 071 260 8000)

PALLISTER, Anthony Gilbert Fitzjames; s of Rev J Pallister (d 1949), of Gt Dunham, and Elizabeth Mary, *née* Feast; *b* 11 Feb 1915; *Educ* King Alfred's Sch Wantage, Brighton Tech Coll; *m* 22 Aug 1942, Barbara Millecent, da of Adm George Bowes Hutton (d 1948), of Belton House, Rutland; 1 s (Julian Guy b 6 Dec 1943), 1 da (Jacqueline Ann (Mrs Robinson) b 14 Jan 1949); *Career* RASC 1940, cmmnd 2 Lt posted 11 Armd Div 1942, Capt 1943, Staff Capt HQ L of C 21 Army Gp 1944, Staff Capt HQ 21 Army Gp 1944, Maj DADST 1944, head of ST5 21 Army Gp 1945; asst D Winton Thorpe Consulting Engrs 1936-37, commercial asst Electric Power Co Shrops Worcs and Staffs 1937, educn and trg mangr Midlands Electricity Bd; county magistrate Worcs 1963-80, chm of magistrates and memb Magistrates Cts Ctee, vice chm and memb Hereford and Worcester Probation Ctee 1963-80; sec Birmingham Outward Bd Assoc 1951-61, memb VSO Ctee Worcs 1970-, ILO expert Malaysia 1960 and 1971, pt/t advsr UPDEA W Africa 1974-76, memb governing bodies of Birmingham Poly and Worcs Coll of Higher Educn; fndr chm: Midlands Ctee for Trg of Probation Staff, Community Serv Ctee Hereford and Worcs; gen commr Income Tax 1974-90; FIPM (chm Birmingham branch); *Recreations* tennis, hockey, golf; *Clubs* Union & County (Worcs); *Style—* Anthony Pallister, Esq; The Grove House, Sytchampton, Stourport on Severn, Worcs (☎ 0905 620371)

PALLISTER, Julian Guy; s of Anthony Gerald Fitzjames Pallister, JP, of The Grove House, Sytchampton, nr Stourport-on-Severn, Worcs, and Barbara Millicent, *née* Hutton; *b* 1 Dec 1943; *Educ* Wellington, Univ of Bristol (BA); *m* 20 Sept 1968, Serena Gay, da of Maj Ernald Richardson (d 1967); 2 s (Andrew Bowes b 13 July 1970, Mark Greville b 5 Jan 1972), 1 da (Louise Ann b 5 Oct 1974); *Career* CA 1968; md Tyndall & Co Ltd 1986-87 (joined 1969, sec and fin controller 1974-86, fin dir 1985), dir Tyndall Holdings plc 1986-87, sec and fin controller The Burns Anderson Group plc 1987-90; sec Cons Assoc 1974-77, treas Clifton Lawn Tennis Club 1974-, govr Avonhurst Sch 1980-86; FCA; *Recreations* tennis, skiing, golf, gardening; *Clubs* Clifton; *Style—* Julian Pallister, Esq; Applehayes, Easton-in-Gordano, Bristol BS20 0QA (☎ 0275 372944)

PALLISTER, Air Cdre Michael Alan; s of Dr Richard Alan Pallister, OBE, of Berkhamsted, Herts, and Muriel Reay Pallister (d 1976); *b* 5 Oct 1930; *Educ* Guildford GS and Hale Sch Aust, Sedbergh, St John's Coll Cambridge (BA, MB BChir), St Thomas's Hosp, Univ of Liverpool (DTM&H), Univ of London (DPH, DIH); *m* 16 July 1955, Shelagh Patricia; 1 s (Simon Richard b 29 May 1956), 1 da (Julia b 26 July 1957); *Career* med branch RAF 1957-89; MOD 1965-69; offr i/c: RAF Inst of Community Med 1976-78, RAF Hosp Akrotiri Cyprus 1978-80; dep dir med orgn (RAF) and asst surgn gen personnel and trg MOD 1980-85, offr i/c Princess Alexandra Hosp RAF Wroughton 1986-89; conslt advsr in community med to RAF 1987-89; BMA 1956, MRCS and LRCP 1956, FRSTM&H 1960, MRCGP 1975, MFOM 1981, FFCM 1988; *Recreations* cabinet making; *Clubs* RAF, Leander; *Style—* Air Cdre Michael Pallister

PALLISTER, Timothy John Barry; s of John C.Pallister (d 1973), of Woodbastwick, Norfolk, and Doreen Barry, *née* Drew (d 1984); *b* 2 July 1940; *Educ* Bloxham Sch; *m* 20 June 1970, Christine, da of The Hon RN Cabbell-Manners; 2 s (James b 10 July 1971, Richard b 22 Nov 1976), 1 da (Charlotte b 16 June 1972); *Career* articled clerk Mills & Reeve 1958-62, ptnr Slaughter and May 1972- (asst slr 1963-71, Paris office 1973-80); memb: Law Soc, Int Bar Assoc, UK Environmental Law Assoc; *Recreations* motoring, tennis, theatre, country pursuits, golf; *Clubs* RAC, Norfolk, Sheringham Golf; *Style—* Timothy Pallister, Esq; Slaughter and May, 35 Basinghall St, London EC2V 5DB (☎ 071 600 1200)

PALLOT, Dr (Doreen) Betty; da of Arthur Charles Pallot, MBE (d 1967), of Sutton, Surrey, and Dorothy Elizabeth Victoria, *née* Hickish (d 1985); *b* 2 Sept 1924; *Educ* Sutton HS, King's Coll London, W London Hosp Med Sch (MB BS); *Career* conslt anaesthetist: Royal Nat Throat Nose and Ear Hosp 1964, Moorfields Eye Hosp 1969; MRCS, LRCP, FFARCS; *Recreations* gardens, music; *Clubs* Royal Soc of Med; *Style—* Dr Betty Pallot; 36 Parkway, Welwyn Garden City, Herts AL8 6HG (☎ 0707 323115)

PALMAR, Sir Derek James; o s of Lt-Col Frederick James Palmar (d 1978), and Hylda, *née* Smith; *b* 25 July 1919; *Educ* Dover Coll; *m* 1946, Edith (d 1990), da of William Brewster (d 1948); 1 s (Alastair), 1 da (Caroline); *Career* Nat Serv RA and Staff 1941-46, psc, Lt-Col 1945; Peat Marwick Mitchell & Co 1937-57, dir Hill Samuel Group 1957-70, advsr Dept of Econ Affrs 1965-67, memb BR Bd 1969-72, chm BR Southern Regnl Advsy Bd 1972-79; Bass plc: chm 1976-87, dir 1970-76, chief exec 1976-84, pres 1987-89; chm: Yorkshire Television 1982-, Boythorpe 1986-, Zoological Soc of London Development Tst 1986-88, Univ of Leeds Fndn 1986-88, Nat Econ Devpt Ctee for Food and Drink Packaging Equipment 1986-88; dir: Grindlays Bank 1973-85, Grindlays Hldgs 1979-85, Drayton Consolidated Tst 1982-, Consolidated Venture Tst 1984-; CM Gp Hldgs 1985-; tstee Civic Tst 1982-89; memb Ct Brewers' Co 1980-87; vice-pres The Brewers' Soc 1982- (chm 1980-82, vice-chm 1978-80); Freeman City of London; FCA 1957 (ACA 1947), CBIM; kt 1986; *Recreations* shooting, gardening; *Clubs* Boodle's; *Style—* Sir Derek Palmar; Yorkshire Television, Leeds

PALMER *see also*: Prior-Palmer

PALMER, 4 Baron (UK 1933), of Reading, Co Berks; Sir Adrian Bailie Nottage Palmer; 4 Bt (UK 1916); s of Hon Sir Gordon William Nottage Palmer, KCVO, OBE, TD (d 1989), and Lorna Eveline Hope, DL, *née* Bailie; suc uncle, 3 Baron Palmer 1990; *b* 8 Oct 1951; *Educ* Eton, Univ of Edinburgh; *m* 7 May 1977, Cornelia Dorothy Katharine, da of Rohan Nicholas Wadham, DFC, of The Dog Kennel, Exning, nr Newmarket; 2 s (Hon Hugo Bailie Rohan b 1980, Hon George Gordon Nottage b 1985), 1 da (Hon Edwina Laura Marguerite b 1982); *Heir* s, Hon Hugo Bailie Rohan Palmer b 1980; *Career* mangr Assoc Biscuits Belgium 1974-77; farmer; sec Royal Caledonian Hunt 1989-; memb: cncl Historic Houses Assoc for Scotland 1980-, cncl Historic Houses Assoc 1981-, cncl Scottish Landowners Fedn 1987-; Scottish rep European Landowning Orgn 1986-, memb Queen's Body Guard for Scotland (Royal Company of Archers); *Recreations* hunting, shooting, tennis, gardening; *Clubs* New (Edinburgh), MCC; *Style—* The Rt Hon Lord Palmer; Manderston, Duns, Berwickshire TD11 3PP (☎ 0361 83450, fax 0361 82010)

PALMER, Andrew Eustace; CMG (1987), CVO (1981); s of Lt-Col Rodney H Palmer, MC (d 1987), and Frances Pauline Ainsworth *née* Gordon-Duff; gf and other ancestors, chm of Huntley & Palmer's Biscuits Reading; *b* 30 Sept 1937; *Educ* Winchester, Pembroke Coll Cambridge (MA); *m* 28 July 1962, Davina Cecil, da of Sir Roderick Barclay, GCVO, KCMG, of Gt White End, Latimer, Bucks; 2 s (Rodney b 1963, Michael b 1977), 1 da (Juliet b 1965); *Career* Nat Serv 2 Lt The Rifle Bde 1956-58; HM Foreign Serv later Dip Serv 1961-; American Dept FO 1962-63, comm sec La Paz 1963-65, second sec Ottawa 1965-67, Treasy Centre for Admin Studies 1967-68; Central Dept FO, later Southern Euro Dept FCO 1968-72, first sec (press and information) Paris 1972-76, asst head of Def Dept FCO 1976-77; cnsllr Royal Coll of Def Studies Course 1978, head of chancery and consul-gen Oslo 1979-82, head Falkland Islands Dept FCO 1982-85, fell Harvard Center for Int Affrs 1985-86, HM ambass to Cuba 1986-88, seconded to Royal Household as private sec to TRH The Duke and Duchess of Kent 1988-90; *Recreations* photography, fishing, following most sports; *Clubs* Brooks's, MCC, Vanderbilt Tennis; *Style*— Andrew Palmer, Esq, CMG, CVO; c/o Foreign & Commonwealth Office, London SW1A 2AH

PALMER, Lady Anne Sophia; *née* Walpole; da of 5 and last Earl of Orford (d 1931; fifth in descent from bro of Sir Robert Walpole, the 1 PM & 1 Earl of Orford of 1 cr, and 1 cous four times removed of the litterateur Horace Walpole, 4 and last Earl of Orford of the 1 cr); *b* 11 Dec 1919; *m* 1, 1939, Col Eric Palmer, CBE, TD, DL (d 1980); 2 s; m 2, 1990, Robert James Berry, of Gisborne, New Zealand; *Career* horticulturist, awarded Victoria Medal of Honour the highest award conferred by RHS; hon fell RHS 1988; Hon DSc Univ of Exeter 1990; *Style*— The Lady Anne Palmer; Rosemoor, Great Torrington, Devon EX38 7EG

PALMER, Anthony Wheeler; QC (1979); s of late Philip Palmer; *b* 30 Dec 1936; *Educ* Wrekin Coll Salop; *m* Jacqueline, da of late Reginald Fortnum, of Taunton; 1 s, 2 da; *Career* barr Gray's Inn 1962, rec Crown Ct 1980-; *Style*— Anthony Palmer, Esq, QC; 17 Warwick Ave, Coventry CV5 6DJ (☎ 0203 75340)

PALMER, Arthur Montague Frank; s of Frank Palmer (d 1965), of Northam, Devon, and Emily Palmer (d 1966); *b* 4 Aug 1912; *Educ* Ashford GS, Brunel Tech Coll (now Brunel Univ); *m* 1939, Dr Marion Ethel Frances Woollaston, da of Frank Woollaston, of Chiswick; 2 da; *Career* chartered engr and chartered fuel technologist; MP (Lab) Wimbledon 1945-50; MP (Lab and Co-Op): Cleveland Oct 1952-Sept 1959, Bristol Central 1964-74, Bristol N E 1974-83; did not contest Gen Election 1983; front bench oppn spokesman on energy 1957-59, chm Co-op Parly Gp 1970, vice chm Select Ctee on Energy 1979-; chm: Select Ctee Science and Technol 1966-70 and 1974-79, Parly and Scientific Ctee 1965-68; memb Brentford & Chiswick Cncl 1937-45, editor Electrical Power Engineer 1945-72, chm Red Rose Gp 1982-83 (gp of Lab MPs formed to maintain party commitment to EEC), vice chm Lab Movement in Europe 1983-90; Def Medal, Queen's Coronation Medal; CEng, FIEE, FInstE; *Books* Future of Electricity Supply (1944), Modern Norway (1949), Law and the Power Engineer (1961), Nuclear Power, the Reason Why (1983), Energy Policy in the Community (1985); *Recreations* walking, gardening, conversation; *Clubs* Athenaeum; *Style*— Arthur Palmer, Esq; Manton Thatch, Manton, Marlborough, Wilts SN8 4HR (☎ 0672 513313)

PALMER, Dr Bernard Harold Michael; OBE (1989); s of late Christopher Harold Palmer; *b* 8 Sept 1929; *Educ* St Edmund's Sch Hindhead, Eton, King's Coll Cambridge (BA, MA); *m* 1954, Jane Margaret, da of late E L Skinner; 1 s, 1 da; *Career* ed of the Church Times 1968-89; DLitt Lambeth 1988; *Recreations* cycling, penmanship; *Clubs* Royal Cwlth Soc; *Style*— Dr Bernard Palmer, OBE; Three Corners, 15 East Hill, Charminster, Dorchester, Dorset DT2 9QL (☎ 0305 260948)

PALMER, Bernard Victor; s of Archibald Richmond Palmer, and Phyllis Edith Louise, *née* Beart; *b* 10 Aug 1944; *Educ* Bedford Sch, Downing Coll Cambridge (MA, MB MChir); *m* 5 Jan 1973, (Kathleen) Rosemary, da of Robin Knight (d 1974), of E Africa; 2 s (Robert b 5 Dec 1976, Andrew b 19 March 1984), 2 da (Sharon b 24 Oct 1978, Rachel b 14 March 1982); *Career* house offr posts London Hosp 1969-70, jr surgical registrar St Bart's Hosp 1971-72, surgical registrar Whipps Cross Hosp 1973-75, sr surgical registrar Royal Marsden and Kings Coll Hosps 1976-83, conslt surgn Lister Hosp Stevenage 1983-; res and pubns on: cosmetic treatment of breast cancer by subcutaneous mastectomy and silastic implants, treatment of haemorrhoids by the banding haemorrhoidectomy technique; memb: Br Assoc of Surgical Oncology, Christian Med Fellowship; co-ordinator of On-Line 89 (Christian outreach in Letchworth) 1989; MRCP 1971, FRCS 1973; *Books* Medicine and the Bible (ed, 1986); *Recreations* friends, tennis, squash, showing relevance of Jesus Christ to those disillusioned by the Church; *Style*— Bernard Palmer, Esq; Southacre, 39 Pasture Rd, Letchworth, Herts SG6 3LR (☎ 0462 683064); Lister Hospital, Stevenage, Herts (☎ 0438 314333); Pinehill Hospital, Benslow Lane, Hitchin, Herts (☎ 0462 422822)

PALMER, Hon Lady (Catherine Elizabeth); *née* Tennant; da of late 2 Baron Glenconner by his 2 w; *b* 10 Nov 1947; *m* 1976, Sir Mark Palmer, 5 Bt; 1 da; *Style*— The Hon Lady Palmer; Mill Hill Farm, Sherborne, Northleach, Glos (☎ 045 14 395); 15 Bramerton St, London SW3

PALMER, Charles Stuart William; OBE (1973); s of Charles Edward Palmer, and Emma Byrne; *b* 15 April 1930; *Educ* Drayton Manor Co Sch; *Career* chm Br Olympic Assoc 1983-88 (vice chm 1977-83); represented GB in judo 1949-59, studied judo in Japan 1951-55, 1 Dan 1948, 4 Dan 1955, 8 Dan 1980; pres Int Judo Fedn 1965-79 (hon life pres 1979-), sec gen Gen Assoc of Int Sports Fedns 1975-84, pres Br Judo Assoc 1977 (chm 1962-85), govr Sports Aid Fndn 1979-, memb GB Sports Cncl 1983-, chm Games and Sports Div CCPR, memb IOC Programme Cmmn; Olympic Order 1980, Gold medal Euro Judo Union 1982; memb Cncl Royal Albert Hall; Key of City of Taipei 1974, Key of City of Seoul 1981; *Recreations* judo, skiing, music, languages; *Style*— Charles Palmer, Esq, OBE; 4 Hollywood Road, London SW10 9HY (☎ 071 352 6238, fax 071 386 7766)

PALMER, Charles William; s of Charles James Strachan Palmer (d 1961), of Estate Factor, Inverlochy, Castle Estate, Fort William, and Ida Patricia, *née* Miskimmin; *b* 17 Dec 1945; *Educ* Lochaber HS, Inverness Royal Acad, Univ of Edinburgh (UB); *m* 20 Dec 1969, Rosemary, da of Lt-Col Henry Walter Holt (d 1976), of Grantley Rd, Boscombe, Hants; 1 s (Richard James b 1971), 2 da (Lavinia Jayne b 1973, Emily Sarah b 1974); *Career* ptnr Allan McDougall & Co, slr Supreme Ct Edinburgh 1975; sheriff N Strathclyde at Dunoon and Dumbarton Sheriff Cts 1986; memb Law Soc of Scotland; *Recreations* hill walking, music, photography; *Style*— Charles Palmer, Esq; 6 Great Stuart St, Edinburgh; Craigeniver, Strachur SRG 7CC (☎ 031 225 4962); Dumbarton Sheriff Ct (☎ 0389 63266); Dunoon Sheriff Ct (☎ 0369 4166)

PALMER, Clifford Frederick; s of Charles Norman Palmer (d 1975), and Nora, *née* Drury; *b* 7 Sept 1948; *Educ* Henley-in-Arden HS; *m* 1, 1 June 1974 (m dis 1984), Janet Mary, da of Frank Wilson, of Kettering, Northants; m 2, 22 Sept 1984, Jill Mary, da of Maurice James Steward (d 1980), of Dennington, Suffolk; 4 da (Charlotte b 1984, Victoria b 1985, Kathryn b 1987, Sarah b 1987); *Career* National Farmers, Union Mutual Insurance Society Stratford-upon-Avon 1965-69, SA Meacock & Co at Lloyds 1969-79, dir Clifford Palmer Underwritng Agencies Ltd at Lloyds 1979- (exec dir 1980); exec dir: Ashley Palmer Holdings 1984, Martin Ashley Underwriting Agencies Ltd 1984, Ashley Palmer & Hathaway Ltd 1987; FCII; *Clubs* City of London; *Style*— Clifford Palmer, Esq; Croft Point, Links Rd, Bramley, Guildford, Surrey; 9/13 Fenchurch Buildings, London EC3M 5HR (☎ 071 488 0103, fax 071 481 4995)

PALMER, David Erroll Prior; s of Brig Sir Otho Prior-Palmer DSO, and Mrs Sheila Mary Peers, *née* Weller-Poley; *b* 20 Feb 1941; *Educ* Eton, Christ Church Oxford (MA); *m* 1974, Elizabeth Helen, da of Tom Young, of Chichester; 2 s (James b 1975, Alexander b 1977), 1 da (Marina b 1978); *Career* gen mangr and main bd dir Financial Times (features 1964-67, NY corr 1967-70, mgmnt ed 1970-72, news ed 1972-77, Frankfurt Project 1977-79, foreign ed 1979-80, dep ed 1981-83), chm St Clements Press; first Br finisher (third in class) 1976 Observer Transatlantic Race; *Books* The Atlantic Challenge (1977); *Recreations* sailing (National Swallow 'Archon'); *Clubs* Itchenor Sailing, Oxford and Cambridge Sailing; *Style*— David Palmer Esq; 45 Lancaster Ave, London SE27 9EL (☎ 081 670 0585); Dairy Cottage, W Broyle, Chichester (☎ 0243 789552); Bracken House, 10 Cannon St, EC4P 4BY (☎ 071 248 8000)

PALMER, David Vereker; s of Brig Julian William Palmer (d 1977), and Lena Elizabeth, *née* Vereker (d 1941); *b* 9 Dec 1926; *Educ* Stowe; *m* 10 June 1950, Mildred (Millie), da of Edward Asbury O'Neal (d 1977), of Alabama, USA; 3 da (Melanie (Mrs Rendall) b 29 June 1951, Alice (Mrs Parsons) b 12 May 1959, Katherine b 21 Feb 1962); *Career* Capt Life Gds 1944-49, served in Europe and ME; mangr NY office Edward Lumley & Sons 1953-59 (joined 1949); Willis Faber & Dumas Ltd: joined 1959, dir 1961, ptnr 1965, dep chm 1972, chief exec 1978, chm 1982, ret 1988; cmmr Royal Hosp Chelsea 1980-88, pres Insur Inst of London 1985-86, chm Br Insur and Investmt Brokers Assoc 1987-89; Freeman City of London 1980, memb Worshipful Co of Insurers (Master 1982); ACII 1950, memb Lloyd's 1953; *Recreations* farming, shooting; *Clubs* City of London, Cavalry and Guards'; *Style*— David Palmer Esq; Burrow Farm, Hambleden, nr Henley-on-Thames, Oxon RG9 6LT (☎ 0491 571256); 18 Whaddon House, William Mews, London SW1X 9HG (☎ 071 235 7900)

PALMER, Felicity Joan; *b* 6 April 1944; *Educ* Erith GS, Guildhall Sch of Music and Drama (AGSM, FGSM), Hochschule für Musik Munich; *Career* mezzo-soprano; Kathleen Ferrier Meml Prize 1970; major appearances at concerts in: Britain, America, Belgium, France, Germany, Italy, Spain, Poland, Czechoslovakia, Russia; operatic appearances: London and throughout England, Paris, Bordeaux, Houston USA, Chicago USA, NY USA, Bern, Zürich, Frankfurt, Hanover, Vienna; recordings with maj record cos incl recital records and two Victorian ballad records; *Style*— Miss Felicity Palmer; 27 Fielding Rd, London W4 1HP

PALMER, Geoffrey; *b* 4 June 1927; *Educ* Highgate Sch; *Career* actor; theatre performances incl: Difference of Opinion (Garrick), West of Suez (Royal Ct), Savages (Royal Ct), On Approval (Haymarket), Eden End (National), Private Lives (Globe), St Joan (Old Vic), Tishoo (Wyndhams), Kafka's Dick (Royal Ct), Piano (National); TV incl: The Fall and Rise of Reginald Perrin, Butterflies, The Insurance Man, The Last Song, Absurd Person Singular, Fairly Secret Army, Seasons Greetings; films incl: O Lucky Man, The Honorary Consul, Clockwise, A Zed and Two Noughts, A Fish Called Wanda; *Recreations* fly fishing; *Clubs* Garrick; *Style*— Geoffrey Palmer, Esq

PALMER, Sir Geoffrey Christopher John; 12 Bt (E 1660); s of Lt-Col Sir Geoffrey Frederick Neill Palmer, 11 Bt (d 1951); *b* 30 June 1936; *Educ* Eton; *m* 1957, Clarissa Mary, da of Stephen Villiers-Smith; 4 da; *Heir* bro, Jeremy Charles Palmer; *Career* is a patron of two livings; *Style*— Sir Geoffrey Palmer, Bt; Carlton Curlieu Hall, Leicestershire (☎ 053 759 2656)

PALMER, Cdr Geoffrey Inderwick; s of John Henry Palmer (d 1954), of Rustington, Sussex, and Louisa, *née* Inderwick (d 1964); *b* 2 Jan 1913; *Educ* St Paul's; *m* 3 April 1943, Diana Millicent (d 1985), da of Arthur Cecil Fitzroy Plantagenet Somerset (d 1955), of Castle Goring, Worthing; 3 da (Juliet Elizabeth b 1945, Anthea Somerset b 1947, Catherine Annabella Inderwick b 1952); *Career* joined RN 1930; various sea and shore appts incl: Br mil mission to USSR 1941-43, sec to Adm Sir Geoffrey Miles 1949-57, ret as Cdr 1961; underwriting memb Lloyds, former farmer, currently a picture dealer; *Recreations* shooting, the arts; *Clubs* MCC; *Style*— Cdr Geoffrey Palmer; The Treasurer's House, Martock, Somerset (☎ 0935 823 288)

PALMER, Gerald Marley; s of Percy William Ernest Palmer (d 1932), of Bulawayo, S Rhodesia, and Esther, *née* Marley (d 1974); *b* 20 Jan 1911; *Educ* Milton HS S Rhodesia, Univ of London (BSc); *m* 6 May 1939, Diana Fleetwood, da of Cornelius Percy Varley (d 1936), of Enfield; 1 da (Celia Fleetwood); *Career* Nat Serv Corpl Home Gd; apprenticeship Scammell Lorries Ltd 1927-38, Morris Motors Ltd 1938-42 (designed Oxford vaporiser anaesthetic apparatus), Jowett Cars Ltd (designed Jowett Javelin car) 1942-49, tech dir Morris Motors 1949-55, asst chief engr Vauxhall Motors Ltd 1955-72, dir F J Payne (Manufacturing) Ltd (designing equipment for disabled people) 1972-88; pres and chm Local Cons Assoc; CEng, FIMechE; *Recreations* sailing, vintage car racing; *Style*— Gerald Palmer, Esq; Orchard House, 4 Tree Lane, Iffley, Oxford (☎ 0865 779222)

PALMER, Dr Godfrey Henry Oliver (Geoff); s of Aubrey George Palmer (d 1985), of Jamaica and NY, and Ivy Georgina, *née* Larmond; *b* 9 April 1940; *Educ* Highbury Co Sch London, Univ of Leicester (BSc), Univ of Edinburgh (PhD), Heriot Watt Univ (DSc); *m* 20 June 1969, (Margaret) Ann; 3 c; *Career* sr scientist Brewing Res Fndn 1968, inventor barley abrasion process for accelerating malt prodn in indust 1969, cereal conslt to various cos 1979, reader Heriot Watt Univ 1988; convenor Church of Scotland Educn Ctee (dealing with multicultural educn) 1988-90, chm Scottish section Inst of Brewing 1990; fell Inst of Brewing 1985; memb Edinburgh Lothian Community Relations Ctee 1989, chm E Mid Lothian Boarders of Scot Ctee (involved in multicultural approach to racial incidence) 1990; *Books* Cereal Science and Technology (1989), Contrib Reader Digest: Complete Guide to Cooking (1989); *Recreations* reading, charity work, television; *Clubs* Staff, Univ of Edinburgh; *Style*— Dr Geoff Palmer; 23 Waulkmill Drive, Penicuik, Mid Lothian, Scotland (☎ 0968 75148); Department of Biological Sciences, International Centre for Brewing & Distilling, Heriot Watt Univ, Riccarton, Edinburgh, Scotland (☎ 031 449 5111)

PALMER, Hon Henry William; s of Viscount Wolmer (s of 3 Earl of Selborne (ka 1942), and Priscilla (*see Baron Newton*), and bro of 4 Earl); *b* 12 July 1941; *Educ* Eton, Christ Church Oxford (MA); *m* 1968, Minette, da of Sir Patrick William Donner, of Hurstbourne Park, Whitchurch, Hants; 3 s, 1 da; *Career* Ford Motor Co 1963-66, Associated Industrial Consultants 1966-68, md The Centre for Interfirm Comparison 1985- (joined 1968, dep dir 1975); *Style*— The Hon Henry Palmer; Burhunt Farm, Selborne, Alton, Hants GU34 3LP (☎ 042050 209)

PALMER, Jeremy Charles; s of Lt-Col Sir Geoffrey Frederick Neill Palmer, 11 Bt (d 1951), and hp of bro, Sir Geoffrey Palmer, 12 Bt; *b* 16 May 1939; *Educ* Eton, Univ of Tours; *m* 24 July 1968, Antonia, da of late Astley Dutton; 2 s; *Career* dir Laytons Wine Co; *Recreations* shooting, tennis; *Clubs* Queen's, Pratts; *Style*— Jeremy Palmer, Esq; Manor House, Stoke Abbott, Beaminster, Dorset; Laytons, 20 Midland Rd, London NW1 (☎ 071 388 5081)

PALMER, John; *Career* euro ed The Guardian 1975- (formerly ed, chief econ ldr writer, industl ed), secondment: dir Gtr London Enterprise Bd 1983-86, memb Bd London Tport 1983-86; experienced radio tv broadcaster; *Style*— John Palmer, Esq; c/o International Press Centre, Box 12, No1 Boulevard Charlemagne, 1041 Brussels, Belgium (☎ 010 322 230 6879)

PALMER, John; CB; s of William Nathaniel Palmer (d 1984), and Grace Dorothy May, *née* Procter (d 1974); *b* 13 Nov 1928; *Educ* Heath GS Halifax, Queens Coll Oxford (MA); *m* 17 Dec 1958, Lyliane Anne Marthe, da of Rene Jeanjean (d 1973); 2 da (Catherine b 1959, Sophie b 1962); *Career* joined admin class Home Civil Serv 1952, Cabinet Office 1963-65, asst sec 1965, under sec DOE 1971, ret as dep sec Dept of Tport 1989 (joined 1976-), md Channel Tunnel BR 1990; Freeman City of London 1985, memb Worshipful Co of Carmen 1985; FCIT; *Clubs* United Oxford & Cambridge Univ; *Style*— John Palmer, Esq, CB

PALMER, Sir John Chance; s of Ernest Clephan Palmer (d 1954), and Claudine Pattie Sapey; *b* 21 March 1920; *Educ* St Paul's, St Edmund Hall Oxford (MA); *m* 1945, Mary Winifred, da of Arthur Sidney Ellyatt, OBE (d 1973); 4 s; *Career* WWII RNVR 1939-46, serv Atlantic and Med; slr 1948; conslt Bevan Ashford (Tiverton, Exeter, Crediton, Bristol and Swindon); memb Cncl Law Soc of England and Wales 1963-83 (pres 1978-79); govr Coll of Law 1965-83; pres: Devon and Exeter Law Soc 1972, S Western Law Soc 1973; chm: Govrs Blundells Sch, Cncl Exeter Univ, Tstees Int Technological Univ, Tstees London Sailing Project; memb: Criminal Injuries Compensation Bd 1981-, SW Region Mental Health Tbnl 1983-; DL Devon 1984, Vice Lord-Lt 1991-; hon memb: American Bar Assoc, Canadian Bar Assoc, Florida Defence Lawyers Assoc; Hon LLD Exeter 1980; kt 1979; *Clubs* Athenaeum, Royal Yacht Squadron; *Style—* Sir John Palmer; Hensleigh, Tiverton, Devon EX16 5NJ (☎ 0884 252959); Sunnycote, Riverside, Shaldon, Devon (☎ 0626 87 2350) The Crannach Enochdhu, nr Blairgowrie, Perthshire

PALMER, (Anthony) John Cleeves; s of A A J Palmer, JP (d 1986), of Wychside, Burton Rd, Bridport, Dorset, and Nora Evelyn Flower, *née* Symonds; *b* 26 Sept 1951; *Educ* Grenville Sch; *m* 29 April 1989, Lucille Tonia, da of Antony Curties Jarrold, of Old Hall, Caistor St Edmund, Norwich, Norfolk; *Career* chm and md Palmers Brewery Bridport 1986-; *Recreations* cricket, tennis, golf, shooting, fishing, skiing; *Style—* John Palmer, Esq; J C & R H Palmer Ltd, Old Brewery, Bridport, Dorset (☎ 0308 22396, fax 0308 421149, car 0836 299347)

PALMER, Sir John Edward Somerset; 8 Bt (GB 1791); s of Sir John Palmer, 7 Bt, DL (d 1963); *b* 27 Oct 1926; *Educ* Canford, Pembroke Coll Cambridge, Univ of Durham; *m* 1956, Dione Catharine, da of Charles Duncan Skinner; 1 s, 1 da; *Heir* s, Robert John Hudson Palmer; *Career* Lt RA serv India; Colonial Agric Serv N Nigeria 1952-61; sr exec R A Lister & Co Ltd Dursley Glos 1962-63, min Overseas Devpt 1964-68, ind conslt 1969-79, dir W S Atkins Agriculture 1979-88; *Recreations* sailing, fishing, shooting; *Style—* Sir John Palmer, Bt; Gayton House, Gayton, Northampton (☎ 0604 858336)

PALMER, Prof John Michael; s of Henry William Palmer (d 1974), and Hilda May, *née* Ball (d 1955); *b* 24 April 1936; *Educ* Yeovil GS, Univ of Reading (BSc), Univ of Oxford (DPhil); *m* 29 July 1959, Irene Alice, da of Sidney Arthur Ricketts, of 16 Cromwell Rd, Yeovil, Somerset; 1 s (Stephen John b 1969), 2 da (Alison Hilary b 1965, Helen Melinda b 1967); *Career* NATO res fell Univ of California 1962-64, lectr in plant physiology KCL 1964-71, prof of plant biochemistry Imp Coll London 1985- (reader in enzymology 1971-85); warden Kent Tst for Nature Conservation; memb: Cncl S London Botanical Inst, Br Mycological Soc, Soc for Experimental Biology, Micrological Soc 1984; *Books* The Physiology and Biochemistry of Plant Respiration (1984); *Recreations* photography, natural history, music; *Clubs* Orpington Field, Kent Field; *Style—* Prof John Palmer

PALMER, John William; s of Leonard James Palmer, and Margery Edith, *née* Skinner; *b* 30 June 1950; *Educ* Dr Mogan's GS Bridgwater Somerset, UEA (BA); *m* 31 Aug 1974, Patricia Marion, da of Capt Arthur J Howard (d 1983), of Cambridge; 1 da (Siobhan b 15 Jan 1985); *Career* journalist; S Wales Argus Newport Gwent 1971-73, Coventry Evening Telegraph 1973-77; chief press offr Southern Television Southampton 1978-79 (press offr 1977-78); head of pres and publicity: TVS 1980, Central TV Nottingham 1981-84, Central TV Birmingham 1984-87; chief press and publicity offr Central TV 1987-; organiser of Eileen Anderson/Central TV Annual Drama award, govr Merrivale Sch Nottingham, memb Road Safety Ctee; *Recreations* soccer, rugby, cricket, theatre, films; *Style—* John Palmer, Esq; Central Independent Television, Broad St, Birmingham B1 2JP (☎ 021 643 9898, fax 021 643 9898 ext 4766)

PALMER, Dr Keith Francis; s of Frank Palmer (d 1987), of Cardiff, and Gwenda Evelyn, *née* Merrick; *b* 26 July 1947; *Educ* Howardian HS Cardiff, Univ of Birmingham (BSc, PhD), Univ of Cambridge (Dip Devpt Econ); *m* 10 Aug 1974, Penelope Ann, *née* McDonagh; 4 da (Alexandra b 1977, Georgia b 1979, Katherine b 1981, Megan b 1982); *Career* NATO post doctoral res fell Lamont Geophysical Observatory NY 1971-73, first asst sec fin Miny Papua New Guinea 1974-78, dir corp fin N M Rothschild & Sons Ltd 1984-; memb RIIA 1984, FGS 1987; *Recreations* geology, gemmology, music; *Clubs* IOD; *Style—* Dr Keith Palmer; New Court, St Swithins La, London, EC4 (☎ 071 280 5000)

PALMER, Kenneth Ernest (Ken); s of Harry Palmer, of 62 Warwick Rd, Taunton, Somerset, and Celia, *née* Rapps (d 1988); *b* 22 April 1937; *Educ* South Broom Secdy Modern Sch Devizes; *m* 1962, Joy Valerie, *née* Gilbert; 1 s (Gary b 1 Nov 1965); *Career* first-class cricket umpire; appointed 1972, selected for int panel 1978-, umpired 18 Test matches 1978-89; player Somerset CCC 1955-69: awarded county cup 1958, testimonial 1968, 314 appearances, 7761 runs, 866 wickets; 1 Test cap England v SA 1964-65; coached in SA 1964-65, currently coaches youth teams; winner cricketers' double Somerset 1961, club record 102 not out batting at number eight, single wicket knockout champion Scarborough 1963; former semi-professional footballer: 2 seasons Bristol City, 1 season Exeter City; *Recreations* playing squash, coaching sports (cricket, squash, football); *Style—* Ken Palmer, Esq; Manor Green House, Curry Rivel, Langport, Somerset TA10 0HE (☎ 0458 250900/251554)

PALMER, Lady Laura; *née* Elliot-Murray-Kynynmound; da of 6 Earl of Minto, MBE, *qvqv*; *b* 11 March 1956; *m* 23 Feb 1984, John Reginald David Palmer, yr s of William Alexander Palmer, of Bussockwood House, Newbury, Berks; 2 s; *Style—* The Lady Laura Palmer

PALMER, Malcolm John Frederick; *b* 22 Oct 1933; *Educ* Charterhouse, Queens' Coll Cambridge (MA); *m* 3 Nov 1962, Rachel M Phillips; 2 s (James b 10 Sept 1963, Stephen b 18 Jan 1965), 1 da (Melanie b 21 Feb 1968); *Career* Nat Serv 1952-54; articled Linklaters & Paines 1957-60, asst slr Rickerby & Mellersh Cheltenham 1960-62; Baker & McKenzie : asst slr London 1962-63, conslt Chicago 1963-65, ptnr London 1965-75, sr ptnr Hong Kong 1975-81, ptnr London 1981-, memb Int Exec Ctee and chm Professional Devpt Ctee 1983-85, admin ptnr and chm London Mgmnt Ctee 1987-, memb Int Professional Responsibility and Practice Ctee 1989-); memb Law Soc 1960; *Recreations* bridge, bowls, buying and occasionally reading, books; *Clubs* Reform, Hurlingham, RAC; *Style—* Malcolm Palmer; Baker & McKenzie, Inveresk House, Aldwych, London WC2B 4JP (☎ 071 242 6531)

PALMER, Sir (Charles) Mark; 5 Bt (UK 1886); s of Sir Anthony Frederick Mark Palmer, 4 Bt (ka 1941), and Lady (Henriette Alice) Abel Smith, *qv*; *b* 21 Nov 1941,posthumous; *Educ* Eton; *m* 1976, Hon Catherine Elizabeth Tennant, da of Baron Glenconner; 1 da; *Heir* kinsman, Charles Lionel Palmer; *Career* was a page of honour to HM 1956-59; *Style—* Sir Mark Palmer, Bt; Mill Hill Farm, Sherborne, Northleach, Glos (☎ 045 14 395)

PALMER, Maj-Gen Sir (Joseph) Michael; KCVO; s of late Lt-Col William Robert Palmer, DSO; *b* 17 Oct 1928; *Educ* Wellington, Sandhurst; *m* 1953, Jillean Monica Sherston; 2 s, 1 da; *Career* Def Servs Sec 1982-85; dir: RAC 1978-81, ACS Allied Forces Central Europe 1976-78; Col 14/20 King's Hussars 1981-, Hon Col Duke of Lancasters Own Yeo 1988-; dir Credit Lyonnais Construction Co, chm Copley Marshall & Co; Master Worshipful Co of Salters 1989-90; FBIM; *Recreations* riding, shooting, music, reading; *Clubs* Cavalry and Guards; *Style—* Maj-Gen Sir Michael Palmer, KCVO; c/o The Royal Bank of Scotland plc, Holt's Branch, Kirkland House, Whitehall, London SW1A 2EB

PALMER, Monroe Edward; OBE (1981); s of William Polikoff, of Westcliff, Essex, and Sybil, *née* Gladstein (d 1980); *b* 30 Nov 1938; *Educ* Orange Hill GS; *m* 21 Jan 1962, Susette Sandra, da of Jeanne Hall, of London; 2 s (John b 1963, Andrew b 1965), 1 da (Fiona b 1981); *Career* ptnr Wilson Green Gibbs; cnllr London Borough of Barnet (ldr SLD), treas Lib Pty 1977-83; FCA; *Recreations* politics, riding, fishing, reading; *Clubs* Nat Lib; *Style—* Monroe Palmer; 31 The Vale, London NW11 8SE (☎ 081 455 5140); 5 North End Rd, London NW11 7RJ (☎ 081 458 9281, fax 081 458 9381)

PALMER, Nigel Webb; OBE (1989), JP (1981); s of Capt Wilfrid Ernest Palmer, MBE (d 1962), of Tyndale, Preston Rd, Yeovil, Somerset, and Helen Margaret, of Lyndon House, The Park, Yeovil, Somerset; *b* 28 Jan 1930; *Educ* Bishops Stortford Coll, St Johns Coll Cambridge (MA), Nat Leathersellers Coll (DipLC); *m* 11 July 1953, Betty Loveday, da of Horace Alexander Bradley (d 1964), of Huntingfield Farm, Bradenham, Thetford, Norfolk; 1 s (Simon b 1958), 2 da (Jane b 1956, Clare b 1965); *Career* cmmnd RE 1948; dir Pittard Garnar plc 1963-, md C W Pittard and Co Ltd 1980-; pres Br Leather Confedn 1988-90, chm Br Leather Mfrs Res Assoc 1976-79, memb Wessex Water Authy 1973-79, govr Yeovil Coll 1989-; Liveryman Worshipful Co of Glovers' 1962, FBIM 1988; *Recreations* golf, swimming, music; *Clubs* Hawks; *Style—* Nigel Palmer, Esq, OBE, JP; Pittard Garnar plc, Sherborne Rd, Yeovil, Somerset BA21 5BA (☎ 0935 74321, fax 0935 21745, telex 46141)

PALMER, Hon Mrs (Patricia Margaret); *née* Feather; da of Baron Feather (Life Peer, d 1976), and Baroness Feather, *qv*; *b* 1934; *Educ* Green Sch Isleworth, French Inst London; *m* 1957, Stanley Lawrence Palmer; 1 s (James b 1966), 1 da (Gillian b 1962); *Recreations* music, travel; *Clubs* Harpenden Tangent; *Style—* The Hon Mrs Palmer; 24 Wheathampstead Rd, Harpenden, Herts

PALMER, Gen Sir (Charles) Patrick Ralph; KBE (1987, CBE 1982, OBE 1974); s of Charles Dudley Palmer (d 1965), and Catherine Anne, *née* Hughes-Buller (d 1981); *b* 29 April 1933; *Educ* Marlborough, RMA Sandhurst, Staff Coll Camberley, RCDS; *m* 1, 19 Dec 1960, Sonia (d 1965), da of Hardy Wigglesworth (d 1944); 1 s (Neil Patrick b 1962); m 2, 3 Sept 1966, Joanna, da of Col Peter Stanhope Baines (d 1975); 2 da (Iona Catherine b 1967, Alison Joanna b 1969); *Career* cmmnd Argyll & Sutherland Highlanders 1953; served 1 Bn: Br Guiana, Berlin, Suez Operation, Cyprus, Borneo, Singapore, Aden; reformed & cmd 1 Bn A & SH 1972-74, COS Hong Kong 1974-76, Cdr 7 Armoured Bde 1977-78, Cdr Br Mil Advsy & Trg Team Zimbabwe 1980-82, GOC NE Dist & Cdr 2 Inf Div 1982-84, Cmdt Staff Coll 1984-86, Mil Sec 1986-89, C in C Allied Forces Northern Europe 1989-, Col A&SH 1982-; CBIM 1988; *Recreations* travel, outdoor interests; *Clubs* Army and Navy; *Style—* Gen Sir Patrick Palmer, KBE; c/o Royal Bank of Scotland, Drummond St, Comrie PH6 2DW

PALMER, Philip Stuart; s of Archdale Stuart Palmer (d 1932), of 18 Stanford Ave, Brighton, and Martha Phebe, *née* Ashdown (d 1939), and ggs of John Horsley Palmer (govr Bank of England 1830-32); *b* 2 July 1906; *Educ* Cheltenham, Brighton Tech Coll; *m* 10 July 1931, Sybil Madeline Conway (d 1973), da of the late Reginald Henry Cox, of 49 Tivoli Cres, Brighton; 2 s (Christopher b 1935, Philip b 1939); *Career* Ceylon Engrs CO railway workshop gp, Capt 1942, Maj 1942 (demob); pupil Brighton Locomotive Works 1925-28, asst to works mangr Southern Railway; Ceylon Govt Railway: asst mechanical engr 1931-38, dep mechanical engr 1938-47, actg chief mechanical engr 1945-46; Freeman Fox & Partners: mechanical engr London 1948-68, sr railway engr 1969-71; City & Guilds of London Inst: memb of Cncl 1958-76, jt hon sec 1969-75; Soc of Sussex Downsmen: memb Cncl 1962-70, 1980-88, hon gen sec 1984-88; Freeman City of London 1927, Liveryman Worshipful Co of Mercers' 1927; CEng, FIMechE 1948; *Style—* Philip Palmer, Esq; 46 Berriedale Ave, Hove, East Sussex BN3 4JJ (☎ 0273 725 850)

PALMER, Hon Ralph Matthew; s and h of Baroness Lucas of Crudwell, and Lady Dingwall (in her own right), and Maj Hon Robert Jocelyn Palmer, MC; *b* 7 June 1951; *Educ* Eton, Balliol Coll Oxford; *m* 1978, Clarissa Marie, da of George Vivian Lockett, TD, of Stratford Hills, Stratford St Mary, Colchester; 1 s (b 1987), 1 da (Hannah Rachel Elise b 1984); *Style—* The Hon Ralph Palmer

PALMER, Richard; s of Geoffrey Harvey Palmer, of Sarisbury Green, Southampton, and Wendy, *née* Naylor; *b* 21 April 1961; *Educ* Price's GS Fareham, Univ of Bristol (BA); *Career* reporter; Westminster Press Trg Centre Hastings 1983, Ealing Gazette 1984-86, freelance reporter Sunday Times, Today and London Daily News 1986-88, home affairs corr The Sunday Times 1990- (environment corr 1988-90); commended Young Journalist of the Year Br Press Awards 1984; memb NUJ 1983; *Recreations* football, cricket, eating out; *Clubs* Espree (Gymnasium), Bearcat, Battersea All Stars FC; *Style—* Richard Palmer, Esq; 56 Windermere Rd, Ealing, London W5 4TD (☎ 081 840 2978); The Sunday Times, 1 Pennington St, London E1 9XW (☎ 071 782 5885)

PALMER, Richard John; JP (1961); s of Reginald Howard Reed Palmer (d 1970); *b* 5 Nov 1926; *Educ* Eton; *m* 1951, Sarah Faith Georgina, da of 1 Viscount Churchill, GCVO (d 1934); 3 s, 1 da; *Career* served Grenadier Guards Lt 1944-48; dir Assoc Biscuit Mfrs, chm Thames Valley Bdcasting plc, dep chm GWR Gp plc; pres Met Region YMCA; High Sheriff of Berks 1979-80; *Recreations* shooting, fishing; *Clubs* White's; *Style—* Richard Palmer Esq, JP; Queen Annes Mead, Swallowfield, Berks (☎ 0734 883264)

PALMER, His Hon Judge Robert Henry Stephen; s of Henry Alleyn Palmer (d 1965), and Maud Palmer, *née* Obbard (d 1973); *b* 13 Nov 1927; *Educ* Charterhouse, Univ Coll Oxford (MA); *m* 1955, Geraldine Elizabeth Anne, da of George Evan Evens (d 1950); 1 s (George), 2 da (Nicola, Katharine); *Career* barr 1950; dep chm Berks QS 1970, rec Crown Ct 1972-78, circuit judge 1978-, resident judge Harrow Crown Ct, pres Mental Health Review Tbnl; *Recreations* self sufficiency; *Style—* His Hon Judge Palmer

PALMER, Maj Hon Robert Jocelyn; MC, JP (Hants), DL (1982); s of late 3 Earl of Selborne by 1 w, Hon Grace, da of 1 Viscount Ridley, and Hon Mary Marjoribanks, da of 1 Baron Tweedmouth; *b* 1919; *Educ* Winchester, Balliol Coll Oxford; *m* 1950, Baroness Lucas of Crudwell (in her own right), *qv*; 2 s, 1 da; *Career* late Maj Coldstream Gds, Italy (despatches) 1939-45; *Style—* Major The Hon Robert Palmer, MC, JP, DL; The Old House, Wonston, Winchester, Hants

PALMER, Robert John Hudson; s and h of Sir John Edward Somerset Palmer, 8 Bt, and Dione Catherine Palmer, *née* Skinner, of Gayton, Northampton; *b* 20 Dec 1960; *Educ* St Edward's Sch Oxford, Grey Coll Univ of Durham (BA), Univ of Cambridge (BA); *m* 11 Aug 1990, Lucinda Margaret, da of Michael Barker, of London SW10, and Mrs Bryan Huffner, of London SW7; *Career* chartered surveyor; *Recreations* rowing, yachting, skiing; *Clubs* Lansdowne, Royal Ocean Racing; *Style—* Robert Palmer, Esq; Gayton House, Gayton, Northampton NN7 3EZ; 26 Sackville St, London W1X 2QL (☎ 071 734 8155)

PALMER, Dr Robert Leslie; s of Reginald John Freeman Palmer (d 1987), of Leamington Spa, and Marion May, *née* Sims (d 1988); *b* 15 March 1944; *Educ* Warwick Sch, St George's Med Sch, Univ of London (MB BS); *m* 19 July 1969, Mary Violet, da of Frank Carter, of Stamford Hill, London; 1 da (Rebecca 23 Oct 1971);

Career res worker and hon lectr St Georges hosp Med Sch Univ of London 1971-73, lectr in psychiatry St Marys Hosp Med Sch 1974-75, sr lectr in psychiatry Univ of Leicester 1975-; author of papers on psychiatry and psychosomatic med especially clinical eating disorders; examiner: for membership RCPsych, Univ of London final MB examination, Nat Univ of Singapore M Med Sci; MRCPsych 1972, FRCP 1984; *Books* Anorexia Nervosa: a guide for Sufferers and their families (1980 and 1989); *Recreations* reading, jogging, birdwatching; *Style*— Dr Robert Palmer; Univ Dept of Psychiatry, Leicester General Hospital, Gwendolen Rd, Leicester (☎ 0533 490490 ext 4707, fax 0533 737991)

PALMER, Rodney Hurry; s of Aubrey James Hurry Palmer, of Watton, Norfolk, and Phyllis Collenette, *née* Tier; *b* 3 July 1939; *Educ* Norwich Sch; *m* Jo Evelyn, 1 s (James Hurry b 29 Nov 1969), 1 da (Rebecca Elizabeth Collenette b 28 June 1967); *Career* dir Connell plc, chm Connell Wilson Holdings Ltd, chm and chief exec Connell Wilson London Ltd; Freeman City of London; FRICS 1974; *Style*— Rodney Palmer, Esq; Connell Wilson, Prince Frederick House, 37 Maddox St, London W1R 9LD (☎ 071 493 3675, fax 071 493 4693)

PALMER, Roger James Hume Dorney; s of Lt-Col Philip Dayrell Stewart Palmer (d 1979), of Dorney Ct, Bucks, and Aileen Frances, *née* Cook (d 1983); *b* 21 March 1947; *Educ* Eton, Gonville and Caius Coll Cambridge (BA); *m* 30 June 1979, Teresa Mary (Tsa), da of Maj-Gen Reginald Henry Whitworth, CB, CBE, *qv*; 1 s (Jonathan b 27 Oct 1989), 2 da (Susannah b 28 June 1984, Lara b 28 April 1986); *Career* ptnr Grieveson Grant & Co 1980-86; dir: Kleinwort Benson Limited 1986-, Kleinwort Benson Securities 1988-; Lloyds 1987; fndr: Palmer Milburn Beagles 1971, Berks & Bucks Draghounds 1974; treas Cambridge Sheep Soc; memb: London Stock Exchange 1980, Lloyds 1987; *Recreations* wolves, beagling, draghunting, wildlife photography; *Clubs* Groucho; *Style*— Roger Palmer, Esq; Kleinwort Benson, 20 Fenchurch St, London EC3

PALMER, Hon Mrs (Sarah Faith Georgina); *née* Spencer; da of 1 Viscount Churchill, GCVO (d 1934); *b* 5 June 1931; *m* 17 Dec 1951, Richard John Palmer, JP, yr s of Reginald Howard Reed Palmer, MC, of Hurst Grove, nr Reading, Berks; 3 s, 1 da; *Career* memb Berks CC 1981; *Style*— The Hon Mrs Palmer; Queen Anne's Mead, Swallowfield, Berks

PALMER, Hon Timothy John; s of Baroness Lucas, of Crudwell, and Dingwall; *b* 10 April 1953; *Educ* Eton, Balliol Coll Oxford; *m* 1984, (Adèle Cristina) Sophia, 4 da of Lt-Col Hon Henry Anthony Camillo Howard, CMG (d 1977); 1 s (Henry Jocelyn b 2 Jan 1987), 2 da (Nan Cristina b 9 Sept 1985, Isabella Spring b 8 Feb 1989); *Style*— The Hon Timothy Palmer; West Woodyates Manor, Salisbury, Wilts (☎ 0725 52321)

PALMER, Maj-Gen Tony Brian; CB (1984); s of Sidney Bernard Palmer, and Ann, *née* Watkins; *b* 5 Nov 1930; *Educ* Luton Technol Coll, Gen Motors Inst of Technol (USA); *m* 1953, Hazel Doris Robinson; 2 s; *Career* cmmnd REME 1954, held various cmd and staff appts 1954-74, head of tech intelligence (Army) 1974-76, dir Orgn and Trg 1977-79, Cdr Arborfield Garrison 1979-82, Col Cmdt REME 1985-, dir gen of electrical and mech engrg (Army) 1983-86 (conslt 1986); *Recreations* gardening, history, bird watching; *Clubs* Army and Navy; *Style*— Maj-Gen T B Palmer, CB; c/o Barclays Bank, 6 Market Place, Newbury, Berks

PALMER, (Ann) Veronica Margaret; MBE (1977); da of late Luke Murray, of Stone Hall, Trim, Co Meath, Ireland, and Mary, *née* Neville; *b* 20 March 1940; *Educ* Convent of Mercy Trim; *m* 1976, Barrie Palmer, s of Arthur Alfred Palmer; 3 da (Judith, Susan, Linda); *Career* student teacher 1958-61; WRAF: joined 1961, cmmnd Pilot Offr 1965, admin trg 1966, adj 114 MU Steamer Point Aden 1966-67, accountant RAF Hosp Ely 1967-68, schs liaison offr 1968-70, Flt Cdr RAF Coll Cranwell 1970-72, personnel servs RAF Cosford 1973, asst regnl Cdr (inspectorate of recruiting) 1974-76 (area Cdr 1977-78), ret as Sqdn Ldr 1978; Parly sec Brewers Soc 1981-88, dir gen Bus and Coach Cncl 1989-; Sash of Merit WRAF Offr Training; *Recreations* hill walking, skiing, reading, theatre, horse racing; *Clubs* RAF; *Style*— Mrs Veronica Palmer, MBE; Bus and Coach Council, Sardinia House, 52 Lincoln's Inn Fields, London WC2A 3LZ (☎ 071 831 7546, fax 071 242 0053)

PALMER, William Alexander; CBE (1983); s of Reginald Howard Reed Palmer, MC, DL (d 1970), of Hurst Grove, nr Reading, Berks, and Lena Florence, *née* Cobham (d 1981); *b* 21 June 1925; *Educ* Eton; *m* 1949, Cherry Ann, da of late Arthur Gibbs (d 1945), of Sheffield Terrace, London; 2 s, 2 da; *Career* serv Grenadier Gds 1943-47, Capt, serv NW Europe and Palestine; dir Huntley & Palmers Ltd 1951 (chm 1980-83), dir Huntley & Palmers Foods plc 1971-83, chm Huntley Boorne & Stevens Ltd until 1983; pres: Flour Milling and Baking Res Assoc 1971-84, Royal Warrant Holders Assoc 1976-77; chm Cake & Biscuit Alliance 1980-83; High Sheriff of Berks 1974-75; treas Univ of Reading 1982-; govr: Malvern Girls' Coll 1965-, King Edward's Sch Whitley; Berkshire cncllr Lambourn Valley; *Recreations* shooting, tennis, gardening; *Clubs* Cavalry and Guards'; *Style*— William Palmer, Esq, CBE; Bussock Wood, Snelsmore Common, nr Newbury, Berks RG16 9BT (☎ 0635 248203); Latheronwheel House, Caithness (☎ 05934 206)

PALUMBO, Baron (Life Peer UK 1991), of Walbrook in the City of London; Peter Garth Palumbo; s of late Rudolph Palumbo and Elsie Palumbo; *b* 20 July 1935; *Educ* Eton, Worcester Coll Oxford (MA); *m* 1, 1959, Denia (d 1986), da of late Maj Lionel Wigram; 1 s, 2 da; m 2, 1986, Hayat, er da of late Kamel Morowa; 1 da; *Career* govr LSE 1976-; chm: Arts Cncl of GB 1989-, Tate Gallery Fndn 1986- 87, Painshill Park Tst Appeal 1986-; tstee: Mies van der Rohe Archive 1977-, Tate Gallery 1978-85, Whitechapel Art Gallery Fndn 1981-87; tstee and hon treas Writers' and Scholars' Educnl Tst 1984-; Hon FRIBA; *Recreations* music, travel, gardening, reading; *Clubs* White's, Turf, City Livery; *Style*— The Rt Hon Lord Palumbo; Bagnor Manor, Bagnor, Newbury, Berks RG16 8AG (☎ 0635 40930)

PAMPLIN, Terence Michael; s of Leslie Cecil Pamplin, and Edith Mary, *née* Hayes; *b* 30 May 1941; *Educ* Middx Poly (BA), Hatfield Mgmnt Sch (DMS); *m* 15 March 1969, Elizabeth Ann, da of Richard Webb; 2 da (Iona b 1971, Kim b 1971); *Career* dir Arnold Dolmetsch Ltd 1973-77; head dept of music technol Sir John Cass Faculty City of London Poly 1983- (joined 1977); dir Early Musical Instrument Makers Assoc (former pres); fndr Nonsuch Guitar Soc (former chm); memb: Waverley BC, City & Guilds of London Inst; MIOA, MBIM, LRAM, LTCL, FIMIT (former pres); *Recreations* playing viol and baryton, viol consorts and baroque trio sonatas, hill walking; *Clubs* City Livery, Musician Livery; *Style*— Terence M Pamplin, Esq; Little Critchmere, Manor Crescent, Haslemere, Surrey GU27 1PB (☎ 0428 651158); Dept of Music Technology, Sir John Cass Faculty, City of London Polytechnic, 41 Commercial Rd, London E1 1LA (☎ 071 247 1953 ext 231)

PANAYI, Prof Gabriel Stavros; s of Stavros Panayi, of Cyprus, and Maria, *née* Tarsides; *b* 9 Nov 1940; *Educ* RGS Lancaster, Gonville and Caius Coll Cambridge, St Mary's Hosp Med Sch London (MD); *m* 11 March 1973, Alexandra, da of Alexander Jourrou; 2 s (Stavros b 5 July 1977, Alexander b 8 Feb 1982); *Career* house physician Queen Elizabeth Hosp Welwyn Garden City 1965-66, house surgn St Mary's Hosp London 1966, sr house offr Med Gen Hosp Nottingham 1966, sr house offr of pathology Central Middx Hosp London 1967, jr res fell MRC St Mary's and Kennedy Inst of Pheumatology London 1967-69, clinical res fell Northern Gen Hosp Edinburgh 1970-73; memb Arthritis and Rheumatism Cncl and prof of rheumatology Guy's 1980- (lectr 1973-76, ARC sr lectr and conslt 1976-80); former memb Exec Ctee: Section for Med Experimental Med and Therapeutics RSM, Heberden Soc; educnl rep Section for Clinical Immunology and Allergy RSM; memb: BSI, BSR, RSM, AASI, American Coll Rheumatology; FRCP; *Books* Annual Research Review of Rheumatoid Arthritis (1977-81), Immunopathogenesis of Rheumatoid Arthritis (1979), Essential Rheumatology for Nurses and Therapists (1980), Scientific Basis of Rheumatology (1982), Seronegative Spondyloarthropathies Clinics in Rheumatic Diseases (1985), Immunogenetics (1985); *Recreations* photography, painting, reading; *Style*— Prof Gabriel Panayi; Rheumatology Unit, Division of Medicine, United Medical and Dental Schools of Guy's and St Thomas' Hosps, St Thomas's St, London SE1 9RT (☎ 071 955 4394, fax 071 407 5134)

PANAYIDES, HE Tasos Christou; GCVO (1990); s of Christos Panayides, and Efrosini Papageorghiou; *b* 9 April 1934; *Educ* Paphos Gymnasium, Univ of London (Dip Ed), Univ of Indiana USA (MA, Dip Pub Admin); *m* 1969, Pandora, da of Georghios Constantinides, of Dramas No 8, Nicosia; 2 s (Alexandros b 1971, George b 1972), 1 da (Froso-Elena b 1976); *Career* teacher 1954-59; first sec to pres 1960-68, dir Pres Off 1969; ambass of Cyprus 1969-78 to: Fed Republic of Germany, Switzerland, Austria, Atomic Energy Orgn Vienna; high cmmr of Cyprus in UK (ambass to Sweden, Norway, Denmark, and Iceland) 1979-, sr high cmmr of Cyprus in UK 1988, doyen of Dip Corps 1988-; chm: Cwlth Fndn Grants Ctee 1986-87, Cwlth Fund for Tech Co-operation 1986-88, fin ctee Cwlth Secretariat 1988-; hon fell Ealing Coll Higher Educn; Freeman City of London 1984; Grand Cross with Star and Sash of the Fed Republic of Germany 1978, Grand Cross in Gold with Star and Sash of the Republic of Austria 1979, Golden Cross of the Archdiocese of Thyateira and Gt Britain, Grand Cross in Gold of the Patriarchate of Antioch; *Recreations* reading, history, swimming; *Style*— HE Tasos C Panayides, GCVO; 5 Cheyne Walk, London SW3 (☎ 071 351 3989); Cyprus High Commission, 93 Park Street, London W1Y 4ET (☎ 071 499 2810, fax 491 0691, telex 263 343)

PANDEY, HE Ishwari Raj; Hon GCVO (1986); s of Hemraj Panditgue (d 1953), Royal Preceptor (Raj Guru), of Kathmandu, Nepal, and Khaga Kumari, *née* Rgmi; ggggf resumed position of Royal Preceptor after helping the royal family to safety after the Kot episode, early 18th century; *b* 15 Aug 1934; *Educ* Patna Univ India (BA), Bombay Univ India (MA), Pittsburgh Univ (MPIA); *m* 3 March 1953, Gita, da of Maj-Gen Chet Shumsher Jung Bahadur Rana (d 1948); 3 s (Bidhan, Bigyan, Siddhant), 2 da (Kabita, Amita); *Career* under sec Govt of Nepal 1959-64 (dir under sec 1964-68), under sec to Min of Foreign Affrs 1968-72, dep head of mission Royal Nepalese Embassy London 1968-72, and NY 1972-74, first sec Nepalese Mission to UN 1972 and 1975, head of mission Teheran 1974-79, jt sec Min Foreign Affrs, Kathmandu 1979-80, Min Nepalese Embassy New Delhi 1980-83, Nepalese Ambass London 1983- (also accredited to Denmark, Finland, Norway, Iceland and Sweden); decorated with Prasiddha Probala Gorakha-Dakshina Nepal, Vikhyat Trishakti Patta, Long Service Medal, King of Bhutan Coronation Medal; *Books* Economic Impact of Tourist Industry (1965); *Recreations* reading, travel; *Clubs* Hurlingham, Travellers'; *Style*— HE The Nepalese Ambassador; 12A Kensington Palace Gardens, London W8 4QU (☎ 071 229 4536)

PANK, Maj-Gen (John) David Graham; CB (1988); s of Edward Graham Pank (d 1982), of Deddington, Oxon, and Margaret Sheelah, *née* Snowball (d 1989); *b* 2 May 1935; *Educ* Uppingham; *m* 27 July 1963, Julia Letitia, da of Col Michael Black Matheson, OBE, of Prosperous Farm, Hurstbourne Tarrant, Andover; 2 s (John William David b 1965, Edward Michael b 1970), 1 da (Victoria Katharine b 1964); *Career* cmmnd KSLI 1958, GSO3 ops HQ 99 Gurkha Bde 1965-66, Bde Maj HQ 24 Bde 1969-71, GSO1 Staff Coll 1973-74, CO 3 Bn LI 1974-76, asst dir def policy MOD 1977-79, cmd 33 Armd Bde 1979-81, RCDS 1982, Brig INf BAOR 1982-83, cmd LF 1983-85, dir gen personal servs (Army) 1985-88, Col LI 1987-90, dir of infantry 1988-90; chief exec Newbury Racecourse 1990-; pres: Army Cricket 1987-90, Combined Servs Cricket 1988; dir and chief exec Newbury Racecourse 1990-; *Recreations* racing, cricket, fishing; *Clubs* Army and Navy, IZ, Free Forestrs, Mount, Mounted Inf; *Style*— Maj-Gen David Pank, CB; c/o Royal Bank of Scotland, Holt's Whitehall Branch, Kirkland House, Whitehall, London SW1A 2EB

PANK, Edward Charles; s of Charles Clifford Pank (d 1974), of Norwich, and Marjorie Eira, *née* Bringloe (d 1988); *b* 5 June 1945; *Educ* Framlingham Coll, Trinity Hall Cambridge (MA), St Thomas's Hosp Univ of London (MB BS); *m* 17 Sept 1983, (Judith) Clare, da of Anthony Pethick Sommerville (d 1988) of Minchinhampton; *Career* admitted slr 1969; dir Slater Walker Ltd 1974-76, co slr and sec Exco Int plc 1987-; Liveryman Worshipful Co of Apothecaries 1986; MRCS, LRCP; *Style*— Edward Pank, Esq; Exco Int plc, 80 Cannon St, London EC4N 6LJ

PANK, Philip Durrell; s of Col P E D Pank, RAMC (d 1964), and Anne Roscoe Pank, *née* Thornely; *b* 3 Nov 1933; *Educ* Wellington, Architectural Assoc (Dip Arch); *m* 30 March 1962, Patricia Ann, da of Maj Ralph Maxwell Middleton, Black Watch (d 1967), of Harare, Zimbabwe; 2 s (William b 1965, Philip b 1970), 2 da (Sarah b 1963, Anna b 1970); *Career* Nat Serv, Northumberland Fus 1959-60; architect and painter in private practice 1965-; work incl: nurseries for Save the Children Fund, private houses for Harvey Unna (Highgate) and Harold Cooper (Hampstead Village), Pank Hart Architects, Thermal Power Station for NEKA Iran 1977, Sari apartments complex Iran 1977, Bauchi Technol Univ of Nigeria Masterplan 1981 (winner of limited competition), workshops and offices Mastmaker Court for Pirin Ltd (Isle of Dogs) 1987, shopping complex Barnstaple High Street for Bullsmoor 1987; *Recreations* drawing, nature; *Style*— Philip D Pank, Esq; 15 Torriano Cottages, London NW5 2TA (☎ 071 267 1199); Pank Hart Architects, 116-126 Grafton Road, London NW5 4BA (☎ 071 482 0400, fax 071 284 0539)

PANNELL, Donald Roy; s of Harold Thomas Pannell (d 1973), of Southernlea, Totteridge, London, and Gladys Louisa, *née* Price (d 1980); *b* 14 Jan 1926; *Educ* Highgate Sch, Hertford Coll Oxford; *m* 11 June 1949, Eileen Eunice, da of John Herbert Haynes (d 1969), of Ravenscroft Pk, Barnet, Herts; 1 da (Jacqueline b 31 Aug 1951); *Career* RAC 1944-47; dir A Pannell Ltd Group of Cos 1954-, chm Pannell (Properties) Ltd 1973 (dir 1960); fndr memb Nat Assoc of Waste Disposal Contractors (chm E Anglia Region 1975-85, life memb 1985), memb Nat Assoc of Warehouse Keepers (memb Nat Cncl); Freeman City of London 1967, Liveryman Worshipful Co of Makers of Playing Cards 1967; MCIT, MILDM, MInstD; *Recreations* golf; *Clubs* South Herts GC; *Style*— Donald Pannell, Esq; 42 Lyonsdown Ave, New Barnet, Herts EN5 1DX (☎ 081 440 1568); A Pannell Ltd, 779/781 Finchley Rd, London NW11 8DN (☎ 081 458 9458, fax 081 458 7344)

PANNELL, Gordon Dennis; s of Harold Thomas Pannell (d 1973), and Gladys Louisa, *née* Price (d 1980); *b* 12 Nov 1930; *Educ* Highgate Sch; *m* 28 July 1956, Stella Rose, Frederick Morris Roberts (d 1973); 2 s (Duncan b 1957, Malcolm b 1959), 1 da (Helen b 1963); *Career* Nat Serv REME; co dir (tport) and chm Pannell Group of Cos 1972 (dir 1951); fndr (former capt) Rd Haulage Assoc; Master Worshipful Co of Playing Card Makers 1989-90; memb Inst Tport, life memb IOD, Grand Lodge offr; *Recreations* golf, freemasonry; *Clubs* South Herts Golf, City Livery; *Style*— Gordon D Pannell, Esq; Meadow View, The Pastures, Totteridge, London N20 8AN (☎ 081 445 7580); A Pannell Ltd, 779/781 Finchley Rd, London NW11 8DN (☎ 081 458 9458)

PANNETT, Juliet Kathleen; da of Charles Somers (d 1958), and May Relph, *née* Brice (d 1960); *b* 15 July 1911; *Educ* Harvington Coll Ealing, Wistons Sch Brighton, Brighton Coll of Art; *m* 4 Oct 1938, Maj Maurice Richard Dalton Pannett (d 1980), s of Richard Dalton Pannett, of London; 1 s (Denis b 7 Sept 1939), 1 da (Liz b 31 May 1947); *Career* portrait painter; special artist to the Illustrated London News 1957-64; freelance to: The Times, Daily Telegraph, Radio Times; portraits incl: HM The Queen for Chartered Insurance Institute 1989, HM The Queen cmmnd by HRH The Duke of Edinburgh for Malta 25th anniversary of independence, HRH The Duke of York and HRH Prince Edward for HM The Queen, HRH Princess Marina, Lavinia Duchess of Norfolk for Arundel Castle; official artist Qantas Inaugural Jet Flights 1959 and 1964; London exhibitions: Royal Festival Hall 1957 and 1958, Cooling Gallery 1961, Fine Art Gallery 1969, Brotherton Gallery 1980, Royal Acad, Royal Soc of Portrait Painters, Royal Inst of Painters in Watercolour, Pastel Soc; exhibitions New York and Hong Kong, work in permanent collections: Oxford and Cambridge Colleges, Maudsley Hosp, St Mary's Hosp, Painter's Hall, Edinburgh Univ, Lincoln's Inn, 22 in Nat Portrait Gallery; Freeman: City of London 1960, Worshipful Co of Painter Stainers 1960; FRSA 1960; *Recreations* painting surgical operations; *Style*— Mrs Juliet Pannett; Pound House, Roundstone Lane, Angmering Village, Littlehampton, W Sussex BN16 4AL (☎ 0903 784446)

PANNONE, Rodger John; s of Cyril John Alfred Pannone (d 1982), and Violet Maud, *née* Weekes (d 1987); *b* 20 April 1943; *Educ* St Brendan's Coll Bristol, Manchester Coll of Law, London Coll of Law; *m* 13 Aug 1966, Patricia Jane, da of William Todd; 2 s (Mark b 24 Oct 1969, Richard b 7 Oct 1971), 1 da (Elizabeth b 19 July 1979); *Career* admitted slr 1969; slr Pannone Blackburn; ptnr: Pannone Napier (Britain's first disaster practice), Pannone de Backer; plaintiff's lawyer in the majority of disaster cases that have occurred in the last decade incl: Manchester Aircraft disaster 1985, Zeebrugge disaster 1987, Lockerbie Aircraft disaster 1988; memb: Lord Chllr's Advsy Ctee on Civil Justice 1985-88, Cncl Law Soc for England and Wales 1978-; past memb Supreme Ct Rule Ctee, chm Employment Relations Assocs Ltd; *Recreations* fell walking, wine and food; *Clubs* St James's (Manchester), Northern Lawn Tennis; *Style*— Rodger Pannone, Esq; 5 Darley Ave, West Didsbsury, Manchester (☎ 061 445 4342); Pannone Blackburn, Solicitors, 123 Deansgate, Manchester M3 2BU (☎ 061 832 3000, fax 061 834 2067)

PANTON, Catherine Rita; da of John Panton, MBE, of Larbert, Stirlingshire, Scotland, and Elizabeth Renwick, *née* Seaton; *b* 14 June 1955; *Educ* Larbert HS, Univ of Edinburgh (MA); *Career* golf player; Scot girls champion 1969, Br amateur champion 1976, Scot sportswomen of the year 1976, E of Scotland womens champion 1976; memb Br World Cup Amateur Team 1976, Vagliano Team 1977; winner: 1979 Womens Professional Golf Tour Order of Merit, 14 tournaments on the Womens Professional Golfers European Tour incl Portugese Open in 1986 and 1987 and S Womens Open in 1988; former Ctee memb Womens Professional golfers Assoc; memb: PGA, WPGET 1978; *Recreations* scrabble, circuit training, current affairs, cinema, listening to music, horse racing; *Clubs* Glenbervie Golf, Pitlochry Golf, Twickenham Park Golf, Silloth Golf, S Herts golf; *Style*— Miss Catherine Panton

PANTON, Dr Francis Harry; MBE (1948); s of George Emerson Panton; *b* 25 May 1923; *Educ* City Sch Lincoln, UCL, Univ of Nottingham; *m* 1952, Audrey Mary, *née* Lane (d 1989); 2 s; *Career* MOD: asst chief sci advsr (nuclear) 1969-76, dir Propellants Explosives and Rocket Motors Estab Waltham Abbey and Westcott 1976-80, head of Rocket Motor Exec 1976-80; dir Royal Armament R and D Estab Fort Halstead 1980-84; conslt: Cabinet Office, MOD 1985-; chm: Mgmnt Ctee Canterbury Archaeological Tst, Canterbury Visitor Info Centre Ltd; cncl memb Kent Archaeological Soc; *Recreations* local history, bridge; *Clubs* Reform; *Style*— Dr Francis Panton, MBE; Cantis House, 1 St Peter's Lane, Canterbury, Kent (☎ 0227 452902)

PANTON, John; MBE (1980); s of William Panton (d 1948), of Pitlochry, and Catherine, *née* Irvine (d 1964); *b* 9 Oct 1916; *Educ* Pitlochry HS; *m* 29 Dec 1947, Elizabeth Renwick, da of John Seaton; 2 da (Joan b 8 March 1951, Catherine, *qv* b 14 June 1955); *Career* Army 1939-46; former professional golfer; memb Pitlochry then Glenbervie Golf Club, semi finalist Br Boys' Championship; professional record: Scottish champion 8 times, Northern Open champion 7 times, Br PGA Matchplay champion 1956 (runner up 1968), World Sr Champion 1967, Br Sr champion 1967 and 1969, represented Scotland World Cup 13 times, memb Ryder Cup team 1951, 1953, 1961; Harry Vardon Trophy 1951, Golf Writers' Trophy 1967; hon professional Royal and Ancient Golf Club 1988-; *Style*— John Panton, Esq, MBE

PANTON, Steve; s of John Robert Garner, MR (d 1985), and Frances Mary, *née* Bottomley; *b* 2 Dec 1947; *Educ* City Sch Lincoln; *m* 14 Sept 1968, Sheena Ann Mary, da of Eric Charles Bowler, of Harmston, Lincs; 1 s (James b 1 Sept 1972), 1 da (Lucy b 19 Oct 1974); *Career* prodr BBC Radio Nottingham 1971-77, mangr BBC Radio Solent 1987- (news ed 1977-81, prog organiser 1981-87); *Recreations* country sports; *Style*— Steve Panton, Esq; Lindum, Chapel Lane, Redlynch, Salisbury, Wilts SP5 2HN (☎ 0725 21642); BBC Radio Solent, South Western House, Southampton SO9 4PT (☎ 0703 631311, fax 0703 332972, telex 47420)

PANTRIDGE, Prof James Francis; CBE (1978), MC (1942); s of Robert James Pantridge; *b* 3 Oct 1916; *Educ* Queen's Univ Belfast (MB ChB, BAO, MD, MRCP); *Career* served RAMC; res fell Univ of Michigan 1948-49, hon prof of cardiology Queen's Univ of Belfast 1971, dir of Regnl Med Cardiology Centre NI 1977-82; Hon DSc Univ of Ulster 1981, Hon Doctorate Open Univ 1981; FRCP 1962, FACC 1967, fell RCPI 1970; *Books* The Acute Coronary Attack (1975), An Unquiet Life (1989); *Recreations* fishing; *Clubs* Athenaeum; *Style*— Prof James Pantridge, CBE, MC

PANUFNIK, Sir Andrzej; s of Tomasz Panufnik (d 1951), of Warsaw, Poland, and Matylda, *née* Thonnes (d 1945); *b* 24 Sept 1914; *Educ* Warsaw State Conservatoire, Vienna State Acad of Music (under Felix Weingartner); *m* 27 Nov 1963, Camilla Ruth, da of Cdr Richard Frederick Jessel, DSO, OBE, DSC, RN (d 1988), of Bearsted Kent; 1 s (Jeremy b 1969), 1 da (Roxanna b 1968); *Career* composer and conductor; debut as conductor with Warsaw Philharmonic Orch 1936, conductor Cracow Philharmonic Orch 1945-46; musical dir: Polish State Film Prodns 1945-46, Warsaw Philharmonic Orch 1946-47; guest appearances with leading Euro orchs incl: Berlin Philharmonic, London Philharmonic, l'Orchestre Nationale Paris; settled in England 1954, musical dir City of Birmingham Symphony Orch 1957-59, numerous guest appearances with int and London orchs; music choreographed into ballets by Martha Graham, Sir Kenneth McMillan and David Bintley; compositions incl: 10 Symphonies, 3 Cantatas, 3 concertos, orchestral and chamber works; cmmns incl: Yehudi Menuhin Violin Concerto 1972, LSO 75 Anniversary Concerto Festivo 1979 and Concertino 1980, Boston Symphony Orch Centenary Sinfonia Votiva 1981, Koussevitsky Fndn Arbor Cosmica 1983, Royal Philharmonic Soc Symphony No 9 1987, Chicago Symphony Orch centenary Symphony No 10 1988; recordings of most orchestral music on EMI, Decca, Louisville, Unicorn, Hyperion and Conifer; Hon RAM 1984, Doctorate London Univ Polish Section 1985; memb: Cncl Musicians' Benevolent Fund, Cncl Composers' Guild of GB, Guild of GB, Assoc of Br Composers PRS; kt 1991; *Books* Composing Myself (autobiog 1987); *Recreations* all arts, travelling; *Clubs* Garrick; *Style*— Sir Andrzej Panufnik; Riverside House, Riverside, Twickenham TW1 3DJ (☎ 081 892 1470)

PAO, Sir Yue-Kong; CBE (1976), JP; s of Sui-Loong Pao, JP (d 1982); hon chm World-Wide Shipping Gp, former owner of paper mill in China, moved to Hong Kong to start import-export business 1948); *b* 10 Nov 1918, Chekiang, China; *Educ* Shanghai China; *m* 1940, Sue-Ing Haung; 4 da; *Career* chm: World-Wide Shipping Gp, The Hong Kong and Kowloon Wharf & Godown Co Ltd, Eastern Asia Navigation Co Ltd, World Int (Hldgs) Ltd, World Maritime Ltd, World Shipping and Investmt Co Ltd, Wheelock Marden Gp, Hong Kong Dragon Airline Ltd; dir Hang Seng Bank Ltd; conslt The Hong Kong and Shanghai Banking Corpn; advsr Industl Bank of Japan Ltd Tokyo; memb: Int Advsy Ctee Chase Manhattan Bank NY, Asia/Pacific Advsy Cncl American Telephone and Telegraph Int, Pacific Advsy Cncl of the Utd Technologies Corpn; JP Hong Kong 1971; kt 1978; *Style*— Sir Yue-Kong Pao, CBE, JP; World-Wide Shipping Agency Ltd, Wheelock House, 6-7 Floors, 20 Pedder St, Hong Kong (☎ 5-8423888)

PAOLOZZI, Prof Sir Eduardo Luigi; CBE (1968); s of Rudolpho Antonio Paolozzi (d 1940), and late Carmella, *née* Rossi; *b* 7 March 1924; *Educ* Edinburgh Sch of Art, Slade Sch of Art; *m* 1951 (m dis 1988); 3 da; *Career* sculptor; tutor in ceramics RCA 1968-90 (visiting prof 1989-), lectr St Martin's Sch of Art 1955-56; prof of: ceramics Fachhochschule Cologne 1977-81, sculpture Akademie der Bildenden Kunste Munich 1981-90 (hon 1991-); maj works incl: fountain for Festival of Britain 1951, sculpture playground for Sir Terence Conran at Wallingford 1973, cast aluminium doors for Hunterian Gallery at Glasgow Univ 1977, cast iron sculpture (Piscator) at Euston Sq 1981, mosaics for Tottenham Court Rd underground station 1984, fountain for Garden Exhibition W Berlin 1984, set design for film Herschel and the Music of the Stars 1985, constructed wood relief in Queen Elizabeth II Conf Centre 1986, 26 bronze elements for Rhinegarten cologne 1986, bronze self-portrait for 34-36 High Holborn London 1987, bronze sculpture for Kowloon Park Hong Kong 1988, bronze head for Design Museum London 1990, giant bronze hand and foot with stone for Edinburgh 1991; Br Critics prize 1953, David E Bright award 1960, Purchase prize Solomon Guggenheim Museum 1967, Norma and William Copley Fndn award 1967, first prize Sculpture Carnegie Int Exhibition 1967, Saltire Soc award 1975 and 1981, first prize Rhinegarten Competition Cologne 1980, Grand Prix d'Honneur Int Print Biennale Yugoslavia 1983; tstee Nat Portrait Gallery 1988-, HM Sculptor in Ordinary for Scotland 1986; hon fell UCL 1986, Hon DLett Heriot-Watt Univ 1987; Hon DLitt: Glasgow 1980, London 1987; Hon Dr RCA 1979; ARA, RA; kt 1989; *Clubs* Athenaeum; *Style*— Prof Sir Eduardo Paolozzi, CBE; 107 Dovehouse St, London SW3; Akademie der Bildenden Kunste, Akadmiestrasse 2, 8000 Munchen 4, West Germany

PAPADAKIS, Dr Andreas Constantine; s of Constantine Pavlou Papadakis, of Nicosia, Cyprus, and Natalia Christou (d 1978); *b* 17 June 1938; *Educ* Faraday House (DFH), Imperial Coll London (DIC), Brunel Univ (PhD); *Career* publisher: ed: Architectural Design 1977, Art and Design 1985-; md Academy Group Ltd 1987- (imprint Academy Edns, founded 1968); fndr and jt organiser Academy Forum at the Tate 1987-89, pres Academy Forum 1990-, memb Int Assoc of art Critics, Ctee of Scientific Cmmn (for restoration prog in Bucharest); *Books* edited jointly Post ModernDesign (1989), Deconstruction Omnibus (1989), New Classicism Omnibus (1990), Deconstruction Pocket Guide (1990), Decade of Architecture (1991), New Art - An International Survey (1991); *Recreations* horseriding, boating (Thistle); *Clubs* Chelsea Arts, IOD, Ascot Racecourse; *Style*— Dr Andreas C Papadakis; 7 Holland St, London W8 4NA (☎ 071 937 6996); 42 Leinster Gardens, London W2 3AN (☎ 071 402 2141, fax 071 723 9540, telex 896928); Church Island House, Church Island, nr Staines, Middx (☎ 07844 61271)

PAPADOPOULOS, Achilles Symeon; CMG (1980), LVO (1972), MBE (1954); s of Symeon Papadopoulos (d 1971); *b* 16 Aug 1923; *Educ* The English Sch Nicosia Cyprus; *m* 1954, Joyce Martin, *née* Stark; 1 s, 2 da; *Career* Dip Serv; HM ambass: El Salvador 1977-79, Mozambique 1979-80, Br high cmmr to Bahamas 1981-83; *Style*— Achilles Papadopoulos, Esq, CMG, LVO, MBE; 14 Mill Close, Great Bookham, Surrey KT23 3JX

PAPPIN, David Frederick; TD (1968); s of Eric Reginald Pappin (d 1979), of Eastbourne, and Evelyn Hope, *née* Pickering (d 1940); *b* 10 March 1935; *Educ* Melville Coll, Univ of Edinburgh (MA); *m* 1, 1958 (m dis 1977), Mary Elizabeth (now Mrs M E Towsey), da of George Trevor Norman Prideaux (d 1986), of Petersfield; 2 da (Amanda Ruth (Mrs Borthwick) b 1964, Belinda Claire b 1970); m 2, 30 Oct 1979, Maureen Grace, da of Malcolm Henry Harper (d 1979); *Career* Nat Serv REME 1953-55 (cmmnd 1954); TA REME 1955-73 (Capt 1961); trainee actuary Liverpool & London & Globe Insur Co Ltd 1952-53 and 1958-61, Res Dept D A Bevan Simpson 1961-64; investment mangr: Minerals Separation Ltd 1964-66, Charterhouse Japhet Ltd 1966-67, Banque Belge Ltd 1967-70; ptnr: J & A Scrimgeour 1970-79, De Zoete & Bevan 1979-86; dir: Barclays de Zoete Wedd (Gilts) Ltd 1986-88, Streets Communications Ltd 1988-; managing conslt of investmt servs Reeves Brown Assocs Ltd 1991-, former chm Cobham Conservation Gp, pres Stoke d'Abernon CC; FFA 1963, ASIA 1961; *Recreations* golf, barbershop singing; *Clubs* Gresham (past chm), MCC; *Style*— David Pappin, Esq, TD; Hatchford Farmhouse, Ockham lane, Hatchford, Surrey KT11 1LS (☎ 0932 863020); Pasarro Amarelo, Dunas Douradas, Almancil, Portugal

PAPPIN, Veryan Guy Henry; s of John Henry Pappin, of 2 New Exeter St, Chudleigh, Devon, and Priscilla Cecil, *née* Pilditch; *b* 19 May 1958; *Educ* Dover Coll, Kelly Coll Tavistock, St Luke's Coll Univ of Exeter (BEd); *Career* joined RAF 1980, Flt Lt physical educn branch; station physical educn offr: RAF Kinloss 1981-82, instr RAF Coll Cranwell 1982-84, instr parachute trg 1984-87, RAF Wattisham 1987-89; leisure conslt hockey international; 37 caps for Scotland 1981- (incl Euro Championships Amsterdam 1983, Moscow 1987), 19 int caps for GB 1982-90 (incl Bronze medal Los Angeles Olympics 1984, Gold medal Seoul Olympics 1988); patron BACKUP 1989 (charity providing sporting opportunities for spinally disabled persons), memb Inst Leisure and Amenity Mgmnt, fell Huguenot Soc of GB and Ireland; *Recreations* squash, hockey, outdoor activities, conservation, music, theatre; *Style*— Veryan Pappin, Esq; 3 New Exeter St, Chudleigh, Devon, TQ13 ODB (☎ 0626 853717)

PAPWORTH, Frank; s of James Papworth (d 1977), and Eva, *née* Heap (d 1980); *b* 11 Jan 1926; *Educ* Bacup Central Sch; *m* 1950, Alice, da of John Andrew Almond (d 1955), of Rochdale, Lancs; 3 s (Paul, David, Andrew); *Career* chm and md Bennie Lifts Ltd 1963-86, dep chm and chief exec Biddle Hldgs plc 1983-86, ret; chm: FH Biddle Ltd 1984-86, ret, Mumford Bailey & Preston Ltd 1984-86; co sec Best Western Hotels 1987-; hon gen sec The Berean Publishing Tst, hon sec The Berean Forward Movement, tstee Chapel of the Opened Book; FCIS, ASCA; *Style*— Frank Papworth, Esq; Shalom, 6 Manor Drive, Baston, Peterborough PE6 9PQ (☎ 077 86 328)

PARAMOR, Roger Carlton; QFSM; s of Albert Walter Alexander Paramor, CBE, of Bognor Regis, Sussex, and Marjorie Flora Maud, *née* Carlton; *b* 10 Nov 1938; *Educ* Churchers Coll Petersfield, Univ of Southampton, Warash, Southampton; *m* 30 Dec 1961, Angela Joan, da of Henry Gordon Harris; 1 s (Mark b 13 June 1965), 2 da (Joanna b 8 Dec 1967, Fiona b 1 March 1972); *Career* 2 offr MN 1956-62; fireman London Fire Bde 1962-64, divnl offr Lancashire Fire Bde 1966-72, dep chief fire offr Portsmouth Fire Bde 1972-73 and W Sussex Fire Bde 1973-76 (leading fireman 1964-66), chief offr Warwickshire Fire Bde 1976-79, chief fire offr Essex Co Fire and

Rescue Serv 1979-; Eastern area govr and voluntary relief skipper Ocean Youth Club, chm Squash Section Fire Servs Sports and Athletics Assoc; Freeman City of London 1986, memb Guild of Fire Fighters 1988; FIFireE 1985 (GIFireE 1966, MIFireE 1967); *Recreations* sailing, squash; *Clubs* West Mersea Sailing; *Style*— Roger Paramor, Esq, QFSM; Essex County Fire and Rescue Service, Rayleigh Close, Hutton, Brentwood, Essex CM13 1AL

PARAVICINI, Dennis Stewart; OBE (1977); s of John Paravicini, JP (d 1961), and Winifred Marian, *née* Stewart-Brown (d 1964); *b* 1 Oct 1930; *Educ* Stowe, Gonville and Caius Coll Cambridge (MA); *m* 1963, Sally Vivienne, da of Cdr H L Hayes, OBE, RN; 1 s (James b 1976), 2 da (Georgina b 1964, Olivia (d 1974)); *Career* Nat Serv Cmmn 5 Royal Inniskilling Dragoon Gds; joined Thomas De La Rue & Co Ltd 1953; chm N Hampshire Cons Assoc 1973-76, vice chm Anglo-Swiss Soc 1975-, tstee N Hampshire Med Tst 1978-, co sec the De La Rue Co plc 1980-85, CBI London Regnl cncllr 1980-86; md Royal Mint Servs 1985-; *Recreations* travelling, sailing; *Clubs* Utd Oxford and Cambridge; *Style*— Dennis Paravicini, Esq, OBE; Street House, Bramley, Nr Basingstoke, Hants (☎ 0256 881283); Thomas De La Rue & Co Ltd, Basing View, Basingstoke, Hants (☎ 0256 29122)

PARAVICINI, Nicolas Vincent Somerset; s of Col Vincent Rudolph Paravicini, TD (d 1989), and Elizabeth Mary (Liza) Maugham (now Baroness Glendevon, *qv*); *b* 19 Oct 1937; *Educ* Eton, RMA Sandhurst; *m* 1, 4 April 1966 (m dis 1986), Mary Ann Parker Bowles; 2 s (Charles b 1968, Derek b 1979), 1 da (Elizabeth Ann b 1970); m 2, 18 Dec 1986 (Susan Rose) Sukie, da of Lt Alan Phipps, RN (ka 1943); *Career* The Life Gds 1957-69, served Oman, Cyprus and Malaysia, ret Maj; dir Joseph Sebag & Co 1972-79, chm A Sarasin & Co Ltd 1980-89, chm and chief exec Sarasin Investment Management Ltd 1983, md Sarasin (UK) Ltd 1983-89, consultant Bank Sarasin & Co 1990, chief exec MacIntyre Investments Ltd 1990, dir Grangehouse Investments Ltd 1990; dir Grangehouse Investments Ltd 1990; memb London Stock Exchange 1972-80; Freeman: City of London 1984, Worshipful Co of Bakers 1984; *Recreations* shooting, skiing; *Clubs* White's, Pratt's; *Style*— Nicholas Paravicini, Esq; Glyn Celyn House, Brecon, Powys LD3 0TY (☎ 0874 4836); MacIntyre Investments Ltd, 28 Ely Place, London EC1N 6RL (☎ 071 242 0242, fax 071 236 0867)

PARBHOO, Santilal Parag; s of Parag Parbhoo (d 1964), of Cape Town, and Jasoda Pemi, *née* Ramjee (d 1961); *b* 16 Jan 1937; *Educ* Livingstone HS Capetown, Univ of Cape Town (MB ChB), Queens Univ Belfast (PhD); *m* 8 Jan 1969, (Constance) Ann, da of William Joseph Cedric Craig, of Belfast, NI; 2 s (Mark b 20 July 1970, Alan b 18 Feb 1977), 1 da (Kathryn b 1 Feb 1974); *Career* house surgn New Somerset Hosp Cape Town SA 1961, sr house surgn Edendale Hosp Pietermaritzburg 1961-62, tutor and registrar Royal Victoria Hosp Belfast 1964-65 (clinical asst 1962-64); surgical registrar: NI Hosp NI 1965-68, Frenchay Hosp Bristol 1973-74; sr lectr Royal Free Hosp and Sch London 1974- (res fell and lectr 1968-72), conslt surgn Royal Free Hosp London, conslt Bristol Myers Oncology UK 1984-86, hon conslt surgn St Bart's Hosp London 1988-, chm div of surgery RFH London 1987-89, chm surgical bd of studies RFHSM 1984-; dir: Cancerkin London 1987-, Royal Free Hosp Breast Cancer Appeal; memb Gujerati Arya Assoc London; fell: Surgical Res Soc, Br Assoc for Surgical Oncology; hon fell; Hong Kong Soc of Surgns, Egyptian Soc of Hepatology 1989 (medal received 1989); FRCS 1967; *Books* Bone Metastases: Monitoring and Treatment (with B A Stoll, 1983); *Recreations* walking, gardening, philately; *Clubs* Consultant Staff (RFH); *Style*— Santilal Parbhoo, Esq; University Department of Surgery, Royal Free Hosp, Pond St, London NW3 2QG (☎ 071 794 0500 ext 4651, private sec ext 4650, fax 071 431 4528)

PARDOE, Alan Douglas William; QC (1988); s of William Douglas Ronald Pardoe (d 1985), and Grace Irene, *née* Jones; *b* 16 Aug 1943; *Educ* Victoria Sch Kurseong India, Oldbury GS, St Catharine's Coll Cambridge (LLB, MA, Winchester reading prize); *m* 1972 (m dis 1976), Mary Ensor; *Career* Hardwicke scholar Lincoln's Inn 1964; asst lectr in Law Univ of Exeter, visiting lectr in law Univ of Auckland NZ 1970, lectr in law Univ of Sussex 1970-74; called to the Bar 1971, began practice at the Bar 1973, rec of Crown Ct 1990-; *Recreations* mountain walking, cooking; *Clubs* Travellers'; *Style*— Alan Pardoe, Esq, QC; Devereux Chambers, Devereux Court, Temple, London WC2R 3JJ (☎ 071 353 7534, fax 071 353 1724)

PARDOE, Hon Mrs (Anna Josephine Bridget); da of 2 Baron Darling; *b* 1946; *m* 1971, Anthony Robert Pardoe; 1 s, 1 da; *Style*— The Hon Mrs Pardoe; Sharow Cottage, Sharow, Ripon, N Yorks

PARDOE, Dr Geoffrey Keith Charles; OBE (1988); s of James Charles Pardoe (d 1954), and Ada Violet, *née* Pert (d 1981); *b* 2 Nov 1928; *Educ* Wanstead Co HS, Loughborough Coll (DLC), Univ of London (BSc), Univ of Loughborough (PhD); *m* 20 June 1953, (Dorothy) Patricia; 1 s (Ian Edward Charles b 1964), 1 da (Jane Patricia b 1967); *Career* RAFVR 1946-58, pilot offr 1949; chief aerodynamicist: Armaments Div Armstrong Whitworth 1949-51, Air Weapons Div De Havilland Props Ltd 1951-56 (project mangr Blue Streak) 1956-60, chief engr Weapons and Space Res Hawker Siddeley Dynamics 1960-63, chief project engr Space Div Hawker Siddeley Dynamics Ltd 1963-70, exec dir British Space Development Co Ltd 1960-71, sales exec space Hawker Siddeley Dynamics Ltd 1971-73, dir Eurosat SA Switzerland 1971-82, chm and md General Technology Systems Ltd 1973-, dep chm Surrey Satellite Technology Ltd 1987-; memb Aeronautical Res Cncl 1971-80, pres RAeS 1984-85, chm Watt Ctee on Energy 1985-; FBIS 1958, FRAeS 1968, FRSA 1976, FInstD 1985, FEng 1988; *Books* Challenge of Space (1964), Project Apollo: The Way to the Moon (1969), The Future for Space Technology (1984); *Recreations* flying, skiing, windsurfing, photography, badminton; *Clubs* RAF, IOD; *Style*— Dr Geoffrey Pardoe, OBE; 23 Stewart Rd, Harpenden, Herts, AL5 4QE (☎ 0582 460 719); General Technology Systems Ltd, Brunel Science Park, Kingston Lane, Uxbridge, Middx, UB8 3PQ (☎ 0895 56767, fax 0895 32078, telex 295607 GENTEC G)

PARDOE, John Wentworth; s of Cuthbert B Pardoe; *b* 27 July 1934; *Educ* Sherborne, Corpus Christi Coll Cambridge; *m* 1958, Joyce R Peerman; 2 s, 1 da; *Career* jt md Sight and Sound Educn Ltd 1979-; sr res fell Policy Studies Inst 1979-; presenter Look Here London Weekend TV 1979-81; *Style*— John Pardoe, Esq; Chy-an-Porth, Trevone, Padstow, Cornwall

PARDOE, Rex Aldous George; s of George Ernest Pardoe (d 1970), and Gladys Lily, *née* Waring (d 1946); *b* 21 Nov 1928; *Educ* SW Essex Tech HS; *m* 19 June 1948, Lyn Kathleen; 1 s (Russell Aldous b 17 June 1963), 4 da (Cheryl Laraine b 18 Dec 1950, Janis Elaine b 5 Jan 1952, Karen Susan b 2 May 1953, Brigitte Louise b 8 July 1959); *Career* Nat Serv RN 1946-48; London and Essex Guardian Newspapers (Reed Int) 1949-90: ed, managing ed, md; chm Whitfield Sch Devpt Tst; pres: Rotary Club, Round Table; *Books* 70 Glorious Years (1965), Battle of London (1972); *Recreations* tennis, bridge; *Clubs* Whitehall, Loughton; *Style*— Rex Pardoe, Esq; 40 Keynsham Ave, Woodford Green, Essex (☎ 081 504 4394)

PARDY, Bruce James; s of William Dryden Cribb Pardy (d 1979), and Mavis Irene Denize (d 1984); *b* 25 Nov 1939; *Educ* St Peter's Sch Cambridge NZ, Christ's Coll Christchurch NZ, Otago Univ NZ (MB BMedSc, ChM); *m* 26 April 1980, Kathleen Margaret, da of Leslie George Henry Townsend Robertson; 1 s (Robert James Dryden b 1985), 1 da (Caroline Anne b 1983); *Career* conslt vascular and gen surgn Newham Gen Hosp and St Andrew's Hosp London, late sr registrar in surgery St Mary's Hosp London; memb: Vascular Soc of GB & I, Surgical Res Soc, Assoc of Surgns UK and I, RSM; med advsr The Raynaud's Assoc; FRACS, FRCS; *Recreations* sailing, camping; *Style*— Bruce Pardy, Esq; 49 Abingdon Villas, Kensington, London W8 6XA; 144 Harley St, London W1N 1AH (☎ 071 935 0023)

PAREKH, Prof Bhikhu Chhotalal; s of Chhotalal Ranchhoddas Parekh, of Washington DC, USA, and Gajaraben Parekh; *b* 4 Jan 1935; *Educ* HDS HS India, Univ of Bombay (BA, MA), Univ of London (PhD); *m* 14 April 1959, Pramila Parekh, da of Kanaiyalal Keshavlal Dalal, of Baroda, India; 3 s; *Career* lectr Univ of Glasgow 1963-64; prof Univ of Hull 1982- (lectr, sr lectr, reader 1964-82), vice chllr Univ of Baroda 1981-84 (lectr 1957-59); visiting prof: Univ of Br Columbia 1967-68, Concordia Univ Montreal 1974-75, McGill Univ Montreal 1976-77; active in local Cncl for Racial Equality, dep chm Cmmn for Racial Equality 1985-90; tstee Runnymeda Tst 1986-; memb: Policy Studies Inst 1986-, Inst for Public Policy Res 1988, Gandhi Fndn 1988; *Books* incl: Hannah Arendt (1981), Karl Marx's Theory of Ideology (1982), Contemporary Political Thinkers (1982), Gandhi's Political Philosophy (1989); *Recreations* reading, music; *Style*— Prof Bhikhu Parekh; 211 Victoria Ave, Hull HU5 3EF (☎ 0482 45530); Dept of Politics, University of Hull, Hull HU5 3E5 (☎ 0482 465798)

PARES, Michael; s of Andrew Pares, CBE, of Northwood, Middx, and Joan Pares; *b* 2 Dec 1943; *Educ* Uppingham, Univ of Edinburgh (BSc); *m* 21 Sept 1968, Jennifer Pauline, da of H E White, of Arkley; 2 da (Catriona b 19 May 1971, Julie b 11 June 1973); *Career* Lt 131 Para Regt RE TA 1963-65; CA Arthur Young, McClellard Moores London 1968, mgmnt appts BOC gp Cos 1969-75, dir Bond & White Ltd (currently md); patron Muswell Hill & Highgate Royal Br Legion; keeper of roll Worshipful Co of Builders Merchants (Liveryman 1978, memb Ct 1988); MInstBM; *Style*— Michael Pares, Esq; Bond & White Ltd, 40 Muswell Hill Rd, Highgate N6 5UN

PARFECT, Maj John Herbert; MBE (1957); s of George Frederick Parfect (d 1970), and Hedwig, *née* Jordi (d 1948); *b* 9 April 1924; *Educ* Brentwood Sch, Univ of Manchester, Columbia Univ NY; *m* 14 Aug 1948, (Mercia) Heather, da of Brig John Lawrence Maxwell, CBE, MC (d 1972), 1 s (Jeremy John b 1963), 4 da (Penelope b 1951, Wendy b 1952, Jane b 1954, Louise b 1958); *Career* WWII cmmnd RE serv Sicily and Italy 1943; serv: Bengal Sappers and Miners India 1945-47, Gurkha Engrs Malaya 1948-50, 6 Armd Div Engrs BAOR 1951-53, Staff Coll Camberley 1954, GSO2 Northern Cmd York 1955-57, OC 40 Field Sqdn Cyprus 1957-58, ret 1958; personnel mangr ICI 1958-81, self employed fin planning conslt Allied Dunbar 1981-; N Yorks CC 1977-, chm N Yorks Police Authy 1985; FIPM; *Recreations* beagling, military history, investments; *Clubs* Yorkshire; *Style*— Maj John Parfect, MBE; Colville Hall, Coxwold, York YO6 4AA (☎ 03476 305)

PARFITT, Judy Catherine Clare; da of Laurence Hamilton Parfitt (d 1973), and Catherine Coulton; *Educ* Notre Dame Convent, RADA; *m* 25 Aug 1963, Anthony Francis Steedman, s of Baron Anthony Ward; 1 s (David Lawrence b 29 Sept 1964); *Career* actress; theatre incl: DH Lawrence trilogy at Royal Court, Annie in A Hotel in Amsterdam 1968, Queen Mary in Vivat! Vivat! Regina! Picadilly Theatre 1970, Cleopatra at Young Vic, Duchess of Malfi at Royal Court, Ranyevskya in The Cherry Orchard at Riverside Studio's 1978, Eleanor in Passion Play at Wyndham's 1980; Films incl: Gertrude in Hamlet 1969, Madam Sarti in Galileo 1974, Getting it Right, Daimond Skulls, Maurice 1986; TV incl: Billette, The Edwardians 1973, Shoulder to Shoulder, Malice Aforethought 1979, Pride and Prejudice, Death of a Princess, Secret Orchards, Jewel in the Crown 1984 (BAFTA Best Actress nomination), The Charmer 1987; *Recreations* needlepoint, gardening, antiques, talking; *Style*— Miss Judy Parfitt; 7 High Park Road, Kew, Richmond, Surrey

PARFITT, Richard John (Rick); s of Richard Parfitt (d 1988), of Woking, and Lillian Rose, *née* Miller; *b* 12 Oct 1948; *Educ* Highlands County Secdy Woking Surrey; *m* 1, 1972, Marietta, da of Willie Böker; 1 s (Richard b 18 Oct 1974), 1 da (Heidi); m 2, Patricia, da of Stanley Beeden; 1 s (Harrison b 20 June 1989); *Career* Status Quo (originally known as the Spectres, joined 1966): co-fndr 1967, continual world touring 1967-, Gold and Silver discs every year since 1971; Silver Clef award 1981, Ivor Novello award (for outstanding servs to music indust) 1984; played at: launch of Prince's Tst 1983, Live Aid 1985, Knebworth 1990; *Recreations* collecting miniature rare Porsches, boating; *Style*— Rick Parfitt, Esq; The Handle Group of Companies, 1 Albion Place, Galena Rd, Hammersmith, London W6 0QT

PARFITT, Stuart Ashley; s of Seth William Parfitt, of Bridgend, and Caroline, *née* Owen; *b* 4 March 1966; *Educ* Lewis Boys Comp Sch Ystrad Munach, Bryntirion Comp Sch Bridgend; *Career* Rugby Union centre Swansea RFC and Wales; Welsh Schs U18 Gp (8 caps) 1983-84; clubs: Bridgend RFC 1984-86 (77 appearences), Swansea RFC 1986- (150 appearances to date), Barbarians RFC; rep: Wales U20, Wales U21, Wales Sevens HK 1990; Wales: debut v Namibia 1990; mktg exec, fin sales exec; *Recreations* golf, cricket, other sports, music, good films; *Style*— Stuart Parfitt, Esq

PARGETER, Edith Mary; da of Edmund Valentine Pargeter (d 1940), and Edith, *née* Hordley (d 1956); *b* 28 Sept 1913; *Educ* Coalbrookdale HS for Girls; *Career* Petty Offr WRNS 1940-45; chemist's asst and dispenser 1933-40; full time author 1945-; novels incl: The City Lies Foursquare (1939), She Goes to War (1942), The Eighth Champion of Christendom (1945), Reluctant Odyssey (1946), Warfare Accomplished (1947), The Soldier at the Door (1954), The Heaven Tree (1960), The Green Branch (1962), The Scarlet Seed (1963), A Bloody Field by Shrewsbury (1972), Sunrise in the West (1974), The Dragon at Noonday (1975), The Hounds of Sunset (1976), Afterglow and Nightfall (1977), The Marriage of Meggotta (1979); transl from Czech: A Handful of Linden Leaves, Tales of the Little Quarter, Granny; mystery novels (under the name of Ellis Peters) incl: Death Mask (1959), Death and the Joyful Woman (1961), Flight of a Witch (1964), A Nice Derangement of Epitaphs (1965), The Piper on the Mountain (1966), Black is the Colour of My Truelove's Heart (1967), Mourning Raga (1969), The Knocker on Death's Door (1970), Death to the Landlords (1972), Rainbow's End (1978), A Morbid Taste for Bones (1977), Monk's-Hood (1980), The Leper of St Giles (1981), The Virgin in the Ice (1982), The Sanctuary Sparrow (1983), The Devil's Novice (1983), The Pilgrim of Hate (1984), The Rose Rent (1986), The Confession of Brother Haluin (1988), The Heretic's Apprentice (1989), The Potter's Field (1989), The Summer of the Danes (1991); awarded: Edgar by Mystery Writers of America 1962, Silver Dagger by CWA 1980; fell Welsh Acad 1989; *Recreations* music, reading, the company of friends; *Style*— Miss Edith Pargeter; c/o Agent, Deborah Owen Ltd, 78 Narrow St, London E14 8BP (☎ 071 987 5119)

PARGETER, Ronald Albert; s of Albert Henry Pargeter (d 1963); *b* 3 Oct 1919; *Educ* Archbishop Tenison's GS; *m* 1, 1943, Edna Margaret; 1 s (Simon), 1 da (Julia); m 2, 1978, Iva Patricia, *née* Stones; 2 da (Lindsay, Deborah); *Career* RAF 1939-45; dir Dalgety Chem Ltd 1978-80, dep chm K & K Greeff Chem Ltd 1976-84, pres Fed Euro Commerce Chimique 1980-82, chm BCDTA 1973-75 (pres 1986-88); dir: Chemrite Int (Pty) Ltd 1979-, Br Tar Products plc 1982-90, Sutcliffe Speakman plc 1986-88; chm Rapadex Ltd 1980-; memb: Exec Cncl Br Importers Confedn 1981-84, Cncl IOD (Sussex branch 1983-88); Freeman City of London; *Recreations* golf, cricket, travelling; *Clubs* St Stephen's, RAF, IOD, Cricketers; *Style*— Ronald Pargeter, Esq; Deep Thatch, Rodmell, East Sussex BN7 3HF (☎ 0273 472912, fax 0273 477086)

PARGITER, Hon Russell Ashby; s of Baron Pargiter, CBE (Life Peer, d 1982); *b* 5

May 1924; *Educ* Southall GS, St Thomas's Hosp Med Sch (MB BS, DPM); *m* 1954, Elizabeth Edwina, da of Dr John George Jamieson Coghill; 2 s (Simon, Timothy b 1964), 1 da (Frances June); *Career* sr hon psychiatrist Royal Hobart Hosp 1959, clinical dir Hobart Clinic; pres Nat Marriage Guidance Cncl 1968-74, sr lecturer in psychiatry Tasmania Univ 1972-81, censor Royal Australian and NZ Coll of Psychiatrists 1975-83 (pres 1973-74), memb Family Law Cncl 1975-81, pres Med Protection Soc of Tasmania 1980-, vice pres Med Protection Soc London 1981-; fell Royal Aust and NZ Coll of Psychiatrists (coll Medal of Honour 1988); FRCPsych; *Recreations* cruising under sail (yacht "Sulatu"), bush walking; *Clubs* Derwent Sailing Sqdn; *Style*— The Hon Russell Pargiter; 42 Grays Rd, Ferntree, Tasmania 7054, (☎ 002 391231); 173 Macquarie St, Hobart, Tasmania 7000 (☎ 002 237867)

PARHAM, Adm Sir Frederick Robertson; GBE (1959, CBE 1949), KCB (1955, CB 1951), DSO (1944); s of Frederick James Parham (d 1906), of Bath, Somerset, and Jessie Esther Brooks, *née* Robertson (d 1961); *b* 9 Jan 1901; *Educ* RNC Osborne and Dartmouth; *m* 1, 1926, Kathleen Dobree (d 1973), da of Eugene Edward Carey, of Guernsey; 1 s; m 2, 1978, Mrs Joan Saunders, *née* Charig; *Career* Cdr 1934, Rear Adm 1949, Vice Adm 1952, a Lord Cmmr of the Admty, Fourth Sea Lord and Chief of Supplies and Tport 1954-55, C-in-C The Nore 1955-58, Adm 1956, ret 1959; former vice chm Br Waterways Bd; *Style*— Adm Sir Frederick Parham, GBE, KCB, DSO

PARHAM, John Carey; s of Adm Sir Frederick Robertson Parham, GBE, KCB, DSO, *qv*, and Kathleen Dobree, *née* Carey; *b* 13 June 1928; *Educ* Rugby, Madgalen Coll Oxford; *m* 20 May 1959, Christian Mary, da of Cuthbert Fitzherbert (d 1986), of Berks; 1 s (Philip b 1960) 4 da (Katherine b 1962, Magdalen b 1964, Barbara b 1968, Henrietta (twin) b 1968); *Career* Nat Serv 1947-49, 2 Lt Mercers Troop 5 RHA; local dir Barclays Bank Windsor and London Western; exec chm Close Registrars Ltd 1988-89; ACIB; *Recreations* swimming, gardening, literature, heraldry; *Style*— John Parham, Esq; Ladymead, South Ascot, Berkshire SL5 9HD (☎ 0344 20087)

PARIKH, Anu; da of Debesh Chandra Das, of Calcutta, India, and Kamala, *née* Nag; *b* 16 March 1947; *Educ* Convent of Jesus and Mary New Delhi, Univ of Delhi (BA), King's Coll London (LLB); *m* 15 Feb 1972, Bharat Amritlal Parikh, s of Amritlal Vithaldas Parikh, of 142a Lee Rd, Calcutta, India; *Career* called to the Bar Middle Temple 1971; formerly sub ed Atkins Court Forms Butterworths Ltd, practising barr 1979-, ptnr Parikh Daskalides, memb Social Security Appeals Tbnl London South Region; *Recreations* reading, gardening, theatres; *Style*— Mrs Anu Parikh; 179 Coombe Lane, London SW20 0RG (☎ 081 947 4544); 76 B Chancery Lane, London WC2 (☎ 071 404 5053, fax 071 404 0118)

PARIKH, Bharat Amritlal; s of Amritlal Vithaldas Parikh, of Calcutta, and Padmalaxmi Amritlal, *née* Mehta; *b* 4 Oct 1946; *Educ* Univ of Calcutta (BCom), Univ of London (BSc); *m* 14 Feb 1972, Anuradha, da of Debesh Chandra Das, formerly permanent sec to Govt of India; *Career* dir Castle Keep Hotels Ltd; distrib Belgian handmade chocolates Parikh Daskalides; FCA; *Recreations* snooker, cricket; *Style*— Bharat A Parikh, Esq; 179 Coombe Lane, West Wimbledon, London SW20 0RG (☎ 947 4644); 17 Tottenham Court Road, London W1 (☎ 580 9633, 631 3810)

PARIS, Andrew Martin Ingledew; s of Vernon Patrick Paris, of Sussex, and Heather Constance Ingledew, *née* Dear; *b* 27 Nov 1940; *Educ* London Hosp Med Coll Univ of London (MB BS); *m* 1, 16 May 1964 (m dis), Anne Cardwell, da of Col Alleyn Cardwell Moore (d 1980), of NI; 1 da (Claire Elizabeth Ingledew Paris b 10 April 1966); m 2, 24 Dec 1975, Susan Philippa da of Perys Goodwin Jenkins (d 1969), of London; *Career* conslt urological surgn The Royal London Hosp 1976-, hon conslt surgn The Italian Hosp 1979-90; hon surgn St John Ambulance Air Wing (fndr memb), OStJ 1985; Liveryman Worshipful Soc of Apothecaries 1967, Freeman City of London 1984; FRCS 1971, FRSM (vice pres section of urology 1988, 1989); *Recreations* sailing, skiing; *Clubs* Aldeburgh Yacht; *Style*— Andrew Paris, Esq; 44 Cleaver Square, London SE11 4EA (☎ 071 735 7763); 121 Harley St, London W1N 1DM (☎ 071 486 6324)

PARIS, Cecil Gerard Alexander; TD (1945); s of Lt Col Alexander Lloyd Paris (d 1968), of Bournemouth, and Geraldine Paris, *née* Brooke (d 1974); *b* 20 Aug 1911; *Educ* The King's Sch Canterbury; *m* 11 Sept 1937, Winifred Anna Blanche, da of Thomas Richardson, OBE (d 1969), of Northumberland; 2 s (James b 1945, Thomas b 1947), 1 da (Winifred b 1940); *Career* joined TA March 1939, cmmnd Hants Heavy Regt RA 1939, serv UK and BLA Europe 1944-45 (awarded Czech MC after serv with Czech Ind Armd Bde Gp), demob as Maj 1945; slr 1935-86, ptnr Paris Smith & Randall Southampton 1965-81; hon sec Hants Law Soc; player Hants CCC 1933-48 (Capt 1938, chm selection ctee 1952-67, club chm 1967-68, pres 1983-), govr Kings Sch Canterbury 1979-84, chm Wessex Body Scan Appeal 1983-; memb ctee MCC 1961-83 (chm of registration ctee and genral purposes ctee, pres 1975-76, tstee 1983-84, hon life vice-pres 1985-), chm ctee responsible for organising and running first (Prudential) World Cup Int Cricket Conf 1975; inaugural chm TCCB 1968-75; played for Hants RFU 1934-46 (capped 1935 when Hants won County Championship); pres and hon sec Hants Law Soc 1961; *Recreations* fly-fishing, cricket admin; *Clubs* MCC, Lord's Taverners, Free Foresters, Hampshire Hogs, Trojans, Forty; *Style*— Cecil G A Paris, TD; Lynsted, Southdown Road, Shawford, Winchester, Hants SO21 2BY (☎ 0962 712152)

PARIS, Judith; da of Thomas Henry Franklin (d 1990), of Abbey House, Cirencester, Glos, and Doris Mary, *née* Baker; *b* 7 June 1944; *Educ* Royal Ballet Sch; *m* 1 (m dis 1970), James Walters; m 2, 28 April 1977, John Kyle, s of Maj John Murphy (d 1971); 2 s (Benedict Kyle b 12 Dec 1979, Tallis Kyle b 6 Sept 1986); *Career* actress: twelve years involvement with the NT between 1974 and 1986, leading lady (Dorothy Moore) in Jumpers, character lead (Joy Ferret) in Jean Sebert, Celia in As You Like It with the RSC 1978 (nominated best supporting actress), leading lady in three of Ken Russell's major films; *Recreations* music, painting, rambling; *Style*— Miss Judith Paris

PARISH *see also*: Woodbine Parish

PARISH, Hon Mrs (Elizabeth Campbell); *née* Boot; da of 2 and last Baron Trent (d 1956); *b* 1927; *m* 1947, Maj Michael Woodbine Parish, MC, Notts Yeo; 1 s, 3 da; *Career* dir: Exploration Co plc, El Oro Mining & Exploration Co, General Explorations Ltd; *Style*— The Hon Mrs Parish; Walcot Hall, Lydbury North, Salop

PARISH, Maj Michael Woodbine; MC, DSM; s of Clement Woodbine Parish (d 1966), of Sussex, and Elsie Mary, *née* Bonham-Christie (d 1931); *b* 6 July 1916; *Educ* Eton; *m* 1, 1943 (m dis 1946), Ninette Sgourdeos; m 2, 1947, Hon Elizabeth Campbell Boot, da of 2 Baron Trent of Nottingham (d 1956); 1 s (Clement Robin b 1950), 3 da (Suzanne b 1948, Caroline b 1953, Emma b 1957); *Career* WWII Maj Sherwood Rangers Yeo (despatches twice, POW 1943), repatriated 1944, invalided out of army 1944; chm and md: The Exploration Co, El Oro Mining & Exploration Co; dir Bisichi Tin Co; *Recreations* work, walking, swimming; *Clubs* Beefsteak, Brookes's, East India and Sports, Cavalry and Guards'; *Style*— Maj Michael Parish, MC, DSM; Walcot Hall, Lydbury North, Shropshire; 41 Cheval Place, London SW7 (☎ 071 581 2782)

PARISH, Hon Mrs (Monica Esmé Ebba); *née* Suenson-Taylor; da of 1 Baron Grantchester, OBE; *b* 17 Jan 1926; *Educ* Queen's Coll London, Newnham Coll Cambridge; *m* 1951 (m dis 1965), Graeme Spotswood Parish; 1 s (Andrew, k in an accident 1973), 1 da (Alexandra Francesca Spotswood (Mrs Nicholas Burnell) b 1953); *Style*— The Hon Mrs Monica Parish; 71 Prince's House, Kensington Park Rd, London W11

PARK, Andrew Edward Wilson; QC (1978); s of late Dennis Edward Park; *b* 27 Jan 1939; *Educ* Leeds GS, Univ Coll Oxford; *m* 1962, Ann Margaret Woodhead; 2 s (and 1 s decd), 1 da; *Career* barr Lincoln's Inn 1964, practice at Revenue Bar 1965-; *Style*— Andrew Park, Esq, QC; Blandford Cottage, Weston Green Rd, Thames, Surrey KT7 0HX (☎ 081 398 5349)

PARK, Hon Mrs (Christine Joanna); *née* Coleman; da of Baron Cohen of Brighton (Life Peer, d 1966); *b* 6 May 1942; *Educ* Roedean, Univ of London (BA), Univ of Sussex (MA); *m* 1965, David Maxwell Park; 1 da (Nira b 1967); *Career* writer and ed; *Books* Joining The Grown Ups (1986), Close Company (ed jtly), The Househusband (1989); *Style*— The Hon Mrs Park; 29 Downshire Hill, London NW3 1NT; 4640 West 6th Avenue, Vancouver, BC V6R 1V7, Canada

PARK, George Maclean; s of James McKenzie Park; *b* 27 Sept 1914; *Educ* Onslow Drive Sch Glasgow, Coventry Tech Coll; *m* 1941, Joyce, da of Robert Holt Stead; 1 da; *Career* MP (Lab) Coventry NE 1974-87; PPS to: Dr J Gilbert (Min for Tport) 1975-76, E Varley (Sec of State for Indust) 1976-79; chm W Midland Gp Lab MPs, memb Public Accounts Ctee 1981-87, chm Coventry Community Health Authy 1990-, jt chm All-Pty Motor Indust Gp 1979-87; JP (Coventry 1961-84); *Style*— George Park, Esq; 170 Binley Rd, Coventry CV3 1HG (☎ 0203 458589)

PARK, Dr Gilbert Richard; TD (1985); *b* 17 May 1950; *Educ* Univ of Edinburgh (MB, ChB, BSc); *m* 19 Dec 1976, Ruth Hilary; 1 s (Richard b 1978), 1 da (Helen b 1980); *Career* TA: offr cadet 1968-74, Lt 1974-75, Capt 1975-80, Maj 1980-; Dept Orthopaedic Surgery Royal Infirmary Edinburgh 1974, Dept Med Bangor Gen Hosp 1974; Dept of Anaesthesia: Royal Infirmary Edinburgh 1975-80, Univ of Edinburgh 1980-83, dir Intensive Care and conslt in anaesthesia Addenbrookes Hosp Cambridge; Hon MA Cambridge Univ 1987, Hon MD Univ of Edinburgh (1991); FFARCS 1978; *Books* Intensive Care: A Handbook (1988), The Postoperative Care of Patients after Liver Transplantation, Anaesthesia and Intensive Care (1989), The Management of Acute Pain (1991); *Recreations* photography; *Style*— Dr Gilbert Park; The Intensive Care Unit, Addenbrooke's Hosp, Cambridge CB2 2QQ (☎ 0223 217474, fax 0223 216781, telex 94070972 PARK G, car 0860 228060)

PARK, (James) Graham; s of James Park, OBE, JP (d 1959), of Salford, and Joan Clay, *née* Sharp (d 1987); *b* 27 April 1941; *Educ* Malvern, Univ of Manchester (LLB); *m* 26 June 1969, Susan, da of Dr Charles Sydney Douglas Don (d 1973), of Manchester; 1 s (James b 1973); *Career* slr in partnership; Parly candidate (C) 1974 and 1979, chm Altrincham Sale Constituency 1983-87, dep chm Cons Party NW 1989-; Duchy of Lancaster, memb of Ct of Salford Univ 1987-; *Recreations* cricket, motor racing; *Style*— Graham Park, Esq; HLF Berry & Co, 25 South King Street, Manchester M2 6BB (☎ 061 834 0548)

PARK, Sir Hugh (Eames); s of late William Robert Park; *b* 24 April 1910; *Educ* Blundell's, Sidney Sussex Coll Cambridge; *m* 1938, Beryl Josephine, da of late Joseph Coombe; 3 da; *Career* called to the Bar Middle Temple 1936, QC 1960, bencher 1965, presiding judge Western circuit 1970-75, judge of the High Ct of Justice, Queen's Bench Div 1973-85 (Family Div 1965-73); hon fell Sidney Sussex Cambridge 1968; Hon LLD Univ of Exeter 1984; kt 1965; *Style*— Sir Hugh Park; 34 Ordnance Hill, St John's Wood, NW8 (☎ 071 586 0417); Gorran Haven, Cornwall (☎ 0726 842333)

PARK, Ian Grahame; s of William Park (d 1982), and Christina Wilson, *née* Scott; *b* 15 May 1935; *Educ* Lancaster Royal GS, Queens' Coll Cambridge; *m* 1965, Anne, da of Edward Turner (d 1979); 1 s (Adam); *Career* Nat Serv cmmnd Manchester Regt 1954-56; md Northcliffe Newspapers Group 1982-, dir Associated Newspapers Holdings 1983-, md and ed in chief Liverpool Daily Post and Echo 1972-82, asst literary ed Sunday Times 1960-63; dir: Reuters 1978-82, Press Assoc 1978-83 (chm 1978-79 and 1979-80); pres Newspaper Soc 1980-81; *Clubs* Reform; *Style*— Ian Park Esq; 31 John Street, WC1 (☎ 071 242 7070)

PARK, Hon Mrs (Joanna MacAlister); er da of Baron Baker, OBE (Life Peer, d 1985); *b* 1933; *m* 1962, Prof David Michael Ritchie Park (d 1990), s of James Ritchie Park (d 1952); 1 s (Tobias John b 1966), 1 da (Rebecca Jane b 1964); *Career* physiotherapist; former JP for Warwicks; MCSP; *Style*— The Hon Mrs Park; 15 Rothesay Place, Edinburgh

PARK, (Ian) Michael Scott; CBE (1982); s of Ian Macpherson Park (d 1960), of Aberdeen, and Winifred Margaret, *née* Scott; *b* 7 April 1938; *Educ* Aberdeen GS, Univ of Aberdeen (MA, LLB); *m* 1964, Elizabeth Mary Lamberton, da of Alexander Marshall Struthers, OBE (d 1964), of Edinburgh; 2 s (Sandy b 1965, William b 1972); *Career* slr; ptnr Paull & Williamsons Advocates Aberdeen 1964-; memb: Soc of Advocates Aberdeen 1962-, of Cncl Law Soc of Scotland 1974-84 (vice pres 1979-80, pres 1980-81), Criminal Injuries Compensation Bd 1983-; frequent broadcaster on legal topics; *Recreations* golf, gardening, travel; *Clubs* New (Edinburgh); *Style*— Michael Park, Esq, CBE; Beechwood, 46 Rubislaw Den, South Aberdeen AB2 6AX (☎ 0224 313799); Investment House, 6 Union Row, Aberdeen (☎ 0224 631414)

PARK, Richard Francis Hanbury; s of Jonathan Cyril Park, OBE (d 1979), and Frances Hanbury, *née* Dodds (d 1984); *b* 29 March 1933; *Educ* Winchester, Trinity Coll Cambridge (MA, LLM); *m* 3 July 1959, Patricia Zillah, da of Norman Louis Forrest (d 1988); of Barlaston, Stoke-on-Trent; 2 da (Caroline b 1963, Elizabeth b 1965); *Career* 1 Royal Dragoons 1951-53, Lanarkshire Yeo TA 1953-58; admitted slr 1959; sr ptnr Steavensons Plant & Park Darlington 1986- (ptnr 1959-86); clerk to Gen Cmmrs of Income Tax: Darlington, Bishop Auckland, Northallerton, Barnard Castle; chm Social Security Appeals Tbnl 1984-, pres Notaries Soc 1987-89, memb Slrs Benevolent Assoc, memb Law Soc 1959; *Recreations* golf, tennis, walking, photography, music, pottery, gardening; *Style*— Richard Park, Esq; The Old Rectory, Hurworth, Darlington, Co Durham (☎ 0325 720 321); 12 Houndgate, Darlington (☎ 0325 466 794, fax 0325 55321)

PARK, William Dennis; s of Edward Park (d 1954), of Cockermouth, Cumbria, and Fanny Moyra, *née* Walker (d 1986); *b* 28 May 1934; *Educ* St Bees Cumbria; *m* 1 Jan 1959, Valerie Margaret, da of Wallace Rutherford Bayne, MD (d 1956), of Barrow-in-Furness, Cumbria; 1 s (Adam b 9 July 1961), 1 da (Claire (Mrs Barkes) b 9 Jan 1963); *Career* Nat Serv RAOC, RASC 1955-57 (Army Legal Aid 1956-57); admitted slr 1955, ptnr Morrison & Masters Swindon 1961-66, sr litigation ptnr Linklaters Cates & Paines London 1971-; former pres London Slrs Litigators Assoc, cncl memb London Int Arbn Tst, memb cncl Br Inst of Int & Comparative Law; memb: Bd of London Int Ct of Arbitration, Ct of Arbitration of the Int Chamber of Commerce Paris; memb: Herdwick Sheep Breeders' Assoc, Friends of the Lake Dist, Nat Tst, English Heritage; subscribes: Melbreak Foxhounds, Ennerdale & Eskdale Foxhounds, Black Combe Beagles; Lord of the Manors of Whicham and Whitbeck Cumbria; memb City of London Slrs Co; memb: Law Soc 1955, ACIArb 1980; *Books* Hire Purchase and Credit Sales (1958), Collection of Debts (1962), Discovery of Documents (1966), Documentary Evidence (1985); *Recreations* farming, living in West Cumbria, hunting, shooting, fishing; *Style*— William Park, Esq; Lorton Park, High Lorton, Cockermouth, Cumbria; Linklaters & Paines, Barrington House, 59-67 Gresham St, London EC2 (☎ 071 606 7080)

PARK OF MONMOUTH, Baroness (Life Peer UK 1990), of Broadway in the County of Hereford and Worcester; Daphne Margaret Sybil Désirée Park;

CMG (1971), OBE (1960); da of John Alexander Park (d 1952), and Doreen Gwynneth Park (d 1982); *b* 1 Sept 1921; *Educ* Rosa Bassett Sch, Somerville Coll Oxford, Newnham Coll Cambridge; *Career* WTS (FANY) 1943-47 (Allied Cmmn for Austria 1946-48); FO 1948; second sec Moscow 1954, first sec Leopoldville 1959, first sec Zambia 1964-67, consul-gen Hanoi 1969-70, chargé d'affaires Ulen Bator 1972, FCO 1973-79; princ Somerville Coll Oxford 1980-89, Bd memb Sheffield Devpt Corp 1989-, dir Devpt Tst Zoological Soc of London 1989-90, govr BBC 1982-87, former memb Br Library Bd, chm Legal Aid Advsy Ctee to Lord Chllr 1984-90, pro vice chllr Univ of Oxford, chm Royal Cmmn on the Historical Monuments of Eng 1989-, tstee the Jardine Fndn 1990-; *Recreations* good talk, politics and difficult places; *Clubs* Naval & Military, Royal Cwlth Soc, Special Forces, Oxford and Cambridge; *Style—* The Rt Hon the Lady Park of Monmouth, CMG, OBE; c/o House of Lords, London SW1

PARKE, Simon Armour; s of Ian Armour Parke, of Harrogate, and Janet Christine, *née* Sparks; *b* 10 Aug 1972; *Educ* Ashville Coll Harrogate; *Career* professional squash player; first tournament victory Yorks Under 12 Championship 1983, winner fifteen open under 12 events 1983-84 incl Br Championships, youngest under 19 jr int aged 14, youngest Yorks sr champion aged 16; turned professional 1988-; Br Open jr champion 1989 and 1991, world jr champion Germany 1990, runner up Br Men's Closed Championship 1991; England: 24 jr caps, 6 full caps, winner World Jr Team Championships 1990, played in World Team Championships Singapore 1989, winner Euro Team Championships Zurich 1990, youngest sr int aged 17; ranking: 3 in England 1990, 32 in world 1991; Avia boy of the year 1987, Yorks Sports Cncl men's winner 1989 (boys' winner 1988); *Recreations* various sorts of pop music, most other sports, films and world affairs; *Style—* Simon Parke, Esq; c/o Ian Parke, 53 Millfield Glade, Harrogate (☎ 0423 886769); Harrogate Squash Club, Hookstone Rd, Harrogate (☎ 0423 504309, fax 0423 523355)

PARKER *see also*: Dodds-Parker

PARKER, Adrian Philip; s of Philip Parker, and Doreen Beryl, *née* Catling; *b* 2 March 1951; *Educ* Univ of Sussex (Athletics blue); *m* 24 Dec 1977, Jane Mary, da of Athelstane John Cornforth; 3 da (Emma Jane b 15 Jan 1979, Hazel Martha b 19 April 1981, Clover Elizabeth b 26 Jan 1984); *Career* former pentathlon competitor; represented Surrey jt water polo 1969, nat biathlon champion 1973; first int pentathlon appearance 1973; major appearances: Fontainbleau 1973 and 1974, Heidenheim 1973 and 1976, Budapest 1973, 1974, 1975, 1976, Warendorf 1974 and 1975, Stockholm 1974, Barcelona 1974, Paris 1975, Sandhurst 1975, World Championships Mexico City 1975 and San Antonio Texas 1977, Latin Cup Rome 1976, Crystal Palace 1976, Olympic Games Montreal 1976; honours incl: winner Barcelona 1974, winner Sandhurst 1975, equal first San Antonio 1975, runner up Europa Cup 1975, UK champion 1975, Gold medal Olympic Games 1976; highest individual UK placing and best run-swim combination Olympic Games 1976; dir Phil Parker Ltd; *Recreations* windsurfing, music, sailing, reading, general fitness training; *Style—* Adrian Parker, Esq; c/o Phil Parker Ltd, 26 Chiltern St, London W1M 1PH (☎ 071 486 8206)

PARKER, Alan; s of Sir Peter Parker, MVO, and Gillian, *née* Rowe-Dutton; *b* 3 May 1956; *m* 22 Feb 1977, Caroline Louise, da of Thaddeus Gordon, of Yates; 1 s (Samuel b 1 Oct 1982), 2 da (Jessica Alexandria b 18 Sept 1984, Natasha Rose b 11 Dec 1987); *Career* dep md Broad St Assoc 1982-87, md Brunswick PR Ltd 1987-; dir Charity Projects Ltd; Freeman City of London; *Recreations* friends; *Style—* Alan Parker, Esq; Brunswick PR, 15 Lincoln's Inn Fields, London WC2A 3ED (☎ 071 404 5959, car 0860 391789, fax 071 831 2823

PARKER, (David) Alec; s of David Herbert Parker (d 1983), and Gertrude Alice, *née* Pipes (d 1978); *b* 3 Oct 1931; *Educ* Queen Elizabeth's GS Wimborne Dorset, Imperial Coll Univ of London (BSc, PhD, DSc (Eng)); *m* 24 March 1956, Mary da of Henry John Gibbs (d 1986); 1 s (Adrian John b 17 March 1964), 2 da (Susan Jane b 8 Aug 1958, Helen June b 12 July 1960); *Career* Nat Serv Lieut REME 1950-51; ldr Mechanical Engrg Res Gp Engrg Div BTH Res Laboratory (AEI Central Res Laboratory 1960-) 1954-68, head Machinery Section Prodn Engrg Res Assoc 1968-69; Associated Engineering Developments Ltd (known as AE Developments Ltd 1982-) 1969-87: mangr Mechanical Engrg Dept 1972-77, dir 1977-78, acting md 1978-79, md 1979-87; memb AE Group Exec 1985-87, chm High Precision Equipment Ltd 1985-87, md T & N Technology 1987-, chm DTI Materials Advsy Ctee 1990-; chm: Rugby Sub Branch 1 Mech E 1977-79, Consortium for Ceramic Applications in Reciprocating Engines 1984-89; memb: Engine and Vehicle Ctee DTI 1982-85, Vehicle Advsy Ctee DTI 1985-88; churchwarden All Saints Leamington Hastings Rugby 1969-, chm govrs Leamington Hastings CE First Sch Rugby 1976-; *Awards* Design Cncl Commendation for AE conoguide piston design 1984, Herbert Akroyd Stuart prize of IMechE for the best paper on diesel engines 1985; Design Cncl award for A Econoguide piston design 1989; FInstP 1968 (AInstP 1961), FIMechE 1981 (MIMechE 1968), FEng (1990, CEng 1968), CPhys 1985; *Recreations* campanology; *Style—* Alec Parker, Esq; Orchard Bungalow, Broadwell, Rugby, Warwickshire CV23 8HB (☎ 0926 812548); T & N Technology, Cawston House, Rugby, Warwickshire CV 7SA (☎ 0788 812555, fax 0788 816952, telex 311 259)

PARKER, Allen Mainwaring; s of Eric Parker (d 1954), of Feathercombe, Hambledon, Surrey, and Ruth Margaret, *née* Messel (d 1933); *b* 23 Feb 1915; *Educ* Eton, Trinity Coll Oxford (MA); *m* 24 March 1945, Suzanne Beechey, da of Cdr Beechey Louis Rogers (d 1953), of Woodfield Cottage, Luston, Herefordshire; 1 s (James), 2 da (Suzanne, Tessa); *Career* WWII Maj KOYLI; sr classics master King's Coll Auckland NZ 1938-39, dir of extramural studies Univ of Birmingham 1955-82, vice chm Univ Cncl for Adult and Continuing Educn 1976-82; FRSA; *Books* University Adult Education in the Later Twentieth Century (Report of the Convenor of a Working Party of the Universities Council for Adult Education, 1970), University Studies for Adults (ed with Prof SG Raybould, 1972); *Recreations* gardening; *Style—* Allen Parker, Esq; The Wadhouse, Heightington, Bewdley, Worcs (☎ 02993 2477)

PARKER, Maj Anthony John; s of John Vernham Parker (d 1980), of 9 Golf Links Rd, Broadstone, Dorset, and Freda Oakley, *née* Twitchett (d 1988); *b* 24 Nov 1923; *Educ* Whitgift Sch; *m* 13 Sept 1952, (Elsie) Patricia, da of Lt-Col Clifford Llewellyn Wilson, OBE, MC (d 1974) of Newbrook, Upper Golf Links Rd, Broadstone, Dorset; 3 s (Jeremy (Capt RM) b 1954, Guy b 1955, Timothy b 1962), 1 da (Diana (Mrs Mills) b 1959); *Career* probationary 2 Lt RM 1942, Lt 1943, Home Fleet (HM Ships: Berwick, Anson, Kent) 1943, Med Fleet (HMS Birmingham) 1944, E Indies Fleet (HMS Nigeria) 1944-46, instr commando trg (qualified weapon trg offr and mil parachutist) 1946-49, 40 Commando RM (Malta, Hong Kong, Malaya) 1949-51, Capt 1951, staff offr amphibious trg (qualified landing craft offr) 1952-54, instr NCO's trg 1954-57, RAF Staff Coll 1957, instr Jt Sch Nuclear Def 1958-60, staff offr Depot RM 1960-62, 42 Commando RM (Singapore, Brunei, Sarawak) 1962-64, staff offr amphibious trg 1964-67, Maj 1967, staff offr HQ Far East Cmd 1967-70, chief landing craft offr RM 1970-73, ret 1973; chief fishery offr S Sea Fisheries Dist 1974-88, pres S Sea Fisheries Dist Fishermen's Cncl; memb: RN Soc Rugby Referees, Dorset & Wilts Soc Rugby Referees, Exec Ctee Dorset Marine Ctee, Mgmnt Ctee Brownsea Island Nature Reserve, Ctee Lytchett Matravers Cons Assoc; vice-pres Poole Town Regatta, hon pirate Poole; vice chm Lytchett Matravers Parish Cncl; *Recreations* rugby football (referee assessor); *Clubs* Army and Navy; *Style—* Maj Anthony Parker; Alder Rise, Lytchett Matravers, Dorset (☎ 0202 622427)

PARKER, Anthony Key; s of Frank James Parker (d 1943), and Edith Emma, *née* Gannaway (d 1974); *b* 7 April 1925; *Educ* Stamford Sch, Trinity Coll Cambridge (MA); *m* 1, 19 Feb 1955, Joanna Margaret (d 1975), da of Dr Vernon Edmund Lloyd, MC (d 1973); 2 s (Andrew b 1958, Philip b 1960), 1 da (Elisabeth b 1963); m 2, 15 Dec 1980, Alison Margaret Bagnall, *née* Kynoch; *Career* Midshipman (Sp) RNVR HMS Collingwood 1945-46, Sub Lt (Sp) RNVR HMS Gabbard 1946, HMS St James 1946-47, HMS Aisne 1947; tech offr Zinc Development Association 1949-52, sr asst Publicity Dept Mond Nickel Co 1953-55, ed Butterworth & Co 1955-57, asst sec to the Syndicates of CUP 1957-85; elder Church of Scotland, memb Scripture Union Ctee for Dumfries; *Books* The Fenland (with Denis Pye, 1976); *Recreations* sailing, walking; *Clubs* Solway YC; *Style—* Anthony Parker, Esq; Drumathol, Southwick, Dumfries DG2 8AP (☎ 038 778 629)

PARKER, Barrie Charles; s of Stanley Charles Digby Parker, of Southampton, and Betty Doreen, *née* Calverley; *b* 2 Oct 1940; *Educ* City of London Sch, Charing Cross Med Sch, Univ of London (MB BS); *m* 27 April 1968, Ann Teressa, da of William Rae Ferguson (d 1981), Coventry; *Career* sr registrar Charing Cross and Royal Nat Orthopaedic Hosps 1973-76, conslt orthopaedic surgn Kingston Hosp 1976- (clinical tutor 1981-86); pres Kingston and Richmond div BMA 1978-79; memb: Kingston and Esher Health Authy, regnl advsr orthopaedics RCS England; fell: RSM 1974, Br Orthopaedic Assoc 1976; FRCS; *Recreations* rugby football, swimming, skiing and water skiing; *Clubs* London Irish RFC, Kingston Med; *Style—* Barrie Parker, Esq, Delaval, Furzefield, Oxshott, Surrey KT22 0UR

PARKER, Bruce Rodney Wingate; s of Robert Parker (d 1988), and Doris Maud, *née* Wingate; *b* 20 July 1941; *Educ* Elizabeth Coll Guernsey, Univ of Wales (BA), Univ of Reading (DipEd); *m* 16 Sept 1967 (m dis 1985), Anne, *née* Dorey; 2 s (James b 9 Aug 1968, Charles b 4 Aug 1974), 1 da (Sarah b 28 Dec 1969); *Career* house master Elizabeth Coll Guernsey 1964-67, BBC News and current affrs reporter, presenter and prodr 1967-; progs incl: Nationwide, Antiques Roadshow, Mainstream, Badger Watch, South Today, political & industl corr BBC South 1991-, presenter BBC South & West Out of Wesminster; frequent contribs to numerous radio and TV progs; rifle-shooting corr The Independent; former memb Hampshire CC Educn Advsy Ctee, former chm of govrs Harestock Schs Winchester, cncl memb Friends of Winchester Cathedral; *Books* Everybody's Soapbox (with N Farrell, 1983); *Recreations* travel, gardening, rifle-shooting; *Clubs* United Guernsey, North London Rifle, London & Middx Rifle, Surrey Rifle Assoc; *Style—* Bruce Parker, Esq; Lanham Cottage, Lanham Lane, Winchester SO22 5JS; BBC Television, South Western House, Southampton SO9 1PF (☎ 0962 866399, 0703 226201, fax 0703 339931)

PARKER, Cameron Holdsworth; s of George Cameron Parker, MBE (d 1967), of Uplands, Monifieth, Angus, and Mary Stevenson, *née* Houston (d 1985); *b* 14 April 1932; *Educ* Morrisons Acad Crieff, Univ of Glasgow (BSc); *m* 1, 20 July 1957, Elizabeth Margaret (d 1985), da of Andrew Sydney Grey Thomson (d 1957), of Dundee; 3 s (David b 1958, Michael b 1960, John b 1964); m 2, 23 May 1986, Marlyne, da of William Honeyman (d 1966), of Glasgow; *Career* chm John G Kinlaid & Co Ltd 80 (md 1967-80), chm and chief exec Scott Lithgow Ltd 1980-83, bd memb Br Shipbuilders Ltd 1977-80 and 1981-83, md Lithgows Ltd 1984-; chm: Campbeltown Shipyard Ltd 1984-, J Fleming Engineering Ltd 1984-, Lithgow Electronics Ltd 1984-, Malak Off & Wm Moore Ltd 1984-, McKinlay & Blair Ltd 1984-, Prosper Engrg Ltd 1984-, A Kenneth & Sons Ltd 1985-, Landcatch Ltd 1985-, Glasgow Iron and Steel Co Ltd 1985-; memb cncl CBI Scotland; Freeman City of London, Liveryman Worshipful Co of Shipwrights 1981, FIMarE 1965; *Recreations* golf, gardening; *Clubs* Caledonian; *Style—* Cameron Parker, Esq; The Heath House, Rowantreehill Rd, Kilmacolm, Renfrewshire PA13 4PE (☎ 050 587 3197); Lithgows Ltd, Netherton, Langbank, Renfrewshire PA14 6YG (☎ 0475 54692, fax 0475 54558, telex 779248)

PARKER, Charles David; s of David Parker (d 1961), of Bradford, Yorks, and Jane, *née* Homler (d 1970); *b* 2 May 1929; *Educ* Hanson HS Bradford, Univ of Leeds Dental Sch (BChD, Charles Rippon medalist); *m* 18 Sept 1954, Margaret Joyce, da of Robert Henry Hull Goss (d 1978), of Bournemouth; 2 s (Richard Martin b 1960, William George b 1963), 1 da (Sarah Caroline b 1958); *Career* Nat Serv Capt 1953-54 (1 Lt 1952-53) RADC, 18 Field Ambulance Hong Kong; Chapman Prize essayist Br Soc for the Study of Orthodontics 1963, pt/t memb Dental Estimates Bd Orthodontics 1975-84; conslt orthodontist Leicestershire HA Hosp and Community Dental Serv 1963-, private practice 1966-; memb Cncl Soc for Study of Orthodontics, chm and treas Conslt Orthondontics Gp; author of approximately 25 pubns of papers and letters and reports on orthodontics; LDS 1951, DOth RCS 1957, FDSRCS 1958; memb: BDA, Br Soc for the Study of Orthodontics; *Recreations* skiing, swimming, public speaking, vegetable gardening; *Clubs* Victory Services; *Style—* Charles Parker, Esq; Stoke Dry Cottage, 2 Main St, Stoke Dry, nr Uppingham, Rutland LE15 9JG (☎ 0572 822805); 25 Allandale Rd, Stoneygate, Leicester LE2 2DA (☎ 0533 704051)

PARKER, Charles G A; JP (London W Central 1978, Oxford City 1990); s of Capt C E Parker, MC (d 1962), of Ewelme, Oxfordshire, and Hilda M, *née* Starkey (d 1979); *b* 30 Jan 1924; *Educ* Eton, New Coll Oxford (MA); *m* 3 Nov 1958, Shirley, da of Col Frank Follett Holt, TD (d 1978), of Corrybrough, Tomatin, Inverness-shire; 1 da (Davina (Mrs John Walter)); *Career* Capt Rifle Bde 1942-46, served France (POW Germany); The Times Newspaper 1949-56, Charringtons 1956-61, BMA Pubns 1961-76, chm Court and Judicial Publishing Co Ltd 1976-; chm: Cncl for Oxfordshire Order of St John, Tower Hill Improvement Tst; pres Assoc of Learned and Professional Soc Publishers, vice pres Nettlebed Branch Royal Br Legion; High Sheriff of Oxfordshire 1989-90; Liveryman Worshipful Co of Stationers 1965; FRSA, FRGS; *Recreations* fishing, tennis; *Clubs* Beefsteak, Whites; *Style—* Charles Parker, Esq; The White House, Nuffield, Oxon RG9 5SR

PARKER, Christopher John McKellen; s of Alfred Derek McKellen Parker, of Beltinge, Herne Bay, Kent, and Muriel Joyce, *née* Hargreaves; *b* 25 July 1945; *Educ* Dulwich, LSE (BSc); *m* 27 Dec 1969, Alison Eyre, da of Robin Gordon Miller, of Shepherdswell, Dover, Kent; 3 s (Thomas b 1972, Jonathan b 1974, Samuel b 1980); *Career* dir: Arbuthnot Latham & Co Ltd 1978-82, Caird Cp plc (formerly A Caird & Sons plc) 1982- (chm 1982-87); ACA 1969, FCA 1979; *Style—* Christopher Parker, Esq; Dennes House, Waltham, Canterbury, Kent CT4 5SD (☎ 022 770 389); 163 Andrewes House, Barbican, London EC2Y 8BA (☎ 071 638 5009); 33 Sekforde St, London EC1R 0HH (☎ 071 250 3003, fax 071 250 3001, car 0836 676622)

PARKER, Christopher William Oxley; JP (Essex 1952), DL (Essex 1972); s of Lt-Col John Oxley Parker (d 1979); *b* 28 May 1920; *Educ* Eton, Trinity Coll Oxford; *m* 1947, Jocelyn Frances Adeline, da of Col C G Arkwright, MC (d 1980); 1 s, 2 da; *Career* WWII 1939-45, 147 Field Regt Essex Yeo RA 1940-42; dir: Barclays Bank Chelmsford Local Bd 1950-81, Strutt & Parker (Farms) Ltd, Lord Rayleighs Farms Inc, Lavenham Fen Farms Ltd; High Sheriff Essex 1961, memb Nat Tst Properties Ctee 1972-89, pres Essex branch CLA 1987-; *Recreations* shooting, golf; *Clubs* Boodle's; *Style—* Christopher Parker, Esq, JP, DL; Faulkbourne Hall, Witham, Essex (☎ 0376 513385)

PARKER, Constance-Anne; *b* 19 Oct 1921; *Educ* Poly Sch of Art, Royal Acad Schs (ATD Dip); *Career* librarian Royal Acad of Arts 1974-88 (asst librarian 1958-74);

painter and sculptor; lectr: Royal Acad, NADFAS; FRBS 1983; *Books* Mr Stubbs the Horse Painter (1971), The Royal Academy Cookbook, Stubbs Art Animals Anatomy (1984); *Clubs* Reynolds (chm); *Style*— Miss Constance-Anne Parker; 1 Melrose Rd, Barnes, London SW13 9LG (☎ 081 878 3687)

PARKER, Dr David; s of late Hubert Eric Robert Parker, and Eileen Rose, *née* Goodson, of St Anne's Court, Buckland Rd, Maidstone, Kent; *b* 28 May 1940; *Educ* Maidstone GS for Boys, Univ of Nottingham (BA), Univ of Sheffield (PhD); *m* 24 Sept 1966, Elinor Sheila Halling, da of Joseph Patrick Anthony Cheek, of 17 Church Hill, Combwich, nr Bridgewater, Somerset; 1 s (Daniel b 1969), 1 da (Clare b 1972); *Career* lectr Univ of Sheffield 1966-68, assoc prof Univ of Malaya 1974-75 (lectr 1968-74), curator The Dickens House Museum 1978-; Freedom of Independance Missouri USA 1983; memb Int Cncl of Museums 1978; *Recreations* cooking, guitar playing; *Clubs* Dickens Fellowship; *Style*— Dr David Parker; The Dickens House Museum, 48 Doughty St, London WC1N 2LF (☎ 071 405 2127)

PARKER, Hon David; s of 8 Earl of Macclesfield; *b* 1945; *m* 1968, Lynne Valerie, da of George William Butler; 1 s, 2 da; *Style*— The Hon David Parker

PARKER, Edward; s of Francis Parker (d 1943), and Lucy Maud, *née* Pritchard (d 1969); *b* 9 Aug 1933; *Educ* Manchester Central HS for Boys, Univ of Manchester (BSc, MSc); *m* 6 Aug 1960, Anne Marguerite, da of Alan Ewart Bracewell, of Heysham; 2 da (Susan Elizabeth b 1961, Katherine Jane b 1964); *Career* head of Aerothermodynamics Section A V Roe Woodford 1955-60, lectr Royal Coll of Advanced Technol 1960-67; Univ of Salford: lectr then sr lectr 1971-79, pro vice chllr 1979-, dir of continuing educn 1981-87, dir CAMPUS 1987-; author of forty articles and papers on thermodynamics, continuing educn and industry-univ rels; memb: Engr Cncl Continuing Educn Ctee 1985-, Standing Ctee on Industry 1990-; chm CONTACT Management Bd 1986-88, memb Salford Health Authy 1986-89, govr Bury GS 1987-, chm Salford Family Practitioner Ctee 1988-90, memb Cncl Soc of Family Practitioners Ctees 1989-90, chm Saltford Family Health Serv Authy 1990-; memb: N Western Regnl Health Authy 1990-, Cncl Nat Assoc of Health Authys and Tsts 1990-; CEng 1964, FIMechE 1971; *Recreations* swimming, walking, music, church services, football (watching!); *Style*— Edward Parker, Esq; 12 Cove Rd, Silverdale, Lancs LA5 0RR (☎ 0524 701187); CAMPUS, The University of Salford, 43 The Crescent, Salford M5 4WT (☎ 061 743 1727, fax 061 745 7808, telex 668680 SULIB)

PARKER, Elinor Sheila Halling; da of Joseph Patrick Anthony Cheek, of New Malden, Surrey, and Joan Sheila Maude, *née* Halling; *b* 21 Sept 1940; *Educ* Grey Coat Hosp Westminster, Univ of Sheffield (BDS); *m* 24 Sept 1966, Dr David Parker, s of Hubert Robert Parker (d 1990), Maidstone; 1 s (Daniel b 1969), 1 da (Clare b 1972); *Career* asst lectr Univ of Sheffield 1966-68; gen dental practitioner: Kuala Lumpur Malaysia 1969-74, New Malden Surrey 1975-81, Hersham Surrey 1981-90; pt/t teacher Vocational Training Scheme for dentists; memb: Mgmnt Ctee Kingston Womens Centre 1984-87; womens Ctee Kingston BC 1987-88, Br Dental Editors Forum 1987; chm Govrs Tiffin Girls Sch 1987-88, chm Women in Dentistry 1989-90 (ed 1986-); memb Gen Dental Practitioners Assoc; *Recreations* writing, badminton, music; *Clubs* Kingston Feminists; *Style*— Mrs Elinor Parker; 16 Alric Avenue, New Malden, Surrey KT3 4JN (☎ 081 949 2596); 5 The Green, Hersham, Walton on Thames, Surrey KT12 4HW (☎ 0932 248348)

PARKER, Sir Eric Wilson; s of Wilson Parker (d 1983), and Edith Gladys, *née* Wellings; *b* 8 June 1933; *Educ* The Priory GS for Boys Shrewsbury; *m* 12 Nov 1955, Marlene Teresa, da of Michael Neale (d 1941); 2 s (Ian, Charles), 2 da (Karen, Sally); *Career* Nat Serv RAPC Cyprus 1956-58; articled clerk with Wheeler Whittingham & Kent (CAs) 1950-55; with Taylor Woodrow 1958-64; Trafalgar House plc: joined 1965, fin dir 1969, dep md 1973, md 1977, chief exec 1983, dep chm and chief exec 1988; Trafalgar House Gp directorships incl: Cunard Line Ltd (chm), Cunard Resorts Ltd, John Brown PLC (chm), The Cunard Steam-Ship Company plc (chm), Trafalgar House Construction Holdings Ltd (chm), Trafalgar House Corporate Development Ltd (chm), Trafalgar House Group Services Ltd (chm), Trafalgar House Investment Management Ltd (chm), Trafalgar House Property Ltd (chm), Trafalgar House Trustees Ltd; non Trafalgar House directorships incl: Hardy Oil & Gas PLC, MB Caradon PLC, The Royal Automobile Club Ltd, RAC Motoring Services Ltd; non-exec dir British Rail Investments Ltd 1980-84 (assisted in formation of Sealink and with the disposal to the private sector of a number of British Rail's non-railway interests); memb: Br Contractors Gp, Gp of Eleven, Appeal Ctee RCS, Devpt Bd Univ of Kent, Ctee for Indust and the City Royal Marsden Appeal, Ctee for the Int Year of Shelter for the Homeless 1987, MCC, Lloyds, Seventh Cwlth Study Conf Cncl; kt 1991; FCA 1967 (ACA 1956), FRSA, CBIM; *Recreations* racehorse owner, golf, tennis, cricket, wine; *Clubs* RAC, Tyrrell's Wood Golf (Leatherhead), MCC; *Style*— Sir Eric Parker; Crimbourne Stud, Wisborough Green, Billingshurst, West Sussex RH14 0HR; Trafalgar House plc, 1 Berkeley Street, London W1A 1BY (☎ 071 499 9020, fax 071 493 5484)

PARKER, Garry Stuart; s of Derek John Parker, (d 1972), of Oxford, and Betty Joyce Parker; *b* 7 Sept 1965; *Educ* Oxford Boys Sch; *m* 1 July 1989, Petra Elaine, da of Ray John Timms; 1 s (Jordan Lloyd b 2 Dec 1990); *Career* professional footballer; schoolboy player Queens Park Rangers; Luton Town 1983-86: apprentice then professional, debut v Manchester Utd 1982, 54 appearances; 95 appearances Hull City 1986-88, over 100 appearances Nottingham Forest 1988-; England caps: 6 youth on tour France, 6 under 21 1986-87, 1 B; honours with Nottingham Forest: League Cup 1989 and 1990, Simod Cup 1989; *Recreations* golf, snooker, swimming; *Style*— Gary Parker, Esq; Nottingham Forest FC, City Ground, Nottingham (☎ 0602 822202)

PARKER, (James) Geoffrey; s of Ian Sutherland Parker (d 1973), of Leicester, and Kathleen Lilian, *née* Cave (d 1976); *b* 27 March 1933; *Educ* Alderman Newton's Sch Leicester, Christ's Coll Cambridge (BA), Wadham Coll Oxford (CertEd); *m* 22 Sept 1956, Ruth, da of Edward Major, of Leicester; 2 da (Georgina b 1959, Katherine b 1960); *Career* RA 1954-56, Lance Bombardier 1955, 2 Lt 1955, Actg Capt 1956; asst master Bedford Modern Sch 1957-66, head History Dept Tonbridge Sch Kent 1966-75, head master Queen Elizabeth GS Wakefield 1975-85, high master Manchester GS 1985-; memb: various HMC ctees (chm 1991), Advsy Cncl for Church's Miny; govr various schs and educnl bodies, QMC Conf 1975-; *Recreations* sailing, coarse gardening; *Clubs* East India, Devonshire, Sports and Public Schs; *Style*— Geoffrey Parker, Esq; The Manchester GS, Manchester N13 0XT

PARKER, Geoffrey John; CBE (1984); s of Stanley John Parker (d 1983), of London, and Alice Ellen Parker (d 1984); *b* 20 March 1937; *Educ* Hendon Co GS; *m* 25 Nov 1957, Hazel Mary, da of Lawrence Edward; 2 s (Simon, Andrew), 2 da (Joanne, Amanda); *Career* Nat Serv RAF 1955-57; commercial dir Townsend Car Ferries Ltd Dover 1962-74, md Atlantic Steam Navigation Co Ltd 1974-86, chm and md Port of Felixstow 1976-87, chm European Ferries plc 1986-87 (dir 1981), chief exec Highland Participants plc 1987-89, chm and chief exec Maritime Transport Services Ltd 1989-; dir Nat Bus Co 1979-86; FCIT 1982, FITA 1986; *Recreations* golf, opera; *Clubs* Ipswich Golf; *Style*— Geoffrey Parker, Esq, CBE; 101 Valley Rd, Ipswich, Suffolk (☎ 0473 216 003); 77 Alder Lodge, Stevenage Rd, London SW6 (☎ 071 385 5434); Maritime Transport Services Ltd (☎ 071 584 6144)

PARKER, Prof (Noel) Geoffrey; s of late Derek Geoffrey Parker, and Kathleen Betsy, *née* Symon; *b* 25 Dec 1943; *Educ* Nottingham HS, Christ's Coll Cambridge (BA, MA, PhD, LittD); *m* 1, 1965 (m dis 1980), Angela Maureen; 1 s, 1 da; m 2, 1986, Jane Helen; 1 s; *Career* fell Christ's Coll Cambridge 1968-72; St Andrews Univ: reader in modern history 1978-82 (lectr 1972-78), prof of early modern history 1982-86; Br Acad Exchange Fell Newberry Library Chicago 1981; visiting prof: Vrije Universiteit Brussels 1975, Univ of BC Vancouver Canada 1979-80, Keio Univ Tokyo 1984; Lees Knowles lectr in mil history Univ of Cambridge 1984, Charles E Nowell distinguished prof of history Univ of Illinois at Urbana - Champaign 1986-; corresponding fell Spanish Royal Acad of History 1988-; Hon Doctorate in History and Letters Vrije Universiteit Brussels 1990; Encomienda Order of Isabel the Catholic (Spain 1988); *Books* The Army of Flanders and The Spanish Road 1567-1659 (1972, 3 edn 1990), The Dutch Revolt (1977, 3 edn 1985), Philip II (1978, 2 edn 1988), Europe in Crisis 1598-1648 (1979), Spain and the Netherlands 1559-1659 (1979, 2 edn 1990), The Thirty Years' War (1984), The World: an illustrated history (ed 1986), The Military Revolution: military innovation and the rise of the West 1500-1800 (1988, 2 edn 1990), The Spanish Armada (with Colin Martin 1988, 2 edn 1990), author of numerous articles and reviews; *Recreations* travel, archaeology; *Style*— Prof Geoffrey Parker; Department of History, University of Illinois, 309 Gregory Hall, 810 S Wright St, Urbana, Illinois 61801, USA (☎ 217 333 4193)

PARKER, Prof Graham Alexander; s of Joe Parker (d 1964), of Nuneaton, Warwickshire, and Margaretta Annie, *née* Mawbey (d 1985); *b* 20 Nov 1935; *Educ* King Edward VI GS Nuneaton Warwicks, Univ of Birmingham (BSc, PhD); *m* 7 Nov 1959, Janet Ada, da of Cecil Parsons (d 1963), of Nuneaton, Warwickshire; 2 da (Joanne Marie b 1966, Louise Alessandra b 1968); *Career* Hawker-Siddeley Dynamics Ltd 1957-60, Cincinnati Milacron Inc USA 1963-64, Univ of Birmingham 1964-68, Univ of Surrey 1968- (prof of mech engrg, dean of the faculty of Engrg); cncl memb: Cranleigh Sch, St Catherines, Br Robot Assoc; div memb mfrg systems IMechE; FIMechE, memb ASME; *Books* Fluidics - Components and Circuits (with K Foster, 1970), A Guide to Fluidics (contrib 1971); *Recreations* squash, tennis, walking; *Style*— Prof Graham Parker; Tall Chimneys, Malacca Farm, West Clandon, Guildford, Surrey GU4 7UG (☎ 0483 22328); Department of Mechanical Engineering, University of Surrey, Guildford, Surrey GU2 5XH (☎ 0483 571281, fax 0483 306039, telex 859331)

PARKER, Prof Howard John; s of John Raymond Parker, and Doreen, *née* Taylor; *b* 2 Nov 1948; *Educ* Birkenhead Sch, Univ of Liverpool (BA, MA, PhD); *m* 4 Jan 1972, Diana Lesley; 2 s (James b 1977, Ben b 1980); *Career* reader social work studies Univ of Liverpool 1987-88 (res fell 1972-74, lectr applied social studies 1974-79, sr lectr social work studies 1980-86), prof social work Univ of Manchester 1988-; seconded res work Home Office Res and Planning 1985 and Wirral Borough Cncl 1986; advsr on drugs policies in Local Regnl and Govt Depts; memb Inst Study and Treatment of Delinquency and Br Criminology Soc; *Books* View from the Boys (1979), Social Work and the Courts (1979), Receiving Juvenile Justice (1981), Living with Heroin (1988), Unmasking the Magistrates (1989); *Style*— Prof Howard Parker; University of Manchester, The Dept of Social Policy and Social Work, Manchester M13 9PL (☎ 061 275 4783)

PARKER, Iain George McKim; s of Ernest Parker (d 1971), of Harrogate, and Barbara Core, *née* Hodgson-Hutton (d 1950); *b* 29 Dec 1937; *Educ* Ashville Coll Harrogate, Emmanuel Coll Cambridge (MA); *m* 29 March 1964, Judith Sian, da of Eric Hardman Taylor (d 1972), of Buxton; 1 s (Andrew b 1965), 1 da (Catherine b 1965); *Career* Lt IPWO Nat Serv; chm: Otter Controls Ltd, Montogomery Thermostats Ltd, St Davids Assemblies Ltd, Tarka Controls Ltd 1967; Stockport & High Peak TEC Ltd 1991 (dir 1989), Gen Cmmn of Income Tax High Peak Div; memb Buxton Musical Soc; *Recreations* mountain walking, photography, orchids; *Clubs* United Oxford and Cambridge University; *Style*— Iain Parker, Esq; Otter Controls Ltd, Otters 'Ole, Buxton, Derbyshire SK17 6LA (☎ 0298 71177, fax 0298 70160, telex 668936)

PARKER, James Mavin (Jim); s of James Robertson Parker (d 1983), of Hartlepool, and Margaret, *née* Mavin; *b* 18 Dec 1934; *Educ* Guildhall Sch of Music and Drama; *m* 1; 1 da (Louise b 1964); m 2, 2 Aug 1969, Pauline Ann, da of John George, of Reading; 2 da (Claire b 1974, Amy b 1976); *Career* Musician 4/7 Dragoon Gds; composer and conductor, joined Barrow Poets 1963; composed music for: Banana Blush (John Betjeman), Captain Beaky (Jeremy Lloyd); *printed music* Follow the Star (Wally K Daly); *childrens musicals*: five Childrens Musicals (Tom Stanier), English Towns (flute and piano), A Londoner in New York (suite for brass), All Jazzed Up (oboe and piano), Mississippi Five (woodwind quintet); *film and TV music:* Mapp and Lucia, Wynne and Pekovsky, Good Behaviour, The Making of Modern London, The Blot, Wish Me Luck, Anything More Would be Greedy, House of Cards, Parnell and the Englishwoman; Hon GSM 1985; GSM (Silvermedal) 1959, LRAM 1959; *Recreations* tennis, twentieth century art, literature; *Style*— Jim Parker, Esq; 19 Laurel Road, London SW13 OEE (☎ 081 876 8571)

PARKER, (Diana) Jean; *née* Morley; CBE (1989); da of Capt Lewis William Reeve Morley (d 1988), of Grantham, Lincolnshire, and Amy, *née* Southwood (d 1973); *b* 7 June 1932; *Educ* Kesteven and Grantham Girls' Sch, Univ of Birmingham (BComm); *m* 26 June 1959, Dudley Frost Parker (d 1971), s of Frederick Parker (d 1960), of Rugby; 1 s (Andrew b 1965), 1 da (Alison b 1960); *Career* dir: Vacu-Lug Traction Tyres Ltd 1957-, Langham Industries Ltd 1980-, Central Independent TV plc 1982-, British Steel (Industries) Ltd 1986-90; memb: Bd E Midlands Electricity 1983-90, Eastern Advsy Bd Nat West Bank plc 1985-; CBI: memb Cncl 1985-89, memb Pres Ctee 1985-89, chm Smaller Firms Ctee 1986-88; chm: Lincolnshire Jt Devpt Ctee 1983-, N Lincolnshire Health Authy 1987-90; former chm: Age Concern Grantham, Grantham C of C; dir Lincs Ambulance & Health Tport Tst 1991-, former memb E Midlands Econ Planning Cncl, sec Friends of St Wulfram's Church; CBIM 1986; *Recreations* church architecture, reading fiction; *Style*— Mrs Jean Parker, CBE; Vacu-Lug Traction Tyres Ltd, Gonerby Hill Foot, Grantham, Lincolnshire (☎ 0476 62424, fax 0476 62736, car 0836 693 389)

PARKER, Hon Jocelyn George Dudley; s of 7 Earl of Macclesfield (d 1975); *b* 1920; *m* 1948, Daphne, da of late Maj G Cecil Whitaker, of Britwell House, Watlington, Oxon; 1 s, 1 da; *Career* European War 1939-45 as Lt RNVR; *Style*— The Hon Jocelyn Parker; Pyrton Field Farm, Watlington, Oxon

PARKER, (Anthony) John; s of John Edward Parker (d 1976), of Nantwich, Cheshire, and Winnie May, *née* Bebbington; *b* 2 Oct 1942; *Educ* Nantwich Acton GS; *m* 21 June 1969, (Mary) Elizabeth, da of Frederick Langley (d 1990), of Audlem, Cheshire; 2 s (Simon b 1972, Stephen b 1974), 1 da (Ann-Marie b 1978); *Career* quantity surveyor Brown & Richmond 1959-65, sr quantity surveyor Allott & Lomax 1965-71, dir Sika Contracts Ltd 1974-86 (sr mangr 1971-74), jt md (following mgmnt buy out) Sika Contracts 1986-; fndr memb and first chm Tech Ctee of Concrete Repair Assoc 1988-, memb Working Pty of The Concrete Soc (on repairs to reinforced concrete structures) 1988-, memb EFNARC Euro Trade Fedn on Eurocodes 1989-, memb BSI Ctee on Euro Standards for 1992; ARICS 1968, FInstD 1975; *Recreations* music, piano playing; *Clubs* IOD; *Style*— John Parker, Esq; Churton, Chester; Sika Contracts Ltd, Cuppin St, Chester, Cheshire CH1 2BN (☎ 0244 312 553)

PARKER, John Gordon; s of Henry Gordon Parker, CBE (d 1980), of Gooderstone, Norfolk, and Alice Rose, *née* Bennett (d 1974); *b* 20 May 1929; *Educ* Eton, Christ

Church Oxford (BA), Mons Offr Cadet Sch; *m* 12 April 1958, Veronica Harriet, eld da of Blackburn of Roshven; 2 s (Hugo b 29 Sept 1963, d 1988, Edmund b 16 Nov 1972), 3 da (Sophie b 9 Feb 1959, Camilla b 9 March 1965, Lucinda b 27 Dec 1967); *Career* Nat Serv cmmnd 4/7 RDG 1948, Capt (AER) 1955; called to the Bar Inner Temple 1953; in practice 1953-59; dir: Felixstowe Tank Devpt Ltd 1963-75, Favor Parker Ltd and subsides 1963-; govr Thetford GS, vice pres Hawk Tst (former chm); MBOU; author various papers in ornithological jnls; *Recreations* shooting, bird watching; *Clubs* Cavalry and Guards', British Ornithologists; *Style*— John Parker, Esq; Clavering House, Oxborough, Norfolk (☎ 036 621 781); Favor Parker Ltd, Stoke Ferry, King's Lynn, Norfolk (☎ 0366 500 911)

PARKER, Dr John Richard Robert; s of Richard Robert Parker (d 1987), and Elsie Winifred, *née* Curtis; *b* 5 Nov 1933; *Educ* SE London Tech Coll, Regent St Poly (Dip Arch), UCL (Dip TP), Central London Poly (PhD); *m* 1959, Valerie Barbara Mary, da of Edward James Troupe Duguid (d 1952); 1 s (Jonathan b 1965), 1 da (Joanna b 1968); *Career* Nat Serv 2 Lt RE served Canal Zone, Cyprus 1952-54, TA (Lt) 1954-64; pte architects and commercial firms 1954-59, architect LCC 1961-64, urban designer London Borough of Lambeth 1964-70, head central area team GLC 1970-86; fndr and md Gtr London Conslts 1986- (dir Environmental Appraisal Unit 1989-), princ John Parker Associates (architectural and planning conslts) 1990-; originator of devpt nr Tport interchanges related to pedestrian movement 1967-87, project mangr Piccadilly Circus redevpt 1972-86, planning cnslt for Addis Ababa 1986; Winston Churchill fell 1967; RIBA Pearce Edwards Award 1969, Br Cncl Anglo-Soviet Award 1988; ARIBA, FRTPI, FRSA; *Publications* subjects incl: urban design, environmental planning, pedestrians and security; *Recreations* tennis, golf, drawing; *Clubs* Royal Cwlth, Shortlands Golf, Catford Wanderers Sports (chm); *Style*— Dr John Parker; 4 The Heights, Foxgrove Rd, Beckenham, Kent BR3 2BY (☎ 081 658 6076); Greater London Consultants, St Brides's House, 32 High St, Beckenham, Kent BR3 1BD (☎ 081 663 6330, fax 081 650 3456, telex 262 433 (ref W6861))

PARKER, Dr (Thomas) John; s of Robert Parker (d 1957), and Margaret Elizabeth, *née* Bell; *b* 8 April 1942; *Educ* Belfast Coll of Technol; *m* July 1967, Emma Elizabeth, da of Alexander Blair, of Ballymena, NI; 1 s (Graham b 31 July 1970), 1 da (Fiona b 1 June 1972); *Career* shipbuilder and engr; md Austin & Pickersgill (shipbuilders) Sunderland 1974-78, memb Bd for Shipbuilding Br Shipbuilders Corp 1978-80 (dep chief exec 1980), chm and chief exec Harland & Wolff Belfast 1983; memb: Indust Devpt Bd NI 1983-87, Br Coal Corp 1986-; Hon DSc Queen's Univ of Belfast 1985, Hon ScD Trinity Coll Dublin 1986; FRINA 1978, FIMarE 1979, FEng 1982; *Recreations* sailing, reading, music; *Style*— Dr John Parker; Harland & Wolff Holdings plc, Queen's Island, Belfast BT3 9DU (☎ 0232 457032, telex 748014, fax 0232 458515)

PARKER, John Townley; s of Arthur Townley Parker, of Burnley, Lancashire, and Margaret Elizabeth, *née* Birchall, of Burnley, Lancashire; *b* 26 July 1959; *Educ* Nelson GS, Blackpool Coll of Art; partner, Angela Chung-Man-Fu; *Career* photographer; asst to: Ed Baxter 1980-82, Jerry Oke 1982-85; fndr of own studio 1986-; 2 Gold awards and 2 Silver awards Assoc of Photographers; memb: Assoc of Photographers 1987-, Design and Art Direction 1988-; *Recreations* football; *Style*— John Parker, Esq; (☎ 071 286 3444, fax 071 286 6963)

PARKER, Vice Adm Sir (Wilfred) John; KBE (1969, OBE 1953), CB (1965), DSC (1943); s of Henry Edmond Parker (d 1962), and Ida Mary Parker (d 1955); *b* 12 Oct 1915; *Educ* RNC Dartmouth, RNC Greenwich; *m* 1943, Marjorie Stuart, da of Alfred Nagle Jones (d 1961), of Halifax, Nova Scotia, Canada; 2 da; *Career* Capt RNC Dartmouth 1961-63, flag offr Medway and Adm Supt HM Dockyard Chatham 1966-69, ret 1969; *Clubs* Royal Navy; *Style*— Vice Adm Sir John Parker, KBE, CB, DSC; Flint Cottage, East Harting, Petersfield, Hants GU31 5LT (☎ 073 085 427)

PARKER, Jonathan Frederic; QC (1979); s of Sir (Walter) Edmund Parker (d 1981), and Elizabeth Mary, *née* Butterfield (d 1984); *b* 8 Dec 1937; *Educ* Winchester, Magdalene Coll Cambridge (MA); *m* 1967, Maria-Belen, da of Thomas Ferrier Burns OBE; 3 s (James b 1968, Oliver b 1969, Peter b 1971), 1 da (Clare b 1972); *Career* called to the Bar Inner Temple 1962; bencher 1985, rec 1989, attorney gen Duchy of Lancaster 1989; *Recreations* painting, sailing; *Clubs* Garrick; *Style*— Jonathan Parker Esq, QC; The Grange, Radwinter, Saffron Walden, Essex CB10 2TF (☎ 0799 599375); 11 Old Square, Lincoln's Inn, London WC2A 3TS (☎ 071 430 0341)

PARKER, Joseph Roy; s of Joseph Parker, and Sarah Ellen, *née* Baddeley; *b* 27 Feb 1926; *Educ* Blackpool GS; Univ of Liverpool: Sch of Architecture (BArch), Dept of Civic Design (Master of Civic Design); *m* June 1948, Kathleen Horrocks; 1 da (Jane Louise b 19 Jan 1963); *Career* redevelopment architect Liverpool City Architects Dept 1954-55, ptnr Nelson & Parker (chartered architects and town planners) 1955-74, sometime sr lectr in town planning and urban design, ptnr TACP Design (architects, product designers and planners, historic building and theatre conslts) 1974-; pres Liverpool Architectural Soc 1974-76; chm 1974-76: Merseyside Branch RIBA, N W Branch Royal Town Planning Inst, SW Regn Soc of Industl Artists and Designers; vice pres CSD, chm Professional Practice Bd CSD 1985-, RTPI rep W Lancs Conservation Areas Advsy Ctee 1985-, Br rep Int Design Toronto 1975-, fndr memb Bd Liverpool Everyman Theatre 1975-, memb Designer Selection Serv Advsy Ctee Design Cncl 1990-; *awards* RIBA medal, Tyson prize, Civic Tst award (for Wakefield Opera House) 1987, Design award 1987; FCSD, MRTPI, memb Assoc of Br Theatre Technicians, MRIBA; *Recreations* silversmith; *Style*— Joseph Parker, Esq; 1 Ingestre Rd, Oxton, Wirral, Merseyside (☎ 051 652 1068); TACP Design, South Harrington Building, Sefton St, Liverpool L3 4BQ (☎ 051 708 7014, fax 051 709 1503)

PARKER, Sir Karl Theodore; CBE (1954); s of late Robert William Parker; *b* 1895; *Educ* Bedford, Paris, Zurich (MA, PhD); *m* Audrey (d 1976), da of Henry Ashworth James; 2 da; *Career* keeper of Ashmolean Museum Oxford Univ, ret 1962; tstee Nat Gallery 1962-69; hon fell Oriel Coll Oxford 1962; FBA; kt 1960; *Style*— Sir Karl Parker, CBE; 4 Saffrons Court, Compton Place Rd, Eastbourne

PARKER, Keith John; s of Sydney John Parker, Tywyn, Gwynedd, N Wales, and Phyllis Mary, *née* Marsh; *b* 30 Dec 1940; *m* 25 Aug 1962, Marilyn Ann, da of Wilfred Frank Edwards; 1 s (Nicholas Edward b 18 July 1966); *Career* reporter: Wellington Journal and Shrewsbury News 1957-63, Express and Star Wolverhampton 1963-64; Shropshire Star: reporter, chief reporter, dep news ed 1964-72, ed and dir 1972-77; ed and dir Express and Star 1977-; pres Guild of Br Newspaper Editors 1988-89 (memb Parly and Legal Ctee), memb Assoc of Br Editors; FRSA; *Style*— Keith Parker, Esq; 94 Wrottesley Rd, Tettenhall, Wolverhampton, West Midlands WV6 8SJ (☎ 0902 758595); Express and Star, 51-53 Queen St, Wolverhampton (☎ 0902 313131)

PARKER, Lynne Eleanor; da of Ronald Samuel Parker and Audrey Eleanor, *née* Tyler; *b* 30 June 1956; *Educ* Ashford Co GS Middx, London Coll of Fashion; *Career* journalist 1975-80; PR conslt in own business Parker Lightman Public Relations 1983-90, dir of consumer offrs Ruder Finn UK Ltd 1990-; MIPR; memb: Nat Union of Journalists; *Clubs* Groucho; *Style*— Ms Lynne Parker; 55 Wavendon Ave, London W4 4NT (☎ 071 474 3679); Ruder Finn UK Ltd, 19 Chelsea Wharf, London SW10 0QY (☎ 071 351 5777, fax 071 351 5355)

PARKER, Malcolm Peter (Mal); s of William Harvey Parker, of 13 The Rise, Navenby, Lincs, and Mary Jean, *née* Spinks; *b* 4 June 1946; *Educ* Kings Sch Grantham, Oxford Sch of Architecture (Dip Arch); *m* 21 June 1975, Linda Diane, da of Emmanuel Theodore, of 2 Brunswick Mews, London; 2 da (Charlotte b 1982, Georgina b 1984); *Career* architect; Tom Hancock Assocs 1972-73, John Winter Assocs 1973-74, Pentagram 1974-76, Richard Ellis 1976-78, founding ptnr Dunthorne Parker 1978-; RIBA 1973, MCSD 1985; *Recreations* golf, skiing, theatre, opera, concerts; *Clubs* Reform; *Style*— Mal Parker, Esq; Dunthorne Parker, 8 Seymour Place, London W1H 5AG (☎ 071 258 0411, fax 071 723 1329)

PARKER, His Hon Judge Michael Clynes; s of Herbert Parker; *b* 2 Nov 1924; *Educ* City of London Sch, Pembroke Coll Cambridge; *m* 1950, Molly Leila Franklin; 1 s, 2 da; *Career* barr Gray's Inn 1949, QC 1979, a rec Crown Ct 1972-78, a Circuit judge 1978-; contested (L) S Kensington 1951; *Style*— His Hon Judge Parker; 17 Courtnell St, W2 (☎ 071 229 5249)

PARKER, Michael Joseph Bennett; s of Henry Gordon Parker, CBE, MM, TEM (d 1980), of Toad Hall, Gooderstone, King's Lynn, Norfolk, and Alice Rose, *née* Bennett (d 1975); *b* 22 June 1931; *Educ* Eton, Magdalene Coll Cambridge (BA Agric); *m* 30 April 1960, Tania Henrietta, da of Peter Frank Tiarks (d 1975), of Melplash Court, Beaminster, Dorset; 2 s (Stephen b 1960, Benjamin b 1962), 1 da (Naomi b 1964); *Career* dir: Favor Parker Ltd 1962-, Favor Parker Feeds Ltd 1963-, Favor Parker Farms Ltd 1965-, Sovereign Chicken Gp Ltd 1977-, BCA (Co-operative & Export) Ltd 1983-, British Poultry Fedn Ltd 1984-, British Chicken Assoc Ltd 1988-; memb UKAEA 1985-88; *Recreations* country sports, windsurfing, lying in the sun; *Style*— Michael Parker, Esq; Gooderstone Manor, King's Lynn, Norfolk PE33 9BP (☎ 036 621 255); Favor Parker Ltd, The Hall, Stoke Ferry, King's Lynn, Norfolk PE33 9SE (☎ 0366 500911, fax 0366 500907, telex 81135 FPFEED G)

PARKER, Hon Nigel Geoffrey; yst s of Hon John Holford Parker (d 1955) and bro of 6 Earl of Morley, qv; *b* 18 Nov 1931; *Educ* Eton, Trinity Coll Cambridge (BA); *m* 23 April 1965, Georgina Jane, eld da of Sir Thomas Gordon Devitt, 2 Bt; 1 s (Edward b 1967), 1 da (Theresa b 1966); *Career* Grenadier Gds 1950-52; Shell Petroleum Co Ltd 1955-91; *Style*— The Hon Nigel Parker; Combe Lane Farm, Wormley, Godalming, Surrey

PARKER, Paul William Giles; s of Anthony John Parker, and (Margaret) Edna Parker; *b* 15 Jan 1956; *Educ* Collyers GS Horsham, St Catharine's Coll Cambridge; *m* 25 Jan 1980, Teresa, da of late Czeslaw Zienkiewicz; 1 s (James William Ralph b 6 Nov 1980), 1 da (Jocelyn P Elizabeth b 10 Sept 1984); *Career* cricketer; represented English Schs Cricket Assoc v Indian Schs 1973; capt: English Schs Cricket Assoc 1974, Nat Young Cricketers 1974; Sussex CCC: joined 1975, capped 1979, capt 1988-; 316 First Class matches to date, scorer of 16557 First Class runs; 1 England cap v Aust (6 Test at The Oval); capt MCC tour of Argentina 1990; stockbroker Laing & Cruickshank 1982-87, Deloitte Haskins & Sells 1989-90, estab own cricket-based co 1990; *Recreations* reading, travel, playing guitar; *Style*— Paul Parker, Esq; Sussex County Cricket Club, Eaton Road, Hove, East Sussex BN3 3AN (☎ 0273 732161, fax 0273 771549)

PARKER, Sir Peter; LVO (1985, MVO 1957); s of late Tom Parker and Dorothy Mackinlay Parker; *b* 30 Aug 1924; *Educ* Bedford Sch, Univ of London, Lincoln Coll Oxford, Cornell Univ, Harvard Univ; *m* 1951, Gillian, da of Sir Ernest Rowe-Dutton, KCMG, CB (d 1965); 3 s, 1 da; *Career* Maj Intelligence Corps 1943-47; contested Bedford as Labour candidate 1951; chm Br Rail Bd 1976-83, memb Br Airways Bd 1971-81; chm: Rockware Group 1983- (dep chm 1981, chm 1971-76, dir 1976-83), Art Advisers Ltd 1989-, The Japan Festival 1990-, Evered plc 1989-, Whitehead Mann Group plc 1984-, Mitsubishi Electric UK Ltd 1984-, Oakland Management Holdings Ltd 1986-, Metropolitan Radio 1983-, Holman Wade Group Ltd 1988-, Fidelity Japan OTC and Regional Markets Fund Ltd 1990-, Apricot Computers Ltd 1990-, Arcadian International plc 1990-; vice chm: Friends of the Earth Trust Ltd 1987, tstees of HRH The Duke of Edinburgh's Cwlth Study Conference (UK Fund); dep chm: H Clarkson & Co (Hldgs) 1976- (chm 1975-76), Group Securitas Ltd 1984-; dir: The Social and Liberal Democrats (Trustees) Ltd 1989-, UK - Japan 2000 Gp, The Design Museum 1989-, Royal National Theatre 1986-; dep chm Ct London Univ 1970-, chm Ct Govrs LSE 1988-; CStJ 1982; hon fell: Nuffield Coll Oxford, Westfield Coll Oxford; formerly with Booker McConnell, dir Booker Bros McConnell 1960-70; memb: Cncl BIM, Fndn Automation & Human Devpt 1971-, NEDC 1980-; Hon LLD Bath 1983, Hon Dr Open Univ; kt 1978; *Books* For Starters: The Business of Life (autobiography, 1989); *Style*— Sir Peter Parker, LVO; 5 Chandos Street, London W1M 9DG (☎ 071 637 0369)

PARKER, Sir (William) Peter Brian; 5 Bt (UK 1844), of Shenstone Lodge, Staffordshire; o s of Sir (William) Alan Parker, 4 Bt (d 1990), and Sheelagh Mary, *née* Stevenson; *b* 30 Nov 1950; *Educ* Eton; *m* 1976, Patricia Ann, da of D E Filtness, of Lea Cottage, Beckingham, Lincoln; 1 s (John Malcolm b 1980), 1 da (Lucy Emma b 1977); *Heir* s, John Malcolm Parker b 1980; *Career* FCA; ptnr Stephenson Nuttall & Co Newark Notts; *Style*— Sir Peter Parker, Bt; Apricot Hall, Sutton-cum-Beckingham, Lincoln

PARKER, Peter William; TD (1966); s of William Nichol Parker (d 1978), of Burnley, and Muriel Constantine (d 1965); *b* 13 June 1933; *Educ* Winchester Coll, New Coll Oxford (MA); *m* 5 Oct 1963, Janet Pusey, da of Tom Rymer Till (d 1982), of Caerleon; 2 s (Tom b 1968, Daniel b 1971), 1 da (Lucy b 1966); *Career* Nat Serv; 2 Lt E Lancashire Regt 1952 (actg capt 1953), TA 4 E Lancashire Regt 1953-67 (Maj 1965); Phillips & Drew 1956-85: ptnr 1962, dep sr ptnr 1983; chm Phillips & Drew International Ltd 1980-85; tstee Tower of London Choral Fndn, vice chm Sidney Perry Fndn, treasurer Egypt Exploration Soc, govr Music Therapy Charity; Liveryman Worshipful Co of Actuaries (master 1989-90), memb of Cncl Inst of Actuaries 1977-82 and 1986- (vice pres 1988-91); FIA 1963; *Recreations* music, gardening, travel, typography; *Clubs* City of London, Naval and Military; *Style*— Peter Parker, Esq, TD; 1 Turner Drive, London NW11 6TX (☎ 081 458 2646)

PARKER, Prof Ralph; s of Harry Parker (d 1950), of Swansea, and Dorothy Elizabeth, *née* Wilson; *b* 3 Dec 1926; *Educ* Univ of Wales (BSc, PhD, DSc); *m* 28 April 1951, Betty, da of late Thomas Frank, of Loughborough; 3 da (Susan b 6 Jan 1956, Helen b 22 May 1959, Margaret b 1 Dec 1961); *Career* scientific civil serv MOS 1950-57, Rolls-Royce Ltd 1957-58, English Electric Co Ltd 1958-64; Dept Mechanical Engrg Univ of Wales; former memb Ctee Aeronautical Res Cncl; FIMechE, MRAeS, FIOA, CEng; *Style*— Prof Ralph Parker; Dept of Mechanical Engineering, University of Wales, University College of Swansea, SA2 8PP (☎ 0792 295221, fax 0792 295 701, telex 48149 UICS-G)

PARKER, Viscount; Richard Timothy George Mansfield Parker; s and h of 8 Earl of Macclesfield; *b* 31 May 1943; *Educ* Stowe, Worcester Coll Oxford; *m* 1, 1967 (m dis), Tatiana Cleone, da of Maj Craig Wheaton-Smith; 3 da (Hon Tanya b 1971, Hon Katharine b 1973, Hon Marian (twin) b 1973); m 2, 1986, Mrs Sandra Hope Mead; *Style*— Viscount Parker; Portobello Farm, Shirburn, Watlington, Oxon

PARKER, Sir Richard William; 12 Bt (E 1681), of Melford Hall, Suffolk; *see*: Hyde Parker, Sir Richard William

PARKER, Prof Robert Henry (Bob); s of Henry William Parker (d 1978), of 7 Clitherow Ave, London, and Gladys Mary, *née* Bunkell (d 1939); *b* 21 Sept 1932; *Educ*

Paston Sch North Walsham Norfolk, UCL (BSc); *m* 5 Oct 1955, (Marie) Agnelle Hilda, da of Antoine Yves Laval (d 1962), of Rue Edouard VII, Rose Hill, Mauritius; 1 s (Michael b 1956), 1 da (Theresa b 1959); *Career* accountant Cassleton Elliott and Co Lagos Nigeria 1958-69, lectr in commerce Univ of Adelaide 1960-61, sr lectr in commerce Univ of W Aust 1962-66, PD Leake res fell LSE 1966, reader in mgmnt accounting Manchester Business Sch 1966-68, assoc prof in finance INSEAD Fontainebleau 1968-70; prof of accountancy: Univ of Dundee 1970-76, Univ of Exeter 1976-; memb Res Bd of Inst of CAs in Eng and Wales, ed Accounting and Business Research 1975-; FCA 1968 (ACA 1958); *Books* Topics in Business Finance and Accounting (jtly, 1964), Readings in Concept and Measurement of Income (jtly, 1 edn 1969, 2 edn 1986), Understanding Company Financial Statements (1 edn 1972, 2 edn 1982, 3 edn 1988), British Accountants: A Biographical Sourcebook (1980), Comparative International Accounting (jtly, 1 edn 1981, 2 edn 1985, 3 edn 1991), Macmillan Dictionary of Accounting (1984), Issues in Multinational Accounting (jtly, 1988), Bibliographies for Accounting Historians (1980), Accounting Thought and Education (jtly, 1980), Management Accounting. An Historical Perspective (1969), The Evolution of Corporate Financial Reporting (jtly, 1979), Papers on Accounting History (1984), A Dictionary of Business Quotations (jtly, 1990), The Development of the Accountancy Profession in Britain to the Early Twentieth Century (1986), Accounting in Scotland. A Historical Bibliography (jtly, 1 edn 1974, 2 edn 1976), Accounting in Australia. Historical Essays (1990), Consolidation Accounting (jtly, 1991); *Recreations* genealogy; *Style*— Prof Bob Parker; St Catherines, New North Rd, Exeter EX4 4AG (☎ 0392 55154); Amory Building, Rennes Drive, Exeter EX4 2RJ (☎ 0392 263201, fax 0392 263108, telex 42894 EXUNIV G)

PARKER, Robert John; s of Eric Robert Parker (d 1984), and Joan Marjorie Parker; *b* 22 Feb 1952; *Educ* Whitgift Sch, St John's Coll Cambridge (MA); *m* 28 Aug 1982, Claudia Jane, da of Col Alexander Akerman; 1 s (Felix Alexander b 12 Feb 1987); *Career* asst dir NM Rothschild & Sons Ltd 1976-82, exec dir investmts Credit Suisse First Boston Group 1982-; Freeman City of London, Liveryman Worshipful Co of Farriers; *Style*— Robert Parker, Esq; Credit Suisse First Boston, UK House, 2A Great Titchfield Street, London W1

PARKER, Robert Keith; s of Robert Y Parker of Hexham, Northumberland, and Catherine, *née* Cairns; *b* 6 Dec 1949; *Educ* St Mary's Sch Hexham, Hexham Gen Hosp (SRN) Royal Cornhill Hosp, Forester Hill Coll of Nursing Aberdeen (RMN), Sunderland Poly (Dip in Mgmnt Studies); *m* 24 July 1971, Hazel Marjorie, da of Ian M Lakeman; 1 s (Keith Robert Parker b 22 June 1973), 1 da (Caroline Anne Parker b 3 March 1975); *Career* student nurse Hexham Gen Hosp 1969-71, post registered student Royal Cornhill Hosp Aberdeen 1971-73, charge nurse Hexham Gen Hosp 1973-75, nursing offr S Tyneside Health Authy 1975-79; sr nursing offr: Forth Valley Health Bd 1979-80, Greater Glasgow Health Bd 1980-82, (acting divnl nursing offr 1982-83); dir Patient Care Servs and dep unit gen mangr Sunderland Dist Gen Hosp 1986-90 (dir Nursing Servs 1983-86), dir Patient Care Servs and Quality Assurance and dep unit gen mangr Sunderland Acute Servs Unit 1990-, MBIM 1986; memb RCN, Nat Assoc of Quality Assurance in Health Care 1989, S Tyneside Health Authy 1987-90; *Recreations* jogging, swimming, reading; *Style*— Robert Parker, Esq; Sunderland Health Authority, Acute Services Unit, District General Hospital, Kayll Rd, Sunderland SR4 7TP (☎ 091 565 6256)

PARKER, Robert Stewart; s of Robert Arnold Parker, and Edna, *née* Baines; *b* 13 Jan 1949; *Educ* Brentwood Sch, Trinity Coll Oxford (BA, MA); *Career* called to the Bar Middle Temple 1975, ad Eundem Lincoln's Inn 1977; Office of the Party Cncl 1980, Dep Pty Cncl 1987, Law Cmmn 1985-87; Freeman City of London 1984, Liveryman Worshipful Co of Wheelwrights 1984; MBIM 1984; *Books* Cases and Statutes on General Principles of English Law (with C R Newton, 1980); *Recreations* the livery, cricket, bridge, books, music, computing; *Clubs* Athenaeum, City Livery; *Style*— Robert Parker, Esq; Office of the Parliamentary Counsel, 36 Whitehall, SW1A 2AY

PARKER, Hon Robin Michael; s of late Hon John Holford Parker and bro of 6 Earl of Morley; *b* 1925; *Educ* Eton; *Career* Col KRCC; Palestine 1946-48 (despatches) cmdg 2 Bn R Green Jackets 1967-69; final rank Brigadier; ret 1980; raised to the rank of an Earl's son 1963; *Style*— The Hon Robin Parker; Saltram, Plympton, Devon

PARKER, Roger; s of Horace William Parker (d 1945), and Eliza Margaret, *née* Luckock (d 1959); *b* 27 April 1943; *Educ* King Edward VI Sch Aston Birmingham; *m* 19 Sept 1964, Anne, da of Douglas Archibald Maundrell; 2 s (Robin Gerard b 4 July 1965, Timothy Roger b 12 May 1969); *Career* sports photographer; Midlands Electricity Bd Birmingham 1960, govt serv Bd of Trade then Miny of Pensions (now DHSS) 1960-64, Key account exec then sales trainer Corn Products Co of USA 1965-68, freelance sports photographer for the press incl Daily Mail and Daily Mirror 1965-68, freelance press photographer 1969-74, The Sun Scotland 1974-75, The Sun London 1975-; attended World Cup Soccer Finals 1966-90; memb: NUJ 1969-85, IOJ 1985-, PSPA 1980-85; *Books* SM (1986); *Recreations* golf, wines, Citröen SM cars, languages, American football; *Style*— Roger Parker, Esq; The Barn, Swanbourne, Buckinghamshire (☎ 029672 273); The Sun, News International, 1 Virginia St, London E1 9XP (☎ 071 782 4207)

PARKER, Rt Hon Lord Justice; Rt Hon Sir Roger Jocelyn Parker; PC (1983); s of Capt Hon T T Parker, DSC, RN (d 1975), and Marie Louise Leonie, *née* Kleinwort (d 1949); *b* 25 Feb 1923; *Educ* Eton, King's Coll Cambridge; *m* 1948, Ann Elizabeth Frederika, *née* White; 1 s, 3 da; *Career* serv Rifle Bde 1942-47; called to the Bar Lincoln's Inn 1948, QC 1961, bencher 1969, High Ct judge (Queen's Bench) 1977-83, judge of the Cts of Appeal Jersey & Guernsey 1974-83, lord justice of appeal 1983; kt 1977; *Style*— The Rt Hon Lord Justice Parker; The Old Rectory, Widford, nr Ware, Herts (☎ 027 984 2593)

PARKER, Timothy James; s of Malcolm Topsfield Parker (d 1978); *b* 28 Oct 1942; *Educ* London Coll of Printing, Univ of Bath; *m* 1970, (m dis 1980), Patricia May, da of John Percy Robert Smith, of Dartmouth; 2 da; *Career* chm Springfields Cartons (Holdings) plc, chief exec TJP Mgmnt, dir Forrest Recruitment Ltd; CBIM, FInstD; *Recreations* tennis, skiing, sailing, theatre; *Clubs* Royal Automobile, St James's, Manchester Tennis & Raquet; *Style*— Timothy Parker, Esq; 2 Glenfield, Highgate Rd, Altrincham, Cheshire WA14 4QH (☎ 061 928 6363)

PARKER, William Joseph; s of Roger Noel, and Olive Alice, *née* Deane; *b* 8 Aug 1946; *Educ* Wychwood Bournemouth, Trent Coll Long Eaton; *m* 16 Aug 1969, Hurst, da of Robert Stuart, of Grand Cayman, BWI; 1 s (Andrew b 1971), 1 da (Clare b 1973); *Career* dir numerous cos incl: W & J Parker Ltd, Leicester Slaughtering Co Ltd, Harrison & King Ltd, Marney Firms Ltd, Parker Farms Ltd, Agricaid Ltd, pres Fedn of Fresh Meat Wholesalers 1989-91; *Recreations* boating; *Style*— William J Parker, Esq; 26 Knighton Grange Road, Leicester LE2 2LE (☎ 0533 703758); W & J Parker Ltd, Cattle Market, Leicester LE2 7LU (☎ 0533 548484, fax 558579, car phone 0831 463800)

PARKER-EATON, Robert George; OBE (1986, MBE (Mil) 1966); s of Leonard George Parker-Eaton (d 1956), of Three Oaks Rd, Grimes Hill, Wythall, nr Birmingham, and Phyllis Muriel, *née* Broome (d 1962); *b* 21 Nov 1931; *Educ* Solihull Sch Warwickshire, RAF Staff Coll; *m* 21 Dec 1962, Dorothy Elizabeth, da of Thomas Edgar Sharpe (d 1957), of 61 Tattenhoe Lane, Bletchley, Bucks; 2 s (Stephen Paul b 1963, Timothy Simon b 1968), 1 da (Sarah Frances b 1965); *Career* cmmnd supply branch RAF 1950, Wing Cdr 1966, controller civil air trooping MOD 1966-69, dep dir logistics prog Supreme Allied Cmd Atlantic 1969-72, OC air movements RAF Brize Norton 1972-74; Britannia Airways Ltd: controller customer servs 1974-78, dir customer servs and external affrs 1978-90, dep mangr dir 1990-; swimming rep: Cornwall 1955-56, Cumbria 1959-60, RAF 1959-69, Combined Services 1960-63, Berkshire 1961-62; MBIM 1968, FBIM 1981, MCIT 1982; *Recreations* swimming, model railways, reading; *Style*— Robert Parker-Eaton, Esq, OBE; 1 Kiln Lane, Clophill, Bedford MK45 4DA (☎ 0525 61128); Britannia Airways Ltd, Luton Airport, Luton, Bedfordshire (☎ 0582 424155, fax 0582 428000, telex 82239)

PARKER-JERVIS, Roger; DL (Bucks 1982); s of George Parker-Jervis (himself gs of Hon Edward Parker-Jervis, 2 s of 2 Viscount St Vincent), and Ruth Alice (d 1990), da of Charles Farmer; *b* 11 Sept 1931; *Educ* Eton, Magdalene Coll Cambridge; *m* 1958, his 2 cous once removed Diana, eldest da of Capt Robert St Vincent Parker-Jervis (himself ggs of Hon Edward P-J, *see above*); 2 s (Edward Swynfen b 1959, Guy b 1960), 1 da (Lucy Alice b 1966); *Career* land agent; cmmn Nat Serv The Rifle Bde; ADC to govr of Tasmania 1954-56, memb Bucks Co Cncl 1967-, chm Bucks CC 1981-85, pres Timber Growers Orgn 1981-83, High Sheriff Bucks 1973; *Style*— Roger Parker-Jervis, Esq, DL; The Gardener's Cottage, Great Hampden, nr Great Missenden, Bucks HP16 9RJ (☎ 024 028 531)

PARKES, Sir Basil Arthur; OBE (1966), JP; s of late Sir Fred Parkes; *b* 20 Feb 1907; *Educ* Boston GS Lincs; *m* 1933, May Lewis McNeill (d 1988); 2 s, 1 da; *Career* formerly with family trawler owning co; pres N Br Maritime Gp Ltd (formerly Utd Towing Ltd) 1960-; hon brother Trinity House Kington upon Hull, vice pres Br Tugowners Assoc; memb: Worshipful Co of Fishmongers, Worshipful Co of Poulters; Offr de l'Ordre National de Mérite (France) Ordre de la Couronne; kt 1971; *Style*— Sir Basil Parkes, OBE, JP; Loghan-y-Yuiy, The Garey, Lezayre, nr Ramsey, Isle of Man

PARKES, Dr Colin Murray; s of late Eric William Parkes, of Herts, and Gwyneth Ann, *née* Roberts; *b* 26 March 1928; *Educ* Royal Med Coll Epsom, Westminster Med Sch Univ of London (MD); *m* 22 June 1957, Patricia Margaret Parkes, da of Rev Edmond Whitehall Patrick Ainsworth, CBE (d 1979), of Bromsash, Gloucestershire; 3 da (Elizabeth b 1958, Jennifer b 1960, Caroline b 1963); *Career* RAF Med Corp; memb res staff: Social Psychiatry Unit MRC, The Tavistock Inst of Human Relations; project offr Laboratory of Community Psychiatry Harvard Med Sch USA, sr lectr in psychiatry The London Hosp Med Sch; chm Cncl Cruse Bereavement Care, tstee Psychiatric Rehabilitation Assoc; FRCPsych; *Books* Bereavement: Studies of Grief in Adult Life, Recovery from Bereavement (with R Weiss); *Recreations* collecting antique blue and white transfer wares; *Style*— Dr Colin Parkes; Academic Dept of Psychiatry, The London Hosp Med College, Turner St, London E1 2HD (☎ 071 377 7343, fax 071 377 7677)

PARKES, Cyril; s of Joseph Thomas Parkes (d 1947), of Bell End, Rowley Regis, and Annie Sophia, *née* Bedford (d 1949); *b* 16 Aug 1904; *m* 30 May 1935, Agnes Elizabeth (Betty), da of William Watkins (d 1965) of Cradley Heath, Staffs; 2 s (Jonathon Michael Cyril b 1937, David Dulane b 1939); *Career* electrical engr AEI (now EEC) 1919, engr with Wm Morris (later Lord Nuffield) 1924, hotel mangr 1929, butler to Lady Rose Wyborn; proprietor decorators merchant building business (expanded into chain of paint and wallpaper shops and paint mfr 1933-75; former memb: Staffordshire CC, Rowley Regis BC; fndr memb: Sons of Rest Mens Fellowship, Cradley Heath Speedway and Greyhound Stadium, Cradleigh Physically Handicapped Club; pres Cradley Heath FC; Rotarian for many years still active in many charitable projects; *Style*— C Parkes, Esq; Clent Hall, Clent, nr Stourbridge, W Midlands DY9 9PJ (☎ 0562 882 320)

PARKES, Daniel William; s of John William Parkes (d 1940), of 76 Laurel Grove, Penge, London, and May Emily, *née* Chesterman (d 1964); *b* 12 Dec 1919; *Educ* Northampton Poly; *m* 16 April 1971, Grace Iris, da of Fredrick Harold Simmons (d 1914); *Career* RAFVR 1939-45; proprietor A & H Rowley Parkes & Co 1971-90 (journeyman 1945-47, ptnr 1947-71); fndr memb Antiquarian Horological Soc 1952; Freeman City of London, Liveryman Worshipful Co Clockmakers 1976 (Freeman 1969, by gift); FRSA 1982; *Books* Early English Clocks (1982); *Recreations* singing in the choir, sailing; *Style*— Daniel Parkes, Esq; 95 Beaulie Ave, Sydenham, London SE26 6PW

PARKES, Sir Edward Walter; s of Walter Parkes; *b* 19 May 1926; *Educ* King Edward's Birmingham, St John's Coll Cambridge; *m* 1950, Margaret Parkes, JP (chm Nat Cncl for Educnl Technol, former govr BBC), da of John Parr; 1 s, 1 da; *Career* head Engrg Dept Univ of Leicester 1960-65, prof mechanics Univ of Cambridge 1965-74, vice chllr City Univ 1974-78; memb: Advsy Bd for Res Cncls 1974-83, Univ and Poly Grants Ctee Hong Kong 1974-; chm: University Grants Ctee 1978-83, Advsy Panel to sec of state for Environment on issues relating to Black Country limestone 1983-, Ctee of Vice Chllrs and Princs 1989-; vice chllr Univ of Leeds 1983-; ScD, FEng; kt 1982; *Clubs* Athenaeum; *Style*— Sir Edward Parkes; University of Leeds, Leeds LS2 9JT (☎ 333000)

PARKES, Francis Patrick; s of Alfred Herbert Parkes (d 1978); *b* 26 March 1932; *Educ* Bryanston, Aiglon Coll Switzerland; *m* June, da of James Alfred Coltas (d 1976); 1 s, 1 da; *Career* md Don International (formerly Small and Parkes Ltd) 1965-70, dir Cape Industries 1970-82, mgmnt conslt 1982-88, md Components Eastern Ltd Hong Kong; *Recreations* travel, gardening; *Style*— Francis Parkes, Esq; Cherry Trees, Cane End, nr Reading, Berks (☎ 0734 723416)

PARKES, Timothy Charles; TD (1988); s of Frank Leonard Parkes (d 1955), of Leamington Spa, Warwickshire, and Marie Joan Parkes, *née* Morris; *b* 13 Aug 1954; *Educ* Royal Masonic Sch, Wadham Coll Oxford (MA); *m* 31 Aug 1985, Wendy Patricia, da of Maj Vincent Reginald Hook, of Church Cottage, Steep, Petersfield, Hants; 1 s (Charles Alexander Frederick b 1988); *Career* TACSC 1989 (Maj TA Royal Yeomanry 1984-); admitted slr 1980; currently ptnrs Herbert Smith; Freeman Worshipful Co of Slrs 1982; memb Law Soc; *Recreations* riding, reading; *Clubs* Cavalry & Guards; *Style*— Timothy Parkes, Esq, TD; Tanglewood, Deepcut, Camberley, Surrey GU16 6RQ (☎ 0252 835326); Herbert Smith, Watling House, 35 Cannon St, London EC4M 5SD (☎ 071 489 8000, fax 071 329 0426, telex 886633)

PARKIN, Ian Michael; s of George Harold Parkin, of Lincett Ct, Lincett Ave, W Worthing, W Sussex, and Ethel Mary, *née* Fullerton; *b* 15 Oct 1946; *Educ* Dorking Co GS, Open Univ (BA); *m* 30 April 1977, Patricia Helen, da of Maj Frederick James Fowles, MC (d 1982); 2 s (Andrew b 1978, Richard b 1984), 1 da (Jennifer b 1981); *Career* CA; sr ptnr Pannell Kerr Forster CI, ptnr Pannell Kerr Forster Gibraltar; vice-pres Praxis Panorama A G Zürich Switzerland; FCA; *Recreations* golf, reading, sailing; *Style*— Ian Parkin, Esq; Le Petit Jardin, La Rue a la Pendue, Millais, St Ouen, Jersey (☎ 0534 83218); Pannell Kerr Forster, Trinity House, Bath St, St Helier, Jersey, CI

PARKIN, Jill; da of Leslie Parkin, of Leeds, and Eileen, *née* Wood; *b* 27 Feb 1958; *Educ* Leeds Girls' HS, Univ of Leeds (BA); *m* 5 Jan 1991, David Arscott; *Career* reporter; training on weekly paper Harrogate, reporter Yorkshire Post 1982-88, chief feature writer Daily Express 1988-; winner Regnl Feature Writer of the Year in Nationwide Awards 1988; *Recreations* reading, writing; *Style*— Ms Jill Parkin; The

Daily Express, Ludgate House, 245 Blackfriars Rd, London SE1 9UX (☎ 071 922 7040)

PARKIN, John Mackintosh; s of Thomas Parkin and Emily Parkin; *b* 18 June 1920; *Educ* Nottingham HS, Emmanuel Coll Cambridge (MA); *m* Biancamaria Giuganino; 2 da; *Career* serv RA WWII, Capt; asst under-sec state MOD 1974-80, asst sec Lord Chllr's Dept 1981-82, admin Royal Courts of Justice 1982-85; *Style—* John Parkin, Esq; 35 Little Bornes, London SE21 8SD

PARKIN, Leonard; s of Leonard Parkin (d 1952), and Helena, *née* Wood (d 1975); *b* 2 June 1929; *Educ* Hemsworth GS Yorks; *m* 4 June 1955, Barbara Anne, da of Donald Rowley (d 1971), of York; 1 s (Jeremy b 1957); *Career* journalist and broadcaster; reporter and feature writer Yorkshire Observer and Telegraph and Argus Bradford 1951-54, reporter and sub ed Yorkshire Evening News 1954-65; BBC reporter and foreign corr: Canada 1960, USA 1963-65; reporter Panorama and Twenty Four Hours 1965-67; ITN 1967-87: reporter (later foreign corr and newcaster) News at Ten, News at 5.45, News at One; anchorman special ITN programmes, election specials; presenter corporate video programmes, contrib sporting magazines; dir Hyvision Ltd 1988; former chm Welwyn Soc, fndr memb Welwyn Film Record Soc, pres Herts Fly Dressers' Guild, former pres The Lytton Players Stevenage; *Books* contributor to sporting magazines, The Field; *Recreations* cricket, trout fishing, shooting; *Clubs* MCC, The Lord's Taverners; *Style—* Leonard Parkin, Esq; 17 Hallgarth, Pickering, N Yorks YO18 7AW

PARKIN, Sara Lamb; da of Dr George Lamb McEwan, of Isle of Islay, Argyll, and Marie Munro, *née* Rankin; *b* 9 April 1946; *Educ* Barr's Hill GS Coventry, Bromsgrove Coll, Edinburgh Royal Infirmary (RGN), Univ of Michigan, Leeds Poly; *m* 30 June 1969, Donald Maxwell Parkin, s of Donald Harry Parkin, of Lincolnshire, and Lesley Mary, *née* Tyson; 2 s (Colin McEwan b 28 March 1974, Douglas Maxwell b 12 Sept 1975); *Career* sec to matron Birmingham & Midland Eye Hosp 1965-67, staff nurse and ward sister Edinburgh Royal Infirmary 1970-74, nursing res asst and undergraduate tutor Univ of Edinburgh 1972-73, served as memb Cncl and teacher of sex educn Brook Advsy Serv and self employed 1974-76, family planning nurse and teacher of sex educn Leeds Area Health Authy and self employed 1976-80, self employed writer and speaker on Green Issues 1981-, press offr and newsletter ed Yorks and Humberside Green Pty; Green Pty: memb Cncl 1980-81, int liaison sec 1983-90, speaker (Euro election campaign) 1989-, speaker (int affrs) 1990-; ed newsletter Euro Greens 1986-89, co-sec Euro Greens 1985-90; memb: Green Pty, New Econs Fndn, Charter '88, Friends of the Earth, 300 Gp, Islay Museum Tst, Finlaggan Tst; *Publications* incl: European Green Joint Programme (co-author 1984), Green Party General Election Manifesto (co-author 1987), Green Strategy (in Into the 21st Century, 1988), European Green Common Statement (co-author, 1989), Green Party European Election Manifesto 1989, Green Parties: An International Guide (1989), Green Politics: An International Perspective (in The Rest of The World is Watching) 1990; *Recreations* walking, camping, gardening, DIY, reading, cooking, theatre, opera; *Style—* Ms Sara Parkin; Green Party, 10 Station Parade, Balham High Rd, London SW12 9AZ (☎ 081 675 6701, 081 673 0045)

PARKINS, Brian James Michael; JP; s of Ronald Anthony Parkins (d 1979), of Ilford, Essex, and Adelaide Florence, *née* Percival; *b* 1 Nov 1938; *Educ* St Ignatius Coll London, King's Coll Hosp and Univ of London (BDS), Inst of Dental Surgery and RCS (LDS, FDS), Northwestern Univ Chicago (MS); *m* 1, 20 Oct 1966 (m dis 1980), Jill Elizabeth, da of James Dawson (d 1982), of Lytham St Annes; 1 s (Richard Mark b 1 March 1971), 1 da (Alison) Jane b 14 Nov 1967); m 2, 19 May 1988, Mary Saunders, *née* Burton; *Career* conslt dental surgn; sr clinical lectr Inst of Dental Surgery 1969-81, private practice 1970-, recognised teacher of the Univ of London 1972, conslt in restorative dentistry UCL and Middx Hosp Sch of Dent 1982; pres Br Soc for Restorative Dentistry 1987-88 (cncl memb 1982-84); sec: ADSL and ADSE; examiner 1977-86: BDS, RCS for LDS Final P III FDS and MGDS; hon memb: ADA, Pierre Fauchard Acad; FICD, FACD; *Recreations* reading, music, golf; *Clubs* Lansdowne, Savage; *Style—* Brian Parkins, Esq, JP; 57 Portland Place, London W1N 3AH (☎ 071 580 7146)

PARKINSON, Rt Hon Cecil Edward; PC (1981), MP (C) Hertsmere 1983-; s of Sidney Parkinson, of Carnforth, Lancs; *b* 1 Sept 1931; *Educ* Royal Lancaster GS, Emmanuel Coll Cambridge; *m* 1957, Ann Mary, da of F A Jarvis, of Harpenden; 3 da (Mary, Emma, Joanna); *Career* joined West Wake Price & Co 1956 (ptnr 1961-71); formerly with Metal Box Co, founded Parkinson Hart Securities Ltd 1967; chm: Hemel Hempstead Cons Assoc 1966-69, Herts 100 Club 1968-69; contested (C) Northampton 1970; MP (C): Enfield W Nov 1970-74, Herts S 1974-1983; sec Cons Parly Fin Ctee 1971-72, PPS to Michael Heseltine as min for Aerospace and Shipping DTI 1972-74, asst govt whip 1974, oppn whip 1974-76, oppn spokesman Trade 1976-79, min of state Dept of Trade 1979-81, chm Cons Pty and Paymaster-General 1981-83, chllr Duchy of Lancaster 1982-83, sec of state Trade and Indust June 1983-Oct 1983 (resigned); sec of state for Energy 1987-89, sec of state for Tport 1989-90; govr: Aldenham Sch, Royal Lancaster GS; *Style—* The Rt Hon Cecil Parkinson, MP; House of Commons, London, SW1A 0AA

PARKINSON, Prof Cyril Northcote; s of William Edward Parkinson, princ York Sch of Art, and Rose Emily Mary, *née* Curnow; *b* 30 July 1909; *Educ* St Peter's Sch York, Emmanuel Coll Cambridge (BA), King's Coll London (PhD); *m* 1, 1943 (m dis 1950) Ethelwyn Edith, da of Francis Graves, editor Windsor Express; 1 s (Christopher b 1945), 1 da (Alison b 1943); m 2, 1952, (Elizabeth) Ann (d 1983), da of Lt-Col Fry, MC, RA; 2 s (Charles b 1955, Jonathan b 1961), 1 da (Antonia b 1958); m 3, 1 June 1985, Iris Hilda (Ingrid), da of Norman Victor Waters; *Career* 2 Lt TA Reserve 1932, Lt 22 London Regt (The Queen's) 1933, Capt Blundell's Sch Tiverton OTC, Capt 166 OCTU 1940, Maj Gen Staff 1943, demob 1944; Hon Lt-Col Alabama Militia; author, historian and journalist; sr history master Blundell's Sch Tiverton, master RNC Dartmouth 1938 and 1944-46, lectr Univ of Liverpool 1947-50, Raffles prof of history Univ of Malaya 1950-58, prof emeritus Troy State Univ Alabama USA 1970-; chm Leviathan House (publishers) 1972-; author of numerous books and novels; contribs to: Encyclopaedia Britannica, The Economist, The Guardian, Punch, Saturday Evening Post and other jnls; fell of Emmanuel Coll Cambridge; Hon: LLD, DLitt; Hon Dr of Business Orgns; FRHistS; *Recreations* painting, travel; *Clubs* Army and Navy; *Style—* Prof C Northcote Parkinson; 36 Harkness Drive, Canterbury, Kent CT2 7RW (☎ 0227 452742)

PARKINSON, Lady Elizabeth Mary; *née* Murray; da of 10 Earl of Dunmore (d 1981), and Patricia Mary, *née* Coles, now Mrs Geoffrey Fitze; *b* 1951; *m* 1973, John Michael Parkinson; 1 s, 2 da; *Style—* The Lady Elizabeth Parkinson; RD Tasman Highway, Cambridge, Hobart, Tasmania 7170, Australia

PARKINSON, Ewart West; s of Thomas Edward Parkinson (d 1958), of 48 Belgrave Ave, Leicester, and Lilian Esther West, *née* Hammond (d 1966); *b* 9 July 1926; *Educ* Wyggeston Sch Leicester, Coll of Tech Leicester, Univ of London (BSc, DPA); *m* 21 Aug 1948, Patricia Joan, da of Capt William John Lawson Wood (d 1985), of 30 Eastfield Rd, Leicester; 2 s (Mark b 1951, Michael b 1955), 1 da (Veronica b 1959); *Career* princ engr Bristol 1949-50, chief asst Dover 1954-57, dep borough engr 1957-60, dep city surveyor Plymouth 1960-64, city planning offr Cardiff 1964-74, dir Environment S Glam 1974-85; devpt advsr and co dir 1985-; specialised rebuilding and regeneration war damaged cities; chm and fndr: Star Leisure and Recreation Tst, Wales Sports Centre for the Disabled Tst; managing tstee Norwegian Church Preservation Tst, vice pres Wales Cncl for the Disabled, chm Facilities Ctee Sports Cncl for Wales 1966-78, fndr and first chm Co Planning Offrs Soc for Wales; hon life memb Int Fedn of Housing and Planning (The Hague), Nat Housing and Town Planning Cncl Diamond Jubilee Silver Medal; numerous papers presented world wide; OStJ; FICE, FRTPI (pres 1975-76); *Recreations* working, being with friends and family; *Style—* Ewart Parkinson, Esq; 42 South Rise, Cardiff (☎ 0222 756 394); W S Atkins & Ptnrs, Longcross Court, Cardiff (☎ 0222 485 159, fax 0222 485 138)

PARKINSON, Graham Edward; s of Norman Edward Parkinson (d 1984), of Cliffwood Ave, Birstall, Leicestershire, and Phyllis, (*née* Jaquiss); *b* 13 Oct 1937; *Educ* Loughborough GS; *m* 1963, Dinah Mary, da of Walter Bevan Pyper (d 1969), of Julian Court, Julian Way, Harrow on the Hill, Middx; 1 s (Nicholas b 1967), 1 da (Georgina b 1973); *Career* ptnr Darlington & Parkinson slrs 1969-82, Metropolitan Stipendory Magistrate 1982; MC Crown Ct 1988; *Recreations* music, theatre, reading; *Style—* Graham E Parkinson, Esq; Thames Magistrates Court, 58 Bow Road, London E3 4DJ (☎ 081 980 1000)

PARKINSON, (Thomas) Harry; CBE (1972), DL (Warwicks 1970); s of G R J Parkinson; *b* 25 June 1907; *Educ* Bromsgrove, Univ of Birmingham (LLB); *m* 1936, Catherine Joan, da of C J Douglas-Osborn; 2 s, 1 da; *Career* RAF 1939-45; admitted slr 1930; Birmingham town clerk 1960-72, clerk of the Peace 1970-72; Hon DSc Aston Univ 1972; *Style—* Harry Parkinson, Esq, CBE, DL; Roseland Nursery, Upper Castle Rd, St Mawes, Truro TR2 5AE (☎ 0326 270592); Three Springs Barn, Stanford Bishop, Bringsty (☎ 0836 884314)

PARKINSON, Dr James Christopher; MBE (1963), TD (1962); s of Charles Myers Parkinson (d 1949), of Blackburn, Lancs, and Sarah Louisa, *née* Aspinall (d 1958); *b* 15 Aug 1920; *Educ* Queen Elizabeth's GS Blackburn, Univ Coll Nottingham (BPharm), Sch of Pharmacy, Univ of London (PhD); *m* 11 April 1950, Gwyneth Margot (Bunty), da of Rev John Raymond Harrison (d 1973); 3 s (Andrew John b 1952, David Charles b 1954, Robert James b 1956); *Career* cmmnd Lancs Fusiliers 1943, Lt parachute regt 1944, Capt Camp Cmdt 2 Parachute Bde 1945, Capt GSO 3 6 Airborne Div 1946, Adj 4 Parachute Field Ambulance TA 1948, GSO 3 Air 16 Airborne Div TA 1952, Maj GSO 2 Air 44 Ind Para Gp TA 1958, ret 1963; lectr Sch of Pharmacy Univ of London 1948-54, dep sec Pharmaceutical Soc GB 1964-67, princ Brighton Tech Coll 1967-70 (head Sch of Pharmacy 1954-64), dep dir Brighton Poly 1970-83; memb: Res Degrees Ctee and Bds of Study CNAA 1965-75, Hurstpier-point PCC, Deanery Synod (past chm), Chichester Diocesan Synod (past lay chm), Mid-Downs DHA 1984-87, Gen Synod C of E 1970-85; fell Royal Pharmaceutical Soc of GB 1948; *Recreations* gardening, walking; *Style—* Dr James Parkinson, MBE, TD; Ravensmere, 92 Wickham Hill, Hurstpierpoint, W Sussex BN6 9NR (☎ 0273 833369)

PARKINSON, (Robert) Michael; s of Robert Scott Parkinson, of Lancaster, and Rhoda, *née* Chirnside (d 1964); *b* 9 Aug 1944; *Educ* Wrekin Coll, Coll of Estate Mgmnt London Univ (BSc); *m* 26 Oct 1968, Elizabeth Ann, da of Michael Moore, of Lancaster; 2 s (Duncan b 27 Nov 1969, Andrew b 4 Sept 1971); *Career* ptnr Ingham & York (chartered surveyors, land agents, auctioneers and valuers) 1971-, dir Marsden Building Soc 1984-; memb (formerly sec and chm) Lancs Cheshire & Isle of Man Branch Rural Practice Div of RICS; FRICS 1976; *Recreations* mountaineering, country pursuits; *Clubs* Fell and Rock Climbing, Rotary (Clitheroe), Clitheroe Ex-Tablers (41); *Style—* Michael Parkinson, Esq; Littlemoor House, Littlemoor, Clitheroe, Lancs BB7 1HF (☎ 0200 22660); Ingham & Yorke, Littlemoor, Clitheroe, Lancs BB7 1HG (☎ 0200 23 655)

PARKINSON, Ronald Dennis; s of late Albert Edward Parkinson, and late Jennie Caroline Clara, *née* Meagher; *b* 27 April 1945; *Educ* St Dunstan's Coll, Clare Coll Cambridge (MA); *Career* res asst V & A 1972-74, asst keeper Tate Gallery 1974-78; asst curator V & A 1978-; *Books* Catalogue of British Oil Paintings 1820-1860 in the V & A (1990); *Recreations* reading, shopping; *Clubs* Algonquin; *Style—* Ronald Parkinson, Esq; Victoria And Albert Museum, London SW7 2RL (☎ 071 938 8474)

PARKS, (Robert) Ralph; *Educ* Univ of Colombia NY (MBA), Rice Univ Houston (BA); *m* Gwendoline E (Wendy); 2 s (Gavin b 1979, Grant b 1989), 1 da (Cecily b 1976); *Career* 1 Lt US Army Field Artillery, serv Korea; Merill Lynch 1970-80 (md 1980), ptnr Goldman Sachs & Co NY 1986-88 (vice pres 1981-86), md Goldman Sachs Int Ltd 1988-; *Style—* Ralph Parks, Esq; Goldman Sachs International Limited, 8/10 New Fetter Lane, London EC4A 1DB (☎ 071 489 5832, fax 071 489 5432, telex 887902 GOSAC)

PARKS, Robert James (Bob); s of James Michael Parks (the former England cricketer), of High Salvington, Sussex, and Irene Marian, *née* Young; *b* 15 June 1959; *Educ* Eastbourne GS, Southampton Inst of Higher Educn; *m* 30 Jan 1982, Amanda, da of Capt M Larrive; *Career* professional cricketer; Hampshire CCC 1977-: debut 1980, awarded county cap 1982, 246 first class appearances; English Cos tour Zimbabwe 1985, represented England v NZ (Lords Test match) 1987 (replaced the injured Bruce French during game); Hants wicket-keeping record 10 catches in a match v Derbyshire 1981; honours: Benson & Hedges Cup 1988, Refuge Assurance League 1986; accountant during off season; *Recreations* stamp collecting, watching, Tottenham Hotspur FC; *Style—* Bob Parks, Esq; Hampshire CCC, Northlands Rd, Southampton, Hants (☎ 0703 333788)

PARKYN, Brian Stewart; s of Leslie Parkyn (d 1985), of Whetstone, London, and Gwen, *née* Scott (d 1976); *b* 28 April 1923; *Educ* King Edward VI GS Chelmsford; *m* 17 March 1951, Janet Anne, da of Charles Stormer (d 1971), of Eastbourne, Sussex; 1 s (Nicholas b 1954), 1 da (Jenifer b 1957); *Career* dir Trylon Ltd 1944-56, Scott Bader Co Ltd 1953-83 (joined 1947), dir Halmatic Ltd 1976-87, princ Assoc Engrg Business Mgmnt Sch 1976-80, gen mangr of trg Br Caledonian Airways Ltd 1981-88; chm Reinforced Plastics Gp of Br Plastics Fedn 1959-63, MP for Bedford 1966-70, memb Select Ctee Sci and Technol 1966-70, chm Carbon Fibre Sub-Ctee 1969, memb Cncl Cranfield Inst of Technol 1970-; memb Ct: Univ of Bradford 1972-75, RCA 1974-80; hon treas RSA 1977-82; FRSA 1964, FPRI 1969; *Books* Polyester Handbook (1953), Unsaturated Polyesters (1967), Glass Reinforced Plastics (ed, 1970), Democracy Accountability and Participation in Industry (1979); *Style—* Brian Parkyn, Esq; 9 Clarendon Sq, Leamington Spa, Warwicks CV32 5QJ (☎ 0926 330 066)

PARLETT, Michael Harold James; s of Lyall Mervyn Malzard Parlett, of Belle Hougue, Cote du Nord, Trinity, Jersey, CI, and Catherine McDougall, *née* Gray; *b* 16 Nov 1940; *Educ* Winchester, Millfield, St Andrews Univ (BSc); *m* 2 Sept 1967, Elizabeth Ann, da of Dr Frederick Roy Gusterson; 2 da (Lucinda b 1969, Clare b 1971); *Career* Shell International Petroleum 1965-68, Shell Sekiyu 1968-73; investmt mangr: Stewart Fund Managers 1973-74, Murray Johnstone Ltd 1974-77; exec dir Murray Johnstone Ltd 1977-83, vice pres and dir Kemper Murray Johnstone International Inc 1983-89, md Murray Johnstone International Ltd 1989-; *Recreations* skiing, hill-walking; *Clubs* Western Club Glasgow; *Style—* Michael Parlett, Esq; Glebe House, Manse Rd, Linlithgow (☎ 0506 844247); 7 West Nile St, Glasgow (☎ 041 226 3131, fax 041 221 5632)

PARMINTER, Gail; da of Francis Parminter, of Maidenhead, Berks, and Barbara

Helen, *née* Cox; *b* 29 Nov 1964; *Educ* Holt Sch Wokingham Berks, Berkshire Coll of Art & Design; *partner*, Peter Gunn; 1 s (Joseph William Parminter-Gunn); *Career* copywriter BSB Dorland 1986-; TV commercial and press work; accounts incl: Eden Vale, Ski, Austin Rover, Heinz, Electricity Cncl, Feminax, Castrol, Halifax Building Society, Woolworths; winner: Silver Campaign Poster award for Austin Rover Mini, D & AD award for Flowers Bitter, Clio award for Eden Vale, Campaign Press award for Austin Rover; *Style*— Ms Gail Parminter; BSB Dorland, 121-141 Westbourne Terrace, London W2 6JR (☎ 071 262 5077 ext 2441)

PARMOOR, 4 Baron (UK 1914); (Frederick Alfred) Milo Cripps; s of 3 Baron Parmoor, DSO, TD, DL (d 1977), and of Violet Mary Geraldine (d 1983), da of Sir William Nelson, 1 Bt; *b* 18 June 1929; *Educ* Ampleforth, Corpus Christi Coll Oxford; *Heir* cous, (Matthew) Anthony Leonard Cripps, *qv*; *Style*— The Rt Hon the Lord Parmoor; Dairy Cottage, Duck Street, Sutton Veny, Wilts

PARNELL, Alexandra; da of Cyril Henry Parnell, (d 1985), of Dorking, Surrey, and Heather, *née* Beasley; *b* 3 May 1952; *Educ* Purley Co GS for girls; *m* 20 April 1974, (m dis 1982), Geoffrey Willis; *Career* asst sec to The Hon David Astor ed The Observer 1970-72, sec to Betty Reyburn, features ed Woman's Journal 1972-73, fashion asst Woman's Journal 1973-75, asst fashion ed Country Life 1975-78, fashion ed Woman's Journal 1978-; *Recreations* cats, horses, foreign travel; *Style*— Ms Alexandra Parnell; King's Reach Tower, London SE1 (☎ 071 261 6064, fax 071 261 7061, telex 915748 MAGDNG)

PARNELL, Hon John Patrick Christian; s and h of 8 Baron Congleton, *qv*; *b* 17 March 1959; *m* 1985, Marjorie-Anne, o da of John Hobdell, of The Ridings, Cobham, Surrey; 2 s (Christopher John Edward b 1987, Harry b 1990); *Style*— The Hon John Parnell

PARNWELL, Peter Wilfred; s of Wilfred Horace Parnwell (d 1947), and Ella Edith, *née* Abbott (d 1965); *b* 24 May 1925; *Educ* Merchant Taylors'; *m* 1, 1947, Edna Buchanan; m 2, 1951, Evelyn Taylor; m 3, 1956, Gillian Pickrell; 2 s (Martin b 1956, Adrian b 1961); m 4, 1977, Anne Horsfall; *Career* WWII A & SH served Normandy and NW Europe (wounded); African traveller and safari operator, guide to Legion Etrangère, discovered Tibesti rock paintings, dir several trading cos; memb Legion of Frontiersmen; Freeman City of London; FRGS; *Books* Puritan and Patriot - the life of Robert Blake; *Recreations* tennis, archaeology, cartophily; *Style*— Peter Parnwell, Esq

PARR, Hon Mrs (Caroline Mary); *née* Renton; da of Baron Renton, KBE, TD, PC, QC, DL; *b* 22 Nov 1948; *m* 1, 1970 (m dis 1974), Peter Dodds Parker; m 2, 1977, Robin Warwick Antony Parr; 1 child by each marriage; *Style*— The Hon Mrs Parr; Port Mary House, Dundrennan, Kirkcudbright (☎ 05575 654)

PARR, David; s of Fred Parr, of The Brooklands, Coombs Rd, Bakewell, Derbyshire, and Margaret, *née* Richardson; *b* 7 Feb 1947; *Educ* Bakewell C of E Boys' Sch, Buxton Coll of Further Educn; *m* 29 May 1968, Maureen, da of William Mervyn Clarke, 2 s (Jonathan b 9 July 1972, Christopher b 20 April 1976), 1 da (Charlotte b 13 July 1982); *Career* registered gen nurse training Northern Gen Hosp Sheffield 1965-68, sr nursing offr acute servs Wandsworth Health Authy St George's Hosp 1976-83, dir of nursing servs Acute Elderly and Physically Handicapped Care Gp Maidstone Health Authy 1983-86; Wakefield Health Authy: unit gen mangr Acute Elderly and Maternity Care Gp and chief nursing offr 1986-90, chief exec Provider Unit 1990-; *Recreations* cricket, reading, swimming, DIY; *Style*— David Parr, Esq; Wakefield Health Authy, Pinderfields Gen Hospital, Aberford Rd, Wakefield, W Yorks WF1 4DG (☎ 0924 375217 ext 2601, fax 0924 290812)

PARR, (Thomas) Donald; CBE (1986); s of Thomas Parr (d 1975), of Bramhall, Cheshire, and Elizabeth Parr; *b* 3 Sept 1930; *Educ* Burnage GS; *m* 1954, Gwendoline Mary, da of Frank Lawton Chaplin, of Cheadle, Cheshire (d 1969); 2 s, 1 da; *Career* chm William Baird plc 1981- (textile and industl gp); non exec dir: Dunhill Hldgs plc, Hepworth plc; *Recreations* sailing (yacht Quailo); *Clubs* Royal Yacht Sqdn, Royal Ocean Racing; *Style*— Donald Parr, Esq, CBE; Homestead, Homestead Rd, Disley, Stockport, Cheshire SK12 2JP; Broadstone House, Broadstone Rd, Reddish, Stockport, Cheshire SK5 7DL (☎ 061 442 8118); William Baird plc, 79 Mount St, W1Y 5HJ (☎ 071 409 1785, telex 886376)

PARRACK, Paul Adrian; s of Stanley Herbert Parrack, of Petworth, W Sussex, and Emma Edith, *née* Gibb; *b* 10 March 1940; *Educ* Hove Co GS, Open Univ (BA); *m* 2 Feb 1963, Susan Margaret, da of Gordon Lay, of Horsham, W Sussex; 3 da (Skeeter b 1963, Keely b 1967, Eloise b 1977); *Career* naval airman RN 1958; served as a photographer in: HMS Victorious, HMS Simbang, HMS Protector; cmmnd Sub Lt (X) (aviation) 1970, asst flight deck offr HMS Eagle 1972-73, photo offr HMS Ark Royal 1975-76, exchange duty with US Navy (USN Photo Center Washington DC 1977-79); photo offr: staff of Capt submarine sea training 1979-81, staff of Flag Offr submarines 1981-83; 1 Lt HMS Cochrane 1983, offr cmdg Jt Servs Sch of Photography 1985-86, staff of Dir Gen aircraft (Navy) 1987-90, ret RN in rank of Lt-Cdr 1990; info offr Govt Info Service Working as asst ed Navy News 1990; FBIPP 1986; *Recreations* sailing, photography, walking; *Style*— Paul Parrack, Esq; Navy News, HMS Nelson, Portsmouth PO1 3NN (☎ 0705 294228)

PARRATT, Prof James Roy; s of James John Parratt, and Eunice Elizabeth Parratt; *b* 19 Aug 1933; *Educ* St Clement Danes Holborn Estate GS, Univ of London (BPharm, MSc, PhD, DSc, MD hc); *m* 7 Sept 1957, Pamela Joan Lyndon, da of Stanley Charles Marels; 2 s (Stephen John Lyndon b 14 March 1960, Jonathan Mark b 21 March 1969), 1 da (Deborah Joy b 3 Sept 1965); *Career* sr lectr Dept of Physiology Univ of Ibadan Nigeria 1958-66, chm and head Dept of Physiology and Pharmacology Univ of Strathclyde 1986 (sr lectr then reader Dept of Pharmacology 1966-74, personal chair pharmacology 1975, newly established chair cardiovascular pharmacology 1983); chm Br Soc Cardiovascular Res, hon memb Pharmacological Soc Hungary 1976, medal Polish Physiological Soc 1989; Hon MD Albert Szent Györgyi Univ Szeged Hungary 1989; FRSE, FIBiol, MRCPath, memb Br Cardiac Soc, FRPharmS; *Books* Early Arrhythmias Resulting From Myocardial Ischaemia; Mechanisms and Prevention by Drugs (1982), Calcium Movement and its Manipulation by Drugs (1984); *Recreations* music; *Clubs* Royal Cwlth Soc; *Style*— Prof James Parratt; 16 Russell Drive, Bearsden, Glasgow G61 3BD (☎ 041 942 1461); Dept of Physiology and Pharmacology, Univ of Strathclyde, Royal Coll, 204 George St, Glasgow G1 1XW (☎ 041 552 4400 ext 2858, fax 041 552 2562, telex 77472)

PARRIS, Matthew Francis; s of Leslie Francis Parris; *b* 7 Aug 1949; *Educ* Waterford Sch Swaziland, Clare Coll Cambridge, Yale Univ USA; *Career* FO 1974-76; Cons Research Dept 1976-79, presenter Weekend World LWT 1986; MP (C) West Derbyshire 1979-86; *Recreations* running, travelling, reading; *Style*— Matthew Parris Esq; 41 Bramfield Rd, SW11 6RA

PARRITT, Clive Anthony; s of Allan Edward Parritt, MBE, and Peta, *née* Lloyd; *b* 11 April 1943; *Educ* private; *m* 1, 28 Sept 1968 (m dis 1984), Valerie Joyce, da of Jesse Sears, of Reigate, Surrey; 2 s (James b 1977, Daniel b 1980); m 2, 5 Oct 1985, Deborah, da of Kenneth Jones, of Tenby, Wales; 2 s (Matthew b 1987, Thomas b 1989); *Career* CA; ptnr 1973-82: Fuller Jenks Beecroft, Mann Judd, Touche Ross & Co; managing ptnr Baker Tilly 1987- (ptnr 1982-); memb Nat Assoc of CA Students Soc 1965-67 (chm London branch 1965-66); chm: Redhill and Reigate Round Table 1976-77, London Soc of CAs 1982-83 (treas 1980-82); treas Br Theatre Assoc 1984-87, memb Advsy Panel to Enterprise and Deregulation Unit DTI 1986-88; FCA 1966 (cncl memb 1983-); *Recreations* theatre, entertaining, gardening; *Style*— Clive Parritt, Esq; 50 Northchurch Rd, London N1 4EJ (☎ 071 254 8562); Baker Tilly, 2 Bloomsbury St, London WC1B 3ST (☎ 071 413 5100, fax 071 413 5100)

PARROT, Hon Mrs (Deirdre Barbara Elland); *née* Lumley-Savile; da of late 2 Baron Savile, KCVO (who assumed by Royal licence surname Savile after that of Lumley) by 2 w, Esmé, *née* Wolton; *b* 1928; *m* 1948, Col Kent Kane Parrot, US Air Force (ret); 2 s, 1 da; *Style*— The Hon Mrs Parrot; 5506 Grove St, Chevy Chase, Maryland, USA (☎ 0101 301 656 3114)

PARROTT, (Horace) Ian; s of Horace Bailey Parrott (d 1953), and Muriel Annie, *née* Blackford (d 1958); *b* 5 March 1916; *Educ* Harrow, RCM, New Coll Oxford (MA, DMus); *m* 1 June 1940, Elizabeth Olga, da of Edwin Cox (d 1956); 2 s (Michael b 16 Sept 1942, Richard b 16 Dec 1945); *Career* WWII Capt Royal Signals Africa 1940-45; lectr Univ of Birmingham 1946-50, examiner Trinity Coll of Music 1949-, Gregynog prof of music UCW Aberystwyth 1950-83, prof emeritus; Symphonic Impression Luxor 1947, first prize Royal Philharmonic Soc 1949, Harriet Cohen Int Musicology Medal 1966; recordings incl: String Quartet No 4 1971, Trombone Concerto 1974; vice pres: Elgar Soc 1973-, Guild for the Promotion of Welsh Music 1979-, Peter Warlock Soc 1984-; fell: Trinity Coll of Music London 1953, London Coll of Music 1983; FRSA, ARCO; *Books* Pathways to Modern Music (1947), A Guide to Musical Thought (1955), Method in Orchestration (1957), The Music of An Adventure (1966), The Spiritual Pilgrims (1969), Elgar Master Musicians (1971), The Music of Rosemary Brown (1978), The Story of The Guild for the Promotion of Welsh Music (1980), Cyril Scott and His Piano Music (1991); *Clubs* Savage; *Style*— Prof Ian Parrott; Henblas Abermad, Aberystwyth, Dyfed SY23 4ES (☎ 097 47 660)

PARRY *see also*: Jones-Parry

PARRY, Alan; s of George Henry Edgar James Parry (d 1984), of Upper Gatton Park, Reigate, Surrey, and Jessica, *née* Cooke; *b* 30 Oct 1927; *Educ* Reedham Sch; *m* 17 April 1954, Shirley Ann, da of Esmonde Plunkett Yeoman (d 1962), of Tadworth, Surrey; 1 s (Simon), 1 da (Alannah); *Career* RN 1946-48; dir Sedgwick Gp 1960-81; chm: Carter Brito e Cunha Ltd 1982-87, Johnson & Higgins Ltd 1987-88; pres Johnson & Higgins (Holdings) Ltd 1989-; dep chm Lloyd's 1987-88; Ctee chm City of London Chamber Orch; Freeman City of London, Liveryman Worshipful Co of Insurers 1981; FBIBA, FRSA; *Recreations* fly-fishing, music, drama; *Clubs* Naval and Military; *Style*— Alan Parry, Esq; Upper Gatton Park, Reigate, Surrey, RH2 0TZ (☎ 0737 645388); Lochletter House, Balnain, Inverness-shire IV3 6TJ (☎ 04564 228)

PARRY, Hon Mrs (Amanda Gwyneth Rosemary); *née* Borwick; yst da of 4 Baron Borwick, MC, *qv*; *b* 24 Jan 1965; *m* 16 May 1987, Brian Wynn Parry, eldest s of P Owen Parry, of Llandderfel, Gwynedd; 1 s (Robert James William b 21 Feb 1990), 1 da (Caroline Hyllarie Wynne b 8 Jan 1988); *Style*— The Hon Mrs Parry; 4 Bro Hafesb, Llandderfel, Bala, Gwynedd

PARRY, Hon Mrs Anna Josephine; *née* Banbury; da of 2 Baron Banbury of Southam, DL (d 1981); *b* 1950; *m* 1970, Michael Parry (m dis 1981); *Style*— The Hon Mrs Anna Parry

PARRY, Emyr Owen; s of Ebenezer Owen Parry; *b* 26 May 1933; *Educ* Caernarfon GS, Univ Coll of Wales Aberystwyth; *m* 1959, Enid Griffiths; 1 s, 1 da; *Career* admitted slr 1957, dep circuit judge 1975, rec Crown Ct 1979-; chm Nat Insur Appeals Tbnl Holyhead Area 1969-, slr memb Lord Chllr's Co Ct Rule Ctee 1975; *Style*— Emyr Parry, Esq

PARRY, Erika Anne Blackmore; da of Brig Hugh Vivian Combe, DSO, MC (d 1972), ADC to HM King George VI 1943-52 and to HM The Queen 1952-53, and Phyllis Marjorie (Jill), *née* Durrant (d 1977); *Educ* Tortington Park Arundel Sussex; *m* Croose Parry; 2 da (Marie-Line, Rozelle); *Career* designer, creative design and prodn devpt conslt and author; created and designed 'Wild Tudor' and Somerset tableware and giftware ranges in English Bone China for Aynsley China Ltd; designer of 250 different items for major int cos items incl: china, enamel boxes, kitchenware, wall coverings, textiles, stationery, wrought iron entrance gates, jewellery, silverware; MCSD, memb BEDA; *Recreations* studying wildlife; *Style*— Mrs Erika Parry; Rushbrooke, Wonersh, Surrey GU5 0QS (☎ 0483 892303)

PARRY, Glyn David; s of Albert George Parry, of North Wales, and Drina Margaret Elizabeth, *née* Eveson (d 1988); *b* 29 June 1955; *Educ* Alsop GS for Boys Liverpool, Univ of Manchester; *m* 3 Nov 1984, Jane Catherine Roberts, da of Walter Robert Roberts; 1 s (David John b 7 Aug 1985), 1 da (Laura Eve b 4 Aug 1988); *Career* auditor Inland Revenue 1977-78, advertising mangr Corgi and Bantam Books 1978-81, account dir Barneys Advertising Bristol 1982-85, gp head Ogilvy & Mather Direct Advertising London 1985-87, dir mktg mangr Rank Xerox (UK) Ltd 1987-; pub speaker Mktg and Advertising Confs; Br Direct Mktg awards, PO awards; *Recreations* yoga, my family; *Style*— Glyn Parry, Esq; 36 Salisbury Rd, Carshalton Beeches, Surrey SM5 3HD (☎ 081 669 5265); Rank Xerox (UK) Ltd, Bridge House, Oxford Rd, Uxbridge, Middlesex UB8 1HS (☎ 0895 51133, fax 0895 54095)

PARRY, Baron (Life Peer UK 1975), of Neyland, Co Dyfed; Gordon Samuel David Parry; s of Rev Thomas Lewis Parry, Baptist Minister (d 1965), and Anne Parry (d 1958); *b* 30 Nov 1925; *Educ* Neyland Sch, Pembroke Co Intermediate Sch, Trinity Coll Carmarthen, Inst of Educn, Univ of Liverpool; *m* 1948, Glenys Catherine, da of Jack Leslie Incledon; 1 da (Hon Catherine Anne b 1955); *Career* sits as Lab peer in House of Lords; teacher and journalist; house master and librarian Co Secdy Sch Haverfordwest 1952-68, warden Pembrokeshire Teachers' Centre 1968-78; chm Wales Tourist Bd 1978-83, memb Br Tourist Authy 1978-83, pres Br Inst of Cleaning Sci, chm British Cleaning Cncl, chm Tidy Britain Cncl, chm Britain in Bloom, pres Milford Docks Co, dir Guidehouse; hon fell: James Cook Univ Queensland Australia, Inst of Wastes Management, Trinity Coll Carmarthen; fell: Tourism Soc, Br Inst of Cleaning Sci, Hotel and Catering and Industl Mgmnt Assoc; FRSA; *Recreations* watching rugby football; *Clubs* Neyland Rugby, Neyland Yacht; *Style*— The Rt Hon Lord Parry; Willowmead, 52 Port Lion, Llangwm, Haverfordwest, Pembrokeshire, Dyfed, SA62 4JT (☎ 0646 600667); House of Lords, London SW1 The Milford Docks Company, The Docks, Milford Haven, Pembrokeshire, Dyfed (☎ 0646 692271)

PARRY, Sir (Frank) Hugh Nigel; CBE (1954); s of Charles Frank Parry; *b* 26 Aug 1911; *Educ* Cheltenham, Balliol Coll Oxford; *m* 1945, Ann Maureen, da of Henry Philip Forshaw; 2 da; *Career* entered Colonial Admin Serv 1939, Fedn of Rhodesia and Nyasaland 1953-63, Miny of Overseas Devpt 1965, actg head Middle East Devpt Div 1969-71, ret 1971; kt 1963; *Style*— Sir Hugh Parry, CBE; c/o Grindlays Bank, 13 St James's Square, London SW1

PARRY, John Charles Frederick; s of Brig Richard Frederick Parry, MC, of Mersham, Kent, and Elspeth Stewart, *née* Wilson; *b* 14 May 1950; *Educ* Sherborne; *Career* dir: ANCO Commodities Ltd 1977-80, Conti Commodity Servs 1980-84; md Capcom Fin Servs Ltd 1984-; *Books* Options (1982); *Recreations* cricket, dining; *Clubs* Turf; *Style*— John Parry, Esq; Capcom Financial Services, 107 Grays Inn Rd, London WC1 (☎ 071 831 4866)

PARRY, John Kelsall; s of Edward Parry (d 1983), of Birmingham, and Kathleen Mary, *née* Allen; *b* 28 Aug 1936; *Educ* Loughborough GS, London Sch of Journalism (Dip); *m* 18 Dec 1960, Judy Valerie, da of late Darcy Nigel Barry Cornwell, of

Gympie, Qld, Aust; 1 s (Edward Dylan Parry b 20 June 1965); *Career* reporter Evening Argus Brighton 1960-62, feature writer then William Hickey diarist Daily Express London 1962-67, reporter Tomorrow's World BBC TV 1967-70, arts corr News and Current Affrs BBC Radio 1982- (reporter and presenter World at One, PM and World This Weekend 1971-82); *Recreations* reading, theatre, opera, cooking, reading cookery books; *Style—* John Parry, Esq; News & Current Affrs, BBC Radio, Room 3116, Broadcasting House, Portland Place, London W1A 1AA (☎ 071 927 5920, fax 071 636 4295)

PARRY, John Richard; s of David Parry (d 1957), of Thetford, Norfolk, and Alma Harriet, *née* Fuller (d 1990); *b* 3 May 1934; *Educ* The GS Thetford, Fitzwilliam Coll Cambridge (MA); *m* 9 Sept 1961, Mary, da of William Dorrington, of Pinner, Middx; 1 s (Simon David William b 1964), 1 da (Anne-Louise b 1968); *Career* Nat Serv Bombadier RA 1952-54 (Suez Canal Zone); Commercial Union Properties Ltd: dir 1971, md 1978; Hammerson Property Investmt and Devpt Corpn plc: dir 1984, dep md 1985, jt md 1986, md 1988; memb: Telford Devpt Corpn 1980-82 (dep chm 1982-86), property advsy gp DOE 1980-, cncl Br Property Fedn 1986-; magistrate Gore div Middx Petty Sessions 1980-84; Freeman: City of London, Worshipful Co of Chartered Surveyors 1985; FRICS 1962; Coll of Estate Mgmnt Reading: memb The Charter Soc 1987, hon fell 1988; *Recreations* keeping fit, eating out, opera and ballet; *Clubs* Arts; *Style—* John Parry, Esq; 100 Park Lane, London W1Y 4AR (☎ 071 629 9494, fax 071 629 0498, car 0836 739 549, telex 261837)

PARRY, Robert; MP (Lab) Liverpool Riverside 1983-; s of Robert Parry; *b* 8 Jan 1933; *Educ* Bishop Goss RC Sch Liverpool; *m* 1956, Marie, *née* Hesdon; *Career* MP (Lab): Liverpool Exchange 1970-74, Liverpool Scotland Exchange 1974-1983; fndr memb Campaign Gp Labour MPs 1982-, chm Merseyside Gp of Labour MPs 1976-, memb Lab Delgn Cncl of Europe and Western Euro Union 1984- (chief whip 1987-); *Style—* Robert Parry, Esq, MP; House of Commons, SW1A 0AA

PARRY, Victor Thomas Henry; s of Thomas Parry (d 1957), of Newport, Gwent, and Daisy, *née* Nott (d 1964); *b* 20 Nov 1927; *Educ* Newport (St Julians) HS, St Edmund Hall Oxford (BA, MA), UCL; *m* 16 May 1959, Mavis, da of Charles Russull (d 1958), of London; 2 s (Richard b 1959, Matthew b 1962), 1 da (Katharine b 1968); *Career* Manchester Public Libraries 1950-56, Colonial and Cwlth Relations Office Library 1956-60; librarian: The Nature Conservancy 1960-64, Br Museum (natural history) 1964-74; chief librarian and archivist Royal Botanic Gdns Kew 1974-78, librarian SOAS London 1978-83, dir Central Library Servs and Goldsmiths librarian Univ of London 1983-89, sr examiner The Library Assoc 1959-68; chm: Circle of State Librarians 1966-68, London Gp UCR Library Assoc 1972-76, Govt Libraries Gp 1977-78; ed Soc for Bibliography of Natural History 1975-78; FLA 1959, FRAS 1979, FRSA 1984; *Books* Conservation of Threatened Plants (ed, 1976); *Recreations* reading, ball games, railways; *Clubs* RSA; *Style—* Victor Parry, Esq; 69 Redway Dr, Twickenham TW2 7NN (☎ 081 894 0742); University Library, Senate House, Univ of London, Malet St, London WC1E 7HU

PARRY-CROOKE, David John; s of Maj Charles Philip Parry-Crooke, JP (d 1978), of Friston, Suffolk, and Winifred Rosa Parry-Crooke, JP, *née* Wales (d 1976); *see* Burke's Landed Gentry 18 Ed Vol III 1972; *b* 3 March 1923; *Educ* Radley, Univ Coll Oxford; *m* 1, 22 Jan 1948, Griselda Mary Powell, da of Rev Canon Norman Powell Williams (d 1942), of Christ Church Oxford; 1 s (John Paul b 1953), 2 da (Charlotte Mary b 1950, Georgiana Mary b 1956); m 2, 1 Nov 1979, Elizabeth Dorothea, da of Dr William Crampton Gore, RHA (d 1945), of Enniskillen Co Fermanagh; *Career* WWII 19 King George V's Own Lancers IA 1942-46; Capt: India, Burma, Malaya; sometime rubber planter Malaya, farmer and travel conslt, landowner; voluntary work: The Samaritans, London, Suffolk Cons Pty; involved with church and local cncls; Master Workshipful Co of Tylers and Bricklayers 1976-77; *Recreations* model railways, photography, shooting, travel; *Clubs* MCC, Army and Navy; *Style—* David Parry-Crooke, Esq; 5 Dixwell Rd, Folkestone, Kent (☎ 0303 55 690)

PARRY EVANS, Mary Alethea (Lady Hallinan); da of Dr Evan Parry Evans, MD, JP; *b* 31 Oct 1929; *Educ* Malvern Girls' Coll, Somerville Coll Oxford (BCL, MA); *m* 1955, Sir (Adrian) Lincoln Hallinan, *qv*; 2 s, 2 da; *Career* barr Inner Temple 1953, Wales and Chester circuit, a rec of the Crown Ct 1978-; *Style—* Lady Hallinan; chambers: 33 Park Place, Cardiff (☎ 0222 33313)

PARRY-EVANS, Air Marshal Sir David; KCB (1985), CBE (1978); s of Gp Capt John Parry-Evans (d 1978), and Dorothy Parry-Evans; *b* 19 July 1935; *Educ* Berkhamsted; *m* 1960, Anne, da of Charles Reynolds (d 1966), and Gertrude Reynolds; 2 s; *Career* RAF 1956-: OC 214 Sqdn 1974-75, OC RAF Marham 1975-77, Air Cdre until 1981, dir Def Policy MOD 1979-81, Cmdt RAF Staff Coll Bracknell 1981-82, Air Vice-Marshal 1982, AOC No 1 and 38 Gps 1982-85, CIC RAF Germany, Cdr 2 Allied Tactical Air Force 1985-87, dep chief Defence Staff 1987-; *Recreations* rugby; *Clubs* RAF; *Style—* Air Marshal Sir David Parry-Evans, KCB, CBE; Air House, Royal Air Force, Rheindahlen, BFPO 40 (☎ 02161 47 4027)

PARSLOE, John; s of (Charles) Guy Parsloe (d 1985), and (Mary) Zirphie (Munro), *née* Faiers; *b* 14 Oct 1939; *Educ* Bradfield, Queen's Coll Oxford (MA); *m* 6 Oct 1973, (Helen) Margaret, da of Dr (Daniel) Arnold Rolfe (d 1985); 2 s (Thomas b 1974, William b 1979), 1 da (Alice b 1976); *Career* admitted slr 1971; dir: Mercury Fund Managers Ltd 1981, Mercury Asset Management plc 1990; memb Law Soc 1971; *Style—* John Parsloe, Esq; 33 King William St, London EC4R 9AS (☎ 071 280 2800)

PARSLOW, Robert Edwin; s of William James Parslow (d 1948), of Northwood, Middx, and Winifred Ada, *née* Coles (d 1937); *b* 19 June 1929; *Educ* Harrow, Peterhouse Cambridge (MA); *m* 21 Jan 1956, Shirley Gordon, da of Dr Eric Gordon Fleming (d 1948), of St Johns Wood, London NW8; 2 s (John b 23 March 1959, Roger b 27 Dec 1961); *Career* admitted slr 1955; sr ptnr Hyde Mahon Bridges 1983-; memb Law Soc; *Recreations* foreign travel; *Style—* Robert Parslow, Esq; 42 Granville Rd, Limpsfield, Oxted, Surrey RH8 0DA (☎ 0883 712 493); 52 Bedford Row, London WC1R 4UH (☎ 071 405 9455, fax 071 831 7721, telex 25210)

PARSONS, (Thomas) Alan; CB (1984); s of late Arthur and Laura Parsons; *b* 25 Nov 1924; *Educ* Clifton, Bristol Univ (LLB); *m* 1, 1947, Valerie Vambeck; 1 s; m 2, 1957, Muriel Lewis; 2 s; *Career* served WWII RM 1943-46; called to the Bar Middle Temple 1950, legal asst Miny of Nat Insur 1950, sr legal asst Miny of Pensions and Nat Insur 1955; DHSS: asst slr 1968, princ asst slr 1977-, chief adjudication offr 1984-86; *Style—* Alan Parsons Esq, CB; 11 Northiam St, Pennethorne Place, London E9 7HF

PARSONS, Hon Mrs (Anne Constance); *née* Manningham-Buller; da of 1 Viscount Dilhorne, PC, and Lady Mary Lilian Lindsay, da of 27 Earl of Crawford and Balcarres, KT; *b* 13 Aug 1951; *Educ* Benenden; *m* 1982, John Christopher Parsons, *qv*; 2 s, 1 da; *Style—* The Hon Mrs Parsons

PARSONS, Sir Anthony Derrick; GCMG (1981, KCMG 1975, CMG 1969), LVO (1965), MC (1945); s of late Col H A J Parsons, MC; *b* 9 Sept 1922; *Educ* King's Sch Canterbury, Balliol Coll Oxford; *m* 1948, Sheila Emily, da of Geoffrey Baird, of Goodnestone, Kent; 2 s, 2 da; *Career* HM Forces 1940, asst mil attaché Baghdad 1952-54; HM Dip Serv: FO 1954-55, Ankara 1955-59, Amman 1959-60, Cairo 1960-61, FO 1961-64, Khartoum 1964-65, political agent Bahrain 1965-69, cnsllr UK Mission to UN NY 1969-71, under-sec FCO 1971-74, ambass Iran 1974-79, UK perm rep UN 1979-82; memb Bd British Cncl 1982-86, PM's personal foreign affairs advsr 1983-; lectr and res fell Univ of Exeter 1984-87; Order of the Two Niles Sudan 1965; *Books* The Pride and The Fall (1984), They Say The Lion (1986); *Clubs* MCC, Royal Over-Seas League; *Style—* Sir Anthony Parsons, GCMG, LVO, MC; Highgrove, Ashburton, S Devon

PARSONS, Prof (John) David; s of Oswald Parsons (d 1976), and Doris Anita, *née* Roberts (d 1986); *b* 8 July 1935; *Educ* Ebbw Vale GS, Univ Coll Cardiff (BSc), King's Coll London (MSc Eng, DScEng); *m* 19 July 1969, Mary Winifred Stella, da of Frederick Stanley Tate (d 1959); *Career* Nat Serv RAF 1954-56; GEC Applied Electronics Laboratories 1959-62, Regent St Poly 1962-66, City of Birmingham Poly 1966-68, reader in electronic engrg (former lectr and sr lectr) Univ of Birmingham 1969-82, UN expert in India 1977, hon sr princ scientific offr Royal Signals and Radar Establishment Malvern 1978-82, visiting prof Univ of Auckland 1982; Univ of Liverpool: David Jardine prof of electrical engrg, head Dept of Electrical Engrg and Electronics 1983-86, dean Faculty of Engrg 1986-89, pro vice-chllr 1990-; visiting res engr NTT Japan 1987; memb: Communications sub-ctee Sci and Engrg Res Cncl 1983-87, Cncl Inst of Electronic and Radio Engrs 1985-88, Cncl Inst of Electrical Engrs 1988-89; FIEE 1985, FEng 1988; *Books* Electronic and Switching Circuits (with Bozic and Cheng, 1975), Mobile Communication Systems (with Gardiner, 1989), The Mobile Radio Propagation Channel (1991); *Recreations* golf, bridge, skiing; *Style—* Prof David Parsons; Department of Electrical Engineering and Electronics, University of Liverpool, PO Box 147, Liverpool L69 3BX (☎ 051 794 4503, fax 051 794 4540, telex 627095 UNILPOL G)

PARSONS, Geoffrey Penwill; AO (1990), OBE (1977); s of Francis Hedley Parsons; *b* 15 June 1929; *Educ* Canterbury HS Sydney, State Conservatorium of Music (with Winifred Burston) Sydney; *Career* concert accompanist; recitals worldwide with many of the world's leading singers; int recital series Geoffrey Parsons and Friends, opening season of Barbican Centre 1982, also Sidney 1988 for Australian Bicentenary, twenty-fifth concert tour of Aust (with Dame Janet Baker); has accompanied many of the Worlds greatest recital singers of past 30 years; hon fell RAM 1975, hon fell GSM 1983, FRCM 1987; *Style—* Geoffrey Parsons, Esq, AO, OBE; 176 Iverson Rd, London NW6 2HL (☎ 071 624 0957)

PARSONS, John Anthony; s of Leslie Norman Parsons, of Oxford, and Marian Eunice, *née* Evans; *b* 20 Feb 1938; *Educ* Magdalen Coll Sch Oxford; *Career* journalist; Oxford Mail 1946-64, Daily Mail 1964-80, Daily Telegraph 1980- (Lawn tennis corr); sec Lawn Tennis Writers Assoc 1983- (chm 1980-81), dep chm Int Tennis Fedn Media Cmmn The Championships Wimbledon 1983-90, chm Oxford-Leiden City Link; *awards* Tennis Writer of the Year (Law Tennis Assoc) 1987, Media Person of the Year (Womens Tennis Assoc) 1990; *Recreations* theatre; *Style—* John Parsons, Esq; Daily Telegraph, 181 Marsh Wall, South Quay, London E14 9SR (☎ 071 538 5000, fax 071 538 6242)

PARSONS, John Christopher; s of Arthur Christopher Parsons, of Hatchwood House, Odiham, Hants, and Veronica Rosetta de Courcy, *née* Glover; *b* 21 May 1946; *Educ* Harrow, Trinity Coll Cambridge (BA); *m* 20 Feb 1982, Hon Anne Constance Manningham-Buller, da of 1 Viscount Dilhorne, PC; 2 s (Michael b 1983, David b 1985), 1 da (Lilah b 1988); *Career* CA; Dowty Group Ltd 1968-72, Peat Marwick Mitchell & Co 1972-85; asst treas to HM The Queen 1985, dep keeper of the Privy Purse and dep treas to HM The Queen 1988; FCA, MIMC; *Clubs* Brooks's; *Style—* John Parsons, Esq; 19 Melrose Gardens, London W6 7RN (☎ 071 602 3035); Zion Cottage, Penton Mewsey, Andover, Hants SP11 0RQ; Buckingham Palace, London SW1A 1AA (☎ 071 930 4832)

PARSONS, John William; CBE (1988); s of Frederick John Parsons (d 1988), of Wareham, Dorset, and Dorothy Ellen, *née* Toop; *b* 24 July 1936; *Educ* Poole GS, Porthcurno Engrg Coll; *m* 1, 1958 (m dis 1979); 1 s (Christopher), 1 da (Yasmin); m 2, 1981, Sally-Anne, da of Robert St Vincent Parker-Jervis (d 1972); 1 s (Timothy); *Career* Actg Capt Royal Signals; Cable and Wireless: joined 1960, head of business (Caribbean) 1966-72, md Euro cos 1972-78; md ITR International Time Ltd 1979-82, chm and chief exec Time and Data Systems International Ltd 1982-; memb: BOTB 1985-, CBI Smaller Firms Cncl; chm Talbot Assocs Ltd; dir: Mixsecure Ltd, Dorset TEC, Princes Youth Business Tst; former pres Dorset C of C and Indust; cncllr: Purbeck DC, Corfe Castle Parish Cncl; govr Poole GS; CEng, FIEE, FInstD, FBIM, MInst AM(Dip), MIEE (USA); *Clubs* IOD, Exiles, RAC; *Style—* John Parsons, Esq, CBE; Townsend House, Corfe Castle, Wareham, Dorset BH20 5EG (☎ 0929 480265); Time and Data Systems International Ltd, Crestworth House, Sterte Ave, Poole, Dorset BH15 2AL (☎ 0202 666222, telex 417218 (TDSICO), fax 0202 679730)

PARSONS, Dr Malcolm; s of Rev Dr Eric Parsons, and late Ina, *née* Robson; *b* 3 March 1933; *Educ* Kingswood Sch Bath, St Catharine's Coll Cambridge (MA), UCH (MB BChir), FRCP; *m* 8 June 1972, Diana Margaret, da of late William Hill; 2 da (Fiona b 1973, Georgina b 1975); *Career* Nat Serv cmmnd RAMC 1960-62; Nat Hosp Queen Sq 1964, Hammersmith Hosp 1965, Maida Vale UCH 1966-69, conslt neurologist Gen Infirmary Leeds and Pinderfields Hosp Wakefield 1969-, currently sr clinical lectr in neurology Univ of Leeds; memb: Assoc Physicians, Assoc Br Neurologists; *Books* Colour Atlas of Clinical Neurology (1983), Diagnostic Picture Tests in Clinical Neurology (1987), Tuberculous Meningitis (1988); *Style—* Dr Malcolm Parsons; Dept of Neurology, Gen Infirmary, Gt George St, Leeds LS1 3EX (☎ 0532 432799)

PARSONS, Hon (Desmond Oliver) Martin; 2 s of 6 Earl of Rosse, KBE, and Anne, Countess of Rosse, *qv*; *b* 23 Dec 1938; *Educ* Eton, Aiglon Coll Switzerland; *m* 1965, Aline Edwina, da of Dr George Alexander Macdonald, of Rugby, and Marguerite Louise Edwina Macdonald; 2 s (Rupert Alexander Michael b 3 Sept 1966, Desmond Edward Richard b 30 October 1968); *Style—* The Hon Martin Parsons; Womersley Park, Doncaster

PARSONS, Sir (John) Michael; s of late Rt Rev Richard Godfrey Parsons, DD, Bishop of Hereford (d 1948), and Dorothy Gales Streeter (d 1956); *b* 29 Oct 1915; *Educ* Rossall, Univ Coll Oxford; *m* 1, 1946 (m dis 1964), Hilda Mary Frewen; 1 s, 2 da; m 2, 1964, Caroline Inagh Margaret, da of Col Laton Frewen, DSO (d 1976), of Ross-on-Wye; *Career* Maj IA 1939-46 (POW Singapore); Inchcape & Co Ltd: dir 1971-81, sr md 1976-81, dep chm and chief exec 1979-81; chm and dir Assam Investments 1976-81, dir Commonwealth Development Finance Co Ltd 1973-80; chm Cncl of Royal Cwlth Soc 1976-81, dep chm Utd World Colls 1982-86; kt 1970; *Recreations* golf; *Clubs* Oriental; *Style—* Sir Michael Parsons; Tall Trees, Warren Hill Lane, Aldeburgh, Suffolk IP15 5QB (☎ 0728 452917)

PARSONS, (Christopher) Nicholas; s of Dr Paul Frederick Nigel Parsons (d 1981), of Hampstead, London, and Nell Louise, *née* Maggs (d 1980); *Educ* St Paul's, Univ of Glasgow; *m* 21 Aug 1954 (sep 1983), Denise Pauline Rosalie, da of Claud Bryer; 1 da (Suzy Zuleika b 13 June 1958); 1 s (Justin Hugh b 24 Dec 1960); *Career* actor, solo performer; live work: The Hasty Heart (London), Jack in Charley's Aunt (Palace Theatre), repertory two years (Bromley), cabaret (Quaglinos, Astor, Cafe de Paris, Blue Angel, Society), comedian (Windmill Theatre) 1952, revues (London fringe theatres and Lyric Theatre) 1953, Swing Along with Arthur Haynes (Palladium) 1963, Boeing Boeing (Duchess Theatre) 1967, Say Who You Are (Vaudeville Theatre) 1968, Uproar in the House (Whitehall Theatre) 1968, Darling I'm Home (tour) 1978, Stage

Struck (tour) 1980, Keeping Down with the Jones (tour) 1981, Charlie Girl (Victoria Palace and nat tour) 1987-88, much pantomime work and 3 one-person shows (Edward Lear Show performed at Edinburgh Festival 1990); tv: Comedy Work partnership with Arthur Haynes 1956-66, Benny Hill Show 1969-70, host of Sale of the Century 1971-84 and The Alphabet Game (Night Network) 1988, Mr Jolly Lives Next Door (for Comic Strip) 1988, The Curse of Fenric (Dr Who) 1989, presenter of Laughlines (BSB) 1990; films: Brothers-in-Law, Carlton Browne of the FO, Happy is the Bride, Don't Raise the Bridge Lower the River, Spy Story; writer and dir of 5 comedy documentaries for cinema and tv for own production co; consistent radio work since 1952 incl: for BBC Drama Repertory Company 1953, host of Just a Minute since 1966, presenter of Listen to This Space 1967, Dear Jenny Dear Julie 1990; memb Cncl: The Lord's Taverners, NSPCC; Barker of The Variety Club; memb: Stars' Organisation for Spastics, Sparks and Conservation Charity, Living Earth; author of Egg on the Face; Variety Club Radio Personality of the Year 1967, entered in the Guinness Book of Records for longest after dinner humorous speech 1978; Rector St Andrews Univ 1988-91 8; *Recreations* cricket, golf, gardening, photography; *Style—* Nicholas Parsons, Esq; c/o Billy Marsh Associates Ltd, 19 Denmark St, London WC2H 8NA (☎ 071 379 4004, fax 071 379 0831)

PARSONS, Sir Richard Edmund Clement Fownes; KCMG (1982, CMG 1977); s of Dr Richard A Parsons (d 1960), of Kirkbeck House, Coniston, Cumbria (d 1960), and Mrs Richard Parsons (d 1977); *b* 14 March 1928; *Educ* Bembridge Sch, Brasenose Coll Oxford (BA); *m* 1960, Jenifer Jane (d 1981), da of Charles Reginald Mathews; 3 s; *Career* Nat Serv 1949-51; Dip Serv; joined FO 1951; formerly serv: Buenos Aires, Ankara, Washington, Vientiane; former cnsllr Lagos, head personnel ops dept 1972-76; ambassador: Hungary 1976-79, Spain 1980-84, Sweden 1984-87 (ret); *Clubs* Travellers'; *Style—* Sir Richard Parsons, KCMG; 152 De Beauvoir Road, London N1

PARSONS, Robert Frederick James; OBE (1985); s of Robert Frederick James Parsons (d 1957), of Camberley, and Grace Maude, *née* Hancock; *b* 19 Aug 1935; *Educ* Kingswood Sch Bath, Downing Coll Cambridge (MA); *Career* admitted slr 1961; ptnr Beachcroft & Co 1965- (now Beachcroft Stanleys), dir Property Owners Building Soc 1984-86; Parly candidate (Cons) Holborn and St Pancras South Feb and Oct 1974; chm Fedn of Cons and Unionist Assoc 1957-58, pres Surrey West Euro Constituency Cons Cncl 1984-87, memb Frimley and Camberley UDC 1962-71 and 1972-74 (ldr: 1965-67, 1969-71, 1972-74; chm 1967-69), memb Surrey CC 1970-77; memb: Standing Conf on London and SE Regnl Planning 1974-77, SE Regnl Econ Planning Cncl 1975-78, Surrey Family Practitioner Ctee 1986-90, Surrey Family Health Servs Authy 1990-; pres: Surrey Heath (formerly Camberley) Scout Cncl 1969-, Camberley and Dist Horticultural Soc 1985-, League of the Helping Hand 1989-; chm: Camberley Soc 1967-70 (vice pres 1985-), St Tarcisius RC Parish Pastoral Cncl 1971-89, Woking Deanery RC Pastoral Cncl 1978-80 and 1987-89, Govrs Collingwood Sch Camberley 1979-89, Govrs St Tarcisius RC Middle Sch 1983-; Freeman Worshipful Co of Slrs 1987; memb Law Soc 1961; *Recreations* travel, music, reading; *Clubs* Athenaeum, Travellers, St Stephens Constitutional; *Style—* Robert Parsons, Esq, OBE; Levington, 104 London Rd, Camberley, Surrey GU15 3TJ (☎ 0276 23491); Beachcroft Stanleys, 100 Fetter Lane, London EC4A 1BN (☎ 071 242 1011, fax 071 430 1532, telex 264607 BEALAW G)

PARSONS, Robin Edward; s of Anthony Maxse Parsons, of Kingsbury, Argos Hill, Rotherfield, East Sussex, and Rosamund, *née* Hurst; *b* 30 Dec 1948; *Educ* Uppingham, UCL (LLB); *m* 27 May 1972, Elizabeth Hamilton Floyd; 2 da (Sonia Katharine Elizabeth, Alexandra Geraldine); *Career* asst slr Coward Chance 1973-75 (articled clerk 1971-73); Cameron Markby Hewitt (formerly Cameron Kemm Norden): asst slr 1975-77, ptnr 1977- (estab Paris Office 1980); lectr at numerous legal conferences and seminars incl series given to Chartered Inst of Bankers 1988-91; Freeman and Liveryman Worship Co of Haberdashers, Freeman Worshipful Co of Slrs; memb Law Soc; *Publications* author of articles for legal jls; *Recreations* tennis, squash, French; *Style—* Robin Parsons, Esq; Cameron Markby Hewitt, Sceptre Court, 40 Tower Hill, London EC3N 4BB (☎ 071 702 2345, fax 071 702 2303)

PARSONS, Prof Roger; s of Robert Harry Ashby Parsons (d 1966), and Ethel, *née* Fenton (d 1973); *b* 31 Oct 1926; *Educ* King Alfred Sch, Strathcona HS Edmonton Alberta, Imp Coll London (BSc, PhD, DIC), Univ of Bristol (DSc); *m* 8 June 1953, Ruby Millicent, da of Malcolm Turner (d 1971); 3 s (Gavin Christopher b 1954, Colin Mark b 1959, Magnus Frank b 1961), 1 da (Celia Janet b 1957); *Career* Deedes fell Univ of St Andrews 1951-54, lectr Univ of Bristol 1954-63 (reader in electrochemistry 1963-79), dir Laboratoire d'Electrochimie Interfaciale du CRNS Meudon France 1977-84, prof of chemistry Univ of Southampton 1985-, ed in chief Jl of Electroanalytical Chemistry 1963-; FRS 1980, ARCS 1946; Palladium medal (UK) 1979, Bruno Breyer medal Aust 1980, Paul Pascal prize France 1983, Galvani medal Italy 1986; *Books* Electrochemical Constants (1959), Interfacial Electrochemistry (1972), Electrochemistry in Research and Development (1985), Standard Potentials in Aqueous Solution (1985); *Recreations* listening to music, going to the opera; *Style—* Prof Roger Parsons, FRS; 16 Thornhill Rd, Bassett, Southampton SO1 7AT (☎ 0703 790143); Merrick, Moniaive, Thornhill, Dumfriesshire DG3 4EJ; Department of Chemistry, University of Southampton, Southampton SO9 5NH (☎ 0703 593371, fax 0703 593781, telex 47661 SOTONU G)

PARSONS-SMITH, Dr Basil Gerald; OBE (1945); s of Basil Thomas Parsons-Smith (d 1954), and Marguerite Ida, *née* Burnett; *b* 19 Nov 1911; *Educ* Harrow, Trinity Coll Cambridge (MA, MD), St George's Hosp London; *m* 3 June 1939, Aurea Mary, da of William Stewart Johnston (d 1942), of Wood Hall, Sunningdale; 2 s (James b 1946, Nicholas b 1949), 1 da (Elizabeth Anne Jacobs b 1940); *Career* blood transfusion offr EMS HQ 1939, RAF Coastal Cmd 1941, med specialist to No 3 and No 5 RAF Hosps ME, cmd No 24 MFH Tripoli (despatches twice); neurologist Charing Cross Hosp London 1950-77, examiner in med RCP London; appeared in BBC TV film Hospital 1922; conslt neurologist: Med Appeal Tbnl 1966-83, Vaccine Damaged Tbnl London 1979-83; Liveryman Worshipful Co of Apothecaries; FRSM; *Recreations* horses and Shetland pony stud; *Clubs* Cambridge Univ, Pitt (life memb); *Style—* Dr Gerald Parsons-Smith, OBE; Roughets House, Blechingley, Surrey RH1 4QX (☎ 0883 343929)

PARTINGTON, Alan; s of Arthur Partington, of Oakenclough, Oldham, and Annie, *née* Farrar (d 1977); *b* 23 Sept 1930; *Educ* Hulmegs Oldham; *m* 12 Sept 1953, Marian, da of Fred Smith (d 1964); 1 s (Ian Farrar b 1958), 1 da (Janet Mary Jarvis b 1954); *Career* Nat Serv RAF 1954-56; articled clerk Wm Wrigley & Son 1948-54, sr asst H L & H L Holden 1956-60, ptnr F Howarth & Co 1960-78, sr ptnr Alan Partington & Co 1978-; chm Lancastrian Building Society (formerly Middleton Building Society) 1978- (dir 1969-); chm of Govrs Bluecoat Sch Oldham 1981-87 (govr 1974-87), chm of Tstees Henshaw Tst 1978- (tstee 1976); FCA 1958; *Recreations* crown green bowls, wine, theatre; *Style—* Alan Partington, Esq; Wood Mount, 2 Woodland Park, Royton, Oldham OL2 5UY (☎ 061 624 0734); Alan Partington & Co, Sterling House, 501 Middleton Rd, Chadderton, Oldham OL9 9LA (☎ 061 652 8212)

PARTINGTON, Christopher John; s of George Partington (d 1977), of Merrington Old Hall, Bomere Heath, nr Shrewsbury, and Audrey Jean, *née* Bolton; father's maternal gf John Henry Davies, founded Manchester United FC; *b* 19 May 1953; *Educ* Ellesmere; *Career* angling historian, conslt in antique fishing tackle, fndr Britain's Angling Heritage Tst; memb numerous angling socs; *Recreations* fishing, shooting, rowing, canoeing, country skiing, sailing, swimming, music, reading, writing; *Clubs* Salop; *Style—* Christopher Partington, Esq; The Vintage Fishing Tackle Shop, 103 Longden Coleham, Shrewsbury, Shropshire SY3 7DX (☎ 0743 69373)

PARTINGTON, Prof (Thomas) Martin; s of Thomas Paullet Partington (d 1980), and Alice Emily Mary, *née* Jelly (d 1970); *b* 5 March 1944; *Educ* Kings Sch Canterbury, Univ of Cambridge (BA, LLB); *m* 1, 15 Aug 1969 (m dis 1973), Marcia Carol, *née* Leavey; 1 s (Daniel b 1971); m 2, 21 Oct 1978, Daphne Isobel, *née* Scharenguivel; 1 s (Adam b 1979), 1 da (Hannah b 1980); *Career* lectr: Univ of Warwick 1969-73, LSE 1973-80; dean of faculty of social sciences Brunel Univ 1985-87 (prof of law 1980-87); Univ of Bristol: asst lectr 1966-69, prof of law 1987-, dean of faculty of law 1988-; called to the Bar Middle Temple 1984; memb: Lord Chllr's Advsy Ctee on Legal Aid 1988-, Law Soc Trng Ctee 1989-; chm: Ctee Heads of Univ Law Schs 1990-, Social Security Appeal Tbnls 1990- (p/t); *Books* Landlord and Tenant (1975), Claim in Time (1978), Housing Law (with Andrew Arden, 1983); *Recreations* music, walking, cooking, gardening, foreign travel; *Style—* Prof Martin Partington; Little Court, Grib Lane, Blagdon, Avon BS18 6SA (☎ 0761 62916); Faculty of Law, University of Bristol, Bristol BS8 1RJ (☎ 0272 303372, fax 0272 251870, telex 445938)

PARTINGTON, (William) Rodney; s of Willie Partington (d 1986), of Polstead, Suffolk, and Sarah Alice, *née* Dickinson (d 1974); *b* 17 Jan 1944; *Educ* Derby Sch Bury Lancs, Bolton Tech Coll; *m* 30 July 1966, Glenda Ann, da of Joseph Daintree (d 1989), of Sale, Cheshire; 1 da (Lisa b 24 April 1972); *Career* trainee Halifax Building Society 1961-69, branch mangr Skipton Building Society 1969-76; Chartered Bldg Soc Inst: chm NW Group 1974-75, chm E Anglian Group 1980-81; md Colchester Building Society 1984-87 (sec 1976, gen mangr 1979), gen mangr and local dir Cheltenham & Gloucester Building Society (incl Colchester Building Society) 1987-88; memb Colchester Forum Rotary Club 1977-, dir Colchester Catalyst Charity 1987-; FCIS (1966), FBIM (1980); *Recreations* angling; *Style—* Rodney Partington, Esq; Stratford House, Polstead, Suffolk, (☎ 0206 262850)

PARTON, Nicholas George; s of Maj Michael Henry Parton, and Jean Mary, *née* Saxby; *b* 1 June 1954; *Educ* Haileybury, Grenoble Univ, Liverpool Poly (BA); *m* 12 Sept 1981, (Elizabeth) Querida, da of His Hon Judge John Wilfred da Cunha, of Churchill, nr Bristol, Avon; 1 s (Sam b 1984), 3 da (Amy b 1983, Phoebe b 1986, Felicity b 1988); *Career* admitted slr 1979; articled clerk Bremmer Sons & Corlett 1977, Holman Fenwick & Willan 1980, Middleton Potts 1983; ptnr: Taylor Garrett 1985, Taylor Joynson Garrett 1989; memb Law Soc 1979; *Recreations* skiing and sailing; *Clubs* Landsdowne; *Style—* Nicholas Parton, Esq; 31 Ambleside Ave, London SW16 1QE (☎ 081 769 0127); Bwthyn Cerios, Treardurr Rd, Treardurr Bay Anglesey, N Wales; Taylor Joynson Garrett, 180 Fleet St, London EC4A 2N5 (☎ 071 430 1122, fax 071 528 7145,telex 25516)

PARTRIDGE, Hon Mrs (Caroline Elizabeth Maud); *née* Cust; da of 6 Baron Brownlow; *b* 1928; *m* 1954 (m dis), John Arthur Partridge; 2 s, 1 da; *Style—* The Hon Mrs Caroline Partridge; 68 Scarsdale Villas, London W8 6PP

PARTRIDGE, Prof Derek; *b* 24 Oct 1945; *Educ* UCL (BSc), Imperial Coll London (DIC, PhD); *m* 27 Aug 1971, Mehrazar; 2 da (Mischa b 1974, Morgan b 1976); *Career* lectr computer sci Univ of Nairobi Kenya 1972-74, asst (later assoc, then full prof) Dept Computer Sci New Mexico State Univ USA 1975-86, prof computer sci Univ of Exeter 1987-; visiting: fell Univ of Essex 1981-82, lectr Univ of Queensland 1983-84; involved Nat York Theatre 1966-68; FRSA, AAAI, AISB; *Books* incl: Artificial Intelligence: Applications in the Future of Software Engineering (1986), The Foundations of Artificial Intelligence: a source book (1989), Computers for Society (contrib 1986), The Encyclopaedia of Microcomputers (contrib 1988), Machine Learning (contrib 1989), The Foundations of AI: a source book (contrib 1989); *Recreations* reading, writing, natural history, football; *Style—* Prof Derek Partridge; Warmhill Barton, Hennock, Bovey Tracey, S Devon TQ13 9QH (☎ 0626 832180); Univ of Exeter, Dept of Computer Sci, Exeter EX4 4PT (☎ 0392 264069 fax 0392 2644067)

PARTRIDGE, Derek William; CMG (1987); s of Ernest Partridge (d 1984), of Wembley, Middx, and Ethel Elizabeth, *née* Buckingham (d 1985); *b* 15 May 1931; *Educ* Preston Manor Co GS Wembley; *Career* RAF 1949-51; Dip Serv; FO 1951-54, Oslo 1954-56, Jedda 1956, Khartoum 1957-60, Sofia 1960-62, Manila 1962-65, Djakarta 1965-67, FCO 1967-72, Brisbane 1972-74, Colombo 1974-77; FCO: civil serv 1977-86, head Migration and Visa Dept 1981-83, head Nat and Treaty Dept 1983-86, Br high cmmr Freetown Sierra Leone 1986-; *Style—* Derek W Partridge, Esq, CMG; c/o National Westminster Bank plc, 1 St James's Square, London SW1Y 4JX; c/o FCO, King Charles St, London SW1A 2AH

PARTRIDGE, Frances Catherine; da of William Cecil Marshall (d 1921), of 28 Bedford Sq, London WC1, and Margaret Anna, *née* Lloyd (d 1941); *b* 15 March 1900; *Educ* Bedales Sch, Newnham Coll Cambridge (BA); *m* 2 March 1933, Maj Reginald Sherring Partridge, MC (d 1960); 1 s (Lytton Burgo b 1935, d 1963); *Career* antiquarian bookseller 1922-28; edited Greville diaries with husband 1928-38 (8 vols), translator of French and Spanish works; FRSL; *Books* A Pacifist's War (1978), Memories (1981), Julia (1983), Everything To Lose (1985), Friends in Focus (1987), The Pasque Flower (1990), Hanging On (1990); *Recreations* travel, music, reading, botany; *Clubs* Int PEN; *Style—* Mrs Frances Partridge; 16 West Halkin St, London SW1 (☎ 071 235 6998)

PARTRIDGE, Frank; s of John Partridge, of N Uist, Western Isles, and Flora Partridge; *b* 16 Aug 1953; *Educ* Abbey Sch Fort Augustus Inverness-shire, Edinburgh Univ (BA), Univ Coll Cardiff (Dip in Journalism); *Career* BBC: presenter Newsbeat Radio One 1982-88, sports corr 1988-91, presenter PM Radio 4 1991-; *Recreations* squash, swimming, cricket playing, watching and collecting; *Clubs* Lansdowne; *Style—* Frank Partridge, Esq; PM, BBC Broadcasting House, London W1A 1AA (☎ 071 927 4100)

PARTRIDGE, Ian Harold; s of Harold William (d 1972), and Eugenia Emily, *née* Stinson; *b* 12 June 1938; *Educ* New Coll Oxford (chorister), Clifton, RCM, Guild Sch of Music (LGSM); *m* 4 July 1959, Ann Pauline, da of William Maskell Glover (d 1965), of Bexhill, Sussex; 2 s (Daniel b 1964, Jonathan b 1967); *Career* concert singer and recitalist with wide repertoire from early baroque to new works; opera debut at Covent Gdn as Iopas in Les Troyens 1969, title role Britten's St Nicholas Thames TV (Prix Italia, 1977), regular appearances at London's concert halls with maj orchestras and conductors and at int festivals throughout the world, frequent broadcaster on BBC Radio 3; many recordings incl: Schubert Die Schöne Müllerin, Winterreise Schumann Dichterliebe, Vaughan Williams On Wenlock Edge, Warlock The Curlew, Britten Winter Words; over 200 performances worldwide of An Evening with Queen Victoria (with Prunella Scales), master classes on Lieder, English Song and Early Music at Aldeburgh, Dartington, Trondheim, Vancouver etc; *Recreations* theatre, bridge, horse racing; *Style—* Ian Partridge, Esq; 127 Pepys Rd, Wimbledon, London SW20 8NP (☎ 081 946 7140)

PARTRIDGE, (Walter Michael) James; s of Maj Michael Harry Partridge, of Betchworth, Surrey, and Diana Marjorie, *née* Chamberlain; *b* 14 March 1958; *Educ*

Lancing, Trinity Coll Cambridge (BA); *m* 16 July 1983, Sarah Mercy, da of Wallace Barrie Page, of Killearn, Scotland; 1 s (Harry Michael James b 1989), 1 da (Georgiana Diana Margaret b 1987); *Career* cmmnd RA (Volunteer) 1979, Maj 1990-, 201 (Hertfordshire and Bedfordshire Yeomanry) Field Battery; admitted slr 1983; asst slr Lawrence Graham 1983-86, ptnr Thomson Snell & Passmore 1987-; memb Law Soc; *Recreations* sailing, walking, reading; *Clubs* Cavalry & Guards; *Style—* James Partridge, Esq; Thomson Snell & Passmore, 3 Lonsdale Gardens, Tunbridge Wells, Kent TN1 1NX (☎ 0892 510000, fax 0892 549884)

PARTRIDGE, John Arthur; s of Claude Partridge (d 1958), of 18 Brompton Square, London SW7, and Iris Florence, *née* Franks (d 1982); *b* 6 July 1929; *Educ* Elstree Sch, Harrow; *m* 1, 1954 (m dis), Hon Caroline Elizabeth Maud Cust, da of 6 Baron Brownlow, of Belton House, Lincs (d 1978); 2 s (Frank David Peregrine b 14 Sept 1955, Claude Edward b 29 Aug 1962), 1 da (Sophia Josephine b 12 May 1969); m 2, Rosemary FitzGibbon, da of Maj Robert Tyrrell (d 1975), of Litcham, Norfolk; *Career* ADC to Govr of S Aust Gen Lord Norrie 1952-53; chm and md Partridge Fine Art plc 1958-, chm Fine Art and Antique Export Ctee 1979-; *Recreations* hunting, fishing, shooting, gardening; *Clubs* Brooks; *Style—* John Partridge, Esq; Prebendal House, Empingham, Rutland, Leicestershire (☎ 078 086 234); 144/146 New Bond St, London W1Y 0LY (☎ 071 629 0834)

PARTRIDGE, Dr Martyn Richard; s of Maj Raymond John Bruce Partridge, RA, of Loughton, Essex, and Grace, *née* Darch; *b* 19 May 1948; *Educ* Pocklington Sch, Univ of Manchester (MB ChB, MD); *m* 23 June 1973, Rosemary Jane Emily, da of Lt (John) Dennis Radford, of Hove, Sussex; 1 s (Richard John Oliver b 15 Feb 1979), 2 da (Judith Stephanie Louise b 10 June 1977, Philippa Rachel Jane b 26 Feb 1981); *Career* res med offr Nat Heart Hosp London 1975-76, med registrar Royal Post Grad Med Sch London 1976-78, sr Jules Thorne res fell Middx Hosp 1978-80; sr med registrar: London Chest Hosp 1980-81, UCH 1981-82; conslt physician Whipps Cross Hosp London 1982-, author of various pubns of respiratory med and terminal care; chm Ed Ctee: British Thoracic Soc, Nat Asthma Campaign (memb Bd of Mgmnt); FRCP, FRSM; *Recreations* travel, railways, music, church and family; *Style—* Dr Martyn Partridge; Whipps Cross Hosp, Whipps Cross Rd, London E11 1NR (☎ 081 539 5522 ext 16, fax 081 558 8115)

PARTRIDGE, Michael John Anthony; KCB (1990, CB 1983); s of Dr John Henry Partridge (d 1956), and Ethel Partridge; *b* 29 Sept 1935; *Educ* Merchant Taylors', St John's Coll Oxford (MA); *m* 1968, Joan Elizabeth, da of Trevor Grattan Hughes (d 1953); 2 s, 1 da; *Career* civil servant; dep sec DHSS 1981-83, dep sec Home Office with responsibility for police dept 1983-87; *Recreations* skiing, reading, DIY; *Clubs* United Oxford and Cambridge; *Style—* Sir Michael Partridge, KCB; Richmond House, 79 Whitehall, London SW1 (☎ 071 210 5543 ext 5543)

PARTRIDGE, Neil Russell; s of Wilfred Lincoln (d 1978), and Elizabeth Mary, *née* Dudley (d 1974); *b* 10 Feb 1954; *Educ* Dame Allan's Sch Newcastle Upon Tyne, Univ of Newcastle (BA); *m* 1980, Sheila Anne, da of Gordon Kerr Henderson, of North Yorks; 1 s (William Lincoln b 1981), 1 da (Rebecca Anne b 1976); *Career* fin dir Vibroplant plc 1986; ACA; *Style—* Neil Partridge, Esq; Cranford, Lands Lane, Knaresborough, North Yorks

PARTRIDGE, Simon Harry Wood; OBE (1983); s of Rt Rev Frank Partridge (d 1941), of Bishopswood, Fareham, Hants, and Elizabeth Maud, *née* Barton (d 1965); *b* 17 Aug 1919; *Educ* Uppingham, Trinity Coll Oxford (MA); *m* 26 May 1951, Barbara Dagmar, da of Anton Emil Schou Bech (d 1981), of Copenhagen, Denmark; 2 s (Andrew b 17 March 1954, Jonathan b 8 Jan 1956); *Career* 57 HTR RAC 1939-40; chm and md: Butterworth Law Publishers Ltd 1974-76, Butterworth & Co (UK) Ltd 1976-82; dir Lloyd's of London Press Ltd 1982-90; memb Editorial Bd Statutes in Force 1984-90; Liveryman Worshipful Co of Merchant Taylors 1952; *Recreations* golf, chess; *Clubs* Garrick; *Style—* Simon Partridge, Esq, OBE; High Rede, Kilndown, Cranbrook, Kent TN17 2RT (☎ 0892 890413)

PASCALL, Matthew Stephen; s of Douglas Charles Pascall, DFC, Order of the Bronze Lion (Netherlands), (d 1970), and Catherine Barbara, *née* Sullivan; *b* 9 April 1961; *Educ* Furze Platt Comprehensive Sch Maidenhead, Trent Poly Nottingham (BA); *Career* called to the Bar Middle Temple 1984, memb of Chambers of J Widdup 1986; Freeman City of London, Liveryman Worshipful Co of Drapers; subscribing memb Gen cncl of the Bar; *Recreations* reading, limited tennis; *Clubs* Hon Life Memb W London Aero, Bourne; *Style—* Matthew Pascall, Esq; 22 Verey Close, Twyford, Reading, Berks RG10 0LW (☎ 0734 343 797); 29 High St, Guildford, Surrey GU1 3DY (☎ 0483 39131, fax 0483 300542)

PASCO, Richard Edward; CBE (1977); s of Cecil George Pasco (d 1982), and Phyllis Irene, *née* Widdison (d 1989); *b* 18 July 1926; *Educ* King's Coll Sch Wimbledon, Central Sch of Speech and Drama; *m* 1 (m dis), Greta, *née* Watson; 1 s; m 2, 1967, Barbara, *née* Leigh-Hunt; *Career* Army Serv 1944-48; actor; many leading roles RSC, London, West End Theatre, film, radio and TV, concert and recital work; hon assoc artist RSC, Royal Nat Theatre player; *Recreations* music, gardening, reading; *Clubs* Garrick; *Style—* Richard Pasco, Esq, CBE; c/o Michael Whitehall Ltd, 125 Gloucester Rd, London SW7 4TE

PASCO, Rowanne; da of John Pasco, and Ann, *née* MacKeonis; *b* 7 Oct 1938; *Educ* Ursuline Convent HS, Open Univ (MA); *Career* travel rep Horizon Holidays 1961-66, various radio and TV commercials whilst res in Hollywood California 1964-66; BBC 1966-79 (reporter radio news, TV ed staff newpaper Ariel, prodr religious programmes radio), ed catholic newspaper The Universe 1979-87, first religious ed TV-AM 1987-; *Books* Faith Alive (ed jtly, 1988); *Style—* Ms Rowanne Pasco; TV-AM, Hawley Crescent, London NW1 8EF (☎ 071 267 4300)

PASCOE, Alan Peter; MBE; s of Ernest George Frank Pascoe, of Portsmouth, and Joan Rosina Pascoe; *b* 11 Oct 1947; *Educ* Portsmouth Southern GS, Borough Rd Coll, Univ of London (BEd Hons); *m* 15 Aug 1970, Della Patricia, da of Douglas Charles Albert James; 1 s (Daniel James b 1984), 1 da (Lucy Joanna b 1979); *Career* int athlete 1967-78; GB rep in: 110m hurdles, 400m hurdles, 200m , 4x100 and 4x400m relay; GB team capt 1971 and 1972, Euro indoor champion 1969, bronze medallist 110m hurdles Euro Championships Athens 1969, Olympic silver medallist 4x400m relay 1972, Euro Cup winner 1973 and 1975, Cwlth Games and Euro champion 1974 (set record in both events), Cwlth silver medallist 4x400m 1974, Euro gold medallist 4x400m relay 1974, ranked No 1 in World 1975, Cwlth bronze medallist 400m hurdles 1978; represented Europe in World Cup Cwlth v USA and USSR; memb: Sports Cncl 1974-80, BBC Asvsy Cncl 1975-79, dir WCRS Gp now Aegis Gp 1986-; *Recreations* theatre; *Style—* Alan Pascoe, MBE; 141-143 Drury Lane, London WC2B 5TB

PASCOE, Dr Michael William; s of Canon W J T Pascoe (d 1974), and Daisy, *née* Farlow; *b* 16 June 1930; *Educ* St John's Sch Leatherhead, Selwyn Coll Cambridge (BA, PhD); *m* 1, 24 March 1957 (m dis 1974), Janet, da of John Clark (d 1962), of Naphill, Bucks; 3 da (Katherine Jane (Mrs Burrows) b 1957, Joanna Mary b 1959, Madeline Bridget b 1961); m 2, 23 Dec 1974, Brenda Hale, *née* Reed; 1 da (Josephine Lucy b 1980); *Career* med physicist Mt Vernon Hosp 1955-57, textile scientist Br Nylon Spinners Ltd 1957-60, surface coating scientist ICI Paints 1960-67, lectr in material science Brunel Univ 1967-76; The Br Museum: princ scientific offr 1976-79, keeper of conservation and technical services 1979-81; tutor Open Univ 1973-84, visiting prof ICCROM Rome (conservation centre); author of numerous publications on friction, textiles, engineering, conservation; conslt and advsr: Royal Acad of Arts, Science Museum, Mary Rose Tst, Public Record Off, Cncl for the Care of Churches; former memb Historic Wrecks Ctee, former govr Camberwell Sch of Art and Crafts; FRSA 1969, MInstP 1958-83; *Recreations* painting and drawing, travel, museums; *Style—* Dr Michael Pascoe; 15 Parkfield Rd, Ickenham, Uxbridge UB10 8LN (☎ 0895 674 723); Science Dept, Camberwell Sch of Art & Crafts, Peckham Rd, London SE5 8UF (☎ 071 703 0987, fax 071 703 3689)

PASCOE, Ronald Rowe (Ron); s of Victor Pascoe (d 1975), and Catherine, *née* Rowe (d 1935); *b* 12 Jan 1935; *Educ* Falmouth GS, Fitzwilliam Coll Cambridge (MA); *m* 25 March 1972, Patricia Lilian, da of William Ellis; 2 s (Stephen b 19 Jan 1974, Richard b 1 June 1976); *Career* Nat Serv 1954-56; sales rep Hadfields Ltd 1959-67, called to the Bar 1967; asst co sec: James Booth Aluminium Ltd 1967-70, Alcan Booth Alumimium Ltd 1970-72; legal mangr Ada Halifax Ltd 1972-75, sec Mullard Ltd 1975-80, div sec of maj divs Philips 1980-87, co sec and UK gp counsel Philips UK Ltd 1987- (dir Philips Pension Fund Ltd); jr C of C 1960-65; tstee Pye Fndn; *Recreations* singing, acting, skiing, swimming; *Style—* Ron Pascoe, Esq; Philips Electronic and Associated Industries Ltd, Philips House, 188 Tottenham Court Rd, London W1P 9LE (☎ 071 436 4044, fax 071 436 9842, telex 267518 PHILHS G, car 0836 204 818)

PASFIELD, Jonathan; s of John Alexander Pasfield, OBE (d 1973), and Mary Alys Flower Patten (d 1983); *b* 10 Sept 1940; *Educ* Lancing, Trinity Coll Cambridge (MA), INSEAD Fontainebleau (MBA); *m* 2 Jan 1965, Jacqueline, da of Robert Alec Linford (d 1943); 2 s (James b 1965, Thomas b 1974), 2 da (Katharine b 1967, Lucy b 1972); *Career* dir Clifford's Dairies plc 1982-86; conslt in food industry; *Recreations* vintage Lagondas, landscape gardening; *Style—* Jonathan Pasfield, Esq; Courtlands Farm, Brooks Green, Horsham, Sussex (☎ 0403 741 737)

PASKETT, Graham; s of George Paskett, of Amphion Radford Semele, Leamington Spa, Warwicks, and Joan, *née* McCubbin (d 1980); *b* 15 June 1946; *Educ* Blackdown Sch; *m* 15 June 1968, Jennifer Diana, da of Douglas Hamilton Sidders, of Breinton House, Hereford; 1 s (James Andrew Fergus b 1975), 1 da (Emma Jane Alice b 1970); *Career* chm: Paskett Public Relations Ltd 1976-, Onecolt Ltd 1981-; *Recreations* field sports particularly salmon fishing; *Style—* Graham Paskett, Esq; Roycroft Lodge, Uttoxeter, Staffordshire ST14 7PQ; Paskett Public Relations, 51 Friar Gate, Derby DE1 1DF (☎ 0332 372196, fax 0332 291035)

PASLEY, Sir (John) Malcolm Sabine; 5 Bt (GB 1794), of Craig, Dumfriesshire; s of Sir Rodney Marshall Sabine Pasley, 4 Bt (d 1982), and Aldyth (d 1983), da of Maj Lancelot Hamber; *b* 5 April 1926; *Educ* Sherborne, Trinity Coll Oxford (MA); *m* 1965, Virginia Killigrew, da of Peter Lothian Killigrew Wait, of Kew, Surrey; 2 s; *Heir* s, Robert Pasley; *Career* fellow Magdalen College Oxford; *Style—* Sir Malcolm Pasley, Bt; 25 Lathbury Rd, Oxford

PASLEY, Robert Killigrew Sabine; er s, and h of Sir Malcolm Pasley, 5 Bt; *b* 23 Oct 1965; *Style—* Robert Pasley, Esq; 25 Lathbury Rd, Oxford

PASMORE, (Edwin John) Victor; CH (1982), CBE (1959); s of Edwin Stephen Pasmore, MD, MRCP (d 1926), and Gertrude Eva, *née* Screech (d 1974); *b* 3 Dec 1908; *Educ* Harrow; *m* 3 June 1940, Wendy, da of Capt John Lloyd Blood (d 1956), of The Old Rectory, White Colne, nr Colchester, Essex; 1 s (John b 1941), 1 da (Mary b 1943); *Career* artist; visiting teacher LCC Camberwell Sch of Art 1945-49, Central Sch of Arts and Crafts 1949-53; master of painting Durham Univ 1954-61; conslt urban and architectural designer SW Area Peterlee New Town 1955-77; memb: London Artists Assoc 1932-34, The London Gp 1935-52, Euston Road Gp 1937-40; tstee Tate Gallery 1963-66; Retrospective exhibitions: Venice Biennale 1960, Musee des Arts Decoratifs Paris 1961, Stedelijle Copenhagen 1962, Kestner-Gesellschaft Hanover 1962, Kunsthalle Berne 1963, Tate Gallery 1965, Sao Paolo Biennale 1965, Cartwright Hall Bradford 1980, Royal Acad London 1980, Yale Center of British Art USA 1988; current exhibitions: London, NY, Rome, Milan, Zurich, Lubjlana, Messina, Oslo, Osaka, Tokyo, Delhi, Toronto; works represented in pub museums incl: GB, Canada, Australia, NZ, Holland, Italy, France, Austria, Portugal, Switzerland, S America and the USA; Carnegie Prize, Pittsburgh Int USA 1964; Grand Prix d' Honneur, Graphics Biennale, Lubjlana 1977; Wollaston Award, Royal Acad 1984; hon degrees: Univ of Newcastle 1967, Univ of Surrey 1969, Univ of Warwick 1985, RCA 1969; *Books* Monograph and Catalogue Raisonné 1926-79 (1980), Burning Waters (poem with visual images, 1988); *Publications* Monographs and Catalogue Raisonée (1980); *Recreations* country walking, animals, natural philosophy; *Clubs* Arts; *Style—* Victor Pasmore, Esq, CH, CBE, RA; 12 St Germans Place, Blackheath, London SE3; Dar Gamri, Gudja, Malta; Marlborough Fine Art Ltd 6 Albemarle Street, London W1X 3HF (☎ 01 629 5161); Marlborough Gallery Inc, 40 West 57th Street, New York, NY 10018, USA

PASSEY, Michael Leighton Struth; s of Prof Richard Douglas Passey (d 1971), and Agnes Pattullo Passey *née* Struth (d 1976); *b* 22 Dec 1937; *Educ* Rugby, Trinity Coll Cambridge; *Career* slr 1964-67, lectr: Faculty of Law, Univ of Leeds 1967-; *Recreations* walking, investment; *Style—* Michael Passey, Esq; Faculty of Law, The Univ of Leeds (☎ 0532 431751)

PASSMORE, Gordon Seymour; s of Lt-Col Frank Frederick Seymour Passmore MBE (1975), of Pursers, Bramdean, Hants, and Claire Eileen, *née* Treacher (d 1984)

PASSMORE, John Francis Wolfe; s of Leonard Wolfe Passmore (d 1944), and Winifred, *née* Sladden (d 1981); *b* 9 Oct 1921; *Educ* Cranleigh; *m* 14 May 1949, Pamela Madeline, da of Otto Dunkels (d 1955); 3 s (Nicholas John Wolfe b 1950, Jeremy Cedric b 1952, David William b 1955); *Career* serv RE 1940-46, cmmnd 1941; sr ptnr Thomson Snell and Passmore (Slrs) 1979-86; *Recreations* gardening, photography, bridge; *Clubs* Naval and Military, Piccadilly; *Style—* John Passmore, Esq; Maynards, Groombridge, Tunbridge Wells TN3 9PR (☎ 0892 864335); 3 Lonsdale Gardens, Tunbridge Wells TN1 1NX (☎ 0892 510000, telex 95194, fax 0892 49884)

PASSMORE, Michael Bramwell; s of Brian Alfred Passmore (d 1985), of The Dog and Duck, W Wittering, Sussex, and Eileen Barbara, *née* Church; *b* 18 Sept 1928; *Educ* Bryanston; *m* 14 Sept 1957, Anne Gillian, da of Joseph Hurrell Pillman, CBE (d 1968), of Ballards Corner, Limpsfield, Surrey; 2 s (Christopher b 1959, Stephen b 1960), 1 da (Stella b 1962); *Career* dir Albaster Passmore and Sons Ltd 1955-, chm Passmore International 1981-89; pres Inst of Printing; *Recreations* sailing, walking; *Clubs* Royal Naval Sailing Assoc, Little Ship; *Style—* Michael Passmore, Esq; Scraces, Rectory Lane, Barming, nr Maidstone, Kent ME16 9NE (☎ 0622 726237)

PASTERFIELD, Rt Rev Philip John; s of Bertie James Pasterfield (d 1955), of West Lavington Vicarage, and Lilian Bishop, *née* Flinn (d 1957); *b* 14 Jan 1920; *Educ* Denstone Coll Staffs, Trinity Hall Cambridge (MA), Cuddesdon Theol Coll; *m* 29 July 1948, (Eleanor) Maureen, da of William John Symons (d 1974), of Castlewood, Cheswardine, Salop; 3 s (Stephen b 1949, Andrew b 1951, Mark b 1955), 1 da (Verity b 1959); *Career* cmmnd Somerset LI 1940, India Cmd 1941, NW Frontier 1942, Arakan, Burma, Capt 1943-44, Adj, Maj 1945; curate Streatham London 1951-54, vicar W Lavington and chaplain King Edward VII Hosp Midhurst Sussex 1954-60, vicar Oxton Birkenhead 1960-68, chaplain TA 1961-68, rural dean Birkenhead 1966-68, canon residentiary St Albans Cathedral 1968-74, rural dean St Albans 1972-74, bishop suffragan Crediton 1974-84, asst bishop Dioc of Exeter 1984-; chm Cncl for Christian Care 1976-84, patron Hospicare Exeter 1980-84; *Recreations* ornithology, cricket, rugger, music; *Style*— The Rt Rev Philip Pasterfield; Wasley House, Harberton, nr Totnes, Devon TQ9 7SW (☎ 0803 865093)

PASTINEN, HE Ilkka Olavi; Hon KCMG (1972); s of Martti Mikael Pastinen (d 1968), and Ilmi Saga, *née* Karlström (d 1963); *b* 17 March 1928; *Educ* Abo Akademi Finland (MPolSc), Inst d'Etudes Politiques Paris France, Inst Int des Sciences et Recherches Diplomatiques Paris; *m* 23 July 1950, Eeva Marja, da of Otto Viitanen (d 1958), Inspr General of Schs and Knight White Rose of Finland; 2 da (Kristiina b 1955, Johanna b 1956); *Career* Dip Serv 1952-: Stockholm 1955-57, perm mission to UN 1957-60, Peking 1962-64, London 1966-69, ambass and dep rep of Finland to UN 1969-71, special rep of Sec Gen of UN to Ctee of Disarmament 1971-75, ambass and perm rep of Finland to UN 1977-83, ambass to Ct of St James 1983-; Cdr First Class of the Order of the White Rose of Finland 1986; *Recreations* golf, music, bridge; *Clubs* Athenaeum, Travellers', Swinley Forest Golf; *Style*— HE the Finnish Ambassador; 14 Kensington Palace Gardens, London W8 (☎ 071 221 4433); Embassy of Finland, 38 Chesham Place, London SW1 (☎ 071 235 9531, fax 071 235 3680, telex 24786 Finamb G)

PASTON-BEDINGFELD; see Bedingfeld

PATCH, Donald; s of Samuel Harry Patch, of Seaford Sussex, and Lillian Gertrude, *née* Dean; *b* 19 June 1930; *m* 29 Sept 1956, Pamela Doreen, da of George Ely, *née* Cullingford; 2 s (Trevor Samuel b 5 Sept 1962 d 1963, Matthew John b 21 Oct 1968), 2 da (Deborah Grace (Mrs Kew) b 21 June 1960, Madeleine Louise b 25 Oct 1964); *Career* Nat Serv Air History Branch Chelsea RAF 1952-53; architectural and civil engrg asst Air Miny London and Northwood 1947-53, asst architect Cameroons Development Corp W Africa 1953-56, project architect Mulago Hosp Kampala Uganda Miny of Health 1956-62, assoc architect Watkins Gray London (specialist in hosp design) 1963-73, ptnr Norman & Dawbarn 1977- (joined 1973); projects incl hosps in: Nigeria, Tanzania, Ethiopia, Oman, London (and Inst of Cancer Res Laboratory Site Devpt studies, Chiswick Health Centre, White City Health Centre); TVS Studios Maidstone Kent, TSW Studies Plymouth, Theatre Studies for Elmbridge Arts Cncl; numerous MOD projects incl: Army Med Centre Arborfield, RAF Hospital Ely, RAF Mess Buildings and Airfield Buildings Ascension Island, Flight Simulator Culdrose, Nat Remote Sensing Centre Farnborough; promoter of arts devpts incl Kampala Nat Theatre and arts facilities in Elmbridge, speaker on green belt issues in Surrey; memb: Borough of Elmbridge Arts Forum 1988-90, architectural advsr Elmbridge Arts Cncl 1988-, Malawi Inst of Architects 1983-; ARIBA 1971; *Recreations* walking, music, travel, theatre (both tech and artistic aspects); *Clubs* Walton and Weybridge Amateur Operatic Soc, Kampala, Cameroon Motor and Social, Basingstoke Canal Soc, RHS; *Style*— Donald Patch, Esq; Norman & Dawbarn, College House, Woodbridge Road, Guildford Surrey GU1 4RT (☎ 0483 33551, fax 0483 506459, telex 859265 NORBAR)

PATCHETT, Terry; MP (Lab) Barnsley E 1983-; s of Wilfred and Kathleen Patchett; *b* 11 July 1940; *Educ* Univ of Sheffield; *m* 1961, Glenys Veal; 1 s, 2 da; *Style*— Terry Patchett, Esq, MP; 71 Upperwood Rd, Darfield, nr Barnsley, S Yorks

PATEL, Atulkumar Bhogilal; s of Bhogilal I Patel, of 9 Bath Rd, Southsea, Hampshire, and Sarojben, *née* Chandubhai Patel; *b* 24 Feb 1958; *Educ* Southern GS, Portsmouth, Univ of Sussex (BA); *m* 21 Feb 1981, Ritaben, da of Chhotubhai Gopalji Naik (d 1982); *Career* youth worker Self Help Project Leicester 1979-81, dir Asra Housing Assoc 1982-88, area mangr Housing Corpn 1988-90; chm Ethnic Arts Ctee E Midlands Arts Assoc 1982-84, dir Tara Arts Gp Ltd 1987-, tstee Housing Assoc Charitable Tst 1986-; ctee memb: Fedn Black Housing Orgns 1985-86, Nat Assoc Asian Youth 1980-81; memb: Ramakrishna Vedanta Centre 1985-, Asra Gtr London Housing Assoc 1984-, Guardian Housing Assoc 1986-, Anchor Housing Assoc 1986-, Asra Housing Assoc 1988-, Fedn Black Housing Orgns 1988-; *Recreations* playing the sitar and surbahar; *Style*— Atul Patel, Esq; Surbahar, 5 Chrisett Close, Goodwood Park, Leicester LE5 6RD (☎ 0533 418806); The Housing Corporation, Attenborough House, 109-119 Charles St, Leicester LE1 1FQ (☎ 0533 623600, fax 0533 623636)

PATEL, Dr Hasmukh Rambhai; s of Rambhai Patel, of London, and Shardaben Patel; *b* 1 Jan 1945; *Educ* King's Coll London, King's Coll Hosp Med Sch (MB BS, MRCS); *m* 16 July 1969, Mrudula Hasmukh, da of Revabhai Patel, of Baroda India; 1 s (Veran b 31 July 1972), 1 da (Nesha b 7 May 1975); *Career* conslt paediatrician Joyce Green Hosp Kent 1976-, clinical tutor Univ of London 1982-, coll tutor RCP 1986-; memb: Royal Med Benevolent Fund, BPA; FRCPE 1985, FRCP 1986; *Recreations* travel, swimming, photography; *Style*— Dr Hasmukh Patel; 9 Irene Road, Orpington, Kent BR6 0HA; Postgraduate Medical Centre, Joyce Green Hospital, Dartford, Kent (☎ 0322 229414)

PATEL, Dr Indraprasad Gordhanbhai; s of Gordhanbhai Tulsibhai Patel, and Kashiben Jivabhai Patel; *b* 11 Nov 1924; *Educ* Baroda Coll Univ of Bombay (BA), King's Coll Univ of Cambridge (BA, PhD), Harvard Univ Grad Sch; *m* 28 Nov 1958, Alaknanda, da of Prof A K Dasgupta; 1 da (Rishiparna Rehana); *Career* prof econs and head dept Univ of Beroda 1949-50 (princ Baroda Coll), economist (later asst dir chief) res dept Int Monetary Fund Washington DC 1950-54, dep econ advsr Miny of Fin Govt of India 1954-58, alternative exec dir for India Bd IMF Washington DC 1958-61, econ advisor Planning Cmmn 1961-63, visiting prof Delhi Sch of Econs 1964, special sec and sec Dept Econ Affrs Miny Fin 1967-72 (chief econ advsr 1961-63, chief econ advsr 1965-67); alternative govr for India 1967-72; memb: Bd IBRD, Bd IFC, Bd IDA, Asian Devpt Bank; dep admin Utd Nations Devpt Prog NY 1972-77, govr India Bd IMF 1977-82, dir Indian Inst Mgmnt Ahmedabad 1982-84, dir LSE 1984-; 1961-67: memb Monopolies Cmmn, chm Managing Agency Ctee, sec Ctee on Gold Control, memb UN Gp Experts on Int Monetary Reform, memb Gp Exports to advise first UNCTAD Meeting; memb 1967-72: Atomic Energy Cmmn Govt India, Space Cmmn Govt India, Tata Inst Fundamental Res, Nat Cncl Applied Econ Res, Inst Economic Growth, Indian Red Cross; memb: UN Ctee Devpt Planning 1977-86, Gp of Thirty 1978-, governing body Int Inst Econs 1983-, Advsy Gp Gen Agreement Trade and Tariffs 1984-85, Governing Body World Inst Devpt Econs Res 1987-; hon fell King's Coll Cambridge 1986; Hon DLitt Sardar Patel Univ India 1980; *Publications incl:* Inflation in Relation to Economic Developemnet (1952), Monetary Policy in Post-War Years (1953), Selective Credit Controls in Underdeveloped Economies (1954), Limits of Economic Policy (1964), Foreign Capital and Domestic Planning from Capital Movements and Economic Developement (ed J Handler 1967), Essays in Economic Policy and Economic Growth (1986); *Recreations* music, reading, watching cricket; *Style*— Dr Indraprasad Patel; The London Sch of Econs and Political Sci, Houghton St, Aldwich, London WC2A 2AE (☎ 01 405 7686 ext 2006 fax 01 242 0392 telex 24655 BLPES G)

PATEL, Dr Kirit; s of Dr Punjabhai M Patel (d 1982), of Nairobi Kenya, and Mangla P Patel; *b* 18 June 1943; *Educ* Duke of Gloucester Sch Nairobi Kenya, MS Univ Med Sch India; *m* 13 Jan 1971, Dr Rekha Patel, da of Dhirubhai B Patel (d 1984), of Bombay, India; 1 s (Sunil Kirit b 17 April 1979); *Career* sr house offr Kidderminster Gen Hosp 1968-69, med registrar Dudley Rd Hosp Birmingham 1969-73, gen practise in Liverpool 1973-74, sr med res St John's Hosp New Found Land Canada 1974-75, sr registrar in gen and geriatric medicine Royal Devon and Exeter Hosp Exeter 1975-78, conslt physician in gen and geriatric medicine N Staffs Health Authy Stoke-on-Trent 1978-, chief architect of integration between geriatric and gen medicine in Stoke-on-Trent 1983; memb: Crime Prevention Panel Newcastle-under-Lyme, Whitmore CC, Wolstanin Rotary Club; MRCPEd 1973, FRCP 1988; *Recreations* cricket, golf; *Clubs* Whitmore Cricket (Newcastle-under-Lyme); *Style*— Dr Kirit Patel; City General Hospital, Newcastle Rd, Stoke-on-Trent ST4 6QK (☎ 0782 621133)

PATEL, Prof Minoo Homi; s of Homo Edalji Patel, of Hounslow, Middlesex, and Doly Homi Patel; *b* 28 July 1949; *Educ* Univ of London (BSc, PhD); *m* Irene Veronica, da of Harry Kay, of Basildon, Essex; 2 s (Zubin Homi b 1973, Darren Lindsay b 1975); *Career* res engr Queen Mary Coll London 1973-76, UCL 1976- (lectr, reader, currently prof of mechanical engrg and head of dept); dir: BPP Ocean Technology Ltd 1983-, Pamec Technology Ltd 1986-, BPP Technology Ltd 1986-, BPP Technical Services Ltd 1989-; FRINA, FIMechE, CEng; *Books* Dynamics of Offshore Structures (1989), Compliant Offshore Structures (1990); *Recreations* gliding, jogging; *Style*— Prof Minoo Patel; Head Department of Mechanical Engineering, University College London, Torrington Place, London WC1E 7JE (☎ 071 380 7178, fax 071 388 0100, telex 296273)

PATEMAN, Rev Donald Herbert; s of Herbert Pateman (d 1967), of Leicester, and May, *née* Carter (d 1963); *b* 22 Feb 1915; *Educ* Wyggeston Sch Leicester, London Coll of Divinity (ALCD); *Career* RAF 1940-45; ordained (dio London) 1948, vicar of St Mark's Dalston 1956-; *Style*— Rev Donald H Pateman; St Mark's Vicarage, Sandringham Rd, London E8 2LL (☎ 071 254 4741)

PATEMAN, Jack Edward; CBE (1970); s of William Edward Pateman; *b* 29 Nov 1921; *Educ* Gt Yarmouth GS; *m* 1949, Cicely Hope Turner; 1 s, 1 da; *Career* dir Canadian Marconi Co 1971-87 (chm 1978-87), md GEC Avionics Ltd 1971-86; dir: GEC Computers Ltd 1971-89, Elliott Brothers (London) Ltd 1979-89, GEC Marconi (China) Ltd 1979-89, Marconi Electronic Devices Ltd 1980-87, GEC Information Systems Ltd 1982-86, GEC Avionics Projects (UK) Ltd 1984-89, GEC Plc 1986-88; dep chm GEC Avionics Ltd 1986-; chm Kent County Engrg Soc 1989-; Br Gold medal RAeS 1981; FEng; *Style*— Jack Pateman, Esq, CBE, FEng; Spindles, Ivy Hatch, Sevenoaks, Kent TN15 0PG

PATERNÒ CASTELLO DI CÁRCACI, Duke (Duca) Don Gaetano Maria Giuseppe; 12 Duke of Cárcaci, 10 Baron of Placa and Baiana; s of Don Francesco Maria Domenico Paternò Castello, 11 Duke of Cárcaci, 9 Baron of Placa and Baiana; descendant of feudal family from Sicily and of Giovanni Paternò 1398; cr Dukes of Cárcaci in 1648 by King Philip IV; confirmed by Imperial Decree in Vienna in 1725 by Emperor Charles VI and recognised by Italian Govt 1903 and 1906; Duke-Peer of Sicily 1816; *b* 13 Sept 1923; *Educ* Docteur ès Sciences Politiques; *m* 1, 12 July 1960, Marie Regina (d 1973), 2 da of Sir Eugen Millington-Drake, KCMG (d 1972), and Lady Effie Mackay (d 1984), 4 da of 1 Earl of Inchcape; 1 s, 1 da; m 2, 1976, Brenda Mary, da of Dr A W Stafford; *Heir* s, Duke Don Alexander Paternò Castello di Cárcaci, b 27 March 1961; m 19 Dec 1990, Lady Charlotte Legge, only da of the 9 Earl of Dartmouth and Countess Spencer; *Career* Kt Royal Order of St Januarius of Naples; Bailiff GCJ with Collar SM Constantinian Order of St George and memb of the Deputation; *Style*— HE The Duke of Cárcaci; 25 Holland Park Gardens, London W14 8EA

PATERSON *see also*: Jardine Paterson

PATERSON, Prof Alan Keith Gordon; s of Maj Albert Paterson (d 1946), of Kinmundy House, Aberdeenshire, and Helen, *née* Horne; *b* 8 March 1938; *Educ* Aberdeen GS, Univ of Aberdeen (MA), Univ of Cambridge (PhD); *m* 28 June 1965, Anna, da of Tageholm Malmö, of Sweden; 1 s (Andrew); *Career* lectr Queen Mary Coll Univ of London 1964-84, prof of Spanish Univ of St Andrews 1985-; author of specialist pubns on theatre poetry and prose of seventeenth century Spain; memb Scottish Examination Bd; *Books* Tirso De Molina La Venganza De Tamar (1967); *Recreations* cooking, hill-walking, motor-cycling; *Style*— Prof Alan Paterson; Argyll Lodge, Kennedy Gardens, St Andrews, Scotland (☎ 0334 72033); Spanish Department, The Scores, St Andrews, Scotland KY16 9AL (☎ 0334 76161, fax 0334 76474, telex 9312110846 SAG)

PATERSON, Alastair Craig; CBE (1987); s of Duncan McKellar Paterson, and Lavinia, *née* Craig; *b* 15 Jan 1924; *Educ* Glasgow HS, RCST (ARCST), Univ of Glasgow (BSc); *m* 1947, Betty *née* Burley; 2 s 2 da; *Career* cmmnd REME 1944, served India and Burma, attached Indian Army 1944-47; engr; Merz and McLellan 1947-58, Taylor Woodrow 1958-60; Bullen and Partners consulting engrs: ptnr 1960-69, sr ptnr 1969-88, ret; Inst of Structural Engrs: memb Cncl 1976-89, vice pres 1981-84, pres 1984-85; Inst of Civil Engrs: memb Cncl 1978-, vice pres 1985-88, pres 1988-89; chm Br Conslts Bureau 1978-80, pres Br Section Societe des Ingenieurs et Scientifiques de France, 1980-81; memb: Cncl Br Bd of Agrément 1982-, Overseas Projects Bd 1984-87, Engrg Cncl 1987-90; fndr memb: Hazards Forum, Br Nat Ctee for Int Engrg Affairs (currently chm); former Br delegate to Fédération Européenne d'Associations Nationales d'Ingénieurs and WFEO Congresses; Hon DSc Univ of Strathclyde 1989; FICE 1963, FIMechE 1964, FCIArb 1968, FIStructE 1970, FEng 1983; *Style*— Alastair Paterson, Esq, CBE

PATERSON, Alison Bianca; da of Peter Noel Vesey Newsome, BEM, and Valerie Janet Boogerman, *née* Phipps; *b* 12 Oct 1955; *Educ* Peak Sch Hong Kong, Wispers Sch Haslemere Surrey, UCL (BSc, Dip Arch); *m* 15 Sept 1984, Richard O'Donnell Paterson, s of Brian O'Donnell Paterson (d 1977); 1 da (Lucy b 1990); *Career* George Wimpey plc London 1984-86, Regalian Properties plc 1986-90, dir of subsiduary Co's 1986-90 (Regalian Homes Ltd, Regalian Urban Renewal, Regalian Developments Ltd), self employed architect and garden designer 1990-; memb: ARCUK 1983, RIBA 1983; *Recreations* bridge, tennis, garden design; *Clubs* Hurlingham; *Style*— Mrs Alison Paterson; 8 Napier Avenue, London SW6

PATERSON, Anthony John; s of John McLennan Paterson (d 1978), and Isobel Margaret, *née* Reichwald; *b* 16 May 1951; *Educ* Winchester, Worcester Coll Oxford (LLB); *Career* slr; special constable 1976-79; Parly candidate (Lib) for Finchley 1979, press offr Cons Bow Group 1983-84, Parly liaison offr 1984-85, res sec 1985-87, Parly candidate (C) for Brent S 1987; author of 3 Bow Group papers; sec Bow Group Environment Ctee; memb: Cncl Wild Wildlife Fund, exec Green Alliances 1987-90; *Books* The Green Conservative (1989); *Recreations* politics, reading, languages; *Style*— Anthony J Paterson, Esq; c/o Bates Wells & Braithwaite, 61 Charterhouse St, London EC4 (☎ 071 251 1122)

PATERSON, Dame Betty Fraser Ross; DBE (1981, CBE 1973), JP (1950), DL (Herts 1980); da of Robert Ross Russell (d 1934), and Elsie Marian Fraser (d 1918); *b* 14 March 1916; *Educ* Harrogate Coll, Western Infirmary Glasgow (MCSP); *m* 1940, Ian Douglas Paterson, s of George Stanley Vaughan Paterson (d 1935); 1 s (Ross), 1 da (Rosemary); *Career* memb: Chartered Soc of Physiotherapy 1938, Cmmn for the New Towns 1961-74 (dep chm 1970-74), Govrs St Bartholomew's Hosp 1961-73, NE Met Regnl Hosp Bd 1960-73, Govrs Bishop Stortford Coll 1966-81; chm: Herts CC 1969-73 (memb 1952-74, alderman 1959-74), NW Thames RHA 1973-84, Nat Staff Ctee for Nurses and Midwives 1974-84; pres Herts Assoc of Local Cncls 1978-90; vice pres: Herts Magistrates Assoc 1987, Herts Community Cncl 1987; *Recreations* music, cooking, foreign travel; *Style*— Dame Betty Paterson, DBE, JP, DL; 52 Free Trade Wharf, The Highway, London E1 9ES (☎ 071 791 0367)

PATERSON, Christopher John; s of John MacDonald Paterson, of North Petherton,

Somerset, and Mary Kathleen, *née* Body; *b* 9 Jan 1947; *Educ* Peterhouse Marandellas S Rhodesia, Univ of Exeter (BA); *m* 15 Dec 1974, Gillian Diana, da of Geoffrey Piper, of Christchurch, Dorset; 1 s (Timothy b 1981), 1 da (Sarah b 1978); *Career* Nat Serv Royal Rhodesia Regt 1965-66; dep md Macmillan London 1978-79, publisher Nature 1980-81, md The College Press Zimbabwe 1983-85, chm Macmillan Boleswa SA 1983-, md The Macmillan Press 1985-, dir Macmillan Publishers Ltd 1989; memb: Nat Tst, Friends of Lutyens Tst, RHS; *Recreations* tennis, gardening, running, watching rugby football; *Clubs* Harare, Newbury RUFC; *Style—* Christopher Paterson, Esq; Macmillan Publishers Ltd, Stockton House, 1 Melbourne Place, London WC2B 4LF (☎ 071 836 6633, fax 071 379 4980, telex 914690)

PATERSON, His Honour Judge; Frank David; s of David Paterson, of Liverpool (d 1956); *b* 10 July 1918; *Educ* Quarry Bank HS Liverpool, Univ of Liverpool (LLB); *m* 1953, Barbara Mary, da of Oswald Ward Gillow (d 1949), of Formby, Lancs; 1 s, 2 da; *Career* called to the Bar Gray's Inn 1941, asst dep coroner Liverpool 1960-68, chm Miny of Pensions and Nat Insur Tbnl Liverpool 1957-68, Mental Health Review Tbnl SW Lancs and Cheshire 1963-68, Circuit judge (formerly County Court judge) 1968-; pres Merseyside Branch Magistrates' Assoc 1978; *Clubs* Athenaeum (Liverpool); *Style—* His Honour Judge Paterson; Vailima, 2 West Lane, Formby, Liverpool L37 7BA (☎ 07048 74345)

PATERSON, Sir George Mutlow; OBE (1946), QC (Sierra Leone 1950); s of Dr George William Paterson (d 1954), of Grenada, WI, and late Olivia Hannah, *née* Mutlow-Williams; *b* 3 Dec 1906; *Educ* Grenada Boys' Sch, St John's Coll Cambridge (MA, LLM); *m* 1935, Audrey Anita, da of late Maj C C B Morris, CBE, MC; 1 s, 2 da; *Career* Colonial Admin Serv Northern Nigeria 1929; called to the Bar Inner Temple 1933; magistrate Nigeria 1936, crown counsel Tanganyika 1937, War Serv King's African Rifles (wounded 1940, Lt-Col); slr-gen Tanganyika 1946-49, attorney-gen Sierra Leone 1949-54, Ghana 1954-57, chief justice N Rhodesia 1957-61, ret 1961; chm Industl Tbnls SW Region of Eng 1965-79; kt 1959; *Recreations* reading; *Clubs* Bath and County (Bath); *Style—* Sir George Paterson, OBE, QC; St George's, Westbury, Sherborne, Dorset DT9 3RA

PATERSON, Graham Julian; s of Peter James Paterson, and Beryl, *née* Johnson; *b* 7 June 1955; *Educ* Dulwich, Magdalen Coll Oxford (BA); *Career* journalist Daily Telegraph 1977-86, ed 7 Days Section Sunday Telegraph 1988- (assoc ed 1987-88, home ed 1986-87), asst ed The Times 1989-; *Clubs* Travellers'; *Style—* Graham Paterson, Esq; c/o The Times, 1 Pennington St, London E1 9XN

PATERSON, Lt-Col Howard Cecil; TD (two clasps); s of Henry John Paterson (d 1969), of Romanno Bridge, Peeblesshire, and Margaret Isobel, *née* Eunson (d 1983); *b* 16 March 1920; *Educ* Daniel Stewart's Coll Edinburgh, Edinburgh Coll of Art; *m* 21 July 1945, Isabelle Mary, da of Frederick Augustus Edward Upton (d 1960), of 28 College Rd, Southampton; 1 s (Colin Howard b 7 Aug 1948); *Career* Lt-Col RA (TA) serv Europe ret 1970; asst personnel mangr Jute Industries Ltd 1949-51, sr dir Scot Tourist Bd 1966-81, ind tourism conslt 1981- (sr ptnr Tourisms Advsy Servs); dept dir Scot Co Indust Devpt Tst 1951-66; chm: Taste of Scot Scheme 1976-86, Scot Int Gathering Tst 1982-; vice chm: Scot Aircraft Collection Tst 1982-89 (chm 1989-90), John Buchan Soc; memb: Br Horse Soc Scot Ctee, Scot Treking & Riding Assoc Cncl, Edinburgh Area Ctee of Scot Lowland Territorial and Volunteer Reserve Assoc, Scot Landowners Fedn, Rural Forum; FSA Scot, FRSA; *Books* Tourism in Scotland (1969), Flavour of Edinburgh (with Catherine Brown, 1986); *Recreations* fishing, shooting, drawing and painting, writing, wild life study, food; *Clubs* Caledonian; *Style—* Lt-Col Howard Paterson, TD; Dovewood, W Linton, Peeblesshire EH46 7DS (☎ 0968 60346)

PATERSON, Sqdn Ldr Ian Veitch; CBE (1969), JP (Hamilton), DL (Lanarkshire, 1963); s of Andrew Wilson Paterson; *b* 17 Aug 1911; *Educ* Lanark GS, Glasgow Univ; *m* 1940, Anne Weir, da of Thomas Brown; 2 s, 1 da; *Career* dep chm Local Govt Boundary Commission 1974-; *Style—* Sqdn Ldr Ian Paterson, CBE; 35 Stewarton Drive, Cambuslang, Glasgow

PATERSON, James Rupert; s of Maj R E Paterson, MC, of Seaforth Highlanders, late of Palazzo Bonlini, Venice, Italy (d 1964), and Josephine Mary, *née* Bartlett (d 1986); *b* 7 Aug 1932; *Educ* St Augustine's Abbey Sch Ramsgate, The Nautical Coll Pangbourne, RMA Sandhurst; *m* 18 Aug 1956, Kay, da of Patrick Dinneen, of Rathmore, Co Kerry; 2 s (Dominic b 1961, Sean b 1963), 2 da (Sara b 1958, Helen b 1959); *Career* cmmnd RA 1953, serv Hong Kong, Cambridge (attached to Faculty of Slavonic Languages), Paris, Singapore, Berlin (twice); HM Dip Serv 1970-: FCO 1970-71, 1 sec Islamabad 1972-75; dep high cmmr Trinidad and Tobago 1975-78, FCO 1979-81, ambass Ulan Bator 1982-84, consul-gen Istanbul 1985-88, consul-gen Geneva 1988-; *Recreations* reading, writing, golf; *Style—* James Paterson, Esq; c/o FCO, (Geneva) King Charles St, London SW1 2AH

PATERSON, James Veitch; s of John Robert Paterson; *b* 16 April 1928; *Educ* Peebles HS, Edinburgh Acad, Lincoln Coll Oxford, Edinburgh Univ; *m* 1956, Ailie, da of Lt Cdr Sir (George) Ian Clark Hutchison; 1 s, 1 da; *Career* admitted to Faculty of Advocates 1953; Sheriff of the Lothian and Borders (formerly Roxburgh, Berwick and Selkirk) at Jedburgh, Selkirk and Duns 1963-; *Style—* James Paterson, Esq; Sunnyside, Melrose, Roxburghshire (☎ 025 481 2502)

PATERSON, John Mower Alexander; OBE (1985), JP, DL (Bucks 1982); s of Leslie Martin Paterson (d 1969), and Olive Harriette, *née* Mower (d 1980); *b* 9 Nov 1920; *Educ* Oundle, Queens' Coll Cambridge (MA); *m* 1944, Daisy Miriam Ballanger, da of Cdr Hugh Haddow Darroch Marshall, RNR (d 1958), of 18 Castle Hill, Dover; 1 s (Martin), 2 da (Rosemary, Lisa); *Career* Lt RE 1941-46; Cincinnati Milling Machines (Birmingham) 1946-48, dir and works mangr The Bifurcated and Tubular Rivet Co Aylesbury 1948-60 (chm and md 1960-69), chm and md Bifurcated Engrg Ltd 1969-73, chm Bifurcated Engrg plc (now BETEC plc) 1974-85 (dir 1974-88), gen cmmr of Taxes Aylesbury Div 1959-; memb: Governing Body Aylesbury Coll of Further Educn 1961-89 (chm 1977-88), Grand Cncl CBI 1971-84, Southern Regnl Cncl CBI 1971-85 (chm 1974-76), Mgmnt Ctee of Waddesdon Manor 1980-; memb Cncl of Order of St John in Bucks 1980- (chm 1981-); pres Aylesbury Div Cons and Unionist Assoc 1984-85, dir Rickmansworth Water Co 1984-90 (chm 1988-90), dir Three Valleys Water Services PLC 1990; High Sheriff of Bucks 1978, Vice Lord Lt of Bucks 1984-; CStJ 1985 (OStJ 1981), KStJ 1990; *Recreations* sailing (yacht "Gallivanter"), veteran cars, gardening; *Clubs* Royal Ocean Racing, Royal Yacht Squadron (Cowes), Royal Lymington Yacht, St John; *Style—* John Paterson, Esq, JP, DL; Park Hill, Potter Row, Great Missenden, Bucks HP16 9LT (☎ 024 06 2995)

PATERSON, Very Rev John Munn Kirk; s of George Kirk Paterson, and Sarah Ferguson, *née* Wilson; *b* 8 Oct 1922; *Educ* Hillhead HS Glasgow, Edinburgh Univ (MA, BD); *m* 1946, Geraldine Lilian Parker; 2 s, 1 da; *Career* serv RAF WWII; former min St Paul's Milngavie, moderator of General Assembly of Church of Scotland 1984-85; Hon DD Aberdeen 1986; *Style—* The Very Rev John Paterson; 58 Orchard Drive, Edinburgh EH4 2DZ

PATERSON, (Isabel) Margaret; da of August Waldemar Reichwald (d 1929), and Isabel Nancy, *née* Bell (d 1955); *b* 20 Oct 1917; *Educ* Benenden, Inst of Household Mgmnt, City and Guilds Cookery Teaching (Dip); *m* 14 Dec 1949, John McLennan Paterson (d 1978), s of late Alexander Paterson; 2 s (Anthony John b 1951, Nigel b 1952); *Career* cookery author: The Craft of Cooking (1978), Masterclass (contrib chapter, 1982), 1001 Ways to be a Good Cook (1986); *Recreations* travel, bridge, gardening, needlework; *Style—* Mrs Margaret Paterson

PATERSON, Martin James Mower; s of Mr John Mower Alexander Paterson, of Park Hill, Great Missenden, Bucks, and Miriam Ballinger Paterson; *b* 14 March 1951; *Educ* Oundle, Univ of Birmingham (BSc), Cranfield Inst of Techol (MBA, Dip Inst of Mktg); *m* 9 July 1977, Anne Vivien, da of Vivien Errol, DSC; 2 s (David Mower Errol, Andrew James), 1 da (Victoria Katharine); *Career* Metal Box 1973-81: graduate trainee 1973-74, devpt technician 1974-76, mfrg mangr 1975-78, works mangr (Thailand) 1978-81; Betec plc 1981-84; dir and gen mangr Black and Luff Ltd 1981-82 (divnl mfrg dir 1982-84), Cranfield Inst of Tech 1984-85, special assignments exec TI Group plc 1985-86; md: Seals Div Aeroquip Ltd 1986-88, STS Ltd 1988-; MIProdE, MCIM, DipM, CEng; *Recreations* sailing; *Clubs* Royal Lymington Yacht, RORC; *Style—* Martin Paterson, Esq; Crossways House, Cowbridge, S Glamorgan, Wales CF7 7LJ (☎ 04463 3171); STS Ltd, Malvern Drive, Ty-Glas Industrial Estate, Cardiff CF4 5WW (☎ 0222 753 221, fax 0222 755 174, telex 495 255)

PATERSON, Maurice Dinsmore; s of Maurice Sidney Paterson (d 1977), of Glasgow, and Agnes Dinsmore, *née* Joss; *b* 28 Aug 1941; *Educ* Glasgow HS; *m* 3 Oct 1967, Avril Grant, da of John Gordon Barclay (d 1984), of Glasgow; 2 s (Michael b 11 Sept 1970, Colin b 28 May 1974); *Career* Scottish Amicable: joined 1959, asst sec 1968, gen mangr sales and mktg 1978, dir 1985, dep md 1990; chm Glasgow Life and Pensions Group 1972-73, non exec chm Origo Services Ltd 1989, dir LAUTROi 1990; pres Insur and Actuarial Soc of Glasgow 1987-88; FFA 1967; *Recreations* golf, badminton, jogging, genealogy; *Clubs* Caledonian, Pollok Golf, Western Gailes Golf; *Style—* Maurice Paterson, Esq; 8 Merrylee Rd, Glasgow G43 2SH (☎ 041 637 2690); Scottish Amicable Life Assurance Society, 150 St Vincent St, Glasgow G2 5NQ (☎ 041 248 2323)

PATERSON, (James Edmund) Neil; s of James Donaldson Paterson (d 1947), and Nicholas *née* Kerr (d 1956); *b* 31 Dec 1915; *Educ* Banff Acad, Univ of Edinburgh (MA); *m* 6 July 1939, Rosabelle, da of David MacKenzie, MC (d 1938); 2 s (Kerr b 1944, John b 1946), 1 da (Lindsay b 1940); *Career* Lt RNVR (mine-sweepers) 1940-45; author and screenwriter; conslt Films of Scotland (memb 1954-76, dir 1976-79); govr: BFI 1958-60, Pitlochry Festival Theatre 1966-76; chm: Nat Film Sch 1970-80, Lit Ctee Scot Arts Cncl 1967-76; dir Grampian TV 1960-86; memb: Planning Ctee Nat Film Sch 1969, Arts Cncl of GB 1974-76; Atlantic Award in Lit 1946, American Film Acad Award 1959; *Books* The China Run (1948), Behold Thy Daughter (1950), And Delilah (1951), Man on the Tight-Rope (1953), The Kidnappers (1957), short stories and screenplays; *Recreations* golf, fishing, bridge; *Style—* Neil Paterson, Esq; St Ronans, Crieff, Perthshire PH7 4AF (☎ 0764 2615)

PATERSON, Peter James; *b* 4 Feb 1931; *Educ* Spurgeon's Orphan Home, Balham and Tooting Sch of Commerce, LLC evening classes; *Career* reporter: Fulham Gazette 1948-49, Fulham Chronicle 1951-52, Western Daily Press 1952-54; parly reporter Exchange Telegraph News Agency 1954-59, industl corr Daily Telegraph 1959-65, industl corr Sunday Telegraph 1962-69, political columnist Spectator 1970, asst ed New Statesman 1970-72, tv critic Daily Mail 1987- (industl ed 1985-87); *Books* The Selectorate (1967); *Recreations* dog walking, collecting old typewriters; *Clubs* Scribes, Academy, Travellers'; *Style—* Peter Paterson, Esq; Daily Mail, Northcliffe House, 2 Derry St, London W8 5TT (☎ 071 938 6362, fax 071 937 3251)

PATERSON, Robert Andrew (Robin); o s of John Leggat Paterson (d 1983), of Beith, Ayrshire, and Winifred Purdon, *née* Ballantyne (d 1983); *b* 27 Oct 1936; *Educ* Strathallan Sch; *m* 27 July 1963, Diane Margaret, o da of Malcolm George Lillingston (ka 1941; *see* Burke's Landed Gentry, 18 edn, vol I, 1965), and Mary Lyons, yst da of Sir William McLintock, 1 Bt, GBE, CVO; 1 s (Jamie John Lillingston-Paterson (assumed additional surname of Lillingston on 18th birthday) b 6 Aug 1967), 1 da (Joanna Mary Lillingston b 16 May 1965); *Career* CA; ptnr Grieveson Grant & Co 1970-86, dir Kleinwort Benson Securities Ltd 1986-88, chm Paterson Printing Ltd 1988-, memb stock exchange; *Recreations* golf, skiing, gardening; *Clubs* New (Edinburgh); *Style—* Robin Paterson, Esq; Lees Ct, Matfield, Tonbridge, Kent TN12 7JU (☎ 089 272 2892); Paterson Printing Ltd, 21 Chapman Way, Tunbridge Wells, Kent TN2 3EF (☎ 0892 511212)

PATERSON, Ronald McNeill; s of Ian McNeill Paterson, of Glasgow, and Doris MacNicol, *née* Dunnett (d 1980); *b* 1 Aug 1950; *Educ* Hillhead HS Glasgow, Univ of Aberdeen (LLB); *m* 31 Dec 1988, Frances Ann Early, da of Hon Mr Justice Kenneth David Potter, QC (d 1986); *Career* CA 1974; ptnr Arthur Young 1982-89 (joined 1970), ptnr and dir of accounting Ernst & Young 1989-; memb: Accounting Standards Ctee 1987-90, Urgent Issues Task Force Accounting Standards Bd 1991-; *Books* UK GAAP - Generally Accepted Accounting Practice in the United Kingdom (jt author 1989); *Recreations* rowing, tennis, travel; *Clubs* Deeside Scullers; *Style—* Ronald Paterson, Esq; 5 Sudeley St, Islington, London N1 8HP (☎ 071 278 2789); Ernst & Young, Rolls House, 7 Rolls Buildings, Fetter Lane, London EC4A 1NH (☎ 071 928 2000)

PATERSON-BROWN, Dr June; CBE (1991), DL (Roxburgh, Ettrick and Lauderdale 1990); da of Wing-Cdr Thomas Clark Garden (d 1978), of South Esk Lodge, Temple, Gorebridge, Midlothian, and Jean Martha Garden, BEM, *née* Mallace (d 1976); *b* 8 Feb 1932; *Educ* Esdaile Coll Edinburgh, Univ of Edinburgh Med Sch (MB ChB); *m* 29 March 1957, Peter Neville Paterson-Brown s of Keith Paterson-Brown (d 1981), of 17 Blackfolrd Rd, Edinburgh; 3 s (Simon b 1958, Timothy b 1960, William b 1965), 1 da (Sara b 1959); *Career* med offr Family Planning and Well Woman Clinics Hawick 1960-86, non-exec dir Border TV plc 1979-; former memb Roxburghshire Co Educn Ctee; chm: Roxburghshire Co Youth Ctee, Roxburgh Dist Duke of Edinburgh Award Ctee; co cmmr: Roxburghshire Girl Guides Assocs 1971-77, Peebleshire Girl Guides Assoc 1973-75; chief cmmr UK and Cwlth Girl Guides 1985-90 (Scot chief cmmr 1977-82); chm: Borders Region Childrens' Panel Advsy Ctee 1982-85, Scot Standing Conf Voluntary Youth Orgns 1982-85; vice chm and tstee Princes Tst 1980-, tstee MacRoberts Tsts 1987-, Queen's Silver Jubilee Medal 1977; *Recreations* skiing, golf, tennis, music, reading, fishing; *Clubs* Lansdowne; *Style—* Dr June Paterson-Brown, CBE, DL; Norwood, Hawick, Roxburghshire TD9 7HP (☎ 0450 72352, fax 0450 77521)

PATEY, Mark; MBE; s of David Howard Patey (d 1978), and Gladys Joyce, *née* Summers (d 1981); *b* 17 Feb 1930; *Educ* Bryanston, Trinity Hall Cambridge (MA); *m* 16 Nov 1957, Cecile O'Connell, da of William Leil Cock (d 1966); 3 da (Helen b 1958, Claire b 1960, Mary-Ann b 1966); *Career* Nat Serv RAF 1948-50 (pilot offr 1949-50); judicial cmmr Colonial Serv Swaziland 1967-70 (dist offr 1954, dist cmmr 1957), chief adjudicator Immigration Appeals UK 1984- (adjudicator 1970); *Recreations* gardening; *Style—* Mark Patey, Esq, MBE; Immigration Appeals (UK), Thanet House, 231 The Strand, London WC2

PATHY, Prof (Mohan Sankar) John; OBE (1991); s of Dr Conjeveram Pathy (d 1977), and Agnes Maud Victoria, *née* Purchel; *b* 26 April 1923; *Educ* King's Coll Univ of London, King's Coll Hosp London; *m* 26 Sept 1949, Norma Mary, da of John Gallwey (d 1959); 2 s (Aidan b 13 May 1951, Damian b 3 Nov 1963), 3 da (Anne b 21 April 1952, Sarah b 29 Nov 1956, Helen b 4 May 1959); *Career* asst physician Oxford

Regnl Hosp Bd 1958-60, conlst physician in geriatric med S Glamorgan Health Authy 1960-79, prof of geriatric med Univ of Wales Coll of Med 1979-; memb: Exec Ctee Int Assoc of Gerontology, Scientific Ctee Fedn Int des Assoc de Personnes Agées; chm Age Concern Wales; memb: BMA 1943, BGS 1959; FRCPE 1967, FRCP 1973, memb BSRA 1976; *Books* Principles and Practice of Geriatric Medicine (1985), Geriatric Medicine: Problems and Practice (1989); *Recreations* creative gardening; *Style*— Prof John Pathy, OBE; Mathern Lodge, Cefn Coed Crescent, Cardiff CF2 6AT (☎ 0222 755476); University of Wales College of Medicine, Heath Park, Cardiff CF4 4XN (☎ 0222 755944, fax 0222 762208)

PATIENT, Matthew Lemay; s of Cyril Mortimer Patient (d 1981), and Joan Mary Christine Grace Lemay; *b* 16 March 1939; *Educ* Brighton Coll; *m* 10 June 1967, Susan Elizabeth (Sue), da of Geoffrey Ernest Soar; 1 s (Jonathan b 1 Feb 1971), 2 da (Joanna Elizabeth b 1 April 1969, Alexandra Louise b 23 Nov 1973); *Career* CA; sr tech ptnr Coopers & Lybrand Deloitte 1981- (ptnr 1966-); memb Co Affrs Ctee IOD 1974-; ICAEW: memb Parly and Law Ctee 1974-81, memb Cncl 1984-88; CCAB: memb Accounting Standards Ctee 1981-86, memb Auditing Practices Ctee 1981-88 (chm 1986-88); memb Urgent Issues Task Force Accounting Standards Bd 1991-; ind memb Retail Trades (non-food) Wages Cncl 1982-, nominated memb Cncl Lloyd's of London 1989-; govr and vice pres Brighton Coll, govr St Andrews Sch Woking; FCA 1973 (ACA 1963), ATII; *Books* Licensed Dealers Rules & Regulations 1983 (1983), Accounting Provisions of The Companies Act 1985 (1985), Auditing Investment Businesses (1989), Manual of Accounting (1990), various professional articles; *Clubs* RAC; *Style*— Matthew Patient, Esq; 128 Queen Victoria St, London EC4P 4JX (☎ 071 583 5000, fax 071 489 9597, direct 071 454 5083, telex 894941)

PATON, Sir (Thomas) Angus Lyall; CMG (1960); s of Thomas Lyall Paton (d 1962), of Valley House, St John, Jersey, CI, and Janet, *née* Gibb (d 1959); *b* 10 May 1905; *Educ* Cheltenham, UCL (BSc); *m* 7 June 1933, (Eleanor) Joan Medora (d 1964), da of Maj George Arthur Delmé-Murray, DSO (d 1944); 2 s (Alan b 1942, John b 1952), 2 da (Janet b 1934, Anne b 1937); *Career* sr conslt Sir Alexander Gibb & Ptnrs 1977-84 (sr ptnr 1955-57); pres Inst of Civil Engrs 1970-71, vice pres Royal Soc 1977-78; fell: UCL 1962, Imperial Coll London 1978; Hon DSc: London 1978, Bristol 1981; Hon FICE 1975, FIStructE, FRSA, Foreign Assoc Nat Acad of Engrg (USA) 1979; kt 1973; *Books* Power From Water (jtly, 1960); *Recreations* gardening, DIY; *Style*— Sir Angus Paton, CMG; L'Epervier, Route Orange, St Brelade, Jersey, CI (☎ 0534 45619)

PATON, David Romer; s of John David Paton, JP (d 1982), of Grandhome, Aberdeen, and Mary Fenella, *née* Crombie (d 1949); *b* 5 March 1935; *Educ* Gordonstoun, Keble Coll Oxford; *m* 2 July 1975, Juliette, da of Capt Christopher Arthur Geoffrey Burney (d 1980), of 35 Edwardes Square, London W8; 2 s (William John Burney b 1976, (Christopher) Matthew George b 1979); *Career* trainee surveyor Southesk Estates Brechin 1961-64; surveyor John Sale & Ptnrs Wooler Northumberland 1964-67, conslt agent Marquess of Bristol Ickworth Suffolk 1967-72; ptnr: Donaldsons London 1972-75, Walker Son & Packman Edinburgh 1975-79; dir Leslie Lintott & Assoc Aberdeen 1979-89; princ practising on own account 1989-; pres Aberdeen C of C 1987-89; chm: Gordon Cons and Unionist Assoc 1986-88, Royal Northern and Univ Club 1984-85, Aberdeen Civic Soc, NE Scotland Preservation Tst, Don Dist Salmon Fishery Bd, Scottish Cs of C, Aberdeen beyond 2000, Grampian Cancer Care Project, pres Friends of Grampian's Stones, vice chm Grampian-Houston Assoc; Min of State appointee HMG Salmon Advsy Ctee, Sec of State appointee NE River Purification Bd; memb: Aberdeen Harbour Bd, Architectural Heritage Soc of Scotland Ctee, Cncl Assoc of Scottish Dist Salmon Fishery Bds, Grampian Initiative Working Party; Tstee Piper Alpha Disaster Fund 1988-89; dir: Aberdeen Maritime Museum Appeal Co Ltd, Aberdeen Salmon Co Ltd; Burgess of Guild, City of Aberdeen 1983; FRICS 1976, FRVA 1971, FSA Scot 1989; *Recreations* fishing, photography, bridge, conservation; *Clubs* Royal Northern and Univ (Aberdeen); *Style*— David Paton, Esq; Grandhome, Aberdeen AB2 8AR (☎ 0224 722202); Estates Office, Grandhome, Aberdeen AB2 8AR (☎ 0224 722202)

PATON, Maj-Gen Douglas Stuart; CBE (1983); s of Stuart Paton, and Helen Kathleen, *née* Hooke (d 1953); *b* 3 March 1926; *Educ* Sherborne, Univ of Bristol (MB ChB, FFCM); *m* 1957, Jennifer Joan, da of Maj Edward Loxley Land (d 1968), of Losely, Lower Rd, Great Bookham, Surrey; 2 da; *Career* cmmnd RAMC 1952, CO CMH Aldershot 1973-76, RCDS 1977, DDMS HQ 1 (BR) Corps 1978-80, DDGAMS MOD 1981-83, cdr med servs BAOR in the rank of Maj-Gen 1983-86; QHP 1981-86, chm RAMC Assoc 1988-, govr Moorfields Eye Hosp 1988-90; CStJ 1986; *Recreations* skiing, opera, gardening, travel; *Style*— Maj-Gen Douglas Paton, CBE; Brampton, Springfield Rd, Camberley, Surrey GU15 1AB

PATON, (Alexander) Frank; s of Alec Paton, of Cheshire, and Gillian, *née* Carey; *b* 14 May 1929; *Educ* Oundle, Pembroke Coll Cambridge; *m* 10 Sept 1959, Dawn, *née* Wood; 2 s, 3 da; *Career* farmer and landowner; pres Int Farm Mgmnt Assoc, memb Cncl Euro Movement, fndr Somerset SDP; *Recreations* gardening, travel, wine; *Clubs* Farmers', 75; *Style*— Frank Paton, Esq; Smocombe House, Enmore, Bridgwater, Somerset TA5 2ED (☎ 027 867 384)

PATON, (Robert) Grant; s of Charlton Paton (d 1972), of Glasgow, and Mary Irene, *née* Grant; *b* 18 May 1939; *Educ* Strathallan Sch, Kelvinside Acad Glasgow, Chesters Business Sch, Univ of Strathclyde (Dip Man); *m* 16 March 1963, Pamela Edith Mary, da of Albert George West, of 31 Hackington Crescent, Beckenham, Kent; 1 da (Fiona b 13 June 1964); *Career* 2 Lt RA 1960-62, Lt TA 1962-65; md Grant Educnl Co Ltd Glasgow 1971-77, md Dillons Univ Bookshops London 1977-82, jt md Univ Bookshops (Oxford) Ltd Oxford 1983-89, dir Blackwell Retail Ltd Oxford 1989-90; memb Retail (non-food) Wages Cncl 1978-85, pres Booksellers Assoc of GB and I 1984-85; Freedom City of London 1986, Liveryman Worshipful Co of Stationers and Newspapermakers 1988; FBIM 1970, FCIS 1972; *Books* Booksellers Charter Economic Survey (ed, 1986-90); *Recreations* motor boating and cruising, map collecting, travel; *Clubs* Thames Motor Yacht; *Style*— Grant Paton, Esq; Odell Cottage, Queens Lane, Eynsham, Oxford OX8 1HL (☎ 0865 880321)

PATON, Maureen; *see*: Paton Maguire, Maureen Virginia

PATON, Hon Mrs (Rachel Audrey); *née* Eden; da of 9 Baron Auckland and Dorothy Margaret, JP, yr da of Henry Joseph Manser, of Beechwood, Friday St, Eastbourne, Sussex; *b* 9 June 1959; *m* 20 June 1981, Bramwell Paton, s of John Paton, of Maidenhead; 2 s (Alexander Robert b 11 March 1983, Joe Bramwell b 13 Nov 1986), 1 da (Charlotte Jane b 2 March 1985); *Style*— The Hon Mrs Paton; 22 Penwortham Road, Streatham London SW16 6RE

PATON, Prof Sir William Drummond Macdonald; CBE (1968); s of Rev William Paton, DD (d 1943), of St Albans, Herts, and Grace Mackenzie, *née* Macdonald (d 1967); *b* 5 May 1917; *Educ* Repton, New Coll Oxford (BA), UCH London (BM BCh, MA, DM); *m* 22 Aug 1942, Phoebe Margaret, da of late Thomas Rooke, of Shinfield, nr Reading; *Career* house physician UCH 1942, pathologist Midhurst Sanatorium 1943-44, staff Nat Inst for Med Res MRC 1944-52; prof pharmacology: RCS 1954-59, Oxford Univ (and fell Balliol Coll) 1959-84; hon dir Wellcome Inst for History of Med 1983-87; serv for various orgns incl: MRC, Royal Soc, Res Def Soc, Physiological Soc, Pharmacological Soc, Br Toxicological Soc; del Clarendon Press 1967-72; tstee: Rhodes Tst 1968-87, Wellcome Tst 1978-87; chm Ctee on Suppression of Doping Jt Racing Bd 1970-71, advsr HO on Intoximeter Breathtesting 1984-85, memb Advsy Cncl for Sci and Technol 1970; JP 1956; Freeman City of London 1976, memb Soc of Apothecaries 1976; Hon DSc: London 1985, Edinburgh 1987; Hon DUniv Surrey 1986, hon fell New Coll Oxford; FRS 1956, FRCP 1969, FRSA 1973, Hon FFARCS 1975, hon FRSM 1982; kt 1979; *Books* Pharmacological Principles and Practice (1968), Man and Mouse (1984); *Recreations* music, old books, geology; *Style*— Prof Sir William Paton, CBE; 13 Staverton Rd, Oxford OX2 6XH (☎ 0865 58355)

PATON MAGUIRE, Maureen Virginia; da of William Harney, and Blanche, *née* Maynard (later Mrs Paton); *Educ* Watford Tech HS, Univ of Leicester (BA); *m* 21 May 1977, William Michael Maguire, s of William Maguire; *Career* journalist; trainee with British Printing Corporation on various pubns 1973-76; journalist: IPC Business Press 1976-79, Daily Express 1979- (sub ed, show business writer, TV critic, video critic, drama critic); freelance work incl: BBC Radio broadcaster GLR, presenter What the Papers Say Granada TV, Daily Mail & Daily Mirror 1978-79, drama critic The Stage & Television Today, Woman, Woman's Own, TV Times, Thames Reports, Pebble Mill at One, Breakfast TV, UK Press Gazette; memb: NUJ 1974, Critics Circle (formerly the Broadcasting Press Guild) 1989; *Recreations* theatre, writing; *Clubs* Scribes; *Style*— Mrs Maureen Paton Maguire; Daily Express, Ludgate House, 245 Blackfriars Rd, London SE1 9UX (☎ 071 922 7036)

PATON-PHILIP, Philip; VRD (1957); s of Dr Wilfrid Paton-Philip, MC, MA, MB, DPH, DMRE, FCCP (USA) (d 1956), of Cambridge, and Mary Isobel, *née* Simpson (d 1985); *b* 12 Sept 1922; *Educ* St John's Coll Cambridge (MA, MB BChir, MChir, FRCS, LRCP); *m* 1, 1959 (m dis 1970), Julia, da of Stephen Vaux (d 1985), of Birchington, Kent; 1 s (Charles Philip b 1960); m 2, 1978, Christina, da of Dr Carl Henri Bernhardson, of Stockholm, Sweden; 2 s (Richard b 1980, James b 1982); *Career* Lt Cmdr RN and RNVR 1947-52, surgn in charge RN Surgical Chest Unit; consulting urological surgn: St George's Hosp, St Helier Hosp Carshalton, Epsom Dist Hosp; teaching at: St Bartholomew's Hosp, St Thomas's Hosp, Denver Med Coll Colorado USA; hon sr lectr St George's Med Sch Univ of London; *Recreations* riding, showjumping, skiing, sailing, carriage driving; *Clubs* Garrick, Savage, BHS, BSJA, British Driving Soc, Royal Naval Med; *Style*— Philip Paton-Philip, Esq, VRD; The Ship, Hurst Drive, Walton-on-the-Hill, Tadworth, Surrey; 149 Harley St, London W1 (☎ 071 935 4444)

PATON-SMITH, Carolin Mary; da of Alexander Ludovic Grant, TD, JP, DL (d 1986), of Marbury Hall, Whitchurch, Shropshire, and Elizabeth Langley, da of late Maj Robert Barbour, of Bolesworth Castle, Tattenhall, Cheshire; *b* 24 Feb 1947; *Educ* Heathfield, Univ of Florence; *m* 19 Aug 1967, William Richard Paton-Smith, s of Norman William Paton-Smith, of Clevelands, Felsted, nr Dunmow, Essex; 2 s (Ben b 21 July 1968, Harry b 9 Aug 1972); *Career* dairy farmer and landowner; *Recreations* hunting, countryside conservation; *Style*— Mrs William Paton-Smith; Marbury Hall, Whitchurch, Shropshire SY13 4LP (☎ 0948 3731 and 0948 5459)

PATON WALSH, Gillian (Jill); da of John Llewellyn Bliss (d 1979), and Patricia, *née* Dubern (d 1977); *b* 29 April 1937; *Educ* St Michael's Convent Sch N Finchley, St Anne's Coll Oxford (BA, MA, DipEd); *m* 1961, Anthony Edmund Paton Walsh; 1 s (Edmund Alexander b 1963), 2 da (Margaret Anne b 1965, Helen Clare b 1966); *Career* teacher Enfield Girls GS 1959-62, Arts Cncl Creative Writing Fellowship 1976-78, perm visiting faculty memb Centre for Childrens Literature Simmons Coll Boston Mass 1978-86, Gertrude Clarke Whittall lectr Library of Congress 1978, judge Whitbread prize 1984, chm Cambridge Book Assoc 1987-89, ptnr Green Bay Pubns; memb: Ctee Children's Writers Gp, Mgmnt Ctee Soc of Authors; adjunct Br Bd Memb Children's Literature New England; *Books* Hengest's Tale (1966), The Dolphin Crossing (1967), Wordhoard (1969), Fireweed (1970), Farewell, Great King (1972), Goldengrove (1972), Toolmaker (1973), The Dawnstone (1973), The Emperor's Winding Sheet (1974), The Butty Boy Macmillan (1975), The Island Sunrise: Prehistoric Britain (1975), Unleaving (1976), Crossing to Salamis, The Walls of Athens, Persian Gold (1977-78), A Chance Child (1978), The Green Book (1981), Babylon (1982), Lost & Found (1984), A Parcel of Patterns (1984), Gaffer Samson's Luck (1985), Five Tides (1986), Lapsing (1986), Torch (1987), A School for Lovers (1989), Birdy and The Ghosties (1989), Can I Play ? (1990); *Recreations* reading, walking, sewing, photography; *Style*— Mrs Jill Paton Walsh; 72 Water Lane, Histon, Cambridge CB4 4LR (☎ 0223 233034); Bruce Hunter, David Higham Associates, 5-8 Lower John Street, Golden Square, London W1R 3PE

PATRICK, Andrew Graham McIntosh; s of Dr James McIntosh Patrick, of Dundee, Angus, Scotland, and Janet, *née* Walterston (d 1983); *b* 12 June 1934; *Educ* Harris Acad Dundee; *Career* The Fine Art Soc: joined 1954, dir 1966, md 1976-; has presented hundreds of exhibitions, mostly of Br artists but covering all aspects of the visual arts; memb: Exec Ctee Soc of London Art Dealers (chm 1983-86), Cncl The Br Antique Dealers' Assoc 1986-, Curatorial Ctee Nat Tst for Scot 1986-89; *Recreations* collecting: pictures, Japanese prints, camels, works by Christopher Dresser, old shoes, etc; *Clubs* Garrick, Marks; *Style*— Andrew McIntosh Patrick, Esq; The Fine Art Society Plc, 148 New Bond St, London W1Y 0JT (☎ 071 629 5116)

PATRICK, (Katherine) Emily (Mrs Michael Perry); da of William Pitt Patrick, of Ladwood Farm, Acrise, Folkestone, Kent, and Rosemary Marther, *née* Pulvertaft; *b* 4 Oct 1959; *Educ* Folkestone GS, Architectural Assoc, Cambridge Univ (MA); *m* 16 Oct 1986, Michael Luke Perry, s of David Edward Perry, of 20 Benslow Rise, Hitchin, Herts; 1 da (Beatrice Lillian b 8 Sept 1987); *Career* exhibited at: King St Gallery, Wraxall Gallery, Sarah Long's, Maire Gallery, Mall Galleries, Lefevre Gallery; one man shows at Agnew's 1986 and 1989; painted HRH The Princess of Wales, portrait for Royal Hants Regt 1987; first winner of Royal Soc of Portrait Painters' Caroll Prize 1988; *Recreations* walking; *Style*— Miss Emily Patrick; 2 St John's Park, London SE3 7TG

PATRICK, Harley Maxwell; s of Lt-Col Alfred Noel Patrick (d 1987), and Elisa Joyce Hyslop, *née* Maxwell (d 1970); *b* 20 Jan 1929; *Educ* Trinity Coll Glenalmond, CCC Cambridge (MA); *m* 1, 19 Oct 1961 (m dis 1990), Caroline Heather, da of Cdr Louis Francis Cowell (d 1957); 3 da (Sophie b 1963, Elisa b 1965, Camilla b 1969); m 2, 17 Nov 1990, Christine Mary, da of Christopher Patrick Downes, MRCVS (d 1984); *Career* serv KOSB 1947-49; acting Capt and ADC to HE the Acting Govr of Cyprus 1969; dep gen mangr The Mercantile and General Reinsurance Co 1976-82, chm of Reinsurance Offices Assoc 1978-80, gen mangr of Tokio Reinsurance Co Ltd 1982-91; memb of Ct of Assts of Worshipful Co of Insurers; *Recreations* gardening, shooting; *Clubs* Lansdowne; *Style*— Harley M Patrick, Esq; Sattenham House, Rake Lane, Milford, Godalming, Surrey GU8 5AB (☎ 0483 421889); 25 Elvaston Place, London SW7 5NL (☎ 071 584 3103)

PATRICK, John; s of George Edward Patrick, of 27 Mytton Villa, Mytton Oak Road, Shrewsbury, Shropshire, and Emmeline Swindells, *née* Brierley; *b* 17 April 1943; *Educ* Haberdashers' Aske's, St Thomas' Hosp Med Sch Univ of London; *m* 9 Sept 1972, Patricia da of Geoffrey Thornton-Smith, of 203 Reading Rd, Woking, Berks; 3 da (Tamsyn b 1975, Abigail b 1977, Bryony b 1989); *Career* RAF 1963-72 (ret sqdn ldr); housejobs St Thomas' Hosp, sr lectr and hon conslt orthopaedic surgn Univ of Liverpool, dir Orthotic Res and Locomotion Assesment Unit, conslt orthopaedic surgn

1980-; papers published in med jls incl British Medical Journal; memb Engrg Sub Ctee BSI, warden Shrewsbury Drapers Co; FRCS 1972; *Recreations* skiing, sailing, travel; *Clubs* RAF Piccadilly; *Style*— John Patrick, Esq; Orthotic Res and Locomotion Assessement Unit, Robert Jones and Agnes Hunt Orthopaedic Hosp, Oswestry, Shrops SY10 7AG (☎ 0691 655311)

PATRICK, Margaret Kathleen; OBE (1976); da of late Roy Patrick and Rose Laura Patrick; *b* 5 June 1923; *Educ* Godolphin and Latymer Girls' Sch, Guy's Hosp Sch of Physiotherapy, Open Univ (BA); *Career* dist supt physiotherapist Central Birmingham Health Authy (formerly United Birmingham Hosps Mgmnt Ctee) Teaching 1951-88; former memb Birmingham AHA; vice chm Bromsgrove and Redditch Health Authy 1982-90; Hon Fell Chartered Soc of Physiotherapy 1988; *Style*— Miss Margaret Patrick, OBE; Cobbler's Cottage, Holy Cross Green, Clent, W Mids DY9 0HG

PATRICK, Peter Laurence; s of Anthony Frederick Herbert Patrick, of St Peters, Broadstairs, Kent, and Joyce Stanley, *née* Sowerby; *b* 11 July 1946; *Educ* Alleyne's Sch Stevenage, Univ Coll Durham (BA); *m* 22 April 1972, Teresa Mary Patrick, JP, da of William Roland Mills, MBE, of Billericay, Essex; 1 s (Edward William b 4 Nov 1973), 1 da (Frances Elizabeth b 10 July 1975); *Career* CA 1972; Price Waterhouse & Co: Newcastle 1967-70, London 1970-73, Paris 1973-76; computer audit mangr Howard Tilly & Co 1976-78, head of inspection Hambros Bank Ltd 1978-86, co sec Hambros plc and Hambros Bank Ltd 1986-; cncllr Billericay East Basildon DC 1984- (dep ldr Cons Gp of cncllrs 1985-90); chm Billericay Cons Assoc 1990-, chm Towngate Theatre Co Basildon Essex 1988-89, tstee Adventure Unlimited (Chelmsford Dio Youth Charity), govr Quilters Sch Billericay, memb choir St Mary Magdalene Gt Burstead Essex; memb Inst of Bankers, assoc memb Br Computer Soc; *Recreations* singing, gardening, politics, history, architecture; *Style*— Peter Patrick, Esq; 6 Highland Grove, Billericay, Essex (☎ 0277 651137); Hambros Bank Ltd, 41 Tower Hill, London EC3N 4HA (☎ 071 480 5000)

PATTEN, Brian; *b* 7 Feb 1946; *Career* poet and author; poems: Little Johnny's Confessions (1967), Penguin Modern Poets (1967), Notes to the Hurrying Man (1969), The Irrelevant Song (1971) The Unreliable Nightingale (1973), Vanishing Trick (1976), The Shabby Angel (1978), Grave Gossip (1979), Love Poems (1981), Clares Countryside (1978), New Volume (1983), Storm Damage (1988), Grinning Jack (Selected Poems, 1990); novels: Mr Moon's Last Case (1975); plays: The Pig and the Junkle (1975), The Mouth Trap (with Roger McGough, 1982), Blind Love (1983), Gargling with Jelly - The Play! (1989); for younger readers: The Elephant and the Flower (1969), Jumping Mouse (1971), Emma's Doll (1976), The Sly Cormorant and the Fish (1977), Gangsters Ghosts and Dragonflies (1981), Gargling with Jelly (1985), Jimmy Tag-along (1988), Thawing Frozen Frogs (1990), The Puffin Book of 20 Century Childrens Verse (ed, 1991); *Clubs* Chelsea Arts; *Style*— Brian Patten, Esq; c/o Penguin Books, 27 Wrights Lane, London W8

PATTEN, Christopher Francis (Chris); MP (C) Bath, 1979-; s of late Francis Joseph Patten; *b* 12 May 1944; *Educ* St Benedict's Ealing, Balliol Coll Oxford; *m* 1971, Mary Lavender St Leger Thornton; 3 da; *Career* CRD 1966-70, dir 1974-79; worked in Cabinet Off 1970-72, Home Off 1972, pa to chm Cons Party 1972-74; PPS to: Norman St John-Stevas as Chllr Duchy of Lancaster and Leader House of Commons 1979-81, Patrick Jenkin Sec of State for Soc Servs 1981; jt vice-chm Cons Fin Ctee Nov 1981-83, under-sec State NI Office 1983-85; min of state DES 1985-86, min of state for Overseas Devpt 1986-July 1989, sec of state for the Environment July 1989-Nov 1990; Chancellor of the Duchy of Lancaster 1990-; *Recreations* reading, learning Spanish, tennis; *Clubs* Beefsteak; *Style*— Chris Patten, Esq, MP; 47 Morpeth Mansions, Morpeth Terrace, SW1 (☎ 071 828 3082); Cromwell's Rest, 207 Conkwell, nr Winsley, Wilts (☎ 022 122 3378)

PATTEN, H; s of Hubert Patten, of Birmingham, and Agnes, *née* Johnson (d 1986); *b* 20 Jan 1961; *Educ* Lea Mason C of E Sch Birmingham, Bournville Sch of Art and Craft Birmingham (City & Guilds Pt 1), South Glamorgan Inst of Higher Educn Cardiff (BA Hons), Univ of Legon Ghana; *m* 1 s (Kwesi Yaadi b 26 July 1987), 1 da (Mawuena Esi b 16 March 1986); *Career* dancer; Danse de L'Afrique 1982-86: fndr memb, princ male dancer, drummer English tour 1983, Moroccan tour 1984 organised and performed Midlands tour with Jean Binta Breeze 1985; participant Mayfest Festival Glasgow with Pepsi Poet and Benjamin Zephonia 1983; Inst of African Studies Univ of Legon Ghana 1983: trg with Ghana National Danse Ensemble, tutor of Caribbean dance, participant in Accra and Hogbetsocho Festival Anloga Volta Region; dep dir and community arts worker The CAVE (Community and Village Entertainment) Birmingham 1983-86; freelance artiste, tutor of Caribbean and African music and dance and visual arts, painter, sculptor, photographer, storyteller 1986-; Adzido Pan African Dance Esemble: joined 1986, re-joined 1987, In the Village of Africa tour 1987, Coming Home tour 1988, performances at Queen Elizabeth Festival Hall South Bank 1988, Edinburgh Festival 1988 performances at Sadlers Wells 1988, Irish tour 1989, Montpellier Dance, Festival France 1989, Under Africa Skies tour 1990, educn outreach liasion offr 1990; Black Dance Development Trust: tstee Bd 1987, performed at first and second annual awards 1987 and 1989, planned and co-ordinated prog for Summer School III 1988, received Creativity in Music & Dance award 1989, East Midlands educn outreach devpt worker 1989; choreographer of: Carnival Fire (Third Dimension Theatre Co) 1987, Devil Going to Dance (Staunch Poets & Players) 1988, Mother Poem (Temba Theatre Co) 1989, Round Heads and Peak Heads (Tara Arts Theatre Co) 1989, Soul-Less-Game (Kokuma Performing Arts) 1989; involved with: UK Black by Karen Wheeler (music video) 1990, Black Voices film 1990, Ama (Efirititi Film Co) 1990, British Council Sponsored tour to Malawi 1990; also extensive teaching in UK and abroad, work with numerous nat and int tutors of African and Caribbean dance; Black Dance Devpt Tst Summer Schs 1 2 3 4 & 5; solo storytelling performance Guildhall Gloucester 1989; has exhibited extensively in Britain and the Caribbean; *Recreations* basketball, music, research into Folk Culture; *Style*— H Patten, Esq; 28A Tressillian Rd, Brockley, London SE4 1YB (☎ 081 692 0297)

PATTEN, James; s of James Arthur Patten (d 1973), and Edith Veronica Patten (d 1989); *b* 30 July 1936; *Educ* St Mary's Coll Liverpool, Trinity Coll of Music London (FTCL, GTCL, LTCL), Die Hochschule für Musik Berlin; *m* (m dis 1990); 3 s (Clovis, Dominic, Samuel); *Career* Duke of Wellington's Regt 1956-59; Die Hochschule Fur Music Berlin DAAD Scholarship, Royal Philharmonic Composition Prize 1963, lectr in theory of music Ealing Coll of Further Educn 1965-69, prof of composition Trinity Coll of Music London 1965-70, tutor Open Univ 1970-76, freelance lectr and composer 1970-79, head of music SWGS Salisbury 1976-78; examiner Univ of Oxford Delegacy 1979 (chief examiner and sr moderator 1989); music tutor and composer in residence Downside Sch 1988-90; compositions incl works for guitar, piano, string quartet, saxophone, choir and orchestra; memb: Ctee SEAC, Univ of Oxford Delegacy Music Panel, Horningham Parish Cncl, Creys Charity; PRS 1965, Composers' Guild of GB 1965, MCPS 1987, BASCA 1987, RSM 1987; *Recreations* playing 1930's & 1940's music; *Clubs* Halley's; *Style*— James Patten, Esq; Homestead Cottage, Edgarley, Glastonbury, Somerset BA6 8LD (☎ 0458 32390); Music Dept Edgarley Hall, Glastonbury, Somerset BA6 6LD (☎ 0458 32446)

PATTEN, Rt Hon John Haggitt Charles; PC (1990), MP (C) Oxford West and Abingdon 1983-; s of Jack Patten, and Maria Olga, *née* Sikora; *b* 17 July 1945; *Educ* Wimbledon Coll, Sidney Sussex Coll Cambridge (MA, PhD); *m* 1978, Louise Alexandra Virginia, da of late John Rowe; 1 da (Mary-Claire b 10 June 1986); *Career* fell Hertford Coll Oxford 1972- (Univ of Oxford lectr 1969-79); author and writer; MP (C) Oxford 1979-83, PPS to Leon Brittan and Timothy Raison, Min of State HO 1980-81; Parly under sec of state: NI 1981-83, Health and Social Security 1983-85; min of state: Housing Urban Affrs and Construction 1985-87, HO 1987-; *Books* The Conservative Opportunity (with Lord Blake), The Penguin Guide to the Landscape of England and Wales (with Paul Coones), three other books; *Recreations* talking to wife; *Clubs* Beefsteak; *Style*— The Rt Hon John Patten, MP; House of Commons, London SW1A 0AA (☎ 071 219 4436)

PATTEN, Prof Thomas Diery (Tom); CBE (1981); s of William Patten (d 1965), of Midlem, Selkirkshire, and Isabella, *née* Hall (d 1986); *b* 1 Jan 1926; *Educ* Leith Acad, Univ of Edinburgh (BSc, PhD); *m* 29 March 1950, Jacqueline McLachlan; 1 s (Colin), 2 da (Diane, Gail); *Career* Capt REME 1946-48, served Palestine and Greece; chartered mechanical engr; prof and head Dept of Mechanical Engrg Heriot Watt Univ 1967-82, dir Inst of Offshore Engrg 1972-79, actg princ Heriot-Watt Univ 1980-81; princ dir: Pict Petroleum plc 1981, Melville St Investments plc 1983, Sealand Industries plc 1987-; Hon DEng Heriot-Watt Univ; FEng, FIMechE, FRSE; *Recreations* music, squash; *Clubs* New (Edinburgh), Caledonian; *Style*— Prof Tom Patten, CBE; 146/4 Whitehouse Loan, Edinburgh EH9 2AN (☎ 031 447 0769)

PATTENDEN, Prof Gerald; s of Albert James Pattenden, and Violet Eugene, *née* Smith; *b* 4 March 1940; *Educ* Brunel Univ, Univ of London (BSc, PhD, DSc); *m* 3 Aug 1969, Christine Frances, da of Charles Leo Doherty; 3 da (Caroline Sarah b 1971, Rebecca Jane b 1974, Katherine Rachel b 1977); *Career* lectr Univ Coll Cardiff 1966, Sir Jesse Boot prof Univ of Nottingham 1988- (lectr 1972, reader 1975, prof 1980); chem conslt; author of 250 res pubns and editor of over 20 books; FRSC, CChem; *Recreations* sport, entertainment; *Style*— Prof Gerald Pattenden; Chemistry Dept, The Univ of Nottingham NG7 2RD (☎ 0602 484848)

PATTERSON; *see*: Stewart-Patterson

PATTERSON, Maj-Gen Arthur Gordon; CB (1969), DSO (1964), OBE (1961), MC (1945); s of late Arthur Abbey Patterson; *b* 24 July 1917; *Educ* Tonbridge, RMC Sandhurst; *m* 1949, Jean Mary Grant; 2 s, 1 da; *Career* dir of Army Trg 1969-72, ret; *Style*— Maj-Gen Arthur Patterson, CB, DSO, OBE, MC; Burnt House, Benenden, Cranbrook, Kent

PATTERSON, Edward McWilliam; s of Samuel Patterson (d 1962), of Kirkbymoorside, and Emily Elisabeth Wright (d 1975); *b* 30 July 1926; *Educ* Univ of Leeds (BSc, PhD); *m* 1, 10 Aug 1950, Joan Sibald (d 1981), da of Thomas Maddick (d 1965), of Goole; 1 da (Christine b 1952); m 2, 16 Sept 1982, Elizabeth McAllan, da of George James Hunter (d 1967), of Aberdeen; *Career* res demonstrator in mathematics Univ of Sheffield 1949-51; lectr: Univ of St Andrews 1951-56, Univ of Leeds 1956-59; prof Univ of Aberdeen 1965-89 (sr lectr 1960-64); Royal Soc visiting prof Univ of Malaya 1973, pres Edinburgh Mathematical Soc 1964-65, chm AUT Scotland 1964-66, vice pres IMA 1973-74, chm Scottish Mathematical Cncl 1974-80; FRSE 1959, FIMA 1964; *Books* Topology (1959), Elementary Abstract Algebra (jtly 1965), Solving Problems in Vector Algebra (1968); *Recreations* music, walking, mathematical problems; *Clubs* Commonwealth Trust; *Style*— Edward Patterson, Esq, FRSE; Dept of Mathematical Sciences, University of Aberdeen, The Edward Wright Building, Dunbar St, Aberdeen AB9 2TT (☎ 0224 272758)

PATTERSON, Hon Mrs (Fiona Elizabeth Cameron); *née* Corbett; da of 2 Baron Rowallan, KT, KBE, MC, TD (d 1977), and Gwyn Mervyn, *née* Grimond (d 1971); *b* 14 Nov 1942; *Educ* Southover Manor Sussex; *m* 1, 1966 (m dis 1972), as his 1 w, David Cecil, yr twin s of Hon Henry Cecil (bro of 3 Baron Amherst of Hackney); 2 s (Rupert b 1967, Benjamin b 1968); m 2, 1974, W G Patterson; 1 s (Joseph b 1981); *Style*— The Hon Mrs Patterson; Kisby's Farm, Ecchinswell, Newbury, Berks RG15 8TS; 43 Holland Villas Road, London W14

PATTERSON, George Benjamin (Ben); MEP (EDG) 1979-; s of Prof Eric James Patterson (d 1972), of Stonehedge, Alphington Cross, Exeter, Devon, and Dr Ethel Patterson, *née* Simkins; *b* 21 April 1939; *Educ* Westminster, Trinity Coll Cambridge (MA), LSE; *m* 5 Dec 1970, Felicity Barbara Anne, da of Gordon W Raybould, of Little Combe Bank, Sundridge, Sevenoaks, Kent; 1 s (Alexander b 6 Dec 1974), 1 da (Olivia b 15 April 1977); *Career* tutor Swinton Coll Masham Yorks 1961-65, ed CPC Monthly Report 1965-73, dep head Euro Parly London Office 1973-79, dir Wiltenbridge Ltd 1980-; EDG spokesman on economic monetary and industl policy in the Euro Parl 1984-89, policy co-ordinator EDG 1989-; cncllr London Borough of Hammersmith 1968-71; MInstD; *Books* The Character of Conservatism (1973), Direct Elections to the European Parliament (1974), The Purse-strings of Europe (1979), Vredeling and All That (1984), VAT: The Zero Rate Issue (1988), A Guide to EMU (1990); *Recreations* squash, walking; *Clubs* IOD, Bow Group; *Style*— Ben Patterson, Esq, MEP; Elm Hill House, Hawkhurst, Kent TN18 4XU (☎ 0580 753260); European Parliament, 89-91 rue Belliard, 1090 Brussels, Belgium (☎ 010 32 2 284 5296, fax 010 32 2 284 9296)

PATTERSON, John Allan; CB (1989); s of Dr William Gilchrist Patterson (d 1956), of Newcastle-upon-Tyne, and Mary Murray, *née* Eggie; *b* 10 Oct 1931; *Educ* Epsom Coll, King's Coll Univ of Durham, Clare Coll Cambridge (BA); *m* 1956, Anne Marie, da of Folke Urban Lasson (d 1947), of Halmstad, Sweden; 1 s (Thomas b 1962), 2 da (Caroline b 1958, Christina b 1963); *Career* HM Dip Serv 1954-65 (Bangkok 1957-61, Rome 1961-64); HM Treasy 1965-81 (on loan to Cabinet Office 1974-78); dir Savings, head of Dept for Nat Savings 1986- (dep dir 1981-86), bd memb Money Mgmnt Cncl 1990; *Recreations* church, gardening, walking, languages; *Style*— John A Patterson, Esq, CB; Department for National Savings, Charles House, 375 Kensington High St, London W14 8SD (☎ 071 605 9462)

PATTERSON, Mark; s of Donald Patterson, of Lilac Cottage, 8 Crabtree Rd, Stockfield, Northumberland, and Angela Elizabeth, *née* Starkey; *b* 13 Sept 1968; *Educ* Prudhoe Co HS; *m* Fiona Donna, da of John Rankin; *Career* professional footballer; Carlisle Utd: apprentice 1985-87, turned professional 1987, 22 league appearances; transferred to Derby County for a fee of £60,000 1987- (over 20 appearances); *Recreations* golf; *Style*— Mark Patterson, Esq; Derby County Football Club, Shaftesbury Crescent, Derby DE3 8NB (☎ 0332 40105)

PATTERSON, Dr Mark Jonathan David Damian Lister; s of Alfred Patterson (d 1972), and Frederica Georgina Mary Hammersley, *née* Lister Nicholson; *b* 2 March 1934; *m* 25 Oct 1958, Jane Teresa Mary Scott, da of David Dominic Scott Stokes, of 5 Cochrane St, London NW8; 1 s (Damian b 1967), 2 da (Rebecca b 1972, Victoria b 1977); *Career* NHS, Univ of London and MRC 1959-67, conslt NHS and sr lectr Univ of London 1967-84; Parly candidate (Cons) Ealing N 1974, memb GLC 1969-73 and 1977-81; memb Worshipful Soc of Apothecaries 1965; MB BS, MRCS, LRCP, MRCP; *Recreations* historic restoration of ancient buildings; *Style*— Dr Mark Patterson; Wolverton Manor, Shorwell, Newport, Isle of Wight PO30 3JS (☎ 0983 740604)

PATTERSON, Neil Michael; s of Robin Shanks Patterson (d 1964), and Nancy Mearns, *née* Milne; *b* 22 March 1951; *Educ* Trinity Coll Glenalmond, Watford Art Sch; *m* 23 July 1983, Doris Karen, da of Ceferino William Boll, of Saguier, Province of Santa Fe, Argentina; *Career* sr writer Saatchi & Saatchi 1973; river columnist: Trout

& Salmon 1976-78, Trout Fisherman 1982; creative dir: TBWA 1983-85, Young & Rubicam 1985-; creative ptnr Mitchell Patterson Aldred Mitchell 1990-; *Books* The Complete Fly Fisher; *Recreations* fly fishing, guitar, cooking; *Clubs* Flyfishers, DA & D; *Style—* Neil Patterson, Esq; Rose Cottage, 59 Bute Gdns, London W6 7DX (☎ 071 603 6931); Wilderness Lodge, Elcot Turn, Bath Rd, Kintbury, Berks; Young & Rubicam, Gtr London House, Hampstead Rd, London NW1 7QP (☎ 071 387 9366, fax 071 380 6570)

PATTERSON, Paul Leslie; s of Leslie Patterson, of Exeter, and Lilian Anne, *née* Braund; *b* 15 June 1947; *Educ* RAM; *m* 12 Dec 1981, Hazel Rosemary, da of Dr Alexander Wilson, of Winchester; 1 s (Alastair b 1986), 1 da (Philippa b 1983); *Career* dir twentieth century music Univ of Warwick 1976-81, head composition RAM 1985- (prof composition 1972-), guest prof Yale Univ 1989; composer of large-scale choral music incl: Mass of the Sea, Stabat Mater, Te Deum, Requiem, Voices of Sleep; other compositions incl: orchestral music, symphony, concertos, chamber music, organ music, film and TV music; performances world-wide by leading musicians; featured composer at festivals incl: Llandaff 1985, Greenwich 1985, PLG 1987, Cheltenham 1988, Three Choirs 1988, Patterson South Bank 1988, Peterborough 1989, Southwark 1989-91, Cheltenham 1990, Exeter 1991; composer in residence: Eng Sinfonia Nottingham 1969-70, SE Arts Canterbury 1981-83; cmmns incl: BBC, RPO, Polish Chamber Orchestra, Kings Singers, Eng Chamber Orchestra, London Sinfonietta; memb: Arts Cncl Recordings Ctee, BBC Reading Panel; ARAM 1978, memb SPNM, FRAM 1982, FRSA 1989; Medal of Honour Miny of Culture Poland 1987; *Recreations* sailing, swimming; *Style—* Paul Patterson, Esq; 31 Cromwell Ave, Highgate, London N6 5HN (☎ 081 348 3711); Royal Academy of Music, London NW1 5HT (☎ 071 935 0782, fax 071 487 3342, telex COUNTER POINT)

PATTERSON, Hon Mrs (Sandra Debonnaire); *née* Monson; da of 10 Baron Monson (d 1958); *b* 1937; *m* 1958 (m dis 1971), Maj William Garry Patterson; 1 s, 3 da; *Style—* The Hon Mrs Patterson; 23 Lamont Rd, London SW10

PATTIE, Sir Geoffrey Edwin; PC (1987), MP (C) Chertsey and Walton Feb 1974-; s of Alfred Edwin Pattie; *b* 17 Jan 1936; *Educ* Durham Sch, St Catharine's Coll Cambridge; *m* 1960, Tuëma Caroline, *née* Eyre-Maunsell; 1 s (and 1 da decd); *Career* served TA Queen Victoria's Rifles, later Queen's Royal Rifles then 4 Royal Green Jackets (Capt); called to the Bar Gray's Inn 1964, Parly candidate (C) Barking 1966 and 1970; former memb GLC (Lambeth) and chm ILEA Fin Ctee; vice chm: All-Pty Ctee on Mental Health 1977-79, Cons Parly Def Ctee 1978-79; Parly under-sec of state: Def and RAF 1979-81, Procurement MOD 1981-83; min of state: MOD (Def Procurement) 1983-84, Indust and Info Technol 1984-87; dir Fairey Gp 1987, dep chm Cambridge Instruments 1988; chm: CDP Nexus 1988, GEC Marconi 1990; kt 1987; *Clubs* Reform, Royal Green Jackets; *Style—* The Rt Hon Sir Geoffrey Pattie, MP; House of Commons, London SW1A 0AA (☎ 071 219 4055)

PATTINSON, Maj Derek Armstrong; OBE (1985), JP (1956); s of Maj J W Pattinson (d 1931), and Isobel, *née* Armstrong (d 1951); *b* 8 Aug 1918; *Educ* Cockermouth; *m* 4 Sept 1952, Eileen Veronica, da of John Harrison (d 1986), of Penrith, Cumbria; 2 s (Nigel John b 1956, David Derek b 1960), 1 da (Julia b 1954); *Career* Gunner 1939, Maj 1946, served Far East; land agent to Earl of Lonsdale 1951-86; dir Tallantire Properties Ltd (chm 1987), conslt Lowther Scott-Harden; FRICS, Dip Forestry; *Recreations* hunting, shooting, fishing; *Style—* Maj Derek A Pattinson, OBE, JP; Corrie, Watermillock, Penrith, Cumbria CA11 OJH (☎ 0768 486582); Scott-Harden, Estate Office, Lowther, Penrith, Cumbria (☎ 09312392)

PATTINSON, Sir (William) Derek; s of Thomas William Pattinson (d 1970), and Elizabeth, *née* Burgess (d 1986); *b* 31 March 1930; *Educ* Whitehaven GS, Queen's Coll Oxford (BA, MA); *Career* Civil Serv 1952-70: Inland Revenue Dept 1952-62 and 1965-68, HM Treasy 1962-65 and 1968-70, asst sec 1961; sec-gen of the Gen Synod of the C of E 1972-90 (assoc sec-gen 1970-72); memb: Parish Clerks' Co (Master 1986-87), Woolmans' Co; kt 1990; *Clubs* Savile; *Style—* Sir Derek Pattinson; 4 Strutton Ct, Great Peter St, London SW1 (☎ 071 222 6307); Church House, Deans Yard, London SW1 (☎ 071 222 9011)

PATTINSON, Mark; 2 s of Geoffrey Pearson Pattinson, of Colchester, Essex, and Mary Agnes Borthwick, *née* Greig; *b* 13 May 1930; *Educ* Rugby, Trinity Coll Cambridge (MA); *m* 22 June 1963, Gillian Katharine, da of Sir William Mather, of Whirley Hall, Cheshire; 1 s (John b 1965), 3 da (Fiona b 1964, Diana b 1969, Rebecca b 1972); *Career* 5 Royal Inniskilling Gds 1951, 2 Lt 1952-56, Capt 41 RTR TA; gen cmmr Inland Revenue 1965-77, dir Manchester Liners Ltd 1970-80, chm Booths charities (Manchester) 1972-88, pres Marine Transport International (Saudi Arabia) 1978-85; chm: Kinloch Damph Ltd 1985-, Kishorn Shellfish Ltd 1989-; Freeman: Worshipful Co of Vintners' 1953, Worshipful Co of Shipwrights' 1978; FCA 1955; *Recreations* skiing, stalking, fishing; *Clubs* Ski Club of GB; *Style—* Mark Pattinson, Esq; Couldoran Kishorn, Strathcarron, Ross-shire IV54 8UY (☎ 05203 227)

PATTISON, Anthony Ryder; s of Maj Douglas Ryder Pattison, TD (d 1976), of The Brown House, Worplesdon Hill, Surrey, and Joan, *née* Berry; *b* 3 Sept 1937; *Educ* Winchester; *m* 2 July 1960 (m dis 1982), Frances Margaret Esterford, da of Capt James William Pearce (d 1948), of London; 3 da (Nicola b 1961, Tracy b 1962, Samantha b 1966); *Career* Nat Serv midshipman (submarines) 1956-58, Sub Lt RNR 1958-64; Berry Magicoal Ltd 1958-71 (sales and mktg dir 1965-71), chm and md Ryderglyde Ltd 1971-77, proprietor Pattison Assoc 1977-88; memb local Cons Assoc; CDipAF (1979), MInstMSM (1964); *Recreations* sailing, golf, bridge; *Clubs* MCC, RNSA; *Style—* Anthony Pattison, Esq; Golf House, Staverton, Northamptonshire NN11 6AJ (☎ 0327 78538, car 0860 597683)

PATTISON, Prof Bruce; s of Matthew Pattison (d 1935), and Catherine, *née* Bruce (d 1949); *b* 13 Nov 1908; *Educ* Gateshead GS, Armstrong Coll Newcastle upon Tyne (BA, MA), Fitzwilliam Coll Cambridge (PhD); *m* 10 Aug 1937, Dorothy (d 1979), da of Ernest Graham; *Career* teacher: Henry Mellish Sch Nottingham 1933-35, Hymer's Coll Hull 1935-36; lectr in English UCL 1936-48, prof of educn Univ of London Inst of Educn 1948-76; *Books* Music and Poetry of the English Rennaissance (2 edn, 1970), Special Relations (1984); *Recreations* music, chess; *Clubs* Athenaeum, Nat Lib; *Style—* Prof Bruce Pattison

PATTISON, Dr David Arnold; s of David Pattison (d 1957), and Christina Russell Bone (d 1988); *b* 9 Feb 1941; *Educ* Kilmarnock Acad, Univ of Glasgow (BSc, PhD); *m* 1967, Anne, da of William Wilson (d 1974); 2 s (David b 1972, Graeme b 1974), 1 da (Isla b 1975); *Career* lectr Univ of Strathclyde 1967-70; dir Tourism Highlands and Islands Devpt Bd 1970-81, chief exec Scottish Tourist Bd 1981-85; dir leisure and tourism consulting Ernest & Young 1985-90, ptnr Cobham Resource Conslts 1990-; *Recreations* watching soccer and rugby, reading, gardening; *Style—* Dr David Pattison; 7 Cramond Glebe Gardens, Edinburgh EH4 6NZ

PATTISON, David Charles; s of Charles Francis Alan Pattison (d 1987), of Victoria Cottage, Warkworth, Northumberland, and Edith, *née* Scott (d 1985); *b* 19 Jan 1937; *Educ* St Peter's Sch York; *m* 19 Nov 1966, (Margaret) Rachel, da of Kenneth Owen Leathard; 2 s (Simon Charles, Richard Thomas), 1 da (Sophie Victoria); *Career* admitted slr 1961, ptnr Hewitt Brown-Humes and Hare; chm SW Durham branch of NSPCC; memb Law Soc; *Recreations* flying and windsurfing; *Style—* David Pattison, Esq; The Orchard, West End, Wolsingham, Bishop Auckland, Co Durham DL13 3AP (☎ 0388 527647); 5 Market Place, Bishop Auckland, Co Durham DL14 7NW (☎ 0388 60469, fax 0388 607899)

PATTISON, Ian Frank; s of Frank Marsden Pattison, of Bradford, West Yorkshire, and Esther, *née* Williams (d 1958); *b* 8 Dec 1943; *Educ* Thornton GS Bradford; *m* 1, 1966 (m dis 1988), Kathleen Brenda Terry; 1 da (Annabel Claire b 29 July 1971); m 2, 1988, Maralyn Fox, da of Leslie Bould; *Career* articled clerk Williamson Butterfield & Roberts (now Grant Thornton) 1960-66, ptnr Grant Thornton 1971-; pres: Kirkless Jr C of C 1975, Kirkless & Wakefield C of C and Indust 1985 (memb Cncl 1980-); chm: Dewsbury Heath Authy 1986-, Kirkless Enterprise Agency 1987-89, Wakefield Enterprise Agency 1987-89; memb Exec N Kirkless Enterprise Gp 1987-, dir Enterprise House Ltd 1989-, dep chm Assoc of Yorks & Humberside Cs of C 1987; ACA 1966, ATII 1962; *Recreations* golf, cricket, rugby; *Clubs* Cleckheaton and District Rotary; *Style—* Ian Pattison, Esq; Hollybank, 81 Bramley Lane, Lightcliffe, Halifax, West Yorkshire HX3 8NS (☎ 0422 201212); Grant Thornton, Eildon Cleckheaton, West Yorkshire BD19 3LS (☎ 0274 876701, fax 0274 851169); Dewsbury Health Authority, 28 Oxford Rd, Dewsbury, West Yorkshire WF13 4LL (☎ 0924 465111, fax 0924 458867)

PATTISON, Michael Ambrose; s of Osmond John Pattison, of Charlecote Mill House, Hampton Lucy, Warwickshire, and Eileen Susannah, *née* Cullen; *b* 14 July 1947; *Educ* Sedbergh, Univ of Sussex; *m* 16 July 1975, Beverly Jean, da of Hugh E Webber (d 1988), of Florida, USA; 1 da (Jennifer b 1977); *Career* civil serv: Miny of Overseas Devpt 1968, asst private sec to Minister for Overseas Devpt 1970-72, 1 sec UK perm mission to the UN NY 1974-77, private sec to successive PMs 1979-82, estab offr ODA 1983-85; sec gen RICS 1985-, dir Surveyors Hldgs Ltd 1985-; dir Battersea Arts Centre Tst 1988-, govr Thames Poly 1989-, memb advsy bd Univ of Nottingham Inst of Engrg Surveying and Space Geodesy; *Recreations* cricket, real tennis, countryside, cinema; *Style—* Michael Pattison, Esq; 12 Great George St, Parliament Square, London SW1P 3AD (☎ 071 222 7000, fax 071 222 9430, telex 915443 RICS G)

PATTISSON, John Harmer; s of Frederick Edward Pattisson (d 1946), of Meyricks Bidborough, Tunbridge Wells, and Louise Mary, *née* Dalton (d 1973); *b* 24 April 1931; *Educ* Radley, Trinity Coll Oxford (MA); *m* 29 March 1958 (m dis 1975), Julia Jane, da of Maj Percy Montagu Nevile (d 1957), of Skelbrooke Park, Yorks and Yerdley House, Long Compton, Warwicks; 2 s (Edward b 1960, William b 1963); *Career* Nat Serv 2 Lt Oxford & Bucks LI 1950-52, Capt TA 1952-63; Dawnay Day Gp 1955- (dir 1964-, md 1969-80), exec dir Hanson Tst Ltd (formerly Wiles Gp Ltd) 1960-74; dir: Target Tst Gp Ltd 1973-81, J Rothschild & Co Ltd 1980-81, Hanson plc 1981-89, New Ct Property Fund Mangrs Ltd 1984-, Wassall plc 1988-; memb Cncl Radley Coll 1965-, vice chm govrs City Technol Coll Kingshurst 1988-; *Clubs* Boodles, City Of London; *Style—* John Pattisson, Esq; 1C Elm Place, London SW7 3QH (☎ 071 370 4652); Hanson plc, 1 Grosvenor Place, London SW1X 7JH (☎ 071 245 1245, fax 071 823 2015, car 0836 224 626, telex 917698)

PATTISSON, Patrick Henry; s of R D M Pattisson, of Chapel House, Selborne, Hants, and P Pattisson, *née* Wise; *b* 21 Dec 1932; *Educ* Rugby, St George's Hosp Med Sch (MB BS); *m* 11 May 1957, Elizabeth Mary, da of Dr W G M Mackay (d 1977); 3 s (Douglas b 1958, John b 1962, Alexander b 1965), 1 da (Rosemary b 1960); *Career* Surgn Lt RN 1959-62; conslt surgn gen and vascular surgery: W Middx Univ Hosp, RFU, Royal Masonic Hosp; hon sr lectr: Charing Cross Hosp, Westminster Med Sch; former chm S Middx Div BMA; FRCS (Eng), FRCS (Ed); *Recreations* rugby, skiing; *Style—* Patrick Pattisson, Esq; Chesterfield House, 32 Broad Lane, Hampton TW12 3AZ

PATTISSON, Rodney; MBE (1969); s of Lt Cdr Kenneth Pattisson, DSC, RN, of Poole, and Margaret, *née* Collett; *b* 5 Aug 1943; *Educ* Pangbourne Coll, Br Royal Naval Coll Dartmouth; *Career* international yachtsman; achievements incl: Cadet world champion 1960, public schs Firefly champion 1960-61, Gold medal Flying Dutchman Olympic Games Mexico and W Germany 1972 (Silver Canada 1976), Flying Dutchman World champion (1969, 1970, 1971) , Flying Dutchman Euro champion (1968, 1970, 1972, 1975), Quarter Ton World Cup champion Finland 1976, co-skipper Victory '83 Americas Cup 1983, One Ton World Cup champion England 1984; in Guinness Book of Records for lowest number of penalty points by winner of any class in Olympic Games (3 points 1968); RN Submariner Lt 1961-71, co dir Marine Yachting Conslts 1971; *Books* Tactics, Boat Speed; *Recreations* aero and nautical modelling, squash, skiing; *Style—* Rodney Pattisson, Esq, MBE

PATTMAN, Dr Richard Stewart; s of Robert Pearson Pattman, VRD, of Milngavie, and Joyce Mary, *née* Long (d 1989); *b* 19 April 1950; *Educ* Glasgow Acad, Sedbergh, Univ of Glasgow (MB ChB); *m* 27 April 1976, (Mary) Geraldine, da of John Purcell (d 1983), of Glasgow; 1 s (Stewart John b 1979); *Career* house offr and registrar in gen med Western Infirmary Gartnavel Glasgow 1976-76, sr registrar in genito-urinary med Royal Infirmary Glasgow 1976-79, conslt in genito-urinary med and clinical lectr to Univ of Newcastle-upon-Tyne 1979-; memb: coll ctee on genito-urinary med, editorial ctee of genito-urinary med; MRCP 1976, FRCP Glas 1986; *Recreations* gardening, fishing; *Style—* Dr Richard Pattman; Dept of Genito-Urinary Medicine, Newcastle General Hosp, Westgate Rd, Newcastle-upon-Tyne NE4 6BE (☎ 091 2733320)

PATTON, Edwin Galbraith; s of Hugh Ferguson Patton, of Newtownards, Co Down, NI, and Sarah, *née* Galbraith (d 1987); *b* 29 June 1942; *Educ* Sullivan Upper Sch Holywood NI, Queen's Univ Belfast (LLB); *m* 1965, Margaret Elizabeth Victoria, da of Samuel Simpson Smyth (d 1979); 1 s (Dominic Edwin b 29 March 1973), 2 da (Sibohan Victoria b 4 Jan 1971, Susannah Jane b 11 April 1978); *Career* lectr in law Univ of Bristol 1964-67; Clifford Chance (formerly Coward Chance) 1987-: articled clerk 1968-70, slr 1970-, ptnr 1974- memb City of London Solicitors Co; supporting memb London Maritime Arbitrators Assoc, memb Law Soc 1970; *Recreations* theatre, golf, skiing; *Style—* Edwin Patton, Esq; 10 Park Hill, Ealing, London W5 2JN (☎ 081 997 1541); Clifford Chance, Blackfriars House, 19 New Bridge St, London EC4V 6BY (☎ 071 353 0211, fax 071 489 0046)

PATTON, Dr Michael Alexander; s of Henry Alexander Patton, of 4 The Trees, Donaghadee, and Margaret Murray, *née* Drennan; *b* 15 April 1950; *Educ* Campbell Coll Belfast, Pembroke Coll Cambridge (MA), Univ of Edinburgh (MB ChB, MSc); *m* 4 June 1977, Jaqueline Heidi, da of John Pickin, OBE, of Keepers Cottage, Siddington, Cheshire; 1 s (Alistair b 10 April 1979), 1 da (Rebecca b 21 Sept 1983); *Career* dir Regnl Genetics Serv SW Thames RHA, conslt and sr lectr St Georges Hosp Med Sch 1986-; med advsr to various parent gps for inherited disease, chm Scientific Ctee Birth Defects Fndn, examiner RCPath; MRCP 1979; *Recreations* skiing, sailing; *Style—* Dr Michael Patton; 126 Woodlands Rd, Little Bookham, Surrey KT23 4HJ (☎ 0372 56327); SW Thames Regnl Genetic Serv, St Georges Hosp Med School, Cranmer Terrace, London SW17 0RE (☎ 081 767 8150)

PATTON, Dr (John) Terence; RD (1970); s of Francis Patton, JP (d 1983), and Winefride, *née* Myhan (d 1977); *b* 18 May 1926; *Educ* St Francis Xavier's Coll Liverpool, Univ of Liverpool; *m* 16 April 1966, Belinda Richmond, da of Edwin Latham Black, of Hendre Uchaf, Abergele, N Wales; 1 s (James Terence (Sam) b 1967), 2 da (Philippa Mary b 1968, Rachel Belinda b 1971); *Career* RNVR and RNR 1952-78, ret Surgn Capt; conslt radiologist Manchester Royal Infirmary 1965-90, civilian conslt radiologist to RN 1982-89, examiner in Fellowship RCR 1974-78; examiner in radiology: Univ of Baghdad 1976, Univ of Aberdeen 1982-85, Malaysia 1986, Edinburgh 1988-90; ed Br Jl of Radiology 1984-89; hon FRCPE 1984, MRCS, LRCP, memb Br Inst Radiology 1962, FRCR 1963, FRCP 1984; *Books* Diagnostic Radiology (contrib and ed, 1986), Multiple Myeloma and other Paraproteinaemias (contrib); *Recreations* sailing, music; *Clubs* Naval; *Style*— Dr Terence Patton, RD; Fallows Hall, Chelford, Macclesfield, Cheshire SK10 4SZ (☎ 0625 861 252)

PATTULLO, (David) Bruce; s of Colin Arthur Pattullo; *b* 2 Jan 1938; *Educ* Rugby, Hertford Coll Oxford; *m* 1962, Fiona Jane Nicholson; 3 s, 1 da; *Career* Bank of Scotland: dep treas 1978-79, treas and chief exec 1979-88, gp chief exec and dep govr 1988-; dir: Standard Life Assur Co 1985-, British Linen Bank Ltd 1977-, Bank of Wales plc 1986-, NWS Bank plc 1986-; *Clubs* New (Edinburgh), Caledonian; *Style*— Bruce Pattullo, Esq; 6 Cammo Rd, Edinburgh EH4 8EB (☎ 031 339 6012)

PAUK, Gyorgy; s of Imre Pauk (d 1944), and Magda Pauk; *b* 26 Oct 1936; *Educ* Franz Liszt Music Acad Budapest; *m* 19 July 1959, Susan, *née* Mautner; 1 s (Thomas b 19 April 1962), 1 da (Catherine b 13 June 1966); *Career* violinist; as the youngest pupil of the Franz Liszt Music Acad toured numerous countries incl Hungary and Eastern Europe; first prize winner: The Paganini Competition, Marguerite Long/Jacques Thibauld Competition, Munich Sonata Competition; London orchestral and recital debuts 1961; currently performs with maj orchestras of the world under such conductors as: Piere Boulez, Sir Colin Davies, Antal Dorati, Kondrashin, Lorin Maazel, Rozhdestvensky, Rattle, Previn, Tennstedt, Haitink, Sir George Solti; American debut with the Chicago Symphony Orch leading to subsequent return visits playing with: Cleveland Philadelphia, Los Angeles Philharmonic, Boston Symphony Orch; festival appearances incl: Aspen, Ravinia, Hollywood Bowl, Saratoga; many prizewinning recordings incl works by Bartok, Schubert, Mozart, Brahms; hon memb Guidhall Sch, prof of music RAM 1986; artistic dir Mozart Festival in London Wigmore Hall 1991; hon memb and princ prof RAM; recordings: all orchestral concertos for violin by Mozart, 3 Brahms sonatas, Mozart Quintets; *Style*— Gyorgy Pauk, Esq; c/o Artist Management International, 12-13 Richmond Buildings, London W1V 5AF (☎ 071 439 5715, fax 071 439 8021)

PAUL, Dr David Manuel; s of Kenneth Paul (d 1960), and Rachel, *née* Favell (d 1965); *b* 8 June 1927; *Educ* Selhurst GS Croydon, St Bartholomew's Hosp Med Coll, London Hosp Med Coll (DRCOG, DA, DMJ); *m* 14 Feb 1948, (Gladys) Audrey, da of William Garton, of The Wallhatch Hotel, Forest Row, Sussex; 2 da (Judith Audrey (Mrs Stevens) b 25 Nov 1948, Alison Jane (Mrs Putman) b 4 July 1950); *Career* GP Drs Duncan & Ptnrs 1955-67; Purley War Meml Hosp: clinical asst anaesthetist 1956-68, clinical asst obstetrician 1958-68; clinical asst anaesthetist Croydon Gp of Hosps 1956-68, divn surgn Met Police 1956-68; coroner: City of London 1966-, Northern Dist London 1968-; Dept of Forensic Med Guy's Hosp: hon lectr, hon conslt in clinical forensic med and ct practice 1966-; hon conslt in clinical forensic med Surrey Constabulary 1967, hon sr lectr in clinical forensic med Dept of Forensic Med and Toxicology Charing Cross and Westminster Hosp Med Sch 1990-, pres Br Acad of Forensic Sciences 1987-88 (chm Med Section 1983-87 and Exec Cncl 1984-87); chm Warlingham and Dist Horse Club 1964-68; Freeman City of London 1966, Liveryman Worshipful Soc of Apothecaries 1966; MRCS, LRCP, memb Assoc of Police Surgns 1956, BAFS 1964; memb: Medico Legal Soc 1964, Forensic Sci Soc 1964, RSM; *Books* chapters in Gradwohl's Legal Medicine (3 edn, 1976), Modern Trends in Forensic Medicine (1973), Taylor's Principles and Practice of Medical Jurisprudence (13 edn, 1984); *Recreations* travel, photography, equitation, fishing, work; *Style*— Dr David Paul; Cobhambury Farm, Edenbridge, Kent TN8 5PN (☎ 0732 863280); Coroner's Court, Milton Court, Moor Lane, London EC2 7BL (☎ 071 260 1598); Coroner's Court, Myddelton Rd, Hornsey, London N8 7PY (☎ 081 348 4411); Shirley Oaks Hospital, Poppy Lane, Shirley Oaks, Croydon, Surrey CR9 8AB (☎ 081 655 2255, fax 081 656 2868)

PAUL, Geoffrey David; s of Reuben Goldstein; *b* 26 March 1929; *Educ* Liverpool, Kendal, Dublin; *m* 1, 1952 (m dis 1972), Joy Stirling; 1 da; *m* 2, 1974, Rachel Mann; 1 s; *Career* ed Jewish Chronicle 1977-90; *Books* Living in Jerusalem; *Style*— Geoffrey Paul, Esq; 25 Furnival St, London EC4A 1JT (☎ 071 405 9252)

PAUL, George William; s of William Stuart Hamilton Paul (d 1984), of Freston Lodge, Ipswich, and Diana Violet Anne, *née* Martin; *b* 25 Feb 1940; *Educ* Harrow, Wye Coll Univ of London (BSc); *m* 1963, Mary Annette (d 1989), da of Col Frank Mitchell, DSO, MC (d 1985); 2 s (Stuart, Oliver), 1 da (Bridget); *Career* chm Pauls plc 1985-; chief exec Harrisons and Crosfield plc 1987- (dir 1985-), ptnr William Paul and Sons Farming (2,000 acres); master Essex and Suffolk Foxhounds 1978-85, High Sheriff Suffolk 1990; *Recreations* farming, hunting, shooting, fishing; *Clubs* Boodle's, Farmers'; *Style*— George Paul, Esq; Harrisons & Crosfield plc, 20 St Dunstan's Hill, London EC3R 8LQ (☎ 071 626 4333, fax 071 782 0113, telex 885636)

PAUL, Prof John Poskitt; s of William Boag Paul (d 1962), of Old Kilpatrick, and Maude Meikle, *née* Poskitt (d 1972); *b* 26 June 1927; *Educ* Aberdeen GS, Allan Glens Sch Glasgow, Royal Tech Coll Glasgow (BSc, PhD), Univ of Glasgow; *m* 7 Sept 1956, Elizabeth Richardson, da of James Richardson Graham (d 1962), of Dalmuir; 1 s (Graham William b 1962), 2 da (Gillian Anne b 1960, Fiona Helen b 1968); *Career* Univ of Strathclyde Glasgow: lectr in mechanical engrg 1952, sr lectr 1964, personal prof of bioengrg 1972, prof and head of Bioengrg Unit 1980; memb Ctee: BSI, MRC, SERC, SHHD; CEng, FIMechE 1971, FISPO 1979, FRSA 1974, CFBOA 1975, FRSE 1984, Eur Ing 1990; pres Int Soc of Biomechanics 1987-89; membre d'Honneur Societé de Biomecanique, Medal of Honour Czechoslovak Soc for Mechanics 1990-; *Books* Disability (co-ed, 1979), Computing in Medicine (sr-ed, 1982), Biomaterials in Artificial Organs (sr-ed, 1984), Influence of New Technology in Medical Practice (sr-ed, 1984), Total Knee Replacement (co-ed, 1988), Progress in Bioengineering (sr-ed, 1989); *Recreations* gardening, bridge, formerly rugby and refereeing; *Style*— Eur Ing Prof John P Paul, FRSE; 25 James Watt Rd, Milngavie, Glasgow G62 7JX (☎ 041 9563221); Bioengineering Unit; Wolfson Centre, Univ of Strathclyde, Glasgow G4 ONW (☎ 041 5524400, fax 041 5526098, telex 77472 UNSLIBG)

PAUL, Sir John Warburton; GCMG (1965, KCMG 1962), OBE (1959), MC (1940); s of Walter George Paul; *b* 29 March 1916; *Educ* Weymouth Coll Dorset, Selwyn Coll Cambridge; *m* 1946, Kathleen Audrey, da of Dr A D Weeden, of Weymouth; 3 da; *Career* called to the Bar Inner Temple 1947; govr and C-in-C: The Gambia 1962-65 (govr gen 1965-66), Br Honduras 1966-72, The Bahamas 1972-73; govr gen The Bahamas July-Oct 1973, Lt-govr Isle of Man 1974-80; dir of overseas rels St John Ambulance 1981-89, chm St Christopher's Motorists' Security Assoc 1980-; hon fell Selwyn Coll Cambridge; chapter gen OStJ 1981- (memb Cncl Hampshire 1990-), KStJ 1962; *Clubs* Athenaeum, MCC, Hawks (Cambridge); *Style*— Sir John Paul, GCMG, OBE, MC; Sherrens Mead, Sherfield-on-Loddon, Hampshire

PAUL, Julian Braithwaite; s of Michael Braithwaite Paul, MD, of Orchard House, Newchurch, Burton-on-Trent, Staffs, and Patricia Elisabeth Ann, *née* Mumm; *b* 18 May 1945; *Educ* Wrekin Coll Shrops, St John's Coll Oxford (BA, MA); *m* 3 Nov 1973, Diana, da of Ernest Trevor Davies (d 1981), of Epsom, Surrey; 1 s (Rupert b 1981), 2 da (Arabella b 1975, Henrietta b 1978); *Career* Arthur Andersen & Co CAs 1966-71, Citibank NA 1971-74, dep md Banco Hispano Americano Ltd 1974-87, md Guinness Mahon & Co Ltd 1989-90 (dir 1987-90), sr ptnr Julian Paul & Co Chartered Accountants 1990-; chm of govrs Valence Sch Westerham Kent, govr Sundridge and Brasted C of E Primary Sch; pres: Sundridge and Brasted Horticultural Soc, Brasted Cons Assoc; cnllr Kent County Cncl (Sevenoaks West) 1985-; FCA 1979; *Recreations* politics, travel; *Clubs* Carlton, Coningsby, Bow Gp; *Style*— Julian Paul, Esq; The Mount House, Brasted, Westerham, Kent (☎ 0959 63617, fax 0959 61296)

PAUL, Dr (Peter) Michael; s of Thomas James Paul, of 3 Blaizefield Close, Woore, Shropshire, and Nora, *née* Wilcox; *b* 26 Sept 1947; *Educ* Queen Elizabeth GS Wakefield Yorkshire, St Andrew's Univ Scotland (MB), Univ of Manchester (MB ChB), DObstRCOG, FPA Cert, MRCGP; *m* 22 June 1974, Susan Margaret, da of Frank Pickles; *Career* house offr Wythenshaw Hosp Manchester 1973-74, sr house offr Casualty Dept Westminster Hosp London 1974, vocational trg scheme Aylesbury Buckinghamshire 1974-77, ptnr in practice White Bungalow Surgery 1977-86, private GP and med dir Gen Med Clinics Ltd Wimpole St London 1986; memb Ctee Ascot Volunteer Bureau 1981-86, med offr Ascot Priory Convent 1977-86, memb Ctee and hon treas Thames Valley Faculty RCGP 1980-86, fndr and hon sec Independent Doctors Forum 1989-, gen practice trainer, pt/t lectr Red Cross; FRSM, memb BMA; *Recreations* theatre, reading, walking; *Clubs* RAC; *Style*— Dr Michael Paul; 14 Vincent Terrace, London N1 8HJ (☎ 071 837 7565); Gen Med Clinics Ltd, 67 Wimpole St, London W1M 7DE (☎ 071 636 5145, mobile 0836 276868)

PAUL, Nancy Catherine Trask; da of Frank Stone Trask (d 1983), of Deer Lodge, Montana, USA, and Cora Nichols (d 1964); *b* 1 June 1936; *Educ* Powell County HS, DL Montana, Univ of Montana USA (BA, MA); *m* 17 Sept 1960 (m dis 1982), William J Paul, Jr; 2 s (William James Paul, III b 24 Nov 1962, Michael Justine Paul b 18 June 1971), 1 da (Elisa Anne Paul b 7 Sept 1969); *Career* lectr psychology Univ of Montana 1958-60, assoc mgmnt prof Brunel Univ 1979-; dir: Paul Mgmnt Ltd 1979-89, Excel International Ltd 1989-; author of pubns on: the effects of divorce on men and women, orgns and work in the UK and USA; fndr memb Inst Transactional Analysis, hon memb Inst Transactional Analysis Assoc; memb: American Acad of Mgmnt, Int OD Network; *Books* The Right to Be You (1985); *Videos* Constructive Criticism (1988), Body Talk (1989); *Recreations* mountaineering, classical music; *Style*— Mrs Nancy Paul; Excel International Ltd, Excel House, 35 Lind Rd, Sutton, Surrey SM1 4PP (☎ 081 770 0465)

PAUL, Robert Cameron (Robin); s of Dr Francis William Paul (d 1964), of Ealing, and Maureen Kirkpatrick, *née* Cameron; *b* 7 July 1935; *Educ* Rugby, Corpus Christi Coll Cambridge (BA, MA); *m* 1 May 1965, Diana Kathleen, da of Sir Arthur Bruce, KBE, MC, of Beaconsfield, Bucks; 2 da (Caroline b 1966, Juliet b 1968); *Career* Nat Serv 2 Lt RE BAOR 1953-55; ICI Gen Chemicals Div 1959: dir ICI Fibres 1976, dep chm ICI Mond Div 1979; dep chm and md Albright & Wilson Ltd 1986-; tstee Duke of Edinburgh Cwlth Study Conf Fund; pres Inst of Chemical Engrs 1990-91; FEng, Hon DEng Univ of Birmingham; *Recreations* music, golf; *Clubs* Oriental; *Style*— R C Paul, Esq; Albright & Wilson Ltd, 1 Knightsbridge Green, London SW1X 7QD (☎ 071 589 6393, fax 071 225 0839)

PAUL, Swraj; s of Payare Paul (d 1944), and Mongwati, *née* Lal; *b* 18 Feb 1931; *Educ* Univ of Punjab (BSc), MIT (BSc, MSc); *m* 1 Dec 1956, Aruna; 3 s (Ambar b 20 Dec 1957, Akash (twin) b 20 Dec 1957, Angad b 6 June 1970), 2 da (Anjli b 12 Nov 1959, Ambika b 1964, d 1968); *Career* dir family owned Apeejay-Surrendra Gp India 1952-66; came to England 1966 and estab Natural Gas Tubes Ltd; chm: Caparo Gp Ltd 1978-, Caparo Industs plc 1980-, United Merchant Bar plc 1984-, Bull Moose Tube Co USA 1988-, Armstrong Equipment plc 1989; Hon PhD American Coll of Switzerland 1986; Order of Padma Bhushan India 1983; *Books* Indira Gandhi (1985); *Clubs* MCC, RAC; India: Royal Calcutta Turf, Royal Calcutta Golf, Cricket of India (Bombay); *Style*— Swraj Paul, Esq; Caparo House, 103 Baker St, London W1M 1FD (☎ 071 486 1417, fax 071 935 3242, telex 8811343)

PAUL, William Halkerston Clunie; s of John Litster Wallace Paul (d 1979), of Fife, Scotland, and Margaret White, *née* Clunie (d 1982); *b* 21 March 1955; *Educ* Bell Baxter HS, Univ of Aberdeen (MA); *m* 2 Nov 1978, Linda Anne, *née* Forsyth; 2 s (Andrew Halkerston Clunie b 26 March 1983, William James Forsyth b 18 Sept 1985); *Career* trainee reporter Press and Journal Aberdeen 1976-80, sr reporter The Scotsman Edinburgh 1980-88, chief reporter Scotland on Sunday Edinburgh 1988-; memb Soc of Authors; *Books* Seasons of Revenge (1985), Mummy's Boy (1987), The Hindmost (1988), The Lion Rampant (1989); *Recreations* rugby, golf; *Style*— William Paul, Esq; Scotland on Sunday, 20 North Bridge, Edinburgh EH1 1YT (☎ 031 243 3593, fax 031 220 2443)

PAULET, Lord Timothy Guy; raised to rank of Marquess's son 1970; s of George Paulet and bro of 18 Marquess of Winchester; *b* 1944; *m* 1973, Gilian Margaret (Jill), da of Capt Thomas Preacher (d 1969); 2 s (Timothy b 1975, Michael b 1976); *Style*— The Lord Timothy Paulet

PAULSON-ELLIS, Jeremy David; s of Christian William Geoffrey Paulson-Ellis (d 1982), and Vivien Joan Paulson-Ellis (d 1966); *b* 21 Sept 1943; *Educ* Sherborne; *m* 27 April 1973, Jennifer Jill, da of Harry Milne (d 1958); 2 s (Nicholas b 1976, Matthew b 1984), 1 da (Vivien b 1974); *Career* Citicorp Scrimgeour Vickers International Ltd (formerly Vickers da Costa & Co): joined 1964, ptnr 1970, dir 1974, chm 1985-88; chm: Genesis Investment Management Ltd, Genesis Emerging Markets Fund Ltd, Genesis Chile Fund Ltd, Genesis Malaysia Maju Fund Ltd; dir Korea Asia Fund Ltd; memb Investmt Advsy Cncl: Korea International Trust 1982-87, Seoul International Trust (chm) 1985-87, Thailand Fund 1986-88; ind memb Heathrow Airport Consultative Ctee 1984-88; memb London Stock Exchange 1970; AMSIA; *Recreations* tennis, travel; *Style*— Jeremy Paulson-Ellis, Esq; Broomlands, Langton Green, Tunbridge Wells, Kent TN3 0RA (☎ 0892 863 555); Genesis Investment Management Ltd, 21 Knightsbridge, London SW1X 7LY (☎ 071 235 5090, fax 071 235 8065, telex 919062 GIML, car 0860 534 116)

PAULUSZ, Jan Gilbert; s of Jan Hendrik Olivier Paulusz, of Tanglewood, Westbury, Wiltshire, and Edith, *née* Gilbert; *b* 18 Nov 1929; *Educ* The Leys; *m* 18 April 1973, Luigia Maria, da of Luigi Attanasio; *Career* Nat Serv 2 Lt 1 Bn S Lancs Regt 1951-53, Lt TA 1953-60 (Capt 1955); called to the Bar Lincoln's Inn 1957, rec of the Crown Ct 1980-; *Recreations* photography, mountain walking; *Style*— Jan Paulusz, Esq; 50 Royston Gardens, Redbridge, Ilford, Essex 1G1 3SY (☎ 081 554 9078); 10 Kings Bench Walk, Temple, London EC4Y 7EB (☎ 071 353 7742)

PAUNCEFORT-DUNCOMBE, David Philip Henry; s and h of Sir Philip Digby Pauncefort-Duncombe, 4 Bt; *b* 21 May 1956; *Educ* Gordonstoun, RAC Cirencester; *m* Sarah Ann, er da of late Reginald T G Battrum; 1 s (Henry Digby b 16 Dec 1988), 1 da (Laura Mary b 15 Jan 1991); *Style*— David Pauncefort-Duncombe, Esq; Westfield Farm, Great Brickhill, Bletchley, Bucks MK17 9BG (☎ 0525 261479)

PAUNCEFORT-DUNCOMBE, Sir Philip Digby; 4 Bt (UK 1859), of Great Brickhill, Buckinghamshire, DL (Bucks 1971); s of Maj Sir Everard Philip Digby Pauncefort-Duncombe, 3 Bt, DSO (d 1971); *b* 18 May 1927; *Educ* Stowe; *m* 4 April 1951, Rachel Moyra, yr da of Maj Henry Gerald Aylmer, gggs of 2 Baron Aylmer; 1 s, 2 da; *Heir* s, David Philip Henry Pauncefort-Duncombe; *Career* 2 Lt Grenadier Guards 1946, Hon Maj (ret 1960), RARO, Co Cmdt Bucks ACF 1967-70, memb HM Body Guard of Hon Corps of Gentlemen-at-Arms; High Sheriff of Buckinghamshire 1987-88; KASG; OStJ 1986; *Style*— Sir Philip Pauncefort-Duncombe, Bt, DL; Great Brickhill Manor, Milton

Keynes, Bucks (☎ 0525 261205)

PAUSON, Prof Peter Ludwig; s of Stefan Pauson (d 1964), and Helene Dorothea, *née* Herzfelder (d 1989); *b* 30 July 1925; *Educ* Univ of Glasgow (BSc), Univ of Sheffield (PhD); *m* 7 June 1952, Lai-ngau, da of Pak Yun Wong (d 1971); 1 s (Alfred b 1956), 1 da (Hilary b 1954); *Career* asst prof Duquesne Univ Pittsburgh PA 1949-51; res fell: Univ of Chicago 1951-52, Harvard Univ 1952-53; reader Univ of Sheffield 1959 (lectr 1953-59), Freeland prof of chemistry Univ of Strathclyde (formerly Royal Coll of Sci and Technol) 1959-; memb Deutsche Akademie der Naturforscher Leopoldina 1976; FRSE 1961; *Books* Organometallic Chemistry (1967); *Recreations* skiing, hill-walking, gardening, listening to music; *Clubs* Scottish Ski, Eagle Ski, Glasgow Glenmore; *Style*— Prof Peter Pauson; 40A Station Road, Bearsden, Glasgow G61 4AL (☎ 041 942 5213); Department of Pure and Applied Chemistry, University of Strathclyde, Glasgow G1 1XL (☎ 041 552 4400, fax 041 552 5664)

PAVEY, Martin Christopher; s of Archibald Lindsay Pavey, MC (d 1977), of Sherborne, Dorset, and Margaret Alice, *née* Salsbury; *b* 2 Dec 1940; *Educ* Magdalen Coll Sch Oxford, UCL (BA), Univ of Cambridge (PGCE), Univ of Nottingham (MA); *m* 9 April 1969, Louise Margaret, da of Dr Joseph Charles Henry Bird (d 1985), of Cambridge; 2 s (Nicholas b 1972, Robert b 1974); *Career* headmaster: Fairham Sch Nottingham 1976-81, Cranbrook Sch Kent 1981-88, Latymer Upper Sch London 1988; memb: SHA, HMC; *Clubs* East India; *Style*— Martin Pavey, Esq; Latymer Upper Sch, London W6 (☎ 071 741 1851)

PAVITT, Prof Keith Leslie Richard; *b* 13 Jan 1937; *Educ* Hackney Downs GS, Trinity Coll Cambridge (BA), Harvard Univ; *m* 29 March 1964, Michelle Simone, *née* Rouffignac; 1 s (Richard Robert b 21 Aug 1965), 1 da (Isabelle Catherine b 6 April 1969); *Career* PO RAF 1955-57; staff memb OECD Paris 1961-70; visiting prof: Princeton Univ USA 1970, Université Louis Pasteur Strasbourg 1983, Univ of Padua 1986; actg dir sci policy res unit Univ of Sussex 1988 (sr fell 1971, prof of sci and technol policy 1984); vice-chm Res Grants Bd, memb Econ and Social Res Cncl; memb Schumpeter Soc 1989; *Books* Technical Innovation and British Economic Performance (ed, 1980), The Comparative Economics of Research, Development And Innovations in East and West: A Survey (with P Harrison, 1987); *Recreations* tennis, food, visits to France; *Clubs* Royal Air Force; *Style*— Prof Keith Pavitt; 7 Gundreda Road, Lewes, Sussex BM7 1PJ (☎ 0273 473528); Science Policy Research Univ, Mamtell Building, Univ of Sussex BN1 9RF (☎ 0273 678173, telex 0771 59 BHVTXS G RECEMIRE, fax 0273 685865)

PAVORD, Anna; da of Arthur Vincent Pavord (d 1989), of Abergavenny, Gwent, and Christabel Frances, *née* Lewis (d 1978); *b* 20 Sept 1940; *Educ* Abergavenny HS for Girls, Univ of Leicester (BA); *m* Trevor David Oliver Ware, s of John Ronald Ware; 3 da (Oenone b 15 Dec 1967, Vanessa b 7 June 1970, Tilly b 8 Dec 1974); *Career* copywriter Lintas Advertising Agency 1962-63, Line-Up BBC TV 1963-70 (prodn asst rising to dir), contrib Observer 1970-, gardening corr Independent 1970-, Flowering Passions (TV prog C4) 1991; memb Pubns Ctee RHS 1990-; *Books* Growing Things (1982), Foliage (1990), The Flowering Year (1991); *Recreations* gardening, sailing, rainforests in Central America, Evelyn Waugh, black and white films; *Style*— Ms Anna Pavord; The Independent, 40 City Rd, London EC1Y 2DB (☎ 071 253 1222, fax 071 962 0017)

PAWLE, Lady Mary Clementine; da of 5 Marquess Camden (d 1983), and 1 w, Marjorie, Countess of Brecknock, DBE (d 1989); *b* 5 Aug 1921; *m* 1, 1940, Flt Lt the Hon (Herbert) Oswald Berry (d 1952); m 2, 1953, (Shafto) Gerald Strachan Pawle; *Career* pres St John Ambulance Bde Cornwall, hon life pres St Ives Cons and Unionist Assoc; *Clubs* Army and Navy; *Style*— Lady Mary Pawle; Trehiven House, Madron, Penzance, Cornwall TR20 8SR (☎ 0736 64158)

PAWLEY, Margaret Grozier; da of James John William Herbertson, MVO, OBE (d 1974), of Folkestone, and Lilian Annie Charlotte, *née* Rawlinson Wood (d 1985); *b* 22 March 1922; *Educ* Stratford House Sch Bickley, St Anne's Coll Oxford (MA), St Hugh's Coll Oxford; *m* 11 Jan 1958, Ven Bernard Clinton Pawley (d 1981), formerly Archdeacon of Canterbury, s of Lt Cdr Sylvester George Pawley, RN (d 1975), of Southwold; 1 s (Matthew James b 1962), 1 da (Felicity Ann b 1961); *Career* Lt Special Op Exec FANY Corps 1943-46, ME and Italy; tutor Open Univ 1975-84; *Books* Rome and Canterbury Through Four Centuries (with B C Pawley, 1974), Donald Coggan, Servant of Christ (1987), One Light for One World and The Unity we Seek (The Sermons of Archbishop Runcie, ed, 1988 and 1989), Praying with the English Tradition (1990), Prayers for Pilgrims (1991); *Recreations* reading, foreign travel; *Style*— Mrs Bernard Pawley; 3 North Court Oast, Old Wives' Lees, Canterbury, Kent (☎ 0227 730818)

PAWLEY, Prof (Godfrey) Stuart; s of George Charles Pawley (d 1956), of Bolton, Lancs, and Winifred Mary, *née* Wardle (d 1989); *b* 22 June 1937; *Educ* Bolton Sch, Univ of Cambridge (MA, PhD); *m* 29 July 1961, Anthea Jean, da of Rev Alan Miller (d 1981), of Northwich, Cheshire; 2 s (Philip b 1963, Graham b 1967), 1 da (Alison b 1965); *Career* prof of computational physics Univ of Edinburgh 1985- (lectr 1964-69, reader 1970-85), guest prof AÅrhus Univ of Denmark 1969-70; FRSE 1975; *Books* An Introduction to OCCAM-2 programming (jtly); *Recreations* choral singing, hill-walking; *Style*— Prof Stuart Pawley, FRSE; Physics Department, Edinburgh University, Kings Building EH9 3JZ (☎ 031 6505300 ext 2699, fax 031 6624712, telex 727442 UNIVED G)

PAWLOWSKI, Mark; s of Kazimierz Pawlowski, of 22 Cranley Gradens, London SW7, and Maria Zwienislawa, *née* Konkol; *b* 15 Sept 1953; *Educ* Wetherby Sch, St Benedicts Sch Ealing, Univ of Warwick (LLB), Wadham Coll Oxford (BCL); *m* 19 April 1986, Lidia Maria, da of Capt Jerzy de Barbaro; 1 da (Joanna Veronica b 9 Feb 1980); *Career* called to the Bar Middle Temple 1978; practice at Chancery Bar 1980-; Thames Poly: pt/t lectr 1980-83, lectr 1983-84, sr lectr 1984-; visiting lectr UCL 1990, memb convocation Wadham Coll Oxford 1983; ed law reports Journal of Rent Review and Lease Renewal; author numerous articles in learned jls on property landlord and tenant law 1984-; Sweet & Maxwell Law prize winner 1974; memb: Middle Temple, Soc of Public Teachers of Law, Br Polish Legal Assoc; ACIArb 1990; *Books* Casebook on Rent Review and Lease Renewal (with Diana Brahams, 1986); *Recreations* beekeeping, scuba diving, gardening, walking, travel; *Style*— Mark Pawlowski, Esq; 5 New Sq, Lincoln's Inn, London WC2A 3RJ (☎ 071 4056171/4797)

PAWLYN, (Doyran) Allen David; s of Clifford Peter Pawlyn, of Oxshott, Surrey, and Betty Winifred Mima, *née* Jones; *b* 11 April 1949; *Educ* Aldenham, Queen Elizabeth Coll London (BSc); *m* 24 Sept 1977, Celia Elizabeth, da of Antony Faraday Sandeman, of Winchelsea, East Sussex; 3 da (Katherine b 1980, Charlotte b 1982, Henrietta b 1987); *Career* ptnr Clark Whitehill CAs 1975; FCA 1973; *Recreations* photography, wine; *Style*— Allen Pawlyn, Esq; 30 Lower Green Rd, Esher, Surrey

PAWSEY, James Francis (Jim); MP (Cons) Rugby and Kenilworth 1983-; s of Capt William John Pawsey (d 1941), of 24 Moseley Avenue, Coventry, and Mary Victoria, *née* Mumford (d 1958); *b* 21 Aug 1933; *Educ* Coventry Tech Sch, Coventry Tech Coll; *m* 1956, Cynthia Margaret, da of Arthur James Francis, of Earlsdon Ave, Coventry; 6 s (Mark, Michael, Gregory, Clive (twin), Philip, Adrian (twin)); *Career* MP (C) Rugby 1979-83, memb: Exec Ctee 1922 Ctee 1989-, Select Ctee of the Parly Cmmn for Admin, vice chm Anglo Portuguese Gp; treas Br Bangladesh Parly Gp 1984-; memb: Rugby RDC 1964-73, Rugby Borough Cncl 1973-75, Warwickshire CC 1974-79; pps: DES 1982-83, DHSS 1983-84, NI Office 1984-86; vice chm Int Parly Union; chm Cons Backbench Educn Ctee 1985-; *Books* The Tringo Phenomenon; *Recreations* gardening; *Clubs* Carlton; *Style*— Jim Pawsey, Esq, MP; Shilton House, Shilton, Warwicks (☎ 0203 612922); Rugby and Kenilworth Cons Assoc, Albert Buildings, Albert St, Rugby (☎ 0788 569556); House of Commons, London SW1A 0AA (☎ 071 219 5127)

PAWSEY, Karol Anne; da of Hubert Sydney Pawsey, of Thurrock, Essex, and Kathleen Ada, *née* Jordan; *b* 26 July 1963; *Educ* Grays Sch Essex, Glos Coll of Art Cheltenham (BA, CNAA distinction for thesis); *Career* Fischer Fine Art London 1985-87, dir Curwen Gallery 1988- (joined 1987), work incl staging maj exhibitions featuring important Br and Euro artists and sculptors and commissioning of maj pub sculptures; *Style*— Ms Karol Pawsey; 361 Queenstown Rd, Battersea, London SW8 (☎ 071 627 1659); Curwen Gallery, 4 Windmill St, off Charlotte St, London W1P 1HF (☎ 071 636 1459, fax 071 436 3059)

PAWSON, Henry Anthony (Tony); OBE (1988); s of Albert Guy Pawson, CMG, of Nassau, and Helen Humphrey, *née* Lawson; *b* 22 Aug 1921; *Educ* Winchester, Ch Ch Oxford (MA); *m* Hilarie Anne, da of Lt-Col Tarn Prichard Bassett, DSO (d 1977), of Chilcomb; 2 s (Anthony James, John Henry), 1 da (Sarah Anne); *Career* Rifle Bde N Africa 1940-46, finished war as Maj (despatches); master at Winchester 1949-50, personnel dir Reed Paper Gp 1950-71, Southern sec Paper and Board Employers Fedn 1972-74, arbitration final stage HMSO procedure 1974-75, industl rels advsr Brewers Soc 1976-87, memb Southampton Industl Tbnl 1977-89, corr for Observer on cricket, soccer and angling, world and Euro flyfishing champion, only man since WWII to play as an amateur in Co Cricket (Kent) and First Div Soccer (Charlton); played in: MCC v S Africa 1947, Gentlemen v Players 1948; 12 rep caps for England amateur soccer team, 1982 GB Olympic soccer team; *Books* 100 Years of FA Cup, Official History (1971), Football's Managers, The Goalscorers, Runs and Catches, Competitive Worlds; *Recreations* fishing, cricket; *Style*— Tony Pawson, Esq, OBE; Manor House, Chilcomb, nr Winchester, Hants SO21 1HR (☎ 0962 861482)

PAWSON, Kenneth Vernon Frank; s of Capt Arnold Gilderdale Pawson (d 1937), and Freda Eunice Pawson; *b* 24 Sept 1923; *Educ* Rugby, Trinity Hall Cambridge; *m* 1950, Nicolette Vivian, da of Mervyn Thoresby (d 1965); 1 s, 2 da; *Career* Capt RB BAOR 1942-47; called to the Bar Gray's Inn 1949; md Joseph Hobson & Son Ltd (Brewers) 1954-74, dir Mount Charlotte Investments plc 1974-, chm and md Gale Lister & Co Ltd 1975-; *Recreations* shooting, fishing, farming, old cars; *Style*— Kenneth Pawson, Esq; Haggas Hall, Weeton, nr Leeds, Yorkshire (☎ 0423 734200); 59 St Dunstans Rd, London W6; 2 The Calls, Leeds 2 (☎ 0532 439111, telex 557934, fax 0532 442038)

PAWSON, Michael Edward; s of Edward Basil Pawson (d 1942), of Dyserth, Gwent, and Mary Bertha Batson, *née* Stephens (d 1979); *b* 10 June 1937; *Educ* Marlborough, St Thomas's Hosp Med Sch (MB BS); *m* 10 Aug 1961, Carolyn, da of Robert Cruickshank Handasyde (d 1979), of Kingsmead Cottage, Weybridge, Surrey; 1 s (Robert b 5 Nov 1964), 2 da (Alexandra b 8 Sept 1966, Lara b 23 Jan 1968); *Career* sr lectr Univ of London; conslt obstetrician and gynaecologist Charing Cross Hosp London 1974 (lectr 1970-74), examiner Univ of London and RCOG; memb: Br Fertility Soc, Br Holistic Med Assoc; MRCOG 1970, FRCOG 1981, LRCP, MRCS; *Books* numerous pubns on infertility; *Recreations* first edition book collecting, gardening; *Style*— Michael Pawson, Esq; 55 Wimpole St, London W1 (☎ 071 935 1964)

PAXMAN, Jeremy Dickson; s of Arthur Keith Paxman, of Queensland, Aust, and Joan McKay, *née* Dickson, of Bramhope, Yorkshire; *b* 11 May 1950; *Educ* Malvern, St Catharine's Coll Cambridge; *Career* reporter: Northern Ireland 1974-77, BBC Tonight 1977-79, Panorama 1979-84; presenter Six O'Clock News 1985-86, presenter and interviewer Breakfast Time 1986-89 and Newsnight 1989-; numerous contribs to newspapers and magazines; Royal TV Soc Award 1984; *Books* A Higher Form of Killing (jtly, 1982), Through the Volcanoes (1985), Friends in High Places (1990); *Recreations* fly fishing, mountains; *Style*— Jeremy Paxman, Esq; c/o David Higham Assocs, 5-8 Lower John St, London W1R 4HA

PAXMAN, Philip John; s of Edward Philip Paxman, JP (d 1949), and Dora Emily, *née* Bowen (d 1985); *b* 24 Oct 1941; *Educ* Oundle, St Johns Coll Cambridge (MA, Vet MB); *m* 13 Dec 1968, Mary Elizabeth, da of A E Witherow (d 1988); 2 s (Jeremy Edward b 1972, James Philip b 1977); *Career* lectr RVC 1966-69, fndr and chief exec Volac Ltd 1970-87, fndr and chm Animal Biotechnology Cambridge Ltd 1985-, chm Championship Foods Ltd; dir: Scottish Beef Developments Ltd, Cria Ovina de Malpica SA (Spain), Ovamass Ltd, Eurogen SRL Italy; RAS Technol prize 1985; tstee Univ of Cambridge Vet Sch Tst, memb Advsy Gp AFRC Inst of Animal Physiology and Genetics Res, chm Euro Assoc for Advanced Animal Breeding; Liveryman Worshipful Co of Farriers; MRCVS; *Recreations* fishing; *Clubs* Farmers; *Style*— Philip Paxman, Esq; South Farm, Shingay Cum Wendy, Royston, Herts SG8 0HR (☎ 0223 207581); Animal Research Station, Univ of Cambridge, 307 Huntingdon Rd, Cambridge CB3 0JQ (☎ 0223 277222, fax 277605)

PAXMAN, Hon Mrs (Rosetta Anne); *née* O'Neill; 2 da of 2 Baron Rathcavan (but eldest by his 2 w); *b* 14 Sept 1954; *m* 1977, Capt John Michael Anthony Paxman, Coldstream Gds; 1 s (Truscote Phelim b 1985), 2 da (Musidora b 1980, Zena b 1982); *Style*— The Hon Mrs Paxman

PAXTON, (Peter) Robin; s of Richard Gordon Paxton (d 1962), and Ilse Marianne Gertrud, *née* Grün; *b* 14 April 1951; *Educ* Leighton Park Sch Reading, Univ of Sussex, LSE, Nuffield Coll Oxford (BA, MSc); *m* 20 March 1987, Linda Jane, da of Raymond Edward John French, of Bournemouth; 2 s (Conrad b 1988, Caspar b 1990); *Career* LWT: dep ed Weekend World 1982-84, ed network features 1984-87, ed The London Programme 1987, head regnl programmes 1987-90, controller features and current affrs 1990-; *Recreations* skiing, arguing; *Style*— Robin Paxton, Esq; LWT, South Bank TV Centre, London SE1 (☎ 071 261 3434, telex 918123)

PAYKEL, Prof Eugene Stern; s of Joshua Paykel (d 1962), and Eva, *née* Stern; *b* 9 Sept 1934; *Educ* Auckland GS NZ, Univ of Otago (MB ChB, MD), Univ of Cambridge (MD), Univ of London (DPM); *m* 7 July 1969, Margaret, da of John Melrose (d 1966); 2 s (Nicholas b 1971, Jonathan b 1973); *Career* registrar then sr registrar Maudsley Hosp 1962-65, asst prof of psychiatry and co dir (later dir) Depression Res Unit Yale Univ 1966-71, prof of psychiatry St George's Hosp Med Sch Univ of London 1977-85 (conslt and sr lectr 1971-75, reader 1975-77), prof of psychiatry Univ of Cambridge and fell Gonville and Caius Coll 1985-; chief scientist advsr Mental Illness Res Liaison Gp DHSS 1984-88, memb Neuro Sciences Bd MRC 1981-85, hon sec Jt Ctee on Higher Psychiatric Trg 1988-, ed Jl of Affective Disorders 1979-; former examiner: Univ of Edinburgh, Univ of Nottingham, Univ of Manchester, Univ of London; RCPsych: examiner, chm Social and Community Psychiatry Section 1984-88, Cncl memb, memb Exec and Fin Ctee, memb Public Policy, Educn and Res Ctees; pres Br Assoc for Psychopharmacology 1982-84 (hon sec 1979-82); tstee Mental Health Fndn 1988-; Foundations Fund Prize for res in psychiatry 1978, second prize Anna Monika Stiftung 1985; Maudsley lectr RCPsych 1988; MRCPEd 1960, MRCP 1961, MRCPsych 1971, FRCP 1977, FRCPEd 1978, FRCPsych 1977; *Books* The Depressed Woman (1971), Psychopharmacology of Affective Disorders (1979), Monoamine Oxidase Inhibitors: the state of the art (1981), Handbook of Affective Disorders

(1982), Community Psychiatric Nursing for Neurotic Patients (1983), Depression: an Integrated Approach (1989); *Recreations* opera, music, theatre; *Clubs* Athenaeum; *Style—* Prof Eugene Paykel; Department of Psychiatry, Univ of Cambridge, Addenbrooke's Hosp, Hills Rd, Cambridge CB2 2QQ (☎ 0223 336961, fax 0223 336968)

PAYLING, Roger; *b* 18 Oct 1950; *Educ* Bournemouth & Poole Coll of Art (Dip Design); *Career* photographer 1975-; specialist in still life, cmmnd by many London advtg agencies; clients incl: American Express, British Gas, Liberty, Marks and Spencer, Salvador Dali; *Style—* Roger Payling, Esq; c/o Roger Payling Partnership, 27 Heddon St, London W1R 7L (☎ 071 734 3277)

PAYMASTER, Dr Nalin Jagmohandas; s of Jagmohandas Varajdas Paymaster, of 151 Buena Vista Apts, Genl Jagannath Bhosle Marg, Bombay, 400021, India, and Champa, *née* Shah; *b* 13 April 1933; *Educ* St Teresa's HS Bombay, Univ of Bombay (MB BS, DA), Univ of London (DA); *m* 30 Sept 1967, (Marjorie) Elaine, *née* Bankes; 1 s (Rajan b 1972), 1 da (Asha b 1969); *Career* res physician KEM Hosp Bombay 1957-59 (house physician 1956-57), sr house offr in anaesthesia United Liverpool Hosps 1959-60, anaesthetic registrar Liverpool Regnl Hosp Bd 1960-61, sr anaesthetic registrar Newcastle Regnl Hosp Bd 1961-62, fell in anaesthiology Univ of Pennsylvania Philadelphia 1962-63 and Univ of Washington Seattle 1963-64, conslt anaesthetist Mersey RHA 1965-; author on: pre medication, intravenous nutrition, post-operative pain, magnesium metabolism, intra cellular pH; *Recreations* photography, mountain walking, chess, bridge, swimming, cricket, table tennis; *Style—* Dr Nalin Paymaster; The Close, Chantry Walk, Lower Heswall, Wirral, Merseyside L60 8PX (☎ 051 3424143); Clatterbridge Hospital, Clatterbridge Rd, Bedington, Wirral, Mersyside L63 4JY (☎ 051 3344000, fax 051 3349299)

PAYNE, Alan Jeffrey; CMG (1988); s of Sydney Ellis Payne (d 1967), of Enfield, Middx, and Lydia Ethel, *née* Sweetman (d 1980); *b* 11 May 1933; *Educ* Enfield GS, Queens' Coll Cambridge (exhibitioner); *m* 6 June 1959, Emily Letitia, da of Frank Hodgkinson Freeman (d 1985); 3 s (Richard Andrew b 1960, David Jeffrey b 1963, Jeremy Martin b 1966); *Career* Nat Serv RN 1955-57; EMI Ltd 1957-62, NATO Secretariat Paris 1962-64; Dip Serv 1964-: first sec Kuala Lumpur 1967-70, asst head SW Pacific Dept FCO 1970-72, head Commercial Dept Br Embassy Budapest 1972-75, dep head Mission on promotion to cnsllr 1975-79, head Mexico and Caribbean Dept FCO 1979-82, consul general Lyons 1982-87, Br high cmmr Kingston Jamaica and non resident ambass Port-au-Prince Haiti 1987-89, sec gen International Primary Aluminium Inst (IPAI) 1989-; FIL 1962; *Recreations* theatre, music, restoring old cars; *Style—* Alan Payne, Esq, CMG; IPAI, 11 Floor, New Zealand House, Haymarket, London SW1Y 4TE

PAYNE, Anthony Edward; s of Edward Alexander Payne (d 1958), and Muriel Margaret Elsie, *née* Stroud; *b* 2 Aug 1936; *Educ* Dulwich, Univ of Durham (BA); *m* 24 Sept 1966, Jane Marian, da of Gerald Manning (d 1987); *Career* visiting Milhaud prof of music Mills Coll Oakland California 1983, teacher in composition NSW Conservatorium Sydney Aust 1986; composer; princ works incl: Phoenix Mass 1968-72, Paean (for solo piano, 1971), Concerto for Orchestra (1974), The World's Winter (for soprano and 8 players, 1976), Sting Quartet (1978), The Stones and Lonely Places Sing (for 7 players, 1979), The Song of the Clouds (for oboe and orchestra, 1980), A Day in the life of a Mayfly (for 6 players 1981), Evening Land (for soprano and piano, 1981) Spring's Shining Wake (for orchestra 1981), Songs and Seascapes (for strings 1984), The Spirit's Harvest (for orchestra 1985), The Song Streams in the Firmament (for 6 players 1986), Half Heard in the Stillness (for orchestra, 1987), Consort Music for string quintet (1987), Sea Change (for 7 Players, 1988), Time's Arrow (for orchestra, 1990); memb: Soc for the Promotion of New Music (chm 1969-71), Macnaghten Concerts Soc (chm 1965-67), Myra Hess Tst, Boise Mendelssohn Fndn; memb: Composers Guild of GB, Assoc of Professional Composers; *Books* Schoenberg (1988), Frank Bridge Radical and Conservative (1984); *Recreations* films, British countryside; *Style—* Anthony Payne, Esq; 2 Wilton Square, London N1 3DL (☎ 071 359 1593)

PAYNE, Christopher Frederick; CBE (1987), QPM (1975), DL (Cleveland 1983); s of Cdr Gerald Frederick Payne, OBE, BEM, QPM (d 1979), of Wallington, Surrey, and Amy Florence Elizabeth, *née* Parker (d 1989); *b* 15 Feb 1930; *Educ* Christ's Coll Finchley, Hendon Tech Coll; *m* 4 Oct 1952, Barbara Janet, da of Herbert Charles Saxby (d 1944), of Hampstead Way, Hampstead; 1 s (Roger b 1961), 3 da (Gillian b 1954, Adrianne b 1956, Valerie b 1965); *Career* Nat Serv Intelligence Corps 1948-50; Met Police: joined 1950, chief inspector Ops Branch 1963, supt and chief supt Hammersmith 1965-68, sr command course 1965, HO R and D Branch 1968-70, chief supt D Dist 1970-71, cdr X Dist 1971-74, cdr Airport Dist 1974-76, chief constable of Cleveland Constabulary 1976-90, dep regnl police cdr (designate) no 2 Home Def Region 1984-90, conslt Disaster Planning & Mgmnt 1990-, advsr Queensland Govt Chemical Hazards Unit 1989-90, memb UNDRO External Servs 1990-, emergency planning advsr Br Red Cross Cleveland 1990-; dep chm Met Police Friendly Soc 1971-76, police advsr to ACC Social Servs Ctee 1979-90, cdr St John Ambulance Cleveland 1985-89 (co dir 1978-85); chm: Cleveland Mental Health Support Gp 1981-86, St John Cncl Cleveland 1986-89; vice pres Cleveland Youth Assoc 1983-, vice chm Royal Jubilee and Prince's Tsts Ctee for Durham and Cleveland 1984-90, memb Editorial Bd Disaster Management Journal 1987-; author of various articles on contingency planning and management; CStJ 1985; Freeman City of London 1987; CBIM 1988; *Recreations* painting, philately, gardening; *Clubs* Royal Cwlth Tst, Cleveland; *Style—* Christopher Payne, Esq, CBE, QPM, DL; Lynwood, Hutton Rudby, North Yorkshire (☎ 0642 700296)

PAYNE, Lady Cynthia Lettice Margaret; *née* Bernard; da of late Lt-Col Ronald Percy Hamilton Bernard, ggs of 2 Earl Bandon; sis of 5 Earl Bandon, GBE, CVO, DSO (d 1979, when title became extinct); raised to the rank of an Earl's da 1925; *b* 1905; *m* 1, 1925 (m dis 1936), Lt-Col Francis Christian Darby Tothill, RB; 1 da; m 2, 1947, Air Cdre Lionel Guy Stanhope Payne, CBE, MC, AFC (d 1965); *Style—* Lady Cynthia Payne; 7 Thurloe Sq, London SW7

PAYNE, David John Allen; s of late Harry Payne, and late Edith Mary, *née* Kirby; *b* 29 July 1928; *Educ* Canterbury, Farnham, Brighton Coll of Art, Royal Acad Schs; *m* 11 Aug 1951, Iris Jean, da of late James Freeman; 1 s (Mark Allen b 21 April 1961), 1 da (Mary Anne b 30 Dec 1956); *Career* oil and watercolour artist; former sr lectr Bedford Coll of Higher Education; exhibited: Ash Barn Gallery Petersfield 1978-80, Bedford Sch 1973-76, The Gallery Wellingborough 1983-85, Ellingham Mill 1979-82, sponsored exhibition at Sotheby's 1981, Portal Gallery 1986, RA 1976 and 1978-87 and 1989, New Ashgate Gallery Farnham 1987; work in permanent collections incl Beds CC Educn Loan Serv; work reproduced and reviewed: ITV Folio 1982, BBC RA review 1983, BBC Academy Illustrated 1983-84; painter of triptychs many sold at RA; *Style—* David Payne, Esq

PAYNE, Harold Lloyd; OBE (1972); s of Horace Frederick Payne (d 1956), of Blackheath, and Dora Kate, *née* Lloyd (d 1972); *b* 16 Oct 1920; *Educ* City of London Sch; *m* 12 June 1942, Mary Mildred, da of William George Hill (d 1951), of Blackheath; 1 da (Lorna b 1949); *Career* TA HAC 1939, II Regt RHA 1939, cmmnd 137 FD Regt RA 1941 (Japanese POW 1942-45); dir Lloyd's Insurance Brokers 1937-80, memb Lloyd's 1949-88; forest owner 1974-; vice chm: Far East Fund, Cncl Br Serv Ex-Serv Orgns; tstee Queen Mary's Roehampton Hosp Tst, pres Nat Fedn of Far Eastern POW Assocs; memb: Bd Govrs Westminster Hosp Gp 1970-74, Central Advsy Ctee War Pensions, chm Kent War Pensions Ctee, Br Membs Cncl World Veterans Fedn, BMC/NUF Med Advsy Ctee; Freeman City of London 1951, Liveryman Worshipful Co of Carmen 1952; *Recreations* rugby, gardening; *Clubs* City Livery, Guild of Freemen; *Style—* Harold L Payne, Esq, OBE; Long View, 18 Whybourne Crest, Tunbridge Wells, Kent TN2 5BS (☎ 0892 27024); Foresters, Girnwood, Hawick, Roxburghshire, Scotland TD9 7PN (☎ 045088 203)

PAYNE, James Gladstone; s of Ralph Arthur Payne (d 1945), of NZ, and Mary Phillot, *née* Gladstone (d 1986); *Educ* Kings PS Auckland NZ, Wanganui Collegiate Sch NZ; *m* 24 July 1954, Margaret, da of Ronald Arthur Vestey (d 1988), of Thurlow Hall, Haverhill, Suffolk; 1 s (Micheal b 1959), 2 da (Nichola (Mrs McArthur) b 1955, (Philippa) Shirley (Mrs Beavan) b 1963); *Career* Nat Serv 1951-53 cmmnd 17/21 Lancers; md Assoc Container Transportation (Aust) Ltd 1969-73 (joined Blue Star Line 1953); dep chm 1974-79: Blue Star Line, Lamport and Holt Line, Booth Line; salmon farmer 1980-; chm Cncl of Euro and Japanese Shipowners Assoc 1977-79; *Recreations* swimming, sailing, stalking, scuba diving; *Clubs* Cavalry; *Style—* James Payne, Esq; Ardvar, Drumbeg-by-Lairg, Sutherland IV27 4NJ (☎ 057 13 260, fax 057 13 303)

PAYNE, Hon Mrs (Joan); *née* Spring Rice; o da of 5 Baron Monteagle of Brandon (d 1946), and Emilie de Kosenko; *b* 16 Aug 1928; *m* 15 May 1953, Michael Shears Payne, MC, o surv s of Rawdon Shears Payne; 1 s, 1 da; *Style—* The Hon Mrs Payne; Scotlands Farm, Cockpole Green, nr Wargrave, Berks RG10 8QP

PAYNE, Keith; VC (1969); s of Henry Thomas Payne; *b* 30 Aug 1933; *Educ* State Sch Ingham N Qld; *m* 1954, Florence Catherine Payne, *née* Plaw; 5 s; *Career* Aust Army Trg Team Vietnam 1969 (Warrant Offr), WO instr RMC Duntroon ACT 1970-72, 42 Bn Royal Qld Regt, Mackay 1973-75, Capt Oman Army 1975-76; *Style—* Keith Payne Esq, VC; St Bees Ave, Bucasia, via Mackay, Queensland, 4741, Australia (☎ 079 546125)

PAYNE, Keith Howard; s of Sydney William John Payne (d 1990), and Jean Emily, *née* Blower (d 1966); *b* 16 July 1937; *Educ* Shooters Hill GS; *m* 1, Dec 1972 (m dis); m 2, 23 Nov 1984, Tania Jeannette, da of Frank John Trevisani; 1 da (Francesca Jean b 13 April 1987); *Career* Nat Serv personal staff Dep SACEUR SHAPE Paris 1955-57; fin journalist The Times 1958-68 (first banking 1965-68); Charles Barker City 1968-91: dir 1970-74, asst md 1974-76, md 1976-80, dep chief exec and vice chm 1980-84, dep chm 1984-; dir Charles Barker Ltd 1988-, dep chm Charles Barker Financial Div 1991-; Freedom Nova Scotia Province (following journalistic visit with The Times) 1965; MInstPR; *Recreations* swimming, walking, theatre; *Style—* Keith Payne, Esq; Charles Barker Ltd, 30 Farringdon St, London EC4A 4EA (☎ 071 634 1310, fax 071 248 3582)

PAYNE, Kevin Jacques; s of Arthur Harold Payne (d 1982), and Margarita, *née* Bussell; *b* 6 May 1956; *Educ* Chelsea Coll London (BSc); *m* 5 May 1990, Jacqueline Kim, *née* Setchell; *Career* scientific res Immunology Dept Chelsea Coll 1977-80, asst ed Golf Illustrated 1980-82, md Kempsters PR 1987- (joined 1982); MIPR 1985 (vice chm Wessex branch 1990-91); *Recreations* scouting; *Style—* Kevin Payne, Esq; Kempsters PR, Essex House, Essex Rd, Basingstoke, Hants RG21 1SU (☎ 0256 842274, fax 0256 469308)

PAYNE, Lady; Maureen Ruth; da of William Charles Walsh; *m* 1951, as his 2 w, Sir Robert Frederick Payne (fndr memb British Acad of Forensic Sciences; d 1985), s of late Frederick Charles Payne; 1 s, 1 step s, 1 step da; *Style—* Lady Payne; Longview, 26 Swanland Hill, North Ferriby, N Humberside HU14 3JJ (☎ 0482 631533)

PAYNE, Michael Anthony; s of Albert John Payne, and Beryl Kathleen Cavey, *née* Slater; *b* 2 Sept 1939; *Educ* Stowe, City of Westminster Coll, Open Univ (BA); *m* 1965, Elizabeth Harvieston, da of Alan Brown, of Scotland; 1 s (Toby b 1970), 1 da (Sophie b 1968); *Career* Nat Serv 2 Lt Royal Regt of Artillery 1960-62, gunner HAC TA, Capt 254 FD Regt RA TA; co sec: Hill Samuel and Co (Jersey) Ltd 1978-88, Hill Samuel Investmt Servs Gp (Jersey) Ltd 1984-; dir: Hill Samuel (CI) Tst Co Ltd 1979-, Hill Samuel Fund Mangrs (Jersey) Ltd 1982-; MBIM, fell Chartered Assoc of Certified Accountants; Hon ADC to Lieut Govr of Jersey 1990-; *Recreations* historical reading, glass engraving; *Clubs* Honorable Artillery Co, United (Jersey); *Style—* Michael Payne, Esq; 3 Ashley Close, Bagatelle Rd, St Saviour, Jersey, CI; 7 Bond St, St Helier, Jersey C1 (☎ 0535 419 2167, fax 0534 79018)

PAYNE, Michael William; s of Albert Leonard Payne, MM, RFC (d 1955), of Orpington, Kent, and Grace Maud, *née* Lyon (d 1974); *b* 18 April 1927; *Educ* Dulwich; *m* 2 June 1951, Angela Margaret Westmacott, da of Hugh Sherwood Leary (d 1955); 2 s (Thomas b 1965, William b 1968), 2 da (Susan b 1952, Sally b 1956); *Career* Sgt RAF 1945-48; trainee underwriter 1948-50, dep underwriter 1950-57, gen mangr 1957-68, sr ptnr Michael Payne & Ptnrs 1967-; active underwriter: Sir William Garthwaite & Others 1969-71, Michael Payne & Others 1973-; exec chm: Janson Payne Mgmnt Ltd 1986-90, Michael Payne Syndicates Pty Ltd 1987-; chm Michael Payne Agencies Ltd 1989-, dep chm Janson Green Hldgs Ltd 1990-; memb Lloyds Law Reform Ctee 1968- (jt chm 1973-84), vice pres Insur Inst of London 1969-; Freeman City of London 1979, memb Worshipful Co of Insurers 1980; *Books* Modern Requirements in Liability Insurance (1968); *Recreations* golf, opera, music; *Clubs* City of London; *Style—* Michael Payne, Esq; Wroughton, 47 Sundridge Ave, Bromley, Kent (☎ 081 460 4924); Shene Cottage, Vicarage St, Colyton, Devon (☎ 0297 52621); 85 Gracechurch St, London EC3V OBH (☎ 081 623 6423, fax 081 283 4531, telex 8813816)

PAYNE, (Geoffrey John) Nicholas; s of John Laurence Payne (d 1961), and Dorothy Gwendoline, *née* Attenborough; *b* 4 Jan 1945; *Educ* Eton, Trinity Coll Cambridge (BA); *m* 6 Jan 1986, Linda Jane, da of Donald Wallace Adamson, of Bristol; 2 s (Ralph John Anthony b 1986, Oliver Nicholas Pearsall b 1988); *Career* fin asst Royal Opera House 1968-70, subsid offr Arts Cncl of GB 1970-76, fin controller WNO 1976-82, gen admin Opera North 1982-; artistic co-ordinator Leeds Festival 1990; *Style—* Nicholas Payne, Esq; Opera North, Grand Theatre, 46 New Briggate, Leeds LS1 6NU (☎ 0532 439 999, fax 0532 435 745)

PAYNE, Sir Norman John; CBE (1976, OBE 1956, MBE 1944); s of late Frederick Payne, of Folkestone; *b* 9 Oct 1921; *Educ* John Lyon Sch Harrow, City and Guilds Coll London; *m* 1946 (sep), Pamela Vivien, *née* Wallis; 4 s, 1 da; *Career* Capt RE (despatches twice), served India and Burma; ptnr Sir Frederick Snow & Ptnrs 1955 (joined 1949); chm Br Airports Authy 1977- (chief exec 1972-77); Hon DTech Loughborough Univ, fell Imperial Coll 1989; FRS, FENG, FCGI, FICE, FCIT, FIHT, CIMB, Companion RACS 1987; kt 1985; *Recreations* amateur photography; *Clubs* Reform, RAC; *Style—* Sir Norman Payne, CBE, FRS; BAA plc, Corporate Office, 130 Wilton Rd, London SW1V 1LQ

PAYNE, Raef John Godfrey; s of Lt-Col Lancelot Hugo Humphrey Payne (d 1955), of Pentre Uchaf Hall, and Gwendolyn Marguerite, *née* Philpot (d 1981); *b* 17 Aug 1929; *Educ* Eton, Trinity Coll Cambridge; *Career* master-in-coll Eton 1957-65 (asst master 1952), asst master Kilquhanity House Kirkcudbrightshire 1966, housemaster Eton

1967-84; *Recreations* retirement; *Style—* Raef Payne, Esq; Pentre Uchaf Hall, Maesbrook, Oswestry, Shropshire (☎ 0691 830 483)

PAYNE, Richard; s of Capt Matt Payne (d 1937), and Ellen Rosina, *née* Burdett (d 1989); *b* 26 June 1935; *Educ* Lancing, De Havilland Aeronautical Sch; *m* 30 Nov 1957, Ann Helen, da of Cyril Philip de Muschamp Porritt (d 1976); 2 s ((Peter) Matt, (Alexander) Richard de Muschamp), 1 da ((Helen) Annabel); *Career* supplies engr De Havilland's 1958-60, design and project engr Norris Bros (consulting engrs) 1961-62, tech mangr Kluber GmbH 1963-65, consulting engr 1966-68, fndr Thurne Engrg Co Ltd 1969 (md 1969-85, chm 1970-), md Edward Hines (engrs) Ltd 1970-89, md and chm Bronpole Gp 1975-; fndr: Thurne GmbH Germany 1985, Thurne Corpn 1985; chm Estuary Engrg 1989 (bought out by Thurne Engrg Co 1975); Queens Award for Technol 1988; memb MIMechE; *Recreations* sailing, skiing, gardening, reading; *Clubs* Norfolk; *Style—* Richard Payne, Esq; Bale Hall, Bale, Norfolk NR21 9DA (☎ 032 877 467); Bronpole Ltd & Thurne Engrg Co Ltd, Delta Close, Norwich (☎ 0603 41071, 0603 624281, fax 0603 487767, car 241878)

PAYNE, Richard William Newth; s of Stuart Dean Payne (d 1954), of Surrey, and Kathleen Amelia, *née* Newth (d 1981); *b* 14 Dec 1930; *Educ* Tonbridge, Univ of Bristol (BA); *m* 30 May 1964, Ann, da of David Windover Millard, of Surrey; 2 s (William b 1965, Timothy b 1967), 1 da (Annabel b 1971), 1 step s (Andrew Payne b 1956), 1 step da (Sarah b 1959); *Career* sr ptnr W H Payne & Co 1974- (ptnr 1955), dir Marlowe Investments (Kent) Ltd 1962-, dir Millard Estates Ltd 1980-; *Recreations* golf, gardening, bridge; *Clubs* MCC; *Style—* Richard Payne, Esq; Broadway, 11 Landscape Rd, Warlingham, Surrey CR3 9JB; 5 Los Almendros, Moraira, Teulada, Alicante, Espana; Sandringham House, 199 Southwark, Bridge Rd, London SE1 0HA

PAYNE, Lt-Col Robert Arnold; JP (1963); s of Robert William Tom Payne (d 1974), and Esther Victoria, *née* Elliott (d 1967); *b* 21 Sept 1919; *Educ* Finchley HS, Finchley Co GS; *m* 20 May 1950, Audrey Mary Jean, da of David Bradford, of 13 Russell Close, Little Chalfont, Bucks; 2 da (Jean Elizabeth b 6 July 1952, Patricia Mary (twin) b 6 July 1952); *Career* WWII Duke of Cornwall's LI 1939-40, cmmnd Beds Herts Regt 1940, Inf Signals Instr 1940, Orkney & Shetland Def Force 1941-42, Instr 160 Sp Gp OCTU 1942-43, 2 Bn Essex Regt 1944-45, Q staff 49 Inf Div HQ 1945-46; RARO 1949, Herts ACF 1953-61; Dep Co Cadet Cmdt 1958-61; memb: ACF Nat Trg Ctee 1961-63, advsy panel ACF Duke of Edinburgh's award 1963-87; hon first aid trg advsr Army and Combined Cadet Forces 1961-87, sr sec and accountancy asst Br Iron and Steel Corpn 1948-52, gp sec and dir subsid cos Int Aeradio Ltd 1952-77 (sec and fin conslt 1977-84); memb: Middx branch Magistrates Assoc Exec Ctee 1977-87 (chm 1984-87), St John Ambulance 1936- (dep cmmr London (Prince of Wales's) Dist 1969-78); Cdr Co of Buckinghamshire 1978-, Branch Ctee Royal Br Legion 1983-(chm 1985-89); hon treasurer: Middlesex Victoria Fund 1989-, Middlesex King Edward VII Meml Fund 1989-; Freeman City of London 1974, Liveryman Worshipful Co of Scriveners 1978; FCIS 1952, FBIM 1970, FFA 1977; Offr Cross of Merit Sovereign Military Order of Malta 1971; KStJ 1975; *Recreations* St John Ambulance, stamp collecting; *Style—* Lt-Col R A Payne, JP; 72 Amersham Rd, Little Chalfont, Amersham, Bucks HP6 6SL, (☎ 0494 764900)

PAYNE, Robert Gardiner; s of Dr Robert Orlando Payne (d 1989), and Frances Elisabeth, *née* Jackson (d 1987); *b* 12 July 1933; *Educ* Lady Barn House Sch, Packwood Haugh, Clifton, Trinity Hall Cambridge (MA); *m* 11 April 1964, Diana Catalina, da of Rupert Henry Marchington, of Wilton Crescent, Alderley Edge, Cheshire; 1 s (Philip Robert b 1968), 2 da (Frances Patricia b 1967, Emily Diana b 1972); *Career* Nat Serv 2 Lt RA 1952-54; admitted slr 1961; ptnr: Skelton and Co (Manchester) 1963-66, March Pearson and Skelton 1966-; chm: Family Welfare Assoc of Manchester, Lady Barn House Sch; dep chm David Lewis Centre for Epilepsy; memb Law Soc; *Recreations* opera, tennis, skiing, walking; *Clubs* St James' (Manchester); *Style—* Robert Payne, Esq; The Coach House, Brook Lane, Alderley Edge Cheshire SK9 7QJ (☎ 0625 583156); 41 Spring Gardens Manchester M2 2BB (☎ 061 832 7290, fax 061 832 2655, telex 669689)

PAYNE, Roger Jeremy; JP; s of Gordon Edgar Payne, OBE, JP (d 1988), and Dorothy Esther Payne; *b* 14 Dec 1937; *Educ* Wycliffe Coll Stonehouse Glos, Birmingham Sch of Architecture (DipArch); *m* 22 Aug 1964, Mary Nanette, da of William Henry Davis (d 1984); 1 s (Mark b 1969), 1 da (Sarah b 1972); *Career* sr ptnr Preece Payne Ptnrship; dir: Abbeybridge Property Gp Ltd, Claremont Rd Investmt Co Ltd, W Country Motor Hotel Servs, Preece Payne Conslt (Gibraltar); memb Br Equity, RIBA; *Recreations* theatre, power boating; *Clubs* Royal Yachting Assoc; *Style—* Roger Payne, Esq, JP; Little Gransmoor, Sussex Gardens, Hucclecote, Gloucester GL3 3ST; 39 Garbinell, Punta Montgo, L'Escala, Gerona, Spain; Bearland House, Longsmith St, Gloucester GL1 1HJ (☎ 24471, fax 300354, mobile 0860 553164)

PAYNE-GALLWEY, Sir Philip; 6 Bt (UK 1812); s of Lt-Col Lowry Philip Payne-Gallwey, OBE, MC, ggs of 1 Bt; suc kinsman, Sir Reginald Frankland-Payne-Gallwey, 5 Bt, 1964; assumed by Royal Licence 1966 the additional surname of Frankland before that of Payne and Gallwey; *b* 15 March 1935; *Educ* Eton; *Career* late Lt 11 Hussars; dir British Bloodstock Agency Ltd; *Style—* Sir Philip Payne-Gallwey, Bt; 1 Chapel View, High St, Lambourn, Newbury, Berks RG16 7XL

PAYNTER, Cecil de Camborne Pendarves; s of late Col E Pendarves Paynter, TD, of Fernchase Manor, Ashurst Park, Fordcombe, Kent, and late Cicely Marion, *née* Hadow; *b* 17 July 1930; *Educ* Summer Fields, Wellington, RMA Sandhurst; *m* 29 July 1961, Fiona Marion Naismith; 2 s (Michael John Pendarves b 1963, Andrew Francis de Camborne b 1965); *Career* Capt 3 Kings Own Hussars, airborne trg offr N Somerset Yeo; regnl mangr Rank Hovis McDougal, md Magnet Signs and Joinery, chm LGT Vending, dir English Wine Consortium; dir: Wine Standards Bd, Bd of Tstees Wine and Spirits Educn Tst; memb Cncl England Agric Show and Soc, gp chm Royal Br Legion W Kent; Swan Warden Ct Vintners' Co; *Recreations* country pursuits, golf, cricket, growing vines; *Clubs* Army and Navy; *Style—* C de C P Paynter, Esq; Rookery Cottage, Hever, nr Edenbridge, Kent (☎ 034 286 350)

PAYNTER, Prof John Frederick; OBE (1985); s of Frederick Albert Paynter (d 1968), and Rose Alice, *née* Garbutt (d 1963); *b* 17 July 1931; *Educ* Emanuel Sch London, Trinity Coll of Music London, Univ of York (DPhil); *m* 25 July 1956, Elizabeth, da of Matthew George Hill; 1 da (Catherine Elizabeth b 12 Aug 1957); *Career* teacher primary and secdy schs 1954-62, lectr in music City of Liverpool Coll of Educn 1962-65, princ lectr in music Bishop Otter Coll Chichester 1965-69; Dept of Music Univ of York: lectr 1969, sr lectr 1974-82, prof 1982, head of dept 1983; dir Schs Cncl Project Music in the Secdy Sch Curriculum; int lectures in music educn, books translated into numerous languages; compositions incl: Landscapes (1972), The Windhover (1972), Galaxies for Orchestra (1977), String Quartet (1981), The Inviolable Voice (1982), Piano Sonata (1987); Hon GSM Guildhall Sch of Music London; FRSA 1987; *Books* Sound and Silence (1970), Hear and Now (1972), The Dance and the Drum (1974), Music in the Secondary School Curriculum (1982), Sound and Structure (1990); *Style—* Prof John Paynter, OBE; Dept of Music, Univ of York, Heslington, York YO1 5DD (☎ 0904 432 444)

PAYTON, Robert Michael (Bob); s of Matthew Payton (d 1984), of Miami, and Frances, *née* Rosenzweig; *b* 25 May 1944; *Educ* Univ of N Carolina (BS), North Western Univ Chicago (MS); *m* 31 Dec 1987, Wendy Becker; *Career* advertising exec Chicago 1967, transferred London 1973; restaurant owner; fndr and proprietor My Kinda Town Group incl: The Chicago Pizza Pie Factory (his first restaurant, opened London 1977), The Chicago Rib Shack, Chicago Meatpackers with restaurants in Britain, Ireland, France, Spain; currently owner Stapleford Park Hotel Leicestershire; reg appearances on TV and radio and featured in newspapers worldwide; has published 12 edns of the Chicagoan Guide to London; *Recreations* song and dance, contemporary music and lifestyles; *Style—* Bob Payton, Esq; Stapleford Park, Stapleford, nr Melton Mowbray, Leics LE14 2EF (☎ 057 284 522, office 057 284 522, fax 057 284 651, car 083621 6779)

PAYTON, Roger Louis; s of Leonard Joseph Payton (d 1984), and Vera Mary, *née* Crepin; *b* 18 Oct 1930; *Educ* Caterham Sch London (LLB); *m* 10 May 1958, Geraldine Eyre, da of Wilfrid Farley (d 1974); 1 s (Christopher b 1961), 1 da (Jane b 1959); *Career* admitted slr 1958; dir: Baring Bros & Co Ltd 1969-84, Davies & Newman Holdings plc, Morland & Co plc, Stewart Underwriting plc 1985-, Roskel plc; dep chm Great Portland Estates plc; chm: Richardsons Westgarth plc 1988-(dir 1971), Waycom Holdings Ltd 1987-; Master Worshipful Co of Gardeners 1981-82; FRSA, FInstD; *Recreations* gardening, tennis; *Clubs* Savile; *Style—* Roger L Payton, Esq; Little Bedwell, Essendon, Hatfield, Herts AL9 6JA (☎ 0707 42623); 8 Bishopsgate, London EC2N 4AE (☎ 071 280 1000, fax 071 280 1181)

PEACE, Dr David Brian; MBE (1977); s of Herbert W F Peace (d 1951), of Sheffield, and Mabel, *née* Hammond (d 1915); *b* 13 March 1915; *Educ* Mill Hill Sch, Univ of Sheffield; *m* 2 Sept 1939, Jean Margaret, da of Rev McEwan Lawson, of Mill Hill; 2 da (Rachel (Mrs D Davies) b 1942, Juliet (Mrs C R Johnson) b 1946); *Career* WWII Sqdn Ldr Airfield Construction Serv RAF 1942-46; town planner: Staffs CC 1948-61, dep co planning offr and head of environmental planning Cambs CC 1961-80; glass engraver; 11 one man shows since 1956; work in 13 public collections incl: V & A, Fitzwilliam & Kettles Yard Cambridge, Broadfield House Nat Museum of Glass Stourbridge, Corning Museum USA, Keatley Tst collection; windows, screens, and doors in many churches incl: St Nicholas Liverpool, St Albans Cathedral, Westminster Abbey, St Nicholas Whitehaven, St Botolph Aldgate; retrospective exhibition 1990; memb: Ely Diocesan Advsy Ctee 1963, Cncl for Br Archaeology 1965-85; Master Art Workers Guild 1973, Liveryman Worshipful Co of Glaziers 1977, pres Guild of Glass Engravers 1980-86; Hon DScTech Univ of Sheffield 1991; ARIBA 1938, RTPI 1948 (memb Cncl 1961-62 and 1972-73), FSA 1975; *Books* Glass engraving: Lettering and Design (1985), The Engraved Glass of David Peace: the Architecture of Lettering (1990), Historic Buildings Maps and Guides: Peak District (1954), North Wales (1958), A Guide to Historic Buildings Law (1965), various publications on historic conservation and work of Eric Gill; *Recreations* townscape, heraldry; *Clubs* Arts; *Style—* Dr David Peace, MBE; Abbots End, Hemingford Abbots, Huntingdon, Cambs PE18 9AA, (☎ 0480 62472)

PEACE, Prof Richard Arthur; s of Herman Peace, of 24 Cross Green, Otley, W Yorks, and Dorthy, *née* Wall; *b* 22 Feb 1933; *Educ* Ilkley GS, Keble Coll Oxford (MA, BLitt); *m* 18 Oct 1960, (Shirley Mary) Virginia, da of Capt William George Wright (d 1969), of London; 1 s (Henry Richard b 24 April 1964, d 25 Sept 1975), 2 da (Mary b 7 April 1967, Catherine b 14 Jan 1969); *Career* prof of Russian: Univ of Hull 1975-84, Univ of Bristol 1984- (lectr 1963, sr lectr 1972-75); pres Br Univs Assoc Slavists 1977-80; *Books* Dostoyevsky: An Examination of The Major Novels (1971), The Enigma of Gogol (1981), Chekhov: A Study of The Four Major Plays (1983); *Recreations* fishing; *Style—* Prof Richard Peace; Dept of Russian Studies, Univ of Bristol, 17 Woodland Rd, Bristol BS8 1TE (☎ 0272 303030 ext 3516)

PEACEY, Col John Capel (Charles); *b* 11 Dec 1928; *Educ* Marlborough, Bournemouth Municipal Coll (Dip Mech Eng); *m* 17 July 1954, Dr Jean Menzies Peacey, *née* Thirlby; 2 da (Susan (Mrs Graves), Diana (Mrs Taine)); *Career* cmmnd RE 1949; various appts mainly of professional engrg interest UK Malaya Germany and Singapore 1950-71, SO I Logistics Petroleum AFSOUTH Naples Italy 1971-73, chief instr Electrical and Mechanical Sch RSME Chatham 1973-75, CRE specialist team RE acting as consltg engrs for Govt of Malta 1975-77, cdr RE team Br Mil Mission to Saudi Nat Gd Riyadh Saudi Arabia 1978-80, chief infrastructure progs and SACEURS rep on NATO Infrastructure Ctee 1980-83, ret; dep sec ACE (asst sec from 1984); Freeman City of London, Liveryman Worshipful Co of Engrs 1986; FICE, FIMechE; *Recreations* golf, family bridge, gardening, conservation, local history; *Style—* Col Charles Peacey; 11 Prospect Row, Brompton, Gillingham, Kent ME7 5AL (☎ 0634 843123); 46 Riverside Court, Nine Elms Lane, London SW8 5BY (☎ 071 627 2818); Association of Consulting Engineers, Alliance House, 12 Caxton St, London SW1H 0QL (☎ 071 222 6557)

PEACH, Denis Alan; s of Richard Peach (d 1979), of Worthing, and Alice Ellen, *née* Fraser (d 1982); *b* 10 Jan 1928; *Educ* Selhurst GS; *m* 1957, Audrey Hazel, da of Allan Chamberlain (d 1970); *Career* Home Office 1946-82 (asst under-sec state 1974-82); chief charity cmmr 1982-; *Recreations* painting, gardening; *Clubs* Reform; *Style—* Denis Peach, Esq; 36 The Vale, Coulsdon, Surrey CR3 2AW (☎ 081 660 6752; office: 071 214 6069)

PEACH, Sir Leonard Harry; s of Harry Peach (d 1985), of Walsall, Staffs, and Beatrice Lilian, *née* Tuck (d 1978); *b* 17 Dec 1932; *Educ* Queen Mary's GS Walsall, Pembroke Coll Oxford (MA), LSE (Dip Personnel Mgmnt); *m* 15 March 1958, Doreen Lilian, da of John Roland Barker (d 1979), of W Molesey, Surrey; 2 s (Mark Philip b 1964, David John b 1967); *Career* Nat Serv 1951-53, 2 Lt 1 Bn S Lancs Regt 1952; Capt TA S Bn 5 Staffs Regt 1953-65; res asst to Randolph S Churchill 1956, various personnel mgmnt appts 1956-71; dir IBM: UK Rentals 1971-76, UK Holdings 1976-85 and 1989-, Pensions Trust 1976-85 and 1989-; gp dir personnel IBM (Europe, Africa, Middle East) 1972-75, dir of personnel and corp affrs IBM UK Ltd 1975-85 and 1989 (dir of personnel 1971-72), pres IPM 1983-85, seconded to DHSS as dir of personnel NHS Mgmnt Bd 1985-86, chief exec NHS Mgmnt Bd 1986-89, dir Nationwide Building Soc 1990-; chm: NHS Trg Authy 1986-, chm Skillbase Ltd 1990-; memb: Data Protection Tbnl 1985-, NHS Supervisory Bd 1986-89; chm IPM Servs Ltd, vice chm PCL, govr Portsmouth GS; FRSA 1979, CIPM 1983, CIBM 1988; *Recreations* opera, theatre, cricket, gardening; *Style—* Sir Leonard Peach; Crossacres, Meadow Rd, Wentworth, Virginia Water, Surrey GU25 4NH (☎ 099 04 2258); IBM UK Ltd, PO Box 41, North Harbour, Portsmouth, Hants PO6 3AU (☎ 0705 321 212, telex 86741 IBM FOR G) 86741 (IBM PQR G)

PEACOCK, Prof Sir Alan Turner; DSC (1945); s of Prof Alexander David Peacock (d 1976), and Clara Mary, *née* Turner (d 1983); *b* 26 June 1922; *Educ* Dundee HS, Univ of St Andrews (MA); *m* 23 Feb 1944, Margaret Martha, da of Henry John Astell Burt (d 1960); 2 s (David Michael b 1945, Richard Alan b 1947); 1 da (Helen Mary Charlton b 1950); *Career* Lt RNVR 1943-45; prof of econs: Univ of Edinburgh 1956-62, Univ of York 1962-77, Univ of Buckingham 1978-84 (princ vice chllr 1980-84); chief econ advsr and dep sec DTI 1973-76, chm Ctee on Financing BBC 1985-86; res prof public fin Heriot-Watt Univ; chm Scottish Arts Cncl 1986-, exec dir David Hume Inst Edinburgh 1985-90, managing tstee Inst of Econ Affrs 1987-, memb Panel of Econ Advsrs Sec of State for Scotland 1987-; hon doctorate: Stirling 1974, Zurich 1984, Buckingham 1986, Brunel 1989, Univ of St Andrews; FBA 1979, FRSE 1989; kt 1987;

Books numerous books and publications in professional journals mainly on economics topics and occasionally on music; *Recreations* trying to write serious music, wine spotting; *Clubs* Reform, Naval; *Style*— Prof Sir Alan Peacock, DSC, FRSE; 8 Gilmour Rd, Edinburgh EH16 5NF (☎ 031 667 0544); David Hume Institute, 21 George Sq, Edinburgh EH8 9LD (☎ 031 667 7004)

PEACOCK, Annette; da of Miles Coleman (d 1969), and Frieda, *née* Morell (d 1990); *b* 8 Jan 1941; *Educ* El Cajon HS, LACC, Mill Brook, Julliard Sch of Music; *m* 1, 1960 (m dis 1967), Gary Peacock; 1 da (Solo b 5 Aug 1966); m 2, 31 Aug 1983, Jeremy Belshaw, s of Prof DGR Belshaw; 1 da (Avalon b 15 Oct 1983); *Career* originator of Free-Form Songform and Philosetry and voice plus band through prototype synthesizers, electronic arranger, prodr, record company proprietor; works incl LPs: Revenge 1969, Improvisie 1971, Dual Unity 1972, I'm The One 1972, X-Dreams 1978, The Perfect Release 1979, Sky-Skating 1982, Been in the Streets Too Long 1983, I Have No Feelings 1986, Abstract-Contact 1988; performances incl: Wired For Sound, Philharmonic Hall, Lincoln Center NYC 1970, Montreux Jazz Festival 1972, holographic actress in show with Salvador Dali on Broadway NYC 1973; WOMAD 1982 and 1986, MCPS, PRS; *Style*— Ms Annette Peacock; Ironic Records, PO Box 58, Wokingham, Berks RG11 7HN (☎ 0344 772061)

PEACOCK, Elizabeth Joan; MP (C) Batley and Spen 1983-, JP (1975); da of late John William Gates, and Dorothy Gates; *b* 4 Sept 1937; *Educ* St Monica's Convent Skipton; *m* 1963, Brian David Peacock, s of late David Peacock, of East Marton, Skipton, N Yorks; 2 s (Jonathan, Nicholas); *Career* memb Select Ctee on: Employment 1983-87, House of Commons Services 1988-; vice chm Back Bench Party Orgn Ctee 1984-86, memb Exec Ctee 1922 Ctee 1987-, hon sec Yorks Cons Membs Gp 1983-87, vice pres Yorkshire Area Young Cons 1984-87; memb UK Fedn of Business and Professional Women 1965-; hon pres Nat Assoc of Approved Driving Instrs 1984-88, pres Yorkshire Cons Trade Unionists 1988-; chm: All Party Wool Textile Gp 1989-, All Party Transpennine Gp 1989-; vice pres: Yorkshire and Humberside Devpt Assoc, W Yorkshire Pre-Retirement Assoc; dir: Transpennine Ltd, Shilton Investments Ltd; memb BBC Gen Advsy Cncl; *Recreations* motoring, theatre; *Clubs* House of Commons Motor (sec); *Style*— Mrs Elizabeth J Peacock, MP, JP; House of Commons, London SW1A OAA (☎ 071 219 4092)

PEACOCK, Sir Geoffrey Arden; CVO (1977); s of Warren Turner Peacock (d 1966), of Crowthorne, and Elsie, *née* Naylor (d 1965); *b* 7 Feb 1920; *Educ* Wellington, Jesus Coll Cambridge (MA); *m* 1949, Mary Gillian Drew, da of Dr Harold Drew Lander (d 1967), of Cornwall; 2 da; *Career* served RA and Royal Lincoln Regt 1939-46, Lt-Col AA Cmd and Burma; pres War Crimes Ct Singapore; called to the Bar Inner Temple, legal asst Treasy Slr's Dept 1949, princ Treasy 1954, sr legal asst Treasy Slr's Dept 1958; Remembrancer City of London 1968-81; Master: Worshipful Co of Watermen and Lightermen of the River Thames 1986, Worshipful Co of Pewterers 1985, 1986 and 1988; kt 1981; *Recreations* sailing, rowing, beagling; *Clubs* Leander, London Rowing, Cruising Assoc, City Livery; *Style*— Sir Geoffrey Peacock, CVO; Haymarsh, Duncton, nr Petworth, West Sussex GU28 0JY

PEACOCK, Graham John; s of John Eward Peacock (d 1946), of 60 Herne Hill Rd, London, and Grace Hendry, *née* Samdison; *b* 21 Dec 1944; *Educ* Sedgehill Sch Beckenham Kent; *m* 26 April 1969 (m dis 1981), Outi-Maija, da of Paavo Hietanen (d 1970); 2 s (John Edward b 19 Dec 1969, Angus Graham b 14 July 1971); m 2, 23 March 1985, Georgina Barbara, da of Walter Albert Lloyds (d 1984); 1 s (Ross Graeme Mathew b 13 June 1982), 1 da (Hannah Rose Grace b 12 Sept 1986); *Career* memb Met Police 1964-; memb: London branch Royal Order of St George, Farringdon Without Ward; Police Long Serv and Good Conduct Medal; Freeman City of London 1976, Liveryman Worshipful Co Loriners 1977; *Recreations* rugby, shooting; *Clubs* City Livery, United Wards; *Style*— Graham Peacock, Esq; 80 Chapel Green, Reedham Drive, Purley, Surrey CR2 4DS (☎ 081 660 5497); Norbury Police Station, 1516 London Rd, Norbury SW16 4EU (☎ 081 680 6100)

PEACOCK, Ian Douglas; s of Andrew Inglis Peacock (d 1981), of Sevenoaks, Kent, and Minnie Maria, *née* King (d 1978); *b* 9 April 1934; *Educ* Sevenoaks Sch; *m* 21 July 1962, Joanna Hepburn, da of George Milne MacGregor, of Strathaven, Lanarkshire; 1 s (Colin Michael b 8 Sept 1963), 1 da (Susan Jean b 2 May 1965); *Career* PO RAF 1953-54, Flying Offr RAuxAF 1955-58; md: Slazenger Ltd 1976-83 (mktg dir 1973-76), Sports Mktg Surveys Ltd 1983-85; exec dir Lawn Tennis Assoc 1986-; chm Golf Ball 1975-, pres Br Sports and Allied Industs Fedn 1983-85, cncllr and dir Golf Fndn 1984-; *Recreations* golf, skiing; *Clubs* RAF, Royal Ashdown Forest Golf, Queens; *Style*— Ian Peacock, Esq; Moat End House, Church Lane, Burstow, Surrey (☎ 034284 2262), The Lawn Tennis Assoc, Queens Club, Palliser Rd, London W14 (☎ 071 3852366)

PEACOCK, Ian Rex; s of Mervyn George Peacock, of Bristol, and Evelyn Joyce, *née* Gay; *b* 5 July 1947; *Educ* Trinity Coll Cambridge; *m* 31 March 1973, Alyanee, da of Lt-Gen Amnuay Chya-Rochana; 1 s (Christopher b 5 May 1982); *Career* economist Unilever Ltd 1968-72, Cripps Warburg Ltd 1972-75; Kleinwort Benson Limited: asst mangr Credit Dept 1976-77, mangr Hong Kong Office 1978-81, asst dir of corporate banking London 1981-82, dir North American Dept London 1984-85 (asst dir 1983-84), dir NY Office 1985-87, dir of corporate banking London 1987-; *Clubs* United Oxford and Cambridge Univ; *Style*— Ian Peacock, Esq; Kleinwort Benson Limited, 20 Fenchurch St, London EC3P 3DB (☎ 071 623 8000)

PEACOCK, Prof Joseph Henry; s of Harry James Peacock, OBE (d 1975), and Florence, *née* Milton (d 1979); *b* 22 Oct 1918; *Educ* Reading Sch, Bristol GS, Univ of Birmingham (MB ChB); *m* 24 June 1950, Gilliam Frances, da of Frederick George Augustus Pinckney (d 1951), of The Old Vicarage, Fisherton De La Mere, Wylye, Wilts; 1 s (Colin Henry b 1954), 1 da (Christabel Phyllis b 1958); *Career* WWII RAMC 1942-47, RMO 19 Royal Fus 1943, served hosps India and Malaya; demonstrator in anatomy Univ of Birmingham 1947, prof of surgical sci Univ of Bristol 1972 (lectr 1953, reader 1965); conslt surgn: United Bristol Hosps 1955, SW Regnl Hosp Bd 1960; memb: Gen Med Cncl 1975-85 (chm Overseas Sub Ctee F 1980-85), SW Regnl Hosp Bd 1975-84 (chm res ctee 1981-84), pres Vascular Surgical Soc GB 1976 (fndr memb), memb Surgical Res Soc and Euro Soc of Surgical Res; Rockefeller fell Ann Arbor Michigan 1950; examiner LDS 1958-63, primary FRCS 1965-71 (memb Ct of Examiners 1976-82, chm 1982); examiner in surgery: Univ of Bristol, Univ of Birmingham, Univ of London, Univ of Wales, Univ of Liverpool, Univ of Ghana, Univ of Sudan; Jacksonian prize RCS 1954 and 1967, Hunterian prof 1956, Arris and Gale lectr 1960; memb of Ct: Univ of Bath, Univ of Bristol; MRCS 1941, LRCP 1941, FRCS 1949, memb BMA, fell Assoc Surgns GB, hon memb Coller Surgical Soc USA; *Books* Liver Transpantation & Vascular Surgery (contrib, 1960), Colston Symposium (1967), Liver Transplantation (1988); *Recreations* short wave radio, gardening, travel; *Clubs* Army and Navy; *Style*— Prof Joseph Peacock; The Old Manor, Ubley, Nr Bristol BS18 6PJ (☎ 0761 62733)

PEACOCK, (Ian) Michael; s of Norman Henry Peacock (d 1973), and Sara Barbara Turnbull, *née* Muir (d 1989); *b* 14 Sept 1929; *Educ* Kimball Union Acad USA, Welwyn Garden City GS, LSE; *m* 1956, Daphne Joyce Lee; 2 s (Adam Michael b 1960, Caspar David b 1963), 1 da (Emma Jane Sylvia b 1969); *Career* md Video Arts TV Ltd 1978-, chm Monitor Enterprises Ltd 1970-; dir: Video Arts Ltd, Greater Manchester Ind Radio Ltd; yachtsman; memb: UK team for Admiral's Cup 1987 (Juno III), 1989 (Juno IV), 1990 (Juno V), UK Kenwood Cup team 1988, UK Southern Cross team 1989 (capt), UK Sardinia Cup team 1990; *Clubs* Royal Thames Yacht, Royal Lymington Yacht, Royal Southern Yacht, Royal Ocean Racing; *Style*— Michael Peacock, Esq; 21 Woodlands Rd, Barnes, London SW13 0JZ (☎ 081 876 2025)

PEACOCK, Prof Raymond Dixon; s of James Archibald Peacock (d 1980), and Hilda, *née* Dixon (d 1989); *b* 24 May 1927; *Educ* Newcastle-upon-Tyne Royal GS, Univ of Durham (BSc, PhD), Univ of Birmingham (DSc); *m* 15 April 1961, Dorine, da of Alan Niven Ainsworth (d 1976); 2 s (Malcolm b 1962, Duncan b 1966), 1 da (Helen b 1965); *Career* asst lectr and lect Imperial Coll 1953-58, lectr and sr lectr Univ of Birmingham 1958-65; Univ of Leicester: prof inorganic chemistry 1965-68, pro vice chllr 1970-73 and 1983-87, prof emeritus 1988-; FRSC 1974; *Recreations* mountain-walking, cycling, mucic, place names; *Style*— Prof Raymond Peacock; Dept of Chemistry, Univ of Leicester, Leicester LE1 7RN (☎ 0533 522522)

PEACOCK, Trevor Edward; s of Victor Edward Peacock (d 1970), of Enfield, Middx, and Alexandra Victoria, *née* Mathews (d 1986); *b* 19 May 1931; *Educ* Enfield GS, Univ of Oxford (Dip Ed); *m* 1, Sept 1957 (m dis 1978), Iris, da of Charles Jones; 1 s (Daniel b 2 Oct 1958), 1 da (Sally Georgia b 16 Feb 1960); m 2, 10 Aug 1979, Victoria Tilly, *née* Sanderson; 1 s (Harry Lemuel Xavier b 25 Aug 1978), 1 da (Maudie Mary b 21 Jan 1982); *Career* Nat Serv 1949-51; actor: Titus in Titus Andronicus, Nathan Detroit in Guys and Dolls, Willy Mossop in Hobsons Choice, Estragon in Waiting for Godot, Tony Lumplein in She Stoops To Conquer; TV series: Born and Bred (Thames TV), The Old Curiosity Shop (BBC), Wish Me Luck (LWT); composer: Erb, Leaping Ginger, Andy Cap, Class K; fndr memb Royal Exchange Theatre Manchester, Ivor Novello award; memb: Amnesty Int, Oxfam, Performing Rights Soc, Writer's Guild; *Recreations* cricket, music, reading, rolling (down grassy slopes); *Style*— Trevor Peacock, Esq; 33 Queens Road, Richmond, Surrey TW10 6JX

PEACOCKE, Rev Dr Arthur Robert; s of (Arthur) Charles Peacocke (d 1961), of Watford, Herts, and Rose Elizabeth, *née* Lilly (d 1967); *b* 29 Nov 1924; *Educ* Watford Boys' GS, Exeter Coll Oxford (BA, BSc, MA, DPhil, DSc, DD), Univ of Cambridge (ScD by incorporation), Univ of Birmingham (BD); *m* 7 Aug 1948, Rosemary Winifred, da of Edgar Mann (d 1970), of Cheltenham; 1 s (Christopher b 1950), 1 da (Jane b 1953); *Career* Univ of Birmingham 1948-59: asst lectr, lectr, sr lectr; lectr in biochemistry Univ of Oxford, fell and tutor St Peter's Coll Oxford 1959-73; Clare Coll Cambridge 1973-84: dean, fell, tutor and dir of studies in theology; prof Judeo-Christian Studies Tulane Univ 1984, dir Ian Ramsey Centre St Cross Coll Oxford 1985-88; lay reader Oxford Dio 1960-71, ordained 1971, vice pres Science and Religion Forum 1978- (chm 1972-78), warden Soc of Ordained Scientists 1987-; Hon Chaplain Christ Church Cath Oxford 1988-; Univ of Oxford: Bampton lectr 1978, select preacher 1973 and 1975; Hulsean preacher Univ of Cambridge 1976; sec then chm Br Biophysical Soc 1965-69; Lecomte du Nouy Prize 1983; Hon DSc De Pauw Univ Indiana 1983, Academic fell Inst on Religion in an Age of Sci 1986; *Books* Molecular Basis of Heredity (with JB Drysale, 1965), Science and the Christian Experiment (1971), Osmotic Pressure of Biological Macromolecules (with M P Tombs, 1974), From Cosmos to Lovê (with J Dominian, 1974), Creation and the World of Science (1974), Intimations of Reality (1984), God and the New Biology (1986), The Physical Chemistry of Biological Organization (1983), Persons and Personality (ed with G Gillet, 1987), Theology for a Scientific Age (1990); *Recreations* music, hill walking, churches; *Style*— The Rev Dr Arthur Peacocke; 55 St John St, Oxford, OX1 2LQ (☎ 0865 512 041); St Cross College, Oxford, OX1 3LZ

PEACOCKE, Prof Christopher Arthur Bruce; s of Arthur Robert Peacocke, and Rosemary Winifred Mann; *b* 22 May 1950; *Educ* Magdalen Coll Sch Oxford, Exeter Coll Oxford (MA, BPhil, DPhil); *m* 3 Jan 1980, Teresa Anne, *née* Rosen; 1 s, 1 da; *Career* jr res fell Queens Coll Oxford 1973, prize fell All Souls Coll Oxford 1975, fell and tutor and CUF lectr in Philosophy, New Coll Oxford 1979, Susan Stebbing Prof of Philosophy KCL 1985-88; visiting prof: Univ of Berkeley 1975, Ann Arbor Univ 1978, UCLA 1981, Univ of Maryland 1987; visiting fell ANU 1981, fell Centre for Advanced Study in the Behavioural Sciences Univ of Stanford 1983, Waynflete prof of metaphysical philosophy Univ of Oxford 1989-, fell Magdalen Coll Oxford 1989-; papers on philosophy of mind, language and logic; pres Mind Assoc 1986, current vice pres Mind Assoc; FBA 1990; *Books* Holistic Explanation: Action, Space, Interpretation (1979), Sense and content (1983), Thoughts: an Essay on Content (1986); *Recreations* music, visual arts; *Style*— Prof Christopher Peacocke; Magdalen Coll, Oxford (☎ 0865 276000)

PEACOCKE, Col Christopher Gaussen; s of Rt Rev Bishop Cuthbert Irvine Peacocke, TD, of Cromlyn Cottage, Hillsborough, Co Down, and Helen Louise, *née* Gaussen (d 1988); *b* 11 March 1938; *Educ* Marlborough, RMCS, Univ of London (BSc); *m* 13 Feb 1965, Virginia Gay, da of Col Alexander James Henry Cramsie, OBE, DL (d 1987), of O'Harabrook, Ballymoney, Co Antrim; 1 s (Henry b 1972), 2 da (Emma b 1967, Louise b 1968); *Career* cmmnd to 1 Queen's Dragoon Gds 1959, Army staff course 1970-71, Col 1985; *Recreations* shooting, fishing; *Clubs* Cavalry and Guards; *Style*— Col Christopher Peacocke; Glentoran, Penton Grafton, Andover, Hampshire (☎ 0264 773110); Ministry of Defence, 23-24 Soho Square, London W1V 5FJ (☎ 071 6324872, fax 071 6324776)

PEAFORD, Alan James; s of James William Thomas Peaford (d 1986), and Iris Maud, *née* Tustain; *b* 31 Oct 1952; *Educ* Ockendon Court, Harlow Coll Cranfield (Mktg Mgmnt Dip); *m* 17 Dec 1978, Jane Elizabeth, da of John Donald Saxton; 1 s (Thomas James Charles b 16 Feb 1982), 2 da (Sara Jane b 20 Aug 1980, Victoria Lesley b 28 March 1985); *Career* journalist; Express Newspapers 1971-74, Westminster Press 1975-76, Times Newspapers 1977-, night ed Arab Times 1977-78, dep ed Gulf Daily News 1978-79, PR and communications mangr British Petroleum 1980-88, md Charles Barker 1988-90, chief exec Barkers Trident Communications 1990-; awards: Foreign Corr of the Year 1977, Safety Writer of the Year 1982; nat chm BAIE 1989-90 (memb 1981, fell 1986), memb Bd Nat Youth Theatre 1988, chm Cornelia de Lange Syndrome Fndn 1990; *Recreations* cricket, debating, eating, theatre, tennis, watching West Ham; *Clubs* Wig & Pen, Oil Industries, Round Table; *Style*— Alan Peaford, Esq; Barkers Trident Communications, The Smokehouse, 44-46 St John St, London EC1M 4DT (☎ 071 253 1514, fax 071 253 4740)

PEAKE, Brig (Anthony) Brian Lowsley; QHS (1983-85); s of Col Henry Gilbert Peake (d 1972), and Ethel Ruie, *née* Lowsley (d 1977); *b* 18 March 1925; *Educ* Epsom Coll, Univ of Cambridge (MA), St Thomas's Hosp; *m* 23 May 1959, Barbara Grace, da of Dr William Alexander Lister (d 1981); 1 s (David b 1960), 3 da (Dinah b 1961, Gillian b 1966, Rachael b 1968); *Career* RAMC 1953-85, Brig, CO BMH Hannover 1972-73, CO LMMH Aldershot 1983-85, conslt advsr to MOD in Obstetrics and Gynaecology; memb postgrad ctee RCOG 1983-85; MRCS, LRCP, FRCOG; *Recreations* fly fishing, game shooting, stalking; *Style*— Brig Brian Peake, QHS; Parsonage House, Hampstead Norreys, nr Newbury, Berks

PEAKE, David Alphy Edward Raymond; s of Sir Harald Peake (d 1978), and his 1 w Resy, OBE, *née* Countess de Baillet Latour; *b* 27 Sept 1934; *Educ* Ampleforth, ChCh Oxford; *m* 1962, Susanna, da of Sir Cyril Kleinwort (d 1980); 1 s, 1 da; *Career* 2 Lt Royal Scots Greys 1953-55; banker; chm: Hargreaves Gp plc 1974-86, Kleinwort Benson Gp plc 1989-; dir: Kleinwort Benson Ltd 1971-, BNP plc; *Clubs* Brooks's,

Cavalry and Guards', Pratt's; *Style—* David Peake, Esq; Sezincote House, Moreton-in-Marsh, Glos (☎ 0386 700 444); 15 Ilchester Place, London W14 (☎ 071 602 2375)

PEAKE, Air Cdre Dame Felicity Hyde (Lady Peake); DBE (1949, MBE 1941), AE, JP; da of late Col Humphrey Watts, OBE, TD; *b* 1 May 1913; *Educ* St Winifred's Eastbourne, Les Grands Huguenots (Vaucresson, Seine et Oise, France); *m* 1, 1935, John Charles Mackenzie Hanbury (ka 1939); m 2, 1952, as his 2 w, Sir Harald Peake, AE (d 1978); 1 s (Andrew, b 1956); *Career* joined ATS Co of RAF 1939, cmmnd WAAF 1939, served at home and M East; dir: WAAF 1946-49, WRAF (from its inception) 1949-50; ret 1950; hon ADC to King George VI 1949-50; memb RAF Benevolent Fund 1946- (vice-pres 1978), tstee Imperial War Museum 1963-85, re-elected govr London House 1978-; pres The Friends of the Imperial War Museum 1988- (fndr memb and chm 1986-88); *Style—* Air Cdre Dame Felicity Peake, DBE, AE, JP; Flat 5, 35 Bryanston Square, London W1H 7LP; Court Farm, Tackley, Oxford OX5 3AQ (☎ 086 983 221)

PEAKE, John Morris; CBE (1986); s of Albert Edward Peake (d 1977), of Cambridge, and Ruby, *née* Morris (d 1978); *b* 26 Aug 1924; *Educ* Repton, Clare Coll Cambridge (mech sci tripos, MA), RNC Greenwich (Dip Naval Arch); *m* 9 May 1953, Elizabeth, da of Arthur Rought, MC (d 1972), of Lympstone, Devon; 1 s (Christopher b 1956), 1 da (Catharine b 1954); *Career* AANC 1944-50; Personnel Admin Ltd 1950-51, dir Baker Perkins 1956-87 (joined 1951), jt md Baker Perkins Ltd 1963-66, md Baker Perkins Pty Aust 1969-74, pres Baker Perkins Inc USA 1975-77, md Baker Perkins Hldgs 1980-85 (dep md 1978-79), chm Baker Perkins PLC 1984-87; Hockey Silver Medal London Olympics 1948; memb Chemicals and Minerals Requirements Bd 1978-81; CBI Cncl 1980: chm Overseas Scholarships Bd 1981-87, chm Educn and Trg Ctee 1986-88, chm Bd for Engrg BTEC 1985 (memb BTEC Cncl 1986-89); chm: Nene Park Tst Peterborough 1988, RSA Examinations Bd 1989 (joined 1987); vice chm Greater Peterborough Trg and Enterprise Cncl 1990-, vice pres RSA Cncl 1989, chm Design Cncl Educn and Trg Ctee 1990; memb: Design Cncl 1991, British Library Advsy Cncl 1990; Hon DTech CNAA 1986; FInstD 1956, FIMA 1967, FIMechE 1969, CBIM 1978, FRSA 1984; *Recreations* sport, travel; *Clubs* East India, MCC; *Style—* John Peake, Esq, CBE; Old Castle Farmhouse, Stibbington, Peterborough PE8 6LP (☎ 0780 782683)

PEAKE, Michael I'Anson; s of Alfred I'Anson Peake (d 1981), of Hillside, Benllech, Anglesey, and Eileen Constance Peake; *b* 25 Nov 1949; *Educ* Rydal Sch, Univ of London (LLB); *m* 11 July 1981, Mrs Dilys Shone; 2 s (Christopher I'Anson b 1981, Daniel Michael b 1984), 1 step s (Richard Arthur Shone b 1977); *Career* slr, ptnr Forshaw Spittles; dep dist judge; chm Contentious Sub Ctee of local Law Soc, memb Slrs' Complaints Panel; *Recreations* golf; *Clubs* Warrington Golf; *Style—* Michael Peake, Esq; Forshaw Spittles, 1 Palmyra Square, Warrington, Cheshire WA1 1BZ (☎ 0925 230000)

PEAKE, Peter Lowsley; s of Col Henry Gilbert Peake (d 1973), of Parsonage House, Hampstead Norreys, Berks, and Mary Ethel Ruie, *née* Lowsley (d 1977); *b* 15 July 1923; *Educ* Haileybury ISC, Sandhurst; *m* 1 March 1952, Mary Gildroy, da of Edward Philip Shaw (d 1970), of Commoners, Englefield Green, Surrey; 2 s (Simon b 1953, Anthony b 1960), 1 da (Philippa b 1957); *Career* cmmnd The Life Gds 1943, ret 1955 Maj; ptnr stockbroking firm Menter of London; memb Stock Exchange 1960, ret 1983; memb Worshipful Co of Blacksmiths 1968; Chevalier of the Order of the Dannebrog Denmark 1951; *Style—* Peter Lowlsey Peake, Esq; Chantry Dene, Fort Rd, Guildford, Surrey (☎ 0483 60697)

PEAKE, Trevor; s of William John Thomas Peake, of 462 Tutle Hill, Nuneaton, and Marie Eileen, *née* Ghent; *b* 10 Feb 1957; *Educ* King Edward VI GS Nuneaton; *m* 5 Feb 1984, Haiddwen, da of Lesley Phillips; 1 s (Callum b 3 Sept 1984); *Career* professional footballer; amateur Nuneaton Borough 1975-79 (229 appearances), 171 league appearances Lincoln City 1979-83, over 300 appearances Coventry City 1983-; 2 England semi-professional caps; FA Cup Winners Coventry City 1987; *Recreations* golf, comedy films; *Style—* Trevor Peake, Esq; Coventry City FC, Highfield Rd, West Midlands (☎ 0203 257171)

PEAKER, Prof Malcolm; s of Ronald Smith Peaker, of Stapleford, Nottingham, and Marian, *née* Tomasin; *b* 21 Aug 1943; *Educ* Henry Mellish GS Nottingham, Univ of Sheffield (BSc), Univ of Hong Kong (PhD); *m* 23 Oct 1965, Stephanie Jane, da of Lt-Cdr J G Large, DFC; 3 s (Christopher James Gordon, Alexander John, Nicholas Edward); *Career* ARC Inst of Animal Physiology 1968-78, head Dept of Physiology Hannah Res Inst 1978-81, dir and Hannah prof Univ of Glasgow 1981-; FZS 1969, FIBiol 1979, FRSE 1983; *Books* Salt Glands in Birds and Reptiles (1975), Avian Physiology (ed, 1975), Comparative Aspects of Lactation (ed 1977), Physiological Strategies in Lactation (ed); *Recreations* zoology, natural history, golf; *Clubs* Farmers, Turnberry GC, Zoological; *Style—* Prof Malcolm Peaker, FRSE; 13 Upper Crofts, Alloway, Ayr KA7 4QX; Hannah Research Inst, Ayr KA6 5HL (☎ 0292 76013, 0292 671052)

PEARCE, (John) Allan Chaplin; yr s of John William Ernest Pearce (d 1951), and Irene, *née* Chaplin; bro of Baron Pearce (Life Peer, d 1990); *b* 21 Oct 1912; *Educ* Charterhouse, Brasenose Coll Oxford; *m* 18 Nov 1948, Raffaella Elizabetta Maria, da of Avv Umberto Baione, of Florence; 2 s (Laurence b 1949, Charles b 1952); *Career* 2 Lt 4 Co of London Yeo, serv Libya, Egypt, Sicily, Italy 1941-44, Maj, mil mission to Italian Army Rome 1945-46; admitted slr 1947; ptnr Sandilands Williamson Hill & Co 1952-70, asst Church Cmmrs for England Legal Dept 1970-78; ctee memb Br Italian Soc 1967-, hon treas of Venice in Peril Fund 1986-, fndr memb, chm & vice pres Turner Soc 1976-85 (whose call for a Turner Gallery was answered in 1987); Liveryman Worshipful Co of Skinners 1937, Freeman City of London; memb Law Soc 1947; Cavaliere of the Order of Merit (Italy) 1978; *Recreations* travel, reading, painting; *Clubs* Travellers, Hurlingham; *Style—* Allan Pearce, Esq; 32 Brompton Square, London SW3 2AE (☎ 071 584 9429); 59 Via Ghibellina, Florence, Italy

PEARCE, Andrew; s of Henry Pearce (d 1964); *b* 1 Dec 1937; *Educ* Rydal Sch Colwyn Bay, Univ of Durham; *m* 1966, Myra, da of Kevin Whelan, of Co Wexford; 3 s, 1 da; *Career* formerly mgmnt servs exec; princ admin Cmmn of the Euro Communities Brussels 1974-79, contested (C) Islington North 1969 and 1970; MEP (C) Cheshire West 1979-89; euro community advsr Littlewoods Orgn Liverpool; *Style—* Andrew Pearce, Esq; 13 Lingdale Rd, W Kirby, Wirral, Merseyside L48 5DG (☎ 051 632 3191)

PEARCE, Sir Austin William; CBE (1974); s of William Thomas Pearce (d 1970); *b* 1 Sept 1921; *Educ* Devonport HS for Boys, Univ of Birmingham (BSc, PhD); *m* 1, 1947, Maglona Winifred Twinn (d 1975); 3 da; m 2, Dr Florence Patricia Grice, da of John Walter Forsythe; *Career* chm and chief exec Esso Petroleum Co Ltd 1972-80 (joined Esso when called Agwi Petroleum 1945, dir 1963, md 1968-71), dir Williams & Glyn's Bank 1974-85 (chm 1983-85), Royal Bank of Scotland Group 1978- (vice-chm 1985-); chm: Br Aerospace 1980-87 (dir 1977-, memb Organising Ctee 1976), Oxford Instruments 1987-, CBI Industl Policy Ctee 1982-86; non-exec dir: Pearl Assurance plc 1985-, Jaguar plc 1986-, Smiths Industries plc 1986-; former pres Inst of Petroleum, chm UK Petroleum Indust Assoc, pt/t memb NRDC 1973-76, memb Standing Cmmn on Energy and Environment 1978-81, pres Soc of Br Aerospace Cos 1982-83, pro chllr Univ of Surrey 1985-, chm Bd of Tstees Sci Museum 1986-, treas Royal Soc of Arts Mfrs and Commerce (RSA) 1988-; Br Assoc of Industl Eds Communicator of the Year Award 1983; Hon DSc Southampton 1978, Hon DSc Exeter 1985; Hon DEng Birmingham 1986, Hon DSc Salford 1987, Hon DSC Cranfield 1987; kt 1980; *Clubs* Athenaeum, Royal Wimbledon GC, R & A GC; *Style—* Sir Austin Pearce, CBE; c/o Royal Bank of Scotland, 67 Lombard St, London EC3 (☎ 071 623 4356)

PEARCE, Brian Harold; s of (John) Harold George Pearce (d 1982), of Sevenoaks, and Dorothy Elsie Pearce; *b* 30 July 1931; *Educ* Tonbridge, UCL (BSc); *m* 1, 3 Sept 1955, Jean Isabel, *née* Richardson (d 1985); 2 s (Nicholas Michael John b 1959, Jonathan Brian Miles b 1966), 1 da (Gillian Sarah (Mrs Mueller-Pearce) b 1961); m 2, 2 Aug 1988, Veronica Mary, *née* Maund, formerly Mrs Magraw; *Career* Nat Serv RE 1953-55 (cmmnd 2 Lt 1954); gp chm Pearce Signs Ltd and subsids 1981- (joined 1955, gp md 1975); vice chm Royal London Soc for the Blind, Bd memb Deptford Enterprise Agency; Cncl memb: Goldsmith Coll London, Business in the Community; memb Bd London C-of-C and Indust (and other offices); pres: Br Sign Assoc, Euro Fedn of Illuminated Signs; govr New Beacon Sch Sevenoaks; Freeman: City of London, Worshipful Co of Lightmongers; *Recreations* sailing; *Clubs* RAC, Little Ship, Royal Cornwall Yacht; *Style—* Brian Pearce, Esq; Pearce Signs Ltd, Insignia House, London SE14 6AB

PEARCE, (John) Brian; s of George Frederic Pearce (d 1963), of Wakefield and Sidmouth, and Constance Josephine, *née* Seed (d 1967); *b* 25 Sept 1935; *Educ* Queen Elizabeth GS Wakefield, Brasenose Coll Oxford (BA); *m* 30 June 1960, Michelle, da of Alfred Starr Etcheverry (ka 1944); 4 s (Christopher David b 1963, Colin Alexander b 1965, Jonathan Edward b 1969, James Frederic Lauriston b 1970); *Career* Nat Serv RAF 1954-56, Pilot Offr 1955-56; Miny of Power 1959-60, Colonial Office 1960-67, Dept of Econ Affrs 1967-69, Civil Serv Dept 1969-81, HM Treasy 1981-84 (under sec 1976-84), dir Inter Faith Network for UK 1987-; *Recreations* reading (mainly theology), travel; *Style—* Brian Pearce, Esq; 124 Court Lane, London SE21 7EA; 5-7 Tavistock Place, London WC1 (☎ 071 388 0008)

PEARCE, Hon Mrs (Constance Ada); *née* Caulfield; da of late 11 Viscount Charlemont; *b* 1918; *m* 1943, Henry Edward Pearce; 2 s, 3 da; *Style—* The Hon Mrs Pearce; 254 Mooroondu Rd, Thorneside, Queensland 4158, Australia

PEARCE, David John; s of Dr Raymond Maplesden Pearce (d 1976), and Ivy, *née* Shingler (d 1960); *b* 25 March 1928; *Educ* Manchester GS, Univ of Manchester (BSc); *m* 1, 24 Feb 1954, Doreen (d 1977), da of John Valentine (d 1964), of Brindle Heath, Salford; 1 s (Andrew b 1959), 1 da (Shiela b 1962); m 2, 7 June 1986, Eileen, da of John Alfred Corlett (d 1961), of Wigan; 2 step s (Paul b 1953, Barry b 1954), 1 step da (Tina-Ann b 1959); *Career* Nat Serv Lance Corpl HQ RE BAOR 1951-53; graduate engr Oscar Faber and Ptnrs (consltg engrs) 1949-51, res engr Spillers Ltd 1949-51, asst engr Merz and McLellan 1953-54, sr devpt engr Matthews and Mumby Ltd (asst engr, pt/t lectr) 1954-71; ptnr: Dennis Matthews and Ptnrs 1972-79 (sr engr 1971-72), Pearce Matthews Partnership 1979-88, res ptnr Wallace Evans and Ptnrs Northern office (incorporating Pearce Matthews) 1988-90, divnl md Wallace Evans Ltd N Western Office 1990-; chm Lancs and Ches branch IStructE 1983; AMIStructE 1953, MICE 1958, FIStructE 1969, MConsE 1970; *Recreations* travel, walking, swimming, crafts; *Clubs* Rotary (Worsley); *Style—* David Pearce, Esq; The Chimes, 19 Bellpit Close, Ellenbrook Grange, Worsley M28 4XH; Wallace Evans and Ptnrs, Bruntwood Hall, Schools Hill, Cheadle, Cheshire SK8 1JD (☎ 061 491 1608, fax 061 491 3151)

PEARCE, Prof David William; s of William Henry Pearce, and Gladys Muriel, *née* Webb; *b* 11 Oct 1941; *Educ* Harrow Weald Co GS, Lincoln Coll Oxford; *m* 27 Aug 1966, Susan Mary, da of William Federick Reynolds; 2 s (Daniel Benjamin b 1972, Corin Gareth b 1976); *Career* lectr in econs Univ of Lancaster 1964-67, sr lectr Univ of Southampton 1967-74, dir Pub Sector Econs Res Centre Univ of Leicester 1974-77; prof: Univ of Aberdeen 1977-83, UCL 1983-; dir London Enviromental Econs Centre 1988-, special advsr to the Sec of State for the Enviroment 1989-; winner of UN Global 500 Award for servs to enviromental improvement; bd memb of Nat Radiological Protection Bd; FRSA 1988; *Books* Economic Analysis (with S G Sturmey, 1966), Cost Benefit Analysis (1971), The Economics of Natural Resource Depletion (ed, 1975), Decision Making for Energy Futures: A Case Study of the Windscale Inquiry (with L Edwards and G Beuret, 1979), Waste Paper Recovery (1979), Social Projects Appraisal (with C A Nash, 1981), The MacMillan Dictionary of Economics (gen ed, 1981), Economics and the Enviroment: A Contribution to the National Conservation Strategy for Botswana (with C Perrings, J Opschoor, J Arntzen and A Gilbert, 1988), Blueprint for a Green Economy (with A Markandya and E Barbier, 1989), Economics of Natural Resources and the Enviroment (with R K Turner, 1989), Sustainable Development (with A Markandya and E Barbier, 1990), Blueprint 2 (jtly, 1991); *Recreations* bird watching in Africa, collecting English porcelain; *Style—* Prof David Pearce; 90 Kimbolton Road, Bedford MK40 2PE (☎ 0234 341946), Department of Economics, University College London, Gower St, London WC1E 6BT (☎ 071 380 7037, fax 0234 215 528)

PEARCE, Gary Stephen; s of Allan Cecil Pearce, and Gwendoline Ruby, *née* Woodford; *b* 2 March 1956; *Educ* The Mandeville Co Secdy Sch Aylesbury Bucks; *m* 29 July 1978, Susan Jean, da of Francis Lewis Eldred; 2 c (Daniel Edward b 30 Nov 1980, Matthew Stephen b 17 May 1983); *Career* Rugby Union prop forward Northampton RFC and England (35 caps); clubs: Aylesbury RFC 1973-77, Buckinghamshire RFC 1974-80, Northampton RFC 1977- (capt: 1988-89, 1989-90, 1990-91; 325 appearances), Barbarians RFC; rep Midland Div; England: debut v Scotland 1979, tour Japan Fiji and Tonga 1979, tour Argentina (2 tests) 1981, tour Canada and US 1982, tour S Africa (1 test) 1984, tour NZ (2 tests) 1985, memb World Cup squad (3 appearances) 1987, tour Aust and Fiji (1 test) 1988, most capped Eng prop; quantity surveyor As Friend and Partners 1975-; *Style—* Gary Pearce, Esq; Northampton Rugby Football Club, Franklins Gardens, Weedon Rd, Northampton NN5 5BG (☎ 0604 751543, fax 0604 750061)

PEARCE, Sir (Daniel Norton) Idris; CBE (1982), TD (1972), DL (Greater London 1986); s of Lemuel George Douglas Pearce (d 1988), and Evelyn Mary Pearce (d 1987); *b* 28 Nov 1933; *Educ* West Buckland Sch, Coll of Estate Mgmnt; *m* 1 June 1963, Ursula Helene, *née* Langley; 2 da (Sara b 30 April 1965, Clare b 8 Dec 1968); *Career* Nat Serv RE 1957-59, Hon Col cmd 135 Int Topographic Sqdn TA 1989-; chartered surveyor; with Richard Ellis 1959 (ptnr 1961, managing ptnr 1981-87); RICS: memb bd mgmnt 1984-, memb gen cncl 1980-, chm Parly and pub affrs 1984-, vice pres 1986-90, pres 1990-91; chm int asset valuation standards ctee 1981-86, memb advsy panel for instn fin in new towns 1974-80, sec of state health and social security inquiry into surplus land in NHS 1982, property advsr NHS 1985-89; memb: advsy bd PSA 1981-86, advsy panel on diplomatic estate 1985-; chm Eng Estate 1989-, contested Neath (C) 1959; memb: court City Univ 1987-, Univs Funding Cncl 1991-; chm bd govrs Stanway Sch Dorking 1982-85; hon fell Coll Estate Mgmnt; Hon DSc City Univ, Centenary fell Thames Poly; Freeman: Worshipful Co of Tylers and Bricklayers 1973, Chartered Surveyors 1973, FRICS, FRSA; Kt 1990; *Recreations* reading, opera, ballet, travel; *Clubs* Brooks's, City of London; *Style—* Sir Idris Pearce, CBE, TD, DL; Richard Ellis, 55 Old Broad St, London EC2M 1LP (☎ 071 256 6411, fax 071 256 8328, telex 887732)

PEARCE, Dr John Dalziel Wyndham; s of John Alfred Wyndham Pearce (d 1951), of Edinburgh, and Mary Logan, *née* Dalziel (d 1933); *b* 21 Feb 1904; *Educ* George Watson's Coll, Univ of Edinburgh (MA, MB ChB, MD); *m* 1, 19 Oct 1929 (m dis), Grace, da of Robert Fowler (d 1959), of Edinburgh; m 2, 20 March 1964, (Ellinor) Elizabeth Nancy Draper, da of Ernest Isaac Lewis (d 1961), of Harrow; *Career* Lt-Col RAMC 1940-45, cmd psychiatrist NI, cmd psychiatrist Northern Cmd, OC Northfield Mil Hosp, advsr in psychiatry AFHQ CMF (despatches); former: physician i/c Depts of Psychiatry St Mary's Hosp and Queen Elizabeth Hosp for Children, conslt psychiatrist Royal Masonic Hosp, hon physician Tavistock Clinic and W End Hosp for Nervous Diseases, med co dir Portman Clinic (Inst for Study and Treatment of Delinquency), medico-psychologist LCC remand homes; memb Academic Bd: Inst of Child Health, St Mary's Hosp Med Sch (Univ of London); examiner in med: RCP, Univ of London, Royal Coll of Psychiatrists; consulting psychiatrist: St Mary's Hosp, Queen Elizabeth Hosp for Children; chm Advsy Ctee on Delinquent and Maladjusted Children Int Union for Child Welfare; memb: cncl Nat Assoc for Mental Health, Home Sec's Advsy Cncl on Treatment of Offenders, Royal Burgess Golfing Soc; FRCP, FRCPE, FRCPsych, FBPsS; *Books* Juvenile Delinquency (1952); *Recreations* golf, painting; *Clubs* Caledonian, New (Edinburgh); *Style—* Dr John Pearce; Flat 28, 2 Barnton Avenue West, Edinburgh EH4 6EB (☎ 031 317 7116)

PEARCE, Dr John Michael Schofield; s of Dr Wilfred Pearce (d 1975), of Leeds, Yorks, and Hannah Ruby, *née* Lyons; *b* 19 Aug 1936; *Educ* Bootham Sch York, Univ of Leeds (MB ChB, MD); *m* 25 Oct 1965, Iris, da of John Swanson (d 1976), of Ashington, Northumberland; 2 s (Simon b 23 Aug 1966, David b 30 June 1968), 1 da (Elizabeth b 20 June 1971); *Career* house physician Royal Postgrad Med Sch London 1960-61, res fell and neurological registrar Newcastle Gen Hosp 1962-64, sr neurological registrar Leeds Gen Infirmary 1964-67 (house physician 1960-61, Fullbright fell Harvard Med Sch 1965-66), conslt neurologist Hull Royal Infirmary and physician i/c Headache and Parkinson's Disease Clinics 1967-; memb: exec Cncl Assoc Br Neurologists, Neurology Ctee RCP London, Editorial Bd and book reviews ed Jnl Neurology Neurosurgery and Psychiatry; pres elect N of England Neurological Assoc 1991 (memb 1983-); RSM 1967 (memb Cncl and sec), FRCP; *Books* Migraine (1969), Clinical Aspects of Dementia (1973), Modern Topic in Migraine (1975), Dementia: A Clinical Approach (1984), Parkinson's Disease (1991); *Recreations* gardening, theatre, natural history and boat rocking; *Style—* Dr J M S Pearce

PEARCE, (George) Malcolm; MBE (1987), JP; s of (Edward) Ewart Pearce, MBE, JP (d 1963), Lord Mayor of Cardiff 1961-62, and Winifred Constance, *née* Blackmore (d 1970); *b* 3 Feb 1926; *Educ* Howard Gardens HS; *m* 4 June 1949, Thelma Mavis, da of Albert John Jones (d 1987), of Cardiff; 2 s (Lester b 1954, Mark b 1967), 3 da (Patricia b 1950, Christine b 1951, Carol b 1958); *Career* Lt Paymaster RAPC Palestine 1945-47; CA; hon vice pres Boys Bde, pres Cardiff Bde 1960-87, treas Wales Festival of Remembrance 1980-; *Recreations* golf, bridge; *Clubs* Cardiff and County, Cardiff Golf, Cardiff E Rotary; *Style—* Malcom Pearce, Esq, MBE, JP; Whitefriars, Westminster Crescent, Cardiff CF2 6SE (☎ 0222 754339)

PEARCE, (Ann) Philippa; da of Ernest Alexander Pearce; *Educ* Perse Girls' Sch Cambridge, Girton Coll Cambridge; *m* 1963, Martin James Graham Christie (decd); 1 da; *Career* prodr/scriptwriter sch's bdcasting BBC Radio 1945-58, ed Educn Dept Clarendon Press 1958-60, children's ed Andre Deutsch Ltd 1960-67, freelance writer of children's fiction 1967-; *Books Incl:* Tom's Midnight Garden (Carnegie medal, 1959), A Dog So Small, The Elm Street Lot, The Battle of Bubble and Squeak (Whitbread award, 1978), The Way to Sattin Shore (1983); *Style—* Miss Philippa Pearce; c/o Viking-Kestrel Books, 27 Wrights Lane W8 5TZ

PEARCE, Thomas Neill; OBE (1979), TD; s of Thomas Henry Pearce (d 1944), and Amelia Harriet, *née* Neill (d 1954); *b* 3 Nov 1905; *Educ* Christ's Hosp; *m* 1935, Stella Mary (d 1978), da of Thomas Rippon (d 1934), of Chelmsford; 1 s (Christopher), 2 da (Valerie, Rosemary); *Career* Maj RA ADGB; Capt Essex Co Cricket Club 1933-50, mangr MCC to India, Pakistan and Ceylon 1961-62; dir Finsbury Distillery Co Ltd; int referee rugby football Middlesex and London Counties, Old Blues RFC; *Recreations* watching cricket and rugby football; *Clubs* MCC, Essex CCC, Lord's Taverners, Br Sportsman's; *Style—* Thomas Pearce, Esq, OBE, TD; 10 Fontwell Close, Findon Valley, Worthing, Sussex BN14 0AD

PEARCE, William James; s of Flt-Lt Stanley James Pearce, DFC, and Sybil Renee Genvieve, *née* Hannaford (d 1987); *b* 8 April 1950; *Educ* Warwick Sch, Univ of Surrey (BSc); *m* 1 July 1977 (m dis 1989), Cheryn Dianna, da of Capt T A Warwick (d 1984); *Career* pupil to C H Davis of Oak Grove St Arvans nr Chepstow 1973-74, asst trainer RC Sturdy of Elston House Shrewto Wilts 1974-75, asst trainer Epsom Trg Centre (principally asst trainer to M Goswell of Mkanna Mead Stables) 1976-79, trainer Lambourn House Lambourn Berks 1979-84, Nat Hunt and flat jockey 1973-84, trainer Hambleton House Nr Thirsk N Yorks 1984-; best season 1989 (23 winners); horses trained incl: Monarch O' The Glen, Premier Lad, Victory; memb NTF; *Recreations* reading, cinema, swimming; *Clubs* Savile; *Style—* William Pearce, Esq; Hambleton House, Hambleton, Thirsk, North Yorks (☎ 0845 597373, fax 0845 597643, car 0836 224099)

PEARCEY, Leonard Charles; s of Leonard Arthur Pearcey, of Dorset, and Jessie Sinclair, *née* Millar (d 1965); *b* 6 June 1938; *Educ* Christ's Hosp, CCC Cambridge (MA); *Career* PA to md Hargreaves Gp 1957-59, dir studies Rapid Results Correspondence Coll 1962-63, teacher Wimbledon 1964-65, arts admin Harold Holt Ltd 1965-66, music dir Guildhall Sch of Music and Drama 1966-70, competition sec Int Violin Competition 1966-70, dir Merton Festival 1972-76, involved in numerous major arts and religious radio and TV programmes, also own series singer and guitarist (Gold disc 1990), composer numerous songs and arrangements; prodr and presenter: P & O Lines Naming Ceremonies, Eng Tourist Bd Awards, inaugural and other major presentations conferences award ceremonies; admin BBC Radio Times Drama Awards and Comedy Awards, stage coordinator and compere World Travel Market (memb advsy cncl), artistic dir Trusthouse Forte Music at Leisure 25 Anniversary Series, ed Music Teacher Magazine 1980-85, feature columnist Classical Music Magazine 1979-85, contrib Radio Times; pres Polruan Regatta Carnival and Children's Sports; Mayoress (sic) London Borough of Merton 1973-74; memb Actors Equity; *Books* The Musician's Survival Kit (1979); *Recreations* travel; *Style—* Leonard Pearcey, Esq; 53 Queens Rd, London SW19 8NP (☎ 081 947 2555)

PEAREY, Capt Michael Alan; s of William Scott Pearey (d 1940), of Newcastle upon Tyne, and Harriet Pringle, *née* Rochester (d 1972); *b* 3 June 1933; *Educ* Christ's Hosp; *m* 1957, Thelma Joy, da of Edward Hugh Owen, of Portsmouth; 3 s (Michael Scott b 1959, Richard Pringle b 1960, Alan Quentin b 1964), 2 da (Susan Adrienne (Mrs White) b 1957, Julia Heriot b 1966); *Career* joined RN 1951, Cdr 1970, Trg Cdr RN Supply Sch 1971-74, HMS Fearless 1974-75, catering advsr RN 1976-78, Cmd Supply Offr Naval Home Cmd 1978-79, Capt 1979, Chief Staff Offr (personal and admin) to Flag Offr Naval Air Cmd 1980-81, dir Fleet Supply Duties 1982-84, dir Naval Offr Appts (S and S Offrs and WRNS) 1984-86, ret 1986; clerk Christ's Hosp Horsham 1986-; chm London HCIMA 1983-85; pres RFU 1990-91 (memb Ctee 1968-); represented at rugby: RN, Combined Servs, Northumberland, Hants, Devon, Barbarians; Freeman: Newcastle upon Tyne 1952, City of London 1986; memb HCIMA 1978; *Recreations* rugby union, tennis; *Clubs* Devonshire, East India and Public Sch Sports; *Style—* Capt Michael Pearey; Itchingfield, W Sussex; Christ's Hosp, Horsham, W Sussex (☎ 0403 211297, fax 0403 211580)

PEARL, David Brian; s of Leonard Pearl (d 1983); *b* 6 Aug 1944; *Educ* Wellington; *m* 1972, Rosamond Mary Katharine, da of Lt-Cdr C G de L'isle Bush, of Frampton-upon-Severn, Glos; 2 s, 1 da; *Career* CA; articled Coopers & Lybrand; chm London Securities plc; underwriting memb Lloyds 1977-89, vice chm Medway Ports Authy 1987-, non-exec chm The Crown Suppliers 1989-90; involvement in local govt: cncllr Westminster City Cncl 1974-82, served numerous ctees, sch govr, rep London Tourist Bd, dep Lord Mayor, chief whip, vice chm Fin and Scrutiny Ctee, chm Contracts Sub Ctee, chm Investmts Sub Ctee; former chm: St Marylebone Cons Assoc, London Central Euro Cons Assoc; FCA, MInstM; *Recreations* private pilot's licence (helicopters), sports, travel; *Clubs* White's, Reform, Royal St George's Golf; *Style—* David Pearl, Esq; Mill Ride Estate, Mill Ride, North Ascot, Berks SL5 8LT (☎ 0344 88 5444)

PEARL, Prof David Stephen; s of Chaim Pearl, and Anita, *née* Newman; *b* 11 Aug 1944; *Educ* George Dixons Sch Birmingham, Univ of Birmingham (LLB), Queens Coll Cambridge (LLM, MA, PhD); *m* 1, 7 April 1967 (m dis 1983), Susan, da of Joseph Roer, of Croydon, Surrey; 3 s (Julian Kim b 1969, Daniel Benjamin Meir b 1971, Marcus Alexander Jethro b 1974); m 2, 4 Oct 1985, Gillian, da of Ryzard Maciejewski, of Melbourn, Royston, Herts; *Career* called to the Bar Gray's Inn 1968, fell and dir studies in law Fitzwilliam Coll Cambridge 1969-89 (life fell), univ lectr 1972-89, prof law and dean Sch of Law UEA 1989-; city cncllr Cambridge 1972-74, co cncllr Cambridge 1974-77, asst dep coroner Cambridge 1978-89, pt/t adjudicator Immigration Act 1980-, asst rec 1985-91, gen sec Int Soc on Family Law 1985-; *Books* A Textbook on Muslim Personal Law (1979, 2 edn 1987), Social Welfare Law (with K Gray, 1981), Interpersonal Conflict of Laws (1981), Family Law and Society (with B Hoggett, 1983, 2 edn 1987), Family Law and Immigrant Communities (1986), Blood Testing, Aids and DNA Profiling (with A Grubb, 1990); *Recreations* long distance running (badly); *Style—* Prof David Pearl; 183 Huntingdon Rd, Cambridge CB3 ODL (☎ 0603 592834)

PEARL, Prof Valerie Louise; da of Cyril R Bence and Florence Bence (d 1974); *b* 31 Dec 1926; *Educ* King Edward VI HS Birmingham, St Anne's Coll Oxford (BA, MA, DPhil); *m* 1949, Morris Leonard Pearl, s of Nathan Pearl (d 1961); 1 da; *Career* prof of history of London UCL 1976-81, pres New Hall Coll Cambridge 1981-; govr Museum of London 1978-; syndicate: Cambridge Univ Library 1983-, CUP 1984-; cmmr Royal Cmmn on Historical Manuscripts 1984-; *Style—* Prof Valerie Pearl; The President's Lodge, 16 Madingley Rd, Cambridge CB3 0EE (☎ 0223 351721 ext 272)

PEARLMAN, Hon Mrs (Esther); *née* Jakobovits; eldest da of Baron Jakobovits (Life Peer), Chief Rabbi of the British Cwlth, *qv*; *b* 1953; *m* 21 Feb 1971, Rev Rabbi Chaim Zundel Pearlman, s of Ralph David Pearlman, of 11 Langport Road, Sunderland; 5 s (Yehuda b 2 Oct 1972, Eliezer b 24 Feb 1974, Ephraim b 20 June 1978, Eliyohu b 2 April 1982, Daniel b 31 July 1985), 3 da (Zipporah b 9 March 1976, Adina b 20 Jan 1980, Sarah b 10 Sept 1988); *Style—* The Hon Mrs Pearlman; 14 Mayfield Gardens, London NW4 2QA (☎ 081 202 8864)

PEARLMAN, Joseph Joshua (Jerry); s of Samuel Myer Pearlman, MM (d 1981), and Sarah Rachael Pearlman (d 1983); *b* 26 April 1933; *Educ* Keighly GS, St James VI GS Bishop Auckland, Univ of London (LLB); *m* 18 June 1962, Bernice; 2 da (Kate, Debbie); *Career* Nat Serv Lt RASC; admitted slr 1956; fndr Pearlman Grazin & Co 1958, advsr to Omukama Bunyoro-Katara Uganda 1960-61, hon slr Sikh temple Leeds 1965-; pres: Leeds and W Riding Medico Legal Soc 1975-, Leeds Law Soc 1985-86; hon slr Ramblers Assoc 1980-, ministerial appointed memb Yorkshire Dales Nat Park Ctee 1983-, memb Adjudicaton Ctee Slrs Complaints Bureau 1986-88, chm Open Spaces Soc 1988; *Recreations* rambling, eating, drinking; *Clubs* Royal Cwlth Soc; *Style—* Jerry Pearlman, Esq; 10 Lakeland Cres, Leeds LS17 7PR (☎ 0532 671114); Bells Cottage, Stalling Busk, Askrigg via Leyburn, N Yorks; 5-6 Park Place, Leeds LS1 2RU (☎ 0532 431534, fax 0532 445718, car 0860 311600)

PEARLMAN, Her Honour Judge; Valerie Anne Pearlman; da of Sidney Pearlman, and Marjorie Pearlman; *b* 6 Aug 1936; *Educ* Wycombe Abbey; *m* 1972; 1 s, 1 da; *Career* called to the Bar Lincolns Inn 1958, rec SE Circuit 1982-85, circuit judge 1985-; memb Parole Bd 1989-; memb Cncl Marlborough Coll 1989-; patron Suzy Lamplugh Tst; *Style—* Her Honour Judge Pearlman; Crown Ct, Southwark, English Ground, London SE1 2HU

PEARS, David; s of Reginald Pears (d 1979); *b* 6 Dec 1967; *Educ* Moorclose Secdy Workington, Workington GS; *Career* Rugby Union fly-half Harlequins FC and England (2 caps); clubs: Aspatria RUFC 1984-88, Sale FC 1989, Harlequins FC 1990-; rep: Eng U21 1989, Eng B 1989-91 (6 caps); England: debut v Argentina 1990, tour Argentina 1990; building project mangr; *Recreations* canoeing, golf, squash; *Style—* David Pears, Esq; 121 Rusthall Avenue, Chiswick, London W4 (☎ 081 994 5179); Harlequins FC, Stoop Memorial Ground, Craneford Way, Twickenham, Middlesex

PEARSALL, Phyllis Isobel; MBE (1986); da of late Alexander Grosz, and late Isobel, *née* Crowley; *b* 25 Sept 1906; *Educ* Roedean, Collège de Jeunes Filles Fécamp, Sorbonne; *m* 1926, (m dis 1938), Richard Montague Stack Pearsall; *Career* artist; one woman exhibitions 1924-90 incl: Brooke St Gallery London 1926, Upper Grosvenor Galleries London 1967-69, Arts Club 1977-79, RGS 50 Anniversary Geographers' A-Z Map Co 1986, Arundel 1983, 1984, 1985, 1988 and 1990; work exhibited with: Orléans 1924, Art Inst Chicago 1931, RA 1935-39, Leicester Galleries London 1938, Upper Grosvenor Galleries 1967-72, Brighton Art Gallery 1970-71, Chilham Gallery Kent 1975, Rye Art Gallery Sussex 1976, Nevill Gallery Canterbury 1976-82, V&A Museum and Museum of London; represented in private art collections UK, USA, France, Canada, Aust, Turkey; Geographers' A-Z Map Co Ltd: fndr and dir 1936-, chm and md 1958-; Geographers Map Tst: fndr and dir 1966-, chm 1987; FRGS; *Books* Castillian Ochre (1934), Fleet Street, Tite Street, Queer Street (1983), Only the Unexpected Happens (1985), Women 1939-40 (1985), Women at War (1990), From Bedsitter to Household Name - the personal story of A-Z Maps (1990); *Recreations* cooking, opera, theatre; *Clubs* Arts, Univ Women's; *Style—* Mrs Phyllis Pearsall, MBE; Geographers' A to Z Map Co Ltd, Vestry Rd, Sevenoaks, Kent TN14 5EP (☎ 0732 41152)

PEARSE, Brian Gerald; *b* 23 Aug 1933; *Educ* St Edwards Coll Liverpool; *m* 5 Jan 1959, Patricia Monica; 2 da, 1 s; *Career* Martins Bank Ltd 1950-69; Barclays Bank: joined 1969, local dir Birmingham 1972-79, gen mangr UK 1979-82, chief exec North America 1982-87, fin dir 1987-; non exec dir 3i Group, chm Assoc of Payment and Clearing Systems, memb Cncl Kings Coll London; FCIB; *Recreations* golf, opera, rugby football; *Clubs* RAC; *Style—* Brian Pearse, Esq; Barclays Bank PLC, 4 Royal Mint Court, London EC3N 4HH (☎ 071 696 4263)

PEARSE, William Richard George (Bill); s of Richard John Pearse (d 1946), of Taunton, and Daisy May, *née* Thomas (d 1982); *b* 23 Feb 1924; *Educ* Taunton Sch; *Career* RASC 1944-46; CA 1951, memb Exec Ctee Robson Rhodes 1981-84, managing ptnr Apsleys 1987-90 (conslt 1990-); pres and co-fndr SW Soc of CAs 1978-79, rec Taunton Ct Leet; govr Bishop Foxes Sch, memb Cncl Taunton Sch, vice pres Somerset CCC, memb Mgmnt Ctee Somerset Co RFU, chm SW Div RFU 1988-89, Somerset rep RFU; Freeman: City of London 1978, Worshipful Co of CAs in England

& Wales 1978; FCA (1961, ACA 1951); *Recreations* sport, cricket, rugby football; *Clubs* E India, Victory Service; *Style—* Bill Pearse, Esq; 11 Highlands, Taunton, Somerset TA1 4HP (☎ 0823 284 701); Apsleys, Apsley House, Billet St, Taunton, Somerset TA1 3TX (☎ 0823 259 101, fax 0823 334 459)

PEARSE WHEATLEY, Robin John; s of John Edward Clive Wheatley, MC, JP, *qv*, of Belenden, Wreford's Lane, Exeter, Devon, and Rosemarie Joy, *née* Malet-Veale; *b* 23 May 1949; *Educ* Leys Sch Cambridge, Inns of Court Sch of Law; *m* 9 April 1979, Victoria Eugenia Perez de Ascanio y Zuleta de Reales, da of Nicolas Perez de Ascanio Ventoso, Duke of Sedavi, Kt of the Holy Sepulchre, of Tenerife, Spain; 1 s (Edward Victor Francisco de Borga b 23 Dec 1988), 2 da (Victoria Eugenia Amabel b 16 Dec 1983, Rafaela Eleanor b 11 Jan 1986); *Career* called to the Bar Inner Temple 1971; asst rec Crown Ct 1987-; councillor RBK and C 1974-78; Cons Parly candidate Lewisham Deptford 1983; chm London Area Nat Fedn Self Employed and Small Business 1989-90; Cons Euro candidate London South Inner 1989; Knight of Grace Constantinian Order of St George; *Recreations* wind surfing, squash, bridge; *Clubs* Annabel's; *Style—* Robin Pearse Wheatley, Esq; 30 Edenhurst Ave, London SW6 3PB (☎ 071 736 7060); 2 Paper Buildings, London EC4Y 7ET (☎ 071 936 2611, fax 071 583 3423, car 0836 787834)

PEARSON, Brig Alastair Stevenson; CB (1958), DSO, OBE (1953), MC, TD; *b* 1 June 1915; *Educ* Kelvinside Acad, Sedbergh; *m* 1944, Mrs Joan Morgan Weld-Smith; 3 da; *Career* farmer; Lord Lt of Dunbartonshire 1979-90; keeper Dunbarton Castle 1981-; KStJ 1980; *Style—* Brig Alastair Pearson, CB, DSO, OBE, MC, TD; Tullochan, Gartocharn, by Alexandria, Dunbartonshire (☎ Gartocharn 205)

PEARSON, Brig Barclay Andrew; DSO (1945), DL (Stirlingshire 1965); s of Andrew Pearson, WS (d 1921), of Johnston Lodge, Laurencekirk, Kincardineshire, and Mary Henrietta Dorothea, *née* Bowden-Smith; *b* 13 Jan 1912; *Educ* Sherborne, Brasenose Coll Oxford (BA); *m* 5 April 1944, Heather, da of Lewis Campbell Gray (d 1947), of Green Island, Co Antrim, NI; 1 da (Richenda b 1953); *Career* 2 Lt Argyll & Sutherland Highlanders 1934, WWII served ME and NW Europe (despatches thrice), ME Staff Coll 1942, DA QMG HQ 30 Corps 1942-44, 2 i/c 2 Bn Argyll & Sutherland Highlanders, Lt-Col 1944, Cmd 8 Bn The Royal Scots 1944-45, AA QMG HQ 51 Div 1945-46, AQMG HQ BAOR 1946, GSOII (Intelligence) BJSM Washington USA 1946-48, GSO1 (asst mil attache) Br Embassy Paris 1948-50, GSO1 (Ops and SD) HQ Scot Cmd Edinburgh 1950-51, Col (SD) HQ AFCENT Fontainebleau 1951-53, cmd 1 Bn Argyll & Sutherland Highlanders 1954-57 (British Guyana, Berlin, Suez Campaign), cmd 154 Highland Bde 1957-60; ret 1960; sec Territorial Assoc Stirlingshire 1960-68, Lanarkshire Productivity Assoc 1968-69; Scottish sec Public Schs Appts Bureau (ISCO) 1969-78; chm: Regtl Museum Ctee Stirling Castle 1975-89, Stirling Dist Scout Cncl 1965-85; awarded Silver Acorn (for servs to scouting) 1985; Chevalier French Legion of Honour (1949); *Recreations* shooting, golf, curling, gardening, croquet; *Clubs* Army and Navy; *Style—* Brig Barclay Pearson, DSO, DL; Spinneyburn, Rumbling Bridge, Kinross-Shire (☎ 05774 270)

PEARSON, Barrie; s of Albert James Pearson (d 1987), of Selby, Yorks, and Mary Pearson (d 1980); *b* 22 Aug 1939; *Educ* King's Sch Pontefract Yorks, Univ of Nottingham (BSc); *m* 1, 1962 (m dis), Georgina Ann; 1 s (Gavin b 1968), 1 da (Philippa b 1965); m 2, 1984, Catherine Campbell; *Career* The De la Rue Co, The Plessey Co, Dexion-Comino Int Ltd, non-exec chm Info Transmission Ltd 1985-87; md Livingstone Fisher plc 1976-; visiting fell in corporate aqcuisitions and disposals City Univ Business Sch; seminar presenter for: Inst of CAs, City Univ, Strategic Planning Soc, Ashridge Mgmnt Coll; video film Business Strategy 1989, Time Management 1990; *Books* Successful Acquisiton of Unquoted Companies (1983, 3 edn 1989), Common Sense Business Strategy (1987), Common Sense Time Management for Personal Success (1988), Realising The Value of a Business (1989), The Profit Driven Manager (1990); *Recreations* food guide inspector, theatre, outstanding hotels, travel; *Style—* Barrie Pearson, Esq; Campbell House, Weston Turville, Bucks HP22 5RQ (☎ 0296 613 828); Livingstone Fisher plc, 11-15 William Rd, London NW1 3ER (☎ 071 388 7000)

PEARSON, David; s of Judge Maurice Pearson, of Beverley Hills, California; *b* 7 March 1942; *Educ* Sir William Turner's Sch Redcar Yorks, King's Coll London; *m* 1972, Christine Faith, da of Douglas Littlejohn, of Paris, France; 7 children; *Career* dep chm: Novelty Doll (Taiwan) Ltd, Philip Littlejohn Personal Services (UK) Ltd; chm: Broadmeadows Ltd, Pearson & Hogan, The Pearson Partnership, Broadmeadows in France, Suddenly With One Bound Jack Was Free; MIPA; *Recreations* skiing, scuba diving, mountaineering, micro-light flying, taxidermy, hot air ballooning; *Style—* David Pearson, Esq; Coleswood House, Harpenden, Herts AL5 1DF; PO Box 1, Harbour Island, Bahamas; Le Caraquet, Boursin 62132, France; 8743 Pacific Hwy, Gold Coast, Queensland, Australia

PEARSON, David Compton Froome; s of Compton Edwin Pearson, OBE (d 1977); *b* 28 July 1931; *Educ* Haileybury, Downing Coll Cambridge; *m* 1966, Venetia Jane, *née* Lynn; 2 da; *Career* admitted slr 1957; ptnr Linklaters & Paines 1961-69 (memb 1957-69); dir: Robert Fleming & Co Ltd 1969-90, The Fleming Enterprise Investment Trust plc 1971-84, Blue Circle Industries plc 1972-1987, Robert Fleming Holdings Ltd 1974-90, Lane Fox & Partners Ltd 1987-; chm: The Fleming Property Unit Trust 1971-90, Channel Tunnel Investments plc 1981-1986, Gill & Duffus Group plc 1982-85 (dir 1973-85), Robert Fleming Securities 1985-90; dep chm: Austin Reed Group plc 1977- (dir 1971-), Robert Fleming Holdings Ltd 1986-90; memb Fin Act 1960 Tbnl; *Recreations* walking, gardening; *Clubs* Brooks's; *Style—* David C F Pearson, Esq; The Manor, Berwick St John, Shaftesbury, Dorset SP7 0EX (☎ 0747 828363)

PEARSON, Sir (James) Denning; JP; s of James Pearson, and Elizabeth Henderson; *b* 8 Aug 1908; *Educ* Canton Secdy Sch Cardiff, Cardiff Tech Coll (BSc); *m* 1932, Eluned Henry; 2 da; *Career* chief exec Rolls-Royce Ltd 1958-70, chm Gamma Associates 1972-80; pres SBAC 1963, memb NEDC 1964-67; govr: Repton Coll until 1982, Trent Coll, Manchester Business Sch; kt 1963; *Style—* Sir Denning Pearson, JP; Green Acres, Holbrook, Derbyshire (☎ 0332 881137)

PEARSON, Dr Donald William Macintyre; s of William Clark Gilmour Pearson (d 1982), of New Cumnock, Ayshire, and Morag Macrae, *née* Macintyre (d 1961); *b* 5 Sept 1950; *Educ* Cumnock Acad Cumnock Ayrshire, Univ of Glasgow (BSc, MB ChB, MRCP); *m* 26 Sept 1972, Margaret Jessie Kennedy, da of James Harris, of Auchenleck, Ayrshire; 2 s (Andrew b 1979, Donald b 1984), 1 da (Gillian b 1977); *Career* registrar Univ Dept of Med Glasgow Royal Infirmary 1979-81, sr registrar in med diabetes and endocrinology Grampian Health Authy 1982-84, hon sr lectr Univ of Aberdeen 1984- (lectr in med 1981-82), conslt physician Grampian Health Bd 1984-; memb: Br Diabetic Assoc, Euro Assoc for the Study of Diabetes, Scottish Soc for Experimental Med, Cncl Aberdeen Medico-Chirurgical Soc; hon sec Scottish Soc of Physicians; memb BMA, MRCP 1979, FRCP (Glasgow) 1988, FRCP(Ed) 1990; *Books* Carbohydrate Metabolism in Pregnancy and the New Born (ed with Sutherland and Stowers, 1989); *Recreations* golf; *Style—* Dr Donald Pearson; Diabetic Clinic, Woolman Hill, Aberdeen Royal Infirmary, Aberdeen, Scotland (☎ 0224 681818)

PEARSON, Lady Frances Elizabeth Ann; *née* Hay; da of 11th Marquess of Tweeddale (d 1967), by his 1 w Marguerite; *b* 1926; *m* 1956, Nigel Arthur Pearson (d 1975), s of Sir Neville Arthur Pearson, 2 Bt; *Style—* The Lady Frances Pearson

PEARSON, Hon Mrs (Francesca Mary); *née* Charteris; o da of Baron Charteris of Amisfield, GCB, GCVO, QSO, OBE, PC (Life Peer), *qv*; *b* 27 Sept 1945; *m* 1977, Malcolm Everard MacLaren Pearson; 2 da (Marina b 1980, Zara Alexandra Mary b 1984); *Style—* The Hon Mrs Pearson; 3 Shepherd's Close, London W1Y 3RT (☎ 071 629 2569)

PEARSON, Graham Scott; CB (1990); s of Ernest Reginald Pearson, and Alice, *née* Maclachlan (d 1987); *b* 20 July 1935; *Educ* Woodhouse Grove Sch Bradford Yorks, Univ of St Andrews (BSc, PhD); *m* 10 Sept 1960, Susan Elizabeth Meriton, da of Dr John Meriton Benn, CB; 2 s (Gavin b 1963, Douglas b 1965); *Career* Univ of Rochester NY 1960-62, princ scientific offr Rocket Propulsion Estab 1967-69 (sr sci offr Westcott 1962-67), explosives and propellants liaison offr Br Embassy Washington DC 1969-72, asst dir Naval Ordnance Servs Bath 1973-76, tech advsr explosives and safety Chevaline 1976-79, princ superintendent Perme Westcott 1979-80, dep dir 1 and 2 Rarde Fort Halstead 1980-83, dir gen R & D Royal Ordnance Factories 1983-84, dir Chemical Def Estab Porton Down 1984-; FBIS 1967, CChem, FRSC 1985, FRSA 1989; *Books* contrib: Advances in Inorganic and Radiochemistry Vol 8 (1966), Advances in Photochemistry Vol 3 (1964), Oxidation and Combustion Reviews Vol 3 and 4 (second edn, 1969); *Recreations* reading, long distance walking, foreign travel; *Style—* Dr G S Pearson, CB; MOD Chemical Def Estab, Porton Down, Salisbury, Wilts SP4 OJQ (☎ 0980 610211)

PEARSON, Hon Graham Thomas; s of Baron Pearson, CBE, PC (Life Peer, d 1980); *b* 1935; *m* 1963, Diana, da of Vice Adm Sir Maxwell Richmond, KBE, CB, DSO; *Style—* The Hon Graham Pearson

PEARSON, John C; s of Francis John Pearson (d 1978), of Newick House, Rottingdean, Sussex, and Mabel Alice, *née* Turley (d 1960); *b* 11 Nov 1932; *Educ* King's Sch Canterbury, Trinity Coll Dublin (MA, LLB); *Career* admitted slr 1960; sr ptnr John Pearson; involved: Malden and Dist C of C, CAB, old peoples' welfare orgns, Mid-Surrey Law Soc, Kingston Heritage; memb Law Soc 1960; *Recreations* walking, rowing, canoeing, opera; *Clubs* London Rowing; *Style—* John Pearson, Esq; 4 Kingston Rd, New Malden, Surrey (☎ 01 942 9193); 2 Kingston Rd, New Malden, Surrey (☎ 01 942 9191)

PEARSON, (Hugh) John Hampden; s of Lt-Col Hugh Henry Pearson (d 1975), and Sybil Monica, *née* Dunn; *b* 22 March 1947; *Educ* Charterhouse, King's Coll London (LLB); *m* 12 Oct 1974, Jacqueline Anne, da of Maj Harold Arthur Bird, of Goring, Sussex; 1 s (Daniel b 1982), 2 da (Alice b 1976, Juliet b 1978); *Career* admitted slr 1971, Stephenson Harwood 1971-73, Coward Chance 1973-86; ptnr: Durrant Piesse 1986-88, Lovell White Durrant 1988-; memb Cncl S African Townships Health Fund; memb: City of London Slrs Co 1982, Law Soc, Assoc of Pension Lawyers; *Recreations* reading, hill walking, squash, bridge, opera; *Clubs* MCC, Roehampton; *Style—* John Pearson, Esq; 15 Howard's Lane, London SW15 6NX; Providence Cottage, Buckland Newton, Dorset DT2 7BU; Lovell White Durrant, 65 Holborn Viaduct, London EC1A 2DY (☎ 071 236 0066, fax 071 248 4212, telex 887122)

PEARSON, Keith Philip; s of Fred Goring Pearson (d 1979), of Preston Lancs, and Phyllis, *née* Fryer; *b* 5 Aug 1941; *Educ* Preston GS, Madrid Univ, Univ of Cambridge (MA, DipEd); *m* 26 Aug 1965, Dorothy, da of Albert Edward Atkinson, of Woolley, Wakefield; 2 da (Lisa b 20 Nov 1968, Sally 13 May 1970); *Career* asst teacher then head of languages Rossall Sch 1964-72, dep princ George Watson's Coll 1979-83 (head of languages 1964-79), head-master, George Heriot's Sch 1983-; memb Scottish Consultative Cncl; memb HMC, SHA; *Recreations* sport, hill-walking, music, DIY, foreign travel; *Style—* Keith Pearson, Esq; George Heriot's School, Lauriston Place, Edinburgh EH3 9EQ (☎ 031 2297263)

PEARSON, Hon Michael Orlando Weetman; s and h of 3 Viscount Cowdray, TD, DL, and his 1 w, Lady Anne, *née* Bridgeman, da of 5 Earl of Bradford; *b* 17 June 1944; *Educ* Gordonstoun; *m* 1, 1977 (m dis), Ellen (Fritzi), da of Hermann Erhardt, of Munich; m 2, 1 July 1987, Marina Rose, da of John Howard Cordle, of Malmesbury House, The Close, Salisbury, and Mrs Venetia Caroline Ross Skinner, *née* Maynard; 3 da (Eliza Anne Venetia b 31 May 1988, Emily Jane Marina b 13 Dec 1989, Catrina Sophie Lavinia b 13 March 1991); *Career* non-exec dir Beckenham Group; *Clubs* White's; *Style—* The Hon Michael Pearson; Greenhill House, Vann Road, Fernhurst, nr Haslemere, Surrey (☎ 0428 53725)

PEARSON, Sir (Francis) Nicholas Fraser; 2 Bt (UK 1964), of Gressingham, Co Palatine of Lancaster; o s of Sir Francis Fenwick Pearson, 1 Bt, MBE (d 1991), and Katharine Mary, *née* Fraser; *b* 28 Aug 1943; *Educ* Radley; *m* 1978, Henrietta, da of Cdr Henry Pasley-Tyler, of Coton Manor, Guilsborough, Northants; *Heir* none; *Career* 3 Bn RB 1961-69 (ADC to C-in-C Far East 1969); Cons party candidate Oldham West 1975-78; dir: Saison Holdings BV, Inter-Continental Hotels Group Ltd, Voyager Travel Holdings Ltd; *Recreations* shooting, fishing, tennis, opera; *Clubs* Carlton; *Style—* Sir Nicholas Pearson, Bt; 9 Upper Addison Gardens, Holland Park, London W14 8AL

PEARSON, Richard John Crewdson; s of Maj R A R B Pearson (d 1983), and Evelyn Katherine, *née* Crewdson; *b* 4 May 1940; *Educ* Packwood Haugh, St Edward's Oxford, Univ of St Andrews (MA); *m* 30 Nov 1968, Catriona Wallace, da of Robert S Angus; 1 s (Richard b 25 Sept 1971), 1 da (Sarah Catriona b 13 April 1973); *Career* CA; ptnr Pannell Kerr Forster 1962-; auditor Corp of London; cmmr of taxes 1988; Freeman City of London, Liveryman Worshipful Co of Barbers 1971; FCA 1975 (ACA 1965), ICEAW; *Recreations* windsurfing, walking, sporting and country pursuits; *Clubs* Reform; *Style—* Richard Pearson, Esq; 6 The Lindens, Stock, Essex; 78 Hatton Garden, London EC1 (☎ 071 831 7393)

PEARSON, Dr Richard Martin; s of Leonard Louis Pearson, of Bournemouth, and late Anne, *née* Tobias; *b* 9 April 1943; *Educ* Royal GS High Wycombe, Gonville and Caius Coll Cambridge, St Mary's Hosp London; *Career* house surgn Addenbrooke's Hosp Cambridge 1967, house physician St Mary's Hosp London 1968, res fell and registrar Hammersmith Hosp 1971-73, sr registrar Royal Free Hosp 1977-80; conslt physician: Harold Wood and St Bart's Hosps 1981-, Musicians' and Keyboard Clinic 1986-; memb Library Ctee RSM; *Recreations* music, ballet, ornithology; *Clubs* Savile; *Style—* Dr Richard Pearson; The Musicians' and Keyboard Clinic, 7 Park Crescent, London W1N 3HE (☎ 071 436 5961)

PEARSON, Baroness; Sophie Grace Hermann; da of Arthur Hermann Thomas, MC, of Worthing; *m* 1931, Baron Pearson, CBE, PC (Life Peer, d 1980); 1 s, 1 da; *Style—* The Lady Pearson; 2 Crown Office Row, 3rd Floor West, Temple, London EC4Y 7HJ (☎ 071 353 5391)

PEARSON, (Geoffrey) Stuart; s of Geoffrey William Pearson, of Chapel House, Chantry Drive, Ilkley, W Yorkshire, and Joan, *née* Richardson; *b* 17 Aug 1947; *Educ* Bradford GS; *m* 27 June 1970, Jean Barbara, da of Capt Charles Raymond Clegg, of Ilkley; 1 s (James Stuart b 1974), 1 da (Emma Jane b 1972); *Career* sr ptnr: Rawlinsons CAs 1976-85, G S Pearson & Co CAs 1989-; chm: Moss Tst 1986-89, Hepburn plc 1989-; govr Bradford Girls GS; FCA 1970, FCCA 1974; *Recreations* reading, opera, squash; *Style—* Stuart Pearson, Esq; Glenside, Askwith, nr Otley, West Yorkshire (☎ 0943 466565); Realtex House, Leeds Rd, Rawdon, Leeds, W Yorkshire LS19 6AX (☎ 0532 500550, fax 0532 500566)

PEARSON, Gen Sir Thomas Cecil Hooke; KCB (1967, CB 1964), CBE (1959, OBE 1953), DSO (1940, and bar 1943), DL (Hereford and Worcester 1983); s of Vice Adm

J L Pearson, CMG (d 1965), and Phoebe Charlotte, *née* Beadon (d 1973); *b* 1 July 1914; *Educ* Charterhouse, RMC Sandhurst; *m* 1947, Aud, da of Alf Skjelkvale (d 1953), of Oslo; 2 s (Anthony, Thomas); *Career* cmmnd RB 1934, Staff Coll 1942, Cdr 2 Bn RB 1942-43, Dep Cdr 2 Para Bde and 1 Airlanding Bde 1944-45, Cdr 1 and 7 Para Bns 1945-47, dir staff Jt Servs Staff Coll 1950, Cdr 45 Para Bde (TA) 1955-56, Nat Def Coll Canada 1957, Cdr 16 Para Bde 1957-59, chief Br Mil Mission to Soviet Forces in Germany 1960-61, Maj-Gen cmd 1 Div BAOR 1961-63, COS Northern Army Gp 1963-67, Cdr FARELF 1967-68, mil sec MOD 1969-72, C-in-C Allied Forces Northern Europe 1972-74, Col Cmdt Royal Green Jackets 1973-77, ADC Gen to HM The Queen 1974, ret; fisheries memb Welsh Water Authy 1980-83; Haakon VII Liberty Cross 1945, Norwegian Defence Association Medal 1973; *Recreations* yachting, shooting, fishing; *Clubs* Naval and Military, Kongalig Norsk Seilforenning; *Style—* Gen Sir Thomas Pearson, KCB, CBE, DSO, DL

PEARSON LUND, Peter Graham; s of Douglas Pearson Lund, CBE (d 1974), of Springfields, Fetcham, Surrey, and Honor Winifred; *b* 9 Sept 1947; *Educ* Shiplake Coll Henley, Guildford Sch of Art; *m* 16 Nov 1968, Isabelle McLachlan; 2 s (Piers b 19 Oct 1969, Oliver b 10 Dec 1971); *Career* Tilney & Co 1969-70, Cazenove and Co 1970-73, Antony Gibbs 1973-75; md: Henderson Unit Trust Management (dir Henderson Administration Ltd) 1975-85, Gartmore Fund Managers Ltd (dir Gartmore Investment Management Ltd) 1985-; *Recreations* tennis, skiing, sailing; *Style—* Peter Pearson Lund, Esq; Gartmore Investment Management Ltd, Gartmore House, 16-18 Monument St, London EC3R 8QQ (☎ 071 623 1212, fax 071 782 2075)

PEARSON OF RANNOCH, Baron (Life Peer UK 1990), of Bridge of Gaur in the District of Perth and Kinross; Malcolm Everard MacLaren Pearson; *b* 20 July 1942; *Career* chm PWS Holdings plc; exec chm Lloyd's Insurance Brokers; *Style—* The Rt Hon Lord Pearson of Rannoch; c/o PWS Holdings plc, 52-56 Minories, London EC3N 1JJ

PEART, Baroness; Sarah Elizabeth; da of Thomas Lewis, of Aberystwyth; *m* 1945, Baron Peart, PC (Life Peer, d 1988); 1 s; *Style—* The Rt Hon Lady Peart

PEART, Prof Sir (William) Stanley; s of John George Francis Peart (d 1950), of London, and Margaret Joan, *née* Fraser (d 1977), of London; *b* 31 March 1922; *Educ* King's Coll Sch Wimbledon, St Marys Hosp Med Sch, Univ of London (MB BS, MD); *m* Peggy, da of Col Walter Parkes, DSO, MC; 1 s (Robert b 1955), 1 da (Celia b 1953); *Career* MRC res student Dept of Pharmacology Univ of Edinburgh 1946-48; St Mary's Hosp Med Sch: lectr in med 1950-54, sr lectr 1954-56, prof of med 1956-87; res fell Nat Inst Med Res 1950-52, master Hunterian Inst RCS 1988-; tstee: Wellcome Tst, Beit Tst; fell Imperial Coll 1988, FRS 1969, FRCP, kt 1985; *Recreations* walking, skiing, reading, gardening; *Style—* Prof Sir Stanley Peart; 17 Highgate Close, Highgate, London N6 4SD (☎ 081 341 3111), Hunterian Inst, Royal College of Surgeons (England), Lincoln's Inn Fields, London WC2A 3PN (☎ 071 405 3474 4104, fax 071 831 9438)

PEART, Susan Rhona; da of John Andrew Peart, of Lion's Gate, Itton, Chepstow, Gwent, and Hylda Craig, *née* Martin; *b* 31 July 1956; *Educ* Felixstowe Coll Suffolk; *m* 11 June 1988, John Anthony Francis Smythe, s of late Francis Smythe; *Career* Cosmopolitan: editorial asst 1979-81, sub ed 1981-82, asst features ed 1982-83, features ed 1983-84; dep features ed Daily Express 1985-87 (dep women's ed 1984-85), ed Sunday Express Magazine 1989- (dep ed 1987-89); runner up Catherine Pakenham Award 1981; memb Br Soc Magazine Eds 1987; *Recreations* entertaining, theatre, films, cooking, reading; *Style—* Ms Susan Peart; Express Newspapers plc, Ludgate House, 245 Blackfriars Rd, London SE1 9UX (☎ 071 928 8000, 071 928 7262)

PEART, Tony Christopher; s of Maj Brian Leonard Howard Peart, of Hawkshead, Ambleside, Cumbria, and Janet Elizabeth, *née* Shaw-Taylor; *b* 23 June 1951; *Educ* Oundle Sch, Univ of Leeds (BA), Univ of Newcastle (MA); *m* 4 April 1978, Sharynn Patricia, da of James William Brown (d 1987), of The Hollies, Battle Hill, Charlton Kings, Cheltenham; 3 s (Charles b 1979, Hector b 1981, Hermione b 1985); *Career* one man exhibitions incl: Marian Goodman Gallery NY 1978, LA Louver Venice California 1978, Bugdahn and Szeimies Dusseldorf 1980, Arnolfini Gallery Bristol 1982, Helene Spiro Paris 1983, Akademie Der Kunste Berlin 1985, Kunstueren Zurich 1988; memb: RSA, ROI, RSWA; *Books* A Whiter Shade of Pale The Modernist Gallery Space (1981), Trouble at the Edge - The History of the Frame (1983); *Recreations* reading, brick-laying, cooking; *Clubs* RSA; *Style—* Tony Peart, Esq; 4 Beanley Avenue, Lemington, Newcastle upon Tyne NE15 8SP (☎ 091 264559*6), 31 Rue Du Helder, Paris 9, France (☎ 47 03 92 91)

PEASE, Alexander Michael; s of Nicholas Edwin Pease (d 1975), and Anne Raikes (d 1985); *b* 14 March 1956; *Educ* Malvern, Mansfield Coll Oxford (MA); *m* 22 April 1989, Lucy Jane, da of (George) Anthony Slater, of Guildford; *Career* ptnr Allen & Overy 1989 (asst slr 1981); memb: Law Soc Int Bar Assoc, City of London Law Soc; *Style—* Alexander Pease, Esq; Allen & Overy, 9 Cheapside, London EC2V 6AD (☎ 071 2489898, fax 071 236 2192, telex 8812081)

PEASE, Hon Mrs (Elizabeth Jane); *née* Ormsby Gore; da of 4 Baron Harlech, KG, GCMG, PC (d 1964); *b* 1929; *m* 1962, Hon William Simon Pease, *qv*; *Style—* The Hon Mrs Pease; 29 Upper Addison Gardens, London W14 8AJ; Lepe House, Exbury, Southampton SO4 1AD

PEASE, Hon George; s of 2 Baron Gainford, TD (d 1971), and Veronica, Baroness Gainford, *qv*; hp of bro, 3 Baron Gainford; *b* 20 April 1926; *Educ* Eton, Edinburgh Coll of Art (DipArch, Dip TP); *m* 1958, Flora Daphne, da of Dr Neville Dyce Sharp; 2 s (Adrian Christopher b 1960, Matthew Edward b 1962), 2 da (Olivia Daphne b 1958, Samantha Rachel b 1965); *Career* served WWII RNVR; county planning offr Ross and Cromarty 1967-75, Scottish Office Inquiry Reporter 1979-89; chm The Saltire Soc 1987-90, dir Lothians Bldg Preservation Tst; ARIBA, ARIAS, MRTPI; *Style—* The Hon George Pease; Naemoor Gardens, Rumbling Bridge, Kinross KY13 7PY (☎ 05774 261)

PEASE, Hon Joanna Ruth Miriam; da of 3 Baron Gainford; *b* 22 Aug 1959; *Style—* The Hon Joanna Pease; c/o 1 Dedmere Court, Marlow, Bucks SL7 1PL (☎ 062 84 4679)

PEASE, Hon John Michael; s of 2 Baron Gainford, TD, and Veronica, Baroness Gainford, *qv*; *b* 22 Sept 1930; *Educ* Gordonstoun; *m* 1962, Catherine, da of Duncan Shaw; 3 s (David b 1964, Andrew b 1967, Daniel b 1973); *Career* farmer; *Recreations* shooting, painting, gardening; *Style—* The Hon John Pease; Auchentenavil, Tayvallich, Lochgilphead, Argyll

PEASE, Joseph Gurney; s of Sir Alfred Edward Pease, 2 Bt (d 1939), and hp of bro, Sir (Alfred) Vincent Pease, 4 Bt; *b* 16 Nov 1927; *Educ* Bootham Sch York; *m* 1953, Shelagh Munro, da of Cyril G Bulman; 1 s, 1 da; *Career* memb Guisborough UDC 1950-53; Lib candidate (gen elections): Bishop Auckland 1959, Darlington 1964, Westmoreland 1970, Penrith and the Border 1974; pres NE Young Lib Fedn 1961, memb Cncl Lib Pty 1969, pres NW Regnl Lib Pty 1970 and 1971; *Style—* Joseph Pease, Esq; Oak Tree House, Woodhall, Askrigg, Leyburn, N Yorks DL8 3LB

PEASE, Richard Peter; s and h of Sir Richard Thorn Pease, 3 Bt, of Hindley House, Stocksfield, Northumberland and Anne, *née* Heyworth; *b* 4 Sept 1958; *Educ* Eton, Univ of Durham; *Career* investmt fund mangr with Central Bd of Fin for the C of E; *Recreations* chess, bridge, backgammon, tennis, squash; *Clubs* Queen's; *Style—* Richard Pease, Esq; 7 St Dionis Rd, London SW6; Central Bd of Finance, Winchester Ho, 77 London WC11 EC2 (☎ 01 588 1815)

PEASE, Sir Richard Thorn; 3 Bt (UK 1920); s of Sir Richard Arthur Pease, 2 Bt (d 1969); *b* 20 May 1922; *Educ* Eton; *m* 9 March 1956, Anne, o da of Lt-Col Reginald Francis Heyworth (d 1941), and formerly w of David Henry Lewis Wigan; 1 s, 2 da; *Heir* s, Richard Peter Pease b 4 Sept 1958, *qv*; *Career* served WW II, 60 Rifles 1941-46; vice chm Barclays Bank Ltd 1970-82, vice chm Barclays Bank UK Mgmnt 1971-82, chm Foreign & Colonial High Income Trust, dir Grainger Tst plc; *Recreations* fishing; *Clubs* Brooks's, Pratt's; *Style—* Sir Richard Pease, Bt; Hindley House, Stocksfield-on-Tyne, Northumberland (☎ 0661 842361)

PEASE, Hon Mrs (Rosemary); *née* Portman; da of 5 Viscount Portman (d 1942); *b* 1931; *m* 1951, Derrick Allix Pease, s of Sir Richard Arthur Pease, 2 Bt (d 1969); 3 s, 1 da; *Style—* The Hon Mrs Pease; 2 Britten St, SW3; Upper Woodcott, Whitchurch, Hants

PEASE, Dr (Rendel) Sebastian; s of Michael Stewart Pease, OBE, JP (d 1966), of Reynolds Close, Girton, Cambridge, and Hon Helen Bowen, *née* Wedgwood, JP (d 1981); *b* 2 Nov 1922; *Educ* Bedales, Trinity Coll Cambridge (MA, ScD); *m* 9 Aug 1952, Susan, da of Capt Sir Frank Todd Spickernell, KBE, CB, CVO, DSO, RN (d 1956), of Deane, Kintbury, Berkshire; 2 s (Christopher b 1956, Roland b 1959), 3 da (Rosamund (Mrs Chalmers) b 1953, Sarah (Mrs Kimbell) b 1955, Rowan b 1963); *Career* asst sci offr op res Miny Aircraft Prodn 1942-46, Sci Civil Serv Harwell 1947-54; UKAEA 1954-87: sci offr 1954-61, dir Culham laboratories 1967-81, dir fusion res programme 1981-87; press Inst of Pyysics 1978-80; conslt: Progressive Engrg Conslts, Pease Ptnrs 1988-; visiting prof Univ of NSW 1991; playing memb Newbury Symphony Orch, chm Br Pugwash Gp 1988-; memb: Euro Physical Soc, Royal Soc, Fabian Soc; Hon D Univ Surrey 1973, Hon ScD Aston 1981, Hon DSc City 1987; Hon FINucE, FInstP 1967 (pres 1978-80), Hon FEns, CPhys, FIEE 1978, FRS 1977 (vice-pres 1986-87); *Recreations* music; *Style—* Dr Sebastian Pease, FRS; The Poplars, W Ilsley, Newbury, Berks (☎ 063528 237)

PEASE, Sir (Alfred) Vincent; 4 Bt (UK 1882); s of Sir Alfred (Edward) Pease, 2 Bt (d 1939), of Pinchinthorpe House, Guisborough, Cleveland, and Emily Elizabeth, *née* Smith (d 1979); half-bro of Sir Edward Pease, 3 Bt (d 1963); *b* 2 April 1926; *Educ* Bootham Sch York, Durham Sch of Agric; *Heir* bro, Joseph Gurney Pease; *Style—* Sir Vincent Pease, Bt; Flat 13, Hamilton House, Belgrave Road, Seaford, E Sussex BN25 2EL

PEASE, Hon William Simon; s of 1 Baron Wardington (d 1950), and Dorothy Charlotte (d 1983), da of 1 Baron Forster (d 1936, when title became extinct); hp of bro, 2 Baron Wardington; *b* 15 Oct 1925; *Educ* Eton, New Coll Oxford (MA), St Thomas's Hosp Medical Sch (MB BS); *m* 27 Oct 1962, Hon Elizabeth Jane Ormsby Gore, *qv*, da of 4 Baron Harlech, KG, GCMG, PC (d 1964); *Career* Capt Grenadier Gds 1944-47; former conslt surgn ENT Dept Central Middx and Northwick Park Hosps; FRCS; *Recreations* sailing, gardening; *Clubs* Royal Yacht Sqdn; *Style—* The Hon William Pease; 29 Upper Addison Gardens, London W14 8AJ (☎ 071 371 1776); Lepe House, Exbury, Southampton (☎ 0703 893724); 10 Upper Wimpole Street, London W1M 7TD (☎ 071 935 0147)

PEAT, Sir Gerrard Charles; KCVO (1988); s of Charles Urie Peat, MC, MP (d 1979), and Ruth Martha, *née* Pulley (d 1979); *b* 14 June 1920; *Educ* Sedbergh; *m* 17 June 1949, Margaret Josephine Collingwood, da of Cyril Wylam-Walker (d 1965); 1 s (Michael Charles Gerrard b 1949); *Career* served WWII pilot RAF and ATA 1940-45, pilot 600 City of London Aux Sqdn 1948-51; ptnr Peat Marwick Mitchell & Co 1956-87, underwriting memb Lloyds 1973-, auditor to Queen's Privy Purse 1980-88 (asst auditor 1969-80); memb: Ctee of Assoc of Lloyds Membs 1983-88, Corp of City of London 1973-78, cncl Lloyds of London 1989-; hon treas Assoc of Cons Clubs 1971-79; Liveryman Worshipful Co of Turners; FCA 1951; *Recreations* travel, shooting, fishing, golf, flying; *Clubs* Boodle's, City Livery; *Style—* Sir Gerrard Peat, KCVO; Home Farm, Mead Lane, Upper Basildon, Berks RG8 8ND (☎ 0491 671241); Flat 10, 35 Pont Street, London SW1X OBB (☎ 071 245 9736); Suite 607, Britannia House, Glenthorne Rd, London W6 0LF (☎ 081 748 9898, telex 916107, fax 081 748 4250)

PEAT, Sir Henry; KCVO (1980, CVO 1973), DFC; s of late Sir Harry (William Henry) Peat, GBE, KCVO; *b* 1913; *Educ* Eton, Trinity Coll Oxford; *Career* served WWII, Flt Lt RAF Bomber Cmd Europe 1939-45; FCA; *Style—* Sir Henry Peat, KCVO, DFC; c/o Cadenham Manor, nr Chippenham, Wiltshire SN15 4NL

PEAT, (William Wood) Watson; CBE (1972), JP (Stirlingshire, 1963); s of William Peat (d 1988), of Kirkland Farm, Denny, and Margaret, *née* Hillhouse (d 1986); *b* 14 Dec 1922; *Educ* Denny Public Sch; *m* 4 Oct 1955, Jean Frew Paton, da of James McHarrie, JP (d 1966), of Westwood, Stranraer; 2 s (James, William), 1 da (Margaret); *Career* served Lt RCS 1940-46 in NW Europe and India; farmer 1946-86 (ret); memb Nat Cncl of Scottish Assoc of Young Farmers' Club 1949-85 (chm 1953-54, pres 1979-81); gen cmmr of Income Tax 1962-; memb: Cncl of Nat Farmers' Union of Scotland 1959-78 (pres 1966-67), Stirling CC 1955-74 (vice-convenor 1967-70); chm BBC Scottish Agric Advsy Cmmn 1971-77; dir: Agri-Finance (Scotland) Ltd 1968-79, FMC plc 1974-83, Islay Farmers Ltd 1974-86; pres Cncl Scottish Agric Orgns Ltd 1974-77, vice-pres Assoc of Agric 1978-; chm: West of Scotland Agric Coll 1983-88 (govr 1964), Scottish Agric Coll 1986-; memb: Scottish River Purification Advsy Ctee 1960-79, cncl Hannah Res Inst 1963-82, Br Farm Produce Cncl 1964-87 (vice-chm 1974), Central Cncl for Agric and Horticultural Co-operation 1967-83, Br Agric Cncl 1974-83, Co-operative Devpt Bd Food From Britain 1983-89; govr W of Scotland Agric Coll 1964- (vice-chm 1975-, chm 1984-88); chm: bd of dirs Scottish Agric Colleges Ltd 1987-, BBC Scottish Agric Advsy Ctee 1971-75, Scottish Advsy Ctee Assoc of Agric 1974-79 (vice-pres 1979-); dir Fedn of Agric Co-operatives (UK) Ltd 1974-77; memb: Brit Agric Cncl 1974-84, govt ctee of enquiry into acquisition and occupancy of agric land 1977-79; BBC nat govr for Scotland, chm Broadcasting Cncl for Scotland 1984-89; pres Ariel Radio Gp BBC 1985-; FRAgS 1987, MRTS, memb Radio Soc of GB; OStJ 1987; *Recreations* amateur radio, flying, photography, gardening; *Clubs* Farmers', BBC; *Style—* Watson Peat, Esq, CBE, JP; Carbro, 61 Stirling Rd, Larbert, Stirlingshire FK5 4SG (☎ 0324 562420)

PECHELL, Dora, Lady; Dora Constance; da of late John Crampthorne; *m* 1949, Sir Ronald Horace Pechell, 9 and last Bt (d 1984); *Style—* Dora, Lady Pechell; 26 Burley Road, Summerley Private Estate, Felpham, West Sussex PO22 7NF

PECHELL, Doris, Lady; Doris Margery; da of late T Drewitt Lobb; *m* 1 (m dis), Lt-Col Arthur Thomas Begg Green, ED (d 1982); 1 da (Felicity Ann (Mrs Irwin), *qv*); *m* 2, 1971, as his 2 w, Sir Paul Pechell, 8 Bt, MC (d 1972); *Style—* Doris, Lady Pechell; 25 Marchwood, 8 Manor Rd, Bournemouth, Dorset

PECK, David Arthur; s of Frank Archibald Peck, of Sunningdale, Hatton Park, Wellingborough, Northants, and Molly, *née* Eyels; *b* 3 May 1940; *Educ* Wellingborough Sch, Univ of Cambridge (MA); *m* 3 Feb 1968, Jennifer Mary, da of Frederick William Still, of 7 Locke Rd, Liphook, Hants; 1 s (Mark b 12 June 1975), 2 da (Emma b 2 Oct 1970, Sophie b 11 Oct 1973); *Career* admitted slr 1966, sr ptnr Birkbeck Montagu's 1985- (ptnr 1967-); memb: Law Soc, Euro Slrs GP, Int Bar Assoc; *Clubs* Hawks, MCC; *Style—* David Peck, Esq; 26 Chepshow Place, London W2 (☎ 01 229 9674);

Pages, Brinton, Norfolk; 7 St Bride St, London EC4 (☎ 01 353 3222, fax 01 353 4761, telex 265068 BIRMON G)

PECK, His Honour Judge; David Edward; s of late William Edward Peck; *b* 6 April 1917; *Educ* Charterhouse, Balliol Coll Oxford; *m* 1, 1950 (m dis), Rosina Seton Glover Marshall; 1 s, 3 da; m 2, 1973, Frances Deborah Redford, *née* Mackenzie; 1 s; *Career* served WW II Cheshire Regt; barr Middle Temple 1949, circuit judge (formerly judge of Co Courts) 1969-; chm Co Court Rule Ctee 1981- (memb 1978-); *Style—* His Honor Judge Peck; 8 New Square, Lincoln's Inn, WC2A 3QP

PECK, Dennis Ralph; s of Ralph Denoon Peck (d 1961), and Florence Scott, *née* Campbell (d 1962); *b* 12 Aug 1914; *Educ* Rugby, London Sch of Printing; *m* 22 Oct 1938, Jean Corbett, da of Harvey Wiley Corbett (d 1954), of NYC, USA; 2 s (John Forbes Steuart b 1943, Christopher Wallace b 1949), 1 da (Ann Harvey (Mrs Gover) b 1940); *Career* writer and composer; over 700 songs, 2 operas, musical pieces, performed as soloist and with other singers in own Scot song programmes in London, Edinburgh and Oxford, recitals in Purcell Room South Bank London; apprenticed to Worshipful Co of Stationers; former memb NFU, memb Soc of Authors; *Books* Bess The Story of Horse (1960), Poems and Translations (1962), Suzanne the Elephant (1968), Jottings of a Genuis (1986); *Recreations* listening to opera, re-reading great literature, admiring Glencoe; *Style—* Dennis Peck, Esq; Flat 2, 167 Woodstock Road, Oxford OX2 7NA (☎ 0865 53694), The Woodstock Press, 167 Woodstock Rd, Oxford OX2 7NA (☎ 0865 53694)

PECK, Sir Edward Heywood; GCMG (1974, KCMG 1966, CMG 1957); s of Lt-Col Edward Surman Peck, IMS (d 1934), and Doris Louise Heywood (d 1934); *b* 5 Oct 1915; *Educ* Clifton, Queen's Coll Oxford (MA); *m* 1948, Alison Mary, da of late John MacInnes, of Sevenoaks; 1 s, 2 da; *Career* entered Consular Serv 1938, served Turkey, Greece, India and Singapore 1940-60, dep cmdt Br Sector Berlin 1955-58; asst under sec of state for SE Asia and Far Eastern Affrs FCO 1960-65, high cmmr Kenya 1966-68, dep under sec of state FCO 1968-70, Br perm rep to N Atlantic Cncl 1970-75, ret; hon visiting fell Def Studies Univ of Aberdeen 1976-85; memb Cncl of Nat Tst for Scot 1982-87; *Publications* North-East Scotland, Avonside Explored; *Recreations* hill walking, skiing, reading history, writing guide-books; *Clubs* Alpine, Royal Geographical Soc; *Style—* Sir Edward Peck, GCMG; (☎ 080 74 318)

PECK, Sir John Howard; KCMG (1971, CMG 1956); s of late Howard Peck, and Dorothea Peck; *b* 16 Feb 1913; *Educ* Wellington, Corpus Christi Coll Oxford; *m* 1, 1939, Mariska Caroline (d 1979), da of Josef Somlo; 2 s; m 2, 1987, Catherine, yst da of Edward McLaren; *Career* asst private sec to: First Lord of the Admty 1937-39, Min for Co-ordination of Def 1939-40, PM 1940-46; UK perm rep to the Cncl of Europe, consul-gen Strasbourg 1959-62; ambass to: Senegal 1962-66, Mauritania 1962-65; asst under-sec of state FO then FCO 1966-70; ambass to the Repub of Ireland 1970-73; *Books* Dublin from Downing Street (memoirs, 1978); *Style—* Sir John Peck, KCMG; Stratford, Saval Park Rd, Dalkey, Co Dublin (☎ 0001 806315)

PECK, Maj-Gen Richard Leslie; CB (1990); s of Frank Archibald Peck, of Wellingborough, Northants, and Molly, *née* Eyels; *b* 27 May 1937; *Educ* Wellingborough Sch, RMA Sandhurst, RMCS Shirvenham (BSc); *m* 4 Aug 1962, Elizabeth Ann (Liz), da of Maj Denis James Bradley, of Shrivenham; 2 s (David b 1967, Simon b 1972), 1 da (Sarah b 1965); *Career* cmmnd RE 1957, Troop Cdr Cyprus 1962, instr RMAS 1965, Staff Coll 1968, Bde Maj 1969, Sqdn Cdr BAOR 1972, DS Staff Coll 1973, CO BAOR 1977, MOD Col (MS) 1979, Bde Cdr 1981, RCDS 1984, Engr-in-Chief MOD 1988- (personnel dir 1985); CEng, FICE, FRGS; *Recreations* cricket, golf, shooting, swimming; *Clubs* Army and Navy, Royal Mid-Surrey Golf, MCC, Free Foresters; *Style—* Maj-Gen Richard Peck, CB; Engineer in Chief (Army), Northumberland House, Northumberland Ave, London WC2N 5BP (☎ 071 218 4524)

PECK, Stanley Edwards; CBE (1974), BEM (1954), QPM (1964), DL (Staffs 1962); s of Harold Edwards Peck, of Shanghai and Edgbaston (d 1962), and Mabel Beatrice Bevan, *née* Bell (d 1966); *b* 24 Jan 1916; *Educ* Solihull Sch, Univ of Birmingham; *m* 1939, Yvonne Sydney Edwards, da of John Edwards Jessop (d 1965); 2 s (John, Timothy), 2 da (Josephine, Angela); *Career* Flt Lt RAF 1941-45; Met Police 1935-54, supt New Scotland Yard 1950, chief constable Staffs 1960-64 (asst and dep chief constable 1954-60), HM inspector of constabulary 1964-78, memb Br Rail Bd Police Ctee 1978-87; pres Royal Life Saving Soc (UK) 1969-74; OStJ; *Recreations* golf, dog walking; *Clubs* RAF; *Style—* Stanley Peck, Esq, CBE, BEM, QPM, DL; Lodge Gdns, Walnut Grove, Radcliffe-on-Trent, Notts (☎ 0602 332361)

PECKER, Morley Leo; s of Alec Pecker (d 1975), of London; *b* 7 April 1937; *Educ* Epsom Coll; *Career* Nat Serv 2 Lt RA 1960-63; CA; articles Charles Eves Lord and Co 1954-60, mangr RF Frazer & Co 1963-65, sr advsr accountant Bd of Inland Revenue 1965-73, princ admin Cmmn Euro Communities Brussels 1973-; memb Int Hockey Fedn, hon treas Euro Hockey Fedn, memb Br Olympic Assoc, hon life memb The Cricket Soc, past hon treas Middx Cricket Union; Olympic Hockey judge: Munich 1972, Montreal 1976, Moscow 1980, Los Angeles 1984; memb Inst of Taxation 1964; ACA 1960, FCA 1970; *Recreations* hockey, cricket, music, photography; *Clubs* Chateau St Anne Belgium, MCC, The Cricket Society; *Style—* Morley Pecker, Esq; Le Grand Forestier, Ave du Grand Forestier 26 (Box 10),B-1160 Brussels, Belgium (☎ Brussels 672 57 85); Commission of the European Communities, 200 Rue de la Loi, B-1049 Brussels, Belgium (☎ Brussels 235 53 79, fax Brussels 235 95 85)

PECKHAM, Prof Catherine Stevenson; da of Dr Alexander King, CBE, CMG, of 168 Rue de Grenelle, Paris, and Sarah Maskell, *née* Thompson; *b* 7 March 1937; *Educ* St Paul's Girls' Sch London, Univ of London (MB BS, MD); *m* 7 Oct 1958, Prof Michael John Peckham, qv, s of William Stuart Peckham (d 1981); 3 s (Alexander b 1962, Daniel Gavin b 1964, Robert Shannan b 1965); *Career* reader in community med Charing Cross Hosp Med Sch 1977-85, prof of paediatric epidemiology Inst of Child Health and hon conslt Hosp for Sick Children Great Ormond St 1985- (sr lectr and hon conslt 1975-77), hon conslt Public Health Laboratory 1985-; memb US Fulbright Cmmn 1987-; FRCP 1988, FFCM 1980; *Recreations* flute; *Style—* Prof Catherine Peckham; 35 Brook Green, London W6 7BL (☎ 071 602 2347); Institute of Child Health, Guilford St, London WC1

PECKHAM, Prof Michael John; s of William Stuart Peckham (d 1981), and Gladys Mary, *née* Harris; *b* 2 Aug 1935; *Educ* William Jones W Monmouthshire Sch, St Catharine's Coll Cambridge (MA, MD), UCH Med Sch; *m* 7 Oct 1958, Catherine Stevenson, qv, da of Dr Alexander King, CMG, CBE, of 168 Rue de Grenelle, Paris; 3 s (Alexander b 1962, Daniel Gavin b 1964, Robert Shannan b 1965); *Career* Capt RAMC 1960-62; clinical res cncl scholar MRC Paris 1965-67, dean Inst of Cancer Res London 1984-86 (sr lectr 1972-74, prof 1974-86), civilian conslt to RN 1975-, dir Br Postgrad Med Fedn 1986, dir of res and devpt Dept of Health 1991; pres: Euro Soc of Therapeutic Radiology and Oncology 1984-85, Br Oncology Assoc 1986-88, Fedn of Euro Cancer Socs 1989; ed in chief European Journal of Cancer 1990-, fndr Bob Champion Cancer Tst; memb special health authy: Hosps for Sick Children Gt Ormond St, Brompton and Nat Heart Hosp, Hammersmith Hosp Imperial Cancer Res Fund (vice chm cncl); FRCP, FRCR, FRCPG; *Recreations* painting; *Style—* Prof Michael Peckham; Department of Health, Richmond House, 79 Whitehall, London SW1

PECKOVER, Richard Stuart; s of Rev Cecil Raymond Peckover, and Grace Lucy, *née* Curtis; *b* 5 May 1942; *Educ* King Edward VII Sch King's Lynn, Wadham Coll Oxford (MA), CCC Cambridge (PhD); *Career* UKAEA 1969-: res scientist Culham Laboratory 1969-81, res assoc MIT 1973-74, branch head Safety and Reliability Directorate 1983-87 (gp ldr 1982), dir Winfrith 1990- (asst dir 1987, dep dir 1989), chm SIESO 1989-; FIMA, FInstP, FRAS, FRMetS, FSaRS; *Recreations* walking, talking, listening to music; *Clubs* United Oxford and Cambridge; *Style—* Richard Peckover, Esq; 6 The Square, Puddletown, Dorset DT2 8SL; Atomic Energy Establishment, Winfrith, Dorchester, Dorset DT2 8DH (☎ 0305 251 888)

PEDDER, Vice Adm Sir Arthur (Reid); KBE (1959), CB (1956); s of Sir John Pedder, KBE, CB (d 1954), and Frances Evelyn Sharpe (d 1952); *b* 6 July 1904; *Educ* RNC Osborne, RNC Dartmouth; *m* 1934, Dulcie, da of Oscar Bickford (d 1954); 2 s; *Career* joined RN 1917, naval observer 1930, Cdr Admty 1937-40; served: HM Penelope, HM Mauritius; cmd: HM Khedive, HM Phoebe; Capt 1944, returned to Admty, dep dir of Plans 1949-50, fourth Naval Memb Aust Cwlth Naval Bd 1950-52, Rear Adm 1953, Asst Chief of Naval Staff (Warfare) Admty 1953-54, Flag Offr Aircraft Carriers 1954-56, Vice Adm 1956, Cdr Allied Naval Forces Northern Europe 1957-59; ran beef cattle farm on retirement; *Recreations* keeping alive; *Clubs* Athenaeum, Ski of GB; *Style—* Vice Admiral Sir Arthur Pedder, KBE, CB; Langhurst, Barn Cottage, Hascombe, Godalming, Surrey (☎ 048 632 294)

PEDDER, Air Marshal Sir Ian Maurice; KCB (1982), OBE (1963), DFC (1949); s of Maurice Albert Pedder (d 1967), and Elsie Pedder (d 1981); *b* 2 May 1926; *Educ* Royal GS High Wycombe, Queen's Coll Oxford; *m* 1949, Jean Mary, da of Tom Kellett; 1 s, 2 da; *Career* served in sqdns in Far East, Germany and UK 1944-64, directing staff RAF Staff Coll 1964-67, staff and cmd appts 1967-80, dep controller Nat Air Traffic Servs 1977-81 controller 1981-85; Air Marshal 1981; memb Bd CAA 1981-85; co dir Davies and Newman plc; *Clubs* Royal Air Force, Victory Services; *Style—* Air Marshal Sir Ian Pedder, KCB, OBE, DFC; The Chestnuts, Cheddar, Somerset

PEDDIE, Hon Ian James Crofton; s of Baron Peddie (Life Peer) (d 1978); *b* 1945; *Educ* Gordonstoun, UCL (LLB); *m* 1976, Susan Renée, da of Edmund John Brampton Howes; *Career* barr Inner Temple 1971; *Style—* The Hon Ian Peddie; 36 Chiswick Staithe, Hartington Road, London W4 3TP

PEDDIE, Peter Charles; CBE (1983); s of Ronald Peddie, CBE, JP (d 1986), of Springwater Farm, Mudgley, Wedmore, Somerset, and Vera, *née* Nicklin (d 1981); *b* 20 March 1932; *Educ* Canford, St John's Coll Cambridge (MA); *m* 25 June 1960, Charlotte Elizabeth, da of Ernest Pierce Ryan (d 1982), of Sunny Cottage, Betchworth, Surrey; 2 s (Andrew b 20 Sept 1963, Jonathan b 5 May 1968), 2 da (Emma b 20 June 1961, Rachel b 9 Aug 1965); *Career* admitted slr 1957, ptnr Freshfields 1960- (asst slr 1957-60); govr Canford Sch 1981-, special tstee Middx Hosp 1977-, memb Cncl Middx Hosp Med Sch 1977-88; Freeman Worshipful Co of Slrs; memb: Law Soc, Slrs Benevolent Assoc; *Recreations* gardening; *Clubs* City of London; *Style—* Peter Peddie, Esq, CBE; Whitefriars, 65 Fleet St, London EC4Y 1HT (☎ 071 936 4000, fax 071 248 3487/8/9, telex 889 292)

PEDDIE, Robert Allan; s of Robert Allan Peddie (d 1966), of Hillside, Sutton, Kingston upon Hull, and Elizabeth Elsie, *née* Sharp (d 1988); *b* 27 Oct 1921; *Educ* Hull Tech Coll, Univ of Nottingham (BSc); *m* 6 April 1946, Ilene Ivy (d 1990), da of John Sillcock (d 1956); 1 da (Barbara Elizabeth b Jan 1952); *Career* CEGB: asst regnl dir NW Regn 1962-65, dep dir gen Midland Region 1966-70, dir gen SE Region 1970-72, memb Bd 1972-77; memb Bd UKAEA 1973-77, chm South Eastern Electricity Bd 1977-83 (conslt 1983-); first station mangr Bradwell Nuclear Power Station, reactor design engr (all nuclear power stations) CEGB; chm Sovereign Youth and Community Centre; Freeman City of London 1981; FIMechE 1961, FInstE 1962, FIEE 1963; *Recreations* swimming, golf, DIY; *Style—* Robert Peddie, Esq; 5 The Mount Drive, Reigate, Surrey RH2 0EZ (☎ 0737 244996)

PEDERSEN, Cecil Ivan; s of Ivan Pedersen (d 1963), of London, and Ethel Mary, *née* McCormick; *b* 31 May 1931; *Educ* Owen's Sch London; *m* 4 June 1960, (Anne) Isabel, da of Samuel James Curry, OBE, JP, of Coleraine, Co Londonderry NI; 2 da (Catherine b 1961, Hilary b 1964); *Career* RAF: Nat Serv Cmmn 1949, short serv cmmn, sponsored to study Russian London Univ 1953, instr in Russian Jt Servs Sch for Linguists 1956-58; sr ed asst The Iron and Steel Inst 1959-61; press offr: DSIR 1961-62, PR Prodn Engrg Res Assoc (PERA) 1962-66, Decca Radar ltd 1966-67; asst sec The Inst of Physics 1967-84 (managing ed 1967-70, dir of publishing 1970-84), md Adam Hilger Ltd 1976-84, publishing conslt 1985-, chief exec Br Assoc Industl Eds 1986-; FInst D, FAIE (Fell Br Assoc of Idustl Eds); *Recreations* bridge, outdoor activites, photography; *Clubs* Danish, Royal Cwlth Soc, Remenham (Henley); *Style—* Cecil Pedersen, Esq

PEDERSEN, Vagn Sondergaard; s of Holger Pedersen (d 1988), of Denmark, and Dorthea, *née* Jensen; *b* 27 April 1943; *Educ* Arhus Graduate Sch of Mgmnt Denmark (Cand Merc); *m* 27 June 1970, Helle Skovridder, da of Albert Jorgensen, of Denmark; 2 s (Christian b 19 March 1972, Steffen b 4 Sept 1975); *Career* asst gen mangr and sec to Bd of Mgmnt Provinsbanken Denmark 1973-81, regnl gen mangr Sparekassen SDS Denmark 1981-84, md and chief exec SDS Bank Ltd London (formerly London Interstate Bank Ltd) 1987-90 (dir and gen mangr 1984, dep md 1985), exec vice pres and dir Int Div Unibank A/S Denmark 1990; memb: ctee Assoc of Int Savings Banks in London 1986-90 (chm 1987-88), ctee Danish Club in London 1989-90, Anglo-Danish Trade Advsy Bd 1987-90, cncl Danish Church in London 1989-90; memb Bd: Unibank SA Luxembourg, Unileasing A/S Denmark, Unibors Borsmaglerselskab A/S Denmark; *Books* Fremtidens Sparekasse System (1972), Pantebreve Effektiv Rente for og efter Skat (1973); *Recreations* skiing, tennis, family life; *Clubs* Danish, Foreign Bankers; *Style—* Vagn Pedersen, Esq; 34 Calonne Rd, Wimbledon, London SW19 5HJ (☎ 081 946 2002)

PEDLER, Sir Frederick Johnson; s of Charles Henry Pedler (d 1935), and Lucy Marian, *née* Johnson; *b* 10 July 1908; *Educ* Watford GS, Gonville and Caius Coll Cambridge; *m* 1935, Esther Ruth, da of Henry F Carling (d 1949), of Peppard Common, Oxon; 2 s (Robin, Martin), 1 da (Esther); *Career* chief Br econ rep Dakar 1942, fin dept Colonial Off 1944, chm Cncl for Tech Educn in Overseas Countries 1959-71, dep chm United Africa Co 1965-68; dir: Unilever Ltd and NV 1956-68, William Baird Ltd 1969-75; treas SOAS 1969-81 (hon fell); kt 1969; *Books* West Africa (1951), Economic Geography of West Africa (1957), The Lion and the Unicorn in Africa (1974), Main Currents of West African History 1940-78 (1979), A Pedler Family History (1984), A Wider Pedler Family History (1989); *Clubs* Reform; *Style—* Sir Frederick Pedler; 36 Russell Rd, Moor Park, Northwood, Middx HA6 2LR

PEDLER, Garth; s of Thomas Wakeham Pedler (d 1984), of Exeter, and Ruby, *née* Cornish; the 2000 or so Pedlers/Pedlars alive today and scattered round the world descend from just three families in 1542 in Wadebridge, Boyton and Okehampton, all in turn descended from ancestors in Clawton, Devon in the 13th century; the earliest record of the name is that of Roger Pedelevre (Pie-de-Lièvre) in 1148 (Buckfast Abbey cartulary); *b* 21 Feb 1946; *Educ* King's Coll Taunton; *Career* Touche Ross & Co 1969-73, taxation cnslt; FCA, ATII; *Books* The 9.5 mm Vintage Film Encyclopaedia (ed and jt-author), biography of Joan Morgan; regular contributor to Classic Images USA 1982-; *Recreations* vintage film research and associated journalism, genealogy, history of transport, alpine hiking in summer; *Style—* Garth Pedler, Esq; Hay Hill, Totnes, Devon TW9 5LH

PEDLEY, Roger Keith; s of Thomas Kenneth Fitzgeorge Pedley (d 1976), and Winifred Gordon, *née* Smith; *b* 12 Oct 1944; *Educ* King's Sch Worcester; *m* 26 Oct 1970, Paula Lesley, da of George Holland; 1 s (Rupert b 1980), 1 da (Helen b 1977); *Career* CA; Peat Marwick Mitchell 1968-; PMM: Paris 1969-72, Nottingham 1973-75, London 1975-76, ptnr 1976 in Nottingham; managing ptnr Peat Marwick McLintock Derby off 1980; *Recreations* flyfishing, windsurfing; *Style—* Roger K Pedley, Esq; Pear Treehouse, Church Street, Ockbrook, Derbyshire DE7 3SL (☎ 0332 662368); Peat Marwick McLintock, 1/2 Irongate, Derby DE1 3FJ (☎ 0332 49268, car 0860 712000)

PEDLEY, Rev (Geoffrey) Stephen; QHC (1985); s of Rev Prebendary Geoffrey Heber Knight Pedley (d 1974), and Muriel, *née* Nixon (d 1972); *b* 13 Sept 1940; *Educ* Marlborough, Queen's Coll Cambridge (MA), Cuddesdon Coll Oxford; *m* 9 Jan 1970, Mary Frances, da of Rev Canon Alexander Macdonald (d 1980); 2 s (Mark Alexander b 1974, Andrew Francis b 1976), 1 da (Philippa Rose b 1979); *Career* asst curate: Liverpool Parish Church 1966, Holy Trinity Coventry 1969; rector Kitwe Zambia 1971-77, vicar St Peter's Stockton 1977-88, rector Whickham 1988-; memb Gateshead Metropolitan Educn Ctee; *Style—* The Rev Stephen Pedley, QHC; The Rectory, Church Chare, Whickham, Newcastle upon Tyne NE16 4SH (☎ 091 488 7397)

PEEBLES, Hon Mrs (Annabel); *née* Elton; da of 2 Baron Elton; *b* 24 Oct 1960; *m* 5 July 1986, Donald M Peebles, er s of Dr R Anthony Peebles, of Hampton Court, Surrey; 2 da (Emma Richenda b 11 July 1988, Rosalie b 10 Jan 1990); *Style—* Hon Mrs Peebles

PEEBLES, Robert Andrew (Andy); s of Robert Peebles (d 1961), and Mary Jean, *née* Simmonds; *b* 13 Dec 1948; *Educ* Bishop's Stortford Coll Herts, Bournemouth Coll Of Tech; *Career* BBC Radio Manchester 1973, Piccadilly Radio Manchester 1974-78, BBC World Serv 1978-88, BBC Radio One 1978-, BBC Schools Radio 1983-87, BBC Radio Sport 1983-; *Books* The Lennon Tapes (1981), The Elton Jones Tapes (1981); *Recreations* sport, cinema, photography; *Clubs* Harlequins Rugby Football Club, Lancashire County Cricket Club; *Style—* Andy Peebles, Esq; BBC Radio, Broadcasting House, London W1A 4WW (☎ 01 927 4847)

PEECH, Neil Malcolm; s of Albert Orlando Peech; *b* 27 Jan 1908; *Educ* Wellington, Magdalen Coll Oxford; *m* 1932, Margaret Josephine, da of Richard Coningsby Smallwood, CBE (d 1933), of Mile Path House, Hook Heath, Surrey; 1 s, 1 da; *Career* Steetley Co Ltd: md 1935-68, chm 1935-76, pres 1976-; dir Albright & Wilson Ltd 1958-79; Lloyd's underwriter 1950-69; High Sheriff Yorks 1959; *Style—* Neil Peech, Esq; Park House, Firbeck, Worksop (☎ 0909 730338)

PEEK, Sir Francis Henry Grenville; 4 Bt (UK 1874); s of Sir Wilfrid Peek, 3 Bt, DSO (d 1927); *b* 16 Sept 1915; *Educ* Eton, Trinity Coll Cambridge; *m* 1, 1942 (m dis 1949), Ann, da of late Capt Gordon Duff and wid of Sir Charles Mappin (she m 1951, Sir William Rootes, later 1 Baron Rootes); m 2, 1949 (m dis 1967), Marilyn, da of Dr Norman Kerr (she m 1967, Peter Quennell); 1 s (decd); m 3, 1967, Mrs Caroline Kirkwood, da of Sir Robert Lucien Morrison Kirkwood, *qv*; *Heir* kinsman, William Grenville Peek; *Career* ADC to Govr of Bahamas 1938-39, served Irish Guards 1939-46; *Style—* Sir Francis Peek, Bt; Los Picos, Nagueles, Marbella, Spain (☎ 774736); 60 Grosvenor Close, Nassau, Bahamas

PEEK, Capt William Grenville; s of late Capt Roger Grenville Peek (2 s of 2 Bt) and hp of kinsman, Sir Francis Peek, 4 Bt; *b* 15 Dec 1919; *Educ* Eton; *m* 1950, Lucy Jane, da of late Maj Edward Dorrien-Smith; 1 s, 3 da; *Career* Capt late 9 Lancers WWII serv 1939-45 (despatches); *Clubs* Royal Western Yacht; *Style—* Capt William Peek; Weekemoor, Loddiswell, S Devon

PEEL, Hon Mrs (Ann Katharine); *née* de Yarburgh-Bateson; o child of 6 Baron Deramore; *b* 10 Aug 1950; *m* 15 May 1982, Jonathan Henry Maconchy Peel, er s of Walter Peel, of Knockdromin, Lusk, Co Dublin; 1 s (Nicholas Richard Yarburgh b 1987), 1 da (Katharine Diana b 1985); *Style—* The Hon Mrs Peel; Sturdy Cottage, High Street, Thornborough, Buckinghamshire

PEEL, (Edmund) Anthony; s of Sir Jonathan Peel, CBE, MC, DL (d 1979), and Daphne Margaret Holwell, *née* Pakenham; *b* 4 Feb 1933; *Educ* Malvern, Pembroke Coll Cambridge (BA, MA); *m* 30 May 1964, Marion Julia, da of Lister Percy Redfern Bass (d 1989), of Fivecorners, Wickham Bishops, Essex; 1 s (Richard b 1969), 1 da (Verity b 1965); *Career* admitted slr 1962, Asher Prior Bates & Ptnrs Colchester; memb: Maldon DC 1973-83, Essex CC 1981-85 and 1989-; dep chm Maldon and Rochford Cons Assoc 1975-77, treas S Colchester and Maldon Cons Assoc 1984-86, chm Colne Housing Soc 1988-; memb: Law Soc 1962, Cncl Univ of Essex 1990; legal memb Royal Town Planning Inst 1967; *Style—* Anthony Peel, Esq; Elm House, Tolleshunt D'Arcy, Maldon, Essex; Blackburn House, 32 Crouch St, Colchester (☎ 0206 768 331, fax 0206 760 096)

PEEL, Gp Capt Geoffrey William; s of Capt Lawrence Peel (ka 1914), of Knowlmere Manor, Clitheroe, Lancs, and Hon Lady (Ethel Laura) Martin (d 1967), da of 2 Baron Crawshaw; *b* 20 Dec 1913; *Educ* Winchester, Magdalene Coll Cambridge (MA); *m* 3 Aug 1938, (Grace) Marjorie, da of Rev Canon Frank Rupert Mills (d 1955), of The Vicarage, Liskeard, Cornwall; 1 s (Anthony b 1941), 2 da (Anne b 1947, Rosemary b 1952); *Career* cmmnd pilot Gen Duties Branch RAF 1935, 16 Sqdn (Army Co-operation) 1936-38, Special Engr Course Home Aircraft Depot Henlow 1938-40, station engr offr RAF West Freugh 1940-41, Wing Cdr Engr Air HQ Iraq 1941, chief tech offr Aircraft Depot Iraq 1942, CO HQ Maintenance Unit Iraq 1942, CO RAF Shaibah Iraq 1943, engr SO HQ 206 Gp Middle East 1943-45, Gp Capt engr HQ Bomber Cmd 1945, HQ 8 Gp (pathfinder) 1945, ret 1946; co dir 1947-55, freelance industl conslt 1955-60, sec and industl conslt to Trade Assoc 1960-85; *Recreations* rifle shooting, tennis, shooting, foreign travel; *Style—* Gp Capt Geoffrey Peel; The Mews, Sherborne Court, Bourton-on-The-Water, Gloucs GL54 2BY (☎ 0451 20881)

PEEL, Jack Armitage; CBE (1972), DL (W Yorks 1971); s of George Henry Peel, of 8 Locherbe Green, Allerton, and Martha Peel; *b* 8 Jan 1921; *Educ* Ruskin Coll Oxford (Dip SocSci); *m* 1950, Dorothy Mabel, da of Walter Dobson, of 18 Melton Terrace, Bradford; 1 s, 1 da; *Career* trade union offr Nat Union of Dyers Bleachers and Textile Workers 1951-73, TUC gen cnsllr 1966-73, pt/t dir NCB 1968-73; div industl rels EEC 1973-79 (chief advsr 1979-81); writer, industl rels conslt 1981-, special advsr industl rels to Sec of State for Tport 1983-84, sr visiting fell industl rels Univ of Bradford 1984-; JP Bradford 1960-72; Hon MA Bradford 1979; *Books* The Real Power Game, What Price Europe?; *Style—* Jack Peel, Esq, CBE, DL; Timberleigh, 39 Old Newbridge Hill, Avon, Bath (☎ 0225 423959)

PEEL, Prof John David Yeadon; s of Prof Edwin Arthur Peel, of Birmingham, and Nora Kathleen, *née* Yeadon (d 1988); *b* 13 Nov 1941; *Educ* Kings Edward's Sch Birmingham, Balliol Coll Oxford (MA), LSE (PhD), Univ of London (DLit); *m* 4 Sept 1969, Jennifer Christine Ferial, da of Maj Kenneth Nathaniel Pare; 3 s (David Nathaniel Yeadon b 16 March 1972, Timothy James Olatokunbo b 30 Jan 1974, Francis Edwin b 27 March 1977); *Career* asst lectr and lectr in sociology Univ of Nottingham 1966-70, lectr in sociology LSE 1970-73, visiting reader in sociology and anthropology Univ of Ife Nigeria 1973-75, Charles Booth prof of sociology Univ of Liverpool 1975-89 (dean of faculty of social and environmental studies 1985-88), visiting prof of anthropology and sociology Univ of Chicago 1982-83, prof of anthropology and sociology with reference to Africa SOAS Univ of London 1989-; ed Africa (jl of Int African Inst) 1979-86, gen ed Int African Library 1985-, advising ed African Studies Series 1986-; writer of numerous scholarly articles in Africanist, anthropological and sociological jls; Amaury Talbot Prize for African Anthropology 1983, Herskovits Award for African Studies (USA) 1984; memb Assoc Social Anthropologists 1979; *Books* Aladura: A Religious Movement among the Yoruba (1968), Herbert Spencer: The Evolution of a Sociologist (1971), Ijeshas and Nigerians: The Incorporation of a Yoruba Kingdom (1985); *Recreations* gardening, walking, old churches; *Style—* Prof J D Y Peel; Bryn Tirion, 23 Mount Rd, Upton, Wirral, Merseyside L49 6JA (☎ 051 678 6783); Dept of Anthropology and Sociology, School of Oriental and African Studies (University of London), Thornhaugh St, London WC1H 0XG (☎ 071 323 6217)

PEEL, Sir John Harold; KCVO (1960); s of Rev John Edward Peel and Katherine Hannah Peel; *b* 10 Dec 1904; *Educ* Manchester GS, Queen's Coll Oxford (MA, BM BCh), King's Coll Hosp Med Sch; *m* 1, 1935 (m dis 1945), Muriel Elaine Pellow; 1 da; m 2, 1947, Freda Margaret Mellish; *Career* obstetric and gynaecological surgn King's Coll Hosp 1936-69, surgn-gynaecologist Princess Beatrice Hosp 1936-66, emeritus lectr King's Coll Hosp Med Sch 1969-, surgn-gynaecologist to HM The Queen 1961-73; fell King's Coll London; pres: RCOG 1966-69 (hon treas 1959-66), BMA 1970-71, Int Fedn of Obstetrics and Gynaecology 1970-73; HonDSc Birmingham 1971, HonDM Southampton 1973, HonDCh Newcastle 1980; Hon FACOG, Hon FACS, Hon FRCS (Canada), Hon FCM (SA), Hon FRSM, FRCS, FRCOG, FRCP; *Books* Textbook of Gynaecology (1943), Lives of the Fellows of Royal College of Obstetricians and Gynaecologists (1976), William Blais-Bell Father and Founder (1988); *Recreations* fishing, gardening; *Clubs* Naval and Military; *Style—* Sir John Peel, KCVO; Flat 2, The Old House, Rougemont Close, Salisbury, Wiltshire

PEEL, Sir (William) John; s of late Sir William Peel, KCMG, KBE; *b* 16 June 1912; *Educ* Wellington, Queens' Coll Cambridge; *m* 1936, Rosemary Mia Minka, da of late Robert Readhead; 1 s, 3 da; *Career* colonial admin serv 1933-51, Br resident Brunei 1946-48, res cmmr Gilbert and Ellice Islands 1949-51; Parly candidate (C) Meriden Div of Warwicks 1955, MP (C) Leicester SE 1957-74; PPS to: Econ Sec to Treasy 1958-59, Min State BOT 1959-60; asst govt whip (unpaid) 1960-61, Lord Cmmr Treasy Nov 1961-64; pres: N Atlantic Assembly 1972-73, WEU Assembly 1972-74; memb Br Delgn to Euro Parl 1973-74, hon dir Cons Party Int Office 1975-76; kt 1973; *Style—* Sir John Peel; 51 Cambridge St, London SW1 (☎ 071 834 8762)

PEEL, Jonathan Sidney; MC (1957), DL (1976); s of Maj David Arthur Peel (ka 1944, s of late Rev the Hon Maurice Berkeley Peel, MC, 4 s of 1 Visc Peel) and Hon Sara Vanneck, da of 5 Baron Huntingfield; *b* 21 June 1937; *Educ* Norwich Sch, Eton, St John's Coll Cambridge (MA); *m* 20 Jan 1965, Jean Fulton, da of Air Chief Marshal Sir Denis Hensley Fulton Barnett, GCB, CBE, DFC, *qv*; 1 s (Robert b 1976), 4 da (Ruth b 1966, Emily b 1967, Anne b 1970, Delia b 1974); *Career* cmmnd RB Royal Green Jackets 1956, served Malaya 1956-57, UN Forces Congo (Zaire) 1960-61, Cyprus 1962-63, Capt 1966, resigned; page of honour to HM King George VI 1951-52 and to HM the Queen 1952-53; dir Norwich Union Insur Gp 1973-, chm Pleasureworld 1985-89; memb Nat Tst: Cncl, Exec Ctee, Properties Ctee (chm 1990-); memb Ctee for E Anglia (chm 1980-90); memb Norfolk CC 1974-; vice-pres Norfolk Naturalists Tst 1982-; chm: How Hill Tst for Environmental Studies 1985-, Norwich Sch 1985-, Police Authy 1985-89, Broad Authy 1985-, Planning and Transport Ctee 1989-; Vice Lord Lt Norfolk 1981-, High Sheriff; *Books* Towards a Rural Policy (with M J Sayer, 1973); *Recreations* music, forestry; *Clubs* Norfolk, Boodle's; *Style—* Jonathan Peel, Esq, MC, DL; Barton Hall, Barton Turf, Norwich NR12 8AU

PEEL, Michael David; s of James Peel (d 1978), of Gildersome, Morley, Leeds, and Kathleen, *née* Horbury; *b* 29 April 1946; *Educ* Queen Elizabeth GS Wakefield; *m* 1973 (m dis 1981), Deirdre Burrows, da of Alec Harrowsmith; *Career* articled clerk Starkie and Naylor 1964-69, CA 1969, audit sr Price Waterhouse 1969-71, chief accountant Richmond Tool Co 1971-72, co sec River Don Stamping Ltd 1972-74, mgmnt conslt Peat Marwick Mitchell and Co 1974-77, ptnr Broadhead Peel Rhodes CAS 1978-; involved coaching and team selection Halifax RUFC; FCA; *Recreations* rugby union, cricket; *Style—* Michael Peel, Esq; 9 Dawson Lane, Tong, Bradford, BO4 0ST; Albion House, Albion St, Morley, Leeds LS27 8DT (☎ 0532 526122)

PEEL, Richard Martin; s of Robert Horace Peel, of 26 Solway Ave, Boston, Lincs and Joan Ella, *née* Martin; *b* 23 April 1952; *Educ* Boston GS, Lanchester Poly (BA); *m* 26 May 1984, Diane Joan, da of Laurie Almond, of Perth, Ontario, Canada; 1 da (Charlotte Emma b 1976); *Career* cricket corr Northampton Chronicle and Echo 1976-79 (journalist 1973-79), press offr Milton Keynes Devpt Corp 1979-83, head of publicity and PR news and current affairs BBC 1988- (press offr 1983, sr press offr 1983-85, chief press offr 1985-87, chief asst of info 1987-88); memb: Media Soc, Royal TV Soc; *Recreations* golf, walking, reading, music; *Style—* Richard Peel, Esq; Pinetree Cottage, 30 Startops End, Marsworth, Bucks (☎ 044 2827568), Room 3331, BBC Television Centre, Wood Lane, London W12 7RJ (☎ 081 743 5138, fax 081 740 7766, car 0860 317785)

PEEL, Hon Robert Michael Arthur; s of 2 Earl Peel (d 1969), and Kathleen, da of Michael McGrath, of Ballyculane, Co Cork; *b* 5 Feb 1950; *Educ* Eton, Hertford Coll Oxford, UCL; *m* 1973, Fiona Natalie, da of Charles Davidson, of Dunhampstead House, Droitwich, Worcs; 3 da; *Style—* The Hon Robert Peel; Berryhill Farm, Coedkernew, Newport, Gwent

PEEL, 3 Earl (UK 1929); Sir William James Robert Peel; 8 Bt (GB 1800); Viscount Peel (UK 1895) and Viscount Clanfield (UK 1929); s of 2 Earl Peel (d 1969, himself gs of 1 Viscount, who was in turn 5 s of Sir Robert Peel, 2 Bt, the distinguished statesman); *b* 3 Oct 1947; *Educ* Ampleforth, Tours Univ, RAC Cirencester; *m* 1, 1973, Veronica Naomi Livingston, da of Alastair Timpson; 1 s (Viscount Clanfield), 1 da (Lady Iona b 1978); m 2, 1989, Hon Charlotte, *née* Soames, da of Baron Soames, GCMG, GCVO, CH, CBE, PC (Life Peer, d 1987), and formerly w of (Alexander) Richard Hambro, *qv*; *Heir* s, Viscount Clanfield; *Style—* The Rt Hon the Earl Peel; Gunnerside Lodge, Richmond, N Yorks

PEERLESS, Brian Read; s of Gordon Read Peerless (d 1977), and Ida Constance Holdup (d 1965); *b* 8 Aug 1934; *Educ* Ampleforth; *m* 1 Feb 1964, Caroline Margaret, da of Richard Leather (d 1977), of Berks; 1 s (Charles b 1968), 1 da (Jane-Emma b 1965); *Career* ptnr: W M Morris & Whiteheads 1963-72, Scott Goff Layon 1973-86; memb Ctee Stock Exchange Members Mutual Reference Soc 1964-88 (chm 1982-85); FInstD; *Recreations* lawn tennis, music; *Clubs* Hurlingham, Honourable Artillery Co; *Style—* Brian Peerless, Esq; 34 Smith Terrace, London SW3 4DH; Smith New Court plc, Smith New Court House, 20 Farringdon Road, London EC1M 3NH

PEERS, Charles; s of (Charles John) Jack Peers (d 1977), of Stadhampton, Oxford, and Rotha, *née* de Selincourt; *b* 16 Oct 1937; *Educ* Wennington Sch Wetherby Yorks, Northamptonshire Coll of Agric; *m* 8 Oct 1963, Heather Myrtle, da of William James Ridgway (d 1975), of Waterstock, Oxon; 2 s (Robert b 1967, Thomas b 1973); *Career* Nat Serv NCO 1956-58; farmer 1963; chm Stadhampton and Great Milton Parish Cncls 1968-82, dist cncllr 1970-78, chm NFU Parly Ctee 1980-87 (branch chm 1979-80) chm Bd of Govrs Peers Sch Littlemore Oxford 1978 (govr 1971-), hon treas Berks Bucks and Oxon Co Branch NFU 1989-; *Recreations* shooting, classic vehicle restoration, agricultural buildings preservation; *Style—* Charles Peers, Esq; Views Farm, Great Milton, Oxford 0X9 7NW (☎ 0844 279 352)

PEET, Frank Antony (Tony); s of Brig Lionel Meredith Peet (d 1967), of The Old

Rectory, Lesnewth, Boscastle, Cornwall, and Elinor Marian, *née* Hayward (d 1988); *b* 5 May 1922; *Educ* Charterhouse, St John's Coll Cambridge, Brasenose Coll Oxford (MA); *m* 25 Nov 1950, June Rosemary, da of Thomas Graham Weall (d 1969), of Foursome, Maple Ave, Cooden Beach, Sussex; 2 s (John Graham b 8 May 1954, Ronald Arthur b 28 June 1957), 1 da (Vanessa b 21 Oct 1951); *Career* WWII, cmmnd RE 1942, Capt 1945, serv Africa, 42 FD Co RE Italy 1944-45 (despatches 1945); Colonial Serv Kenya 1949-62; admin cadet 1949, dist cmmr Garissa 1951, dist off Embu 1952, dist off Wundanyi Voi Dist 1952-54, Off Municipal African Affrs Mombasa 1954, dist off Kandara 1955, seconded to Sp B Nairobi 1956; dist cmmr: Nakuru 1957-59, Kiambu 1959, Fort Hall 1960-62; sr dist cmmr Mombasa 1963; called to the Bar Gray's Inn 1952 (disbarred 1964), admitted slr 1964, ptnr Marshall & Galpin 1965-88; clerk cmmrs of taxes Oxfordshire West 1979-88, Under Sheriff Oxfordshire 1986-88; treas Stadhampton PCC 1964-87, churchwarden 1966-70 and 1987-; *Recreations* golf, riding; *Clubs* Pegasus AFC, Harlequins CC, Vincent's (Oxford), Huntercombe Golf; *Style—* Tony Peet, Esq; The Mill House, Stadhampton, Oxford

PEET, Ronald Hugh; CBE (1974); s of late Henry Leonard Peet, and late Stella Peet, of Manchester; *b* 12 July 1925; *Educ* Doncaster GS, Queen's Coll Oxford; *m* 1, 1949, Winifred Joy (d 1979), da of late Ernest Adamson; 2 s, 2 da; m 2, 1981, Lynette Judy Burgess Kinsella; *Career* Legal & General Assurance Soc Ltd: dir 1969- 1984, chief exec 1972-80, chm 1980- 1984; Legal & General Group plc: gp chief exec 1979-84, dir 1979-84; chm Aviation & General Insurance Co Ltd 1978-80, dir Watling Streets Properties 1971-84, chm City Arts Trust Ltd 1980-87; dir: Royal Philharmonic Orch Ltd 1977-88, ENO 1978-; chm Stockley plc 1984-87, dir AMEC plc 1984-; chm The Howard Group plc 1985-86, dep chm PWS Holdings plc 1986-88, dir New Scotland Insurance Group plc 1987-; FIA; *Recreations* music, opera; *Clubs* Hurlingham, City of London; *Style—* Ronald Peet, Esq, CBE; 9 Marlowe Court, Petyward, London SW3 3PD (☎ 071 581 3686)

PEET, Vanessa Mary (Mrs Norman); *née* NORMAN; da of Frank Antony Peet, of The Mill House, Stadhampton, Oxfordshire, and June Rosemary, *née* Weall; *b* 21 Oct 1951; *Educ* The Abbey Sch Malvern Wells Worcs, St Hughs Coll Oxford (PPE); *m* 17 April 1982, Archibald John (Archie) Norman, s of Dr Archibald Percy (Archie) Norman, of White Lodge, Heather Close, Kingwood, Surrey; 1 da (Florence); *Career* teacher ILEA 1974-76, ed The Diplomat 1979, dir Diplomatist Assocs Ltd 1981, publisher The Diplomat Magazine and Foreign Service Magazine 1988; *Books* Bakery (1978), Garage (1979); *Style—* Ms Vanessa Peet; Diplomatist Associates Ltd, 58 Theobalds Rd, London WC1X 8SF (☎ 071 405 4874, 071 405 4903, fax 071 831 0667)

PEGG, Dr Michael Anstice; s of Benjamin Daniel Pegg (d 1951), and Rose, *née* Anstice; *b* 3 Sept 1931; *Educ* Burton-on-Trent GS, Univ of Southampton (BA, MA, PhD); *m* 1, 31 August 1955, Jean Williams; 3 s (Paul b 1957, Richard b 1959, Timothy b 1962); m 2, 1 April 1986, Margaret Rae; *Career* Capt RAEC Educn Office SHAPE Paris 1959-61; sec and estab offr Nat Library of Scotland Edinburgh 1967-76 (asst keeper 1961-67), librarian Univ of Birmingham 1976-80, dir and univ librarian John Rylands Univ Library of Manchester 1980-90; memb: Br Library Bd 1981-84, Standing Conference of Nat and Univ Libraries Cncl 1981-83; *Books* Les Divers Rapports d'Eustorg de Beaulieu (1964), Catalogue of German Reformation Pamphlets in Libraries of Great Britain and Ireland (1973), Catalogue of Sixteenth-Century German Pamphlets in Collections in France and England (1977), Catalogue of Reformation Pamphlets in Swiss Libraries (1983), Catalogue of Early Sixteenth Century Books in the Royal Library Copenhagen (1989); *Recreations* tennis, music, railways; *Style—* Dr M A Pegg; c/o John Rylands University Library of Manchester, Oxford Rd, Manchester M13 9PP (☎ 061 275 3700)

PEGG, Dr Michael Stuart; s of Gilbert Seaton Pegg, of Reigate, Surrey and Waldy Greta, *née* Jonsson; *b* 15 June 1948; *Educ* The Grammar Sch Reigate Surrey, UCL, Westminster Med Sch (BSc, MB BS); *m* 17 Jan 1983, Kaija Kaarina, da of Niilo Sarolehto, of Espoo, Finland; 1 s (Justing William b 12 June 1986), 1 da (Antonia Alexandra b 9 Aug 1984); *Career* conslt annaesthetist Royal Free Hosp 1981-, hon sr lectr Royal Free Hosp Med Sch 1981-; memb: BMA, Assoc Anaesthetists; *Style—* Dr Michael Pegg; Newstead, 3 Canons Close, Radlett, Herts WD7 7ER (☎ 0923 056640)

PEGGIE, Robert Galloway Emslie; CBE (1986); s of John Masterton Peggie (d 1966), of Loanhead, Midlothian, and Euphemia Glendinning, *née* Emslie (d 1956); *b* 5 Jan 1929; *Educ* Lasswade HS; *m* 27 June 1955, Christine Jeanette, da of William Cumming Simpson (d 1943); 1 s (David b 11 Feb 1962), 1 da (Alison b 13 Feb 1958); *Career* Nat Serv RAF 1947-49; mgmnt accountant Brush Electrical Engineering 1955-57, dep city chamberlain Edinburgh Corp 1966-72 (O & M team 1957), seconded to PA Management Consultants 1972-74, chief exec Lothian Regnl Cncl 1974-86, cmmr local admin Scotland 1986-; memb: Ct Heriot-Watt Univ, Cncl Royal Scottish Geographical Soc, Devpt Ctee Scottish Museums Cncl; ACCA 1954; *Style—* R G E Peggie, Esq, CBE; 54 Liberton Drive, Edinburgh EH16 6NW (☎ 031 664 1631); Princes House, 5 Shandwick Place, Edinburgh EH2 4RG (☎ 031 229 4472)

PEGLER, James Basil Holmes; TD (and bar 1946); s of Harold Holmes Pegler (d 1963), of Greystones, Heathhurst Rd, Sanderstead, Surrey, and Dorothy Cecil, *née* Francis (d 1957); *b* 6 Aug 1912; *Educ* Charterhouse, Open Univ (BA); *m* 11 Sept 1937, Enid Margaret, da of Leonard Dell (d 1952), of Sanderstead, Surrey; 1 s (Stephen b 1951), 3 da (Judith b 1939, Valerie b 1941, Audrey b 1945); *Career* cmmnd 2 Lt 4 Bn The Queen's Royal Regt TA 1935, Maj 4 Bn Queen's Royal Regt (63 Searchlight Regt RA) TA 1941, GSO 2 WO LM5 1944, 2 i/c 127 LAA Regt RA TA 1948-50; gen mangr and actuary Clerical Medical and General Life Assurance Society 1950 (investmt sec 1948); visiting prof City Univ 1980-86 (prof of actuarial sci 1975-79); chm Life Offices Assoc 1959-61, pres Comité Européen des Assurs Life Gp 1964-70, govr Fyling Hall Sch Robin Hood's Bay 1977-90; FIA 1939 (hon sec 1951-59, pres 1968-70), FSS 1948, FIS 1951, FIMA 1971; *Recreations* mathematics, tap dancing; *Clubs* Army and Navy; *Style—* James B H Pegler, Esq, TD; Dormers, 28 Deepdene Wood, Dorking, Surrey RH5 4BQ (☎ 0306 885955)

PEGNA, Hon Mrs (Elizabeth Ruth Frances); da of 1 Baron Layton (d 1966); *b* 1923; *m* 1944 (m dis 1965), Edward William Guttiers (Bobbie) Pegna; 2 s, 2 da; *Style—* The Hon Mrs Pegna; 2 Farmington, Cheltenham, Glos GL5 3NQ

PEIERLS, Sir Rudolf Ernst; CBE (1946); s of Heinrich Peierls (d 1945), of Berlin, and Elisabeth, *née* Weigert (d 1921); *b* 5 June 1907,Berlin; *Educ* Humboldt Sch Oberschöneweide Berlin, Berlin Univ, Munich Univ, Leipzig Univ (DPhil), Univ of Manchester (DSc), Univ of Cambrige (MA); *m* 1931, Eugenia (d 1986), da of Nikolai Kannegiesser (d 1910), of St Petersburg; 1 s, 3 da; *Career* asst Fed Inst of Technol Zurich 1929-32, Rockefeller fell Rome and Cambridge 1932-33, hon res fell Univ of Manchester 1933-35, res asst Royal Soc Mond Laboratory Cambridge 1935-37, prof of applied maths (later mathematical physics) Univ of Birmingham 1937-63, worked on Atomic Energy Project 1940-43 (USA 1943-45), Wykeham prof of physics Univ of Oxford and fell New Coll 1963-74 (later hon fell), pt/t prof of physics Univ of Washington Seattle 1974-77; FRS, FInstP; kt 1968; *Clubs* Athenaeum; *Style—* Sir Rudolf Peierls, CBE; 2B Northmoor Rd, Oxford OX2 6UP (☎ 0865 56497); Nuclear Physics Laboratory, Keble Rd, Oxford OX1 3RH

PEIL, Prof Margaret; da of Francis Peil (d 1965), and Alice Mary, *née* Clancy (d 1947); *b* 18 June 1929; *Educ* Milwaukee-Downer Coll (BS), Fordham Univ (MA), Univ of Chicago (PhD); *Career* lectr in sociology Univ of Ghana 1963-68, prof of the sociology of W Africa Univ of Birmingham 1983- (former lectr, sr lectr and reader in sociology), visiting lectr Univ of Lagos 1971-72, visiting sr lectr Univ of Sierra Leone 1980; memb: Royal African Soc, American Sociological Assoc, Harbourne Soc; *Books* The Ghanaian Factory Worker (1972), Nigerian Politics: The People's View (1976), Consensus and Conflict in African Societies (1977), Cities and Suburbs: Urban Life in West Africa (1981), Social Science Research Methods (with D Rimmer and P K Mitchell 1982), African Urban Society (with P O Sada, 1985), Lagos: The City is the People (1991); *Recreations* gardening, travel; *Style—* Prof Margaret Peil; Birmingham University, Centre of W African Studies, Birmingham B15 2TT (☎ 021 414 5123)

PEILE, George Howard; MC (1943 and bar 1944), TD, DL; s of Henry Peile, CBE (d 1935), of Broomshiels Hall, Satley, Co Durham, and Eva Ethel, *née* Beckingham (d 1964); *b* 10 Sept 1910; *Educ* Eton, Trinity Coll Cambridge (BA); *m* 23 March 1946, Rosemary Margherita Cecilia, da of Maj George Cecil Whitaker (d 1959), of Watlington, Oxon; 2 s (Charles b 1954, 1 s decd), 1 da (Margaret b 1949); *Career* WWII serv 1939-45: Surrey & Sussex Yeo (QMR) 98 Fd Rgt RA France, Italy; barr 1932; dir The Priestman Collieries Ltd, asst md The Newcastle Breweries Ltd, ret 1956; JP Northumberland 1959-79, memb Northumberland CC 1968-84; *Recreations* shooting; *Clubs* Northern Counties; *Style—* George H Peile, Esq, MC, TD, DL; Kirsopp House, Great Whittington, Northumberland, Newcastle-upon-Tyne NE19 2HA (☎ 0434 672241)

PEIRCE, Rev Canon (John) Martin; s of Martin Westley Peirce (d 1966), and Winifred Mary, *née* Bennett; *b* 9 July 1936; *Educ* Brentwood Sch, Jesus Coll Cambridge (MA, CertEd), Westcott House Cambridge; *m* 8 June 1968, Rosemary Susan, da of George Duncan Nicholson Milne, of Kingston upon Thames; 2 s (Richard b 1969, Michael b 1971); *Career* RAF 1954-56, PO; teacher and housemaster St Stephen's Coll Hong Kong 1960-64; asst curate: St John the Baptist Croydon 1966-70, Holy Trinity Fareham 1970-71; team vicar St Columba Fareham 1971-76, team rector of Langley Slough 1976-85, diocesan dir of ordinands Oxford 1985-, canon residentiary of Christ Church Oxford 1987-; memb Gen Synod C of E 1985; *Recreations* walking, gardening; *Style—* The Rev Canon Martin Peirce; Christ Church College, Oxford OX1 1DP

PEIRSE, Air Vice-Marshal Sir Richard (Charles Fairfax); KCVO (1988), CB (1984); s of late Air Chief Marshal Sir Richard Peirse, KCB, DSO, AFC (d 1970), and late Lady (Mary Joyce) Peirse, *née* Ledgard; the Peirses were once great landowners in N Riding of Yorks, being descended from Peter Peirse, who fought for the House of York as a standard-bearer at Bosworth Field 1485 (where he lost a leg); the pedigree is first recorded in the Visitation of 1634; John Peirse (1593-1658) is thought to have been the purchaser of the manor of Bedale, where the family resided for many generations, until it descended through m to the Beresford-Peirse family, *qv*; *b* 16 March 1931; *Educ* Bradfield, RAF Coll Cranwell; *m* 1, 1955 (m dis 1963), Karalie Grace Cox; 2 da (Amanda, Susan); m 2, 1963, Deirdre Mary O'Donovan (d 1976); 1 s (Richard d 1989); m 3, 1977, Anna Jill Margaret Long, da of Rt Hon Sir John (Brinsmead) Latey, MBE, of Roehampton, qv; *Career* cmmnd 1952, serv various sqdns and HQ in Germany, UK, Malta 1952-68, graduate RAF Staff Coll Andover 1963, Jt Servs Staff Coll 1968, cmd No 51 Sqdn 1968-69, Dep Capt of the Queen's Flight 1969-72, cmd RAF Waddington 1973-75, MOD 1975-82, AOC and Cmdt RAF Coll Cranwell 1982-85, Defence Servs Sec 1985-88, ret 1988; qualified flying instr (1956); RCDS 1972; Gentleman Usher of the Scarlet Rod Order of the Bath 1990-; *Clubs* RAF; *Style—* Air Vice-Marshal Sir Richard Peirse, KCVO, CB; The Old Mill House, Adderbury, nr Banbury, Oxon (☎ 0295 810196)

PEIRSON, Margaret Ellen; eld da of late David Edward Peirson, CBE, and Norah Ellen, *née* Corney; *b* 28 Nov 1942; *Educ* N London Collegiate Sch Canons Edgware Middx, Somerville Coll Oxford (BA), Yale USA; *Career* joined HM Treasy 1965, seconded to Bank of England 1982-84, under sec HM Treasy 1986-, seconded to DSS 1990-; *Recreations* choral singing, theatre; *Style—* Miss Margaret Peirson; DSS, Adelphi, John Adam Street, London WC2

PEIRSON, Richard; s of Geoffrey Peirson (d 1986), of Purley, Surrey, and Beryl Joyce, *née* Walder; *b* 5 March 1949; *Educ* Purley GS, Univ of Liverpool (BSc); *m* 31 May 1975 (m dis), Jennifer Margaret, da of late F E Fernie; 1 s (James Richard b 1978), 1 da (Caroline Jane b 1980); *Career* Arthur Andersen & Co 1970-72, Colegrave & Co 1972-73, J & A Scrimgeour Ltd 1973-75, Carr Sebag & Co (formerly W I Carr Sons & Co) 1975-82, Grieveson Grant & Co 1982-86, Kleinwort Benson Investment Management Ltd 1986-; govr Denmead Sch; memb Stock Exchange; *Recreations* tennis, squash, reading, collecting watercolours; *Style—* Richard Peirson, Esq; 51 Mount Ararat Rd, Richmond, Surrey TW10 6PL (☎ 081 940 2013); Kleinwort Benson Investment Management Ltd, 10 Fenchurch St, London EC3M 3LB (☎ 071 623 8000, fax 9413545)

PEISER, Graham Allan; s of Eric George Peiser, of Bucks, and Honor, *née* Greenwood (d 1988); *b* 26 March 1940; *Educ* Coll of Estate Mgmnt Aldenham; *m* 26 Sept 1970, Jennifer Ann, da of Dr John Richard Cooper, of W Sussex; 2 da (Georgina b 1972, Lucy b 1976); *Career* chartered surveyor; ptnr Fuller Peiser 1970-; FRICS; *Style—* Graham A Peiser, Esq; Pear Tree Cottage, The Green, Sarratt, Rickmansworth, Herts WD3 6BL (☎ 0923 269136); Thavies Inn House, 3-4 Holborn Circus, London EC1N 2HL (☎ 071 936 2233)

PELHAM, Hon Mrs Anthony; Barbara Clare; da of former Col J E D Taunton, late DQMG, Aust Mil Forces; *m* 1928, as his 2 w, Hon Anthony Ashley Ivo Pelham, s of 5 Earl of Chichester (d 1951); *Style—* The Hon Mrs Anthony Pelham; Halland, Clyst St Mary, Exeter, Devon

PELHAM, Hugh Reginald Brentnall; s of Reginald Arthur Pelham, (d 1981), and Pauline Mary, *née* Brentnall; *b* 26 Aug 1954; *Educ* Marlborough, Christ's Coll Cambridge (MA, PhD); *m* 26 March 1976 (m dis 1989), Alison Mary, *née* Slowe; *Career* res fell Christ's Coll Cambridge 1978-84, postdoctoral fell Dept of Embryology Carnegie Inst of Washington Baltimore Maryland 1979-81, staff memb MRC Laboratory of Molecular Biology Cambridge 1981-, visitor Univ of Zürich Switzerland 1987-88; awards: Colworth medal of the Biochemical Soc 1988, EMBO medal 1989, Louis Jeantet prize for med 1991; memb: Euro Molecular Biology Orgn 1985, Academia Europaea 1990; FRS 1988; *Style—* Hugh Pelham, Esq, FRS; MRC Laboratory of Molecular Biology, Hills Rd, Cambridge CB2 2QH (☎ 0223 248011, fax 0223 412142)

PELHAM, Michael Alan; s of Harry Alan Pelham (d 1971), and Doris Millicent, *née* Taunton (later Mrs Eccles, d 1959); *b* 23 Sept 1926; *Educ* Sherborne, King's Coll Cambridge (BA, MA); *m* 25 Oct 1958, Lucy Helen, da of Cyril R Egerton, of Hall Farm, Stetchworth, Newmarket; 1 s (Charles Peregrine b 27 July 1959), 1 da (Laura Mary b 15 May 1962); *Career* Nat Serv Capt RE 1946-48, RAFVR (Cambridge Univ Air Sqdn); Wiggins Teape & Co 1951-58; md: Abitibi Sales Co UK 1958, Abitibi-Bathurst Ltd 1962, Consolidated Bathurst (Overseas) Ltd 1967, Bridgewater Paper Sales Ltd 1983-87, Bridgewater Newsprint Ltd 1988; vice chm Bridgewater Paper Co Ltd 1990-; JP Inner London Area 1961, London Juvenile Ct Panel 1961-78, vice chm London Fedn of Boy's Clubs 1963-66; Freeman City of London 1964, Liveryman Worshipful Co of Newspaper Makers & Stationers 1964 (memb Ct 1991-); *Recreations* sailing, gardening, fishing, shooting, music; *Clubs* Brooks's, Hurlingham, Royal Yacht Squadron, Royal Ocean Racing; *Style—* Michael Pelham, Esq; Old Ways House, Beaulieu, Hants SO42 7YT (☎ 0590 612 264); 41 Yeomans Row, London SW3; 195 Knightsbridge, London SW7 (☎ 071 581 7676, fax 071 589 6514, car 0836 260 832, telex 25863)

PELHAM, Michael Leslie; s of Cyril Hall (d 1967), and Clare Elizabeth Hall (d 1981); *b* 27 Dec 1939; *Educ* St Edward's Sch Oxford, St Edmund Hall Oxford (BA); *m* Elizabeth Vivien; 1 s (Hugh b 1967), 1 da (Georgina b 1970); *Career* Richard Costain Limited 1961-69: grad engr, posts overseas, asst to Chief Exec UK; mgmnt conslt McKinsey & Co Inc 1969-72, responsible for industl acquisitions and jt ventures between consolidated African Selection Tst and Baird & Lane Ltd 1972-76, md Seltrust CBO (subsid of Selection Trust Ltd) 1976-78, chm and md CBO International 1978-86, md Conder Group plc 1988- (dir gp devpt 1987-88); chm and fndr Br Int Rowing Fund, tstee Oxford Univ Boat Club; *Recreations* sculling, squash, reading; *Clubs* Leander, Vincent's; *Style—* Michael Pelham, Esq; Conder Group plc, Kingsworthy Court, Kings Worthy, Winchester, Hants SO23 7QA (☎ 0962 882222, fax 0962 882610)

PELHAM, Richard Anthony Henry; s of Maj Anthony George Pelham (d 1969); kinsman and hp of 9 Earl of Chichester; *b* 1 Aug 1952; *Educ* Eton; *m* 1987, Georgina, da of David Gilmour, of Ringshall, Suffolk; 2 s (Duncan b 1987, Christopher b 1990); *Recreations* vintage motor cycle racing; *Clubs* Vintage Motor Cycle; *Style—* Richard Pelham, Esq; c/o Coutts & Co, 162 Brompton Rd, London SW3

PELHAM, Hon Mrs (Valery); yr da of Baron Segal (Life Peer; d 1985), and Molly, *née* Rolo (d 1989); *b* 14 Feb 1943; *Educ* Badminton Sch Bristol; *m* 1967, Paul Nicholas David Pelham; 1 s, 3 da; *Career* SRN St Thomas' Hosp; *Style—* The Hon Mrs Pelham; 24 Frognal Lane, London NW3

PELHAM BURN, Angus Maitland; JP (Kincardine and Deeside 1984), DL (1978); s of Brig-Gen Henry Pelham Burn, CMG, DSO (d 1958), and Katherine Eileen, *née* Staveley-Hill (d 1989); *b* 13 Dec 1931; *Educ* Harrow, N of Scotland Coll of Agric; *m* 19 Dec 1959, Anne Rosdew, da of Sir Ian Algernon Forbes-Leith, 2 Bt, KT, MBE (d 1973); 4 da (Amanda b 1961, Lucy b 1963, Emily b 1964, Kate b 1966); *Career* Hudson's Bay Co 1951-58; chm and dir: Macrobert Farms (Douneside) Ltd 1970-87, Pelett Admin Ltd 1973-; dir: Aberdeen and Northern Marts Ltd 1970-86 (chm 1974-86), Aberdeen Meat Mktg Co Ltd 1973-86 (chm 1974-86), Bank of Scotland 1977- (chm Aberdeen Local Bd 1973-), Scottish Provident Inst 1975-, Prime Space Design Ltd 1981-87, Taw Meat Co 1984-86, Skeendale Ltd 1987-88, Aberdeen Tst Hldgs Ltd (formerly Aberdeen Fund Mangrs) 1985-, Status Timber Systems 1986-90, Abtrust Scotland Investment Co plc 1989-; memb: Kincardine CC 1967-75 (vice convener 1973-75), Grampian Regnl Cncl 1974-; memb: Aberdeen Assoc for the Prevention of Cruelty to Animals 1975- (dir 1984-, chm 1984-89), Accounts Cmmn 1980- (dep chm 1987-), Cncl Winston Churchill Mem Tst 1984-; chm Aberdeen Airport Consultative Ctee 1986-; memb Queen's Body Guard for Scotland (The Royal Co of Archers) 1968-; Vice Lord Lt for Kincardineshire 1978-; Liveryman Worshipful Co of Farmers until 1988; Hon FInstM 1987; *Recreations* vegetable gardening, stalking, shooting, fishing; *Clubs* New (Edinburgh), Royal Northern & Univ (Aberdeen); *Style—* Angus Pelham Burn, Esq, JP, DL; 68 Station Rd, Banchory, Kincardineshire AB31 3YJ (☎ 033 023343); Knappach, Banchory, Kincardineshire AB31 3JS (☎ 033 044 555)

PELHAM-CLINTON-HOPE, Lady Kathleen Marie Gabrielle; yr da of 9 Duke of Newcastle, OBE (d 1988); *b* 1 Jan 1951; *m* 1, 27 Feb 1970 (m dis), Edward Vernon Reynolds, s of Henry Reynolds, of The Mall, Kenton, Middlesex; *m* 2 (m dis), a Thai; resumed her maiden name; *Style—* The Lady Kathleen Pelham-Clinton-Hope; c/o Diana, Duchess of Newcastle, Cortington Manor, Warminster, Wilts BA12 OSY

PELHAM-CLINTON-HOPE, Lady Patricia; *née* Pelham-Clinton-Hope; da of 9 Duke of Newcastle, OBE (d 1988); *b* 20 July 1949; *m* 1, 1971 (m dis 1974), Alan Pariser; resumed surname of Pelham-Clinton-Hope 1974; m 2, 1981 (m dis 1983), Nick Mancuso, of Toronto; resumed maiden name again; 1 s (Dorian Henry Navarre Pelham-Clinton-Kole b 17 Nov 1990); *Career* actress; films: The Killing of a Chinese Bookie 1976, Mask 1985; *Style—* The Lady Patricia Pelham-Clinton-Hope; 13947 Chandler Blvd, Van Nuys, California 91401, USA

PELL, Marian Priscilla; *née* Leak; da of Anthony Edward Leak, and Elsie Ellen, *née* Chellingworth; *b* 5 July 1952; *Educ* Watford GS for Girls, Univ of Southampton (LLB); *m* 4 Aug 1973, Gordon Francis Pell, s of Lt-Col Denis Herbert Pell (d 1987); 2 s, 1 da; *Career* asst slr Herbert Smith 1976-84 (ptnr 1984-); memb Law Soc; *Recreations* music, walking; *Style—* Mrs Marian Pell; Exchange House, Primrose St, London EC2A 2HS (☎ 071 374 8000, fax 071 496 0043)

PELLEREAU, Maj-Gen Peter John Mitchell; s of Col John Cyril Etienne Pellereau (d 1973), of Tebbs Corner, Ightham, Kent, and Aileen Nora Vidal, *née* Betham (d 1990); family became Br following ceding of Isle de France to Britain becoming Mauritius; *b* 24 April 1921; *Educ* Wellington, Trinity Coll Cambridge (BA, MA); *m* 1949, Rosemary, da of Sydney Robert Garnar (d 1981), of Wrotham, Kent; 2 s (Matthew, David); *Career* cmmnd RE 1942, serv NW Europe, Maj OC 26 Armd Engr Sqdn RE (Hameln) 1946-47, Tech Staff Offr Fighting Vehicles Design Estab Chobham 1948-49, Dep Cdr Engr Base Installations Singapore 1953-55, sec Def Res Policy Ctee MOD 1959-60, Lt-Col Mil Sec's Dept MOD 1960-62, cmdg 131 Parachute Engr Regt RE TA 1963-64, Col Mil Dir of Studies RMCS Shrivenham 1965-67, asst dir RE Equipment Devpt MOD 1967-70, Brig Sr Mil Offr Royal Armament Res and Devpt Estab Fort Halstead Sevenoaks 1970-73, pres Ordnance Bd 1975-76; sec ACE 1976-87; past pres: RE Lawn Tennis Club, Oxted Hockey Club; memb: Ctee Wolfe Soc, Sevenoaks Cons Assoc; CEng, FIMechE, FBIM; *Clubs* Knole; *Style—* Maj-Gen Peter Pellereau; Woodmans Folly, Crockham Hill, Edenbridge, Kent (☎ 0732 866309)

PELLEW, Mark Edward; LVO (1980); s of Anthony Pownoll Pellew, of Wimbledon, and Margaret Julia Critchley, *née* Cookson; *b* 28 Aug 1942; *Educ* Winchester, Trinity Coll Oxford (BA); *m* 1965, Jill Hosford, da of Prof Frank Thistlethwaite, CBE, of Cambridge; 2 s (Adam Lee b 1966, Dominic Stephen b 1968); *Career* HM Dip Serv 1965-; FO 1965-67, Singapore 1967-69, Saigon 1969-70, FCO 1970-76, first sec Rome 1976-80, asst head Personnel Ops Dept FCO 1981-83; cnsllr (political) Washington DC 1983-89, on secondment to Hambros Bank Ltd 1989-; *Recreations* tennis, singing, playing the horn; *Clubs* Hurlingham; *Style—* Mark Pellew, Esq, LVO; 51 St George's Square, London SW1V 3QN)

PELLEW DE LLANSO, Hon Mrs (Mary Rose); *née* Pellew; da of 9 Viscount Exmouth (d 1970); *b* 1938; *m* 1974, D Roman Llanso, of Madrid; *Style—* The Hon Mrs Pellew de Llanso; Urb. Los Pinos, 28220-Majadahonda, Madrid, Spain

PELLING, Anthony Adair; s of Brian Pelling, and Alice, *née* Lamb; *b* 3 May 1934; *Educ* Purley GS, LSE (BSc), NW Poly London, Wolverhampton Coll of Technol (MIPM); *m* 1, Margaret Rose, *née* Lightfoot; 1 s (Andrew John), 1 da (Sarah Margaret); m 2 Virginia, *née* Glen-Calvert; *Career* ROAC WO 1955-57; NCB 1957-67, Civil Serv 1967-; Miny Public Bldgs & Works: princ 1967-69, asst sec 1969-81, under sec 1981; dep dir Business in the Community 1981-83; dir DTp Highways Contracts and Maintenance 1983-85, construction indust, sports and recreation directorates DOE 1985-87, dir London Region DOE 1987-; *Clubs* Reform, Surrey CC; *Style—* Anthony Pelling, Esq; London Region, Dept of the Environment, Millbank Tower, Millbank, London SW1P 4QU

PELLING, Dr Henry Mathison; s of late Douglas Langley Pelling, of Birkenhead, Cheshire, and late Maud Mary, *née* Mathison; *b* 27 Aug 1920; *Educ* Birkenhead Sch, St John's Coll Cambridge (BA, MA, PhD, LittD); *Career* RA 1941-42, cmmnd 2 Lt then Lt RE 1942, Capt Educn Corps 1945; Queen's Coll Oxford: fell 1949-65, tutor 1950-65, dean 1963-64, supernumerary fell 1980; St John's Coll Cambridge: fell 1966, asst dir of res History Faculty 1966-77, reader in recent Br history 1977-80; Smith-Mundt Sch Univ of Wisconsin USA 1953-54, fell Woodrow Wilson Center Washington DC 1983, author of pieces written for various jls; Hon DLitt New Sch for Social Res NY 1983; *Books* Origins of the Labour Party (1954), Challenge of Socialism (1954), America and the British Left (1956), British Communist Party (with Frank Bealey, 1958), Labour and Politics (1958), American Labour (1960), Modern Britain 1885-1955 (1960), Short History of the Labour Party (1961, 9 edn 1991), History of British Trade Unionism (1963, 4 edn 1987), Social Geography of British Elections (1967), Popular Politics and Society in Late Victorian Britain (1968, 2 edn 1979), Britain and the Second World War (1970), Winston Churchill (1974, 2 edn 1989), The Labour Governments 1945-51 (1984), Britain and the Marshall Plan (1988); *Recreations* theatre, cinema; *Clubs* Nat Lib, Royal Cwlth Soc; *Style—* Dr Henry Pelling; St John's College, Cambridge CB2 1TP (☎ 0223 338600)

PELLY, Derek Roland (Derk); s of Arthur Roland Pelly (d 1966), of Ballygate House, Beccles, Suffolk, and Phyllis Elsie, *née* Henderson (d 1973); *b* 12 June 1929; *Educ* Marlborough, Trinity Coll Cambridge (MA); *m* 20 June 1953, Susan, da of John Malcolm Roberts (d 1986), of Felpham, Sussex; 1 s (Sam b 1960), 2 da (Rosemary b 1955, Catherine b 1958); *Career* 2 Lt RA 1947-49; Barclays Bank 1952-88: local dir Chelmsford Dist 1959-68 (asst to chm 1968-69), local dir Luton Dist 1969-79, dir Barclays Int 1974 (vice chm 1977-86, chm 1986-87), dir Barclays plc 1974 (vice-chm 1984-86, dep chm 1986-88); dir Private Bank and Tst Co Ltd 1989-, memb Ctee Family Assur Soc 1988-, chm City Commuter Gp 1987-88, dir Milton Keynes Devpt Corpn 1976-85, memb Cncl Overseas Devpt Inst 1984-89; govr London House for Overseas Graduates 1985-, treas Friends of Essex Churches 1989-, memb Chelmsford Diocesan Bd of Fin 1989-; JP Chelmsford 1965-68; FCIB, FRSA; *Recreations* painting; *Clubs* Commonwealth; *Style—* Derk Pelly, Esq; The Bowling Green, The Downs, Gt Dunmow, Essex CM6 1DT (☎ 0371 872662)

PELLY, Sir John Alwyne; 6 Bt (UK 1840), of Upton, Essex, JP (Hants 1966), DL (Hants 1972); s of Sir (Harold) Alwyne Pelly, 5 Bt, MC (d 1981), and Caroline Earle, da of Richard Heywood-Jones (d 1976), of Badsworth Hall, Yorks; *b* 11 Sept 1918; *Educ* Canford, RMC, RAC; *m* 1, 1945, (Ava) Barbara Ann, da of Brig Keith Frederick William Dunn, CBE, DL; m 2, 1950, Elsie May (Hazel) (d 1987), da of late Louis Thomas Dechow, of Rhodesia (now Zimbabwe); 1 da (Margaret b 1952) and 2 da decd; m 3, 3 Aug 1990, his 1 w, Mrs (Ava) Barbara Ann Cazenove; *Heir* n, Richard John Pelly b 1951; *Career* Coldstream Gds 1938-50, serv WWII (Egypt and Libya) POW 1942, Malayan Campaign 1948-50, ret Maj; High Sheriff Hants 1970-71, memb Lands Tbnl 1982-88; *Recreations* shooting, skiing; *Clubs* Royal Overseas; *Style—* Sir John Pelly, Bt, JP, DL; The Manor House, Preshaw Park, Upham, nr Southampton, Hants SO3 1HP (☎ 0962 771757, office 0962 771758)

PELTZER DUNN, Garry Ian Michael; s of Richard Michael Fallows Dunn, and Bettine, *née* Primrose Smith; *b* 2 Feb 1943; *Educ* Hove Coll; *m* 9 April 1966, Elaine Louise Bole, da of Maj Anton Peltzer (d 1976); 2 da (Katharine b 1967, Elizabeth b 1971); *Career* chartered surveyor; (ARICS), ldr Hove Borough Cncl (elected chm Policy and Resources Ctee 1974); former vice chm: Hove C Assoc, SE Area Young C; former memb E Sussex CC, life memb Hove Civic Soc, former Ctee memb Hove Civic Soc; memb: Preston Nomads CC; Hove and Kingsway; *Recreations* animal welfare, sport, travel; *Clubs* Hove Conservative, Hove Deep Sea Anglers; *Style—* Garry Peltzer Dunn, Esq; 234 New Church Rd, Hove, E Sussex (☎ 0273 414615); 5 St George Place, Brighton, E Sussex (☎ 0273 680874, fax : 0273 607021)

PEMBERTON, Sir Francis Wingate William; CBE (1970), DL (Cambs 1979); s of late Dr William Warburton Wingate (assumed Arms of Pemberton, by Royal Licence, 1921), and Viola Patience, *née* Campbell; *b* 1 Oct 1916; *Educ* Eton, Trinity Coll Cambridge; *m* 19 April 1941, Diana Patricia, da of late Reginald Salisbury Woods and late Irene Woods, CBE, TD; 2 s; *Career* former sr conslt Bidwells Chartered Surveyors; dir: Agric Mortgage Corp Ltd 1969-, Barclays Bank UK Mgmnt Ltd 1977-81; High Sheriff Cambs and Isle of Ely 1965-66; FRICS; kt 1976; *Style—* Sir Francis Pemberton, CBE, DL; Trumpington Hall, Cambridge (☎ 0223 841941); Business: Enterprise House, Maris Lane, Trumpington, Cambridge (☎ 0223 840840)

PEMBERTON, Dr James; s of Tom Winstanley Pemberton, of 114 Norton Park View, Sheffield, and Marjorie, *née* Chesney; *b* 21 Dec 1940; *Educ* King Edward VIII Sch Sheffield, St Bartholomew's Hosp Med Sch (MB BS, MRCP, BSc scholarship, Hayward prize); *m* Sylvia Ann, *née* Finnigan; 4 c (Philippa Louise b 18 Sept 1968, Tom Winstanley b 12 Oct 1969, James Wentworth b 25 June 1971, Sam b 28 April 1981); *Career* St Bartholemew's Hosp: house physician 1968, house surgn 1969, registrar Pathology Dept 1970, registrar in Med 1970-71, registrar diagnostic radiology 1971-73; sr registrar diagnostic radiology King's Coll Hosp 1973-74, conslt radiologist St Thomas's Hosp 1974-; admin head Radiology Dept Lambeth and S Western Hosps 1975-77; memb Prog Ctee BIR 1976-79, Med Ctee BIR 1977-79; organiser Scientific Exhibition JL Annual Congress of the Combined Royal Colls of UK, Netherlands and BIR 1978 and 1979; chm Radiology Sub Ctee St Thomas's Hosp 1978-80 and 1984-86, Dist Working Pty on Jr Hosp Med and Dental Staff Hours of Work 1988; St Thomas's Hosp: vice chm Med and Surgical Offrs Ctee 1988-89, chm Dist Working Pty Jr Drs Rotas-Safety Nets, memb Dist Manpower Ctee, pres Sch of Radiography; memb: Regnl Radiography Working Pty 1984-, Regnl Manpower Ctee 1986-, Regnl Radiology Specialists Sub Ctee 1984-90; BIR: memb Cncl 1990, memb Med Ctee 1990, memb Radiation Protection Ctee 1990; med lectr for: RCR, Br Cncl, FRCS Course and FRCR Course in radiotherapy St Thomas's Hosp; author numerous pubns in learned jls; MRCS 1967, LRCP 1967, DMRD 1972, FFR 1974, FRCR 1976; *Recreations* watching Arsenal FC, horseracing; *Clubs* Carlton, St Thomas's Hosp Soccer (vice pres); *Style—* Dr James Pemberton; 18 Village Way, Dulwich, London SE1 7AN (☎ 071 737 2220); St Thomas's Hospital, London SE1 (☎ 071 928 9292); 148 Harley St, London W1 (☎ 071 486 8685)

PEMBERTON, Jeremy; s of Sidney Charles Pemberton (d 1974), and Levina Beatrice (d 1974); *b* 17 Oct 1948; *Educ* Hampton GS; *m* 25 July 1969, Anne Marie Therese Antoinette, da of Adrien Croughs; *Career* dep chm Yellowhammer plc 1987- (creative dir 1972-87); *Recreations* squash, chess; *Clubs* RAC; *Style—* Jeremy Pemberton, Esq; Yellowhammer, 76 Oxford St, London W1

PEMBROKE, Ann Marjorie Francesca; *née* Gorman; da of Reginald William Gorman (d 1979), of Bromley, Kent, and Ethel, *née* Lamb-Shine (d 1979); *b* 1 Jan 1938; *Educ* Holy Trinity Convent, Sorbonne; *m* 18 June 1960, Mark Pembroke, s of Geoffrey Vernon Worth Pembroke (d 1983), of Bexhill-on-Sea, Sussex; 2 s (Guy Richard b 1963, James Robert b 1966); *Career* FO London and Paris 1956-58; Pembroke & Pembroke London 1969-; memb: Ct of Common Cncl City of London, Care, IOW Soc; Dep Ward of Cheap, asst Irish Soc, govr City of London Sch, tstee Dr Johnson's House, rep Nat Assoc for Maternal and Child Welfare; Freeman City of London 1977,

Liveryman Worshipful Co of Horners 1980; *Recreations* travel, horticulture, country pursuits; *Clubs* City Livery, Guildhall; *Style*— Mrs Mark Pembroke

PEMBROKE AND MONTGOMERY, 17 Earl of (E 1551) and 14 Earl of (E 1605) respectively; Henry George Charles Alexander Herbert; also Baron Herbert of Cardiff (E 1551), Baron Herbert of Shurland (E 1605), and Baron Herbert of Lea (UK 1861); o s of 16 Earl of Pembroke and Montgomery, CVO (d 1969), and Mary Countess of Pembroke, *qv*; *b* 19 May 1939; *Educ* Eton, Ch Ch Oxford; *m* 1, 1966 (m dis 1981), Claire Rose, o da of Douglas Gurney Pelly; 1 s, 3 da (Lady Sophia b 1966, Lady Emma b 1969, Lady Flora b 1970); m 2, 16 April 1988, Miranda J, da of Cdr J S K Oram, of Bulbridge House, Wilton, Salisbury, Wilts; 1 da (Lady Jemima b 4 Oct 1989); *Heir* s, Lord Herbert, *qv*; *Career* hereditary grand visitor of Jesus Coll Oxford; Royal Horse Gds 1958-60; owner of Wilton House (Inigo Jones, built around 1650, with additional work by James Wyatt 1810); *Style*— The Rt Hon the Earl of Pembroke and Montgomery; Wilton House, Salisbury, Wilts (☎ 0722 743211)

PEMBROKE AND MONTGOMERY, Mary, Countess of; Lady Mary Dorothea; *née* Hope; CVO (1947) DL; da of 1 Marquess of Linlithgow, KT, GCMG, GCVO, PC (d 1908); *b* 31 Dec 1903; *m* 27 July 1936, 16 Earl of Pembroke and Montgomery, CVO (d 1969); 1 s (17 Earl of Pembroke), 1 da; *Career* hon first offr WRNS; lady-in-waiting to HRH the Duchess of Kent 1934-49, extra lady-in-waiting 1949-68; *Style*— The Rt Hon Mary, Countess of Pembroke and Montgomery, CVO, DL; The Old Rectory, Wilton, Salisbury, Wilts SP2 0HT (☎ 0722 743157)

PENDER, 3 Baron (UK 1937); John Willoughby Denison-Pender; s of 2 Baron Pender, CBE (d 1965), and Camilla Lethbridge, da of late Willoughby Arthur Pemberton; *b* 6 May 1933; *Educ* Eton; *m* 1962, Julia, da of Richard Nevill Cannon, OBE, of Coombe Place, Lewes, Sussex; 1 s, 2 da (Hon Emma Charlotte b 1964, Hon Mary Anne Louise b 1965); *Heir* s, Hon Henry John Richard Denison-Pender b 19 March 1968; *Career* formerly Lt 10 Royal Hussars and Capt City of London Yeo; former dir Globe Trust Ltd, chm J J & D Frost plc; sits as Cons in House of Lords; *Recreations* golf, racing, gardening; *Clubs* White's, Pratt's; *Style*— The Rt Hon The Lord Pender; North Court, Tilmanstone, Kent

PENDER, Reginald Robinson; s of Reginald George Pender (d 1967); *b* 23 March 1934; *Educ* Harrow; *m* 1958, Elizabeth, da of Charles Joseph Meager (d 1968); 2 s, 1 da; *Career* Nat Serv Capt (Army) 1952-54; co sec; dir Standard Building Soc; FICS, ACIArb; *Recreations* gardening; *Clubs* Challoner; *Style*— Reginald Pender, Esq; 10 Beverley Gardens, Cullercoats, N Shields, Tyne & Wear NE30 4NS (☎ 091 2521282); Bark Mill, West Hall, Brampton, Cumbria (☎ 069 72 289)

PENDRILL, (Alfred) Malcolm; s of A A Pendrill (d 1970), of Redhill, Surrey, and Olive Rose, *née* Sutton (d 1989); *b* 14 Feb 1926; *Educ* Reigate GS; *m* 11 Dec 1948, Phyllis Margaret, *née* Bryant; 1 da (Christine Ann b 8 June 1986); *Career* photographer; aerial photographer, staff photographer for a gp of engrg cos; fndr Malcolm Pendrill Ltd 1963 (offering serv to industl clients in aerial photography, industl photography and documentary films); lectr to various professional bodies and amateur gps; former external assessor at various colls: former memb Bd of Govrs Reigate Sch of Art and Design; hon memb Rotary Club of Reigate (memb 1967); FBIPP 1972, FRPS 1973, FRSA 1987; *Books* Reflections of Yesterday (1982), Memories of Yesterday (1983); *Recreations* music, films; *Style*— Malcolm Pendrill, Esq; Malcolm Pendrill Ltd, Chivalry House, Battersea Rise, London SW11 1HP

PENDRY, Prof John Brian; s of Frank Johnson Pendry (d 1978), and Kathleen, *née* Shaw; *b* 4 July 1943; *Educ* Ashton-under-Lyne GS, Downing Coll Cambridge (BA, MA, PhD); *m* 15 Jan 1977, Patricia, da of Frederick Gard, of London; *Career* res fell in physics Downing Coll Cambridge 1969-75, memb tech staff Bell Laboratories USA 1972-73, sr res asst Cavendish Lab Cambridge 1973-75 (postdoctoral fell 1969-72), SPSO and head Theory Gp SERC Daresbury Laboratory 1975-81, prof of theoretical solid state physics and assoc head of dept Imperial Coll London 1981-; memb SERC Physics Ctee (chm panel Y) 1985-88; FRS 1984, FInstP 1984; *Recreations* music, piano playing, gardening; *Style*— Prof John Pendry, FRS; Metchley, Knipp Hill, Cobham, Surrey KT11 2PE (☎ 0932 64306); The Blackett Laboratory, Imperial College, London SW7 2BZ (☎ 071 589 5111, fax 071 589 9463, telex 929484)

PENDRY, Thomas (Tom); MP (Lab) Stalybridge and Hyde 1987-; s of L E Pendry, of Broadstairs; *b* 10 June 1934; *Educ* St Augustine's Ramsgate, Univ of Oxford; *m* 1966, Moira Anne, da of A E Smith, of Derby; 1 s, 1 da; *Career* serv RAF 1955-57; joined Lab Pty 1950, NUPE official 1960-70, memb Paddington Cncl 1962-65, chm Derby Lab Pty 1966, MP (Lab) Stalybridge and Hyde 1970-, oppn whip 1971-74, lord cmmr of Treasy (govt whip) 1974-77 (resigned), parly under-sec state NI Office 1978-79; oppn spokesman: NI 1979-81, Overseas Devpt 1981-82, Devolution and Regnl Affrs 1982; chm: PLP Sports Ctee, All Pty Football Ctee, NUPE Gp of Lab MP's; steward of the BBB of C; *Recreations* sports of all kinds; *Clubs* Reform, Stalybridge Labour; *Style*— Tom Pendry, Esq, MP; 2 Cannon St, Hollingworth, Hyde, Cheshire

PENFOLD, David Jon; s of Maj Arthur Jon Penfold, RA (d 1978), and May Dalglish, *née* Wardrop; *b* 26 April 1935; *Educ* Highgate Sch, and in France; *m* 19 June 1968 (m dis 1980), Susan, da of William Elliott (d 1978); 1 s (Jonathan David b 1970); *Career* Nat Serv RA 1953-55, Lt 1955; dir WB Darley Ltd 1958-63, ptnr Thompson Scheduling Ltd 1964-75; conslt KH Publicity Ltd 1975-81, Streets Fin Ltd 1981-87; (assoc dir 1985-87), dir Mountain & Molehill Ltd 1988-; chm: Burton-on-Trent Constitutional Club 1960-63, W Midlands Area Young Cons 1960-63, Windsor and Maidenhead Cons Assoc 1986-89; party candidate (Cons): W Nottingham 1966, Derby N Feb and Oct 1974; cllr: Burton-on-Trent Cncl 1960-63 and 1967-71, Windsor and Maidenhead DC 1983-87; chm Colne Valley Groundwork Tst 1988-; *Books* The Young Idea (co-author 1963); *Recreations* skiing, golf, gardening, reading; *Style*— David Penfold, Esq; 10 Courtenay Square, London SE11; The Thatch, Littlewick Green, Berkshire; Mountain & Molehill Ltd, 56 Britton St, London EC1 (☎ 071 253 2268, fax 071 251 1939)

PENFOLD, Derek John; s of Joseph Penfold, of Tiverton, Devon, and Catherine, *née* O'Sullivan; *b* 17 July 1948; *Educ* Clapham Coll, City of Westminster Coll, NW London Poly (LLB); *Career* features ed Estates Times 1975-78, dep ed Estates Gazette 1980-86 (news ed 1978-80), property analyst Alexanders Laing & Cruickshank 1986-87, dir Streets Communications 1987-89, Phillips Communications 1990-; chm Greenwich Theatre 1980-88 (dir 1975-90), dir Greenwich Young People's Theatre 1980-88 (tstee 1990); former chm Greenwich Festival; London Borough of Greenwich cncllr 1971-78, chm Leisure Ctee, chief whip; vice pres The Story of Christmas Charity Appeal; Freeman City of London; *Recreations* theatre; *Clubs* Wig & Pen, Gresham; *Style*— Derek Penfold, Esq; 42 Owenite St, Abbey Wood, London SE2 0NQ (☎ 081 311 6039); Oliver House, 51-53 City Rd, London EC1Y 1AU (☎ 071 490 4595, fax 071 490 3202)

PENLEY, Francis Charles; s of Reginald Herbert Penley, of Rockstowes Hill, Dursley, Gloucs, and Geraldine, *née* Murray-Browne; *b* 28 Dec 1915; *Educ* Marlborough, Christ's Coll Cambridge (BA, LLM); *m* 7 Dec 1940, Katharine, da of Lt Col Archibald Nelson Gavin-Jones, DSO (d 1967); 1 s (John b 1948, *qv*), 2 da (Prudence b 1946, Nicola b 1953); *Career* WWII: Lt TA 1936, Capt 1940, Adj 73 Medium Regt RA 1940-41, GSO 3 8 Army HQ 1942, serv Western Desert 1941-42 (POW 1942-45); admitted slr 1945-, Notary Public 1957-90; clerk: Gen Cmmrs of Taxes 1950-80, Justices Dursley, Whitminister, Berkeley Divs 1951-67; chm Stroud Bldg Soc (now Stroud and Swindon Bldg Soc) 1982-86 (dir 1970-86); town cncllr Dursley 1962-78; fndr pres Dursley Rotary Club 1952-53 (memb 1952-), pres Gloucs and Wilts Law Soc 1977-78, tstee and chm Gloucs Historic Churches Preservation Tst 1982-, fndr tstee Stinchcombe Hill Recreation Ground Tst 1983-, Paul Harris fell 1988; *Recreations* book binding, gardening; *Style*— Francis Penley, Esq; 26 Long St, Dursley, Gloucs GL11 5TE (☎ 0453 542357)

PENLEY, Lt Col John Francis; TD (1984); s of Capt Francis Charles Penley, RA, *qv*, and Katharine, *née* Gavin-Jones; *b* 22 Dec 1948; *Educ* Marlborough Coll of Law; *m* 25 Jan 1978, Caroline Anne Myfanwy, da of George William Harris James (surgn Lt RNVR); 1 s (Matthew John b 1982), 1 da (Eleanor Anne b 1984); *Career* cmmnd Wessex Yeo 1971, Capt 1978, Maj OC A (Royal Glos Hussars) Sqdn The Royal Wessex Yeo 1984, 2 i/c The Royal Wessex Yeo 1987, cmdg The Royal Wessex Yeo 1989; slr 1973, asst slr Clifford Turner 1973-78, ptnr Penleys 1978, NP 1979; sec: Stinchcombe Hill Recreation Ground Tst, Dursley United Charities, Dursley Church Houses and Torchacre Charity, Henry Vizard Charity; vice chm Uley Parish Cncl 1991; memb: Bow Gp 1975-80, exec Glos Ctee Country Landowners Assoc 1987-; memb: Law Soc 1974, Soc of Notaries 1979, Agric Lawyers Assoc 1984; *Recreations* hunting, shooting, walking, gardening; *Style*— Lt Col John Penley, TD; The Royal Wessex Yeomanry, Highfield House, Cirencester, Glos (☎ 0285 654771)

PENMAN, Caroline Elizabeth; da of Reginald Geoffrey Filmer (d 1967), and Lucy Kathleen, *née* Long (d 1982); *b* 4 Feb 1944; *Educ* educated privately; *m* 28 June 1969, Richard Howard Browne Penman, s of Donald Penman; *Career* owner antiques shop 1964-74, organiser circuit of antiques fairs (incl S of England Antiques Trade Fair Ardingly 1974-85) 1970-85; owner of: W London Antiques Fair 1976-, Chelsea Antiques Fair 1985-; organiser City of London Antiques Fair 1987-88, dir London and Provincial Antique Dealers Assoc 1983-; *Recreations* antiques; *Style*— Mrs Caroline Penman; Cockhaise Mill, Lindfield, Sussex (☎ 0444 482514); P O Box 114, Haywards Heath, Sussex (☎ 0444 484531, fax 0444 483412)

PENN, Christopher Arthur; s of Lt-Col Sir Eric Penn, GCVO, OBE, MC, *qv*; *b* 13 Sept 1950; *Educ* Eton; *m* 1976, Sabrina Mary, 2 da of Timothy Colman, DCL, of Bixley Manor, Norwich; 1 s (Rory b 1980), 1 da (Louisa b 1983); *Career* chartered surveyor; ptnr Jones Lang Wootton; *Clubs* Buck's; *Style*— Christopher Penn, Esq; 70 Lyford Rd, London SW18 3JW (☎ 081 874 8200)

PENN, Dr Christopher Robert Howard; s of John Howard Penn (d 1977), of Southend-on-Sea, Essex, and Kathleen Mary, *née* Dalton; *b* 24 Aug 1939; *Educ* Felsted, QMC, Trinity Hall Cambridge (MA, MB BCh); *m* 27 May 1966, Elizabeth, da of John Henry Griffin, of Bishopsteignton, Devon; 3 da (Katherine Clare, Sarah Elizabeth, Charlotte Mary); *Career* sr house offr in med Lincoln Co Hosp 1966-67, sr house offr in surgery Scartho Rd Infirmary Grimsby 1967-68; The London Hosp Dept of Radiotherapy 1968-73: sr house offr, registrar, sr registrar; sr conslt Dept of Radiotherapy and Oncology Royal Devon and Exeter and Torbay Hosps 1982- (conslt 1973-83); numerous pubns in jls; govr Trinity Sch Teignmouth; memb: PCC St Gregory's Dawlish, Br Inst Radiology; Freeman City of London 1960; FRCR 1972; *Books* Radiotherapy in Modern Clinical Practice (contrib 1975); *Recreations* sailing, naval history; *Style*— Dr Christopher Penn; 1 Holcombe Road, Teignmouth, Devon TQ14 8UP (☎ 0626 778448), Dept of Radiotherapy and Oncology, Royal Devon and Exeter Hosp (Wonford), Barrack Rd, Exeter (☎ 0392 402101)

PENN, Christopher William Milner; s of late William Henry Milner Penn, of Westholms, Bisley, nr Stroud, Glos, and Ruth Adeline Mary, *née* Pendleton; *b* 6 June 1937; *Educ* Sherborne; *m* 1, 12 Oct 1963 (m dis 1983), Angela Edith Margeret, da of Louis Edward Peacock (d 1978); 3 s (Jonathan b 1965, William b 1967, Edward b 1969); m 2, 16 Dec 1988, Maureen Janice, da of Larry Edward Reeve (d 1965); *Career* Nat Serv RN 1955-57, cmmnd 1956, RNR 1957-77; Gabriel Wade & English Ltd 1957-70, William Brown & Co (Ipswich) Ltd 1970-73, Paul Frost Ltd 1973-90 (dir 1975-); memb Ipswich Borough Cncl 1958-78, memb Suffolk CC 1979- (ldr 1986-); *Recreations* sailing, fishing; *Clubs* Waldringfield; *Style*— Christopher Penn, Esq; Cherry Bank, Church Lane, Playford, Ipswich IP6 9DS (☎ 0473 622 636); Paul Frost Ltd, Tolleshunt Major, Maldon, Essex CM9 8LW (☎ 0621 860 323)

PENN, David John; s of late Surgn Capt Eric Arthur Penn, DSC, of 9 New Orleans, Coast Rd, W Mersea, Essex, and Catherine, *née* Dunnett; *b* 2 Jan 1945; *Educ* Dulwich, St Catherine's Coll Oxford (MA); *Career* keeper Imp War Museum: Dept of Info Retrieval 1970-77, Dept of Firearms 1973-76, Dept of Exhibits and Firearms 1976-; vice chm Nat Pistol Assoc, vice pres Muzzle-Loaders Assoc of GB, hon sec Hist Breechloading Smallarms Assoc; memb: Br Shooting Sports Cncl, Home Office Firearms Consultative Ctee 1989; fell Soc of Antiquaries 1989; Freeman: City of London 1982, Worshipful Co of Gunmakers 1982; *Books* Imperial War Museum Film Cataloguing Rules (with R B N Smither, 1976); *Recreations* shooting; *Clubs* Reform; *Style*— David Penn, Esq; Imperial War Museum, Lambeth Rd, London SE1 6HZ (☎ 071 416 5270, fax 071 416 5374)

PENN, Lt-Col Sir Eric Charles William Mackenzie; GCVO (1980, KCVO 1972, CVO 1965), OBE (1960), MC (1944); s of Capt Eric Frank Penn (ka 1915, eldest s of William Penn, of Taverham Hall, Norwich), by his w Gladys, yr da of Charles John Ebden, JP, DL, of Newton House, Lanarks; *b* 9 Feb 1916; *Educ* Eton, Magdalene Coll Cambridge; *m* 29 Jan 1947, Prudence Stewart-Wilson, da of Aubyn Wilson (d 1934), and Muriel Stewart-Stevens (d 1982), of Balnakeilly, Pitlochry, Perthshire; 2 s (David, Christopher, *qv*), 1 da (Fiona); *Career* Grenadier Gds 1938-60; serv: France and Belgium 1939-40, Italy and Austria 1943-45, Germany 1945-46, Libya, Egypt 1950-52, Germany 1954-55; comptroller Lord Chamberlain's Office 1964-81 (asst comptroller 1960-64), extra equerry to HM The Queen 1963-; *Clubs* White's, Pratt's; *Style*— Lt-Col Sir Eric Penn, GCVO, OBE, MC; 6 Rosscourt Mansions, 4 Palace St, London SW1E 5HZ

PENN-SMITH, Derek John; s of Major Sydney Penn-Smith, RE, FRIBA (d 1987), of Leicester, and Olive Amelia, *née* Kinton; *b* 21 Feb 1934; *Educ* Wyggeston Sch Leics, Sch of Architecture Leicester (DipArch), Univ of Durham (Dip Town Planning); *m* 1, 19 July 1968 (m dis), Eva Margaret; 2 da (Fiona b 1964, Sally b 1966); m 2, 2 Dec 1972, Molly, da of John Berkin (d 1985), of Leics; *Career* Nat Serv 2 Lt RE Gibraltar; ptnr and conslt: Penn-Smith & Wall Peterborough 1961-87, Penn-Smith & Weston Derby 1961-88; ptnr S Penn-Smith Son & Ptnrs Leicester 1961-88 (sr ptnr 1980-88), dir Douglas Smith Stimson Ptnrship Ltd (inc S Penn-Smith Son & Ptnrs) 1988-89, town planning conslt 1989-; Freeman City of London, Liveryman Worshipful Co of Pewterers; FRIBA, FRTPI; *Recreations* sailing, (Univ of Durham colours), aviation (gliding), orchid growing; *Style*— Derek J Penn-Smith, Esq; Delphi, High St, Naseby, Northants NN6 7DD (☎ 0604 740326)

PENNA, Colin Eric; s of John Henry Penna (d 1988), of 16 Park St, Willington, Crook, Co Durham, and Ruth, *née* Collin (d 1966); *b* 1 Nov 1935; *Educ* King James I Sch Bishop Auckland Co Durham, King's Coll London (LLB); *Career* slr; ptnr Marquis Penna & Hewitt Brown-Humes & Hare of Co Durham; HM coroner S Dist Durham Co 1980; *Recreations* music, theatre; *Clubs* RAC; *Style*— Colin Penna, Esq; 28 Briardene, Durham City (☎ 091 386 8030); 5 Market Place, Bishop Auckland, Co Durham (☎ 0388 604 691)

PENNANT-REA, Hon Mrs (Helen); *née* Jay; er (twin) da of Baron Jay, PC (Life Peer), *qv*; *Educ* N London Collegiate Sch, Sussex Univ (BA); *m* 1, 1975 (m dis 1982), David Kennard; 2 da (Amanda b 1976, Juliet b 1979); m 2, 24 June 1986, Rupert Lascelles Pennant-Rea, *qv*; 1 s (Edward b 1986), 1 step s, 1 step da; *Style*— The Hon Mrs Pennant-Rea

PENNANT-REA, Rupert Lascelles; s of Peter Athelwold Pennant-Rea, MBE, of Guiting Power, Glos, and Pauline Elizabeth, *née* Creasy; *b* 23 Jan 1948; *Educ* Peterhouse Zimbabwe, Trinity Coll Dublin (BA), Univ of Manchester (MA); *m* 1, 3 Oct 1970 (m dis 1975), (Elizabeth) Louise, da of Rt Rev William Derrick Lindsay Greer (d 1972), sometime Bishop of Manchester; m 2, 18 Aug 1979 (m dis 1986), Jane Trevelyan, da of John Hamilton, of Isles of Scilly; 1 s (Rory b 1983), 1 da (Emily b 1982); m 3, 24 June 1986, Hon Helen (*qv*), er (twin) da of Baron Jay, PC (Life Peer), and former w of David Kennard; 1 s (Edward b 1986), 2 step da; *Career* with Confedn of Irish Indust 1970-71, Gen & Municipal Workers Union 1972-73, Bank of England 1973-77; The Economist: economics ed 1981-85, economics corr 1977-81, ed 1986-; *Books* Gold Foil (1978), Who Runs The Economy? (jtly, 1979), The Pocket Economist (jtly, 1982), The Economist Economics (jtly, 1986); *Recreations* music, tennis, fishing, family; *Clubs* MCC, Reform; *Style*— Rupert Pennant-Rea, Esq; 25 St James's St, London SW1A 1HA

PENNEY, Hon Christopher Charles; yr s of Baron Penney, OM, KBE, FRS (Life Peer, d 1991), and his 1 w, Adele Minnie, *née* Elms (d 1944); *b* 1941; *Educ* Cranleigh, Gonville and Caius Coll Cambridge (MA), Guy's Hosp; *m* 1968, Margaret, da of Henry Bell Fairley, of Stockport; 1 s (Richard William b 1970); *Career* MRCP, FRCP; *Style*— The Hon Christopher Penney; 39 Beaulieu Ave, Sydenham SE26

PENNEY, Jennifer Beverly; da of James Beverley Guy Penney (d 1989), of Canada, and Gwendolyn Florence, *née* McKie; *b* 5 April 1946; *Educ* Kelowna HS, Royal Ballet Sch; *m* 22 June 1983 (m dis 1984), Philip Ian Porter; *Career* memb Royal Ballet Co 1963-88, soloist 1966-88, princ 1970-88, ret 1988; maj roles incl: Titania in The Dream, The Ballerina in Petrushka, Tatiana in Anastasia, Autumn in The Four Seasons, The Golden Hours in Elite Syncopations, Princess Aurora and Princess Florine in The Sleeping Beauty, Clara in The Nutcracker, Odette and Odile in Swan Lake, title roles in Manon and Cinderella, Nikiya in La Bayadère, Marie Larisch, Mitzi Caspar and Mary Vetsera in Mayerling, The Aristocrat in Mam'zelle Angot, Sacred Love in Illuminations, title role in Giselle, Juliet in Romeo and Juliet; various roles in: Liebeslieder Waltzer, My Brother, My Sisters, The Seven Deadly Sins, Dance of Albion; *Awards* New Standard Ballet award 1980; *Recreations* pottery, water colours, gardening, DIY; *Style*— Ms Jennifer Penney

PENNEY, Malcolm Olaf; s of John William Penney (d 1983) of Shipton Gorge, Bridport, Dorset, and Phyllis Gertrude, *née* Radnor; *b* 24 June 1939; *Educ* City of London Sch; *m* 28 Dec 1973, Marian Joyce, da of Leslie Edward Johnson, 1 s (Martin Edward b 19 Aug 1976), 1 da (Caroline Phyllis b 10 Sept 1980); *Career* Lord Foster & Co: articled clerk 1956-61, sr clerk 1961-64, ptnr 1964-86 (latterly ptnr i/c Int Tax); ptnr i/c Newbury office and tax ptnr Thames Valley Dearden Farrow (latterly Binder Hamlyn) 1986-88, tax ptnr Reading office Ernst & Young 1988-; chm Fiscal Ctee of the Confédération Fiscal Européenne 1991-, memb Tax Ctee ICAEW 1978-, memb Cncl Inst of Taxation 1987-; Plender prize ICAEW 1959, Stephens prize ICAEW 1961; Freeman City of London 1973, memb Court of Assistants Worshipful Co of Glovers 1986- (Liveryman 1973-); FCA (ACA 1961), FTII (ATII 1964); *Books* Capital Transfer Tax Planning (with E K Wright and others, 1974) Taxation of Capital Gains (with P W Elliott 1982); *Recreations* travelling, walking; *Clubs* City Livery, Berkshire Athaneum; *Style*— Malcolm Penney, Esq; Maple Cottage, Stanbrook Close, Southend Bradfield, Reading, Berkshire RG7 6HZ (☎ 0734 744449); Ernst & Young, Apex Plaza, Reading RG1 1YE (☎ 0734 500611, fax 0734 507744)

PENNEY, Hon Martin Charles; er s of Baron Penney, OM, KBE, FRS (Life Peer, d 1991), and his 1 w, Adele Minnie, *née* Elms (d 1944); *b* 13 March 1938; *Educ* Cranleigh, Gonville and Caius Coll Cambridge (MA); *m* 1961, Margaret Heather, da of Sqdn Ldr H Almond, DSO, DFC, of Ramsdell, nr Basingstoke; 2 da (Claire Virginia b 1962, Kathryn Jane (Mrs Christopher J Coleman) b 1964); *Career* headmaster Bearwood Coll Wokingham 1980-; *Style*— The Hon Martin Penney; Bearwood College, Wokingham, Berks (☎ 0734 786915)

PENNEY, Flt Lt Ronald Frederick; s of John Henry Penney, of Belmont Lodge, Belmont Rd, Bushey, Herts, and Ivy Kathleen Penney (decd); *b* 7 June 1924; *Educ* Glendale GS; *m* 26 July 1973, Mrs Joan Rebecca Jacobs; 1 da (by previous m, Marilyn (Mrs Bishop) b 1947), 1 step s (Jeremy Jacobs b 1955), 1 step da (Jacqueline (Mrs Barnett) b 1948, d 1988); *Career* cmmnd RAF 1941 as Pilot Offr, Flt Lt 1944 (demobilised 1946), joined RAFVR, ret 1951; navigator Lancaster Aircraft with 626 Sqdn on Bomber Cmd, and 100 Sqdn; held private pilot's licence until 1982; CA 1954; former ptnr F G Jenkins Wood Co, dir PJB Ltd; memb: Sqdn Assoc, The Wickenby Register, Air Crew Assoc, Bomber Cmd Assoc, Hendon Old People's Welfare Ctee, Rotany Int; chm Elderly Accommodation Bureau; Liveryman: Worshipful Co of Poulters, Worshipful Co of Bakers; Freeman City of London, memb Guild of Freemen; FICA, MInstD; *Recreations* flying, sailing, riding; *Clubs* RAF, City Livery; *Style*— Fl Lt Ronald Penney; 5 March Close, Mill Hill, London NW7 4NY (☎ 081 959 4083)

PENNIE, John Anthony; s of Terence Edward Pennie, of 9A Cavendish Avenue, Cambridge, and Denise Judith, *née* Watkins; *b* 18 Feb 1955; *Educ* Marlborough, Univ of Cambridge (MA), Universite Libre De Bruxelles; *m* 12 Feb 1983, Annette Francine, da of Raymond Charles Rendall (d 1981); 1 s (Wilfred Oscar Norleigh b 29 Oct 1987), 1 da (Celia Mary b 18 Oct 1984); *Career* slr; ptnr Dickinson Dees 1984; Sandhoe Parish cncllr, sch govr, chm Tynedale Environmental Gp memb Law Soc; *Recreations* gardening; *Style*— John Pennie, Esq; Beaufront Hill Head, Hexham, Northumberland (☎ 0434 603508); Cross House, Westgate Rd, Newcastle-upon-Tyne (☎ 091 261 1911, fax 091 261 5855)

PENNINGTON, Malcolm Read; s of Capt Stanley Read Pennington (d 1975), and Esther Elsie, *née* Hall; *b* 6 Feb 1947; *Educ* Repton Sch; *m* 24 April 1971, Jillian Elizabeth, da of James Shepherd (d 1977); 1 s (James b 1976), 1 da (Sarah b 1977); *Career* CA fndr ptnr Pennington Williams CAs of Bromborough and Chester 1975; Chevalier de l'Ordre des Coteaux de Champagne 1982-; FCA 1979; *Recreations* golf, cricket, badminton, gastronomy; *Clubs* Delamere Forest Golf, Heswall Golf, Oxton CC, Wirral Wine Soc; *Style*— Malcolm Pennington, Esq, Horbury, 74 Osmaston Rd, Prenton, Birkenhead, Merseyside L42 8LP (☎ 051 608 1578)

PENNINGTON, Michael Vivian Fyfe; s of Vivian Maynard Cecil Pennington (d 1984), and Euphemia Willock Fyfe (d 1987); *b* 7 June 1943; *Educ* Marlborough, Trinity Coll Cambridge (BA); *m* 10 Oct 1964 (m dis 1967), Katharine, da of Peter Barker; 1 s (Mark Dominic Fyfe b 12 Aug 1966); *Career* memb Royal Shakespeare Co 1964-67; freelance West End and TV, plays incl: The Judge, Hamlet, A Woman of No Importance, Savages 1967-73; leading memb Royal Shakespeare Co 1974-81, roles incl: Angelo in Measure for Measure, Mercutio in Romeo and Juliet, Edgar in King Lear, Berowne in Love's Labours Lost, Mirabell in Way of the World, title role Hippolytus, title role Hamlet, Donal Davoren in Shadow of a Gunman; Nat theatre 1984: title role in Strider, Jaffier in Venice Preserved, title role in Anton Chekhov; The Real Thing (West End, 1985), Oedipus The King (BBC TV), 1985; artistic dir English Shakespeare Co (fndr and leading actor 1986-90, participated in four round the world tours) roles incl: Richard II, Henry V, Coriolanus, Leontes in The Winter's Tale; Summer's Lease (BBC TV) 1989, Playing with Trains (RSC Barbican) 1989, Vershinin in Three Sister (Gate Theatre Dublin) 1990; *Books* Rossya: A Journey Through Siberia (1977), English Shakespeare Company: The Story of the Wars of The Roses (1990); *Recreations* reading, music; *Style*— Michael Pennington, Esq; English Shakespeare Company, 369 St John St, London EC1 (☎ 071 278 7970, fax 071 278 7978)

PENNINGTON, Prof Robert Roland; s of Roland Alexander Pennington (d 1952), of Warley, W Mids, and Elsie Davis (d 1977); *b* 22 April 1927; *Educ* Holly Lodge Smethwick W Mids, Univ of Birmingham (LLB, LLD); *m* 14 March 1968, Patricia Irene, da of Cecil Allen Rook (d 1968), of Alcester, Worcs; 1 da (Elisabeth Anne b 1974); *Career* admitted slr 1951; reader Law Soc's Sch of Law London 1955 (sr lectr 1951), memb Bd of Mgmnt Coll of Law London 1962, prof in commercial law Univ of Birmingham 1968- (sr lectr 1962-68), govt advsr on co legislation Trinidad 1967 (Seychelles 1970), special legal advsr on commercial law Harmonisation Cmmn of the Euro Communities 1973-79; memb Law Soc 1951; *Books* Company Law (1959, 6 edn 1990), Companies in the Common Market (1962, 3 edn as Companies in the European Communities 1982), The Investor and the Law (1967), Stannary Law: A History of the Mining Law of Cornwall and Devon (1973), Commercial Banking Law (1978), The Companies Acts 1980 and 1981 - a practitioner's manual (1983), Stock Exchange Listing - the new requirements (1985), Directors' Personal Liability (1987), Company Liquidations: the Substantive Law, the Procedure (2 vols, 1987), The Law of Investment Marketing (1990), Insolvency Law (1990); *Recreations* travel, walking, history, archaeology; *Style*— Prof Robert Pennington; Gryphon House, Langley Road, Claverdon, Warwicks (☎ 092 684 3235); Faculty of Law, Univ of Birmingham, Birmingham B15 2TT (☎ 021 414 6296)

PENNOCK, Dr Charles Anthony; s of Sydney Pennock, and Edith Anne, *née* Oliver; *b* 26 Dec 1937; *Educ* Varndean Sch Brighton, Univ of Bristol (MB ChB, MD); *m* 1 April 1961, Patricia Ann (Paddy), da of Charles Ross Haller; 1 s (Christopher b 3 March 1965), 1 da (Sarah b 30 Sept 1963); *Career* conslt Paediatric Chem Path Dept Bristol and Weston Health Authy 1972-, sr lectr in child health Univ of Bristol 1975-; govr Inst of Child Health Univ of Bristol, chm Br Inherited Metabolic Disease Gp, sec Bristol Ctee on Action Res for the Crippled Child; FRCPath 1982 (MRCPath 1970); *Recreations* photography, fiscal philately; *Style*— Dr Charles Pennock; Warners Cottage, Chewton Keyncham, Avon BS18 2SU (☎ 0272 862320); Paediatric Chem Pathology Dept, Bristol Maternity Hosp, Southwell St, Bristol BS2 8EG (☎ 0272 285318)

PENNOCK, Hon David Roderick Michael; o s of Baron Pennock (Life Peer); *b* 1944; *Educ* Rugby, Merton Coll Oxford; *m* 1969, Jane Pinhard; 3 s, 1 da; *Career* chm Astell Scientific Ltd; *Recreations* tennis, farming, theatre; *Style*— The Hon David Pennock; Iridge Place, Hurst Green, Sussex TN19 7PN

PENNOCK, Baron (Life Peer UK 1982), of Norton in the Co of Cleveland; Raymond William Pennock; s of Frederick Henry Pennock and Harriet Anne, *née* Mathison; *b* 16 June 1920; *Educ* Coatham Sch, Merton Coll Oxford (MA); *m* 1943, Lorna, da of Percival Pearse, of Morpeth; 1 s (Hon David Roderick Michael b 1944), 2 da (Hon Susan Lorna (Hon Mrs Selby) b 1948, Hon Claire Elizabeth (Hon Mrs Walford) b 1958); *Career* served RA 1941-46, Capt (despatches 1945); dep chm ICI 1975-80 (joined 1947, dir 1972), chm BICC plc 1980-84, pres CBI 1980-82 (pres 1979-80); memb: Plessey Bd 1979-89, Standard Chartered plc Bd 1982- (dep chm), Willis Faber Bd 1985-90, Eurotunnel 1986-; hon fell Merton Coll Oxford; kt 1978; *Recreations* tennis, music, ballet, travel; *Clubs* AELTC, Queen's, Boodle's, Vincent's; *Style*— The Rt Hon the Lord Pennock; Morgan Grenfell Gp plc, 23 Great Winchester St, London EC2P 2AX (☎ 071 588 4545)

PENNY, Joseph Noel Bailey; QC (1971); s of Joseph A Penny, JP; *b* 25 Dec 1916; *Educ* Worksop Coll, Christ Church Oxford; *m* 1, 1947, Celia (d 1969), da of R H Roberts; 3 s, 1 da; m 2, 1972, Sara Margaret, da of Sir Arnold France; 1 da; *Career* Maj Royal Signals 1939-46; called to the Bar Gray's Inn 1948, Nat Insurance (now Social Security) cmmr 1977-89; *Style*— Joseph Penny, Esq, QC; Fair Orchard, Lingfield, Surrey (☎ 0342 832191)

PENNY, Hon Patrick Glyn; s of 2 Viscount Marchwood, MBE (d 1979); *b* 3 July 1939; *m* 1, 1968 (m dis 1974), Sue Eleanor Jane, da of late Charles Phipps Brutton, CBE; 1 da; m 2, 1979, Mrs Lynn Vanessa Knox, da of John Leslie Wyles, of Wimbledon; *Style*— The Hon Patrick Penny; 33 Wellington Sq, London SW3 4NR

PENNY, Hon Peter George Worsley; s and h of 3 Viscount Marchwood; *b* 8 Oct 1965; *Educ* Winchester; *Career* assoc dir The HMG Gp plc 1990-; *Recreations* racing, tennis, cricket, shooting; *Style*— The Hon Peter Penny; 37 Coniger Road, London SW6 (☎ 071 736 6834); The HMG Group plc, Plaza 535, Kings Road, London SW10 OSZ (☎ 071 823 3838, fax 071 823 3194)

PENRHYN, 6 Baron (UK 1866); Malcolm Frank Douglas-Pennant; DSO (1945), MBE (1943); s of 5 Baron Penrhyn (d 1967, himself gn of 17 Earl of Morton and ggs of Lady Frances Lascelles, da of 1 Earl of Harewood), and Alice Nellie (d 1965), da of Sir William Charles Cooper, 3 Bt; *b* 11 July 1908; *Educ* Eton, RMC Sandhurst; *m* 1954, Elisabeth Rosemary, da of late Brig Sir Percy Laurie, KCVO, CBE, DSO, JP; 2 da (*see* Thomas Richard Troubridge); *Heir* bro, Hon Nigel Douglas-Pennant; *Career* Col (ret) KRRC, served WWII 1939-45 in N Africa and NW Europe; *Style*— The Rt Hon the Lord Penrhyn, DSO, MBE; Littleton Manor, Winchester, Hants SO22 6QU (☎ 0962 880205)

PENRICE, Geoffrey; CB (1978); s of Harry Penrice; *b* 28 Feb 1923; *Educ* Thornes House GS, LSE; *m* 1947, Janet Gillies Allardice; 3 s; *Career* dir of statistics and dep sec Dept of Employment 1978-; *Style*— Geoffrey Penrice Esq, CB; 10 Dartmouth Park Ave, NW5 (☎ 071 267 2175)

PENROSE, Prof Oliver; s of Lionel S Penrose, FRS, and Margaret, *née* Leathes; *b* 6 June 1929; *Educ* Central Collegiate Inst London, UCL (BSc), Univ of Cambridge (PhD); *m* 1953, Joan Lomas, *née* Dilley; 2 s (and 1 s decd), 1 da; *Career* mathematical physicist English Electric Co Luton 1952-55, res asst Yale Univ 1955-56, lectr rising to reader in mathematics Imperial Coll London 1956-69, prof of mathematics: Open Univ 1969-86, Heriot-Watt Univ 1986-; author of numerous papers in physics jls; FRS 1987, FRSE; *Books* Foundations of Statisical Mechanics (1970); *Recreations* making music, chess; *Style*— Prof Oliver Penrose, FRS; 29 Frederick St, Edinburgh EH2 2ND (☎ 031 225 5879); Department of Mathematics, Heriot-Watt University, Riccarton, Edinburgh EH14 4AS

PENROSE, Dr Richard James Jackson; s of Walter James Pace (d 1944), (name changed by deed poll from Pace, 1968) and Gertrude May, *née* Penrose (d 1981); *b* 12 Oct 1941; *Educ* Haberdashers' Aske's, Charing Cross Hosp Med Sch Univ of London (MB BS, LRCP, MRCP); *m* 1 May 1976, Lynda Elizabeth, da of Dr Reginald John Alcock, of The Pigeon House, Kemble; 2 s (James b 1977, William b 1980); *Career* Charing Cross Hosp: house surgn ENT 1966, house physician gen med 1967, sr house offr in psychiatry 1968; sr registrar in psychiatry St Georges Hosp 1971-75 (sr house offr and registrar 1968-71); conslt psychiatrist: St George's Hosp 1975-89, West Park Hosp Epsom 1975-81, Springfield Hosp 1981-89, Epsom Dist Hosp 1989-; memb: Assoc of Behavioral Clinicians, Br Assoc for Social Psychiatry; fndr Br Assoc for

Psychopharmacology; MRCS 1966, DPM 1970; *Books* various articles in jls on life events, brain haemorrhage, depression and drug treatment; *Recreations* music, gardening, reading; *Style—* Dr Richard Penrose; Dept of Psychiatry, Epsom District Hospital, Epsom, Surrey (☎ 0372 726100)

PENROSE, Roger Ian; s of Edward Charles Penrose, of Plymouth, and Grace Feltis, *née* Bond; *b* 15 Sept 1953; *Educ* Plymouth Coll, Univ of Bath (BSc, BArch); *m* 7 Aug 1976, Janet Elaine, da of Richard Alan Harvey, RN; 2 s (Richard Merrick b 1984, Simon Tristan b 1987), 1 da (Laura Jane b 1989); *Career* princ Ian Penrose and Associates (chartered architects), md Ian Penrose Architects Ltd 1987-; *Recreations* motorcycling, sailing, cycle, swimming; *Clubs* OPM, IMTC, Exeter Golf and Country; *Style—* Roger I Penrose, Esq; Red Ridges, Cheriton Bishop, Devon (☎ 0647 24435, 392 5300, fax 0392 410265); Mamhead House, Mamhead, nr Exeter, Devon EX6 8HD; Pynes Hill, Rydon Lane, Exeter EX2 5AZ

PENRY, (William) Cedric Rhys; s of Benjamin William Penry (d 1972), and Ethel Evelyn Penry (d 1972); descended from John Penry, Christian martyr (1563-1593); *b* 21 June 1927; *Educ* Gowerton GS, Univ of Wales (BSc), Stanford, INSEAD Fontainblea; *m* 1952, Margaret Winifred, da of Charles Starvington Cetta (d 1978); 1 s, 1 da; *Career* RAF 1945-48; works mangr Richard Thomas and Baldwins 1951-63; dir: Halivourgiki Athens 1963-69, Br Steel Corp (Int) Ltd 1977-, Br Steel Corp (Overseas Services) 1976-87, Slater Steel Corp Canada 1977-86; int business conslt 1987-; FIM; *Recreations* golf, gardening; *Clubs* Directors'; *Style—* Cedric Penry, Esq; Swallows Corner, Islet Road, Maidenhead, Berks SL6 8LG (☎ 0628 72701)

PENRY-DAVEY, David Herbert; QC (1988); s of Samuel Saunders Watson Penry-Davey, and Almary Lorna, *née* Patrick, of 37 Church St, Hoo, Rochester, Kent; *b* 16 May 1942; *Educ* Hastings GS, King's Coll London (LLB); *m* 1970, Judith Ailsa Nancy, da of John Walter, of Firgrove, Morley St, Botolph, Norfolk; 2 s (Matthew b 1972, James b 1979), 1 da (Caroline b 1974); *Career* called to the Bar Inner Temple 1965; rec Crown Ct 1986; *Recreations* music, golf, cycling; *Style—* David Penry-Davey, Esq, QC; 8 New Square, Lincoln's Inn, London WC2A 3QP (☎ 071 242 4986, fax 071 405 1166)

PENSON, Alan Anthony; *b* 30 Jan 1952; *Educ* Dulwich, St Catharine's Coll Cambridge (MA); *m* 1976, Jane; 1 s (Alexander b 1983), 1 da (Mary b 1985); *Career* Price Waterhouse 1974-85, fin dir Clarke Hooper plc 1986-; ACA; *Style—* Alan Penson, Esq; Clarke Hooper plc, 10 The Grove, Slough Berks SL1 1QP (☎ 0753 77767, fax 0753 811776)

PENTELOW, Jack Owen; s of John Owen Pentelow (d 1959), of 321 Brincliffe Edge Rd, Sheffield, and Margaret Anne Scott, *née* Bailey (d 1951); *b* 29 Nov 1915; *Educ* King Edward VII Sch Sheffield; *m* 5 Oct 1940, Joan Elizabeth, da of John Hadfield Topham (d 1957), of 6 Kenwood Bank, Sheffield; 2 s (Michael b 1946, Guy b 1949); *Career* cmnd 1944, Flying Offr 1945 RAF Aircrew; asst cost accountant John Fowler & Co Ltd Leeds 1939, cost accountant Br Jeffrey Diamond Ltd 1940-47; Smiths Industs Ltd: chief cost accountant 1947, div chief acct Clock and Watch Div 1948 (prodn dir 1957), dir and gen mangr 1967-80; Liveryman Worshipful Co Clockmakers 1970; FCMA; *Clubs* Hove Conservative, Hove Deep Sea Anglers; *Style—* Jack Pentolow, Esq; 11 Welbeck Ave, Hove, E Sussex BN3 4JP (☎ 0273 734 219)

PENTIN, David John; s of Sydney Edward Pentin (d 1971), of Canterbury, Kent, and Amelia, *née* Winkel (d 1989); *b* 26 June 1935; *Educ* Kent Col Canterbury, Univ of London (LLB); *m* 11 June 1960, Alicia Pentin, JP, da of Gp Capt Ivor Morgan Rodney, OBE, RAF (d 1954); 3 s (John b 11 Feb 1964, Richard b 16 Aug 1969, Edward b 23 Feb 1971), 1 da (Caroline b 23 April 1962); *Career* Nat Serv RAF; sr ptnr Pentins CAs; memb Canterbury City Cncl: memb 1983-, chm Fin and Gen Purposes Ctee 1985-90, dep ldr of Cncl 1987-90, ldr of Cncl 1990-; FCA 1959; *Recreations* walking, skiing, cycling, music; *Style—* David Pentin, Esq; Ashley House, Brewery Lane, Bridge, Canterbury, Kent CT4 5LD (☎ 0227 830278); Lullingstone House, 5 Castle St, Canterbury, Kent CT1 2QF (☎ 0227 763400, fax 0227 762416, telex 888781)

PENTLAND, Baroness; Lady Lucy Elisabeth Babington; *née* Babington Smith; da of Sir Henry Babington Smith; *m* 1941, 2 Baron Pentland; 1 da; *Style—* The Rt Hon Lady Pentland; 4670 Independence Ave, New York City 10471, USA

PENTON, John Howard; MBE (1987); s of Richard Howard Penton (d 1960), of 33 Clephane Rd, London N1, and Ciceley Urmson, *née* Heinekey (d 1966); *b* 12 Feb 1938; *Educ* Merchant Taylors', Architectural Assoc Sch of Architecture (AAdip), Open Univ (BA); *m* 2 Nov 1963, (Elizabeth) Diana, da of (Henry) Harold King (d 1985), of 1 Summerhill Ct, Avenue Rd, St Albans, Herts; 1 da (Ciceley Rebecca Clare b 1975); *Career* chartered architect; assoc D E Pugh & Assocs 1963-72, fndr ptnr Penton Smart & Grimwade 1972-; consultancies: LT, London Housing Consortium, Irish Nat Rehabilitation Bd, The Inst for Rehabilitation & Res Houston Texas, The English Tourist Bd, Perkins Sch & Inst for the Blind Boston USA, The Nordic Ctee on Deaf/ Blindness Dronninglund Denmark, St Alban's Cathedral; hon architect Herts Assoc for Disabled; awards: RIBA/DOE Housing Design 1985 special award, RIBA res fellowship 1984-85; Liam McGuire Memorial Lecture Dublin 1986, res fell Hull Sch of Architecture 1987, expert witness damage actions of disabled; fndr chm Herts and Beds Constructions Indust Liaison Gp, former chm Herts Assoc of Architects, chm Centre for Accessible Environments, fndr memb The Access Ctee for England; Asst: Worshipful Co of Merchant Taylors, Liveryman Worshipful Co of Chartered Architects; RIAS, ACIArb, FCSD, FRSA; *Recreations* reading, sketching, swimming, target rifle shooting, carving chessmen; *Clubs* Reform, Nat Lib; *Style—* John Penton, Esq, MBE; 1 Batchwood Gardens, St Albans, Hertfordshire AL3 5SE (☎ 0727 53854); Penton, Smart & Grimwade, 8 Spicer St, St Albans, Herts AL3 4PQ (☎ 0727 40911, fax 0727 44148); 4 Rutland Square, Edinburgh EH1 2AS (☎ 031 228 4137, fax 031 228 4540)

PENTY, Michael Harvey; s of Arthur Joseph Penty (d 1937), of Church St, Old Isleworth, Middx, and Violet Leonard, *née* Pike (d 1978); *b* 6 Nov 1916; *Educ* St Benedict's Ealing; *m* da of Col Laurence Sebastian Cecil Roche, MC (d 1968), of Castle Barton, Tiverton, Devon; 4 s (John Christopher Mathew b 22 Sept 1950, Stephen Michael Philip b 2 May 1952, Andrew Penty Laurence b 29 June 1954, Blaise Gerard Nicholas b 30 April 1956) 2 da (Frances Mary Cecilia (Mrs Walker) b 22 Nov 1948, Joanna Hilary Ruth b 2 March 1965); *Career* RA 1940-46, Capt Adj 40 (Highland) LAA Regt 1942-43, jr staff course Sarafand 1943, GSO3 (SD) HQ 13 Corps 1945-46; admitted slr 1939, attorney Supreme Ct SA 1949; co fndr Whitefriar's Sch Cheltenham 1957-58, ed Law and Justice (formerly Quis Custodiet?) 1964-84, hon sec Plowden Legal Soc 1969-75, vice pres Isleworth Civic Tst (memb 1960-, formerly chm and hon sec); sr vice pres Newman Assoc 1961-63 (memb 1955-); Lord of the Manor of the Rectory of Isleworth; memb Law Soc; KSG; *Recreations* lawn tennis, gardening; *Clubs* Wig and Pen, Victory Servs, Ealing Lawn Tennis; *Style—* Michael Penty, Esq; The Manor House, 59A Church St, Old Isleworth, Middx TW7 6BE (☎ 081 560 8524); 35 Ashley Road, Hampton, Middx TW12 2JA (☎ 081 979 4333, fax 081 979 1393)

PENYCATE, John William (Jack); CBE (1988); s of Walter John Penycate (ka Jutland 1916), and Emily, *née* Puttock (1944); *b* 10 March 1913; *Educ* Royal GS Guildford; *m* 1, 9 Sept 1939, Dorothy Gladys Crawt (d 1969); 1 s (John), 1 da (Prudence (Mrs Goodwin)); m 2, 10 Jan 1970, Mary Doreen (Mollie) Liggett, MBE; *Career* journalist; gp editorial dir The Surrey Advertiser 1960-74 (ed); playwright; plays: Peacock in a Dovecot, Ordeal by Marriage, A Killing in Oils; Yvonne Arnaud Theatre Guildford: tstee Bldg Appeal Ctee 1958-61 (memb), chm Bd of Dirs 1972-88 (vice chm 1961-72); Nat Fedn of Playgoer's Socs: jt fndr, hon sec 1957-75, vice pres; memb Co Sound Radio, chm Middx and Surrey League for the Hard of Hearing, chm Broadcasting Ctee Br Assoc for the Hard of Hearing; Hon D Univ Surrey 1974; *Recreations* formerly cricket, currently The Times and The Independent crosswords; *Style—* Jack Penycate, Esq, CBE; 11 Josephs Road, Guildford, Surrey GU1 1DN (☎ 0438 66943)

PEPLOE, Guy; s of Denis Frederick Neil Peploe, RSA, and Elizabeth Marion, *née* Barr; *b* 25 Jan 1960; *Educ* The Edinburgh Acad, Univ of Aberdeen (MA); *Career* exhibition offr Royal Scottish Acad 1983, res asst Scottish Nat Gallery of Modern Art 1983-85, The Scottish Gallery 1984-; *Recreations* golf, sex; *Clubs* Scottish Arts (Pictures Convenor 1988-89); *Style—* Guy Peploe, Esq; The Scottish Gallery, 94 George Street, Edinburgh EH2 3DF (☎ 031 225 5955, fax 031 226 2312)

PEPPARD, Nadine Sheila; CBE (1970); da of Joseph Anthony Peppard (d 1960), of Tunbridge Wells, and May, *née* Barber (d 1963); *b* 16 Jan 1922; *Educ* Macclesfield HS, Univ of Manchester (BA, Dip in teaching); *Career* teacher Maldon GS 1943-46, Spanish ed George G Harrap & Co 1946-55, Training Dept Marks & Spencer 1955-57, dep gen sec London Cncl of Social Service 1957-64, nat advsy offr for cwlth immigrants 1964-65, gen sec Nat Ctee for Cwlth Immigrants 1965-68, chief offr Community Rels Cmmn 1968-72, race rels advsr Home Office 1972-83, race rels conslt 1983-89, dir of admin Equalities Associates 1989-90, race relations conslt 1991-; *Publications* Primitive India (trans 1954), Toledo (trans 1955); author of: various professional articles on race rels 1957-, race rels training articles for New Community 1972-85; *Recreations* writing, travel, cookery; *Style—* Ms Nadine Peppard, CBE

PEPPER, Donald John; s of Cdr Frank Sydney Charles Pepper (d 1940), of Plymouth, and Beatrice Mary, *née* Trevor (d 1952); *b* 7 Aug 1921; *Educ* Devonport HS; *m* 7 June 1946, Maureen, da of Robert MacKenzie im Thurn (d 1956), of Friern Barnet; 3 s (John Robert b 1948, David MacKenzie b 1952, Mark im Thurn b 1957); *Career* RN 1939-47; Frobisher RN Coll Dartmouth 1939, RN Engrg Coll Plymouth 1940-43, HMS King George V serv Med and Home Flt 1943-44, RNC Greenwich 1944-46, HMS Indefatigable 1946-47, staff RN Engrg Coll 1947, invalided out 1947; designer naval and merchant ship propulsion Foster Wheeler Ltd 1950-55, head nuclear energy dept Foster Wheeler Ltd 1955-59, md Rolls Royce & Assocs 1962-66 (fndr dir 1959-62); Rolls Royce HQ: main bd 1969, reappointed dir 1974, vice-chm 1976, ret 1983; currently: chm Met Safe Deposits Ltd, chm Port Solent Ltd, dir Chilworth Centre Ltd, advsr to Lockheed Air Terminal Inc; memb: Def Industs Cncl 1977-81, cncl Royal Soc of Aerospace Contractors; devpt fund tstee Southampton Univ, memb exec ctee Hants Devpt Assoc; gold medal winner for paper on nuclear propulsion to NICES 1961; Freeman City of London 1982, memb Worshipful Co of Coach Makers and Coach Harness Makers 1982; MIMechE 1959, MIMarE 1960, memb NICES 1961, CBIM 1969; *Recreations* golf, sailing; *Clubs* Royal Mid-Surrey Golf, Royal Southern Yacht, RNC and RAYC, Army and Navy; *Style—* Donald Pepper, Esq; Hard Cottage, Swanwick Shore, Southampton SO3 7EF (☎ 048 95 2107)

PEPPER, Gordon Terry; CBE; s of Harold Terry Pepper (d 1973), and Jean Margaret Gordon, *née* Furness (d 1963); *b* 2 June 1934; *Educ* Repton, Trinity Coll Cambridge (MA); *m* 30 Aug 1958, Gillian Clare, da of Lt-Col William Helier Huelin (d 1978); 3 s (Alasdair b 1960, Harry b 1967, Mark b 1969), 1 da (Linda (Ninna) b 1961); *Career* Nat Serv cmmnd RCS 1952-54; Equity and Law Life Assurance Soc 1957-60; W Greenwell & Co: joined 1960, ptnr 1962, jt sr ptnr 1980; chm Greenwell Montagu & Co 1986-87, dir and sr advsr Midland Montagu (Holdings) Ltd 1987-90, chm Payton Pepper & Sons Ltd 1987 (dir 1986), prof City Univ Business Sch 1991- (hon visiting prof 1987-90), dir Centre For Financial Markets 1988-; memb: Ctee on Indust and Fin Nat Econ Devpt Cncl 1988-90, Econ and Social Res Cncl 1989-; author of articles in various econ and fin jls; memb Stock Exchange; FIA 1961, fell Soc Investmt Analysts, CBIM; *Recreations* sailing, tennis, walking, family; *Clubs* Reform, Royal Ocean Racing, Royal Channel Islands Yacht; *Style—* Gordon Pepper, Esq, CBE; Staddleden, Sissinghurst, Cranbrook, Kent TN17 2AN (tel and fax 0580 714853); City University Business School, Frobisher Crescent, Barbican Centre, London EC2Y 8HB (☎ 071 920 0111, fax 071 588 2756)

PEPPER, Hon Mrs ((Elizabeth) Jane Graham); *née* Guest; o da of Baron Guest, PC (Life Peer); *b* 25 May 1945; *m* 8 June 1968, G Willing Pepper, of Philadelphia, USA; *Style—* The Hon Mrs Pepper; 128 Springton Lake Rd, Media, Pa 19063, USA

PEPPER, John Douglas; s of Douglas Ernest Pepper (d 1979), and Kathleen Mary, *née* Taylor; *b* 11 Jan 1932; *Educ* Scarborough HS for Boys; *m* 9 April 1955, Shirley Mary, da of Jack Wade, of Barrington Court, Staines, Middx; 2 s (David b 1956, Michael b 1965), 2 da (Brigitte b 1958, Vivien b 1959); *Career* chm Plaxton Group plc 1987 (dir 1972, conslt 1988); FCA; *Recreations* golf (Ganton and Filey Golf), Rotary; *Clubs* Rotary (pres Filey 1978-79); *Style—* John D Pepper, Esq; White Lodge, Gristhorpe, Filey, N Yorks (☎ 0723 512959); Plaxton Group plc, Castle Works, Eastfield, Scarborough, N Yorks (☎ 0723 581500, fax 0723 581328)

PEPPER, Prof Michael; s of Morris Pepper (d 1982), and Ruby, *née* Bloom; *b* 10 Aug 1942; *Educ* St Marlebone GS, Univ of Reading (BSc, PhD); *m* 22 Oct 1973, Dr Jeannette Denise, da of Albert Josse, of London; 2 da (Judith Leah, Ruth Jennifer); *Career* res physicist The Plessey Co Ltd 1969-82, res Cavendish Lab 1973-, Warren res fell Royal Soc 1978-86, princ res fell GEC plc 1982-87, prof of physics Univ of Cambridge 1987-, fell Trinity Coll Cambridge 1982-; md Toshiba Cambridge Research Centre Ltd 1990-; awarded: Guthrie Prize and Medal Inst of Physics 1985, Hewlett-Packard Europhysics Prize 1985, Hughes Medal of Royal Soc 1987; ScD Cambridge 1989; FRS 1983; *Recreations* travel, music, walking, whisky tasting; *Style—* Prof Michael Pepper, FRS; Cavendish Laboratory, Madingley Rd, Cambridge CB3 0HE (☎ 0223 337 330, fax 0223 632 63); Toshiba Cambridge Research Centre, 260 Cambridge Science Park, Milton Rd, Cambridge CB4 4WE (☎ 0223 424 666, fax 0223 424341)

PEPPERCORN, David James Creagh; s of James Kenneth Peppercorn, and Ida Alice Knight (d 1985); *b* 25 Aug 1931; *Educ* Beaumont Coll, Trinity Coll Cambridge (MA); *m* 1, 11 April 1959, Susan Mary Sweeney; 3 da (Caroline b 1961, Sarah b 1963, Frances b 1964); m 2, 10 June 1977, Serena Gillian, da of Michael Sutcliffe; *Career* int wine conslt; dir: Wine Standards Bd of the Vintners Co 1987, Morgan Furze & Co Ltd 1958-74, Peter Dominic 1964-74, Gilbey Vintners 1969-79; Inst of Masters of Wine 1968-76 (chm 1968-70); judge at Premier Concours Mondial (Budapest 1972); Liveryman Worshipful Co of Vintners 1952, memb Worshipful Co of Waterman; Chevalier de l'Ordre des Arts et des Lettres 1988; *Books* Bordeaux (1982, 2 edn 1991), Pocket Guide to the Wines of Bordeaux (1986) (translations into: German (1986), French (1987), Danish (1987), Swedish (1988), Japanese (1990); American edn Simon & Schuster (1987)), Drinking Wine (with Bryan Cooper, 1979); *Recreations* music, walking, travelling; *Clubs* Garrick, MCC, Saintsbury; *Style—* David Peppercorn, Esq; 2 Bryanston Place, London W1H 7FN (☎ 071 262 9398)

PEPPERELL, Peter Frederick; s of Amos Victor Pepperell (d 1947), and Elizabeth Sarah Gower (d 1943); *b* 12 May 1926; *Educ* Newport GS, Leeds Univ; *m* 1 Oct 1955, Joyce Johnston, da of David Henderson Adamson (d 1975); 1 s (David 1958), 1 da (Susan b 1960); *Career* serv Royal Hampshire Regt 1944-48; with Duncan Bros &

Co Ltd Calcutta 1950-73, with Walter Duncan Gp UK 1973-; dir: Western Dooars Hldgs plc 1973, Walter Duncan & Goodricke plc 1982, Lawrie Gp plc 1985, Assam-Dooars Hldgs plc 1986; chm Lawrie Plantation Servs Ltd 1979, etc; *Recreations* golf; *Clubs* Oriental, Bengal (Calcutta); *Style*— Peter Pepperell, Esq; Lawrie Plantation Service Ltd, Wortham Place, Wrotham, Sevenoaks, Kent TN15 7AE

PEPPIATT, Michael Henry; s of Edward George Peppiatt (d 1983), of Stocking, Pelham, Herts, and Elsa Eugène, *née* Schlaich; *b* 9 Oct 1941; *Educ* Brentwood Sch, Göttingen Univ, Trinity Hall Cambridge (MA); *m* 1989, Jill Patricia Lloyd, da of Dr John Barnes; 1 da (Clio Patricia b 16 Feb 1991); *Career* art critic The Observer 1964, arts ed Réalités Paris 1966-68, art and literary ed Le Monde 1969-71; Paris arts corr: New York Times, Financial Times 1972-76, Art News 1973-86; ed and publisher Art International 1987- (Paris corr and sr ed 1972-85, bought and relaunched the magazine 1986); regular contrib to: Sunday Times, Connoisseur, Architectural Digest, Connaissance Des Arts; fndr The Archive Press Fine Art Publishers 1987-; author: Imagination's Chamber: Artists and Their Studios, of over 200 catalogue introductions and essays on modern and contemporary art, Conversations with Francis Bacon (French version with Michelleiris); art film conslt and script writer Musée D'Art Moderne Paris, exhibition organiser; memb Vasari Prize Jury Paris 1988-; memb: Int Art Critics Assoc, Foreign Press Assoc; *Recreations* squash, real tennis; *Clubs* Jeu de Paume (Paris), Oxford and Cambridge, RAC; *Style*— Michael Peppiatt, Esq; Art International, 77 Rue des Archives, 75003 Paris, France (☎ 48048454, fax 48048200)

PEPPITT, John Raymond; QC (1976); s of Reginald Peppitt, MBE (d 1962), and Phyllis Claire, *née* French (d 1978); *b* 22 Sept 1931; *Educ* St Paul's, Jesus Coll Cambridge (BA); *m* 2 April 1960, Judith Penelope, da of Maj Lionel Frederick Edward James, CBE; 3 s (Matthew b 1962, William b 1964, Edward b 1968); *Career* Nat Serv 2 Lt RA 1950-51; called to the Bar Gray's Inn 1958; rec Crown Court 1976-, bencher 1982; *Recreations* collecting watercolours, rearing sheep; *Style*— John Peppitt, Esq, QC; Chegworth Manor Farm, Chegworth, Harrietsham, Kent ME17 1DD (☎ 0622 859313); Chambers: 3 Gray's Inn Place, London WC1 (☎ 071 831 8441, fax 071 831 8479, telex 295 119 LEXCOL G)

PEPYS, Hon Mrs (Pamela Sophia Nadine); *née* Stonor; da of 5 Baron Camoys (d 1968), and Mildred (d 1961), da of William Watts Sherman, of New York; *b* 1917; *m* 1941, Lt-Col Charles Donald Leslie Pepys (King's Own Yorks LI; ggs of 1 Earl of Cottenham), eld s of late Col Gerald Leslie Pepys; *Style*— The Hon Mrs Pepys; 30/31 Lyefield Ct, Kidmore End Rd, Emmer Green, Reading, Berks RG4 8AP (☎ 0734 482981)

PEPYS, Lady (Mary) Rachel; *née* Fitzalan Howard; DCVO (1968, CVO 1954); da of 15 Duke of Norfolk, KG, PC, GCVO (d 1917); *b* 27 June 1905; *m* 1, 1939, Lt-Col Colin Keppel Davidson, CIE, OBE, RA (ka 1943), s of Col Leslie Davidson, CB, RHA, and Lady Theodora, da of 7 Earl of Albemarle; 1 s, 1 da; m 2, 1961, Brig Anthony Hilton Pepys, DSO (d 1967); *Career* Lady-in-Waiting to HRH Princess Marina, Duchess of Kent 1943-68; *Style*— The Lady Rachel Pepys, DCVO; Highfield House, Crossbush, Arundel, W Sussex (☎ 0903 883158)

PEPYS, Lady Rose Edith Idina; da of late 6 Earl of Cottenham, and the Countess of Devon, *née* Sybil Venetia Taylor, of Powderham Castle, Exeter; ggggda of Capt William Bligh of the Bounty; *b* 5 Nov 1927; *Educ* Beatchington Court Seaford Sussex, St Mary's Hosp London; *Career* pt/t medical receptionist, formerly nurse; *Recreations* reading, cooking, writing poetry, theatres, music and films; *Clubs* RCN; *Style*— The Lady Rose Pepys; Flat B, 101 Earls Court Road, London W8

PEPYS, Victoria; da of John Charles Geoffrey Pepys, of Kilpin, N Humberside, and Joyce Lillian, *née* Harvey; *b* 14 July 1955; *Educ* Beverley HS for Girls, Goole GS, Hull Regnl Sch of Art, St Martins Sch of Art (BA); *m* 23 May 1987, Simon Cranmer, s of Ernest Young, of Preston, Lancs; *Career* fashion stylist; PA to Jasper Conran 1977-79, account dir Lynne Franks PR 1980-90; *Style*— Ms Victoria Pepys; (☎ 081 677 2544)

PERA, Mary; da of Lt-Col Ralph Blewitt, DSO (d 1958), and Denys Beatrix, *née* Henderson (d 1972); *b* 20 July 1922; *Educ* Hayes Court Sch Kent; *m* Giovanni Battista Pera; *Career* WAAF 1940-45; yachtswoman; extensive offshore racing in Med and UK waters; called to the Bar Lincoln's Inn 1948; sec Royal Ocean Racing Club 1972-78, chm RYA Racing Rules Ctee 1979-, memb IYRU Racing Rules Ctee 1983-; FRIN; *Books* Surveys of the Seas (1955), The Yacht Racing Rules (2 edn, 1989), Navigation for Yachtsmen (5 edn, 1984), Celestial Navigation for Yachtsmen (10 edn, 1990); *Style*— Mrs Mary Pera

PERCEVAL, Hon Mrs (Joanna Ida Louisa); er da of 5 Baron Hatherton (d 1969), by his 1 w, Ida Gwendolyn (d 1969), formerly wife of Capt Henry Burton Tate and only child of Robin Legge; *b* 14 Oct 1926; *m* 1948, Robert Westby Perceval, s of Francis Westby Perceval (d 1956); 1 s, 2 da; *Style*— The Hon Mrs Perceval; Pillaton Hall, Penkridge, Stafford

PERCEVAL, John Dudley Charles Ascelin; s of Lt-Col John Francis George Perceval (d 1981), of Vancouver, Br Columbia, and Diana Madeleine Scott, *née* Pearce; *b* 8 April 1942; *Educ* Eton; *m* 11 Sept 1971, Tessa Mary, da of Geoffrey Bruce Dawson, OBE, MC (d 1984), of Caerleon; 2 s (Oliver Charles b 1972, Christopher Geoffrey John b 1978), 1 da (Candida Mary b 1974); *Career* Unilever 1961-69; exec dir Save & Prosper Gp Ltd 1985- (joined 1969); *Style*— John Perceval, Esq; The Forge House, Monk Sherborne, Basingstoke, Hants RG26 5HS (☎ 0256 850 073); Save & Prosper Gp Ltd, Finsbury Ave, London EC2 (☎ 071 588 1717)

PERCEVAL, Viscount; Thomas Frederick Gerald Perceval; s of 11 Earl of Egmont; *b* 17 Aug 1934; *Style*— Viscount Perceval

PERCHARD, Colin William; OBE (1985); s of William George Perchard, of La Chasse, St Martin, Jersey, CI, and Winifred Sarah, *née* Horn; *b* 19 Oct 1940; *Educ* Victoria Coll Jersey, Univ of Liverpool (BA), Int Inst for Educn Planning UNESCO Paris (Advanced Dip Educn Planning and Admin); *m* 4 April 1970, Elisabeth Penelope Glynis, da of Sir Glyn Jones, GCMG, MBE, QV, of Brandfold Cottage, Goudhurst, Kent; 3 s (Nicholas b 1972, Jonathan b 1976, Adam b 1985); *Career* Br Cncl: asst rep Blantyre Malawi 1964-68, regnl offr Africa S of Sahara 1968-71, asst rep Calcutta 1971-72, offr i/c Dhaka 1972, rep Seoul 1973-76, dir Tech Coop Trg Dept 1976-79, Int Inst for Educn Planning Paris 1979-80, rep Harare 1980-86, controller Africa Div 1986-90, dir Turkey 1990-; *Recreations* theatre, music, cooking; *Style*— Colin Perchard, Esq, OBE; The British Council, 10 Spring Gardens, London SW1A 2BN (☎ 071 930 8466, fax 071 839 6347, telex 8952201)

PERCIVAL, Prof Alan; s of Harold Percival (d 1948), and Hilda, *née* Twyford (d 1970); *b* 22 May 1932; *Educ* Manchester GS, BNC Oxford (MA, BM), St Mary's Hosp Med Sch (BCh); *m* 1, 15 Sept 1962, Audrey Gillian, *née* Hughes (d 1979); 1 s (David b 1963), 1 da (Sally b 1964); m 2, 14 Oct 1983, (Pauline) Jill, *née* Gillett; 2 step da (Alison b 1962, Karen b 1964); *Career* house surgn Radcliffe Infirmary Oxford 1958-59, house physician med unit St Mary's Hosp London 1959, registrar in pathology Edgware Gen Hosp 1959-63, lectr in bacteriology Wright-Flemming Inst St Mary's Hosp 1963-67; Univ of Liverpool: sr lectr in bacteriology 1967-79, prof in clinical bacteriology 1979-81 and 1988-; prof of bacteriology Univ of Manchester 1981-88; memb: Assoc Med Microbiologists (chm 1985-87), W Lancs Health Authy 1985-88, Southport and Formby DHA 1988-; Hon MSc Univ of Manchester 1982; MRC Path 1970 (cncl memb 1982-85); *Recreations* golf, music; *Clubs* Royal Birkdale Golf; *Style*— Prof Alan Percival; 3 Coudray Road, Hesketh Park, Southport, Merseyside PR9 9NL (☎ 0704 34530), Dept of Medical Mircobiology, Duncan Building, Royal Liverpool Hosp, PO Box 147, Liverpool L69 3BX (☎ 051 7090141, ext 2876)

PERCIVAL, Allen Dain; CBE (1975); s of Charles Percival; *b* 23 April 1925; *Educ* Bradford GS, Magdalene Coll Cambridge; *m* 1952, Rachel Hay; *Career* principal Guildhall Sch of Music and Drama 1965-78, exec chm Stainer & Bell Publishers 1978-, Gresham Prof of Music City Univ 1980-; conductor, professional continuo player, broadcaster; *Style*— Allen Percival, Esq, CBE; 7 Park Parade, Cambridge (☎ 0223 353953)

PERCIVAL, Gordon Edward; s of Alan Percival (d 1981); *b* 20 Sept 1933; *Educ* Manchester GS; *m* 1989, Maureen Shirley; 2 s (Nicholas, Mark), 1 da (Jacqueline); *Career* dir Quartet plc and various other cos; landowner; *Style*— Gordon Percival, Esq; The Old Post House, Old Minster Lovell, nr Witney, Oxon OX8 5RN

PERCIVAL, Rt Hon Sir Ian; PC (1983), QC (1963); s of Eldon Percival (d 1947), and Chrystine, *née* Hoyle (d 1979); *b* 11 May 1921; *Educ* Latymer Upper Sch, St Catharine's Coll Cambridge (MA); *m* 1942, Madeline Buckingham, da of Albert Cooke (d 1928); 1 s (Robert), 1 da (Jane); *Career* serv WWII Maj The Buffs N Africa and Burma 1940-46; called to the Bar Inner Temple 1948; bencher 1970, rec of Deal, later of the Crown Court 1971-, slr gen 1979-83, master treas Inner Temple 1990; memb Sidley and Austin USA and Int Attorneys 1984-; MP (C) Southport 1959-87; landowner; memb Royal Econ Soc, pres Masonic Trust for Girls and Boys 1989-; Liveryman and memb Worshipful Co of Arbitrators; FTII, FCIArb; kt 1979; *Recreations* golf, parachuting, windsurfing, tennis; *Clubs* Carlton, Beefsteak, Royal Birkdale Golf, Rye Golf, City Livery; *Style*— The Rt Hon Sir Ian Percival, QC; Oxenden, Stone-in-Oxney, nr Tenterden, Kent (☎ 023 383 321); 2 Harcourt Buildings, Temple, London EC4 (☎ 071 583 2939); 5 Paper Buildings, Temple, London EC4 (☎ 071 583 4555, telex 8956431 ANTON G, fax 071 583 1926)

PERCIVAL, Prof John; s of Walter William Percival, and Eva, *née* Bowers; *b* 11 July 1937; *Educ* Colchester Royal GS, Hertford and Merton Colls Oxford (MA, DPhil); *m* 1, 11 Aug 1962, Carole Ann (d 1977), da of Eric John Labrum; 2 da (Alice Mary Ann b 28 June 1963, Jessica Jane b 29 Dec 1964); m 2, 10 Sept 1988, Jacqueline Anne, da of Terence Donavan; *Career* Univ Coll Cardiff: (asst lectr 1962, lectr 1964, sr lectr 1972, reader 1979, prof 1985, dep princ 1987-90, currently head of Sch of History and Archaeology; vice pres The Classical Assoc; FSA; *Books* The Reign of Charlemagne (with H R Loyn, 1975), The Roman Villa (2 edn, 1988); *Recreations* music; *Style*— Prof John Percival, FSA; 26 Church Road, Whitchurch, Cardiff CF4 2EA (☎ 0222 617869), Sch of History and Archaeology, Univ of Wales Coll of Cardiff, PO Box 909, Cardiff CF1 3XU (☎ 0222 874260)

PERCIVAL, Michael John; s of John William Percival (d 1971), of Northampton, and Margery Edith, *née* Crawford; *b* 11 July 1943; *Educ* Berkhamsted Sch Herts; *m* 11 June 1966, Jean Margaret, da of Vincent Everard Dainty, of Northampton; 3 da (Katie b 1968, Alison b 1970, Linda b 1973); *Career* admitted slr London 1966, ptnr Howes Percival Slrs (sr ptnr 1984); memb Cncl of Northants Law Soc 1982, pres Northampton and Dist Branch MS Soc 1988; tstee: Northants Nat Hist Soc and Field Club, St Christopher's Church of England Home for the Elderly Northampton; registrar High Ct and Co Ct 1983-88, memb Northampton DHA 1987-90, clerk to Gen Cmmrs of Taxes for Northampton Dist 1 and 2 1988-; memb Law Soc 1966-; *Recreations* rugby, tennis, sailing; *Clubs* Northampton, Dallington Lawn Tennis, Brancaster Staithe Sailing; *Style*— Michael Percival, Esq; Messrs Howes Percival Solicitors, Oxford House, Cliftonville, Northampton NN1 5PN (☎ 0604 230400, fax 0604 20956, telex 311445)

PERCY, Lady Richard; Hon Clayre; *née* Campbell; 2 da (by 1 m) of 4 Baron Stratheden and Campbell, CBE; *b* 1927; *m* 1, 17 Aug 1950 (m dis 1974), Rt Hon Nicholas Ridley, MP; 3 da (Jane b 1953, Susanna b 1955, Jessica b 1957); m 2, 1979, as his 2 w, Lord Richard Charles Percy (d 1989), 3 s of 8 Duke of Northumberland, KG, CBE, MVO (d 1930); *Style*— The Lady Richard Percy; 212 Lambeth Rd, London SE1 7JY (☎ 071 928 3441)

PERCY, Humphrey Richard; s of Adrian John Percy of Wadhurst E Sussex and Maisie, *née* Gardner; *b* 2 Oct 1956; *Educ* Winchester; *m* 27 April 1985, Suzanne Patricia Spencer, da of Maj Bruce Holford-Walker of London SW3; 2 s (Luke, Christopher), 2 da (Daisy, Emma); *Career* J Henry Schroder Wagg & Co Ltd 1974-80, dir Barclays Merchant Bank Ltd 1985-86 (joined 1980); dir Barclays de Zoete Wedd Ltd 1986-; *Recreations* squash, reading, travel; *Clubs* Cannons; *Style*— Humphrey Percy, Esq; The Old House, Goodley Stock Rd, Crockham Hill, Edenbridge, Kent TN8 6SU (☎ 0732 865737); Barclays de Zoete Wedd Ltd, Ebbgate House, 2 Swan Lane, London EC4R 3TS (☎ 071 623 2323, fax 071 623 6075, telex 923120)

PERCY, Lord James William Eustace; 3 and yst s of 10 Duke of Northumberland, KG, GCVO, TD, PC (d 1988); *b* 18 June 1965; *Educ* Eton, Univ of Bristol; *Style*— The Lord James Percy; Alnwick Castle, Alnwick, Northumberland

PERCY, Prof John Pitkeathly (Ian); s of John Percy (d 1984), of Edinburgh, and Helen Glass, *née* Pitkeathly (d 1988); *b* 16 Jan 1942; *Educ* Edinburgh Acad, Univ of Edinburgh; *m* 26 June 1965, Sheila Isobel, da of Roy Toshack Horn (d 1957), of Edinburgh; 2 da (Jill Sheila b 12 April 1969, Sally Charlotte b 24 Dec 1972); *Career* CA; asst Graham Smart & Annan 1960-68, ptnr Martin Currie & Scott 1969-71; Grant Thornton: ptnr 1971-81, London managing ptnr 1981-88, sr ptnr 1988-; hon prof of accountancy Univ of Aberdeen; pres Inst CAs of Scot 1990-91; elder St Cuthbert's Church of Scotland; Freeman: City of London 1982, Worshipful Co of Painter Stainers 1982; CA 1967, FRSA 1989; *Recreations* golf, trout fishing; *Clubs* Hon Co of Edinburgh Golfers, RAC, Hazard's, Golfing Soc, Royal and Ancient Golf, New (Edinburgh), Caledonian; *Style*— Prof Ian Percy; 30 Midmar Drive, Edinburgh EH10 6BU (☎ 031 447 3645); Grant Thornton, Grant Thornton House, Melton St, Euston Square, London (☎ 071 383 5100, fax 071 383 4334) and 1/4 Atholl Crescent, Edinburgh (☎ 031 229 9181, fax 031 229 4560)

PERCY, Keith Edward; s of Cyril Edward Percy, of London, and Joyce Rose Percy; *b* 22 Jan 1945; *Educ* Wanstead Co HS, Univ of Manchester (BA); *m* 14 Feb 1970, (Rosemary) Pamela, da of Thomas William Drake, of London; 1 s (Nicholas b 1977), 1 da (Elizabeth b 1974); *Career* head res Phillips & Drew 1976-83 (joined 1967), exec chm Phillips & Drew Fund Management 1983-90; chief exec: UBS Asset Management (UK) Ltd 1989-90; non-exec dir: Smiths Industries Med Systems 1977-, Imro 1987-; memb Cncl Soc of Investmt Analysts 1976-87; *Recreations* tennis, rugby, music; *Clubs* The City; *Style*— Keith Percy, Esq; Morgan Grenfell Asset Management, 20 Finsbury Circus, London EC2M 1NB (☎ 071 256 7500, fax 071 826 0331, telex 920286 MGAM G)

PERCY, Lady Geoffrey; Mary Elizabeth; *née* Lea; o da of Ralph Lea, of Teddington, Middx; *m* 27 May 1955, Lord Geoffrey William Percy (d 1984), 4 and yst s of 8 Duke of Northumberland (d 1930); 1 da (Diana Ruth b 1956); *Style*— The Lady Geoffrey Percy

PERCY, Lord Ralph George Algernon; 2 s of 10 Duke of Northumberland, KG, GCVO, TD, PC (d 1988); hp of bro 11 Duke of Northumberland, *qv*; *b* 16 Nov 1956; *Educ* Eton, Christ Church Oxford; *m* 1979, (Isobel) Jane, da of John Walter Maxwell Miller Richard, of Edinburgh; 2 s (George Dominic b 1984, Max Ralph b 1990), 2 da

(Catherine Sarah b 1982, Melissa Jane b 1987); *Career* chartered surveyor, publisher, landowner; *Recreations* shooting, fishing, painting, skiing, tennis, snooker; *Style*— The Lord Ralph Percy; Chatton Park, Chatton, nr Alnwick, Northumberland

PERCY, His Hon Judge; Rodney Algernon; 3 s of late Hugh James Percy, of Alnwick; *b* 15 May 1924; *Educ* Uppingham, BNC Oxford (MA); *m* 1948, Mary Allen, da of late J E Benbow, of Aberystwyth; 1 s, 3 da; *Career* Lt RCS 1942-46; serv: Burma, India, Malaya, Java; called to the Bar: Middle Temple 1950, Lincoln's Inn 1987; dep coroner N Northumberland 1957, asst rec Sheffield QS 1964, dep chm Co Durham QS 1966-71, rec Crown Ct 1972-79, circuit judge NE Circuit 1979-; fndr memb Conciliation Serv for Northumberland and Tyneside 1982, pres Northumberland and Tyneside Marriage Guidance Cncl 1983-87; *Publications* ed: Charlesworth on Negligence (4 edn 1962, 5 edn 1971, 6 edn 1977), Charlesworth & Percy on Negligence (7 edn 1983, 8 edn 1990); *Recreations* golf, gardening, hill walking, beachcombing, King Charles Cavalier spaniels; *Style*— His Hon Judge Percy; Brookside, Lesbury, Alnwick, Northumberland NE66 3AT (☎ 0665 830326)

PERCY-ROBB, Prof Iain Walter; s of Capt Ian Ernest Percy-Robb (d 1967), and Margaret Drysdale Carrick, *née* Galbraith; *b* 8 Dec 1935; *Educ* George Watsons Coll Edinburgh, Univ of Edinburgh (MB ChB, PhD); *m* 22 May 1961, Margaret Elizabeth, da of Dr Ronald Leslie Cormie, of 22 Glencairn Drive, Pollokshields, Glasgow; 2 s (Michael Iain b 1964, Stephen Leslie b 1966), 2 da (Jane Elizabeth b 1962, Claire Margaret b 1971); *Career* MRC int travelling res fell Cornell Univ 1972-73; Univ of Edinburgh: res scholar 1963-65, lectr 1965-68, sr lectr 1968-76, reader 1976-84; prof of pathological biochemistry Univ of Glasgow 1984-, chm Informed Software Ltd 1987-; memb: Chief Scientist Ctee, Scottish Home and Health Dept; ed-in-chief Clinica Chimica Acta Scottish Health Management Gp; memb Scot Swimming Team Empire and Cwlth Games Cardiff 1958; FRCPE, FRCPath; *Books* Lecture Notes on Clinical Chemistry (jtly 1984), Diseases of the Gastrointestinal Tract and Liver (jtly 1989); *Recreations* golf; *Clubs* Royal Burgess Golfing Soc (Edinburgh), The Glasgow Golf; *Style*— Prof Iain Percy-Robb; Rossendale, 7 Upper Glenburn Road, Bearsden, Glasgow G41 4DW (☎ 041 9431481), Dept of Pathological Biochemistry, Western Infirmary, Glasgow G11 6NT (☎ 041 3398822, fax 041 3574547)

PEREGRINE, Prof (Dennis) Howell; *b* 30 Dec 1938; *Educ* Univ of Oxford (BA), Univ of Cambridge (PhD); *Career* prof Univ of Bristol 1987- (lectr 1964-77, reader 1977-87); FIMA; *Style*— Prof D H Peregrine; School of Mathematics, University Walk, Bristol BS8 1TW (☎ 0272 303312, fax 0272 303497, telex 445938 BSUNIV G)

PEREIRA, Sir (Herbert) Charles; s of Herbert John Pereira (d 1952); *b* 12 May 1913; *Educ* St Alban's Sch, Univ of London (BSc, PhD, DSc); *m* 1941, Irene Beatrice, da of David James Sloan (d 1916); 3 s, 1 da; *Career* RE 1939-46; Colonial Serv 1946-67, dep dir E Africa Agric and Forestry Res Orgn 1955-61; dir: ARC of Rhodesia and Nyasaland 1961-63, ARC of Central Africa (Rhodesia Zambia and Malawi) 1963-67; chm ARC of Malawi 1967-74, dir E Malling Res Station 1969-72, chief scientist (dep sec) MAFF 1972-77, res conslt in tropical agric to World Bank and other orgns 1978-, memb Bd of Tstees Royal Botanic Gdns Kew 1983-86; Haile Selassie Prize for Res in Africa 1966; FRS 1969; kt 1977; Hon DSc Cranfield 1977; *Books* Land Use and Water Resources (1973), Policy and Practice in the Management of Tropical Watersheds (1989); *Recreations* sailing, swimming, mountain walking; *Clubs* Athenaeum, Harare; *Style*— Sir Charles Pereira, FRS; Peartrees, Nestor Court, Teston, Maidstone, Kent ME18 5AD (☎ 0622 813333)

PEREIRA, Dr (Raul) Scott; s of Dr Helio Gelli Pereira, and Dr Marguerite, *née* Scott (d 1988); *b* 14 April 1948; *Educ* Mill Hill Sch, Trinity Coll Cambridge, Univ of Oxford Med Sch; *m* 14 April 1972, Hilary Glen, da of Prof Vernon Rycroft Pickles, of Oxford; 1 s (Thomas b 1979), 1 da (Penelope b 1977); *Career* pathology trainee Northwick Park Hosp Harrow 1973-76, res sr registrar Westminster Hosp and Med Sch 1976-79, clinical scientist MRC Clinical Res Centre Harrow 1979-83, res fell West Middlesex Univ Hosp 1983-86; conslt and sr lectr in immunology: St Helier Hosp, Carshalton and St Georges Hosp Med Sch Tooting 1986-; chm Residential Boat Owners Assoc; *Recreations* boating; *Style*— Dr Scott Pereira; 3 Ducks Walk, Twickenham, Middlesex TW1 2DD (☎ 01 892 5086), Division of Immunology, Dept of Cellular & Molecular Sci, St George's Hosp Medical Sch, Tooting, London SW17 ORE (☎ 081 672 9944 ext 55752, telex 945291 SAGEMS G, fax 081 672 4864)

PEREIRA GRAY, Prof Denis John; OBE (1981); s of Dr Sydney Joseph Pereira Gray (d 1975), of Exeter, and Alice Evelyn, *née* Cole; *b* 2 Oct 1935; *Educ* Exeter Sch, St John's Coll Cambridge (MA), St Bart's Hosp Med Sch (MB BChir); *m* 28 April 1962, Jill Margaret, da of Frank Carruthers Hoyte (d 1976), of Exeter; 1 s (Peter b 1963), 3 da (Penelope b 1965, Elizabeth b 1968, Jennifer b 1970); *Career* gen med practice 1962-, prof of gen practice Univ of Exeter 1986- (sr lectr 1973-86), advsr in gen practice Univ of Bristol 1975-, ed Med Annual 1983-87, conslt advsr in gen practice to CMO DHSS 1984-87, dir PGMS Exeter 1987-; hon ed RCGP journal 1972-80 and pubns 1976-; Hunterian Soc Gold Medal 1966 and 1969, Sir Charles Hastings Prize 1967 and 1970, James Mackenzie Lecture 1977, George Abercrombie Award 1978, Gale Memorial Lecture 1979, RCGP Fndn Cncl Award 1980, Sir Harry Platt Prize 1981, Haliburton Hume Memorial Lecture 1988, Northcott Memorial Lecture 1988, Harvard Davis Lecture 1988; Murray Scott Lecture 1990; chm cncl RCGP 1987-90; MRCGP 1967, FRCGP 1973, FRSA 1989; *Books* Training for General Practice (1981), Running a Practice (jtly, 1978); *Recreations* reading, walking; *Style*— Prof Denis Pereira Gray, OBE; Alford House, 9 Marlborough Rd, Exeter, Devon EX2 4TJ (☎ 0392 218080); 34 Denmark Rd, Exeter, Devon EX1 1SF (☎ 0392 51661, fax 0392 413449)

PERELMAN, Alan Steven; s of Arthur Perelman, of 12 Woodlands Close, Harrogate, Yorks, and Evelyn, *née* Beraha; *b* 30 April 1948; *Educ* Ashville Coll Harrogate, Christ's Coll Cambridge (MA), London Business Sch (MSc); *m* 30 Jan 1977, Christine, da of Godfrey Thomas; 1 s (Richard b 1 March 1978), 1 da (Elizabeth); *Career* controller Bougainville Copper 1980-82, dep gen mangr mktg and devpt Hamersley Iron 1984-85 (controller ops 1982-84); gp fin dir: The Gateway Corporation 1986-89, Whitbread and Co 1989-; govr Tetherdown Primary Sch; *Recreations* theatre, bridge, squash; *Style*— Alan Perelman, Esq; Whitbread and Co plc, The Brewery, Chiswell St, London EC1Y 4SD (☎ 071 606 4455)

PERERA, Dr Bernard Sarath; s of Vincent Perera (d 1985), of Colombo, Sri Lanka, and Patricia, *née* Fernando; *b* 20 Feb 1942; *Educ* St Joseph's Coll Colombo Sri Lanka, Univ of Ceylon (MB BS), Univ of Manchester (Dip Bact); *m* 1 June 1971, late Dr Piyaseeli Perera, da of Piyasena Jayatilake, of Colombo; 1 s (Shamira b 10 Aug 1973), 1 da (Lakshika b 7 June 1975); *Career* registrar Med Res Inst Colombo 1972-75, registrar in pathology Manchester Royal Infirmary 1976-78, sr registrar Northwest Regnl HA 1978-82; conslt microbiologist: Scarborough Hosp 1983, Royal Oldham Hosp 1984-; memb: BMA, Assoc of Med Microbiologists, Assoc of Clinical Pathologists, Manchester Med Soc; MRCPath 1982, FFPath RCPI 1985; *Clubs* St Josephs Coll Old Boys, Sri Lankan Doctors; *Style*— Dr Bernard S Perera; Consultant of Microbiologist, Dept of Microbiology, Royal Oldham Hospital, Oldham OL1 2JH (☎ 061 6240420)

PERERA, S Brandon Jayalath; s of Edward A Perera (d 1956), of Sri Lanka, and Elsie Lilian; *b* 2 Jan 1938; *Educ* St Benedict's Coll Colombo; *m* 13 Oct 1962, Ingrid Helen, da of Alfred Bohm (d 1972), of Switzerland; 2 s (Eugene b 1965, Adrian b 1970), 1 da (Sonia b 1967); *Career* CA in private practice; co dir and investor; FCA (1974); *Recreations* tennis, travel, languages; *Style*— Brandon Perera, Esq; Caerleon, Ruxley Crescent, Claygate, Esher, Surrey KT10 0TZ (☎ 0372 64432); Perera Fraser & Reeves, 6 Harwood Rd, London SW6 4PH (☎ 071 731 3462)

PERFECT, Geoffrey William; s of Frank George Perfect (d 1976), and Miriam Agnes, *née* Evans (d 1969); *b* 4 Feb 1922; *Educ* Royal GS, High Wycombe Bucks; *m* 8 April 1930, Eileen Mary, da of Lawrence Liddall (d 1970); 2 da (Anna (Mrs Duncan) b 1954, Sarah (Dr Marshall) b 1955); *Career* WWII RAF 1940-45; engr asst Amersham Rural Dist Cncl 1945; chm: Frank Perfect & Sons Ltd (dir 1950), Frank Perfect & Sons Retail Ltd 1965, Geoffrey Perfect Ltd (Hldgs, Homes, Investmts, Film and TV Prodns) 1987; govr Sports Aid Fndn Southern; chm: Alde House, Elderley Persons Home Bucks, Village Recreation Tstees, Methodist Church Tstees; JP 1972; Freeman City of London 1981, Liveryman Worshipful Co of Fanmakers 1982, Master Worshipful Co of Constructors 1989 (Freeman 1981); FCIOB 1980, FFB 1982; *Recreations* collector of vintage and sports cars; *Clubs* RAC; *Style*— Geoffrey Perfect, Esq; Glen More, Church Rd, Penn, Bucks (☎ 049481 2679); Casa Volante, Los Mojones, Puerto del Carmen, Lanzarote; Geoffrey Perfect Holdings Ltd, Church Rd, Penn, Bucks HP10 3LY (☎ 049481 4123)

PERHAM, Prof Richard Nelson; s of Cyril Richard William Perham (d 1948), of London, and Helen Harrow, *née* Thornton; *b* 27 April 1937; *Educ* Latymer Upper, St John's Coll Cambridge (BA, MA, PhD, ScD), MRC Laboratory of Molecular Biology Cambridge (MRC scholar); *m* 22 Dec 1969, Nancy Jane, da of Maj Temple Haviland Lane; 1 s (Quentin Richard Haviland b 1973), 1 da (Temple Helen Gilbert b 1970); *Career* Nat Serv RN 1956-58; fell St John's Coll Cambridge 1964- (res fell 1964-67, tutor 1967-77), Helen Hay Whitney fell Yale Univ 1966-67; Univ of Cambridge: lectr in biochemistry 1969-77 (demonstrator 1964-69), reader biochemistry of macromolecular structures 1977-89, head of dept 1985-, pres St John's Coll 1983-87, prof of structural biochemistry 1989-; govr: Bishop's Stortford Coll, Syndic CUP; pres Lady Margaret Boat Club; memb Sci Bd SERC 1985-90; chm Biological Sci Ctee SERC 1987-90, pres Section D Br Assoc for Advancement of Sci 1987-88, memb Exec Cncl CIBA Fndn 1989-; Fogarty int scholar Nat Insts of Health USA 1990-; memb: Biochemical Soc 1965, Euro Molecular Biology Orgn 1983, Royal Inst of GB 1986; FRS 1984, FRSA 1988; *Books* Instrumentation in Amino Acid Sequence Analysis (ed 1975), numerous papers in scientific jls; *Recreations* gardening, theatre, rowing, nosing around in antique shops; *Clubs* Hawks (Cambridge); *Style*— Prof Richard Perham, FRS; 107 Barton Rd, Cambridge CB3 9LL (☎ 0223 63752); Dept of Biochemistry, Univ of Cambridge, Tennis Ct Road, Cambridge CB2 1QW (☎ 0223 333663/7, fax 0223 333345, telex 81240 CAMSPL G)

PERKIN, (George) David; s of Alan Spencer Perkin, of Leeds, and Vera Perkin (d 1958); *b* 16 Aug 1941; *Educ* Leeds Modern Sch, Pembroke Coll Cambridge, Kings Coll Hosp; *m* 11 July 1964, Louise Ann, da of Sqdn Ldr John Boston, of Sevenoaks; 2 s (Michael b 1967, Matthew b 1971), 1 da (Emma b 1968); *Career* conslt neurologist Charing Cross Hosp 1977-; FRCP, FRSM; *Books* Optic Neuritis and its Differential Diagnosis (1978), Basic Neurology (1986), Slide Atlas of Neurology (1986), Diagnostic Tests in Neurology (1988); *Recreations* music; *Style*— David Perkin, Esq; Department of Neurology, Charing Cross Hospital, London W6 (☎ 081 846 1153)

PERKINS *see also*: Steele-Perkins

PERKINS, Hon Mrs (Celia Mary); *née* Sandys; da (by 1 m) of Baron Duncan-Sandys, CH, PC (d 1987), and Diana Churchill (d 1963); da of Sir Winston Churchill; *b* 18 May 1943; *m* 1, 1965 (m dis 1970), George Michael Kennedy; 1 s (Justin b 1967); m 2, 1970 (m dis 1979), Dennis Walters, MBE, MP, *qv*; 1 s (Dominic b 1971); m 3, 1985, Maj-Gen Kenneth Perkins, CB, MBE, DFC, *qv*; 1 s (Alexander b 1986), 1 da (Sophie b 1988); *Style*— The Hon Mrs Perkins; Carscombe, Stoodleigh, Devon EX16 9PR

PERKINS, David Charles Langrigge; s of Charles Samuel Perkins, OBE (d 1987), of Newcastle upon Tyne, and Victoria Alexandra Ryan; *b* 31 May 1943; *Educ* Uppingham, Univ of Newcastle (LLB); *m* Sept 1971, Sandra Margaret, da of Frank Gerard Buck; 4 s (Benedict William Charles Heritage b 21 June 1972, Rory Philip Francis b 12 Oct 1979, Guy Ranulf David Westbury b 27 Jan 1983, Rupert Alexander David Langrigge b 19 Nov 1973, d 1981), 1 da (Davina Helen Alexander b 20 May 1978); *Career* admitted slr 1969; Theodore Goddard & Co 1967-72, Clifford-Turner 1972-, Clifford Chance 1987-; dir Common Law Inst of Intellectual Property; memb Law Soc, City of London Slrs Co, Patent Slrs Assoc, Int Bar Assoc, Euro Communities Trade mark Practitioners Assoc, Union of Euro Practitioners Assoc, Union of Euro Practitioners in Industl Property, Association Internationale pour la Protection de la Propriète Industrielle, American Bar Assoc; assoc memb: Chartered Inst of Patent Agents, Inst of Trade Mark Agents; foreign memb US Trade Mark Assoc, American Intellectual Property Law Assoc; memb Cncl Common Law of Intellectual Property; *pubns incl* Rights of Employee Inventors in the United Kingdom under the Patents Act 1977 (1979), Intellectual Property Protection for Biotechnology (1983), Copyright and Industrial Designs (1985), Intellectual Property and the EEC: 1992 (1988), Intellectual Property Aspects of 1992 (1989), Transnational Legal Practise in Europe (1991); *Recreations* golf, tennis; *Clubs* Northumberland Golf, Northern RFC, Hurlingham; *Style*— David Perkins, Esq; Clifford Chance, Blackfriars House, 19 New Bridge St, London EC4V 6BY (☎ 071 353 0211, fax 071 489 0046, fax 0285 720 766, car 0860 578652)

PERKINS, Francis Layton; CBE (1977), DSC (1940); s of Montague Thornton Perkins, and Madge Perkins; *b* 7 Feb 1912; *Educ* Charterhouse; *m* 1, 1941 (m dis 1971), Josephine Brice Miller; 1 s, 2 da; m 2, 1971, Jill Patricia Greenish; *Career* slr 1937; ptnr Clifford Turner & Co 1946, dir Hogg Robinson & Capel-Cure 1962; chm Hogg Robinson Group, dir Transport Holding Co, pres Corpn Insur Brokers, chm UK Insur Brokers European Ctee; memb Cncl and treas Industl Soc 1976-; chm: Br Insur Brokers' Assoc 1976-80, Insur Brokers' Registration Cncl 1977-83, Barts (Hosp) Fndn for Res Ltd 1980-; cncl memb Common Law Inst of Intellectual Property 1983; Master of Worshipful Co Skinners' 1967; *Style*— Francis Perkins, Esq, CBE, DSC; Flat 4, 34 Sloane Court West, London SW3

PERKINS, Ian Richard Brice; s of Francis Layton Perkins, CBE, DSC, of London, and Josephine Louise, *née* Brice; *b* 15 Nov 1949; *Educ* Charterhouse; *m* 5 April 1975, Melissa Anne, da of Sir John Milne; 1 s (Roderick John Bloomfield b 2 Oct 1984), 2 da (Lisa Elizabeth b 5 Feb 1980, Tania Catherine Brice 29 Jan 1982); *Career* W I Carr 1968-70 and 1971-72, Fergusson Bros Johannesburg 1970-71, Greenshields Inc 1972-79; James Capel and Co: joined 1979, pres James Capel Inc NY 1986-88, dir 1988-; Freeman: City of London 1973, Worshipful Co of Skinners 1975; *Recreations* golf, tennis, skiing; *Clubs* Boodle's, Royal St Georges, The Berkshire, The Honourable of Edinburgh Golfers (Muirfield), Swinley Forest; *Style*— Ian Perkins, Esq; Moth House, Brown Candover, Alresford, Hants SO24 9TT (☎ 025 687 260); James Capel & Co Ltd, James Capel House, PO Box 551, 6 Bevis Marks, London EC3A 7JQ (☎ 071 621 0011)

PERKINS, Prof (Michael) John; s of George Karl Perkins (d 1987), and Eva, *née* Richardson (d 1990); *b* 29 Sept 1936; *Educ* Warwick Sch, King's Coll Univ of London (BSc, PhD, DSc); *m* 24 March 1962, Pauline Mary, da of Herbert Edwin Attwood (d 1948); 3 da (Inger b 1963, Georgina b 1964, Alexandra b 1971); *Career* lectr Kings

Coll London 1960-72; prof: Chelsea Coll London 1972-84, Royal Holloway and Bedford New Coll 1985- (head of dept 1985), author of papers published in various jls incl Journal of the Chemical Soc, sometime co author and co ed Organic Reaction Mechanisms series; Corday-Morgan medallist Chem Soc 1972; FRSC, CChem; *Recreations* hill walking, photography; *Style*— Prof John Perkins; Department of Chemistry, Bourne Laboratory, Royal Holloway and Bedford New College, Egham, Surrey TW20 0EX (☎ 0784 443403, fax 0784 437520, telex 935504)

PERKINS, Maj-Gen Kenneth; CB (1977), MBE (1955), DFC (1953); s of George Samuel Perkins and Arabella Sarah, *née* Wise; *b* 15 Aug 1926; *Educ* Lewes Co Sch for Boys, New Coll Oxford; *m* 1, 1949 (m dis 1984), Anne Theresa, da of John Barry (d 1960); 3 da; m 2, 1985, Hon Celia Mary, 2 da of Baron Duncan-Sandys (Life Peer, *qv*); 1 s (b 1986), 1 da (b 1988); *Career* enlisted in the ranks 1944, cmmnd RA 1946, held various appts worldwide 1946-66 (incl army aviation during Korean War and Malayan Emergency); cmd: 1 Regt Royal Horse Artillery 1967-69, 24 Airportable Bde 1971-72, Sultan of Oman's Armed Forces 1975-77; ACDS (Ops) 1977-79, dir Mil Assistance Office 1980-82, Col Cmdt RA 1980-82, ret 1982; Order of Oman 1977, Hashemite Order of Independence 1975, Selangor Distinguished Conduct medal 1955; *Books* Weapons and Warfare (1987), A Fortunate Soldier (1988), Khalida (1991); *Recreations* writing, painting; *Clubs* Army and Navy; *Style*— Maj-Gen Kenneth Perkins, CB, MBE, DFC; Carscombe, Stoodleigh, Devon EX16 9PP

PERKINS, Michael John; s of Phillip John Broad Perkins, OBE, DL (d 1982), of Lymington, Hants, and Jane Mary, *née* Hope; *b* 31 Jan 1942; *Educ* Eton, RNC Dartmouth; *m* 9 Nov 1968, Nicola Margaret, da of Air Cdre William Vernon Anthony Denney, of Amersham, Bucks; 1 s (Robert b 1971), 1 da (Caroline b 1973); *Career* RN 1961-66, Sub Lt 1963, Lt 1965; CA; ptnr Westlake Clerk CA's 1981, dir Southern Newspapers plc 1981; Freeman City of London 1956, Liveryman Worshipful Co of Haberdashers 1964; FCIS 1982; *Recreations* sailing, skiing, shooting; *Clubs* Royal Lymington Yacht; *Style*— Michael Perkins, Esq; Critchells Farmhouse, Lockerley, Romsey, Hants SO51 0JD (☎ 0794 40281); Westlake Clark & Co CAs, Newcourt House, New St, Lymington, Hants SO41 9BQ (☎ 0590 672674, fax 0425 621220)

PERKINS, Patricia; da of Charles Henry Victor Brown (d 1980), and Sarah Elizabeth, *née* Jones (d 1984); *b* 24 May 1935; *Educ* Putney HS for Girls, Girls Public Day Sch Tst; *m* 1, June 1960 (m dis), Stanley Edward Stewart Perkins (d 1984), s of Stanley Perkins (d 1968), of London; 1 s (Shane Charles Stewart b 22 July 1961), 1 da (Samantha Elizabeth Stewart b 21 Sept 1963); m 2, June 1982, Beau Maurice Gill; *Career* md Harlee Ltd 1979- (dir 1969-79), dir Helene plc 1979-; chm Nat Childrens Wear Assoc of GB and NI 1981-84, cncl memb Br Knitting Export Cncl 1983-85; *Recreations* sailing, riding, fishing; *Style*— Mrs Patricia Perkins; 407/409 Hornsey Rd, London N19 4DZ (☎ 071 272 4331, fax 071 281 4298, telex 8951059)

PERKINS, Robert James; s of John Howard Audley Perkins, MBE (d 1969), of Bristol, and Muriel May, *née* Bates (d 1957); *b* 27 June 1942; *Educ* Clifton, Fitzwilliam Coll Cambridge (MA); *m* 3 Aug 1968 (m dis 1991), Catherine Elizabeth, *née* Robertson; 1 s (Matthew b 1972), 1 da (Clare b 1971); *Career* admitted slr 1967, managing ptnr Moore and Blatch Lymington Hants 1976-89, dir John Perkins and Son Ltd 1968-, NP 1986; memb Ctee Hants Law Soc 1984-88 (hon sec New Forest Area Ctee 1984-88); chm: Milford on Sea Neighbourhood Cncl 1974-76, Milford on Sea Parish Cncl 1976-78 (memb 1976-87); memb: Law Soc 1967, Int Bar Assoc 1978; *Recreations* sailing, singing, rowing; *Clubs* Bristol Commercial Rooms, Stewards Enclosure Henley, Keyhaven YC; *Style*— Robert Perkins, Esq; 15 Broad Lane, Lymington, Hants SO41 9QN (☎ 0590 670306); Moore and Blatch, 48 High St, Lymington, Hants SO41 9ZQ (☎ 0590 72371, fax 0590 71224)

PERKS, Hon Mrs (Betty Quenelda); *née* Butler; 2 da of 28 Baron Dunboyne, *qv*; *b* 23 June 1956; *Educ* Benenden, Girton Coll Cambridge (BA, MA); *m* 1985, Edward Roland Haslewood Perks, s of Judge Clifford Perks MC, of 32 Melbury Close, Chislehurst, Kent; 1 s (Lawrence Patrick Haslewood b 1989), 1 da (Candida Anne Quenelda b 1986); *Career* teacher: at Francis Holland London 1980-83, Headington Sch Oxford 1983-85; *Recreations* photography, tennis, swimming, skiing, squash; *Clubs* Hurlingham; *Style*— The Hon Mrs Perks; 45 Heathfield Rd, London SW18 2PH

PERKS, His Hon (John) Clifford; MC (1944), TD; s of late John Hyde Haslewood Perks; *b* 20 March 1915; *Educ* Blundell's, Balliol Coll Oxford; *m* 1940, Ruth Dyke, *née* Appleby; 2 s (1 s and 2 da decd); *Career* called to the Bar Inner Temple 1938, dep chm Devon QS 1965-71, circuit judge 1970-85; *Style*— His Hon Clifford Perks, MC, TD; 32 Melbury Close, Chislehurst, Kent

PERKS, David Rowland; s of Rowland Loftus Perks, OBE, of Leeds, and Doris Mary, *née* Whitfield; *b* 16 May 1948; *Educ* The Leys Sch Cambridge, Univ of Bristol (LLB); *m* 4 Jan 1975, Susan Lesley, da of Ernest Riddlough, MBE, of Heysham, Lancs; 2 da (Emma, Clare); *Career* admitted slr 1973; ptnr Ashurst Morris Crisp 1980; *Recreations* shooting; *Clubs* Lysander Boat, Castle Camps Gun; *Style*— David Perks, Esq; Broadwalk House, 5 Appold St, London EC2A 2HA (☎ 071 6381111, fax 071 9727990, telex 887067)

PEROWNE, Hon Lady (Agatha Violet); *née* Beaumont; da of 1 Viscount Allendale (d 1923); *b* 1903; *Educ* privately; *m* 1933, Sir John Victor Thomas Woolrych Tait Perowne, KCMG (d 1951); 1 s (John Florian Canning b 1942); *Career* OStJ; *Recreations* music, reading, Girl Guides; *Style*— The Hon Lady Perowne; 1 Sandringham Court, Norwich, Norfolk NR2 2LF (☎ 0603 624746)

PEROWNE, Rear Adm Benjamin Cubitt; CB (1978); s of late Bernard Cubitt Perowne, and Gertrude Dorothy Perowne; *b* 18 Feb 1921; *Educ* Culford Sch; *m* 1946, Phyllis Marjorie, da of late Cdre R D Peel, RNR, of Southampton; 2 s, 1 da; *Career* RN; dir Mgmnt and Support Intelligence 1976-78, chief Naval Supply and Secretariat Offr 1977-78; dir Royal UK Beneficent Assoc 1978-88, DAG ML Holdings plc 1988; *Recreations* shooting, gardening, fishing; *Clubs* Army & Navy; *Style*— Rear Adm B C Perowne, CB; c/o Barclays Bank, Haslemere, Surrey

PEROWNE, Capt James Francis; OBE (1983); s of Lt Cdr John Herbert Francis Perowne, of Saundersfoot, Dyfed, and (Mary) Joy, *née* Dibb; *b* 29 July 1947; *Educ* Sherborne, BRNC Dartmouth; *m* 22 May 1971, Susan Anne, da of Cdr Peter John Holloway, of Western Australia; 4 s (Julian b 1972, Samuel b 1975, Roger b 1977, Timothy b 1977); *Career* CO: HMS Opportune 1976-77, HMS Superb 1981-83, HMS Boxer 1986-88; *Recreations* shooting, gardening, classic cars; *Clubs* Army and Navy; *Style*— Capt James Perowne, OBE; The Captain Submarines, Second Submarine Sqdn, HM Naval Base, Plymouth

PEROWNE, John Florian Canning; s of Sir Victor Perowne, KCMG (d 1951), and Hon Agatha, *née* Beaumont, da of 1 Viscount Allendale; *b* 20 Aug 1942; *Educ* Eton, Corpus Christi Coll Cambridge (MA); *m* 12 Oct 1968, Elizabeth Mary, da of Rev S B Freeman,a formerly Rector of Long Bredy, Dorset; 1 s (Matthew b 1983), 2 da (Anastasia b 1975, Clementine b 1979); *Career* admitted slr 1968, ptnr Daynes Hill & Perks Norwich; *Clubs* Norfolk (Norwich); *Style*— John Perowne, Esq; The White House, Bramerton, Norwich NR14 7DW (☎ 050 88 673), Paston House, 13 Princes St, Norwich NR31 1BD (☎ 060 366 0241)

PEROWNE, Stewart Henry; OBE (1943); s of Arthur William Thomson, Bishop of Worcester, and the late Helena Frances, *née* Oldnall-Russell; *b* 17 June 1901; *Educ* Haileybury, Corpus Christi Coll Cambridge (BA), Harvard (MA); *m* 10 Oct 1947, Freya Madeleine Stark, DBE, qv; *Career* joined Palestine Govt Educn Serv 1927, Admin Serv 1930 (pres offr 1931), asst dist cmmr Galilee 1934, asst sec Malta 1934, political ofr Aden Prot 1937, Arabic programme organiser BBC Radio 1938, info offr Aden 1939, PR attaché Br Embassy Baghdad 1941, oriental cnsllr 1944, colonial sec Barbados 1947-51, seconded as princ advst (interior) Cyrenaica 1950-51, ret 1951; discovered ancient city of Ajiris 1951, advst UK Delgn to UN Assembly Paris 1951, designer and supervisor of refugee model villages; helped in the design of stamps and backnotes for various countries; hon fell Corpus Christi Coll Cambridge 1981; memb C of E Foreign Relations Cncl; Coronation Medal 1937, FRSA; Iraq Coronation Medal 1953; *Books* The One Remains (1954), Herod the Great (1956), The Later Herods (1958), Hadrian (1960), Caesars and Saints (1962), The Pilgrim's Companion in Rome (1964), The Pilgrim's Companion in Jerusalem (1964), End of the Roman World (1966), The Death of the Roman Republic (1969), The Journeys of St Paul (1973), Roman Mythology (second edn 1983); *Recreations* archaelogy of Greece and the Aegean, Holy Places of Christendom; *Clubs* Travellers', London; *Style*— Stewart Perowne, Esq, OBE; Vicarage Gate House, Vicarage Gate, London W8 4AQ (☎ 01 229 1907)

PERRAUD, Michel Bernard; s of René Perraud (d 1989), of Vendée France, and Jeanne, *née* Brebion; *b* 30 Jan 1957; *m* 17 Oct 1981, Anne, da of Maurice Roul; 1 s (Cédric b 16 Dec 1985), 1 da (Sabrina b 23 Oct 1987); *Career* chef; French Nat Serv 1978-79; apprentice Restaurant Dagorno Paris France 1975-77; commis de cuisine: Hotel St Paul Noirmoutier France 1977, Restaurant Chez Albert Cassis France 1977-78; chef de partie: Hotel St Paul Noirmoutier France 1979, Restaurant Trois Gros Roanne France 1979-80; demi-chef de partie Restaurant Taillerent Paris France 1980-81; chef de cuisine: Hotel St Paul Noirmoutier 1981, Restaurant Le Bressan London 1981, Waterside Inn Restaurant Bray Berkshire Eng 1982-87; assistant de direction conseiller en sous vide Ecole de Cuisine Georges Pralus Briennon France 1988, chef de cuisine Les Alouettes Restaurant Claygate Surrey Eng 1988; *awards* First prize Mouton Cadet Rothschild Menu Competition 1983-84, 3 Stars Michelin (at Waterside Inn) 1985, Diplôme MOGB (Meilleur Ouvrier de Grande Bretagne), 1 Star Michelin (at Les Alouettes); memb Académie Culinaire de France in UK 1983-; *Style*— Michel Perraud; Les Alouettes Restaurant, 7 High St, Claygate, Surrey KT10 0JW (☎ 03724 67289 or 03724 64882)

PERRETT, Desmond Seymour; QC (1980); s of His Honour Judge Perrett *qv*; *b* 22 April 1937; *Educ* Westminster; *m* 1961, Pauline Merriel, da of late Paul Robert Buchan May, ICS; 1 s, 1 da; *Career* RN 1955-57; called to the Bar Gray's Inn 1962, bencher 1989, rec of Crown Ct 1978-; *Style*— Desmond Perrett, Esq, QC; The Old Tap House, Upper Wootton, Basingstoke, Hants (☎ 0256 850027); 2 Crown Office Row, Temple, London EC4Y 7HJ (☎ 071 353 9337)

PERRETT, His Hon John Perrett; JP Warwicks 1970; s of late Joseph Perrett; *b* 22 Oct 1906; *Educ* St Anne's RC, Stratford Rd Schs Birmingham, King's Coll London; *m* 1931, Elizabeth Mary, da of late William Seymour; 2 s, 2 da; *Career* RAPC 1939-45, RASC 1945; called to the Bar Gray's Inn 1946; dep chm Warwicks QS 1970-71, circuit judge 1969-81; *Style*— His Hon John Perrett, JP; 5B Vicars Close, Lichfield, Staffs (☎ 0543 252320); Farrar's Building, Temple, London EC4 (☎ 071 583 9241)

PERRIN, Arthur Stanley; s of Walter William Perrin (d 1961); *b* 7 April 1920; *Educ* Southgate Co Sch; *m* 1954, Enid Beatrice, *née* Harvey; 1 s, 1 da; *Career* Sgt RASC WWII; md: Diecasting Machine Tools Ltd 1973-83, Lone Star Products Ltd 1973-83 Wheatrade Ltd 1983-84; chm: Californian Screen Blocks Ltd 1974-83, Eaglet Industries Ltd 1975-, British Toy & Hobby Manufacturer's Assoc 1980-82 (currently memb); chm Mayfield Athletic Club Ltd 1970-89; *Recreations* golf; *Clubs* Brookman's Park Golf, Mayfield Athletic, The Sportsman's, Hadley Wood Golf; *Style*— Arthur Perrin, Esq; Hadley, 3 Anthorne Close, Potters Bar, Herts EN6 1RW (☎ 0707 50563)

PERRIN, Charles John; s of late Sir Michael Perrin, CBE, of London (d 1988), and Nancy May, *née* Curzon; *b* 1 May 1940; *Educ* Winchester, New Coll Oxford; *m* 1966, Gillian Margaret, da of late Rev M Hughes-Thomas (d 1969); 2 da (Felicity Margaret Roche b 1970, Nicola May Roche b 1973); *Career* joined Hambros Bank 1963- (dir 1973, dep chm 1986-); dir: Hambros plc, Hambro Pacific Ltd Hong Kong (chm), Hambros Bank Executor & Tstee Co Ltd, Harland & Wolff plc Belfast (non-exec 1984-89); memb Exec Ctee UK Ctee UNICEF 1970- (vice chm 1972-); hon treas UK Assoc for Int Year of the Child 1979, memb Cncl and Mgmnt Ctee Zoological Soc of London 1981-88; govr Queen Anne's Sch Caversham 1981-; *Clubs* Athenaeum; *Style*— Charles Perrin, Esq; 4 Holford Rd, Hampstead NW3 1AD (☎ 071 435 8103); 41 Tower Hill, London EC3N 4HA (☎ 071 480 5000, fax 071 702 9262)

PERRING, Dr Franklyn Hugh; OBE (1988); s of Frank Arthur Perring (d 1982), of Oundle, and Avelyn Millicent Newsum (d 1987); *b* 1 Aug 1927; *Educ* Forest Sch, Snaresbrook London, Harlow Coll, Earls Colne GS, Queens' Coll Cambridge; *m* 1, 16 June 1951 (m dis 1972), Yvonne Frances Maud, da of Harold Matthews; 1 s (Neil Stephen b 1954); m 2, Margaret Dorothy, da of Harold Barrow; 1 da (Emma Frances b 1972); *Career* Nat Serv 1945-48 (2 Lt RA 1947-48); dir Botanical Soc of Br Isles Distribution Maps Scheme Botanic Garden Cambridge 1959-64 (asst 1954-59), head of Biological Records Centre Monks Wood Experimental Station Huntingdon 1964-79, gen sec Royal Soc for Nature Conservation Lincoln 1979-87; botanical sec of Linnean Soc 1972-78; memb: Cncl Inst of Biology 1973-77, Cncl for Ray Soc 1990-; vice pres Botanical Soc of Br Isles 1987-; chm: Exec Cambridgeshire Wildlife Tst 1968-70, Northamptonshire Wildlife Tst 1985-87, Peterborough Wildlife Gp 1987-90, pres Peterborough Wildlife Gp 1990-; Hon DSc Univ of Leicester 1989; FLS 1964, FIBiol 1979; *Books* Atlas of British Flora (co-ed, 1962), Critical Supplement to the Atlas of British Flora (1968), English Names of Wild Flowers (co-ed, 1974), RSNC Guide to Wild Flowers (1984), Conservation Heritage (1991); *Recreations* opera going, poetry reading, plant hunting in the Mediterranean; *Style*— Dr Franklyn Perring, OBE; 24 Glapthorn Rd, Oundle, Peterborough PE8 4JQ (☎ 0832 273388)

PERRING, John Raymond; TD (1965); s and h of Sir Ralph Edgar Perring, 1 Bt, by his w Ethel Mary, da of Henry Theophilus Johnson, of Putney; *b* 7 July 1931; *Educ* Stowe; *m* 1961, Ella Christine, da of late Maj Anthony George Pelham; 2 s (John b 1962, Mark b 1965), 2 da (Emma b 1963, Anna b 1968); *Career* chm: Perring Furnishings Ltd 1981-88, Perrings Fin Ltd, Ave Trading Ltd 1986-; chm Non-Food Ctee of Retail Consortium; Master Worshipful Co of Merchant Taylors' 1988-89; one of HM Lts of City of London 1963-; FRSA; *Style*— John Perring, Esq, TD; 21 Somerset Rd, Parkside, Wimbledon, London SW19 5JZ

PERRING, Sir Ralph Edgar; 1 Bt (UK 1963) JP (London 1943); s of Col Sir John Ernest Perring, JP, DL (d 1948), and Florence, *née* Higginson (d 1960); *b* 23 March 1905; *Educ* Univ Coll Sch London; *m* 20 June 1928, (Ethel) Mary, OStJ (d 1991), da of late Henry Theophilus Johnson; 2 s (and 1 s decd); *Heir* s John Raymond Perring, *qv*; *Career* Lt RA (TA) 1938-40; memb Ct of Common Cncl (Ward of Cripplegate) 1948-51, alderman City of London (Langbourn Ward) 1951-75, one of HM Lts of City of London and Sheriff 1958-59, Lord Mayor of London 1962-63, chm Perring Furnishings Ltd 1948-81, memb bd of govrs E-SU 1976-81, dir Confedn Life Insur Co of Canada 1969-82, vice-pres: Royal Bridewell Hosp 1964-73; tstee Morden Coll Blackheath 1970-, chm 1979-; former Master Worshipful Co of: Tin Plate Workers, Painters-Stainers, Furniture Makers; FeSA, KStJ; kt 1960; *Clubs* City Livery (sr former pres);

Style— Sir Ralph Perring, Bt, JP; 15 Burghley House, Somerset Rd, Wimbledon, London W19 (☎ 081 946 3433)

PERRIS, Sir David Arthur; MBE (1970), JP (Birmingham 1961); s of Arthur Perris; *b* 25 May 1929; *Educ* Sparkhill Commercial Sch Birmingham; *m* 1955, Constance Parkes; 1 s, 1 da; *Career* sec Birmingham Trades Cncl 1966-83; chm: Birmingham RHB 1970-74, W Midlands RHA 1974-82; regnl sec TUC W Midlands 1974-, chm Nat Trg Cncl NHS 1975-82; vice chm ATV Midlands Ltd 1980-81, dir Central Independent TV plc and vice chm W Midlands Regnl Bd 1981-83, pres Community Media Assoc 1983-, chm Birmingham Hosp Saturday Fund 1985-, pres Birmingham Magistrates Assoc 1986 (chm 1975-86), chm Central Telethon Tst 1988-; Hon LLD Univ of Birmingham; kt 1977; *Style*— Sir David Perris, MBE, JP; Broadway, Highfield Rd, Moseley, Birmingham B13 9HL (☎ 021 449 3652)

PERROT, Emile Georges; s of Emile Georges Adolphus Perrot (d 1978), and Lilian May, *née* de Carteret; *b* 9 March 1949; *Educ* Guernsey GS, Univ of Hull (Dip Arch); *m* 24 Nov 1979, Carole Ann; 1 s (Emile b 1981), 1 da (Adele-Marie b 1978); *Career* architect; States of Guernsey Civil Serv Architects Dept 1966-70, Deneuil Marty & Paoli Paris 1974-75, Krikor Baytarian London 1976-77, D Y Davies Assoc Richmond Surrey 1977-79, princ Emile Perrot Chartered Architects 1979-; FRIBA; *Style*— Emile G Perrot, Esq; 2 Clifton, St Peter Port, Guernsey, CI; Les Buttes, Rue De L'Eglise, St Pierre Du Bois, Guernsey

PERROTT, Prof Ronald Henry; *b* 27 Dec 1942; *Educ* Queen's Univ Belfast (BSc, PhD); *m* 4 April 1974, Valerie Mary Perrott; 1 s (Simon b 2 March 1976); *Career* prof of sotfware engrg; Univ of Wisconsin 1968-69, NASA Ames Res Centre California 1977-78, Cern Geneva 1984-85; FBCS, FRSA; *Books* Operating Systems Techniques (1972), Software Engineering (1978), Pascal for Fortran Programmers (1983), Parallel Programming (1987); *Recreations* skiing, squash; *Style*— Prof Ronald Perrott; Dept of Computer Sciences, David Bates Building, Coll Park, The Queen's Univ of Belfast, Belfast BT7 1NN Northern Ireland (☎ 0232 245133 ext 3246)

PERRY, Alan Joseph; s of Joseph George Perry (d 1957), of London, and Elsie May, *née* Lewis (d 1963); *b* 17 Jan 1930; *Educ* John Bright Sch, LLandudno; Dartford GS, Kent; *m* 1961, Vivien Anne, da of Lt-Col Ernest Charles Ball, of London (d 1968); 2 s (Howard b 1968, Myles b 1974); *Career* serv RE 1948-50; HM Treasy 1951-86, (princ 1968, asst sec 1976), cnsllr (Econ) Br Embassy Washington 1978-80, chm Review of BBC Ext Serv 1984, dir Public Sector Servs Ernst & Young Accountants and Consultants 1986-; *Recreations* tennis, painting; *Style*— Alan Perry, Esq; c/o Ernst & Young, 1 Lambeth Palace Rd, London SE1 7EV (☎ 071 928 2000)

PERRY, Hon Alan Malcolm; s of Baron Perry of Walton (Life Peer) of Walton House, Whittlebury, Northants, and Anne Elizabeth, *née* Grant; *b* 6 Feb 1950; *Educ* George Heriot's Sch Edinburgh, Trinity Coll Oxford (MA); *m* 1976, Naomi Melanie, da of Dr Abraham Freedman, MD, FRCP, of 21b Chesterford Gardens, London NW3; 3 s (Daniel b 1980, Guy b 1982, Edmund b 1986); *Career* slr; *Recreations* painting, making music, gardening; *Style*— The Hon Alan Perry; 43 Meadway, London NW11 7AX; D J Freeman & Co, 43 Fetter Lane, London EC4A 1NA (☎ 071 583 4055, telex 894579)

PERRY, Barrie Edward; s of Edward Perry; *b* 5 June 1933; *Educ* Surbiton Modern Sch, King's Coll Durham; *m* 1961 (m dis); 1 s; *Career* naval architect; former chm and md Proctor Masts, former md The Marine Devpt Gp plc, owner Hartford Marina; *Recreations* sailing; *Clubs* Royal Southern YC; *Style*— Barrie Perry, Esq; Waters Edge, Hartford Marina, Huntingdon, Cambs PE17 2AA

PERRY, Colin Heywood; s of John Philip Perry (d 1972), and Barbara, *née* Heywood; *b* 14 Dec 1940; *Educ* Winchester, Clare Coll Cambridge (MA), INSEAD Fontainebleau (MBA); *m* 1966, Rebecca Mary, da of John S Barclay (d 1968); 1 s (Alexander b 1970), 1 da (Georgina b 1968); *Career* chm and md Birmingham Mint Gp plc; *Style*— Colin Perry, Esq; Birmingham Mint Gp plc, Icknield St, Birmingham B18 6RX (☎ 021 236 7742, telex 336991); Great Blakes, Shelsley Beauchamp, Worcester WR6 6RB

PERRY, David Andrew; s of Peter Nelson Perry, of Bridport, Dorset, and Margaret Adeleine, *née* Murrell; *b* 10 Nov 1945; *Educ* Colfox Sch Bridport, LSE (BScEcon); *m* 1970, Mary Jane, *née* Pratt; 1 s ((Anthony John) Julian b 1976), 1 da (Helen Elizabeth b 1985); *Career* Arthur Andersen & Co: articled clerk 1967-70, qualified chartered accountant 1970, ptnr 1979-, fndr and managing ptnr Reading office 1984; Freeman City of London 1982, memb Worshipful Co of Weavers 1982; FCA (ACA 1970); *Recreations* music, choral singing, reading, family pursuits; *Clubs* City Livery; *Style*— David Perry, Esq; Arthur Andersen & Co, Abbots House, Abbey Street, Reading, Berkshire RG1 3BD (☎ 0734 508141, fax 0734 508101, car 0860 223090)

PERRY, David Gordon; s of Elliott Gordon Perry, of Kemble, nr Cirencester, and Lois Evelyn, *née* Allen; *b* 26 Dec 1937; *Educ* Clifton, Christ's Coll Cambridge (Rugby blue); *m* 16 Sept 1961, Dorne Mary, da of Edwin Timson Busby (d 1980), of Braybrooke, Market Harborough; 4 da (Belinda b 1963, Philippa b 1964, Rebecca b 1967, Joanna b 1970); *Career* Nat Serv 2 Lt Parachute Regt 1956-58; Br Printing Corp (BPC) Ltd: md Fell & Briant Ltd (subsid) 1966-78, chief exec Packaging and Paper Products Div 1978-81, dir 1981; chief exec John Waddington plc 1988- (md 1981-88); fifteen caps England Rugby XV 1963-66 (Capt 1965); CBIM 1986; *Recreations* golf, tennis, music; *Clubs* United Oxford & Cambridge, MCC; *Style*— David Perry, Esq; Deighton House, Deighton, Nr Escrick, York YO4 6HQ; John Waddington plc, Wakefield Rd, Leeds LS10 3TP (☎ 0532 712244, fax 0532 713503)

PERRY, Sir David Howard; KCB (1986); s of Howard Dace Perry (d 1971), and Annie Evelyn (d 1976); *b* 13 April 1931; *Educ* Berkhamsted Sch, Pembroke Coll Cambridge (MA); *m* 1961, Rosemary, da of Alfred Seymour Grigg (d 1982); 1 s, 2 da; *Career* Royal Aircraft Estab 1954-78; MOD: procurement exec Air Systems Controllerate 1978-82, chief of Def Procurement 1983-85, chief of Def Equipment Collaboration 1985-87; FRAeS; *Style*— Sir David Perry, KCB

PERRY, George Cox; s of George Cox Perry (d 1962), of Berkhamsted, Herts, and Hortense Irene Emily Sadler (d 1983); *b* 7 Jan 1935; *Educ* Tiffin Sch, Trinity Coll Cambridge (BA, MA, ed Varsity); *m* 1 (m dis 1976), Susanne Puddefoot; m 2, 1976, Frances Nicola, da of Sidney Murray Scott (d 1987); 1 s (Matthew Richard Scott b 1977); *Career* advtg (creative) T Eaton Co Montreal 1957, sub ed The Sphere 1957-58, copywriter J Walter Thompson 1958-62; The Sunday Times: sub ed 1962-63, asst to the ed 1963-65, projects ed 1965-69, asst ed 1967-77, sr ed 1977-85, films ed 1985-; managing ed Crossbow 1965-70; film critic: The Illustrated London News 1982-88, Jazz-FM 1990-; presenter Radio 2 Arts 1990-, dir Cinema City 1970; external examiner photography examinations 1979-89; memb: Cncl Minnesota Symposium of Visual Communication Univ of Minnesota 1974-80, Validation Bd Degree Scheme in Communications Media The London Inst 1991-; vice chm (film) The Critics' Circle 1987-; *books incl* The Films of Alfred Hitchcock (1965), The Penguin Book of Comics 1967, The Great British Picture Show (1974), Movies from the Mansion (1976), Forever Ealing (1981), Life of Python (1983), Rupert - A Bear's Life (1985), Bluebell (adapted as BBC drama serial, 1986), The Complete Phantom of the Opera (1987); *Recreations* watching movies, travelling, taking pictures; *Style*— George Perry, Esq; The Sunday Times, 1 Pennington St, London E1 9XW (☎ 071 782 5776, fax 071 782 5120)

PERRY, Dr Ian Charles; s of Capt Sidney Charles Perry (d 1984), of Bush Hill Park, Enfield, Middx, and Marjorie Ellen, *née* Elliott; *b* 18 April 1939; *Educ* Highgate, Guy's Hosp (MB BS, LRCP), RAF Inst of Aviation Med (DAV Med), Univ of London (MFOM), RCP; *m* 27 July 1963, Janet Patricia, da of Maj Albert Edward Watson, of Burton Bradstock, Dorset; 2 da (Johanna Elizabeth b 18 Oct 1964, Helen b 7 July 1967); *Career* Lt RAMC 1963, Capt 2 i/c 24 Field Ambulance Aden 1965 and 1967 (SMO Aden Bde 1966), SMO (specialist Aviation Med) Army Air Corps Centre 1967-68, 200 Army Pilots Course 1968-69, Maj SMO Conslt Aviation Med Army Air Corps Centre 1969, chm NATO (AG ARD) Aircrew Fatigue Panel 1969-72, ret 1973, RARO 1973-; TA 1989-, princ aviation med practice (accident investigator) 1973-; sr conslt Avimed Ltd, sr conslt Occumed Ltd, chm Fireseal Ltd; former chm Br Assoc of Aviation Conslts, hon conslt Br Helicopter Advsy Bd; former chm: Grateley PC, Grateley PTA; memb: Army Air Corps Museum Friends, Preservation of Rural Eng; sec Nurdling Assoc of England; Freeman City of London 1973, Ct Asst and Liveryman Guild of Air Pilots and Navigators 1984; MRCS, FRSM, FRAeS, FAMA, MBIM 1986, MIOSH 1988; *Books* numerous papers on aviation med; *Recreations* orchids, golf, shooting; *Clubs* Sloane, Helicopter GB, Tidworth Golf; *Style*— Dr Ian Perry; The Old Farm House, Grateley, Hants SP11 8JR (☎ 026488 659/639, fax 026488 639, mobile 0836 664670); 19 Cliveden Place, London SW1W 8HD (☎ 071 730 8045/9328, fax 071 730 1985)

PERRY, Prof Jack; s of Abraham Perisky, and Rebecca Goldstein; *b* 31 March 1915; *Educ* Dame Alice Owen GS; *m* 5 Feb 1939, Doris Kate, da of Maurice Shaer, of Myddleton Rd, Golders Green; 3 s (Graham, Stephen, Jonathan); 2 da (Jillian, Vivien); *Career* chm London Export Corpn Hldgs Ltd 1952-88; vice pres: 48 Gp of Br Traders with China 1978-, Soc for Anglo-Chinese Understanding 1988-; prof of business studies Univ of Int Business and Econs Beijing 1986, visiting prof Foreign Trade Univ Tietsin 1988-; *Recreations* football, golf, cricket; *Clubs* Wentworth Golf, RAC; *Style*— Prof Jack Perry; 49 Fairacres, Roehampton Lane, London SW15; Weavers, Down House, Liphook, Hants; London Export Corporation (Holdings) Ltd, 7 Swallow Place, London W1 (☎ 071 493 7083, fax 071 629 5585, telex 297335 LLCM G)

PERRY, Prof John Grenville; s of Frederick Perry (d 1974), of Stoke-on-Trent, and Elsie, *née* Till; *b* 21 May 1945; *Educ* Longton HS Stoke-on-Trent, Univ of Liverpool (BEng, MEng), Univ of Manchester (PhD); *m* 20 April 1968, Ruth Katharine, da of Eric Stanley Forrester (d 1989), of Fulford, Staffs; 2 s (Jonathan b 17 Nov 1970, Timothy b 10 June 1972); *Career* engr Costain Ltd 1967-70, project engr ICI Ltd 1970-74, sr lectr UMIST 1984-88 (lectr 1974-84), Beale Prof and head of Sch of Civil Engrg Univ of Birmingham 1988-; former chm local branch Lib Pty; MICE 1975, MAPM 1988; *Recreations* tennis, squash, golf, fell walking; *Style*— Prof John Perry; School of Civil Engineering, The Univ of Birmingham, Edgbaston, Birmingham B15 2TT (☎ 021 4145048)

PERRY, John Hill; s of Archie John Hill Perry (d 1982), and Evelyn Blanche, *née* Dalton (d 1978); *b* 11 May 1928; *Educ* Charterhouse, École Hôtelière Lausanne Switzerland; *m* 12 April 1958, Patricia Stuart, da of Frederick Charles Gatcombe Fry; 2 s (James Hill b 5 April 1963, Andrew Hill b 29 Oct 1965); *Career* asst mangr Imperial Hotel Torquay 1950-53, P & H Hotels Ltd: Raven Hotel Shrewsbury 1953-60, Livermead House Hotel Torquay 1960-89, Livermead Cliff Hotel Toquay 1968-; West Country Tourist Bd: memb Exec Ctee 1974, vice chm 1978, first chm of the commercial membs; fndr govr Sports Aid Fndn (SW region); memb: Rotary Club of Torquay 1972-, Nat Cncl Br Hotels Restaurants and Caterers Assoc 1972-86 and 1990-, BHRCA/AA Liaison Ctee, Hotel and Catering Advsy Ctee Torquay Tech Coll, Howell Ctee of Inquiry into Sponsorship in Sport (CCPR) 1981-83, Econ Planning Cncl for SW DOE (cncl terminated 1979); former nat chm Best Wetsern Hotels (formerly Interchange Hotels), pres Skal Club of Devon and Cornwall 1980, dir Torquay United FC 1970-87; Master Innholder 1981-; Freeman City of London 1981, Liveryman Worshipful Co of Butchers 1981; fell Tourism Soc, FHCIMA; *Recreations* golf, watching sports, collecting; *Clubs* MCC, Churston Golf; *Style*— John Perry, Esq; P & H Hotels (Torquay) Ltd, Livermead Cliff Hotel, Seafront, Torquay, Devon TQ2 6RQ (☎ 0803 299666, fax 0803 294496, telex 42424)

PERRY, Jonathan Peter Langman; s of Thomas Charles Perry, and Kathleen Mary Perry; *b* 6 Sept 1939; *Educ* Peter Symonds Sch Winchester; *Career* chartered accountant; articles Butler, Viney & Childs (CA's) 1956-62, Coopers & Lybrand 1962-66; Morgan Grenfell Group plc: joined 1966, dir Morgan Grenfell & Co Limited 1973, jtly i/c banking 1973-77, i/c New York Office 1977-80, i/c banking and capital markets 1980-87, i/c overseas offices 1987-88, dir 1987; memb Cncl of Int Stock Exchange 1986-88, fin advsr and proprietor Perry & Associates 1988-90, chm and chief exec Ogilvy Adams & Rinehart Ltd 1990-; capt Br Team Int 14s 1973, 1977 and 1983, team capt Br America Cup 1986; FCA; *Recreations* sports (yacht racing, tennis, golf), music, painting, writing; *Clubs* Itchenor Sailing, Vanderbilt Racquet, Royal Yacht Squadron; *Style*— Jonathan Perry, Esq; Ogilvy Adams & Rinehart Limited, Chancery House, Chancery Lane, London WC2A 1QU (☎ 071 405 8733)

PERRY, Margaret Strachan; *née* Maclaren; da of William Anderson Maclaren, of Inverness, Scotland, and Elizabeth, *née* Strachan; *b* 7 March 1934; *Educ* Inverness Royal Acad, Univ of Edinburgh (MA); *m* 14 Feb 1964 (m dis 1988), Brian Evelyn Perry, s of Arthur Raymond Perry (d 1983), of Arborfield Cross, Berks; 2 s (Guy Robert Maclaren b 17 June 1966, Gregory Stuart b 10 Nov 1968); *Career* teacher London and Scotland 1954-64; dir Liftrucs Ltd 1970-90 (md 1984-90); fndr Artemis Equipment Ltd 1990; *Recreations* the arts, good food and wine, motor racing; *Style*— Mrs Margaret Perry; The Smithy, The Cross, Bramhope, Leeds (☎ 0532 842 791); Artemis Equipment Ltd, Aberford Rd, Garforth, Leeds LS25 2ET (☎ 0532 874 874, fax 0532 869 158)

PERRY, Ven Michael Charles; s of Charlie Perry (d 1972), and Kathleen Farmer; *b* 5 June 1933; *Educ* Ashby-de-la-Zouch Boys' GS, Trinity Coll Cambridge (MA), Westcott House Cambridge; *m* 13 July 1963, Margaret, da of Maj J M Adshead (d 1965); 2 s (Andrew b 1965, David b 1968), 1 da (Gillian b 1973); *Career* archdeacon of Durham and canon residentiary of Durham Cathedral 1970-, sub dean 1985-; chm: Churches' Fellowship for Psychical and Spiritual Studies, Lord Crewe's Charity; memb: Cncl Soc for Psychical Res 1984-89, General Synod 1974-90; author; ed: The Church Quarterly 1968-71, The Christian Parapsychologist 1978-; *Books* incl: The Easter Enigma (1959), Sharing in One Bread (1973), The Resurrection of Man (1975), The Paradox of Worship (1977), Handbook of Parish Finance (1981), Psychic Studies (1984), Deliverance (1987); *Style*— The Ven the Archdeacon of Durham; 7 The College, Durham DH1 3EQ (☎ 091 386 1891)

PERRY, Hon Michael John; s of Baron Perry of Walton (Life Peer); *b* 1948; *m* 1970, Kathleen Elliott; *Style*— The Hon Michael Perry; 5 Corstorphine Park Gdns, Edinburgh

PERRY, Michael Sydney; CBE (1990, OBE 1973); s of Lt Cdr Sydney Albert Perry, RNVR (d 1979), of Douglas, IOM, and Jessie Kate, *née* Brooker; *b* 26 Feb 1934; *Educ* King William's Coll IOM, St John's Coll Oxford (MA); *m* 18 Oct 1958, Joan Mary, da of Francis William Stallard (d 1948), of Worcester; 1 s (Andrew b 1967), 2 da (Carolyn b 1962, Deborah b 1963); *Career* Nat Serv RN 1952-54; dir Unilever 1985- (joined 1957), vice chm Unilever plc 1991-; memb Br Overseas Trade Bd 1986-, chm Japan Trade Advsy Gp BOTB 1986-, jt chm Netherlands Br C of C 1988-; *Recreations* music (choral), golf; *Clubs* Oriental; *Style*— Michael Perry, Esq, CBE; Bridges Stone Mill,

Alfrick, Worcs WR6 5HR (☎ 0886 332 90); 35/3 Queen's Gate Gardens, London SW7 5RR (☎ 071 581 9839); Unilever, Unilever House, Blackfriars, London EC4P 4BQ (☎ 071 822 5252 telex 28395)

PERRY, Hon Niall Fletcher; s of Baron Perry of Walton (Life Peer); *b* 1953; *m* 1978, Sandra Buchanan; *Style*— The Hon Niall Perry; 57 Rowney Croft, Hall Green, Birmingham

PERRY, Nick; *b* 1961; *Educ* Univ of Hull, Nat Film and TV Sch; *Career* playwright and dramatist; TV dramas and stage plays incl: Arrivederci Millwall (produced 1985, jt winner of Samuel Beckett award 1986), Smallholdings (performed Kings Head 1986), Rockliffe Babies (contrib to BBC series), Tales of Sherwood Forest (for Central TV), Mamma (for BBC); awarded Euro Script Fund devpt prize for screen adaptation of Paddy The Cope; *Style*— Nick Perry, Esq; Rochelle Stevens & Co, 2 Terretts Place, Upper Street, London N1 1QZ (☎ 071 359 3900, fax 071 354 5729)

PERRY, Dr Norman Henry; s of Charles Perry (d 1984), of London, and Josephine, *née* Ehrlich (d 1986); *b* 5 March 1944; *Educ* Quintin Sch London, UCL (BA, PhD); *m* 7 Aug 1970, Barbara Ann, da of James Harold Marsden, and Margaret, *née* Lütkemeyer, of Sheffield; 2 s (Ben b 1974, Tom b 1977); *Career* lectr in geography UCL 1965-69, sr res offr GLC 1969-73, sr res fell Social Sci Res Cncl Survey Unit 1973-75; DOE: princ London & Birmingham 1975-79, princ London 1979-80, asst sec W Midlands 1980-86; Grade 4 head of Inner Cities Unit Dept of Employment and DTI 1986-88, Grade 3 regnl dir DTI W Midlands 1988-90; chief exec Wolverhampton Metropolitan Borough Cncl 1990-; chm Third Olton (Solihull) Scout Gp 1985-88; FBIM 1983; *Books* Demands for Social Knowledge (with Elisabeth Crawford, 1976), Vols in European Glossary of Legal and Administrative Terminology: German/English, Vol 18 Regional Policy (1974), Vol 29 Environmental Policy (1979), Public Enterprise (1989); *Recreations* reading, history, gardening, occasional jogging; *Clubs* Civil Service (Arden Solihull); *Style*— Dr Norman Perry; Civic Centre, St Peter's Square, Wolverhampton WV1 1SH (☎ 0902 314000, fax 0902 314006)

PERRY, Pauline; *née* Welch; da of John George Embleton Welch (d 1963), of Sunderland, and Elizabeth, *née* Cowan (d 1982); *b* 15 Oct 1931; *Educ* Girls HS Wolverhampton, Girton Coll Cambridge (BA, MA); *m* 26 July 1952, George Walter Perry, s of Percy Walter Perry (d 1939), of Wolverhampton; 3 s (Christopher b 1952, Timothy b 1962, Simon b 1966), 1 da (Hilary (Mrs Hayward) b 1955); *Career* teacher various secdy schs UK USA and Canada 1953-56 and 1959-61; lectr in philosophy: Univ of Manitoba 1956-59, Univ of Mass 1961-62; lectr in educn: Univ of Exeter (pt/t) 1963-66, Univ of Oxford 1966-70; Access Course tutor 1966-70, HM Chief Inspr Schs 1981-86 (inspr 1970-74, staff inspr 1975-81), dir South Bank Poly 1987- freelance journalist and broadcaster; memb: ESRC, Fndn for Educn Business Partnership, Greater London Enterprise, bd IDS, Br Cncl CICHE, bd of South Bank Technopar Ltd; chm teacher educn gp SRHE; conslt to OECD on Higher Educn and professional devpt of teachers 1976-81, nat corr in serv trg Cncl of Europe; Hon FCP 1987, FRSA 1988; *Books* Your Guide to the Opposite Sex (1970), Case-Studies in Adolescence (with G Perry, 1970), Case-Studies in Teaching (with G Perry, 1969); *Recreations* music, walking; *Clubs* Nat Lib; *Style*— Pauline Perry; South Bank Polytechnic, Borough Rd, London SE1 0AA (☎ 071 620 0046, fax 071 261 9115)

PERRY, Peter George; CB (1983); s of Joseph George Perry (d 1958), and Elsie Lewis (d 1963); *b* 15 Dec 1923; *Educ* Dartford GS, Univ of London (LLB); *m* 1957, Marjorie Margaret, da of J J Stevens (d 1970); *Career* Civil Service 1947-84; under sec DHSS 1974-84; memb: Industl Tbnls 1984-, Parole Bd 1988-; chm Investigation Ctee Slrs Complaints Bureau 1989-; JP City of London 1974-87; *Recreations* sailing (Hestia of Hamble), opera, theatre, skiing; *Clubs* Little Ship; *Style*— Peter Perry, Esq, CB; 50 Great Brownings, College Rd, Dulwich, London SE21

PERRY, Dr Robert Henry; s of Frank Perry, of Carlton House, Quaker Road, Sileby, Loughborough, Leics, and Lois Ellen, *née* Harriman; *b* 20 Aug 1944; *Educ* Loughborough GS, Univ of St Andrews; *m* 5 June 1971, Elaine King, da of James Cyril King Miller, WS, (d 1979), of 16 Gillespie Road, Collinton, Edinburgh; 1 s (Jonathan b 1972), 1 da (Nicolette b 1973); *Career* Newcastle Gen Hosp: sr registrar in neuropathology 1975-79, clinical scientist MRC neuroendocrinology unit, conslt neuropathologist 1980-; sr lectr neuropathology Univ of Newcastle-upon-Tyne 1986-; author of res pubns on neuropathological correlations of dementia Alzheimer's disease, Parkinson's disease and related topics; memb Br Neuropathological Soc; MRCP, FRCPath; *Recreations* sailing, skiing; *Style*— Dr Robert Perry; Dilston Mill House, Corbridge, Northumberland NE45 5QZ (☎ 0434 6232308), Neuropathology Dept, Newcastle General Hosp, Westgate Rd, Newcastle-upon-Tyne NE45 5QZ (☎ 091 2738811 ext 22373)

PERRY, Robert John; s of Idris James Perry (d 1975), and Betty, *née* Davies; *b* 23 March 1948; *Educ* Exeter Sch, Univ of Warwick (BSc); *Career* Arthur Anderson & Co 1969-76, N M Rothschild & Sons Ltd 1976- (dir 1987-), dir Bumiputra Merchant Bankers Berhad Malaysia 1988-; FCA; *Recreations* tennis, travel; *Clubs* Hurlingham; *Style*— Robert Perry, Esq; N M Rothschild & Sons Limited, New Court, St Swithin's Lane, London EC4P 4DU (☎ 071 280 5000, fax 071 283 2426)

PERRY, Rodney Charles Langman (Rod); s of Thomas Charles Perry, of 60 Felpham Way, Felpham, Bognor Regis, West Sussex, and Kathleen Mary, *née* Moojen; *b* 23 July 1941; *Educ* Peter Symonds Sch Winchester; *m* 5 March 1965, Susan Geraldine, da of John Reginald Quertier, of 24 Wellington Court, Spencers Wood, Reading; 1 s (James Quertier b 20 Sept 1968), 1 da (Sarah De Moulpied b 23 Feb 1967); *Career* CA; articles Charles Comins & Co 1960-65, Coopers & Lybrand Zimbabwe 1965-69, ptnr Coopers & Lybrand UK 1976; ICAEW: memb C£cl 1984-86, chm Technology Gp 1984-86; Freeman: City of London, The Co of Information Technologists; FCA 1975; *Books* An Audit Approach To Computers (1986); *Recreations* squash, golf, boating, painting; *Clubs* Royal Lymington, Calcot Park Golf; *Style*— Rod Perry, Esq; Orchard House, Swallowfield St, Swallowfield, Reading, Berks; Flat 19, 87 St George's Court, St George's Drive, Pimlico, London SW1 (☎ 0734 883 666, 071 630 7968); Coopers & Lybrand, Deloitte, Plumtree Court, London (☎ 071 822 4575, telex 887470)

PERRY, Prof Roger; s of Charles William Perry, of Newquay, Wales, and Gladys, *née* Cooper; *b* 21 June 1940; *Educ* King Edward's GS Birmingham, Univ of Birmingham (BSc, PhD); *m* ; 1 s (Jonathan b 1965), 1 da (Deborah b 1968); *Career* appts in chem indust until 1964, Dept of Chem and Chem Engrg Univ of Birmingham 1964-70, prof of environmental control and waste mgmnt Imperial Coll 1981- (memb academic staff 1970-); conslt to: UK and Int Chem and Engrg Insts, WHO, UNEP; memb Senate and Academic Cncl Univ of London 1984-; FRSH 1984, FIEWM 1972, FRCS 1970, CChem; *Books* Handbook of Air Pollution Analysis (1977, 2 edn 1986); *Recreations* cooking, gardening, building and travel; *Clubs* Athenaeum; *Style*— Prof Roger Perry; Centre for Toxic Waste Management, Imperial College, London SW7 2BU (☎ 071 589 5111, fax 071 823 8525, telex 918351)

PERRY, Simon James; s of James Anthony Perry, of Oxfordshire and Pauline, *née* Bezani; *b* 9 June 1962; *Educ* Croydon Sch of Art, Chelsea Sch of Art (BA), Royal Acad Sch (MA); *m* 14 Oct 1986, Elise, da of Andrew Terry Fraser; 1 s (Oscar Fraser b 15 April 1988), 1 da (Mathilda Fraser b 6 Feb 1991); *Career* artist and sculptor; solo exhibition Nicola Jacobs Gallery London 1988; gp exhibitions incl: ILEA at the Barbican (London) 1983, Portland Bill Sculpture Park 1983, Quarries Exhibition (Camden Art Centre London) 1983, Christie's Inaugural Exhibition (London) 1983, Summer Exhibition (Nicola Jacobs Gallery London) 1983, New Sculpture Exhibition (Royal Acad London) 1984, Interbuild Exhibition (NEC Birmingham) 1985, Nicola Jacobs Gallery London 1986, 1987 and 1990, Germinations IV (touring) 1988, Work in Progress (Br Sch at Rome) 1988, Dieci Artisti (Br Sch at Rome) 1988, Ten Years of the Br Sch at Rome (RCA London) 1990, Lynne Stern Associates Gallery London 1990; author of several catalogues and other pubns incl The History of the British School at Rome (1990); *Awards* Landseer scholarship award 1985, Edward Stott Tst travel scholarship 1986, Royal Acad Gold medal for sculpture 1986, Rome scholar in sculpture Br Sch at Rome 1987; *Style*— Simon Perry, Esq; Flat 5, 59 Sutherland Ave, Maida Vale, London W9 (☎ 071 289 5206); Nicola Jacobs Gallery, 9 Cork St, London W1 (☎ 071 437 3868)

PERRY, Stephen Laurence Andrew; s of Jack Perry, of London, and Doris Kate Perry (d 1985); *b* 12 Sept 1948; *Educ* UCL (LLB); *m* 24 Dec 1980, Wendy Janet, da of Joseph Bond (d 1957), and Lillian Bond; 1 s (Jack b 1984), 1 da (Jodie b 1981); *Career* md: London Export Corp (Holdings) Ltd, London Export Corp (Marketing) Ltd; dir: Tienshan Ltd, China Business Servs Ltd; pres Academicals Football Club, dir International Shakespeare Globe Tst Ltd; *Recreations* football, tai-chi; *Clubs* RAC, Wentworth, IOD; *Style*— Stephen Perry, Esq; 4 Floor, 7 Swallow Place, London W1R 7AD (☎ 071 493 7083, telex 297335)

PERRY, Dr Wayne; s of William Perry (d 1947), of Hayes, Middlesex, and Margery Rideley, *née* Wilson; *b* 30 June 1944; *Educ* Royal Hosp Sch Ipswich, Univ of Birmingham Med Sch (MB ChB, MRCP), Accreditation by Jt Ctee on Higher Med Trg (RCP) in Gen (Internal) Med with a special interest in Metabolic Med; *m* 1980, Siew Mui Lee; *Career* house physician Queen Elizabeth Hosp Birmingham 1968, house surgn Dudley Rd Hosp Birmingham 1969; sr house offr: Dept of Med Harari Hosp Univ of Salisbury Rhodesia 1969 (Dept of Paediatrics), Chest Diseases King Edward VII Hosp Warwick 1971; registrar in med The Med Professorial Unit King's Coll Hosp London 1972, sr med registrar Dept of Metabolic Med Royal Nat Orthopaedic Hosp Stanmore 1974, asst prof Dept of Internal Faisal Univ Saudi Arabia 1979 (conslt physician and endocrinologist King Fahad Univ Hosp, hon conslt endocrinologist King Fahad Univ Hosp, hon conslt endocrinologist King Abdul Aziz Airbase Hosp); conslt endocrinologist: Harley St 1983, Metabolism and Bone Disease The Endocrine and Dermatology Centre Harley St 1987; author numerous learned articles in med jls; Sir Herbert Seddon Gold Medal and prize for origional res (Inst of Orthopaedics Univ of London and Royal Nat Orthopaedic Hosp); medals awarded at VI and VII Saudi Med Confs 1981, 1982, and for the first graduating students from King Faisal Fahad Univ Dammam Saudi Arabia; FRSM; memb: BMA, Med Defence Union, registered Med Practioner Gen Med Cncl; approved conslt for UK: BUPA, PPP; *Recreations* violincello, poetry, arcadian landscapes, France; *Style*— Dr Wayne Perry; The Endocrine and Dermatology Centre, 140 Harley St, London W1N 1AH (☎ 071 935 2440)

PERRY OF WALTON, Baron (Life Peer UK 1979), of Walton, Co Bucks; Walter Laing Macdonald Perry; OBE (1957); s of Fletcher Smith Perry (d 1960), and Flora Macdonald Macdonald (d 1966); *b* 16 June 1921; *Educ* Ayr Acad, Dundee HS, Univ of St Andrews; *m* 1, 1946 (m dis 1971) Anne Elizabeth Grant; 3 s (Hon Michael John b 1948, Hon Alan Malcolm b 1950, Hon Niall Fletcher b 1953); m 2, 1971, Catherine Hilda, da of Ambrose Crawley; 2 s (Hon Robin Charles Macdonald b 11 June 1973, Hon Colin Stuart Macdonald b 12 Aug 1979), 1 da (Hon Jennifer Joan b 6 Feb 1981); *Career* dep leader SDP in House of Lords 1981-83; dir Dept of Biological Standards Nat Inst for Med Res 1952-58; prof of pharmacology Univ of Edinburgh 1958-68 (vice princ 1967-68); vice chllr The Open Univ 1969-80 (fell 1981-); FRCPE, FRCP, FRSE, FRS; kt 1974; *Recreations* making music and playing games; *Clubs* Savage, Scottish Arts; *Style*— The Rt Hon the Lord Perry of Walton, OBE, FRS; The Open University Scotland, 60 Melville St, Edinburgh EH3 7HF (☎ 031 226 3851)

PERRYMAN, Stephen John (Steve); MBE (1986); s of Ronald Edward Perryman, and Joyce, *née* Barwick; *b* 21 Dec 1951; *Educ* Elliots Green GS Northolt; *m* 25 March 1973, Cherrill Anne, da of Ronald Frederick Tarrant; 1 s (Glenn Richard b 29 Sept 1977), 1 da (Loren Ann b 5 Feb 1974); *Career* professional football manager; schoolboy player: Ealing District, Middlesex County, London and England Schs; professional player: 864 appearances Tottenham Hotspur 1969-86, 17 appearances Oxford Utd 1986, 66 appearances Brentford 1986-90; manager: Brentford 1987-90, Watford 1990-; England caps: under 18, 17 under 23, 1 full v Iceland 1982; honours as player Tottenham Hotspur: FA Cup twice, League Cup twice, UEFA Cup twice, capt for 10 years; records: most appearances Tottenham Hotspur, most England under 23 caps; Football Writers' player of the year 1982; *Books* A Man For All Seasons (autobiography, 1985); *Recreations* own sports shops, tennis, travel; *Style*— Steve Perryman, Esq, MBE; Watford FC, Vicarage Rd, Watford WD1 8ER (☎ 0923 30933, fax 0923 39759)

PERSSE, Richard Henry; s of Brig Reginald Barry Lovaine Persse, KSLI (d 1985), of Taunton, Somerset, and Sheeleh Patricia, *née* Battersby (d 1979); *b* 22 Oct 1937; *Educ* Eton; *m* 3 May 1969, Susan Royale, da of Cdr Anthony Kennett, RN (ret), of Somerset; 2 s (Edward b 1971, James b 1972); *Career* cmmnd 1 Kings Dragoon Gds, served Malaya 1957-58; dir: Morgan Furze & Co (wine merchants) 1968-79, Morans of Bristol 1979-84; md J B Reynier Ltd (wine shippers) 1987-; *Recreations* fishing; *Clubs* Flyfishers; *Style*— Richard Persse, Esq; 64a Tachbrook St, Pimlico, London SW1V 2NA (☎ 071 630 8639); JB Reynier Ltd, 18 Upper Tachbrook St, London SW1 (☎ 071 834 2917)

PERSSON, Rt Rev William Michael Dermot; *see*: Doncaster, Bishop of

PERTH, 17 Earl of (S 1605); (John) David Drummond; PC (1957); also Lord Drummond of Cargill and Stobhall (S 1488), Lord Maderty (S 1609), Viscount Strathallan (S 1686), and Lord Drummond of Cromlix (S 1686); s of 16 Earl of Perth, GCMG, CB, PC (d 1951), and Hon Angela Constable-Maxwell (d 1965), da of 11 Lord Herries of Terregles; *b* 13 May 1907; *Educ* Downside, Trinity Coll Cambridge; *m* 4 Aug 1934, Nancy Seymour, da of Reginald Fincke, of New York City; 2 s; *Heir* s, Viscount Strathallan; *Career* Lt Intelligence Corps, seconded to War Cabinet Offices 1942-43 and to Min of Production 1944-45; a representative peer for Scotland 1952-63, Hereditary Thane of Lennox and Hereditary Steward of Menteith and Strathearn; min of state for Colonial Affairs 1957-62, first crown estate cmmr 1962-77, chm of the Reviewing Ctee on the Export of Works of Art 1972-76, tstee Nat Library of Scotland; Hon LLD St Andrew's Univ; Hon FRIBA 1978, Hon FRIAS 1988; *Clubs* White's, Puffin's (Edinburgh); *Style*— The Rt Hon the Earl of Perth, PC; 14 Hyde Park Gardens Mews, London W2 (☎ 071 262 4667); Stobhall, by Perth (☎ 082 14 332)

PERTWEE, Anthony Nigel Ferens; s of Norman Frank Pertwee; *b* 4 Nov 1942; *Educ* Tonbridge; *m* 1965, Margaret Joan, da of Ronald George Gammer; 1 s, 2 da; *Career* chm Pertwee Anfood Ltd, former dir Pertwee Holdings Ltd; fndr Anglo Alpine Balloon Sch; involved in corporate entertaining with Chateau Ballooning (France) and Alpine Ballooning (Austria); *Recreations* sailing, hot air ballooning, water sports, skiing; *Style*— Anthony Pertwee, Esq; 5 Baynards Crescent, Frinton on Sea, Essex CO13 0QS (☎ 0255 673 709)

PERTWEE, Christopher Ferens; s of Norman Frank Pertwee, of Frinton-on-Sea, Essex, and Eileen Pertwee (d 1982); *b* 25 Nov 1936; *Educ* Tonbridge; *m* 1960, Carole, da of Alfred George (Jim) Drayson, of Sutton Valence, Kent; 3 s (Mark, Julian, Nicholas); *Career* chm and co dir Pertwee Holdings Ltd, pres UK Agric Supply Trade Assoc 1982-83; dir: Rosenlew MiniBulk Ltd, East Trust Ltd; memb Cncl Univ of Essex; memb Ct Worshipful Co of Farmers; *Recreations* hunting, gardening, antiques; *Clubs* Farmers; *Style—* Christopher Pertwee, Esq; The Bishops House, Frating, Colchester, Essex CO7 7HQ (☎ 0206 250706); office: Harbour House, Colchester, Essex CO2 8JF (☎ 0206 577991, telex 98121)

PERTWEE, Richard James Charles Drury; s of Capt James Waddon Martyn Pertwee, CBE, of Cintra House, 5 Christchurch Rd, Winchester, Hants, and Margaret Alison, *née* Elliott; *b* 2 May 1955; *Educ* Sherborne, Worcester Coll Oxford (BA); *m* 15 Aug 1981, Gail, da of Wilfred McBrien Swain, OBE (d 1983); 2 da (Laetitia b 1984, Sophie b 1987); *Career* joined RNR 1978, Sub Lt 1980, res 1982; Richards Butler & Co: articled clerk 1978-80, slr 1980-82; asst then ptnr: Trevor Robinson & Co 1982-85, Joynson-Hicks 1985-89; ptnr Taylor Joynson Garrett (merger of Joynson-Hicks and Taylor Garrett) 1989-; *Recreations* hockey, tennis, squash, shooting, cricket; *Clubs* Sherborne Pilgrims, Vincent's (Oxford), MCC; *Style—* Richard Pertwee, Esq; 180 Fleet St, London EC4 (☎ 071 430 1122, fax 081 528 7145, telex 25516)

PERUTZ, Gerald; s of Dr Georg Perutz (d 1935); *b* 8 Sept 1929; *Educ* Loughborough Coll; *m* 1953, Dinah Fyffe, *née* Pope; 3 children; *Career* gen mangr Rank Precision Industs 1957-63; chm Bell & Howell Co Chicago USA to 1983 (ret); chm Nimlor Gp Chicago USA; *Recreations* tennis, skiing; *Clubs* Glenview; *Style—* Gerald Perutz Esq; c/o National Westminster Bank Ltd, 115 Old Brompton Rd, London SW7; 223 Melrose, Kenilworth, Illinois USA

PERUTZ, Max Ferdinand; OM (1988), CH (1975), CBE (1963); s of Hugo Perutz, and Adele Perutz; *b* 19 May 1914; *Educ* Theresianum Vienna, Vienna Univ, Peterhouse Cambridge (hon fell 1962); *m* 1942, Gisela Peiser; 1 s, 1 da; *Career* chm med Research Cncl Laboratory of Molecular Biology Cambridge 1962-79 (memb Scientific Staff 1979-), Fullerian prof of physiology at the Royal Institution 1973-79, Nobel prize for Chemistry 1962, Royal medal of Royal Society 1971, Copley medal of Royal Soc 1979; Pour le Mérite 1988, OM; *Style—* Dr Max Perutz, OM, CH, CBE, FRS; 42 Sedley Taylor Rd, Cambridge CB2 2PN (☎ 0223 246041); MRC Laboratory of Molecular Biology, Cambridge CB2 2QH (☎ 0223 248011, telex 81532)

PERY, Hon Michael Henry Colquhoun; s of 5 Earl of Limerick, GBE, CH, KCB, DSO, TD (d 1967), and Angela Olivia, GBE, CH (d 1981), da of Lt-Col Sir Henry Trotter, KCMG, CB; bro of 6 Earl, *qv*; *b* 8 May 1937; *Educ* Eton, New Coll Oxford (BA); *m* 1963, Jennifer Mary, eldest da of John Anthony Stuart-Williams (d 1978), of Braughing, Herts; 2 s, 2 da; *Career* Lt XII Royal Lancers; Inns of Court, City Yeomanry; md: Alginate Industries Ltd 1974-82, Sifam Ltd 1983-; dir London Life Assoc 1983-; *Recreations* sailing, skiing, tennis; *Clubs* Garrick; *Style—* The Hon Michael Pery; Ardtur, Appin, Argyll PA38 4DD (☎ (063 173) 223); Sifam Ltd, Woodland Rd, Torquay, Devon (☎ (0803) 63822)

PERYER, Roger Norman; s of Frederick Grey Peryer (d 1988), of Bexhill-on-Sea, and Edna, *née* Watt (d 1987); *b* 27 Feb 1937; *Educ* King's Coll Sch Wimbledon, Law Soc Coll of Law; *m* 6 Oct 1973 (m dis 1989), (Joan) Juliet, da of Peter Landymore Green; 1 s (Guy Roger Frederick b 2 Sept 1977), 1 da (Holly Juliet b 25 March 1975); *Career* admitted slr 1959; ptnr: Stileman Neate & Topping 1961-75, D J Freeman & Co 1975-; memb negligence panel Slrs Complaint Bureau 1988; Freeman City of London 1984, Liveryman Worshipful Co of Slrs 1985; memb Law Soc 1960, CIArb 1987; *Recreations* golf, shooting, boating; *Clubs* RAC, Leander, MCC, Temple Golf; *Style—* Roger Peryer, Esq; 43 Fetter Lane, London EC4A 1NA (☎ 01 583 4055, fax 01 353 7377, telex 894579)

PESCHARDT, Michael Mogens; s of Mogens Jan Hagbarth Peschardt, and Betty Joyce, *née* Foster; *b* 17 Nov 1957; *Educ* Merchant Taylors', Univ of Sussex; *m* 9 July 1977, Sarah Louise, da of Tom James Vaughan; 3 s (Joseph Mogens b 1980, Jack Oliver b 1982, Samuel Thaddeus b 1984); *Career* news prodr BBC Radio Manchester 1980-82, chief parly journalist BBC Regnl Broadcasting until 1986, sports reporter BBC TV News, stories incl: 1986 World Cup England v Argentina, Umpire Rhanàs row with Mike Gatting (lead story), 1988 Olympics; contributor to the Listener and New Statesman; *Recreations* walking, children, holidays; *Style—* Michael Peschardt, Esq; Holly Cottage, N Chailey, E Sussex; Social Affrs Unit, BBC TV Centre, London W12 (☎ 01 743 8000)

PESCOD, Peter Richard; s of Philip Pescod (d 1965), of Darlington, and Elsie, *née* Parnaby; *b* 29 June 1951; *Educ* Queen Elizabeth GS Darlington, Univ of Newcastle (LLB); *m* 15 April 1978, Barbara Jane, da of John Magoveny King, of 11 Kings Ave, Morpeth, Northumberland; 1 s (Henry b 12 April 1983), 1 da (Jennifer b 21 May 1981); *Career* admitted slr 1975; ptnr Hay and Kilner 1976-; memb: Standing Ctee Newcastle Law Soc 1985-88, Northumberland CC 1989-; chm Sub Ctee Legal Aid 1986-87; parly candidate (C) Blaydon 1987; memb: Exec Ctee Hexham Cons Assoc 1988-, Northumberland FPC 1985-90 (chm Med Serv Ctee 1988-), Nat Tst, Eng Heritage, Law Soc; *Recreations* politics, auction sales, building, landscape gardening, architecture; *Clubs* Anglo Belgian, Newcastle upon Tyne Lit and Phil; *Style—* Peter Pescod, Esq; Ovington Cottage, Ovington, Northumberland NE42 6DH (☎ 0661 32358); Hay & Kilner, 33 Grey St, Newcastle upon Tyne NE1 6EH (☎ 091 2328345, telex 537879)

PESCOD, Prof (Mainwaring Bainbridge) Warren; OBE (1977); s of Bainbridge Pescod (d 1979), and Elizabeth, *née* Brown (d 1973); *b* 6 Jan 1933; *Educ* Stanley GS Co Durham, King's Coll Univ of Durham (BSc), MIT (SM); *m* 16 Nov 1957, (Mary) Lorenza, da of John Francis Coyle (d 1970); 2 s (Duncan Warren b 1959, Douglas James b 1961); *Career* teaching and res assoc MIT 1954-56, res assoc Dept of Civil Engrg King's Coll Univ of Durham 1956-57, lectr and actg head Dept of Engrg Fourah Bay Coll, Univ Coll of Sierra Leone W Africa 1957-61, asst engr Babtie Shaw and Morton Glasgow 1961-64, prof and chm Environmental Engrg Div Asian Inst of Technol Bangkok 1964-76; Univ of Newcastle upon Tyne: Tyne & Wear prof of environmental control engrg 1976-, head Dept of Civil Engrg 1983-; memb Northumbrian Water Authy 1986-89, dir Northumbrian Water Group PLC 1989-, chm and md Environmental Technology Consultants Ltd 1988-; CEng, FICE 1973, FIWEM (formerly FIPHE) 1962, MIWM 1985, MRSH 1964; *Books* Water Supply and Wastewater Disposal in Developing Countries (ed, 1971), Treatment and Use of Sewage Effluent for Irrigation (ed with A Arar, 1988); *Recreations* squash, golf, reading; *Clubs* British and Royal Bangkok Sports (Bangkok); *Style—* Professor Warren Pescod, OBE; Tall Trees, High Horse Close Wood, Rowlands Gill, Tyne & Wear NE39 1AN (☎ 0207 542 104); Dept of Civil Engrg, University, Newcastle upon Tyne NE1 7RU (☎ 091 222 6000 ext 6410, fax 091 261 1182, telex 53654 UNINEW G)

PESKIN, Barry; s of Samuel Peskin (d 1965), of 14 Bryanston Square London W1, and Gladys, *née* Ward (d 1975); *b* 24 May 1931; *Educ* Cheltenham; *m* 1 (m dis 1966), Elaine Segal; 1 s (Stephen Mark b 13 March 1957), 1 da (Linda Ruth b 5 May 1954); m 2, Feb 1968, Janet, da of Leonard Nicholson (d 1982), of Grassmere Ave, Telscobe, Sussex; 1 da (Emma Leah b 24 Dec 1970); *Career* dir Finewood Products Ltd 1952-60; md: Insection Instruments Ltd 1967-85, A and B Indsutrial Supplies Ltd 1962-73, B T Wood Products Ltd 1969-73; dir 1985-; Pontis Consumables Ltd, Iberian Corporate Finance Ltd, Trimvain Ltd, Software for Professional Educn Ltd, Engrg Trade Co Ltd, OB One Ltd; JP 1969-70, cncllr Camden Cncl 1970-74, chief whip Ruling Gp 1973-74; memb: American Soc of Materials Testing, Br Inst of Non Destructive Testing; FInstD; *Recreations* golf, cricket, theatre; *Clubs* Elstree Golf, Middlesex Cricket; *Style—* Barry Peskin, Esq; 4 Crediton Hill, London NW6 (☎ 071 435 2277); Lieudit Longeroy, Pierrecourt Blangy, France; Heriot House, Heriot Rd, London NW4

PESKIN, Richard Martin; s of Leslie Peskin (d 1980), and Hazel Pauline Peskin (d 1980); *b* 21 May 1944; *Educ* Charterhouse, Univ of Cambridge (MA,LLM); *m* 6 Feb 1979, Penelope Ann Elizabeth *née* Howard; 1 s (Michael b 1966), 2 da (Elizabeth b 1969, Virginia b 1979); *Career* Great Portland Estates PLC: dir 1968, dep md 1972, md 1985, chm and md 1986; FRSA 1989, CBIM 1989; *Recreations* golf, theatre, wine; *Clubs* MCC, RAC, Mark's, Annabel's, Wentworth; *Style—* Richard Peskin, Esq; 41 Circus Rd, London NW8 9JH (☎ 071 289 0492); Knighton House, 56 Mortimer St, London WIN 8BD (☎ 071 580 3040)

PESTELL, Catherine Eva; CMG (1984); da of Edmund Ernest Pestell (d 1965), and Isabella Cummine, *née* Sangster (d 1987); sister of John Pestell, *qv*; *b* 24 Sept 1933; *Educ* Leeds Girls' HS, St Hilda's Coll Oxford (MA); *Career* 3 sec The Hague 1958, 2 sec Bangkok 1961, FO 1964, 1 sec UK Delgn to OECD Paris 1969, FCO 1971, St Antony's Coll Oxford 1974, cnsllr E Berlin 1975-78, Cabinet Office 1978-80, Dip Serv inspr 1980-82, min (econ) HM Embassy Bonn 1983-87, asst (public depts) FCO 1987-89; princ Somerville Coll, Oxford; *Style—* Miss Catherine Pestell, CMG; Somerville College, Oxford OX2 6HD

PESTELL, John Edmund; s of Edmund Ernest Pestell (d 1965), and Isabella Cummine, *née* Sangster (d 1987); brother of Catherine Pestell, *qv*; *b* 8 Dec 1930; *Educ* Roundhay Leeds, New Coll Oxford (MA); *m* 19 April 1958, Muriel Ada, da of William Norman Whitby (d 1971); 3 s (James b 1962, Hugh b 1963, Charles b 1966); *Career* admin Staff Coll Henley 1963; MOD 1953-72: private sec to Parly Under sec of State 1958-60, private sec to Min of Equipment 1969-70; pres sec (co-ordination) PMs Office 1972-74, under sec Civil Service Dept 1976-81 (asst sec 1974-76), HM Treasy 1981-84, MOD 1984-88, chm Civil Service Selection Bd, Cabinet Office 1988-90, partnership sec Linklaters & Paines 1990-; govr Cranleigh Sch 1975-; *Clubs* Athenaeum; *Style—* John Pestell, Esq; New House, Bridge road, Cranleigh, Surrey GU6 7HH

PESTELL, Sir John Richard; KCVO (1969); s of late Lt-Cdr Frank Lionel Pestell, RN (d 1947), and Winifred Alice Pestell (d 1983); *b* 21 Nov 1916; *Educ* Portsmouth Northern Secdy Sch; *m* 1951, Betty, da of Reuben Parish (d 1955); 3 da; *Career* Br SA Police S Rhodesia 1939-65, Cyrenaica Def Force 1944-49, Maj; sec and comptroller to Govr of S Rhodesia (Rt Hon Sir Humphrey Gibbs) 1965-69, adjudicator Immigration Appeals Harmondsworth 1970-87; *Recreations* walking; *Style—* Sir John Pestell, KCVO; Batch Cottage, North Rd, Charlton Horethorne, Sherborne, Dorset DT9 4NS (☎ 0963 22719)

PESTON, Baron (Life Peer UK 1987), of Mile End, Greater London; Maurice Harry Peston; s of Abraham Peston; *b* 19 March 1931; *Educ* Bellevue Bradford, Hackney Downs London, LSE (BSc), Princeton Univ USA (BScEcon); *m* 17 Nov 1958, Helen, da of Joseph Conroy; 2 s (Hon Robert James Kenneth b 1960, Hon Edmund Charles Richard b 1964), 1 da (Hon Juliet Claire Elaine b 1961); *Career* prof of economics Queen Mary Coll Univ of London; *Style—* The Rt Hon Lord Peston; c/o Queen Mary College, Mile End Rd, London E1 (☎ 081 980 4811)

PETCH, Barry Irvine; s of Charles Reginald Petch and Edith Anne, *née* Fryer (d 1952); *b* 12 Oct 1933; *Educ* Doncaster GS; *m* 1966, Anne Elisabeth, da of Dr F Johannessen, of Trondheim, Norway; 2 s, 1 da; *Career* RAPC (Capt) 1957-59; former finance dir IBM United Kingdom Holdings Ltd and subsidiaries; vice pres finance IBM Europe; FCA; *Recreations* sailing, golf; *Clubs* Reform, Country Club de Fourqueux; *Style—* Barry Petch, Esq; Les Moukelins, Chemin des Hauts de Grisy, St Nom La Breteche, France; IBM Europe, Tour Pascal, 22 route de la Demi-Lune, Puteaux - Hauts de Seine, France (☎ (767) 78 40)

PETCH, Dr Michael Charles; s of Dr Charles Plowright Petch (d 1987), of The Manor House, Wolferton, Norfolk, and Edna Margaret, *née* Stirling; *b* 15 July 1941; *Educ* Gresham's, St John's Coll Cambridge, St Thomas's Hosp (MA, MD, MB, BChir); *m* 19 April 1965, Fiona Jean Shepheard, da of Cdr David George Fraser Bird, of the White House, Nyewood, Sussex; 2 s (Tom b 1966, Simon b 1968), 1 da (Amanda b 1971); *Career* sr registrar Nat Heart Hosp 1971-77, conslt cardiologist Papworth and Addenbrooke's Hosps 1977-, assoc lectr Univ of Cambridge; memb: cncl Br Cardiac Soc 1985-89, various ctees Coll of Physicians; contrib: BMJ, Lancet, British Heart Journal; MRCP 1967, FRCP 1980, fell American Coll of Cardiology 1980; *Books* Heart Disease (1989); *Recreations* natural history, sailing, opera; *Style—* Dr Michael Petch; 20 Brookside, Cambridge CB2 1JQ (☎ 0223 65226); Papworth Hosp, Cambridge CB3 8RE (☎ 0480 830541, fax 0480 831083)

PETCH, Simon Geoffrey Filby; s of Eric Petch (d 1986), of Cirencester, Glos, and Nancy Mary, *née* Lamplough; *b* 6 May 1943; *Educ* Dean Close Sch Cheltenham, St Peter's Coll Oxford; *m* 1969, Patricia Ann, da of William James Burton (d 1983); 1 s (Jack b 1975); *Career* research offr Union of Construction Allied Trades and Technicians 1969-73, research Nat offr Electrical Power Engrs Assoc 1973-76; dep gen sec: Engrs Managers Assoc, Electrical Power Eng Assoc 1976-85; gen sec Soc of Telecom Executives 1986; *Recreations* horse racing, reading, walking; *Style—* Simon Petch, Esq; 3 Walpole Gardens, Strawberry Hill, Twickenham, Middx (☎ 01 894 1316); 1 Park Road, Teddington, Middx TW11 0AR (☎ 01 943 5181, telex 927162 STE G)

PETER, John (Anthony); s of Dr András Peter (d 1944), and Veronika, *née* Nagy (d 1977); *b* 24 Aug 1938; *Educ* various state schools in Hungary, Campion Hall Oxford (MA), Lincoln Coll Oxford (BLitt); *m* 1978, Linette Katharine, da of Rai Bahadur Amar Math Purbi; *Career* reporter and editorial asst Times Educational Supplement 1964-67; The Sunday Times: editorial staff 1967-79, dep arts ed 1979-84, chief drama critic 1984-; *Books* Vladimir's Carrot: Modern Drama and the Modern Imagination (1987); *Style—* John Peter, Esq; The Sunday Times, 1 Pennington St, London E1 9XW (☎ 071 782 5000)

PETERBOROUGH, 36 Bishop of (cr 1541), 1984-; Rt Rev William John Westwood; patron of 101 livings, the chancellorship, the archdeaconries of Northampton and Oakham, and the canonries of his cathedral; Bishopric created by Henry VIII from the proceeds of the dissolved land holdings of the Abbey of St Peter (founded by Saxulf, a Thane of Mercia, 653), whose last Abbot became the first Bishop of the new see; s of Ernest, and Charlotte Westwood; *b* 28 Dec 1925; *Educ* Grove Park GS Wrexham, Emmanuel Coll Cambridge (MA), Westcott House Cambridge; *m* 1954, Shirley Ann, yr da of Dr Norman Jennings; 1 s, 1 da; *Career* served Army 1944-47; rector of Lowestoft 1957-65, vicar of St Peter Mancroft Norwich 1965-75, hon canon Norwich Cathedral 1969-75, rural dean of Norwich 1966-70, city dean of Norwich 1970-73, area bishop of Edmonton 1975-84; memb Archbishop's Cmmn on Church and State 1966-70, church cmmr 1973-78 and 1985-; memb Press Cncl 1975-81, chm of govrs Coll of All Saints Tottenham 1976-78, chm C of E Ctee for Communications 1979-86; memb IBA Panel of Religious Advrs 1983-87, pres Church Housing Assoc (formerly chm 3 housing assocs); memb: BBFC Video Consultative Cncl 1985-89, Bdcasting Standards Cncl; hon fell Emmanuel Coll Cambridge Freeman City of London 1988-; *Recreations* the countryside, wine bars, art galleries; *Style*— The Rt Rev the Lord Bishop of Peterborough; The Palace, Peterborough PE1 1YA (☎ 0733 62492)

PETERKEN, Hon Mrs (Hyacinthe Ann); da of 7 Baron Hatherton, TD; *b* 1934; *m* 1954, Patrick Peterken; 2 s, 1 da; *Career* LLB Newcastle, solr 1978; *Style*— The Hon Mrs Peterken; Claypool Farm, Hutton Henry, Castle Eden, Durham

PETERKEN, Laurence Edwin; CBE (1990); s of Edwin James Peterken (d 1971), of Banstead, Surrey, and Constance Fanny, *née* Giffin (d 1973); *b* 2 Oct 1931; *Educ* Harrow, Peterhouse Cambridge (MA); *m* 10 Dec 1955, (Hanne) Birgithe (d 1968), da of Harald von der Recke (d 1960), of Copenhagen; 1 s (Oliver b 1956), 1 da (Camilla b 1959); m 2, 29 May 1970, Margaret Raynal Blair; 1 s (Alexander b 1974), 1 da (Jemima b 1977); *Career* Nat Serv 1950-52, Pilot Offr RAF Regt, Sqdn Adjt No 20 LAA Sqdn 1952; mangr Serv Div 1961-63 and commerical dir Hotpoint Ltd 1963-66, gp md Br Domestic Appliances 1966-68, dir Br Printing Corp Ltd 1969-73; mgmnt auditor Debenhams Fashion Multiple Div 1975-77 (md 1974-75) controller of operational servs GLC 1977-85, gen mangr Gtr Glasgow Health Bd 1986-; *Recreations* golf, opera; *Clubs* Athenaeum; *Style*— Laurence Peterken, Esq, CBE

PETERKIN, Hon Sir Neville Allan Mercer; s of Joseph and Evelyn Peterkin; *b* 27 Oct 1915; *Educ* Wellington Sch Somerset; *m* 1942, Beryl Thompson; 2 s, 1 da; *Career* barr Middle Temple 1939, registrar St Lucia 1943, magistrate Trinidad and Tobago 1944, res magistrate Jamaica 1954, high ct judge Trinidad 1957; West Indies Associated States: high ct judge 1967, Justice of Appeal 1975, Chief Justice 1980-88; kt 1981; *Style*— The Hon Sir Neville Peterkin; Requit, St Lucia, West Indies

PETERS, Brian Henry; s of Harry Peters; *b* 13 June 1933; *Educ* Edmonton County GS; *m* 1957, Moyra Bowes; 2 s; *Career* admin dir Allied Hambro Unit Trust Gp; *Recreations* badminton, motoring, compiling crossword puzzles; *Style*— Brian Peters, Esq; 74 Mayfield Rd, Writtle, Chelmsford, Essex (☎ 0245 420936)

PETERS, Hon Mrs (Corynne Lesley); 2 da of 2 Baron Burden; *b* 1 April 1955; *Educ* La Retrait W-S-M, St Brandons Clevedon, Taunton Sch; *m* 1977, William D-Day Peters, s of late Leonard Thomas Peters; 1 s (Alexander b 1983), 1 da (Lindsey Jane b 1988); *Career* nurse; *Style*— The Hon Mrs Peters; Greenland, Royston Water, Churchinford, Taunton, Somerset TA3 MEF (☎ 0823 60 484)

PETERS, Prof David Keith; s of Herbert Lionel Peters, of 16 Fernfield, Baglan, Port Talbot, and Olive Manwaring, *née* Hare; *b* 26 Sept 1938; *Educ* Glanafan GS Port Talbot, Welsh Nat Sch of Med Univ of Wales (MB, BCh); *m* 1, 1961 (m dis 1976) Jean Mair Garfield; 1 s (Andrew b 1961), 1 da (Katharine b 1969); m 2 1979, Pamela, da of Norman Wilson Ewan, of Cambridge; 2 s (James b 1980, William b 1989), 1 da (Hannah b 1982); *Career* prof of med Royal Postgraduate Med Sch 1977- (lectr 1969, reader 1975) regius prof of physic Univ of Cambridge Sch of Clinical Med 1987-, fell Christ's Coll; memb: MRC 1984-88, Advsy Cncl Sci and Technol 1988-, chm Nat Kidney Res Fund 1980-86; hon MD Wales 1986; FRCP 1975; *Books* Clinical Aspects of Immunology (jt ed 1982); *Recreations* tennis; *Clubs* Garrick; *Style*— Prof D K Peters; Office of the Regius Prof of Physics, Univ of Cambridge, Sch of Clinical Medicine, Addenbrookes Hosp, Hills Rd, Cambridge CB2 2QQ (☎ 0223 336738, fax 0223 336709)

PETERS, Ellis; *see*: Pargeter, Edith Mary

PETERS, Kenneth Jamieson; CBE (1979), JP (City of Aberdeen 1961), DL (Aberdeen 1978); s of William Jamieson Peters (d 1966), and Edna Rosa, *née* Hayman (d 1980); *b* 17 Jan 1923; *Educ* Aberdeen GS, Univ of Aberdeen; *m* 1951, Arunda Merle Jane Jones; *Career* serv WWII, Capt/Adj 2 Bn King's Own Scottish Borderers; ed: Evening Express Aberdeen 1953-56, The Press and Journal Aberdeen 1956-60; dir Highland Printers Ltd (Inverness) 1968-83, md Aberdeen Journals Ltd 1960-80, chm 1980-81; dir: Thomson Regional Newspapers 1974-81, Thomson North Sea 1981-88 and Thomson Scottish Petroleum Ltd 1981-86, Aberdeen Journals Ltd 1960-90, National Girobank Scotland 1984-90; chm Aberdeen and NE Scotland Ctee The Scottish Cncl Devpt and Industry 1982-88; memb Bd: British Rail (Scotland) 1982-, Peterhead Bay Authority 1983- (vice chm 1989-); assoc memb CInstT 1985, FSA (Scot) 1980, FRSA 1989; *Clubs* MCC, Royal Northern and University (Aberdeen); *Style*— Kenneth Peters Esq, CBE, JP, DL; 47 Abergeldie Rd, Aberdeen AB1 6ED (☎ 0224 587647)

PETERS, Mary Elizabeth; CBE 1991 (MBE 1973); da of Arthur Henry Peters (d 1990), of Australia, and Hilda Mary Ellison (d 1956); *b* 6 July 1939; *Educ* Ballymena Acad, Portadown Coll, Belfast Coll of Domestic Science; *Career* former Home Economics teacher Graymount Girls' Secondary Sch; Int athlete 1961-74, represented N Ireland at every Cwlth Games 1958-74, 1964 Olympics (Pentathlon 4th), 1966 Cwlth games (Shot 2nd), 1970 Cwlth games (Pentathlon 1st, Shot 1st), 1972 Olympics (Pentathlon 1st, world record), 1974 Cwlth Games (Pentathlon 1st); memb NI Sports Cncl 1973-, vice chm NISC 1977-80, chm NI Ctee of Sport for the Disabled 1984-91, memb Sports Cncl (GB) 1974-77, re-elected 1987, memb Sports Aid Fndn, Patron NI amateur Athletic Fed past pres NI Womens' AAA, team mangr Br Womens' Athletics Team 1979-84 (inc Moscow and LA Olympic Teams); md Mary Peters Sports Ltd, tstee Ulster Sports & Recreation Tst; chm Ulster Games Fndn, Belfast 1991 Sports Ctee; patron Friends of The Royal (Royal Victoria Hosp); hon DSc New Univ of Ulster (1974); *Recreations* fitness training; *Style*— Mary E Peters, CBE; Willowtree Cottage, River Rd, Dunmurry, Belfast; Mary Peters Health Club, 37 Railway Street, Lisburn (☎ 084 66 76411)

PETERS, Michael Edmund du Thon; s of Edmund Lind du Thon Peters (d 1986), of Ryde, IOW, and Raymonde Marie, *née* Stempfer (d 1985); *b* 19 March 1939; *Educ* Clayesmore Sch, Dorset Coll of Agric (NCA); *m* 1964, Judith Joy, da of Donald George Harris (d 1982), of Minehead, Somerset; 2 da (Emma, Charlotte); *Career* agric journalist, farmer and stockbreeder 1959-62, fndr and jt md Agripress Publicity Ltd 1963-70 (relinquished directorship 1975), md A O Smith Harvestore Products Ltd 1971-86, currently fndr and chm Merston Peters Ltd (mgmnt and recruitment consltss); tstee Central Suffolk Conservation Assoc 1984-; *Recreations* shooting, gardening, livestock, writing; *Style*— Michael Peters, Esq; Mead House, Drinkstone Green, Bury St Edmunds, Suffolk IP30 9TL (☎ 0449 736570); Merston Peters Ltd, Mead House, Drinkstone Green, Bury St Edmunds, Suffolk IP30 9TL (☎ 0449 736002, fax 0449 737539)

PETERS, Robert Byron; MBE (1977); s of Geoffrey Halsted Peters, of Eddington Mill House, Hungerford, Berks RG17 0HL, and Edith Frances *née* Scott; *b* 3 May 1926; *Educ* Marlborough, RAF Short Course Trinity Coll Oxford; *m* 15 Jan 1959, Jean Eileen Meredith, da of George Thomas Edwards, of Hornsey; 1 s (Laurence Geofrey Byron b 1963); 2 da (Rebecca Frances b 1965, Victoria Louise b 1967); *Career* served RAF aircrew 1942-47; chief exec and sec Inst of Advanced Motorists; dir and sec: Advanced Mile-Posts Publications Ltd, IAM Fleet Training Ltd; dir Clearshift Ltd; chm Kentex Estates Ltd; chm Holborn & Metropolitan Cos Friendly Soc; *Books* amateur radio, swimming, tennis, computers, travel, aviation; *Style*— Robert Peters, Esq, MBE; IAM House, 359 Chiswick High Rd, London W4 4HS (☎ 081 994 4403, fax 081 994 9274, car 0860 516 313)

PETERS, Stanley Eric; s of late Thomas Peters, of Glos, and Fanny Ethel, *née* Hawtin; *b* 4 May 1918; *Educ* private; *m* 1952, Pauline, da of Mr Besson, of Dublin; *Career* WWII Capt Royal Warwicks Regt; design conslt in: historic domestic architecture, decoration and gardens; advsr on architecturally famous houses; *Recreations* music, literature, travel, arts; *Style*— Stanley Peters, Esq; 26A Camberwell Rd, London SE6 0EN (☎ 071 703 0150)

PETERS, Prof Timothy John; s of Stanley Frederick Peters, of Uley, Dursley, Gloucester, and Paula, *née* March (d 1973); *b* 10 May 1939; *Educ* King's Sch Macclesfield Cheshire, Univ of St Andrews (MB ChB, MSc, DSc), Univ of London (PhD), Rockefeller Univ NY USA; *m* 21 Sept 1965, Judith Mary, da of Dr William Basil Bacon (d 1983), of Manchester; 1 s (Christopher b 1983), 2 da (Carolyne b 1967, Sarah b 1969); *Career* successively lectr, sr lectr, reader Royal Postgrad Med Sch Univ of London 1972-79, head of Div of Clinical Cell Biology Clinical Res Centre Harrow 1979-88, prof and head of Dept of Clinical Biochemistry King's Coll London 1988-; FRCP 1974, FRCPE 1981, FRCPath 1984; *Recreations* baroque recorders; *Clubs* RSM; *Style*— Prof Timothy J Peters; Dept Clinical Biochemistry, King's Coll Sch of Medicine and Dentistry, Bessemer Rd, London SE5 9PJ (☎ 071 3263008, fax 071 7377434)

PETERS, William; CMG (1980), LVO (1961), MBE (1959); s of John William Peters (d 1983), of Morpeth, Northumberland, and Louise, *née* Woodhouse (d 1965); *b* 28 Sept 1923; *Educ* King Edward VI GS Morpeth, Balliol Coll Oxford (MA), LSE, SOAS; *m* 1944, Catherine Bertha, da of Daniel Bailey (d 1928), of Edinburgh and Paisley; *Career* WWII serv Britain and Far East Queen's Royal Rifles, KOSB, 9 Gurkha Rifles, demob as Capt 1946; joined Colonial Serv, asst dist cmmr Gold Coast (now Ghana) 1950, ret as acting sec regnl cmmr (Cabinet rank) Northern Ghana; joined CRO as asst princ 1959, princ CRO 1959; 1 sec: Dacca 1960-63, Cyprus 1963-67; head Zambia and Malawi Dept CRO 1967-68, head Central African Dept FCO 1968-69, dir Int Affrs Div Cwlth Secretariat 1969-71, cnsllr and head Chancery Canberra 1971-73, dep high cmmr Bombay 1974-77, ambass Uruguay 1977-80, high cmmr Malawi 1980-83; chm: LEPRA, Tibet Soc of UK; pres Royal Br Legion (Downs Branch), hon treas Tibet and China Ctee; memb: Abbeyfield (Walmer) Soc, Editorial Bd Royal Soc for Asian Affairs; past pres Deal Rotary Club 1989-90, govr Walmer Secdy Sch; *Books* Diplomatic Service: Formation and Operation (1972); *Recreations* music, walking, archaeology; *Clubs* Oxford & Cambridge, Royal Commonwealth Soc, Royal Soc for Asian Affrs; *Style*— William Peters, Esq, CMG, LVO, MBE; 12 Crown Court, Middle St, Deal, Kent (☎ 0304 362822)

PETERSEN, Sir Jeffrey Charles; KCMG (1978, CMG 1968); s of Charles Petersen; *b* 20 July 1920; *Educ* Westcliff HS, LSE; *m* 1962, Karin Kristina Hayward; 2 s, 4 da; *Career* RN 1939-46; HM Dip Serv 1948-80; ambass to: Republic of Korea 1971-74, Romania 1975-77, Sweden 1977-80; chm: Barclays Bank SAE (Spain) 1982-87, British Materials Handling Board, North Sea Assets plc, Ake Larson Ltd; pres: Anglo-Korean Soc, Anglo-Swedish Soc; vice pres Swedish C of C for the UK; Knight Grand Cross Royal Order of the Polar Star Sweden 1984, Order of Diplomatic Merit South Korea 1984; *Clubs* Travellers', Kent and Canterbury; *Style*— Sir Jeffrey Petersen, KCMG; 32 Longmoore St, London SW1 (☎ 071 834 8262); Crofts Wood, Petham, Kent (☎ 022 770 537)

PETERSEN, Prof Ole Holger; s of Rear Adm Jorgen Petersen (d 1986), and Elisabeth, *née* Klein; *b* 3 March 1943; *Educ* Med Sch Copenhagen Univ (MB ChB, MD); *m* 4 May 1968, Nina Bratting, da of Wilhelm Jensen, of Copenhagen, Denmark; 2 s (Jens b 26 May 1969, Carl b 25 Dec 1970); *Career* Lt Royal Danish Army Med Corps 1970-71; sr lectr in physiology Univ of Copenhagen 1973-75 (lectr 1969-73), prof of physiology Univ of Dundee 1975-81, field ed Pflügers Archiv euro jl of physiology 1978-, George Holt prof of physiology Univ of Liverpool 1981-; memb Bd and Scientific Advsy Bd Max Plank Inst for Biophysics Frankfurt Am Main FRG 1980-, fndn memb Academia Europaea; memb Royal Danish Acad of Sciences and Letters 1988; *Books* The Electrophysiology of Gland Cells (1980); *Recreations* music; *Style*— Prof Ole Petersen; MRC Secretary Control Research Group, The Physiological Laboratory, Univ of Liverpool, Brownlow Hill, Liverpool L69 3BX (☎ 051 7945322, fax 051 7945327)

PETERSEN, Richard Eli; s of Eli Ezra Petersen, and Alice Margaret, *née* Wolfe; *b* 22 Oct 1940; *Educ* Lewiston Senior HS Idaho, Univ of Idaho (BArch); *m* 28 Dec 1968, Hylda Margaretta, da of James Noel Green; 1 s (Christian James b 30 Nov 1972), 1 da (Anna Sophia b 14 Jan 1971); *Career* architect: Payne & Settecase Salem Oregon 1963-66, Borough Architect's Dept Southend-on-Sea 1966-67, Noel Tweddle & Park London 1967-68, Shavey & Schmidt Seattle 1968-69; architect and interior designer Benaroya Co Seattle 1969-71, interior designer Henry End Assoc London 1971-72, architectural assoc Tributus Design Group 1972-75, architect and interior design assoc Michael Aukett Assoc 1975-79, architect and interior design ptnr Knox Design Bremerton Washington 1979-81, interior design ptnr Aukett Assocs; dir: architecture and design BAAC 1988-89, design mgmnt BAA plc 1989-; FCSD, FRSA; *Recreations* golf, swimming, weight-training, squash; *Clubs* RAC, Pall Mall, Epsom; *Style*— Richard Petersen, Esq; The Garden House, Burley Orchard, Staines Lane, Chertsey, Surrey KT16 8PS (☎ 0932 560508); BAA plc, Masefield House, Gatwick Airport, West Sussex RH6 0HZ (☎ 0293 595499, fax 0293 595710)

PETERSHAM, Viscount; Charles Henry Leicester Stanhope; s and h of 11 Earl of Harrington and Eileen, *née* Grey; *b* 20 July 1945; *Educ* Eton; *m* 1, 1966 (m dis), Virginia Alleyne Freeman, da of Capt Harry Freeman Jackson, of Cool-na-Grena, Co Cork; 1 s (William b 1967), 1 da (Serena b 1970); m 2, 1984, Anita, formerly w of 21 Earl of Suffolk and Berkshire, and yr da of Robin Fuglesang, of Lacock, Wiltshire; *Recreations* shooting, sailing (circumnavigation 1983-85 sy Surama), hunting (Master of the Limerick Hounds 1974-77), skiing, fishing; *Clubs* House of Lords Yacht; *Style*— Viscount Petersham; Baynton House, Coulston, Westbury, Wiltshire (☎ 0380 830273, fax 0380 830988); 5 Stanhope Mews West, London SW7 (☎ 071 244 6611, fax 071 373 8003)

PETERSON, Col Christopher Matthew; CBE (1983), TD (1956), JP (1973), DL (1978); s of Oscar Peterson (d 1923); *b* 22 Feb 1918; *Educ* St Illtyd's Coll Cardiff; *m* 1945, Grace Winfred, da of John McNeil (d 1940); 3 children (and 1 child decd); *Career* co dir; Lloyd's underwriter; High Sheriff S Glamorgan 1981; *Clubs* Cardiff County, Army and Navy; *Style*— Col Christopher Peterson, CBE, TD, JP, DL; 51 Rannoch Drive, Cyncoed, Cardiff CF2 6LP (☎ 0222 754062); 15 Castle Pill Crescent, Milford Haven

PETERSON, Colin Vyvyan; CVO (1982); s of late Sir Maurice Drummond Peterson, GCMG; *b* 24 Oct 1932; *Educ* Winchester, Magdalen Coll Oxford; *m* 1966, Pamela Rosemary Barry; 2 s, 2 da; *Career* HM Treasy 1959, sec for appts to Prime Minister and ecclesiastical sec to Lord Chllr 1974-82, under sec Mgmnt and Personnel Office 1985-, lay asst to Bishop of Winchester 1985-; *Style*— Colin Peterson, Esq, CVO; Balldown Farmhouse, Sparsholt, Hants (☎ 0962 72 368)

PETERSSON, Lars Urban Leonard; s of Robert Leonard Petersson, and Birgit Valborg Petersson; *b* 29 Oct 1938; *Educ* Stockholm Univ (MA), Harvard Business Sch (MBA); *m* 10 Sept 1965, Elisabeth Margaret, da of Erik Rutger Smith (d 1970), of

Sweden; 3 s (Magnus b 1966, Thomas b 1968, Philip b 1973); *Career* mgmnt conslts McKinsey & Co (London, NY, Zurich) 1965-72; dir: ITEL Corp 1972-73, of corporate diversification Hunter Douglas 1973-75; vice pres Trans Ocean Leasing 1975-83; fndr and md: Leasing Ptnrs Int 1983-87, Golden Golf Fin NV, Chateau Golf Int NV, Chateau des Vigiers Golf & Country Club SA; *Recreations* golf, boating; *Clubs* Harvard, Harewood Down; *Style—* Lars Petersson, Esq; The Third House, West Witheridge, Beaconsfield (☎ 0494 676 537); Chateau des Vigiers, 24240 Monestier, France (☎ 53279272)

PETHER, Dr John Victor Sebastian; s of Dr Geoffrey Charles Pether, TD (d 1972), of South Petherton, Somerset, and Margaret Joan, *née* Broderick (d 1985); *b* 13 Aug 1934; *Educ* Haileybury, ISC, Pembroke Coll Oxford (MA, BMBCh, DipBact, DTM&H); *m* 1, 12 April 1961, Anne (d 1984), da of George Boys (d 1953), of Huddersfield; 2 s (Michael b 1963, Thomas b 1969), 1 da (Suky b 1965); m 2, Sonia Jane, *née* David; *Career* house physician St Luke's Hosp Guildford 1960, pathologist Middx Hosp 1961-64 (house surgn 1960), Public Health Laboratory Serv Colindale 1965-68, dir Taunton Public Health Laboratory 1969-; FRCPath; *Recreations* climatology, travel; *Style—* Dr John Pether; Public Health Laboratory, Taunton & Somerset Hospitals, Musgrove Park Branch, Taunton, Somerset TA1 5DB (☎ 0823 335557)

PETHERICK, Christopher; DL (1982); yr s of George Gerald Petherick (d 1946), and his w, Lady Jeane Pleydell-Bouverie (d 1976), eldest da of 6 Earl of Radnor; *b* 29 March 1922; *Educ* Harrow; *m* 1951, Countess Charlotte Raben-Levetzau, da of Count Raben-Levetzau (d 1965; cr as Lehnsgreve of Christiansholm, by Christian VI, King of Denmark 1734); 2 s (Martin, Thomas), 2 da (Catherine, Harriet); *Career* served in WWII as Capt Life Gds; High Sheriff of Cornwall 1978-79; *Clubs* White's; *Style—* Christopher Petherick, Esq, DL; Porthpean House, St Austell, Cornwall (☎ 0726 72888)

PETHICK, Jan Stephen; s of Maj Thomas Francis Henry Pethick (d 1981), of Trewartha, Ventnor, IOW, and Denise Joyce, *née* Clark; *b* 16 Sept 1947; *Educ* Clifton, Jesus Coll Oxford (MA); *m* 20 Dec 1974, Belinda Patricia, da of Douglas Collins, of Hare Hatch House, Hare Hatch, Reading, Berks; 1 s (Benjamin b 18 May 1981), 2 da (Emily b 26 May 1975, Nancy b 15 April 1977); *Career* stock jobber trader Pinchin Denny & Co 1969-74, Midland Doherty Eurobond Trading 1975-77, head of Eurobond sales Lehman Bros Kuhn Loeb 1974-84, md Shearson Lehman Hutton Int Inc 1986-; tstee The Peper Harow Foundation; *Recreations* golf, tennis, squash; *Clubs* NZ Gold, Roehampton; *Style—* Jan Pethick, Esq; 71 Kew Green, Kew, Richmond, Surrey TW9 3AH (☎ 01 940 2426); Shearson Lehman Hutton International, One Broadgate, London EC2M 7HA (☎ 01 260 3123, fax 01 382 9598, telex 888881)

PETHIG, Prof Ronald; s of Charles Edward Pethig, of Sanderstead, Surrey, and Edith Jane, *née* Jones; *b* 10 May 1942; *Educ* Purley GS, Univ of Southampton (BSc, PhD, DSc), Univ of Nottingham (PhD); *m* 10 Aug 1968, Angela Jane, da of John Bryon Sampson, of Tibshelf, Derbyshire (d 1973); 1 s (Richard John b 16 June 1971), 1 da (Helen Jane b 17 Jan 1976); *Career* ICI Fell Univ of Nottingham 1968-71, corpn memb Marine Biological Laboratory Woods Hole USA 1982-, adjunct prof of physiology Med Univ S Carolina USA 1984-; Univ of Wales: reader 1982-86, personal chair 1986-, dir Inst of Molecular and Biomolecular Electronics 1986-, chm Gyros Technology Ltd 1989; CEng 1975, FIEE 1986; *Books* Dielectric and Electronic Properties of Biological Materials (1979); *Recreations* mountain walking, restoring old scientific instruments; *Style—* Prof Ronald Pethig; Lleyn, Telford Rd, Menai Bridge, Gwynedd LL59 5DT (☎ 0248 714362); Inst of Molecular and Biomolecular Electronics, Univ of Wales at Bangor, Dean St, Bangor, Gwynedd LL57 1UT (☎ 0248 351151, fax 0248 361429)

PETHYBRIDGE, Hon Mrs (Olivia Mary); *née* Hawke; da of 9 Baron Hawke (d 1985); *b* 5 April 1955; *Educ* Heathfield; *m* 1983, Timothy John Pethybridge, s of J H Pethybridge, of Barn Park, Bodmin, Cornwall; 1 s (Henry b 1989), 2 da (Maryrose b 1985, Flora b 1987); *Style—* The Hon Mrs Pethybridge; 64 Hendham Rd, London SW17 7DQ (☎ 071 682 0680)

PETHYBRIDGE, Prof Roger William; s of Arthur Pethybridge (d 1981), and Sadie Isobel, *née* Renshaw; *b* 28 March 1934; *Educ* Sedbergh, Univ of Oxford (MA), Univ of Geneva; *Career* prof and dir centre of Russian studies Univ of Swansea 1974, visiting professorships incl: Australian Nat Univ at Canberra; former memb ESRC Politics Ctee, Nat Assoc for Soviet & E European Studies, Br Cncl Ctee for Cultural Exchange with Russia, various ed boards; fell Kennan Inst; pubns incl: A Key to Soviet Politics- The Crisis of the Anti-Party Group (1962), Witnesses to the Russian Revolution (ed 1964), The Development of the Communist Bloc (ed 1965), A History of Postwar Russia (1966), The Spread of the Russian Revolution: Essays on 1917 (1972), The Social Prelude to Stalinism (1974), One Step Backwards, Two Step Forwards, Soviet Society and Politics under the New Economic Policy (1990), over 30 chapters and papers; *Clubs* Athenaeum; *Style—* Prof Roger Pethybridge; Centre of Russian Studies, University, Swansea (☎ 0792 205678)

PETIT, (Joseph) Adrien Letierė; s of Capt Joseph Paris Sydney Petit (d 1967), and Florence Georgina May, *née* Hawthorne (d 1959); *b* 6 May 1921; *Educ* Warwick Sch, Univ of Nottingham (BSc), Univ of Birmingham (Dip Eng); *m* 25 April 1959, Carroll Foster, da of Henry Alan Gould (d 1986); 1 s (Adam b 6 Nov 1963), 1 da (Marie-Louise b 9 Dec 1961); *Career* chm: C Brandauer & Co 1959-, Brandauer Holdings Ltd 1964-, Assmann Electronics Ltd 1976-85; regnl dir PE Consulting Gp 1971-73 (1952-73) former cncllr Leamington Borough Cncl (vice chm various ctees incl fin), chm men's branch Leamington Cons Pty, fell Huguenot Soc GB, treas Inst of Mgmnt Conslts (pres 1979-80); memb Soc of Genealogists, FCIS, FIMC; *Recreations* travel, music, genealogy; *Clubs* IOD; *Style—* Adrien Petit, Esq; C Brandauer & Co Ltd, 401-414 New John St West, Birmingham B19 3PF (☎ 021 359 2822)

PETIT, Sir Dinshaw Manockjee; 4 Bt (UK 1890), of Petit Hall, Island of Bombay; né Nasserwanjee Dinshaw Petit but obliged, under a trust created by Sir Dinshaw Manockjee Petit, 1 Bt, to adopt the name of the first Bt; s of Sir Dinshaw Manockjee Petit, 3 Bt (d 1983), and Sylla (d 1963); *b* 13 Aug 1934; *m* 1, 1964 (m dis 1985), Nirmala Mody (surname of stepfather assumed by Deed Poll 1964), *née* Nanavati; 2 s, (Jehangir b 1965, Framjee b 1968); m 2, Elizabeth Maria Tinkelenberg; *Heir* s, Jehangir b 21 Jan 1965; *Career* Pres: NM Petit Charities, Sir D M Petit Charities, F D Petit Sanatorium, Persian Zoroastrian Amelioration fund, Petit Girls' Orphanage, D M Petit gymnasium, JN Petit Inst, Native Gen Dispensary; tstee Soc for Prevention of Cruelty to Animals and memb managing ctee B D Petit Parsi Gen Hosp; *Style—* Sir Dinshaw Petit, Bt; Petit Hall, Nepean Sea Rd, Bombay

PETIT, Jehangir; s and h to Sir Dinshaw Manockjee Petit, 4 Bt, *qv*; *b* 21 Jan 1965; *Style—* Jehangir Petit, Esq

PETO, Barbara, Lady; Barbara; da of Edwyn Thomas Close, of Woodcote, Camberley, Surrey; *m* 1935, Sir Christopher Henry Maxwell Peto, DSO, 3 Bt (d 1980); *Style—* Barbara, Lady Peto; Grey Walls, Chadlington, Oxford OX7 3NQ

PETO, Henry Christopher Morton Bampfylde; s and h of Sir Michael Henry Basil Peto, 4 Bt, of Childesden, Basingstoke, and Sarah Susan Worthington, *née* Stucley; *b* 8 April 1967; *Educ* Eton; *Recreations* tennis, psychology, football; *Style—* Henry Peto, Esq; Court Hall, North Molton, Devon EX36 3HP (☎ (059 84) 224)

PETO, Sir Henry George Morton; 4 Bt (UK 1855); s of Cdr Sir Henry Francis Morton Peto, 3 Bt, RN (d 1978); *b* 29 April 1920; *Educ* Sherborne, CCC Cambridge; *m* 1947, Frances Jacqueline, JP, da of late Ralph Haldane Evers; 2 s; *Heir* s, Francis Michael Morton Peto; *Career* RA 1939-46; manufacturing industry 1946-80; *Style—* Sir Henry Peto, Bt; Stream House, Selborne, Alton, Hants (☎ 042 050 246)

PETO, Sir Michael Henry Basil; 4 Bt (UK 1927); s of Brig Sir Christopher Henry Maxwell Peto, 3 Bt, DSO (d 1980); *b* 6 April 1938; *Educ* Eton, Ch Ch Oxford (MA); *m* 1, 1963 (m dis 1970), Sarah Susan, da of Maj Sir Dennis Stucley, 5 Bt; 1 s, 2 da; m 2, 1971, Lucinda Mary, da of Maj Sir Charles Douglas Blackett, 9 Bt; 2 s; *Heir* s, Henry Christopher Morton Bampfylde Peto b 8 April 1967; *Career* called to the bar Inner Temple 1960, memb Stock Exchange 1965-; dir Barnett Consulting Group 1985-; *Clubs* Pratt's; *Style—* Sir Michael Peto, Bt; Lower Church Cottage, Cliddesden, Basingstoke, Hants

PETO, Hon Mrs (Selina Lillian); *née* Hughes-Young; da of late 1 Baron St Helens, MC; *b* 1944; *m* 1969, Jonathan Basil Morton Peto (gs of Sir Basil Edward Peto, 1 Bt); 2 s, 3 da; *Style—* The Hon Mrs Peto

PETRE, His Hon Judge; Francis Herbert Loraine; s of late Maj-Gen R L Petre, CB, DSO, MC; *b* 9 March 1927; *Educ* Downside, Clare Coll Cambridge; *m* 1958, Mary Jane, da of Everard White, of Masterton, NZ; 3 s, 1 da; *Career* called to the Bar Lincoln's Inn 1952, dep chm E Suffolk QS 1970, dep chm Agric Lands Tbnl (Eastern area) 1972, a circuit judge 1972-, regular judge central criminal court 1982; chm Police Complaints Authy 1989; *Style—* His Honour Judge Petre; The Ferriers, Bures, Suffolk CO8 5DL (☎ 0787 227254)

PETRE, 18 Baron (E 1603); John Patrick Lionel Petre; o s of 17 Baron Petre (d 1989), and Marguerite Eileen, *née* Hamilton; *b* 4 Aug 1942; *Educ* Eton, Trinity Coll Oxford (MA); *m* 16 Sept 1965, Marcia Gwendolyn, o da of Alfred Plumpton, of Portsmouth; 2 s (Hon Dominic William, Hon Mark Julian b 1969), 1 da (Hon Clare Helen b 1973); *Heir* s, Hon Dominic William Petre b 9 Aug 1966; *Style—* The Rt Hon Lord Petre; Writtle Park, Essex

PETRI, Dr Michael Philip; s of Philip Ludvis Carr Petri (d 1977), and Beryl Katherine, *née* Wood; *b* 17 April 1956; *Educ* Univ of London (MB BS); *m* 22 May 1976, Linda Mary, da of Alan Powell; 1 s (Robert b 1988), 2 da (Lydia b 1982, Marissa b 1983); *Career* currently conslt physician Polle; MRCP 1980; *Style—* Dr Michael Petri; Poole General Hosptial, Poole, Dorset ☎ 0202 675100

PETRIE, Charles James; s and h of Sir Peter Petrie, 5 Bt, CMG; *b* 16 Sept 1959; *Educ* American Coll Paris (BA), INSEAD Fontainebleau (MBA); *m* 1981, France, yr da of Comte Bernard de Hauteclocque, of Châ- teau d'Etrejust, Picardie; 2 s (Arthur Cecil b 15 Feb 1987, Oliver Bernard b 12 July 1989), 1 da (Cecilia Marie Bernard b and d 1985); *Career* 2 Lt 67 French Inf Regt; devpt conslt Coopers & Lybrand 1987-; *Style—* Charles Petrie, Esq; c/o Sir Peter Petrie, Bt, CMG, 16a Cambridge Street, London SW1V 4QH

PETRIE, James Colquhoun; s of Dr James Beattie Petrie (d 1966), of London, and Dr Cairine Ross Petrie; *b* 18 Sept 1941; *Educ* Robert Gordon's Coll Aberdeen, Univ of Aberdeen (MB, ChB); *m* 16 July 1964, Dr (Margaret) Xanthe Patricia, da of Col Sir John Stewart Forbes, 6 Bt, DSO (d 1984); 2 s (John b 1965, Mark b 1969), 2 da (Rachel b 1967, Paula b 1970); *Career* hon conslt physician Aberdeen Teaching Hosps 1971-, prof of clinical pharmacology Univ of Aberdeen 1985-; chm Lecht Ski Co; FRCP, FRCPE (memb cncl), FFPM; *Books* The Problem Orientated Medical Record (with N McIntyre, 1979), Clinically Important Adverse Drug Interactions vol 1-3 (1985), Textbook of Medical Treatment (ed with R H Girwood, 1988); *Recreations* ski, golf, fishing; *Clubs* Royal Aberdeen Golf; *Style—* Prof James Petrie; Clinical Pharmacology Unit, University of Aberdeen, Polwarth Building, Fosterhill, Aberdeen AB2 4DQ (☎ 0224 681818, fax 0224 685157)

PETRIE, Dowager Lady; Jessie Ariana Borthwick; *née* Campbell; da of late Cdr Patrick Straton Campbell, JP, RN, of Westleton, Saxmundham, Suffolk; *m* 27 Nov 1962, Lt-Col Sir (Charles) Richard Borthwick Petrie, 4 Bt, TD (d 1988); *Style—* Dowager Lady Petrie; 3 Northmoor Road, Oxford

PETRIE, Sir Peter Charles; CMG (1980); 5 Bt (UK 1918); s of Sir Charles Petrie, 3 Bt (d 1977), and of Cecilia, Lady Petrie (d 1987); suc his half-bro, Sir Richard Petrie, 4 Bt 1988; *b* 7 March 1932; *Educ* Westminster, Ch Ch Oxford (MA); *m* 1958, Countess Lydwine Maria Fortunata, da of Count Charles Alphonse Von Oberndorff, of The Hague and Paris; 2 s, 1 da; *Heir* s, Charles James Petrie b 16 Sept 1959; *Career* 2 sec UK Delegation NATO Paris 1958-61, 1 sec New Delhi 1961-64, chargé d'affaires Katmandu 1963, Cabinet Office 1965-67, UK Mission to UN (NY) 1969-73, cnsllr (head of Chancery) Bonn 1973-76, head of Euro Integration Dept (Int) FCO 1976-79, min Paris 1979-85; ambass to Belgium 1985-89; Euro advsr to govr Bank of England 1989-; *Clubs* Brooks's, Jockey (Paris); *Style—* Sir Peter Petrie, Bt, CMG; 16A Cambridge St, London SW1V 4QH

PETSOPOULOS, Lady Charlotte Mary Roberte Paul; *née* Ponsonby; da of 10 Earl of Bessborough; *b* 1949; *m* 1974, Yanni Petsopoulos; 1 s; *Style—* The Lady Charlotte Petsopoulos; 43 Pembridge Villas, London W11 3EP (☎ 071 727 8809)

PETTERSSON, Dr Rosemary Winifred; da of Arthur Reginald Atkinson (d 1980), and Marjorie Edith Sarah, *née* Orchard (d 1985); *b* 23 May 1939; *Educ* St Joseph's Convent Wanstead, Wanstead Co HS, Royal Free Hosp, Univ of London (MB BS); *m* 9 May 1964, Dr Michael Jollius Pettersson, s of Dr Max Leopold Robert Pettersson, of 19 Joy Lane, Whitstable, Kent; 2 da (Hannah b 1 Dec 1966, Elizabeth b 20 July 1968); *Career* conslt physician in med for the elderly; memb Hosp and Health Bd Ctees; memb Soc of Med and Dental Hypnosis, LRCP, MRCS; *Recreations* reading, walking, cooking, gardening, cats; *Style—* Dr Rosemary Pettersson; Greenrig, Hawksland, Lesmahagow, Lanark ML11 9QB (☎ 0555 4866); Department of Medicine for the Elderly, Law Hospital, Carluke, Lanarkshire ML8 5ER (☎ 0698) 351100)

PETTIFER, Brian Warren Bowers; s of Fred Tyler Pettifer (d 1965), of Alfryn House, Grimsby, S Humberside, and Chrystine, *née* Thompson; *b* 10 Oct 1935; *Educ* Oundle; *m* 2 Oct 1965, Veronica Mary, da of Dr Georg Tugendhat (d 1973), of Greensted Hall, Greensted, Ongar, Essex; 3 s (Crispin b 1967, Adam b 1969, Daniel b 1970), 1 da (Teresa b 1974); *Career* served HAC 1963-66, admitted slr 1963; fndr own practice 1966, underwriter Lloyd's 1977-; CCncllr: Lindsey 1970-74, Humberside 1974-77; chief whip cons pty and shadow chm for planning 1974-77; chm: Humberside Youth Assoc 1974-75, Barton on Humber Youth Centre Mgmnt Ctee 1974-88, Humberside Euro Cons Cncl 1983-86; capt Law Soc GC 1985-86; *Recreations* skiing, golf, tennis; *Clubs* Oriental; *Style—* Brian Pettifer, Esq; Cob Hall, Priestgate, Barton-on-Humber, S Humberside DN18 5ET (☎ 0652 32248); Pettifer & Co, 26 Priestgate, Barton-on-Humber, S Humberside DN18 5ET (☎ 0652 660660, fax 0652 660077)

PETTIFER, Julian; s of Stephen Henry Pettifer (d 1980), of Malmesbury, Wilts, and Diana Mary, *née* Burton; *b* 21 July 1935; *Educ* Marlborough, St John's Coll Cambridge (BA); *Career* Nat Serv 1953-55, basic trg with Rifle Bde, cmmnd Northamptonshire Regt, served as 2 Lt in Korea and Hong Kong; tv broadcaster and author; tv series include: BBC Tonight, Panorama, 24 Hours, Diamonds in the Sky, The Living Isles, Missionaries, ITV's Nature Watch, Automania; awarded BAFTA Reporter of the Year 1968-69; memb cncl World Wide Fund for Nature; vice-chm British Wildlife Appeal; hon pres Malmesbury Civic Tst; *Books* Diamonds in the Sky (with Kenneth Hudson, 1979), Automania (with Nigel Turner, 1984), Nature Watch (with Robin Brown, 1981),

Missionaries (with Richard Bradley, 1990); *Recreations* music, theatre, tennis, gardening, books; *Clubs* Queen's; *Style—* Julian Pettifer, Esq; c/o Curtis Brown, 162-168 Regent St, London W1R 5TB

PETTINGELL, (Peter) John Partington; s of Hubert Edmund Pettingell (d 1980), and Avril Leah Nancy Pettingell (d 1985); *b* 28 Jan 1934; *Educ* Leeds GS, London Univ (BD); *m* 31 July 1965, Phyllis Margaret, da of Charles Chamberlain (d 1983); 1 s (John Stephen Edmund b 3 Jan 1973), 2 da (Julie Margaret b 5 Oct 1966, Susan Jane b 2 April 1968); *Career* Nat Serv RAF 1956-58; audit mangr WL Gallant & Co 1958-60, audit supervisor Price Waterhouse 1960-63, chief accountant GLC London 1963-65, sr lectr SW London Coll 1973-77, princ lectr Hong Kong Poly 1977-80, sr lectr Dorset Inst Higher Educn 1980-86, princ Partington Pettingell & Co 1983-; min Stockwell Baptist Church 1973-77; Lord of the Manor of Donhead Wilts; FCA 1956; *Books* Then the Spirit Came (1975), Jesus is Coming (1974); *Recreations* sailing, badminton, tennis; *Style—* John Pettingell, Esq; 41A Southern Rd, Bournemouth, Dorset (☎ 0202 431 406)

PETTIT, Sir Daniel Eric Arthur; s of Thomas Edgar Pettit (d 1940), of Liverpool, and Pauline Elizabeth, *née* Kerr (d 1957); *b* 19 Feb 1915; *Educ* Quarry Bank HS Liverpool, Fitzwilliam Coll Cambridge (MA); *m* 1940, Winifred, da of William Standing Bibby, of Liverpool (d 1951); 2 s (Richard, *qv*, Michael); *Career* Mil Serv 1940-46, RA; serv: UK, Africa, India, Burma; Major (RA) TA, Hon Col (movement); UK team Olympic Games 1936; sch master 1938-39, 1946-47; Unilever MGT 1948-59; chm: SPD Ltd (Unilever) 1960-70, Nat Freight Corp 1970-78; dir: Bransford Farmers Ltd 1973-, Bransford Leisure Ltd 1973-, Lloyd's Bank Ltd 1977-78; chm Birmingham and W Midlands Lloyd's Bank Ltd 1978-85, dir Lloyd's Bank (UK) Ltd 1979-85; pres and chm: Incpen 1979-90, PosTel Investmt Ltd 1982-83; dir: Black Horse Ltd 1984-85, Lloyd's Bank Unit Tst 1984-85; chm RDC Properties Ltd 1987-; memb: Nat Ports Cncl 1971-80, Freight Integration Cncl 1971-78, Fndn of Mgmnt Educn 1973-78; chm: Econ Devpt Ctee for Distributive Trades 1974-78, Post Office Staff Superannuation Fund 1979-83; Freeman City of London 1971, Liveryman Worshipful Co of Carmen 1971; hon fell Fitzwilliam Coll Cambridge 1985; pres CInst of Tport 1972, CBIM, FCIT, FRSA, MIPM; kt 1974; *Recreations* cricket, football, fishing, shooting; *Clubs* Hawks (Cambridge), MCC, Farmers'; *Style—* Sir Daniel Pettit; Bransford Court Farm, Worcester WR65 5JL (☎ 0905 830098)

PETTIT, Richard William; s of Sir Daniel Pettit *qv*, and Winifred, *née* Bibby; *b* 11 Nov 1941; *Educ* Westminster, St John's Coll Oxford (MA); *m* 1967, Jane Anne, da of Wing Cdr Duncan Basset McGill, of Ruthin Castle, Clwyd; 1 s, 1 da; m 2, Alicia Margaret, da of Albert Ernest Stone, of Bristol; *Career* md Vaux Brewery Sunderland (formerly operations dir); md DRG Cartons Bristol, memb CBI northern regn Cncl 1978-83; CEng, MIMechE, MIProdE, MBIM; *Recreations* farming, fishing, model railways; *Clubs* RAC; *Style—* Richard Pettit Esq; Blackmountain Farm, Newcastle-on-Clun, Craven Arms, Shropshire SY7 8PL

PETTIT, Rosemary; da of G H N Pettit, and Ruby, *née* Garner; *b* 22 May 1944; *Educ* Bury St Edmunds GS, Bedford Coll London (BSc); *Career* copy ed Penguin Books 1971-73, researcher LWT 1973-74, section ed Marshall Cavendish 1974-75; sec: Ind Publishers Guild 1979-89, Book Packagers Assoc 1985-, Dir Publishers Assoc 1989-; jt ed Traditional Acupuncture Journal 1982-90; memb Liberal Party 1979, Social and Liberal Democrat candidate for By Election 1989 (Cncl elections 1982); *Books* The Craft Business (1975), Occupation Self Employed (2 edn, 1981); *Style—* Ms Rosemary Pettit; 93A Blenheim Crescent, London W11 2EQ (☎ 071 221 9089)

PETTMAN, Prof Barrie Owen; s of Matthew Mark Pettman (d 1967), and Ivy, *née* Warcup; *b* 22 Feb 1944; *Educ* Hull GS, Hull Tech Coll (BSc), City Univ Business Sch (MSc, PhD); *m* 1, 1970 (m dis 1986), Heather Richardson; m 2, 1987, Norma, da of Walter Albert Bonser (d 1974); *Career* lectr Dept of Social Admin Univ of Hull 1970-82, dir Manpower Unit Univ of Rhodesia 1978-79, registrar Int Mgmnt Centres 1983-; dir: MCB Univ Press 1970-, Int Inst of Social Econ 1972-; ed: Management Research News 1981-, International Journal of Sociology & Social Policy 1984-, International Journal of Social Economics 1973-79, International Journal of Manpower 1980-84, Industrial Relations News 1982-84; jt ed Managerial Law 1975-; asst ed: Employee Relations 1978-82, Equal Opportunities International 1982-; visiting prof Canadian Sch of Mgmnt 1983-, hon vice pres Br Soc of Commerce 1975-; chm: Inst of Sci Business 1972-79, Inst of Trg and Devpt Humberside Branch 1990-; memb: Manpower Soc 1977-, Int Inst of Social Econs, FCI, FRGS, FRSA, FITD, MBIM; *Books* Training and Retraining (1973), Labour Turnover and Retention (1975), Equal Pay (1975), Manpower Planning Workbook (1976, 1984), Industrial Democracy (1984), Discrimination in the Labour Market (1980), Management: A Selected Bibliography (1983); *Recreations* golf, shooting; *Clubs* The Reform; *Style—* Prof Barrie Pettman; Enholmes Hall, Patrington, Hull HU12 0PR (☎ 0964 630033); MCB University Press, 62 Toller Lane, Bradford, W Yorkshire BD8 9BY (☎ 0274 499821, telex 51317, fax 0274 547143, car 0860 813688)

PETTY, Very Rev John Fitzmaurice; s of Dr Gerald Fitzmaurice Petty, TD, MRCS, LRCP, FRCGP (d 1986), and Edith Stuart, *née* Knox (d 1977); *b* 9 March 1935; *Educ* King's Sch Bruton, RMA Sandhurst, Trinity Hall Cambridge (MA), Cuddesdon Theol Coll Oxford; *m* 10 Aug 1963, Susan, da of Sir Geoffrey Peter Shakerley (d 1982); 3 s (Simon b 1967, Mark b 1969, Jeremy b 1972), 1 da (Rachel b 1965); *Career* cmmnd RE 1955, seconded Gurkha Engrs Malaya/Borneo 1959-62, resigned cmmn as Capt 1964; ordained Sheffield Cath: deacon 1966, priest 1967; curate St Cuthbert's Fir Vale Sheffield 1966-69, p-in-c Bishop Andrewes' Church Southwark 1969-75, area dean Ashton-Under-Lyme 1975-87, vicar St John's Hurst Ashton-under-Lyne 1983-87, hon canon Manchester Cathedral 1986, provost of Coventry 1988-; hon chaplain RAPC (Offrs Accounts) Ashton-under-Lyne 1977-87; memb Ctee St Helier Artificial Kidney Fund (SHAK) 1967-69, chm Tameside Aids and Services for the Handicapped (TASH) 1981-87; co-ordinator: Home for Homeless Girls Tameside 1977-87, Ambulance for the Elderley 1976-87, Holidays for Belfast Families 1977-86; *Recreations* squash, skiing; *Style—* The Very Rev the Provost of Coventry; Provost's Lodge Priory Row, Coventry CV1 5ES (☎ 0203 221835); Coventry Cathedral, 7 Priory Row, Coventry CV1 5ES (☎ 0203 227 597)

PEVSNER, Dieter; s of Sir Nikolaus Pevsner, CBE (d 1983); *b* 2 Aug 1932; *Career* jt dep md André Deutsch Ltd 1981-; formerly sr ed Penguin; fndr and jt owner Wildwood House (publishers) 1971-81; *Style—* Dieter Pevsner, Esq; c/o André Deutsch Ltd, 105 Gt Russell St, WC1 (☎ 01 580 2746)

PEYRONEL, Alexandra Louise; *née* Rubens; da of Col Ralph Alexander Rubens, of 27 Gertrude St, London SW10, 3 husb of Lady Rosemary (d 1963), *née* Eliot, er da of 6 Earl of St Germans, MC, and Lady Blanche Douglas, *née* Somerset, da of 9 Duke of Beaufort; through Lady Blanche she is co-heiress (with Samantha Cope and Lady Cathleen Hudson, *qqv*) to the Baronies of Botetourt and Herbert, which went into abeyance on the death of 10 Duke of Beaufort, KG, GCVO, PC (1984); *b* 9 Oct 1951; *Educ* St Martin's and Byam Shaw Schs of Art (BA); *m* 1976, Daniel Augusto Peyronel, s of HE Vice-Adm Aldo Peyronel, of Buenos Aires and Mar del Plata; 1 s; *Recreations* tennis, swimming, riding, hunting; *Style—* Mrs Daniel Peyronel

PEYSSON, Hon Mrs (Elizabeth Cecilia); *née* Shaw; *née* Shaw yst da of Baron Kilbrandon, PC (Life Peer), *qv*; *b* 1948; *m* 1984, Jean-Marc Peysson; 1 s (Jean-Christophe b 1986); *Style—* The Hon Mrs Peysson; La Gautrivière, 03160 Bourbon l'Archambault, Allier, France

PEYTON, Kathleen Wendy; da of William Joseph Herald, and Ivy Kathleen, *née* Weston; *b* 2 Aug 1929; *Educ* Wimbledon HS, Manchester Sch of Art (ATD, Carnegie medal, Guardian award); *m* Sept 1950, Michael Peyton; 2 da (Hilary b 1956, Veronica b 1958); *Career* author; art teacher Northampton HS 1953-55; *Publications incl* as Kathleen Herald: Sabre the Horse from the Sea (1947), The Mandrake (1949), Crab the Roan (1953); as K M Peyton: Flambards (Guardian award, 1967), The Edge of the Cloud (Carnegie medal, 1969), Flambards in Summer (1969), Pennington's Seventeenth Summer (1970), A Pattern of Roses (1972), Prove Yourself a Hero (1977), A Midsummer Night's Death (1978), Flambards Divided (1981), Dear Fred (1981), Who, Sir? Me, Sir? (1983), The Sound of Distant Cheering (1985), Darkling (1989), No Roses Round the Door (1990), Poor Badger (1990); memb Soc of Authors; *Recreations* riding, walking, gardening; *Style—* Mrs Kathleen Peyton; Rookery Cottage, North Fambridge, Chelmsford, Essex CM3 6LP (☎ 0621 828 545)

PEYTON, Hon Thomas Richard Douglas; o s of Baron Peyton of Yeovil, PC (Life Peer); *b* 5 April 1950; *Educ* Eton; *m* 1981, Vivien, da of Dr Jack Birks, CBE; 1 s (Joseph Anthony Charles b 1986); *Style—* The Hon Thomas Peyton; BP Oil Middle East, PO Box 299, Manama, Bahrain

PEYTON OF YEOVIL, Baron (Life Peer UK 1983), of Yeovil, Co Somerset; John Wynne William Peyton; PC (1970); s of Ivor Eliot Peyton (d 1938), of Englemere Wood, Ascot, and Dorothy Helen, *née* Elphinstone (d 1977); *b* 13 Feb 1919; *Educ* Eton, Trinity Coll Oxford (MA); *m* 1, Dec 1947 (m dis 1966), Diana, da of Douglas Clinch, of Durban, S Africa; 1 s (Hon Tom), 1 da (Hon Sarah (Hon Mrs Graham-Campbell)), and 1 s decd; m 2, 27 July 1966, Mary Constance, only da of Col Hon Humphrey Wyndham, MC (6 s of 2 Baron Leconfield), and former w of Ralph Hamilton Cobbold; *Career* served 15/19 Hussars WWII (POW 1940-45); called to the Bar Inner Temple 1945; MP (C) Yeovil 1951-83, Parly sec Miny of Power 1962-64, min of Transport 1970, min for Transport Industries DOE 1970-74, chm Texas Instruments Ltd 1974-90; dir: British Alcan Aluminium plc 1974 (chm 1987-91), Alcan Aluminium Ltd 1985-91; treas Zoological Soc of London 1984-, chm Zoo Operations Ltd 1988-; pres Devon Guild of Craftsmen 1988-; *Clubs* Boodle's, Pratt's; *Style—* The Rt Hon the Lord Peyton of Yeovil, PC; The Old Malt House, Hinton St George, Somerset TA17 8SE (☎ 0460 73618); 6 Temple West Mews, West Sq, London SE11 4TJ (☎ 071 582 3611)

PFEFFER, Dr Jeremy Michael; s of Maurice Leslie Pfeffer, of Manchester, and Hannah, *née* Posen; *b* 23 Sept 1946; *Educ* Manchester GS, UCH London (MB BS, BSc); *m* 5 Sept 1972, Vivian Barbara, da of Dr Eric Norman, of Liverpool; 2 s (James b 1978, Paul b 1979); *Career* house surgn Professorial Surgical Unit UCH London 1972, house physician Newmarket Gen Hosp 1972-73, sr house offr and registrar chest med Papworth Hosp Cambridge 1973-74, sr house offr psychiatry Fulbourn Hosp Cambridge 1974-75, sr house offr and registrar psychiatry Bethlem Royal and Maudsley Hosp 1975-78, sr registrar psychiatry The London and Bethlem Royal and Maudsley Hosps 1978-80, conslt psychiatrist The Royal London Hosp 1980-, hon conslt psychiatrist Royal Brompton Hosp; examiner RCPsych, offr and memb of Med and Psychiatric Ctees at local regnl and nat level; MRCP UK 1974, MRCPsych 1977, FRCPsych 1988, FRCP 1990, memb RSM; *Books* Medicine and Psychiatry: A Practical Approach (ed with Francis Creed, 1982), Psychiatric Differential Diagnosis (with Gillian Waldron, 1987); *Recreations* music, reading, food, football; *Style—* Dr Jeremy Pfeffer; The London Hosp, London E1 1BB (☎ 071 377 7168)

PHAIR, Michael Keith; s of George Carlton Phair, of Ontario, Canada, and Mary Lucille, *née* Munro; *b* 24 June 1950; *Educ* Univ of Western Ontario (BA), Graduate Sch of Business Univ of Western Ontario (MBA); *m* 21 July 1973, Margaret Noreen (Margot), da of Charles Alexander Joseph Rogers, of Buenos Aires; 1 s (Nicholas b 20 Aug 1982), 1 da (Stephanie b 16 Aug 1978); *Career* sr rep Mexico Toronto Dominion Bank 1975-79, pres Banque Anval S America Panama 1979-84, sr investmts offr Capital Mkts Dept Int Fin Corp Washington DC 1984-87, dir corp fin NM Rothschild & Son Ltd 1988-; memb: Latin American Ctee London C of C, Canning Club, Canada and UK C of C; *Recreations* squash, tennis, sailing; *Style—* Michael K Phair, Esq; PO Box 185, New Court, St Swithin's Lane, London EC4P 4DN (☎ 071 280 5494, fax 071 626 0799)

PHAM, Prof Duc-Truong; s of Van-Xam Pham, of Hochiminh City, Vietnam and ThiNinh, *née* Vu; *b* 16 Feb 1952; *Educ* Univ of Canterbury NZ (BEng, PhD); *m* 19 May 1979, Paulette Thi Nga, da of Pierre Laforet, of Lyon, France; 1 da (Kim-Anh b 1982); *Career* lectr Univ of Birmingham 1979-88, prof of engrg Univ of Wales 1988-; *Books* Robot Grippers (ed with WB Heginbotham, 1986), Expert Systems in Engineering (ed, 1988), Artificial Intelligence in Design (ed, 1990); *Style—* Prof Duc-Truong Pham; School of Electrical Electronic and Systems Engineering, University of Wales, PO Box 904, Cardiff CF1 3YH (☎ 0222 874429, fax 0222 874192, telex 497 368)

PHARO-TOMLIN, Col John Axel; s of Axel Christian Pharo-Tomlin (d 1965), of Dane Court, St Peters-in-Thanet, Kent, and Edith Madelaine Quayle, *née* Tomlin (d 1974); *b* 8 April 1934; *Educ* Radley, RMA Sandhurst; *m* 19 Dec 1964, Joanna Marguerite Kate, da of Lt-Col John Boileau Pemberton (d 1974), of Coaxdon Hall, Axminster, Devon; 1 s (Edward b 1968), 2 da (Sally b 1965, Alice b 1975); *Career* cmmnd 14/20 King's Hussars 1954, Adj 1961, instr RMA Sandhurst 1963, RNSC 1966, Sqdn Ldr 14/20 King's Hussars 1967, GSO 2 Singapore Dist 1968, Second-in-Cmd Duke of Lancaster's Own Yeo 1971, Bde Major 11 Armoured Bde 1972, GSO 1 Operational Requirements MOD 1975, CO 14/20 King's Hussars 1977 (despatches 1979), Col AG 16/17/18 MOD 1980, Col M1 (A) MOD 1984, ret 1986; mangr Banque Paribas London 1986-; Freeman City of London 1987; FBIM 1984; *Recreations* country pursuits, music; *Clubs* Cavalry and Guards'; *Style—* Col John Pharo-Tomlin; Banque Paribas, 68 Lombard St, London EC3V 9EH (☎ 071 9294545/071 9555367, fax 071 7266761, telex 945881/886055)

PHAROAH, Prof Peter Oswald Derrick; s of Oswald Higgins Pharoah (d 1941), and Phylis Christine, *née* Gahan; *b* 19 May 1934; *Educ* Lawrence Meml Royal Mil Sch Lovedale India, Palmers Sch Grays Essex, Univ of London (MD, MSc); *m* 17 May 1960, Margaret Rose, da of James McMinn (d 1979); 3 s (Paul b 1962, Mark b 1966, Timothy b 1975), 1 da (Fiona b 1961); *Career* med offr Dept of Public Health Papua New Guinea 1963-74, sr lectr London Sch of Hygiene and Tropical Med 1974-79, prof community health Univ of Liverpool 1979-; FFCM 1980; *Recreations* philately, squash, walking; *Style—* Prof Peter Pharoah; 11 Fawley Road, Liverpool L18 9TE (☎ 051 724 4896); Dept of Community Health, University of Liverpool, Liverpool L69 3BX (☎ 051 794 5577)

PHAYRE, Maj Robert Dermot Spinks (Robin); s of Col Robert Desmond Hensley Phayre, and Barbara Charlton, *née* Spinks; *b* 3 Nov 1949; *Educ* Rugby, Trent Poly (BA); *m* 11 Dec 1976, Jane Elisabeth Stirling, da of Maj Michael Ranulph Vincent; 2 da (Katherine b 1980, Jemma b 1983); *Career* Adj LI Depot 1978-80, platoon instr RMA Sandhurst 1980, Army Staff Coll Camberley 1981-82, Co Cdr 2 Bn LI 1983-84, S02 GI OPS HQ (BR) Corps 1985-86, 2 i/c 1 Bn LI 1987-89, chief instr Signal Wing Sch of Inf 1989-; Freeman: City of London, City of Shrewsbury; Liveryman Worshipful Co of

Haberdashers; MITD 1989; *Recreations* sailing, tennis, squash, Hash House Harrier; *Style—* Major Robin Phayre; c/o Lloyds Bank, 30 High St, Crediton, Devon

PHEASANT, Victor Albert; MBE (1983); s of Albert George Pheasant (d 1976), of Bexleyheath, Kent, and Margaret, *née* Williams; *b* 2 July 1940; *Educ* Erith Technical Sch; *m* 21 Oct 1961, Susan Mary, da of Arthur Waldron Slade, of Rothwell, Northamptonshire; 2 s (Andrew Victor b 1962, Richard Michael b 1965); *Career* RAF 1960-84: air crew Strike Cmd 1960-80, RAF Central Tactics and Trials Orgn CTTO 1980-84, ret as Sqdn Ldr; projects dir Chemring Gp plc 1985-; *Recreations* carpentry; *Clubs* RAF; *Style—* Victor A Pheasant, Esq, MBE; Heathcote, Purbrook Heath, Portsmouth, Hants PO7 5RX (☎ 0705 263249); Chemring Gp plc, Rodney Rd, Fratton, Portsmouth, Hants (☎ 0705 735457, fax 0705 817509)

PHELAN, His Hon Judge Andrew James; s of Cornelius Phelan, of Clonmel, Ireland; *b* 25 July 1923; *Educ* Clongoweswood Co Kildare, Nat Univ of Ireland, Trinity Coll Cambridge; *m* 1950, Joan Robertson, da of John McLagan (d 1978), of Callender, Perthshire; 1 s, 2 da; *Career* barr: (Ireland) King's Inn 1945, Gray's Inn 1949; jr fell Univ of Bristol 1948-50, circuit judge 1974-; *Recreations* skiing, sailing (yacht 'Sarakiniko'); *Clubs* Royal Cruising, Bar YC; *Style—* His Hon Judge Phelan; 17 Hartington Rd, Chiswick, London W4 3TL (☎ 081 994 6109)

PHELAN, Dr Martin Kennedy; s of John Lazarian Phelan (d 1986), of Balleymullen, Abbeyleix, Eire, and Mary Prisca, *née* Kennedy (d 1964); *b* 24 Oct 1938; *Educ* Finchley Catholic GS, UCH London (BDS, LDSRCS, DOrth, capt and colours for football), Clare Coll and Addenbrookes Hosp Cambridge (LMSSA, MB BChir), London Coll of Osteopathic Med (MLCOM); *m* 10 June 1968, Almut Brigitte, da of Johannes Karl Wünsche; 3 s (Sean b 22 May 1968, Timothy b 11 Nov 1970, Patrick b 24 July 1976), 2 da (Marianne b 8 Sept 1969, Annette b 13 Jan 1981); *Career* various hosp jobs London and Univ of Cambridge, asst surgn Queen Elizabeth II Hosp Welwyn Garden City 1970, osteopathic physician UCH and Middlesex Hosp 1978-90; current appts: osteopathic physician Royal London Homeopathic Hosp, tutor London College of Osteopathic Medicine, private practitioner in orthopaedic osteopathic and sports medicine Harley St, med offr Newmarket Race Course, lectr in psychosomatic med and history of med; sr memb list Clare Coll Cambridge, sec then vice pres Anglo American Med Soc; FDSRCS, FRSM; Freeman City of London 1979, Yeoman then Liveryman Worshipful Soc of Apothecaries 1984; memb: BMA, Ctee Byron Soc, Euro Atlantic Gp, Anglo American Med Soc, Inst of Agric Med, Br Assoc of Manipulative Med, Br Osteopathic Assoc, Cambridge Med Soc, Cambridge Philosophical Soc, Hunterian Soc, Inst of Sports Med, Chelsea Clinical Soc; Cons Med Soc, Cncl Inst of Orthopaedic Med; *Recreations* horse riding, skiing, tennis, fishing, farming, country sports; *Clubs* Royal Society of Medicine London; *Style—* Dr Martin Kennedy Phelan; 137 Harley St, London W1N 1DJ (☎ 071 224 0557, fax 071 935 5972)

PHELIPS, David Edward; s of Cdre Harry Phelips, of Southampton, and Irene Woolcock (d 1943); formerly of Montacute House, Somerset, built by Sir Edward Phelips (1551-1614), Speaker of House of Commons and Master of the Rolls; *b* 6 Dec 1924; *Educ* Taunton Sch; *m* 4 Dec 1965, Claudie, da of Marcel Cambier, of Paris; *Career* RNVR 1943-46; dir: Harrisons & Crossfield Ltd S India 1951-60, Drix Plastics Ltd 1964-79, Montacute Estate Ltd 1979-; *Recreations* sailing; *Clubs* Naval, Master Mariners' (Southampton); *Style—* David E Phelips, Esq; Barn Close House, Itchen Abbas, Hampshire (☎ 096278 464); Montacute Estate Office

PHELPS, Charles Frederick; s of Capt Seth Arthur Rose Phelps, MBE (d 1978), of Peaslake, Surrey, and Rigmor Louise, *née* Kaae (d 1984); *b* 18 Jan 1934; *Educ* Bromsgrove, BNC Oxford (BSc, MA, DPhil, DSc); *m* 29 Feb 1960, Joanna, da of Eric Lingeman, CBE (d 1966), of Eaton Square, London; 1 s (Anthony John Rose b 8 Sept 1960), 1 da (Amanda Louise Barnett b 20 Sept 1962); *Career* Univ of Bristol: lectr in chem physiology 1960-63, reader in biochemistry 1970-74 (lectr 1963-70); prof of biochemistry Univ of Lancaster 1974-80, princ Chelsea Coll Univ of London 1980-84, pro-rector Imp Coll of Sci Technol and Med 1984-89 (advsr to rector on int affrs); memb: Res Ctee Arthritis and Rheumatism Cncl 1974-78, Ctee Br Biophysical Soc 1974-84 (chm 1983-84), editorial Bd Biochem Biophys ACTA 1976-80, Ctee Biochemical Soc 1980-84, editorial Bd Int Res Common Systems 1980-; govr: Furzedown Sch Battersea 1980-85, King Edward's Sch Witley 1984-, Mill Hill Sch 1985-, Royal GS Guildford 1988-, Royal Postgrad Med Fndn 1986-; fell King's Coll London 1985; *Books* Messenger RNA (ed with H R V Arnstein), Biotechnology (ed with P Clarke), Molecular Variants of Proteins (with P Campbell); *Recreations* landscape gardening, cooking, birdwatching; *Clubs* Athenaeum; *Style—* Prof Charles Phelps; Brockhurst, The Green, Chiddingfold, Surrey GU8 4TU (☎ 042 868 3092, fax 042 868 5297)

PHELPS, Hon Mrs (Helen Rosemary); da of late 3 Baron Cozens-Hardy; *b* 1918; *m* 1953, Brig Douglas Vandeleur Phelps, TD, JP, DL (d 1988); 1 adopted s (John Edward Vandeleur b 1961), 1 adopted da (Laura Douglas b 1959); *Style—* The Hon Mrs Phelps; Grove Farm House, Langham, Holt, Norfolk

PHELPS, Howard Thomas Henry Middleton; s of Ernest Henry Phelps (d 1981), of Gloucester, and Harriet Maria Ann, *née* Middleton (d 1978); *b* 20 Oct 1926; *Educ* Crypt GS Gloucester, Hatfield Coll Univ of Durham (BA); *m* 1949, Audrey, da of Thomas Ellis (d 1972); 1 da; *Career* dep dir industl rels NCB until 1972, dir of ops BA 1979-86 (personnel dir 1972-79); dir P & O Steam Navigation Co 1986-89, chm QA Training Ltd 1989-, dir Alden Press Ltd 1990-; chm: Earls Court and Olympia Ltd 1986-89, Sutcliffe Catering Gp Ltd 1986-89; FRAeS, FIPM, FCIT, CBIM; *Recreations* music, gardens; *Clubs* Royal Over-Seas; *Style—* Howard Phelps, Esq; Tall Trees, Chedworth, nr Cheltenham, Glos (☎ 0285 720324)

PHELPS, John Christopher; s of Anthony John Phelps, CB, of London, and Sheila Nan, *née* Rait (d 1967); *b* 25 May 1954; *Educ* Whitgift Sch S Croydon, Univ of Liverpool (LLB); *m* 13 April 1985, Isabelle Michele Jeanine, da of Maurice Albert Haumesser (d 1987), of Nancy, France; 1 s (Christopher b 1988); *Career* admitted slr 1978; ptnr Beachcroft Stanleys 1986; Freeman City of Oxford; *Books* Solicitors and VAT (with Julian Gizzi, 1986); *Recreations* football, rugby and cricket spectator, squash; *Clubs* MCC; *Style—* John Phelps, Esq; 20 Furnival St, London EC4A 1BN (☎ 071 242 1011, fax 071 430 1532, fax 071 430 1532, telex 264607 (BEALAW G)

PHELPS, Maurice; s of Harry Thomas Phelps (d 1973), and Lilian Carter; *b* 17 May 1935; *Educ* Wandsworth Sch, CCC Oxford (BA); *m* 1960, Elizabeth Anne; 2 s, 1 da; *Career* personnel dir Heavy Vehicle Div Leyland Vehicles 1977-80; Bd memb Personnel British Shipbuilders 1980-87, Br Ferries Ltd 1987-89; *Recreations* surfing, sailing, squash; *Style—* Maurice Phelps, Esq; Abbotsfield, Goring Heath, South Oxfordshire (☎ 0491 681916); Maurice Phelps Assocs & Emslie Phelps Assocs, Abbotsfield House, Goring Heath, Reading RG8 7SA (☎ 0491 682031)

PHELPS, Dr Peter David; s of Donald Percy (d 1944), of Little Chalfont, Bucks, and Phyllis Mabel, *née* Willis; *b* 22 May 1939; *Educ* Merchant Taylors', Charing Cross Hosp Med Sch Univ of London (MB BS, DMRD, MD); *Career* Charing Cross Hosp 1962-63, sr house offr of surgery Leicester Royal Infirmary 1964, radiology trg Radcliffe Infirmary Oxford 1969-72 (surgical training ENT 1966-68), conslt radiologist to Coventry Gp Hosp for Nervous Diseases 1974-, conslt radiologist to Royal Nat ENT Hosp 1987- (hon conslt to Gt Ormond St Children's Hosp London 1988-); contrib numerous chapters in radiology and ENT text books; memb: Inland Water Ways Assoc, Avon Canal Tst; FRCS 1968, FRCR 1973, MDU, memb BMA; *Books* Radiology of the Ear (with Dr G A S Lloyd, 1983); *Recreations* vintage cars, canals, rugby football; *Clubs* Vintage Sports; *Style—* Dr Peter Phelps; Doric House, Easenhall, Rugby, Warwickshire CV23 0JA (☎ 0788 832347); Dept of Radiology, Royal National Throat Nose and Ear Hosp, Gray's Inn Rd, London (☎ 071 837 8855); Radiology Dept, Walsgrave Hosp, Clifford Bridge Rd, Coventry

PHELPS, Richard Lawson; s of John Graham Phelps, and Barbara Phelps; *b* 19 April 1961; *Career* athlete (modern pentathlon); jr nat champion 1979, 1981 and 1982; sr nat champion 1979, 1981-84, 1986 and 1988; Team Bronze medalist (modern pentathlon) Seoul Olympics 1988; life memb: Modern Pentathlon Assoc of GB 1984, Gloucester City Swimming Club 1988; *Style—* Richard Phelps, Esq; c/o British Olympic Assoc, 1 Wandsworth Plain, London SW18 1EH

PHELPS, Richard Wintour; CBE (1986); s of late Rev H Phelps, of Sidmouth, Devon, and Elsie, *née* Pearce; *b* 26 July 1925; *Educ* Kingswood Sch Bath, Merton Coll Oxford (MA); *m* 12 Feb 1955, Pamela Marie Phelps; 2 da (Hilary Susan b 25 Oct 1957, Diana Gillian b 15 March 1961); *Career* Lt 14 Punjab Regt Indian Army 1944-46; HM Overseas CS Nigeria 1948-57 and 1959-61, princ home CS HM Treasy 1957-59 and 1961-65, gen mangr Skelmersdale New Town Devpt Corp 1967-71, gen mangr Central Lancs Devpt Corp 1971-86, sr admin Hants CC 1963-65; pt/t advsr on housing to: Govt of Vanuatu 1986-88, Govt of Falkland Islands 1988 and 1989; Parly candidate (Alliance) Barrow in Furness 1987, chm Examinations in Public of Derbyshire and Nottinghamshire Co Cncl Structure Plans 1989-90; *Recreations* travel, reading, bridge; *Clubs* Royal Cwlth Soc; *Style—* Richard Phelps, Esq, CBE; Fell Foot House, Newby Bridge, Ulverston, Cumbria LA12 8NL (☎ 053 95 312 74)

PHILIP SORENSEN, (Nils Jorgen) Philip; s of Erik Philip Sorensen, of Lillon, Skane, Sweden, and Brita Hjordis Bendix, *née* Lundgren (d 1984); *b* 29 Sept 1938; *Educ* Herlufsholm Kostskole Naerstved Denmark, Niels Brock Commercial Sch (CPH); *m* 1962, Ingrid, da of Eigil Baltzer-Andersen (d 1965); 1 s (Mark b 1973), 3 da (Annette b 1963, Christina b 1965, Louisa b 1968); *Career* estab modern security indust in Europe; chm and fndr Group 4 Securitas cos: UK, Ireland, Belgium, Cyprus, India, Luxembourg, Malta, Netherlands, Greece, Spain, Portugal; memb Bd various security cos in: Sweden, Australia, France, Japan, Thailand; pres Ligue Internationale des Societes de Surveillance; memb Cncl Br Security Indust Assoc; owner: Dormy House Hotel Broadway, Strandhotellet Skagen Denmark; Soldier of the Year award Sweden; hon citizen of Cork 1985; *Recreations* sailing (fishing vessel "Oke"), photography, travelling, book collecting; *Clubs* Bucks, Hurlingham, Annabel's, Harry's Bar, Mossimanns; *Style—* P Philip Sorensen, Esq; Farncombe House, Broadway, Worcestershire (☎ 0386 858585, fax 0386 858254)

PHILIPP, Elliot Elias; s of Oscar Isaac Philipp (d 1965), of Geneva, Switzerland, and Clarisse, *née* Weil (d 1971); *b* 20 July 1915; *Educ* St Paul's, St John's Coll Cambridge (MA), Middlesex Hosp (MB BCh, MRCS, LRCP), Univ of Lausanne; *m* 22 March 1939, Lucie Ruth (d 1988), da of Zacharias Max Hackenbroch (d 1937); 1 s (Alan Henry b 24 Oct 1943), 1 da (Ann Susan (Mrs Hills) b 7 Jan 1941); *Career* Sqdn Ldr (med) RAFVR 1940-46, Bomber Cmd (despatches twice); registrar Addenbrooke's Hosp 1947, anatomical demonstrator Middlesex Hosp 1948 (house surgn 1939-40, house surgn and registrar in obstetrics and gynaecology 1946-47); sr registrar: St Thomas's Hosp 1948-49, Royal Free Hosp 1949-50; first asst Dept of Obstetrics and Gynaecology Univ Coll Hosp 1951; conslt obstetrician and gynaecologist: Old Church Hosp Romford 1952-64, Royal Northern Hosp and City of London Maternity Hosp 1964-80, Whittington Hosp 1980-; pres Hunterian Soc 1988-89 (orator 1987); FRCS, FRCOG; chev Legion d'Honneur 1971, Gold Medal of City of Milan 1972; Freeman of City London, Liveryman Worshipful Soc of Apothecaries; memb RSM; *Books* Scientific Foundations of Obstetrics and Gynaecology (co-ed 1970, 4th edn 1990), Infertility (1981), Caesareans (1988), Obstetrics and Gynaecology Combined for Students (1st edn 1962, 2nd edn 1970); *Recreations* walking (particularly along sea walls), formerly mountaineering and skiing; *Style—* Elliot Philipp, Esq; 78 Nottingham Terrace, York Gate, London NW1 4QE (☎ 071 486 1075); 46 Harley St, London W1N 1AD (☎ 071 935 5007)

PHILIPPE, His Excellency André J; Hon GCVO 1972; *b* 28 June 1926,Luxembourg City; *Career* barr Luxembourg 1951-52, Luxembourg ambass to UK, perm rep to Council of WEU, and concurrently ambass to Ireland and Iceland 1972-78, ambass to France 1978-84, ambass United Nations New York 1984-87, ambass to United States 1987-; Cdr Order of Adolphe of Nassau; Grand Officer Order of Daken Crown and Order of Merit (Lux), Cdr Légion d'Honneur (France); *Style—* His Excellency M André Philippe, GCVO; 801 Second Ave, New York, NY 10017, USA (☎ 212 370 9850)

PHILIPPS, Hon Colwyn Jestyn John; s (by 1 m) and h of 2 Viscount St Davids, *qv*; *b* 30 Jan 1939; *m* 1965, Augusta Victoria Correa Larrain, da of late Don Estantislao Correa Ugarte of Santiago, Chile; 2 s; *Style—* The Hon Colwyn Philipps

PHILIPPS, Hon Mrs (Elizabeth Joan); da of 1 Baron Kindersley, GBE (d 1954); *b* 1911; *m* 1930, Maj the Hon James Perrott Philipps, TD; *Style—* The Hon Mrs Philipps; Dalham Hall, Newmarket, Suffolk

PHILIPPS, Hon Gwenllian; OBE (1962); da of 1 Baron Milford (d 1962); *b* 1916; *Career* Subaltern ATS; former JP Radnorshire; memb CC Radnorshire 1959-64; High Sheriff 1970-71; *Style—* The Hon Gwenllian Philipps, OBE; The Old Rectory, Boughrood, Llyswen, Brecon

PHILIPPS, Hon (Richard) Hanning; MBE (1945); s of 1 Baron Milford (d 1962), and Ethel Georgina, JP, only da of late Rev Benjamin Speke; *b* 14 Feb 1904; *Educ* Eton; *m* 1930, Lady Marion, JP, *qv*, da of 12 Earl of Stair; 1 s, 1 da; *Career* served NW Europe 1944-45, Maj Welsh Gds (Reserve), Hon Col Pembroke Yeo; chm: Schweppes Ltd 1940-68, Northern Securities Trust Ltd 1950-80, Dun & Bradstreet Ltd 1945-68, Milford Haven Conservancy Bd 1963-75; memb Civic Tst for Wales , JP; Lord-Lt for: Pembrokeshire 1958-74, Dyfed 1974-79; keeper of the Rolls for Dyfed 1974-; contested (Nat) Brecon and Radnor 1939; *Recreations* painting, forestry, gardening; *Clubs* Boodle's; *Style—* The Hon Hanning Philipps, MBE; Picton Castle, The Rhos, Haverfordwest, Dyfed SA62 4AS (☎ 0437 751 201)

PHILIPPS, Hon Hugo John Laurence; s and h of 2 Baron Milford; *b* 27 Aug 1929; *Educ* Eton, King's Coll Cambridge; *m* 1, 1951 (m dis 1958), Margaret, da of Capt Ralph Heathcote, DSO, RN; 1 da; m 2, 1959 (m dis 1984), Hon Mary Makins, da of 1 Baron Sherfield, GCB, GCMG; 3 s, 1 da; m 3, 26 Jan 1989, Mrs Felicity Leach; *Career* memb Lloyd's; farmer; *Clubs* Boodle's; *Style—* The Hon Hugo Philipps; Llanstephan House, Llanstephan, Brecon, Powys

PHILIPPS, Lady Jean Meriel; *née* McDonnell; da of 7 Earl of Antrim (d 1932); *b* 1914; *m* 1939, Capt the Hon William Speke Philipps, CBE (d 1975); 2 s, 2 da; *Style—* The Lady Jean Philipps; Slebech Park, Haverfordwest, Dyfed

PHILIPPS, Lady Marion Violet; *née* Dalrymple; JP (Dyfed 1965); da of 12 Earl of Stair, KT, DSO (d 1961); *b* 1 Feb 1908; *Educ* privately; *m* 1930, Hon (Richard) Hanning Philipps, MBE, *qv*; 1 s, 1 da; *Career* memb Narberth Rural Dist Cncl 1970-73; chm Picton Land & Investment Pty Ltd WA; tstee The Graham and Kathleen Sutherland Fndn (at Picton Castle Gallery) 1976-, fndr memb and first pres British Polled Hereford Soc 1950, pres Royal Welsh Agric Soc 1979; FRAgS; CStJ; Order of

Mercy 1926; *Style*— The Lady Marion Philipps, JP; Picton Castle, The Rhos, Haverfordwest, Dyfed SA62 4AS (☎ 043786 751201)

PHILIPS, Prof Sir Cyril Henry; s of William Henry Philips; *b* 27 Dec 1912; *Educ* Rock Ferry HS, Univ of Liverpool (MA), Univ of London (PhD); *m* 1, 1939, Dorcas (d 1974), da of John Rose Wallasey; 1 da (1 s decd); m 2, 1975, Joan Rosemary, da of William George Marshall; *Career* chm Police Complaints Bd, prof of oriental history Univ of London 1946-80, dir Sch of Oriental and African Studies London 1957-76, vice-chllr Univ of London 1972-76; chm: Cncl on Tribunals 1986-, Royal Cmmn on Criminal Procedure 1978-80; kt 1974; *Clubs* Athenaeum; *Style*— Prof Sir Cyril Philips; School of Oriental and African Studies, Malet St, London WCIE 7HP (☎ 071 637 2388)

PHILIPS, John Anthony Burton; VRD (1979); s of Anthony Burton Capel Philips (d 1983), of The Heath House, Tean, Stoke-on-Trent, Staffs, and Margaret, JP, *née* Elletson; the Philips family has been prominent in Staffs for many centuries and seated at Tean, nr Cheadle from at least the mid 16 century, when Francis Phylype of Nether Tean died. They built up their estates around Heath House and Heybridge and put the small village of Tean on the map from the mid 18 century with the fndn of the well-known tape manufacturing firm of J and N Philips at Tean Mall Mills. From this period many members of the family have served as high sheriffs, members of the lieutenancy, JPs, offrs in volunteer forces and membs of the CC. John Burton Philips, High Sheriff of Staffs 1826, rebuilt Heath House from 1836, creating one of the county's finest houses in a magnificent parkland setting; *b* 8 March 1936; *Educ* Eton; *m* 2 Oct 1965, (Elizabeth) Flavia, JP, da of Maj Ronald Russell Pelham Burn, MC, TD (d 1967), of 17 Flood St, Chelsea, London; 2 s (Benjamin Maitland Capel b 28 June 1967, Justin Ronald Burton b 10 June 1969); *Career* Nat Serv RN 1955-57, RNR 1958-84; chm and md of Charles Harbage Ltd 1979-; *Recreations* classical music, sailing, gardening; *Clubs* Royal Cruising, Birmingham Book; *Style*— John Philips, Esq, VRD; Radford Fruit Farm, Inkberrow, Worcestershire WR7 4LR (☎ 0386 792 110); The Heath House, Tean, Stoke-on-Trent, Staffs ST10 4HA (☎ 0538 722 212); Charles Harbage Ltd, Heath St South, Birmingham 18 (☎ 021 454 5421)

PHILIPSON, Maj Christopher Roland; s of Major Thirlwell Philipson, MC (d 1952), of Fordham Abbey, Cambridgeshire, and Daphne, *née* Gladstone (d 1971); *b* 4 March 1929; *Educ* Eton, Sandhurst; *m* 1 Jan 1958, Mary, da of Sir Reginald MacDonald-Buchanan, KCVO, MC (d 1981), of Cottesbrooke Hall, Northampton; 2 da (Caroline b 1959, Joanna b 1961); *Career* Maj Life Gds, served in Germany, Cyprus, Egypt, Aden 1947-61; md British Bloodstock Agency plc 1980-; *Recreations* shooting, gardening; *Clubs* Turf; *Style*— Maj Christopher Philipson; Queensberry House, Newmarket, Suffolk (☎ 0638 665021)

PHILIPSON, Garry; DFC (1944); s of George Philipson, and Marian Philipson, of Stockton-on-Tees; *b* 27 Nov 1921; *Educ* Stockton GS, Univ of Durham (BA, Jubilee prize 1947); *m* 27 Aug 1949, June Mary Miller, da of Lt-Col James Miller Somerville (d 1975); 1 da (Diana Chloe Joan b 9 Sept 1952); *Career* Flt-Lt RAFVR 1941-46, 2 Gp Bomber Cmd; Overseas Admin Serv 1949-60, princ Scottish Office 1961-66, under sec RICS 1966-67, dir Smith & Ritchie Ltd 1967-70, sec New Towns Assoc 1970-74, md Aycliffe and Peterlee Devpt Corp 1974-85; vice chm North Housing Assoc 1985-, tstee Dales Care 1988-; *Books* Aycliffe and Peterlee: Swords into Ploughshares and Farewell Squalor (1988); *Recreations* country pursuits, history, archaeology; *Clubs* RAF; *Style*— Garry Philipson, Esq, DFC; Tunstall Grange, Tunstall, Richmond, N Yorks (☎ 0748 833327)

PHILIPSON, Sir Robert James (Robin); s of James Philipson; *b* 17 Dec 1916; *Educ* Whitehaven Secdy Sch, Dumfries Acad, Edinburgh Coll of Art; *m* 1, 1949, Brenda Mark; m 2, 1962 (m dis 1975), Thora Clyne; m 3, 1976, Diana Mary Pollock; *Career* head of Sch of Drawing and Painting The College of Art Edinburgh 1960-, pres Royal Scottish Academy 1973-; FRSA, FRSE, Hon RA, PRSA; Hon DUniv Stirling 1976, Hon LLD Aberdeen 1977; kt 1976; *Style*— Sir Robin Philipson, FRSE; 23 Crawfurd Rd, Edinburgh EH16 5PQ (☎ 031 667 2373)

PHILIPSON, (John) Trevor Graham; QC (1989); s of William Arnold Philipson, of Morpeth, Northumberland, and Rosalind Amy, *née* Mood; *b* 3 March 1948; *Educ* Newcastle Royal GS, Wadham Coll Oxford (BA, BCL); *m* 13 July 1974 (m dis 1982), Victoria Caroline, da of Oliver Haskard, of Vermont, USA; *Career* called to the Bar Middle Temple 1972; *Recreations* The Pyrenees; *Clubs* RAC; *Style*— Trevor Philipson, QC; 239 Knightsbridge, London SW7 1DJ (☎ 071 581 2214); Fountain Court, Temple, London Ec4Y 9DH (☎ 071 583 3335, fax 071 353 0329, telex 8813408 FONLEG G)

PHILIPSON-STOW, Sir Christopher; 5 Bt (UK 1907), of Cape Town, Cape of Good Hope, and Blackdown House, Lodsworth, Co Sussex, DFC; s of late Henry Matthew Philipson Philipson-Stow, JP (3 s of Sir Frederic Philipson-Stow, 1st Bt) by his w Elizabeth (herself da of Sir Thomas Chitty, 1st Bt); suc 1 cous, Sir Edmond Cecil Philipson-Stow, 4th Bt, MBE, 1982; *b* 13 Sept 1920; *Educ* Winchester; *m* 1952, Elizabeth Nairn, da of late James Dixon Trees, of Toronto, and widow of Maj Frederic George McLaren, of the Canadian 48 Highlanders; 2 s (Robert Matthew b 29 Aug 1953, Rowland Frederic b 2 Sept 1954); *Heir* er s, Robert; *Career* late Flt-Lt RAFVR, served WWII; *Style*— Sir Christopher Philipson-Stow, Bt, DFC; RR2, Port Carling, Ontario, Canada POB 1JO

PHILIPSON-STOW, Lady; Cynthia Yvette; da of late William Robertson Jecks, of Johannesburg, S Africa, and formerly w of Francis Romaine Govett; *m* 1951, as his 2 w, Sir Frederic Lawrence Philipson-Stow, 3 Bt (d 1976); *Style*— Lady Philipson-Stow; Na Xencha, Villa Carlos, Menorca, Spain; Apartado 211, Mahon, Menorca, Spain

PHILIPSON-STOW, Robert Nicholas; o s of Guyon Philipson Philipson-Stow (d 1983); 6 and yst s of Sir Frederick Samuel Philipson Stow, 1 Bt), and Alice Mary, *née* Fagge (d 1989); *b* 2 April 1937; *Educ* Winchester; *m* 25 Sept 1963, Nicolette Leila, er da of Hon Philip Leyland Kindersley, *qv*; 2 s (Robert Rowland b 23 Sept 1970, Edward Miles b 30 April 1972), 1 da (Georgina Mary b 26 Oct 1976); *Career* Nat Serv 2 Lt RHG 1955-57; co sec Miles Druce & Co Ltd 1966-68; ptnr: George Henderson & Co stockbrokers 1970-74, Henderson Crosthwaite & Co stockbrokers 1974-86; head of admin Guinness Mahon Holdings plc 1986-; chm Crown and Manor Boys' Club Hoxton; memb HAC 1983; FCA 1963; *Clubs* White's; *Style*— Robert Philipson-Stow, Esq; Priors Court, Long Green, Gloucester (☎ 068 481 221); c/o Guinness Mahon Holdings plc, 32 St Mary-at-Hill, London EC3P 3AJ (☎ 071 623 9333)

PHILLIMORE, Hon Mrs Anthony; Anne Julia; da of Maj-Gen Sir Cecil Edward Pereira, KCB, CMG; *m* 1934, Capt the Hon Anthony Francis Phillimore (ka 1940, s of 2 Baron Phillimore); 1 s (3 Baron Phillimore d 1990), 1 da; *Style*— The Hon Mrs Anthony Phillimore; Coppid Hall, Henley-on-Thames, Oxon

PHILLIMORE, 4 Baron (UK 1918); Sir Claud Stephen Phillimore; 5 Bt (UK 1881); 2 s of 2 Baron Phillimore, MC (d 1947); suc nephew, 3 Baron 1990; *b* 15 Jan 1911; *Educ* Winchester, Trinity Coll Cambridge (BA); *m* 17 Feb 1944, Anne Elizabeth, eldest da of late Maj Arthur Algernon Smith-Dorrien-Smith, DSO, of Tresco Abbey, Isles of Scilly; 1 s (Hon Francis Stephen, *qv*), 1 da (Hon (Marion) Miranda b 9 May 1946); *Heir* s, Hon Francis Stephen Phillimore b 25 Nov 1944; *Career* Capt and Acting Maj 11 (City of London Yeo) Light Anti-Aircraft Brig RA (TA); architect; *Style*— The Rt Hon the Lord Phillimore; 39 Ashley Gdns, London SW1; Rymans, Apuldram, Chichester, W Sussex

PHILLIMORE, Hon Francis Stephen; o s and h of 4 Baron Phillimore, *qv*; *b* 25 Nov 1944; *Educ* Eton; *m* 1971, Nathalie, da of late Michel Anthony Pequin, of Paris, France; 2 s (Tristan Anthony Stephen b 18 Aug 1977, Julian Michel Claud b 1981), 1 da (Arabella Maroussia Eleanor b 1975); *Style*— The Hon Francis Phillimore; Coppid Hall, Binfield Heath, nr Henley-on-Thames, Oxon

PHILLIMORE, Maria, Baroness; Maria; da of Ilya Slonim and Tatiana, *née* Litvinov; *m* 1983, as his 2 w, 3 Baron Phillimore (d 1990); *Style*— The Rt Hon Maria, Lady Phillimore; Crumplehorn Barn, Corks Farm, Dunsden Green, nr Reading, Berks

PHILLIMORE, Cdr Richard Augustus Bagot; s of Adm Sir Richard Fortescue Phillimore, GCB, KCMG, MVO (d 1940), and Violet Gore, *née* Turton (d 1963); *b* 9 Jan 1907; *Educ* RNS Osborne and Dartmouth; *m* 28 June 1948, Pamela Mary, da of Lt-Col John A Darlington, DSO; 4 s (Peter Richard b 10 Feb 1950, Roger Henry b 28 Aug 1951, Charles Robert b 28 June 1953, Mark Augustus b 26 April 1956); *Career* RN: HMS Frobisher 1924-25, HMS Hood 1925-27, Sub Lt courses 1928, HM Yacht Victoria & Albert 1929, HMS Repulse 1930, HMS Dragon 1930-32, HMS Vortigern 1933, observers' course 1934, HMS Eagle 1934, HMS Hermes 1935-37, RAF Sch of Photograhy Farnborough 1937, HMS Cornwall 1938, HMS Rodney 1939, 3 Bomber Gp RAF Mildenhall 1939-40, trg naval observers 1940-41, HMS Biter 1942, staff of C in C Western Approaches 1943, jt A/U Sch Maydown 1943-44, Staff Flag Offr Air East Indies 1945, cmd HMS Argonaut 1946, cmd HMS Dido 1947, fleet aviation offr Staff of C in C Med 1948-50, Naval Air Div Admty 1951-53, ret 1953; church warden 1954-79, deanery rep 1979-85; pres Waltham Chase Boys Motor Cycle Club 1971-; High Sheriff and DL Hants 1960; *Style*— Cdr Richard Phillimore; Shedfield House, Shedfield, Southampton SO3 2HQ (☎ 0329 833 116)

PHILLIMORE, Hon Mrs Robert; Sheila Bruce; da of John Farquhar MacLeod, JP, MB ChB; *m* 1944, Hon Robert George Hugh Phillimore, OBE (d 1984), s of late 2 Baron Phillimore, MC; 4 da; *Style*— The Hon Mrs Robert Phillimore; Brook Cottage, Mill Road, Shiplake, Oxon RG9 3LW

PHILLIPPS, Ian Hugh; DL (Notts 1990); s of Dr Frederick Alfred Phillipps, MBE (d 1975), of Jersey, and Gwendolen Herbert, *née* Smith (d 1980); *b* 15 Nov 1924; *Educ* Winchester, Trinity Coll Cambridge (MA); *m* 14 Oct 1958, Jennifer, da of Capt Harold Freeman Robinson, of Little Hallingbury, Essex; 1 s (Vere b 1961), 2 da (Victoria (Mrs Sargent) b 1959, Christina b 1968); *Career* dir: Humphreys & Glasgow Ltd 1960-67, Radiation Group Ltd 1967-70, Tube Investments Ltd 1970-81, Chamberlain Phipps plc 1982-89; chm and chief exec Raleigh Industries Ltd Nottingham 1974-81; chm: Wests Group International plc 1983-86, The BSS Group plc 1986-; chm Cncl Soc of Br Gas Industs 1970-72, pres The Bicycle Assoc of GB 1977-79, chm E Midlands Regnl Cncl CBI 1983-84; memb Cncl; CBI 1980-, Univ of Nottingham 1979-; govr Welbeck Coll MOD 1987-, chm Indust Year E Mids 1986; memb: Pay Review Body for Nurses Midwives and the Professions Allied to Med 1984-91, Probation Ctee for Notts 1990-; treas Quorn Hunt 1978-, pres CUBC 1945; FEng 1982, FICE 1950, FIGE 1950; *Recreations* fishing, brass band playing; *Clubs* Leander, London Rowing; *Style*— Ian Phillipps, Esq, DL; Grange Farm, Rempstone, Loughborough, Leics LE12 6RW (☎ 0509 880071); The BSS Group plc, Fleet House, Lee Circle, Leicester LE1 3QQ (☎ 0533 623232, telex 342761 BSS G)

PHILLIPPS, Karen; da of David Malcolm Phillipps, and Audrey Vivienne, *née* Mothersole; *Career* called to the Bar Gray's Inn 1980; memb Senate of The Inns of the Court; *Recreations* theatre, travel tennis, riding, golf; *Style*— Miss Karen Phillipps; 2 Kings Bench Walk, Temple, London EC4 (☎ 071 3539276, fax 071 7944909)

PHILLIPS, Adrian Alexander Christian; s of Eric Lawrance Phillips, CMG, of 46 Platts Lane, London, and Phyllis Mary, *née* Bray; *b* 11 Jan 1940; *Educ* The Hall Sch, Westminster, Ch Ch Oxford (MA), UCL (DipTP); *m* 16 Feb 1963, Cassandra Frances Elais, da of David Francis Hubback, CB, of 4 Provost Rd, London; 2 s (Oliver b 1965, Barnaby b 1968); *Career* planning serv Miny of Housing 1962-68, sr res offr then asst dir Countryside Cmmn 1968-74, exec dir then head Programme Co-ordination Univ UN Environment Programme Nairobi 1974-78, programme dir Int Union for Conservation of Nature & Natural Resources Switzerland 1978-81, dir gen Countryside Cmmn 1989- (dir 1981-), dep chm Int Cmmn on Nat Parks and Protected Areas 1988-; MRTPI 1966, RSA 1982, FRGS 1983; *Recreations* walking, stroking the cat; *Clubs* Royal Overseas League; *Style*— Adrian Phillips, Esq; 2 The Old Rectory, Dumbleton, nr Evesham WR11 6TG (☎ 0386 881 973); The Countryside Commission, John Dower House, Crescent Place, Cheltenham GL50 3RA (☎ 0242 521 381, fax 0242 224 962)

PHILLIPS, Alan Bransby; s of David Henry Phillips (d 1984), of Ilford, Essex, and Lilian, *née* Hertzberg; *b* 7 June 1947; *Educ* Beal GS for Boys, Coll of Distributive Trades; *m* 8 April 1973, Bernice Janet, da of Joel Winter (d 1985), of Buckhurst Hill, Essex; 3 da (Julia b 3 Dec 1976, Claire b 7 July 1978, Wendy b 5 April 1981); *Career* Lintas 1966-68, Sharp MacManus Advertising 1968-71, media mangr Gerald Green Assoc 1971-72, dep media dir Osborne Advertising 1972-74, dir Media and Mktg Consultancy Gp 1974-76, chm and md Phillips Russell plc 1976-; MIPA 1976, MBIM 1977, MCIM 1977; *Recreations* photography, playing musical instruments (sax, flute, clarinet), pistol shooting; *Clubs* EFPC; *Style*— Alan Phillips, Esq; Phillips Russell plc, 58 Wardour St, London W1V 3HN (☎ 071 439 0431, fax 071 734 7406, telex 296502)

PHILLIPS, His Hon Judge (David) Alan Phillips; s of Stephen Thomas Phillips, MC (d 1971), and Elizabeth Mary Phillips, *née* Williams (d 1963); *b* 21 July 1926; *Educ* Llanelli GS, Univ Coll Oxford (MA); *m* 1960, Jean Louise, da of Frederick Edmund Godsell (d 1963); 2 s (Stephen, David); *Career* served WWII 1944-48, Capt GS (Far East); lecturer 1952-59; called to the Bar Gray's Inn 1960, barr 1960-75, a rec of the Crown Court 1974, stipendiary magistrate for Mid-Glamorgan 1975-83; circuit judge Wales and Chester Circuit 1983-; *Recreations* music, computers, swimming; *Style*— His Honour Judge Alan Phillips; The Crown Court, The Castle, Chester CH2 2PA

PHILLIPS, Rev Canon Dr Anthony Charles Julian; s of Arthur Reginald Phillips (d 1965), of Mawnan Smith, Falmouth, Cornwall, and Esmee Mary, *née* Aikman (d 1987); *b* 2 June 1936; *Educ* Kelly Coll Tavistock, King's Coll London (BD, AKC), Gonville and Caius Coll Cambridge (PhD), Coll of the Resurrection Mirfield; *m* 11 April 1970, Victoria Ann, da of Vernon Bruce Stainton, OBE (d 1946), of Rawalpindi, Punjab; 2 s (Christopher Charles Withiel b 6 Aug 1971, James Alexander Withiel b 27 June 1973), 1 da (Lucy Karenza Withiel b 10 Feb 1975); *Career* curate of Good Shepherd Cambridge 1966-69, dean chaplain and fell of Trinity Hall Cambridge 1969-74; St John's Coll Oxford: chaplain and fell 1975-86, domestic bursar 1982-84; lectr in theol: Jesus Coll Oxford 1975-86, Hertford Coll Oxford 1984-86; SA Cook Bye fell Gonville & Caius Coll Cambridge 1984, hon chaplain to Bishop of Norwich 1970-71; examining chaplain to: Bishop of Oxford 1979-86, Bishop of Manchester 1980-86, Bishop of Wakefield 1984-86; inter faith conslt for Judaism Archbishops of Canterbury and York 1984-86; headmaster The King's Sch Canterbury 1986-, canon theologian Dio of Truro 1986-, hon canon of Canterbury Cathedral 1987-; author of various articles in learned jls; *Books* Ancient Israel's Criminal Law (1970), Deuteronomy (1973), God BC (1977), Israel's Prophetic Tradition (ed, 1982), Lower than the Angels (1983), Preaching from the Psalter (1987); contributor: Words and Meanings (ed P R Ackroyd and B Lindars, 1968), Witness to the Spirit (ed W Harrington, 1979), The Ministry of the World (ed

G Cuming, 1979), Heaven and Earth (ed A Linzey and P Wexler, 1986), Tradition and Unit (1991); *Recreations* gardening, beachcombing; *Clubs* Athenaeum; *Style*— The Rev Canon Dr Anthony Phillips; The King's School, Canterbury, Kent CT1 2ES (☎ 0227 475501)

PHILLIPS, (William) Bernard; s of Stanley George Phillips (d 1968), of Sutton Coldfield, and Enid Effie, *née* Eades; *b* 26 April 1944; *Educ* Bishop Vesey GS Sutton Coldfield, Hertford Coll Oxford (MA); *m* 1, 13 May 1967 (m dis 1986), Christine Elizabeth, da of Arthur Charles Wilkinson, of Maidstone; 3 s (Andrew b 1968, Simon b 1972, William b 1974); m 2, 1 Aug 1987, Deborah Grace, da of Ellis Green (d 1975), of Sheffield; *Career* schoolmaster 1966-67, lectr 1967-70, called to the Bar Inner Temple 1970, in practice NE Circuit 1971-, rec 1989-; asst rec 1984-89; memb Inner Temple 1964; *Recreations* cookery, woodwork, collecting books; *Style*— Bernard Phillips, Esq; Padley Croft, Nether Padley, Grindleford, Derbyshire (☎ 0433 31359); 12 Paradise Square, Sheffield (☎ 0742 738951, fax : 0742 760848)

PHILLIPS, Brian Harold; s of Charles Douglas Phillips (d 1958); *b* 30 Aug 1930; *Educ* Luton GS; *m* 1952, Margaret June, da of Stanley Archibald Wilkins (d 1977); 1 s, 1 da; *Career* sr local govt fin appts to 1967; Nationwide Building Society: fin controller 1967-71, gen mangr 1972-85, dir 1985-, dep chief gen mangr 1986-87; non-exec dir Nationwide Anglia Building Society 1988- (dir and dep chief exec 1987-88); cncl memb Assoc of Certified Accountants 1985; FCCA, FRSA, IPFA, FBIM; *Style*— Brian Phillips, Esq; Treetops, 17 Silverthorn Drive, Longdean Park, Hemel Hempstead, Herts HP3 8BU

PHILLIPS, Prof Calbert Inglis; s of Rev David Horner Phillips, and Margaret Calbert Phillips; *b* 20 March 1925; *Educ* Glasgow HS, Robert Gordon's Coll Aberdeen, Univ of Aberdeen (MB ChB, MD), Univ of Edinburgh (DPH), Univ of Bristol (PhD), Univ of Manchester (MSc); *m* 1962, Christina Anne, *née* Fulton; 1 s; *Career* Nat Serv Lt and Capt RAMC 1947-49; house surgn: Aberdeen Royal Infirmary 1946-47 (house physician 1951), Aberdeen Maternity Hosp 1949, Glasgow Eye Infirmary 1950-51; asst Anatomy Dept Univ of Glasgow 1951-52, resident registrar Moorfields Eye Hosp 1953-54, sr registrar St Thomas' Hosp (and res asst Inst of Ophthalmology) 1954-58, conslt surgn Bristol Eye Hosp 1958-63, Alexander Piggott Wernher travelling fell Dept of Ophthalmology Harvard Univ 1960-61, conslt ophthalmic surgn St Goerge's Hosp 1963-65, prof of ophthalmology Univ of Manchester 1965-72, hon conslt ophthalmic surgn to United Manchester Hosps 1965-72, prof of ophthalmology Univ of Edinburgh 1972-90, ophthalmic surgn Royal Infirmary Edinburgh 1972-90; Hon FBOA 1975; FRCS 1955, FRCSE 1973; *Books* Clinical Practice and Economics (jt ed, 1977), Basic Clinical Ophthalmology (1984), author of numerous papers on ophthalmological and related topics for Br and American jls; *Style*— Prof Calbert Phillips; Princess Alexandra Eye Pavilion, Chalmers St, Edinburgh, Lothian EH3 9HA (☎ 031 229 2477)

PHILLIPS, Dr Celia Mary; da of Percival Edmund Phillips (d 1989) and Marjorie, *née* Hughes; *b* 16 Dec 1942; *Educ* Dunferline HS, Windsor Sch, High Wycombe HS, LSE (BSc, PhD); *m* 23 June 1973, Ronald Frederick, s of Frederick William Swan (d 1975), of Broadlands Rd, Southampton; 1 s (Toby b May 1978), 1 da (Elly b Dec 1974); *Career* lectr LSE 1967-; memb Educn Ctee ILEA 1975-78, tstee St Catherines Cumberland Lodge Windsor 1987, dean undergrad studies LSE 1986-89; FRSS; *Books* Changes in Subject Choices at School and University (1969), Statistical Sources in Civil Aviation (1979), The Risks in Going to Work (with J Stockdale, 1989); *Recreations* choral singing (Chelsea Opera Group and others), walking, reading; *Style*— Dr Celia Phillips; Statistics Dept, London School of Economics, Houghton St, London WC2A 2AE (☎ 071 955 7644)

PHILLIPS, Capt Christmas (Chris); s of Albert Phillips, and Mary Ann, *née* Stephens; *b* 25 Dec 1920; *Educ* Porth Co Sch, Birmingham Centl Tech Coll (BSc); *m* 20 March 1945, Mary, da of Edward Williams, of Mansfield, Notts; 2 s (Christoper b 1949, Ian b 1958), 2 da (Carol b 1949, Anne b 1961); *Career* Capt REME, cmmnd 1943; serv: Syria, Lebanon, Palestine, N Africa, Italy, France, Belgium, Holland, Germany, demoblised 1947; jt md Redman Tools Worcester, md John Barnsley Ltd Netherton, dep chm Williams (Hldgs) plc Caerphilly, chm Holdens Bromyard, ret; pres Worcester & Hereford C of C and Indust, chm Mercia Industrialists Assoc, pres Worcester Industrialists Assoc; CEng, FIMechE, FIProdE; *Recreations* mountaineering, swimming; *Style*— Capt Chris Phillips; Severncroft, 95 Park Ave, Worcester NR3 7AQ (☎ 0905 21386)

PHILLIPS, Prof David; s of Stanley Phillips (d 1979), of South Shields, Tyne and Wear, and Daphne Ivy, *née* Harris; *b* 3 Dec 1939; *Educ* South Shields Grammar Tech Sch, Univ of Birmingham (BSc, PhD); *m* 21 Dec 1970, (Lucy) Caroline, da of Clifford John Scoble, of Plymouth, Devon; 1 da (Sarah Elizabeth b 1975); *Career* Fullbright fell Univ of Texas Austin USA 1964-66, exchange fell Royal Soc/Acad of Sciences USSR 1966-67; Univ of Southampton: lectr 1967-73, sr lectr 1973-76, reader 1976-80; The Royal Inst of GB: Wolfson prof of natural philosophy 1980-89, dep dir 1986-89; prof of physical chemistry, Imperial Coll London 1989-; res scientist in applications of lasers in chemistry biology and med, author of 300 scientific papers reviews and books in this field, various appearances on BBC TV and Radio incl Royal Inst Christmas Lectures for Young People with JM Thomas 1987 and 1988; vice pres and gen sec Br Assoc for the Advancement of Science 1988-89; FRSC 1976; *Books* Time-correlated Single-photon Counting (with DV O'Connor), Time-resolved Vibrational Spectroscopy (with GH Atkinson); *Recreations* music, theatre, popularisation of science; *Clubs* Athenaeum; *Style*— Prof David Phillips; 195 Barnett Wood Lane, Ashtead, Surrey KT21 2LP (☎ 0372 274385); Dept of Chemistry, Imperial College of Science Technology and Medicine, Exhibition Rd, London SW7 2A2 (☎ 071 589 5111 ext 4508, fax 071 581 9973)

PHILLIPS, Sir David Chilton; KBE (1989); s of Charles Harry Phillips (d 1963), of Ellesmere, Shropshire (d 1963), and Edith Harriet, *née* Finney (d 1972), da of Samuel Finney, MP 1916-22; *b* 7 March 1924; *Educ* Oswestry Boys' HS, Univ Coll Cardiff (BSc, PhD); *m* 1960, Diana Kathleen, da of Maj Edward Maitland Hutchinson, RA (d 1957), of Chalfont St Giles; 1 da (Sarah); *Career* Sub Lt RNVR 1944-47; post doctoral fell Nat Res Cncl of Canada 1951-53, res offr Nat Res Labs Ottawa Canada 1953-55, res worker Royal Instn London 1956-66, prof of molecular biophysics Oxford Univ 1966-90, fell CCC Oxford 1966-90 (hon fell 1990-), Fullerian prof physiology Royal Instn 1979-83; dir Celltech Ltd 1982, biological sec The Royal Soc 1976-83; memb Medical Res Cncl 1974-78; Royal Soc assessor 1976-83, chm Advsy Bd Res Cncls 1983-; Hon DSc: Univ of Leicester 1974, Univ of Wales 1975, Univ of Chicago 1978, Univ of Warwick 1982, Univ of Exeter 1982, Univ of Birmingham 1987, Univ of Glasgow 1990; Hon DUniv Univ of Essex 1983; Biochemical Soc CIBA medal 1971, Royal Soc Royal medal 1975, Prix Charles Léopold Mayer French Académie des Sciences (jtly, 1979), Wolf prize (jtly, 1987); hon memb American Soc Biological Chemists, foreign hon memb American Acad Arts and Sciences; foreign associate, US Nat Acad of Sciences, foreign memb Royal Swedish Acad; FInstP, FRS 1967 (vice pres 1972-73 and 1976-83); kt 1979; *Style*— Sir David Phillips, KBE; 35 Addison Court, Holland Villas Road, London W14 8DA (☎ 071 602 0738); Advisory Board for Research Councils, Elizabeth House, York Road, London SE1Y 7PH (☎ 071 934 9851)

PHILLIPS, David John; s of Arnold Phillips, and Sylvia Marie Phillips, *née* Mendoza; *b* 5 May 1952; *Educ* William Hulme's GS Manchester, Leeds Univ (LLB); *m* 23 June 1974, Ruth, da of Elias Edelstein; 2 s (Daniel b 1979, Richard b 1981), 1 da (Emma b 1983); *Career* slr (admitted 1978); proprietor: Phillips & Co, Slrs Manchester, Phillips Import Agents; dir Briton Finance Ltd; cncl memb Hale Synagogue; *Recreations* backgammon, bridge, watching Manchester City FC; *Clubs* Valley Lodge Country, Wilmslow; *Style*— David J Phillips, Esq; 8A Talbot Road, Old Trafford, Manchester (☎ 061 872 1458, telex via Prestel 618721458)

PHILLIPS, Prof Dewi Zephaniah; s of David Oakley Phillips (d 1978), of 70 Bath Rd, Morriston, Swansea, and Alice Frances, *née* Davies (d 1982); *b* 24 Nov 1934; *Educ* Swansea GS, Univ Coll of Swansea (BA, MA), St Catherine's Coll Oxford (BLitt); *m* 2 Sept 1959, (Margaret) Monica, da of Frederick John Hanford (d 1951), of Swansea; 3 s (Aled b 1962, Steffan b 1965, Rhys b 1971); *Career* lectr in philosophy: Queen's Coll Dundee 1964-65 (asst lectr 1963-64), Univ Coll Bangor 1963-65, Univ Coll of Swansea 1965-67 (sr lectr 1967-70, prof 1971-); *Books* The Concept of Prayer (1969), Faith and Philosophical Enquiry (1970), Death and Immortality (1970), Moral Practices (with H O Mounce, 1970), Sense and Delusion (with Ilham Dilman, 1971), Athroyddu am Grefydd (1974), Religion Without Explanation (1976), Through a Darkening Glass (1982), Dramau Gwenlyn Parry (1982), Belief Change and Forms of Life (1986), R S Thomas: Poet of the Hidden God (1986), Faith After Foundationalism (1988), From Fantasy to Faith (1991); *Recreations* lawn tennis, supporting Swansea City AFC; *Style*— Prof D Z Phillips; 45 Queen's Rd, Sketty, Swansea (☎ 0792 203 935); Dept of Philosophy, Univ Coll of Swansea, Singleton Park, Swansea (☎ 0792 29 5189)

PHILLIPS, Lt-Col Edward Courtenay; MC (1945), JP (Hereford 1965), DL (Hereford 1987); s of Gerald Courtenay Phillips (d 1938), of St Ct, Kingsland, Leominster, Hereford, and Dorothy Phillips (d 1975); *b* 6 June 1922; *Educ* Marlborough; *m* 9 Aug 1947, Anthea Mary, da of Capt R F J Onslow, MVO, DSC, RN, of The Cat and Fiddle, Presteigne, Radnorshire; 2 da (Sarah (Mrs Corbett) b 1948, Harriet (Mrs Cheney) b 1953); *Career* KRRC: joined 1940, cmmnd 1941, Capt 1945, Temporary Maj 1946-54, mil attache Khartoum 1959-61, ret 1961, Co Cmdt ACF Hereford 1970-75; conslt dir Sun Valley Poultry 1987- (joined 1961, chm 1983-87); chm: Herefordshire Co PSD 1987, South Hereford PSD 1988-90, Hereford Diocesan Appeal 1976-81; High Sheriff Hereford and Worcester 1977-78; *Recreations* field sports, racing; *Clubs* Army and Navy, MCC; *Style*— Lt-Col Edward Phillips, MC, JP, DL; Chase House, Monnington-on-Wye, Hereford HR4 7NL (☎ 098 17 282); Sun Valley Poultry Ltd, Hereford HR4 9PB (☎ 0432 352400)

PHILLIPS, Edward Thomas John (Jack); CBE (1985); s of Edward Emery Kent Phillips (d 1984), and Margaret Elsie, *née* Smith (d 1986); *b* 5 Feb 1930; *Educ* Exmouth GS Devon, UCL (BA), Inst of Educn London Univ (postgraduate Cert Ed), SOAS (Dip Linguistics); *m* 27 Sept 1952, Sheila May, da of Thomas Henry Abbott (d 1978); 2 s (Christopher b 11 Dec 1957, Jonathan b 8 May 1965), 2 da (Nicola b 11 Sept 1960, Deborah b 3 July 1962); *Career* Nat Serv RAF 1948-49; educn offr Colonial Serv Nigeria 1953-62; The British Cncl: head of centre unit London overseas students dept 1962-65, trg at SOAS 1965-66, English language offr Enugu Nigeria 1966-67, sr lectr dept of educn Lagos Univ Nigeria 1967-70, English language teaching advsr Miny of Educn Nicosia Cyprus 1970-72, chief inspr English teaching div inspectorate 1974-75 (inspr 1972-74), rep Bangladesh 1975-77, dir personnel dept and dep controller personnel and staff recruitment div 1977-80, rep Malaysia 1980-85, controller English language and lit div 1985-89, ret 89; conslt on recruitment British Exec Serv Overseas 1990-; memb: IATEFL, Br-Malaysia Soc, Anti-Slavery Soc; *Books* Organised English Books I and II (jt ed 1973); *Recreations* sport, music, theatre; *Style*— Edward Phillips, Esq, CBE; 1 Bredune, Kenley, Surrey; Westcott, Westwood, nr Starcross, Devon

PHILLIPS, Elaine; da of James Curran (d 1954), of Dublin, Ireland, and Mary Louise Curran, *née* Mallinson (d 1970); *b* 24 Aug 1934; *Educ* Longley Hall Huddersfield Yorks; *m* 18 Nov 1959, Colin Phillips, s of Victor Phillips (d 1976), of Yorks; 1 da (Louise b 22 Feb 1962); *Career* shop keeper; chm Elaine Phillips Antiques Ltd; owner: Sarah Curran, Lane Phillips Mktg; fndr memb Harrogate NADFAS; memb Br Antique Dealers Assoc; *Recreations* shops and shopping and the north of England; *Style*— Mrs Elaine Phillips; Elaine Phillips Antiques Ltd, 1-2 Royal Parade, Harrogate, N Yorks (☎ 0423 569745)

PHILLIPS, Sir Fred Albert; CVO (1966), QC; s of Wilbert A Phillips, of Brighton, St Vincent; *b* 14 May 1918; *Educ* Univ of London (LLB), Toronto Univ, McGill Univ (MCL); *Career* called to the Bar Middle Temple; cabinet sec West Indies Fedn 1958-62, govr St Kitts, Nevis & Anguilla 1967-69; sr legal advsr Cable & Wireless 1969-; dir: Trinidad External Telecommunications 1970-, Jamaica External Communications 1971-, Barbados External Telecommunications, Barbados Telephone Co, Telecommunications of Jamaica, Jamaica Telephone Co; chm Grenada Telecommunications Ltd, vice chm Offshore Keyboarding Corporation; LLD Univ of the WI honoris causa; KStJ 1968; kt 1967; *Recreations* writing; *Style*— Sir Fred Phillips, CVO, QC; P O Box 206, Bridgetown, Barbados (☎ 42 90448/42 90427)

PHILLIPS, Mrs Harold (Georgina); *née* Wernher; er da of Maj-Gen Sir Harold Augustus Wernher, 3 and last Bt, GCVO, TD (d 1973), and Lady Zia Wernher, CBE, *née* Countess Anastasia de Torby (d 1977), da of HIH Grand Duke Mikhail Mikhailovitch of Russia; *b* 17 Oct 1919; *m* 10 Oct 1944, Lt-Col Harold Pedro Joseph Phillips, Coldstream Gds (d 1980), 2 s of Col Joseph Harold John Phillips (d 1953), of Broome Cottage, Sunningdale, Berks; 1 s (Nicholas Harold b 1947), 4 da (Alexandra Anastasia (Duchess of Abercorn) b 1946, Fiona Mercedes (Mrs Burnett of Leys) b 1951, Marita Georgina (Mrs Randall Crawley) b 1954, Natalia Ayesha (Duchess of Westminster) b 1959); *Career* chief pres St John Ambulance; DGStJ 1987-90; *Recreations* racing; *Style*— Mrs Harold Phillips; 13 Burton Court, Franklins Row, London SW3; Ardhuncart Lodge, Alford, Aberdeenshire

PHILLIPS, (Gerald) Hayden; CB (1989); s of Gerald Phillips, of 30 Rydal Drive, Tunbridge Wells, and Dorothy Florence, *née* Joyner; *b* 9 Feb 1943; *Educ* Cambridgeshire HS Clare Coll Cambridge (MA), Yale USA (MA); *m* 1, 23 Sept 1967, Dr Ann Watkins, da of Prof S B Watkins (d 1966); 1 s (Alexander b 1970); 1 da (Rachel b 1974); m 2, 11 July 1980, Hon Laura Grenfell, da of 2 Baron St Just (d 1984); 1 s (Thomas Peter b 1987), 2 da (Florence b 1981, Louisa Henrietta b 1984); *Career* princ private sec to Home Sec 1974-76, dep chef de cabinet to Pres the Euro Communities 1977-79, asst sec Home Office 1979-81, under sec of state Home Office 1981-86, dep under sec of state Cabinet Office 1986-88, dep sec HM Treasy 1988; *Clubs* Brooks's; *Style*— Hayden Phillips, Esq, CB; HM Treasury, Parliament St, London SW1 (☎ 071 270 5939)

PHILLIPS, Lady; Hazel Bradbury; JP (1961); only da of Thomas John Evans, OBE (d 1972), of Stavros, Cyncoed Crescent, Cardiff, and Elsie Rosina Evans, *née* Bradbury (d 1985); *b* 26 Nov 1924; *Educ* Howell's Sch Llandaff, Roedean, King's Coll London (LLB); *m* 8 Aug 1951, Sir (John) Raymond Phillips, MC (Hon Mr Justice Phillips, d 1982), s of Rupert Phillips, JP (d 1952), of The Greenway, Radyr, nr Cardiff; 2 s (David b 4 May 1953, Richard b 26 April 1955); *Career* called to the Bar Inner Temple 1948, memb Wales and Chester Circuit, lawyer memb London Rent Assessment Panel 1966- (vice pres 1972, pres 1973-79), memb Parole Bd 1979-82, chm Richmond upon Thames PSD 1985-88; *Recreations* walking, riding, reading, gardening; *Clubs* United Oxford and Cambridge Univ; *Style*— Lady Phillips, JP; The

Elms, Park Rd, Teddington, Middx TW11 0AQ (☎ 081 977 1584)

PHILLIPS, Capt Hedley Joyce; OBE (1980), QPM 1972, DL (Hants 1987); s of Francis Hedley Joyce Phillips (d 1928), and Constance Daisy, *née* Bigg (d 1986); *b* 12 March 1925; *Educ* Aldworth's Hosp (Reading Blue Coat Sch); *m* 22 March 1947, Brenda Marjorie, da of Herbert Walter Horner (d 1968); 1 s (Michael Hedley Joyce Phillips b 1948); *Career* WWII serv: enlisted RM 1942, cmmnd 1944, 48 RM Commando NW Europe 1944-45, 44 RM Commando SE Asia 1945-46, demobbed with rank of Capt 1946; cmmnd RM Forces Vol Res 1948, ret Capt 1953; Berks Constabulary 1946-64, asst chief constable Hants Constabulary 1964-67 (dep chief constable 1967-83), ret 1983; chm Winchester & Dist VSO Ctee 1965-70, vice pres RLSS 1985- (chm S Region 1980-89), treas Southampton Traveller's Aid 1972-80; *Recreations* golf, swimming, chess, military history; *Clubs* Naval & Military, Bramshaw Golf; *Style—* Capt Hedley Phillips, OBE, QPM, DL

PHILLIPS, Sir Henry Ellis Isidore; CMG (1960), MBE (Mil 1946); s of Harry Joseph Phillips, MBE (d 1961), and Rachel Love Trachtenberg (d 1961); *b* 30 Aug 1914; *Educ* Haberdashers' Sch Hampstead, UCL (MA), Inst of Historical Res; *m* 1, 1941 (m dis 1965), Vivien, da of Albert M Hyamson, OBE (d 1954); 2 s, 1 da; m 2, 1966, Philippa, da of Michael Cohen (d 1965); *Career* cmmnd Beds and Herts Regt 1939, Capt and Adj 5 Bn (POW Singapore 1942-45); Colonial Admin Serv 1946: devpt sec Nyasaland 1952, seconded to Fed Treasy Rhodesia and Nyasaland 1953-57 (dep sec 1956-57); fin sec Nyasaland Govt 1957-64, min of fin Nyasaland 1961-64; md Standard Bank Finance and Development Corporation 1966-72, dir SIFIDA Investment Co SA 1970-; chm: Assured Property Trust plc 1988, Ashley Industrial Trust 1986-88; advsr Air Tport Users Ctee 1981-; bd memb: Civil Aviation Authy 1975-80, Nat Bank of Malawi 1983-88; vice chm Stonham Housing Assoc; hon treas: Stonham Meml Tst 1977-, SOS Sahel Int UK 1987-; Fell UCL (memb Fin Ctee 1986-); FRHistS; kt 1964; *Clubs* MCC, Royal Cwlth; *Style—* Sir Henry Phillips, CMG, MBE; 34 Ross Ct, Putney Hill, London SW15 (☎ 081 789 1404)

PHILLIPS, Sir Horace; KCMG (1973, CMG 1963); s of Samuel Phillips; *b* 31 May 1917; *Educ* Hillhead HS Glasgow; *m* 1944, Idina Doreen Morgan; 1 s, 1 da; *Career* Br later Indian Army (Maj) 1940-47; Dip Serv 1947-; ambass to Indonesia 1966-68, high cmmr in Tanzania 1968-72, ambass to Turkey 1973-77; resident rep Taylor Woodrow International Ltd: Iran 1978-79, Hong Kong 1979-83, Bahrain 1983-84, China (at Peking) 1985-87; visiting lectr in diplomacy Bilkent Univ Ankara Turkey 1988-; Hon LLD Glasgow 1977; Order of the Taj (Iran) 1961; *Recreations* languages, long distance car driving; *Clubs* Travellers', Hong Kong; *Style—* Sir Horace Phillips, KCMG; 34a Sheridan Rd, Merton Park, London SW19 3HP (☎ 081 542 3836)

PHILLIPS, Lt-Col Hugh Beadnell Jeremy; MBE (1978); s of Surgn Rear Adm George Phillips, CB (d 1980), of Yelverton, Devon, and Ernestine Sabina, *née* Orwin; *b* 18 Sept 1936; *Educ* Kelly Coll, RMA Sandhurst, Staff Coll Camberley; *m* 22 Aug 1964, Angela Patricia, da of Claude Hillyard; 3 da (Lucy, Detta, Becky); *Career* nat serv 1955-56, offr RTR In Hong Kong, Germany, Aden, Berlin 1957-68; army rep Jt Planning Staff to Flag Office Malta 1969-71, OC Armd Sqdn Rhine Army 1971-73, SO and instr on armour Sch of Inf 1973-75, co cdr and instr RMA Sanhurst 1975-77, CO Jr Ldrs Regt RAC 1978-80, SO to dir of personal servs MOD 1980-82, project offr MOD Trial on Chem Warfare 1982-83, cdr Recruiting and Liaison Staff NW Dist 1983-85, sr admin offr Def Nuclear Biological and Chem Centre 1986-89; *Recreations* cricket, golf, squash, watercolours; *Clubs* Landsdowne; *Style—* Lt-Col Hugh Phillips, MBE

PHILLIPS, Ian; s of Wilfrid Phillips (d 1976), and Dorothy McLellan, *née* Taylor (d 1963); *b* 16 July 1938; *Educ* Whitgift Sch Croydon; *m* 21 Oct 1961, Fay Rosemary, da of George Sharpe Stoner (d 1986); 2 s (Jonathan Peter b 13 April 1964, Simon James b 3 Sept 1966); *Career* bd memb (fin) London Tport Exec 1980-84, dir fin and planning BR Bd 1985-88, dir fin BBC 1988-; FCA; *Recreations* golf; *Style—* Ian Phillips, Esq; 113 Lower Camden, Chislehurst, Kent BR7 5JD (☎ 081 467 0529); Bakers Cottage, Church Rd, Quenington, Cirencester, Glos; BBC, Broadcasting House, London W1A 1AA (☎ 071 927 4312, fax 071 323 6820, telex 265781, car 0860 748109)

PHILLIPS, Prof Ian; s of Stanley Phillips (d 1942), of Whitworth, Lancashire, and Emma, *née* Price (d 1960); *b* 10 April 1936; *Educ* Bacup and Rawtenstall GS, St John's Coll Cambridge (MA, MD), St Thomas's Hosp Med Sch; *Career* prof med microbiology United Med and Dental Schs of Guy's and St Thomas's Hosps, hon conslt microbiologist St Thomas's Hosp, civil conslt microbiology RAF 1979-; memb Cncl Royal Coll of Pathologists 1974-76 and 1987-90, chm Dist Med Team St Thomas's Hosp 1978-79, chm Br Soc for Antimicrobial Chemotherapy 1979-82, memb Veterianry Products Ctee 1981-85, chm elect Assoc of Med Microbiologists 1989; memb S London Botanical Inst; Freeman City of London 1975, Liveryman Worshipful Soc of Apothecaries; FRCP, FRCPath; *Books* Laboratory Methods in Antimicrobial Chemotherapy (ed with D S Reeves, J D Williams and R Wise, 1978), Microbial Disease (with D A J Tyrell, GS Goodwin and R Blowers, 1979); *Clubs* Royal Soc of Med; *Style—* Prof Ian Phillips; Dept of Microbiology, St Thomas's Hospital, Lambeth Palace Rd, London SE1 7EH (☎ 071 928 9292)

PHILLIPS, John; s of John Tudor Phillips (d 1981), of Finchley, London N12, and Bessie Maud, *née* Cork (d 1989); *b* 25 Nov 1926; *Educ* Christ's Coll Finchley, Northern Poly Holloway; *m* 24 Sept 1955, Eileen Margaret, da of Lt-Col Robert Fryer (d 1946), of Finchley; *Career* Nat Serv 1945-48, cmmnd 2 Lt RE 1947; studied under Romilly B Craze architect 1948-52; surveyor to the fabric: Truro Cathedral 1960-79 (conslt architect 1979-), Westminster Cathedral 1976-, RIBA 1979-; conslt architect Brisbane Cathedral 1988-; pres Ecclesiastical Architects' and Surveyors' Assoc 1982, chm Christian Enterprise Housing Assoc 1964-82; memb RIBA 1954; *Recreations* steeple crawling, choral singing; *Style—* John Phillips, Esq; 8 Friary Way, N Finchley, London N12 9PH (☎ 081 445 3414); 208-209 Upper St, London N1 1RL (☎ 071 359 2299, fax 071 359 0187)

PHILLIPS, John Christopher; s of James Stacey Phillips (d 1980), of Torquay, Devon, and Emma, *née* England (d 1976); *b* 26 June 1935; *Educ* Sherborne; *m* 19 April 1969, Judith Ann, da of Thomas Ronald Biggart, MBE, TD (d 1990); 2 s (David b 1972, Mark b 1974); *Career* fin dir Tarmac Bricks & Tiles Ltd (formerly Westbrick Ltd) 1979-90, conslt 1990-, vice chm Exeter Chamber of Commerce, cmmr Income Tax; govr Exeter Coll pres South Western Soc of Chartered Accountants 1985-86; FCA 1958; *Recreations* golf, sailing, gardening; *Style—* John Phillips, Esq; Willowgarth, Sunhill Lane, Topsham, Exeter (☎ 0392 873 828)

PHILLIPS, John Douglas Parnham; s of Maj Douglas Middleton Parnham Phillips (d 1958), and Sheila Esme, *née* Wilkinson; *b* 3 May 1934; *Educ* Harrow, Pembroke Coll Cambridge (BA, MA); *m* 30 March 1968 (m dis 1982), Diana Phyllis Frances, da of John Stratton; 2 s (Douglas Hugh Parnham b 27 March 1970, Alexander Patrick Middleton b 31 Jan 1972); *Career* conslt in wildlife mgmnt concerned with uplands - UK and Europe; CBiol, MIBiol 1988; *Recreations* field sports, countryside, dogtraining; *Style—* John Phillips, Esq; Arngibbon House, Kippen, Stirlingshire (☎ 0360 85420)

PHILLIPS, John Edward; s of Stanley Edward Phillips (d 1987), of London, and Elsie Evelyn Ruth, *née* Wilson; *b* 12 May 1938; *Educ* Haileybury, ISC; *m* 29 Dec 1967, Mary Isabelle, da of Colin Bootra-Taylor; 1 s (Michael John b May 1972 d 16 Oct 1980), 1 da (Sarah Jane b 14 Sept 1969); *Career* Trade Indemnity plc: joined 1961, mangr Aust 1969-73, dep gen mangr UK 1973-78, gen mangr and dir 1978-90 (amended chm 1989-90); dir Gen Surety & Guarantee Co Ltd, dep chm Trade Indemnity Group plc 1991-; pres Int Credit Insur Assoc 1986-88, memb Bd Mgmnt and dep chm Nat Head Injuries Assoc (Headway), tstee Old Haileyburians RFC; Freeman City of London 1980, memb Ct Assts Worshipful Co of Insurers; FBIM, fell Inst of Credit Mgmnt, memb IOD 1987; *Recreations* tennis, golf; *Clubs* MCC, Worplesdon Golf, Royal Melbourne Golf, Athenaeum (Melbourne); *Style—* John Phillips, Esq; Trade Indemnity plc, Trade Indemnity House, 12-34 Great Eastern St, London EC2A 3AX (☎ 071 739 4311, fax 071 739 4397, telex 21227)

PHILLIPS, John Francis; CBE (1977, OBE 1957), QC (1981); s of late F W Phillips; *b* 1911; *Educ* Cardinal Vaughan Sch, Univ of London, Trinity Hall Cambridge (LLB, LLM); *m* 1937, Olive M Royer; 1 s, 2 da; *Career* arbitrator; called to the Bar Gray's Inn 1944; chm London Ct of Int Arbitration 1985-88; pres (formerly chm) Private Patients Plan 1977-, dep chm Eggs Authy 1971-80; DCL 1985, chm Associated Examining Bd 1976-; OStJ 1985; *Clubs* Athenaeum, Oxford and Cambridge; *Style—* John Phillips, Esq, CBE, QC; 17 Ossulton Way, Hampstead Gdn Suburb, London N2 0DT (☎ 071 455 8460)

PHILLIPS, Josephine Marian (Jose); da of late William Norman Phillips, of Durban, South Africa, and Eileen Helen, *née* Callaghan; *b* 21 Oct 1947; *Educ* Convent HS Durban South Africa, Univ of Natal; *Career* info offr SE Arts 1975-78; Sadler's Wells Royal Ballet: press offr 1978-82, press and mktg 1983-87; mktg mangr Royal Opera House 1987-; vice chm Exec Ctee Convent Garden Marketing Group until 1990; *Recreations* theatre, music, reading, cooking, gardening; *Style—* Ms Jose Phillips; Royal Opera House, Convent Garden, London WC2E 9DD (☎ 071 240 1200, fax 071 836 0231, telex 27988 COVGAR G)

PHILLIPS, Lady Katharine Mary; *née* Fitz-Alan-Howard; da of 15 Duke of Norfolk, KG, PC, CVO (d 1917); *b* 1912; *m* 1940, Lt-Col Joseph Anthony Moore Phillips, DSO, MBE, DL (d 1990); 1 s (Anthony Bernard Moore Phillips b 1953, lost at sea on Whitbread Round the World Race 1989); *Career* Order of Mercy; *Clubs* Royal Corinthian Yacht, Burnham on Crouch, Royal Thames YC London; *Style—* The Lady Katharine Phillips; Lund House, Lund, Driffield, East Yorks

PHILLIPS, Hon Mrs (Laura Claire); *née* Grenfell; da of 2 and last Baron St Just (d 1984) and his 1 w Leslie, Lady Bonham Cauver, da of Condé Nast; *b* 17 July 1950; *Educ* Univ of London (BA); *m* 1980, Hayden Phillips, CB, *qv*; 1 s (Thomas Peter b 1987), 2 da (Florence b 1981, Louisa Henrietta b 1984); *Career* with Private Office of Rt Hon Lord Jenkins of Hillhead Brussels Euro Cmmn 1977-79, ed Becket Pubns (Beckets Directory of the City of London 1984-90, dir Devpt Bd Rambent Dance Company 1990-; *Style—* The Hon Mrs Phillips

PHILLIPS, Leslie Samuel; s of Frederick Arthur Phillips (d 1934), and Cecelia Margaret, *née* Newlove (d 1984); *b* 20 April 1924; *Educ* Chingford Sch, Italia Conti; *m* (m dis), Penelope Noel, da of Richard Thorpe Bartley (d 1963); 2 s (Andrew Richard Bartley b 21 Nov 1954, Roger Quentin b 16 Nov 1959), 2 da (Caroline Elizabeth b 30 Oct 1949, Claudia Mary b 4 Oct 1951); m 2, 31 July 1982, Angela Margaret, da of Lt-Col Alexander Scoular (d 1978); *Career* Mil Serv DLI; actor, dir and prodr; career started as a child 1935, enjoys continuing success in comedy and serious roles alike; radio: The Navy Lark; TV: Our Man At St Marks, Summer's Lease, Chancer, Life After Life, Who Bombed Birmingham?, Rumpole, Thacker; theatre: Dear Octopus, On Monday Next, For Better For Worse, The Man Most Likely To..., Chapter 17, The Cherry Orchard, Passion Play; over one hundred films incl: Ferdinando, The Longest Day, Out Of Africa, Empire of the Sun, Scandal, King Ralph; dir Royal Theatrical Fund; *Style—* Leslie Phillips, Esq; c/o Julian Belfrage, 68 St James St, London SW1 (☎ 071 491 4400)

PHILLIPS, Dr Marisa; da of Dr Joseph Fargion (d 1963), of Rome, and Bice, *née* Sacerdoti (d 1963); *b* 14 April 1932; *Educ* Henrietta Barnett Sch Univ of Rome (PhD), Redlands Univ USA; *m* 1 Dec 1956, Philip Harold Phillips; 1 s (Adrian Brune b 21 July 1963), 1 da (Suzanne Julia b 29 June 1959); *Career* US Info Serv 1957-59, Penguin Books, legal advsr Police Complaints Bd 1977-81, princ asst dir Public Prosecutions 1984-87 (legal asst 1964-70, sr legal asst 1970-77, asst dir 1981-), dir of legal servs Crown Prosecution Serv, ret 1990; sr legal advsr banking ombudsman and pres of Mental Health Review Tbnl NE and NW Thames Area; memb: NSPCC, Anglo-Italian Soc; memb Hon Soc Lincoln's Inn; *Recreations* music, travel, theatre; *Style—* Dr Marisa Phillips; Dane Court, Kidderpore Avenue, Hampstead, London NW3; Les Galets D'Or, Ville Pranche-sur-Mer, Cote D'Azur, France

PHILLIPS, Capt Mark Anthony Peter; CVO (1974), ADC(P); s of Maj Peter William Garside Phillips, MC, late 1 King's Dragoon Gds, and Anne Patricia, *née* Tiarks; *b* 22 Sept 1948; *Educ* Marlborough, RMA Sandhurst; *m* 1973, HRH The Princess Royal (*see* Royal Family section); 1 s (Peter b 15 Nov 1977), 1 da (Zara b 15 May 1981); *Career* 1 The Queen's Dragoon Gds 1969, Regtl Duty 1969-74, co instr RMA Sandhurst 1974-77, Army Trg Directorate MOD 1977-78, ret; student RAC Cirencester 1978-79; personal ADC to HM The Queen 1974-; in Three Day Equestrian Event GB winning teams; team championships: World 1970, European 1971, Olympic Gold Medallists (Team) Olympic Games Munich 1972, memb Equestrian Team (Reserve) Olympic Games Mexico 1968 and Montreal 1976, Olympic Silver Medal (Team) Olympic Games Seoul 1988; dir Gleneagles Mark Phillips Equestrian Centre 1988-; second person ever to win Badminton Horse Trials four times; memb Royal Caledonian Hunt; patron: Glos Youth Assoc, Everyman Theatre Cheltenham; farmer; Liveryman Worshipful Co of: Farriers, Farmers, Saddlers, Loriners; Freeman: Worshipful Co of Carmen, City of London; *Clubs* Buck's (hon memb); *Style—* Captain Mark Phillips, CVO, ADC(P); Gatcombe Park, Minchinhampton, Stroud, Glos

PHILLIPS, Mark Paul; s of Norman John Phillips, of Balagan, 35 Stratton Rd, Beaconsfield, Bucks, and Wendy Sharon, *née* Cashman; *b* 28 Dec 1959; *Educ* The John Hampden Sch High Wycombe, Univ of Bristol (LLB, LLM); *m* 11 Aug 1984, Deborah Elizabeth, da of Norman Fisher, of The Barn, Burrows Fold, Castleton, Derbs; 1 da (Kathryn Mary b 22 Oct 1990); *Career* called to the Bar Inner Temple 1984; practising commercial law and specialising in insolvency and city work at the chambers of Michael Crystal, QC 1986-; memb: Nat Youth Theatre of GB 1977-82, Br Debating Team to USA Speaking Union 1983; *Books* Byles on Bills of Exchange (contrib, 1988), Paget's Law of Banking (contrib, 1989), Butterworth's Insolvency Law Handbook (co ed, 1990); *Recreations* theatre; *Style—* Mark Phillips, Esq; 3/4 South Square, Gray's Inn, London WC1R 5HP (☎ 071 696 9900, telex 920757 COSOL G, fax 071 696 9911)

PHILLIPS, Mark Trevor; s of George Milton Phillips (d 1972), of Georgetown, Guyana and New York, and Marjorie Eileen Phillips, *née* Canzius; *b* 31 Dec 1953; *Educ* Wood Green Sch N London, Queens Coll Georgetown Guyana, Imperial Coll London (BSc); *m* 25 July 1981, Asha Aline Francine, da of Padmashree Jehangir Bhownagary, of Bombay and Paris; 2 da (Sushila Melody b 11 July 1984, Holly May b 7 Jan 1988); *Career* pres NUS 1978-80; LWT: researcher (Skin, The London Programme) 1980-82, prodr (Black on Black, Club Mix, The Making of Britain) 1982-86; reporter This Week Thames TV 1986-87; LWT: presenter The London Programme 1987-, ed in chief regnl progs 1987-88, anchor reporter Eyewitness 1988-90; ed: Special Inquiry 1990, The London Programme 1991; US Prized Pieces Winner (pub affrs/news) 1985, RICS

Journalist and Broadcasters Award 1988, Royal Television Soc Regnl Current Affairs Award 1988; memb RTS 1990, ARCS; *Books* Partners In Progress (1986); *Recreations* music, theatre, America; *Clubs* The Groucho; *Style—* Trevor Phillips, Esq; London Weekend Television, Kent House, Upper Ground, London SE1 9LT (☎ 071 261 3144, fax 071 261 8047)

PHILLIPS, Max; *b* 31 March 1924; *Educ* Colston's Sch Bristol, Christ's Hosp, Magdalene Coll Cambridge (MA); *m* 1953, Patricia, da of late Cecil Moore; 2 s (Nicholas b 1953, James b 1962), 2 da (Alison b 1955, Gillian b 1959); *Career* WWII RA 1943-46; princ Colonial Office 1953-59 (asst princ 1949-53), sec Nigeria Fiscal Cmmn 1957-58; UKAEA: Overseas Rels Branch 1959-61, Health and Safety Branch 1961-64, Econs and Programming Branch 1964-69 (dep head 1967-69); chief personnel offr AWRE Aldermaston 1969-74, asst sec HM Treasy 1974-77, asst under sec State MOD 1977-84, sec AWRE 1984-87; Govnr and Almoner of Christ's Hosp; *Recreations* walking, swimming, travel; *Style—* Max Phillips, Esq; 2 Wilderness Farm, Onslow Village, Guildford, Surrey

PHILLIPS, Michael David; s of Frank Philips, and Cynthia Margaret, *née* Bond; *b* 22 June 1955; *Educ* Rickmansworth GS, Univ of Bath (BSc), PCL (DipArch); *m* 23 Aug 1986, Jane Louise, *née* Hamon; *Career* architect; DeVerre Urban Design prize PCL 1981; Casson Conder 1974, Ralph Erskine 1975, Moxley Jenner 1978, Powell Moya 1978-79, Hutchison Locke & Monk 1981-85; ptnr: Michael Phillips Assocs 1985-, McFarlane Phillips Architects 1989; prize winner IBA Int Soc Housing Competition Berlin; RIBA; *Style—* Michael Phillips, Esq; Welsbach Hse, Broomhill Rd, London SW18 4JQ (☎ 081 871 5178)

PHILLIPS, Michael George; s of Walter George Phillips (d 1958); *b* 31 Oct 1931; *Educ* Steyning GS; *m* 1957, Elizabeth Ann, da of Harold Stanley Batten (d 1959); 1 da; *Career* chm and md UBM Gp Ltd 1975-82, dep chm MK Electric Gp 1976-88; *Style—* Michael Phillips, Esq; Maysmead Place, Langford, nr Bristol BS18 7HX (☎ 0934 862343)

PHILLIPS, Michael Lothian Elliott; s of Cdre Jo Allan Phillips, RN (d 1985), of the Old Forge, West Meon, nr Petersfield, Hants, and Pansy Myra Edith, *née* Bonham Carter; *b* 30 Jan 1940; *Educ* Westbury House, Winchester; *m* 6 Dec 1975, Sarah Lindsay, da of James Palmer Tomkinson (d 1953); 2 s (Patrick James Elliott b 8 June 1980, David William b 11 Nov 1984), 1 da (Rebecca Jane b 7 Feb 1979); *Career* Short Serv Cmmn with KRRC, later 2 Greenjackets Lt 1958-61; Warren Hill Sporting Life 1962-65, racing corr The Times 1965-84 (Mandarin 1984-); *Recreations* gardening, tennis, skiing, shooting; *Clubs* Jockey Club Rooms; *Style—* Michael Phillips, Esq; Barndown House, Shefford Woodland, Nr Newbury, Berks RG16 7AE (☎ 048839 260); c/o The Times - Racing Desk, PO Box 481, Virgina Street, London E1 9BD

PHILLIPS, Hon Morgan David; s of Baroness Phillips; *b* 1939; *Educ* St Paul's, Downing Coll Cambridge, London U; *Style—* The Hon Morgan Phillips

PHILLIPS, Prof Neville Crompton; CMG (1973); 2 s of Samuel Phillips, of Christchurch, NZ, and Clara Phillips; *b* 7 March 1916; *Educ* Dannevirke HS, Palmerston North Boys' HS, Canterbury Univ Coll NZ, Merton Coll Oxford; *m* 1940, Pauline Beatrice, 3 da of Selby Palmer, of Havelock North, NZ; 1 s, 2 da; *Career* serv RA 1939-45, Maj, N Africa, Italy (despatches); emeritus prof Univ of Canterbury Christchurch NZ 1966 (prof of history 1949-66, vice chllr and rector 1966-77), ret; chm: Mgmnt Ctee Canterbury Archaeological Tst 1980-83, Canterbury Dist Country Paths Gp 1981-85; Hon LittD Univ of Canterbury NZ 1977; presented with Festschrift 1984; *Books* Italy, vol I (Sangro to Cassino), NZ Official War Histories (1957), History of University of Canterbury (ed and contrib, 1973), Yorkshire and English National Politics 1783-84 (1961); *Recreations* walking, cricket, wine, things Italian; *Style—* Professor Neville Phillips, CMG; Tyle House, Hackington Rd, Tyler Hill, Canterbury, Kent CT2 9NF (☎ 0227 471708)

PHILLIPS, Hon Mr Justice; Sir Nicholas Addison; QC (1978); *b* 21 Jan 1938; *Educ* Bryanston Sch, King's Cambridge; *m* 1972, Christylle Marie-Thérèse Rouffiac, nee Doreau; 2 da, and 1 step s, 1 step da; *Career* RNVR 1956-58; called to the Bar Middle Temple 1962, jr counsel to MOD and to Treasy in Admty matters 1973-78, rec Crown Ct 1982-, judge of High Ct Queen's Bench Div 1987-; govr Bryanston Sch 1975- (chm 1981); kt 1987; *Style—* The Hon Mr Justice Phillips; Royal Courts of Justice, Strand, London WC2A 2LL

PHILLIPS, (David) Nicholas; s of (David) Cecil Phillips (d 1988), of Sandwich, Kent, and Megan, *née* Davey; *b* 13 Jan 1953; *Educ* Dover Coll; *m* 13 Sept 1980, Anne Rosemary, da of Ernest Frank Robert Cross (d 1980), of Salford, Surrey; 1 s (Oliver b 1984), 1 da (Lucy b 1987); *Career* admitted slr 1977; ptnr Stephenson Harwood 1987-; Freeman Worshipful Co of Slrs 1980; memb Law Soc 1977; *Recreations* sailing, tennis; *Style—* Nicholas Phillips, Esq; The Thatched House, The Street, Bolney, W Sussex (☎ 0444 881405); Stephenson Harwood, 1 St Pauls Churchyard, London EC4 (☎ 071 329 4422, fax 071 606 0822, telex 886789)

PHILLIPS, Baroness (Life Peer UK 1964), of Fulham, Co London; Norah Phillips; JP (Co of London); o da of William and Catherine Lusher, of Fulham; *b* 12 Aug 1910; *Educ* Marist Convent, Hampton Trg Coll; *m* 1930, Morgan Walter Phillips (d 1963; sometime Gen Sec Labour Pty); 1 s (Hon Morgan David b 1939), 1 da (Hon Gwyneth Patricia (Hon Mrs Dunwoody) b 1930); *Career* sits as Labour Peer in House of Lords; a baroness-in-waiting (Govt whip) 1965-70; dir Assoc for the Prevention of Theft in Shops; pres: The Pre-Retirement Assoc, The Nat Assoc of Womens' Clubs (former gen sec), The Keep Fit Assoc, The Assoc for Research into Restricted Growth, The Industrial Catering Assoc, The Int Professional Security Assoc, Early Accomodation Counsel, The Inst of Safety and Public Protection, Beaufort Opera, All Party Parly Gp on Home Safety; vice pres: Nat Assoc for Maternal and Child Welfare, Fair Play for Children, Nat Chamber of Trade, Employment Fellowship, Women's Nat Cancer Control Campaign; memb: Home Office Standing Ctee on Crime Prevention, Consumer Forum, London Tourist Bd, London Heritage Tst; former memb: Cncl of Europe, Nat Consumer Cncl, Advertising Standards Authy, Women's Nat Cmmn, Snowdon Working Pty (integration of the disabled); HM Lord Lieut of Gtr London 1978-85, jr min in Govt 1945-70; *Style—* The Rt Hon the Baroness Phillips, JP; 115 Rannoch Rd, London W6 9SY

PHILLIPS, (Jeremy) Patrick Manfred; QC (1980); s of Manfred Henry Phillips (d 1963), and Irene Margaret, *née* Symondson (d 1970); *b* 27 Feb 1941; *Educ* Charterhouse; *m* 1970, Virginia Gwendolyn Dwyer; 2 s (Rufus b 1969, d 1989, Marcus b 1970); m 2, 1976, Judith Gaskell Hetherington; 2 s (Tobias b 1982, Seamus b 1985), 2 da (Rebekah b 1979, Natasha b 1980); *Career* barr 1964; owner of Kentwell Hall; contrib to successive ed of Coopers Manual of Auditing and Coopers Students Manual of Auditing; deviser and originator of Kentwell Hall's Annual Re-Creation of Tudor Domestic Life 1978-; landowner (130 acres); dir Care Br (pt of Care Int, the Third World devpt agency); *Books* author of various articles and pamphlets on Kentwell Hall Tudor Domestic Life and Heritage Educn; *Recreations* Kentwell Hall, Tudor bldgs, Tudor domestic life; *Style—* Patrick Phillips, Esq, QC; Kentwell Hall, Long Melford, Suffolk; 2 Temple Gardens, London EC4

PHILLIPS, Peter Anthony; s of Thomas George Phillips, of Cardiff, and Hilda Maud, *née* Connolly (d 1962); *b* 21 June 1938; *Educ* Howardian HS Cardiff, Cardiff Coll of Art (Cert commercial art), Welsh Coll of Advanced Technol (HNC Building); *Career* Nat Serv Gunner RA 1960-62; trainee Co Design Studio 1955-60, designer for int co 1962-63; BBC: design asst 1963-66, designer 1966-80, sr designer 1980-82, mangr TV prodn servs Wales 1982-; TV design credits incl: Hawkmoor, Dylan, Enigma Files; theatre design credits incl: My People and Solidarity (Theatre Clwyd), War Music and Pity of War (Lyric Theatre Hammersmith); winner Wales award for the design of a TV opera (The Rajah's Diamond) RTS; MCSD 1970 (licentiate 1960), memb Nat Cncl CSD 1989; *Recreations* gardening, travel; *Style—* Peter Phillips, Esq; Telynfa, Gwaelod-y-Garth, nr Cardiff CF4 8HJ (☎ 0222 810791); BBC, B H Llandaff, Cardiff CF5 2YQ (☎ 0222 572851)

PHILLIPS, (Ian) Peter; JP (Inner London); s of Bernard Phillips, of 7 South Drive, Ferring-on-Sea, Sussex, and Constance Mary Clayton (d 1984); *b* 13 Oct 1944; *Educ* Highgate Sch London, Sorbonne; *m* 2 May 1970, Wendy, da of Maurice Samuel Berne, of London NW11; 1 s (Leo b 1972), 1 da (Kira b 1974); *Career* ptnr Bernard Phillips & Co London 1968-82, ptnr Arthur Andersen & Co 1982-88, UK head corporate recovery services Arthur Andersen 1982-88, sr ptnr Buchler Phillips 1988-; treas North Kensington Neighbourhood Law Centre 1972, pres Insolvency Practitioners Assoc 1988-89; FCA 1968, FIPA 1981, FCCA 1983, MICM 1974; *Recreations* horse riding, skiing, modern jazz, baroque music, photography; *Style—* Peter Phillips, Esq, JP; Buchler Phillips, 84 Grosvenor St, London W1X 9DF (☎ 071 493 2550, fax 071 629 6444)

PHILLIPS, Sir Peter John; OBE (1983); s of Walter Alfred Phillips (d 1972), of Cardiff, and Victoria Mary Phillips (d 1974); *b* 18 June 1930; *Educ* Radley, Pembroke Coll Oxford (MA); *m* 9 June 1956, Jean Gwendoline, da of Sydney Essex Williams of Cardiff; 1 s (Jeremy Essex b 30 May 1957), 1 da (Louise Victoria b 7 May 1960); *Career* Nat Serv 2 Lt Welch Regt 1948-49; md Aberthaw & Bristol Channel Portland Cement plc 1964-83, chm AB Electronic Product Group plc 1987-, dep chm Principality Building Society 1988, memb Bd S Wales Electricity, chm CBI Wales 1982-83 (memb Cncl); chm Welsh Indust Devpt Advsy Bd, memb Cncl UCW Cardiff; kt 1990; *Recreations* fishing, walking, reading; *Clubs* Cardiff & County; *Style—* Sir Peter Phillips, OBE; Great House, Llanblethian, Cowbridge S Glamorgan CF7 7JG (☎ 0446 775163); AB Electronic Products Group plc, Abercynon, Mid Glam CF45 4SF (☎ 0443 740 331, fax 0443 741 676, telex 498606)

PHILLIPS, Richard Charles Jonathan; QC (1990); s of Air Cdre M N Phillips (d 1986), and Dorothy Ellen, *née* Green (d 1987); *b* 8 Aug 1947; *Educ* King's Sch Ely Cambridge (King's scholar), Sidney Sussex Coll Cambridge (exhibitioner); *m* 9 Sept 1978, Alison Jane (Annie) Phillips, OBE, da of David Arthur Francis; *Career* barr 1970, specialising in town and country planning and local govt; *Recreations* natural history, travel, photography; *Style—* Richard Phillips, Esq, QC; 2nd Floor, 2 Harcourt Bldgs, Temple, London EC4Y 9DB (☎ 071 353 8415, fax 071 353 7622)

PHILLIPS, Robert Sneddon; s of William James Phillips (d 1982), and Mary Jane Sneddon (d 1983); *b* 15 Sept 1932; *Educ* George Heriot's Sch Edinburgh, Univ of Edinburgh (MB ChB); *m* 2 Oct 1957, Isabella Newlands (Ella), da of George Forrest (d 1969); 1 s (Graeme Robert b 2 Nov 1964), 1 da (Gillian Moir b 16 March 1961); *Career* Surgn Lt RNVR 1957-59; conslt orthopaedic surgn 1967-, contrib numerous pubns on orthopaedic matters; memb: Cons Party, Methodist Church, Leonard Cheshire Fndn, local ctee Oakwood Home; pub speaker on works of Robert Burns; FRCSEd, memb Br Orthopaedic Assoc; *Recreations* cricket, golf; *Clubs* Heaton Mersey Cricket, Hazel Grove Golf, Forty, MCC; *Style—* Robert Phillips, Esq; 3 Milverton Drive, Bramhall, Stockport SK7 1EY (☎ 061 440 8037); Manchester Hosp, 11 St John St, Manchester M3 4DW (☎ 061 832 9999)

PHILLIPS, Sir Robin Francis; 3 Bt (UK 1912); s of Sir Lionel Francis Phillips, 2 Bt (d 1944); *b* 29 July 1940; *Educ* Aiglon Coll Switzerland; *Heir* none; *Career* owner of Ravenscourt Theatre Sch Ltd Hammersmith London; *Style—* Sir Robin Phillips, Bt; 12 Manson Mews, Queen's Gate, London SW7

PHILLIPS, Sian (Mrs Robin Sachs); da of David Thomas Phillips (d 1961), and Sally Thomas (d 1985); *Educ* Pontardawe GS, Cardiff Coll Univ of Wales (BA), RADA (Meggie Albanesi scholarship, Bancroft Gold medal); *m* 1, 1959 (m dis 1979), Peter O'Toole,*qv* ; 2 da (Kate b 1961, Pat b 1964); m 2, 24 Dec 1979, Robin David Sachs, s of Leonard Sachs (d 1990); *Career* actress; BBC News reader/announcer Wales 1953-55; London prodns incl: Hedda Gabler 1959, Ondine, Duchess of Malfi 1961, Lizard on the Rock 1961, Gentle Jack 1963, Maxibules 1964, Night of the Iguana 1964 (best actress nomination), Ride a Cock Horse 1965, Man and Superman (best actress nomination), Man of Destiny 1966, The Burglar 1967, Epitaph for George Dillon 1972, A Nightingale in Bloomsbury Square 1973, The Gay Lord Quex 1975, Spinechiller 1978, You Never Can Tell 1979, Pal Joey 1979-80 (best actress (musical) nomination), Dear Liar 1982, Major Barbara (NT) 1983, Peg 1984, Gigi 1985, Thursday's Ladies 1987, Brel 1988, Paris Match 1989, Vanilla 1990; TV drama series incl: Shoulder to Shoulder, How Green was my Valley (BAFTA Best Actress award), Crime and Punishment, Tinker Tailor Soldier Spy, Barriers, The Oresteiaa of Aescylus, I Claudius (BAFTA Best Actress award and Best Performance Royal TV Soc), Vanity Fair, Shadow of the Noose, Snow Spider, Emlyns Moon (1990), Perfect Scoundrels (1991); *Films* Becket 1963, Goodby Mr Chips 1968 (Best Supporting Actress award), Murphy's War 1970, Under Milk Wood 1971, Dune 1984, Valmont 1989, Dark River, A Painful Case (C4); Welsh Arts Cncl, BBC Rep Co, dir Film Wales, ITV, BBC; *Radio* incl: Bequest to a Nation, Anthony and Cleopatra, Henry VIII, All's Well That Ends Well, Oedipus, Phaedra, The Maids; *Records* Pal Joey (LP), Gigi (LP), Peg (LP), Bewitched Bothered and Bewildered (single), I Remember Mama (LP); journalism incl: Vogue, Cosmopolitan, Radio Times; memb: Gorsedd of Bards 1960, Drama Ctee Arts Cncl 1970-75; former govr St David's Theatre Tst; Hon DLitt Univ of Wales 1983; hon fell: Cardiff Coll Univ of Wales 1980, Polytechnic of Wales 1988; *Books* Sian Phillips' Needlepoint (1987); *Recreations* gardening, drawing, needlepoint; *Style—* Miss Sian Phillips; Saraband Ltd, 265 Liverpool Rd, London N1 (☎ 071 609 5313)

PHILLIPS, Dr Simon Jeremy; s of Basil Montagu Phillips, LVO, of Astley Close, Pewsey, Wilts, and Sheila Monica, *née* Redding; *b* 13 April 1943; *Educ* Sherborne, St Bartholomews Hosp and Univ of London (MB BS, MRCS, LRCP, DCH, DObstRCOG), Univ of Bath (M Phil); *m* 30 Sept 1967, (Susan) Jennifer, da of Albert Hugh Thompson (d 1969), of Leeds, Yorkshire; 2 s (Jeremy David Hugh b 29 Oct 1970, Charles James Aston b 24 Oct 1973); *Career* GP 1970-, currently ptnr in practice; res grant from Bath Area Med Res Tst for work with refugees from Indo-China 1981-83; author of numerous papers, articles in major journals and contribns to med books; Freeman City of London 1968, Liveryman Worshipful Co of Gardeners 1976 (Freeman 1968); memb: BMA 1966, Clinical Soc of Bath; *Recreations* cooking, fishing, walking and mountaineering, backpacking, cross country skiing, photography, painting; *Style—* Dr Simon Phillips; Church Holding, Etchilhampton, Devizes, Wilts SN10 3JL (☎ 0380 086 291); Lansdowne Surgery, Waiblingen Way, Devizes (☎ 0380 722278)

PHILLIPS, Hon Mrs (Sophia Rosalind); *née* Vane; 3 da of 11 Baron Barnard, TD, JP, *qv*; *b* 24 Jan 1962; *Educ* Cobham Hall, Westfield Coll London (BSc); *m* 20 Sept 1986, Simon Benjamin Phillips, yst s of late Peter J Phillips, of Gustard Wood, Wheathampstead, Herts; 1 s (Oliver John b 2 Sept 1989); *Style—* The Hon Mrs Phillips; The Yellow House, Copt Hewick, Ripon, N Yorkshire

PHILLIPS, Thomas Bernard Hudson; s of Prof Arthur Phillips OBE, of Otterbourne, nr Winchester, Hants, and Kathleen, *née* Hudson; *b* 12 Aug 1938; *Educ* King's Sch Canterbury; *m* 14 July 1979, Rosemary Eleanor, da of Maj RAD Sinclair (ret), of Burnham-on-Crouch, Essex; 1 s (Roland b 12 Dec 1980), 1 da (Laura b 9 May 1982); *Career* slr; State Counsel Kenya 1967-70, Herbert Smith 1970- (ptnr 1977-); memb Law Soc; *Recreations* sailing, skiing, golf; *Style—* Tom Phillips, Esq; Watling House, 35 Cannon St, London EC4M 5SD (☎ 071 489 8000)

PHILLIPS, Trevor Thomas (Tom); s of David John Phillips, and Margaret Agnes, *née* Arnold; *b* 24 May 1937; *Educ* Henry Thornton GS, St Catherines Coll Oxford (MA), Camberwell Sch of Arts and Crafts (NDD); *m* 12 Aug 1961 (m dis 1988), Jill Purdy; 1 s (Conrad Leofric (Leo) b 26 Jan 1965), 1 da ((Eleanor) Ruth b 25 Jan 1964); *Career* artist; works in collections of: Tate Gallery, V & A Museum, Br Museum, Nat Portrait Gallery, Br Cncl, MOMA NY, Philadelphia Museum, Library of Congress, Bibliotheque Nationale Paris, Aust Nat Gallery Canberra, Museum of Fine Arts Budapest; exhibitions worldwide since 1969 incl retrospective exhibition 1974-75: Kunsthalle Basel, Germeente Museum, The Hague, Serpentine Gallery London, portrait retrospective Nat Portrait Gallery 1989, N Carolina Museum 1990; designer of tapestries: St Catherine's Coll Oxford, HQ Channel 4, Morgan Grenfell Office, The Ivy Restaurant; book artist: translated, illustrated, printed and published Dantes Inferno 1983; composer of the opera IRMA (recorded twice by Obscure Records 1977 and Matchless Recordings 1988), performed at Bordeaux Festival, Istanbul Festival, ICA; writer and critic for TLS and regular writer for The Independent and RA Magazine; TV dir for A TV Dante for Channel 4 with Peter Greenaway (first prize Montreal Festival 1990); chm Royal Academic Library, vice chm copywright Cncls 1984-88, hon pres S London Art Soc 1988-; ARA 1984, RE 1987, RA 1989; *Books* Trailer (1971), Works and Texts to 1974 (1975), A Humument (revised edn, 1987), Heart of a Humument (1985), Where are they now: The Class of '47 (1990); *Recreations* watching cricket, collecting African art; *Clubs* Chelsea Arts, The Groucho, SCCC; *Style—* Tom Phillips, Esq; 57 Talfourd Rd, London SE15 (☎ 071 701 3978)

PHILLIS, Michael John; s of Francis William Phillis, and Gertrude Grace, *née* Pitman; *b* 6 March 1948; *Educ* Archbishop Tennysons GS Croydon; *m* 30 Aug 1969, Janice Susan, da of George Horne (d 1963); 1 s (Marc Weston b 26 Aug 1973), 1 da (Michelle b 18 Feb 1976); *Career* Bank of London & S America Ltd 1967-73, asst dir London & Continental Bankers 1973-81, regnl vice pres Marine Midland Bank 1981-83, dep gen mangr (Treasy) Kansallis Osake Pankki 1983-; dir: Kansallis Gota Securities Ltd 1989-90, Kansallis Securities Ltd 1990-; memb Chicago Mercantile Exchange Interest Rate Advsy Ctee (London) 1990-; *Recreations* golf, music, family, gardening; *Clubs* Warley Park Golf, St James'; *Style—* Michael Phillis, Esq; Kansallis-Osake-Pankki, Kansallis House, 19 Thomas More Street, London E1 9YW (☎ 071 265 3333 and 071 860 1763, fax 071 588 9121, telex 267173 KOPLON)

PHILLIS, Robert Weston; s of Francis William Phillis, and Gertrude Grace Phillis; *b* 3 Dec 1945; *Educ* John Ruskin GS, Univ of Nottingham; *m* 16 July 1966, Jean, da of Herbert William Derham; 3 s (Martin b 1971, Benjamin b 1974, Timothy b 1974); *Career* lectr Univ of Edinburgh and Scottish Business Sch 1971-75; md: Sun Printers Ltd 1976-79, Ind TV Pubns Ltd 1979-81, Central Ind TV plc 1981-87; dir: ITCA 1982-87, ITN 1982-87; chm: Zenith Prodns Ltd 1984-91, ITV Network Programming Ctee 1984-86; gp md Carlton Communications plc 1987-91; dir and tstee TV Tst for the Environment 1984-, dir Int Cncl of Nat Academy of TV Arts and Socs 1985-, chm RTS 1989-; *Recreations* golf, home and garden, theatre; *Style—* Robert Phillis, Esq; Independent Television News Ltd, 200 Gray's Inn Rd, London WC1X 8XZ (☎ 071 833 3000, fax 071 430 4305)

PHILLPOTTS, Simon Vivian Surtees; s of Christopher Louis George Phillpotts, CMG (d 1985), and Vivian Chanter, *née* Bowden; *b* 9 Feb 1947; *Educ* Abberley Hall, Harrow, Georgetown Univ USA; *Career* mangr: Shiro (China) Ltd Hong Kong 1968-74, Jardine Matheson & Co Hong Kong 1974-82; gen mangr Anglo Swiss Trading Hong Kong 1982-84, dir Daks-Simpson Ltd UK 1985-; *Clubs* Whites; *Style—* Simon Phillpotts, Esq; 11 Hanbury House, Regents Bridge Gdns, Rita Rd, London SW8 (☎ 071 735 6323); Daks-Simpson, 34 Jermyn St, London SW1 6HS (☎ 071 439 8781, fax 071 437 3633, telex 22466 DAKS M)

PHILP, (Dennis Alfred) Peter; s of Alfred Thomas Philp, MBE (d 1959), and Elsie May *née* Whitt (d 1981); *b* 10 Nov 1920; *Educ* Penarth Co Sch; *m* 25 Sept 1940, Pamela Mary, da of William Alfred Coxon-Ayton (d 1980); 2 s (Paul b 1941, Richard b 1943); *Career* WWII RAF 1940-42; playwright and author; plays: The Castle of Deception (winner Arts Cncl Award, 1951), Love and Lunacy (1954); *Books* Books Antique Furniture for the Smaller Home (1962), Furniture of the World (1974); contrib to: jls incl The Times, Antique Dealer and Collectors Guide, Sotheby's Encyclopedia of Furniture 1989; memb Soc of Authors; *Recreations* literature, theatre, music; *Clubs* East India; *Style—* Peter Philp, Esq; 77 Kimberley Rd, Cardiff CF2 5DP (☎ 0222 493826)

PHILPOT, Elizabeth; *née* Massey; da of William Edmund Devereux Massey, CBE, of Dorking, Surrey, and Ingrid, *née* Glad-Block; *b* 8 April 1943; *Educ* Heathfield, Courtauld Inst Univ of London (BA), Johann Wolfgang Goethe-Universität Frankfurt am Main (Dip); *m* 10 Sept 1977, Timothy Stephen Burnett Philpot, s of Christopher Burnett Philpot (d 1971), of Pickering, Yorks; *Career* local govt offr LCC (later GLC and ILEA) 1962-65; asst keeper of the muniments Westminster Abbey 1968-69; admin asst Bedford Coll London 1969-70, HM Dip Serv 1970-82: third sec Brasilia Embassy, info attaché Paris Embassy; lectr and art historian 1982-; chm Reigate branch Nat Cncl of Women of GB; Freeman City of London 1975, Liveryman Worshipful Co of Clockmakers 1983 (Steward 1989); *Recreations* art history, travel, photography, horology, theatre, swimming, sailing, skiing; *Style—* Mrs Timothy Philpot; Ivinghoe, 9 Croft Ave, Dorking, Surrey RH4 1LN (☎ 0306 882739)

PHILPOT, Robert James; s of Maj R H Philpot, MC (d 1969), of Sherfield Manor, Romsey, Hants, and Miriam, *née* Hopkinson (d 1979); *b* 24 Oct 1925; *Educ* Wellington; *m* 8 Sept 1956, Sylvia Mavis Rita, da of (William Alexander) Thomas (d 1934); *Career* served 1943-47, cmmnd Queens Royal Regt; dir Asprey plc 1983- (gen mangr 1975); *Recreations* gardening, sport; *Style—* Robert Philpot, Esq; Madeira Road, Mitcham, Surrey; Asprey plc, 165-169 New Bond St, London W1Y 0AR (☎ 071 493 6767, fax 071 491 0384, telex 25110)

PHILPOTT, Brian; s of Harold Edmund Philpott (d 1961), of London, and Nellie Edith Philpott (d 1986); *b* 22 June 1933; *Educ* Roan Sch for Boys Greenwich, Nat Coll for Heating, Ventilating, Refrigeration and Fan Engrg; *m* 12 June 1959, Vivienne Joan, da of Horace Percy Winder (d 1949), of Dorking; 1 s (David b 1963), 2 da (Diane b 1962, Sally b 1966); *Career* Nat Serv RAF 1951-53; trg Benham & Sons Ltd 1949-51 and 1953-55, project engr Matthew Hall & Co Ltd 1955-61, sr design engr then head of Environment Engrg Dept WS Atkins & Partners 1961-68, ptnr Building Design Partnership 1973- (joined 1968, appointed assoc 1969); memb assoc Inst Heating and Ventilating Engrs 1961; CEng, FCIBSE 1969, MConsE 1981; *Recreations* badminton, gardening, photography, walking; *Style—* Brian Philpott, Esq; Watchwood House, Watchwood Drive, Lytham St Annes, Lancs FY8 4NP (☎ 0253 735385); Building Design Partnership, Vernon St, Moor Lane, Preston, Lancs PR1 3PQ (☎ 0772 59383, fax 0772 201378 GROUP 3, telex 677160)

PHILPS, Dr (Frank) Richard; MBE (1946); s of Francis John Philps (d 1915), and Matilda Ann, *née* Healey (d 1963); *b* 9 March 1914; *Educ* Christ's Hospital Horsham Sussex, UCL (MB BS, DPH, MD); *m* 26 April 1941, Emma Lilla Florence Mary, da of Frederick William Schmidt, Order of Franz Josef (d 1934); 2 s (William, James), 1 da (Victoria (Mrs Taylor)); *Career* WWII, med offr RAFVR 1940, captured by Japanese Java 1942; pathologist St Pancras Hosp 1952-54, conslt pathologist Eastbourne Gp of Hosps 1954-64, res asst Surgical Unit UCH 1955-60, conslt cytologist UCH 1960-73, hon conslt in cytology Royal Free Hosp 1972-73, dir Jt Royal Free and UCH Dept of Cytology 1972-73; memb: Nat Tst, RSPB, Devon Tst for Nature Conservation; memb BMA 1940, FRC Path 1964, fell Int Acad of Cytology USA 1967; *Books* A Short Manual of Respiratory Cytology (1964), Watching Wildlife (1968); *Recreations* watching and filming wild animals (BBC nature film prize 1963), watercolour painting (exhibited RI 1980-84); *Style—* Dr Richard Philps, MBE; Woodlands, Sydenham Wood, Lewdown, Okehampton, Devon EX20 4PP (☎ 082 286 347)

PHIPP, Peter John; s of Reginald John Phipp, and Hilda Emily Silk, *née* Edwards; *b* 4 March 1942; *Educ* Bournemouth GS; *Career* BBC TV 1962-72; advertising photographer at studios in Bedford Gardens Kensington specialising in work for beauty and cosmetics indust and travel indust 1972-; dir Bartok Mgmnt; *Recreations* tennis; *Style—* Peter Phipp, Esq; 30 Lansdowne Walk, London W11 3LT; Studio 11A, 79 Bedford Gardens, London W8 7EG (☎ 071 727 0100)

PHIPPIN, Eric Thomas; s of Thomas William Phippin (d 1979), and Margaret Anne, *née* Preston; *b* 9 Oct 1931; *Educ* Loughborough Central Sch London, City of London Coll; *m* 18 July 1953, Patricia Ann, da of Sidney Henry Collins (d 1982), of London; 3 s (Paul Jeremy b 31 Aug 1957, Stephen Christopher b 2 May 1960, Andrew Michael b 7 Sept 1966); *Career* Nat Serv RAF (movement control) 1950-52; RAFVR: Pilot Offr 1952, Flying Offr (orgn and supply) 1955; mgmnt trainee Union-Castle Mail Steamship Co Ltd 1952-63 (seconded to S and E Africa 1956-58); dir: Ocean Travel Devpt 1967-77, Chandris Cruises Ltd 1963-77 (passenger mangr 1963), Chandris Tours 1971-77, CTC Lines 1977-89, CTC (Air Sea Holidays) Ltd 1977-89, Passenger Shipping Assoc 1977-, CTC (Hellas) SA 1984-89, Chandris Ltd 1989-; Freeman: City of London 1974, Worshipful Co of Basket Makers 1974; FCIT 1963; *Recreations* tennis, cricket, music; *Style—* Eric Phippin, Esq; Chandris Ltd, 5 St Helen's Place, London EC3A 6BJ (☎ 071 588 7021, fax 071 628 0171, telex 884111 LONDON)

PHIPPS, Antony Bourne; s of Thomas Edward Phipps (d 1971), of Farndish Manor, Wellingboro, N Hants and Cicely Radcliffe, *née* Bourne (d 1988); *b* 18 Feb 1931; *Educ* Radley; *m* 30 Aug 1958, Virginia Margaret Jimpson, da of Harry Jimpson Greenhalgh (d 1966), of Santon House, Holmrook, Cumbria; 2 da (Cicely b 27 June 1959, Elizabeth b 11 Aug 1960); *Career* Nat Serv RN; chm and md: Storland plc, Skeltools Ltd, Novoguage Ltd, Harris Lifting and Shipping Tackle Co Ltd, David Willets Ltd, EMC Engrg Co (London) Ltd, Medifield Ltd; tstee Letchworth Centre of Holistic Med Rosehill Hosp Hitchin; *Recreations* breeding racehorses, farming, hunting; *Clubs* Worcs Hunt; *Style—* Antony Phipps, Esq; Stoke House Farm, Stoke Hammond, Bucks (☎ 0908 644498)

PHIPPS, Dr Colin Barry; s of Edgar Reeves Phipps; *b* 23 July 1934; *Educ* Acton Co Sch, Swansea GS, UCL, Univ of Birmingham; *m* 1956, Marion May, da of Clifford Harry Lawrey; 2 s, 2 da; *Career* dep chm and chief exec Clyde Petroleum Ltd 1979-83, non-exec chm Clyde 1983-, Greenwich Resources plc 1989-; MP (Lab) Dudley W 1974-79; memb: Cncl of Europe 1976-79, Western Euro Union 1976-79; chm Falkland Islands Fndn 1990-; FGS 1956, FInstPet 1972, memb Inst of Geologists 1978; *Clubs* Reform; *Style—* Dr Colin Phipps; Mathon Court, Mathon, Malvern WR13 5NZ (☎ 0684 892267); 38 Cheyne Walk, London SW3 (☎ 071 352 5381)

PHIPPS, Air Vice-Marshal Leslie William; CB (1983), AFC (1959); s of late Frank Walter Phipps; *b* 17 April 1930; *Educ* SS Philip and James Sch Oxford; *Career* dir of Air Def and Overseas Ops 1978-79, dir-gen Personnel Mgmnt RAF 1980-82, sr directing staff RCDS 1983-; British Aerospace (Mil Aircraft Div) 1984-; *Style—* Air Vice-Marshal Leslie Phipps, CB, AFC; 33 Knole Wood, Devenish Rd, Sunningdale, Berks SL5 9QR

PHIPPS, Lady (Evelyn) Patricia Mary; *née* Scudamore-Stanhope; da of late 12 Earl of Chesterfield; *b* 7 May 1917; *m* 1, 28 Sept 1938 (m dis 1947), Lt Cdr Ian McDonald, RAN; m 2, 24 Oct 1947, as his 3 w, John Harford Stanhope Lucas-Scudamore, DL (d 1976); 1 s, 1 da; m 3, 1983, Leckonby John Alexander Phipps; *Style—* The Lady Patricia Phipps; Newcote, Moccas, Hereford (☎ 09817 291)

PHIPPS, Lady Phoebe; *née* Pleydell-Bouverie; 3 da of 7 Earl of Radnor, KG, KCVO, JP, DL, by his 1 w; *b* 25 Jan 1932; *Educ* Greenvale Sch Long Island USA, Godolphin Sch Salisbury, Queen's Secretarial Coll, Powderham Castle Sch of Domestic Sci; *m* 1955 (m dis 1963), Hubert Beaumont, s of John Sheaffer Phipps, of Long Island; 1 s, 1 da; *Career* artist; *Clubs* Lansdowne; *Style—* The Lady Phoebe Phipps; Water's Edge, 1 New Bridge Rd, Salisbury, Wilts (☎ 0722 28978)

PHIPPS, Rosemary Carolanne Tecla; da of James Fawcett Shirtcliffe (d 1985), and Tecla Lilli, *née* Behrmann; *b* 3 Aug 1944; *Educ* Parktown Girls HS, Pharmacy Sch SA (Dip Pharm), Newland Park (DMS, DipM); *m* 1975 (m dis 1987), John-Francis Phipps, s of late Sir Eric Phipps; 1 s (William b 1978), 1 da (Sophie b 1976); *Career* business mgmnt mktg conslt, lectr, author and publisher; dir Phipps Radburn Publishing Ltd 1986-90; chm: Oxford Area Bd Young Enterprise 1989-, IBA Advsy Ctee Oxford and Banbury 1989-; *Books* Coming up Trumps (1986), Keep on the Safe Side (1989), Discover Windsor Castle (1991); *Recreations* painting, music, gardening; *Style—* Ms Rosemary Phipps; 43 Leckford Rd, Oxford OX2 6HY

PHIPPS, Rt Rev Simon Wilton Phipps; MC (1945); s of Capt William Duncan Phipps, CVO, RN (d 1967); *b* 6 July 1921; *Educ* Eton, Trinity Coll Cambridge; *m* 1973, Mary, widow of Rev Dr James Welch and da of Sir (Charles) Eric Palmer (d 1948); *Career* ordained 1950, curate of Huddersfield Parish Church 1950-53, chaplain of Trinity Coll Cambridge 1953-58, industl chaplain in Coventry Diocese and chaplain of Coventry Cathedral 1958-68 (hon canon 1965-68), first bishop suffragan of Horsham (Diocese of Chichester) 1968-74, bishop of Lincoln 1974-86; *Style—* The Rt Rev Simon Phipps; Sarsen, Shipley, West Sussex RH13 8PX

PHIPSON, John Norman; TD (1975); s of N H W Smith, and Margaret Helen, *née* Brown; descendant of Oliver Cromwell, via mother,s family; *b* 29 Nov 1940; *Educ* Rugby; *m* 2 Feb 1984, Harriet Jane Maxwell, da of late Hugh Hamilton McCleery; 2 s, 2 da; *Career* slr; ptnr Linklaters & Paines Slrs, London, Paris, New York, Hong Kong, Brussels, Tokyo; Maj HAC (TA) 1959-75, Court of Assts HAC 1972, treas 1984-87, vice pres 1988-90; *Recreations* family; *Clubs* Players Theatre; *Style—* John N Phipson, Esq, TD; Barrington House, 59-67 Gresham St, London EC2V 7JA (☎ 071 606 7080, fax 071 606 5113, telex 884 349)

PHIZACKERLEY, Ven Gerald Robert; s of John Dawson Phizackerley (d 1980), and Lilian Mabel Ruthven, *née* Falloon (d 1983); *b* 3 Oct 1929; *Educ* Queen Elizabeth GS Penrith, Univ Coll Oxford (MA), Wells Theol Coll; *m* 1959, Annette Catherine, da of Cecil Frank Baker, MBE (d 1982); 1 s (David b 1963), 1 da (Mary b 1961); *Career* curate St Barnabas Carlisle 1954-57, chaplain Abingdon Sch 1957-64, rector Gaywood with Bawsey & Mintlyn Norwich 1964-78, rural dean Lynn 1968-78, hon canon Norwich Cathedral 1975-78, archdeacon Chesterfield and hon canon of Derby Cathedral 1978-; fell Woodard Corpn 1981-; JP Norfolk 1972-78; *Recreations* theatre, travel, border collies; *Style—* The Ven the Archdeacon of Chesterfield; The Old Parsonage, Taddington, Buxton, Derbyshire SK17 9TJW (☎ 0298 85607)

PHYLACTOU, Christodoulos Pindar (Chris); s of Maj Pindar Phylactou, MBE, RE, and Kroustallo, *née* Skyrianides; *b* 26 Oct 1930; *Educ* privately, Pancyprian Gymnasium, Trinity Coll Cambridge (BA, MA); *m* 14 May 1956, (Eugenie) Youli, *née* Papadopoulos (d 1985); 1 da (Maria Christina b 3 Oct 1958); *Career* chm: Cyprus Cold Stores Ltd 1970-75 (dir 1956), Textiles Manufacturing Co Ltd Cyprus 1970-75 (dir 1957), Moorgate Merchants Ltd 1985-90 (md 1981-85); projects dir Industrial Development & Services Ltd Iran 1975-78; vice pres: Georgia Industrial Incorporated Georgia USA 1981-85, Granite Holdings Inc Delaware USA 1983-; dir Travel Buff Ltd 1990-; fell IOD, FICSA; *Recreations* travelling, motoring, Byzantine studies; *Style—* Chris Phylactou, Esq; 55 Brompton Square, London SW3 2AG (☎ 071 589 7155, fax 071 589 6972); Villa Giulia, Platres, Cyprus (☎ 054 21869)

PHYSICK, Dr John Frederick; CBE (1984); s of Nino William Physick (d 1946), of London, and Gladys, *née* Elliott (d 1978); *b* 31 Dec 1923; *Educ* Battersea GS, DrRCA; *m* 28 May 1954, Eileen Mary, da of Cyril Walter Walsh (d 1970), of London; 2 s (Alastair b 2 Dec 1955, Nigel b 9 June 1958), 1 da (Helen b 6 Jan 1960); *Career* WWII RN 1942-46, AFHQ Algiers/Caserta 1942-45, RNVR until 1956; V & A Museum: joined 1948, sec to Advsy Cncl 1973-83, asst to Dir 1974-83, keeper of museum servs 1975-83, dep dir 1983; memb: Drawings Ctee RIBA 1975, Cathedrals Advsy Ctee 1977-81; pres Church Monuments Soc 1984-86, chm Monuments Sub-Ctee Cncl for the Care of Churches 1984- (memb 1978-); memb: Westminster Abbey Architectural Advsy Panel 1985-, Rochester Cathedral Fabric Ctee 1987-, Canterbury and Rochester Jt Diocesan Books and Documents Ctee, Canterbury and Rochester Jt Diocesan Archaeological Sub Ctee; vice chm: Rochester Diocesan Advsy Ctee for the Care of the Churches 1987- (memb 1965-), Friends of Kent Churches (chm Grants Ctee); FSA, FRSA; *Books* Catalogue of the Engravings of Eric Gill (1965), Designs for English Sculpture 1680-1860 (1969), The Wellington Monument (1970), Marble Halls (1975), The Victoria and Albert Museum, the History of its Building (1982), Sculpture in Britain 1530-1830 (ed 2 edn, 1988), The Royal College of Art (contrib, 1987), Westminster Abbey, The Monuments (jtly, 1989); *Style—* Dr John Physick, CBE, FSA; 49 New Rd, Meopham, Kent DA13 0LS; 14 Park St, Deal, Kent CT14 6AG

PIATKUS, Judith; da of Raphael Emmanuel Assersohn (d 1988), and Estelle Freda, *née* Richenberg; *b* 16 Oct 1949; *Educ* South Hampstead HS; *m* 1, 5 Dec 1971 (m dis 1985), Brian John Piatkus; 1 s, 2 da; m 2, 30 Dec 1990, Cyril Bernard Ashberg; 1 step da; *Career* md and publisher Piatkus Books 1979-; *Recreations* golf, bridge, reading; *Style—* Ms Judith Piatkus; 5 Windmill St, London W1P 1HF (071 631 0710, fax 071 436 7137, telex 266082 PIATKS G)

PICK, Charles Samuel; s of Samuel Pick; *b* 22 March 1917; *Educ* Masonic Sch Bushey; *m* 1938, Hilda Beryl Hobbs; 1 s, 1 da; *Career* serv war 1939-46, cmmnd RA, AA Cmd, apptd Staff Capt; served ALFSEA: India, Ceylon, Singapore; started in publishing with Victor Gollancz Ltd 1933, fndr memb Michael Joseph Ltd 1935 (jt md 1959-62), md William Heinemann Ltd 1962, dir Heinemann Group of Publishers 1962 (md 1979-85), dir Pan Books 1968, chm Secker & Warburg 1973, ret from Heinemann in 1985; started Charles Pick Consultancy 1985 acting as sole literary agent for Wilbur Smith; chm and pres Heinemann Holdings Inc 1980-85, memb Cncl Publishers' Assoc 1950-83; *Recreations* walking, reading, theatre; *Clubs* Savile, MCC; *Style—* Charles Pick, Esq; Littlecot, Lindfield, Sussex (☎ 04448 2218); 3 Bryanston Place, London W1 (☎ 071 402 8043)

PICK, Joan Margaret; da of William Pick (d 1985), of Cumbria, and Harriet Rhodes, *née* Bancroft; *b* 9 Dec 1940; *Educ* Barrow in Furness County GS for Girls, Univ of Bristol (BSc); *Career* scientific writer Understanding Science 1962-64, market researcher and business planner conslt Product Planning Ltd 1964-67, business planning conslt and dir Interplan 1967-73; *Books* The Earth Enterprise Project (1973); *Recreations* keeping mentally and physically fit for the job; *Clubs* Mensa; *Style—* Miss Joan Pick; 23 Maybourne Grange, Turnpike Link, Croydon CR0 5NH (☎ 081 686 5089)

PICK, Prof John Morley; s of John Mawson Pick, of Ripon, Yorks, and Edith Mary, *née* Morley; *b* 12 Oct 1936; *Educ* King Edward VI Sch Retford, Univ of Leeds (BA, PGCE), Univ of Birmingham (MA), City Univ London (Phd); *m* 19 April 1960, Ann Clodagh, da of Sydney Simmons Johnson (d 1983), of Eastbourne; 1 s (Martyn b 1963), 1 da (Catherine b 1965); *Career* dir Dillington House Coll of Adult Educn and Arts Centre 1973-76, head arts policy and govt studies City Univ 1976-90, Gresham prof rhetoric Gresham Coll City Univ 1983-88, prof arts mgmnt City Univ 1985-91, dir Gresham Coll Res Project 1988-; prof emeritus City Univ 1991-; FRSA 1987; *Books* Arts Administration (1980), The State of The Arts (1981), The West End: Mismanagement And Snobbery (1983), The Theatre Industry (1984), The Modern Newspeak (1985), Managing The Arts? (1987), Arts in a State (1988), Vile Jelly (1991); *Recreations* gardening, theatre, writing, comedy; *Style—* Prof John Pick; Willow Cottage, 20 High St, Sutton on Trent, Newark NG23 6QA (☎ 0636 822102); Department Arts Policy and Management, Level 12, Frobisher Cres, The Barbican, Silk St, London EC2Y 8HB (☎ 071 253 4399, 071 628 5641/2)

PICK, (Frederick) Michael; s of Frederick William Leopold Walter Pick (d 1949), and Helene Alice, *née* Julissen; *b* 21 June 1949; *Educ* England and Germany, Gonville and Caius Coll Cambridge (MA); *Career* civil servant 1975-77; dir Stair & Co Ltd (London and NYC); antique dealer, designer and decorator; hon UK advsr to Perm Consulate Gen and Legation Republic of Estonia USA; fndr ctee memb The Thirties Soc 1979; memb: Br Antique Dealers Assoc, Royal Soc for Asian Affrs; author, lectr, designer i/c of reconstruction of Norman Hartnell Ltd 1989; contrib to numerous periodicals and newspapers; *Books* The English Room (1985), The National Trust Guide to Antiques (1985), The English Country Room (1988); *Recreations* pottering to music, conversation, literature, languages; *Clubs* Lansdowne; *Style—* Michael Pick, Esq; 120 Mount St, London W1Y 5HB (☎ 071 499 1784, fax 071 629 1050)

PICK, (Rachel Anne); *née* Bridge; 2 da of Baron Bridge of Harwich, PC; *b* 15 April 1946; *Educ* BA (Hons); *m* 1975, Martin Pick; 1 s (Oliver b 1984), 1 da (Katharine b 1977); *Career* child psychotherapist; *Style—* Mrs R Pick

PICKARD, Brian Harold; s of Alfred Harold Pickard (d 1954), of London, and Winifred Sarah, *née* Cockrill (d 1982); *b* 14 Feb 1922; *Educ* Eltham Coll, Guy's Hosp and London Univ (MB BS, DLO); *m* 1, 13 May 1944, Joan Daisy, da of Harry Packham, of London; 2 s (Geoffrey b 1952, William b 1958), 2 da (Diane (Mrs Yeo) b 1945, Celia (Mrs Greetham) b 1947); m 2, Diana Sylvia, da of John William Stokes, of Frinton; 1 da (Lucy b 1981); *Career* RAF 1948-50, ENT specialist RAF Hosp Cosford; Sqdn Ldr RAFVR 1950-55; sr registrar ENT: Hosp for Sick Children Great Ormond St, Kings Coll Hosp London; conslt surgn ENT: St Georges Hosp London, Moorfields Eye Hosp London, Dreadnought Seamans Hosp London, Dispensaire Francais London visiting ENT specialist St Helena; med advsr Guild of Air Pilots and Air Navigators, conslt Br Airways; private pilot 1948-, colours for swimming Guy's and King's (cap Guy's swimming club); memb Med Panel CAA; Freeman: City of London, Worshipful Soc of Apothecaries; Past Master Guild of Air Pilots and Air Navigators; FRCS, LMSSA, FRSM, FRSA, MRAeS, memb Br Med Pilots Assoc (former pres); Chevalier de l'Ordre National du Merite; *Recreations* sailing, flying; *Clubs* RAF, RAC, United Hosps Swimming (vice cdre), St Georges Hosp Swimming (former cdre); *Style—* Brian Pickard, Esq; Shandon, 19 Waltham Way, Frinton-on-Sea Essex CO13 9JE (☎ 0255 674808); Cromwell Hospital, Cromwell Rd, SW5; Blackheath Hospital, 40 Lee Terrace, SE3 (☎ 0255 674808, telex 8951182 GECOMS G)

PICKARD, Sir Cyril Stanley; KCMG (1966, CMG 1964); s of G W Pickard; *b* 18 Sept 1917; *Educ* Alleyn's Sch Dulwich, New Coll Oxford; *m* 1, 1941, Helen Elizabeth (d 1982), da of G F Strawson, of Horley, Surrey; 3 s, 1 da, and 1 s decd; m 2, 1983, Mary Cecilia Rosser, wid of David Rosser, of Crawley, and da of Basil Cozens-Hardy, of Leatheringsett; *Career* served RA 1940-41, Capt; Br high cmmr Pakistan 1966-71, Br high cmmr Nigeria 1971-74, ret; *Style—* Sir Cyril Pickard, KCMG; 3 Orwell Rd, Norwich NR2 2ND

PICKARD, (John) Michael; s of John Stanley Pickard (d 1979), of Epsom, Surrey, and Winifred Joan Pickard; *b* 29 July 1932; *Educ* Oundle; *m* 1959, Penelope Jane, da of Christopher Catterall; 3 s, 1 da; *Career* fin dir Br Printing Corp Ltd 1965-68, md Trust House Forte 1968-71; chm: St Paul's Fin Investmt Co Ltd 1963-86, Michael Pickard Ltd 1972-86, Happy Eater Ltd 1972-86, Grattan plc; chm and chief exec Imperial Brewing & Leisure Ltd, dir Imperial Gp plc 1981, chief exec Sears plc 1986-, non exec dir: Brown Shipley Hldgs Ltd 1986-, Electra Investmt Tst 1988-, Nationwide Anglia 1991-; chm Roedean Cncl 1981-90, govr Oundle 1987-; FCA; *Recreations* sport, education; *Clubs* Walton Heath, MCC, Pilgrims; *Style—* Michael Pickard, Esq; 40 Duke St, London W1A 2HP (☎ 071 408 1180)

PICKARD, Michael John; s of Denis Luther Pickard; *b* 9 July 1939; *Educ* Christ's Hosp; *m* 1965, Heather Jill, da of John Hallsworth (d 1969); 1 s, 1 da; *Career* The Royal London Mutual Insurance Society Ltd: actuary 1974-82, dir 1977-, chief gen mangr 1983-87, chm 1988-; chm Life Insur Cncl of Assoc of Br Insurers 1990-; FIA; *Recreations* squash, golf, reading; *Style—* Michael Pickard, Esq; Tyndals, Groton, nr Boxford, Suffolk CO6 5EE (☎ 0787 210692); The Royal London Mutual Insurance Soc Ltd, Royal London House, Middlesborough, Colchester, Essex CO1 1RA (☎ 0206 761761)

PICKARD, Willis Ritchie Sturrock; s of William Sturrock Pickard (d 1973), and Anne Ogilvy Gall, *née* Ritchie; *b* 21 May 1941; *Educ* Daniel Stewart's Coll Edinburgh, Univ of St Andrews (MA); *m* 27 Dec 1969, Ann Marie; 2 da (Gillian Fleur b 1970, Rebecca Jane b 1974); *Career* leader writer and features ed The Scotsman 1963-77, ed Times Scottish Education Supplement 1977-; rector Univ of Aberdeen 1988-90, memb Scottish Arts Cncl 1982-88, chm Childrens Book Ctee for Scotland; *Clubs* Scottish Lib; *Style—* Willis Pickard, Esq; Times Scottish Education Supplement, 37 George St, Edinburgh (☎ 031 220 1100, fax 031 220 1616)

PICKEN, Ralph Alistair; s of Dr David Kennedy Watt Picken, TD, JP, DL, of Cardiff, and Liselotte Lore Inge, *née* Regensteiner; *b* 23 May 1955; *Educ* Shrewsbury, Univ of Birmingham (LLB); *Career* admitted slr 1980; ptnr Trowers & Hamlins London 1984- (joined 1981), res Muscat 1981-86; memb Law Soc 1980; *Recreations* bridge and The Baroque, Bordeaux and Bangkok; *Style—* Ralph Picken, Esq; 3 Gloucester Cres, London NW1 7DS (☎ 071 485 5121); 6 New Sq, Lincoln's Inn, London WC2A 3RP (☎ 071 831 6292, fax 071 831 8700, telex 21422)

PICKERING, Brian Neil; *b* 31 Dec 1929; *Educ* Cheltenham, Univ of London (MB BS); *Career* Nat Serv RAMC 1949-51; conslt cardio thoracic surgn: Harefield and Colindale Hosps 1972-79, Derriford Hosp Plymouth 1979-90; author chapters in med books; FRCS; *Recreations* sea-fishing, gardening; *Style—* Brian Pickering, Esq

PICKERING, Prof Brian Thomas; s of Thomas Pickering (d 1952), and Dorothy May, *née* Rourk (d 1983); *b* 24 May 1936; *Educ* Haberdashers' Aske's, Hatcham, Univ of Bristol (BSc, PhD, DSc); *m* 4 Sept 1965, Joan, da of Frederic Charles Robinson Perry (d 1984), of Gävle, Sweden; 2 da (Francesca b 1966, Veronica b 1969); *Career* jr res biochemist Hormone Research Laboratory Univ of California 1962 (Wellcome Res travelling fell 1961), memb Scientific Staff MRC Nat Inst for Med Res Mill Hill 1963-65, memb MRC Gp for Res in Neurosecretion, visiting prof Dept of Physiology Univ of Geneva Switzerland 1977; Univ of Bristol: lectr in biochemistry and pharmacology 1965-70, lectr in anatomy and biochemistry 1970-72, reader 1972-78, prof of anatomy and head of dept 1978-, dean Faculty of Med 1985-87, pro vice chllr 1990-; contrib numerous papers on neuroendocrinology in scientific jls; memb United Bristol Healthcare NHS Tst, pres Euro Soc for Comparative Endocrinology, sec Br Neuroendocrine Gp, ctee memb (former chm) Westbury on Trym Conservation Soc, annual review lectr Anatomical Soc of GB and Ireland 1984; memb: Anatomical Soc, Biochemical Soc, Physiological Soc, Soc for Endocrinology (Society medallist 1977), Euro Neuroscience Assoc, Euro Soc for Comparative Endocrinology; *Books* ed: Pharmacology of the Endocrine System and Ralted Drugs: The Neurohypophysis (with H Heller, 1970), Stimulus Secretion Coupling in Neuroendocrine Systems (with D Ganten and D Pfaff, 1988), Neurosecretion: Cellular Aspects of the Production and Release of Neuropeptides (with J B Wakerley and A J S Summerlee, 1988); *Recreations* gardening; *Style—* Prof Brian Pickering; Department of Anatomy, University of Bristol, Bristol BS8 1TD (☎ 0272 303488, fax 0272 303497)

PICKERING, Donald Ellis; s of John Joseph Pickering (d 1978), of Newcastle-upon-Tyne, and Edith, *née* Ellis (d 1983); *b* 15 Nov 1933; *Educ* private; *Career* actor; trained Old Vic Theatre Sch under Michel St Denis 1950-52, Old Vic Co 1952, Stratford 1954, Bristol Old Vic 1957-59; West End appearances incl: Poor Bitos, School for Scandal (and NY), Case in Question, Conduct Unbecoming (nominated Tony Award), Male of the Species, Hay Fever; Nat Theatre 1987-89; TV appearances incl: The Pallisers, Private Lives, Irish RM, Yes Prime Minister, Return to Treasure Island; films incl: Nothing but the Best, Thirty Nine Steps, Half Moon St; *Recreations* gardening, riding, tennis; *Style—* Donald Pickering, Esq; Back Court, Manor House, Eastleach Turville, Cirencester, Glos GL7 3NQ; (☎ 036 785 476)

PICKERING, Dr Errol Neil; s of Russell Gordon Pickering (d 1985), of Australia, and Sylvia Mary, *née* Bennett; *b* 5 May 1938; *Educ* York Univ Toronto (BA), Univ of Toronto (Dip Hosp Admin, Robert Wood Johnston award), Univ of NSW (PhD); *Career* exec dir: Aust Cncl on Hosp Standards 1974-80, Aust Hosp Assoc 1980-87; dir gen Int Hosp Fedn 1987-; past pres UNICEF Aust, chm Int Assoc Forum RSM; *Recreations* classical music, reading biographies; *Style—* Dr Errol Pickering; International Hospital Federation, 4 Abbots Place, London NW6 1NP (☎ 071 372 7181, fax 071 328 7344)

PICKERING, Prof John Frederick; s of William Frederick Pickering (d 1973), of Slough, and Jean Mary, *née* Clarke; *b* 26 Dec 1939; *Educ* Slough GS, UCL (BSc, PhD, DSc); *m* 25 March 1967, Jane Rosamund, da of Victor William George Day, of Bristol; 2 da (Rachel b 1970, Catherine b 1974); *Career* industl market res exec 1961-62; lectr: Univ of Durham 1964-66, Univ of Sussex 1966-73; sr directing staff Admin Staff Coll Henley 1974-75; UMIST: prof industl econ 1975-88, vice princ 1983-85, dean 1985-87; vice pres Portsmouth Poly 1988-; memb: Royal Econ Soc 1973, Retail Prices Index Advsy Ctee 1974-, Gen Synod C of E 1980-90; church cmmr 1983-90, pres BCMS Crosslinks 1986-; memb MMC 1990-; non exec dir Staniland Hall Ltd; FBIM 1987; *Books* Resale Price Maintenance in Practice (1967), The Small Firm in the Hotel and Catering Industry (jtly, 1971), Industrial Structure and Market Conduct (1974), The Acquisition of Consumer Durables (1977), The Economic Management of the Firm (jt ed, 1984); *Recreations* family life, cricket, classical music; *Clubs* Royal Cwlth Soc; *Style—* Prof J F Pickering; 1 The Fairway, Rowlands Castle, Hants PO9

6AQ ; Portsmouth Poly, Ravelin House, Museum Rd, Portsmouth, Hants PO1 2QQ (☎ 0705 843 203, fax 0705 843 319)

PICKERING, His Hon Judge; John Robertson; s of late J W H Pickering; *b* 8 Jan 1925; *Educ* Winchester, Magdalene Cambridge; *m* 1951, Hilde, widow of E M Wright; 1 s, 2 step s; *Career* barrister Inner Temple 1949, dep chm NE London QS 1971, circuit judge 1972-; *Clubs* MCC; *Style*— His Honour Judge Pickering; 35 Eaton Terrace, London SW1 (☎ 071 730 4271)

PICKERING, His Hon Judge; Richard Edward Ingram; s of Richard Pickering (d 1961), and Dorothy Pickering; *b* 16 Aug 1929; *Educ* Birkenhead Sch, Magdalene Coll Cambridge (MA); *m* 1962, Jean Margaret, *née* Eley; 2 s; *Career* called to the Bar Lincoln's Inn 1953; elected jr of N Circuit 1960, cncllr Hoylake UDC 1961-64, legal chm Miny of Pensions and Nat Insurance Appeals Tbnl Liverpool 1967-77, hon memb Manx Bar (Summerland Fire Enquiry) 1973-74, pt/t chm Liverpool Industl Tbnl 1977-79, rec Crown Ct 1977-81, regnl chm Merseyside Mental Health Review Tbnl 1979-81, circuit judge (N Circuit) 1981-, N Circuit rep on Cncl HM Circuit Judges 1984-89, nominated judicial memb Merseyside Mental Health Review Tbnl 1984-; *Recreations* study of military history, gardening; *Clubs* Athenaeum (Liverpool), United Oxford & Cambridge Univ; *Style*— His Hon Judge Pickering; Crown Court, Derby Square, Liverpool

PICKERING, Hon Mrs (Veronica Mary); da of Baroness Fisher of Rednal (Life Peeress) and Joseph Fisher (d 1978); *b* 24 Nov 1944; *Educ* Bournville Grammar Tech Sch, Bordesley Coll of Educn; *m* 1968, John Adrian Pickering, s of Alfred Walter Pickering, of Birmingham; 1 s (John Joseph b 1979), 1 da (Lyndsey Jane b 1974); *Career* teacher; *Style*— The Hon Mrs Pickering; Redlands, 8 Marlborough Ave, Bromsgrove, Worcs (☎ 0527 75190)

PICKETT, Joy Rosina; da of James William Bishop Woodford (d 1982), of Bushey, Herts, and Ivy, *née* Maskell; *b* 15 April 1950; *m* 28 March 1978, (m dis), Graham John Pickett; *Career* Friends Provident Life Office 1969-71, Sun Alliance Insurance Group 1971-76 (life and pensions), sr pensions admin Noble Lowndes Pension Consultants 1977-79, pensions funds mangr British Waterways Board 1979-87, co sec British Waterways Pensions Trustees Ltd, IMC plc 1988- (gp pensions mangr, dir IMI Pensions Trust Ltd, dir IMI Investment Management Ltd); Nat Assoc of Pensions Funds: co-opted memb Membership Ctee 1983-88, memb Sifting Panel of Golden Pen awards 1986 (chm 1989), memb Ctee W Midlands Gp 1988-, memb Cncl NAPF 1989-, memb Parly Ctee 1990-; Nationalised industs Pension Gp: memb 1980-87, memb Gen Purposes Ctee 1982-87, sec 1985-87; Occupational Pensions Advsy Serv: regnl organiser London NW Region 1987-88, advisor W Midlands region 1988-; memb CBI Pensions Panel 1989-; assoc Pensions Mgmnt Inst (prizewinner), Bushey GS, Cassio Coll, Universite de Nanterre, Watford Coll of Technol; *Recreations* voluntary work, literature, music, art; *Style*— Mrs Joy Pickett; IMI plc, Kynoch Works, PO Box 216, Birmingham B6 7BA (☎ 021 356 4848, fax 021 344 3392)

PICKETT, Hon Mrs (Patricia Margaret); da of 2 Baron Kershaw (d 1961); *b* 1943; *m* 1968, David Anniss Pickett, BSc, BMus; 2 da; *Style*— The Hon Mrs Pickett

PICKETT, Hon Mr Justice; Thomas Pickett; CBE (1972); s of John Joseph Pickett (d 1985), and Caroline, *née* Brunt (d 1970); *b* 22 Nov 1912; *Educ* Glossop GS, Univ of London (LLB); *m* 29 June 1940, (Winifred) Irene, yr da of Benjamin Buckley (d 1945); *Career* served Army 1939-50, Maj; dep asst dir Army Legal Servs 1948, called to the Bar Lincoln's Inn 1948; Judge Pres of Ct of Appeal for Zambia 1965-71; sr regional chm NW Area Industl Tbnls (England and Wales) 1972-85 (ret); *Recreations* walking, swimming; *Clubs* County (Llandudno), Victoria (Llandudno); *Style*— Hon Mr Justice Pickett, CBE; Bryn Awelon, Aber Place, Craigside, Llandudno, Gwynedd LL30 3AR (☎ 0492 44244)

PICKFORD, Anthony James; s of Frederick Pickford, and Ethel Alice, *née* Hart; *b* 12 May 1925; *Educ* Univ Coll Sch Hampstead, King's Coll London (LLB); *m* 1 Sept 1956, Bettine Eleanor Marion Casson, da of Kenneth Casson Smith; *Career* Served Army 1943-49; called to the Bar Lincoln's Inn 1951; practice in: London 1951-57, Nigeria 1957-59; legal asst George Wimpey & Co Ltd 1959-64, legal advsr Smithkline & French Laboratories Ltd 1964-90; practising barrister dir Penn Chemicals BV; memb: Standing Advsy Ctee (trade marks) DTI 1970-88, Ctees ABPI 1964-, Ctees UNICE; assoc memb Chartered Inst of Patent Agents; memb (formerly sec) Cons Ctee for W Africa Affrs, Parly candidate (C) East Ham Gen Election 1955, former chm and pres Harlow Cons Assoc; *Recreations* conservative politics; *Clubs* East India; *Style*— Anthony Pickford, Esq; Smithkline & French Labs Ltd, Mendells Welwyn Garden City, Herts AL7 1EX (☎ 07073 25111, fax 07073 25600)

PICKFORD, David Michael; s of Aston Charles Corpe Pickford (d 1945); *b* 25 Aug 1926; *Educ* Emanuel Sch London, Coll of Estate Mgmnt; *m* 1956, Elizabeth Gwendoline, da of John Hooson, of Segrwyd Hall, Denbigh (d 1972); 1 s (Charles John Norcliffe b 1960), 2 da (Penelope Anne b 1952, Elizabeth Jane b 1958); *Career* chartered surveyor; chm: Haslemere Estates plc 1983-86 (md until 1983), Lilliput Property Unit Trust, Compco Holdings plc, Gulliver Developments Property Unit Trust; dir: Youth with a Mission, Care Campaigns Ltd, Louth Estates Ltd, London and Nationwide Missions Ltd, and many others; vice pres Drug and Alcohol Fndn; chm: Prison Fellowship England & Wales, Mission to London; pres Christians In Property, organizer of Residential Christian Conference Centre for 15-25 year-olds (2000 visitors each year); *Recreations* sheep farming, youth work; *Style*— David Pickford, Esq; Elm Tree Farm, Mersham, nr Ashford, Kent TN25 7HS (☎ 023 3720 200); 33 Grosvenor Sq, London W1X 9LL (☎ 071 493 1156)

PICKFORD, Prof John Aston; OBE (1964); s of late Aston Charles Pickford, of London, and Gladys Ethel, *née* May (d 1981); *b* 28 Dec 1924; *Educ* Emanuel Sch London, Imperial Coll London (BSc, MSc); *m* 27 Sept 1947, Daphne Annie, da of William Edumund Ransom (d 1972), of London; 3 s (Robert Aston b 1950, William John b 1952, Ian Charles b 1952), 1 da (Helen Dorothy (Mrs Sheard) b 1959); *Career* REME 1943-47, Lt 1944, Capt 1946; boroughs of Sutton and Cheam, Southall and Gravesend 1945-54, town engr Sekondi-Tahoradi Municipal Cncl Ghana 1954-60; Loughborough Univ: lectr 1960-66, sr lectr, dir Water Engrg and Development Centre 1971-, head of Dept of Civil Engrg 1983-87, prof 1985-; pres IPHE 1981-82 (memb Cncl 1971-87)-; hon FIWEM 1987, FICE 1977; *Books* Analysis of Surge (1969), Developing World Water (Volumes 1-5 ed, 1985-90); *Recreations* travel, DIY, history of the Indian subcontinent; *Style*— Prof John Pickford, OBE; 5 Forest Rd, Loughborough, Leics LE11 3NW (☎ 0509 215035); WEDC (Water, Engineering and Developement Centre), Loughborough University of Technology, Leicestershire LE11 3TU (☎ 0509 222390, fax 0509 610231, telex 24319 UNITEC G)

PICKFORD, Robert William Granville; s of late Col Richard Ellis Pickford, TD, DL, of Hathersage, Derbyshire, and Mary Avice, *née* Glossop; *b* 26 Nov 1941; *Educ* Rugby, Univ of Sheffield (LLB); *m* 11 Oct 1980, Heather Elizabeth, da of Francis Ernest Woodings, of Chesterfield, Derbyshire; 1 s (Bartholomew b 9 Sept 1985), 1 da (Olivia b 21 Dec 1981); *Career* admitted slr 1966; ptnr W & A Glossop Sheffield, NP 1966; vice pres The Notaries Soc (dir 1979-), memb Slrs Benevolent Soc, former chm RNLI Sheffield Branch; memb Law Soc; *Style*— Robert Pickford, Esq; 66 Wilkinson St, Sheffield S10 2GQ (☎ 0742 737776)

PICKIN, Joseph Peter George; s of John Edmondson (Jack) Pickin, of Brookland's Road, Manchester, and Avril Maureen, *née* Rushforth; *b* 9 April 1956; *Educ* Ampleforth Coll Yorkshire, St Luke's Coll Exeter (BEd), St Thomas' Hosp London (Grad Dip Phys); *m* 21 Dec 1985, Heather Ann, da of Henry Chee Ting; 1 s (John Joseph Henry (Jack) b 18 May 1990), 1 da (Josie Teresa Pickin b 1 May 1986); *Career* asst master Ampleforth Coll 1977-80; chartered physiotherapist: St Thomas' Hospital London (also Royal Free Hosp, The London Hosp and St Leonard Hosp) 1983; King Khaled Hosp Jeddah 1983-84; in private practice 1984-; attendant physiotherapist: Starlight Express 1984-, Cats 1986-, Miss Saigon 1989-; memb Med Advsy Panel Nat Orgn Dance & Mime; played Rugby Union for: England under 23 squad 1976-77, Yorkshire 1977-76, Middx 1980-81; memb: Chartered Soc of Physiotherapy 1983-, Metropolitan Private Practitioners Assoc 1984-, Orgn Chartred Physiotherapists in Private Practice 1984; *Recreations* sailing, windsurfing, squash, tennis, skiing; *Style*— Joseph Pickin, Esq; Kersall, 189 Peckham Rye, London SE15 3HZ (☎ 071 639 5611); Central London Injuries Clinic, Ground Floor Suite, 27 Weymouth St, London W1N 3FJ (☎ 071 636 4890, 081 884 3344 pager A354)

PICKLES, His Hon Judge; James; s of Arthur Pickles, OBE, JP; *b* 18 March 1925; *Educ* Worksop Coll, Leeds Univ, Ch Ch Oxford; *m* 1948, Sheila Ratcliffe; 2 s, 1 da; *Career* barr Inner Temple 1948, rec Crown Ct 1972-76, circuit judge 1976-; contested (Lib) Brighouse and Spenborough 1964; *Books* Straight from the Bench (1987); *Style*— His Honour Judge Pickles; c/o Leeds Crown Court, Leeds

PICKLES, John George; s of William Pickles (d 1972), of N Wales, and Kathleen Pickles, *née* Cathcart; *b* 29 Nov 1935; *Educ* Ruthin Sch, Univ of Liverpool (MCD, BArch); *m* 15 July 1961, Susan Rosemary (d 1985), da of Dr William Webb (d 1955), of Liverpool; 1 s (Charles b 1965), 1 da (Caroline b 1962); *Career* architect and town planner; ptnr in Holford Associates 1972-, dir Meridian Office Servs; artist exhibitions in NW England 1984-; ARIBA, MRTPI, MSAI, FRSA; *Recreations* watercolour painting, skiing, travel; *Style*— John G Pickles, Esq; Derby Cottage, 29 Derby Road, Formby, Merseyside; Holford Associates, Queen Building, 8 Dale Street, Liverpool (☎ 051 227 2881, fax 051 236 1329)

PICKSTOCK, Samuel Frank (Sam); CBE (1989); s of Francis John Pickstock (d 1981), of Stafford, and Hilda Jane, *née* Billington; *b* 10 Aug 1934; *Educ* King Edward VI GS Stafford; *m* 1957, Edith, da of Joseph Lawton (d 1980), of Hanley; *Career* dir: John McLean & Sons Ltd and its subsids 1976, Tarmac Properties Ltd and its subsids 1977, Tarmac plc 1984, Tarmac East Bute Dvpts Ltd 1985; md John McLean & Sons Ltd (chm subsids) 1981; *Recreations* weeding and thinking (occasionally); *Style*— Sam Pickstock, Esq, CBE; The Crows Nest Holding, Coton End, Gnosall, Stafford (☎ 0785 822755); Crestwood House, Birches Rise, Willenhall, West Midlands, (☎ 0902 368511)

PICKTHORN, Sir Charles William Richards; 2 Bt (UK 1959); s of Rt Hon Sir Kenneth William Murray Pickthorn, 1 Bt (d 1975); *b* 3 March 1927; *Educ* Eton, CCC Cambridge; *m* 1951, Helen Antonia, da of late Sir James Mann, KCVO; 1 s, 2 da; *Heir* s, James Francis Mann Pickthorn; *Career* called to the Bar Middle Temple 1952, dir J Henry Schroder Wagg & Co Ltd 1971-79, chm R S Surtees Soc 1980-; *Style*— Sir Charles Pickthorn, Bt; Manor House, Nunney, nr Frome, Somerset (☎ 037 384 574); 3 Hobury St, London SW10 (☎ 071 352 2795)

PICKTHORN, Lady; Helen Antonia; da of Sir James Gow Mann, KCVO (d 1961), and Mary, *née* Cook (d 1956); *b* 31 July 1927; *Educ* privately, Univ of Cambridge (MA); *m* 4 July 1951, Sir Charles William Richards Pickthorn, 2 Bt, *qv*; 1 s (James b 1955), 2 da (Caroline b 1958, Frances b 1960); *Career* teacher Fidelis Sch London 1950-56, dir of Studies Kensington Sch of Languages 1956-61, res asst Lord Gladwyn House of Lords 1963-83; ed newsletter Cncl for Educn in the Cwlth 1956-76, Cwlth and Parly Liaison offr 1974-89, memb and ball chm Br-Italian Soc 1976-86; govr and chm More House Sch 1972-75, life memb Chelsea Soc; *Books* Student Guide to Britain (1965), Locked Up Daughters (with Felicia Lamb 1967), Alexander Mann: Sketches and Correspondence (1985); *Recreations* design and decoration; *Clubs* National Liberal (non political memb); *Style*— Lady Pickthorn; Manor House, Nunney, nr Frome, Somerset BA11 4NJ

PICKTHORN, Henry Gabriel Richards; s of Rt Hon Sir Kenneth William Murray Pickthorn, 1 Bt (d 1975), and Nancy Catherine Lewis, *née* Richards (d 1982); *b* 29 Sept 1928; *Educ* Eton, Trinity Coll Cambridge (BA); *m* 9 July 1955, Mary, da of Juxon Barton, CMG, OBE (d 1980); 3 s (John b 1957, Andrew b 1961, Thomas b 1967), 1 da (Henrietta b 1959); *Career* Nat Serv 1946-48, 2 Lt Northants Regt; TA 1952-61, Capt Queen's Westminsters (KRRC); admitted slr 1955; ptnr Linklaters & Paines 1959-90; *Style*— Henry Pickthorn, Esq; 54 Chelsea Park Gdns, London SW3 6AD (☎ 071 352 8905)

PICKTHORN, James Francis; s and h of Sir Charles William Richards Pickthorn, 2 Bt; *b* 18 Feb 1955; *Educ* Eton; *Style*— James Pickthorn, Esq; 45 Ringmer Ave, London SW6 5LP

PICKUP, Col Christopher John; OBE (1984); s of Wing Cdr K H Pickup, of 34 High St, Budleigh Salterton, Devon, and Vera, *née* Halliwell (d 1943); *b* 26 Aug 1942; *Educ* Abingdon Sch, RMA Sandhurst; *m* 16 Dec 1967, Elizabeth Anne, da of Robert Geoffrey Spencer (d 1971); 1 s (Charles b 1970), 1 da (Lucy b 1971); *Career* cmmnd RA 1962, transferred Army Air Corps 1972, Army Staff Coll 1972-74; various cmd and staff appts: UK, Borneo, Germany; *Recreations* sailing, skiing, fishing; *Style*— Col Christopher Pickup, OBE; Regt Col Army Air corps, Middle Wallop, nr Stockbridge, Hants SO20 8DY (☎ 0264 384211, fax 0264 384418)

PICKUP, Ronald Alfred; s of Erick Pickup (d 1981), of Chester, and Daisy, *née* Williams; *b* 7 July 1940; *Educ* Kings Sch Chester, Leeds Univ (BA), RADA; *m* 9 Aug 1964, Lans Talbot, da of Claude Traverse, of Encino, CA, USA; 1 s (Simon b 1971), 1 da (Rachel b 1973); *Career* actor; performed: Repertory Leicester 1964, Royal Ct first title role Shelley 1965; Nat Theatre 1966-72: Rosalind in all male As You Like It, Esmond in Long Days Journey Into Night, title role in Richard II; TV incl: Jennie, Orwell, Fortunes of War; films incl: Day of the Jackel, The Mission, Eleni; memb Global Co-op for a Better World; *Recreations* walking, reading, listening to music; *Clubs* BAFTA; *Style*— Ronald Pickup, Esq; London Management, 235/241 Regent St, London W1R 7AG (☎ 071 493 1610, fax (2&3) 071 408 0065)

PICKWOAD, Michael Mervyn; s of William Mervyn Pickwoad (d 1976), of Windsor and Ludham, and Anne Margaret, *née* Payne Cook; *b* 11 July 1945; *Educ* Charterhouse, Univ of Southampton (BSc); *m* 27 Oct 1973, Vanessa Rosemary, da of Leslie William Orriss, of Cookham, Berks; 3 da (Zoë b 1975, Katharine b 1977, Amy b 1979); *Career* film production designer; films incl: Comrades 1985, Withnail and I 1986, The Lonely Passion of Judith Hearne 1987, How to Get Ahead in Advertising 1988, The Krays 1989, Let Him Have It 1990; memb: Georgian Gp, ACTT 1968; *Recreations* architectural history, drawing, photography, sailing, history of transport; *Clubs* Rolls Royce Enthusiasts; *Style*— Michael Pickwoad, Esq; 3 Warnborough Rd, Oxford (☎ 0865 511106)

PICOZZI, Gerard Louis; s of Louis Picozzi, of Coatbridge, and Madaleine, *née* Lagorio; *b* 2 Oct 1949; *Educ* St Patrick's HS, Univ of Glasgow (MB ChB); *m* 20 Sept 1975, Joan, da of Joseph McCue, of Glasgow; 1 s (Christopher b 1977, d 1981), 2 da (Natalie b 1976, Madeleine b 1983); *Career* registrar ENT surgery Glasgow Royal Infirmary 1978-80, sr registrar ENT surgery Gtr Glasgow Health Bd 1980-84, conslt otolaryngolgist Lanarkshire Health Bd 1984; FRCS 1980, RCPSGlas 1980, RSM 1980; *Recreations* running, cycling, motoring, skiing, shooting; *Style—* Gerard Picozzi, Esq; 8 Muir St, Coatbridge, Lanarkshire ML5 1NH (☎ 0236 21556); Department of Ear Nose & Throat Surgery, Law Hospital, Carluke, Lanarkshire ML8 5ER (☎ 0698 351100)

PICTON, Jacob Glyndwr (Glyn); CBE (1972); s of David Picton (d 1960), of Aberdare, and Elen Evans (d 1937); *b* 28 Feb 1912; *Educ* Aberdare Boys' Co Sch, Univ of Birmingham (MCom); *m* 2 Sept 1939, Rhiannon Mary (d 1978), da of late Arthur James, of Swansea; 1 s (Arthur b 1943), 1 da (Eira b 1946); *Career* Chance Bros Ltd 1933-47 (asst sec 1945-47); Univ of Birmingham: sr lectr in industl econs 1947-79, sub dean Faculty of Commerce and Social Scis 1952-58; govr United Birmingham Hosps 1953-74 (vice chm 1958-74), chm Birmingham Children's Hosp 1956-66, vice chm W Midlands RHA 1974-82; pres W Midlands Rent Assessment Panel, teaching hosps rep on Whitley Cncls of NHS, vice chm Nat Staff Ctee NHS; chm Birmingham Industl Therapy Assoc Ltd, chm several wages cncls; sole cmmr of enquiry into S Wales Coalfield Dispute 1965; *Books* South Wales Coalfield Strike (1965); *Recreations* music, gardening, Pembrokeshire history; *Clubs* Univ of Birmingham Academic Staff; *Style—* Glyn Picton, Esq, CBE; 54 Chesterwood Rd, Birmingham B13 0QE

PICTON, John Douglas; RD (1969, Clasp 1979); s of Dr Norman Picton (d 1960), of Saltcoats, Ayrshire, and Margaret Brown, *née* McGinn (d 1988); *b* 8 April 1934; *Educ* Loretto, Univ of St Andrews (BSc); *m* 23 Sept 1960, Elizabeth Mary, da of Douglas Clark Wallace, OBE (d 1989), of Lundin Links, Fife; 1 s (Simon b 1970), 3 da (Jane b 1961, Nicola b 1963, Sarah b 1966); *Career* Nat Serv RN 1955-57, CO Tay Div RNR 1978-81 (joined 1952, former cdr); md Robert L Fleming Ltd 1974- (joined 1957); *Recreations* hockey, golf; *Clubs* Naval; *Style—* John Picton, Esq, RD; Robert L Fleming Ltd, 2 Perth Rd, Dundee DD1 4LW (☎ 0382 27801, fax 0382 22967, telex 76194)

PICTON-TURBERVILL, Richard Charles Quentin; JP (Glamorgan 1959), DL (Mid Glamorgan 1982); s of Col Charles Thomas Edmondes, of Old Hall, Cowbridge, Glamorgan, by his w Eleanor, o child of Charles Grenville Turbervill, JP, Lord of the Manor of Ewenny (whose maternal gf was Sir Grenville Temple, 10 Bt, of the family which at one time enjoyed the Dukedom of Buckingham and a branch of which still has the Earldom of Temple of Stowe); *b* 6 July 1924; *Educ* Radley, RAC Cirencester; *m* 1, 1950 (m dis 1971), Catherine Vivian Lindsay, da of Col E D Corkery; 3 s; m 2, 1972, Ann Elizabeth, da of Geoffrey Field Arthur (d 1960), of Ranskill, Notts; *Career* WWII mobile radar RA 1942-46; cncllr 1951-82, High Sheriff Glamorgan 1965; chm: Gen Cmmrs of Income Tax, Petty Sessional Div Newcastle and Ogmore 1982-87, Political Pty Assoc; pres Bridgend Show Soc 1965-86; memb: Industl Cncl for Wales, Agric Land Tbnl (Wales); former memb Welsh Water Authy; *Recreations* shooting, stalking, sailing, gardening, skiing, reading, music; *Clubs* Royal Overseas, Farmers', County (Cardiff); *Style—* Richard Picton-Turbervill Esq, JP, DL; Ewenny Priory, Bridgend, Mid Glamorgan CE35 5BW (☎ 0656 2913)

PIDD, Michael; s of Ernest Pidd, of Sheffield, and Marion, *née* Clark; *b* 3 Aug 1948; *Educ* High Storrs GS Sheffield, Brunel Univ (BTech), Univ of Birmingham (MSc); *m* 2 Jan 1971, Sally Anne, da of Eric Victor Nutt, of London; 2 da (Karen b 18 Aug 1977, Helen b 22 Jan 1981); *Career* team leader operational res Cadbury Schweppes Ltd 1971-75, lectr in operational res Univ of Aston 1975-79, lectr and sr lectr in operational res Univ of Lancaster 1979-; memb: St Thomas Church Lancaster, Lancashire Against Nuclear Dumping, Operational Res Soc; Fell Inst Mgmnt Sciences; *Books* Computer Simulation in Management Sciences (1984, 1988), Computer Modelling for Disease Simulation (1989); *Recreations* squash, swimming, church activities; *Style—* Michael Pidd, Esq; The Management School, Univ of Lancaster, Bailrigg, Lancaster LA1 4YX (☎ 0524 65201 ext 3870, fax 0524 381454, telex 6511 LANCUL G)

PIDGLEY, Anthony William; s of William Pidgley (d 1967), of Hersham, Surrey, and Florence, *née* Smith; *b* 6 Aug 1947; *Educ* Ambleside Sch, Hersham Surrey; *m* 7 May 1966, Ruby Theresa Pidgley, da of Walter John Williams, of East Molesey, Surrey; 1 s (Tony b 17 Sept 1968), 1 da (Tania b 12 June 1966); *Career* fndr P & J Plant Hire 1963 (sold business 1968), dir Crest Nicholson plc (formerly Crest Homes) 1968-75, jt fndr Berkeley Gp plc 1976-, appt serv bro Order of St John 1987, appt govr Brooklands Tech Coll Weybridge 1989; *Recreations* gardening; *Clubs* Ritz, RAC, Willows, Peak Carlton Towers, Dorchester; *Style—* Anthony Pidgley, Esq; The Old House, 4 Heath Rd, Weybridge, Surrey KT13 8TB (☎ 0932 847222, fax 0932 858596)

PIERCE, David Glyn; s of Gwilym John Pierce, of London, and Hilda Alice, *née* Webster; *b* 25 July 1942; *Educ* Stationers' Co Sch London, Univ of Exeter (BA); *m* 1, 1963, Anne Valerie Sherwood; 1 s (Adam b 7 Dec 1967), 1 da (Rebecca b 18 Aug 1970); m 2, 9 Feb 1991, Victoria Isobel, da of Samuel Seymour, of Seattle Washington USA; *Career* TV time buyer Garland Compton 1964-68 (media trainee 1963), head Media Gp Foote Cone & Belding 1968-77, head of TV buying Everetts 1977-82; Media Campaign Services: joined 1982, Bd dir 1986, dir planning and res 1987; occasional lectr Coll for Distributive Trades; MCAM 1981, memb Publicity Club of London 1982; *Recreations* competitive cycling, memb Soho CC; *Style—* David Pierce, Esq; Media Campaign Services, 3 St Peter's St, Islington Green, London N1 8JD (☎ 071 359 6696, fax 071 354 5735)

PIERCY, Dr David MacLennan; s of Capt William Norman Piercy (d 1958), and Margaret Florence, *née* MacLennan (d 1985); *b* 5 Oct 1930; *Educ* Arbroath HS, Univ of St Andrews (MB ChB); *m* 8 Aug 1953, Gillian Gertrude, da of Ernest Martin Vine, of Norfolk; 2 s (David b 12 Aug 1956, Christopher b 28 April 1970), 2 da (Susan Rose b 7 March 1960, Lesley Smith b 6 May 1963); *Career* RAF 1950-54, cmmnd 1951, pilot, Glen Flying Trophy 1951, jet Instructor 1952 (Cat A2), 870 aircraft dep ldr Coronation Review Flypast Odiham 1953; registrar neonatal paediatrics Dundee Univ Hosp 1961-63, sr registrar and hon lectr in pathology Dundee Royal Infirmary and Ninewells Hosp and Med Sch 1965-74, conslt histopathologist Hull and E Yorks Health Authys 1975-, chm Div of Pathology 1988-; memb: ACP 1970, Pathological Soc of GB and Ireland 1970, BMA 1972; FRCPath 1982 (MRCPath 1970); *Books* Diagnostic Manual of Tumours of Central Nervous System (contrib, 1988); *Recreations* music, art; *Clubs* Rotary (Hull Kingston, former pres); *Style—* Dr David Piercy; 32 Westella Rd, Kirkella, N Humberside HU10 7QE; Dept of Histopathology and Cytology, Hull Royal Infirmary, Hull (☎ 0482 28541)

PIERCY, 3 Baron (UK 1945); James William Piercy; s of 2 Baron Piercy (d 1981), and Oonagh Lavinia, JP (d 1990), da of Maj Edward John Lake Baylay, DSO; *b* 19 Jan 1946; *Educ* Shrewsbury, Univ of Edinburgh (BSc); *Heir* bro, Hon Mark Edward Pelham Piercy; *Career* AMIEE, ACCA; *Style—* The Rt Hon the Lord Piercy; 13 Arnold Mansions, Queen's Club Gdns, London W14 9RD

PIERCY, Hon Mark Edward Pelham; s of 2 Baron Piercy (d 1981), and hp of bro, 3 Baron; *b* 30 June 1953; *Educ* Shrewsbury, New Coll Oxford (BA); *m* 1979, Vivien Angela, da of His Hon Judge Monier-Williams, *qv*; 1 s (William Nicholas Pelham b 1989), 3 da (Katherine Henrietta b 1982, Olivia Charlotte b 1984, Harriet Lavinia b 1987); *Career* barr Lincoln's Inn; *Style—* The Hon Mark Piercy; 39 Carson Rd, W Dulwich, London SE21 8HT

PIERCY, Prof Nigel Francis; s of Gilbert Piercy (d 1984), of Cambridge, and Helena Gladys, *née* Sargent; *b* 13 Jan 1949; *Educ* Cambridge GS for Boys, Heriot-Watt Univ (BA), Univ of Durham (MA), Univ of Wales (PhD); *m* 1, 26 Sept 1971 (m dis 1985), (Patricia) Jean Piercy; 1 s (Niall Christopher b 1979); m 2, Stephanie Monica, da of Eric James Oscar Burges; *Career* planner Amersham International 1974-77; sr lectr Newcastle Poly 1977-81 (lectr 1972-74); Univ of Wales: lectr 1981-83, sr lectr 1983-86, reader 1988-; prof of mktg and strategy Cardiff Business Sch 1988-; Author of the Year UK Inst of Mktg 1980-82; FCIM 1988; *Books* Export Strategy (1982), Managing Marketing Information (with M Evans, 1983), The Management Implications of New Information Technology (ed, 1984), Marketing Organisation (1985), Management Information Systems (ed 1986), Marketing Budgeting (1986); *Recreations* cycling, badminton; *Style—* Prof Nigel Piercy; 9 The Green, Radyr, Cardiff CF4 8BR (☎ 0222 842185); Marketing and Strategy Group, Cardiff Business School, University of Wales College of Cardiff, Colum Drive, Cardiff CF1 3EU (☎ 0222 874275, fax 0222 874419, car 0836 751042)

PIERCY, Hon Penelope Katherine; CBE (1968); da of 1 Baron Piercy, CBE (d 1966), and Mary Louisa, OBE (d 1953; da of Hon Thomas Pelham, CB, who was 3 s of 3 Earl of Chichester); *b* 15 April 1916; *Educ* St Paul's Girls' Sch, Somerville Coll Oxford (MA); *Career* under sec Miny of Technol 1964-68, ret; *Recreations* gardening; *Style—* The Hon Penelope Piercy, CBE; Charlton Cottage, Tarrant Rushton, Blandford Forum, Dorset (☎ 0258 52072)

PIERCY, Baroness; Veronica; da of late John Hordley Warham; *Educ* St Paul's Girls Sch; *m* 1964, as his 2 w, 1 Baron Piercy, CBE (d 1966); *Style—* The Rt Hon Veronica, Lady Piercy; Fair View House, Marton, Sinnington, York YO6 6RD

PIERS, Sir Charles Robert Fitzmaurice; 10 Bt (I 1661), VRD; s of Sir Charles Piers, 9 Bt (d 1945); *b* 30 Aug 1903; *Educ* RNCs Osborne and Dartmouth; *m* 1936, Ann Blanche Scott (d 1975), da of late Capt Thomas Ferguson; 1 s, 1 da (decd); *Heir* s, James Desmond Piers; *Career* mangr Midland Doherty Ltd of Duncan BC, ret; *Style—* Sir Charles Piers, Bt; PO Box 748, Duncan, British Columbia V9L 3Y1, Canada

PIERS, James Desmond; s and h of Sir Charles Robert Fitzmaurice Piers, 10 Bt, *qv*; *b* 24 July 1947; *m* 1975, Sandra Mae Dixon; 1 s (Stephen James b 1979); 1 da (Christine Sarah b 1976); *Style—* James Piers, Esq

PIERS, Martin James; s of Karl Piers, of Ewell, Surrey, and Meryl Menzies; *b* 12 Sept 1954; *Educ* Hertford GS, Univ of Southampton (LLB); *m* 4 June 1983, Nicola Susan, da of Geoffrey Stewart Walker, of Lemington Spa, Warwicks; *Career* admitted slr 1979, ptnr Gouldens 1983-; lectr on dir personal liability at insur and insolvency confs; contrib business law section Financial Times; memb insurance ctee section of business law Int Bar Assoc; memb: Int Bar Assoc, Br Insur Law Assoc, Br and American Chamber of Commerce, Soc Eng and American Lawyers, Insol, The City Forum; *Books* Guide to Directors and Officers Liability and Loss Prevention (1989); *Recreations* skiing, tennis, walking; *Clubs* Roof Garden; *Style—* Martin Piers, Esq; 22 Tudor St, London EC4Y 0JJ (☎ 071 583 7777, fax 071 583 3051, telex 21520)

PIESSE, Hugh Montagu Roper; s of Denys Montagu Roper Piesse (d 1973), of 29 Trevor Square, London SW7, and Elizabeth Loveday, *née* Melvill; *b* 10 Jan 1939; *Educ* Wellington, Aix-En-Provence Univ France; *m* 1 June 1963, Angela Mary, da of Joseph Anthony Martin (d 1974), of The Howe, Aughton, Lancashire; 1 s (James b 1964), 2 da (Emma b 1966, Kate b 1970); *Career* RMVR 1957-62; slr; Piesse & Sons slrs 1962-72, Durrant Piesse slrs 1973-75, Roper Piesse slrs 1975; memb Nat Art Collections Fund; Freeman Worshipful Co of Slrs 1973; memb Law Soc 1962; *Recreations* the arts, cricket, tennis, literature; *Clubs* several sporting clubs; *Style—* Hugh Piesse, Esq; 19 Blenheim Rd, St Johns Wood, London (☎ 071 624 8730); Duckleston Mill, Sherborne, Gloucestershire (☎ 045 14 203); Roger Piesse, 9 Staple Inn, Holborn, London WC1V 7RH (☎ 071 405 5959, fax 071 430 1494)

PIGGOT, (Thomas) Alan; TD (1967); s of Thomas Piggot (d 1957), and Elizabeth Winifred, *née* Spence; *b* 8 March 1930; *Educ* Methodist Coll Belfast, Queens Univ Belfast (MB ChB, BAO), RCS Edinburgh; *m* 16 Sept 1961, Mary Simpson, da of Robert Sprott, of Randalstown, Co Antrim, N Ireland; 1 s (Alan b 1962), 1 da (Dawn b 1964); *Career* joined TA: Queens Univ OTC 1950-68, Lt-Col 201(N) Gen Hosp RAMC(V) 1969-80; sr registrar plastic surgn Wythenshave Hosp Manchester 1966-68, clinical lectr in plastic surgery Univ of Newcastle upon Tyne 1968-, conslt plastic surgn Newcastle Health Authy 1968-; memb: BMA 1953, Br Assoc Plastic Surgns 1976, Br Assoc Aesthetic Plastic Surgns 1981, Br Med Laser Assoc 1984; FRCS 1961; *Recreations* golf, photography; *Style—* Alan Piggot, Esq, TD; Ardlui, 3 Osbaldeston Gardens, Gosforth, Newcastle upon Tyne, Tyne & Wear NE3 4JE (☎ 091 285 8934); Dept Plastic Surgery, Newcastle General Hospital, Westgate Rd, Newcastle upon Tyne, Tyne & Wear NE4 6BE (☎ 091 273 8811, fax 091 272 264)

PIGGOTT, Donald James; s of James Piggott (d 1962), and Edith, *née* Tempest (d 1968); *b* 1 Sept 1920; *Educ* Bradford, Christs Coll Cambridge (MA), LSE; *m* 15 June 1974, Kathryn Jessie Courtenay-Evans, *née* Eckford; *Career* Army Serv 1941-46, NW Europe and India; PA to fin dir London Tport 1947-50, distributor mgmnt Shell-Mex and BP Ltd 1951-58, mktg devpt BP Co Ltd 1958-73, dir gen Br Red Cross Soc 1980-85 (int dir 1973- 80); memb central appeals advsy ctees BBC and IBA 1980-83, tstee memb Jt Ctee of St John and Red Cross 1980, dep pres Suffolk Branch Br Red Cross 1987; OStJ 1983; Freeman City of London 1988, Liveryman Worshipful Co of Carmen 1988; FRSM 1982; *Recreations* music, theatre; *Style—* Donald Piggott, Esq; 18 Elm Lodge, River Gardens, London SW6 6NZ (☎ 071 385 5588); Beech House, The Green, Tostock, Bury St Edmunds

PIGGOTT, Harold Ebenezer; s of Percy Henry Heath Piggott (d 1979), and Mary Gertrude, *née* Saunders (d 1962); *b* 14 April 1937; *Educ* Worthing HS for Boys, Brighton Tech Coll (City & Guilds); *m* 5 Sept 1959, Barbara Ethel, da of William John Tunbridge, of Cornwall; 3 da (Susan b 17 July 1960, Clare b 8 Aug 1965, Amanda b 29 April 1968); *Career* fndr Harold E Piggott Ltd 1962, dir Hearts of Oak Benefit Soc 1978- (dep chm Staff Pension Scheme), dir Hearts of Oak Tstee Ltd London 1982-, chm Aberdeen & Northern Mutual Assur Soc Ltd, investmt dir Hearts of Oak Insur Gp 1983-; pres Worthing Hard of Hearing Club, govr C of E Sch; chm: Sussex Parkinson Disease Soc, fndr chm City of London Freeman Assoc of Sussex; rotarian, life memb Guild of Freeman of City of London, Nat Tst and Worthing Civic Soc; elected Exec Bd Nat Conf Friendly Socs, sec Sussex regn Assoc, Worthing Borough Sussex Police Conslt Ctee; co cncllr W Sussex 1974-85, chm catering Co Hall 1980-85, cncllr Worthing BC, Mayor of Worthing 1982-83, chm Policy & Resources Ctee, Worthing Centenary Ctee; elected memb Assoc of Dist Cncls W Sussex Branch, memb DHSS Appeals Tbnl 1975-87; auditor Worthing Heene Cons, Lord of the Manor of Netherhall Old Newton Sussex; Liveryman City of London 1977 (Freeman 1972), Steward Worshipful Co of Basketmakers 1988; Fell IOD 1965, FBIM 1983, FCEA 1983, FFA 1987, FRSA 1988; *Books* Beauty & History in the South East (article in Hearts of Oak Magazine, 1978); *Recreations* swimming, chess, snooker, golf, reading; *Clubs* The Manorial Soc of GB, The United Wards of City of London; *Style—* Harold Piggott, Esq; Netherhall, Upper Brighton Rd, Worthing, W Sussex BN14 9HY (☎ 0903 35510); Apartment at Playa Sol, Avenida Gola D'estany, 11-15 Santa Margarita,

Rosas; Hearts of Oak House, Registered Office, 84 Kingsway, London WC2B 6NF (☎ 071 404 0393)

PIGGOTT, (Francis John) Richard; s of Maj-Gen F J C Piggott, CB, CBE, DSO, *qv*; *b* 8 March 1943; *Educ* Ullenwood Manor, Battisborough; *m* 2, 1980, Jennifer Anne; 2 s (James b 1970, Benjamin b 1981), 1 da (Sarah b 1968); *Career* chm and fndr Guildbourne Hldgs Gp (UK), Sociètè Immobilière de Guildbourne SARL (France), Guildbourne Hldgs BV (Holland), Guildbourne Texas Inc (USA); *Recreations* shooting, fishing, sailing; *Clubs* Army and Navy; *Style—* Richard Piggott, Esq

PIGNATELLI, Frank; *b* 22 Dec 1946; *Educ* Jordanhill Coll, Univ of Glasgow (Dip Ed, Med, MA); *m* 23 Aug 1969, Rosetta; 1 s (Paul b 4 Sept 1970), 1 da (Angela b 13 Oct 1973); *Career* Strathclyde Dept of Educn: teacher of French and Italian, asst princ teacher, head Dept of Modern Languages, asst head teacher, educn offr, asst dir of educn, dep dir of educn, visiting prof of educn Univ of Glasgow, dir of educn; chm Scottish Advsy Gp on Tech and Vocational Educn Initiative (memb UK Nat Steering Gp); memb: UK Policy Gp on Understanding British Industry CBI, Scottish Nat Task Gp on 16s-18s, Nat Ctee for In-Service Trg of Teachers, numerous nat ctees on all aspects of teaching and educn, Bd Scottish Cncl for Res Educn, Scottish Educnl Res Assoc, Schools Assessment Res Support Unit; conslt: Egyptian Govt on vocational educn, Queensland Catholic Educn Cmmn; FBIM; *Books* World Yearbook of Education (contrib, 1987); *Recreations* genealogy, reading, swimming, DIY; *Style—* Frank Pignatelli, Esq; Dept of Education, Strathclyde Regional Council, Strathclyde House, 20 India St, Glasgow G2 4PF (☎ 041 227 2359, fax 041 227 2676)

PIGOT, Sir George Hugh; 8 Bt (GB 1764), of Patshull, Staffordshire; s of Maj-Gen Sir Robert Anthony Pigot, 7 Bt, CB, OBE (d 1986), and his 1 w, Honor, *née* Gibbon (d 1964); *b* 28 Nov 1946; *Educ* Stowe; *m* 1, 2 Dec 1967 (m dis 1973), Judith Sandeman, er da of late Maj John Hele Sandeman Allen, RA; 1 da (Melanie Barbara b 4 Dec 1969); m 2, 2 Feb 1980, Lucinda Jane, yr da of Donald Charles Spandler, of Chiddingfold, Surrey; 2 s ((George) Douglas Hugh b 17 Sept 1982, (Robert) Richard b 26 Sept 1984); *Heir* s, (George) Douglas Hugh Pigot b 17 Sept 1982; *Career* with Coutts & Co 1965-67, Hogg Robinson & Gardner Mountain 1967-69; freelance photographer (fashion) 1970-77; founded Padworth Fisheries (trout farm) 1977, chm and md Padworth Fisheries Ltd 1981-; memb: Cncl British Trout Assoc 1986- (hon treas 1990); *Recreations* promotion of fish farming, trout, classic cars, golf; *Clubs* British Trout Assoc, NFU; *Style—* Sir George Pigot, Bt; Mill House, Mill Lane, Padworth, nr Reading, Berks RG7 4JX; Padworth Fisheries Ltd, Mill Lane, Padworth, nr Reading, Berks RG7 4JX (☎ 0734 712322, fax 0734 713015)

PIGOT, His Hon Judge Thomas Herbert; QC (1967); s of late Thomas Pigot, and late Martha Ann Pigot; *b* 19 May 1921; *Educ* Manchester GS, Brasenose Coll Oxford (BA, BCL, MA); *m* 19 Aug 1950, Zena Marguerite, da of Thomas Wall; 3 da (Diana Marguerite b 1953, Clare Rowena b 1956, Anne Rosalind b 1959); *Career* 2 Lt Welsh Regt 1941, transfd to Lincs Regt 1942, served N Africa (POW 1943-45); barr 1947, Northern Circuit, circuit judge 1972, dep sr judge in Sovereign Base areas of Cyprus 1971, sr judge (chief justice), Common SJT in City of London 1984, HM Lt in the City of London 1984, bencher of the Inner Temple 1985; memb Worshipful Co of Cutlers 1985; *Style—* His Hon Judge Pigot, QC; c/o Central Criminal Court, London EC4M 7EH

PIGOTT, Anthony Charles Shackelton (Tony); s of Thomas Adrian McaWean Pigott, of Groombridge, Sussex, and Juliet, *née* Strong; *b* 4 June 1958; *Educ* Harrow; *m* Feb 1984 (m dis 1987); 1 s (Elliot Sebastian b 15 March 1983); *Career* professional cricketer; Sussex CCC 1976-: first class debut 1978, awarded county cap 1982; overseas teams: Waverley CC Aust 1976, 1977, 1979, Wellington NZ 1982 and 1983, Claremont SA 1980 and 1981; England: Young Eng v Aust 1976, under 23 tour Aust 1979, 1 Test match v NZ 1984; public schs raquets champion 1975; proprietor squash club Sussex; *Recreations* spending time with my son, squash; *Style—* Tony Piggott, Esq; 82 Old Shoreham Rd, Hove, Sussex BN3 6HL (☎ 0273 24209); Sussex CCC, Eaton Rd, Hove, Sussex BN3 3AN (☎ 0273 732161, fax 0273 771549)

PIGOTT, David John Berkeley; er s and h of Sir (Berkeley) Henry Sebastian Pigott, 5 Bt; *b* 16 Aug 1955; *Educ* Moor Park Ludlow, Hurn Court Bournemouth; *m* 1, 1981 (m dis 1984), Alison Fletcher; m 2, 19 Nov 1986, Julie, da of Eric Gordon Wiffen, of 28 Fitzroy Close, Bassett, Southampton; 1 da (Christabel Maria b 18 Aug 1989); *Career* neon glassbender Pearce Signs 1980-87; production mangr Signwise (Scotland) Ltd 1987-89; proprietor Neon Light Co 1989-; memb: local Conservative Assoc, Model Helicopter/Plane Club, Jensen Owners' Club; *Recreations* flying model helicopter/plane, rebuilding Jensen cars; *Style—* David Pigott, Esq; 91 Bellemoor Road, Upper Shirley, Southampton SO1 2QW (☎ 0703 777168)

PIGOTT, Sir (Berkeley) Henry Sebastian; 5 Bt (UK 1808), of Knapton, Queen's County; s of Maj Sir Berkeley Charles Pigott, 4 Bt (d 1982), and Christabel, *née* Bowden-Smith (d 1974); *b* 24 June 1925; *Educ* Ampleforth; *m* 4 Sept 1954, (Olive) Jean, o da of John William Balls (d 1975), of Holly Lodge, Surlingham, Norfolk; 2 s (David John Berkeley b 1955, Antony Charles Philip b 1960), 1 da (Sarah Jane Mary b 1964); *Heir* s, David John Berkeley Pigott, *qv*; *Career* served WWII RM 1944-45; farmer; Freeman of City of Baltimore USA; *Recreations* sailing (in Guinness Book of Records (1988 edn) for smallest single-handed circumnavigation); *Style—* Sir Henry Pigott, Bt; Brook Farm, Shobley, Ringwood, Hants BH24 3HT

PIGOTT, Hugh Sefton; s of Alfred Sefton Pigott, OBE (d 1979), of Dean Hill, Wilmslow, Cheshire, and Frances Ann, *née* Mills (d 1984); *b* 21 Dec 1929; *Educ* Oundle, King's Coll Cambridge (BA, MA); *m* 1, 31 Aug 1957 (m dis 1984), Venetia Caroline Mary, da of Derric John Stopford Adams, of Ansty Hall, Coventry, Worcs; 4 s (Charles b 1958, Francis b 1960, Edward b 1963, Philip b 1966); m 2, 1 Nov 1986, Fiona Margaret Miller, da of John McDermid, of The Old Rectory, Hickling, Norfolk; *Career* Clifford Chance (formerly Coward Chance): articled clerk 1952-55, asst slr 1955-60, ptnr 1960-; memb: Law Soc's Standing Ctee on Co Law 1972-85, Advsy Working Pty on Europe 1976-79; hon legal advsr to Accounting Standards Ctee 1986-90, memb Top Salaries Review Body 1988; Liveryman Worshipful Co of Slrs; *Recreations* poetry, the visual arts, piano playing, cooking; *Style—* Hugh Pigott, Esq; Clifford Chance, Royex House, Aldermanbury Square, London EC2V 7LD (☎ 071 600 0808, fax 071 726 8561)

PIHL, Brig the Hon Dame Mary Mackenzie; *née* Anderson; DBE (1970, MBE 1958); da of 1 Viscount Waverley, PC, GCB, OM, FRS (d 1958), and Christina, *née* Mackenzie (d 1920); *b* 3 Feb 1916; *Educ* Sutton HS, Villa Brillantmont Lausanne Switzerland; *m* 8 July 1973, Frithjof Pihl (d 1988), s of Carl Pihl (d 1936); *Career* joined ATS 1941, transfd WRAC 1949; dir WRAC 1967-70; Hon ADC to HM The Queen 1967-70, ret 1970; *Clubs* Naval, English Speaking Union; *Style—* Brig the Hon Dame Mary Pihl, DBE

PIKE, Claude Drew; OBE (1970), DL (Devon 1979); s of Ivan Samuel Pike (d 1934), and Alice, *née* Goodhead (d 1956); bro of Baroness Pike of Melton (Life Peer), *qv*; *b* 4 July 1915; *Educ* Silcoates Sch Wakefield, Jesus Coll Cambridge (MA, LLM); *m* 23 May 1941, Margaret, da of George Thomas Hirst (d 1965); 1 s (John), 1 da (Penelope); *Career* WWII serv 1940-45, promoted Capt Paymaster; chm Watts Blake Bearne plc 1964-86 (dir 1945); dir: Hepworth Ceramic Holdings plc 1974-87, Lloyds Bank (Devon and Cornwall) 1973-86, Morwellham Recreational Tst 1979-90; chm Exeter Cathedral Preservation Tst, former pres Men of the Trees Devon, chm Torbay Hosp Med Res Tst, govr Blundell's; pres: and former dir Devon Historic Buildings Trust Ltd, Devon Co Agric Assoc 1988; landowner; Hon LLD Exeter 1988; CBIM 1976; *Recreations* forestry, dendrology; *Clubs* Oxford & Cambridge Univ; *Style—* Claude Pike, Esq, OBE, DL; Dunderdale Lawn, Penhurst Rd, Newton Abbot TQ12 1EN (☎ 0626 544 04); Manwood, Heathercombe, Newton Abbot, Devon TQ13 9XE; Watts Blake Bearne & Co plc, Park House, Courtenay Park, Newton Abbot, Devon TQ12 4PS (☎ 0626 523 45, telex 428 24 WBB G)

PIKE, Derek; s of Harold Pike, of Cheltenham and Frances Christina, *née* Williams (d 1990); *b* 24 Jan 1944; *Educ* Harrow Weald Co GS, Univ of Leeds (BSc, PhD); *m* 14 Dec 1979, Thirza Guté, da of Lionel Kotzen, of Johannesburg, SA; *Career* jr engr Harris & Sutherland London 1970-73, engr Arup Associates 1973-77; project engr: John Herrick CSE Oregon USA 1977-79, Michael Barclay Partnership London 1979-82, assoc Ove Arup & Partners 1982-90; ptnr Building Design Partnership; visiting lectr Liverpool Sch of Architecture; registered civil engr USA; MICE, MIStructE, MASCE; *Recreations* pottery, travel; *Style—* Dr Derek Pike; Building Design Partnership, PO Box 4WD, 16 Gresse St, London W1A 4WD (☎ 071 631 4733, fax 071 631 0393)

PIKE, Prof Edward Roy; s of Anthony Pike (d 1968), of Abercarn, Monmouth, and Rosalind, *née* Davies (d 1982); *b* 4 Dec 1929; *Educ* Southfield Sch Oxford, Univ Coll Cardiff (BSc, PhD); *m* 1955, Pamela, da of William Henry Spearing Sawtell (d 1978); 1 s, 2 da; *Career* serv RCS (SHAPE HQ France) 1948-50; Fulbright scholar faculty of physics MIT USA 1958-60, chief scientific offr Scientific Civil Serv 1960-, Clerk Maxwell prof of theoretical physics King's Coll London 1986-; chm Adam Hilger Ltd 1981-85, dir Richard Clay plc 1985-86; vice pres Inst of Physics 1981-85; FRS, FRSA; *Recreations* languages, music; *Style—* Prof E R Pike; 8 Bredon Grove, Malvern, Worcs WR14 3JR (☎ 0684 574910)

PIKE, Francis Bruce; s of Esmund Francis Victor Wallace Pike, of Old Brow, Bimport, Shaftesbury, Dorset, and Elizabeth Rosemary, *née* Dun; *b* 13 Feb 1954; *Educ* Uppingham, Univ of Paris, Selwyn Coll Cambridge (MA); *Career* md MIM Tokyo KK 1983-87; dir: OUB Investment Management Ltd 1986-, MIM Britannia Okasan Investment Management Ltd 1986-, MIM Ltd 1987-, Nippon Warrant Fund 1987-, Drayton Far Eastern Trust plc 1988-, Drayton Asia Tst plc 1989-, Euro Warrant Fund 1990-, East Europe Development Fund; chm: Asia Supergrowth Fund 1987-, Asia Tiger Warrant Fund 1990-, Central European Asset Management 1990; *Recreations* reading; *Style—* Francis Pike, Esq; 15 The Cooperage, Horsley Down Sq, London SE1; MIM Ltd, 11 Devonshire Square, London EC2 (☎ 071 626 3434, fax 071 623 3339, telex 886108)

PIKE, Baroness (Life Peer UK 1974), of Melton, Co Leics; Irene Mervyn Parnicott Pike; DBE (1981); da of Ivan Samuel Pike (d 1934), and Alice Pike (d 1956); sis of Claude Drew Pike, *qv*; *b* 16 Sept 1918; *Educ* Hunmanby Hall, Univ of Reading; *Career* MP (C) Melton, Leics Dec 1956-Feb 1974, asst postmaster-gen 1959-63, jt parly under-sec state Home Office 1963-64; chm: IBA Gen Advsy Cncl 1974-79, WRVS 1974-81, Broadcasting Complaints Ctee 1981-86; dir Dunderdale Investmts; *Style—* The Rt Hon the Lady Pike, DBE; Hownam, nr Kelso, Roxburgh

PIKE, John Douglas; s of Rev Horace Douglas Pike, of Rufforth, nr York, and Phyllis Joyce, *née* Langdon; *b* 4 Oct 1947; *Educ* QEGS Wakefield, Keighley Sch, Jesus Coll Cambridge (MA); *m* 11 Oct 1975, Rosemary Elizabeth, da of Archibald Richard Harlow (d 1985), of Wetherby; 2 s (Richard b 28 April 1983, Stephen b 18 July 1985), 1 da (Alison b 23 July 1981); *Career* Booth and Co: articled clerk 1969-71, slr 1972-76, ptnr 1976, practice devpt ptnr 1989-91, head Commercial Property Dept 1991-; NP; memb Law Soc, Slrs Benevolent Assoc; *Recreations* walking, swimming, rugby football, skiing, gardening; *Style—* John Pike, Esq; Booth & Co, Sovereign House, South Parade, Leeds LS1 1HQ (☎ 0532 832000, fax 0532 832060, car 0860 500507, telex 557439)

PIKE, Michael Edmund; KCVO, CMG (1984); *b* 4 Oct 1931; *Educ* Wimbledon Coll, LSE, BNC Oxford (MA); *m* 1962, Catherine, *née* Lim; 1 s, 2 da; *Career* former cnsllr Washington and Tel Aviv, RCDS, ambass to Vietnam 1982-85, min and dep perm rep NATO 1985-87, high cmmr Singapore 1987-90 (ret); *Style—* Sir Michael Pike, KCVO, CMG

PIKE, Peter Leslie; MP (Lab) Burnley 1983-; s of Leslie Henry Pike (d 1980), and Gladys Pike (d 1971); *b* 26 June 1937; *Educ* Hinchley Wood Secdy Sch; *m* 1962, Sheila Lillian, da of Hubert John Bull (d 1964); 2 da; *Career* served RM 1955-57; Midland Bank 1954-62, pty organiser Lab Pty 1963-73, Mullard (Simonstone) 1973-83, memb Environment Select Ctee 1985, chm Lab Pty Environment Ctee 1987-90, front bench spokesperson Rural Affrs 1990-; vice pres Burnley Youth Theatre; memb: Nat Tst, CND, Anti-Apartheid; *Recreations* Burnley FC supporter; *Clubs* Byerden House Socialist, Philips Sports and Social; *Style—* Peter Pike, Esq, MP; 73 Ormerod Rd, Burnley, Lancs BB11 2RU (☎ 0282 34719); House of Commons, London SW1A 0AA (☎ 071 219 33514/6488)

PIKE, Lady Romayne Aileen; *née* Brabazon; da of 14 Earl of Meath, and his w Elizabeth Mary, only da of Capt Geoffrey Vaux Salvin Bowlby, RHG; *b* 1943,May; *m* 1968, Robert Eben Neil, s of Lt-Col Godfrey Eben Pike (d 1967); 1 s (Harry), 1 da (Tamsin); *Career* sculptor; *Style—* Lady Romayne Pike; Kidborough House, Danehill, Sussex RH17 7HQ

PIKE, Lt-Gen Sir William Gregory Huddleston; KCB (1961, CB 1956), CBE (1952), DSO (1943); s of Capt Sydney Royston Pike, RA (d 1907), and Sarah Elizabeth, *née* Huddleston (d 1963); bro of Marshal of the RAF Sir Thomas Pike (d 1983); *b* 24 June 1905; *Educ* Bedford Sch, Marlborough, RMA Woolwich; *m* 1939, Josephine Margaret, da of Maj-Gen Reginald Henry Dalrymple Tompson, CB, CMG, DSO (d 1937); 1 s, 2 da; *Career* Br and Indian Artillery 1925-36, Staff Coll Camberley 1937-38, cmd and staff appts in France, Belgium, N Africa, UK, USA, Far East 1939-50, CRA 1 Cwlth Div Korea 1951-52, dir staff duties WO 1954-57, COS FARELF 1957-60, Vice CIGS 1960-63, Hon Col 277 Highland Field Rgmt RA (TA) 1960-67, Col Cmdt RA 1962-70; Lt of HM Tower of London 1963-66; jt hon pres Anglo Korean Soc 1963-69, chief cdr St John Ambulance 1969-75; chm Lord Mayor Treloar Tst and Governing Body Treloar Coll until 1982; memb HAC, govr Corps of Commissionaires; Legion of Merit (USA) 1953; GCStJ 1976; *Recreations* field sports, gardening; *Style—* Lt-Gen Sir William Pike, KCB, CBE, DSO; Ganwells, Bentley, Hants (☎ 0420 22152)

PIKESLEY, Richard Leslie; s of Leonard Leslie Pikesley, and Gwendolen Eleanor, *née* Read; *b* 8 Jan 1951; *Educ* St Nicholas GS Northwood, Harrow Sch of Art, City of Canterbury Coll of Art, Univ of London; *m* 4 May 1974, Susan Margaret, da of Sidney James Stone; 2 da (Caroline b 1984, Elzabeth b 1987); *Career* artist; contribs to mixed exhibitions incl: Royal Acad Summer Exhibition, New English Art Club, Academician's Choice London and Bristol, Laing Prize Exhibition, Royal Inst of Painters in Watercolours, New Grafton Gallery London, Jonleigh Gallery Guildford, WH Patterson Fine Art London, Brian Sinfield Fine Paintings, Minton Fine Art Toronto; one man shows incl: New Grafton Gallery London, Butlin Gallery Somerset, Linfield Gallery, St James's Gallery Bath; rep in various collections incl: St Johns Coll Cambridge, Hambro's Bank, S G Warburg; awards: finalist Hunting Gp prize 1981 and 1989, EF Hutton prize 1987, W H Patterson prize 1988; memb NEAC 1974 (memb Exec Ctee); *Recreations* horses, gardens, riding; *Style—* Richard Pikesley, Esq; Middlehill Farm,

Marrowbone Lane, Bothenhampton, Bridport, Dorset DT6 4BU (☎ 0308 221 81)

PIKETT, Christopher; s of Maj Cecil Charles Pikett, and Joan Madeleine Pikett; *b* 15 Oct 1952; *Educ* West Bridgford GS Nottingham, Univ of Southhampton (LLB); *m* 18 Sept 1976, Geraldine Barbara, da of Derek Alan Stopps; 2 s (Oliver James b 1980, Edward Guy b 1983); *Career* barr middle Temple 1976, legal advsr in indust 1976-82; dir legal servs and co sec Varity Hldgs and subsidaries 1987-89; co sec and gen mangr Legal Affairs 3M United Kingdom PLC 1989-; memb Hon Soc of Middle Temple; FRSA; *Style—* Christopher Pikett, Esq; 3M United Kingdon PLC, 3M House, Bracknell, Berks RG12 1JU (☎ 0344 58565, fax 0344 860635)

PILBROW, Richard Hugh; Cranbrook Sch, Central Sch of Speech and Drama; s of Arthur Gordon Pilbrow; *b* 28 April 1933; *Educ* Cranbrook Sch, Central Sch of Speech and Drama; *m* 1, 1958, Viki Brinton; 1 s, 1 da; m 2, 1974, Molly Friedel; 1 da; *Career* chm Theatre Projects Consultants 1957-, theatre conslt prodr and lighting designer for prods in London, Moscow, New York, Paris; vice pres: Assoc of Br Theatre Technicians, memb: Cncl Nat Youth Theatre, Cncl London Acad of Music and Drama; FRSA; *Books* Stage Lighting (1970); *Clubs* Garrick; *Style—* Richard Pilbrow, Esq; Theatre Projects Consultants Inc, 78 Barrack Hill Road, Ridgefield, Connecticut 06877, USA (☎ 010 1 203 431 3949)

PILCH, (Anthony) Michael; CBE (1984); s of Lt-Col George Harold Pilch (d 1943); *b* 6 July 1927; *Educ* Shrewsbury, Balliol Coll Oxford (BA); *m* 1950, Betty Christine, da of Franklin John Skinner (d 1976); 1 da; *Career* dir Noble Lowndes & Partners Ltd 1968-85 (ret); chm: Nat Assoc of Pension Funds 1979-81 (vice pres 1981-83), New Horizon Tst; *Recreations* theatre, photography, writing; *Style—* Michael Pilch, Esq, CBE; 10 Timber Hill Rd, Caterham, Surrey CR3 6LD (☎ 0883 46671)

PILCHER, Anthony David; s of Lt-Col William Spelman Pilcher, DSO (d 1970), and Diana, *née* Lawrence (d 1987); *b* 7 Sept 1935; *Educ* Eton; *m* 4 Feb 1964 (Margaret) Ann, da of Maj Gerald Borland Walker (ka 1941); 2 s (Harry b 4 Oct 1968, Sam b 16 Oct 1973); *Career* sr ptnr FLP Secretan 1977-87 (previously ptnr), chm FLP Secretan & Co Ltd 1987-90, chm Secretan (underwriting agencies) Ltd; Freeman: City of London, Worshipful Co of Pewterers; Liveryman and memb Ct Worshipful Co of Haberdashers; *Recreations* fishing, sailing, viticulture; *Clubs* Bembridge SC; *Style—* Anthony D Pilcher, Esq; 8 Victoria Rd, Kensington, London W8 5RD (☎ 071 937 3711); Upper North Wells House, Bembridge, IOW PO35 5NF; F L P Secretan & Co Ltd, Suite 776, Lloyd's, Lime St, London EC3M 7DQ (☎ 071 623 8084, fax 071 626 8066, telex 987321 LLOYDS G)

PILCHER, David Richard; s of Archibald Bertram Pilcher, of 23 Haglands Copse West Chiltington Sussex, and Sylvia, *née* Adlard; *b* 26 March 1937; *Educ* Aldenham; *m* 4 April 1970, Veronica Betty, da of George Brown (d 1983), of Wimborne; 1 s (Jonathan David b 21 July 1973), 1 da (Sarah Elizabeth b 26 Feb 1972); *Career* CA with Pridie Brewster & Gold 1957-67, chief accountant of The Royal Opera House 1968-; ACA 1966, ATII 1966, FCA 1977; *Recreations* music, theatre, amateur dramatics; *Style—* David Pilcher, Esq; 16 Church Lane, Kimpton, Hitchin, Herts SG4 8RS (☎ 0438 832 439); Royal Opera House, Covent Garden, 45 Floral St, London WC2 (☎ 071 240 1200, fax 071 836 1762, telex 27988 COVGAR G)

PILCHER, Sir (Charlie) Dennis; CBE (1968); s of Charlie Edwin Pilcher; *b* 2 July 1906; *Educ* Clayesmore Sch, The Coll of Estate Mgmnt; *m* 1929, Mary Allison, da of William Aumonier; 2 da (*see* The Earl of Strafford); *Career* served RA 1940-45, Normandy 1944 (despatches), Maj; chartered surveyor; conslt Graves Son & Pilcher Chartered Surveyors (ptnr 1930 subsequently sr ptnr), Hemel Hempsted Devpt Corp 1949-56; chm: Bracknell Devpt Corp 1968-71 (joined 1956), Cmmn for the New Towns 1971-78; advsr to govt on: housing rent assessment, control of business rents, commercial property devpt 1965-76; dir: Sun Life Assur Soc 1968-77, Save and Prosper Gp Ltd 1970-80; memb cncl Glyndebourne Festival Opera 1969-; FRICS; kt 1974; *Style—* Sir Dennis Pilcher, CBE; Brambles, Batts Lane, Mare Hill, Pulborough, W Sussex (☎ 079 82 2126)

PILCHER, (Anthony) Julian; s of Col Alan Humphrey Pilcher, CIE, MC, ED (d 1957), and Dorothy Eileen, *née* Parrington; *b* 7 Feb 1936; *Educ* Shrewsbury; *m* 26 Oct 1963, Sally Louise, da of Herbert John Murray Cook, of Tilford, Surrey; 1 s (Simon b 1966), 2 da (Rebecca b 1967, Sophie b 1969); *Career* qualified CA 1959; ptnr: Harmood Banner & Co 1963-74, Deloitte Haskins & Sells 1974-82; founding ptnr Lyon Pilcher & Co 1983-; dir: Coll Servs Ltd, Solent Pensions Ltd; past pres Southampton C of C, govr Rookesbury Park Sch; *Recreations* sailing, shooting, skiing; *Clubs* Cavalry and Guards, Royal Southern Yacht; *Style—* Julian Pilcher, Esq; The Garden House, Steventon, Basingstoke, Hampshire (☎ 0256 398270); Lyon Pilcher, 102-108 Above Bar, Southampton (☎ 0703 636915, fax 0703 339369)

PILCHER, Roger Anthony; s of Walter Pilcher (d 1967); *b* 11 April 1931; *Educ* Tonbridge, RMA Sandhurst; *m* Lydia; 5 s , 1 da; *Career* The Buffs; Colonial Serv Kenya; mgmnt Int Factors Ltd (md 1967-68), md Credit Factoring Int Ltd 1968-84, Chm Assoc Br Factors 1980-83, memb of cncl CBI 1983-84, chief exec The Export Fin Co Ltd 1984-; MIEX 1975; *Recreations* wildlife, hillwalking, photography; *Style—* Roger Pilcher, Esq; Ash House, Lea, Malmesbury, Wilts (☎ 0666 824 884); The Export Finance Co Ltd, Exfinco House, Swindon SN1 1QQ (☎ 0793 614 404)

PILDITCH, James George Christopher; CBE (1983); s of Frederick Henry Pilditch (d 1952), and his w, Marie-Thérèse, *née* Priest (d 1982); *b* 7 Aug 1929; *Educ* Slough GS, Univ of Reading, INSEAD; *m* 1, 1952 (m dis) Molly; m 2, 1970, Anne Elisabeth, da of Osborne Wilhemson Johnson, of Stockholm; 1 da; *Career* Nat Serv RA and RCA (Res); fndr AIDCOM International plc; chm: Design Bd BTEC, Cncl Mktg Gp of GB; memb Design Cncl; memb Cncl RSA 1984, memb Cncl Heritage of London Tst 1986; chm: Furniture EDC NEDO 1985, Design Working Pty NEDO 1985; memb: Design Panel Br Airports Authy 1987, Advsy Panel Design Mgmnt Unit London Business Sch 1982 (chm Financial Times award 1987), Cncl and treas RCA 'I'll be over in the morning'; awarded CHEAD medal (Conf for Higher Educn in Art and Design) 1988; first fell Design Mngmt Inst USA; FRSA, Hon FCSD; *Publications* The Silent Salesman, The Business of Product Design, Communication by Design, Talk about Design, Winning Ways; *Recreations* writing, drawing, watching the Lord's Test; *Clubs* MCC, Army & Navy, Travellers'; *Style—* James Pilditch, Esq, CBE; 62 Cadogan Sq, London SW1 (☎ 071 584 9279); Brookhampton House, N Cadbury, Somerset (☎ 096 340 225)

PILDITCH, John Richard; s and h of Sir Richard Edward Pilditch, 4 Bt , qv; *b* 24 Sept 1955; *Style—* John Pilditch, Esq; c/o 4 Fisherman's Bank, Mudeford, Christchurch, Dorset

PILDITCH, Sir Richard Edward; 4 Bt (UK 1929); s of Sir Philip Harold Pilditch, 2 Bt, and bro of Sir Philip John Frederick Pilditch, 3 Bt (d 1954); *b* 8 Sept 1926; *Educ* Charterhouse; *m* 7 Oct 1950, Pauline Elizabeth Smith; 1 s, 1 da; *Heir* s, John Richard Pilditch, qv; *Career* RN 1944-45 India and Ceylon; *Style—* Sir Richard Pilditch, Bt; 4 Fishermans Bank, Mudeford, Christchurch, Dorset

PILE, Anthony John Devereux; er s of Sir John Pile (d 1982), and Lady Pile, *qv*; hp to unc, Sir Frederick Pile, 3 Bt; *b* 7 June 1947; *Educ* Durham Sch; *m* 1977, Jenny Clare, da of Peter H Youngman, of Fenn St, Westleton, Suffolk; 2 s (Thomas b 6 April 1978, Hugh b 1980), 1 da (Harriet b 1983); *Career* cmmnd Durham LI 1966, served in Dhofar, Oman (despatches), NI, Cyprus, GSO3 (Ops) HQ 3 Armd Div 1979-80, Maj 1980, ret; attended Sloan Fellowship Programme London Business Sch, prodn mangr Hygrade (Meats) London 1982-85, prodn dir Mayhew Foods Ltd Uckfield E Sussex 1985-, md Crossley Ferguson Ltd Stockholm-on-Tees; *Recreations* squash, politics; *Style—* Anthony Pile, Esq; 23 The Green, Norton, Cleveland; Crossley Ferguson Ltd, Riverside House, 33 Bridge Rd, Stockton-on-Tees, Cleveland TS18 3AE (☎ 0642 612592)

PILE, Col Sir Frederick Devereux; 3 Bt (UK 1900), of Kenilworth House, Rathgar, Co Dublin; MC (1945); s of Gen Sir Frederick Alfred Pile, 2 Bt, GCB, DSO, MC (d 1976), and his 1 w Vera, da of Brig-Gen Frederick Lloyd, CB; *b* 10 Dec 1915; *Educ* Weymouth Coll, RMC Sandhurst; *m* 1, 1940, Pamela (d 1983), da of late Philip Henstock; 2 da; m 2, 1984, Violet Josephine Andrews, da of Alfred Denys Cowper; *Heir* n, Anthony John Devereux Pile; *Career* served WWII 1939-45, Col Royal Tank Regt; Br Jt Servs Mission Washington DC 1957-60, Cmdt RAC Driving and Maintenance Sch 1960-62; *Recreations* fishing, cricket, travelling; *Clubs* MCC; *Style—* Col Sir Frederick Pile, Bt, MC; Beadles, Cowbeech, nr Hailsham, East Sussex

PILE, Sir William Dennis; GCB (1978, KCB 1971, CB 1968), MBE (1944); s of James Edward Pile; *b* 1 Dec 1919; *Educ* Royal Masonic Sch, St Catharine's Coll Cambridge; *m* 1, 1939 (m dis 1947), Brenda Skinner; m 2, 1948, Joan Marguerite Crafter; 1 s, 2 da; *Career* chm Bd of Inland Revenue 1976-79, dir Nationwide Building Society 1980-89; memb Distillers' Co Ltd 1980-86; *Clubs* United Oxford & Cambridge, Hawks (Cambridge); *Style—* Sir William Pile, GCB, MBE; The Manor House, Riverhead, nr Sevenoaks, Kent TN13 2AS (☎ 0732 54498)

PILGRIM, Lawrence William; DFC (1943); s of Harold Evelyn Pilgrim (d 1941), and Margaret, *née* Aldrich (d 1981); *b* 30 Sept 1921; *Educ* Owens Sch, City of London Coll (pt/t); *m* 1 Oct 1977, Angela, da of Donald Marks, of 103 Victoria Rd, Warminster, Wilts; *Career* joined RAF 1941, qualified pilot, Bomber cmd 1943, instr Heavy Con Unit 1944-45, Flt Cdr operations (Sqdn Ldr); CA 1948; asst co sec Evans & Ridler Gp Hereford 1948-51, commercial airline pilot Br Euro Airways 1952; co sec and chief accountant: Evans & Ridler Gp 1952-61, Ushers Wilts Brewery 1961 (fin dir 1970); fin controll Grand Metropolitan Ltd 1974, fin conslt in private practice 1980-; dir: Roux Waterside Inn Ltd, Roux Continuation Ltd, Home Rouxl Ltd; vice chm Bomber Cmd Assoc; FCA; *Recreations* golf, photography; *Clubs* West Wilts Golf; *Style—* Lawrence Pilgrim, Esq, DFC; Sandstones, 18 Church Hill, Camberley, Surrey GU15 2HA (☎ 0276 27545)

PILKINGTON, Sir Alastair Lionel Alexander Bethune; s of Col Lionel George Pilkington, MC (d 1955), and Evelyn Carnegie (d 1985), da of Sir Alexander Sharp Bethune, 9 Bt; *b* 7 Jan 1920; *Educ* Sherborne, Trinity Coll Cambridge; *m* 1, 1945, Patricia Nicholl (d 1977), da of Rear Adm Frank Elliott, OBE; 1 s, 1 da; m 2, 1978, Kathleen, wid of Eldridge Haynes; *Career* inventor floating glass process; chm and dir: Bank of England 1974-84, BP 1976-; chm Chloride Gp Ltd 1979-87, hon pres Pilkington Bros Ltd 1985- (chm 1973-80, dir 1980-85); dir: Hambros Advanced Technol Tst, Banque Nationale de Paris Wellcome Fndn Ltd; memb bd of govrs Technical Change Centre, pro-chllr Univ of Lancaster 1980-90, chm cncl Nat Academic Awards 1984-87; Hon FUMIST 1969; hon fell: Imperial Coll 1974, LSE 1980, Poly of Wales 1980, Trinity Coll Cambridge; Hon DTech Loughborough 1968, Hon DEng Liverpool 1971, Hon LLD Bristol 1979, Hon DSc (Eng) London 1979, Hon DSc East Anglia 1988, Hon Engr Birmingham 1988, DSc Alfred Univ NY 1990, LLD Univ of Lancaster 1990; FBIM, CNAA, FRS; kt 1970; *Clubs* Athenaeum; *Style—* Sir Alastair Pilkington, FRS; 74 Eaton Place, London SW1X 8AU (☎ 071 235 5604); Goldrill Cottage, Patterdale, nr Penrith, Cumbria (☎ 085 32 263)

PILKINGTON, Sir Antony Richard; DL; only s of Maj Arthur Cope Pilkington, MC (yr bro of late Sir Richard Pilkington, KBE, MC), and Otilia Dolores, *née* Reed-Cook; *b* 20 June 1935; *Educ* Ampleforth, Trinity Coll Cambridge; *m* 1960, Alice Kirsty, er da of Sir Thomas Calderwood Dundas, 7 and last Bt (d 1970), MBE; 3 s (Jerome b 1961, David b 1963, Simon b 1972), 1 da (Miranda b 1966); *Career* chm Pilkington plc 1980-; non-exec dir: GKN plc 1982-, National Westminster Bank plc, Nat West Investment Bank Ltd; chm Community of St Helen's Tst; kt 1990; *Style—* Sir Antony Pilkington, DL; Pilkington plc, Prescot Rd, St Helens, Merseyside WA10 3TT (☎ 0744 28882)

PILKINGTON, (Richard) Godfrey; s of Col Guy Reginald Pilkington, DSO, TD (d 1970), of Fairfield, Crank, St Helens, Merseyside, and Margery, *née* Frost (d 1973); *b* 8 Nov 1918; *Educ* Clifton, Trinity Coll Cambridge (MA); *m* 14 Oct 1950, Evelyn Edith (Eve), da of Philip Robert Stanley Vincent (d 1933), of Gerrards Cross, Bucks; 2 s (Andrew b 1955, Matthew b 1964), 2 da (Penny b 1956, Clarissa (Dr Arscott) b 1958); *Career* WWII Lt (Temp Actg Capt) Anti-Tank and Medium Gunners RA, served BNAF I Army and CMF Italy 1940-46; art dealer Frost and Reed Ltd 1947-53, fndr and ptnr Piccadilly Gallery London 1953-, ed Pictures and Prints 1951-60; Master Fine Art Trade Guild 1964-66, chm Soc London Art Dealers 1974-77; *Recreations* walking, gardening, tennis, golf, boating; *Clubs* Athenaeum, Garrick, Hurlingham; *Style—* Godfrey Pilkington, Esq; 45 Barons Court Rd, London W14 9DZ (☎ 071 385 8278); The Old Vicarage, Lamb Lane, Buckland, Faringdon, Oxfordshire; Piccadilly Gallery, 16 Cork St, London W1X 1PF (☎ 071 499 4632/071 629 2875)

PILKINGTON, Rev the Hon John Rowan; o s of Baron Pilkington (Life Peer, d 1983), and his 1 w, Rosamond Margaret, *née* Rowan (d 1953); *b* 15 March 1932; *Educ* Rugby, Magdalene Coll Cambridge (MA); *m* 4 April 1964, Celia, da of Robert Ian Collison; 2 da, 1 adopted s; *Career* vicar of St Mark with St Paul Darlington Co Durham; *Style—* The Rev the Hon John Pilkington; St Mark's Vicarage, 394 North Rd, Darlington, Co Durham DL1 3BH

PILKINGTON, Baroness; Mavis Joy Doreen; er da of Gilbert Caffrey, of Woodleigh, Lostock Park, Bolton; formerly Mrs Wilding; *m* 2, 17 Feb 1961, as his 2 w, Baron Pilkington (Life Peer, d 1983); *Career* Dep Lt Merseyside 1985; vice-patron Nat Rose Soc; *Style—* The Rt Hon the Lady Pilkington; Windle Hall, St Helens, Merseyside

PILKINGTON, Norman; s of Norman Pilkington, of Great Harwood, Blackburn, Lancs, and Bessie, *née* Ashworth; *b* 25 April 1936; *Educ* Accrington GS, Balliol Coll Oxford (BA), Univ of Oxford (Cert in Stats); *m* 6 Aug 1960, Margaret Gordon, da of Reginald Neville; 1 s (Simon Richard b 16 June 1965), 1 da (Jane Katharine b 23 Oct 1963); *Career* Flt Lt Educn Branch RAF 1959-62; investmt analyst Phillips & Drew 1962-65, asst investmt mangr Pilkington Brothers Ltd 1965-67, investmt mangr Shell International Petroleum Co Ltd 1970-73 (asst investmt mangr 1967-70), vice pres Euro res Baker Weeks & Co Inc (NYSE Stockbrokers) 1973-77; Geoffrey Morley & Partners Ltd (pension fund portfolio mangrs): dir 1977-79, dep chm 1979-84, chm and md 1984-88, chief exec Globe Morley Ltd (after co acquired by Globe Investment Trust plc) 1988-91, md Commercial Union Morley Ltd (after co acquired by Commercial Union Assurance plc) 1991; Soc of Investmt Analysts: memb 1965-, memb Cncl 1969-78, chm 1975-78, fell 1985; *Recreations* reading, theatre, crosswords; *Clubs* United Oxford & Cambridge University; *Style—* Norman Pilkington, Esq; High Orchard, 17 Chantry View Rd, Guildford, Surrey GU1 3XW (☎ 0483 38917); Commercial Union Morley Ltd, St Helen's 1 Undershaft, London EC3P 3DQ (☎ 071 283 7500, fax 071 283 7517)

PILKINGTON, Rev Canon Peter; s of Frank Pilkington (d 1977), and Doris Pilkington (d 1985); *b* 5 Sept 1933; *Educ* Dame Allans Sch Newcastle upon Tyne,

Jesus Coll Cambridge (BA, MA); *m* 1966, Helen, da of Charles Wilson, of Risholme, Lincoln and Elleron Lodge, N Yorks; 2 da (Celia b 1970, Sarah b 1972); *Career* schoolmaster St Joseph's Coll Chidya Tanganyika 1955-58, ordained 1959, curate of Bakewell Derbys 1959-62, schoolmaster Eton Coll 1965-75, headmaster King's Sch Canterbury 1975-86, high master St Pauls Sch London 1986; hon canon of Canterbury Cathedral 1975-; *Clubs* Garrick, Beefsteak; *Style—* The Rev Canon Peter Pilkington

PILKINGTON, Raymond; s of William Pilkington (d 1962), and Doris Pilkington (d 1975); *b* 30 April 1932; *Educ* Blackpool GS, St Bartholomew's Hosp (MB BS), Univ of London (MD); *m* 5 Sept 1959, Phyllis Mary, da of James Worsley (d 1968); 2 s (Gareth Mark b 11 Aug 1960, Martin Simon b 20 Dec 1962), 1 da (Clare Joanne b 21 Sept 1964); *Career* Nat Serv 1951-53; obstetrician and gynaecologist: St Bartholomew's Hosp 1959, St Mary's Hosp Manchester 1960, Queen Charlotte's Hosp London 1961, Princess Mary Hosp and Royal Victoria Infirmary Newcastle upon Tyne 1962-63, St Mary's Hosp Manchester 1963-65 and 1980, Mill Rd Maternity Hosp Liverpool 1966-67; conslt Southend DHA 1967-; FRCOG 1978 (MRCOG 1964); *Books* Aetiological aspects of Foetal-Maternal Transfusion (1964); *Recreations* golf, sport, music, books, antique collecting; *Clubs* Thorpe Hall Golf, Nondescripts Cricket; *Style—* Raymond Pilkington, Esq; 74 Parkanaur Ave, Thorpe Bay, Essex SS1 3NB (☎ 0702 588408); Wellesley Hospital, Eastern Ave, Southend-on-Sea (☎ 0702 469244)

PILKINGTON, Dr Roger Windle; s of (Richard) Austin Pilkington (d 1951), of St Helens, and The Hon Hope Cozens-Hardy (d 1947); *b* 17 Jan 1915; *Educ* Rugby, Univ of Freiburg, Magdalene Coll Cambridge (MA, PhD); *m* 1, 27 July 1937 (m dis 1973), Theodora Miriam, da of Dr Farris Nasser Jaboor (d 1940); 1 s (Hugh Austin b 1942, d 1986), 1 da (Cynthia Miriam b 1939); m 2, 11 Oct 1973, Ingrid Maria, da of Herman Gustaf Geijer (d 1961), of Brattfors; *Career* res in genetics 1937-45; freelance writer and author of 56 books; contrib to: Time and Tide, Family Doctor, Sunday Telegraph; chm: London Missionary Soc 1962, of tstees Homerton Coll Cambridge 1962-74, The Hall Sch 1962-73; life memb Eugenics Soc 1951; master Worshipful Co of Glass Sellers 1967 (memb 1957); Chevalier Confrèrie du Minervois (France 1987); *Books* incl: Scientific works: The Ways of the Sea (1957), Robert Boyle, Father of Chemistry (1959); for children: The Boy from Stink Alley (1966), The Ormering Tide (1974), I Sailed on the Mayflower (1990); The Small Boat Series in 20 volumes, Small Boat in the Midi (1988), Small Boat Down The Years (1988); *Recreations* inland navigation, walking; *Style—* Dr Roger Pilkington; La Maison Du Coti, St Aubin, Jersey (☎ 0534 43760); Les Cactus, Montouliers, France (☎ 67 89 49 98)

PILKINGTON, Ruth; s of Ian Everard Pilkington, of Sycamore Farm, High Lane, Ormskirk, Lancashire, and Arabella Lynda, *née* Penny; *Educ* Merchant Taylors' Sch for Girls Liverpool, Univ of Birmingham; *Career* hockey player; Hightown Ladies Hockey Club 1985-89, First Personnel Sutton Colefield Ladies Hockey Club 1989-91 (currently playing for club at nat level); Eng under 18 team 1986-88: forward position, 15 caps, Home Countries Competition (Largs 1987, winners Swindon 1988), Easter Euro Tournaments (Largs 1987, Germany 1988 third place); Eng under 21 team 1988-90: forward position, 24 caps, Home Countries Competition (winners Glasgow 1988, winners Nottingham 1989, runners-up Cork 1990), Silver medallists Euro Championships Paris 1989, Eighth position World Cup Ottawa 1989; memb: Eng Sr Trg Squad 1990-91, Eng Indoor Team 1990-91; *Recreations* poultry fancier, cooking, shooting, music; *Style—* Miss Ruth Pilkington; Sycamore Farm, High Lane, Ormskirk, Lancashire L40 7SW (☎ 0695 573169); The Secretary, First Personnel Sutton Coldfield Ladies HC, Rectory Park, Rectory Rd, Sutton Coldfield, West Midlands

PILKINGTON, Lady Sophia Frances Anne; *née* Vane-Tempest-Stewart; er da of 9 Marquess of Londonderry; *b* 23 Feb 1959; *m* m 24 Oct 1987, Jonathan Mark Pilkington, yst s of Ronald Charles Leslie Pilkington, of Hill House, Stanstead Abbots, Herts; 1 da (Hermione Alice b 10 Jan 1989); *Style—* The Lady Sophia Pilkington

PILKINGTON OF REAY, Maj Thomas Douglas; s of Alan Douglas Pilkington, DL (d 1973), and Edith Winifred, *née* Turner (d 1937); land and titles confiscated after Battle of Bosworth 1485; *b* 23 Oct 1912; *Educ* Eton, Worcester Coll Oxford, RAC; *m* 1, 1937 (m dis 1961), Vivien Mary, da of Walter Bernard Baker (d 1955); 3 s (Ian b 1938, Christopher b 1947, Nigel b 1951), 2 da (Fiona b 1941, Jane b 1943); m 2, 1962, Jane St Clare Carden, da of Lt-Col Thomas Edward St Clare Daniell, OBE, MC (d 1948); *Career* served RE (TA) 1937-39, WWII Major RA in N Africa, Italy 1939-45 (despatches); stockbroker 1934-39; farmer; JP (Hants) 1954-62; Gen Cmmr Inland Revenue: Hants 1955-62, Glos 1962-87; *Recreations* fishing, shooting, cricket, point to point racing, NH racing since 1948 (twice winner Belgian Grand Nat and many other races); *Clubs* MCC; *Style—* Maj Thomas D Pilkington of Reay; Hyde Mill, Stow on the Wold, Cheltenham, Glos GL54 1LA (☎ 0451 30641)

PILL, Hon Mr Justice; Sir Malcolm Thomas; s of Reginald Thomas Pill, MBE (d 1987), and Anne Elizabeth, *née* Wright (d 1982); *b* 11 March 1938; *Educ* Whitchurch GS, Trinity Coll Cambridge (MA, LLM), Hague Acad of Int Law (Dip); *m* 19 March 1966, Roisin Mary, da of Dr Thomas Prior Riordan, of Swansea; 2 s (John b 1967, Hugh b 1968), 1 da (Madeleine b 1971); *Career* serv RA 1956-58, Glamorgan Yeo (TA) 1958-67; called to the bar Gray's Inn 1962; third sec FO 1963-64, rec Crown Ct 1976-87, QC 1978, bencher Gray's Inn 1987, judge of the High Ct (Queen's Bench Div) 1988-, presiding judge Wales and Chester Circuit; chm: UNA (Welsh Centre) Tst 1969-77 and 1980-87, Welsh Centre for Int Affairs 1973-76, UK Ctee Freedom from Hunger Campaign 1978-87; kt 1988; *Clubs* Royal Cwlth Soc, Cardiff and Co; *Style—* The Hon Mr Justice Pill; Royal Courts of Justice, Strand, London WC2A 2LL

PILLAR, Rt Rev Kenneth Harold; *see*: Hertford, Bishop of

PILLAR, Adm Sir William Thomas; GBE (1983), KCB (1980); s of William Thomas Pillar (d 1960), of Dartmouth, and Lily, *née* Woolnough (d 1932); *b* 24 Feb 1924; *Educ* Blundell's, RNEC; *m* 1946, Ursula Winifred, da of Arthur Benjamin Ransley, MC (d 1965); 3 s, 1 da; *Career* joined RN 1942, Capt RNEC 1973-75, Port Adm Rosyth 1976-77, Asst Chief Fleet Support 1977-79, Chief Fleet Support and memb Admty Bd 1979-82, Adm 1982, Cmdt RCDS 1982-83, Lt Govr and C-in-C Jersey 1985-90, memb Cncl RUSI 1984-87 (vice chm 1986-87), vice pres Blundell's Sch 1987-, pres Square Rigger Club (support of training ship Royalist) 1988-; KStJ 1985; FIMechE, CEng, FIMarE; *Recreations* sailing (yacht 'Shrimp II'), rough gardening, fixing things; *Clubs* Army and Navy, Royal Naval Sailing Assoc (Cdre 1980-83, Life Vice Cdre 1990), Royal Yacht Sqdn; *Style—* Adm Sir William Pillar, GBE, KCB; Selwood, Zeals Row, Zeals, Warminster, Wilts BA12 6PE (☎ 0747 840577)

PILLEY, John Cyril Dorland; s of Capt Eric Charles Pilley, and Elsa Celeste, *née* Henderson; *b* 25 Jan 1935; *Educ* Charterhouse, Ch Ch Oxford; *m* 1 Feb 1985, Caroline Yvonne, da of Ian Gillett Gilbert; *Career* ADC to CINC Far East 1960-61, ADC to CIGS 1961-62, Adj 1 Bn Coldstream Guards 1964-66, ret as Capt; dir: Henderson Unit Trust Management 1982, Henderson Administration Ltd 1987; chm Russell Wood Ltd 1989; *Recreations* tennis, fishing, riding; *Clubs* Boodles, City of London; *Style—* John Pilley, Esq; Trotton Old Rectory, Petersfield, Hampshire (☎ 0730 813612); Russell Wood Ltd, 30 Great Guildford St, London SE1 (☎ 071 928 0505, fax 071 928 8931, telex 927665)

PILLMAN, Joseph Charles; s of Lt-Col Joseph Robert Pillman, TD (d 1977), of Clwyd; *b* 7 July 1952; *Educ* Rugby, Cambridge (MA); *m* 28 May 1983, Briony Susan, da of Alan Lethbridge, of Henley on Thames; 2 da (Katherine Avril b 1985, Harriet Emma b 1987); *Career* admitted slr 1977-, ptnr Cole and Cole Oxford 1983-; *Clubs* MCC; *Style—* Joseph Pillman, Esq; The Cottage, Islip Rd, Bletchingdon, Oxon (☎ 0869 50513); St George's Mansions, George St, Oxford OX1 2AR (☎ 0865 841222, fax 0865 841444, telex 837628)

PILSWORTH, Michael John; s of Alwyne Pilsworth, of Gringley-on-the-Hill, Yorks, and Catherine, *née* Silverwood; *b* 1 April 1951; *Educ* King Edward VI GS Retford Notts, Univ of Manchester (BA, MA); *m* 7 Oct 1972, Stella Frances, da of Donald Lionel Hore, of Bristol; 1 s (Thomas James b 18 Dec 1984), 1 da (Rosa Grace b 8 March 1977); *Career* res asst Inst of Advanced Studies Manchester Poly 1972-73, lectr in adult educn Univ of Manchester 1976-78 (res fell 1973-75), res assoc Centre for TV Research Univ of Leeds 1979, prog devpt exec London Weekend TV 1983-84 (researcher 1979-82), gp devpt controller TVS Entertainment plc 1987-88 (head of prog planning and devpt 1985-86), chief exec MGMM Communications Ltd 1988-89, dir Select TV plc 1990, md Alomo Productions Ltd 1990-; memb: BAFTA, RTS; *Books* Broadcasting in The Third World (1977); *Recreations* swimming, cinema, reading; *Clubs* Groucho; *Style—* Michael Pilsworth, Esq; 74 Trinity Court, Grays Inn Road, London WC1X 8JY (☎ 071 837 6940); Bailey Cottage, Whipsnade, Beds LU6 2LG (☎ 0582 872752); Alomo Productions Ltd, Elstree Studios, Shenley Rd, Borehamwood, Herts (☎ 081 953 1600, fax 081 905 1427, car 0836 585 894)

PIMLOTT, Prof Benjamin John (Ben); s of John Alfred Ralph Pimlott, CB (d 1969), of Wimbledon, London SW19, and Ellen Dench, *née* Howes (d 1976); *b* 4 July 1945; *Educ* Marlborough, Worcester Coll Oxford; *m* 2 July 1977, Jean Ann, da of Albert William Seaton; 3 s; *Career* lectr Univ of Newcastle 1970-79 (Br Acad Thank Offering to Britain fell 1972-73, Nuffield Fndn res fell 1977-78), res assoc LSE 1979-81, prof of politics and contemporary history Birkbeck Coll Univ of London 1987- (lectr 1981, reader 1986); columnist: Today 1986-87, The Times 1987-88, New Statesman 1987-88, Sunday Times 1988-89; ed Samizdat 1988-90; Parly candidate (Lab): Arundel 1974, Cleveland and Whitby 1974 and 1979; exec The Fabian Soc 1987-; *Books* Labour and the Left in the 1930s (1977), Hugh Dalton (Whitbread Biography award, 1985); *Style—* Ben Pimlott; Birkbeck College, Malet St, London WC1 (☎ 071 580 0198)

PINCHER, (Henry) Chapman; s of Maj Richard Chapman Pincher (d 1964), and Helen, *née* Foster (d 1960); *b* 29 March 1914; *Educ* Darlington GS, Kings Coll London (BSc, Carter medallist), Inst of Educn; *m* 16 Nov 1965, Constance Sylvia Wolstenhome; 1 s (Michael b 1949), 1 da (Patricia b 1947); *Career* RAC 1940, Mil Coll of Sci 1942, Tech SO Rocket Div Min of Supply 1943-46; staff Liverpool Inst 1936-40, defence sci and medical ed Daily Express 1946-73 (Journalist of the Year 1964, Reporter of the Decade 1966), asst ed Daily Express and chief def corr Beaverbrook Newspapers, freelance writer and business conslt 1979-; Hon DLitt Univ of Newcastle, fell King's Coll London 1979; *Books* Breeding of Farm Animals (1946), A Study of Fishes (1947), Into the Atomic Age (1947), Spotlight on Animals (1950), Evolution (1950), It's Fun Finding Out (with Bernard Wicksteed, 1950), Sleep and how to get more of it (1954), Not with a Bang (1965), The Giantkiller (1967), The Penthouse Conspirators (1970), Sex in our Time (1973), The Skeleton at the Villa Wolkonsky (1975), The Eye of the Tornado (1976), The Four Horses (1978), Inside Story (1978), Dirty Tricks (1980), Their Trade is Treachery (1981), The Privatè World of St John Terrapin (1982), Too Secret Too Long (1984), The Secret Offensive (1985), Traitors (1987), A Web of Deception (1987), Contamination (1989), The Truth About Dirty Tricks (1990), One Dog and Herman (1990); *Recreations* fishing, shooting, natural history, music; *Style—* Chapman Pincher, Esq; The Church House, 16 Church St, Kintbury, nr Hungerford, Berks RG15 0TR (☎ 0488 58855)

PINCHES, Rosemary Vivian; *née* Bidder; da of Lt-Col Harold Francis Bidder, DSO, JP (d 1971), formerly of Ravensbury Manor, Morden, Surrey, and Lilias Mary Vivian, *née* Rush (d 1973); ggf was George Parker Bidder 'The Calculating Boy', illustrious engineer with Robert Stephenson and others, pres Inst of Civil Engineers, etc (*see* DNB and George Parker Bidder, by E F Clark (1983)); *b* 19 Jan 1929; *Educ* Glendower Sch London, Westonbirt Sch Glos; *m* 26 July 1952, John Harvey Pinches, MC, s of John Robert Pinches (d 1968), of 19 Holland Park Ave, London W11; 2 da (Joanna Harriet (Hon Mrs Edward Orlando Charles Wood) b 1954, Sarah Carolann Rosemary b 1956); *Career* personal asst to Sir John Heaton-Armstrong Chester Herald Coll of Arms 1948-52; Heraldic publisher and author, genealogist, proprietor of Heraldry Today London (a publishing house and bookshop specializing in heraldry and genealogy) 1954-; memb: Heraldry Soc, AGRA, Wilts Archaeological Inst, Wilts Family History Soc; *Books* Elvin's Mottoes Revised (1971), A European Armorial (with Anthony Wood, 1971), The Royal Heraldry of England (with John H Pinches, 1974), A Bibliography of Burke's 1876-1976 (1976); *Recreations* horse-racing, browsing in old bookshops, playing bridge; *Style—* Mrs John Pinches; Parliament Piece, Ramsbury, Marlborough, Wiltshire SN8 2QH (☎ 0672 20613, 20617, fax 0672 20183)

PINCHES, Stuart John Allison; s of George Arthur Pinches, of 610 Howard House, Dolphin Square, London, and Marjorie Allison; *b* 2 April 1947; *Educ* Friern Barnet GS, Poly of Central London (Dip Photography & Film); *m* 18 Dec 1970, (Brigid) Imelda, da of Patrick Behan (d 1969), of Edenderry, Co Offaly, Eire; *Career* gen mgmnt exec United Artists Corporation Ltd 1968-70, project mangr Organon International bv Holland 1971-73, md Viscom Ireland Ltd Dublin 1974-77, assoc dir Purchasepoint Group London 1978-79, divnl md Viscom Group London 1979-81, head of Programme Servs TVS plc 1981-85; md: AKA Ltd London 1986-87, Interface Design Ltd 1988; jt md Roach and Partners Ltd 1989-; memb IPPA; *Recreations* photography, personal fitness, collecting music; *Style—* Stuart Pinches, Esq; Flat 6, 106 Oxford Gardens, London W10 6NG (☎ 081 968 6562); Roach & Partners Limited, 2 Goldhawk Mews, London W12 8PA (☎ 081 746 2000, fax 081 740 4838, car 0836 369 389)

PINCKNEY, David Charles; s of Dr Charles Percy Pinckney (d 1982), of Park House, Ascot, Berks, and Norah Manisty, *née* Boucher (d 1988); *b* 13 Sept 1940; *Educ* Winchester, New Coll Oxford (MA); *m* 25 May 1974, Susan Audrey, da of Col Austin Richards (d 1974), of Pump House, Writtle, Essex; 1 s (Charles b 1977), 2 da (Katherine b 1974, Caroline b 1976); *Career* sr audit ptnr Peat Marwick Mitchell CAs France 1977-83 (London 1963-67, Paris and Lyons 1968-83), md Wrightson Wood Financial Services Ltd 1984-86, gp fin dir Thornton and Co Ltd 1987-; govr Br Sch Paris 1981-83; ACA 1966; *Recreations* skiing, tennis, foreign travel, opera; *Clubs* Brooks's, The Hurlingham, Vincent's (Oxford); *Style—* David Pinckney, Esq; Rake Hanger House, Hill Brow, Liss, Hampshire (☎ 0730 893775); Thornton Management Ltd, 33 Cavendish Square, London W1M ODH (☎ 071 493 7262, fax 071 409 0590, telex 923061 THORN G)

PINCKNEY, Jeremy Gerald; s of Gerald Henry Pinckney; *b* 17 Oct 1935; *Educ* Eton; *m* 1960, Helen Belinda, da of Maj M H Gold, MC; 2 s, 1 da; *Career* served 9 Lances; dir: Guardian Corp Fin Ltd, English Nat Investment Co Ltd, Risk Decisions Ltd and other cos; *Style—* Jeremy Pinckney Esq; 45 Black Lion Lane, London W6; Garden House, Balthayock, Perth PH2 7LG

PINCOTT, Leslie Rundell; CBE (1978); s of Hubert George Pincott; *b* 27 March 1923; *Educ* Mercers' Sch Holborn; *m* 1944, Mary Mae Tuffin; 2 s, 1 da; *Career* oil industrialist 1950-78, md Esso Petroleum Co Ltd 1970-78; dep chm Price Cmmn 1978-80, pres Dist Heating Assoc 1977-79; vice chm Remploy Ltd 1970-87, chm Edman Communications Group plc 1983-87, tstee London Devpt Capital Fund (Guiness

Mahon) 1985-; chm: Printing Indust Econ Devpt Ctee 1982-87, Stone-Platt Industs 1980-82; Canada Permanent Trust Co (UK) Ltd 1978-79, BR SR Bd 1977-89; dir: George Wimpey & Co Ltd 1978-85, Highlands Fabricators Ltd 1985-, FCA, CBIM, MInstM; *Recreations* tennis; *Clubs* Hurlingham (chm 1988), Arts; *Style*— Leslie Pincott, Esq, CBE; 6 Lambourne Ave, Wimbledon, London SW19 7DW

PINCUS, George Bernard; s of Dr Joseph Victor Pincus (d 1946), of Brighton, and Ruth, *née* Burns; *b* 13 Nov 1942; *Educ* Epsom Coll; *m* 21 May 1965 (m dis); 2 s (Benjamin b 1969, Damian b 1970); *Career* md: PVAF 1974-84, BBDO Ltd 1984-90, Interpartners 1990-; vice chm THP Group 1990-; memb Cncl Epsom Coll 1965- (chm Devpt Ctee 1986-); *Recreations* visual arts, theatre, history, travel; *Style*— George B Pincus, Esq; Willoughbys West, Wrens Hill, Oxshott, Surrey; Inner Court, 48 Old Church St, London SW3 5BY (☎ 071 351447)

PINDER, Margaret Lilian; o da of Brig Harold Senhouse Pinder, CBE, MC, Royal Leics Regt (d 1973), of Burghclere Grange, Newbury, Berks, and Lilian Edith Murray (d 1975); *b* 4 May 1920; *Educ* Privately; *Career* vice-chm and vice-pres Arthritis Care (formerly Br Rheumatism and Arthritis Assoc), memb since 1953; fndr of first recuperative holiday hotel for arthritis (later names Margaret Pinder House by Arthritis Care) 1960; fndr and tstee of Pinder Centre for the treatment of physically disabled 1973; tstee the Lady Hoare Tst 1985; *Recreations* painting, racing (first owner to have horses trained under Nat Hunt in France after war); *Style*— Margaret Pinder; Summerfield House, Hatt Common, Newbury, Berkshire G15 0NH (☎ 0635 254354); Pinder Centre, Old Coach House, Avington, nr Winchester, Hants SO21 1DD (☎ 096 278 498)

PINDLING, Rt Hon Sir Lynden Oscar ; KCMG (1983), PC (1976); s of Arnold Franklin Pindling; *b* 22 March 1930; *Educ* Western Sr Sch, Nassau Govt HS, London Univ; *m* 1956, Marguerite McKenzie; 2 s, 2 da; *Career* barr Middle Temple 1953, PM and min of econ affairs The Bahamas 1969-; *Style*— The Rt Hon Sir Lynden Pindling, KCMG; Office of the Prime Minister, Rawson Sq, Nassau, Bahamas

PINE-COFFIN, Lt-Col Trenchard John; OBE, DL (Devon 1982); s of Lt-Col Edward Claude Pine-Coffin (whose mother Louisa, *née* Beresford, ggda of Rt Hon John Beresford, yr bro of 1 Marquess of Waterford); *b* 12 June 1921; *Educ* Malvern, RMC Sandurst; *m* 1952, Susan Therese, er da of Col A D Bennett, OBE, MC; 1 s (John b 1961), 2 da (Julia b 1953, Sarah b 1956); *Career* serv WWII Para Regt; High Sheriff Devon 1973-74; *Style*— Lt-Col Trenchard Pine-Coffin, OBE, DL; Portledge, Fairy Cross, Bideford, Devon

PINHORN, Malcolm Alan; s of Malcolm Herbert Pinhorn (d 1961), Morton House, Hatfield, Hertfordshire, and Florence Louisa, *née* Wicks; *b* 26 March 1932; *Educ* Ardingly, Fitzwilliam Coll Cambridge (BA), Portsmouth Poly (Dip); *m* 22 June 1962, Siobhan Joan Sara Philomena, da of Malachi John Keegan (d 1988); 2 s (Richard b 1963, Thomas b 1964); *Career* Flying Offr RAF 1951-53; exec dir Phillimore and Co Ltd 1961-66, proprietor Pinhorns 1966-, lectr Univ Extra Mural Studies 1973-, admin dir Conservative Central Office 1975-78; sec Br Leather Fedn 1979-81, chm Kent Assoc for the Disabled 1965-66; memb Ctee IOW Record Series, fndr and vice pres IOW Soc, memb Cncl Harleian Soc; FSG (chm 1960-61); *Books* Historical Archaeological and Kindred Societies in the United Kingdom: a list (1986); *Recreations* local history, walking, gardening; *Style*— Malcolm Pinhorn, Esq; Norman's Place, Calbourne, Isle of Wight PO41 0TY

PINHORN, Margaret (Maggie) (Mrs Martin Dyke-Coomes); da of George Herbert Pinhorn, of Woodside, Comp Lane, St Mary's Platt, nr Sevenoaks, Kent, and Mary Elizabeth Suther (d 1963); *b* 1 Nov 1943; *Educ* Walthamstow Hall Sch for Girls (Sevenoaks), Central Sch of Art and Design (London); *m* 24 June 1978, Martin Dyke-Coomes, *qv*, s of Ernest Thomas Dyke-Coomes, of 67 Furzefield, West Green, Crawley, Sussex; 1 s (Ned Alexander b 1981), 1 da (Amy Elizabeth b 1983), 2 adopted s (Anthony b 1967, Claude b 1973); *Career* artist, dir, designer, prodr; fndr of Alternative Arts and dir: Covent Garden St Theatre 1975-88, Soho St Theatre from 1988; started career in films in 1968 at Pinewood Studios in Art Dept of James Bond movie; worked on Br feature films incl: Chitty Chitty Bang Bang, Otley, Till Death Us Do Part; ind film maker, made Dynamo (1970), and Tunde's Film (1973); started Basement Community Arts Workshop in Cable Street 1972; made one of the first 'Open Door' progs for BBC, TV and went on to res and present the first BBC TV series 'Grapevine' for Community Programmes Unit; nat co-ordinator of the Assoc of Community Artists 1974-79; vice-chm Tower Hamlets Arts Ctee 1975-79; memb: Arts Cncl Community Art Ctee 1975-79, Gtr London Arts Community Arts Ctee 1979-81; dir of Circus UK 1985-; *Recreations* playing with my children, creative cooking, collecting wines, travel, philosphy, the arts; *Clubs* West Ham Football, Covent Garden Community Centre; *Style*— Ms Maggie Pinhorn; Alternative Arts, 49-51 Carnaby St, West Soho, London W1V 1PF (☎ 071 287 0907)

PININSKI, Count Peter James; s of Stanislaw Hieronim Mieczyslaw Aleksander 8 Count Pininski, of Surrey and Devonshire, and Jean Isobel Margaret, da of James Wells Graham (of Montrose), OBE, and Jessie Cameron, *née* Paul; is 9 Count Pininski, in direct descent from Count Jerzy of Krasiczyn (d 1793), Kt of St Stanislaw, cr Count in 1778 by Empress Maria Theresia, and from Andrzej Jastrzebiec, Lord of Pinino and Judge of the Lands of Dobrzyn 1379; *b* 23 Aug 1956; *Educ* Downside, Whitgift Sch, Sotheby Works of Art Course; *m* 18 June 1983, Countess Mary Sophie Teresa Matylda, da of Sqdn Ldr Count Jan Jozef Badeni, of Norton Manor, Norton, Wilts, and Isita June, *née* Wilson; 1 s (Aleksander Leon Jan Stanislaw b 15 June 1988); *Career* jr ptnr Hoare Govett (stockbrokers) 1984; dir: Laing & Cruickshank (stockbrokers) 1986, Barclay de Zoete Wedd (stockbrokers) 1989; tstee Ciechanowiecki Fndn 1988; *Recreations* history, literature, art and antiques; *Style*— Count Pininski; 4a Campden Hill Gardens, London W8; Orchard House, Norton, Wilts; U2 Polna 44m 6, Warszawa, Poland

PINK, Lady Dora Elizabeth; JP (London); raised to the rank of a Marquess's da 1973; da of George Leonard Tottenham, ggs of Rt Rev Lord Robert Ponsonby Tottenham, Bishop of Clogher (s of 1 Marquess of Ely); sis of 8 Marquess; *b* 9 Nov 1919; *Educ* Queen's Univ Kingston Ontario (BA); *m* 1, 1946, Lt (E) Bernard Edgar Hall, RN (d 1947); m 2, 1950, Sir Ivor Thomas Montague Pink, KCMG (d 1966), er s of Leonard Montague Pink, of Port Iona, Sandbanks, Bournemouth; 1 da (Celia Elizabeth b 1952); *Career* served as Lt WRCNS 1939-45; *Clubs* The Hurlingham; *Style*— The Lady Dora Pink, JP; 24 The Gateways, Chelsea, London SW3 3JA

PINKER, Sir George Douglas; KCVO (1990, CVO 1983); s of late Ronald Douglas Pinker; *b* 6 Dec 1924; *Educ* Reading Sch, St Mary's Hosp London Univ (MB BS), DObst; *m* Dorothy Emma, nee Russell; 3 s, 1 da; *Career* surgn-gynaecologist to the Queen 1973-90, consltg gynaecological surgn and obstetrician St Mary's Hosp Paddington and Samaritan Hosp 1958-90, consltg gynaecological surgn Middx and Soho Hosps 1969-80, conslt gynaecologist King Edward VII Hosp for Officers 1974 -; chief med advsr BUPA 1983-; pres Royal Coll of Obstetricians and Gynaecologists 1987- (hon treas 1970-77, vice pres 1980-83), memb bd Modern Med 1980 (chm 1988); chief med advsr BUPA 1983-90; cncl memb Winston Churchill Tst, vice pres London Choral Soc 1988; Hon FRCSI 1987, hon memb British Paediatric Assoc 1988; Hon FRACOG (Aust) 1989, Hon FACOG (America) 1990, MRCOG, FRCS(Ed), FRCOG, FRSocMed, FRCS 1989; *Clubs* Garrick; *Style*— Sir George Pinker, KCVO; Top Flat, 96 Harley St, London W1N 1AF (☎ 071 935 2292)

PINKER, Maj Richard Walrond; s of Henry George Pinker (d 1961), and May Simcoe (d 1963), da of Rev Walrond Clarke (*see* Burke's Landed Gentry, 1871 edn, Clarke of Tremlett); *b* 19 July 1913; *Educ* Wrekin Coll Sherborne; *m* 16 Sept 1940, Caroline Mary, da of Charles Gordon Darroch Farquhar (d 1946) (*see* Burke's Landed Gentry, 18 edn, Vol I, 1965, Farquhar of Acheron); 1 s (Charles), 1 da (Anne (wid of Lt-Col David Blair, Queens Own Highlanders, ka 1979 NI)); *Career* cmmnd Devonshire Regt 1932, served India, Malta, UK (acting Lt-Col), ret from Army 1947; in wine trade with Mentzendorff & Co, dir (late md) Simon Bros & Co Ltd, wine buyer NAAFI (ret 1973); *Recreations* shooting, golf, gardening; *Clubs* Army and Navy; *Style*— Maj Richard W Pinker; Pilgroves, Brasted Chart, Westerham, Kent TN16 1LY (☎ 0959 62579)

PINKER, Prof Robert Arthur; s of Joseph Pinker (d 1976), and Dora Elizabeth, *née* Winyard (d 1987); *b* 27 May 1931; *Educ* Holloway Co Sch, LSE (Cert Soc Sc), Univ of London (BSc, MSc); *m* 24 June 1955, Jennifer Farrington, da of Fred Boulton (d 1941); 2 da (Catherine b 1963, Lucy b 1965); *Career* Nat Serv, 2 Lt Royal Ulster Rifles 1951-52; TA, Lt London Irish Rifles 1952-54; head of Sociology Dept Goldsmiths Coll 1964-72, Lewisham prof of social admin Goldsmiths and Bedford Colls 1972-74, prof of social studies Chelsea Coll 1974-78, prof of social work studies LSE 1978- (pro-dir 1985-88), pro vice chllr for social sci Univ of London 1988-90; chm: Social Admin Assoc 1974-77, Br Library Project on Family and Social Res 1983-86, Advsy Cncl Centre for Policy on Ageing 1971-81 (chm of govrs 1981-), Jl of Social Policy 1981-86 (ed 1977-81), Editorial Bd Ageing and Soc 1981-; scientific advsr Nursing Res DHSS 1974-79 and 1980-82; memb: Social Sci Res Cncl 1972-76, Working Pty on Role and Tasks of Social Workers Barclay Ctee 1981-82, Cncl Advertising Standards Authy 1988-; govr: LSHTM 1990-, Br Post Grad Med Sch 1990-; *Recreations* reading, writing, travel, unskilled gardening; *Style*— Prof Robert Pinker; 76 Coleraine Rd, Blackheath, London SE3 7PE (☎ 081 858 5320); LSE, Houghton St, Aldwych, London WC2A 2AE (☎ 071 405 7686)

PINNER, Hayim; OBE (1989); s of late Simon Pinner, and Annie, *née* Wagner; *b* 25 May 1925; *Educ* Davenant Fndn Sch, Univ of London, Yeshiva Etz Hayim, Bet Berl Coll Israel; *m* 1956 (m dis 1980), Rita, *née* Reuben; 1 s, 1 da; *Career* RAOC 1944-48; ed Jewish Vanguard 1950-74, exec dir B'nai B'rith 1957-77, hon vice pres Zionist Fedn of GB and Ireland 1975- (hon treas 1971-75), sec gen Bd of Deputies of Br Jews 1977-, vice pres Lab Zionist Movement; memb: Jewish Agency and World Zionist Orgn, Exec Cncl Christians and Jews, Inter-Faith Network, Advsy Cncl World Congress of Faiths, Trades Advsy Cncl, Hillel Fndn, jt Israel Appeal, Lab party Middle East Ctee, B List Parly Candidates, UNA, Imperial War Museum; contrib to: BBC radio and TV, LBC, Radio London; Freeman City of London; *Recreations* travelling, swimming, reading, talking; *Style*— Hayim Pinner, Esq, OBE; c/o Board of Deputies of British Jews, Woburn House, Tavistock Square, London WC1H OEZ (☎ 071 387 3952, fax 071 388 5848, telex 262666 BOD G)

PINNEY, Frederick Arthur Charles (Ted); OBE (1987); s of Arthur Pinney (d 1972), of Barrington, Sidmouth, Devon, and Edith Mina Jessie, *née* Hart; *b* 9 July 1917; *Educ* Sidmouth Woolbrook Sch; *m* 13 Nov 1943, Betty Louise (d 1986), da of Bruce Langton (d 1955), of 1 Winslade, Sidmouth, Devon; *Career* ROC; cnllr Sidmouth Urban 1946, chm Pinney Properties Ltd 1966, dir Langton Pinney Ltd 1991; leader E Devon 1975- (cnllr 1973), leader Devon CC 1988- (cnllr 1972); memb: Exec and Recreation Ctees Assoc of CC's, Standing Advsy Ctees local authys and the Arts SACLAT, Round Table, 41 Club, various football and cricket clubs; *Recreations* countryside and conservation; *Style*— Ted Pinney, Esq, OBE; 11 Primley Gardens, Sidmouth, Devon EX10 9LE (☎ 0395 513292); Langton Pinney Ltd, 10 Primley Gardens, Sidmouth, Devon (☎ 0395 577501); Pinney Properties Ltd, Woodlands Hotel, Sidmouth Devon (☎ 0395 513120, fax 0395 579163)

PINNIGER, Cherry Janet; da of Edward James Pinniger (d 1978), of Salisbury, Wilts, and Eileen Nancy, *née* Perkins; *b* 26 Aug 1955; *Educ* Godolphin Sch Salisbury, Bristol Poly; *Career* CA; sr Ball Baker Carnaby Deed 1978-79 (trainee 1974-78), supervisor Fraser Thelford 1979-80, audit sr and supervisor Ernst & Whinney 1980-83 (latterly in Training Dept), Internal Audit Dept Manufacturers Hanover Trust 1983-85; Finnie & Co: nat training mangr 1985-, ptnr responsible for training 1988-, currently ptnr in London Office; memb: Educn and Training Ctee LSCA, Post Qualification Ctee ICAEW, Mgmnt Bd CA Student Introductory Serv, London Accountants Training Discussion Gp; FCA 1988 (ACA 1978); *Recreations* wine, walking, sailing, theatre; *Clubs* International Exhibition Cooperative Wine Soc Stevenage (co-opted memb Mgmnt Ctee 1989-90); *Style*— Miss Cherry Pinniger; Finnie & Co, Kreston House, 8 Gate St, London WC2A 3HJ (☎ 071 831 9100, fax 071 831 2666)

PINNINGTON, Geoffrey Charles; s of Charles Pinnington; *b* 21 March 1919; *Educ* Harrow Co Sch, Rock Ferry HS Birkenhead, King's Coll London; *m* 1941, Beryl, da of Edward Clark; 2 da; *Career* serv WWII RAF, Sqdn Ld 1943; journalist; ed Sunday People 1972-82, ret; dir Mirror Gp Newspapers 1976-82; jt vice chm Press Cncl 1983- (memb 1982-); *Style*— Geoffrey Pinnington Esq; 23 Lauderdale Drive, Richmond, Surrey TW10 7BS

PINNINGTON, Roger Adrian; TD; s of William Austin Pinnington (d 1979), of Oakhurst, Alderley Edge, Cheshire, and Elsie Amy Pinnington (d 1983); *b* 27 Aug 1932; *Educ* Rydal Sch Colwyn Bay, Lincoln Coll Oxford (MA); *m* 16 April 1961, (Marjorie) Ann, da of George Alan Livingstone Russell, of Beverley, Yorks; 1 s (Andrew b 1967), 3 da (Suzanne b 1963, Sally-Ann b 1964, Nikki b 1975); *Career* 2 Lt RA 1952, Maj Royal Mil Police 1960; dir: William E Cary Ltd 1964-74, Jonas Woodhead & Sons plc 1968-74, Cam Gears Ltd 1974-82; vice-pres TRW Europe Inc 1980-82; dep chm and chief exec UBM Group plc 1982-85; dir Norcros plc 1985-86; dir and chief exec: Royal Ordnance plc 1986-87, Pilgrim House Group 1987-89; chm: Blackwood Hodge plc 1988-90, Bath and Bristol Estates Ltd, Aqualisa Ltd, Harford Consultancy Services Ltd, Petrocon plc; Freeman City of London, Liveryman Worshipful Co of Glaziers 1977; CBIM 1988, FRSA 1983; *Recreations* gardening, debate, collecting sad irons; *Clubs* Vincent's, RAC, St James's; *Style*— Roger Pinnington Esq, TD; 46 Willoughby Rd, Hampstead, London NW3 (☎ 071 431 3999, fax 071 431 4064, car 0836 244464); Jardines del Puerto, Puerto Banus, Spain

PINNINGTON-HUGHES, Prof John; *see*: Hughes, John Pinnington

PINNOCK, Trevor David; s of Kenneth Alfred Thomas Pinnock, of Canterbury, Kent, and Joyce Edith, *née* Muggleton; *b* 16 Dec 1946; *Educ* Canterbury Catheral Choir Sch, Simon Langton GS Canterbury, RCM (winner maj performance prizes organ and harpsichord); *m* 2 Aug 1988, Pauline Heather, *née* Nobes; *Career* London debut with Galliard Harpsichord Trio (jt fndr) 1966; solo debut Purcell Room London 1968, formed The English Concert 1972, London debut English Bach Festival 1973; recordings: CRD Records 1974-78, Polydor (Archiv) 1978-; tours of Europe, USA, Canada, Japan, South America, solo with The English Concert, and as orchestral conductor; Metropolitan Opera debut Handel, Gvilio Cesare 1988, formed NY based Classical Band in 1989; hon RAM; *Style*— Trevor Pinnock, Esq; 35 Gloucester Crescent, London NW1 7DC (☎ 071 485 7765, fax 071 267 4478)

PINSENT, Sir Christopher Roy; 3 Bt (UK 1938); s of Sir Roy Pinsent, 2 Bt (d 1978); *b* 2 Aug 1922; *Educ* Winchester; *m* 27 June 1951, Susan Mary, da of John

Norton Scorer, of Walcot Lodge, Fotheringhay; 1 s, 2 da; *Heir* s, Thomas Benjamin Roy Pinsent b 21 July 1967; *Career* lectr Camberwell Sch of Art; *Style—* Sir Christopher Pinsent, Bt; The Chestnuts, Castle Hill, Guildford, Surrey

PINSENT, David Hume; s of Basil Hume Pinsent, of Lingfield, Surrey, and Patricia Arbery Mary, *née* Atteridge; fifth in descent from David Hume, the Scottish philosopher; *b* 2 April 1943; *Educ* Downside, Imperial Coll London; *m* 1974, Alexandra Therese Emblyn, da of Capt Charles Edward Kendall (d 1978), of Gt Nineveh, Benenden, Kent; 2 s, 1 da; *Career* chm and md Anglo American Agric plc 1981-89; dir: David Hume Securities, Cronite Gp plc, The Plantation Tst Co plc 1985-88; *Recreations* hunting, bridge, music, politics; *Style—* David Pinsent, Esq; Old Chellows, Crowhurst, Lingfield, Surrey RH7 6LU (☎ 0342 832049, fax 0342 833659)

PINSON, Barry; QC (1973); s of Thomas Alfred Pinson; *b* 18 Dec 1925; *Educ* King Edward's Sch, Univ of Birmingham; *m* 1, 1950, Miriam Mary; 1 s, 1 da; m 2, 1977, Anne Kathleen Golby; *Career* called to the Bar Gray's Inn 1949, bencher 1981; tstee RAF Museums 1980-; *Publications* Revenue Law (17 edns); *Recreations* music, photography; *Clubs* Arts; *Style—* Barry Pinson, Esq, QC; 11 New Square, Lincoln's Inn, London WC2 (☎ 071 242 3981, fax 071 831 2391)

PINTER, Harold; CBE (1966); s of J Pinter; *b* 10 Oct 1930; *Educ* Hackney Downs GS; *m* 1, 1956 (m dis 1980), Vivien Thompson (Vivien Merchant) (d 1982); 1 s; m 2, 1980, Lady Antonia Fraser, *qv*; *Career* actor 1949-57; directed: The Collection (Aldwych) 1962, The Birthday Party (Aldwych) 1964, Exiles (Mermaid) 1970, Butley 1970 (film 1973), Next of Kin (NT) 1974, Otherwise Engaged (Queens) 1975 (NY 1977), Blithe Spirit (NT) 1977, The Rear Column (Globe) 1978, Close of Play (NT) 1979, The Hothouse (Hampstead) 1980, Quartermaine's Terms (Queens) 1981, Incident at Tulse Hill (Hampstead) 1981, The Trojan War Will Not Take Place (NT) 1983, The Common Pursuit (Lyric, Hammersmith) 1984, Sweet Bird of Youth (Haymarket) 1985, Circe and Bravo (Hampstead, Wyndham's) 1986, Vanilla (Lyric) 1990; *Plays* The Room (1957), The Birthday Party (1957), The Dumb Waiter (1957), The Hothouse (1958), A Slight Ache (1958), A Night Out (1959), The Caretaker (1959), Night School (1960), The Dwarfs (1960), The Collection (1961), The Lover (1962), Tea Party (1964), The Homecoming (1964), The Basement (1966), Landscape (1967), Silence (1968), Old Times (1970), Monologue (1972), No Man's Land (1974), Betrayal (1978), Family Voices (1980), Victoria Station (1982), A Kind of Alaska (1982), One For the Road (1984), Mountain Language (1988); *Screenplays* The Caretaker (1962), The Servant (1962), The Pumpkin Eater (1963), The Quiller Memorandum (1965), Accident (1966), The Birthday Party (1967), The Homecoming (1969), The Go-Between (1969), Langrishe Go Down (1970), A la Recherche du Temps Perdue (1972), The Last Tycoon (1974), The French Lieutenant's Woman (1980), Betrayal (1981), Turtle Diary (1984), The Handmaid's Tale (1987), Reunion (1988), The Heat of The Day (1988), The Comfort of Strangers (1988), The Trial (1989), The Remains of the Day (1990); has also published volumes of poetry; *Clubs* Groucho; *Style—* Harold Pinter, Esq, CBE; Judy Daish Associates Ltd, 83 Eastbourne Mews, London W2 6LQ

PINTO, George Richard; s of Maj Richard James Pinto, MC (d 1969), of London, and Gladys, *née* Hirsch (d 1985); *b* 11 April 1929; *Educ* Eton, Trinity Coll Cambridge (MA); *Career* Nat Serv 2 Lt Coldstream Gds 1947-49; Cooper Bros and Co (now Coopers & Lybrand Deloitte) 1953-56, Model Roland and Stone 1957-58, banker Kleinwort Benson Ltd 1958- (dir 1968-85, advsr 1985-); hon treas Anglo-Israel Assoc 1987-, chm Central Cncl for Jewish Soc Serv 1975-78 (vice chm 1972-75), chm of Fin Ctee Jewish Blind Soc 1962-89, vice pres Jewish Care 1990-; govr Oxford Centre for Postgraduate Hebrew Studies 1987-; FCA; *Recreations* reading, listening to classical music, golf, bridge; *Clubs* Brooks's, Cavalry and Guards', Portland; *Style—* G R Pinto, Esq; 20 Fenchurch St, London EC3P 3DB (☎ 071 623 8000, telex 888531, fax 071 623 4069)

PIPER, Geoffrey Steuart Fairfax; s of Sqdn Ldr Donald Steuart Piper (d 1972), of Bakewell, and Nancy Fairfax, *née* Robson (d 1990); *b* 8 June 1943; *Educ* Repton, Pembroke Coll Cambridge (MA); *m* 29 July 1967, Susan Elizabeth, da of Roswell Douglas Arnold; 1 s (Charles b 1980), 3 da (Jennifer b 1968, Angela b 1970, Caroline b 1973); *Career* ptnr i/c Deloitte Haskins & Sells: CI 1980-86, Liverpool 1986-90; pres Jersey Soc of Chartered and Certified Accountants 1983-85, chm Business Opportunities on Merseyside 1987-; dir: Eldonian Devpt Tst 1988-, INWARD 1989-; chief exec NW Business Leadership Team 1990-; FCA 1973; *Recreations* golf, cricket, choral music; *Clubs* Royal and Ancient, MCC; *Style—* Geoffrey Piper, Esq; The Croft, Thornton Hough, Wirral, Merseyside L63 1JA (☎ 051 336 4830); Business Opportunities on Merseyside, PO Box 87, Liverpool L69 3NX (☎ 051 236 4510, fax 051 227 4575)

PIPER, John Egerton Christmas; CH (1972); s of late C A Piper; *b* 13 Dec 1903; *Educ* Epsom Coll, RCA; *m* 1937, Mary Myfanwy Evans; 2 s, 2 da; *Career* painter and writer; memb Oxford Diocesan Advsy Ctee 1950-, vice pres Turner Soc; Hon ARIBA 1957, Hon FRIBA 1971, Hon ARCA 1959; (sr fell 1987); Hon DLitt: Leics 1960, Oxon 1966, Sussex 1974, Reading 1977, Univ of Wales 1981, Essex 1984, Leeds 1985; *Clubs* Athenaeum; *Style—* John Piper, Esq, CH; Fawley Bottom Farmhouse, nr Henley-on-Thames, Oxon (☎ 0491 572494)

PIPER, Dr Mary Elizabeth; da of Kenneth Banks Piper, of Farnborough, Kent, and Beryl June, *née* Hornblow; *b* 17 May 1947; *Educ* Beckenham GS for Girls, Royal Free Hosp Sch of Med, Univ of London (MB BS, LRCP); *Career* lectr in geriatric med: Dept of Geriatric Med, UCH Sch of Med 1977-79; conslt physician in geriatric med Northwick Park Hosp Harrow 1979- (sr registrar 1975-77); chm Policy Ctee Br Geriatrics Soc 1987-89 (hon sec 1982-84), memb Attendance Allowance Bd DSS 1988-; FRCP 1986, MRCS 1971; *Recreations* literature, good friends and humour; *Style—* Dr Mary Piper; Northwick Park Hospital, Watford Rd, Harrow, Middx (☎ 081 869 2600, 081 869 3232, fax 081 423 0046)

PIPPARD, Prof Sir (Alfred) Brian; s of Prof Alfred John Sutton Pippard (d 1969), and Frances Louisa Olive Field (d 1964); *b* 7 Sept 1920; *Educ* Clifton, Clare Coll Cambridge (MA, PhD, ScD, hon fell 1973); *m* 1955, Charlotte Frances, da of Francis Gilbert Dyer (d 1948); 3 da; *Career* Cambridge Univ: demonstrator, lectr, reader, J H Plummer prof, Cavendish prof of physics 1971-82; pres Clare Hall Cambridge 1966-73; FRS; kt 1975; *Recreations* music; *Style—* Prof Sir Brian Pippard, FRS; 30 Porson Rd, Cambridge CB2 2EU (☎ 0223 358713)

PIPPARD, Prof Martin John; s of Dr John Sutton Pippard, of Woodford Green, Essex, and Kathleen Marjorie, *née* Fox; *b* 16 Jan 1948; *Educ* Buckhurst Hill Co HS Essex, Univ of Birmingham (BSc, MB ChB); *m* 15 May 1976, Grace Elizabeth, da of Wallace Swift, of Guisley, Leeds; 2 s (Timothy b 1980, Benjamin b 1983), 1 da (Helen b 1977); *Career* conslt haematologist MRC Clinical Res Centre Harrow 1983-88, prof of haematology Univ of Dundee 1989-; memb: Br Soc for Haematology, Assoc Clinical Pathologists, Ed Bd British Journal of Haematology; MRCPath 1982, FRCP 1988; *Recreations* hill walking, gardening; *Style—* Prof Martin Pippard; 10 Balnacarron Avenue, 118 Hepburn Gardens, St Andrews, Fife KY16 9LF (☎ 0334 76234); University of Dundee, Dept of Haematology, Dundee DD1 9SY (☎ 0382 60111, fax 0382 645748)

PIRIE, David Alan Tarbat; s of Maj Halyburton Berkeley Pirie, MC, TD, DM (d 1984), and Joyce Elaine, *née* Tarbat; *b* 4 Dec 1946; *Educ* Trinity Coll Glenalmond, Univ of York (BA); *m* 21 June 1983, Judith Leslie, da of Maj William Leslie Harris (d 1985); 1 s (Jack b 1987), 1 da (Alice b 1984); *Career* writer, film and TV critic; Time Out: TV critic 1970-74, film critic 1974-80, film ed 1981-84; film critic 1976-: Kaleidoscope (BBC Radio 4), BBC World Service, Capital Radio; contrib 1976-: The Times, Sunday Times, The Media Show, Did You See?, The South Bank Show, Sight and Sound, Movie Magazine; film columnist Options Magazine 1981-, literary ed Event Magazine 1980-81; film and TV screenwriter 1984-; works incl: Rainy Day Women 1984 (winner Drama Prize NY Film and TV Fest), Total Eclipse of the Heart (screenplay), Mystery Story (screenplay from own novel), Wild Things (BBC TV film) 1989, Never Come Back (TV series) 1990; sr tutor Br Film and TV Prodrs Assoc Advanced Screenwriting Course 1990; *Books* Heritage of Horror (1973), Mystery Story (1980), Anatomy of the Movies (1981); *Recreations* running, walking; *Clubs* Writers Guild; *Style—* David Pirie, Esq; c/o Stephen Durbridge, Lenon and Durbridge, 24 Pottery Lane, Holland Park, London W11 (☎ 071 727 1346, fax 071 727 9037, telex 27618 AUTHOR G)

PIRIE, Gp Capt Sir Gordon Hamish; CVO (1987), CBE (1946), JP (London 1962), DL (London 1962); s of Harold Victor Campbell Pirie; *b* 10 Feb 1918; *Educ* Eton, RAF Coll Cranwell; *m* 1, 1953, Margaret Joan Bomford (d 1972); m 2, 1982, Joanna Marian, wid of John C Hugill; *Career* perm cmmn RAF 1938, serv WWII (despatches), Gp Capt 1946, ret; contested (LNat&U) Dundee W 1955; memb Westminster City Cncl 1949-82 (Mayor 1959-60, ldr 1961-69, alderman 1963-78, Lord Mayor 1974-75); dep high bailiff Westminster 1978-87; chm Servs Sound and Vision Corp 1979-90, dir Parker Gallery; KStJ 1969; Cdr Cross of Merit SMO Malta 1971; kt 1984; *Recreations* motoring, bird-watching; *Clubs* Carlton, RAF; *Style—* Gp Capt Sir Gordon Pirie, CVO, CBE, JP, DL; Cottage Row, Tarrant Gunville, Blandford, Dorset DT11 8JJ (☎ 025 889 212)

PIRIE, Sheriff Henry Ward; s of William Pirie (d 1922), of Leith; *b* 13 Feb 1922; *Educ* George Watson's Coll Edinburgh, Univ of Edinburgh (MA, LLB); *m* 1948, Jean Marion, da of Frank Jardine (d 1956), former pres RCS Edinburgh; 4 s; *Career* cmmnd Bombay Grenadiers 1944; advocate 1947, jr counsel to the Admiralty in Scotland 1950; sheriff substitute of Lanarkshire: Airdrie 1954-55, Glasgow (later sherriff) 1955-74; ret 1974; crossword compiler, journalist and broadcaster; OStJ 1967; *Recreations* opera, bridge, walking; *Style—* Sheriff H W Pirie; 16 Poplar Drive, Lenzie, Glasgow G66 4DN (☎ 041 776 2494)

PIRIE, Dr (Duncan) Madsen; s of Douglas Gordon Pirie, and Eva, *née* Madsen; *b* 24 Aug 1940; *Educ* Univ of Edinburgh (MA), Univ of St Andrews (PhD); *Career* prof of philosophy and logic Hillsdale Michigan USA 1975-78, pres Adam Smith Inst 1978-; sec MENSA; *Books* Trial and Error & The Idea of Progress (1978), Test Your IQ (with Eamonn Butler, 1983), Boof of the Fallacy (1985), Micropolitics (1988), Privatization (1988), Boost Your IQ (with Eamonn Butler, 1991); *Recreations* calligraphy; *Style—* Dr Madsen Pirie; 23 Great Smith St, London SW1P 3BL (☎ 071 222 4995, fax 071 222 7544)

PIRIE-GORDON OF BUTHLAW, (George) Patrick; yr s of Lt-Col Charles Pirie-Gordon, OBE, DSC, GCStJ, FSA, FRGS, sometime ed *Burke's Landed Gentry* and Dir of Ceremonies Ven Order of St John, by his w Mabel, CStJ, herself da of George Buckle, sometime ed *The Times*; suc er bro as 15th Laird of Buthlaw 1980; *b* 24 May 1918; *Educ* Winchester, Oriel Coll Oxford; *m* Catherine Grace, da of Alfred Rickard Taylor, of Lymington, and widow of Maj Jack Childerstone Colebrooke; 2 da (Penelope b 1948, Jean b 1950); *Career* serv WWII RA, rising to Lt-Col 2 Survey Regt (despatches twice); local dir Glyn Mills & Co bankers (now Royal Bank of Scotland) 1949-78; dir: Anglo-American Securities Corp 1973-80, Montagu Boston Investmt Tst 1982-85; tstee Transantarctic Assoc 1962-, chm Mount Everest Fndn 1966, vice pres Queens Nursing Inst 1980-, hon vice pres RGS 1982-, memb Royal Co Archers (Queen's Bodyguard for Scotland) 1948-; Master Worshipful Co of Skinners 1963-64; hon fell Oriel Coll Oxford 1988; KStJ, FRGS; *Recreations* gardening, cooking, bird-watching; *Clubs* Athenaeum; *Style—* Patrick Pirie-Gordon of Buthlaw; Waterton, Paddock Field, Chilbolton, Stockbridge, Hants SO20 6AU

PISSARIDES, Prof Christopher Antoniou; s of Antonios Pissarides, Cyprus, and Eudokia, *née* Georgiades; *b* 20 Feb 1948; *Educ* Pancyprian Gymnasium Nicosia Cyprus, Univ of Essex (BA, MA), LSE (PhD); *m* 24 July 1986, Francesca Michela, da of Antonio Cassano, of Rome; 1 s (Antony b 1987), 1 da (Miranda b 1988); *Career* LSE: lectr 1976-82, reader 1982-86, prof 1986-; res dir Centre for Labour Economics; *Books* Labour Market Adjustment (1976), Equilibrium Unemployment Theory (1990); *Recreations* father; *Style—* Prof Christopher Pissarides; London School of Economics, Houghton St, London WC2A 2AE (☎ 071 955 7513, fax 071 831 1840, telex 24655 BLPES G)

PITBLADO, Sir David Bruce; KCB (1967, CB 1955), CVO (1953); s of Robert Bruce Pitblado, and Mary Jane, *née* Sear; *b* 18 Aug 1912; *Educ* Strand Sch, Emmanuel Coll Cambridge; *m* 1941, Edith (d 1978), da of Capt J T Rees Evans; 1 s, 1 da; *Career* civil servant 1935-71: Dominions Office, Treasy, private sec to PM 1951-56, Miny of Power (perm sec); Comptroller and Auditor Gen 1971-76, ret; hon treas SSAFA 1978-90, chm Davies's 1979-89; hon fell Emmanuel Coll Cambridge 1972; memb Middle Temple; *Clubs* Athenaeum; *Style—* Sir David Pitblado, KCB, CVO; 23 Cadogan St, London SW3 2PP (☎ 071 589 6765); Pengoitan, Borth, Dyfed

PITCHER, Desmond Henry; s of George Charles Pitcher (d 1968), of Liverpool, and Alice Marion, *née* Osborne (d 1985); *b* 23 March 1935; *Educ* Liverpool Coll of Technol; *m* 1, 1961 (m dis 1973), Patricia, *née* Ainsworth; 2 da (Stephanie b 18 May 1965, Samantha (twin) b 18 May 1965); m 2, 1978 (m dis 1984), Carol Ann, *née* Rose; 2 s (George b 1 Oct 1978, Andrew b 1 March 1981); *Career* devpt engr A V Roe & Co 1957-58, systems engr Automatic Telephone & Electrical Co 1958-60, nat mangr engrg Sperry Univac Ltd 1961-66 (md 1971-73), md MDS (Data Processing) Ltd 1966-71, dir Sperry Rand Ltd 1971-73 (dep chm 1973-76), vice pres Euro Div Sperry Univac Corp 1973-76, md Truck and Bus Div BL Ltd 1976-78, md Plessey Telecommunications and Office Systems 1978-83, dir Plessey Co 1979-83, chief exec The Littlewoods Orgn 1983-, chm Mersey Barrage Co Ltd 1986-, non-exec dir Nat West Bank (Northern Advsy Bd) 1989, dir N W Water PLC 1990-, dep chm Everton FC Ltd 1990-; Faraday lectr 1973-74; Freeman: City of London 1987, Worshipful Co of Info Technologists 1987; CEng, FIEE 1968, FBCS 1975, HFIDE 1977, CBIM 1985, FRSA 1987; *Recreations* music, opera, golf; *Clubs* Brooks's, Royal Birkdale Golf, RAC, Moor Park Golf; *Style—* Desmond Pitcher, Esq; Aguarda, 4 Granville Rd, Birkdale, Southport, Merseyside (☎ 0704 63531); Middle Dell, Bishopsgate Rd, Englefield Green, Egham, Surrey; The Littlewoods Organisation, JM Centre, Old Hall St, Liverpool (☎ 051 235 2222, fax 051 235 4900, telex 628501)

PITCHER, Edward Archibald; s of Archibald Alfred Ernest Pitcher (d 1949), of Lee Park, Blackheath SE3, and Amy Caroline Lucy, *née* Clifton (d 1969); *b* 13 Sept 1920; *m* 20 Aug 1945, Rita, *née* Carr; 2 da (Barbara b 1946, Nan b 1953); *Career* Flt-Lt 38, 70, 99 and 192 sqdns RAF Bomber Cmd 1940-46; chartered engr 1946-53, consltg engr Edward A Pitcher & Ptnrs 1953-80, sr ptnr Barnan industrial Devpts 1964-, dir of devpts Fourth Thames Ltd 1968-71; chief exec: Land & Estate Conslts Ltd 1971-88, Essex Industl Devpts 1979-; external name Lloyds of London 1978-, dir De Havilland Aircraft Museum Trust Ltd 1985-; Liveryman City of London 1977,

Worshipful Co of Constructors; FIStructE 1950, MConsE 1968; *Recreations* flying, current affairs, reading non-fiction; *Style—* Edward Pitcher, Esq; 17 Cedar Heights, Petersham Rd, Richmond, Surrey TW10 7AE (☎ 081 940 7031); Hurst Mount, 31 High St, Hampton Middlesex TW12 2SA (☎ 081 941 7201, fax 081 941 7203)

PITCHFORD, His Hon Charles; *Career* called to the Bar Middle Temple 1948, circuit judge Wales and Chester Circuit 1972-87 (ret); *Style—* His Hon Charles Pitchford; Llanynant, Coed Morgan, Abergavenny, Gwent

PITCHFORD, John Hereward; CBE (1971); s of John Pitchford; *b* 30 Aug 1904; *Educ* Brighton Coll, Christ's Coll Cambridge; *m* 1930, Teresa Agnes Mary Pensotti; 1 s, 2 da (one of whom, Elizabeth m Sir John Leahy, KCMG, *qv*); *Career* chm Ricardo Consulting Engrs Ltd 1962-76, pres 1976-; pres IMechE 1966; *Clubs* RAC; *Style—* John Pitchford, Esq, CBE; Byeways, Ditchling, E Sussex (☎ 079 18 2177)

PITCHFORD, Margot Walker; da of James Riley (d 1985), of Chelsea, London, and Joanna, *née* Walker; *b* 1 July 1943; *Educ* Queenswood, Herts; *m* 1, 1965 (m dis 1975), David Robert Wilkinson; m 2, John Pitchford; 3 s (Piers b 1967, Adam b 1970, Guy b 1975); *Career* fashion model 1962-67, restaurateur Edwards Restaurant Bristol 1982-88, hotelier Penhallow Manor 1989-90, restaurateur with husb 1990-; *Recreations* ballet, needlepoint, interior design; *Style—* Mrs John Pitchford; Sandy Park Place, Arracott, nr Lewdown, Okehampton, Devon (☎ 0566 83254)

PITCHFORK, Air Cdre Graham Ralph; MBE (1972); s of Ralph Pitchfork, of Sheffield, and Margaret Agnes, *née* Wragg; *b* 4 Feb 1939; *Educ* High Storrs GS Sheffield, RAF Coll Cranwell (BA); *m* 5 June 1965, Marlane Margaret-Rose, da of Gareth Weadick (d 1939), of Dublin; 1 s (Paul b 1971), 2 da (Siobhan b 1966, Joanna b 1968); *Career* RAF: navigator, Air Cdre; Malay Peninsula 1965-66, S Arabia 1965-66; CO: 208 Sqdn 1979-81, RAF Finningley 1987-89; AOC and COMDT DASC Biggin Hill 1989-; *Recreations* gliding, ornithology; *Clubs* RAF; *Style—* Air Cdre Graham Pitchfork, MBE; Barclays, Commercial St, Sheffield

PITFIELD, Michael; s of Edward George Pitfield (d 1976), and Robina Heslop; *b* 22 May 1945; *Educ* Univ of London (BSc), Univ of Reading (MA); *m* 12 Aug 1972, Angela May, da of Albert Victor McCallin (d 1969); 2 s (Alexander b 1975, Alastair b 1982), 1 da (Anna b 1979); *Career* asst dir Inst of Personnel Mgmnt 1978-89, dir Thames Valley Business Sch 1989-90, dir of corp mktg Henley-The Mgmnt Coll 1990-; memb CNAA, IPM, MCI; FIPM 1980; *Recreations* genealogy, history, swimming, travel; *Style—* Michael Pitfield, Esq; Henley-The Management College, Greenlands, Henley-on-Thames, Oxon RG9 3AU (☎ 0491 571454, fax 0491 571635, telex 849026 HENLEY G)

PITFIELD, Thomas Baron; s of Thomas Baron Pitfield (d 1925), and Mary, *née* Fallows; *b* 5 April 1903; *Educ* Bolton Municipal Sch, Bolton Tech Coll, Royal Manchester Coll of Music, Bolton Sch of Art; *m* 26 Dec 1934, Alice Maud, da of William Astbury (d 1945); *Career* millwright draughtsman 1917-24, teacher of cabinet work to unemployed Wolverhampton Cncl of Social Serv 1934-36, p/t and supply teacher, later sr art and music master Tettenhall Coll 1935-47, 26 years freelance designer and composer and prof of composition Royal Northern and Manchester Coll of Music 1947-73; Br Music Heritage 26 songs; exhibits in Royal Acad of Art, numerous one man exhibitions in municipal and other galleries; articles in: The Listener, Country Life, The Countryman, The Artist, Musical Times, Musical Opinion; numerous broadcasts; numerous musical pubns for chorus, orchestra chamber, piano and other arrangements; memb: Bd of Profs Royal Manchester Coll of Music, Cheshire Community Cncl, SCAM, Composers Guild of GB, Performing Right Soc, NRD; hon fell: Royal Manchester Coll of Music, Vegetarian Soc UK; Hon FRMCM; *Books* The Poetry of Trees (1945), Words without Songs, Musicianship for Guitarists, Art Teaching Course, No Song No Supper (autobiography, Vol 1), A Song after Supper (autobiography, Vol 2), A Cotton Town Boyhood (autobiography), My Words (50 poems), Limusics (40 limericks and linocuts); *Recreations* country walking, bird watching, wood carving; *Clubs* Penn; *Style—* Thomas Pitfield, Esq; Lesser Thorns, 21 East Downs Road, Bowdon, Altrincham, Cheshire WA14 2LG (☎ 061 928 4644)

PITHER, Jon Peter; s of Philip John Pither (d 1965), and Vera, *née* Roth (d 1980); *b* 15 June 1934; *Educ* Dauntsey's, Queens' Coll Cambridge (MA); *m* 1961, Karin Jutta, da of Werner Gropp; 1 s (Michael Gordon Carsten b 1963), 1 da (Brigitte Clare b 1965); *Career* cmmnd Royal Sussex Regt 1969-; dir Suter plc, chm Charles David Ltd, underwriter Lloyds of London; *Recreations* sailing, skiing, golf; *Clubs* Athenaeum, Royal Thames Yacht, N Z Golf; *Style—* Jon P Pither, Esq; South House, Claremont Park, Esher, Surrey; Tides Reach, Rookwood, Sussex; Amari plc, Amari House, 52 High St, Kingston upon Thames KT1 1HN (☎ 081 549 6122, telex 262937, fax 081 546 0637, car 0836 220426)

PITHER, Hon Mrs (Pauline Ruth); da of 1 and last Baron Lambury (d 1967); *b* 1931; *m* 1954 (m dis 1972), John Pither; 2 s (Steven Edward b 1957, Gary John b 1959); *Style—* The Hon Mrs Pither; Appletree Farm House, Chorley Wood Common, Herts WD3 3EW (☎ 0923 282118)

PITMAN, Brian Ivor; s of Ronald Ivor Pitman, and Doris Ivy, *née* Short; *b* 13 Dec 1931; *Educ* Cheltenham GS; *m* 1954, Barbara Mildred Ann; 2 s (Mark, David), 1 da (Sally); *Career* dir: Lloyds Bank California 1982-86, The Nat Bank of NZ 1982-, Lloyds Bank plc 1983- (dep chief exec 1982-83, then chief exec 1983-), Lloyds Bank Int Ltd 1985-87 (dep chief exec 1978-81), Lloyds Merchant Bank Holdings Ltd 1985-88; *Recreations* golf, cricket, music; *Style—* Brian Pitman, Esq; Lloyds Bank Plc, 71 Lombard Street, London EC3P 3BS (☎ 071 626 1500)

PITMAN, Giles William; s of Capt John Pitman (ka 1943), and Elizabeth Cattanach Pitman; *b* 5 Sept 1938; *Educ* Eton, ChCh Oxford (MA); *m* 1961, da of Maj George De Pree; 2 s, 1 da; *Career* jt gp md Pitman plc 1981-85; dir: Marine & General Mutual Life Assurance Society 1976, Bath Press Ltd 1981; Sir Isaac Pitman Ltd 1985; chief exec Summer International plc 1989-; dep chm Pitman Examinations Inst 1985; FCA, ACMA; *Style—* Giles Pitman, Esq; Heath House, Albury, Ware, Herts SG11 2LX (☎ 027 974 293)

PITMAN, Mark Andrew; s of Richard Thomas Pitman, of Weathercock House, Upper Lambourn, Berks, and Jennifer Susan, *née* Harvey; *b* 1 Aug 1968; *Educ* Wycliffe Coll; *Career* jockey; debut 1983, professional 1984-; 2 yst jockey to complete the National Course 1984, 2 place Conditional Jockey Championship 1986-87; retained jockey to Mrs J Pitman 1988-89; career best of 57 winners in a season 1989-90 (incl 2 place in Cheltenham Gold Cup and won Ritz Club Jockey of the Meeting Aintree); maj races won incl: The Martell Cup Steeple Chase, The Mumm Club Novices Steeple Chase, The Larchlap Chase, The Midlands Grand National, The EBF Hurdle Final, The Charterhouse Mercantile Chase, The Swish Hurdle, The John Bull Chase, The Sporting Life Weekender HCP Chase, The Old Road Securities Novice Chase, The Souter of Stirling Novices Chase; *Recreations* keeping fit incl aerobics and circuit training, squash, water-skiing; *Style—* Mark Pitman, Esq; 21 Child St, Lambourn, Newbury, Berks (☎ 0488 71425); Weathercock House, Upper Lambourn, Berkshire (☎ 0488 71714, fax 0488 721986)

PITOI, Sir Sere; CBE (1975); s of Pitoi Sere Orira; *b* 11 Nov 1935; *Educ* Sogeri, Queensland Univ, Birmingham Univ; *m* 1957, Daga Leva; 2 s, 3 da; *Career* chm Public Services Commission of Papua New Guinea 1971-; fell PNG Inst of Management MACE; kt 1977; *Style—* Sir Sere Pitoi, CBE; P O Box 6029, Boroko, Papua New Guinea

PITT, Barrie William Edward; yr s of John Pitt, and Ethel May, *née* Pennell; *b* 7 July 1918; *Educ* Portsmouth Southern GS; *m* 1, 1943, Phyllis Kate, *née* Edwards; 1 s (decd); m 2, 1953 (m dis 1971), Sonia Deirdre, *née* Hoskins; m 3, 1983, Frances Mary, *née* Moore; *Career* WWII army 1939-45; bank clerk 1935, surveyor 1946, info offr UKAEA 1961, historical conslt to BBC series The Great War 1963; author and ed of mil histories, contrib to Enclycopaedia Britannica and The Sunday Times; *Books* The Edge of Battle (1958), Zeebrugge, St George's Day 1918 (1958), Coronel and Falkland (1960), 1918 The Last Act (1962), Purnell's History of the Second World War (ed, 1964), Ballantine's Illustrated History of World War 2 (ed-in-chief, 1967), Purnell's History of the First World War (ed, 1969), Ballantine's Illustrated History of the Violent Century (ed-in-chief, 1971), British History Illustrated (ed, 1974-78), The Battle of the Atlantic (1977), The Crucible of War: Western Desert 1941 (1980), Churchill and the Generals (1981), The Crucible of War: Year of Alamein 1942 (1982), Special Boat Squadron (1983), The Military History of World War II (1986), The Chronological Atlas of World War II (with Frances Pitt, 1989); *Recreations* golf; *Clubs* Savage; *Style—* Barrie Pitt, Esq; Fitzhead Ct, Fitzhead, Somerset TA4 3JP (☎ 0823 400923)

PITT, Barry Winston; s of Charles William Pitt, and Rhoda Grace, *née* Fenn; *b* 16 Aug 1942; *Educ* Dane Sch Nat Coll (Dip Environmental Studies); *m* 22 Aug 1967, Yvonne Dianne, da of Arthur Henry, of Woking, Surrey; 2 s (Antony Arthur Charles Winston, James Alexander Winston); *Career* sr ptnr The BPA Partnership 1983-, md CJ Jeffries Ltd until 1986 (chm until 1987), chm Wocad Ltd (until 1988); chm: Coastal and Countryside plc 1987-, QA Servs Ltd 1988-; former chm Bisley Cons Assoc; Freeman City of London, Liveryman Worshipful Co of Feltmakers; FCIBSE, MIHospE, MIP; *Recreations* yachting; *Clubs* Wig and Pen; *Style—* Barry Pitt, Esq; Vinyard Haven, 5 Allen House Park, Hook Heath, Woking, Surrey GU22 0DB; Premier House, Victoria Way, Woking, Surrey (☎ 04862 72053, fax 04862 29200, car 0836 702218)

PITT, Hon Bruce Michael David; o s of Baron Pitt, of Hampstead (Life Peer), *qv*; *b* 18 June 1945; *Educ* King Alfred Sch Hampstead, Univ Coll London (LLB); *Career* called to the Bar Gray's Inn 1970; memb: Sub-ctee Criminal Bar Assoc Advsy Body to Law Cmmn on Special Def - Duress and Entrapment Coercion 1974, Bar Cncl Young Barristers' Ctee 1974-75, Senate Inns of Court and Bar Cncl 1975-76, Attorney-Gen's List of Counsel 1981-, Race Relations Ctee Bar Cncl 1990-; asst rec S Eastern Circuit 1985-; memb: Hampstead Lab Pty 1960-69, Campaign Against Racial Discrimination 1964-67; memb Bars of Jamaica, Trinidad and Tobago, Barbados, and West Indies Associated States; *Recreations* swimming, arts, watching cricket; *Clubs* MCC, St Katherine's Yacht; *Style—* The Hon Bruce Pitt; 6 Heath Drive, London NW3; 2 Stone Buildings, Lincolns Inn, London WC2 (☎ 071 405 4232)

PITT, David Arthur; s of Frank Arthur Pitt (d 1954), of Alderley Edge, and Beatrice Ellen Pitt (d 1956); *b* 4 Oct 1927; *Educ* St Edward's Sch Oxford, Queens' Coll Cambridge (MA); *m* 30 May 1964, Margaret Helen Crichton, da of James Burnett Budge (d 1962), of Tanganyika; 3 s (James David Crichton, Andrew Alan, Jonathan Michael); *Career* RN 1946-48; Credit Insurance Association 1954-56, Henry Cooke Lumsden plc 1956-89 (dep chm 1981-88); memb: Lords Taverners NW Ctee; Assoc of Soc Investment Analysts 1961; *Recreations* real tennis, lawn tennis, sailing, skiing; *Clubs* MCC, Hawks', St James's (Manchester), Manchester Tennis and Racquet; *Style—* David Pitt, Esq; Thornycroft Lodge, Pexhill, Macclesfield, Cheshire SK11 9PT

PITT, Hon Mrs (Deborah Elspeth); da of 2 Viscount Leathers; *m* 1, 1966 (m dis), Thomas Richard Chadbon; 2 s (Dominic Thomas b 1966, Nicholas Richard b 1968); m 2, 1980, Richard William Pitt, yst s of late George Stanhope Pitt, of Rowbarns Manor, Horsley, Surrey; 1 da (Isabelle b 1981); *Style—* The Hon Mrs Pitt; 6 Bassingham Road, London SW18 3AG

PITT, Desmond Gordon; s of late Archibald George Edward William Pitt, and Amy Gertrude Lander; *b* 27 Dec 1922; *Educ* Bournemouth GS; *m* 14 Sept 1946, Barbara Irene, da of William Hollott; 1 s (Andrew Nigel b 7 Nov 1953), 2 da (Marilyn Anne b 28 Feb 1950, Jane Barbara b 15 Nov 1960); *Career* HM Customs and Excise: offr 1947, inspr 1958, asst sec 1973, under sec 1979, cmmr 1979-83 (now ret); memb Conservative Assoc Bournemouth, govr Portfield Sch for Autistic Children, hon treas Wessex Autistic Soc Bournemouth Dorset; FCCA, ACIS, AIB; *Style—* Desmond Pitt, Esq; 4 Ken Road, Southbourne, Bournemouth, Dorset (☎ 0202 426380)

PITT, Brig John Keith; OBE (1979); s of Herbert William Pitt (d 1972), of Quinnings Barn, East Ashling, Chichester, and Beatrice Irene, *née* Reeve; *b* 5 April 1934; *Educ* Highgate Sch; *m* 21 Dec 1968, Yvette Anne Barbara, da of Charles Edward Emile Cormeau (d 1940), of London; 1 s (Keith Charles William b 8 April 1970), 1 da (Natasha Anne Barbara b 10 Nov 1971); *Career* enlisted RCT 1952, ret Brig 1988 (despatches 1981); dep dir Wandsworth Borough Cncl 1988-; Freeman City of London 1988, Liveryman Worshipful Co of Carmen 1988; FCIT; *Recreations* marathon running, music, military history; *Clubs* Landsdowne; *Style—* Brig John Pitt, OBE; Robin House, Old Park Lane, Farnham, Surrey GU10 5AA (☎ 0252 714965); Wandsworth Borough Cncl, The Town Hall, Wandsworth High St, London SW18 2PU (☎ 01 871 6354, car 0860 461523, fax 01 871 7560)

PITT, Peter Clive Crawford; TD (1976); s of Norman Pitt (d 1987), of High Trees Ct, High Trees, Reigate, and Emily, *née* Crawford; *b* 7 Sept 1933; *Educ* Epsom Coll, Guy's Hosp (MB BS, DTM&H, MRCP); *m* 23 Jan 1965, Anna Catherine, da of Frederick William Markham Pratt (d 1965), of Pewsey, Wilts; 2 s (James Peter William b 22 Jan 1966, Daniel Crawford b 12 Sept 1969), 1 da (Rachel Louise b 6 Sept 1967); *Career* (mentioned in despatches 1956), QA Mil Hosp 1959-61; surgical specialist Br Mil Hosp Kaduna Nigeria 1961-63, Cambridge Mil Hosp Aldershot 1963-65; sr surgical specialist: Br Mil Hosp Rinteln BAOR 1965-66, Br Mil Hosp Dharan Nepal 1966-68; Regtl MO TA 1969-; house surgn: Guy's 1957, (Paediatric) Guy's 1958; house physician Addenbrooks Cambridge 1958, registrar Redhill 1968-70, sr registrar Guy's and Chase Farm 1970-72, conslt surgn Oldchurch Hosp 1972-, dir Garnish Hall Tutorial Centre 1983-; pres Barking and Brentwood branch BMA 1981; cmmr Inland Revenue 1988; memb: BMA, Hunterian Soc; fell PEN 1985; FRCS 1963; *Books* Surgeon in Nepal: John Murray (1970); *Recreations* gardening, tennis; *Style—* Peter Pitt, Esq, TD; Garnish Hall, Margaret Roding, Dunmow, Essex (☎ 024 531 209); 3 Lake Rise, Romford, Essex (☎ 07087 47255)

PITT, William Henry; *b* 17 July 1937; *Educ* Heath Clark Sch Croydon, London Nautical Sch, South Bank Poly London (BA); *m* 1961, Janet, *née* Wearn; 1 da (Jane); *Career* housing offr; joined Lib Party 1960, contested Croydon NW 1974 and 1979, First Alliance MP Croydon NW 1981-83; memb Inst of Trg and Devpt; *Style—* William Pitt, Esq; 10 Inverness Terrace, Broadstairs, Kent CT10 1QZ

PITT-KETHLEY, (Helen) Fiona; da of Rupert Singleton Pitt-Kethley (d 1975), of England, and Olive, *née* Banfield; *b* 21 Nov 1954; *Educ* Haberdasher's Aske's Girls' Sch Acton, Chelsea Sch of Art (BA, Biddulph painting prize); *Career* poet, travel writer, novelist and journalist; memb: Film Artiste's Assoc, Soc of Sussex Authors; *Books* poetry collections: Sky Ray Lolly (1986), Private Parts (1987); Journies to the Underworld (1988), The Perfect Man; *Recreations* opera, weight-training, herbalism, painting, sex; *Clubs* Chelsea Arts; *Style—* Ms Fiona Pitt-Kethley; 7 Ebenezer Rd, Hastings, East Sussex TN34 3BS (☎ 0424 718658, 0424 440996); c/o Agent, Giles

Gordon, Anthony Sheil Associates Ltd, 43 Doughty St, London WCN 2LF (☎ 071 405 9351)

PITT OF HAMPSTEAD, Baron (Life Peer UK 1975), of Hampstead, Greater London, and Grenada; David Thomas Pitt; JP (1966), DL (1988); s of Cyril S L Pitt, of St David's Grenada, WI; *b* 3 Oct 1913; *Educ* St David's RC Sch Grenada, Grenada Boys' Secdy Sch, Edinburgh Univ (MB ChB); *m* 1943, Dorothy Elaine, da of Aubrey Alleyne; 1 s (Hon Bruce Michael David), 2 da (Hon Phyllis Leonora, Hon Amanda); *Career* takes Labour Whip in House of Lords; GP London 1947-, pres W Indian Nat Party (Trinidad) 1943-47, memb LCC 1961-64, memb GLC 1964-77 for Hackney (dep chm 1969-70, chm 1974-75), chm Campaign Against Racial Discrimination 1965, dep chm Community Relations Commission 1968-77 (chm 1977-), memb Standing Advsy Council on Race Relations 1977-79, part time memb PO Bd 1975-77, chm Shelter 1979-90 (currently vice pres); contested (Lab) Hampstead 1959, Clapham (Wandsworth) 1970; Hon DSc Univ of WI 1975, Hon DLitt Bradford 1977, Hon LLD Bristol 1977, Hon LLD Hull 1983, Hon LLD Shaw Univ N Carolina 1985; *Style*— The Rt Hon Lord Pitt of Hampstead, JP; 6 Heath Drive, London NW3

PITTAM, Robert Raymond; MBE (1991); s of Rev Raymond Gerald Pittam (d 1986), and Elsie Emma, *née* Sale (d 1978); *b* 14 June 1919; *Educ* Colne GS, Bootle GS, Pembroke Coll Cambridge (MA); *m* 14 Sept 1946, Gwendoline Lilian, da of Albert George Brown (d 1967); 1 s (Michael Robert b 1948), 1 da (Christine Margaret (Mrs Richardson) b 1953); *Career* WWII RAOC 1941-42; temp serv with Civil Serv during war; joined HO 1946, princ private sec to Home Sec 1955-57, serv Treasy and Civil Serv Dept 1966-72, asst under sec of state HO 1972-79, fndr chm HO Retired Staff Assoc; lay preacher and chm Gp of Churches Welfare Orgn; FBIM 1965; *Recreations* cricket, reading; *Style*— Robert Pittam, Esq, MBE; 14 Devonshire Way, Shirley, Croydon CR0 8BR

PITTAWAY, David Michael; s of Eric Michael Pittaway, of Coventry, and Heather Yvette, *née* Scott; *b* 29 June 1955; *Educ* Uppingham, Sidney Sussex Coll Cambridge (MA); *m* 26 March 1983, Jill Suzanne, da of Dr Ian Douglas Bertie Newsam, of Cambridge; 2 s (James Frederick Henry b 9 July 1986, Charles Edward Bennet b 22 July 1989); *Career* called to the Bar 1977, practising Midland and Oxford circuit 1979-; *Recreations* shooting, skiing, travel; *Clubs* RAC, Lansdowne; *Style*— David Pittaway, Esq; 43 Canonbury Park N, London N1 (☎ 071 226 3060); 6 Kings Bench Walk, Temple, London EC4 (☎ 071 353 9901)

PITTEWAY, Prof Michael Lloyd Victor; s of Lloyd Sydney Pitteway (d 1990), and Elsie Maud, *née* Hall (d 1947); *b* 10 Feb 1934; *Educ* Felsted, Queens' Coll Cambridge (MA, PhD, ScD); *m* 2 April 1955, Cynthia Ethel Paplicia, da of Percival Henry Wilkins (d 1955), of Leicester; *Career* Harkness fell USA 1959-61, sr res fell Space and Sci Res Lab Slough 1961-63, computer dir Univ of Nottingham 1963-67, res prof Brunel Univ 1985- (head of Computer Sci Dept 1967-85); FBCS 1968, FIMA 1972, FInstP 1978; *Recreations* music, duplicate bridge; *Style*— Prof Michael Pitteway; Hedgerows, Star Lane, Knowl Hill, Berks RG10 9XY; Brunel Univ, Computer Sci Dept, Uxbridge UB8 3PH (☎ 0895 74000 ext 2233, fax 0895 32806, telex 261173 G)

PITTS, David; s of Tom Farrar Pitts (d 1974), and Florence Pitts, *née* Crossley (d 1983); *b* 27 April 1929; *Educ* Woodhouse Grammar, Bradford Coll; *m* 6 July 1957, Shirley Moira, da of Percy William Walker (d 1974); 1 s (William D b 1926); *Career* dir: David Pitts & Holt Ltd, P M Electronics Ltd, Pitts Energy Ltd; pres Electrical Contractors Assoc 1979-80; chm N Midland Centre IEE 1973-74; JP 1967; Freeman: City of London, Worshipful Co of Lightmongers; FIEE; *Recreations* yachting, golf, opera; *Clubs* Bradford; *Style*— David Pitts, Esq; Miramar, Ryelands Grove, Bradford BD9 6HJ (☎ 0274 491223); 413 Cutler Heights Lane, Bradford BD4 9JL (☎ 0274 662871, fax 0274 660 686, car 0860 223 953)

PITTS, John Kennedy; s of Thomas Alwyn Pitts (d 1968); *b* 6 Oct 1925; *Educ* Trowbridge, Univ of Bristol; *m* 1, 1957, Joan Iris (d 1986), da of Henry Charles Light (d 1963); m 2, 1990, Julia, da of Frank Bentall; *Career* dir ICI Mond Division 1969-71, chm Richardson Fertilizers Ltd 1972-76, dep chm ICI Agricultural Div 1972-77, vice pres Compagnie Neerlandaise de l'Azote 1975-77, chm Hargreaves Fertilizers Ltd 1975-77, chm and chief exec Tioxide Group plc 1978-87, memb Tees and Hartlepool Port Authy 1976-78, vice chm Shildon and Sedgefield Devpt Agency Ltd 1986-; pres Chemical Industs Assoc 1984-86, chm Legal Aid Board 1988-; *Clubs* RAC; *Style*— John Pitts, Esq

PITTS, (James) Michael; s of James Walter Pitts (d 1956); *b* 20 July 1929; *Educ* Shrewsbury; *m* 1955, Jean Hilarie; 2 s, 1 da; *Career* CA; sr ptnr Hodgson Impey 1979-90, dir Smalley Excavators Ltd; dir: Tuke and Bell Ltd, Lydiate Securities Ltd; pres Birmingham & W Midlands Soc of CAs 1979-80, memb ct Univ of Birmingham 1980-90, tstee Cannon Hill Tst; *Recreations* gardening, golf; *Clubs* Copt Heath Golf; *Style*— Michael Pitts, Esq; Hickecroft, Mill Lane, Rowington, Warwick

PIZEY, Adm Sir (Charles Thomas) Mark; GBE (1957, KBE 1953), CB (1942), DSO (and bar, 1942), DL (Somerset 1962); s of late Rev C E Pizey; *b* 1899; *m* Phyllis, da of Alfred D'Angibau; 2 da; *Career* WWI joined RN 1916 served HMS Revenge Battle of Jutland, HMS Danae Special Serv Sqdn World Cruise 1921-22, Flag Lt to Vice Adm Sir Howard Kelly Med Fleet 1929-30, cmd destroyers Med and Home fleets 1930-39, WWII Capt HMS Campbell Channel and North Sea op 1940-42 (despatches twice), Capt HMS Tyne and chief staff offr to Rear Adm Destroyers Russian Convoys 1942-43 (despatches twice), dir Ops (Home) Admty Naval Staff 1944-45, chief of staff to C-in-C Home Fleet 1946, Imperial Defence Coll 1947, chief UK servs liaison staff Aust 1948-49, Flag Offr cmdg 1 Cruiser Sqdn Med Fleet 1950-51, chief of naval staff and C-in-C Indian Navy 1951-55, Admiral 1954, C-in-C Plymouth 1955-58, ret; *Style*— Adm Sir Mark Pizey, GBE, CB, DSO; 1 St Ann's Drive, Gore Rd, Burnham on Sea, Somerset TA8 2HR (☎ 0278 785 770)

PLACE, Rear Adm (Basil Charles) Godfrey; VC (1944), CB (1970), DSC (1943); s of Maj Charles Godfrey Morris Place, DSO, MC (d 1931), and Anna Margaret, *née* Stuart-William (d 1949); descended from Archbishop Ussher (17th century), who dated bible and aquired Book of Kells for Trinity Dublin; *b* 19 July 1921; *Educ* The Grange Folkestone, RNC Dartmouth; *m* 1943, Althea Anningson, da of late Harry Tickler; 1 s (Charles), 2 da (Andrea, Melanie); *Career* Capt 1958, Adm cmd Reserves and dir gen Naval Recruiting 1968-70; chm VC and GC Assoc 1971-, lay observer 1975-78; Polish Cross of Valour 1941; *Style*— Rear Adm Godfrey Place, VC, CB, DSC; The Old Bakery, Corton Denham, Sherborne, Dorset

PLAISTER, Sir Sydney; CBE (1972); s of Herbert Plaister; *b* 15 Jan 1909; *Educ* Acton and Chiswick Poly, Coll of Estate Mgmnt; *m* 1937, Coralie Fraser Steele; 1 s, 1 da; *Career* chartered quantity surveyor 1930-; memb Exec Ctee Nat Union of Cons Assocs 1967-82, chm Midlands Central Cons Euro-Constituency Cncl 1978-83, pres W Midlands Cons Cncl 1980-83; Freeman City of London; FRSA, FRICS; kt 1980; *Style*— Sir Sydney Plaister, CBE; Turnpike Close, Old Warwick Rd, Lapworth, Warwicks B94 6AP (☎ 0564 782792)

PLAISTOWE, Alan David; s of David Plaistowe, of Connemara, Co Galway, and Rhona Elizabeth, *née* French; *b* 18 June 1932; *Educ* Marlborough, Ramsey Labs UC London (BSc); *m* 14 June 1957, Jane, da of Donovan Candler, of London; 1 da (Victoria b 1966); *Career* Lt RE Libya 1950-52; with Design Engrs (gas processing, oil refining) 1955-58; Stone and Webster Engrg 1958-65; fndr and md Chem Systems Int 1965, pres Chem Systems Gp 1986-; FIChemEng, FIPet; *Recreations* flying, golf, gardening, jazz; *Clubs* RAC; *Style*— Alan Plaistowe, Esq; Wanden, Egerton, Kent; Chem Systems Ltd

PLAISTOWE, (William) Ian David; s of David William Plaistowe (d 1975), Julia, *née* Ross Smith; *b* 18 Nov 1942; *Educ* Marlborough Queens' Coll Cambridge; *m* 1968, Carolyn Anne Noble, da of Tom Kenneth Noble Wilson; 2 s (Richard William Ian b 1969, Peter David Alexander b 1972), 1 da (Nicola Louise b 1977); *Career* Arthur Andersen & Co: joined 1964, ptnr 1976, head of Accounting & Audit Practice London 1984-87, practice dir Accounting and Audit UK and Ireland 1987-; chm: London Soc of Chartered Accountants 1981-82 (memb Cncl 1985), Practice Regulation Directorate ICAEW 1987-90 (vice pres 1990); FCA; *Recreations* golf, tennis, squash, skiing, gardening; *Clubs* Carlton, Moor Park Golf; *Style*— Ian Plaistowe, Esq; Arthur Andersen & Co, 1 Surrey St, London WC2R 2PS (☎ 071 438 3572, fax 071 831 1133)

PLANE, Marjorie; da of Reginald Shepherd, and Frances Miriam, *née* Wren; *b* 18 Feb 1950; *Educ* Rochdale Girls' Central Sch; *m* 18 Feb 1950, Geoffrey James Plane, s of Fred Plane (d 1970); 1 s (Garry James b 21 Dec 1950); *Career* jr clerk 49 Eclipse Mill Co Ltd 1947-49, costing clerk Samuel Heap & Sons Ltd 1949-50, payroll supervisor Samuel O'Neill Ltd 1951-52; Ratcliffe Industs plc: cashier bookeeper 1952-56, co sec 1956-77, main bd dir 1977-88; pres Rochdale C of C 1980-82, dir and sec Rochdale C of C Trade & Indust 1988-; chm Rochdale Enterprise Tst; memb: Saiwbal Rochdale Twinning Ctee, TVEI Steering Gp, bd Trg and Enterprise Cncl; chm: Friends of High Birch Ctee, Safe City Steering Gp; co delegate CBI 1965-86, sec Rochdale Continental Travellers Club 1965; MBIM 1967; *Recreations* sailing, travel; *Clubs* Home Base-Glass Glasson Yacht Basin, Misty Two Lancaster; *Style*— Mrs Marjorie Plane; Knowlewood, 68 Woodhouse Lane, Norden, Rochdale OL12 7SD (☎ 0706 41407); Lewis House, 12 Smith St, Rochdale OL16 1TX (☎ 0706 343810, fax 0706 31777)

PLANER, Nigel George; s of George Victor Planer, and (Margaret) Lesley, *née* Weeden; *b* 22 Feb 1953; *Educ* Westminster, Univ of Sussex, LAMDA; *m* 19 Aug 1989, Anna, da of Michael Lea; 1 s (Stanley b 5 Step 1988); *Career* actor; theatre work incl: Leeds Playhouse, Lyric Theatre, Young Vic, Oxford Playhouse, memb original cast Evita, Man of the Moment Globe Theatre; leading roles in tv incl: Shine on Harvey Moon, Rollover Beethoven, King and Castle, The Young Ones, Filthy Rich and Catflap, Number Twenty Seven, Blackeyes, Frankenstein's Baby, The Comic Strip Presents, The Naked Actor; films incl: The Supergrass, Brazil, Yellowbeard, More Bad News, The Strike; written work incl: Radio 4 sketches, Not the Nine O'Clock News, Funseekers (Channel 4 film); comic appearances: fndr memb Comic Strip, Comedy Store, Edinburgh Festival, MTV NY, Adelaide Festival (Aust), Hammersmith Odeon; other work incl two comedy LPs; winner BPI award Best Comedy Record 1984; memb: Equity 1977, Writers Guild 1987, Musicians Union 1987; *Books* Neil's Book of the Dead (1983), I, An Actor (1987); *Style*— Nigel Planer, Esq; Fraser & Dunlop & Peters, 5th Floor, The Chambers, Chelsea Harbour, Lots Road, London SW10 0XF

PLANK, Hon Mrs (Marion Rose); *née* Blyton; 2 da of Baron Blyton (Life Peer; d 1987); *b* 1926; *m* 1948, John Plank; children; *Style*— The Hon Mrs Plank; 36 Gerald St, S Shields, Tyne and Wear

PLANT, Hon Christopher Victor Howe; s of Baron Plant (d 1986, Life Peer); *b* 1945; *m* 1966 (m dis 1980), Marian, da of John Parkes; m 2, 1986, Linda Louisa, da of Albert John Pike, 2 da; *Style*— The Hon Christopher Plant; Laural Bank, 7 St Michael's Terrace, Lewes, E Sussex BN7 2HX

PLANT, (Ronald Arthur) Derek; s of Arthur Plant (d 1982), and Edith Frances, *née* Brock (d 1985); *b* 13 Jan 1935; *Educ* Rothesay Acad Isle of Bute, Scottish Hotel Sch Glasgow (Dip Hotel Mgmnt); *m* 22 Dec 1960, Christina Ann Murray, da of John Craig, of Cardross, Scotland; 2 da (Alison Christina (Mrs Carlton) b 1964, Isla Edith b 1966); *Career* Nat Serv 1955-57; Br Tport Hotels Ltd 1957-83: hotel gen mangr 1964-79, div dir 1979-80, company ops dir 1980-83; joint md Compass Hotels Ltd 1983-; Freeman: City of London 1978, Worshipful Co of Distillers 1979-; FHCIMA 1975; *Recreations* music, cricket, travel, reading; *Clubs* MCC; *Style*— Derek Plant, Esq; 9 Bishops Rd, Tewin Wood, Herts AL6 0NR (☎ 043879 493)

PLANT, Baroness; Gladys; *née* Mayers; da of Sampson Mayers; *m* 1931, Baron Plant, CBE (Life Peer UK (1978), d 1986); 2 s, 1 da; *Style*— The Rt Hon Lady Plant; 8 Apple Tree Close, North Street, Barming, Maidstone, Kent ME16 9HQ

PLANT, (Edward) Nicholas; s of Maj Raymond Plant (d 1990), of St Georges Meadows, West Drayton, Middx, and Margery Grace, *née* Windsor; *b* 11 Oct 1941; *Educ* Prior Park Coll Bath, Kings Sch Chester, Univ of Sheffield (LLB); *m* 30 March 1967, Patricia Mary, da of Percival Lee (d 1978), of Liverpool; 2 s (Edward b 1970, James b 1972); *Career* admitted slr 1966, Middleton & Upsall 1968- (managing ptnr Trowbridge Office), NP 1974; former: sec Trowbridge C of C, memb Round Table, Cons Branch sec and pres; sec Trowbridge Rotary Club, GDBA Branch; govr St Augustines Sch, Almshouse Tstee; memb: Law Soc 1966, Br Legal Assoc, Provincial Notaries Soc 1974; *Recreations* antiques, reading, things French, working; *Clubs* Royal Overseas League; *Style*— Nicholas Plant, Esq; 2 Fore St, Trowbridge, Wiltshire (☎ 0225 762 683, fax 0225 760 555)

PLANT, Prof Raymond; s of Stanley Plant (d 1983), and Marjorie Plant; *b* 19 March 1945; *Educ* Havelock Sch Grimsby, King's Coll London (BA), Univ of Hull (PhD); *m* 27 July 1967, Katherine Sylvia, da of Jack Dixon (d 1989); 3 s (Nicholas b 1969, Matthew b 1971, Richard b 1976); *Career* sr lectr (former lectr) in philosophy Univ of Manchester 1967-69, prof Univ of Southampton 1979-, Stevenson lectr Univ of Glasgow 1981, Agnes Cumming lectr Univ Coll Dublin 1988, Stanton lectr Univ of Cambridge 1989, Sarum lectr Univ of Oxford 1990; contribs to New Statesman and The Independent, columnist The Times 1988-; memb: Fabian Soc, Political Studies Assoc UK; *Books* Social and Moral Theory in Social Work (1970), Hegel: An Introduction (1973), Community and Ideology (1974), Political Philosophy And Social Welfare (1981), Philosophy Politics and Citizenship (1984), Equality Markets And the State (1984), Conservative Capitalism in Britain And The United States: A Critical Appraisal (1988), Citizenship Rights and Socialism (1989), Modern Practical Thought (1991); *Recreations* ornithology, opera, Bach, Mozart; *Style*— Prof Raymond Plant; 6 Woodview Close, Bassett, Southampton SO2 3P2 (☎ 0703 769529); Dept of Politics, University of Southampton (☎ 0703 592511)

PLANTEROSE, Rowan Michael; s of Anthony Ernest Charles Planterose, of Chedworth, Gloucs, and Jean D'Arcy, *née* Palmer; *b* 19 Feb 1954; *Educ* Eastbourne Coll, Downing Coll Cambridge (MA, LLB); *Career* called to the Bar 1978; FCIArb 1989; *Recreations* squash, skiing; *Style*— Rowan Planterose, Esq; 12 Grays Inn Square, Grays Inn, London WC1R 5JP (☎ 071 404 4866, fax 071 831 0713, telex 262433 Ref M 3011, car 0860 593743)

PLASKETT, Maj-Gen Frederick Joseph; CB (1980), MBE (1966); s of Frederick Joseph Plaskett (d 1982), and Grace Mary Plaskett (d 1988); *b* 23 Oct 1926; *Educ* Wallasey GS, Chelsea Poly; *m* 1, 9 Sept 1950, Heather (d 1982), da of Maurice William Kington (d 1976), of Salisbury, Wilts; 4 da (Helen b 1951, Wendy b 1954, Kate b 1960, Lucy b 1965); m 2, 1984, Mrs Patricia Joan Healy, da of Richard Upton, of Wimborne, Dorset; *Career* Army 1945-81; regtl and staff appts: India, Korea, Japan,

Malaya, W Africa, Germany, UK; ret as Maj-Gen; dir gen Tport and Movements (Army) 1981; Col Cmdt RCT 1981-; cmmr Royal Hosp Chelsea 1985-88; dir gen Road Haulage Assoc Ltd 1981-88; dir: Paccar UK (Foden Trucks) 1981-, Road Haulage Insurance Services 1983-88, Br Road Fedn 1982-88, BR London Midland Regn 1986- (chm 1989-); FCIT; *Recreations* sailing, fishing, gardening; *Clubs* Army and Navy; *Style*— Maj-Gen Frederick Plaskett, CB, MBE; c/o National Westminster Bank plc, The Commons, Shaftesbury, Dorset SP7 8JY

PLASSON, Michel; *Educ* studied piano with Lazare Levy, studied at Conservatorie of Music Paris (winner first prize for percussion and conducting); *Career* conductor; worked with Eric Leinsdorf, Pierre Monteux and Leopold Stokowski, musical dir Metz, dir Theatre du Capitole de Toulouse 1968-83, dir Orchestre Nat du Capitole de Toulouse 1968-; conducted in converted Halle aux Grains Toulouse: Fidelio by Lavalli 1977, Salome, Aida, Die Meistersinger, Faust, Parsifal, Carmen and Montsegur (world premiefe of Marcel Landowcki's opera 1985); conducted at Palais Ominsport de Paris-Bercy: Adia 1984, Turandot 1985, Verdi's Requiem 1986, Nabucco 1987; has worked with several int orchestras incl: Berlin Philharmonic, London Philharmonic, La Suisse Romande, Gewandhaus of Leipzig, Paris Opera, Geneva Opera, Vienna Opera, Munich Opera, Hamburg Opera, Zurich Opera, Covent Garden, Metropolitan Opera (Chicago and San Francisco); recorded maj French works with Orchestre Nat du Capitole de Toulouse for Pathe Marconi EMI; *awards* first prize in int competition 1962, many int prizes for recordings; *Style*— Michel Plasson, Esq

PLASTOW, Sir David Arnold Stuart; s of James Stuart Plastow (d 1987), of Grimsby, Lincs, and Marie Plastow (d 1975); *b* 9 May 1932; *Educ* Culford Sch Bury St Edmunds; *m* 1954, Barbara Ann, da of Ralph May, of Luton, Beds; 1 s, 1 da; *Career* mktg dir Motor Car Div Rolls-Royce Ltd 1967-70 (md 1971), md Rolls-Royce Motors Ltd 1972 (gp md 1974-80); chief exec Vickers plc 1980- (chm 1987-, non-exec dir 1975-80), pres: Soc of Motor Manufacturers and Traders 1976-78, Motor Indust Res Assoc 1978-81; non-exec dir: GKN plc 1978-84, Legal and Gen Gp plc 1985-87, memb: Bd Tenneco Inc Houston 1985-, Offshore Energy Technol Bd 1985-86, Engrg Cncl 1980-83; non-exec dir Guinness plc 1986- (dep chm 1987); dep chm Listed Cos Advsy Ctee 1987-; chm: Cncl Indust Soc 1983-87, MRC 1990-; Hon DSc Cranfield 1978; kt 1986; *Recreations* golf, music; *Clubs* Royal and Ancient (St Andrews), Royal St George's (Sandwich); *Style*— Sir David Plastow; Vickers plc, Vickers House, Millbank Tower, Millbank, London SW1P 4RA (☎ 071 828 7777, telex 27921)

PLASTOW, Norman Frederick; s of Frederick Stephen William Plastow (d 1958), and Helena Florence Plastow (d 1974); *b* 27 March 1929; *Educ* King's Coll Sch Wimbledon; *m* 4 April 1953, Audrey Ruth, da of Donald S Prosser (d 1977); 2 da (Hazel Anne b 1958, Wendy Jane b 1961); *Career* RAF (F/O) 1953-55; architect works incl: schs for Notts CC, Cornwall CC, ILEA (Finsbury Coll of Advanced Technol 1962), offices for Weidenfeld & Nicholson (1978) and Dominion Ins Co (1985); memb SIAD 1953-83; vice pres and chm Wimbledon Soc 1975-, hon curator Wimbledon Windmill Museum 1976-, local sec Surrey Archaeological Soc 1978-, Wimbledon and Putney Commons Conseruator 1979-, vice chm Conservation Areas Advsy Ctee to Borough of Merton; Time/RICS Conservation Award 1972; FRIBA, FBIS; *Books* ed Architects Standard Catalogue (annual); books inc: Safe as Houses (1972), The Trees of Wimbledon (1975), Wimbledon Windmill (1977), A History of Wimbledon and Putney Common (1986); *Recreations* archaeology, local history, photography, molinology; *Style*— Norman Plastow, Esq; Far House, Hillside, Wimbledon, London SW19 4NL (☎ 081 947 2825)

PLATER, Alan Frederick; s of Herbert Richard Plater, and Isabella Scott Plater; *b* 15 April 1935; *Educ* Kingston HS Hull, King's Coll Newcastle upon Tyne; *m* 1, 1958 (m dis 1985), Shirley Johnson; 2 s, 1 da; m 2, 1986, Shirley Rubinstein; 3 step s; *Career* architect until 1961, writer 1961-; *theatre* A Smashing Day, Close the Coalhouse Door And a Little Love Besides, Swallows on the Water, Trinity Tales, The Fosdyke Saga, Fosdyke Two, On Your Way, Riley!, Skyhooks, A Foot on the Earth, Prez In Blackberry Time, Rent Party, Sweet Sorrow, Going Home, I Thought I Heard A Rustling; *television* plays: So Long Charlie, See the Pretty Lights, To See How Far It Is (trilogy), Land of Green Ginger, Willow Cabins, The Party of the First Part, The Blacktoft Diaries, Thank You, Mrs Clinkscales; biographies: The Crystal Spirit, Pride of our Alley, Edward Lear - On the edge of the sand, Coming Through; series and serials: Z Cars, Softly Softly, Shoulder to Shoulder, Trinity Tales, The Good Companions, The Consultant, Barchester Chronicles, The Beiderbecke Affair, The Fortunes of War, The Beiderbecke Tapes, A Very British Coup, The Beiderbecke Connection; *radio* the Journal of Vasilije Bogdanovic; *films* The Virgin & the Gypsy, It Shouldn't Happen to a Vet, Priest of Love; co chm Writer's Guild of GB 1986-87, Writer in Residence Aust Film Television & Radio Sch Sydney 1988; *awards* Writer's Guild Radio award 1972, Sony Radio award 1983, RTS Writer's award 1984/5, Broadcasting Press Guild award 1987 and 1988, BAFTA Writer's award 1988, Banff Television Festival (Canada) Grand Prix 1989; hon fell Humberside Coll Furthur Educn 1983, Hon DLitt Univ of Hull 1985; FRSL 1985; *Books* The Beiderbecke Affair (1985), The Beiderbecke Tapes (1986), Misterioso (1987), plays and short pieces in various anthologies, contrib The Guardian, Listener, New Statesman & others; *Recreations* reading, theatre, jazz, snooker, dog-walking, talking, listening; *Clubs* Dramatists', Ronnie Scott's; *Style*— Alan Plater, Esq; c/o Margaret Ramsay Ltd, 14A Goodwin's Court, St Martin's Lane, London WC2N 4LL (☎ 071 240 0691)

PLATT, Adrian; s of Clifford Lowe Platt, OBE (d 1982), of Chislehurst, Kent, and Katharine Eileen, *née* Everington (d 1975); *b* 28 Nov 1935; *Educ* Marlborough, Univ of Lyons; *m* 24 Sept 1960, Valerie, da of Richard Bois (d 1956); 2 da (Emma b 1965, Katie b 1967); *Career* Nat Serv 4 RHA 1954-56, TA HAC 1956-62; dir Sedgwick Collins Ltd 1964-; chm: Sedgwick Forbes Marine Ltd 1968-69, Sedgwick Forbes Bland Payne Marine Ltd 1969-; dir Sedgwick Gp plc 1981; chm: Sedgwick Marine and Aviation Gp 1986-88, Sedgwick Ltd Devpt Gp 1988-, Sedgwick James Overseas Cos Ltd 1990-; tstee Mary Rose Tst; Liveryman: Worshipful Co of Vintners 1956, Worshipful Co of Shipwrights 1988; *Recreations* skiing, tennis, golf, shooting, reading; *Clubs* HAC, IOD; *Style*— Adrian Platt, Esq; Rosehill, Ockham Rd South, E Horsley, Surrey KT24 6SL (☎ 04865 3448); Sedgwick Ltd, Sedgwick House, 10 Whitechapel High St, London E1 (☎ 071 377 3411, fax 071 377 3199, telex 882131)

PLATT, Anthony Michael Westlake; CBE (1991); s of James Westlake Platt, CBE (d 1972), and Veronica Norma Hope, *née* Arnold (d 1987); *b* 28 Sept 1928; *Educ* St George's Coll and Belgrano Day Sch Buenos Aires, Stowe, Institut auf dem Rosenberg St Gallen, Balliol Coll Oxford (BA); *m* 1, 12 April 1952 (m dis 1982), (Jennifer) Susan, *née* Scott-Fox; 3 s (Michael b 1953, Timothy b 1961, Robin b 1962); m 2, 14 April 1984, Heather Mary (formerly Mrs Stubbs), *née* McCracken (d 1986); 1 step s (Rupert Stubbs b 1960), 1 step da (Imogen Stubbs b 1961); m 3, 18 Dec 1987, Sarah Elizabeth, *née* Russell; *Career* 2 Lt RA 1947-49, pilot offr RAFVR 1949-51; FO 1951-52, 3 sec (commercial) Br Embassy Prague 1953-54, private sec to Br Ambass to UN 1955-56; various positions Shell Group (UK and Abroad) 1957-84: vice pres Public Affrs Shell Internationale Petroleum Maatschappij 1973-74, chm and chief exec Billiton UK Ltd 1975-77, vice pres Secondary Metals Billiton International Metals (Hague) 1977-79, md Consolidated Petroleum Co Ltd 1979-84, area co-ordinator Shell International Petroleum Co 1979-84, chief exec London C of C and Indust 1984-, admin London Chamber Commercial Educn Tst; chm: Br Mexican Businessmen's Ctee 1988-, CEMAI (Consejo Empresarial Mexicano para Asuntos Internacionales) Euro Ctee Chm 1989-; memb: East Euro Trade Cncl, Euro Trade Cncl; *Recreations* gliding, walking, opera, languages; *Style*— Anthony Platt, Esq, CBE; London Chamber of Commerce and Industry, 69 Cannon St, London EC4N 5AB (☎ 071 248 4444, fax 071 489 0391, telex 888941 LCCI G)

PLATT, Prof Colin Peter Sherard; s of James Westlake Platt, CBE (d 1972), of Jersey, CI, and Veronica Norma Hope, *née* Arnold (d 1987); *b* 11 Nov 1934; *Educ* Collyers Sch Horsham Sussex, Balliol Coll Oxford (BA, MA), Univ of Leeds (PhD); *m* 8 Feb 1963, Valerie, da of Thomas Ashforth (d 1976), of Cannock, Staffs; 2 s (Miles b 9 April 1965, Theo b 20 Dec 1971), 2 da (Emma b 17 July 1963, Tabitha b 3 Jan 1967); *Career* Nat Serv RN Leading Coder Special 1953-54; lectr in medieval archaeology Univ of Leeds 1962-64; Dept of History Univ of Southampton: lectr 1964-74, sr lectr 1974-79, reader 1979-83, prof 1983-; FSA 1968, FRHistS 1971; *Books* The Monastic Grange in Medieval England (1969), Medieval Southampton: The Port and Trading Community, AD 1000-1600 (1973), Excavations in Medieval Southampton 1953-1969 (1975), The English Medieval Town (1976), Medieval England: A Social History and Archaeology from the Conquest to 1600 AD (1978), The Atlas of Medieval Man (1979), The Parish Churches of Medieval England (1981), The Castle in Medieval England and Wales (1982), The Abbeys and Priories of Medieval England (1984), Medieval Britain from the Air (1984), The Traveller's Guide to Medieval England (1985), The National Trust Guide to Late Medieval and Renaissance Britain (1986), The Architecture of Medieval Britain: A Social History (1990); *Recreations* reading fiction, visiting antiquities; *Style*— Prof Colin Platt, FSA; Department of History, Univ of Southampton, Southampton SO9 5NH (☎ 0703 595 000, fax 0703 593 939, telex 47661)

PLATT, David Andrew; s of Frank Platt, and Jean, *née* Jackson; *Educ* South Chadderton Comp Sch; *Career* professional footballer; Manchester Utd 1983-85 (no appearances), Crewe Alexandra 1985-88 (145 appearances, 60 goals), Aston Villa 1988- (over 125 appearances, over 60 goals); England: 3 under 21 caps, 3 B caps, 14 full caps (appeared in World Cup 1990 in Italy scoring 3 goals); Professional Footballers' Assoc Player of the Year 1990; *Recreations* horse racing, films; *Style*— David Platt, Esq; Aston Villa FC, Villa Park, Birmingham B6 6HE (☎ 021 327 6604)

PLATT, David Wallace; s of Christopher Platt, of Knock, Ulster, and Susan Harriette La Nauze, *née* Wallace; *b* 13 Sept 1964; *Educ* Campbell Coll, Trinity Hall Cambridge (MA); *Career* barr Middle Temple 1987, chm CUCA 1986; vice chm Westminster Cons Assoc, former political res asst and aide House of Commons and Cons Central Office, memb exec Cncl for Protection of Rural England; *Books* Educating Our Future (1986); *Recreations* politics, skiing, architecture, conservation; *Style*— David Platt, Esq; 44 Denbigh St, London SW1 (☎ 071 630 7089); 1 Harcourt Bldgs, Temple, London EC4 (☎ 071 353 0375, fax 071 583 5816)

PLATT, Denise; da of Victor Platt (d 1980), of Cheshire, and May, *née* Keeling; *b* 21 Feb 1945; *Educ* Congleton GS for Girls, Univ Coll Cardiff (BSc Econ); *Career* social worker Middx Hosp 1968-73, sr social worker Guy's 1973-76, gp ldr Southwark Social Servs 1976-78, princ social worker Hammersmith Hosp 1978-83; dir of Social Serv London Borough Hammersmith and Fulham 1986-(asst dir 1983-86); tstee Nat AIDS Tst; memb: advsy gp Policy Studies Inst, ed bd Info Tech in Local Govt, Exec Cncl Assoc of Dirs of Social servs (chair London branch); memb exec ctee The Old Water Colour Soc Club; AIMSW 1968; *Recreations* music, watercolours, walking; *Style*— Miss Denise Platt; 13 Hillmore Court, Belmont Hill, Lewisham, London SE13 5AZ (☎ 081 852 9556); Social Services Department, 145 King St, London W6 (☎ 081 748 3020, fax 081 741 3408)

PLATT, Derek William; s of Thomas Platt (d 1933), and Eliza, *née* Ford (d 1947); *b* 30 Dec 1927; *Educ* London Univ (BSc); *m* 30 July 1949, Barbara Mary, da of Wilfred Walker (d 1973); 2 s (Derek Andrew Jonathan b 1954, Michael William b 1955), 1 da (Penelope Mary Jane b 1951); *Career* chartered engr civil, mechanical and electrical; chm Highplaced Ltd 1963-; FICE, FIMechE, FIEE; *Recreations* sailing; *Clubs* Royal Thames YC, Royal Ocean Racing; *Style*— Derek Platt, Esq; The Old Vicarage, Hambledon, Hants PO7 6RP (☎ 070 132 432)

PLATT, Eleanor Frances; QC (1982); er da of Dr Maurice Leon Platt (d 1966), of Sussex, and Sara, *née* Stein (d 1983); *b* 6 May 1938; *Educ* Univ of London (LLB); *m* 1963, Frederick Malcolm; 1 s (Jonathan b 1969), 1 da (Amanda b 1965); *Career* called to the Bar Gray's Inn 1960; rec SE circuit 1982-, memb Matrimonial Causes Rule Ctee 1986-90, treas Family Law Bar Assoc 1990-; *Recreations* the arts, travel, skiing; *Style*— Miss Eleanor Platt, QC; 1 Garden Court, Temple, London EC4Y 9BJ (☎ 071 353 5524, fax 071 583 2029)

PLATT, Martin Philip; s and h of Hon Prof Sir Peter Platt, 2 Bt; *b* 9 March 1952; *m* 1971, Frances Corinne Moana, da of Trevor Samuel Conley; 2 s, 2 da; *Style*— Martin Platt, Esq; 9 Glenross St, Dunedin, New Zealand

PLATT, Norman; OBE (1985); s of Edward Turner Platt (d 1956), and Emily Jane Platt (d 1972); *b* 29 Aug 1920; *Educ* Bury GS, King's Coll Cambridge (BA); *m* 1, 1942, Diana Franklin, da of Sir Charles Travis Clay, CB (d 1975); 1 s (Tristan), 1 da (Marianna); m 2, 1963, Johanna Sigrid, da of Jesse Stewart Bishop; 1 s (Benjamin b 1965), 2 da (Rebecca b 1966, Lucinda b 1969); *Career* singer, actor, teacher; translator of: The Coronation of Poppea, Don Giovanni, Fidelio; opera prodr: L'Incoronazione di Poppea (Lisbon), Iphigenia in Tauris (Edinburgh Festival), Il Seraglio (Metz), Agrippina (Sadler's Wells), Don Giovanni (Singapore and Valencia), Peter Grimes (Bath Festival); princ: Sadler's Wells Opera 1946-48, Eng Opera Gp 1948; memb Deller Consort, fndr and artistic dir Kent Opera 1969-89; co-fndr (with Robin Jessel) The Canterbury Theatre and Festival Tst, chm Canterbury Festival Planning Ctee 1984-86; dir: Acting in Opera course 1989-, Kent Opera A Celebration 1990-, ed of Opera in Perfomance for Bristol Classical Press 1991, began Kent Opera Concert Series 1991-; Hon DCL Kent; *Recreations* listening to music, being read to by my wife; *Style*— Norman Platt, Esq, OBE; Pembles Cross, Egerton, Ashford, Kent TN27 9EN (☎ 023 376 237)

PLATT, Hon Mrs (Pauline Mary); da of Baroness Fisher of Rednal and Joseph Fisher; *b* 1940; *m* 1961, Michael James Platt; *Style*— The Hon Mrs Platt

PLATT, Hon Sir Peter; 2 Bt (UK 1959); s of Baron Platt (Life Peer and 1 Bt, d 1978), and Margaret Irene, *née* Cannon (1987); *b* 6 July 1924; *Educ* Abbotsholme Sch Derbyshire, Magdalen Coll Oxford (MA, BMus, BLitt), RCM; *m* 1948, Jean Halliday, da of late Charles Philip Brentnall, MC; 1 s (Martin), 2 da (Margaret, Katherine); *Heir* s, Martin Philip Platt, b 9 March 1952; *Career* served WWII RNVR (despatches), ret 1989; prof of music: Univ of Otago NZ 1957-75, Univ of Sydney 1975-89; hon FGSM 1973; *Style*— The Hon Sir Peter Platt, Bt; 1 Ellison Place, Pymble, NSW 2073, Australia (☎ 010 612 4494372)

PLATT, Hon Roland Francis; s of Baroness Platt of Writtle, CBE (Life Peer); *b* 1951; *Educ* Felsted; *m* 1982, Louise M, yr da of Lionel B B Jackson, of Sheffield; 1 s (James b 1987), 2 da (Ann b 1985, Harriette b 1990); *Career* FCA (ACA 1976); *Style*— The Hon Roland Platt; Fremnells, 10 Westbury Rd, Brentwood, Essex

PLATT, Ronald Thomas George; OBE (1969); s of Arthur Thomas Platt (d 1986), of Torquay, and Henriette Jessie, *née* Collins; *b* 18 Sept 1926; *Educ* Bancrofts Sch, Univ of Glasgow, LSE (BSc); *m* 4 Aug 1953, Kathleen; 4 s (Simon b 1957, David b 1962, Stephen b 1964, Andrew b 1960 (decd)); 2 da (Johanna b 1963, Alison b 1968); *Career* dir Ford Cos in: Belgium, Finland, France, Ireland, Italy, Netherlands, Portugal, Switzerland (chm France); English Ford line mangr Ford US 1963-70, dir car sales Ford of Britain, vice pres Euro sales ops and export Ford of Europe 1974- (mktg dir 1973-74); *Recreations* sailing, crosswords, grass cutting; *Style—* Ronald T G Platt, Esq, OBE; Higher Barton, Hallwood Crescent, Brentwood, Essex (☎ 0277 223172); Ford of Europe Inc, Eagle Way, Brentwood, Essex

PLATT, Sylvia, Lady; Sylvia Jean; da of late Sidney Charles Caveley, and formerly w of John Alfred Haggard; *m* 1974, as his 2 w, 1 Baron Platt (Life Peer and 1 Bt; d 1978); *Style—* The Rt Hon Sylvia, Lady Platt; 53 Heathside, Hinchley Wood, Esher, Surrey

PLATT, Hon Victoria Catherine; da of Baroness Platt of Writtle; *b* 1953; *Educ* Marlborough, Girton Coll Cambridge (MA); *m* 1984, Rhodri Davies, s of His Hon Judge John Davies, QC, of Teddington, Middx; 3 da (Rachael Catherine b 1985, Joanna Megan b 1987, Jessica Polly b 1990); *Career* accountant and lectr in private practice; ACA, ATII; *Recreations* running, hill walking, sailing; *Clubs* Thames, Hare and Hounds; *Style—* The Hon Vicky Platt

PLATT OF WRITTLE, Baroness (Life Peer UK 1981), of Writtle, Co Essex; Beryl Catherine Platt; CBE (1978), DL (Essex 1983); da of Ernest Myatt (d 1950); *b* 18 April 1923; *Educ* Westcliff HS for Girls, Girton Coll Cambridge (MA); *m* 1949, Stewart Sydney Platt, s of Sydney Rowland Platt (d 1946); 1 s (Hon Roland Francis b 1951), 1 da (Hon Victoria Catherine (Hon Mrs Davies) b 1953); *Career* aeronautical engr; tech asst Hawker Aircraft Ltd 1943-46, BEA 1946-49; Chelmsford RDC 1959-74; Essex CC elected 1965 (alderman 1969-74, vice chm and chm co-ordinating and Fin Ctee 1980-83, vice chm Educn Ctee 1969-71, chm 1971-80, chm Further Educn Sub Ctee 1969-71); non-exec dir Br Gas plc 1988, fell Smallpiece Tst 1988; memb: Court Univ of Essex 1968-, City Univ 1968-78, Cncl City and Guilds of London Inst 1974-, Univ of Cambridge Appts Bd 1975-79, Engrg Cncl 1982-90, Cncl Royal Soc of Arts 1983-88, Cncl Careers Res and Advsy Ctee 1983-, Engrg Trg Authy 1990-; chm Equal Opportunities Cmmn 1983-88; memb: House of Lords Select Ctee on Murder and Life Imprisonment 1988-89, House of Lords Select Ctee on Sci and Technol 1990 and 1982-85; memb Ct: Brunel Univ 1985, Cranfield Inst 1989-; vice pres UMIST 1985-; Freeman City of London 1988, Liverman Worshipful Co of Engrs 1988; hon fell: Womens Engrg Soc 1988, Girton Coll Cambridge, Poly of Wales, Poly of Manchester; Hon Insignia Award City and Guilds London Inst 1988; Hon LLD Univ of Cambridge 1988; Hon DSc: Cranfield Inst, City Univ; Hon D: Univ of Salford, Open Univ, Univ of Bradford (Eng), Univ of Essex, Brunel Univ (Tech); FEANI 1988, Hon FCP, Hon FIMechE, FEng 1987, FRAeS, FRSA, FITD; *Recreations* reading, gardening, cooking, (yacht 'Corydalis'); *Style—* The Rt Hon the Baroness Platt of Writtle, CBE, DL; House of Lords, London SW1

PLATTS, David Ernest; s of John Ernest Platts (d 1977), of Halifax, Yorks, and Emma Crossley, *née* Crossland (d 1990); *b* 8 July 1936; *Educ* Crossley and Porter GS Halifax; *m* 20 June 1959, Judith Beryl, da of Stanley Priestley, of Halifax, Yorks; 2 s (Charles John Savile b 1962, Mark Howard David b 1967), 1 da (Sarah Judith Rachel b 1966); *Career* slr; currently conslt Summers Platts, former legal asst to Registrar-Gen Hong Kong; former in-house lawyer: Abbey National Building Society, Trafalgar House Gp, Hammerson Gp; *Recreations* gardening, sailing, wine; *Clubs* Rotary; *Style—* David Platts, Esq; Seeleys Orchard, Penn Rd, Beaconsfield, Bucks HP9 2LN (☎ 0494 675833)

PLATTS, Nigel Landsbrough; s of Francis Arthur Platts and Mabel Landsbrough, *née* Williams; *b* 20 Oct 1945; *Educ* Whitgift Sch, Oriel Coll Oxford (MA); *m* 26 July 1969, Anne Christine, da of Samuel Walker; 1 s (Thomas b 22 May 1978), 2 da (Philippa b 8 Feb 1972, Hannah b 8 April 1980); *Career* CA 1970; KPMG Peat Marwick McLintock (formerly Peat Marwick Mitchell & Co): articled clerk, sr mangr, ptnr, currently gen practice ptnr; FCA; *Recreations* watching rugby, playing, coaching and organising cricket; *Style—* Nigel Platts, Esq; KPMG Peat Marwick McLintock, 1 Puddle Dock, Blackfriars, London EC4V 3PD (☎ 071 236 8000, fax 071 583 1938)

PLATTS-MILLS, John Faithful Fortescue; QC (1964); s of John F W Mills, of NZ, and Dr Daisy Platts-Mills; *b* 4 Oct 1906; *Educ* Nelson Coll Victoria Univ NZ (LLM), Balliol Coll Oxford (MA, BCL); *m* 1936, Janet Katherine Cree; 6 s; *Career* serv WWII, pilot offr RAF; collier 1944-45; called to the Bar New Zealand 1928, Inner Temple 1932; bencher Inner Temple 1970; MP (Lab) Finsbury 1945-48, (Lab Ind) 1948-50; pres: Haldane Soc, Soc for Cultural Relations with USSR; vice-pres Int Assoc of Democratic Lawyers; memb: TGWU, NUM; *Clubs* Athenaeum, Vincent's (Oxford), Leander; *Style—* John Platts-Mills, Esq, QC; Cloisters, Temple, London EC4Y 7AA (☎ 071 583 0303); Terrible Down Farm, Halland, E Sussex (☎ 082 584 310)

PLAYER, Edward; s of Edward Player, CBE (d 1968), and Mary Edith; *b* 25 March 1920; *Educ* Wrekin, Univ of Birmingham (Dip Engrg Prodn Mgmnt); *m* 15 Dec 1945, Joan, da of Walter Guy (d 1934), of Fiji; 2 da (Susan b 1947, Virginia b 1952); *Career* Capt RTR 1941-50, serv WWII N Africa (POW); chm Sterling Metals Ltd 1973-74 (md 1962-73); dir many assoc cos incl: Birmid Industries 1964-69, Birmid Qualcast (Foundries) Ltd 1969-73; mgmnt conslt (specialising ferrous and non ferrous indus) 1975-; Liveryman Worshipful Co of Coachmakers' and Coach Harness Makers'; fell Inst of Br Foundrymen; *Recreations* fishing, shooting; *Style—* Edward Player, Esq; 9 The Maltings, Lillington Ave, Leamington Spa (☎ 0926 339378)

PLAYFAIR, Sir Edward Wilder; KCB (1957, CB 1949); s of late Dr Ernest Playfair; *b* 17 May 1909; *Educ* Eton, King's Coll Cambridge; *m* 1941, Dr Mary Lois Rae; 3 da; *Career* serv Treasy 1934-46 and 1947-56, control office Germany and Austria 1946-47, perm under sec of state for War 1956-59, perm sec MOD 1960-61; chm Int Computers and Tabulators Ltd 1961-65; tstee National Gallery 1967-74 (chm 1972-74), fell Imperial Coll of Science and Technol 1972; hon fell: UCL 1969, King's Coll Cambridge 1986; Hon FBCS; *Clubs* Brooks's; *Style—* Sir Edward Playfair, KCB; 62 Coniger Rd, London SW6 3TA (☎ 071 736 3194)

PLAYFAIR, Lt-Col Hugh George Lyon; OBE (1989); s of John Maxwell Playfair (d 1983), of Baltilly, Ceres, Fife, and Marjory Jean Playfair-Hannay, MBE, *née* Armour-Hannay; *b* 5 Dec 1939; *Educ* Oundle, King's Coll Cambridge (MA), New Coll Oxford (Dip Ed); *m* 22 Aug 1970, Bridget Ingledew Jane, da of Edward Andrew Garland (d 1953), of India; 2 s (Patrick b 1971, Edward b 1972), 1 da (Elizabeth b 1974); *Career* Nat Serv 2 Lt King's Own Scottish Borderers attached to Somaliland Scouts 1957-59; asst master: Marlborough Coll 1960-68, Cranbrook Sch Sydney 1969-73 (housemaster, sr history master 1970-73), Canford Sch 1974-; lay reader Diocese of Bath and Wells, MBIM 1979; *Books* The Playfair Family (1984); *Recreations* golf, gardening, shooting, stamp collecting; *Clubs* Royal & Ancient, Sherborne Golf; *Style—* Lt-Col Hugh Playfair, OBE; Canford School, Wimborne, Dorset (☎ 0202 881 254)

PLAYFAIR - HANNAY OF KINGSMUIR, Patrick Armour; s of John Maxwell Playfair (d 1983), of Baltilly, Ceres, Fife, and Majory Jean, *née* Armour-Hannay, MBE (d 1983); *b* 12 July 1929; *Educ* Oundle; *m* 15 May 1954, Frances Ann, da of Robert James Roberton, of Morebattle Tofts, Kelso; 1 s (James Patrick Lyon b 4 March 1957), 1 da (Freda Mary Caroline b 27 April 1962); *Career* Nat Serv 2 Lt RASC 1946-48 (Suez Canal Zone with Air Despatch Co); tea and rubber planter Rosehaugh & Co Ltd Ceylon 1948-55, landowner and farmer at Clifton-on-Bowmont Kelso Fife 1956-; chm Assoc for Protection of Rural Scotland, memb Ctee Nat Sheep Assoc, elder Church of Scotland; *Recreations* shooting, archery; *Clubs* Royal Company of Archers, Farmers; *Style—* Patrick Playfair - Hannay of Kingsmuir, Esq; Clifton-on-Bowmont, Kelso (☎ 057 382 227)

PLAYFORD, Jonathan Richard; QC (1982); s of Maj Cecil Roche Bullen Playford (d 1977), of London, and Euphrasia Joan, *née* Cox; *b* 6 Aug 1940; *Educ* Eton, Univ of London (LLB); *m* 1978, Jill Margaret, da of William Herbert Dunlop, MBE (d 1982), of Doonside, Ayr; 1 s (Nicholas b 1981), 1 da (Fiona b 1985); *Career* called to the Bar Inner Temple 1962; rec Crown Ct 1985; *Recreations* golf, music, country pursuits; *Clubs* Garrick; *Style—* Jonathan Playford, Esq, QC; 2 Harcourt Buildings, Temple EC4Y 9DB (☎ 071 583 9020)

PLEASANCE, Roy Thomas; s of James Harold Pleasance (d 1981), and Mary Catherine, *née* Harris (d 1982); *b* 11 Feb 1926; *Educ* Rutlish Sch Merton; *m* 1, 12 June 1948, Gwendoline May; m 2, 3 Oct 1964, Anne; m 3, 29 June 1984, Norman Mary Germaine, da of Sir Norman King, KCMG (d 1963); *Career* CA taxation specialist; head of taxation dept BP Co Ltd 1958-73, chm UK Oil Ind Taxation Ctee 1964-74; *Books* UK Taxation of Offshire Oil and Gas (with R Hayllar, 1977); *Recreations* opera, architecture, history; *Style—* Roy Pleasance, Esq; Arden's House, Abbey St, Faversham, Kent ME13 7BH (☎ 0795 534 124); 80 Preston St, Faversham, Kent (☎ 0795 535 249)

PLEASENCE, Donald; s of Thomas Stanley Pleasence (d 1964), and Alice Armitage (d 1964); *b* 5 Oct 1919; *Educ* Ecclesfield GS Sheffield; *m* 1, 1941, Miriam Raymond; 2 da; m 2, 1956, Josephine Crombie; 2 da; m 3, 1970, Meira Shore; 1 da; m 4, 1989, Linda Woollam; *Career* RAF 1942-46, POW 1944-46; first stage appearance 1939, London debut in Twelfth Night (Arts Centre) 1942; Birmingham Repertory Theatre 1948-50, Bristol Old Vic Co 1950-51; stage appearances incl: The Brothers Karamazou 1946, Peter Pan (Perth Repertory Theatre) 1947, Right Side Up and Saints Day (London) 1951, NY with Lawrence Olivier's Co 1951-52, Hobson's Choice (Arts Theatre) 1952, Ebb Tide (own play, Edinburgh Festival and Royal Court Theatre 1952), Stratford-on-Avon season 1953, Anthony and Cleopatra (London) 1953, The Rule of the Game 1955, The Lark 1955, Misalliance 1956, Restless Heart 1957, The Caretaker (London and NY) 1960, Poor Bitos (co-producer), The Man in the Glass Booth (co-producer) 1967, Tea Party, The Basement 1970, Wise Child (NY) 1972, Reflections (London) 1980; film appearances incl: The Beachcomber, Manuela, Heart of a Child, The Caretaker, The Greatest Story Ever Told, Fantastic Voyage, The Hallelujah Trail, The Great Escape, Doctor Crippin, Cul-de-sac, Will Penny, The Mad Woman of Chaollot, Arthur! Arthur?, Soldier Blue, Jerusalem File, Pied Piper, Oustback, The Black Windmill, Wedding in White, The Rainbow Boys, Mutations, Henry VIII, Malachi's Cove, Escape to Witch Mountain, Journey into Fear, The Count of Monte Cristo, Doctor Jekyll and Mr Hyde, Hearts of the West, I Don't Want to be Born, Trial by Combat, The Devil's People, The Eagle Has Landed, The Last Tycoon, Telefon, Devil Cat, Sergent Pepper's Lonely Hearts Club Band, Blood Relatives, Power Play, Halloween 1, 2, 4 and 5, Centennial, A Breed Apart, Escape From New York, All Quiet in the Western Front, The French Atlantic Affair, The Monster CLub, The Corsican Brothers, Black Arrow, Pleasure of the Amazon, Warrior of the Lost, A Breed Apart, Ground Zero, Where is Parcifal?, Hanna's War; numerous TV appearances; awarded: Television Actor of the Year award 1958, London Critics' Best Stage Performance award 1960, Variety Club Stage Actor of 1967 award; *Books* Scouse the Mouse (1977), Scouse in New York (1978); *Style—* Donald Pleasence, Esq; Joy Jameson Ltd, The Plaza, 2-19 the Plaza, 535 Kings Rd, London SW10 0SZ (☎ 071 351 3971, fax 071 352 1744)

PLEAT, David John; *b* 15 Jan 1945; *Educ* Mundella GS Nottingham; *m* 14 June 1969, Maureen, *née* Brown; 1 s (Jonathan b 8 Oct 1970), 1 da (Joanne b 26 April 1973); *Career* professional football manager; player: debut Nottingham Forest v Cardiff 1962 (youngest debutant at time aged 17), transferred to Luton Town for a fee of £8,000 1964, Shrewsbury Town 1967-68, Exeter City 1968-70, Peterborough Utd 1970-71; mangr: Nuneaton 1971-74 (also player), Luton Town 1978-86 (coach 1975-78), Tottenham Hotspur 1986-87, Leicester City 1987-91; England: 5 schoolboy caps 1959-60, youth caps 1961-63 (memb World Cup Youth Winner's Squad 1963); FA full coaching award 1968; Div 2 Championship Luton Town 1982, FA Cup runners-up Tottenham Hotspur v Coventry City 1987; various Bell's Mangr of the Month Awards, Sportsman of the Year award Canon Football League 1983; commentator and analyst: ITV 1983-89, Sky TV 1990, BBC Radio 2 and 5, covered World Cup Mexico 1986 and Italy 1990; judge Barclay's performance of the week award, memb Football League Exec Staff Assoc 1982- (dep chm 1984); contrib football articles: Inside Football 1965-68, Luton News 1978-86, Sports Argus Birmingham 1985-87, Leicester Mercury 1988-90; *Style—* David Pleat, Esq

PLEETH, William; OBE (1989); s of John Pleeth, né Plicht (d 1973), of Warsaw, and Edith, *née* Gold (d 1971); *b* 12 Jan 1916; *Educ* Leipzig Conservatoire Germany; *m* 28 Jan 1944, (Alice) Margaret, da of Frank Leonard Good; 1 s (Anthony Michael b 1948), 1 da (Janet Elizabeth b 1946); *Career* concert cellist until 1980; debut in Leipzig 1931, London debut 1933; prof of cello Guildhall Sch of Music 1948-78; visiting prof: Menuhin Sch 1981-, Royal Coll of Music 1986-; frequent broadcasts and recordings 1933-80; FGSM 1952 (emeritus 1978), FRCM 1988; *Books* Cello (1982); *Recreations* cooking, researching antiques, reading; *Style—* William Pleeth, Esq, OBE

PLENDER, (William) John Turner; s of William Plender (d 1977), of Wiltshire, and Avril Maud, *née* Turnbull; *b* 9 May 1945; *Educ* Downside, Oriel Coll Oxford; *m* 1 (m dis 1989), Sophia Mary, *née* Crombie; 1 s, 2 da; *Career* CA and writer; Deloitte Plender Griffiths & Co 1967-70, Investors' Chronicle 1970-71, The Times 1972-74, fin ed The Economist 1979, FCO 1980-81, freelance journalist publisher and broadcaster (leader writer Financial Times) 1982-; FCA 1970; *Books* That's The Way The Money Goes (1981), The Square Mile (with Paul Wallace, 1985); *Clubs* Travellers'; *Style—* John Plender, Esq

PLENDER, Richard Owen; QC (1989); s of George Plender, and Louise Mary, *née* Savage; *b* 9 Oct 1945; *Educ* Dulwich, Queens' Coll Cambridge (BA, LLB, Rebecca Squire Prize), Univ of Illinois (LLM, JSD, Coll of Law Prize), Univ of Sheffield (PhD); *m* 16 Dec 1978, Patricia Clare, da of Wing Cdr John Lawson Ward (d 1976); 1 da (Sophie Clare b 31 Aug 1986); *Career* called to the Bar Inner Temple 1972; referendaire Euro Ct 1980-83; dir Centre of Euro Law Kings Coll London 1988-90, assoc prof Univ of Paris II; hon sr memb Robinson Coll Cambridge; *Books* International Migration Law (1972, 2 edn 1988), Fundamental Rights (1973), Cases and Materials on the Law of the European Communities (1980, 2 edn 1989), A Practical Introduction to European Community Law (1980), Introduccion al Derecho Comunitario (1985), Legal History and Comparative Law (1990); *Recreations* classical music, writing light verse; *Style—* Richard Plender, Esq; 3 Essex Court, Temple, London EC4Y 9AL (☎ 071 583 9294, fax 071 583 1341, telex 893468 SXCORT G)

PLENDERLEITH, Ian; s of Raymond William Plenderleith, and Louise Helen, *née* Martin; *b* 27 Sept 1943; *Educ* King Edward's Sch Birmingham, Christ Church Oxford (MA), Columbia Business Sch NY (MBA); *m* 1 April 1967, Kristina Mary, da of John Hardy Bentley, OBE (d 1980); 1 s (Giles b 1972), 2 da (Melanie b 1969, Cressida b

1976); *Career* joined Bank of Eng 1965, seconded as tech asst to UK Exec Dir International Monetary Washington DC 1972-74, private sec to govr 1976-79, alternate dir Euro Investment Bank 1980-86, head Gilt Edged Div 1982-90, govt broker 1989-, assoc dir 1990-; hon sec Tillington CC; memb Advsy Bd Inst of Archaeology Devpt Tst UCL; Liveryman Worshipful Co of Innholders 1977-; *Recreations* archaeology, theatre, cricket; *Clubs* Tillington CC; *Style—* Ian Plenderleith, Esq; Bank of England, London EC2R 8AH (☎ 071 601 4444)

PLESS, Mary, Princess of; (Dorothea) Mary Elizabeth; da of Lt-Col Richard George Edward Minchin (d 1985), of Busherstown, Co Offaly and Annagh, Co Tipperary, and Elizabeth Eve, *née* McKerrell-Brown (d 1985); *b* 1928; *Educ* St Leonards Sch St Andrews; *m* 23 July 1958 (m dis 1971), Henry, Prince of Pless (d 1984), eld s of Hans Heinrich XV, 3 Prince of Pless, Imperial Count of Hochberg by his 1 w Daisy, *née* Cornwallis-West; *Recreations* theatre, animal life; *Style—* Mary, Princess of Pless; 14 Campden House, Sheffield Terrace, London W8

PLEWES, Jeremy John Lawrence; s of Lawrence William Plewes, CBE, of Kensworth, Beds, and Faith Sybil Etrenne, *née* Downing; *b* 5 Sept 1940; *Educ* Marlborough, ChCh Oxford (MA, BM BCh); *m* 12 Feb 1966, Jenna Rose, da of Lt Cdr Vernon Judge Glassborow (d 1971), of Yelverton, Devon; 1 da (Caryl Robin b 1969), 1 s (Andrew Burns b 1970); *Career* conslt orthopaedic surgn Central Birmingham Health Authy 1982-, sr clinical lectr Surgery Univ of Birmingham 1982-; FRCS, FRSM; *Recreations* photography, oenology, sailing; *Style—* Jeremy Plewes, Esq; Selvas Cottage, Withybed Green, Alvechurch, Worcs B48 7PR (☎ 021 445 1624); 81 Harborne Rd, Edgbaston, Birmingham B15 3HG; Gen Hosp, Birmingham B4 6NH (☎ 021 455 9496)

PLEWS, Nigel Trevor; s of Isaac Plews (d 1981), of Nottingham, and Minnie, *née* Stanley (d 1968); *b* 5 Sept 1934; *Educ* Mundella GS Nottingham; *m* 24 Sept 1956, Margaret Mary, da of Francis George Ley; 1 s (Douglas b 21 April 1964), 1 da (Elaine b 24 Feb 1961); *Career* cricket umpire; former club and league cricketer Nottinghamshire; appointed to: First Class Cricket Umpires List 1982, Int Panel 1986, Test Panel 1988; umpire: 5 Test Matches (England v West Indies Old Trafford 1988, England v Australia Lords and Trent Bridge 1989, England v India Lords and The Oval 1990), 4 One Day Internationals (England v New Zealand Old Trafford 1986, England v West Indies Lords 1988, England v Australia Lords 1989, England v New Zealand Headingly 1990), 3 Cup Finals Lords 1988 1989 and 1990; former detective sgt Company Fraud Squad Nottingham City Police Force, currently employed off season in insolvency work Touche Ross; *Recreations* hill walking, reading, travel; *Style—* Nigel Plews, Esq

PLEYDELL-BOUVERIE, Hon Mrs Peter; Audrey; *née* Kidston; yst da of Capt Archibald Glen Kidston, JP, of Breconshire; *b* 11 July 1906; *Educ* private; *m* 1, 1929 (m dis 1946), Anthony Seymour Bellville; m 2, 1947, as his 2 w, Maj Hon Peter Pleydell-Bouverie (d 1981), late KRRC and 5 s of 6 Earl of Radnor; 1 s (James b 1950); *Style—* The Hon Mrs Peter Pleydell-Bouverie; Bodenham House, Bodenham, Salisbury, Wilts (☎ 0722 29735)

PLEYDELL-BOUVERIE, Hon Mrs Edward; (Alice) Pearl; da of Maj Edward Barrington Crake, Rifle Bde, by his 2 w, Clara Alice, da of George William Plunkenett Woodroffe, RHG; *m* 1, 1920 (as his 2 w), 2 Baron Montagu of Beaulieu, KCIE, CSI, JP, DL (d 1929); 1 s (3 Baron *qv*), 3 da (Anne Rachel Pearl, m 1, Howel Moore-Gwyn (d 1948); m 2, Sir John Chichester, Bt; Caroline Cecily, m (m dis) Grainger Weston; Mary Clare, m 1, Viscount Garnock; m 2, Timothy Horn); m 2, 1936, Capt the Hon Edward Pleydell-Bouverie, MVO, DL, RN (d 1951), 2 s of 6 Earl of Radnor; 1 s (Robin); *Style—* The Hon Mrs Edward Pleydell-Bouverie; The Lodge, Beaulieu, Hampshire SO42 7YB (☎ 0590 612356)

PLEYDELL-BOUVERIE, Hon Peter John; 2 s of 8 Earl of Radnor and his 1 w Anne, *née* Seth-Smith; *b* 14 Jan 1958; *Educ* Harrow, Trinity Coll Cambridge; *m* 14 June 1986, Jane Victoria, da of Rt Hon Sir Ian Hedworth John Little Gilmour, 3 Bt, MP; 2 s (Timothy b 1987, Jamie b 1989); *Career* dir: Fidelity Investment Services Ltd, Fidelity Pension Ltd (Investment Management Co); *Recreations* fishing, skiing, shooting, photography; *Clubs* Pratt's; *Style—* The Hon Peter Pleydell-Bouverie; Longford Castle, Salisbury, Wilts; 38 Queensdale Road, London W11 4SA (☎ 071 602 0394)

PLEYDELL-BOUVERIE, Hon Reuben; 2 s of 7 Earl of Radnor, KG, KCVO, JP, DL (d 1968), and his 1 w Helena Olivia, *née* Adeane; *b* 30 Dec 1930; *Educ* Harrow; *m* 28 Jan 1956, Bridget Jane, da of Maj John Fowell Buxton (ggs of Sir Thomas Buxton, 1 Bt); 2 s, 1 da; *Career* late 2 Lt Royal Scots Greys; prospector; industrial designer; *Recreations* beekeeping, windsurfing, sailing, shooting, fishing; *Style—* The Hon Reuben Pleydell-Bouverie; The Dower House, Slindon, Arundel, Sussex BN18 0RP

PLEYDELL-BOUVERIE, Hon Richard Oakley; s of 7 Earl of Radnor, KG, KCVO, JP, DL (d 1968), by his 2 w Isobel, OBE, da of Lt-Col Richard Oakley, DSO, JP; *b* 25 June 1947; *Educ* Harrow, RAC Cirencester; *m* 1978, Victoria, yr da of late Frank Waldron, of Pond House, Kidmore End, nr Reading; 2 s (David b 1979, Bartholomew b 1981); 1 da (Harriot b 1984); *Style—* The Hon Richard Pleydell-Bouverie; Lawrence End, Peters Green, Luton, Beds (☎ 0582 21082)

PLIATZKY, Sir Leo; KCB (1977, CB 1972); s of Nathan Pliatzky; *b* 1919; *Educ* Manchester GS, City of London Sch, CCC Oxford; *m* 1948, Marian Jean (d 1979), da of late Capt James Elias, MN; 1 s, 1 da; *Career* Sgt REME and Capt RAOC in ME and Central Med 1940-45 (despatches); second perm sec Treasy 1976-77, perm sec Dept of Trade 1977-79, ret, retained for special duties 1979-80; non-exec dir: BA 1980-85, Assoc Communications Corp plc 1980-82, Central Independent TV 1981-89, Ultramar plc 1981-90; visiting prof City Univ 1980-84, assoc fell LSE 1982-85, hon fell CCC Oxford 1980; *Books* Getting and Spending: Whitehall memoirs (revised edn 1984), Paying and Choosing - The Intelligent Person's Guide to the Mixed Economy (1985), The Treasury Under Mrs Thatcher (1989); *Clubs* Reform; *Style—* Sir Leo Pliatzky, KCB; 27 River Ct, Upper Ground, London SE1 9PE (☎ 071 928 3667)

PLINCKE, John Richard; s of John Frederick Plincke (d 1969), and Norah Mary, *née* Pollard; *b* 29 Oct 1928; *Educ* Stowe, Architectural Assoc Sch of Arch (AADip); *m* 5 Dec 1970, Rosemary Drummond, da of Col Peter Halley Ball, of Hants; 2 da (Katherine b 1971, Anna b 1974); *Career* architect; set up practice 1961, ptnr Plincke, Leaman and Browning Architects and Project Mgmnt Consultants (Winchester) 1971-87, dir Tropical Plants Display Ltd 1977; Civic Tst awards 1984 and 1986; professional artist; notable works incl: Runic Cross Series (I to XIV), Tapestries, Stained Glass Windows at St Marks Church Kempshott 1987; Freeman City of London 1959, Liveryman Worshipful Co of Plaisterers 1975-; MRIBA, RI; *Recreations* sailing, skiing; *Style—* J Richard Plincke, Esq; Plincke, Leaman and Browning Architects, 5 The Square, Winchester, Hants SO23 9ES (☎ 0962 842200)

PLINSTON, John Anthony; s of Capt Harold Plinston, RAMC, and Ruth, *née* Mihalop; *b* 9 Jan 1947; *Educ* Battersea GS; *m* 1, 1969 (m dis 1989), Jean Barbara *née* Candy; 1 s (Adam b 1972), 1 da (Sharon b 1969); m 2, 1989, Susan Margaret, *née* Southwell; 1 da (Natasha b 1989); *Career* articled clerk: Burgess Hodgson & Co 1964-70, with Coopers & Lybrand 1971-73; ptnr: Daeche Dubois & Plinston 1974-, Burgess Hodgson & Co 1981-90, Westbury Schotness & Co 1988-89, dir: Ibex Holdings Ltd and subsid cos 1988-, Coastfront International Ltd 1989-, Sebastian Christian Group and subsid cos 1989-; chm: Merlin Financial Consultants Ltd 1988-, SP Associates Ltd and subsid 1986-; FCA 1971; *Recreations* sport, music, travel; *Style—* John Plinston, Esq; 7 Homefield Road, Warlingham, Surrey CR3 9HU (☎ 0883 627514); 45 Bedford Row, London WC1R 4LR (☎ 071 242 8381, fax 071 405 1904, telex 27460)

PLINT, Dennis Arthur (Jock); BEM 1945; s of Cyril Arthur Plint (d 1944), of Capetown, S Africa, and Dorothy Kate Allnutt (d 1968); *b* 9 March 1924; *Educ* Observatory Boys High Sch Capetown, Cape Town and Witwatersrand Univ (BDS); *m* 16 Dec 1950, Moira Jean, da of Johannes S S Martens (d 1983), of Pieter Maritzburg, S Africa; 2 s (Simon John b 1956, Andrew Charles b 1959); *Career* served S African Forces 1942-46; non resident dental surgn Soweto 1951-52, house surgn St Thomas Hosp London 1952-54, private practice Durban S Africa 1958-60, conslt dental surgn in orthodontics Hastings, Eastbourne and Tunbridge Wells 1961-67, conslt dental surgn in orthodontics and children's dentistry Great Ormond St Hosp 1967-86, conslt dental surgn in orthodontics Royal Dental Hosp 1967-86 (sr registrar and lectr 1957, sr lectr 1960-61); conslt dental surgn: UCH 1987-89, Great Ormond St Children's Hosp 1987-89 (sr house offr 1954-55, registrar 1955-57); ret 1989; FDSRCS, DOrthRCS; *Books* chapters in: Walter's Orthodontic Notes (1975), Scott Brown's ENT (1987); *Recreations* gardening, travel; *Style—* Jock Plint, Esq; Tillingham, Beckley Furnace, nr Brede, Rye, E Sussex (☎ 0424 882 497); Hospital for Sick Children, Gt Ormond St, London WC1; University College Hospital and Dental School

PLOUVIEZ, Peter William; s of Charles Plouviez; *b* 30 July 1931; *Educ* Sir George Monoux GS, Hasting GS; *m* 1978, Alison Dorothy Macrae; 2 da (by former m); *Career* gen sec Br Actors' Equity Assoc 1974-; chm: Radio and TV Safeguards Ctee 1974-, Festival of Br Theatre 1983-90; cncllr St Pancras 1962-65, Parly candidate (Lab) St Marylebone by-election 1963; vice chm Confedn of Entertainment Unions 1974-, vice pres Int Fedn of Actors, treas Entertainment Charities Fund, memb Theatres Tst; *Style—* Peter Plouviez, Esq; 8 Harley St, London W1 (☎ 071 637 9311)

PLOWDEN, Hon Anna Bridget; da of Baron Plowden (Life Peer); *b* 1938; *Educ* Newhall Chelmsford, Inst of Archeology London Univ; *Career* md Plowden & Smith Ltd 190 St Ann's Hill London SW18 2 RT, dir Recollections Ltd; chm Conservation Ctee Crafts Cncl 1979-83, memb Ctee Conservation Unit Museums and Galleries Cmmn, assessor of the Ceramic Restoration Course West Dean Coll Sussex; tstee: St Andrews Conservation Tst Wells, Br Sch of Archaeology Iraq, V&A Museum, Edward James Fndn; memb Cncl Royal Warrant Holders Assoc, fell Int Inst for Conservation of Historic and Artistic Works; *Books* Looking after Antiques (co-author, 1987); *Style—* The Hon Anna Plowden; 46 Brixton Water Lane, London SW2 1QE

PLOWDEN, Baroness; Bridget Horatia; *née* Richmond; DBE (1972); da of late Adm Sir Herbert Richmond, KCB, and Elsa Florence, 2 da of Sir Hugh Bell, 2 Bt, CB, JP, DL, by his 2 w Florence, DBE, JP, da of Sir Joseph Olliffe; *Educ* Downe House; *m* 1933, Baron Plowden, *qv*; 2 s, 2 da; *Career* dir Trust Houses Forte Ltd 1961-72; govr and vice-chm BBC 1970-75, chm IBA 1975-80; vice-chm ILEA Schools Sub-Ctee 1967-70; Advsy Ctee for the Educn of Romany and Other Travellers: memb 1969- (chm 1969-84, pres 1984); pres: Pre-School Playgroups Assoc 1972-82 (vice-pres 1982-), Nat Assoc of Adult Educn 1980-88, Nat Marriage Guidance Cncl 1983-, Voluntary Orgn Liaison Cncl for Under-Fives 1984 (chm 1974-83, pres 1983-); memb Nat Theatre Bd 1976-88; pres Br Accreditation Cncl for Independent Further and Higher Educn 1985-90; Liveryman Worshipful Co of Goldsmiths' 1979-, vice-pres Coll of Preceptors 1983 (pres 1987), JP Inner London Area Juvenile Panel 1962-71, fell Royal TV Soc 1980; Hon LLD: Leicester 1968, Reading 1970, London 1976; Hon DLitt Loughborough 1976, DUniv Open 1974; *Style—* The Rt Hon the Lady Plowden, DBE; Martels Manor, Dunmow, Essex (☎ 0371 2141); 11 Abingdon Gardens, Abingdon Villas, London W8 6BY (☎ 071 937 4238)

PLOWDEN, Baron (Life Peer UK 1959), of Plowden, Co Shropshire; Edwin Noel Plowden; GBE (1987, KBE 1946), KCB (1951); s of late Roger H Plowden; *b* 6 Jan 1907; *Educ* Switzerland, Pembroke Coll Cambridge (hon fell 1958); *m* 1933, Bridget Horatia (*see* Plowden, Baroness); 2 s, 2 da; *Career* sits as Independent in House of Lords; temp civil servant Miny of Econ Warfare 1939-40, Miny Aircraft Prodn 1940-46 (chief exec and memb Aircraft Supply Cncl 1945-46), chief planning offr and chm Econ Planning Bd, HM Treasy 1947-53, vice chm Temp Cncl Ctee of NATO 1951-52; chm: UKAEA 1954-59, various Ctees of Inquiry 1959-79, Tube Investments Ltd 1963-76 (pres 1976-90), London Graduate Sch of Business Studies 1964-76 (pres 1976-), Equity Capital for Indust Ltd 1976-83, Police Complaints Bd 1976-81, Top Salaries Review Body 1981-89 (memb 1977-); independent chm Police Negotiating Bd 1979-83; memb: Ford Euro Advsy Cncl 1976-83, Engrg Industs Cncl 1976, Int Advsy Bd Southeast Bank NA 1982-86; visiting fell Nuffield Coll Oxford 1956-64, hon fell Pembroke Coll Cambridge; Hon DSc Pennsylvania State Univ 1958, Hon DSc Aston 1972, Hon DLitt Loughborough 1976; *Books* An Industrialist in the Treasury: The Post War Years; *Style—* The Rt Hon the Lord Plowden, GBE, KCB; Martels Manor, Dunmow, Essex (☎ 0371 872141); 11 Abingdon Gardens, Abingdon Villas, London W8 6BY (☎ 071 937 4238)

PLOWDEN, Hon Francis John; s of Baron Plowden (Life Peer); *b* 1945; *Educ* Eton, Trinity Coll Cambridge; *m* Geraldine *née* Wickman; *Career* CA 1969; seconded to Fin Mgmnt Unit HM Treasy/MPO 1981-82, ptnr i/c Govt Servs Div Cooper Lybrand Assocs Ltd 1986- (dir 1983-); govr Royal Ballet Sch 1989-, tstee Royal Armouries 1989-; *Style—* The Hon Francis Plowden; 63 St John's Avenue, London SW15 6AL

PLOWDEN, William Francis Godfrey; JP (1953 Shropshire); o s of Roger Edmund Joseph Plowden, JP (d 1946), and his 1 w, Mary Florence, *née* Cholmondeley (d 1930); the Plowden family has been seated at Plowden since the C12, when Roger de Plowden is believed to have been present at the siege of Acre 1191 (*see* Burke's Landed Gentry, 18 edn, vol III, 1972); *b* 4 Dec 1925; *Educ* Beaumont, RAC Cirencester; *m* 17 July 1951, Valerie Ann, o da of Cdr Athelstan Paul Bush, DSO, RN (d 1970), of Tockington Court, nr Bristol; 3 s (Roger Godfrey Paul b 8 Feb 1953, Francis Richard Piers b 12 Jan 1957, Charles Edmund Philip b 31 Dec 1960), 1 da (Jacqueline Mary Prudence b 27 Feb 1954); *Career* serv WWII in Rifle Bde 1943-46; farmer on family estate; High Sheriff of Shropshire 1967; *Recreations* hunting, fishing, shooting; *Style—* William Plowden, Esq, JP; Plowden Hall, Lydbury North, Shropshire (☎ 058 88246)

PLOWDEN, Hon William Julius Lowthian; s of Baron Plowden (Life Peer); *b* 1935; *Educ* Eton, King's Coll Cambridge, California Univ; *m* 1960, Veronica Mary, da of Lt-Col Derek Ernest Frederick Orby Gascoigne; 2 s, 2 da; *Career* under sec Dept of Indust 1977-78, dir-gen Royal Inst of Public Adm 1978-88; visiting prof Dept of Govt LSE 1982-88; exec dir UK Harkness Fellowships New York 1988-; *Style—* The Hon William Plowden; 49 Stockwell Park Rd, London SW9 (☎ 071 274 4535)

PLOWDEN ROBERTS, (Hugh) Martin; s of Stanley Plowden Roberts, OBE (d 1968), and Joan Aline Mary, *née* Mawdesley; *b* 6 Aug 1932; *Educ* St Edwards Sch Oxford, St Edmund Hall Oxford (BA, MA); *m* 22 Sept 1956, Susan Jane, da of Andrew Patrick (d 1979), of Melton Grange, Ferriby, Humberside; 2 da (Alexandra b 1961, Caroline b 1964); *Career* dir Payne & Son Meat Group Ltd 1958-60, asst gen mangr CWS Meat Group 1960-67; dir: Allied Suppliers Ltd 1967-82, Cavenham Ltd 1979-82 (chm 1981-82); dep chm Argyll Stores Ltd 1983-85; dir: Argyll Group plc 1983-, Plowden Roberts Association Ltd 1984-; chm Dairy Crest Ltd 1985-88, dir Lawson

Mardon Group Ltd 1987-, memb Milk Mktg Bd 1983-89; Liveryman Worshipful Co of Butchers 1958; fell Inst of Grocery Distribution 1983; *Clubs* Farmers; *Style*— Martin Plowden Roberts, Esq; Barn Cottage, Fulking, Henfield, West Sussex BN5 9NH (☎ 0273 857622); Argyll Group plc, 6 Millington Rd, Hayes, Middx UB3 4AY (☎ 081 848 8744, fax 081 573 1865, telex 934888)

PLOWMAN, John Patrick; s of Robert Gilbee Plowman, of Bolter End, Bucks, and Ruth Wynn, *née* Dutton; *b* 20 March 1944; *Educ* St Edward's Sch Oxford, Univ of Grenoble, Univ of Durham (BA); *m* 8 Sept 1973, Daphne Margaret, Dr Alexander Kennett (d 1984), of Swanage, Dorset; 2 s (Hugo b 1977, William b 1981), 1 da (Katherine b 1974); *Career* Lt Royal Marines Res 1967-70; MOD: joined 1967, Private Office Ministers of State for Def 1969-71; on secondment: Civil Service Selection Bd 1975, Cabinet Office 1976-78; memb Bd of Supplies Property Servs Agency 1982-84, DOE 1984-87 and 1990-, UK permanent rep to the European Communities 1987-90; FBIM 1984; *Recreations* skiing, tennis, cricket, fly fishing, choral singing; *Clubs* Royal Overseas League; *Style*— John Plowman; Department of Environment, Romney House, Marshal St, London SW1P 3PY

PLOWMAN, Sir John Robin; CBE (1970, OBE 1949); s of Owen Plowman; *b* 18 Sept 1908,Bermuda; *Educ* Bermuda and England; *m* 1936, Marjorie Hardwick (d 1989); 2 s; *Career* various Govt boards and cmmns 1942-68; Miny: Organisation 1968-77 and 1980-82, Marine & Air 1977-80; govt leader Legislative Cncl (now Senate) 1968-82; kt 1979; *Style*— Sir John Plowman, CBE; Chiswick, Paget, Bermuda

PLOWRIGHT, David Ernest; s of William Ernest Plowright; *b* 11 Dec 1930; *Educ* Scunthorpe GS; *m* 1953, Brenda Mary, *née* Key; 1 s, 2 da; *Career* Granada TV: joined as news ed 1958 (from Yorkshire Post), progr prod 1960, exec prod of news and current affrs 1966 (in charge World In Action), prog controller 1969-79, jt md Granada TV Ltd 1976-81 (md 1981-87, chm 1987-), dir Granada Gp 1981- (exec responsibility for drama including Brideshead Revisited and Laurence Olivier's King Lear); dir: Br Screen Ltd, Inward; memb: Tate in the North Advsy Ctee, Civic Tst in the NW, Euro Film and TV Forum, Manchester Olympic Bid Ctee, Int Cncl; vice pres Royal TV Soc, tstee of BAFTA; *Recreations* sailing, theatre, television; *Style*— David Plowright; Westways, Wilmslow Rd, Mottram St Andrew, Prestbury, Cheshire; Granada TV Ltd, Manchester M60 9EA (☎ 061 832 7211); Granada TV, 36 Golden Square, W1 (☎ 071 734 8080)

PLOWRIGHT, Joan Ann; (Lady Olivier), CBE (1970); da of William Ernest Plowright; *b* 28 Oct 1929; *Educ* Scunthorpe GS, Laban Art of Movement Studio, Old Vic Theatre Sch; *m* 1, 1953 (m dis) Roger Gage; m 2, 1961, Sir Laurence Olivier, later Baron Olivier (Life Peer, d 1989); 1 s, 2 da; *Career* leading actress stage, film and TV; memb Cncl RADA; *Recreations* reading, music, entertaining; *Style*— Miss Joan Plowright, CBE; c/o LOP Ltd, 33-34 Chancery Lane, WC2A 1EN (☎ 071 836 7932)

PLOWRIGHT, Rosalind Anne; da of Robert Arthur Plowright, and Celia Adelaide Plowright; *b* 21 May 1949; *Educ* Notre Dame HS Wigan, Royal Northern Coll of Music Manchester; *m* 1984, James Anthony Kaye; 1 s (Daniel Robert), 1 da (Katherine Anne); *Career* soprano; London Opera Centre 1974-75, debut as Agathe in Der Freischutz (Glyndebourne Chorus and Touring Co) 1975, with ENO, WNO and Kent Opera 1975-78, Miss Jessel in Turn of the Screw (END) 1979, Ortlinde in Die Walküre (Royal Opera House debut) 1980; 1980-81: Bern Opera (Adriadne, Alceste), Frankfurt Opera (Ariadne, Aida, Il Trovatore), Munich Opera (Ariadne); debuts: 1982 (USA, Paris, Madrid, Hamburg), 1983 (La Scala, Milan, Edinburgh Festival, San Francisco, Carnegie Hall NY), 1985 (Berlin, Houston, Pittsburgh, Vernon), 1986 (Rome, Florence, Holland), 1987 (Tulsa, NY Philharmonic, Buenos Aires, Santiago, Chile, Israel, Paris Opera, Bonn), 1988 (Lausanne, Geneva, Oviedo, Bilbao), 1989 (Zurich, Copenhagen, Lisbon), 1990 (Vienna); principal roles include: Aida, Amelia in Un Ballo in Maschera, Desdemona in Otello, Elizabetta in Don Carlos, Leonora in Il Trovatore and La Forza del Destino, Violetta in La Traviata, Abigaille in Nabucco, Giorgetta in Il Tabarro; First Prize Int Competition for Opera Singers (Sofia 1979), Prix Fndn Fanny Heldy (Nat Acad du Disque Lyrique 1985); *Recreations* fell walking; *Style*— Ms Rosalind Plowright; c/o Kaye Artists Management Ltd, Kingsmead House, 250 Kings Rd, London SW3 5UE (☎ 071 376 3456)

PLOWRIGHT, Dr Walter; CMG (1974); s of Jonathan Plowright; *b* 20 July 1923; *Educ* Moulton and Spalding GS, RVC London; *m* 1959, Dorothy Joy, *née* Bell; *Career* with Colonial Vet and Res Servs (Kenya and Nigeria) 1950-63, Animal Virus Res Inst Pirbright 1963-71, prof of vet microbiology RVC 1971-78, head Dept of Microbiology Inst for Res on Animal Diseases 1978-83; King Baudouin Int Devpt prize 1984; Hon DSc: Univ of Nairobi 1984, Univ of Reading 1986; Gold award Office Int des Epizooties 1988; FRCVS, FRS; *Style*— Dr Walter Plowright, CMG, FRS; Whitehill Lodge, Reading Rd, Goring, Reading RG8 OLL ☎ (0491 872891)

PLOWS, Fiona Kay; da of Harold William Plows (d 1984), of Bournemouth, and Sarah, *née* Burgess; *b* 3 May 1938; *Educ* Bromley HS, UCL (LLB); *m* 1, 4 Sept 1965 (m dis 1972), (Michael) Jeremy Brown, s of Norman Marcus Brown (d 1969), of Chislehurst, Kent; m 2, 14 July 1977, David Michael Huntington Alderson, s of Nathan Alderson (d 1984), of Burnley, Lancs; *Career* admitted slr 1963; currently sr ptnr Godfrey Davis & Baldwin (Mitcham); life govr Imp Cancer Res Fund;Freeman City of London; memb Law Soc; *Recreations* theatre, travel, opera, wining, dining, history, archaeology; *Style*— Miss Fiona Plows; 19a Upper Green East, Mitcham, Surrey CR4 2XD (☎ 081 648 5221, fax 081 648 6830)

PLUMB, Baron (Life Peer UK 1987), of Coleshill, Co Warwicks; (Charles) Henry Plumb; DL (Warwicks 1977), MEP (EDG) The Cotswolds 1979-; s of Charles Plumb, of Ansley, Warwicks, and Louise, *née* Fisher; *b* 27 March 1925; *Educ* King Edward VI Sch Nuneaton; *m* 1947, Marjorie Dorothy, da of Thomas Victor Dunn, of Bentley, Warwicks; 1 s (Hon John Henry b 1951), 2 da (Hon Mrs Holman, Hon Mrs Mayo, *qqv*); *Career* ldr (Cons) EDG Euro Parl 1982-87, pres Euro Parl 1987-89; pres NFU 1970-79 (dep pres 1966-69, vice pres 1964-66, memb Cncl 1959-), chm Br Agric Cncl 1975-79; pres Warwicks County Fedn of Young Farmers' Clubs 1974-, pres Nat Fedn 1976-86; memb Cncl: CBI, Animal Health Tst; pres: COPA 1975-77, RASE 1977 (dep pres 1978), Int Fedn of Agric Prodrs 1979-; chm Agric Ctee Euro Parl 1979-82, hon pres Ayrshire Cattle Soc; non-exec dir: United Biscuits, Lloyds Bank, Fisons; Liveryman Worshipful Co of Farmers; Hon Fell Wye Coll, Hon DSc Cranfield 1983; FRSA 1970, FRAgS 1974; Order of Merit (Federal Republic of Germany) 1976, Gd Cross Order of Merit (Portugal) 1987, Order of Merit (Luxembourg) 1988, Grand Cross Order of Civil Merit (Spain) 1989; kt 1973; *Clubs* Farmers', St Stephens, Coleshill Rotary (hon memb); *Style*— The Rt Hon Lord Plumb, DL, MEP; Maxstoke, Coleshill, Warwickshire B46 2QJ (☎ 0675 63133, telex 0675 464156); 2 Queen Anne's Gate, London SW1 (☎ 071 222 0411)

PLUMB, Prof Sir John Harold; s of late James Plumb, of Leicester; *b* 20 Aug 1911; *Educ* Alderman Newton's Sch Leicester, Univ Coll Leicester, Christ's Coll Cambridge (PhD, LittD); *Career* historian; prof of modern English history Univ of Cambridge 1966-74, master Christ's Coll Cambridge 1978-82, chm Centre of E Anglian Studies 1979-82; tstee Nat Portrait Gallery 1961-82; Hon DLitt: Univ of Leicester 1968, UEA 1973, Bowdoin Coll 1974, Univ of S California 1978, Westminster Coll 1983, Washington Univ, St Louis 1983, Bard Coll 1987; FRHistS, FSA, FRSL, FBA; kt 1982; *Clubs* Brooks's; *Style*— Sir John Plumb, FSA; Christ's College, Cambridge (☎ 0223 334900); The Old Rectory, Westhorpe, Stowmarket, Suffolk (☎ 0449 781235)

PLUMBE, (Philip) Graham; s of John Philip Hubert Plumbe (d 1980), of Crundall House, Crookham Village, Fleet, Hants, and Winifred, *née* Roberts; *b* 28 Sept 1933; *Educ* Berkhamsted Sch, Coll of Estate Management Univ of Reading; *m* 6 Nov 1965, Rachel Mary, da of Noel Cattell Kemp; 1 s (Timothy Guy b 28 June 1970), 1 da (Joanna Mary b 28 Oct 1967); *Career* RAF pilot Fighter Cmmd then Flt Lt 1952-56; clerk Dalgety & Co Ltd 1950-51, trainee surveyor Edward Erdman & Co 1957-63; Gooch & Wagstaff (Chartered Surveyors): joined 1963, ptnr 1972, chm Management Bd 1988-90, sr ptnr 1990; regular arbitration appointments and memb sundry professional ctees and working parties; Freeman City of London 1976, Liveryman Worshipful Co of Gold and Silver Wyre Drawers 1976; FRICS 1973, FCIArb 1975; *Recreations* golf, squash, gardening; *Clubs* North Hants Golf; *Style*— Graham Plumbe, Esq; Gooch & Wagstaff, 73 Watling St, London EC4M 9BL (☎ 071 248 2044, fax 071 236 4659)

PLUMBE, (Edwin) John Astley; s of Edwin Raymond Plumbe (d 1963), and Jessie Louisa, *née* Avis (d 1964); *b* 24 Dec 1914; *Educ* Weymouth Coll; *m* 1, 29 Dec 1948, Eleanor Burleigh (d 1956), da of Harry L Pope (d 1956), of Fairhaven, USA; 1 s (John Lawrence b 26 Oct 1952), 1 da (Robin Cornelia (Mrs Wood) b 25 Nov 1949); m 2, 2 Dec 1960, Katherine Bethune, *née* Macdonald; 2 da decd; *Career* Lt-Col 4/10 Baluch 1A, AA and QMG 10 Indian Div; former exec insur co, conslt and dir Antigua, Singapore, Jamaica, Kenya, India, Italy; dir Norfolk Boat (Sail Trg) Ltd, pres Wells branch Cons Assoc; *Recreations* enjoying old age; *Clubs* HAC, Oriental, Norfolk; *Style*— John Plumbe, Esq; Yew Tree House, Wells-next-the-Sea, Norfolk NR23 1EZ (☎ 0328 710357)

PLUMBLEY, Philip Rodney; s of Alfred Daniel Plumbley (d 1970), of Freshwater, and Emily Amelia, *née* Jackson (d 1962); *b* 29 Aug 1931; *Educ* Co GS Newport IOW, Univ of Bristol (BA); *m* 13 April 1957, Shelagh Morell, da of Capt Howard Morell Holmes (d 1963); 1 s (Peter b 1964), 1 da (Rachel b 1962); *Career* Sgt Air Signaller 220 Sqn RAF Coastal Cmd 1951-53; NIIP 1964-65, MSL/ASL 1965-70, md Compton Ptnrs Recruitment and Fin Advertising and Consultancy Div 1970-72, co founder and dir Plumbley Endicotte Assoc Ltd (1973) Executive Search Consultancy; chm high Wycombe Operatic Soc 1985-; *Recreations* music, sailing; *Clubs* IOD; *Style*— Philip R Plumbley, Esq; Easterton, Ellesborough Rd, Wendover, Bucks (☎ 0296 622116); Premier House, 150 Southampton Row, London WC1B 5AL (☎ 071 278 3117)

PLUMBLY, Derek John; s of John Cecil Plumbly (d 1987), and Jean Elizabeth, *née* Baker; *b* 15 May 1948; *Educ* Brockenhurst GS, Magdalen Coll Oxford (BA); *m* 10 Nov 1979, Nadia, da of Youssef Gohar, of Cairo, Egypt; 2 s (Samuel b 1985, Joseph b 1987), 1 da (Sara b 1983); *Career* VSO Pakistan 1970-71, FCO 1972, second sec Jedda 1975, first sec Cairo 1977, FCO 1980, first sec Washington 1984, cnsllr and dep head mission Riyadh 1988; *Style*— Derek Plumbly, Esq; FCO, King Charles Street, London SW1

PLUME, John Trevor; s of William Thomas Plume, and Alice Gertrude, *née* Edwards; *b* 5 Oct 1914; *Educ* City of London Sch; *m* 5 April 1947, Christine Mary, da of Samuel Albert Wells; 1 da (Katherine Mary); *Career* enlisted Army 1940, demobbed Capt RA 1946; called to the Bar Gray's Inn 1936; bencher Gray's Inn 1969, regnl chm Indust Tbnls 1984-87 (chm 1976-); legal assoc memb Royal Town Planning Inst 1939; Liveryman Worshipful Co of Clockmakers 1977; *Recreations* bee keeping, gardening, fishing, carpentry; *Style*— John Plume, Esq; Mulberry Cottage, Forest Side, Epping, Essex CM16 4ED (☎ 0378 72389)

PLUMMER, Maj-Gen Leo Heathcote; CBE (1974); s of Lt-Col Edmund Waller Plummer, DSO (d 1958), of Farnham, Surrey, and Mary Dorothy, *née* Brookesmith (d 1984); *b* 11 June 1923; *Educ* Canford Sch, Queen's Coll Cambridge; *m* 13 April 1955, Judyth Ann, da of Edward Victor Dolby, OBE (d 1973), of Eardisley, Hereford and Worcester; 3 da (Virginia, Sara, Nicola); *Career* cmmnd RA 1943, 17 Field Regt served N Africa, Sicily, Italy, Austria 1943-47, Adj LAA Regt RA TA 1947-49, 66 Airborne Light Regt 1949-50, 4 RHA 1950-51, Staff Coll Camberley 1952, GSO 2 HQ Anti-Aircraft Cmd 1953-54, BMRA 7 Armd Div 1957-59, Jt Servs Staff Coll 1959, battery cdr 39 Missile Regt 1960-61, brevet Lt-Col 1961, directing staff Staff Coll Camberley 1961-63, Cmdt Sudan Armed Forces Staff Sch 1963-65, CO 20 Heavy Regt 1965-67, Col Gen Staff MOD 1967, Brig Cdr 1 Artillery Bde 1967-70, dep dir Manning Army MOD 1971-74, asst chief staff ops HQ Northern Army Gp 1974-76, ADC to HM the Queen 1974-76, Maj-Gen chief Jt Servs Liaison Orgn Bonn 1976-78, ret 1979; chm Civil Serv Cmmn Panel 1983-90; churchwarden: All Saints' Cologne 1976-78, All Saints' Icklesham E Sussex 1981-85; memb SSAFA Canterbury 1987-; *Recreations* gardening; *Clubs* Army and Navy; *Style*— Maj-Gen Leo Plummer, CBE; 1 High St, Wingham, Canterbury, Kent CT3 1AY (☎ 0227 720 538)

PLUMMER, Hon Sally Jane; da of Baron Plummer of St Marylebone (Life Peer); *Educ* Francis Holland Sch for Girls, Roedean, London Univ; *Career* human resources mgmnt conslt; *Recreations* animal welfare; *Style*— The Hon Sally Plummer; 33 Huntsworth Mews, Regent's Park, London NW1 6DD

PLUMMER OF ST MARYLEBONE, Baron (Life Peer UK 1981), of the City of Westminster; Sir (Arthur) Desmond (Herne) Plummer; TD (1950), JP (London 1958), DL (Greater London 1970); s of late Arthur Herne Plummer, and late Janet McCormick; *b* 25 May 1914; *Educ* Hurstpierpoint Coll, Coll of Estate Mgmnt; *m* 1941, Ella Margaret (Pat), da of Albert Holloway, of Epping; 1 da (Hon Sally Jane); *Career* sits as Cons peer in House of Lords; Mayor St Marylebone Borough Cncl 1958-59 (memb 1952-65), LCC St Marylebone 1960-65, ILEA 1964-76, GLC (memb for Cities of London and Westminster 1964-73, for St Marylebone 1973-76), ldr of oppn 1966-67, ldr of Cncl GLC 1967-73; pres: Portman Bldg Soc 1990- (chm 1983-90), Nat Employers' Life Assur Co 1983-88, Horserace Betting Levy Bd 1974-82, Epsom and Walton Downs Trg Grounds Mgmnt Bd 1974-82; Nat Stud 1975-82, pres: Met Assoc of Bldg Socs 1983-89, London Anglers' Assoc 1976-; FAI 1948, FRICS 1970, FRSA 1974, Hon FFAS 1966, KStJ 1986; kt 1971; *Clubs* Carlton, RAC; *Style*— The Rt Hon the Lord Plummer of St Marylebone, TD, DL; 4 The Lane, Marlborough Place, St Johns Wood, London NW8 OPN

PLUMPTON, Alan; CBE (1980), JP (Monmouthshire 1971); s of John Plumpton (d 1978), of Sunderland, Co Durham, and Doris, *née* Barrett; *b* 24 Nov 1926; *Educ* Sunderland Tech Sch, Univ of Durham (BSc), Henley Admin Staff Coll; *m* 9 Dec 1950, Audrey; 1 s (Nigel b 5 July 1953), 1 da (Jill (Mrs Stiel) b 3 Oct 1956); *Career* N Eastern Electricity Bd: graduate engr 1948-49, asst distribution engr 1949-57, dist commercial engr Stockton 1957-60; S Wales Electricity Bd: dist mangr E Monmouthshire Dist 1961-64, dep chief commercial engr 1964-67, chief commercial engr 1967-72; London Electricity Bd: dep chm 1972-76, chm 1976-80; dep chm Electricity Cncl 1981-86, dir Schlumberger Measurement and Systems (UK) Ltd 1985-87; chm: Manx Electricity Cncl 1985-, Ewbank Preece Group Ltd 1986-, Schlumberger Measurement and Control (UK) Ltd 1988-; memb: Cncl Inst of Electrical Engrs UK 1983-87, Jt Ctee of Princs Electricity Bd/Br Electrical & Allied Mfrs Assoc UK 1981-86, Br Nat Ctee of CIGRE 1981-85, Directing Ctee of UNIPEDE 1975-81, Br Nat Ctee and Exec Ctee World Energy Conf 1981-, Industl Policy Ctee CBI Industs 1981-85; chm Euro Panel of Nationalised Industs 1983-85; former chm Pontypool RDC, former memb Gwent Water Authy; Freeman and

Liveryman Worshipful Co of Gardeners 1978; FIEE, FCIBSE, CBIM, FRSA; *Recreations* golf, gardening; *Clubs* City Livery, IOD, Harewood Downs Golf; *Style*— Alan Plumpton, Esq, CBE, JP; Lockhill, Stubbs Wood, Amersham, Bucks HP6 6EX (☎ 024 03 3791); Ewbank Preece, North Street, Brighton BN1 1RW (☎ 0273 724533, fax 0273 200483, telex 878102 EPLBTN G)

PLUMPTRE, Hon Francis Charles; yst s of 21 Baron FitzWalter, and Margaret Melisina, *née* Deedes; *b* 30 May 1963; *Educ* St Edmund's Sch Canterbury Kent; *Style*— The Hon Francis Plumptre; Goodnestone Park, Canterbury, Kent

PLUMPTRE, Hon (Wyndham) George; s of 21 Baron FitzWalter, *qv*, and Margaret Melesina, *née* Deedes; *b* 24 April 1956; *Educ* Radley, Jesus Coll Cambridge; *m* 1984, Alexandra Elizabeth, da of Prince Michael Cantacuzene, Count Speransky and Mrs James Edwards; 2 s (Wyndham James Alexander b 1986, Piers Harry Constantine b 1987); *Career* Sotheby's rep in Kent 1991-; author; *Books* Royal Gardens (1981), Collins Book of British Gardens (1985), The Fast Set (1985), Homes of Cricket (1988), The Latest Country Gardens (1988), Cricket Caricatures and Cartoons (1989), Garden Ornament (1989), The Golden Age of Cricket (1990), Barclays World of Cricket (ed, 1986), Back Page Cricket (ed, 1987), Back Page Racing (ed, 1989); *Clubs* Beefsteak; *Style*— The Hon George Plumptre; Rowling House, Goodnestone, Canterbury, Kent CT3 1QB (☎ 0304 813287)

PLUMPTRE, Hon Henry Bridges; 2 s of 21 Baron FitzWalter; *b* 18 Feb 1954; *m* 1981, Susie, only da of F T Payne, of Waverley Station, Scone, NSW; 1 s (Sam b 1982), 1 da (Camilla b 1984); *Style*— The Hon Henry Plumptre; Lordship Stud, Newmarket, Suffolk

PLUMPTRE, Hon Julian Brook; s and h of 21 Baron FitzWalter, and Margaret Melesina, *née* Deedes; *b* 18 Oct 1952; *Educ* Radley, Wye Coll London (BSc); *m* March 1988, Alison Sally, *née* Quiney; 1 s (Edward Brook b 26 April 1989); *Career* land agency; *Style*— The Hon Julian Plumptre; Crixhall Court, Staple, Canterbury, Kent

PLUMPTRE, Hon William Edward; s of 21 Baron FitzWalter, and Margaret Melesina, *née* Deedes; *b* 23 July 1959; *Educ* Milton Abbey Sch Dorset; *Style*— The Hon William Plumptre; Fell Yeat, Martsop, Patterdale, Penrith, Cumbria

PLUNKET, Aileen Sibell Mary; resumed use of first husband's surname; da of Arthur Ernest Guinness, JP, DL (d 1949, 2 s of 1 Earl of Iveagh, KP, GCVO), and Marie Clotilde (d 1953), da of Sir George Russell, 4 Bt; Mrs Aileen Plunket's wedding present from her f was Lutrellstown Castle and estate, in Co Dublin, Ireland, which she sold at auction in Oct 1983; *b* 16 May 1904; *m* 1, 16 Nov 1927 (m dis 1940), Flt Lt Hon Brinsley Sheridan Bushe Plunket, RAFVR (ka 1941), 2 s of 5 Baron Plunket, GCMG, KCVO, KBE; 3 da (1 decd); m 2, 1956 (m dis 1965), Valerian Stux-Rybar, s of Geza Stux-Rybar; *Style*— Mrs Aileen Plunket

PLUNKET, Hon Mrs (Denis) Kiwa; Pamela Mary; da of late James Watherston, of Christchurch, NZ; *m* 1962, the Hon (Denis) Kiwa Plunket (d 1970), s of 5 Baron Plunket, GCMG, KCVO, KBE (d 1920); *Style*— The Hon Mrs Kiwa Plunket; 16 Town Hill, W Malling, Kent ME19 6QN (☎ 0732 841197)

PLUNKET, 8 Baron (UK 1827); Robin Rathmore Plunket; s of 6 Baron Plunket (d 1938), and bro of 7 Baron (d 1975); *b* 3 Dec 1925; *Educ* Eton; *m* 1951, Jennifer, da of late Bailey Southwell, of S Africa; *Heir* bro, Hon Shaun Albert Frederick Sheridan Plunket; *Career* formerly Capt Rifle Bde; *Style*— The Rt Hon the Lord Plunket; Rathmore, Chimanimani, Zimbabwe; 39 Lansdowne Gdns, London SW8 (☎ 071 622 6049)

PLUNKET, Hon Shaun Albert Frederick Sheridan; s of 6 Baron Plunket, and Dorothé, *née* Lewis (both died in aircrash in USA 1938); hp of bro, 8 Baron Plunket; *b* 5 April 1931; *Educ* Eton, L'Institut de Touraine; *m* 1, 1961, Judith Ann, er da of late Gerard Patrick Power, of Lapworth, Warwickshire; 1 s (Tyrone Shaun Terence b 1966), 1 da (Loelia Dorothé Alexandra b 1963); m 2, 1980, Mrs Elisabeth de Sancha, da of late Helge Drangel, of Stockholm, formerly w of T de Sancha (d 1986); m 3, 1989, Mrs Andrea Reynolds, da of late André Milos; *Career* formerly Lt Irish Gds, ADC to GOC Rhine Army 1951-52, dist cmdt Kenya Police Res (Mau Mau) 1953; Hambros Bank, dir Garrod & Lofthouse Ltd 1956-66, chm and md Wilmington Overseas Security Ltd 1978-, memb Lloyd's, vice chm Arthritis Care; tstee Lady Hoare Tst; FIOD; *Clubs* White's, Vanderbilt, Mark's; *Style*— The Hon Shaun Plunket; 11 Ennismore Gardens, London SW7 5AA (☎ 071 584 1099)

PLUNKETT, Hon Edward Carlos; s (by 1 m) and h of Randal Arthur Plunkett, 19 Baron Dunsany, and Vera de Sá Sotto Maior; *b* 10 Sept 1939; *Educ* Eton, Slade Sch, Ecole des Beaux Arts Paris; *m* 1982, Maria Alice Villela de Carvalho; 2 s (Randal b 1983, Oliver b 1985); *Career* artist and architectural designer, princ de Marsillac Plunkett Architecture PC (architects); *Recreations* chess; *Style*— The Hon Edward Plunkett; 45 East 89th St, New York, NY 10028 (☎ 212 410 0795); 38 East 57th St, New York, NY 10022 (☎ 212 750 6145, fax 212 980 1025)

PLUNKETT, Hon Jonathan Oliver; s and h of 16 Baron Louth; *b* 4 Nov 1952; *Educ* De La Salle Coll Jersey, Hautlieu Sch Jersey, Hull Univ (BSc); *m* 1981, Jennifer, da of Norman Oliver Hodgetts, of Weston-super-Mare; 1 s (Matthew Oliver b 22 Dec 1982), 1 da (Agatha Elizabeth b 17 Aug 1985); *Career* electronics engr; AMIEE; *Style*— The Hon Jonathan Plunkett; Les Sercles, La Grande Pièce, St Peter, Jersey, CI

PLUNKETT, Patrick Trevor; s of Oliver Plunkett Judge of the Supreme Ct Colonial Serv and Judge in Mixed Courts of Egypt (Order of the Nile 1945) and half bro of late George Noble, Count Plunkett (d 1971), and Cordelia Edmée (d 1988 aged 100), da of Lt Col Sir Edward Wheler, 12 Bt (E 1660); *b* 13 June 1908; *Educ* St Gerards Bray Co Wicklow Ireland, Douai Sch Woolhampton Berks; *m* 18 May 1939, Penelope Mary, da of late Raymond Dumas (chm Willis Faber & Dumas), of Hill Deverill Manor, Hill Deverill, Wilts; 2 s ((Oliver) David b 1939, Peter Nicholas b 1948), 3 da (Davinia (Mrs Sainthill) b 1945, (Rosalyn) Lindy (Mrs Charles Spencer Bernard) b 1947, Georgina (Mrs Ian Agnew) b 1949); *Career* WWII 1940-45: IA, Adj Scinde Horse, ADC to GOC Waziristan Dist NW Frontier (Datta Khel Ops 1941), Staff College Quetta 1943, Staff Capt Br Heavy Armoured Bde, Major DAAG CHQ MEF, Aux Cavalry India Southern Provinces Mounted Rifles 1930-40; tea estate mgmnt S India 1930-40; farmer 1945-63; memb: Exec Ctee Cornwall Co NFU, Far-West Area Ctee Milk Mktg Bd; mktg conslt NRDC 1958-59, farming journalist; govr Liskeard Secdy Mod Sch; Bachelor Robinson & Co Ltd Birmingham 1963-73 (overseas mktg dir, factory md, ret 1973); Somerset Co BRCS: a centre organiser, memb Co Branch Ctee; *Recreations* racing, reading, contemplation of pretty girls!; *Clubs* Army and Navy; *Style*— Patrick Plunkett, Esq; Wyatts Leaze, Seend, Melksham, Wiltshire SN12 6PN (☎ 0380 828330)

PLUNKETT, Hon Stephanie Patricia; da of 16 Baron Louth; *b* 1963; *Educ* Beaulieu Convent Jersey; *Career* equine technician; *Recreations* reading, travel, equitation; *Style*— The Hon Stephanie Plunkett; Les Sercles, La Grande Piece, St Peter, Jersey CI

PLUNKETT, Hon Timothy James Oliver; s of 16 Baron Louth; *b* 1956; *Educ* de la Salle Coll Jersey; *m* 20 Oct 1984, Julie Anne Cook; 1 s (Joseph Timothy Oliver b 16 Oct 1989), 1 da (Sophie Louise b 7 Sep 1987); *Recreations* sailing, diving (sub aqua); *Style*— The Hon Timothy Plunkett

PLUNKETT-ERNLE-ERLE-DRAX, Henry Walter; JP (1971), DL (1979); s of Adm the Hon Sir Reginald Aylmer Ranfurly Plunkett-Ernle-Erle-Drax (2 s of 17 Baron Dunsany); *b* 18 March 1928; *Educ* RNC Dartmouth; *m* 1957, Hon Pamela Rose, *qv*; 5 s; *Career* served RN 1945-68; landowner, farmer, forester; co dir; govr: Milton Abbey Sch, Canford Sch; *Recreations* skiing, shooting, fishing, tennis, golf; *Style*— Henry Plunkett-Ernle-Erle-Drax, Esq, JP, DL, RN; Charborough Park, Wareham, Dorset BH20 7EW (☎ 0258 857368, office 0258 857484)

PLUNKETT-ERNLE-ERLE-DRAX, Hon Mrs (Pamela Rose); *née* Weeks; da of Lt-Gen 1 and last Baron Weeks, KCB, CBE, DSO, MC, TD (d 1960), and his 2 w, Cynthia Mary, *née* Irvine (d 1985); *b* 9 Nov 1931; *m* 6 April 1957, Lt-Cdr Henry Plunkett-Ernle-Erle-Drax, RN, *qv*; 5 s; *Style*— The Hon Mrs Plunkett-Ernle-Erle-Drax; Charborough Park, Wareham, Dorset BH20 7EW (☎ 0258 857368)

PLURENDEN, Baroness; Dorothee Monica; da of Maj Robert Bateman Prust, OBE, of Vancouver, BC, Canada; *m* 1951, 1 and last Baron Plurenden (d 1978); 2 da (Rosanne, Francesca); *Style*— The Rt Hon the Lady Plurenden; Plurenden Manor, High Halden, Ashford, Kent; Lidostrasse 63, 6314 Unterägeri, Switzerland

PLYMOUTH, 3 Earl of (UK 1905); Other Robert Ivor Windsor-Clive; DL (Salop 1961); Viscount Windsor (UK 1905), Baron Windsor (E 1529); s of 2 Earl of Plymouth, DL, PC (d 1943), and Lady Irene Corona, *née* Charteris (d 1989), da of 11 Earl of Wemyss; *b* 9 Oct 1923; *Educ* Eton; *m* 1950, Caroline Helen, da of Edward Rice, of Dane Court, Eastry, Kent; 3 s, 1 da; *Heir* s, Viscount Windsor; *Career* late Coldstream Gds; memb Standing Cmmn on Museums and Galleries 1972-82, chm Reviewing Ctee on Export of Works of Art 1982-85; FRSA; KStJ; *Style*— The Rt Hon the Earl of Plymouth, DL; Oakly Park, Ludlow, Shropshire (☎ 0584 77243)

PLYMOUTH, Bishop of 1988-; Rt Rev Richard Stephen Hawkins; s of John Stanley Hawkins (d 1965), and Elsie, *née* Briggs; *b* 2 April 1939; *Educ* Exeter Sch, Exeter Coll Oxford (MA), St Stephen's House Oxford, Univ of Exeter (BPhil); *m* 1966, Valerie Ann, da of Leonard William Herneman; 2 s (Simon b 1967 decd, Daniel b 1973), 2 da (Rebecca b 1968, Caroline b 1972 decd); *Career* team vicar Clyst Valley Team Ministry 1966-78, jt dir Exeter-Truro Min Trg Sch and Bishop of Exeters Offr for Ministry 1978-81, Diocesan dir of Ordinands 1979-81, archdeacon of Totnes 1981-88; *Style*— The Rt Rev the Bishop of Plymouth; 31 Riverside Walk, Tamerton Foloit, Plymouth, Devon PL5 4AQ (☎ 0752 769836)

POBERESKIN, Louis Howard; *b* 16 Aug 1948; *Educ* Case Western Reserv Univ (BS, MD); *m* 28 Nov 1980; 2 da (Sarah b 1983, Lisa b 1983); *Career* sr registrar in neurosurgery Addenbrooks Hosp Cambridge 1981-85, conslt neurosurgeon Derriford Hosp 1985-; FRCSEd 1987; *Style*— Louis Pobereskin, Esq; Dept of Neurosurgery, Derriford Hospital, Plymouth (☎ 0752 792593)

POCKNEY, Penrhyn Charles Benjamin; s of Maj Ronald Penrhyn Pockney (d 1969), of Bishopthorpe, York, and Catherine Helen Margaret, *née* Dodsworth; *b* 22 May 1940; *Educ* Winchester; *m* 15 May 1965, (Patricia) Jane, da of Sir Richard William de Bacquencourt des Voeux, Bt (d 1944), of Burghclere, Newbury, Berks; 2 s (Richard b 1968, James b 1969); *Career* dir J & A Scrimgeour Ltd 1972- (ptnr 1968-72), ptnr Mullens & Co 1980-86, dir S G Warburg Akroyd Rowe & Pitman Mullens Securities Ltd 1986-; Liveryman Worshipful Co Skinners 1977 (Freeman 1963); FCA; *Recreations* gardening, fishing, golf; *Clubs* Boodles, Lansdowne, MCC; *Style*— Penrhyn Pockney, Esq; 1 Finsbury Ave, London EC2M 2PA (☎ 071 606 1066)

POCOCK, Air Vice-Marshal Donald Arthur; CBE (1975, OBE 1957); s of Arthur Pocock (d 1970), of Hampstead, and E Pocock, *née* Broad; *b* 5 July 1920; *Educ* Crouch End; *m* 1947, Dorothy Monica, da of D Griffiths; 2 s, 3 da; *Career* cmmnd RAF 1941; cmd RAF Regt Wing 1957-58, MOD 1958-59, HQ AAFCE 1959-62, sr ground def SO NEAF 1962-63, MOD 1963-66, sr ground def SO FEAF 1966-68, ADC to HM The Queen 1967, Cmdt-Gen RAF Regt 1973-75; gen mangr (Iran) British Aerospace Dynamics Group 1976-79; dir Br Metallurgical Plant Constructors' Assoc 1980-85; *Style*— Air Vice-Marshal Donald Pocock, CBE; 16 Dence Park, Herne Bay, Kent CT6 6BQ (☎ 0227 374773)

POCOCK, Gordon James; s of Leslie Pocock; *b* 27 March 1933; *Educ* Royal Liberty Sch Romford, Keble Coll Oxford; *m* 1959, Audrey Singleton; *Career* sr mktg dir Br Telecom 1979-; *Style*— Gordon Pocock, Esq; 2 Queensberry Place, Friars Lane, Richmond, Surrey TW9 1NW (☎ 081 940 7118)

PODMORE, William; OBE (1985), JP (1965); s of William Podmore, JP (d 1958), of Consall Hall, Wetley Rocks, Stoke-on-Trent, and Alberta, *née* Grainger (d 1958); *b* 12 Nov 1918; *Educ* Leek HS, Loughborough Univ of Technol (DLC); *m* 30 Aug 1947, Edna May, da of Benjamin Atkinson (d 1966); 1 s (William b 1948), 1 da (Helen b 1952); *Career* mechanical engrg dir, test engr Power Jets Ltd 1941-46; chm: Podmores (Engrs) Ltd 1946, Consall (Hldgs) Ltd 1965; memb: Stoke-on-Trent Assoc of Engrs 1947-, Inst of Quarry Engrs 1948-65; pres Cheadle Rotary Club 1958-59; chm: Staffs Moorlands Cons Assoc 1965-, Cheadle RDC 1966-67; tax cmmr 1967; memb Exec Ctee CPRE Staffs Branch 1970-; memb Nat Tst Ctee for Mercia 1982-89; CEng, MIMechE 1941; *Recreations* landscape gardening, photography; *Style*— William Podmore, Esq, OBE, JP; Consall Hall, Wetley Rocks, Stoke-on-Trent (☎ 0782 550203); Winton House, Stoke Rd, Stoke-on-Trent (☎ 0782 45361)

POETON, William George; s of George Edward Poeton (d 1963), and Gladys Maude, *née* Jewill (d 1974); *b* 24 Dec 1926; *Educ* Bristol GS; *m* 1, 1947 (m dis 1970), Jean Rankin Poeton; 3 s (Anthony b 1948, Barrie b 1952, Timothy b 1956); m 2, 21 Oct 1971, Barbara, da of Frederick Bevis; *Career* fndr A T Poeton and Son Ltd (high tech electro plating) 1954-, dir of admin and lab affrs HTV Ltd 1969-72, currently chm and chief exec Eddington Poeton Video Productons Ltd; special advsr to the dir gen Inst Dirs; pres Bristol W of England Mfrs Assoc 1960, regnl chm SW CBI 1974-76, Nat Cncl memb CBIs President's Advsrs Panel 1974-76; memb: Mgmnt Bd W England Employers Assoc 1974-83, SWRHA; vice pres Econ and Social Ctee of the Euro Communities 1986-89 (memb 1982-89), former pres Gloucester Cons Assoc, former cncllr Univ of Bristol, fndr Bristol Arts Centre; former chm: Bristol-Hanover Soc, Bristol Round Table, The Everyman Theatre Cheltenham; former int convenor Round Table, current pres Union of Ind Cos, current dep chm Small Business Bureau; MInstD; *Recreations* sailing, theatre; *Clubs* Reform, Royal Thames Yacht; *Style*— William Poeton, Esq; 9 Pelham Place, London SW7 2NW (☎ 071 589 2120, 071 589 1945, telex 43278, fax 071 225 0444)

POETT, Gen Sir (Joseph Howard) Nigel; KCB (1959, CB 1952), DSO (1944) and bar (1945); s of Maj-Gen Joseph Howard Poett, CB, CMG, CBE (d 1929), and Julia Caswell (d 1937), of Providence, Rhode Island, USA; *b* 20 Aug 1907; *Educ* Downside, RMC Sandhurst; *m* 1937, Ethne Julia, da of late Edward Jasper Herrick, of Hawkes Bay, NZ; 2 s, 1 da; *Career* cmmnd Durham LI 1927, Cdr 11 Bn Durham LI 1942, Cdr 5 Para Bde 1943-46; ops: Normandy to the Baltic 1944-45, Far East 1945-46, dir of Plans WO 1946-48, COS Far East LF 1950-52, Maj-Gen 1951, GOC 3 Inf Div 1952-54, dir Military Ops War Office 1954-56, Cmdt Staff Coll Camberley 1957-58, Lt-Gen 1958, GOC-in-C Southern Cmd 1958-61, Gen 1962, C-in-C Far East Land Forces 1961-63; Col Durham LI 1956-65; dir Br Productivity Cncl 1966-72; Silver Star (USA) 1944; *Clubs* Army and Navy; *Style*— Gen Sir Nigel Poett, KCB, DSO; Swaynes Mead, Great Durnford, Salisbury, Wilts

POGMORE, Dr John Richard; s of Edward Richard Fry Pogmore, MBE (d 1986), and Edith Mary, *née* Trevitt; *b* 12 June 1989; *Educ* Southwell Minster GS, Univ of

London (MB BS); *m* 18 June 1966, Trina Ann Leigh, da of Frederick Waterman; 2 s (Simon b 1970, James b 1972); *Career* cmmnd RAF 1963, ret 1980 with rank of Wing Cdr; currently conslt obstetrician and gynaecologist Selly Oak Hosp Birmingham; chm Hosp Recognition Ctee RCOG; FRCOG 1988; *Recreations* rugby, cartography, wine; *Clubs* Moseley Rugby Football; *Style—* Dr John Pogmore; Selly Oak Hospital, Raddlebarn Rd, Selly Oak, Birmingham B29 6JD (☎ 021 472 5313)

POHL, Erich Harald; s of Erich Franz Adolf Pohl, of Wiesbaden, Germany, and Kreszeuz, *née* Dolp; *b* 7 Nov 1956; *Educ* Werner-von-Siemens-Schule Wiesbaden Germany, Bankakademie Mainz-Frankfurt Germany; *Career* Deutsche Bank: private accounts and cashier Wiesbaden 1975-76 (bank trg 1973-75), investmt advsr and security salesman Russelsheim 1976-81, bond trader and salesman DM Bonds Frankfurt 1981-84; Morgan Stanley London: DM bond trader 1984-85, vice pres 1985-, sr trader in non US dollar currencies, exec dir 1986-; *Style—* Erich Pohl, Esq; Morgan Stanley Int, Colegrave House, 70 Berners St, London W1P 3AE (☎ 071 872 2890, telex 081 881 2564)

POHL, Dr Jürgen Ernst Friedrich (George); s of Dr Ernst Richard Albert Pohl (d 1985), of Kronberg Germany, and Hildegard Anneliese, *née* Gorschlüter; *b* 14 March 1935; *Educ* Melbourne Boys HS, Univ of Melbourne (BSc, MB BS); *m* 24 Aug 1963, Irene Jean, da of Thomas Wickham, of London; 2 s (John b 1964, David b 1971), 3 da (Julia b 1966, Andrea b 1969, Deborah b 1975); *Career* lectr in therapeutics and materia medica Univ of Manchester 1968-74, conslt physician Manchester Royal Infirmary 1972-74, sr lectr in med Univ of Leicester 1974-, conslt physician United Leicester Hosps 1974-, univ memb South Lincs Dist Health Authy 1982-90; memb: MENSA 1966-, Assoc of Physicians, Med Res Soc, Br Cardiac Soc, Int and Br Hypertension Soc, Renal Assoc; MRCP, FRCP; *Recreations* chess, bridge, reading; *Style—* Dr George Pohl; 9 Woodland Ave, Stoneygate, Leicester LE2 3HG (☎ 0533 708 129); Dept of Medicine, Leicester General Hospital, Gwendolen Rd, Leicester LE5 4PW (☎ 0533 490490)

POINTER, Simon Nicholas Peter; s of Peter Albert Pointer, of Shillingford Court, Shillingford, Oxon, and Mary Rosamund, *née* Slay; *b* 15 July 1950; *Educ* St Paul's, Exeter Coll Oxford (BA); *Career* dir The Map House 1978-; *Books* author of numerous articles in arts jls on the subject of antique maps and engravings; *Style—* Simon Pointer, Esq; 35 Cornwall Gdns, Kensington, London SW7 4AP (☎ 071 937 1382); The Map House, 54 Beauchamp Place, Knightsbridge, London SW3 1NY (☎ 071 589 4325, fax 071 589 1041)

POIRIER, Lady Anne Thérèse; *née* Bennet; da of 9 Earl of Tankerville (d 1980); *b* 18 Oct 1956, (twin sis of 10 Earl); *m* 1981, Timothy, s of Joseph Poirier, of Comox, BC, Canada; *Style—* The Lady Anne Poirier

POLAK, Prof Julia Margaret; da of Carlos Polak, and Rebeca, *née* Mactas; *b* 29 June 1939; *Educ* Univ of Buenos Aires Argentina (MD, Dip Histopathology), Univ of London (DSc); *m* 1961, Daniel Catovsky, s of Felix Catovsky; 2 s (Elliot Sebastian b 1973, Michael David b 1976), 1 da (Marina b 1963); *Career* Buenos Aires: demonstrator 1961-62, SHO in surgery and med 1962, sr registrar 1963-67 (registrar); London Royal Postgrad Med Sch: res asst Dept of Histochemistry 1968-69, asst lectr 1970-73, lectr 1973-79, sr lectr 1979-82, reader 1982-84; Dept of Histopathology Hammersmith Hosp: hon conslt 1979-, prof of endocrine pathology 1984-, dep dir 1988-; ed of numerous med jls and organiser of int and nat med meetings; memb numerous ctees within Royal Postgrad Med Sch; external ctees incl: chm Immunocytochemistry Club, chm Br Endocrine Pathologists Club, sec Bayliss & Starling Soc, memb Exec Ctee Cncl Circulation of American Heart Assoc, memb Cncl Histochemical Soc of GB 1984-86, memb Bd of Studies on Pathology; memb learned socs incl: American Thoracic Soc, Br Cardiac Soc, Br Neuroendocrine Gp, Cwlth Assoc for Devpt, IBRO, NY Acad of Sciences; memb: BMA, RSM, American Assoc of Pathologists; FRCPath 1986 (memb 1974); Benito de Udaondo Cardiology prize 1967; *Books* incl: Gut Hormones (with S R Bloom, 1981), Basic Science in Gastroenterology, Vol I: Structure of the Gut (jtly, 1982), The Systematic Role of Regulatory Peptides (with S R Bloom and E Lindenlaub, 1983), Immunolabelling for Electron Microscopy (with I M Varndel, 1984), Endocrine Tumours - The Pathobiology of Regulatory Peptide-producing Tumours (with S R Bloom, 1985), Regulatory Peptides (1989); *Style—* Prof Julia Polak; Department of Histochemistry, Royal Postgraduate Medical School, Du Cane Rd, London W12 0NN (☎ 081 740 3231, fax 081 740 3231)

POLAND, Michael Desmond; s of Kenneth Gordon Poland (d 1970), of Downlands, Liphook, Hants, and Hester Mary Beatrice, *née* Chicheli-Plowden; *b* 9 Aug 1937; *Educ* Downside; *m* 1, (m dis 1981), Elizabeth, da of late Philip Asprey; 4 da (Lara b 1969, Emma b 1970, Lisa b 1973, Anna b 1974); m 2, 20 Feb 1981, Carolyn Mary, da of late Wing Cdr William James Maitland Longmore, CBE (d 1988), of Strete End House, Bishops Waltham, Southampton; *Career* dir: Ajax Insur Hldgs Ltd (formerly The Ajax Insur Assoc Ltd) 1964-91, John Poland & Co Ltd 1968-89; The Ajax Insur Assoc Ltd 1980-91; chief exec HP Motor Policies at Lloyd's 1974-82; chm: Poland Insur Brokers Ltd (formerly Cannon Rogers Ltd) 1974-, Radio Victory Ltd 1984-85 (dir 1982-85), Beechbourne Ltd 1989, Poland Estate Agents Ltd 1990-; dir: Thomas P Stackhouse & Son Ltd 1990-, A H Worth Ltd 1990-; jt Master IOW Foxhounds; *Recreations* foxhunting, thoroughbred horse breeding; *Style—* Michael Poland; Lower Preshaw House, Upham, Southampton SO3 1HP (☎ 0489 892652)

POLAND, Rear Adm (Edmund) Nicholas; CB (1967), CBE (1962); s of Maj Raymond Alfred Poland, RMLI (ka 1918), and Frances Olive Bayly Jones, *née* Weston (d 1976); *b* 19 Feb 1917; *Educ* RNC Dartmouth; *m* 1 Sept 1941, Pauline Ruth Margaret, da of Maj Hugh Charles Pechell (d 1955), of Manor Close, Felpham, Bognor Regis, Sussex; 3 s (Raymond Anthony b 1942, Roger b 1949, Andrew b 1960), 2 da (Elizabeth b 1944, d 1948, Celia b 1947); *Career* Midshipman HMS Hood and Shropshire 1935-37, Sub Lt HMS Beagle and Hermes 1938-40, Lt HMS Eclipse Norwegian Campaign 1940, MTB serv in Channel and Med 1940-43, qualified torpedo offr HMS Vernon 1943, HMS Furious 1943-44, staff offr ops to Naval Force Cdr Burma HMS Nith 1944, HMS Royalist 1945, MTB's HMS Hornet 1945-46, Lt Cdr HMS Osprey 1946, Flotilla Torpedo Anti-Submarine Offr 3 Submarine Flotilla 1947-50, Cdr 1950, Naval Staff Course Admty Naval Staff Air Warfare Div 1950-53, Br Jt Servs Mission Washington DC 1953-55, Jt Servs Staff Course 1956, Admty Tactical and Ship Requirements Div 1957, Capt 1957, Cmd RN Air Station Abbotsinch 1957-59, NATO Standing Gp Washington DC 1959-62, dir of underseas warfare MOD 1963-66, Rear Adm 1966, Chief of Staff to C in C Western Fleet 1966-68, ret 1968; md: Wellman Incandescant (Africa) pty Ltd Johannesburg 1968-70, John Bell Fabrics of Scot Ltd Biggar Lanarkshire 1970-72; vice pres Scot Assoc for the Care and Resettlement of Offenders 1979 (dir 1974-79), vice pres Int Prisoners Aid Assoc 1980; pres local branch Royal Br Legion 1982-88; Alliance candidate CC; FBIM 1958-70, MBIM 1958-70; *Recreations* golf; *Style—* Rear Adm Nicholas Poland, CB, CBE; Yew Tree Lodge, Shaftesbury Rd, Wilton, Wilts, SP2 0DR (☎ 0722 742 632)

POLANI, Prof Paul Emanuel; s of Enrico Polani (d 1945), of Trieste, Italy, and Elsa, *née* Zennaro (d 1962); *b* 1 Jan 1914; *Educ* Classical Lyceum F Petrarca Trieste, Univ of Siena, Scuola Normale Superiore Pisa (MD); *m* 24 Aug 1944, Nina Ester, da of Samuel Sullam, of London; *Career* ships surgn 1939-40, MO i/c First Aid Post Borough of Southwark 1941-45; sr med and surgical offr Evelina Childrens Hosp London 1941-48; Guy's Hosp and Med Sch London: Nat Birthday Tst Res fell 1948-50, asst dir of paediatrics 1950-55, hon conslt paediatrician 1960-83, Prince Philip prof of paediatric res 1960-80, dir res unit 1960-83, geneticist paediatric res unit 1961; res physician and dir res unit The Spastics Soc London 1955-60, seconded WHO conslt Nat Inst of Health USA 1959-60, visiting prof of human genetics and devpt Coll of Physicians and Surgns Columbia Univ NY 1977-85; Int Sanremo award for Genetic Res 1984, Baly medal RCP 1985, Gold medal Int Cerebral Palsy Soc 1988; chm Bd of Studies in Genetics Univ of London 1976-78, chm Ctee of Mutagencity DHSS 1978-86, memb Study Gp on Med Biology GEC 1984-87; FRCP 1961, FRCOG 1971, FRS 1973, FRCPath 1984, FRCPI 1989; cdr Order of Merit Italian Republic 1981; *Recreations* reading, horse riding; *Style—* Prof Paul Polani; Little Meadow, The Street, West Clandon, Guildford, Surrey GU4 7TL (☎ 0483 222436); Paediatric Research Unit, The Prince Philip Research Laboratories, Division of Medical and Molecular Genetics, United Schools of Guy's and St Thomas's Hospitals, Guy's Tower, London SE1 9RT (☎ 071 955 5000 ext 2524, fax 071 407 1706)

POLE *see also*: Carew Pole

POLE, Prof Jack Richon; s of Joseph Pole (d 1985), and Phoebe Louise, *née* Rickards (d 1989); *b* 14 March 1922; *Educ* King Alfred Sch London, Kings Coll London, Queen's Coll Oxford (BA), Princeton (PhD); *m* 31 May 1952 (m dis 1988), Marilyn Louise, da of John Glenn Mitchell (d 1968); 1 s (Nicholas), 2 da (Ilsa, Lucy); *Career* RCS 1941-42, 2 Lt RA 1942, served E Surrey Regt seconded to Somali Scouts 1944-46, ret Capt; instr in history Princeton Univ 1952-53, asst lectr (later lectr) in American history UCL 1953-63, lectr Commonwealth Fund American Studies 1957; visiting prof: Berkeley 1960-61 (Jefferson Meml lectr 1971), Ghana 1966, Chicago 1969, Peking 1984; fell Center for Advanced Study in Behavioural Sciences Stanford California 1969; Univ of Cambridge: reader in American history and govt 1963-78, fell Churchill Coll 1968-78, vice master Churchill Coll 1975-78, memb Cncl of Senate 1970-74; guest scholar Woodrow Wilson Int Center Washington 1978-79; Univ of Oxford: Rhodes prof of American history and institutions, fell of St Catherine's Coll 1979-; memb Amnesty Int, hon vice pres Int Cmmn for the History of Representative and Parly Inst (1990); New Jersey prize Princeton Univ 1953, Ramsdell prize Southern Hist Assoc USA 1960; hon fell Hist Soc of Ghana; FBA 1985, FRHistS; *Books* Political Representation in England & The Origins of the American Republic (1966), The Advance of Democracy (ed, 1967), The Seventeenth Century: The Origins of Legislative Power (1969), Foundations of American Independence (1972), The Revolution in America: Documents of the Internal Development of America in the Revolutionery Era (1971), The Decision for American Independence (1975), The Pursuit of Equality in American History (1978), Paths to the American Past (1979), The Gift of Government (1983), Colonial British America (co-ed, 1983), The American Constitution For and Against (ed, 1987), An Encyclopedia of the American Revolution (co-ed, 1991); *Recreations* playing cricket, organising, writing, painting; *Clubs* MCC, Trojan Wanderers Cricket; *Style—* Prof Jack Pole; 20 Divinity Rd, Oxford OX4 1LJ (☎ 0865 246950); St Catherine's Coll, Oxford OX1 3UJ (☎ 0865 271 700)

POLE, Leslie Hammond; s of Reginald Hammond Pole (d 1978), of Syston, Leics, and Harriet, *née* Taylor (d 1985); *b* 10 Dec 1930; *Educ* Loughborough Coll; *m* 26 Aug 1961, Kay, da of Walter Kenneth Bentley (d 1984); 2 s (Timothy Bentley b 1962, Michael Hammond b 1966), 1 da (Nicola Lesley b 1970); *Career* Actg Pilot Offr RAF 1954-56; CA; sr ptnr Pole Arnold (largest ind Leicester firm), chm Raithby Lawrence & Co Ltd Printers 1978-; treas Br Show Pony Soc, sec Leics Local Pharmaceutical Ctee; FCA 1954; *Recreations* motor rallies (incl Monte Carlo), horses, soccer; *Style—* Leslie H Pole, Esq; The Homestead, Old Woodhouse, Leicester (☎ 0509 890038)

POLE, Sir Peter Van Notten; 5 Bt (GB 1791); s of late Arthur Chandos Pole and kinsman of Sir Cecil Pery Van-Notten-Pole, 4 Bt (d 1948); *b* 6 Nov 1921; *Educ* Guildford GS; *m* 1949, Jean Emily, da of late Charles Douglas Stone; 1 s, 1 da; *Heir* s, Peter John Chandos Pole; *Career* 1939-45 war as Flt-Sgt RAAF; accountant; FASA, ACIS; *Style—* Sir Peter Pole, Bt; 5 Sandpiper Mews, 10 Perina Way, City Beach, WA 6015, Australia

POLITEYAN, Ronald Chrysostom; s of Rev J Politeyan (d 1957), of Ferncliffe, Meadvale, Redhill, Surrey, and Mabel Louisa Helena Augusta, *née* Beckingsale (d 1939); *b* 29 April 1908; *Educ* St Lawrence Coll, Queens' Coll Cambridge (BA, MA); *m* 5 Nov 1941, Beryl Marguerite Richards, widow of Lt Hugh Richards RN, and da of Albert Clifford Owen (d 1937); *Career* cmmnd RAFVR 1940-45, reached rank of Sqdn Ldr; asst slr: Pringle & Co 1936-37, Edward Mackie & Co 1937-40; princ Edward Mackie & Co 1946-72; pres Ealing Chamber of Commerce 1947-48 (memb 1937-), Ealing Borough Cncl 1947-72, Central and S Middlesex Law Soc 1962-63; Mayor of Ealing Borough 1962-63, ruling cncllr Ealing Branch Primrose League 1965, pres Ealing and Acton Constituency Cons Assoc 1971-76, chm W Sussex Branch Primrose League 1979, pres Middlesex Co Assoc 1982-84; Liveryman Worshipful Co of Slrs 1960; *Recreations* cricket, soccer, hockey, badminton, lawn tennis; *Clubs* various; *Style—* Ronald Politeyan, Esq; 6 Marechal, 101 Elmer Rd, Elmer, Middleton, Bognor Regis, West Sussex PO22 6LH (☎ 0243 582576)

POLIZZI DI SORRENTINO, Hon Mrs (Olga); *née* Forte; CBE (1990); eldest da of Baron Forte (Life Peer), *qv*; *b* 1947; *Educ* St Mary's Ascot; *m* 26 Sept 1966, Marchese Alessandro Polizzi di Sorrentino, s of Gen Polizzi di Sorrentino (d 1980); 2 da (Alexandra b 28 Aug 1971, Charlotte b 8 April 1974); *Career* dir Trusthouse Forte plc; elected to Westminster City Cncl 1989, Cons cncllr Lancaster Gat Ward; govr: St Mary Sch Ascot, Hallfield Sch Westminster; co-chm The Grosvenor House Antiques Fair, ctee memb The Keats-Shelley Meml Assoc; *Style—* The Hon Mrs Olga Polizzi, CBE; 166 High Holborn, London WC1 (☎ 071 836 7744)

POLKINGHORNE, Rev Dr John Charlton; s of George Baulkwill Polkinghorne (d 1981), and Dorothy Evelyn, *née* Charlton (d 1983); *b* 16 Oct 1930; *Educ* Elmhurst GS Street Somerset, Perse Sch Cambridge, Trinity Coll Cambridge (BA, PhD, MA, ScD), Westcott House Cambridge; *m* 26 March 1955, Ruth Isobel, da of Hedley Gifford Martin (d 1979); 2 s (Peter b 1957, Michael b 1963), 1 da (Isobel Morland b 1959); *Career* Nat Serv RAEC 1948-49; fell Trinity Coll Cambridge 1954-86; lectr: Univ of Edinburgh 1956-58, Univ of Cambridge 1958-65 (reader 1965-68, prof mathematical physics 1968-79); ordained: deacon 1981, priest 1982; curate: Cambridge 1981-82, Bristol 1982-84; vicar Blean Kent 1984-86, fell dean and chaplain Trinity Hall Cambridge 1986-89 (hon fell 1989), pres Queen's Coll Cambridge 1989-; chm: Ctee on Use of Foetal Material 1988-89, Nuclear Physics Bd 1978-79; memb: SRC 1975-79, Doctrine Cmmn 1989-, Proctor in Convocation 1990-; chm govrs Perse Sch 1972-81; FRS 1974; *Books* The Analytic S-Matrix (1966), The Particle Play (1979), Models of High Energy Processes (1980), The Quantum World (1984), The Way the World Is (1983), One World (1986), Science and Creation (1988), Science and Providence (1989), Rochester Roundabout (1989); *Recreations* gardening; *Style—* The Rev Dr John Polkinghorne, FRS; The President's Lodge, Queens' College, Cambridge CB3 9ET (☎ 0223 335532)

POLL, Prof (David) Ian Alistair; s of Ralph Poll, of Macclesfield, Cheshire, and Mary, *née* Hall; *b* 1 Oct 1950; *Educ* Heckmondwike GS Yorks, Imperial Coll London (BSc), Cranfield Inst of Technol (PhD); *m* 31 May 1975, Elizabeth Mary, da of Ewart John Read (d 1968), of Painswick, Gloucestershire; 2 s (Edward b 1977, Robert b

1980), 1 da (Helen b 1984); *Career* Future Projects Dept Hawker Siddeley Aviation 1972-75, sr lectr in aerodynamics Cranfield Inst of Tech 1985-87 (res asst 1975-78, lectr 1978-85), prof of aeronautical engrg and dir Goldstein Laboratory Univ of Manchester 1987-, md Flow Science Ltd 1990-; visiting scientist: DFVLR Göttingen W Germany 1983, NASA Langley Res Centre Virginia USA 1983, 1989 and 1990; retained consIt BAe Commercial Aircraft Divs; conslt: Marconi Space Defence Systems Ltd, Thorn EMI Electronics Ltd, Ferranti Instrumentation Ltd, Avions Marcel Dassault (France), BT; author of over 100 papers on aerodynamics; chm Accreditation Panel Royal Aeronautical Soc 1989- (memb Cncl 1987-89), memb Manchester Literary and Philosophical Soc 1989-; ACGI 1972; CEng 1978, MAIAA 1983, FRAeS 1987; *Recreations* fell walking, DIY, political debate; *Style—* Prof Ian Poll; 4 Beech Court, Macclesfield Rd, Wilmslow, Cheshire SK9 2AW (☎ 0625 528673); Dept of Engineering, Simon Building, The University of Manchester, Oxford Rd, Manchester M13 9PL (☎ 061 275 4306, fax 061 275 3844)

POLLACCHI, Derek Albert Paterson; s of Dr Alberto Giovanni Pollacchi (d 1969), and Kathleen Mary, *née* Paterson (d 1980); *b* 23 July 1951; *Educ* St Mungo's Acad Glasgow, Dip Inst of Health Servs Mgmnt; *m* 25 July 1975, Jean Lindsay, da of John Charles Mullan; 2 da (Christine Maria b 7 June 1980, Julie Kathleen Margaret b 12 Jan 1982); *Career* higher clerical offr 1972-74, gen admin asst 1974-75, sr admin asst 1975-79; sector admin: Mearnskirk Gen Hosp Glasgow 1979-83, Leverndale Hosp Glasgow 1983-84; dir Admin Servs Lennox Castle Hosp Stobhill Gen Hosp and assoc community health servs 1984-87, unit gen mangr Mental Handicap Servs Forth Valley Health Bd 1987-; assoc memb Inst Health Servs Mgmnt; *Style—* Derek Pollacchi, Esq; Forth Valley Health Board, Mental Handicap Services, Royal Scottish National Hospital, Old Denny Rd, Larbet FK5 4SD (☎ 0324 556131, fax 0324 562367)

POLLACK, Anita Jean; MEP (Lab) London SW 1990-; da of John Samuel Pollack, of Sydney, Australia, and Kathleen, *née* Emerson; *b* 3 June 1946; *Educ* Sydney Tech Coll (Dip in Advertising), City of London Poly (BA), Birkbeck Coll London (MSc); *m* Philip Stephen Bradbury; 1 da (Katherine Louise Pollack Bradbury b 4 Sept 1986); *Career* former advertising copywriter Australia, book ed London 1970-74, res asst to Rt Hon Barbara Castle 1981-89; *Recreations* family, reading, cinema, travel; *Style—* Ms Anita Pollack, MEP; 177 Lavender Hill, London SW11 5TE (☎ 071 228 0839, fax 071 228 0916)

POLLARD, Andrew Garth; s of Rev George Pollard, of 44 Vernon Rd, Sheffield, and Elizabeth Beatrice, *née* Briggs; *b* 25 April 1945; *Educ* Queen's Coll Taunton, King's Coll London (LLB); *m* 26 May 1973, Lucy Petica, da of Prof Charles Martin Robertson, of Cambridge; 3 s (Finn b 1978, Tam b 1980, Liam b 1982); *Career* admitted slr 1969; ptnr: Clifford-Turner 1975-87 (slr 1969-75), Clifford Chance 1987-; AKC; *Recreations* music, walking; *Style—* Garth Pollard, Esq; Clifford Chance, Royex House, Aldermanbury Sq, London EC2V 7LD (☎ 071 600 0808, fax 071 726 8561, telex 895991)

POLLARD, Prof Arthur; s of George Arthur Pollard, of Clitheroe, Lancs, and Nellie, *née* Smith (d 1977); *b* 22 Dec 1922; *Educ* Clitheroe Royal GS, Univ of Leeds (BA), Lincoln Coll Oxford (BLitt); *m* 1, 2 Sept 1948, Ursula Ann Egerton (d 1970), da of Nathan Jackson (d 1973), of Congleton, Cheshire; 2 s (John Stanley b 1952, Andrew Michael b 1958); m 2, 9 April 1973, Phyllis Mary, da of John Richard Pattinson (d 1958), of Cartmel, Cumbria; *Career* 161 (RMC) OCTU 1943, cmmnd E Lancs Regt, served 1 Bn 1943; overseas serv, seconded on intelligence to FO 1943-45, Staff Capt (Movements), Kilindi E Africa 1945-46; Univ of Manchester: asst lectr in Eng literature 1949-52, lectr 1952-64, sr lectr 1964-67, dir of gen studies Faculty of Arts 1964-67; Univ of Hull: prof of Eng 1967-84, dean Faculty of Arts 1976-78; conslt prof of Eng Univ of Buckingham 1983-89; Congleton BC: cncllr 1952-65, ldr 1963-67, alderman 1965-67; Humberside CC: cncllr 1979, Cons educn spokesman 1981-, dep ldr 1990-; memb: Secdy Examinations Cncl 1983-88, Assoc of CCs Educn Ctee 1985-89; contrib to Black Papers on educn; reader: St Peter's Congleton 1951-67, All Saints North Ferriby 1968-74, All Saints South Cave 1974-; memb Cncl Gen Synod C of E 1990-; Hon DLitt Univ of Buckingham 1982; *Books* Charles Simeon 1759-1836 (with M M Hennell, 1959), New Poems of George Crabbe (1960), English Hymns (1960), English Sermons (1963), Mrs Gaskell Novelist and Biographer (1965), Richard Hooker (1966), The Letters of Mrs Gaskell (with J A V Chapple, 1966), The Victorians (1970, revised and enlarged 1987), Satire (1970), Crabbe: The Critical Heritage (1972), Anthony Trollope (1978), The Landscape of the Brontes (1988), Complete Poetical Works of George Crabbe, 3 vols (with Norma Dalrymple-Champneys, 1988), Richard Hooker: Ecclesiastical Polity (1990); *Recreations* cricket, railway history; *Style—* Prof Arthur Pollard; Sand Hall, North Cave, Brough, E Yorks (☎ 0430 422 202); County Hall, Beverley, E Yorks

POLLARD, Maj-Gen (Charles) Barry; s of Leonard Charles Pollard (d 1980); *b* 20 April 1927; *Educ* Ardingly, Selwyn Coll Cambridge; *m* 1954, Mary, da of Jack Sydney Heyes (d 1970); 3 da; *Career* RE 1947, GSO 1 MOD 1967, DS Staff Coll 1967-68, CRE 3 Div 1969-71, Col GS 3 Div 1971-72, CCRE 1 (Br) Corps 1972-74, RCDS 1975, chief engr BAOR 1976-79, Col Cmdt RE 1982-87; nat dir Project Trident (Trident Tst) 1980-84, dir Solent Business Fund 1984-, md Westgate Fund Mgmnt Ltd 1985-; chm Douglas Haig Meml Homes; *Recreations* ocean sailing, golf; *Style—* Maj-Gen Barry Pollard; Yateley, Coombe Rd, Salisbury, Wilts (☎ 0722 335493)

POLLARD, Christopher Leslie; OBE (1989); s of Sidney Samuel Pollard (d 1975), and Gertrude Winifred, *née* Skipper (d 1987); *b* 18 June 1939; *Educ* Thames Valley GS Twickenham, Ealing Sch of Hotel Mgmnt, post graduate City & Guilds Technical Teachers Certificate (UWIST); *m* 13 April 1963, Vivien Mary, da of Edwin Hornby (d 1982); 1 da (Rebecca b 27 June 1966); *Career* lectr hotel management and assoc studies Cardiff Coll of Food Technol and Commerce 1960-63; proprietor Mount Sorrel Hotel Barry 1963-74; md Hamard Catering Gp 1968-86 (chm 1974-86), dir Hamard Catering Saudi Arabia Ltd 1978, chm and md Dramah Investmts Ltd and Dramah Devpts ltd 1986; dir: Middlepatch Ltd 1987, Cardiff Mktg Bureau Ltd 1987; memb Wales Tourist Bd appointed by Sec of State for Wales 1983-; chm: Taste of Wales - Blas ar Gymru Ltd, attractions advsy ctee Wales Tourist Bd 1986, hotels advsy ctee Wales Tourist Bd 1986; memb Help the Aged Jubilee Appeal for Wales 1986, hon treas UK Freedom from Hunger Campaign 1977-87; High Sheriff of South Glamorgan 1989-90; Freeman City of London 1986, Liveryman Worshipful Co of Tinplate Workers alias Wire Workers 1986; FHCIMA; *Clubs* RAC, Leander Rowing, City Livery, Guards' Polo; *Style—* Christopher Pollard, Esq, OBE; Penarth House, Cliff Parade, Penarth, South Glamorgan CF6 2BP (☎ 0222 709065)

POLLARD, Dr Corinna Mary; da of Air Vice-Marshal Henry Lindsay Roxburgh, CBE (d 1989), and Hermione Babington, *née* Collard; *b* 16 Oct 1951; *Educ* Farnborough Hill Convent Coll, St George's Hosp Med Sch London (MB BS); *m* 16 Aug 1975, Timothy William, s of Kenneth John Pollard (d 1979); 2 da (Amy b 1984, Sophie b 1986); *Career* currently conslt haematologist Mayday Hosp Surrey; memb Br Soc for Haematology 1985; MRCP 1979, MRCPath 1983; *Recreations* art, skiing; *Style—* Dr Corinna Pollard; Dept of Haematology, Mayday Hospital, Mayday Rd, Thornton Heath, Surrey CR4 7YE (☎ 081 684 6999)

POLLARD, Eve (Lady Lloyd); da of Ivor Pollard, and Mimi Pollard; *m* 1, 8 Dec 1968, (m dis), Barry Lester David Winkleman; 1 da (Claudia b 15 Jan 1972); m 2, 23 May 1978, Sir Nicholas Markley Lloyd; 1 s (Oliver b 6 Aug 1980); *Career* fashion ed: Honey 1967-68, Daily Mirror Magazine 1968-69; womens ed: Observer Magazine 1970-71, Sunday Mirror 1971-81; asst ed Sunday People 1981-83, features ed and presenter TV-am 1983-85; ed: Elle (USA) 1985-86, Sunday Magazine (News of the World) 1986, You Magazine (Mail on Sunday) 1986-88; Sunday Mirror and Sunday Mirror Magazine; devised two series Frocks on the Box for ITV 1985; *Books* Jackie: Biography of Mrs J K Onassis (1971); *Style—* Miss Eve Pollard; Sunday Mirror, 33 Holborn Circus, London EC1P 1DQ (☎ 071 353 0246, fax 071 822 3405, telex 27286 MIRROR G)

POLLARD, George; s of George Charles William Pollard (d 1935), and Thirza Elizabeth, *née* Wilson (later Mrs Walter Leonard Freeman; d 1979); *b* 12 Nov 1929; *Educ* St Pauls; *m* 22 May 1956, Jean Eileen, da of William George Simmonds (d 1970), of London SW14; 2 da (Barbara Ann b 27 Feb 1957, Sally Jane b 14 June 1960); *Career* Nat Serv 2 Lt Northants Regt, served Greece 1948-49; admitted slr 1955; sr ptnr Shoosmiths & Harrison 1981-89; Cons memb: Northampton Co Borough 1962-71 and 1972-74, Northampton Borough Cncl 1974-79, Northamptonshire CC 1973 (chm 1985-89); chm Northampton Central Cons Cncl 1985-88, pres Northampton S Cons Assoc 1986 (chm 1982-86); *Recreations* snooker, swimming, gardening, walking; *Clubs* Northampton and County; *Style—* George Pollard, Esq; 5 Favell Way, Weston Favell, Northampton (☎ 0604 405924); Shoosmiths & Harrison, PO Box 2, Compton House, Abington St, Northampton (☎ 0604 29977, fax 0604 20229, telex 32167 SAND HG)

POLLARD, Ian Douglas; s of Douglas Pollard, DFC (d 1945), and Peggy, *née* Murfitt (d 1989); *b* 9 June 1945; *Educ* Perse Sch Cambridge; *m* 25 July 1964, Dianna, da of Prof Alexander Deer, of Cambridge; 3 da (Juliette b 1964, Samantha b 1966, Arushka b 1987); *Career* chm and md Flaxyard plc 1972-; architectural designer of: Marcopolo (Observers Bldg) 1987, Sainsbury's Homebase Kensington 1988; memb Nat Gdns Scheme; ARICS; *Recreations* gardening, cycling, diving; *Style—* Ian Pollard, Esq; Hazelbury Manor, Nr Box, Corsham, Wilts SN14 9HU (☎ 0225 810715)

POLLARD, John Stanley; s of Prof Arthur Pollard, of Sand Hall, Station Rd, N Cave, Humberside, and Ursula Ann Egerton, *née* Jackson (d 1970); *b* 4 Jan 1952; *Educ* Kings Sch Macclesfield, Hymers Coll Hull, Univ of Leeds (LLB); *m* 14 Sept 1974, Clare Judith, da of Arnold Walter George Boulton, of White House, Winter Hill, Cookham Dean, Berkshire; 3 s (Samuel John b 1979, Joseph William b 1981, Edward George b 1984); *Career* admitted slr 1977; HM dep coroner West and Central Cheshire; memb: Congleton Borough Cncl (elected as SDP candidate 1987, now Cons), Congleton Town Cncl (7 yrs), SDP Parly Candidate for Crewe and Nantwich 1983; *Recreations* walking, gardening, politics; *Style—* John Pollard, Esq; Toft Green Cottage, Toft Green, Congleton, Cheshire; Hibbert & Co Slrs, 144 Nantwich Rd, Crewe, Cheshire

POLLARD, Kenneth Charles; s of Hubert George Pollard (d 1970), and Georgina Elizabeth, *née* Durman; *b* 21 Dec 1945; *Educ* Saltash S M; *m* 5 Oct 1974 (m dis 1986); 1 s (James b 1981); *Career* with RAF 1961-74: active serv 8 and 208 Sqdns, 2 tours of duty para test unit RAE Farnborough; sr ptnr Air Decor (aircraft interior consIts) 1987-; *Recreations* sailing (flying fifteen), golf; *Style—* Kenneth Pollard, Esq; Willow Cottage, Water End, Cople, Beds (☎ 02303 559, fax 02303 8121, car 0860 382796)

POLLARD, Michael Trent; s of George Edward Pollard (d 1974), and Flora, *née* Wise (d 1985); ggf Midshipman (later Lt) John Pollard serv in Victory at Trafalgar and shot dead the French sniper who had killed Nelson, John Pollard was known as 'Nelson's Avenger'; *b* 16 June 1931; *Educ* Queen Elizabeth's GS Wimborne, Westminster, Univ of London; *m* 1, 1957, Joyce; 2 s (Nicholas b 1958, Simon b 1964); m 2, 1969, Anna Jane; *Career* Nat Serv RAF 1949-51; teacher 1956-66; ed: Read Magazine 1967-69, Pictorial Education 1969-71; dep ed Teachers World 1969-71, ed Resources in Education 1971-72; freelance journalist, author 2nd PR Conslt 1972-; dir Topic Records Ltd 1966-73; *Books* North Sea Surge (1978), Walking the Scottish Highlands: General Wade's Military Roads (1984), The Hardest Work Under Heaven (1984), and numerous non-fiction books for children; *Recreations* writing unpublishable novels; *Style—* Michael Pollard, Esq; Orchard House, Great Cressingham, Thetford, Norfolk IP25 6NL (☎ 076 06 297)

POLLARD, Prof Sidney; s of Moses Pollak (d 1942), and Leontine, *née* Katz (d 1942); *b* 21 April 1925; *Educ* Univ of London (BSc, PhD); *m* 1, 13 Aug 1949 (m dis 1982), Eileen, da of Stanley Andrews (d 1961); 2 s (Brian Joseph b 12 Feb 1951, David Hugh b 20 May 1955), 1 da (Veronica Ruth b 22 March 1957); m 2, 6 Nov 1982, Helen, da of James Alfred Swift Trippett, of 9 Upper Ley Court, Chapeltown; *Career* Reconnaissance Corps 1943-47; prof in economic history Univ of Sheffield 1963-80 (lectr in economics 1952-57, sr lectr in economic history 1957-63), prof Univ of Bielefeld 1980-90; memb Cncl Economic History Soc 1970-80; corresponding FBA 1989; *Books* incl: History of Labour in Sheffield 1850-1939 (1959), The Idea of Progress (1968), The Economic Integration of Europe 1815-1870 (1974), Peaceful Conquest (1981), Development of the British Economy (1983), Britain's Prime and Britain's Decline (1988); *Recreations* walking, music; *Style—* Prof Sidney Pollard; 34 Bents Rd, Sheffield S11 9RJ (☎ 0742 368543)

POLLARD, Walter; s of David Pollard (d 1976), and Jane, *née* Hammond (d 1981); *b* 18 Nov 1927; *Educ* Clitheroe Royal GS, Univ of Dublin (BA, MB BCh); *m* 1, 23 Aug 1956, Rosemary Ann, da of F F Pinnock, CMG (d 1979), of Charlwood; 1 s (Rupert Francis b 1958), 2 da (Sophia Jane b 1957, Rebecca Mary b 1982); m 2, 29 Oct 1982, Joy Yvonne, da of S Pegler (d 1948), of Stroud; 1 da (Victoria Jane b 1983); *Career* RA 1946-47, RANC 1947-48; obstetrician and gynaecologist 1968-; examiner: Univ of Southampton, Univ of Bristol, GMC, RCOG; main interests: new surgical techniques, cynosurgery and laser in gynaecology; *Recreations* gardening, carpentry, travel; *Clubs* Fothergill; *Style—* Walter Pollard, Esq; Fosse House, Midford Road, Combe Down, Bath, Avon (☎ 0225 835312); Royal United Hospital Bath (☎ 0225 28331)

POLLEN, Arabella Rosalind Hungerford (Mrs Giacomo Algranti); da of Peregrine Michael Hungerford Pollen, of Norton Hall, Mickleton, Glos, and Patricia Helen, *née* Barry; *b* 22 June 1961; *Educ* St Swithun's Winchester, Queen's Coll London; *m* 5 Aug 1985, Giacomo Dante Algranti, s of Gilberto Algranti, of Milan, Italy; 2 s (Jesse Gilberto b 4 Jan 1986, Samuel Peregrine b 25 Feb 1989); *Career* fashion designer; chm and head of design Arabella Pollen Ltd (exporting to 20 countries worldwide); *Recreations* piano, literature, travelling, art; *Style—* Ms Arabella Pollen; Block 20, Avon Trading Estate, Avonmore Rd, London W14 8TS (fax 071 602 8772, telex 8952022)

POLLEN, Sir John Michael Hungerford; 7 Bt (GB 1795), of Redenham, Hampshire; s of late Lt Cdr John Francis Hungerford Pollen, RN; suc father's 2 cous, Sir John Lancelot Hungerford Pollen, 6 Bt, 1959; *b* 6 April 1919; *Educ* Downside, Merton Coll Oxford; *m* 1, 1941 (m dis 1956), Angela Mary Oriana, da of Maj F J Russi, MC; 1 s, 1 da; m 2, 1957, Mrs Diana Alice Jubb, da of late A E Timbrell; *Heir* s, Richard John Hungerford Pollen; *Career* served WW II (despatches), Capt RA; *Style—* Sir John Pollen, Bt; Manor House, Rodbourne, Malmesbury, Wilts; Lochportain, Isle of North Uist, Outer Hebrides

POLLEN, Peregrine Michael Hungerford; s of Sir Walter Michael Hungerford Pollen, MC, JP (d 1968); 1 cous of Sir John Pollen, 7 Bt; *b* 24 Jan 1931; *Educ* Eton, Ch Ch Oxford; *m* 26 June 1958, Patricia Helen, 3 da of Lt-Col Gerald Barry, MC; 1 s,

2 da; *Career* exec dep chm Sotheby Parke Bernet & Co 1975-82 (joined 1957, dir 1961), with former responsibility for Sotheby Parke Bernet New York (pres 1965-72); ADC to Sir Evelyn Baring as govr of Kenya 1955-57; *Clubs* Brooks's, Beefsteak; *Style*— Peregrine Pollen, Esq; Norton Hall, Mickleton, Glos (☎ 0386 438 218)

POLLEN, Richard John Hungerford; s and h of Sir John Michael Hungerford Pollen, 7 Bt, *qv*; *b* 3 Nov 1946; *Educ* Worth Abbey; *m* 2 Oct 1971, Christianne Mary, da of Sir (William) Godfrey Agnew, KCVO, CB; 4 s (William b 1976, Jonathan b 1979, Andrew b 1982, Alexander b 1986), 2 da (Isabel b 1975, Alice b 1984); *Career* Capel-Cure Myers 1964-68; overseas 1969-70; Charles Barker 1971-79, Valin Pollen 1979-89, Richard Pollen & Company (Corporate Communications) 1989-; memb: BHS, CGA; MInstD, IPR; *Recreations* riding (eventing); *Style*— Richard J H Pollen, Esq; Dunsfold Ryse, Chiddingfold, Surrey GU8 4YA (☎ 048 649 354); Richard Pollen & Company, Dunsfold Ryse, Chiddingfold, Surrey (☎ 048 649 866, fax 048 649 596)

POLLER, Prof Leon; s of Nathan Kristian Poller (d 1975), of Southport, Lancs, and Helena, *née* Minshull (d 1987); *b* 16 April 1927; *Educ* Univ of Manchester (DSc, MD); *m* 9 July 1955, Jean Mavis, da of James Albert Dier, MBE (d 1989), of Bolton, Lancs; 2 s (David b 1962, John b 1965); *Career* Lt, Capt, Maj RAMC 1953-55, CDEE Porton Down Miny of Supply; jr hosp appts Manchester 1957-61, conslt haematologist and dir UK ref lab for anticoagulant reagents and control collaborating centre WHO 1961-, prof Univ of Manchester; over 200 published papers and reviews on blood coagulation and thrombosis; chm: Int Ctee Standardization in Haematology Task Force Blood Coagulation 1972-, nat and internat med scientific ctees; sec Manchester Thrombosis Res Fndn; chm Manchester and Dist Home for Lost Dogs; FRCPath 1968; *Books* Theory and Practice of Anticoagulant Treatment (1962), Recent Advances in Blood Coagulation (ed, 1968-), Recent Advances in Thrombosis (ed, 1972); *Recreations* forestry, cricket (playing), music (listening); *Clubs* Athenaeum; *Style*— Prof Leon Poller; 5 Oakwood Ave, Gatley, Cheadle, Cheshire SK8 4LR (☎ 061 428 7621); Withington Hosp, UK Ref Lab for Anticoagulant Reagents and Control, Manchester M20 8LR (☎ 061 447 3630, fax 061 428 0763/447 3629)

POLLINGTON, Viscount; John Andrew Bruce Savile; s and h of 8 Earl of Mexborough; *b* 30 Nov 1959; *Style*— Viscount Pollington; Arden Hall, Hawnby, York YO6 5LS

POLLINS, Martin; s of Harry Pollins (d 1969), of London, and Hetty Pollins; *b* 11 Dec 1938; *Educ* Brighton Tech Sch; *m* 1, March 1963 (m dis 1980); m 2, 13 Dec 1980, Susan Elizabeth, da of Arthur Edwin Hines, of Brighton; 4 s (Andrew, Richard, Nicholas, Matthew), 1 da (Anna); *Career* CA; ptnr PRB Martin Pollins 1968, chm Professional Enterprise Gp plc 1986-; cncl memb ICAEW 1987-, memb C of C; FCA 1964, ATII 1964; *Recreations* spectator of sport; *Style*— Martin Pollins, Esq; Forest Ridge, Maresfield, E Sussex TN22 3ER; PRB Martin Pollins, 5 Bridge Rd Business Park, Bridge Rd, Haywards Heath, W Sussex RH16 1TX (☎ 0444 458252, fax 0444 458184)

POLLITT, Dr John Deryk; s of Charles Edwin (d 1968), of Plumstead, London, and Sarah Jane, *née* Fisher (d 1976); *b* 24 Aug 1926; *Educ* City of London Sch, St Thomas' Hosp Med Sch Univ of London (Peacock scholar, MB BS, MD, DPM Planck prize in Psychiatry); *m* 1953, Erica Elizabeth da of Arthur Ratzkowski; 2 da (Angela Elizabeth b 10 Feb 1957, Daphne Jane b 26 June 1958); *Career* chief asst to Sr Registrar Dept of Psychological Med St Thomas' Hosp London 1958-59, Rockefeller travelling res fell in med 1959-60, res fell Harvard Med Sch, Mass Mental Health Centre Boston (resident conslt and memb Advsy Bd Drug Res Project); St Thomas' Hosp London: physician in psychological med 1972-79, physician i/c Dept Psychological Med 1979-83; regnl postgraduate dean SE Thames RHA 1979-83, asst dir Br Postgraduate Med Fedn 1983-86; dir of med educn and hon clinical advsr Hayes Grove Priory Hosp 1988- (med dir 1986-88); recognised teacher of psychological med Univ of London 1961-85, advsr in psychiatry to chief med offr Metropolitan Police 1977-82, postgrad advsr RCP SE Thames Region 1977-79; memb: Bd of Postgrad Studies in Med Univ of London 1972-85, Advsy Cmmn of Deans Cncl of Postgrad Med Educn 1979-83, Conf of Postgrad Deans and Dirs of Postgrad Educn in UK 1979-83, Jt Med Advsy Ctee of Academic and Collegiate Cncls Univ of London 1979-83; chm Regnl Postgrad Ctee of SE Thames Region 1979-83, advsr in psychiatry to chief med offr Imperial Chemical Industries 1986-; pres Section of Psychiatry RSM 1976-77 (vice pres 1973-76), vice pres Br Assoc for Social Psychiatry 1974-76; *Books* Depression and its Treatment (1965), Psychological Medicine for Students (1973), Psychiatric Emergencies in Family Practice (1987); *Recreations* landscape, painting in watercolour, architectural drawing, letterpress printing, etching and drypoint, antiquarian horology (memb Antiquarian Horological Society); *Style*— Dr John Pollitt; 152 Harley Street, London W1N 1HH; Hayes Grove Priory Hospital, Prestons Rd, Hayes, Kent BR2 7AS (☎ 081 462 7722, fax 081 462 5028)

POLLITT, Dr Norman Travers; s of Ellis Pollitt (d 1949), of Palmers Green, London N13, and Rose Malvina, *née* Graves (d 1962); *b* 25 May 1918; *Educ* Southgate Co Sch, St Mary's Hosp Med Sch Univ of London (MB BS, LRCP, MRCS); *m* 5 June 1953, Rosemary Lucy, da of Herbert Bexon Spencer (d 1989), of Manor Cottage, Horton, Wimborne, Dorset; 2 s (Michael b 1955, Timothy b 1959), 1 da (Clare b 1963); *Career* Friends' Ambulance Unit 1940-46: Ethiopia 1942-45, NW Europe 1945-46; princ gen practice NHS 1956-60, med advsr Vitamins Group 1961-68, res physician Roche Products 1968-79, conslt in vitaminology Hoffmann-La Roche 1979-82; chm Med Bds DHSS 1979-89; med ed Pears Cyclopaedia 1980-86; author of numerous pubns on nutrition and vitaminology; memb: Med Journalists Assoc, Assoc of Br Sci Writers; Freeman City of London 1979, Liveryman Worshipful Soc of Apothecaries 1978; FRSM 1960, MRCGP 1961; *Books* Which? Guide to Family Health (jtly, 1980); *Recreations* musical appreciation, photography, oenology; *Style*— Dr Norman Pollitt; 70 Royston Park Rd, Hatch End, Pinner, Middx; Springhead Cottage, Swallowcliffe, Salisbury, Wilts

POLLOCK; *see*: Montagu-Pollock

POLLOCK, Alexander; s of Robert Faulds Pollock, OBE, and Margaret Findlay, *née* Aitken; *b* 21 July 1944; *Educ* Rutherglen Acad, Glasgow Acad, BNC Oxford (Domus exhibitioner, MA), Univ of Edinburgh (LLB), Perugia Univ; *m* 1975, Verena Francesca Gertraud Alice Ursula, da of J Reginald Critchley, of Patmore Lodge, Patmore Heath, Albury, Ware, Herts; 1 s (Andrew b 1979), 1 da (Francesca b 1976); *Career* slr 1970-73, advocate Scottish Bar 1973-; MP (C): Moray and Nairn 1979-1983, Moray 1983-87; memb Commons Select Ctee on Scottish Affrs 1979-82; PPS to George Younger: as Sec of State for Scotland 1982-86, as Sec of State for Def 1986-87; sec Br Austrian Parly Gp 1979-87, Advocate Depute 1990-; memb Queen's Bodyguard for Scotland (Royal Co of Archers) 1984-; *Clubs* New (Edinburgh), Highland (Inverness); *Style*— Alexander Pollock, Esq; Drumdarrach, Forres, Moray, Scotland IV36 ODW

POLLOCK, His Hon Judge (Peter) Brian; s of Brian Treherne Pollock, of Dial Cottage, Rolvenden Layne, Kent, and Helen Evelyn, *née* Holt-Wilson; *b* 27 April 1936; *Educ* St Lawrence Coll; *m* 1, 1966 (m dis 1981), Joan Maryon, da of late Maj Charles Eustace Maryon Leggett; 2 s (Robin b 1967, Guy b and d 1969, Richard b 1971); m 2, 22 June 1988, Jeannette Mary Nightingale, da of Cdr Wilfrid Farrell, MBE, RN; *Career* called to the Bar Middle Temple 1958; rec Crown Court 1986, circuit judge 1987-; *Recreations* playing tennis, watching cricket, travel, walking, cooking, gardening; *Clubs* MCC, Roehampton; *Style*— His Hon Judge Pollock; 17 Gilpin Ave, Sheen, London SW14 8QX (☎ 081 876 9704); Snaresbrook Crown Court, Hollybush Hill, London E11

POLLOCK, David (Charles) Treherne; s of Brian Treherne Pollock, and Helen Evelyn, *née* Holt-Wilson; *b* 7 April 1938; *Educ* St Andrew's Pangbourne, Nowton Ct, St Lawrence Coll; *m* 1961, Lisbeth Jane, *née* Scratchley; 2 s, 1 da; *Career* 2 Lt The Gordon Highlanders 1956-59; The Economist 1961-69; dir: Mathers & Streets Ltd 1968-69, Charles Barker (City) Ltd 1969-70, Dewe Rogerson Ltd 1970-88, Dewe Rogerson Gp Ltd 1975-88, Dewe Rogerson Aust 1985-87, Dewe Rogerson Japan 1987-88, Maxwell Stamp plc 1988-; chm: IMS Ltd 1988-, Corporate Television Broadcasting Ltd 1988-; *Recreations* the arts, shooting; *Clubs* City of London; *Style*— David Treherne Pollock, Esq; Maxwell Stamp plc, 2 Hat and Mitre Court, St John St, London EC1M 4EL (☎ 071 251 0147)

POLLOCK, David Frederick; s and h of Sir George Frederick Pollock, 5 Bt, *qv*; *b* 13 April 1959; *m* 14 Sept 1985, Helena R, o da of L J Tompsett, OBE, of Tadworth, Surrey; *Career* md Pollock Audio Visual Ltd 1983-, dir Cloud 9 (Video Film Prodns) Ltd 1987; *Style*— David Pollock, Esq; Camelot Cottage, 43 Chequers Lane, Walton-on-the-hill, Surrey KT20 7SF (☎ 0737 81 3155)

POLLOCK, David Raymond John; s of Eric John Frank Pollock, of Dulwich, and Beryl Olive, *née* Newens (d 1982); *b* 22 Oct 1949; *Educ* Dulwich, Univ of Keele (BA); *m* 30 July 1975, Barbara Ann, da of Henry Chambre, MBE, of Hendon; 1 s (Thomas Hugo John b 19 March 1984), 1 da (Sarah Charlotte Chambré b 23 Aug 1980); *Career* MOD: admin trainee 1972, higher exec offr 1975 (private sec to Chief Sci Advsr), princ 1978; asst dir Primary Mkts Div Int Stock Exchange 1989- (head of Industry Policy Unit 1986, head of Business Devpt Primary Mkts Div 1988); memb: Fin Ctee Royal Inst of GB, City of London Branch Ctee BIM; *Recreations* squash, walking, drawing and painting, books, convivialty; *Clubs* Snuffers Dining; *Style*— David Pollock, Esq; 46 Dacres Rd, London SE23 (☎ 081 699 3883); The International Stock Exchange, Old Broad St, London EC2 (☎ 071 588 2355, telex 886557)

POLLOCK, Hon David Stephen Geoffrey; s of 2 Viscount Hanworth; *b* 16 Feb 1946; *Educ* Wellington Coll, Guildford Tech Coll, Sussex Univ; *m* 1968, Elizabeth Vambe; 2 da; *Career* lectr, QMC, Univ of London; *Style*— The Hon David Pollock

POLLOCK, Ellen Clara; da of Hedwig Elizabeth Kahn (d 1958); *Educ* St Mary's Coll W2, Convent of The Blessed Sacrament Brighton; *m* 1, 13 July 1928, Lt-Col Leslie Frank Coventry Hancock, OBE (d 1944); 1 s (Michael Coventry); m 2, 1945, James Proudfoot (d 1971); *Career* actress 1920-; theatre incl: Hit the Deck 1927, Her First Affaire 1930, The Good Companions 1931, Finished Abroad 1934, The Dominant Sex 1935; seasons of Shaw's plays 1944-53, Six Characters in Search of an Author 1963, Lady Frederick 1969-70, Pygmalion 1974, Tales from Vienna Woods (NT) 1976, The Dark Lady of the Sonnets 1977, The Woman I Love 1979, Country Life 1980; Harlequinade (NT); numerous film and TV appearances incl: Forsyte Saga, The Pallisers, The Nightingale Saga, The Old Men at the Zoo; pres The Shaw Soc; *Recreations* antiques; *Style*— Miss Ellen Pollock; 9 Tedworth Square, Chelsea, London SW3 4DU (☎ 071 352 5082)

POLLOCK, Sir George; QC (1951); s of William Mackford Pollock; *b* 15 March 1901; *m* 1, 1922, Doris Evelyn (d 1977), da of Thomas Main, of Leamington Spa, Warwicks; 1 s, 1 da; m 2, 1977, Mollie, *née* Pedder, (d 1988) wid of J A Van Santen; *Career* barr Gray's Inn 1928, bencher 1948, recorder of Sudbury 1946-51, dir Br Employers' Confedn 1954-65, sr consult to CBI on Int Labour Affrs 1965-69; kt 1959; *Style*— Sir George Pollock, QC; 62 Staveley Court, Eastbourne, East Sussex

POLLOCK, Sir George Frederick; 5 Bt (UK 1866), of Hatton, Middx; s of Sir (Frederick) John Pollock, 4 Bt (d 1963); *b* 13 Aug 1928; *Educ* Eton, Trinity Coll Cambridge (MA); *m* 1951, Doreen Mumford, da of Norman Ernest Keown Nash, CMG (d 1966); 1 s, 2 da; *Heir* s, David Frederick Pollock b 13 April 1959; *Career* 2 Lt 17/21 Lancers 1948-49; slr 1956; artist-photographer and audio-visual creator 1963-; Hon FRPS (pres 1978), FBIPP, FRSA, AFIAP; *Clubs* DHO; *Style*— Sir George F Pollock, Bt; Netherwood, Stones Lane, Westcott, nr Dorking, Surrey RH4 3QH

POLLOCK, Prof Griselda Frances Sinclair; da of Alan Winton Seton Pollock (d 1986), and Kathleen Alexandra, *née* Sinclair (d 1964); *b* 11 March 1949; *Educ* Queen's Coll London, Lady Margaret Hall Oxford (BA), Courtauld Inst of Art (MA, PhD); *m* 30 Oct 1981, Dr Antony Bryant, s of Paul Bryant, of London; 1 s (Benjamin b 22 March 1983), 1 da (Hester b 7 Feb 1986); *Career* lectr art history and film Univ of Leeds 1977-85 (sr lectr 1985-90), prof Social and Critical Histories of Art Univ of Leeds 1990-; author of numerous articles in jnls; memb Yorkshire Arts Cncl and Exec, memb Tate Gallery Liverpool Advsy Bd; *Books* Millet (1977), Vincent Van Gogh (1978), Mary Cassatt (1980), Old Mistresses Women Art and Ideology (1981), The Journals of Marie Bashkirtseff (1985), Framing Feminism Art and the Women's Movement (1987), Vision and Difference Feminism, Femininity and the Histories of Art (1988); *Recreations* running, skiing, opera, music; *Style*— Professor Griselda Pollock; Department of Fine Art, University of Leeds, Leeds LS2 9JT (☎ 0532 335260, fax 0532 336017, telex 556473 UNILDS G)

POLLOCK, John C; s of Alfred Kenneth Pollock, of Cooden, Sussex, and Ruby Nora Kathleen, *née* Briggs; *b* 4 June 1940; *Educ* Dulwich; *m* 3 March 1972, Renee Mary Desborough; 1 s (James Martin b 2 June 1978); *Career* sr Layton Bennett Billingham & Co CAs 1963-64 (articled clerk 1958-63), chartered accountant Ernst & Whinney The Hague 1965-66 (London 1966-67), Litton Industries Zurich 1968-70, md MCA/Universal Pictures Amsterdam 1970-74, estab Netherlands office Josolyne Layton Bennet & Co 1974-82 (ptnr UK firm), following merger estab Leeds office Arthur Young 1982-85 (returned as UK desk ptnr in the Netherlands 1985-89), equity ptnr Moret Ernst & Young Netherlands 1990- (following merger with Ernst & Whinney 1989); memb Cncl Netherlands/Br C of C, chm UK Accountants in the Netherlands ICAEW 1979, fndr memb BCS, numerous articles published and lectures given; FCA, MBCS; *Recreations* skiing, walking, photography, travel, formerly a keen alpinist; *Clubs* Rotary; *Style*— John C Pollock, Esq; Moret Ernst & Young (register accountants), Drentestraat 20, 1083 HK Amsterdam, The Netherlands (☎ 020 5497 500, fax 020 462553)

POLLOCK, Rev John Charles; s of Robert Pollock (d 1957), of Syresham Priory, Brackley, Northants, and Ethel Mary Purefoy, *née* Powell (d 1970); *b* 9 Oct 1923; *Educ* Charterhouse, Trinity Coll Cambridge (MA); *m* 4 May 1949, Anne, da of Sir Richard Barrett-Lennard, Bt, OBE, of Horsford Manor, Norwich, Norfolk (d 1977); *Career* Coldstream Gds 1943-45, 2 Lt 1943, Lt 1944, Capt 1945, GSO III Staff of Supreme Allied Commander's SE Asia (Mountbatten); asst master Wellington 1947-49; ordained C of E: deacon 1951, priest 1952; curate St Paul's Portman Square London 1951-53, rector Horsington Somerset 1953-58; biographer and historian; *Books incl* Hudson Taylor and Maria (1962), Moody without Sankey (1963), Billy Graham (3 edn, 1984), The Apostle (1969), Wilberforce (1977), Amazing Grace (1981), Shaftesbury (1985), John Wesley (1989); *Recreations* tennis, mountain and moorland walking; *Clubs* English-Speaking Union; *Style*— The Rev John Pollock; Rose Ash House, South Molton, Devonshire EX36 4RB (☎ 07697 403)

POLLOCK, John Craig Stuart; s of Ian Stuart Pollock (d 1954), and Lois, *née* Harris (d 1956); family has been in the Paper Trade, f to s for five generations; *b* 1 July 1927;

Educ Selwyn House Canada, Lower Merion Sr HS USA; *m* 21 Jan 1961, da of Margaret Elizabeth, da of Ernest George Willmot, of W Sussex; 1 s (David John Stuart b 1962), 1 da (Katharine Lois Milton b 1963); *Career* pres (formerly chm) Pollock & Searby Ltd; co fndr (with wife) and proprietor of The Penny Royal Open-Air Theatre Bosham Sussex 1983; trained as journalist 1944 on The Philadelphia Inquirer, asst ed 'American Outlook'; *Recreations* sailing, theatre; *Clubs* Lansdowne; *Style*— John C S Pollock, Esq; Trippet Meadow, Canute Rd, Bosham, Chichester, W Sussex (☎ 0243 573288, fax 0243 573889)

POLLOCK, Adm of the Fleet Sir Michael Patrick; GCB (1971, KCB 1969, CB 1966), LVO (1952), DSC (1944); s of Charles Albert Pollock (d 1937), of The Lane House, Lydham, Shrops, and Gladys Mason; *b* 19 Oct 1916; *Educ* RNC Dartmouth; *m* 1, 1940, Margaret Steacy (d 1951); 2 s, 1 da; m 2, 1954, Marjory Helen Reece, *née* Bisset; 1 step da; *Career* RN 1930, Cdr 1950, Capt 1955, cmd HMS Ark Royal 1963-64, Rear Adm 1964, Asst Chief of Naval Staff 1964-66, 2 i/c Home Fleet 1966-67, Vice Adm 1968, Flag Offr Submarines and NATO Cdr Submarines Eastern Atlantic 1968-69, Adm 1970, Controller of the Navy 1970-71, Chief of Naval Staff and First Sea Lord 1971-74, first and princ Naval ADC to The Queen 1972-74, Adm of the Fleet 1974; chm Naval Insur Tst 1975-85; Bath King of Arms 1976-85; *Style*— Adm of the Fleet Sir Michael Pollock, GCB, LVO, DSC; c/o National Westminster Bank, 8 Mardol Head, Shrewsbury, Shropshire SY1 1HE

POLLOCK, Peter Glen; s of Jack Campbell Pollock (d 1953), and Rebecca Shields Marshall, *née* Clarke (d 1985); *b* 6 Sept 1946; *Educ* Nautical Coll Pangbourne, Univ of St Andrews (MA); *m* 3 Sept 1977, Nicola Sara, da of Derek William Bernard Clements, of Cirencester, Glos; 2 s (Jonathan William Campbell b 1982, Matthew Charles Simon b 1984); *Career* fin dir: Hawker Siddeley Power Transformers Ltd 1978-83, Fisher Controls Ltd 1983-85; gp chief exec ML Holdings plc 1985; memb: Ctee RUKBA 1985-, Cncl SBAC 1989-; FCA; *Recreations* golf, shooting, fishing, skiing, sailing; *Clubs* Knole, Knole Park Golf; *Style*— Peter Pollock, Esq; Hamilton House, Temple Ave, London EC4Y 0HA (☎ 071 353 4212)

POLLOCK, Hon Richard Charles Standish; TD (1986); yr s of 2 Visc Hanworth; *b* 6 Feb 1951; *Educ* Wellington, Trinity Coll Cambridge (MA); *m* 1982, Annette Louise, da of Peter Lockhart, of Daisy Cottage, Studham, Common Lane, nr Dunstable, Beds; 2 s (Harold William Charles b 30 April 1988, Frederick Thomas Charles (twin) b 30 April 1988); *Career* Maj Royal Yeo TAVR; slr; *Recreations* TAVR; *Style*— The Hon Richard Pollock, TD; 135 Thurleigh Rd, London SW12 8TX; office: 14 Dominion St, London EC2M 2RJ (☎ 071 628 2020, telex 888562)

POLLOCK, Hon Mrs (Rosemary Tyrwhitt); da and co-heiress of Baroness Berners, *qv*; *b* 20 July 1931; *Educ* Stonar Sch Cottles Park nr Melksham Wilts, Dorset House Sch of Occupational Therapy Oxford; *m* 1959, Kelvin Alexander Pollock, s of Kelvin Clayton Pollock; 2 s (Simon b 1962, Alastair b 1964); *Career* practising occupational therapist 1952-59; *Recreations* gardening, bird watching, walking, travel, music; *Style*— The Hon Mrs Pollock; Malt House, Hollingbourne, Kent

POLLOCK-HILL, Stephen David; s of Malcolm William Lyttleton Pollock-Hill, of San Pedro, Malaga, Spain, and Jeanne, *née* Beale; *b* 22 March 1948; *Educ* Harrow, Sorbonne, Univ de Madrid, Univ de Vienna, Hatfield Poly (HND); *m* 18 June 1983, Samantha Ann Maria Russell, da of Sir William Russell Lawrence, QC; 1 s (Robert b 1977), 1 da (Talitha Louise b 1985); *Career* documentalist Mead Carney France (mgmnt conslts) 1970-71; Nazeing Glass Works: sales liaison offr 1972, sales rep 1973, sales mangr 1975, export mangr 1976, sales dir 1980-; memb Euro Domestic Glass Ctee 1978-, chm Sci Museum Glass Gallery Ctee 1978-, cncl memb Glass Mfrs Cncl 1980-88, chm GMF Domestic and Handmade Glass Ctee 1980-88, euro domestic glass advsr EEC-CPIV Ctee Brussels 1985-; exec ctee memb Herts Conservation Soc; life memb: Nat Tst, Int Wine & Food Soc, Lutyens Tst, RHS and Rose Soc, Soc of Glass Technol; Freeman City of London, Liveryman Worshipful Co of Glass Sellers; *Recreations* lawn tennis, read tennis, gardening, fine wine; *Clubs* Hatfield House Real Tennis, The October (hon sec); *Style*— Stephen Pollock-Hill, Esq; Nazeing Glass Works Ltd, Broxbourne, Herts EN10 6SU (☎ 0992 464485, fax 0992 450966)

POLLOK-MCCALL, Maj Robert George; JP (1960), DL (Ross-shire 1964); s of Brig-Gen John Buchanan Pollok-McCall CMG, DSO, DL, JP (d 1951), of Kindeace, and Frances Catrina, *née* McCall; *b* 22 March 1912; *Educ* Harrow, Sandhurst; *m* 1, 26 July 1941, Pamela Mary (d 1983), da of Sir Kenneth Lloyd Gibson, Bt (d 1967), late of Gt Warley; 1 s (Angus John Kenneth), 2 da (Camilla b 1942, Juliet Fiona b 1946 decd); m 2, 27 Aug 1986, Jeanette Karen Julie, da of Baron Juel Brockdorff, of Hindemaye Fyn, Denmark; *Career* The Black Watch (ret 1954) served Palestine (despatches) and WWII; Queens Body Gd for Scotland (Royal Co of Archers); DL (Ross-shire 1964); *Recreations* shooting, fishing, skiing; *Clubs* Army and Navy, Royal Perth Golfing Soc; *Style*— Maj Robert Pollok-McCall, JP; Machany, Auchterarder, Perthshire (☎ 076 481343)

POLONIECKI, Piotr Bernard Hammersley; *b* 15 July 1948; *Educ* Ampleforth, Oriel Coll Oxford (BA); 3 s (Leo b 1975, Dominic b 1979, Luke b 1980); *Career* dir Morgan Grenfell Co Ltd 1982, md Midland Montagu Asset Management 1987-; memb Soc Investmt Analysts; *Recreations* skiing, tennis, photography; *Style*— Piotr Poloniecki, Esq; Midland Montagu Asset Management, 10 Lower Thames St, London EC3R 6AE (☎ 071 260 9163, fax 071 260 9140, telex 8956886)

POLTIMORE, 7 Baron (UK 1831); Sir Mark Coplestone Bampfylde; 12 Bt (E 1641); s of Capt the Hon Anthony Gerard Hugh Bampfylde (d 1969), er s of 6 Baron, and Brita Yvonne (now Mrs Guy Elmes), *née* Baroness Cederström; suc his gf 6 Baron, Poltimore 1978; *b* 8 June 1957; *Educ* Radley; *m* 12 June 1982, Sally Anne, da of Dr Norman Miles, of The Old House, Caythorpe, Lincs; 2 s (Hon Henry, Hon Oliver Hugh Coplestone b 15 April 1987), 1 da (Lara Fiona Brita b 14 May 1990); *Heir* s, Hon Henry Anthony Warwick Bampfylde, b 3 June 1985; *Career* Christie's: associate dir Picture Dept 1984, dir and head of 19th Century Picture Dept 1987; *Books* Popular 19th Century Painting, A Dictionary of European Genre Painters (1986, co-author with Philip Hook); *Clubs* White's; *Style*— The Rt Hon the Lord Poltimore; 55 Elsynge Rd, London SW18 2HR (☎ 081 870 6053); Christie's, 8 King St, St James's, London SW1Y 6QT (☎ 071 839 9060, telex 916429)

POLUNIN, Prof Nicholas; CBE (1975); s of Vladimir Polunin (d 1957), of Chiswick Mall, London, and Elizabeth Violet, *née* Hart; *Educ* Latymer Upper Sch, ChCh Oxford (BA, MA, DPhil, DSc), Yale Univ (MS), Harvard Univ; *m* 3 Jan 1948, Helen Eugenie, da of late Douglas Argyle Campbell, of Toronto; 2 s (Nicholas Vladimir Campbell, Douglas Harold Hart), 1 da (April Xenia); *Career* WWII Intelligence Offr Home Guard E Oxford; New Coll Oxford 1939-47: univ demonstrator and lectr in botany, sr res fell, Fielding curator & keeper of univ herbaria; Macdonald prof of botany McGill Univ Montreal Canada 1947-52, various appts Harvard and Yale Univs 1952-55, prof of plant ecology and taxonomy and head of Dept of Botany while helping to plan Univ of Baghdad Iraq until revolution 1956-58; guest prof Univ of Geveva 1959-61 and 1975-76, fndr prof and head Dept of Botany Univ of Ife Nigeria 1962-66 (founding dean Faculty of Science), established Fndn for Environmental Conservation 1975, fndr and pres World Campaign for the Biosphere 1982-, sec gen and ed fourth Int Conf on Environmental Future Budapest 1990 (fndr first 1971, organiser second 1977, sec gen and ed third 1987); fndr and ed: Environmental Conservation 1974- (Biological Conservation 1967-74), Environmental Monographs of Synposia 1979-, Cambridge Studies in Environmental Policy; discovered: descendants of plants introduced to Greenland from North America by Vikings two thousand years previously 1936, in arctic Canada the last major islands to be added to the world map (later named Prince Charles Island and Air Force Island) 1946; demonstrated the existence of microbial life over North Pole and correlated spora with air mass provenance 1948; awards: US Order of Polaris 1948, Canadian Marie Victorin Medal 1957, Indian Ramdeo Medal for Environment Sci 1986, Int Sasakawa Environment Prize 1987, UN sec gen illuminated and signed certificate for outstanding contribution in the field of the environment, Chinese Academy of Sciences' Pres Quo Mo-Jo Medal 1987, USSR Academy of Sciences' Vernadsky Medal 1988 and 1989, Hungarian Academy of Sciences' Founder's (Zéchenyi) Medal 1990, Netherlands Order of the Golden Ark (Officer) 1990; *Books* author of over 500 res and sci papers, editorials and books, incl: Botany of the Canadian Eastern Arctic (3 vols 1940, 1947, 1948), Circumpolar Arctic Flora (1959), Introduction to Plant Geography and some Related Sciences (1960), Eléments de Géographie Botanique (1967), The Environmental Future (ed 1972), Growth without Ecodisasters? (ed 1980), Ecosystem Theory and Application (1986), Maintenance of The Biosphere (ed with Sir John Burnett, 1990), Surviving With The Biosphere (ed with Sir John Burnett, 1991); *Recreations* mountain scrambling, maintaining a multiplicity of serious joblets; *Clubs* Reform, Harvard NY USA; *Style*— Prof Nicholas Polunin, CBE; Environmental Conservation, 7 Chemin Taverney, 1218 Grand-Saconnex, Geneva, Switzerland (☎ 010 41 022 798 2383 and 4, fax 010 41 022 798 2344)

POLWARTH, Master of; Hon Andrew Walter Hepburne-Scott; s and h of 10 Lord Polwarth; *b* 30 Nov 1947; *Educ* Eton, Trinity Hall Cambridge; *m* 1971, (Isabel) Anna, da of Maj John Freville Henry Surtees, OBE, MC; 2 s, 2 da; *Career* asst dir Baring Bros 1982-; *Style*— The Master of Polwarth; 72 Cloncurry St, London SW6; Harden, Hawick

POLWARTH, 10 Lord (S 1690); Henry Alexander Hepburne-Scott; TD, DL (Roxburgh 1962); s of Master of Polwarth, JP, DL (d 1942), and Elspeth, JP (da of Rt Rev Archibald Campbell, DD, DCL, sometime Bishop of Glasgow and Galloway, by his w, Hon Helen, *née* Brodrick, da of 8 Visc Midleton, JP); suc gf (9 Lord Polwarth, CBE, JP, DL) 1944; *b* 17 Nov 1916; *Educ* Eton, King's Coll Cambridge; *m* 1, 1943 (m dis 1969), Caroline (d 1982), da of Capt Robert Hay (d 1939), er bro of Sir Bache Hay, 11 Bt (d 1966, since when Btcy dormant); 1 s, 3 da; m 2, 1969, Jean, da of Adm Sir Angus Cunninghame Graham of Gartmore and of Ardoch, KBE, CB, and formerly w of Charles Jauncey, QC; 2 step s, 1 step da; *Heir* s, Master of Polwarth; *Career* sits as Cons Peer in House of Lords, Rep Peer for Scotland 1945-63; Maj Lothians and Border Horse NW Europe 1944-45; CA; govr Bank of Scotland 1966-72 (dir 1974-), chm General Accident Gp 1968-1972, min of State for Scotland 1972-74; dir: ICI 1974-81, Canadian Pacific Ltd 1975-, Sun Life Assur of Canada 1975-84, Halliburton Co (USA) 1974-; memb Royal Co of Archers (Queen's Bodyguard for Scotland), Vice Lord-Lieut Borders Region (Roxburgh, Ettrick and Lauderdale) 1975-, chllr Aberdeen Univ 1966, memb Franco-Br Cncl (Br section); Hon LLD: St Andrews, Aberdeen; Hon DLitt Heriot-Watt, DUniv Stirling, FRSE, FRSA, Hon FRIAS; *Recreations* country pursuits and the arts; *Clubs* Brooks's, Pratt's, Army and Navy, New (Edinburgh); *Style*— The Rt Hon the Lord Polwarth, TD, DL; Harden, Hawick, Roxburghshire TD9 7LP (☎ 0450 72069); 37 St James's Place, London SW1 (☎ 071 499 9789)

POMEROY, Brian Walter; *b* 26 June 1944; *Educ* The King's Sch Canterbury, Magdalene Coll Cambridge (MA); *m* 7 Aug 1974, Hilary Susan; 2 da (Gabriela b 1975, Alisa b 1977); *Career* ptnr Touche Ross & Co 1975, seconded as under sec in DTI 1981-83, ptnr i/c of Touche Ross Mgmnt Conslts 1987-; dir Centrepoint Soho, non-exec dir BL 1985-88 (now known as The Rover Gp plc); memb Ctee of Enquiry into Regulatory Arrangements of Lloyd's 1986-, nominated memb of Cncl of Lloyd's 1987; FCA 1978; *Recreations* photography, tennis, running; *Style*— Brian Pomeroy, Esq; c/o Touche Ross & Co, Hill House, 1 Little New St, London EC4 3TR (☎ 071 936 3000)

POMEROY, Maj Hon Robert William; yst s of 8 Viscount Harberton, OBE (d 1956), and Mary Katherine, *née* Leatham (d 1971); bro of 9 Visc (d 1980) and bro and hp of 10 Visc; *b* 29 Feb 1916,(twin); *Educ* Eton; *m* 28 April 1953, (Winifred) Anne, da of Sir Arthur Colegate, MP (d 1956); 2 s (Henry Robert b 1958, Richard Arthur b 1960); *Career* Maj Welsh Gds 1945, ret 1960; *Books* Nunney Church; *Recreations* beagling; *Clubs* Bembridge Sailing; *Style*— Maj The Hon Robert Pomeroy; Rockfield House, Nunney, nr Frome, Somerset (☎ 037 384 208)

POMEROY, Hon Rosamond Mary; da of 8 Viscount Harberton, OBE (d 1956); *b* 29 Feb 1916; *Career* served WWII 1944-45 with ATS; *Clubs* Sailing; *Style*— The Hon Rosamond Pomeroy; 38 Thurloe Sq, SW7; The Cottage in the Lane, Swaines Lane, Bembridge, IOW

POMPA, Leonardo (Leon); s of Dominic Albert Pompa (d 1976), of Edinburgh and Maria Annunziata Pompa (d 1956); *b* 22 Feb 1933; *Educ* Bournemouth Sch, Univ of Edinburgh (MA, PhD); *m* 9 Aug 1962, (Juliet) Caroline, da of Rupert Leigh Sich, KCB, CB, of Norfolk House, Chiswick Mall, London; 1 s (Nicholas b 1963), 1 da (Antonia b 1965); *Career* lectr in philosophy Univ of Edinburgh 1961-77; Univ of Birmingham: prof of philosophy 1977-, dean of arts 1984-87 and 1989-, pres Hegel Soc of GB; memb: Cncl Nat Ctee for Philosophy, mgmnt Ctee Br Soc for History of Philosophy, Aristotelian Soc 1964-; *Books* Vico: A Study of the New Science (1975, 2 edn 1990), Substance and Form in History (ed with W H Dray, 1982), Vico: Selected Writings (trans and ed, 1982), Human Nature and Historical Knowledge: Hume Hegel Vico (1990); *Recreations* music, sport, literature, foreign travel, wine; *Clubs* Edgbaston Golf, Murrayfield Golf; *Style*— Prof Leon Pompa; 155 Russell Rd, Moseley, Birmingham B13 8RR (☎ 021 449 3623); University of Birmingham, Birmingham B15 2TT (☎ 021 414 5657)

PONCIA, Dr John; s of Anthony Edward Poncia (d 1982), of Warks, and Mary Winifred, *née* Tams; *b* 15 April 1935; *Educ* Ratcliffe Coll, Univ of Edinburgh Med Sch (MB ChB); *m* Elizabeth Madaleine (d 1972), da of Alexander Birrell Grosset, of Fife; 4 s (Jonathan b 1960, Gavin b 1962, Fergus b 1964, Hugo b 1970); *Career* house offr Royal Infirmary Edinburgh, registrar St George's Hosp London, sr registrar Westminster Hosp, conslt psychotherapist Broadmoor Hosp; DPM, MRCPsych; *Recreations* yachting; *Clubs* Savile, Royal Thames Yacht, Lloyds Yacht, Royal Ocean Racing; *Style*— Dr John Poncia; 109 Harley St, London W1N 1DG (☎ 071 935 1621, fax 0273 734836)

POND, Edward Charles (Eddie); s of Nathan James Pond (d 1965), and Mary Elizabeth, *née* Seabrook (d 1983); *b* 12 March 1929; *Educ* Royal Coll of Art (Royal Scholar Silver medal); *m* 1954, Grace Nina Primrose, *née* Sparks; 1 s (Christopher b 1960), 2 da (Rebecca b 1963, Hannah b 1965); *Career* Nat Serv Parachute regt; dir: Bernard Wardle (Everflex) Ltd 1958-61, Bernard Wardle (Fabrics) Ltd 1961-65, The Wall Paper Manufacturers Ltd 1965-76, Polycell Products Ltd, Polypops Products Ltd 1969-71; owner and dir Paperchase Products Ltd; fndr Edward Pond Associates Ltd 1976-; Awards: COID Design of the Year award 1959, Pub Arts Devpt Tst competition winner 1988, prizewinner Nat Paperbox and Packing Assoc of America, 3 Excellence awards 1988, Bronze medal NY Advertising Festival 1990; design projects incl: BR Network SE, Boots The Chemist plc, Defeat of the Armada (ceramic mural, Plymouth) fabric hangings BAA; author of various articles in jls and magazines; pres CSD 1981-83 (memb 1959), memb DIA; FRSA; *Recreations* painting, writing, police liaison, jazz; *Clubs* Blackheath FC; *Style—* Eddie Pond, Esq; Edward Pond Associates Ltd, Coach House Studio, 99 Blackheath Park London SE3 OEU (☎ 081 297 0432)

PONSONBY, Arthur Mountifort Longfield; s of late Maj the Hon Cyril Myles Brabazon Ponsonby, MVO, Grenadier Gds (ka 1915, 2 s of 8 Earl of Bessborough) and his 1 w, Rita Narcissa (d 1977), da of late Lt-Col Mountifort John Courtenay Longfield (to all titles except UK Earldom) of 10 Earl of Bessborough; *b* 11 Dec 1912; *Educ* Harrow, Trinity Coll Cambridge; *m* 1, 1939, Patricia (d 1952), da of Col Fitzhugh Lee Minnigerode, of Virginia, USA; 1 s (Myles), 1 da (Sarah); m 2, 1956 (m dis 1963), Princess Anne Marie Galitzine, da of late Lt-Gen Sir Rudolf Carl Slatin (Baron von Slatin), GCVO, KCMG, CB; m 3, 1963, Madeleine Lola Margaret, da of Maj-Gen Laurence Douglas Grand, CB, CIE, CBE; 2 s (Matthew, Charles); *Career* served Welsh Gds 1940-46, Capt; company dir, ret; *Clubs* White's; *Style—* Arthur Ponsonby, Esq; Roche Court, Winterslow, Salisbury, Wilts (☎ 0980 862204)

PONSONBY, Sir Ashley Charles Gibbs; 2 Bt (UK 1956), of Wootton, Co Oxford; MC (1945); s of Col Sir Charles Edward Ponsonby, 1 Bt, TD, DL (d 1976), and Hon Winifred Gibbs, da of 1 Baron Hunsdon (d 1935); *b* 21 Feb 1921; *Educ* Eton, Balliol Coll Oxford; *m* 14 Sept 1950, Lady Martha, *qv*, *née* Butler, da of 6 Marquess of Ormonde, CVO, MC (d 1971); 4 s; *Heir* s, Charles Ashley Ponsonby b 10 June 1951; *Career* Schroder Wagg & Co Ltd (dir 1962-80); chm Colville Estate Ltd; dir: Equitable Life Assur Soc 1969-86, Rowntree Mackintosh Ltd 1974-86, Schroder Global Tst plc 1963-89 (chm 1964-87); church cmmr 1963-80; memb Cncl Duchy of Lancaster 1979-; Lord-Lieut of Oxfordshire 1980-; *Clubs* Pratt's; *Style—* Sir Ashley Ponsonby, Bt, MC; Woodleys, Woodstock, Oxon (☎ 0993 811422); 120 Cheapside, London EC2V 6DS (☎ 071 382 6000)

PONSONBY, Charles Ashley; s and h of Sir Ashley Charles Gibbs Ponsonby, 2 Bt, MC, of Woodleys, Woodstock, Oxford, and Lady Martha Ponsonby, yr da of 6 Marquess of Ormonde; *b* 10 June 1951; *Educ* Eton, Ch Ch Oxford (MA); *m* 1983, Mary Priscilla, yr da of Arthur Bromley Davenport (d 1982); 2 s (Arthur Ashley b 1984, Frederick Edward b 1986), 1 da (Alice Elizabeth b 1988); *Heir* s, Arthur Ashley Ponsonby; *Career* CA; Deloitte Haskins & Sells 1973-77, Price Waterhouse 1977-79, Kleinwort Benson 1980-87, Barclays de Zoete Wedd 1987-; non-exec dir South Uist Estates Ltd 1985- (non-exec chm 1985-89); FCA; *Clubs* Pratt's, Beefsteak; *Style—* Charles Ponsonby, Esq; Flat 3, 5 Ralston St, London SW3 4DT (☎ 071 376 4178); Grim's Dyke Farm, Woodstock, Oxon OX7 1HJ; Barclays de Zoete Wedd Ltd, Ebbgate House, 2 Swan Lane, London EC4R 3TS (☎ 071 956 4640, fax 071 956 4663)

PONSONBY, Hon Mrs Bertie B; Constance Evelyn; da of late Rev Horace Rollo Meyer, Hon Canon of St Albans, and Arabella (d 1960), da of John Hamilton Ward (who was ggs of 1 Viscount Bangor); *b* 17 Nov 1907; *m* 1933, Hon Bertie Brabazon Ponsonby (d 1967), s of late 8 Earl of Bessborough, KP, CB, CVO; *Career* vice pres SSAFA (Herts); *Style—* The Hon Mrs Bertie Ponsonby; 44 Hallmores, St Catharine's Rd, Broxbourne, Herts (☎ 0992 465676)

PONSONBY, Hon Laura Mary; da of 2 Baron Ponsonby of Shulbrede (d 1976); *b* 1935; *Educ* Langford Grove, Guildhall Sch of Music (AGSM); *Career* guide lectr Royal Botanic Gdns Kew; pres Haslemere Natural History Soc 1983-, vice pres Haslemere Recorded Music Soc 1986-; hon botanist Haslemere Educnl Museum; *Books* A List of Flowering Plants and Ferns of Haslemere and District (1978), Marianne North at Kew Gardens (1990); *Recreations* music, gardening, natural history; *Style—* The Hon Laura Ponsonby; 17 South End, Kensington Sq, London W8

PONSONBY, Lady Martha; *née* Butler; da of 6 Marquess of Ormonde, CVO, MC (d 1971), and Jessie Carlos (d 1969), da of late Charles Carlos Clarke; *b* 14 Jan 1926; *m* 1950, Capt Sir Ashley Charles Gibbs Ponsonby, 2 Bt, MC, *qv*; *Style—* The Lady Martha Ponsonby; Woodleys, Woodstock, Oxon

PONSONBY, Myles Walter; CBE (1966); s of Victor Coope Ponsonby, MC (d 1966), of Tackley, nr Oxford, and Gladys Edith, *née* Walter, ggda of John Walter, fndr of The Times; *b* 12 Sept 1924; *Educ* St Aubyn's Rottingdean, Eton; *m* 20 May 1950, Anne Veronica Theresa, da of Brig Francis Herbert Maynard, CB, DSO, MC (d 1979), of London; 1 s (John b 1955), 2 da (Belinda (Mrs Mitchell) b 1951, Emma (Mrs Parry) b 1959); *Career* cmmnd KRRC 1943; active serv: Normandy 1944 (wounded), Tripolitania 1945-46, Palestine 1946-47, GHQ M East (Canal Zone) 1947-49; HMFO (later HM Dip Serv) 1951-80; served in: Egypt, Cyprus, Beirut, Indonesia, Kenya, N Vietnam (consul-gen), Rome, Mongolia (HM ambass); hon sec Salisbury Branch RUKBA, memb Advsy Cncl for CARE Br, pres S Wilts Export Assoc 1990, councillor Wilts CC 1988; *Style—* Myles Ponsonby, Esq, CBE; The Old Vicarage, Porton, nr Salisbury, Wilts SP4 0LH

PONSONBY, Robert Noel; CBE (1985); s of Noel Edward Ponsonby (d 1928), and Mary Adela, *née* White-Thomson; *b* 19 Dec 1926; *Educ* Eton, Trinity Coll Oxford (MA); *Career* Glyndebourne 1951-55, dir Edinburgh Festival 1955-60, gen mangr Scottish Nat Orchestra 1964-72, controller music BBC 1972-85; artistic dir Canterbury Festival 1986-88; admin Friends of Musicians Benevolent Fund 1987, chm London Choral Soc 1990-; *Recreations* walking, bird watching, photography, music; *Style—* Robert Ponsonby, Esq, CBE; Flat 4, 11 St Cuthbert's Rd, London NW2 3QJ (☎ 071 452 1715)

PONSONBY, Hon Thomas Maurice; TD, DL (Glos); s of 5 Baron de Mauley; hp to bro, 6 Baron; *b* 2 Aug 1930; *Educ* Eton; *m* 1956, Maxine Henrietta, da of late William Dudley Keith Thellusson; 2 s; *Career* Lt-Col The Royal Wessex Yeo 1970-72, Brevet Col TA 1972-; High Sheriff of Glos 1978; *Style—* The Hon Thomas Ponsonby, TD, DL; The Common, Little Faringdon, Lechlade, Glos

PONSONBY OF SHULBREDE, 4 Baron (UK 1930), of Shulbrede, Sussex; Frederick Matthew Thomas Ponsonby; o s of 3 Baron Ponsonby of Shulbrede (d 1990), and his 1 w, Ursula Mary, *née* Fox-Pitt; *b* 27 Oct 1958; *Educ* Holland Park Sch, Univ Coll Cardiff, Imperial Coll London; *Heir* none; *Career* cllr London Borough of Wandsworth 1990-; *Style—* The Rt Hon Lord Ponsonby of Shulbrede; c/o House of Lords, London SW1

PONSONBY OF SHULBREDE, Baroness; Maureen Estelle Ponsonby; da of Alfred William Windsor; *m* 1 (m dis), Dr Paul Campbell-Tiech; m (2) 1973, as his 2 w, 3 Baron Ponsonby of Shulbrede (d 1990); *Style—* The Rt Hon Lady Ponsonby of Shulbrede; 261 Kennington Road, London SE11 6BY

PONTE, Lady Jennifer Jane; *née* Curzon; da of 6 Earl Howe, CBE; *b* 1941; *m* 1962, Alan Joseph Ponté; 4 s, 1 da; *Style—* The Lady Jennifer Ponté; Ardeley Bury, nr Stevenage, Herts

PONTEFRACT, Bishop of 1971-; Rt Rev (Thomas) Richard Hare; *b* 29 Aug 1922; *Educ* Marlborough, Trinity Coll Oxford, Westcott House Cambridge; *m* 1963, Sara, da of Lt Col J E Spedding, OBE, (d 1969), of Keswick; 1 s (William), 2 da (Rosamund, Alice); *Career* RAF 1942-45; curate of Haltwhistle 1950-52, domestic chaplain to Bishop of Manchester 1952-59, canon residentiary Carlisle Cathedral 1959-65, archdeacon of Westmorland and Furness 1965-71; vicar: St George with St Luke Barrow in Furness 1965-69, Winster 1969-71; *Style—* The Rt Rev the Bishop of Pontefract; 306 Barnsley Rd, Wakefield WF2 6AX

PONTER, Prof Alan Robert Sage; s of Arthur Tennyson Ponter (d 1964), of Abergavenny, and Margaret Agatha Ponter (d 1974); *b* 13 Feb 1940; *Educ* King Henry VIII GS Abergavenny, Imperial Coll London (BSc, ARCS, PhD), Univ of Cambridge (MA); *m* 14 Sept 1962, Sonia, da of Robert Hutchinson Valentine, of Leigh, Lancs; 1 s (David Robert Arthur b 25 Nov 1964, d 1986), 3 da (Ruth Virginia b 1964, Kathryn Emma b 1968, Alexandra Margaret Valentine b 1980); *Career* visiting lectr Iowa Univ 1964, res fell Brown Univ USA 1964-65, lectr Univ of Glasgow 1965-66, sr asst researcher Engrg Dept Univ of Cambridge 1966-69, fell Pembroke Coll Cambridge 1967-69, prof engrg Brown Univ USA 1976-78; Univ of Leicester: lectr 1969-74, reader 1974-76, prof engrg 1978-, pro-vice chllr 1987-; memb several SERC ctees and working parties on mechanical engrg, conslt to EEC and others on structural integrity of nuclear structures; *Books* Creep of Structures (1982), about 100 articles in applied mathematics and engrg literature; *Recreations* reading, music and walking; *Style—* Prof Alan Ponter; 10 Elmsleigh Ave, Stoneygate, Leicester LE2 2DF (☎ 0533 704395); University of Leicester, University Rd, Leicester LE1 7RH (☎ 0533 522323, fax 0533 558691, telex 347250 LEICHN G)

PONTIFEX, Brig David More; CBE (1977, OBE 1965, MBE 1956); s of Cdr John Weddall Pontifex, (d 1977), of Cloudes Lodge, Lilliput, Poole, Dorset, and Monica Melangell Rosewall, *née* Matthews (d 1970); *b* 16 Sept 1922; *Educ* Downside; *m* 6 Aug 1968, Kathleen Betsy (Kate), da of Maxwell Heron Matheson (d 1978), of Widelands, Waldringfield, Woodbridge, Suffolk; 1 s (John b 1975), 4 da (Catherine b 1969, Emily b 1971, Louise b 1973, Rosalind b 1975); *Career* cmmnd Rifle Bde 1942, Lt then Capt 10 and 2 Bn Italy 1944-45 (despatches 1945), Capt adjt 2 Bn BAOR 1946-48, Capt instr Eaton Hall OCS 1948-50, Staff Coll Camberley 1951, Maj DAA and QMG 16 Ind Para Bde Gp Egypt 1952-54, 1 Bn Kenya, WO (MO 4) 1956-58, Armed Forces Staff Coll Norfolk Virginia 1958-59, 1 Bn BAOR 1959-61, Bde Maj 63 Gurkha Bde Gp Malaya 1961-62, Lt-Col 1 Bn Fed Regular Army Aden 1962-64, GSO1 2 Div BAOR 1965-67, Col GS Staff Coll Camberley 1967-69, Brig the Light Div Winchester 1969-73, DDSD Army 1973-75, Dep Cdr and COS SE Dist Aldershot 1975-77; ADC to HM The Queen 1975-77, gen sec ACF Assoc, sec CCF Assoc, ed The Cadet Journal 1977-87; govr Farnborough 6 Form Coll 1977-81; *Recreations* travel, history; *Clubs* Naval and Military; *Style—* Brig David Pontifex, CBE; 68 Shortheath Rd, Farnham, Surrey (☎ 0252 723 284)

PONTIN, Sir Fred - Frederick William (Fred); *b* 24 Oct 1906; *Educ* Sir George Monoux GS Walthamstow; *m* Dorothy Beatrice Mortimer; 1 da; *Career* work in catering and welfare for Admty WWII; Pontins Ltd: chm and md 1946-79, currently dir and hon fndr pres 1987-; dir: Pontinental Ltd 1963-79, Belhaven Brewery until 1981; dep chm Kunick Leisure Gp plc 1985-87 (chm 1983-85); memb: Variety Club of GB (chief barker 1968), Grand Order of Water Rats; first pres Hotel and Catering Benevolent Assoc 1979; Lloyd's underwriter; memb IOD; kt 1976; *Clubs* Farmers Club, IOD, Saints and Sinners, Lords Taverners; *Style—* Sir Fred Pontin; Flat 64, 3 Whitehall Court, London SW1A 2EL (☎ 071 839 5251)

POOLE, Anne Avril Barker; *b* 11 April 1934; *m* John Poole; *Career* asst chief nursing offr City of Westminster 1967-69, chief nursing offr London Borough of Merton 1969-74, area nursing offr Surrey Area Health Authy 1974-81, dep chief nursing offr Dept of Health 1981-82; memb NHS Policy Bd, expert advsr to WHO; memb: Royal Coll of Nursing, Health Visitors' Assoc, Br Inst of Mgmnt; RSM; CBIM; *Recreations* gardening, embroidery, entertaining; *Style—* Mrs Anne Poole; Ancaster House, Church Hill, Merstham, Surrey RH1 3BL (☎ 0734 4332); Department of Health, Richmond House, 79 Whitehall, London SW1A 2NS (☎ 071 210 5597, fax 071 210 5572)

POOLE, Hon Mrs (Anne Rosemary Dorothea); da of 1 Baron Croft, CMG, TD, PC (d 1947), and Hon Nancy, da of 1 Baron Borwick; *b* 2 April 1918; *Educ* private; *m* 1946, Flt Lt (Herbert) Edmund Poole, RAF (d 1984), s of Herbert Poole (d 1966), of Norwich; 3 s; *Career* nursing 1939-46; social work 1966-83; *Style—* The Hon Mrs Poole; Dower House, 17a Knight St, Sawbridgeworth, Herts (☎ 0279 723146)

POOLE, David Anthony; QC (1984); s of William Joseph Poole (d 1956), and Lena Thomas; *b* 8 June 1938; *Educ* Ampleforth, Jesus Coll Oxford (MA), Univ of Manchester (Dip Tech Sci); *m* 1974, Pauline, da of James O'Flaherty; 4 s (William, Alexander, Gareth, Simon); *Career* called to the Bar Middle Temple 1968, rec 1982; chm Assoc of Lawyers for the Def of the Unborn, govr St Bede's Coll Manchester; *Recreations* reading, walking, watching rugby; *Clubs* Vincent's, London Irish, Northern Lawn Tennis, Heaton Mersey Cricket; *Style—* David Poole, Esq, QC; 1 Priestnall Rd, Stockport, Cheshire SK4 3HR; 1 Deans Ct, Crown Sq, Manchester 3; 1 Crown Office Row, Temple, London EC4Y 7HH

POOLE, David Arthur Ramsay; s of Arthur Poole, of Cobham, Surrey, and late Viola Isbol, *née* Ramsay; *b* 30 Sept 1935; *Educ* Kings Canterbury, St Edmund Hall Oxford (MA); *m* 11 March 1961, Jean Mary, da of the late Norman Percy Male; 3 da (Nicola, Julia, Vanessa); *Career* 2 Lt RA 1955-57; with Baring Bros & Co Ltd 1960-65, APCM Ltd (now BCI) 1965-70, William Brandts & Co Ltd 1970-73, Br Caledonian Gp 1973-75; Blue Circle Industs plc: joined 1976, appt Bd 1984, gp md 1987, ret 1989; Freeman City of London 1976, Liveryman Worshipful Co of Fanmakers; *Recreations* shooting, skiing, travel; *Clubs* E India, Sports and Social; *Style—* David Poole, Esq; Fairhaven, Fairmile Ave, Cobham, Surrey KT11 2JA (☎ 0932 864830)

POOLE, Hon David Charles; s and h of 1 Baron Poole, CBE, TD, PC; *b* 6 Jan 1945; *Educ* Gordonstoun, ChCh Oxford, Insead Fontainebleau; *m* 1, 21 Sept 1967, Fiona, da of John Donald; 1 s (Oliver John); m 2, 1975, Philippa, da of late Mark Reeve; *Career* memb Stock Exchange; *Clubs* Brooks's, Buck's, Royal Yacht Squadron, Groucho's; *Style—* The Hon David Poole; Rectory Farm, East Woodhay, nr Newbury, Berks (☎ 0635 253923)

POOLE, David James; s of Thomas Herbert Poole (d 1978), and Catherine, *née* Lord (d 1980); *b* 5 June 1931; *Educ* RCA; *m* 5 April 1958, Iris Mary, da of Francis Thomas Toomer (d 1968); 3 s (Edward b 1959, Vincent b 1960, Bruce b 1964); *Career* served RE 1949-51; sr lectr of painting and drawing Wimbledon Sch of Art 1961-77; portraits incl: HM The Queen, HRH Prince Philip, HM Queen Elizabeth the Queen Mother, HRH the Princess Royal, HRH Prince Charles, HRH Prince Andrew, HRH Prince Edward, Lord Mountbatten, distinguished membs of govt, HM Forces, industry, commerce, medical, the academic and legal professions; featured in BBC TV series Portrait 1976; cmmnd by the City of London Corp to paint the official portrait group of the Royal Family to commemorate Her Majesty Queen Elizabeth II's Silver Jubilee Luncheon; one man exhibitions: London 1978, Zürich 1980; featured in magazine 'Frankfurter Allgemeine' W Germany 1986; work in private collections: Her Majesty The Queen, Aust, Bermuda, Canada, France, W Germany, Italy, S Africa, Saudia Arabia, Switzerland, USA; ARCA 1954; RP 1968 (pres 1983); *Recreations* travel, being in the country; *Style—* David J Poole, Esq; The Granary, Oxton Barns, Kenton, Exeter, Devon EX6 8EX (☎ 0626 891611); Studio 6, Burlington Lodge, Rigault Rd, Fulham, London SW6 4JJ (☎ 071 736 9288)

POOLE, Henry Michael (Francis); s of Charles Frederick John Kaitting Poole (d 1976), of Mixtow House, Lanteglos-By-Fowey, Cornwall, and Stella Mary Grant, *née* Morris; *b* 23 Sept 1949; *Educ* Summer Fields Oxford, Eton Coll Windsor, Trinity Hall,

Cambridge (MA); *m* 20 Sept 1975, Diana Mary Olga, da of Eric Arthur Parker; 1 s (Henry b 1983), 2 da (Lucy b 1978, Antonia b 1980); *Career* joined Laing & Cruickshank 1971 (ptnr 1979, dir Institutional Equities 1987), non-exec dir Rockware Gp 1986-87; *Books* European Paper directory (1988); *Recreations* bridge, mountain walking, history; *Style—* Henry Poole, Esq; Laing Cruickshank, Broadwalk House, 5 Appold St, London EC2A 2DA (☎ 071 588 4000); 74 Hornton St, London W8 4NY; Gibbet Oast, Appledore Rd, Leigh Green, Tenterden, Kent

POOLE, (Francis) Henry Michael; s of Charles Frederick John Kaitting Poole (d 1976), of Mixtow House, Lanteglos-by-Fowey, Cornwall, and Stella Mary Grant, *née* Morris; *b* 23 Sept 1949; *Educ* Eton, Trinity Hall Cambridge; *m* 20 Sept 1975, Diana Mary Olga, da of Eric Arthur Parker (d 1983), of Summerhill Farm House, Headcorn, Kent; 1 s (Frederick Henry Eric b 1983), 2 da (Angelica Lucy Daphne, Stella Antonia Felicity); *Career* dir Laing and Cruickshank Institutional Equities 1985- (joined 1971, ptnr 1979), non-exec dir Rockware Gp 1986-87; memb: Kensington Cons Assoc, London Stock Exchange 1979-; *Books* European Paper Directory (1988); *Recreations* bridge, riding, mountain walking; *Style—* Henry Poole, Esq; 74 Hornton St, London W8 4NU; Gibbet Oast, Leigh Green, Tenterden, Kent TN30 7DH; Laing & Cruickshank, Broadwalk House, 5 Appold St, London EC2A 2DA (☎ 071 588 4000, telex 888397/8, fax 071 588 0290)

POOLE, Sheriff Isobel Anne; da of John Cecil Findlay Poole (d 1985), and Constance Mary, *née* Gilkes; *b* 9 Dec 1941; *Educ* Oxford HS for Girls, Univ of Edinburgh (LLB); *Career* advocate 1964, former standing jr cncl to the Registrar Gen for Scot; Sheriff of: the Lothian and Borders 1979-, Edinburgh 1986; memb: Sheriffs' Cncl 1980-85, Scot Lawyers Euro Gp; *Recreations* country, the arts, house, gardens, friends; *Clubs* Scottish Arts; *Style—* Sheriff Isobel Anne Poole

POOLE, Hon Mrs (Jean); *née* Bruce; da of late 7 Lord Balfour of Burleigh; *b* 1924; *m* 1, 1949 (m dis 1971), John Shirley Ward; 1 s, 2 da; m 2, 1974, John Herbert Poole; *Style—* The Hon Mrs Poole; 1030 South El Molino Ave, Pasadena, Calif 91106, USA (☎ 213 796 4905)

POOLE, Matthew David; s of (Peter) David Poole, of The Cottage, Main St, Keyham, Leicestershire, and Ainsley Jane, *née* Bunney; *b* 6 Feb 1969; *Educ* Roundhill Secdy Sch Leics, Laurel's Acad and Coll Leics; *Career* Rugby Union lock forward Leicester FC; clubs: Syston RUFC, Leicester FC 1988-; rep: England Colts (3 caps, tour Italy) 1987-88, England U21 (3 caps, tour Romania, tour France & Holland) 1988-90; England: memb squad Argentina tour (3 appearances); business systems sales in family business; *Recreations* crewing and racing yachts, water sports, music; *Style—* Matthew Poole, Esq; The Cottage, Main St, Keyham, Leicestershire (☎ 053 750 235, 0533 517 777); Leicester FC, Welford Rd, Aylestone Rd, Leicester LE2 7LF (☎ 0533 541 607, fax 0533 511 854)

POOLE, 1 Baron (UK 1958); Oliver Brian Sanderson Poole; CBE (1945), TD (1945), PC (1963); s of late Donald Louis Poole, whose family connections with Lloyd's stretch back two centuries to when Henry Poole (d c 1793) did business at Lloyd's Coffee House; *b* 11 Aug 1911; *Educ* Eton, Ch Ch Oxford; *m* 1, 1933 (m dis 1951), Betty Margaret, da of Capt Dugald Gilkison and Janet, *née* Harcourt Vernon (ggggda of 1 Baron Vernon); 1 s, 3 da; m 2, 1952 (m dis 1965), Daphne Wilma Kenyon, da of late Eustace Bowles (himself gs of 6 Earl of Macclesfield), and formerly w of Brig Algernon Heber Percy, DSO; m 3, 1966, Barbara Ann, da of E A Taylor; *Heir* s Hon David Charles Poole; *Career* Warwicks Yeo 1934, MP (C) Oswestry Div of Salop 1945-50; chm Cons Pty Orgn 1955-57 (vice-chm 1963-64); memb of Lloyd's, formerly dir S Pearson & Son Ltd, Hon DSc City Univ 1970; *Style—* The Rt Hon The Lord Poole, CBE, TD; 24 Campden Hill Gate, Duchess of Bedford's Walk, W8 (☎ 071 937 6466)

POOLE, (Jeremy) Quentin Simon; s of Graham Poole, of Kingswear, S Devon, and Dr Jill Poole, *née* Prichards; *b* 7 Jan 1955; *Educ* Epsom Coll, Univ of Warwick (LLB); *Career* admitted slr 1981: ptnr Wragge & Co 1985-; memb Birmingham Law Soc 1981; memb Law Soc 1981; *Recreations* cricket; *Style—* Quentin Poole, Esq; Wragge & Co, Bank House, 8 Cherry St, Birmingham B2 5JY (☎ 021 632 4131, fax 021 643 2417, telex 338728 WRAGGE G)

POOLE-CONNOR, Murray; s of Murray Poole-Connor (d 1969), and Mary, *née* Bodkin (d 1990); *b* 24 March 1939; *Educ* Kent Coll Canterbury; *m* 23 June 1965, Jennifer Blanche, da of William Thomas Waterlow (d 1985); 2 s (Murray b 1971, Duncan b 1973), 2 da Lara b 1968, Karyn b 1969); *Career* CA 1960; private practice 1963, sr ptnr Orr Shotliff 1969-; memb private charitable orgn and various W Sussex voluntary assocs; FCA 1972, ATII; *Recreations* rugby football, restoration; *Clubs* East India, Eccentric, Wig & Pen; *Style—* Murray Poole-Connor, Esq; Furzefield House, Cowfold, West Sussex RH13 8BU (☎ 0403 864213); Orr Shotliff, 160 Piccadilly, London W1V 0NQ (☎ 071 493 3903, fax 071 495 1094, telex 849668)

POOLE-WILSON, Denis Smith; CBE (1969); s of Alexander Poole Wilson, MBE (d 1934), and Jessie Maude, *née* Smith (d 1960); *b* 22 Sept 1904; *Educ* St Andrew's Coll Dublin, Trinity Coll Dublin, Middx Hosp, London Hosp (BA, MB BCh, BAO, FRCS(Eng), FRCS, MCh); *m* 14 Oct 1939, Monique Michell (d 1985), da of Charles Philip Goss (d 1959), of The Home Farm, Sunningdale, Berks; 2 s (Peter Nicholas b 1941, Philip Alexander b 1943); *Career* Lt-Col RAMC 1939-45, served N Africa and Italy; conslt urological surgn: Royal Manchester Children's Hosp 1935-69, Salford Royal Hosp 1935-69, Christie Hosp and Holt Radium Inst 1946-69, N Manchester Gen Hosp 1939-69; lectr in urology Univ of Manchester 1951-69; Hunterian prof RCS 1946; memb Int Soc Urology 1947-69, hon memb Manchester Med Soc 1934- (pres 1967-68), fndr memb Urological Club 1946-, fndr and hon memb Br Assoc of Urological Surgns (pres 1965-67); St Peter's medal for notable contribs to urology 1971; FRSM (pres Section of Urology 1959-60); *Recreations* gardening, fishing, reading; *Style—* Denis Poole-Wilson, Esq, CBE; Cockspur Thorns, Berwick St James, Salisbury, Wilts SP3 4TS (☎ 0722 790445)

POOLE-WILSON, (Peter) Nicholas; s of Denis Smith Poole-Wilson, CBE, of Cockspur Thorns, Berwick St James, Salisbury, Wilts, and Monique Michelle, *née* Goss (d 1985); *b* 7 Sept 1941; *Educ* Marlborough, Trinity Coll Cambridge (BA); *m* 3 July 1965, Mary Raeburn, da of late John Gemmell; 2 s (Peter, Alexander); *Career* md Bernard Quaritch Ltd antiquarian booksellers 1975-; memb: Friends of Br Library (memb Cncl 1988-), Friends of Lambeth Palace Library (memb Ctee 1987-), Bibliographical Soc (memb Cncl 1989-); *Recreations* gardening, old porcelain, boomerangs; *Clubs* Grolier (NY); *Style—* Nicholas Poole-Wilson, Esq; 26 Ringwood Ave, London N2 9NS (☎ 071 883 8358); c/o Bernard Quaritch Ltd, 5-8 Lower John St, Golden Square, London W1R 4AU (☎ 071 734 2983, fax 071 437 0967, telex 8955509)

POOLE-WILSON, Prof Philip Alexander; s of Denis Smith Poole-Wilson, CBE, and Monique Michelle Poole-Wilson (d 1985); *b* 26 April 1943; *Educ* Marlborough, Trinity Coll Cambridge (MA), St Thomas's Med Sch (MB BChir, MD); *m* 25 Oct 1969, Mary Elizabeth, da of Dr William Horrocks Tattersall; 2 s (William, Michael), 1 da (Oenone); *Career* prof of cardiology Nat Heart and Lung Inst Univ of London 1984-(sr lectr and reader 1976-84, vice dean 1981-84), Simon Marks Br Heart Fndn prof of cardiology 1988-, hon conslt physician Royal Brompton Nat Heart & Lung Hosp 1976-, visiting prof Charing Cross and Westminster Med Sch 1988-; memb Cncl Br Heart Fndn, sec Euro Soc of Cardiology 1990- (memb Bd 1988-90); FRCP 1978; *Recreations* sailing, gardening, countryside, opera; *Style—* Prof Philip Poole-Wilson; 174 Burbage Rd, London SE21 7AG (☎ 071 274 6742); National Heart and Lung Institute, Dovehouse St, London SW3 6LY (☎ 071 352 8121, fax 071 376 3442)

POOLEY, Dr Derek; s of Richard Pike Pooley (d 1988), of Port Isaac, Cornwall, and Evelyn, *née* Lee (d 1985); *b* 28 Oct 1937; *Educ* Sir James Smiths Sch Camelford, Univ of Birmingham (BSc, PhD); *m* 1961, Jennifer Mary, da of William Arthur Charles Davey (d 1980), of Birmingham; 2 s (Michael Bruce b 1967, Benjamin John b 1969), 1 da (Miriam Jane b 1973); *Career* head Materials Devpt Div Harwell 1976-81, dir energy res Harwell 1981-83, chief scientist Dept of Energy 1983-86, dir Winfrith 1989-90, chief exec AEA Thermal Reactors 1990-91, md EAE Nuclear Business Group 1991-; *Recreations* photography, walking, history, gardening; *Style—* Dr Derek Pooley; 11 Halls Close, Drayton, Abingdon, Oxfordshire 0X14 4LU; Hartwell Laboratory, Oxfordshire OX11 0RA (☎ 0235 821111)

POOLEY, Prof Frederick David; s of Frederick Pooley (d 1964), and Ellen, *née* Dix; *b* 3 Feb 1939; *Educ* Univ of Wales Coll of Cardiff (BSc, MSc, PhD); *m* 18 Aug 1962, Patricia Mary, da of John Boyt Williams, of Abergavenny, Gwent; 2 s (Anthony John b 1964, Andrew David b 1966), 1 da (Susan Elizabeth b 1968); *Career* res fell MRC 1966-69; Univ of Wales Coll of Cardiff: lectr in minerals engrg Dept of Mineral Exploitation 1969-76, sr lectr 1976-77, reader 1977-87, prof Sch of Engrg 1987-; author of numerous papers and articles in dust disease res and biological treatment of minerals; fell Minerals Engrg Soc 1986; CEng 1977, MIMM 1977, MAIME 1979; *Recreations* sailing, squash; *Clubs* PH Yacht; *Style—* Prof Frederick Pooley; School of Engineering, University of Wales College of Cardiff, Newport Rd, PO Box 917, Cardiff CF2 1XH (☎ 0222 874000, fax 0222 371921, telex 498635)

POOLEY, Graham Howard John; s of John Henry William Pooley, of Loughton, Essex, and Joan Margaret, *née* Price (d 1983); *b* 11 March 1949; *Educ* Brentwood Sch, Oriel Coll Oxford (MA); *m* 8 May 1971, Moira Helen *qv*, da of Roger Francis Lewis (d 1978), of Chadwell Heath; 1 s (Oliver b 1973), 1 da (Laura b 1976); *Career* Nat & Grindlays Bank 1970-73, asst dir Chem Bank Int Ltd 1974-80, head Syndicate and Trading County Bank Ltd 1980-82, exec dir Bank of America Int Ltd 1982-86, dir and head int primary mkts Barclays de Zoete Wedd Ltd 1986-89, md and head UK capital markets Chase Investment Bank 1989-; memb SLDP; *Recreations* bridge, croquet, ski-ing, home improvement, music; *Style—* Graham HJ Pooley, Esq; 4 Pratts Farm Cottages, Pratts Farm Lane, Little Waltham, nr Chelmsford, Essex CM3 3PR; Chase Investment Bank Ltd, PO Box 16, Woolgate House, Coleman St, London EC2P 2HD (☎ 071 726 5367)

POOLEY, Moira Helen; *née* Lewis; da of Roger Francis Lewis (d 1978), of Chadwell Heath, Essex, and Kathleen, *née* Kingseller; *b* 17 June 1950; *Educ* Ursuline Convent Brentwood Essex, QMC London (LLB); *m* 8 May 1971, Graham Howard John Pooley *qv*, s of John Henry William Pooley, of Loughton, Essex; 1 s (Oliver Edward b 24 March 1973), 1 da (Laura Kathleen May b 10 Nov 1976); *Career* called to the Bar Middle Temple 1974; memb local govt and planning bar assocs; vice chm: Little Baddow Parish Cncl 1981-84, Barnston Parish Cncl 1988-; chm: Social Security Appeal Tbnl 1986-, Nat Insur Tbnl 1986-; *Recreations* poultry keeping, archaeology, cookery; *Style—* Mrs Moira Pooley; Barnston Old Rectory, Great Dunmow, Essex CM6 3PA (☎ 0371 820329); Temple Gardens, London EC4Y 9AU (☎ 071 353 0832)

POOLEY, Peter; *b* 1936; *m* 1966, Janet Mary, er da of Jack Pearson, of Banbury; 1 s, 1 da; *Career* agric min Office of UK Perm Rep to Euro Community Brussels 1979-82, fisheries sec Miny of Agric London 1982-83, dep dir gen (Agric) Euro Cmmn Brussels 1983-89, dep dir gen (Devpt) 1989-; *Style—* Peter Pooley, Esq; Commission of the European Communities, Rue de la Loi 200, B1049, Brussels, Belgium; Dereymaekerlaan 53, 3080 Tervuren, Belgium

POOLEY, Robert John; s of Sydney John Pooley (d 1972), and Hilda Vera, *née* Salmon; *b* 9 Feb 1935; *Educ* Medburn Sch; *m* 1, 24 Feb 1962 (m dis 1973), Yvonne Margaret, da of William Pereiva (d 1976), of Hatfield, Herts; 1 s (Julian David b 26 Feb 1964), 1 da (Katharine Yvonne 12 March 1966); m 2, 5 July 1974, Carolyn, da of Dr J Alfred Lee, of Westcliff, Essex; 1 s (Sebastian Robert John b 3 May 1979), 1 da (Samantha Carolyn Merlyn b 30 July 1974); *Career* RAF SAC 4 Sqdn 1953-57; De Havilland Aircraft Co 1957-61, chm Airtour Int Gp, Airtour Flight Equipment Ltd, Airlife Publishing Ltd, Robert Pooley Ltd, World Expeditions Ltd, Airtour Balloon Co Ltd, ed and publisher Pooley Flight Guides 1961; chm Soc of the St John Opthalmic Hosp Jerusalem, tstee Museum of Army Flying Devpt Tst; vice pres: Helicopter Club of GB, Guild of Aviation Artists, Br Precision Pilots Assoc; vice chm Royal Aero Club, tstee Boxmoor Tst, pres 1187 Sqdn ATC, St Johns Ambulance Bde Hemel Hampstead; memb St Johns Cncl for Herts OStJ 1986, chm The Ballon Club; Freeman City of London 1971, Liveryman Guild of Air Pilots and Air Navigators 1971 (Master 1987-88); FRIN 1979, FRAS 1981; *Books* Air Touring Flight Guides (1962-1991), Pilots Information Guide (1982 and 1986); *Recreations* flying, ballooning, riding, sub-aqua, skiing; *Clubs* Royal Aero, City Livery; *Style—* Robert Pooley, Esq; Felden Grange, Felden, Herts HP3 0BL (☎ 0442 65764, fax 0442 234228); Forter Castle, Glenisla, Angus PH11 8QW (☎ 057 582305); Airtour International, Elstree Aerodrome, Herts WD6 3AW (☎ 081 953 4870/6064, fax 081 953 5219, car 0860 643203)

POORE, Lady; Amelia; da of Senor Santiago Guliemone, of Estancia La Blanca, Estacion Acuna, Corrientes, Argentine Republic; *m* 1922, Sir Edward Poore, 5 Bt (d 1938); *Style—* Lady Poore; Curuzu Cuatia, Corrientes, Argentina

POORE, Dr (Martin Edward) Duncan; s of Thomas Edward Deverell Poore (d 1966), of Coshieville, Aberfeldy, and Elizabeth, *née* MacMartin (d 1965); *b* 25 May 1925; *Educ* Trinity Coll Glenalmond, Clare Coll Cambridge (MA, PhD), Oxford (MA by incorpn); *m* 3 Sept 1949, Judith Ursula (Judy), da of Gen Sir Treffry Thompson, KCSI (d 1979), of Chulmeigh, N Devon; 2 s (Robin b 1952, Alasdair b 1954); *Career* prof of botany Univ of Malaya 1959-65, dir Nature Conservancy 1966-74, sci dir then DG IUCN 1974-78, prof of forest sci and dir Cwlth Forestry Inst Univ of Oxford 1980-83, conslt in land use and conservation 1983-, sr fell IIED; Thames Water Authy 1981-84, chm Advsy Ctee on Sci Nature Conservancy Cncl 1982-84 chm Cwlth Forestry Assoc 1986-88; FIBiol, FRGS 1967, FRSA 1974; *Books* No Timber Without Trees: Substainability in The Tropical Forest (1989); *Recreations* gardening, hill walking, music; *Clubs* Royal Cwlth Soc; *Style—* Dr Duncan Poore; Balnacarn, Glenmoriston, Inverness-shire (☎ 0320 40261)

POORE, Sir Herbert Edward; 6 Bt (GB 1795); s of Sir Edward Poore, 5 Bt (d 1938); *b* 1930,April; *Heir* unc, Nasionceno Poore; *Style—* Sir Herbert Poore, Bt; Curuzu Cuatia, Corrientes, Argentine Republic

POORE, Nasionceno; s of Herbert Poore (d 1905) and bro of 5 Bt (d 1938); hp of n, Sir Herbert Edward Poore, 6 Bt; *b* 1900; *m* Juana Borda (d 1943); 3 s, 3 da; *Style—* Nasionceno Poore Esq

POOT, Anton; *b* 23 Nov 1929; *Educ* HS Holland; *m* 1983, Jesmond, *née* Masters; by former m 1 s (Anton b 1958), 1 da (Marietta b 1954); *Career* worked for: NV Phillips Holland 1946-51, Phillips S Africa and Fedn of Rhodesia and Nyasaland 1951-63, NV Phillips Eindhoven Holland 1963-66; chm and md Phillips E Africa 1967-71, md: Ada (Halifax) Ltd, Phillips Electrical Ltd UK 1971-76; divnl md NV Phillips Holland 1976-

78, chm and md: Phillips Appliances Div Holland 1978-83, Phillips Electronics and Assoc Industs Ltd 1984-; FBIM, FRSA; *Recreations* golf, sailing, skiing; *Clubs* Buck's, Wimbledon Park Golf; *Style*— Anton Poot, Esq; Arundel Great Court, 8 Arundel Street, London WC2R 3DT (☎ 071 689 2166, telex 267518, fax 071 379 0992)

POPAT, Surendra (Andrew); s of Dhirajlal Kurji Popat (d 1989), of Putney, London, and Kashiben Chitalia (d 1963); *b* 31 Dec 1943; *Educ* Govt Secdy Sch Dar Es Salaam Tanzania, Univ of London (LLB), Univ of California (LLM); *Career* called to the Bar Lincoln's Inn 1969, apptd list of the dir of public prosecutions by the then attorney gen Sir Michael Havers 1984, admitted memb Inner Temple 1985; contested Palewell Ward E Sheen as Cons candidate 1978, Cons Parl candidate for Durham N election 1983, treas Surbition Cons Assoc 1985, dir John Patten's election campaign 1987; selected as Parly Candidate (C) Bradford South 1990; Freedom City of London 1987, Liveryman Worshipful Co of Plaisterers 1987; *Recreations* travel, theatre, cricket, tennis; *Clubs* Carlton; *Style*— Andrew Popat, Esq; 9 King's Bench Walk, Temple, London EC4Y 7DX (☎ 071 353 7202, fax 071 583 2030)

POPE, Andrew Lancelot; CMG (1972), CVO (1965), OBE (1959); s of Maj Andrew Noble Pope, OBE (d 1941); *b* 27 July 1912; *Educ* Harrow; *m* 1, 1938 (m dis); m 2, 1948, Ilse, da of late K Pipperger, of Frayn, Austria (d 1988); 1 step da; *Career* cncllr Bonn 1962-72, dir Conference Board NY 1972-80, Gerling Global Gen and Reinsurance Co Ltd; *Style*— Andrew Pope, Esq, CMG, CVO, OBE; Goldhill Grove, Lower Bourne, Farnham, Surrey (☎ 0252 721662)

POPE, Anthony; s of Lt Col Albert Victor Pope (d 1976), and his w, Barbara, *née* Shaw (d 1982); *b* 25 April 1933; *Educ* Melbourne GS Victoria Aust; *m* 1965, Cynthia Margaret, da of Wing-Cdr Alexander Walker (d 1976); 1 s, 1 da; *Career* dir: Eldridge Pope & Co plc 1960-, Hants & Dorset Mineral Water Co Ltd 1977-, Barnham Broom Golf and Country Club 1979-; FHCIMA, FRSH; *Recreations* shooting, farming; *Clubs* Cavalry and Guards; *Style*— Anthony Pope, Esq; Hamlet House, Hamlet, nr Sherborne, Dorset (☎ 0935 872325); Eldridge Pope & Co plc, Dorchester Brewery, Dorchester, Dorset (☎ 0305 251251)

POPE, Dudley Bernard Egerton; s of Sidney Broughton Pope (d 1926), and Alice Egerton, *née* Meehan; *b* 29 Dec 1925; *Educ* Ashford GS; *m* 17 March 1954, Kathleen Patricia, da of Edward Reginald Hall (d 1983); 1 da (Jane Clare Victoria b 17 Feb 1965); *Career* Midshipman MN 1942-43 (wounded invalided); London Evening News: naval corr, sub-ed, dep foreign ed 1944-59; naval historian and author 1959-; *Books* non-fiction: Flag 4, the Battle of Coastal Forces in the Mediterranean (1954), The Battle of the River Plate (1956), 73 North (1958), England Expects (1959), At 12 Mr Byng Was Shot (1962), The Black Ship (1963), Guns (1965), The Great Gamble (1972), Harry Morgan's Way (1977), Life in Nelson's Navy (1981), The Devil Himself (1987); fiction: the Ramage series: Ramage (1965), Ramage and the Drum Beat (1967), Ramage and the Freebooters (1969), Governor Ramage, RN (1973), Ramage's Prize (1974), Ramage and the Guillotine (1975), Ramage's Diamond (1976), Ramage's Mutiny (1977), Ramage and the Rebels (1978), The Ramage Touch (1979), Ramage's Signal (1980), Ramage and the Renegades (1981), Ramage's Devil (1982), Ramage's Trial (1984), Ramage's Challenge (1985), Ramage at Trafalgar (1986), Ramage and the Saracens (1988), Ramage and the Dido (1989); The Yorke Series: Convoy (1979), Buccaneer (1981), Admiral (1982), Decoy (1983), Galleon (1986), Corsair (1987); *Recreations* sailing, shell collecting; *Style*— Dudley Pope, Esq; Le Pirate 379, BP 296, 97150 Marigot, St Martin, French West Indies (☎ 590 87 78 37)

POPE, Vice Adm Sir (John) Ernle; KCB (1976); s of Cdr R K C Pope; *b* 22 May 1921; *Educ* RNC Dartmouth; *Career* RN 1935, Capt 1960, Flag Offr Flotillas Western Fleet 1969-71, COS to C-in-C Western Fleet 1971-74, Rear Adm 1969, Vice Adm 1972, COS to Cdr Allied Naval Forces S Europe 1974; *Clubs* Army and Navy; *Style*— Vice Admiral Sir Ernle Pope, KCB; Homme House, Much Marcle, Herefordshire

POPE, Dr Geoffrey George; CB (1986); s of Sir George Reginald Pope (d 1982), and Lady Pope, *qv*; *b* 17 April 1934; *Educ* Epsom Coll, Imperial Coll London (MSc, PhD); *m* 1961, Rosemary Frances Harnden (d 1989); 2 s; *Career* dep dir (Weapons) Royal Aircraft Estab 1979-81, asst chief scientific advsr (Projects) MOD 1981-82, dep controller and advsr (Res and Technol) MOD 1982-84; dir Royal Aircraft Estab (now Royal Aerospace Estab) 1984-89; dep chief scientific advsr MOD 1989-; FEng, FRAeS, FCGI; *Recreations* music, photography, walking; *Style*— Dr Geoffrey Pope, CB; Ministry of Defence, Rm 6310 Main Building, Whitehall, London SW1A 2HB (☎ 071 218 2848)

POPE, Hon Mrs (Jacqueline Dorothy Mametz); *née* Best; yr da of 8 Baron Wynford, MBE, DL; *b* 9 Nov 1946; *Educ* St Mary's Wantage; *m* 7 June 1969, Jeremy James Richard Pope, s of Philip Pope, of Dorchester; 3 s; *Career* social sec to Lady Erskine of Rerrick 1966-68 (wife of former govr of NI); internal and external landscape gardener and horticulturist; *Recreations* gardening, skiing; *Style*— The Hon Mrs Pope; Field Cottage, Compton Abbas West, Maiden Newton, Dorset (☎ 030 0 20469); work: The Winterbourne Hospital, Dorchester, Dorset (☎ 0305 263252)

POPE, Jeremy James Richard; OBE (1985); s of Philip William Rolph Pope, of Dorset, and Joyce Winifred Harcourt, *née* Slade; *b* 15 July 1943; *Educ* Charterhouse, Trinity Coll Cambridge (MA); *m* 1969, Jacqueline Dorothy Mametz, da of Lt-Col the Lord Wynford, MBE, DL, of Dorchester; 3 s (Rory b 1970, Rupert b 1973, Toby b 1977); *Career* admitted slr 1969-; dir: Eldridge Pope & Co plc 1969- (md 1988, dep chm 1987-), Winterbourne Hosp plc 1981-89 (fndr chm), JB Reynier Ltd 1984-; chm Realstream Ltd 1987-, Highcliff Hotel (Bournemouth) Ltd 1988-; memb Exec Ctee Brewers' Soc 1977-88, memb Dept of Trade Advsy Panel on Co Law 1980-81, chm Smaller Firms' Cncl CBI 1981-84, memb NEDC 1981-85, govr Forres Sch Swanage 1983-; memb: Royal Cmmn on Environmental Pollution 1984-, Exec Ctee Food and Drinks Fedn (dep pres 1987-90), Top Salary Review Body 1986-; memb Law Soc, FRSA 1989; *Recreations* gardening, field sports, cooking; *Style*— Jeremy Pope, Esq, OBE; Field Cottage, West Compton, nr Dorchester, Dorset DT2 0EY; Eldridge, Pope & Co plc, The Dorchester Brewery, PO Box 2, Dorchester, Dorset DT1 1QT (☎ 0305 251251)

POPE, Sir Joseph Albert; s of Albert Henry Pope, and Mary Pope; *b* 18 Oct 1914; *Educ* Sch of Arts and Crafts Cambridge, King's Coll London; *m* 1940, Evelyn Alice, da of Rev Robert Henry Gallagher; 1 s, 2 da; *Career* Whitworth scholarship 1935, prof of mechanical engrg Nottingham Univ 1949-60, vice chllr Univ of Aston in Birmingham 1969-79, chm TecQuipment Gp Nottingham 1975-88; dir John Brown plc 1970-82, gen treas Br Assoc 1975-82, chm W Midlands Econ Planning Cncl 1977-79, dir Royal Worcester plc 1979-84; Hon LLD Birmingham Univ 1979, Hon DUniv Heriot-Watt 1979; Hon DSc: Aston 1979, Belfast 1980, Salford 1980, Nottingham 1987; FBIM, CEng, FIMechE; kt 1980; *Style*— Sir Joseph Pope; 3 Mapperley Hall Drive, Nottingham NG3 5EP (☎ 0602 621146); TecQuipment Ltd, Bonsall St, Long Eaton, Nottingham NG10 2AN (☎ 0602 722611, telex 377 828)

POPE, Michael Henry Burges; s of Maj John Edward Buckingham Pope (d 1978), and Elizabeth Burges, *née* Watson; *b* 28 June 1940; *Educ* Aiglon Coll Switzerland; *m* 1, 6 Feb 1969, Edwina Elizabeth, da of Maj John Francis Yates, of Codsall Wood, nr Wolverhampton; 2 s (Henry b 1972, Charles b 1973); m 2, 17 Aug 1982, Jane Philippa, da of George Raikes, of The Ark, Coleman's Hatch, nr E Grinstead, Sussex; *Career* sales dir Golf-o-Tron UK Ltd 1964-66; mktg field promotions: conslt Ulysses Group 1972-77, chm FPS Field Marketing Ltd 1977-90, chm Swiftwash Ltd 1962-89; memb Lloyds (1973); team mangr Br World Gliding Team 1983; MInstM; *Recreations* gliding, skiing (Ski Club of GB gold, Kandahar gold); *Clubs* Lansdowne, SCGB, Avon Gliding; *Style*— Michael Pope, Esq; 123 Woodsford Square, Addison Road, London W14 8DT (☎ 071 603 8769)

POPE, Philip William Rolph; s of Alfred Rolph Pope (d 1951), of Dorchester, and Kate Rendall (d 1967); *b* 19 March 1907; *Educ* Charterhouse, Trinity Coll Cambridge (BA); *m* 1939, Joyce Winifred, da of James Harcourt Slade (d 1962); 1 s (Jeremy James Richard b 1943), 2 da (Philippa Rachel b 1940, Nicola Jane b 1948); *Career* actg Capt RA 1939-46, Capt (actg) ADGB England, Main HQ BAOR Belgium and Germany; slr 1931; Eldridge Pope & Co plc: dir 1931, md 1951, chm 1974, pres 1982; dir Co of Proprietors Weymouth Waterworks; chm Weymouth Waterworks until taken over by Water Bd; cmmr for taxes Dorchester; chm Weymouth Div; *Clubs* ESJ; *Style*— Philip Pope, Esq; The Garden House, Tenantrees, West Stafford, Dorchester, Dorset DT2 8AW (☎ 0305 262811); The Brewery, Dorchester (☎ 0305 251251)

POPE, Hon Dr (Rachel Trixie); *née* Gardner; 2 da of Baroness Gardner of Parkes, *qv*; *b* 8 April 1961; *Educ* Univ of London (MB BS); *m* 24 Sept 1988, Dr Alvan John Pope, s of Kenneth Pope, of The Old Rectory, Chastleton, Glos; *Style*— The Hon Dr Pope; 20 Bark Place, London W2 4AR

POPE, Very Rev Robert William; OBE (1970); s of Jonas George Pope (d 1970), and Marjorie Mary, *née* Coates (d 1978); *b* 20 May 1916; *Educ* Harvey GS Folkestone, Maidstone GS, St Augustine Coll Canterbury, Univ of Durham (LTh); *m* 12 Aug 1941, Elizabeth Beatrice Matilda, da of Robert James Bressey; 2 s (David Robert b 1942, Patrick John b 1943), 1 da (Hilary Mary Elizabeth b 1948); *Career* ordained Rochester Cathedral: deacon 1939, priest 1940; curate: Holy Trinity Gravesend 1939-41, St Nicholas Guildford 1942-43, Peaslake Parish of Shere 1943-44; chaplain RN 1944-71; HMS Chinkara 1944-46, HMS Daedalus 1946-47, RM Barracks Chatham 1947-50, HMS Gambia 1950-52, RM Commando 1955-57, RM Barracks ITC Lympstone 1957-59, HMS Tiger 1959-60, HMS Sultan 1960-63, HMS Phoenecia 1963-65 (acting chllr St Pauls Anglican Cathedral Malta), HMS Dockyard Chatham 1965-67, RM Barracks Eastney 1967-69, HM Dockyard Portsmouth 1969-71; vicar Whitchurch Hants 1971-77, dean of Gibraltar 1977-82; minister gen Third Order Soc of St Francis 1987-90 (memb 1963, minister provincial Euro Province 1985-); *Style*— The Very Rev Robert Pope, OBE; West Wood, Wreath Green, Tatworth, Chard, Somerset TA20 2SN (☎ 0460 209 87)

POPE, Timothy Patrick; s of Bryan George Patrick Pope, of Walton-on-Thames, and Mary Margaret, *née* Knoyle; *b* 23 March 1948; *Educ* Glynn GS; *m* Dec 1980, Gerda Hendrika Maria, da of L T M Rokebrand; 3 s (Alexander b Sept 1983, Michael b Aug 1985, William b Feb 1988); *Career* ptnr Deloitte Plender Haskins & Sells 1979- (articled clerk 1966-70), ptnr Coopers & Lybrand Deloitte (following merger); FCA (ACA 1970); *Recreations* golf, photography; *Clubs* Brooks's, RAC, The Wisley Golf; *Style*— Timothy Pope, Esq; Coopers & Lybrand Deloitte, 128 Queen Victoria St, London EC4P 4JX (☎ 071 583 5000)

POPE-HENNESSY, Sir John Wyndham; CBE (1959, MBE 1944); s of Maj-Gen Ladislaus Herbert Richard Pope-Hennessy, CB, DSO (d 1942), and Dame Una Pope-Hennessy, DBE (d 1949); *b* 13 Dec 1913; *Educ* Downside, Balliol Coll Oxford; *Career* dir and sec V and A Museum 1967-73, dir Br Museum 1974-76, consultative chm Dept of Euro Paintings Metropolitan Museum New York 1977-86, prof of fine arts New York Univ 1977-; FBA, FSA, FRSL; kt 1971; *Style*— Sir John Pope-Hennessy, CBE, FSA; 28 via del Bardi, 50125 Florence, Italy

POPHAM, Maj-Gen Christopher John; CB (1982); s of Gordon F B Popham (d 1949), and Dorothy A L, *née* Yull (d 1990); *b* 2 April 1927; *Educ* Merchant Taylors'; *m* 1950, Heather Margaret, da of Lt-Col H Reginald W Dawson (d 1937); 2 s; *Career* asst COS (Intelligence) Supreme HQ Allied Powers Europe 1979-82, ret 1982, Col Cmdt Corps of RE 1982-87; dir Br Atlantic Ctee 1982-; *Recreations* photography, railways, music; *Style*— Maj-Gen Christopher Popham, CB; c/o Barclays Bank plc, High St, Andover, Hants

POPPER, Prof Sir Karl Raimund; CH (1982); s of Dr Simon Siegmund Carl Popper, of Vienna, and Jenny, *née* Schiff; *b* 28 July 1902; *Educ* Vienna Univ (PhD); *m* 1930, Josefine Anna, da of Josef Henninger (d 1985), of Vienna; *Career* prof of logic and scientific method LSE 1949-69, emeritus prof 1969-; memb Acad Int de Philosophie des Sciences 1949, hon memb Royal Soc of NZ 1965, foreign hon memb American Acad of Arts and Sciences 1966, assoc memb Académie Royale de Belgique 1976, memb d'Honneur Académie Int d'Histoire des Sciences 1977, hon memb Deutsche Akademie für Sprache and Dichtung 1979, memb de l'Académie Européenne des Sciences 1980, hon fell Darwin Coll Cambridge, memb de l'Institut de France 1980, Socio Straniero dell'Accademia Nazionale dei Lincei 1981, hon memb Austrian Akademie der Wissenschaften 1982; foreign associate of the Nat Acad of Sciences, Washington; sr res fell of the Hoover Inst Stamford Univ; Hon LittD Univ of Cambridge 1980, Hon DLitt Univ of Oxford 1982, Hon DSc Univ of London 1986; and many other hon degrees from British, NZ, US, Canadian, Austrian and German Univs; Grand Decoration of Honour in Gold (Austria) 1976, Ehrenzeichen für Wissenschaft & Kunst (Austria) 1980, Order Pour le Mérite (W Germany) 1980, Grand Cross with Star of the Order of Merit (W Germany) 1983, First Int prize of Catalonia 1989; FRS, FBA; *Publications incl*: The Logic of Scientific Discovery, The Open Society and Its Enemies, Conjectures and Refutations, Objective Knowledge, Unended Quest, The Self and Its Brain (with Sir John Eccles), Postcript to the Logic of Scientific Discovery (3 vols, ed W W Bartley III); *Style*— Prof Sir Karl Popper, CH, FRS; c/o London School of Economics and Political Science, Houghton St, London WC2A 2AE

POPPLEWELL, Nicholas James; s of Newton J Popplewell, of Gory, Co Wexford, and Olive, *née* Gregory; *b* 6 April 1964; *Educ* Newtown Sch Waterford; *Career* Rugby Union prop forward Greystones RFC and Ireland (2 caps); clubs: Gorey RFC, Greystones RFC 1984-, Barbarians RFC (v Newport 1989); rep: Leinster 1987-, Ireland U25 (debut v Italy 1988); Ireland: tour France 1988, tour USA and Canada 1989, debut v NZ 1989, reserve Five Nations 1990; retail mangr Argus Furniture; *Recreations* golf, squash, reading, eating; *Style*— Nicholas Popplewell, Esq; 90 Richmond Park, Bray, Co Wicklow (☎ 862614); Greystones Rugby Club, Greystones, Co Wicklow (☎ 874640/874814)

POPPLEWELL, Hon Mr Justice; Hon Sir Oliver Bury Popplewell; s of Frank Popplewell, OBE (d 1965), and Nina, *née* Sydney (d 1979); *b* 15 Aug 1927; *Educ* Charterhouse, Queens' Coll Cambridge (exhibitioner, MA, LLB); *m* 1954, Catharine Margaret, da of Alfred John Storey (d 1941); 4 s (and 1 s decd); *Career* served RN 1946-48; called to the Bar Inner Temple 1951, QC 1969, dep chm Oxon QS 1970-71; rec: Burton-on-Trent 1970-71, Crown Court 1972-83; bencher Inner Temple 1978, High Court Judge (Queen's Bench) 1983-; memb: of Home Office Advsy Bd on Restricted Patients 1980-82, Parole Bd 1985, Carlisle Ctee of Inquiry into Parole 1988; chm and ind memb Wages Cncls, vice chm of Parole Bd 1986-1987 (memb 1985), pres Employment Appeal Tbnl 1986-88, chm Ctee of Inquiry into Crowd Control Safety and Control at Sports Grounds 1985; kt 1983; *Recreations* sailing, tennis, bridge; *Clubs* MCC (memb Ctee 1972 and 1987-, tsteė 1983-), Hawks (Cambridge), Blakeney Sailing, Garrick; *Style*— The Hon Mr Justice Popplewell; Royal

Courts of Justice, Strand, London WC2

PORCHER, Michael Somerville; CMG (1962), OBE (1960); s of late Geoffrey Lionel Porcher; *b* 9 March 1921; *Educ* Cheltenham, St Edmund Hall Oxford; *m* 1955, Mary Lorraine, *née* Tweedy; 2 s; *Career* dep chief sec Br Guyana 1956, colonial sec Br Honduras 1960, chief sec 1961, ret 1964; sec Ops Div RNLI 1964-83, ret; *Style—* Michael Porcher Esq, CMG, OBE; Bladon, Worth Matravers, nr Swanage, Dorset BH19 3LQ

PORCHESTER, Lord; George Reginald Oliver Molyneux Herbert (Geordie); s and h of 7 Earl of Carnarvon, *qv*; *b* 10 Nov 1956; *Educ* Eton, St John's Coll Oxford (BA); *m* 16 Dec 1989, Jayne M, eldest da of K A Wilby, of Cheshire, and Princess Prospero Colonna di Stigliano, of Ashford, Co Wicklow; *Career* a page of honour to HM The Queen 1969-73; computer conslt and horticulturalist 1976-79; *Style—* Lord Porchester

PORRITT, Baron (Life Peer UK 1973), of Wanganui, NZ, and of Hampstead, Greater London; Sir Arthur Espie Porritt; 1 Bt (UK 1963), GCMG (1967), GCVO (1970), CBE (1945); s of Ernest Edward Porritt, VD, MD, FRCS (d 1950), of Wanganui, NZ; *b* 10 Aug 1900; *Educ* Wanganui Collegiate Sch NZ, Otago Univ NZ, Magdalen Coll Oxford, St Mary's Hosp London; *m* 1, 1926, Mary Frances Wynne, da of William Bond; m 2, 1946, Kathleen Mary, da of late Alfred Sidney Peck, of Spalding, Lincs; 2 s (Hon Jonathan Espie b 1950, Hon Jeremy Charles b 1953), 1 da (Hon Joanna Mary (Hon Mrs Hardy) b 1948); *Heir* (to Btcy only) s, Hon Jonathon Espie Porritt; *Career* sits as Independent in House of Lords; Sgt Surgn to HM The Queen 1952-67, Govr-Gen of New Zealand 1967-72; pres: RSM 1966-67, RCS 1960-63, BMA 1960-61 (Gold Medal); formerly hon surgn: St Mary's Hosp, Royal Masonic Hosp (chm 1973-82; Grand Master's Order of Service to Masonry 1981), King Edward VII Hosp for Offrs, Hosp of St John and Elizabeth; consulting surgn: King Edward VII Convalescent Home for Offrs, Osborne and Royal Hosp Chelsea; hon consulting Surgn to the Army 1954-67, chm Medical Advisory Ctee Miny of Overseas Devpt, memb Int Olympic Ctee 1934, chm Empire Games Fedn 1948-67, vice pres 1968-; Red Cross cmmr for NZ in UK; chm African Med and Res Fndn 1973-82; pres Arthritis and Rheumatism Cncl 1973-88; KStJ; Order Legion of Merit (USA); *Clubs* Buck's; *Style—* Brig the Rt Hon the Lord Porritt, GCMG, GCVO, CBE; 57 Hamilton Terrace, NW8 (☎ 071 286 9212)

PORRITT, Hon Jeremy Charles; s of Baron Porritt, GCMG, GCVO, CBE (Life Peer and 1 Bt); *b* 19 Jan 1953; *Educ* Eton; *m* 1980, Penny, da of J H Moore, of London, Ontario; 2 s (Andrew b 1981, Hugo b 1986); *Style—* The Hon Jeremy Porritt

PORRITT, Hon Jonathon Espie; s and h of Baron Porritt, GCMG, GCVO, CBE (Life Peer and 1 Bt); *b* 6 July 1950; *Educ* Eton, Magdalen Coll Oxford; *m* 1986, Sarah, da of Malcolm Staniforth, of Malvern, Worcs; *Career* dir Friends of the Earth 1984-90; author; *Books* Seeing Green: the Politics of Ecology Explained, The Friends of the Earth Handbook, The Coming of the Greens, Where on Earth Are We Going; *Style—* The Hon Jonathon Porritt; 17a Laurier Road, London NW5 1SD

PORRITT, Sheila; da of Lt Cdr Geoffrey Arthur Stephen Cowley, MBE (d 1979), and Linda, *née* Dessberg; *b* 14 June 1948; *Educ* Portsmouth HS for Girls, Univ of Bristol (BSc); *m* 11 April 1970 (m dis 1988), Stephen John Porritt, s of Sidney Sherwood Porritt (d 1966); 1 s (Eliot b 1979), 1 da (Luisa b 1987); *Career* scientific asst nuclear physics statistical res CEGB 1969-72, dept head of radio programming IBA 1987-89 (broadcasting exec: TV scheduling 1972-77, radio programming 1977-89), prog mangr Channel Four TV 1989-90, station mangr Melody Radio 1990-; memb Radio Acad Festival Ctee 1989; *Recreations* tennis, film, theatre, gardening, interior design; *Style—* Ms Sheila Porritt; The Sycamores, 131 Haverstock Hill, Hampstead, London NW3 4RU (☎ 071 722 5693); Channel Four Television, 60 Charlotte St, London W1P 2AX (☎ 071 927 8522, telex 892355, fax 071 637 1495)

PORTAL, Sir Jonathan Francis; 6 Bt (UK 1901), of Malshanger, Church Oakley, Co Southampton; s of Sir Francis Spencer Portal, 5 Bt (d 1984), and his 2 w, Jane Mary, da of late Albert Henry Williams, OBE; *b* 13 Jan 1953; *Educ* Marlborough, Edinburgh Univ (BCom); *m* 9 Oct 1982, Louisa Caroline, er da of John Hervey-Bathurst, *qv*; 1 s (William Jonathan Francis); *Heir* s, William Jonathan Francis Portal b 1 Jan 1987; *Career* chartered accountant (ACA); chief accountant Seymour Int Press Distributors; govr Old Malthouse School, Swanage, Dorset; Liveryman Clothworkers Co; *Recreations* travel, sailing, country sports; *Style—* Sir Jonathan Portal, Bt; 21 Yeomans Row, London SW3 2AL; office: (☎ 071 733 0022)

PORTARLINGTON, 7 Earl of (I 1785); George Lionel Yuill Seymour Dawson-Damer; Baron Dawson (I 1770), Viscount Carlow (I 1776); s of Air Cdre Viscount Carlow (k on active ser 1944) and gs of 6 Earl of Portarlington (d 1959); *b* 10 Aug 1938; *Educ* Eton; *m* 26 July 1961, Davina, eldest da of late Sir Edward Henry Windley, KCMG, KCVO; 3 s (Viscount Carlow, Hon Edward Lionel Seymour b 1967, Hon Henry Lionel Seymour b 1971), 1 da (Lady Marina Davina b 1969); *Heir* s, Viscount Carlow; *Career* Page of Honour to HM The Queen 1953-55; dir: G S Yuill & Co Ltd Sydney, Australian Stock Breeders Co Ltd Brisbane, Yuills Australia Ltd Sydney; *Recreations* skiing, fishing; *Clubs* Union (Sydney); *Style—* The Rt Hon the Earl of Portarlington; 19 Coolong Rd, Vaucluse, NSW 2030, Australia (☎ Sydney 010 61 2 337 3013)

PORTCH, Peter Ernest; s of Ernest Cecil Protch (d 1938), of Liverpool, and Edith Beatrice, *née* D'Abreu; *b* 14 Sept 1927; *Educ* Addleby Cumbria; *m* 23 Nov 1974, Joyce, da of Norman R Nicholson; *Career* RM 1945; joined head office Provincial Insur Co Lt 1948 (Leicester branch 1959-63), ptnr Black Patch & Swan 1963-74, cmmr Inland Revenue 1974-; memb bd tstees Loros Hospice Leicester, chm Br Insur and Investmt Policies Assoc 1986 (vice pres 1981); Freeman Worshipful Co of Insurers; ACII 1957; *Recreations* golf, sailing, tennis, shooting; *Clubs* Leicestershire Golf, St Enodoc Golf, Leicester Tennis; *Style—* Peter Portch, Esq; Sandbank Cottage, Stoughton Lane, Stoughton, Leicestershire LE2 2FH (☎ 0533 717633); 1 West Walk, Leicester LE1 7NG (☎ 0533 553 676, fax 0533 548 145)

PORTEN, Anthony Ralph; QC (1988); s of Ralph Charles Porten (d 1976), and Joan, *née* Edden; *b* 1 March 1947; *Educ* Epsom Coll, Emmanuel Coll Cambridge (BA); *m* 17 Oct 1970, Kathryn Mary, da of John Rees Edwards, JP (d 1988); 2 da (Lucinda b 1973, Deborah b 1976); *Career* called to the Bar Inner Temple 1969; *Recreations* family, walking, motoring; *Clubs* RAC; *Style—* Anthony Porten, Esq, QC; Clive Cottage, Claremont Drive, Esher, Surrey KT10 9LU (☎ 0372 467513); 8 New Square, Lincoln's Inn, London WC2A 3QP (☎ 071 242 4986, telex 21785 ADVICE G, fax 071 405 1166, car 0836 215935)

PORTEOUS, Christopher Selwyn; s of Selwyn Porteous (d 1972), of Dulwich, and Marjorie Irene, *née* Glover (d 1958); *b* 8 Nov 1935; *Educ* Dulwich; *m* 27 Feb 1960, Brenda, da of William Stanley Wallis (d 1977); 4 da (Catherine b 1961, Judith b 1963, Gillian b 1965, Anne b 1969); *Career* admitted slr 1960; articled clerk local Govt 1954-60, slr London CC 1960-62; New Scotland Yard: legal asst 1962-68, sr legal asst 1968-76, asst slr 1976-86, slr to the Cmmr of Police 1987-; author of articles in law magazines; reader of C of E, former memb pastoral ctee Rochester Dio; memb Law Soc; *Recreations* writing, gardening, walking, listening to music; *Style—* Christopher Porteous, Esq; The Solicitor, Solicitors Department, New Scotland Yard, Broadway, London SW1H 0BG (☎ 071 230 7353, fax 071 230 7215)

PORTEOUS, George Ross Dalziel; s of Prof Alexander James Dow Porteous (d 1981), of Birkenhead, Merseyside, and Eliza Murray Dalziel, *née* Ross (d 1972); *b* 19 July 1934; *Educ* Birkenhead Sch, Univ of Liverpool (LLB); *m* 23 Feb 1963, (Constance) Ursula, da of Hubert Kerridge (d 1969), of Irby Wirral, Merseyside; 1 s (Michael b 1965), 2 da (Lyn b 1963, Fiona b 1968); *Career* slr 1960, sr ptnr Warburton Porteous and Co; NP; pres The Cheshire Co Lawn Tennis Assoc 1989-90, rep Lawn Tennis Assoc Cncl; memb: Law Soc, Liverpool Law Soc, Soc of Notaries; *Recreations* tennis, squash, photography; *Clubs* Heswall Lawn Tennis, Heswall Squash Racquets; *Style—* George Porteous, Esq; Kinross, 8 Church Meadow Lane, Heswall, Wirral, Merseyside L60 4SB (☎ 051 342 1713); 90-92 Telegraph Rd, Heswall, Wirral, Merseyside L60 0AQ (☎ 051 342 6116)

PORTEOUS, John Robin; s of Charles Frederick Porteous (d 1941), of London, and Mary Grace, *née* Wooster; *b* 29 July 1934; *Educ* Westminster, ChCh Oxford (MA); *m* 16 June 1956, Catherine Eleanor, da of John Traill Christie; 2 s (Matthew b 1957, Tom b 1960), 1 da (Rebecca b 1969); *Career* Baring Bros & Co Ltd 1955-57, Philip Hill Higginson Ltd 1957-60, ptnr Pember & Boyle Stockbrokers 1966-86 (joined 1960), dir Morgan Grenfell Govt Securities Ltd 1986; memb Stock Exchange 1966-87, fell and bursar Gonville and Caius Coll Cambridge 1987-; memb: Cncl of Ancient Monuments Soc, Royal Mint Advsy Ctee 1968, Syndicate of Fitzwilliam Museum Cambridge 1989; Liveryman Worshipful Co of Skinners 1956; FSA 1980; *Books* Coins (1963), Coins in History (1969), Aangemunt En Nagemunt (Amsterdam 1970); *Recreations* numismatics, foreign travel, second hand bookshops; *Style—* John Porteous, Esq, FSA; 52 Elgin Cres, London W11 (☎ 071 727 6915); 7 Summerfield, Newnham, Cambridge (☎ 0223 63947); Gonville and Caius College, Cambridge CB2 1TA (☎ 0223 332455, fax 0223 332456)

PORTEOUS, Col Patrick Anthony; VC (Dieppe 1942); s of Brig-Gen C McL Porteous (d 1936); *b* 1 Jan 1918; *Educ* Wellington, RMA Woolwich; *m* 1, 1943, Lois Mary (d 1953), da of Maj-Gen Sir Horace Roome, KCIE (d 1970); 1 s, 1 da; m 2, 1955, Deirdre, da of late Eric King; 3 da; *Career* 2 Lt RA 1937, 6 AA Regt 1938, served France, Belgium, Dunkirk 1939-40, joined Commandos 1940, Dieppe 1942, Normandy 1944; instr RMA Sandhurst 1950-53, DAQMG FARELF 1953-56, 14 Field Regt RA 1956, RAF Staff Coll 1958, AMS HQ Southern Cmd 1959-60, Col Junior Leaders Regt RA 1960-63, Col Gen Staff War Off later MOD 1963-66, Cdr Rheindahlen Garrison 1966-69, ret 1970; *Recreations* sailing, gardening; *Style—* Col Patrick Porteous, VC; Christmas Cottage, Funtington, Chichester, W Sussex (☎ 0243 58315)

PORTER *see also*: Horsbrugh-Porter

PORTER, Alastair Robert Wilson; CBE (1985); s of James Porter (d 1974), of 40 Backwoods Lane, Lindfield, Haywards Heath, Sussex, and Olivia, *née* Duncan (d 1968); *b* 28 Sept 1928; *Educ* Irvine Royal Acad, Glasgow Acad, Merton Coll Oxford (MA); *m* 28 Aug 1954, Jennifer Mary Priaulx, da of Capt Philip Charles Forman, RN (d 1965); 2 s (Angus b 1957, Duncan b 1961), 1 da (Francis b 1955); *Career* Nat Serv Royal Scot Fus and RASC 1947-49 (2 Lt 1948); barr 1952-54, res magistrate N Rhodesia 1954-61, registrar of High Ct of N Rhodesia 1961-64, perm sec Min of Justice N Rhodesia (later Zambia) 1964-65, sec and registrar RCVS 1966-91; Haywards Heath Round Table until 1968, class ldr Perrymount Road Methodist Church, sec gen Fedn of Veterinarians of the EEC 1973-79, chm EEC'S Advsy Ctee on Veterinary Training 1986, vice chm Euro Secretariat for the Lib Professions; hon Akademische Ehrenbürger Hanover Veterinary Sch 1988; memb Gray's Inn 1952; Hon Assoc RCVS 1979; *Books* An Anatomy of Europe (jtly, 1972); *Recreations* watching soccer; *Clubs* Caledonian; *Style—* Alastair Porter, Esq; 4 Savill Rd, Lindfield, Haywards Heath, Sussex, RH16 2NX (☎ 0444 482001)

PORTER, Alistair Campbell; s of Robert William Porter, OBE, of 73 Beaumont Rd, Cambridge, and Marion Audrey, *née* Glascock; *b* 26 March 1950; *Educ* The Leys Sch, Univ of Exeter (LLB), Coll of Law; *m* 31 Aug 1985, Leila, da of Adel Assassa (d 1972); 2 da (Francesca Lauren b 1987, Melissa Claire b 1989); *Career* sr ptnr Alistair Porter & Co slrs 1981-; memb Law Soc; *Recreations* sailing; *Clubs* Royal Ocean Racing, Royal Corinthian Yacht; *Style—* Alistair Porter, Esq; 16-18 Empress Place, West Brompton London SW6 (☎ 071 405 8855, fax 071 386 9570, car tel 0836 711 030)

PORTER, Arthur Thomas; s of Guy Hazeley Porter (d 1982), of Sierra Leone, and Aoina Agnes, *née* Cole (d 1949); *b* 26 Jan 1924; *Educ* Fourah Bay Coll (BA), Cambridge Univ (BA, MA), Boston Univ USA (PhD); *m* 1 Sept 1953, Rigmor Sondergaard, da of Christian Malling Rasmussen (d 1971); 1 s (Arthur Thomas b 1956), 1 da (Emma Adina b 1958); *Career* asst lectr Edinburgh Univ 1952-53; Univ of Sierra Leone: lectr Fourah Bay Coll 1953-58 (sr lectr 1958-61), prof 1962-64, vice chllr 1974-84; princ Univ Coll Nairobi Kenya 1964-70, staff memb UNESCO 1970-74, Fulbright scholar USA 1986-87; memb Sierra Leone Historical Soc; Hon Citizen Kansas City Kansas Missouri USA; Hon LHD Boston Univ USA 1969, Hon LLD Univ of Malta 1969, Hon DLitt Univ of Sierra Leone 1988; memb Order of the Republic of Sierra Leone (MRSL) 1978; *Books* Creoledom (1963); *Clubs* Royal Cwlth Soc; *Style—* Arthur Porter, Esq; 81 Fitzjohn Ave, Barnet, Herts EN5 2HN; 266 Spur Rd, PO Box 1363, Freetown, Sierra Leone

PORTER, Bruce Scott; s of Eric Andrew Porter (d 1981), and Helen, *née* Spooner (d 1964); *b* 12 Dec 1937; *Educ* Christ's Hosp, Trinity Coll Oxford (BA, MA, 1st XV Rugby); *m* Jan 1963, Marion, da of Sydney Herbert Allard; *Career* Baker & McKenzie: articled clerk 1961-64, admitted slr 1965, admitted slr New South Wales and Victoria 1967, slr Sydney 1967-72, ptnr 1969, admitted slr Hong Kong 1977, slr Hong Kong 1977-80, admin ptnr London 1975, 1977 and 1982, memb Exec Ctee 1985-88, chm Policy Ctee 1990-91; memb Law Soc; *Recreations* tennis, walking, travel; *Style—* Bruce Porter, Esq; Stanbridge House, Staplefield, Sussex (☎ 0444 400209); Baker & McKenzie, Aldwych House, Aldwych, London WC2B 4JP (☎ 071 242 6531, fax 071 831 8611)

PORTER, Colin Blanchard; s of Harry Colin Porter (d 1969), and Eveline Porter (d 1976); *b* 16 Sept 1937; *Educ* Hull GS, Shuttleworth Agric Coll (CDA, NDA); *m* 24 Aug 1963, Pauline Margaret, da of Keneth Walter Ekins (d 1949); 2 s (Andrew James b 1967, Simon John b 1969); *Career* ICI: devpt mangr agrochemicals ICI Australasia 1965-69, mangr agrochemicals 1973-75, territorial mangr PPD 1976-78 (1970-73); mangr agrochemicals ICI: SA 1983-86, Pakistan 1986-88; dir gen ICI Romania 1989 (1978-82); memb Nat Tst; *Recreations* wine appreciation, squash, tennis, gardening; *Clubs* Diplomatic (Bucharest); *Style—* Colin Porter, Esq; Uplands, Brandy Hole Lane, Chichester, W Sussex (☎ 0243 527798); Hotel Bucharest, Scara E appt 17, Bucharest, Romania (☎ 131063); ICI Romania, 1 Edgar Quinet St, Sector 1, Bucharest, Romania (☎ 131250, fax 133178, telex 11672 ICIRO R)

PORTER, Colin Grant; s of William Graham Porter (d 1973), and Edna May, *née* Wilson; *b* 18 March 1951; *Educ* Syon Sch Isleworth, Harrow Sch of Art, Wolverhampton Sch of Art (BA); *m* 15 July 1972, Janice Ann, da of Albert Edward Manning; 4 s (Joel Edward William b 26 Oct 1976, James Henry b 30 Aug 1978, William Alexander b 11 Feb 1982, Theo Hugh b 2 April 1989); *Career* jr graphic designer Fitch & Company 1977, graphic designer Murdoch Design Associates 1973-74, assoc dir Fitch & Company 1978-79 (sr designer 1974-79), founding ptnr Coley

Porter Bell 1979; clients incl: Guinness, Marks & Spencer, United Biscuits, Tesco, Jacksons of Piccadilly, A & P, Woolworths, RHM, Sainsburys; regular tutor and speaker on design and design management for various orgns incl Design Cncl and Market Res Soc; awarded: 3 CLIOs (US) 1989, 1 CLIO (US) 1990, Design Business Assoc Design Effectiveness award 1990, D & ADA awards; one man painting exhibition (Smith's Gallery Covent Garden) 1991; fndr memb Design Business Assoc; memb: D & ADA 1975, CSD 1986; *Recreations* painting, collecting anything that looks good (especially paintings and ephemera); *Style*— Colin Porter, Esq; Coley Porter Bell, 4 Flitcroft Street, London WC2 (☎ 071 379 4355)

PORTER, David Andrew; s of Michael Robert Porter, OBE, of Hereford, and Cecile Jane Graeme, *née* Stuart (d 1988); *b* 22 April 1960; *Educ* Dulwich; *Career* media exec Westbourne Ltd 1977-78, media mangr Woolward Royds (Edinburgh) Ltd 1980-82, co dir Yellowhammer Advertising Co 1986-89 (media exec 1978-80, dep md 1982-89), md Axle Media Ltd 1989-90; media dir: Generator Advertising and Marketing Ltd 1989-90, The Leisure Process Ltd 1990-; MIPA 1987; *Recreations* music, cinema, passive smoking; *Style*— David Porter, Esq; The Leisure Process Ltd, 126 Great Portland St, London W1N 5PH (☎ 071 631 0666)

PORTER, David John; MP (C) Waveney 1987-; s of George Edward Porter (d 1964), of Lowestoft, and Margaret Elizabeth, *née* Robinson; *b* 16 April 1948; *Educ* Lowestoft GS, New Coll of Speech and Drama London; *m* 25 March 1978, Sarah Jane, da of Rev Peter Shaw (d 1979); 2 s (Thomas Edward b 1982, Samuel George b 1986), 2 da (Victoria Louise b 1979, Alice Elizabeth b 1988); *Career* dist cncllr Waveney; *Recreations* writing, Waveney past present and future, family; *Style*— David Porter, Esq, MP; House of Commons, Westminster, London SW1A OAA (☎ 071 219 6235)

PORTER, Dorothea Noelle Naomi (Thea); da of Rev M S Seale, of Limassol, Cyprus, and Rene, *née* Attal; *b* 24 Dec 1927; *Educ* Lycée Francais Damascus, Fern Hill Manor, Royal Holloway Coll; *m* (m dis 1967), Robert Stanley Porter, CB, OBE, s of S R Porter; 1 da (Venetia Ann); *Career* embassy wife Beirut, painter; six exhibitions Beirut 1954-64; interior designer London 1964-67, fashion and fabric designer 1967-; Designer of the Year 1972 (with Zandra Rhodes); *Books* author various articles in Harpers & Queen Magazine; *Recreations* cooking, travelling, music, painting, collecting antique Islamic fabrics, consulting clairvoyants; *Clubs* Colony Room, The Ottoman Picnic; *Style*— Mrs Thea Porter; 13 Bolton Street, London W1

PORTER, George Barrington (Barry); MP (C) Wirral South 1983-; s of Kenneth William Porter; *b* 11 June 1939; *Educ* Birkenhead Sch, Univ Coll Oxford; *m* 1965, Susan Carolyn James; 2 s, 3 da; *Career* slr 1965, cncllr Birkenhead County Borough Cncl 1967-74, Wirral Borough 1975-79, MP (C) Bebington and Ellesmere Port 1979-1983; *Clubs* RAC, Artists (Liverpool); *Style*— Barry Porter, Esq, MP; House of Commons, London SW1 (☎ 071 219 3000)

PORTER, Henry Christopher Mansel; s of Maj Harry Robert Mansel Porter, MBE, of Pershore, Worcs, and Anne Victoria, *née* Seymour; *b* 23 March 1953; *Educ* Wellington, Univ of Manchester (BA), Perugia Univ Italy; *m* Elizabeth Mary Elliot; 2 da (Miranda Victoria Elliot b 30 Oct 1985, Charlotte Mary Clementine Elliot b 22 Oct 1988); *Career* journalist; Evening Standard 1979-81, feature writer Sunday Times 1981-83 (columnist 1983-87); ed: Illustrated London News 1987-89, Sunday Correspondent Magazine 1989-90, assoc ed Independent on Sunday 1990-, dir Media Interviews; *Books* Lies, Damned Lies and Some Exclusives (1984); *Recreations* sailing, sleeping in the afternoon, reading; *Style*— Henry Porter, Esq; c/o Lloyds Bank plc, Pershore, Worcs; The Independent on Sunday, 40 City Rd, London EC1Y 2DB (☎ 071 253 1222)

PORTER, James (Henry) Newton; TD; s of Col James Herbert Porter, CBE, DSO (d 1973), of Pigdon Hall, Morpeth, Northumberland, and Ellen, *née* Newton (d 1947); *b* 23 Feb 1926; *Educ* Eton; *m* 12 April 1950, Violet Anne Bates (Wendy), da of Sir Ralph George Elphinstone Mortimer, KT, OBE (d 1955), of Milbourne Hall, Ponteland, Newcastle upon Tyne; 1 s (Timothy b 1952), 1 da (Lucinda b 1954); *Career* Capt Grenadier Gds 1944-47, Maj Northumberland Hussars 1948-59; dir: John Rowell & Sons Ltd 1959, Scottish & Newcastle Breweries Ltd 1960; The Newcastle Breweries Ltd: joined 1947, asst md 1954, jt md 1961, md 1964, chm and md 1967, ret 1976; farmer 1976-; memb: Ct Univ of Newcastle upon Tyne, Cncl for the Disabled Newcastle upon Tyne; Northumberland Boy Scouts: chm fin ctee, chm West Castle Dist; *Recreations* shooting; *Clubs* Northern Counties (Newcastle upon Tyne); *Style*— Henry Porter, Esq, TD; The Woll, 46 Runnynede Rd, Ponteland, Newcastle upon Tyne NE20 9HG (☎ 0661 227 42); Pigdon Farm, Morpeth, Northumberland NE61 3SE (☎ 0670 513 511)

PORTER, James Forrest; s of Ernest Porter, and Mary Violetta Porter; *b* 2 Oct 1928; *Educ* Salford GS, Dudley Trg Coll, LSE, London Univ Inst of Educn; *m* 1952, Dymphna, da of Leo Francis Powell; 2 da (Louise, Alison); *Career* princ Bulmershe Coll of Higher Educn 1967-78, dir gen Cwlth Inst 1978-; chm World Educ Fellowship 1979-, Cwlth fell Aust 1977, conslt UN 1975-; memb: UGC 1970-76, James Ctee on Teacher Educn 1972-, IBA 1973-80, BBC Educn Cncl 1987-; chm Newsconcern Int 1983-, memb Bd Cwlth Magazine; FRSA, Hon FCP, FRGS; *Clubs* Royal Commonwealth Soc, Athenaeum; *Style*— James Porter, Esq; Commonwealth Institute, Kensington High St, London W8 6NQ (☎ 071 602 3252); House by the Water, Bolney Ave, Shiplake, Oxon (☎ 073 522 2187)

PORTER, James William; OBE (1990), MC (1945); s of Edward William (d 1932), of 14 Ernest Place, Fenton, Stoke-on-Trent, and Annie Louisa Porter (d 1977); *b* 22 Sept 1910; *Educ* St Thomas RC Stoke-on-Trent; *m* 1937, Mabel (d 1961), da of Herbert Brittan (d 1964), of Stoke-on-Trent; 2 da (Patricia, June); *Career* Capt, served Dunkirk, N Africa, Italy, Austria; exec co rels 1970, dir Michelin Tyre UK Group 1975; vice pres: Staffs Assoc of Boys Clubs, Stoke-on-Trent branch Dunkirk Veterans Assoc; *Style*— James Porter, Esq, OBE, MC; 425 New Inn Lane, Trentham, Stoke-on-Trent ST4 8BN (☎ 0782 657965); Michelin Tyre plc, Campbell Rd, Stoke-on-Trent ST1 4EY (☎ 0782 48101, telex 36299)

PORTER, Air Vice-Marshal John Alan; OBE (1971); s of Alan Porter (d 1979), and Etta, *née* Ward (d 1952); *b* 29 Sept 1934; *Educ* Lawrence Sheriff Rugby, Bristol Univ (BSc), Southampton Univ; 2 s (Alan, David); *Career* Procurement Exec MOD 1984-89, ret RAF 1989; dir Communications-Electronics Security Group GCHQ; *Recreations* the arts, skiing; *Style*— Air Vice-Marshal John Porter, OBE; GCHQ, Oakley, Cheltenham, Glos

PORTER, John Andrew; TD, JP (Kent 1952), DL (Kent); s of Horace Augustus Porter, DFC, JP (d 1948), of Kent, and Vera Marion, *née* Andrew (d 1967); *b* 18 May 1916; *Educ* Radley, Sidney Sussex Coll Cambridge (MA); *m* 1941, Margaret Isobel, da of Samuel Alexander Wisnom (d 1944), of London; 2 da (Jocelyn, Angela); *Career* served WWII, Lt-Col RA; past chm: Anglia Building Society, Hastings and Thanet Building Society; sr ptnr Porter & Cobb Chartered Surveyors 1948-81, chm Gravesham PSD 1976-83; pres Gravesend Cons Assoc 1966-78, cmmr of Income Tax; FRICS; *Recreations* cricket, gardening, reading; *Clubs* RAC, Hawks (Cambridge), Kent CCC (pres 1985-86); *Style*— John Porter, Esq, TD, JP, DL; Leader, Hodsoll St, nr Wrotham, Kent TN15 7LH (☎ 0723 822260); 178-182 Parrock St, Gravesend, Kent (☎ 0474 64400)

PORTER, Air Marshal Sir (Melvin) Kenneth Drowley; KCB (1967, CB 1959), CBE (1945, OBE 1944); s of Flt Lt Edward Ernest Porter, MBE, DCM (d 1927), and Helen Porter (d 1920); *b* 19 Nov 1912; *Educ* No 1 Sch of Tech Trg Halton, RAF Coll Cranwell; *m* 1940, Elena, da of F W Sinclair (d 1961); 2 s, 1 da; *Career* RAF 1928, cmmnd 1932, served WWII 1939-45 (despatches 3); chief signals offr: Balloon Cmd 11 Gp, 2 Tactical AF 1943-45 (Actg Air Cdre 1944), Bomber Cmd 1945-46, 2 TAF 1955-56, Fighter Cmd 1956-59 (Air Cdre 1958), IDC 1959, Cmdt No 4 Sch of Tech Trg RAF St Athan and Air Offr Wales 1960-61, dir-gen of Ground Trg Air Miny 1961-63, Air Vice-Marshal 1962, dir-gen of Signals (Air) MOD 1963-66, AOC-in-C Maintenance Cmd 1966-70, Air Marshal 1966, ret 1970; dir Tech Educn Projects Dept of Educn Univ Coll Cardiff 1970-74, conslt 1975; CEng, FRAeS, FIEE, CBIM; Offr Legion of Merit (USA); *Recreations* reading; *Clubs* RAF; *Style*— Air Marshal Sir Kenneth Porter, KCB, CBE; c/o Lloyds Bank, Redland Branch, 163 Whiteladies Rd, Clifton, Bristol BS8 8RW

PORTER, Sir Leslie; s of Henry Alfred Porter (d 1955), and Jane, *née* Goldstein (d 1983); *b* 10 July 1920; *Educ* Holloway Co Sch; *m* 1949, Shirley, da of Sir John Edward Cohen (d 1980); 1 s (John), 1 da (Linda); *Career* Nat Serv WWII Army 1 Bn KRRC TQMS; served: Egypt, Greece, Lybia, Algeria, Sicily, Italy; chm Tesco plc 1973-85 (pres 1985-90), landowner (8200 acres); memb Lloyds 1964- (John Poland and other syndicates), chm Euro-Consultants London Ltd 1990-; hon vice pres Sports Aid Fndn, Hon chm Bd of Govrs Tel Aviv Univ, govr Hong Kong Baptist Coll, vice pres Age Concern NPFA, pres UK Boys' Town Jerusalem; past pres Inst of Grocery Distribution; CBIM, FIGD; *Recreations* yachting, golf, bridge, swimming; *Clubs* City Livery, Coombe Hill Golf, Dyrham Park Co, Frilford Heath Golf, RAC, Valderrama Golf; *Style*— Sir Leslie Porter

PORTER, Hon Mrs (Linda Carol); *née* Bellow; yr da of Baron Bellwin, JP (Life Peer); *b* 1956; *m* 1, 1976 (m dis 1988), Leslie Harris; m 2, June 1990, Steven Porter; *Style*— The Hon Mrs Harris; Flat 8, 20 Crediton Hill, London NW6 1HP

PORTER, Luke St George Fehling; s of John Vivian Porter, and Henrietta, *née* Fehling; *b* 6 May 1972; *Educ* Bournemouth Sch, Brockenhurst Coll, Bournemouth Poly; *Career* trampolinist; clubs: KATS, Poole Trampoline Club, Littledown Trampoline Club; under 11 World Champion; Br Champion: under 11, under 13, under 15, under 18; Br Men's Champion 1989 (youngest ever), jr int (first appearance aged 13, capt Br team 1988-90), sr int (first appearance aged 15); first Nissen Cup (under 15) 1985, fourth European Youth Championships (under 18) 1988, first GB v W Germany (under 18) 1989, thirty fifth European Championships Denmark 1989, third Dobrovolski Cup Russia 1989, eleventh World Championships Germany 1990; second Br Gymnastic Championship (under 11); *Recreations* snooker, diving, ten pin bowling; *Style*— Luke Porter, Esq; 11 Malmesbury Park Place, Bournemouth, Dorset BH8 8PH (☎ 0202 396278)

PORTER, Marguerite Ann (Mrs Henson); da of William Albert Porter, and Mary Maughan; *b* 30 Nov 1948; *m* 1, 1970 (m dis 1978), Carl Myers; m 2, 1 Aug 1986, Nicholas Victor Leslie Henson, s of Leslie Henson; 1 s (Keaton Leslie b 24 March 1988); *Career* Royal Ballet Co 1966-: soloist 1973, princ 1978-85, guest artist 1985-; *Books* Ballerina, A Dancers Life (1989); *Recreations* motherhood, reading, friends, theatre, teaching Balletcise (a ballet-based exercise class); *Style*— Ms Marguerite Porter; c/o Richard Jackson, 59 Knightsbridge, London SW1

PORTER, Peter Neville Frederick; s of William Ronald Porter (d 1982), of Brisbane, Australia, and Marion, *née* Main (d 1938); *b* 16 Feb 1929; *Educ* C of E GS Brisbane, Toowoomba GS; *m* 24 March 1961, Shirley Jannice, da of Dr Richard Nichol Henry; 2 da (Katherine Sybilla Marion b 1962, Clarissa Jane b 1965); *Career* poet; journalist Brisbane 1947-48, warehouseman Brisbane until 1951, clerk London 1951-53 and 1955-56, bookseller London 1956-59, advertising copywriter 1959-68, freelance writer 1968-; author of: Collected Poems (1983, contents of 9 previously published volumes), Fast Forward (1984), The Automatic Oracle (1987), Possible Worlds (1989); awarded: London Magazine Poetry prize 1962, Duff Cooper Memorial prize 1984, Whitbread Poetry award 1988; DLitt hc: Univ of Melbourne 1985, Univ of Loughborough 1986; Australian Literature Gold medal 1990; former memb Literature Panel Arts Council; *Recreations* music, Italy; *Style*— Peter Porter, Esq; Flat 3, 42 Cleveland Square, London W2 6DA (☎ 071 262 4289)

PORTER, Richard James; s of Capt James Graham Porter, of Conwy, Gwynedd, and Ann, *née* Wharry; *b* 28 Nov 1951; *Educ* Eton, Univ Coll Oxford (MA, MSc, BM BCh); *m* 26 July 1974, Diana Isabel, da of Douglas James Roper Austin (d 1979); 2 da (Charlotte b 1977, Alice b 1980); *Career* sr registrar in obstetrics and gynaecology St Mary's Hosp London and Addenbrookes Hosp Cambridge 1984-88, conslt in obstetrics and gynaecology Bath DHA 1989-; MRCOG 1982; *Recreations* wine, theatre; *Style*— Richard Porter, Esq; Weston Lea, Weston Park, Bath BA1 4AL (☎ 0225 425618); Bath Clinic, Claverton Down Rd, Bath BA2 7BR (☎ 0225 835555)

PORTER, Richard William; s of Dr W A Porter, of Hove, Sussex, and Phyllis May, *née* Richardson; *b* 25 March 1946; *Educ* Brighton Coll; *m* 1 Oct 1988, Tracy Jane Vallis-Porter, da of Stanley Vallis; *Career* insur broker: Halford Shead Lloyd's Broker 1965-71, G P Turner 1971-73; Alexander Stenhouse UK Ltd: joined 1973, mangr Reading Branch 1974-78, unit dir City Branch 1978-81, exec dir mktg London and Lloyd's 1981-82, devpt dir City Branch 1983-86, divnl dir Central Insur 1987-88, exec dir 1989-; memb: Canada-UK C of C, Royal Inst of Int Affairs, CBI; FCII 1971, MBIM 1984; *Recreations* squash, rugby; *Style*— Richard Porter, Esq; Holmgarth, Betchworth Ave, Earley, Berks RG6 2RJ (☎ 0734 65637); Alexander Stenhouse UK Ltd, 10 Devonshire Square, London EC2M 4LE (☎ 071 621 9990, fax 071 621 9950)

PORTER, Prof Richard William; s of Joseph Luther Porter, and Mary, *née* Field; *b* 16 Feb 1935; *Educ* Oundle, Univ of Edinburgh (MD); *m* Christine Margaret, da of Wilfred Brown; 4 s (Daniel, William, Matthew, James); *Career* former conslt orthopaedic surgn Doncaster; pres Br Soc for Back Pain Res; FRCS, FRCSEd; *Books* Understanding Back Pain (1985), Management of Back Pain (1986); *Style*— Prof Richard Porter; Department of Orthopaedics, Forester Hill Hospital, Aberdeen

PORTER, Rt Hon Sir Robert Wilson; PC (NI 1969), QC (NI 1965); s of late Joseph Wilson Porter; *b* 23 Dec 1923; *Educ* Model Sch, Foyle Coll Londonderry, Queen's Univ Belfast (LLB); *m* 1953, Margaret Adelaide, da of late F W Lynas; 1 s, 1 da (and 1 da decd); *Career* RAFVR 1943-46, RA (TA) 1950-56; called to the Bar: NI 1950, Repub of I 1975, Middle Temple 1988; counsel to Attorney-Gen for NI 1963-64 and 1965; min of Health and Social Services NI 1969, Parly sec 1969 and min of Home Affairs NI 1969-70; chm War Pensions Appeal Tbnl for NI 1961-66 (vice chm 1959-61); MP (U): Queen's Univ of Belfast 1966-69, Lagan Valley 1969-73; County Court Judge NI 1978-; kt 1971; *Clubs* RAF; *Style*— The Rt Hon Sir Robert Porter, QC; Larch Hill, Ballylesson, Belfast, N Ireland BT8 8JX

PORTER, Robin Anthony; s of Maurice Malcolm Porter (d 1986), and Danuta, *née* Monitz; *b* 15 Sept 1945; *Educ* Highgate Sch, Univ of Leeds (LLB); *m* 14 Sept 1974, Monica Joeán, da of Péter Dénes Halász, of Munich, Germany; 2 s (Adam b 1978, Nicholas b 1983); *Career* articled clerk Titmuss Sainer & Webb 1968-70; asst slr: Commercial Property Dept Clifford-Turner & Co 1971-72, Company and Commercial Dept McKenna & Co 1972-73, Company and Commercial Dept Penningtons 1974; Wilde Sapte 1974-: asst slr Commercial Property Dept 1974-75 (ptnr Commercial Property Dept 1975-84 and 1987-), ptnr i/c New York Office 1984-87; Freeman City of

London 1987, Liveryman Worshipful Company of Musicians 1990; memb: Law Soc 1971, Int Bar Assoc 1984, British-Hungarian Law Assoc 1990; *Recreations* music, theatre, tennis, skiing, cycling; *Clubs* English Speaking Union, Cumberland Lawn Tennis; *Style*— Robin Porter, Esq; 200 Walm Lane, London NW2 3BP (☎ 081 208 1465); Wilde Sapte, Queensbridge House, 60 Upper Thames St, London EC4V 3BD (☎ 071 236 3050, fax 071 236 9624, telex 887793)

PORTER, Ronald Robert; s of Maj Kenneth Russell Porter, of 34 Dawson Ave, Brighton, Victoria, Australia, and Laura Maria, *née* Terenzi; *b* 10 Nov 1951; *Educ* Melbourne C of E Boys GS, Securities Inst of Australia (Cert, Dip), Coll of Mktg UK, Australian Admin Staff Coll (Advanced Mgmnt); *m* 2 Feb 1974, Helen Mary, da of Dr John J Bourke (d 1985); 2 s (Nicholas James b 1979, William Charles b 1986), 2 da (Stephanie Jane b 1980, Alexandra Elizabeth b 1984); *Career* ptnr and dir JB Were & Son 1983, memb Melbourne Stock Exchange 1983, md JB Were & Son Ltd London 1987-; ASIA, memb ASX; *Recreations* tennis, golf, rugby, rowing; *Clubs* Riverside Old Oarsmen's Assoc, NSW GC, White City TC (NSW); *Style*— Ronald Porter, Esq; JB Were & Son Ltd, 10 Old Jewry, London TW10 6HG (☎ 071 606 2261, fax 071 606 2452, telex 885201)

PORTER, Prof The Rev Canon (Joshua) Roy; s of Joshua Porter (d 1945), of Marple, Cheshire, and Bessie Evelyn, *née* Earlam (d 1976); *b* 7 May 1921; *Educ* King's Sch Macclesfield, Merton Coll Oxford (BA), St Stephen's House Oxford (BA, MA); *Career* ordained: deacon 1945, priest 1946; curate St Mary Portsea 1945-47, resident chaplain to Bishop of Chichester 1947-49, fell chaplain and tutor Oriel Coll Oxford 1949-62, prof of theology and head of dept Univ of Exeter 1962-86 (emeritus prof 1986-), dean of arts Univ of Exeter 1968-71, canon and prebendary Wightring and theol lectr Chichester Cath 1965-88, Wiccamical canon and prebendary of Exceit 1988-, visiting prof South Eastern Seminary Wake Forest N Carolina 1967, Ethel M Wood lectr Univ of London 1979, Michael Harrah Wood lectr Univ of the S Sewanee 1984, lectr in Holy Scriptures Holyrood Seminary New York 1986-; examining chaplain to: Bishop of London, Bishop of Gibraltar in Europe 1989-; Proctor in Convocation Canterbury Exeter Diocese 1964-75 (and other Univs incl Canterbury) 1975-90; memb: Gen Synod 1970-90 (Panel of chm 1984-86), Soc for Old Testament Study 1952 (pres 1983), Folklore Soc (hon memb 1988), Soc of Biblical Lit 1967, Anglican Assoc (pres), Prayer Book Soc (vice chm); *Books* World in the Heart (1944), Moses and Monarchy (1963), The Extended Family in the Old Testament (1967), Proclamation and Presence (with J I Durham, 1970), The Non-Juring Bishops (1973), Leviticus (1976), Animals in Folklore (with W M S Russell, 1978), C Westermann, The Living Psalms (translated 1989); *Recreations* theatre, opera, book collecting, travel; *Clubs* Royal Over-Seas League; *Style*— Prof The Rev Canon Roy Porter; 36 Theberton St, Barnsbury, London N1 OQX (☎ 071 354 5861); 68 Sand St, Longbridge Deverill, nr Warminster, Wilts BA12 7DS (☎ 0985 40311)

PORTER, Dame Shirley; DBE (1991), DL; da of Sir John Edward Cohen (d 1980), and Sarah Fox; *b* 29 Nov 1930; *Educ* Warren Sch Worthing, La Ramée Lausanne Switzerland; *m* 1949, Sir Leslie Porter, s of Henry Alfred Porter (d 1955); 1 s (John), 1 da (Linda); *Career* dir and memb Bd TBG (Tidy Britain Group); former dir: Capital Radio, English National Ballet; vice-pres LUYC; past Master Worshipful Co of Environmental Cleaners; JP (Inner London) 1972-84; ldr Westminster City Cncl 1983-91; *Recreations* golf, boating, ballet, theatre, travel, efficiency in local govt; *Clubs* Queen's, Coombe Hill, Frilford Heath, Wentworth, Dyrham Park Golf, RAC; *Style*— Dame Shirley Porter, DBE, DL; Westminster City Council, City Hall, Victoria St, London SW1 (☎ 071 828 8070)

PORTER OF LUDDENHAM, Baron (Life Peer 1990), of Luddenham in the Co of Kent; Sir George; OM (1989); s of late John Smith Porter, and Alice Ann, *née* Roebuck; *b* 6 Dec 1920; *Educ* Thorne GS, Univ of Leeds (BSc), Emmanuel Coll Cambridge (MA, PhD, ScD); *m* 12 Aug 1949, Stella Jean, da of Col George Brooke (d 1973), of Caring, Leeds, nr Maidstone, Kent; 2 s (John Brooke b 22 Sept 1952, Andrew Christopher George b 17 Aug 1955); *Career* Radar Offr RNVR Western Approaches and Med 1941-45; demonstrator physical chemistry Univ of Cambridge 1949-52, asst dir of res physical chemistry and fell Emmanuel Coll Cambridge 1952-54, asst dir Br Rayon Res Assoc 1954-55, Firth prof of chemistry and head Dept of Chemistry Univ of Sheffield 1963-66 (prof of physical chemistry 1955-63); The Royal Instn of GB: dir 1966-85, dir The Davy Faraday Res Laboratory 1966-85, Fullerian prof of chemistry 1966-87; chllr Univ of Leicester 1986-, res prof and fell Imperial Coll London 1987-, Gresham prof of astronomy and physical sciences 1990-; visiting prof: Pennsylvania State Univ 1961, UCL 1967-86, Caltech 1974, Univ of California at Berkeley 1978, Imperial Coll London 1978-; hon fell: Emmanuel Coll Cambridge 1967, Royal Scot Soc of Arts 1975, Royal Med Soc Edinburgh 1987, Imperial Coll London 1987; foreign fell Indian Nat Acad of Sciences 1990; fell: Royal Soc of Edinburgh 1983, Queen Mary and Westfield Coll London 1986; awarded: Corday-Morgan Medal of Chem Soc 1955, Nobel Prize for Chemistry 1967, Silvanus Thompson Medal of Br Inst of Radiology 1968, Davy Medal of Royal Soc 1971, 1976, Kalinga Prize (UNESCO) for Popularisation of Sci 1977, Robertson Prize of Nat Acad Sci 1978, Rumford Medal of Royal Soc 1978, Communications Award of Euro Physical Soc 1978, Faraday Medal of Chem Soc 1980, Longstaff Medal of RSC 1981, Melchett Medal of Inst of Energy 1987, Porter Medal 1988; author of over 300 scientific papers, many lectures given on scientific subjects, numerous TV and radio appearances, producer of scientific films and videos; pres: Comité International de Photobiologie 1968-72, Chem Soc 1970-72 (Faraday Div 1973-74), Nat Assoc for Gifted Children 1975-80, Res and Devpt Soc 1977-82, Assoc for Sci Educn 1985, Br Assoc for Advancement of Sci 1985-86, Royal Soc 1985-90, London Int Youth Sci Fortnight 1987-89; vice pres UK Soc for Promotion of Sci and Technol in Pakistan 1989-; hon memberships incl: NY Acad of Sciences 1968, Chem Soc of Japan 1982, Royal Inst GB 1988; memberships incl: Res Grants Ctee DSIR 1963-65, Aeronautical Res Cncl 1964-66, BBC Sci Consultative Gp 1967-75, Open Univ Cncl 1969-75, Advsy Cncl Sci Museum 1970-73, Pontifical Acad of Sciences 1974, Euro Acad of Arts Sciences and Humanities 1980, Cncl RSA 1978-80; foreign memberships incl: Soviet Acad of Sciences, Japan Acad, Academia Lincei, La Real Academia de Ciencias Madrid 1978, Indian Nat Acad of Sciences 1986; foreign assoc Nat Acad of Sciences Washington 1974; tstee: Br Museum 1972-74, The Bristol Exploratory 1986-; Hon Liveryman Worshipful Co of Salters 1981, Freeman City of London 1981; Hon Doctorate of 30 Univs, Hon Professorship of 2 Univs and 2 Insts; FRS 1960, PRS 1985; kt 1972; *Books* Chemistry for the Modern World (1962); *Recreations* sailing; *Clubs* Athenaeum; *Style*— The Rt Hon Lord Porter of Luddenham, OM, PRS; The Old Rectory, Luddenham, nr Faversham, Kent ME13 0TE; Chairman of the Centre for Photomolecular Sciences, Department of Biology, Imperial College of Science and Technology, South Kensington, London SW7 2AZ (☎ 071 589 5111, fax 071 584 7596)

PORTES, Prof Richard David; s of Herbert Portes; *b* 10 Dec 1941; *Educ* Yale Univ, Balliol and Nuffield Colls Oxford; *m* 1963, Barbara Frank; children; *Career* fell Balliol Coll 1965-69; econ prof: Princeton Univ 1969-72, London Univ 1972-; head Econ Dept Birkbeck Coll 1975-77 and 1980-83, dir Centre for Econ Policy Res 1983-; *Books* Planning and Market Relations (1971), Deficits and Detente (1983), Threats to International Financial Stability (1987), Global Macroeconomics (1987), Blueprints for Exchange Rate Management (1989); *Recreations* swimming, squash; *Clubs* Groucho; *Style*— Prof Richard Portes; Department of Economics, Birkbeck College, 7-15 Gresse St, London W1P 1PA

PORTILLO, Michael Denzil Xavier; MP (Cons) Enfield Southgate 1984-; s of Luis Gabriel Portillo, and Cora Waldegrave, *née* Blyth; *b* 26 May 1953; *Educ* Harrow Co Sch for Boys, Peterhouse Cambridge (MA); *m* 12 Feb 1982, Carolyn Claire, da of Alastair G Eadie; *Career* Ocean Transport and Trading Co 1975-76, Cons Res Dept 1976-79, special advsr to Sec of State for Energy 1979-81, Kerr McGee Oil (UK) Ltd 1981-83, special advsr to Sec of State for Trade and Indust 1983, special advsr to Chllr of the Exchequer 1983-84, asst govt whip 1986-87, Parly under sec of state for Health and Social Security 1987-88, min of state for Tport 1988-90, min for Local Govt 1990-; *Clubs* Carlton; *Style*— Michael Portillo, Esq, MP; House of Commons, Westminster, London SW1A 0AA (☎ 071 219 6595)

PORTLAND, 11 Earl of (GB 1689); Henry Noel Bentinck; also Viscount Woodstock, Baron Cirencester (both GB 1689), and Count Bentinck (Holy Roman Empire); s of Capt Count Robert Bentinck (d 1932), and Lady Norah Ida Emily Noel (d 1939), da of 3 Earl of Gainsborough; suc his kinsman 9 and last Duke (and 10 Earl) of Portland, CMG (d 1990); *b* 2 Oct 1919; *Educ* Harrow; *m* 1, 1940, Pauline (d 1967), da of late Frederick William Mellowes, of Penn House, Renolds Close, Hampstead, London NW; 1 s, 2 da; m 2, 1974, Jenifer, o da of late Reginald Hopkins, of 91 Kingsley Way, London N2; *Heir* s, Viscount Woodstock, *qv*; *Career* formerly Lt Coldstream Guards; served WWII (twice wounded); *Style*— The Rt Hon the Earl of Portland

PORTMAN, Hon Christopher Edward Berkeley; s and h of 9 Viscount Portman; *b* 30 July 1958; *m* 30 July 1983, Caroline, da of Terence Ivan Steenson, of Caversham, Berks; 1 s (Luke Oliver Berkeley b 31 Aug 1984); m 2, 7 Dec 1987, Patricia Martins, da of Bernardino Pim, of Rio de Janeiro, Brazil; 1 s (Matthew Bernardo Berkeley b 24 Sept 1990); *Style*— The Hon Christopher Portman; Clock Mill, Clifford, Herefs

PORTMAN, 9 Viscount (UK 1873); Edward Henry Berkeley Portman; Baron Portman (UK 1873); s of Hon Michael Berkeley Portman (d 1959) (yr s of 7 Viscount) and n of 8 Viscount (d 1967); *b* 22 April 1934; *Educ* Canford, RAC Cirencester; *m* 1, 1956 (m dis 1965), Rosemary Joy, er da of Charles Farris, of Coombe Bissett, Wilts; 1 s, 1 da; m 2, 1966, Penelope Anne Hassard, yr da of Trevor Robert William Allin, of North Moreton, Berks; 4 s (Hon Alexander b 1967, Hon Justin b 1969, Hon Piers b 1971, Hon Matthew b 1973, d 1990); *Heir* s, Hon Christopher Edward Berkeley Portman, *qv*; *Career* farmer; *Recreations* music, motorsport, fishing, shooting; *Clubs* White's, British Racing Drivers'; *Style*— The Rt Hon the Viscount Portman; Clock Mill, Clifford, Herefordshire (☎ 049 73 235)

PORTMAN, Viscountess Nancy Maureen; da of Capt Percy Herbert Franklin, RN (ret); *m* 1946, as his 2 w, 8 Viscount Portman (d 1967); *Style*— The Rt Hon Nancy, Viscountess Portman; Sutton Waldron House, Blandford, Dorset

PORTMAN, Rodney John Berkeley; s of Berkeley Portman, and Sheila Margaret Penelope, *née* Mowat; *b* 15 Dec 1947; *Educ* Wellington, Trinity Coll Cambridge (MA); *m* 9 March 1976, Angela Theresa, da of Maj John Pringle, MC; 2 s (Guy Seymour Berkeley b 12 Sept 1977, John Berkeley b 21 Aug 1982), 1 da (Oliva Joan b 1 Nov 1979); *Career* land agent 1970-73; estab Mander Portman Woodward Independent Sixth Form Coll 1973; estab Berkeley Reafforestation Tst (charity dedicated to promoting Third World tree planting and tree mgmnt 1987); Freeman City of London 1977, Liveryman Worshipful Co of Gunmakers; ARICS 1972; *Recreations* forestry, travel, countryside; *Clubs* Chelsea Arts; *Style*— Rodney Portman, Esq; 3 Harley Gdns, London SW10 9SW

PORTMANN, Dr Bernard Claude; s of late Henry Paul Portmann, and Emilie Emma, *née* Jaques; *b* 6 Feb 1940; *Educ* Calvin Coll Geneva Switzerland, Geneva Univ (MB, Swiss Med Dip, MD); *m* 1, 11 Sept 1963 (m dis 1969), Arlette Andree, da of Walter Ernst Kress; 1 da (Sandra b 7 Aug 1964); m 2, 23 Sept 1970, Hermine Elisabeth, da of Leo Bertholdt Neumann; 2 c (Barbara b 8 Feb 1971, Jan b 26 Oct 1972); *Career* Univ Hosp Geneva: lectr in pathology 1968-72 (house offr 1966-67); KCH London: conslt, hon sr lectr 1978- (res fell Liver Unit 1973-75, res histopathologist 1975-78); hon sr lectr Univ of London 1978; travelling fellowship Mount Sinai Med Center NY 1982; former memb Ctee Br Assoc for Study of the Liver; MRCPath 1977, FRCPath 1989; *Recreations* skiing, woodwork; *Style*— Dr Bernard Portmann; 20 Ewelme Rd, Forest Hill, London SE23 3BH (☎ 081 699 6717); Institute of Liver Studies, King's College Hospital, Denmark Hill, London SE5 9RS (☎ 071 326 3369)

PORTNOY, Leslie Reuben; s of Israel Portnoy, and Miriam Portnoy; *b* 27 May 1939; *Educ* Manchester GS, Univ of Manchester (LLB); *m* 7 March 1961, Stephanie, da of Nathan Swift; 1 s (Jonathan b 10 May 1966), 1 da (Naomi b 25 Oct 1969); *Career* called to the Bar Gray's Inn 1961; dep circuit judge 1978, memb Panel and Jewish Tbnl (Shops Act) 1980, asst rec 1981, rec 1988; govr King David Schs Manchester; *Style*— Leslie Portnoy, Esq; 95 Cavendish Rd, Salford, Manchester M7 0NB (☎ 061 740 2286); Crown Square Chambers, 1 Deans Court, Crown Square, Manchester M3 3HA (☎ 061 833 9801, fax 061 835 2483)

PORTSMOUTH, Archdeacon of; *see*: Crowder, Ven Norman Harry

PORTSMOUTH, Bishop of (RC) 1988-; Rt Rev (Roger Francis) Crispian Hollis; s of (Maurice) Christoper Hollis (d 1977), of Mells, Somerset, and Margaret Madelaine, *née* King (d 1984); *b* 17 Nov 1936; *Educ* Stonyhurst, Balliol Coll Oxford, Pontifical Gregorian Univ Rome; *Career* Nat Serv 2 Lt Somerset LI 1954-56; ordained priest 1965, asst priest Amesbury Wilts 1966-67, asst RC chaplain Oxford Univ 1967-70 (sr RC chaplain 1970-77), RC asst to head of religious broadcasting BBC 1977-81, admin Clifton Cathedral and vicar gen Clifton Diocese 1981-87, auxiliary bishop Archdiocese of Birmingham 1987-88; *Recreations* golf, cricket-watching; *Style*— The Rt Rev the Bishop of Portsmouth; Bishops House, Edinburgh Rd, Portsmouth PO1 3HG (☎ 0705 820 894)

PORTSMOUTH, Dr (Owen Henry) Donald; s of Oliver Spencer Portsmouth (d 1970), of Swansea, and Gwendolen Anne, *née* Trevor Owen (d 1991); *b* 24 May 1929; *Educ* Blundell's, St Thomas's Med Sch Univ of London (MB BS, DTM and H); *m* 1, 18 Sept 1954, Moira Heloise (d 1979), da of Alan John Sinclair (d 1967), of Kenya; 3 s (Charles b 1956, Richard b 1958, Andrew b 1961), 1 da (Helen b 1964); m 2, 3 Jan 1981, Glennis Cook, *née* Weddle; 1 step da (Esther b 1975); *Career* jr hosp appointments 1953-56; med serv Kenya Govt 1956-66 (med specialist 1960-66), conslt physician geriatric med E Birmingham Hosp 1966-; dir W Midlands Inst of Geriatric Med 1975-, vice chm Solihull Health Authy 1984-90, tstee Solihull Frail Ambulant Unit, Dawson meml lectr Queens Univ Kingston Ontario 1984; FRCP 1977, FRCPE 1971; *Recreations* heraldry, architecture, history, foreign travel; *Style*— Dr Donald Portsmouth; Oakfield, 12 Paddock Drive, Dorridge, Solihull, W Midlands B93 8BZ (☎ 0564 775032); Department of Geriatric Medicine, Arden Lodge, East Birmingham Hospital, Yardley Green Rd, Birmingham B9 5TX (☎ 021 766 6611 ext 2149)

PORTSMOUTH, 10 Earl of (GB 1743); Quentin Gerard Carew Wallop; also Baron Wallop (GB 1720), Viscount Lymington (GB 1720); Hereditary Bailiff of Burley in the New Forest; s of Viscount Lymington (d June 1984) and his 2 w Ruth Violet, née Sladen (d 1978); suc gf 9 Earl (d Sept 1984); *b* 25 July 1954; *Educ* Eton, Millfield; *m* 1, 1981 (m dis 1985), Candia Frances Juliet, only da of Colin McWilliam, and

Margaret, *née* Henderson; 1 s (Oliver Henry Rufus b 1981), 1 da (Lady Clementine Violet Rohais b 1983); m 2, 16 March 1990, Annabel, eldest da of Ian Fergusson, of Tudor Place, Richmond Green, Surrey; 1 da (b 23 Oct 1990); *Heir* s, Viscount Lymington, *qv*; *Career* vice pres Basingstoke Cons Assoc; patron SE Region of Nat Childrens' Home; dir Grainger Tst plc; *Recreations* shooting, sailing; *Clubs* Bucks, Royal Yacht Sqdn, Int Assoc of Cape Horners; *Style*— The Rt Hon the Earl of Portsmouth; Estate Office, Farleigh Wallop, Basingstoke, Hants RG25 2HS (☎ 0256 21026)

PORTSMOUTH, Bishop of 1985-; Rt Rev Timothy John Bavin; s of Lt-Col Edward Sydney Durrance Bavin, RASC (d 1979), and Marjorie Gwendoline, *née* Dew; *b* 17 Sept 1935; *Educ* St George's Sch Windsor Castle, Brighton Coll, Worcester Coll Oxford, Cuddesdon Coll Oxford; *Career* Nat Serv RASC 1957-59, cmmnd 1958, Platoon Offr (2 Lt) 90 Co Aden 1958-59; curate St Alban's Cathedral Pretoria SA 1961-63, chaplain St Alban's Coll Pretoria 1963-69, curate Uckfield with Litte Horsted 1969-71, vicar Parish of the Good Shepherd Brighton 1971-72, dean of Johannesburg and rector of the Cathedral Parish 1971-74, bishop of Johannesburg 1974-84; *Books* Deacons in the Ministry of the Church (ed, 1988); *Recreations* music, victoriana, country life; *Clubs* Athenaeum, Royal Yacht Squadron (Cowes), Royal Naval (Portsmouth); *Style*— The Rt Rev the Bishop of Portsmouth; Bishopswood, Fareham, Hants PO14 1NT (☎ 0329 280 247)

PORTWIN, Guy Lyster; s of Edwin Thomas Portwin, of Herts, and Elizabeth Emily Louise, *née* Gadd; *b* 28 Dec 1949; *Educ* Merchant Taylors'; *m* 6 May 1979, Kathleen, da of John Joseph Skerritt, of Eire; 4 children (Liza, Emma, Guy, John); *Career* dir: Wheatland Journals Ltd 1973-, Turret Press (Holdings) Ltd 1979-84; md Turret-Wheatland Ltd 1984-88, chm Turret Group plc 1988-90, chm Hill Media Ltd 1991-; *Recreations* riding, reading; *Clubs* Durrants; *Style*— Guy L Portwin, Esq; Hill Media Ltd, 118-120 Broad St, Chesham, Bucks (☎ 0494 792888)

POSFORD, John Albert; s of Capt Benjamin Ashwell Posford (d 1915); *b* 3 Sept 1914; *Educ* The Oratory Sch, King's Coll Cambridge; *m* 1, 1940, Nell Margaret (d 1966), da of Capt Augustus Knight (d 1950); 1 s, 4 da; m 2, 1970, Jean Davidson, da of Col Alastair Gordon, MC, Royal Scots Fus (d 1968); 2 s; *Career* sr ptnr and fndr (1944) Posford, Pavry & Ptnrs (consulting engrs to the ports of Felixstowe, Milford Haven and Sheerness); Queen's Award for Export Achievement 1979; chm Maritime Gp Br Conslts Bureau 1979; FRSA; *Recreations* gardening; *Clubs* United Oxford and Cambridge Univ; *Style*— John Posford, Esq; Falkenham Lodge, Ipswich, Suffolk (☎ 039 48 246); 49 Eaton Mews South, London SW1 (☎ 071 235 7446)

POSNANSKY, Jeremy Ross Leon; s of Anthony Victor Posnansky, of Switzerland, and Evelyn, Leon, JP; *b* 8 March 1951; *Educ* St Paul's, Coll of Law London; *m* 31 Dec 1974, Julia Mary, da of Richard Sadler, MBE (d 1967), of Bournemouth; 2 da (Charlotte b 1976, Zoë b 1979); *Career* called to the Bar Gray's Inn 1972; memb hon socs: Gray's Inn, Lincoln's Inn; *Recreations* golf, classic motor cars, computers; *Clubs* Roehampton; *Style*— Jeremy Posnansky, Esq; 22 Old Buildings, Lincoln's Inn, London WC2A 3JU (☎ 071 831 0222, fax 071 831 2239)

POSNER, Michael Vivian; CBE (1983); s of Jack Posner; *b* 1931; *Educ* Whitgift Sch, Balliol Coll Oxford; *m* 1953, Prof Rebecca Posner, da of William Reynolds; 1 s, 1 da; *Career* dir econs Miny of Power 1966-67, conslt IMF 1971-72, reader econs Univ of Cambridge 1974-75 (fell Pembroke Coll 1960-83), memb Energy Conservation Advsy Cncl 1974-76, dep chief econ advsr Treasy 1975-76 (econ advsr 1967-69, econ conslt 1969-71); memb: BR bd 1976-84, Standing Cmmn on Energy and Environment 1978-82; chm SSRC 1979-83, dir Tech Change Centre 1981-86, econ dir Nat Econ Devpt Office 1984-86, sec gen Euro Sci Fndn Strasbourg 1986-; *Style*— Michael Posner, Esq, CBE; Rushwood, Jack Straw's Lane, Oxford

POSNER, Prof Rebecca; da of William Reynolds (d 1958), and Rebecca, *née* Stephenson (d 1988); *b* 17 Aug 1929; *Educ* HS for Girls, Somerville Coll Oxford (BA, DPhil); *m* 5 Aug 1953, Michael Vivian Posner, s of Jack Posner (d 1978); 1 s (Christopher Nicholas b 14 Sept 1965), 1 da (Barbara Virginia b 7 July 1968); *Career* res fell Girton Coll Cambridge 1960-63, prof of French studies and head of dept of mod languages Univ Ghana 1963-65, reader in linguistics Univ of York 1965-78, prof of the romance languages Univ of Oxford 1978-; memb: Philological Soc, Linguistics Assoc of GB, Mod Humanities Res Assoc, Soc for French Studies, Assoc for French Language Studies, Nat Conference of Univ Profs; *Books* Consonantal Dissimilation in the Romance Languages (1960), The Romance Languages (1966), Introduction to Romance Linguistics (1970), Trends in Romance Linguistics and Philology (with J N Green, 1980-); *Recreations* gardening, walking, music, travel; *Style*— Prof Rebecca Posner; Rushwood, Jack Straw's Lane, Oxford (☎ 0865 63578); St Hugh's College, Oxford (☎ 0865 274995, fax 0865 274912)

POSNER, Richard Max Stanley; JP (Middx Cmmn Area 1988); s of Claude Joseph Posner (d 1969), and Betty, *née* Lee; *b* 16 Aug 1944; *Educ* Christ's Coll Finchley; *m* 30 Aug 1974, Barbara Susan, da of Jan Konrad Szwenk (d 1971), of London; *Career* dir F66 Danish Design Ltd 1973-76; md: Richard Posner Assocs 1970-75, Baric Clothing Ltd 1976-80, Pappagalli's Pizza Inc Ltd 1980-89; dir Pozzitive TV Productions Ltd 1988; md: Mirrotech Video Systems Ltd 1989-, Expco (London) Ltd 1989; vice-chm Cunningham Ct Residents Assoc; *Recreations* sport fishing, winter sports, food and wine, pistol and clay pigeon shooting; *Clubs* RAC, Marylebone Rifle & Pistol; *Style*— R M S Posner, Esq, JP; 30 Cunningham Ct, Blomfield Rd, Little Venice, London W9 1AE (☎ and fax 071 286 0816)

POSNETT, Sir Richard Neil; KBE (1980, OBE 1963), CMG (1976); s of Rev Charles Walker Posnett, K-i-H of Medak, India, and Phyllis, *née* Barker; *b* 19 July 1919; *Educ* Kingswood, St John's Coll Cambridge (MA); *m* 1; 2 s, 1 da; m 2, 1959, Shirley Margaret, da of Claude Hudson; 2 s, 1 da; *Career* lawyer, colonial admin, diplomat; admin offr Uganda 1941, called to the Bar Gray's Inn 1951, Uganda Olympics Ctee 1955, Colonial Office London 1958, perm sec for External Affrs Uganda 1962-63; joined Foreign Serv 1964, UK mission to UN 1965-70, govr and C-in-C of Belize 1972-76, Dependent Territories advsr FCO 1977-79, UK cmmr Br Phosphate Cmmrs 1978-81, Br high cmmr Kampala 1979, govr and C-in-C of Bermuda 1980-83; memb Lord Chllr's Panel of Ind Insprs 1984-89, pres Kingswood Assoc 1980; govr Kingswood Sch 1985; memb RIIA; KStJ 1972; *Recreations* skiing, golf, trees; *Clubs* Royal Commonwealth Soc, Achilles, West Surrey GC, Privateers Hockey; *Style*— Sir Richard Posnett, KBE, CMG; Timbers, Northway, Godalming, Surrey GU7 2RE (☎ 048 68 6869)

POSNETTE, Prof Adrian Frank (Peter); CBE (1976); s of Frank William Posnette (d 1956), of Cheltenham, Glos, and Edith Mary, *née* Webber (d 1969); *b* 11 Jan 1914; *Educ* Cheltenham GS, Christ's Coll Cambridge (BA, MA, ScD), Imp Coll of Tropical Agric (AICTA), Univ of London (PhD); *m* 15 July 1937, Isabelle, da of Dr Montgomery De Forest La Roche (d 1958), of New York City; 1 s (John b 1950), 2 da (Jane b 1939, Suzanne b 1942); *Career* Colonial Agric Serv Gold Coast 1937-55: appointed botanist 1937-44, head of botany and plant pathology W African Cocoa Res Inst 1944-49, seconded to E Malling Res Station Maidstone Kent 1949, appointed princ scientific offr 1955; dir E Malling Res Station 1972-79 (head Plant Pathology Section 1957-69, dep dir 1969-72, dir 1972-79), hon prof of plant sciences Wye Coll Univ of London 1971-78; author of: series of eight res pubns on virus diseases of cocoa trees 1947-55, numerous pubns on virus diseases of fruit trees and strawberries 1953-80; govr Redhill Sch E Sutton; awarded Ridley medal of the Worshipful Co of Fruiterers 1978 (Hon Freeman 1982); FIBiol 1963, FRS 1971, VMH 1982; *Recreations* ornithology; *Clubs* Farmers, CU Hawks; *Style*— Prof Adrian Posnette, CBE, FRS; Walnut Tree, East Sutton, Maidstone, Kent ME17 3DR (☎ 0622 843282)

POST, Herschel; s of Herschel E Post (d 1973), and Marie, *née* Connelly; *b* 9 Oct 1939; *Educ* Yale (AB), New Coll Oxford (BA, MA), Harvard Law Sch (LLB); *m* 24 Aug 1963, Peggy, da of Charles H Mayne (d 1963); 1 s (Herschel Day b 1969), 3 da (Clarissa b 1975, Eliza b 1977, Olivia b 1982); *Career* dep admin Parks Recreation and Cultural Affrs Admin City of NY 1972-73, vice pres Morgan Guaranty Trust Co Brussels and London 1974-84; pres and dir 1984-: Posthorn Global Asset Management, Shearson Lehman Global Asset Management; chief operating offr 1990-: Lehman Bros International Ltd, Lehman Bros Securities; dep chm The International Stock Exchange of GB and the Repub of Ireland 1988-; *Clubs* Vauderbilt Racquet, Knickerbocker (NY); *Style*— Herschel Post, Esq; c/o Lehman Bros, 1 Broadgate, London EC2M 7HA (☎ 071 601 0011, fax 071 260 2332, telex 888881 SLHLON G)

POSTAN, Lady Cynthia Rosalie; *née* Keppel; da (by 1 m) of late 9 Earl of Albemarle, MC; *b* 25 June 1918; *m* 1944, Prof Sir Michael Moissey Postan (d 1981, prof of economic history Cambridge and fell of Peterhouse), s of Efim Postan, of Tighina, Bessarabia; 2 s (Basil David b 1946, Alexander Henry Keppel b 1948); *Style*— The Lady Cynthia Postan; 84 Barton Road, Cambridge CB3 9LH

POSTGATE, Prof John Raymond; s of Raymond William Postgate (d 1971), of Canterbury, and Daisy (d 1971); *b* 24 June 1922; *Educ* Kingsbury Co Sch and others, Balliol Coll Oxford (BA, MA, DPhil, DSc); *m* 20 Oct 1948, (Muriel) Mary, da of Leslie Gordon Stewart (d 1963), of Whetstone, London; 3 da (Selina b 1955, Lucy b 1956, Joanna b 1958); *Career* Nat Chem Laboratory: sr res investigator 1949-50, sr and later princ sci offr 1950-59; princ then sr princ sci offr Microbiological Res Estab 1959-63, asst dir ARC Unit of Nitrogen Fixation Royal Vet Coll 1963-65 (Univ of Sussex 1965-80); Univ of Sussex: dir AFRC Unit of Nitrogen Fixation 1980-87, prof of microbiology 1965-87, emeritus prof 1987-; visiting prof: Univ of Illinois 1962-63, Oregon State Univ 1977-78; hon memb: Soc for Applied Bacteriology 1981, Soc for Gen Microbiology 1988 (pres 1984-87); FIBiol (pres 1982-84), FRS 1977; *Books* Microbes and Man (1969, 1986), The Fundamentals of Nitrogen Fixation (1982), The Sulphate - Reducing Bacteria (1979, 1984), A Plain Man's Guide to Jazz (1973); *Recreations* hearing and playing jazz music, scientific, jazz and biographical writing, reviewing records; *Style*— Prof John Postgate, FRS; Houndean Lodge, 1 Houndean Rise, Lewes, E Sussex BN7 1EG (☎ 0273 472 675)

POSTLETHWAITE, William; s of William Postlethwaite (d 1971), and Alice Julia, *née* Bernie; *b* 28 Dec 1932; *Educ* St Anselm's Coll Cheshire; *m* 6 Sept 1958, Mary Louise, da of Eric Apter (d 1978); 1 s (John Andrew b 1962), 1 da (Diana Mary b 1961); *Career* md Kwik Save Gp plc 1983-88, chm Plastech Ext Co Ltd, chm and chief exec Leaguewood Ltd Co; FInstM; *Recreations* reading, sport, gardening; *Clubs* Lancs CC, pres Rotary West Wirral, St Melyd GC; *Style*— William Postlethwaite, Esq; Plastech Exturusions Ltd, The Barkin Centre, Widnes, Cheshire (☎ 051 495 1424, fax 051 495 1727); Leaguewood Ltd Co, Wilson Rd, Liverpool (☎ 051 480 4929, fax 051 480 6296)

POSWILLO, Prof David Ernest; CBE (1989); s of Ernest Joseph Poswillo, JP (d 1979), of Gisborne, NZ, and Amelia Mary, *née* McCormick; *b* 1 Jan 1927; *Educ* Gisborne Boys' HS, Univ of Otago NZ (BDS, DDS, DSc), Westminster Med Sch Univ of London (MRCPath), Univ of Zurich (MDhc); *m* 27 June 1956, Elizabeth Alison, da of John Whitworth Russell (d 1982), of Nelson, NZ; 2 s (Stephen b 22 Nov 1962, Mark b 10 Dec 1964), 2 da (Jane (Mrs Caton) b 13 Oct 1958, Jill (Mrs Battye) b 8 Jan 1960); *Career* OC Southern Dists Hosp RNZDC 1948-50, 30 Field Ambulance RAMC BAOR 1951; dir oral surgery N Canterbury Hosp Bd NZ 1953-68, prof of teratology RCS 1969-77, conslt oral surgn Queen Victoria Hosp E Grinstead 1969-77, prof of oral pathology and oral surgery Univ of Adelaide South Aust 1977-79, sr oral and maxillofacial surgn Royal Adelaide and Childrens Hosp South Aust 1977-79; prof: of oral Surgery Royal Dental Hosp London 1977-83, of oral and maxillofacial surgery Guy's Hosp London 1983-; memb: Human Task Force WHO 1976-78, Cncl Royal Dental Hosp London 1977-83; conslt advsr to chief MO DHSS 1979-86, tstee Tobacco Prods Res Tst 1980-, memb Bd of Faculty of Dental Surgery RCS 1981-89; vice pres and memb Cncl Med Def Union 1983- (chm Dental Ctee), sec gen Int Assoc of Oral and Maxillofacial Surgeons 1983-90, memb Govrs Cncl UMDS of Guys and St Thomas' Hosps 1983-89; pres: Odontology Section Royal Soc of Med 1989-90, Br Assoc Oral and Maxillofacial Surgns 1990-91; chm Dept of Health Anaesthesia, Sedation and Resuscitation in Dentistry (Poswillo Report) 1990; Hunterian prof RCS 1968 and 1976, Regent's prof Univ of California 1987; lectures: Arnott demonstrator 1972, Erasmus Wilson 1973, Darwin-Lincoln and Johns Hopkins 1975, Waldron (Harvard) 1976, Richardson (Harvard) 1981, Tomes RCS 1982, President's BAOMS 1985, Sarnat (UCLA) 1989, William Guy RCS of Ed 1990; RNZADC prize 1948, Tomes prize 1966, Down medal 1973, Kay-Kilner prize 1975, ASOMS res award 1976, Hunter medal and Triennial prize 1976, Orthog Surgery award Univ of Texas 1982, Edison award Univ of Michigan 1987, Colyer Gold medal RCS of Eng 1990; memb: German Acad of Natural Scis (Leopoldina) 1988, Inst of Med Nat Acad of Sci Washington USA 1989; hon FFDRCSI 1974; FDSRCS 1952, FRACDS 1966, FIBiol, CBiol, FRCPath 1981; *Recreations* gardening, DIY, skiing, sailing; *Style*— Prof David Poswillo, CBE; Ferndale, Oldfield Rd, Bickley, Kent BR1 2LE (☎ 081 467 1578); Floor 24 Guy's Hospital Tower, London SE1 9RT (☎ 071 955 4338)

POTEZ, Richard Julian; s of Andrew Louis Potez (d 1977), of Knights Manor, Dedham, Essex, and June Rosemary, *née* Avila; *b* 14 July 1949; *Educ* Ampleforth; *m* 6 Aug 1977, Mary Josephine, da of Geoffrey Peter Rickards, of Bijou, Church Street, Willingdon, Eastbourne, Sussex; 1 s (Christopher b 1980), 1 da (Rebecca b 1982); *Career* RN 1967-88, Lt Cdr Far East, Middle East, Europe, Falklands; with Citicorp Scrimgeour Vickers stockbrokers and market makers 1988-90, with Denton Hall Burgin & Warrens 1990-; MNI, MBIM, MIAM, MISM; *Recreations* shooting, fishing, dinner parties; *Style*— Richard Potez, Esq; Sharnden Manor, Rushers Cross, Mayfield, Sussex; Denton Hall Burgin & Warrens, Five Chancery Lane, Cliffords Inn, London EC4A 1BU

POTTER; *see*: Lee Potter

POTTER, David Roger William; s of William Edward Potter, of Durweston, Dorset, and Joan Louise, *née* Frost; *b* 27 July 1944; *Educ* Bryanston, Univ Coll Oxford (MA); *m* 1991, Jill, da of James Benson; 2 da (Louise b 1969, Antonia b 1971); *Career* md: Credit Suisse First Boston 1969-81, Samuel Montagu and various subsidiaries 1981-87, Midland Montagu Corporate Banking 1987-89, David Potter Consultants 1989-90; dep chm and chief exec Guinness Mahon & Co Limited 1990-; non-exec dep chm Tyndall Holdings plc 1990-; non-exec dir The Thomas Cook Group Limited 1989-; govr and chm of Fin Ctee Guy's & St Thomas's Med Sch; govr Bryanston; tstee ORBIS; *Recreations* shooting, theatre, wine; *Clubs* Oxford and Cambridge, City, Vincents Oxford; *Style*— David R W Potter, Esq; 32 St Mary at Hill, London EC3P 3AJ (☎ 071 623 6222, fax 071 528 0935)

POTTER, Donald Charles; QC (1972); s of late Charles Potter; *b* 24 May 1922; *Educ*

St Dunstan's Coll, LSE; *Career* barr Middle Temple 1948, bencher Lincoln's Inn 1979, asst lectr in law LSE 1947-49; *Clubs* Garrick; *Style—* Donald Potter Esq, QC; 37 Tufton St, London SW1P 3QL

POTTER, Edward; s of Flt Lt Edward Josef Data (d 1974), of Krakow, Poland, and Eleanor, *née* Bolton (d 1976); *b* 15 Sept 1941; *Educ* Bolton Tech Sch, Manchester Regnl Coll of Art, Oxford Sch of Arch (Dip Arch); *Career* architect; RIBA Thesis Prize Winner 1968; ptnr Edward Potter Assocs (architects), specialists in restoration of historic buildings; RIBA, FFAS; *Recreations* railways; *Clubs* Chelsea Arts; *Style—* Edward Potter, Esq; 59 Westover Rd, London SW18 2RF (☎ 081 870 8683, fax 081 870 7595)

POTTER, Ernest Frank; s of Frank William Potter; *b* 29 April 1923; *Educ* Dr Challoner's GS Amersham; *m* 1945, Madge, *née* Arrowsmith (d 1990); 1 s; *Career* dir mgmnt consulting servs Coopers & Lybrand 1959-71, head of info servs Br Steel Corp 1972, fin dir Cammell Laird Shipbuilders Ltd 1973-76, dir fin and corp planning Cable and Wireless Ltd 1977-79 (fin dir 1979-87); dir: Bahrain Telecommunications Corp 1981-89, Gen Hybrid Ltd 1987-, The Telecom Corp 1988-, The Cable Corp 1989-, Micrelec Group plc 1989-; chm Holmes Protection Inc 1990-; memb Accountancy Standards Ctee 1985-90; FCMA, FCIS; *Clubs* Wentworth, RAF; *Style—* Ernest Potter, Esq; Long Meadow, Gorse Hill Rd, Virginia Water, Surrey GU25 4AS

POTTER, Jennifer; da of Desmond Potter (d 1961), and Mavis, *née* Sutter; *b* 24 Jan 1949; *Educ* Univ of Sussex (BA); *m* 24 Jan 1981, Dennis Svoboda, s of Emil Svoboda; *Career* public relations exec; PR offr: Hong Kong Tourist Association 1972, Peter Whelpton Associates 1973, FJ Lyons (acquired by Charles Barker 1976) 1975; md Charles Barker-Marketing 1988, dir Charles Barker Holdings Ltd 1989; *Style—* Ms Jennifer Potter; Charles Barker, 30 Farringdon St, London EC4A 4EA (☎ 071 634 1025, fax 071 236 0170, mobile 0831 349 782)

POTTER, (Ronald) Jeremy; s of Alistair Richardson Potter; *b* 25 April 1922; *Educ* Clifton, Queen's Coll Oxford; *m* 1950, Margaret, da of Bernard Newman; 1 s, 1 da; *Career* formerly dep chm New Statesman, md ITV Pub Ltd 1970-79, chm ITV Books Ltd 1971-79, gp dir of Corporate Affrs LWT 1979-; dir Hutchinson Ltd 1978- (dep chm 1980-81, chm 1981-); pres Periodical Publishers Assoc 1978-79, chm Richard III Soc 1971-; author; FRSA; *Books* Hazard Chase, Death in Office, Foul Play, The Dance of Death, A Trail of Blood, Going West, Disgrace and Favour, Death in the Forest, Good King Richard?; *Style—* Jeremy Potter Esq; 41 Woodsford Sq, London W14 8DP (☎ 071 602 0982)

POTTER, Dr John McEwen; s of Alistair Richardson Potter, JP (d 1951), of Hazeldene, Bexley, Kent, and Mairi Chalmers, *née* Dick (d 1954); *b* 28 Feb 1920; *Educ* Clifton, Emmanuel Coll Cambridge (BA, MB BChir, MA), Univ of Oxford (MA, BM, BCh, DM); *m* 21 April 1943, Kathleen, da of Rev Dr Herbert Shaw Gerrard (d 1969), of Manchester; 3 s (James b 1944, Andrew b 1949, Simon b 1953); *Career* RAMC 1944-47, Lt 1944, active serv 8 Army Europe, Capt 1945, served India and Burma, graded neurosurgeon 1946; lectr in physiology and jr chief asst professorial surgical unit Bart's 1948-51, graduate asst to Nuffield prof of surgery Oxford 1951-56, EG Fearnsides scholar Cambridge 1954-56, Hunterian prof RCS 1955; conslt neurosurgeon: Manchester Royal Infirmary 1956-61, Radcliffe Infirmary Oxford 1961-87; clinical lectr in neurosurgery Univ of Oxford 1962-68, fell Linacre Coll 1967-69, univ lectr in neurosurgery 1968-87; Wadham Coll Oxford: fell 1969, professorial fell 1974-87, sub warden 1978-81, dean of degrees 1983-, emeritus fell 1987-; dir of postgrad med educn Oxford Univ 1972-87, memb Bd of Govrs Utd Oxford Hosps 1973; memb: Gen Med Cncl 1973-89 (chm Registration Ctee 1979-89), Gen Bd of Faculties Univ of Oxford 1975-83, Oxon Health Authy 1982-89, Hebdomadal Cncl Univ of Oxford 1983-89, Med Appeals Tbnl 1987-; former examiner Univs of Oxford and Cambridge; vice pres Fourth Int Congress of Neurological Surgery; FRCS 1951, memb BMA, FRSM (pres Neurology Section 1975-76), archivist Soc of Br Neurological Surgns (former hon sec), corr memb American Assoc of Neurological Surgns; memb: Deutche Gesellschaft für Neurochirurgie, Sociedad Luso-Espanhola de Neurocirurgia; hon memb Egyptian Soc of Neurological Surgns; FRCS; *Books* The Practical Management of Head Injuries (fourth edn 1984), contrib books and jls on subjects mostly relating to neurology and med educn; *Recreations* fishing; *Style—* Dr John Potter; 47 Park Town, Oxford OX2 6SL (☎ 0865 57875); Myredykes, Newcastleton, Roxburghshire TD9 OSR

POTTER, Maj-Gen Sir (Wilfrid) John; KBE (1968, CBE 1963, OBE 1951), CB (1966); s of late Maj Benjamin Henry Potter, OBE, MC; *b* 18 April 1913; *m* 1, 1943, Vivienne Madge (d 1973), da of late Capt Henry D'Arcy Medlicott Cooke; 1 s, 1 da; m 2, 1974, Mrs D Ella Purkis; 1 step s, 1 step da; *Career* Maj-Gen 1962, dir of Supplies and Tport (Army) 1963-65, Tport Offr in Chief (Army) 1965-66, dir of movements (Army) MOD 1966-68, ret; chm Traffic Cmmrs and Licensing Authy Western Traffic Area 1973-83; *Style—* Maj-Gen Sir John Potter, KBE, CB; Orchard Cottage, The Orchard, Freshford, Bath, Avon (☎ 0225 722594)

POTTER, Jon Nicholas; s of Robert Edward Potter, and June, *née* Rosemeyer; *b* 19 Nov 1963; *Educ* Burnham GS, Univ of Southampton (BA), MBA; *Career* sr product mangr KP Foods; hockey player: Olympic Bronze LA 1984, World Cup Silver London 1986, Euro Cup Silver Moscow 1987, Olympic Gold Seoul 1988, Capt Barcelona 1988, 164 int caps, Hockey Player of the Year 1987-88; *Recreations* most sports, films, music; *Clubs* Hounslow Hockey, Ladykillers; *Style—* Jon Potter, Esq; Spiral Cottage, 42 Hamilton Rd, Twickenham, Middx TW21 6SN (☎ 081 755 4023); KP Foods Ltd, Heathgate House, 57 Colne Rd, Twickenham, Middx (☎ 081 894 5600, fax 081 894 6715, telex 936246)

POTTER, Laurie; s of Ronald Henry Ernest Potter, of Perth, WA, and Audrey Megan, *née* Stainton; *b* 7 Nov 1963; *Educ* Kelmscott Sr HS Perth WA; *m* 26 Sept 1989, Helen Louise, da of Francis Michael Turner; 1 s (Michael Laurie b 14 March 1990); *Career* professional cricketer; 48 appearances Kent CCC 1981-85, 104 appearances Leicestershire CCC 1986- (awarded county cap 1988), Griqualand West SA 1984-86 (capt 1985-86), Orange Free State SA 1987-88; capt Aust under 19 tour of Pakistan 1981 (scored 108 not out in youth Test match), capt England under 19 v W Indies 1982 (6 young England Test matches); youth devpt offr Leicestershire CCC 1989-90; *Recreations* hockey, rugby, family; *Style—* Laurie Potter, Esq; Leicestershire CCC, Grace Rd, Leicester (☎ 0533 832128)

POTTER, Leila Oriel; da of Leslie Gordon McConomy (d 1964), of London, and Amelia Kessler; *Educ* Birkenhead High Sch (GPDST); *m* George Potter, s of Patrick Potter (d 1970); 3 da (Sarah b 1954, Lucy b 1965, Emily b 1967); *Career* md Bunbury Domestic/Equestrian Employment Agency 1968-; chm Ladies Circle 1964-65, cnclr Crewe and Nantwich Borough and Dist 1968-75, chm Local Govt Advsy Ctee 1988-89, memb Women's Enterprise Network (WEN) and Women Into Business 1988-89; govr Kingsway Sch Crewe 1970-75; *Style—* Mrs Leila Potter; Foxdale, Bunbury, Nr Tarporley, Cheshire (☎ 0829 260 357/148)

POTTER, His Hon Judge (Francis) Malcolm; s of Francis Martin Potter; *b* 28 July 1932; *Educ* Rugby, Jesus Coll Oxford; *m* 1970, Bertha Villamil; 1 s, 1 da; *Career* called to the Bar Lincoln's Inn 1956, rec of the Crown Ct 1974-78, circuit judge 1978-; *Style—* His Hon Judge Malcolm Potter; Queen Elizabeth II Law Courts, Birmingham

POTTER, Hon Mr Justice; Hon Sir Mark Howard; s of Prof Harold Potter (d 1951), and Beatrice Spencer, *née* Crowder (d 1978); *b* 27 Aug 1937; *Educ* Perse Sch Cambridge, Gonville and Caius Coll Cambridge (MA); *m* 1962, Undine Amanda Fay, da of Maj James Eric Miller (Rajputana Rifles); 2 s (Nicholas b 6 Sept 1969, Charles b 27 Dec 1978); *Career* cmmnd 15 Medium Regt RA 1958, Lt 2 Sqdn Para Regt RHA (TA) 1960-65; asst supervisor legal studies Univ of Cambridge (Gonville and Caius, Queen's, Sydney Sussex) 1961-68; called to the Bar Gray's Inn 1961, QC 1980, bencher 1987, judge of the High Ct Queen's Bench Div 1988; chm Bar Public Affrs Ctee 1987; memb: Cncl of Legal Educn 1982-, Advsy Ctee Lord Chllrs Civil Justice Review 1985-88; kt 1988; *Recreations* family, sporting; *Clubs* Garrick; *Style—* The Hon Mr Justice Potter; Royal Courts of Justice, Strand, London WC2 (☎ 071 936 6000)

POTTER, Melissa Mary; da of Wilfrid Humble Gibson, of Linnel Hill, Hexham, Northumberland, and Joan Margaret, *née* Gair; *b* 9 Feb 1958; *Educ* Colegio Santa Maria Del Camino Puerto De Heirro Madrid, New Hall Convent of The Holy Sepulchre Chelmsford, Queen Elizabeth GS Hexham; *m* 1 June 1965, Ian Jeffrey Potter, s of Cyril David Potter, of Ormskirk, Lancs; *Career* sr sales exec: Woman's Jl (IPC) 1982-83, Over 21 (Morgan Grampian) 1983-85; fndr Gibson & Co 1985 (works under maiden name as headhunter specialising in media depts within advertising agencies, co is unique in London for dealing with media); *Recreations* entertaining (a lot), cooking, flower arranging; *Clubs* The Farmers; *Style—* Mrs Melissa Potter; 28 Grosvenor Rd, Chiswick, London W4 4EG (☎ 081 994 7643); Casa León, Camino De La Maquivilla, Frigiliana, Spain

POTTER, Raymond; CB (1990); *b* 26 March 1933; *Career* joined Lord Chancellors Dept Central Office Royal Courts of Justice 1950, Western Circuit of Assize 1962; called to the Bar Inner Temple 1971; chief clerk Bristol Crown Ct 1972, dep circuit admin Western Circuit 1976, circuit admin Northern Circuit 1982, dep sec Cts and Legal Servs 1986, dep clerk of the Crown in Chancery 1989-; *Recreations* painting; *Clubs* Athenaeum; *Style—* Raymond Potter, Esq, CB; Lord Chancellor's Department, Trevelyan House, Great Peter Street, London SW1P 2BY (☎ 071 210 8719)

POTTER, Sir (Joseph) Raymond Lynden; s of Rev Henry Lynden Potter, and Mabel Boulton Potter; *b* 21 April 1916; *Educ* Haileybury, Clare Coll Cambridge; *m* 1939, Daphne Marguerite, da of Sir Crawford Douglas-Jones, CMG; 3 s, 1 da; *Career* served WWII Queen's Own Royal W Kent Regt, UK and Middle East, subsequently Asst QMG WO; chm Halifax Building Society 1974-83 (joined 1951, gen mangr 1956, chief gen mangr 1960-74, dir 1968-83); vice-pres Bldg Socs Assoc 1981- (formerly memb Cncl then chm 1974-83); memb Bd: Warrington and Runcorn New Town Development Corporation 1969-86, Wakefield Diocesan Bd of Fin 1960-65; life govr Haileybury Sch, sec RIIA 1947-51; Freeman City of London 1981; kt 1978; *Clubs* Hawks (Cambridge); *Style—* Sir Raymond Potter; Oakwood, Chilbolton, Stockbridge, Hants SO20 6BE (☎ 026 474 523)

POTTER, Hon Mrs (Vanessa Jane); *née* Robson; da of Sir Lawrence William Robson (d 1982), and Baroness Robson of Kiddington, J P; *b* 2 Sept 1949; *Educ* Wycombe Abbey, St Thomas's Medical Sch; *m* 1973, Jonathan Martin Potter; 1 s, 2 da; *Career* medical practitioner; *Style—* The Hon Mrs Potter; Tyler Hall, Tyler Hill, Canterbury, Kent

POTTERTON, Homan; s of Thomas Edward Potterton (d 1960), and Eileen, *née* Tong (d 1990); *b* 9 May 1946; *Educ* Kilkenny Coll, Trinity Coll Dublin (BA, MA); *Career* cataloguer Nat Gallery of Ireland 1971-73, asst keeper Nat Gallery London 1974-80, dir Nat Gallery of Ire 1980-88, contrib to Burlington Magazine, Apollo, Connoisseur, Country Life, Financial Times; FSA, HRHA; *Books* Irish Church Monuments 1570-1880 (1975), A Guide to the National Gallery (1976), The National Gallery, London (1977), Reynolds and Gainsborough: themes and painters in the National Gallery (1976), Pageant and Panorama: the elegant world of Canaletto (1978), Irish Art and Architecture (1978), Venetian Seventeenth Century Painting (1979), Dutch Seventeenth and Eighteenth Century Paintings in the National Gallery of Ireland - a complete catalogue (1986) The Golden Age of Dutch Paintings from the National Gallery of Ireland (exhibition catalogue, 1986; *Style—* Homan Potterton, Esq; 119 West 71 St, NY 10023 (☎ 212 721 0510); 3 Westmoreland Terrace, London SW1V 4AG (☎ 071 834 8279)

POTTINGER, Alan Derek; JP (1985); s of Dr JH Pottinger (d 1961), and Winifred, *née* Bradley (Lady Kirby (d 1989), wid of Sir Arthur Kirby, CMG, KBE); *Educ* Taunton Sch, Exeter Coll Oxford (MA); *m* 15 Aug 1953, Elizabeth Jean Laurie, *née* Gay; 1 s (Timothy Stuart b 8 Dec 1956), 1 da (Sally Anne Laurie b 16 Aug 1954); *Career* serv Royal Marines 44 Commando 1944-46; Smith Mackenzie & Co Ltd E Africa 1949-62 (latterly shipping mangr), Shell Mex & BP Ltd 1962-76, Shell UK Oil Ltd 1976-84 (latterly mangr distribution planning); advsr to Coll of Petroleum Studies Oxford 1986-; FCIS 1954; *Recreations* sailing; *Clubs* Naval; *Style—* Alan Pottinger, Esq, JP; 2 Church Cottages, Aldbury, Nr Tring, Herts HP23 5RS (☎ 044 285 207)

POTTINGER, Martin Neil; s of Peter Jamieson Henry Pottinger (d 1987), of Edinburgh, and Gladys May, *née* Crafer; *b* 14 March 1948; *Educ* Royal HS Edinburgh, Scott Sutherland Sch of Architecture Aberdeen, Thames Poly London (Dip Arch); *m* 1, 10 Sept 1976 (m dis 1985), Caroline Mary, *née* Moresco; m 2, 30 Sept 1985, Harriet St Bride Ram, da of Capt David Burdett Money-Coutts, of Magpie House, Peppard Common, Henley on Thames; 3 s (William b 19 Nov 1985, Thomas b 6 Jan 1989, Robin b 2 Sept 1990), 1 da (Flora b 2 April 1987); *Career* architect; ptnr Hutchinson & Ptnrs 1979-81, princ Martin Pottinger Chartered Architect 1982-85, princ Martin Pottinger Assoc Architects 1986-; memb RIBA 1980; *Recreations* carpentry, gardening, walking, my children; *Style—* Martin Pottinger, Esq; Mount Pleasant Cottage, Upottery, Honiton, Devon EX14 9PF (☎ 040 486 483); Martin Pottinger Assoc, 150 Regents Park Rd, Primrose Hill, London NW1 8XN (☎ 071 586 9372, fax 071 586 9373, car 0836 284036)

POTTS, Archibold (Archie); s of Ernest Wilkinson Potts (d 1979), of Sunderland, Tyne and Wear, and Ellen, *née* Simpson (d 1980); *b* 27 Jan 1932; *Educ* Monkwearmouth Central Sch Sunderland, Ruskin Coll Oxford, Oriel Coll Oxford (MA), Univ of London (external PGCE), Univ of Durham (external MEd); *m* 17 Aug 1957, Marguerite Elsie (d 1983), da of Gabriel Elliott (d 1983), of Sunderland; 1 s (Michael b 1965), 1 da (Margaret b 1963); *Career* RAF Corpl 1950-53, serv Second Tactical Air Force Germany 1951-53; railway clerk 1947-50 and 1953-56; lectr in economics and econ history: N Oxfordshire Tech Coll 1961, York Tech Coll 1962-65, Rutherford Coll of Tech and Newcastle Upon Tyne Poly 1965-80; head Sch of Business Admin 1980-86, assoc dean Faculty of Business and Professional Studies 1987; pt/t case worker: Nat Prices and Income Bd 1967-68, Cmmn on Industl Rels 1970; chm NE Labour History Soc 1990-, memb Exec Ctee Assoc of Northumberland Local History Socs 1987-, sec Newcastle and Gateshead Co-op Pty 1988- (treas 1983-88), sec Newcastle TS Nelson Sea Cadet Corps 1988-; Lab candidate Westmorland constituency general election 1979; Tyne and Wear CC 1979-86: vice chm 1983-84, chm 1984-85; memb Exec Ctee Soc for Study of Lab History 1987-; *Books* Stand True (1976), Bibliography of Northern Labour History (ed, 1982), Shipbuilders and Engineers (ed, 1988), contrib to Dictionary of Labour Biography (Vol 2 1974, Vol 4 1977, Vol 5 1979); *Recreations* local history and military modelling; *Clubs* Victory Service; *Style—* Archie Potts, Esq; 41 Kenton Avenue, Kenton Park, Newcastle upon Tyne NE3 4SE (☎ 091 2856361)

POTTS, Michael Stuart; s of Thomas Edmund Potts, ERD, of Bray on Thames, and Phyllis Margaret, *née* Gebbie; *b* 2 Sept 1938; *Educ* Hilton Coll S Africa, Repton; *m* 23 May 1964, Virginia May Lindsay, da of Gp Capt Hugh Whittall Marlow, OBE, AFC, of Cape Town, S Africa; 3 s (Andrew b 1966, Alexander b 1968, Rupert b 1970); *Career* CA; ptnr Coopers & Lybrand Deloitte: Ireland 1968-70, UK 1970- (sr) Liverpool Office 1971-; pres Liverpool Soc of CAs 1982-83; cncl memb: Merseyside C of C and Indust 1974- (hon treas 1974-82), Univ of Liverpool 1979-89 (dep treas 1986-89); ICAEW 1988-; *Recreations* sailing, golf, motoring, horology; *Clubs* Dee Sailing (Commodore 1979-80), Royal Liverpool Golf, Aston Martin Owners, Antiquarian Horological Soc; *Style—* Michael Potts, Esq; Brooke House, The Parade, Parkgate, Cheshire L64 6RN (☎ 051 336 1494); Coopers & Lybrand Deloitte, Richmond House, 1 Rumford Place, Liverpool L3 9QS (☎ 051 227 4242, fax 051 227 4575, telex 628724, car 0860 649097)

POTTS, Robin; QC (1982); s of Flt Lt William Potts (d 1971), and Elaine Muriel, *née* Winkle (d 1958); *b* 2 July 1944; *Educ* Wolstanton GS, Magdalen Coll Oxford (BA, BCL); *m* 1 (m dis 1982), Eva Rebeca, *née* Giwercer; 1 s (James Rupert b 1970); m 2, 8 March 1985, Helen Elizabeth, da of Neville Duncan Sharp, of IOW; 2 s (Timothy Edward b 1986, Christopher William b 1988), 1 da (Emma Clarke b 1990); *Career* called to the Bar Gray's Inn 1968; *Recreations* gardening, reading, wine; *Style—* Robin Potts, Esq, QC; The Grange, Church Lane, Pinner, Middx HA5 3AB; Windmill Cottage, Queen's Rd, Freshwater, IOW PO40 9ES

POTTS, Prof William Taylor Windle; s of Ronald Windle Potts (d 1983), and Kathleen Anne, *née* Cole (d 1983); *b* 10 July 1928; *Educ* The Perse Sch Cambridge, St Catharines Coll Cambridge (MA, PhD); *m* 17 Sept 1955, Margaret Taylor; 3 s (Aidan b 1957, Thomas b 1959, Malcolm b 1963); *Career* lectr Univ of Birmingham 1955-56, prof Univ of Lancaster 1966-; *Books* Osmotic & Ionic Regulation in Animals (1964); *Recreations* archaeology; *Style—* Prof William Potts; The Nook, Caton, Lancaster (☎ 0524 770500); Dept Biological Sciences, University, Lancaster LA1 4YQ (☎ 0524 65201, fax 0524 63806, telex 65111 LANCUL G)

POTWOROWSKI, Tadeusz Krzysztof; s of Jan Jozef Zygmunt Potworowski, and Jadwiga Stefania, *née* Jaroszynska; family landowners in Poland since 14th centry, gs of Senator Tadeusz Potworowski, memb of Upper House in 1930s; *b* 10 Jan 1947; *Educ* Gunnersbury Catholic GS; *m* 28 Dec 1974, Irena Izabella, da of Count Konstanty Lukasz Maria Bninski, of Warsaw, Poland; 1 s (Dominik b 1980), 1 da (Gabriela b 1983); *Career* CA; ptnr Tad Potworowski & Kinast (formerly Jeffreys, Ubysz & Co) 1973-; dir: Robinski & Co Ltd 1986-88, Andrews Delicacies Ltd 1986-88, TP & K Consultants Ltd 1990-; chm W London CA 1986-89; FCA; *Recreations* travelling, skiing, swimming, gardening; *Clubs* The Polish Hearth; *Style—* Tadeusz K Potworowski, Esq; Copperfield, Wayside Gardens, Gerrards Cross, Bucks SL9 7NG; 2 Bamborough Gardens, London W12 8QN (☎ 081 749 2821)

POULETT, Countess; Margaret Christine; *née* Ball; da of Wilfred John Peter Ball, of Reading; *m* 12 Sept 1968, as his 3 w, 8 Earl Poulett (d 1973, when the Earldom became ext, and the Barony became ext or dormant); *Style—* The Rt Hon the Countess Poulett; Le Cercle, Rue du Croquet, St Aubin, Jersey, C I

POULTER, Graham George; s of George Henry Poulter (d 1980), and Mavis Kathleen, *née* Shipman; *b* 5 May 1942; *Educ* Art Coll Wakefield; *m* 29 March 1967 (m dis), Patricia Ann, *née* Dickinson; 2 s (Jason b 1970, James b 1975); *Career* art dir/copywriter Kidds Advertising, account mangr Cravens Advertising, branch mangr Taylor Advertising (London), dir Leeds Office Goddard Watts; chm and chief exec Graham Poulter Ptnrship plc (fndr memb 1969); *Recreations* skiing, squash, gym; *Style—* Graham G Poulter, Esq; Flat 1, The Mews, Oakhampton Court, Park Avenue, Roundhay, Leeds 8 (☎ 0532 733011); Poulter House, 2 Burley Road, Leeds LS3 1NJ (☎ 0532 469611, fax 0532 448796)

POULTON, Christopher Geoffrey; s of Sqdn Ldr Geoffrey Poulton, DFC, and Margery, *née* Hillman; *b* 4 June 1943; *Educ* Dulwich Coll, Churchill Coll Cambridge (MA); *m* 2 Sept 1967, Judith, *née* Barton; 3 da (Annabel, Rebecca, Victoria); *Career* Baring Bros & Co 1972-75, asst dir Charterhouse Japhet 1975-84, dir Cadogan Oakley 1984-86, divnl md Credit Lyonnais Securities 1986-; *Recreations* fishing, music, sailing; *Style—* Christopher G Poulton, Esq; Belle Farm, Belle Farm Lane, Hadlow, Kent; Broadwalk House, 5 Appold St, London EC2A 2DA

POULTON, Richard Christopher; s of Rev Christopher John Poulton (d 1988), and Aileen Muriel, *née* Sparrow (d 1977); *b* 21 June 1938; *Educ* Kings Coll Taunton, Wesleyan Univ Middleton Connecticut USA, Pembroke Coll Cambridge (DipEd, MA); *m* 3 April 1965, Zara Irene Mary, da of Prof Peter Charles Crossley-Holland, of Llangeler, Llandysul; 2 s (Anthony b 1969, Benedict b 1971), 1 da (Elizabeth b 1966); *Career* asst master: Bedford Sch 1962-63, Beckenham and Penge GS 1963-66; head of dept and housemaster Bryanston Sch 1966-80; headmaster: Wycliffe Coll 1980-86, Christs Hosp 1987-; JP S Glos 1985-86, govr Oxford and Cambridge Exam Bd 1987-90; memb: Head Masters Conf 1980, Secdy Heads Assoc 1980; Freeman City of London 1987; *Books* Victoria, Queen of a Changing Land (1975), Kings and Commoners (1977), A History of the Modern World (1980); *Recreations* choral music, walking, watching sport, writing; *Clubs* East India, Public Schs; *Style—* Richard Poulton, Esq; The Headmaster's House, Christ's Hospital, Horsham, W Sussex RH13 7LS (☎ 0403 52547)

POULTON, William Dacres Campbell; s of Maj Arthur Stanley Poulton (d 1981), of Battle, Sussex, and Winifred Evelyn, *née* Montgomery Campbell; *b* 15 Dec 1937; *Educ* Dover Coll, New Coll Oxford (BA, MA); *m* 3 Jan 1970, Carolyn Frances, da of Flt Lt Francis Macken (d 1961); 2 s (Charles b 1970, Andrew b 1976), 1 da (Elinor b 1972); *Career* Nat Serv 1956-58, 2 Lt Royal Sussex Regt 1957, Somaliland Scout 1957-58; lectr in law New Coll Oxford 1963-68; called to the Bar Middle Temple 1965, in practice S E circuit, asst rec 1987; memb Sevenoaks Deanery Synod; *Recreations* gardening, walking, skiing; *Style—* William Poulton, Esq; Quarry Chase, Seal Hollow Rd, Sevenoaks, Kent (☎ 0732 451 389); 12 New Square, Lincolns Inn, London WC2 (☎ 071 405 3808, fax 071 831 7376)

POUND, Guy Peter; s of Ernest John Pound, of Poole, Dorset; *b* 26 Jan 1933; *Educ* Brentwood Public Sch, Bartlett Sch of Arch, UCL (Dip Arch); *m* 8 March 1982, Deborah, *née* Hall; *Career* architect; md of The Guy Pound Gp Practice (Architects and Planners) Ltd 1986, dir Anglo Continental Casinos Ltd 1987, chm Macs Rainwear Ltd 1983; works incl: Hythe Marina Village Hants, Milbay Docks Plymouth, Supreme Law Cts Canberra; competitions incl runner up Cwlth Bank Canberra; ARIBA, fell RAIA; lawn tennis umpire all major tournaments incl: centre ct Wimbledon, Wembley, Davis Cup; Freeman City of London 1989; *Recreations* squash, tennis; *Clubs* Royal Southampton Yacht, Lawn Tennis Umpires Assoc of GB; *Style—* Guy Pound, Esq; The Studio, 11 Ravine Rd, Canford Cliffs, Poole, Dorset BH13 7HS; The Loft, Rear of 13 Ravine Rd, Canford Cliffs, Poole, Dorset BH13 (☎ 0202 707655, fax 0202 707076)

POUND, Joan, Lady; Joan Amy; da of James Woodthorpe; *m* 1942, Sir Derek Allen Pound, 4 Bt (d 1980); *Style—* Joan, Lady Pound; Corner Farmhouse, Watton Road, Shipdham, nr Thetford, Norfolk IP25 7RL

POUND, Sir John David; 5 Bt (UK 1905), of Stanmore, Co Middlesex; s of Sir Derek Allen Pound, 4 Bt (d 1980); Sir John Pound, 1 Bt, was head of the firm John Pound & Co, Portmanteau Manufacturers, and Lord Mayor of London 1904-05; *b* 1 Nov 1946; *m* 1, 20 July 1968 (m dis 1978), Heather Frances O'Brien, o da of Harry Jackson Dean; 1 s; m 2, 1978, Penelope Ann, da of Grahame Arthur Rayden; 2 s (Christopher b 1982, Nicholas Edward b 1986); *Heir* s, Robert John Pound b 2 Feb 1973; *Career* Liveryman Leathersellers' Co; *Style—* Sir John Pound, Bt; Dunaway, 29 Alton Road, Pownall Park, Wilmslow, Cheshire SK9 5DY

POUND, Ven Keith Salisbury; s of Percy Salisbury Pound (d 1946), of Charlton, London SE1, and Annie Florence, *née* Button (d 1979); *b* 3 April 1933; *Educ* Roan Sch for Boys Blackheath, St Catharine's Coll Cambridge (BA, MA), Cuddesdon Coll Oxford; *Career* curate St Peter and St Helier Morden Surrey 1957-61, trg offr Hollowford Training Centre 1961-64, warden Dioceste of Sheffield 1964-68, rector Holy Trinity with St Mathew Southwark 1968-78, rural dean Southwark and Newington 1973-78, team rector Thamesmead 1978-86, sub-dean of Woolwich 1984-86, dean of Greenwich 1985-86, hon canon Southwark Cathedral 1985-, chaplain gen and archdeacon to HM Prison Serv 1986-, chaplain to HM The Queen 1988-; *Books* Creeds and Controversies (1966); *Recreations* theatre, music, reading, crosswords; *Clubs* Civil Service; *Style—* The Ven Keith Pound; 7 Vanbrugh Court, Wincott St, London SE11 4NS; 28 Tackleway, Hastings, E Sussex; HM Prison Service, Cleland House, Page St, London SW1P 4LN (☎ 071 217 6266)

POUNDER, Prof Derrick John; s of Wilfred Pounder, of Penycoedcae, Wales, and Lilian, *née* Jones; *b* 25 Feb 1949; *Educ* Pontypridd Boys GS, Univ of Birmingham (MB, ChB); *m* 28 Nov 1975, Georgina, da of Patrick Kelly, of Tullamore, Co Offaly, Ireland; 1 s (Emlyn b 18 May 1989), 1 da (Sibéal b 30 March 1985); *Career* lectr then sr lectr in forensic pathology Univ of Adelaide S Aust, dep chief med examiner Edmonton Alberta Canada and assoc prof Univs of Alberta and Calgary 1985-87, prof of forensic med Univ of Dundee Scotland 1987-; memb SNP; Freeman Llantrisant; FRCPA, FFPathRCPI, FCAP, MRCPath; *Recreations* photography, medieval architecture, almost-lost causes; *Style—* Prof Derrick Pounder; 12 Hill St, Broughty Ferry, Dundee, Scotland DD5 2JL; Department of Forensic Medicine, The Royal Infirmary, Dundee, Scotland DD1 9ND (☎ 0382 200794, fax 0382 22094)

POUNDER, Rafton John; s of late Cuthbert C Pounder; *b* 13 May 1933; *Educ* Charterhouse, Christ's Coll Cambridge; *m* 1959, Valerie Isobel, da of late Robert Stewart, MBE; 1 s, 1 da; *Career* MP (UU) Belfast S Oct 1963-Feb 1974; sec NI Bankers' Assoc 1977-; *Style—* Rafton Pounder, Esq; Gunpoint, Coastguard Lane, Orlock, Bangor, Co Down BT19 2LR

POUNDS, Prof Kenneth Alwyne; CBE (1984); s of Harry Pounds (d 1976), and Dorothy Louise, *née* Hunt (d 1981); *b* 17 Nov 1934; *Educ* Salt Sch Shipley Yorks, UCL (BSc, PhD); *m* 1, 29 Dec 1961, Margaret Mary (d 1976), da of Patrick O'Connell (d 1969); 2 s (David Edwin b 12 May 1963, John Michael b 13 April 1966), 1 da (Jillian Barbara b 12 June 1964); m 2, 10 Dec 1982, Joan Mary, da of Samuel Millit (d 1983); 1 s (Michael Andrew b 5 Aug 1983), 1 da (Jennifer Anne b 22 Feb 1987); *Career* Univ of Leicester: asst lectr 1960, lectr 1962, sr lectr in physics 1989, dir X-Ray astronomy gp 1969-, reader in physics 1971, prof of space physics 1973-, head of physics 1986-; author of over 150 publications world-wide; playing memb: Oadby Town CC, Oadby Wyvern FC; fndr memb BNSC Mgmnt Bd; cncl memb: SERC (chm Astronomy, Space and Radio Bd 1980-84), Royal Soc 1986-87; pres Royal Astronomical Soc 1990-; Hon DUniv of York 1984; FRS 1981; *Recreations* cricket, football, music; *Style—* Prof Kenneth Pounds, CBE, FRS; 12 Swale Close, Oadby, Leics (☎ 0533 719 370); Dept of Physics, Univ of Leics LE1 7RH (☎ 0533 523 509, telex 341664)

POUNTAIN, Christopher Charles; s of Charles Alfred Pountain, of Edinburgh, and Jean Mary, *née* Stanfield; *b* 4 May 1953; *Educ* Royal High Sch Edinburgh, St Andrews (BSc); *m* 29 July 1988, Joyce Margaret, da of William Thomson, of Balrownie nr Brechin; *Career* actuary student Scottish Widows Fund 1975-79, insur analyst Wood Mackenzie 1979 (dir 1985, merger with County Nat West 1988), with London Office County Nat West 1988; FFA 1978; *Recreations* hill walking, skiing, cinema going, reading; *Style—* Christopher Pountain, Esq; County Nat West Securities, Drapers Gardens, 12 Throgmorton Ave, London EC2P 2ES (☎ 071 382 1549, fax 071 382 1001)

POUNTAIN, Sir Eric John; DL (Staffs); *b* 5 Aug 1933; *Educ* Queen Mary's GS Walsall; *m* 1960, Joan Patricia, *née* Sutton; 1 s, 1 da; *Career* chm Tarmac plc; non exec chm: James Beattie plc, IMI plc; non exec dir Midland Bank plc; patron Staffs Agric Soc; hon fell Wolverhampton Poly; MBIM, FIHE, FRSA; kt 1985; *Style—* Sir Eric Pountain, DL; Edial House, Edial, nr Lichfield, Staffordshire; c/o Tarmac plc, Hilton Hall, Essington, Wolverhampton WV11 2BQ

POUNTNEY, David Willoughby; s of Edward Willoughby Pountney, of Clevedon, Avon, and Dorothy Lucy, *née* Byrt (d 1984); *b* 10 Sept 1947; *Educ* St Johns Coll Choir Sch Cambridge, Radley, St Johns Coll Cambridge (MA); *m* 23 Feb 1980, Jane Rosemary, da of Maj James Emrys Williams (d 1978); 1 s (James b 1984), 1 da (Emilia b 1981); *Career* dir of productions: Scottish Opera 1976-80, ENO 1983-; dir of operas in: Ireland, Holland, Germany, Italy, Aust and USA, all maj Br cos; princ productions incl: the Janacek cycle (Scot Opera, WNO), Bussoni's Dr Faust (ENO, Deutsche Opera), The Lady Macbeth of Mtensk (ENO), Hansel and Gretel (ENO, received the Evening Standard award), Wozzeck, Pelleas at Mélesande; *Books* numerous opera translations incl: Smetana's The Bartered Bride, Two Widows, Die Fledermaus, From the House of the Dead, The Flying Dutchman, La Traviata, Christmas Eve, Seraglio; *Recreations* croquet, cooking, gardening; *Clubs* Garrick; *Style—* David Pountney, Esq; 35 Brookfield Mansions, Highgate West Hill, London N6 6AT (☎ 081 342 8900); ENO, London Coliseum, St Martin's Lane, London WC2 (☎ 071 836 0111)

POUT, Harry Wilfred; CB (1978), OBE (1959); *b* 11 April 1920; *Educ* East Ham GS, Imperial Coll London; *m* 1949, Margaret Elizabeth, *née* Nelson; 3 da; *Career* dep controller (MOD): Guided Weapons 1973, Guided Weapons and Electronics 1973-75, Air Systems 1975-79, Aircraft Weapons and Electronics 1979-80; def conslt 1980-82, Marconi Underwater Weapons Systems Ltd 1982-1986; def conslt 1986-; *Recreations* mountaineering, geology; *Style—* Harry Pout, Esq, CB, OBE; Oakmead, Fox Corner, Worplesdon, nr Guildford, Surrey GU3 3PP (☎ 0483 232223)

POVER, Alan John; CMG (1990); s of John Pover (d 1978), and Anne, *née* Hession, of Woodland House, Atherton, Manchester; *b* 16 Dec 1933; *Educ* Salesian Coll Bolton; *m* 31 Oct 1964, Doreen Elizabeth, da of James Dawson (d 1988); 1 s (David b 1966), 2 da (Jane b 1965, Claire b 1971); *Career* Nat Serv Army 1952-54; Civil Serv Miny Pensions and Nat Insur 1954-61; HM Dip Serv: CRO London 1961-62, second sec Lagos 1962-66 (Tel Aviv 1966-69), first sec and consul Karachi and Islamabad 1969-73, FCO 1973-76, consul Cape Town 1976-80, cnsllr and consul gen Washington DC 1986-90, high cmmr Banjul 1990-; *Recreations* golf, historical research. gardening, cricket; *Style—* Alan Pover, Esq, CMG; British High Commission, Atlantic Rd, Fajara, Banjul, The Gambia; c/o Foreign & Commonwealth Office, King Charles St, London SW1A 2AH

POVER, Hon Mrs (Joan Vera); *née* Brockway; 3 da of Baron Brockway (Life Peer), and his 1 w, Lilla, *née* Harvey-Smith; *b* 1921; *m* 29 April 1944, Capt Everett Samuel Pover, s of Samuel Pover, of Bushey, Herts; 3 s, 1 da; *Style—* The Hon Mrs Pover

POVEY, Robert Frederick Donald; s of Donald James Frederick Povey (d 1987), and Ellen Lillian, *née* Nye (d 1987); *b* 8 July 1944; *Educ* Strand GS, Brixton Sch of Bldg; *m* 23 March 1966 (m dis 1970), Pauline, da of Ernest John Wise; m 2, 22 June 1974,

Karen Moira, da of late Arthur Reginald Whitfield; *Career* engr; ptnr Mitchell McFarlane and Ptnrs (dir and co sec); former chm Surrey Branch of Inst Structural Engrs, memb ctees of CIRIA and SCI producing pubns for structural engrs; FIStructE, MConsE; *Recreations* golf, amateur dramatics; *Clubs* Puttenham Golf; *Style—* Robert Povey, Esq; Mitchell McFarlane & Ptnrs, Old Inn House, 2 Carshalton Rd, Sutton, Surrey SM1 4RA (☎ 081 661 6565, fax 081 643 9136)

POWELL, Albert Edward; JP (1961); s of Albert Edward Powell (d 1938), of Morden Surrey, and Mrs Mary Daisy Fewtrell; *b* 20 May 1927; *Educ* Holy Family RC Sch Morden Surrey; *m* 1947, Margaret da of Thomas Neville (d 1942); 1 s (Michael), 2 da (Susan, Deirdre); *Career* London organiser Nat Union Printing, Bookbinding and Paperworkers 1957, organising sec SOGAT 1967 (gen pres 1973-83); dep chm Bexley Magistrates and Bexley Juvenile Bench of Magistrates; memb: Indust Trg Bd 1968 (chm 1974), Central Arbitration Ctee 1978, Industl Tribunal 1984, Parole Bd 1986, Social Security Appeal Tribunal 1985, MTM Assoc of UK; former govr London Coll of Printing; tstee: Bookbinders Charitable Assoc, Mgmnt Ctee of Printers Charitable Assoc; former memb: London Electricity Consultative Ctee, NEDO Printing Industs Ctee; FIMS, HM The Queens Silver Jubilee medal; *Recreations* golf, chess, gardening, music (classical); *Style—* Albert Powell Esq, JP; 31 Red House Lane, Bexley Heath, Kent DN6 8JF (☎ 081 304 7480)

POWELL, Albert Paul; s of late Albert Edward Powell; *b* 1 March 1940; *Educ* St Luke's Portsmouth, Law Society's Coll; *m* 1972, Avril Moira, *née* Wylie; 1 s, 2 da; *Career* Capt Mid & Near E; slr; co dir: Trafalgar House Offshore & Structural Ltd, Cleveland Alloys Ltd, Cleveland Engineering Design Services Ltd; dep dist judge; Freeman of the City of London; *Recreations* rifle shooting, medal collecting; *Clubs* English XX; *Style—* Albert Paul Powell, Esq; 20 Edinburgh Dve, Darlington, Co Durham (☎ 0325 357909)

POWELL, Anthony Dymoke; CH (1988), CBE (1956); s of late Lt-Col P L W Powell, CBE, DSO; *b* 21 Dec 1905; *Educ* Eton, Balliol Coll Oxford; *m* 1934, Lady Violet Pakenham, 3 da of 5 Earl of Longford, KP, MVO (ka 1915); 2 s (Tristram, John); *Career* served Welch Regt and Intelligence Corps WWII, Maj; tstee Nat Portrait Gallery 1962-76; hon fell: Balliol Coll Oxford 1974, Modern Language Assoc of America 1981; hon memb American Acad of Arts and Letters 1977; Hon DLitt: Univ of Sussex 1971, Univ of Leicester 1976, Univ of Kent 1976, Univ of Oxford 1980, Univ of Bristol 1982; Order of the White Line (Czech), Order of the Oaken Crown and Croix de Guerre (Luxembourg), Order of Leopold II (Belgium); *Books Incl:* Agents and Patients (1936), Music of Time (12 Vol series), A Question of Upbringing (1951), At Lady Molly's (1957, James Tait Black Memorial Prize), Temporary Kings (1973, W H Smith Prize), Hearing Secret Harmonies (1975), To Keep the Ball Rolling (memoirs; 4 Vol series, Vol I 1976, Vol IV 1982), The Fisher King (1986), *Plays* Afternoon Men (adapted from book of 1931), Arts Theatre Club, The Garden God, The Rest I'll Whistle, The Album of Music of Time (ed Violet Powell) (1987), Miscellaneous Verdicts (1990); *Clubs* Travellers', Pratt's; *Style—* Anthony Powell, Esq, CH, CBE; The Chantry, nr Frome, Somerset (☎ 037 384 314)

POWELL, Hon Mrs (Beryl); *née* Davies; o da of Baron Davies of Penrhys (Life Peer), *qv*; *b* 1947; *m* 1965, Colin James Powell; 1 s; *Style—* The Hon Mrs Powell; Maesgwyn, Ton Pentre, Rhondda

POWELL, Dr Brian David; s of T D L Powell (d 1970); *b* 20 Feb 1926; *Educ* Saltley Birmingham, Coleshill Warwicks, Trinity Coll Cambridge (MA, PhD), Univ of NSW Aust; *m* 1957, Jean Mary, *née* Stephenson; 3 da; *Career* Nat Res Cncl of Canada 1952-53; fell: Royal Soc of Chemistry 1962, Inst of Food Sci and Technol 1971; mastership in Food Control 1980; dir: Cadbury Ltd 1969-86, Cadbury Schweppes plc 1980-86, Int Scientific Standards, Ghana Cocoa Growing Res Assoc Ltd 1980-86; memb Cncl Br Industl Biological Res Assoc 1966-86, vice pres Int Office of Cocoa and Chocolate 1976-86, dir Edgbaston C of E Coll for Girls 1985-; *Recreations* silversmithing, ind archaeology, walking, photography, community services; *Style—* Dr Brian Powell; 427 Heath Rd South, Northfield, Birmingham B31 2BB (☎ 021 475 4983)

POWELL, Sir Charles David; KCMG (1990); s of John Frederick Powell, and Geraldine Ysolda, *née* Moylan; *b* 6 July 1941; *Educ* Kings Sch Canterbury, New Coll Oxford (BA); *m* 24 Oct 1964, Carla, da of Domingo Bonardi, of Italy; 2 s (Hugh b 1967, Nicholas b 1968); *Career* memb HM Dip Serv, Helsinki, Washington, Bonn and EEC Brussels, private sec to PM 1984- (under sec 1987); kt 1990; *Recreations* walking; *Clubs* Turf; *Style—* Sir Charles Powell; c/o 10 Downing Street, London SW1

POWELL, (John) Christopher; s of Air Vice Marshal John Frederick Powell, and Geraldine Ysolda Moylan; *b* 4 Oct 1943; *Educ* Canterbury Cathedral Choir Sch, St Peter's, York, LSE (BSc); *m* 1973, Rosemary Jeanne, da of Ralph Symmons; 2 s (Ben b 1974, Jamie b 1977), 1 da (Lucy b 1980); *Career* account mgmnt trainee Hobson Bates 1965-67, account mangr Waseys 1967-69; BMP DDB Needham: account mangr 1969-75, jt md 1975-, chief exec 1988; *Recreations* tennis, walking, riding, reading; *Style—* Christopher Powell, Esq; BMP DDB Needham, 12 Bishops Bridge Rd, London W12 (☎ 071 258 3979)

POWELL, Daryl Anthony; s of Garry Powell, and Jean, *née* Simpson; *b* 21 July 1965; *Educ* Carlton HS Pontefract, Castleford HS; partner, Janice Collins; *Career* rugby league player; amateur Redhill Castleford, professional Sheffield Eagles 1984- (over 200 appearances); represented Yorkshire v Lancashire 1988; GB: debut v France 1990, toured NZ and Papua New Guinea 1990, 3 Test matches v Aust 1990, 10 full caps; overseas clubs: Glenora NZ 1986, Balmain Aust 1988; Player of the Year Sheffield Eagles 1985, Players' Player of the Year Sheffield Eagles 1988-89, Fellow Professionals' Div 2 player of the year 1988-89, Journalists Div 2 Star Man of the Year 1988-89; rugby league coaching scheme: regnl coach 1989-90, staff coach 1990-; *Recreations* golf, squash, football, physical training, spending time with Janice; *Style—* Daryl Powell, Esq; Sheffield Eagles Rugby League Club, Don Valley Stadium, Sheffield (☎ 0742 510326)

POWELL, David Beynon; s of David Eynon Powell (d 1942), and Catherine Ada, *née* Beynon; *b* 9 Feb 1934; *Educ* Gowerton GS, Christ's Coll Cambridge (MA, LLB), Yale Law Sch (LLM), Harvard Business Sch (SMP 18); *m* 18 Sept 1973 (m dis 1983), Pamela Susan, *née* Turnbull; *Career* Nat Serv Flying Offr RAF 1952-54; slr Supreme Ct, dep legal advsr BLMC Ltd 1970-73, dir legal servs BL Ltd 1974-83, gp legal dir Midland Bank plc 1984-; *Recreations* reading, music, bridge; *Style—* David Powell, Esq; 20c Randolph Crescent, London W9 1DR (☎ 071 289 2326); Midland Bank plc, Head Office, Poultry, London EC2P 2BY (☎ 071 260 8239, fax 071 260 8461)

POWELL, His Hon Judge Watkin Dewi Watkin; JP (Mid Glamorgan); s of W H Powell; *b* 29 July 1920; *Educ* Penarth GS, Jesus Coll Oxford; *m* 1951, Alice, da of William Williams; 1 da; *Career* called to the Bar Inner Temple 1949, dep chm Merioneth and Cardigan QS 1966-71; dep rec 1965-71: Cardiff, Birkenhead, Merthyr Tydfil, Swansea; a circuit judge and official referee for Wales and Chester 1972-, liaison judge for Dyfed 1974-84 and Mid Glamorgan 1984-, designated judge for Merthyr Tydfil 1986-90; Univ Coll Cardiff: memb of Ct and Cncl 1976-88, vice pres 1982-88, hon fell and chm of Cncl 1987-88; vice pres hon fell and vice chm Cncl UCW Cardiff 1988-; memb: Ct and Cncl Univ Coll of Wales Aberystwyth 1972-, Cncl Univ of Wales Coll of Med 1989-, Ct Univ of Wales 1974-, Cncl Univ of Wales 1990; chm Cncl of Hon Soc of Cymmrodorion 1979-86 (vice pres 1986-), pres Cymdeithas Theatr Cymru 1983-89, memb Gorsedd of Bards; *Style—* His Hon Judge Watkin Powell, JP; Crown Court, Law Courts, Cathays Park, Cardiff

POWELL, (Elizabeth) Dilys; CBE (1974); da of late Thomas Powell and late Mary Powell; *b* 20 July 1901; *Educ* Bournemouth HS, Somerville Coll Oxford; *m* 1, 1926, Humfry Payne (d 1936); m 2, 1943, Leonard Russell (d 1974); *Career* film critic The Sunday Times 1939-76, TV film critic 1976-; film critic Punch 1979-; FRSL; *Books* Descent from Parnassus, Remember Greece, The Traveller's Journey is Done, Coco, An Affair of the Heart, The Villa Ariadne; *Style—* Miss Dilys Powell, CBE; 14 Albion St, Hyde Park, London W2 (☎ 071 723 9807)

POWELL, Rt Hon (John) Enoch; MBE (1943), PC (1960); s of Albert Enoch Powell; *b* 16 June 1912; *Educ* King Edward's Birmingham, Trinity Coll Cambridge (MA); *m* 1952, Margaret Pamela, *née* Wilson; 2 da; *Career* fell of Trinity Coll Cambridge 1934-38, prof of Greek Sydney Univ NSW 1937-39; serv Royal Warwickshire Regt WWII, Brig 1944; MP (C): Wolverhampton SW 1950-74, Down S 1974-83, S Down 1983-87; parly sec Miny of Housing and Local Govt 1955-57, fin sec to the Treasy 1957-58, min of Health 1960-63; author; *Clubs* Athenaeum; *Style—* The Rt Hon Enoch Powell, MBE; 33 South Eaton Place, SW1 (☎ 071 730 0988)

POWELL, Geoffrey; s of Owen Thomas Powell, of Stoke-on-Trent, and Ethel Mary, *née* Woollam; *Educ* Stanfield HS Stoke-on-Trent, London Univ (BSc, MSc); *m* 30 Nov 1968, Penelope Elizabeth, da of Maj George Eastlake; 1 s (Adam b 1971), 1 da (Nina b 1973); *Career* chief exec Imperial Foods (General Products) Ltd 1984-86 (personnel dir 1979-82, planning dir 1982-84); md: Granada TV Rental Ltd 1986-88, Granada UK Rental and Retail Ltd 1988-; dir Granada Gp plc 1987, dir Kingfisher plc (responsible for B&Q, Comet and Charlie Browns Autocentres) 1989; *Recreations* skiing, squash, reading; *Style—* Geoffrey Powell, Esq; Granada TV Rental Ltd, PO Box 31, Ampthill Rd, Bedford MK42 9QQ (☎ 0234 55233, fax 0234 226006, telex 82303)

POWELL, Col Geoffrey Stewart; MC (1944); s of Owen Welch Powell (d 1964), of Scarborough, and Ada Jane, *née* King (d 1968); *b* 25 Dec 1914; *Educ* Scarborough Coll, Open Univ (BA); *m* 7 July 1944, (Anne) Felicity, da of Maj Walter William Wadsworth, MC (d 1972), of West Grimstead; 1 s (Col John Stewart Wadsworth), 1 da (Rosemary Anne Felicity (Mrs Anderson)); *Career* 2 Lt TA 1936-39, 2 Lt The Green Howards (regular army) 1939; WWII serv Parachute Regt India, ME, NW Europe 1942-45; Staff Coll Camberley 1946, Bde Maj Java and Malaya 1946-49 (despatches), US Cmd and Gen Staff Coll Fort Leavenworth 1951, CO II Bn KAR Kenya 1957-59, Col gen staff WO 1959-62, Bde Col Yorks Bde 1962-64, ret 1964; attached to MoD 1964-76; Dep Col The Green Howards 1982-84; vice pres Campden and Dist Hist and Archaeological Soc; FRHistS; *Books* The Green Howards (1968), The Kandyan Wars: The British Army in Ceylon 1803-1818 (1973), Men at Arnhem (1976), Suez: The Double War (with Roy Fullick 1979), The Book of Campden: History in Stone (1982), The Devil's Birthday: The Bridges to Arnhem (1984), Plumer: The Soldiers' General (1990); *Recreations* hill walking, writing, books, beagling; *Clubs* Army & Navy; *Style—* Col Geoffrey Powell, MC; Leysbourne, Chipping Campden GL55 6AE (☎ : 0386 840300)

POWELL, (Richard) Guy; s of Richard Albert Brakell Powell (d 1957), of 2 Kings Bench walk London EC4, and Stella Float, *née* Young; *b* 28 April 1927; *Educ* The King's Sch Canterbury, Hertford Coll Oxford (MA); *Career* admitted slr 1953; ptnr: Rooper & Whately 1960-70, Lee & Pembertons 1970-; clerk Prowdes Educnl Fndn 1974-; memb cncl of Private Libraries Assoc 1963-; Freeman City of London 1948, Liveryman Worshipful Co of Drapers' 1952; FRSA 1952, memb Vereinigung Der Freunde Antiker Kunst (Switzerland) 1960; *Recreations* book collecting, gardening; *Clubs* Travellers, United Oxford and Cambridge; *Style—* R Guy Powell, Esq; 45 Pont St, London SW1X 0BX (☎ 071 589 1114, fax 071 589 0807)

POWELL, (Michael) James Joseph; s of Brian Joseph Powell, of Cardiff, S Wales, and Rita, *née* Mahoney; *b* 22 March 1962; *Educ* Lady Mary HS Cardiff, Mountview Theatre Sch London; partner Jo-Anna Lee; *Career* actor; roles incl: Proteus in Two Gentlemen of Verona (Theatre Museum), Boltam in A Midsummer Nights Dream and Parolles in Alls Well That Ends Well (Open Air Theatre Holland Park), Ratty in Toad of Toad Hall (Winchester Theatre Royal), Idwal in The Corn is Green (Yvonne Arnaud, Old Vic, UK tour), Jack in Jack The Giant Killer (The Theatre Chipping Norton), Edek in The Silver Sword (Phoenix Arts Theatre, Leicester), Bombur-Thorin in The Habbit (Fortune Theatre, nat tour), Benjamin in Joseph and the Amazing Technicolour Dreamcoat (nat tour), Priscilla Goose in Mother Goose (Bridge Lane Theatre), Godspell (nat tour), James and The Giant Peach (nat tour), Oliver (nat tour), Rick in A Slice of Saturday Night (Arts Theatre Club and Kings Head Theatre Club); *Recreations* clowning, juggling; *Style—* James Powell, Esq; Rossmore Associates, 1a Rossmore Rd, Marylebone, London NW1 6NJ (☎ 071 258 1953, fax 071 723 1040)

POWELL, James Richard Douglas; s and h of Sir Nicholas Folliott Douglas Powell, 4 Bt, and his 1 w, Daphne Jean, *née* Errington; *b* 17 Oct 1962; *Educ* Peterhouse Zimbabwe, RAC Cirencester; *Career* dir Petrunella Coffee Estate; *Style—* James Powell, Esq; Petrunella Coffee Estate, Box 58, Chipinge, Zimbabwe

POWELL, Jane; da of Anthony Alfred Edward Powell, of Sheffield, and Barbara, *née* Jackson; *b* 19 Jan 1957; *Educ* Abbeydale Girls GS Sheffield, Chelsea Coll of PE, Univ of Sussex (BEd); *Career* memb Eng Women's Cricket Squad 1979-, Eng Women's Cricket Capt 1988-, memb Eng Women's Hockey Squads 1978-80; hockey coach: Eng Univs, Midland Under 21; memb: Christians in Sport, Nat Coaching Fndn, Inst of Leisure and Amenity Mgmnt; *Books* all sports, golf, active Christian work; *Style—* Miss Jane Powell; Flat 4, 79 Albert Road South, Malvern, Worcestershire WR14 3DX (☎ 0684 565361); The Chase High School, Geraldine Rd, Malvern, Worcestershire WR14 3NZ (☎ 0684 572096)

POWELL, Jeffrey Richard (Jeff); s of Alfred William John Powell, of Canvey Island, Essex, and Dorothy Faith, *née* Parkin; *b* 21 Feb 1942; *Educ* Buckhurst Hill Co HS, The Poly Regent St; *m* 1 (m dis); 2 da (Natalie Jane b 22 May 1972, Natasha Dawn b 14 April 1974); m 2, 20 Feb 1987, Maria del Consuelo Ortiz de Powell, da of Gen Jose Ortiz Avila; 1 s (Jeffrey Jose b 17 March 1988); *Career* Walthamstow Guardian 1959-66 (jr reporter, sports ed); Daily Mail: sports sub-ed 1966-69, football reporter 1969-71, chief soccer corr 1971-89, chief sports feature writer 1989-; Br Sports Reporter of the Year 1978 1983 1985; Br Sports Journalist of the Year 1985; memb: Football Writers Assoc 1969- (chm 1982-83 and 1989-90), Sportswriters Assoc 1969-; *Recreations* golf, tennis, chess; *Clubs* RAC, Scribes, Morton's; *Style—* Jeff Powell, Esq; Daily Mail, Northcliffe House, 2 Derry St, Kensington, London W8 5TT (☎ 071 938 6229, fax 071 937 3745)

POWELL, John Frederick; s of Alfred John Powell, of Greenford, Middlesex, and Ethel Mary, *née* Levy; *b* 22 Sept 1934; *Educ* Univ Coll Sch; *m* 1, 5 Oct 1957, Ena Deirdre, *née* Leeland; 2 s (Richard John, Neil Andrew), 2 da (Sandra Jane, Susan Mary); m 2, 25 April 1980, Cecilia Mary Theresa, *née* Relph; 1 da (Danielle Ida); *Career* Nat Serv RAPC; articled clerk Elles Reeve; Coopers & Lybrand (merged with Cork Gully 1980): joined 1963, ptnr 1977, sr insolvency ptnr West Midlands 1986; FCA (ACA 1957), fell Insolvency Practitioners Assoc; *Books* Liquidation Manual (1988); *Recreations* golf, football (spectator), walking; *Clubs* Copt Heath Golf, The Birmingham; *Style—* John Powell, Esq; Cork Gully, the insolvency practice of Coopers

& Lybrand Deloitte, 43 Temple Row, Birmingham B2 5JT (☎ 021 236 9966, fax 021 200 4040, car 0836 230437)

POWELL, Air Vice-Marshal John Frederick; OBE (1956), AE (1946); s of Rev Morgan Powell (d 1951), of Limpley Stoke, nr Bath, and Edith Susannah, *née* David (d 1964); *b* 12 June 1915; *Educ* King's Coll Choir Sch Cambridge, Lancing, King's Coll Cambridge (BA, MA); *m* 16 Sept 1939, (Geraldine) Ysolda, da of Sir John Moylan, CB, CBE (d 1967), of Church Lane Cottage, Bury, Sussex; 4 s (Charles b 1941, *qv*, Christopher b 1943, Roderick b 1948, Jonathan b 1956); *Career* lectr RAF Coll Cranwell 1938, controller coastal cmd (ops) RAFVR 1939-45, (despatches), RAF (Educn Branch) 1946, instr later sr tutor RAF Coll 1946-59, educn staff FEAF 1959-62, MOD 1962-64, Gp Capt 1964, cmd educn offr HQ Bomber Cmd 1964-66, OC RAF Sch of Educn 1966-67, Air Cdre 1967, dir RAF Educn Servs 1967-72, Air Vice-Marshal 1968; warden and dir of studies Moor Park Coll Farnham 1972-77; *Recreations* choral music, gardening, walking; *Clubs* RAF; *Style*— Air Vice-Marshal John Powell, OBE, AE; Barkers Hill Cottage, Donhead St Andrew, Shaftesbury, Dorset SP7 9EB (☎ 074 788 505)

POWELL, John Lewis; QC (1990); s of Gwyn Powell (d 1981), of Ammanford, Dyfed and Lilian Mary, *née* Griffiths; *b* 14 Sept 1950; *Educ* Christ Coll Brecon, Amman Valley GS, Trinity Hall Cambridge (MA, LLB); *m* 1 Sept 1973, Eva Zofia, da of Dr Adam J Lomnicki; 3 c (Sophie Anna b 14 Feb 1980, Catrin Eva (Katie) b 3 Jan 1982, David John b 3 Feb 1985); *Career* called to the Bar Middle Temple (Harmsworth scholar) 1974; Parly candidate (Lab) Cardigan 1979; vice pres Soc of Construction Law 1988-, memb Commercial Bar Assoc; *Books* Encyclopedia of Financial Services Law (with Eva Lomnicki), Professional Negligence (with R Jackson, 2 edn 1987), Palmer's Company Law (jt ed, 24 edn 1987), Issues and Offers of Company Securities: The New Regimes (1988); *Recreations* travel, sheep farming in Black Mountains Dyfed, walking; *Style*— John Powell, Esq, QC; 2 Crown Office Row, Temple, London EC4Y 7HJ (☎ 071 583 8155, fax 071 583 1205)

POWELL, (Geoffrey) Mark; s of Francis Turner Powell, MBE, of Tanglewood, Oak Grange Rd, W Clandon, Surrey, and Joan Audrey, *née* Bartlett; *b* 14 Jan 1946; *Educ* Tonbridge, St Chad's Coll Univ of Durham (BA); *m* 24 July 1971, Veronica Joan, da of Paul Frank Rowland, of Langford, Clymping, Sussex; 2 da (Jessica b 1973, Catriona b 1976); *Career* ptnr Powell Popham Dawes & Co 1972-77, dir Laing & Cruickshank 1977-86; chief exec: CL-Alexanders Laing & Cruickshank Hldgs Ltd 1987-89 (dir 1986-89), Laurence Keen 1989-; Freeman City of London 1967, Memb of Ct Worshipful Co of Haberdashers 1989-; memb Int Stock Exchange 1971, FRSA; *Clubs* MCC, City of London; *Style*— Mark Powell, Esq; Creedhole Farm, High Button, Thursley, Surrey GU8 6NR (☎ 0428 683163); Laurence Keen Ltd, 49/51 Bow Lane, London EC4M 9LX (☎ 071 489 9493, fax 071 489 8638, telex 916966)

POWELL, Michael Leslie; s of Harold Edwin Powell, of Tiverton Devon, and Dolores Barbara Powell; *b* 10 Feb 1950; *Educ* Tiverton GS; *m* 24 May 1975, Jean Sylvia, da of Alfred John William Owen (d 1979), of Exeter; 2 s (Steven Owen Michael b 1988, James John Harry b 1990); *Career* head of news Devonair Radio 1982-83, md County Sound Radio 1986- (head of news 1983-84, prog controller 1984-85, prog dir 1985-86), dir and co sec of First Oxfordshire Radio Co (Fox FM) 1988-; *Recreations* railway modelling, writing, music; *Style*— Michael Powell, Esq; County Sound Radio, Chertsey Rd, Woking, Surrey GU21 5XY (☎ 0483 740066, telex 859537 COUNTY, fax 0483 740753, car 0860 368041)

POWELL, Neil Ashton; s of Ian Otho James Powell, of Orford, Suffolk, and Dulcie Delia, *née* Lloyd; *b* 11 Feb 1948; *Educ* Sevenoaks Sch Kent, Univ of Warwick (BA, MPhil); *Career* English teacher Kimbolton Sch Huntingdon 1971-74, head of English St Christopher Sch Letchworth 1978-86 (English teacher 1974-78), owner The Baldock Bookshop 1986-90; ed Tracks 1967-70, winner Soc of Authors Gregory Award 1969, writer in residence Samuel Whitbread Sch Shefford 1988, res tutor Arvon Fndn Totleigh Barton Devon 1989, tutor Bd of Extra Mural Studies Univ of Cambridge 1991; contrib of poetry, fiction, essays and reviews to: Critical Quarterly, Encounter, The Guardian, The Listener, London Magazine, New Statesman, PN Review, Poetry Review, Times Literary Supplement, various anthologies, BBC Radio Three; memb Soc of Authors 1974; *Books* Suffolk Poems (1975), At the Edge (1977), Carpenters of Light (1979), Out of Time (1979), A Season of Calm Weather (1982), Selected Poems of Fulke Greville (ed, 1990), True Colours: New and Selected Poems (1991); *Recreations* food and wine, landscape and seascape, good music and bad boys; *Style*— Neil Powell, Esq; Carcanet Press Ltd, 208-212 Corn Exchange, Manchester M4 3BQ (☎ 061 834 8730)

POWELL, Sir Nicholas Folliott Douglas; 4 Bt (UK 1897); s of Sir Richard George Douglas Powell, MC, 3 Bt (d 1980); descends from Walter Powell (d 1567), descendant of Rhys ap Tewdwr Mawr, King of South Wales (*see also* William R Powell, MP); *b* 17 July 1935; *Educ* Gordonstoun; *m* 1, 26 May 1960 (m dis 1987), Daphne Jean, yr da of Maj George Henry Errington, MC; 1 s (James Richard Douglas b 17 Oct 1962), 1 da (Catherine Mary b 1961); m 2, 10 July 1987, Davina Hyacinth Berners, er twin da of Michael Edward Ranulph Allsopp; 2 s (Benjamin Ranulph Berners b 5 Jan 1989, Oliver Michael Folliott b 4 Nov 1990); *Heir* s, James Richard Douglas Powell; *Career* Lt Welsh Gds 1953-57; co dir; *Style*— Sir Nicholas Powell, Bt; Petrunella Coffee Estate, Box 58, Chipinga, Zimbabwe

POWELL, Peter William George; s of Albert Victor Powell (d 1960), of London, and Jessie May Graveney (d 1981); *b* 18 Feb 1926; *Educ* Christ's Coll London, Northern Poly (Dip Arch), UCL (Dip Civic Arch and Town Planning); *m* 16 Feb 1962, Jamila Akhter Jabeen, da of Mohd Amin Malik (d 1987); 1 s (William Ahmed b 1964), 2 da (Jessima Elizabeth b 1968, Sophia Elizabeth (twin) b 1968); *Career* chartered architect and chartered town planner 1950-; private practice London and Govt Serv 1959-66, advsr town planning and housing to the Govt of Pakistan under the Tech Cooperation Scheme of the Columbo Plan; author of two reports for Pakistan Govt on urban improvements and housing legislation; fndr memb Pakistan Inst of Architects 1959 and the Pakistan Inst of City of Regnl Planning 1960; professional serv: Overseas Relations Ctee RIBA 1967-73, Herts Assoc of Architects cncl memb and hon treas 1973-80, RIBA Eastern Region memb Cncl and hon treas 1979-84, memb Cncl of Architects Registration Cncl of the UK 1987-91, memb Organising Ctee RTPI 1970 to estabish a Cwlth Assoc of Planners; FRIBA, FRTPI; *Recreations* watching cricket, book collecting; *Clubs* Marylebone Cricket, Middlesex CCC and Surrey CCC, Cricketers (London); *Style*— Peter Powell, Esq; 8 Longdean Park, Hemel Hempstead, Herts HP3 8BS

POWELL, Sir Philip; CH (1984), OBE (1957); s of late Canon A C Powell, of Epsom, and late Mary Winnifred, *née* Walker; *b* 15 March 1921; *Educ* Epsom Coll, AA Sch of Architecture (Hons Dip); *m* 1953, Philippa, da of Lt-Col C C Eccles, of Tunbridge Wells; 1 s, 1 da; *Career* ptnr Powell and Moya Architects 1946- (now Powell Noya and Ptnrs); works incl: Skylon for festival of Britain 1951 (won in open competition), Mayfield Sch Putney 1956, Plumstead Manor Sch Woolwich 1970, dining rooms Bath Acad of Art Corsham 1970 and Eton Coll 1974, Br Pavilion Expo 70 Osaka Japan; houses and flats at: Churchill Gdns flats Westminster 1948-62 (won in open competition), Chichester 1950, Gospel Oak St Pancras 1954, Toys Hill 1954, Oxshott 1954, Baughurst Hants 1954, Vauxhall Park Lambeth 1972, Covent Gdn 1983; extension to: Brasenose Coll Oxford 1961, Chichester Festival Theatre 1961, picture gallery and undergraduate rooms Christ Church Oxford 1967, Cripps Bldg St John's Coll Cambridge 1967, Swimming Baths Putney 1967, Corpus Christi Coll Oxford 1969, Wolfson Coll Oxford 1974, Cripps Court Queen's Coll Cambridge 1976, Museum of London 1976, London and Manchester Assurance HQ nr Exeter 1978, Sch for Advanced Urban Studies Univ of Bristol 1981, NatWest Bank Shaftesbury Ave London 1982, Queen Elizabeth II Conf Centre Westminster 1986, laboratories incl Queen's Bldg Royal Holloway and Bedford New Coll Egham 1986; work to hosps in: Swindon, Slough, High Wycombe, Wythenshawe, Woolwich, Maidstone; has won numerous medals and awards for architectural work incl Royal Gold Medal for Architecture RIBA 1974; memb Royal Fine Art Cmmn 1969-, treas RA 1985-; RA 1977 (ARA 1972), memb RIBA; kt 1975; *Recreations* travel, listening to music; *Style*— Sir Philip Powell, CH, OBE; 16 The Little Boltons, London SW10 9LP (☎ 071 373 8620); 21 Upper Cheyne Row, London SW3 15JW (☎ 070 351 3882)

POWELL, Sir (Arnold Joseph) Philip; CH (1984), OBE (1957); s of Rev Canon Arnold Cecil Powell (d 1963), of Chichester, and (Mary) Winnifred, *née* Walker (d 1954); *b* 15 March 1921; *Educ* Epsom Coll, AA Sch of Architecture; *m* 17 Jan 1953, (Philippa) June, da of Lt-Col Charles Chevalier Eccles (d 1977), of Tunbridge Wells; 1 s (Benjamin James b 1957), 1 da ((Harriet) Dido b 1955); *Career* architect in private practice, ptnr Powell Moya and Ptnrs; works incl: Churchill Gdns Housing Pimlico and Skylon for 51 Festival of Britain (both of which won in open competition), new buildings at St John's and Queens' Colls Cambridge, Wolfson Coll Oxford, Chichester Festival Theatre, Museum of London, Queen Elizabeth II Conf Centre, Westminster and several new hosps; memb: Royal Fine Art Cmmn 1969-, RA 1977- (treas 1985); FRIBA (Royal Gold medal for Architecture 1974); kt 1975; *Recreations* travel, listening to music; *Style*— Sir Philip Powell, CH, OBE; 16 The Little Boltons, London SW10 9LP (☎ 071 373 8620); office: Powell Moya & Ptnrs, 21 Upper Cheyne Row, London SW3 5JW (☎ 071 351 3882, fax 071 351 6307)

POWELL, Raymond; MP (Lab) Ogmore 1979-; s of Albert Powell; *b* 19 June 1928; *Educ* Pentre G S, Nat Cncl of Labour Colls, LSE; *m* 1951, Marion Grace Evans; 1 s, 1 da; *Career* chm Lab Pty Wales 1977-78, chm S Wales Euro-Constituency Lab Pty 1979-80, sec Anglo-Bulgaria All Pty Parly Gp 1982-, sec Welsh Gp Lab MP's 1985-, vice-chm PLP Agriculture Ctee 1987-88, Paiting Whip 1987-; *Style*— Raymond Powell Esq, MP; 8 Brynteg Gdns, Bridgend, Mid-Glam (☎ 0656 2159)

POWELL, Sir Richard Royle; GCB (1967, KCB 1961, CB 1951), KBE (1954), CMG (1946); s of Ernest Hartley Powell; *b* 30 July 1909; *Educ* Queen Mary's GS Walsall, Sidney Sussex Coll Cambridge; *Career* dep sec: Admty 1948-50, MOD 1950-56; perm sec: MOD 1956-59, BOT 1960-68; dep chm Perm Ctee on Invisible Exports 1968-76; chm: Alusuisse (UK) Ltd 1969-84, Sandoz Gp of cos 1972-1987, Wilkinson Match Ltd 1979-80 (hon pres 1981-83); dir: Whessoe plc 1968-87, Ladbroke Gp plc 1980-1986, Bridgewater Paper Co Ltd 1983-90, Aero-Print Ltd 1969-84, Clerical, Medical and Gen Life Assurance Soc 1972-85, BPB Industries plc 1973-83, Philip Hill Investmt Tst until 1981, Philip Hill & Partners 1981-1986; chm Civil Service Security Appeals Panel until 1982; hon fell Sidney Sussex Coll Cambridge 1972; *Clubs* Athenaeum; *Style*— Sir Richard Powell, GCB, KBE, CMG; 56 Montagu Sq, London W1H 1TG (☎ 071 262 0911)

POWELL, Robert James; s of John Ernest Powell Jones, CMG, of Cranleigh, Surrey, and Ana Elizabeth, *née* Murray; *b* 6 Jan 1954; *Educ* Winchester, Wadham Coll Oxford (MA); *m* 29 March 1980, Flora Elizabeth, da of Rt Hon Maj Sir Hugh Charles Patrick Joseph Fraser, MBE, MP, PC (d 1984); 1 da (Stella Elizabeth b 1987); *Career* called to the Bar Middle Temple 1978; *Style*— Robert Powell, Esq; 13 Old Square, Lincoln's Inn, London WC2 (☎ 071 404 4800, fax 071 405 4267)

POWELL, Roy Colin; s of Fred Johnson, of Florida, and Mildy Powell (d 1986); *b* 30 April 1965; *Educ* Batley HS for Boys; *Career* Rugby League second row forward Leeds RLFC and GB (17 caps); rep: Yorkshire (3 appearances), GB U21 (5 appearances); GB: toured 1988 and 1990; Carryfast 1981-82, Co-op Maintenance Dept 1982-83, Cave and Gerrald 1983, Walter West Builders 1983, Plastering Div Miller Construction 1983-85, Simmons & Wainwright Plasterers 1985-86, self-employed plasterer 1986-; *Recreations* photography, learning to play the piano; *Style*— Roy Powell, Esq

POWELL, Sandy; *b* 7 April 1960; *Educ* St Martin's Coll of Art and Design, Central Sch of Art; *Career* designer; film costume design incl: A Midsummer Nights Dream Cobachan (dir Lindsay Kemp), The Last of England (dir Derek Jarman), Didn't You Kill My Brother (Comic Strip), Stormy Monday (dir Mike Figgis), Stalking Tigers (dir Mitsuo Yanagamachi), The Pope Must Die (dir Peter Richardson), Edward II (dir Derek Jarman), Caravaggio (dir Derek Jarman), Venus Peter (dir Ian Sellar), The Miracle (dir Neil Jordan); theatre set design: Orders of Obedience (Rational Theatre), Hidden Grin (ICA), Mr Punch's Pantomime (Lindsay Kemp Co), Edward II (RSC), Rococo (Rational Theatre), Brightside (Lumière and Son), The Big Parade (Lindsay Kemp Co), Nijinsky (Lindsay Kemp Co), A Midsummer Night's Dream (Lindsay Kemp Co); costume designer for Mick Jagger on The Rolling Stones European Urban Jungle tour 1990 and for all shows by The Cholmondoleys; *Style*— Ms Sandy Powell; c/o Hope & Lyne, 108 Leonard St, London EC2 4RH (☎ 071 739 6200, fax 071 739 4101)

POWELL, Stephen Joseph; s of Joseph Thomas Powell (d 1958), of Goffs Oak, Herts, and Dorothy May, *née* Welch; *b* 26 May 1943; *Educ* Cheshunt GS, The Royal Dental Hosp of London Sch of Dental Surgery (BDS); *m* 6 July 1968, Yvonne Heather, da of Sydney Frederick Williams, of Puckle Church, nr Bristol; 1 da (Rebecca b 1986); *Career* sr registrar in orthodontics Hosp for Sick Children Gt Ormond St and The Royal Dental Hosp London 1972-74; conslt in orthodontics: The Royal Dental Hosp London and St Georges Hosp London 1975-, Kings Coll Hosp Sch of Med and Dentistry 1986-; memb: BDA, Br Soc for the Study of Orthodontics, American Assoc of Orthodontists; cncl memb Soc of St Augustine of Canterbury; FDS RCS, MOrth RCS; *Recreations* swimming, music, theatre, French culture; *Clubs* Athenaeum; *Style*— Stephen Powell, Esq; 5 Hood Rd, Wimbledon, London SW20 0SR (☎ 081 946 3401); St Georges Hospital, Blackshaw Rd, Tooting, London SW17 0LT; 2A Barham Rd, Wimbledon, London SW20 0EV (☎ 081 672 1255, car 0836 216595)

POWELL, Tim Harry Allan Rose; MBE (1944), TD (1973); s of William Allan Powell (d 1954); *b* 15 Feb 1912; *Educ* Winchester, Pembroke Coll Cambridge; *m* 1936, Elizabeth North, da of Leonard W North Hickley (d 1932); 2 da; *Career* Herts Yeo 1938, Col S E Asia 1944-45 (head of Secretariat to Supreme Allied Cdr); md Massey-Ferguson Hldgs Ltd 1962-78 (chm 1970-80), chm Holland & Holland Ltd 1983-87; *Recreations* fishing, lapidary; *Clubs* Bucks, MCC; *Style*— Tim Powell, Esq, MBE, TD; Ready Token, nr Cirencester, Gloucs (☎ 028 574 219); 12 Shafto Mews, Cadogan Sq, SW1 (☎ 071 235 2707)

POWELL, Victor George Edward; s of George Richard Powell; *b* 1 Jan 1929; *Educ* Beckenham GS, Univ of Durham, Univ of Manchester; *m* 1956, Patricia Copeland Allen; 3 s, 1 da; *Career* sr ptnr Victor G Powell Assocs (mgmnt conslts) 1963-, dir and chief advsr ILO 1977-88, dir Mosscare Housing Assoc Ltd 1974-; assoc memb BIM 1957; MIMC 1968; *Style*— Victor Powell Esq; Knowles House, Hollin Lane, Sutton, Macclesfield, Cheshire SK11 0HR (☎ 02605 2334)

POWELL, Lady Violet Georgiana; *née* Pakenham; da of 5 Earl of Longford, KP, MVO (d 1915); *b* 1912; *m* 1934, Anthony Dymoke Powell, CH, CBE; 2 s; *Style*— The Lady Violet Powell; The Chantry, Nr Frome, Somerset

POWELL, William Rhys; MP (C) Corby 1983-; yst s of Rev Canon Edward Powell, formerly Vicar and Lord of the Manor of Belchamp St Paul, Sudbury, Suffolk, and Anne Woodhouse, *née* Newton; descends from Walter Powell (d 1567), of Bucknell, Salop who descended from Rhys ap Tewdwr Mawr, King of South Wales; *see also* Sir Nicholas Powell, 4 Bt; *b* 3 Aug 1948; *Educ* Lancing, Emmanuel Coll Cambridge (MA); *m* 1973, (Mary) Elizabeth, da of Adolphus Henry Vaudin, Great Bookham, Surrey; 3 da; *Career* called to the Bar Lincoln's Inn 1971; *Clubs* Corby Cons; *Style*— William Powell Esq, MP; House of Commons, London SW1; Lynch House, Fowlmere, Cambs; 1 Crown Office Row, Temple, London EC4 (☎ 071 583 3724)

POWELL-COTTON, Christopher; CMG (1961), MBE (1951), MC (1945), JP; s of Maj P H G Powell-Cotton; *b* 23 Feb 1918; *Educ* Harrow, Trinity Coll Cambridge; *Career* Uganda Admin: dist cmmr 1950, prov cmmr 1955, min of Security and External Rels 1961, ret 1962; dir Powell-Cotton Museum of Natural History and Ethnography; landowner; *Clubs* MCC; *Style*— Christopher Powell-Cotton, Esq, CMG, MBE, MC, JP; Quex Park, Birchington, East Kent CT7 0BH (☎ 0843 41836)

POWELL-JONES, John Ernest; CMG (1974); s of late Walter James Powell-Jones and Gladys Margaret, *née* Taylor; *b* 14 April 1925; *Educ* Charterhouse, Univ Coll Oxford; *m* 1, 1949 (m dis 1967), Ann Murray; 2 s, 1 da; *m* 2, 1968, Pamela Sale; *Career* HM Foreign Serv 1949-; ambass at Phnom Penh 1973-75, RCDS 1975; ambass to: Senegal, Guinea, Mali, Mauritania and Guinea-Bissau 1976-79, Cape Verde 1977-79; ambass and perm rep UN Conference on Law of the Sea (concluded Dec 1982) 1979-82; ambass Switzerland 1982-85, ret 1985; chm Inter Counsel (UK) Ltd 1986; elected cnclIr Waverley Borough 1987; *Clubs* Travellers'; *Style*— John Powell-Jones, Esq, CMG; Gascons, Gaston Gate, Cranleigh, Surrey (☎ 0483 274313)

POWELL-TUCK, Dr Jeremy; s of Dr Geoffrey Alan Powell-Tuck, of Cleeve Hill nr Cheltenham, Glos, and Catherine Gwendoline Powell-Tuck, *née* Kirby; *b* 20 May 1948; *Educ* Epsom Coll, Univ of Birmingham (MB ChB, MD); *m* Fiona Caroline, da of Charles William Sandison Crabbe (d 1969); 1 s (Thomas b 1984), 2 da (Amy b 1987, Rosie b 1988); *Career* res fell St Marks Hosp 1974-80, res fell dept of nutrition London Sch of Hygiene and Tropical Med 1980-81, sr registrar of med and gastroenterology Charing Cross, W Middx and Westminster Hosps 1981-88, sr lectr Rank dept of human nutrition London Hosp Med Coll and conslt physician The Royal London Hosp 1988-; contrib chapters on nutritional therapy and gastro-intestinal disease; memb: Ctee WHO steering gp, Network for Nutrition Educn in Med Schs; MRCP 1973, FRSM 1976; *Recreations* opera, squash; *Style*— Dr Jeremy Powell-Tuck; 9 Horbury Crescent, London W11 3NF (☎ 071 727 2528); Department of Human Nutrition, London Hospital Medical College, Turner St, London E1 (☎ 071 377 7794)

POWER, Sir Alastair John Cecil; 4 Bt (UK 1924), of Newlands Manor, Milford, Southampton; s of Sir John Patrick McLannahan Power, 3 Bt (d 1984), and Melanie, adopted da of Hon Alastair Erskine (d 1987; s of 6 Baron Erskine); *b* 15 Aug 1958; *Style*— Sir Alastair Power, Bt; c/o Ashwick House, Dulverton, Somerset

POWER, Lady; Barbara Alice Mary; *née* Topham; elder da of His Honour Judge Alfred Frank Topham, KC, of Cracknells, Yarmouth, IOW; *b* 4 Dec 1904; *Educ* Manor House Sch Lympsfields; *m* 1930, Adml Sir Manley Power, KCB, CBE, DSO, DL (d 1981), sometime C-in-C Portsmouth, Allied C-in-C Channel and C-in-C Home Station designate (RN), seventh in descent from John Power (d 1659), whose elder bro Sir Henry Power, PC, was 1 & last Viscount Valentia of the 1620 cr; 1 s (decd), 1 da; *Recreations* reading, conservation; *Clubs* Royal Solent Yacht; *Style*— Lady Power; Eden House, Eden Rd, Totland, IOW (☎ 0983 754898)

POWER, Christopher Danvers (Kit); s of Piers Danvers Power (d 1960), and Margaret, *née* Chilton; *b* 5 May 1934; *Educ* Eton, Trinity Coll Cambridge (MA); *m* 26 March 1968, Penelope Joyce, da of Capt Robert Shaw, RN; 2 s (Nicholas b 1973, Julian b 1975); *Career* Nat Serv RN; Rootes Motors Ltd 1958-69, chm Spencer Stuart and Associates Ltd (joined 1969, md 1975-81); *Recreations* sailing; *Clubs* Royal Cruising, Royal Yacht Sqdn; *Style*— Kit Power, Esq; Dudley House, Montpelier Row, Twickenham, Middx; Brook House, Park Lane, London W1 (☎ 071 493 1238, fax 071 491 8068)

POWER, Prof Edwin Albert; s of Lewis Frank Power (d 1977), of Honiton, and Edith May, *née* Skinner (d 1986); *b* 12 Feb 1928; *Educ* The King's Sch Ottery St Mary, UCL (DSC), Univ of Glasgow (Phd); *m* 7 July 1962, (Elizabeth) Anne, da of Leonard Harry Roberts (d 1980), of Thorpe Satchville; 2 s (William Lawrence b 1969, Robert John Max b 1971); *Career* UCL: lectr, reader and prof 1951-86, head of dept of mathematics 1986-90, vice dean faculty of sci 1988-90; visiting fell: Cwlth Fund fell Cornell Univ 1953-54, Cwlth Fund fell Princeton Univ 1954-55, Univ of Waikato NZ 1979; visiting prof of physics: Univ of Colorado 1962-63, Univ of Chile 1963, Univ of Arizona 1976, Univ of Southern California 1978-79; visiting prof of chemistry: Univ of Wisconsin 1966, Australian Nat Univ 1968-69, Univ of Western Ontario 1970; fell American Physical Soc; *Books* Nuclear Forces and Few Nucleon Problem (1960), Introductory Quantum Electrodynamics (d 1964), The Vacuum in Non-relativistic Matter Radiation Systems (1988); *Recreations* orienteering, organ; *Style*— Prof Edwin Power; 6 Mallard Close, New Barnet, Herts EN5 1DH (☎ 081 449 5984); Department of Mathematics, University College London, Gower St, London WC1E 6BT (☎ 071 387 7050)

POWER, Eugene Barnum; Hon KBE (1977); s of Glenn Warren Power (d 1955), and Annette Barnum Power (d 1941); *b* 4 June 1905; *Educ* Michigan Univ (AB, MBA, LHD), St John's Univ (LHD); *m* 1929, Sadye Lillian, da of Clarence Abraham Harwick (d 1949); 1 s (Philip Harwick); *Career* microphotographer, ret 1970; organised 1936 first large microfilming project for libraries, to copy all books printed in England before 1640; dir of first large-scale copying operation of important Br MSS and enemy documents during WWII; special rep and co-ordinator Library of Congress London 1942, Offr of Strategic Servs 1943-45; fndr: Univ Microfilms Ann Arbor Michigan (merged with Xerox Corp 1962, sold to Bell & Howell 1986) 1938-70, Univ Microfilms Ltd London 1952; dir: Xerox Corp 1962-68, Domino's Pizza Inc 1978-; pres: Eskimo Art Inc 1953-, Power Fndn 1967-; chm and tstee Ann Arbor Summer Festival Inc 1978- (chm emeritus 1988), regent Univ of Michigan 1956-66; memb Cncl of Nat Endowment for the Humanities 1968-74; co-fndr and first pres and fell Nat Microfilm Assoc (now Assoc for Info and Image Mgmnt) 1944-54, co-fndr and first pres Int Micrographic Congress (now Int Info Mgmnt Congress) 1964-65; Alumni Achievement award Univ of Michigan Sch of Business Admin 1990; hon fell Magdalene Coll Cambridge 1967; *Recreations* water polo, swimming, music, theatre, sailing, fishing; *Clubs* The American (London), Ann Arbor Rotary (Ann Arbor Michigan); *Style*— Mr Eugene Power, KBE; 989 Forest Rd, Barton Hills, Ann Arbor, Mich 48105, USA (☎ 313 662 2886); 2929 Plymouth Rd, Suite 300, Ann Arbor, Mich 48105, USA (☎ 313 769 8424)

POWER, John Christopher; TD (1980); s of Geoffrey William Power; *b* 7 Dec 1945; *Educ* BA (Hons); *m* 1969, Ann Marie; 1 da; *Career* Maj Para Regt (TA); formerly dir NEI Parsons Peebles Transformers Ltd 1980, dir Hawker Siddeley Petter Diesels Ltd & Petter Diesels Inc (USA) 1984; Min of Def 1987; hon treas Round Table; CDipAF, FBIM, FIMEMME, FIElecIE; *Recreations* squash, running, swimming, parachuting, shooting; *Style*— John Power, Esq, TD; Harwood, 2 Oakwood Ave, Purley, Surrey

POWER, Jonathan Richard Adrian; s of Patrick Power, of Little House, Lincombe Lane, Boars Hill, Oxford, and Dorothy Power (d 1984); *b* 4 June 1941; *Educ* Liverpool Inst HS, Univ of Manchester (BA), Univ of Wisconsin (MA); *m* 22 Dec 1964 (m dis 1988), Anne Elizabeth, da of Dennis Hayward, of Southampton; 3 da (Carmen b 18 Jan 1966, Miriam b 23 May 1968, Lucy b 24 Nov 1978); *ptnr* Jean-Christine, da of Arvid Eklund, of Gothenburg, Sweden; 1 da (Jenny b 25 June 1990); *Career* columnist: International Herald Tribune (column syndicated to 30 princ US and Canadian papers and 20 African, Asian and Australasian papers) 1973-; film: It's Ours Whatever They Say (Silver medal Venice Film Festival 1972); memb Int Inst for Strategic Studies 1980; *Books* Development Economics, World of Hunger, The New Proletariat, Against Oblivion; *Recreations* walking, cycling, opera; *Style*— Jonathan Power, Esq; Houseboat Esperance, 106 Cheyne Walk, London SW10 (☎ 071 351 6344)

POWER, Michael Charles; s of Maj Charles Alfred Power (d 1974), of Wadhurst, Sussex, and Margaret Henley; *b* 31 Dec 1935; *Educ* Dover Coll, Lincoln Coll Oxford (MA); *m* 1, 6 Oct 1962 (m dis 1976), Margaret Katherine, da of Lt Col John Anthony Dene, of Kitleelagh, Nenagh, Co Tipperary; 1 s (George b 1968), 2 da (Katherine b 1965, Erica b 1967); *m* 2, 1 July 1976, Ann Genevieve, da of Ronald Dayas Just of Kensington; *Career* Nat Serv cmmn RAF 1954-56; J Walter Thompson Co Ltd London 1959-63, W D & H O Wills Bristol 1964-68, Michael Power Research Ltd London 1971-; memb Hon Soc of The Inner Temple 1969, MRS 1969, FInstD 1972; *Books* UK Franchising (1984/85/86/87/88/89/90); *Recreations* music, literature, art, travel; *Clubs* RAF; *Style*— Michael Power, Esq; Lizard Farm Cottage, Foulsham, Dereham, Norfolk NR20 5RN (☎ 0362 84288); 17 Wigmore St, London W1H 9LA (☎ 071 580 5816, fax 071 491 0607, telex 24637 WIGMOR G)

POWERS, George Dale; s of George Powers, of Chicago, Illinois, USA, and Harriette Elizabeth, *née* Bonyata (d 1977); *b* 13 Dec 1941; *Educ* Art Inst of Chicago (Interior Design), Univ of Chicago; *m* 20 June 1964, Enid, da of John Wilson Willison (d 1975), of New Farm, Worksop, Notts; 2 da (Caroline b 1965, Alexandra b 1969); *Career* interior designer, trainee Jack Denst Designs 1962-63; interior designer: John M Smyth & Co 1963-64, Sir Percy Thomas & Son 1965-66, William McCarty Assocs 1966-67; freelance 1967-71 clients incl: David Hicks, Billy McCarty, Colefax and Fowler, private clientele; George Powers Assocs 1971-, clients incl: Schlumberger Oil, NBC News (offices), restoration work St James Church Piccadilly, Ferguson & Partners, state bedroom Hatfield House for Marchioness of Salisbury, interior for Lord Charles Cecil; churchwarden St James Church Piccadilly 1982-87; memb Nat Tst for Historic Preservation 1986; IDDA 1979, ASID 1986; *Books* The Revolving Kitchen (1966); *Recreations* reading, swimming, cooking, ecclesiastical architecture, music, historic restoration; *Clubs* East India, Lansdowne; *Style*— George Powers, Esq; George Powers Assocs, 27 Rosebury Rd, London SW6 2NQ (☎ business 071 736 9016, home 071 731 4547)

POWERS, Dr Michael John; s of Reginald Frederick Powers, of Parkstone, Poole, and Kathleen Ruby, *née* Whitmarsh; *b* 9 Feb 1947; *Educ* Poole GS, London Univ, The Middx Hosp Med Sch (BSc, MB BS, DA), Poly of Central London (Dip Law); *m* 16 Nov 1968, Meryl Julia, da of Frank Edward Hall of Queen's Park Bournemouth; 1 s (Andrew b 1982), 1 da (Julia b 1972); *Career* registered med practitioner 1972-, house surgn Middx Hosp 1972-73, house physician Royal S Hants Hosp 1973-74, sr house offr Royal Utd Hosp Bath 1974-75, registrar (anaesthetics) Northwick Park Hosp Harrow 1975-77; called to the Bar Lincoln's Inn 1979, practising at Common Law Bar specialising in med and pharmaceutical law, pres SE Eng Coroners Soc 1987-88; students' cnsllr to Hon soc Lincoln's Inn 1983-, HM asst dep coroner Westminster 1981-87; memb: BMA, Medico-Legal Soc; FRSM 1972; *Books* The Law and Practice on Coroners (with Paul Knapman 1985), Casebook on Coroners (with Paul Knapman, 1989), Medical Negligence (with Nigel Harris, 1990); *Recreations* sailing, hill walking, painting, and music; *Clubs* Bar YC, Royal Yachting Assoc; *Style*— Dr Michael Powers; 1 Paper Buildings, Temple, London, EC4Y 7EP, (☎ 071 583 7355, fax 071 353 2144)

POWERS, William; MBE (1982), JP, DL; s of Capt John Powers (d 1974), and Doris Gladys, *née* Rickard; *b* 2 Sept 1924; *m* 27 June 1953, Janet Elsie Elisabeth, da of Archibald Fletcher; 2 da (Lynda Elisabeth b 1954, Jane Alison b 1957); *Career* Beds & Herts Regt 1942, 9 Commando 2 Special Serv Bde 1942-45 (despatches 1943), Mounted Police Palestine 1945-47, appointed Dist Supt 1947, Trans-Jordan Frontier Force 1947-49, seconded Maj; chief exec Shaw & Kilburn Luton 1968-86, chm Station Motors Group 1986-; patron: Luton & Dist Royal Br Legion, Luton & Dunstable Burma Star Assoc; vice pres: Luton Household Div Assoc, Luton Royal Naval Assoc; dir Luton Musical Pageant, pres Luton and Dunstable Operatic Soc, JP and dep chm Luton Magistrates Ct, chm S Beds Cmmrs of Taxes, memb The Lord Chancellors Advsy Ctee, High Sheriff of Beds; FIMI 1965; *Clubs* The Household Div Luton; *Style*— William Powers, Esq, MBE, JP, DL; Old Bedford Rd, Luton, Beds, LU2 7BL

POWERSCOURT, 10 Viscount (I 1743); Mervyn Niall Wingfield; also Baron Wingfield (I 1743), and Baron Powerscourt (UK 1885, title in House of Lords); s of 9 Viscount Powerscourt (d 1973), and Sheila, Viscountess Powerscourt *qv*; *b* 3 Sept 1935; *Educ* Stowe; *m* 1, 1962 (m dis 1974), Wendy Ann Pauline, da of Ralph C G Slazenger; 1 s, 1 da; *m* 2, 1979, Pauline, da of W P Van, of San Francisco, Calif; *Heir* s, Hon Mervyn Anthony Wingfield; *Style*— The Rt Hon the Viscount Powerscourt

POWERSCOURT, Sheila, Viscountess; Sheila Claude; da of Lt-Col Claude Beddington (who fought, and was wounded, in the Boer War, and WWI and who was ka in WWII in 1939), of London, Italy and Hampshire, and late (Frances) Ethel, er da of Francis Berry Homan-Mulock, JP; *b* 23 May 1906; *Educ* Roedean Sch; *m* 1932, Hon Mervyn Wingfield, later 9 Viscount Powerscourt (d 1973); 2 s (10 Viscount, Hon Guy Wingfield), 1 da (Hon Lady Langrishe); *Career* writer of poetry and prose (all as Sheila Wingfield, with one exception); *Prose Publications* Real People (1952), Sun Too Fast (1978, as Sheila Powerscourt); *Poetry* Poems (1938), Beat Drum, Beat Heart (1946), A Cloud Across The Sun (1949), A Kite's Dinner (1954), The Leaves Darken (1964), Her Storms (1974), Admissions (1977), Collected Poems of Sheila Wingfield (1983), Ladder to the Loft (1987); *Recreations* country pursuits, sailing (small boats), travelling, voracious reading; *Style*— The Rt Hon Sheila, Viscountess Powerscourt; Palma au Lac, CH-6600 Locarno, Switzerland (☎ 093 33 01 71)

POWIS, 7 Earl of (UK 1804); George William Herbert; Baron Powis, of Powis Castle, Co Montgomery, Baron Herbert of Chirbury, Co Salop, and Viscount Clive, of Ludlow, Co Salop (all UK 1804; Baron Clive, of Walcot, Co Salop (GB 1794); Baron Clive of Plassey, Co Limerick (I 1762); eldest s of Rt Rev Percy Mark Herbert, KCVO, DD, sometime Bishop of Norwich (d 1968), and Hon Elaine Letitia Algitha Orde-Powlett (d 1984), o da of 5 Baron Bolton; ggs of 2 Earl of Powis; s his kinsman the 6 Earl 1988; *b* 4 June 1925; *Educ* Eton, Trinity Coll Cambridge (MA); *m* 26 July 1949, Hon Katharine Odeyne de Grey, yst da of 8 Baron Walsingham, DSO, OBE; 4 s (Viscount Clive, Hon Michael Clive b 1954, Hon Peter James b 1955, Hon Edward David b 1958), 2 adopted da (Lorraine Elizabeth b 1961, Nicola Wendy b 1962); *Heir* s, Viscount Clive, *qv*; *Career* served army 1943-47; former chartered land agent; farmer; FRICS; patron of twelve livings; *Style*— The Rt Hon the Earl of Powis; Marrington Hall, Chirbury. Montgomery, Powis (☎ 093 872 256)

POWIS, Russell John; s of George Henry Powis, of Birmingham, and Nellie, *née* Croft; *b* 6 Aug 1947; *Educ* Yardley GS; *m* 30 May 1970, Susan Mary, da of Ernest John Cotterill; 3 s (Richard James Andrew b 27 Feb 1973, David Russell James b 1 Oct 1974, Stephen Robert Edward b 1 Jan 1983); *Career* articled clerk Russell Durie Kerr Watson and Co 1965-70; Coopers & Lybrand Deloitte (formerly Coopers and Lybrand): joined 1976 (Birmingham), tax ptnr (Cardiff) 1982-, ptnr i/c tax practice 1990-; FCA (ACA 1970); *Recreations* spectator sports, golf; *Clubs* Cardiff and County; *Style—* Russell Powis, Esq; Coopers & Lybrand Deloitte, Churchill House, Churchill Way, Cardiff CF1 4XQ (☎ 0222 237000, fax 0222 223361)

POWLES, Prof David Graham; s of John Howard Powles, of Minehead, Somerset, and Gwyneth Mary, *née* Price; *b* 6 March 1946; *Educ* Minehead GS, UCL (LLB, LLM); *m* 1, 29 July 1969 (m dis 1975), Juliet Mary, da of David Merrifield (d 1971), of Bishops Tawton, nr Barnstaple; m 2, 4 Sept 1981, Christina Stella, da of Horace Avory Cook (d 1976), of Bath; 1 da (Rhiannon Mair b 1983); *Career* called to the Bar Middle Temple 1971; lectr: UCL 1971-72 (asst lectr 1968-71), Univ of Bristol 1972-74, Univ of Exeter 1974-77, Univ of Wales 1977-82; sr lectr Univ of Wales 1982-85, prof commercial law Univ of Glasgow 1986-; memb Exec Cncl Dumbarton Cons Assoc; memb SPTL 1986; *Books* Encyclopaedia of European Community Law Vol C1 (1975), The Mareva Injunction (1985); *Recreations* gardening, reading, music; *Style—* Prof David Powles; Cawdor Lodge, 109 Sinclair Street, Helensburgh, Dunbartonshire G84 9QD (☎ 0436 72931); Centre for Commercial Law, The University, Glasgow G12 8QQ (☎ 041 339 8855, fax 041 330 4920, telex 77070 UNIGLA)

POWLETT; *see:* William-Powlett

POWLEY, John Albert; s of Albert Powley (d 1984), of 151 Green End Rd, Cambridge, and Evelyn Mary, *née* Fulcher; *b* 3 Aug 1936; *Educ* Cambridge Central Sch, Cambs Coll of Arts and Technol; *m* 13 July 1957, Jill, da of Lt Cdr Herbert Henry Palmer, RNVR (d 1985), of Fen Ditton, Cambridge; 2 s (Stephen John b 1961, Stewart Wayne b 1965), 1 da (Amanda Jane b 1963); *Career* Nat Serv 1957-59; radio and tv serv engr Pye Ltd Cambridge 1959-60, md John Powley (Radio & TV) Ltd 1960-84; memb Cambs CC 1967-77, ldr Cambridge City Cncl 1976-79 (memb 1967-79); Parly candidate (C) Harlow 1979, MP (C) Norwich South 1983-87; *Recreations* golf; *Style—* John Powley, Esq; 32 Sunningdale, Eaton, Norwich, Norfolk NR4 6AN (☎ 0603 504437)

POWLEY, Roger Peter; s of Frank William Powley (d 1991), of 17 King's Court, Beddington Gardens, Wallington, Surrey, and Jessie Ethel, *née* Shaw; *b* 6 May 1947; *Educ* St Joseph's Coll London; *m* 26 July 1975, Diana Mary, da of George Harrison Wray; 1 s (Adam Oliver b 18 Aug 1984), 2 da (Imogen Louise b 15 Sept 1982, Alannah Corinne b 2 June 1988); *Career* PA to sr ptnr Hays Allan (chartered accountants) 1973-75 (articled clerk then jr accountant 1966-73), asst to Gp Chief Accountant Courtaulds 1975-76, fin controller Mktg Servs Subsids Kimpher plc 1976-1978, fin dir TMD Advertising Ltd 1978-88, gp fin dir TMD Advertising plc 1985-; dir: Manning Gottlieb Media Ltd, Meridian Outdoor Ltd; FCA 1971; *Recreations* motor boating, sailing; *Clubs* Chichester Yacht; *Style—* Roger Powley, Esq; 9 Alleyn Park, Dulwich, London SE21 8AU (☎ 081 670 9847); TMD Advertising Holdings plc, 28/30 Litchfield St, London WC2H 9NJ (☎ 071 836 5817)

POWLING, Wing Cdr Ronald Henry Charles; DL; s of George William Powling (d 1987), of Tankerton, Kent, and Amelia Powling (d 1968); *b* 2 Nov 1920; *Educ* Simon Langton Sch Canterbury; *m* 15 Nov 1941, Silvia, da of Harold Marshall (d 1973), of Southport; 3 s (Neil Patrick, Nicholas Michael, Mark Adrian Rufus), 1 da (Katrina Beverley); *Career* WWII Fighter Pilot RAFVR 1939-46, Flying and Admin Cmd RAF 1946-73; chm: Kent CC, SE Provincial Cncl of Local Authorities; memb Jt Cncl Local Authorities; pres Tankerton Cons Assoc; *Recreations* golf, gardening, swimming, walking; *Style—* Wing Cdr Ronald Powling, DL; Browndown, 73 Bennells Ave, Tankerton, Whitstable, Kent CT5 2HP (☎ 0227 274 893)

POWNALL, His Hon Judge Henry Charles; QC (1979); s of John Cecil Glossop Pownall, CB (d 1967); *b* 25 Feb 1927; *Educ* Rugby, Trinity Coll Cambridge; *m* 1955, Sarah Bettine, da of Maj John Latham Deverell (d 1978); 1 s, 1 da (and 1 da decd); *Career* called to the Bar Inner Temple 1954; jr prosecuting counsel to the Crown at the Central Criminal Ct 1964-71, rec Crown Ct 1972-84, bencher 1976, sr and second sr prosecuting counsel 1976-79, hon legal advsr ABA 1976-86, judge Cts of Appeal Jersey and Guernsey 1980-86, circuit judge 1984 (sr judge Knightsbridge Crown Ct 1984-88); pres Orders and Medals Res Soc 1971-75 and 1977-81 (memb Ctee 1961-69, 1970-71 and 1981-); *Recreations* travel, medals and medal ribbons; *Clubs* Pratt's, Ebury Court; *Style—* His Honour Judge Henry Pownall QC; Central Criminal Court, Old Bailey, London EC4M 7EH

POWNALL, Brig John Lionel; OBE (1972); s of John Cecil Glossop Pownall, CB (d 1967), and Margaret Nina, *née* Jesson; *b* 10 May 1929; *Educ* Rugby, RMA Sandhurst; *m* 1962, Sylvia Joan Cameron, da of James Cameron Conn, WS (d 1957), of Hawick, Roxburghshire; 2 s (Richard b 1967, Edward b 1972); *Career* enlisted 1947, cmmnd 16/5 Lancers 1949, served in Egypt, Cyrenaica, Tripolitania, BAOR, Hong Kong, Cyprus, cmd 16/5 The Queen's Royal Lancers 1969-71, Adj-Gen's Secretariat 1971-72, offr i/c RAC Manning and Records 1973-75, Col GS Near East Land Forces/Land Forces Cyprus 1975-78, asst dir def policy MOD 1978-79, Brig RAC UK Land Forces 1979-82, Brig MOD 1982-84, ret 1984, Col 16/5 The Queen's Royal Lancer's 1985-90; dep chm Police Complaints Authy 1986-(memb 1985-); *Recreations* country pursuits, opera, arts; *Clubs* The Cavalry and Guards; *Style—* Brig John Pownall, OBE; Police Complaints Authority, 10 Great George St, London SW1P 3AE

POWNALL, Philip John; s of Alexander Pownall, and Lilian Pownall; *b* 22 Feb 1937; *Educ* Lymm GS, Manchester Univ (MB ChB); *m* 20 April 1963, Margaret, da of E G Sadler, of Cheshire; 2 s (Christopher Alexander b 1969, Timothy Philip b 1983), 2 da (Helen Margaret b 1964, Suzanne b 1970); *Career* tutor Orthopaedic Surgery Leeds Univ 1972-75, conslt orthopaedic surgn Bolton Hosps 1975-, vice-chm Bolton Ind Hosp 1984-87 ("The Beaumont") (dir 1983-87); pres Bolton and District Med Soc 1986-88, memb Manchester Med Soc 1961-; FRCS (1971 London, Edinburgh 1972); *Recreations* photography, engrg, boats; *Clubs* The Country Gentleman's, Gourmet; *Style—* Philip J Pownall, Esq; 22 Bottom o'th Moor, Horwich, Bolton BL6 6Q7 Consulting Rooms, 11 Chorley Hill Road, Bolton (☎ 0204 384404 & 0204 22444)

POWNER, Prof Edwin Thomas; s of Thomas Powner (d 1989), of Stoke on Trent, and Evelyn, *née* King; *b* 22 April 1938; *Educ* Univ of Durham (BSc), Univ of Manchester (MSc, PhD); *m* 8 Sept 1962, Barbara, da of William Henry Turner (d 1963), of Stoke on Trent; 2 s (Stephen John b 25 Dec 1966 d 13 March 1987, Peter David b 30 May 1972), 1 da (Suzanne b 18 March 1969); *Career* Inst of Sci and Technol Univ of Manchester: electronics engr 1960-63, lectr 1963-74, sr lectr 1974-79, reader 1979-80, prof of electronic engrg 1980-, vice princ 1986-88, dean of technol 1989-; author of numerous tech pubns; Inst Nat Electrical Engrs: memb cncl, chm Library Ctee, memb professional bd, memb qualifications bd, memb membership bd, memb accreditation bd, local chm NW centre 1988-89; CEng, FIEE 1987 (memb 1965); *Books* Digital Simulation (jtly), Digital Signal Processing (jtly); *Recreations* photography, mechanisms and clocks, railways; *Style—* Prof Edwin Powner; University of Manchester Institute of Science & Technology, Sackville St, Manchester M60 1QD (☎ 061 200 4702, telex 666094, fax 061 228 7040)

POYNDER, Col Anthony John Irvine (Tony); MC; s of late Lt-Col Frederick Sinclair Poynder, DSO, OBE, MVO, MC, and Grace Muriel, *née* Campbell; *b* 10 Feb 1920; *Educ* Wellington, RMA Woolwich, Peterhouse Cambridge (MA); *m* 15 Dec 1945, Anne, da of late Maj-Gen James Francis Harter, DSO, MC, DL; 2 da (Jennifer (Mrs Parks) b 28 Nov 1946, Patricia (Lady Francis Seymour) b 7 Oct 1958), 2 step s (Charles David Stancomb b 30 April 1942, Anthony James Stancomb b 2 Feb 1944); *Career* cmmnd RE 1939, WWII served France, N Africa, NW Europe, 6 Amd Div RE and 82 Assault Engrs Sqdn RE (despatches); Staff Coll and Jt Servs Staff Coll appts incl 1945-66: Cdr 9 Para Sqdn RE, MA to Adj Gen, Cdr 4 Div Engrs, chief instr Field Engrg RSME, sr Army memb Def Operational Requirements Staff MOD; mktg mangr Br Hovercraft Corp 1966-70, sr mktg devpt exec Westland Aircraft 1970-71, head Crane Dept Sea Containers Gp 1971-81, md Sea Container Atlantic Services Ltd 1974-81; dir: Sea Container Services Ltd 1972-74, Sea Co Holdings Ltd 1981-85, Orient Express Hotels Holdings Ltd; Freeman City of London, Liveryman Worshipful Co of Coachmakers and Coach Harness Makers; *Books* Wahid The Little Camel; *Clubs* Hawks, Army and Navy, REYC; *Style—* Col A J I Poynder, MC; Gassons, Slindon Village, Arundel, W Sussex (☎ 0243 65 395)

POYNTER, Kieran Charles; s of Kenneth Reginald Poynter, of Sanderstead, Surrey, and Catherine Elizabeth, *née* Reilley; *b* 20 Aug 1950; *Educ* Salesian Coll, Imperial Coll of Sci and Technol, Univ of London (BSc, ARCS); *m* 20 Aug 1977, Marylyn, da of Cmdt Thomas Melvin (d 1968), of Athlone, Ireland; 3 s (Dominic b 1979, Benedict b 1980, Andrew b 1983), 1 da (Louise b 1981); *Career* CA 1974; ptnr Price Waterhouse 1982 (joined 1971, now responsible for servs to insur sector in Europe and memb PW World Firm Insurance Group); memb: Insur Ctee ICAEW 1983-, Standing Inter Professional Liaison Gp Accounting and Actuarial Professions 1987-, Accounting and Auditing Standards Ctee Lloyd's of London 1988-99; memb Catenian Assoc; FCA 1979; *Recreations* golf, skiing, tennis; *Clubs* Surrey Tennis and Country; *Style—* Kieran Poynter, Esq; Cranbrook, The South Border, Woodcote, Purley, Surrey CR8 3LL (☎ 081 660 4723); Price Waterhouse, Southwark Towers, 32 London Bridge St, London SE1 9SY (☎ 071 939 3000, fax 071 403 8382, telex 884657/8)

POYNTON, Lady Finola Dominique; *née* Fitz-Clarence; da of 7 Earl of Munster by his 1 w; *b* 6 Dec 1953; *m* 1981, Jonathan Terence Poynton, s of Lt Col D R Poynton, of Woodford, Cheshire; 1 s (Oliver Maximillian Christo b 1984), 1 da (Chloë Nona b 1982); *Style—* The Lady Finola Poynton; 153 Wellfield Road, London SW16

POYNTON, Sir (Arthur) Hilton; GCMG (1964, KCMG 1949, CMG 1946); s of Arthur Blackburne Poynton (d 1944, formerly master of Univ Coll Oxford), and Mary (d 1952), da of late J Y Sargent, fell of Hertford Coll Oxford; *b* 20 April 1905; *Educ* Marlborough, Brasenose Coll Oxford; *m* 1946, Elisabeth Joan, da of late Rev Edmund Williams; 2 s, 1 da; *Career* entered Civil Serv 1927, Dept of Scientific and Industl Res, transfd to Colonial Office 1929; private sec to: Min of Supply (Lord Beaverbrook) 1941, Min of Production (Oliver Lyttelton later Lord Chandos) 1942-43; reverted to Colonial Office 1943, dep under sec state 1948-59, perm under sec state 1959-66; hon fell Brasenose Coll Oxford 1964, KStJ 1968; *Recreations* music, travel, gardening; *Style—* Sir Hilton Poynton, GCMG; Craigmillar, 47 Stanhope Rd, Croydon CRO 5NS (☎ 081 688 3729)

POYNTON, Robert Alan (Joe); s of Alan Poynton, of Lelant, Cornwall, and Mabel Winifred, *née* Evans; *b* 28 Jan 1943; *Educ* King Edwards Sch Bath, Univ of Bath (BSc); *m* 14 Aug 1970, Jane Elizabeth, da of Leonard East, of The Manor, Cannington, Somerset; 3 da (Susan b 1971, Jenny b 1973, Sally b 1976); *Career* architect; sr ptnr Poynton Bradbury Assocs St Ives Cornwall; architect: the Barbara Hepworth Museum 1975, Lands End Visitor Centre 1982, Isles Of Scilly Centre 1984, Nat Lighthouse Museum 1987; architect to Curry Mallet Village Community Project initiated by HRH The Prince of Wales 1985; memb The Nat Community Architecture Gp 1982-87, chm Cornwall Branch RIBA 1984-86; winner: CPRE/RIBA Housing Design award 1987, Cwlth Fndn award 1989, RIBA Regnl Design award 1991; *Recreations* sailing, wind surfing; *Clubs* St Ives Sailing (pres), RIBA Sailing; *Style—* Robert Poynton, Esq; The Old Sail Lofts, The Harbour, St Ives, Cornwall TR26 1PB (☎ 0736 797828)

PRAG, Derek Nathan; MEP (EDG) Herts 1979-; s of Abraham J Prag; *b* 6 Aug 1923; *Educ* Bolton Sch, Emmanuel Coll Cambridge (MA); *m* 1948, Dora Weiner; 3 s; *Career* econ journalist Reuters 1950-55, freelance ed Financial Times Business Letter from Europe 1975-76, in charge of Anglo-American Section of Info Serv of High Authy of the Euro Coal and Steel Community 1955-59, head Pubns Div Euro Communities 1959-67, dir London Office Jt Info Serv of Euro Communities 1965-73; ran own consultancy on rels with EEC 1973-79; Cons spokesman and first vice chm EDG Instl Ctee 1987- (1982-84), Cons spokesman Political Affrs Ctee 1984-86, sr vice chm Ctee of Enquiry into Facism and Racism 1986; memb: Political Affrs Ctee, Euro Parl Israel Delgn; rapporteur on Seat of the EC Insts and working-place of the Euro Parl; chm: Euro Parl's All-Party Gp on Disablement, London Europe Soc; hon dir EEC Cmmn, Silver Medal of Euro Merit; *Recreations* listening to music, reading, swimming, gardening; *Clubs* Carlton, RAC (Brussels); *Style—* Derek Prag, Esq, MEP; Pine Hill, 47 New Rd, Digswell, Herts AL6 0AQ (☎ 043781 2999)

PRAG, (Andrew) John Nicholas Warburg; s of Adolf Prag, of The Old Prebendal House, Shipton-under-Wychwood, Oxon, and Dr Frede Charlotte, *née* Warburg; *b* 28 Aug 1941; *Educ* Westminster, BNC Oxford (Domus Exhibitioner, Hon Scholar, BA, Dip Classical Archaeology, sr Hulme Scholar, MA, DPhil); *m* 6 July 1969, Dr Kay Prag, da of Douglas James Wright (d 1979), of Sydney, NSW; 1 s (Jonathan Ralph Warburg b 1975), 1 da (Kate Susannah b 1977); *Career* temp asst keeper Dept of Antiquities Ashmolean Museum Oxford 1966-67; Univ of Manchester: keeper of archaeology Manchester Museum 1969-, sr lectr 1977, hon lectr Dept of History 1977-83, hon lectr in archaeology 1984-; visiting prof Dept of Classics McMaster Univ Hamilton Ontario 1978, ed Archaeological Reports 1975-87; memb: Cncl Soc for the Promotion of Hellenic Studies, Managing Ctee Br Sch Athens; family rep Mgmnt Ctee Warburg Inst Univ of London, ind assessor Office of Arts & Libraries Review Ctee for the Export of Works of Art; FSA 1977; *Books* The Oresteia: Iconographic & Narrative Tradition (1985); *Recreations* walking, music, cooking, travel; *Style—* Dr A J N Warburg, FSA; The Manchester Museum, The University, Manchester M13 9PL (☎ 061 275 2665, fax 061 275 2676)

PRAGNELL, Anthony William; CBE (1982, OBE 1960), DFC (1944); s of late William Hendley Pragnell, and late Silvia Mary Pragnell; *b* 15 Feb 1921; *Educ* Cardinal Vaughan Sch London, Univ of London (LLB external); *m* 1955, Teresa Mary (d 1988), da of late Leo Francis Monaghan, of Maidstone; 1 s, 1 da; *Career* served RAF 1942-46, Flt Lt Bomber Cmd; civil servant; asst examiner Inland Revenue 1939-50, GPO 1950-54; dep dir gen Independent TV Authority (became IBA 1972) 1961-83 (joined 1954, sec 1955-61), dir Channel 4 TV 1983-88; fell: RTV Soc 1980, Euro Inst for the Media, Univ of Manchester 1983-; Emile Noël Euro prize 1987; memb BBC Radio Kent Religious Advsy Gp 1988-, chm Sevenoaks and Dist Cncl of Churches 1990-; *Recreations* reading, listening to music, watching TV; *Clubs* RAF, Kent CCC; *Style—* Anthony Pragnell, Esq, CBE, DFC; Ashley, Grassy Lane, Sevenoaks, Kent TN13 1PL (☎ 0732 451463)

PRAIN, Philip James Murray; s of (John) Murray Prain, DSO, OBE, TD, DL (d

1985), and Lorina Helen Elspeth, *née* Skene; *b* 14 Nov 1936; *Educ* Eton, Clare Coll Cambridge (MA); *m* 28 Sept 1972, Susan Ferrier, da of Andrew Munro Marr (d 1955); 1 da (Philippa Victoria b 1975); *Career* 2 Lt Black Watch 1955-57, Lt TARO, memb The Queen's Body Guard for Scot, Royal Co of Archers 1966; called to the Bar Inner Temple 1963; asst dir Kleinwort Benson Ltd Hong Kong (joined 1962); chm Manor Gardens Enterprise Centre Islington, vice chm Westminster Amalgamated Charity, memb Cncl Nat Canine Def League, tstee St Clement Danes Holborn Estate Charity, All Saints' Fndn Margaret St; Freeman City of London 1978, Liveryman Worshipful Co of Founders 1978; *Recreations* travel, photography; *Clubs* MCC, Royal and Ancient Golf, Leander (Assoc), Hong Kong, Royal Hong Kong Jockey; *Style—* Philip Prain, Esq; 73 Woodsford Square, London W14 8DS (☎ 071 603 7767); Kleinwort Benson Ltd, 20 Fenchurch St, London EC3P 3DB (☎ 071 956 5828, fax 071 621 1481)

PRAIN, Sir Ronald Lindsay; OBE (1946); s of Arthur Lindsay Prain, and Amy Gertrude, *née* Watson; *b* 3 Sept 1907, Iquiqui, Chile; *Educ* Cheltenham Coll; *m* 1938, Esther Pansy (d 1987), da of late Norman Brownrigg; 2 s (Graham b 1940, Angus b 1952); *Career* controller Miny of Supply: diamond die and tool control 1940-45, quartz crystal control 1943-45; chm exec Roan Selection Tst (RST) Int Gp of Copper Mining Companies 1943-68 (chm 1950-72); dir: Metal Market & Exchange Co Ltd 1943-65, Selection Trust Ltd 1944-78, San Francisco Mines of Mexico Ltd 1944-68, Int Nickel Co of Canada Ltd 1951-72, Wankie Colliery Co Ltd 1953-63, Monks Investment Tst 1960-83, Minerals Separation Ltd 1962-78, Foseco Minsep Ltd 1969-80, Barclays Bank Int 1971-77, Pan-Holding SA and other cos; first chm: Merchant Bank of Central Africa Ltd 1956-66, Agric Res Cncl of Rhodesia and Nyasaland 1959-63, Merchant Bank (Zambia) Ltd 1966-72; pres: Br Overseas Mining Assoc 1952, Inst of Metals 1960-61, Cheltenham Coll 1972-80; memb cncl Overseas Devpt Inst 1960-80; tstee Inst for Archaeo-Metallurgical Studies; hon pres Copper Devpt Assoc; Hon FIMM; kt 1956; *Publications* Selected Papers (4 vols), Copper, The Anatomy of an Industry (1975, Japanese edn 1976, Spanish edn 1981), Reflections on an Era (1981); *Recreations* cricket, real tennis, travel; *Clubs* White's, MCC; *Style—* Sir Ronald Prain, OBE; Waverley, Granville Rd, St George's Hill, Weybridge, Surrey KT13 0QJ; (☎ 0932 842776)

PRAIS, Prof Sigbert Jon; s of Samuel Prais, and Bertha Prais; *b* 19 Dec 1928; *Educ* King Edward's Sch Birmingham, Univ of Birmingham (MCom), Univ of Cambridge (PhD, ScD), Univ of Chicago; *m* 1971, Vivien Hennessy; 1 s, 3 da; *Career* Dept of Applied Economics Cambridge 1950-57, res offr NIESR 1953-59, UN Tech Assistance Orgn 1959-60, IMF Washington 1960-61, fin dir Elbrief Co 1961-70, sr res fell NIESR 1970-, visiting prof of econ City Univ 1975-; memb: Cncl Royal Econ Soc 1979-83, Cncl City Univ 1990-; Hon DLitt City Univ 1989; FBA 1985; *Books* Analysis of Family Budgets (co-author, 1955), Evolution of Giant Firms in Britain (1976), Productivity and Industrial Structure (1981), articles in economics and statistical jls; *Style—* Prof Sigbert Prais; 83 West Heath Rd, London NW3 (☎ 081 458 4428, office 071 222 7665)

PRANCE, Prof (Ghillean) Iain Tolmie; s of Basil Camden Prance, CIE, OBE (d 1947), and Margaret Hope, *née* Tolmie (d 1970); *b* 13 July 1937; *Educ* Malvern, Univ of Oxford (BA, MA, DPhil); *m* 13 July 1961, Anne Elizabeth, da of The Rev Archibald MacAlister Hay (d 1980); 2 da (Rachel b 1963, Sarah b 1966); *Career* NYBG: res asst 1963-68, BA Krukoff curator Amazonian Botany 1968-75, dir res 1975-81, vice pres 1977-81, sr vice pres 1981-88, dir Inst Econ Botany 1981-88; adjunct prof City Univ NY 1968-; visiting prof: tropical studies Univ of Yale, Univ of Reading 1988-; dir Royal Botanic Gdns Kew 1988-; author of numerous papers and books; memb Bd of Dirs: Margaret Mee Amazon Tst 1988-, Lovaine Tst 1989-, Royal Botanic Gardens Kew Fndn 1990-; exec dir Orgn Flora Neotropica (UNESCO) 1975-88, memb Mayor's Cmmn on Cable TV White Plains NY 1981-88; tstee: Au Sable Inst of Environmental Studies 1984-, WWF for Nature Int 1989-; Horniman Museum 1990-; ldr Amazonian Exploration Prog 1965-88; FIL, DR (hc) Goteborgs Univ 1983; FLS 1963, FRGS 1989; foreign memb Royal Danish Acad Scis and Letters 1988, corr memb Brazilian Acad of Scis 1976, foreign memb Royal Swedish Acad Sci 1989; *Books* Arvores De Manaus (1975), Extinction Is Forever (1977), Biological Diversification in the Tropics (1981), Leaves (1986), Amazonia (1985), Wild Flowers for all Seasons (1988), White Gold (1989); *Recreations* squash, music; *Clubs* Explorers (fell 1978); *Style—* Prof Iain Prance, Esq; Royal Botanic Gardens, Kew, Richmond, Surrey, TW9 3AB, (☎ 081 940 1171 fax 081 948 1197)

PRANKERD, Prof Thomas Arthur John; s of Horace Arthur Prankerd (d 1958), of Shanklin, IOW, and Julia Dorothy, *née* Shorthose (d 1978); *b* 11 Sept 1924; *Educ* Charterhouse, Bart's (MB BS, MD); *m* 18 Feb 1950, Margaret Vera Harrison, da of William Harrison Cripps (d 1960), of Horley, Surrey; 3 s (Richard b 1951, d 1982, Henry b 1953, Stephen b 1960), 1 da (Nicola b 1958, d 1982); *Career* Nat Serv, Maj RAMC 1949-51; conslt physician UCH 1960-82, prof of clinical haematology 1965-79, dean Univ Coll Med Sch 1972-79; univ examiner: London, HK, Ibadan, Malaysia, Tripoli; examiner RCP; visiting prof: Univ of W Aust 1972, Univ of Cape Town 1978; memb: Bd of Govrs UCH 1969-73, Camden and Islington AHA 1973-76, NE Thames RHA 1976-79; FRCP 1962; *Books* The Red Cell (1961), Haematology in Diagnosis and Treatment (1968); *Recreations* watercolour painting, gardening; *Style—* Prof Thomas Prankerd; Milton Lake, Milton Abbas, Blandford, Dorset DT11 0BJ (☎ 0258 880278)

PRASHAR, Usha; *b* 29 June 1948; *Educ* Univ of Leeds (BA), Univ of Glasgow (Dip in Social Admin); *m* 21 July 1973, Vijay Sharma; *Career* conciliation offr Race Rels Bd 1971-76, dir Runnymede Tst 1976-84, res fell Policy Studies Inst 1984-86, dir Nat Cncl for Voluntary Orgns 1986-; memb: Arts Cncl of GB 1979-81, Study Cmmn on the Family 1980-83, Social Security Advsy Ctee 1980-83, Exec Ctee Child Poverty Action Gp 1984-85, Gtr London Arts Assoc 1984-86; tstee Thames Help Tst 1984-86, memb London Food Cmmn 1984-, tstee Charities Aid Fndn 1986-, vice pres Cncl for Overseas Student Affrs 1986-, patron Sickle Cell Soc 1986-, memb BBC Educnl Broadcasting Cncl 1987-88, tstee Independent Broadcasting Telethon Tst 1987-; memb Open Call Advsy Cncl 1987-88, vice chm Br Refugee Cncl 1987-90, memb Elfrida Rathbone Soc 1988-, chm English Advsy Ctee Nat Aids Tst 1988-89; memb: Slrs Complaints Bureau 1989, vice pres Patients' Assoc 1990-, hon assoc Nat Cncl of Women of GB 1989-; FRSA 1989; *Books* contrib to: Britain's Black Population (1980), The System: a study of Lambeth Borough Council's race relations unit (1981), Scarman and After (1984), Sickle Cell Anaemia Who Cares? a survey of screening counselling training and educational facilities in England (1985), Routes or Road Blocks a study of consultation arrangements between local authorities and local communities (1985), Acheson and After: primary health care in the inner city (1986); *Recreations* painting, country walks, squash, music; *Style—* Miss Usha Prashar; National Council for Voluntary Organisations, 26 Bedford Square, London WC1B 3HU (☎ 071 636 4066, fax 071 436 3188)

PRATLEY, Alan Sawyer; s of Frederick Pratley (d 1970), and Hannah, *née* Sawyer (d 1981); *b* 25 Nov 1933; *Educ* Latymer Upper Sch, Sidney Sussex Coll Cambridge (BA); *m* 1, 29 Aug 1960 (m dis 1979), Dorothea, da of Walter Rohland; 2 da (Christiane b 14 Nov 1961, Alexa b 5 Jan 1963); m 2, 22 Dec 1979, Josette Kairis; 1 da (Fiona b 3 Feb 1981); *Career* head of German Dept Stratford GS 1958-60, asst dir examinations Civil Service Cmmn 1960-68, asst sec Home Office 1971-73 (princ 1968-71); Cmmn Euro Communities: head of Individual Rights Div 1973-79, dep head cabinet to Christopher Tugendhat 1979-80, advsr to Michael O'Kennedy 1981, dir gen admin 1981-86, dir fin control 1986-90, dep fin controller Fin Control 1990-; *Recreations* tennis, gardening; *Clubs* Travellers'; *Style—* Alan Pratley, Esq; 3 Avenue de l'Abbaye d'Affligem, 1300 Wavre, Belgium (☎ 010 22 66 06); Commission of the European Communities, 200 rue de la Loi, 1049 Brussels, Belgium (☎ 235 2686, fax 235 0141)

PRATLEY, David Illingworth; s of Arthur George Pratley, of Dorset, and Olive Constance, *née* Illingworth; *b* 24 Dec 1948; *Educ* Westminster, Univ of Bristol (LLB); *Career* PR offr Thorndike Theatre Leatherhead 1970-71, press and publicity offr Queen's Univ Belfast 1971-72, dep dir Merseyside Arts Assoc 1972-76, dir Gtr London Arts Assoc 1976-81, regnl dir Arts Cncl of GB 1981-86, arts mgmnt conslt 1986-87, dir Dance Umbrella Ltd 1986-, chief exec Royal Liverpool Philharmonic Soc 1987-88, chm Nat Campaign for the Arts 1988-, md Trinity Coll of Music 1988-; memb SDP Arts Ctee 1987 (chm Alliance Arts and Broadcasting Panel 1986-88); *Books* Culture for All (1981), Cumbria Arts & Museums Strategy (1987), The Pursuit of Competence - the Arts and the European Community (1987); *Recreations* arts, travel, gardens, countryside; *Clubs* Athenaeum; *Style—* David Pratley, Esq; 13 St James St, London W6 9RW (☎ 071 741 3513); Trinity Coll of Music, Mandeville Place, London W1M 0AU (☎ 071 935 5773)

PRATT, Anthony Richard (Tony); s of Arthur Edward Pratt (d 1976), of Brentwood, Essex, and Marjorie Louise, *née* Wright; *b* 21 June 1940; *Educ* Brentwood Sch; *m* 9 Sept 1961, Barbara Ann Grace, da of Herbert Edward Richardson; 1 da (Susan b 1 Aug 1965), 1 s (David b 21 Jan 1967); *Career* reporter: Brentwood Review 1956-62, Romford Recorder 1962-64, sub ed then diary writer Sun 1964-70; Daily Mirror: diary writer 1970-76, TV and showbusiness feature writer and TV critic 1976-84, TV critic and TV listings ed 1984-89; TV listings ed and critic Mirror Group (incl Daily Mirror, Sunday Mirror, The People) 1989-, memb NUJ; *Recreations* cricket, reading, gardening, music, walking; *Clubs* Wig and Pen, Essex County Cricket; *Style—* Tony Pratt, Esq; Mirror Group Newspapers Limited, Holborn Circus, London EC1P 1DQ (☎ 071 353 0246, fax 071 822 2254, direct 071 822 3496)

PRATT, (Richard) Camden; s of Richard Sheldon Pratt, of 108 Manthorpe Rd, Grantham, Lincs, and Irene Gladys, *née* Whalley; *b* 14 Dec 1947; *Educ* Boston GS, Westcliff HS, Lincoln Coll Oxford (MA); *m* 4 Aug 1973, Dorothy Jane Marchia, da of Capt William Paul Allsebrook, of Tichis 15, Glyfada, Athens, Greece; *Career* called to the Bar Grays Inn 1970; *Recreations* sailing, shooting, walking,theatre; *Style—* Camden Pratt, Esq; 1 Kings Bench Walk, Temple, London EC4 (☎ 071 583 6266, fax 071 583 2068)

PRATT, (Ewart) George; CVO (1986); s of George William Pratt (d 1955), of Harrow on the Hill, and Florence Edith, *née* Redding (d 1957); *b* 10 Oct 1917; *Educ* LSE (Dip); *m* 9 Oct 1948, Margaret, da of William Heath (d 1977), of Letchworth; 2 s (Christopher John Ewart b 1950, Martin Andrew b 1953); *Career* Inner London Probation Serv 1949-81 (probation offr, sr probation offr, asst chief probation offr, dep chief probation offr 1970-), chm Assoc of Social Workers 1959-70, treas Br Assoc of Social Workers 1970-73, fndr govr Nat Inst for Social Work 1961-71, sec Voluntary Housing Assoc 1964-81, memb Ctee on the Voluntary Worker in the Social Servs 1966-69, memb Home Office Working Pty on Community Serv by Offenders 1971-72; The Prince's Tst: tstee 1976-, hon admin 1976-78, chm 1978-86; tstee REACT 1990-; UK delegate to World Cncl of Churches, elder United Reformed Church 1985-, memb Social Responsibility Ctees of the Baptist Union and the Br Cncl of Churches; memb numerous governmental, professional and charitable advsy gps; *Recreations* music, theatre, travelling, lecturing and talking about the needs of disadvantaged and terminally-ill children and young people; *Clubs* RAC; *Style—* George Pratt, Esq, CVO; 14 The Squirrels, The Avenue, Branksome Park, Poole, Dorset BH13 6AF (☎ 0202 767552)

PRATT, George Henry; s of Joseph Henry Pratt, and Hannah Carruthers, *née* Briggs (d 1949); *b* 15 Jan 1929; *Educ* Whitehaven GS; *m* 20 Sept 1952, Elsie, da of John Lawson (d 1955), of Glenesk, Vulcans Lane, Workington; 1 s (Michael J b 26 Jan 1956); *Career* sr ptnr R Gibbons & Co CAs 1955-89, chief exec West Cumbria Building Soc 1963, memb local Tbnl of Dept of Health & Social Security; former pres: Cumberland Soc of CAs, Round Table, Rotary Club; pres Cumbria Union of Golf Clubs 1989-90; FICA 1952; *Recreations* gardening, golf, all sports; *Clubs* Workington Golf (former capt and pres); *Style—* George Pratt, Esq; Lynthwaite, 45 Stainburn Rd, Workington, Cumbria CA14 1SW (☎ 0900 603119); West Cumbria Building Society, Cumbria House, Murray Road, Workington, Cumbria CA14 2AD (☎ 0900 605717)

PRATT, (Edward Roger) Michael; JP (Norfolk 1969), DL (Norfolk 1974); s of Lt-Col Edward Roger Pratt, MC (d 1966), and Beatrix Elaine, *née* Thynne (d 1969); *b* 28 Sept 1926; *Educ* Eton, Univ of Cambridge; *m* 28 July 1955, Sarah Constance Neville, da of The Very Rev Dean Hedley Robert Burrows (d 1983); 2 s ((Edward Roger) Piers b 1956, Nicholas Julian Hedley b 1958), 1 da ((Lavinia Mary) Claire (Mrs Bunting)); *Career* Nat Serv Lt in Coldstream Gds 1944-47; chm Downham Bench 1984-89 (dep chm 1976), memb Lord Chllr's Advsy Sub Ctee 1986; Downham Rural Dist Cncl: elected 1952, vice chm 1964, chm 1967-74; memb Norfolk CC 1970-74, dep chm Norfolk Valuation and Community Charge Tribunal 1973-, W Norfolk Dist Cncl Hon Alderman 1976 (memb 1975-76), Lord Chllr's Advsy Ctee for Gen Cmmrs 1980- (joined as gen cmmr for Income Tax 1965, dep chm Kings Lynn Div); *Recreations* shooting, photography; *Clubs* Army & Navy; *Style—* Michael Pratt, Esq, JP, DL; Stonehills House, Ryston, Downham Market, Norfolk PE35 0AB (☎ 0366 382059); Estate Office, Ryston Hall, Downham Market, Norfolk PE38 0AA (☎ 0366 383322)

PRATT, Michael John; QC (1976); o s of W Brownlow Pratt; *b* 23 May 1933; *Educ* West House Sch Edgbaston, Malvern Coll (LLB Birmingham); *m* 1960, Elizabeth Jean Hendry; 2 s, 3 da; *Career* 2 Lt 3 Carabiniers (Prince of Wales's Dragoon Gds), Staff Capt; called to the Bar Middle Temple 1954, rec of the Crown Ct 1974-, bencher 1986; *Clubs* Cavalry and Guards, Birmingham Cons; *Style—* Michael Pratt, Esq, QC; 9 Moorland Rd, Edgbaston, Birmingham B16 9JP (☎ 021 454 1071)

PRATT, Lord Michael John Henry; s of 5 Marquess Camden (d 1983), and 2 w, Averil (d 1977), da of late Col Henry Sidney John Streatfield, DSO (through whom she was ggda of 2 Earl of Lichfield); *b* 15 Aug 1946; *Educ* Eton, Balliol Coll Oxford; *Career* author and researcher; *Clubs* White's, Pratt's, MCC, Beefsteak; *Style—* The Lord Michael Pratt; 16 Coulson St, London SW3 (☎ 071 581 2200); Bayham Manor, Lamberhurst, Kent (☎ 0892 890500)

PRATT, Peter Charles; s of Charles Frederick Pratt (d 1982), of Sunningdale, and Edith Hilda, *née* Appleton (d 1983); *b* 24 Sept 1931; *Educ* Salesian Coll, Clapham Coll, Univ of Reading (BSc); *m* 1 29 Sept 1956, Pamela Mary (d 1969), da of Alfred Smith (d 1960) of Colchester; 1 s (Julian b 1957), 1 da (Nicola b 1961); m 2, 8 July 1982, Fay Jameson, *née* Wright; *Career* Nat Serv Lance-Corpl RE 1950-52 (works servs Cyprus 1951-52); Overseas Civil Serv 1955-60: trainee surveyor Sch of Mil Survey 1955-56, surveyor Dept of Lands and Surveys Govt of Tanganyika 1956-60; Ellerman Lines plc: investmt mgmnt and admin 1960-74, co sec 1967-84, divnl chief exec 1979-82, dir Main Bd 1982-84; chm and md New Cavendish St Investmt Co Ltd 1990 (dir 1984); memb: Investmt Ctee Merchant Navy Ratings Pension Fund 1982-, MNOPF Tstees Ltd (chm Investmt Ctees 1991-), dir Argosy Asset Management plc 1989-91; tstee and sec: Moorgate Tst Fund, New Moorgate Tst Fund; tstee Burgh House Tst

Hampstead (chm Mgmnt Ctee 1990-); Freeman City of London 1967, Liveryman Worshipful Co of Shipwrights 1968; FRGS 1952, FCIS 1966; *Recreations* swimming, clay-pigeon shooting, theatre, music, reading, watching cricket; *Clubs* Carlton, Royal Automobile, Surrey CCC; *Style*— Peter Pratt, Esq; 25 Willoughby Rd, Hampstead, London NW3 1RT (☎ 071 794 9040); Suite 10, Aria House, 23 Craven St, London WC2N 5NT (☎ 071 930 8566, fax 071 839 3654)

PRATT, Lord Roderic Arthur Nevill; s of 4 Marquess of Camden (d 1943); *b* 1915; *Educ* Eton, Trinity Coll Cambridge; *m* 1945, Ursula Eva, da of Capt the Hon Valentine Maurice Wyndham-Quin, RN (d 1983), s of late 5 Earl of Dunraven and Mount-Earl); 1 s (Capt Adrian Pratt b 1952, m 1984, Leonora Murray Lee), 1 da (Zara b 1955, m 1988, John Weir Johnstone); *Career* Maj late Life Gds; underwriting memb Lloyd's; *Style*— The Lord Roderic Pratt; The Garden House, Dewhurst, Wadhurst, E Sussex TN5 6QB (☎ 089 288 3179)

PRATT, Sandy Robert Gammack

PRAWER, Prof Siegbert Salomon; s of Marcus Prawer, and Eleanora Prawer; *b* 15 Feb 1925; *Educ* King Henry VIII Sch Coventry, Jesus Coll and Christ's Coll Cambridge (MA, LittD), Univ of Birmingham (PhD), Univ of Oxford (MA, DLitt); *m* 1949, Helga Alice; 1 s, 2 da; *Career* Univ of Birmingham 1948-63: asst lectr, lectr, sr lectr; prof of German Westfield Coll Univ of London 1964-69; visiting prof: City Coll NY 1956-67, Univ of Chicago 1963-64, Harvard 1968, Univ of Hamburg 1969, Univ of Calif Irvine 1975, Univ of Otago 1976, Univ of Pittsburgh 1977; visiting fell: Knox Coll Dunedin 1976, Humanities Res Centre ANU 1980, Tauber Inst Univ of Brandeis 1981-82, Russell Sage Fndn 1988; hon dir Univ of London Inst of Germanic Studies 1966-68, pres Br Comparative Lit Assoc 1984-87 (hon fell 1987), hon memb Modern Language Assoc of America 1986, pres English Goethe Soc 1990-; co-ed: Oxford German Studies 1971-75, Anglica Germanica 1973-79; Univ of Oxford: prof of German Lit and Lang 1969-86 (now Emeritus), professorial fell Queen's Coll 1969-86 (dean of degrees 1978-, now hon fell); Hon DPhil Cologne 1984, Hon DLitt Birmingham 1988, Goethe medal 1973, Friedrich Gundolf Prize 1986; hon fell: Br Acad 1981, German Acad of Language and Literature 1988; *Books* German Lyric Poetry (1952), Mörike und Seine Leser (1960), Heine: The Tragic Satirist (1962), The Penguin Book of Lieder (1964), The Romantic Period in Germany (1970), Comparative Literary Studies (1973), Karl Marx and World Literature (1976, Isaac Deutscher meml Prize, 1977), Caligari's Children (1980, 2 edn 1989), Heine's Jewish Comedy (1983), Frankenstein's Island (1986); *Recreations* portrait drawing; *Style*— Prof Siegbert Prawer; 9 Hawkswell Gardens, Oxford OX2 7EX

PREBBLE, David Lawrence; s of George Wilson Prebble (d 1983), of Eastbourne, Sussex, and Margaret Jessie, *née* Cuthbertson; *b* 21 Aug 1932; *Educ* Cranleigh Sch, ChCh Oxford (MA); *m* 9 May 1959, Fiona Winifred, da of Thomas Hudspith Melville (d 1986); 3 da (Sarah Lorne Melville (Mrs Kollias) b 1960, Catriona Jean b 1963, Alison Fiona b 1966); *Career* Nat Serv cmmnd 3 Carabiniers Prince of Wales Dragoon Guards 1950-52; barr in private practice 1957-81, master of The Queen's Bench Div Supreme Court of Justice 1981-; Capt TA 1952-61, City of London Yeomanry (Rough Riders); *Recreations* wine, food, music, horses, hounds and dogs (especially Salukis and Border Collies), books; *Clubs* Royal Wimbledon Golf; *Style*— David Prebble, Esq; 16 Wool Rd, Wimbledon, London SW20 (☎ 081 946 1804); Royal Courts of Justice, Strand, London WC2

PREBBLE, Stuart Colin; s of Dennis Stanley, of 25 Priory Close, Beckenham, Kent, and Jean Margaret, *née* McIntosh (d 1981); *b* 15 April 1951; *Educ* Beckenham & Penge GS, Univ of Newcastle upon Tyne (BA); *m* 25 Aug 1978, Marilyn Anne, da of George Charlton, of 15 Weardale Ave, Forest Hall, Newcastle upon Tyne; 2 da (Alexandra Juliette b 1979, Claire Samantha b 1982); *Career* reporter BBC TV 1973-79; Granada TV: ed World in Action 1986-89 (prodr 1981-86), head of regnl progs 1989-; fndr Campaign for Quality TV; memb BAFTA; *Books* A Power in the Land (1988), The Lazarus File (1989); *Recreations* music, writing, travel, unicycling; *Style*— Stuart Prebble, Esq; Granada Television, Quay St, Manchester M60 9EA (☎ 061 832 7211, fax 061 953 0285)

PREECE, Andrew Douglas; s of Bernard Charles Preece, of 2 Knowle Rd, Weeping Cross, Stafford, and Joyce Mary, *née* Clayton; *b* 28 Sept 1944; *Educ* King Edward VI GS Stafford, Selwyn Coll Cambridge (MA); *m* 5 Oct 1968, Caroline Jane, da of Edmund Arthur Bland (d 1988); 1 s (James Douglas b 4 Aug 1976), 2 da (Victoria Jane b 31 March 1972, Joanna Mary b 19 Jan 1981); *Career* articled clerk asst slr Hall Collins 1968-71, ptnr Herbert Smith 1977- (asst slr 1971-74, assoc ptnr 1974-77); memb UK Oil Lawyers Gp; Freeman Worshipful Co of Slrs; memb: Law Soc, IBA; *Recreations* sailing, golf; *Clubs* Moor Park Golf, RAF Yacht, RNVR Yacht; *Style*— Andrew Preece, Esq; The Red House, Dog Kennel Lane, Chorleywood, Hertfordshire WD3 5EL; Flat 20, Presidents Quay House, 72 St Katherines Way, London E1; Exchange House, Primrose St, London EC2A 2HS (☎ 071 374 8000, fax 071 496 0043)

PREECE, Annette Susan; da of Evan André Preece, and Margery, *née* Phillips; *b* 30 July 1956; *Educ* Univ of Liverpool (BSc); *Career* pres offr RSPB 1986-88 (ed Birdlife 1980-83), head of pubns and ed-in-chief Birds Magazine 1986-; *Recreations* gardening, painting, birdwatching, eating out, reading; *Style*— Ms Annette Preece; Royal Society for the Protection of Birds, The Lodge, Sandy, Beds SG19 2DL (☎ 0767 680551, fax 0767 692365, telex 82469 RSPB G)

PREECE, Anthony John; s of John Henry Preece (d 1977), and Ivy, *née* Rhodes; *b* 11 May 1945; *Educ* Batley GS, Univ of Loughborough; *m* 1, 30 Sept 1967 (m dis 1986), Caroline Betty, da of Thomas Harold Keston Edwards (d 1962); 3 s (David b 23 Nov 1971, Christopher b 6 March 1975, Adam b 23 March 1977); m 2, Esme Irene, da of Jacques Sadler (d 1971); 1 da (Sarah b 18 June 1986); *Career* asst dir Stock Exchange 1972-85, md Scrimgeour Vickers Services 1985-86; ops dir Citicorp Scrimgeour Vickers 1986-, dir Stock Exchange 1989-; *Recreations* wine, food, travel, theatre; *Clubs* Royal Institution, IOD; *Style*— Anthony J Preece, Esq; Little Sunningdale, London Rd, Harrow-on-the-Hill Middx HA1 3LX (☎ 081 422 1643); International Stock Exchange, Old Broad St, London EC2 1HP (☎ 071 588 2355)

PREECE, David Henry Gunston; s of Reginald Preece (d 1935), and Elizabeth Gwen, *née* Jenkins (d 1981); *b* 4 Aug 1933; *Educ* Barry GS, Welsh Sch of Architecture, UWIST (DipArch with Distinction 1956); *m* 27 Aug 1983, Denise Celia, da of Bill Upward (d 1982); 1 step s (Marcus Livermore b 1971); *Career* CA, princ ptnr David Preece Assocs; major cmmns include: New Civic Centres for Boroughs of Islwyn, Vale of Glam, Lliw Valley, Afan and HQ for SW Water Authy Exeter, Welsh Water Brecon, Palace for Sheikh Mohammed Bin Saleh in Riyadh; currently engaged on projects in Hong Kong, China and SE Asia; *Recreations* sketching, travel; *Clubs* IOD; *Style*— David H G Preece, Esq; Cliff House, Cliff Walk, Penarth, S Glamorgan; 48 Elm Grove Road, Dinas Powys, S Glamorgan CF6 4AB (☎ (0222) 514037, fax (0222) 514120)

PREECE, David William; s of Wilfred George Preece, of Bridgnorth, Shropshire, and Margaret Anne, *née* Pyke; *b* 28 May 1963; *Educ* Oldbury Wells Secdy Modern Bridgnorth Shropshire; *m* 11 Dec 1989, Louise Elizabeth, da of Michael John Brown; 1 da (Tabitha Jane b 17 Jan 1989); *Career* professional footballer; Walsall: schoolboy 1977-79, apprentice 1979-80, professional 1980-84, debut 1981, 111 league appearances; over 200 appearances Luton Town 1984-; memb England B tour 1988-89 (Switzerland, Iceland, Norway); represented Shropshire football and cricket (capt under 14 and under 16); League Cup winners Luton Town 1988 (runners up 1989); *Recreations* cricket, golf, horse racing, sport in general, being a good father; *Style*— David Preece, Esq; Luton Town FC, Kenilworth Rd, Luton, Bedfordshire LU4 8AW (☎ 0582 411622)

PREECE, Michael John Stewart; s of Lt-Col James Preece, OBE, TD, of Broadeaves, Les Ruisseaux, St Brelade, Jersey, CI, and Margaret, *née* Paterson; *b* 29 Dec 1934; *Educ* Rugby, Emmanuel Coll Cambridge (MA); *m* 20 Sept 1958, Tessa Gillian Rosamond (MBE), da of Sir Francis John Watkin Williams, BT, QC, of Llys, Middle Lane, Denbigh, Clwyd; 2 s (James b 1964, Hugh b 1969), 2 da (Emily b 1961, Rosamond b 1963); *Career* Nat Serv 2 Lt 1953-55 (Korea, Hong Kong), Capt Cheshire Yeo 1963-70; slr; registrar Diocese of Bangor, clerk to Dean and Chapter of Bangor Cathedral; under sheriff Anglesey; *Recreations* shooting, squash, golf, Roman remains; *Clubs* Lansdowne; *Style*— Michael Preece, Esq; Plas Llanddyfnan, Talwrn, Llangefni, Anglesey, Gwynedd LL77 7TH (☎ 0248 750659); 282A High Street, Bangor, Gwynedd LL57 1UL (☎ 0248 352387)

PREECE, Ralph Stephen; s of John Raymond Preece, of 1 Ashgrove, Dinas Powis, South Glamorgan, and Doris, *née* Derrick; *b* 14 May 1946; *Educ* Kings College Sch, Cathays HS Cardiff; *m* 27 Dec 1969, Marilyn, da of Edwin Ralph Gardener Thomas; 2 da (Justine Claire b 28 Sept 1973, Natalie Jane b 27 Feb 1976); *Career* articled clerk Richard Davies & Co Cardiff 1965-70, qualified chartered accountant 1970, Coopers & Lybrand 1970-76 (Johannesburg, London, Cardiff), insolvency specialist Mann Judd Cardiff 1976-79; Touche Ross: moved to Birmingham Office 1979, ptnr 1983, ptnr i/c Corp Special Servs 1983-; memb Transvaal Soc of CAs 1972, FCA 1979 (ACA 1970), MICM 1986, MIPA 1988, memb Assoc Européene des Practiciens des Procedures Collectives 1988, MSPI 1990; *Recreations* gardening; *Clubs* Leeds; *Style*— Ralph Preece, Esq; Keldholme, Linton Lane, Linton, W Yorks LS22 4HL (☎ 0937 586683); Touche Ross, 10-12 East Parade, Leeds LS1 2AJ (☎ 0532 439021, fax 0532 448942, car 0836 617279)

PREECE, William Royston; s of Horace Preece, and Gladys, *née* Gravenor; *b* 26 April 1933; *m* 8 Nov 1958, Dorothy Vivien Carrington, da of Herbert Kitchener Evans, DCM; 1 s (Jeffrey b 1960), 1 da (Diana b 1964); *Career* Steel Co of Wales 1951-58, chm and md A Watkinson Ltd (footwear retailers) 1960-, chm Ind Footwear Retailers Assoc (Northern England) 1975-76 (exec memb Nat Assoc 1975-80); memb: City of York Worshipful Co of Cordwainers (clerk 1977-79, master 1980-81), Worshipful Co of Merchant Taylors; FID; *Recreations* gardening, spectator sports, family, dogs, photography; *Clubs* Royal Overseas League, York 41; *Style*— William Preece, Esq; c/o A Watkinson Ltd, 53 Goodramgate, York (☎ 0904 23388)

PREEDY, Ronald Alan; OBE (1977); s of William Frank Preedy (d 1969), of St Agnes, Cornwall, and Rose Esther, *née* Chubb; *b* 30 Sept 1935; *Educ* Truro Sch; *m* 20 June 1959, (Lillian) Mary, da of late Henry Russell Richards, of St Agnes, Cornwall; 1 s (Mark b 1960); *Career* cmmnd RA 1954, posted 33 Para Lt Regt 1954-61, Troop Cdr 45 Fd Regt BAOR 1961-63, Gunnery Staff Course Larkhill 1963-64 (Instr-in-Gunnery 1964-66), RAF Staff Coll 1967, Bde Maj RA 5 Div Wrexham 1968-70, Battery Cdr 29 Commando Regt RA Poole 1970-73, Nat Def Coll 1973-74, Instr Jr Div Staff Coll Warminster 1974-75, CO 29 Commando Regt Plymouth 1975-77, Princ Staff Offr (Ops) Royal Brunei Malay Regt 1977-80, ret (voluntary) 1980; commenced yacht delivery 1981-, completed single-handed double transatlantic in aid of RNLI 1984-85, awarded Alex Rose trophy and RNVR Cruise Challenge Cup by RN Sailing Assoc; SDLJ Brunei 1980; *Books* Sail and Deliver (1989); *Recreations* sailing, golf, drawing, painting; *Clubs* RN Sailing Assoc, Ocean Cruising; *Style*— Ronald Preedy, Esq, OBE; 34 Trevaunance Rd, St Agnes, Cornwall TR5 OSQ (☎ 087 255 3110)

PREISKEL, Harold Wilfred; s of David Preiskel (d 1983), of 27 Aylestone Avenue, London NW6, and Lili, *née* Wick; *b* 1 June 1939; *Educ* St Paul's, Guy's Med and Dental Sch (LDSRCS, BDS, FDSRCS, MDS), Ohio State Univ (MSc); *m* 22 Aug 1962, Nira, da of Joshua Orenstein (d 1977), of Tel Aviv; 3 s (Daniel b 1965, Ronald b 1969, Alon b 1976), 1 da (Daphne b 1979); *Career* house surgn 1962, lectr restorative dentistry Royal Dental Hosp Sch of Surgery 1966-69, hon conslt Guy's Hosp 1971, chm London Dental Study Club 1971, examiner in dental prosthetics RCS 1972, appointed to the Ed Bd of Jl of Dentistry 1972, staff examiner in prosthetic dentistry Univ of London 1974 (examiner 1969), pt/t conslt in prosthetic dentistry Guy's Hosp Dental Sch 1974 (sr lectr 1969, lectr 1962-66); Thomas Hinman award Atlanta Georgia 1975, Int Circuit Course award of the American Coll of Prosthodontists 1988; pres: Int Coll of Prosthodontists, The American Dental Soc of London, BDA metropolitan branch 1981-82; chm: Ed Bd of Int Jl of Prosthodontists 1988, tstees of Alpha Omega Charitable Tst; fell Int Coll of Dentists; memb: Br Soc for Restorative Dentistry, Br Soc for Study of Prosthetic Dentistry, Euro Prosthodontic Assoc, Euro Dental Soc, American Dental Soc of London, American Dental Soc of Europe, Carl O Boucher Prosthodontic Soc, (fndr) American Acad Esthetic Dentistry, American Equilibration Soc, Federation Dentair International; hon citizen of New Orleans 1978; *Books* author of numerous pubns in the field of prosthodontic dentistry incl Precision Attachments in Dentistry (1968, 1973, 1979); *Recreations* classical music, general aviation; *Style*— Harold Preiskel, Esq; 25 Upper Wimpole St, London W1M 7TA (Practice) (☎ 071 935 4525, fax 071 487 3971, car 0836 223194); Department of Prosthetic Dentistry, United Medical and Dental Schools of Guy's and St Thomas', London Bridge SE1 9RT (☎ 081 955 4027)

PRENDERGAST, (Christopher) Anthony; CBE, DL (1980); s of Maurice Prendergast; *b* 4 May 1931; *Educ* Falmouth GS; *m* 1959, Simone Ruth Laski, DBE, OBE, JP, DL; 1 s; *Career* chm Dolphin Sq Tst Ltd 1967-, dir London Electricity plc 1990-; Lord Mayor and dep high steward of Westminster 1968-69, High Sheriff of Gtr London 1980, DL Gtr London 1988; Lloyd's underwriter; *Recreations* shooting, fishing, photography; *Clubs* Carlton, Brooks's, Irish, MCC; *Style*— Anthony Prendergast, Esq, CBE, DL; Flat C, 52 Warwick Sq, London SW1V 2AJ (☎ 071 821 7653)

PRENDERGAST, Brig John Hume; DSO (1946), MC (1937, bar 1940); s of Maj-Gen Charles Gordon Prendergast, CB (d 1930), of Jersey, and Marguerite Eghertha, *née* Hume (d 1973); *b* 15 Nov 1910; *Educ* Victoria Coll Jersey; *m* 3 April 1939, (Rose Ann) Peggy, da of Henry Norton Hutchinson, OBE, ICS (d 1947); 2 s (John b 1942, Rollo b 1947), 1 da (Caroline (Mrs Priestly) b 1944); *Career* cmmnd Royal Sussex Regt 1931, 4/15 Punjab Regt Razmak Waziristan 1932, seconded N Wajiristan Transborder Armed Police 1936-39, active serv Ipi Ops, Capt 1939, mountain warfare advsr Norway Expedition 1940, returned IA 1940, Maj 1940, instr in mountain warfare Sch of Inf Poona 1941-42, raised and cmmd 1 Western Tribal Legion in NWFP 1943-43, 2 i/c 1/15 Punjab Regt in first Arakan ops 1943-44, joined 19 (Dagger) Indian Div in reconquest of Burma 1944, cmd first river recrossing of Irawaddy (despatches), recapture of Mandalay, CO 3/6 Rajputana Rifles 1945, continued in Burma until 1947, Staff Coll Quetta 1947, 1 Yorks and Lancaster Regt 1948, mil attaché Abul Embassy Afghanistan 1948-50, 1 Yorks and Lancaster Regt Brunswick 1951 (cmd 1952), served Khartoum and Canal Zone 1952, GSO1 BAOR 1955, cmd 147 Midland Bde TA 1957-60, ret 1960; long distance motor exploration (incl voluntary work for wild life conservaton): Iran, Afghanistan, Pakistan, India; pres 15 Punjab Regt Assoc 1983-88;

Books The Road to India (1977), Prender's Progress (1979); *Recreations* long distance motor travel, fly-fishing, painting, writing; *Style—* Brig John Prendergast, DSO, MC; Barton Mead, Tisbury, Wilts SP3 6JU (☎ 0747 870542)

PRENDERGAST, Sir John Vincent; KBE (1977, CBE 1960), CMG (1968), GM (1955), CPM (1955), QPM (1963); yst s of late John and Margaret Prendergast; *b* 11 Feb 1912; *Educ* Ireland, Univ of London (extnl); *m* 1943, Enid Sonia, yr da of Percy Speed; 1 s, 1 da; *Career* served WWII, Maj; local govt London 1930-39, asst dist cmmr Palestine 1946-47, Colonial Police Serv Palestine and Gold Coast 1947-52, seconded Army Canal Zone 1952-53, Kenya 1953-58 (dir of Intelligence and Security 1955-58), chief of Intelligence Cyprus 1958-60, dir Special Branch Hong Kong (ret as Dep Cmmr of Police) 1960-66, dir Intelligence Aden 1966-67, dep cmmr and dir of ops Ind Cmmn Against Corruption Hong Kong 1973-77, dir G Heywood Hill Ltd 1982-; *Clubs* East India, Hong Kong, Royal Hong Kong Jockey; *Style—* Sir John Prendergast, KBE, CMG, GM CPM, QPM; 20 Westbourne Terrace, London W2 3UP (☎ 071 262 9514)

PRENDERGAST, (Walter) Kieran; s of Lt Cdr Joseph Henry Prendergast, and Maj, *née* Hennessy (d 1988); *b* 2 July 1942; *Educ* St Patrick's Coll Sydney Aust, Salesian Coll Chertsey Surrey, St Edmund Hall Oxford; *m* 10 June 1967, Joan, da of Patrick Reynolds (d 1974); 2 s (Damian b 1968, Daniel b 1976) 2 da (Siobhain b 1971, Brigid b 1973); *Career* FO 1962, Istanbul (Turkish language student) 1964, Ankara 1965, FO 1 967, second sec Nicosia 1969, Civil Serv Coll 1972, first sec FCO 1972, first sec (info later econs), The Hague 1973, asst private sec to 2 foreign secs (Rt Hon Anthony Crosland, MP, and Rt Hon Dr David Owen, MO) 1976, UK Minion to UN New York 1979, cnsllr head of chancery and consul-gen Tel Aviv 1982, head of Southern African dept FCO 1986-89; *Recreations* family, walking, reading, sport, wine; *Clubs* Travellers'; *Style—* Kieran Prendergast, Esq; c/o Foreign and Commonwealth Office, King Charles St, London SW1A 2AH

PRENDERGAST, His Hon Judge Robert James Christie Vereker; s of Capt Richard Henry Prendergast (d 1965), of Roehampton, London, and Jean, *née* Christie (d 1988); *b* 21 Oct 1941; *Educ* Downside, Trinity Coll Cambridge (MA); *m* 16 Apr 1971, Berit, da of Wilburg Thauland (d 1982), of Oslo, Norway; 1 da (Victoria b 1973); *Career* called to the Bar Middle Temple 1964, S Eastern circuit, rec 1987, circuit judge 1989; *Recreations* most gentle pursuits, keeping friends mildly amused; *Style—* His Hon Judge Prendergast; 9 King's Bench Walk, Temple, London EC4, (☎ 071 353 5638, fax 071 353 6166)

PRENDERGAST, Dame Simone Ruth; DBE (1986, OBE 1981), DL (Greater London 1982), JP (Inner London 1971); da of Norman Laski (d 1968), and Elaine Blond, *née* Marks, OBE (d 1985); *b* 2 July 1930; *Educ* Queens Coll London, Cheltenham Ladies Coll; *m* 1, 1953 (m dis 1957), Albert Kaplan; m 2, 21 Sept 1959, (Christopher) Anthony Prendergast, CBE, *qv*, s of Maurice Anthony Prendergast (d 1961); 1 s (Christopher Hugh b 6 June 1960); *Career* chm: Cities London and Westminster Cons Assoc 1971-75, London Central-Euro Constituency 1976, Gtr London Area Nat Union of Cons Assocs 1984-87; dep chm Gtr London Area Cons Party Non Union 1981-84; pres Westminster Homes 1985-90; chm: Blond McIndee Centre Med Res 1986-, Jewish Refugees Ctee 1980-, Westminster Childrens Soc 1980-90; vice chm Age Concern Westminster 1988; memb: Cncl Central Br Fund for Jewish Relief 1969, St John Cncl for London 1975-82, Bethnal Green and E London Housing Assoc 1990-; Lady Mayoress Westminster 1968; memb: Lord Chllr Advsy Ctee 1981-91, Slrs Disciplinary Tbnl 1986-; asst cmmr St John 1982; memb Ct of Patrons RCS 1987, hon FRSA 1988; *Recreations* reading, walking, gardening; *Style—* Dame Simone Prendergast, DBE, JP, DL; 52 Warwick Square, London SW1V 2AJ (☎ 071 821 7653); Quilter Cottage, Broadway, Worcs

PRENN, Oliver Simon; *b* 26 Sept 1937; *Educ* St Paul's, Hertford Coll Oxford (MA); *m* 27 Sept 1958, Nyda Margaret McDonald; 1 s (Alexis b 18 March 1962), 1 da (Natasha b 11 April 1964); *Career* private family cos 1959-65, dep md Controls & Communications Ltd 1965-69, dep chm Racal Electronics Ltd (now plc) 1974-77 (dep md 1969-77); chm: Derritron plc 1980-82, Celestion Industries plc 1988-; vice chm Serpentine Gallery, memb Devpt Cncl Royal Nat Theatre, Hon patron of New Art Tate Gallery, FRSA; Jr Wimbledon Tennis Champion 1955, played Wimbledon Championships 1956-59; *Recreations* spectator, listener and occasional patron of theatre, music and art; *Clubs* Queen's; *Style—* Oliver Prenn, Esq; 47 Hyde Park Gate, London SW7 5DU (☎ 071 584 8870); 24-25 New Bond St, London W1Y 9HD (☎ 071 491 2443)

PRENTICE, Hon Mrs (Eve-Ann); da of Baron Whaddon (Life Peer); *b* 1952; *m* 1972, Patrick Prentice; *Career* journalist Guardian 1978-87; production ed Sunday Telegraph 1988-89 (dep prodn ed 1987-88); production ed The Sunday Correspondent 1989-90 (asst ed 1990); The Times Foreign Dept 1991-; *Recreations* science, foreign affairs; *Style—* The Hon Mrs Prentice

PRENTICE, Graham Noel; *b* 7 March 1955; *Educ* Peter Symonds Winchester, Churchill Coll Cambridge (BA); *m* 15 Sept 1975, Beverley Annette Prentice; 2 da (Katy b 1987, Alice b 1989); *Career* admitted slr 1980; articled clerk Wragge & Co 1978-80, ptnr Freshfields 1986 (joined 1981); *Pubns* Irregular Resolution of Unincorporated Association May Not be a Nullity (1980), The Enforcement of Outsider Rights (1980), Protected Shorthold Tenancies: Traps for the Unwary (I, II, III, 1982), Remedies of Building Sub-Contractors against Employers (1983); *Recreations* photography, reading; *Style—* Graham Prentice, Esq; Freshfields, Whitefriars, 65 Fleet St, London EC4Y 1HT (☎ 071 936 4000, fax 071 832 7001)

PRENTICE, Hon Mrs (Helen); *née* Chilver; er da of Baron Chilver (Life Peer), *qv*; *b* 30 May 1960; *Educ* Bedford HS; *m* 1979, Geoffrey Prentice; *Style—* The Hon Mrs Prentice; 125 Wood Street, London EC2V 7AQ

PRENTICE, James Kniveton; s of Oscar Prentice (d 1959), of Birkenhead, Cheshire, and Hester Alice Owen, *née* Kniveton (d 1987); *b* 21 Jan 1927; *Educ* Bradfield Coll, Univ of Liverpool (LLB); *m* 27 April 1957, Maria Theresa, da of Reginald Porter (d 1930), of Godalming; 2 s (David James Kniveton b 20 Feb 1958, Peter Hugh b 15 Jan 1961), 1 da (Tessa Mary b 3 Sept 1959); *Career* served HAC 1951-55; dir Bleichroeder Bing & Co 1951-69, exec dir Willis Faber & Dumas Ltd 1970-87; dir: Willis Faber Belgium Ltd 1974-87, Willis Faber (Int) Ltd 1985-87, Willis Faber Hellas 1982-87, Kentriki Insurance Co Ltd Nicosia 1987-; Freeman City of London, Liveryman Worshipful Co of Insurers 1984; *Books* Time Chance and Change (1984), The Memory is Green (1987); *Recreations* sailing, music, voyaging, writing, photography; *Clubs* Travellers, Emsworth Sailing; *Style—* James Prentice, Esq; Cranberry, Westbourne, Emsworth, Hants (☎ 0243 372 608); 312 Willoughby House, Barbican, London EC2Y 8BL (☎ 071 623 0478)

PRENTICE, John Oscar ; s of Oscar Prentice (d 1957), of The Green Cottage, Langstone, Hants, and Hester Alice Owen, *née* Kniveton (d 1987); *b* 15 Dec 1925; *Educ* Bradfield, Clare Coll Cambridge; *m* 1, 5 Feb 1954, Geraldine Ildiko, da of Capt Humphrey Ridley Tomalin (d 1976), of London; 3 da (Juliet b 1956, Kate b 1959, Jessica b 1961); m 2, 1987, Catherine; *Career* Lloyd's broker and underwriter; dep chm Willis Faber plc 1972-84, chm: Willis Faber & Dumas (Agencies) Ltd 1977-85, Wellington Underwriting Agencies Ltd 1985-; yachtsman; Britannia Cup (Royal Yacht Sqdn) 1974, Admiral's Cup (Victorious Br Team) 1975, second Euro Championship (Int 6 Metre Class) 1988; FRGS; *Recreations* yacht racing (yacht 'Battlecry'), fishing, farming, music; *Clubs* Royal Thames Yacht, City of London, Imperial Poona Yacht, Royal Southern Yacht; *Style—* John Prentice, Esq; Gentilshurst, Fernhurst, Haslemere, Surrey GU27 2HQ (☎ 0428 53010); 29 Wilton Row, London SW1; Wellington, 120 Fenchurch St, London EC3M 5BA (☎ 071 929 2811, car 0836 204 4611, telex 268892 WELTN g)

PRENTICE, Rt Hon Sir Reginald Ernest; PC (1966), JP (Croydon 1961); s of Ernest George Prentice; *b* 16 July 1923; *Educ* Whitgift Sch, LSE; *m* 1948, Joan Godwin; 1 da; *Career* MP (Lab): East Ham North 1957-74, Newham North East 1974-77; MP (C): Newham North East 1977-79, Daventry 1979-87 (ret 1987 election); min of state Dept of Educn and Sci 1964-66, min for Public Building and Works 1966-67, min for Overseas Devpt 1967-69, alderman GLC 1970-71, oppn spokesman on Employment 1972-74, sec of state Educn and Sci 1974-75, min Overseas Devpt 1975-76, min of state (min for Social Security) DHSS 1979-81; memb Exec Ctee Nat Union of Cons Assocs, pres Assoc of Business Execs; co dir and conslt on public affrs; kt 1987; *Clubs* Marlborough Golf; *Style—* The Rt Hon Sir Reginald Prentice, JP, DL

PRENTICE, Hon Sir William Thomas; MBE (1945); s of Claud Stanley Prentice (d 1931); *b* 1 June 1919; *Educ* St Joseph's Coll Sydney, Univ of Sydney (BA, LLB); *m* 1946, Mary Elizabeth Beresford, da of Frank Beresford Dignam (d 1946); 3 s, 1 da; *Career* Staff Capt 25 Aust Inf Bde PNG Campaigns 1942-43 and 7 Aust Inf Bde Bougainville Campaign 1944-45; barr NSW 1947-70, Judge Supreme Ct PNG 1970, sr puisne judge 1975, dep chief justice on independence PNG 1975, chief justice 1978-80; kt 1977; *Recreations* bush walking, swimming, reading; *Clubs* Tattersall's (Sydney), Cricketers; *Style—* The Hon Sir William Prentice, MBE; 16 Olympia Rd, Naremburn, NSW 2065, Australia

PRENTICE, Dame Winifred Eva; DBE (1977, OBE 1972); da of Percy John Prentice, and Anna Eva Prentice; *b* 2 Dec 1910; *Educ* Northgate Sch for Girls Ipswich E Suffolk and Ipswich Hosp, W Middx Hosp, Queen Elizabeth Coll Univ of London; *Career* principal tutor Stracathro Hosp 1947-61, matron 1961-72; pres Royal Coll of Nursing 1972-76; *Style—* Dame Winifred Prentice, DBE, OBE; Marleish, 4 Duke St, Brechin, Angus (☎ 035 62 2606)

PRENTIS, Henry Barrell; s of Stanley William Prentis (d 1974), of London, and Elizabeth Maxwell, *née* MacDonald (d 1970); *b* 16 Oct 1944; *Educ* St Olaves and St Saviour's GS; *m* 1 July 1967, Lilia Doris Nelson, da of Efstratios Kyriacou Sotirkati, of London; 1 s (Henry b 14 May 1975), 1 da (Miranda b 15 July 1972); *Career* dir: Leslie & Goodwin Ltd (and subsid cos) 1975-80, Frank B Hall (Holdings) plc 1981; dep chm Leslie & Goodwin (Lloyds insur brokers); Freeman: City of London 1983, Worshipful Co of Insurers 1983; FCA 1969; *Recreations* numismatic, bibliophile, fishing; *Clubs* RAC, The City; *Style—* Henry Prentis, Esq; Cherry Lawn, Nunnery St, Castle Hedingham, Essex CO9 3DP (☎ 0787 61100); Leslie & Godwin Ltd, 6 Braham St, London E1 8ED (☎ 071 480 7200, fax 071 480 7450, car 0836 741 353, telex 8950221 CORPCO G)

PRENTIS, Nigel Anthony; s of James Martin Prentis, and Megan, *née* Jones; *b* 2 Dec 1951; *Educ* Perse Sch Cambridge; *m* 9 March 1974, Caroline Sylvia, da of Victor Stephen Plumb (d 1985); 2 s (Daniel b 1979, Matthew b 1982), 1 da (Louisa b 1977); *Career* trg Spicer & Pegler 1969-75, audit mangr Charter & Myhill 1975-77, fndr Prentis & Co 1977; FCA 1974; *Books* Self Employment Fact Book (1982); *Recreations* soccer, voluntary work with children; *Style—* Nigel Prentis, Esq; 115c Milton Rd, Cambridge CB4 1XE (☎ 0223 352024, fax 0223 64317, telex 817936 CAMTEL)

PRESCOT, Kenrick Warre; s of late Brig C P Prescot, CBE; *b* 21 Nov 1920; *Educ* Eton, Worcester Coll Oxford; *m* 1948, Angharad Joanna, da of Brig C R M Hutchison, DSO, MC (ka 1942); 2 s, 1 da; *Career* served WWII RA, India, Burma and UK 1942-46, Capt; Bank of England 1947-59, vice pres Bankers Trust Company 1959-83; dir: Bankers Trust Int Ltd 1970-76, AMEV Life Assurance Ltd 1973-80, AMEV (UK) Ltd 1980-, Bankers Tstee Co Ltd 1983-; *Recreations* tennis, beagling, croquet; *Clubs* Gresham, MCC, Hurlingham; *Style—* Kenrick Prescot, Esq; 13 The Little Boltons, London SW10 9LJ

PRESCOTT, Jeremy Malcolm; s of Malcolm Crosby, CF, QHC, of Prescott, and Mary, *née* Webber (d 1974); *b* 26 March 1949; *Educ* Ampleforth, Fitzwilliam Coll Cambridge; *m* 20 May 1982, Jacqueline Mary Elizabeth, *née* Kirk; 1 s (John Edmund Philip), 1 da (Katherine Mary); *Career* CA; asst mangr Peat Marwick Mitchell & Co 1970-76, dir Samuel Montagu & Co Ltd 1987- (joined 1976); FCA 1979; *Books* How to Survive the Recession (1982); *Recreations* fishing; *Style—* Jeremy Prescott, Esq; Samuel Montagu & Co Ltd, 10 Lower Thames St, London EC3R 6AE (☎ 071 260 9249, fax 071 623 5512)

PRESCOTT, Prof John Herbert Dudley; s of Herbert Prescott (d 1959), of Barrow-on-Humber, Lincs, and Edith Vera, *née* Crowder; *b* 21 Feb 1937; *Educ* Haileybury, Univ of Nottingham (BSc, PhD); *m* 23 July 1960, Diana Margaret, da of Frank Mullock, of Poulton Hall, Chester; 2 s (Ian b 26 May 1961, Tony b 22 Aug 1962), 2 da (Joanna b 8 July 1965, Sarah-Vivien b 24 April 1968); *Career* dir H Prescott (Goxhill) Ltd 1959-78 (chm 1970-78), demonstrator in agric Univ of Nottingham 1960-63, lectr in animal prodn Univ of Newcastle-upon-Tyne 1963-74, animal prodn offr FAO UN (Argentina) 1972-74, head of animal prodn and devpt East of Scotland Coll of Agric 1974-78, prof of animal prodn Univ of Edinburgh 1978-84, dir Grassland Res Inst Hurley 1984-86, dir Animal & Grassland Res Inst 1986, dir of res Grassland & Animal Prodn 1986-88, princ Wye Coll Univ of London 1988-; memb Cncl Br Grassland Soc 1984-87, pres Br Soc Animal Prodn 1988; FIBiol 1983, FRAgS 1986; *Recreations* walking, wildlife, country pursuits; *Clubs* Farmers; *Style—* Prof John Prescott; Court Lodge, Brook, Ashford, Kent TN25 5PF (☎ 0233 812341); Wye College (University of London), Wye, Ashford, Kent TN25 5AH (☎ 0233 812401, fax 0233 813320, telex 94017832)

PRESCOTT, John Leslie; MP (Lab) Kingston upon Hull, E 1970-; s of John Herbert Prescott, JP, of Chester, by his w Phyllis; *b* 31 May 1938; *Educ* Ellesmere Port Secondary Modern, WEA, Ruskin Coll Oxford, Hull Univ; *m* 1961, Pauline, da of Ernest Tilston, of Chester; 2 s; *Career* joined Lab Pty 1956; former trainee chef & merchant seaman (NUS official 1968-70); contested (Lab) Southport 1966, PPS to Sec of State for Trade 1974-76, ldr Lab Pty Delegn European Parl 1976-79 (memb 1975-79); oppn spokesman: on Tport 1979-81, Regional Affrs 1981-Nov 1983; memb shadow cabinet and front bench spokesman Tport Nov 1983-84; front bench spokesman Employment 1984-; *Style—* John Prescott, Esq, MP; 365 Saltshouse Rd, Sutton-on-Hull, North Humberside (☎ 0482 702698)

PRESCOTT, Prof Laurie Francis; s of Dr F Prescott (d 1989), of Coombe Ridge, Churt, Surrey, and J Prescott, *née* Raison (d 1983); *b* 13 May 1934; *Educ* Hitchin Boys GS Herts, Downing Coll Cambridge (MA, MB BChir, MD); *m* 1, 21 Dec 1957 (m dis 1978), Josephine Anne, da of Nicholas Carpentieri, of 88 Wayne Ave, White Plains, NY, USA; 1 s (Nicholas David b 8 Jan 1962), 3 da (Katherine Elizabeth b 16 Oct 1964, Caroline Fiona b 8 Jan 1967, Christina Rachel b 26 July 1970); m 2, 11 Sept 1980, Jennifer Anne, da of Charles Gorvin, of Garden Cottages, Tapeley Park, Westleigh, N Devon; *Career* cmmnd pilot RAF 1952-54; res fell The John Hopkin's Hosp Baltimore USA 1963-65, lectr Univ of Aberdeen 1965-69, prof in clinical pharmacology Univ of Edinburgh 1985- (sr lectr and conslt physician 1969-74, reader 1974-85); memb Home Office Poisons Bd, former memb Ctee on Safety of Med; FRCPE, FRSE, memb RSM; *Books* Drug Absorption (ed 1981), Handbook of Clinical Pharmacokinetics (ed 1983), Rate Control in Drug Therapy (1985), Novel Drug Delivery (1989); *Recreations* gardening, flying, sailing, music; *Style*— Prof Laurie Prescott, FRSE; 24 Colinton Road, Edinburgh EH10 5EQ (☎ 031 447 2571); University Department of Clincial Pharmacology, The Royal Infirmary, Edinburgh EH3 9YW (☎ 031 229 2477)

PRESCOTT, Sir Mark; 3 Bt (UK 1938), of Godmanchester, Co Huntingdon; s of Maj (William Robert) Stanley Prescott (d 1962, yr s of Col Sir William Prescott, 1 Bt), by his 1 w Gwendolen, *née* Aldridge, and n of Sir Richard Stanley Prescott, 2 Bt (d 1965); *b* 3 March 1948; *Educ* Harrow; *Career* racehorse trainer; *Style*— Sir Mark Prescott, Bt; Heath House, Moulton Rd, Newmarket, Suffolk CB8 8DU (☎ 0638 662117)

PRESCOTT, Peter John; s of Wentworth James Prescott (d 1983), and Ellen Marie, *née* Burrows; *b* 6 April 1936; *Educ* Windsor GS, Pembroke Coll Oxford (MA); *m* 15 Sept 1971, Gillian Eileen, da of late Harold Lowe, and of Eddie Lowe, *née* Pennack; *Career* Nat Serv 2 Lt RA 1957-59; asst cultural attaché HM Embassy Cairo 1964 (London 1967-70), Univ of Sussex 1970-71; Br Cncl: asst then dep rep Paris 1971-75, dir E Europe and N Asia Dept London 1975-79, seconded to Dept of Educn and Sci 1979-81, rep Aust 1981-84, rep and cultural cnsllr HM Embassy Paris 1984-90, dir Arts Div London 1990-; *Recreations* reading, music, walking, swimming; *Style*— Peter Prescott, Esq; British Council, 11 Portland Place, London W1N 4EJ (☎ 071 389 3044, fax 071 389 3199, telex 8952201, BRICOUN G)

PRESCOTT, Peter Richard Kyle; s of Capt Richard Stanley Prescott (d 1987), of Cordoba, Argentina, and Sarah Aitchison, *née* Shand; *b* 23 Jan 1943; *Educ* St George's Coll Argentina, Dulwich, UCL (BSc), QMC (MSc); *m* 23 Sept 1967, Frances Rosemary, da of Wing Cdr Eric Henry Bland (d 1980), of Tonge Corner, Sittingbourne; 2 s (Richard Julyan Kyle b 1973, Thomas Alexander Kyle b 1975), 1 da (Miranda Katherine b 1971); *Career* called to the Bar Lincoln's Inn 1970; *Books* The Modern Law of Copyright (with Hugh Laddie and Mary Victoria, 1980); *Recreations* flying, music, reading, sub-aqua diving; *Style*— Peter Prescott, Esq; Arlington Square, London N1 (☎ 071 359 4580); Isle of Purbeck, Dorset; Francis Taylor Building, The Temple, London EC4 (☎ 071 353 5657, fax 071 353 3588/8715)

PRESCOTT THOMAS, John Desmond; RD (1977, clasp 1987); s of William Prescott Thomas (d 1973), and Beatrice Isobel, *née* Jones; *b* 28 May 1942; *Educ* Rhyl GS Clwyd, Whitchurch GS Glamorgan, Jesus Coll Oxford (BA, MA); *m* 7 Oct 1967, Bridget Margaret, da of Rev Canon Adrian Denys Somerset-Ward (d 1976); 2 da (Viveka Ruth b 1969, Bronwen Jane b 1971); *Career* BBC: gen trainee 1963-65, asst prodr sch TV 1965-68, prodr 1968-76, sr prodr modern languages and euro studies 1976-81, head sch bdcasting TV 1981-84, head Bristol network prodn centre 1984-86, head of bdcasting South and West 1986-; wrote and produced: radiovision prog on Stanley Spencer's Burghclere paintings (Japan Prize nomination 1965), TV adaptation of Peter Carter's The Black Lamp; three BAFTA RTS award nominations, twelve Euro documentary and language series; articles in: TES, Br Language Teaching Jl, Le Français dans le Monde; Bolland Lecture (Bristol Poly 1984); govr Bristol Poly, memb Court Univ of Bath, vice pres Bristol-Oporto assoc, tstee and dep chm Bath Int Festival; tstee: TV Tst for the Environment, The Exploratory, St George's Music Tst Bristol, Bristol Cathedral Tst; memb: Mgmnt Ctee SW Arts, Publicity Ctee Royal Bath and West Show, Friends Ctee Arnolfini Gallery Bristol, Policy Advsy Ctee Univ of Bristol Vet Sch, Communications Gp, Diocese of Bath and Wells, Royal TV Soc, Assoc for Language Learning; RNR: cmmnd 1963, qualified ocean cmd 1974, Cdr 1978, exec offr London div 1983-84, Severn div 1984-; *Books* Two EFL stories for children, Encounter: France (1980), Dès le Début, Dicho y Hecho, Alles Klar (1983); *Recreations* languages, sailing, photography, industrial archaeology, model engineering, heraldry, playing the alto saxophone; *Clubs* Naval; *Style*— John Prescott Thomas, Esq, RD; Earl's Pool, Ladymead Lane, Lower Langford, Avon BS18 7EQ (☎ 0934 852606); BBC South and West, Broadcasting House, Whiteladies Rd, Bristol BS8 2LR (☎ 0272 732211, fax 0272 739331, telex 265781 BSA)

PRESLAND, Frank George; *Educ* Univ of London (BSc), Univ Coll of Rhodesian and Nyasaland; *m* 16 April 1968, Julia Mary Bronwer; 1 s (Anthony Charles b 1980), 1 da (Linda Mary b 1975); *Career* admitted slr 1973; ptnr Frere Cholmeley 1976-; memb Law Soc; *Recreations* yachting; *Style*— Frank Presland, Esq; Frere Cholmeley, 28 Lincolns Inn Fields, London WC2 (☎ 071 405 7878, telex 27623, fax 071 405 9056)

PRESLAND, John David; s of Leslie Presland; *b* 3 July 1930; *Educ* St Albans Sch, LSE; *m* 1969, Margaret Brewin; *Career* exec vice chm Port of London Authy 1978-82; memb Br Computer Soc; memb IPFA, FCA; *Clubs* Oriental; *Style*— John Presland, Esq; Pilots National Pension Fund, New Premier House, 150 Southampton Row London WC1B 5AL

PRESLEY, Prof John Ralph; s of Ralph Presley, of 12 South St, Dinnington, Sheffield, and Doris, *née* Edson; *b* 17 Sept 1945; *Educ* Woodhouse GS Sheffield, Univ of Lancaster (BA), Univ of Loughborough (PhD); *m* 15 July 1967, Barbara, da of Kenneth Mallinson, of 7 Burley Rise, Kegworth, Derby; 1 s (John Robert Ralph b 9 June 1981), 2 da (Joanne Marie 29 July 1968, Catherine Jane b 2 Sept 1972); *Career* sr lectr Univ of Loughborough 1976-81 (lectr 1969-76), sr econ advsr Miny of Planning Saudi Arabia 1979-80, visiting scholar Harvard 1982-; Univ of Loughborough: reader 1981-84, prof econs 1984-, dir Banking Centre 1985-89; visiting professorial fellow Univ of Nottingham 1989-90; *Books* European Monetary Integration (with P Coffey, 1971), Currency Areas: Theory and Practice (with G E J Dennis, 1976), Robertsonian Economics (1978), Pioneers of Modern Economics Vol 1 (ed with D O'Brien , 1983), Pioneers of Modern Economics Vol 2 (ed with D Greenaway, 1989), Directory of Islamic Financial Institutions (1989), A Guide to the Saudi Arabian Economy (with A J Westaway, 1983, 2 edn 1989); *Recreations* gardening, reading, music, travel; *Style*— Prof John Presley; Dept of Economics, Loughborough University, Loughborough, Leics (☎ 0509 222711, telex 34319)

PRESS, John Bryant; s of Edward Kenneth Press (d 1951), and Gladys Mary Smith, *née* Cooper (d 1980); *b* 11 Jan 1920; *Educ* King Edward VI Sch Norwich, CCC Cambridge (MA); *m* 20 Dec 1947, Janet Nellie, da of Oliver Crompton (d 1982), of Cardiff; 1 s (Roger b 1948), 1 da (Judith b 1953); *Career* WWII RA 1940-45: Gunner 1940-41, 2 Lt 1942, Lt 1943, Staff Capt 1944-45; Br Cncl 1946-80: Athens 1946, Salonika 1947-50, Madras 1950-51, Colombo 1951-52, Birmingham 1952-54, Cambridge 1955-62, London 1963-65, Paris 1966-71, Oxford 1972-78, London 1979-80; FRSL 1959; *Books* The Fire and the Fountain (1955), Uncertainties (1956), The Chequer'd Shade (1958), Guy Fawkes Night (1959), Rule and Energy (1963), A Map of Modern English Verse (1969), The Lengthening Shadows (1971), A Girl with Beehive Hair (1986); *Recreations* the arts, travel; *Style*— John Press, Esq; 5 South Parade, Frome, Somerset BA11 1EJ (☎ 0373 611 42)

PRESS, Dr (Christopher) Martin; s of Gp Capt Charles Henry Press, of Gt Gormellick, Liskeard, Cornwall, and Christina, *née* Hindshaw; *b* 24 Jan 1944; *Educ* Bedales Sch, King's Coll Cambridge (BA), UCH (MB BChir, MA), Chelsea Coll London (MSc); *m* 10 June 1967, Angela Margaret, da of Charles Douglas Lewis, of Church Farm, Dibden, Southampton; 5 s (Matthew b 1970, Joseph b 1972, Samuel b 1974, Benjamin b 1980, Daniel b 1984); *Career* med registrar Royal Post Grad Med Sch Hammersmith Hosp 1971-73, Med Res Cncl res fell Univ of California 1973-75, asst prof of med and paediatrics Yale Univ Sch of Med 1981-87, conslt physician Dept of Endocrinology Charing Cross Hosp London 1986-; memb: BMA, Br Diabetic Assoc, American Diabetic Assoc, Southampton Canal Soc; *Recreations* orienteering, bell ringing, canal cruising; *Style*— Dr Martin Press; 99 Highfield Lane, Southampton SO2 1NN (☎ 0703 55 1617); Department of Endocrinology, Charing Cross Hospital, London W6 8RT (☎ 081 846 1065)

PRESSEY, Hon Mrs (Rachel Jean); da of The Rt Hon the Viscount Galway, CD of 583 Berkshire Drive, London, Ontario, Canada N67 353 and Fiona Margaret, *née* Taylor; Gen Robert Monckton, govr of New Brunswick and New York State; *b* 21 June 1957; *m* 1978, (m dis), Ronald John Pressey; 2 s (Michael b 1980, Christopher b 1981); *Style*— The Hon Mrs Pressey; 583 Berkshire Drive, London, Ontario, Canada N6J 3S3

PREST, (Edward) Charles; OBE (1986), DFC (1944); s of Gerald Stanley Prest (d 1956), of Eastbourne, and Margaret Sabine, *née* Pasley (d 1967); *b* 11 May 1920; *Educ* Rugby Sch, RMA Woolwich; *m* 6 Nov 1944, Joyce Marjorie, da of John Perks (d 1969), of London; 1 s (Richard Jullion b 1946), 1 da (Jennifer Mary (Mrs John Brinkley) b 1957); *Career* cmmnd in RA 1939, served with 99 Field Regt (Royal Bucks Yeomanry) RA in France (until Dunkirk) and England 1939-42, Army (Air Observation Post) pilot 1942; flying instructor 1942-43, Flight Cdr in 659 AOP Sqdn RAF Attached to 11 Armoured Divn Normandy to the Rhine 1943-45 (Capt 1945); Slag Reduction Co Ltd (now Faber Prest plc): joined 1946, sec 1948, dir 1952, md 1963-83, chm 1966-86, pres 1986; former dir of all subsidiary Cos; dir associated cos: The Slag Reduction Co NZ Ltd 1979-84, Appleby Slag Reduction Co Ltd 1976-83, Appley Slag Co Ltd 1981-84; Freeman City of London 1963, memb Ct Worshipful Co of Paviors 1986 (Liveryman 1963); *Recreations* golf, walking, computers; *Clubs* Army and Navy, Seaford Golf, Sea View Yacht; *Style*— Charles Prest, Esq, OBE, DFC; Henleys, High St, Seaview, Isle of Wight PO34 5EU (☎ 0983 617310)

PREST, Nicholas Martin; s of Prof Alan Richmond Prest (d 1984), of Wimbledon, and Pauline Chasey, *née* Noble; *b* 3 April 1953; *Educ* Manchester GS, ChCh Oxford (MA); *m* 1985, Anthea Joy Elisabeth, da of Stuart John Guthrie Neal, of Wales; 1 s (Frederick George Alan b 1989), 1 da (Clementine Joy Chasey b 1987); *Career* entered civil serv MOD 1974 admin trainee, princ offr 1979; joined United Scientific Instruments Ltd 1982, chief exec United Scientific Holdings plc 1989 (dir 1985); *Recreations* tennis; *Style*— Nicholas Prest, Esq; 16 Leamington Rd Villas, London W11 1HS (☎ 071 727 7704); United Scientific Holdings plc, United Scientific House, 215 Vauxhall Bridge Rd, London SW1 (☎ 071 821 8080)

PRESTIGE, Colin Gwynne; s of Harold Haldane Calder Prestige, CBE (d 1982), of Chislehurst, Kent, and Lydia Ellen Neville, *née* Edwards (d 1983); *b* 19 Nov 1926; *Educ* Bradfield Coll, Oriel Coll Oxford (BA, MA); *Career* Supply and Secretarial Div RN 1945-48; admitted slr 1954; second sr ptnr Lawrence Graham London 1987-89 (ptnr 1959-89, conslt 1989-), chm Young Slrs Gp Law Soc 1960-61, memb Cncl Law Soc 1967-, chm Non-contentious Business Ctee 1974-77, vice chm Professional Purposes Ctee 1980-82 and 1983-84 (father of Cncl 1987-); fndr memb Holborn Law Soc 1962 (memb Ctee 1962-, hon treas 1963-71, vice pres 1971-73, pres 1973-74); chm Rent Assessment Appeals Ctee Greater London 1965-68; memb Cncl: Incorporated Cncl of Law Reporting England and Wales 1984-, The Selden Soc 1988-, Slrs Staff Pension Fund 1988-; memb: Law Soc Working Pty Modernisation of Conveyancing 1964-69, Land Registration Rules Ctee 1972-, Investigation Ctee Slr's Complaints Bureau 1987-, Br Records Assoc (Records Preservation Section) 1988-, Disciplinary Bd Br Psychological Soc 1990-; dir Royal Theatrical Fund 1967-79 and 1989-; tstee: D'Oyly Carte Opera Tst 1964-, Friends of D'Oyly Carte 1981-; memb Worshipful Co of Slrs 1988; FRSA 1967; *Books* D'Oyly Carte and the Pirates; Original New York Productions 1875-96 (1971), Conveyancing; Who Buys Your House ? (1977); *Recreations* Gilbert and Sullivan, literary research; *Clubs* Garrick; *Style*— Colin Prestige, Esq; c/o Lawrence Graham, 190 Strand, London WC2R 1JN (☎ 071 379 0000, fax 071 379 6854, telex 22673 LAWGRA G)

PRESTON, Allan; s of Thomas Raymond Preston, and Jeanie Duncan Smith, *née* West; *b* 16 Aug 1969; *Educ* Leith Acad; *Career* professional footballer; debut Dundee Utd 1987 v Falkirk (over 35 appearances), represented Scotland at all levels from under 15-under 21; *Recreations* golf, snooker; *Style*— Allan Preston, Esq; 13/3 Kirkgate House, Leith, Edinburgh, Scotland EH6 6AF (☎ 031 553 2684); Dundee Utd FC, Tannadice St, Dundee, Tayside (☎ 0382 819888, fax 0382 826289)

PRESTON, Hon Mrs (Caroline Anne); *née* Cecil; er da of 3 Baron Rockley; *b* 27 March 1960; *m* 1985, Mark G Preston, yr s of Simon Preston, of Lowfield Farm, Tetbury, Glos; 2 s (Hugh Simon b 1987, Edward James b 1989), 1 da (Lucy Camilla b 1991); *Style*— The Hon Mrs Preston; 92 Elms Rd, London SW4

PRESTON, Dr Frank Samuel; OBE (1988), VRD (1963); s of Frank Anderson Baillie Preston (d 1978), of Milngavie, Scotland, and Rachel, *née* McDonald (d 1968); *b* 13 March 1923; *Educ* Glasgow Acad, Univ of Glasgow (MB ChB, DA); *m* 2 Oct 1954, Margaret, da of Norman McGregor (d 1974), of Falkirk, Scotland; 1 s (Frank Alan b 1955), 2 da (Jacqueline Ann b 1961 (Mrs G Murray), Katherine Frances b 1962); *Career* marine engr small vessels pool Admlty 1943-45, Surgn Lt RNVR - Surgn Capt RNR 1947-73, regn med offr BEA 1954-65, princ air med offr BEA and BOAC 1965-78, dir med serv BA 1981-87 (dep dir med serv 1978-81), med spokesman Br Heart Fndn 1987-90, conslt in aviation and space med 1987-, memb med cmmn for accident prevention 1987-, govr LSHTM 1987-; QHP 1972-73; sr med examiner CAA and Fed Aviation Authy USA; memb Anglo-American Med Soc (former pres); numerous articles on aviation and travel; co surgn St John Ambulance, diving med examiner UK and Norwegian govts, Freeman Guild of Air Pilots and Air Navigators 1979, memb Int Acad Aviation and Space Med (former vice pres); fell Aerospace Med Assoc, FRAeS, FFOM RCP; *Books* contrib to: Oxford Textbook of Medicine (1988), Textbook of Aviation Medicine (1988); *Recreations* golf, diving, sailing; *Clubs* RNSA; *Style*— Dr Frank Preston, OBE, VRD; Wynn Institute for Metabolic Research, 21 Wellington Rd, St John's Wood, London NW8 9SQ (☎ 071 9352266)

PRESTON, (John) Hugh Simon; JP (West Berkshire 1990); s of Rev Cecil George Armitage Preston (d 1966), and Dr Maureen Evans; *b* 28 April 1937; *Educ* Marlborough; *m* 10 Oct 1964, Julia Deborah, da of Richard Glover Hubbard (d 1969); 1 s (Guy b 1968), 1 da (Olivia b 1972); *Career* chartered surveyor, ptnr Strutt & Parker; FRICS; *Recreations* reading, gliding, gardening, music; *Clubs* Farmers'; *Style*— Hugh Preston, Esq, JP; Summerdown House, Malshanger, Basingstoke, Hampshire; 55 Northbrook St, Newbury, Berks

PRESTON, Ian Mathieson Hamilton; s of John Hamilton Preston (d 1978), and Edna Irene Paul; *b* 18 July 1932; *Educ* Kilmarnock Acad, Univ of Glasgow (BSc, PhD); *m* 5 Aug 1958 Sheila Hope, da of Robert Johnston Pringle; 2 s (Colin John b 10 Feb 1960, Ewan Robert b 5 Dec 1961); *Career* asst lectr Univ of Glasgow 1957-59; South of Scotland Electricity Bd: asst reactor physicist 1959-65, sr asst engr 1965-67, res projects mangr 1967-69, tech servs mangr 1969-70, mangr generation and design Tech Servs Div 1970-72, chief engr Generation Design and Construction Div 1972-77, dep chm 1983-90; dir gen Generation Devpt and Construction Div CEGB 1977-83, chief exec Scottishpower 1990-; MInstP 1959, FIEE 1974, FEng 1982; *Recreations* fishing, gardening; *Clubs* RAC; *Style—* Ian Preston, Esq; ScottishPower, Cathcart House, Spean St, Glasgow G44 4BE (☎ 041 637 7177, fax 041 637 9647)

PRESTON, Jeffrey William; CB (1989); s of William Preston, and Sybil Grace, *née* Lawson; *b* 28 Jan 1940; *Educ* Liverpool Collegiate Sch, Hertford Coll Oxford (MA); *Career* asst princ Miny of Aviation 1963, private sec to perm sec BOT 1966, princ BOT 1967, HM Treasy 1970, DTI 1973, asst sec Dept of Trade 1975-82, under sec and regnl dir Yorks and Humberside Reg DTI 1982-85, dep sec Welsh Off 1985-90, dep dir gen OFT 1990-; chm Hertford Soc 1986-; *Recreations* motoring, opera, swimming; *Clubs* United Oxford and Cambridge Univ; *Style—* Jeffrey Preston, Esq, CB; Office of Fair Trading, Field House, Bream's Buildings, London EC4A 1PR (☎ 071 269 8921)

PRESTON, Hon Mrs (Judith Susanna); *née* Briggs; yr da of Baron Briggs (Life Peer); *b* 1961; *m* 1985, Philip G F Preston, only s of W Preston, of Folkestone, Kent; *Style—* Hon Mrs Preston

PRESTON, Sir Kenneth Huson; s of late Sir Walter Preston; *b* 19 May 1901; *Educ* Rugby, Trinity Oxford; *m* 1, 1922, Beryl Wilmot (d 1979), da of Sir William Wilkinson; 1 s, 1 da; m 2, 1984, Mrs Violet Evelyn Dumont; *Career* dir Midland Bank Ltd 1945-76, pres Stone-Platt Inds Ltd 1968-82; memb: S Area Bd BR, Br Olympic Yachting team 1936 and 1952, Capt 1960; kt 1959; *Clubs* Royal Yacht Sqdn (Vice Cdre 1965-71), Thames Yacht (Vice Cdre 1953-56); *Style—* Sir Kenneth Preston; Court Lodge, Avening, Tetbury, Glos (☎ 045 383 4402)

PRESTON, Michael David; s of Richard Preston, and Yetta, *née* Young (d 1958); *b* 12 Dec 1945; *Educ* St Paul's, Exeter Coll Oxford (Sr Open scholar, MA); *m*·13 April 1969, Stephanie Ann, *née* Levy; 2 s (Matthew b 1972, Robert b 1975); *Career* articled clerk Price Waterhouse London; fndr shareholder and dir The Sterling Publishing Group plc (dep chm 1990-), dir Debrett's Peerage Ltd; playing memb Royal Amateur Orchestra; former pres Oxford Univ Cons. Assoc; FCA 1971; *Recreations* music, wine, tennis, golf; *Clubs* Utd Oxford and Cambridge, MCC; *Style—* Michael Preston, Esq; 91 Redington Rd, London NW3 7RR (☎ 071 431 2530, fax 071 794 8654); The Sterling Publishing Gp plc, 53 Grosvenor St, London W1X 9FH (☎ 071 495 1262, fax 071 491 0049)

PRESTON, Michael Richard; s of Maj Frederick Allen Preston, MC, TD (d 1972), of Carshalton, Surrey, and Winifred Gertrude, *née* Archer (d 1987); *b* 15 Oct 1927; *Educ* Whitgift Sch, Sutton and Cheam Sch of Art Surrey, Guildford Sch of Art (NDD), Goldsmith's Coll London (ATD, Dip Humanities); *m* 1, 13 Aug 1955 (m dis 1975), Anne, da of Dr Ralph Gillespie Smith (d 1959), of Kirdford, Sussex; m 2, 22 Aug 1980, Judith Gaye James, da of Alec Warden Hopkins (d 1989), of Blenheim, NZ; *Career* volunteer Queen's Royal Regt 1944-48, Queen's Royal Regt TA 1948-52, HAC 1952-61; asst master Whitgift Sch 1954-55, drawing master Dulwich Coll 1955-64, head of design and later keeper Dept of Museum Servs Science Museum 1964-87; exhibitions designed incl: Centenary of Charles Babbage 1971, A Word to the Mermaid's 1973, Tower Bridge Observed 1974, The Breath of Life 1974, Science and Technology of Islam 1976, Stanley Spencer in the Shipyard 1979, Science and Technology of India 1982, The Great Cover-Up Show 1982, Beads of Glass 1983, Louis Pasteur and Rabies; designed many exhibitions in permanent galleries incl: Science Museum 1964-86, Nat Railway Museum York 1971-75, Wellcome Museum of the History of Medicine 1975-80, Nat Museum of Photography Film and Television Bradford 1977-83; advsy assignments on museum projects: Iran 1976-79, Spain 1977-80, Germany 1978-79, Canada 1979-82, Expo '86 Vancouver BC 1984-86, Trinidad 1982-83, Turkey 1984-, Hong Kong 1985, ret; conslt designer 1987-; consultancies to: The Wellcome Fndn 1986-, Dean and Chapter of Canterbury 1987-, TAVRA 1988-, Design Expo '89 Nagoya Japan 1988-89; Nat Inst of Design India 1989-, Bank of England Museum 1989, Tricycle Theatre 1989-, Royal National Theatre 1988-90, Norwich Tourist Agency 1989-90 (Scottish Off 1990), Norwich Tourist Agency 1989-90 (Scottish Office 1990), Richmond Theatre Surrey 1990, Academia Italiana 1990-, English Heritage 1990-; chm Greenwich Soc 1961-64, examiner UEI 1959-64, examiner first degrees Univ of London 1970-74, Panel memb BTEC 1982-, memb Int Advsy Panel Tubitak (Sci Res Cncl of Turkey) 1984-; visitng prof NID Ahmedabad 1989, tstee Vivat Tst 1989-; FRSA 1955-68, memb ICOM 1964-, memb CSD 1953 (fell 1972-), hon memb Guild Glass Engravers 1976- (hon fell 1980-, pres 1986-); *Recreations* looking at buildings, travel, food, jazz; *Clubs* Arts; *Style—* Michael Preston, Esq; 37 Walham Grove, London SW6 1QR (☎ fax 071 381 6955, telex 23491 DOON G)

PRESTON, (Christopher) Miles (Cary); s of Alan Tomlinson Preston, TD, of Shrewsbury, Shropshire, and Audrey Anne Flint, *née* Wood; *b* 12 April 1950; *Educ* Shrewsbury; *m* 5 June 1974, Jane Mowbray, da of Norman Seddon Harrison (d 1988), of Blackheath, London SE3; 2 da (Caroline Mowbray b 28 Dec 1978, Georgina Clare b 20 Nov 1986); *Career* admitted slr 1974; ptnr Radcliffes & Co 1980-, serv on Sir Gervase Sheldon's Family Law Liaison Ctee 1982; Slrs' Family Law Assoc: fndr memb 1982, memb Main Ctee 1982-88, chm Working Pty on procedure 1982-88; Int Acad of Matrimonial Lawyers: fndr memb 1986, govr 1986-, pres Eng chapter 1989, pres Euro chapter 1989-, parliamentarian to Main Ctee 1989; *Recreations* food and travel; *Clubs* Turf, Leander; *Style—* Miles Preston, Esq; Blackheath, London SE3; Radcliffes & Co, 5 Great College St, Westminster, London SW1P 3SJ (☎ 071 222 7040, fax 071 222 6208, telex 919302)

PRESTON, (Bryan) Nicholas; OBE (1985); s of Bryan Wentworth Preston, MBE (d 1965); *b* 6 Feb 1933; *Educ* Eton, RAC Cirencester; *m* 1955, Elsbeth, *née* Hostettler; 1 s, 2 da; *Career* farmer; dir Stone Manganese Marine Ltd, chm Br Marine Equipment Cncl 1966-68 and 1976-78; memb: BOTB E Euro Trade Cncl 1979-82, BOTB Euro Trade Ctee 1972-89; *Recreations* field sports, skiing; *Clubs* Boodle's, Farmers'; *Style—* Nicholas Preston, Esq, OBE; Park Farm, Beverston, nr Tetbury, Glos GL8 8TT (☎ 0666 502688)

PRESTON, Peter John; s of John Whittle Preston; *b* 23 May 1938; *Educ* Loughborough GS, St John's Coll Oxford; *m* 1962, Jean Mary Burrell; 2 s, 2 da; *Career* editor The Guardian 1975-; *Style—* Peter Preston Esq; The Guardian, 119 Farringdon Rd, London EC1 (☎ 071 278 2332)

PRESTON, Sir Peter Sansome; KCB (1978), CB (1973); s of Charles Guy Preston; *b* 18 Jan 1922; *Educ* Nottingham HS; *m* 1951, Marjory Harrison; 2 s, 3 da; *Career* served WWII RAF; joined BOT as exec offr 1947, trade cmmr New Delhi 1959, under sec BOT (subsequently DTI) 1969-72, dep sec Dept of Trade 1972-76, perm sec Miny of Overseas Devpt (subsequently Overseas Devpt Admin FCO) 1976-82; int advsr Land Rover-Leyland 1983-87, dir Wellcome International Trading 1985-; vice chm CARE Br 1985-; *Style—* Sir Peter Preston, KCB; 5 Greville Park Avenue, Ashtead, Surrey (☎ 0372 72099)

PRESTON, Hon Robert Francis Hubert; s of late 15 Viscount Gormanston; *b* 1915; *Educ* Downside; *m* 1, 1941 (m dis 1955), Jean Helen o child of late Capt Charles Shaw, 15 Hussars; 2 da; m 2, 1970, Daphne Helen Anne, da of late Col Robert Hanbury Brudenell-Bruce, DSO (*see* Peerage Marquess of Ailesbury), and formerly w of (1) late Lt-Cdr Reginald Hughes-Onslow, RN (*see* Peerage Earl of Onslow), and (2) late Maj John Edward Mountague Bradish-Ellames; *Career* formerly Capt 11 Hussars, served WWII (wounded); hon sec Northamptonshire Branch CPRE; *Style—* The Hon Robert Preston; Thatched Cottage, Dingley, Market Harborough, Leics

PRESTON, Brig Roger St Clair; CBE (1986, OBE 1979); s of Col Geoffrey William Preston (d 1976), of Menethorpe, Malton, N Yorks, and Daphne Jane Preston, OBE, *née* St Clair-Ford; *b* 24 Oct 1935; *Educ* Eton, RMA Sandhurst; *m* 29 Aug 1964, Polly Mary, da of Robin George Marriott (d 1943), of Malton, N Yorks; 2 s (Mark b 20 Jan 1968, Hugh b 21 Oct 1970), 1 da (Sarah b 5 March 1966); *Career* cmmnd KOYLI 1955, serv in Kenya Cyprus Malaya Brunei Germany 1955-66, Indian Staff Coll 1966, CO 2 LI 1976-79, Col AG2 1981-84, Brig CO UDR 1984-86; Br Heart Fndn 1986, pt/t farmer 1986, Hon Col 8 (Yorkshire) Bn LI 1989; local chm CPRE, church warden, FBIM 1985; *Recreations* shooting, gardening, fishing; *Clubs* Army & Navy; *Style—* Brig Roger Preston, CBE; British Heart Foundation, 4 Bridge St, Tadcaster, North Yorkshire LS24 9AL (☎ 0937 835421)

PRESTON, Sir Ronald Douglas Hildebrand; 7 Bt (UK 1815); s of Sir Thomas Hildebrand Preston, OBE, 6 Bt (d 1976), and Ella Lady Preston (d 1989); *b* 9 Oct 1916; *Educ* Westminster, Trinity Cambridge, Ecole des Sciences Politiques Paris; *m* 1, 1954 (m dis 1971), Smilya Stefanovic; m 2, 1972, Pauleen Jane, da of late Paul Lurcott; *Heir* kinsman, Philip Charles Henry Hulton Preston; *Career* served WW II, with 8 Army in Mid East and Italy, Austria and Allied Control Cmmn to Bulgaria, late Maj Intelligence Corps; Reuters corr in Belgrade 1948-53; Times corr: Vienna and E Europe 1953-60, Tokyo 1960-63; HM Dip Serv 1963-76; *Recreations* tennis, shooting; *Clubs* Travellers', Norfolk (Norwich), Tokyo (Tokyo); *Style—* Sir Ronald Preston, Bt; Beeston Hall, Beeston St Lawrence, Norwich NR12 8YS (☎ 0692 630771)

PRESTON, Simon Douglas Nelson; s of Jocelyn Panizzi Preston (d 1970), of Romsey, and Emily Geraldine Morval Kirby, *née* Nelson; *b* 5 Aug 1933; *Educ* Sherborne, Trinity Coll Cambridge (MA); *m* 30 June 1962, Celia Mary, da of Frank Bodenham Thornely, MC (d 1958), of Tunbridge Wells; 4 s (Rupert b 1963, Adam b 1966, John b 1975, Charles b 1975), 1 da (Emma b 1965); *Career* Nat Serv Lt RM Commandos Austria special duties 1952-54; PR offr Stock Exchange 1959-64, info offr Lazard Bros & Co Ltd 1964-66; dir: Fin PR Ltd 1966-68, Charles Barker City Ltd 1968-71, Mixed Media Ltd 1982-87; fin dir Leo Burnett Ltd 1971-74, md and dir Dewe Rogerson Ltd 1974-81, dep chm St James PR Ltd 1987-90; chm: City Liaison Gp 1973-74 and 1979-83, Br Enterprise Award Ctee 1981-84; memb Cncl Assoc Ind Business 1978-79, dir Think Br Campaign 1982-; memb Inst PR (hon treas 1981-82); *Recreations* farming, sailing, entomology; *Clubs* Travellers; *Style—* Simon Preston, Esq; Badsell Park Farm, Matfield, Tonbridge, Kent (☎ 0892 832 549); Financial Public Relations Ltd, 76 Shoe Lane, London EC4 (☎ 071 353 8907, fax 071 353 7550)

PRESTON, Thomas Davis; s of Thomas William Samuel Lane Preston (d 1952), of Eastbourne, Sussex, and Madeleine Irene, *née* Davis (d 1966); *b* 1 Dec 1932; *Educ* Gillingham Sch; *m* 23 March 1963, Jennifer Katherine, da of Dr James Anderson, OBE; 2 da (Carolyn b 1969, Lesley b 1971); *Career* Colonial Serv Kenya: dist offr 1954-62, dist cmmr 1962-63, ret 1963; Phillips Harrisons & Crosfield Kenya: mktg mangr 1963-69, mktg dir 1970-73, chm and md 1974-79, chm 1979-88; dir Harrisons & Crosfield plc London 1981-, chm and chief exec Harrisons & Crosfield Aust 1982-; chm: Harcros Chemicals Aust 1982-, Harcros Timber Aust 1982-, Harrisons & Crosfield Papua New Guinea 1982-, New Britain Palm Oil Development Papua New Guinea 1982-, Linatex Aust 1984-, Kapiura Plantations Papua New Guinea 1986-; *Recreations* golf; *Style—* Thomas Preston, Esq; High St, Sevenoaks, Kent; Melbourne Mansions, Queens Club Gardens, London; Elemang Ave, Kirribilli, Sydney, Australia; 20 St Dunstans Hill, London EC3R 5AB (☎ 071 626 4333, fax 071 929 3785, telex 885 636)

PRESTON, Timothy William; QC (1982); s of Charles Frank Preston; *b* 3 Nov 1935; *Educ* Haileybury, Jesus Coll Oxford; *m* 1965, Barbara Mary Haygarth; *Career* called to the Bar Inner Temple 1964, rec Crown Ct 1979-; *Clubs* Cavalry and Guards; *Style—* Timothy Preston, Esq, QC; 2 Temple Gardens, London EC4Y 9AY (☎ 071 583 6041)

PRESTON-DUNLOP, Dr Valerie Morthland; *née* Preston; da of Arthur Llewellyn Preston (d 1936), Bishop of Woolwich, and Nancy Robina, *née* Napier (d 1977); *b* 14 March 1930; *Educ* Downe House Newbury, Art of Movement Studio (Dip), Univ of London (Dip Ed, MA), Laban Centre (PhD); *m* 16 Sept 1961, John Henderson Dunlop, s of Sir John Kinninmont Dunlop, KBE, CMG, MC (d 1976), of Ridge Lea, Sevenoaks; 1 s (Roger Napier b 1965), 1 da (Emma Preston b 1971); *Career* sr lectr Dartford Coll of PE 1954-63, dir Beechmont Movement Study Centre 1965-73, sr post grad tutor Laban Centre for Movement and Dance 1978-, int lectr and writer on dance (princ areas of res Rudolf Laban and Choreology), pioneer of dance scholarship, fndr Beechmount Action Centre Tst for the Disadvantaged, govr Walthamstow Hall Sch; FICKL 1961, fndr memb Dance Res Soc 1982; *Books* Practical Kinetography (1969), Dancing and Dance Theory (1979), Dance in Education (1980), Point of Departure (1984), Schrifttanz: a view of German dance in the Weimar Republic (1990), Rudolf Laban: an introduction; *Recreations* gardening, music; *Clubs* Royal Society of Arts; *Style—* Dr Valerie Preston-Dunlop; Corners, The Street, Ightham, Kent (☎ 0732 884882); Laban Centre, Newcross, London SE14 (☎ 081 692 4070)

PRESTT, His Hon Arthur Miller; QC (1970); s of Arthur Prestt (d 1959); *b* 23 April 1925; *Educ* Bootham Sch York, Trinity Hall Cambridge; *m* 1949, Jill Mary, da of Graham Richards Dawbarn, CBE (d 1977); 1 s, 1 da; *Career* served WWII 13 Bn Parachute Regt: NW Europe, Malaya, Java; war crimes prosecutor Far E, hon Maj Parachute Regt; called to the bar Middle Temple 1949; JP Cumberland 1966, chm Cumberland QS 1969-70 (dep chm 1966-69), circuit judge 1971-90, sr circuit judge Manchester (N Circuit) and rec of Manchester 1982-90; previously active in Scout Assoc (Silver Acorn 1970); *Recreations* golf, gardening; *Style—* His Hon Arthur Prestt, QC; 10 Heigham Grove, Norwich, Norfolk NR2 3DQ (☎ 0603 622631)

PRESTT, Ian; CBE (1986); s of Arthur Prestt (d 1959), and Jessie, *née* Miller (d 1978); bro of His Hon Judge Prestt QC, circuit Judge, Hon Rec of Manchester and Sr Circuit Judge, Manchester 1982; *b* 26 June 1929; *Educ* Bootham Sch York, Liverpool Univ (BSc, MSc, FIBiol); *m* 8 Sept 1956, Jennifer Ann, da of Reginald Wagstaffe, of Southport, Lancs (d 1983); 1 s (Duncan b 1 March 1959, d 1979), 2 da (Julie b 1959, Alexandra b 1968); *Career* 2 Lt RA 1947-49; joined Nature Conservancy 1956, dep dir Central Unit Environmental Pollution Cabinet Off & DOE 1968, dept dir NCC 1974; dir gen RSPB 1975-; vice pres Int Cncl for Bird Preservation 1990- (chm 1982-90); pres CPRE (Cambridge Branch) 1990-; memb of exec ctee Wildfowl Tst 1976-90; NCC Advsy Ctee Birds 1981-; *Recreations* sketching, reading, architecture; *Clubs* Athenaeum; *Style—* Ian Prestt, Esq, CBE; Eastfield House, Tuddenham Rd, Barton Mills, Bury St Edmonds IP28 6AG (☎ 0638 715139); RSPB, The Lodge, Sandy, Beds SG19 2DL (☎ 07676 80551)

PRESTWICH, Prof Michael Charles; s of John Oswald Prestwich, of Oxford, and Menna, *née* Roberts (d 1990); *b* 30 Jan 1943; *Educ* Charterhouse, Magdalen Coll Oxford, ChCh Coll Oxford (MA, D Phil); *m* 11 May 1973, Margaret Joan, da of Herbert Daniel (d 1980), of Glossop; 2 s (Robin b 1974, Christopher b 1976), 1 da (Kate b 1980); *Career* res lectr Christ Church Oxford 1965-69, lectr medieval history Univ of St Andrews 1969-79, prof history Univ of Durham 1986- (reader in medieval history 1979-86); FRHistS 1972, FSA 1980; *Books* War, Politics and Finance under

Edward I (1972), The Three Edwards: War and State in England 1272-1377 (1980), Documents Illustrating the Crisis of 1297-8 in England (1980), Edward I (1988), English Politics in the Thirteenth Century (1990); *Recreations* skiing; *Style—* Prof Michael Prestwich, FSA; 46 Albert Street, Western Hill, Durham DH1 4RJ (☎ 091 3862539); Department of History, 43/46 North Bailey, Durham DH1 3HX

PRETOR-PINNEY, Anthony Robert Edmund; o s of Lt Cdr Giles Robert Pretor-Pinney, RN (ka 1942), and Lucy Theodosia Gascoigne, *née* Fowle (who m 2, Capt John Domvile Auchmulty Musters, DSC, RN, and d 1980); descended from John Pretor (d 1818), who assumed the additional surname and arms of Pinney by Royal Licence on succeeding to the estates of his kinsman John Frederick Pinney (d 1762), of Bettiscombe, Dorset (*see* Burke's Landed Gentry, 18 edn, vol I, 1965); *b* 7 May 1930; *Educ* Winchester, RNC Dartmouth, RAC Cirencester (MRAC 1957); *m* 22 Aug 1963, Laura Uppercu, eld da of George Winthrop Haight (d 1983), of New York, USA; 2 s (Giles b 3 July 1964, Gavin b 11 May 1968), 1 da (Jennifer b 11 March 1966); *Career* RN 1947-1954; agriculturalist; memb Lloyd's 1955; MSTA 1987; *Style—* Anthony Pretor-Pinney; Somerton Erleigh, Somerset; 25 Church Rd, London SW13

PREVETT, Geoffrey James; s of James William Prevett, of Ewell, Surrey, and Helen Lillian, *née* Luckett; *b* 30 Nov 1944; *Educ* Westminster; *m* 25 June 1966, Joan, da of Thomas Bevan, of Maesteg, South Wales; 1 s (Christopher b 31 Jan 1980), (Melanie b 6 Feb 1973); *Career* admitted slr 1978; Travers Smith Braithwaite 1963-79, Lewis Lewis and Co 1979-82 (ptnr 1981), ptnr Jaques and Lewis 1982-; memb: Law Soc, Holborn Law Soc, Ecclesiastical Law Soc; *Recreations* music, theatre, reading; *Style—* Geoffrey Prevett, Esq; 22 Northcliffe Close, Worcester Park, Surrey KTF4 7DS (☎ 081 3373377), 2 South Square, Grays Inn, London WC1R 5HR (☎ 081 2429755, fax 081 4054464)

PREVETT, John Henry; OBE (1974); s of Frank George Harry Prevett (d 1981), and Florence Emily, *née* Wilson (d 1968); *b* 6 April 1933; *Educ* Oxted Co GS, John Ruskin GS; *m* 28 March 1959, Joy Maureen, da of Martin Josiah Goodchild (d 1947); 2 s (David b 1961, Steven b 1962); *Career* actuary; ptnr Bacon & Woodrow Consultants 1962-; chm: Assoc of Consltg Actuaries 1983-85, Br Def and Aid Fund for Southern Africa 1983-; memb: (lab) Reigate Borough Cncl 1963-69 and 1971-73, Reigate and Banstead Borough Cncl 1973-84 and 1986-; Freeman: City of London 1980, Worshipful Co of Actuaries 1980; FIA 1955, FPMI 1977; *Books* Actuarial Valuations of Interests in Settled Property (with C O Beard, 1973); *Recreations* wining and dining; *Clubs* Lunchtime Comment; *Style—* John Prevett, Esq, OBE; 62 Gatton Rd, Reigate, Surrey (☎ 0737 246629); Bacon & Woodrow, St Olaf House, London Bridge City, London SE1 2PE (☎ 071 357 7171, fax 071 378 8428 and 071 378 8470)

PREVETTE, Kenneth George Charles; OBE (1983); s of George William Prevette (d 1966), and Rosina Hannah, *née* Gray (d 1966); *b* 17 May 1917; *m* 1946, Sheila, da of Herbert Henry Spencer (d 1949), of North Shore, Blackpool; 1 s (Martin), 1 da (Linda); *Career* TA (Queen's Own Royal W Kent Regt) 1939-46, Colour Sgt 1939, POW 1940-45; dir: The London Cremation Co plc 1971-, Kent Co Crematorium plc 1973-, Norwich Crematorium plc 1978-83, Golders Green Crematorium Ltd 1984-; sec The Pharos Press 1946-83, clerk Golders Green Fndn 1959-83, gen sec Cremation Soc of GB 1964-83 (exec sec 1963-64), chm The Pharos Assur Friendly Soc 1978-80 (sec 1967-72), tstee Golders Green Fndn 1983-; Int Cremation Fedn: sec gen 1979-81, vice pres 1981-84, hon life memb 1984; Freeman City of London 1974; *Recreations* photography, growing trees from seeds, roses; *Style—* Kenneth Prevette, Esq, OBE; 80 Ware St, Bearsted Green, Maidstone, Kent ME14 4PG (☎ 0622 38261)

PREVITE, Hon Mrs (Phyllida); *née* Browne; da of 6 Baron Kilmaine, CBE (d 1978); *b* 1935; *m* 1959, John Edward Previté, QC; 2 s; *Style—* The Hon Mrs Previté; The Wilderness, Hampton Wick, Kingston upon Thames, Surrey

PREVOST, Brian Trevor George; s of Raymond George Prevost (d 1974), and (Winifred) Grace, *née* White (d 1981); *b* 2 May 1932; *Educ* Bradfield, Imede Lausanne Switzerland; *m* 16 June 1956, Margaret Anne, da of Lt-Col John Douglas Allder Vincent (d 1964); 3 da (Sally b 1958, Wendy b 1960, Jacky b 1964); *Career* 2 Lt RA 1951-53, Lt HAC (RHA) 1955-63; dir Sedgwick Collins & Co Ltd 1964-72, underwriting memb Lloyds 1969-79, dir Sedgwick Forbes Ltd and chm Sedgwick Forbes Reins Brokers Ltd 1972-79; Swiss Reins Co (UK) Ltd: dep chief exec 1979-83, dir and gen mangr 1983-89, md 1989-; chm and chief exec Swiss Re GB Mgmnt Ltd 1989-; chm Reins Off Assoc 1988-90 (memb Exec Ctee 1983-90, dep chm 1987-88), memb Cncl London Insurance and Reinsurance Market Assoc; *Recreations* yachting, golf, bridge; *Clubs* Royal Southern Yacht, Little Ship, Lloyds Yacht, Insur Golfing Soc of London; *Style—* Brian T G Prevost, Esq; Rickstones, 8 Orchard Way, Esher, Surrey KT10 9DY (☎ 0372 462318); Swiss Re House, 71-77 Leadenhall St, London EC3A 2PQ (☎ 071 623 3456, fax 071 929 4282, telex 884380)

PREVOST, Sir Christopher Gerald; 6 Bt (UK 1805); s of Sir George James Augustine Prevost, 5 Bt (d 1985), and Muriel Emily, *née* Oram (d 1939); *b* 25 July 1935; *Educ* Cranleigh; *m* 1964, Dolores Nelly, o da of Dezo Hoffmann; 1 s, 1 da; *Heir* s, Nicholas Marc Prevost b 13 March 1971; *Career* late 60 Regt; fndr Mailtronic Ltd, manufacturers and suppliers of mailroom equipment, chm and md 1977-; memb Business Equipment Trade Assoc 1982-; *Recreations* squash, skiing; *Style—* Sir Christopher Prevost, Bt; Highway Cottage, Berry Grove Lane, Watford, Herts WD2 8AE

PRICE *see also*: Rugge-Price, Tudor Price

PRICE, (Alan) Anthony; s of Walter Longsdon Price (d 1942), and Kathleen Lawrence (d 1937); *b* 16 Aug 1928; *Educ* The King's Sch Canterbury, Merton Coll Oxford (MA); *m* 1953, Ann, da of Norman George Stone (d 1968); 2 s (James, Simon), 1 da (Katherine); *Career* mil serv 1947-49, Capt; journalist and author; ed The Oxford Times 1972-88; *Books* The Labyrinth Makers (1970, CWA Silver Dagger), The Alamut Ambush (1971), Colonel Butler's Wolf (1972), October Men (1973), Other Paths to Glory (1974, CWA Gold Dagger 1974, Swedish Acad of Detection Prize 1978), Our Man in Camelot (1975), War Game (1976), The '44 Vintage (1978), Tomorrow's Ghost (1979), The Hour of the Donkey (1980), Soldier No More (1981), The Old Vengeful (1982), Gunner Kelly (1983), Sion Crossing (1984), Here Be Monsters (1985), For the Good of the State (1986), A New Kind of War (1987), A Prospect of Vengenance (1988), The Memory Trap (1989), The Eyes of The Fleet (1990); *Recreations* military history; *Clubs* Detection; *Style—* Anthony Price, Esq; Wayside Cottage, Horton-cum-Studley, Oxford OX9 1AW (☎ 0865 735 326)

PRICE, Barrie; s of Albert Price (d 1978), of Bradford and Mary, *née* Melvin (d 1982); *b* 13 Aug 1937; *Educ* St Bede's GS Bradford; *m* 15 April 1963, Elizabeth, da of William Murphy (d 1979); 4 s (Nicholas Becket b 1963, Joseph b 1965, Gerard b 1968, Mark b 1974), 1 da (Catherine b 1966); *Career* trainee accountant 1953-58, sr ptnr Lishman Sidwell Campbell and Price 1974- (joined 1962), chm and md Slouand Ltd (mgmnt conslts) 1968-; chm: Ripon Life Care and Housing Tst, Ripon City and Dist Devpt Assoc 1969-90; govr St Wilfrids RC Sch Ripon; memb: Ripon City Cncl (Mayor 1980-81, dep Mayor 1974-75, 1982-83 and 1987-88), Harrogate Borough DC (dep leader 1987-88, chm Econ Devpt Ctee); tstee: City of Ripon Festival (chm 1981), Yorks Film Archive, Ripon Cathedral Appeal; memb: Friends of the Venerable, Harrogate Int Festival; FCA 1968 (ACA 1959), FCCA, FBIM; *Recreations* opera, theatre, football, racing; *Clubs* Opera North, Ripon Race Course Members; *Style—* Barrie Price, Esq; Prospect House, Palace Road, City of Ripon, North Yorks HG4 1HA (☎ 0765 2058); Becket's House, Market Place, Ripon (☎ 0765 700681)

PRICE, Barry David Keith; CBE (1991), QPM (1981); s of John Leslie Price, and Lena, *née* Morgan; *b* 28 June 1933; *Educ* Southall GS; *m* 4 July 1953, Evelyne Jean; 3 da (Gaynor b 8 Aug 1954, Alison b 29 Aug 1956, Kathryn b 28 Aug 1964); *Career* Constable through ranks to Detective Chief Supt Metropolitan Police 1954-75, Asst Chief Constable Northumbria Police 1975-78, Dep Chief Constable Essex Police 1978-80, Chief Constable Cumbria Constabulary 1980-87, coordinator Nat Drugs Intelligence Unit 1987-; author articles in law enforcement and med pubns; co dir St John Ambulance Assoc 1981-87, pres English Police Golf Assoc 1981-, memb Advsy Cncl on Misuse of Drugs 1982-87, advsr to ACPO Crime Ctee on Drugs Matters 1985- (former chm and sec), memb Drug Intelligence Steering Gp 1987-; *Recreations* golf, painting, gardening; *Style—* Barry Price, Esq, CBE, QPM; National Drugs Intelligence Unit, New Scotland Yard, Broadway, London SW1H 0BG (☎ 071 2303823, fax 071 2304056, telex 918056)

PRICE, (William Frederick) Barry; OBE (1976); s of William Thomas Price (d 1984), of Hanley Swan, and Vera Evelyn, *née* Burt; *b* 12 Feb 1925; *Educ* King Edward's Sch Birmingham, Worcester Royal GS; *m* 20 March 1948, Lorraine Elisabeth Susanne, da of Maj Archibald Hoather (d 1960), of Epsom; 3 s (Adam b 1956, Matthew b 1963, Ashley b 1968), 2 da (Caroline b 1949, Amanda b 1960); *Career* joined Bd of Trade 1950: asst trade cmmr Delhi 1954-57 (Nairobi 1958-61, Dar es Salaam 1961-63), trade cmmr Accra 1963-67; FCO: first sec Sofia 1967-71, consul gen Rotterdam 1973-77, cnsllr Br Embassy Bangkok 1981-83, consul gen Amsterdam 1983-85, ret 1985; chm Anglo-Netherlands Soc 1989-; sec (now hon sec) William and Mary Tercentenary Tst 1986-; Cdr of Order of Orange-Nassau 1989; *Recreations* Open Univ student, cycling, computers; *Clubs* Oriental; *Style—* Barry Price, Esq, OBE; 46 Finchley Park, London N12 9JL (☎ 081 445 4642)

PRICE, Bernard Albert; s of Albert Price (d 1952), of Calverhall, Shrops, and Doris, *née* Whittingham (d 1959); *b* 6 Jan 1944; *Educ* Whitchurch GS Shrops, Kings Sch Rochester Kent, Merton Coll Oxford (MA); *m* 4 June 1966, Christine Mary, da of Roy William Henry Combes (d 1979), of Chelmsford, Essex; 2 s (David b 1971, John b 1976), 1 da (Emma b 1973); *Career* co clerk and chief exec Staffs CC 1983- (sr dep clerk 1980-83), clerk to the Lieutenancy Staffs 1983-, sec W Mids Forum of Strategic Local Authys 1985-; *Recreations* sailing, walking; *Style—* Bernard Price, Esq; The Cottage, Yeatsall Lane, Abbots Bromley, Rugeley, Staffs (☎ 0283 840269); County Buildings, Martin St, Stafford, Staffs (☎ 0785 223121)

PRICE, Brian Derek; s of Gp Capt Derek Price (d 1988), and Lorna Mary MacMullen, *née* Bulleid; *b* 2 Oct 1939; *Educ* Tonbridge; *m* 18 June 1966, Juliet Elisabeth Rosamund, da of Maj Sir Reginald Lawrence William Williams, Bt, MBE, ED (d 1970); 2 s (Edmund Hugh Owain b 1969, Henry William Frederick b 1973); *Career* CA; ptnr Kidsons Impey (formerly Hodgson Impey and Hodgson Harris) 1974-90, seconded as dep sec DOE 1988-89; chm London Soc of CAs 1979-80 (ctee memb 1967-80), tstee and treas Fight for Sight 1980-, treas Fight for Sight Special Appeal 1987-, govr Royal Nat Coll for the Blind Hereford 1982-90, memb cncl ICAEW 1987-; ACA 1962, FCA 1967; *Recreations* history, walking; *Clubs* Athenaeum, City of London, Leander, London Rowing; *Style—* Brian Price, Esq; 52 Hazlewell Rd, Putney, London SW15 6LR

PRICE, Charles Beaufort; s of Mervyn Beaufort Price, and Jessie, *née* Price; *b* 7 Nov 1945; *Educ* King's Coll Taunton, Queen Mary Coll London (BA); *m* 29 May 1971, Patricia Ann Price; 1 s (Gareth Charles b 29 March 1978), 1 da (Isabelle Louise b 8 Sept 1981); *Career* md N M Rothschild & Sons (Singapore) Limited 1976-79, dir N M Rothschild & Sons Limited 1985-; memb Lombard Assoc; AIB; *Recreations* gardening, rugby, opera; *Clubs* Tanglin (Singapore); *Style—* Charles Price, Esq; N M Rothschild & Sons Ltd, New Court, St Swithins Lane, London EC4 (☎ 071 280 5000)

PRICE, The Hon Charles H; s of Charles Harry Price and Virginia, *née* Ogden; *b* 1 April 1931; *Educ* Univ of Missouri; *m* Carol Ann, *née* Swanson; 2 s, 3 da; *Career* pres Linwood Securities 1960-81; chm: Price Candy Co 1969-81, American Bank Corpn 1973-81, American Bank and Tst Co 1973-81, American Mortgage Co 1973-81, Ameribanc Inc 1989-; US ambass: Belgium 1981-83, UK 1983-89; dir: BA, Hanson plc London, New York Times Co, Texaco Inc NY, United Telecommunications Inc Kansas City; chm Midwest Res Inst Kansas City, hon Fell Regent's Coll 1986, Hon Dr Westminster Coll Missouri; Salvation Army's William Booth award 1985; Tstee Citation award Midwest Res Inst 1987; *Recreations* golf, tennis, shooting; *Clubs* White's, Mark's, Swinley Forest Golf, The Brook (NY), Metropolitan (Washington); *Style—* The Hon Charles H Price II; 5049 Wornall Rd, Apt 1011 C-D, Kansas City, Missouri 64112, USA

PRICE, Christopher; s of Stanley Price (d 1988), of Sheffield, and Katherine Phyllis, *née* Thornton; *b* 26 Jan 1932; *Educ* Leeds GS, Queen's Coll Oxford; *m* 26 June 1956, Annie Greirson, da of James Ross (d 1987), of Edinburgh; 2 s (Anthony Ross b 1959, Michael John b 1962), 1 da (Jennifer Margaret b 1957); *Career* ed New Education 1966-68, educn corr New Statesman 1968-74, dir Leeds Poly 1986-; MP (Lab): Birmingham Perry Barr 1966-70, Lewisham West 1974-83; chm Select Ctee on Educn Sci and the Arts 1979-83; fell Int Inst of Biotechnology 1984, FRSA 1987; *Books* The Confait Confessions (1979); *Clubs* Athenaeum; *Style—* Christopher Price; Churchwood, Beckett Park, Leeds LS6 3QS (☎ 0532 755508); Leeds Polytechnic, Leeds, LS1 3HE (☎ 0532 832600)

PRICE, Christopher James (Chris); s of Alan James Price, of 3 Frome Ave, Redhill, Hereford, and Constance Mary, *née* Preedy; *b* 30 March 1960; *Educ* Haywood HS; *m* 12 April 1980, Linda Mary, da of Alan Edmund Thomas Payne; 1 da (Natasha Louise b 5 Sept 1980); *Career* professional footballer; Hereford Utd: debut v Notts County 1977, 330 league appearances, 27 goals; 83 league appearances Blackburn Rovers (11 goals), currently Aston Villa (over 90 appearances); 1 England youth cap v Norway 1977; Full Member's Cup Winner's medal with Blackburn Rovers 1987; *Recreations* snooker, ten pin bowling, darts; *Style—* Chris Price, Esq; Aston Villa FC, Villa Park, Trinit Rd, Birmingham (☎ 021 327 6604)

PRICE, Christopher John Stuart; s of John Eric Price, of Weymouth Park, Salcombe, S Devon, and Mary Stuart, *née* Hicks; *b* 16 March 1939; *Educ* Brentwood Sch; *m* 8 Sept 1962, Elizabeth Kay, da of Geoffrey Egerton Gilbert; 1 s (Matthew Stuart b 28 Dec 1965), 1 da (Emma Ruth b 22 Jan 1968); *Career* chm Sedgwick James Credit Ltd, dir Sedgwick James Europe Ltd; Freeman City of London, Liveryman Worshipful Co of Insurers; CBIM; *Recreations* gardening, walking, hunting, music; *Clubs* City of London; *Style—* Christopher Price, Esq; The Oasts, Lower Cousley Wood, Wadhurst, East Sussex TN5 6HF (☎ 089 288 3106); Sedgwick James Credit Ltd, Sedgwick House, The Sedgwick Centre, London E1 8DX (☎ 071 481 5229, fax 071 377 3199, telex 882131)

PRICE, Lt-Col Christopher Keith; s of Col David Keith Price, MC, TD (d 1981), of Upper Sydenhurst, Chiddingfold, Surrey, and Barbara Christian, *née* Naumann; *b* 12 July 1947; *Educ* Charterhouse; *m* 6 April 1974, Michele, da of Edward Asa-Thomas, TD (d 1983), of Whitethorn House, Crawley, Winchester, Hants; 1 s (Andrew b 2 Nov 1980); *Career* cmmnd 4/7 Royal Dragoon Guards 1966, Troop Ldr 1966-70, Regtl Signals Offr/Asst Adj 1970-71, ADC to Cdr Land Forces NI 1971-73, 2 i/c Sqdn 4/7

DG 1973-75, GSO3 3 Div 1975-77, Staff Offr to Res Cmmr Designate to Rhodesia 1977-78, chief of staff HQ 33 Amd Bde 1980-81, Sqdn Cdr 4/7 DG 1982-83, Directing Staff Army Coll 1984-86, CO 14/20 King's Hussars 1987-; memb Grand Mil Race Ctee; Freeman: City of London, Worshipful Co of Grocers 1977; *Recreations* hunting, shooting, polo, fishing; *Clubs* Cavalry & Guards; *Style*— Lt-Col Christopher Price

PRICE, Cyril; s of Ieuan Penry Price (d 1975), and Elsie (d 1980); *b* 26 Feb 1924; *Educ* Cathays Cardiff; *m* 1946, Nancy Joy, da of Fredric Seaton, JP, of Australia (d 1966); 1 s, 1 da; *Career* Fleet Air Arm Lt RNVR (A) 828 Sqdn HMS Formidable, HMS Implacable; dir: Tennant Guaranty Ltd 1964-83 (renamed The Royal Bank of Canada Trade & Finance Ltd 1982), Orford Trading Co Ltd 1964-83, Tennant Guaranty Trust Ltd 1969-83, Tennant Guaranty Int Ltd 1976-83; sr int exec AMCA Netherlands BV 1983-84, int business consult 1984-; chm High Wycombe Centre Inst of Dir's 1988-, cncl memb Econ League (SE Region) 1985-; *Clubs* Hazlemere Golf and Country, IOD; *Style*— Cyril Price, Esq; 11 Hubert Day Close, Beaconsfield, Bucks HP9 1TL (☎ 0494 670321)

PRICE, Sir David Ernest Campbell; DL (Hants 1982), MP (C) Eastleigh 1955-; s of Maj Villiers Price (d 1982), and Margaret Campbell Currie (d 1930); *b* 20 Nov 1924; *Educ* Eton, Trinity Coll Cambridge, Univ of Yale USA; *m* 1960, Rosemary Eugénie Evelyn, da of Cyril F Johnston, OBE (d 1950); 1 da (Arabella); *Career* WWII served 1 Bn Scots Gds, HQ 56 (London) Div, Italy; ICI 1949-62; Parly sec BOT 1962-64, oppn front bench spokesman on Sci and Technol 1964-70, Parly sec Miny of Technol June-Oct 1970, Parly sec Miny of Aviation Supply 1970-71, Parly under sec state Aerospace DTI 1971-72; memb Select Ctee on: Tport 1979-83, Social Servs 1984-, Health 1991-; conslt Western United Investment Company Ltd 1973-, vice pres Inst of Industl Mangrs 1973-, chm Parly & Scientific Ctee 1973 and 1979-82; kt 1980; *Recreations* wine, history of art, music, cooking, gardening; *Clubs* Beefsteak; *Style*— Sir David Price, DL, MP; 16 Laxford House, London SW1W 9JU; Forest Lodge, Moonhills Lane, Beaulieu, Hampshire SO42 7YW; The House of Commons, London SW1

PRICE, David George; s of Lt Cdr Rodney Athelstan Price, RN (ka 1943), and Elizabeth Peace, *née* Cole-Hamilton; *b* 22 March 1940; *Educ* Wellington, Univ of Cambridge (MA), London Coll Estate Mgmnt; *m* 14 March 1970, Diana Catherine, da of T A S Davie (d 1978), of Grangehill, Beith, Ayrshire; 2 s (Toby Charles Rodney b 18 Oct 1972, Simon James Edward b 26 June 1974); *Career* 2 Lt Black Watch (TA) 1964, Lt 1966; md Titan Tanks Ltd 1966-74, chm and md Power Plastics Ltd 1974-87; Liveryman Worshipful Co Merchant Taylors; pres Made Up Textiles Assoc 1989; *Recreations* tennis, opera, gardening; *Style*— David Price, Esq; Woodcock, Thirsk, N Yorks YO7 2AB

PRICE, David William James; s of Richard J E Price (d 1983), of Quinta da Romeira, Bucelas, Portugal, and Miriam Joan, *née* Dunsford; *b* 11 June 1947; *Educ* Ampleforth, CCC Oxford (MA); *m* 1971, Shervie Ann Lander, da of Sir James Whitaker, 3 Bt, *qv*; 1 s (William b 1973), 1 da (Hesther b 1971); *Career* merchant banker; dir: Warburg Investmt Mgmnt Ltd 1978-, S G Warburg & Co Ltd 1982-87; chm Mercury Asset Mgmnt plc 1983-, dep chm Mercury Asset Mgmnt Gp plc 1987-; cncllr London Borough of Lambeth 1979-82; *Clubs* Brooks's; *Style*— David Price, Esq; 39 Old Town, Clapham, London SW4 (☎ 071 720 4359); Harrington Hall, Spilsby, Lincs; Mercury Asset Management plc, 33 King William St, London EC4 (☎ 071 280 2800)

PRICE, Edgar Charles Vincent; TD (1969); s of Charles James Price (d 1958), of Erith, Kent, and Ellen Mable, *née* Fort (d 1963); *b* 16 Sept 1927; *Educ* Dulwich, Middx Med Sch (MB BS); *m* 3 May 1958, Diane Audrey, da of Arthur Smith (d 1974), of Birmingham; 1 s (Julian b 1961), 1 da (Susan b 1964); *Career* TA 1968-87 (Nat Serv 1954-56, AER 1956-68); conslt orthopaedic surgn York Hosps 1967-; chm: Yorkshire Regnl Orthopaedic Sub Ctee 1981-, York Div BMA 1986-88; pres Hosp Conslts and Specialists Assoc 1986-88, memb York Health Authy 1987-90, RCS regnl advsr in orthopaedics Yorkshire 1987-, chm Yorkshire Orthopaedic Trg Sub Ctee 1989-; FRSM 1959, FRCSEd 1962 (ad eundem Eng 1990), FBOA 1967; *Recreations* hill walking, idleness; *Clubs* Yorkshire; *Style*— Edgar Price, Esq, TD; Orthopaedic Dept, York District Hosp, Wiggington Rd, York (☎ 0904 631313)

PRICE, Eric Hardiman Mockford; s of Frederick Hardiman Price, and Florence Nellie Hannah; *b* 14 Nov 1931; *Educ* St Marylebone GS, Christ's Coll Cambridge (BA, MA); *m* 3 Feb 1963, Diana Teresa Anne Mary Stanley, da of Stanley Joseph Leckie Robinson (d 1962), of Harbury Hall, Warwicks; 1 s (Julian b 27 Feb 1969), 3 da (Caroline b 29 Jan 1964, Nichola b 28 March 1966, Ashling b 6 July 1970); *Career* Nat Serv Army 1950-52, HAC 1952-57; economist: Central Electricity Authy Electricity Cncl 1957-58, Br Iron and Steel Fedn 1958-62; chief economist Port of London Authy 1962-67; Miny of Tport: sr econ advsr 1966-69, chief econ advsr 1967-71, dir of econs 1971-75; DOE: under sec econs 1972-76, dir of econs and statistics 1975-76; under sec econs and statistics: Depts of Trade Indust and Consumer Protection 1977-80, Dept of Energy 1980-; dir Robinson Bros Ltd Ryders Green 1985-; Br Inst of Energy Econs: memb Cncl 1980-, vice chm 1981-82 and 1988-89, chm 1982-85; memb BIEE, FREconS, FSS, FInstD; *Recreations* squash, tennis, local history; *Clubs* Moor Park Golf; *Style*— Eric Price, Esq; Batchworth Ho, Batchworth Heath Farm, London Rd, Rickmansworth, Herts WD3 1QB (☎ 09274 24471); Department of Energy, 1 Palace St, London SW1 (☎ 071 211 3440)

PRICE, Lady; Eva Mary; *née* Dickson; *m* 1939, as his 2 w, Sir Henry Philip Price, 1 and last Bt (d 1963); *Career* chm Nat Liberal Cncl 1952-53 and cr Bt 1953; *Style*— Lady Price; c/o Midland Bank, 60 Broadway, Hayward's Heath, Sussex

PRICE, Sir Francis Caradoc Rose; 7 Bt (UK 1815); s of Sir Rose Francis Price, 6 Bt (d 1979), and Kathleen June, yr da of Norman William Hutchinson, of Melbourne, Aust; *b* 9 Sept 1950; *Educ* Eton, Trinity Coll Univ of Melbourne, Univ of Alberta; *m* 1975, The Hon Madam Justice Marguerite Jean, da of Roy Samuel Trussler, of Victoria, BC; 3 da; *Heir* bro, Norman William Rose Price; *Career* barr and slr Canada, ptnr Reynolds Mirth Richards & Farmer; *Books* Pipelines in Western Canada (1975), Mortgage Actions in Alberta (1985); *Recreations* cricket, jogging, theatre, opera; *Clubs* Centre, Faculty; *Style*— Sir Francis Price, Bt; 9677 95 Ave, Edmonton, Alberta T6C 2A3, Canada (☎ home 403 469 9555, work 403 425 9510)

PRICE, Sir Frank Leslie; DL (Hereford and Worcs and Co of W Midlands 1977); s of George Frederick Price (d 1978), and Lucy Price (d 1978); *b* 26 July 1922; *Educ* St Mathias Sch Birmingham, Vittoria St Arts Sch; *m* 1, 1944 (m dis 1976), Maisie Edna, da of Albert Davis, of Handsworth Wood, Birmingham; 1 s (Noel Bayley); m 2 (m dis 1984), Veronica, da of Zubadri Singh; m 3, Daphne, da of John Ling (d 1947), of Highgate; *Career* md Murrayfield Real Estate Co Ltd 1958-68; chm: Midlands Arts Centre for Young People 1960-66, Birmingham and Midlands Investmts Ltd 1967-74, Telford New Town Corp 1968-72, Br Waterways Bd 1968-84, Wharf Holdings 1968-72, ML Alkan Ltd 1972-75, Sir Frank Price and Compania Sociedad Colectiva 1985-; dir: Comp Devpts Assoc 1968-80, Nat Exhibition Centre Ltd 1970-76, Butlers and Colonial Wharfs Ltd 1971-76; cncllr and alderman Birmingham City Cncl 1949-84, DL Warwickshire 1969-77; memb: Birmingham Cncl Town and Country Planning Assoc 1954-74, Nat Water Cncl 1975-79, Eng Tourist Bd 1975-82; pres Br Assoc Industl Eds 1979-83; FSVA, FCIT, FRSA; kt 1966; *Clubs* Reform; *Style*— Sir Frank Price, DL; Pueblo Diana Apartado, 534 Mojacar Playa, Almeria 04638, Spain (☎ 51 478 915, fax 51 478 963)

PRICE, Frederick Enoch; s of Frederick William Rayner Price (d 1975), and Gladys May, *née* Shingleton (d 1979); *b* 4 May 1930; *Educ* Dudley GS Worcs, Hertford Coll Oxford (BA, MA); *m* 19 June 1965, Margaret Ann, da of Norman Forsyth Wilson (d 1961); 1 s (Christopher Forsyth b July 1966), 1 da (Joanna b Sept 1970); *Career* graduate trainee Martins Bank 1953- 57, articled clerk Cooper Bros and Co 1957-60, sr ptnr Blackham Cox Taylor and Co 1971-, underwriting memb Lloyds 1981-; memb Edgbaston Rotary Club; FCA, ACMA; *Recreations* reading, travels; *Style*— Frederick Price, Esq; Blackham Cox Taylor and Co, First Floor, Calthorpe House, Hagley Rd, Birmingham B16 8QY (☎ 021 455 9060, fax 021 455 0854)

PRICE, Rt Hon George Cadle; PC (1982); s of William Price, by his w Irene Cecilia Escalante de Price; *b* 15 Jan 1919; *Educ* Holy Redeemer Primary Sch Belize City; *Career* city cncllr Belize City 1947-65 (intermittently mayor), fndr People's Utd Pty 1950 (leader 1956-), memb Nat Assembly 1954-, PM Belize 1981- (Premier 1964-81 when independence granted); *Style*— The Rt Hon George Price; Office of The Prime Minister, Belmoplan, Belize

PRICE, Hugh Maxwell; s of Capt Denis Lewin Price, of Crossways House, Cowbridge, S Glamorgan, and Patricia Rosemary, *née* Metcalfe; *b* 25 April 1950; *Educ* Haileybury; *m* 14 June 1975, Sarah Anne, da of Royden Eric Snape; 1 s (Andrew b 17 March 1979), 1 da (Emma b 10 May 1982); *Career* admitted slr 1975; ptnr Morgan Bruce (formerly Morgan Bruce & Hardwickes) Cardiff 1978-, dep dist judge; hon asst sec Cardiff Law Soc; memb Law Soc; *Recreations* squash, tennis, gardening; *Clubs* Cardiff Athletic, Cowbridge Squash and Tennis; *Style*— Hugh Price, Esq; Orchard House, Llanblethian, nr Cowbridge, South Glamorgan C87 7EY (☎ 04463 3590); Morgan Bruce, Bradley Court, Park Place, Cardiff CF1 3DP (☎ 0222 233 677, fax 0222 399 288)

PRICE, Janet Esson Grace (Jinty); da of Dr Duncan McKenzie Stewart, of Scotland, and Janet Elizabeth Stewart (d 1980); *b* 8 Dec 1957; *Educ* Merchant Taylors Sch for Girls, Newnham Coll Cambridge (MA); *m* 25 Aug 1984, (Owen) David Boucher Price, s of Henry George Boucher Price, of Midlands; 1 s (Cameron Owen Stewart b 12 July 1989); *Career* ptnr de Zoete & Bevan 1986 (joined 1980), dir BZW Res 1986-; AMSIA, memb Stock Exchange; *Recreations* hillwalking, foreign travel, horse riding; *Style*— Mrs Jinty Price; BZW, Ebbgate Hse, 2 Swan Lane, London EC4R 3TS (☎ 071 623 2323)

PRICE, Hon Mrs (Joanna Mary); *née* Cavendish; er da of 5 Baron Chesham, PC, TD (d 1989); *b* 20 July 1938; *m* 1960, Peter Henry Mabille Price; 1 s, 1 da; *Style*— The Hon Mrs Price; Avington Manor, Alresford Road, Winchester, Hants

PRICE, John Alan (Jack); QC (1980); s of Frederick Leslie Price (d 1976); *b* 11 Sept 1938; *Educ* Stretford GS, Univ of Manchester (LLB Hons); *m* 1, 1964 (m dis 1982), Elizabeth Myra, da of Stanley Priest; 1 s, 1 da; m 2, 1984, Alison Elizabeth, da of Stanley Ward; *Career* called to the bar Gray's Inn 1961, in practice on Northern Circuit, rec Crown Ct 1980-; *Recreations* tennis, golf; *Style*— Jack Price, Esq, QC; 25 Byrom St, Manchester M3 4PF (☎ 061 834 5238); 5 Essex Court, Temple, London EC4Y 9AH (☎ 071 353 4363)

PRICE, John Philip; s of Eifion Wyn Price, of Rhayader, Powys, and Kathleen, *née* Woodfield; *b* 11 Dec 1949; *Educ* Monmouth Sch, CCC Oxford (MA, BPhil); *Career* called to the Bar Inner Temple 1974-; dir gen Dairy Trade Fedn 1986-; *Books* The English Legal System (1979); *Style*— John Price, Esq; 36 Rossmore Court, Park Rd, London NW1 6XX (☎ 071 402 6658); Dairy Trade Federation, 19 Cornwall Terrace, London NW1 4QP (☎ 071 486 7244, fax 071 487 4734, telex 262027)

PRICE, Air Vice-Marshal John Walter; CBE (1979, OBE 1973); s of Henry Walter Price (d 1984), and Myrza, *née* Griffiths (d 1958); *b* 26 Jan 1930; *Educ* Solihull Sch, RAF Coll Cranwell; *m* 1956, Margaret Sinclair (d 1989), da of John McIntyre (d 1960), of Sydney, Aust; *Career* cmmnd from RAF Coll Cranwell 1950; Sqdn flying appts: Vampires and Venoms Germany, Meteors with 77 Sqdn RAAF Korea (despatches 1953), Vampires and Meteors Aust; staff appts in Air Miny 1961-64, cmd No 110 Sqdn Sycamores and Whirlwinds Malaya and Borneo 1964-66, PSO to CAS 1968-70, cmd No 72 Sqdn Wessex 1970-72, dep dir Ops MOD Air 1973-75, cmd RAF Laarbruch (Buccaneers and Jaguars) Germany 1976-78, Gp Capt Ops HQ Strike Cmd 1979, dir Ops Strike MOD Air 1980-82, ACAS Ops 1982-84, ret as Air Vice-Marshal 1984; Clyde Petroleum plc 1984- (mangr external rels 1986); memb Bd of Govrs Solihull Sch 1979- (elected chm 1982); *Recreations* golf, cabinet making, motor cycling; *Clubs* RAF; *Style*— Air Vice-Marshal John Price, CBE; 2 Palace Yard, Hereford (☎ 0432 272292); Coddington Ct, Coddington Ledbury, Herefordshire (☎ 053 186811)

PRICE, June, Lady; (Kathleen) June; da of late Norman W Hutchinson, of Toorak, Melbourne, Australia; *m* 1949, Sir Rose Francis Price, 6 Bt (d 1979); 2 s; *Style*— June, Lady Price; Dormer Cottage, Park Rd, Stoke Poges, Bucks

PRICE, (Arthur) Leolin; QC (1968, Bahamas 1969, NSW 1987); s of Evan Price (d 1959), and Ceridwen Price (d 1974); *b* 11 May 1924; *Educ* Judd Sch Tonbridge, Keble Coll Oxford (scholar, MA); *m* 1963, Hon Rosalind, *qv*; 2 s, 2 da; *Career* called to the Bar Middle Temple 1949; *ad eundem* Lincoln's Inn 1959; bencher Middle Temple 1970 (treas 1990); govr Gt Ormond St Hosp for Sick Children 1972-, chm Ctee of Mgmnt Inst of Child Health 1976-, govr Christ Coll Brecon 1977-, chllr Diocese of Swansea and Brecon 1982-; dir: Marine Adventure Sailing Trust plc 1982-89, Thornton Asian Emerging Markets Investment Trust plc 1989-; vice chm Soc of Cons Lawyers 1987-, chm Child Health Res Investment Trust plc (now Thornton Pan-European Investment Trust) 1987 (dir 1980-); *Clubs* Carlton; *Style*— Leolin Price, Esq, QC; 32 Hampstead Grove, London NW3 6SR (☎ 071 435 9843); 10 Old Sq, Lincoln's Inn, London WC2A 3SU (☎ 071 405 0758); Moor Park, Llanbedr, Crickhowell, Powys NP8 1SS (☎ 0873 810443)

PRICE, Leonard Sidney; OBE (1974); s of late William Price, and late Dorothy Price; *b* 19 Oct 1922; *Educ* Central Fndn Sch London; *m* 1958, Adrienne Mary, *née* Wilkinson; *Career* WWII 1942-45; Dip Serv 1939-81; FO 1939-42 and 1945-48, Chungking (later vice consul) 1948, Mexico City 1950, Rome 1953, vice consul (later second sec) Katmandu 1954, consul Split 1960, consul and first sec Copenhagen 1963, FO (later FCO) 1967, first sec Kuching 1970, Suva 1972, Parly clerk FCO 1975, cnsllr (admin) Canberra 1977-81, ret 1981; hon treas St John Ambulance in Somerset 1983-88; *Recreations* carpentry; *Clubs* Civil Serv; *Style*— Leonard Price, Esq, OBE; 5 Staplegrove Manor, Taunton, Somerset TA2 6EG (☎ 0823 337 093)

PRICE, Lionel Dennis Dixon; s of Flt Lt Harold Price (d 1988), of Birkenhead, and Florence Mitchley, *née* Thompson; *b* 2 Feb 1946; *Educ* Bolton Sch, CCC Cambridge (MA); *m* 19 Oct 1968, Sara Angela, da of Flt Lt Ronald William Holt, of Gerrards Cross, Bucks; 3 s (Matthew b 1972, Edward b & d 1974, James b 1975); *Career* Bank of England 1967-79, alternate exec dir IMF 1979-81; Bank of England: head Info Div 1981-84, head Int Div 1985-90, head Economics Div 1990-; *Recreations* genealogy, golf; *Clubs* Overseas Bankers; *Style*— Lionel D D Price, Esq; Bank of England, London EC2R 8AH (☎ 071 601 4418, fax 071 601 5288)

PRICE, Margaret Berenice; CBE (1982); da of late Thomas Glyn Price; *b* 13 April 1941; *Educ* Pontllanfraith Secondary Sch, Trinity Coll of Music London (hon fellow); *Career* opera singer; debut 1962 with Welsh Nat Opera, since then has appeared in all the major opera houses: La Scala, Vienna State, Munich, Paris, Hamburg, San Francisco, Metropolitan (New York), Chicago; also concert and Lieder career, renowned for her interpretation of Mozart; Elizabeth Schumann Prize for Lieder, Ricordi Prize for Opera, Silver Medal Worshipful Co of Musicians; Bayerische Kammersängerin 1979; Hon DMus Wales 1983; *Style—* Miss Margaret Price, CBE; Bayerisch Staatsoper München, Max-Joseph-Platz 2, 8000 München 22, W Germany

PRICE, Hon Mrs (Margaret Joan); *née* Nelson; JP (Warwicks); da of 1 Baron Nelson of Stafford (d 1962); *b* 1915; *m* 1941, Edward Michael Price; 3 da; *Style—* The Hon Mrs Price, JP; Frankton Manor, Frankton, Warwickshire

PRICE, Mary Elizabeth; da of David Oglesby, of Slough, Berks, and Dora, *née* Mason; *b* 27 Aug 1943; *Educ* Bishop Otter Teacher Training Coll; *m* 5 April 1969, Peter Edwin Price, s of Herbert George William Price, of Burnham, Bucks; *Career* teacher: Bartholomew Tipping Sch Stokenchurch Bucks 1964-65, Lynch Hill Sch Slough 1965-79; self employed supplier and engraver of sports trophies 1979-; memb: Eng Women's Bowls Assoc, Eng Women's Indoor Bowls Assoc; *Recreations* bowls; *Clubs* Burnham (Bucks), Desborough (Maidenhead); *Style—* Mrs Peter Price

PRICE, (John) Maurice; QC (1976); s of Edward Samuel Price; *b* 4 May 1922; *Educ* Grove Park Sch Wrexham, Trinity Coll Cambridge; *m* 1945, Mary, da of Dr Horace Gibson, DSO; 2 s; *Career* RN 1941-46, Lt RNVR, barr Gray's Inn 1949, memb Senate of Inns of Ct and the Bar 1975-78; *Clubs* Flyfishers'; *Style—* J Maurice Price, Esq, QC; Bowzell Place, Weald, Sevenoaks, Kent TN14 6NF; 2 New Sq, Lincoln's Inn, WC2A 3RU (☎ 071 242 6201)

PRICE, Dr (Rhys) Michael John; s of Lt-Col Rhys Neville Griffiths Price, MBE, ERD, of 30 Chancellor House, MT Ephraim, Tunbridge Wells, Kent, and Marjory, *née* Body; *b* 25 Feb 1944; *Educ* Blundells, Selwyn Coll Cambridge (MA), Middx Hosp Med Sch (MB BChir); *m* 17 Aug 1968, Hilary, da of Norman Butters, TD (d 1979), of Aldeburgh, Suffolk; 2 s (Rupert b 1970, Jeremy b 1973); *Career* Surgn Lt Cdr HMS President RNR 1977-83; princ gen practice 1970-, memb Herts Local Med Ctee 1974-77, assoc regnl advsr gen practice NW Thames 1982-; RCGP: hon sec and chm Herts and Beds faculty 1978-84, ed News and Views RCGP journal 1983-84, memb occasional papers ed bd 1983-; Freeman City of London 1976, Liveryman Worshipful Co of Apothecaries; 1972; MRCGP 1976, FRCGP 1984; *Recreations* travel, fitness training; *Clubs* BMA, Royal Naval Med; *Style—* Dr Michael Price; 38 Oakwood, Berkhamsted, Herts (☎ 0442 866871); The Surgery, Parkwood Drive, Hemel Hempstead, Herts (☎ 0442 50117)

PRICE, Norman George; JP (1961); s of George Strongitharm Price (d 1942); *b* 14 Nov 1922; *Educ* Rockferry HS, Univ of Liverpool, Univ of London (MSc); *m* 1945, Grace Dorothy, da of Sydney Russell Barratt-Melling; 2 da; *Career* Merchant Navy 1940-46, Miny of Supply 1950-54, Colonial Serv Fiji 1954-58, Granada Group Ltd 1958-62; personnel dir: Carreras Ltd 1962-71, J Bibby Sons Ltd 1971-81; educn conslt Assoc of Business Exec 1981-82; chm: Dunmow Bench Domestic Ct, Boleyns Estate Ltd 1971-; memb: Essex Magistrates Cts Ctee, Essex Probation Ctee, Central Cncl Magistrates Cts Ctees; Dr res LSE 1985-, govr Birkbeck Coll London Univ 1990-; sec Donkey Breed Soc 1982-85; *Recreations* racing, gardening, reading; *Clubs* Reform, Newmarket Race; *Style—* Norman Price, Esq, JP; Boleyns, Duton Hill, Dunmow, Essex CM6 2DU (☎ 0371 870419)

PRICE, Norman William Rose; s of Sir Rose Francis Price, 6 Bt (d 1979), and Kathleen June, yr da of Norman William Hutchinson, of Melbourne, Australia; hp of bro, Sir Francis Caradoc Rose, 7 Bt; *b* 17 March 1953; *Educ* Eton, Gordonstoun; *m* 1987, Charlotte Louise, da of Randolph Rex Bivar Baker, of Yelverton, Devon; 1 s (Benjamin William Rose b 16 Sept 1989); *Career* restaurateur; *Style—* Norman Price, Esq; 73 Fawnbrake Avenue, London SE24 0BE

PRICE, Dr Paul Anthony; s of Wolf Price, of London, and Dinah, *née* Shafar; *b* 15 May 1949; *Educ* Christ's Coll GS Finchley, UCL (BSc), UCH Med Sch (MB BS); *m* 15 March 1985, Sandra Margaret, *née* Miller; *Career* sr house offr physician: Brompton Hosp, Enfield Dist Gen Hosp 1973-75; hon registrar and Parkinson's Disease Soc res fell KCH 1977-78, registrar UCH 1978-79, hon sr registrar Bart's 1979-83, sr registrar St George's Hosp Gp London 1983-85, conslt physician Princess Margaret Hosp Swindon 1985-; MRCP, FRSM, memb BMA; *Books* chapters in books on neurology and endocrinology; *Recreations* music, playing the bassoon; *Style—* Dr Paul Price; Department of Medicine, Princess Margaret Hospital, Okus Rd, Swindon SN1 4JU (☎ 0793 536231 ext 3343)

PRICE, Peter Nicholas; MEP (EDG) Lancs W 1979-84, London SE 1984-; s of late Rev Dewi Emlyn Price; *b* 19 Feb 1942; *Educ* Worcester Royal GS, Aberdare Boys' GS, Southampton Univ; *Career* slr; sr ptnr Peter Price & Ptnrs 1969-80; chm Budgetary Control Ctee Euro Parl 1989- (vice chm 1979-84); EDG spokesman: on Legal Affrs Ctee 1984-87, on Budgets Ctee 1986-89; rapporteur for several budgetary and legal reports; former nat vice chm: Young Cons, Cons Political Centre; former sec Foreign Affrs Forum; former memb Cons Nat Exec Ctee; memb: EDG, ACP-EEC Jt Assembly, RIIA; *Recreations* theatre, music, photography; *Style—* Peter Price, Esq, MEP; 60 Marlings Park Ave, Chislehurst, Kent BR7 6RD (☎ 0689 820681, fax 0689 890622); European Parliament, 97-113 Rue Belliard, 1040 Bruxelles, Belgium (☎ 010 32 2 284 3610)

PRICE, (Llewelyn) Ralph; CBE (1972); s of Llewelyn David Price (d 1962); *b* 23 Oct 1912; *Educ* Quarry Bank Sch Liverpool; *m* 1939, Vera Patricia, da of C H Harrison (d 1935); 1 s, 2 da; *Career* chm: Honeywell Ltd 1972-88, ML Hldgs Ltd 1975-87, Honeywell Advsy Cncl 1981-88, Enborne Foods Ltd 1989-; dir American Chamber of Commerce 1976-81; former memb NEDC Electronics Ctee, pres Br Indust Measurement and Control Trade Assoc 1972-77; FCA; *Recreations* golf, music, bridge; *Clubs* RAC, Temple Golf; *Style—* Ralph Price, Esq, CBE; Nascot, Pinkneys Drive, Pinkneys Green, Maidenhead, Berks (☎ 0628 28270)

PRICE, Richard Henry; s of Henry George Price, of Monmouth, Gwent, and Nesta Suzanne, *née* Jones (d 1986); *b* 13 July 1944; *Educ* Monmouth Sch, UCL (BSc Econ), Univ of Cambridge (PGCE); *m* 29 March 1969, Sally Josephine, da of Col John Lewis McCowen, of Devon; 3 s (Guy b 1970, Toby b 1972, Tom b 1980); *Career* sch master Queens Coll Taunton 1968-70; CBI 1970-: head of Indust Trends Dept 1973-79, dep then dir of regions 1979-83, dir of employment affrs 1983-87, exec dir for govt rels 1987-90, dep DG 1990-; memb: Cncl of ACAS 1984-, MSC Trg Cmmn 1988-89, Soc of Business Economists; *Recreations* golf, bridge, skiing, cricket, gardening; *Clubs* Oxford and Cambridge; *Style—* Richard Price, Esq; 10 Beechwood Grove, East Acton Lane, London W3 (☎ 081 740 8357); Kingscot, The Parade, Monmouth, Gwent; CBI Centre Point, 103 New Oxford St, London WC1A 1DU (☎ 071 379 7400)

PRICE, Richard Stephen; s of Dr David Brian Price, OBE, of The Croft, 81 Park St, Bridgend, Mid Glamorgan, and Menna Myles, *née* Jones (d 1988); *b* 27 May 1953; *Educ* Cowbridge GS, Univ of Leeds (Hons); *m* 3 May 1980, Nicola Mary, da of Philip Griffin, of 7 Virginia Close, Henstridge, Nr Templecombe, Somerset; 1 s (Nicholas b 13 Sept 1988), 1 da (Roseanna b 4 Dec 1986); *Career* admitted slr 1977; McKenna and Co (ptnr 1984 i/c ME practice 1984-88); memb City of London Slrs Co; memb Law Soc; *Recreations* golf; *Style—* Richard Price, Esq; Mitre House, 160 Aldersgate St, London EC1A 4DD (☎ 071 606 9000, fax 071 606 9100, telex 27251)

PRICE, Air Vice-Marshal Robert George; CB (1983); *b* 1928; *Career* RAF Coll Cranwell 1950; AOA HQ Strike Command 1981-; *Style—* Air Vice-Marshal Robert Price, CB; c/o Barclays Bank, Easingwold, Yorks

PRICE, Robert Thomas; s of Richard James Price (d 1978), of Monfa, Beach Bank, Criccieth, Gwynedd, and Laura Jane, *née* Thomas; *b* 10 Oct 1932; *Educ* Porthmadog GS, Univ Coll of Wales Aberystwyth (LLB); *m* 14 Oct 1978, Ann Wyn, da of Hugh John Hughes (d 1978), of Bryneglwys Ynys Talsarnau, Gwynedd; 1 da (Anna Eluned b 1981); *Career* RAF 1958-60; admitted slr 1957, ptnr William George & Son Porthmadog Gwynedd, coroner Lleyn and Eifion Dist of Gwynedd 1984-; capt Criccieth GC 1968; chm: Criccieth Town Cncl 1967, 1973, 1980, 1989, Dwyfor DC 1980; vice pres Gwynedd Law Soc; *Recreations* yachting, golf, angling; *Style—* Robert Price, Esq; Monfa, Beach Bank, Criccieth, Gwynedd LL52 0HW (☎ 0766 522717); 103 High St, Porthmadog, Gwynedd (☎ 0766 512474, fax 0766 514363)

PRICE, Robin John; JP (1980); s of Lt-Col Kenrick Jack Price, DSO, MC (d 1982), of Bala Gwynedd, and Juliet Hermione de Laszlo, *née* Slessor; *b* 7 March 1947; *Educ* Millfield; *m* 15 April 1972, Diana Mary, da of William Paige Gilbert Lyon, of Victoria, Australia; 1 s (Richard b 1976), 2 da (Annabel b 1974, Charlotte b 1982); *Career* chm Merioneth Branch CLA 1973-75, pres Int Sheep Dog Soc 1980; landowner; *Recreations* shooting, fishing, tennis; *Clubs* MCC, Turf; *Style—* Robin Price, Esq, JP; Rhiwlas, Bala, Gwynedd LL23 7NP (☎ Bala 520612); Estate Office, Rhiwlas, Bala, Gwynedd LL23 7NP (☎ Bala 520387)

PRICE, Robin Mark Dodgson; s of Wilfred Barrie Price, of Knowle, West Midlands, and Jocelyn Mary, *née* Berry; *b* 30 April 1956; *Educ* The Leys Sch Cambridge, Univ of Bristol (LLB); *m* 27 Sept 1986, Jane, da of Vyvian Hugh Reginald Rawson; 1 s (Joe Gulliver b 19 Nov 1990); *Career* Arthur Young McClelland Moores 1978-82 (articled clerk, chartered accountant), md Frontline Video Ltd 1983-87, jt managing ptnr Howell Henry Chaldecott Lury 1987-; ACA, MIPA; *Recreations* tennis, golf, swimming; *Clubs* Roehampton; *Style—* Robin Price, Esq; Howell Henry Chaldecott Lury, Kent House, 14-17 Market Place, London W1N 7AJ (☎ 071 436 3333, fax 071 436 2677)

PRICE, Roland John Stuart; s of Philip Stuart Price, of Tamworth, and Rowena Mary, *née* Jones; *b* 29 July 1961; *Educ* Sydney GS Aust, Royal Ballet Sch London; *Career* ballet dancer; Gold Medal Adeline Genée award 1978, Sadler's Wells Royal Ballet 1979- (princ dancer 1984-), princ dancer Boston Ballet USA 1990-; princ roles incl: The Two Pigeons, La Fille Mal Gardee, Coppelia, Swan Lake, The Sleeping Beauty, The Snow Queen, Abdallah, The Nutcracker, Etudes, many one act ballets incl creations by Macmillan and Bintley; *Style—* Roland Price, Esq

PRICE, Brig Rollo Edward Crwys; CBE (1967), DSO (1961); s of Eardley Edward Carnac Price, CIE (d 1972), and Frances Louisa, *née* Crwys (d 1980); *b* 6 April 1916; *Educ* Canford, RMC Sandhurst, Staff Coll Camberley; *m* 28 July 1945, Diana, da of Maj John Austen Budden (d 1967), of Sutton, Bingham Manor, nr Yeovil, Somerset; 3 da (Angela b 1947, Gillian b 1951, Tessa b 1955); *Career* cmmnd 2 Lt 24 Regt SWB 1936, 2 SWB active serv Palestine 1936, 2 Lt 2 SWB UK 1937-38, Lt 1 SWB India 1938-41, WWII serv Actg Capt 1 SWB Iraq 1941-42, 1 SWB Western Desert 1943, POW Italy 1942-43, escaped and returned UK 1943, Actg Maj Co 161 (RMC) OCTU UK, 1 SWB active serv Palestine 1945-46, Cyprus 1946-47, Staff Coll UK 1948, Maj DAAG HQ Western Cmd 1949-51, Maj 1 SWB Eritrea and BAOR 1952-53, Bde Maj 5 Inf Bde 1954-55, Maj 1 SWB active serv Malaya 1956-58, Maj 2 in Cmd 1 SWB UK; Lt-Col Cmd 4 Bn Queen's Own Nigeria Regt 1959-61: Nigeria, S Cameroons, UN Force Belgian Congo, Lt-Col AA & QMG HQ 43 Inf Div UK 1962-63, Actg Brig Cdr 160 Inf Bde S Wales 1964-66, Brig Dep Cdr Malta and Libya 1967, Cdr Br Troops Malta 1968-69, ret 1969; *Recreations* travel, reading, writing; *Style—* Brig Rollo Price, CBE, DSO; Elsford, Netherton, Yeovil, Somerset

PRICE, Hon Mrs (Rosalind Helen Penrose); *née* Lewis; da of 1 Baron Brecon, PC (d 1976, when title became extinct), and Baroness Brecon, CBE, *qv*; *b* 1938; *Educ* Cheltenham Ladies' Coll; *m* 1963, (Arthur) Leolin Price, QC, *qv*; 2 s, 2 da; *Career* Conservative Central Office Radio and TV Dept 1959-61; Br Consul-Generals Office NY 1962; dir: Bulldog Manpower Servs Ltd 1975-87, Norland Nursery Trg Coll 1964-86; chm: Powys Dist Health Authy 1986-, Governing Body of N London Collegiate Sch 1968-87; co chm of the Fndn 1975-87; memb: Social Security Advsy Ctee DHSS 1987-, Midwifery Ctee of UK Central Cncl 1983-88, Governing Body of the Frances Mary Buss Fndn 1969-87, Police Complaints Bd 1983-85, Cons Party Ctee 1977, Jellicoe Ctee 1974-75 (and vice-chm), Cncl of Nat Assoc for the Care and Resettlement of Offenders 1974-79, Parole Bd for England and Wales 1969-74, The Griffins Soc 1965-79 (hon sec 1966-70, vice-chm 1970-74, chm 1974-79); dep chm Camden Sch for Girls 1981; memb 1972-80 and later chm Bd of Visitors Brixton Prison; co-opted memb Inner London Probation Ctee 1971-; memb sub ctees regarding community service; *Style—* The Hon Mrs Price; 32 Hampstead Grove, London NW3 6SR (☎ 071 435 9843); Moor Park, Llanbedr, Crickhowell, Powys NP8 1SS (☎ 0873 810443)

PRICE, Hon Mrs (Sarah Theresa Mary); *née* Butler; da of Baron Butler of Saffron Walden, KG, CH, PC (Life Peer, d 1982), and his 1 w, Sydney Elizabeth (d 1954); *b* 1944; *m* 1969, Anthony John Willis Price; 3 s; *Style—* The Hon Mrs Price

PRICE, Lady Susan; *née* Murray; da of 10 Earl of Dunmore; *m* 1980, Graham Price, of Bunbury, W Aust; *Style—* Lady Susan Price; 15 Wandoo Rd, Duncraig, W Aust 6023

PRICE, (Benjamin) Terence; s of Ben Price (d 1955), of Gloucester, and Nelly Elizabeth Caroline, *née* Barnes (d 1973); *b* 7 Jan 1921; *Educ* Crypt Sch Gloucester, Queens' Coll Cambridge (MA); *m* 9 July 1947, Jean Stella, da of John Vidal (d 1971); 1 s (Jeremy b 1951), 1 da (Nicola b 1954); *Career* Lt RNVR 1945-46; head Reactor Devpt Div AERE Harwell 1947-60, asst chief sci advsr MOD 1960-65, dir DOAE 1965-68, chief sci advsr Miny of Tport 1968-71, dir of devpt Vickers Ltd 1971-73, sec-gen Uranium Inst 1974-87; memb: Int Inst for Strategic Studies, Int Sci Policy Fndn; *Books* Radiation Shielding (1954), Political Electricity (1990); *Recreations* making music, flying, skiing; *Clubs* Athenaeum; *Style—* Terence Price, Esq; Seers Bough, Wilton Lane, Jordans, Beaconsfield, Bucks HP9 2RG (☎ 02407 4589)

PRICE, Dr Timothy James Carlyle; s of Dr James Alan Price, and Elizabeth, *née* Donnan; *b* 3 Dec 1941; *Educ* Rugby, Clare Coll Cambridge (BA, MB BChir), Middx Hosp Med Sch (DMRD); *m* 26 June 1970, Anne, da of Frederick Robinson (d 1984); 1 s (Henry James b 3 May 1976), 1 da (Melissa Catherine b 23 Dec 1970); *Career* conslt radiologist Calderdale Health Authy 1974-; *Recreations* gardening, tapestry; *Clubs* Hebden Bridge Constitutional; *Style—* Dr Timothy Price; Hollinsgate, Broad Lane, Luddenfoot, Halifax, West Yorkshire HX2 6JY (☎ 0422 882955)

PRICE, Victor Henry John; s of John Herbert Price, and Doreen, *née* Purdy; *b* 10 April 1930; *Educ* Methodist Coll Belfast, Queens Univ Belfast (BA); *m* 20 Oct 1956, Colette, da of Frederick-Bertrand Rodot; 2 s (Martin b 1957, Eric b 1960); *Career* teaching posts in Ireland and Germany 1952-56; various posts in BBC and Radio Hong Kong head of BBC German Service until 1990; *Books* The Death of Achilles (1963), The Other Kingdom (1964), Caliban's Wooing (1966), The Plays of Georg Büchner (1975), Apollo in Mourne (1978), Two Parts Water (1980); *Recreations* languages, tennis, music; *Style—* Victor Price, Esq; 33 Pembridge Square, London W2 4DT (☎ 071 229 1704)

PRICE, Hon Mrs (Virginia Yvonne Lloyd); *née* Lloyd-Mostyn; da of 5 Baron Mostyn, MC; *b* 24 March 1946; *m* 1, 1973, John Robert Hodgkinson; 2 s (Dominic, Thomas b 1976); m 2, 1983, James R K Price; *Style—* The Hon Mrs Price; c/o Capt

Rt Hon Lord Mostyn, MC, Mostyn Hall, Mortyn, Flintshire

PRICE, Vivian William Cecil; QC (1972); s of late Evan Price; *b* 14 April 1926; *Educ* Judd Sch Tonbridge, Trinity Coll Cambridge, Balliol Coll Oxford; *m* 1961, Elizabeth Anne, da of late Arthur Rawlins; 3 s, 2 da; *Career* RN 1946-49; called to the Bar Middle Temple 1954, Hong Kong 1975, Singapore 1979, bencher Middle Temple 1979, dep high ct judge (Chancery Div) 1975-; *Clubs* Travellers'; *Style—* Vivian Price, Esq, QC; Redwall Farmhouse, Linton, Kent (☎ Maidstone 743682)

PRICE, Vivienne Lola; da of Eric Heyward Price (d 1932), of Upminster, Essex, and Edith Corrie, *née* Bolton (d 1972); *b* 9 Jan 1931; *Educ* Rosebery GS Epsom, RCM (ARCM); *m* 14 March 1959 (m dis 1988), Anthony Howard Carter, s of John Leonard Carter, MBE (d 1979), of Fitznells, Ewell, Surrey; 2 s (Julian b 1961, Vernon b 1965); *Career* teacher: Tiffin Girls Sch 1948-50, Central Fndn Girls Sch 1950-61; dir Jr Dept Fitznells Sch of Music 1959-88 (fndr 1959); fndr: Nat Children's Orchestra 1978 (dir), Epsom Childrens Orchestra 1983 (conductor); teacher violin and conductor Jr Orchestras at Guildhall School of Music and Drama 1985-; *Books* The Young Violinist's Book of Theory (1963); *Recreations* walking, gardening, crosswords, reading; *Style—* Ms Vivienne Price; 157 Craddocks Ave, Ashtead, Surrey KT21 1NU (☎ 0372 276857)

PRICE, William Barclay; s of Edward Cuthbert Barclay Price (d 1968), and Doris, *née* Thompson (d 1975); *b* 21 Nov 1931; *Educ* Marling Sch Stroud Gloucs, Wycliffe Coll Stonehouse Gloucs; *m* 29 Oct 1955, Rosemary Joyce, da of James William Vaile (d 1972); 1 s (Stephen b 1959), 1 da (Jacqueline b 1956); *Career* Nat Serv cmmnd Pilot Offr 1954, RAF 1954-56, Pilot Offr 501 (County of Gloucester) Sqdn Royal Auxiliary Air Force 1956-57; CA 1953; ptnr S J Dudbridge & Sons 1964- (articled clerk 1948-53, rejoined 1956); tstee Stroud United Charities; former: hon treas Stroud branch CAB, hon treas South Cerney Sailing Club, memb Minchinhampton PCC; FCA 1964; *Recreations* sailing, reading; *Style—* William Price, Esq; Jastene, 33 Sheppard Way, Minchinhampton, Stroud, Gloucs GL6 9BZ (☎ 0453 883114); Dudbridges Chartered Accountants, 8/9 Lansdown, Stroud, Gloucs GL5 1BD (☎ 0453 764488)

PRICE, William Frederick Ernest; *b* 25 Nov 1947; *Educ* Durrants Sch Croxley Green; *m* 1 s (Alexander b 1980), 2 da (Victoria b 1978, Charlotte b 1982); *Career* chm and md Avica Equipment Ltd 1970-80; gp md: Balterley Bathrooms plc 1981-, chm Arrowhead Properties Ltd; *Style—* William Price Esq; c/o Balterley Bathrooms plc, Silverdale Rd, Newcastle-under-Lyme, Staffs ST5 6EL (☎ 0782 711118)

PRICE, (Robert) William Watson; s of Harold William Watson Price (d 1984), of Brighouse, W Yorks, and Adelaide Mearns, *née* Neely (d 1984); *b* 26 March 1940; *Educ* St Edwards Sch Oxford; *m* Alethea Jane Price, JP, da of John Doughton Allen, of Harrogate; 1 s (Timothy William Watson b 22 Feb 1968), 1 da (Nicola Jane (Mrs Durham) b 18 April 1966); *Career* Armitage Norton: articled clerk 1958-63, qualified chartered accountant 1963, ptnr 1969-, head Bradford office 1978-87; ptnr KPMG Peat Marwick McLintock 1987-; FCA (ACA 1963); *Recreations* golf, fell walking; *Clubs* Bradford, Bradford Golf (capt 1980); *Style—* William Price, Esq; Westridge, Esholt Ave, Guiseley, Leeds, W Yorks (☎ 0943 74159); KPMG Peat Marwick McLintock, Peat House, Forster Square, Bradford, W Yorks (☎ 0274 725546)

PRICHARD, Brian Justin; s of Bernard A'Bear Prichard (d 1957), of Epsom, and Florence Eveline, *née* Smith (d 1966); *b* 2 Sept 1925; *Educ* Wimbledon Coll, Keble Coll Oxford, King's Coll London (LLB); *m* 1 May 1954, Patricia Margaret Oldham, da of Reginald Garforth Cooke, of Christchurch; 1 s (Jonathan Mark b 1957), 3 da (Gillian Mary (Mrs Theokritoff) b 1956, Nicola Anne (Mrs Boath) b 1960, Susan Elizabeth (Mrs Mac Carroll) b 1964); *Career* Sub Lt RNVR 1944-47; slr; sr ptnr Rooks Rider; chm Walter Lawrence plc 1964-; fndr memb Westminster Advsy Ctee on Alcoholism; memb Law Soc 1951; Freeman: City of London, Worshipful Co of Barbers; *Recreations* travel, reading; *Clubs* City Livery; *Style—* Brian Prichard, Esq; Drakes Hide, Windsor Bridge Court, Brocas St, Eton, Windsor, Berks (☎ 0753 856015); 8 and 9 New Square, Lincoln's Inn, London WC2A 3QJ (☎ 071 242 8023)

PRICHARD, Prof Brian Norman Christopher; s of Sir Norman George Mollett Prichard (d 1972), of 4 Rusham Rd, London SW12, and Winifred, *née* Just (d 1989); *b* 7 Nov 1932; *Educ* Merton House Sch, Battersea GS, St George's Hosp Univ of London (BSc, MSc, MB BS); *m* 8 Sept 1956, Denise Margaret, da of Edward Stoneham (d 1982), of 9 Lakehurst Rd, Ewell; 2 s (Andrew, Ian), 2 da (Ruth, Catherine); *Career* sr house offr surgery Dorking Gen Hosp 1958-59, registrar St George's Hosp 1959-61 (house offr posts 1957-58); Univ Coll Hosp Med Sch: res asst 1961-62, lectr in clinical pharmacology 1962-68, sr lectr 1968-75, reader 1975-80, prof 1980-, conslt physician 1973-; author of about 150 reviews and papers, winner of Astra Award Int Soc of Hypertension (for the introduction of beta adrenergic blocking drugs into the treatment of Hypertension) 1979; memb: Br Pharmacological Soc, Med Soc of London, Assoc of Physicans, Med Res Soc, Int Soc of Hypertension; chm Action on Drinking and Driving, treas Cons Med Soc, pres Wandsworth Tooting Cons Assoc, cncllr London Borough of Wandsworth; memb RSM, MRCP 1966, FRCP 1977, FFPM 1989; *Books* Biological Effects of Drugs in Relation to their Plasma Concentration (ed with DS Davies, 1973), Prescribing - What, When, Why? (with J Fry and M Godfrey, 1986), Beta Blockers in Clinical Practise (with J M Cruickshark, 1988); *Recreations* photography, walking; *Clubs* Carlton; *Style—* Prof B N C Prichard; 24 Lyford Road, Wandsworth Common, London SW18 3LG (☎ 081 870 3066); Dept of Clinical Pharmacology, University College and Middlesex School of Medicine, University College, 5 University St, London WC1E 6JJ (☎ 071 380 9677)

PRICHARD, David Colville Mostyn; s of Rev George Mostyn Prichard (d 1972), of 12 Palace Ct, Kensington, and Joan Mary, *née* Wild (d 1978); *b* 26 May 1934; *Educ* Radley, Pembroke Coll Oxford (MA); *Career* CO CCF Monkton Combe Sch 1955, fndr first UK Volunteer Police Cadets 1965, headmaster Port Regis Sch 1969-, organiser Nat Conf of Govrs Bursars and Heads 1981-87 (lectr 1974-, Aust Bicentenary lectr 1988), chm Inc Assoc of Prep Schs 1990- (memb cncl 1986); memb ctee Pembroke Coll Oxford, fndr memb Sci Exploration Soc, dir Smallpiece Tst, chm Smallpiece Enterprises Ltd, tstee of Parnham, memb mgmnt ctee Hooke Park Coll; govr: Wycliffe Coll, Hordle House, Swanbourne House, Holmwood House; memb bd of visitors Guys Marsh Detention Centre; Freeman Worshipful Co of Lorriners FBIM, FRSA, FCP; *Books* Training for Service (1968); *Recreations* travel, management, gardening; *Clubs* Leander, National (Carlton); *Style—* David Prichard, Esq; Castleton House, Sherborne, Dorset DT9 3SA (☎ 0935 816539); Villa Roca, Mijas 1Km Malaga, Spain; Port Regis, Motcombe Park, Shaftesbury, Dorset SP7 9QA (☎ 0747 52566, fax 0747 54684)

PRICHARD, Francis Anthony; s of Capt Francis Leo Prichard, of The Old Crown, Moelfre, Anglesey, and Dorothy Joanne; *b* 10 June 1949; *Educ* Ratcliffe Coll Leicester, Univ of Liverpool (LLB); *m* 21 Dec 1974, Elizabeth Ann, da of Jospeh Prescott, of Holmdove House, Blundellsands Rd East, Blundellsands, Liverpool; 3 s (Mark b 10 Aug 1979, Paul b 6 April 1981, James b 28 Dec 1983); *Career* admitted slr 1974; ptnr Weightman Rutherfords Liverpool 1976-; Notary Public; memb Law Soc; *Recreations* tennis, skiing, squash; *Clubs* Racquet, Blundellsands Lawn Tennis; *Style—* Anthony Prichard, Esq; Merrywood, Dowhills Road, Blundellsands, Liverpool L23 8SP (☎ 051 931 2315); Weightman Rutherfords, Richmond House, 1 Rumford Pl, Liverpool L3 9QW (☎ 051 227 2601, fax 051 227 3223, telex 627538)

PRICHARD, Jonathon Simon; s of Francis Leo Prichard, of Liverpool, and Dorothy Joan, *née* Wilkinson; *b* 9 May 1957; *Educ* Radcliffe Coll Syston Leicester, Poly of Liverpool (BAArch, DipArch); *m* 4 Jan 1982, Brigette Jane, da of John Blades, of Lincoln; 1 s (Robert b 17 Nov 1984), 1 da (Sara b 7 Sept 1986); *Career* sr ptnr Jonathon Prichard Partnership (architect for Liverpool RC Archdiocese 1989); commissions incl: community care projects, secondary and primary schs, urban renewal housing devpt; memb: Cons Assoc, Royal Windermere Yachting Assoc; RIBA 1982; *Clubs* Liverpool Racquets; *Style—* Jonathon Prichard, Esq; Hodge Hill, Cartmel Fell, Grange-over-Sands, Cumbria; 25 Marine Crescent, Waterloo, Liverpool; Georges Dock Building, Pierhead, Liverpool (☎ 051 236 0712, fax 051 236 298); Kendal, Cumbria (☎ 0539 730448)

PRICHARD, Mathew Caradoc Thomas; s of Maj Hubert de Burgh Prichard, of Pwllywrach, Cowbridge (ka 1944), and Rosalind Margaret Clarissa Hicks, *née* Christie; *b* 21 Sept 1943; *Educ* Eton, New Coll Oxford (BA); *m* 20 May 1967, Angela Caroline, da of Thomas Craddock Maples, of Symonds Farm House, Childrey, nr Wantage; 1 s (James b 1970), 2 da (Alexandra b 1968, Joanna b 1972); *Career* chm Agatha Christie Ltd and Booker Entertainment; chm Welsh Arts Cncl 1986-, memb Arts Cncl GB 1983-, advsr local div Barclays Bank S Wales; High Sheriff Co of Glam 1973-74; *Recreations* golf, cricket, bridge; *Clubs* Boodle's, Cardiff and County, R & A, Royal Porthcawl Golf, MCC; *Style—* Mathew Prichard, Esq; Booker Entertainment, 141 Sloane St, London SW1X 9AY (☎ 071 730 7778)

PRICHARD, Sir Montague Illtyd; CBE (1965), MC (1944); s of George Montague Prichard (d 1929), and Elsie Honoriah, *née* Farrow (d 1968); *b* 26 Sept 1915; *Educ* Felsted; *m* 1942, Kathleen Georgana Hamill; 2 s (James, Roger), 1 da (Anne); *Career* served RE: India, Somaliland, Malaya, Burma, Lt-Col as CRE 20 Indian Div; chm and chief exec Perkins Engine Group Ltd and subsids 1957-75; chm: Brown Bros Corpn 1977-82, Tozer Kemsley & Millbourn (Holdings) plc 1982-85; dir Polysius Ltd; chm: Scientific Applied Res plc 1984, Belgrave Holdings plc 1985-; FBIM, FIPE, FInstMSM; kt 1972; *Recreations* work, people, gardening; *Clubs* East India, Sports, Devonshire; *Style—* Sir Montague Prichard, CBE, MC; Willowdale House, Apethorpe, Peterborough, Cambs

PRICHARD, Robert David Caradoc; s of Lt-Col David Prichard and Elizabeth , 2 da of Sir David Llewellyn, 1 Bt; Col Prichard is ninth in descent from Matthew Prichard, whose epitaph claims him to be desended from 'Cradocke Vraich Vras, Earle of Hereford, and Prince between Wye and Seaverne'; *b* 17 Nov 1947; *Educ* Wellington, CCC Cambridge; *Career* merchant banker; asst dir Kleinwort Benson Investment Management 1981-; *Recreations* bridge, croquet; *Style—* Robert Prichard Esq; 25 Longmoore St, SW1 (☎ 071 828 0919)

PRICHARD JONES, Kenneth Victor; s of John Victor Jones, MBE (d 1981), and Eunice Aldwyn Marie, *née* Prichard (d 1976); *b* 12 Sept 1946; *Educ* Clifton, Univ of Kent at Canterbury (BA); *m* 26 Sept 1967, Dagmar Eva, da of Capt Pavel Svoboda, of 29 Gwendolen Ave, Putney, London; 3 s (Sebastian b 1973, Piers b 1975, Christian b 1980), 1 da (Lucy b 1978); *Career* admitted slr 1972; chm: Clifton Charterhouse Securities Ltd 1976-, Radio Mercury plc 1987-; dir City Trust Limited Bankers 1978-; chm: Ctee Keats-Shelley Meml Assoc, Devpt Bd Univ of Kent; memb Law Soc; *Books* The Law and Practice of Franchising (with Prof John Adams, 3 edn 1990) F is for Franchising (2 edn, 1983), Agency Documents in Encyclopaedia of Forms and Precedents (1984); Merchandising (contrib, 1987), Commercial Hiring and Leasing (contrib, 1989); *Recreations* skiing, shooting; *Style—* Kenneth Prichard Jones, Esq; Field Place, Warham, West Sussex RH12 3PB (☎ 0403 65004); 34 James Street, London W1M 5HS (☎ 071 486 9957, car 0836 768596)

PRICHARD-JONES, David John Walter; s and h of Sir John Prichard-Jones, 2 Bt, by his 1 w, Heather, da of Sir Walter Nugent, 4 Bt; *b* 14 March 1943; *Educ* Ampleforth, ChCh Oxford (BA); *Style—* David Prichard-Jones, Esq

PRICHARD-JONES, Lady; Heather Vivian Mary; da of Sir Walter Richard Nugent, 4 Bt, MP (d 1955) and sis of Sir Peter Nugent, 5 Bt, *qv*; *m* 1937, Sir John Prichard-Jones, 2 Bt, *qv*; 1 s (David); *Style—* Lady Prichard-Jones

PRICHARD-JONES, Sir John; 2 Bt (UK 1910); s of Sir John Prichard-Jones, 1 Bt, JP, DL (d 1917); *b* 20 Jan 1913; *Educ* Eton, ChCh Oxford (MA); *m* 1, 1937 (m dis 1950), Heather, da of late Sir Walter Nugent, 4 Bt; 1 s; m 2, 1959, Helen Marie Therese, da of J F Liddy; 1 da (Susan); *Heir* s, David John Walter Prichard-Jones; *Career* called to the Bar Gray's Inn 1936; former Capt The Queen's Bays; farmer and bloodstock breeder; *Style—* Sir John Prichard-Jones, Bt; Allenswood House, Lucan, Co Dublin, Republic of Ireland

PRICKETT, Prof (Alexander Thomas) Stephen; s of Rev William Ewart Prickett (d 1975), of Canterbury, Kent, and Barbara Browning, *née* Lyne; *b* 4 June 1939; *Educ* Kent Coll Canterbury, Trinity Hall Cambridge (scholar, BA, MA, PhD, T H prize for Eng, Edward George Harwood prize for Eng, Cambridge Univ Membs' prize), Univ Coll Oxford (DipEd); *m* 17 Aug 1966 (m dis 1981), Diana Joan, da of George Mabbutt; 1 s (Mark Thomas b 1974), 1 da (Ruth Charlotte b 1970); m 2, 1984, Maria Angelica; *Career* teacher of English: Methodist Coll Uzuakoli E Nigeria 1962-64, Univ of Sussex 1967-82, Aust Nat Univ Canberra Australia 1983-89; regius prof of English language and literature Univ of Glasgow 1990-; govr Bishop Otter Coll of Educn 1974-77, tstee Fernley Hartley Tst 1978-83; chm: Higher Educn Gp 1971-82, Higher Educn Fndn 1991-; *Books* Do It Yourself Doom (1962), Coleridge and Wordsworth: The Poetry of Growth (1970), Romanticism and Religion (1976), Victorian Fantasy (1979), Words and the Word (1986); *Recreations* walking, skiing, tennis, attending conferences; *Style—* Prof Stephen Prickett; Department of English Literature, University of Glasgow, Glasgow G12 8QQ (☎ 041 339 8855, fax 041 330 4601)

PRICKETT, Air Chief Marshal Sir Thomas Other; KCB (1965, CB 1957), DSO (1943), DFC (1942); s of late Eric G Prickett, of Bedford; *b* 31 July 1913; *Educ* Stubbington House Sch, Haileybury Coll; *m* 1942, Elizabeth Gratian (d 1984), da of late William Galbally, of Laguna Beech, California, USA; 1 s, 1 da; m 2, 1985, Shirley Westerman, w of William Westerman; *Career* joined RAF 1937, served 1939-45 (Desert Air Force and Bomber Cmd), Gp Capt 1952, Air Cdre 1956, COS special air task force (Suez Operations), SASO 1 Group, Air Vice-Marshal 1960, asst chief Air Staff (Ops) Air Miny 1960-63 (Policy and Planning 1963-64); AOC-in-C NEAF and Cdr Br Forces Cyprus (admin Sovereign Base Area) 1964-66, Air Marshal 1966, AOC-in-C RAF Transport and Air Support Cmds 1967-68, Air Chief Marshal 1969, Air memb for Supply and Organisation MOD (RAF) 1968-70, ret; *Clubs* RAF; *Style—* Air Chief Marshal Sir Thomas Prickett, KCB, DSO, DFC; 46 Kingston Hill Place, Kingston Upon Thames, Surrey KT2 7GY

PRIDAY, Charles Nicholas Bruton; s of Christopher Bruton Priday, and Jill, *née* Sergeant; *b* 17 July 1959; *Educ* Radley, Univ Coll Oxford, City Univ London; *m* 17 July 1982, Helen Elizabeth, da of M M Jones; 2 da (Elizabeth b 1987, Emma b 1989); *Career* called to the Bar Middle Temple 1982; *Recreations* escaping to the Cotswolds, golf, tennis; *Clubs* St Enodoc Golf, Oxford Unicorns Real Tennis, Moreton Morrell Real Tennis; *Style—* Charles Priday, Esq; 7 King's Bench Walk, Temple EC4Y 7DS (☎ 071 583 0404, fax 071 583 0950, telex 887491 KBLAW)

PRIDAY, Christopher Bruton; QC (1986); s of Arthur Kenneth Priday (d 1968), of Cheltenham, and Rosemary, *née* Bruton (d 1982); *b* 7 Aug 1926; *Educ* Radley, Univ Coll Oxford (MA); *m* 24 Oct 1953, Jill Holroyd, da of John Holroyd Sergeant, MC (d

1965), of Rottingdean, Sussex; 2 s (Edward b 1957, Charles b 1959); *Career* called to the Bar Gray's Inn 1951, bencher 1991 (hon ad eundum Middle Temple 1985); Fell Central Assoc of Agric Valuers 1988; ARICS 1987; *Books* Milk Quotas: Law and Practice (jtly, 1986), A Handbook of Milk Quota Compensation (jtly, 1987); *Recreations* opera, golf; *Clubs* St Enodoc Golf; *Style—* Christopher Priday, Esq, QC; 61 Chiddingstone St, London SW6 4TQ (☎ 071 736 4681); Falcon Chambers, Falcon Ct, London EC4Y 1AA (☎ 071 353 2484, fax 071 353 1261)

PRIDAY, Helen Elizabeth; da of Michael Montague Jones, of Radley, Oxon, and Alison Priscilla, *née* Shepherd; *b* 24 Sept 1957; *Educ* Dragon Sch, Radley; *m* 17 July 1982, Charles Nicholas Bruton Priday, s of Christopher Bruton Priday, QC, of London; 2 da (Elizabeth b 1987, Emma b 1989); *Career* publicity and promotions mangr W H Freeman & Co Oxford 1978-82, ed Pitkin Pictorials London 1982-83, mktg and publicity dir Times Books Angus and Robertson London 1983-, promotions dir The Times Supplements 1990- (The Times Literary Supplement, The Times Educational Supplement, The Times Higher Educational Supplement); *Recreations* opera, tennis, golf, good food and wine, travelling in France; *Clubs* St Enodoc Golf; *Style—* Mrs Helen Priday; The Times Supplements, Priory House, St John's Lane, London EC1M 4BX (☎ 071 253 3000, fax 071 253 0731)

PRIDDEN, Lady Maria; *née* Noel; da of 5 Earl of Gainsborough, JP; *b* 3 Feb 1951; *Educ* St Mary's Convent, Ascot; *m* 1971, Robert Pridden; 1 s, 1 da; *Style—* The Lady Maria Pridden; Fort Henry House, Exton, Oakham, Leics

PRIDEAUX, Sir Humphrey Povah Treverbian; OBE (1945), DL (Hants 1983); s of Walter Treverbian Prideaux; bro of Sir John Prideaux and Walter Prideaux, *qqv*; *b* 13 Dec 1915; *Educ* St Aubyns Rottingdean, Eton, Trinity Coll Oxford; *m* 1939, Cynthia, da of late Lt-Col H Birch Reynardson, CMG; 4 s; *Career* Jt Planning Staff War Office 1945, Naval Staff Coll 1948, Cmdt Sch of Admin 1948, Chiefs of Staff Secretariat 1950-53, ret; dir: NAAFI 1956-73 (chm 1963-73), The London Life Assoc Ltd 1964-88 (vice pres 1965-72, pres 1973-84), Brooke Bond Liebig Ltd 1968-81 (chm 1972-81), W H Smith & Son Ltd 1969-77 (vice chm 1977-81), Morland & Co 1981- (chm 1983-), Grindlays Bank 1982-85; chm Lord Wandsworth Fndn 1966-; kt 1971; *Clubs* Cavalry & Guards; *Style—* Sir Humphrey Prideaux, OBE, DL; Summers Farm, Long Sutton, Basingstoke, Hants (☎ 0256 862295)

PRIDEAUX, John Denys Charles Anstice; s of Denys Robert Anstice Prideaux (d 1966), and Francis Hester Dorethy, *née* Glaze; *b* 8 Aug 1944; *Educ* The Hall Hampstead, St Paul's, Univ of Nottingham (BSc, PhD); *m* 3 June 1972, Philippa Mary Anstice; 1 s (John Piers Grahame Anstice b 1976), 1 da (Sophia Mary Louise Anstice b 1974); *Career* BR: area mangr Newton Abbot 1972-74, strategic planning offr BR Bd 1974-80, divnl mangr Birmingham 1980-83, dir Policy Unit BR Bd 1983-86, dir InterCity, md (designate) Intercity 1990; memb: Advsy Ctee on Trunk Road Assessment 1977, Transport Ctee Science & Engrg Research Cncl 1982, Environment Ctee ESRC 1985, Cncl Manchester Business Sch; MCIT, FRSA; *Books* Five Railway Histories (1964-1980), author of many professional papers; *Recreations* riding, hunting, shooting, skiing, design; *Style—* John Prideaux, Esq; InterCity, British Rail HQ, Euston House, 24 Eversholt St, London NW1 1DZ (☎ 071 922 6343, fax 071 922 4163)

PRIDEAUX, Sir John Francis; OBE (1945), DL (Surrey 1976); s of Walter Treverbian Prideaux, of Elderslie, Ockley, Dorking, Surrey (d 1958), and Marion Fenn, *née* Arbuthnot (d 1958); bro Sir Humphrey Prideaux and Walter Prideaux, *qqv*; *b* 30 Dec 1911; *Educ* St Aubyn's Rottingdean, Eton; *m* 1934, Joan Terrell, da of Capt Gordon Hargreaves Brown, MC, Coldstream Gds (missing, presumed ka 1915), of Doddershall Park, Quainton, Aylesbury, Bucks; 2 s (Michael, *qv*), 1 da; *Career* joined Middx Yeo 1933, served WWII, Col Q, 2 Army 1944; Arbuthnot Latham & Co Ltd Merchant Bankers: joined 1930, dir 1936-69, chm 1964-69; Arbuthnot Latham Holdings: chm 1969-74, dir 1969-82; chm Arbuthnot Latham Bank 1983-85, memb London Advsy Bd Bank of New South Wales 1948-74; dir: Westminster Bank Ltd (later National Westminster Bank Ltd) 1955-81 (chm 1971-77), Westminster Foreign Bank Ltd (later Int Westminster Bank Ltd) 1955-81 (chm 1969-77); chm Ctee of London Clearing Banks 1974-76, dir Dow Scandia Banking Corp 1982-85; vice pres British Bankers Assoc 1972-77, pres Inst of Bankers 1974-76, memb Wilson Ctee to Review Functioning of Fin Insts in the City 1977-80; dep chm Cwlth Devpt Corp 1960-70, chm Victoria League for Cwlth Friendship 1977-82, memb Lambeth Southwark and Lewisham AHA (T) 1974-82 (cmmr 1979-1980); treas and chm bd of govrs St Thomas' Hosp 1964-74 and chm Special Tstees 1974-88, prime warden Worshipful Co of Goldsmiths' 1972; Legion of Merit USA 1945; kt 1974; *Recreations* all country pursuits; *Clubs* Brooks's; *Style—* Sir John Prideaux, OBE, DL; Elderslie, Ockley, Dorking, Surrey RH5 5TD (☎ 0306 711263)

PRIDEAUX, Julian Humphrey; s of Sir Humphrey Prideaux, OBE, DL, of Summers Farm, Long Sutton, Basingstoke, Hampshire, and Cynthia, *née* Birch-Reynardson; *b* 19 June 1942; *Educ* St Aubyns Rottingden, Eton, RAC Cirencester (Dip); *m* 5 Aug 1967, Rosamund Jill, da of Richard Patrick Roney Dougal, of 19 East Castle St, Bridgnorth, Shropshire; 2 s (Adam b 1968, Nigel b 1971); *Career* land agent; Burd and Evans Chartered Surveyors Shrewsbury 1964-67; Col the Hon GC Cubitt and Others 1967-69; The Nat Tst: land agent Cornwall Region 1969-77, dir Thames and Chilterns Region 1978-86, chief agent 1987-; FRICS 1974; *Recreations* walking, fishing; *Clubs* Farmers; *Style—* Julian Prideaux, Esq; The National Trust, 36 Queen Annes Gate, London SW1H 9AS (☎ 071 222 9251, fax 071 222 5097)

PRIDEAUX, Michael Charles Terrell; s of Sir John Francis Prideaux, *qv*; *b* 23 Oct 1950; *Educ* Eton, Trinity Coll Cambridge (BA); *m* 1975, Susan Henriette, da of Charles Peto Bennett (d 1977); 1 s (John b 1979), 1 da (Laura b 1976); *Career* fin advertisment mangr Financial Times 1979-80 (UK advertisment dir 1980-83), chief exec Charles Barker City 1983-89; dir: Charles Barker Gp 1983-89, Charles Barker plc 1987-89, gp public affrs BAT Industries plc 1989-; *Recreations* gardening, shooting; *Style—* Michael Prideaux Esq; Selehurst, Lower Beeding, nr Horsham, Sussex (☎ 0403 891501); Windsor House, 50 Victoria St, London SW1 (☎ 071 222 7979)

PRIDEAUX, Col Nicholas Mark; s of Sir Humphrey Povah Treverbian Prideaux, OBE, DL, of Summers Farm, Long Sutton, Basingstoke, Hants, and Cynthia Violet, *née* Birch-Reynardson; *b* 23 July 1940; *Educ* St Aubyns, Eton, Army Staff Coll, US Armed Forces Staff Coll; *m* 23 July 1966, Amanda Fiona, da of Cdr Donald Cameron, VC (d 1961); 1 s (William James Nicholas b 1974), 2 da (Victoria b 1967, Henrietta b 1970); *Career* cmmd 1 Green Jackets 43 and 52 1959, ADC to GOC Northumbrian Dist 1961-63, MOD 1975-77, second in cmd and CO 2 Bn The Royal Green Jackets 1979, CO The Rifle Depot The Royal Green Jackets 1980-82, Mil Asst to Dsaceur shape 1982-85, Col GS Live Oak 1985-88, Army Dir NAAFI Bd of Mgmnt 1988-; Freeman: Worshipful Co of Goldsmiths 1986, City of London 1987; FBIM 1989; *Recreations* outdoor pursuits; *Style—* Col Nicholas Prideaux; Summers Farm, Long Sutton, Basingstoke, Hants RG25 1TQ (☎ 0256 862295); Imperial Court, Kennington Lane, London SE11 5QX (☎ 071 735 1200, fax 071 793 4326)

PRIDEAUX, Walter Michael Cokayne; er s of Walter Arbuthnot Prideaux, CBE, MC, TD, *qv*; *b* 19 Nov 1937; *Educ* Eton, Trinity Coll Cambridge (BA, MA); *m* 19 Sept 1964, Lenore Mary Jaqueline, da of Brig Richard Hugh Rossiter Cumming (d 1982), of Abbotswood Lodge, Weybridge, Surrey; 1 s (Walter Edward Cumming b 25 July 1971), 2 da (Rebecca Lenore b 20 Aug 1965, Belinda June b 20 June 1969); *Career* 2 Lt Queen's Royal Rifles (TA) 1961, Lt 1963, TARO 1964-87; admitted slr 1964, sr ptnr White Brooks & Gilman Winchester Southampton and Eastleigh 1983 (asst slr 1964, ptnr 1966); memb Winchester City Cncl 1976-90; govr: Perin's Community Sch Alresford 1976- (chm 1981-88), Peter Symond's Sixth Form Coll Winchester 1981-; Freeman City of London 1958, Liveryman Worshipful Co of Goldsmiths 1961; memb Law Soc 1964; *Clubs* Hampshire; *Style—* Walter Prideaux, Esq; High Stoke, Beauworth, Alresford, Hants (☎ 096 279 434); 19 St Peter St, Winchester, Hants (☎ 0962 844440, fax 0962 842300)

PRIDEAUX-BRUNE, Peter John Nicholas; s of John Charles Fulke Prideaux-Brune (d 1988), of Prideaux Place, Padstow, Cornwall, and Margaret Mary, *née* Hearne (d 1982); *b* 21 Aug 1944; *Educ* Downside, Christ Church Oxford (MA); *m* 1, 14 Oct 1971, Vivien Patricia (d 1983), da of Maj Arthur Creagh Gibson, MC (d 1970), of Glenburn Hall, Jedburgh, Roxburghshire; 2 s (Nicholas Pagan b 2 May 1975, William Anthony b 4 Nov 1978); m 2, 27 Oct 1988, Elisabeth, da of Maj William Conon Grant Peterkin (d 1978), of Hillside House, Ceres, Fife; *Career* called to the Bar Inner Temple 1972, in practice Western circuit; underwriting memb Lloyd's 1977; landowner Prideaux Place (family estate); pres Padstow branch RNLI; Freeman City of London 1972, Liveryman Worshipful Co of Vintners 1972; memb Criminal Bar Assoc; kt SMOM 1983; *Recreations* skiing, music; *Clubs* Turf; *Style—* Peter Prideaux-Brune, Esq; Prideaux Place, Padstow, Cornwall (☎ 0841 532411); 46 The Quadrangle, Chelsea Harbour, London SW10 0UG; Queen Elizabeth Building, Temple, London EC4 (☎ 071 353 7181)

PRIEST, Christopher McKenzie; s of Walter Mackenzie Priest, and Millicent Alice, *née* Haslock; *b* 14 July 1943; *Educ* Cheadle Hulme Sch; *m* Laura Lee, *née* McClure; 1 s (Simon Walter b 23 Oct 1989), 1 da (Elizabeth Millicent (twin) b 23 Oct 1989); *Career* writer; books: Indoctrinaire (1970), Real-Time World (short stories, 1971), Fugue for a Darkening Island (1972), Inverted World (1974),The Space Machine (1976), A Dream of Wessex (1977), An Infinite Summer (short stories, 1979), The Affirmation (1981), The Glamour (1984), The Quiet Woman (1990); memb Soc of Authors; *Style—* Christopher Priest, Esq; Maggie Noach Literary Agency, 21 Redan St, London W14 0AB (☎ 071 602 2451, fax 071 603 4712)

PRIEST, David James; s of James George Priest (d 1945), and Phoebe Young, *née* Logan; *b* 20 March 1937; *Educ* Kingston Coll; *m* 23 May 1959, Carol-Ann, da of Arthur Basham, of 425 Westborough Rd, Westcliff-on-Sea, Essex; 1 s (Christopher David b 1961), 1 da (Melanie Jayne (Mrs Constable) b 1966); *Career* engr: Vicker Armstrongs Aircraft Ltd Weybridge 1954-61, Br United Airways 1961-65, various positions Standard Telephones and Cables Ltd (ITT) 1965-75; md: Barking-Grohe Ltd (ITT) 1975-79, ITT Jabsco Ltd 1979-83, Woods of Colchester Ltd (GEC) 1983-; immediate past pres: Fedn of Environmental Trade Assocs, Heating and Ventilation Mfrs Assoc; memb Rotary Int, vice chm Essex Trg and Enterprise Cncl; cncl memb: Colchester Business Enterprise Agency, Univ of Essex; vice chm Colchester Govrs Inst; local advsy bd memb Community Hospitals Ltd; tstee Winsley's Charity (Alms Houses); CEng, FIMechE, FBIM; *Recreations* swimming, tennis; *Clubs* Colchester Garrison Officers; *Style—* David Priest, Esq; 44 Lexden Rd, Colchester, Essex CO3 3RF (☎ 0206 48398); Woods of Colchester Ltd, Tufnell Way, Colchester, Essex CO4 5AR (☎ 0206 44122, fax 0206 574434)

PRIEST, Prof Eric Ronald; s of Ronald Priest, of Halesowen, Worcs, and Olive Vera, *née* Dolan; *b* 7 Nov 1943; *Educ* King Edward VI Birmingham, Univ of Nottingham (BSc), Univ of Leeds (MSc, PhD); *m* 25 June 1970, Clare Margaret, da of Rev William Henry Wilson, of St Andrews; 3 s (Andrew Nicholas b 1973, David Mark b 1978, Matthew Aidan b 1978), 1 da (Naomi Clare b 1982); *Career* prof of theoretical solar physics Univ of St Andrews 1983- (lectr in applied mathematics 1969, reader 1977); FRSE 1985, FInstP 1989, FRAS; *Books* Solar Flare Magnetohydrodynamics (1981), Solar Magnetohydrodynamics (1982), Solar System Magnetic Fields (1985), Dynamics and Structure of Solar Prominences (1989), Magnetic Flux Ropes (1990), Basic Plasma Processes on the Sun (1990), Advances in Solar System MHD (1991); *Recreations* bridge, swimming, hill walking, aerobics, children; *Style—* Prof Eric Priest; Mathematical & Computational Sciences Dept, The University, St Andrews, Scotland KY16 9SS (☎ 0334 76161)

PRIEST, Margaret Diane (Mrs Tony Scherman); da of Arthur Edmund Priest, of Toronto, Ontario, Canada, and Gertrude, *née* Tommason; *b* 15 Feb 1944; *Educ* Dagenham Co HS Essex, S W Essex Tech Coll and Sch of Art Walthamstow, Maidstone Coll of Art (DipAD), RCA (John Minton scholar, MA, Silver medallist); *m* 1 Sept 1972, Tony Scherman, s of Paul Scherman; 1 s (Leo b 2 April 1975), 2 da (Georgia Donna b 13 Jan 1978, Claudia Eve b 3 April 1980); *Career* artist; teacher of art: Harrow Sch of Art 1970-74, St Martin's Sch of Art London 1972-76, Univ of Waterloo Sch of Architecture Ontario 1982-83, Univ of Toronto Sch of Architecture 1983-; currently tenured assoc prof of fine art Univ of Guelph Ontario (joined Dept of Fine Art 1983), visiting critic to schs of art and architecture England and Canada; major solo exhibitions: Arnolfini Gallery Bristol 1970 and 1974, Garage Art Limited London 1974, Felicity Samuel gallery London 1976, Theo Waddington Gallery London 1980, Theo Waddington Galleries Toronto 1981, Theo Waddington & Company Inc New York 1982, Parchment Suite Theo Waddington Galleries Toronto 1982, Theo Waddington Inc Montreal 1983, Marianne Friedland Gallery Toronto 1985 and 1987, Albemarle Gallery London 1989; numerous gp exhibitions 1969- in England, Yugoslavia, Switzerland, Belgium, Canada, USA, West Germany; work in numerous public and private collections in UK USA and Canada; *awards* Arts Cncl of GB 1969, Ontario Arts Cncl Drawing award 1981; artist with winning team Toronto Bay/Adelaide competition 1990; memb: Univ Art Assoc of Canada, Bd Gershon Iskowitz Fndn 1988-; *Style—* Ms Margaret Priest; 38 Dunvegan Rd, Toronto, Ontario M4V 2P6, Canada (☎ 416 922 9699, fax 416 944 0814); Department of Fine Art, University of Guelph, Guelph, Ontario NIG 2WI, Canada (☎ 519 824 4120 ext 2413, fax 519 837 1315)

PRIEST, Prof Robert George; s of James George Priest (d 1945), of South Benfleet, Essex, and Phoebe, *née* Logan; *b* 28 Sept 1933; *Educ* Westcliff HS, UCL (MB BS, MD); *m* 24 June 1955, Marilyn, da of Baden Roberts Baker, JP (d 1979), of Westcliff-on-Sea; 2 s (Ian b 1956, Roderick b 1960); *Career* Capt RAMC 1958-61 (acting Maj 1960-61), Sch of Infantry Warminster 1958-59, GHQ Far ELF Singapore 1960-61; house physician to Lord Amulree 1956-57, house surgn Edgware Gen Hosp 1957, SHO registrar Royal Edinburgh Hosp 1961-64, lectr in psychiatry Univ of Edinburgh 1964-67, visiting lectr Univ of Chicago 1966-67, sr lectr St Georges Hosp Med Sch Univ of London 1967-73, prof of psychiatry St Mary's Hosp Med Sch Imperial Coll Univ of London 1973-, chm Bd of Studies in Med Univ of London 1987-89, senator Univ of London 1989-; chm Psychiatric Advsy Ctee NW Thames RHA 1976-79, memb cncl Br Assoc for Psychopharmacology (chm Membership Ctee) 1977-81, pres Soc for Psychosomatic Res 1980-81, vice chm Regnl Manpower Ctee NW Thames RHA 1980-83, chm Mental Health Gp Ctee BMA 1982-85, memb Ctee World Psychiatric Assoc 1985- (memb Cncl 1989-); Int Coll of Psychosomatic Med: fell 1977, memb Governing Body and UK delegate 1978-81, treas 1981-83, sec 1981-85, vice pres 1985-87; Royal Coll of Psychiatrists: memb of Cncl 1982-88, registrar 1983-88, chm

Public Policy Ctee 1983-88, memb Ct of Electors 1983-88, chm Gen Psychiatry Ctee 1985-88 (chm Fellowship Sub-Ctee); memb Central Ctee for Hosp Med Servs 1983- (chm Psychiatric Sub Ctee 1983-87); FRCP (Edin) 1974, FRCPsych 1974; *Books* Insanity: A Study of Major Psychiatric Disorders (1977), Sleep Research (jt ed, 1979), Benzodiazepines Today and Tomorrow (jt ed, 1980), Psychiatry in Med Practice (ed, 1982), Anxiety and Depression (1983), Sleep: An International Monograph (1984), Nomifensine Pharmacologial and Clinical Profile (jt ed, 1984), Psychological Disorders in Obstetrics and Gynaecology (ed, 1985), Handbook of Psychiatry (jtly, 1986); *Recreations* squash, tennis, foreign languages, nature study; *Style—* Prof Robert Priest; Academic Dept of Psychiatry, St Mary's Hospital, Praed St, London W2 1NY (☎ 071 725 1648)

PRIESTLAND, Dr Gerald Francis; s of Francis Edwin Priestland (d 1962) of Berkhamsted, and Ellen Juliana, *née* Renny (d 1965); *b* 26 Feb 1927; *Educ* Charterhouse, New Coll Oxford (MA); *m* 14 May 1949, (Helen) Sylvia, da of Hugh Rhodes (d 1939), of London; 2 s (Andreas Edward, Oliver Francis), 2 da (Jennet Ann, Diana Elizabeth); *Career* BBC: sub ed BBC News 1949-54, asst corr BBC Paris 1954, corr New Delhi 1954-58, asst corr Washington 1958-60, corr Beirut 1960-62, foreign ed TV News 1962-64, chief corr Washington 1965-69, newscaster 1970-76, religious affrs corr 1976-82; freelance author and broadcaster 1982-; hon fell Manchester Poly 1982, hon master Open Univ; DD: Univ of St Andrews 1987, Univ of Hull 1988; Coronation Medal (Nepal) 1956; *Books* America the Changing Nation (1968), Frying Tonight: the Saga of Fish and Chips (1971), The Future of Violence (1976), Yours Faithfully Vol 1 (1979), Dilemmas of Journalism (1979), Priestland's Progress (1981), Gerald Priestland at Large (1983), Priestland Right and Wrong (1983), The Case Against God (1984), For all the Saints (Backhouse lecture, 1985), Something Understood (autobiography, 1986), The Unquiet Suitcase (1988); *Recreations* baking; *Clubs* Oxford Union; *Style—* Dr Gerald Priestland; 4 Temple Fortune Lane, London NW11 (☎ 081 455 3297); The Old Sunday School, Carfury, Penzance, Cornwall (☎ 0736 69191)

PRIESTLEY, Clive; CB (1983); s of Albert Ernest Priestley (d 1985), of Bournemouth, Dorset, and Annie May Priestley (d 1974); *b* 12 July 1935; *Educ* Loughborough GS, Univ of Nottingham (BA MA), Harvard Univ; *m* 1, 1961 (m dis 1984), Barbara Anne, da of George Gerard Wells; 2 da (Rebecca, Alison); m 2, 1985, Daphne June Challis, da of Walter Challis Franks, JP (d 1969); *Career* civil serv 1960-83 (under sec PM's off 1979-83); HQ dir BT plc 1983-88; conslt on orgn and mgmnt; govr RSC 1984-, memb St Bart's Med Coll 1990; chm London Arts Bd 1991; Freeman City of London 1989, Liveryman Worshipful Co Glaziers 1989; *Clubs* Army and Navy; *Style—* Clive Priestley, Esq, CB; 80 Thomas More House, Barbican, London EC2Y 8BU (☎ 071 628 9424)

PRIESTLEY, Hugh Michael; s of James Frederick Priestley, MC, of Upton Manor, Upton, Nr Andover, Hants, and Honor Purefoy, *née* Pollock; *b* 22 Aug 1942; *Educ* Winchester, Worcester Coll Oxford (MA); *m* 9 July 1968, Caroline Clarissa Duncan, da of Brig John Hume Prendergast, DSO, MC, of Barton Mead, Taramah Gardens, Tisbury, Wilts; 2 da (Alexandra b 1971, Susannah b 1974); *Career* The Times Newspaper 1964-66; dir Henderson Admin 1972- (joined 1966); md: Witan Investment Co plc, Greenfriar Investment Co plc, Highland Investment Co plc; treas UCL 1981-; *Recreations* shooting, skiing, fishing; *Clubs* City of London, Hurlingham, MCC; *Style—* Hugh Priestley, Esq; 52 Stanford Rd, London W8 5PZ (☎ 071 937 5554); Henderson Administration plc, 3 Finsbury Ave, London EC2M 2PA (☎ 071 638 5757, fax 071 377 5742, telex 884616)

PRIESTLEY, (Jessie) Jacquetta; OBE (1952); da of Sir Frederick Gowland Hopkins OM, FRS (d 1947), and Jessie Anne Stephens; f second cousin of Gerard Manley Hopkins the poet; *b* 5 Aug 1910; *Educ* Perse Girls Sch Cambridge, Newnham Coll Cambridge (MA); *m* 1, 1933 (m dis 1953), Prof Christopher Hawkes; 1 s (Charles Nicolas b 1937); m 2, 1953, J B Priestley, OM (d 1984); *Career* author and archaeologist; entered admin grade of Civil Serv 1941, princ and sec of the UK Nat Cmmn of UNESCO 1943-49, archaeological advsr Festival of Britain 1951, formerly archaeological corr to The Observer and Sunday Times; has excavated in England, Ireland, France and Palestine; Hon D Litt Warwick Univ; FSA; *Books* as Jacquetta Hawkes: Archaeology of Jersey (1939), Prehistoric Britain (with Christopher Hawkes), A Land (Kensley award, 1951), Fables (1953), Man on Earth (1954), Journey Down a Rainbow (with J B Priestley, 1955), Providence Island, Man and the Sun (1962), UNESCO History of Mankind Vol 1, Part 1 (1963), The Dawn of the Gods (1968), The First Great Civilizations (1973), Atlas of Early Man (1976), A Quest of Love (1980), Mortimer Wheeler: An Adventurer in Archaeology (1982); *Recreations* natural history, walking; *Style—* Mrs Jacquetta Priestley, OBE; Littlecote, Leysbourne, Chipping Campden, Gloucs GL55 6HL

PRIESTLEY, James Frederick; MC (1944); s of Hugh William Priestley, MC (d 1932), and Elizabeth Grainger, *née* Hall (d 1974); *b* 22 Feb 1915; *Educ* Horris Hill, Winchester, Western Reserve Acad Ohio USA; *m* 9 Sept 1939, Honor Purefoy, da of Robert Pollock (d 1957); 2 s (Hugh b 1942, Richard b 1947), 2 da (Sarah (Mrs Bond) b 1945, Julia b 1952, d 1975); *Career* 1 Bn Herts Regt (TA) 1939, 1 Bn Coldstream Guards 1940, Maj and Co Cdr Guards Armoured Div from formation until 1945; jobber Wedd Jefferson (later Wedd Durlacher) 1933 (ptnr 1944-74), ret; pres NW Hants Cons Assoc 1958-62; *Recreations* shooting, fishing; *Style—* James Priestley, Esq; Invergeldie, Comrie, Perthshire; Little Blackhall, Banchory, Kincardineshire; Upton Manor, Upton, nr Andover, Hampshire (☎ 026 476 250)

PRIESTLEY, John Philip; s of Walter Priestley (d 1980), and Edith, *née* Moss; *b* 4 July 1937; *Educ* Barnsley GS, Univ of Oxford (BA); *m* Kathleen Margaret, da of late Raymond Arthur Foord; 1 s (Julian b 1985), 2 da (Alison b 1978, Jennifer b 1980); *Career* CA 1965; Arthur Anderson & Co: ptnr London 1972, managing ptnr Bristol Office 1978-85, managing ptnr Manchester Office 1985; FCA; *Style—* John Priestley, Esq; Arthur Andersen & Co, Bank House, 9 Charlotte St, Manchester M1 4EU (☎ 061 228 2121)

PRIESTLEY, Leslie William; TD (1974); s of George Priestley (d 1947), and Winifred, *née* Young; *b* 22 Sept 1933; *Educ* Shooters Hill GS; *m* 8 Oct 1960, Audrey Elizabeth, da of Sidney Humber (d 1978); 1 s (Ian b 1967), 1 da (Jane b 1970); *Career* hd mktg Barclaycard 1966-73, local dir Barclays Bank 1978-79 (asst gen mangr 1974-77), sec gen Ctee of London Clearing Bankers 1979-83, dir Banker's Automated Clearing Servs Co 1983, md Barclays Insurance Services 1983-84, regnl gen mangr Barclays Bank 1984-85; chief exec TSB England & Wales plc 1985-89; dir: dir LEB 1984-, TSB Group 1985-89 (Trustcard 1985-89), Hill Samuel Group plc 1988-89; chm: Hill House Hammond Ltd 1988-89, Mortgage Express 1988-89; dir: Civil Aviation Authy 1990-, Pearce Group Holdings Ltd 1989-, Pinnacle Insurance Co Ltd 1990-; memb Monopolies & Mergers Commision 1990-, visiting fell Univ Coll of N Wales 1989-, conslt ed Bankers Magazine 1972-81; FCIB, CBIM, FInstM; *Recreations* reading, gardening, swimming, theatre; *Clubs* Wig and Pen, RAC; *Style—* Leslie Priestley, Esq, TD; CAA House, 45-59 Kingsway, London WC2B 6TE (☎ 071 832 5371, fax 071 379 3264)

PRIESTLEY, Prof Maurice Bertram; s of Jack Priestley, of Manchester, and Rose Priestley (d 1966); *Educ* Manchester GS, Jesus Coll Cambridge (MA, Dip Math Stat), Univ of Manchester (PhD); *m* 24 June 1959, Nancy, da of Ralph Norman Nelson (d 1959); 1 s (Michael Richard b 1963), 1 da (Ruth Nicola b 1961); *Career* scientific offr Royal Aircraft Estab 1955-56, lectr Univ of Manchester 1960-65 (asst lectr 1957-60), prof UMIST 1970- (sr lectr 1965-70, hd Dept of Mathematics 1973-75, 1980-85, 1986-), dir of Manchester-Sheffield Sch of Probability and Statistics 1976-79 and 1988-, visiting prof Univs of Princeton and Stanford USA 1961-62; Cncl memb Manchester Statistical Soc; hon prof of probability and statistics Univ of Sheffield; fell of Royal Statistical Soc 1955, memb Int Statistical Inst 1972, fell Inst of Mathematical Statistics 1978; *Books* Spectral Analysis and Time Series (vols I and II, 1981), Essays in Time Series and Allied Processes (jt ed 1986), Non-Linear and Non-Stationary Time Series Analysis (1988); *Recreations* music, Hi-Fi, amateur radio, golf; *Style—* Prof Maurice Priestley; Department of Mathematics, UMIST, Manchester, M60 1QD (☎ 061 236 3311)

PRIESTLEY, His Excellency Philip John; Frederick Priestley (d 1963), and Caroline, *née* Rolfe (d 1982); *b* 29 Aug 1946; *Educ* Boston GS Lincs, Univ of E Anglia (BA); *m* 14 Nov 1972, Christine, da of Mrs M Sanders (d 1987); 1 s (Max b 1 Nov 1978), 1 da (Maya b 30 March 1976); *Career* Foreign & Commonwealth Office 1969-71, 3 sec Sofia 1971-73, 3 later 2 sec Kinshasa 1973-76, 1 sec FCO 1976-79, head of Chancery Wellington 1979-83, 1 sec FCO 1984-87, commercial cnsllr/dep head of mission Manila 1987-90, HM ambass Libreville 1990-; memb Rotary Club of Libreville; *Recreations* golf, tennis, bridge, theatre; *Style—* His Excellency Philip Priestley; c/o Foreign & Commonwealth Office (Libreville), King Charles St, London SW1A 2AH (☎ 071 233 3000); British Embassy, B P 476, Immeuble CK2, Libreville, Gabon (☎ 740707, telex 5538 PRODROM GO)

PRIESTMAN, Jane; OBE (1991); da of Reuben Stanley Herbert (d 1986), and Mary Elizabeth, *née* Ramply (d 1957); *b* 7 April 1930; *Educ* Northwood Coll, Liverpool Coll of Art (NDD, ATD); *m* 1954 (m dis), Arthur Martin Priestman; 2 s (Matthew Temple b March 1958, Paul Dominic b June 1961); *Career* designer; own design practice 1954-75, design mangr BAA 1975-86, dir of architecture and design BR Bd 1986-; govr: Cwlth Inst, Kingston Poly; memb: Jaguar Styling Panel, Design Mgmnt Gp CSD, Cncl Architectural Assoc, Percentage for Art Steering Gp Arts Cncl; hon fell RIBA, FCSD, FRSA; *Recreations* opera, city architecture, textiles, food; *Clubs* Architecture; *Style—* Mrs Jane Priestman, OBE; 30 Duncan Terrace, London N1 8BS (☎ 071 837 4525); British Railways Board, Euston House, 24 Eversholt St, London NW1 1DZ (☎ 071 922 6981, fax 071 922 4158)

PRIESTMAN, Richard John; s of Cecil Priestman, of Liverpool, and Mary, *née* Gray; *b* 16 July 1955; *Educ* Maghull GS, Liverpool Poly; *Career* bank clerk Nat West Bank plc, Br record holder 1988, Olympic Games Seoul 1988 Bronze Medallist Archery Team Event, ranked Number 1 in GB 1989; *Clubs* Nethermoss Archers, Grand National Archery Soc; *Style—* Richard Priestman, Esq; 20 Haymans Green, Maghull, Liverpool L31 6DA (☎ 051 526 6523)

PRIMAROLO, Dawn; MP (Lab Bristol South 1987-); *b* 2 May 1954; *Educ* Thomas Bennett Comprehensive Sch Crawley, Bristol Poly (BA), Univ of Bristol; *m* 7 Oct 1972 (sep), Michael Primarolo; 1 s (Luke b 24 Jan 1978); m 2, 29 Nov 1990, Ian Ducat; *Career* legal sec and advice worker 1972-75, sec Resources for Learning Avon CC 1975-78 (cncllr 1985-87); *Style—* Ms Dawn Primarolo, MP; 272 St Johns Lane, Bedminster, Bristol BS3 5AU (☎ 0272 635 948)

PRIME, Brian Salisbury; s of George Henry Luke Prime (d 1975), of Northwood, Middx, and Dilys Salisbury, *née* Jones (d 1978); *b* 14 Aug 1932; *Educ* Harrow GS, LSE (BSc); *m* 10 March 1962, Susan Mary Eveline, da of Thomas Holdstock (d 1983), of Redhill; 2 s (Jonathan b 1965, Richard b 1967), 1 da (Sally-Ann b 1963); *Career* Lt RA 1954-56; trained as CA and mgmnt accountant; md Kingsway Gp plc (dir 1967-), Celcon Blocks Ltd 1975-, Ryarsh Brick Ltd 1980-, Compton Aggregates Ltd 1978-, Eurospace Furniture Packs Ltd 1983-, New Horizon Furniture Ltd 1985-, Nymoelle Stenindustri Ltd 1986-, Bushboard Parker Ltd 1986-, Brantham Engrg Ltd 1987-, Elremco Products Ltd 1987-, Hormigones Celulares SA 1989-, Essex Electronics Ltd 1989-, Earthspan plc 1990-, Brlynco BV (Netherlands) 1990-, Bald BV (Netherlands) 1990-, Bald NV (Belgium) Kayplan Windows Ltd 1990-; memb: Cncl Chartered Inst of Mgmnt Accountants, Lloyds 1982; CBIM, FCA, FCMA; *Recreations* skiing, gardening; *Clubs* Directors, Danish; *Style—* Brian S Prime, Esq; White Gables, 18 Bromley Common, Bromley, Kent (☎ 081 460 9245); Kingsway Gp plc, Celcon House, 289-293 High Holborn, London WC1V 7HU

PRIMROSE, Lady Caroline Sara Frances; da of 7 Earl of Rosebery, DL; *b* 20 Nov 1964; *Educ* Royal Agric Coll Cirencester; *Career* slr; *Recreations* racing, music; *Style—* The Lady Caroline Primrose

PRIMROSE, James Smith Arthur; s of James Smith Arthur Primrose, and Emily, *née* Sturdy; *b* 1 July 1924; *Educ* Kelvinside Acad, Glasgow Acad, Glasgow Univ (BSc); *m* 19 Feb 1952, Bethia Smart Anderson, da of late Thomas Forrest Mathieson Leishman; 2 s (Haold Robert Stuart b 2 April 1954, Robert Thomas Anderson b 20 July 1960), 1 da (Catherine Bethia Mary b 16 Feb 1956); *Career* RE Trg Unit 1944, cmmd 2 Lt off trg QVO Sappers and Miners Bangalore 1945-46, Lt 1 Indian Sapper & Miners M&E Burma Meiktila 1946-47, Capt GHQ Singapore 1947; precedent ptnr Ramsay & Primrose Consulting Engrs, Scotland Curling Team Switzerland 1980; St Pauls Church of Scotland, Soc Building Contracts Ctee, Nat Cncl for Electrical Contractors, Glasgow High/Kelvinside RFC; memb Incorporation of Bakers; CEng, FIEE, FCIBS, MConsE; *Recreations* yachting, curling, golf; *Clubs* Royal Northern & Clyde YC, Glasgow Rotary, Buchanan Castle GC; *Style—* James Primrose, Esq; Carfax, 14 Baldernock Rd, Milngavie G62 8DU (☎ 041 956 2095); 18 Lynedoch St, Glasgow G3 6EY (☎ 041 332 4015, fax 041 333 9197)

PRIMROSE, Lady Jane Margaret Helen; da of 7 Earl of Rosebery, DL; *b* 11 July 1960; *Educ* New Coll Oxford (BA); *m* 13 May 1989, Michael Kaplan; *Career* slr; *Recreations* racing, art, music, photography; *Style—* The Lady Jane Primrose; 137 Holland Park Avenue, London W11

PRIMROSE, John Ure; s and h of Sir Alasdair Primrose, 4 Bt, and Elaine Noreen, da of Edmund Cecil Lowndes, of Buenos Aires, Argentina; *b* 1960; *Style—* John Primrose Esq

PRIMROSE, Sir (Alasdair) Neil; 4 Bt (UK 1903), of Redholme, Dumbreck, Govan, co of City of Glasgow; s of Sir John Ure Primrose, 3 Bt (d 1984), and Enid, da of Late James Sladen, of Br Columbia, Canada; *b* 11 Dec 1935; *Educ* St Georges Coll, Teachers Trg Coll; *m* 1958, Elaine Noreen, da of Edmund Cecil Lowndes, of Buenos Aires, Argentina; 2 s (John, Andrew), 2 da (Doris, Deborah); *Heir* s, John Ure, *qv*; *Career* teacher; head master St Peter's 1965-72; head of Middle Sch St Andrews 1973-; landowner (200 acres); *Recreations* bowls, golf; *Clubs* Old Georgian, Boulogne Golf, San Isidro Bowls; *Style—* Sir Neil Primrose, Bt; Ada Elflein 3155, 1642 San Isidro, Buenos Aires, Argentina (☎ 766 9438); St Andrew's Scots School; R S Pena 691, 1636 Olivos, Buenos Aires, Argentina (☎ 781 8031/2/3)

PRIMROSE, Robert William; ISO (1977), MBE (1969); s of Neville Arthur Primrose (d 1972), of Trunch, Norfolk, and May Edith, *née* Martin (d 1951); *b* 3 July 1921; *Educ* Co Sch for Boys Gillingham Kent; *m* 28 Dec 1948, Elizabeth Katherine Maud, da of Preston Wong; *Career* Civil Serv (Admty) 1938-44, Lt RNVR, Br Assault Area Normandy 1944, Br Pacific Fleet 1945, Hong Kong 1946; admin offr Colonial Admin

Serv Hong Kong 1947-77 (appts incl clerk of exec and legislative cncls, first admin sec UMELCO off, staff grade admin offr), partnership sec Johnson Stokes and Master Slrs Hong Kong 1977-88, ret; FCIS 1955; *Recreations* music, philately, reading; *Clubs* Royal Cwlth Soc, Royal Overseas League, Civil Serv; *Style—* Robert Primrose, Esq, ISO, MBE; 52 Beechwood Ave, Kew Gardens, Surrey TW9 4DE (☎ 081 878 6756)

PRINCE, Prof Alan; s of Harold Bernard Prince (d 1971), and Amy, *née* Williamson (d 1975); *b* 9 Sept 1927; *Educ* Holgate GS Barnsley, Univ of Sheffield (BMet); *m* 27 Jan 1951, Shelia Mary, da of William Foster Jacklin (d 1969); 4 s (Neil b 1957, Ian b 1958, Simon b 1961, Howard b 1965), 1 da (Christine (Mrs Maltby) b 1955); *Career* tech offr ICI 1949-52, lectr Univ of Southampton 1953-55; chief metallurgist: Simon Carves Atomic Energy Div GEC 1956-61, Hirst Res Centre GEC 1961-87; prof assoc Brunel Univ 1987-; FIM 1954 (pres 1972-73), FEng 1986; *Books* The Constitution of Alloys: a Bibliography (1956), Alloy Phase Equilibria (1966), Multicomponent Alloy Constitution Bibliography 1955-73 (1978), Multicomponent Alloy Constitution Bibliography 1974-77 (1981), Handbook of Precious Metals (ed, 1989), Phase Diagrams of Ternary Gold Alloys (jtly, 1990); *Style—* Prof Alan Prince; 90 Station Road, Harpenden, Herts AL5 4TY (☎ 0582 712335); Brunel University, Uxbridge, Middlesex UB8 3PH (☎ 0895 74000)

PRINCE, Harold Smith; s of Milton Prince (d 1966), and Blanche Stern (d 1984); *b* 30 Jan 1928; *Educ* Univ of Pennsylvania (BA); *m* 26 Oct 1962, Judith Chaplin Prince, da of Saul Chaplin; 1 s (Charles b 1963), 1 da (Daisy b 1965); *Career* theatre dir and prodr; *co-produced:* The Pajama Game (Tony) 1954, Damn Yankees (Tony) 1955, New Girl in Town 1957, West Side Story 1957, A Swim In the Sea 1958, Fiorello! (Tony and Pulitzer) 1959, Tenderloin 1960, A Call On Kuprin 1961, They Might Be Giants 1961, Side By Side by Sondheim 1977; *produced:* Take Her, She's Mine 1961, A Funny Thing Happened on the Way to the Forum (Tony) 1962, Fiddler on the Roof 1964, Poor Bitos 1964, Flora, The Red Menace 1965, Follies (co-dir, Tony) 1971; directed: Family Affsir 1962, Baker Street 1965, The Great God Brolon 1972, The Visit 1973, Love for Love 1974, Some of My Best Friend 1977, On the Twentieth Century 1978, Evita (London 1979, NY 1980, LA 1982, Chicago, Detroit, Aust, Vienna; Tony award best dir) 1978, Sweeney Todd (Tony award best dir) 1979, Merrily We Roll Along (co-prodr) 1981, Play Memory 1984, End of the World 1984, Diamonds 1984, Grind (co-prodr), Phantom of the Opera NY 1988, Tokyo 1989, Vienna, LA, Toronto (Tony award best dir) 1986, roza 1987, Cabaret 1987; *produced and directed:* Superman 1966, Cabaret (Tony award: best dir, best musical) 1966, Zorba 1968, Company (Tony award best musical) 1973, Candide (co-prodr, Tony award best dir) 1974, Pacific Overtures, A Doll's Life 1982; opera directed at NY City Opera: Ashmedai 1976, Silverlake 1980, Candide 1982, Sweeny Todd 1984, Don Giovonni 1989; opera directed: La Fanciulla del West (Chicago Lync Opera) 1978, Willie Stark (Houston Grand Opera) 1981, Madam Butterfly (Chicago Lync Opera) 1983, Turandot (Vienna Staatsoper) 1983, Faust (Metrepolitan Opera) 1990; film co-prodr: The Pajama Game 1957, Damn Yankees 1958; film dir: Something for Everyone 1970, A Little Night Music 1978; memb Nat Cncl for the Arts 1976-82, pres League of NY Theatres; Drama Critics Circle award, Obi awards, Plays & Players Best Dir award, Evening Standard award, Pulitzer prize, Commonwealth award; Hon DFA: Univ of Pennsylvania, Pratt Inst, Wagner Coll; Hon DLitt Franklin & Marshall Emerson Coll; *Books* Contradictions (1974); *Clubs* Players, SSD & C; *Style—* Harold Prince, Esq; 10 Rockefeller Plaza, Suite 1009, New York, NY 10020 (☎ 212 399 0960, fax 212 974 8426)

PRINCE, Dr John Anthony; s of Flt Lt Allan Leslie Prince (ka 1944), and Mary Pamela, *née* Paul; *b* 5 Nov 1941; *Educ* Giggleswick, ChCh Oxford (MA, BM BCh, DIH, MRCGP, MFOM); *Career* conslt occupational physician: Occidental Oil Inc 1977-83, London Borough of Tower Hamlets 1983-, Tower Hamlets Health Authy London Hosp 1983, News International 1985-86; memb Tower Hamlets DHA, sr ptnr Tower Med Centre, special advsr on disablement to DSS; memb: BMA, Soc of Occupational Med; *Recreations* literature, history, antiquarianism, natural history, walking; *Style—* Dr John Prince; 69 Philpot St, London E1 2JH

PRINCE, Michael Eliot Gerald; s of Leslie Barnett Prince, CBE (d 1985; s of Sir Alexander Prince, KBE (fndr of NAAFI)), of London, and Norah Millie, *née* Lewis (d 1979); *b* 16 Dec 1927; *Educ* Marlborough, Magdalene Coll Cambridge; *m* 1, 2 May 1955 (m dis), Lore, da of Henry Meyer (d 1948), of London; 1 s (Andrew b 1957), 2 da (Carolyn b 1956, Jennifer b 1960); m 2, 10 June 1969, Rosemary June (Tremayne), da of Sir Oliver Hart Dyke, 8 Bt (d 1969); *Career* CA; co-fndr Target Trust Group (dir 1962-84); chm: Dulwich Coll Prep Sch 1986-, Bembridge Sch 1977-; FCA; *Recreations* walking; *Clubs* Carlton, City Livery, MCC; *Style—* M E G Prince, Esq; 5 Knott Park House, Wrens Hill, Oxshott, Leatherhead, Surrey KT22 0HW

PRINCE, Oscar Peter; s of Peter E Prince, MBE (d 1972), of Heliopolis St, Nicosia, Cyprus, and Minnie Prince; *b* 3 Sept 1934; *Educ* Mount St Mary's Coll Spinkhill, Univ of Hull; *m* 12 June 1976, Patricia, da of Donald Reilly, of 20 Howard St, Macandrew Bay, Dunedin, NZ; *Career* called to the Bar Gray's Inn 1966; Thos R Miller & Son Lonon 1960-64, BISC London 1965-66, Constructors John Brown Ltd London 1966-68, RMC Gp plc (legal advsr) 1968-; memb: Int Bar Assoc 1982-, Gen Ctee BACFI 1985-, Cncl of Legal Educn 1987-, Gen Cncl of the Bar 1988-; *Recreations* walking, gardening, theatre; *Style—* Oscar Prince, Esq; The First House, Midway, Walton-on-Thames, Surrey KT12 3HY (☎ 0932 228472); RMC Gp plc, RMC House, Coldharbour Lane, Thorpe, Egham, Surrey TN20 8TD (☎ 0932 568833, fax 0932 568933, telex 918150)

PRINCE, Roger Graham; s of Graham Stanley Prince, of Norwich, and Lilian Mary, *née* Gee; *Educ* City of Norwich Sch, Downing Coll Cambridge (MA, LLB); *Career* called to the Bar Inner Temple 1977, assoc Prince de Pinna foreign and int lawyers 1988-, called to the Bar of New South Wales 1989; practice devoted to establishing rule of law over judiciary and govt and so the independence of the Bar from the judiciary and the judiciary from itself; teaching 1987; fndr World Law Centre 1988; MENSA 1983; *Books* The Law of Fact (1990); *Recreations* instr Amateur Rowing Assoc, riding, sailing; *Clubs* Downing Coll Boat, London Rowing, Bar Yacht, Inner Temple Boat; *Style—* Roger Prince, Esq; 76B Chancery Lane, Lincoln's Inn, London WC2A 1AA (☎ 071 404 5053)

PRINCE, William Herbert Carriss; s of Charles William Carriss Prince (d 1972), and Mary, *née* Redden (d 1983); *b* 8 Feb 1934; *Educ* Denstone, Univ of Birmingham (BSc); *m* 1959, Janet Christine Mary, da of Frank Livingstone Haworth (d 1984); 1 s (Christopher b 1963), 1 da (Nicola b 1965); *Career* Lt REME, Nat Serv BAOR; dep md Walsall Conduits Ltd 1988-; *Recreations* sailing; *Style—* William Prince, Esq; 125 Little Sutton Rd, Four Oaks, Sutton Coldfield, W Midlands (☎ 021 308 5174); Walsall Conduits Ltd, Dial Lane, Hill Top, West Bromwich, W Midlands (☎ 021 557 1171)

PRINCE-SMITH, James William; s and h of Sir (William) Richard Prince-Smith, 4 Bt, *qv*; *b* 2 July 1959; *Educ* Wellesley House, Gresham's Sch Holt, Univ of Buckingham; *Career* Capt 13/18 Royal Hussars (Queen Mary's Own) 1979-87, Yorks Sqdn QOY; *Recreations* farming, mountaineering, photography, riding, travelling; *Clubs* Cavalry and Guards'; *Style—* James Prince-Smith, Esq; Morton Hall, Norwich NR9 5JS (☎ 0603 880165)

PRINCE-SMITH, Sir (William) Richard; 4 Bt (UK 1911), of Hillbrook, Keighley, W Riding of Yorks; s of Sir William Prince-Smith, 3 Bt, OBE, MC (d 1964), and Marian Marjorie (d 1970); *b* 27 Dec 1928; *Educ* Charterhouse, Clare Coll Cambridge (MA); *m* 1, 11 Oct 1955, Margaret Ann, da of late Dr John Carter; 1 s (James, *qv*), 1 da; m 2, 1975, Ann Christina, da of Andrew Faulds, OBE, of Lee Wick Farm, St Osyth, Colchester, Essex; *Career* former farmer and agric landowner; fin investor; *Clubs* The Springs (Rancho Mirage); *Style—* Sir Richard Prince-Smith, Bt; 40-735 Paxton Drive, Rancho Mirage, Calif 92270, USA (☎ 619 321 1975)

PRING, David Andrew Michael; CB (1980), MC (1943); s of Capt John Arthur Pring (d 1957), of Rochester, Kent, and Gladys Pring (d 1955); *b* 6 Dec 1922; *Educ* King's Sch Rochester, Magdalene Coll Cambridge (MA); *m* 1962, Susan Margaret, da of A W B Brakspear (d 1972), of Henley; 1 s, 1 da; *Career* serv RE 1941-46 (N Africa, Sicily, Italy, Austria), Capt 1945; clerk of the House of Commons 1948-87, clerk of ctees House of Commons 1976-87; *Books* Parliament and Congress (with Sir Kenneth Bradshaw, 1972); *Clubs* Athenaeum; *Style—* David Pring, Esq, CB, MC; Bushy Platt, Stanford Dingley, nr Reading, Berks RG7 6DY (☎ 0734 712585)

PRING-MILL, Dr Robert Duguid Forrest; s of Maj Richard Pring-Mill, RA (d 1961), and Nellie, *née* Duguid (d 1967); *b* 11 Sept 1924; *Educ* Colegio de Montesión Palma de Mallorca, New Coll Oxford (Heath Harrison scholar (Spanish), Arteaga prize essayist, BA, MA); *m* 19 July 1950 (Maria) Brigitte, da of Ludwig Heinsheimer (d 1960); 1 s ((Andrew) Francis b 1952), 1 da ((Mary) Monica Sophia b 1954); *Career* The Black Watch RHR: enlisted 1941, cmmnd 1942, temp Capt 1945, despatches 1947, demobbed 1947; sr Demyship Magdalen Coll Oxford 1950-52, lectr in Spanish Univ of Oxford 1952-88 (New Coll 1956-88, Exeter Coll 1963-81); English ed: Romanistisches Jahrbuch 1953-, Estudios Lulianos 1957-; corresponding memb Inst d'Estudis Catalans 1966, fell (by special election) St Catherine's Coll Oxford 1988-91 (fell and tutor 1965-88); Magister Maioricensis Schola Lullistica 1957; Premi Pompeu Fabra 1956, Premi Ciutat de Palma 1979, DLitt (Oxon) 1986; FBA 1988; Creu de Sant Jordi (Generalitat de Catalunya) 1990, Comendador Orden de Isabel la Católica (Spain) 1990; *Books* Chinese Triad Societies (1946), Lope de Vega: Five Plays (ed, 1961), El Microcosmos Lul·liá (1961), Neruda: The Heights of Macchu Picchu (with N Tarn, 1966), Neruda Poems (with Katya Kohn, 1969), Lullus: Quattuor Libri Principiorum (ed, 1969), Neruda: A Basic Anthology (1975), Cardenal: Marilyn Monroe & Other Poems (ed and trans, 1975), The Scope of Spanish-American Committed Poetry (1977), Studies in Honour of P E Russell (jt ed, 1981), Hacia Calderón (jt ed, 1982), Cantas - Canto - Cantemos (1983), Gracias a la vida: The Power and Poetry of Song (1990); *Recreations* travel, field-recording & photography in Latin America, glass engraving; *Style—* Dr Robert Pring-Mill; 11 North Hills, Brill, Bucks HP18 9TH (☎ 0844 237481); St Catherine's College, Oxford OX1 3UJ

PRINGLE, Air Marshal Sir Charles Norman Seton; KBE (1973, CBE 1967); s of Seton Pringle, OBE (d 1955), of Dublin, and Ethel Louisa, *née* McMunn (d 1938); *b* 6 June 1919; *Educ* Repton, St John's Coll Univ of Cambridge (MA); *m* 1946, Margaret Elisabeth, da of Bertie Sharp (d 1956), of Baildon, Yorks; 1 s (Andrew Charles Seton b 30 April 1949); *Career* RAF: joined 1941, dir gen of Engrg MOD 1969-70, AO Engrg Strike Cmd 1970-73, dir gen Engrg 1973, controller Engrg and Supply 1973-76, ret 1976; sr exec Rolls Royce Ltd 1976-78, dir Hunting Engrg 1976-78, dir and chief exec Soc of Br Aerospace Cos 1979-85; dir: FR Gp plc 1985-89, Aeronautical Tsts 1987-; Cncl memb: RAeS 1968-87 (pres 1975-76), Air League 1976-, CBI 1978-84, RSA 1978-83 and 1986-; memb Def Industs Cncl 1978-84, pres Inst of Mechanical & Gen Tech Engrs 1979-82; chm: CEI 1977-78 (treas 1980-83), governing body Repton Sch 1987- (memb 1985-); CBIM, FEng 1977, Hon FRAeS 1989; *Recreations* photography, ornithology; *Clubs* Buck's, RAF, Inst of Dir; *Style—* Air Marshal Sir Charles Pringle, KBE; K9 Sloane Ave Mansions, London SW3 3JP; Appleyards, Fordingbridge, Hants SP6 3BP (☎ 0425 652357)

PRINGLE, Derek Raymond; s of Donald James Pringle (d 1975) of Nairobi, Kenya, and Doris May, *née* Newton; *b* 18 Sept 1958; *Educ* St Mary's Sch Nairobi Kenya, Felsted Sch Essex Fitzwillian Coll Cambridge; *Career* Cambridge Univ Cricket Club 1979-82, Essex CCC debut 1978, toured India with England Schs 1978, England Debut 1982 v India; 21 Test Caps, 24 One-Day Internationals, 2 Man of Match Awards v West Indies; author of several articles for Telegraph, Times, The Cricketer; *Recreations* art, music, conchology, photography, travel; *Style—* Derek Pringle, Esq; Essex County Cricket Club, New Writtle St, Chelmsford, Essex (☎ 0245 252420)

PRINGLE, Hamish Patrick; s of Robert Henry Pringle, of Nassau, Bahamas, and Pamela Ann, *née* Molloy; *b* 17 July 1951; *Educ* Trinity Coll Glenalmond Perthshire, Trinity Coll Oxford (BA); *m* 24 July 1977, Vivienne Elizabeth, da of Dr H Michael Lloyd (d 1976), of West Byfleet, Surrey; 3 s (Sebastian b 1983, Benedict b 1985, Tristan b 1989); *Career* assoc dir Boasc Massimi Pollitt 1978-79, new business dir McCormick Publicis 1979-82, dir Abbott Mead Vickers 1982-86, md Madell Willmot Pringle 1986-; cncl memb IPA 1985-86, memb IPA Advertising Effectiveness Awards ctee 1985-; MIPA 1985; ctee memb Hartswood Tennis Club; *Recreations* sport, gardening, property development, art, family; *Style—* Hamish Pringle, Esq; Madell Wilmot Pringle & Ptnrs Advertising Ltd, 140 Gt Portland St, London W1N 5TA (☎ 071 631 4464, fax 071 631 0361)

PRINGLE, Margaret Douglas (Maggie); da of John Douglas Pringle, of Sydney, Australia, and Celia, *née* Carroll; *Educ* Convent of the Holy Child London, Convent of the Sacred Heart Sydney, Lady Margaret Hall Oxford (MA); *Career* journalist; former asst on: diary Evening Standard, Pendennis column Observer; former fiction ed: Nova, Woman; London Ed Doubleday 1979-81, sr ed John Murray 1981-82, commissioning ed Michael Joseph 1983-, literary ed Today 1987-; *Books* Dance Little Ladies (1977); *Recreations* reading, travel; *Clubs* Academy; *Style—* Ms Maggie Pringle; Today, Virginia St, London E1

PRINGLE, (Arthur) Michael; TD (and Bar 1951); s of Dr John Pringle (d 1953), of 153 Withington Rd, Manchester, and Dorothy Emily, *née* Beney, MBE (d 1985); *b* 11 Feb 1914; *Educ* Rugby; *m* 17 May 1941, Ruth Margaret (Peggy), da of Cdr Alfred Bernard Stairs Townend, OBE, RN; 2 da (Katherine Margaret (Mrs Thorogood) b 23 Jan 1945, Harriet Mary (Mrs Cripps) b 10 Aug 1948); *Career* cmmnd 42 E Lancs Div RASC TA 1936, served France and Belgium 1940, Normandy Landing 1944; jt fndr and dir British Tufting Machinery Ltd 1954-61; farmer at Gt Leighs 1962-; underwriting memb Lloyd's 1971-; *Style—* Michael Pringle, Esq, TD; Longlands Farm, Gt Leighs, Chelmsford, Essex CM3 1PR (☎ 0245 361 274)

PRINGLE, Dr Robert William; OBE (1967); s of Robert Pringle (d 1973), of Edinburgh, and Lillias, *née* Hair (d 1976); *b* 2 May 1920; *Educ* George Heriot's Sch Edinburgh, Univ of Edinburgh (BSc, PhD); *m* 1948, Carol, da of John Foster Stokes (d 1937), of Ontario, Canada; 3 s (Robert, David, Andrew), 1 da (Vivien); *Career* prof and chm of physics Univ of Manitoba 1949-56; pres: Nuclear Enterprises Ltd Winnipeg 1949-, Nuclear Enterprises Ltd Edinburgh 1976- (chm and md 1956-76); Queen's award to Indust 1966 and 1979); memb: Ct Univ of Edinburgh 1967-75, Econ Cncl for Scot 1971-75, Bd Scot Sch for Business Studies 1972-82; SRC: memb Bd Astronomy Space and Radio 1970-72, memb Cncl 1972-76, memb Bd Nuclear Physics 1972-76; hon advsr Nat Museum of Antiquities of Scot 1969-, tstee Scot Hosps Endowment Res Tst 1976-88; FInstP, FRS (Canada), FRSE, fell American Inst Physics, hon FRSA (Scot) 1972; *Recreations* golf, book-collecting, rugby; *Clubs* Athenaeum, New (Edinburgh), Yacht de Monaco; *Style—* Dr Robert Pringle, OBE, FRSE; 27 Avenue

Princesse Grace, Monaco (☎ 93 50 71 30)

PRINGLE, Simon Robert; s and h of Sir Steuart Robert Pringle, 10 Bt; *b* 6 Jan 1959; *Educ* Worth Abbey, Trinity Coll Oxford (BA); *Career* oil and gas insur broker; *Clubs* Oxford & Cambridge; *Style—* Simon Pringle, Esq; 4 Brand Street, Greenwich, London SE21 8SR; Newmand and Martin Ltd, London EC3; Insurance Services Ltd, Woodruff House, Cooper's Row, London EC3 (☎ 071 488 3288; telex 833133)

PRINGLE, Lt-Gen Sir Steuart Robert; 10 Bt (NS 1683), KCB (1982); o s of Sir Norman Hamilton Pringle, 9 Bt (d 1961), and Winifred Olive, *née* Curran; *b* 21 July 1928; *Educ* Sherborne; *m* 5 Sept 1953, Jacqueline Marie, o da of late Wilfrid Hubert Gladwell; 2 s, 2 da; *Heir* s, Simon Robert Pringle b 6 Jan 1959; *Career* Lt RM 1949, Capt 1957, Maj 1964, Lt-Col 1971, Col 1975, Maj-Gen RM Commando Forces 1978-79, COS to Cmdt Gen RM 1979-81, Cmdt Gen RM 1981-84, Col Cmdt RM 1989-90, Rep Col Cmdt RM 1991-; chm and chief exec Chatham Historic Dockyard Tst 1984-; pres: St Loyes Coll Exeter 1984-, City of London Branch RM Assoc 1984-; vice-pres Royal Naval Benevolent Tst 1984-, dir Medway Enterprise Agency 1986-89; Hon DSc City Univ 1982; Man of the Year Awards 1982; CBIM 1984-; *Clubs* Royal Thames Yacht, MCC, Army and Navy; *Style—* Lt-Gen Sir Steuart Pringle, Bt, KCB; 76 South Croxted Rd, Dulwich, SE21

PRINGLE OF TORWOODLEE, James William; *b* 3 Dec 1956; *Style—* James Pringle of Torwoodlee

PRIOR, Venerable Christopher; CB (1968); s of Ven William Henry Prior (d 1969), and Mary Prior (d 1956); *b* 2 July 1912; *Educ* King's Coll Taunton, Keble Coll Oxford (MA), Cuddesdon Coll; *m* 1945, Althea Stafford, da of Lt-Col Cuthbert Harold Coode, RM; 2 da; *Career* clerk in Holy Orders; chaplain RN 1941-, chaplain of the Fleet and archdeacon for the RN 1966-69, archdeacon of Portsmouth 1969-77, emeritus 1977-; QHC 1966-69; *Style—* The Venerable Christopher Prior, CB; Ponies End, West Melbury, Shaftesbury, Dorset SP7 OLY (☎ 0747 811239)

PRIOR, Hon David Gifford Leathes; eld s of Baron Prior, PC (Life Peer), *qv*; *b* 3 Dec 1954; *m* 1987, Caroline, da of Peter Holmes, of The Old Rectory, Shotesham, Norwich; 1 s (Nicholas James Peter b 1988), 1 da (Helena Caitlin Elizabeth b (twin) 1988); *Style—* The Hon David Prior; 6 Ashchurch Terrace, London W12 9SL

PRIOR, Baron (Life Peer UK 1987), of Brampton, Co Suffolk; James Michael Leathes Prior; PC (1970); 2 s of Charles Bolingbroke Leathes Prior (d 1964), of Norwich; *b* 11 Oct 1927; *Educ* Charterhouse, Pembroke Coll Camb; *m* 30 Jan 1954, Jane Primrose Gifford, 2 da of Air Vice-Marshal Oswin Gifford Lywood, CB, CBE (d 1957); 3 s (Hon David, Hon Simon, Hon Jeremy), 1 da (Hon Mrs Roper); *Career* farmer and land agent in Norfolk and Suffolk; MP (C): Lowestoft (Suffolk) 1959-83, Waveney 1983-87; PPS to: Pres of BOT 1963, Min of Power 1963-64, Rt Hon Edward Heath (leader of the oppn) 1965-70; min of Agric Fisheries and Food 1970-72, a dep chm Cons Pty 1972-74 (vice chm 1965), lord pres of Cncl and ldr of House of Commons 1972-74, oppn front bench spokesman on employment 1974-79; sec of state: Employment 1979-81, NI Sec 1981- 84; chm The General Electric Co plc 1984-; dir: United Biscuits, J Sainsbury plc, Allders Ltd, Allders International Ltd (non-exec chm); *Books* A Balance of Power; *Recreations* cricket, gardening, philately, field sports, golf; *Style—* The Rt Hon Lord Prior, PC; House of Lords, London SW1

PRIOR, Baroness; Jane Primrose Gifford Prior; da of Air Vice-Marshal Oswin Gifford Lywood, CB, CBE (d 1957), and Hilda Jessie, *née* Foster; *b* 5 Oct 1930; *Educ* St Agnes Sch Alexandria Virginia USA, St Felix Southwold; *m* 30 Jan 1954, Baron Prior (Life Peer), *qv*; 3 s, 1 da; *Career* non-exec dir: Tate & Lyle plc 1984-, TSB Group plc 1984; JP 1977-89; memb Cncl Prince's Youth Business Tst 1987-, tstee Charities Aid Fndn 1990-; govr: Atlantic Coll 1986-, Bradfield Coll 1989-; chm Govrs St Felix Sch Southwold; *Style—* The Rt Hon Lady Prior; 36 Morpeth Mansions, Morpeth Terrace, London SW1

PRIOR, Hon Jeremy James Leathes; 3 and yst s of Baron Prior, PC (Life Peer), *qv*; *b* 9 April 1962; *m* 16 April 1988, Camilla Sarah, er da of Julian Riou Benson, of The Old Rectory, Abbots Ann, Andover, Hants; 1 s (Oliver James Leathes b 11 March 1991); *Style—* The Hon Jeremy Prior; 19 Crofton Rd, London SE5 (☎ 071 584 9219)

PRIOR, Michael John; JP (1983); s of Harold Prior (d 1989), and Nellie, *née* Cochrane; *b* 22 July 1945; *Educ* St Ambrose Coll; *m* 19 June 1976, Angela Elizabeth, wid of John Elland, da of Roger Stephen Popplewell; 4 c (Catherine Mary b 21 Aug 1966, Mathew Roger Percy b 5 April 1969, David Michael Harold b 13 July 1977, Elizabeth Margaret Helen b 25 Nov 1978); *Career* articled clerk Joseph W Shepherd & Co 1961-66, qualified CA 1966, ptnr Heywood Shepherd 1969-89, chm Manchester area Kidsons Impey 1990- (ptnr 1989-), chm Manchester Business Venture 1990-; pres: Manchester CAs Students Soc 1979-80, Manchester Soc of CAs 1988-89; FCA (ACA 1966); *Recreations* my family, golf, walking in the Lake District, watching Manchester Utd; *Clubs* St James's, Portico Library, Ringway Golf; *Style—* Michael Prior, Esq, JP; Rooftree, Arthog Rd, Hale, Altrincham, Cheshire WA15 0LU (☎ 061 980 4906); Kidsons Impey, Devonshire House, 36 George St, Manchester M1 4HA (☎ 061 236 7733, fax 061 236 7020, car 0860 578983)

PRIOR, Peter James; CBE (1980), DL (1983); s of Percy Prior (d 1954), and Eleanora Prior (d 1976); *b* 1 Sept 1919; *Educ* Royal GS High Wycombe, Univ of London (BSc); *m* 1957, Prinia Mary, da of Reginald Ernest Moreau (d 1970); 2 s; *Career* fin dir Br Aluminium Co 1961-64, chm H P Bulmer Holdings 1973-82, dep chm Holden Hydroman plc 1982-87, dir Trebor Ltd 1982-86; named Communicator of the Year by Br Assoc of Industrial Editors 1982; chm Govt Inquiries into: Potato Processing 1970, Motorway Servs 1980, Prison Discipline 1984; Croix de Guerre 1944; FCA, FRSA, CBIM, FIMC, FIIM; *Books* Leadership is not a Bowler Hat; *Recreations* flying, motorcycling, music, sub-aqua; *Clubs* Army & Navy, Special Forces; *Style—* Peter J Prior Esq, CBE, DL; Rathays, Sutton St Nicholas, Hereford HR1 3AY (☎ 0432 72 313)

PRIOR, Hon Simon Gifford Leathes; 2 s of Baron Prior, PC (Life Peer), *qv*; *b* 17 July 1956; *m* 30 March 1985, Vivien Ann, da of Peter George Keely, of 48 Lowestoft Road, Worlingham, Beccles, Suffolk; 1 da (Alice Rebecca b 2 May 1986); *Style—* The Hon Simon Prior; Moat House, Brampton, Beccles, Suffolk NR34 8EE

PRIOR-PALMER, Lady Doreen (Hersey Winifred); *née* Hope; yst da of 2 Marquess of Linlithgow, KG, KT, PC, GCSI, GCIE, OBE, TD (d 1952); *b* 17 June 1920; *m* 9 Jan 1948, as his 2w, Maj-Gen George Erroll Prior-Palmer, CB, DSO (d 1977), s of late Prior Spunner Prior-Palmer, of Dublin; 1 s, 1 da (*see* Green, Lucinda); *Style—* The Lady Doreen Prior-Palmer; Appleshaw House, Andover, Hants

PRIOR-PALMER, Lady Julia Margaret Violet; *née* Lloyd George; da of 3 Earl Lloyd George of Dwyfor, by his 1 w; *b* 19 May 1958; *m* 1984, Simon Erroll Prior-Palmer, only s of Maj-Gen George Erroll Prior-Palmer, CB, DSO (d 1977), by his 2 w, Lady Doreen *qv*; 1 s (George Erroll Owen b 25 Nov 1988); *Style—* The Lady Julia Prior-Palmer

PRIOR-WANDESFORDE, Peter MacDonell; s of Capt Richard Cambridge, of Ireland, and Doreen Emily, *née* Handcock (d 1949); *b* 12 Nov 1934; *Educ* Cothill House Abingdon, Stowe, Univ of Bangor (BSc); *m* 15 Nov 1982, Jennifer Wendy, da of Algernon Stuart Bligh (d 1952); *Career* farmer; breeder and judge of poll Hereford cattle, throughbred breeder of national hunt horses; *Recreations* national hunt racing, hunting, fishing, cricket; *Style—* Peter M Prior-Wandesforde, Esq; Well Farm, Timberscombe, Minehead, Somerset TA24 7UB (☎ 0643 841 334)

PRIOR-WILLEARD, Christopher Howard; s of Peter Arnold Prior-Willeard, of Kent, and Anne Jocelyn, *née* Prior; *b* 7 March 1956; *Educ* Gresham's; *m* 18 Oct 1980, Penelope Jane, da of David John Steen, of Sevenoaks, Kent; 1 s (Mark b 1982), 1 da (Annabel b 1984); *Career* MN 1974-80; fndr London Meat Futures Exchange, sr mangr UK Equities Stock Exchange, European Divisional Executive Corporate Trust, Chase Manhattan Bank, dir Chase Manhattan Trustees Ltd; govr Cage Green Sch Tonbridge; *Books* Farming Futures; *Recreations* farming; *Clubs* Farmers'; *Style—* Christopher H Prior-Willeard, Esq; Crookfoot, Rye Lane, Otford, Kent TN14 5JF

PRISINZANO, Hon Mrs (Helen Margaret); *née* Macdonald; da of 2 Baron Macdonald of Gwaenysgor; *b* 1950; *m* 1974, James Edward Richard Prinsinzano; *Style—* The Hon Mrs Prisinzano

PRITCHARD, (Arthur) Alan; CB (1979), JP (1981); s of Arthur Henry Standfast Pritchard; *b* 3 March 1922; *Educ* Wanstead HS Essex; *m* 1949, Betty Rona Nevard, *née* Little; 2 s, 1 da; *Career* BOT 1939, pilot RAFVR 1941-52, Admty 1952, asst under sec of State Naval Personnel and Op Requirements MOD 1972-76, seconded as dep sec NI office 1976-78, dep under sec of state (Navy) MOD 1978-81; mgmnt conslt 1984-; chm Ringwood Bench 1991-; *Style—* Alan Pritchard, Esq, CB, JP; Courtlands, Manor Farm Rd, Fordingbridge, Hants

PRITCHARD, Prof Colin; s of Sydney William Pritchard (d 1986), and Doris (d 1947); *b* 24 Feb 1936; *Educ* Univ of Manchester (Post grad Cert), Univ of Bradford (MA); *m* 15 Sept 1962, Beryl, da of Ivor William Harrison (d 1968); 2 da (Rebecca Anne Harrison b 26 Feb 1967, Claire Elizabeth b 23 Dec 1968); *Career* RAF 1954-56, serv in Cyprus and Suez 1956; lectr Dept of Psychiatry Univ of Leeds 1970-76, dir social work Univ of Bath 1976-80, fndn prof of social work Univ of Southampton 1980-; memb: Central Cncl Educn and Training in Social Work 1974-81, Southampton Health Authy 1981-86; chm: Jt Univ Cncl Social Work Educn 1985-88, Southampton Fabian Soc; memb: Assoc of Child Psychiatry and Psychology 1965, Br Assoc of Social work 1970, American Assoc of Suicidology 1988, Int Assoc of Social Work (BR rep and Bd Memb 1988-); *Books* Social Work Reform or Revolution? (with R K S Taylor, 1978), The Protest Makers: The British Anti-Nuclear Movement Twenty Years On (with R K S Taylor, 1980), Social Work with Adolescents (with R Jones, 1980), Social work with the mentally ill (with A J W Butler, 1986), Maintaining Staff Morale (1987); contrib to comparisons of: Suicide and Violet Death in the Western World 1964-86, Suicide and Unemployment in UK and EEC, Elderly Suicide: Salutary or Disregarded Neglect 1964-88; *Recreations* family, friends, fell walking, squash, mourning Yorkshire and English Cricket; *Clubs* Hemsworth Miners Welfare, Fitzwilliam (hon life memb); *Style—* Prof Colin Pritchard; 33 Bassett Avenue, Bassett, Southampton SO1 7DP (☎ 0703 769169); Dept of Social Work Studies, University of Southampton, Southampton SO9 5NH (☎ 0703 594000, fax 0703 593939, telex 47661)

PRITCHARD, David Peter; s of Norman Pritchard, of Brampton, Cambs, and Peggy, *née* Fotherby; *b* 20 July 1944; *Educ* Read GS, Univ of Southampton (BSc); *m* (m dis); 1 s (James b 1978), 1 da (Louisa b 1971); *Career* Hawker Siddeley Aviation 1966-71, Wm Brandt's Sons & Co 1971-72, Edward Bates & Sons Ltd 1972-78, md Citicorp Investment Bank Ltd 1978-86, sr vice pres and gen mangr Euro Royal Bank of Canada 1986-; FRSA; *Recreations* bicycle racing, cross country skiing, photography; *Style—* David Pritchard, Esq; 17 Thorney Crescent, London SW11 3TR (☎ 071 585 2253); The Royal Bank of Canada Centre, 71 Queen Victoria St, London EC4V 4DE (☎ 071 489 1188, fax 071 329 6144, telex 8811837)

PRITCHARD, Baron (Life Peer UK 1975), of West Haddon, Northants; Derek Wilbraham Pritchard; DL (Northants); s of Frank Wheelton Pritchard, of Didsbury, Lancs, and Ethel Annie, *née* Cheetham; *b* 8 June 1910; *Educ* Clifton; *m* 1941, Denise Arfor, da of Frank Huntbach; 2 da (Hon Rosemary Gail (Hon Mrs Barby) b 1946, Hon Diana Gillian Amanda (Hon Mrs Johnson) b 1948); *Career* serv WWII, Col; md E Halliday & Son Ltd (family business wine merchants) 1930-51; dir: Ind Coope Ltd 1951 (md Grants St James's 1949, later Ind Coope Tetley Ansell Ltd following merger 1961), Midland Bank Ltd 1968-85, Samuel Montagu Ltd 1969-85, Adelaide Assoc Ltd 1970-, Rothmans Int Ltd 1972-86 (chm 1972-75), Rothmans Gp Servs Ltd 1972-80, Rothmans Int Advsy Bd 1980- (chm 1986-), Carreras Gp (Jamaica) Ltd 1972-, Paterson Zochonis & Co Ltd 1977-, Philips Electronic & Assoc Indus Ltd 1978-86, Templeton Investmts Int Inc 1980-, Tiedemann-Goodnow Int Capital Corpn 1984-; chm: Chalk's Int Airline 1984-, Euro-Canadian Bank Inc 1984-, Age Action Tst 1975-, Dorchester Hotel Bd of Tstees 1980-87, advsy bd Rothmans World Gp 1980-, UK-Jamaica Ctee 1981-, Salamon Bros NY 1980-84, Thoroughbred Hldgs Int Ltd 1984-, Pytchley Hunt, Wine & Spirit Assoc of GB 1964- (pres 1962- 64), Northants Youth Club Assoc 1965-, E of England Agric Soc 1974- (vice-pres), Inst of Export 1976- (pres 1974-76); pres: Br Export Houses Assoc 1976-82, Northants Branch Royal Agric Benevolent Inst 1981-; patron: Abbeyfield Soc for the Aged 1971- (pres 1970-79), Northants C of C and Indust 1978- (pres), Three Shires Ind Hosp 1978-; memb: Br Overseas Trade Advsy Cncl 1976-86, Royal Coll of Surgns Fund Raising Ctee 1976-85; govr: Clifton Coll Bristol 1969-, Lyford Cay Club Nassau 1975-85, Nene Coll Northampton 1976-, Br Fndn for Age Research; kt 1968; *Recreations* farming, golf, swimming, hunting; *Style—* The Rt Hon Lord Pritchard, DL; West Haddon Hall, Northampton NN6 7AU (☎ 078 887 210); 15 Hill St, London W1 (☎ 071 491 4366)

PRITCHARD, Capt Eric; s of Robert Pritchard (d 1980), of Rhos-on-Sea, and Catherine, *née* Roberts (d 1962); *b* 24 Jan 1921; *Educ* George Dixon GS; *m* 20 March 1946, Bernice Catherine, da of William Frederick Stuart Henderson (d 1963), of Calgary, Alberta, Canada; 2 da ((Mary Catherine) Erica (Mrs Bryant) b 16 Aug 1947, (Elizabeth Anne) Sherran (Mrs Tye) b 25 May 1951); *Career* RAFVR serv wireless operator 1939, pilot 1941, pilot No 45 Gp Tport Cmnd Montreal (ferrying aircraft across N and S Atlantic) 1942, Cmmnd Flt-Lt RAFVR 1943-, posted to No 46 Gp on close support air tport 1944 (despatches 1945), Tport Cmnd Trg Gp detached to Central Flying Sch Little Rissington, completed serv as Flying Instr Tport Cmnd 1945; 1 Offr BOAC 1946, transferred to Euro div (later BEA) 1946, appointed to Cmd BEA 1950; aircraft flown incl: Vickers Viking, Douglas Dakota, Vickers Viscount, A W Argosy, DH Comet IVB, HS Trident, Boeing 707; ret 1976; memb: BEA modification ctee and mgmnt/pilot tech liason ctee, tech ctee Br Airline Pilots Assoc for 25 years (chm accident investigation study gp for 7 years), panel World Aerospace Med Conf Miami 1976; chm accident investigation study gp Int Fedn Airline Pilots Assoc for 7 years (sec tech sub-ctee D at 6 int confs, rep at Accident Investigation Panel Meeting Int Civil Aviation Orgn Montreal), currently chm Air Safety Gp; visiting lectr on accident investigation and prevention Coll Aeronautics Cranfield, presented various papers at air safety and tech confs; awards: Certificate of Appreciation Flight Safety Fndn 1969, Master Air Pilot Certificate No 500, Guild Air Pilots and Air Navigators 1972, Scroll of merit IFALPA 1974, Silver Medal BALPA 1976; Freeman City of London 1976, Liveryman Guild of Air Pilots and Air Navigators 1976; *Recreations* walking, gardening; *Style—* Capt Eric Pritchard

PRITCHARD, (Iorwerth) Gwynn; s of Rev Robert Islwyn Pritchard (d 1988), and Megan Mair, *née* Lloyd; *b* 1 Feb 1946; *Educ* schs in Eng and Wales, King's Coll Cambridge (MA), Chelsea Coll London; *m* 17 Oct 1970, Marilyn Patricia; 2 s (Matthew Osian b 1975, Dafydd Islwyn b 1989), 1 da (Nia Siân b 1977); *Career* prodr and dir BBC OU Productions 1970-77; prodr: BBC Wales 1977-82, HTV Wales 1982-85; commissioning ed Channel 4 TV 1985-88, sr commissioning ed educn Channel 4 TV 1989-; tstee: Broadcast Support Servs, Welsh Writers Tst; memb Bd: Nat Inst of Adult and Continuing Educn, INPUT; memb: RTS 1985, BAFTA 1985; Chevalier de L'Ordre des Lettres et des Arts France 1990; *Recreations* reading, swimming, walking; *Style*— Gwynn Pritchard, Esq; Channel 4 TV Ltd, 60 Charlotte St, London W1P 2AX (☎ 071 927 8929, fax 071 580 2617, telex 892355)

PRITCHARD, Kenneth William; WS; s of Dr Edward Kenneth Pritchard (d 1976), of Uxbridge, and Isobel Mary, *née* Broom (d 1948); *b* 11 Nov 1933; *Educ* Dundee HS, Fettes, Univ of St Andrews (BL); *m* 18 Oct 1962, Gretta, da of late Robert Broadfoot Stitt Murray, of Lochranza, Isle of Arran; 2 s (Kenneth b 1963, Gavin b 1964), 1 da (Katharine b 1968); *Career* Nat Serv Argyll & Sutherland Highlanders 1955-57, Capt TA 1957-62; sr ptnr J & J Scrimgeour Dundee 1970-76 (joined 1957); memb: Sheriff's Court & Rules Cncl 1973-76, Lord Dunpark's Ctee on Reparation Reporting, Nat Tst for Scotland Jubilee Ctee 1980-82; pres Dundee HS Old Boy's Club 1975-76 (capt RFC 1959-62), sec Law Soc of Scot 1976-, Hon Sheriff Dundee 1978, govr Moray House Coll of Educn 1978-80; hon visiting prof of law Univ of Strathclyde, memb Ct Univ of Dundee; *Recreations* golf; *Clubs* New (Edinburgh), Hon Co of Edinburgh Golfers, Bruntsfield Links Golfing Soc; *Style*— Kenneth Pritchard, Esq, WS; 36 Ravelston Dykes, Edinburgh EH4 3EB (☎ 031 332 8584); Law Society of Scotland, 26 Drumsheugh Gdns, Edinburgh (☎ 031 226 7411, telex 72436 LAWSCOG, fax 031 225 2934)

PRITCHARD, Dr Michael John; s of Alfred Wiliam Pritchard (d 1968), of Shirley, Croydon, Surrey, and Margaret Constance, *née* Dixie (d 1975); *b* 20 July 1929; *Educ* Selhurst GS Croydon, Trinity Hall Cambridge (MA), St Thomas' Hosp (MB BChir); *m* 31 March 1956, Mary Veronica, da of Walter James Hanover Derham (d 1960), of Brisbane, Aust; 2 s (Mark b 1957, Jeremy b 1958); *Career* Nat Serv RAMC Capt MO to 16/5 Queens Royal Lancers; registrar, then sr registrar Maudsley Hosp London1958-63, sr lectr and hon conslt psychiatrist The London Hosp Med Coll 1964-75, reader and hon conslt psychiatrist St Thomas' Hosp Med Sch 1983-89 (house offr 1954-55, sr lectr and hon conslt psychiatrist 1975-83), pt/t reader in psychiatry at UMDS and St Thomas's Hosp 1989-, advsr in psychiatry to CMO Met Police 1983-89; FRCPsych 1974, FRCP 1977; *Books* Medicine and the Behavioural Sciences: An Introduction for Students of the Health and Allied Professions; *Recreations* music, architecture, home computing, photography; *Style*— Dr Michael Pritchard; UMDS Dept of Psychiatry, St Thomas' Hospital Campus, Lambeth Palace Rd, London SE1 7EH (071 928 9292)

PRITCHARD, Sir Neil; KCMG (1962, CMG 1952); s of late Joseph Pritchard; *b* 14 Jan 1911; *Educ* Liverpool Coll, Worcester Coll Oxford; *m* 1943, Mary Borroughes (d 1988); *Career* high cmmr Tanganyika 1961-63, dep under sec state Cwlth Office 1963-67, ambass Bangkok 1967-70, ret; *Style*— Sir Neil Pritchard, KCMG; Little Garth, Daglingworth, Cirencester, Glos GL7 7AQ (☎ 0285 652 353)

PRITCHARD, Prof Robert Hugh; s of Henry Ambrose Pritchard, OBE (d 1931), of London, and Fiorenza Rozina, *née* Napolitano (d 1981); *b* 25 Jan 1930; *Educ* Emmanuel Sch London, Kings Coll London (BSc), Univ of Glasgow (PhD); *m* 1, (m dis), Jacqueline, *née* Thompson; 2 s (John David b 1960, Simon Niel b 1961); m 2, 3 Nov 1974, Susan Beth, da of Sidney Rosenberg (d 1983), of Chicago; 1 step da (Naomi Rose b 1966); *Career* lectr in genetics Univ of Glasgow 1956-59, Scientific Staff MRC 1959-64, prof of genetics Univ of Leicester 1964-84; City cncllr (leader of Lib Democrats) Leicester, co cncllr Leicestershire; memb: Genetic Soc, Soc for Genetic Microbiology, American Soc for Microbiology; *Books* Basic Cloning Techniques (1985); *Recreations* politics, gardening; *Style*— Prof Robert Pritchard; 8 Knighton Grange Rd, Leicester LE2 2LE (☎ 0533 705210); University of Leicester, University Rd, Leicester LE1 7RH

PRITCHARD, Robin Alistair; s of John Ernest Pritchard (d 1984), of Southport, and Ethel, *née* Goodwin; *b* 22 July 1948; *Educ* Liverpool Bluecoat Sch, Lanchester Poly (BA); *m* 1, 9 Aug 1975 (m dis 1982), Linda Jane, *née* Street; m 2, 30 April 1983 (m dis 1990), Margaret Ruth, da of Kenneth Buckley Drennan, of Cheltenham; *Career* product promotions offr Gerrard Industs 1971, account handler Garland Compton 1972, account exec Roe Compton 1973, account dir Central and Whites Advertising 1978, co fndr Pritchard Williams Ltd (now Solomon Oakley Pritchard Williams Ltd) 1979, proprietor Ruberoid Insulation Services (Shrewsbury) 1991; MInstM 1973, FCIM 1989; *Recreations* cycling, walking, flying, reading; *Clubs* The Squadron (N Weald); *Style*— Robin Pritchard, Esq; Downton Farm House, Upton Magna, Shrewsbury SY4 4PL (☎ 0743 77660); Solomon Oakley Pritchard Williams Ltd, Priory House, 223 Bristol Rd, Birmingham B5 7UB (☎ 021 440 3300, fax 021 440 2668); Ruberoid Insulation Services (Shrewsbury) (☎ 0743 232700, fax 0743 271275)

PRITCHARD, Lt-Col Steven Charles George; TD (1976, bar 1984); s of Dennis Pritchard, QPM, and Gwendoline Cecilia, *née* Marshall; *b* 4 July 1938; *Educ* Sir George Monoux Sch, Univ of London (BA); *m* 1 June 1963, Christine Patricia, da of Sydney Royston Bent; 1 s (Hadley Barrington Charles b 16 Oct 1974); *Career* TA serv: Herts and Beds Yeo, 100 Medium Regt RA, 95 Commando Fou RA, 6 FD Force, 617 Sqdn RAF; dir Hill Samuel 1971-74, vice-pres Rapidata Inc 1974-76, md Systel Telematics 1976-85; conslt to Sultanate of Oman and Emirate of Kuwait 1985-87; Freeman City of London 1982, Liveryman Worshipful Co of Turners 1983; FBIM, ACEA; *Recreations* tennis, scuba diving, parachuting; *Clubs* HAC; *Style*— Lt-Col Steven Pritchard, TD; The Towers, Sewards End, Essex; 192 Sloane St, London SW1

PRITCHARD-BARRETT, Christopher; s of Stanley Pritchard-Barrett (d 1962), of Tiggins House, Kelsale, Saxmundham, Suffolk, and Winifred Mary, *née* Ransom (d 1976); *b* 24 Sept 1931; *Educ* Eton; *m* 1, 27 Sept 1957 (m dis 1966), Diana Joan Tower, da of Surgn Cdr E R Sorley, RN (ka HMS Barham 1941), of Pangbourne; 1 s (James Robert b 1 Dec 1962), 1 da (Sara b 13 Jan 1959); m 2, 21 March 1970, Susan Hulda Monica, da of Robert Bald (d 1962), of Wallington, Baldock, Herts; 1 s (Jonathan Christopher b 6 April 1972), 1 da (Kate b 10 April 1974); *Career* Nat Serv cmmnd 12 Royal Lancers 1950-52; Furness Withy & Co Ltd 1955-61, West of England Steamship Owners Protection and Indemnity Assoc Ltd 1961 (gen mangr 1969), dir West of England Insur Servs (successor co) 1978; chief exec: The Shipowners Protection and Indemnity Assoc Ltd 1981, The Shipowners Protection Ltd 1987; memb: Exec Ctee Br Motorship Owners Assoc, S Devon Herd Book Soc; Liveryman Worshipful Co of Shipwrights, Freeman Worshipful Co of Watermen and Lightermen of the River Thames; memb: Inst Chartered Shipbrokers 1959, NFU, RASE; *Recreations* off shore sailing; *Clubs* Royal Cruising, Aldeburgh Yacht Thames Barge Sailing; *Style*— Christopher Pritchard-Barrett, Esq; 10 Mariners Way, Aldeburgh, Suffolk IP15 5QH; The Shipowners Protection Ltd, St Clare House, 30-33 Minories, London EC 3N 1BP (☎ 071 488 0911, fax 071 480 5806, telex 928 525 SOPCL)

PRITCHARD-GORDON, Giles William; s of William Herbert Alexander Pritchard-Gordon (d 1987), and Lesley Pamela Joy, *née* Blackburn; *b* 22 May 1947; *Educ* Radley; *m* 19 Nov 1971, Veronica, da of Ronald Victor Smyth, of Clear Height, Downs Rd, Epsom, Surrey; 4 da (Alice Clare b 1974, Emily Kate b 1979, Lucy Clementine b 1983, Eliza Mary 1986); *Career* dir H Clarkson & Co Ltd 1972-73, fndr Giles W Pritchard-Gordon & Co Ltd 1973; Giles W Pritchard-Gordon Ltd dir subsids: Shipbroking 1981, Farming 1981, Property 1984, Futures 1985; pres Staplefield CC; Freeman City of London, Liveryman Worshipful Co of Fishmongers 1983; *Recreations* horse racing and breeding, stalking, golf; *Clubs* R & A, MCC, Seaview YC; *Style*— Giles Pritchard-Gordon, Esq; Slaugham Park, Slaugham, Sussex (☎ 0444 400 388); 11/15 Arlington St, St James's, London SW1 (☎ 071 408 0585, telex 261143)

PRITCHETT, Sir Victor Sawdon; CBE (1968); s of Sawdon Pritchett; *b* 16 Dec 1900; *Educ* Alleyn's; *m* 1936, Dorothy, da of Richard Samuel Roberts; 1 s, 1 da; *Career* author and literary critic; Christian Gauss Lectr Univ of Princetown 1953, Beckman Prof Univ of California Berkeley 1962, writer-in-residence Smith Coll Mass 1966; visiting prof: Univ of Brandeis Mass, Univ of Columbia (Clark Lectr 1969); foreign memb: American Acad and Inst 1971, American Acad Arts and Sci 1971; pres: Int PEN 1974-76, Soc of Authors 1977-; companion Royal Soc of Lit 1987; Hon DLitt Univ of Leeds, Hon DLitt Univ of Columbia and Sussex, Hon DLitt Harvard Univ 1985; kt 1975; *Clubs* Savile, Beefsteak; *Style*— Sir Victor Pritchett, CBE; 12 Regent's Park Terr, London NW1 (☎ 071 485 8827)

PRITTIE, Hon (Henry) Francis Cornelius; s and h of 6 Baron Dunalley; *b* 30 May 1948; *Educ* Gordonstoun, Trinity Coll Dublin (BA); *m* 1978, Sally Louise, da of late Ronald Vere, of Heaton Chapel, Cheshire; 1 s (Joel Henry b 1981), 3 da (Rebecca Louise b 1979, Hannah Beatrice b 1983, Rachel Sarah b 1987); *Career* probation offr with Oxfordshire Probation Serv; *Style*— The Hon Francis Prittie; 25 Stephen Rd, Oxford OX3 9AY (☎ 0865 61914)

PRITTY, Dr Paul Edmund; s of Charles Pritty, and Kathleen, *née* Ellenthorpe; *b* 29 Nov 1945; *Educ* Spalding GS, St Georges Med Sch, Selwyn Coll Cambridge (MB BChir, MA); *m* 1 Dec 1973, Carole, da of William Thomas; 2 da (Emma Louise b 5 Nov 1976, Amy Clare b 27 Feb 1979); *Career* conslt in accident and emergency med Derbyshire Royal Infirmary 1980-, jt site med offr Kegworth M1 air crash 1989; conslt in charge Flying Squad Emergency Med Team; Derbyshire Red Cross: MO Derby City Centre, asst branch MO; FRCS 1978, memb Casualty Surgns Assoc 1980; *Recreations* DIY, butterfly breeder; *Style*— Dr Paul Pritty; Accident and Emergency Department, Derbyshire Royal Infirmary, London Rd, Derby DE1 2QY (☎ 0332 47141)

PRIZEMAN, John Brewster; s of Donald John Charles Prizeman (d 1952), of 73 Whiteknights Rd, Reading, Berks, and Mary Elizabeth, *née* Brewster (d 1984); *b* 15 Nov 1930; *Educ* Leighton Park Sch, AA Sch of Architecture (Dip Arch); *m* 8 Feb 1958, Jennifer Willow, da of Horace Milner Bentley (d 1965), of The Mill House, Elstead, Surrey; 1 s (Mark b 1959), 2 da (Camilla b 1963, Oriel b 1969); *Career* architect; past pres Architectural Assoc 1981-83; RIBA; *Books* Kitchens, Living Rooms, European Interior Design, Your House: The Outside view; *Recreations* reading, drawing, painting, photography, gardening; *Clubs* Surveyor's, The Architecture; *Style*— John Prizeman, Esq; The Old Rectory, Church Lane, Albourne, Hassocks, West Sussex BN6 9BY

PROBERT, David Henry; s of William David Thomas Probert, of Birmingham, and Doris Mabel, *née* Mayell (d 1987); *b* 11 April 1938; *Educ* Bromsgrove HS; *m* 14 June 1968, Sandra Mary, da of John Howard Prince (d 1988); 1 s (Russell b 1979), 1 da (Jane b 1974); *Career* various posts: ICI Metals Div 1960-66, Coopers & Lybrand 1966-71; gp fin dir: BSA Ltd 1971-73, Mills & Allen International Ltd 1974-75, W Canning plc 1976- (chief exec 1979-85, chm and chief exec 1986-); non-exec dir: Linread plc 1983-90, ASD plc 1984-90, Sandvik Ltd 1986-90, Beatson Clark plc 1987-88, Rockwool Ltd 1988-90, Private Patients Plan Ltd 1988-; chm Crown Agents 1990- (dep chm 1985-90, crown agent 1981-); memb: W Midlands Regnl Cncl CBI 1978-84 and 1984-90, Br Hallmarking Cncl 1983-, Ctee W Midlands Lord Taverners 1985-, Cncl Birmingham C-of-C 1990-; Freeman: City of London, Worshipful Co of Secs and Administrators; CBIM, MIMC, FCMA, FCCA, FCIS; *Recreations* reading, music, theatre; *Clubs* RAC, City Livery; *Style*— David Probert, Esq; W Canning plc, Canning House, St Paul's Square, Birmingham B3 1QR (☎ 021 236 8224, fax 021 236 3320)

PROBERT, Lt-Col Richard Harlackenden Carwardine; OBE (1959), DL (Suffolk 1983); s of Col Geoffrey Oliver Cardwardine Probert, CBE (d 1987), of Bevills, Suffolk, and Ruby Margaret Alexandra, *née* Marc; descendant in the male line from Ynyr, King of Gwent (11 century) and the Proberts of Pantglas and The Argoed, Mon, Gentlemen Ushers to the King and High Sheriffs of Mon, with collateral family links with Bures and Earls Colne dating back to 14 century (*see* Burke's Landed Gentry 18 edn, Vol I, 1965); *b* 19 April 1922; *Educ* Eton, RMCS; *m* 25 April 1945, Elisabeth Margaret, da of Donald Boase Sinclair, OBE, WS, of 9 Belgrave Place, Edinburgh; 1 s (Geoffrey b 1953), 2 da (Camilla b 1946, Anne b 1948); *Career* serv WWII RHA 1940-45, Normandy and NW Europe 1944-45, instr in gunnery 1945-46, Royal Armament Res and Design Estab 1948-51 (Tripartite Conf Washington 1951), 3 RHA BAOR 1951-54, staff Dir-Gen of Artillery 1954-56, Br Nuclear Def Trials Australia 1957; Dir Staff Lt-Col RMCS 1956-59; md Bexford Ltd (a subsid of ICI 1968) 1962-76; Queen's award to Industry 1966, 1969, 1971, 1973; farmer; Freeman City of London 1956, Liveryman Worshipful Co of Ironmongers (Master 1977-78); High Sheriff Suffolk 1980-81; hon lay canon St Edmundsbury Cathedral 1984-; memb: Ct of Essex Univ 1966-, Suffolk TAVR 1980-, Suffolk Ctee CLA 1981- (pres 1991-); FRSA 1964; *Recreations* countryside, conservation, walking, travel; *Clubs* Army and Navy; *Style*— Lt-Col Richard Probert, OBE, DL; Great Bevills, Bures, Suffolk

PROBY, Sir Peter; 2 Bt (UK 1952), of Elton Hall, Cambs; s of Sir Richard George Proby, 1 Bt, MC (d 1979), and Betty Monica (d 1967), er da of Alexander Henry Hallam Murray, of Sandling, Hythe, Kent; *b* 4 Dec 1911; *Educ* Eton, Trinity Coll Oxford; *m* 15 Jan 1944, Blanche Harrison, da of Col Henry Harrison Cripps, DSO (d 1960), of Bath Lodge, Ballycastle, Co Antrim; 1 s (and 1 s decd), 3 da (Sarah (Mrs Mills) b 1945, Charlotte (Mrs Hay) b 1957, Christine (Mrs Dobbs) b 1957); *Heir* s, William Henry Proby, *qv*; *Career* serv WWII 1939-45 Capt Irish Gds; bursar of Eton Coll 1953-71; land agent; Lord-Lt Cambs 1981-85 (DL 1980); FRICS; KStJ 1983; *Clubs* Travellers'; *Style*— Sir Peter Proby, Bt; Pottle Green, Elton, Peterborough PE8 6SG (☎ 0832 280434)

PROBY, William Henry; s and h of Sir Peter Proby, 2 Bt; *b* 13 June 1949; *Educ* Eton, Univ of Oxford (MA), Brooksby Coll of Agric; *m* 1974, Meredyth Anne Brentnall, da of Dr Timothy David Brentnall; 3 da (Alexandra b 1980, Alice b 1982, Frances b 1986); *Career* CA 1975-; farmer; asst dir Morgan Grenfell 1980-82, md M W P Ltd 1980-82; dir: M M & K Ltd 1986, Ellis & Everard plc 1988; chm Taxation Ctee, dep chm Historic Houses Assoc 1988; FCA 1975; *Recreations* skiing, shooting, music; *Clubs* Brook's; *Style*— William Proby, Esq; Elton Hall, Elton, nr Peterborough PE8 6SH (☎ 0832 280310); Flat 3, 4 Lyall St, London SW1 (☎ 071 235 7801)

PROBYN, Jeffrey Alan (Jeff); s of Charles Probyn, of Winchelsa View, Udimore, Sussex, and late Patricia Rachel Thomas; *b* 27 April 1956; *Educ* London Nautical Sch; *m* 27 December 1975, Jennifer Christine Probyn, Victor Gordon Thomas (father-in-law); 3 c (Jeffrey-Paul Probyn 8 July 1976, Steven James Victor Charles Probyn 3 September 1977, Rebecca Faye Jennifer Probyn 14 May 1980); *Career* Rugby Union prop forward Wasps and England (17 caps); Surrey Sch U15 and U18, London Cos U15 and U18m U15 Eng traillist; clubs: Old Albanians 1971-77, Streatham & Croydon 1977-80, Richmond 1980-84, Wasps 1984- (110 appearances); county: Hertfordshire

1976, Surrey Club 1979, Middlesex 1982, Surrey 1984-85; London Division: vs Aust as replacement, appeared in every game in Divnl Championship 1985-; England: reserve World Cup 1987, debut vs France Parc des Princes 1988, toured Australia 1988, first try vs Queensland 1988, first test try vs Romania 1989, first Five Nations try vs Ireland Twickenham 1990; toured South Africa with World XV 1989, memb British Lions vs France bicentennial 1989; litigation clerk Durrant Pierce Solicitors 1975-77, dir Probros Ltd 1977-; *Recreations* sailing, shooting, scuba diving; *Style*— Jeff Probyn, Esq; Probros Ltd, 2-4 Chance St, Bethal Green, London E1 6JT (☎ 071 739 3887, fax 071 729 4403)

PROBYN-JONES, Lady; Eileen; da of late James Evans, of The Old Hall, Helsby, Cheshire; *m* 1919, Sir Arthur Probyn Probyn-Jones, 2 and last Bt (d 1951); Sir Robert Jones, KBE, CB, the eminent orthopaedic surgn cr 1 Bt 1926; *Style*— Lady Probyn-Jones; Spur Cottage, South Lodge, Ham Common, Surrey

PROCHASKA, Dr Alice Marjorie Sheila; da of John Harold Barwell (d 1983), of Cambridge, and The Hon Sheila Margaret Ramsay, *née* McNair; *b* 12 July 1947; *Educ* Perse Sch for Girls Cambridge, Somerville Coll Oxford (BA, MA, DPhil); *m* 25 June 1971, Franklyn Kimmel Prochaska, s of Franklin Anton Prochaska (d 1952), of Cleveland, Ohio, USA; 1 s (William b 1982), 1 da (Elizabeth b 1980); *Career* asst keeper Public Record Office 1975-84 (London Museum 1971-73), sec & librarian Inst of Historical Res Univ of London 1984-; author of numerous articles on archives and various aspects of Br history c 1800 to present; organiser of special expos incl: London in the Thirties 1973, Young Writers of the Thirties 1976; memb: Cncl Br Records Assoc, Nat Archives Cncl (chm 1991), Steering Gp History at the Univs Def Gp, Nat Curriculum History Working Gp Dept of Educn and Sci 1989-90; FRHistS 1987; *Books* London in the Thirties (1973), History of the General Federation of Trade Unions, 1899-1980 (1982), Irish History from 1700: A guide to sources in the Public Record Office (1986), Margaretta Acworth's Georgian Cookery Book (ed with Frank Prochaska, 1987); *Recreations* family life, cookery, travel, reading; *Style*— Dr Alice Prochaska; Institute of Historical Research, University of London, Senate House, Malet St, London WC1E 7HU (☎ 071 636 0272)

PROCKTOR, Patrick; s of Eric Christopher Procktor (d 1940), and Barbara Winifred, *née* Hopkins; *b* 12 March 1936; *Educ* Highgate Sch, Slade Sch of Fine Art, UCL; *m* 1973, Kirsten Bo (d 1984), da of Nils Bo Andersen, of Copenhagen; 1 s (Nicholas b 1974); *Career* painter, etcher, illustrator, stage designer; since 1963 14 one man exhibitions at Redfern Gallery; Monograph with 42 colour plates 1985; *Recreations* bridge, Russian ballet; *Style*— Patrick Procktor, Esq; 26 Manchester St, London WIM 5PG

PROCTER, Gordon Heslop; s of Frederick Adlington Procter (d 1970), and Elizabeth, *née* Heslop (d 1974); *b* 11 Oct 1924; *Educ* Public Sch Whitgift Surrey; *m* 1949, Florence Henrietta (Floss), da of Harold Bibby (d 1960); 1 s (John Howard Adlington b 1950), 2 da (Sarah Jane (Sally) b 1953, Jane Hilary Elizabeth (Mrs Goldstaub) b 1954 *qv*); *Career* air crew trg 1943, cmmnd pilot 1944, 6 Airborne Div 1944, took part in Op Varsity 1945, Air Force of Occupation Japan 1946, demob 1947; Erwin Wasey 1947-52, Samson Clark 1952-53, Pembertons 1954-71, GPP Ltd 1971-80, Barrett Communications Gp 1981-89, Dorland Business Communications 1989-; former: pres Solus Club of London, chm Nat Advertising Benevolent Soc, chm Regent Advertising Club of London, chm Media Exec Soc; memb: Croydon Advertising Assoc, Freeman City of London 1960, Liveryman Worshipful Co of Upholders (past Master 1987); fell Inst of Practitioners in Advertising, memb Inst of Public Relations; *Recreations* motor sport (drove for Ford of Europe on int rallies), classic cars, off-shore power boat racing, rugby; *Clubs* City Livery, RAF, Royal London YC, Royal Solent YC, Aston Martin Owners, Rolls Royce MC, Daimler CC, Jowett Javelin CC, Jenson CC; *Style*— Gordon Procter, Esq; Falcon Field, Cherry Garden Hill, Groombridge, East Sussex TN3 9NY (☎ 0892 864050); Dorland Business Communications, 141 Westbourne Terrace, London W2 6JR (☎ 071 262 0828, fax 071 402 3346)

PROCTER, Herbert Gerald; s of Herbert George Procter (d 1974), of N Ferriby, Humberside, and Phyllis, *née* Charlesworth (d 1985); *b* 28 May 1931; *Educ* Hull GS; *m* 14 April 1956, Pauline, da of Frederick Charles McKeigh Heath (d 1964); 2 s (Andrew b 1958, Nicholas b 1964), 1 da (Deborah b 1960); *Career* Capt (TA) 1959-61, Flying Offr RAF 1955-57; slr; sr ptnr Stamp Jackson & Procter 1968-, coroner for Holderness 1965-74; dep chm Humberside CC 1980-81 (chm Planning and Tport Ctee 1977-81); pres: Kingston upon Hull Cons Fedn 1980-89, Hull Incorporated Law Soc 1978-79, Hull Jr C of C & Shipping 1966-67; dir W A Holdings plc 1973-87; *Recreations* flying, music, languages; *Clubs* Carlton; *Style*— H Gerald Procter, Esq; The Paddock, Southtergate, Hedon, Hull HU12 8JS (☎ 0482 897 640); 5 Parliament St, Hull HU1 2AZ (☎ 0482 24591, telex 597 001, fax 0482 224 048)

PROCTER, Jane Hilary Elizabeth (Mrs Goldstaub); da of Gordon Heslop Procter, and Florence Henrietta Procter; *Educ* Queen's Coll Harley St; *m* 4 June 1985, Thomas Charles Goldstaub, s of Werner Fritz Goldstaub; 1 s (Rollo Alexander b 1989), 1 da (Tabitha Sophie b 1985); *Career* fashion asst Vogue 1974-75, asst fashion ed Good Housekeeping 1975-77, actg fashion ed Woman's Journal 1977-78, fashion writer Country Life 1978-80; freelance fashion ed: Times, Sunday Times, Daily Express 1980-87; ed British W 1987-88, ed Tatler 1990-; *Books* Dress Your Best (1983), Celebrity Knitting (1984), What do you call a kid? (1985), Savoy Centenary 1889-1989 (1989); *Style*— Miss Jane Procter; 2 Hannington Rd, London SW4 ONA (☎ 071 622 9634)

PROCTER, John Howard Adlington; s of Gordon Heslop Procter, of Falcon Field, Cherry Orchard Hill, Groombridge, W Sussex, and Florrence Henrietta Procter; *b* 11 June 1950; *Educ* Downside, Hurstpierpoint Coll; *m* 5 Nov 1977, Glenda Kathryn, da of Sqdn Ldr (Cecil) Bertram Hislop, of 34 Roslyn Park, Weybridge, Surrey; 1 s (David Jonathan Howard b 13 Oct 1983), 1 da (Vanessa Kathryn Hislop b 22 Sept 1986); *Career* stockbroker and trading dealer 1969-74, insurance broker JH Minet 1974-78, exec dir EW Payne 1978-87, dir CE Heath Aviation Ltd 1987-; area rep Local Community Security; Freeman: City of London 1979, Worshipful Co of Upholders 1979; memb BIBA; *Recreations* sailing, motor racing; *Clubs* Bewel Valley Sailing, Inst of Advanced Motorists, Royal Solent Yacht, Royal Yachting Assoc, Lloyds Motor; *Style*— John Procter, Esq; 25 Great Footway, Langton Green, Tunbridge Wells, Kent TW3 ODT (☎ 0892 86 3355); CE Heath Aviation Ltd, Cuthbert Heath House, 150 Minories, London EC3N 1NR (☎ 071 488 2488, telex 8813001, fax 071 481 4561, car 0860 639259)

PROCTER, (Mary) Norma; da of John Procter (d 1977), of Grimsby, and Edith Clarice, *née* Hockney; *b* 15 Feb 1928; *Educ* Wintringham Secdy Sch; *Career* int concert singer (contralto); vocal studies with Roy Henderson, musicianship with Alec Redshaw, lieder with Hans Oppenheim and Paul Hamburger, London debut at Southwark Cathedral 1948, specialist in concert works oratorio and recitals, appeared with all the major orchestras and in all the major festivals in UK; operatic debut Lucretia in Britten's Rape of Lucretia Aldenburgh Festival 1957-58, Covent Garden debut in Gluck's Orpheus 1960; performed in: Germany, France, Spain, Portugal, Norway, Holland, Belgium, Sweden, Denmark, Finland, Austria, Israel, Luxembourg, S America; recording's incl: Messiah, Elijah, Samson, Mahler's 2, 3 and 8 Symphonies, Das Klagende Lied, Hartmann 1 Symphony, Juluis Caeser Jones, Nicholas Maw's Scenes and Arias, Hermann Suter Le Laudi, BBC Last Night of the Proms; pres Crimsby Philharmonic Soc; Hon RAM; *Recreations* sketching, painting, tapestry, TV; *Style*— Miss Norma Procter; 194 Clee Rd, Grimsby, S Humberside DN32 8NG (☎ 0472 691 210)

PROCTER, (Sarah Jane) Sally; da of Gordon Procter, of Falcon Field, Cherry Garden Hill, Groombridge, E Sussex, and Florence, *née* Bibby; *b* 11 Feb 1953; *Educ* Croydon HS; *Career* market res Lindsay Smithers Johannesburg 1973, indust market res Indust Facts and Forecasting London 1974; Leith's School of Food and Wine: student 1975, teacher 1976-80, princ 1980-89; gp mktg mangr Leith's Good Food 1989; certified memb of Int Assoc of Cooking Professionals; cooking demonstrations in: London, UK, NY, Sydney; *publications* contrib to food sections of various newspapers and magazines; *Recreations* skiing, yachting, power boat racing, gliding, eating out; *Style*— Miss Sally Procter; 27 Sisters Avenue, Battersea, London SW11 5SR (☎ 071 223 2369); Leiths Good Food, 86 Bondway, London SW8 1SF (☎ 071 735 6303, fax 071 735 1170)

PROCTER, Sidney; CBE (1986); s of Robert Procter; *b* 10 March 1925; *Educ* Ormskirk GS; *m* 1952, Isabel, *née* Simmons; 1 da; *Career* RAF 1943-47; dir: Williams & Glyn's Bank 1976- (chief exec 1978-82), Royal Bank of Scotland 1979-85; Royal Bank of Scotland Group: dir 1978-86, dep gp md 1979-82, gp chief exec 1982-85, vice chm 1986-87; advsr to Govr Bank of England 1985-87; chm Exeter Trust Ltd 1985-, dir Provincial Group 1985-, cmmr Bldg Socs Cmmn 1986-; FIB; *Style*— Sidney Procter, Esq, CBE; The Piece House, Bourton-on-the-Water, Glos

PROCTOR, His Hon Judge Anthony James; s of James Proctor (d 1967), of Harrogate, Yorks, and Savina Maud, *née* Horsfield (d 1981); *b* 18 Sept 1931; *Educ* Mexborough GS Yorkshire, St Catharine's Coll Cambridge (BA, LLB, MA, LLM); *m* 12 Sept 1964, Patricia Mary, da of George William Bryan, of Sheffield (d 1981); 1 da (Susan Jane b 1966); *Career* Nat Serv Flying Offr RAF 1953-55; articled clerk to Sir Bernard Kenyon, clerk W Riding CC 1955-58, admitted slr 1958, asst slr Barnsley Corporation 1958-60, sr prosecuting and Common Law slr Sheffield Corporation 1960-64, ptnr Neals and Shelley Barkers Slrs 1964-74, dist registrar and registrar of Co Ct 1974-88, recorder Crown Ct 1985-88, circuit judge 1988-; memb Law Soc 1958-, pres Soc of Dist and Co Registrars 1985; *Recreations* fell walking, photography, genealogy; *Style*— His Hon Judge Anthony Proctor; Courts of Justice, Crown Square, Manchester (☎ 061 932 8393)

PROCTOR, Gillian Mary; da of John Hargreaves Turner, of Dorset, and Amy Winifred Turner, *née* Herring (d 1975); *b* 9 Nov 1947; *Educ* Church HS Newcastle on Tyne, Harrogate Ladies Coll, Wentworth Milton Mount; *m* 4 Oct 1969 (m dis 1986), David, s of Stanley Budleigh, of Devon; 2 da (Victoria Jane b 1972, Clare Louise b 1976); *Career* property restoration 1969-, md & chm Longmeadow Homes Ltd specialising in care 9 nursing homes 1982-; *Recreations* vintage cars, gardening; *Clubs* Rolls-Royce Enthusiasts, Daimler & Lanchester, Reg Residential Care Homes Assoc, Royal Horticultural Soc; *Style*— Mrs Gillian M Proctor; Allington, Honiton, Devon; Hay House, Broadclyst, Exeter, Devon (☎ 0392 61779)

PROCTOR, Ian Douglas Ben; s of Douglas McIntyre Proctor (d 1951), and Mary Albina Louise Proctor (d 1975); *b* 12 July 1918; *Educ* Gresham's Sch Holt, Univ of London; *m* 1943, Elizabeth Anne, da of Air Vice-Marshal Oswyn Gifford Lywood, CB, CBE (d 1960); 3 s (Keith, Brian, Roger), 1 da (Jill); *Career* Flying Offr RAF VR 1941-45; md Gosport Yacht Co 1947-48, jt ed Yachtsman Magazine 1948-50, Yachting corr Daily Telegraph 1950-64, freelance industl designer 1950-, chm Ian Proctor Metal Masts Ltd 1962-76 and 1980-86 (dir 1959-86); Cncl Industl Design Award 1967, Design Cncl Award 1977 and 1979; Yachtsman of the Year 1965; RDI 1969, FCSD 1969, FRSA 1971; *Books* Racing Dinghy Handling, Sailing Strategy, Racing Dinghy Maintenance, Boats for Sailing; *Recreations* sailing, photography, bird watching; *Clubs* Int Yacht Racing Union, Stoke Gabriel Sailing; *Style*— Ian Proctor, Esq; Ferry House, Duncannon, Stoke Gabriel, nr Totnes, Devon TQ9 6QY (☎ 080 428 589)

PROCTOR-BEAUCHAMP, Sir Christopher Radstock; 9 Bt (GB 1745); s of Rev Sir Ivor Cuthbert, 8 Bt (d 1971); *b* 30 Jan 1935; *Educ* Rugby, Trinity Coll Cambridge; *m* 1965, Rosalind Emily Margot, da of Gerald Percival Wainwright, of St Leonards-on-Sea; 2 s, 1 da; *Heir* s, Charles Barclay Proctor-Beauchamp b 7 July 1969; *Style*— Sir Christopher Proctor-Beauchamp, Bt; The White House, Harpford, nr Sidmouth, Devon

PRODDOW, Nigel Norman; s of William Norman Proddow (d 1954), and Elsie Gladys Mumford (d 1981); *b* 6 Sept 1929; *Educ* Stowe, Jesus Coll Oxford (MA); *m* 25 May 1968, Caroline Alexandra, da of David William Stanley, of S Africa; 2 s (Charles b 1969, Guy b 1971); *Career* chief gen mangr & dir Pearl Assurance plc 1984-89 (dir 1983-89); dir: Pearl Group plc 1985-89, Pearl Assurance (Unit Funds) Ltd 1983-89, Pearl Trust Managers Ltd 1983-89, Pearl Assurance (Unit Linked Pensions) Ltd 1983-89, Hallmark Insurance Co Ltd 1985-89, Insur Orphans' Fund 1985-90, Watling St Properties Ltd 1985-89, St Helen's Trust Ltd 1986-89; memb: Bd Royal Nat Orthopaedic Hosp, Policyholders' Protection Bd; FIA, ACIS; *Recreations* tennis, golf, sailing, skiing; *Clubs* Roehampton, Sea View Yacht; *Style*— Nigel Proddow, Esq; 27 Hertford Avenue, East Sheen, London SW14 8EF; 252 High Holborn, London WC1V 7EB (☎ 071 405 8441, telex 296350 PEARL G, fax 071 831 6251)

PRODGER, John Alan; ERD (1964), JP (Bucks 1982); s of Alan St George Cuthbert Prodger (d 1983), and Rona Ethel Prodger; *b* 19 Jan 1932; *Educ* Merchant Taylors', Worcester Coll Oxford (BA); *m* 1971, Tessa Mary Colthurst, da of Capt Gerald Oulton Colthurst Davies, RN (d 1989); 1 s, 1 da; *Career* served 9 Queen's Royal Lancers (now 9/12 Royal Lancers); Tate and Lyle Ltd 1957-73; dir: personnel bd Carreras Rothmans Ltd 1973-84, dir personnel Rothmans International plc 1984-88; mgmnt conslt 1988-; chm Tobacco Indust Employers' Assoc 1979-84, CBI Cncl, Southern region CBI 1979-88, chm Cncl Centre for Judaism Selly Oak Colls 1988-; memb Area Manpower Bd Herts and Bucks 1985-1988, gen cmmr for income tax 1989-, chm Oxford Diocesan Bd of Fin 1990-, govr Aylesbury GS 1990-; tstee: Open Univ Fndn 1990-, Maj Stanley's Tst OURFC 1990-; FIPM, FInstD, FRSA; *Recreations* fishing, cricket, gardening, watching rugby (former Oxford blue); *Clubs* Cavalry and Guards, MCC, Vincent's; *Style*— John Prodger, Esq, ERD, JP; Granborough Lodge, Granborough, Buckingham MK18 3NJ (☎ 029 667 349)

PROES, Capt Richard Geoffrey; s of Maj Geoffrey Ernest Sullivan Proes (ka 1942), and Nancy Madeleine, *née* Churcher (d 1983); *b* 18 Aug 1937; *Educ* Wellington, RMA Sandhurst; *m* 28 May 1970, Victoria Margaret, da of Maj Arthur Michael Temple Trubshawe (d 1985); *Career* Capt Grenadier Gds 1958-68; salmon farmer; dir Kyles of Bute Salmon Ltd 1981-; *Recreations* shooting, fishing; *Style*— Capt Richard G Proes; West Glen Caladh, Tighnabruaich, Argyll PA21 2EH (☎ 0700 811224)

PROFUMO, John Dennis; CBE (1975, OBE (Mil) 1944); 5 Baron of the United Kingdom of Italy; s of Baron Albert Peter Anthony Profumo, KC (d 1940), and Martha Thom, *née* Walker; bro of Mary Baroness Balfour of Inchrye; *b* 30 Jan 1915; *Educ* Harrow, BNC Oxford (MA); *m* 1954, Valerie Louise, da of late Cdr Robert Gordon Hobson, RN, and former w of Anthony James Allan Havelock-Allan (now 4 Bt); 1 s; *Career* MP (Cons): Kettering Div Northants 1940-45, Stratford-on-Avon Div Warwicks 1950-63; jt Parly sec Miny of Tport and Civil Aviation 1952-57, Parly under sec state Colonies 1957-58, Parly under sec state Foreign Affrs 1958-59, min state Foreign Affrs 1959-60, sec state for War 1960-63; dep chm Provident Life Assoc of London

1978-82 (dir 1975-), pres Toynbee Hall 1985 (chm 1982-84); *Clubs* Boodle's; *Style*— John Profumo, Esq, CBE

PROLA, Hon Mrs (Julia Margaret); yr da of 8 Baron Grey of Codnor, CBE, AE, DL, *qv*; *b* 4 Dec 1939; *m* 1978, Max Prola, DPhil (Psych); *Style*— The Hon Mrs Prola; The Croft, High Leigh, Knutsford, Cheshire

PROOPS, Marjorie; OBE (1969); da of Alfred Rayle, and Martha Rayle; *Educ* Dalston Secdy Sch; *m* 1935; 1 s; *Career* journalist: The Daily Mirror 1939-45 and 1954-, The Daily Herald 1945-54; currently dir Mirror Gp Newspapers; Woman Journalist of the Year 1969; memb: Royal Commn on Gambling 1976-78, Cncl for One-Parent Families; *Books* Pride, Prejudice and Proops (1975), Dear Marje (1976); *Style*— Ms Marjorie Proops, OBE; 9 Sherwood Close, London SW13

PROSSER, David John; s of Ronald Thomas Prosser, of Penarth, S Wales, and Dorothy, *née* Denham; *b* 26 March 1944; *Educ* Ogmore GS, Univ Coll Wales; *m* Nov 1971, Rosemary Margaret, da of Alan Snuggs; 2 da (Charlotte Jane b Aug 1976, Claire Elizabeth b July 1979); *Career* Sun Alliance Group 1965-69, Hoare Govett 1969-73, CIN Management 1973-88, Legal & General 1988-; FIA 1971; *Recreations* golf, family tennis, watching my children grow up; *Clubs* RAC; *Style*— David Prosser, Esq; Legal & General Group, Temple Court, 11 Queen Victoria St, London EC4N 4TP

PROSSER, Ian Maurice Gray; s of Maurice and Freda Prosser; *b* 5 July 1943; *Educ* King Edward's Sch Bath, Watford GS, Univ of Birmingham (BComm); *m* 1964, Elizabeth Herman; 2 da; *Career* Coopers and Lybrand (accountants) 1964-69, joined Bass Charrington Ltd (later Bass) 1969: memb Bd 1978, vice chm 1982-87, gp md 1984-87, chm and chief exec 1987-; dir: Boots Co 1984-, Brewers' Soc 1983-, Lloyds Bank plc 1988-; FCA; *Recreations* bridge, squash, gardening; *Clubs* RAC; *Style*— Ian Prosser, Esq; Bass plc, 66 Chiltern Street, London W1M 1PR (☎ 071 486 4440)

PROSSER, (Elvet) John; QC (1978); s of David Prosser; *b* 10 July 1932; *Educ* Pontypridd GS, King's Coll London; *m* 1957, Mary Louise Cowdry; 2 da; *Career* Flt Lt RAF 1957-59; barr Gray's Inn 1956, rec Crown Ct 1972-, pt/t chm of Industl Tbnls 1975-81, asst boundary cmmr for Wales 1977-; ldr Wales and Cheshire Circuit 1984-87; *Recreations* cricket, golf; *Clubs* East Inuim, Cardiff and Co (Cardiff); *Style*— John Prosser, Esq, QC; 78 Marsham Court, Westminster, London SW1 (☎ 071 834 9779); Hillcroft, Mill Rd, Lisvane, Cardiff CF4 5XJ (☎ 0222 752380)

PROSSER, Brig (William) Keith Lloyd; CBE (1982, MBE 1973), MC (1958); s of William George Prosser (d 1985), of Bath, and Maud, *née* Lloyd (d 1989); *b* 7 March 1936; *Educ* City of Bath Sch, Sandhurst, Army Staff Coll Camberley, RCDS London; *m* 10 Feb 1962, May Ruth, da of Jacob Elias (d 1973), of Singapore; 1 s (David b 1963), 1 da (Amanda b 1966); *Career* cmmnd The 22 (Cheshire) Regt 1956, CO 1 Bn The 22 (Cheshire) Regt 1976-78, Bde Cdr 8 Inf Bde 1980-82, dir Army Reserves and cadets MOD (A) 1986-89, Col The 22 (Cheshire) Regt 1985-91, ADC 1988; Clerk Worshipful Co of Tallow Chandlers 1990; *Recreations* rugby, skiing, tennis, walking; *Style*— Brig Keith Prosser, CBE, MC; Tallow Chandlers' Hall, 4 Dowgate Hill, London EC4R 2SH (☎ 071 248 4726)

PROSSER, Margaret Theresa; s of Frederick James (d 1973), of London, and Lilian Mary, *née* Barry (d 1983); *b* 22 Aug 1937; *Educ* St Philomena's Convent Carshalton Surrey, NE London Poly (post graduate dip); *m* 15 Feb 1957 (m dis); 1 s (Jeffrey Jonathan b 1958), 2 da (Carol Ann b 1960, Stella Jane b 1963); *Career* advice centre organiser Home Office Funded Community Devpt Project 1974-77, law centre advsr 1977-83, nat women's sec TGWU 1984- (dist organiser 1983-84), memb Gen Cncl TUC, Equal Ops Cmmr; assoc memb Inst of Legal Execs 1981-83; *Recreations* walking, cooking; *Style*— Mrs Margaret Prosser; 154 Moffat Rd, Thornton Heath, Surrey CR7 8PX (☎ 081 771 5487); Transport House, Smith Square, Westminster, London SW1P 3JB (071 828 7788, fax 071 630 5861)

PROSSER, Robert; s of Harold Llewelyn Prosser, of Pont-y-Waun, and Winifred May, *née* Morgan; *b* 23 Sept 1951; *Educ* The Grammar Sch Newbridge Gwent, Univ of Liverpool (Cert Ed, BEd); *Career* asst master: Fairfield HS Widnes 1975-89, Heath Sch Runcorn 1989-; sec: Regina Coeli Ward Soc of Mary, Liverpool Diocesan Church Union, Fanworth Widnes Youth Club, N Eng Catholic League; govr St Matthew's Sch St Helens; memb Coll Preceptors 1980; ACP 1976, FRSH 1986, MRIPHH 1988, MREHIS 1988, MIHE 1989; *Books* The Influence of Thomism on the Second Vatican Council; *Recreations* bellringing, writing, theological and philosophical research; *Clubs* Lunt's Heath, S Basil's; *Style*— Robert Prosser, Esq; 13 Allerton Rd, Widnes, Cheshire WA8 6HP; 136 North Rd, Pont-y-Waun, Cross Keys, Newport, Gwent NP1 7FW (☎ 051 420 7654); The Heath School, Clifton Rd, Runcorn, Cheshire WA7 4SY (☎ 0928 5 76664)

PROSSER, Hon Lord; William David Prosser; s of David G Prosser, MC, WS, of Edinburgh; *b* 23 Nov 1934; *Educ* Edinburgh Acad, Corpus Christi Oxford (MA), Univ of Edinburgh (LLB); *m* 1964, Vanessa, da of Sir William O'Brien Lindsay, KBE; 2 s, 2 da; *Career* advocate 1962, QC (Scot) 1974; vice dean of the Faculty of Advocates 1979-83 (dean 1983-86); Senator of the Coll of Justice in Scotland 1986-; chm: Royal Fine Art Cmmn for Scotland 1990-, Royal Lyceum Theatre Co Edinburgh 1987-, Scottish Historic Bldgs Tst 1988-; *Clubs* New (Edinburgh), Scottish Arts; *Style*— The Hon Lord Prosser; 7 Randolph Crescent, Edinburgh EH3 7TH (☎ 031 225 2709); Netherfoodie, Dairsie, Fife (☎ 0334 870438)

PROTHERO, Dr David; s of Lewis Thomas Prothero, of Church Stretton, Shropshire, and Gwyneth Mary, *née* Jenkyn-Owen (d 1986); *b* 10 April 1937; *Educ* Bembridge Sch IOW, Univ Coll London, UCH Sch (MB BS, MRCS, LRCP, DPM); *m* 1, 1963 (m dis), Dr Yolanda Glaser; 1 s (Alan Neil b 6 July 1964), 1 da (Caroline Marion (Mrs Kelly) b 16 Sept 1966); m 2, 5 Sept 1973, Dianne, da of William Wells; 1 s (William b 8 Sept 1989), 2 da (Claudia Elizabeth b 10 Oct 1981, Louise b 17 Oct 1984); *Career* UCH and Shenley Hosp Herts 1960-66, clinical lectr in psychiatry London Hosp Med Coll 1966-69, conslt psychiatrist Claybury Hosp Woodford Green Essex 1969-86, conslt psychiatrist and med dir Grovelands Priory Hosp 1986-; memb BMA 1969, FRCPsych 1985 (MRCPsych 1972); *Style*— Dr David Prothero; 152 Harley St, London W1N 1HH (☎ 071 935 8868); Grovelands Priory Hospital, The Bourne, London N14 6RA (☎ 081 882 8191, fax 081 447 8138)

PROTHERO, Dr William Bernard Francis; s of Huw Prothero (d 1986), of Haverford West, Pembrokeshire, and Hannah Facmai Mary, *née* Mathias; *b* 12 July 1953; *Educ* Aberaeron CS, Univ of Wales Cardiff (MB BCh); *Career* registrar Guys Hosp London 1980-83; sr registrar: Westminster Hosp 1983-85, Charing Cross Hosp 1986-88, conslt psychiatrist Ashford Hosp 1986-88, conslt psychiatrist Ashford Hosp 1988-; MRCPsych; *Recreations* theatre, reading, golf, travel; *Style*— Dr William Prothero; 13 Seymour Road, Chiswick, London W4 (☎ 081 742 1722; Department of Psychiatry, Ashford Hospital, Ashford Middx (☎ 0742 251188)

PROTHEROE, Col Alan Hackford; CBE (1991, MBE 1980), TD (and Bar); s of Rev B P Protheroe (d 1971); *b* 10 Jan 1934; *Educ* Maesteg GS Glam; *m* 1956, Anne Miller, da of late H M Watkins (d 1984); 2 s; *Career* Nat Serv 2 Lt Welch Regt 1954-56, Col TA; reporter: Glamorgan Gazette 1951-53, BBC Wales 1957-70; industl corr Wales BBC 1959-64, ed Wales News and Current Affrs 1964-70, asst ed BBC TV News 1970-72 (dep ed 1972-77, ed 1977-80), asst dir BBC News and Current Affrs 1980 (asst dir-gen 1982-87); dir: Visnews Ltd 1982-87, Def Public Affrs Conslts Ltd 1988-, Europac Gp 1989-; dep chm Eastern Wessex Reserve Forces Assoc, md The Services Sound and Vision Corp 1988-; memb Cncl RUSI 1984-87, fndr memb Assoc of Br Eds (chm 1987); lectr and contrib to jls on def and media affrs; hon Col Pool of Army Information Offrs; FBIM; *Recreations* pistol and rifle shooting; *Clubs* Savile; *Style*— Col Alan Protheroe, CBE, TD; Chalfont Grove, Gerrard's Cross, Bucks SL9 8TN (☎ 02407 4461)

PROTHEROE, Dr David Trevelyan; s of Dr Harry Trevelyan Protheroe, of Gilwern, Gwent, and Ruby, *née* Davies; *b* 22 Feb 1937; *Educ* King Edwards Sch Sheffield, Trinity Coll Oxford, St Thomas' Hosp Med Sch (BA, MA, BM BCh); *m* 22 Oct 1963, Margaret Catherine, *née* Cooke; 2 s (Richard Trevelyan b 22 June 1965, Andrew Simon b 21 Sept 1966); *Career* sr registrar in anaesthetics Bristol 1968-72, conslt anaesthetist Bath 1972; memb Br Standard Inst Ctee on Infusion Pumps, rep and del of Int Electrotechnical Commission 65D; memb: BMA, Assoc of Anaesthetics 1966, RCS 1968, Intensive Care Soc 1974, RSM 1985; FFARCS 1968; *Recreations* golf; *Clubs* Bath & County; *Style*— Dr David Protheroe; Long Barn, Charlton, Kilmersden, Somerset BA3 5TN (☎ 0761 323226); Royal United Hospital, Combe Park, Bath (☎ 0225 428331) The Bath Clinic, Claverton Down Rd, Bath (☎ 0225 8355555)

PROUD, Hon Mrs (Fiona Janice); *née* Brain; 2 da of 2 Baron Brain, *qv*; *b* 1958; *m* 1977, Rev Andrew John Proud; 1 s (Justin Dominic Edward b 1979), 1 da (Emma Jane Chrysogen b 1977); *Style*— The Hon Mrs Proud; St Michael's Vicarage, Brook Rd, Boreham Wood, Herts

PROUD, George; s of Albert Proud (d 1972), of Durham, and Frances, *née* Sigworth; *b* 23 Aug 1943; *Educ* Newcastle Royal GS, Univ of Durham (BDS), Univ of Newcastle (MB BS, MD); *m* 25 July 1970, Janet Mary, da of Joseph Davies (d 1978), of Worthing; 1 s (Stuart James b 1 April 1976), 1 da (Kathryn Siân b 8 Sept 1973); *Career* conslt surgn Royal Victoria Infirmary Newcastle 1981- (and clinical director of Surgery), gen sec Br Transplantation Soc; memb: Euro Soc for Organ Transplantation, Assoc of Surgns of GB and 1, Vascular Surgical Soc, Euro Soc for Vasular Surgery, Exec Ctee Northern Cos Kidney Res Fund, fndr Weardale Ski Club, fndr NE Ski Assoc; former pres Heaton on Tyne Rotary Club; Hunterian prof of Surgery RSC 1979; winner Jacksonian Prize for Surgery RCS 1981; FRCS, memb BMA; *Books* many papers on surgical topics; *Recreations* skiing, fell walking, photography; *Style*— George Proud, Esq; Royal Victoria Infirmary, Queen Victoria Rd, Newcastle upon Tyne NE1 4LP (☎ 091 2325131, car 0860 440290)

PROUDFOOT, Prof (Vincent) Bruce; s of Bruce Falconer Proudfoot, of Westgate, Wardlaw Gardens, St Andrews, Fife, and Cecilia, *née* Thompson; *b* 24 Sept 1930; *Educ* Royal Belfast Academical Inst, Queen's Univ Belfast (BA, PhD); *m* 16 Dec 1961, Edwina Valmai Windram, da of Edwin Alexander Field, of 15 Liberton Brae, Edinburgh; 2 s (Bruce b 1962, Malcolm b 1964); *Career* lectr in geography: Queen's Univ Belfast 1958-59 (res offr Nuffield Quaternary Res Unit 1954-58), Univ of Durham 1959-67; coll librarian Hatfield Coll Univ of Durham 1963-64 (tutor 1960-63), visiting fell Univ of Auckland NZ 1966, prof Univ of Alberta Canada 1970-74 (assoc prof 1967-70), co-ordinator and staff conslt Alberta Human Resources Res Cncl 1971-72, prof of geography Univ of St Andrews 1974- (head Dept of Geography 1974-85); Br Assoc Advancement of Sci: jt sec Section H (Anthropology and Archaeology) 1958-62 (memb Ctee 1957-58), rec 1962-65, pres 1985; tstee Nat Museum of Antiquities of Scotland 1982-85, vice chm Royal Scot Geographical Soc 1980-81 (hon ed 1978-, memb Cncl 1975-78); Royal Soc of Edinburgh: memb Cncl 1982-85, 1990-, convenor Earth Sciences Ctee 1983-85, memb Awards Ctee 1984-85, vice pres 1985-88, convenor Grants Ctee 1988-; FSA 1963, FRSE 1979, FRGS, FSA Scotland 1979; *Books* The Downpatrick Gold Find (1955), Frontier Settlement Studies (jtly, 1974), Site, Environment and Economy (ed, 1983); *Recreations* gardening; *Style*— Prof Bruce Proudfoot, FRSE; Westgate, Wardlaw Gardens, St Andrews, Scotland KY16 9DW (☎ 0334 73293); Dept Geography, University of St Andrews, St Andrews, Scotland KY16 9ST (☎ 0334 76161, fax 0334 74487)

PROUDFOOT, (George) Wilfred; *b* 19 Dec 1921; *Educ* Crook Cncl Sch, Scarborough Coll; *m* 1950, Margaret Mary, da of Percy Clifford Jackson; 2 s, 1 da; *Career* MP (Cons): Cleveland Div of Yorkshire 1959-64, Brighouse and Spenborough 1970-74; md Radio 270 1975-, owner supermarkets, conslt in distribution, hypnotherapist (chm Br Cncl of Hypnotist Examiners), master practitioner NLP, former chm Cleveland Euro Constituency Cons Assoc; *Style*— Wilfred Proudfoot, Esq; 278 Scalby Rd, Scarborough, N Yorkshire (☎ 0723 367027)

PROUDMAN, Kenneth Oliphant; s of Percy Chesters Proudman (d 1950), of Birkenhead, and Olive, *née* Oliphant (d 1975); *b* 2 Aug 1915; *Educ* Birkenhead Inst, Henley Business Sch; *m* 30 May 1945, Sati, da of Ivan Hekimian (d 1931), of Cairo; 1 da (Sonia); *Career* RASC (TA) UK and MEF 1939-46, staff and regtl duties incl appts as DAAG and DADST (Plans) GHQ MEF, Actg Cdr RASC 15 Area (despatches 1944), awarded C-in-C Middle East's commendation 1944; District Bank Ltd 1932-39; Esso Petroleum Co Ltd: mangr salary admin and labour rels 1946-58, dep employee rels advsr 1958-60, various appts in sales and ops 1961-67 (mangr industl sales 1964-65, mktg mangr SE 1966-67), UK gp co-ordinator mgmnt devpt 1967-77, ret; memb: Oil Cos Conciliation Ctee 1949-60 (chm Employer's Panel 1958-60), Grand Cncl Br Employers Confedn 1957-60, Consumer Panel Manchester Business Sch 1971-75; chm Esso Tst for Tertiary Educn 1978-90; Freeman City of London 1974, Liveryman Worshipful Co of Coachmakers and Coach Harness Makers 1974; AIB 1936; *Recreations* cricket, reading, music, motoring; *Clubs* MCC, Hurlingham; *Style*— Kenneth O Proudman, Esq

PROUDMAN, Sonia Rosemary Susan; da of Kenneth Oliphant Proudman, of London, and Sati, *née* Hekimian; *b* 30 July 1949; *Educ* St Paul's Girls' Sch, Lady Margaret Hall Oxford (MA); *m* 19 Dec 1987, David Crispian Himley, s of Himley Cartwright, of Henley-on-Thames; *Career* called to the Bar Lincoln's Inn 1972, in practice at the Chancery Bar 1972; *Recreations* cinema, jazz, food, fashion, writing romantic fiction; *Clubs* Hurlingham, CWIL; *Style*— Miss Sonia Proudman; 11 New Square, Lincoln's Inn, London WC2A 3QB (☎ 071 831 0081, fax 071 405 2560/0798)

PROUT, Sir Christopher James; TD (1987), QC (1988), MEP (Cons) Shrops and Stafford 1979; s of Frank Yabsley Prout, MC and bar (d 1980), and Doris Lucy, *née* Osborne (d 1983); *b* 1 Jan 1942; *Educ* Sevenoaks Sch, Univ of Manchester (BA), Queen's Coll Oxford (BPhil, DPhil); *Career* TA Offr (Maj) OU OTC 1966-74, 16/5 The Queen's Royal Lancers 1974-82, 3 Armd Div 1982-88; called to the Bar Middle Temple 1972; English Speaking Union fell Columbia Univ 1963-64, Int Bank for Reconstruction and Devpt (UN) Washington DC 1966-69, Leverhulme fell and lectr in law Univ of Sussex 1969-79; dep whip Euro Democratic (C) Gp 1979-82, chm Parly Ctee on Electoral Disputes 1982-83, chief whip of the Euro Democratic Gp 1983-87, chm Parly Ctee on Legal Affrs 1987, ldr of the Euro Democratic Gp 1987-; La Grande Medaille de la Ville de Paris 1988; kt 1990; *Books* Market Socialism in Yugoslavia (1985), Halsbury's Laws of England, (contrib 4 edn Vols 51 and 52, 1986); *Recreations* riding, sailing; *Clubs* Pratt's, Beefsteak, Royal Ocean Racing; *Style*— Sir Christopher Prout, QC, MEP; 2 Queen Anne's Gate, London SW1 (☎ 071 222 1722); 2 Paper Buildings, Temple, London EC4 (☎ 071 353 5835)

PROUT, David John; s of Donald Cornell Prout, of Budleigh, Salterton, Devon, and Kethleen Susan Constance, *née* Miller; *b* 13 Nov 1947; *Educ* Rugby, Hatfield Coll Durham, Univ of Reading (BA); *m* 17 July 1971, Amanada Jane, da of late Clifford

Sherwood Nell; 2 s (Oliver Samuel b 13 June 1981, Jonathan Benedict b 9 Dec 1984); *Career* photographer; photographic asst AEI 1965, phototypesetter Graphic Systems 1971-72, started Creed Lane Studio 1975; clients incl: BMA, William Collins, Jonathan Cape, Grant Thornton, Schlumberger, Touche Ross, Arthur Anderson, Vauxhall Motors, British Telecom, Esso, Rank Xerox; Creed Lane nominated for Eurobest and AGR Graduate Recruitment awards; former teacher Canterbury Coll of Art; FCSD 1985 (MCSD 1971, memb Graphics Gp and various ctees 1976-), memb AFAEP; *Recreations* restoring pre-war cars, skiing, golf (just a beginner), shopping at Tesco on Friday night; *Clubs* MG Car, Octagon Car; *Style—* David Prout, Esq; Creed Lane, Graphic Communications, 82-84 Clerkenwell Rd, London EC1M 5RJ (☎ 071 608 1122, ax 071 608 1127)

PROVAN, James Lyal Clark; s of John Provan (d 1981), and Jean, *née* Clark; *b* 19 Dec 1936; *Educ* Ardvreck, Oundle, RAC Cirencester; *m* 1960, Roweena Adele, da of Andrew Holmes Spencer Lewis; 2 s (Lyal, Andrew (twin)), 1 da (Pepita); *Career* farmer 1958-, business mangr and dir 1966-, former MEP NE Scotland 1979-89, EDG spokesman on agric and fisheries Euro Parl 1981-87, parly quaestor 1987-89; exec dir Scottish Financial Enterprise 1990-, chm McIntosh Donald 1989-, chm McIntosh of Dyce 1990-; area pres Scottish NFU 1965 and 1971; memb: Tayside Regnl Cncl 1978-81, Tay River Purification Bd 1978-81, Lloyds; *Recreations* country pursuits, sailing, flying, music; *Clubs* Royal Perth Golfing Soc, East India, Farmers'; *Style—* James Provan, Esq; Wallacetown, Bridge of Earn, Perth PH2 8QA, Scotland (☎ 0738 812243, fax 0738 812944)

PROWSE, Dr Keith; s of Valentine Prowse, of Rugby, and Irene Ellen, *née* Rogers (d 1989); *b* 23 Dec 1937; *Educ* Lawrence Sheriff GS Rugby, Univ of Birmingham (BSc, MB ChB, MD); *m* 22 Sept 1962, Hilary Ann, da of Reginald Varley (d 1971), of Sutton Coldfield; 1 s (Robert b 1975), 1 da (Carolyn b 1972); *Career* lectr in med Univ of Birmingham 1968-71, Inserm res fell unité 14 Centre Hospitalier Universitaire Nancy France 1971-72, conslt physician N Staffs Hosps Centre 1972-, sr lectr in respiratory med dept of post grad med Univ of Keele 1986-; hon asst treas Br Thoracic soc, fndr memb of cncl Br Lung Fndn, memb thoracic servs ctee RCP, UK rep UEMS monospeciality ctee respiratory diseases; FRCP 1977; *Recreations* castles, owls, walking, music, France; *Clubs* Y; *Style—* Dr Keith Prowse; Kyriole Pinewood Road, Ashley Heath, Nr Market Drayton, Shropshire TF9 4PP (☎ 0630 87 2879); Department of Respiratory Medicine, City General Hospital, Newcastle Rd, Stoke on Trent, Staffs ST4 6QG (☎ 0782 621133)

PROWTING, Peter Brian; s of Arthur Edwin Alfred Prowting (d 1977), of Littlehampton, and Edith Kate, *née* Jones (d 1987); *b* 19 Dec 1924; *Educ* Ickenham HS, Frays Coll Uxbridge; *m* 1, 22 Oct 1948 (m dis 1965), Phyllis; 1 da (Wendy b 9 Sept 1956); m 2, 24 Nov 1966, Elizabeth Anne (Liz), da of Wing Cdr Leslie George Mobsby, RAF (d 1966), of Chenies, Bucks; *Career* chm: Prowting plc 1955- (dir 1948-), Estates & General plc 1982- (dir 1974-); *Recreations* gardening, golf, jazz; *Clubs* Gerrards Cross Golf, Beaconsfield Golf, Mill Reef (Antigua); *Style—* Peter Prowting, Esq; Prowting plc, Breakspear House, Bury St, Ruislip, Middx HA4 7SY (☎ 0895 633344, fax 0895 677190, telex 935106)

PRYCE, G Terry; s of Edwin Pryce (d 1961), and Hilda, *née* Price; *b* 26 March 1934; *Educ* Welshpool GS, Nat Coll of Food Technol; *m* 1957, Thurza Elizabeth, da of Arthur Denis Tatham (d 1942); 2 s (Simon Charles Conrad b 1961, Timothy John Robert b 1965), 1 da (Sarah Jane b 1970); *Career* chm Solway Foods Ltd 1970-89; Dalgety plc: dir 1972, md 1978, chief exec and md 1981; dir H P Bulmer Holdings plc 1981, chm Horticulture Res Int 1991; govr Nat Coll of Food Technol 1986, chm Bd of Ford Studies Univ of Reading; memb Cncl AFRC, CBIM, FIFST; *Recreations* sport (golf), reading; *Style—* G Terry Pryce, Esq

PRYCE, Jonathan; s of Isaac Price (d 1976), of N Wales, and Margaret Ellen, *née* Williams (d 1986); *b* 1 June 1947; *Educ* Holywell GS, Sch of Art Kelsterton, Edge Hill Coll of Educn, RADA; *Career* actor; Everyman Theatre Liverpool 1972, Nottingham Playhouse 1974, RSC 1979 and 1986, Royal Court Theatre 1980, Nat Theatre 1981, Lyric Hammersmith, Queens Theatre, Vaudville Theatre, Drury Lane Theatre Royal 1989-90, Music Box and Belasco NY; roles incl: Richard III, Hamlet, Macbeth, Petruchio, Angeloa, Octavius Caesar, Mick in the Caretaker, Gethin Price in Comedians, Tallys Folly, Trigorin, Astrov, Engineer in Miss Saigon; TV: Daft as a Brush, Playthings, Glad Day, Roger Doesn't Live Here Anymore, The Caretaker, Comedians, Timon of Athens, Martin Luther Heretic, Praying Mantis, Two Weeks in Winter, The Man from the Pru; films: Voyage of the Damned, Breaking Glass, Loophole, Ploughmans Lunch, Something Wicked This Way Comes, Brazil, Man on Fire, Jumpin' Jack Flash, Doctor and the Devils, Haunted Honeymoon, Consuming Passions, The Adventures of Baron Munchausen, The Rachel Papers; Recordings: Under Milk Wood, Miss Saigon; awards: Tony award and Theatre World award for Comedians 1977, SWET/Olivier award for Hamlet 1980, Olivier award for Miss Saigon 1990, Variety Club of GB Stage Actor of 1990; *Style—* Jonathan Pryce, Esq; James Sharkey Associates, 3rd Floor Suite, 15 Golden Square, London W1R 3AG (☎ 071 434 3801-6, fax 071 494 1547)

PRYCE-JONES, Hon Mrs (Clarissa Sabina); er da of Baron Caccia, GCMG, GCVO (Life Peer, d 1990), and Anne Catherine, *née* Barstow; *b* 26 May 1939; *m* 29 July 1959, David Eugene Henry Pryce-Jones, s of Alan Payan Pryce-Jones, TD, of Newport, Rhode Island, USA; 1 s (Adam b 1973), 3 da (Jessica (Mrs David Roderick Shukman) b 1961, Candida (Mrs Owen William Luxado Mostyn-Owen) b 1963, Sonia b 1970 d 1972); *Style—* The Hon Mrs Pryce-Jones; Phillimore Lodge, 1 Phillimore Terrace, Allen St, London W8

PRYCE-JONES, Lady; Syra Roantree; o da of late Francis O'Shiel, of Omagh, Co Tyrone; *m* 10 Sept 1938, Capt Sir Pryce Victor Pryce-Jones, 2 and last Bt (d 1963); *Style—* Lady Pryce-Jones; The Manor Cottage, Great Ryburgh, Norfolk NR21 0DX (☎ 032 878 238)

PRYER, (Eric) John; CB (1986); s of Edward John Pryer (d 1970), of Pickhurst Mead, Hayes, Kent, and Edith Blanche, *née* Jordan (d 1943); *b* 5 Sept 1929; *Educ* Beckenham & Penge County GS, Birkbeck Coll, Univ of London BA (Hons); *m* 20 Oct 1962, Moyra Helena, da of James Townley Cross (d 1942), of Blackburn, Lancs; 1 s (Andrew b 26 May 1968), 1 da (Sarah b 23 Aug 1971); *Career* called to the Bar Gray's Inn 1957; exec offr Treasy Slrs Dept 1948, legal asst HM Land Registry 1959, asst land registrar 1965, dist land registrar Durham 1976, dep chief land registrar 1981-83, chief land registrar 1983-90, legal offr Cncl for Licensed Conveyancers 1991-; assoc memb RICS; *Publications* Ruoff & Roper's The Law and Practice of Registered Conveyancing (co-ed fifth edn), Land Registration Handbook, articles in professional jls; *Recreations* reading; *Style—* John Pryer, Esq, CB; Council for Licensed Conveyancers, Suite 3, Cairngorm House, 203 Marsh Wall, London E14 9YT (☎ 071 537 2953, fax 071 537 3847)

PRYKE, Sir David Dudley; 3 Bt (UK 1926); s of Sir (William Robert) Dudley Pryke, 2 Bt (d 1959), and Dame Majorie Pryke (d 1936); gf Lord Mayor of London 1925-26; *b* 16 July 1912; *Educ* St Lawrence Coll Ramsgate; *m* 1945, Doreen Winifred, da of late Ralph Bernard Wilkins; 2 da (Madge, Anita); *Heir* bro, William Dudley Pryke; *Career* dir: Pryke & Palmer Ltd 1945-62, Pryke & Scott Ltd 1963-86; former common cnclman Queenhithe Ward 1960-74; Liveryman Worshipful Co of Turners 1961 (Renter Warden 1983, Upper Warden 1984, Master 1985); *Recreations* photography; *Clubs* Guildhall, Queenhithe Ward (former chm); *Style—* Sir David Pryke, Bt; Flatholme, Brabant Rd, N Fambridge, Chelmsford, Essex CM3 6LY (☎ 0621 740227)

PRYKE, William Dudley; s of Sir (William Robert) Dudley Pryke, 2 Bt (d 1959), and hp of bro, Sir David Pryke, 3 Bt; *b* 18 Nov 1914; *Educ* Highgate Sch; *m* 1940, (Lucy Irene) Peggy (d 1984), da of late Frank Madgett, of Whetstone; 1 s (Christopher), 1 da (Rosemarie); *Career* formerly Capt Duke of Cornwall's LI (India, M East, Italy); former Capt Co of Pikemen and Musketeers; Liveryman Worshipful Co of Plumbers (Master 1969-70); *Recreations* golf; *Clubs* United Sports; *Style—* William Pryke, Esq; 30 Hadley Highstone, Barnet, Herts EN5 4PU (☎ 081 449 8527)

PRYNNE, Andrew Geoffrey Lockyer; s of Maj-Gen Michael Whitworth Prynne, CB, CBE (d 1977), and Jean Violet, *née* Stewart (d 1977); *b* 28 May 1953; *Educ* Marlborough, Univ of Southampton (LLB); *m* 30 July 1977, Catriona Mary, da of Maj Henry Gordon Brougham (d 1958); 3 da (Jessica Jean, Miranda Wendy, Natasha Sally); *Career* called to the Bar Middle Temple 1975; *Recreations* sailing, fishing, shooting, theatre, music; *Clubs* Royal Solent Yacht, Island Sailing; *Style—* Andrew Prynne, Esq, Mount Le Hoe, Benenden, Kent (☎ 0580 241583); 107 Elm Park Mansions, Park Walk, London SW10

PRYOR, John Pembro; s of (William) Benjamin Pryor, and Kathleen Martha Amelia, *née* Pembro (d 1959); *b* 25 Aug 1937; *Educ* Reading Sch, King's Coll London, King's Coll Hosp Medical Sch (MS); *m* 25 July 1959, Marion, da of Illtyd Thomas Hopkins; 4 s (Andrew b 1962, Damian b 1964, Justin b 1966, Marcellus b 1968); *Career* conslt urological surgn with special interest in andrology King's Coll Hosp and St Peter's Hosp 1974-; dean Inst of Urology London Univ 1978-85; first chm Br Andrology Soc 1978-85, memb Ctee British Assoc of Urological Surgeons 1979-82; FRCS; *Books* Andrology (1985); *Style—* John Pryor, Esq; The Lister Hospital, Chelsea Bridge Rd, London SW1W 8RH (☎ 071 730 3417)

PRYOR, Robert Charles; QC 1983; s of Charles Selwyn Pryor (d 1977), of Suffolk, and Olive, *née* Woodall (d 1977); *b* 10 Dec 1938; *Educ* Eton, Trinity Coll Cambridge (BA); *m* 1969, Virginia, da of Lt-Col Peter Thomas Wellesley Sykes, of Wilts; 1 s (Michael b 1969), 1 da (Caroline b 1971); *Career* Nat Serv 2 Lt KRRC 1957-59; dir Sun Life Assur plc 1977-; *Recreations* fishing; *Style—* Robert Pryor, Esq, QC; Chitterne House, Warminster, Wilts; 11 King's Bench Walk, London EC4

PRYS-DAVIES, Baron (Life Peer UK 1982), of Llanegryn in the Co of Gwynedd; Gwilym Prys Prys-Davies; s of William and Mary Matilda Davies; assumed by deed poll 1982 the surname Prys-Davies in lieu of his patronymic; *b* 8 Dec 1923; *Educ* Towyn Sch, Univ Coll of Wales Aberystwyth; *m* 1951, Llinos, da of Abram Evans; 3 da (Hon Catrin Prys (Hon Mrs Waugh) b 1957, Hon Ann Prys b 1959, Hon Elin Prys b 1963); *Career* RN 1942-46; slr 1956, ptnr Morgan Bruce and Nicholas slrs 1957-87, special advsr to Sec of State for Wales 1974-78; chm Welsh Hosp Bd 1968-74; memb: Welsh Cncl 1967-69, Econ and Social Ctee EEC 1978-82; oppn asst spokesman on health 1985, oppn spokesman on NI 1986, oppn asst spokesman on Welsh affrs 1986-; OStJ; *Publications* A Central Welsh Council 1963, Y Ffermwr a'r Gyfraith (1967); *Style—* The Rt Hon The Lord Prys-Davies; Lluest, 78 Church Rd, Tonteg, Pontypridd, Mid Glam; c/o House of Lords, London SW1

PSYLLIDES, Milton Nicholas; s of Nicholas Milton Psyllides, of Chislehurst, Kent, and Loulla, *née* Christophides; *b* 30 Oct 1953; *Educ* Brockley Co GS, Univ of Liverpool (LLB); *m* 16 April 1976, Lynne Josephine, da of Horace Walter Rutherford, of Birmingham; 2 s (Paul b 4 Oct 1986, d 27 July 1988, Andrew b 11 May 1989), 1 da (Louise b 11 Aug 1984); *Career* slr; Evershed & Tomkinson (now Evershed Wells & Hind following merger with Wells & Hind 1989): asst slr 1978, assoc 1981, ptnr 1984; chm: First Roman Property Trust plc 1988, Roman Rentals 001-055 plc, Drayton Hotels plc; non-exec dir: Shire plc, Burgmann (UK) Ltd; memb Co and Commercial Law Ctee Birmingham Law Soc; memb Law Soc 1978; *Recreations* family life, keep fit; *Style—* Milton N Psyllides, Esq; 4 Richmond Rd, Sutton Coldfield, West Midlands B73 6BJ (☎ 021 354 7694); Evershed Wells & Hind, 10 Newhall St, Birmingham B3 3LX (☎ 021 233 2001, fax 021 236 1583, telex 336688)

PUCKRIN, Arthur William; s of Thomas William Puckrin (d 1977), of Middlesbrough, and Eleanor Mary, *née* Cumiskey; *b* 5 May 1938; *Educ* Middlesbrough HS, Univ of London (LLB Hons, BL); *m* 2 April 1966, Patricia Ann, da of Charles Henry Dixon (d 1972), of Middlesbrough; 2 s (Geoffrey Arthur b 1984, James William b 1986); *Career* called to the Bar 1966; legal advsr Dorman Long Steel Ltd 1966-71, Parly advsr to City of London Corp 1971; memb: Bar Assoc for Commerce Fin and Indust 1967-, BIM 1980; athlete and long distance runner; record holder for: Pennine Way 250 miles, Southern Highlands of Scotland 170 miles, Welsh 14 Peaks over 3000 feet, N Yorks Moors 80 miles, Lyke Walk N Yorks Moors 120 miles; defeated 50 horses over 44 miles at Wolsingham Horse Trials, record holder for 110 mile walk Middlesborough to York and back in 23 hours 40 mins; represented GB playing bridge on 8 occasions incl 2 World Championships and four Euro Championships; life master English Bridge Union; FCIS 1977; *Clubs* Hartlepool Bridge, Middlesbrough and Cleveland Harriers, Lyke Wake; *Style—* Arthur W Puckrin, Esq; 3 Romanby Gdns, Middlesbrough (☎ 0642 593807); 257 Acklam Rd, Middlesbrough (☎ 0642 240215)

PUDNEY, Hon Mrs (Carolyn); da of late Baron Delacourt-Smith (Life Peer, d 1972) and Baroness Delacourt-Smith (Life Peer); *b* 1944; *m* 1969, Roger Martin Pudney; 1 s (Christopher b 1977), 1 da (Louise b 1975); *Style—* The Hon Mrs Pudney

PUDNEY, Hon Mrs (Janet Victoria); *née* Stoddart; da of Baron Stoddart of Swindon (Life Peer) and his 1 w, Doreen, *née* Maynard; *b* 1947; *m* 1967, Jack Pudney, of W Australia; 2 s (Christopher John b 1967, Adam Keith b 1970); *Style—* The Hon Mrs Pudney

PUGH, Alastair Tarrant; CBE (1986); s of Sqdn Ldr Rev Herbert Cecil Pugh, GC (d 1941), and Amy Lilian Pugh (d 1956); *b* 16 Sept 1928; *Educ* Tettenhall Coll Staffs, De Havilland Aeronautical Tech Sch; *m* 1957, Sylvia Victoria Marlow; 2 s (Giles, Duncan), 1 da (Emma); *Career* md British Caledonian Airways 1978-85, exec vice chm British Caledonian Group 1985-88, conslt Goldman Sachs International Ltd; pres Chartered Inst of Tport 1988-89; *Recreations* vintage sports cars; *Style—* Alastair Pugh, Esq, CBE; England's Cottage, Sidlow Bridge, Reigate, Surrey (☎ 0737 243456)

PUGH, Andrew Cartwright; QC; s of Lewis Gordon Pugh (d 1989), and Erica, *née* Cartwright; *b* 6 June 1937; *Educ* Tonbridge, New Coll Oxford (MA); *m* 28 April 1984, Chantal Helene, da of Andre Langevin (d 1987); 2 da (Alexandra b 21 Nov 1985, Sophie b 16 Sept 1987); *Career* Nat Serv Royal Sussex Regt 1955-57; called to the Bar Inner Temple 1961; SE Circuit: bencher 1989, rec 1990; Liveryman Worshipful Co of Skinners; *Recreations* tennis, gardening, reading; *Clubs* United Oxford and Cambridge; *Style—* Andrew Pugh, Esq, QC; 2 Hare Ct, Temple, London EC4, (☎ 071 583 1770, fax 2 & 3 071 583 9269, telex 27139 LIN LAW)

PUGH, Hon Mrs Caroline Mary Stewart; *née* Maud; da of Baron Redcliffe-Maud, GCB, CBE (Life Peer, d 1982); *b* 29 May 1939; *m* 1967, The Very Rev Joel Wilson Pugh, yr s of late Robert Dean Pugh, of Portland, Arkansas, USA; *Style—* The Hon Mrs Pugh; The Dean's House, 320 W 18th Street, Little Rock, Arkansas 72206, USA

PUGH, Dennis; OBE (1988), JP (1982); s of Rhys Pugh (d 1963), and Elizabeth, *née* Vaughan (d 1971); *b* 27 July 1930; *Educ* Ffestiniog Co Sch; *m* 20 Dec 1952, Annie Lloyd, da of William George Rees (d 1951); 2 da (Carolyn b 1958, Judith b 1961);

Career Nat Serv RAF 1948-50, BAFO Berlin 1949-50; entered Civil Serv 1947; Miny of Pensions: Blackpool, Newcastle upon Tyne and Wales 1947-66; DTI (formerly Bd of Trade) 1966-72, Customs and Excise 1972-76, Welsh Office 1976-90; special advsr Welsh Devpt Int 1990-, dep dir Business in the Community in Wales 1990-; JP Gwynedd 1982 (dep chm Llandudno Div); *Recreations* tennis, hill walking, swimming; *Style*— Dennis Pugh, Esq, OBE, JP; Moelwyn, Tyn y Groes, Conwy, Gwynedd LL32 8SZ (☎ 0492 650438); Welsh Office, Industry Dept, Government Buildings, Rhos on Sea, Clwyd (☎ 0492 44261)

PUGH, Edward Gwynne; s of Arthur Gwynne Pugh (d 1979), and Alice, *née* Trotter; *b* 26 Aug 1948; *Educ* Tulse Hill Sch, LAMDA; *m* 29 Sept 1973, Lorraine Alice Elfrida, da of William Ivan Ronald Sansom; 3 da (Eleanor Claire b 1978, Laura Geraldine b 1979, Rhiannon Beth b 1982); *Career* BBC TV: studio mgmnt 1970-79, dir and prodr Children's Dept 1979-86; ed children's progs: BBC North West 1987-90, Granada TV Manchester 1991-; *Recreations* listening to music, walking, photography; *Style*— Edward Pugh, Esq; Granda TV, Quay St, Manchester M60 9EA (☎ 061 832 7211)

PUGH, Sir Idwal Vaughan; KCB (1972, CB 1967); s of late Rhys Pugh; *b* 10 Feb 1918; *Educ* Cowbridge GS, St John's Coll Oxford (hon fell 1979); *m* 1946, Mair Lewis (d 1985); 1 s, 1 da; *Career* second perm sec DOE 1971-76, Parly cmmr for admin and health serv, cmmr for England Wales and Scotland 1976-79; chm Chartered Trust Ltd 1979-88; dir: Standard Chartered Bank 1979-88, Halifax Building Soc 1979-88; chm Devpt Corp of Wales 1980-83, vice pres Univ Coll Swansea 1988-, chm Cncl RNCM 1988-, pres Coleg Harlech 1990-; Hon LLD Univ of Wales 1988; *Clubs* Brooks's; *Style*— Sir Idwal Pugh, KCB; Flat 1, The Old House, Cathedral Green, Llandaff, Cardiff

PUGH, Ivor Evans; DL (1975); s of Lt Col Archibald John Pugh OBE, VD (d 1923), and Marion Fraser (Nina), *née* Arundell; *b* 3 Aug 1916; *Educ* Charterhouse; *m* 28 June 1941, Jean Barclay, da of Morton Howell Llewellyn, of Wernoleu, Ammanford, Carmarthenshire; 2 s (Anthony Ivor b 15 June 1943, Michael Duncan b 15 Feb 1946), 1 da (Susan Elizabeth b 16 Oct 1948); *Career* 24 Regt SWB 1940-45, Capt 1943; slr 1939-88; dep Licensing Authy and dep chm Traffic Cmmrs S Wales Traffic Area (and later W Midlands Traffic Area) 1975-88; chm Bridgend Dist Old Comrades' Assoc Royal Regt of Wales, govr Christ Coll Brecon; memb Law Soc 1939; *Recreations* golf, gardening, cricket; *Clubs* Cardiff and Co, Royal Porthcawl GC, South Wales Hunts CC; *Style*— Ivor E Pugh, Esq, DL; 1 Court Drive, Llansannor, Cowbridge, S Glam CF1 7SD (☎ 0446 772891)

PUGH, John Arthur; OBE (1968); s of Thomas Arthur Pugh (d 1958), and Dorothy Susannah Baker Pugh (d 1972); *b* 17 July 1920; *Educ* Brecon GS, Univ of Bristol (DPA); *Career* RN 1941-45; Home Civil Serv 1950-54, Gold Coast admin serv 1955-58, advsr to Govt of Ghana 1958-60; HM Dip Serv: first sec Br High Cmmn Lagos 1962-65, first sec (econ) HM Embassy Bangkok, Br perm rep to Econ Cmmn for Asia 1965-68, dep high cmmr Ibadan 1971-73, inspr HM Dip Serv 1973-76, high cmmr Seychelles 1976-80; *Recreations* travel, ornithology, writing; *Clubs* Royal Cwlth Soc; *Style*— John Pugh, Esq, OBE; Pennybrin, Hay-on-Wye, Hereford HR3 5RS (☎ 0497 820 695)

PUGH, Hon Mrs (Judith Alexandra Anne); *née* Serota; da of Baroness Serota, *qv*; *b* 1948; *Educ* Royal Manchester Coll of Music; *m* 1973, Francis John Pugh; 2 da (Rebecca Sarah b 1975, Ellen Martha b 1978); *Career* arts administrator; *Style*— The Hon Mrs Pugh

PUGH, Michael James; s of Patrick James Pugh (d 1974), of Redruth, and Daphne Pamela, *née* Webber; *b* 23 April 1948; *Educ* Downside; *m* 11 July 1970, Shirley Condliffe, da of Matthew Douglas Reginald Legg (d 1990), of Wimbledon; *Career* articled clerk G C Davies & Ptnrs Redruth 1967-72, admitted slr 1972, ptnr Barlow Lyde and Gilbert 1975- (asst slr 1972-75); chm: Insur Ctee of Int Bar Assoc 1984-88, Br Insur Law Assoc 1990-92; admitted slr Hong Kong 1986; vice chm Ctee on Int Tort and Insur Law American Bar Assoc; memb Worshipful Co of Solicitors; memb: Law Soc 1972, Int Bar Assoc 1981, Br Insur Law Assoc 1982, Law Soc of Hong Kong 1986; *Recreations* mountain walking, bird watching, music, classic motor cars, wine; *Clubs* Reform, RAC; *Style*— Michael Pugh, Esq; Beaufort House, 15 St Botolph St, London EC3A 7NJ (☎ 071 247 2277, fax 071 782 8500, telex 913281)

PUGH, Hon Mrs (Petrina Frances Anne); *née* Mitchell-Thomson; da of 3 Baron Selsdon; *b* 1945; *Educ* Queen's Gate Sch London; *m* 1967, James Geoffrey Lennox Pugh, late Grenadier Gds; 1 s, 1 da; *Career* dir Ranvet Ltd (equine feed supplements and medications); *Recreations* real tennis; *Style*— The Hon Mrs Pugh; Whitelands, Rudford, Glos GL2 8ED (☎ 045 279 204)

PUGH, Richard Henry Crommelin; s of John James Edgar Pugh (d 1944), of Buxton, Derbyshire, and Charlotte Winifred Crommelin, *née* Sadler (d 1977); *b* 9 Sept 1927; *Educ* Buxton Coll, Univ of London (LLB); *m* 15 Aug 1953, Ann, da of Roy Waddington Swales (d 1979), of Fernilee, Derbyshire; 1 s (Stephen b 1958), 1 da (Helen b 1956); *Career* Nat Serv RAF 1947-49; CA; Grattan Warehouses Ltd 1951-56, chm Home Shopping Div Great Universal Stores 1956-, dep chm GUS plc; govr and fell Worcester Coll of Further Educn, chm Worcester Cathedral Appeal; memb Worshipful Co of Chartered Secretaries 1984, Freeman City of London 1984; FCA 1951, ACIS 1951, ACMA 1959; *Recreations* golf, swimming, motor cruising, genealogy; *Clubs* City Livery; *Style*— Richard Pugh, Esq; Elgar Suite, 250 Bransford Rd, Worcester WR2 5ES (☎ 0905 23411)

PUGH, Sheenagh Myfanwy; da of John Richard Pugh, of Swansea, and Moira Eveleen Sara, *née* Neil; *b* 20 Dec 1950; *Educ* Mundella GS Nottingham, Univ of Bristol (BA); *m* 17 Sept 1977, Michael John Hugh Burns, s of Daniel Burns (d 1980), of Chester-Le-Street; 1 s (Anthony b 1979), 1 da (Samantha b 1980); *Career* writer; awards: Br Comparative Literature Assoc Translation Prize 1986, Cardiff Int Poetry Competition 1988, Nat Poetry Competition (commended) 1987 and 1988; *Books* Crowded by Shadows (1977), What a Place to Grow Flowers (1979), Earth Studies and Other Voyages (1982), Prisoners of Transience (1985), Beware Falling Tortoises (1987); *Recreations* reading, playing pool, watching snooker; *Style*— Ms Sheenagh Pugh; Maengwyn, Bridge St, Lower St Clears, Dyfed SA33 4EN (☎ 0994 230945)

PUGH-COOK, Richard Gerald; s of Cdr George Garnet Pugh-Cook, OBE, RN (d 1969); *b* 15 Dec 1937; *Educ* Felsted; *m* 1963, Elizabeth Ann, da of Capt Michael William Allday; 2 s, 1 da; *Career* dir: Mid-Wales Yarns Ltd, Steeles Carpets Ltd; gp mktg dir Tomkinsons Carpets Ltd; *Recreations* tennis, cricket; *Style*— Richard Pugh-Cook, Esq; The Old Vicarage, Elmbridge, Droitwich, Worcs (☎ 029 923 214, office 0562 820006, fax 0562 820030, telex 337577)

PUGH-THOMAS, Anthony; s of Dr John Pugh-Thomas (d 1968), of The Wirral, and Gladys, *née* Dugdale (d 1989); *b* 14 July 1939; *Educ* Repton, Jesus Coll Cambridge (MA, LLM); *m* 20 May 1967, Rosemary Dennys, da of Michael Bernard Clarke Butler-Cole; 2 da (Antonia Francesca b 18 June 1970, Claudia Rachel b 19 Oct 1972); *Career* admitted slr 1965; articled clerk Simmons & Simmons Solicitors, ptnr Durrant Cooper & Hambling 1967 (joined as asst slr), currently ptnr Lovell White Durrant (formerly Durrant Cooper Hambling and then Durrant Piesse); author of various articles on topics of legal interest; memb: Cncl and treas Justice, Law Soc (co-opted memb Civil Litigation Ctee), Ctee City of London Law Soc, Int Bar Assoc (memb Banking Law Sub Ctee); nominated memb Ct of Appeal (Civil Div) Users' Ctee, pres London Slrs' Litigation Assoc 1980-82; *Recreations* collecting eighteenth century mezzo-tints and nineteenth century pottery, growing unusual plants; *Clubs* Oriental, Travellers'; *Style*— Anthony Pugh-Thomas, Esq; Lovell White Durrant, 65 Holborn Viaduct, London EC1A 2DY (☎ 071 236 0066, fax 071 236 0084)

PUGHE, Brig Neville Morris; s of Maj Morris George Pughe (d 1950), and Dorothy Edith, *née* Goss; *b* 10 Jan 1936; *Educ* Exeter Sch, RMA Sandhurst, RMCS Shrivenham, Staff Coll Bracknell; *m* 19 Jan 1963, Linda Jane, da of Denis Carr Chetwood (d 1974); 3 s (David Michael Stephen b 9 Jan 1964, Richard Neville Iain b 31 July 1965, Jonathan Owen b 7 Feb 1967); *Career* cmmnd RA 1955, Maj 16 Parachute Bde 1972-74, instr Staff Coll 1974-76, CO 26 Field Regt RA 1976-78, Col GS MOD 1980-82, AMA Washington 1983-85, def attaché Bonn 1986-88, dep cdr SW England 1988-89; currently chief exec Surrey Heath Borough Cncl; warden Woodland Tst; FBIM 1988, MITD 1989; *Recreations* walking, gardening, music, writing, environment, sport; *Style*— Brig Neville Pughe; The Fieldings, Ham Meadows, Marnhull, Dorset (☎ 0258 820930); Surrey Heath Borough Council, Knoll Rd, Camberley, Surrey (☎ 0276 686252, fax 0276 22277)

PUGSLEY, Sir Alfred Grenvile; OBE (1944); s of Herbert William Pugsley, of Wimbledon, and Marian, *née* Clifford; *b* 1903,May; *Educ* Rutlish Sch, Univ of London; *m* 1928, Kathleen Mary (d 1974), da of Laban Warner, of Aldershot; *Career* Royal Airships Works Cardington 1926-31, RAE Farnborough 1931-45, prof of civil engrg Univ of Bristol 1944-68 (pro vice chllr 1961-64, emeritus prof); hon fell Univ of Bristol; Hon DUniv Surrey; Hon DSc: Belfast 1965, Cranfield 1978; emeritus memb Smeatonian Soc of Civil Engrs 1989; Structural Engrs Gold Medal 1968, Civil Engrs Ewing Gold Medal 1979; FRS 1952; Hon: FRAeS 1963, FICE 1981; kt 1956; *Clubs* Athenaeum; *Style*— Sir Alfred Pugsley, OBE, FRS; 4 Harley Ct, Clifton Down, Bristol BS8 3JU (☎ 0272 739400)

PUGSLEY, Peter Vivian Rupert; s of Vivian Stanley Pugsley; *b* 2 March 1933; *Educ* Cranleigh; *m* 1971, Carolyn, da of Sidney Francis Morgann; 1 child; *Career* md Green Shield Trading Stamp Co Ltd; *Recreations* hockey, golf; *Clubs* MCC; *Style*— Peter Pugsley, Esq; Herons Hollow, North St, Westbourne, Emsworth, Hants PO10 85N (☎ 0243 377529)

PULESTON JONES, Haydn; s of Iago Oliver Puleston Jones (d 1971), and Elizabeth Ann, *née* Morris; *b* 16 Sept 1948; *Educ* Welshpool HS, King's Coll London (LLB, AKC); *m* 9 June 1973, Susan Elizabeth, da of Lt Cdr George Karn (d 1970); 2 s (Simon b 1975, Nicholas b 1978); *Career* ptnr Linklaters & Paines 1979- (joined 1971); memb: Banking Law Sub Ctee City of London Law Soc 1980-, Ctee Montgomery Soc 1974-; tstee Montgomeryshire Charitable Tsts 1983-; memb: Law Soc 1973-, City of London Slrs' Co 1980-; *Recreations* gardening, classical music, genealogy; *Style*— Haydn Puleston Jones, Esq; Ducks Farm, Dux Lane, Plaxtol, nr Sevenoaks, Kent TN15 ORB; Linklaters & Paines, Barrington House, 59/67 Gresham St, London EC2V 7JA (☎ 071 606 7080, fax 071 606 5113, telex 884349)

PULFER, Hon Mrs (Margaret Hilary Diana); *née* Brooke; da of Baron Brooke of Cumnor, CH, PC (Life Peer, d 1984), and Baroness Brooke of Ystradfellte (Life Peer); *b* 1944; *m* 1971, James Douglas Pulfer; *Style*— The Hon Mrs Pulfer

PULL, William; s of Stanley Herbert Pull, and Suzanne, *née* Birnie; *b* 5 May 1942; *Educ* Malvern, Oriel Coll Oxford (MA); *m* 1981, Andrea, da of Henry Michael Cairns-Terry; 2 s (Richard b 1983, Jonathan b 1985); *Career* Baring Bros & Co Ltd 1969-79, Harrisons & Crosfield plc 1979-87 (dir 1985-87), head of corporate fin Italian International Bank 1988-; *Recreations* history, walking, paintings; *Clubs* Savile; *Style*— William Pull, Esq; 30 Poplar Grove, London W6 (☎ 071 602 7833); Brook Farm, Pulham St Mary, Norfolk

PULLEIN-THOMPSON, Josephine Mary Wedderburn; MBE (1984); da of Harold James Pullein-Thompson (d 1958), and Joanna Cannan (novelist, d 1961); *Educ* Wychwood Sch Oxford, and educated at home; *Career* author; Eng Centre of Int PEN: elected gen sec 1976- (official delegate of many int confs); published 40 books from 1946, first novel It Began with Picotee (juvenile work, written jtly with sisters); crime novels: Gin and Murder (1959), They Died in the Spring (1960), Murder Strikes Pink (1963); Ernest Benn award (for All Change) 1961; horsewoman; has competed in horse trials, showjumping and dressage judge; memb: Ctee Crime Writers' Assoc 1971-73, Ctee of Children's Writers' Group (Soc of Authors) 1973-78; *Recreations* reading, travel; *Style*— Miss Josephine Pullein-Thompson, MBE; Jennifer Luithlen Agency, 88 Holmfield Rd, Leicester LE2 1SB (☎ 0533 738863, fax 0533 735697)

PULLEN, Janice Annette; da of Albert Henry Pullen, of Bow, London, and Joan, *née* Morgan (d 1985); *b* 3 Jan 1951; *Educ* Lewes County GS for Girls; *Career* wardrobe sec Glyndbourne Festival Opera 1966-72, wardrobe mistress Scottish Opera 1974-77, wardrobe dir Royal Opera House 1979-; *Recreations* reading, cooking and entertaining, DIY, photography; *Style*— Miss Janice Pullen; Muffin Cottage, 6 Little East St, Lewes, East Susex BN7 2NU (☎ 0273 479373); Royal Opera House, Covent Garden, London WC2E 9DD (☎ 071 240 1200, telex 27988 COVGAR G, fax 071 497 1075)

PULLEN, Sir (William) Reginald James; KCVO (1987, MVO 1966, CVO 1975), JP (Inner London); s of William Pullen (d 1964), of Falmouth, and Lily Rhoda Chinn (d 1990); *b* 17 Feb 1922; *Educ* Falmouth GS, King's Coll London (LLB); *m* 1948, Doreen Angela, da of Tom Hebron, CBE, MVO; 2 da (Rosalind b 1951, Sandra b 1953); *Career* Flt Lt RAFVR (admin and special duties SE Asia); Westminster Abbey: asst to chief accountant 1947, dep registrar 1951-64, receiver gen 1959-87, chapter clerk 1963-87, registrar 1964-84; memb Westminster City Cncl 1962-65; tstee: The Passage RC Day Centre for Homeless People 1983-, St Marylebone Almshouses 1990-, Abbey Community Centre 1990-; clerk to tstees of the Utd Westminster Almshouses Gp of Charities 1987-, jt hon treas Cncl Christians and Jews 1988-; Dep High Bailiff Westminster 1987-; OStJ 1969, CStJ 1981, KStJ 1987; Freeman: City of London, Worshipful Co of Waxchandlers; Liveryman Worshipful Co of Fishmongers; FCIS; *Recreations* travelling, dog walking, gerentology; *Clubs* MCC, Royal Air Force; *Style*— Sir Reginald Pullen, KCVO, JP; 42 Rochester Row, London SW1P 1BU (☎ 071 828 3131)

PULLEN, Trevor Keith; s of Ronald Pullen, of Bexley, Kent, and Pamela Ann, *née* Berry; *b* 22 Nov 1948; *Educ* Roan GS Greenwich, Lanchester Poly Coventry (BA); *m* 1, 13 Sept 1969 (m dis 1980), Glenise May; 1 s (Andrew b 1973), 1 da (Samantha b 1971); m 2, 31 March 1988, Pauline; *Career* Prudential Portfolio Mangrs: UK equity dir 1982, global securities dir 1988; investmt dir Prudential Holborn 1987, chm Barnard Enterprises 1987, Prudential Funeral Services 1991; *Recreations* golf, squash, skiing; *Clubs* Addington GC; *Style*— Trevor Pullen, Esq; 9 Prince Consort Drive, Chislehurst, Kent (☎ 071 467 9522); 142 Holborn Bars, London EC1N 2NH (☎ 071 548 3145, telex 265082, car 0860 811309)

PULLEY, (Henry John) Campbell; s of William Laurie Pulley, of Shenfield, Essex, and Janet Fairley, *née* Jackson (d 1985); *b* 26 Oct 1939; *Educ* Lancing, Magdalene Coll Cambridge (MA); *m* 25 April 1964, Margaret Anne (Nan), da of Walter Roy Nieland (d 1962), of Hutton, Essex; 2 da (Nicola b 8 April 1965, Deborah b 3 Nov 1967); *Career* memb Lloyd's 1972-, dir Anderson Finch Villiers Ltd 1977-80, dir of gp insur Minet Group 1985-, chm Hutton Mount Ltd; Freeman City of London 1961, memb Ct Worshipful Co of Saddlers 1988 (Liveryman 1961); FCII 1975; *Style*— H J C Pulley, Esq; Bow End, 9 Bowhay, Hutton Mount, Brentwood, Essex CM13 2JX (☎ 0277 214

072),. Minet House, 100 Leman St, London E1 8HG (☎ 071 481 0707, fax 071 488 9786, telex 8813901)

PULLIN, Peter Charles; s of William John Pullin (d 1984), and Dorothy Hilda Pullin; *b* 3 May 1952; *Educ* Cheltenham GS; *m* 26 April 1980, Shane, da of Harold Heyes; *Career* Marcus Hazlewood and Co Certified Accountants 1970-76, asst mangr Chelsea Bldg Soc 1976-80 (accountant 1980-81), treasy accountant TSB Tst Co Ltd 1981-84; treas: Derbyshire Bldg Soc 1984-86, Cheltenham and Gloucester Bldg Soc 1986-; FCCA 1975, MCT 1987; *Recreations* golf, photography; *Style*— Peter Pullin, Esq; Cranlea, Malleson Rd, Gotherington, Cheltenham, Glos (☎ 0242 67 6322); Cheltenham and Gloucester Bldg Soc, Cheltenham House, Clarence St, Cheltenham, Glos GL50 3JR (☎ 0242 36161)

PULLINGER, Sir (Francis) Alan; CBE (1970), DL (Herts 1982); s of William Pullinger; *b* 22 May 1913; *Educ* Marlborough, Balliol Coll Oxford; *m* 1, 1946, Felicity Charmian Gotch Hobson (decd); 2 s, 1 da; m 2, 1966, Jacqueline Louise Anne Durin; *Career* chm Haden Carrier Ltd 1961-79, pres Inst of Heating and Ventilating Engrs 1972-73; vice chm Cncl of Benenden Sch, chm Herts Scout Cncl; Hon FCIBS 1977; kt 1977; *Recreations* mountaineering, sailing, beagling; *Clubs* Alpine, Travellers'; *Style*— Sir Alan Pullinger, CBE, DL; Barnhorn, Meadway, Berkhamsted, Herts (☎ 0442 863206)

PULLINGER, Anthony Giles Broadbent; s of Sir Alan Pullinger, CBE, *qv*, of Barnhorn, Meadway, Berkhamstead, Herts, and Felicity Charmian Gotch, *née* Hobson (d 1964); *b* 24 May 1955; *Educ* Dragon Sch, Marlborough, Balliol Coll Oxford; *m* 2 Oct 1982, Henrietta Mary Conyngham, da of Maj Richard Conyngham Corfield, of Hill Cottage, Radway, Warwicks; 1 s (Jack b 1985), 1 da (Rosanna b 1988); *Career* stockbroker Laing & Cruickshank 1978-90, seconded to the Panel on Takeovers and Mergers 1982-84, ptnr Laing & Cruickshank 1984-87, dir Alexanders Laing & Cruickshank 1985-89, sec to Panel on Takeovers and Mergers 1990-; Freeman: City of London 1986, Worshipful Co of Grocers 1986; *Recreations* fishing, shooting, walking, music, travel, natural history; *Style*— Anthony Pullinger, Esq; 3 Thurleigh Ave, London SW12 8AN (☎ 081 673 3724); The Panel on Takeovers and Mergers, PO Box No 26, The Stock Exchange Building, London EC2P 2JX (☎ 071 382 9026, fax 071 638 1554)

PULLMAN, Bruce John; s of Bernard John Pullman, of Brockenhurst, Hants, and Dorothy Jean, *née* Hayes; *b* 4 April 1957; *Educ* Canford, Merton Coll Oxford (BA); *m* 14 July 1979, Joanna Alexis Hamilton, da of John Edward Hamilton Davies, of Whitby, N Yorks; 1 s (Joshua b 1989), 2 da (Rebecca b 1984, Abigail b 1985); *Career* NM Rothschild & Sons Ltd 1979-81, dir County NatWest Investmt Mgmnt (CNIM) 1987- (joined 1981, responsible for quantitative investmt res); *Books* contrib Portfolio Insur (ed Donald L Luskin, 1988); *Recreations* Baptist Church; *Style*— Bruce Pullman, Esq; County Nat West Investment Management Ltd, Fenchurch Exchange, 43/44 Crutched Friars, London EC3N 2NX (☎ 071 374 3000, fax 071 373 3277)

PULVERMACHER, (Francis) Michael; s of Francis Howard Pulvermacher (d 1978), of Pentyrch, Glamorgan, and Marjorie Constance Denman, *née* Wheatley; *b* 26 July 1938; *Educ* Framlingham, Univ of London (LLB, LLM); *m* 17 Sept 1966, Diana, da of Lt-Col James William Randall Penrose (d 1966), of Shernal Green, Droitwich, Worcs; 1 s (Francis b 1975), 3 da (Joanna b 1968, Isobel b 1969, Helen b 1971); *Career* admitted slr 1961; ptnr Alms and Young 1968-; hon sec Somerset Law Soc 1971-84, lectr Notaries Soc 1983- (memb Cncl); NP 1961; memb: Scout Assoc, Lord Chllr's Legal Aid Advsy Ctee 1986-; pres Assoc of SW Law Socs 1977-78, tstee St James Pool Taunton Charity; memb Law Soc 1961; *Recreations* hill walking, sailing, beekeeping, campanology; *Style*— Michael Pulvermacher, Esq; Causeway Cottages, West Buckland, Wellington, Somerset

PULVERTAFT, Rear Adm David Martin; CB (1990); s of Captain William Godfrey Pulvertaft, OBE, RN (d 1971), and Annie Joan Martin (d 1988); *b* 26 March 1938; *Educ* Canford, Brittania RNC Dartsmouth, RN Engrg Coll Manadon (BSc); *m* 25 July 1961, Mary Rose, da of Frederick John Jeacock (d 1973), of Hong Kong; 1 s (Rupert James b 1964), 2 da (Sarah Jane b 1965, Lucy Michelle b 1966); *Career* HMS Anchorite 1963-66, HMS Dreadnought 1967-71, 10 Submarine Sqdn 1971-72, HM Dockyard Devonport 1973-75 and 1979-82, NDC Latimer 1975-76, MOD 1976-78, RCDS 1983, chm Naval Nuclear Tech Safety Panel 1984-85; dir: Ship Refitting 1986-87, Gen Aircraft (Navy) 1987-90, Gen Procurement and Support Orgn (Navy) 1990-; FIMechE 1989 (MIMechE 1974), FBIM 1990; *Recreations* genealogy, printing and bookbinding; *Clubs* Naval; *Style*— Rear Adm David Pulvertaft, CB; c/o Naval Secretary, Ministry of Defence (Navy), Whitehall, London SW1A 2BL

PUMPHREY, Christopher Jonathan; TD; s of Col Jonathan Moberly Pumphrey, OBE, TD, DL, and Violet Frances, *née* Bosanquet (d 1984); *b* 2 Nov 1933; *Educ* Winchester, Magdalene Coll Cambridge (MA); *m* 1960, Joanna Jane, da of (Frederic) Howard Aykroyd (d 1978), of The Lodge, Kirkby Overblow, nr Harrogate; 2 s (Edward b 1963, Andrew b 1965), 1 da (Sara Rose (Mrs Alexander) b 1962); *Career* chm Wise Speke & Co stockbrokers 1987- (ptnr 1960-87); *Clubs* Northern Counties (Newcastle upon Tyne), Leander; *Style*— Christopher Pumphrey, Esq, TD; Bolam West House, Middleton, Morpeth, Northumberland (☎ 0661 881232)

PUMPHREY, Sir (John) Laurence; KCMG (1973, CMG 1963); s of late Charles Ernest Pumphrey (d 1950), of W Bitchfield, Belsay, Northumberland, and Iris Mary, *née* Moberly-Bell (d 1968); *b* 22 July 1916; *Educ* Winchester, New Coll Oxford; *m* 1945, Jean, da of Sir Walter Riddell, 12 Bt, of Hepple, Morpeth, Northumberland; 4 s (Matthew b 1946, Charles b 1948, Jonathan b 1954, James b 1964), 1 da (Laura b 1951); *Career* served WWII, Lt Northumberland Hussars (POW 1941-45); joined Foreign Serv 1945, dep high cmmr Nairobi 1965-67, high cmmr Zambia 1967-71, ambass to Pakistan 1971-76, ret; *Recreations* walking, fishing; *Clubs* Royal Cwlth Soc; *Style*— Sir Laurence Pumphrey, KCMG; Caistron, Thropton, Morpeth, Northumberland NE65 7LG (☎ 0669 40244)

PUNCH, Michael Richard Talbot; s of James William Punch (d 1989), and Madeline Mary Punch, MBE, *née* Talbot; *b* 22 May 1944; *Educ* Magdalen Coll Sch Brackley, Magdalen Coll Oxford (BA); *m* 7 June 1973, Johanna Catherine, da of Richard Patrick Lowe (d 1987); 1 s (Thomas Richard Talbot b 8 Jan 1981), 1 da (Lucy Alice Talbot b 30 Dec 1977); *Career* copywriter: Foote Cone & Belding, London Press Exchange, Grey Advertising 1965-73; dep creative dir: Lonsdale Crowther Osborn 1973-76, David Williams & Ketchum 1976-78; creative dir and dep md JR Foote Cone & Belding Hong Kong 1979-82, creative dir Nicklin Advertising 1983-; *Style*— Michael Punch, Esq; Nicklin Advertising Ltd, 56 Marsh Wall, London E14 (☎ 071 538 5521)

PUNT, Jonathan Arthur Gilbert; s of Norman Arthur Punt (d 1986), of London, and Gwendolen Phyllis, *née* Moore (d 1986); *b* 14 Sept 1948; *Educ* Epsom Coll Surrey, Guy's Hosp Med Sch Univ of London (MB BS); *m* 7 Aug 1970, Susan Elizabeth, da of Norman Poyntz-Roberts (d 1983), of Sussex; 1 s (Robin b 10 Aug 1974), 1 da (Emma b 15 July 1977); *Career* conslt neurosurgeon Univ Hosp Nottingham and Leicester Royal Infirmary 1984; memb UK Childrens Cancer Study Group, sec Brain Tumour Gp of Euro Orgns for Res into Treatment of Cancer; FRCS 1976, FRSM; *Books* Fetal and Neonatal Neurology and Neurosurgery (co ed and contrib, 1988); *Recreations* wine & food, motorsport, travel; *Style*— Jonathan Punt, Esq; Department of Neurosurgery, University Hospital, Nottingham NG7 2UH (☎ 0602 709103)

PUNUKOLLU, Dr Nageswara Rao; s of Gopalakrishnaiah Punukollu, of India, and Bhaskaramba Punukollu; *b* 28 Dec 1942; *Educ* Osmania Univ India (MB BS), Univ of Dublin (DPM); *m* 22 May 1972, Krishna Kumaria Parvataneni, da of Venktaratnan Parvataneni (d 1980); 1 s (Bhaskar b 4 July 1976), 1 da (Mallika b 21 July 1973); *Career* conslt psychiatrist NHS UK 1980- (trainee 1973-80), dir Nat Inst of Crisis Intervention 1988-; developed: crisis intervention team in Huddesfield, comprehensive community based mental health services in Huddersfield dist, transcultural psychiatry in Huddersfield dist; estab: Nat Inst of Crisis Intervention Therapy and Res In UK, Mental Handicap Prevention Gp Huddersfield; memb Health Advsy Serv England; MRCPsych 1979; *Style*— Dr Nageswara Punukollu; National Institute of Crisis Intervention Therapy and Research, 63 Nabcroft Lane, Crosland Moor, Huddersfield (☎ 0484 654711, fax 0484 654777)

PURBECK, Luca G; s of Herbert Gutmann (d 1942, former dir of Dresdner Bank Berlin, and London stockbroker), and Daisy (d 1959), da of Maj Kurt von Frankenberg und Ludwigsdorf (d 1932); Mr Purbeck's (1) paternal gf Gutmann founded Dresdner Bank 1872; (2) maternal gggf Gen von Porbeck was ka at Talavera on Napoleon's side, whilst (3) maternal gggf Frankenberg fought under the Duke of Brunswick with Wellington in Spain and at Waterloo and was severely wounded; *b* 13 July 1914; *Educ* Realgymnasium Potsdam, Berlin Univ; *m* 1, 1954, Vera (d 1979), da of Arthur Doughty, of London (d 1961); 1 s (and 1 s decd); m 2, 1982, Monica Pelissier, da of Arthur Greey (d 1974), of Birmingham; *Career* Hambros Bank Ltd London 1936-37, dir Brieger & Co Ltd London 1938-39, news ed Assoc Press of America (London) 1944-46, fndr md Mayborn Products Ltd London and Dylon Int Ltd, pres Dylon-France Safco SA; dir: Dylon-Japan KK, Dylon-Nederland NV 1946-79, Mayborn Gp Ltd 1983-86 (non exec vice chm 1980-82); silver medallist Soc of Dyers and Colourists; paintings and sculpture accepted by Royal Acad; FCIM, FInstD; *Publications* Selected Poems (1982), Ausgewaehlte Gedichte (1982); *Recreations* golf, painting, sculpting, writing; *Clubs* Wentworth, RAC, Directors'; *Style*— Luca Purbeck, Esq; 14 Langford Place, St John's Wood, London NW8 0LL (☎ 071 624 9492)

PURCELL, Roger Bernard Allan; s of Bernard George Purcell (d 1982), of Leatherhead, and Hazel Cecily, *née* Roseberry; *b* 27 April 1945; *Educ* Shrewsbury, Pembroke Coll Cambridge (MA); *Career* CA; Binder Hamlyn 1966-72, First Investors and Savers 1972-74, Save & Prosper Gp 1974-86; dir: County Securities 1986-87, Securities and Investmts Bd 1987-; FCA 1969; *Recreations* walking, jogging, bridge, singing; *Style*— Roger Purcell, Esq; 202 Old Brompton Rd, London SW5 (☎ 071 370 3028); Gavrelle House, 2-14 Bunhill Row EC1 (☎ 071 638 12409, fax 071 382 5900)

PURCHAS, Christopher Patrick Brooks; QC (1990); s of The Rt Hon Sir Francis Purchas, and Patricia Kathleen, *née* Milburn; *b* 20 June 1943; *Educ* Marlborough, Trinity Coll Cambridge; *m* 7 Dec 1974, Bronwen Victoria Mary, da of Lt-Col Charles Peter Vaughan, DSO, DL (d 1975); 2 da (Léonie Melissa b 2 Aug 1978, Domino Octavia b 5 April 1983); *Career* called to the Bar Inner Temple 1966; recorder 1986; *Recreations* tennis, shooting; *Style*— Christopher Purchas, Esq, QC; 2 Crown Office Row, Temple London EC4 (☎ 071 353 9337)

PURCHAS, Rt Hon Lord Justice; Sir Francis Brooks; PC (1982); s of late Capt Francis Purchas; *b* 19 June 1919; *Educ* Summerfields Sch Oxford, Marlborough, Trinity Coll Cambridge; *m* 1942, Patricia Mona Kathleen, *née* Milburn; 2 s; *Career* called to the Bar Inner Temple 1948, QC 1965, cmmr Central Criminal Ct 1970-71, bencher 1972, rec Canterbury 1969-72, ldr S Eastern Circuit 1972-74, High Court judge (Family Div) 1974-82, presiding judge S Eastern Circuit 1977-82, Lord Justice of Appeal 1982-; kt 1974; *Recreations* shooting, golf, fishing; *Clubs* Hawks (Cambridge); *Style*— The Rt Hon Lord Justice Purchas; Parkhurst House, nr Haslemere, Surrey GU27 3BY (☎ 0428 78280); 1 Temple Gdns, Temple, London EC4Y 9BB (☎ 071 353 5124)

PURCHAS, Robin Michael; QC (1987); s of Rt Hon Sir Francis Brooks Purchas, *qv*; *b* 12 June 1946; *Educ* Marlborough, Trinity Coll Cambridge (MA); *m* 3 Sept 1970, (Denise) Anne Kerr, da of Capt David Finlay, RN; 1 s (James Alexander Francis b 27 Sept 1973), 1 da (Charlotte Robin b 3 Nov 1975); *Career* called to the Bar Inner Temple 1968, rec 1989; *Recreations* tennis, skiing, sailing, opera, theatre, shooting; *Clubs* Queens, Lansdowne; *Style*— Robin M Purchas, QC; 2 Harcourt Buildings, Temple, London EC4 (☎ 071 353 8415, fax 071 353 7622)

PURDEN, Roma Laurette (Laurie); MBE (1973); da of George Cecil Arnold Purden (d 1964), and Constance Mary Sheppard (d 1952); *b* 30 Sept 1928; *Educ* Harecroft Sch Tunbridge Wells; *m* 1957, John Keith Kotch (d 1979), s of Harold James Kotch, OBE (d 1962); 2 da (Emma, Sophie); *Career* asst ed Homes Notes 1951-52 (fiction ed 1948-51), asst ed Woman's Own 1952, sr asst ed Girl 1952-54; ed: Housewife 1954-57, Home 1957-62, House Beautiful 1963-65, Good Housekeeping 1965-73; ed-in-chief: Good Housekeeping and Womancraft 1973-77, Woman's Journal 1978-88, (Woman's Journal won Periodical Publishers Assoc Consumer Magazine of the Year award 1985), Woman & Home 1982-83; dir Brickfield Pubns Ltd 1978-80; Magazine Editor of the Year 1979 (Br Soc of Magazine Editors); *Style*— Laurie Purden, MBE; 174 Pavilion Road, London SW1 (☎ 071 730 4021)

PURDIE, Prof David Wilkie; s of Robert Wilkie Purdie, and Jean Wilson Purdie; *b* 13 Aug 1946; *Educ* Ayr Acad, Univ of Glasgow (MB ChB); *m* 24 June 1983, Dr Katherine Ann, da of Maj Thomas Arklay Guthrie, of Wind Edge Farm, by Tibbermore, Perthshire; 1 s (Arklay b 1984), 2 da (Catriona b 1986, Mhairi-rose b 1988); *Career* ships surgn SS Canberra RNR 1970-72; MRC res fell Univ of Glasgow 1973-75, registrar Queens Mother's Hosp and W Infirmary Glasgow 1975-78, lectr Univ of Dundee 1978-83, sr lectr Univ of Leeds 1983-89, prof and dir of post grad med educn Univ of Hull 1989-; exec memb Assoc Study of Med Educn; FRCOG 1988, FSA Scot 1981; *Books* Scientific articles on med educn and menopause related subjects; *Recreations* Golf; *Clubs* Savage; *Style*— Prof David Purdie; Rowley Rectory, Rowley, Little Weighton, N Humberside HU20 3XR; Centre for Postgraduate Education, Hull Royal Infirmary, Anlaby Road, Hull HU3 2KZ (☎ 0482 586024)

PURDIE, Robert Anthony James; s of Red Anthony Watson Purdie, of Shearwater, Popes Lane, Colyford, Colyton, Devon, and Erica Margaret Gertrude Helen, *née* Roberts; *b* 15 April 1956; *Educ* Harrow, Seaford Coll, Univ Coll Cardiff (LLB); *m* 5 Feb 1983, Elisabeth Jean, da of Roy Maclean Calman (d 1976); *Career* barr Middle Temple 1979, practicing South Eastern circuit; churchwarden Parish of St Cross or Holywell with St Peter-in-the-East cum St John Baptist Oxford 1988; memb Family Law Bar Assoc; *Books* Matrimonial and Domestic Injunctions (jtly, second edn 1987), contrib to Atkins Encyclopedia of Court Forms, Husband and Wife (1985); *Recreations* fishing, collecting books and antiques; *Clubs* Lansdowne; *Style*— Robert Purdie, Esq; Francis Taylor Building, Temple, London EC4Y 7BY (☎ 071 353 9942, fax 071 353 9924)

PURDON, Maj-Gen Corran William Brooke; CBE (1970), MC (1945), CPM (1982); s of Maj-Gen (William) Brooke Purdon, DSO, OBE, MC, and Dorothy Myrtle, *née* Coates; *b* 4 May 1921; *Educ* Rokeby Sch Wimbledon, Campbell Coll Belfast, RMC Sandhurst; *m* 28 July 1945, (Maureen) Patricia, da of Maj James Francis Petrie (d 1952); 2 s (Patrick b 1947, Timothy b 1949), 1 da (Angela b 1958); *Career* cmmnd Royal Ulster Rifles 1939, Army Commandos, France and Germany 1940-45 (wounded, MC), Palestine Emergency 1945-46, Egypt 1949-51, Malayan Emergency 1956-58,

Cyprus Emergency 1958; CO 1 Bn Royal Ulster Rifles, BAOR and Borneo War 1962-65, GSO1 and chief instr Sch of Inf Warminster 1965-67, Cdr Sultan's Armed Forces Sultanate of Oman and Dir of Ops Dhofar War 1967-70, Cmdt Sch of Inf Warminster 1970-72; GOC: NW Dist 1972-74, Near East Land Forces 1974-76, ret as Maj-Gen; dep cmmr Royal Hong Kong Police 1978-81; dir: Falconstar Ltd (Mil Trg Teams) 1983-85, Defence Systems Ltd 1985-89; govr Royal Humane Soc 1984-, Hon Col Queen's Univ Belfast OTC 1975-78, pres Army Gymnastic Union 1973-76, patron Small Arms Sch Corps Old Comrades Assoc 1985-90; memb Cncl St John Ambulance Bde Wiltshire 1981-86; Hon Col D Co (London Irish Rifles) 4 (V) Bn Royal Irish Rangers 1986-; KstJ 1983; MBIM; Bravery Medal (Oman) 1968, Distinguished Service Medal (Oman) 1969; *Recreations* physical fitness, running, swimming, military biographies, reviewing military books; *Clubs* Army and Navy, Hong Kong; *Style—* Maj-Gen Corran Purdon, CBE, MC, CPM; Old Park House, Devizes, Wiltshire SN10 5JR (☎ 0380 724876); Lightweight Body Armour Ltd, Hinton Hse, Daventry, Northamptonshire NN11 6OG (☎ 0327 61282, fax 0327 60656, telex 312112 Armour G)

PURDUM, Richard Curtis; s of Rufus Purdum (d 1970), of Blawenberg, New Jersey, USA, and Mary Louise, *née* Reed (d 1970); *b* 26 Feb 1943; *Educ* Princeton HS Princeton New Jersey, Chouinard Art Inst Los Angeles; *m* 6 Dec 1976, Jill, da of Ralph Thomas; *Career* served US Navy 1965-69; MGM Animation/Chuck Jones Enterprises 1965, dir and animator Richard Williams Animation London 1969-79, fndr Richard Purdum Productions 1980 (studio produces traditional character animation primarily for advertising and title sequences); awards for animated commercials incl: Grand Prix Cinema 24 Int Advertising Festival 1977, Clio Award for Craftsmanship in Animation 1977, Gold award Int Film and TV Festival of New York 1984, Br Animation Awards for best design in animation and best advertising concept in animation 1988, Br Animation Award best animated commercial 1990; *Recreations* cats; *Style—* Richard Purdum, Esq; Richard Purdum Productions, Kings Court, 2-6 Goodge St, London W1P 1FF (☎ 071 636 5162, fax 071 436 5628)

PURDY, Dr Martin Terence; s of Gordon Purdy, OBE (d 1976), and Margaret Mary Purdy (d 1950); *b* 22 Feb 1939; *Educ* Oakham Sch, Lancing Coll, Poly of Central London, Univ of York (MA), Univ of Birmingham (PhD); *Career* ptnr Apec Architects 1969-; formerly teaching and res positions at Birmingham Sch of Architecture and Univ of Aston; foremost designs incl: Ecumenical Centre Skelmersdale, St Bartholomew's Church and Centre East Ham, Froud Centre Manor Park; currently architect to Sheffield Cathedral; memb RIBA; *Books* Housing on Sloping Sites (with Barry Simpson 1984), Churches and Chapels - a design and development guide (1991), author of numerous articles on church architecture; *Style—* Dr Martin Purdy; APEC Architects, 2 Sailsbury Rd, Moseley, Birmingham B13 8JS (☎ 021 4424747, fax 021 4224050)

PURDY, Quentin Alexander; s of Gordon Purdy, OBE (d 1976), and Margaret Dorothy Annie, *née* Stokes; *b* 23 Aug 1960; *Educ* Gresham's, Leicester Poly (BA), UCL (LLM); *m* 3 Sept 1988, Elizabeth Audrey, da of William Alfred Hazelwood, of Paddock Wood, Kent; *Career* called to the Bar Gray's Inn 1983; practising in Common Law Chambers London and on S Eastern circuit; memb Criminal Bar Assoc; *Recreations* reading, foreign travel, walking, sailing; *Style—* Quentin Purdy, Esq; 14 Gray's Inn Square, Gray's Inn, London WC1R 5JP (☎ 071 242 0858, fax 071 242 5434)

PUREFOY, Geoffrey; GSM Malaya (1949); s of Rev Canon Brian Purefoy (d 1963), and Mary Lillias Geraldine Purefoy (d 1989); family connected with Shalstone Manor since 1400 AD, see Purefoy Letters, Eland Sidgwick and Jackson 1931; *b* 3 March 1929; *Educ* Rugby, Ecole Hotelière Lausanne; *m* 1, 28 April 1956, Marcia Lamond; m 2, 1 March 1984, Wendy Allison; 2 da (Caroline Mews, Alison Bryony), 1 s (Simon Henry); *Career* farmer, vice chm Nat Sheep Assoc 1973-76, chm Bd of Govrs Buckingham Sch 1979-82; pres: Buckingham Horticultural Soc 1970-90, Brackley Farming Club 1963-84; gen cmmr of taxes Buckingham & Winlaw 1964-; memb Ct of Assts Worshipful Co of Clothworkers; *Style—* Geoffrey Purefoy, Esq; Shalstone Manor, Buckingham MK18 5LT (☎ 0280 704854)

PURKIS, Dr Andrew James; s of Clifford Henry Purkis, OBE, of Trevone, N Cornwall, and Mildred Jeannie, *née* Crane; *b* 24 Jan 1949; *Educ* Highgate Sch, CCC Oxford (BA), St Antonys Coll Oxford (DPhil); *m* 18 July 1980, Jennifer Harwood, da of Francis Harwood Smith, of Willaston, Wirral, Cheshire; 1 s (Henry b 1982), 1 da (Joanna b 1980); *Career* princ NI Office 1977-80 (admin trainee 1973-76, private sec 1976- 1977), asst dir Nat Cncl for Voluntary Orgns 1986-87 (head of policy analysis 1980-84, head of policy planning 1984-86); dir: Cncl for the Protection of Rural England 1987-, dir Contact a Family; FRSA 1989; *Books* Housing and Community Care (jtly, 1982), Health in the Round (jtly, 1984); *Recreations* walking, birdwatching, surf riding, travel, theatre, music; *Style—* Dr Andrew Purkis; 38 Endlesham Rd, Balham, London SW12 8JL (☎ 081 675 2439); Council for the Protection of Rural England, Warwick House, 25 Buckingham Palace Road, London SW1W OPP (☎ 071 976 6433, fax 071 976 6373)

PURNELL, Prof John Howard; s of Walter John Purnell (d 1968), of Ferndale, Rhondda, Mid Glamorgan, and Sarah Ceridwen, *née* Davies (d 1972); *b* 17 Aug 1925; *Educ* Maesydderwen Co Sch, Pentre Secdy Sch, Univ Coll Cardiff (BSc, PhD), Univ of Cambridge (MA, PhD, ScD); *m* 24 Aug 1954, Elizabeth Mary, da of Stanley Edwards (d 1989), of Bishopston, Swansea, W Glamorgan; 1 s (Nicholas b 1960), 1 da (Rachel b 1957); *Career* lectr: Univ Coll Cardiff 1947-52, Univ of Cambridge 1960-65 (demonstrator 1955-60); prof Univ Coll of Swansea 1965-, bd chm Swansea Sound Ltd 1974-; author 200 sci papers; memb Rotary Club of Swansea 1984-, chm Swansea Rugby Patrons; FRSC (hon treas 1985-90); *Books* Gas Chromatography (1961); *Recreations* sport, gardening, music; *Clubs* Savage; *Style—* Prof Howard Purnell; 1 Bishopston Rd, Bishopston, Swansea, West Glam SA3 3EH (☎ 044 128 2407); Department of Chemistry, University College of Swansea, Singleton Park, Swansea SA2 8PP (☎ 0792 295257, fax 0792 295618, telex 48358, ULSWAN G)

PURNELL, Kenneth Benjamin; CBE (1970); s of Sidney Harold Purnell (d 1934), of Birmingham, and Edith, *née* Bevan (d 1962); *b* 21 Aug 1923; *Educ* Blue Coat Sch Birmingham, Commercial Coll Birmingham; *m* Beryl, da of W Bradburn (d 1942); 2 s (Andrew b 1962, Trevor b 1962), 1 da (Jacqueline b 1964); *Career* memb Lloyds; chm: KBP Hldgs Ltd 1962-86, Rentcroft Investmts Ltd 1964-90, Peter Reeves Co Ltd 1970-; dir: Nationwide Rental Gp plc 1986-88, Birmingham Midland Investments, Merchant Bankers 1964-72, Birmingham Freehold Investments Ltd 1964-72, Birmingham Leasehold Investments Ltd 1964-72, Industrial Metal Services 1989-; chm Dvpt Ctee Birmingham Assoc of Youth Clubs 1963-66 (memb Exec Cncl 1963-72), vice pres Br Olympic Assoc 1965; pres: W Midlands Sports Cncl 1965-72, Birmingham Radio Cncl 1972-74, Birmingham Sporting Club 1965-80, vice-pres Cwlth Games Ctee Scotland 1970, pres Birmingham Engrg & Building Centre 1971-82; ldr Trade Missions to: Far East 1974 (1979 and 1982), America 1976, S America 1977, Zimbabwe, S Africa and Kenya 1980; memb Cncl Birmingham Chamber of Industry & Commerce 1971-83; vice chm Variety Club of GB, memb Midland Region Ctee 1971-75 (chm Appeals Ctee 1977-79, sec 1980-86), dir Sports Aid Fndn 1977-90, chm W Midlands Regnl Sports Cncl 1977-80; govr The Birmingham Blue Coat Sch 1971, dir Malvern Festival 1978, memb Appeals Ctee RCS 1978-, pres Haematology Unit E Birmingham Hosp 1979-84; Liveryman Worshipful Co of Patternmakers, Freeman City of London; *Recreations* all sports; *Clubs* Reform, RAC, Lloyds; *Style—* Kenneth B Purnell, CBE; 54 Somerset Road, Edgbaston, Birmingham B15 2PD

PURSEGLOVE, Prof John William; CMG (1973); s of late Robert Purseglove; *b* 11 Aug 1912; *Educ* Lady Manners Sch Bakewell, Univ of Manchester, Gonville and Caius Coll Cambridge, Imperial Coll of Tropical Agric Trinidad; *m* 1947, Phyllis Agnes Adèle, da of late George Turner, of Falkland Islands; 1 s, 1 da decd; *Career* tropical crops specialist ODA E Malling Res Station Kent 1967-75; memb Green Alliance, friend of Royal Kew Gardens; FLS 1944, FIBiol 1970; *Books* Tobacco in Uganda (1951), Tropical Crops Dicotyledons (2 vols, 1968), Monocotyledon (2 vols, 1972), Spices (1981, Japanese edn 1986); *Recreations* natural history; *Style—* Prof John Purseglove, CMG; Walnut Trees, Sissinghurst, Cranbrook, Kent TN17 2JL (☎ 0580 712836)

PURSER, George Robert Gavin; s of Dr Joseph Alexander Purser (d 1968), of Charlwood, Surrey, and Constance Katherine, *née* Back; *b* 31 May 1936; *Educ* Lancing; *m* 4 June 1966, Mary-Ruth, da of Harold Lowe, of Charlwood Surrey; 2 da (Harriet b 1968, Philippa b 1969); *Career* Lt served Cyprus; sr ptnr Lawrence Graham slrs; *Recreations* tennis, golf, shooting, gardening; *Clubs* Athenaeum; *Style—* G R G Purser, Esq; Halesbridge House, Blanks Lane, Newdigate, Surrey RH5 5ED Lawrence Graham, 190 Strand, London WC2R 1JN (☎ 071 379 0000, fax 071 379 6854, telex 22673)

PURSER, Dr John Whitley; s of John William Richard Purser (d 1988), and Elizabeth Henrietta, *née* Jellett; *b* 10 Feb 1942; *Educ* Fettes, RSAMD (DRSAM), Univ of Glasgow (MA, PhD); *m* 1, 1965 (m dis 1987), Wilma McLeod Thomson, da of William Paterson; 1 s (Sean b 16 Sept 1967), 1 da (Sarah b 9 June 1969); m 2, 9 Oct 1987, Barbara Ann, da of Prof Elliott Forbes; *Career* composer and writer; compositions incl: numerous orchestral and chamber works, operas, vocal works; plays incl: Papageno, Heartwood, Girl at a Window, Carver; author of books of poetry and literary criticism; *Books* The Counting Stick (1976), A Share of the Wind (1980), Amoretti (1985), Is the Red Light On (1986), The Literary Works of Jack B Yeats (1991); *Recreations* climbing; *Style—* Dr John Purser; 3 Drinan, Isle of Skye, Scotland (☎ 04716 262); 29 Banavie Rd, Glasgow G11 5AW (☎ 041 339 5292)

PURSER, Simon Edmund Kinross; s of Lt Edmund Kinross Purser, RN (ret), of Exeter, Devon, and Pamela Mary, *née* Scanes; *b* 21 Feb 1947; *Educ* Sherborne; *Career* audit supervisor Cooper Bros 1971-73, exec Old Broad St Securities 1973-75, dir County NatWest Ltd 1975-89, chief exec Buckland Corp Fin Ltd 1990-; tstee the John McCarthy Fndn; FCA 1970; *Recreations* sailing, squash, skiing, flying; *Style—* Simon Purser, Esq; 10d Belvedere Drive, Wimbledon, London SW19 (☎ 081 947 4224); 16 Monmouth Hill, Topsham, Devon (☎ 0392 877013); Buckland Corporate Finance Ltd, Buckland House, Portland Mews, Portland Place, Plymouth (☎ 0752 265816)

PURSLOW, Christopher George (Chris); s of George Ellis Purslow (d 1985), and Lillian Rose, *née* Embrey; *b* 27 March 1946; *Educ* The High Sch Newcastle under Lyme, Univ of Bristol (BA, BArch); *m* 12 Aug 1970 (m dis 1977), (Sally) Louise, da of Dr Carl Basch, of South Orange, New Jersey; *Career* architect; Courtaulds Ltd Coventry 1967, Tarmac Ltd Wolverhampton 1968, Philip Johnson (Architect) NY 1969, Rice/Roberts (Architects) London 1972, London Borough of Islington 1974, borough architect Islington 1983-88, dir of architecture Glasgow 1988-; memb RIBA, FRSA; *Recreations* theatre, music, architecture, rocking the boat; *Style—* Chris Purslow, Esq; Rosslyn House, 1a Victoria Circus, Glasgow G12 9LH (☎ 041 334 8162); 20 Trongate, Glasgow G1 6EY (☎ 041 227 5379, fax 041 227 5551)

PURSLOW, Louise; da of Carl Lorenz Basch, of S Orange, New Jersey, USA, and Helen, *née* Feldstein; *b* 13 May 1944; *Educ* Barnard Coll Columbia Univ NY (AB); *m* 3 May 1984, Harold Salmond Greenberg, s of Rev Barry Greenberg (d 1965); 2 s (Jonathan Barry b 22 Aug 1976, Alexander Solomon b 22 Nov 1985), 2 da (Naomi Philippa b 22 June 1974, Judith Beila (twin) b 22 Nov 1985); *Career* prodr: WNBC and WABC NY USA, Radio Bristol 1970-72; BBC Radio: prodr Today and Kaleidoscope (original team), sr prodr Talks and Documentaries Dept, acting chief prodr sci progs 1981, chief prodr documentaries 1982, currently chief prodr features, arts and educn; *Recreations* music, theatre, books, galleries; *Style—* Miss Louise Purslow; Room 7089, Broadcasting House, London W1A 1AA (☎ 071 580 4468)

PURSSELL, Anthony John Richard; *b* 5 July 1926; *Educ* Oriel Coll Oxford; *m* 1952, Ann Margaret Batchelor; 2 s, 1 da; *Career* jt vice chm Arthur Guinness Son & Co Ltd 1981-83 (md 1975-81), regnl dir Lloyds Bank (S Midlands Bd) 1981-91 (chm 1989); hon treas Oxfam 1987-; memb: IBA 1976-81, Bd CAA 1984-90; *Clubs* Leander (Henley); *Style—* Anthony Purssell, Esq; Allendale, Bulstrode Way, Gerrards Cross, Bucks SL9 7QT

PURTON, Peter John; s of Arthur John Purton (d 1970), of Watford, Herts, and Olive May Purton (d 1991); *b* 18 July 1933; *Educ* Aldwickbury Harpenden Herts, Aldenham; *m* 6 Sept 1958, Mary, da of Lawrence Fone, of Chipperfield, Herts; 2 s (William b 1962, Thomas b 1965), 1 da (Catherine b 1960); LRAD; *Career* 3 Regt RHA 2 Lt Germany 1951-53, 290 (City of London) Field Regt RATA, Capt UK 1953-60; admitted slr 1958, Norton Rose 1953- (ptnr 1961-), memb: Cncl Law Soc 1969-86, Wine Standards Bd of the Vinters 1990-; chm: Law Reform Ctee 1972-75, Planning and Devpt Law Ctee 1979-86; memb: Scott Ctee on Property Linked Unit Tsts 1973, Lord Chllrs Law Reform Ctee 1975-, American Bar Assoc, Int Bar Assoc, Anglo-American Real Property Institute; dep pres Family Welfare Assoc 1990- (chm 1983-90), memb bd of govrs Aldenham Sch 1981-; former Master Worshipful Co of Slrs 1983-84, Liveryman Worshipful Co of Tallow Chandlers 1983; FRSA, LMRTPI; *Books* The Organisation and Management of a Solicitors Practice (gen ed 1979), Planning Law and Practice (jt gen ed, 1990); *Recreations* swimming, shooting, stalking, walking, heritage, jigsaw puzzles and family; *Clubs* Union Soc of Westminster, Royal Overseas League; *Style—* Peter Purton, Esq; The Old Rectory, Dunton, nr Winslow, Bucks MK18 3LW (☎ 0525 240 228); Kempson House, Camomile Street, London EC3A 7AN (☎ 071 283 2434, fax 071 588 1181)

PURVES, Elizabeth Mary (Libby); da of James Grant Purves, CMG (d 1984), of Suffolk, and Mary, *née* Tinsley; *b* 2 Feb 1950; *Educ* Sacred Heart Tunbridge Wells, St Annes Coll Oxford; *m* 1980, Paul Heiney, s of Norbert Wisniewski (d 1970), of Sheffield; 1 s (Nicholas b 1982), 1 da (Rose b 1984); *Career* journalist & broadcaster; presenter: Radio 4 Today, Midweek; radio documentaries incl Street Gospel, Holy Bones, Seven about Seven; *Books* Britain at Play (1982), Adventures Under Sail (1982), Sailing Weekend Book (with Paul Heiney, 1985), How Not To Be A Perfect Mother (1986), One Summer's Grace (1989), How Not to Raise a Perfect Child (1991); *Recreations* yachting, walking, writing; *Clubs* Roy Thames YC, Ocean Cruising, Royal Cruising; *Style—* Ms Libby Purves; Vale Farm, Middleton, nr Saxmundham, Suffolk; c/o A P Watt, 26-28 Bedford Row, London WC1

PURVES, (Andrew) Geoffrey; s of Maj Andrew Purves (d 1967), of 9 Winchcombe Place, High Heaton, Newcastle upon Tyne, and Blanche, *née* Lawson; *b* 12 June 1944; *Educ* Heaton GS, Univ of Durham (BA), Univ of Newcastle (BArch); *m* 12 Oct 1968, (Elizabeth) Ann, da of James Campbell Finlay, of 20 Lodore Rd, Newcastle upon Tyne; *Career* architect; sr ptnr Geoffrey Purves and Ptnrs; chm: Northumbria Branch RIBA 1981-83, Northern Regn RIBA 1988-89; dir: Newcastle Arch Workshop Ltd, Saunders and Purves Ltd, Power Factors Ltd, Purves Ltd, Geoffrey Purves and Ptnrs (Project Mgmnt) Ltd; RIBA, ARIAS, FRSA; *Recreations* sailing; *Clubs* Royal Cwlth Soc, Clyde Cruising; *Style—* Geoffrey Purves, Esq; Hawthorn House, Kirkwhelpington, Northumberland NE19 2RT (☎ 0830 40376); 8 North Terrace, Newcastle upon Tyne NE2 4AD (☎ 091 232 0424, fax 091 232 8131)

PURVES, Peter John; s of (John) Kenneth Purves (d 1987), of Swanage, Dorset, and Florence, *née* Patton (d 1976); *b* 10 Feb 1939; *Educ* Arnold Sch Blackpool, Alsager Teachers Training Coll (DipEd); *m* 1, 29 Sept 1962 (m dis 1981), Gillian Diane Emmet; 1 s (Matthew b 1963), 1 da (Lisa b 1963 adopted); m 2, 5 Feb 1983, Kathryn Lesley Evans; *Career* prodr, writer, dir, actor and presenter; began in repertory theatre Barrow in Furness 1961-63, London Theatre and TV 1963-65; TV credits incl: Dr Who BBC 1965-66), Blue Peter (BBC 1967-78), Special Assignments (BBC 1976-79), Crufts Dog Show (BBC 1976-), We're Going Places (BBC 1978-80), Stopwatch (BBC 1978-81), Darts Presenter (BBC 1979-84), Makers (HTV 1983-84), Work Out (HTV 1985), Babble (Ch 4 1985-87), Superdogs (BBC 1990-91), Crimewatch Midlands (BBC 1989-91); theatre: various pantomines 1978-, Once in a Lifetime (Blackpool, 1981); md Purves Wickes Video Projects Ltd 1984-; author of Tess, The Story of a Guide Dog (1980); *Clubs* Vaudeville Golf Soc, Rugby, Golf; *Style—* Peter Purves, Esq; Purves Wickes Video Projects Ltd, 1 Hyde Park Place, London W2 2LH (☎ 071 262 3449, fax 071 262 3450, car 0860 370155)

PURVES, William; CBE (1988), DSO (1951); s of Andrew Purves (d 1943), and Ida Purves; *b* 27 Dec 1931; *Educ* Kelso HS; *m* 1958 (m dis 1988), Diana Troutbeck, da of Nicholas Gosselin Pepp Richardson (d 1944); 2 s, 2 da; m 2, 9 Feb 1989, Rebecca Jane, *née* Lewellen; *Career* chm: The Hongkong and Shanghai Banking Corporation Limited, The Br Bank of The ME; chm HSBC Holdings plc; vice pres and fell Chartered Inst of Bankers, assoc memb Inst of bankers Scotland; Hon DUniv Stirling; ACIB (Scotland), FCIB; *Recreations* golf; *Clubs* Hong Kong, Royal Hong Kong Jockey, Royal Hong Kong Golf, New (Edinburgh); *Style—* William Purves, Esq, CBE, DSO; The Hongkong and Shanghai Banking Corporation Limited, PO Box 64, Hong Kong (☎ 8221122, telex 73201 HKBG HX, fax 8680244)

PURVIS, Christopher Thomas Bremner; s of Dr Victor Bremner Purvis, of Upper Town Farm, Clifton Hampden, Abingdon, Oxon, and Joanna Isabel, *née* Gibbs; *b* 15 April 1951; *Educ* Bradfield Coll, Keble Coll Oxford (MA); *m* 21 June 1986, Phillida Anne, *née* Seaward; 2 da (Kerensa Toura Isabel b 26 March 1988, Xeuobe Eva Wendela b 8 March 1990); *Career* S G Warburg & Co Ltd: joined 1974, dir Warburg Investmt Mgmnt Int Ltd 1980, chief rep Tokyo 1982, dir 1983, branch mangr Tokyo 1985, dir S G Warburg Securities 1986, London office 1987, branch mangr Tokyo 1989-; *Clubs* Oriental; *Style—* Christopher Purvis, Esq; Akasaka Hillside House II C, 9-5-14 Akasaka, Minato-Ku, Tokyo (☎ 03 37462988); S G Warburg Securities (Japan), Inc, New Edobashi Building, 1-7-2, Nihombashi Honcho, Chuo-Ku, Tokyo, Japan (☎ 03 32464111)

PURVIS, John Robert; CBE (1990); s of Lt-Col Robert William Berry Purvis, MC; *b* 6 July 1938; *Educ* Cargilfield Barnton Edinburgh, Glenalmond Coll Perths, St Salvator's Coll, Univ of St Andrews; *m* 1962, Louise S Durham; 1 s, 2 da; *Career* md Gilmerton Mgmnt Servs Ltd 1973-, managing ptnr Purvis & Co 1986-, dir James River (UK) Holdings Ltd 1988-; MEP (EDG) Mid Scotland and Fife 1979-84; memb IBA London (chm for Scotland) 1985-89, chm SCUA Econ Ctee 1986-, vice pres Scottish Cons & Unionist Assoc 1987-89; *Clubs* Cavalry and Guards, Farmers', New (Edinburgh), Royal and Ancient (St Andrews); *Style—* John Purvis, Esq, CBE; Gilmerton, Dunino, St Andrews, Fife KY16 8NB (☎ 0334 73275)

PURVIS, Brig Richard Hopkins (Dick); CBE; s of Albert Hopkins Purvis (d 1968), and Mabel Hope, *née* Fendick (d 1931); *b* 16 Dec 1920; *Educ* Aldenham; *m* 2 Oct 1948, Jean, da of William Douglas Walker (d 1957); 2 s (Nicholas Hopkins b 1952, Paul Richard b 1956); *Career* memb HAC 1938-40, cmmnd Royal Regt of Artillery 1940, Royal Artillery pilot Air Observation Post 654 Sqdn RAF 1942-44, ME Staff Coll 1945, Royal Naval Staff Coll 1957, CO 1963-65, Cmdt Sch of Artillery Manorbier 1969-70, Def Sales Orgns MOD 1970-75; fndr Def Mfrs Assoc of GB 1976 (dir gen 1976-87, life vice pres 1987) chm Euro Def Mfrs Assoc Gp; Freeman City of London 1947, Liveryman Worshipful Co of Painters and Stainers 1947-88; MInstD, RUSI; *Clubs* Army & Navy; *Style—* Brig Richard H Purvis, CBE; c/o Army and Navy Club, 36 Pall Mall, London SW1Y 5JN

PURVIS, Stewart Peter; s of Peter Purvis, and Lydia, *née* Stewart; *b* 28 Oct 1947; *Educ* Dulwich, Univ of Exeter (BA); *m* 2 Sept 1972, Mary, da of Arthur Presnail; 1 da (Helen b 1974); *Career* ITN 1972-: joined 1972, prog ed News at Ten 1980, ed Channel Four News 1983, dep ed ITN 1983, ed ITN 1989-; prodr of 2 exclusive documentaries about Prince and Princess of Wales; winner: two Royal TV Soc awards, Bdcasting Press Guild Award for Best News or Current Events Prog (Channel Four News), BAFTA award for Best News or Outside Broadcast (Channel Four News) 1987 and 1988; *Style—* Stewart Purvis, Esq; ITN, 48 Wells St, London W1 (☎ 071 637 2424, fax 071 636 0349, telex 22101)

PUTTERGILL, Graham Fraser; s of Henry William Puttergill (d 1984), of Gonubie, SA, and Elizabeth Blanche, *née* McClelland; *b* 20 March 1949; *Educ* St Patrick's Coll Port Elizabeth SA; *m* 7 Aug 1976, Susan Jennifer, da of Victor James Wilkinson, of Dorchester; 2 s (Miles b 1982, David b 1987), 2 da (Robyn b 1985, Lucy b 1989); *Career* 1 Lt Capt Town Highlanders 1967-68; chm Antony Gibbs Pension Servs Ltd 1982- (md 1977-82), exec chm Gibbs Hartley Cooper Ltd 1985-, dir HSBC Hldgs UK Ltd 1986; ACII 1973, FPMI 1983; *Style—* Graham Puttergill, Esq; Kisdon, Puers Lane, Jordans, Bucks; Bishops Ct, Artillery Lane, London E1

PUTTNAM, David Terence; CBE (1983); s of Capt Leonard Arthur Puttnam, RA (d 1981), of Winchmore Hill, and Marie Beatrice, *née* Goldman; *b* 25 Feb 1941; *Educ* Minchenden GS London; *m* 22 Sept 1961, Patricia Mary, da of Maj John Frederick Jones, of Folkestone, Kent; 1 s (Alexander David b 5 April 1966), 1 da (Deborah Jane (m, Lloyd Grossman, *qv*) b 25 Jan 1962); *Career* film prod; dir: British Film & TV Producers Association Ltd, Enigma Productions Ltd; chm Hamuni Ltd, Nat Film & TV Sch Ltd, dir Anglia TV Group plc; pres Cncl for Protection of Rural England 1985; tstee: Tate Gallery, National Energy Foundation; Special Jury Prize (Cannes) for The Duellists 1977, two Academy Awards and four Br Academy Awards for Midnight Express 1978, four Acadamy Awards (incl Best Film) and three Br Academy Awards (incl Best Film) for Chariots of Fire 1981, three Academy Awards and eight Br Academy Awards (incl Best Film) for The Killing Fields 1985, Michael Balcon Award for outstanding contrib to the BFI, Br Academy Award 1982; Hon LLD Bristol 1983, Hon DLitt Leicester 1986, hon fell Manchester Poly; Chevalier des Arts et des Lettres (France) 1986; chm and chief exec offr Columbia Pictures 1986-88; visiting prof Film Dept Univ of Bristol 1985; FRGS, FRSA; *Books* The Third Age of Broadcasting (co-author, 1982), Rural England (co-author, 1988); *Recreations* fishing, reading, cinema, watching cricket; *Clubs* MCC; *Style—* David Puttnam, Esq, CBE; Enigma Productions, 13-15 Queen's Gate Place Mews, London SW7 5BG (☎ 071 581 0238, fax 071 584 1799)

PUXLEY, James Christopher Lavallin; s of Capt William Lavallin Puxley, RN (d 1969), and Margaret Jessie Lavallin Puxley, *née* Burgess, of Dunboy Castle, Co Cork; *b* 24 Dec 1930; *Educ* Upper Canada Coll, RN Coll Dartmouth; *m* 1955, Alys Jean Marie, da of Dr Cyril Rickword Lane (d 1984); 1 s (Patrick), 1 da (Victoria); *Career* chm: County Bisgood Ltd, Bisgood Int Ltd, Bisgood Int Futures Ltd; dir: County Hldgs Ltd, County Bank Ltd; memb: Stock Exchange 1963, cncl of Stock Exchange, (Cncl's vice-chm membership ctees); vice-chm Cncl's Markets Ctee; *Recreations* animal husbandry; *Style—* James Puxley Esq; Charity Farm, Goring Heath, Oxon (☎ 0491 680331); County Bisgood & Co Ltd, Copthall House, 48 Copthall Avenue, London EC2R 7DN (☎ 071 628 3033)

PUXLEY, Maj John Philip Lavallin; TD (with two clasps); s of Rev H L Puxley (d 1950), of The Whitehouse, Chaddleworth, Newbury, Berks, and Dorothy Florence Mary, *née* Wroughton (d 1971); *b* 28 June 1915; *Educ* Eton, Brasenose Coll Oxford (BA); *m* 21 June 1947, Aline Carlos, da of Carlos Butler Wilson (d 1934), Of Welford Farmhouse, Newbury, Berks; 2 s (James Henry Lavallin b 1948, Charles John Lavallin b 1950); *Career* Berkshire Yeo 1939-60, WWII served India, Malaya and Java; slr of the Supreme Ct 1947; High Sheriff of Berkshire 197l, gen cmmr of Income Tax 1982-; pres Newbury Agric Soc 1969, life memb Royal Agric Soc of Eng; *Recreations* stamp collecting; *Style—* Maj John Puxley, TD; Llethr Llestry, Carmarthen, Dyfed (☎ 048 838 203); Welford Park Newbury, Berks

PUXTY, Prof Anthony Grahame; s of Eric Harry Puxty, and Joan, *née* Brooks (d 1979); *b* 17 May 1946; *Educ* Southend-on-Sea HS, Open Univ (BA), Univ of Lancaster (MA), Univ of Sheffield (PhD); *Career* chief accountant Advertising Agency Poster Bureau Ltd 1971-73, fin accountant Ruberoid Contracts Ltd 1973-74, lectr Univ of Sheffield 1976-87, prof accounting and fin Univ of Strathclyde 1987-; ACIS 1973, MBIM 1976; *Books* Critiques of Agency Theory in Accountancy (ed, 1985), Organization and Management (1986), Multinational Enterprise: An Encyclopedic Dictionary of Concepts and Terms (1987), Financial Management: Method and Meaning (1988), Critical Perspectives In Management Control (ed, 1989); *Recreations* swimming, music; *Style—* Prof Anthony Puxty; The Lindens, 9 Victoria Rd, Helensburgh, Dunbartonshire G84 7RT (☎ 0436 76878); Dept of Accounting and Finance, Univ of Strathclyde, 100 Cathedral St, Glasgow G4 OLN (☎ 041 552 4400, fax 041 552 3547, telex UNSLIB 77472)

PYBUS, William Michael; s of Sydney James Pybus (d 1972), and Evelyn Mary, *née* Wood (d 1976); *b* 7 May 1923; *Educ* Bedford Sch, New Coll Oxford (MA); *m* 12 Sept 1959, Elizabeth Janet, da of Peter Percy Whitley (ka 1942); 2 s (Peter b 1961, Charles b 1965), 2 da (Sarah b 1962, Elizabeth b 1967); *Career* WWII cmmnd 1 King's Dragoon Gds 1942, attached II Hussars: Normandy (wounded), Egypt, Middle East; admitted slr 1950; ptnr Herbert Oppenheimer Nathan & Vandyk 1953-88; chm: AAH Holdings plc 1968-, British Fuel Co 1968-88, Inter-Continental Fuels Ltd 1975-88, Overseas Coal Developments Ltd 1979-88, Leigh Interests plc 1982-89, British Rail (London Midland) 1977-89 (pt/t memb BR Midlands and W Bd 1975- 77); dir: National Westminster Bank plc (Outer London Region) 1977-88, Cornhill Insurance plc 1977-, Bradford & Bingley Building Society 1983-, Siebe plc 1990-(chm 1980-90); dep chm R Nansell Ltd 1980-85; dir: Coal Trade Benevolent Assoc 1969-, Homeowners Friendly Soc 1980-, pres Coal Indust Soc 1976-81 (vice pres 1981-), conslt Denton Hall Burgin & Warrens 1988-; Master Worshipful Co of Pattenmakers 1972-73, asst Worshipful Co of Fuellers; CBIM, FCIM, FRSA; *Recreations* fishing; *Clubs* Cavalry and Guards', MCC, RAC, YCCC; *Style—* William Pybus, Esq; 5 Chancery Lane, London WC2A 1LF (☎ 071 242 1212, fax 071 831 2085, telex 263567)

PYE, Prof (John) David; s of Wilfred Frank Pye (d 1972), of Mansfield, Notts, and Gwenllian, *née* Davies; *b* 14 May 1932; *Educ* Queen Elizabeths GS for Boys Mansfield, UCW Aberystwth (BSc), Bedford Coll for Women Univ of London (PhD); *m* 27 Dec 1958, Ade, da of August Kuku, of Valga, Estonia; *Career* Univ of London: res asst inst laryngology and otology 1958-64, lectr in zoology King's Coll 1964-70, reader zoology King's Coll 1970-73, prof of zoology Queen Mary Coll 1973-, head Dept Zoology and Comparative Physiology Queen Mary Coll 1977-82; fndr dir QMC Instruments Ltd 1976-89, delivered the six televised Royal Inst Christmas Lectures 1985-86 and two Friday Evening Discourses 1979 and 1983, memb IEE Professional Gp Ctee E15 (Radar, Sonar, Navigation and Avionics) 1983-86; Ed Bds: Zoologic Soc 1985-90 (1972-77, 1978-83), Journal of Experimental Biology 1974-78, Journal of Comparative Physiology 1978-, Bioacoustics 1987-; ed of the Zoological Journal 1981-85 (ed sec 1985-91, vice pres 1987-90); memb: Linnean Soc Zoological Soc 1957, Soc for Experimental Biology 1958, Assoc for Study of Animal Behaviour 1963, Mammal Soc 1964, Royal Hort Soc 1988; *Books* Bats (1968), Ultrasonic Communication by Animals (with G D Sales, 1974), Sound Reception in Mammals (ed with R J Bench and A Pye, 1975); *Recreations* brewing, baking, DIY, arts and travel; *Style—* Prof David Pye; 24 St Mary's Ave, Finchley, London N3 1SN (☎ 081 346 6869); Sch of Biological Sciences, Queen Mary and Westfield Coll, Mile End Rd, London E1 4NS (☎ 071 975 5555 ext 4102)

PYE, Brig Hugh William Kellow; s of Brig Randall Thomas Kellow Pye DSO, OBE, of Horsted Keynes, W Sussex, and Peggy Muriel, *née* Sagar-Musgrave- Brooksbank; *b* 23 May 1938; *Educ* Wellington Coll, RMA Sandhurst; *m* 8 June 1968, Mary Ann, da of Cdr The Hon David Edwardes, DSC, RN (d 1983), of Wincanton, Somerset; 1 s (Robert Alec Kellow b 1970), 1 da (Victoria Ann b 1973); *Career* cmmnd 12 Royal Lancers (POW) 1958, Cdr Berlin Armd Sqdn 1968, Staff Coll Camberley 1971, GSO2 INT JSIS Hong Kong 1972, Armed Forces Staff Coll Norfolk Virginia USA 1976, cmdg 9/12 Royal Lancers (POW) 1977-79 (despatches), AMS MS 4 1979, dep Chief of Staff (DCOS) and Cdr Br Contingent UNFICYP 1982, Col Coordination Staff Coll Camberley 1984, proj mangr, Dep Cdr and advsr Oman Cmd and Staff Coll 1986, Dep Cdr SW dist and Cdr Br Element AMF (L) 1990; awarded Sultan of Oman's Commendation medal 1989; *Recreations* shooting, fishing; *Clubs* Cavalry and Guards; *Style—* Brig Hugh Pye; Deputy Commander, South West District, Bulford Camp, Salisbury, Wilts SP4 9NY (☎ 0980 33371 ext 2392)

PYE, Nigel Lindsay; s of Herbert Francis Pye, of The Tower House, London Rd, Cuckfield, Sussex, and Doreen Mary, *née* Star; *b* 1 May 1945; *Educ* Whitgift Sch Croydon; *m* 1, 1972 (m dis 1985), Frances Jean Fermor; 1 s (Matthew Francis b 1976), 1 da (Alexandra Claire b 1978); m 2, 1988, Hilary, da of John Thomas Carroll; *Career* articled clerk James Edwards Dangerfield & Co London 1964-69, admitted chartered accountant 1969, assigned to Alexander Grant & Co Chicago 1970-71, London office Tansley Witt & Co (successor firm of James Edwards Dangerfield & Co) 1971-79 (ptnr 1976), ptnr Arthur Andersen & Co London office 1979-85, managing ptnr Arthur Andersen and Co Cambridge office 1985-; chm Croydon Soc of Chartered Accountants 1984-85, dir S Cambridge Training and Enterprise Cncl 1989-, memb Cncl CBI 1989-, dir Cambridge Arts Theatre 1991; *Recreations* squash, country walking, travel, theatre; *Style—* Nigel Pye, Esq; Avenue House, High St, Madingley, Cambridge CB3 8AB (☎ 0954 210457); Arthur Andersen & Co, Betjeman House, 104 Hills Road, Cambridge CB2 1LH (☎ 0223 353906, fax 0223 66287, car 0836 762942)

PYE, (William) Roger; s of William Ernest Pye, (d 1985) of Staunton-on-Arrow, Hereford, and Daisy Grace, *née* Lewis; *b* 6 Dec 1938; *Educ* Hereford Cathedral Sch; *m* 28 Oct 1961, Barbara Ann Juanita, da of Arthur Edgar Wall (d 1988); 2 da (Nicola Susan b 26 Jan 1963, Dawn Louise b 21 June 1967); *Career* forestry conslt and nurseryman, md WE Pye (Forestry) Ltd 1985-88 (dir 1961-85); capt Kington CC 1960; fndr: Silurians RFC 1961, Radnorshire Soc Field Res Section (chm 1976-80, ed

1988); dir of excavation: Dorstone Hill (Neolithic) Herefordshire 1965-71, Fron Dyrys (Neolithic) Radnorshire 1976, Hindwell Fort (Roman) Radnorshire 1976-79, Old Radnor (Neolithic) Radnorshire 1990; fndr memb and chm Woolhope Archaelogical Field Section 1973, vice chm Gp II CBA 1980-83 (liaison offr), tstee Rankin Lecture Tst 1974-81 (sec 1976-81); memb Ctee Kington Twinning Assoc, chm Kington Primary Sch PTA 1976; winner Folk Songwriter's Contest Folk Show Radio Salop 1989; *Recreations* ethnology, art, archaelogy, folklore; *Style*— Roger Pye, Esq; The Cressyn, Old Radnor, Presteign, Radnorshire (☎ 054421/634); Beech Grove Nursery, Rushock, Kington, Herefordshire (☎ 0544 231422)

PYE, William Burns; s of Sir David Pye, CM, FRS, (d 1959), of Elstead, Surrey, and Virginia Frances, *née* Kennedy; *b* 16 July 1938; *Educ* Charterhouse, Wimbledon Sch of Art, Sch of Scupture RCA; *m* 1963, Susan Marsh; 1 s (Tristram b 18 March 1966), 2 da (Rebecca Jane b 2 June 1968, Alexandra Virginia b 4 Aug 1973); *Career* sculptor; cmmns and sculptures on pub sites: Ganglion (Loughborough Tech Coll), Zemran (Southbank London), Kings Cross House Cmmn (Pentonville Rd London), Charioteer (Rufford Sculpture Garden Ollerton Notts), Water Sculpture Trent Polytechnic Notts, mural at Vauxhall railway station London, Slipstream and Jetstream water sculptures (N Terminal Gatwick), Curlicue (Greenland Dock London); one man exhibitions incl: Rufford Craft Centre Nottingham 1981, Parnham House Beaminster Dorset 1984, London Business Sch Regents Park London 1986, The Rotunda Hong Kong 1987; selected gp exhibitions: British Sculpture 1950-65 New Art Centre Glasgow Garden Festival 1988, 6 Henry Moore Grand Prize Exhibition (Br nomination) Utsukushi-ga-hara Museum Japan 1989, Sculpture in a Rose Garden Royal Nat Rose Soc Garden St Albans 1989, The Cultivated Garden High Wall Oxford 1989; pub collections incl: Arts Cncl of GB, Museum of Modern Art NY, Contemporary Art Soc, Royal Albert Museum Exeter, Leicestershire Educn Authy, Graves Art Gallery Sheffield, Birmingham City Art Gallery; visiting prof California State Univ 1975-76; Prix de Sculpture Budapest Int Sculpture Exhibition 1981-, winner: Vauxhall Mural competition 1983, Peace Sculpture competition for Ackers Park Small Heath Birmingham 1984; Art at Work award Wapping Arts Tst for sculpture at Gatwick airport 1988, Assoc of Business Sponsorship of the Arts award 1988, Royal VENO award Japan 1989; films: Reflections 1971, From Scrap to Sculpture 1971; *Recreations* playing the flute; *Style*— William Pye; 43 Hambalt Rd, Clapham, London SW4 9EQ (☎ 081 673 2318); studio (☎ 081 767 3588, office 081 675 3491, fax 081 675 7667)

PYM, Hon Andrew Leslie; yr s of Baron Pym, MC, PC (Life Peer), *qv*; *b* 30 Nov 1954; *Educ* Eton, RAC Cirencester; *m* 1976, Ruth Alison, da of Benjamin Peter Skelton; 1 s (Benjamin Ruthven b 1979), 1 da (Jessica Mary b 1982); *Career* FRICS; *Style*— Andrew Pym, Esq; The Elms, Everton, Sandy, Beds SG19 2JU

PYM, Baron (Life Peer UK 1987), of Sandy, Co Beds; Francis Leslie Pym; PC (1970), MC (1945), DL (Cambs 1973); Lord of the Manor of Sandy and Girtford, and patron of one living (Sandy); o s of Leslie Ruthven Pym, JP, DL (d 1945), sometime MP for Monmouth and Lord Cmmr of the Treasy, and Iris Rosalind (d 1982), da of Charles Somerville Orde; *b* 13 Feb 1922; *Educ* Eton, Magdalene Coll Cambridge (hon fell); *m* 25 June 1949, Valerie Fortune, er da of Francis John Heaton Daglish; 2 s (Hon (Francis) Jonathan, Hon Andrew Leslie, *qqv*), 2 da (Hon Charlotte Hazell (Hon Mrs Lightbody) b 1950, Hon Sarah Lucy (Hon Mrs Walton) b 1958); *Career* served WWII, 9 Queen's Royal Lancers (despatches twice), Capt; former gen mangr Merseyside Dairies Ltd, then ran tent-making co in Hereford; memb Herefordshire CC 1958-62; contested (C) Rhondda 1959, MP (C) Cambs 1961-83 and SE Cambs 1983-87; parly sec to the Treasy and govt chief whip 1970-73, sec of state NI 1973-74; oppn spokesman: agric 1974-76, House of Commons affrs and devolution 1976-78, foreign and cwlth affrs 1978-79, Sec of State for Def 1979-81; chllr of the Duchy of Lancaster, paymaster gen and ldr House of Commons 1981, lord pres of the Cncl and Ldr House of Commons 1981-82, Foreign and Cwlth sec 1982-83; pres Atlantic Treaty Assoc 1985-88, chm English Speaking Union 1987-; *Books* The Politics of Consent (1984); *Clubs* Cavalry and Guards', Buck's; *Style*— The Rt Hon the Lord Pym, PC, MC, DL; Everton Park, Sandy, Beds SG19 2DE (☎ 0767 681640)

PYM, (Hon) (Francis) Jonathan; er s of Baron Pym, MC, PC (Life Peer), *qv*; does not use courtesy prefix of Hon; *b* 21 Sept 1952; *Educ* Eton, Magdalene Coll Camb (MA); *m* 25 June 1981, Laura Elizabeth Camille, yr da of Robin Alfred Wellesley, *qv*; 2 s ((Francis) Matthew b 1984, Oliver Quintin b 1988), 1 da (Katie Camille b 1985); *Career* ptnr Travers Smith Braithwaite slrs 1984-; memb: Law Soc, City of London Law Soc; *Clubs* Garrick; *Style*— Jonathan Pym, Esq; 53 Ridgway Place, London SW19 4SP (☎ 081 946 3583); 10 Snow Hill, London EC1A 2AL (☎ 071 248 9133, fax 071 236 3728, telex 887117 TRAVER G)

PYRAH, Malcolm John; s of lat flt-Lt Stanley Pyrah, and Joyce Evelyne, *née* Hall; *b* 26 Aug 1941; *Educ* Kingston HS Hull; *m* 22 Oct 1973, (Suzanne) Judy, da of Leigh Boulter, of Manor Farm, Queniborough, Leics; 1 da (Niki Jane b 1982); *Career* showjumper; team world gold 1978, team Euro gold 1979, individual Euro silver 1981, individual world silver 1982, team Euro gold 1985 and 1987; exec memb and memb Br show jumping Assoc; *Style*— Malcolm Pyrah, Esq; Keyworths Farm, Granby, Nottingham NG13 9PS (☎ 0949 50599, fax 0949 51246, car 0860 353946)

PYTCHES, Rt Rev (George Edward) David; 6 s of Rev Thomas Arthur Pytches (d 1953), of The Little Grange, Woodbridge, Suffolk (see Burke's Landed Gentry 1937 edn), and Eirene Mildred, *née* Welldon (d 1947); *b* 9 Jan 1931; *Educ* Old Buckenham Hall Norfolk, Framlingham Coll Suffolk, Univ of Bristol (BA), Univ of Nottingham (MPhil), Trinity Coll Bristol; *m* 8 Jan 1958, Mary, da of Albert Trevisick (d 1984), of Highclere, Chestwood, Bishopstawton, N Devon; 4 da Charlotte Mary (Mrs Cocksworth) b 24 Dec 1958, Deborah Jane (Mrs Wright) b 13 Dec 1961, Rebecca Anne (Mrs Hopper) b 10 July 1963, Natasha Clare (Mrs Shaw) b 18 Feb 1965); *Career* ordained: deacon 1955, priest 1956; asst curate: St Ebbe's Oxford 1955-58, Holy Trinity Wallington 1958-59; missionary priest: Chol Chol Chile 1959-62, Valparaiso Chile 1962-68 (rural dean 1966-70); asst bishop and vicar-gen Diocese of Chile Bolivia and Peru 1972-77 (bishop 1970-72), vicar St Andrew's Chorleywood 1977; *Books* Come Holy Spirit (1985), Does God Speak Today? (1989), Some Said It Thundered (1990); *Recreations* travel, pottering about, collecting semi-precious stones; *Style*— The Rt Rev David Pytches; The Vicarage, Quickley Lane, Chorleywood, Herts WD3 5AE (☎ 092 78 2391)

PYTEL, Walenty; s of Wladislaw Pytel, of Bath, and Jadwiga Pytel; *b* 10 Feb 1941; *Educ* Leominster Minster Sch, Hereford Coll of Art (NDD); *m* 7 Oct 1963, Janet Mary, da of William Sidney Spencer (d 1973), of Westington Court; 1 s (Jeremy Walenty Spencer b 1964), 1 da (Victoria Catharine Mary b 1968); *Career* sculptor in steel, bronze, bone china; works incl: mural Lord Montague Beaulieu 1972, Le Perroquet Berkeley Hotel London 1973, Chanel Perfume Paris 1975, Sculpture cmmnd by MPs to commemorate Queen's Silver Jubilee New Palace Yard Westminster 1977, unicorn from HRH Princess Anne to Portuguese Govt 1979, Cwlth beasts for Sir Edward du Cann MP and Sir John Hall MP 1980, Take Off Birmingham Int Airport 1985, unicorn representing coat of arms for Lord and Lady Leigh Stoneleigh Abbey 1989; exhibitions: Marbella 1985, New Jersey 1987, San Diego 1987, Tokyo 1987, Soc of Wildlife Artists Mall Galleries 1988 (award winner) and 89; work in various private collections; *Recreations* salmon fishing, game shooting, sailing; *Style*— Walenty Pytel, Esq; Terrace Hall, Woolhope, Hereford HR1 4QJ (☎ 0432860 373, 0432 50722)

Q

QUAGLIA, Pietro Giovanni Battista; s of Giovanni Quaglia (d 1966), of Turin, Italy, and Margherita Garelli Quaglia (d 1985); *b* 30 Nov 1937; *Educ* Turin Business Mgmnt Sch, Int Univ of Social Studies Turin; *m* 1964, Maria, da of Cav Antonio Troso, of Pescara; 2 da (Gianna b 1968, Silvana b 1969); *Career* vice pres Fiat UK Ltd, formerly md Fiat Auto (UK) Ltd, dir Fiat Fin Ltd, vice pres Fiat USA Inc, dir Hesston Corpn, chm and md Fiat Aust Pty Ltd, pres Italian C of C (Sydney Aust); FInstD; Kt of Order of Italian Repub 1987; *Recreations* riding, tennis, fencing; *Clubs* Guards' Polo; *Style—* Pietro Quaglia, Esq; Thorney Court, Palace Gate, London W8; Fiat Auto (UK), Riverland UK House, Putney Bridge Approach, London SW6 (☎ 071 371 0006)

QUAILE, Peter; JP (Surrey); s of Charles Thompson Quaile (d 1958), of Birkenhead, Cheshire, and Elsie May, *née* Crickmore (d 1958); Manx family, Sir William Quaile Lord Mayor of Dublin 1700, s-in-law Sir James Sumerville, 1 Bt, Lord Mayor of Dublin 1736, Mark Hildesley Quaile, of Castletown was elected memb of House of Keys 1842; *b* 4 March 1927; *Educ* Birkenhead Sch; *m* 3 Nov 1951, Eileen Elizabeth Olive, da of Aubrey Alford Gifford Toone (d 1963), of Bowden, Cheshire; 2 s (Andrew b 1954, Michael b 1958 d 1989), 2 da (Helen b 1957, Penelope b 1960); *Career* Pilot Fleet Air Arm; Alliance of Liverpool & Manchester: asst underwriter 1948, marine rep 1951, underwriter 1959; mangr and underwriter Sea Elders of Liverpool 1971 (dep mangr 1967), dep chief gen mangr of Sun Alliance Insur Gp 1984 (asst gen mangr 1975, gen mangr 1979), chm DAS Legal Expenses Insur Co Ltd 1985; dir: London and Co Glazing Co Ltd 1985, Fire Protection Assoc 1985, Br Aviation Insur Co Ltd 1987, Sun Insur Co (Bermuda) Ltd 1987, Sun Insur Co (NY) 1987, McGee (New York) 1987, Alliance Assur Co Ltd 1980, Sun Alliance and London Insur plc 1980, Phoenix Assur plc, Sun Alliance and London Assur Co Ltd 1980, Sun Insur Off Ltd 1980, The London Insur 1980; FCII; *Recreations* shooting, fishing, rugby; *Style—* Peter Quaile, Esq, JP; Springfold, Lawbrook Lane, Peaslake, Guildford, Surrey GU5 9QW (☎ 048 641 2501); Sun Alliance Insurance Gp, 1 Bartholomew Lane, London EC2N 2AB (☎ 071 588 2345, fax 071 638 3728/1103, telex 888310 G, car 0860 314 503)

QUAILE, Capt Roger Thompson; TEM (1950); s of Charles Thompson Quaile (d 1958), of Birkenhead, and Elsie May, *née* Crickmore (d 1958); *b* 6 Oct 1920; *Educ* Birkenhead Sch, Park High Sch Birkenhead; *m* 31 May 1952, Patricia Elizabeth, da of Robert Beck Jones (d 1952); 2 s (Jonathan Robert Charles b 1958, William Roger b 1964), 1 da (Elizabeth Mary b 1953); *Career* TA 1939, RA 1939, cmmnd 2 Lt 1941, 1 Lt 8 Army Western Desert 1942-43, 2 Bn King's (Liverpool) Regt Italy and Greece 1944-46 Capt 1945-46 (Raiding Support Regt Land Forces Adriatic 1944); md WT Oversy and Co Ltd 1963 (dir 1954-), dep chm Morice Tozer and Beck Ltd 1970 (dir 1967), md Alexander Howden Insurance Brokers Ltd 1976-78; underwriting memb Lloyd's 1976, chm and dir various minor cos; life vice pres Warlingham Rugby FC; FCII 1950, FInstD 1956, FCIB 1967, FCIArb 1971; *Recreations* shooting, rugby football administration, gardening; *Clubs* Gresham; *Style—* Capt Roger Quaile, TEM; Hillsborough, 8 Searchwood Rd, Warlingham, Surrey CR6 9BA (☎ 0883 622413)

QUALLINGTON, (Herbert) Timothy; s of Herbert Edward Quallington, (d 1959), and Dorothy, *née* Smith (d 1971); *b* 2 Nov 1935; *m* 16 Sept 1961, Jean Frances, da of Frank Loudonsack Barker; 1 s ((Herbert) Philip b 20 Sept 1962), 2 da ((Brenda) Elizabeth 4 Jan 1965, Rachel Mary b 16 March 1966); *Career* Nat Serv Armanemt Fitter RAF 1954-57; asst Scout master and asst Rover Scout ldr 1st Oxshott Scout Gp 1957-60; photographer: Jack Harley Ltd Cranleigh 1961-62, Central Electricity Res Laboratories Leatherhead 1961-63, The Cncl of Industl Design (now The Design Cncl) 1963-64 (then sr photographer and studio mangr 1964-88); self employed commercial social and editorial photographer 1988-, lectr in photography Farnborough Coll of Technol 1988-; work published in various local and nat newspapers and magazines incl Design Magazine and Engineering magazine, paper on The Photography of Lighting Installation presented to Illuminating Engineering Soc 1971; former external course and student assessor SIAD and external assessor for BIPP at W Surrey Coll of Art Farnham; memb RSA 1969, FBIPP 1970, FRPS 1971, FCSD 1974; *Recreations* family, local church, interior design, gardening, caravaning and photography; *Clubs* Rotary Int (past pres local Rotary); *Style—* Timothy Quallington, Esq; 2 Woodland Grange, Cranleigh, Surrey GU6 7HY (☎ 0483 273361)

QUANCE, Gordon William; s of Frederick William Quance (d 1984), and Alice May, *née* Holden; *b* 7 March 1931; *Educ* Queen Mary's GS W Midlands, Univ of Birmingham (LLB, LLM); *m* 30 Aug 1962, Sylvia, da of John Bertram Grice (d 1969); *Career* admitted slr 1956, in private practice 1956-; memb Law Soc; *Recreations* music, books; *Style—* Gordon Quance, Esq; Talbot House, Talbot Ave, Little Aston Park, Streetly, Staffordshire; 31 High St, West Bromwich, W Midlands (☎ 021 553 0314/2681)

QUANJER, Johan Henri; s of Cdre Adriaan Johan Quanjer, RNN, and Johanna Mathilde, *née* van Zelm van Eldik; *b* 23 May 1934; *Educ* HBS The Hague; *Career* publisher and ed New Humanity Jl 1975-; lectr on: philosophy, psychology, history, politics; author of numerous papers; fndr of pneumatocratic, social, philosophical and political principles 1973; *Books* One World One Truth (1964); *Recreations* collecting antique books, gardening, classical music; *Style—* Johan Quanjer, Esq; 51A York Mansions, Prince of Wales Drive, London SW11 4BP (☎ 071 622 4013)

QUANT, Air Cdre (John) Antony; s of John Henry Quant (d 1968), and Mildred Gwenllian, *née* Jones; *b* 19 Jan 1933; *Educ* Taunton Sch, Eltham Coll, Univ of London, Guy's Hosp (BDS, MB BS); *m* 11 Feb 1956, Valerie Kathleen, da of Ernest James Goose (d 1970); 2 da (Sarah (Mrs Allen) b 1958, Amanda (Mrs Chandler) b 1961); *Career* Nat Serv RAF 1957, perm cmmn Dental Offr 1958, Prince Rupert Sch Wilhelmshaven 1958, RAF Sundern 1959, RAF Guterslah 1961, RAF Halton 1961, oral surgn PMRAF Hosp Halton 1962, RAF Hosp Nocton Hall 1962, registrar oral surgn RAF Hosp Cosford 1963, sr registrar TPH RAF Hosp Akrotiri 1965; med student Guy's 1966-70, house surgn Guy's 1971, house physician Willesborough Hosp Ashford Kent, sr registrar/conslt (oral surgery and med) RAF Hosp Wegberg 1972, conslt PM RAF Hosp Halton 1978, conslt advsr (oral surgery and med) RAF 1979-; memb (former sec and chm) Def Med Servs Post Grad Cncl Speciality Bd in Oral Surgery and Oral Med, dental advsr RAF Aviation Forensic Pathology Team, chm RAF LTA 1985-88; CStJ 1987; FDSRS 1963, MRCS 1970, LRCP 1970, fell BAOMS, memb Oral Surgery Club of GB; *Recreations* tennis, shooting, bridge; *Clubs* RAF; *Style—* Air Cdre Antony Quant; Witsend, Clay Lane, Wendover, Bucks HP22 6NS (☎ 0296 624714); The Paddocks Private Hosp, Princes Risborough, Bucks HP17 0JS (☎ 08444 6951); BMH Hanover, BFPO 40 (☎ 010 49 511 67440)

QUANT, Mary (Mrs A Plunket Greene); OBE (1966); da of Jack Quant and Mildred Quant; *b* 11 Feb 1934; *Educ* Goldsmiths' Coll of Art; *m* 1957, Alexander Plunket Greene; 1 s; *Career* fashion designer, dir Mary Quant Gp of Cos 1955-; memb: Design Cncl 1971, Br and USA Bicentennial Liaison Ctee 1973, Advsy Cncl V & A 1976-78; winner: Maison Blanche Rex award 1964, Sunday Times Int award 1964, Piavola d'Oro award 1966, Annual Design medal Inst of Industl Artists and Designers 1966, Hall of Fame award Br Fashion Cncl 1990; FSIA 1967, RDI 1969; *Style—* Miss Mary Quant, OBE; 3 Ives St, London SW3 (☎ 071 584 8781)

QUANTRILL, Prof Malcolm William Francis; s of Arthur William Quantrill (d 1976), of Norwich, and Alice May, *née* Newstead (d 1979); *b* 25 May 1931; *Educ* City of Norwich Sch, Univ of Liverpool (BArch), Univ of Pennsylvania (MArch), Tech Univ of Wroclaw (DSc); *m* 1 (m dis 1965), Arja Irmeli Nenonen; m 2, 18 Dec 1971, Esther Maeve, da of James Brignell Dand (d 1983), of Chester; 2 s (Christopher b 1961, Jan b 1962), 2 da (Francesca b 1974, Alexandra b 1978); *Career* dir Architectural Assoc London 1967-69, dean Sch of Architecture London Poly 1973-80, prof of architecture Univ of Jordan Amman 1980-83, distinguished prof of architecture Texas A & M Univ 1986-; dep ed Art International Lugano 1978-83, ed-in-chief The Cubit 1988-; fndr memb The Thomas Cubitt Tst London (tstee 1977, sec 1977-80), memb Rotary Int 1988; memb RIBA 1961; Cdr of the Order of Knights of the Finnish Lion 1988; *Books* Gotobed Dawn (1962), Gotobedlam (1964), John Gotobed Alone (1965), Ritual and Response in Architecture (1974), Monuments of Another Age (1976), On the Home Front (novel, 1977), Alvar Aalto: a critical study (1983), Reima Pietilä: architecture, context and modernism (1985), The Environmental Memory (1987), Reimě Pietilä: One Man's Odyssey in Search of Finnish Architecture (1988); *Recreations* photography, travel, tennis, broadcasting; *Clubs* Garrick; *Style—* Prof Malcolm Quantrill; College of Architecture, Texas A & M Univ, Texas 77843-3137 (☎ 409 845 7878, fax 409 845 4491)

QUARMBY, Arthur; s of Harold Quarmby (d 1981), of Lane House, Holmfirth, and Lucy May, *née* Barrow; *b* 18 March 1934; *Educ* Pocklington Sch, Leeds Sch of Architectural Town Planning (Dip Arch); *m* 13 Aug 1957, Jean Valerie, da of Herbert Mitchell, of Hebble Drive Holmfirth; 1 s (Jonathan Hugh, b 1961), 1 da (Rachel Jane b 1964); *Career* architect; plastics structures in Europe and the Antarctica, worlds largest transparent inflated dome (for 20th Century Fox), assault craft for Rotork Marine, conslt on structural plastics, world authy on earth-sheltered architecture, architectural journalist; chief constable of the Graveship of Holme; memb: Huddersfield Choral Soc, Colne Valley Male Voice Choir, Holme Valley Choir; memb RIBA 1959, FRIBA 1985, FRSA; *Books* The Plastics Architect (1974); *Recreations* music, archaeology, watersports, hill walking; *Clubs* Inigo Jones; *Style—* Arthur Quarmby, Esq; Underhill, Holme, W Yorks (☎ 0484 682372); 83 Fitzwilliam St, Huddersfield (☎ 0484 536553, fax 0484 432586)

QUARMBY, David Anthony; s of Frank Reginald Quarmby (d 1983); *b* 22 July 1941; *Educ* Shrewsbury, King's Coll Cambridge (MA), Univ of Leeds (PhD, Dip Industl Mgmnt); *m* 1968, Hilmary, da of Denis Hilton Hunter; 4 da; *Career* md London Tport Exec Buses 1978-84 (memb 1975-84), jt md J Sainsbury plc 1988- (dir 1984); FCIT, FILDM, FRSA, CBIM; *Recreations* music, singing; *Style—* David Quarmby, Esq; J Sainsbury plc, Stamford St, London SE1 9LL (☎ 071 921 6000)

QUARREN EVANS, His Hon Judge; John Kerry; s of Hubert Royston Quarren Evans, MC (d 1967), and Violet Soule Quarren Evans; *b* 4 July 1926; *Educ* King Henry VIII Sch Coventry, Cardiff HS, Trinity Hall Cambridge (MA, LLM); *m* 1958, Jane Shaw, da of Neil Lawson (d 1985); 1 s, 1 da; *Career* Army 1944-48, Capt Royal Welch Fus; slr of Supreme Ct 1953; ptnr: Lyndon Moore & Co of Newport Gwent 1954-71, T S Edwards & Son 1971-80; rec Wales and Chester circuit 1974-80, a circuit judge S Eastern circuit 1980-; *Recreations* music, golf, rugby football, staurologosophy, oenology, old things; *Clubs* Denham Golf, Newport Golf, Royal Porthcawl Golf, Crawshays Welsh RFC; *Style—* His Honour Judge Quarren Evans; c/o Acton Crown Ct, Armstrong Rd, London W3 7BJ (☎ 081 740 8888)

QUASTEL, Dr Anthony Stephen; s of Gerald Quastel, of London, and Rita Joy Leonora Quastel; *b* 14 Nov 1955; *Educ* St Dunstan's Coll Catford, Middlesex Hosp Med Sch Univ of London (MB BS); *Career* princ in gen practice 1984; res appts in med and surgery 1980-81, sr house offr in psychiatry The Middlesex Hosp 1982, currently med dir of four private practices covering SE England; *Recreations* gardening, politics, talking; *Style—* Dr Anthony Quastel; Hightrees House, Highclere Close, Kenley, Surrey CR8 5JU (☎ 081 668 1998); 204 High St, Bromley, Kent (☎ 081 464 4599, fax 081 464 3471, car 0836 201 725); 12 Parsons Mead, Croydon, Surrey (☎ 081 680 9853); 100-104 King St, Maidstone, Kent (☎ 0622 688188); 67 Victoria Way, Woking, Surrey (☎ 0483 750465)

QUAYLE, Anthony John; *b* 3 March 1946; *Educ* King's Coll London, Sloan Sch of Mgmnt (BSc), MIT (SM); *Career* appts in BR Engrg Ltd 1968-76, mfrg mangr Brush Electrical Machines Ltd 1976-79, md Alvis Ltd 1979- (a United Scientific Gp Co; mfr of armoured vehicles, Scorpion range best known; Queen's Award for Export 1982), dir United Scientific Holdings PLC 1981-; CEng, MIMechE; *Style—* Anthony Quayle, Esq; Alvis Ltd, Holyhead Rd, Coventry CV5 8JH, W Midlands (☎ 0203 595501, telex 31459); Miralago, Church Lane, Norton Lindsey, Warwick CV35 8JE (☎ Claverdon 092684 2842)

QUAYLE, (Thomas) David Graham; CB (1990); s of Dr Thomas Quayle, CIE (d 1962), and Phyllis Gwendolen, *née* Johnson (d 1977); *b* 7 April 1936; *Educ* Repton, Trinity Coll Oxford (BA); *m* 2 Aug 1962, Susan Jean, da of Brig FWP Bradford, MBE (d 1977); 3 da (Lucy b 1963, Sophie b 1964, Emma b 1966); *Career* served in Germany, Kenya, Aden and UK 1958-66, RMCS 1967, IA Staff Coll 1968, Staff HQ 1 Br corps 1969-70, cmdg The Chestnut Troop RHA 1971-72, Staff MOD 1972-74, instr Staff Coll Camberley 1974-76, cmdg 40 Field Regt (The Lowland Gunners) RA 1976-79, Royal Sch of Artillery 1979-81, Cdr artillery 4 Armd Div and Herford Garrison 1981-83, def Attaché Br Embassy Bonn 1983-86, Cdr Artillery 1 Br Corps 1987-90, ret as Maj-Gen 1990; ombudsman for corporate estate agents 1990-; *Recreations* shooting, fishing, racing, bridge, travel; *Style*— David Quayle, Esq, CB; PO Box 1114, Salisbury SP1 1YQ (☎ 0722 33 3306)

QUAYLE, John Bryant; s of George Quayle, and Christina, *née* Lonsdale; *b* 13 Oct 1945; *Educ* Llandovery Coll, Fitzwilliam Coll Cambridge (MA, MB BChir), St George's Hosp Med Sch London (MChir); *m* 4 March 1972, Prudence Margaret, da of (John) Denis Smith; 3 da (Tamsin Elinor b 4 Jan 1975, Ruth Elizabeth b 26 Oct 1976, Anna Margaret 27 March 1979); *Career* sr surgical registrar (rotation) St George's Hosp London 1978-82 (house physician 1970), conslt surgn Royal Shrewsbury Hosp 1982-89, conslt surgn Princess Royal Hosp Telford 1989-; memb Cncl Surgical Section RSM 1980-; memb Worshipful Soc of Apothecaries 1974; FRCS 1974; *Recreations* riding, sailing, music, walking; *Clubs* RSM; *Style*— John Quayle, Esq; Salop Nuffield Hospital, Shrewsbury; Princess Royal Hospital, Telford (☎ 0743 53441)

QUAYLE, John Douglas Stuart; s of Douglas Quayle (d 1957), of London, and Katherine, *née* Parke; *b* 21 Dec 1937; *Educ* Challoners St Albans, RADA; *m* 20 Oct 1966, Petronell Emily, da of Arthur Thomas Pickard (d 1972), of Torquay; *Career* Nat Serv RCS 1956-58, Cyprus and NI; Pitlochry Festival Theatre 1966; repertory: in Colchester, Salisbury, Richmond, Tours, London plays incl Donkeys Years and Habeas Corpus 1967-78; Nat Theatre player 1980-82, Noises Off Savoy Theatre 1983-85, Theatre of Comedy Ambassadors and Criterion 1986-88; various radio, TV and film performances; *Recreations* riding, shooting, walking; *Clubs* Garrick, Farmers'; *Style*— John Quayle, Esq; c/o Barry Burnett, Suite 42/43, Grafton House, 2/3 Golden Square, London W1R 4AA

QUAYLE, Robert Brisco MacGregor; s of John Pattinson Quayle, of Fontmell Magna, Dorset, and Doreen Helen MacGregor, *née* MacMullen; *b* 6 April 1950; *Educ* Monkton Combe Sch, Selwyn Coll Cambridge (MA); *m* 30 Sept 1972, (Deborah) Clare, da of Sir (Francis) Alan Pullinger, CBE, of Barnhorn, Meadway, Berkhamsted, Herts; 3 s (Jonathan b 1981, William b 1985, Thomas b 1988), 2 da (Hannah b 1976, Eily b 1978); *Career* admitted slr 1978; Linklaters & Paines 1974-76, clerk of Tynwald and sec House of Keys 1976-87, ptnr Travers Smith Braithwaite 1987-90 (conslt 1990-); dir: Singer & Friedlander (IOM) Ltd, TSB Overseas Bank (IOM) Ltd; memb Manx Heritage Fndn, dir Manx Radio; author of various articles on Parly affrs and history of IOM; *Recreations* family, church (licensed lay reader); *Clubs* Manx Automobile (IOM); *Style*— Robert Quayle, Esq; Mullen Beg, Patrick, IOM (☎ 0624 842912); 4 Upper Church St, Douglas, IOM (☎ 0624 625515, fax 0624 624625)

QUAYLE, Prof (John) Rodney; s of John Martin Quayle, and Mary Doris Quayle; *b* 18 Nov 1926; *Educ* Alun GS, UCNW Bangor (BSc, PhD), Univ of Cambridge (PhD); *m* 1951, Yvonne Mabel, da of Albert Sanderson; 1 s, 1 da; *Career* West Riding prof of microbiology Univ of Sheffield 1965- (sr lectr biochemistry 1963-65), vice chllr Univ of Bath 1983-; FRS; *Style*— Prof Rodney Quayle, FRS; The Lodge, North Rd, Bath BA2 6HE; Bath Univ, Claverton Down, Bath, Avon BA2 7AY

QUEENSBERRY, 12 Marquess of (S 1682); Sir David Harrington Angus Douglas; 11 Bt (S 1668); also Viscount Drumlanrig, Lord Douglas of Hawick and Tibbers (both S 1628), and Earl of Queensberry (S 1633); s of 11 Marquess (d 1954), by his 2 w Cathleen, *née* Mann; *b* 19 Dec 1929; *Educ* Eton; *m* 1, 1956 (m dis 1969), Ann, da of Maurice Jones and formerly w of George Radford; 2 da; m 2, 1969, Alexandra, da of Guy Wyndham Sich; 2 s (Viscount Drumlanrig, Lord Milo b 1978), 1 da (Lady Kate b 1969); *Heir* s, Viscount Drumlanrig; *Career* late 2 Lt RHG; prof of ceramics RCA 1959-83; pres Design and Industs Assoc 1976-78; *Style*— Prof the Most Hon the Marquess of Queensbury; 24 Brook Mews North, London W2 3BW (☎ 071 724 3701, telex 24224 REF 750)

QUEENSBERRY, Mimi, Marchioness of; Muriel Beatrice Margaret Françoise; da of Arthur John Rowe-Thornett (d 1936), of Villa Ginetta, Monte Carlo, and Ella Margaret Teresa, *née* March (d 1961); *b* 5 April 1911; *Educ* Inst Massena Nice, Inst des Essarts Montreux Switzerland, Broomfield Hall Sunningdale; *m* 1, Albert Sydney Gore Chunn; 1 da (Yosky Rowena b 1931); m 2, 1947, as his 3 wife, Francis Archibald Keihead, 11 Marquess of Queensberry (d 1954), s of Percy Sholta Douglas, 10 Marquess of Queensberry; 1 s (Lord Gawain Douglas, *qv*); *Style*— The Most Hon Mimi, Marchioness of Queensberry; 2 Archery Square, Walmer, Deal, Kent (☎ 0304 375813)

QUELCH, John Anthony; s of Norman Quelch, of Stratford St Mary, Suffolk, and Laura Sally, *née* Jones; *b* 8 Aug 1951; *Educ* King Edward VI Sch Norwich, Exeter Coll Oxford (BA), Univ of Pennsylvania (MBA), Harvard Univ (MS, DBA); *m* 17 June 1978, Joyce Ann, da of Harold Loring Huntley; *Career* asst prof Univ of Western Ontario Canada 1977-79; Harvard Business Sch: asst prof 1979-84, assoc prof 1984-88, prof of business admin 1988-; dir: Reebok International Ltd, WPP Group plc; *Books* Advertising and Promotion Management (1987), Multinational Marketing Management (1988), Sales Promotion Management (1989), How to Market to Consumers (1989), The Marketing Challenge of Europe 1992 (1991); *Recreations* tennis, squash; *Clubs* Harvard (Boston); *Style*— John Quelch, Esq; Harvard Business School, Soldiers Field, Boston, Massachusetts 02163, USA (☎ 010 1 617 495 6433, fax 010 1 617 496 8678)

QUENBY, John Richard; s of Richard Quenby (d 1942), of Bedford, and Margaret, *née* Wyse; *b* 30 Oct 1941; *Educ* Bedford Modern Sch, Open Univ (BA); *m* 9 April 1965, Sandra, da of Col Noel Frederick Charles King (d 1974), of Sydney, Aust; 2 da (Georgia Margaret b 1970, Fiona Elizabeth b 1971); *Career* dir Granada Computer Servs Ltd 1983-85, md Granada Overseas Hldgs Ltd 1985-89, chm GL Distrib France 1986-89; dir and chm: Granada France SA 1986-87, Telerent Italiana SPA 1986-87, Telerent Iberica 1986-87, Telerent Denmark 1986-87; dir Kapy SA Spain 1988-89, chief exec and dir RAC Motor Sports Assoc 1990-; *Recreations* rowing, photography; *Clubs* Bedford, Bedford Rowing; *Style*— John Quenby, Esq; 22 St Georges Rd, Bedford (☎ 0234 62192); Motor Sports House, Colnbrook (☎ 0753 681736)

QUENINGTON, Viscount; Michael Henry Hicks Beach; s and h of 2 Earl St Aldwyn, KBE, TD, PC; *b* 7 Feb 1950; *Educ* Eton, Univ of Oxford (MA); *m* 1982, Gilda Maria, o da of Barão Saavedra, of Rua Paula Freitas 104, Copacabana, Rio de Janeiro, Brazil; 2 da (Atalanta Maria b 1983, Aurora Ursula b 1988); *Career* commodity broker; *Clubs* Leander, White's; *Style*— Viscount Quenington; 17 Hale House, 34 de Vere Gardens, London W8 5AQ (☎ 071 937 6223); E D & F Man Int Ltd, Sugar Quay, Lower Thames St, London EC3R 6DU

QUICK, Anthony Oliver Hebert; s of Rev Prof Oliver Chase Quick (d 1944), of Christ Church, Oxford, and Frances Winifred, *née* Pearson; *b* 26 May 1924; *Educ* Shewsbury, SOAS London, Univ of Oxford (MA); *m* 20 Dec 1955, (Eva) Jean, da of Walter Carruthers Sellar (d 1951); 3 s (Oliver b 1959, James b 1962, Jonathan b 1968), 1 da (Ruth b 1957); *Career* RNVR 1943-46, Midshipman, Lt; asst master Charterhouse 1949-61; headmaster: Rendcomb Coll 1961-71, Bradfield 1971-85; *Books* Britain 1714-1851 (1961), Britain 1851-1945 (1967), 20th Century Britain (1968), Charterhouse: A History of the School (1990); *Style*— Anthony Quick, Esq; Corbin, Scorriton, Buckfastleigh, Devon TQ11 OHU (☎ 036 43 383)

QUICKE, Sir John Godolphin; CBE (1978), DL (Devon 1985); s of Capt Noel Arthur Godolphin Quicke (d 1943), and Constance May Quicke; *b* 20 April 1922; *Educ* Eton, New Coll Oxford; *m* 1953, Prudence Tinné, da of Rear Adm Charles Pierre Berthon, CBE (d 1965); 3 s, 3 da; *Career* farmer and landowner; chm SW Regnl Panel Miny of Agric SW 1972-75, pres CLA 1975-77, memb SW Regnl Bd Natwest Bank 1973-, chm Exeter Local Bd Commercial Union Assur Co 1980-; memb: Consultative Bd Jt Consultative Orgn for R & D, Food & Agric 1980-84, Countryside Cmmn 1981-88, Properties Ctee Nat Tst 1984-; vice chm N Devon Meat Ltd 1982-86; chm: Agric EDC, NEDO 1983-88, Agric Sector Gp NEDO, Soc for the Responsible Use of Resources in Agric and on the Land 1983-, Estates Panel Nat Tst 1984-, memb Bd SW Poly 1989; pres Royal Bath and West of England Soc 1989-90, hon fell Royal Agric Soc of England 1989; Hon DSc Univ of Exeter 1989; RASE Bledisloe Gold medal 1985; kt 1988; *Recreations* music, gardening, travel; *Clubs* Boodle's; *Style*— Sir John Quicke, CBE, DL; Sherwood, Newton St Cyres, Exeter, Devon (☎ 039 2851 216)

QUIGLEY, Desmond Francis Conor; s of Dr Thomas Francis Quigley, and Eleanor, *née* Blachford; *b* 20 May 1947; *Educ* Downside, The Coll Swindon; *m* 6 Jan 1973, Johanna Mary, da of John Foley; *Career* The Financial Times 1973-75, The Times 1975-79, Financial Weekly 1979-81; dir: Dewe Rogerson 1989-, Grandfield Rork Collins Finance 1981-82, Streets Finance 1982-86; chm Quigley & Associates 1986-89; *Style*— Desmond Quigley, Esq; 3 1/2 London Wall Bldgs, London Wall, London EC2M 5SY (☎ 071 638 9571)

QUIGLEY, Dr (William) George Henry; CB (1982); s of William George Cunningham Quigley (d 1969), and Sarah, *née* Martin (d 1987); *b* 26 Nov 1929; *Educ* Ballymena Acad, Queen's Univ Belfast (fndn scholar, BA, PhD); *m* 5 May 1971, Moyra Alice, da of Frank Munn (d 1970); *Career* NI Civil Serv: joined 1955, perm sec Dept of Manpower Servs 1974-76, perm sec Dept of Commerce 1976-79, perm sec Dept of Fin 1979-82, perm sec Dept of Fin and Personnel 1982-88; chm Ulster Bank Ltd 1989- (dep chm 1988-89), dir: Short Brothers PLC 1989-, National Westminster Bank PLC 1990-; professorial fell Queen's Univ Belfast 1988-; memb: Fair Employment Cmmn for NI 1989-, Cncl NI C of C and Indust 1989-, Cncl CBI (NI div) 1990-; chm IOD (NI div) 1990-; CBIM 1977; *Books* Registrum Johannis Mey (co-author with Dr EFD Roberts, 1972); *Recreations* historical research, reading, music, gardening; *Style*— Dr George Quigley, CB; Ulster Bank Limited, 47 Donegall Place, Belfast BT1 5AU (☎ 0232 320222, fax 0232 322097)

QUILLEY, Denis Clifford; s of Clifford Charles Quilley (d 1968), and Ada Winifred, *née* Stanley; *b* 26 Dec 1927; *Educ* Bancroft's Sch Woodford Essex; *m* 1949, Stella Jean, *née* Chapman; 1 s, 2 da; *Career* actor; first stage appearance Birmingham Repertory Theatre 1945; Nat Theatre 1971-76; theatre work incl: Privates on Parade (Aldwych 1977 (SWET award 1977), Piccadilly 1978), Morell in Candida (Albery Theatre) 1977, Deathtrap (Garrick) 1978, title role in Sondheim's Sweeney Todd (Drury Lane, SWET award 1980), Molokov in Chess (Barbican) 1985, Antony in Antony and Cleopatra (Chichester) 1985, Fatal Attraction (Haymarket) 1985, La Cage aux Folles (Palladium 1986 and NT 1990-91); films incl: Murder on the Orient Express, Evil Under the Sun, Privates on Parade, Mister Johnson; TV plays and series incl: The Merchant of Venice, The Crucible, Masada, Anno Domini, Rich Tea and Sympathy; *Recreations* playing the piano, flute and cello, walking; *Style*— Denis Quilley, Esq; c/o Bernard Hunter Associates, 13 Spencer Gardens, London SW14 7AH

QUILLIAM, Prof Juan Pete (Peter); OBE (1986); s of Thomas Alfred Quilliam (d 1953), of N Finchley, London, and Caroline Maude, *née* Pavitt (d 1958); *b* 20 Nov 1915; *Educ* Univ Coll Sch Hampstead, UCL (BSc, MSc, MB BS, DSc); *m* 1, Melita Kelly (d 1957); 1 s (Jonathan Peter b 1953), 1 da (Penelope Sally Ann (Mrs Walker) b 1950); m 2, 28 March 1958, Barbara Lucy, da of Rev W Kelly, of Pelynt, Cornwall; *Career* MO RAFVR 1942-46; Univ of London: prof of pharmacology St Bartholomew's Hosp Med Coll 1962-83, memb Senate 1968-90 memb Ct 1973-90, memb Mil Educn Ctee, chm Convocation 1973-90, chm Convocation Tst 1973-90; memb: Advertising Advsy Ctee IBA 1984-, Jt Charity Appeals Advsy Ctee IBA/BBC 1987-; dep chm Gen Optical Cncl 1975-88 (memb 1960-88), tstee City Parochial Fndn 1977-89, chm Crouch Harbour Authy 1988-, tstee and co-chm Help the Hospices Tst 1986-; BMA: chm of Med Academic Staff Ctee 1978, 1980, 1982, memb Cncl 1971-85, chm Bd of Sci 1982-85, vice-pres 1988-; memb: Physiological Soc 1948, Br Pharmacological Soc 1950; Univ of London Rowing Purple 1938-40, pres Univ of London Boat Club 1939-40; FRCP (London) 1975; *Books* Experimental Pharmacology (1954, 1989), Medical Effects of Nuclear War (jtly, 1983); *Recreations* sailing; *Clubs* United Hosps SC (Essex); *Style*— Prof Peter Quilliam, OBE; Hornbeams, 34 Totteridge Common, London N20 8NE

QUILTER, David Cuthbert Tudway; DL (Somerset 1970); s of Percy Cuthbert Quilter (d 1947), and Gladys Clare Alice, *née* Tudway (d 1973); *b* 26 March 1921; *Educ* Eton; *m* 30 Oct 1953, Elizabeth Mary, da of Col Sir John Carew Pole, Bt, DSO, TD, JP, DL, *qv*; 1 s (Simon b 26 March 1955), 2 da (Susan b 9 July 1957, Lucy b 6 May 1961); *Career* served WWII, Coldstream Gds, Capt; Barclays Bank Ltd: local dir Pall Mall Dist 1957-62, Bristol Dist 1962-84, dir 1971-81; dir Bristol Evening Post 1982-; chm of tstees Wells Cathedral Preservation Tst 1976-, treas Univ of Bristol 1976-88, govr Wells Cathedral Sch 1968-; memb: cncl Outward Bound Tst 1959-, Garden Soc 1973-; life tstee Carnegie UK Tst 1981-, tstee The American Museum in Br 1986-; master Soc of Merchant Venturers Bristol 1984; JP London Juvenile Courts 1959-62, Mayor of Wells 1974-75, High Sheriff Somerset 1974-75, Vice Lord-Lt Somerset 1978-; Liveryman Worshipful Co of Fishmongers 1964; Hon LLD Univ of Bristol; *Books* No Dishonourable Name (1947), History of Wells Cathedral School (1985); *Recreations* gardening, shooting, tennis, golf; *Clubs* Boodle's, Pratt's; *Style*— David Tudway Quilter, Esq, DL; Milton Lodge, Wells, Somerset (☎ 0749 72168)

QUIN, Joyce Gwendolen; MEP (Lab) S Tyne and Wear 1979-; *b* 1944; *Style*— Miss Joyce Quin, MEP; 5 Grange Crescent, Sunderland, Tyne and Wear

QUINE, Hector; s of Herbert Leigh Quine (d 1951), of London, and Gladys, *née* Foster (d 1934); *b* 30 Dec 1926; *Educ* Hextable Coll Kent; *m* 10 Oct 1960, Penelope Mary, da of Francis Henry Arnold Engleheart (d 1963), of The Priory, Stoke-by-Nayland, Suffolk; 1 s (Adrian b 1967), 1 da (Francesca b 1972); *Career* serv RASC 1944-48, Norway, Egypt, Palestine; guitarist Royal Opera House Covent Garden 1958-; prof: RAM 1959-87, Guildhall Sch of Music and Drama 1967-78, Trinity Coll of Music London 1958-78; advsr Assoc Bd of the Royal Schs of Music 1967- (examiner); Hon RAM, Hon FTCL; *Recreations* cricket, carpentry, photography; *Clubs* Chelsea Arts, Royal Philharmonic Soc, Royal Soc of Musicians, Performing Rights Soc; *Style*— Hector Quine, Esq; 22 Limerston St, Chelsea, London SW10 0HH (☎ 071 352 4419)

QUINION, David William; s of Frederick William Quinion (d 1984), and Muriel Elizabeth, *née* Price (d 1980); *b* 29 Sept 1926; *Educ* Watford GS for Boys, Northampton Engrg Coll (Hons Dip), Univ of London (BSc); *m* 1951, Joan Leonora, da of Percival Philip Parker; 2 s (Graham Robert b 3 June 1953, Malcolm David b 25 April 1956), 1 da (Sharon Fiona b 11 Jan 1965); *Career* indentured engr Sir Robert McAlpine 1946-49, design engr Oscar Faber Ptnrs 1949, section engr Marples Ridgway 1950-52, contracts mangr Taylor Woodrow Construction 1952-67, chief engr Tarmac Construction Ltd 1967-88, conslt Tarmac Construction 1988-; vice pres: Concrete Soc 1982-84 (chm W Midlands Branch 1976-77), Int Assoc for Bridge & Structural Engrg 1990- (chm Br Gp 1988); chm Tech Advsy Ctee FCEC 1984-; memb Cncl: BBA 1982-, CIRIA 1978-88, IStructE 1975-80 (chm Midland Cos Branch 1975-76); memb Standing Ctee on Structural Safety 1989-; FIStructE 1963, FICE 1963, FEng 1988, FRSA 1987; *Recreations* walking and countryside; *Clubs* RSA; *Style*— David Quinion,

Esq; 4 Netheravon Close, Salisbury, Wiltshire SP1 3BE (☎ 0722 333378); Tarmac Construction Limited, Birch St, Wolverhampton WV1 4HY (☎ 0902 22431)

QUINLAN, Chris Charles; s of Edward Charles Quinlan, of Betchworth, Surrey, and June, *née* Richiardi; *b* 21 Dec 1954; *Educ* Alleyn's Sch Dulwich London, Univ of Sheffield (LLB); *m* 4 April 1987, Catriona, da of Ronald F McDonald, of Fulham, London; *Career* slr Wilkinson Kimbers 1981-83, advtg control offr IBA 1983-84, asst sec Beecham Gp plc 1984-85, controller of advtg The Cable Authy 1985-90, mktg dir Cabletime Limited (subsid of Carlton Communications plc) 1990-; memb: Jt Indust Ctee for Cable Audience Res, Cable TV Assoc Mktg Gp, Bd of Mgmnt Gp 64 Theatre London; memb: Law Soc 1981, MRS 1988; *Recreations* ballooning, directing plays, games inventing; *Style—* Chris Quinlan, Esq; Cabletime, Newbury Business Park, London Road, Newbury, Berkshire RG13 2PZ (☎ 0635 35111)

QUINLAN, Sir Michael Edward; GCB (1991, KCB 1985, CB 1980); s of late Gerald Andrew Quinlan, of Hassocks, Sussex, and late Roseanne Quinlan; *b* 11 Aug 1930; *Educ* Wimbledon Coll, Merton Coll Oxford; *m* 1965, Margaret Mary, *née* Finlay; 2 s, 2 da; *Career* RAF 1952-54; civil servant 1954-: def cnsllr UK delgn to NATO 1970-73, under sec Cabinet Office 1974-77, dep under sec of State (policy and programmes) MOD 1977-81, dep sec Treasy 1981-82, perm sec Dept of Employment 1983-88, MOD 1988-; author of various articles on nuclear deterrence; *Recreations* cricket, squash, listening to music; *Clubs* RAF; *Style—* Sir Michael Quinlan, GCB; Ministry of Defence, Whitehall, London SW1A 2HB

QUINLAN, Timothy Edward; s of Edward John Quinlan (d 1959), of Essex, and Emma Louise, *née* Norrie (d 1974); *b* 12 Aug 1935; *Educ* St Ignatius Coll, Harvard Business Sch; *m* 1961 (m dis 1981), Maryann, da of Arthur Barron (d 1976), of Essex; 2 s (James b 1962, Edward b 1975), 1 da (Sarah b 1964); m 2, 22 July 1988, Susan, da of Raymond Lindley, of Moorland House, Epworth, nr Doncaster, South Yorkshire; 1 da (Emma Louise b 1989); *Career* dir and gp gen mangr: Brent Walker Gp plc, Basildon Astrodome Ltd, Radio Mercury, Essex Radio, Widcombe Basin Ltd, Brent Walker Hldgs plc, Brent Walker Ltd 1978, Brent Walker Casinos Div Ltd, Brent Walker Catering Div Ltd, Brent Walker Film Distributors Ltd, Brent Walker Film Prodns Ltd, Brent Walker Restaurants Ltd, Curzon Restaurants Ltd, Peter Evans Hldgs Ltd, Peter Evans Eating Houses Ltd, La Boheme (Chelsea) Ltd, Focus Cinemas Ltd, Garons Agencies Ltd, Isow's Restaurants Ltd, Marlowe Rooms Ltd, Network Cinema (UK) Ltd, Waldair (Chancery Lane) Ltd, Waldair (Foster Lane) Ltd, Waldair (High Holborn) Ltd, Waldair (Tower Hill) Ltd, Westcliff Leisure Centre Ltd, Brent Walker Concessionaires Ltd, Manorlike Ltd, Brent Walker Fin Ltd, Brent Walker Casinos Northern Ltd, Fillfore Ltd; *Recreations* skiing, golf, tennis; *Clubs* Thorpe Hall Golf, Thorpe Bay Tennis, St James's; *Style—* Timothy Quinlan, Esq; 121 Thorpe Bay Gdns, Thorpe Bay, Southend on Sea, Essex SS1 3NW (☎ 0702 296310); Brent Walker House, 19 Rupert Street, London W1V 7FS (☎ 071 465 0111, fax 071 465 8101)

QUINN, (James Steven) Brian; s of James Joseph Quinn (d 1977), of Lancs, and Elizabeth, *née* Thomas; *b* 16 June 1936; *Educ* Waterpark S Ireland, Univ Coll Dublin, King's Inn Dublin (LLB, BCL); *m* 1963, Blanche Cecilia, da of Richard Francis James (d 1986), of Spain; 2 s (James b 1963, Alexander b 1969), 1 da (Susannah b 1965); *Career* head of Industl Activities Prices and Incomes Bd 1969-71, dir M L H Conslts 1971-79, corporate devpt advsr Midland Bank Int 1977-80, chief industl advsr Price Cmmn 1977-80; chm: Brightstar Communications 1983-85, B A J Hldgs 1985-87, Harmer Holbrook 1987-88; memb Exec Ctee Inst of Euro Trade and Technol 1983-, pres Int Inst of Communications 1988- (tstee 1982-87, chm Exec Ctee 1984-87), chm Gtr London Regnl Cncl BIM 1990-; *Recreations* golf, reading, veteran vehicles; *Clubs* Athenaeum; *Style—* Brian Quinn, Esq; Craiglea House, Austenwood Lane, Gerrards Cross, Bucks; Network House, Oxford Rd, Uxbridge, Middx (☎ 0895 74141)

QUINN, James Charles Frederick; s of Rev Chllr James Quinn (d 1962), and Muriel Alice May, *née* MaGuire (d 1973); *b* 23 Aug 1919; *Educ* Shrewsbury, Trinity Dublin, ChCh Oxford (MA); *m* 1941, Hannah, da of Rev Robert Malcolm Gwynn (Vice Provost Trinity Dublin); 1 s (Gough), 1 da (Christina); *Career* served WWII Maj Irish Gds Italy and NW Europe 1941-46, Br Army Staff France, and Town Major Paris 1946; film prodr and exhibitor; dir BFI 1955-64, memb BBC Gen Advsy Cncl 1960-64; Foreign Leader award US State Dept 1962, Cncl of Europe fellowship 1966; tstee: Imperial War Museum 1968-78, Nat Life Story Collection 1986-; chm Nat Panel for Film Festivals 1966-83; films produced incl: Herostratus 1966, Overlord 1975 (Silver Bear Berlin Film Festival); memb Br Cncl Film TV and Video Advsy Ctee 1984-90; chm The Minema Ltd 1984-; Chevalier de l'Ordre des Arts et des Lettres (France 1979); *Recreations* lawn tennis; *Clubs* Cavalry and Guards', Vincents (Oxford); *Style—* James Quinn, Esq; 108 Marine Parade, Brighton, Sussex

QUINN, Niall; s of William Quinn, of Dublin, and Mary, *née* Condon; *b* 6 Oct 1966; *Educ* Drumnagh Castle Catholic Boys' Sch Dublin; *Career* professional footballer; 93 appearances Arsenal 1983-90 (20 goals), transferrerd for a fee of £800,000 to Manchester City 1990-; Republic of Ireland: 2 under 21 caps, 23 full caps 1986-91, played in World Cup Italy 1990; League Cup winners' medal Arsenal 1987; *Recreations* golf, tennis, horseracing; *Style—* Niall Quinn, Esq; Manchester City FC, Maine Rd, Moss Side, Manchester M14 7WN (☎ 061 226 1191)

QUINN, Peter Herbert; s of H S Quinn (d 1983), and Mrs I Quinn, *née* Shephard (d 1979); *b* 11 Dec 1931; *Educ* Bishopshalt Sch; *m* 1958, Ann Veronica, da of H V Beecroft (d 1985); 1 s (Paul b 1962), 2 da (Deborah b 1959, Caroline b 1967); *Career* chm and md Tizer Ltd 1970-72, md Thornbers Holdings Ltd 1973, chief exec Planet Group plc 1973-1985, chm The Phoenix Timber Group plc 1985-; Freeman City of London 1986; FCA; *Recreations* golf, squash, rugby; *Style—* Peter Quinn, Esq; The Phoenix Timber Group plc, Arisdale Ave, South Ockendon, Essex RM15 5TR (☎ 0708 851801, fax 0708 851850)

QUINN, Dame Sheila Margaret Imelda; DBE (1987, CBE 1978); da of Wilfred Amos Bairstow Quinn (d 1963); *b* 16 Sept 1920; *Educ* Layton Hill Convent Sch Blackpool, Univ of London; *Career* regnl nursing offr Wessex RHA 1978-83, UK rep Standing Ctee of Nurses EEC 1979-, pres Royal Coll of Nursing 1982-86 (chm Cncl 1974-79, dep pres 1980-82), nursing advsr Br Red Cross 1983-88; memb EEC Advsy Ctee on Trg in Nursing 1983-90 (pres 1979-82), first vice pres Int Cncl of Nurses 1981-85 (memb Bd of Dirs 1977-81); Hon DSc Univ of Southampton 1986; *Recreations* reading, walking, gardening; *Clubs* New Cavendish, St John's House; *Style—* Dame Sheila Quinn, DBE; 31 Albany Park Court, The Avenue, Southampton, Hants SO2 1EN (☎ 0703 676592)

QUINNEN, (Paul) Nigel Andrew; s of John Norman Quinnen (d 1986), of Ealing, London, and Elisabeth, *née* Clark; *b* 10 Oct 1953; *Educ* St Benedict's Ealing, Wadham Coll Oxford (Rugby blue); *m* 16 Dec 1977, Dinah Mary, da of Rear Adm Derek Hetherington, of Christmas Common, Oxon; 1 s (Bruno b 1986), 1 da (Romy b 1987); *Career* articles Coopers & Lybrand 1976-80, fund mangr J Henry Schroder Wagg 1980-85, investmt dir Lazard Investors 1985; ACA 1980; *Recreations* golf; *Clubs* Royal Mid Surrey Golf; *Style—* Nigel Quinnen, Esq; 11 Blakesley Avenue, Ealing, London W5 2DN (☎ 081 997 6049)

QUINNEN, Peter John; s of John Norman Quinnen (d 1986), of Ealing, London, and Mabel Elisabeth, *née* Clark; *b* 4 April 1945; *Educ* St Benedict's Sch Ealing, ChCh Oxford (MA); *m* 26 Aug 1972, Pammy, da of Gordon Urqhart, of Ayr, Scotland; 2 s (Thomas b 1974, Henry b 1977); *Career* stockbroker; dir James Capel and Co 1982-, chm and chief exec James Capel and Co 1986-; *Recreations* golf, opera, music; *Clubs* Royal Automobile, St George's Hill Wednesday; *Style—* Peter Quinnen, Esq; James Capel & Co, James Capel House, PO Box 551, 6 Bevis Marks, London EC3A 7JQ (☎ 071 621 0011)

QUINTON, Baron (Life Peer UK 1982), of Holywell in City of Oxford and Co of Oxfordshire; Anthony Meredith Quinton; s of Surgn Capt Richard Frith Quinton, RN (d 1935), and Gwenllyan Letitia Quinton; *b* 25 March 1925; *Educ* Stowe, Christ Church Oxford (BA); *m* 1952, Marcelle, da of late Maurice Wegier, of New York; 1 s, 1 da; *Career* RAF, served WWII; fell: All Souls Coll Oxford 1949-55, New Coll Oxford 1955-78; pres Trinity Coll Oxford 1978-87, memb Arts Cncl of GB 1979-82; vice pres Br Acad 1985-86, chm Br Library Bd 1985-90; FBA; *Books* Political Philosophy (ed, 1967), The Nature of Things (1973), Utilitarian Ethics (1973), K Ajdukiewicz - Problems and Theories of Philosophy (trans with H Skolimowski, 1973), The Politics of Imperfection (1978), Francis Bacon (1980), Thoughts and Thinkers (1982); *Clubs* Garrick, Beefsteak, United Oxford and Cambridge Univ; *Style—* The Rt Hon the Lord Quinton; The Mill House, Turville, Henley-on-Thames, Oxon RG9 6QL

QUINTON, Hon Edward Frith; o s of Baron Quinton (Life Peer), *qv*; *b* 24 Dec 1957; *Educ* Winchester, Imperial Coll of Science and Technol London (BSc); *m* 22 June 1987, Sarah Eve, da of A W Travis, of Western Samoa; *Career* mechanical engr; *Recreations* vintage motoring; *Style—* The Hon Edward Quinton; Leslie Hartridge Ltd, Buckingham MK18 1EF (☎ 0280 813661)

QUINTON, Sir John Grand; s of William Grand Quinton (d 1968), and Norah May, *née* Nunn (d 1969); Freeman City of Norwich (by inheritance since 1702); *b* 21 Dec 1929; *Educ* Norwich Sch, Univ of Cambridge (MA); *m* 1954, Jean Margaret, da of Donald Chastney (d 1950); 1 s (Michael), 1 da (Joanna); *Career* Barclays Bank: sr gen mangr 1982-84, dep chm 1985-87, chm 1987-; kt 1990; *Recreations* gardening, opera; *Clubs* Reform; *Style—* Sir John Quinton; Chenies Place, Chenies, Bucks; Barclays Bank, 54 Lombard St, London EC3P 3AH (☎ 071 626 1567)

QUINTON, Kenneth Charles; MBE (1988); s of Charles Henry Quinton (d 1968), and Kate, *née* Rowcliffe (d 1971); *b* 21 Dec 1923; *Educ* East Barnet GS, Northampton Poly London (BSc); *m* 1948, Vera Joyce, da of Charles Bull; 1 s (Hedley Charles b 1953), 1 da (Janet Clare b 1955); *Career* served apprenticeship in radio engrg at STC, sr engr BBC 1949-58, dir of res Rediffusion Engineering (now British Cable Services) 1974-87 (joined 1958), ret 1987; hon memb Cable TV Assoc 1987; FIEE, FEng 1984, FRTS 1984; *Recreations* cabinet making; *Style—* Kenneth Quinton, Esq, MBE; Cobbins, 20 The Barton, Cobham, Surrey KT11 2NJ (☎ 0932 863013)

QUIRICI, Daniel; s of Ernest Quirici, of Cannes, France, and Candide, *née* Postai; *b* 8 June 1948; *Educ* Ecole des Hautes Etudes Commerciales Paris (MBA), Stanford Univ California (PhD); *m* 1 Sept 1972, Margaret, da of Donald Wright Mann, of NY; 2 s (Alexandre b 15 Aug 1973, Francois b 23 May 1979), 1 da (Florence b 14 Feb 1978); *Career* assoc prof HEC 1970-76, assoc Arthur D Little 1976-82, sr vice pres Credit Commercial de France Paris 1983-, md Laurence Prust & Co Ltd (a subsidiary of CCF) 1986-; memb Traffic Ctee Knightsbridge Assoc; *Recreations* tennis, golf; *Clubs* RAC; *Style—* Daniel Quirici, Esq; 8 Montpelier Square, London SW7; Laurence Prust & Co Ltd, 27 Finsbury Square, London EC2 1LP (☎ 071 982 7531, 071 628 1111, fax 071 638 7660)

QUIRK, Hon Mrs (Carol Ann); *née* Penny; da of 2 Viscount Marchwood, MBE (d 1979); *b* 1948; *m* 1978, Patrick J Quirk; 2 s; *Style—* The Hon Mrs Quirk; 9 Lambourn Rd, London SW4 0LX

QUIRK, Eric Randolph; s of Prof Sir Randolph Quirk, CBE, and Jean, *née* Williams; *b* 30 Dec 1951; *Educ* Highgate Sch, UCL (LLB); *m* 30 July 1977, Patricia Anne, da of Stanley Lawrence Hemsworth, of 70 Wood Lane, Ashenhurst, Huddersfield, W Yorks; 1 s (Richard b 2 April 1983), 2 da (Catharine b 25 May 1979, Sara b 14 Nov 1980); *Career* admitted slr 1975; asst slr: Slaughter & May 1973-77, Alexander Tatham & Co Manchester 1978-81; ptnr Alsop Wilkinson (formerly Lee Lane-Smith) 1981- (trg ptnr 1982-); memb: Legal Resources Gp Educn Ctee 1988-90, UCL Alumnus Soc, Univ of Manchester Careers Cncl, Law Soc; corp memb CBI; *Recreations* violin, string quartets, squash, fell walking, reading bedtime stories; *Style—* Eric Quirk, Esq; Alsop Wilkinson, 11 St James's Square, Manchester M2 6DR (☎ 061 834 7760, fax 061 831 7515)

QUIRK, (Jonathan) Piers; s of Dudley Cecil Quirk, JP, of Chiddingstone, Kent, and Joan Mary, *née* Salmon; *b* 27 Dec 1943; *Educ* Winchester, Coll of Estate Mgmnt Univ of London (BSc); *m* 3 Sept 1983, Sally, da of (Arthur) Richard Kemp, of Chiddingstone, Kent; 2 s (Frederick b 1986, Augustus William (Gus) b 1990), 1 da (Zoe b 1988); *Career* ptnr Messrs Parris & Quirk Chartered Surveyors of Tunbridge Wells and London 1971-87; pres Royal Tunbridge Wells C of C 1986; Freeman City of London 1984, Liveryman Worshipful Co of Chartered Surveyors 1984; FRICS 1974; *Recreations* photography, woodwork, paintings, rugs, travel; *Style—* Piers Quirk, Esq; The Oasts, Chiddingstone, Kent TN8 7AQ (☎ 0892 870 701); Fox & Sons, 27 Mount Pleasant, Tunbridge Wells, Kent TN1 1PP (☎ 0892 515 252, fax 0892 515 868)

QUIRK, Prof Sir (Charles) Randolph; CBE (1976); s of Thomas Quirk; *b* 1920; *Educ* Cronk y Voddy Sch, Douglas HS IOM, UCL (MA, PhD, DLitt), Yale Univ; *m* Prof Gabriele Stein; *Career* prof of Eng language: Univ of Durham 1958-60, Univ of London 1960-68, Quain prof of Eng language and lit UCL 1968-81, vice chllr Univ of London 1981-85; memb: Bd Br Cncl 1983-, Cncl RADA; govr English Speaking Union, hon master of Bench Gray's Inn 1983; pres: Br Acad 1985-89, Inst of Linguists 1983-36, Coll of Speech Therapists 1987-; chm: Br Library Advsy Ctee, Hornby Educnl Tst; tstee Wolfson Fndn; ed English Language Series (Longman); hon doctorates: Lund, Uppsala, Paris, Liège, Nijmegen, Salford, Reading, Leicester, Newcastle, Durham, Bath, Open, Essex, Bar Ilan, Southern California, CNAA, Brunel, Sheffield, Glasgow; foreign fell: Royal Belgian Acad of Sci, Royal Swedish Acad; fell and res fell UCL; FBA, fell Academia Europaea; kt 1985; *Books* A University Grammar of English (1973), Style and Communication in the English Language (1982), English in the World (1985), A Comprehensive Grammar of the English Language (1985), Words at Work (1986), English in Use (1990), A Student's Grammar of the English Language (1990); *Clubs* Athenaeum; *Style—* Prof Sir Randolph Quirk, CBE; University College London, Gower St, London WC1E 6BT (☎ 071 387 7050)

QUIRKE, Patrick Adair; s of John Patrick Quirke, of Itchenor, W Sussex, and Elizabeth, *née* Naismith; *b* 26 June 1951; *Educ* Westminster, Kingston Coll of Technol; *m* 15 Oct 1988, Suzanna Angela, da of John David Anthony Willis, of Bath, Avon; *Career* film dept BBC TV: asst sound recordist 1973-85, film sound recordist 1985-, BAFTA award for film sound The Duty Men 1988; ptnr The Chance Band (high soc dance band) 1974-; *Recreations* tennis, skiing, sub-aqua; *Clubs* Roof Garden; *Style—* Patrick Quirke, Esq; BBC TV, Ealing Film Studios, Ealing Green, London W5 (☎ 081 567 6655 ext 647)

QURAISHY, Dr Ehsanullah; s of M M Quraishy, of Lucknow, India, and S K Quraishy; *b* 1 July 1942; *Educ* Univ of Gorakhpur India (BSc), Univ of Lucknow India (MB BS), Univ of London (Dip Derm, DPM); *m* 2 June 1968, Nargis Ara, da of Nazir Ahmad (d 1989), of Jharmahui, India; 2 da (Ghazala b 1973, Aalia b 1977); *Career* MO

Prov Med Serv Uttar Pradesh India 1967-68, registrar Manchester & Salford Skin Hosp 1971-73, registrar psychiatry Mid Wales Hosp 1973-77, sr registrar psychiatry Sefton Gen and Royal Liverpool Hosps 1978-81, conslt psychiatrist NW Regnl Health Authy 1981-; author of pubn Erythema Multiforme During Treatment with Mianserin; memb NW Dermatological Soc; memb: BMA, Soc of Clinical Psychiatrists; *Recreations* music, cricket, tennis; *Style—* Dr Ehsanullah Quraishy; 303 Bramhall Lane South, Bramhall, Stockport, Cheshire SK7 3DW (☎ 061 439 5272); Stepping Hill Hospital, Poplar Grove, Stockport, Cheshire SK2 7JE (☎ 061 4195735 Ext 36)

QURESHI, Dr (Mohammed) Jafer Hossain; s of Baquer Hossain Qureshi, of Offrs Mess House, Hyderabad, and Ahmed Unissa Begum; *b* 19 April 1945; *Educ* Osmania Univ (MB BS), Univ of Liverpool (DTM and H), Univ of London (DPM); *m* 13 Aug 1971, Fouzia Qureshi, da of late Mohammed Ali, of Jubilee Hills, Hyderabad; 1 s (Mohammed Salman), 1 da (Ayesha Salma); *Career* conslt psychiatrist Wolverhampton and Woodbourne Clinic Birmingham, hon lectr in psychiatry Univ of Birminghamn, specialist in sexual med and res in the area of erectile dysfunction (impotence); sec to Psychiatric Med Staff Ctee in Wolverhampton hosps, advsr to Princess Durr-Shehvar Childrens Hosp Hyderabad, tstee Hyderabad Charitable Tst London, sec Nat Assoc of Behaviour Therapists, memb of psychotherapy and community psychiatric section of RCPsych; co-fndr Steering Ctee Soc for Investigation of Male Sexual Dysfunction (SIMSED), fndr pres Surdhwani soc for the promotion of Asian arts; coordinator for developing servs for elderly mentally infirm patients for Borough of Wolverhampton; MRCPsych; *Recreations* Indian classical music, swimming, travelling; *Style—* Dr Jafer Qureshi; 136 Linden Lea, Compton, Wolverhampton, West Midlands WV3 8BE (☎ 0902 771674); 50 Maple St, London W1; 8 Summerfield Road, Chapel Ash, Wolverhampton, West Midlands WV1 4PR (☎ 0902 29044, fax 021 771 1193)

QURESHI, (Abdul) Saleem; s of Sheikh Muhammad Qureshi Qadi (d 1969), of Khanpur, Pakistan, and Amina Begum, *née* Ameer (d 1972); *b* 15 Jan 1938; *Educ* Punjab Univ (BA), Karachi Univ (LLB); *m* 1, 15 Sept 1970 (m dis 1978), Joy Edith, da of Thomas Gordon Falconer (d 1945), of Chichester, Essex; m 2, 6 Jan 1980, Khadeer Unnisa Sajida, da of Mohammed Ehsan-ul-Haq (d 1970), of Hyderabad, India; 1 s (Arif b 25 May 1986), 2 da (Sara b 7 Oct 1981, Asma b 12 April 1983); *Career* asst ed weekly Satluj Bahawalpur Pakistan 1955-57, ed Nationalism and Internationalism Pakistan 1957, teacher govt sch Noorpur Pakistant 1958-59, sub ed Daily Rehbar Bahalvapur Pakistan 1959; teacher: Mary Claco Sch for Girls and Boys Karachi 1961-62, Cantonment Public Sch Karachi Cantonment 1962-64; called to the Bar Middle Temple 1972, practising SE Circuit 1973-; memb Exec Ctee of Asian Lawyers, hon advsr to UK Pakistan Cultural Fndn, convenor and sec gen Nat Youth Cncl Bahawalpur Pakistan 1957, author of law articles and lectures and contrib Hum Log magazine; sec Public Speaking Union and memb Drama Club SM Law Coll Karachi 1963-64, fndr memb World Assoc Muslim Jurists Lahore Pakistan 1978, fndr and sec gen MA Jinnah Soc London 1984, chm Police Monitoring Gp Waltham Forest London 1982-83; memb Gen Cncl of the Bar; *Recreations* swimming, lawn tennis, badminton, participation in poetic symposia; *Clubs* Nat Lib; *Style—* Saleem Qureshi, Esq; 74 Acacia Rd, London E11 3QG (☎ 081 558 2289); 12 Old Square, Lincoln's Inn, London WC2 3TX (☎ 071 404 0875)

QURESHI, Dr Shakeel Ahmed; s of Mohammed Aslam Qureshi, of 14 Filmer Rd, Luton, Beds, and Sara Begum Qureshi; *b* 20 March 1952; *Educ* Thomas Rotherham Coll, Rotherham GS, Univ of Manchester Med Sch (MB ChB); *m* 29 Dec 1968, Azra Siddique, da of Mohammed Siddique Qureshi, of 97 Millat Colony, Rawalpindi, Pakistan; 3 s (Sajid Shakeel b 21 May 1977, Abid Shakeel b 14 Feb 1980, Imran Shakeel b 29 July 1982), 1 da (Noreen b 14 April 1971); *Career* house physician Luton and Dunstable Hosp Luton 1976-77, house surgn Manchester Royal Infirmary Feb-July 1977, sr house physician Joyce Green Hosp Dartford 1977-79, med registrar Barnet Gen Hosp Herts 1979-80, cardiology res registrar Harefield Hosp Middx 1980-83, conslt paediatric cardiologist Rawalpindi Pakistan 1983-85, sr registrar paediatric cardiology Royal Liverpool Children's Hosp June-Dec 1986, conslt paediatric cardiologist 1987-88, Guy's Hosp 1988-; memb: BMA 1976, Br Cardiac Soc; MRCP 1979; *Recreations* squash, cricket; *Style—* Dr Shakeel Qureshi; Department of Paediatric Cardiology, Guy's Hospital, St Thomas St, London SE1 9RT (☎ 071 955 4616)

QUYSNER, David William; s of Charles William Quysner, of Mildenhall, Suffolk, and Marjorie Alice, *née* Partington; *b* 26 Dec 1946; *Educ* Bolton Sch, Selwyn Coll Cambridge (MA), London Business Sch; *m* 11 Sept 1971, Lindsay Jean Parris, da of Sir Norman Biggs, of Hurstpierpoint, Sussex; 1 s (Simon James b 1980), 2 da (Sarah Louise b 1976, Deborah Helen b 1977); *Career* Investors in Indust plc 1968-82, dir Abingworth plc 1982-, non exec dir The Melville Gp plc 1986-; *Recreations* opera, golf; *Style—* David Quysner, Esq; Abingworth plc, 26 St James's St, London SW1A 1HA (☎ 071 839 6745, fax 071 930 1891)

R

RABAGLIATI, Duncan Charles Pringle; s of Brig (Charles) Ian Evershed Rabagliati, of Menston, Yorkshire, and Joan, *née* Pringle; *b* 3 Jan 1945; *Educ* Sedbergh; *m* Mair Alethea, da of (Christopher) Ivor Williams; 2 s (Alastair James b 15 Jan 1974, Jonathan Stuart b 5 Oct 1975), 1 da (Sarah Louise b 9 June 1980); *Career* articled clerk Booth & Co Leeds 1964-69, ptnr McKenna & Co London 1973 (asst slr 1969-73); *Books* The Formula One Record Book (jtly, 1971), The History of Grand Prix and Voiturette Racing (VII vols, jtly, 1985); contrib to numerous motoring books and magazines; *Recreations* motoring history, classic motor racing, genealogy; *Style—* Duncan C P Rabagliati, Esq; McKenna & Co, Mitre House, 160 Aldersgate St, London EC1A 4DD (☎ 071 606 9000, fax 071 606 9100)

RABAN, Jonathan; s of Rev Peter J C P Raban, and Monica, *née* Sandison; *b* 14 June 1942; *Educ* Univ of Hull (BA); *m* 1985, Caroline Cuthbert; *Career* lectr in Eng and American Lit UCW 1965-67, UEA 1967-69, professional writer 1969-; *Booksi* The Technique of Modern Fiction (1969), Mark Twain: Huckleberry Finn (1969), The Society of the Poem (1971), Soft City (1973), Arabia Through The Looking Glass (1979), Old Glory (1981, Heinemann award RSL 1982, Thomas Cook award 1982), Foreign Land (1985), Coasting (1986), For Love and Money (1987), God, Man and Mrs Thatcher (1989); FRSL; *Recreations* sailing; *Clubs* Groucho, Cruising Assoc; *Style—* Jonathan Raban, Esq; c/o Aitken & Stone Ltd, 29 Fernshaw Rd, London SW10 0TG

RABEN-LEVETZAU, Lady Rosanagh Mary; *née* Crichton; Baroness Michael Raben-Levetzau; da of late 5 Earl of Erne and Lady Davidema Katherine Cynthia Mary Millicent Bulwer Lytton, da of 2 Earl of Lytton; *b* 12 Aug 1932; *m* 1956, Baron Michael Paul Raben-Levetzau (d 1990), of Rathmore Park, Tullow, Co Carlow; 4 s (Matthew b 1962 m Sarah Jane Stratton 1987, Alexander b 1964, Victor b 1968, Seamus b 1970); *Style—* The Lady Rosanagh Raben-Levetzau; Rathmore Park, Tullow, Co Carlow, Republic of Ireland (☎ 0503 61179)

RABIN, Prof Brian Robert; s of Emanuel Rabin (d 1973), and Sophia, *née* Neshaver (d 1982); *b* 4 Nov 1927; *Educ* Latymer's, UCL (BSc, MSc, PhD); *m* 29 Aug 1954, Sheila Patricia, da of Charles Patrick George (d 1972); 1 s (Paul Robert b 27 Jan 1958), 1 da (Carol (Mrs Costa) b 23 Sept 1959); *Career* UCL 1954-: asst lectr then lectr 1954-63, reader in biochemistry 1963-67, prof of enzymology 1967-70, head of Biochemistry Dept 1970-88, fell UCL 1984, prof of biochemistry 1988-; fndr dir London Biotechnol Ltd 1985-, dir Cogent Ltd and Cogents Hldgs Ltd 1986-89; FZS 1972, FIBiol 1972, EMBO 1980, memb Academie FurUmuweltfragen 1987; *Recreations* travel, carpentry; *Clubs* Athenaeum; *Style—* Prof Brian Rabin; 34 Grangewood, Potters Bar, Herts EN6 1SL (☎ 0707 54576); Dept of Biochemistry, University College, Gower St, London WC1E 6BT (☎ 071 388 1604)

RABINOWITZ, Harry; MBE (1978); s of Israel Rabinowitz (d 1960), and Eva, *née* Kirkel (d 1971); *b* 26 March 1916; *Educ* Athlone HS SA, Witwatersrand Univ, London Guildhall Sch of Music; *m* 15 Dec 1944, Lorna Thurlow, da of Cecil Redvers Anderson (d 1970); 1 s (Simon Oliver b 1951), 2 da (Karen Lesley b 1947, Lisa Gabrielle b 1960); *Career* Corpl SA Forces 1942-43; conductor BBC radio 1953-60; head of music: BBC TV Light Entertainment 1960-68, LWT 1968-77; now freelance conductor/composer; conductor: Hollywood Bowl 1983-84, Boston Pops 1985-89, London Symphony Orchestra, Royal Philharmonic Orchestra; conductor films: Chariots of Fire, Manhattan Project, Heat & Dust, The Bostonians, Maurice, Time Bandits, Return to Oz, L'Argent, Camile Claudel, etc; TV: New Faces 1987/8, Paul Nicholas Special 1987-88, Julia MacKenzie Special 1986, Nicholas Nickleby, Drummonds, The Insurance Man, Absent Friends, Simon Wiesenthal Story, Marti Caine Special; composer TV: Agatha Christie Hour, Reilly Ace of Spies; conductor theatre: World Premieres of "Cats" and "Song and Dance"; Discs: Michael Crawford, Sarah Brightman, John Mathis; awards: Br Acad of Songwriters, Composers and Authors (BASCA) Gold Award 1986, Radio and TV Industries Award 1986; *Recreations* wine tasting, gathering edible fungi; *Clubs* Holmbury St Mary Village; *Style—* Harry Rabinowitz, Esq, MBE; Yellow Cottage, Walking Bottom, Peaslate, Surrey GU5 9RR (☎ 0306 730605)

RABSON, John; s of Rev Alban Rabson (d 1966), and Kathleen Muriel, *née* Blackshaw; *b* 8 Sept 1942; *Educ* Newport GS Essex, Colchester Royal GS, Harlow Tech, Enfield Tech, Univ of Essex (MPhil, Dip EE); *m* 9 Dec 1972, Rosemary Margaret, da of Thomas Border (d 1985); 1 s (Hugo b 1975); *Career* chartered electrical electronic and radio engr; res offr Univ of Essex Jan-Sept 1973, exec engr PO (now BT) 1973-; CEng, MIEE, MIERE; *Recreations* amateur radio (licence G3PAI held since 1961), codes and ciphers, science fiction; *Style—* John Rabson, Esq; Limes Farm House, Eyke, Woodbridge, Suffolk (☎ 0394 460298); BTRL, Martlesham, Ipswich (☎ 0473 643210, telex 98376)

RABUKAWAQA, Sir Josua Rasilau; KBE (1977, CBE 1974, MBE 1968), MVO (1970); s of Dr Aisea Rasilau; *b* 2 Dec 1917; *Educ* Suva Methodist Boys' Sch, Queen Victoria Sch, Teachers' Training Coll Auckland (NZ); *m* 1944, Mei Tolanivutu; 3 s, 2 da; *Career* served Fijian Armed Forces 1953-55; ambass-at-large Fiji & chief Protocol 1978-; first high commnr Fiji to UK 1970-76, awarded R B Bennett Cwlth Prize 1981 by RSA; *Style—* Sir Josua Rabukawaqa, KBE, MVO; 6 Vunivivi Hill, Nausori, Fiji

RABY, Derek Graham; s of Sir Victor Harry Raby, KBE, CB, MC (d 1990), and Dorothy Alys, *née* Buzzard; *b* 18 May 1927; *Educ* King's Sch Bruton, Somerset; *m* 14 July 1956, Elsa Jean, da of H White (d 1969), of Felpham, Sussex; 1 s (Charles b 1959); *Career* RAF 1945-48; appeals dir PDSA, dir PDSA Trading Ltd; conslt memb Charities Effectiveness Review Tst 1990-; writer of plays, articles, and occasional broadcaster 1973-; Freeman City of London; *Books* incl: We Need a Man (1975); *Recreations* gardening, wine; *Style—* Derek Raby, Esq; The Little House, Elm Grove Rd, Cobham, Surrey KT11 3HB (☎ 0932 864465)

RACE, Russell John; s of Russell Edgar Race (d 1982), and Winifred Olive, *née* Clissold; *b* 28 May 1946; *Educ* Sir Joseph Williamson's Mathematical Sch Rochester, Univ of Liverpool (BA); *Career* economist White Fish Authy 1967-70, dir Hoare Govett 1985- (investmt analyst 1970-76, corp fin 1976-); memb: Soc of Business Economists, Soc of Investmt Analysts; *Recreations* hockey, cricket, music; *Style—* Russell Race, Esq; 86 Ingle Rd, Chatham, Kent ME4 5SE (☎ 0634 406 347); Hoare Govett Corporate Finance Ltd, 4 Broadgate, London EC2M 7LE (☎ 071 374 1861, fax 071 374 1587)

RACE, Stephen Russell (Steve); s of Russell Tiniswood Race (d 1926), of Lincoln, and Robina Race (d 1964); *b* 1 April 1921; *Educ* Christ's Hosp Sch (formerly Lincoln Sch), RAM; *m* 1, 7 June 1944, Clair Leng (d 1969); 1 da (Nicola b 1946); m 2, 14 April 1970, Leonie Rebecca Govier Mather; *Career* RAF 1941-46; freelance pianist arranger and composer 1946-55, light music advsr Assoc-Rediffusion Ltd 1955-60, TV conductor Tony Hancock and Peter Sellers Shows; radio and TV appearances incl: My Music, A Good Read, Jazz in Perspective, Any Questions?, Music Now, Music Weekly, Kaleidoscope, Look What They've Done to My Song, Jazz Revisited, With Great Pleasure, Desert Island Discs, Steve Race Presents The Radio Orchestra Show, Gershwin Among Friends, Irving Berlin Among Friends; compositions incl: Nicola (Ivor Novello Award), Faraway Music, The Pied Piper, incidental music for Richard III, Cyrano de Bergerac, Twelfth Night (BBC); Cantatas: Song of King David, The Day of the Donkey, Song of Praise, My Music - My Songs; numerous other works incl: ITV advertising soundtracks (Venice Award 1962, Cannes Award 1963); film music: Calling Paul Temple, Three Roads to Rome, Against The Tide, Land of Three Rivers; author of radio reviews in The Listener 1975-80; Wavenden Allmusic Media Personality of the Year 1987, TV and Radio Industs Club Award 1988; dep chm Performing Rights Soc 1966-68, memb Royal Albert Hall Cncl of Arts and Sci 1976-, govr Tokyo Metropolis Prize for Radio 1979, memb Exec Cncl Musicians' Benevolent Fund 1985-; Freeman City of London 1982; ARAM 1968, FRSA 1975, FRAM 1978; *Books* Musician at Large (autobiography 1979), My Music (1979), Dear Music Lover (1981), Steve Race's Music Quiz (1983), The Illustrated Counties of England (1984), You Can't be Serious (1985), The Penguin Masterquiz (1985), With Great Pleasure (1986), The Two Worlds of Joseph Race (1988); *Style—* Steve Race, Esq; Martins End Lane, Great Missenden, Bucks HP16 9HS

RACK, Prof Peter Michael Horsman; s of Ralph Skinner Rack, and Elsie, *née* Horsman; *b* 27 Oct 1928; *Educ* Ackworth Sch, Bootham Sch, Univ of Cambridge (MA, MB BCh); *m* 17 Nov 1956, Brenda Mavis, da of Frank Hemsley; 4 da (Mary b 1959, Jane (Mrs Fenna) b 1960, Lucy b 1965, Eleanor b 1967); *Career* MO Nat Serv RAMC 1954-56; house offr London Hosp 1953-54, registrar and sr registrar posts in NHS Hosps in London Cardiff and Birmingham 1957-65, lectr Univ of Birmingham 1965-83, prof of experimental neurology Univ of Birmingham 1984, author of numerous papers in jls on med topics; ed for Physiological Soc 1977-84; memb Physiological Soc; FRCS; *Recreations* music, mountaineering; *Style—* Prof Peter Rack; The Medical School, Edgbaston, Birmingham B15 2TJ (☎ 021 414 6920, fax 021 414 6924)

RADA, Prof Roy; s of Col Roy Rada, of Denver, Colorado; *b* 13 June 1951; *Educ* Univ of Illinois Urbana (PhD), Univ of Yale (BA), Univ of Houston (MD), Baylor Coll of Med (MD); *Career* instr in computer sci Univ of Houston 1977, asst prof computer sci Wayne State Univ 1981-84, ed Index Medicus Nat Library of Med 1985-88 (res offr 1984-85), chair of computer sci Univ of Liverpool 1988; memb Assoc of Computing Machinery; *Books* Machine Learning (1986), Hypertext (1990); *Style—* Prof Roy Rada; Department of Computer Science, Chadwick Tower, University of Liverpool, Liverpool L69 3BX (☎ 051 794 3669, fax 051 794 3759, telex 627095 UNILPL G)

RADCLIFFE, David Andrew; s of Clinton Bower Radcliffe, and Margaret, *née* Turnbull; *b* 13 June 1942; *Educ* The Leys Sch Cambridge, Univ of Cambridge (MA); *m* 22 May 1971, Elisabeth Mary, da of David Scotson Bramley; 2 s (James b 11 Nov 1975, Matthew b 5 Jan 1981), 1 da (Emily b 7 Feb 1978); *Career* cmmnd RM Reserve 1967, ret 1971; called to the Bar Inner Temple 1966; recorder Crown Court 1987-; vice pres Putney Soc 1987- (chm 1983-85); *Recreations* golf, tennis, squash, swimming, walking; *Clubs* Roehampton; *Style—* David Radcliffe, Esq; 5 King's Bench Walk, Temple, London EC4Y 7DN (☎ 071 353 4713, fax 071 353 5459)

RADCLIFFE, Hugh John Reginald Joseph; MBE (1944); s of late Sir Everard Radcliffe, 5 Bt; hp of nephew, Sir Sebastian Radcliffe, 7 Bt; *b* 3 March 1911; *Educ* Downside; *m* 15 April 1937, Marie Thérèse, yst da of Maj-Gen Sir Cecil Edward Pereira, KCB, CMG; 5 s, 1 da; *Career* served WWII London Scottish, G1 (technical) AA cmd Lt Col; co dir; dep chm London Stock Exchange 1967-70; Kt Order of St Gregory the Great (Papal) 1984; Kt Cdr Order of St Silvester (Papal) 1965; *Style—* Hugh Radcliffe, Esq, MBE; The White House, Stoke, Andover, Hants

RADCLIFFE, Julian Guy Yonge; TD; s of Maj G L Y Radcliffe, MBE; *b* 29 Aug 1948; *Educ* Eton, New Coll Oxford; *m* Francis Harriet Thompson; 2 s, 1 da; *Career* Lloyd's broker and underwriting memb of Lloyd's; md: Investmt Insurance Int 1973, Control Risks Ltd; dir: Credit Insurance Assoc Ltd 1975, Hogg Group plc; cmmnd Royal Yeomanry 1971, Maj 1980; *Recreations* farming, shooting, military and strategic studies; *Clubs* City of London, Carlton, Cavalry and Guards; *Style—* Julian Radcliffe, Esq, TD; 32 Brynmaer Rd, SW11 4EW; Lower Stanway, Much Wenlock, Shropshire TF13 6LD (☎ 06943 223)

RADCLIFFE, Mark Hugh Joseph; s of Hugh John Reginald Joseph Radcliffe, MBE, of Andover, Hants, and Marie Therese, *née* Pereira; *Educ* Downside; *m* 20 Feb 1963, Anne, da of Maj-Gen A E Brocklehurst, CB, DSO; 3 da (Lucinda b 1964, Emily Marie Louise b 1968, Camilla Mary b 1971); *Career* 2 Lt Coldstream Gds 1956-58; mktg mangr Cape Asbestos Ltd plc 1958-68, chief exec Lancer Boss Gp Ltd 1968-74, md Triang Pedigree Ltd 1974-78, dir TI Gp plc 1978-, currently pres and md John Crane Int; FInstD; *Recreations* shooting, golf, tennis, gardening; *Clubs* Guards and Calvalry; *Style—* Mark Radcliffe, Esq; The Malt House, Upton, nr Andover, Hants (☎ 026 476 266); Foxcombe Court, Abingdon Business Park, Abingdon, Oxon OX14 1D2 (☎ 0235 555757, fax 0235 555818)

RADCLIFFE, Michael Francis; s of John Maurice Radcliffe (d 1949), of Almondsbury, nr Bristol, and Margery Bloomfield, *née* Lumsden (d 1974); *b* 8 March 1940; *Educ* Cheltenham, Clare Coll Cambridge (MA), Carnegie Mellon Univ Pittsburgh USA (MSc); *m* 13 June 1964, Gillian Mary, da of Reginald Harvey (d 1985), of Bishops Cleeve; 2 da (Abigail Sarah b 20 Sept 1968, Jessica Jane b 21 May 1970); *Career* Br Oxygen Co Ltd 1962-71, fin controller Plessey Telecommunications Ltd 1971-78, fin dir Brush Electrical Machines Ltd 1978-85, md Brush Transformers Ltd 1985-; dir: Crompton Greaves Ltd Bombay 1986-, Brush Electrical Engrg Co Ltd 1989-; FBIM 1979, FIMEMME 1985, FInstD 1986; *Recreations* golf; *Style—* Michael Radcliffe, Esq; 1 Manor Park, Ruddington, Nottingham NG11 6DS (☎ 0602 213776); Brush Transformers Ltd, PO Box 20, Loughborough, Leics LE11 1HN (☎ 0509 611411, fax

0509 610721, telex 341094 BTZ G)

RADCLIFFE, Neville Browne; s of James Radcliffe (d 1961), of Nelson, Lancs, and Edith Elizabeth Radcliffe (d 1984), of Nelson, Lancs; *b* 21 Aug 1932; *Educ* Colne GS Victoria, Univ of Manchester (LLB); *m* 5 April 1958, Mabel, da of John William Taylor Holmes (d 1961), of Nelson Lancs; 2 da (Jacqueline Ann (Jackie) b 1965, Nicola Jane Radcliffe (Nikki) b 1969); *Career* admitted slr 1957; Messrs Browne Jacobson Slrs Nottingham: litigation asst 1957, ptnr 1961, sr litigation ptnr and sr ptnr; pres Nottinghamshire Law Soc 1988-89, inaugural pres Nottinghamshire Medico-Legal Soc 1988, area chm (E Midlands) Area Legal Aid Ctee; former visiting lectr in law Univ of Nottingham, former memb Cncl of Legal Studies Univ of Nottingham and Poly, memb Univ of Nottingham Hosp Ethical Cmmn; vice pres Nottingham RFC; memb Law Soc; *Recreations* fell-walking, gardening, music, travel, sport, reading; *Clubs* Nottingham & Notts Utd Services; *Style—* Neville Radcliffe, Esq; 58 Firs Rd, Edwalton, Nottinghamshire (☎ 0602 233612); 44 Castle Gate, Nottingham NG1 6EA (☎ 0602 500055, fax 0602 475246)

RADCLIFFE, Percy; JP; s of Arthur and Annie Radcliffe; *b* 14 Nov 1916; *Educ* Ramsey GS; *m* 1942, Barbara Frances, da of William Cannell Crowe; 2 s, 1 da; *Career* farmer; elected IOM Govt 1963, chm Local Govt Bd 1966-76, chm Finance Bd 1976-81, chm Govt Exec Cncl (prime minister) Isle of Man 1981-; *Recreations* horse driving (Holypark Sensation); *Style—* Percy Radcliffe Esq, JP, MLC; Kellaway, Sulby, Isle of Man (☎ 064 89 7257); Government Office, Douglas, Isle of Man (☎ 0786 26262)

RADCLIFFE, Sir Sebastian Everard; 7 Bt (UK 1813); s of Capt Sir (Joseph Benedict) Everard Henry, 6 Bt, MC (d 1975); *b* 8 June 1972; *Heir* unc, Hugh Radcliffe, MBE; *Style—* Sir Sebastian Radcliffe, Bt

RADCLYFFE, Sarah; da of Capt Charles Raymond Radclyffe, of Lew House, Lew, Nr Bampton, Oxon, and Helen Viola Egerton, *née* Cotton; *b* 14 Nov 1950; *Educ* Heathfield Sch Ascot Berks; *Career* film prodr 1978-; films incl: My Beautiful Laundrette 1985, Caravaggio 1985, Wish You Were Here 1986, Sammy and Rosie Get Laid 1987, A World Apart 1988, Paperhouse 1989, Fools of Fortune 1990, Robin Hood 1991; *Style—* Miss Sarah Radclyffe; 15 Shirlock Rd, London NW3 2HR; 1 Water Lane, Kentish Town Rd, London NW1 8NZ (☎ 071 911 6100, fax 071 911 6150, telex 914106 WORKING)

RADFORD, Prof Colin Buchanan; s of Walter Buchan Radford, of London, and Elizabeth Robertson, *née* Collie; *b* 28 May 1931; *Educ* Ashby-de-la-Zouch Boys GS, RMA Sandhurst, Univ of Nottingham (BA, MA, PhD); *m* 5 April 1958, Ingeborg Sara (Inge), da of Chaim Frenkel (d 1938), of Vienna; 1 s (Tim b 23 Feb 1963), 1 da (Katy b 24 April 1961); *Career* cmmnd RA 1952, served 1952-57; asst head of recruitment for employee rels Esso Petroleum 1961-62, head of modern languages Up Holland GS 1962-66; Queen's Univ Belfast: prof of French 1975-, dir Sch of Modern and Medieval Languages 1987-; author of books incl four on French Lit; memb: Arts Cncl of NI, Br Inst in Paris; memb and hon treas Soc French Studies 1972-; Commandeur dans l'Ordre des Palmes Acadèmiques France 1989 (Officier 1986); *Recreations* squash, theatre, gardener's mate; *Style—* Prof Colin Radford; The Hill, Woburn Rd, Millisle, Co Down (☎ 0247 861361); Queen's University, Belfast BT7 1NN (☎ 0232 245133)

RADFORD, David Wyn; s of Robert Edwin Radford, CB, of Guildford, Surrey, and Eleanor Margaret, *née* Jones; *b* 3 Jan 1947; *Educ* Cranleigh Sch, Selwyn Coll Cambridge (MA, LLM); *m* 23 Sept 1972, Nadine, da of Joseph Poggioli, of London; 2 s (Simon b 1982, Peter b 1983), 2 da (Carina b 1975, Lauren b 1986); *Career* called to the Bar Gray's Inn 1969, asst rec 1988-; Lib Parly candidate Hampstead 1975-83; *Recreations* following soccer, politics, theatre; *Style—* David Radford, Esq; 1 Gray's Inn Sq, Gray's Inn, London WC1R 5AG (☎ 071 404 5416, fax 071 405 9942)

RADFORD, John Davenport; s of Vaughan Nattrass Radford (d 1988), of Epperstone, Notts, and Beatrice Mary, *née* Bullivant; *b* 8 Sept 1923; *Educ* Oundle; *m* 10 Nov 1948, Angela, da of Maj Frederick William Cooper (d 1960), of Carcolston Notts; 1 s (Stephen b 1959), 2 da (Diana b 1952, Philippa b 1954); *Career* RN 1943-46; md Stag Furniture plc 1970-83 (joined 1947); chm Convent Hosp Nottingham, cncl memb Southwell Minster; High Sheriff Notts; Master Worshipful Company of Furniture Makers 1987; *Recreations* yachting, country sports; *Clubs* Royal Thames Yacht, Royal Lymington Yacht, Nottingham & Notts United Services; *Style—* John D Radford, Esq; Stag Furniture Holdings plc, Haydn Road, Nottingham (☎ 0602 605007)

RADFORD, Jonathan Vaughan; s of Patrick Vaughan Radford, CBE, MC, TD, DL, of Langford Hall, Newark, Notts, and Evelyn, *née* Wilkinson; *b* 11 June 1959; *Educ* Eton, Univ of Bristol (BA); *Career* accountant; Peat Marwick Mitchell and Co London 1981-86, Stag Furniture Holdings plc 1986-; former memb Governing Bd Young NACF; Freeman City of London 1987, Liveryman Worshipful Co of Furniture Makers 1987; ACA 1984, ACIS 1990; *Recreations* shooting, skiing, tennis, art, travel; *Clubs* Annabels; *Style—* Jonathan Radford, Esq; Stag Furniture Holdings plc, Haydn Rd, Nottingham NG5 1DU (☎ 0602 605007)

RADFORD, (Oswald) Michael James; s of Oswald Charles Radford, of Haslemere, Surrey, and Ruth, *née* Presser; *b* 24 Feb 1946; *Educ* Bedford Sch, Worcester Coll Oxford (BA), Nat Film and TV Sch; *m* 4 Aug 1990, Iseult Joanna, *née* St Aubin de Teran; *Career* freelance film dir 1979-; documentary films for BBC TV incl: The Madonna and The Volcano (Grand Prix Nyon Documentary Film Festival 1979), The Last Stronghold of the Pure Gospel, La Belle Isobel, The White Bird Passes (Scot Acad award 1980); Feature Films: Another Time, Another Place (Best Film award Cannes Film Festival 1983, Special Jury prize Celtic Film Festival 1983, George Sadoul prize Paris for Best Foreign Film 1982, Nineteen Eighty Four (Standard Best Film of the Year award 1984) 1984, White Mischief 1988; govr Nat Film and TV Sch 1982-90; memb BAFTA; *Recreations* fishing, skiing, snooker; *Clubs* Groucho's; *Style—* Michael Radford, Esq; Linaa Siefert Associates, 18 Ladbroke Terrace, London W11 3PG (☎ 071 229 5163, fax 071 221 0637)

RADFORD, Neal Victor; s of Victor Reginald Radford, of Johannesburg, SA, and Joyce Edith, *née* Osler; *b* 7 June 1957; *Educ* Athlone Boys HS Johannesburg SA; *m* 20 April 1985, Lynne Mary, da of Lawrence Middleton; 2 s (Luke Anthony b 3 June 1988, Josh Deckland b 12 Feb 1990); *Career* professional cricketer; schoolboy teams: Transvaal SA 1974-75, SA Schs 1975-76; SA Army 1978, first class Transvaal 1978-89; Lancs League: Bacup 1979-80, Nelson 1981, Ramsbottom 1983; Lancashire CCC 1980-84; Worcestershire CCC 1985-: awarded county cap 1985, 113 first class appearances (214 career), 121 one day appearances (240 career), 452 first class wickets (787 career); England: 3 Test matches (v India Edgbaston 1986, NZ Lords 1986, NZ Auckland 1987), 6 one day Ints (4 v NZ 1987, 1 v Aust 1987, 1 v W Indies 1988); honours with Worcestershire CCC: Co Championship 1988 and 1989, NatWest Trophy runners up 1988, Refuge Assurance League 1987 and 1988; record for most wickets in a season 1985 (101) and 1987 (109); Esso/Mail on Sunday bowler of the year 1985, Cricketers' cricketer of the year 1985, Wisden cricketer of the year 1985, Mail on Sunday bowler of the year 1987, Worcestershire CCC player of the year 1987; Army SA 1977-78, auditor SA 1979-81, cricket coach SA 1981-89, PR and promotional work Spectrum Organisation Wilts 1990-91; *Recreations* enjoying home comforts with my family, pottering around in the garden, playing golf and other sports; *Style—* Neal Radford, Esq; Worcestershire CCC, County Ground, New Rd, Worcester (☎ 0905 422 694)

RADFORD, Patrick Vaughan; CBE (1983), MC (1945), TD, DL (1987); s of Vaughan Nattras Radford (d 1988), and Beatrice Mary, *née* Bullivant (d 1978); *b* 16 Nov 1920; *Educ* Oundle; *m* 1, 1945 (m dis 1956), Nancy Madeline, *née* Shaw; 1 da (Carol b 1946); m 2, 1956, Evelyn Lily, da of George Herbert Wilkinson (d 1971); 4 s (Nicholas b 1957, Jonathan b 1959, Timothy b 1960, Anthony b 1962), 1 step da (Anthea b 1947); *Career* Nat Serv WWII, joined RAC 1941, cmmnd 2 Lt 1942, served 1 Derby Yeo in UK, N Africa, Italy, Austria 1942-46, joined Derby Yeo TA 1947 (Maj), 2i/c Leics and Derbys Yeo TA 1956, Lt-Col 1958-61; called to the Bar Grays Inn 1954; chm Stag Furniture Holdings PLC 1971-; govr Trent Coll; gen cmmr for Income Tax; Liveryman Worshipful Co of Furniture Makers 1963 (Master 1982-83); FCIS; *Recreations* country sports, fishing, shooting; *Clubs* Cavalry & Guards, Nottingham United Servs; *Style—* Patrick Radford, Esq, CBE, MC, TD, DL; Langford Hall, Newark, Notts NG23 7RS (☎ 0636 76802); Stag Furniture Holdings PLC, Haydn Rd, Nottingham (☎ 0602 605007)

RADFORD, Sir Ronald Walter; KCB (1976, CB 1971), MBE (1947); s of George Leonard Radford (d 1959), and Ethel Mary Radford (d 1971); *b* 28 Feb 1916; *Educ* Southend-on-Sea HS, St John's Coll Cambridge (MA); *m* 1949, Jean Alison Dunlop, da of Lawrence Harold Strange (d 1954); 1 s, 1 da; *Career* served with Indian Civil Serv 1939-47; HM Customs and Excise: asst princ 1947, princ 1948, asst sec 1953-65, cmmr and sec 1965-70, dep chm 1970-73, chm 1973-77; sec-gen Customs Co-op Cncl 1978-83 (hon sec gen 1983-); *Clubs* Reform, MCC, Civil Service; *Style—* Sir Ronald Radford, KCB, MBE; 4 Thomas Close, Brentwood, Essex CM15 8BS (☎ 0277 211567)

RADICE, Giles Heneage; MP (Lab) North Durham 1983-; s of Lawrence Radice (himself s of Evadio Radice) and Patricia (eldest da of Sir Arthur Pelham Heneage, DSO, JP, DL, sometime MP for Louth); *b* 4 Oct 1936; *Educ* Winchester, Magdalen Coll Oxford; *m* 1959, Penelope, er da of late Robert Angus, JP, DL, of Ladykirk, Ayrshire, by his w (subsequently Lady Moore); 2 da (Adele b 1961, Sophia b 1964); *Career* former head GMWU Res Dept, MP (Lab) Chester-le-Street March 1973-1983, chm Manifesto Gp in Labour Party, memb Cncl Policy Studies Institute 1978-, oppn front bench spokesman Employment 1981-Nov 1983, memb Shadow Cabinet Nov 1983-; *Style—* Giles Radice Esq, MP; 40 Inverness St, London NW1

RADLEY, (Herbert) Arthur Farrand; MBE (1946); s of John Charles Radley (d 1927), of Rusholme, Manchester, and Helen Louise, *née* Howell (d 1959); *b* 16 June 1916; *Educ* Friends' Sch Saffron Walden, Leighton Park, St Edmund Hall Oxford (MA), Sorbonne Paris; *m* 17 May 1947 (m dis 1950), Gisela, da of Stefan Fritz Ingenieur (d 1980), of Weiz, Austria; *Career* English asst Lycée Lakanal Sceaux Paris 1938-39, asst modern language master Watford GS 1939; enlistment TA, Rifleman (Artists Rifles) 1939, served Malta GC 1941-44 (incl ADC to GOC), memb Special Forces Exec SOE ops in France and Italy 1944-45, HQ Eighth Army and V Corps; involved: Mil Govt Land Steiermark 1945-46, Allied Cmmn for Austria, Political Div Vienna 1946-47, released as Maj XX Lancs Fus 1947; asst head Visitors Dept Br Cncl 1947-50; BBC 1950-76: orgn and methods 1950-60, organiser TV music 1960-65, TV gen features 1965-70, mgmnt servs 1970-76; has broadcast on: French radio, BBC German Serv, BBC World Serv; lectr 1976, subjects incl: architecture (Georgian and Euro baroque), industl archaeology (Royal Dockyards and Victualling Yards); Grosses Goldenes Ehrenzeichen (Grand Gold medal) of Styria Austria 1985; memb: Exec Ctee Anglo-Austrian Soc, London Gp Ctee, Railway and Canal Historical Soc; vice pres London Branch Inland Waterways Assoc; MIPM (exec memb Cncl 1952-55), FInstAM 1967 (chm London Branch 1961-63); *Recreations* travel and photography, chess, chamber music and choral singing, archiving, protocol; *Clubs* Special Forces; *Style—* Arthur Farrand Radley, Esq, MBE; 157 Holland Park Ave, London W11 4UX (☎ 071 603 6062)

RADLEY, Eric John; s of Rev John Benjamin Radley (d 1942), and Florence Sophia, *née* Roberts; *b* 12 June 1917; *Educ* Eltham Coll, London Univ (BA); *m* 28 Aug 1948, Margaret Elisabeth, da of Leonard Munro Cobb (d 1958), of Cliftonville; 1 s (Peter Benjamin b 1949), 3 da (Helen Margaret (Mrs Penfold) b 1953, Mary Elisabeth b 1954, Rosemary Ann (Mrs Whittle) b 1959); *Career* farm business Elton Newham Glos, lectr W Glos Coll 1962-79; sec: Littledean Utd Reform Church 1951-88, Forest of Dean Utd Reform Church 1962-88; parly candidate 1959; memb: Glos RDC 1955-62, Glos CC 1981- (chm 1985-); *Books* Notes on Economic History (1967), Objective Tests in Economic History (1979), A Country Diary from the Forest of Dean (1984); *Recreations* gardening for flowers, literature, theatre, cricket; *Style—* Eric Radley, Esq; Elton Farm, Newnham on Severn, Glos GL14 1JJ (☎ 045 276 239)

RADLEY, Gordon Charles; s of Ronald Neterfield Radley, and Diana, *née* Nairn; *b* 26 March 1953; *Educ* Bromley GS, Stockwell Coll of Educn, Highbury Coll; *m* 4 May 1985, Joan Elizabeth, da of Keith Smith, of Polegate, Sussex; *Career* promotion scriptwriter HTV 1974-76, promotion prodr Anglia TV 1977-78; presenter: Grampian TV 1979, Points West BBC TV West 1979-81, TVS 1981-85; presenter and reporter South Today BBC TV South, presenter, newsreader and reporter Anglia News Anglia TV 1988-90; freelance presenter, reporter and prodr: satellite TV, BBC, ITV; *Recreations* country pursuits, horticulture, cycling, keeping fit, entertaining at home; *Style—* Gordon Radley, Esq; 22 Bassett Row, Bassett, Southampton (☎ 0703 760322)

RADNOR, Dowager Countess of; Anne Isobel Graham Pleydell-Bouverie; OBE (1961), DL (Wiltshire 1987); da of Lt-Col Richard Oakley, DSO, JP (d 1948), and Enid Elizabeth (d 1980), da of James Noble Graham, JP, DL (of the senior cadet branch of the Ducal family of Montrose); *b* 6 Sept 1908; *m* 1, 1931, Richard Sowerby (d 1939), er s of Lt-Col Thomas Sowerby, JP, of The Manor House, Lilley, Herts; m 2, 1943, as his 2 w, 7 Earl of Radnor, KG, KCVO, JP, DL (d 1968); 1 s (Richard Oakley); *Career* memb: Historic Buildings Cncl for England 1953-68, advsy bd for Redundant Churches 1969-79; tstee Historic Churches Preservation Tst; pres: Health Visitors' Assoc 1963-84, Wilts Tst for Nature Conservation, Wilts Community Cncl, Salisbury-South Wilts Museum; former pres: Assoc of Wilts Parish Cncls, Wilts Assoc of Youth Clubs; *Style—* The Rt Hon the Dowager Countess of Radnor, OBE, DL; Avonturn, Alderbury, Salisbury (☎ 0722 710235)

RADNOR, 8 Earl of (GB 1765); Sir Jacob Pleydell-Bouverie; 11 Bt (GB 1714); also Viscount Folkestone, Baron Longford (both GB 1747), and Baron Pleydell-Bouverie (GB 1765); patron of two livings; s of 7 Earl of Radnor, KG, KCVO (d 1968), and his 1 w, Helena (who m 2, 1943, Brig Montacute William Worrell Selby-Lowndes, and d 1985), da of late Charles Adeane, CB (whose w Madeline, CBE, JP, was gda of 1 Baron Leconfield); *b* 10 Nov 1927; *Educ* Harrow, Trinity Coll Cambridge; *m* 1, 1953 (m dis 1962), Anne, da of Donald Seth-Smith, MC; 2 s; m 2, 1963 (m dis 1985), Margaret, da of Robin Fleming, of Catter House, Drymen; 4 da; m 3, 1986, Mrs A C Pettit; *Heir* s, Viscount Folkestone; *Career* landowner and farmer; chm Br Dyslexia Assoc 1971-76, pres Dyslexia Fndn 1975-, memb House of Lords Select Ctee (agriculture, food and consumer affrs) 1985-90; *Recreations* field sports; *Clubs* White's, Farmers; *Style—* The Rt Hon the Earl of Radnor; Longford Castle, Salisbury, Wilts SP5 4EF (☎ 0722 411515)

RADOMIR, Hon Mrs (Sarah Elizabeth); *née* Marks; da of 2 Baron Marks of Broughton; *b* 1953; *m* 1979 (m dis 1989), Nicholai Radomir; 2 s (Michael Richard b 1981, Leo Mark b 1985); *Style—* The Hon Mrs Radomir

RAE, Allan Alexander Sinclair; CBE (1973); s of John Rae (d 1969), of Ayr, and Rachel Margaret, *née* Sinclair (d 1969); *b* 26 Nov 1925; *Educ* Ayr Acad, Univ of Glasgow (LLB); *m* 1, 1 June 1955, Shelia Grace (d 1985), da of Capt Geoffrey Saunders, OBE, RN (d 1948); 2 s (Nigel b 1956, David b 1961), 1 da (Susan b 1962); m 2, 7 April 1986, Gertrud, da of Arnold Dollinger (d 1972), of Basle, Switzerland; *Career* Staff Capt RA JAG Dept 1944-47; slr; sr ptnr Crawford Bayley & Co Bombay 1959-64 (joined 1948, ptnr 1950-59), dir and head of Legal and Patents Dept CIBA Ltd Basle 1964-69, dir and head of Regnl Servs CIBA-GEIGY Ltd Basle 1969-72, memb Exec Ctee CIBA-GEIGY AG Basle 1972-88, chm CIBA-GEIGY Gp of Cos UK 1972-90, Ilford Ltd 1972-88; dir: ABB Power Ltd 1973-89, Williams & Glyn's Bank 1974-85, T & N plc 1979-, ABB Kent (Hldgs) plc 1980-, Mettler Instruments Ltd 1985-89, Riggs AP Bank Ltd 1986-; pres Chemical Industs Assoc Ltd 1986-88 (vice pres 1984-86, memb Cncl 1975-); vice pres Business and Industry Advsy Ctee OECD 1985-; companion BIM; *Recreations* sailing, skiing, golf; *Clubs* Buck's, Royal Thames Yacht, Sunningdale Golf; *Style—* Allan Rae, Esq, CBE; Bryn Dulas, Llanddulas, Clywd LL22 8NA (☎ 0492 517501, fax 0492 518088)

RAE, Barbara Davis; da of James Rae, Provost Crieff, of Perthshire (d 1982), and Mary, *née* Young; *b* 1943; *Educ* Morrisons Acad Crieff, Edinburgh Coll of Art, Moray House Coll of Educn (Scot Int Fencer; winner of several Scot championships, Br Jr Foil title, Baptiste Bertrand Cup); *Career* artist; art teacher: Ainsie Park Comp Edinburgh 1968-69, Portobello Secdy Sch Edinburgh 1969-72; lectr in drawing painting and printmaking Aberdeen Coll of Educn 1972-74, lectr in drawing and painting Glasgow Sch of Art 1975, exchange teacher Fine Art Dept Univ of Maryland 1984; solo exhibitions incl: New '57 Gallery Edinburgh 1967 and 1971, Univ of York 1969, Univ of Aberdeen and Aberdeen Art Gallery 1974, Peterloo Gallery Manchester 1975, Stirling Gallery Stirling 1976, Greenock Arts Guild 1976, Gilbert Parr Gallery London 1977, Univ of Edinburgh 1978 and 1979, The Scottish Gallery Edinburgh 1979, 1983, 1987, 1988 and 1990, Wright Gallery Dallas Texas USA 1985, Leinster Fine Art London 1986, Glasgow Print Studio 1987, The Scottish Gallery London and Edinburgh 1989-90; gp exhibitions incl: Contemporary Art from Scotland (touring exhibiton organised by The Scottish Gallery 1981-82), Basle Int Art Fair (with The Scottish Gallery) 1981, Bath Art Fair (with The Scottish Gallery) 1981-83 and 1987-89, Int Contemporary Art Fair (London with Leinster Fine Art) 1984-86, Scottish Landscapes (Santiago Chile) 1985, The Athena Competition Exhibition 1987, 5th Biennial of European Graphic Art (Heidelberg) 1988, ARCO Art Fair Madrid (with The Scottish Gallery) 1990, Monotypes (Glasgow Print Studio) 1990; work in numerous private and pub collections incl: Bank of England, Scot Arts Cncl, HRH Prince Philip, Br Museum, Royal Bank of Scotland, Soc Nat Gallery of Modern Art; *awards* Arts Cncl award 1968, maj Arts Cncl award 1975-81, Guthrie medal RSA 1977, May Marshall Brown award (RSW Centenary Exhibition) 1979, RSA Sir William Gillies prize 1983, Calouste Gulbenkian Printmaking award 1983, Alexander Graham Munro award RSW 1989, Hunting Gp prizewinner 1990, Scottish PO Bd award RSA 1990, Scottish Amicable award RGI 1990; memb: Art Panel CNAA 1986-, RSW Cncl 1986-90; tstee Arts Educn Tst 1986-90; assoc: RSW, RGI; ARSA; *Style—* Ms Barbara Rae; William Jackson Fine Art, 28 Cork St, London

RAE, Dr John; s of John Rae (d 1976), of Rutherglen, Lanarkshire, and Marion, *née* Dow; *b* 29 Sept 1942; *Educ* Rutherglen Acad, Univ of Glasgow (BSc, PhD); *m* 11 May 1968, Irene Isabella, da of William Cassels, of Glasgow; 1 s (Philip John b 23 March 1974), 1 da (Helen Janet b 13 May 1976); *Career* teaching and res in theoretical physics: Univ of Glasgow 1964-68, Univ of Texas Austin 1968-70, Univ Libre Brussels 1970-72, QMC London 1972-74; acting div head theoretical physics div Harwell 1985 (industl fell 1974-76, gp leader theory of fluids 1976-86), chief scientist Dept of Energy 1986-89; chief exec AEA Environment and Energy 1990-; memb: SERC 1986-89, NERC 1986-89; BNES 1985, FInstE 1986; *Recreations* music (singing), gardening; *Style—* Dr John Rae; B551 Harwell Laboratory, Oxon OX11 0RA (☎ 0235 432986, fax 0235 434361)

RAE, Dr John Malcolm; s of Dr Lawrence John Rae, of Walton on the Hill, Surrey, and Annie Blodwen, *née* Williams (d 1977); *b* 20 March 1931; *Educ* Bishop's Stortford Coll, Sidney Sussex Coll Cambridge (MA), King's Coll London (PhD); *m* 31 Dec 1955, Daphne Ray, da of John Phimester Simpson (d 1939), of Edinburgh; 2 s (Shamus, Jonathan (twins)), 4 da (Siobhan, Penelope, Alyce, Emily); *Career* 2 Lt Royal Fus 1950-51; history master Harrow Sch 1955-66, headmaster Taunton Sch 1966-70, headmaster Westminster Sch 1970-86, dir The Laura Ashley Fndn 1986-89, Gresham prof of rhetoric 1988-90; dir: The Portman Group 1989-, The Observer Ltd; author of film script Reach for Glory 1961 (UN award), contrib to nat newspapers; JP Middx 1961-66, memb Ethics Ctee Humana Hosp London, govr of Schs and Colls; Freeman City of London; Hon FCP 1984, FRSA 1988; *Books* The Custard Boys (1960), Conscience and Politics (1970), The Public School Revolution (1980), Letters from School (1987), Too Little, Too Late? (1989); five books for children; *Recreations* cinema, swimming; *Clubs* Hawks (Cambridge), RAC; *Style—* Dr John Rae; 101 Millbank Court, 24 John Islip St, London SW1P 4LG (☎ 071 828 1842)

RAE, John William; er s of Lt-Col William Rae, DSO, VD, CD (d 1973), and Edith Marion, *née* Brodrick (d 1988); *b* 16 Dec 1938; *Educ* Charterhouse, Queen's Coll Oxford (MA); *Career* TA: 2 Lt 5 Bn Queen's Royal Regt 1959-60, Lt 3 Bn Queen's Royal Surrey Regt 1961-63, TA Reserve of Offrs 1963-67; Regular Army Reserve of Offrs (II) 1967-85 and 1988-, HAC (HSF) 1985-88; called to the Bar Inner Temple 1961 (worked way around world 1962-64), int commercial lawyer (German speaker) 1965-78, practising barr 1979-; memb: Exec Ctee Oxford Soc (chm West London Branch 1968-), Guild Church Cncl and Ctee of Friends of St Botolph-without-Aldersgate Church London, Aldersgate Ward Club, St Bart's Hosp Choral Soc, Friends of Holland Park Kensington; Freeman City of London, Master Worshipful Co of Plumbers 1982-83, memb Ct of City Univ, Liveryman Worshipful Co of Painter-Stainers; *Recreations* beagling, cycling, skiing, walking, travel, current affairs, music, photography; *Clubs* Athenaeum, Beefsteak, Coningsby, Canada; *Style—* John W Rae, Esq; 16A Campden Hill Court, Campden Hill Rd, London W8 7HS (☎ 071 937 3492); 2 Paper Buildings, Temple, London EC4Y 7ET (☎ 071 936 2611, fax 071 583 3423, telex 885358 TEMPLE G)

RAE, Kenneth St John; s of Lt Col William Rae, DSO (d 1973), and Edith Marion, *née* Brodrick (d 1988); *b* 2 Oct 1940; *Educ* Charterhouse, Univ of Br Columbia (BCom); *m* 21 March 1969, Sarah Hine, da of Lt Col Phillip Anthony Egerton Dumas, of Matfield, Kent; 1 s (Angus William Brodrick b 1970), 1 da (Isobel Julie Egerton b 1972), 1 step s (James Henry George Pollard b 1964); *Career* Sub Lt Univ Naval Trg Div Canada 1962; economist P & O 1964-68; PA to: chm Anglo Norness 1968-70, gen md JH Fenner 1970-71; dir Davies & Newman 1977- (joined 1971); Freeman: City of London, Worshipful Co of Plumbers (1965); *Recreations* gardening; *Style—* Kenneth Rae, Esq; Wyck House, Wood's Green, Wadhurst, Sussex TN5 6QS (☎ 089 288 2609); Davies & Newman Ltd, New City Ct, 20 St Thomas' St, London (☎ 071 378 6867, fax 071 403 2025, telex 892141)

RAE, Hon Mrs (Penelope Ann); *née* Rippon; yst da of Baron Rippon of Hexham, PC, QC (Life Peer); *b* 5 Oct 1953; *m* 1984, Simon Rae; 1 da (Albertine Helen Yorke b 1985); *Style—* The Hon Mrs Rae

RAE SMITH, David Douglas; CBE (1976), MC (1945); s of Sir Alan Rae Smith, KBE (d 1961), of Copynsfield, Westerham, Kent, and Mabel Grace *née* Eales (d 1963); *b* 15 Nov 1919; *Educ* Radley, ChCh Oxford (MA); *m* 12 April 1947, Margaret Alison, da of James Watson (d 1968), of Holyrood House, Hedon, E Yorks; 3 s (James b 1949, John b 1952, Alan b 1960), 1 da (Katherine b 1957); *Career* Capt RA 1939-46 (despatches), served ME, Italy, France and Germany; CA; sr ptnr Deloitte Haskins & Sells 1973-82 (ptnr 1954-82), Thomas Tilling plc 1982-83, Sandoz Products Ltd 1983-, Bankers Trustee Co Ltd 1984-; hon treas RIIA 1961-81, memb Licensed Dealers Tbnl 1974-88, chm Radley Coll 1976- (memb Cncl 1966-); *Recreations* horse racing, golf; *Clubs* Gresham; *Style—* David Rae Smith, Esq, CBE, MC; Oakdale, Crockham Hill, Edenbridge, Kent (☎ 0732 866220)

RAEBURN, Ashley Reinhard George; CBE (1976); s of Dr Adolf Alsberg (d 1933), of Kassel, Germany, and Elisabeth, *née* Hofmann (d 1949); *b* 23 Dec 1918; *Educ* UCS, Balliol Coll Oxford (MA); *m* 6 Nov 1943, Esther Letitia Vivonne, da of Alfred Johns, of Goodwick, Pembs (d 1957); 1 s (Richard b 1946), 3 da (Ursula b 1944, Joanna b 1949, Charlotte b 1954); *Career* WWII RA (Capt) served in UK and India 1940-46; MOF and HM Treasy 1946-54, Royal Dutch Shell Group 1955-77 (gp treas 1962), dir Shell International Petroleum Co Ltd (responsible for Africa, India and Pakistan) 1968-72, chief rep Shell Cos in Japan 1972-77, dir Rolls Royce Ltd 1978-82 (vice chm rep 1979-), dir Boosey & Hawkes plc 1983-88 (chm 1984-86), dir Amalgamated Metal Corporation plc 1983-; endowment tstee Balliol Coll Oxford 1965-, memb Cncl of Mgmnt Studies Oxford 1965- (now Templeton Coll, chm 1978-85), dir Euro Centre for Pub Affrs 1987-; *Recreations* walking, gardening, music; *Clubs* United Oxford and Cambridge Univs; *Style—* Ashley Raeburn, Esq, CBE

RAEBURN, David Antony; s of Walter Augustus Leopold Raeburn, QC (d 1972), of London, and Dora Adelaide Harvey, *née* Williams; *b* 22 May 1927; *Educ* Charterhouse, ChCh Oxford (MA); *m* 8 April 1961, Mary Faith Fortescue, da of Arthur Hubbard (d 1977), of Harare, Zimbabwe; 2 s (Mark b 1965, Martin b 1967), 1 da (Fiona b 1964); *Career* Nat Serv 1949-51 cmmnd RAEC 1950; asst master: Bristol GS 1951-54, Bradfield Coll 1955-58; head of classics Alleyns Sch Dulwich 1958-62; headmaster: Beckenham and Penge GS (renamed Langley Pk Sch for Boys 1969) 1963-70, Whitgift Sch Croydon 1970-91; treas of HMC 1983-89, pres Jt Assoc of Classical Teachers 1983-85 (dir summer sch in ancient greek 1968-85); FRSA 1969; *Recreations* play production; *Style—* David Raeburn, Esq; Haling House, 38 Haling Park Rd, S Croydon CR2 6NE (☎ 081 688 8114); Whitgift Sch, Haling Park, S Croydon CR2 6YT (☎ 081 688 9222)

RAEBURN, Maj-Gen Sir (William) Digby Manifold; KCVO (1979), CB (1966), DSO (1945), MBE (1941); s of late Sir Ernest Manifold Raeburn, KBE, s of 1 Bt; *b* 6 Aug 1915; *Educ* Winchester, Magdalene Coll Cambridge; *m* 1960, Adeline Margaret, da of late Thomas Selwyn Pryor, MC; *Career* Maj-Gen (ret) late Scots Gds; dir of Combat Devpt (Army) 1963-65, Chief of Staff Allied Forces N Europe 1965-68, Chief Army Instructor Imperial Defence Coll 1968-70, resident govr and keeper of Jewel House of HM Tower of London 1971-79; *Style—* Maj-Gen Sir Digby Raeburn, KCVO, CB, DSO, MBE; 25 St Ann's Terrace, London NW8

RAEBURN, Prof John Alexander; TD (1978); s of Lt-Col Hugh Adair Raeburn, RAMC (d 1975), and Christine Constance, *née* Forbes; *b* 25 June 1941; *Educ* Loretto, Univ of Edinburgh (MB ChB, PhD); *m* 1, 12 Aug 1967 (m dis 1980); 1 s (Hugh Alasdair b 1974), 2 da (Morag Elspeth Jean b 1969, Alison Forbes b 1971); m 2, 17 May 1980, Arlene Rose, da of George Conway, MBE, of Edinburgh ; 2 s (Kenneth Robert Aitchison b 1970, Ian George Aitchison b 1972); *Career* Maj TA & VR RAMC; sr res fell Univ of Leiden 1972-73, sr lectr in human genetics Univ of Edinburgh 1973-89; prof clinical genetics Univ of Nottingham; former chm: Scot Downs Syndrome Assoc, Scot Cncl Cystic Fibrosis Res Tst; FRCPE 1976; *Recreations* Scottish literature, fishing; *Style—* Prof John Raeburn, TD; Centre for Medical Genetics, City Hospital, Hucknall Rd, Nottingham (☎ 0602 627728)

RAEBURN, (Sir) Michael Edward Norman; (4 Bt, UK 1923, but does not use his title); s of Sir Edward Alfred Raeburn, 3 Bt (d 1977), and Joan, da of Frederick Hill, of Boston, USA; *b* 12 Nov 1954; *m* 1979, Penelope Henrietta Theodora, da of Alfred Louis Penn (d 1963), of London; 2 s, 2 da; *Heir* s, Christopher Edward Alfred Raeburn b 4 Dec 1981; *Career* civil servant; *Style—* Michael Raeburn, Esq; Little Spring Cottage, Fletching Street, Mayfield, East Sussex TN20 6TN; HM Land Registry, Curtis House, Forest Rd, Hawkenbury, Tunbridge Wells, Kent

RAFFAN, Keith William Twort; MP (C) Delyn 1983-; s of Alfred William Raffan, TD, and Jean Crampton, *née* Twort; *b* 21 June 1949; *Educ* Robert Gordon's Coll Aberdeen, Trinity Coll Glenalmond, Corpus Christi Coll Cambridge (MA); *Career* Parly corr Daily Express 1981-83; Parly candidate (C): Dulwich Feb 1974, E Aberdeenshire Oct 1974; memb Select Ctee on Welsh Affrs 1983-, introduced Controlled Drugs (Penalties) Act 1985; pres: Wales Young Cons 1987-90, Wales Cons Trade Unionists 1984-87; memb NUJ; *Clubs* Carlton, Chelsea Arts, RAC, Flint Cons, Prestatyn Cons; *Style—* Keith Raffan, Esq, MP; House of Commons, London SW1A 0AA

RAFFAN, Mark Thomas; s of Albert Smith Raffan, of Maidstone, Kent, and Joan, *née* Martin; *b* 18 May 1963; *Educ* Knoll Sch for Boys Hove Sussex, Brighton Tech Coll (catering certs); *Career* apprentice Eaton Restaurant Eaton Gardens Hove 1978-81, commis chef then chef de partie Gravetye Manor Hotel 1981-85, chef de partie Walper Terrace Hotel Kitchener Ontario Canada 1985, training Le Gavaroche London 1985-86, chef de cuisine Gravetye Manor Hotel 1989- (jr sous chef 1986, sous chef 1987-88); winner: Gold medal South Eastern Salon culiner 1979, Acorn award 1990, 1 star Arrow Egon Ronay 1991, 3 out of 5 Good Food Guide 1991, Clover award Ackerman Guide 1991; *Recreations* shooting, skiing, squash; *Style—* Mark Raffan, Esq; Apartment 2, The Abbey, Hammerwood Road, Ashurstwood, nr East Grinstead, West Sussex RH19 3SA (☎ 034282 3617); Gravetye Manor Hotel, Vowles Lane, nr East Grinstead, West Sussex RH19 4LJ (☎ 0342 810496, fax 0342 810080, telex 957239)

RAFIQUE, (Syed) Tariq Daud; s of Syed Ahmad Rafique, of Ealing, London, and Margaret Eddy, *née* Hawes; *b* 27 Sept 1937; *Educ* Karachi GS, Christ's Coll Cambridge (BA); *m* 1, 27 April 1964 (m dis 1988); 1 s (Zafar b 15 Jan 1982), 2 da (Johanara b 28 Aug 1973, Hafsa b 27 March 1980); m 2, 7 Aug 1989, Farida Hayyati, da of Abdul Mohamed, of Malaysia; *Career* called to the Bar Lincoln's Inn 1961; in practice: Pakistan High Ct 1961-71, London civil and criminal law 1971-; memb Lab Pty (candidate local elections Finchley); vice-chm: E London Mosque Tst, Race Rels Ctee Bar; chm Moslem Lawyers Assoc; *Recreations* tennis, swimming, golf; *Clubs* Royal Cwlth Soc; *Style—* Tariq Rafique, Esq

RAFTERY, Andrew Thomas; s of Andrew Raftery (d 1987), of York, and Nora Maria, *née* Kelly; *b* 29 June 1943; *Educ* St Michaels Jesuit Coll, Univ of Leeds Sch of Med (BSc, MB ChB, MD); *m* 6 Aug 1980, Anne Christine, da of Norman Turnock, of Buxton; 2 s (Andrew b 1985, Dominic b 1989), 1 da (Catherine b 1981); *Career* lectr in anatomy Univ of Leeds 1970-73, surgical registrar Yorkshire Health Authy 1974-75, lectr in surgery Univ of Manchester 1976-80, lectr in surgery and hon conslt Univ of Cambridge 1980-83, conslt surgn (vascular surgery and transplantation) Sheffield Health Authy 1983-, external examiner in surgery Univ of Cambridge 1983-; examiner primary: FRCS England 1985-, FRCS Glasgow 1989-; numerous contribs to books and jls; MI Biol, FRCS (Eng); *Recreations* horse racing, theatre, water colour painting;

Style— Andrew Raftery, Esq; Renal Unit, Northern General Hospital, Herries Rd, Sheffield S5 7AU (☎ 0742 434343)

RAGEH, His Excellency Ahmed Abdo; *Career* The Republic of Yemen ambassador to the Ct of St James 1987-; His Excellency Ahmed Rageh, Ambassador of the Republic of Yemen; Embassy of the Republic of Yemen, 41 South Street, London W1Y 5PD (☎ 071 629 9905, 071 499 1521)

RAGLAN, 5 Baron (UK 1852); FitzRoy John Somerset; JP (Monmouthshire, now Gwent, 1958), DL (1971); s of 4 Baron Raglan, JP (d 1964; who was descended from 5 Duke of Beaufort), and Hon Julia Hamilton, da of 11 Lord Belhaven and Stenton; *b* 8 Nov 1927; *Educ* Westminster, Magdalen Coll Oxford, RAC Cirencester; *m* 1973 (m dis), Alice (who m 1981, Ian, s of Capt Evan Williams, of Co Limerick), yr da of Peter Baily, of Gt Whittington, Northumberland; *Heir* bro, Hon Geoffrey Somerset; *Career* sits as SDP peer in House of Lords; Capt Welsh Gds; chm: Cwmbran New Town Devpt Corpn 1970-83, Courtyard Arts Tst 1974-, Bath Preservation Trust 1975-77, Bath Soc 1977-, Bugatti Owners' Club 1988-; pres: Bath Centre Nat Tst, UK Housing Trust 1982- (chm S Wales Region 1976-89), Usk Civic Soc; memb Sub-Ctee D (Food and Agric) of House of Lords Ctee on European Communities 1974-85 and 1987- (chm 1976-78); patron: Usk Farmers' Club, Raglan Baroque Players; *Style—* The Rt Hon the Lord Raglan, JP, DL; Cefntilla, Usk, Gwent (☎ 029 13 2050)

RAI, Dr Gurcharan Singh; s of Gurdev Singh Rai, of London, and Kartar Kaur Rai; *b* 30 July 1947; *Educ* Tollington GS London, Univ of Newcastle-upon-Tyne (MBBS, MD), Univ of London (MSc); *m* 8 Nov 1977, Harsha da of Shon Lal Bhetie (d 1980), of India; 2 s (Sandeep b 30 Sept 1978, Gordeep b 18 Nov 1981); *Career* house offr Nottingham Gen Hosp 1971-72, registrar in med Newcastle Univ Hosp 1974-76 (sr house offr 1972-73), sr res assoc Univ of Newcastle-upon-Tyne 1976-78, sr registrar gen med Chesterton Hosp Cambridge 1978-80; conslt physician: Whittington Hosp 1980-, Royal Northern Hosp 1980-, Middx Med Sch 1980-; chm Regnl Advsy Cmmn Geriatric Med NE Thames Region; FRCP 1988; *Books* Databook On Geriatrics (1980), Case Presentations In Clinical Geriatric Medicine (1987), Manual of Geriatric Medicine (1991); *Recreations* chess, stamp collecting; *Style—* Dr Gurcharan Rai; Whittington Hosp, Highgate Hill, London N19 5NF (☎ 071 272 3070)

RAIKES, Vice Adm Sir Iwan Geoffrey; KCB (1976), CBE (1967), DSC (1943), DL (Powys 1983); s of Adm Sir Robert Henry Taunton Raikes, KCB, CVO, DSO (d 1953), and Ida Guinevere, *née* Evans (d 1983); *b* 21 April 1921; *Educ* RNC Dartmouth; *m* 1947, Cecilia Primrose, da of Philip Gerald Benedict Hunt (d 1958), of Woodhayes, Woodlands, Southampton; 1 s, 1 da; *Career* RN 1935, HMS Beagle Atlantic convoys 1941, submarines Atlantic, Mediterranean and North Sea 1942-45; cmd HM Submarines: H43 1943-44, Varne 1944-45, Virtue 1945-46, Talent 1948-49, Aeneas 1951-52; Cdr 1952, staff of C-in-C Allied Forces Mediterranean 1953-55, exec offr HMS Newcastle (Far East) 1955-57, JSSC 1957, Capt 1960, cmd HMS Loch Insh (Persian Gulf) 1961-62, dep dir Undersurface Warfare MOD 1962-64, dir plans and Operations (Singapore) on staff of C-in-C Far East 1965-66, IDC 1967, cmd HMS Kent 1968-69, ADC to HM The Queen 1969-70, Rear Adm 1970, naval sec MOD 1970-72, flag offr First Flotilla 1973-74, flag offr Submarines and cdr Submarines Eastern Atlantic 1974-76, Vice Adm 1973, ret 1977; *Recreations* fishing, shooting, gardening; *Clubs* Naval & Military; *Style—* Vice Adm Sir Iwan Raikes, KCB, CBE, DSC, DL; Aberyscir Ct, Brecon, Powys

RAILTON, Dame Ruth; DBE (1966, OBE 1954); da of Rev David Railton, MC (d 1955; rector of Liverpool and originator of the idea of the Unknown Warrior Tomb, his flag, used in WW I, hangs in the Warriors Chapel in Westminster Abbey), and Ruby Marion de Lancey Willson; *b* 14 Dec 1915; *Educ* St Mary's Sch Wantage, Royal Acad of Music London (FRAM); *m* 1962, Cecil Harmsworth King (d 1987); *Career* dir of music or choral work for many schools and societies 1937-49, adjudicator Fedn of Music Festivals 1946-74, fndr and musical dir of the Nat Youth Orchestra of GB and Nat Jr Music Sch 1946-65, pres Ulster Coll of Music 1960-, govr Royal Ballet Sch 1966-74, vice pres Cork Int Fest 1960, fndr and pres Irish Children's Theatre 1978-81, memb bd of dirs Nat Concert Hall Dublin 1981-86; patron European Pianoforte Teachers Assoc, fndr Cecil King Meml Fndn 1991; Hon LLD Aberdeen Univ 1960; hon prof: Chopin Conservatoire Warsaw 1960, Conservatoire of Azores (Lisbon) 1966; Hon RMCM; FRCM, FTCL; *Style—* Dame Ruth King, DBE; 54 Ardoyne House, Pembroke Park, Dublin 4 (☎ 0001 617262)

RAINBOW, (James) Conrad Douglas; CBE (1979); s of Jack Conrad Rainbow (d 1956), of Edgware, Middx, and Winifred Edna, *née* Mears (d 1973); *b* 25 Sept 1926; *Educ* William Ellis Sch Highgate London, Selwyn Coll Cambridge (MA); *m* 13 April 1974, Kathleen Margaret, da of Robert Holmes (d 1947); 1 s (James b 14 April 1975), 1 da (Nicola b 8 June 1977); *Career* Nat Serv 1946-48, Flt Lt RAF VR (T); asst master St Paul's Sch London 1951-60, HM inspr of schs 1960-69, chief educn offr Lancs 1974-79 (dep chief 1969-73), princ private tutorial coll 1979-, visiting prof Univ of Wisconsin; former memb: Ct and Cncl Univ of Lancaster, Advsy Ctee Duke of Edinburgh Awards Scheme; former chm Steering Gp Understanding Br Indust; current memb Exec Ctee Cncl of Br Int Schs in the Euro Community; *Recreations* music, rowing (now as observer); *Clubs* Leander, IOD; *Style—* Conrad Rainbow, Esq, CBE; Freefolk House, Laverstoke, Whitchurch, Hants RG28 7PB (☎ 0256 892 634)

RAINE, Dr Anthony Evan Gerald; s of John Wellesley Evan Raine, OBE, of Wellington, NZ, and Eleanor Josephine, *née* Luke (d 1978); *b* 21 July 1949; *Educ* Wellington, Univ of Otago, Univ of Oxford (BA, BMed Sc, MB ChB, DPhil); *m* 18 Oct 1975, June Munro, da of David Harris, of Saffron Walden, Essex; 1 s (Charles b 1984), 1 da (Juliet b 1986); *Career* sr res fell Dept of Med Univ of Oxford 1987-88 (Rhodes scholar 1974-76, lectr Merton Coll 1974-, lectr 1981-87), conslt physician Bart's 1988-; memb Assoc of Physicians of GB and I, treas Hypertension Soc; MRCP 1979; *Recreations* golf, skiing, music; *Clubs* Vincents (Oxford); *Style—* Dr Anthony Raine; Dept of Nephrology, St Bart's Hospital, West Smithfield, London EC1A 7BE (☎ 071 601 8273, fax 071 796 3753)

RAINE, Craig Anthony; s of Norman Edward Raine, and Olive Marie Raine, *née* Cheeseborough; *b* 3 Dec 1944; *Educ* Barnard Castle Sch, Exeter Coll Oxford; *m* 1972, Elisabeth Ann Isabel, da of Dr Eliot Slater, OBE (d 1982); 3 s (Isaac b 1979, Moses b 1984, Vaska b 1987), 1 da (Nina b 1975); *Career* poet; The Onion Memory (1978), A Martian Sends A Postcard Home (1979), Rich (1984), The Electrification of the Soviet Union (1986), 1953 (1990), Haydn and the Valve Trumpet (1990); *Recreations* publishing; *Style—* Craig Raine, Esq; c/o Faber and Faber, 3 Queen Square, London WC1N 3AR (☎ 071 278 6881)

RAINE, George Edward Thompson; s of Reginald Thompson Raine, MC (d 1960), of Stocksfield, Northumberland, and Mary Dorothy, *née* Tomlinson (d 1976); *b* 1 Aug 1934; *Educ* Rugby, Emmanuel Coll Cambridge, St Thomas' Hosp Med Sch (MA, MB B Chir, FRCS); *m* 11 June 1960, Ena Josephine, da of Joseph Noble; 1 da (Meriel b 1965); *Career* sr conslt Orthopaedic Surgn W Middlesex Univ Hosp 1974-, assoc surgn Royal Masonic Hosp London; formerly sr orthopaedic registrar: St George's Hosp London, Rowley Bristow Orthopaedic Hosp Pyrford Surrey, Centre for Hip Surgery Wrightington; orthopaedic surgn to Rambert Dance Co Sch; orthopaedic surgn Crystal Palace Football Club; govr The Lady Eleanor Holles' Sch Hampton; Freeman City of London 1987; *Recreations* English Lake District, foreign travel; *Clubs* Whitefriars; *Style—* George E T Raine, Esq; Pelham's View, 32 Pelhams Walk, Esher, Surrey KT10 8QD (☎ 0372 466656); 144 Harley St, London W1N 1AH (☎ 071 935 0023)

RAINE, (Harcourt) Neale; s of Harold Raine (d 1966), and Gertrude Maude, *née* Healey (d 1972); *b* 5 May 1923; *Educ* Dulwich, London Univ (MSc); *m* 1947, Eileen; 1 s (Antony b 1954); *Career* divnl md and board memb Associated Engrg Ltd 1965-70; md Alfred Herbert Ltd 1971-75, consultant engr 1975-; chm Technician Educn Cncl 1976-82; chm Business & Technician Education Cncl 1983-; dir Stothert & Pitt plc 1978-; MInstD; CEng, MICE, FIMC, FIProdE, FRSA; *Recreations* saloon car racing, painting (pastels); *Style—* Neale Raine Esq; Penn Lea, The Avenue, Charlton Kings, Cheltenham, Glos GL53 9BJ (☎ 0242 526185)

RAINEY, Christopher John (Chris); s of Alec Barnard Rainey, of Bishops Lydeard, Taunton, and Hilda Edith, *née* Edmonds; *b* 22 Jan 1946; *Educ* Westwoods GS, Polytechnic of the South Bank (HNC); *m* 20 July 1967, Christel, da of late Hermann Carl Wilhelm Laarta; 2 s (Mark Andrew b 23 Dec 1970, Paul Simon b 24 Feb 1973); *Career* Signal Dept London Transport Board (involved with design of trackside electronics for world's first automatic passenger train Victoria Line) 1964-69, devpt of UK's first cash dispensers with Burroughs Machines and Lead Electronics Team (patent assigned relating to Credit Card security) 1969-72, whilst self-employed jtly invented and patented Endfield/Rainey keyboard (now called Microwriting System) 1973, conslt on Microwriter projects; currently engineer, inventor, problem solver; awarded British Design Award 1990 for design of Agenda electronics (current microwriters machine); *Recreations* vintage car restoration, video production, scouting; *Style—* Chris Rainey, Esq; Bellaire Electronics, 4 Broadgate, Pilton, Barnstaple, N Devon EX31 1QZ (☎ 0271 43296, fax 0271 24759)

RAINEY, Hon Mrs (Jane Teresa Denyse); *née* Ormsby Gore; da of 5 Baron Harlech, PC, KCMG (d 1985); *b* 1942; *m* 1966 (m dis 1984), Michael Sean O'Dare Rainey, s of Maj Sean Rainey, and Mrs Marion Wrottesley; 2 s, 2 da; *Style—* The Hon Mrs Rainey; Brogyntyn Home Farm, Oswestry, Salop

RAINEY, Simon Piers Nicholas; s of Peter Michael Rainey, of Calverley Park Crescent, Tunbridge Wells, and Theresa Cora, *née* Heffernan; *b* 14 Feb 1958; *Educ* Cranbrook Sch Kent, Corpus Christi Coll Cambridge (MA), Univ of Brussels (Lic Sp Dr Eur); *m* Pia Maria Clemence Fulbert, da of Karel Johanna Maria Witlox, of Taalstraat, Vught, The Netherlands; 2 s (Nicholas b 1989, Alexander (twin) b 1989), 1 da (Venetia b 1988); *Career* called to the Bar Lincoln's Inn 1982, in practice 1984-, advsr to UN Ctee for Trade and Devpt (Minconmar Project) 1984-85; *Publications* Halsbury's Laws: European Communities (jtly), Marsden: Law of Collisions at Sea (jtly), Maritime Laws of Anglophone Countries of West Africa (1985); *Recreations* classical music, opera, drawing, riding, Italy; *Style—* Simon Rainey, Esq; 38 Halton Rd, London N1 2EU; 2 Essex Ct, Temple, London EC4 (☎ 071 583 8381, 071 353 2918, fax 071 353 0998, telex 8812528 ADROIT)

RAINEY, (John) Stanley; s of John Rainey (d 1987), of Belfast, and Mary Lilian, *née* Ross (d 1971); *b* 30 Aug 1923; *Educ* Royal Belfast Academical Inst, Queen's Univ Belfast (BSc); *m* 21 Aug 1951, (Margaret) Ann Bruce, da of Bruce Slipper (d 1966), of Groomsport, Co Down; 4 s (John b 1952, David b 1954, Stephen, Neil (twins) b 1958); *Career* Capt RE 1944-47; John Rainey & Son Ltd 1948-: dir 1948-, md and chm 1968-87, chm 1987-; chm TSB NI 1983-86 (dep chm 1977-78 and 1980-83); dir: TSB Gp plc 1983-, TSB Pension Tst Ltd 1984-89, TSB Trustcard Ltd 1985-89; chm TSB NI plc 1986-; Capt Instonians CC 1956-57; pres: Rotary Club Belfast 1969-70, Ulster Reform Club 1983; C Eng, MIMechE 1958, MIProdE 1964; *Recreations* golf, shooting, music, painting; *Clubs* Royal Co Down Golf, Malone Golf, Ulster Reform; *Style—* Stanley Rainey, Esq; Long Thatch, 33 Bally Morran Rd, Co Down, N Ireland (☎ 0238 541302); TSB Northern Ireland plc, 4 Queen's Sq, Belfast (☎ 0232 325599, telex 743665, fax 0232 221754)

RAINFORD, John; s of Robert Sutter Rainford (d 1959), of Nelson House, The Beacon, Exmouth, Devon, and Monica, *née* Tamblyn (d 1987); *b* 20 July 1935; *Educ* Exeter Sch, Pembroke Coll Cambridge (BA, LLB); *m* 9 Sept 1959, Shelia, da of Reginald Walter Charles Pile (d 1975), of Parkway, Exmouth, Devon; 2 s (Justin b 1965, Kyle b 1966), 1 da (Helen b 1963); *Career* Nat Serv RA 1954-56, cmmnd 2 Lt 20 Field Regt 1956; slr, ptnr Messrs Richards Butler 1967-; memb Law Soc 1963; *Clubs* United Oxford & Cambridge University; *Style—* John Rainford, Esq; The Courtyard, Windhill, Bishop's Stortford, Herts CM23 2NG (☎ 0279 652854); Beaufort House, 15 St Botolph St, London EC3A 7EE (☎ 071 247 6555, fax 071 247 5091, telex 949494)

RAINGER, Peter; CBE (1982); s of Cyril Frederick Rainger (d 1973), and Ethel, *née* Wilson (d 1983); *b* 17 May 1924; *Educ* Northampton Engrg Coll, Univ of London (BSc); *m* 1, 1953, the late Josephine Dorothy, da of Joseph Campbell, of Northolt, London; 2 s (John b 1957, David b 1960); m 2, Barbara Gibson; 1 step da (Pamela b 1946); *Career* Nat Serv RAF 1942-47; engr BBC 1951-: designer TV equipment 1951-69, head Designs Dept 1969-71, head Res Dept 1971, ret dep dir engrg responsible for all R & D 1984 (devpts incl: conversion of TV pictures between different tech standards, introduction of teletext broadcasting); currently conslt to broadcasting indust; Freeman City of London, memb Worshipful Co of Engineers; FRS, FEng, FIEE, FRTS, SMPTE; *Books* Satellite Broadcasting (1985); *Recreations* computing, model engineering, sailing; *Style—* Peter Rainger, Esq, CBE, FRS; Applehurst, West End Ave, Pinner HA5 1BJ; Denham Court, 4 Wortley Rd, Highclyffe BH23 5DT

RAINGOLD, Gerald Barry; s of Henry Raingold (d 1979), of 19 Hanover House, London NW8, and Frances Raingold; *b* 25 March 1943; *Educ* St Paul's, Inst of CAs, London Graduate Sch of Business Studies (MBA); *m* 12 July 1978, Aviva, da of Henry Petrie (d 1962), of London; 1 s (Andrew b 18 Sept 1981), 2 da (Nina b 2 Aug 1979, Karen b 23 July 1983); *Career* CA; Cole Dicken & Hills (articles) 1963-68, Cooper Bros 1968-72 (mangr 1972), sr mangr corporate fin Wallace Brothers Bank 1972-76, sr conslt Midland Montagu Group 1976-78, dep md Banque Paribas London 1978- (formerly mangr, sr mangr, asst gen mangr); memb: London Business Sch Alumni, City Ctee Inst of Mgmnt 1980-83, IOD City Branch, Royal Inst Int Affrs, Bus Graduates Assoc; dir Br Francophone Business Group (trade assoc); Freeman City of London 1987; FCA 1968, FInstD 1987; *Recreations* opera, ballet, tennis, reading; *Clubs* Overseas Bankers; *Style—* Gerald Raingold, Esq; 12 Marston Close, London NW6 4EU (☎ 071 328 5800); Paribas Limited, 33 Wigmore St, London W1H 0BN (☎ 071 355 2000, fax 071 895 2555, car 0860 622149)

RAINS, Prof Anthony John Hardins; CBE (1986); s of Robert Harding Rains (Capt RAMC, d 1920), of Bexhill, and Florence Eleanor, *née* Rapson (d 1962); *b* 5 Nov 1920; *Educ* Christs Hosp, St Marys Hosp Med Sch, Univ of London (MB BS, MS); *m* 30 Oct 1943, Mary Adelaide, da of Edward Henry Lillywhite (d 1963), of London; 3 da (Margaret b 1944, Diana b 1948, Charlotte b 1963); *Career* med offr RAF 1944-47; lectr in surgery Univ of Birmingham 1950-59, hon conslt surgn Utd Birmingham Hosps 1954-59, prof of surgery Charing Cross Hosp Med Sch (Univ of London) 1959-81, hon conslt surgn Charing Cross, West London and Fulham Hosps 1959-81, dean Inst Basic Med Sci RCS 1976-83, postgrad dean SW Met RHA 1981-85, asst dir Br Postgrad Med Fedn 1981-85, ed J1 RSM 1986-; chm Med Cmmn Accident Prevention 1972-84, tstee Smith and Nephew Fndn 1974, first chm Child Accident Prevention Ctee, cncllr

Kings Norton Birmingham 1953-59; Freeman Worshipful Soc of Apothecaries 1965; FRCS 1948; *Books* The Treatment of Cancer in Clinical Practice (with PB Kunkler, 1959), Bailey and Loves Shorts Practice of Surgery (ed 13-20 edns, 1965-88), Joseph Lister and Antisepsis (1977); *Recreations* reading; *Style—* Prof Anthony Rains, CBE; 42 Sydney Buildings, Bath BA2 6 DB (☎ 0225 63148)

RAISMAN, John Michael; CBE (1983); s of Sir Jeremy Raisman GCMG, GCIE, KCSI (d 1978), and Renée Mary, *née* Kelly (d 1989); *b* 12 Feb 1929; *Educ* Dragon Sch Oxford, Rugby, Queen's Coll Oxford (MA); *m* 22 Aug 1953, (Evelyn) Anne, da of Brig James Ingram Muirhead, CIE, MC (d 1964); 1 s (Andrew Jeremy b 1969), 3 da (Angela (Mrs Denniss) b 1955, Valerie (Mrs Kelleher) b 1957, Alison (Mrs Brady) b 1960); *Career* Nat Serv 1951-53, Lieut Kings Dragoon Guards; dep chm British Telecom plc 1987-, chm Shell UK Ltd 1979-85 (chief exec 1978-85); dir: Vickers plc 1981-90, Glaxo Holdings plc 1982-90, Lloyds Bank plc 1985-; chm: Oil Indust Emergency Ctee 1980-85, Advsy Cncl London Enterprise Agency 1980-85, Cncl Indust for Mgmnt Educ 1979-85; CBI: memb Cncl, chm Europe Ctee 1980-88, memb Presidents Ctee 1980-88; memb: Governing Body Business in the Community 1982-85, Cncl Inst for Fiscal Studies , Royal Cmmn on Environmental Pollution 1985-87; chm: Electronics EDC 1985-87, Bd of Tstees Royal Acad, Investmt Bd Electra Candover Ptnrs; govr Henley Mgmnt Coll, pro chllr Aston Univ; Hon D Univ Stirling 1983; Hon LLD Aberdeen 1985; Hon LLD Manchester 1986; CBIM 1980; *Recreations* golf, skiing, travel, opera; *Clubs* Brooks's, Royal Mid-Surrey, Sunningdale Golf; *Style—* John Raisman, Esq, CBE; c/o British Telecom, BT Centre, 81 Newgate St, London EC1A 7AJ (☎ 071 356 5251)

RAISON, Dr John Charles Anthony; s of Cyril Alban Raison, MB, FRCS (d 1948), and Ceres Constance Mary, *née* Johnson; *b* 13 May 1926; *Educ* Malvern, Trinity Hall Cambridge (MA, MD), Univ of Birmingham; *m* 1, 3 April 1951 (m dis 1982), Rosemary, da of Edgar H Padmore, MC (d 1958); 1 s (Charles Christopher John b 3 April 1957), 2 da ((Marie) Louise b 15 June 1953, Camille Annette b 29 Oct 1954); m 2, 13 Sept 1983, Mrs Ann Alexander, da of Capt (John Henry) Roy Faulkner, MN (d 1982); 3 step da (Kate Helen Alexander b 12 Dec 1964, Jane Susan Alexander b 12 Nov 1966, Lucy Ann Alexander b 9 May 1969); *Career* Sqdn Ldr Royal Auxiliary Air Force 605 Sqdn 1950-52; house surgn and physician Queen Elizabeth's Hosp Birmingham 1951, visiting prof in cardiac surgery Gulbenkian Fndn Lisbon 1962, conslt clinical physiologist Regnl Cardiothoracic Surgical Unit Birmingham Regnl Hosp Bd 1962-66, clinical physiologist and chief planner Cardiac Surgical Unit Presbyterian Pacific Med Cantre San Francisco USA 1966-69, sr princ med offr then chief sci offr Dept of Health London 1969-79, dep dir Nat Radiological Protection Bd 1978-81, specialist in community med Wessex Regnl Health Authy 1982-91 (acting regnl med dir 1989), ret 1991; memb Southern Warwicks RDC 1955-60; MFCM 1972, FFPHM 1987; *Recreations* tennis, gardening, sailing; *Style—* Dr John Raison; Broom Cottage, Easton, nr Winchester, Hants SO21 1EF (☎ 0962 78 723)

RAISON, Patrick Nicolas; s of Rev Herbert Chaplin Raison (d 1952); *b* 30 Oct 1933; *Educ* Harrow, Magdalen Coll Oxford, Sch of Business Stanford Univ USA; *m* 1962, Françoise Yvonne, da of Maitre Fernand Haissly, of Switzerland; 1 s, 2 da; *Career* barr Grays Inn, md Oxford Controls Co Ltd; *Recreations* travel, aviation (Cessna GBFGY); *Clubs* Carlton; *Style—* Patrick Raison Esq; Farncombe Hill, Broadway, Worcs (☎ 0386 852465)

RAISON, Rt Hon Sir Timothy Hugh Francis; PC (1981), MP (C) Aylesbury 1970-; s of Maxwell Raison, of Theberton; *b* 3 Nov 1929; *Educ* Eton, Christ Church Oxford; *m* 1956, Veldes Julia, er da of John Arthur Pepys Charrington (himself yr s of Arthur Charrington by Dorothea Lethbridge, ggda of Sir Thomas Lethbridge, 2 Bt); 1 s, 3 da; *Career* former journalist with: Picture Post, New Scientist; former ed: Crossbow, New Society; PPS to NI Sec 1972-73, Parly under sec DES 1973-74, oppn spokesman Environment 1975-76, min of state Home Office 1979-83, min for overseas devpt 1983-86; memb: ILEA 1967-70, Richmond Cncl 1967-71, Home Office Advsy Cncl on Penal System 1970-74, Central Advsy Cncl on Educn 1963-66, Cncl Policy Studies Inst 1978-79; kt 1991; *Clubs* Beefsteak, MCC; *Style—* The Rt Hon Sir Timothy Raison, MP; House of Commons, London SW1

RAITT, Dr Alan William; s of William Raitt (d 1968), of Morpeth, Northumberland, and Mary Davison (d 1970); *b* 21 Sept 1930; *Educ* King Edward VI GS, Morpeth, Magdalen Coll Oxford (MA, DPhil); *m* 1, 29 July 1959, Janet Suzanne Taylor (m dis 1971); 2 da (Suzanne b 1961, Claire b 1964); m 2, 16 Dec 1974, Lia Noèmia Rodrigues Correia, da of Cdr Virgilio Lopes Correia (d 1985), of Parede, Portugal; *Career* fell by examination Magdalen Coll Oxford 1953-55, fell and lectr Exeter Coll Oxford 1955-66, fell and tutor Magdalen Coll Oxford 1966-, reader in French literature Oxford Univ 1979-, gen ed French studies 1987-, prof associè à La Sorbonne 1987-88, memb Exec Ctee Soc for French Studies 1987-, FRSL 1971, Officier de l'Ordre des Palmes Acadèmiques (France) 1987, Grand Prix du Rayonnement de la Langue Française (Mèdaille D'Argent), French Acad 1987; *Books* Villiers de l'Isle-Adam et le Movement Symboliste (1965), Life and Letters in France, The Nineteenth Century (1966), Prosper Mèrimèe (1970), The Life of Villiers de l'Isle-Adam (1981), Villiers de l'Isle-Adam: Oeuvres Complétes (ed with P G Castex, 1986), Villiers de l'Isle-Adam Exorciste Du Rèel (1987); *Recreations* music, watching football; *Style—* Dr Alan Raitt; Magdalen College, Oxford OX1 4AU (☎ 0865 276024)

RAJA RAYAN, Raj Kumar; s of Ramanathan Chelvarayan Raja Rayan, of Ceylon, and Lingamani, *née* Suntharalingam; *b* 6 April 1953; *Educ* Harrow, Guy's Hosp Dental Sch (BDS), Eastmans Dental Hosp (MSc); *m* Ahila, da of Sanmugam Arumugam, of Ceylon; 1 da (Dipa Lakshmi b 3 Nov 1980), 2 s (Darshan Kumar b 3 Aug 1982, Ravi Kumar b 11 Dec 1987); *Career* currently: lectr Royal London Hosp Dental Sch, general practice Harley St, dental practice advsr Kensington and Chelsea and Westminster FHSA, assoc advsr Br Postgrad Med Fedn, res fell Inst Dental Surgery; examiner: RCS for memb in Gen Dental Surgery, Examining Bd for Dental Surgery Assistants; chm BDA Metropolitan Branch Study Circle (ed and memb Branch Cncl); memb: Ctee of Dentists Provident Soc, North West Thames Regnl Postgrad Dental Educn Ctee, Inter Regnl Working Pty for Gen Practitioners, Ed Ctee Probe Dental Magazine; former fndr memb and ed: Anglo Asian Odontological Gp, BDA Young Practioner Gp; former treas; Clindent, Br Soc for Gen Dental Surgery; Cottrell award 1990; memb: BDA, Br Soc for Gen Dental Surgery, Br Endodontic Soc, Br Soc for Periodontology, Br Soc for Restorative Dentistry, Br Soc for the Study of Prosthetic Dentistry; life memb: Music Acad of India, Int Inst of Tamil Studies; memb Lord Chancellor's Advsy Ctee on JPs; LDS RCS, MGDS RCS, DRD RCS (Edinburgh); *Recreations* cricket, chess, bridge, golf; *Clubs* MCC, Magpies Cricket; *Style—* Raj K Raja Rayan, Esq; 46 Harley St, London W1N 1AD (☎ 071 631 5213)

RAJAGOPALAN, Narayanaswami; MBE (1976); s of Narayanaswami Subramania Ayyar (d 1966), of Nagapattinam, S India, and Muthuswami Ayyar, *née* Rajammai; *b* 28 Oct 1930; *Educ* Educated at home; *m* 30 Nov 1956, Parvatham Vasntha, da of Chidambara Subramaniam Krishnamoorthy; 1 s (Ravikrishnan b 24 July 1956); *Career* pro consul and acting vice consul Mina Al Ahmadi Kuwait 1950-66, vice consul Br Embassy Consular Section Kuwait 1966-, worked for a yr in legislative assembly secretatiat and as stenographer Madras, India; parents memb in Indian Sch Kuwait 1972-74; *Recreations* tennis, billiards, bridge, swimming; *Clubs* Unity (Ahmadi, Kuwait); *Style—* Narayanaswami Rajagopalan, Esq, MBE; British Embassy Consular Section, PO Box 2, Arab Gulf St, 13001 Safat, Kuwait (☎ 965 2432046/7, fax 965 2407395, telex 446314 KT A/B PRODROM)

RAJAKUMAR, Rajaratnam; *b* 27 Dec 1947; *Educ* Univ of Ceylon Colombo (MB BS); *m* 29 March 1978, Rajakumar Rajakulamathy; 1 s (David), 2 da (Rebecca, Anna); *Career* conslt genito-urinary med Derbyshire Royal Infirmary; LRCP (Edin), LRCP and S (Glasgow), MRCP; memb: BMA 1984, Med Soc for Study of Venereal Diseases 1984; *Style—* Rajaratnam Rajakumar, Esq; 18 Wirksworth Rd, Duffield, Derby DE6 4GZ (☎ 0332 840969); Derbyshire Royal Infirmary, Genitourinary Medicine Dept, London Rd, Derby (☎ 0332 47141)

RAKOFF, Alvin Abraham; s of Samuel Rakoff (d 1970), of Toronto Canada, and Pearl Himmelspring (d 1986); *Educ* Ryerson Public Sch Toronto Canada, Harbord Collegiate, Univ of Toronto (BA); *m* 4 June 1958, Jacqueline Hill; 1 s (John Dmitri b 27 Jan 1970), 1 da (Sasha Victoria b 27 Aug 1967); *Career* journalist: New Toronto Advertiser, The Globe and Mail Toronto; memb BBC Contract Staff 1954-57; freelance: dir, writer, prodr in TV Film and Theatre; directed: Requiem for a Heavyweight (Sean Connery, Michael Caine) 1957, On Friday at Eleven (Rod Steiger) 1960, The Comedy Man (Kenneth More) 1963, The Seekers 1964, Hamlet (Bristol Old Vic) 1965, Call Me Daddy (Donald Pleasance), Hoffman (Peter Sellers) 1969, Say Hello to Yesterday (Jean Simmons) 1970, Summer and Smoke (Lee Remick) 1971, The Adventures of Don Quixote (Rex Harrison) 1972, Shadow of a Gunman 1973, Cheap in August 1974, In Praise of Love (Claire Bloom, Kenneth More) 1975, The Dame of Sark (Celia Johnson) 1976, The Kitchen (BBC) 1977, Mr Halpen and Mr Johnson (Lawrence Oliver, Jackie Gleeson) 1981, A Voyage Round My Father (Lawrence Olivier, Alan Bates) 1982, Paradise Postponed, The First Olympics (Angela Lansbury, Louis Jordan) 1983, Royal Albert Hall Cruise Charity Concert (before HM Queen) 1984; *Awards* Nat TV award 1964, Emmy int award Nat Acad of TV Arts and Scis US 1967 and 1982, Best in Festival award and Best Film award Banff TV Festival 1982; various nominations incl: Monte Carlo Festival, BAFTA, Prix Italia; memb: Dirs Guild of GB (pres 1988-90), Dirs Guild of Canada, Writers Guild of GB; *Recreations* photography, literature, music, skiing, boats, swimming, cricket, baseball; *Style—* Alvin Rakoff, Esq; Table Top Productions, Alvin Rakoff Productions Ltd; c/o Nyman Libson Paul, 124 Finchley Rd, London NW3 5JS (☎ 071 794 5611, fax 071 431 1109)

RALLI, David Charles; s and h of Sir Godfrey Ralli, 3 Bt, TD; *b* 5 April 1946; *Educ* Eton, Harper Adams Agric Coll; *m* 1975, Jacqueline Cecilia, da of David Smith; 1 s (Philip Neil David b 31 March 1983), 1 da (Marina Louise b 15 May 1980); *Career* farmer; chm Dereham Farm Servs 1985-87, dir Mid Norfolk Farmers 1985-, cncllr Breckland DC 1987-; memb Worshipful Co of Farmers 1985-; *Recreations* golf, shooting, fishing; *Clubs* White's, Farmers; *Style—* David Ralli, Esq; The Old Hall, Hardingham, Norwich, Norfolk NR9 4EW

RALLI, Sir Godfrey Victor; 3 Bt (UK 1912), TD; s of Sir Strati Ralli, 2 Bt, MC (d 1964); *b* 9 Sept 1915; *Educ* Eton; *m* 1, 24 June 1937 (m dis 1947), Nora Margaret, o da of late Charles Forman, of Lodden Court, Spencers Wood, nr Reading; 1 s, 2 da; m 2, 24 March 1949, Jean, da of late Keith Barlow; *Heir* s, David Charles Ralli; *Career* Ralli Brothers Ltd 1936-62 (apart from Army Serv 1939-45); chm: G & L Ralli Investment & Tstee Co Ltd 1962-75, Greater London Fund for the Blind 1962-82; *Recreations* golf, fishing, gardening; *Clubs* White's, Naval and Military; *Style—* Sir Godfrey Ralli, Bt, TD; Great Walton, Eastry, Sandwich, Kent CT13 0DN

RALLING, (Antony) Christopher; s of Harold St George Ralling, and Dorothy Blanche, *née* Williams; *b* 12 April 1929; *Educ* Charterhouse, Wadham Coll Oxford (BA); *m* Angela Norma, da of John Henry Gardner (d 1985); 1 da (Joanna Margaret b 1965); *Career* TV writer, prodr and dir; British Memorial Foundation Fellowship in Australia 1959; BBC: radio scriptwriter and prodr External Services 1955-59, radio and tv prodr West Region Bristol 1960-62, dep ed Panorama 1965-66 (prodr 1962-65); BBC TV Documentary Department 1966-82: prodr and dir Revolution in Hungary 1966, prodr One Pair of Eyes 1967, dir Tokyo - the Fifty First Volcano 1969 (Blue Ribbon, NY Film Festival), prodr Australia - Last of Lands 1970, prodr and dir The Search for the Nile 1972 (2 US Emmys, UK Critic's Guild Award), prodr and dir The Fight Against Slavery 1973 (Martin Luther King Award), prodr and dir Everest The Hard Way 1975, prodr The Voyage of Charles Darwin 1978 (2 Br Acad Awards), Head of Documentaries 1980-82; fndr Dolphin Productions 1982; freelance: scriptwriter Shackleton BBC 1983, prodr Everest the Unclimbed Ridge 1983, dir The History of Africa Channel Four 1984 (Gold medal, NY Film Festival), writer and dir Chasing a Rainbow 1985 (US Emmy, Gold medal NY Film Festival), dir Vintage Channel Four 1987, dir Charles At Forty LWT 1988. contrib Kaleidoscope BBC 1988, writer and prodr The Kon-Tiki Man BBC 1989, dir The Buried Mirror BBC (2 episodes) 1990; FRGS 1978; *Books* Muggeridge Through the Microphone (1967), The Voyage of Charles Darwin (1987), Shackleton (1983), The Kon-Tiki Man (1990); *Recreations* tennis, skiing; *Clubs* BAFTA, Alpine; *Style—* Christopher Ralling, Esq

RALPH, Prof Brian; s of Reginald James (d 1960), of Norwich, and Gwenthellian Anne, *née* Thomas (d 1990); *b* 4 Aug 1939; *Educ* City of Norwich Sch, Jesus Coll Cambridge (BA, MA, PhD, ScD); *m* 22 June 1961, Anne Mary, da of Leslie Ernest Perry, of Bath; 1 da (Zoanna); *Career* lectr Dept of Metallurgy and Material Sci Univ of Cambridge 1966-83 (demonstrator 1964-66, fell and tutor Jesus Coll 1964-83); prof and head of Dept: Metallurgy and Material Sci Univ Coll Cardiff 1984-87, Materials Technol Brunel Univ 1987-; co-ed over twenty res monographs in the field of microscopy and physical metallurgy; FIM, FInstP, hon FRMS, CEng, CPhys; *Recreations* sailing, woodwork, music; *Clubs* Cardiff and Country; *Style—* Prof Brian Ralph; Ty Carrog, St Bride's-super-Ely, Cardiff CF5 6EY (☎ 0446 760469); Dept of Materials Technology, Brunel, The University of W London, Uxbridge, Middx UB8 3HP (☎ 0895 74000, fax 0985 32806, telex 0895 261173 G)

RALPH, Colin John; s of Harold Ernest Ralph, and Vining, *née* Bromley; *b* 16 June 1951; *Educ* Royal W Sussex Hosp (RGN), Royal Coll of Nursing Univ of London (DN), Brunel Univ (MPhil); *Career* staff nurse and student Nat Heart Hosp 1974, charge nurse Royal Free Hosp 1974-77, nursing offr The Royal London Hosp 1978-83, dir of nursing Westminster Hosp and Westminster Children's Hosp 1983-86, chief nursing advsr Glos Health Authy 1986-87, registrar and chief exec UK Central Cncl for Nursing, midwifery and health visiting 1987-; contrib to professional jls and books; memb: Nat Ctee Br Red Cross Soc 1974-76, Professional Servs Ctee Royal Coll of Nursing 1986-87, Nat Florence Nightingale Ctee Cncl of Mgmt 1983; memb: Euro Cmmn Advsy Ctee on Trg in Nursing 1990, Int Ctee Royal Coll of Nursing 1990; *Recreations* friends, the arts, travel; *Style—* Colin Ralph, Esq; 23 Portland Place, London W1N 3AF (☎ 071 637 7181)

RALPH, Philip Pyman; s of Leslie Philip Ralph, of Rossland, Hatch Beauchamp, Somerset, and Christian Doreen, *née* Pyman (d 1973); *b* 4 Aug 1931; *Educ* Fettes, Clare Coll Cambridge; *m* 20 Aug 1960, Joan Francis (Jill), da of Dr John Scott Brown; 2 s (Charles Ralph b 1962, Nicholas Ralph b 1963); *Career* Nat Serv 1950-52; articled clerk Albert Goodman & Company 1955-58, accoutant Peat Marwick Mitchell & Company 1958-62, exec Corp Fin Dept Hill Samuel & Company Ltd 1962-71 (dir 1968-71), jt md Spey Investments Ltd 1971-76; dir and head Corp Fin Dept: William Brandt & Company Ltd 1973-76, Charterhouse Japhet Ltd 1976-81; assoc dir The

General Electric Company plc 1981-88; non-exec dir: Chamberlin & Hill plc 1971-, Olim Convertible Trust plc 1989-; vice chm The Summit Group plc 1988-; FCA 1958; *Recreations* tennis, skiing, sailing; *Style—* Philip Ralph, Esq; The Summit Group plc, 84 St Katharine's Way, London E1 9YS (☎ 071 867 8400, fax 071 867 8667, telex 920906)

RALPHS, Lady; Enid Mary; CBE (1984), JP, DL (Norfolk 1981); da of Percy William Cowlin (d 1929), and Annie Louise, *née* Willoughby (d 1977); *b* 20 Jan 1915; *Educ* Camborne GS, Exeter Univ (BA; DipEd Cambridge); *m* 1938, Sir Lincoln Ralphs (d 1978), sometime chief educn offr Norfolk; 1 s, 2 da; *Career* teacher Penzance GS 1937-38; staff tutor Univ of Oxford 1942-44, pt/t sr lectr Keswick Hall Coll of Educn 1948-80; chm Norwich Bench 1977, vice pres Magistrates' Assoc of England and Wales, chm Cncl of Magistrates' Assoc 1981-84, memb Home Office Advisory Bd on Restricted Patients 1985-; ret; Hon DCL Univ of E Anglia 1989; *Books* co author The Magistrate as Chairman (1987); *Recreations* gardening, travel; *Clubs* Royal Overseas League; *Style—* Lady Ralphs, CBE, JP, DL; Jesselton, 218 Unthank Rd, Norwich NR2 2AN (☎ 0603 53382); The Magistrates' Association, 28 Fitzroy Sq, London W1P 6DD (☎ 071 387 2353)

RAM, Edward David Abel (Ned); s of Sir Lucius Abel John Granville Ram, KCB, QC (d 1952), and Elizabeth Lady Ram, *née* Mitchell-Innes; *b* 5 Dec 1934; *Educ* Eton, Worcester Coll Oxford (BA); *m* 2 Dec 1960, Sheliagh Ann, da of Lt Col James Albert Lewis, MC (ka 1942); 1 s (Henry b 1967); *Career* Nat Serv 2 Lt Rifle Brigage; slr; ptnr Withers 1962; dir: Daily Mail and Great Trust 1977-, QS Holdings plc 1989-; *Recreations* shooting, sailing; *Clubs* Brooks's, Royal Fowey Yacht; *Style—* Ned Ram, Esq; 52 St Augustines Road, London NW1 9RN (☎ 071 485 3255); Messrs Withers, 20 Essex Street, Strand, London WC2

RAMAGE, Richard; s of Richard Ramage (d 1971), of London, and Elizabeth Maud, *née* Sims (d 1982); *b* 13 Aug 1927; *Educ* Haberdashers' Askes's, Cubitt Town Sch; *m* 15 March 1952, Sylvia Mavis, da of Sydney John Eary (d 1986); 3 s (Colin Richard b 1953, Kevin John b 1957, Christopher James b 1968); *Career* Esso Petroleum Gp 1948-64, dir and controller Conoco Europe 1964-72, dep md Conoco Ltd 1972-; memb Tport Users Consultative Ctee for Eastern England; FCIS, ATII; *Style—* Richard Ramage, Esq; 3 Roundwood Grove, Hutton Mount, Shenfield, Brentwood, Essex CM13 2NE (☎ 0277 219128); Conoco Ltd, 230 Blackfriars Rd, London SE1 (☎ 071 408 6192)

RAMEL, Baron (Axel) Knut Stig Malte; yr (twin) s of Baron Stig Urban Malte Ramel, of Stockholm, Sweden, and Ann-Marie, *née* Wachtmeister; *b* 4 April 1954; *Educ* Stockholm Sch of Economics; *Career* Beijer Invest AB Stockholm 1978-80, Credit Suisse First Boston Ltd 1980-84, exec dir Merrill Lynch Int & Co 1984-; *Style—* Baron Knut Ramel; 49A Britannia Rd, London SW6 (☎ 071 384 1081); 25 Ropemaker St, London EC2 (☎ 071 867 2805, fax 071 867 2040)

RAMM, Rev Canon Norwyn MacDonald; s of Rev Ezra Edward Ramm, and Dorothy Mary Ramm; *b* 8 June 1924; *Educ* Berkhamstead Sch Herts, St Peter's Coll Jamaica WI, Univ of Oxford (MA); *m* 23 June 1962, Ruth Ellen, da of Robert James Kirton, CBE (d 1988), of Byron Cottage, North End Ave, London; 2 s (Peter Kay MacDonald b 1965, David Oliver Kirton b 1967), 1 da (Selina Angela Susan b 1963); *Career* curate St James Montego Bay Jamaica 1951-53, rector Stony Hill with Mount James Jamaica 1953-57, curate St Michael at the North Gate Oxford 1957-61, p-in-c St Martin and All Saints Oxford 1961-71, vicar St Michael at the North Gate Oxford 1961-88; chaplain to HM The Queen 1985, hon canon Christ Church Cathedral Oxford 1985-88 (hon canon emeritus 1988); chaplain: Br Fire Servs Assoc 1980, Oxford City Police Assoc; pres Isis Dist Scout Assoc 1984, fndr and pres Samaritans of Oxford; *Recreations* gardening, skiing, collecting graces; *Clubs* Clarendon (Oxford), Frewen (Oxford), Oxford Rotarian; *Style—* The Rev Canon Norwyn Ramm; Fairlawn, Church La, Harwell, nr Abingdon, Oxon OX11 0EZ (☎ 0235 835 454)

RAMPHAL, Sir Shridath Surendranath; CMG (1966), QC (Guyana 1965); s of James I Ramphal and Grace Ramphal; *b* 3 Oct 1928; *Educ* Queen's Coll Georgetown, King's Coll London, Harvard Law Sch; *m* 1951, Lois Winifred, *née* King; 2 s, 2 da; *Career* called to the Bar Gray's Inn 1951, crown counsel Br Guyana 1953-54, asst to attorney-gen 1954-56, legal draftsman Br Guyana 1956-58, slr-gen 1959-61, asst attorney-gen W Indies 1961-62, attorney-gen Guyana 1965-73, memb Nat Assembly 1965-75, min state External Affrs 1967-72, min Foreign Affrs 1972-75 (held concurrently with attorney-generalship until 1973), min Justice 1973-75, sec-gen Cwlth 1975-90; memb: South Cmmn, Brandt Cmmn on Int Devpt Issues, Palme Cmmn on Disarmament and Security Issues, Independent Cmmn on Int Humanitarian Issues, World Cmmn on Environment and Devpt, Int Cmmn Jurists, and many other bodies; chllr: Univ of Guyana 1988, Univ of Warwick 1989, Univ of W Indies 1989; hon master of bench Gray's Inn 1981; Hon FRSA 1981; hon fell: King's Coll London 1975, LSE 1979, Magdalen Coll Oxford 1982; visiting prof: Univ of Exeter 1986, faculty of laws Kings Coll London 1988; Hon LLD: Southampton 1976, Aberdeen 1979, Hull 1983; Cambridge 1985, Warwick 1988; Hon DLitt Bradford 1985; Hon DUniv: Surrey 1979, Essex 1980; Hon DCL: Oxford 1982, East Anglia 1983; Durham 1985; Hon DSc Cranfield Inst of Technol 1987; and hon degrees from many Cwlth univs; Int Educn Award Richmond Coll London 1988, RSA Albert Medal 1988; sr counsel Guyana 1966, Hon AC 1982, AC 1982, OE 1983, ONZ 1990, Order of Excellence Guyana 1983; kt 1970; *Books* One World to Share: selected speeches of the Commonwealth Secretary-General 1975-79, Inseparable Humanity: An Anthology of Reflections of Shridath Ramphal (ed R Sanders, 1988); *Recreations* photography, cooking; *Style—* Sir Shridath Ramphal, CMG, QC; Commonwealth Secretariat, Marlborough House, Pall Mall, London SW1Y 5HX (☎ 071 839 3411, telex 27678)

RAMPLING, Dr Roy Peter; s of Alan William Rampling (d 1984), and Lorenza, *née* Camilleri (d 1966); *b* 13 Sept 1946; *Educ* Clacton Co HS, Imperial Coll (BSc, PhD, DIC), Chelsea Coll (MSc), UCL (MB BS); *m* 27 Dec 1975, Susan Mary, da of Richard Erskine Bonham-Carter, *qv*, of Knebworth; 2 s (Thomas William b 1979, Jack Richard b 1984), 1 da (Laura Elizabeth b 1977); *Career* currently sr lectr dept of radiation oncology Univ of GLasgow; ARCS, memb Inst of Physics 1972, MRCP 1981, FRCR 1984; *Style—* Dr Roy Rampling; Beatson Oncology Centre, Western Infirmary, Glasgow G11 6NT (☎ 041 339 8822)

RAMPLY, David Temple; s of George Temple Ramply, OBE, and Mary Betty Grosvenor, *née* Jarvis (d 1962); *b* 1 March 1944; *Educ* Oundle; *m* 4 July 1968, Patricia Jane, da of Capt Gavin Miller Hunter (d 1978), of Huntingdon, Cambs; 3 da (Katherine Jane b 1970, Emma Clare b 1971, Suzanna Elizabeth b 1976); *Career* former md R & T Agric Group of Companies 1972-87; former dir R & T Agric Ltd, dir R & T Agric Liming Ltd; *Recreations* rugby, tennis; *Clubs* Huntingdon RUFC (pres); *Style—* David T Ramply, Esq; Paxton Place, Gt Paxton, Huntingdon, Cambs PE19 4RG (☎ 0480 72123, fax 0480 403555)

RAMPTON, Sir Jack Leslie; KCB (1973, CB 1969); s of Leonard Wilfrid Rampton, and Sylvia, *née* Davies; *b* 10 July 1920; *Educ* Tonbridge, Trinity Coll Oxford (MA); *m* 1950, Eileen Joan, *née* Hart; 1 s, 1 da; *Career* joined Treasy 1941, asst private sec to Chllrs of the Exchequer 1942-43, private sec to Fin Sec 1945-46, econ and fin advsr to Cmmr Gen SE Asia and Br High Cmmr Malaya 1959-61, under sec 1964-68; dep sec: Mintech 1968-70, DTI 1970-72, second perm sec DTI 1972-74, perm under sec Dept of Energy 1974-80; dir: London Atlantic Investment Trust 1981-, Sheerness Steel Co 1982-87 (dep chm 1985-87), ENO 1982-88, Carnarvon Mining 1984, Flextech 1985-; pt/t conslt Sun Oil 1982-87; memb: Cook Soc 1977 (chm 1987-88), Honeywell Advsy Cncl 1981-, Cncl Victoria League (dep chm 1985-), Cncl Br-Aust Soc 1986- (dep chm 1989-); govr: Cwlth Tst 1988- (dep chm 1989-); London House for Overseas Students 1990-; Hon DSc Univ of Aston; CBIM, FInstPet, FInstGasE; *Recreations* gardening, travel, photography; *Style—* Sir Jack Rampton, KCB; 17 The Ridgeway, Tonbridge, Kent (☎ 0732 352117); c/o Britain Australia Society, Borax House, Carlisle Place, London (☎ 071 976 5611)

RAMPTON, (Anthony) James Matthew; s of John Richard Anthony Rampton, of London, and Carolyn Mary, *née* Clarke; *b* 22 May 1964; *Educ* St Paul's Davidson Coll N Carolina US (scholar), Exeter Coll Oxford (BA); *Career* dep film ed (listings) The Independent 1988-89, TV ed The Independent on Sunday 1990-; *Recreations* rugby, cricket, *not* watching television; *Style—* James Rampton, Esq; The Independent On Sunday, 40 City Rd, London EC1Y 2DB (☎ 071 253 1222, fax 071 415 1333)

RAMSAY, Alexander William; s of Sir William Clark Ramsay, CBE (d 1973), and Sarah Nora, *née* Evans (d 1982); *b* 3 Aug 1931; *Educ* Mill Hill, BNC Oxford (MA); *m* 15 Aug 1957, Patricia, da of late William Hague; 2 s (William Alexander b 26 Dec 1958, Sholto David Hague b 7 May 1965), 2 da (Araminta Mary b 24 June 1961, Bonella Ann b 11 March 1964); *Career* 2 Lt Middx Regt, served in Korea 1950, Capt TA; called to the Bar Gray's Inn; company dir, vice chm Portman Building Soc; Westminster City cncllr for six years, dep Lord Mayor of Westminster, JP (resigned), High Sheriff of Gtr London 1976-77; Freeman of City of London, Liveryman of Worshipful Co of Fuellers; pres The Rugby Football Union 1979-81; *Recreations* sport, reading; *Clubs* Carlton, East India, City Univ, Vincent's, RLYC; *Style—* Alexander Ramsay Esq; Etna House, 350 Kennington Rd, London SE11 4LG (☎ 071 735 8811, fax 071 820 1936, telex 919349, car 0836 242308

RAMSAY, Sir Alexander William Burnett; 7 Bt (UK 1806); s of late Sir Alexander Burnett Ramsay, 6 Bt (d 1965); is the presumed heir to the Baronetcy of Burnett of Leys (cr 1626); *b* 4 Aug 1938; *m* 1963, Neryl Eileen, da of J C Smith Thornton Trangie; 2 s; *Heir* s, Alexander David Ramsay b 20 Aug 1966; *Style—* Sir Alexander Ramsay, Bt; 30 Brian St, Balgownie, NSW 2519, Australia

RAMSAY, Alison Gail; da of William John Buckingham, of Chorley, and Jean Sybil Bouttell; *b* 16 April 1959; *Educ* Leeds Girls HS, St Margaret's Sch Edinburgh, Univ of Edinburgh (LLB); *m* 7 July 1982, David Shanks Ramsay; *Career* hockey player, former capt: Univ of Edinburgh, Scottish Univs, Br Univs, Scotland under 23; 88 Scottish caps, 69 GB caps; Silver medal Euro Clubs Outdoor Tournament 1989 and 1990 (Bronze medal 1988) with Glasgow Western Ladies Hockey Club; ptnr legal practice Perth 1986-; *Recreations* dog walking, gardening, cars; *Style—* Mrs Alison Ramsay

RAMSAY, Hon Anthony; s of 16 Earl of Dalhousie, KT, GCVO, GBE, MC; *b* 1949; *Educ* Ampleforth, Magdalen Coll Oxford; *m* 1973 (m dis), Georgina Mary, da of the late the Hon Michael Langhorne Astor (s of late 2 Visc Astor); 1 s; *Style—* The Hon Anthony Ramsay

RAMSAY, Maj-Gen Charles Alexander; CB (1989), OBE (1979); s of Adm Sir Bertram Home Ramsay, KCB, KBE, MVO (Allied Naval C in C Invasion of Europe 1944, ka 1945), and Helen Margaret Menzies; descended from Sir Alexander Ramsay, 2nd Bart of Balmain Kincardineshire; *b* 12 Oct 1936; *Educ* Eton, Sandhurst; *m* 1967, Hon Mary Margaret Hastings, da of 1 Baron MacAndrew, TD, PC (d 1979); 2 s, 2 da; *Career* cmmnd Royal Scots Greys 1956, Staff Coll, Canada 1967-68, cmd Royal Scots Dragoon Gds 1977-79, Cdr 12 Armd Bde and Osnabruck Garrison 1980-82, dep DMO MOD 1983-84, GOC Eastern Dist 1984-87; dir gen TA and Army Orgn 1987-89, resigned from Army 1990; dir John Menzies plc 1990-; farmer and landowner; memb Royal Co of Archers (Queen's Body Gd for Scotland); *Recreations* field sports, equitation, travel; *Clubs* Boodle's, Cavalry & Guards, New (Edinburgh), Farmers, Pratt's; *Style—* Maj-Gen C A Ramsay, CB, OBE; Bughtrig, Coldstream, Berwickshire (☎ 089 084 221); Chesthill, Glenlyon, Perthshire (☎ 088 77 224)

RAMSAY, Col George Patrick Maule; s of Capt Archibald Henry Maule Ramsay (d 1955), and Ismay Lucretia Mary, *née* Hon Ismay Preston (d 1975); *qv* Dalhousie; *b* 15 Nov 1922; *Educ* Eton, RMA Sandhurst; *m* 1, 1947; 2 s (Alexander, Patrick), 3 da (Catherine, Diana, Fiona); m 2, 1980, Bridget, da of Ronald Hornby (d 1984); *Career* WWII serv Scots Gds: Italy (wounded), Malaya, Egypt, Kenya, Germany; Col cmdg Scots Gds 1964-67; dir: Hill Samuel 1968-79, Kornferry International 1979-82, Goddard Kay Rogers 1982-87; memb Royal Co of Archers (Queens Body Guard for Scotland); *Recreations* shooting, fishing, gardening; *Clubs* Boodle's, Army and Navy, Pratt's; *Style—* Col George Ramsay; The Old School House, The Square, Elham, Canterbury, Kent CT4 6TJ

RAMSAY, Lord; James Hubert Ramsay; s and h of 16 Earl of Dalhousie, KT, GBE, MC, by his w Margaret, da of late Brig-Gen Archibald Stirling of Keir (2 s of Sir John Stirling-Maxwell, 10 Bt, KT, DL, which Btcy has been dormant since 1956) and Hon Margaret Fraser, OBE, da of 13 Lord Lovat; *b* 17 Jan 1948; *Educ* Ampleforth; *m* 1973, Marilyn, yr da of Maj David Butter, MC, and Myra (da of Sir Harold Wernher, 3 and last Bt, GCVO, TD, by his w Lady Zia, *née* Countess Anastasia Mikhailovna, er da of HIH Grand Duke Mikhail of Russia; Lady Ramsay is hence 1 cous of the Duchesses of Abercorn and Westminster, *qqv*); 1 s, 2 da (Hon Lorna b 1975, Hon Alice b 1977); *Heir* s, Hon Simon David Ramsay b 18 April 1981; *Career* cmmnd 2 Bn Coldstream Gds 1968-71; dir Hambros Bank 1981-82; exec dir Enskilda Securities 1982-87; dir: Jamestown Investments Ltd 1987-, Central Capital Ltd 1987-, Capel-Cure Myers 1987-; chm William Evans 1990-; pres: The British Deer Soc 1987, The Caledonian Club 1990-; *Clubs* White's, Pratt's, Turf; *Style—* Lord Ramsay; Dalhousie Lodge, Edzell, Angus; 3 Vicarage Gdns, London W8 (T 071 727 2800)

RAMSAY, Hon John Patrick; yst s of 16 Earl of Dalhousie, KT, GCVO, GBE, MC, *qv*; *b* 9 Aug 1952; *Educ* Ampleforth; *m* 1981, Louisa Jane, only da of late Robert Erland Nicolai d'Abo, of W Wratting Park, Cambs; 1 s (Christopher b 1984), 1 da (Lucy b 1985); *Heir* Christopher Ramsay; *Clubs* Turfs, Whites; *Style—* The Hon John Patrick Ramsay; 1 Kassala Rd, London SW11

RAMSAY, Dr Lawrence Eccles; s of William Ramsay (d 1970), of Ayrshire, Scotland, and Margaret Cables, *née* Eccles (d 1989); *b* 11 June 1943; *Educ* Cumnock Acad, Univ of Glasgow (MB ChB); *m* 17 Sept 1965, Mary Helen, da of Harry Hynd (d 1971), of Lanark, Scotland; 3 s (William b 1972, Alan b 1974, Iain b 1983), 1 da (Helen b 1970); *Career* Surgn Lt RN 1968-73, HMS Osprey 1968-69, HMS Jufair 1969-70, Admty Med Bd 1970-71, RNH Haslar 1971-73; lectr in medicine Univ of Glasgow 1977-78, conslt physician Royal Hallamshire Hosp 1978-, reader in clinical pharmacology Univ of Sheffield 1985-, ed British Journal of Clinical Pharmacology 1988-; visiting memb to Australasia for Br Pharmacological Soc 1989-; memb: cncl World Hypertension League 1989, Br Pharmacopoeia Cmmn 1980-, ctee on Review of Medicines 1982-, Assoc of Physicians 1987; sec Br Hypertension Soc 1985-89; FRCP 1985 (memb 1970); *Recreations* soccer, golf, travel; *Style—* Dr Lawrence Ramsay; 85 Redmires Rd, Lodge Moor, Sheffield S10 4LB (☎ 0742 766222)

RAMSAY, Norman James Gemmill; WS (1939); s of James Ramsay (d 1940), of Buenos Aires, and Kilmarnock, Scotland, and Christina Emma, *née* Sheppard (d 1950); *b* 26 Aug 1916; *Educ* Merchiston Castle Sch, Univ of Edinburgh (MA, LLB); *m* 5 Jan

1952, Rachael (Ray) Mary Berkeley, da of Sir Herbert Charles Fahie Cox; 2 s (David James b 10 Jan 1954, Alexander Malcolm b 4 March 1957); *Career* WWII RN 1940-46; serv: E Indies Station, Eastern Fleet Aden; writer, leading writer, Petty Offr Writer, Paymaster Sub Lt, Paymaster Lt, Lt (S) RNVR; admin gen Northern Rhodesia 1947-56, advocate (Scotland) 1956-, res magistrate 1956-58, sr res magistrate 1958-64, puisne judge High Ct of Northern Rhodesia (later Zambia) 1964-68; Hon Sheriff: S Strathclyde, Dumfries and Galloway (Hon Sheriff 1970-); *Recreations* gardening; *Clubs* Royal Cwlth Soc; *Style—* Sheriff Norman Ramsay; Mill of Borgue, Kirkcudbright DG6 4SY (☎ 05577 211)

RAMSAY, Patrick George Alexander; s of Rt Rev Ronald Erskine Ramsay (d 1953), and Winifred, *née* Partridge (1985); *b* 14 April 1926; *Educ* Marlborough, Jesus Coll Cambridge (MA); *m* 22 Dec 1948, Hope Seymour Dorothy, da of Rt Rev Algernon Markham (d 1948); 2 s (Alexander b 1950, Jamie b 1953); *Career* RN Fleet Air Arm 1944-46; BBC: report writer Eastern Euro Desk, Monitoring Serv 1949, liaison offr US for broadcasts info serv Cyprus 1951-52, sr admin asst external broadcasting 1956-58, head of news admin 1958-64, planning mangr to programme planning 1964-66, controller prog servs 1972-79 (asst controller 1966-69), asst controller programme planning 1969-72, controller BBC Scotland 1979-83; mgmnt advsr Oman Broadcasting Servs 1984-85; chm Windsor and Eton Soc 1971-76; FRSA; *Clubs* National Liberal, New (Edinburgh); *Style—* Patrick Ramsay, Esq; Abcott Manor, Clungunford, Shrops

RAMSAY, Raymond; MBE (1946); s of Alexander Ramsay (d 1963), of Cape Province, S Africa, and Florence E Ramsay, MBE, *née* Tanner (d 1957); *b* 19 Aug 1916; *Educ* St Marylebone GS, St Bart's Hosp Med Coll (LRCP); *m* 4 Oct 1952, Lillian Jane, da of Lt-Col W H Bateman, MC, TD, of Little Court, Batheaston, Bath; 3 s (Jonathan b 1953, William b 1956, Alasdair b 1961); *Career* vol RAMC 1939, cmmnd Lt 1939, Capt 1940, Maj 1942; active serv: Burma 1940, retreat to India 1942, sr MO first Wingate Expdn (wounded POW, i/c Hosp Barracks no 6 Block Rangoon Central Jail 1943-45); demonstrator in anatomy St Bart's Hosp Med Coll 1946-47, jr surgical registrar St Bart's Hosp 1947-48, surgical registrar Norfolk and Norwich Hosp 1948-51, sr surgical registrar Bristol Royal Infirmary 1951-53, conslt surgn to E Berks Dist (formerly Windsor Gp of Hosps) 1953; FRCS, fell Hunterian Soc, memb RSM; *Recreations* sailing; *Clubs* Royal Solent YC; *Style—* Raymond Ramsay, Esq, MBE

RAMSAY, Richard Alexander McGregor; s of Alexander John McGregor (d 1986), of Ramsay, and Beatrice Kent, *née* De La Nauze; *b* 27 Dec 1949; *Educ* Trinity Coll Glenalmond, Univ of Aberdeen (MA); *m* 19 July 1975, Elizabeth Catherine Margaret, da of Robert Cecil Blackwood (d 1969); 1 s (Alistair Robert Blackwood b 19 Feb 1983), 1 da (Catherine Anne Blackwood b 1 Feb 1981); *Career* CA; articled clerk Price Waterhouse 1972-75, exec mangr Grindlay Brandts Ltd 1975-78, Hill Samuel and Co Ltd 1979-88 (dir 1984-88, seconded as dir Industl Devpt Unit DTI 1984-86), dir Barclays de Zoete Wedd Ltd 1988-; FCA; *Recreations* skiing, mountain walking, gardening, historic cars; *Style—* Richard Ramsay, Esq; Ebbgate house, 2 Swan Lane, London EC4R 3TS (☎ 071 623 2323, 0737 822329)

RAMSAY, William Marcus Raymond; s of Raymond Ramsay, MBE, of Long Meadow, Farnham Common, Bucks, and Lillian, *née* Bateman; *b* 24 July 1956; *Educ* Univ of London (BA), Henley Mgmnt Coll, Brunel Univ (MPhil); *m* 11 Oct 1980, Fiona, da of P H Gray, of Lothersdale, N Yorks; 2 s (William b 1981, James b 1985), 1 da (Sophie b 1989); *Career* asst dir Morgan Grenfell & Co Ltd 1985 (grad entrant 1979, mangr 1984), memb Exec Ctee N M Rothschild Asset Mgmnt 1988 (joined 1986, dir 1987), memb Occupational Pensions Bd (appointed by Sec of State) 1989; dir: Capoco Ltd, Theatre Royal Windsor 1987, Berkeley Medical Investments Ltd 1990; Freeman: City of London 1980, Worshipful Co of Fletchers 1980-; *Recreations* the theatre, swimming; *Clubs* Brooks's; *Style—* William Ramsay, Esq; Five Arrows House, St Swithin's Lane, London EC4N 8NR (☎ 071 280 5000, fax 071 929 1643, telex 888031)

RAMSAY OF MAR, Capt Alexander Arthur Alfonso David Maule; DL (Aberdeenshire 1971); s of Adm Hon Sir Alexander Ramsay, GCVO, KCB, DSO (d 1972, s of 13 Earl of Dalhousie), and Lady Patricia (d 1974, da of HRH 1 Duke of Connaught and Strathearn, 3 s of Queen Victoria), who on her marriage renounced, by Royal permission, the style and title of HRH and Princess and assumed that of Lady; *b* 21 Dec 1919,(King Edward VIII and King Alfonso XIII of Spain sponsors); *Educ* Eton, Trinity Coll Oxford (MA); *m* 1956, Lady Saltoun, *qv*; 3 da; *Career* Grenadier Gds 1938-47 (wounded N Africa 1943), Capt 1941, ADC to HRH the Duke of Gloucester 1944-47; page of honour at Coronation of George VI 1937; chartered surveyor; memb Forestry Soc of GB 1957- (now Inst of Chartered Foresters), vice patron Braemar Royal Highland Soc 1959-, Laird of Mar 1963, chm Exec Ctee Scottish Life Boat Cncl RNLI 1965-89, Hon Life Govr RNLI 1989; memb Nat Bd SWOA (later TGUK) 1966- (chm NE Region 1967-82); FRICS; *Recreations* shooting, sailing, travel, Scottish and family history, heraldry; *Clubs* Cavalry and Guards', Turf (London), Royal Northern and Univ (Aberdeen), New (Edinburgh), Household Div YC (Warsash), Island SC (Cowes); *Style—* Capt Alexander Ramsay of Mar, DL; Cairnbulg Castle, Fraserburgh, Aberdeenshire AB4 5TN (☎ 0346 23149); Inverey House, Braemar, Aberdeenshire AB3 5YB; Flat 8, 25 Onslow Sq, London SW7 3NJ

RAMSAY OF MAR, Hon Elizabeth Alexandra Mary; yst da of Lady Saltoun, *qv*; *b* 15 April 1963; *Style—* The Hon Elizabeth Ramsay of Mar

RAMSAY RAE, Air Vice-Marshal Ronald Arthur; CB (1960), OBE (1947); s of George Ramsay Rae (d 1949), of Lindfield, NSW, Aust, and late Alice, *née* Haselden; *b* 9 Oct 1910; *Educ* N Sydney HS, Sydney Tech Coll; *m* 19 Sept 1939, Rosemary Gough, da of Charles Gough Howell, QC, Attorney Gen of Singapore; 1 s (Ian Wallace b 1956), 1 da (Philippa Anne b 1958); *Career* Cadet RAAF 1930, cmmnd 1931, transfrd RAF 1932, 33 Sqdn Bicester 1932-1936, 142 Sqdn Air Armament Sch Eastchurch 1936, Singapore 1937 (POW Java 1942-45, despatches 1946), Empire Air Arm Sch 1946, CO Central Gunnery Sch 1946-47, RAF Staff Coll Andover 1948, ME 1948-50, CO N Luffenham 1950, CO Oakington 1951-53, Air Min DD of Flt Trg 1954-55, Cmdt Aircraft and Arm Ex Estab Boscombe Down 1955-57, Air Min Dep Air Sec 1957-59, AOC 224 GP Malaya Singapore 1959-62 (ret 1962); gen sec Nat Playing Fields Assoc 1962-71, sec St Moritz Tobogganing Club 1971-78; MRAES; *Recreations* cricket, golf, cresta; *Clubs* RAF, St Moritz Tobogganing (pres 1978-84), MCC, W Sussex Golf (Pulborough); *Style—* Air Vice-Marshal Ronald A Ramsay Rae, CB, OBE; Little Wakestone, Fittleworth, W Sussex RH20 1JR (☎ 079 882 217)

RAMSAY-FAIRFAX-LUCY, Hon Lady; *see*: Fairfax-Lucy

RAMSAY-STEEL-MAITLAND, Lady; Matilda Brenda; *née* Doughty; da of late Thomas Doughty, of Coalbrookdale; *b* 2 Dec 1907; *Educ* Clewer Windsor, Coalbrookdale Sch of Art; *m* 1942, as his 2 w, Sir (Arthur) James (Drummond) Ramsay-Steel-Maitland, 2 Bt (d 1960); *Career* pianist; served Dept of Lab 1939-45, Nat Serv Melbourne Aust; county cmdt Scottish Girls Trg Corps Edinburgh for 7 yrs; exhibited pictures in Africa, Edinburgh, London and Paris; gave 1 man exhibition Edinburgh 1980; past pres Corstophine Art Gp; owned and controlled an orange grove Marrakesh, Morocco until liberation; *Style—* Lady Ramsay-Steel-Maitland; Castle Gogar, Edinburgh 12 9BQ (☎ 031 339 1234); Royal Bank of Scotland, 36 St Andrews Sq, Edinburgh

RAMSBOTHAM, Gen Sir David John; KCB (1987), CBE (1980, OBE 1974); s of Rt Rev Bishop John Alexander Ramsbotham (d 1989), of Hexham, Northumberland, and Eirian Morgan, *née* Morgan Owen (d 1988); *b* 6 Nov 1934; *Educ* Haileybury, CCC Cambridge (BA, MA); *m* 26 Sept 1958, Susan Caroline, da of Robert Joicey Dickinson, of Corbridge, Northumberland (d 1980); 2 s (James David Alexander b 30 Aug 1959, Richard Henry b 8 June 1962); *Career* cmmnd Rifle Bde 1958, Royal Green Jackets CO 2 RGJ 1974-76, Cdr 39 Inf Bde 1978-80, RCDS 1981, dir PR (Army) 1982-84; Cdr: 3 Armd Div 1984-87, UK Field Army 1987-90; inspr gen TA 1987-90, Adj Gen 1990-; *Recreations* shooting, gardening, sailing; *Clubs* MCC; *Style—* Gen Sir David Ramsbotham, KCB, CBE

RAMSBOTHAM, Hon Sir Peter Edward; GCMG (1978, KCMG 1972, CMG 1964), GCVO (1976); yr s of late 1 Viscount Soulbury, GCMG, GCVO, OBE, MC, PC (d 1971), and his 1 w, Doris Violet (d 1954), da of Sigmund de Stein; hp of bro, 2 Viscount; *b* 8 Oct 1919; *Educ* Eton, Magdalen Coll Oxford; *m* 1, 30 Aug 1941, Frances Marie Massie (d 1982), da of late Hugh Massie Blomfield; 2 s, 1 da; m 2, 1985, Dr Zaïda Hall, da of Maurice Henry Megrah, QC; *Career* FO 1950, Br high cmmr Cyprus 1969-71, ambass to Iran 1971-73, ambass to USA 1974-77, govr Bermuda 1977-80; dir: Commercial Union Assurance Co 1981-90, Lloyds Bank plc 1981-90; chm Southern Regnl Bd Lloyds Bank 1983-89; tstee Leonard Cheshire Fndn 1981-, chm Ryder-Cheshire Mission for Relief of Suffering 1982-; KStJ 1976; *Style—* The Hon Sir Peter Ramsbotham, GCMG, GCVO; East Lane, Ovington, nr Alresford, Hants SO24 0RA (☎ 096 273 2515)

RAMSBOTTOM, Roy Frederic; s of Harry Ramsbottom, of The Paddocks, Davenham, Northwich, Cheshire, and Stella, *née* Walton; *b* 11 Aug 1943; *Educ* Sir John Deanes GS Northwich; *m* 21 Oct 1972, Susan Mary (Su); *Career* sr ptnr Murray Smith and Co CAs Northwich Ches 1985- (ptnr 1970-85), dir Walthamstow Building Soc 1985-90, local div Cheltenham & Gloucester Building Society 1990-; hon treas Cheshire Agric Soc 1977, chm Chester and N Wales Soc of CAs; memb ICEAW; *Recreations* cricket; *Style—* Roy Ramsbottom, Esq; Helensmere, Little Budworth, Tarporley, Cheshire CW6 9EL; Murray Smith and Co, Darland House, 44 Winnington Hill, Northwich, Cheshire CW8 1AU (☎ 0606 79411, fax 0606 782878)

RAMSBURY, Bishop of 1989-; Rt Rev Peter St George Vaughan; s of late Dr Victor St George Vaughan, of 50 Sedlescombe Road South, St Leonards-on-Sea, E Sussex, and Dorothy Marguerite, *née* Longworth-Dames; *b* 27 Nov 1930; *Educ* Dean Close Jr Sch, Charterhouse, Selwyn Coll Cambridge (MA), Ridley Hall Cambridge, Univ of Oxford (MA); *m* 2 Sept 1961, Elisabeth Fielding, da of late Dr Fielding Parker, of Selwyn Village, Auckland, NZ; 1 s (Richard b 1969), 2 da (Sarah b 1963, Merle b 1966); *Career* Army NS RHA and RAPC (Lt) 1949; asst curate Birmingham Parish Church 1957-62; chaplain: Oxford Pastorate, Brasenose Coll Oxford 1963-67; vicar Christ Church Galle Face Colombo Sri Lanka 1967-72, precentor Auckland Cathedral NZ 1972-75, princ Crowther Hall Selly Oak Coll 1975-83, archdeacon of Westmorland and Furness 1983-89; *Recreations* swimming, walking, gardening, reading; *Style—* The Rt Rev the Bishop of Ramsbury; Bishop's House, High St, Urchfont, Devizes, Wilts SN10 4QH (☎ 0380 840373)

RAMSDEN, Anne, Lady; Anne; *née* Wickham; er da of Lt-Col Sir Charles George Wickham, KCMG, KBE, DSO (d 1971), and his 1 w, Phyllis Amy, *née* Rose (d 1924); *m* 6 Oct 1945, Sir Caryl Oliver Imbert Ramsden, 8 Bt, CMG, CVO (d 1987); 1 s (Sir John, 9 Bt, *qv*); *Style—* Anne, Lady Ramsden; Vallance Cottage, Upper Chute, nr Andover, Hants SP11 9EH

RAMSDEN, Rt Hon James Edward; PC (1963); only s of Capt Edward Ramsden, MC, JP, and Geraldine Ramsden, OBE, yst da of Brig-Gen John Wilson, CB, JP, DL, and great n of 13 Baron Inchiquin; *b* 1 Nov 1923; *Educ* Eton, Trinity Coll Oxford; *m* 1949, Juliet Barbara Anna, yst da of Col Sir Charles Ponsonby, 1 Bt, TD, by his w Hon Winifred Gibbs, eld da of 1 Baron Hunsdon; 3 s (Thomas b 1950, George b 1953, Richard b 1954), 2 da (Emma b 1957, Charlotte b 1960); *Career* KRRC, served WWII NW Europe, with RB (despatches); MP (C) for Harrogate 1954-74, PPS to Home Sec 1959-60, under-sec and fin Sec WO 1960-63, sec State War 1963-64, Min Def (Army) April-Oct 1964; dir: Colonial Mutual Life Assur (UK Bd) 1966-72, Standard Telephones & Cables 1971-81, Prudential Assur 1972- (dep chm 1976-82), London Clinic 1973- (chm 1984-), Prudential Corpn 1979- (dep chm 1979-82); memb Historic Bldgs Cncl England 1971-72; *Recreations* foxhunting, forestry, woodturning; *Clubs* Pratts; *Style—* The Rt Hon James Ramsden; Old Sleningford Hall, Ripon, N Yorks (☎ 0765 85229)

RAMSDEN, Lady; (Jennifer) Jane; *née* Bevan; yr da of Rear Adm Christopher Martin Bevan, CB, and Patricia Constance, *née* Bedford; *b* 4 Jan 1953; *Educ* Winchester County HS, Newnham Coll Cambridge (MA); *m* 14 Dec 1985, Sir John Charles Josslyn Ramsden, 9 Bt, *qv*; 2 da (Isobel Lucy b 27 April 1987, Stella Evelyn b 4 Aug 1989); *Career* professional musician (solo violinist) 1974-79; memb HM Dip Serv 1979-85 (3 to 1 sec); prodr Music Dept BBC Radio 3 1985-; *Recreations* music, writing, family; *Style—* Lady Ramsden

RAMSDEN, Sir John Charles Josslyn; 9 Bt (E 1689), of Byram, Yorks; o s of Sir Caryl Oliver Imbert Ramsden, 8 Bt, CMG, CVO (d 1987), and Anne, Lady Ramsden, *qv*; *b* 19 Aug 1950; *Educ* Eton, Trinity Coll Cambridge (MA); *m* 14 Dec 1985, (Jennifer) Jane, *qv*, da of Rear Adm Christopher Martin Bevan, CB; 2 da (Isobel Lucy b 27 April 1987, Stella Evelyn b 4 Aug 1989); *Heir* undetermined; *Career* Dawnay Day & Co Ltd (merchant bankers) 1972-74, entered HM Dip Serv 1975; second Sec Dakar 1976-78, first Sec Delgn to MBFR Talks Vienna 1979, head of chancery and HM consul Hanoi 1980-82, FCO 1982-90 (cnsllr and dep head of Mission Embassy to GDR 1990, cnsllr and dep head of Br Embassy Berlin Office); *Style—* Sir John Ramsden, Bt; c/o Foreign and Commonwealth Office, King Charles St, London SW1

RAMSDEN, (John) Michael; s of John Leonard Ramsden (d 1967), and Edith Alexandra, *née* Hartley (d 1979); *b* 2 Oct 1928; *Educ* Bedford Sch, de Havilland Aeronautical Tech Sch; *m* 26 Sept 1953, Angela Mary, da of Walter Mortimer; 1 s (James b 1956), 1 da (Annabel b 1960); *Career* ed in chief Flight 1981-89 (ed 1964-81), ed Aerospace 1989-; vice chm D-Notice Ctee 1980-89, dir de Havilland Aircraft Museum; CEng, FRAeS; *Books* The Safe Airline (1978), Caring for the Mature Jet (1981); *Recreations* flying, water-colour painting, squash; *Clubs* London Sch of Flying; *Style—* Michael Ramsden, Esq; The Royal Aeronautical Soc, Hamilton Place, Park Lane, London W1 (☎ 071 499 3515)

RAMSDEN, Richard Thomas; s of Thomas William Ramsden, of Balmerino, Fife, and Elaine Napier, *née* Meikle; *b* 30 Dec 1944; *Educ* Madras Coll St Andrews, Univ of St Andrews (MB ChB); *m* 1, 1968 (m dis 1984), Wendy Margaret, *née* Johnson; 1 s (Alistair b 1974), 2 da (Helen b 1972, Fiona b 1977); m 2, 21 June 1985, (Eileen) Gillian, da of Clifford Whitehurst, of Knutsford, Cheshire; *Career* conslt otolaryngologist Manchester Royal Infirmary and Booth Hall Children's Hosp Manchester; hon lectr: dept of surgery Victoria Univ of Manchester, dept of audiology speech pathology and educn of the deaf Victoria Univ of Manchester 1977; author of articles on aspects of ear surgery; cncl memb and treas otology section RSM 1985-; memb ct examiners RCPSGlas 1987-, chm Br Cochlear Implant Gp 1989-; FRCS 1973, memb BMA 1977; *Books* chapters on aspects of ear surgery; *Recreations* golf, otology; *Clubs* Mere, St Andrews New; *Style—* Richard Ramsden, Esq; Lake House, Legh Rd, Knutsford, Cheshire WA16 8LP (☎ 0565 50936); 9,11 Lorne St, Manchester M13 0EZ (☎ 061

273 4231)

RAMSDEN, Prof Stuart Abbott; s of Arnold Richardson Ramsden (d 1984), of Walkington, Humberside, and Helen, *née* Abbott (d 1979); *b* 17 Sept 1930; *Educ* West Leeds HS Leeds, Keble Coll Oxford (BA, DPhil); *m* 17 Dec 1955, Eileen Nancy, da of Vernon Harcourt Richardson (d 1988), of Leconfield, Humberside; 2 s (Nigel Christopher b 1957, Simon Nicholas b 1960), 1 da (Caroline Jane b 1963); *Career* sr scientific offr AERE Harwell 1956-62, gp leader laser and plasma physics section Nat Res Cncl Ottowa Canada 1962-67, prof of applied physics Univ of Hull 1986- (prof 1967-86), co-ordinator of x-ray laser prog Rutherford Appleton Laboratory, memb Defence Scientific Advsy Cncl; govr Pocklington Sch; MAPS, memb Euro Physical Soc, FInstP; *Recreations* walking, sailing, piano and organ; *Style—* Prof Stuart Ramsden; Sarren House, Buckland, Faringdon, Oxon (☎ 036787 381); 23 Les Hameaux de Valcros, La Londe Les Maures, 83250 France; Dept of Applied Physics, Hull University, Cottingham Rd, Hull, Humberside HU6 7RX (☎ 0482 465501, fax 0482 466205, telex 592592); Rutherford Appleton Laboratory, Chilton, Didcot, Oxon OX11 0QX

RAMSDEN, Veronica Mary; da of James Edgar Ramsden, and Pamela Mary, *née* Cox; *b* 15 Oct 1956; *Educ* Ursuline Convent Brentwood Essex, Univ of Wales (LLB); *Career* called to the Bar Gray's Inn 1979; practising barr 1982-; *Recreations* chess, horse-racing, reading, pool, snooker, fringe theatre; *Clubs* Presscala Fleet St; *Style—* Miss Veronica Ramsden; Blounts Court Lodge, Potterne, Wiltshire (☎ 0380 721705); 4 Studley Rd, London E7 (☎ 071 470 0467); 59 Temple Chambers, Temple Ave, London EC4Y OHP (☎ 071 353 3111, fax 071 353 4581)

RAMSEY, Hon Mrs (Alice Elizabeth Margaret); 2 da of Capt Alexander Ramsay of Mar, and Lady Saltoun, *qv*; *b* 8 July 1961; *m* 28 July 1990, David Ramsey, yr s of Ronald Ramsey, of St James, Barbados; *Style—* The Hon Mrs David Ramsey

RAMSEY, Mark DeCourcey; s of Carlisle DeCourcey Ramsey, and Olive Elizabeth, *née* Denton; *b* 24 Jan 1968; *Educ* Saltley Secdy Sch; *Partner* Tina Maria Tábone; *Career* lightweight boxer; jr ABA finalist 1984, NABC champion 1985 and 1987; ABA: lightweight finalist 1987-88, lightweight champion 1988-89; represented: Young England in Euro Championships 1986-87, England 1987-89 (Silver medalist in Felix Stam Poland and Tammer Tour Finland), World Championships Moscow 1989; turned professional 1989; entered for Sports Personality of the Year in Birmingham Evening Mail; *Recreations* running; *Style—* Mark Ramsey, Esq

RAMSEY, Prof Peter Herbert; s of Stanley Churchill Ramsey (d 1968), and Cecilia Violet, *née* Plumridge (d 1968); *b* 19 Nov 1925; *Educ* Mill Hill Sch, Worcester Coll Oxford (MA, DPhil); *m* 11 April 1966, Priscilla Jean, da of Rev David Cecil Patrick Telford (d 1967); 3 da (Margaret b 1966, Helen b 1967, Elizabeth b 1970); *Career* asst Univ of Glasgow 1951-55; Univ of Bristol: lectr 1955-65, sr lectr 1965; prof Univ of Aberdeen 1966-; FRHistS 1973; *Books* Tudor Economic Problems (1963), The Price Revolution in Sixteenth Century England (1971); *Recreations* reading, music; *Style—* Prof Peter Ramsey; Dept of History, King's College, Aberdeen AB9 2UB

RAMSEY, Vivian Arthur; s of Ian Thomas Ramsey (d 1972 former Bishop of Durham), and Margretta, *née* McKay; *b* 24 May 1950; *Educ* Abingdon Sch, Harley Sch Rochester NY USA, Oriel Coll Oxford (MA), City Univ (Dip Law); *m* 14 Aug 1974, Barbara, da of Lt-Col Gerard Majella Walker, of Farnborough, Hants; 2 s (Nicholas b 1981, James b 1986), 2 da (Helen b 1980, Katharine b 1984); *Career* graduate engr Ove Arup & Ptnrs 1972-77, called to the Bar Middle Temple 1979; practising barr 1981-, ctee official referee Bar Assoc 1986-, arbitrator (incl ICC arbitration) 1988-; ed Construction Law Jl 1984-; treas: St Swithuns Hither Green 1977-84, Swanley Village Sports and Social Club 1986-; MICE 1977; *Recreations* pantomime, building renovation; *Style—* Vivian Ramsey, Esq; 10 Essex St, Outer Temple, London WC2R 3AA (☎ 071 240 6981, fax 071 240 7722, telex 8955650)

RAMSEY-FAIRFAX-LUCY; *see*: Fairfax-Lucy

RAMSHAW, Alec; JP (1982); s of John Robert Ramshaw (d 1969), of Beverley, E Yorks, and Olive, *née* Ackrill (d 1968); *b* 4 July 1931; *Educ* St Mary's Beverley, Woods Coll Hull; *m* 1 (m dis), Patricia Margaret; m 2, 5 Dec 1980, Sheila Patricia, da of Alfred Albert Fox (d 1964); 2 s (Simon James, Nicholas Mark), 1 da (Claire Alexandra); *Career* Nat Serv RAF; estate agent and insur broker 1963-, insur inspr 1963-52; memb Humberside Fin Ctee Br Red Cross Soc 1963 (chm 1976), fndr memb Hull Hosp League of Friends, cncllr Swanland Beverley Borough Cncl, cncllr S Hunsley Humberside CC (former ldr Cons Gp); Mayor Borough of Beverley E Yorkshire 1991-92; FNAEA 1977; *Recreations* golf; *Style—* Alec Ramshaw, Esq, JP; Owl Cottage, Spinney Croft Close, N Ferriby, Hull HU14 3EQ (☎ 0482 631 421); 3 Spinney Croft Close, N Ferriby, Hull HU14 3EQ

RAMSHAW, Colin; *b* 12 Oct 1936; *Educ* Univ of Newcastle (BSc, Hons PhD); *Career* sr scientific offr Miny of Aviation 1962-66, scientific offr Central Instrument Res Laboratories ICI Plc 1966-74, sr staff and section mangr ICI Corporate Laboratory 1974- (res assoc, memb Fluid Separation Panel); fndr jt res scheme (with John Porter) Univ of Newcastle 1981, jt fndr ICI/ETSU project Heriot Watt Univ (with Prof K Cornwell), conslt EEC Joule 1 programme on energy conservation 1990-; visiting prof chem Engrg Dept Univ of Newcastle 1989-; lecturer; author of various papers in learned journals; memb Inst of Chemical Engrs Res Ctee 1984-86; FENG 1989; *Style—* Dr Colin Ramshaw; 4 The Spinney, Norley, Warrington, Cheshire WA6 8LS (☎ 0928 88829); (☎ office 0928 511363)

RAMSLAND, Johan Fleming; s of Johan Marius Ramsland (d 1974), and Jean Kirkwood, *née* Fleming; *b* 29 Oct 1942; *Educ* Brighton GS Melbourne Australia; *m* 1, 19 June 1971 (m dis 1985), Carole, da of John Ronald Whiting, of London; 2 s (Johan-James b 1977, Benjamin b 1982); m 2, 6 Feb 1988 Susan, da of Arthur Haw, of Somerset; 1 s (Nicholas b 1990); *Career* dep ed MacQuarie Nat News Australia 1965-67, newsroom ed BBC World Serv News 1988-90 (sub ed 1968-88), ed BBC World Serv TV News 1990-; *Recreations* golf, swimming, travel; *Clubs* Foxhills Golf and Country, Wig and Pen; *Style—* Johan Ramsland, Esq; BBC World Service, Bush House, Strand, London WC2 (☎ 071 257 2016, fax 071 836 1810, telex 265 781)

RAND, Gerald Frederick; s of William Frederick Rand (d 1960), of Herts, and Elsie Mary White (d 1926); *b* 10 Nov 1926; *Educ* Merchant Taylors'; *m* 1, 13 July 1949, Eileen Margaret, da of William Alexanda Winson (d 1975), of Herts; 1 s (Stephen b 1953); m 2, 1 Nov 1972, Clarissa Elizabeth, da of Thomas William Barker (d 1956), of Hull; *Career* landowner and master builder, ret; chm Rand Contractors Ltd 1952-68, md Power Plant Int 1962-71, chm Manor Minerals (UK) Ltd 1985-; elected to Société Jersiaise 1967, memb governing cncl The Manorial Soc of GB 1985, regnl chm Domesday Nat Ctee 1986, memb Country Landowners Assoc; owner of the Lynford Hall Estate Norfolk; Lord of the Manor of: Lynford, Mundford, Cranwich Norfolk; *Recreations* shooting, hunting, studies in medieval history, historic buildings; *Style—* Gerald F Rand, Esq; Lynford Hall, Thetford, Norfolk IP26 5HW (☎ 0842 878351); Westmill, Ashwell, Herts (☎ 046 274 2568)

RANDALL, Adrian John Laurence; s of Robert Bennet Randall (d 1950), of London, and Ivy Ellen, *née* French (d 1986); *b* 4 Dec 1944; *Educ* Harrison Coll Barbados, Univ of Hull (BSc); *m* 1, 5 Sept 1970 (m dis 1990), Suzanne, da of William Marshall, of Morpeth; 2 da (Nicola Jane b 6 Oct 1973, Emma Louise b 3 June 1976); partner Jennifer LesBirel, da of Cecil Henry Sturgess; *Career* articled clerk Harper Smith Bennet & Co Norwich 1964-68; Tate & Lyle plc: accountant Zambia Sugar Co Ltd 1971-76, accountant Tate & Lyle Ltd 1976-78, fin controller Tate & Lyle Agribusiness Ltd 1978-79, fin mangr Unalco Div 1980-84; Hays Chemicals Ltd: IT chief exec Anti Pollution Chemicals Ltd 1984-85, gen mangr Gen Chemicals Div London 1985-87 (fin mangr 1985-86); fin dir Cancer Research Campaign 1987-; pres Essex Socl of CA 1988-89, fndr chm The Charity Fin Dirs Gp, Cancer Res campaign rep Charity Tax Reform Gp, chm ICAEW Career Devpt Gp, memb Bd Chartered Accountants in Business; ACA 1968; *Recreations* camping, swimming, cricket, reading, theatre, music, charity activities; *Clubs* Essex CCC; *Style—* Adrian Randall, Esq; 23 Plumberow Mount Ave, Hockley, Essex SS5 5AU; Cancer Research Campaign, 2 Carlton House Terrace, London SW1Y 5AR (☎ 071 930 8972, 071 839 4150, fax 071 321 0838, mobile 0831 251986)

RANDALL, Jeff William; s of Jeffrey Charles Randall, and Grace Annie Randall; *b* 3 Oct 1954; *Educ* Royal Liberty GS Romford, Univ of Nottingham (BA), Univ of Florida; *m* 8 Feb 1986, Susan Diane, da of H W Fidler; 1 da (Lucy Susan b 10 Jan 1989); *Career* research economist Wolverhampton Poly 1980-82, Hawkins Publishers 1982-85, asst ed Financial Weekly 1985-86, city corr The Sunday Telegraph 1986-88, city ed The Sunday Times 1989- (joined 1988); *Recreations* golf, horseracing; *Clubs* Warley Park Golf; *Style—* Jeff Randall, Esq; The Sunday Times, 1 Pennington St, London E1 (☎ 071 782 5766, fax 071 782 5658)

RANDALL, John Alexander; s of Alec Charles Randall (d 1975), of Worcester, and Elizabeth, *née* Harber (d 1977); *b* 30 Dec 1944; *Educ* Worcester Royal GS; *m* 1968, Linda Mary, da of late Geoffrey St Leger Chambers; 2 s (Geoffrey Thomas b 1974, Matthew Alexander b 1975); *Career* CA 1967; articled clerk EHB Butler & Co Worcester, ptnr Crumpton Homer & Co Kidderminster until 1981, sole practitioner Worcester 1981-90, merged with Pannel Kerr Foster 1990; dir Wolverhampton Speedway; ATII 1967; *Recreations* watching cricket, football, speedway; *Style—* John Randall, Esq; Pannell Kerr Forster, Virginia House, The Butts, Worcester (☎ 0905 24437, fax 0905 29006)

RANDALL, Stuart Jeffrey; MP (Lab) Kingston upon Hull W 1983-; *b* 22 June 1938; *Educ* Univ of Wales (BSc); *m* 1963, Gillian Michael; 3 da (Jennifer, Joanna, Emma); *Career* PPS to Roy Hattersley (dep ldr Lab Pty and shadow chllr of the Exchequer); front bench spokesman: Agric and Fisheries and 1985-87, Home Affrs 1987-; *Style—* Stuart Randall, Esq, MP; House of Commons, London SW1 (☎ 071 219 3583)

RANDALL, William Edward; CBE (1978), DFC (1944), AFC (1945); s of William George Randall, and Jane Longdon, *née* Pannell; *b* 15 Dec 1920; *Educ* Tollington Sch London; *m* 1, 1943, Joan Dorothea Way; 2 s, 1 da; m 2, 1975, Iris Joyce Roads; *Career* chm: Chubb & Son plc 1981-84, The Br Security Indust Assoc 1981-85; *Style—* William Randall Esq, CBE, DFC, AFC; Villa Oleander, Vale de Milho, 8400 Lagoa, Portugal

RANDLE, Guy Hawksworth; s of James Randle (d 1965), and Emma, *née* Hawksworth (d 1978); *b* 10 July 1937; *Educ* Hitchin GS, St Bartholomew's Hosp Med Coll (MB BS), Liverpool Med Sch; *m* 26 June 1965, Diana Suzanne, da of Brian Wright (d 1971); 1 s (Marcus b 1970), 2 da (Katherine b 1966, Louisa b 1975); *Career* conslt obstetrician and gynacologist Beverley E Yorks; memb Worshipful Soc of Apothecaries, hon memb Med Soc MRCS (Eng), LRCP (Lond), LMSSA (London), DOSSE RCOG, MRCOG, FRCOG; *Recreations* squash, golf; *Clubs* Squash (Beverley), Golf (Beverley and Ganton); *Style—* Guy Randle, Esq; Walkington Grange, Walkington, E Yorkshire HJ17 852; 61 North Bar, within Beverley

RANDLE, James Neville; s of James Randle (d 1989), and Florence, *née* Wilkins (d 1980); *b* 24 April 1938; *Educ* Waverley GS Birmingham, Aston Tech Coll Birmingham; *m* 1963, Jean Violet, da of Alfred Robert Allen; 1 s (Steven James b 1966), 1 da (Sally Joanne b 1968); *Career* Rover Co Ltd: apprentice 1954-61, tech asst 1961-63, project engr 1963-65; Jaguar Cars Ltd: project engr 1965-72, chief vehicle research engr 1972-78, dir vehicle engrg 1978-80, dir product engrg 1980-90, dir vehicle and concept engrg 1990-; leader of team that produced: Jaguar XJ40 (winner Top Car award 1986), Jaguar XJ220 (winner Turin and Horner prize 1988); chm Automobile Div/MechE 1987-88, fndr memb Autotech; *Awards* Crompton Lanchester medal 1986, James Clayton prize 1986, Sir William Lyons International award 1987; FEng, FIMechE, FInstD, FRSA; *Recreations* flying, sailing, skiing, hill walking; *Clubs* Coventry Flying Club; *Style—* James Randle, Esq; Jaguar Cars Ltd, Engineering Centre, Abbey Road, Whitley, Coventry CV3 4LF (☎ 0203 303080, fax 0203 639059)

RANDLE, Prof Sir Philip John; s of Mr Alfred John Randle (d 1952), of Nuneaton, and Nora Annie, *née* Smith (d 1968); *b* 16 July 1926; *Educ* King Edward VI GS Nuneaton, Univ of Cambridge (MA, PhD), UC Hosp Med Sch; *m* 1952, Elizabeth Ann, da of Dennis Arthur Harrison (d 1974); 1 s (Peter d 1971), 3 da (Rosalind, Sally, Susan); *Career* res fell Sidney Sussex Coll Cambridge 1954-57, fell Trinity Hall Cambridge 1957-64, lectr in biochemistry Univ of Cambridge 1955-64, prof of biochemistry Univ of Bristol 1964-75, prof of clinical biochemistry Univ of Oxford (fell Hertford Coll 1975-); FRCP, FRS; kt 1985; *Style—* Prof Sir Philip Randle; 11 Fitzherbert Close, Iffley, Oxford (☎ 0865 773115); Dept of Clinical Biochemistry, John Radcliffe Hospital, Oxford (☎ 0865 817395)

RANDOLPH, Denys; s of Harry Beckham Randolph (d 1980); *b* 6 Feb 1926; *Educ* St Paul's, Queen's Univ Belfast (BSc); *m* 1951, Marjorie, *née* Hales; 2 da; *Career* chm: Wilkinson Sword 1972-1980 (pres 1980-85), Wilkinson Match Ltd 1974-80, Woodrush Investments 1980-; chm IOD 1976-79; Master: Worshipful Co of Scientific Instrument Makers 1977, Worshipful Co of Cutlers 1985; CEng, AFRAeS, FIProdE, CBIM, FIOD; *Recreations* viticulture, golf, boating (La Russhe); *Clubs* City Livery, Little Ship; *Style—* Denys Randolph, Esq; 6 Atherstone Mews, London SW7 (☎ 071 584 5121); Clapcot House, Rush Court, Wallingford, OX10 8lJ (☎ 0491 36586)

RANDOLPH, Hugh Thomas; s of Ven Thomas Berkeley Randolph (d 1987), and Margaret, *née* Jenner; for Randolph and Jenner families see Burke's Landed Gentry 18th edn, Vol III, 1972; *b* 27 Sept 1936; *Educ* Marlborough, Sidney Sussex Coll Cambridge (MA); *Career* asst master: King Edward VI Sch Southampton 1959-63, Abingdon Sch 1963- (housemaster 1978-90); *Recreations* history, music, rural pursuits, theology; *Style—* Hugh Randolph, Esq; 30 Park Rd, Abingdon, Oxfordshire OX14 1DS (☎ 0235 522887); Abingdon Sch, Abingdon, Oxfordshire OX14 1DE (☎ 0235 521563)

RANFURLY, 7 Earl of (I 1831); Gerald Francoys Needham Knox; also Baron Welles (I 1781), Viscount Northland (I 1791), and Baron Ranfurly (UK 1826, which he sits as in House of Lords); er s of Capt John Needham Knox, RN (d 1967, ggs of Hon John Knox, 3 s of 1 Earl of Ranfurly), and Monica, *née* Kitson (d 1975); suc kinsman, 6 Earl of Ranfurly, KCMG 1988; *b* 4 Jan 1929; *Educ* Wellington; *m* 22 Jan 1955, Rosemary Beatrice Vesey, o da of Air Vice-Marshal Felton Vesey Holt, CMG, DSO (d 1931); 2 s (Viscount Northland, *qv*, Hon Rupert Stephen b 5 Nov 1963), 2 da (Lady Elizabeth Marianne (Mrs Empson) b 24 Feb 1959, Lady Frances Christina (Mrs Gordon-Jones) b 13 Feb 1961); *Heir* s, Viscount Northland, *qv*; *Career* former Lt Cdr RN; memb London Stock Exchange 1963-, chm Brewin Dolphin & Co Ltd Stockbrokers; *Style—* The Rt Hon the Earl of Ranfurly; Maltings Chase, Nayland, Colchester, Essex (☎ 0206 262224)

RANFURLY, Dowager Countess of; Hermione; *née* Llewellyn; OBE (1970); eldest da of Griffith Robert Poyntz Llewellyn, of Baglan Hall, Abergavenny, Mon (er bro of

Sir Godfrey Llewellyn, 1 Bt, CB, CBE, MC, TD, JP, DL); *m* 17 Jan 1939, 6 Earl of Ranfurly, KCMG (d 1988); 1 da (Lady Caroline Simmonds, *qv*); *Career* WWII PA to Supreme Allied Cdr Med; fndr pres Ranfurly Library Serv, which sends donated books to developing countries; received Rotary Award for World Understanding 1987; CStJ; *Style—* The Hon Dowager Countess of Ranfurly; Great Pednor, Chesham, Bucks HP5 2SU (☎ 024 06 2155)

RANGER, Sir Douglas; s of William Ranger, and Hatton Thomasina Ranger; *b* 5 Oct 1916; *Educ* Brisbane CEGS, Middx Hosp Med Sch (MB BS); *m* 1943, Betty, da of Capt Sydney Harold Draper; 2 s; *Career* temp maj and surgical specialist RAMC 1945-48; surgical registrar Middx Hosp 1942-44; otolaryngologist: Middx Hosp 1950-82, Mt Vernon Hosp 1958-74, London Chest Hosp 1952-75; dean Middx Hosp Med Sch 1974-83; memb: Cncl RCS 1967-72, Ct of Examiners 1966-72; civil conslt in otolaryngology RAF 1965-83, advsr in otolaryngology to DHSS 1971-83, hon civil conslt RAF 1983-; hon sec Br Assoc of Otolaryngologists 1965-71, dir Ferens Inst of Otolaryngology 1965-83; FRCS 1943; kt 1978; *Books* The Middlesex Hospital Medical School, Centenary to Sesquicentary; *Style—* Sir Douglas Ranger; The Tile House, Chipperfield, King's Langley, Herts WD4 9BH

RANK, John Rowland; s of Capt Rowland Rank, RFA (d 1939), of Aldwick Place, W Sussex, and Margaret, *née* McArthur (d 1988); n of late J Arthur Rank (Baron Rank, d 1972), fndr of Rank Orgn, and gs of late Joseph Rank, fndr of Rank Flour Milling; *b* 13 Jan 1930; *Educ* Stowe; *Career* property owner; Lord of Manor of Saham Toney Norfolk; Rank Ltd 1948-50; patron Pallant House Gallery Tst; tstee: Stanstead Park Fndn, Chichester Festival Theatre, Chichester Centre of Arts (former chm); sometime on Ct: of Corpn of Sons of Clergy, of Sussex Diocesan Cncl; former memb Cncl Friends of Chichester Cathedral, memb Sennicotts Church Advsy Cncl; Freeman City of London 1989; *Recreations* theatre, architectural, gardening, travelling, art exhibitions; *Clubs* Georgian Gp, Regency Soc of Brighton and Hove; *Style—* John Rank, Esq; Sennicotts, Chichester

RANK, Hon Mrs (Moira); *née* Hopwood; only da of 3rd Baron Southborough (d 1982); *b* 13 Dec 1919; *m* 1, 1940, Fl Lt Peter Anthony Stanley Woodwark (ka 1943), s of late Col Sir (Arthur) Stanley Woodwark, CMG, CBE; 1 da (Caroline Nicola b 1943); m 2, 1946, Joseph McArthur Rank, *qv*; 1 s (Colin Rowland Hopwood b 1948), 1 da (Camilla Moira b 1953); *Recreations* gardening; *Style—* The Hon Mrs Rank; Landhurst, Hartfield, Sussex TN7 4DH (☎ 0892 770293)

RANK, Nicholas John; s of John Stephen Rank, OBE, of Cheshire, and Hilda, *née* , Hammerton; *b* 5 Nov 1950; *Educ* Stockport Sch, Univ of Manchester (BA, BArch); *m* 28 July 1973, Janet Elizabeth, da of Sidney Silcock, of Cheshire; 3 da (Naomi b 1976, Anna b 1978, Sarah b 1981); *Career* architect: ptnr Nicholas Rank Assocs (architects, designers, historic bldgs conslts) 1983, conslt architect Manchester Dio, sr lectr in architecture Manchester Poly 1978-79; chm Assoc of Christians aid Planning and Architecture, memb Ecclesiastical Architects and Surveyors Assoc; memb RIBA; *Recreations* music, reading; *Style—* Nicholas Rank, Esq; 68 Parsonage Rd, Heaton Moor, Stockport, Cheshire SK4 4JR (☎ 061 442 7086, 061228 7414)

RANK, Peter Michael; s of Ernest Adrian Rank (d 1980), of Collingham, Newark, Notts, and Vera Eileen, *née* Burrage (d 1986); *b* 18 May 1947; *Educ* Univ of Hull (LLB), Queen's Coll Oxford (BCL), Inns of Court Sch of Law; *m* 5 Aug 1970, Valerie, da of John William Hayward, of Newark, Nottinghamshire; 2 s (James b 1976, Christopher b 1985), 1 da (Caroline (twin) b 1985); *Career* called to the Bar Middle Temple 1976; princ lectr in law Staffordshire Poly 1977, practising barr Oxford and Midland circuit 1984-, property law corr Solicitors Journal; numerous articles and book reviews in: Solicitors Journal, The Conveyancer, Law Socs Gazette, New Law Journal; govr two schs in Staffs 1985-, memb Legal Studies Bd of CNAA 1984-87, specialist property advsr 1987-89; Assoc Law Teacher 1975-, memb Middle Temple 1971-; *Books* You and Your Home (jtly, 1982); *Recreations* gardening, family life, judo; *Style—* Peter Rank, Esq; Rowchester Chambers, 4 Whittall St, Birmingham B4 6DH (☎ 021 233 2327, 021 236 1951, fax 021 236 7645)

RANKEILLOUR, Baroness; Mary Sibyl; da of Lt-Col Wilfred Ricardo, DSO (gn of David Ricardo, the celebrated political economist); *b* 5 April 1910; *m* 1933, 3 Baron Rankeillour (d 1967); 1 s (4 Baron), 1 da (Hon Mrs Dobson); *Style—* The Rt Hon Lady Rankeillour; 106 Headley Road, Liphook, Hants GU30 7PT (☎ 0428 722177)

RANKEILLOUR, 4 Baron (UK 1932); Peter St Thomas More Henry Hope; s of 3 Baron Rankeillour (d 1967; descended from Gen the Hon Sir Alexander Hope, of Craighall, in the Kingdom of Fife, GCB, 4 s of 2 Earl of Hopetoun, ancestor of the Marquesses of Linlithgow), and Mary Sybil, da of late Col Wilfred Ricardo, DSO; *b* 29 May 1935; *Educ* Ampleforth and privately; *Heir* kinsman, Michael Hope; *Career* farming and landowner; grand-scale landscaping; agricultural and horticultural equipment inventor and designer, freelance; former dep chm Br Sailors' Soc (North of Scotland); currently rear cdre House of Lords Yacht Club; *Style—* The Rt Hon the Lord Rankeillour; Achaderry House, Roy Bridge, W Inverness-shire (☎ 039 781 206); House of Lords, London SW1

RANKI, Dezso; *b* 1951; *Educ* Franz Liszt Acad; *Career* pianist; has played most important musical centres in Europe, Japan and America; orchs appeared with incl: Berlin Philharmonic, London Philharmonic, Concertgebouw Amsterdam, Eng Chamber Orch, Orchestre National de France, NHK Tokyo; conductors worked with incl: Zubin Mehta, Kurt Sanderling, Sir Georg Solti, Vaclav Neumann, Kyrill Kondrashin, Jeffrey Tate; regular guest London, Paris, Amsterdam, Berlin, Vienna and Milan as well as Lucerne, Vienna, Prague Spring, Berlin, Helsinki and Bath Festivals; frequent appearances at the Proms Albert Hall (most recently 1990) and Queen Elizabeth Hall; many recordings made with Hungaraton, Teldec and Quint Records Awards; first prize: Robert Schumann Competition Zwickau 1969, Int Liszt Competition Budapest 1973; Kossuth prize (Hungary's top cultural award) 1978, Grand Prix de l'Academie Charles-Cros; *Style—* Deszo Ranki, Esq; Sue Lubbock Concert Management, 25 Courthope Road, London NW3 2LE (☎ 071 485 5932, fax 071 267 0179)

RANKIN, Alick Michael; CBE (1987); s of Col Niall Rankin (d 1965), and Lady Jean Margaret Rankin, DCVO, *qv*, da of 12 Earl of Stair; *b* 23 Jan 1935; *Educ* Eton, Univ of Oxford; *m* 1, 1958 (m dis 1976), Susan, da of Hugh Dewhurst, of Dungarthill, Dunkeld; 1 s, 3 da; m 2, 1976, Suzetta, da of Patrick Nelson, of Seafield, IOM; *Career* served Scots Gds 1953-55; investmt banking Toronto Canada 1956-59, joined Scottish & Newcastle Breweries 1960 (gp md 1983-, chief exec 1985, dep chm 1987, chm 1989); dir: Bank of Scotland 1987, Christian Salveson plc 1986; chm The Brewers Soc 1990; memb Brewers' Co; *Recreations* fishing, shooting, golf, tennis; *Clubs* Royal and Ancient (St Andrews), Hon Co of Edinburgh Golfers (Muirfield), Boodle's, New (Edinburgh), I Zingari (cricket), Eton Ramblers, Butterflies, Lansdowne; *Style—* Alick Rankin Esq, CBE; 3 Saxe Coburg Place, Edinburgh (☎ 031 332 3684); Scottish & Newcastle Breweries, Abbey Brewery, Holyrood Rd, Edinburgh EH8 8YS (☎ 031 556 2591)

RANKIN, Andrew; QC; s of William Locke Rankin (d 1963), and Mary Ann, *née* McArdle; *b* 3 Aug 1924; *Educ* Royal HS Edinburgh, Univ of Edinburgh (BL), Downing Coll Cambridge (BA); *m* 1, 1944 (m dis 1963), Winifred, da of Frank McAdam, of Edinburgh; 5 children, 1 decd; m 2, 1964, Veronica (d 1990), da of George Aloysius Martin, of Liverpool (d 1965); *Career* lectr faculty of law Univ of Liverpool 1948-52; called to the Bar Gray's Inn 1950, rec of the Crown Ct 1970-; *Style—* Andrew Rankin, Esq, QC; Chelwood, Pine Walks, Prenton, Birkenhead, Merseyside L42 8LQ; 69 Cliffords Inn, Fetter Lane, London EC4A 1BZ (☎ 071 405 2932); Strand Chambers, 218 Strand, London WC2R 1AP (☎ 071 353 7825, fax 071 583 2073, telex 265871)

RANKIN, (Herbert) David; s of Walter Rankin (d 1980), of Newtownards, Co Down, and Anna, *née* Douglas; *b* 21 June 1931; *Educ* Belfast Royal Acad, Tinity Coll Dublin (BA); *m* 1 Nov 1957, Anne Margaret Isobel, da of Ebenezer Vannan (d 1964), of Ewell, Surrey; 1 s (Aidan b 1966); *Career* asst lectr in classics QMC 1955-58, asst lectr and lectr in classics Univ of Sheffield 1958-65, fndn prof of classical studies and chm of Dept Monash Univ Aust 1965-72, head Dept of Philosophy Univ of Southampton 1989- (prof of classics and head of Dept 1972-88, prof of ancient philosophy 1988); *Books* Plato and the Individual (1964), Petronius the Artist (1971), Archilochus of Paros (1978), Sophists Socratics and Cynics (1983), Antisthenes Sokratikos (1985), Celts and the Classical World (1987); *Recreations* Celtic studies, model railways, photography; *Style—* David Rankin, Esq; Dept of Philosophy, Univ of Southampton, Southampton S09 5NH (☎ 0703 595000 ext 3400, telex 47661)

RANKIN, Gavin Niall; s and h of Sir Ian Niall Rankin, 4 Bt; *b* 19 May 1962; *Educ* Eton, Buckingham Univ (LLB); *Career* 2 Lt Scots Gds 1981; Price Waterhouse 1984-88, CA Panfida Gp 1989-90, md Lonpra Prague 1991-; page of Honour to HM Queen Elizabeth The Queen Mother 1977-79; memb ICA, FRGS; *Clubs* Annabels, Brooks's; *Style—* Gavin Rankin, Esq; 52 Bassett Rd, London W10 6JL; Rasinovo Nabrezi 42, Prague 2, Czechoslovakia

RANKIN, Sir Ian Niall; 4 Bt (UK 1898), of Bryngwyn, Much Dewchurch, Co Hereford; s of late Lt-Col (Arthur) Niall Talbot Rankin, yr s of 2 Bt; s unc, Sir Hugh Rankin, 3 Bt 1988; *b* 19 Dec 1932; *Educ* Eton, ChCh Oxford (MA); *m* 1, 1959 (m dis 1967), Alexandra, da of Adm Sir Laurence George Durlacher, KCB, OBE, DSC; 1 s (Gavin Niall), 1 da (Zara Sophia b 1960); m 2, 1980, June, er da of late Capt Thomas Marsham-Townshend, and former w of Bryan Montagu Norman; 1 s (Lachlan John b 1980), 1 step da; *Heir* s, Gavin Niall Rankin b 19 May 1962; *Career* Lt Scots Gds (Res); dir of Indust Cos; FRGS; *Recreations* tennis, shooting, yachting; *Clubs* Royal Yacht Sqdn, Pratt's, Car Clamp Recovery, Beefsteak, White's; *Style—* Sir Ian Rankin, Bt; 63 Marlborough Place, London NW8 0PT (☎ 071 286 0251)

RANKIN, James Deans (Hamish); s of James Deans Rankin (d 1963), of Barnoldswick, Yorks, and Florence Elizabeth, *née* Wight; *b* 17 Feb 1943; *Educ* Merchiston Castle Sch, Gonville and Caius Coll Cambridge (BA, MA); *m* 6 Oct 1973, Susan Margaret, da of Francis Eric Adams; 1 s (Andrew Deans b 15 May 1975), 1 da (Sally Margaret b 5 May 1977); *Career* Agric div ICI: res 1965-68, projects and engineering 1968-71, plant commissioning and management Ammonia Works 1971-77, res management 1977-83; process technol gp mangr ICI New Science Gp 1983-88, Res & Devpt mangr ICI Films 1988- FEng 1987, FIChE 1987; *Recreations* domestic engineering, motoring, church bell ringing, photography; *Style—* Hamish Rankin, Esq; ICI Films, PO Box 90, Wilton Centre, Middlesborough, Cleveland TS6 8JE (☎ 0642 432692, fax 0642 432762)

RANKIN, Lady Jean Margaret; *née* Dalrymple; DCVO (1969), CVO (1957); da of late 12 Earl of Stair, KT, DSO; *b* 15 Aug 1905; *m* 1931, Lt-Col (Arthur) Niall Talbot Rankin, Scots Gds (d 1965), s of Lt-Col Sir (James) Reginald (Lea) Rankin, 2 Bt; 2 s (*see* Rankin, Ian Niall and Rankin, Alick Michael); *Career* woman of the bedchamber to HM Queen Elizabeth The Queen Mother 1947-; govr: Thomas Coram Fndn, Magdalen Tst; *Style—* Lady Jean Rankin, DCVO; House of Treshnish, Dervaig, Isle of Mull (☎ 068 84 249)

RANKIN, Dr Robert Alexander; s of Prof Oliver Shaw Rankin (d 1954), of Edinburgh, and Olivia Theresa, *née* Shaw (d 1963); *b* 27 Oct 1915; *Educ* Fettes, Clare Coll Cambridge (BA, MA, PhD, ScD); *m* 25 July 1942, Mary Ferrier, da of William Morgan Llewellyn, (d 1959), of Cardiff; 1 s (Charles Richard Shaw b 1947), 3 da (Susan Mary Llewellyn b 1943, Fenella Kathleen Clare b 1950, Olivia Roberta Mary b 1954); *Career* WWII work on rockets MOS 1940-45; asst tutor and praelector Clare Coll Cambridge 1947-51 (res fell 1939-47), lectr Univ of Cambridge 1947-51 (former asst lectr), Mason prof of maths Univ of Birmingham 1951-54, dean of faculties Univ of Glasgow 1985-88 (prof of maths 1954-82, clerk of Senate 1971-78); chm: Scot Maths Cncl 1967-73, Clyde Estuary Amenity Cncl 1969-81; memb Glasgow Incorporation of Hammermen 1984; FRSE 1955, FRSAMD 1982; *Books* Introduction to Mathematical Analysis (1969), Lectures on The Modular Group (1969),Modular Forms and Functions (1969); *Recreations* hill walking, organ music, gaelic studies; *Style—* Dr Robert Rankin, FRSE; 98 Kelvin Ct, Glasgow G12 0AH (☎ 041 339 2641); Univ of Glasgow, Dept of Maths, Glasgow G12 8QW (☎ 041 339 8855)

RANKIN, Robina, Lady; Robina; da of Stewart Finlay, of Comrie, Perthshire; *m* 1946, as his 2 w, Sir Hugh Charles Rhys Rankin, 3 Bt (d 1988); *Career* SRN, Swedish masseuse, ret; FSA (Scot); *Style—* Robina, Lady Rankin; Bracken Cottage, Kindallochan, Pitlochry, Perthshire

RANKIN-HUNT, Maj David; TD (1990); s of James Rankin-Hunt, of Wales, and Edwina Anne, *née* Blakeman; *b* 26 Aug 1956; *Educ* Christ Coll Brecon, St Martin's Sch; *Career* Lt Scots Gds, Maj The London Scot Regt (51 Highland Vol) 1989-; Lord Chamberlain's Office 1981-: registrar 1987-89, employed in The Royal Collection 1989-; dir The Highland Soc, lay steward St George's Chapel Windsor Castle; Order of Isabella The Catholic Fifth Class Spain; *Recreations* military history, heraldry, conservation issues, Welsh affairs; *Clubs* Army and Navy, Highland Brigade; *Style—* Maj David Rankin-Hunt, TD; Flat 5, Henry III Tower, Windsor Castle, Berkshire, SL4 1NJ (☎ 0753 851408); The Royal Collection, Stable Yard House, St James' Palace, London SW1 (☎ 071 930 4832)

RANKINE, Jean Morag; da of Alan Rankine (d 1988), of Whitley Bay, and Margaret Mary Sloan, *née* Reid; *b* 5 Sept 1941; *Educ* Central Newcastle HS, UCL (BA, MPhil), Copenhagen Univ; *Career* British Museum: res asst Dept of Printed Books 1967-73, asst keeper Dir's Office 1973-78, head of public servs 1978-83, (dep dir 1983-); fell UCL 1990; *Recreations* rowing, skiing, walking, opera; *Clubs* Thames Rowing; *Style—* Miss Jean Rankine; British Museum, London WC1B 3DG (☎ 071 323 8490, fax 071 323 8480)

RANNIE, Prof Ian; s of James Rannie (d 1954), of Troon, and Nichola Denniston, *née* McMeekan (d 1971); *b* 29 Oct 1915; *Educ* Ayr Acad, Univ of Glasgow (Bsc, MB ChB, BSc); *m* 3 July 1943, Flora, da of William Welch (d 1954), of Gateshead; 2 s (Bruce b 1944, Gordon b 1946); *Career* lectr in pathology Med Sch Univ of Durham 1942-, conslt pathologist Royal Victoria Infirmary Newcastle upon Tyne 1948-81; prof of pathology Dental Sch: Univ of Durham 1960-63, Univ of Newcastle 1963-81; active in Univ affairs and NHS, memb BMA Ctees (Cncl and Jt Conslt Ctee), pres Int Soc of Geographical Pathology 1970-73, vice pres Int Angiology Soc 1970-77, chm Central Manpower Ctee 1976-81; hon membership awarded by Hungarian Atherosclerosis Soc 1976; FRCPath 1963, FIBiol 1963; *Recreations* golf; *Clubs* East India, Royal Overseas League; *Style—* Prof Ian Rannie; 5 Osborne Villas, Newcastle upon Tyne NE2 1JU (☎ 091 281 3163)

RANSFORD, Andrew Oliver; s of Doctor Oliver Neil Ransford (med and hist author), of Bulawayo, Zimbabwe, and Doris Irene, *née* Galloway; *b* 25 April 1940; *Educ* Emmanuel Coll Cambridge (BA), Univ Coll Hosp Med Sch (MB BChir); *m* 21 Sept

1968, Penelope Jane, da of Peter Albert Nigel Milmo (d 1968), of Caterham, Surrey; 2 s (Mark b 1971, Christopher b 1977), 2 da (Philippa b 1969, Helen b 1980); *Career* conslt orthopaedic surgn: Univ Coll Hosp London 1977, Royal Nat Orthopaedic Hosp 1978; hon conslt orthopaedic surgn Nat Hosps for Nervous Diseases London 1989; multiple orthopaedic publications in journals and medical text books; FRCS 1970; *Recreations* antiques; *Clubs* BMA, RCS; *Style—* Andrew Ransford, Esq; 5 Fordington Rd, London N6 4TD (☎ 081 883 3317); 107 Harley St, London W1N 1DG (☎ 071 486 1088)

RANSOM, David; s of Wallace Charles Ransom, of Ilkeston, Derbyshire, and Betty Florence, *née* Goodson; *b* 2 Sept 1947; *Educ* Hallcroft Sch, City of Sheffield Coll, Univ of Nottingham, Sheffield Poly; *m* 5 Jan 1978, Susan; 1 s (Joseph b 11 Jan 1987), 1 da (Jessica b 1 Dec 1981); *Career* basketball coach; Nat Basketball League coach 1976-87; clubs: Doncaster Panthers, Leeds Athletic Inst, Calderdale, Nottingham; head coach English Basketball Team 1989- (asst coach 1987-89); nat dir of coaching 1990-; 53 int caps, team qualified for semi-finals Euro Championships Turkey 1987 and Norway 1989; college lectr 1970-79 and 1984-87, projects mangr MSC 1980-82, local govt mangr 1982-84, dir of mktg 1987-88, asst princ with responsibility for mktg 1988-90; *Recreations* management training and consultancy; *Style—* David Ransom, Esq; 41 Mylor Rd, Sheffield S11 7PF (☎ 0742 661895); English Basketball Association, 48 Bradford Rd, Stanningley, Leeds LS28 6DF (☎ 0532 361166, fax 0532 361022)

RANSOM, Robert Stephen; s of Donald Hibbert Ransom (d 1963), of Bushey, and Dora Millicent, *née* Lewis (d 1970); *b* 26 Nov 1929; *Educ* Bradfield; *m* 28 Dec 1963, Alice, da of Poul Emil Kronmann (d 1979), of Copenhagen; 2 da (Anne-Marie b 1966, Julia b 1970); *Career* Lt RA 1948-50; CA 1957, sr ptnr Macnair Mason 1980- (ptnr 1958-); FCA; *Recreations* literature, travel, gardening; *Clubs* City of London; *Style—* Robert Ransom, Esq; Rampyndene House, Burwash, Sussex (☎ 0435 882248); Macnair Mason, 30-33 Minories, London EC3N 1DU (☎ 071 481 3022, fax 071 488 4458, telex 886189)

RANSOME, Hon Mrs; Hon (Shirley) Elizabeth; *née* Macpherson; da of 2 Baron Macpherson of Drumochter by his 1 w Ruth; *b* 31 March 1953; *m* 1978, Mark William Ransome; *Style—* The Hon Mrs Ransome; 101, 18th Street, Parkhurst 2193, Johannesburg, S Africa

RANT, His Hon Judge James William; QC (1980); s of Harry George Rant (d 1989), of Gerrards Cross, Bucks, and Barbara, *née* Veale (d 1989); Grant of Arms to William Rant of Yelverton 1574 (Robert Cooke, Clarenceaux King of Arms); *b* 16 April 1936; *Educ* Stowe, Univ of Cambridge (MA, LLM); *m* 1963, Helen, da of Percival George Adnams (d 1964), of IOM; 2 s, 2 da; *Career* called to the Bar Gray's Inn 1961, pupillage with the late J N Dunlop 1962-63, in chambers of Dorothy Waddy QC until 1968, head of Chambers 1968-84, dep circuit judge 1975, rec of the Crown Ct 1979, circuit judge 1984, judge of Central Criminal Ct 1986, judge advocate general of the Army and RAF 1991; Freeman: City of London, Worshipful Co of Clockmakers; *Recreations* cookery, music, family life; *Style—* His Hon Judge James Rant, QC; 3 Temple Gdns, Middle Temple Lane, Temple, London EC4

RANTZEN, Esther Louise (Mrs Desmond Wilcox); OBE; da of H B Rantzen, of London, and Katherine, *née* Leverson; *b* 22 June 1940; *Educ* N London Collegiate Sch, Somerville Coll Oxford (MA); *m* 22 Dec 1977, Desmond Wilcox, s of John Wilcox; 1 s (Joshua b 1981), 2 da (Emily b 1978, Rebecca b 1980); *Career* television prodr and presenter; studio mangr BBC Radio 1963; BBC TV: researcher 1965, dir 1967, researcher and reporter Bradens Week 1968, presenter and prodr That's Life 1973-; prodr documentary series The Big Time 1976; presenter: That's Family Life, Hearts of Gold 1988, Drugwatch, Childwatch; chm Childline; pres Meet-a-Mum Assoc; vice pres ASBAH; hon memb NSPCC 1989; memb: Consumer Cncl 1981-90, Health Educn Authy 1989-, Health Visitors Assoc, Spastics Soc, Contact-a-Family (families of disabled children), DEMAND (furniture for the disabled), Downs Children Assoc; patron Addenbrookes Kidney Patients Assoc, tstee Ben Hardwick Meml Fund; Special Judges Award RTS 1974, BBC Personality of 1975 Variety Club of GB, Euro Soc for Organ Transplant Award 1985, Richard Dimbleby award BAFTA 1988; *Books* Kill the Chocolate Biscuit (with D Wilcox, 1981), Baby Love (with D Wilcox, 1985), Ben - the Story of Ben Hardwick (with Shaun Woodward) 1985; *Recreations* walking the dogs; *Style—* Ms Esther Rantzen, OBE; BBC TV, Wood Lane, London W12 7RJ; Childline, London N1 0QJ; c/o Noel Gay Artists, 24 Denmark St, London WC2 (☎ 071 836 3941)

RAPER, Dr Alan Humphrey; CBE (1989); s of Frederick George Raper (d 1977), and Beatrice May, *née* Humphrey; *b* 11 Aug 1927; *Educ* Acklam Hall Middlesbrough, Univ of Leeds (BSc, Akroyd scholar); *m* 1955, Audrey, *née* Baker; 1 s, 2 da; *Career* dir: Glaxo Holdings Ltd, Glaxo Nigeria Ltd, Glaxo Group Ltd, Glaxochem (Pte) Ltd Singapore, Glaxo Nigeria Ltd, Glaxo Laboratories (India) Ltd, Glaxo Far East (Pte) Ltd, Glaxo Orient (Pte) Ltd, Glaxo Australia Pty Ltd, Glaxo Bangladesh Ltd, Glaxo Canada Ltd, Glaxo Laboratories (Pakistan) Ltd, Glaxo Philippines Inc, Glaxo NZ Ltd, Glaxo (1972) Charity Tst, Scholeds Ltd; chm Macfarlan Smith Ltd (ret 1987), pres Br & S Asian Trade Assoc 1986-88; memb: Cncl Chemical Industs Assoc 1974-87, Health and Safety Cmmn 1983-90; *Recreations* skiing, hill walking, history; *Clubs* The Oriental; *Style—* Dr Alan Raper, CBE; The White House, Husthwaite, York YO6 3TA

RAPHAEL, Adam Eliot Geoffrey; s of Geoffrey George Raphael (d 1969), of London, and Nancy May, *née* Rose; *b* 22 April 1938; *Educ* Charterhouse, Oriel Coll Oxford (MA); *m* 16 May 1970, Caroline Rayner, da of George Ellis (d 1954), of Cape Town, SA; 1 s (Thomas Geoffrey b 1971), 1 da (Anna Nancy b 1974); *Career* 2 Lt RA 1956-58; political corr The Guardian 1974-76 (foreign corr Washington 1969-73 and S Africa 1973), exec ed The Observer 1988- (political corr 1976-81, political ed 1981-87), presenter Newsnight BBC TV 1987-88; *Recreations* tennis, skiing; *Clubs* RAC, Hurlingham, SCGB; *Style—* Adam Raphael, Esq; 50 Addison Ave, London W11 4EP (☎ 071 603 9133); The Observer, Chelsea Bridge House, Queenstown Rd, London SW8 4NN (☎ 071 350 3435)

RAPHAEL, Derek Neale; s of Capt Maurice Raphael, of Lausanne, Switzerland, and Mirri, *née* Blusgar (d 1986); *b* 3 Sept 1938; *Educ* Kingswood Coll Grahamstown SA (BCom), Univ of Cape Town (BCom); *m* 26 Oct 1965, Inks, da of Maj Phil Baron, of Bulawayo, Zimbabwe; 3 s (Gavin b 1967, Andrew b 1969, Peter b 1971); *Career* md Continental Ore Euro Ltd 1965-73, chm Derek Raphael and Co Ltd 1973; *Recreations* cricket, real tennis, skiing, riding, golf; *Clubs* MCC; *Style—* Derek Raphael, Esq; 99 Clifton Hill, London NW8 0JR (☎ 071 328 0978); 18 Spring St, London W2 3RA (☎ 071 486 9931, fax 071 935 0179, telex 261916)

RAPHAEL, Frederic Michael; s of Cedric Raphael Raphael, TD (d 1979), and Irene Rose, *née* Mauser; *b* 14 Aug 1931; *Educ* Charterhouse, St John's Coll Cambridge (MA); *m* 17 Jan 1955, Sylvia Betty, da of Hyman Glatt; 2 s (Paul b 1958, Stephen b 1967), 1 da (Sarah b 1960); *Career* author; *Books* Obbligato (1956), The Earlsdon Way (1958), The Limits of Love (1960), A Wild Surmise (1961), The Graduate Wife (1962), The Trouble with England (1962), Lindmann (1963), Orchestra and Beginners (1967), Like Men Betrayed (1970), Who Were You With Last Night? (1971), April, June and November (1972), Richard's Things (1973, screenplay 1981), California Time (1975), The Glittering Prizes (1976, TV plays 1976, Writer of the Year award), Heaven and Earth (1985), After The War (1988), The Hidden I (1990); short stories: Sleeps Six (1979), Oxbridge Blues (1980, TV plays 1984), Think of England (1986); screenplays: Nothing but the Best (1964), Darling (Acad award 1965), Two for the Road (1967), Far From the Madding Crowd (1967), A Severed Head (1972), Daisy Miller (1974), Rogue Male (1976), Something's Wrong (dir 1978), School Play (1979), The Best of Friends (1979), Oxbridge Blues (1984), After the War (1989); biography: Somerset Maugham and his World (1977), Byron (1982); essays: Bookmarks (ed, 1975), Cracks in the Ice (1979); From the Greek (play, 1979); translations (with Kenneth McLeish): Poems of Catullus (1976), The Oresteia (1978, televised as The Serpent Son BBC 1979), Complete plays of Aeschylus (1991); FRSL 1964; *Recreations* tennis, skiing; *Clubs* Savile, The Queen's; *Style—* Frederic Raphael, Esq; The Wick, Langham, Colchester, Essex CO4 5PE; Lagardelle, St Laurent-La-Vallée 24170 Belves, France; c/o A P Watt Ltd, 20 John St, London WC1

RAPLEY, Hon Mrs (Heather); *née* McLeavy; da of Baron McLeavy (Life Peer, d 1976); *b* 1929; *m* 1955, Patrick William Rapley; *Style—* The Hon Mrs Rapley; 7 Salcombe Drive, Earley, Reading

RAPLEY, Raymond Herbert; s of Richard Herbert Rapley (d 1928), and Olive Evelyn, *née* Riddiford (d 1979); *b* 13 Jan 1929; *Educ* Huntingdon GS, Open Univ (BA); *m* 6 May 1950, Betty, da of Harry Gregory, MM (d 1946) of Dronfield, Derbys; 2 s (Martin b 1957, David b 1965), 2 da (Elizabeth Frances, b 1955, Yvonne Linda b 1958); *Career* Rapleys Surveyors and Planning Conslts London 1951-89, md Yelcon Ltd Housebuilders Cambs 1961-; former memb Cncl Int Soc of Valuers and Auctioneers 1968-69, regnl pres Housebuilders Fedn (E Anglia regn) 1986-87, pres Bldg Employers Confedn (Cambridge branch) 1986-87; *Style—* Raymond Rapley, Esq; Misty Meadows, Gore Tree Rd, Hemingford Grey, Cambs

RAPPORT, Cecil Herbert; MBE, JP, DL (South Glamorgan); s of Maurice Aaron Rapport (d 1953), and Phoebe Annie, *née* Jacobs (d 1960); *b* 12 Oct 1915; *Educ* Monkton House Coll Cardiff, City of Cardiff Tech Coll; *m* 25 Nov 1942, Audrey Rachel, da of Sidney Fligelstone; 1 s (Derek Ivor), 2 da (Valerie Avery Gee, Heather Hockley); *Career* Welch Regt 1939-45; pres: Cardiff Inst for the Blind, Royal Br Legion Cardiff, Friends of Cardiff Royal Infirmary, Cardiff Central Cons Assoc; chm Wales Festival of Rememberance; High Sheriff S Glamorgan 1984-85, former Dep Lord Mayor City of Cardiff; former Alderman City Cardiff, Freeman City of London 1959; memb: Worshipful Co of Horners 1958, Guild of Freemen of the City of London 1969; memb IOD; KStJ; *Recreations* swimming, sailing, music; *Clubs* City Livery, RAC; *Style—* Cecil Rapport, Esq, MBE, JP, DL; Cefn Coed House, Cefn Coed Rd, Cyncoed, Cardiff, South Glam CF2 6AP (☎ 2222 757375); Ivor House, Bridge St, Cardiff, South Glam CF1 2TH (☎ 02222 373737/02222 231444, fax 0222 220121)

RASCH, Maj Sir Richard Guy Carne; 3 Bt (UK 1903); s of Brig Guy Elland Carne Rasch, CVO, DSO (d 1955; s of 1 Bt), and Phyllis Dorothy Lindsay, *née* Greville (d 1977); suc unc, Col Sir Frederic Carne, 2 Bt, TD, 1963; *b* 10 Oct 1918; *Educ* Eton, RMC Sandhurst; *m* 1, 1947 (m dis 1959), Anne Mary, eld da of late Maj John Henry Dent-Brocklehurst, OBE, of Sudeley Castle, Glos; 1 s, 1 da; m 2, 1961, Fiona Mary, eld da of Robert Douglas Shaw, and former w of Humphrey John Rodham Balliol Salmon; *Heir* s, Simon Anthony Carne Rasch, *qv*; *Career* former Maj Grenadier Gds; memb HM Bodyguard of Hon Corps of Gentlemen-at-Arms 1968-88; memb London Stock Exchange; *Recreations* fishing, shooting; *Clubs* White's, Pratt's, Cavalry and Guards'; *Style—* Major Sir Richard Rasch, Bt; The Manor House, Lower Woodford, Salisbury, Wilts SP4 6NQ; 30 Ovington Square, London SW3 1LR

RASCH, Simon Anthony Carne; s and h of Sir Richard Rasch, 3 Bt, by his 1 w, Anne Mary, eld da of late Maj John Henry Dent-Brocklehurst, OBE, of Sudeley Castle, Winchcombe, Glos; *b* 26 Feb 1948; *Educ* Eton, RAC Cirencester; *m* 31 Oct 1987, Julia, er da of Maj Michael and Lady Joanna Stourton, *qv*; 1 da (b 10 Sept 1990); *Career* page of honour to HM 1962-64; chartered surveyor; *Style—* Simon Rasch Esq; The White House, Manningford Bruce, nr Pewsey, Wilts (☎ 098 063 0200)

RASH, Dr Ramakant Maganlal; s of Maganlal Bhanji Rash, of Heaton Moor, Stockport, and Kasturben Maganlal, *née* Mirani; *b* 20 Jan 1937; *Educ* Govt Secdy Sch Kampala Uganda, Plymouth and Davenport Coll, Univ of Manchester (BSc, MB ChB); *m* 6 June 1964, Bena Aruna, da of Narshidas Liladhar Ghelani (d 1962); 1 s (Amar b 28 Jan 1971); *Career* conslt physician in geriatric med Wythenshawe Hosp Manchester 1975- (house physician 1962-63, house surgn 1963, sr house offr 1963-66, med registrar 1966-70, sr registrar 1971-75), hon assoc lectr in geriatric med 1985-; memb Br Geriatric Soc, fell Manchester Med Soc; memb BMA, MRCP 1967, FRCP 1984; *Recreations* gardening, reading, watching football (supporter of Manchester City FC); *Style—* Dr Ramakant Rash; 46 Leegate Rd, Heaton Moor, Stockport SK4 4AX (☎ 061 432 1085); Rehabilitation Unit, Area A, Wythenshawe Hospital, Southmoor Rd, Manchester M23 9LT (☎ 061 946 2877/8)

RASHBASS, Dr Barbara; da of Leonard Cramer (d 1972), and Sarina, *née* Klinger; *Educ* Godolphin Sch Salisbury, Univ Coll London (MB BS); *m* 9 Oct 1956, Cyril Rashbass (d 1982); 2 s (Jem b 1961, Andrew b 1965), 1 da (Pen b 1964); *Career* called to the Bar 1969, sec Wolfson Family Charitable Tst 1989-, dir Wolfson Fndn 1990- (dep dir 1987-90), PMO MRC 1983-87, dept chm Harrow Health Authy 1982-84; memb Med Legal Soc; DCH 1961, DPH 1968; FRSM 1989; *Recreations* tennis, cello, gardening; *Style—* Dr Barbara Rashbass; Universal House, 251-256 Tottenham Court Rd, London W1A 1BZ (☎ 071 580 6441, fax 071 631 3641)

RASHID, Dr Abutaleb Muhammed Fazlur (Faz); s of Dr A M M A Rouf (d 1972), of Barisal, Bangladesh, and Shamse Ara, *née* Ahmed; *b* 29 Dec 1937; *Educ* Univ of Dhaka Bangladesh (MB BS, MSc); *m* 9 June 1968, Faozia Sultana, da of M Habibullah (d 1987), of Chandpur, Bangladesh; 2 da (Tina Farzana b 1971, Samantha Fahima b 1972); *Career* various trg posts in pathology Dhaka Med Coll and Hosp Bangladesh 1962-70, asst prof of pathology Inst of Post Grad Med and Res Dhaka Bangladesh 1970-74, asst in pathology Inst of Pathology Free Univ of Berlin W Ger 1974-75, registrar in pathology Royal Sussex Co Hosp 1975-78, sr registrar in pathology Southampton Gen Hosp and Poole Gen Hosp 1978-80, conslt pathologist Joyce Green Hosp 1980-; coll tutor and currently chm RCPath; past pres Dartford Bengali Assoc, past treas London and SE Branch Bangladesh Med Assoc in UK; past memb: Central Exec Ctee Bangladesh Med Assoc in UK, Regnl Exec Ctee BMA Dartford and Medway, ACP, BSCC, ODA; FRCPath; *Recreations* swimming, jogging, snooker, gardening, DIY, computers; *Style—* Dr Faz Rashid; Joyce Green Hospital, Dartford, Kent DA1 5PL (☎ 0322 227242 ext 325)

RASHLEIGH, Jonathan; s of Vernon Leslie Rashleigh, (d 1936), and Flora Marian, *née* Leitch (d 1925); *b* 7 June 1913; *Educ* Lancing; *m* 1943, Margaret, da of Philip James Stoneman; 1 da (Carolyn Vivien b 1944); m 2, 1956, Lavinia Mary Ellert, da of Lt-Col Richard Leslie Agnew; 1 s (Julian Philip b 1957), 1 da (Elizabeth b 1961); *Career* RAF: Gen Duties Branch India 1941-45, B flight cmd 5 sqdn India 1942-44, sqdn ldr Tech Trg Cmd Reading 1945; asst chief accountant Assam Railways & Trading Co India 1939-40, sec International Refrigeration Co Brixton 1946, sr ptnr Phillips & Drew 1961-72 (joined 1947); author of paper Portfolio Investments - Aids to Decision Taking 1968; FCA 1938; *Recreations* eventing with my daughter Elizabeth; *Style—* Jonathan Rashleigh, Esq; Dumbledore, Warren Row, nr Reading, Berkshire RG10 8QS (☎ 0628822723)

RASHLEIGH, Jonathan Michael Vernon; s of Nicholas Vernon Rashleigh, of

Rodmell, Lewes, Sussex, and Rosalie Mary, *née* Matthews; *b* 29 Sept 1950; *Educ* Bryanston; *m* 5 April 1975, Sarah, da of John Norwood, of Knowle, Solihull, W Midlands; 3 s (Charles b 1979, Hugh b 1986, Philip b 1988), 1 da (Julia b 1982); *Career* Ernst and Whinney 1968-76, 3i Group 1976-90 (dir 3i plc 1986-90), dir Legal & General Ventures Ltd 1991; Freeman City of London, Liveryman Worshipful Co of Tobacco Pipe Makers and Tobacco Blenders 1972; FCA 1979 (ACA 1974); *Recreations* chess, theatre, cricket, music; *Style—* Jonathan Rashleigh, Esq; Longeaves, Norton Lindsey, Warwick CV35 8JL (☎ 092684 2523); Bucklersbury House, 3 Queen Victoria St, London EC4N 8EL

RASHLEIGH, Sir Richard Harry; 6 Bt (UK 1831); s of Sir Harry Evelyn Battie Rashleigh, 5 Bt (d 1984), and Honora Elizabeth, *née* Sneyd; *b* 8 July 1958; *Educ* All Hallows Sch Dorset; *Heir* none; *Career* mgmnt accountant; with Arthur Guinness Son & Co plc 1980-82, Dexion-Comino Int Ltd 1982-84, United Biscuits plc 1985-; *Recreations* sailing, tennis, shooting; *Clubs* Naval; *Style—* Sir Richard Rashleigh, Bt; Stowford Grange, Lewdown, nr Okehampton, Devon EX20 4BQ; office: UBFF, North Rd Industrial Estate, Okehampton, Devon (☎ 0837 3261)

RASKIN, Susan; da of John Cary Abbatt (d 1988), of Bath, and Sybil Eileen, *née* Lympaney; *b* 28 March 1942; *Educ* Plymouth HS, Tiffin Girls' Sch Kingston upon Thames; *m* 18 Aug 1966, James Leo Raskin, s of Meyer Raskin (d 1971); 2 s (Benjamin Leo 1969, Thomas John b 1972), 1 da (Joanna b 1967); *Career* admitted slr 1967; ptnr: Raskin & Raskin 1969-88, Russell Jones & Walker 1988-; sr law lectr Bristol Ploy 1980-83 (lectr 1974-80); Bath Assoc of Graduate Women Slrs, Bristol Medico-Legal Assoc; govr Bath HS, GPDST 1983-; *Recreations* singing, foreign languages, reading, hill-walking, swimming; *Style—* Mrs Susan Raskin; Tanglewood, Claverton, Bath (☎ 0225 723366); Russell Jones & Walker, 15 Clare St, Bristol (☎ 0272 273098)

RASTALL, (Walter) Guy; s of Herbert Guy Rastall (d 1968), and Madge Eveline Rastall, *née* Haggar (d 1985); gs of Walter Haggar the S Wales film pioneer; *b* 29 April 1938; *Educ* Lydney GS, Univ of Birmingham (BA); *m* 5 Sept 1966, Jane, da of Hector Ardern, MBE, of Gwent; 1 s (Andrew b 1967), 2 da (Felicity b 1969, Penelope b 1972); *Career* CA; sr lectr Bristol Poly 1965-70, chief cost and mgmnt accountant (military engines) Rolls-Royce plc 1970-; FCA; *Recreations* golf; *Clubs* St Pierre Golf and Country; *Style—* Guy Rastall, Esq; Keep House, Castle View, Tutshill, Chepstow, Gwent (☎ 0291 622680); Rolls Royce plc, Filton, Bristol (☎ 0272 797734)

RATCLIFF, Christopher John Raven; s of John Henry Raven Ratcliff, (d 1989), of Bengeo, Hertford, Herts, and Kathleen Mary, *née* Viall (d 1956); *b* 4 July 1931; *Educ* The Leys Sch Cambridge, Clare Coll Cambridge (MA), Architectural Assoc Sch of Architecture (AA Dipl); *m* 29 Oct 1955, Josephine Celia, da of Alexander Delap (d 1962), of Patnor House, Eastergate, Chichester; 2 s (Jeremy b 1959, Jonathan b 1961), 2 da (Diana b 1956, Melanie b 1963); *Career* Nat Serv 2 Lt RE 1957-59; architect; ptnr Building Design Ptnrship 1980- (architect 1959, assoc 1963), examiner Sch of Architecture Univ of Liverpool 1986-; memb: Cncl ARCUK 1980-82, Cncl RIBA 1982-88; chm RIBA NW region 1988-90, govr Beaumont Coll (Spastics Soc) Lancaster 1989-; MRIBA; *Recreations* genealogy, calligraphy, music, fell-walking; *Clubs* Sloane; *Style—* Christopher Ratcliff, Esq; Building Design Partnership, Vernon St, Moor Lane, Preston, Lancs PR1 3PQ (☎ 0772 59383)

RATCLIFFE, Anne Kirkpatrick; da of John Kirkpatrick Ratcliffe, and Alice Margaret, *née* Vaughan-Jones; *b* 19 April 1956; *Educ* Cheltenham Ladies' Coll, Univ of Southampton (BSc), City Univ (Dip Law); *Career* called to the Bar Inner Temple 1981, in practice 1981-; memb: Soc of Cons Lawyers, Bow GP, London Borough of Wandsworth Cons; treas Graveney Ward; *Recreations* collecting modern art, gardening; *Style—* Miss Anne Ratcliffe; 34 Valnay St, London SW17; Ty Fry Manor, Pentraeth, Anglesey; 5 Pump Ct, Temple, London EC4 (☎ 071 353 2532, fax 071 353 5321)

RATCLIFFE, Dr Frederick William; JP (Cambridge 1981); s of Sidney Ratcliffe (d 1964), of Leek, Staffs, and Dora, *née* Smith (d 1975); *b* 28 May 1927; *Educ* Leek HS, Univ of Manchester (BA, MA, PhD), Univ of Cambridge (MA); *m* 20 Aug 1952, Joyce, da of Thomas Edwin Brierley, of Harrogate; 2 s (R George, R John), 1 da (Helen L); *Career* WWII N Staffs Regt 1945-48; asst librarian Univ of Manchester Library 1954-62, sub librarian Univ of Glasgow Library 1962-63, dep univ librarian Univ of Newcastle Upon Tyne 1963-65, librarian Univ of Manchester 1965-80 (dir John Rylands Univ Library of Manchester 1972-80), hon lectr historical bibliography Univ of Manchester 1970-80, univ librarian Univ of Cambridge and fell Corpus Christi Coll 1980-, visiting prof Univ of Loughborough 1982-86, Sandars reader bibliography Univ of Cambridge 1989; JP Stockport 1972-80; tstee: St Deiniol's Library Hawarden, George Fearn Tst Stockport, FC Pybus Tst Newcastle, Cambridge Fndn; fell Woodard Corp 1981-; chm: Cambridgeshire Library and Info Jt Ctee, Advsy Ctee Nat Preservation Office, Wellcome Inst for the History of Med Library Panel; memb UK Delgn CSCE Cultural Forum Budapest 1985, patron Soc of Bookbinders and Restorers; memb: Library Assoc, Bibliographical Soc, Cambridge Bibliographical Soc; hon FLA 1987; FRSA 1986; Comendador de la Orden del Merito Civil (Spain) 1988; *Books* numerous articles in literary jnls; *Recreations* book collecting, gardening, handprinting; *Clubs* Sette of Odd Volumes; *Style—* Dr Frederick Ratcliffe, JP; Ridge House, Rickinghall Superior, Diss, Norfolk IP22 1DY (☎ 0379 898 232); 84 Church Lane, Girton, Cambridge CB3 0JP (☎ 0223 277 512); University Library, West Rd, Cambridge CB3 9DR (☎ 0223 333045, fax 0223 334 748, telex 81395); Corpus Christi College, Cambridge

RATCLIFFE, Prof John Graham; s of Stuart Graham Ratcliffe (d 1973), of Sheffield, and Mary Gladys, *née* Hargreaves; *b* 3 Nov 1938; *Educ* King Edward VII Sch Sheffield, St John's Coll Oxford (BA, BM, BCh, DM), Middx Hosp Med Sch; *m* 10 Sept 1969, Wendy Anne Smith; *Career* lectr in chem pathology St Bart's Hosp Med Coll 1968-72, conslt in pathological biochemistry Royal Infirmary Glasgow 1973-81, prof of chem pathology Univ of Manchester 1981-86, prof of clinical chemistry Univ of Birmingham, dir Wolfson Res Laboratories and hon conslt Central Birmingham Health Authy 1986-; memb: Bd Nat Inst of Biological Standards and Control, Scientific Grants Ctee Cancer Res Campaign, Cncl Assoc of Clinical Biochemists; FRCPath 1985, FRCP (Glasgow)1982, author of various pubns in med and scientific literature; *Style—* Prof John Ratcliffe; Wolfson Research Laboratories, Dept of Clinical Chemistry, Queen Elizabeth Hospital, Edgbaston, Birmingham B15 2TH (☎ 021 472 1311 ext 4559)

RATCLIFFE, (John) Michael; s of Donald Ratcliffe (d 1988), and Joyce Lilian, *née* Dilks; *b* 15 June 1935; *Educ* Cheadle Hulme Sch, Christ's Coll Cambridge (BA); *Career* journalist; graduate trainee Sheffield Telegraph 1959-61, asst literary and arts ed Sunday Times 1962-67, chief book reviewer The Times 1972-82 (literary ed 1967-72), freelance writer 1982-83, literary ed The Observer 1990- (theatre critic 1984-89); commended in critic of the year section Br Press Awards 1989; memb NUJ 1959-; *Books* The Novel Today (1967), The Bodley Head 1887-1987 (with J W Lambert, 1987); *Recreations* music, travel, walking, architecture, gardening; *Style—* Michael Ratcliffe, Esq; 4 Elia St, London N1 8DE (☎ 071 837 1687); The Observer, Chelsea Bridge House, Queenstown Rd, London SW8 4NN (☎ 071 350 3209/3210, fax 071 627 5570-2)

RATCLIFFE, Col Peter Jocelyn Carne; OBE (1972); s of Jocelyn Vivian Ratcliffe (d 1973), of Helston, Cornwall, and Daphne Naylor, *née* Carne; *b* 17 Nov 1926; *Educ* Harrow; *m* 7 Oct 1950, Ann Pamela, da of Leonard Forsell, of Bosrhyn, Port Navas, Cornwall; 1 s (David b 1953), 1 da (Susan b 1956); *Career* Grenadier Gds 1944, cmmnd 2 Lt 1945; serv: Germany, Egypt, Cyprus (despatches 1958), Belgium; Adj Gds Depot 1952, Adj 2 Bn Gren Gds 1954, SD Directorate WO and MOD 1962-64, Regtl Adj Gren Gds 1964, 2 i/c 1 Bn 1967, Cmdt Gds Depot 1967, GSOI HQ London Dist 1970, Dep Cdr 3 Inf Bde 1973, chief Mil Personnel Branch SHAPE 1974, ret 1974; City Marshal 1974; stock exchange firm (admin) 1978, exec dir Cinema and TV Benevolent Fund 1983-; Freeman City of London 1974; *Recreations* sailing, gardening, radio; *Clubs* Royal Yacht Sqdn, Household Division Yacht; *Style—* Col Peter J C Ratcliffe, OBE; c/o Barclays Bank Ltd, 1 Chertsey Rd, Woking, Surrey GU21 5AA; 72 Dean St, London W1V 6LT

RATCLIFFE, (James) Terence; MBE (1987), JP (1972); s of John Ratcliffe, Bury, and Alice, *née* Bennet (d 1981); *Educ* Bury HS, Univ of Manchester (DipArch); *m* 8 Sept 1956, Mary Grundy (Molly), da of Reginald Victor Adlem (d 1990), of Bury; 3 s (Mark b 1961, Jonathon b 1964, Nicholas b 1965), 1 da (Elisabeth (twin) b 1965); *Career* architect, md Ratcliffe Groves Partnership, dir Carter Design Consultants; pres Euro Area of YMCA's; ARIBA; *Recreations* athletics, YMCA; *Style—* Terence Ratcliffe, Esq, MBE, JP; Ivy House, Bolton Rd, West, Holcombe Brook, Bury, Lancs (☎ 020 488 2519); 105 Manchester Rd, Bury, Lancs (☎ 061 797 6000); 83/84 Long Acre, Covent Garden, London (☎ 071 240 9827)

RATFORD, David John Edward; CMG (1984), CVO (1979); s of late George Ratford, and Lilian, *née* Jones; *b* 22 April 1934; *Educ* Whitgift Middle Sch, Selwyn Coll Cambridge; *m* 1960, Ulla Monica, da of late Oskar Jerneck, of Stockholm; 2 da; *Career* Nat Serv Intelligence Corps 1953-55; joined FO 1955, 3 sec Prague 1959-61, 2 sec Mogadishu 1961-63, 2 then 1 sec FO 1963-68, 1 sec (commercial) Moscow 1968-71, FCO 1971-74, cnsllr (agric and econ) Paris 1974-78, cnsllr Copenhagen 1978-82, min Moscow 1983-86, asst under-sec of state (Europe) and dep political dir FCO 1986-90, HM ambass Oslo 1990-; Cdr Order of The Dannebrog Denmark 1979; *Recreations* music, tennis; *Clubs* Travellers'; *Style—* David Ratford, Esq, CMG, CVO; c/o Foreign & Commonwealth Office, London SW1A 2AH

RATFORD, William Frederick (Bill); s of Job Lewis Ratford (ka 1941), and Emma Louisa Green (d 1981); *b* 2 Feb 1930; *Educ* Raine's Foundation GS for Boys; *m* 22 Aug 1953, Rose Patricia, da of Henry Woodward; 3 s (David John b 30 July 1954, Michael Christopher b 3 Sept 1956, Ian Nicholas b 15 July 1958); *Career* Nat Serv RAF 1948-50; Peat Marwick Mitchell & Co: joined as jr clerk 1946, qualified incorporated accountant 1955, chartered accountant 1957, ptnr insolvency 1975; Insolvency Practitioners Assoc: memb Cncl 1982, vice pres 1984-85, pres 1985-86; ACA 1957, Insolvency Practitioners Assoc 1976; *Books* Employees' Rights in Receiverships and Liquidations (1979), A Guide to the Involvency Act (1985), Insolvency - Understanding The New Law (1987); *Recreations* golf (badly!), church, charitable work; *Style—* William Ratford, Esq; KPMG Peat Marwick McLintock, 20 Farringdon St, London EC4A 4PP (☎ 071 236 8000, fax 071 248 1790)

RATH, James Winston; s of Maj Joseph Rath (d 1983), and Mary, *née* Futterweit (d 1988); *b* 12 May 1944; *Educ* St Marylebone GS, Univ of St Andrews (MA); *Career* CA; Coopers & Lybrand Deloitte (formerly Coopers & Lybrand) 1969-73; sec Assoc Investmt Tst Cos 1988- (asst sec 1973-88); ACA 1972, FCA 1978; *Style—* James Rath, Esq; 6 Atherton Heights, Bridgewater Rd, Wembley, Middx HA0 1YD (☎ 081 902 3123); Park House (6th Floor), 16 Finsbury Circus, London EC2M 7JJ (☎ 071 588 5347, fax 071 638 1803)

RATHBONE, Brian Benson; s of Brig Reginald Blythe Rathbone, OBE (d 1987), of Arreton, Blockley, Glos, and Eileen, *née* Wakeley (d 1930); *b* 15 Oct 1924; *Educ* Bradfield Coll Berks, Trinity Coll Dublin; *m* 20 Feb 1971 (m dis 1974), (Amelda) Jane, da of late Cdr Redvers Prior, DSO, RN, of Highland, St Lawrence, Jersey, CI; *Career* joined RE 1943, cmmnd RASC 1947, ret as Lt 1950; in business 1952-57, called to the Bar Lincoln's Inn 1960; in practice: Oxford Circuit 1960-71, Western Circuit 1972-; examiner of the court 1977-87, pt/t judge advocate 1981-, joined the chambers of Mr Andrew Parsons in Portsmouth 1990-; Parly candidate (C) Smethwick 1970; memb: Birmingham City Cncl 1967-70, Camden Borough Cncl 1982-86; *Recreations* riding, swimming, travelling, bridge, chess; *Clubs* Carlton, Hamshire (Winchester); *Style—* Brian Rathbone, Esq; 33 Colley Court, Winchester, Hants SO23 7ES (☎ 0962 866779); Victory House, 7 Bellevue Terrace, Portsmouth, Hants PO5 3AT (☎ 0705 831292, fax 0705 291262, DX 2239)

RATHBONE, John Rankin (Tim); MP (C) Lewes 1974-; s of J Rathbone, MP (ka 1940), and Beatrice, later Lady Wright (m Sir Paul Wright, *qv*); *b* 17 March 1933; *Educ* Eton, Ch Ch Oxford, Harvard Business Sch; *m* 1, 1960 (m dis 1981), Margarita Sanchez y Sanchez; 2 s (John Paul, Michael), 1 da (Tina); m 2, 1982, Susan Jenkin, da of Jenkin Coles (d 1969) and former w of Lionel Geoffrey Stopford Sackville, *qv*; 2 step s (Charles, Thomas), 1 step da (Lucinda); *Career* 2 Lt KRRC 1951-53; Robert Benson Lonsdale & Co 1956-58; trainee to vice pres Ogilvy & Mather Inc NY 1958-66; chief publicity & PRO Cons Central Office 1966-68; dir: Charles Barker Gp 1968-87, Ayer Barker Ltd (md 1970-74, dep chm 1974-79), Charles Barker City 1981-87; PPS to: Min of Health 1979-82, Min for Trade (consumer affrs) 1982-83, Min for the Arts 1985; chm Advsy Ctee Inst of Mgmnt Resources 1987-; fndr memb and chm All Pty Drug Misuse Gp 1984, fndr memb Cons Gp for Fundamental Change in SA 1985, vice chm Br-Japanese Gp; memb: All Pty Franchise Gp, Br-SA Gp, Br S American Gp, Parly Engrg Devpt Gp, Br American Gp, Euro Movement; delegate to Cncl of Euro and Western Euro Union 1987-; FRSA (memb Cncl 1984-88); *Publications* Nursery Schooling-Too long the overlooked ingredient in education for life (Tory Reform Group, 1990); *Clubs* Brooks's, Pratt's, Sussex, Soc of Sussex Downsmen; *Style—* Tim Rathbone, Esq, MP; House of Commons, London SW1A 0AA (☎ 071 219 3460)

RATHBONE, Julian Christopher; s of Christopher Fairrie Rathbone (d 1960), and Decima Doreen,*ne´e* Frost (d 1984); *b* 10 Feb 1935; *Educ* Clayesmore Sch Dorset, Magdalene Coll Cambridge (BA); *Career* author; English teacher: Ankara Coll and Univ of Ankara 1959-62, various Schs UK 1962-73 (head English Dept Bognor Regis Comp Sch 1970-73); full time author 1973-; books incl: Diamonds Bid (1967), Trip Trap (1971), Bloody Marvellous (1975), King Fisher Lives (1976) A Raving Monarchist (1977), Joseph (1979), A Last Resort (1980), A Spy of the Old School (1982), Wellington's War (1984), Lying in State (1985), ZDT (1986), The Crystal Contract (1988), The Pandora Option (1990); radio play Albert and the Truth About Rats (Suddeutscher Rundfunk 1990); contrib: The Guardian, New Statesman, Literary Review; Southern Arts bursary 1977, literary advsr Royal Berks Library Servs 1981; nominated for Booker Prize for Fiction 1976 (King Fisher Lives) and 1979 (Joseph), Deutsches Krimi Preis (Grñfinger) 1989; memb: Crime Writers Assoc, Assoc Int des Ecrivains Policiers; *Recreations* painting, music, skiing, cycling; *Style—* Julian Rathbone; Sea View, School Rd, Thorney Hill, Christchurch, Dorset BH23 8DS (☎ 0425 73313); c/o Margaret Hanbury, 27 Walcot Square, London SE11 4UB (☎ 071 735 7680, fax 071 793 0316)

RATHBONE, Robert; s of Roger Anthony Rathbone, of Keswick, Cumbria, and Jean, *née* Sander; *b* 19 Aug 1962; *Educ* Keswick GS Cumbria, Teeside Poly Middlesborough, Richmond Coll Sheffield; *m* 23 July 1990, Lorraine Susan, da of John

Broadley; 1 s (Robert Anthony b 24 June 1988); *Career* photographer; trainee press photographer West Cumberland Times and Star Workington Cumbria 1983-85, freelance photographer working through East Midlands Picture Service Nottingham 1986-87, chief photographer East Midlands Picture Service Nottingham 1987, photographer News Team Birmingham 1988, self-employed Robert Rathbone Photography Nottingham 1988-; *awards* Sports Picture award Kodak Black and White Photography awards 1987, Photographic Printer award (Sport Section) Kodak Black and White Photography awards 1987, Sports Photographer of the Year British Press awards 1989; memb NUJ 1983; *Recreations* football, cricket, squash, music, walking; *Clubs* Derwent, Keswick; *Style—* Robert Rathbone, Esq; Robert Rathbone Photography, 15 Dorchester Gardens, West Bridgford, Nottingham NG2 7AW (☎ 0602 452335, car 0836 660935)

RATHBONE, Sebastian David; s of Richard Reynolds Rathbone (d 1969); *b* 6 Jan 1932; *Educ* Rugby, Trinity Coll Cambridge; *m* 1964, Susan Kennedy, da of late Robert Kennedy Rathbone; 4 s, 1 da; *Career* CA, ptnr Rathbone Bros & Co 1960-88, dep chm Rathbone Bros plc 1988-; *Recreations* sport; *Style—* Sebastian Rathbone, Esq; c/o Rathbone Bros & Co Ltd, Port of Liverpool Bldg, Pier Head, Liverpool

RATHCAVAN, 2 Baron (UK 1953); Hon Phelim Robert Hugh O'Neill; 2 Bt (UK 1929), PC (NI 1969); er s of 1 Baron Rathcavan (d 1982), by his w Sylvia (d 1972), da of Walter Sandeman of the sherry and port family; 1 Baron Rathcavan was only surv s of 2 Baron O'Neill, JP, DL (descended from the O'Neills who, as High Kings of Ireland, are the earliest traceable family in Europe); *b* 2 Nov 1909; *Educ* Eton; *m* 1, 1934 (m dis 1944), Clare Désirée (d 1956), er da of Detmar Jellings Blow, JP (d 1910), of Carlos Place, Mayfair, and Hilles House, Stroud (sometime Lord of the Manor of Painswick) by his w Winifred, ggda of 1 Baron Tollemache; 1 s, 1 da; m 2, 1953, Bridget Doreen, yst da of late Maj Hon Richard Coke (3 s of 2 Earl of Leicester) and formerly w of Thomas Ewards-Moss (yr bro of Sir John E-M, 4 Bt); 3 da (1 da decd); *Heir* s, Hon Hugh O'Neill; *Career* Maj RA; MP (UU) for N Antrim (UK Parl) 1952-59, NI Parl (U and later Alliance) 1959-73 (Parl suspended March 1972); min: of Educn 1969, of Agric 1969-71; *Clubs* Brooks's; *Style—* Maj the Rt Hon the Lord Rathcavan, PC; Killala Lodge, Killala, Co Mayo, Ireland

RATHCREEDAN, 3 Baron (UK 1916), of Bellehatch Park, Oxon; Christopher John Norton; s and h of 2 Baron Rathcreedan, TD (d 1990), and Ann Pauline, *née* Bastian; *b* 3 June 1949; *Educ* Wellington, RAC Cirencester; *m* 1978, Lavinia Anne Ross, da of Alan George Ross Ormiston, of Coln Orchard, Arlington, Bibury, Glos; 2 da (Hon Jessica Charlotte b 13 Nov 1983, Hon Serena Clare b 12 Aug 1987); *Heir* br, Hon Adam Gregory Norton, *qv*; *Career* pedigree livestock auctioneer; *Recreations* horse racing, gardening; *Clubs* Turf; *Style—* The Rt Hon Lord Rathcreedan; Waterton Farm House, Ampney Crucis, Cirencester, Gloucestershire GL7 5RR (☎ 0285 654282)

RATHDONNELL, 5 Baron (I 1868); Thomas Benjamin McClintock-Bunbury; s of 4 Baron Rathdonnell (d 1959); *b* 17 Sept 1938; *Educ* Charterhouse, RNC Dartmouth; *m* 2 Oct 1965, Jessica Harriet, o da of George Gilbert Butler (eighth in descent from 2 Baron Dunboyne) and Norah Pomeroy Colley, gggda of 4 Viscount Harberton; 3 s (Hon William, Hon George b 26 July 1968, Hon James b 21 Feb 1972), 1 da (Hon Sasha b 1976); *Heir* s, Hon William Leopold McClintock-Bunbury, b 6 July 1966; *Style—* The Rt Hon the Lord Rathdonnell; Lisnavagh, Rathvilly, Co Carlow, Republic of Ireland (☎ 0503 61104)

RATIU, Indrei Stephen Pilkington; s of Ion Augustin Nicolae Ratiu de Nagylak, of Zermatt, Switzerland (pres World Union Free Romanians), and Elisabeth Balnche, *née* Pilkington; *b* 12 July 1946; *Educ* Bryanston Sch, St John's Coll Cambridge (MA), INSEAD (MBA); *m* 28 Sept 1974, Ioana Maria, da of George Georgescu (d 1964) (conductor, Bucharest Philharmonic Orchestra 1929-64); 1 s (Alexandru b 2 Aug 1986); *Career* scriptwriter BBC Overseas Servs 1967-69, memb faculty INSEAD 1971-75, mgmnt conslt 1976-, dir Regent House Properties 1976-. managing ptnr Inter Cultural Mgmnt Assoc 1982-88; tstee: Rainford Tst 1985-, Ratiu Family Fndn 1987-; memb World Union of Free Romanians 1984-; memb: Int Consits Fndn, Int Soc for Intercultural Educn Trg and Res; *Books* Leads Sans Frontiers (with F Gauthey et al 1988), numerous articles on mgmnt devpt and cross-cultural mgmnt; *Recreations* skiing, walking, swimming; *Style—* Indrei Ratiu, Esq

RATLEDGE, Prof Colin; s of Fred Ratledge (d 1975), of Preston, Lancs, and Freda Smith Proudlock (d 1986); *b* 9 Oct 1936; *Educ* Bury HS, Univ of Manchester (BSc, PhD); *m* 25 March 1961, Janet Vivien, da of Albert Cyril Bottomley (d 1977), of Preston, Lancs; 1 s (Stuart b 15 March 1968), 2 da (Alison b 7 July 1964, Jane b 15 July 1971); *Career* res fellowship MRC Ireland 1960-64, res scientist Unilever plc 1964-67, prof of microbial biochemistry Univ of Hull 1988- (lectr 1967-73, sr lectr 1973-77, reader 1977-83, personal chair 1983, head of Dept of Biochemistry 1986-88; memb Euro Fedn of Biotechnol (Sci Advsy Ctee 1984-90); chm: Food Res Grant Bd and memb Food Res Ctee AFRC, Soc of Chemical Industry and Inst of Biology Biotechnol Gps 1989- (memb Int Union of Biochemistry Biotechnol Ctee), Br Co-ordinating Ctee for Biotechnol 1989-91; memb: Soc for Gen Microbiology, Soc of Chem Industry, Biochemical Soc, American Microbiological Soc, American Oil Chemists Soc; FRSC 1970, FIBiol 1983, FRSA 1987; *Books* The Mycobacteria (1977), Microbial Technology: Current State, Future Prospects (1979), The Biology of the Mycobacteria (vol 1 1982, vol 2 1983, vol 3 1989), Biotechnology for the Oils and Fats Industry (1984), Microbial Technology in the Developing World (1987), Microbial Lipids (vol 1 1988, vol 2 1989), Microbial Physiology and Manufacturing Industry (1988), Biotechnology: Economic and Social Aspects, World Journal of Microbiology and Biotechnology, Biotechnology Techniques; *Recreations* walking, gardening; *Style—* Prof Colin Ratledge; 49 Church Drive, Leven, Beverley, E Yorks (☎ 0964 542690); Dept of Applied Biology, Univ of Hull, Hull HU6 7RX (☎ 0482 465243, fax 0482 466205, telex 592592 KHMAIL G)

RATLIFF, John Harrison; s of Anthony Hugh Cyril Ratliff, and Jean *née* Harrison; *b* 13 Jan 1957; *Educ* Clifton, Univ Coll Oxford (BA), Univ of Amsterdam (DIEI); *m* 27 July 1985, Pascale, da of Pierre Bourgeon; *Career* called to the Bar Middle Temple 1980; winner of Hon Sir Peter Bristow Award 1981, young lawyers prog Germany 1981-82, J C Goldsmith and Assoc Paris 1983-84, ptnr Stanbrook and Hooper Brussels 1987-; memb; Int Bar Assoc, Anglo Germany Lawyers Assoc, Rheinischer Internationaler Juristen Verein; *Recreations* music, travel; *Style—* John Ratliff, Esq; 42 Rue Du Taciturne, 1040 Brussels, Belgium (☎ 02 2305059, fax 02 2305713, telex 61975 STALAW)

RATNAYAKE, Anton Maürice; s of Noel Mervyn Abeykoonge-Ratnayake (d 1959), of Ceylon, and Bertha Muriel, *née* Heyn (d 1987); *b* 27 Aug 1942; *Educ* St Peters Coll Colombo Ceylon, Univ of Ceylon (BSc), Harvard Business Sch Boston, USA; *m* 9 Dec 1964, da of Henry Kenneth (Harry) Butler-Clark (d 1982), of Camden Rd, London; *Career* accountant Universal Sky Tours 1964-65, computer programmer Thomason Holidays & ACT Ltd 1965-68, chief programmer ACT Ltd 1969-72, sr analyst ACT & OCL Ltd 1973-75, projects mangr computer systems OCL Ltd 1983-85 (systems devpt mangr 1978-80, data centre mangr 1980-83), gp gen mangr P&O Containers Ltd 1983-, dir Community Network Servs Ltd Southampton 1986- (chm bd 1988-89); rep memb Nat Computing Centre (UK) 1979, sec Ind Computer Users Assoc (Europe) 1983-84, visiting lectr info technol mgmnt Ashridge Magmnt Coll and Cambridge Acad Tport; numerous articles in computer and tech pubns; corp memb Br Computer Soc 1978, MBIM 1983; *Recreations* cricket (charity matches), theatre, collecting antique French and English paper weights; *Style—* Anton Ratnayake, Esq; Rose Cottage, Layer Marney, Essex C05 9UP (☎ 0206 330736); P & D Containers Ltd, Beagle House, Braham St, London E1 8EP (☎ 071 488 1313/071 873 1286, car 0836 224207, fax 071 480 5749, telex 883947)

RATNER, Gerald Irving; s of Leslie Manuel Ratner, and Rachelle Ezra, *née* Moses; *b* 1 Nov 1949; *Educ* Hendon County GS; *m* 1, (m dis 1989), Angela Nadine Trupp; 2 da (Suzanne b 1975, Lisa Karen b 1977); m 2, Kathleen Moira, *née* Day; 1 da (Sarah Charlotte b 1989); *Career* Ratners: dir 1970, jt md 1978, md 1984, chm and chief exec 1986-; memb: Crime Concern, Business in the Community; *Recreations* tennis, scrabble; *Style—* Gerald Ratner, Esq; 15 Stratton St, London W1 (☎ 071 499 1000, fax 071 408 0901)

RATNER, Richard Anthony; s of Jack Lewis Ratner (d 1970), of Bryanston Court, London, and Vivienne, *née* Salbstein (d 1976); *b* 21 Sept 1949; *Educ* Epsom Coll, Univ of Leeds (LLB); *m* 1975, Silvia Jane, da of Maj AC Hammond, TD, JP; 2 s (James Anthony Mark b 1976, Christopher Piers Alexander b 1980), 1 da (Katie Emma Jayne b 1979); *Career* textile indust (latterly chm U U Textiles plc) 1972-81, dir institutional sales and ptnr Kitcat & Aitken & Co 1981-, dir and dep head of institutional sales Carr Kitcat & Aitken Ltd 1981-; dir: Owen & Robsinson plc 1986-, Seasons Garden Centres 1988-; ptnr Philip Spormer Antiques Dorking 1990-; Maj The Queens Own Hussars (TA) 1968-85; memb Court of Common Cncl for the Ward of Broad St 1981-; former chm: Broad St Ward Club, Soc of Young Freeman, Bd of Govrs City of London Sch; govr Bridewell Royal Hosp and Christ's Hosp; memb: City Branch TA & VRA, HAC; Freeman City of London 1976, Liveryman Worshipful Co of Gunmakers 1979; memb: Lloyds 1975-84, Stock Exchange 1984; *Books* The English Civil War (contrib, 1971); *Recreations* antique firearms, antiques, model railways; *Clubs* Cavalry and Guards; *Style—* Richard Ratner, Esq; Hill House, Hammerfield, Abinge Hammer, Dorking, Surrey (☎ 0306 730182); Carr Kitcat & Aitken, 10th Floor, No 1 London Bridge, London SE1 (☎ 071 528 0100, fax 071 403 0755)

RATSEY, Dr David Hugh Kerr; s of Capt Franklin, and Mary Gwendoline Lucy, *née* Walduck; *b* 7 June 1944; *Educ* Sherbourne, St Bartholomew's Hosp (MB BS, MRCS, LRCP); *m* 6 Sept 1969, Christine, da of Arthur William Tutt-Harris; 3 s (Matthew David, Timothy James, Nicholas Paul), 1 da (Anna Mary); *Career* appts 1968-69: pre-registration post Prince of Wales Hosp Tottenham, house surgn Whipps Cross Hosp Leytonstone; sr house offr anaesthesia St Bartholomew's Hosp 1970-71, Alwyn bursar and res registrar in anaesthesia St Bartholomew's Hosp 1971-72, anaesthetic registrar St George's Hosp 1973-75, trainee then princ Gen Practice 1975-80, pt/t clinical asst Royal Homeopathic Hosp 1975-82 and 1986-, acquired consltg Homopathic practice Kensington 1980-; recognised as having consit status for benefit payment purposes by following: PPP 1984, BCWA 1987, BUPA 1988, Orion and Sun Alliance 1989; Faculty of Homeopathy: elected Cncl 1983, offr 1984, external examiner 1984, founder memb of first official Ct of Examiners 1987, vice pres 1987 and 1988; *Recreations* sailing; *Clubs* Walton and Frinton Yacht; *Style—* Dr David Ratsey; 2 Harley St, London W1N 1AA (☎ 071 589 2776, fax 071 323 5743)

RATTANSI, Prof Pyarally Mohamedally (Piyo); s of Mohamedally Rattansi (1958), of Nairobi, Kenya, and Mani Hirji, *née* Ladha (1965); *b* 15 Oct 1930; *Educ* Duke of Gloucester Sch Nairobi, LSE (BSc, PhD), Univ of Cambridge (MA); *m* 11 June 1966, Zarin Pyarally, da of Mirali Bhimji Charania (d 1953), of Kisumu, Kenya; 2 s (Afshin b 13 Jan 1968, Shihab b 25 Aug 1971); *Career* lectr Dept of Philosophy Univ of Leeds 1964-67 (Leverhulme Res Fell 1962-64), visiting assoc prof Univ of Chicago 1966, fell Kings Coll Cambridge 1967-71, visiting lectr Princeton Univ 1969-70, memb Inst for Advanced Study Princeton 1969, prof and head of Dept of History and Philosophy UCL 1971-; Univ of London: chm Bd of Studies in history of Sci Medicine and Technol and Philosophy of Sci 1988- (also 1975-78 and 1983-86), vice pres Br Soc for History of Sci 1974-77 (memb 1972-74), advsy ed Isis jl of the American History of Sci Soc 1971-75, UK delegate to numerous int scientific confs and symposia; *Books* incl: Science and Society 1600-1900 (contrib, 1972), Isaac Newton and Gravity (1974), History and Imagination Essays in Honour of HR Trevor-Roper (contrib, 1981), The Physical Sciences Since Antiquity (contrib, 1986), Revolutions in Science-Their Meaning and Relevance (contrib, 1988), Let Newton Be! (contrib, 1988), Teaching the History of Science (contrib, 1989); *Recreations* swimming; *Style—* Prof Piyo Rattansi; 6 Hillersdon Avenue, Edgware, Middx, HA8 7SQ (☎ 081 958 9442), Dept of History & Philsophy of Science, Univ Coll London, Gower St, London WC1E 6BT (☎ 071 387 7050)

RATTEE, The Hon Sir Donald Keith; QC (1977-); *b* 9 March 1937; *Career* called to the Bar Lincoln's Inn 1962, QC 1977, bencher Lincoln's Inn 1985, attorney gen Duchy of Lancaster 1986-89, rec Crown Ct 1989-, Justice of the High Ct (Family Div) 1989-; kt 1989; *Style—* The Hon Sir Donald Rattee; Royal Courts of Justice, Strand, London WC2A 2LL

RATTRAY, Andrew; s of James Dewar Rattray (d 1971), and Martha Topley, *née* Gray (d 1966); *b* 14 April 1925; *Educ* Leith Acad Edinburgh, Heriot Watt Coll Edinburgh, Glasgow Coll of Commerce; *m* 21 July 1953, Margaret Ann Todd, da of John Burns (d 1966); *Career* Sgt Queens Own Cameron Highlanders 1943-47; co sec Rest Assured (Northern) Ltd 1964-79, md Airsprung Scotland Ltd 1981-90 (dir gen mangr 1979-81), ret 1990; FSCA 1972, MBIM 1979; *Recreations* hill walking, music, theatre; *Style—* Andrew Rattray, Esq; 6 Fair Oaks, Carmunnock, Glasgow G76 (☎ 041 644 3913)

RATTRAY OF RATTRAY, Hon Mrs (Elizabeth Sophia); *née* Sidney; da (by 1 m) of 1 Viscount De L'Isle, VC, KG, GCMG, GCVO, PC; *b* 1941; *m* 1, 1959 (m dis 1966), George Silver Oliver Annesley Colthurst; m 2, 1966 (m dis 1971), Sir (Edward) Humphry Tyrell Wakefield, 2 Bt; m 3, 1972, Capt James Silvester Rattray of Rattray; 1 s; *Style—* The Hon Mrs Rattray of Rattray; Craighall-Rattray, Blairgowrie, Perthshire

RAVEN, (Anthony) David; s of Harry Raven (d 1967), of Bournemouth, and May Louise, *née* Fletcher (d 1982); *b* 12 July 1934; *Educ* Ermysted's, Yeovil Technical Coll, Univ of London (BSc); *m* 3 April 1965, Elizabeth, da of Ronald Spence Allen (d 1969), of Loughborough; 2 da (Louisa Elizabeth b 21 July 1971, Natasha Mary b 11 Aug 1977); *Career* with: Westland Aircraft Ltd, English Electric Co Ltd, Perkins Ltd 1965-68, Jaguar Cars Ltd 1968-71; tech dir Willowbrook Ltd 1971-73; chm and md: Diplomat Technico Ltd 1973-90, Diplomat Projects Ltd 1986-88, Debdale Consultancy Ltd 1984-, C H Technology Ltd 1988-90, chm: Bruce Engrs Ltd 1986-88, Hallite Diplomat Ltd 1988-90, Milsco Diplomat Ltd 1987-, Diplomat Ltd 1988-; dir Remora Textiles Ltd 1980-82, non-exec dir Roger Staton Assocs Ltd 1978-; PSV Tech Ctee SMMT, govr Lutterworth HS, chm Leicester Symphony Orchestra Tst; CEng, MIMechE, MBIM, FInstD; *Books* Profit Improvement by Value Analysis Value Engineering and Purchase Analysis (1971); *Recreations* antique clocks, choral singing, historic buildings, pretending to garden; *Style—* David Raven, Esq; c/o Debdale Consultancy Ltd, Shawell, Lutterworth, Leics LE17 6AL

RAVEN, Peter Leo; s of Norman Joseph Raven (d 1987), of Blackheath, London, and Christina Mary Louise Guilly (d 1947); *b* 7 Jan 1939; *Educ* Downside; *m* 6 Oct 1962,

Jane Doe, da of William Gummer Castell (d 1978), of Limpley Stoke, Wiltshire; 2 s (Timothy b 1964, Jonathan b 1966); *Career* fin dir Ultramar plc 1981- (gp fin coordinator 1978-80); American Ultramar Ltd: sr vice pres fin 1980-84, exec vice pres 1984-88, pres and gp chief fin offr 1988-; FCA 1972, FCT 1978; *Recreations* fishing, golf, antiques, music; *Clubs* MCC, City of London, Wallabue Country; *Style—* Peter Leo Raven, Esq; Ultramar plc, 141 Moorgate, London EC2M 6TX (☎ 071 256 6080, fax 071 256 8556), American Ultramar Ltd, 120 White Plains Rd, Tarrytown NY 10591 USA (☎ 914 3332151, fax 914 33220930)

RAVEN, Ronald William; OBE (Mil 1946), TD (1953); s of Fredric William Raven (d 1952), and Annie Williams, *née* Mason (d 1973), who was a direct descent of Miles Mason (1752-1822), originator of Mason's Patent Ironstone China; bro of Dame Kathleen Raven, *qv*; *b* 28 July 1904; *Educ* Ulverston GS, St Bartholomew's Hosp and Med Coll London; *Career* RAMC 1941-46 served: N Africa, Italy, Malta (despatches); Hon Col RAMC 1946-; consulting surgn Westminster and Royal Marsden Hosp 1969-; pres Epsom Coll 1990- (vice pres 1954-90), Marie Curie Memorial Fndn 1990 (chm Exec Ctee 1948-61, chm Cncl 1960-90); fndr pres: Assoc Head and Neck Oncologists for GB 1968-71, Br Assoc Surgical Oncology 1973-77; life pres Hellennic Soc Oncology 1990-; author of papers on surgical subjects (esp relating to cancer) in Br and foreign jls; memb ct of patrons RCS 1976- (memb cncl 1968-76), vice pres Malta Meml Dist Nursing Assoc 1982-; created the Ronald William Raven Room Museum Royal Crown Derby Porcelain Co 1987 (hon life memb Derby Porcelain Int Soc 1988); Ronald Raven Chain Clinical Oncology (Univ of London) estab at Royal Free Hosp London 1990; Master Worshipful Co of Barbers 1980-81; Hon MD Cartagena 1949, foreign memb Acad of Athens 1983-; hon FRSM, FRSA, MRCS, LRCP 1928, FRCS 1931; awarded G Papanicoladu Gold medal (Greece) 1990, Chev de la Légion d'Honneur 1952; OStJ 1946; *Books* Treatment of Shock (trans Russian, 1942), Surgical Care (second edn 1952), Cancer and Allied Diseases (1955), Cancer of Pharynx, Larynx and Oesophagus and its Surgical Treatment (1958), Cancer (ed and contrib, 7 vols 1958-60), Modern Trends in Oncology (1973), The Dying Patient (trans Dutch and Japanese, 1975), Principles of Surgical Oncology (1977), Foundations of Medicine (1978), Rehabilitation and Continuing Care in Cancer (1986), The Gospel of St John (1987), Death Into Life (1990), Theory and Practice of Oncology (1990), Rehabilitation Oncology (1991); *Recreations* philately (medallist int stamp exhib 1950), music, ceramics, paintings, travel; *Clubs* MCC, Pilgrims; *Style—* Ronald Raven Esq, OBE, TD; 29 Harley St, London W1N 1DA (☎ 071 580 3765)

RAVEN, Capt Simon Arthur Noel; s of Arthur Godart Raven, and Esther Kate, *née* Christmas; *b* 28 Dec 1927; *Educ* Charterhouse, King's Coll Cambridge (MA); *m* 1951 (m dis), Susan Mandeville, *née* Kilner; 1 s (Adam); *Career* novelist, dramatist & critic; The Pallisers (BBC); Edward & Mrs Simpson (Thames); *Books* Arms for Oblivion (10 vols), The First-Born of Egypt (7 vols, 6 vols complete); *Style—* Simon Raven, Esq; c/o Curtis Brown, 162-168 Regent St, London W1R 5TB

RAVEN (INGRAM), Dame Kathleen Annie; DBE (1968); da of Fredric William Raven (d 1952), and Annie Williams, *née* Mason (d 1973); sis of Ronald William Raven, *qv*; *b* 9 Nov 1910; *Educ* Ulverston GS, privately, St Bartholomew's Hosp London, City of London Maternity Hosp; *m* 1959, Prof John Thornton Ingram (d 1972); *Career* asst matron St Bartholomews Hosp 1946-49, matron The General Infirmary Leeds 1949-57, chief nursing offr DHSS 1958-72; memb: Gen Nursing Cncl for England and Wales 1950-57, Exec Ctee Assoc of Hosp Matrons for England and Wales 1955-57, Cncl Royal Coll Nursing 1950-57, Cncl Central Health Services 1957-58, Cncl and Nursing Advsy Bd BRCS 1958-72, Nat Florence Nightingale Meml Ctee of GB and NI 1958-72, WHO Expert Advsy Panel on Nursing 1961-79 (fell 1960); vice pres Royal Coll of Nursing 1972-, chm Interviewing Panels Civil Serv Cmmn 1974-80, chief nursing advsr United Medical Enterprises 1973-, fndn govr Aylesbury GS 1986-, memb Distressed Gentlefolks Aid Assoc 1973-89 (chm Exec Ctee 1981-87); Hon Freewoman Worshipful Co of Barbers 1981, Freeman City of London 1986; SRN 1936, SCM 1938, FRSA 1970 FRCN 1986; OStJ 1963; *Recreations* painting, reading; *Clubs* Royal Commonwealth Soc; *Style—* Dame Kathleen Raven, DBE; Jesmond, Burcott, Wing, Leighton Buzzard, Beds LU7 OJU (☎ 0296 688 244); 29 Harley St, London W1N 1DA

RAVENSCROFT, Ven Raymond Lockwood; s of Cecil Ravenscroft, and Amy Gwendoline, *née* Beatty; *b* 15 Sept 1931; *Educ* Sea Point Cape Town, Univ of Leeds (BA), Coll of the Resurrection Mirfield; *m* 24 June 1957, Ann, da of James Peter Stockwell; 1 s (David b 1960), 1 da (Gillian b 1958); *Career* ordained 1955; asst curate: St Alban's Goodwood Cape SA 1955-58, St John's Pro-Cathedral Bulawayo S Rhodesia 1958-59; rector Francistown Bechuanaland 1959-62, asst curate St Ives Cornwall 1962-64; vicar: All Saints Falmouth 1964-68, St Stephen by Launceston with St Thomas 1968-74; team rector Probus Team Miny 1974-88, rural dean Powder 1977-81, hon canon Truro Cathedral 1982-88, archdeacon of Cornwall 1988-, canon librarian of Truro Cathedral 1988-; *Style—* The Ven the Archdeacon of Cornwall; Archdeacon's House, Knights Hill, Kenwyn, Truro, Cornwall TR1 3UY (☎ 0872 72866)

RAVENSDALE, 3 Baron (UK 1911); Sir Nicholas Mosley; 7 Bt (GB 1781), of Ancoats, Lancashire, and of Rolleston, Staffordshire, MC (1944); s of Sir Oswald Mosley, 6 Bt (d 1980), and (first w) Lady Cynthia Blanche, *née* Curzon, da of 1 Marquess of Curzon Kedleston and 1 Baron Ravensdale (she d 1933); suc aunt, Baroness Ravensdale (who was also cr a Life Peer as Baroness Ravensdale of Kedleston 1958) 1966; suc father as 7 Bt 1980; *b* 25 June 1923; *Educ* Eton, Balliol Coll Oxford; *m* 1, 1947 (m dis 1974), Rosemary Laura (d 1991), da of Marshal Sir John Salmond, GCB, CMG, CVO, DSO, RAF, by his 2 w, Hon Monica Grenfell (da of 1 Baron Desborough and Ethel, da of Hon Julian Fane, 4 s of 11 Earl of Westmorland, by Julian's w Lady Adine Cowper, da of 6 Earl Cowper); 3 s, 1 da; m 2, 1974, Verity, 2 da of John Raymond, of Winslade House, Basingstoke, and former w of John Bailey; 1 s (Hon Marius b 1976); *Heir* s, Hon Shaun Mosley; *Career* Capt Rifle Bde WW II; author (as Nicholas Mosley); *Books Incl:* Accident (1964, filmed by Joseph Losey), The Assassination of Trotsky (1972, also filmed), Rules of the Game: Sir Oswald and Lady Cynthia Mosley 1896-1933 (1982), Beyond the Pale, Sir Oswald Mosley 1933-80 (1983), Hopeful Monsters (Whitbread Book of the Year, 1990); *Style—* The Rt Hon the Lord Ravensdale, MC; 2 Gloucester Crescent, London NW1 7DS (☎ 071 485 4514)

RAVENSWORTH, 8th Baron (UK 1821); Sir Arthur Waller Liddell; 13th Bt (E 1642), JP (Northumberland 1959); s of Hon Cyril Liddell, JP, DL (2 s of 5th Baron Ravensworth); suc cous, 7th Baron, 1950; is 2 cous once removed of late Guy Liddell, CB, CBE, MC, sometime civil asst War Office. Lord Ravensworth's gf, the 5th Baron, was second cousin to Alice Liddell, whose Adventures in Wonderland and through the Looking Glass were immortalised by Lewis Carroll; *b* 25 July 1924; *Educ* Harrow; *m* 1950, Wendy, adopted da of J Stuart Bell, of Cookham; 1 s, 1 da; *Heir* s, Hon Thomas Liddell; *Career* former radio engr BBC; *Style—* The Rt Hon The Lord Ravensworth, JP; Eslington Park, Whittingham, Alnwick, Northumberland (☎ 066 574 239)

RAW, Peter Michael; s of George Raw, of Ewell, and Florence May, *née* Elliott (d 1990); *b* 17 May 1939; *Educ* Queen Elizabeth's GS Wakefield, Downing Coll Cambridge (BA, MA); *m* 1 July 1972, Mary Angela, da of John Smith (d 1977), of Leicester; 3 s (James Edward b 1973, Simon David b 1975, John Peter b 1977), 1 da (Catherine Jane b 1981); *Career* devpt dir Engelhard Ltd Chessington Surrey 1983-; vice pres Esher RFC; MIM 1970, CEng 1984; *Recreations* long distance running, cricketer, scouting; *Clubs* Capital Road Runners; *Style—* Peter Raw, Esq; Orchard House, Bushy Rd, Bookham, Surrey KT22 9SX (☎ 0372 57546); Engelhard Ltd, Engineered Materials Division, Davis Rd, Chessington, Surrey KT9 1TD (☎ 081 397 5292, fax 081 914 1412, telex 28720)

RAWCLIFFE, Rt Rev Derek Alec; OBE (1971); s of James Alec Rawcliffe (d 1947), and Gwendoline Alberta, *née* Dee; *b* 8 July 1921; *Educ* Sir Thomas Rich's Sch Gloucester, Univ of Leeds (BA), Coll of the Resurrection Mirfield; *m* 10 Sept 1977, Susan Kathryn (d 22 July 1987), da of William Arthur Rawson Speight, of Kitkatts, Wetherby Rd, Bardsey, Leeds LS17 9BB; *Career* ordained priest 1945, asst priest St George's Claines, Worcester 1944-47, All Hallow's Sch Pawa Solomon Is 1947-56 (headmaster 1953-56), St Mary's Sch Maravovo Sol Is 1956-58, archdeacon of Southern Melanesia 1958-74, asst bishop Melanesia 1974-75, bishop of New Hebrides 1975-80, bishop of Glasgow and Galloway 1981-91; *Recreations* music, numismatics; *Style—* The Rt Rev Derek Rawcliffe, OBE; Kitkatts, Wetherby Rd, Bardsley, Leeds LS17 9BB (☎ 0937 72201)

RAWCLIFFE, Roger Capron; s of Brig James Maudsley Rawcliffe, OBE, MC, TD (d 1965), and Margaret Duff Capron (d 1982); *b* 2 Aug 1934; *Educ* Rossall Sch, Trinity Coll Cambridge (Open Exhibitioner, Henry Arthur Thomas Travelling Scholarship, BA, MA); *m* 1960, Mary Elizabeth White, da of Maurice White; 1 s (James Maurice b 1966); *Career* Nat Serv 1952 Grenadier Guards and E Lancs Regt, 2 Lt 1953, Lt 1954, Capt Stowe CCF 1963, Maj 1964, OC 1966, Hon Col IOM ACF 1987; articled to Sir Thomas Robson at Price Waterhouse; Stowe Sch: asst master 1960-80, head of dept 1967, housemaster 1969, OC CCF 1966; lectr School of Extension Studies Univ of Liverpool 1981-, guest later Swan Hellenic Cruises 1967-, ptnr Pannell Kerr Forster 1982- (joined Ponnell Fitzpatrick & Co IOM 1980); govr Rossall Sch 1981-, tstee King William's Coll 1987; memb Hon Artillery Co 1960; FCA 1970 (ACA 1960); *Style—* Roger Rawcliffe, Esq; Pannell Kerr Forster, Exchange House, 54/58 Athol St, Douglas, Isle of Man (☎ 0624 673811)

RAWDON-LEEFE, Christopher Timothy; s of Maj Thomas Leefe (d 1968), of Langton, Malton, Yorks, and Sylvia Paola, *née* Roden, TD (d 1989); *b* 7 Oct 1926; *Educ* Branksome Hall, Worksop Coll; *m* 1, 1952 (m dis 1963), Dorothé Gisela (d 1970), da of Dr Paul Goerz; m 2, 18 April 1964, Joanna Elizabeth, da of John Edward Buxton (d 1981), of Surrey; 2 s (Mark, Tom); *Career* Army 1944-62, 1 Bn Green Howards, RASC NW Egypt, Europe, Far East, ret Maj 1962; tport mangr Br Oxygen 1964-67, personnel and admin mangr RF White 1967-70, gen mangr Advertising Euromoney Publications Ltd 1970-84, chm Money Media 1984-; dir Rolls-Royce Enthusiasts' Club; Freeman City of London 1977, memb Worshipful Co of Coachmakers and Coach Harness Makers 1977; *Books* Rolls-Royce Alpine Compendium (1973); *Recreations* restoration of vintage Rolls-Royce cars, music, antiques, opera, travel; *Clubs* RREC, RROC of America, 20 Ghost, Silver Ghost Assoc; *Style—* Christopher Rawdon-Leefe, Esq; West Farm House, Harriotts Lane, Ashtead, Surrey KT21 2QE (☎ 0372 275337, office 0372 278127)

RAWLENCE, Lorna Marjorie; da of Henry Augustus Ralph Chapman, CBE (d 1958), and Hilda Winifred, *née* Barfoot (d 1970); *Educ* Cheltenham Ladies' Coll; *m* 5 May 1945 (m dis 1973), Michael Fitzgerald Rawlence, s of (George) Norman Rawlence, MBE (d 1967); 2 s (Simon Edward Fitzgerald b 5 Aug 1947, Nigel John Randal b 6 Sept 1954), 2 da (Justine Diana b 31 March 1946 d 11 Jan 1950, Anthea Justine b 14 Oct 1950); *Career* called to the Bar Inner Temple 1979; practising: Southampton 1981-87, Portsmouth 1987-; memb Inner Temple 1963; *Recreations* riding, theatre, travel; *Style—* Ms Lorna Rawlence; 22 Ennismore Gdns, London SW7 1AB; The Bell House, Charlton All Saints, Salisbury SP5 4HQ (☎ 0725 20089); 7 Bellevue Terrace, Southsea, Portsmouth Hants P05 3AT (☎ 0705 831292, fax 0705 291262)

RAWLENCE, Simon Edward Fitzgerald; s of Michael Fitzgerald Rawlence, and Lorna Marjorie Rawlence; *b* 5 Aug 1947; *Educ* Eton, Clare Coll Cambridge; *m* 26 July 1969, Suzanna Elaine, da of Cuthbert Neil Kirkus; 2 s (Ben b 1974, Leo b 1976), 2 da (Zoe b 1979, Eleanor b 1982); *Career* CA; sole practitioner 1977-87, sr ptnr Rawlence & Browne 1987-; *Recreations* tennis, amateur dramatics; *Style—* Simon Rawlence, Esq; Riversfield, 159 Lower Rd, Bemerton, Salisbury, Wilts SP2 9NL; Rawlence & Browne, 65 St Edmunds Church St, Salisbury SP1 1EF (☎ 0722 24853)

RAWLINGS, Keith John; s of Jack Frederick Rawlings (d 1985), and Eva, *née* Mullis; *b* 24 April 1940; *Educ* Kent Coll Canterbury; *m* 21 Dec 1963, Susan Mary, da of Thomas Johnson (d 1967); 1 s (Jonathan James Ashley b 27 March 1965), 1 da (Sarah Louise (Mrs Watson) b 15 Feb 1967); *Career* insur broker and ind fin advsr, chm Burlington Insurance Group 1969-; dir: London & Edinburgh Trust plc 1986-87, Rutland Trust plc 1987-, Whitehouse Moorman & Partners Ltd 1988-, Greville Baylis & Parry Ltd 1988-, Norminster Associates Ltd 1988-, Atticus Financial Services Ltd 1988-; *Recreations* golf, tennis, skiing, sailing, bridge, travel; *Clubs* St James's; *Style—* Keith Rawlings, Esq; Summerhayes, Cliff Rd, Hythe, Kent CT21 5XQ (☎ 0303 267014); Burlington Insurance Services Ltd, Westbourne House, Coolinge Lane, Folkestone, Kent CT20 3RH (☎ 0303 850555, fax 0303 44914, telex 96240, car 0836 274010)

RAWLINGS, Margaret Lilian; da of late Rev George Wiliam Rawlings, and late Lilian Amelia, *née* Boddington; *b* 5 June 1906; *Educ* Oxford HS for Girls, Lady Margaret Hall Oxford; *m* 1, 3 July 1928 (m dis 1936), Gabriel, s of Francis Toyne, of Brighton, Sussex; m 2, 14 Feb 1942, Robert Barlow (kt 1943, d 1976); 1 da (b 16 July 1943); *Career* professional actress; Macdona Players Bernard Shaw Repertory Co 1927, Bianca Capello in The Venetian 1931, Elizabeth Baret Browning in The Barrets of Wimpole St, Liza Doolittle in Pygmalion 1935, Mary and Lily in Black Limelight, Kate O'Shea in Parnell, Lady Macbeth for OUDS 1936, Helen in Trojan Women 1938-39, Mrs Dearth in Dear Brutus (with John Gielgud) 1941-42, Gwendolen Fairfax in The Importance of Being Ernest (with Edith Evans) 1946, Titania in Purcell's Fairy Queen 1946, Victoria Corombona in The White Devil (with Robert Helpmann) 1947, Germain in A Woman in Love 1949, Zabina in Tamburlain (with Donald Wolpit) 1951-52, title role in Racine's Phedre 1957-58, Jocasta in Oedipus (with John Neville) 1964, Gertrude in Hamlet 1965, Mrs Bridgenorth in Getting Married (all star cast, Strand London) 1967, Cats Play (with Elizabeth Bergner and Penelope Keith) 1973, Mixed Economy 1977, solo performance Empress Eugenie (by Jason Lindsey) 1979, Lord Arthur Savilles Crime 1980, Uncle Vanya (with Donald Sinden) 1982; films: Roman Holiday, Beautiful Stranger, No Road Back, Hands of the Ripper, Jekyll's Mother in Dr Jekyll and Mr Hyde 1989; television: Somerset Maughan Hour, Maigret, Black Limelight, Armchair Theatre, Wives and Daughters, Folio; radio broadcasts incl: We Beg to Differ, Desert Island Discs, Tumbledown Dick, Golouliovo; memb cncl and tstee Actor's Equity; vice pres: Poetry Soc, Voluntary Euthanasia Soc, Browning Soc of London, Actor's Charitable Tst; memb exec and tstee Dancers Resettlement Tst, memb and Arts Educnl Tst Sch Tring; *Books* Racine's Phédre (translation, 1961); *Recreations* poetry; *Clubs* Arts Theatre; *Style—* Miss Margaret Rawlings

RAWLINGS, Patricia Elizabeth; MEP (C) Essex South West 1989-; da of late Louis Rawlings, and Mary, *née* Boas de Winter; *b* 27 Jan 1939; *Educ* Oak Hall Surrey, Le

Manoir Lausanne Switzerland, Univ of Florence, UCL (BA Hons), LSE (Post grad Dip Int Rels); *m* 1962 (m dis 1967), Sir David Wolfson, s of Charles Wolfson; *Career* Parly candidate (C): Sheffield 1983, Doncaster 1987; spokesperson Women's Rights, jr whip, special advsr to Miny on Inner Cities DOE 1987-88; memb Euro Parl's Ctee on: Youth, Educn, Culture, Media, Sport, Women; vice pres Euro Parl's Delgn to Romania and Bulgaria; BRCS: memb 1964-, chm Appeals London Branch 1964-88, hon vice pres 1988; memb: Children's Care Ctee LCC 1959-61, WHNR Nursing Westminster Hosp to 1968, Br Bd of Video Classification, Peace Through NATO Cncl, IISS, RIIA, Euro Union Women, Cons Women's Nat Ctee; dir Eng Chamber Orchestra and Music Soc; *Recreations* music, art, golf, skiing, travel; *Clubs* Queen's; *Style—* Ms Patricia Rawlings, MEP; 97-113 Rue Belliard, 1040 Brussels, Belgium (☎ 010 32 2 284211)

RAWLINS, Capt Christopher Stuart; s of Maj Gen Stuart Blundell Rawlins, CB, CBE, DSO, MC (d 1955), of St Georges Island, Looe, Cornwall, and Millicent Olivia Burges (d 1930); *b* 21 April 1926; *Educ* Eton, Univ of Aberdeen; *m* 7 May 1949, June Rosemary, da of Brig William Thomas Gill, MC (d 1975), of Allington House, Allington, nr Salisbury, Wilts; 1 s (Nigel b 1951); *Career* cmmnd Gloucester Regt 1946, Capt 1950, Staff Capt 3 Div 1951-52, Adj 5 Gloucester Regt (TA) 1953-54, Co Cdr 1956; called to the Bar Gray's Inn 1957, advocate Supreme Ct of Kenya 1957-64, practising barr Albion Chambers Bristol 1964- (dept circuit judge, asst recorder, head of Chambers); memb Western Circuit; *Recreations* field sports (especially shooting and fishing); *Clubs* Army & Navy; *Style—* Capt Christopher Rawlins; Little Sodbury House, Chipping Sodbury, Bristol BS17 6QA (☎ 0454 312269); Albion Chambers, Broad St, Bristol BS1 1DR (☎ 0272 272144, fax 0272 262469)

RAWLINS, Colin Guy Champion; OBE (1965), DFC (1941); s of Capt Richard Seymour Champion Rawlins, DCM (d 1949), and Yvonne Blanche, *née* Andrews (d 1925); *b* 5 June 1919; *Educ* Prince of Wales Sch Nairobi Kenya, Charterhouse, Queen's Coll Oxford (BA, MA), LSE; *m* 25 May 1946, Rosemary, da of Capt Jens Jensen (d 1972); 2 s (Robert Champion b 1949, Andrew Champion b 1957), 1 da (Susan Champion b 1947); *Career* Pilot Offr RAFVR 1938, WWII Actg Sqdn Ldr 1941, served in 5 Gp Bomber Cmd, Flt Cdr 144 Sqdn (shot down Holland 1941, POW Germany 1941-45); HM Overseas Civil Service served in N Rhodesia and Zambia, cadet provincial admin 1946, dist offr 1948, res cmmr 1963-66, other appts in field and Govt HQ; dir of zoos and chief exec Zoological Soc of London 1966-84, pres Int Union of Directors of Zoological Gdns and Aquaria 1977-80, chm and memb many statutory and voluntary orgns in N Rhodesia and Zambia, dir and assoc ed Aircraft Owners and Pilots Assoc of UK 1985-; chm and pres local branch of Amersham and Chesham Cons Assoc 1967-; FCSA; *Recreations* gardening, aviation, travel; *Style—* Colin Rawlins, Esq, OBE, DFC; Birchgrove, 64 Earl Howe Rd, Holmer Green, nr High Wycombe, Bucks HP15 6QT (☎ 0494 712249)

RAWLINS, Gordon John; OBE (1986); s of Arthur James Rawlins, of New Milton, Hants, and Joyce Rosemary, *née* Smith; *b* 22 April 1944; *Educ* Welbeck Coll, RMA Sandhurst, RMCS (BSc); *m* 1, 28 Aug 1965, Ann Rose (d 1986), da of Alfred George Beard (d 1981); 1 s (Richard James b 1968); m 2, 25 Oct 1986, Margaret Anne (Meg), da of James Martin Edward Ravenscroft; 1 step s (Hamish Richmond Haddow b 1970), 1 step da (Islay Elizabeth Haddow b 1972); *Career* cmmnd REME 1964; recent career: Staff Coll (Maj) 1977-78, Maj GSO2 ASD 1 MOD 1978-80, Maj 21C 5 ARMD WKSP 1981-82, Lt-Col CO 7 ARMD WKSP 1982-84, Lt-Col Mil Asst to MGO MOD 1984-86, Col PB21 MOD 1986, Col Sec to COS Ctee MOD 1987, Brig Comd Maint 1 (BR) Corps 1988, serv Aden, Oman, Jordan, UK, Hong Kong and BAOR, ret 1989 as Brig; Sec IProdE and chief exec Inst of Indust Mangrs 1988-; MRAeS, CEng 1982, FIProdE, FIIM 1989; *Recreations* rugby, cricket, music; *Clubs* Army and Navy; *Style—* Gordon Rawlins, Esq, OBE; Instns of Prodn Engrs and Industl Mngrs, Rochester House, 66 Little Ealing Lane, London W5 4XX (☎ 081 579 9411, fax 081 579 2244)

RAWLINS, Surgn Vice Adm Sir John Stuart Pepys; KBE (1978, OBE 1960, MBE 1956); s of Col Cmdt Stuart William Hughes Rawlins, CB, CMG, DSO (d 1927), and Dorothy Pepys, *née* Cockerell (d 1937); *b* 12 May 1922; *Educ* Wellington, Univ Coll Oxford (MA), St Bartholomew's Hosp (BM BCh); *m* 1944, Diana Margaret Freshney, da of Charles Freshney Colbeck, ISO (d 1966); 1 s, 3 da; *Career* Surgn Lt RNVR 1947, Surgn Lt RN, RAF Inst Aviation Med 1951, RN Physiology Laboratory 1957, Surgn Cdr RAF Inst Aviation Med 1961, HMS Ark Royal 1964, US Naval Med Res Inst 1967, Surgn Capt 1969, Surgn Cdre dir of health and res (Naval) 1973, Surgn Rear Adm 1975, Dean of Naval Medicine and MO i/c Inst of Naval Medicine 1975-77, Actg Surgn Vice Adm 1977, Med Dir-Gen (Navy) 1977-80; Queens Hon Physician 1975-80; chm: Deep Ocean Technology Inc, Deep Ocean Engineering Inc, Trident Underwater (Systems) Ltd, Medical Express Ltd; dir: Under Sea Industs Inc 1981-83, Diving Unlimited Int Ltd; past pres Soc for Underwater Technology; conslt in underwater technol, conslt to CDE/MOD, hon fell Univ of Lancaster Dept of Psychology, chm External Advsy Ctee Survival Centre Robert Gordons Inst of Technol; CStJ, FRCP, FFCM, FRAeS; *Recreations* stalking, shooting, riding, judo; *Clubs* Vincent's (Oxford), Explorer's (New York); *Style—* Surgn Vice Adm Sir John Rawlins, KBE; Little Cross, Holne, Newton Abbott, S Devon TQ13 7RS (☎ 036 43 249/400)

RAWLINS, Prof Michael David; s of Rev Jack Rawlins (d 1947), of Kingswinford, Staffs, and Evelyn Daphne, *née* Douglas-Hamilton; *b* 28 March 1941; *Educ* Hawtreys nr Marlborough Wilts, Uppingham, St Thomas's Hosp, Univ of London (BSc, MB BS, MD); *m* 3 Aug 1963, Elizabeth Cadbury JP, da of Edmund Hambly (d 1985), of Seer Green, Bucks; 3 da (Vicky b 1964, Lucy b 1965, Suzannah b 1972); *Career* lectr med St Thomas's Hosp Med Sch London 1968-71, sr registrar Hammersmith Hosp London 1971-73, visiting res fell MRC Karolinska Inst Stockholm 1972-73, Ruth and Lionel Jacobsen prof clinical pharmacology Univ of Newcastle upon Tyne 1973-, visiting prof Royal Perth Hosp Western Aust 1980, Bradshaw lectr RCP London 1987, pub orator Univ of Newcastle upon Tyne 1990-; papers clinical pharmacology and therapeutics: memb: Nat Ctee Pharmacology 1977-83, Cncl St Oswalds Hospice 1977-, Ctee Safety of Meds 1980-; chm: Sub Ctee Safety Efficacy and Adverse Reactions 1987-, Ctee on Toxicity of Chemicals in Food Consumer Prods & Environment 1989-, Northern Regnl Health Authy 1990-; MRCP 1968, FRCP London 1977, FRCP Edinburgh 1987, FFPM 1989, fell RSM; *Books* Variability in Human Drug Response (with S E Smith 1973); *Recreations* music, golf; *Style—* Prof Michael Rawlins; 29 The Grove, Gosforth, Newcastle-upon-Tyne, NE3 1NE; Shoreston House, Shoreston, Seahouses, Northumberland; The University, Wolfson Unit of Clinical Pharmacology, Newcastle-upon-Tyne NE1 7RU (☎ 091 222 8041 fax 091 232 3613)

RAWLINS, Peter Jeremy; s of Leslie Rawlins; *b* 14 May 1941; *Educ* Warwick Sch, Univ of Nottingham (BA); *m* 1967, Gillian Lister, da of Cyril Goddard (d 1980); 4 s (Thomas b 1970, James b 1973, John b 1980, Tim b 1982); *Career* fin dir Tunstell Group plc 1989; FCA; *Recreations* sport; *Style—* Peter Rawlins Esq; Beech Cottage, Apperley Lane, Rawdon, Leeds LS19 6LW (☎ 0532 502363); Tunstall Group plc, Whitley Lodge, Whitley Bridge, Yorks DN14 0HR (☎ 0977 661234)

RAWLINS, Hon Mrs (Rachel Elizabeth Cecily); *née* Irby; eld da of 7 Baron Boston (d 1958); *b* 30 Aug 1914; *m* 15 June 1940, Lt Darsie Rawlins, RNVR, s of George Edward Hawkes Rawlins, of King's Lane, Great Missenden, Bucks; 2 s (Adrian b 1942, Anthony b 1944), 2 da (Diana b 1949, Christina b 1955); *Style—* The Hon Mrs Rawlins; Red Tiles, Kingswood Ave, Penn, Bucks

RAWLINS, Richard Duddingston; s of Donald Frank Rawlins, of 33 Whitfield Hill, Kearsney, Dover, Kent, and Eileen Muriel Rawlins, MBE; *b* 3 Oct 1944; *Educ* King's Sch Canterbury, Middx Hosp Univ of London (MB BS); *m* 3 Oct 1981, Jayne Margaret Dale, da of Douglas Brownsword (d 1973); 2 s (Alexander b 29 March 1984, Digby b 3 April 1986); *Career* Surgn Lt Cdr RNR 1978-; lectr King's Coll London 1971-73, sr orthopaedic registrar Guy's Hosp 1978-85, conslt orthopaedic surgn Bedford Gen Hosp 1985-; former: pres Br Orthopaedic Trainee's Assoc, chm Hosp Doctor's Assoc; co surgn St John Ambulance Bde Bedfordshire; FRCS 1975; *Recreations* sailing, skiing, family; *Clubs* Naval; *Style—* Richard Rawlins, Esq; 13 Pemberley Ave, Bedford MK40 2LE (☎ 0234 211882)

RAWLINSON, Alexander Noel; s and h of Sir Anthony Rawlinson, 5 Bt; *b* 15 July 1964; *Style—* Alexander Rawlinson Esq

RAWLINSON, Sir Anthony Henry John; 5 Bt (UK 1891); s of Sir (Alfred) Frederick Rawlinson, 4 Bt (d 1969), and Bess, Lady Rawlinson, *qv*; *b* 1 May 1936; *Educ* Millfield; *m* 1, 1960 (m dis 1967), Penelope Byng, da of Rear Adm Gambier John Byng Noel, CB; 1 s, 1 da; m 2, 1967 (m dis 1976), Pauline Strickland, da of John Holt Hardy, of Sydney, NSW; 1 s; m 3, 1977, Helen Leone, da of Thomas Miller Kennedy, of Glasgow; 1 s; *Heir* s, Alexander Rawlinson; *Career* fashion photographer (portraits); *Recreations* tennis, cricket; *Style—* Sir Anthony Rawlinson, Bt; Heath Farm, Guist, Dereham, Norfolk

RAWLINSON, Hon Anthony Richard; 2 s of Baron Rawlinson of Ewell, PC, QC, by his 2 w, Elaine; *b* 28 Dec 1963; *Educ* Foreign Service Sch at Georgetown Univ (BSc), Worth School; *Career* corporate financier with Jardine Fleming Holdings Ltd Hong Kong; formerly with N M Rothschild & Sons Ltd London; *Recreations* theatre, music and cricket; *Style—* The Hon Anthony Rawlinson; 9 Priory Walk, London SW10

RAWLINSON, Charles Frederick Melville; s of Capt Rowland Henry Rawlinson (d 1980); *b* 18 March 1934; *Educ* Canford, Jesus Coll Cambridge; *m* 1962, Jill Rosalind, da of John Wesley; 3 da (incl Julia Caroline b 1964, m 1988, James Ogilvy, s of Hon Sir Angus Ogilvy, and HRH Princess Alexandra); *Career* banker; chm API Group plc 1979-, dir Willis Faber plc 1981-89, jt chm Morgan Grenfell & Co Ltd (London) 1983-87 (dir 1970-85, former vice chm); sr advsr Morgan Grenfell Group plc 1988- (vice chm 1985-88), hon pres Morgan Grenfell Asia Ltd Singapore 1989-, dir Cambridge Symphony Orchestra Ltd, dep chm and jt hon treas Nat Assoc of Boys Clubs 1980-; chm: The Hundred Gp 1985-86, chm The Peache Advowson Tst 1982-; MAFCA, FCT; *Recreations* music, sailing; *Clubs* Brooks's, Leander; *Style—* Charles Rawlinson, Esq; 23 Great Winchester St, London EC2P 2AX (☎ 071 588 4545)

RAWLINSON, Hon Michael Vincent; er s of Baron Rawlinson of Ewell, PC, QC, and his 2 w, Elaine Angela, *née* Dominguez; *b* 24 Jan 1957; *m* 1982, Maria Alexandra Hilda Madeline de Lourdes (b 14 Dec 1953), only da of late Anthony Garton, by his w Hilda Isabella Maria (Anita), whose bro Juan m HRH Princess Hilda of Bavaria, and who was herself da of Garstang Bradstock Lockett, of Lima, Peru, by his w Hilda Luz Dora, yr da of late Juan Leovigilde de Loayza, of Lima and Santiago, Chile; *Style—* The Hon Michael Rawlinson; The Willowpond, 314 Fulham Rd, London SW10

RAWLINSON, William; CBE (1978); s of David Rawlinson (d 1950), of London, and Ann Markus (d 1974); *b* 10 Sept 1916; *Educ* Balliol Coll Oxford (MA); *m* 29 July 1954, Marietta, *née* Pordes; *Career* Nat Serv Flt Lt RAF 1941-46; called to the Bar Inner Temple 1939; memb Govt Legal Serv 1948-81; since 1972 dealing with EEC Law and policy, lectr on EEC Civil Serv Coll; lectr: Univ of Southern California, California State Univ 1982, Bar Ilan Univ; contrib Fordham Int Law Jl and Int Fin Law Review, sitting periodically stipendiary Met Magistrate London; *Books* European Community Law; *Recreations* reading, music; *Clubs* Reform; *Style—* William Rawlinson, Esq, CBE; 11 Kings Bench Walk, Temple, London EC4Y 7EQ (☎ 071 583 0610, fax 071 583 9123)

RAWLINSON OF EWELL, Baron (Life Peer UK 1978), of Ewell, Co Surrey; Peter Anthony Grayson Rawlinson; PC (1964), QC (1959, NI 1972); s of Lt-Col Arthur Richard Rawlinson, OBE (d 1984), of Ferring, Sussex, and Ailsa, eldest da of Sir Henry Grayson, 1 Bt, KBE; *b* 26 June 1919; *Educ* Downside, Christ's Coll Cambridge (exhibitioner 1938, hon fellow 1981); *m* 1, 1940 (m annulled by Sacred Rota Rome 1954), Haidée, da of Gerald Kavanagh, of Dublin; 3 da; m 2, 1954, his 1 cous, Elaine, da of Vincent Dominguez, of Rhode Island, and Angela, 6 da of Sir Henry Grayson, 1 Bt, KBE; 2 s, 1 da; *Career* sits as Cons peer in House of Lords; Maj Irish Gds WWII (despatches); barr 1946; MP (C): Epsom 1955-74, Epsom and Ewell 1974-78; slr-gen 1962-64, attorney gen 1970-74, rec Kingston 1975-, chm of the Bar 1975-76, ldr Western Circuit 1975-82, reader Inner Temple 1983, treas Inner Temple 1984; pres Senate Inns of Courtland Bar 1986-87; kt 1962; *Clubs* White's, Pratt's, MCC; *Style—* The Rt Hon the Lord Rawlinson of Ewell, PC, QC; Priory Walk, London SW10

RAWNSLEY, Andrew Nicholas James; s of Eric Rawnsley, and Barbara, *née* Butler; *b* 5 Jan 1962; *Educ* Rugby, Sidney Sussex Coll Cambridge (MA); *Career* writer and broadcaster; BBC 1983-85, The Guardian 1985- (political columnist 1987-), presenter Channel 4 TV series A Week in Politics 1989-; Student Journalist of the Year 1983, Young Journalist of the Year 1987; *Recreations* House of Commons; *Style—* Andrew Rawnsley, Esq; The Guardian Newspaper, 119 Farringdon Rd, London EC1R 3ER (☎ 071 278 2332, fax 071 837 2114, telex 8811746 GUARDN G)

RAWSON, Christopher Selwyn Priestley; JP (City of London Bench 1972, Inner London 1967-72); s of Cdr S G C Rawson, OBE, RN (d 1974), and Dr Doris Rawson, *née* Brown (d 1979); *b* 25 March 1928; *Educ* The Elms Sch Colwall Worcs, The Nautical Coll Pangbourne; *m* 24 Jan 1959, Rosemary Ann, da of Alex R Focke (d 1983); 2 da (Gina b 16 Jan 1961, Caroline b 22 March 1964); *Career* navigating apprentice Merchant Serv T & J Brocklebank Ltd 1945-48, mangr John Crossley & Sons Ltd Halifax 1948-53, London rep of Milford Docks Ltd 1953-60, chm and md Christopher Rawson Ltd 1960-80, dir London Underwriters First Fin Servs Ltd 1983-; underwriting memb Lloyds 1973; JP City of London Bench 1972- (Inner London 1967-72), Sheriff City of London 1961-62, common councilman Ward of Bread St 1963-72, Alderman Ward of Lime St 1972-83, HM Lt City of London 1980-83, CStJ; Master Worshipful Co of Clothworkers 1988 (Liveryman 1952, Asst 1977), Master Co of Watermen and Lightermen 1982-84 (Freeman 1966, Asst 1974), Yr Bro Trinity House 1988; assoc Textile Inst 1953; Cdr Order of: Senegal 1961, Ivory Coast 1961, Liberia 1962; *Recreations* shooting, sailing; *Clubs* Garrick, Royal London Yacht (Cdre 1989-); *Style—* Christopher Rawson, Esq, JP; 56 Ovington St, London SW3 2JB; Prince Rupert House, 64 Queen St, London EC4R 1AD

RAWSON, Jessica Mary; *née* Quirk; da of Roger Nathaniel Quirk, CB (d 1964), and Paula, *née* Weber; *b* 1 Jan 1943; *Educ* St Paul's Girls Sch, New Hall Cambridge (BA, MA), SOAS London (BA); *m* May 1968, John Graham Rawson, s of Graham Stanhope Rawson (d 1953); 1 da (Josephine b 1972); *Career* asst princ Miny of Health 1965-67; Dept of Oriental Antiquities Br Museum: asst keeper II 1967-71, asst keeper I 1971-76, dep keeper 1976-87, keeper 1987-; FBA 1990; *Books* Animals in Art (1977), Ancient China, Art and Archaeology (1980), Chinese Ornament, the Lotus and the Dragon (1984), Chinese Bronzes, Art and Ritual (1987), Ancient Chinese Bronze in the Collection of Bella and PP Chiu (1988), Western Zhou Bronzes from the Arthur M Sackler Collections (with Emma Bunter, 1990), Ancient Chinese and Ordos Bronzes

(1990); *Style*— Mrs John Rawson; 3 Downshire Hill, London NW3 1NR (☎ 071 794 4002); Dept of Oriental Antiquities, British Museum, Great Russell St, London WC1 (☎ 071 323 8444, fax 071 323 8480)

RAWSON, John Oliver; s of Harry Rawson (d 1983), and Olive May, *née* Buckle; *b* 23 Nov 1948; *Educ* Ripon GS N Yorkshire, St John's Coll Oxford (BA, DPhil, HWC Davis prize for history); *m* 24 Feb 1985, Jonquil Margaret, da of Stephen Christopher Naish; 1 da (Madeleine Naomi b 29 Jan 1986); *Career* copywriter Christian Brann Ltd 1973-78, chief copywriter Kays of Worcester (mail order) 1978-82; creative gp head Christian Brann Ltd 1984-86 (sr copywriter 1982-84), creative dir Chapter One Direct plc 1986-; memb: Cheltenham Borough Cncl 1980-87, Gloucestershire CC 1981-; chm Social Services Ctee Gloucestershire CC 1985-90; *Recreations* family, local government, studying humanity; *Style*— John Rawson, Esq; 18 The Grove, Cheltenham, Gloucestershire GL52 6SX (0242 242738); Chapter One Direct plc, Green Lane, Tewkesbury, Glos GL20 8EZ (☎ 0684 850040, fax 0684 850113)

RAWSON, Prof Kenneth John; s of Arthur William Rawson (d 1949), and Beatrice Annie, *née* Standing; *b* 27 Oct 1926; *Educ* Northern GS Portsmouth, RNC Greenwich, UCL, Brunel Univ (MSc); *m* 29 July 1950, Rhona Florence, *née* Gill, da of William Henry Gill MBE, of Manor Farm House, Norton St Philip; 2 s (Christopher John b 1955, Timothy James b 1981), 1 da (Hilary Anne b 1958); *Career* at sea 1950-51, structural research 1951-53, forward design Admty 1953-57, with Lloyds Shipping Register 1957-59, ship designer MOD 1959-69, naval staff 1969-72, prof UCL 1972-77, head of forward design MOD 1977-79, chief naval architect MOD 1979-83; Brunel Univ 1983-89: prof, dean of educn and design, pro vice-chllr; vice pres RINA 1982; FEng 1983, FRINA 1961, FCSD 1984, FRSA 1984; *Style*— Prof Kenneth Rawson; Moorlands The Street, Chilcompton, Bath BA3 4HB (☎ 0761 232 793)

RAWSON, Dr Malcolm David; s of Stanley Ronald Rawson, OBE (d 1977), and Phyllis Elizabeth, *née* Birkin (d 1988); *b* 26 June 1933; *Educ* Leeds GS, Univ of Leeds Med Sch (MD); *m* 8 June 1963 (m dis 1988), Janet Elizabeth Rees, da of Clifford Lodge (d 1981); 1 s (James b 1966), 2 da (Edwina b 1965, Felicity b 1970), 2 step da (Clare b 1956, Caroline b 1961); *Career* sr registrar in neurology (former registrar) Manchester Royal Infirmary 1963-70, sr res fell in neurology Yale Univ Med Sch New Haven Conn USA 1966-67, conslt neurologist Hull Royal Infirmary Yorks RHA 1969-; memb Cncl N of England Neurological Assoc, pres Hull Med Soc 1980, dir Postgrad Educn Hull 1984-89; FRCR 1976, FRCP 1977; *Recreations* salmon and trout fishing, fell walking, skiing; *Style*— Dr Malcolm Rawson; Ravenspur, Davenport Ave, Hessle, North Humberside HU13 0RP (☎ 0482 648863), Hull Royal Infirmary, Anlaby Rd, Hull HU3 2KZ (☎ 0482 28541)

RAWSON OF SOWERBY, John Hugh Selwyn; er s of Frederick Philip Selwyn Rawson, JP (d 1947), of Brockwell, Triangle, Sowerby, and Sarah Katharine, *née* Mitchell (d 1960); descended from John Rawson, of Ingrow, Yorks (b 1505) (*see* Burke's Landed Gentry, 18 edn, vol III, 1972); *b* 28 April 1915; *Educ* Loretto, Huddersfield Tech Coll; *m* 1, 30 Jan 1939 (m dis), Mary Elizabeth (d 1980), o da of Harold Whitaker (d 1955), of Hopewell House, Lightcliffe, Halifax; 1 da (Margaret Elizabeth Ann b 1945); m 2, 25 March 1965, Marjorie Louis, 2 da of George Nelson Bories (d 1930), of The Stubbins, Triangle; *Career* Lt 4 Duke of Wellington's Regt, 58 Anti-Tank Regt 1935-38, 3/7 How Mountain Battery FMSVF 1939-40, 1 Perak Bn FMSVF 1940-41, escaped after fall of Singapore, invalided out; rubber planter in Malaya 1939- 42; agriculture and property owner 1942-, shipping mangr 1958-75; memb: Royal Br Legion, British Field Sports Soc, Sowerby Conservative Assoc, Yorks Agric Soc, Lorettonian Soc; Sowerby St Peter's Church Archivist, Master of Otterhound Assoc; *Recreations* hunting, gardening, writing under nom de plume Isoceles, building; *Style*— John Rawson, Esq; The Stubbins, Triangle, Sowerby Bridge, West Yorks HX6 3DR

RAY, Cyril; s of Albert Benson Ray, and Rita, *née* Caminetsky; *b* 16 March 1908; *Educ* Manchester GS, Jesus Coll Oxford; *Career* war corr Manchester Guardian 1939-45: 5 Destroyer Flotilla 1940, HMS Victorious N African Landings 1942, 8 Army Italy 1942-3 (despatches); war corr BBC: US 82 Airborne Div (US Army citation Nijmegen 1944), US 3 Army 1944-45; trustee of Albany 1967- (chm 1981-86); Freeman City of London, Liveryman Worshipful Co of Fanmakers 1975, Hon Citizen of Cognac 1985, Burgess of St Emilion 1973; hon life memb: NUJ, Circle of Wine Writers (fndr and former pres); Commendatore Italian Order of Merit 1981 (Cavaliere 1972), Chevalier French Order of Merit 1985 (Mérite Agricole 1974); *Books* Scenes and Characters from Surtees (ed 1948), From Algiers to Austria The History of 78 Division in Italy (1952),The Compleat Imbiber (ed, 1956; first André Simon Prize, 1965), The Pageant of London (1958), Merry England (1960), Regiment of the Line: The Story of the Lancashire Fusiliers (1963), The Gourmet's Companion (ed 1963), Morton Shand's Book of French Wines (ed 1964), The Wines of Italy (1966, Bologna Trophy 1967), In a Glass Lightly (1967), Mouton: The Story of Mouton Rothschild (1974), Wine and Food (with Elizabeth Ray 1975), The Wines of France (1976), The Wines of Germany (1977), The Complete Book of Spirits and Liqueurs (1978), The Saint Michael Guide to Wine (1978), Ruffino: The Story of a Chianti (with C Mozley 1979), Lickerish Limericks with Filthy Pictures by Charles Mozley (1979), Ray on Wine (Glenfiddich Wine Book of the Year, 1979), The New Book of Italian Wines (1982), Bollinger: The Story of a Champagne (revised edn 1982) Lafite: The Story of Château Lafite - Rothschild (revised edn 1985), Cognac (revised edn 1985); *Clubs* Athenaeum, Brooks's, MCC, Special Forces; *Style*— Cyril Ray, Esq; K 1 Albany, Piccadilly, London W1V 9RQ (☎ 071 734 0270)

RAY, Edward Ernest; CBE (1988); s of Walter James Ray (d 1968), of London, and Cecilia May, *née* Hampton; *b* 6 Nov 1924; *Educ* Holloway Co Sch, Univ of London (BCom); *m* 2 July 1949, Margaret Elizabeth, da of (Stanley) George Bull (d 1964), of Kettering, Northants; 2 s (Andrew John b 26 Nov 1952, Patrick Charles b 17 March 1956); *Career* Petty Offr RN 1943-46; CA, sr ptnr Spicer and Oppenheim (formerly Spicer and Pegler) 1984-88 (ptnr 1957-88), chm London CAs 1972-73, inspr DTI, bd memb Securities and Investmt Bd 1984-90, chm Investors Compensation Scheme 1988-90; memb: Worshipful Co of CAs 1975-, Freeman City of London; FCA (pres 1982 and 1983); *Books* VAT for Businessmen (1972), Partnership Taxation (3 edn 1987); *Recreations* golf, tennis, walking and bird watching; *Clubs* City of London; *Style*— Edward Ray, Esq, CBE; Southgate, Wiveton Rd, Blakeney, Norfolk NR25 7NJ (☎ 081 360 0028)

RAY, Elizabeth Mary; JP (Kent 1968-81; E Sussex 1981-); da of Rev Henry Cleeve Brocklehurst (d 1942), of Chalfont St Giles, Bucks, and Gwenna Maud, *née* Jones (d 1971); *b* 1 Oct 1925; *Educ* Private, LSE (Dip Soc Sci and Admin 1956); *m* 22 May 1953, Cyril Ray, s of Albert Benson Ray (d 1954), of Lytham St Annes; 1 s (Jonathan Cleeve b 1960); *Career* social worker LCC 1956-60, GLC 1964-68; Kent CC Social Servs 1972-83; freelance study supervisor Social Servs Course 1983-87; memb: bd of visitors HM Prison Lewes 1984-89, mgmnt cncl Kent Opera 1970-89; author (with husband): Wine with Food (1976), Best of Eliza Acton (1968), Resourceful Cook (1975), Country Cooking (1978); contrib: Homes and Gardens, A La Carte, and many other magazines; cookery corr Observer 1969-79; *Recreations* travel, listening to music, cooking; *Clubs* University Women's; Lansdowne; *Style*— Mrs Elizabeth Ray, JP; K I Albany, Piccadilly, London W1V 9RQ (☎ 071 734 0270)

RAY, George William; s of late George William Ray, of High Wycombe, and Agnes Mary, *née* Pryke (d 1973); *b* 6 May 1905; *Educ* Royal GS High Wycombe; *m* 31 Aug 1940, (Ellen) Eileen, da of Harry Saunders (d 1974); 1 s (John Stewart); *Career* Furniture Industs Ltd (later Ercol Furniture Ltd) 1923-: co sec 1932, dir 1944; dir Ercol Hldgs Ltd; vice-chm Govrs Royal GS High Wycombe, memb High Wycombe CC, cncl memb Thames Chiltern C of C and Indust, Furnishing Trades Benevolent Assoc (nat pres 1989), formerly memb Nat Savings Ctee; chm: Consultative Ctee of TSB, Mgmnt and Languages Consultative Ctee of Bucks Coll; Warden of local church; Freeman City of London, Liveryman Worshipful Co of Furniture Makers 1963; FInstD; *Style*— George Ray, Esq; Ramsdale, 8 School Close, High Wycombe, Bucks HP11 1PH (☎ 0494 206 55); Ercol Holdings Ltd, London Rd, High Wycombe, Bucks HP13 7AE (☎ 0494 212 61, fax 0494 462 467, telex 83616)

RAY, Malcolm John; s of George Henry Ray (d 1985), and Lucy, *née* Roberts (d 1985); *b* 27 Aug 1938; *Educ* Bilston GS, Univ of Aston (BSc, MSc); *m* 6 Sept 1962, Betty Maria, da of Whitmore Nicholls (d 1968), of Staffs; 1 s (Jonathan b 1974); *Career* GKN Technology Ltd 1953-70, Hycast Ltd (tech dir) 1970-75, sales dir Rylands Whitecross Ltd Warrington 1976-81, Catton & Co Ltd Leeds 1981-87; chm and md: Birmid Holdings Ltd 1990-, Birmid Industrial Products Ltd; chm: Birmal Components Ltd 1987, PBM Components Ltd 1987, Darcast Components Ltd 1987, Thyssen Industrie Holdings (UK) Ltd 1990, Birmid Holdings Pension Trustees Ltd 1990; MIBF 1964, MBIM 1974, FIM 1975, CEng 1976, MInstM 1976; *Recreations* game fishing, walking; *Style*— Malcolm Ray, Esq; Thatched Cottage, Hill Wootton, Warwick CV35 7PP (☎ 0926 50 309); Birmid Holdings Ltd, 6 The Quadrangle, Cranmore Ave, Shirley, Solihull, West Midlands B90 4LE (☎ 021 711 4555, fax 021 711 4447)

RAY, Robin; s of Ted Ray, and Sybil, *née* Stevens; *Educ* Highgate Sch, RADA; *m* 1960, Susan, da of Alan Stranks; 1 s (Rupert b 1979); *Career* actor, author, broadcaster; West End debut The Changeling (Royal Court Theatre) 1960, extensive work in radio and TV, especially music and arts, stage play Cafe Puccini (Wyndham's Theatre) 1986, drama critic Punch 1986-87, artistic dir Classic FM Radio 1989-91; *Books* Words on Music (1985); *Style*— Robin Ray, Esq; c/o David Wilkinson Associates, 115 Hazlebury Road, London SW6 2LX (☎ 071 371 5188)

RAY, Sidney; *b* 5 Oct 1939; *Educ* Owen's Sch London, North London Poly (BSc), The Polytechnic Regent St, City Univ London (MSc); *m* 2 s; *Career* cadet instr and RAF civilian instr ATC 1956-68; photographer and lectr in photography; asst chemist Res Laboratories Gas Cncl 1959-60, photographic chemist Johnsons of Hendon Ltd 1960-66; pt/t lectr 1962-66; lectr Poly of Central London 1966-; examiner various colls and courses 1972-, organiser confs 1978-; conslt for govt depts, industry, publishers and others; reg contrib to Br Jl of Photography, contrib ed Photoresearcher magazine; reg book reviewer for: British Book News, The Photographer, The Photogrammetric Record Jl of Photographic Science, Photoresearcher, Professional Photographer; numerous articles in photographic jls; many hundreds of photographs published; author of 14 photographic textbooks and contrib to 8 others; memb: NATFHE, Photogrammetric Soc, Euro Soc for the Hist of Photography, The Steroscopic Soc, Photographic Educn Gp, Cinema Theatre Assoc, Greater London Industl Archaeology Soc, Assoc of Hist and Fine Art Photographers; FRPS 1972; fell: BIPP 1974, Master Photographers Assoc 1986; *Style*— Sidney Ray, Esq

RAYFIELD, Tom; s of Alfred John Rayfield and Doris Caryl, *née* Lyons; *b* 15 Feb 1941; *Educ* Watford GS, Queens' Coll Cambridge (exhibitioner, MA); *m* 15 Oct 1971, Rosemary Jean, da of John Fearon; 2 s (Tobias Stephen Fearon b 3 Jan 1974, Joe Daniel Fearon b 9 June 1977); *Career* J Walter Thompson: copywriter 1963, transferred NY office 1966-67, creative gp head London 1967, creative dir and memb Bd 1973, creative dir and Bd dir 1978-, chm and creative dir JWT Direct 1988-; creative dir and Bd dir: Lintas 1974-75, The Kirkwood Company 1975-77; memb and former vice pres Advertising Creative Circle, memb: D & AD Assoc 1969, BDMA, MIPA 1973; *Recreations* collecting modern first editions, golf; *Clubs* The Naval; *Style*— Tom Rayfield, Esq; The Blacksmiths, Radnage Common, Bucks HP14 4DH (☎ 0494 483 986); J Walter Thompson Company Ltd, 40 Berkeley Square, London WIX 6AD (☎ 071 499 4040, fax 071 629 3054, car phone 0860 713 851)

RAYLEIGH, 6 Baron (UK 1821) John Gerald Strutt; s of Hon Charles Richard Strutt (d 1981; s of 4 Baron Rayleigh), and Hon Mrs Charles Strutt, *qv*; suc uncle 5 Baron Rayleigh 1988; *b* 4 June 1960; *Educ* Eton, RAC Cirencester; *Heir* uncle, Hon Hedley Vicars Strutt, *qv*; *Career* Lt Welsh Guards (ret); *Style*— The Rt Hon The Lord Rayleigh; Terling Place, Chelmsford, Essex

RAYMAKERS, Roeland Leonard; s of Karel Raymakers (d 1967), of Helmond, Holland, and Dymphna Hubertina (Tiny), *née* Keulen; *b* 3 Feb 1933; *Educ* Stonyhurst, Univ of London Westminster Hosp (MB BS); *m* 11 June 1960, Joan Susan, da of John Creasey, of Lambeth; 2 s (Christopher b 1961, Dominic b 1964), 2 da (Katharine b 1963, Susanna b 1968); *Career* RMO Westminster Hosp 1960-61, registrar Royal Nat Orthopaedic Hosp 1965-67, sr registrar Harlow Wood Orthopaedic Hosp 1967-71, conslt orthopaedic surgn Leicester Dist Hosp 1971-, clinical head of orthopaedic serv Leicester Royal Infirmary 1986-; memb: BMA, Hosp Conslts and Specialists Assoc; FRCS 1965; *Recreations* game shooting, fishing, skiing; *Style*— Roeland Raymakers, Esq; Crowbank, 31 Chapel Lane, Knighton, Leicester LE2 3WF (☎ 0533 708660); Leicester Royal Infirmary, Leicester LE1 5WW (☎ 0533 541414)

RAYMENT, Lt-Col Clifton Herbert; MBE (1951); s of Lionel Herbert Rayment (d 1979), and Mary Charlotte Gertrude, *née* Clifton (d 1972); *b* 24 Dec 1919; *Educ* Berkhamsted Sch, Coll of Estate Mgmnt, Quetta Staff Coll; *m* 1, 14 Feb 1942, Patricia; 1 da (Sarah b 1945); m 2, 21 Sept 1957, Aileen, da of William Vans Agnew, of Fairacre, Shermanbury, W Sussex; 1 s (Alastair b 1958), 1 da (Lucinda b 1960); *Career* Probyn's House (Indian Army) 1939-46, Royal Tank Regt 1946-62, Regtl sec, Royal Tank Regt 1962-86; sec RAC Benevolent Fund; *Recreations* shooting, beagling, sailing, cricket, tennis, squash; *Clubs* Army and Navy, MCC, Parkstone Yacht; *Style*— Lt-Col Clifton Rayment, MBE; Briarswood House, Wareham, Dorset (☎ 0929 552993)

RAYMENT, William Alfred; s of William Charles Rayment (d 1958), of Finchley, London, and Daisy Catherine Rayment (d 1976); *b* 23 Jan 1917; *Educ* Tollington Park Central, Northern Poly; *m* 1, 25 Jan 1941 (m dis 1946), Gladys Florence, da of late George Stockham, of Islington, London; m 2, 28 Aug 1948, Marjorie Lily, da of William Whiteway (d 1924), of Hornsey, London; 1 da (Margaret Ann b 7 June 1949); *Career* WWII RA, enlisted 1940, cmmnd 1944, seconded IA 1945, Maj 1 Indian anti-Tank Regt 1946, hon Capt 1946; nat pres Display Prodrs and Screen Printers Assoc 1967-69, pres Fedn of Euro Screen Printers Assoc 1975-79, memb Lloyds 1977; Freeman: City of London 1977, Worshipful Co of Farriers 1977; FInstD 1965; *Recreations* flat green bowls; *Style*— William A Rayment, Esq; Kerswell, 4 Upland Drive, Brookmans Park, Hatfield, Herts AL9 6PS (☎ 0707 53056)

RAYMER, Garth Anthony; s of Charles Robert Peyton Raymer (d 1968), and Christine Joyce, *née* Spaul; *b* 28 Aug 1945; *Educ* Prince Henry's GS Evesham; *m* 5 Sept 1970, Lynne Margaret; 3 s (Martin b 1973, Peter b 1975, Michael b 1976); *Career* CA; ptnr Clement Keys Rabjohns Birmingham Worcs and Evesham 1970-; *Recreations* sport, public service, architecture; *Style*— Garth Raymer, Esq; Woodwards House, Cooks Hill, Wicks, Pershore, Worcestershire; 113 High St,

Evesham, Worcs (☎ 0386 765567)

RAYMOND, Diana Joan; da of Lt William Thomas Young, RA (d 1917), and Hilda Joan Drummond, *née* Black (d 1952); *b* 25 April 1916; *Educ* Cheltenham Ladies' Coll; *m* 12 Aug 1940, Ernest Raymond, s of Maj-Gen George Frederic Blake, RM (d 1904); 1 s (Peter John Franics b 1 June 1941); *Career* author; *Books* Joanna Linden (1952), The Small Rain (1954), Between the Stirrup and the Ground (1956), Strangers' Gallery (1958), The Five Days (1959), Guest of Honour (1960), The Climb (1962), People in the House (1967), Are You Travelling Alone? (1969), The Best of the Day (1972), Incident on a Summer's Day (1974), Horseman Pass By (1977), The Dark Journey (1978), Emma Pride (1981), The Dancers All Are Gone (1983), House of the Dolphin (1985), Lily's Daughter (1988); *Recreations* reading, travel, walking; *Style*— Mrs Diana Raymond; 22 Pryors, East Heath Rd, London NW3 1BS (☎ 071 435 3716)

RAYMOND, Hon Mrs (Gay); da of 4 Visc Hardinge (d 1979); *b* 1938; *m* 1963, Pierre Raymond; 1 s; *Style*— The Hon Mrs Raymond; Stage Coach Road, Brome, Québec J0E 1K0, Canada

RAYMOND, Michael Murray John; MC (1945), DL (Essex 1982); only s of Samuel Raymond; *b* 9 Jan 1923; *Educ* Sherborne, Trinity Coll Oxford; *m* 1, 1951 (m dis 1960), Madeline June, da of Brig Sidney Lucey, MC; 2 s (Richard b 1952, Philip b 1953), 1 da (Virginia b 1955); m 2, 1962, Daphne, da of R Alexander, of Worcs; 1 s (Charles b 1965); *Career* served as Capt WWII 60 Rifles and Rifle Bde; dir Henry Head & Co 1964-73; memb Lloyd's; *Style*— Michael Raymond, Esq, MC, DL; Belchamp Hall, Belchamp Walter, Sudbury, Suffolk (☎ 0787 72744)

RAYMOND, Paul; *b* 15 Nov 1925; *Educ* St Francis Xaviers Coll Liverpool, Glossop GS Glossop Derbyshire; 1 s (Howard b 23 Nov 1959), 1 da (Deborah b 28 Jan 1956); *Career* RAF 1944-47; musician, music hall artiste, impresario, night club proprietor, publisher, West End property owner; memb Grand Order of Water Rats; *Style*— Paul Raymond, Esq; Arlington St, London SW1; Paul Raymond Organisation Ltd, 2 Archer St, London W1V 7HE (☎ 071 734 9191, fax 071 734 5030, telex 22638)

RAYMOND, William Francis (Frank); CBE (1978); s of Capt Leonard William Raymond, ISO (d 1973), of Maidenhead, Berks, and May Raymond, MBE, *née* Bennett (d 1973); *b* 25 Feb 1922; *Educ* Bristol GS, Queen's Coll Oxford (BA, MA); *m* 13 Aug 1949, Amy Elizabeth (Betty), da of Maj Charles Kingston Kelk, of Ludshott Manor, Liphook, Hants; 3 s (Christopher b 1950, Robin b 1954, Charles b 1959), 1 da (Karen b 1952); *Career* res scientist: MRC 1943-45, Grassland Res Inst 1945-72 (asst dir 1962-72); chief scientist MAFF London 1980-82 (dep chief scientist 1972-80); agric sci conslt: EEC, FAO, World Bank; visiting prof of agric Wye Coll London 1978-83; hon treas Soc for the Responsible use of Resources in Agric and on the Land (Rural), chm Stapledon Meml Tst; FRSC, CCHEM 1962; *Books* Forage Conservation and Feeding (with Redman and Waltham, fourth edn 1987); *Recreations* gardening; *Clubs* Farmers; *Style*— Frank Raymond, Esq, CBE; Periwinkle Cottage, Christmas Common, Watlington, Oxon OX9 5HR (☎ 0491 612 942)

RAYMONT, Timothy; s of Richard Kenneth Raymont (d 1970), and Patricia Parris, *née* Goodenough; *b* 26 July 1946; *Educ* Radley, Univ of East Anglia (BA); *Career* jt md Holmes of Reading Ltd 1972-; dir: GG Furniture Ltd 1979-82 (chm 1980-81), Minty plc and subsidiaries 1983-88; memb of Design Index Selection Ctee 1978-88; *Recreations* opera, squash, motor cycling; *Style*— Timothy Raymont, Esq; 32 Hartismere Rd, London SW6 7UD (☎ 071 381 1134); Chatham St, Reading RG1 7JX (☎ 0734 586421)

RAYNAR, Hon Mrs (Sarah Elizabeth Ann); *née* Butler; da of 16 Viscount Mountgarret (d 1966); *b* 1932; *m* 1955 (m dis 1976), Geoffrey Kenneth Raynar; 2 s; *Style*— The Hon Mrs Raynar; 52 St Anne's Road, Headingley, Leeds LS6 3NX

RAYNE, Sir Edward; CVO (1977); s of Maj Joseph Edward Rayne (d 1951), of Park Lane, London, and Meta Elizabeth, *née* Reddish (d 1967); *b* 19 Aug 1922; *Educ* Harrow; *m* 10 Oct 1952, Phyllis, da of William Cort (d 1977), of Worcester Park, Surrey; 2 s (Edward Anthony Claude b Sept 1953, Nicholas Edward b 3 June 1957); *Career* ladies shoe mfr & retailer; chm & md H & M Rayne Ltd 1951-87, pres Rayne-Delman Shoes Inc 1961-72, exec chm Rayne-Delman Shoes Inc 1972-87, dir Debenhams plc 1975-88, pres Debenhams Inc 1976-87; exec chm Harvey Nichols & Co Ltd 1978-88; chm: Lotus Ltd 1978-86, Br Fashion Cncl 1985-90; pres Royal Warrant Holders Assoc 1964, (hon treas 1974-91); Master Worshipful Co of Pattenmakers 1981; FRSA 1971; Chevalier de l'Ordre National du Mérite (France) 1984; kt 1988; *Recreations* bridge, golf; *Clubs* Portland, White's; *Style*— Sir Edward Rayne, CVO; 29 Hartfield Rd, Cooden, nr Bexhill-on-Sea, Sussex (☎ 04243 2175)

RAYNE, Baroness; Lady Jane Antonia Frances; *née* Vane-Tempest-Stewart; da of 8 Marquess of Londonderry (d 1955); *b* 1932; *m* 1965, as his 2 w, Baron Rayne (Life Peer), *qv*; 2 s, 2 da; *Career* patron Guardee Ctee Jewish Care (formerly Jewish Welfare Bd) 1965-; memb Cncl of Management Chiswick Family Rescue 1986-; tstee Chicken Shed Theatre Co 1989-; *Style*— The Rt Hon the Lady Rayne; 33 Robert Adam St, London W1M 5AH

RAYNE, John; s of Percy Claude Rayne (d 1980), of King's Langley, Herts, and Hilda Rose, *née* Bradfield (d 1988); *b* 18 May 1935; *Educ* Univ Coll Sch Hampstead, Royal Dental Hosp (LDS RCS), Univ of Oxford (DPhil); *m* 20 Oct 1962, Norma Vanda Faith, da of Leonard Victor George Honey, of Hammersmith; 1 s (Timothy John Charles b 1965), 1 da (Philippa Valerie Faith b 1964); *Career* Flt Lt RAF Dental Branch 1956-59, GSM, civil conslt in dental surgery RAF 1985-; house surgn Royal Dental Hosp 1955-56, gen dental practice 1959-60, registrar Stoke Mandeville Hosp 1960-63, sr registrar United Oxford Hosps 1963-68; conslt oral surgn: Mount Vernon & Wexham Park Hosps 1968-72, John Radcliffe Hosp 1972-; scientific advsr: Br Dental Jl, Int Dental Jl; clinical lectr Maxillo-Facial Surgery 1972-, visiting fell Green Coll Oxford; examiner: Oxford (MSc), Sheffield (BDS, MDS, MSc), RCS (FDS), Colombo (MS), Bristol (BDS, MSc); chm DHSS Standing Dental Advsy Ctee 1980-84, memb Cncl RCS 1983-, pres BDA 1989-90; MA Univ of Oxford 1972; fell Br Assoc of Oral and Maxillo-Facial Surgns FDSRCS 1960; ed: Gen Dental Practice, Gen Dental Treatment; *Recreations* watching rowing; *Clubs* Leander; *Style*— John Rayne, Esq; Tudor Lodge, Buckland, Faringdon, Oxfordshire SN7 8PY (☎ 036 787215), John Radcliffe Hosp, Headley Way, Headington, Oxford OX3 9DU (☎ 0865 817270, fax 0865 69223)

RAYNE, Baron (Life Peer UK 1976), of Prince's Meadow in Greater London; Max Rayne; er s of Phillip and Deborah Rayne; *b* 8 Feb 1918; *Educ* Central Fndn Sch, UCL; *m* 1, 1941 (m dis 1960), Margaret, da of Louis Marco; 1 s (Hon Robert Anthony b 1949), 2 da (Hon Madeleine Barbara (Hon Mrs Rayner) b 1943, Hon Susan Ann (Hon Mrs Rubin) b 1945); m 2, 1965, Lady Jane Antonia Frances Vane-Tempest-Stewart, *qv*, da of 8 Marquess of Londonderry, JP, DL; 2 s (Hon Nicholas Alexander b 1969, Hon Alexander Philip b 1973), 2 da (Hon Natasha Deborah b 1966, Hon Tamara Annabel b 1970); *Career* served WWII RAF; chm: London Merchant Securities plc 1960-, Westpool Investment Trust plc 1980-, London Festival Ballet Trust 1967-75, Nat Theatre Bd 1971-88; dep chm First Leisure Corporation plc 1984-; govr: St Thomas' Hosp 1962-74 (special tstee 1974-), Royal Ballet Sch 1966-79, Yehudi Menuhin Sch 1966-87 (vice pres 1987-), Malvern Coll 1966-, Centre for Environmental Studies 1967-73; memb: Gen Cncl King Edward VII's Hosp Fund for London 1966-, Cncl RADA 1973-, South Bank Bd 1986-, Cncl of Govrs United Medical Sch of Guy's and St Thomas's Hosps 1982-89; hon vice-pres Jewish Care (formerly Jewish Welfare Bd) 1966-; fndr patron Rayne Fndn 1962-; hon fellow: Darwin Coll Cambridge 1966, UCL 1966, LSE 1974, King's Coll Hosp Med Sch 1980, Univ Coll Oxford 1982, King's Coll London 1983; Hon FRCPsych 1977, Hon LLD Univ of London 1968; Officier Legion d'Honneur 1987 (Chevalier 1973); kt 1969; *Style*— The Rt Hon the Lord Rayne; 33 Robert Adam St, London W1M 5AH (☎ 071 935 3555)

RAYNE, Hon Robert Anthony; s of Baron Rayne by his 1 w, Margaret; *b* 1949; *m* Jane, da of late Robert Blackburn, the aviation pioneer; 1 s; *Career* memb Bd London Merchant Securities 1983-, First Leisure Corporation plc 1983-, Westpool Investment Trust plc 1984-, chm Cullens Holdings plc; govr Eastman Dental Hosp Special Health Authy 1990-; *Recreations* art, cycling; *Style*— The Hon Robert A Rayne

RAYNER, Prof Anthony John; s of Cyril Spencer Rayner, of E Markham, Newark, Notts, and Lucy Mary, *née* Boothroyd; *b* 27 Aug 1943; *Educ* King Edward VI GS Retford, Univ of Cambridge (BA, MA), Univ of Manchester (PhD); *m* 1 July 1967, Patricia Florence, da of James Leonard Kester, of Radcliffe-on-Trent, Notts; 1 s (John b 1977), 2 da (Catherine b 1971, Clare b 1973); *Career* lectr Univ of Manchester 1969 (asst lectr 1967), prof Univ of Nottingham 1980- (reader 1973); author of numerous scientific papers; memb AES; *Books* contrib: Resource Structure of Agriculture An Economic Analysis (1970), The Demand for Food An Exercise in Household Budget Analysis (1972), Agricultural Marketing Boards An International Perspective (1979), Forecasting Milk Supply (1982), Price and Market Policies in European Agriculture (1984), Current Issues in Development Economics (1991); *Recreations* cricket, badminton, gardening; *Style*— Prof Anthony Rayner; The University of Nottingham, Dept of Economics, University Park, Nottingham NG7 2RD (☎ 0602 4848488)

RAYNER, Claire Berenice; *b* 2 Jan 1931; *Educ* City of London Sch for Girls, Royal Northern Hosp Sch of Nursing (SRN 1954, awarded Hosp Gold medal for outstanding achievement), Guy's Hosp; *m* 1958, Desmond Rayner; 2 s (Adam, Jay), 1 da (Amanda); *Career* sister Paediatric Dept Whittington Hosp; writer, broadcaster and public speaker; Ruth Martin of Woman's Own 1966-75 (own by-line 1975-88); Woman Magazine 1988-; radio appearances incl: Woman's Hour, Schools, Today, Contact BBC Wales, Mike Aspel Show Capital Radio London 1982-85; TV appearances incl: Pebble Mill at One, Kitchen Garden, Claire Rayner's Casebook BBC 1980-84, TV AM, Sky TV 1989-90; former advice columnist: Petticoat, The Sun, Today, The Sunday Mirror 1980-88; awarded Best Specialist Columnist Publisher Magazine 1988; hon fell Poly of North London 1988; Freeman City of London 1981; *Books* Over 80 (some under the pseudonyms of Sheila Brandon and Ann Lynton) incl: The Meddlers, A Time to Heal, The Running Years, Clinical Judgement, The Performers (12 vol family sequence, translated into several languages); contrib: Design magazine (the journal of the Design Council), The Lancet, Medical World, Nursing Times, Nursing Mirror, UK National newspapers and leading magazines; *Clubs* Royal Soc of Medicine; *Style*— Claire Rayner; PO Box 125, Harrow, Middx HA1 3XE

RAYNER, Colin Robert; s of Charles Wilfred Rayner, of Brighton, and Helen Patricia, *née* Rolling; *b* 28 Oct 1938; *Educ* St George's Coll Weybridge Surrey, Middx Hosp Univ of London (MB BS, MS); *m* 1 Jan 1966, Margaret Mary, da of Harold Salt (d 1973), of Cheltenham; 1 s (Dominic James b 5 Feb 1969), 2 da (Clare Rachel b 9 Nov 1967, Suzannah Louise b 15 March 1971); *Career* Ethicon res fell 1974, John Lawson fell Westminster Hosp 1975, currently conslt plastic surgn Aberdeen Royal Infirmary and Royal Aberdeen Childrens Hosp; over 30 scientific pubns, Pulvertaft prize (hand surgery) 1976, Assoc of Surgns special educnl award 1981; chm ethical ctee and memb nat disaster planning ctee Br Assoc of Plastic Surgns, advsr to Soviet Govt at time of train disaster 1989; memb: Br Soc Surgery of Hand, Br Assoc Head and Neck Oncologists, Br Assoc of Plastic Surgns; FRCS 1969, FRCSEd 1980; *Recreations* skiing, opera, developing international medical relationships; *Style*— Colin Rayner, Esq; 14 Church St, Helmsley, York (☎ 0439 70001), The St John Hospital, 21 Albyn Place, Aberdeen (☎ 0224 595993 ext 262), Ward 39, Aberdeen Royal Infirmary, Foresterhill, Aberdeen, Scotland

RAYNER, Baron (Life Peer UK 1983), of Crowborough in Co of East Sussex; Derek George Rayner; s of George William Rayner; *b* 30 March 1926; *Educ* City Coll Norwich, Selwyn Cambridge; *Career* adviser to PM on improving efficiency in Civil Service 1979-82; jt md Marks & Spencer 1973 and jt vice-chm 1982, chm 1984- (dir 1967-, joined 1953); special advsr to Govt 1970, chief exec Procurement Exec Mgmnt Bd MOD 1971-72, memb UK Perm Security Cmmn 1977-; dep chm Civil Service Pay Board 1978-80, former memb Design Cncl, Cncl of Royal Coll of Art; kt 1973; *Style*— The Rt Hon the Lord Rayner; c/o Marks & Spencer, Michael House, Baker St, London W1; 29 Connaught Sq, London W2 (☎ 071 935 4422)

RAYNER, Hon Mrs; Hon Madeleine; *née* Rayne; da of Baron Rayne by his 1 w, Margaret; *b* 1943; *m* 1964, Alan Rayner; *Style*— The Hon Mrs Rayner

RAYNER, Maj Michael Staney; s of Rupert Rayner (d 1934), and Ida Feodora, *née* Pickles (d 1977); *b* 11 July 1916; *Educ* Roundhay Sch Leeds; *m* 12 June 1941, Margaret Olivia, da of Frederick Owen Lighton (d 1967); 2 s (John Michael b 1942, Paul Rupert b 1946); *Career* enlisted RA 1940, cmmnd 2nd Lt RA 1941-, London Div 1941-42, transferred to RE 1942, Capt India Cmd RE 1943, XIV Army Burma 1943-46, Arakan Burma Campaign 1944, Imphal to Rangoon Campaign 1944-45, Maj RE 1945 (despatches twice 1946); dir Victoria Court Mgmnt (Filey) Ltd 1982-; chm Yorkshire Region Chartered Inst of Bldg 1967-68, chm Bd of Govrs Leeds Coll of Building 1976-80; FCIOB; *Recreations* sailing; *Clubs* Ullswater Yacht; *Style*— Maj Michael Rayner; 5 Victoria Court, Filey, N Yorks YO14 9LJ (☎ 0723 514748); Smithy Cottage, Stainton, Penrith Cumbria CA11 (☎ 0768 64200)

RAYNER, Patrick Brear; s of Wing Cdr Michael Oliver Rayner, OBE, of Skipton, N Yorks, and Kathleen, *née* Brear; *b* 11 Nov 1951; *Educ* Woolverstone Hall, Univ of St Andrews (MA); *m* 1, 29 Dec 1976 (m dis 1986), Susan Mary, da of James Gill of Carlisle; m 2, 30 April 1987, Stella Joanna, da of Andrew Murray Forge; 1 s (Edward b 24 April 1988), 1 da (Margot b 30 Jan 1990); *Career* prodr drama BBC Radio; memb bd dirs Royal Lyceum Theatre Edinburg; handlist of records for the study of crime in early modern Scottish history to 1747 (1982); *Recreations* cricket, golf, theatre; *Clubs* Scottish Arts, North Berwick Golf; *Style*— Patrick Rayner, Esq; BBC Broadcasting House, 5 Queen St, Edinburgh (☎ 031 2431200)

RAYNER, Maj Ranulf Courtauld; s of Brig Sir Ralph Herbert Rayner, MBE (d 1977), of Ashcombe Tower, nr Dawlish, S Devon, and Edith Elizabeth, *née* Courtauld; *b* 25 Feb 1935; *Educ* Eton, RMA; *m* 2 July 1970, Annette Mary, da of Brig Angus Binny, CBE, MICE, of Skilgate, Somerset; 2 s (Ralph b 8 Sept 1971, Giles b 25 June 1975); *Career* cmmnd 9 Queen's Royal Lancers 1955, instr RMA Sandhurst 1962, Army FLying Sch 1964, Royal Horse Gds 1965, cmd Ind Sqdn Cyprus 1967, ret 1969; local steward Devon and Exeter Steeplechases; represented Army at: Polo, Skiing, Cresta run (capt Cresta Team 1959-69); *Books* The Painting of the America's Cup (1986), The Story of Yachting (1988), The Story of Skiing (1989); *Recreations* yachting, shooting, fishing, flying, skiing, tobogganing, painting; *Clubs* Starcross; *Style*— Maj Ranulf Rayner; Ashcombe Tower, nr Dawlish, S Devon EX7 0PY (☎ 0626 863 178, office 0626 862 484, fax 0626 867 011)

RAYNES, Prof (Edward) Peter; s of Edward Gordon Raynes, of 8 Monnow Close, Malvern, Worcs, and Ethel Mary, *née* Wood; *b* 4 July 1945; *Educ* St Peter's York, Gonville and Caius Coll Cambridge (MA, PhD); *m* 19 Sept 1970, Madeline, da of Cecil

Ord (d 1967); 2 s (Michael b 1974, Andrew b 1977); *Career* dep chief scientific offr Royal Signals and Radar Establishment Malvern (joined 1971); hon prof Sch of Chem Univ of Hull 1990-; FRS 1987, MInstP; *Books* Liquid Crystals: Their Physics, Chemistry and Applications (with C Hilsum 1983); *Recreations* choral and solo singing; *Style—* Prof Peter Raynes, FRS; 23 Leadon Rd, Malvern, Worcs WR14 2XF (☎ 0684 565497); Royal Signals and Radar Establishment, Malvern, Worcs WR14 3PS (☎ 0684 894873, fax 0684 894540)

RAYNES, Lady (Frederica) Rozelle Ridgway; *née* Pierrepont; da of 6 Earl Manvers (d 1955); *b* 1925; *Educ* Queen Elizabeth's GS Mansfield Notts; *m* 1, 1953 (m dis 1961), Maj Alexander Montgomerie Greaves Beattie; m 2, 1965, Richard Hollings Raynes, MB BS, DPH, MFCM; *Career* served 1939-45 war as Leading Wren Stoker WRNS; writer, school care worker (ILEA), asst purser Merchant Navy; *Books* North in a Nutshell, Maid Matelot, The Sea Bird, The Tuesday Boys; *Recreations* sailing; *Clubs* Royal Cruising, Royal Naval Sailing Assoc, Royal Cinque Ports Yacht; *Style—* The Lady Rozelle Raynes; Dolphin's Leap, St Margaret's Bay, Kent; 88 Narrow St, London E14 8BP

RAYNHAM, Viscount; Charles George Townshend; s and h of 7 Marquess Townshend; *b* 6 Sept 1945; *Educ* Eton, Royal Agricultural College Cirencester; *m* 1, 1975, Hermione (d 1985), da of Lt-Cdr Robert Martin Dominic Ponsonby; 1 s, 1 da (Hon Louise b 1979); m 2, 6 Dec 1990, Mrs Alison Marshall, yr da of Sir Willis Ide Combs, KCVO, CMG, *qv*; *Heir* s, Hon Thomas Charles Townshend b 2 Nov 1977; *Style—* Viscount Raynham; 22 Ebury St, London SW1 (☎ 071 730 3388)

RAYNSFORD, Capt Antony Edward Montague; DL (Northants); er s of Lt-Col Richard M Rainsford, DSO, DL (d 1965), of Milton Malsor Manor, Northampton, and Daphne, *née* Pemberton, OBE (d 1976); sr descendant of Henry Raynsford, of Rainford Hall, Lancs, and of the Manor of Great Tew, Oxon (d ca 1430); *b* 22 Sept 1914; *Educ* RNC Dartmouth; *m* 18 March 1944, Hon Joan Rosemary Wakefield (*qv*), eldest da of 1 and last Baron Wakefield of Kendal (d 1983); 1 s (Richard), 1 da (Julia); *Career* served WWII with Home Fleet (Despatches), Force H Med, radar devpt and trg, S Pacific, Western Approaches; ret 1958; *Style—* Capt A E M Raynsford, DL, RN; Milton Malsor Manor, Northampton NN7 3AR (☎ 0604 858251)

RAYNSFORD, Hon Mrs (Joan Rosemary); *née* Wakefield; OBE (1981); eldest da of 1 and last Baron Wakefield of Kendal (d 1983), and Rowena Doris, *née* Lewis (d 1981); the Wakefield family can trace its lineage to Roger Wakefield, of Challon Hall, near Kendal, Westmorland, *temp* Elizabeth I. The family is recorded in the first generation of Kendal money men and was contemporary with London Bankers listed in the first London Directory of 1677. Wakefield's Bank was established in 1788 in the Old House, Kendal, which the family still occupies, and subsequently became the Kendal Bank. This was taken over by the Bank of Liverpool in 1831 which amalgamated with Martins Bank in 1918 and is now Barclays Bank; *b* 18 Nov 1920; *Educ* Francis Holland Sch London, Downe House Newbury, Univ of Berlin; *m* 18 March 1944, Capt Antony Edward Montague Raynsford, DL, RN (ret), er s of Lt-Col Richard Raynsford, DSO, JP, DL; 1 s (Richard), 1 da (Julia (Mrs John Boyd)); *Career* chm: Battlefields (Hldgs) Ltd, Shapland & Petter Hldgs Ltd, Lake District Estates Co Ltd, Ullswater Navigation & Transit Co Ltd, Ravenglass & Eskdale Railway Co Ltd; vice-chm Cons National Women's Ctee 1971-72 (chm Gtr London Women's Ctee 1968-71); memb Int Exec Ctee European Union of Women 1979-81; vice-pres British Ski Fedn 1966-69; *Recreations* skiing, walking in mountains; *Clubs* Lansdowne, Ski of GB (chm 1972-75, pres 1981), Kandahar Ski (chm 1977-82); *Style—* The Hon Mrs Raynsford, OBE; Milton Malsor Manor, Northampton NN7 3AR (☎ 0604 858251); The Old House, Kendal, Cumbria LA9 4QG (☎ 0539 720861)

RAYNSFORD, Wyvill Richard Nicolls (Nick); s of Wyvill John Macdonald Raynsford (Capt Northants Yeo, ka 1944), and Patricia Howell, *née* Dunn (d 1956); *b* 28 Jan 1945; *Educ* Repton, Sidney Sussex Coll Cambridge (MA), Chelsea Sch of Art (Dip Art and Design); *m* 30 Aug 1968, Anne Elizabeth, da of Col Marcus Jelley, of Northampton; 3 da (Catherine Patricia b 1979, Laura Anne b 1982, Helen Daphne b 1984); *Career* market res A C Neilsen Co Ltd 1966-68, Student Co-operative Dwellings 1972-73, SHAC (London Housing Aid Centre) 1973-86 (dir 1976-86), dir Raynsford & Morris Ltd (housing and Parly conslts) 1987-; cncllr London Borough of Hammersmith and Fulham 1971-75; MP (Lab) Fulham 1986-87; prospective Parly candidate (Lab) Greenwich 1990-; memb Inst of Housing 1978; *Books* A Guide to Housing Benefit (1982); *Style—* Nick Raynsford, Esq; 31 Cranbury Rd, Fulham, London SW6 2NS (☎ 071 731 0675); London House, 271-3 King St, Hammersmith, London W6 9LZ (☎ 081 741 8011)

RAZ, Prof Joseph; s of Shmuel Zaltsman Raz, and Sonya, *née* Alterkovski; *b* 21 March 1939; *Educ* Hebrew Univ Jerusalem (MJuris), Oxford Univ (DPhil 1967); *m* 8 Sept 1963 (m dis 1979), Yael; 1 s (Noam b 1969); *Career* lectr and sr lectr in Hebrew Univ of Jerusalem 1967-77; Balliol Coll Oxford: fell and tutor in jurisprudence 1972-85, prof of philosophy of law 1985-; FBA 1987; *Books* The Concept of a Legal System (1970, 1980), Practical Reason and Norms (1975), The Authority of Law (1979), The Morality of Freedom (1986); *Style—* Prof Joseph Raz; Balliol College, Oxford OX1 3BJ (☎ 0865 277721, fax 0865 277803)

RAZZALL, (Edward) Timothy; s of Leonard Humphrey Razzall, of Barnes, London, a Master of the Supreme Court 1954-81, and Muriel, *née* Knowles (d 1968); *b* 12 June 1943; *Educ* St Paul's, Worcester Coll Oxford (BA); *m* 1 (m dis); 1 s (James Timothy b 8 Nov 1972), 1 da (Katharine Mary b 31 Oct 1970); m 2, 30 Sept 1982, Deirdre Bourke, da of Duncan Taylor-Smith (d 1985); *Career* admitted slr 1969; ptnr Frere Cholmeley 1973-; dir: Cala plc 1973-, Wea Records Ltd, ISS Holdings Ltd; London Borough of Richmond upon Thames: cllr 1974-, chm Policy and Resources Ctee and dep ldr 1983-; treas: Lib Pty 1987-88, Lib Democrats 1988-; memb Law Soc 1969-; *Recreations* all sports; *Clubs* Nat Lib, MCC; *Style—* Timothy Razzall, Esq; 28 Lincoln's Inn Fields, London WC2A 3HH (☎ 071 405 7878, fax 071 405 9056, telex 27623 FRERES G)

REA, Christopher William Wallace (Chris); s of William Wallace Rea, TD, DL, of Meigle Perthshire, and Helen Chalmers, *née* Bissett; *Educ* HS of Dundee, Univ of St Andrews (MA); *m* 18 Sept 1974, Daphne Theresa (Terri), da of George James Manning (d 1973); 1 da (Alison Jane b 2 July 1981); *Career* rugby union footballer and broadcaster; 13 caps for Scotland 1968-71; memb: Br Lions tour party to NZ 1971, 4 major overseas tours; played for Barbarians RFC; BBC: joined admin 1970, rugby corr Radio Sports Dept 1972, presenter TV's Rugby Special 1988-, radio golf commentator 1985; rugby and golf corr The Scotsman, ed Rugby News; *Books* Illustrated History of Rugby Union (1977), Injured Pride (1980), Scotland's Grand Slam (1984); *Recreations* golf, walking; *Clubs* Luffenham Heath Golf; *Style—* Chris Rea, Esq

REA, Hon Daniel William; s of 3 Baron Rea; *b* 30 Dec 1958; *Educ* William Ellis Sch, Bristol Univ, Univ Coll Hosp London; *m* 1983, Hon Rebecca, *qv*, da of Baron Llewelyn Davies; *Style—* The Hon Daniel Rea; 3 Benn St, London E9

REA, Rev Ernest; s of Ernest Rea (d 1975), of Belfast, NI, and Mary Wylie, *née* Blue (d 1973); *b* 6 Sept 1945; *Educ* Methodist Coll Belfast, Queen's Univ Belfast (BA, BD); *m* 13 Sept 1973, Kathleen (Kay), da of Robert Kilpatrick (d 1987), of Belfast, NI; 2 s (Stephen Ernest b 28 April 1975, Jonathan Robert b 17 April 1978); *Career* prodr religious progs BBC NI 1979-84; BBC South and West: sr prodr religious progs 1984-88, editor Network Radio 1988-89; head of religious bdcasting BBC 1989; *Recreations* theatre, reading, playing tennis; *Style—* Ernest Rea, Esq; 8 Bannetts Tree Crescent, Alveston, Bristol, Avon (☎ 0454 415127), BBC Broadcasting House, Portland Place, London W1A 1AA (☎ 071 580 4468)

REA, Hon Mrs Findlay; Helen Margaret; *née* Richardson; da of Bernhard Hermann Richardson (decd), of Edinburgh; *m* 1, 1936, Donald Crawford Reid; m 2, 1959, as his 3 w, Hon Findlay Russell Rea (d 1984), 3 and yst s of 1 Baron Rea; *Style—* The Hon Mrs Findlay Rea; Weald Cottage, Weald, Sevenoaks, Kent

REA, Hon (Charles) Julian; s of Hon James R Rea (d 1954), and Betty Marion Rea, *née* Bevan (d 1965); *b* 7 June 1931; *Educ* Bryaston, Downing Coll Cambridge (MA); *m* 1, 1952, Bridget, da of Montague Slater (d 1956); 1 s (Steven b 1956), 1 da (Julia b 1952); m 2, 1963, Anne, da of William Robson (d 1978); 2 s (William b 1965, James b 1968), 2 da (Lucy b 1966, Kate b 1972); *Career* publisher; exec dir Longman Group Ltd (formerly Longman Holdings), Longman Group (Overseas Holdings) Ltd, Longman Group Far East Ltd, Longman Nigeria Ltd, Maskew Miller Longman (Pty) Ltd SA, Longman Zimbabwe Ltd; chm: The Egyptian International Publishing Longman Egypt, Goodlife Foods Ltd, International Book Development Ltd; *Recreations* fishing, pottery, theatre, music; *Clubs* Garrick; *Style—* The Hon Julian Rea; 62 Dukes Avenue, London N10 2PU; Mitchells, West Chiltington, Pulborough, Sussex; Longman Gp Ltd, Longman House, Burnt Hill, Harlow, Essex CM20 2JE (☎ 0279 426721, fax 0279 431060, telex 81259)

REA, Hon Matthew James; s and h of 3 Baron Rea; *b* 28 March 1956; *Educ* William Ellis Sch, Sheffield Univ; 1 da (Ellis Kelsey Haslam Rea b 2 Feb 1989); *Style—* The Hon Matthew Rea; 12 St Leonards Bank, Edinburgh

REA, 3 Baron (UK 1937); Sir (John) Nicolas Rea; 3 Bt (UK 1935); s of Hon James Rea (d 1954; 2 s of 1 Baron Rea), by his 1 w, Betty, *née* Bevan (d 1965); suc unc, 2 Baron, 1981; *b* 6 June 1928; *Educ* Dartington Hall, Dauntsey's Sch, Christ's Coll Cambridge (MA, MD), Univ Coll Hosp London; *m* 1951, Elizabeth Anne, da of William Robinson (d 1944), of Woking; 4 s (Matthew, Daniel, Quentin, Nathaniel); *Heir* s, Hon Matthew Rea; *Career* Actg Sergeant Suffolk Regt; sits as Labour peer in House of Lords; research fellow Paediatrics Ibadan Univ Nigeria 1952-55, lectr in Social Medicine St Thomas's Hosp Med Sch 1966-68, medical practitioner in NHS general practice (Kentish Town Health Centre); DPH, DCH, DObst; MRCGP; *Recreations* music (bassoon), travel, maintaining crumbling houses; *Clubs* Royal Soc of Medicine; *Style—* The Rt Hon the Lord Rea; House of Lords, London SW1

REA, Hon Mrs (Rebecca); da of Baron Llewelyn-Davies, PC (Life Peer); *b* 21 Dec 1957; *m* 1983, Hon Daniel William, *qv*, s of 3 Baron Rea; *Style—* The Hon Mrs Rea; 3 Benn St, London E9

READ, Prof Alan Ernest; CBE (1988); s of Ernest Arthur Read, BEM (d 1957), of Wembley, Middx, and Annie Lydia Read (d 1971); *b* 15 Nov 1926; *Educ* Kilburn GS, Wembley Co GS, Preston Manor Co GS, St Marys Hosp Med Sch London (MB BS, MD, MRCP); *m* 9 Aug 1952, Enid, da of Harold Arthur Malein, of Bristol; 1 s (Simon Andrew b 4 April 1956), 2 da (Sara Jane b 11 May 1957, Lousia Mary b 28 Dec 1965); *Career* Nat Serv med specialist BMH Trieste 1952-54; Univ of Bristol: reader in med 1965-69, prof of med 1969, head of Academic Med Unit 1969-, dean of Faculty of Med 1984-86, pro vice chllr 1987-90; vice pres RCP (sr censor) 1985-86; memb: Assoc of Physicians, Br Soc of Gastroenterology; Freeman City of London, Liveryman Worshipful Soc of Apothecaries; FRCP 1965; *Books* Basic Gastroenterology (jtly, 1965), The Clinical Apprentice (1966), Modern Medicine (1975), The Liver (jtly, 1984), Gastroenterology (jtly, 1988); *Recreations* riding, boating, fishing, golf; *Style—* Prof Alan Read, CBE; Riverbank, 77 Nore Rd, Portishead, Bristol, Avon BS20 9JZ (☎ 0272 843 543); Department of Medicine, University of Bristol, Bristol Royal Infirmary, Avon (☎ 0272 279 220)

READ, Bryan Colman; CBE (1984), JP (1965), DL (1986); s of L Hector Read (d 1963), of Norwich, and Ena P Read (d 1985); *b* 1 Oct 1925; *Educ* Bishop's Stortford Coll, St John's Coll Cambridge (MA); *m* 1949, Sheila Mary, da of Frank Oliver Winter, of Norwich; 1 s (James b 1953), 3 da (Joanna b 1950, Susan b 1950, Rebecca b 1960); *Career* flour miller; R J Read (Hldgs) Ltd 1954-87, Pasta Foods Ltd 1955-85; pres Nat Assoc of Br and Irish Flour Millers 1968 and 1983; chm: Nat Inst of Agricultural Botany 1976-78, Cncl Flour Milling and Baking Res Assoc 1989-; memb: Home Grown Cereals Authy 1966-, AFRC 1983; chm: Norfolk and Norwich Festival 1982, Broads Authy; *Recreations* sailing, music; *Clubs* Farmers'; *Style—* Bryan Read, Esq; 21 Upton Close, Norwich NR4 7PD (☎ 0603 54281)

READ, Douglas Melville; s of Alfred Melville Read (d 1918), and Edith Ella, *née* Payne (d 1978); *b* 10 Feb 1917; *Educ* Dulwich Coll; *m* 26 June 1957, Olga Patricia Lily; *Career* WWII RAF 1939-45 (RAuxAF 601 Sqdn 1935-39); Simmonds Aerocessories and assoc co 1936-39, MAP 1943-45; fndr dir: Société de Fabrication d'Instruments de Mésure (GB) Ltd 1945-57, Electro Mechanisms Ltd 1957-89 (later Schaevitz EM Ltd, now Lucas Gp); memb Cncl and hon offr Scientific Instruments Mfrs' Assoc 1974-84; memb: Ctee Advanced Tech Trg and Educn EEF, Industl Panel Standing Conf on Schs Sci and Technol; vice chm Thames Trg Gp Ltd; tstee: London Projects Office, Worcester Poly Inst USA; memb Ct of City Univ; Freeman City of London 1976, Liveryman Worshipful Co of Engrs, Master Worshipful Co of Sci Instumental Makers 1989 (FRAeS, FRSA); *Books* A History, The Worshipful Company of Scientific Makers (1988); *Recreations* equestrianism, gardening, reading, music, art; *Clubs* City Livery, Anglo Belgian; *Style—* Douglas Read, Esq; Weybourne, Fulmer Rd, Gerrards Cross, Buckinghamshire SL9 7EF (☎ 0753 883202)

READ, Prof Frank Henry; s of Frank Charles Read (d 1976), and Florence Louisa, *née* Wright; *b* 6 Oct 1934; *Educ* Haberdashers' Aske's Hampstead Sch, Univ of London (ARCS, BSc), Univ of Manchester (PhD, DSc); *m* 16 Dec 1961, Anne Stuart, da of Neil Stuart Wallace; 2 s (Jonathon Hugh Tobias b 16 June 1965, Sebastian Timothy James b 18 Aug 1970), 2 da (Kirsten Victoria b 17 Oct 1962, Nichola Anne b 12 Feb 1964); *Career* Univ of Manchester: lectr 1959-68, sr lectr 1968-74, reader 1974-75, prof of physics 1975-; vice pres Inst of Physics 1984-; memb: Cncl of Royal Soc 1987-, Sci Bd Sci and Engrg Res Cncl (SERC) 1987-; FRS 1984, FInstP 1973; *Books* Electrostatic Lenses (1976), Electromagnetic Radiation (1980); *Recreations* farming, stone-masonry; *Style—* Prof Frank Read, FRS; Hardingland Farm, Macclesfield Forest, Cheshire SK11 0ND (☎ 0625 25759); Dept of Physics, University of Manchester, Manchester M13 9PL (☎ 061 275 4125, fax 061 273 5867, telex 668932 MCHRULG)

READ, Imelda Mary (Mel); da of Robert Alan Hoching, and Teresa Mary Hocking; *b* 8 Jan 1939; *Educ* Bishopshalt Sch Hillingdon, Univ of Nottingham (BA); *m* 1 s, 1 da, 1 step s; *Career* laboratory technician Plessey 1963-74; teacher 1977-84: Trent Poly, Leicester Poly, WEA, Beeston Coll of Further Educn, Clarendon Coll of Further Educn; employment worker Community Relations Council Nottingham 1984-89; chair Euro Parly Lab Party 1990-; Lab spokesperson Euro Parly: Econ Monotary and Idust Ctee, Social Affairs Ctee, Women's Ctee, South Asia Delgn; Parly candidate (Lab): Melton 1979, NW Leics 1983; memb: MSF (elected NEC 1975-), Child Poverty Action GP, Rural Revival, Cradock No 1 Allotment Soc; former chair: Notts Area Manpower Bd, TVC Regnl Women's Ctee; *Recreations* bee-keeping, gardening; *Style—* Ms Mel Read; Labour Euro Office, 81 Great Central Street, Leicester LE1 4ND (☎ 0533

532035, fax 0533 532038)

READ, Janet Mary; da of Richard Charles Read (d 1969), of Staffordshire, and Ivy, *née* Watkiss; *b* 21 Jan 1947; *Educ* Univ of London, Univ of Birmingham, Univ of Warwick (MA); *m* 17 April 1976 (m dis 1985), John Barry O'Shea; 1 s (Luke b 1977), 1 da (Chiade b 1977); *Career* social worker Birmingham City Cncl 1969-74, trg offr Coventry City Cncl 1974-76, lectr Univ of Warwick 1978-90, tutor Fndn for Conductive Educn Budapest Centre 1990-; nat sec Rapid Action for Conductive Educn (Race) 1986-88; *Books* Come Wind, Come Weather (1988), Going to Budapest (1990); *Recreations* embroidery, running; *Style—* Ms Janet Read; The Fndn for Conductive Educn, Budapest Centre, Virányos út 15B, Budapest XII, Hungary (☎ 01036 1760017)

READ, Gen Sir John Antony Jervis; GCB (1972, KCB 1967, CB 1965), CBE (1959, OBE 1957), DSO (1945), MC (1941); s of John Dale Read, of Heathfield, Sussex (d 1940), and Evelyn Constance Bowen; *b* 10 Sept 1913; *Educ* Winchester, RMC Sandhurst; *m* 14 June 1947, Sheila, da of Frederick G C Morris, of London NW8; 3 da; *Career* 2 Lt Oxford and Bucks LI 1934, served Africa and Burma WWII, dep asst mil sec WO 1947-49, Co Cdr Sandhurst 1949-52, Lt-Col 1952, Temp Brig 1957, Cmdt Sch of Inf Warminster 1959, Brig 1961, GOC 50 Inf Div TA and Northumbrian Dist 1962-64, Maj-Gen 1962, Vice QMG 1964-66, Lt-Gen 1966, GOC-in-C Western Cmd 1966-69, Gen 1969, QMG 1969-72, ADC (Gen) to HM The Queen 1971-73, Cmdt RCDS 1973-74; Col Cmdt: Army Catering Corps 1966-76, Light Div 1968-73, Small Arms Sch Corps 1970-75; special cmmr Duke of York's Royal Mil Sch 1974-90; pres: Ex-Services Fellowship Centre 1974-, TA Rifle Assoc 1974-90; chm: Army Cadet Force Assoc 1973-82 (pres 1982-), Royal Sch for Daughters of Offrs 1975-82 (govr 1966); govr: St Edward's Sch Oxford 1972-87, Royal Hosp Chelsea 1975-81; *Clubs* Army & Navy; *Style—* Gen Sir Antony Read, GCB, CBE, DSO, MC; Brackles, Little Chesterton, nr Bicester, Oxon OX6 8PD (☎ 0869 252189)

READ, Sir John Emms; s of William Emms Read, of Brighton (d 1952); *b* 29 March 1918; *Educ* Brighton Hove and Sussex GS, Admin Staff Coll Henley; *m* 1942, Dorothy Millicent, da of Thomas Alfred Berry; 2 s; *Career* Cdr (S) RN 1939-46; CA; Ford Motor Co Ltd 1946-64 (dir of sales 1961-64), dir EMI Ltd 1965-; EMI Gp: jt md 1967, chief exec 1969-79, dep chm 1973-74, chm 1974-79; dep chm Thorn-EMI 1979-81; dir: Thorn EMI plc 1981-1987, Capital Industs-EMI Inc 1970-83; dep chm: Thames TV 1981-88 (dir 1973-), Wonder World, FI Group plc 1989-; chm: CBI Fin & GP Ctee 1978-84, TSB Hldgs Ltd 1980-88, Central Bd TSB 1980-88, TSB Group plc 1986-88, Utd Dominions Tst 1981-85; chm Cncl of Mgmnt Inst of Neurology, memb and dep chm Governing Body Br Post Grad Med Fedn London Univ, pres Sussex Assoc of Boys' Clubs, govr Henley Mgmnt Coll 1974-; tstee: Westminster Abbey Tst 1979-86, Community Action Tst 1985-, Utd Westminster Almshouses, Brighton Festival Tst 1985-, London Symphony Orchestra Tst 1985-91; chm: Charities Aid Fndn 1990-, Barn Research Tst 1882-; memb Ct Univ of Surrey 1986-, Hon DUniv Surrey 1987; FCA, FRSA, CBIM, FIB CompIERE; kt 1976; *Recreations* music; *Clubs* MCC, Royal Over-Seas League; *Style—* Sir John Read; Muster House, 12 Muster Green, Haywards Heath, W Sussex RH16 4AG; 41 Portman Sq, London W1H 9FH (☎ 071 935 7888)

READ, Leonard Ernest (Nipper); QPM (1976); s of Late Leonard Read, of Nottingham, and Ida, *née* Morris (d 1929); *b* 31 March 1925; *Educ* Bramshill Nat Police Coll; *m* 1, 4 June 1951 (m dis 1979), Marion, *née* Millar; 1 da (Maralyn b 1955); m 2, 3 April 1980, Patricia Margaret, *née* Allen; *Career* WWII petty offr RN 1943-46; Met Police 1947-70: served every rank CID to Detective Chief Supt Murder Squad, seconded to Bucks Constabulary 1963 to assist investigation to Gt Train Robbery, formed squad to enquire into activities of Kray Bros 1968 (Kray twins convicted of murder 1969); appt Asst Chief Contable Notts 1970, appt nat co-ordinator Regnl Crime Squads England and Wales 1972, ret 1967; nat security advsr Museums and Galleries Commission 1976-83; vice pres World Boxing Assoc, vice chm Br Boxing Bd of Control; Freeman City of London 1983; *Recreations* swimming, keyboard playing, computers; *Clubs* Nat Sporting; *Style—* Nipper Read, Esq, QPM; 23 North Barn, Broxbourne, Herts EN10 6RR (☎ 0992 440902), British Boxing Board of Control, 70 Vauxhall Bridge Rd, London SW1V 2RP (☎ 071 839 3321, fax 071 931 0989)

READ, Martin; s of Charles Enderby Read, of Nine Acres, Ulceby, Alford, Lincs, and Lillian Clara, *née* Chambers; *b* 24 July 1938; *Educ* Queen Elizabeth's GS Alford, Wadham Coll Oxford (MA); *m* 27 April 1963, Laurette, da of J T Goldsmith (d 1960), of Green Walk, Hendon, London; 2 da (Robyn Lisa b 7 Sept 1966, Abigail Kim b 14 May 1970); *Career* articled clerk A V Hammond & Co Bradford 1959-62, ptnr Slaughter and May 1971- (asst slr 1963-70); vice chm Law Soc Standing Ctee on Co Law, past chm Co Law Sub Ctee City of London Law Soc; memb City of London Slrs' Co; memb Law Society 1963; *Recreations* theatre, literature, golf, cricket, tennis; *Clubs* MCC, Royal St George's; *Style—* Martin Read, Esq; Michaelmas House, Bois Avenue, Chesham Bois, Amersham, Bucks HP6 5NS; 35 Basinghall St, London EC2V 5DB (☎ 071 600 1200, fax 071 726 0038, 071 600 0289, telex 883486, 88889260)

READ, Martin Peter; s of Philip Peter Lennox Read, and Patricia Mary, *née* Ireland; *b* 22 Oct 1944; *Educ* St Mary's Sch Nairobi, Bexhill-on-Sea GS; *m* 14 June 1975, Nicolette Evelyn Marianne, da of Guy William Willett, of Alderney, Channel Islands; 3 da (Isabel b 1979, Louise b 1981, Juliet b 1984); *Career* served HM Forces Aden BAOR 1963-69; md: Petty Wood & Co Ltd 1985 (dir 1979), Tastemasters & Co Ltd 1989; asst appeals sec Help the Aged 1969; MICM 1977, FBIM 1984; *Recreations* admiring beauty, lateral thought, sailing, fireworks; *Style—* Martin Read; The Telegraph House, Pains Hill, Lockerley, Hants SO51 0JE (☎ 0794 41082)

READ, Michael Philip; s of Leslie Gustave Read, of Essex, and Joyce Eleanor, *née* Barker (d 1974); *b* 3 Feb 1944; *Educ* Westcliff-on-Sea GS, Southend Sch of Architecture; *m* 11 Aug 1973, Sandra Jean, da of Frederick George Hedges, of Herts; 2 s (Robert b 1974, Simon b 1976); *Career* chief exec Harpenden Building Soc; lectr on Building Soc law at Luton Coll of Higher Educn and refresher courses for the Chartered Building Societies Inst; MBIM, FCBSI; *Recreations* sailing, antique map collecting; *Style—* Michael Read, Esq; Aberdeen House, 14/16 Station Rd, Harpenden, Herts AL5 4SE (☎ 0582 765411)

READ, Prof Nicholas Wallace; s of Wallace Frederick Read, of Restwarrow, Blagdon Hill, Taunton, Somerset, and Doris Vera, *née* Scriven; *b* 7 July 1945; *m* 27 Nov 1976, Maria Grazyna, da of Capt Alexander Zaga-Pietkiewicz (d 1959), of London; 1 s (Alexander b 1980), 3 da (Esther b 1973, Katherine b 1978, Emily b 1982); *Career* conslt gastroenterologist Trent RHA Sheffield 1981, prof gastrointestinal physiology and nutrition Univ of Sheffield 1988, dir Centre Human Nutrition 1988; memb: Physiological Soc 1980, Nutrition Soc 1986; FRCP 1987; *Books* Irritable Bowel Syndrome (1984), BDS Textbook of Physiology (1988), Gastrointestinal Motility, Which Test (1989); *Recreations* hill walking, cycling, writing; *Style—* Prof Nicholas Read; 3 Victoria Rd, Broomhall, Sheffield S10 2DJ (☎ 0742 660908); Centre for Human Nutrition, Northern General Hospital, Sheffield S5 7AU (☎ 0742 738917)

READ, (Charles) Patrick Wilson; s of Sir Charles David Read (d 1957), of London, and Frances Edna, *née* Wilson; *b* 17 March 1942; *Educ* Harrow; *m* 1966, Susan Viner, da of Brian Viner Edsall, of Wisborough Green, W Sussex; 1 s (Jason b 1968); *Career* md Young & Co's Brewery plc 1976-, dir B Edsall & Co Ltd 1984-; *Recreations* shooting, fishing; *Style—* Patrick Read, Esq; Malthouse Cottage, Little Bognor, nr Fittleworth, Pulborough, W Sussex (☎ 079 882 260); Young & Co's Brewery plc, Ram Brewery, Wandsworth, London SW18 (☎ 081 870 0141, telex 8814530, fax 870 9444)

READ, Paul Graham; s of Henry Graham Read (d 1968), and Norah Lilian, *née* Barnett; *b* 4 April 1947; *Educ* Prices GS; *m* 15 April 1972, Patricia Jacqueline, da of George Henry Lovell, of Hampshire; 1 s, (Matthew Paul Henry b 1988), 1 da (Natalie b 1985); *Career* md Berkeley Homes (N London) Ltd 1980-83, commercial dir and md Camper & Nicholas Ltd 1974-80, commercial dir The Berkeley Gp plc 1983-; *Recreations* sailing, music, karate, photography; *Clubs* Porchester Sailing; *Style—* Paul Read, Esq; Greenhill Cottage, Stoner Hill Road, Froxfield, Hampshire GU32 1DX (☎ 07308 65 475); 4 Heath Rd, Weybridge, Surrey KT13 8TB (☎ 0932 847 222, fax 0932 858 596)

READ, Piers Paul; s of Sir Herbert Edward Read, DSO, MC (d 1968), and Margaret, *née* Ludwig; *b* 7 March 1941; *Educ* Ampleforth, St John's Coll Cambridge (BA, MA); *m* 29 July 1967, Emily Albertine, da of E B Boothby, KCMG, of 23 Holland Park Avenue, London W11; 2 s (Albert b 1970, William b 1978), 2 da (Martha b 1972, Beatrice b 1981); *Career* author; artist in residence Ford Fndn Berlin 1963-64, sub ed Times Literary Supplement London 1965, Harkness fell Cwlth Fund NY 1967-68, adjunct prof of writing Univ of Columbia 1980; memb: Ctee of Mgmnt Soc of Authors 1973-76, Literature Panel Arts Cncl London 1975-77; govr Cardinal Manning Boys Sch London 1985-90; FRSL 1972; *Books* Games in Heaven with Tussy Marx (1966), The Junkers (1968), Monk Dawson (1969), The Professor's Daughter (1971), The Upstart (1973), Alive: the story of the Andes Survivors (1974), Polonaise (1976), The Train Robbers (1978), A Married Man (1979), The Villa Golitsyn (1981), The Free Frenchman (1986), A Season in The West (1988), On the Third Day (1990); *Style—* Piers Read, Esq; 50 Portland Rd, London W11 4LG (☎ 071 727 5719)

READ, Richard Michael Hodgson; s of Lt Richard Hodgson Read (d 1936), of Eastbrook Hall, Dinas Powis, and Dorothy Jessie, *née* Penwarden (d 1985); *b* 24 Dec 1936; *Educ* Clifton Coll, St James' Sch Maryland USA, Univ of London (BSc); *m* 21 July 1964 (m dis 1969), Jennifer Diane, da of Marcus Leaver (d 1966), of Mill Hill; *Career* CA; RH March Son & Co and Mann Judd & Co 1962-79, ptnr Touche Ross & Co 1979-81, dir various cos affiliated to Lloyd's 1981-90; chm: D G Durham Group plc 1988-, Zelix Corporation Ltd 1989-; underwriting memb Lloyd's; memb CBI: Smaller Firms Cncl 1973-79, Cncl 1978-79, Welsh Cncl; FCA; *Recreations* skiing, tennis, swimming; *Clubs* Cardiff & County; *Style—* Richard Read, Esq; Llanmaes, St Fagans, Cardiff CF5 6DV (☎ 0222 553511, car 0836 564 132)

READ, Thomas Bonamy; s of Sir Herbert Read, DSO, MC (d 1969), and Margaret, *née* Ludwig; *b* 21 Dec 1937; *Educ* Ampleforth, Univ of Leeds (BA); *m* Celia Mary, da of Charles Guy Vaughan-Lee, DSC (d 1984); 3 s (Alexander Paul b 26 April 1968, James Herbert b 6 Dec 1969, Matthew Charles b 16 April 1974); *Career* reporter and educn correspondant Daily Mirror 1962-67, BBC Radio 1967-; prodr Reith Lectures 1981, ed Analysis Radio 4 1982-84; World Serv 1984-: head of Central Talks and Features 1987, acting ed World Serv in English 1989, acting gen mangr BBC Monitoring 1991-; winner Sony Award for best documentary 1984; RIIA; *Recreations* travel, growing avacados; *Style—* Thomas Read, Esq; 31 St Albans Road, London NW5 1RG (☎ 071 485 0256), c/o BBC World Service, Bush House, Strand, London WC2B 4PH (☎ 071 240 3456, telex 265 781)

READE, Sir Clyde Nixon; 12 Bt (E 1661); s of late Sir George Reade, 10 Bt; suc bro, Sir John Stanhope Reade, 11 Bt, 1958; *b* 1906; *m* 1, 1930, Trilby (d 1958), da of Charles McCarthy; m 2, 1960 (m dis 1968), Alice Martha, da of Joseph Asher, of Ohio; *Heir* kinsman, Robert Reade; *Style—* Sir Clyde Reade, Bt; 408 East Columbia St, Mason, Michigan 48854, USA

READE, Robert Ward; s of late Leverne Elton Reade, 5 s of 9 Bt; hp of kinsman, Sir Clyde Reade, 12 Bt; *b* 11 Oct 1923; *Style—* Robert Reade Esq

READER HARRIS, Dame (Muriel) Diana; DBE (1972); da of Montgomery Reader Harris (d 1945), and Frances Mabel Wilmot, *née* Wilkinson (d 1915); (*see also* Hon Mrs Reader-Harris); *b* 11 Oct 1912; *Educ* Sherborne Sch for Girls, Univ of London (BA); *Career* Sherborne Sch for Girls: asst mistress 1934, house mistress 1938, headmistress 1950-75 (i/c group evacuated from Sherborne to Canada 1940); asst educn sec and dep gen sec Nat Assoc of Youth Clubs 1943-49; pres: Assoc of Headmistresses 1964-66, Church Missionary Soc 1969-82; chm: Christian Aid 1978-83, Royal Fndn St Katharine 1979-88, Royal Soc of Arts 1979-81 (vice pres 1981-88, vice pres emeritus 1989-), and various other organizations; FRSA; *Clubs* University Women's; *Style—* Dame Diana Reader Harris, DBE; 35 The Close, Salisbury, Wilts SP1 2EL (☎ 0722 26889)

READER-HARRIS, Hon Mrs (Henrietta Marguerite Jean); *née* Loder; da of 2 Baron Wakehurst (d 1970), and Dame Margaret Wakehurst, *née* Tennant; *b* 5 Feb 1922; *Educ* Sydney Univ (Dip Soc Studies); *m* 1953, John Wilmot Reader-Harris (d 1975), s of Montgomery Reader-Harris (d 1945) (*see also* Dame Diana Reader-Harris); 1 s (Michael), 1 da (Sarah Van Hove); *Career* hosp almoner; voluntary social servs; FRSA; *Recreations* visiting places of historical and archaeological interest; *Clubs* ESU; *Style—* The Hon Mrs Reader-Harris; 35 The Close, Salisbury, Wilts SP1 2EL (☎ 0722 26889)

READER-HARRIS, Dr Michael John; s of John Wilmot Reader-Harris (d 1975), and The Hon Henrietta Marguerite Jean, *née* Loder; *b* 26 Oct 1957; *Educ* Harrow, BNC Oxford (BA), Univ of St Andrews (PhD); *m* 6 July 1985, Susan Mary, da of Lt-Col John Logan Wilson Smith, OBE, of Cumledge, Duns, Berwickshire; 1 s (Peter b 1989); *Career* Grade 7 (princ sci offr) Nat Engrg Laboratory 1990- (sr sci offr 1981-85); lay reader Scot Episcopal Church; *Recreations* hill walking, railway history; *Style—* Dr Michael Reader-Harris; 26 Mansefield Avenue, Cambuslang, Glasgow, Scotland G72 8NZ (☎ 041 6413987), National Engineering Laboratory, East Kilbride, Glasgow G75 0QU (☎ 03552 72302)

READING, Anthony John; MBE (1978); *b* 8 Aug 1943; *Educ* Brighton Coll Sussex; *m* 1966; 1 s; *Career* articled clerk Spain Bros Dalling and Co Brighton 1962-66, audit sr and asst mangr Whinney Murray Ernst and Ernst Brussels 1966-70, md Donaldson Europe Belgium 1978-80 (dir of fin 1970-76, dir of mfrg 1976-77), gp exec Thomas Tilling plc London 1980-83, divnl gp chief exec BTR plc 1983-87, gp md Polly Peck International plc 1987-89, gp md Pepe Group plc 1989-90, divnl dir Tomkins plc 1990-; FCA 1966, FBIM 1989; *Recreations* family, music, tennis, watersports; *Clubs* Naval and Mil; *Style—* Anthony Reading, Esq, MBE; Tomkins plc, East Putney House, 84 Upper Richmond Rd, London SW15 2ST (☎ 081 871 4544, fax 081 874 4510)

READING, Bishop of 1989-; Rt Rev John Frank Ewan Bone; s of Jack Bone (d 1944), and Herberta Blanche, *née* Ewan (d 1984); *b* 28 Aug 1930; *Educ* Monkton Combe Sch, St Peter's Hall Oxford (MA), Ely Theol Coll, Whitelands Coll of Educn; *m* 26 June 1954, Ruth Margaret, da of Wilfrid John Crudgington (d 1968); 3 s (Nicholas b 1961, Stephen b 1964, Patrick (adopted) b 1972), 2 da (Sarah b 1955, Elizabeth b 1958); *Career* asst curate: St Gabriel's Pimlico 1956-60, St Mary's Henley-on-Thames 1960-63; vicar St Mary's Datchet 1963-76, rural dean Burnham 1974-77, rector St Mary's Slough 1976-78, archdeacon of Buckingham 1978-89; memb General Synod 1980-85; *Style—* The Rt Rev the Bishop of Reading; Greenbanks, Old Bath Road,

Sonning, Reading RG4 0SY (☎ 0734 692187); 24 New St, Padstow, Cornwall

READING, Dowager, Marchioness of; Margot Irene; da of Percival Augustus Duke, CBE, of Walton-on-the-Hill, and Violet Maud, *née* Mappin; *b* 11 Jan 1919; *Educ* Benenden; *m* 7 June 1941, 3 Marquess of Reading, MBE, MC (d 1980); 3 s (4 Marquess, Lord Anthony Rufus-Isaacs, Lord Alexander Rufus-Isaacs), 1 da (Lady Jacqueline Thomson); *Style*— The Most Hon the Dowager Marchioness of Reading; Glebe Farm House, Cornwell, nr Chipping Norton, Oxon (☎ 060 658 523)

READING, Peter; s of Wilfred Gray Reading, of Liverpool, and Ethel Mary, *née* Catt; *b* 27 July 1946; *Educ* Liverpool Coll of Art (BA); *m* 5 Oct 1968, Diana Joy, da of Edward Thomas Gilbert; 1 da (Angela b 14 April 1977); *Career* poet; schoolteacher 1967-68, lectr in art history Liverpool Coll of Art 1968-70; publications: Water and Waste (1970), For the Municipality's Elderly (1974), The Prison Cell & Barrel Mystery (1976), Nothing for Anyone (1977), Fiction (1979), Tom O'Bedlam's Beauties (1981), Diplopic (1983), 5 x 5 x 5 x 5 x 5 (1983), C (1984), Ukulele Music (1985), Stet (1986), Essential Reading (1986), Final Demands (1988), Perduta Gente (1989), Shitheads (1989); writer in residence Sunderland Poly 1980-82, Cholmondeley award for poetry 1978, Dylan Thomas award 1983, Whitbread award poetry category 1986; fell RSL 1988, literary fellowship award Lannan Fndn USA 1990; *Style*— Peter Reading, Esq; Ragleth View, Little Stretton, Shropshire SY6 6RF

READING, 4 Marquess of (UK 1926); Simon Charles Henry Rufus Isaacs; also Baron Reading (UK 1914), Viscount Reading (UK 1916), Earl of Reading and Viscount Erleigh (both UK 1917); s of 3 Marquess of Reading, MBE, MC (d 1980); *b* 18 May 1942; *Educ* Eton, Univ of Tours; *m* 1979, Melinda, yr da of Richard Dewar; 1 s, 2 da (Lady Sybilla b 3 Nov 1980, Lady Natasha b 24 April 1983); *Heir* s, Julian Michael Rufus, Viscount Erleigh b 26 May 1986; *Career* Lt 1 Queen's Dragoon Gds 1961-64; chm and chief exec: Abbey Hickman Gp, Abbey Corporate Events Ltd; dir Shepherd Insur Hldgs, memb Stock Exchange 1971-74; pres Dean Close Sch; *Clubs* Cavalry and Guards', MCC, All England; *Style*— The Most Hon the Marquess of Reading; Jayne's Court, Bisley, Glos GL6 7BE

READMAN, (Eleanor Maysie) Hope; *née* Bowser; OBE (1990); da of David Charles Bowser, CBE, JP (d 1979), of Argaty and The Kings Lundies, Doune, Perthshire, and Maysie Murray, *née* Henderson (d 1974); *b* 18 April 1929; *Educ* privately in Scotland, Southover Manor Sch Sussex; *m* 29 April 1950, Lt-Col Ian Richard Readman, MC, JP (d 1980), s of Lt-Col John Jeffrey Readman, DSO (d 1951), of Broadholm, Lockerbie, Dumfriesshire; 2 s (John Charles Jeffrey b 1951, Alexander Hubert (Sandy) b 1954), 1 da (Jane Hope b 1958); *Career* BRCS: memb Perth Branch 1959, pres Perth and Kinross Branch 1974-84, chm Scottish Central Cncl 1986-90 (vice chm 1984-86); elder and memb choir Dunblane Cathedral, memb Perth Ctee Scottish Veterans Garden Assoc 1981-; Vol Med Serv medal 1975 (with 3 Bars), Jubilee medal 1980; *Recreations* music, reading, sewing; *Clubs* Cavalry and Guards; *Style*— Mrs I R Readman, OBE; Gateside of Glassingall, Dunblane, Perthshire FK15 0JG (☎ 0786 824 248)

READY, Nigel Peter; s of Colin Peter Ready (d 1986), and Monica Isabel Elms, *née* Tapper; *b* 13 July 1952; *Educ* Wycliffe Coll, Jesus Coll Cambridge (MA); *m* 29 Dec 1973, Marisa, da of Germano Brignolo, of Asti, Italy; 2 s (Oliver James b 1976, Thomas Nigel b 1985), 1 da (Natasha Isabella b 1975); *Career* ptnr Cheeswrights 1981-, Notary Public 1980; hon sec Soc of Public Notaries of London 1988-, special agent for Dep Cmmnr of Maritime Affrs Repub of Vanuatu 1986-; Freeman City of London, Liveryman Worshipful Co of Scriveners; *Books* The Greek Code of Private Maritime Law (jtly, 1982), Brooke's Notary (10 edn, 1988); *Recreations* wine, opera, reading; *Style*— Nigel Ready, Esq; 206 Denmark Hill, London SE5 8DX; c/o Cheeswrights, 24 St Mary Axe, London EC3A 8HD (☎ 071 623 9477, fax 071 623 5428, telex 883806)

REARDON, John Michael; s of J F J Reardon (d 1987), of Greenford, Middx, and Geerdina, *née* Theodore; *b* 8 July 1938; *Educ* Salvatorian Coll Harrow; *m* April Anne; 2 s (Paul Philip, Michael John); *Career* Nat Serv; gen trainee then trainee tv camera man Associated Redifusion 1955-68, joined LWT 1968 and became tv dir; series incl: Whoops Apocalypse, Agony, Two's Company, Me & My Girl, Drummonds, Bust; currently directing London's Burning; BAFTA nominations for Two's Company and Agony; memb Dir's Guild of GB; *Style*— John Reardon, Esq

REARDON, Rev Canon Martin Alan; s of Ernest William Reardon, CBE (d 1981), and Gertrude Mary, *née* Pyne; *b* 3 Oct 1932; *Educ* St Edward's Sch Oxford, Selwyn Coll Cambridge (BA, MA), Cuddesdon Coll; *m* 22 July 1964, Ruth Maxim, da of (Henry) George Slade; 1 s (John Paul b 1970), 1 da (Sarah Mary b 1972); *Career* ordained: deacon 1958, priest 1959; curate: Rugby St Andrew Coventry 1958-62, Wicker with Neepsend Sheffield 1962-65; sec Sheffield Cncl of Churches 1962-71, licence to officiate 1965-71, sub warden Lincoln Theol Coll 1971-78, sec Gen Synod Bd for Mission and Unity C of E 1978-89, canon and prebendary Lincoln Cathedral 1979-89, rector Plumpton Dio of Chichester 1989-; *Style*— The Rev Canon Martin Reardon; The Old Bakery, Danehill, Haywards Heath, W Sussex RH17 7EZ

REARDON SMITH, (William) Antony John; s and h of Sir William Reardon-Smith, 3 Bt; *b* 20 June 1937; *Educ* Wycliffe Coll; *m* 1962, Susan, da of Henry W Gibson, of Cardiff; 3 s, 1 da; *Style*— Antony Reardon Smith, Esq; 26 Merrick Square, London SE1 4JB

REARDON-SMITH, Sir William Reardon; 3 Bt (UK 1920); s of Sir Willie Reardon-Smith, 2 Bt (d 1950); *b* 12 March 1911; *Educ* Blundell's Sch; *m* 1, 1935 (m dis 1954), Nesta (d 1959), da of Frederick J Phillips; 3 s, 1 da; m 2, 1954, Beryl, da of William H Powell; 1 s, 3 da; *Heir* s, (William) Antony Reardon-Smith; *Career* Maj RA (TA); *Style*— Sir William Reardon-Smith, Bt; Rhode Farm, Romansleigh, South Molton, N Devon

REASON, Eric Frank; s of Frank Wesley Reason (d 1937), of 15 Evelyn Rd, Worthing, and Agnes, *née* Anders (d 1955); *b* 24 Aug 1904; *Educ* Steyning GS Sussex; *m* 7 Feb 1942, Violet Edith, da of Robert Richard Walker (d 1939), of 1 A'Becket Gdns, West Worthing; 1 s (David b 1947), 1 da (Janet b 1942); *Career* RA 1942, FD Security Section Sgt Intelligence Corps 1944; dep overseas mangr Guardian Assurance Co Ltd 1950-65 (asst mangr Paris Branch 1931-45, overseas inspector 1945-50); chm and md: Reason & Ptnrs Ltd 1965-, Insurance Consultancy Servs Ltd Gibraltar 1978-; memb: Friendship Assoc for the Blind, memb Br Tunisian Soc; Freeman City of London 1959, Liveryman Worshipful Co of Wheelwrights 1959; FCII; *Clubs* City Livery, British Commonwealth; *Style*— Eric Reason, Esq; 83 The Chine, Grange Park, London N21 2EG (☎ 081 360 9413 and 081 360 0374)

REASON, (Bruce) John; s of Claude Leon Reason (d 1980), of Dunstable, Bedfordshire, and Gladys May Reason (d 1976); *Educ* Dunstable GS, Univ of London; *m* Joan, da of William Wordsworth (d 1938), of Penistone, Yorkshire; 3 s (Ross George b 1961, Mark John b 1963, William b 1968, d 1974); *Career* journalist author and publisher; News Chronicle Manchester and News of the World Manchester 1953, The Recorder Fleet St 1953-54, sports news ed News of the World London 1955-63 (asst sports ed Manchester 1954-55), prodn ed The Cricketer magazine 1966-76; rugby corr: The Daily Telegraph 1964-79, The Sunday Telegraph 1979-; memb: NUJ, Inst of Journalists; *Books* The 1968 Lions (1968), The Victorious Lions (1971), The Lions Speak (1972), The Unbeaten Lions (1974), Lions Down Under (1977), The World of Rugby (1978), Backs to the Wall (1980); *Recreations* golf, gardening, property devpt, political work for Conservative Party until Nov 1990; *Clubs* MCC; *Style*— John Reason, Esq; The Sunday Telegraph, 181 Marsh Wall, London E14 9SR (☎ 071 538 5000)

REAY, Master of; Hon Aeneas Simon Mackay; also Baron Aeneas Mackay; s and h of 14 Lord Reay (and h to S Btcy, Netherland Baronies and Jonkheership), and his 1 w, Hon Annabel Thérèse Fraser, da of 17 Lord Lovat; *b* 20 March 1965; *Educ* Westminster Sch, Brown Univ USA; *Style*— The Master of Reay

REAY, Lt-Gen Sir (Hubert) Alan John; KBE (1981); s of Rev John Reay; *b* 19 March 1925; *Educ* Lancing, Edinburgh Univ; *m* 1960, Ferelith Haslewood Deane; 2 s (and 1 s decd), 2 da; *Career* formerly post graduate dean Royal Army Med Coll, dir Medical Services HQ BAOR 1979-81, dir-gen Army Medical Services 1981-85; chief hon steward Westminster Abbey 1985-, govr and chm Med Ctee Royal Star and Garter Home Richmond 1986-; QHP, FRCP, FRCPE; *Style*— Lt-Gen Sir Alan Reay, KBE; 63 Madrid Rd, Barnes, London SW13 4PQ

REAY, Charlotte, Lady; Charlotte Mary; *née* Younger; da of William Younger, of Ravenswood, Melrose (d 1925, 4 s of James Younger, of Alloa; bro of George Younger, cr a Bt and 1 Viscount Younger of Leckie); sis of Sir William Younger, 1 Bt, DSO, of Fountainbridge, and Maj-Gen Ralph Younger, CB, CBE, DSO, MC, JP, DL; 1 cous twice removed of Rt Hon George Younger, Sec of State for Scotland; *m* 14 April 1936, 13 Lord Reay (d 1963); 1 s, 2 da; *Style*— The Rt Hon Charlotte, Lady Reay; Southbank, Melrose, Roxburghshire

REAY, David William; s of Stanley Reay, of Sunderland, Tyne & Wear, and Madge, *née* Hall (d 1990); *b* 28 May 1940; *Educ* Monkwearmouth GS, Newcastle upon Tyne Poly; *m* 21 Nov 1964, Constance Susan, da of William Gibney, of London; 2 da (Alison Ann b 10 Sept 1969, Stephanie Sarah b 18 Nov 1972); *Career* engr; Independent Television Authority 1960-62, Alpha Television (ATV & ABC) Ltd Birmingham 1962-64, Tyne Tees Television Limited 1964-72, HTV Cardiff & Bristol 1972-84 (chief engr, engrg mangr, dir of engrg), md Tyne Tees Television Holdings plc 1984-91, chief exec Tyne Tees Television Holdings PLC 1991-; currently dir: Tyne Tees Enterprizes, ITVA, The Wearside Opportunity, Business In The Community Tyne & Wear and Northumberland, ITN; currently chm: Hadrian Television, Legend Television; memb Cncl Univ of Newcastle upon Tyne; CPhys, CEng, FIEE 1980, FRTS 1984, FInstP 1984, CBIM 1987; *Recreations* walking, reading, music, watching soccer; *Clubs* Savile; *Style*— David Reay, Esq; Tyne Tees Television Holdings plc, Television Centre, City Rd, Newcastle upon Tyne NE1 2AL (☎ 091 261 0181, fax 091 232 6724, telex 53279, car 0860 711 755)

REAY, 14 Lord (S 1628); Sir Hugh William Mackay; 14 Bt (NS 1627); also Chief of Clan Mackay, Jonkheer Mackay (Netherlands 1816), Baron Mackay van Ophemert (Netherlands 1822), and Baron Mackay (Netherlands 1858); s of 13 Lord Reay (d 1963, having been naturalised a British subject 1938), by Charlotte, da of William Younger (bro of 1 Viscount Younger of Leckie); *b* 19 July 1937; *Educ* Eton, Ch Ch Oxford; *m* 1, 1964 (m dis 1978), Hon Térèse Fraser, da of 15 Lord Lovat; 2 s (Master of Reay b 1965, Hon Edward b 1974), 1 da (Hon Laura b 1966); m 2, 1980, Hon Victoria Isabella Anne, *née* Warrender, da of 8 Baron Bruntisfield; 2 da (Hon Antonia b 1981, 1 da b 1985); *Heir* s, Master of Reay; *Career* memb of European Parly 1973-79; vice chm Cons Gp European Parl; delegate to Cncl of Europe and WEU 1979-; sits as Conservative in House of Lords; a Lord in Waiting 1989-; *Clubs* Turf, Beefsteak, Pratt's; *Style*— The Rt Hon The Lord Reay; Kasteel Ophemert, Ophemert in Gelderland, The Netherlands; House of Lords, London SW1

REAY, John Ridley; s of John Ridley Reay (d 1990), of Belford, Northumberland, and Evelyn, *née* Browell; *b* 16 April 1936; *Educ* Sedbergh, Emmanuel Coll Cambridge (MA); *m* 29 July 1961, Hilary Mayman, da of John Edmund Torrance Smith (d 1984), of Berwick-upon-Tweed; 3 s (John b 1962, Peter b 1966, David b 1974), 1 da (Katherine b 1965); *Career* admitted slr 1963, sr ptnr TC Smith & Sons Berwick-upon-Tweed; sec: Berwick and Dist Soc of Arts 1964-75, Berwick Freemans' Guild 1974-; clerk to Berwick-upon-Tweed Corp Acad Fndn 1979-, dir The Maltings (Berwick) Tst 1988-; chm Berwick: Round Table 1971-72, 41 Club 1981-82; Sheriff Berwick-upon-Tweed 1989-90 (Under Sheriff 1975-86 and 1990); memb Law Soc 1963; *Recreations* fell walking, genealogy; *Clubs* Rotary; *Style*— John R Reay, Esq

REAY, William Robert; s of Michael Errington Reay (d 1979), and Agnes Clara, *née* Heslop; *b* 15 March 1925; *Educ* Heaton GS Newcastle Upon Tyne; *m* 20 Sept 1952, Mary Alison, da of Charles Lane (d 1928); 1 da (Susan Margaret b 1956); *Career* Sub Lt RNVR 1943-46 (combined ops and minesweeping); Joseph Miller and Co CA's: ptnr 1952-73, sr ptnr 1973-87, conslt 1987-; Tynemouth Bldg Soc: dir 1978-85, chm 1985-; dir Northern Indust Improvement Tst plc 1987-, dir Talawakelle Estates Hldgs Ltd 1987-, dir Talawakelle Hldgs Ltd 1987-; Warden St Mary's Church, Monkseaton, Whitley Bay; ACA 1952, FCA 1957; *Recreations* painting, music, caravanning; *Clubs* Pen & Palette (Newcastle), Constitutional (Newcastle); *Style*— William Reay, Esq; 5 Grasmere Crescent, Monkseaton, Whitley Bay NE26 3TB (☎ 091 252 4265); Joseph Miller & Co, 31 Mosley St, Newcastle upon Tyne (☎ 091 232 8065, fax 091 222 1554)

REBBECK, Dr Denis; CBE (1952), JP (1949), DL (Belfast 1960); s of Sir Frederick Ernest Rebbeck, KBE, JP, DL (d 1964), of Belfast and Amelia Letitia, *née* Glover (d 1955); *b* 22 Jan 1914; *Educ* Campbell Coll Belfast, Univ of Cambridge (MA), Univ of Dublin (MA, BLitt), Univ of Belfast (MSc, PhD); *m* 1938, Rosamond Annette Kathleen, da of Henry Boal Jameson (d 1932); 4 s; *Career* shipbuilder; dir: National Shipbuilders Security Ltd 1952-58, Colvilles (Scottish steelmakers) 1963-67, Shipbuilding Corporation Ltd 1963-73, Royal Bank of Scotland 1969-84 (Nat Commercial Bank 1965-69), Nordic Business Forum for Northern Britain 1980-84, Nationwide Building Society 1980-89; chm: Harland and Wolff Ltd Belfast 1965-66 (dir 1946-70, md 1962-70), John Kelly Ltd Shipowners Belfast 1969-79 (dir 1968-79), Iron Trades Insurance Group 1972-84 (dir 1950-84), Belships Co Ltd 1972-76 (dir 1970-76), General Underwriting Agencies (dir 1984-); pres: Shipbuilding Employers' Fedn 1962-63, World Ship Soc 1978-81; cmmr Belfast Harbour 1962-85; memb: Gen Ctee Lloyd's Register of Shipping 1962-85, Mgmnt Bd Engrg Employers' Fedn 1963-75, NI Econ Cncl 1965-70, Res Cncl Br Ship Res Assoc 1965-73; chm Pilotage Cmmn 1979-83; Prime Warden Worshipful Co of Shipwrights London 1980-81; *Recreations* sailing (10 ton sloop 'Drommedaris'); *Clubs* Royal Yacht Sqdn, Royal Norwegian Yacht, City Livery; *Style*— Dr Denis Rebbeck, CBE, JP, DL; The White House, Craigavad, Holywood, Co Down BT18 0HE (☎ 023 17 2294); General Underwriting Agencies Ltd, 33 Massey Ave, Belfast BT4 2JT (☎ 0232 760725, telex 747478)

RECKITT, Basil Norman; TD (1946); s of Maj Frank Norman Reckitt (d 1940); *b* 12 Aug 1905; *Educ* Uppingham, King's Coll Cambridge; *m* 1, 1928, Virginia, da of late Maj Meredith Carre-Smith; 3 da; m 2, 1966, Mary, *née* Peirce, wid of Paul Holmes, OBE; *Career* Lt-Col Home & Germany (Mil Govt); co dir; chm Reckitt & Colman Ltd 1966-70; Sheriff of Kingston upon Hull 1970-71, pro-chllr Univ of Hull 1971-; Hon LLD Hull 1967; *publications*: Charles I and Hull, The History of Reckitt & Sons Ltd, Diary of Military Government in Germany, The Journeys of William Reckitt, Diary of Anti-Aircraft Defence; *Recreations* hunting, ornithology; *Style*— Basil Reckitt, Esq, TD; Haverbrack, Milnthorpe, Cumbria; Holoman Hse, Isle of Raasay, By Kyle of Lochalsh, Ross-shire, Scotland

RECORD, Norman John Ronald; s of George Ronald Record (d 1967), of 26 Windsor Ave, Newton Abbot, Devon, and Dorothy Millie Rowland; *b* 19 May 1934; *Educ* Wembley Co GS, UCL (BSc); *m* 1 April 1961, Susan Mary, da of Ernest Samuel Weatherhead (d 1969), of Grosvenor Rd, Paignton, Devon; 2 s (Guy b 1964, Justin b 1966); *Career* 2 Lt RAOC 1955-57; economist; sr ptnr Business Economics Management Consultants 1991-, corp planning dir C & J Clarkk Ltd 1980-91; formerly held planning and mktg posts in C & J Clark Ltd since 1964, and Perkins Engines Ltd 1957-64; CBI: Cncl memb 1982-, SW regnl memb Cncl 1979-85, memb Econ Situation Ctee 1973-83, SW Econ Planning Cncl 1973-79; memb: The Strategic Planning Soc, The Mktg Soc, The Lab Fin and Indust Gp, The Lab Econ Strategies Gp, Ct of Govrs Univ of Bath; fell Soc Business Economists, FBIM; author of papers on Macro-Economics; originator of The Theory of Capacity Utilisation in the Control of The Economy; *Recreations* current affrs, theatre, local history, swimming; *Clubs* Royal Overseas League; *Style—* Norman Record, Esq; The Old Vicarage, Wedmore, Somerset BS28 4AA (☎ 0934 712326); C & J Clark Ltd, Street, Somerset BA16 0YA (☎ 0458 43131, telex 44102)

RECORDON, Hon Mrs (Dinah); da of Baron Baker, OBE (Life Peer, d 1985), and Fiona Mary MacAlister Baker (d 1979); *b* 2 April 1936; *Educ* Perse Sch for Girls, Homerton Coll Cambridge; *m* 1960, Nigel Esmond Recordon, s of Esmond Gareth Recordon (d 1958); 1 s (Benedict), 3 da (Emma, Clare, Martha); *Style—* The Hon Mrs Recordon; Bush Farm, Colwall, nr Malvern, Worcs WR13 6HH (☎ 0684 40393)

RECORDON, Nigel Esmond; s of Esmond Gareth Recordon (d 1957), of Cambridge, and Frieda, *née* Robertson (d 1973); *b* 5 March 1934; *Educ* Oundle, St John's Coll Cambridge (MA); *m* 25 June 1960, Hon Dinah, yr da of late Baron Baker, OBE, (Life Peer), of Cambridge; 1 s (Benedict), 3 da (Emma, Clare, Martha); *Career* Nat Serv 2 Lt RA 1952-54, TA Suffolk Yeo; admitted slr 1960, ptnr Recordon & Lister; *Recreations* farmer, beekeeper, long distance walking; *Style—* Nigel Recordon, Esq; Bush Farm, Colwall, Malvern (☎ 0684 40393); 12 Worcester Rd, Malvern, Worcs WR14 4QU (☎ 0684 892939)

REDCLIFFE-MAUD, Baroness; Jean; yr da of late John Brown Hamilton, of Melrose, Roxburghshire; *m* 1932, Baron Redcliffe-Maud, GCB, CBE (d 1982), sometime Master Univ Coll Oxford; 1 s (Hon Humphrey Maud), 2 da (Hon Mrs Pugh, Hon Mrs Nicholls); *Clubs* University Women's; *Style—* The Rt Hon the Lady Redcliffe-Maud; 221 Woodstock Rd, Oxford (☎ 0865 515354)

REDDAWAY, Prof (William) Brian; CBE (1971); s of William Fiddian Reddaway (d 1949), of 2 Buckingham Rd, Cambridge, and Kate Waterland, *née* Sills (d 1966); *b* 8 Jan 1913; *Educ* King's Coll Sch Cambridge, Lydgate House Hunstanton, Oundle, King's Coll Cambridge (BA, MA); *m* 17 Sept 1938, Barbara Augusta, da of Edward Bennett (d 1916), of Lydbrook, Glos; 3 s (Peter b 1939, Stewart b 1941, Lawrence b 1943), 1 da (Jacqueline b 1947); *Career* asst Bank of England 1934-35, res fell Univ of Melbourne 1936-37, fell Clare Coll Cambridge 1938, statistician Bd of Trade 1940-47, dir Dept of Applied Econs Univ of Cambridge 1955-70 (lectr 1939-55); memb Royal Cmmn on the Press 1961-62; FBA 1967; *Books* Russian Financial System (1935), Economics of a Declining Population (1939), Measurement of Production Movements (1948), Development of the Indian Economy (1962), Effects of UK Direct Investment Overseas (1968), Effects of the Selective Employment Tax (1973), Some Key Issues for the Development of the Economy of Papua New Guinea (1986); *Recreations* chess, skating, swimming, walking; *Style—* Prof Brian Reddaway, CBE; 12 Manor Court, Grange Rd, Cambridge CB3 9BE (☎ 0223 350041); Economics Faculty, Sidgwick Ave, Cambridge CB3 9DD (☎ 0223 335228); Clare Coll, Cambridge (☎ 0223 333200)

REDDAWAY, (George Frank) Norman; CBE (1965, MBE (Mil) 1946); s of William Fiddian Reddaway (d 1949), of King's College, Cambridge, and Kate Waterland, *née* Sills (d 1966); *b* 2 May 1918; *Educ* Oundle, King's Coll Cambridge (MA), Staff Coll Camberley, IDC; *m* 19 Feb 1944, Jean Muriel, OBE, da of (William) Harold Brett (d 1981), of Southport; 2 s (John b 1946, David b 1953), 3 da (Helen b 1948, Catharine b 1951, Lucy b 1960); *Career* Lance-Corpl Suffolk Regt 1939, 2 Lt No 3 Mil & Air Mission 1940, Capt GHQ Liaison Regt (Phantom) 1941-44, Maj Military Govt 1944, maj/actg Lt-Col Greater Berlin Mil Govt 1945-46; FO: German Dept 1946, priv sec to Parly under-sec 1947-49, HM Embassy Rome 1949-52, UK High Cmmn Ottawa 1952-55, Info Res Dept FO 1955-59, IDC 1960, regnl info offr HM Embassy Beirut 1961-65, Singapore 1965-66, Khartoum 1967-69, asst under-sec FCO 1970-74, HM ambass Warsaw 1974-78; chm International House; dir Stearns Catalytic Int Ltd, tstee Thomson Fndn; Cdr Order of Merit (Polish People's Republic) 1985; *Recreations* int affairs, gardening, family history; *Clubs* Athenaeum, Oxford and Cambridge, Royal Cwlth Soc; *Style—* Norman Reddaway, Esq, CBE; 51 Carlton Hill, London NW8 (☎ 071 624 9238)

REDDIHOUGH, John Hargreaves; s of Frank Hargreaves Reddihough, of Manchester, and Mabel Grace, *née* Warner; *b* 6 Dec 1947; *Educ* Manchester GS, Univ of Birmingham (LLB); *m* 26 June 1981, Sally Margaret, da of Bert Fryer, of Crawley, 1 s (Alex b 1984), 1 da (Gayle b 1981); *Career* called to the Bar Grays Inn 1969; *Recreations* skiing, running, gardening, music, reading; *Style—* John Reddihough, Esq; Clyde House, Coley Avenue, Woking, Surrey GU22 7BT (☎ 071 353 5371, fax 071 353 1344)

REDDISH, John Wilson; s of Frank Reddish, of Middleton, Gtr Manchester, and Elizabeth, *née* Hall; *b* 19 Jan 1950; *Educ* Manchester GS, Lincoln Coll Oxford (MA); *m* 20 May 1978, Dawn Marian, da of Edward Henry John McKenzie Russell (d 1963); 1 da (Helena b 1987); *Career* teaching assoc NorthWestern Sch of Law Chicago 1971-72, called to the Bar Middle Temple 1973, in practice 1974-; memb: Family Law Bar Assoc, London Commercial and Common Law Bar Assoc; *Recreations* cricket, squash; *Clubs* Old Gowers Cricket, Dulwich Hamlet Squash Rackets; *Style—* John Reddish, Esq; 1 Kings Bench Walk, Temple, London EC4Y 7DB (☎ 071 583 6266, fax 071 583 2068)

REDDY, Joanne Elizabeth; da of John William Thomas Staley, of Tythe Barn Farm, Norton, nr Evesham Worcs, and, Jean Elizabeth, *née* Heighway; *b* 19 Feb 1969; *Educ* Prince Henry's HS Evesham Worcs; *m* 25 Aug 1990, (Vuchuru) Sadhana Reddy, s of Drs V V and V K Reddy; *Career* athlete; Worcestershire Schs Co javelin champion (jr, intermediate and sr), capt Worcestershire Nat Schs Athletics Championships 1983-86; hockey career: Evesham Ladies Hockey Club 1983-88, Olton and West Warwicks Hockey Club 1988-; repres; Worcestershire U21 1983-89 (capt 1989), Worcester Seniors 1983-, Midlands Seniors 1990- (U18 1987, U21 1987-90); England U21 appearances 1989-90 (vice capt 1990): Holland BMW Four Nations Tournament 1989, Home Countries Tournament Nottingham July 1989, U21 Jr World Cup Ottawa Canada 1989, home Countries Tournament Ireland Cork; memb England Sr Training Squad 1990-; trainee accountant HDA Forgings Redditch (Hawker Siddeley Group) 1989-91, mgmnt accountant GKN Axles Birmingham 1991-; *Style—* Mrs Joanne Reddy; 42 Sandhills Crescent, Solihull, West Midlands B91 3UE (☎ 021 711 2967)

REDDY, Thomas; s of Thomas Reddy (d 1973), of Poulton-le-Fylde, and Charlotte Winifred Teresa, *née* Hickey (d 1987); *b* 6 Dec 1941; *Educ* Baines's Sch Poulton; *m* 30 Aug 1969, Phyllis Wendy, da of Stanley Smith (d 1969), of Manchester and Lytham St Annes; 1 s (Christian b 1973), 1 da (Verity b 1971); *Career* journalist 1968-70; dir and exec creative dir Royds McCann 1970-87, chief exec Tom Reddy Advertising 1987-; broadcaster on advertising TV and radio; chm Creative Club Manchester, fndr Manchester Creative Circle; guest lectr on advertising Univ of Manchester Inst of Sci and Technol; memb Br Direct Marketing Assoc (BDMA), Manchester Publicists Assoc (MPA); *Recreations* book collecting; *Clubs* Portico Library, Manchester Literary and Philosophical Society; *Style—* Thomas Reddy, Esq; Byeways, White House Lane, Great Eccleston, Lancs (☎ 0995 70568); Tom Reddy Advertising, Old Colony House, 6 South King St, Manchester (☎ 061 832 0182)

REDER, Dr Peter; s of Jack Mannie Reder, of London, and Beatrice *née* Kantor; *b* 29 June 1946; *Educ* Kilburn GS, Birmingham Univ Med Sch (MB, ChB), MRCPsych, DPM, DCH, D Obst, RCOG; *m* 15 Aug 1979, Dr Geraldine Sarah Mary, *née* Fitzpatrick; 1 s (Nicholas b 17 Jan 1984); *Career* sr conslt child psychiatrist Charing Cross Hosp 1985-; author pubns: psychotherapy, family therapy, child psychiatry and child abuse; MRC Psych 1975; *Style—* Dr Peter Reder; Dept of Child and Family Psychiatry, Charing Cross Hosp, 2 Wolverton Gdns, London W6 (☎ 081 748 2603)

REDESDALE, 6 Baron (UK 1902), of Redesdale, Co Northumberland; Rupert Bertram Mitford; o s of 5 Baron Redesdale (d 1991), and Sarah Georgina Cranstoun, *née* Todd; *b* 18 July 1967; *Heir* none; *Style—* The Rt Hon Lord Redesdale; The School House, Rochester, Newcastle-upon-Tyne NE19 1RH; 2 St Mark's Square, London NW1 7TP

REDFERN, Thomas Stathis; s of Arthur John Redfern, of Richmond, Surrey, and Maria, *née* Chionidon; *b* 25 Sept 1955; *Educ* Ratcliffe Coll Leics, King's Coll London (LLB); *m* 15 July 1988, Diane Alison, da of Frederick Alwyn Wilcox (d 1989), of Stourport on Severn, Worcs; 1 da (Madeleine Clare b 4 July 1990); *Career* A E Hamlin & Co 1977-79, Taylor Woodrow Construction Ltd 1980-82, Staveley Industries plc 1983-87, Ashby and Horner Group plc 1987-88, dir and co sec H Young Holdings plc 1989-; memb Law Soc 1975; *Recreations* football, rugby, cricket, golf, tennis, theatre; *Style—* Thomas S Redfern, Esq; H Young Holdings plc, Old Dominion House, 5 Gravel Hill, Henley on Thames, Oxon RG9 2EG (☎ 0491 578988, fax 0491 572360, car 0831 129760)

REDFERN, Prof Walter David; s of Walter Barton Redfern (d 1968), of Liverpool, and Charlotte, *née* Jones (d 1986); *b* 22 Feb 1936; *Educ* Bootle GS, Cambridge (MA, PhD); *m* 30 March 1963, Angela, da of John Robert Kirkup (d 1978), of Chester-Le-Street, Co Durham; 1 s (Sam b 9 Dec 1970), 1 da (Kate b 20 Sept 1968); *Career* prof of French Univ of Reading 1980- (lectr 1963, reader 1972), visiting prof Univ of Illinois 1981-82; memb Assoc For French Studies; *Books* Private World of Jean Giono (1968), Paul Nizan (1972), Queneau: Zazie Dans le Métro (1980), Puns (1984), Georges Darien (1985), A Calm Estate (1986), Clichés and Coinages (1989); *Recreations* jazz, cinema, writing; *Style—* Prof Walter Redfern; 8 Northcourt Ave, Reading RG2 7HA (☎ 0734 871083); Univ of Reading, French Dept, Whiteknights, Reading RG6 2AA (☎ 0734 875123 ext 7323)

REDFORD, Donald Kirkman; CBE (1980), DL (Lancs 1983); s of Thomas Johnson Redford (d 1965), of Whetstone, London; *b* 18 Feb 1919; *Educ* Culford Sch, King's Coll London (LLB); *m* 1942, Mabel, 2 da of Wilfrid Wilkinson, of Humberston, Lincs; 1 s, 1 da; *Career* Wing Cdr RAFVR; called to the Bar, practising barr until 1946; Manchester Ship Canal Co: joined 1946, md 1970, chm 1972-86; chm: Nat Assoc of Port Employers 1972-74, British Ports Assoc 1974-78; memb Ctee of Mgmnt RNLI 1977-; Univ of Manchester Court and Cncl: dep treas 1980-82, treas 1982-83, chm of Cncl 1983-87; *Clubs* Oriental; *Style—* Donald Redford Esq, CBE, DL; 8 Harrod Drive, Birkdale, Southport, Lancs PR8 2HA

REDGRAVE, John Albert Bryan; s of John Albert Redgrave (d 1985), of Felixstowe, Suffolk, and Lily Maria Redgrave (d 1986); *b* 2 Aug 1931; *Educ* Holloway GS, Open Univ (BA); *m* 27 March 1954, May Florence Lillian, da of Walter Jennings (d 1955); 2 da (Lynn b 1958, Jane b 1966); *Career* served RAF (Bomber Commd) 1955-57; md and chm Bellrock Gypsum Indust 1958-70, chief exec Powell Duffryn Pollution Control and Powell Duffryn Process Engrg 1970-72; chm and chief exec: Grimshaw Holdings 1972-74, Walter Lawrence plc 1974-85; chm Hunting Gate Group 1990- (chief exec 1985-90); JP (Bucks) 1971-76; Worshipful Master the Fletchers' Co (1990-91), Freeman City of London 1972; *Recreations* golf, archery, swimming, game fishing; *Clubs* Carlton, City Livery, Royal Toxophilite Society, Flempton Golf, Sheringham Golf, Norfolk, Strangers, Blickling Fly Fishing; *Style—* John Redgrave, Esq; Crowsteps, Church Lane, Wroxham, Norfolk NR12 8SH; Hunting Gate Group, 4 Hunting Gate, Hitchin, Herts, SG4 0TB (☎ 0462 434444, fax 0462 455924)

REDGRAVE, Lady; Rachel (Rachel Kempson); da of Eric William Edward Kempson (d 1954), and Beatrice Hamilton, *née* Ashwell (d 1960); *b* 28 May 1910; *Educ* privately, RADA; *m* 18 July 1936, Michael Redgrave; 1 s (Corin William b 16 July 1939), 2 da (Vanessa b 30 Jan 1936, Lynn b 20 March 1942); *Career* theatre, TV and film actress; first stage appearance Much Ado About Nothing (Stratford) 1933, first London appearance The Lady from Alfaqueque (Westminster) 1933; most recent stage appearance incl: The Seagull, St Joan of the Stockyards (Queens) 1964, Samson Agonistes, Lionel and Clarissa (Guildford) 1965, A Sense of Detachment (Apollo) 1975, The Old Country (Queens) 1977, Savannah Bay (Royal Court) 1983, Chekov's Women (Queens) 1986, The Cocktail Party (Phoenix) 1986, Uncle Vanya (Vaudeville) 1988, Coriolanus (Young Vic) 1989; films incl: Charge of the Light Brigade, Jane Eyre, Out of Africa 1985; TV appearances incl: Elizabeth R, Love for Lydia 1981, The Bell 1981, The Jewel in the Crown 1984, The Black Tower 1985, Small World 1988; *Books* A Family and Its Fortunes (1987); *Recreations* reading, theatre going; *Style—* Lady Redgrave; c/o Hutton Management, 200 Fulham Rd, London SW10

REDGRAVE, Maj Gen Sir Roy Michael Frederick; KBE (1979), MC (1945); s of Robin Roy Redgrave (d 1972), of Rye, Sussex, and Jean Micheline, *née* Capsa (d 1977); *b* 16 Sept 1925; *Educ* Sherborne; *m* 1953, Valerie, da of Maj (Richard) Arthur Colley Wellesley (d 1984); 2 s (Alexander, Robin); *Career* joined RHG as trooper 1943, Cmd RHG 1964-67; Nat Def Coll Canada 1973, Cmdt RAC Centre 1974-75, British Cmdt Berlin 1975-78, Cdr British Forces Hong Kong and Maj-Gen Bde of Gurkhas 1978-80, Hon Col 31 Signal Regt Volunteers 1982-86; DG Winston Churchill Mem Tst 1980-82; chm: Hammersmith and Fulham Dist Health Authy 1981-85, special tstees Charing Cross W London Hosps, Cncl Victoria League for Cwlth Friendship; memb Cncl: Med Sch Charing Cross & Westminster, Br Nepal Soc; govr Cwlth Tst; FRGS; *Style—* Maj-Gen Sir Roy Redgrave, KBE, MC; c/o Lloyd's Bank, Wareham, Dorset BH20 4LX

REDGRAVE, Steven Geoffrey; MBE (1986); s of Geoffrey Edward Redgrave, of Marlow Bottom, Bucks, and Sheila Marion, *née* Stevenson; *b* 23 March 1962; *Educ* Marlow C of E First Sch, Holy Trinity Sch Marlow, Burford Sch Marlow Bottom, Great Marlow Sch; *m* 12 March 1988, (Elizabeth) Ann, da of Brian John Callaway, of Cyprus; *Career* sports conslt, amateur rower; notable achievements: Olympic gold coxed pairs 1988, Olympic bronze coxed pairs 1988, World Champs winner coxless pairs and second coxless pairs 1987, World Champs winner coxless pairs, Cwlth Games gold single sculls, gold coxed fours, gold coxless pairs 1986, Olympic gold coxed fours 1984, Jr World Champs second double sculls 1980, 8 wins Henley Royal Regatta 1981-87, Wingfield Sculls Champ 1985-88; *Clubs* Marlow Rowing, Leander Henley; *Style—* Steven G Redgrave, Esq, MBE; c/o Olympic British Assoc, 1 Wandsworth Plain, London, SW18 1EH

REDGRAVE, Vanessa; CBE (1967); da of Sir Michael Redgrave (d 1985), and Rachel, *née* Kempson; sis of Corin Redgrave, actor, and Lynn Redgrave, actress; *b* 30 Jan 1937; *Educ* Queensgate Sch, Central Sch of Speech and Drama; *m* 1962 (m dis 1967), Tony Richardson (*qv*), s of Clarence Albert Richardson; 2 da; *Career* actress, numerous stage and film performances; memb WRP; *Style—* Miss Vanessa Redgrave, CBE; c/o James Sharkey Assocs Ltd, 3rd Floor Suite, 15 Golden St, London W1R 3AG

REDGROVE, Peter; s of late Gordon James Redgrove and late Nancy Lena, *née* Cestrilli-Bell; *b* 2 Jan 1932; *Educ* Taunton Sch Somerset, Queens' Coll Cambridge; *m* 2, Penelope Shuttle; *Career* scientific journalist and ed 1954-61, won Fulbright award to travel to US as visiting poet to Univ of Buffalo NY 1961, Gregory fell in poetry Univ of Leeds 1962-65, resident author and sr lectr in complementary studies Falmouth Sch of Art Cornwall 1966-83, O'Connor prof of lit Colgate Univ NY 1974-75; freelance writer, poet, analytical psychologist; broadcaster BBC 1956-, writer of radio and TV drama (Imperial Tobacco prize for Radio Drama 1978, Giles Cooper award for Radio Drama 1981, Prix Italia 1982); FRSL; *Books* playbooks incl: Miss Carstairs Dressed for Blooding and other plays (1976), In the Country of the Skin (1973); psychology and sociology: The Wise Wound (with Penelope Shuttle, 1978), The Black Goddess and the Sixth Sense (1987); novels incl: The Beekeepers (1980), The Facilitators (1982); poetry incl: The Collector and Other Poems (1960), Penguin Modern Poets II (1968), Dr Faust's Sea-Spiral Spirit and Other Poems (1972), The Apple-Broadcast and Other New Poems (1981), The Working of Water (1984), The Mudlark Poems and Grand Buveur (1986), The Moon Disposes: Poems 1954-87, In the Hall of the Saurians (1987), The First Earthquake (1989), Poems 1954-87 (1989), Dressed as For a Tarot Pack (1990); anthologies incl: Lamb and Thundercloud (1975), Poets' Playground (1963); reviewer for the Guardian 1975-, numerous prose articles for other jls; contrib to: TLS, Spectator, New Statesman, Observer and Listener; *Recreations* work, photography, yoga; *Style—* Peter Redgrove, Esq; c/o David Higham Associates, 5-8 Lower John St, Golden Square, London W1R 4HA

REDHEAD, Prof Michael Logan Gonne; s of Robert Arthur Redhead, of Oak Cottage, Cooden Beach, Sussex, and Christabel Lucy Gonne, *née* Browning (d 1966); *b* 30 Dec 1929; *Educ* Westminster, UCL (BSc, PhD); *m* 3 Oct 1964, Jennifer Anne, da of Montague Arthur Hill; 3 s (Alexander b 1965, Julian b 1968, Roland b 1974); *Career* dir Redhead Properties Ltd 1962, ptnr Galveston Estates 1970; prof: philosophy of physics Chelsea Coll London 1984-85, philosophy of physics King's Coll London 1985-87, history and philosophy of sci Univ of Cambridge 1987-; fell Wolfson Coll Cambridge 1988; pres Br Soc Philosophy of Sci 1989; Lakatos award 1988; FInstP; *Books* Incompleteness Nonlocality and Realism (1987); *Recreations* tennis, music, poetry; *Clubs* Hurlingham, Queen's; *Style—* Prof Michael Redhead; 34 Coniger Rd, London SW6 (☎ 071 736 6767); Dept of History and Philosophy of Science, Univ of Cambridge, Free Sch Lane, Cambridge (☎ 0223 334540, car 0865 263199)

REDMAN, Lady (Barbara Ann); *née* Wharton; da of late J R Wharton, of Haffield, nr Ledbury, Herefordshire; *b* 15 April 1919; *Educ* Benenden; *m* 1953, as his 2 w, Lt-Gen Sir Harold Redman, KCB, CBE (d 1986); 1 s, 1 da; *Career* 3 offr WRNS Lord Mountbatten's staff SACSEA; priv sec to Capt Anthony Kimmins (author and film producer); patron Royal Homeopathic Soc; *Recreations* gardening, environmental protection, painting, music; *Style—* Lady Redman; Stair House, West Lulworth, Dorset

REDMAN, Dr Christopher Willard George; s of Pro Roderick Oliver Redman (d 1975), and Annie Kathleen Redman; *b* 30 Nov 1941; *Educ* Perse Sch Cambridge, Cambridge Univ (MA, MB BChir); *m* 8 Aug 1964, Corinna Susan, da of Prof Sir Denys Lionel Page, KBE (d 1978); 4 s (Paul b 1967, Andrew b 1969, George b 1972, Oliver b 1982), 1 da (Sophie b 1972); *Career* intern and resident dept of pathology John Hopkins Hosp Baltimore USA 1967, house offr Childrens Hosp Sheffield 1969, sr house offr Jessop Hosp Sheffield 1969, lectr Regius Dept of Med Radcliffe Infirmary Oxford 1970 (house offr 1968), clinical reader Nuffield Dept of Obstetrics John Radcliffe Hosp Oxford 1988 (univ lectr 1976); FRCP 1982; *Recreations* walking; *Style—* Dr Christopher Redman; Nuffield Dept of Obstetrics and Gynaecology, John Radcliffe Hosp, Oxford OX3 9DU (☎ 0865 64711, fax 0865 69141)

REDMAN, Jean; da of Alan Havelock, of 64 Sish Lane, Stevenage, Herts, and Clara, *née* Anderson (d 1990); *b* 23 Nov 1932; *Educ* St Saviours and St Olaves GS For Girls London; *m* 1, 31 Jan 1953 (m dis 1962), Peter Gilbert Wenham; 1 s (Nicholas James b 1954), 1 da (Candida b 1958); m 2, 23 March 1963 (m dis 1974), Kenneth Victor Redman; 2 s (Oliver b 1963, Callum b 1969); *Career* W J Rendell Ltd 1959- (product mangr, int regulatory affairs mangr, prodn controller, chief exec); chm Westmill Residents Assoc, memb Romani Assoc, involved with The Samaritans; WIWM 1977; *Publications* Sex Without Fear (1969), Responsible Sex (1975), various technical manuals; *Recreations* chess, reading, magic, walking; *Clubs* Hitchin Conservative; *Style—* Mrs Jean Redman; Apartment 8, Cannon House, Queen Street, Hitchin, Herts SG4 9TX (☎ 0462 437326); W J Rendell Ltd, Ickleford Manor, Hitchin, Herts SG5 3XE (☎ 0462 432596, fax 0462 420423, telex 82311 RENHYD G)

REDMAN, Maurice; s of Herbert Redman (d 1974), and Olive, *née* Dyson; *b* 30 Aug 1922; *Educ* Hulme GS Oldham, Univ of Manchester (BSc); *m* 17 Sept 1960, Dorothy, da of James Appleton (d 1936); 2 da (Pamela b 19 July 1961, Philippa b 2 March 1964); *Career* various appts Co Borough of Oldham Gas Dept 1943; N Western Gas Bd: asst prodn engr, dep prodn engr 1951, chief devpt engr 1957; dir of engrg Southern Gas Bd 1970 (chief engr 1966), dep chm Scottish Gas Bd 1970, chm Scottish Regn Br Gas Corpn 1974 (dep chm 1973); various offices Methodist Church; CEng, CChem, FIGasE, MRSC, MIChemE; *Recreations* music, gardening, swimming, photography; *Clubs* New (Edinburgh); *Style—* Maurice Redman, Esq; Avington, 3 Cramond Regis, Edinburgh EH4 6LW (☎ 031 312 6178)

REDMAN, Timothy Stewart; s of Dudley Stewart Redman (d 1960), and Josephine Mary, *née* Baker (d 1952); *b* 4 June 1940; *Educ* Cheltenham; *m* 23 May 1964, Gillian Judith, da of John Pillar (d 1974); 2 s (Jonathan Stewart b 1967, Nicholas Timothy b 1970); *Career* Brewer; dir Greene King plc 1975-; memb Lloyd's of London 1984-; *Recreations* gardening, fishing, shooting; *Style—* Timothy Redman, Esq; Orchard House, Comberton, Cambridge CB3 7EE; Chalet le Caribou, Les Carroz d'Araches, France; Westgate Brewery, Bury St Edmunds, Suffolk IP33 1QT (☎ 0284 63222, telex 817589, fax 0284 706502)

REDMAN-BROWN, Geoffrey Michael; s of Arthur Henry Brown, of Newport, Gwent, and Marjorie Frances Joan, *née* Redman (d 1969); *b* 30 March 1937; *Educ* Newport HS, Balliol Coll Oxford (MA); *m* 23 Feb 1988, Mrs Jean Wadlow, da of Leslie James Wilkinson (d 1986), of Essex; *Career* Nat Serv RAF 1956-58; memb Stock Exchange 1967, ptnr Phillips & Drew 1970-90 (joined 1961), dir press and PR UBS Phillips & Drew Ltd 1989-90, dir Wadlow Grosvenor 1990-; Prov Grand Master for Oxfordshire, United Grand Lodge of Eng; Freeman City of London, Liveryman Worshipful Co of Broderers; ASIA 1972; *Recreations* swimming, gardening, travel; *Clubs* City of London, RAC; *Style—* Geoffrey Redman-Brown, Esq; 5 Three Kings Yard, Mayfair, London W1Y 1FL (☎ 071 629 2638); Priestfield, Hook Norton, Banbury, Oxon OX15 5NH (☎ 0608 737 738); Wadlow Grosvenor, 19-20 Grosvenor St, London W1X 9FD (☎ 071 409 1225, fax 071 409 8135)

REDMAYNE, Clive; s of Procter Hubert Redmayne (d 1965), of 9 Grenville Rd, Hazel Grove, Stockport, Cheshire, and Emma, *née* Torkington (d 1976); *b* 27 July 1927; *Educ* Stockport Sch, Univ of London (BSc); *m* 19 July 1952, Vera Muriel, da of Wilfred Toplis, MM (d 1983), of 35 Wellfield Rd, Stockport, Cheshire; 1 s (John Clive James b 27 July 1959), 1 da (Jane Susan (Mrs Goodwin) b 6 April 1956); *Career* apprentice Fairey Aviation Co Stockport 1944-48; stress offr: Fairey Aviation Co 1948-50, Eng Electric Co Warton 1950-51, A V Roe & Co Chadderton 1951-55; head of structural analysis Weapons Div Woodford 1955-62, Structures Dept Royal Aircraft Estab Farnborough 1962-67, asst dir Miny of Technol 1967-70; MOD(PE): AD/MRCA 1970-74, dir Harrier 1978-80, dir gen Future Projects 1980-81, dir gen Aircraft 3 1981-84; div ldr systems engrg Namma Munich 1974-76, chief supt A & AEE Boscombe Down conslt aeronautical engr 1985-; MIMechE 1956, CEng 1970, FRAeS 1981; *Recreations* caravanning, walking, skiing, chess, bridge, reading; *Clubs* Caravan; *Style—* Clive Redmayne, Esq; Bowstones, 5 Westbrook View, Stottingway St, Upwey, Weymouth, Dorset (☎ 0305 814691)

REDMAYNE, Hon Sir Nicholas John; 2 Bt (UK 1964); s of Baron Redmayne, DSO, TD, PC, DL (Life Peer and 1 Bt, who d 1983); *b* 1 Feb 1938; *Educ* Radley, Sandhurst; *m* 1, 7 Sept 1963 (m dis 1976), Anne (d 1985), da of Frank Birch Saunders, of Kineton, Warwicks; 1 s, 1 da; m 2, 1978, Mrs Christine Diane Wood Hewitt, da of late Thomas Wood Fazakerley; *Heir* s, Giles Martin Redmayne b 1 Dec 1968; *Career* cmmnd Grenadier Gds 1958-62; stockbroker; md Kleinwort Benson Securities; dir: Kleinwort Benson Ltd, Kleinwort Benson Group plc; *Recreations* shooting, tennis, skiing; *Style—* The Hon Sir Nicholas Redmayne, Bt; Walcote Lodge, Walcote, Lutterworth, Leics (☎ 0455 55 2637, business tel 071 623 8000)

REDMAYNE, Simon Mark; s of Richard Taubman Redmayne, of Cambridge, and Mary Katherine, *née* Tidd; *b* 23 Feb 1960; *Educ* Oundle, Worcester Coll Oxford (BA); *Career* called to the Bar Inner Temple 1982; *Recreations* fishing, skiing, walking; *Clubs* Lansdowne; *Style—* Simon Redmayne, Esq; 134 Fulham Rd, London SW10 9PY (☎ 071 835 1720); Strand Chambers, 218 The Strand, London WC2R 1AP (☎ 071 353 7825, fax 071 583 2073)

REDMON, Vincent William; s of David Redmon, and Mavis Cordilia, *née* James; *b* 8 May 1965; *Educ* White Lodge Royal Ballet Lower Sch, St Joseph's Coll Ipswich, Arts Educnl Sch Royal Ballet Upper Sch; *Career* Ursular Morteon Choreographic Award 1982 and 1983, Award at Prix de Lausanne 1983, graduated with dip of distinction from Royal Ballet Sch 1984; Sadlers Wells Royal Ballet: joined 1984, soloist 1988, 1st soloist 1990; roles incl: Petrushka and Franz in Coppelia, Puck in The Dream, Will Mosiop in Hobson's Choice; choreographed: Auras 1989, Meridian of Youth for SWRB 1990, Yesterday, Today, Tomorrow for London City Ballet 1990; *Style—* Vincent Redmon, Esq; Sadler's Well's Theatre, Rosebury Ave, London

REDMOND, Dr Aileen Oonagh Beatrice; da of Dr William Alexander Redmond (d 1948), of Ballyward, Co Down, NI, and Sheila Arabella, *née* Badger (d 1986); *b* 17 Oct 1936; *Educ* Alexandra Coll Dublin, Rainey Endowed Sch, Magherafelt Co Derry, Univ Trinity Coll Dublin (MB BCh, BAO, BA); *Career* assoc chief res Hosp for Sick Children Toronto 1966-67, clinical fell Harvard Med Sch Boston Mass 1967-68, clinical res fell Nutrition Unit Red Cross Childrens Hosp Capetown SA 1970-71, conslt paediatrician Royal Belfast Hosp for Sick Childrean And Belfast City Hosp 1971-; hon med advsr Cystic Fibrosis Res Tst NI regn, memb Children In Need Appeals Ctee and NI Appeals Advsy Ctee BBC; memb Br Paediatric Assoc; *Recreations* gardening, travel; *Style—* Dr Aileen Redmond; 4 Rosevale Close, Drumbeg, Dunmurray, Belfast BT17 9LQ (☎ 0232 612024); Royal Belfast Hospital For Sick Children, Belfast (☎ 0232 240503)

REDMOND, Dr Anthony Damien; s of Gerard Redmond (d 1976), and Kathleen, *née* Bates; *b* 18 Nov 1951; *Educ* Cardinal Langley Sch, Univ of Manchester (MB ChB, MD); *m* 22 Dec 1972, Caroline Ann, da of Dr John Arthur Howarth, of Devon; 3 da (Katherine Mary b 12 Dec 1978, Sarah Michelle b 15 Sept 1980, Helen Margaret b 24 April 1982); *Career* conslt in charge S Manchester A/E Serv 1987-, dir S Manchester Accident Rescue Team 1987 (attended Armemian Earthquake 1988, Lockerbie Air Crash 1988, Iranian Earthquake 1990); fdr ed Archives of Emergency Med 1984; memb: Resuscitation Cncl UK, Fontmell Gp for Disaster Relief; Soviet Order for Personal Courage 1989 (for work in Armenian Earthquake); fell Royal Soc of Med; MRCP UK 1981, FRCSEd 1982, MBIM 1985; *Books* Lecture Notes on Accident and Emergency Medicine (1984), Accident and Emergency Medicine (jtly 1989); *Recreations* music; *Style—* Dr Anthony D Redmond; Silverwood, Ladybrook Road, Bramhall, Cheshire SK7 3NE; Univ Hosp of S Manchester, Nell Lane, W Didsbury, Manchester M20 8LR (☎ 061 445 8111)

REDMOND, Geraldine Melaine; da of Jerome Anthony Wilson, of Liverpool, and Dorothy Kathleen, *née* Hoult; *b* 20 Jan 1953; *Educ* Notre Dame Convent Woolton, Upton RC Convent Wirral, Cygnets House London; *m* (m dis); 1 da (Melaine Francesca); *Career* md Famous Army Stores Ltd; dir Limocoat Ltd, Famous Army Stores (Holdings) Ltd, Tenglow Ltd, Betterpoise Ltd, Harmond Investments Ltd; chllr Alder Hey Childrens Hosp Appeal; *Recreations* cookery, swimming, classic vintage car driving; *Style—* Mrs G M Redmond; Sunbeam House, Woolton Rd, Garston, Liverpool L19 5PH (☎ 051 427 5151, fax 051 427 3918, 0831 299299)

REDMOND, Sir James; s of Patrick and Marion Redmond; *b* 8 Nov 1918; *Educ* Graeme HS Falkirk; *m* 1942, Joan Morris; 1 s, 1 da; *Career* radio offr Merchant Navy 1937-38 and 1939-45; BBC Television Alexandra Palace 1937-39; BBC: installation engr 1949, supt engr Television Recording 1960, sr supt engr TV 1963, asst dir of engrg 1967, dir of engrg 1968-78; pres IEE 1978-79; memb: cncl Brunel Univ 1980-88, cncl Open Univ 1981-, bd Services Sound & Vision Corp 1983-90; FEng, Hon FIEE; kt 1979; *Recreations* golf; *Clubs* Athenaeum; *Style—* Sir James Redmond; 43 Cholmeley Crescent, Highgate, London N6 5EX (☎ 081 340 1611)

REDMOND, John Vincent; s of Maj Robert Spencer Redmond, TD, of Knutsford, Cheshire, and Marjorie Helen, *née* Heyes; *b* 10 April 1952; *Educ* Wrekin Coll, Western Reserve Acad Ohio USA, Univ of Kent at Canterbury (BA); *m* 21 May 1977, Tryphena Lloyd (Nina), da of Jenkin John Lloyd Powell, of Carmarthen, Dyfed; 2 s (William b 1981, Samuel b 1985); *Career* admitted slr 1976; Cobbetts Manchester 1974-75, Clyde & Co Guildford and London 1975-78, Laytons Bristol and London (ptnr) 1978-; memb: Bristol Jr Chamber 1978-, Soc of Construction Law; memb Law Soc 1976, FFB; *Recreations* squash, sailing; *Style—* John Redmond, Esq; Hafod, Scot Lane, Chew Stoke, Avon BS18 8UW (☎ 0272 333181); Laytons, St Bartholomews, Lewins Mead, Bristol BS1 2NH (☎ 0272 291626, fax 0272 293369, car 0836 533382)

REDMOND, Martin; MP (Lab) Don Valley 1983-; *b* 15 Aug 1935; *Style—* Martin Redmond Esq, MP; House of Commons, London SW1

REDMOND, Robert Spencer; TD; s of Frederick Redmond (d 1937), of Croxteth Rd, Liverpool, and Eliza, *née* MacKenzie (d 1976); *b* 10 Sept 1919; *Educ* Liverpool Coll; *m* 19 May 1949, Marjorie Helen, da of Abraham Vincent Heyes, of Tanhouse Lane, Parbold, N Wigan, Lancs; 1 s (John Vincent b 10 April 1952); *Career* Liverpool Scot (TA) 2 Lt 1938, RASC 1941, Special Ops 1943-45, ME Staff Coll 1943, released with rank Maj 1946; Cons constituency agent: Wigan 1947-49, Knutsford 1944-56; md Heyes & Co Ltd 1956-66, md Ashley Associates 1969-70 (commercial mangr 1966-69 and pt/t commercial dir 1970-72), MP (Cons) Bolton W 1970-74 (vice chm

Employment Ctee, memb Select Ctee on Nat Industs, spokesman on problems of small business), private practise as exec selection conslt 1972-76, dir Nat Fedn of Clay Industs 1976-84; freelance journalist 1984-; fndr (and chm) NW Export Club 1960, NW regnl cncllr FBI and CBI 1958-66 (memb cncl CBI 1976-84); *Books* How to Recruit Good Managers (1989); *Recreations* writing, gardening; *Clubs* Army and Navy; *Style*— Robert S Redmond, Esq, TD; 194 Grove Park, Knutsford, Cheshire WA16 8QE (☎ 0565 2657)

REDWAY, Maj Paul Warwick; TD (1950); s of Warwick Richard Redway, FAI (d 1958), of Princes Risborough, and Eva Gladys, *née* Burr; *b* 7 June 1918; *Educ* Royal GS High Wycombe; *m* 22 June 1940, Jacqueline Kelleway, da of John Paul Line (d 1959); 2 s (Marcus Vaughan b 15 Nov 1943, Hugh Warwick b 1 Oct 1948), 1 da (Robina Paulina b 25 Jan 1946); *Career* TA 2 Lt Queen Victoria's Rifles 1937, Maj 1942, served with KRRC UK and Normandy; md Skinningrove Iron Co Ltd 1966-; JP 1955; *Recreations* skiing, shooting, fishing; *Clubs* London, The Royal Green Jackets; *Style*— Maj Paul Redway, TD; Bugle Cottage, Egton, Whitby, N Yorks YO21 1UT (☎ 0947 85363)

REDWOOD, David Robert; s of Edward James Redwood (d 1967); and Florence Maude Elizabeth, *née* Harper; *b* 4 Nov 1935; *Educ* King's Sch Worcester, Jesus Coll Cambridge (MA, MB BChir); *m* 1, 1960, Mehranguise (d 1980), 3 s (Michael b 1961, Simon b 1963, David b 1970); m 2, 1 May 1982, Janet Elizabeth, da of George Young, CBE; 1 s (Jamie b 1987), 1 da (Katherine b 1984); *Career* head of cardiovascular diagnosis Nat Inst of Health Bethesda Maryland USA 1973-76 (visiting scientist 1968-76), head of cardiology Cedars of Lebanon Hosp Miami Florida USA 1976-77; conslt cardiologist: St Georges Hosp London, Harley St, St Anthony's Hosp Cheam Surrey 1977-; author chapters in cardiology textbooks and numerous papers in scientific jls; FRCP; *Recreations* sailing, walking, photography, golf; *Style*— David Redwood, Esq; St Anthony's Hospital, London Rd, Cheam, Surrey (☎ 081 337 6691)

REDWOOD, John Alan; MP (C) Wokingham 1987-; s of William Charles, Kent, and Amy Emma Champion; *b* 15 June 1951; *Educ* Kent Coll Canterbury, Magdalen Coll Oxford (BA), St Anthony's Coll 1971-72 (DPhil, MA); *m* 1974, Gail Felicity, da of Robert Stanley Chippington; 1 s (Richard b 1982), and 1 da (Catherine b 1978); *Career* fell All Souls Coll Oxford 1972-87; investmt analyst Robert Fleming & Co 1974-77; Oxfordshire County Cncllr 1973-77; clerk mangr dir NM Rothschild Asset Mgmnt 1977-83; head Prime Minister's Policy Unit 1983-86; dir Overseas Corporate Finance NM Rothschilds 1986-87; non-exec dir Norcros 1986-87; min of state for Industry and Enterprise 1990-; *Recreations* village cricket, water sports; *Style*— John Redwood, Esq, MP; 506 Queen's Quay, Upper Thames Street, London EC4V 3EH; House of Commons SW1

REDWOOD, Sir Peter Boverton; 3 Bt (UK 1911); s of Sir Thomas Boverton Redwood, 2 Bt (d 1974); *b* 1 Dec 1937; *Educ* Gordonstoun; *m* 22 Aug 1964, Gilian Waddington, o da of John Lee Waddington Wood, of Limuru, Kenya; 3 da; *Heir* half-bro, Robert Redwood; *Career* Col KOSB, ret 1987; memb Queen's Body Guard for Scotland (Royal Co of Archers); Liveryman Worshipful Co of Goldsmiths; *Recreations* shooting; *Clubs* Army and Navy; *Style*— Sir Peter Redwood, Bt; c/o National Westminster Bank, Millbank Branch, Thames House, Millbank, SW1

REDWOOD, Robert Boverton; s of Sir Thomas Boverton Redwood, 2 Bt (d 1974); hp of half-bro, Sir Peter Redwood, 3 Bt; *b* 24 June 1953; *Educ* Truro Cathedral Sch; *m* 1978, Mary Elizabeth Wright; 1 s (James b 1985), 1 da (Morwenna b 1982); *Career* police offr; *Style*— Robert Redwood, Esq

REECE, Sir Charles Hugh; s of Charles Reece (d 1962), and Helen Yuille Reece; *b* 2 Jan 1927; *Educ* Pocklington Sch, Huddersfield Coll, Univ of Leeds (BSc, PhD); *m* 1951, Betty, *née* Linford; 2 da (Ann Heather b 1954, Pamela Janet b 1957); *Career* ICI plc (formerly ICI Ltd): res chemist 1949-69, res dir Mond Div 1969-72, dep chm Mond Div 1972-75, chm Plant Protection Div 1975-79, res and technol dir 1979-89, dir Finnish Chemicals Oy 1971-75, chm Teijin Agricultural Chemicals Ltd 1975-78, chm Robens Inst of Industl and Environmental Health 1984-; non-exec dir: APV plc 1984-, British Biotechnology plc 1989; memb: ACOST 1983-89, SERC 1984-89, Advsy Bd of Res Cncls 1989-, Univs Funding Cncl 1989-, Ctee for the Euro Devpt of Sci and Technol 1989-, Soc of Chem Indust; Hon DSc: Univ of St Andrews, Queens Univ Belfast, Univ of Bristol, Univ of Surrey; MRI, FRSC, FRSA; kt 1988; *Recreations* sailing, gardening; *Style*— Sir Charles Reece; Heath Ridge, Graffham, Petworth, W Sussex (☎ 0798 6274); APV plc, 2 Lygon Place, London SW1W 0JR (☎ 071 730 7244, fax 071 730 2660, telex 925465)

REECE, His Hon Judge (Edward Vans) Paynter; s of Clifford Mansel Reece, QC (d 1973), and Catherine Barbara, *née* Hathorn (d 1974); *b* 17 May 1936; *Educ* Blundell's, Magdalene Coll Cambridge (MA); *m* 23 Sept 1967, Rosamund Mary, da of Thomas Vaughan Roberts; 3 s (Rupert Vaughan Paynter b 6 July 1968, William Hugh Hathorn b 11 April 1970, Henry John Mansel b 25 March 1975), 1 da (Alexandra Catherine b 2 July 1973); *Career* RA 1954-56 (2 Lt 1955); called to the Bar Inner Temple 1960, rec Crown Court S Eastern Circuit 1980-82, circuit judge S Eastern Circuit 1982-; *Recreations* fishing; *Style*— His Hon Judge Paynter Reece; 2 Harcourt Buildings, Temple, London EC4Y 9DB

REECE-SMITH, Gregory; s of Gordon Reece-Smith, of Spain, and Joyce Constance, *née* Baxter; *b* 22 March 1948; *Educ* KCS Wimbledon, LSE (BSc); *m* 22 June 1973, Caroline Mary, da of Basil Arthur Buche, of Surrey; 2 s (Gavin Robert b 1977, Duncan Paul b 1980); *Career* CA; joined Peat Marwick Mitchell 1970 (resigned as sr mangr 1983), chief fin offr Dubilier America Inc NY 1984, mgmnt engr to medium sized cos facing the problems of high growth and change 1985-; dir: Blue Chip Systems Gp plc, Blue Chip Microsystems Ltd, Overview Films Ltd, St Christopher's Sch Tst (Epsom) Ltd; *Recreations* squash, rugby, educn; *Clubs* RAC; *Style*— Gregory Reece-Smith, Esq; 2 The Ridings, Epsom, Surrey KT18 5JQ (☎ 03727 25437, work 071 434 9829)

REED, Alec Edward; s of Leonard Reed (d 1953), of London, and Anne, *née* Underwood (d 1983); *b* 16 Feb 1934; *m* 16 Sept 1961, Adrianne Mary, da of Harry Eyre (d 1943); 2 s (James b 12 April 1963, Richard b 27 March 1965), 1 da (Alexandra b 22 Jan 1971); *Career* Nat Serv 1952-54; fndr and chm and chief exec: Reed Exec plc 1960-, Inter-Co Comparisons Ltd 1969-70, Reed Coll of Accountancy 1971, Medicare Ltd 1975-86; chm and chief exec Andrews and Ptnrs Ltd 1985-89; pres: Inst of Employment Conslts 1974-78, Int Confedn of Private Employment Agencies Assoc 1978-81; chm Employment Think Tank 1979; memb: Cncl Royal Holloway Coll 1979-85, Bd of Govrs Thomas Coram Fndn for Children 1981-91, Helpage Exec Ctee 1983-88; fndr and memb Bd of Tstees: Womankind Worldwide 1988-, Ethiopiaid 1989-; memb Oxfam Fundraising Ctee 1989, elected hon fell Royal Holloway and Bedford New Coll 1988; FCIS 1957, FCMA 1967, FECI 1971; *Books* Returning to Work (1989); *Recreations* family, theatre, cinema, tennis, riding; *Clubs* Royal Over-Seas League; *Style*— Alec Reed, Esq; Reed Executive plc, 114 Peascod St, Windsor, Berks SL4 1DN (☎ 0753 850441, fax 0753 841688)

REED, April Anne; Air Cdre; RRC (1981); da of Capt Basil Duck Reed, RN (d 1969), and Mignon Ethel Nancy, *née* Neame (d 1976); *b* 25 Jan 1930; *Educ* Sherborne House Chandlersford, Channing Sch Highgate, Middx Hosp London, Royal Maternity Hosp Belfast; *Career* Princess Mary's RAF Nursing Serv: joined as Flying Offr 1954, Flt Offr 1958, Sqdn Ldr dep matron 1970, Wing Cdr sr matron 1976, Gp Capt princ matron 1980, Air Cdre dir nursing servs 1984; ret due to serv reorganistaion 1985; memb charity exec RAF Benevolent Fund 1985-89; *Recreations* gardening, wildlife, hill walking, antiques, oriental rugs; *Clubs* RAF; *Style*— Air Cdre April Reed, RRC; 3 Edieham Cottages, Angle Lane, Shepreth, Royston, Herts (☎ 0763 61329); 3 Garners Row, Burnham Thorpe, Norfolk; 2 Murlaggan, Roy Bridge, By Fort William, Inverness

REED, Bernard William Douglas; *b* 21 Aug 1935; *Educ* Sutton GS Surrey, St Peter's Coll Oxford (MA), City of London Coll (Dip), Harvard Business Sch (MBA); *m* 25 March 1961, Terry; 3 s (Ian Michael b 1963, Neil Malcolm b 1966, Duncan James b 1969), 1 da (Julia Louise b 1964); *Career* Sub Lt RN 1954-56; Phillips & Drew 1959-62, McKinsey & Co 1964-68, BOC Group 1973-78, London Int Fin Futures Exchange 1981-84, exec dir of mktg Int Stock Exchange 1985-90; Freeman Worshipful Co of Wheelwrights; AMSIA 1961; *Recreations* windsurfing, running; *Style*— Bernard Reed, Esq; Haldem Securities Ltd, Malverley, The Warren, Ashtead, Surrey KT21 2SP (☎ 0372 272374)

REED, David; s of Dr George Norman Reed (d 1954), Surg Lt Cdr RN, and Phyllis Maude, *née* Cave (later Mrs Dawson, d 1969); *b* 31 July 1947; *Educ* St Edward's Sch Oxford; *m* 19 Jan 1974, Jennifer Carol, da of Dennis George Sandford Loudon, of Michael Bournes, West meston, Sussex; 3 s (Jonathan b 16 Jan 1977, Nicholas b 8 March 1982, Bemjamin b 17 Jan 1987), 1 da (Emily b 3 Sept 1979); *Career* with Whinney Murray (now Ernst and Whinney) 1967-71; with Peat Marwick Mitchell and Co Sydney 1972-73; County Bank Ltd (now County Nat West Ltd) 1974- (dir 1979, md 1986); memb: FCA 1976 (ACA 1971); *Recreations* shooting, sailing, tennis; *Style*— David Reed, Esq; 8 Holtwood Road, Oxsholt, Surrey (☎ 0372 842180); County Natwest Ltd, Drapers Gardens, 12 Throgmorton Avenue, London EC2 (☎ 071 382 1000)

REED, Derek Sydney; s of Sydney Richard Reed, of Town Barton, Ilsington, Devon, and Margaret Annie Reed; *b* 8 Sept 1946; *Educ* Newton Abbot GS, Univ of Liverpool (LLB); *m* 26 May 1973, Carole, da of William Brunswick Whiting; 2 s (James b 1976, Mark b 1980), 1 da (Vanessa b 1974); *Career* admitted slr 1971, ptnr Woollcombe Beer Watts; *Recreations* walking, gardening, sport, music; *Style*— Derek Reed, Esq; Church House, Newton Abbot, Devon (☎ 0626 331199)

REED, Gavin Barras; s of Lt-Col Edward Reed (d 1953), and Greta Milburn, *née* Pybus (d 1964); *b* 13 Nov 1934; *Educ* Eton, Trinity Coll Cambridge (BA); *m* 28 June 1957, Muriel Joyce, da of late Humphrey Vaughan Rowlands; 1 s (Christopher b 1964), 3 da (Fiona b 1958, Joanna b 1960, Lucinda b 1962); *Career* Nat Serv Pilot Fleet Air Arm; dir Scottish & Newcastle Breweries plc; other directorships incl Independent Investment Co, Milburn Estates Ltd; *Recreations* shooting, tennis; *Clubs* Naval, New (Edinburgh); *Style*— Gavin Reed, Esq; Whitehill, Aberdour, Burntisland, Fife KY3 0RW; Broadgate, West Woodburn, Northumberland; Scottish & Newcastle Breweries plc, 111 Holyrood Rd, Edinburgh EH8 8YS (☎ 031 556 2591)

REED, Glenn; s of John Wilfred James Reed, of Westbury-on-Trym, Bristol, and Jean, *née* Arnold; *b* 25 Dec 1955; *Educ* Henbury Sch, Univ of Southampton (LLB); *m* 31 July 1985, Dr Deborah Lyn Reed, da of Denis Raymond, of Knowle, Bristol; *Career* called to the Bar Michaelmas 1982; memb Hon Soc of the Inner Temple (Duke of Edinburgh scholar) 1978; *Recreations* karate, cooking, reading, ancient history, the occult; *Clubs* Commerical Rooms (Bristol); *Style*— Glenn Reed, Esq; All Saints Chambers, Holbeck House, 9-11 Broad St, Bristol BS1 2HP (☎ 0272 211966, fax 0272 276493); 1 Gray's Inn Square, Gray's Inn, London WC1R 5AA (☎ 071 405 8946)

REED, Ian Malcolm; *b* 16 Nov 1947; *Educ* Tiffin Sch Kingston Upon Thames, Univ of Bradford (BSc); *m* Hilary Anne, da of Donald Ralph Fife, of Worthing, W Sussex, 1 s; *Career* Touche Ross & Co 1972-74 (articled clerk 1969-72, Plantation Holdings 1974-76, fin dir and md TVI Ltd 1976-85, gp md Limehouse TV Ltd 1985-, chm Trilion plc 1987- (gp md 1986-); FCA 1972, memb IOD 1988; *Recreations* rugby, golf, cricket, music; *Clubs* RAC; *Style*— Ian Reed, Esq; Trilion plc, Limehouse Studios, 128 Wembley Park Drive, Middx HA9 8HQ (☎ 081 900 1199, fax 081 900 2800, car 0836 691641)

REED, Jane Barbara; da of William Charles Reed, and Gwendoline Laura, *née* Plaskett; *b* 31 March 1940; *Educ* Royal Masonic Sch for Girls; *Career* ed Woman's Own 1969-79, publisher Quality Monthly Gp IPC 1979-81, ed-in-chief Woman 1981-83, md Holborn Publishing Gp IPC 1983-85, managing ed (features) Today Newspaper 1985-86, managing ed News UK Ltd 1986-89, dir of corporate relations News Int 1989-; memb Ctee for the Public Understanding of Science (Copus) Royal Society 1986-; *Books* Girl about Town (1964), Kitchen Sink or Swim (with Dierdre Saunders, 1981); *Recreations* music, writing, work; *Clubs* Groucho's; *Style*— Miss Jane Reed; News International, 1 Virginia Street, London E1 9XY

REED, John Edward; s of John William Reed, of Devon, and Gladys Lavinia Williams, *née* Silk (d 1982); *b* 7 April 1946; *Educ* Dulverton Secondary, Aston Univ (BSc) RIBA (DipArch); *m* 7 Aug 1976, Christine Anne, da of Richard Foley (d 1966), of Worthing; 2 da (Joai Jane b 1983, Chloë Yi-Fen b 1985); *Career* Chartered Architect ptnr; Reed Holland Associates 1981-; *Recreations* family and Christian orientated; *Style*— John E Reed, Esq; Reed Holland Associates, Chartered Architects, 4 Middle St, Taunton, Somerset TA1 1SH (☎ 0823 336479)

REED, Dr John Langdale; s of John Thompson Reed (d 1966), of Northampton, and Elsie May, *née* Abbott (d 1962); *b* 16 Sept 1931; *Educ* Oundle, Cambridge Univ (MA, MB BChir), Guy's Hosp; *m* 7 Jan 1959, Hilary, da of Lt-Col John Freeman Allin, MC (d 1976), of Kings Norton; 1 s (John Richard b 1967), 1 da (Alison b 1960); *Career* Nat Serv RAMC 1958-60; conslt psychiatrist Bart's London 1967-, sr lectr Bart's Med Coll 1967-; dir Community Psychiatry Res Unit 1979-86, sr princ med offr mental health and the elderly div Dept of Health London 1986-; chm Vanguard Housing 1981-86; FRCP 1974, FRCPsych 1974; *Books* Psychiatric Services in the Community (jtly 1984); *Recreations* genealogy, bridge, walking; *Style*— Dr John Reed; Dept of Health, Alexander Fleming House, Elephant & Castle, London SE1 (☎ 071 407 5522)

REED, Malcolm Edward; s of Colin Reed, of Barnsley, Yorks, and Lilian, *née* Dixon; *b* 5 May 1947; *Educ* Penistone GS, Hollings Coll Manchester (HND), Univ of Durham (MSc); *Career* joined Trust House Hotels 1966; trained in Weston-super-Mare, Nice and Edinburgh; mangr: George Hotel Huddersfield 1971, Tyneside Post House 1973, Randolph Hotel Oxford 1976; dir Swallow Hotels 1982- (joined as central area mangr 1978); lay reader C of E 1976; Freeman City of London 1978; memb Assoc of MBAs 1966, FHCIMA 1979; *Recreations* church music, opera, walking, cooking; *Clubs* Wig & Pen; *Style*— Malcolm Reed, Esq; Clough Cottage, Cathill, nr Sheffield, Yorkshire S30 6JB (☎ 0226 767328); Swallow Hotels Ltd, Southern Regional Office, Kenwood Road, Sheffield, Yorkshire S7 1NQ (☎ 0742 583811, fax 0742 509450, car 0836 538147)

REED, Dr May; da of Joseph Henry George Reed (d 1970), of The Grange, Ingatestone, Essex, and Edith May, *née* Leech (d 1966); *b* 22 April 1914; *Educ* Brentwood Co HS, Bedford Coll London (BSc, PhD); *Career* WWII nurse Br Red Cross 1939-42; res sci MRC 1958-77, sr res fell Somerville Coll Oxford 1972-79; hon res advsr Chartered Soc of Physiotherapy 1966-75, fndr memb and first hon sec The Brill Soc, vice chm Brill Royal Br Legion Women's Section, chm Vale of Aylesbury Decorative and Fine Arts Soc, pres Brill Sports and Social Club; memb: Soc for Endocrinology, Soc for Study of Fertility 1960; FRSA 1959, FRSM 1965; *Recreations* fly-fishing; *Clubs* Royal Commonwealth Soc; *Style—* Dr May Reed; Old Post Office House, Brill, Bucks HP18 9RP (☎ 0844 238226)

REED, Paul; s of Donald Henry Reed, of 2 Mercer Court, Exeter, Devon, and Irene, *née* Vanstone; *b* 18 Aug 1956; *Educ* Ladysmith Secdy Modern Sch, Exeter Coll Catering Dept; *m* Sheridan Elizabeth, da of Alan Woodman; 2 da (Harriet b 6 April 1987, Emily 20 October 1990); *Career* commis chef rising to head chef Buckerell Lodge Hotel 1974-79, commis chef rising to sous chef Hilton Hotel Park Lane London 1979-82, sr chef de partie Dorchester Hotel Park Lane London 1982-83, chef and owner London House Restaurant Broad Clyst Devon 1983-84, head chef Copper Inn Pangbourne Berks 1984-85, sr sous chef The Dorchester Hotel Park Lane London 1985-86, exec chef The Chester Grosvenor Hotel Chester 1986-; Gold medallist Culinary World Cup 1986; *Recreations* golf; *Clubs* Upton by Chester Golf; *Style—* Paul Reed, Esq; 4 Westway, Trevalyn Estate, Rossett, Clwyd LL12 ODX (☎ 0244 570614); Chester Grosvenor Hotel, Eastgate St, Chester, Cheshire CH1 1LT (☎ 0244 324024, fax 0244 313246)

REED, Piers Knowle Moorhouse; s of Gerald Basil Moorhouse Reed, and Madeleine, *née* Deverill; *b* 15 Aug 1952; *Educ* Haileybury; *m* 7 Aug 1976, Vicky Ann Maguerite, da of William Alexander Edwards; 2 da (Pierrette Babette Madeleine b 2 June 1980, Tanya Daniele Marguerite b 2 Sept 1982); *Career* called to the Bar Lincoln's Inn 1974; memb Bar Assoc: England and Wales, NI; *Style—* Piers Reed, Esq; 9 Farm Close, Cuffley, Herts EN6 4RQ (☎ 0707 875433); 4 New Square, Lincoln's Inn, London WC2A 3RJ (☎ 071 242 8508, fax 071 404 3139)

REED, Dr William Leonard; s of William Alfred Reed (d 1949), of Dulwich, and Alice Kate, *née* Bloxam (d 1964); *b* 16 Oct 1910; *Educ* Dulwich, Guildhall Sch of Music, Jesus Coll Oxford (MA, DMus), RCM; *Career* Nat Fire Serv 1941-44; music lectr Br Cncl in Scandinavia and Finland 1937-39, music master Sloane Sch Chelsea 1945, tutor adult educn classes in music appreciation for Oxford Delegacy for Extra Mural Studies ILEA and WEA 1962-, dir music Westminster Theatre Arts Centre 1967-80; compositions (with date of first BBC broadcasts) incl: Idyll for Small Orchestra (1936), Saraband for Orchestra (1936), Hornpipe for Orchestra (1938), Two Short Pieces for Orchestra (1938), Three Dance Movements (1938), Six Facets for Orchestra (1939), Lady Nevell Suite (1939), Fantasy for Piano Quartet (1940), Waltz Fantasy for Orchestra (1949), A Reflection for Small Orchestra (1969), Scherzo for Orchestra (1970), Concert Overture for Orchestra (1981), five Spiritual Songs for Baritone and Piano (1981), Fantasy for String Quartet (1985), Three Surrey Impressions for Two Pianos (1985), Prelude, Nocturne and Rhapsody for Piano (1988), Piano Trio (1990), Child Portraits for Piano (1990); Musicals: Annie (1967), Love All (1978); with other composers: The Vanishing Island (1955), The Crowning Experience (1958), High Diplomacy (1969); Freeman Worshipful Co of Musicians 1944; PRS; memb Soc: Elgar, Delius, Sibelius, Dvořák, Sullivan, Haydn, Grainger, Howells, Rachmaninoy; *Books* ed: The Treasury of Christmas Music (1950), Music of Britain (1952), The Treasury of Easter Music (1963), The Second Treasury of Christmas Music (1967); jt ed: The Treasury of English Church Music (1965), The Treasury of Vocal Music (1969), National Anthems of the World (1978, 1985, 1987); *Recreations* photography; *Style—* Dr William L Reed; Upper Suite No 7, The Quadrangle, Morden College, London SE3 OPW (☎ 081 305 0380)

REED-PURVIS, Air Vice-Marshal Henry; CB (1982), OBE (1972); *b* 1 July 1928; *Educ* King James I Sch, Univ of Durham (BSc); *m* 1951, Isabel Price; 3 da (Jane, Sara, Shona); *Career* served RAF Regt in: Iraq, Persian Gulf, Oman, Malaya, Borneo, Europe, N America; dir RAF Regt 1976-79, Cmdt-Gen RAF Regt and Dir-Gen Security (RAF) 1979-83, ret; sales dir Br Aerospace Army Weapons Div 1983-89; vice pres Cncl for Cadet Rifle Shooting; memb: Exec Ctee The Forces Help Soc, Lord Roberts' Workshops; *Recreations* golf, archaeology, bridge; *Clubs* RAF; *Style—* Air Vice-Marshal Henry Reed-Purvis, CB, OBE; Cobb House, Bampton, Oxon OX8 2LW (☎ 0993 851032)

REEDAY, Thomas Geoffrey; s of Thomas Cockcroft Reeday (d 1947), and Marion, *née* Johnson (d 1975); *b* 20 July 1924; *Educ* Queen Elizabeth GS Wakefield, Univ of London (LLB); *Career* Nat Serv WWII Army 1943-47, NW Europe RASC 1944-47; banker, lawyer, lectr; called to the Bar Lincoln's Inn 1954; head dept law Poly Central London 1977-85, chief examiner in law relating to Banking Inst of Bankers 1973-86; Freeman City of London 1977, Liveryman Worshipful Co of Chartered Secs and Admin 1978; FCIS 1978, Hon FCIB 1989; *Books* Law Relating to Banking (5 edn, 1985), Legal Decisions Affecting Bankers (co-ed vols 9 and 10, 1988); *Recreations* railway preservation; *Style—* Geoffrey Reeday, Esq; 66 Lamorna Grove, Stanmore, Middx HA7 1PG (☎ 081 952 4591)

REEDER, Frederick John; s of Frederick Reeder, of Gravesend, Kent, and Susan Elizabeth, *née* Evans (d 1982); *b* 19 Nov 1936; *Educ* Coopers' Company's Sch; *m* 31 March 1962, Judy Barbara, da of Frank William Smith; 2 s (Paul b 1968, Mark b 1974), 1 da (Tracy b 1965); *Career* Nat Serv Br Army Singapore and Malaya 1955-57; Commercial Union Properties Ltd: dir 1974-82, chm 1976-82 (UK); dir property invstmt Postel Investment Management 1982-90, ptnr Jones Lang Wootton 1990-; FCIS 1970, FRICS 1974, FSVA 1986; *Recreations* sailing; *Clubs* Les Ambassadeurs; *Style—* Frederick Reeder, Esq; 22 Hanover Square, London W1A 2BN

REES, Alan Martin; s of William Thomas Owen Rees, of Newport, Gwent, and Margaret Alice, *née* Martin; *b* 29 July 1952; *Educ* Llandovery Co HS, Univ Coll Cardiff (BSc), Univ of Wales Coll of Med (MB BCh); *m* 25 Sept 1976, Susan Ann, da of William Joseph Payne, of Tredegar, Gwent; 1 s (Peter b 1983), 1 da (Alison b 1979); *Career* house offr Llanelli Gen Hosp 1976-77; Univ Hosp of Wales: sr house offr of pathology 1977-78, registrar 1978-80, sr registrar 1980-83; conslt pathologist Princess of Wales Hosp Bridgend 1983-; memb, then fell Br Interplanetary Soc 1974, MRCPath 1982; *Style—* Alan Rees, Esq; Pathology Dept, Princess of Wales Hospital, Coity Rd, Bridgend, Mid Glamorgan (☎ 0656 662166)

REES, Allen Brynmor; s of Allen Brynmor Rees, of 74 Coleridge Ave, Penarth, S Glamorgan (d 1941), and Elsie Louise, *née* Hitchcock, (d 1956); *b* 11 May 1936; *Educ* Monmouth Sch, Univ of Wales Aberystwyth (LLB); *m* 26 Aug 1961, Nerys Eleanor, da of Wynne Evans, (d 1977), of Upper Maen, Meifod, Powys; 2 da (Meriel Anne Brynmor b 7 Oct 1968, Eleanor Haf Brynmor b 22 Aug 1975); *Career* sr ptnr: Rees Page (incorporating Darbey-Scott-Rees and Pages and Skidmore Hares & Co) Slrs, (incl internal Legal Dept of Midland News Assoc); chm W Mids Rent Assesment Panel 1968-, head office slr to Birmingham Midshires Building Society 1976-; chm: Social Security Tbnls 1980-, Industl Tbnls 1982- (pt/t); author of The Solicitors Notebook for the Slrs Jl 1968-, chm Bilston Round Table 1974 (memb 1966-77), memb Legal Aid Area Ctee 1975-, pres Exec Ctee Old Monmothians 1977 (memb 1966-), Negligence Panel rep for Wolverhampton Area of Law Soc 1982-, pres Bilston Rotary Club 1984 and 1985 (memb 1974-); memb Law Soc 1962; *Recreations* squash, canoeing, shooting, skiing, gardening; *Style—* Allen Rees, Esq; Rossleigh, Shaw Lane, Albrighton, Wolverhampton WV7 3DS; Yr Hen Ystabl, Meifod, Powys (☎ 0902 372423); 17 Wellington Rd, West Midlands WV14 6AD; 44 Queen St, Wolverhampton WV1 3BN (☎ 0902 353535/0902 21241, fax 0902 353088/0902 25136, telex 338490 CHACOM G)

REES, Andrew Merfyn; s of Peter Donald Rees, and Rita Clarice, *née* Coleshaw; *b* 20 July 1954; *Educ* Culford Sch, FitzWilliam Coll Cambridge (MA); *m* 11 Sept 1981, Monica, da of Rosman Gordon; 2 s (Richard b 1983, Charles b 1987); *Career* admitted slr 1981; head of corporate servs Eversheds Wells & Hind 1988 (associate 1983, ptnr 1985); memb Law Soc; *Recreations* shooting, travel; *Style—* A M Rees, Esq; 10 Newhall St, Birmingham B3 3LX (☎ 021 233 2001, fax 021 236 1583)

REES, Wing Cdr Arthur Morgan; OBE (1963, CBE 1970), QPM (1970), DL (Staffs 1967); s of Thomas Rees, of S Wales; *b* 20 Nov 1912; *Educ* Llandovery Coll, St Catharine's Coll Cambridge (BA, MA, Rugby blue); *m* 1943, Dorothy, *née* Webb (d 1988); 1 da (Rosemary); *Career* RAF Pilot 1941-46, Substantive Sqdn Ldr and actg Wing Cdr; chief constable: Denbighshire Constabulary 1956-64, Staffordshire & Stoke on Trent Police 1964-77; conslt dir: Wedgwood 1977-80, Royal Dalton 1980-83, Armitage Shanks 1980-83, Wales Britannia Building Soc 1983-87, Inter Globe Security Servs Ltd 1985-; chm: Crawshays RFC 1962-, Midlands Sport Cncl 1967-77 (life memb Midlands Sports Advsy Cncl), Staffs St John Cncl 1967-88, Queens Silver Jubilee Appeal Sports Ctee, Prince's Tst 1974-88, English Karate Bd, Br Karate Bd, Hanks Dinner Ctee 1986; dep pres Staffs Boys Club 1970-; pres: (fndr) Ex Police in Indust and Commerce Soc, pres Eccleshall RFC 1979-, Staffs Playing Fields Assoc 1986; former Wales Rugby Union Int rugby referee for London Soc; KstJ; *Recreations* rugby, karate, hockey; *Clubs* RAF, Hawks (Cambridge); *Style—* Wing Cdr Arthur Rees, CBE, QPM, DL; 18 Broom Hall, Oxshott, Surrey KT22 OJ2 (☎ 037 284 3500)

REES, Brian; s of Frederick Thomas Rees (d 1966), of Ashbrooke Road, Sunderland, and Anne, *née* Keedy (d 1976); *b* 20 Aug 1929; *Educ* Bede GS Sunderland, Trinity Coll Cambridge; *m* 1, 17 Dec 1959, Julia (d 1978), da of Sir Robert Birley, KCMG, FSA (d 1983), of Somerton, Somerset; 2 s (Robert Hugh Corrie b 13 April 1961, Philip Timothy b 28 Aug 1964), 3 da (Jessica Margaret Anne b 19 April 1963, Natalia Rachel b 24 Jan 1966, Camilla Marion b 2 April 1969); m 2, 3 Jan 1987, Juliet Mary Akehurst, da of C D O Gowan; *Career* Nat Serv RASC 1948-49; housemaster Eton 1963-65 (asst master 1952-63); headmaster: Merchant Taylors' 1965-73, Charterhouse 1973-81, Rugby 1981-84; dir Argentine-Br Conf 1989-; chm ISIS 1982-83, patron Conf for Ind Educ 1983- (former pres); Liveryman Worshipful Co of Merchant Taylors; *Books* A Musical Peacemaker (Biography of Sir Edward German, 1987), History of Idealism Essays and Addresses of Sir Robert Birley (ed 1990); *Recreations* music, painting, travel; *Style—* Brian Rees Esq; 52 Spring Lane, Flore, Northants NN7 4LS (☎ 0327 41330); Le Manoir de Subarroques, Viens, 84750 Vaucluse, France

REES, Prof Brinley Roderick; s of John David Rees (d 1947), of Port Talbot, Wales, and Mary Ann, *née* Roderick (d 1976); *b* 27 Dec 1919; *Educ* Christ Coll Brecon, Merton Coll Oxford (MA, PhD); *m* 23 Aug 1951, Zena Muriel Stella, da of Alfred Reginald Mayall, of Leominster; 2 s ((Idris John) Mark b 1954, (Alan) Hugh b 1957); *Career* Welch Regt 1940-45, Capt 4 Welch Regt 1943, Capt/Adj 15 Welch Regt 1945; Univ Coll Cardiff: prof of Greek 1958-70, dean of arts 1963-65, dean of students 1968-69, hon lectr 1980-88, vice pres 1986-88; Univ of Birmingham: prof of Greek 1970-75, dean of arts 1973-75, life memb Univ Ct 1982-; St David's Univ Coll Lampeter: princ 1975-80, pres classical assoc 1978-79, emeritus prof 1981; Rotarian 1966-75, hon Rotarian 1975-; Hon LLD Univ of Wales 1981, Leverhulme emeritus fell 1984-86; *Books* The Merton Papyri, II (with Bell and Barns, 1959), Papyri from Hermopolis and Elsewhere (1964), Lampas (with Jervis, 1970), Classics for the Intending Student (ed, 1970), Pelagius: A Reluctant Heretic (1988); *Recreations* walking, reading; *Style—* Prof Brinley Rees; 31 Stephenson Ct, Wordsworth Ave, Cardiff, S Glam CF2 1AX (☎ 0222 472 058)

REES, Prof Charles Wayne; s of Percival Charles Rees (d 1963), and Daisy Alice, *née* Beck (d 1941); *b* 15 Oct 1927; *Educ* Farnham GS, Univ Coll Southampton, Univ of London (BSc, PhD, DSc); *m* 19 Dec 1953, Patricia Mary, da of George Walter Francis; 3 s (David Charles b 1958, George Wayne b 1959, Michael Francis b 1961); *Career* lectr in organic chemistry: Birkbeck Coll London 1955-57, King's Coll London 1957-63 (reader 1963-65); prof of organic chemistry: Univ of Leicester 1965-69, Univ of Liverpool 1969-77 (Heath Harrison prof 1977-78); Hofmann prof of organic chemistry Imperial Coll London 1978-, visiting prof Univ of Würzburg 1968, lectr Royal Soc of Chemistry Tilden 1973-74, Pedler lectr 1984-85, Award in Heterocyclic Chemistry 1980; Andrews lectr Univ NSW 1988, lectured widely in Australia, China, Japan and USA; pres Perkin Div 1981-83, pres chemistry section Br Assoc for the Advancement of Sci 1984; written and edited about 30 books and 300 res papers on organic chemistry; FRSC 1966, FRS 1974; *Recreations* food and wine, music, London; *Style—* Prof Charles Rees, FRS; 67 Hillgate Pl, London W8 7SS (☎ 071 229 5507); Chemistry Dept, Imperial Coll, London SW7 2AY (☎ 071 225 8334)

REES, David Albert; s of David John Rees (d 1980), of Manchester, and Sarah Elizabeth, *née* Searle (d 1967); *b* 22 March 1936; *Educ* William Hulme GS Manchester, Univ of Manchester Med Sch (MRCS, FRCOG); *m* 10 Aug 1963, Marlene Elizabeth, da of Henry Illingworth (d 1983), of Bradford; 1 s (David b 1965); *Career* house offr in med and surgery Bury Gen Hosp 1962-63; registrar in obstetrics and gynaecology: Sefton Gen Hosp Liverpool 1967-70, Mill Road Hosp Liverpool 1970-72 (admin med offr 1973-74); conslt obstetrician and gynaecologist St Helens and Knowsley AHA 1974-; memb: Br Med and Dental Hypnosis Assoc, North of England Obstetrics and Gynaecological Soc, Br Music Soc, St Helens Med Soc, Long Distance Walkers Assoc; *Recreations* music, long distance walking, fell walking; *Clubs* St Helens Med Soc; *Style—* David Rees, Esq; 8 Downham Close, Liverpool L25 4TY (☎ 051 428 3905); Whiston Hospital, Maternity Department, Prescot, Liverpool L35 5DR (☎ 051 426 1600)

REES, David Bartlett; s of Gerald Bartlett Rees (d 1981), of Surbiton, Surrey, and Margaret Elizabeth Belinda, *née* Healy (d 1990); *b* 18 May 1936; *Educ* King's Coll Sch Wimbledon, Queens' Coll Cambridge (exhibitioner, BA, MA); *m* 1966 (m dis), Jenny Lee, da of Charles Watkins; 2 s (Stephen Andrew b 24 Dec 1968, Adam Aaron b 24 Nov 1970); *Career* writer; schoolmaster: Wilson's GS Camberwell London 1960-65, Vyners Sch Ickenham Middx 1965-68; lectr: St Luke's Coll Exeter 1968-77, Sch of Educn Univ of Exeter 1977-84; distinguished visiting prof San Jose State Univ Calif USA 1985 and 1987; freelance writer 1984-; co-fndr Third House (publishers) 1987-; children's books: Landslip (1977), The Exeter Blitz (Carnegie medal, 1978), The House That Moved (1979), The Night Before Christmas Eve (1980), A Beacon for the Romans (1981), Holly, Mud and Whisky (1981), The Mysterious Rattle (1982), The Burglar (1987), Friends and Neighbours (1987), The Flying Island (1988); novels for teenagers: Storm Surge (1975), Quintin's Man (1976), The Missing German (1976), The Spectrum (1977), The Ferryman (1977), Risks (1978), In The Tent (1979), Silence (1979), The Green Bough of Liberty (The Other award, 1980), The Lighthouse (1980), Miss Duffy Is Still With Us (1980), Waves (1983); novels for adults: The Milkman's on His Way (1982), The Estuary (1983), Out of The Winter Gardens (1984), The Hunger (1986), Watershed (1986), Twos and Threes (1987), The Wrong Apple (1988), Quince (1988), The Colour of His Hair (1989); short story collections: Islands (1984), Flux (1988), Letters to Dorothy (1990); other books: A Better Class of Blond (travel book, 1985), Dog Days, White Nights (essays, 1991); *Style—* David Rees, Esq; 69 Regent St, Exeter EX2 9EG (☎ 0392 432479)

REES, Frederick Thomas (Tom); s of Thomas Percy Rees, OBE (d 1963), and Adeline Isabel, *née* Stephens (d 1986); *b* 18 Oct 1933; *Educ* Harrow; *m* 28 April 1962, Anna, da of Charles Carnes, VRD, of Littlehampton, W Sussex; 3 da (Sarah b

13 March 1963, Rachel b 7 June 1965, Lucy b 14 March 1969); *Career* Nat Serv York and Lancaster Regt Sudan 1952-54; memb Stock Exchange; jt treas Wealden Cons Assoc 1983-86; memb: Rotherfield Community Assoc, Abbeyfield Soc; Freeman City of London (Upholder 1968); *Recreations* travel, swimming, tennis; *Style*— Tom Rees, Esq; Willinghurst, Rotherfield, E Sussex (☎ 082 585 312); Central House, Medwin Walk, Horsham, W Sussex

REES, Gareth Mervyn; s of Joseph Rees (d 1981), of Llangadog, Wales, and Gwen Rees (d 1988); *b* 30 Sept 1935; *Educ* Llandovery HS, St Mary's Hosp Univ of London (MB BS, MS); *m* 1, 1962 (m dis 1968), Anne Frisby Richards; 1 s (Philip b 1964); m 2, 21 Dec 1968, Prof Lesley Rees, *née* Davis, da of Howard Leslie Davis (d 1942); *Career* house surgn and house physician St Marys Hosp 1960, int res fell Dept of Heart Surgery Univ of Oregon Portland USA 1970, conslt i/c Dept of Cardio-thoracic Surgery St Bartholomews Hosp London 1984- (conslt heart surgn 1973-); memb: Cardiac Soc, Int Coll of Surgns, Assoc of Thoracic Surgns UK; FRCS 1966, FRCP 1983; *Recreations* fishing, skiing, rugby, football; *Clubs* Garrick, RAC; *Style*— Gareth Rees, Esq; 10 Upper Wimpole St, London W1 (☎ 071 487 3598)

REES, Harland; s of Dr David Charles Rees, of Port Elizabeth, SA, and Myrtle May, *née* Dolley (d 1950); *b* 21 Sept 1909; *Educ* St Andrews Coll Grahamstown SA, Oxford Univ (BA, MA, BM BCh, MCh); *m* 20 May 1950, Helen Marie, da of John Ronald Tulloch Tarver (d 1963), of Wing, Bucks; 2 s (David b 1951, Martin b 1956), 1 da (Annabel b 1954, d 1976); *Career* WWII Capt RAMC 1942, Maj 1944, Lt-Col 1945; served: India, Burma, Thailand; conslt surgn: St Peter's Hosp 1947-62, Hampstead Gen Hosp 1947-74, King's Coll Hosp 1948-74; South Beds DC: parish cncllr, dist cncllr, chm 1986; chm Kensworth Cons Assoc; FRCS, BA US; *Recreations* golf (previously rugby Oxford Univ); *Clubs* Vincent's (Oxford); *Style*— Harland Rees, Esq; Kensworth Gorse, Kensworth, nr Dunstable, Bedfordshire LU6 3RF (☎ 0582 872 411)

REES, (Thomas Morgan) Haydn; CBE (1975), JP (Mold 1977), DL (Flints 1969, Clwyd 1974); s of late Thomas Rees, of Gorseinon, Swansea, and Mary, *née* Bowen; *b* 22 May 1915; *Educ* Swansea Business Coll; *m* 12 July 1941, Marion, da of A B Beer, of Mumbles, Swansea; 1 da ((Elizabeth) Maryon Haydn (Mrs Hughes)); *Career* serv WWII 1939-45; slr 1946, asst slr Caernarvonshire CC 1947; Flints CC 1948-74: dep clerk, clerk of the peace (until office abolished 1971, formerly dep clerk), clerk Police Authy (until merger with N Wales Police Authy 1967, formerly dep clerk), clerk Magistrates Cts Ctee (formerly dep clerk), clerk Probation Ctee (formerly dep clerk), clerk Justices Advsy Ctee, chief exec, Clerk to Lieutenancy; Clwyd CC 1974-77: chief exec, clerk Magistrates Cts Ctee, clerk Justice Advsy Ctee, Clerk to Lieutenancy; clerk N Wales Police Authy 1967-77, sec Welsh Counties Ctee 1968-77, asst cmmr Royal Cmmn on Constitution 1969-73; memb: Welsh Cncl 1968-79, Welsh Arts Cncl 1968-77 (memb Regl Ctee 1981-), Lord Chllr's Ctee for Wales and Chester circuit 1972-77, Prince of Wales Ctee 1976-79, Gorsedd Royal National Eisteddfod of Wales, Nat Water Cncl 1977-82, Water Space Amenity Cmmn 1977-82, Severn Bridge Ctee 1978-81, Theatre Clwyd Govrs 1983-(clerk 1974-77), North Wales Music Festival 1983-; pt/t memb Bd BSC (Indust) Ltd 1979-83; chm: Govt Quality of Life Experiment in Clwyd 1974-76, Welsh Water Authy 1977-82, New Jobs Team Shotton Steelworks 1977-82, N Wales Arts Assoc 1981-, Deeside Enterprise Tst Ltd 1982-89; pres: Clwyd Voluntary Servs Cncl 1980-, Clwyd Pre-Retirement Assoc 1986-; *Recreations* the arts, golf; *Clubs* Mold Golf; *Style*— Haydn Rees, Esq, CBE, JP, DL; Cefn Bryn, Gwernaffield Rd, Mold, Clwyd CH7 1RQ (☎ 0352 2421)

REES, Dr Helene Ceredwyn; da of Delwyn Garland Rees, of 346 Toorak Rd, South Yarra, Victoria, Aust, and Jean Helene, *née* Höette; *b* 8 April 1948; *Educ* Presbyterian Ladies Coll Melbourne Aust, Univ of Melbourne (MB BS); *m* 17 Dec 1971 (m dis 1984), David Alan McDonald, s of Alan McDonald; 2 s (Lachlan James b 11 March 1974, Alexander Rhys b 25 April 1980), 1 da (Kate Helene b 17 July 1975); *Career* annual appts in gen med and surgery in maj teaching hosps in Melbourne 1972-73; in trg in pathology 1973-81: The Royal Childrens Hosp, Fairfield Infectious Diseases Hosp, Alfred Hosp and Prince Henry's Hosp, all in Melbourne Australia; sr registrar in histopathology Hammersmith Hosp 1984-86 (registrar 1981-84), sr lectr and hon conslt in histopathology St Bartholomews Hosp Med Coll 1986-; memb: Kew Soc, Aust and NZ Med and Dental Assoc 1984, Hunterian Soc 1984, Graduate Union of Univ of Melbourne 1980; vice pres Med Soc of London 1990-91 (fell 1984); Freeman City of London 1986, Liveryman Worshipful Soc of Apothecaries 1989 (Yeoman 1985); FRCPA (Aust) 1980, MRCPath 1984; *Recreations* gymnastics, golf, classical music; *Clubs* Hogarth, Meon Valley Country; *Style*— Dr Helene Rees; Histopathology Dept, St Bartholomews's Hospital Medical College, West Smithfield, London EC1A 7BE (☎ 071 601 8532)

REES, (William) Howard Guest; CB (1988); s of Walter Guest Rees (d 1967), of S Wales, and Margaret Elizabeth, *née* Harries (d 1978); *b* 21 May 1928; *Educ* Llanelli GS, Royal Veterinary Coll, Univ of London (BSc, MRCVS, DVSM); *m* 1952, Charlotte Mollie, da of Enoch Collins (d 1979), of S Wales; 3 s (Michael, Nicholas, Alan), 1 da (Amanda); *Career* vet surgn; chief vet offr; min of agric fisheries & food 1980-88; hon Fell RASE 1988, memb Cncl Royal Vet Coll London 1989; *Recreations* golf; *Clubs* Pennard Golf (S Wales), Tyrrells Wood (Leatherhead); *Style*— Howard Rees, Esq, CB; Taliesin, Paddocks Way, Ashtead, Surrey KT21 2QY (☎ 0372 276 522)

REES, Prof Hubert; DFC (1944); s of Owen Rees (d 1970), and Evelyn Tugela, *née* Bowen; *b* 2 Oct 1923; *Educ* Llanelli Co and Llanelli Co Sch, Univ Coll Wales (BSc), Univ of Birmingham (PhD, DSc); *m* 26 Dec 1946, Mavis Rosalind, da of Roland Hill; 2 s (Wynne d 1977, Hubert), 2 da (Gwyneth, Judith); *Career* RAFVR 1942-46; lectr Genetics Dept Univ of Birmingham 1950-59; Dept of Agric Botany University College of Wales: sr lectr 1959, reader 1966, prof 1967-; FRS 1976; *Recreations* fishing; *Style*— Prof Hubert Rees, DFC, FRS; Irfon, Llanbadarn Rd, Aberystwyth (☎ 0970 623 668); Univ Coll of Wales, Abertstwyth (☎ 0970 623 111)

REES, Rt Rev (John) Ivor; s of David Morgan Rees (d 1928), and Cecilia Maria Perrott (d 1955), *née* Evans; *b* 19 Feb 1926; *Educ* Llanelli GS, Univ Coll of Wales (BA), Westcott House Cambridge; *m* 5 Aug 1954, Beverley, da of Henry Albert Richards, Co Sergeant-Major, (d 1946); 3 s ((Christopher) Meirion b 1956, (David) Mark b 1958, Stephen (Wynne) b 1963); *Career* RN, Coastal forces and Pacific fleet 1943-47; curate: Fishguard 1952-55, Llangathen 1955-57; vicar: Slebech & Uzmaston 1957-65 (priest in charge 1957-59), Llangollen 1965-74; rector Wrexham 1974-76; canon St Asaph 1975-76; dean of Bangor Cathedral 1976-88, vicar of the cathedral parish of Bangor 1979-88, appointed arch deacon of St Davids 1988, consecrated assistant Bishop of St Davids 1988; OStJ 1981; *Books* The Parish of Llangollen and its Churches (1971), Keeping Forty Days - Addresses for Lent (1989); *Recreations* good music, light reading; *Style*— The Rt Rev the Assistant Bishop of St Davids; Llys Dewi, 45 Clover Park, Uzmaston Rd, Haverfordwest, Dyfed SA61 1UE (☎ 0437 767750)

REES, Jeremy John; s of John Louis Rees, of Gloucestershire, and June Rosamond, *née* Lloyd; *b* 13 Feb 1955; *Educ* Felsted, Univ of Southampton (LLB); *m* 26 April 1980, Fiona Michelle, da of Michael Hudelist, of Perth, Aust; 2 s (James b 1984, David b 1987); *Career* Peat Marwick Mitchell & Co 1976-81, dir IBJ International Ltd 1986- (joined 1981); ACA 1979; *Recreations* cricket, hockey, squash, skiing (snow and water), gardening; *Style*— Jeremy Rees, Esq; Bucklersbury House, 3 Queen Victoria St, London EC4N 8HR (☎ 071 236 1090)

REES, John Samuel; s of John Richard Rees, and Mary Jane Rees; *b* 23 Oct 1931; *Educ* Cyfarthfa Castle GS Merthyr Tydfil; *m* 1 June 1957, Ruth Jewell; 1 s (Paul b 1961), 1 da (Diane b 1962); *Career* Nat Serv Welch Regt and RAEC 1950-52; sports ed Merthyr Express 1952-54 (reporter 1948-50); The Star Sheffield: reporter 1954-56, sub ed 1956-58, dep chief sub ed 1958-60, dep sports ed 1960-62, asst ed 1962-66; dep ed Evening Echo Hemel Hempstead 1966-69; ed: Evening Mail Slough & Hounslow 1969-72, The Journal Newcastle upon Tyne 1972-76, Evening Post-Echo Hemel Hempstead 1976-79; asst md Evening Post-Echo Ltd 1979-81, ed Western Mail Cardiff 1981-88; editorial conslt 1988-; *Recreations* marquetry, watching cricket and rugby, walking, gardening; *Style*— John Rees, Esq; Timbertops, St Andrew's Road, Dinas Powys, S Glam CF6 4HB (☎ 0222 513254)

REES, Jonathan Michael; s of Robert Bruce Rees (d 1981), and Evelyn Foy *née* Puckey; *b* 25 Feb 1965; *Educ* Edgbarrow Sch Crowthorne, Univ of Southampton (BSc); *Career* hockey player; capt Wales Hockey Team 1989- (rep 1986-), rep GB 1988; *Recreations* films, music, books; *Clubs* Hounslow Hockey; *Style*— Jonathan Rees, Esq; 76 Bedfordshire Way, Woosehill, Wokingham, Berks RG11 9BA (☎ 0734 794149); Andersen Consulting, 2 Arundel St, London WC2R 3LT (☎ 071 438 5000)

REES, Prof Lesley Howard; da of Howard Leslie Davis (d 1942), and Charlotte Patricia Siegrid, *née* Young (d 1960); *b* 17 Nov 1942; *Educ* Pates Girls GS Cheltenham, Malvern Girls Coll, Med Coll Bart's Univ of London (MB BS, MD, MSc); *m* 21 Dec 1969, Gareth Mervyn Rees, s of Joseph Philip Rees; *Career* ed Clinical Endocrinology 1979-84, public orator University of London 1984-86, sub dean Bart's Med Coll 1983-87, chm Soc for Endocrinology 1984-87, sec gen Int Soc for Endocrinology 1984-, prof chem endocrinology Barts Med Coll (dean 1989); FRCP 1979, FRCPath 1988; *Books* author numerous papers on endocrinology; *Recreations* reading, music, art, skiing, cooking; *Clubs* Mosimann's; *Style*— Prof Lesley Rees; 23 Church Row, Hampstead, London NE3 6UP (☎ 071 794 4936); Medical College of St Bartholomew's Hospital, West Smithfiel, London EC1A 7BE (☎ 071 601 7436, 071 606 7404)

REES, Prof (William) Linford Llewelyn; CBE (1977); s of Edward Parry Rees (d 1947), and Mary Rees (d 1952); *b* 24 Oct 1914; *Educ* Llanelli GS, Univ Coll Cardiff (BSc), Welsh Nat Sch of Medicine (MBBCh), Univ of London (DSc); *m* 1940, Catherine Magdalen, da of David Thomas Alltwen (d 1941); 2 s, 3 da; *Career* emeritus prof of psychiatry Univ of London, conslt physician Bart's 1980-, civilian conslt psychiatry to RAF to 1983; treas World Psychiatric Assoc 1966-78, vice pres Psychiatric Rehabilitation Assoc, pres RCPsych 1975-78, pres BMA 1978-79, chm Stress Fndn (vice pres) and Medico-Pharmaceutical Forum 1980, psychiatrist in chief and exec med dir Charter Medical 1984-89; Liveryman: Worshipful Co of Barber Surgns, Worshipful Soc of Apothecaries; Hon LLD Univ of Wales; distinguished fell American Psychiatric Assoc 1968, Hon FRCPsych, hon fell American Coll of Psychiatrists 1977; FRCP; *Recreations* photography, entertaining grandchildren, gardening, swimming; *Clubs* Athenaeum; *Style*— Prof Linford Rees, CBE; 62 Oakwood Ave, Purley, Surrey; 27 Speed House, Barbican, London EC1 (☎ 071 588 4881)

REES, Rt Rev (Leslie) Lloyd; s of Rees Thomas Rees (d 1939), of Trebanos, Swansea, Glam, and Elizabeth Rees (d 1965); *b* 14 April 1919; *Educ* Pontardawe GS, Kelham Theol Coll; *m* 5 Feb 1944, Rosamond (d 1989), da of Thomas Smith (d 1960); 2 s (Christopher Michael b 1946, Gerald Hugh b 1948); *Career* curate St Saviour's Roath Cardiff and asst chaplain HM Prison Cardiff 1942-45; chaplain: HM Prison Durham 1945-48, HM Prison Dartmoor (and vicar of Princetown) 1948-55, HM Prison Winchester 1955-62; chaplain gen of prisons, hon canon of Canterbury, chaplain to HM The Queen 1962-80, bishop of Shrewsbury 1980-86, hon canon Lichfield 1980-86, asst bishop diocese of Winchester 1986-; memb Parole Bd 1987-90; chaplain OStJ; Freeman of the City of London; *Recreations* music; *Style*— The Rt Rev L Lloyd Rees; Kingfisher Lodge, 20 Arle Gardens, Alresford, Hants (☎ 0962 734619)

REES, Prof Lovat Victor Charles; s of Sqdn Ldr Daniel George Rees (d 1960), of Nairn Scotland, and Margaret Jane, *née* Urquhart Stephen (d 1967); *b* 7 Nov 1927; *Educ* Robert Gordon's Coll Aberdeen, Univ of Aberdeen (BSc, PhD, DSc); *m* 12 Aug 1953, Elizabeth Margaret, da of Joseph Main (d 1989), of Stonehaven, Scotland; 1 s (Lovat Michael Graham b 1959), 3 da (Lesley Elizabeth b 1957, Shauna b 1961, Gillian Main b 1963); *Career* asst lectr Univ of Aberdeen 1952-53, sr scientific offr Awre Aldermaston 1953-57, prof Imperial Coll Univ of London 1958-; FRSC, CChem 1984; *Recreations* rifle shooting, golf; *Clubs* St Nicholas Rifle & Pistol, Chislehurst Brechin Golf; *Style*— Prof Lovat Rees; Pantiles, Yester Park, Chislehurst, Kent BR7 5DQ (☎ 081 467 2928); Imperial Coll of Sci Technol and Med, Chemistry Dept, S Kensington, London SW7 2AY (☎ 071 589 5111 ext 4606, fax 071 584 7596, telex 261503)

REES, Prof Martin John; s of Reginald Jackson Rees, and Harriette Joan, *née* Bett (d 1985); *b* 23 June 1942; *Educ* Shrewsbury, Trinity Coll Cambridge (MA, PhD); *Career* prof Univ of Sussex 1972-73, Plumian Prof of astronomy and experimental philosophy Univ of Cambridge 1973-, dir Cambridge Inst of Astronomy 1977-, Regents fell Smithsonian Inst Washington 1984-88, visiting prof Harvard Univ; Foreign Assoc US Nat Acad Sci; foreign hon memb American Acad of Arts and Scis, memb Pontificial Acad of Scis, hon fell Indian Acad of Scis; FRS; *Recreations* rural pursuits; *Style*— Prof Martin Rees, FRS; West Farm House, Orwell, Royston, Herts SG8 5QN; c/o King's College, Cambridge CB2 1ST

REES, Rt Hon Merlyn; PC (1974), MP (Lab) Morley and Leeds S 1983-; s of L Rees; *b* 18 Dec 1920; *Educ* Harrow Weald GS, Goldsmiths' Coll London, LSE, Univ of London Inst of Educn; *m* 1949, Colleen Faith, *née* Cleveley; 3 s; *Career* served WWII RAF; schoolmaster (economics and history) 1949-60, economics lectr 1962-63; fought (Lab) Harrow E 1955, 1959 (twice: general and by-election); MP (Lab) S Leeds 1963-1983, PPS to chllr Exchequer 1964, Parly under sec MOD (Army) 1965-66 and (RAF) 1966-68, Home Office 1968-70, memb Shadow Cabinet 1972-74 and again 1980-, oppn spokesman NI 1972-74, NI Sec 1974-76, Home Sec 1976-79, shadow Home Sec 1979-81, oppn front bench spokesman Energy 1981-83; memb: Franks Ctee on Official Secrets Act 1972, Franks Ctee on Falklands 1982; Hon DLL Univ of Wales; *Books* Northern Ireland, A Personal Perspective (1985); *Style*— The Rt Hon Merlyn Rees, MP; House of Commons, London SW1A 0AA

REES, Canon (Richard) Michael; s of Rev Richard Rees (d 1975), of Bedford, and Margaret Patricia, *née* Head; *b* 31 July 1935; *Educ* Brighton Coll, St Peter's Coll Oxford (MA), Tyndale Hall Bristol; *m* 6 Sept 1958, Yoma Patricia, da of Maj the Rev Cyril Herbert Hampton, of Branksome Park; 2 s (Timothy b 1960, Killadeas b 1961); *Career* ed Missionary Mandate 1956-69; curate: All Saints Crowborough Sussex 1959-62, Christ Church with Emmanuel Clifton Bristol 1962-64; chaplain Bristol ATC 1963-64, vicar Christ Church Clevedon Avon 1964-72, chaplain Clevedon Maternity Hosp, vicar Holy Trinity Church Cambridge 1972-84, chm Cambridge Cncl of Churches, chief sec Church Army 1984-90, canon missioner Chester 1990-; tstee: Disabled Christians Fellowship 1962- (chm 1962-72), Cambridge Work Relations Gp 1984-, Simeon's Tstees 1969-; govr St Brandon's Sch Clevedon 1969-87; *Recreations* photography, tropical fish, classical music; *Style*— The Rev Canon Michael Rees; 103 Five Ashes Rd, Westminster Park, Chester CH4 7QA (☎ 0244 680 804); The Chief Secretary,

Church Army, Independents Road, Blackheath, London SE3 9LG (☎ 081 318 1226, fax 081 318 5258)

REES, Nigel Thomas; s of (John Cedric) Stewart Rees (d 1989), and Frances Adeline, *née* Gleave (d 1982); *b* 5 June 1944; *Educ* Merchant Taylors' Sch (Crosby), New Coll Oxford (MA); *m* 6 May 1978, Susan Mary, da of Raymond Bates (d 1962); *Career* radio and TV presenter, author; BBC Radio 4: Today 1976-78, Quote... Unquote 1976-, Stop Press 1984-86; ITV: Amoebas to Zebras 1985-87, Challenge of the South 1987-88; *Books* Quote...Unquote (3 vols 1978-83), Graffiti (5 vols 1978-86), Sayings of the Century (1984), The Joy of Clichés (1984), Dictionary of Twentieth Century Quotations (1987), Why do We Say...? (1987), The Newsmakers (1987), Talent (1988), A Family Matter (1989), Why Do We Quote...? (1989), Dictionary of Popular Phrases (1990), Dictionary of Phrase and Allusion (1991); *Recreations* listening to music; *Style*— Nigel Rees, Esq; 24 Horbury Crescent, London W11 3NF (☎ 071 727 8535)

REES, Owen; CB (1991); s of John Trevor Rees (d 1970), of Trimsaran Dyfed, and Esther (d 1977), *née* Phillips; *b* 26 Dec 1934; *Educ* Llanelli GS, Univ of Manchester (BA); *m* 17 May 1958, Elizabeth, da of Harold Frank Gosby (d 1955), of Henley-on-Thames and Trimsaran; 1 s (David), 2 da (Philippa, Helen); *Career* Civil Serv: Bd of Trade 1959-69; Cabinet Office 1969-71; Welsh Office 1971-, head Euro Div Welsh Office 1972-75, sec for Welsh Educn 1977-78, head Educn Dept 1978-80, dir Indust Dept 1980-85, head Econ and Regnl Policy Gp 1985-89, head Agriculture Dept 1990-; *Style*— Owen Rees, Esq, CB; Welsh Office, Cathays Park, Cardiff (☎ 0222 823114)

REES, Peter John; s of Leslie Marchant Rees, of St Florence nr Tenby, Dyfed, and Betty, *née* Bass; *b* 21 April 1957; *Educ* Baines Sch Poulton-le-Fylde Lancashire, Downing Coll Cambridge (MA); *m* 15 Aug 1981, Allison Mary, da of Patrick John Williams, of Wallingford Oxon; 1 da (Megan b 7 May 1988); *Career* admitted slr 1981; ptnr Norton Rose 1987-; memb IBA (chm Sub Ctee Arch/Eng Law); Freeman Worshipful Co of Slrs (memb Insurance Sub Ctee); memb: RHS, Law Soc; ACIArb; *Recreations* rugby football, association football, golf, theatre, gardening; *Clubs* Stapleford Abbots Golf, Brentwood RUFC; *Style*— Peter Rees, Esq; Kempson House, Camomile St, London EC3 (☎ 071 283 2434, fax 071 588 1181, telex 883652)

REES, Baron (Life Peer UK 1987), of Goytre, Co Gwent; Peter Wynford Innes Rees; PC (1983), QC (1969); s of Maj-Gen Thomas Wynford Rees, CB, CIE, DSO, MC, Indian Army (d 1959), of Goytre Hall, Abergavenny, and Rosalie, da of Sir Charles Alexander Innes, KCSI, CIE (d 1959); *b* 9 Dec 1926; *Educ* Stowe, ChCh Oxford; *m* 1969, Mrs Anthea Wendell, da of late Maj J M Hyslop, Argyll & Sutherland Highlanders; *Career* served Scots Gds 1945-48; barr 1953, practised Oxford circuit; contested (C): Abertillery 1964 and 1965, Liverpool, West Derby, 1966; MP (C): Dover 1970-74, Dover and Deal 1974-83, Dover 1983-87; PPS to Solicitor-Gen 1972; min of state HM Treasury 1979-81; min for Trade 1981-83, chm sec to Treasury and memb Cabinet 1983-85; memb Ct and Cncl Museum of Wales; chm: Lasmo plc, Economic Forestry Gp plc; dep chm Leopold Joseph plc; *Clubs* Boodle's, Beefsteak, White's; *Style*— The Rt Hon Lord Rees, PC, QC; Goytre Hall, Abergavenny, Gwent; 39 Headfort Place, London SW1X 7DE

REES, Peter Wynne; s of Gwynne Rees, of Virginia Water, Surrey, and late Elizabeth Rodda, *née* Hynam; *b* 26 Sept 1948; *Educ* Pontardawe GS, Whitchurch GS, Bartlett Sch of Architecture, UCL (BSc) Welsh Sch of Architecture, Univ of Wales (B Arch), Poly of the South Bank (BTP); *Career* architectural asst Historic Buildings Div GLC 1971-72, asst to Gordon Cullen CBE 1973-75, architect Historic Areas Conservation Div DOE 1975-79, asst chief planning offr Borough of Lambeth 1979-85; Corp of London: controller of planning 1985-87, city planning offr 1987-; tstee Bldg Conservation Tst, fndr memb and dir Br Cncl Foreign Offices; life memb: SPAB, Nat Tst; Freeman City of London 1985, memb: RIBA 1975, FRTPI 1982, FRSA 1988; *Style*— Peter Wynne Rees, Esq; City Planning Offr, Corp of London, Guildhall, London EC2P 2EJ (☎ 071 260 1700, fax 071 260 1119, telex 265608 LONDON G)

REES, Philip; s of John Trevor Rees, of Ebbw Vale, Gwent, and Olwen Muriel, *née* Jones (d 1982); *b* 1 Dec 1941; *Educ* Monmouth Sch, Univ of Bristol (LLB); *m* 6 Aug 1969, Catherine, da of Joseph Stephen Good, of Cardiff; 1 s (David Stephen b 27 Aug 1970), 1 da (Siân Catrin b 1 Oct 1973); *Career* barr, rec Crown Ct 1983-; *Recreations* music, sport; *Clubs* Cardiff and County; *Style*— Philip Rees, Esq; 35 South Rise, Llanishen, Cardiff CF4 5RF (☎ 0222 754364); 34 Park Place, Cardiff CF1 3BA (☎ 0222 382731, fax 0222 22542)

REES, Dr Richard John William (Dick); CMG (1979); s of William Rees, MVO (d 1952), of London, and Gertrude Ethel, *née* Smith (d 1959); *b* 11 Aug 1917; *Educ* E Sheen County Sch, Univ of London, Guy's Hosp Med Sch (BSc, MB BS, FRCPath, FRCP); *m* 1942, Kathleen, da of Joseph Harris, MVO (d 1967), of Yorks; 3 da (Lorna, Hazel, Diana); *Career* Capt RAMC Army Blood Transfusion Service, served in N Africa and Italy campaigns 1942-46; asst clinical pathologist Guy's Hosp 1946-49, memb Scientific Staff Nat Inst of Med Res London 1949-69, head of Laboratory for Leprosy and Mycubacterial Res Nat Inst Med Res 1969-82, chm Lepra Med Advsy Bd 1963-1987; pres Section of Comparative Med Royal Soc of Med 1975, memb Lepra Exec Ctee 1964-87; vice pres: Lepra 1987-, Int Leprosy Assoc 1988-; memb MRC Tropical Med Res Bd 1968-72, WHO, Advsy Panel on Leprosy 1969-, Editorial Bd of Leprosy Reviews 1960-; hon memb Section of Comparative Med RSM; *Publications* more than 200 Scientific papers on: basic and applied studies on animals and man relevant to pathology, immunology and chemotherapy of leprosy and tuberculosis; *Recreations* theatre, gardening; *Style*— Dr Dick Rees, CMG; Highfield, Highwood Hill, London NW7 4EU (☎ 081 959 2021)

REES, Roger Thomas; s of Aerwyn Howell Rees, of Capel Hendre, Ammanford, Dyfed, S Wales, and Llowella Francis, *née* Roberts; *b* 16 Oct 1943; *Educ* Mercer's Sch, Colfe's GS, Royal Dental Hosp, St Bartholomews Med Coll Univ of London (MB BS, BDS); *m* 10 Aug 1969, Sandra Jones, da of David Williams, of Cross Hands, Dyfed, S Wales; 1 s (Richard Hywell b 9 Dec 1973), 1 da (Sara Jane b 22 June 1977); *Career* sr registrar Kings Coll Hosp London and Queen Victoria Hosp E Grinstead 1974-79, tech advsr to Nigerian Mil Govt in Maxillo-Facial Surgery (seconded by Dept Overseas Admin) 1976; conslt oral surgn: Norfolk and Norwich Health Authy, Gt Yarmouth and Waveney Dist Health Authy 1979-; chm Dist Dental Ctee; memb: Br Dental Assoc, Br Med Assoc; Freedman City of London 1968; fell Br Assoc of Maxillo-Facial Surgns 1979; FDSRCS; *Style*— Roger Rees, Esq; Norfolk & Norwich Hospital, Brunswick Road, Norwich, Norfolk NR1 3SR (☎ 0603 628377)

REES, Dr (Robert) Simon Owen; s of Edward Bertram Rees (d 1985), of Carmarthen, Dyfed, and Dorothy, *née* Owen; *b* 24 May 1933; *Educ* Harrow, Gonville and Caius Coll Cambridge (MA, MB BChir), Westminster Med Sch Univ of London; *m* 13 Dec 1958, Dr Jacqueline Jane Rees, da of James Layton, of Hampstead, London; 3 s (Rupert b 18 Aug 1962, Jasper b 7 Dec 1964, Sheridan b 13 March 1967); *Career* conslt radiologist Nat Heart Hosp London 1966-90, conslt radiologist St Bartholomews Hosp London 1967-88, dean Inst of Cardiology Univ of London 1969-72, dir of radiology Royal Brompton Hosp 1988-, dir and chm Scientific Advsy Ctee CORDA Charity; Liveryman Worshipful Soc of Apothecaries 1964; memb: Br Cardiac Soc, Br Inst of Radiology; FRCP, FRCR, FRSM; *Books* Clinical Cardiac Radiology (1973, 2 ed 1980); *Recreations* hunting, driving, real tennis, choral singing, skiing; *Clubs* Boodle's, MCC; *Style*— Dr Simon Rees; Rubbin Cottage, Treyford, Midhurst, West Sussex GU29 0LD (☎ 0730 825444)

REES, Sir (Charles William) Stanley; TD (1950), QC (1957), DL (Sussex 1968); s of Dr David Charles Rees (d 1917); first supt and med tutor to London Sch of Tropical Medicine (went to S Africa in 1901 at invitation of Cape Govt to deal with outbreak of bubonic plague, where he remained until his death from typhus), and Myrtle May, *née* Dolley (d 1950); *b* 30 Nov 1907; *Educ* St Andrew's Coll Grahamstown S Africa, Univ Coll Oxford (BA, BCL); *m* 1934, Jean Isabel (d 1985), da of Laurence Henry Munro (d 1906), of Melbourne, Aust; 1 s; *Career* 2 Lt 99 Anti-Aircraft RA Regt (London Welsh) 1939, Capt 1940, JAG's Office in Home Cmd 1940-43, Lt-Col 1943, i/c JAG's branch HQ Palestine Cmd 1944-45, ret as Hon Lt-Col 1945; barr Inner Temple 1931, rec of Croydon 1961-62, bencher 1962, Judge of the High Ct of Justice Family Div (formerly Probate, Divorce and Admty Div) 1962-77, chm E Sussex QS 1964-70 (dep chm 1959-64), pt/t memb Ct of Appeal 1979-82; vice patron Brighton Coll 1983- (govr 1954-83, pres 1974-83), chm Statutory Pharmaceutical Soc of GB 1980-81; kt 1962; *Recreations* walking, gardening; *Clubs* United Oxford and Cambridge, Sussex; *Style*— Sir Stanley Rees, TD, DL; Lark Rise, Lyoth Lane, Lindfield, Haywards Heath, W Sussex RH16 2QA (☎ 0444 482049)

REES, William Hurst; s of Richard Rees (d 1956), of Bushey, Herts, and Florence Ada, *née* Bonner (d 1975); *b* 12 April 1917; *Educ* Watford GS, Coll of Estate Mgmnt London (BSc); *m* 15 Feb 1941, Elizabeth Mary, da of Dr A Wight (d 1975), of Reading; 2 s (William Andrew b 6 Feb 1944, John Hurst b 12 Feb 1948), 1 da (Jacqueline (Mrs Padley) b 8 Feb 1950); *Career* Army 1940-46, cmmd 2 Lt RA 1941, transferred RE 1943, liaison offr Belgian Army Engrs SO 2 RE, Maj RE 1946; head of Valuation Dept Coll of Estate Mgmnt 1946-51; princ in private practice: Richard Ellis & Son London 1951-61, Turner Rudge & Turner E Grinstead Sussex 1961-73; memb Lands Tbnl 1973-89; Hon FSVA, hon memb Rating Surveyor's Assoc; FRICS; *Books* Modern Methods of Valuation (co-author, 6 edn 1970), Valuation: Principles into Practice (ed, 3 edn 1988); *Recreations* music, opera; *Style*— W H Rees, Esq; Brendon, Carlton Rd, S Godstone, Surrey RH9 8LD (☎ 0342 892 109)

REES-DAVIES, William Rupert (Billy); QC (1973); s of Sir William Rees-Davies, KC, JP, DL (sometime Lib MP for Pembroke and chief justice Hong Kong, d 1939); *b* 19 Nov 1916; *Educ* Eton, Trinity Coll Cambridge; *m* 1, 1959, Jane Lesa, *née* Mander; 2 da; m 2, 1982, Sharlie Kingsley; *Career* served WWII Welsh Gds; called to the Bar Inner Temple 1939; MP (C): Isle of Thanet 1953-74, Thanet W 1974-83; chm: All Party Ctee for Tourism 1965-68, Cons Ctee for Tourism; Cons ldr Select Ctee Health and Social Servs 1980-83; *Clubs* MCC, Hawks, Turf; *Style*— Billy Rees-Davies Esq, QC; 1 Crown Office Row, Temple, London EC4 (☎ 071 583 3724); 5 Lord North St, London SW1; Gore Street Manor, Monkton, Thanet, Kent

REES-JONES, Elizabeth Helen; da of William Jones (d 1980), of Goring on Thames, Oxon, and Elizabeth, *née* Thomas; *b* 9 Sept 1944; *Educ* The Alice Ottley Sch Worcester, Trinity Coll Dublin (BA); *m* George, s of Anthony G Cambitzi; 1 s (Alexander b 1977), 1 da (Anastasia b 1982); *Career* promotions ed Harpers' Bazaar 1967-71, promotions conslt National Magazine Co 1975-87 (promotions dir 1971-75), md Elle 1987-88, jt chm News International/Hachette 1987-, md Murchoch Magazines 1987-; dir Periodical Publishers Association; memb: Women of the Year Ctee 1972-, Birthright Appeals Ctee 1975-, ICA Appeals Ctee 1987-; *Recreations* travel, spectator sports; *Clubs* The Vanderbilt Racquet; *Style*— Ms Elizabeth Rees-Jones; Murdoch Magazines, King's House, 10 Haymarket, London SW1Y 4BP (☎ 071 839 8272)

REES-MOGG, Baron (Life Peer UK 1988), of Hinton Blewitt, Co Avon; William; s of late Edmund Fletcher Rees-Mogg, JP, of Cholwell House, Somerset, and Beatrice, da of Daniel Warren, of New York State, USA; *b* 14 July 1928; *Educ* Charterhouse, Balliol Coll Oxford (MA); *m* 1962, Gillian Shakespeare, yr da of Thomas Richard Morris, JP, Mayor of St Pancras 1962; 2 s (Hon Thomas Fletcher b 1966, Hon Jacob William b 1969), 3 da (Hon Emma Beatrice b 1962, Hon Charlotte Louise b 1964, Hon Annunziata Mary b 1979); *Career* dir: GEC, J Rothschild Holdings plc, M & G Group; chm: Pickering & Chatto (antiquarian booksellers & publishers), Sidgwick & Jackson (publishers) 1985-88; editor The Times 1967-81; dir: The Times 1968-81, Times Newspapers Ltd 1978, GEC; vice chm BBC 1981-86; chm: Arts Cncl 1982-88, Broadcasting Standards Cncl 1988-, Sinclair-Stevenson Ltd 1989-; High Sheriff Somerset 1978; kt 1981; *Books* An Humbler Heaven (1977), The Reigning Error: The Crisis of World Inflation (1974), Blood in the Streets (1987); *Clubs* Garrick, Carlton; *Style*— The Rt Hon Lord Rees-Mogg; The Old Rectory, Hinton Blewitt, nr Bristol, Avon (☎ 0761 52489); 3 Smith Square, London SW1; Pickering & Chatto Ltd, 17 Pall Mall, London SW1Y 5NB (☎ 071 930 2515)

REES ROBERTS, Tristan William Otway; s of Peter William Rees Roberts, of Hants, and Ursula Vivien, *née* McCannell; *b* 11 April 1948; *Educ* Frensham Heights, Farnham GS, Trinity Hall Cambridge (MA, BArch, DipArch); *m* 21 March 1970, Anna Ingelin, da of Edmund George Noel Greaves, of Cambridge; 1 s (Marcus Lucien Branch b 1975), 2 da (Saria Mona Natascha b 1973, Ariana Lucia Katrina b 1979); *Career* architect in private practice with Henry Freeland 1980-; most important cmmns: Kings Coll, Temple Bar, Thorpe Hall, Bishop's Palace Ely; Freeman City of London 1986; *Books* painting, hill walking; *Style*— Tristan Rees Roberts, Esq; 13 Caius Terrace, Glisson Rd, Cambridge CB1 2HJ (☎ 0223 68101); Freeland Rees Roberts Architects, 25 City Rd, Cambridge (☎ 0223 66555)

REES-WILLIAMS, Hon Morgan; s of 1 Baron Ogmore, TD, PC (d 1976) and hp of bro, 2 Baron; *b* 19 Dec 1937; *Educ* Mill Hill Sch; *m* 1, 1964 (m dis 1970), Patricia, da of C Paris Jones; m 2, 1972 (m dis 1976), Roberta, da of Capt Alec Stratford Cunningham-Reid, DFC; m 3, 1990, Beata, da of Zdzislaw Solski; *Career* Lt R Regt of Wales (TA); *Style*— The Hon Morgan Rees-Williams; 50 Novello St, London SW6 4JB

REESE, Dr Alan John Morris; TD (1958; clasps: 1964, 1970, 1976), JP (Middx 1974); s of Joseph Reese (d 1968), of Plymouth, Devon, and Emily, *née* Brand (d 1984); *b* 26 Aug 1920; *Educ* Plymouth Coll, Bart's Med Coll Univ of London (MB BS, MD); *m* 24 Jan 1959, Margaret Denise, da of Ernest George Turner (d 1969), of Battersea, London; 1 s (Charles b 1962), 1 da (Victoria b 1960); *Career* emergency cmmn RAMC 1945; served: Egypt, Palestine, Cyrenaica, Malta; war substantive Capt 1946, released 1948; TA: Capt 1948, Maj 1953, Lt Col 1966; TAVR 1967, Lt Col RARO; sr registrar in pathology St George's Hosp London 1950-54, lectr in pathology Univ of Bristol 1954-56, sr lectr in pathology Inst of Basic Med Scis Univ of London RCS 1956-82, WHO prof of pathology Univ of Mandalay Burma 1963-64, hon conslt in morbid anatomy Whittington Hosp 1966-82, senate of Univ of London 1974-83; examiner in pathology: RCS 1973-79, RCSEd 1978-;called to the Bar Middle Temple 1955; memb Islington Cons Assoc 1960-, contested seats on Islington Borough Cncl, vice pres Islington S and Finsbury Cons Assoc 1987-, contested Lewisham W on ILEA 1986, Cons cncllr and chm Health Ctee Met Borough of St Pancreas 1959-62; govr Godolphin and Latymer Sch 1976-85 OStJ 1974; Freeman City of London 1944, Liveryman Worshipful Soc of Apothecaries 1948- (Yeoman 1943-48); MRCPath 1963, FRCPath 1968, LMSSA 1943; *Books* The Principles of Pathology (1981); *Recreations* fishing; *Clubs* Army and Navy; *Style*— Dr Alan Reese, TD, JP; 9 Hopping Lane, Canonbury, London N1 2NU (☎ 071 226 2088); 14 Herd St, Marlborough, Wilts SN8 1DF (☎ 0672 512339)

REESE, Colin Bernard; s of Joseph Reese (d 1968), of London, and Emily Reese (d 1984); *b* 29 July 1930; *Educ* Dartington Hall Sch, Clare Coll Cambridge (BA, PhD, MA, ScD); *m* 29 June 1968, Susanne Leslie, da of Joseph Charles Henry Bird (d 1985); 1 s (William Thomas b 11 July 1972), 1 da (Lucy b 13 Aug 1970); *Career* res fell: Clare Coll Cambridge 1956-59, Harvard Univ 1957-58; Univ demonstrator in chemistry Univ of Cambridge 1959-63, official fell and dir of studies in chemistry Clare Coll 1959-73; Univ of Cambridge: asst dir of res 1963-64, lectr in chemistry 1964-73; Daniell prof of chemistry King's Coll London 1973- (fell London 1989); FRS 1981; *Style—* Prof Colin Reese, FRS; 21 Rozel Rd, London SW4 0EY (☎ 071 498 0230); Dept of Chem, King's Coll London, Strand, London WC2R 2LS (☎ 071 873 2260)

REEVE, Adrian Grantley; s of Leonard Alfred Reeve (d 1979), and Margaret Auld Nizbet, *née* Nicol; *b* 14 Jan 1957; *Educ* Peter Symonds GS, Univ Coll of Wales (BSc), Cranfield Sch of Mgmnt (MBA); *m* 3 Jan 1983, Alison Claire, da of John Lionel Jacobs, of Southampton; 2 s (Daniel Jacob, Adam Scott); *Career* sales and mktg dir RH Tech Industries Ltd 1982-86, business devpt exec Bowthorpe Holdings plc 1988-89, md Wessex Advanced Switching Products Ltd 1989-90, sr conslt World Class International Ltd 1990-; tstee Fairfax Tst, memb Lloyd's; MInstD; *Recreations* skiing, swimming, tennis; *Clubs* IOD, Pall Mall; *Style—* Adrian Reeve, Esq; 17 Fairfax Close, Winchester, Hampshire SO22 4LP (☎ 0962 851586); World Class International Ltd, Technology House, Parklands Business Park, Forest Road, Denmead, Hampshire PO7 6XP (☎ 0705 268133, fax 0705 268160)

REEVE, Anthony; CMG (1986); s of Sidney Reeve, of Cheltenham, Glos, and Dorothy, *née* Mitchell; *b* 20 Oct 1938; *Educ* Queen Elizabeth GS Wakefield, Marling Sch Stroud, Merton Coll Oxford (MA); *m* 1 Feb 1964 (m dis 1988), Pamela Margaret Angus; 1 s (James b 1968), 2 da (Emily b 1972, Anna b 1977); *Career* Lever Brothers and Associates 1962-65; HM Dip Serv: joined 1965, MECAS 1966-68, asst political agent Abu Dhabi 1968-70, FCO 1970-73, first sec (later cnsllr) Washington 1973-78, cnsllr FCO 1978-81, cnsllr Cairo 1981-84, cnsllr later asst under sec of state FCO 1984-88, HM ambass to the Hashemite Kingdom of Jordan 1988-; *Recreations* writing, music; *Clubs* United Oxford and Cambridge Univ, Leander; *Style—* Anthony Reeve, Esq, CMG; c/o FCO (Amman), King Charles St, London SW1A 2AH

REEVE, Carol Ann; da of John Reeve, and Hilda, *née* Foxall; *b* 26 May 1950; *Educ* Westcliff HS For Girls; *Career* dir and co sec Talk of the South Ltd 1986- (joined 1972), dir Essex Radio plc 1979-, co sec Manzi Leisure Ltd 1986-, ptnr Reco Shoes; *Style—* Miss Carol Reeve; 42 Springfield Drive, Westcliff On Sea, Essex SSO ORA (☎ 0702 348 707); Talk Of The South, Lucy Rd, Southend-on-Sea SS1 2AU (☎ 0702 467921); Essex Radio, Clifftown Rd, Southend-on-Sea SS1 1SX

REEVE, David Richard; s of Richard Walter Reeve, of Angmering, Sussex, and Constance Katherine, *née* Cullum; *b* 7 April 1937; *Educ* Haileybury & ISC, Bloxham Sch, Eaton Hall OCTU; *m* 1, 15 July 1962 (m dis 1981), Anne, da of Richard Morris, of Capetown, SA; 1 s (Simon Christopher b 1969), 1 da (Johanna Helen b 1966); m 2, Margarita Klara, da of Cyril Gillam, of W Mersea, Essex; *Career* W H Smith & Son 1959-72, dir Courtney Pope Holdings plc 1987-, md Versatile Fittings Ltd 1988; Liveryman Worshipful Co of Ironmongers, Freeman City of London 1958; *Recreations* rugby, golf, shooting; *Clubs* Blue Boar RFC, Beckenham RFC, Kent RFC, Oxfordshire Referees Soc; *Style—* David Reeve, Esq; 1 Lime Grove, Southmoor, Abingdon, Oxon OX13 5DN; Versatile Fittings Ltd, Bicester Rd, Aylesbury, Bucks (☎ 0296 83481, fax 0296 437596)

REEVE, James Ernest; CMG (1982); s of Ernest Stanley Reeve (d 1970), of Surrey, and Margaret Anthea, *née* James (d 1939); *b* 8 June 1926; *Educ* Bishop's Stortford Coll Herts; *m* 20 Aug 1947, Lillian Irene, da of Capt Albert Edward Watkins, OBE, of Epsom, Surrey; 1 s (Christopher b 30 April 1953), 1 da (Sandra b 8 Oct 1955); *Career* HM Dip Serv 1949-83: HM vice consul Ahwaz and Khorramshahr Iran 1949-51, UN Gen Assembly Paris 1951, private sec to Rt Hon Selwyn Lloyd FO 1951-53, HM Embassy Washington 1953-57, HM Embassy Bangkok 1957-59, Northern Dept FO 1959-61, HM consul Frankfurt W Germany 1961-65, 1 sec HM Embassy Libya 1965-69, first sec HM Embassy Budapest 1970-72, chargé d'affaires and csllr for estab of first Br Embassy to GDR E Berlin 1973-75, HM consul gen Zurich and Liechtenstein 1975-80, HM min and consul gen Milan 1980-83; dir Sprester Investmts Ltd 1983-; memb secretariat Int Aluminium Inst London 1983-; *Recreations* theatre, tennis, skiing, travel; *Clubs* RAC; *Style—* James Reeve, Esq, CMG; 20 Glenmore House, Richmond Hill, Richmond, Surrey (☎ 081 948 3153); c/o IPAI, New Zealand House, Haymarket, London SW1 (☎ 071 930 0528)

REEVE, John; s of Clifford Alfred Reeve, and Irene Mary Turnidge; *b* 13 July 1944; *Educ* Westcliff HS; *m* 21 Dec 1974, Sally Diane; 1 da (Emily Virginia Weston b 27 Jan 1979); *Career* articled clerk Selbey Smith & Earle 1962-67, audit sr Peat Marwick Mitchell & Co 1967-68, Vickers Ltd/ Roneo Vickers Group 1968-76 (commercial dir Furniture and Systems Div, mangr Gp Fin Evaluation and Planning), dir Accounting Servs Wilkinson Match Ltd 1976-77, Amalgamated Metal Corporation Ltd 1977-80 (controller Physical Trading Div, corp controller); gp fin dir: The British Aluminium Co plc 1980-83, Mercantile House Holdings Plc 1983-87, gp md Sun Life Corporation plc 1988-; *Recreations* yachting, music, theatre; *Clubs* Essex Yacht; *Style—* John Reeve, Esq; Starvelarks, 85 Warren Road, Leigh on Sea, Essex SS9 3TT (☎ 0702 556769); Sun Life Corporation plc, 107 Cheapside, London EC2V 6DU (☎ 071 606 7788, 071 796 2216, telex 8811871)

REEVE, Kathryn May; da of Frank Evelyn Heppenstall, of Epsom Downs, Surrey, and Doris May, *née* Davison; *b* 22 July 1948; *Educ* Sutton HS GPDST, New Hall Cambridge (MA); *m* 14 April 1971, Peter Joseph Reeve, s of late Joseph Reeve, of Leamington Spa, Warwickshire; *Career* admitted slr 1973; ptnr Shoosmiths & Harrison 1989-; treas Leamington Hastings Parochial Church Cncl, assoc Royal Photographic Soc, pres Dunchurch Photographic Soc; memb Law Soc; *Recreations* natural history, photography, tennis; *Style—* Mrs Kathryn Reeve; 23 Warwick St, Rugby, Warwickshire CV21 3DP (☎ 0788 73111, telex 265871, fax 0788 536651)

REEVE, Michael Arthur Ferard; s of Maj Wilfrid Norman Reeve, OBE, MC (d 1976), of 6 Bramerton St, London, and Agnes Bourdon, *née* Ferard; *b* 7 Jan 1937; *Educ* Eton, Univ Coll Oxford (MA); *m* 30 Dec 1970, Charmian Gay, da of David Roydon Rooper, of 5 Albert Place London; 2 s (Hugo b 10 Dec 1973, Luke b 15 Sept 1977); *Career* dir: Elliott Gp of Peterborough 1969-83, Charterhouse Bank 1970-74, Rea Bros 1977-80, Collins Collins & Rawlence (Hamptons estate agents) 1982-85, underwriter Lloyds 1978; md Copley & Bank 1974-80, Greyhound Bank 1981-87; The Tregeare Company Ltd 1981-, Scottish and Mercantile Investment Trust plc 1990; memb: Royal Inst of Int Affrs, The Pilgrims; FCA 1964; *Recreations* horses, gardening, reading; *Clubs* Institute of Directors, Royal Over-Seas League; *Style—* Michael Reeve, Esq; 138 Oakwood Court, London W14 8JL (☎ 071 602 2624)

REEVE, Robin Martin; s of Percy Martin Reeve, of Lancing, W Sussex, and Cicely Nora, *née* Parker; *b* 22 Nov 1934; *Educ* Hampton Sch, Gonville and Caius Coll Cambridge (BA, MA), Univ of Bristol (PGCE); *m* 25 July 1959, Brianne Ruth, da of Leonard Stephen Hall (d 1953), of Ashford, Middx; *Career* asst master: King's Coll Sch 1958-62 (headmaster 1980-), Lancing Coll 1962-80 (head of History Dept 1962-80, dir of studies 1975); chm Govrs Rosemead Sch W Sussex; HMC 1980-, SHA; *Recreations* gardening, architecture, reading; *Clubs* East India Public Schs; *Style—* Robin Reeve, Esq; 20 Burghley Rd, London SW19 5BH; King's College School, Southside, Wimbledon Common, London SW19 4TT (☎ 081 947 9311)

REEVE, Sir (Charles) Trevor; s of William George Reeve (d 1918), and Elsie, *née* Bowring (d 1952), of Wokingham, Berks; *b* 4 July 1915; *Educ* Winchester, Trinity Coll Oxford; *m* 1941, Marjorie (d 1990), da of Charles Evelyn Browne, of Eccles, Lancs; *Career* served WWII, Maj 10 Royal Hussars (PWO), BEF, MEF and CMF, GSO (2) (SD) 10 Corps (despatches), Staff Coll Camberley 1945; called to the Bar Inner Temple 1946, QC 1965, bencher 1965, county ct judge 1968, circuit judge 1972, judge of the High Court of Justice (Family Div) 1973-88; kt 1973; *Clubs* Garrick, Royal North Devon Golf, Sunningdale Golf; *Style—* Sir Trevor Reeve; 95 Abingdon Rd, Kensington, London W8 6QU

REEVES, Anthony Alan; s of Allen Joseph Reeves, MBE, (d 1976), and Alice Turner, *née* Pointon (d 1966); *b* 5 March 1943; *Educ* Hanley HS; *m* 19 Aug 1967, Jane, da of William Thowless (d 1942); 1 s (Max b 1972), 2 da (Rachel b 1969, Ruth b 1974); *Career* admitted slr 1965; managing ptnr Kent Jones and Done Slrs 1978; non-exec dir: Steelite Int plc 1983-, Bullers plc 1984-86, Butler Woodhouse Ltd 1987-; chm The CAS Gp plc 1985-90; sr tstee The Beth Johnson Fndn 1972-, memb N Staffs Med Inst Cncl 1979-82, non-exec dir Stoke City FC 1984-85, chm Law Soc Working Party coal mining subsidence 1985-; memb Law Soc; *Recreations* fishing, shooting, supporting ballet, contemporary art; *Style—* Anthony Reeves, Esq; Churchill House, 47 Regent Rd, Hanley, Stoke on Trent ST1 3RQ (☎ 0782 202020, fax 0782 202040, car 0836 726633)

REEVES, Anthony Henry; s of Herbert Henry Reeves, of Limpsfield Chart, Surrey, and Kathleen Norah Reeves (d 1963); *b* 8 Sept 1940; *Educ* Sir Walter St Johns; *m* 1972, Jacqueline, da of Herbert Mitchell Newton-Clare, of Edgeworth, Cirencester; 4 s, 2 da; *Career* former dir Alfred Marks Bureau Ltd, founded Graphics Staff Agency (later acquired by Alfred Marks Gp), estab ORS (Overseas Recruitment Servs) Ltd (acquired HCC 1984) as part of Alfred Marks Gp; purchased ORS Ltd 1981, exec md Hosp Capital Corp 1984-86, pres and chief exec Lifetime Corp USA (acquired HCC 1986) 1986-; *Recreations* golf, squash, tennis; *Clubs* Royal Automobile, Royal Wimbledon Golf, Reform, Arts; *Style—* Anthony Reeves Esq; Spur Lodge, 142 Upper Richmond Road West, London SW14 8DS (☎ 081 878 4738)

REEVES, Christopher Reginald; s of Reginald Raymond Reeves (d 1989), and Dora Grace, *née* Tucker (d 1962); *b* 14 Jan 1936; *Educ* Malvern; *m* June 1965, Stella Jane, da of Cdr Patrick Whinney, of Guernsey; 3 s; *Career* Nat Serv cmmnd Rifle Bde (served Kenya and Malaya) 1955-58; merchant banker; Bank of England 1958-63, Hill Samuel & Co Ltd 1963-67; Morgan Grenfell & Co Ltd: joined 1968, dir 1970, head Banking Div 1972, dep chm and dep chief exec 1975, jt chm 1985-87; dep chm and gp chief exec Morgan Grenfell Gp plc (formerly Morgan Grenfell Holdings Ltd) 1985-87, sr advsr to Pres Merrill Lynch Capital Markets 1988; dir: BICC plc 1982-, Andrew Weir & Co Ltd 1982-, Allianz International Insurance Co Ltd 1983-, Oman Int Bank 1984-, Int Freehold Properties (Supervisory Bd) 1988-; vice chm Merrill Lynch International Ltd 1989- (chief exec 1980-87, dep chm 1984-87); *Recreations* sailing, shooting, skiing; *Clubs* Boodle's, Royal Southern Yacht; *Style—* Christopher Reeves Esq; 64 Flood St, London SW3 5TE

REEVES, (Charles) Christopher Seward; s of late Maj Charles Westcott Reeves, OBE, of Enfield, Middx, and Winifred Mary Reeves; *b* 6 Oct 1917; *Educ* Aldenham; *m* 1, 3 April 1948, Betty Rosanne Roberts (d 1987); 1 s (Robert Christopher b 1952), 1 da (Bettina b 1949); m 2, 10 Dec 1988, Elizabeth Mary (Bunty), da of late Arthur Brown; *Career* WWII Home Guard 1941-45; selling and admin Fitch and Son Ltd (now Fitch Lovell Gp) 1939-53, selling EM Denny Ltd 1953-55, selling Danish Bacon Co Ltd 1955-63, sales mangr Mathews and Skailes Ltd London 1963-73, mangr Atalanta (UK) Ltd London (subsid of Atlanta Corpn NY USA), now ret; fndr chm Enfield Young Cons 1946, memb local Cons pty 1946-, pres Chislehurst Cons Commons Branch, chm Bromle Youth Tst, govr four local schs, chm of govrs Kemnal Manor Sch 1982-88; cncllr London Borough of Bromley 1967-, Mayor of Bromley 1986-87, memb Bromley Family Practitioners Ctee, chm Nat Benevolent Inst; Liveryman Worshipful Co of Skinners; *Recreations* bridge, sailing, petanque; *Style—* Christopher Reeves, Esq; 6 Manor Place, Chislehurst, Kent BR7 5QH (☎ 081 467 5247); 114 Bay View, Hermanus Cape, RSA

REEVES, David Arthur; s of Frank Clement Reeves (d 1950), of Southborough, nr Tunbridge Wells, Kent, and Constance Easton, *née* Fisher; *b* 12 July 1934; *Educ* Skinners Sch Tunbridge Wells Kent; *m* 22 March 1958, Margaret Evelyn, da of Thomas James Thrower (d 1975), of Tunbridge Wells, Kent; 2 s (Martin Grahem b 1961, Nigel David b 1964), 1 da (Lisa Marie b 1969); *Career* md Tunbridge Wells Flooring Co Ltd 1978-85; pres Southern Counties Amateur Swimming Assoc 1982, chief exec Amateur Swimming Assoc 1985; memb: BOA, Commonwealth Games Cncl for Eng; fell Inst of Swimming Teachers and Coaches; *Recreations* all sports, photography, philately; *Style—* David Reeves, Esq; 3 Slate Brook Cl, Groby, Leicester LE6 0EE; Amateur Swimming Association, Harold Fern House, Derby Sq, Loughborough, Leics LE11 OAL (☎ 0509 230431, fax 0509 610720, telex 347072 AMSWIM G)

REEVES, David Robert Christopher; s of Harold Charles Reeves (d 1967), of Bristol, and Phylis, *née* Boalch; *b* 19 May 1946; *Educ* Backwell Comprehensive, Bristol Poly (HND, DMS); *m* 1, 10 Oct 1970 (m dis 1977), Dierdre Elizabeth, da of Charles Henry Gravatte (d 1970); 1 da (Zoë Catherine b 24 April 1971); m 2, Elizabeth Jean Barnes; 1 da (Claire Louise Catherine b 14 April 1979); *Career* RAFVR (T) 1962-76; PA to Fin Controller Concorde 1968-69, graduate trainee Esso Petroleum Ltd 1969-71, chief exec G and R Consultants Ltd 1971-77; ptnr: Sapper Atkins Reeves & Co Accountants 1977-81, Featherstone Leach Reeves & Co Accountants 1981-84, Atkin Reeves & Co 1984; chief exec Collegia Ltd; co author: The Care of the Elderly a National Design (paper, with Sir Ronald Gibson), Collegias Answer to an Ageing Society (paper, with J L Firth); *Recreations* flying, swimming, sailing, reading; *Clubs* RAF; *Style—* David Reeves, Esq; Collegia Ltd, Makeney Hall, Makeney Milford, Derby DE5 ORS (☎ 0332 842562, fax 0332 842638, car 0860 218383)

REEVES, Rev Donald St John; s of Henry St John Reeves (d 1984), and Barbara Eugn, *née* Rusbridger (d 1967); *b* 18 May 1934; *Educ* Sherborne, Queens' Coll Cambridge; *Career* lectr Brit Cncl 1957-60, curate All Saints Maidstone 1963-65, domestic chaplain to Bishop of Southwark 1965-68, vicar St Peter's St Helier 1968-80, rector St James's Piccadilly 1980-; memb: Gen Synod of C of E, London Diocesan Synod; *Books* Church and State (ed, 1984), For God's Sake (1988), Making Sense of Religion (1989); *Recreations* playing the organ, gardening, bee-keeping, watching TV soap operas; *Clubs* Arts, RAC; *Style—* Rev Donald Reeves

REEVES, Helen May; OBE (1986); da of Leslie Percival William Reeves, (d 1967), and Helen Edith, *née* Brown; *b* 22 Aug 1945; *Educ* Dartford Girls GS, Univ of Nottingham; *Career* probation offr later sr probation offr Inner London Probation Serv 1967-79, dir Nat Assoc of Victims Support Schemes 1980-; *Recreations* gardening, food, architecture; *Clubs* Soc of Friends; *Style—* Ms Helen Reeves; Victim Support, Cranmer House, 39 Brixton Rd, London SW9 6DZ (☎ 071 735 9166)

REEVES, Jonathan Harvey William; s of Lt-Col William Robert Reeves, DSO, of Whitegate, Cheshire, and Joan Riddell Scudamore, *née* Jarvis; *b* 9 Aug 1937; *Educ*

Monkton Combe, RAC Cirencester; *m* 1, 29 July 1961, Daphne Susan, da of Col Brian Pierson Doughty-Wylie, MC (d 1981), of Pen-y-Graig, St Asaph; 1 s (Thomas b 1969), 2 da (Emma (Mrs Farquahar) b 1963, Katherine b 1966); m 2, 9 Sept 1974, Susan Elizabeth, da of Maj John Frederick Mowat, of Lake House, Ellesmere, Salop; *Career* served RWF 1960-70, Queen's Own Mercian Yeo 1971-74, cmd Shropshire Yeo Sqdn, ret as Maj; ptnr Fisher Hoggarth land agents and chartered surveyors 1983-, surveyor to Diocese of Worcester 1986-; FRICS 1984; *Recreations* shooting, fishing, skiing, gardening; *Clubs* Army and Navy; *Style—* Jonathan Reeves, Esq; Southern Mythe Court, Tewkesbury, Gloucestershire (☎ 0684 292178); Fisher Hoggarth, The Estate Office, Dumbleton, Evesham, Worcestershire (☎ 0386 881214)

REEVES, Dr Marjorie Ethel; da of Robert John Ward Reeves (d 1935), and Edith Saffery, *née* Whitaker (d 1980); *b* 17 July 1905; *Educ* Trowbridge Girls HS Wilts, St Hugh's Coll Oxford (BA, MA, DLitt), Westfield Coll London (PhD); *Career* history teacher Roan Sch Greenwich 1927-29, lectr St Gabriel's Coll of Educn London 1932-38, vice princ St Anne's Coll Oxford 1938-72 (former tutor and fell); hon warden House of St Gregory & St Macrina Oxford, church warden Univ Church Oxford, memb Dante Soc, corr fell Medieval Acad of America; hon fell: St Annes Coll Oxford, St Hugh's Coll Oxford; former memb: Central Advsy Cncl for Educn, Academic Planning Bds Univ of Kent and Univ of Surrey, Br Cncl of Churches; former chm Higher Educn GP; FR HistS 1945, FBA 1972; *Books* The Influence of Prophecy in the Later Middle Ages (1969), The Figurae of Joachim of Fiore (1972), Then and Then Series (gen ed), Why History? (1980), The Myth of the Eternal Evangel in the Nineteenth Century (1987), The Crisis in Higher Education (1988), The Diaries of Jeffrey Whitaker (1989); *Recreations* gardening, music; *Clubs* Univ Womans; *Style—* Dr Marjorie Reeves; 38 Norham Rd, Oxford OX2 6SQ (☎ 0865 57039)

REEVES, Prof Nigel Barrie Reginald; OBE (1987); s of Capt Reginald Arthur Reeves, of Battle, E Sussex, and Marjorie Joyce, *née* Pettifer; *b* 9 Nov 1939; *Educ* Merchant Taylors', Worcester Coll Oxford (BA), St John's Coll Oxford (DPhil); *m* 1, 1964 (m dis 1976), Ingrid, *née* Söderberg; 1 s (Dominic Hans Adam b 1968), 1 da (Anna b 1973); m 2, 3 April 1982, Minou, da of Sadegh Samimi (d 1978); *Career* lectr: in English Univ of Lund 1964-66, in German Univ of Reading 1968-74; Alexander von Humboldt fell Univ of Tübingen 1974-75; Univ of Surrey: prof of German 1975-90, head Linguistic and Int Studies Dept 1979-89, dean Faculty of Human Studies 1986-90, dir Surrey Euro Mgmnt Sch 1989-90; prof of German and head of Modern Languages Dept Univ of Aston 1990-; visiting prof and cncl memb Euro Business Sch London 1983-90; chm Inst of Linguists 1985-88; pres: Nat Assoc of Language Advsr 1986-90, Assoc of Teachers of German 1987-89; chm Nat Congress on Languages in Educn 1986-90, exec vice-pres Conference of Univ Teachers of German 1988-, memb Governing Bd Inst of Germanic Studies Univ of London 1989-; FIL 1981, FRSA 1986, CIEX 1986; Goethe Medauille 1989; *Books* Heinrich Heine, Poetry and Politics (1974), Fr Schiller, Medicine, Psychology and Literature (with K Dewhurst, 1978), The Marquise of O and Other Short Stories by Heinr Kleist (with F D Luke, 1978), Business Studies, Languages and Overseas Trade (with D Liston, 1985), The Invisible Economy, A Profile of Britains Invisible Exports (with D Liston, 1988), Making Your Mark, Effective Business Communication in Germany (with D Luton, M Howarth, M Woodhall, 1988), Franc Exchange, Effective Business Communication in France (with C Sanders, Y Gladkow, C Gordon, 1991); *Style—* Prof Nigel Reeves, OBE; Dept of Modern Languages, University of Aston, Birmingham B4 7ET (☎ 021 359 3611 ext 4228, fax 021 359 6153, telex 336997 UNIAST G)

REEVES, Dr Robert Walter Kingham; s of Frederick Kingham Reeves (d 1975), of 24 Ryecroft Rd, London, and Heather Mary, *née* Gilbert (d 1981); *b* 13 Dec 1932; *Educ* Stowe, London Hosp Med Coll Univ of London (MB BS, DPM); *Career* Nat Serv non-med cmmn RAMC 1952-54; conslt psychiatrist Broadmoor Hosp 1967-73, MO Bristol Prisons 1973-81, conslt psychiatrist Glenside Hosp Bristol 1981-89, med dir of Sub Regnl Secure Unit of Fromeside Clinic 1988-89, conslt forensic psychiatrist Bristol 1989-; former med memb Frenchay Dist Health Authy; memb: of the Parole Bd, Exec Ctee Bristol Drugs Project; memb BMA, FRSPsych 1987; *Recreations* gardening; *Style—* Dr Robert Reeves; The South Cottage, Little Chalfield Manor, Melksham, Wilts; 7 Calle De Sol, Altea, Alicante, Spain; Fig Tree Cottage, Beniaya, Val D'Alcala, Alicante, Spain

REEVES, Roger Howard; s of Cecil Reeves, of Hale, Cheshire, and Nancy, *née* Walker; *b* 4 Aug 1943; *Educ* Altrincham GS; *m* 3 Aug 1968, Catherine Edwards (Kate), da of Maj Thomas Edwards Barry (d 1989), of Altrincham, Cheshire; 2 s (Crispin John b 1970, Francis Paul b 1973); *Career* chm Provincial & City Properties 1980; *Recreations* aerobatics, collecting and flying historic aircraft; *Style—* Roger H Reeves, Esq; PO Box 52, Macclesfield, Cheshire SK10 4QU

REEVES, Steve; s of John Reeves, of 141 Epping New Road, Buckhurst Hill, Essex, and Caryl, *née* Harvey; *b* 16 Dec 1966; *Educ* Wanstead Comp Roding Lane Wanstead, East Ham Art Coll, Watford Copywriting Course (Dip in Copywriting); partner, Karen Young; *Career* copywriter BMPDDB Needham 1988-; winner various awards for creative achievements in print and film advtg; memb NFT; *Recreations* film, art; *Style—* Steven Reeves, Esq; 12 Bishops Bridge Rd, London W2 (☎ 071 258 4422)

REEVES-SMITH, Leonard Edward; OBE (1977), JP (1970); s of Edward Kitchener Reeves-Smith (d 1975), of Mitcham, and Rose, *née* Reeves (d 1979); *Educ* Hampton GS; *m* 6 Feb 1952, Jeannette Avril, da of Henri Askew (d 1981); 1 s (Gary b 22 Feb 1953); *Career* WWII enlisted RAC 1944, served Italy, demob Capt 1948; buyer and gen mangr family retail grocery business 1948-62; chief exec Nat Grocers Fedn 1965 (exec asst 1962, nat sec 1963), dir gen Nat Grocers Benevolent Fund 1980-, dir Nat Grocers Benevolent Fund (Properties) Trust Ltd; gen sec: Grocers Fedn Benevolent Fund, London Grocers and Tea Dealers Benevolent Soc, Grocery Employees Nat Benefits Soc; dep chm Farnham Petty Sessional Div 1975 (Juvenile Panel and Domestic Panel); Freeman City of London 1978, Liveryman Worshipful Co of Chartered Secs and Admins 1978; MIGD 1963, FCIS 1970, FRSA 1970, MBIM 1970; *Recreations* walking, bird watching, conservation; *Style—* Leonard Reeves-Smith, Esq, OBE, JP; Marralomeda, 25 Mount Pleasant Close, Lightwater, Surrey; National Grocers Benevolent Fund, 17 Farnborough St, Farnborough, Hants (☎ 0252 515946)

REFFELL, Adm Sir Derek Roy; KCB (1984), KSPJ (1989); s of Edward Pomeroy Reffell (d 1974), and Murielle Frances (d 1975); *b* 6 Oct 1928; *Educ* Culford Sch, RNC Dartmouth; *m* 1956, Janne Marilyn Gronow, da of Capt William Gronow Davis, DSC, RN (d 1946); 1 s (David, b 1960), 1 da (Jane, b 1962); *Career* Capt HMS Hermes 1974-76, Rear Adm 1980, Asst Chief Naval Staff (Policy) 1980-81, Flag Offr Third Flotilla (Cdr Naval Task Gp South Atlantic July-Oct 1982) 1982-83, Flag Offr Naval Air Cmd 1983-84, Controller of the Navy 1984-89, Adm 1988, Govr and C-in-C Gibraltar 1989; Asst Coachmakers and Coach Harness Makers of London; FNI, CBIH; *Recreations* golf, wine making; *Style—* Adm Sir Derek Reffell, KCB; The Convent, Gibraltar FOREIGN

REGAN, Jack Hugh; s of John Regan (d 1972), of Edinburgh, and Molly Agnes, *née* Sommerville; *b* 10 Jan 1942; *Educ* Scotus Acad Edinburgh, Univ of Edinburgh (MA); *m* 2 Oct 1965, (Isabel) Katrina, da of Stanley Thewlis, of Lancs; 2 s (Dominic b 1967, Quentin b 1980), 3 da (Jane b 1968, Tessa b 1972, Anna-Louise b 1975); *Career* sub-ed The Scotsman Edinburgh 1960-68, chief sub-ed The Daily Nation Nairobi Kenya 1968-70; BBC: TV news reporter 1971-76, prodr Radio Aberdeen 1976, reporter Radio Scotland 1976-78, Scottish affrs corr Radio 4 1978-84, home news ed BBC Radio News London 1984-87, ed news and current affrs Radio Scotland 1987-; *Recreations* reading, writing, sampling Scotch whisky; *Style—* Jack Regan, Esq; 51 Newark Drive, Pollokshields, Glasgow G41 4QA (☎ 041 423 2647); BBC Radio Scotland, Queen Margaret Drive, Glasgow G12 8DG (☎ 041 330 2658, 041 339 8844, fax 041 337 1402, telex 777746)

REGAN, Michael Denis; s of Denis Charles Regan (d 1965), of Westcliff-on-Sea, Essex, and Selina, *née* Webb; *b* 4 Oct 1955; *Educ* Westcliff HS for Boys, Pembroke Coll Oxford (MA); *m* 20 Feb 1987, Henrietta, da of Henry George Richard Falconar (d 1981), of Horsham, W Sussex; 1 s (George b 1987), 1 da (Grace b 1990); *Career* articled clerk Rowe and Maw 1978-80, admitted slr 1980, ptnr in charge of Lloyd's office 1988- (asst slr 1980-85, ptnr 1985-); ACIArb 1984; *Books* JCT Management Contract (jtly); *Recreations* watching cricket; *Style—* Michael Regan, Esq; Rowe & Maw, 20 Black Friars Lane, London EC4; The Lloyd's Building, 1 Lime St, London EC3 (☎ 071 327 4144, fax 071 623 7965, telex 914901)

REGAN, Nils Albert; s of Dr Kenneth Martin Regan (d 1976), of London and Lausanne, and Ruth, *née* Boss (d 1988); *b* 19 Feb 1925; *Educ* King's Coll Wimbledon, Univ of Aberdeen (MB ChB, DObst); *m* 22 Nov 1956, Doreen Thelma, da of Dr Norman S Gurrie (d 1981), of London; 1 s (Andrew b 1967), 2 da (Carolyn b 1957, Gillian b 1959); *Career* Sqdn Ldr RAF med branch 1949-52; princ in gen practice 1957-; hosp practitioner G/U med and family planning: Westminster Hosp, St Stephens Hosp; advsr family planning Riverside Health Authy, vice chm Kensington Chelsea and Westminster Family Practitioner Ctee and Med Servs Ctee; memb BMA, MRCOG 1954, FRCOG 1989; *Recreations* theatre, music, tennis; *Clubs* Hurlingham; *Style—* Nils A Regan, Esq; 36 Shawfield St, London SW3 4BD (☎ 071 351 0307); 15 Denbigh St, London SW1V 2HF (☎ 071 834 6969)

REGER, Janet; da of Hyman Phillips (d 1981), of Reading, Berks, and Rachel, *née* Leven; *b* 30 Sept 1937; *Educ* Kendrick Sch Reading, Leicester Coll of Arts and Technol (Dip); *m* 1 Jan 1961, Peter Reger (d 1985), s of Josef Reger (d 1955), of Munich; 1 da (Aliza b 1961); *Career* freelance designer Zurich 1960-67, fndr Janet Reger exclusive designer lingerie and nightwear 1967-, own boutique Beauchamp Place Knightsbridge 1974-; *Style—* Mrs Janet Reger; 2 Beauchamp Place, London SW3

REGESTER, Michael; s of Hugh Adair Regester, of St George's, 42 Kneesworth St, Royston, Herts, and Monique, *née* Levrey; *b* 8 April 1947; *Educ* St Peter's Sch Guildford Surrey, Newport GS Newport Essex; *m* Christine Mary, da of Denis Harrison; 2 da (Lucinda Jane b 12 April 1971, Alice Mary b 8 Aug 1975); *Career* mangr of pub affrs (Euro, W Africa, ME) Gulf Oil Corporation 1975-80, jt md Traverse-Healy & Regester Ltd 1980-87, dir Charles Barker Public Relations 1987-90, md Regester plc 1990-; memb Bd Int PR Assoc 1988, FIPR 1990, MInstPet 1990; *Books* Crisis Management (1987), Investor Relations (with Neil Ryder, 1990); *Recreations* sailing, opera, cooking; *Clubs* Wig and Pen; *Style—* Michael Regester, Esq; Old Farm, 104 High Street, Melbourn, Royston, Herts SG8 6AL (☎ 0763 260796); Regester plc, 4 The Square, Burwash, East Sussex TN19 7EF (☎ 0435 882803, fax 0435 883713)

REGESTER, Paul John Dinsmore; OBE (1944), TD (1947); s of William Regester, JP (d 1930), Moorside, Westfield, Sussex, and Rose, *née* Horton (d 1919); *b* 14 Jan 1911; *Educ* Oundle; *m* 1, July 1940 (m dis 1960), Barbara, da of Edward Stern (d 1963), of Claydon, Suffolk; 1 s (Michael b 1942); m 2, 1960, Margaret Audrey Constance, da of Maj Frank Naumann, MC (d 1947), of Rydenwood, Cranleigh, Surrey; *Career* cmmnd RA (TA) 1929, TA Res 1932, active list 1939 (Straits Settlement Vol Force 1932-39), France 1940, Staff Capt Q HQ 5 Corps 1940 (DAAG Tport 1940, DAQMG 1941), serv N African invasion 1942; AAG: 1 Army 1943, 2 Army 1943; serv Normandy 1944, Col A Orgn HQ 21 Army Gp 1944, CSO Br Mil Admin Singapore 1945-46; admitted slr 1932; advocate slr Penang 1932-39, advocate and slr Kuala Lumpur 1946-59, judge advocate gen Fedn Malaya Armed Forces 1957-59, memb Ctee Straits Racing Assoc 1954-59, returned UK and recommenced practice 1959; memb Dummer Parish Cncl 1963-71; *Recreations* horse racing and gardening; *Clubs* E India; *Style—* Paul Regester, Esq, OBE, TD; Thatch Cottage, Farley Green, Albury, Guildford, Surrey GU5 9DN (☎ 0486 41 2274)

REGIS, Cyrille; *b* 9 Feb 1958; *m* Beverley Marie; 1 s (Robert Laurent), 1 da (Michelle Marie); *Career* professional footballer; amateur Moseley then Hayes; West Bromwich Albion 1977-84: joined for a fee of £5,000, 300 appearances, 122 goals; Coventry City 1984-: joined for a fee of £300,000, over 250 appearances, over 50 goals; England caps: 6 under 21 1979-83, 3 B, 5 full 1982-88; jt record holder most goals in League Cup match (5 v Chester City 1985); FA Cup winners' medal Coventry City v Tottenham Hotspur 1987; young player of the year Professional Footballers' Assoc 1978; *Style—* Cyrille Regis, Esq; Coventry City FC, Highfield Road, King Richard Street, Coventry CV2 4FW (☎ 0203 257171)

REGIS, John Paul Lyndon; s of Tony Regis, and Agnes Regis; *b* 13 Oct 1966; *Educ* St Austins RC Boys Sch; *Career* sprinter; Euro Jr Championships 1985: Bronze medallist 100m, Gold medallist 4x100m; Bronze medallist 200m: Euro Indoor Championships (Br record), World Championships; Silver medallist 4x100m (Br record) Olympic Games Seoul 1988, Gold medallist 200m World Indoor Championships 1989; Euro Championships 1990: Bronze medallist 100m, Gold medallist 200m, Silver medallist 4x100m, Gold medallist 4x400m; Cwlth record holder 4x200m indoors relay; *Recreations* golf, tennis; *Clubs* Queen's Tennis, Sundridge Park GC; *Style—* John Regis, Esq; 67 Fairby Rd, Courtlands Estate, Lee, London SE12 8JP (☎ 081 852 3670)

REGO, Paula; da of José Fernandes Figueiroa Rego (d 1966), of Portugal, and Maria Des José Paiva; *b* 26 Jan 1935; *Educ* St Julian's Sch Carcavelos Portugal, Slade Sch of Fine Art UCL; *m* 1959, Victor Willing, s of George Willing; 1 s (Nicholas Juvenal b 1961), 2 da (Caroline b 1956, Victoria Camilla b 1959); *Career* artist; solo exhibitions: SNBA Lisbon 1965, Galeria S Mamede Lisbon 1971, Galeria da Emenda Lisbon 1974, Galeria Modulo Oporto 1977, Galeria III Lisbon 1978, Air Gallery London 1981, Edward Totah Gallery London 1982, 1984, 1985, 1987, Arnolfini Bristol 1983, Gallery Espace Amsterdam 1983, Midland Group 1984, The Art Palace NY 1985, Travelling Show 1987, Retrospective Exhibition (Gulbenkian Fndn Lisbon and Serpentine Gallery London) 1988, Nursery Rhymes (Marlborough Graphics) 1989; group exhibitions incl: S Paulo Biennale 1969 and 1985, Br Art Show 1985, Cries and Whispers (Br Cncl) 1988, Br Art (Japan) 1990; pt/t lectr Slade Sch of Fine Art 1983-90, assoc artist Nat Gallery London 1990, Gulbenkian Fndn bursary 1962-63; sr fell RCA; *Style—* Mrs Paula Rego; Marlborough Fine Art, 6 Albemarle St, London W1X 4BY (☎ 071 629 5161, fax 071 629 6338)

REHAAG, Godfrey Claude; s of Claus Walter Rehaag (d 1984), and Hollis Maud, *née* Lehmann; *b* 6 June 1948; *Educ* Harvey GS Folkestone, Univ of Kent (MA); *m* 10 May 1980, Jane, da of Raymond Peter Hitchings, of Cornwall; 1 s (Thomas b 1982), 3 da (Natalie b 1980, Lucie b 1985, Emily b 1988); *Career* CA; sr ptnr Rehaag McGuire & Co 1987-90, dir Biotech Ind Products Ltd 1987-89, dir Incisive Technol 1990; Cncl memb: Sterts Arts and Environmental Centre 1986, Gaia Tst 1987, Marine Biological Assoc UK 1987, Sir Alister Hardy Foundation for Ocean Science 1990; memb MENSA; FCA 1973, ATII 1973; *Recreations* gardening, DIY, rambling, writing, voluntary work; *Clubs* British Mensa, Sterts Theatre Co; *Style—* Godfrey Rehaag, Esq; Frogs Meadow, Milton Combe, Yelverton, Devon PL20 6HL (☎ 0822 854926, fax 0822 852816)

REHDER, Frank Ernest; CVO (1976); s of Ernest A Rehder (d 1955), of Dulwich, London, and Julia Clara Dorothea, *née* Lienau (d 1959); *b* 4 Aug 1918; *Educ* Charterhouse, CCC Oxford (MA); *Career* WWII Capt RA 1940-45, Capt Royal Northumberland Fus 1945-46; admitted slr 1948, ptnr Sinclair Roche & Temperley London 1953-83 (conslt 1984-), maritime and commercial arbitrator 1975; memb and hon slr: London Maritime Arbitrators Assoc 1960 (hon memb 1977-), London Ct of Int Arbitration 1975-; chm: CIArb 1984-86, Dulwich Cons Assoc 1963-67; cncllr Camberwell Borough Cncl 1960-65; Freeman City of London, Liveryman: City of London Solicitors Co, Worshipful Co of Arbitrators (Master 1985-86); FCIArb 1972; *Recreations* gardening, walking; *Style—* Frank E Rehder, Esq, CVO; 152 Court Lane, Dulwich, London SE21 7EB (☎ 081 693 6240)

REID, (Philip) Alan; s of Philip Reid (d 1981), of Glasgow, and Margaret, *née* McKerracher (d 1976); *b* 18 Jan 1947; *Educ* Fettes, Univ of St Andrews (LLB); *m* 14 July 1971, Maureen Anne Reid, da of Alexander Petrie, of Cupar, Fife, Scotland; 1 s (Richard b 1984), 1 da (Caroline b 1981); *Career* sr tax ptnr London Region Peat Marwick McLintock 1979-; chm Int Tax Ctee Inst of CAs of Scot 1982-; memb: Tax Steering Ctee Consultative Ctee of Accountancy Bodies 1982-85, tax practices ctee Inst of CAs of Scot 1982-; govr Eton End Sch Berks; CA 1973, FTII 1981; *Recreations* family, skiing, theatre, travel; *Clubs* RAC; *Style—* Alan Reid, Esq; 1 Puddle Dock, Blackfriars, London EC4V 3PD (☎ 071 236 8000, 071 248 6552, telex 8811541)

REID, Sir Alexander James; 3 Bt (UK 1897), of Ellon, Aberdeenshire, JP (Cambs and Isle of Ely 1971), DL (1973); s of Sir Edward Reid, 2 Bt, KBE (d 1972), and Tatiana, *née* Fenoult; *b* 6 Dec 1932; *Educ* Eton, Magdalene Coll Cambridge; *m* 1955, Michaela, da of Olaf Kier, CBE, of Royston; 1 s, 3 da; *Heir* s, Charles Reid; *Career* 2 Lt 1 Bn Gordon Highlanders 1951 served Malaya; Capt 3 Bn Gordon Highlanders TA, ret 1964; chm: Ellon Castle Estates Co Ltd 1965-, Cristina Securities Ltd 1970-, Cytozyme (UK) Ltd 1985-; govr Heath Mount Prep Sch 1970- (chm 1976-); High Sheriff of Cambridge 1987-88; landowner (1100 acres); *Recreations* shooting, all country pursuits; *Clubs* Caledonian; *Style—* Sir Alexander Reid, Bt, JP, DL; Kingston Wood Manor, Arrington, Royston, Herts (☎ 0954 719231)

REID, Alexander Maynard; s of Alexander Simpson Reid (d 1985), of London, and Kathleen Irene, *née* Maynard (d 1989); *b* 3 May 1943; *Educ* Highgate Sch, Fitzwilliam Coll Cambridge (MA); *Career* admitted slr 1970; ptnr Milne Moser & Sons Kendal 1983, clerk to Gen Cmmrs of Income Tax for S Westmorland Div, Notary Public 1982; chm of govrs Brewery Arts Centre Kendal; memb Law Soc 1970; *Recreations* fellwalking, running, horseriding, tennis, golf, cinema; *Style—* Alexander Reid, Esq; Milne Moser, 100 Highgate, Kendal, Cumbria LA9 4HE (☎ 0539 729 786, fax 0539 723 425)

REID, Alexander Richard (Alec); s of Richard Alan Slade Reid (d 1980), and Lucy, *née* Hallamore; *b* 11 July 1943; *Educ* Ealing Coll; *m* Eleanor, da of John Royston Ward, of Tettenhall, Wolverhampton; 2 s (Duncan b 3 Feb 1977, Kerry b 15 Nov 1980); *Career* BBC radio prodr specialising in: feature documentary, drama, poetry progs; trainee clerk 1961, studio mangr, dir Int Control Room during first moon walk; prodr: Sound Archives Dept Radio 1, World Serv, Kaleidoscope, religious broadcasting, Drama Dept; author and musical dir: Misrule (Radio 3) 1976 and Gilgamesh (Radio 4) 1984; dir: Loose Gags, Sons and Sketches (Bristol Old Vic, Radio 4), Lyrics of the Hearthside (Arts Theatre London); prodr: Time for Verse, With Great Pleasure; moved to Bristol 1984; writer and performer on poetry circuit, broadcast on various poetry progs, poems published in anthologies, broadcaster of own children's stories; *Books* With Great Pleasure (vol 1 1986, vol 2 1988); *Recreations* writing, jogging and keeping fit, theatre, music, cinema, eating out; *Style—* Alec Reid, Esq; BBC, Whiteladies Rd, Bristol BS8 2LR (☎ 0272 742143, fax 0272 744114)

REID, Andrew John; s of Thomas Miller Reid, and Joan, *née* Hunter; *b* 4 Nov 1947; *Educ* Royal GS, Univ of Bradford (BSc); *m* 1970 (m dis 1980), Deborah, *née* Ward; 3 da (Rebekah Esme b 7 Oct 1972, Chloe Eleanor b 2 Jan 1976, Charlotte Jane b 22 Dec 1976); 1983, partner, Elspeth Lynette McTear; *Career* formerly res asst Glaxo, advtg exec then prof mangr Warner Lambert Gp Pontypool 1971-74, advtg exec Design Systems Cardiff 1974-79, mktg exec AH Robins Company 1979-81, co-fndr (with Brian Shields) Matrix 1981- (merger to form Strata 'Matrix 1989); played the Geordie lad in The Long and the Short and the Tall (Pontypool Theatre) 1972; *Recreations* music, tenor saxophone; *Style—* Andrew Reid, Esq; 159 Lake Rd West, Cardiff CF2 5PL; Strata 'Matrix Ltd, 1 Talbot St, Cardiff CF1 9BW (☎ 0222 231231, fax 0222 372798)

REID, Andrew Milton; s of late Rev A A R Reid, DD; *b* 21 July 1929; *Educ* Glasgow Acad, Jesus Coll Oxford; *m* 1953, Norma MacKenzie, da of late Norman Davidson; 2 s; *Career* asst md John Player Sons 1975-77, dir Imperial Gp Ltd 1978-89, chm Imperial Tobacco Ltd 1979-86 (full-time chm and chief exec 1983), dep chm Imperial Gp 1986-89; dir: Trade Indemnity plc 1982-, Renold plc until 1983; memb: Cncl Royal Sch of Church Music 1986-91, Tobacco Advsy Cncl 1977-87, Bristol Urban Devpt Bd, Cncl Univ of Bristol; *Recreations* fishing, golf, sailing; *Clubs* Clifton (Bristol), United Oxford and Cambridge; *Style—* Andrew Reid, Esq; Parsonage Farm, Publow, Pensford, nr Bristol

REID, Hon Mrs (Angela Margaret Amherst); *née* Cecil; o da of 3 Baron Amherst of Hackney, CBE (d 1980), and Margaret Eirene, *née* Clifton Brown; *b* 16 May 1955; *Educ* St Mary's Sch Calne, Froebel Inst Roehampton; *m* 7 June 1980, (Gavin) Ian Reid, s of Col (Percy Fergus) Ivo Reid, of Hill House, Somerton Oxford; 1 s (Nicholas Andrew b 1985), 2 da (Susanna Claire b and d 1987, Jessica Mary b 1988); *Career* primary teacher specialising in dyslexia; *Style—* The Hon Mrs Reid; Lower Dean Farm, Watlington, Oxford OX9 5ET (☎ 049 161 2886)

REID, Beryl Elizabeth; OBE (1986); da of late Leonard Reid, and Anne Burton McDonald Reid (d 1962); *b* 17 June 1921; *Educ* Withington Girl's Sch; *m* 1, 1950, Bill Worsley; m 2 1954, Derek Franklin; *Career* actress; in pantomime and variety 1941-; After the Show (St Martin's) 1951, Watergate Revues March-Nov 1954, Rockin' The Town (Palladium) 1956, The Killing of Sister George (Duke of York's 1965, NY 1966, Tony Award for Best Actress, film of same 1969), Entertaining Mr Sloane (film 1970, play Royal Court 1975), Spring Awakening, and Romeo and Juliet (Nat Theatre) 1974, Il Campiello, and Counting the Ways (Nat Theatre) 1976-77, The Way of the World (RSC Aldwych) 1978, Born in the Gardens (Bristol Old Vic, SWET Award) 1979-80, Joseph Andrews (film) 1977, Smiley's People (BAFTA Award for Best TV Actress) 1982, The School for Scandal (Haymarket and Duke of York's) 1983-84, Gigi (Lyric) 1985-86, Duel of Love (film) 1990; TV: Put on Cunning 1990, Boon 1990, Perfect Scoundrels 1991; *Books* So Much Love (autobiog, 1984), Cats Whiskers (1985), Beryl Food and Friends (1986); *Recreations* painting, cooking, surfing, flying, intensive driving; *Style—* Beryl Reid, OBE; Honeypot Cottage, Wraysbury, nr Staines, Middx

REID, Carolyn Marie; da of Thomas Reid, of 39 Hathaway Rd, Gateacre, Liverpool, and Marie Joan, *née* Doyle; *b* 28 March 1972; *Educ* St Julie's HS Liverpool, Millbrook Coll Liverpool; *Career* hockey player; Hightown Ladies Club 1986-, Merseyside Jrs 1985-89, Lancs Indoor 1987-, North Indoor and Outdoor under 18 1987-90 (capt 1989-90), North Outdoor Srs 1990-; England: 18 under 18 caps 1988-90 (capt 1989-90), 4 under 21 indoor caps 1991 (vice capt), under 21 outdoor 1991-, sr indoor 1989-, sr outdoor training squad 1990-; honours with Hightown: Nat Outdoor Finals 1986-91 (runners up 1988 and 1990), Nat Indoor Finals 1986-91 (runners up 1990), winners Sheffield Indoor Tournament 1986-90, fourth place Typhoo Nat League 1990; nat honours: winners Home Countries Tournament under 18 1989-90, Silver medal under 18 Euro Tournament Antwerp 1989 (Bronze Groningen 1990), Silver medal Euro Under 21 Indoor Cup Vienna 1991, winners HDM Holland sr indoor 1991 (runners up 1989); youngest ever player England sr indoor team 1989, goalkeeper of the tournament HDM Holland 1991, jr player of the year Hightown 1989 and 1990; other sporting achievements: county netball and athletics rep Catholic Students Sports Fedn of GB Vienna 1987; *Recreations* sport in general especially tennis, reading, listening to music, socialising; *Style—* Miss Carolyn Reid; 39 Hathaway Road, Gateacre, Liverpool L25 4ST (☎ 051 428 6074); c/o Miss Monica Rooney, 8 Ellwood Close, Hale , Liverpool L24 4BX (☎ 051 425 2669)

REID, Charles Edward James; s and h of Sir Alexander Reid, 3 Bt; *b* 24 June 1956; *Educ* Rannoch Sch, RAC Cirencester; *Recreations* shooting, fishing; *Clubs* Clifton, Caledonian; *Style—* Charles Reid, Esq

REID, Dr Daniel; OBE (1989); s of John Dinsmore Reid (d 1972), of Glasgow, and Ethel, *née* Cheyne (d 1978); *b* 5 Feb 1935; *Educ* Allan Glen's Sch Glasgow, Univ of Glasgow (MB ChB, MD), Royal Inst of Public Health and Hygiene (DPH); *m* 3 Aug 1963, Eileen, da of William James Simpson (d 1939), of Greenock, Renfrewshire; 2 da (Anne Cheyne b 21 April 1965, Jane Anderson b 25 July 1967); *Career* Nat Serv Capt RAMC 1960-62, attached Royal Northumberland Fus, Hong Kong; registrar Univ Dept of Infectious Diseases Ruchill Hosp Glasgow 1963-65, sr registrar epidemiological res laboratory Central Public Health Laboratory London 1965-69, dir communicable diseases (Scot) unit Ruchill Hosp Glasgow 1969-; chm: Advsy Gp on Infection Scottish Health Servs Planning Cncl 1983-, Glasgow Assoc for the Welfare of the Disabled 1983-87; FFCM 1977, FRSH 1976, FRCP (Glasgow) 1983; Encomienda con placa de la Orden Civil de Sanidad Spain 1975; *Books* Infections in Current Medical Practice (jt ed, 1986); *Style—* Dr Daniel Reid, OBE; 29 Arkleston Rd, Paisley, Strathclyde PA1 3TE (☎ 041 889 4873); Communicable Diseases (Scotland) Unit, Ruchill Hospital, Glasgow G20 9NB (☎ 041 946 7120, fax 041 946 4359, telex 776373)

REID, Dr (Peter) Eric; s of Hans Reid, of 38 Fruin Court, Newton Mearns, Glasgow, and Erica, *née* Friedner; *b* 27 June 1936; *Educ* Hamilton Acad Hamilton, Univ of Glasgow (BSc, PhD); *m* 19 Sept 1962, Linda Anne, da of Richard Terley; 3 s (Mark b 17 March 1964, David b 14 July 1966, Grant b 15 June 1970), 1 da (Kim b 15 Mar 1974); *Career* md: Terleys Ltd 1962-, Glenruth Property Co Ltd 1970-, Semple & Peck Ltd 1971-, Texstyle World 1980-; chm Yorkhill Scanner Appeal Glasgow, tstee Yorkhill Children's Hosp Glasgow; FID; *Recreations* squash, tennis, photography; *Style—* Dr Eric Reid; Terleys Ltd, Farmeloan Estate, Rutherglen, Glasgow G73 1NA (☎ 041 647 9231, telex 777685, fax 041 647 6812, car 0860 614213)

REID, George Newlands; s of George Reid (d 1978), and Margaret (d 1969); *b* 4 June 1939; *Educ* Dollar Acad, Univ of St Andrews (MA, Gold Medal in history, pres students' Rep Cncl); *m* 4 July 1970, Daphne Ann, da of Calum McColl; 2 da (Caroline Lucinda, Morag Marsaili); *Career* reporter: Daily Express 1961-62, political correspondent Scottish TV 1962-64; prodr Granada TV 1964-68, head of News and Current Affrs Scottish TV 1968-74, MP (SNP) Clackmannan and E Stirlingshire 1974-79 (memb Assembly of Cncl of Europe 1976-79 and Assembly of Western Europe Union 1976-79), freelance broadcaster and journalist (BBC TV and Radio and various newspapers) 1979-84, dir Public Affrs League of Red Cross and Red Crescent Socs Geneva 1985-90 (head of information 1984-90), dir Int Red Promotion Bureau 1990-; dir Scottish Cncl Res Inst 1978-81; Pirogor Gold Medal (for work as chief Red Cross Del in American Earthquake) USSR 1989 and 1990; *Books* Red Cross, Red Crescent (ed, 1989), Casualties of Conflict (ed, 1990); *Recreations* gardening, hill walking, cross-country skiing; *Style—* George Reid, Esq; Villa Rosemont, 23 Avenue du Bouchet, 1209 Petit Saconnex, Geneva, Switzerland (☎ 010 41 22 734 6705); International Red Cross (IPB), Chemin de la Vie Des Champs, Geneva, Switzerland (☎ 010 41 22 734 6001, fax 010 41 22 734 6485)

REID, Sir Hugh; 3 Bt (UK 1922); s of Sir Douglas Neilson Reid, 2 Bt (d 1971), and Margaret Brighton Young, *née* Maxtone; *b* 27 Nov 1933; *Educ* Loretto; *Heir* none; *Career* RAF 1952-56, served Egypt and Cyprus, RAF (VRT) 1963-75, Flying Offr; self-employed travel conslt 1961-; *Recreations* travel, skiing, aviation, cooking; *Style—* Sir Hugh Reid, Bt; Caheronaun Park, Loughrea, Co Galway, Ireland

REID, Iain Malcolm Gordon; s of Anthony Gordon Reid, and Virginia Ann, *née* Heredia; *b* 21 April 1956; *Educ* Harrow; *m* 24 April 1980, Susan Macleod; 1 da (Philippa Susanna b 17 Oct 1986); *Career* police offr Northern Constabulary 1978-80, Met police 1980-81, farmer 1983-; memb Cons Ctee; *Recreations* rugby, shooting, flying, skiing; *Clubs* Lansdowne, Fitzmaurice Place; *Style—* Iain Reid, Esq; Tullochcurran, Kirkmichael, Perthshire PH10 7NB (☎ 025 081 230)

REID, Dr (Richard) Ian; s of Richard Morton Reid (d 1971), of Coatbridge, Scot, and Margaret Mackay, *née* McCaul; *b* 12 May 1951; *Educ* Coatbridge HS, Univ of Glasgow (MB ChB, MRCP); *m* 1, 2 Sept 1975 (m dis 1980), Carole Jane Westley; m 2, 28 March 1981, Amanda Jane, da of Maj Peter Munden, of Farm Cottage, Monxton, Andover, Hants; 2 da (Jeannie Isabel b 1982, Eleanor Susan b 1984); *Career* conslt in geriatric med Southampton and SW Hants DHA and hon clinical teacher Univ of Southampton 1982; pres Ashton Club Moorgreen Hosp Southampton, memb Br Geriatrics Soc 1979; *Recreations* windsurfing, walking, swimming, railway modelling; *Style—* Dr Ian Reid; Dept of Geriatric Medicine, Glevel, West Wing, Southampton General Hospital, Southampton, Hants SO9 4XY (☎ 0703 777222) ext 3438)

REID, Dr John; MP (Lab) Motherwell North 1987-; *b* 8 May 1947; *m* Cathie; 2 s (Kevin, Mark); *Career* advsr to Rt Hon Neil Kinnock, MP 1983-86, Scot organiser of Trade Unionists for Lab 1986-87, MP (Lab) Motherwell North 1987-, front bench dep spokesman for children 1989, front bench def spokesman 1990-; *Style—* Dr John Reid, MP; 114 Manse Rd, Newmains, ML2 9BD (☎ 0698 383866, fax 0698 381243)

REID, John (Robson); *b* 1 Dec 1925; *Educ* Wellingborough GS, Sch of Architecture, The Poly (Dip Arch); *m* 1948, Sylvia Mary, *née* Payne; 1 s (Dominic), 2 da (Suzannah, Victoria (twin)); *Career* WWII Capt The Green Howards served West Africa and Middle East 1944-47; architect and industl designer 1950-; architecture incl: Westminster Theatre, Savoy Grill, Barbican Centre Exhibition Halls; industl design incl: furniture and lighting fittings, road and rail tport, consumer durables; ldr Br Delgn on Design Educn USSR 1967, Pageantmaster to the Lord Mayors of London 1972-, Dean art and design Middx Poly 1975-78; UNIDO conslt on industl design 1977-79: India, Pakistan, Egypt, Turkey; advsr to Nat Inst of Design India 1979-, specialist Br Cncl India 1985; winner of four Design Cncl awards and two Milan Trienalle Silver medals; pres: Soc of Industl Artists and Designers 1966-67, Int Cncl of Socs of Industl Design 1969-71; vice pres The Illuminating Engrg Soc 1969-71, chm Nat Inspection Bd for Electricity Installation Contracting; memb Advsy Ctee: Central Sch of Art and Design, Leeds Coll of Art and Design, Newcastle upon Tyne Sch of Art and Design, Carleton Univ; tstee Geffrye Museum, govr Hornsey Coll of Art and Design; lectr for Design Cncl in: Canada, Czechoslovakia, Eire, Hungary, Japan, Poland, USA, USSR;

Master: Worshipful Co of Furniture Makers 1989-90, Worshipful Co of Chartered Architects 1988-89; RIBA, PPSCD, FRSA; *Books* incl: International Code of Professional Conduct for Industrial Design (1969), A Guide to Conditions of Contract for Industrial Design (1969), Industrial Design in India, Pakistan, Egypt and Turkey (1978); *Recreations* music, swimming; *Clubs* City Livery; *Style*— John Reid, Esq; Arnoside House, The Green, Old Southgate N14 7EG; 5 The Green, London N14 7EG (☎ 081 882 1083/4)

REID, Sir John James Andrew; KCMG (1985), CB (1975), TD (1958); s of Alexander Scott Reid (d 1966), of Fife, and Mary Cullen Andrew Reid (d 1970); *b* 21 Jan 1925; *Educ* Bell-Baxter Sch Cupar, Univ of St Andrews (BSc, MB ChB, DSc, MD, DPH); *m* 1949, Marjorie (d 1990), da of Cyril Robins Crumpton (d 1952); 1 s (Jonathan), 4 da (Joanna, Lucinda, Nicola, Morag); *Career* Nat Serv 1948-50; Lt-Col TA; med practitioner; conslt advsr on Int Health (DHSS)1985-89, ret; hon conslt in communtiy med to the Army 1971-90, MOH Northamptonshire, MOH Buckinghamshire 1967-72, dep chief MO DHSS 1972-77, visiting prof of health serv admin London Sch of Hygiene and Tropical Med 1973-78, chief MO Scottish Office 1977-85; memb of Exec Bd WHO 1973-75, 1976-79, 1980-83, 1984-87 (former chm); Hon LLD Univ of Dundee; FRCP, FRCPE, FRCPG, FFCM; *Style*— Sir John Reid, KCMG, CB, TD; The Manor House, Oving, Aylesbury, Bucks HP22 4HW (0296 641 302)

REID, Rev Prof John Kelman Sutherland; CBE (1970), TD (1961); s of David Reid (d 1933), of 11 Braid Rd, Edinburgh, and Georgina Thomson, *née* Stuart (d 1946); *b* 31 March 1910; *Educ* George Watson's Boys' Coll Edinburgh, Univ of Edinburgh (MA, BD); *m* 3 Jan 1950, Margaret Winnifrid, da of Rev WS Brookes (d 1958), of Corrie, Isle of Arran; *Career* Royal Army Chaplains Div, Chaplain Class 4 Royal Signals 1942-43, Parachute Regt 1943-46, TA 1946-62; prof of philosophy Univ of Calcutta 1936-38, min of religion Craigmillar Park Church Edinburgh, prof of theology Univ of Leeds 1952-61, prof of systematic theology Univ of Aberdeen 1961-76; ed (and emeritus) Scottish Jl of Theology 1948-, sec New English Bible 1949-82; memb: World Cncl of Churches Faith and Order Cmmn 1961-82, Br Cncl of Churches 1961-68, Soc for Study of Theology, Societas NT Studiorum, Scottish Church Theology Soc, Church Serv Soc, Scottish Church Soc; Hon DD Edinburgh Univ 1957; *Books* The Authority of Scripture (third edn 1981), Presbyterians and Unity (1962), Life in Christ (1963), Christian Apologetics (1969), Calvin's Concerning the Eternal Predertination of God (trans, second edn 1982), Oscar Cullmann: Baptism in the New Testament (trans 1950); *Style*— The Rev Prof John Reid, CBE, TD; 8 Abbotsford Court, 18 Colinton Road, Edinburgh EH10 5EH (☎ 031 447 6855)

REID, Prof John Low; s of James Reid (d 1961), of Glasgow, and Irene Margaret; *b* 1 Oct 1943; *Educ* Kelvinside Acad Glasgow, Fettes, Univ of Oxford (MA, BM, BCh, DM); *m* 2 May 1964, Randa, da of Naguib Aref Pharaon (d 1987), of London; 1 s (James b 1965), 1 da (Rebecca b 1967); *Career* house offr Radcliffe Infirmary Oxford and Brompton Hosp London 1968-70, res fell sr lectr and reader Royal Postgrad Med Sch London 1970-78, visiting scientist Nat Inst of Health Bethesola Maryland USA 1973-75; Univ of Glasgow: regius prof materia medica 1978-89, regius prof of med and therapeutics 1989-; memb Med Advsy Ctee BBC Scotland; FRCPG 1979, FRCP 1987; *Books* Handbook of Hypertension (1981), Lecture Notes on Clinical Pharmacology (1981), Clinical Science (ed 1982-84), Journal of Hypertension (ed 1987); *Recreations* gardening, books, outdoors; *Style*— Prof John Reid; 1 Whittingehame Gardens, Glasgow G12 (☎ 041 339 4034); Western Infirmary, Glasgow (☎ 041 339 8822)

REID, Lady Laura Louise; *née* Meade; 4 da of 6 Earl of Clanwilliam (d 1989); *b* 11 March 1957; *m* 25 April 1981, W Scott B Reid, s of Howard A Reid, of Bronxville, NY; 1 s (Nicholas b 1982), 2 da (Amelia b 1984, Clementine b 1988); *Style*— The Lady Laura Reid; 524 Purchase St, Rye, New York 10580, USA

REID, Dr Mark McClean; s of E Mayne Reid, CBE (d 1985), and Meta, *née* Hopkins (d 1990); *b* 27 Dec 1937; *Educ* Bangor GS, Queens Univ Belfast (MB BChir); *m* 10 July 1964, Barbara, da of James Cupples (d 1986); 1 s (Alistair b 18 Aug 1966), 2 da (Fiona b 1 Nov 1968, Claire b 20 July 1973); *Career* conslt paediatrician with special interest in new-born Royal Maternity Hosp Belfast 1978-; pres: Irish Perinatal Soc 1979-80, Ulster Paediatric Soc 1987-88; chm NI Postgrad Paediatric Cmmn 1985-; memb: BMA, Br Paediatric Assoc (memb Cncl 1981-84), Ulster Med Soc, Ulster Paediatric Soc, Irish Perinatal Soc, Ulster Obstetric and Gyanaecological Soc; FRCPGlas, FRCPI; *Books* Handbook Neonatal Intensive Care (jtly, first and second edns), various pubns on perinatal or neonatal field in Br Euro and N American jls 1967-; *Recreations* mountain climbing, travel, Alpine gardening, photography; *Style*— Dr Mark Reid; 10 Kensington Gardens, Hillsborough, Co Down BT26 6HP (☎ 682267); Neonatal Intensive Care Unit, Royal Maternity Hospital, Belfast B12 (☎ 240503)

REID, Sir (Harold) Martin Smith; KBE (1987), CMG (1978); s of Marcus Reid (d 1948), and Winifred Mary Reid, *née* Stephens (d 1969); *b* 27 Aug 1928; *Educ* Merchant Taylors', BNC Oxford (MA); *m* 1956, Jane Elizabeth, da of Frank Lester Harwood (d 1975), of Hants; 1 s (Thomas), 3 da (Philippa, Emily, Alice); *Career* RN 1947-49; entered Foreign Serv 1953; served: London, Paris, Rangoon, London; political advsr to Govr Br Guyana 1965-66, dep high cmmnr Guyana 1966-68, no 2 in Bucharest and Blantyre Malawi 1968-73, princ private sec to successive Secs of State for NI 1973-74, head Central and S African Dept FCO 1974-79, min Pretoria 1979-82, seconded as dip serv res chm Civil Serv Selection Bd 1983, Br high cmmr Kingston 1984-87, ambass (non res) Port au Prince 1984-87, special res advsr FCO 1987-88, ret 1988; *Recreations* painting (fourth one-man exhibition 1991); *Style*— Sir Martin Reid, KBE, CMG; 43 Carson Road, London SE21 8HT

REID, Michael (Mike); s of Gp Capt George Frederick Reid, of Stoke Gabriel, nr Totnes, Devon, and Eileen Margaret, *née* Tamplin; *b* 3 Oct 1949; *Educ* Haileybury; *Career* dir: Reed Stenhouse Financial Services Ltd 1980-85, Intel Ltd 1985-86; md: Sentinel Funds Management 1985-86, Sentinel Portfolio Management 1985-86, Commercial Union Trust Managers Ltd 1986-, Commercial Union Prestige Fund Management Ltd 1989-; chief exec: Commercial Union Financial Management International Ltd 1986-, Commercial Union Luxembourg SA 1988-, Commercial Union Financial Management International (Guernsey) Ltd 1988-; chm: Sentinel Life plc 1985-86, Assetmix Advisory 1989-, Assetmix 1989-, Commercial Union Financial Management International (Asia) Ltd 1989-; *Recreations* sailing; *Style*— Mike Reid, Esq; Yew Cottage, Cozens Lane West, Broxbourne, Herts (☎ 0992 446670); Commercial Union Financial Management International Ltd, 1st Floor, Plantation House, 10-15 Mincing Lane, London EC3P 3AL (☎ 071 623 2099, fax 071 623 4279, car 0860 239919)

REID, Sir Norman Robert; s of Edward Daniel Reid (d 1956); *b* 27 Dec 1915; *Educ* Wilson's GS Camberwell, Edinburgh Coll of Art, Univ of Edinburgh (DA); *m* 1941, Jean Lindsay, da of Alexander Taylor Bertram, of Brechin; 1 s, 1 da; *Career* WWII served A & SH, Maj 1946; Tate Gallery: joined 1946, dep dir 1954, keeper 1959, dir 1964-79; memb: Cncl Friends of the Tate Gallery 1958-79, Arts Cncl Panel 1964-74, Advsy Panel ICA 1965-, Advsy Ctee Paintings in Hosps 1965-69, Br Cncl Fine Arts Ctee 1965-77 (chm 1968-75), Cultural Advsy Ctee UK Nat Cmmn for UNESCO 1966-70, Studies in History of Art Bd London Univ 1968, The Rome Centre 1969-77 (pres 1975-77), Burlington Magazine Bd 1971-75, Advsy Cncl Paul Mellon Centre 1971-78, Cncl of Mgmnt Inst of Contemporary Prints 1972-78, Contemporary Arts Soc Ctee 1973-77 (and 1965-72), Cncl RCA 1974-77; pres Penworth Soc of Arts, tstee Graham and Kathleen Sutherland Fndn 1980-86; Hon LittD UEA; FMA, FIIC; Offr of the Mexican Order of the Aztec Eagle; kt 1970; *Clubs* Arts; *Style*— Sir Norman Reid; 50 Brabourne Rise, Park Langley, Beckenham, Kent

REID, Peter; *b* 20 June 1956; *m* Barbara, da of Wilfred Watkinson; 1 da (Louise b 22 July 1983); *Career* professional footballer player and manager; player: 261 appearances Bolton Wanderers 1974-82, transferred to Everton for £60,000 Dec 1982, 234 appearances Everton 1982-89, 32 appearances Queens Park Rangers 1989; Manchester City: joined Dec 1989, player 1989-90, player-manager 1990-; England caps: 6 under 21 1977-78, 13 full 1985-88, played in World Cup Mexico 1986; honours with Everton: League Championship 1985 and 1987, FA Cup 1984 (runners up 1985 and 1986), Euro Cup-Winners' Cup 1985; Player of the Year Professional Footballers' Assoc 1985; *Recreations* reading, horse racing; *Style*— Peter Reid, Esq; Manager, Manchester City FC, Maine Road, Moss Sider, Manchester M14 7WN (☎ 061 226 1191)

REID, Sir Robert Basil; CBE (1980); s of Sir Robert Neil Reid, KCSI, KCIE (d 1963), and Amy Helen Disney (d 1980); *b* 7 Feb 1921; *Educ* Malvern, BNC Oxford (hon fell 1985); *m* 1951, Isobel Jean (d 1976), da of Robert McLachlan (d 1942), of Coruannan, Giffnock, Glasgow; 1 s, 1 da; *Career* WWII cmmnd RTR 1941-46, Capt, hon col 275 Railway Sqdn RCT(V) 1989-; joined London and NE Railway as traffic apprentice (later goods agent, asst dist goods mangr, dist passenger mangr and commercial offr), planning mangr Scottish region BR 1967, divnl mangr Doncaster Eastern Region 1968, dep gen mangr Eastern Region 1972, gen mangr Southern Region 1974; BR bd: full-time memb 1977, chief exec (Railways) 1980, vice chm 1983, chm 1983-90; chm W Lambeth Health Authy 1990; pres Chartered Inst of Tport 1982-83, chm Nationalised Industs Chm's Gp 1987, rep BR Bd on Managing Bd of the Union of Int Railways 1980-90, chm Community of Euro Railways 1988-90, vice pres Inst of Materials Handling 1987, doctor of business admin (honoris causa) Int Mgmnt Centre Buckingham; Freeman City of London; Master: Worshipful Co of Carmen 1990-91 (formerly sr warden), Worshipful Co of Info Technologists 1988-89; Hon DEng Univ of Bristol, hon fell BNC Oxford 1985; CBStJ 1986; CBIM; kt 1985; *Recreations* shooting, fishing, mountaineering; *Clubs* Naval & Military; *Style*— Sir Robert Reid, CBE; West Lambeth Health Authority, St Thomas's Hospital, Lambeth Palace Rd, London SE1 7EH (☎ 071 928 9292)

REID, (James) Robert; s of His Hon Judge John Alexander Reid, MC (d 1969), and Jean Ethel, *née* Ashworth; *b* 23 Jan 1943; *Educ* Marlborough, New Coll Oxford, (MA); *m* 25 May 1974, Anne Prudence, da of John Arkell Wakefield; 2 s (Edward b 1976, David b 1978), 1 da (Sarah b 1980); *Career* called to the Bar Lincoln's Inn 1965; QC 1980, rec 1985, bencher 1988; jt treas Barrs Benevolent Assoc 1986; *Style*— Mr Robert Reid; 9 Old Square, Lincoln's Inn, London WC2

REID, Dr Russell Warwick; s of Donald William Reid (d 1984), of Auckland NZ, and Dorothy Ellen, *née* Stedman (d 1964); *b* 4 Oct 1943; *Educ* Kings HS, Christchurch Boy's HS, Otago Univ Med Sch Duredin NZ (MB ChB); *Career* Capt Royal NZ Army Med Corps, in active service combined Med Servs team Bong Son S Vietnam 1970; conslt psychiatrist Mount Vernon Hosp Northwood (St Bernards Hosp Southall, Hillingdon Hosp Hillingdon), hon conslt psychiatrist Charing Cross Hosp London; MRCPsych; *Recreations* squash, swimming; *Style*— Dr Russell Reid; 10 Warwick Rd, London SE5 (☎ 071 373 0901, car 0836 278926)

REID, Sue; da of Peter Reid, DSC (d 1971), and Vera Reid; *b* 20 May 1950; *Educ* Casterton Sch Cumbria, Brunel Univ; *m* 26 Oct 1974 (m dis 1982), Simon Fulford-Brown; 1 s (Harry Reid Kemble b 19 Nov 1988); *Career* asst ed Mail on Sunday; *Books* Labour of Love (1988); *Style*— Ms Sue Reid; 12 Burnaby Street, London SW10; Mail on Sunday, Northcliffe House, London W8

REID, William; CBE (1987); s of Colin Colquhoun Reid, of Glasgow (d 1978), and Mary Evelyn (d 1987); *b* 8 Nov 1926; *Educ* Eastwood Secdy Sch Glasgow, Univs of Glasgow and Oxford; *m* 1958, Nina Frances; *Career* RAF 1945-48 (cmmnd 1946); memb Br Nat Ctee ICOM 1973-88; hon memb: The American Soc of Arms Collectors 1975, The Indian Army Assoc 1981; hon life pres Int Assoc of Museums of Arms and Military History 1987, hon life memb Friends of the Nat Army Museum 1988 (dir 1970-88); consultative dir The Heralds' Museum 1988-, asst keeper The Armouries HM Tower of London 1956-70; tstee: Florence Nightingale Museum, Museum of Richmond, Museum of the Royal Army Educational Corps, Museum of the Royal Hampshire Regt; memb: founding cncl The Army Records Soc, Cons Ctee for the Arts and Heritage 1987-; The North Parish Washing Green Soc (Glasgow) 1988; Liveryman Worshipful Co of Scriveners; FSA 1965, FMA 1974-88; *Books* The Lore of Arms (1976); *Recreations* music, bird watching, the study of armour and arms; *Clubs* The Athenaeum; *Style*— William Reid, Esq, CBE; 66 Ennerdale Rd, Kew Gdns, Richmond, Surrey TW9 2DL (☎ 081 940 0904); The Heralds' Museum, The College of Arms, Queen Victoria St, London EC4V 4BT (☎ 071 248 1912)

REID, Flt Lt William; VC (1943); s of William Reid (d 1941), and Helena, *née* Murdoch (d 1972); *b* 21 Dec 1921; *Educ* Baillieston Sch, Coatbridge Secdy Sch, W of Scot Agric Coll, Univ of Glasgow (BSc); *m* 28 March 1952, Violet Campbell, da of William George Gallagher (d 1976); 1 s (William Graeme b 1961), 1 da (Susan May b 1963); *Career* RAFVR Bomber Cmd 1941-46: 61 Sqdn 1943, 617 sqdn 1944 (POW 1944), demobbed 1946; farms mangr Macrobert Farms Douneside Ltd 1950-59, nat cattle and sheep advsr Spillers Ltd 1959-81; hon pres Br Legion (Crieff), memb Bd BLESMA, pres Strathallan Aircraft Assoc, hon life pres Air Crew Assoc (chm Scot branch); Freeman City of London 1988; *Recreations* golf, fishing, shooting; *Clubs* RAF; *Style*— Flt Lt William Reid, VC; Cranford Ferntower Place, Crieff, Perthshire, Scotland PH7 3DD (☎ 0764 2462)

REID, William Kennedy; CB (1981); s of late James Reid, and late Elspet Stewart; *b* 15 Feb 1931; *Educ* Robert Gordon's Coll Aberdeen, George Watson's Coll Edinburgh, Univ of Edinburgh (MA), Trinity Coll Cambridge (maj scholar, MA); *m* 1959, Ann, da of Lt-Col The Rev Donald Campbell; 2 s, 1 da; *Career* Miny of Educn 1956, Cabinet Office 1964-67, DES 1976-78, dep sec Scot Office 1978-84, sec Scot Home and Health Dept 1984-89; chm: Govrs Scot Police Coll 1984-89, Tstees James Smart Lecture Fund 1984-89; Parly cmmr for Admin and Health Service Cmmrs for Eng,Scot and Wales 1990-; memb: Cncl on Tbnls, Cmmns for Local Admin in England and in Wales; *Books* Outlook (contrib 1963); *Recreations* hill walking, verse; *Clubs* New (Edinburgh), Utd Oxford and Cambridge Univ; *Style*— William Reid, Esq, CB; Church House, Great Smith St, London SW1P 3BW (☎ 071 276 3000)

REID, William Pollock; s of William Reid (d 1982), of Ruthergten, Glasgow, and Marjorie Evitt, *née* Rainey; *b* 25 May 1942; *Educ* Rutherglen Acad 1954-59; *m* 15 Aug 1964, Dorothy May McNaught; 2 s (Gordon Scott b 3 March 1970, Ian Fraser b 30 May 1971), 1 da (Fiona Margaret b 21 Sept 1973); *Career* Scottish Amicable Life Assurance Soc: joined as actuarial student 1959, transfd to computer programming 1960, progressed during next 30 years to asst gen mangr i/c Computer Devpt 1988, transfd to Pension Div as asst gen mangr 1990; MBCS; *Recreations* sports, scouting, travel; *Clubs* Stirling Golf; *Style*— William P Reid, Esq; Foinavon, 46 Dalmorglen

Park, Stirling FK7 9JL (☎ 0786 71794); Scottish Amicable Life Assurance Society, Craigforth, Stirling FK9 4UE (☎ 0786 73141)

REID ENTWISTLE, Dr Ian; s of John Morton Entwistle, and Mary, *née* Reid; *b* 29 Sept 1931; *Educ* Rivington and Blackrod Sch, Univ of Liverpool Med Sch (MB ChB, KLJ, Cert GAM); *m* 1, 15 May 1969, Anthea Margaret (d 1979), da of Kenneth Evans, of Norfolk House, Meols Dr, West Kirby, Wirral; 2 s (John b 1972, Alexander b 1973); m 2, Rosemary Elizabeth, *née* Harrison; *Career* Surgn Lt HMS Eaglet RNR 1962-65; specialist (EEC accredited) in occupational med Royal Coll of Physicians; princ med offr RMS Queen Mary, Queen Elizabeth and Queen Elizabeth II 1961-; casualty offr David Lewis Northern Hosp Liverpool 1957, house physician to prof of child health Royal Liverpool Children's Hosp 1957, princ in private and NHS practice 1958-, med supt Cunard Ellerman PLC 1966-; pt/t med conslt: Spillers Foods Ltd, Hanson Engrg Ltd, BHS plc, BASS Northern; pt/t authorised assessor and examiner: CAA, Gen Cncl of Br Shipping, Gen Foods Ltd, Trafalgar House plc; conslt: Pre-Retirement Assoc, The Joseph Nelson Group; formerly med conslt Br Eagle Int Airlines 1966-68, sr gp med conslt Utd Gas Industs 1971-80; treas and sec Merseyside and N Wales RCGP 1973-80 (bd memb 1963-), jt treas and sec Soc of Occupational Med (Merseyside) 1961-67, chm Brewing Indust Med Advsrs 1987-, memb cncl Birkenhead Med Soc 1986-89; memb: Aerospace Physiology and Med Working Pty Cncl of Europe 1974-, NASA 1969-; med advsr West Kirby Swimming Club for Disabled; underwriting memb Lloyd's 1978-, assoc fell Aerospace Med Assoc USA 1973-; memb: RAeS, Soc of Occupational Med, Assur Med Assoc; MFOM; FRCGP, FFOM, FBIM 1988; *Books* Exacta Medica (ninth edn, 1989), Exacta Mecanix (fifth edn, 1988), Exacta Paediatrica (1991); *Recreations* motor racing, horticulture, boating, horology, photography, railway modelling; *Clubs* Mid Cheshire Pitt, Manchester Naval Offrs Assoc; *Style*— Dr Ian Reid Entwistle; Knollwood, Well Lane, Gayton, Wirral L60 8NG (☎ 051 342 2332); consultation suite, 27 Banks Rd, West Kirby, Wirral L48 0RA (☎ 051 625 6600)

REID SCOTT, David Alexander Carroll; s of Maj Alexander Reid Scott, MC (d 1960), and Ann, *née* Mitchell (d 1953); *b* 5 June 1947; *Educ* Eton, Lincoln Coll Oxford (MA); *m* 1, 23 April 1972, Anne (d 1988), da of Phillipe Clouet des Pesruches (d 1977); 3 da (Iona b 1975, Camilla b 1976, Serena b 1979); m 2, 7 July 1990, Elizabeth, da of John Latshaw; *Career* 1 vice pres White Weld & Co 1969-77, seconded sr advsr Saudi Arabian Monetary Agency 1978-83, md Merrill Lynch & Co 1983-84, exec dir Phoenix Securities Ltd 1984-, non-exec dir Merrett Holdings plc 1986-; *Recreations* Irish country life, farming, arts, antiques; *Clubs* Turf, Kildare St, Coningsby; *Style*— David Reid Scott, Esq; 2 Brunswick Gardens, London W8 4AJ (☎ 071 221 8004); Ballynure, Grange Con, Co Wicklow, Ireland; Phoenix Securities Ltd, 99 Bishopsgate, London EC2 (☎ 071 638 2191, fax 071 638 0707, car 0836 732 963)

REID SCOTT, Malise; s of Maj Alexander Reid Scott, MC (d 1960), and Ann Mitchell (d 1953); *b* 28 Sept 1948; *Educ* Eton; *m* 11 Sept 1978, Verity Fleur, da of Dudley Austell Comonte (d 1983), of 13 Upper Belgrave St, London SW1; 1 s (Hugo Alexander Carroll b 5 Sept 1985), 1 da (Rebecca b 10 Feb 1981); *Career* 11 Hussars (PAO) 1967-70; Watney Mann Ltd 1970-72, Laurence Prust & Co 1972-86 (ptnr 1983-86), ptnr Laurence Keen & Co 1986-; *Recreations* country pursuits, painting; *Clubs* Hurlingham; *Style*— Malise Reid Scott, Esq; 48 Lyford Rd, London SW18 3LS (☎ 081 874 1629); 49-51 Bow Lane, London EC4M 9LX (☎ 071 489 9493)

REIDHAVEN, Viscount; James Andrew Ogilvie-Grant; also Master of Seafield; er s and h of 13 Earl of Seafield; *b* 30 Nov 1963; *Educ* Harrow; *Style*— Viscount Reidhaven

REIDY, Dr John Francis; s of Frederick Cyril Reidy (d 1957), and Marie Isobel, *née* Smith; *b* 25 Aug 1944; *Educ* Stonyhurst, St Georges Hosp Med Sch and Kings Coll London (MB BS, LRCP, MRCP); *m* 25 Nov 1978, Dianne Patricia, da of Gerald Eugene Murphy, of Launceston, Tasmania, Australia; 1 s (Thomas Edward b 19 Nov 1980), 1 da (Laura Eugenie b 1 June 1982); *Career* conslt radiologist Guys Hosp 1980-; Liveryman Worshipful Soc of Apothecaries; MRCS, FRCR 1975, FRCP 1988; *Books* numerous pubns on cardiovascular and interventional radiology; *Style*— Dr John Reidy; 19 Cumberland St, London SW1V 4LS (☎ 071 834 3021); Radiology Dept, Guys Hosp, London SE1 (☎ 071 955 5000)

REIGATE, Baron (Life Peer UK 1970), of Outwood, Co Surrey; Sir John Kenyon Vaughan-Morgan; 1 Bt (UK 1960), PC (1961); yr s of Sir Kenyon Pascoe Vaughan-Morgan, OBE, DL, sometime MP Fulham East, n of Sir Walter Vaughan Morgan, 1 and last Bt (cr 1906, extinct 1916); *b* 2 Feb 1905; *Educ* Eton, Christ Church Oxford (MA); *m* 1940, Emily Redmond, da of William Redmond Cross, of New York; 2 da (Hon Julia Redmond (Hon Mrs King) b 1943, Hon Deborah Mary (Hon Mrs Whitfeld) b 1944); *Heir* none; *Career* WWII served Welsh Gds; sits as Cons peer in House of Lords; MP (C) Reigate 1950-70, Min of State BOT 1957-59; late memb LCC and pres E Fulham Con Assoc; former co dir; *Clubs* Brooks's, Beefsteak, Hurlingham; *Style*— The Rt Hon the Lord Reigate, PC; 36 Eaton Sq, SW1 (☎ 071 235 6506)

REILLY, Hon Mrs; Hon (Brigid Margaret); *née* Campbell; only da of 3 Baron Glenavy (Patrick Campbell, the raconteur and wit, d 1980) by his 2 w, Cherry, da of Maj George Monro; *b* 8 May 1948; *Educ* Godstowe, Pipers Corner Sch Naphill, E Berks Coll of Further Educn; married; *Style*— Hon Mrs Reilly; 2535 Panorama Drive, N Vancouver, BC, Canada V7G 1V4

REILLY, Lt-Gen Sir Jeremy Calcott; KCB (1987), DSO (1973); s of Lt-Col Julius Frank Calcott Reilly (d 1984), of Chilbolton, Hants, and Eileen Norah, *née* Moreton; *b* 7 April 1934; *Educ* Uppingham, RMA Sandhurst; *m* 12 Nov 1960, Julia Elizabeth, da of William Forrester (d 1984), of Weymouth, Dorset; 3 da (Katherine b 1961, Penelope b and d 1964, Brigid b 1965); *Career* cmmnd Royal Warwicks Regt 1954, CO 2 Bn Royal Regt of Fusiliers 1971-73, instr Staff Coll 1974-75, Col GS MOD 1975-77, PSO to FM Lord Carver and attached to FCO (Rhodesia) 1977-79, Brig 1979, Cdr 6 Field Force and UK Mobile Force 1979-81, Maj-Gen 1981, GOC 4 Armd Div BAOR 1981-83, Dep Col Royal Regt Fusiliers 1981-86, DBD MOD 1983-84, ACDS MOD 1985-86, Col Royal Regt Fusiliers 1986-, Lt-Gen 1986, CTAD 1986-89, Col Cmdt Queen's Div 1988-90, ret 1989; *Style*— Lt-Gen Sir Jeremy Reilly, KCB, DSO; c/o Royal Regt Fusiliers, HM Tower of London, London EC3N 4AB

REILLY, Malcolm John; s of Robert Reilly, of 155 Station Rd, Kippax, nr Leeds, and Annie, *née* Wood; *b* 19 Jan 1948; *Educ* Ashton Rd Secdy Sch Castleford, Whitwood Tech Coll Castleford; *m* 19 Nov 1972, Susan, da of Harold Leonard Sault (d 1982); 1 s (Glen Robert b 26 Jan 1974), 1 da (Lyndsey Clare b 24 May 1978); *Career* rugby league coach; former amateur footballer Kippax Welfare, switched to rugby league with Kippax Amateur Club 1967; professional Castleford 1967-71 and 1975-87 (player-coach then coach), total 330 appearances; transferred for a fee of £15,000 to Manly Warringah Aust 1971-75 (87 appearances); 3 England caps, 9 GB caps incl tour Aust and NZ 1970; coach GB 1987-: 26 matches, 17 wins, won series v NZ 1989 and 1990; honours as player Castleford: Challenge Cup 1969 (awarded Lance Todd Trophy) and 1970, Grand Final winners 1972 and 1973, try of the year 1972; honours as coach Castleford: John Player Final winners 1976 and 1977, Yorkshire Cup winners 3 times, Challenge Cup 1986; mechanic 1963-70, area sales mangr Aust 1970-75, area sales rep Rocol Ltd 1975-80, publican 1980-82, accounts mangr John Smiths Free Trade 1982-90; *Recreations* keeping fit, jogging, strength training, cooking, eating, athletics, nature, sub-aqua diving; *Style*— Malcolm Reilly, Esq; c/o Rugby League HQ, 180 Chapeltown Rd, Leeds LS7 4HT (☎ 0532 624637, fax 0532 623386)

REILLY, Michael Charles Tempest; s of Hugh Tempest Reilly (d 1943), and Jessie Margery, *née* Dunthorne (d 1958); *b* 30 Aug 1913; *Educ* Haileybury, St Mary's Hosp and Univ of London (MB BS, MS); *m* 12 Dec 1945, Katharine Joyce (Joy), da of Gilbert Petrie (d 1955); 3 s (David b 1947, Christopher b 1953, Timothy b 1956), 1 da (Susan b 1946); *Career* WWII med branch RAFVR 1940-46, station med offr UK 1940-44, Station MO Ceylon 1944 and 1945, SMO Cocos Is Expeditionary Force, HQ 222 Gp Columbo, demob war-substantive Sqdn Ldr; surgical first asst The London Hosp 1950-54, conslt surgn Plymouth and Dist Hosps 1954-78, emeritus conslt surgn SW RHA; initiator of new operation sigmoid myotomy for diverticular disease 1964, author of numerous articles in med press on diverticular disease and chapters in three surgical textbooks; pres: section of proctology RSM 1972 (life memb), SW Surgns 1976; memb GMC 1979-83, memb cncl RCS of England 1973-85 (Bradshaw lectr 1985), former memb Plymouth Hosp Mgmnt Ctee (former chm med advsy ctee), sec Plymouth Med Soc 1960-65, pres Devon and Cornwall Ileostomy Assoc 1970-75; hon fell: Medico-Chirugical Soc of Jordan 1978, Medico-Chirugical Soc of Bologna 1980; memb BMA 1938, MRCS 1947, LRCP 1947, FRCS 1949, sr fell Assoc of Surgns of GB and Ireland 1978; *Recreations* pestering politicians about the decline of the NHS; *Style*— Michael Reilly, Esq; Magnolia Cottage, Harrowbeer Lane, Yelverton, Devon PL20 6EA (☎ 0822 852636)

REILLY, Sir (D'Arcy) Patrick; GCMG (1968), OBE (1942); s of Sir D'Arcy Reilly (d 1948), and Margaret Florence, *née* Wilkinson; *b* 17 March 1909; *Educ* Winchester, New Coll Oxford (MA); *m* 1, 27 July 1938, Rachel Mary (d 1984), da of Brig-Gen Sir Percy Sykes, KCIE, CB, CMG; 2 da (Jane b 1939, Sarah b 1941); m 2, 23 Oct 1987, Ruth Margaret, wid of Sir Arthur Norrington; *Career* joined Dip Serv 1933; third sec Tehran 1935, second sec FO 1938, Miny Econ Warfare 1939-42, first sec Algiers 1943 and Paris 1944, cnsllr Athens 1947, Imperial Def Coll 1949, asst under sec 1950-53, min Paris 1953-56, dep under sec FO 1956, ambass to USSR 1957-60, dep under sec FO 1960-64, ambass to France 1965-68; chm: Banque Nationale de Paris plc 1969-80, United Bank for Africa (Nigeria) 1969-74, pres London Chamber of Commerce and Indust 1972-75; chm: Cncl Bedford Coll Univ of London 1970-75, N Kensington Amenity Tst 1971-74; fell All Souls Coll Oxford 1932-39 and 1969-, hon fell New Coll Oxford 1972; Hon LittD Univ of Bath 1982; Commandeur Légion d'Honneur France 1979; *Recreations* gardening, travel; *Clubs* Athenaeum; *Style*— Sir Patrick Reilly, GCMG, OBE; 75 Warrington Crescent, London W9 1EH (☎ 071 289 5384); 12 Lansdowne Crescent, BAth BA1 5EX (☎ 0225 311 412)

REILLY, Lady; Ruth Margaret; *née* Cude; yst da of Edmund Cude (d 1970), and Alice Marian Haswell (d 1974); *b* 17 May 1922; *m* 1, 1946, Frank Davies (d 1959), s of Frederick Davies; 1 da; m 2, 1963, (Peter) Rupert Waterlow (d 1969), s of Sir Philip Waterlow; m 3, 1969, as his 2 w, Sir Arthur Norrington, JP (d 1982), sometime pres Trinity Coll Oxford, vice-chllr Oxford Univ and warden Winchester Coll; m 4, Sir D'Arcy Patrick Reilly, GCMG, OBE, former Ambassador in Moscow and Paris; *Career* physiotherapist, writer; *Books incl:* In the Shadow of a Saint (1983), The Household of St Thomas More (1985); *Recreations* music, painting, reading; *Style*— Lady Reilly; 12, Lansdown Crescent, Bath, Avon BA1 5EX; 75 Worrington Crescent, London, W9; 3 Beach Cottages, Fishguard, Dyfed

REILLY, Wyn Anthony Prowse; s of Dr Noel Marcus Prowse Reilly, CMG, of N Sandwich, USA, and Dolores Albra Thompson, *née* Pratten (d 1982); *b* 17 March 1930; *Educ* Leighton Park Sch, Trinity Hall Cambridge (MA), Univ Coll Oxford; *m* 4 Sept 1965, Annuschka Maria, da of Capt Peterpaul Maria Pilarski (d 1970); 2 s (J Alyosha J b 1968, P M Julian P b 1971), 1 da (S Natasha S b 1972); *Career* ADC and private sec to HE Govr The Gambia 1953-54, admin offr Tanganyika HMOCS 1956-62; sr lectr in public admin Univ of Manchester 1962-; on secondment from Univ of Manchester: prof of admin Univ of Mauritius 1969-71, princ Admin Coll of Papua New Guinea 1973-75, sr planning offr local govt Botswana 1978-79, dir gen Mgmnt Devpt Inst The Gambia 1984-85; *Recreations* sailing, skiing, walking, music; *Style*— Wyn Reilly, Esq; West Cottage, Birtles Rd, Macclesfield, Cheshire SK10 3JG (☎ 0625 431114); IDPM, Crawford House, University of Manchester, Precinct Centre, Oxford Rd, Manchester M13 9QS (☎ 061 275 2817)

REINERT, Richard Arnim; s of Dr Harald Herman Richard Reinert (d 1981), of Le Pinede, Frejuś, France, and Irene Mary, *née* Bridge; *b* 8 Aug 1956; *Educ* Dover Coll, Tours Univ Tours France (Dip), Southampton Univ; *m* 27 April 1979, Brigitte Edgard Therese, da of Dr Hendrik Rene Firmin Verhamme; 2 s (Alexander H R b 24 Oct 1981, Scott R H b 8 Oct 1987), 1 da (Stephanie B M 10 Jan 1983); *Career* dir REFCO SA Paris 1983-, md REFCO Overseas London 1988-; *Recreations* golf, squash, tennis, sailing; *Clubs* Royal St Georges GC; *Style*— Richard A Reinert, Esq; REFCO Overseas Ltd, Europe House, World Trade Centre, London, E1 9AA (☎ 071 488 3232, fax 071 480 7069, telex 887438)

REINHARDT, Max; s of Ernest Reinhardt (d 1942), of Istanbul, Turkey, and Frieda *née* Darr (d 1960); *b* 30 Nov 1915; *Educ* English HS Istanbul, Ecole Des Hautes Etudes Commerciales Paris, LSE; *m* 1957, Joan Dorothy, da of Carlisle MacDonald (d 1972), of NY, USA; 2 da (Alexandra, Veronica); *Career* book publisher; chm and md Bodley Head 1957-87, jt chm Bodley Head Chatto and Jonathan Cape 1973-87; chm: Reinhardt Books Ltd, The Nonesuch Press Ltd; cncl memb RADA; *Recreations* swimming, bridge, reading for pleasure; *Clubs* Garrick, Savile, Beefsteak, RAC; *Style*— Max Reinhardt, Esq; Flat 2, 43 Onslow Square, London SW7 3LR (☎ 071 589 5527)

REISS, Charles Alexander; s of Dr J C Reiss, (d 1979), of London; *b* 23 March 1942; *Educ* Bryanston; *m* 1978, Susan, da of Sir John Newson-Smith; 3 da (Rowan b 10 Sept 1978, Holly b 1 Sept 1980, Bryony b 22 Aug 1986); *Career* political corr and chief leader writer Evening News 1975-80, political editor Evening Standard 1985- (political corr and leader writer 1980-85); *Style*— Charles Reiss, Esq; Evening Standard, Northcliffe House, 2 Derry St, London W8 5EE

REISS, Prof Hans Siegbert; s of Berthold Reiss (d 1950), of Heidelberg, Federal German Republic, and Maria Petri (d 1974); *b* 19 Aug 1922; *Educ* Karl Friedrich Gymnasium Mannheim, Wesley Coll Dublin, Trinity Coll Univ of Dublin (BA, MA, PhD); *m* 8 March 1963, Linda, da of Ludwig Bernard Wahter; 2 s (Thomas b 27 April 1966, Richard b 13 Oct 1969); *Career* asst to prof of German Univ of Dublin 1943-46, lectr LSE 1946-53 (former asst lectr), lectr QMC 1953-58; prof of German: McGill Univ 1958-65, Univ of Bristol 1965-88 (head of dept 1965-88, dean of Faculty of Arts 1976-78); emeritus prof of German Univ of Bristol 1988-; visiting prof: McGill Univ 1968-69 (1957-58), Middlebury Coll 1967, Univ of Munich 1978-79 (1970-71); memb Akademie der Freien Künste Mannheim; Officer's Cross OM FRG; *Books* The Political Thought of the German Romantics (1955), Franz Kafka - Eine Betrachtung seines Werkes (1952, 2 edn 1956), Goethe's Romane (1963), Emmannuel Geibels Briefe an Henriette Nölting (with H Wegener, 1963), Das Politische Denken in der Deutschen Romantik (1966), Goethe's Novels (1969), Kant's Political Writings (1970, 2 edn 1981), Goethe's Die Wahlverwandtschaften (with H B Nisbet, 1971), Goethe und die Tradition (1972), Kant's Politisches Denken (1977) The Writer's Task from Nietzsche to Brecht (1978); *Recreations* walking, music, reading, travel; *Style*— Prof Hans Reiss

REISS, Stephen Charles; OBE (1973); s of Richard Leopold (Dick) Reiss (d 1959), and Celia, *née* Butts; *b* 7 Aug 1918; *Educ* Gresham's Sch, Balliol Coll Oxford, Chelsea Sch of Art; *m* 17 Jan 1942, Elizabeth Ruth (Beth), da of George Moore Gladden (d 1984), of Brunstead, Norfolk; 1 s (Nicholas b 6 May 1943), 1 da (Bridget b 14 April 1946); *Career* Capt Bedfordshire and Hertfordshire Regt 1939-45; gen mangr Aldeburgh Festival of Music and the Arts 1955-71, dir Fanfare For Europe 1972-73, arranged Aelbert Cuyp in Br Collections Exhibition Nat Gallery 1973, admin LSO 1974-75, md Curwen Prints 1975-80, fndr and md Business Art Galleries 1978-85, md Stephen Reiss Fine Art 1985; *Books* Aelbert Cuyp (1975), The Child Art of Peggy Somerville (1990); *Style*— Stephen Reiss, Esq, OBE; 5 Westgate, Thorpeness, Suffolk IP16 4NE (☎ 0728 452499); 14 Bridewell Alley, Norwich NR2 1AQ (☎ 0603 615357)

REITER, Glenn Mitchell; s of Bernard Leon Reiter (d 1968), and Helene Gloria, *née* Edson; *b* 1 Feb 1951; *Educ* Yale Univ (BA), Yale Law Sch (JD); *m* 5 Sept 1976, Marilyn, da of Edward John Beckhorn, of Marco Is, Florida, USA; 1 s (Benjamin Bernard b 1980), 1 da (Diana Elizabeth b 1983); *Career* ptnr Simpson Thacher & Bartlett 1984- (assoc 1978-84); *Clubs* RAC; *Style*— Glenn M Reiter, Esq; Simpson Thacher & Bartlett, 99 Bishopsgate, London EC2M 3XD (☎ 071 638 3851, fax 071 628 0977)

REITH, Barony of (UK 1940);; *see*: Reith, Christopher John

REITH, Christopher John; s of 1 Baron Reith, KT, GCVO, GBE, CB, TD, PC (dir-gen BBC 1926-38); suc f 1971 but disclaimed Peerage for life 1972; *b* 27 May 1928; *Educ* Eton, Worcester Coll Oxford; *m* 1969, Ann Penelope Margaret, da of Henry Morris, of Notts; 1 s (James b 1971), 1 da (Julie b 1972); *Heir* s, Hon James Harry John Reith b 2 June 1971; *Career* served RN 1946-48; subsequently farmer; *Style*— Christopher Reith, Esq; Whitebank Farm, Methven, Perthshire (☎ 073 884 333)

REITH, Robert Davidson; s of Alexander Davidson Reith (d 1974), and Margaret, *née* Hunter (d 1979); *b* 25 July 1938; *Educ* Dulwich; *m* 30 Sept 1961, Stella Ann, da of Francis Joseph Lewis (d 1984); 1 s (Martin Robert Davidson b 1965), 1 da (Catherine Ann b 1963); *Career* dir: Oscar Faber plc, Oscar Faber Consulting Engrs Ltd 1986; ptnr Oscar Faber Partnership 1974; memb: Cncl of Assoc of Consltg Engrs, Watford Borough Cncl 1967-72; vice pres Euro Cncl of Consltg Engrs; memb: Worshipful Co of Plumbers 1980, Worshipful Co of Engrs 1988; CEng, FICE, FIStructE, MConsE; *Recreations* golf, tennis, riding, private flying; *Clubs* Caledonian; *Style*— Robert Reith, Esq; Oscar Faber plc, Marlborough House, St Albans AL1 3UT (☎ 081 784 5784, fax 081 784 5700)

RELLIE, Alastair James Carl Euan; CMG (1987); s of Lt Cdr William Rellie (d 1943), and Lucy Rellie, *née* Modin (d 1974); *b* 5 April 1935; *Educ* Michaelhouse S Africa, Harvard (BA); *m* 1961, Annalisa, da of Maj Clive Modin (d 1944); 1 s (Euan b 1968), 2 da (Jemima b 1970, Lucasta b 1972); *Career* Lt Rifle Bde 1958-60; second sec FCO 1963-64, vice consul Geneva 1964-67, first sec FCO 1967-68, (commercial) Cairo 1968-70, Kinshasa 1970-72, FCO 1972-74; cnsllr: UK Mission to UN, NY 1974-79, FCO 1979-; *Recreations* travel, talk, newspapers; *Clubs* Brooks's; *Style*— Alastair Rellie, CMG; FCO, King Charles St, London SW1 (☎ 071 270 0703)

RELLY, Gavin Walter Hamilton; *b* 6 Feb 1926, of Stellenbosch SA; *Educ* Trinity Coll Oxford (MA); *m* 1951, Jane Margaret, *née* Glenton; 1 s, 2 da; *Career* chm: Anglo-American Corporation of S Africa 1983-90, AECI Ltd 1983-, Cleveland Potash Ltd; dir: Anglo-American Industrial Corporation Ltd, Anglo-American Coal Corporation Ltd, Anglo-American Farms Ltd, Anglo-American Gold Investment Co Ltd, Anglo-American Investment Trust Ltd, ASA Ltd, Charter Consolidated plc, De Beers Consolidated Mines Ltd, De Beers Centenary AG, Highveld Steel and Vanadium Corporation Ltd, Minerals and Resources Corporation Ltd, Standard Bank Investment Corporation Ltd, Transatlantic Holdings plc, Zambia Copper Investments Ltd, Southern Life Association Ltd; chm SA Nature Fndn, Chllr Rhodes Univ; *Recreations* golf, fishing; *Clubs* Rand, River, Country, Western Province; *Style*— Gavin Relly, Esq; c/o Anglo-American Corporation of South Africa Ltd, 40 Holborn Viaduct, London EC1P 1AJ (☎ 071 936 4044); 44 Main St, Johannesburg, South Africa

RELPH, Michael Leighton George; s of George Relph (CBE), and Deborah Caroline, *née* Nanson; *Educ* Bembridge Sch Isle of Wight; *m* 1, 1940 (m dis 1948), Doris, *née* Ringwood; 1 s (Simon); m 2, 1950, Maria Rose, *née* Barry; 1 da (Emma); *Career* stage designer West End 1940-50, asst art dir (originally apprentice) Gaumont Br Studios, art dir Warner Bros Studios, art dir Ealing Studios 1942; assoc prodr to Michael Balcon 1945, prodr-writer in partnership with Basil Dearden (dir) until his death in 1972; Ealing prodns incl: The Captive Heart, Kind Hearts and Coronets, The Blue Lamp (Best Film Award Br Film Acad), Saraband for Dead Lovers; also produced and/or wrote, directed for: Ealing MGM, Rank Orgn, Br Lion, United Artists, Paramount, EMI; fndr dir Allied Film Makers produced: League of Gentlemen, Victim, Man in the Moon; chm Film Prodn Assoc of GB 1971-76, memb Cinematograph Films Cncl 1971-76, govr Br Film Inst (chm Prodn Bd) 1971-78; *Style*— Michael Relph, Esq; The Lodge, Primrose Hill Studios, Fitzroy Rd, London NW1 (☎ 071 586 0249)

RELPH, Simon George Michael; s of Michael George Leighton Relph, and Doris, *née* Ringwood (d 1978); *b* 13 April 1940; *Educ* Bryanston, King's Coll Cambridge (MA); *m* 14 Dec 1963, Amanda Jane, da of Col Anthony Grinling, MC (d 1981), of Hinds Cottage, Dyrham Park, Avon, Wilts; 1 s (Alexander James b 16 June 1967), 1 da (Arabella Kate b 17 Sept 1975); *Career* asst dir feature films 1961-73, prodn admin Nat Theatre 1974-78, prodn supervisor Yanks 1978, exec prodr Reds 1979-80; prodr and co-prodr 1981-85: The Return of the Soldier, Privates on Parade, The Ploughman's Lunch, Secret Places, Wetherby, Comrades; chief exec Br Screen Fin Ltd 1986-90; memb Cncl: BAFTA, Br Screen Advsy Cncl; exec memb Br Film and TV Producers Assoc; *Recreations* golf, photography, fishing; *Style*— Simon Relph, Esq; Skreba Films, 5A Noel St, London W1V 3RB (☎ 071 437 6492, fax 071 437 0644)

REMFRY, David Rupert; s of Geoffrey Rupert Remfry, of Worthing, Sussex, and Barbara, *née* Ede; *b* 30 July 1942; *Educ* Hull Coll of Art; *m* 1, 1963 (m dis 1971), Jacqueline Wayne Alwyn; 3 s (Jacob Rupert b 1967, Samuel b 1968, Gideon Jethro b 1970); m 2, Jackie Crisp; *Career* artist; exhibitions incl: New Grafton Gallery 1973, Editions Graphiques 1974, Ferens Gallery Hull 1975, Folkestone Art Gallery 1976, Mercury Gallery London 1978, 1980, 1982, 1984, 1986, 1988 and 1990, Bohun Gallery Henley-on-Thames 1978, 1981, 1983, 1985, 1987, Galerie de Beerenburght Holland 1979, 1980, 1982, 1983, Ankrum Gallery Los Angeles 1980, 1981, 1983, 1985, 1987 Middlesborough Art Gallery 1981; work in the collections of: Swathmore Coll Pa, Museo Rayo Columbia, Minneapolis Museum of Art USA, Nat Portrait Gallery, V and A Museum, Middlesbrough and Towner Art Galleries; RWS; *Recreations* opera; *Clubs* Chelsea, Groucho's; *Style*— David Remfry, Esq; 19 Palace Gate, Kensington, London W8 5LS

REMINGTON-HOBBS, Lady Clare Charlotte Rosemary; *née* Finch-Knightley; yr da of 11 Earl of Aylesford, *qv*; *b* 13 Sept 1959; *m* 1985, James Remington-Hobbs, s of C Remington-Hobbs, of Normandy, France; 2 s (Johnathon b 1986, Alexander Charles b 1988); *Style*— The Lady Clare Remington-Hobbs

REMINGTON-HOBBS, Col Edward; DSO (1945), OBE (1947); s of A Remington-Hobbs, MD (d 1928), and gs of Sir Joseph Wilkinson (d 1902); *b* 7 Feb 1916; *Educ* Westminster, RMC Sandhurst; *m* 1, 1950, Angela Susan (k in air crash 1953), only da of Capt Marshall Owen Roberts (d 1931), of 15 Grosvenor Sq, London W1; 1 da (Julie Marguerite b 1951); m 2, 1957 (m dis 1967), Ann; m 3, 1972, Susan Mary Sheila, *qv*; *Career* WWII serv Argyll and Sutherland Highlanders: UK, BNAF, NW Europe (wounded), SEAC; instr Staff Coll Camberley 1944, ret 1950; gold staff offr Coronation of HM The Queen 1953, usher (silver stick) Silver Jubilee Thanksgiving Serv 1977; underwriting memb of Lloyd's 1959-; chm & md: Polyseal Ltd 1960-75, Bellfax Int Ltd 1975-84; chm Snuffers Ltd 1984-; memb OStJ Cncl for Sussex 1965-69 (Order Cross Bearer 1966-90); memb Chapter Gen 1972-; Freeman City of London 1960, memb Guild of Freemen 1987, Liveryman Worshipful Co of Gunmakers 1988-; The Pilgrims 1971-; KStJ 1976; *Recreations* cricket, shooting, golf; *Clubs* Boodle's, Pratt's, MCC, I Zingari, Free Foresters, Butterflies, Swinley Forest; *Style*— Col Edward Remington-Hobbs, DSO, OBE; The Maidens' Tower, Leeds Castle, Maidstone, Kent ME17 1PL (☎ 0622 880272); 3 Lyall Mews, London SW1X 8DJ (☎ 071 235 0930); 123-124 Newgate St, London EC1A 7AA (☎ 071 600 8387)

REMINGTON-HOBBS, Mrs Edward; Susan Mary Sheila; *née* Winn; da of Hon Charles Winn (2 s of 2 Baron St Oswald, JP, DL), by his 1 w Hon Olive, da of 1 and last Baron Queenborough, GBE, JP (gs of 1 Marquess of Anglesey); *b* 27 April 1923; *Educ* Owleston Croft, Cambridge, French Sch Paris; *m* 1, 20 July 1946, Hon Geoffrey Denis Erskine Russell (now Baron Ampthill); 3 s (David Whitney Erskine b 1947, James Nicholas Geoffrey b 1948 d 1969, Anthony John Mark b 1952), 1 da (Vanessa Mary Linda b 1960); m 2, 19 Dec 1972, Col Edward Remington-Hobbs, DSO, OBE, *qv*; *Career* joined Red Cross 1939, serv VAD 1941-45; *Recreations* reading, walking, photography; *Style*— Mrs Edward Remington-Hobbs; The Maidens' Tower, Leeds Castle, Maidstone, Kent ME17 1PL (☎ 0622 880272); 3 Lyall Mews, London SW1X 8DJ (☎ 071 235 0930)

REMNANT, Hon Hugo Charles; 3 s of 3 Baron Remnant, CVO; *b* 28 Nov 1959; *Educ* Eton, Univ of Newcastle (BSc), RAC Cirencester; *Career* land agent; *Style*— The Hon Hugo Remnant; c/o Bear Ash, Hare Hatch, Reading RG10 9XR (☎ 0734 402639)

REMNANT, 3 Baron (UK 1928); Sir James Wogan Remnant; 3 Bt (UK 1917), CVO (1979); o s of 2 Baron Remnant, MBE (d 1967), and Norah Susan, *née* Wogan-Browne (d 1990); *b* 23 Oct 1930; *Educ* Eton; *m* 24 June 1953, Serena Jane, o da of Cdr Sir Clive Loehnis, KCMG, RN (ret), and his w, Rosemary Beryl, o da of Maj Hon Robert Dudley Ryder, 4 s of 4 Earl of Harrowby; 3 s, 1 da; *Heir* s, Hon Philip John Remnant, *qv*; *Career* ptnr Touche Ross & Co 1958-70; dir: Australian Mercantile Land and Finance 1957-69, Australia & NZ Banking Group 1965-81 ; chm: Touche Remnant & Co 1980-89 (md 1970-80), TR City of London Trust 1978-90 (dir 1973-), TR Pacific Investment Trust 1987-; dir Bank of Scotland 1989- (chm London Bd 1979-); dep chm Ultramar 1981- (dir 1970-), chm National Provident Inst 1990- (dir 1963-); dir Union Discount Co of London 1969- (dep chm 1970-86) and other cos; pres: Nat Cncl of YMCAs 1983- (previously govr and pres London Central YMCA), Nat Florence Nightingale Memorial Ctee; tstee The Royal Jubilee Trusts 1989- (chm 1980-88, hon treas 1972-80); chm Assoc of Investmt Tst Cos 1977-79; church cmmr 1976-84; FCA; *Clubs* White's; *Style*— The Rt Hon the Lord Remnant, CVO; Bear Ash, Hare Hatch, Reading, Berks RG10 9XR (☎ 0734 402639)

REMNANT, Hon Philip John; s and h of 3 Baron Remnant, CVO; *b* 20 Dec 1954; *Educ* Eton, New Coll Oxford; *m* 1977, Caroline, da of Capt Godfrey Cavendish; 1 s (Edward b 1981), 2 da (Eleanor b 1983, Sophie b 1986); *Career* Peat Marwick Mitchell and Co 1976-82, Kleinwort Benson Limited 1982-90 (dir 1988-90), dir Barclays de Zoete Wedd Limited 1990-; *Style*— The Hon Philip Remnant; 36 Stevenage Rd, London SW6 6ET

REMNANT, Hon Robert James; 2 s of 3 Baron Remnant, CVO; *b* 10 Oct 1956; *Educ* Eton; *m* 1981, Sherrie, da of Frederick Cronn and Mrs Michael Watson, of Los Angeles; 2 s (Christopher Michael b 31 Oct 1982, Jack Preston b 30 June 1989), and 1 adopted s (Shannon Lynn b 19 Jan 1973); *Style*— The Hon Robert Remnant; c/o Jardine Matheson & Co Ltd, PO Box 70, GPO, Hong Kong

RENALS, Sir Stanley; 4 Bt (UK 1895); s of Sir James Herbert Renals, 2 Bt (d 1927), and Susan Emma, *née* Crafter (d 1957); suc bro, Sir Herbert Renals, 3 Bt (d 1961); *b* 20 May 1923; *Educ* City of London Freemen's Sch; *m* 2 Jan 1957, Maria Dolores Rodriguez Pinto, da of José Rodriguez Ruiz (d 1948); 1 s; *Heir* s, Stanley Michael Renals, *qv*; *Career* serv Merchant Navy 1938-60, entered as apprentice and ret with Master Mariner (FG) Certificate World Wide; *Style*— Sir Stanley Renals, Bt; 52 North Lane, Portslade, East Sussex BN4 2HG

RENALS, Stanley Michael; s and h of Sir Stanley Renals, 4 Bt, of Brighton, Sussex, and Maria Dolores Rodriguez, *née* Pinto; *b* 14 Jan 1958; *Educ* Falmer HS, Brighton Poly (BSc); *m* 1982, Jacqueline Ann, da of Roy Denis Riley, of 26 Uplands Rd, Hollingdean, Brighton, Sussex; 1 s (Lloyd James b 1985) 1 da (Frances Emma b 1986); *Career* design engr Kulicke & Soffa 1983-85, sales and marketing mangr Alpha Metals 1988 (area mangr 1985); CEng, MIMechE, MIProdE; *Recreations* golf, squash; *Clubs* Dragons Health and Leisure, Horton Park Country; *Style*— Stanley Renals, Esq; 72 Parsonage Rd, Henfield, W Sussex BN5 9JG; Alpha Metals, 1 The Broadway, Tolworth, Surbiton, Surrey KT6 7DQ (☎ 081 390 7011, fax 081 399 6252, telex 929818)

RENCHER, Derek; s of Walter Samuel Rencher (d 1974), of Birmingham, and Alice Gertrude, *née* Houlton (d 1960); *b* 6 June 1932; *Educ* Handsworth GS, Janet Cranmore Sch of Ballet Birmingham, Bourneville Sch of Arts and Crafts Birmingham, RCA, Barbara Vernon Sch of Russian Ballet, Royal Ballet Sch; *Career* Royal Ballet performances: King of the East in Pas de Six Pagodas, Demophoon in Persephone, Haeman in Antigone, Grey Prince in Lady and the Fool, Lysander in Midsummer Nights Dream, White Boy in Patineurs, Paris in Romeo, Elgar in Enigma Variations, Czar Nicholas in Anastasia, Rothbart in Swan Lake, Duke in Giselle, Prince and King in Beauty, Paris Singer in Isadora, Rakitin in Month in the Country, Ancestor in Shadow Play, Emperor Franz in Josef Mayerling, Lord Capulet in Romeo, Mons G M in Manon, Zeus in Creatures of Prometheus, Brahmin in La Bayadere, Doctor in Winter Dreams; designer of: Swanlake Act III (Philadelphia Ballet), One in Five (Canadian National and Australian Ballet), Lament of the Waves and Siesta (Royal Opera House); *Recreations* gardening, painting, needlework, cooking, swimming, walking; *Style*— Derek Rencher, Esq; The Royal Opera House, Covent Garden, London WC2 (☎ 071 240 1200)

RENDALL, Max; s of Richard Antony Rendall, CBE (d 1957), of Park Square East, London NW1, and Anne, *née* Moinet (d 1960); *b* 2 April 1934; *Educ* Winchester, Trinity Coll Cambridge (MA), Middx Hosp Med Sch (MB BChir); *m* 2 Oct 1963, Mary, da of George Douglass Debevoise (d 1980), of Brookville, Long Island, NY, USA; 1 s (Julian Douglass b 1969); *Career* Guy's Hosp: conslt surgn 1969, clinical supt 1981; memb Lewisham & North Southwark Health Authy; FRCS 1964, fell King's Fund Coll; *Recreations* woodwork, walking, wine; *Style*— Max Rendall, Esq; 4 Ladbroke Square, London W11 3LX (☎ 071 221 4847); Guy's Hospital, London SE1 9RT (☎ 071 955 4169)

RENDALL, Peter Godfrey; s of Godfrey A H Rendall (d 1961), of Bushey Heath, Herts, and Mary Whishaw, *née* Wilson (d 1946); *b* 25 April 1909; *Educ* Rugby, CCC Oxford (BA, MA); *m* 6 Feb 1944, Ann, da of Edward McKnight Kauffer (d 1956), of London and NY; 2 s (Jonathan Godfrey, Edward Simon), 1 da (Helen Grace); *Career* Flt Lt RAF 1943-46; Upper Canada Coll Toronto 1934-35, housemaster Felsted Sch

1935-43 (sr classics master 1931-43), second master St Bees Sch Cumberland 1946-48, headmaster Achimota Sch Gold Coast Ghana 1948-53, classics master Lancing Coll 1954-59, headmaster Bembridge Sch IOW 1959-74; town clerk Burford Oxon 1977-85; asst co cmmr Boy Scouts 1947-48; chm: Lancing branch UNO 1956-59, Tolsey Museum Burford 1976-89; Coronation medal 1951; *Recreations* reading, carpentry, gardening; *Clubs* Royal Cwlth Soc, Oxford Union Soc; *Style*— Peter Rendall, Esq; Chippings, The Hill, Burford, Oxon (☎ 099 382 2459)

RENDELL, Ruth Barbara; da of Arthur Grasemann (d 1973), and Ebba Elise Grasemann, *née* Kruse (d 1963); *b* 17 Feb 1930; *m* 1950 (re-m 1977), Donald John Rendell; 1 s (Simon b 1953); *Career* writer; awards: Arts Cncl Nat Book award Genre Fiction (1981), Crime Writers' Assoc 3 Gold Dagger awards (1976, 1987 and 1987), 1 Silver Dagger (1984), Mystery Writers of America 3 Edgar Allen Poe awards (1974, 1984 and 1987), Sunday Times award for Literary Excellence 1990; FRSL; *Books* From Doon with Death (1964), The Face of Trespass (1971), A Judgement in Stone (1976), Master of the Moor (1982), The Killing Doll (1984), An Unkindness of Ravens (1985), The New Girlfriend (1985), Live Flesh (1986), Talking to Strange Men (1987), The Veiled One (1988), The Bridesmaid (1989); under pseudonym Barbara Vine: A Dark-Adapted Eye (1986), A Fatal Inversion (1987), House of Stairs (1989), Gallowglass (1990); *Recreations* reading, walking, opera; *Clubs* Groucho's, Detection; *Style*— Mrs Ruth B Rendell; Nussteads, Polstead, Suffolk; 26 Cornwall Terrace Mews, London NW1

RENDER, Phillip Stanley; s of Stanley Render, of Bransholme, Hull, and Bessie, *née* Bestwick; *b* 15 Jan 1944; *Educ* Malet Lambet HS Hull; *m* 21 Oct 1967, Patricia Mary, da of Alfred Bernard Rooms, of Parkstone Rd, Hull; 2 s (Adrian b 1973, Andrew b 1978), 1 da (Suzanne b 1982); *Career* chartered surveyor in own practice 1982-, surveyor to tstees of Beverley Consolidated Charity 1973-, dir Beverley Bldg Soc 1986-, memb sub-ctee Northern Assoc of Surveryors 1988-; sec West Beck Preservation Soc 1982-, memb exec ctee Salmon and Trout Assoc (E Yorks Branch) 1982-; CS 1961-71; FRICS 1968; *Recreations* salmon and trout fishing, badminton; *Clubs* West Beck Preservation Soc, Hull and East Riding Sports; *Style*— Phillip Render, Esq; 6 West End Rd, Cottingham, N Humberside (☎ 0482 848 327); 7 North Bar Within, Beverley, N Humberside (☎ 0482 860 169, fax 0482 472 340)

RENDLE, Michael Russel; s of late H C R Rendle, and Valerie Patricia, *née* Gleeson; *b* 20 Feb 1931; *Educ* Marlborough, New Coll Oxford (MA); *m* 1957, Elizabeth Heather, da of J W J Rinkel; 2 s, 2 da; *Career* joined Anglo-Iranian Oil Co (now BP) 1954; md: BP Trinidad 1967-70, BP Australia Ltd 1974-78, BP Trading Ltd 1978-81, BP Co plc 1981-86; chm: BP Chemicals International Ltd 1981-83, BP Nutrition 1981-86, BP Coal Ltd 1983-86; dep chm: IC Gas Association 1986-87, British Borneo Petroleum Syndicate plc 1986-; memb London Advsy Bd Westpac Banking Corporation (Aust) 1978-89; dir: Willis Corroon plc (formerly Willis Faber plc) 1985-, Petrofina SA 1986-87; memb BOTB 1982-86; chm: European Trade Ctee 1982-86, INSEAD Int Cncl and UK Advisory Bd 1984-86; memb: BOTB 1982-86, Social Affairs Ctee UNICEF 1984-87, Cncl Marlborough Coll 1987-; *Recreations* golf, music, outdoor sports, gardening; *Clubs* Vincent's (Oxford); Australian (Melbourne), Royal Melbourne Golf; *Style*— Michael Rendle, Esq; c/o Willis Corroon plc, c/o 10 Trinity Square, London EC3P 3AX (☎ 071 481 7152)

RENDLE, Timothy John; s of Morgan Rendle, of Hove, Sussex, and Joy, *née* Griffith (d 1975); *b* 25 March 1929; *Educ* Brighton Coll, BC, Brighton Coll of Art; *m* 13 Sept 1975, Judith Anne, da of Robert Chalenor Freeman (d 1983), of Liverpool; 1 da (Claudia b 1976); *Career* architect, interior and furniture designer, architectural asst Louis de Soissons & ptnrs 1950-52, architectural assoc to Sir Hugh Casson 1953-60; formed architectural practice 1958; chm WLAS 1983 and WLAS Planning 1984-; ARIBA; *Recreations* music (violin) painting, photography; *Style*— Timothy J Rendle, Esq; 54 Britannia Rd, London SW6 (☎ 071 736 9744)

RENDLESHAM, 8 Baron (I 1806); Charles Anthony Hugh Thellusson; s of Lt-Col Hon Hugh Thellusson, DSO, 3 s of 5 Baron Rendlesham, JP, DL, by his w Lady Egidia Montgomerie (da of 13 Earl of Eglinton and Winton, KT); Hugh was bro of 6 and 7 Barons Rendlesham and m Gwynnydd, da of Brig-Gen Sir Robert Colleton, 1 and last Bt, CB; suc unc 1943; the Thellussons descend from an eighteenth century Swiss Ambass to the court of Louis XV of France, one Isaac de Thellusson; *b* 15 March 1915; *Educ* Eton; *m* 1, 1940 (m dis 1947), Margaret, da of Lt-Col Robin Rome, MC; 1 da (Hon Lady Goring, *qv*); m 2, 1947, Clare (d 1987), da of Lt-Col Douglas McCririck, of Wiveliscombe, Somerset; 1 s, 3 da; *Heir* s, Hon Charles Thellusson; *Career* late Royal Corps of Signals, Capt, served WW II; *Style*— The Rt Hon The Lord Rendlesham; 100b Eaton Square, SW1

RENFREW, Prof (Andrew) Colin; s of Archibald Renfrew (d 1978), and Helena Douglas, *née* Savage; *b* 25 July 1937; *Educ* St Albans Sch, St John's Coll Cambridge (BA, PhD, ScD); *m* 21 April 1965, Jane Margaret, da of Ven Walter F Ewbank; 2 s (Alban b 24 June 1970, Magnus b 5 Nov 1975), 1 da (Helena b 23 Feb 1968); *Career* Nat Serv Flying Offr (Signals) RAF 1956-58; reader in prehistory & archaeology Univ of Sheffield 1965-72 (formerly lectr and sr lectr), res fell St Johns Coll Cambridge 1965-68, Bulgarian Govt scholarship 1966, visiting lectr Univ of California (Los Angeles) 1967, prof of archaeology and head of dept Univ of Southampton 1972-81, Disney prof of archaeology and head of dept Univ of Cambridge 1981-, fell St John's Coll Cambridge 1981-86, master Jesus Coll Cambridge 1986-; memb: Royal Cmmn for Historic Monuments of England 1977-87, Historic Bldgs & Monuments Commn Advsy Bd 1983-, Historic Bldgs & Monuments Cmmn Sci Panel 1983-89; Freeman City of London; Hon DLitt Univ of Sheffield 1987; FSA 1968, FSA (Scotland) 1970, FBA 1980; *Books* The Explanation of Culture Change: Models in Prehistory (ed, 1973), British Prehistory, a new Outline (ed, 1977), Problems in European Prehistory (1979), Approaches to Social Archaeology (1984), The Archaeology of Cult: The Sanctuary at Phylakopi (1985), Archaeology and Language: The Puzzle of Indo-European Origins (1987), The Cycladic Spirit (1991); *Recreations* modern art, numismatics, travel; *Clubs* Athenaeum, United Oxford and Cambridge Universities; *Style*— Prof Colin Renfrew; The Master's Lodge, Jesus College, Cambridge CB5 8QL (☎ 0223 323 934); University of Cambridge, Department of Archaeology, Downing Street, Cambridge CB2 3DZ (☎ 0223 333 520)

RENFREW, Glen McGarvie; *b* 15 Sept 1928; *m* Daphne; 1 s (Barry), 3 da (Susan, Judy, Pamela; also 1 da, Ann, decd); *Career* jt dep md Reuters Ltd to 1981, md Feb 1981-; dir IDR Inc (USA); *Style*— Glen Renfrew Esq; c/o Reuters Ltd, 1700 Broadway, NY 10019, USA; c/o Reuters Ltd, 85 Fleet St, EC4 (☎ 01 353 6060/836 2567); Shorewood Drive, Sands Point, New York, USA

RENNELL, 3 Baron (UK 1933); (John Adrian) Tremayne Rodd; 2 but only surviving s of Cdr Hon Gustaf Rodd (bro of: (1) 2 Baron Rennell, KBE, CB, JP, DL, who d 1978, (2) Hon Peter Rodd, who d 1968, husb of late Nancy Mitford and allegedly the model for Evelyn Waugh's character Basil Seal, (3) late Baroness Emmet of Amberley, and (4) late Hon Mrs (Lt-Col Simon) Elwes, wife of the former Official War Artist); *b* 28 June 1935; *Educ* Downside, RNC Dartmouth; *m* 1977, Phyllis, da of Thomas Neill, of Co Armagh; 1 s, 3 da (Hon Sophie b 1981, Hon Rachel b 1987, Hon Lilias b 28 June 1989); *Heir* s, Hon James Roderick David Tremayne Rodd b 9 March 1978; *Career* served RN 1952-62; Morgan Grenfell & Co 1963-66, former freelance journalist & Scottish Rugby International; dir Tremayne Ltd 1980-; *Clubs* White's, Brooks's, Portland, Queens, Sunningdale; *Style*— The Rt Hon Lord Rennell; c/o White's Club, 37 St James's Street, London SW1

RENNELLS, William John; s of Albert Edward Rennells (d 1975), of Canterbury, and Alice Emily Rennells (d 1970); *b* 25 July 1931; *m* 1, 19 June 1954 (m dis 1988), Lois Brunger; 2 da (Susan b 20 July 1963, Jane b 23 May 1965); m 2, 21 May 1988, Angela Valera, *née* Griffiths; 1 step s (Marcus John b 4 July 1971), 1 step da (Sarah Louise b 4 April 1969); *Career* Nat Serv Pay Corps 1949-51; chief reporter Eastbourne Gazette 1957-61, asst dist news ed Oxford Mail 1961-70, prodr BBC Radio Oxford 1970-78, announcer and presenter BBC Radio 2 1978-; presented: Test Match Special Radio 3 1985-, Sounds of Jazz Radio 1; has deputised for Jimmy Young, Ray Moore, Gloria Hunniford and John Dunn on Radio 2; life pres Abingdon Keyboard Club, vice pres Abingdon Town FC, patron Abingdon Operatic Soc; Inst of Journalists 1955-70, memb of Equity; *Recreations* walking, playing and watching cricket, reading, visiting jazz clubs; *Style*— William Rennells, Esq; The Arbour, Foster Road, Abingdon, Oxon OX14 1YW (☎ 0235 553436)

RENNERT, Jonathan; s of Sidney Rennert, of London, and Patricia, *née* Clack; *b* 17 March 1952; *Educ* St Paul's, RCM, St John's Coll Cambridge (MA); *Career* dir of music: St Jude's Church London 1975-76, St Matthew's Ottawa Canada 1976-78, St Michael's Cornhill City of London 1979-; organ recitalist on four continents, lectr; recordings, radio and TV broadcasts as conductor, solo organist, organ accompanist, harpsichord continuo player; conductor: Cambridge Opera 1972-74, St Jude's Singers 1975-76, St Michael's Singers 1979-, The Elizabethan Singers 1983-88, English Harmony 1988-; fndr and dir Cornhill Festival of Br Music and Lloyds Bank Nat Composers' Award 1982-; examiner: Assoc Bd of the Royal Schs of Music, Royal Coll of Organists; adjudicator Thames TV, course dir Royal Sch of Church Music, admin and chm Exec Ctee Int Congress of Organists 1987; memb: Inc Soc of Musicians, Musicians' Union, cncl Royal Coll of Organists and Organists' Benevolent League; past pres The Organ Club; hon fell Royal Canadian Coll of Organists 1987; Liveryman Worshipful Co of Musicians; FRCO, ARCM, LRAM; *Books* William Crotch 1775-1847 Composer Artist Teacher (1975), George Thalben-Ball (1979); *Style*— Jonathan Rennert, Esq; 74 Pembroke Rd, Kensington, London W8 6NX (☎ 071 602 7483)

RENNIE, Archibald Louden; CB (1980); s of John Rennie Lindores, of Fife (d 1974), and Isabella Mitchell, *née* Louden (d 1979); *b* 4 June 1924; *Educ* Madras Coll St Andrews, Univ of St Andrews (BSc, LLD); *m* 14 Sept 1950, Kathleen, da of John James Harkess (d 1955), of Chingford, Essex; 4 s (Adam b 1951, John b 1953, David b 1956, Simon b 1959); *Career* temp experimental offr Mine Design Dept and Minesweeping Res Div Admty 1944-47; princ Dept of Health for Scotland 1954-62 (asst princ 1947-54), private sec to Sec of State for Scotland 1962-63, asst sec Scottish Home and Health Dept 1963-69, registrar gen for Scotland 1969-73, under sec Scottish Econ Planning Dept 1973-77, sec Scottish Home and Health Dept 1977-84, ret 1984; vice chm NHS Advsy Ctee on Distinction Awards 1985-; assessor Ct St Andrew's Univ 1984-89 (chllrs assessor 1986-89); memb: Scottish Records Advsy Cncl 1985-, Cncl on Tbnls (and Scottish Ctee) 1987-88; chm Hong Kong Disciplined Servs Pay Review Ctee 1988; chm Blacket Assoc (local conservation soc) 1970-73; Vice-Cdre Elie and Earls Ferry SC; tstee Lockerbie Air Disaster Tst; *Recreations* sailing, sea-fishing, gardening, golf, Scottish literature; *Clubs* Scottish Arts (Edinburgh), Elie Golf House; *Style*— Archibald Rennie, Esq, CB; Baldinnie, 10 Park Place, Elie, Leven, Fife (☎ 0333 330741)

RENNIE, Ian George; s of Peter Bruce Rennie, of Eccleston Park, Prescot, Merseyside, and Vera Margaret, *née* Haworth; *b* 10 Nov 1952; *Educ* Prescott GS, Univ of Sheffield (MB ChB); *m* 1, 28 Aug 1976 (m dis 1986), Janet Mary Rennie; m 2, 19 July 1986, Sharon, da of Stanley Herbert Markland, of Waterloo, Liverpool; *Career* lectr Dept of Ophthalmology Univ of Liverpool 1982-85, sr lectr Dept of Ophthalmology Univ of Sheffield 1985-, hon conslt ophthalmic surgn Royal Hallamshire Hosp 1985-; memb RSM, FRCSEd 1981, FC Ophth 1989; *Recreations* astronomy, windsurfing; *Style*— Ian Rennie, Esq; 27 Whirlowdale Crescent, Sheffield, South Yorkshire S7 2NA (☎ 0742 362325); Dept of Ophthalmology, University of Sheffield, Royal Hallamshire Hospital, Sheffield (☎ 0742 766222, fax 0742 766381)

RENNIE, Dr Janet Mary; da of Arthur Ball (d 1965), of Liverpool, and Marjorie Kennerley, *née* Jones; *b* 2 Dec 1954; *Educ* Belvedere Sch GPDST Liverpool, Univ of Sheffield (MB ChB, MD, MRCP), DCH; *m* 28 Aug 1976 (m dis 1986) Ian George Rennie, s of Peter Bruce Rennie; *Career* jr hosp posts 1978-85, sr res asst Univ of Liverpool 1983-85, lectr paediatrics Univ of Cambridge 1985-88, currently conslt neonatal med Rosie Maternity Hosp Cambridge; memb Midwives Advsy Info Resources Cncl, fell Girton Coll Cambridge; memb: Br Paediatric Assoc, Br Assoc Perinatal Paediatricians, Neonatal Soc, Paediatric Res Soc; *Books* Chapters in: Textbook of Paediatrics, Textbook of Neonatology; *Recreations* piano, cooking; *Style*— Dr Janet Rennie; Dept Paediatrics, Level 8, Addenbrooke's Hosp, Hills Rd, Cambridge, CB2 2QQ (☎ 0453 841636)

RENNIE, John Aubery; s of James Rennie (d 1987), and Ethel May Aubrey, *née* Byford; *b* 19 Jan 1947; *Educ* Kings Coll Sch Wimbledon, St Bartholemew's Med Sch London; *m* 12 Aug 1972, Sheelagh Ruth, da of John Robert Winter, of White Cottage, Harmans Cross, Dorset; 1 s (Alexander John b 1982), 3 da (Natasha Louise b 1973, Sara Rosalind b 1976, Rachel Suzannah b 1979); *Career* lectr in surgery Charing Cross Hosp London, resident surgical offr St Mark's Hosp London, sr lectr and conslt Kings Coll Hosp London (formerly sr registrar); fndr memb Bureau of Overseas Med Servs, med dir ME Christian Outreach; FRSM, FRCS; *Style*— John Rennie, Esq; 94 Burbage Road, Dulwich, London SE24 9HE (☎ 071 274 0233); Department of Surgery, Rayne Institute, Kings College Hospital, London SE5 (☎ 071 274 6222)

RENNIE, Sir John Shaw; GCMG (1968, KCMG 1962, CMG 1958), OBE 1955; s of late John Shaw Rennie, of Saskatoon, Saskatchewan, Canada; *b* 12 Jan 1917; *Educ* Hillhead HS Glasgow, Univ of Glasgow, Balliol Coll Oxford; *m* 1946, Mary Winifred Macalpine, da of James Bryson Robertson, of Hillhead, Glasgow; 1 s; *Career* entered Colonial Civil Serv Tanganyika 1940: asst dist offr 1942, dist offr 1949, dep colonial sec Mauritius 1951, Br res cmmr New Hebrides 1955-62, govr and CIC Mauritius 1962-68, govr-gen 1968, dep cmmr gen UN Relief and Works Agency for Palestine Refugees 1968-71, cmmr gen 1971-77; Hon LLD Univ of Glasgow; *Clubs* Royal Cwlth Soc; *Style*— Sir John Rennie, GCMG, OBE; 26 College Cross, London N1 1PR; Via Roma 33, 06050 Collazzone (PG), Italy

RENNIE, Michael Christopher Gibson; s of Thomas Gibson Rennie (d 1970), of Glasgow, and Elizabeth Livingstone, *née* McCorquodale (d 1962); *b* 6 June 1933; *Educ* Fettes, Univ of Glasgow (MB ChB); *Career* Nat Serv RAF 1958-60; med practitioner, princ in gen practice 1968, med advsr and examiner in occupational health and life assurance med 1968; memb: Assurance Med Soc 1960, Scottish Soc of the History of Med 1975, nat exec Epilepsy Assoc of Scotland 1987; Decon Incorporation of Hammermen of Glasgow 1983-84; F Inst Pet 1978; *Recreations* hillwalking; *Style*— Michael Rennie, Esq; 8 Buckingham Terrace, Glasgow G12 8EB (☎ 041 339 0641)

RENNY, Hon Mrs (Nicola Gladys); *née* Moncreiff; da of 4 Baron Moncreiff (d 1942); *b* 1917; *m* 1, 1940, Capt Frederick W Gifford, RA (ka 1943); 1 s; m 2, 1946, Charles John Derek Renny (d 1970); 1 s, 2 da; *Clubs* Royal Channel Islands Yacht (RCIYC);

Style— The Hon Mrs Renny; Greenways, Les Vardes, St Peter Port, Guernsey

RENOUF, Sir Francis Henry; s of Francis Charles Renouf (d 1983), of NZ, and Mary Ellen, *née* Avery (d 1983); *b* 31 July 1918; *Educ* Wellington Coll NZ, Victoria Univ of Wellington (M Com), Oxford Univ (Dip PL); *m* 1, 7 Aug 1954 (m dis 1985), Ann Marie Harkin; 1 s (John b 1956), 3 da (Paula b 1955, Frances b 1957, Catherine b 1957); m 2, 2 Sept 1985 (m dis 1990), Susan, da of Sir John Rossiter (d 1988), and formerly w of Robert Sangster and previously of Andrew Peacock; m 3, 16 Jan 1991, Michele, formerly w of Daniel Griaznoff; *Career* 2 Lt (later Capt) NZEF 1940, (POW Germany 1941-45); chm Renouf Gp 1950-87, ret; Lawn Tennis Victoria Univ blue 1938-40, Oxford blue 1948 and 1949; Order of Merit (first class) West Germany 1986; *Recreations* lawn tennis; *Clubs* Cavalry and Guards'; *Style*— Sir Francis Renouf; 37 Eaton Sq, London SW1 (☎ 071 235 1124)

RENOWDEN, Very Rev Charles Raymond; s of Rev Canon Charles Renowden (d 1964), and Mary Elizabeth, *née* Williams (d 1974); bro of Ven Glyndwr Rhys Renowden, *qv*; *b* 27 Oct 1923; *Educ* Llandysil GS, St David's Univ Coll Lampeter (BA), Selwyn Coll Cambridge (BA, MA); *m* 1951, Ruth Cecil Mary, da of George Edward Cecil Collis (d 1969); 1 s, 2 da; *Career* ordained: deacon 1951, priest 1952; lectr in philosphy and theology St David's Univ Coll Lampeter 1955-57 (head Dept of Philosophy 1957-69, sr lectr philosphy and theology 1969-71); dean of St Asaph 1971-; *Recreations* music, ornithology; *Style*— The Very Rev the Dean of St Aspah; The Deanery, St Asaph, Clwyd, N Wales LL17 0RL (☎ 0745 583597); St Asaph Cathedral Office (☎ 0745 583429)

RENOWDEN, Rev Canon; Air Vice-Marshal (Ret) Glyndwr Rhys; CB (1987), QHC (1980); s of Rev Canon Charles Renowden (d 1964), and Mary Elizabeth Renowden (d 1972); *b* 13 Aug 1929; *Educ* Llanelli GS, St David's Univ Coll Lampeter (BA, LTh); *m* 1956, Mary Kinsey-Jones; 1 da; *Career* Chaplain in Chief RAF 1983-88; *Style*— The Rev Canon Glyndwr R Renowden, CB, QHC; Red Cedars, Kenystyle, Penally, nr Tenby, Dyfed

RENSHALL, (James) Michael; CBE (1991, OBE 1977); s of Arthur Renshall (d 1973), and Ethel, *née* Gardner (d 1970); *b* 27 July 1930; *Educ* Rydal Sch, Clare Coll Cambridge (MA); *m* Aug 1960, Kathleen Valerie, da of Harold Tyson, of Liverpool; 1 da (Susan b 1961); *Career* CA; ptnr KPMG Peat Marwick McLintock, chm Accounting Standards Ctee 1986-; memb Cncl of Inst of CA England and Wales; FCA; *Recreations* theatre, art, economic and military history, gardens; *Clubs* Utd Oxford and Cambridge, City Livery; *Style*— Michael Renshall, Esq, CBE; 5 Ferrings, London SE21 7LU (☎ 081 693 3190); 1 Puddle Dock, Blackfriars, London EC4V 3PD (☎ 071 236 8000, telex 8811541 PMMLONG, fax 071 583 1938)

RENSHAW, John David; s and h of Sir (Charles) Maurice Bine Renshaw, 3 Bt, and Isobel Bassett Popkin (now Mrs L E S Cox); *b* 9 Oct 1945; *Educ* Ashmole Sch Southgate; *m* 1970 (m dis 1988) Jennifer, da of Gp Capt Fredrick Murray, RAF (ret), 1 s (Thomas b 1976), 2 da (Joanna b 1973, Catherine b 1978); *Career* Army 1960-69 Corpl; fatstock offr Meat and Livestock Cmmn 1974-88; *Recreations* skiing, upholstery, DIY; *Style*— John Renshaw Esq; 40 Bromsberrow Way, Meir Park, Meir, Stoke-on-Trent (☎ 0782 393408)

RENSHAW, Sir (Charles) Maurice Bine; 3 Bt (UK 1903); s of Capt Sir (Charles) Stephen Bine Renshaw, 2 Bt (d 1976), and Edith Mary, 4 da of Rear-Adm Sir Edward Chichester, 9 Bt, CB, CMG; *b* 7 Oct 1912; *Educ* Eton; *m* 1, 1942 (m dis 1947), Isobel Bassett, da of late Rev John L T Popkin; 1 s, 1 da; m 2, Winifred Mary, da of H F Gliddon, and formerly w of of James H T Sheldon; 3 s, 3 da; *Heir* s, (John) David Renshaw; *Career* late Flying Offr RAF; *Style*— Sir Maurice Renshaw, Bt; Tom-na-Margaidh, Balquhidder, Perthshire; Linwood, Instow, N Devon

RENSHAW, Peter Bernard Appleton; s of Bernard Artoune Renshaw, Flat 3, Wrayton Lodge, Whitehall Rd, Sale, Cheshire, and Elsie Renshaw, *née* Appleton (d 1954); *b* 23 July 1954; *Educ* Charterhouse, Selwyn Coll Cambridge; *m* 16 Oct 1982, Patricia Ann, da of Robert Vernon Caffrey, of 26 Avonlea Rd, Sale, Cheshire; 1 s (Thomas Peter b 1987); *Career* ptnr Slater Heelis Slrs Manchester 1982- (articled clerk 1977-79, slr 1979-82); Notary Public 1988; memb Law Soc; *Recreations* walking, squash, DIY; *Style*— Peter Renshaw, Esq; Slater Heelis, 71 Princess St, Manchester, Greater Manchester M2 4HL (☎ 061 228 3781, fax 061 236 5282, telex 669568)

RENTON, Andrew; s of Michael Paul Renton, of London, and Yvonne Renee, *née* Labaton; *b* 8 Feb 1963; *Educ* Manchester GS, Univ of Nottingham (BA), Univ of Reading (PhD); *Career* fndr and artistic dir Quite Theatre 1985-88, art critic Blitz magazine, Br corr Flash Art magazine 1989; *Recreations* sleep; *Clubs* RAC; *Style*— Andrew Renton, Esq; 51 Warrington Crescent, London W9 1EJ (☎ 071 289 6868)

RENTON, Hon Clare Olivia; 2 da of Baron Renton, KBE, TD, PC, QC, DL (life peer); *b* 23 Aug 1950; *Educ* St Mary's Wantage, Birkbeck Coll London; *m* 1982, Timothy John Whittaker Scott, s of J D Scott (d 1980); 1 s (Duncan b 1984), 1 da (Helen b 1983); *Career* barr Lincoln's Inn 1972; *Recreations* opera, history, the country; *Style*— The Hon Clare Renton; 5 Raymond Buildings, Gray's Inn, London WC2 (☎ 071 831 0720)

RENTON, Baron (Life Peer UK 1979), of Huntingdon in Co Cambs; David Lockhart-Mure Renton; KBE (1964), TD, QC (1954), PC (1962), DL (Hunts 1962, Huntingdon & Peterborough 1964, Cambs 1974); s of Dr Maurice Waugh Renton; *b* 12 Aug 1908; *Educ* Oundle, Univ Coll Oxford (MA, BCL); *m* 1947, Claire Cicely (d 1986), yst da of late Walter Atholl Duncan; 3 da (Hon Caroline Mary (Hon Mrs Parr) b 1948, Hon Clare Olivia (Hon Mrs Scott) b 1950, Hon Davina Kathleen b 1954); *Career* Maj RA; barr 1933; sits as Cons peer in House of Lords; Maj RA; MP Hunts (Nat Lib 1945-50, Nat Lib & C 1950-68, C 1968-79); min of state Home Office 1961-62; memb Cmmn on the Constitution 1971-74, chm Ctee on Preparation of Legislation 1973-75; pres: Conservation Soc 1971-72, Statute Law Soc 1980-, Nat Cncl for Civil Protection 1980-, Nat Soc of Mentally Handicapped Children 1982-88 (chm 1978-82); dep speaker House of Lords 1982-88, bencher Lincoln's Inn 1963 (treas 1979); patron: Hunts Cons Assoc, Nat Law Library, Ravenswood Fndn, Design and Mfr for Disability (DEMAND), Greater London Assoc for the Disabled; hon fell Univ Coll Oxford; *Recreations* shooting, tennis, gardening; *Clubs* Carlton, Pratt's; *Style*— The Rt Hon Lord Renton, KBE, TD, QC, DL; Moat House, Abbots Ripton, Huntingdon (☎ 048 73 227); 16 Old Buildings, Lincoln's Inn, WC2A 3TL (☎ 071 242 8986)

RENTON, Dr Helen Ferguson; CB (1982); da of John Paul Renton (d 1973), and Sarah Graham, *née* Cook (d 1986); *b* 13 March 1931; *Educ* Stirling HS, Univ of Glasgow (MA); *Career* cmmnd RAF 1955 (Admin Branch); serv UK 1955-60, Cyprus 1960-62, UK 1962-67, HQ Staff Germany 1967, MOD Staff 1968-71, HQ NEAF 1971-73, HQ Trg Cmd 1973-76, MOD Staff 1977-78 and 1980-86; dir WRAF 1980-86; vice pres RAF Assoc 1982-91, ret as Air Cdre; Hon LLD Glasgow Univ; *Publications* Service Women (1977); *Recreations* needlework, travel, gardening; *Clubs* RAF; *Style*— Dr Helen F Renton; c/o Royal Bank of Scotland, 14-15 Hereward Centre, Broadway, Peterborough, Cambridgeshire PE1 1TB

RENTON, (Robert) Ian; s of Col Robert Donald Alexander Renton, MBE, MC (d 1976), and Susan Marion Langdon, *née* Studdy; *b* 1 Nov 1958; *Educ* Shrewsbury, Magdalene Coll Cambridge (MA); *m* 28 Sept 1985, Claire Lindsay, da of Dr James Woods Rentoul, of Cornwall; 1 s (Alec b 29 Sept 1990), 1 da (Ailsa b 9 Jan 1989); *Career* racecourse mangr; asst mangr Cheltenham Racecourse 1985-88, racecourse mangr Warwick Racecourse 1986-88, gen mangr and clerk of course Salisbury and Wincanton Racecourses 1988-; *Recreations* skiing, tennis, wine; *Style*— Ian Renton, Esq; Holywell Farmhouse, Holywell, Dorchester, Dorset DT2 0LQ

RENTON, Rt Hon Ronald Timothy (Tim); PC (1990), MP (C) Mid-Sussex 1974-; yr s of Ronald Kenneth Duncan Renton, CBE (d 1980), by his 2 w Eileen, MBE, yst da of Herbert James Torr, of Morton Hall, Lincs, and gda of John Torr, MP for Liverpool 1873-80; *b* 28 May 1932; *Educ* Eton, Magdalen Coll Oxford (MA); *m* 1960, Alice Blanche Helen, da of Sir James Ferugsson of Kilkerran, 8 Bt; 2 s (Alexander b 1961, Daniel b 1965), 3 da (Christian b 1963, Chelsea (twin) b 1965, Penelope b 1970); *Career* dir: Silvermines Ltd 1967-84, ANZ Banking Gp 1968-75; former md Tennant Trading; contested (C) Sheffield Park 1970, chm Cons Employment Ctee, PPS to John Biffen (as chief sec to Treasy) 1979-81, pres Cons Trade Unionists 1980-84 (vice pres 1978-80), PPS to Sir Geoffrey Howe (as chllr and foreign sec) 1983-84, Parly under sec FCO 1984, min of State FCO 1984-87, min of State Home Off 1987-89, govt chief whip 1989-90, min for the Arts 1990-; memb: Advsy Cncl BBC 1982-84, Governing Cncl Roedean Sch 1982-; chm Cons Foreign and Cwlth Cncl 1983-84, tstee Mental Health Fndn 1985-89; memb APEX; *Recreations* gardening, listening to opera, sea fishing (mv Porage); *Clubs* Garrick; *Style*— The Rt Hon Tim Renton, MP; c/o House of Commons, London SW1A 0AA

RENWICK, Diana, Lady; Diana Mary; da of Col Bernard Cruddas, DSO, of Middleton Hall, Morpeth; *m* 1934, Sqdn Ldr Sir Eustace Renwick, 3 Bt (d 1973); 2 s, 1 da; *Style*— Diana, Lady Renwick; Whalton, Northumberland

RENWICK, George Frederick; s of George Russell Renwick (d 1984), of The Old Parsonage, Sidlesham, Sussex, and Isabella Alice, *née* Watkins; *b* 27 July 1938; *Educ* Charterhouse, New Coll Oxford (MA); *m* 16 March 1974, Elizabeth Zoe, da of Strathearn Gordon, CBE (d 1983); 1 d (Helen b 1978); *Career* Nat Serv Lt RA 1957-59; teaching assoc North Western Univ Sch of Law Chicago 1962-63; admitted slr 1966; ptnr Slaughter and May 1970- (joined 1963); memb Addington Soc; memb: Law Soc 1966, Int Bar Assoc; *Clubs* Athenaeum, MCC; *Style*— George Renwick, Esq; c/o Slaughter and May, 35 Basinghall St, London EC2V 5DB (☎ 071 600 1200, fax 071 726 0038, telex 883486)

RENWICK, 2 Baron (UK 1964), of Coombe, Co Surrey; Sir Harry Andrew Renwick; 3 Bt (UK 1927); s of 1 Baron Renwick, KBE (d 1973), by his 1 w, Dorothy, *née* Parkes; *b* 10 Oct 1935; *Educ* Eton; *m* 1, 1965 (m dis 1989), Susan, da of Capt Kenneth Lucking (decd), and Mrs M Stormonth Darling; 2 s (Hon Robert b 19 Aug 1966, Hon Michael b 26 July 1968); m 2, 1989, Mrs Homayoun Mazandi, da of late Col Mahmoud Yasdanparst (Pakzad); *Heir* s, Hon Robert James Renwick b 19 Aug 1966; *Career* dir Gen Technology Systems 1975-, ptnr W Greenwell and Co 1963-80; vice pres Br Dyslexia Assoc 1982- (chm 1977-82), chm Dyslexia Educnl Tst 1986-; memb House of Lords Select Ctee on the Euro Communities 1988-; *Clubs* White's, Turf; *Style*— The Rt Hon Lord Renwick; House of Lords, Westminster SW1A 0PW

RENWICK, Prof James Harrison; s of Ray Renwick, MBE, (d 1974), of Otley Yorks, and Edith Helen, *née* Harrison (d 1988); *b* 4 Feb 1926; *Educ* Sedbergh, St Andrews Univ (MB ChB), UCL (PhD, DSc); *m* 1, 2 April 1959 (m dis 1979), Helena, da of Albert Verheyden (d 1986), of Ghent; 1 s (Arnold James b 1962), 1 da (Sonia Ruth b 1963), m 2, Kate, da of Vincent James Salafia (d 1967), of Philadelphia; 2 s (Douglas Raymond b 1982, Gregory Hugh b 1984); *Career* Nat Serv Capt RAMC 1951-53, serv Korean War, seconded Atomic Bomb Casualty Cmmn Hiroshima Japan; prof human genetics Univ of Glasgow 1967-68, reader then prof human genetics and teratology Univ of London 1977-; Freeman Worshipful Co of Stationers and Newspaper Makers; FRCP, FRCPath; *Books* contrib scientific appendix to report Royal Cmmn on Civil Liability and Compensation for Personal Injury; *Recreations* music, walking; *Style*— Prof James Renwick; 5 Speed House, Barbican, London, EC2Y 8AT; London School of Hygiene & Tropical Medicine, Keppel St, London WC1E 7HT (☎ 071 637 2839, fax 071 436 5389, telex 8953474); Rue des Coteaux, 1030 Brussels, Belgium (☎ 02 218 7668)

RENWICK, Joan, Baroness; (Edith) Joan; da of Sir Reginald Clarke, CIE; *m* 1, Maj John Ogilvie Spencer (decd); m 2, as his 2 w, 1953, 1 Baron Renwick, KBE (d 1973); *Style*— The Rt Hon Joan, Lady Renwick; Herne's Cottage, Windsor Forest, Berks

RENWICK, Sir Richard Eustace; 4 Bt (UK 1921), of Newminster Abbey, Morpeth, Northumberland; s of Sir Eustace Renwick, 3 Bt (d 1973), and Diana, Lady Renwick, *qv*; *b* 13 Jan 1938; *Educ* Eton; *m* 1966, Caroline, da of Maj Rupert Milburn, JP (2 s of Sir Leonard Milburn, 3 Bt, JP), and Anne, da of Maj Austin Scott Murray, MC; 3 s; *Heir* s, Charles Richard Renwick b 10 April 1967; *Career* late Capt Northumberland Hussars; md and proprietor Master Saddlers Co; *Recreations* tennis, hunting, point-to-pointing; *Clubs* Northern Counties (Newcastle); *Style*— Sir Richard Renwick, Bt; Whalton House, Whalton, Morpeth, Northumberland (☎ 067 075 383)

RENWICK, Sir Robin William; KCMG (1989, CMG 1980); s of Richard Renwick, of Edinburgh, and Clarice, *née* Henderson (d 1958); *b* 13 Dec 1937; *Educ* St Paul's, Univ of Cambridge (MA), Univ of Paris (Sorbonne); *m* 1965, Annie Colette, *née* Giudicelli; 1 s (John), 1 da (Marie-France); *Career* HM Dip Serv, first sec New Delhi 1966-70, Paris 1972-76; head of Chancery Washington 1971-84, cnsllr Cabinet Office 1976-78, head Rhodesia Dept FCO 1978-79, political advsr to Lord Soames as Govr of Rhodesia 1979-80, asst under sec FCO 1984-87, HM ambass to SA July 1987-91; *Books* Economic Sanctions (Harvard 1981); *Recreations* trout fishing, tennis; *Clubs* Hurlingham, Travellers; *Style*— Sir Robin Renwick, KCMG; c/o Foreign and Commonwealth Office, King Charles Street, London SW1

REPARD, Hon Mrs (Peggy); *née* Bowyer; da of late 1 Baron Denham (d 1948); *b* 18 May 1925; *m* 24 April 1947, Cdr John David Latimer Repard, OBE, DSC, RN; s of late William John Repard, of Many Waters, Bexhill; 3 da; *Style*— The Hon Mrs Repard; 18 Friars Field, Northchurch, Berkhamsted, Herts HP4 3XE (☎ 0442 864375)

REPTON, Rt Rev the Bishop of 1986-; (Francis) Henry Arthur Richmond; s of Francis Richmond (d 1985), of Newtownbutler, Co Fermanagh, N Ireland, and Lena, *née* Crawford; *b* 6 Jan 1936; *Educ* Portora Royal Sch Enniskillen, Trinity Coll Dublin (BA, MA), Strasbourg Univ, Linacre Coll Oxford (M Litt), Wycliffe Hall Oxford; *m* 10 Sept 1966, Caroline Mary, da of Herbert Siegmund Berent (d 1988), of Blechingley, Surrey; 2 s (Patrick b 1969, Gerald b 1971), 1 da (Harriet b 1974); *Career* curate All Saints Woodlands Doncaster 1963-66, Sir Henry Stephenson res fell and hon lectr Dept of Biblical Studies Univ of Sheffield 1966-69, vicar of St George's Sheffield 1969-77, hon lectr on New Testament Dept of Biblical Studies Univ of Sheffield 1969-77, anglican chaplain Univ of Sheffield 1974-77, warden Lincoln Theol Coll 1977-85, proctor in convocation 1980-85; *Recreations* music, gardening, walking; *Style*— The Rt Rev the Bishop of Repton; Repton House, Lea, Matlock, Derbyshire DE4 5JP (☎ 0629 534644)

RESUGGAN, Harold Frederick; s of John Henry Resuggan (d 1940), and Hilda Priscilla, *née* Worrall (d 1981); *b* 2 July 1929; *Educ* Handsworth Tech Coll, Aston Tech Coll (HND); *m* 19 March 1960, Dorothy Leone, da of William Edward Kirk (d 1982); *Career* Nat Serv, RAF 1950-52; chief designer Tangyes Ltd 1964, md Webley and Scott Ltd 1982 (tech dir 1972); various patents for hydraulic equipment and air rifles; CEng, MIMechE 1968, FRSA 1976; *Recreations* photography, gardening, cabinet making, painting; *Style—* Harold Resuggan, Esq; Webley & Scott Ltd, Frankley Industrial Park, Tay Rd, Rubery, Rednal, Birmingham B45 0PA (☎ 021 453 1864, fax 021 457 7846)

RETALLACK, James Keith; s of Capt Keith Retallack (d 1975), of Birmingham, and Betty Margery, *née* Heaps (d 1978); *b* 8 July 1957; *Educ* Malvern, Univ of Manchester (LLB); *m* 11 Nov 1989, Carol Krystal, da of Charles Henry Mosley (d 1987), of Birmingham; *Career* slr, articled clerk Lee Crowder & Co 1979-81, admitted 1981; Edge & Ellison: asst slr 1981-84, assoc 1984-88, ptnr 1988-; *Recreations* music, reading, skiing, travel; *Clubs* Club 64; *Style—* James Retallack, Esq; The Gables, 44 Streetly Lane, Four Oaks, Sutton Coldfield, W Midlands B74 4TX (☎ 021 308 3842); Edge & Ellison, Rutland House, 148 Edmund St, Birmingham B3 2JR (☎ 021 200 2001, fax 021 200 1991)

RETTIE, (James) Philip; CBE (1987), TD (1964); s of James Low Rettie (d 1962), of Balcairn, Dundee , and Josephine Rachel, *née* Buist (d 1989); *b* 7 Dec 1926; *Educ* Trinity Coll Glenalmond, Univ of Manchester; *m* 1, 1955 Helen Grant; 2 s (Andrew, Simon), 1 da (Sarah); m 2, 1980, Diana Mary, da of Col Colin John Ballantyne, TD, DL (d 1981); *Career* RE 1945-48, Maj RETA 1949-65 ; William Low & Co plc 1948-85 (chm 1980-85); farmer 1964-; chm Sea Fish Indust Authy 1981-87, ptnr Crossley & Rettie 1989-; tstee: TSB 1967-88, Scottish Civic Tst 1983-; memb: Cncl Saltire Soc 1989-, Highland TA Assoc 1975-; Hon Col 117 Field Sqdn RETA 1982-87, Hon Col 277 Field Sqdn RETA 1983-89; *Recreations* shooting, hill walking; *Clubs* Caledonian (London); *Style—* Philip Rettie, Esq, CBE, TD; Hill House, Ballindean, Inchture, Perthshire, PH14 9QS (☎ 0828 86337)

REUBEN, Arnold; JP (1971); s of Jack Reuben (d 1971); *b* 19 Dec 1929; *Educ* King George V Sch Southport, Exeter Coll Oxford; *m* 1954, Audrey, *née* Cussins; 1 s, 2 da; *Career* dir Waring & Gillow Hldgs Ltd, chm Leeds United Devpt Co Ltd; govr Leeds Playhouse, pres Leeds Jewish Welfare Bd; *Recreations* theatre, lit, wine and food, travel, walking; *Clubs* Royal Cwlth Soc; *Style—* Arnold Reuben, Esq, JP; Stone Acre, Leeds LS17 8EP (☎ 0532 683222)

REUPKE, Michael; s of Dr Willm Reupke (d 1968), and Frances Graham, *née* Kinnear; *b* 20 Nov 1936; *Educ* Latymer Upper Sch, Jesus Coll Cambridge (MA), Coll of Europe Bruges (Dip Euro Studies); *m* (Helen) Elizabeth, da of Edward Restrick (d 1988); 1 s (Peter b 1965), 2 da (Alison b 1968, Rachel b 1971); *Career* Reuters 1962-89: trainee journalist 1962, journalist (Geneva, London, Conakry, Paris, Bonn) 1962-69, euro mgmnt 1970-73, chief rep W Germany 1973-74, mangr Latin America 1975-77, ed-in-chief 1978-89, gen mangr 1989, conslt 1990-; dir Visnews Ltd 1985-89; tstee Reuter Fndn; memb: Int Inst of Communications, Media Law Gp, Int Press Inst; *Recreations* walking, sailing; *Clubs* Leander, Royal Automobile; *Style—* Michael Reupke, Esq; Tippings, The Common, Stokenchurch, Bucks HP14 3UD (☎ 0494 48 23 41, car 0836 201226)

REVANS, Reginald William; s of Thomas William Revans (d 1936), of London, and Ethel Amelia Charlotte Mary, *née* Evans (d 1966); *b* 14 May 1907; *Educ* Battersea GS, UCL (BSc), Emmanuel Coll Cambridge; *m* 1, June 1932 (m dis 1948), Ann-Ida Margareta Aqvist, of Sweden; 3 da (Marina b 31 March 1933, Vendela b 5 June 1935, Barbara b 8 Dec 1938); m 2, 30 Sept 1955, Norah Mary, da of Harold Merritt (d 1950), of Chelmsford, Essex; 1 s (Andrew b 24 Aug 1957); *Career* reserved occupation Essex Civil Def Servs; educn offr: Essex CC 1935-45, Mining Assoc of GB 1945-47, NCB 1947-50; res advsr NCB and Nat Assoc of Colliery Mangrs 1950-55, prof of indust admin Univ of Manchester 1955-65, res advsr Fondation Industrie-Universite Bruxelles Belgium 1965-75; memb Br Olympic Team Amsterdam 1928, Cambridge Univ Long Jump record 1929, Cwlth Games Hamilton Ont Canada 1930 (two silver medals); pres Euro Assoc of (Univ) Mgmnt Trg Centres 1962-64, fndr memb Br Inst of Mgmnt, hon professorial fell Univ of Manchester; Chevalier of the order of Leopold (Belgium) 1972; Hon MSc Univ of Manchester 1965, Hon DSc Univ of Bath 1973; CBIM 1947-; *Recreations* formerly athletics; *Style—* Reginald Revans, Esq; 8 Higher Downs, Altrincham, Cheshire WA14 2Ql

REVELL, Dr Peter Allen; s of William Allen Revell, of Leicester, and Edith Emma, *née* Pitts; *b* 1 Jan 1943; *Educ* Wyggeston GS Leicester, Univ of London (BSc, MB BS, PhD); *m* 11 Nov 1967, Margaret Ruth, da of John Sharples (d 1982), of Exeter; 2 s (Matthew Peter b 14 Jan 1969, David John b 25 Sept 1977), 1 da (Elizabeth Ruth b 23 March 1971); *Career* res fell MRC; presently reader and conslt pathologist Inst Pathology The London Hosp Med Coll (previously lectr, sr lectr), visiting prof Queen's Univ Kingston Ontario; MRCPath 1976-, FRCPath 1988-; memb: Int Skeletal Soc, American Coll of Rheumatology, various scientific socs in pathology, rheumatology and orthopaedics; *Books* Pathology of Bone (1986), contrib twelve chapters in other books, many papers in med jnls; *Recreations* choral singing and music, walking, swimming, photography; *Style—* Dr Peter Revell; The London Hosp Medical Coll, Inst of Pathology, London E1 2AD (☎ 071 377 7347 or 7419, fax 071 377 0949)

REVELL, Stephen Michael; s of Alfred Vincent Revell, of Beardwood Meadow, Blackburn, Lancs, and Doris, *née* Peaty (d 1985); *b* 20 Dec 1956; *Educ* St Mary Coll Blackburn, Christ's Coll Cambridge (MA); *m* 10 Nov 1979, Anne Marie, da of Brian Higgins, of Whitefield, Greater Manchester; *Career* ptnr Freshfields 1987- (asst slr 1979-87); Freeman Worshipful Co of Slrs 1988; memb Law Soc; *Recreations* skiing, fell walking, sugar lump collecting, travelling; *Style—* Stephen Revell, Esq; 42 Canonbury Park South, London N1; Freshfields, Whitefriars, 65 Fleet St, London EC4Y 1HS (☎ 071 936 4000, fax 071 238 3487, telex 889292)

REVELSTOKE, 4 Baron (UK 1885); Rupert Baring; s of 3 Baron Revelstoke (d 1934, through whose sis Susan, the present Lord R is 1 cous once removed to Richard Ingrams, ed of Private Eye); also 1 cous twice removed of HRH The Princess of Wales, n to late Countess (w of 5 Earl) of Kenmare, and bro-in-law of late Guy Liddell, CB, CBE, MC; *b* 8 Feb 1911; *Educ* Eton; *m* 1934 (m dis 1944), Hon Flora Fermor-Hesketh (d 1971; da of 1 Baron Hesketh by his w Florence, gda of Gen J C Breckinridge, sometime Vice-Pres of the USA), sis of Hon Lady Stockdale; 2 s; *Heir* s, Hon John Baring; *Career* late 2 Lt RAC (TA); *Style—* The Rt Hon Lord Revelstoke; Lambay Island, Rush, Co Dublin, Eire

REWSE-DAVIES, Jeremy Vyvyan; *b* 24 Nov 1939; *m* 1, 1961 (m dis) Teri Donn; 1 s (Jason Saul b 1968), 1 da (Jessica Lucy b 1968); m 2, 1975 (m dis), Kezia de Winne; m 3, 1981, Iga Przedrzymirska; 1 s (Alexander Henry Thomas b 1985); *Career* prodn designer BBC TV 1964-74 (jtly designed Dr Who Daleks), freelance interior and TV designer 1974-76; Office Planning Consultants: sr designer 1976-79, design dir 1979-81, md 1981-86; design dir and dep chm Business Design Group 1986-88, dir of design London Transport 1988-; pres elect Chartered Soc of Designers 1990-91; FCSD 1978 (MCSD 1964), FRSA 1980; *Recreations* birdwatching, gardening and trips to Africa; *Style—* Jeremy Rewse-Davies, Esq; The Manor, Steeple Ashton, nr Trowbridge, Wiltshire (☎ 0380 870776); London Transport, 55 Broadway, London SW1 (☎ 071 227 3611)

REX, Prof John Arderne; s of Frederick Edward George Rex, and Winifred Natalie, *née* Arderne; *b* 5 March 1925; *Educ* Grey HS Port Elizabeth SA, Rhodes Univ Grahamstown SA (BA), Univ of Leeds (PhD); *m* 1, 6 July 1949 (m dis 1964), Pamela Margaret Rex; 2 da (Catherine b 1952, Helen b 1955); m 2, 5 June 1965, Margaret Ellen, da of Frank Biggs (d 1977); 2 s (Frederick b 1966, David b 1968); *Career* able seaman SA Naval Forces, seconded to RN 1943-45; lectr: Univ of Leeds 1949-62, Univ of Birmingham 1962-64; prof of social theory and instns Univ of Durham 1964-70, prof of sociology Univ of Warwick 1970-79 (emeritus prof 1990-); dir: Res Unit on Ethnic Rels Aston Univ 1979-84, Centre for Res in Ethnic Rels Univ of Warwick 1984-90; chm Br Sociological Assoc 1969-71; *Books* Key Problems of Sociological Theory (1961), Race Relations in Sociological Theory (1970), Sociology and the Demystification of the Modern World (1973), Colonial Immigrants in a British City (1979), Race and Ethnicity (1985); *Recreations* spectator football; *Clubs* Coventry City FC; *Style—* Prof John Rex; 33 Arlington Ave, Leamington Spa, CV32 5UD (☎ 0926 425781); Univ of Warwick, Centre for Research in Ethnic Relations, Coventry CV4 7AZ (☎ 0203 523523)

REX-TAYLOR, David; s of William Walter Taylor (d 1953); *b* 25 Jan 1947; *Educ* Jt Servs Sch Linguists, Birkbeck Coll London; *Career* asst mangr (Russia) BEA 1969-71, regnl organiser London Nat Fund Res into Crippling Diseases 1971-72; fndr: Bibliagora Publishers and Int Book Mail Order Co (1973), Bridge Book Club and Lineage Res Unit, Evening Standard Bridge Congress; exec ed Int Bridge Press Assoc (md USA); FInstSMM; *Recreations* snooker, bridge; *Style—* David Rex-Taylor, Esq; PO Box 77, Feltham TW14 8JF (☎ 081 898 1234, Cellnet 0860 518507, fax 081 844 1777, telex 935918 BRIDGE G)

REYNOLDS, Alan David; s of Gwynfor Reynolds, and Heulwen, *née* Davies; *b* 24 Jan 1966; *Educ* Ysgol Gruffydd Jones Secdy Sch; *Career* Rugby Union flanker Swansea RFC and Wales (2 caps); clubs: Laugharne RFC, Whitland RFC, Swansea RFC 1988- (70 appearances); rep: Welsh Youth v Eng Colts 1985, Pembrokeshire v American Eagles 1987, Crawshays in Dubai Sevens 1989; Wales: toured Namiba 1990, debut v Namibia 1990, HK Sevens 1990; Heineken League Man of the Month 1990; self employed plastering contractor; *Recreations* squash, swimming, athletics, music, films; *Style—* Alan Reynolds, Esq; Santa Clara Inn, St Clears, Dyfed (☎ 0994 231 251); Swansea RFC, The Pavilion, St Helens Ground, Swansea (☎ 0792 464918)

REYNOLDS, Prof Alan James; s of Russell Hogarth Reynolds (d 1972), of Toronto, Canada, and Edith Edna, *née* Brownlow; *b* 8 Sept 1934; *Educ* Univ of Toronto (BSc), Univ of London (PhD); *m* 31 July 1962, Caroline Mary, da of Albert Wlliam Edwin Bury (d 1985), of Billericay, Essex; 2 s (Andrew Hogarth b 1963, James Haldane b 1967); *Career* res fell Cavendish Laboratory Univ of Cambridge 1960-62, assoc prof Dept of Civil Engrg and Applied Mechanics McGill Univ Montreal Canada 1962-66, pro vice chllr Brunel Univ 1991- (reader 1966-82, prof 1982-, head Dept of Mechanical Engrg 1983-); ed Journal of Power and Energy (Part A of proceedings of Inst of Mechanical Engrs); memb Cncl Inst of Mechanical Engrs (chm Gtr London Branch); FIMechE 1982, FRSA 1983; *Books* Thermofluid Dynamics (1970), Turbulent Flows in Engineering (1974, Russian edn 1976, Romanian edn 1980); *Style—* Prof Alan Reynolds; Dept of Mechanical Engrg, Brunel Univ, Kingston Lane, Uxbridge, Middx UB8 3PH (☎ 0895 74000)

REYNOLDS, Alan Munro; *b* 27 April 1926; *Educ* Woolwich Poly Sch of Art, RCA; *m* 1951, Vana; *Career* teacher Central Sch of Arts and Crafts London 1954-61, sr lectr St Martins Sch of Art London 1985- (teacher 1961-85); solo exhibitions: Redfern Gallery London 1952 (1960, 1972), Durlacher Gallery New York 1954, Leicester Galleries London 1958, Annely Juda Fine Art London 1978, Gallerie Rénee Ziegler Zurich 1980 (with Malcom Hughes and Peter Lowe), Juda Rowan Gallery London 1982 (1986), Galerie Wack Kaiserslauten 1986 (1990), Repères A la Galerie Lahumière Paris; gp exhibitions include: London Gp Exhibition 1950, British Contemporary Painting (British Cncl Exhibition Olso and Coppenhagen) 1955, British Painting 1952-77 (Royal Acad London) 1977, Creation Modern Art and Nature (Scottish National Gallery of Modern Art Edinburgh) 1984, Systematic Constructive Drawings (Univ of York) 1986, Non-Objective World Revisited (Annely Julia Fine Art London) 1988, 1959-1989 30 years (Galerie Renée Ziegler Zurich) 1989; One Man Exhibition Annely Juda Fine Art London 1991; selected public collections: Walker Art Gallery Liverpool, Tate Gallery London, Victoria and Albert Museum London, Nat Gallery of Victoria Melbourne, Cincinnati Art Museum Ohio, Nat Gallery of Canada Ottawa, Bibliothèque Paris; Arts Cncl Purchase Award 1967; *Style—* Alan Reynolds, Esq; Annely Juda Fine Art, 11 Tottenham Mews, London W1P 9PJ (☎ 071 637 5517, fax 071 580 3877)

REYNOLDS, Dr (Eva Mary) Barbara; da of Alfred Charles Reynolds (d 1969), and Barbara, *née* Florac (d 1977); *b* 13 June 1914; *Educ* St Paul's Girls' Sch, UCL (BA, PhD), Univ of Cambridge (MA); *m* 1, 5 Sept 1939, Lewis Guy Melville Thorpe (d 1977); 1 s (Adrian b 1942), 1 da (Kerstin b 1949); m 2, 30 Oct 1982, Kenneth Robert Imeson; *Career* asst lectr in Italian LSE 1937-40, lectr in Italian Univ of Cambridge 1940-62, reader in Italian Univ of Nottingham 1966-78 (warden of Willoughby Hall 1963-69); visiting prof in Italian: Univ of Calif Berkeley 1974-75, Wheaton Coll Illinois 1977-78, Trinity Coll Dublin 1980 and 1981, Hope Coll Michigan 1982; hon reader Univ of Warwick 1975-80; managing ed Seven (an Anglo-American literary review) 1980-90; chm Univ Women's Club 1988-90; Hon DLitt: Wheaton Coll Illinois 1979, Hope Coll Michigan 1982; Silver medal for servs to Italian culture 1964, Silver medal for servs to Anglo-Veneto cultural rels 1971, Cavaliere Ufficiale al Merito Della Repubblica Italiana 1978; *Books* The Linguistic Writings of Alessandro Manzoni (1952), The Cambridge Italian Dictionary (gen ed Vol I 1962, Vol II 1981), Dante: Paradise (trans with Dorothy L Sayers), Guido Farina, Painter of Verona (with Lewis Thorpe, 1967), Dante: Poems of Youth (trans 1969), Concise Cambridge Italian Dictionary (1975), Ariosto: Orlando Furioso (trans Vol I 1975, Vol II 1977), The Passionate Intellect: Dorothy L Sayers' Encounter with Dante (1989); *Recreations* travel; *Clubs* University Women's, Authors; *Style—* Dr Barbara Reynolds; 220 Milton Rd, Cambridge CB4 1LQ (☎ 0223 424 894)

REYNOLDS, Brian Edwin Albert; s of Walter Albert Reynolds (d 1942), and Ann Margaret, *née* Boyce; *b* 5 March 1938; *Educ* Leyton Co HS, West Ham Coll Of Technol; *m* 28 July 1962, Mary Christine, da of William Horace Sherman, of Parkstone, Poole, Dorset; 3 da (Amanda Jennifer b 1964, Sarah Gillian b 1968, Janine Verity b 1979); *Career* prodn mangr Berk Ltd 1963-65, mangr Wax Dept Wynmouth Lehr Fatoils Ltd 1965-70, supervisor BDH Chemicals 1973-75, md Poth Hille & Co Ltd 1989 (gen mangr 1975-77, dir 1977-88), dir Holroyds Oil & Ceresine Co Ltd; church warden (formerly dep church warden) St Marys and All Saints Langdon Hills Essex 1975; Freeman City of London 1980, Liveryman Worshipful Co of Wax Chandlers 1981; *Recreations* music, philately, railways; *Style—* Brian Reynolds, Esq; 28 New Ave, Langdon Hills, Basildon, Essex SS16 6BT (☎ 0268 542566); Poth Hille & Co Ltd, 37 High St, Stratford, London E15 2QD (☎ 081 534 7091, fax 081 534 2291, telex 897300)

REYNOLDS, Brian James; s of Thomas Reynolds, of 19 Ferndale Lodge, Eastbourne, and Beatrice, *née* Rutherford; *b* 22 April 1938; *Educ* Downhills Sch Tottenham; *m* 1, 19 Sept 1959 (m dis 1977), Janet, *née* Gallagher; 1 s (Andrew), 1 da (Suzanne); m 2, 1985, Patricia Ann, da of George McIntyre; *Career* slr's clerk and litigation clerk 1953-59, dir and co sec Financial Information Co 1959-81, Daily Express 1981-85; dir: Money Marketing (Design) Public Relations Ltd 1985-86, Streets Communications Ltd 1986; *Recreations* lifetime supporter Tottenham Hotspur FC; *Style—* Brian Reynolds, Esq; Streets Communications Ltd, 18 Red Lion Court, Fleet St, London EC4A 3HT (☎ 071 353 1090, fax 071 583 0661)

REYNOLDS, David Geoffrey; s of William Oliver Reynolds, OBE, of Follifoot, nr Harrogate, and Eleanor, *née* Gill; *b* 11 June 1948; *Educ* Bedford Sch, LAMDA; *m* 5 Sept 1970, Valerie, *née* Wells; 2 da (Emma b 5 Oct 1973, Tessa b 7 July 1976); *Career* dep stage mangr Spa Theatre Whitby 1967, stage mangr Sheffield Playhouse 1967-68, dir Yorkshire Television 1973-79 (floor mangr 1968-73), freelance dir 1979-86, dep controller of entertainment Yorkshire Television 1986-; TV work incl: Emmerdale, Hadleigh, The Sandbaggers, The Onedin Line, When The Boat Comes In, Juliet Bravo, Give Us a Break, Big Deal, Bergerac, Lovejoy, The Beiderbecke Affair, Room At The Bottom (Int Emmy nomination and Best Comedy award Banff Festival), prodr The New Statesman (Int Emmy winner), prodr and dir Home to Roost (Int Emmy nomination), prodr and co-dir A Bit of a Do (TRIC award for Best Sit-Com, Broadcasting Press and Guild award for Best Entertainment Series, RTS award Best Drama Series and Br Comedy awards Best ITV and Channel 4 Sit-Com and Best Br TV Comedy), prodr and dir Stay Lucky, currently working on Rich Tea and Sympathy; *Recreations* boating, theatre, photography, films, travel; *Style*— David Reynolds, Esq; Pencob House, Scotton, Knaresborough, North Yorkshire HG5 9HZ (☎ 0423 862854); Yorkshire TV, TV Centre, Leeds LS3 1JS (☎ 0532 438283)

REYNOLDS, Sir David James; 3 Bt (UK 1923); s of Lt-Col Sir John Francis Roskell Reynolds, 2 Bt, MBE (d 1956), and Millicent Orr-Ewing (d 1932); gda of 7 Duke of Roxburgh, and ggda of 7 Duke of Marlborough; *b* 26 Jan 1924; *Educ* Downside; *m* 1966, Charlotte Baumgartner; 1 s (James Francis), 2 da (Lara Mary b 1 March 1967, Sofie Josefine b 5 May 1968); *Heir* s, James Reynolds b 10 July 1971; *Career* serv WWII Capt 15/19 Hussars Italy; *Style*— Sir David Reynolds, Bt; Blanchepierre House, rue de la Blanchepierre, St Lawrence, Jersey, CI

REYNOLDS, Dean; s of Robert (Butch) Reynolds, of Grimsby, and Sandra, *née* Bennet; *b* 11 Jan 1963; *Educ* Willer Sch Grimsby, Whitgist Comp Grimsby; *m* 6 Aug 1988, Joanne Maxim, da of John Cyril Gray; 1 s (Dean Reynolds Jr b 6 Jan 1991); *Career* snooker player; turned professional 1981; achievements incl: winner English Professional Championship 1988, runner up Anglian Windows Br Open 1989, runner up Rothams Grand Prix 1989, semi-finalist various other tournaments; former motor mechanic; *Recreations* golf, fishing; *Style*— Dean Reynolds, Esq; c/o IMG Snooker Division, Pier House, Strand on the Green, Chiswick, London W4 3NN (☎ 081 994 1444, fax 081 994 9606)

REYNOLDS, Dr Edward Henry; s of William Henry Reynolds, of Broad Towers, Caerleon, Gwent, and (Mary) Angela, *née* Keane (d 1989); *b* 13 Oct 1935; *Educ* The Oratory, The Welsh Nat Sch of Med Cardiff (MB BCh, MD); *m* 20 July 1968, Angela Pauline, da of John Martin Anthony Sheehan (d 1960), of 28 Manor Rd, Cheam, Surrey; 1 da (Catherine b 1974); *Career* visiting asst prof of neurology Yale Univ Med Sch 1970, conslt neurologist Maudsley and King's Coll Hosps London 1974-; sec MRC Coordinating Gp for Epilepsy 1978-83, memb Ctee Br Neuropsychiatry Assoc 1987-, vice pres Int League Against Epilepsy 1989- (sec Br branch 1979-84); memb BMA, FRCP 1980, FRCPsych 1985; *Books* incl: Folic Acid in Neurology, Psychiatry and Internal Medicine (ed with M I Botez, 1979), Epilepsy and Psychiatry (ed with M R Trimble, 1981), Paediatric Perspectives on Epilepsy (ed with E Ross, 1985), The Bridge Between Neurology and Psychiatry (ed with M R Trimble, 1989); *Recreations* golf, tennis; *Clubs* RAC; *Style*— Dr Edward Reynolds; Buckles, Yew Tree Bottom Road, Epsom Downs, Surrey KT17 3NQ (☎ 0737 360867); Dept of Neurology, King's College Hospital, London SE5 (☎ 071 326 3130)

REYNOLDS, Gillian; da of Charles Beresford Morton (d 1970), of Liverpool, and Ada Kelly (d 1962); *b* 15 Nov 1935; *Educ* Liverpool Inst HS for Girls, St Anne's Coll Oxford (BA), Mount Holyoke Coll South Hadley Mass; *m* 23 Sept 1958 (m dis 1983), Stanley Ambrose Reynolds, s of Ambrose Harrington Reynolds (d 1970), of Holyoke, USA; 3 s (Ambrose Kelly b 12 June 1960, Alexander Charles b 3 Jan 1970, Abel Stanley b 5 Sept 1971); *Career* tv and radio broadcaster 1964-; radio critic: The Guardian 1967-74, The Daily Telegraph 1975-, prog controller Radio City Liverpool 1974-75; memb: Mgmnt Ctee Soc of Authors 1989-, Sr Assoc Ctee St Anne's Coll Oxford 1990-, Mount Holyoke Coll Alumnae Assoc, RTS; first fell Radio Acad 1990; *Recreations* listening to the radio, the company of friends; *Clubs* University Women's; *Style*— Ms Gillian Reynolds; Flat 3, 1 Linden Gardens, London W2 4HA (☎ 071 229 1893)

REYNOLDS, Graham; OBE (1984); s of the late Arthur Thomas Reynolds, and Eva Mullins; *b* 10 Jan 1914; *Educ* Highgate Sch, Queens' Coll Cambridge (BA); *m* 6 Feb 1943, Daphne, da of Thomas Dent, of Huddersfield; *Career* asst keeper V & A Museum 1937, seconded to Miny of Home Security 1939, princ 1942; dep keeper V & A (Dept of Paintings) 1947-58; keeper V & A (Dept of Prints, Drawings and Paintings) 1959-74; tstee William Morris Gallery Walthamstow 1972-75, chm Gainsborough's House Soc Sudbury 1977-79, memb Reviewing Ctee on Export of Works of Art 1984-90; Leverhulme emeritus fellowship 1980-81; *publications incl* Nicholas Hilliard and Issac Oliver (1947,1971), English Watercolours (1959, revised 1988), English Portrait Miniatures (1952, revised 1988), Painters of the Victorian Scene (1953), Constable the Natural Painter (1965), Victorian Paintings (1966,1987), Turner (1969), Catalogue of the Constable Collection V & A Museum (1960, revised 1973), Concise History of Watercolour Painting (1972), Catalogue of Portrait Miniatures Wallace Collection (1980), Constable's England (1983), The Later Paintings and Drawings of John Constable (1984, awarded Mitchell prize 1984); *Clubs* Athenaeum; *Style*— Graham Reynolds, Esq, OBE; The Old Manse, Bradfield St George, Bury St Edmunds, Suffolk IP30 0AZ (☎ 028 486610)

REYNOLDS, Jane Caroline Margaret (Mrs Peter Hall); da of Maj Thomas Reynolds, MC (d 1981), of Richmond, N Yorks, and Cynthia Myrtle Margaret, *née* Eden (later Mrs Witt, d 1982); *b* 4 March 1953; *Educ* Winchester Co HS for Girls, Brighton Poly, Lincoln Meml Clinic for Psychotherapy; *m* 10 Nov 1990, Dr Peter Lawrence Hall; *Career* student teacher St Mary's Westwood Educnl Tst Ltd 1970-72, offr i/c Gary Richard Homes Ltd 1972-76, matron Alison House (St John's Wood) Ltd 1976-81, dir The Westminster Soc for Mentally Handicapped Children and Adults 1983-87 (devpt offr 1981-83); memb Registered Homes Act (1984) Tbnl Panel 1990-; FBIM 1988 (MBIM 1977); *Recreations* travelling, the arts, aerobic exercise; *Style*— Ms Jane Reynolds; Leavesden Hospital, College Rd, Abbots Langley, Watford, Herts WD5 0NU (☎ 0923 674090 ext 1)

REYNOLDS, John Arthur; JP (1972); s of Arthur Reynolds (d 1986), of Buntingford, Herts, and Beatrice Mary, *née* Darton; *b* 23 May 1930; *Educ* Hertford GS; *m* 1, 9 Feb 1952, Joyce Florence (d 1979), da of Arthur James Harvey (d 1986); 1 s (Geoffrey Arthur b 1955), 1 da (Kathryn Louise b 1959); m 2, 18 Oct 1980, Olive (d 1989), da of Flt Offr W C Rasbary (ka 1941); 2 step s (Graham Handy b 1953, Douglas Handy b 1955); *Career* master builder and shopkeeper, ret 1988; currently pre-planning conslt; memb: Buntingford Town Cncl 1961-91 (chm 1973-76 and 1979), Braughing RDC 1964 (chm Housing Ctee 1970-74); E Herts DC 1973: vice chm 1976-79, vice chm Planning Ctee 1979-83, chm Appeals Ctee 1983-; fndr memb and first hon pres Buntingford Civic Soc, ind cncllr on all cncls; *Recreations* travel, music, theatre, antiques; *Style*— John Reynolds, Esq, JP; Aspenden Cottage, Aspenden, Buntingford, Herts SG9 9PE (☎ 0763 71507)

REYNOLDS, John Roderick; s of David Reynolds (d 1988), of Peterborough, and Gwen Reynolds, *née* Roderick; *b* 11 Oct 1948; *Educ* Laxton Sch, Oundle, Imperial Coll London (BSc); *m* 7 Sept 1974, Jane Elizabeth, da of David Berridge, of Cambs; 2 s (Henry b 1980, Guy b 1982), 1 da (Daisy b 1985); *Career* Price Waterhouse 1970-76, dir J Henry Schroder Wagg & Co Ltd 1976-; FCA, ARCS; *Recreations* skiing, tennis, opera, bridge; *Clubs* Annabels, Hurlingham, RAC; *Style*— John Reynolds, Esq; The Manor House, Weston-Sub-Edge, Chipping Campden, Glos; 32 Winchendon Rd, London SW6; 120 Cheapside, London EC2 (☎ 071 382 6000, fax 071 382 6459)

REYNOLDS, (James) Kirk; s of The Hon Mr Justice James Reynolds, of Helen's Bay, Co Down, N Ireland, and Alexandra Mary Erskine, *née* Strain; *b* 25 March 1951; *Educ* Campbell Coll Belfast, Peterhouse Cambridge (MA); *Career* called to the Bar Middle Temple 1974; *Books* Handbook of Rent Review (1981), Renewal of Business Tenancies (1984); *Style*— Kirk Reynolds, Esq; 46 St John's Villas, London N19

REYNOLDS, Martin Paul; s of Cedric Hinton Fleetwood Reynolds, of 38 West Hill Way, Totteridge, London, and Doris Margaret, *née* Bryan (d 1982); *b* 25 Dec 1936; *Educ* Univ Coll Sch, St Edmund Hall Oxford (MA); *m* 17 June 1961, Gaynor Margaret, da of Stuart Morgan Phillips (d 1957); 3 s (Simon Stuart Hinton b 1964, Peter Bryan b 1966, Thomas Edward Barnsbury b 1969); *Career* qualified teacher 1961; called to the Bar Inner Temple 1962, asst rec 1988; cncllr London Borough of Islington 1968-71 and 1973-82; Parly candidate Harrow W Oct 1974; ACIARB 1985; *Books* Negotiable Instruments for Students (1964); *Recreations* sailing, travel in France, music; *Clubs* Savage; *Style*— Martin Reynolds, Esq; 3 Mountfort Crescent, Barnsbury Square, London N1 1JW (☎ 071 607 7357); 1 Paper Buildings, Temple, London EC4 (☎ 071 583 7355, fax 071 353 2144)

REYNOLDS, Dr Mary Angela; da of Dr William Henry Reynolds, of Ladycroft, 118 Marsh Lane, Mill Hill, London NW7 4PE, and Mary Angela, *née* Keane (d 1989); *Educ* St Mary's Convent Shaftesbury Dorset, Charing Cross Hosp Med Sch (MB BS); *Career* MO to US Public Health Serv American Embassy 1967-68, asst gen mangr chief underwriter and chief med offr Canada Life Assur Co (UK and Ireland) 1978-; first lady pres Assur Med Soc 1989, chm med affrs ctee Assoc of Br Insurers, vice-pres London Insur Inst (former cncl memb), dep chm Life Underwriters Club 1988-; memb: steering ctee Women in Mgmnt Insur Project MSC and Industl Soc, gen ctee Insur Benevolent Fund (dir Insur Orphans Fund), Perm Health Insur Club; Assur Med Soc: memb working pty for Chartered Insur Insts Underwriting Dip, first ed bulletin; Freeman City of London 1983, Liveryman Worshipful Co of Insurers 1983; FBIM 1980, FAMS; *Books* Your Health is Your Wealth (1978), Ethics of Modern Life Underwriting (1978); *Recreations* opera, tennis; *Style*— Dr Mary Reynolds; Canada Life Assurance Co, Canada Life Place, Potters Bar, Herts (☎ 0707 51122, fax 0707 46088, telex 25376)

REYNOLDS, Michael Arthur; s of William Arthur Reynolds (d 1981), of Hakin, Milford Haven, Dfyed, Wales, and Violet Elsie, *née* Giddings, (d 1978); *b* 28 Aug 1943; *Educ* Milford Haven GS, Cardiff Coll of Art (Dip Ad); *m* 1, (m dis 1971), Patricia; 1 s (Joseph Michael b 1970); m 2, (m dis 1974), Judith; m 3, 15 April 1983, Jill Caroline, da of Derek Holmes; *Career* creative dir KPS Ltd Nairobi 1968, copywriter J Walter Thompson 1971, gp head Benton & Bowles 1973; creative dir: ABM 1975, McCann Erickson 1979, Interlink 1981, MWK (and shareholder) 1983, Pearson Partnership 1987, Pearson & Hogan 1989; MIPA; *Recreations* gardening, archery, rare books; *Clubs* Chelsea Arts; *Style*— Michael Reynolds, Esq; Winwick Manor, Winwick, Northants NN6 7PD (☎ 078 887 502); 50 Long Acre, London WC2E 9JR (☎ 071 497 9727, fax 071 497 3581, car 0860 864729)

REYNOLDS, Michael Emanuel; CBE; s of Isaac Mark Rosenberg (d 1959), of 16 Palace Ct, Finchley Rd NW3, and Henrietta, *née* Woolf (d 1977); *b* 22 April 1931; *Educ* Haberdashers' Aske's Sch; *m* 1 (m dis 1961), Hazel, *née* Fishberg; m 2, 28 Aug 1964, Susan Geraldine, da of Mervyn Clement Scott Yates (d 1967), of 22 Albany Park Rd, Kingston, Surrey; 2 da (Amanda Jane b 4 July 1965, Michelle b 7 March 1967); *Career* Nat Serv RASC; with Marks & Spencer plc 1951-61, controller Br Home Stores plc 1961-64; Spar UK Ltd: trading controller 1964-67, chm and md 1967-77; BV Intergroup Trading (IGT): fndr memb Bd of Admin, dir 1974-75, chm and dir 1975-77; fndr and owner Susan Reynolds Books Ltd 1977-84; pres Nat Grocers Benevolent Fund 1976-77; FRSA; *Recreations* bridge; *Style*— Michael Reynolds, Esq, CBE; 55 Newlands Terrace, 155 Queenstown Rd, London SW8 3RN (☎ 071 627 5862)

REYNOLDS, Patrick John; s of James Reynolds (d 1969); *b* 20 Aug 1929; *Educ* Latymer Sch Edmonton; *m* 1959, Pauline Claire, *née* Farmer; 2 da; *Career* chm Reynolds Med Ltd; Queen's Award for Export 1980 and 1988, Queen's Award for Technol 1988; *Recreations* cricket, real tennis, tennis; *Style*— Patrick Reynolds, Esq; Old Manor, Little Berkhamsted, Hertford, Herts (☎ 0707 874 071)

REYNOLDS, (Arthur) Paul; s of Capt A C J Reynolds (d 1954), of Cornwall, and Violet Emma, *née* Tuttle (d 1966); *b* 1 May 1917; *Educ* St Austell GS Cornwall, Coll of Estate Mgmnt London; *m* 1, 1945, Joyce (d 1979), da of Flt Lt Harold Arthur Rolls, of Leighton Buzzard (d 1980); 1 s (Christopher b 1946), 1 da (Elizabeth b 1950); m 2, 1981, Diana, da of Edward John Pyman (d 1985), of Leighton Buzzard; *Career* Capt RA 1940-46 attached to Indian Artillery; former ptnr H A Rolls & Ptnrs, specialist in the care & restoration of churches (St Albans & Oxford Dioceses), ret; surveyor to the fabric of All Saints Church Leighton Buzzard; FRICS, MIAS, EASA; *Recreations* music - choral singing, oil painting, golf, cricket, swimming; *Style*— Paul Reynolds, Esq; Sandy Mount, Plantation Rd, Leighton Buzzard, Beds LU7 7HR (☎ 0525 373307)

REYNOLDS, (Christopher) Paul Michel; s of Christopher John Loughborough Reynolds, of Salter's Green, Lymington, Hants, and Elisabeth, *née* Ewart-James; *b* 23 Feb 1946; *Educ* Ardingley Coll, Worcester Coll Oxford (BA); *m* 25 July 1950, Louise, da of Bishop Eric William Bradley Cordingly (d 1976); 1 s (James Edward b 1974), 1 da (Alice Elizabeth b 1976); *Career* joined BBC Norwich 1968, BBC Radio London 1970-78; BBC corr: NY 1978-82, Brussels 1982-85, Jerusalem 1985-87; dip and ct corr BBC 1987; *Recreations* birdwatching, archaeology; *Style*— Paul Reynolds, Esq; BBC Broadcasting House, London W1A 1AA (☎ 071 927 4547)

REYNOLDS, Sir Peter William John; CBE; s of late Harry Reynolds, of Amersham, and Gladys Victoria French; *b* 10 Sept 1929; *Educ* Haileybury; *m* 1955, Barbara Anne, da of Vincent Kenneth Johnson, OBE; 2 s (Mark, Adam); *Career* Nat Serv 2 Lt RA 1948-50; Unilever Ltd 1950-70: trainee, md then chm Walls (Meat & Handy Foods) Ltd; Rank Hovis McDougall plc 1971-: asst gp md 1971, gp md 1972-81, chm 1981-89, dep chm 1989-; memb Consultative Bd for Resources Devpt in Agric 1982-84, dir Ind Devpt Bd for NI 1982-89, chm Resources Ctee Food & Drink Fedn 1983- (fndr memb of Ctee 1974-); dir: Ranks Pension Ltd, RHM Overseas Ltd, RHM Res Ltd, RHM Overseas Fin BV (Holland), RHM Int Fin NV, RHM Holdings (USA) Inc, Purchase Fin Co Ltd, RHM Operatives Pensions Ltd, Avis Europe Ltd, Cilva Holdings plc, The Boots Co plc, Guardian Royal Exchange plc, Pioneer Concrete (Holdings) Ltd, Nationwide Anglia Building Society; memb Covent Garden Market Authy; kt 1985; *Recreations* gardening, beagling; *Clubs* Naval & Military, Farmers; *Style*— Sir Peter Reynolds, CBE; Rignall Farm, Great Missenden, Bucks; PO Box 178, Windsor, Berks SL4 3ST (☎ 0753 857123)

REYNOLDS, Richard Christopher; s of Stanley Reynolds (d 1960), and Christine, *née* Barrow; *b* 2 June 1945; *Educ* Peter Simmons Sch Winchester, Croydon Tech Sch, Croydon Tech Coll; *m* 2 March 1968, Sharon, da of Peter Bragg, of Great Bookham, Surrey; 1 s (Paul), 1 da (Julia); *Career* md: Barratt E London Ltd 1983-, Barratt Urban Renewal E London Ltd 1983-, Barratt Urban Construction E London Ltd 1983-; dir: Barratt Southern Ltd 1983-, Barratt Rosehaugh Co-Ptnrship Ltd 1988-, Countryside Barratt Ltd, Lanhill Road Developments Ltd, Tulip Grey Ltd; *Recreations* clay pigeon shooting, scuba diving; *Style—* Richard Reynolds, Esq; Barratt East London Ltd, Warton House, 150 High St, Stratford E15 2NE (☎ 081 555 3242, fax 081 519 5536)

REYNOLDS, Ruth Evelyn Millicent; da of Lt-Col Charles Ernest White-Spunner Fawcett (d 1944), of Littlewood, Ganghill, Guildford, and Millicent Aphrasia, *née* Sullivan (d 1971); *b* 4 Oct 1915; *Educ* Conamur Sandgate Kent, Guildford Sch of Art, Wycombe Coll of Art; *m* 4 Nov 1939, Lt-Col Dudley Lancelot Collis Reynolds, OBE, s of Maj James Christopher Reynolds (d 1923), of The Lawns, Alveston, Glos; 1 s (John b 1950), 2 da (Jenny b 1941, Diana b 1946); *Career* WWII WAAF Bomber Cmd HQ Langley Bucks 1939; J Stanley Beard & Bennett Architects 1934-37, BBC Admin Dept 1937-39 (six month in News Talks run by Richard Dimbleby, later Talks Dept and Features and Drama); sculptor and artist in oil and water-colour; one man exhibitions incl: Halifax House, Univ of Oxford Graduate Centre 1965, ESU Oxford 1967, Co Museum Aylesbury 1976, Loggia Gallery London 1982, Century Galleries Henley-on-Thames 1986; gp exhibitions: Loggia Gallery, Amnesty Int Sculpture Exhibition Bristol and London 1979, Mall Galleries; work in private collections incl: Anne Duchess of Westminster's Arkle Collection, Rev J Studd, Guinness (Park Royal) Ltd, Mrs Jenny Hopkinson (California), Fuad Mulla Hussein Kuwait Planning Bd, RAF Halton Bucks, G Wright (Iowa), St Dunstan's Church Monks Risborough Aylesbury, Welch Regt Museum, Cardiff Castle, P Van Kuran (dir Tandem Computers Inc, California, A Jarrett vice-pres Syntex Corp (California), BBONT Oxford, Dr T J Goodwin Chorleywood, Mrs M Bohli Berne (Switzerland), Lambeth Palace, Diana R Roome (Mountain View, Calif); fndr memb Aylesbury Decorative and Fine Arts Soc, former tutor Duke of Edinburgh's Award in Art, memb Buckinghamshire Art Soc; asst organizer Millenium Art Exhibition (St Dunstan's Church Monks Risborough Aylesbury) 1988, presented sculpture Beulah Sheep (for Art for Winchester 1993) 1990; former memb: FPS, AFAS; FRSA 1980; *Recreations* sketching, dog-walks in Chilterns, travel; *Clubs* Int Lyceum; *Style—* Mrs Ruth Reynolds; 30 The Retreat, Princes Risborough, Aylesbury, Bucks HP17 OJQ (☎ 08444 3115)

REYNOLDS, Simon Anthony; s of Maj James Reynolds (d 1982), of Leighton Hall, Carnforth, Lancs, and Helen Reynolds (d 1977); *b* 20 Jan 1939; *Educ* Ampleforth, Heidelberg Univ; *m* 1970, Beata Cornelia, da of late Baron Siegfried von Heyl zu Herrnsheim (d 1982), of Schlosschen, Worms, Germany; 2 s, 2 da; *Career* dealer in fine art; *Books* The Vision of Simeon Solomon; *Recreations* writing, collecting fine art, travelling; *Style—* Simon Reynolds, Esq; 64 Lonsdale Rd, Barnes, London SW13 (☎ 081 748 3506)

REYNOLDS, (Thomas) Watson; s of Capt Thomas Reynolds (d 1933), of Cambridge, and Winnifred Jessie, *née* Wells (d 1988); *b* 26 April 1924; *Educ* Harrow, Peterhouse Cambridge; *m* 17 July 1948, Gabrielle Ann, da of Lt-Col Jonathan Richard Greenbank (d 1964), of Galphay, Ripon, N Yorks; 2 s (Thomas, John); *Career* RAFVR 1942-46 (despatches 1945), 37 Sqdn CMF Italy 1944, pilot, shot down 13 June 1944, evaded capture, returned allied lines 8 Nov 1944, 7 Sqdn Bomber Cmd 1945-46; farmer and landowner 1948-; chm: Fen Centre Nat Skating Assoc 1948-, Waterbeach Level Internal Drainage Bd 1977- (cmmr 1948-, vice chm 1966-77); Liveryman Worshipful Co of Curriers 1982, Freeman City of London 1982; *Recreations* outdoor ice speed skating, shooting; *Clubs* RAF; *Style—* Watson Reynolds, Esq; Waterbeach Hall, Waterbeach, Cambridgeshire (☎ 0223 860216); Bank Farm, Waterbeach, Cambridgeshire (☎ 0223 860250)

REYNTIENS, (Nicholas) Patrick; OBE (1976); s of Nicholas Serge Reyntiens, OBE (d 1951), and Janet Isabel, *née* MacRae (d 1975); *b* 11 Dec 1925; *Educ* Ampleforth, Regent St Poly, Edinburgh Coll of Art (DA); *m* 8 Sept 1953, Anne Mary, da of Brig-Gen Ian Bruce, DSO, MBE (d 1956); 2 s (Dominick Ian, John Patrick), 2 da (Edith Mary, Lucy Anne); *Career* WWII Lt 2 Bn Scots Guards 1943-47; artist specialising in stained glass, work includes: Coventry Cathedral, Liverpool Met Cathedral, Derby Cathedral, Eton Chapel, Great Hall Christ Church Oxford, Washington DC Episcopalian Cathedral; other works incl in private collections; co-fndr Burleighfield and Reyntiens Trust 1967-76; memb Panel of Architectural Advsrs to: Westminster Abbey, Westminster Cathedral, Brompton Oratory; fell Br Soc of Master Glass Painters; *Books* The Beauty of Stained Glass (1990), The Technique of Stained Glass (4 edn 1991); *Style—* Patrick Reyntiens, Esq, OBE; Ilford Bridges Farm, Close Stocklinch, Ilminster, Somerset (☎ 0460 52241)

RHEAD, David Michael; s of Harry Bernard Rhead, JP; *b* 12 Feb 1936; *Educ* St Philips GS Edgbaston; *m* 1958, Rosaleen Loretto, *née* Finnegan; 4 da; *Career* chm: LCP Holdings plc 1975-87 (dep chm 1973, fin dir 1968), Hickman Boswell plc; Freeman: City of London, Worshipful Co of CAs; FCA, CBIM; *Recreations* fishing, golf; *Style—* David Rhead Esq; Cherry Trees, 62 Little Sutton Lane, Sutton Coldfield, W Midlands B75 6PE (☎ 021 308 4762)

RHIND, Prof David William; s of William Rhind (d 1976), and Christina, *née* Abercombie; *b* 29 Nov 1943; *Educ* Berwick GS, Univ of Bristol (BSc), Univ of Edinburgh (PhD); *m* 27 Aug 1966, Christine, da of William Frank Young, of Berwick-upon-Tweed; 1 s (Jonathan b 1969), 2 da (Samantha b 1972, Zoe b 1979); *Career* res offr Univ of Edinburgh 1968-69, res fell RCA 1969-73, reader (former lectr) Univ of Durham 1973-81, prof of geography Birkbeck Coll Univ of London 1982-; visiting fell: Int Trg Centre Netherlands 1975, Aust Nat Univ 1979; author of around 100 tech papers; hon sec RGS; chm: Bloomsbury Computing Consortium Mgmnt Ctee, Sci Ctee Royal Soc of Ordnance Survey; vice pres Int Cartographic Assoc; advsr House of Lords Select Ctee Sci of Technol 1984-85, memb Govt Ctee of Enquiry on Handling of Geographic Info 1985-87; FRGS 1970, MIBG; *Books* Land Use (with R Hudson, 1980), A Census User's Handbook (1983), An Atlas of EEC Affairs (with R Hudson and H Mounsey, 1984), Geographical Information Systems (ed, with D Maguire and M Goodchild, 1991); *Clubs* Athenaeum; *Style—* Prof David Rhind; 7 New Place, Welwyn, Herts AL6 9QA (☎ 043 871 5350); Dept of Geography, Birkbeck Coll, Univ of London, Malet St, London (☎ 071 631 6474, fax 071 631 6498)

RHODE, Michael William; *b* 17 Dec 1940; *Educ* Yale Univ; *m* Vanessa Kathleen Rhode; *Career* former dir: Rhode Investments Ltd, Rhode Properties Ltd, The Gardenstore Ltd, Thames Land Ltd, New Demerger Corpn plc, Paget Res Ltd, Gradine plc, Skynet Computer Systems Ltd, Finlan Gp plc, Finlan Property Investments Ltd, Global Food Technologies (UK) Ltd, Merchant Developers Ltd, Midtown Properties Ltd, The Retail Corpn plc, Skybridge Charters Ltd, Skybridge Personnel and Mgmnt Servs Ltd, Valvetab plc; currently dir: Langleyfield plc, Upski Europe; *Clubs* Queens, Vanderbilt Racquet, Wentworth Golf; *Style—* Michael Rhode, Esq; Finlan Group plc, 37 Ixworth Place, London W8 (☎ 071 584 4231, fax 071 603 0798)

RHODES, Anthony John David; s of John Percy Rhodes (d 1985), of Leigh-on-Sea, Essex, and Eileen Daisy, *née* Frith (d 1984); *b* 22 Feb 1948; *Educ* Westcliff GS, Corpus Christi Coll Cambridge (MA); *m* 14 Dec 1974, Elisabeth Marie Agnes Raymonde, da of Lt-Col Pierre Fronteau (ret French Army), of Lisieux, France; 1 s (Christophe b 1978), 1 da (Sophie b 1984); *Career* project mangr Shell Int Petroleum Co 1969-73, dep treas Ocean Transport & Trading Ltd 1975-80, exec dir Bank of America Int Ltd 1980-; *Recreations* opera, classical music, golf, hill walking, philately; *Style—* Anthony Rhodes, Esq; 1 Alie St, London E1 8DE (☎ 071 634 4556, fax 071 634 4532, telex 884552)

RHODES, Sir Basil Edward; CBE (1981, OBE 1945, MBE 1944), TD, DL (S Yorks 1975); s of Col Harry Rhodes, TD, of Lane End House, Rotherham, S Yorks, and Astri Alexandra, *née* Natvig (d 1969); *b* 8 Dec 1915; *Educ* St Edwards Sch Oxford; *m* 21 Sept 1962, Joëlle, da of Robert Vilgard; 1 s (Charles Edward Robert Christian); *Career* serv WWII: W Desert, Greece, Crete, Burma (wounded and mentioned in despatches); Yorks Dragoons and Queen's Own Yeo (Hon Col 1973-81) TA; admitted slr 1946, ptr Gichard & Co Rotherham 1946-; dir: Carlton Main Brickworks Ltd, S H Ward & Co, Wessex Fare Ltd, Duncan Millar & Assocs Ltd; pres Rotherham Cons Assoc, chm S Yorks Cons Fedn; Mayor of Rotherham 1970-71, High Sheriff S Yorks 1982-83, Pres of Sheffield & Dist Law Soc 1983-84; Cons Pty area treas for Yorks 1983-88; *Recreations* field-sports, skiing, gardening; *Clubs* Cavalry and Guards, Sheffield; *Style—* Sir Basil Rhodes, CBE, TD, DL; Bubnell Hall, Baslow, Derbys (☎ 024 688 3266); 31/33 Doncaster Gate, Rotherham S65 1DF (☎ 0709 365 531, fax 0709 829 752)

RHODES, Benjamin; s of Dr Brian William Rhodes, of Wimborne, Dorset, and Joan, *née* Martin (d 1972); *b* 12 Nov 1952; *Educ* Oundle, Univ of Manchester; *m* 1977, Carol, da of Dr Falk Heinz Kroch (d 1983); 2 s (Daniel b 2 March 1979, Xavier b 24 Feb 1984); *Career* opened Benjamin Rhodes Gallery (in partnership with Carol Kroch-Rhodes) July 1985-; *Style—* Benjamin Rhodes, Esq; Benjamin Rhodes Gallery, 4 New Burlington Place, London W1X 1SB (☎ 071 434 1768, fax 071 287 8841)

RHODES, Dr Ellen Linda (Betty); da of Victor Sydney Joynson Wreford, and Dora Winifred Kingscote, *née* Rowland (d 1920); *b* 28 Oct 1920; *Educ* Mill Mount Sch York, Univ of Leeds (MB ChB); *m* Wilfred Harry Rhodes; 1 s (Jonathan Michael b 1949); *Career* conslt dermatologist St Helier and Kingston hosps 1966-85; memb: Br Ass of Dermatologists, RSM; *Books* Dermatology for the Physician (1979); papers incl: Autoimmunity in Chronic Bullous Diseases (1967), Immunity in Herpes Simplex (1975); *Style—* Dr Betty Rhodes; 3 Pelham's Close, Esher, Surrey KT10 8QB (☎ 03724 66127); St Anthony's Hospital, Cheam, Surrey; New Victoria Hospital, Kingston, Surrey

RHODES, Gary; step s of John Smellie, of London, and Jean, *née* Ferris; *b* 22 April 1960; *Educ* Howard Sch Gillingham Kent, Thanet Tech Coll (City and Guilds, Chef of the Year, Student of the Year); *m* 7 January 1989, Yolanda Jennifer, da of Harvey Charles Adkins; 2 s (Samuel James b 24 Sept 1988, George Adam b 17 May 1990); *Career* Amsterdam Hilton Hotel 1979-81 (commis de cuisine, chef de partie), sous chef Reform Club Pall Mall 1982-83, head chef Winstons Eating House Feb 1983- Oct 83, sr sous chef Capital Hotel Knightsbridge 1983-85; head chef: Whitehall Restaurant Essex 1985-86, Castle Hotel Taunton 1986-90, Greenhouse Restaurant Mayfair 1990-; temp appts: Lameloise and La Cote St Jacques (Michelin starred restaurants in France); tv series BSB 1990; runner up: Mumm Champagne Chef of Tomorrow 1978, William Hepinstall award 1979; Michelin star Castle Hotel 1986, finalist Meilleur Ouvrier de Grande Bretagne competition 1987, 30 under 30 award 1988, rep GB at a cooking festival Singapore Hilton Hotel 1989; *Style—* Gary Rhodes, Esq; The Greenhouse Restaurant, 27A Hays Mews, Mayfair, London (☎ 071 409 1017)

RHODES, Sir John Christopher Douglas; 4 Bt (UK 1919); s of Lt-Col Sir Christopher George Rhodes, 3 Bt (d 1964); *b* 24 May 1946; *Heir* bro, Michael Rhodes; *Style—* Sir John Rhodes, Bt

RHODES, Prof John David; *b* 9 Oct 1943; *Educ* Univ of Leeds (BSc, PhD, DSc), Univ of Bradford (DEng); *Career* Dept of Electrical and Electronic Engrg Univ of Leeds: res fell 1966-67, lectr 1969-72, reader 1972-75, prof 1975-81, industl prof 1981-; fndr, chm and tech dir Filtronic Components Ltd 1977-; awards incl: The Microwave prize (USA) 1969, Browder J Thompson award (USA) 1970, The Queen's award for Technol Achievement (UK) 1985, The Queen's award for Export Achievement (UK) 1988; FIEEE 1980, FIEE 1984, FEng 1987; *PS* Theory of Electrical Filters (1976), author of numerous technical papers; *Style—* Prof John Rhodes; Boodles, Thorpe Lane, Tranmere Park, Guiseley, Leeds LS20 8JH

RHODES, John Guy; s of Canon Cecil Rhodes, of Bury St Edmunds, and Gladys, *née* Farlie; *b* 16 Feb 1945; *Educ* King Edward VI Birmingham, Jesus Coll Cambridge (BA); *m* 11 June 1977, Christie Joan, da of Peter Dorrington Batt, MC, of Bury St Edmunds; 2 s (Alexander Luke b 1979, Nicholas Hugh b 1981); *Career* articled clerk Macfarlanes 1968; admitted slr 1970, ptnr Macfarlanes 1975-; *Recreations* woodlands, tennis, skiing; *Clubs* City; *Style—* John Rhodes, Esq; Macfarlanes, 10 Norwich St, London EC4A 1BD (☎ 071 831 9222, fax 071 831 9607)

RHODES, Hon Mrs (Margaret); *née* Elphinstone; da of late 16 Lord Elphinstone, KT, and Lady Mary Bowes-Lyon, DCVO, da of 14 Earl of Strathmore, whereby Mrs Rhodes is first cous of HM The Queen (at whose wedding Mrs Rhodes was a bridesmaid); *b* 9 June 1925; *m* 1950, Denys Gravenor Rhodes (d 1981), er s of Maj Tahu Rhodes, Gren Gds, and Hon Helen (eldest da of 5 Baron Plunket); 2 s, 2 da; *Style—* The Hon Mrs Rhodes; The Garden House, Windsor Great Park, Windsor, Berks (☎ 0784 434617)

RHODES, Marion; da of Samuel Rhodes (d 1930), of Huddersfield, Yorks, and Mary Jane, *née* Mallinson (d 1956); *b* 17 May 1907; *Educ* Greenhead GS Huddersfield, Huddersfield Art Sch, Leeds Coll of Art, The Central Sch of Arts and Crafts London (Art Teachers Cert Univ of Oxford); *Career* teacher 1930-67, pt/t lectr in art Berridge House Trg Coll 1947-55; Paris Salon: hon mention 1952, Bronze medal 1956, Silver medal 1961, Gold medal 1967; exhibited at: Royal Acad 1934-, Royal Scottish Acad, The Paris Salon, Walker Art Gallery, Towner Art Gallery, Atkinson, Southport, Brighton, Bradford, Leeds, Manchester, USA, SA; works purchased by Br Museum and V & A Museum Print Room (amongst many others); illustrasions for Robert Harding's Snettisham; memb: Soc of Graphic Fine Artists 1936 (hon life memb 1969), Acad of Fine Art 1955-81, Accademia Delle Arti E De Lavoro Parma 1979-82; fell: Ancient Monuments Soc, Assoc Artistes Francois 1971-79; hon memb Tommasso Campanella Acad Rome (Silver medal 1979), Academy of Italy (Gold medal 1979), Certificate of Merit Dictionary of Internat Biography 1972; fell Royal Soc of Painter-Etchers and Engravers, life FRSA; *Recreations* gardening, geology; *Clubs* ESU; *Style—* Miss Marion Rhodes; 2 Goodwyn Ave, Mill Hill, London NW7 3RG (☎ 081 959 2280)

RHODES, Michael Philip James; s of late Lt-Col Sir Christopher Rhodes, 3 Bt; hp of bro, Sir John Rhodes, 4 Bt; *b* 3 April 1948; *m* 1973, Susan, da of Patrick Roney-Dougal; 1 da; *Style—* Michael Rhodes Esq

RHODES, Sir Peregrine Alexander; KCMG (1984, CMG 1976); s of Cyril Edmunds Rhodes (d 1966), and Elizabeth Frances (d 1962); *b* 14 May 1925; *Educ* Winchester, New Coll Oxford (BA); *m* 1, 1951 (m dis), Jane Hassell; 2 s, 1 da; *m* 2, 1969, Margaret Rosemary, da of Eric Page (d 1980); *Career* Coldstream Gds 1944-47; HM Dip Serv 1950-: Rangoon, Vienna, Helsinki, Rome, Charge D'Affaires E Berlin (opening Embassy) 1973-75, under sec Cabinet Office 1975-78, high cmmr Cyprus

1979-82, ambass Greece 1982; dir gen Br Property Fedn 1986-90; seconded to Inst for Study of Int Orgn Univ of Sussex 1968-69; chm Anglo Hellenic League 1986-; vice pres Br Sch Athens; FRSA 1988; *Recreations* photography, reading; *Clubs* Travellers'; *Style—* Sir Peregrine Rhodes, KCMG

RHODES, Prof Philip; s of Sydney Rhodes (d 1962), of Sheffield, and Harriett May, *née* Denniff (d 1981); *b* 2 May 1922; *Educ* King Edward VII Sch Sheffield, Clare Coll Cambridge (BA, MA), St Thomas' Hosp Med Sch (MB BChir); *m* 26 Oct 1946, Mary Elizabeth, da of Rev John Kenneth Worley, MC (d 1957), of Barrowden, Rutland; 3 s (Richard, David, Kenneth), 2 da (Susan (Mrs Lutwyche), Frances (Mrs Marshall)); *Career* Maj RAMC 1949-51; St Thomas' Hosp: obstetric physician 1958-64, prof of gynaecology 1964-74, dean of Med Sch 1968-74; dean Faculty of Med Univ of Adelaide S Aust 1974-77, postgrad dean of med Univ of Newcastle upon Tyne 1977-80, postgrad dean and prof of postgrad med educn Univ of Southampton 1980-87; Brontë Soc prize 1972; chm Educn Ctee of King Edward's Hosp Fund for London, memb Gen Med Cncl 1979-89; FRCS, FRCOG, FRACMA, FFOM, FRSA; *Books* Fluid Balance in Obstetrics (1960), An Introduction to Gynaecology and Obstetrics (1967), Woman: A biological study (1969), Reproductive Physiology for Medical Students (1969), The Value of Medicine (1976), Doctor John Leake's Hospital (1977), Letters to a Young Doctor (1983), An Outline History of Medicine (1985); *Recreations* writing, reading; *Style—* Prof Philip Rhodes; 1 Wakerley Court, Wakerley, Oakham, Leicester, LE15 8PA (☎ 057 287 665)

RHODES, Philip John; s of (Osmond) Cyril Rhodes, of Lincoln, and Dorothy, *née* Ibbetson; *b* 23 Aug 1937; *Educ* City Sch Lincoln; *m* 11 Sept 1965, Madeleine Ann, da of Samuel Edward Blaza, of Waltham, Lincs; 2 da (Jane b 1966, Judith b 1969); *Career* Nat Serv Sherwood Foresters 1956, Intelligence Corps 1957; asst gen mangr Gen Accident plc 1988- (city mangr 1985-87); pres Perth C of C 1982-83, vice pres The Insur Inst of London 1988; Freeman City of London, Liveryman Worshipful Co of Insurers 1988; ACII; *Recreations* music, golf, tennis; *Clubs* Royal Cwlth Soc; *Style—* Philip Rhodes, Esq; Dixon House, 1 Lloyds Ave, London, EC3N 3DH (☎ 071 626 8711, fax 071 481 8403, telex 885372)

RHODES, Richard David Walton; JP (Fylde 1978); s of Harry Walton Rhodes (d 1966), of 38 Hill Road, Penwortham, Preston, Lancs, and Dorothy Fairhurst (d 1986); *b* 20 April 1942; *Educ* Rossall Sch Fleetwood, St John's Coll Durham (BA), Hertford Coll (Dip Ed); *m* 11 Aug 1966, Stephanie, da of Frederic William Heyes (d 1978), of 6 Hollinhurst Ave, Penwortham, Preston, Lancs; 2 da (Deborah b 1968, Victoria b 1971); *Career* asst master St John's Sch Leatherhead 1964-75; headmaster: Arnold Sch Blackpool 1979-87 (dep headmaster 1975-79), Rossall Sch Fleetwood 1987-; *Recreations* sports, photography, public speaking, gardening; *Clubs* East India, Devonshire, Sports and Public Schs; *Style—* Richard Rhodes, Esq; The Hall, Rossall Sch, Fleetwood, Lancs FY7 9JW (☎ 025387 3849)

RHODES, Robert Elliott; QC; s of Gilbert Gedalia Rhodes (d 1970), of London, and Elly Brook, *née* Feingold; *b* 2 Aug 1945; *Educ* St Paul's, Pembroke Coll Oxford (MA); *m* 16 March 1971, Georgina Caroline, da of Jack Gerald Clarfelt, of Linhay Meads, Timsbury, Hants; 2 s (Matthew b 1973, James b 1975), 1 da (Emily b 1983); *Career* called to Bar Inner Temple 1968; 1 prosecuting counsel to Inland Revenue at Central Criminal Ct and Inner London Crown Cts 1981 (2 prosecuting counsel 1979), rec Crown Ct 1987, QC 1989; *Recreations* reading, listening to opera, watching cricket, playing real tennis; *Clubs* MCC; *Style—* Robert Rhodes, Esq, QC; 2 Crown Office Row, Temple, London, EC4Y 7HJ (☎ 071 583 2681, fax 071 583 2850, telex 8955733 INLAWS)

RHODES, Prof Roderick Arthur William; s of Keith Firth Rhodes, and Irene, *née* Clegg; *b* 15 Aug 1944; *Educ* Fulneck Boys' Sch, Univ of Bradford (BSc), St Catherine's Coll Oxford (BLitt), Univ of Essex (PhD); *m* 2 Dec 1978, Cynthia Margaret, da of John Marshall; 1 s (Edward Roderick b 25 June 1979), 1 da (Bethan Margaret b 30 Oct 1981); *Career* Univ of Birmingham 1970-76, Univ of Strathclyde 1976-79, Univ of Essex 1979-89, prof of politics Univ of York 1989-; memb: RIPA, dep chm Public Admin Ctee, Jt Univ Cncl for Social and Public Admin, Political Studies Assoc of UK, Society and Politics RDG of Economic and Scocial Res Cncl; *Books* Control and Power in Central-Local Government Relations (1979), The National World of Local Government (1986), Beyond Westminster and Whitehall (1988), Public Admin (ed, 1986-); *Style—* Prof Roderick Rhodes; Dept of Politics, University of York, Heslington, York YO1 5DD (☎ 0904 433540, fax 0904 433433, telex 57933 YORKUL)

RHODES, Timothy (Tim); s of Herbert Bassett Rhodes (d 1977), of Woodgreen, Hants, and Felicity, *née* Woodman; *b* 30 Sept 1940; *Educ* Nottingham HS, Univ of Durham (BA), Université de Lyon France; *m* 15 Jan 1963, Jacquetta Mary Christine, da of Leonard Bryant Lunn (d 1979), of Guildford, Surrey; 1 s (Jonathan b 1965), 2 da (Tracy b 1963, Karen b 1964); *Career* econ conslt and dir 1964-67, pt/t prof of geography Univ of Reading 1967-81, asst mangr South Hampshire Plan 1968-74; Central Info Services Oxfordshire CC: head of R and I 1974-80, asst chief exec 1980-87, head of info serv 1987-89, dir 1989-; rep on statistics groups ACC, chm 1991 Census Local Authy GP, fndr chm CC Chief Executives Support Network, conslt for OECD; MBCS 1968; *Recreations* gardening, travel; *Clubs* Rotary, North Oxford; *Style—* Tim Rhodes, Esq; Oxfordshire County Council, County Hall, Oxford OX1 1ND (☎ 0865 815200, fax 0865 761255)

RHODES, Zandra Lindsey; da of Albert James Rhodes (d 1988), of Chatham, Kent, and Beatrice Ellen, *née* Twigg (d 1968), fitter at Worth, Paris; *b* 19 Sept 1940; *Educ* Medway Technical Sch for Girls Chatham, Medway Coll of Art Rochester Kent, Royal Coll of Art (DesRCA); *Career* started career as textile designer 1964, set up print factory and studio with Alexander McIntyre 1965, transferred to fashion indust 1966, ptnrship with Sylvia Ayton producing dresses using own prints, opened Fulham Rd clothes shop (fndr ptnr and designer) 1967-68, first solo collection US 1969 (met with phenomenal response from Vogue and Women's Wear Daily), thereafter established as foremost influential designer (developed unique use of printed fabrics and treatment of jersey), prodr annual spectacular fantasy shows USA; fndr with Anne Knight and Ronnie Stirling: Zandra Rhodes (UK) Ltd, Zandra Rhodes Shops 1975-86 (md 1975-); first shop London 1975 (others opened in Bloomingdales NY and Marshall Field Chicago), shops and licencees now world wide; Zandra Rhodes designs currently incl: interior furnishing, sheets and pillowcases, sarees, jewellry, rugs, kitchen accessories, fine china figurines; launched fine arts and prints collections Dyanssen Galleries USA 1989; solo exhibitions incl: Texas Gallery Houston 1981, La Jolla Museum of Contemporary Art San Diego 1982, Barbican Centre 1982, Parson's Sch of Design NY 1982, Art Museum of Santa Cruz Co California 1983; work represented in numerous permanent costume collections incl: V & A, City Museum & Art Gallery Stoke-on-Trent, Royal Pavilion Brighton Museum, City Art Gallery Leeds, Met Museum NY, Museum of Applied Arts & Scis Sydney, Nat Museum of Victoria Melbourne; acknowledged spokeswoman and personality of 60s and 70s (famous for green and later pink coloured hair), frequent speaker on fashion and design, subject of numerous documentaries and films; Designer of the Year English Fashion Trade UK 1972, Emmy Award for Best Costume Design Romeo and Juliet on Ice CBS TV 1984, Best Show of the Year New Orleans 1985, Woman of Distinction Award Northwood Inst Dallas Texas 1986; key to City of Miami and City of California; hon DFA Int Fine Arts Coll Miami, hon DRCA Royal Coll of Art, hon DD Cncl for Nat Acad Awards 1987; RDI 1977, FSIAD 1982; *Books* The Art of Zandra Rhodes (1984, US ed 1985); *Recreations* gardening, travelling, drawing, watercolours; *Style—* Miss Zandra Rhodes; 85 Richford St, London W6 7HJ (☎ 081 749 9561, fax 081 749 6411, telex 946561 ZANDRA G)

RHODES JAMES, Robert Vidal; MP (C) Cambridge 1976-; s of William Rhodes James, OBE, MC (d 1972), Indian Army; *b* 10 April 1933; *Educ* Sedbergh, Worcester Coll Oxford; *m* 1956, Angela Margaret, eld da of late Ronald Robertson; 4 da; *Career* clerk House of Commons 1955-64, fell All Souls Coll Oxford 1964-68, dir Inst for Study of Int Orgn Univ of Sussex 1968-73, PA to UN sec-gen 1973-76, PPS FCO 1979-82, Cons liaison offr for higher educn 1979-87, vice chm Home Affrs and Constitutional Ctees; chm History of Parly Tst 1983-, memb Chairman's Panel of House of Commons 1987-, chm Cons Friends of Israel 1988-; Hon DLitt; FRSL, FRHistS; *Books* Lord Randolph Churchill (1959), An Introduction to the House of Commons (1961), Rosebery (1963), Gallipoli (1965), Chips: The Diaries of Sir Henry Channon (1967), JCC Davidson: Memoirs of a Conservative (1968), Churchill, A Study in Failure 1900-1939 (1970), Ambitions and Realities (1972), The Complete Speeches of Sir Winston Churchill (eight volumes, 1974), Victor Cazalet, A Portrait (1975), The British Revolution 1880-1939 (two volumes, 1976, 1977), Albert, Prince Consort (1983), Anthony Eden (1986); *Recreations* sailing; *Clubs* Travellers', Grillions, Pratt's; *Style—* Robert Rhodes James, Esq, MP; The Stone House, Great Gransden, nr Sandy, Beds

RHYL, Baroness; Hon Esmé Consuelo Helen; *née* Glyn; OBE (1946); 2 da of 4 Baron Wolverton, JP, DL, by his w, Lady Edith Ward, CBE (da of 1 Earl of Dudley); sis of late 5 Baron Wolverton and late Lady Hyde (mother of 7 Earl of Clarendon); *b* 20 Sept 1908; *m* 1950, Baron Rhyl, OBE, PC (Life Peer, d 1981), s of Gen Sir Noel Birch, GBE, KCB, KCMG, and Florence (3 da of Sir George Chetwode, 6 Bt, and sis of 1 Baron Chetwode; *Style—* The Rt Hon Lady Rhyl, OBE; Holywell House, Swanmore, Hants

RHYS, Lady Anne Maud; *née* Wellesley; da of 5 Duke of Wellington, and Hon Lilian Coats, da of 1 Baron Glentanar; *b* 2 Feb 1910; *m* 1933 (m dis 1963), Hon David Rhys, 3 s of 7 Baron Dynevor; 1 s, 1 da; *Career* inherited Duchy (Sp) of Ciudad Rodrigo and Grandeeship of 1 Class on death of her bro, 6 Duke, 1943, but ceded them to unc, 7 Duke, 1949; *Style—* The Lady Anne Rhys; Le Bourg, Rue de Tertrie, Castel Parish, Guernsey

RHYS, Col David Lewellin; OBE (1950), MC (1937), DL (Gwent 1975-); s of Owen Lewellin Rhys; *b* 2 April 1910; *Educ* Epsom, RMC Sandhurst; *m* 1949, Doreen, *née* Giles; 2 s; *Career* cmmnd S Wales Borderers 1930, Palestine 1936, Waziristan 1937, Burma 1942-43, Italy 1944-45, Malaya 1955-56, Col; mil attaché Netherlands East Indies 1947-49; sec: Monmouth T and AFA 1957-68, Wales TA and VRA 1968-75, DL Monmouthshire 1963-75; chief cmmr St John Ambulance Bde Wales 1975-79; CStJ 1975, KStJ 1978; *Recreations* fishing, shooting, golf; *Clubs* Army and Navy, Cardiff and Country; *Style—* Colonel David Rhys, OBE, MC, DL; Paradwys, Aberthin, Cowbridge, S Glamorgan (☎ 044 632 056)

RHYS, Hon David Reginald; s of 7 Baron Dynevor (d 1956), and Lady Margaret Child-Villiers (d 1960), da of 7 Earl of Jersey; *b* 18 March 1907; *Educ* Eton, Tours, Frankfurt (AM); *m* 1, 1933 (m dis 1963), Lady Anne Maud Wellesley, da of 5 Duke of Wellington; 1 s, 1 da; m 2, 1963, Sheila Mary d'Ambrumenil (MTC AAGB 1943-46), da of D J Phillips; 1 s; *Career* late Capt Welsh Gds, served 1939-45 war (wounded, Normandy), hotel dir; *Recreations* racing; *Clubs* Farmers'; *Style—* The Hon David Rhys; Southwick Ct, Trowbridge, Wilts BA14 9QB (☎ 0225 75 2469)

RHYS, Hon Mrs Elwyn; Diana; da of Maj Roger Cyril Hans Sloane Stanley, DL, JP of Paultons Park, Hants; *m* 1931, Capt the Hon Elwyn Villiers Rhys (2 s of 7 Baron Dynevor and who d 1966); 1 da; *Style—* The Hon Mrs Elwyn Rhys

RHYS, Prof (David) Garel; OBE (1989); s of Emyr Lewys Rhys, and Edith Phyllis, *née* Williams; *b* 28 Feb 1940; *Educ* Ystalyfera GS, Univ of Swansea (BA), Univ of Birmingham (MCom); *m* (Charlotte) Mavis, da of Edward Colston Walters; 1 s (Jeremy Charles), 2 da (Angela Jayne, Gillian Mary); *Career* lectr Univ of Hull 1967-70 (asst lectr 1965-67); Univ Coll Cardiff 1970-87: lectr, sr lectr, prof; prof Cardiff Business Sch Univ of Wales 1987-; advsr to: select ctees House of Commons, Nat Audit Office; conslt to govt depts; FITA 1987, FIMI 1989; *Books* The Motor Industry: An Economic Survey (1971), The Motor Industry in the European Community (1989); *Recreations* walking, gardening; *Style—* Prof Garel Rhys, OBE; Cardiff Business School, University of Wales, Aberconway Building, Colum Drive, Cardiff CF1 3EU (☎ 0222 874281, fax 0222 874419)

RHYS, (William Joseph) St Ervyl-Glyndwr; s of Edward John Rhys (d 1955), and Rachel, *née* Thomas (d 1986); *b* 6 July 1924; *Educ* Newport HS, Univ of Wales, Guy's Hosp Univ of London, St John's Coll Cambridge (MA, MB BS); *m* 1961, Ann, *née* Rees; 6 da; *Career* Nat Serv Sqdn Ldr RAF Inst Aviation Med & Empire Test Pilot Sch; conslt gynaecologist Welsh Hosp Bd 1962, MOH Cardiganshire 1966-74, conslt physician community med (Dyfed) 1974-82, hon med advsr Welsh Nat Water Devpt Authy 1966-82, Univ of Camb rep on Cncl, rep Ct of Govrs Univ Coll Wales 1979-86, chm tstees St John's Coll Dyfed 1987- (memb 1979-); High Sheriff Co of Dyfed 1979-80; cmmr St John Ambulance Bde Ceredigion 1982-89, pres Scout Assoc Ceredigion 1983-, chm Hospitallers' Club Dyfed 1983-; memb: exec ctee Assoc of Friends of Nat Library of Wales 1984-; chm Governing Body Ceredigion Schs 1987- (memb 1985-); tstee The Two Red Dragons Educn Tst (promotes Japan studies in Europe) 1988-; hon memb (White Robe) Gorsedd of Bards of Wales; Lord of the Barony of Llawhaden, Lord of the Manor of Llanfynydd (Celtic, pre-Norman), Freeman City of London, Liveryman Worshipful Soc of Apothecaries; MRCOG, MFCM; CStJ; *Recreations* medical history, genealogical research, local history, walking; *Clubs* RAF; *Style—* St Ervyl-Glyndwr Rhys, Esq; Plas Bronmeurig, Ystrad Meurig, Dyfed (☎ 09745 650); Minffordd, Llangadog, Dyfed (☎ 0550 777496)

RHYS, William Escott; s of Hubert Ralph John Rhys (d 1972), and Ethel Violet, *née* Sweet-Escott (d 1949); *b* 13 July 1924; *Educ* Shrewsbury; *m* 1 July 1950, Yvette Dorothy Mary, da of Frederick James Box (d 1952); 1 s (John Frederick William b 1958), 2 da (Jane Caroline b 1953, (Yvette) Julia b 1955); *Career* WWII served RN 1943-46: cmmnd midshipman 1943, Sub Lt 1944, CO LCT 7092 1944, Temp Lt 1946; SA Brain & Co: asst brewer 1946-52, dir 1952-65, head brewer 1965-68, jt md 1968-71, chm and md 1971-79, chm and chief exec 1979-89; regnl dir Lloyds Bank 1985-; chm S Wales Brewers Assoc 1973-76; memb: Inst of Brewing, Inc Brewers Guild; *Recreations* golf, shooting; *Clubs* MCC, Royal Porthcawl Golf, Cardiff & Co; *Style—* William Rhys, Esq; 20 Hollybush Rd, Cyncoed, Cardiff CF2 6TA (☎ 0222 762127); S A Brain & Co Ltd, The Old Brewery, St Mary St, Cardiff CF1 1SP (☎ 0222 399022, fax 0222 383 127)

RHYS EVANS, Peter Howell; s of Gwillym Rhys Evans, MC, of Rickledown, Durham, and Jean Marjorie, *née* Foord; *b* 17 May 1948; *Educ* St Martins Sch Yorkshire, Ampleforth, St Bart's (MB BS, cricket and rugby colours), Univ of Paris, Gustave-Roussy Inst (DCC); *m* 6 Jan 1973, Irene Caroline, da of Prof Deryk J Mossop; 2 s (Matthew James b 1 Feb 1976, Marc Givillym b 2 May 1980), 1 da (Melissa Charlotte b 2 March 1984); *Career* qualified Bart's 1971, house physician Whipps Cross Hosp 1972, house surgn Bart's 1972, ENT house Surgn Bart's 1973, anatomy demonstrator Univ of Bristol 1973-74, casualty offr Bristol Royal Infirmary 1973-74, sr house offr Plastic Surgery Hull Royal Infirmary 1975, The Royal Nat Throat Nose and Ear Hosp London 1975-79 (registrar, sr registrar, sr surgical offr), sr ENT registrar Queen Elizabeth Hosp Birmingham 1979-80, consltt and sr lectr ENT surgery Univ of Birmingham 1981-84, consltt ENT surgn Queen Elizabeth Hosp Birmingham 1984-86, consltt ENT and Head Neck Surgn The Royal Marsden Hosp 1986-; examiner RCS 1986-, fndr memb Euro Acad of Facial Surgeons 1978 (vice pres 1987), memb Nat Cncl Otolaryngological Res Soc 1984-88; Freeman City of London 1990; hon ENT surgn St Mary's Hosp, hon sr lectr Univ of London; MRCS 1975, LRCP, FRSM, FRCS 1985, memb BMA; *publications:* Cancer of Head and Neck (ed, 1983), Face and Neck Surgical Techniques-Problems and Limitations (ed, 1983), Facial Plastic Surgery-Otoplasty (guest ed, 1985), contrib to numerous med jls and books, varied presentations, Otoplasty Monograph (1987); *Recreations* skiing, golf, tennis, anthropology; *Style—* Peter Rhys Evans, Esq; The White House, 15 Drax Ave, Wimbledon, London SW20 0EG (☎ 081 946 4499); 106 Harley St, London W1N 1AF; The Royal Marsden Hosp, Fulham Rd, London SW3 6JJ (☎ 071 935 3525, 071 352 8171 ext 2730 and 2731, fax 071 351 3785)

RHYS JONES, Griffith (Griff); s of Elwyn Rhys Jones, and Gwyneth Margaret Jones; *b* 16 Nov 1953; *Educ* Brentwood Sch, Emmanuel Coll Cambridge (MA); *m* 21 Nov 1981, Joanna Frances, da of Alexander James Harris; 1 s (George Alexander b 1985), 1 da (Catherine Louisa b 1987); *Career* actor and writer; BBC radio prodr 1976-79; TV comedy series: Not The Nine O'Clock News 1979-82, Alas Smith and Jones 1984-, The World According to Smith and Jones 1986-87, Small Doses 1989; TV play A View of Harry Clarke 1989; theatre: Charley's Aunt 1983, Trumpets and Raspberries 1985, The Alchemist 1986, Arturo Ui 1987, Thark 1989-90, Wind in the Willows 1990-91; film: Morons From Outer Space 1985, Wilt 1989; opera: Die Fledermaus 1989; dir Twelfth Night RSC 1989; dir: Talkback, Playback, Smith Jones Brown & Cassie; columnist for The Times 1989-90; *Books* The Lavishly Tooled Smith and Jones (1986), Janet Lives with Mel and Griff (1988); *Clubs* Groucho; *Style—* Griff Rhys Jones, Esq; 33 Percy Street, London W1 (☎ 071 637 5302, fax 071 631 4273)

RHYS WILLIAMS, Lady; Caroline Susan; *née* Foster; eldest da of Ludovic Anthony Foster (d 1990), of Greatham Manor, Pulborough, Sussex; *m* 14 Feb 1961, Sir Brandon Meredith Rhys Williams, 2 Bt, MP (d 1988); 1 s (Sir Gareth, 3 Bt, *qv*), 2 da (Elinor Caroline b 21 Oct 1964, Miranda Pamela Cariadwen b 5 Nov 1968); *Career* JP Inner London; vice pres: London Choral Soc, Kensington & Chelsea Arts Cncl; assoc memb Special Health Authy Hosps for Sick Children Gt Ormond St, tstee Wishing Well Appeal, chm Barking and Havering Family Health Servs Authy; *Style—* Lady Rhys Williams; Gadairwen, Groes Faen, Mid-Glamorgan; 32 Rawlings Street, London SW3

RHYS WILLIAMS, Sir (Arthur) Gareth Ludovic Emrys; 3 Bt (UK 1918), of Miskin, Parish of Llantrisant, Co Glamorgan; s of Sir Brandon Rhys Williams, 2 Bt, MP (d 1988), and Caroline Susan, eldest da of Ludovic Anthony Foster (d 1990), of Greatham Manor, Pulborough, Sussex; *b* 9 Nov 1961; *Educ* Eton, Univ of Durham, INSEAD; *Heir* none; *Career* md NFI Electronics Isle of Wight; *Recreations* Bow Group, target shooting, TA, conjuring, travel; *Style—* Sir Gareth Rhys Williams, Bt; Gadairwen, Groes Faen, Mid Glamorgan; 32 Rawlings St, London SW3 (☎ 071 584 0636)

RIBBANDS, Mark Jonathan; s of Henry Stephen Ribbands, of Hornchurch, and Christina Ivy, *née* Saggers (d 1984); *b* 6 Jan 1959; *Educ* Forest Sch Snaresbrook, N E London Poly (BSc); *m* 30 May 1987, Maya, da of Flt Offr Wassoudeve Goriah, DFC (d 1969); *Career* md Ribbands Explosives Ltd 1982-; involved with: explosives disposal, demolition, purchase and supply of arms and ammunition specialising in anti-armour weaponry, supply of explosive ordnance disposal personnel worldwide; memb cncl Inst of Explosives Engrs 1988; FGS 1983, FRGS 1983, MIExpE 1985; *Recreations* scuba diving, flying (helicopters), shooting; *Style—* Mark Ribbands, Esq; 43 Westland Ave, Hornchurch, Essex RM11 3SD (☎ 04024 55805, fax 04024 37093); 18 Kingsgate Castle, Broadstairs, Kent CT10 3PH (☎ 0843 61909)

RICARDO, Lady Barbara Maureen; *née* Montagu Stuart Wortley; da of 3 Earl of Wharncliffe (d 1953), of Wortley Hall, later Carlton House, Wortley, and Lady Maud Lilian Elfreda Mary Wentworth Fitzwilliam (d 1979); *b* 26 Aug 1921; *Educ* privately; *m* 1943, David Cecil Ricardo, s of Maj Louis Ferdinand Ricardo, 8 Hus of Tanganyika, East Africa; 2 s (Dorrien, Richard); *Career* served WW II Women's Land Army, remount depot rider Melton Mowbray Leicestershire 1941-55; *Style—* The Lady Barbara Ricardo; Carlton Lodge, Wortley, Sheffield S30 7DG (☎ 0742 882584)

RICE, Anneka; da of John Rice, of Tudor Hall, Branksome Park Rd, Camberley, Surrey; *b* 4 Oct 1958; *Educ* St Michael's Sch Limpsfield Surrey, Croydon HS for Girls; *m* 5 Aug 1988, Nicholas David Allott, s of Brig David Allott (d 1969); 2 s (Thomas Alexander David b 17 Jan 1989, Joshua James b 20 June 1990); *Career* journalist and broadcaster; principal series: CBTV 1982-85, Treasure Hunt 1983-88, Wish You Were Here 1984-91, TVAM 1985-86, Sporting Chance 1984-85, Challenge Anneka 1989-91; numerous guest appearances on radio and TV; patron: Back Up, Br Deaf Assoc; Cncl memb: WWF, Nat Cncl of Women, Parents for Safe Food; pres Cowbridge Male Voice Choir; *Books* The Adventure Series: Scuba-Diving, Skiing, Sailing; *Recreations* tennis, swimming, scuba-diving, gliding; *Clubs* Riverside Racquets; *Style—* Miss Anneka Rice

RICE, Arthur Gorton; s of Arthur Edwin Rice (d 1967), of Birmingham; *b* 8 April 1929; *Educ* St Georges in the Field Birmingham; *m* 6 June 1953, Joan, da of Thomas Rollason; 3 s (Michael b 23 March 1956, Jonathan b 7 April 1962, Ian b 30 Dec 1967), 2 da (Pamela b 20 Sept 1958, Sarah (twin) b 7 April 1962); *Career* Nat Serv RAF, Berlin airlift 1948-49; sr ptnr Rice & Co Bank House Cannock Staffs; FCA; *Recreations* squash rackets, golf, tennis; *Clubs* Moor Hall Golf, Four Oaks; *Style—* Arthur Rice, Esq; Bank House, Mill St, Cannock, Staffs WS11 3OW (☎ 0543 503846, fax 0543 574250, telex 335622 SPETAL G)

RICE, Maj-Gen Sir Desmond Hind Garrett; KCVO (1989, CVO 1985), CBE (1976, OBE 1970); s of Arthur Garrett Rice (d 1948), of Battle, Sussex; *b* 1 Dec 1924; *Educ* Marlborough; *m* 1954, Denise Anne, da of Stanley Ravenscroft (d 1956), of Budleigh Salterton, Devon; 1 da; *Career* served in: Italy, Egypt, Germany, W Berlin; Vice Adj Gen 1978-79, Col 1 The Queen's Dragoon Gds 1980-86, Maj-Gen; sec The Central Chancery of The Orders of Knighthood 1980-89; *Recreations* field sports, gardening; *Clubs* Cavalry and Guards'; *Style—* Maj-Gen Sir Desmond Rice, KCVO, CBE; Fairway, Malacca Farm, W Clandon, Guildford, Surrey (☎ 0483 222677) F

RICE, His Hon Judge Gordon Kenneth; s of Victor Rice (d 1947); *b* 16 April 1927; *Educ* BNC Oxford; *m* 1967, Patricia Margaret; *Career* called to the Bar Middle Temple 1957, Crown Court judge 1980-; *Style—* His Hon Judge Gordon Rice; 83 Beach Ave, Leigh-On-Sea, Essex (☎ 0702 73485)

RICE, Janet; da of George Robert Whinham, of Amble, Northumberland, and Ella, *née* Grey (d 1972); *b* 14 Dec 1949; *Educ* Duchess's County GS for Girls Alnwick Northumberland, City of Leeds & Carnegie Coll of Educn (Cert Ed); *m* 7 Aug 1971, Martin Graham Rice, s of Alfred Victor Rice; *Career* pensions asst Clarke Chapman-John Thompson Ltd 1972-74, clerical offr DHSS 1974; British Gas: pensions asst northern region 1974-78, pensions offr HQ 1978-85, asst pensions admin mangr 1985-86, pensions admin mangr 1986-89, mangr Pensions and Int Benefits 1989-; assoc Pensions Mgmnt Inst 1979; *Recreations* walking, gardening, reading, music; *Style—* Mrs Janet Rice; British Gas plc, Rivermill House, 152 Grosvenor Rd, London SW1V 3JL (☎ 071 821 1444, fax 071 233 6075)

RICE, Kenric Garrett; s of Charles Robert Rice (d 1958), and Winifred Margaret, *née* Hill (d 1976); *b* 9 Oct 1918; *Educ* Stowe; *m* 1, 23 Nov 1940 (m dis 1978), Rachel Barbara, da of George Robinson (d 1955); 1 s (Nigel b 4 Oct 1945), 2 da (Amanda b 5 June 1948, Nicola b 19 March 1956); m 2, 29 Sept 1978, Anna, da of Edward William Minton Beddoes (d 1952); 1 da (Emma b 21 July 1980); *Career* Princess Louise Regt (Middx Regt) TA, cmmnd 5 BN Argyll and Sutherland Highlanders 1940, Staff Offr GSO III Air 2 Army 1944, GSO III (Int) 56 Ind Bde 1945; Boar Int staff The Hong Kong and Shanghai Banking Corp (Shanghai, Singapore, Penang, Hong Kong, Calcutta, Rangoon, Borneo and London) 1946-71, gp treas Babcock & Wilcox Ltd 1971-78, chm advsr Guinness Mahon Bankers 1979-82, dir Wintrust Securities Ltd Bankers 1982-85, non-exec dir Regency W of England Building Soc 1980-89; MCT 1980; *Recreations* sailing, golf, skiing; *Clubs* MCC, Overseas Bankers (and Golf), East India, Island Sailing; *Style—* Kenric Rice, Esq; The Old Well House, Lodsworth, Petworth, West Sussex GU28 9BZ (☎ 07985 216)

RICE, Ladislas Oscar ; *b* 20 Jan 1926; *Educ* Reading Sch, LSE (BSc), Harvard Grad Sch of Business Admin (MBA); 1 s (Sebastian b 1970), 1 da (Valentina b 1973); *Career* W H Smith & Son Ltd 1951-53, sr ptnr Urwick Orr & Ptnrs 1953-66, md Minerals Separation 1966-69, chm Burton Gp plc 1969-80; current directorships incl: Burton Gp plc (dep chm), Huntingdon Int Hldgs plc, Drayton Cons Tst plc, Polymark Int plc, Heredities Ltd, Stanley Gibbons Hldgs plc, Fndn for Mgmnt Educn, Sovereign High Yield Investmt Co NV, Scudder New Europe Fund Inc; memb E Anglian RHA; CBIM, FIMC; *Recreations* travel, books, pictures; *Clubs* Brooks's, Harvard (New York City); *Style—* Ladislas Rice, Esq; 19 Redington Rd, London NW3 (☎ 071 435 8095); La Casa di Cacchiano, Monti in Chianti, Siena, Italy

RICE, Michael Penarthur Merrick; s of Arthur Vincent Rice (d 1969), of Penarth, Glam, and Dora Kathleen, *née* Blacklock (d 1980); *b* 21 May 1928; *Educ* Challoner Sch; *Career* Nat Serv Royal Norfolk Regt 1946-48; chm Michael Rice Group Ltd 1955-, dir Eastern England TV Ltd 1969-83; consltt: Govt of Saudi Arabia 1960-, Govt of Bahrain 1963-71, Govt of Egypt, Jamaica, Oman, Carreras Marketing Ltd 1965-75; chm The PR Consultants Association 1978-81; The Aga Khan award for Architecture 1980; museum planning and design for: Qatar Nat Museum, The Museum of Archaeology and Ethnography Riyadh Saudi Arabia, 8 prov museums in Saudi Arabia, Oman Nat Museum, The Museum of the Sultan's Armed Forces Oman; co-fndr The PR Consltts Assoc (memb Honoris Causa 1985), tstee The Soc for Arabian Studies; FIPR 1975, FRSA 1987; *Books* Dilmun Discovered The First Hundred Years of the Archaeology of Bahrain (1984), The Temple Complex at Barbar Bahrain (1983), Search for the Paradise Land: the Archaeology of Bahrain and the Arabian Gulf (1985), Bahrain Through the Ages: The Archaeology (1985), The Excavations at Al-Hajjar Bahrain (1988), Egypt's Making (1990); *Recreations* collecting English watercolours, antiquarian books and early Egyptian artefacts, embellishing a garden, the opera and listening to music, writing poetry, the company of friends and animals; *Clubs* Athenaeum; *Style—* Michael Rice, Esq; Odsey Hse, Baldock Rd Odsey, nr Baldock, Herts SG7 6SD (☎ 0462 74 2706); The Glassmill, 1 Battersea Bridge Rd, London SW11 3BG (☎ 071 223 3431, fax 071 228 4229, telex 917343 ORYZA G)

RICE, Olwen Mary; da of James Anthony Rice, of Rugeley, Staffs, and Mary, *née* Wood; *b* 2 Aug 1960; *Educ* Hagley Park Sch Rugeley Staffs, London Coll of Printing (HND, NCTJDip); *m* 16 Nov 1990, Andrew Tilley, s of Raymond Tilley, of Tettenhall, Wolverhampton; *Career* rep Oxford Mail 1980-84, news ed Fitness Magazine 1984-85, health and beauty ed Chat Magazine 1985-87, dep ed Best Magazine 1987-88, ed Living Magazine 1988-; *Recreations* playing cello, swimming, reading; *Style—* Ms Olwen Rice; Living, Kings Reach Tower, Stamford St, London SE1 (☎ 071 261 5854, fax 071 261 6892)

RICE, Peter Anthony; s of John Daniel Rice (d 1981), of Newry, Co Down, NI, and Brigid Tina, *née* McVerry; *b* 25 June 1950; *Educ* Abbey GS Newry, Univ of Lancaster (BA); *Career* ptnr Wood Mackenzie & Co 1981- (joined 1974), dir Hill Samuel & Co 1986-87, gp corporate fin and planning mangr Commercial Union Assur plc 1988-; chm Edinburgh Central Cons Assoc 1977-79, fndr chm Scot Bow Gp 1980-82; memb Stock Exchange 1981, FIA 1974; *Style—* Peter Rice, Esq; The Old Rectory, 6 Redington Rd, Hampstead, London NW3 7RS (☎ 071 431 3176); Commerical Union, St Helens, Undershaft, London EC2 (☎ 071 283 7500)

RICE, Timothy Miles Bindon (Tim); s of Hugh Gordon Rice (d 1988), and Joan Odette, *née* Bawden; *b* 10 Nov 1944; *Educ* Lancing, La Sorbonne; *m* 1974, Jane, da of Col A H McIntosh, OBE (d 1979); 1 da (Eva Jane Florence), 1 s (Donald Alexander Hugh); *Career* writer and broadcaster; lyricist for stage shows: Joseph and the Amazing Technicolour Dreamcoat (music by Andrew Lloyd Webber) 1968, Jesus Christ Superstar (music by ALW) 1970, Evita (music by ALW) 1976, Blondel (music by Stephen Oliver) 1983, Chess (music by Bjorn Ulvaeus and Benny Anderson) 1984, Cricket (music by ALW) 1986, Starmania (music by Michel Beiger) 1991; major songs incl: Don't Cry For Me Argentina, One Night in Bangkok, I Know Him So Well, Superstar, I Don't Know How To Love Him, All Time High; awarded many gold and platinum discs, 8 Ivor Novello awards, 2 Tony awards, 2 Grammys; co-fndr: Pavilion Books, GRRR Books; chm Stars Organisation for Spastics 1983-85, pres Lord's Taverners 1988-90; *publications incl* Guinness Book of British Hit Singles (8 vols) and many related books, Evita (1978), Treasurer of Lord's (1989); *Recreations* cricket, history of popular music; *Clubs* MCC, Garrick, Saints & Sinners (chm 1990-91), Dramatists', Fonograf (Budapest); *Style—* Tim Rice, Esq; c/o Pavilion Books, 196 Shaftesbury Ave, London WC2 (☎ 071 836 1306)

RICE-OXLEY, James Keith; CBE (1981); s of Montague Keith Rice-Oxley (d 1956), and Marjorie, *née* Burrell (d 1929); *b* 15 Aug 1920; *Educ* Marlborough, Trinity Coll Oxford (MA); *m* 1949, Barbara Mary Joan, da of Frederick Parsons (d 1957), of Bull Lane, Gerrards Cross; 2 da; *Career* Maj (despatches) 1944; chm: Nat Sea Trg Tst 1965-80, Shipowners Gp ILO 1969-80; dir: Gen Cncl of Br Shipping 1965-80, Int Shipping Fedn 1969-80; memb: Cncl Dr Barnardo's 1981- (vice chm 1988), Industl Tribunals (Eng and Wales) 1981-88; chm MN Trg Bd 1981-, memb Engrg Bd Business and Technician Educn Cncl 1983-87, UK govr World Maritime Univ 1983-89; Gen Cmmr of Income Tax 1986-; *Recreations* ceramics, squash; *Style—* James Rice-Oxley, Esq, CBE; Ox House, Bimport, Shaftesbury, Dorset SP7 8AX (☎ 0747 52741)

RICH, Allan; s of Norman Rich, and Tessa, *née* Sawyer; *m* 5 June 1966, Vivienne, da of Fred Ostro; 1 s (Jason b 8 May 1970), 2 da (Michaela b 6 May 1967, Natalie b 13 May 1972); *Career* advertising exec; Masius Wynne Williams (now known as DMB & B) 1960-66, fndr and media dir Davidson Pearce Berry & Tuck (bought Spottiswood 1971) 1966-75, fndr The Media Business Group 1975-; MIPA 1968, MAA 1969; *Style—* Allan Rich, Esq; The Media Business Group, Media House, 16 Morwell St, London WC1B 3EY (☎ 071 637 7299, fax 071 636 4145)

RICH, Michael Samuel; QC (1980); s of Sidney Frank Rich, OBE, JP (d 1985), of Streatham, and Erna Babette, *née* Schlesinger (d 1988); *b* 18 Aug 1933; *Educ* Dulwich, Wadham Coll Oxford (MA); *m* 31 July 1983, Janice Sarita, da of Henry Jules Benedictus; 3 s (Benedict b 1966, Jonathan b 1969, Edmund b 1970), 1 da (Sara b 1964); *Career* Lt RASC 1954; called to the Bar Middle Temple 1959, bencher 1985, rec 1986, memb Hong Kong Bar; tstee: Southwark Playgrounds Tst, Brixton Village, S London Liberal Synagogue; *Books* Hills Law of Town and Country Planning (1968); *Style—* Michael Rich, Esq, QC; 18 Dulwich Village, London SE21 7AL (☎ 081 693 1957); 2 Paper Buildings, Temple, London EC4 (☎ 071 353 5835, fax 071 583 1390)

RICH, Owen James; CBE (1987); s of John Alan Frank Rich (d 1953), and Lilian Frances, *née* Mounty (d 1978); *b* 22 Sept 1925; *Educ* Midsomer Norton GS; *m* 12 Nov 1949, Dorothy Edith, da of Samuel Philip Gordon (d 1945); 1 s (Matthew Ashman b 24 May 1960), 1 da (Christine Frances b 11 Dec 1950); *Career* WWII Capt IA; served: India, Burma, French Indo China (Vietnam), Celebes New Guinea; Alfred McAlpine plc 1941-: pupil civil engr 1941-43, contracts engr 1947-58, contracts dir 1958-72, md Main Subsid 1972-76, md 1976-85, dep chm 1985-87; chm of tstees Alfred McAlpine Pension Co 1977-90; involved with: Third World orgns, Homeless in Eng; chm Cncl Fed of Civil Engrg Contractors 1988-89, FCIOB 1978, FRSA 1987; *Recreations* walking, fishing, gardening; *Style—* Owen Rich, Esq, CBE; Villa Julia, Weston Rd, Bath BA1 2XT (☎ 0225 424205)

RICHARD, Cliff; OBE (1980); s of Rodger Oscar Webb (d 1961), and Dorothy Marie Bodkin (formerly Webb), *née* Beazley; *b* 14 Oct 1940; *Educ* Riversmead Sch Cheshunt; *Career* singer and actor; first hit record Move It 1958, own series on BBC and ITV, various repertory and variety seasons; 14 gold records, 35 silver records; films: Serious Charge 1959, Expresso Bongo 1960, The Young Ones 1961, Summer Holiday 1962, Wonderful Life 1964, Finders Keepers 1966, Two a Penny 1968, His Land 1970, Take Me High 1973; vice pres: PHAB, Tear Fund; *Books* Which One's Cliff (1977), Happy Christmas from Cliff (1980), You, Me and Jesus (1983), Jesus, Me and You (1985), Single-Minded (1988); *Recreations* tennis; *Style—* Cliff Richard, Esq, OBE; PO Box 46C, Esher, Surrey KT10 9AA (☎ 0372 467752, fax 0372 462352)

RICHARD, Baron (Life Peer UK 1990), of Ammanford in the County of Dyfed; Ivor Seward Richard; QC (1971); s of Seward Thomas Richard, of Rhiwbina, Cardiff; *b* 30 May 1932; *Educ* St Michael's Sch Llanelly, Cheltenham, Pembroke Coll Oxford; *m* 1; 1 s; m 2, 1 s, 1 da; m 3, 1989, Janet, da of John James, of Oxford; 1 s; *Career* called to the Bar Inner Temple 1955, Parly candidate (Lab) S Kensington Gen Election 1959 and LCC Election 1961, MP (Lab) Barons Court 1964-74, PPS to Sec of State for Def 1966-69, Parly under-sec of state for Def (Army) 1969-70, oppn spokesman Posts and Telecommunications 1970-71, dep oppn spokesman for affrs 1971-74, UK perm rep at the UN 1974-79, chm Rhodesia Conf Geneva 1976; UK cmmr to the Cmmn of the European Communities 1981-85 responsible for: employment, social affrs, educn and vocational trg; memb: Fabian Soc, Lab Lawyers; *Style—* The Rt Hon Lord Richard, QC; 11 South Square, Gray's Inn, London WC2

RICHARD, John Walter Maxwell Miller; s of Col J E M Richard, OBE, of Kaizle, Peebles, and Gaynor Richard (d 1933); *b* 19 April 1933; *Educ* Cargilfield, Eton, Trinity Coll Cambridge (BA); *m* 1977, Christine Margaret, da of Ludwig Christian Saam (d 1954); 1 s, 3 da; *Career* ptnr Bell, Lawrie, Macgregor & Co; memb: Stock Exchange 1959, Cncl of Stock Exchange, Cncl's Markets Ctee; *Style—* John Richard Esq; 8 Braid Hills Approach, Edinburgh EH10 6JY (☎ 031 447 9313); Bell, Lawrie, Macgregor & Co, PO Box No 8, Erskine House, 68-73 Queen St, Edinburgh EH2 4AE (☎ 031 225 2566; telex 72260)

RICHARD, Pierre Ernest Charles Laurent (Peter); DFC (1945); s of Ernest Adolph Richard, MM (d 1960), of London, and Ivy Lilian, *née* Payne (d 1968); *b* 11 April 1921; *Educ* Univ Coll Sch Hampstead, RADA; *m* 14 Dec 1968, Ann Josephine; 2 s (Stephen b 1969, Christopher b 1977), 1 da (Louise b 1972); *Career* WWII serv Flying Offr RAF 1941-46, navigator and bomb aimer 8 (PFF) Gp, Bomber Cmd 1944-45; importer clock and watch indust 1946-, dir subsidiary co of Gt Univ Stores; chm Nat Benevolent Soc Watch and Clock Makers, former chm Watch and Clock Importers Assoc of GB; sec Hampstead Garden Suburb Free Church 1986-, pres The Pathfinder Assoc 1987-89; Freeman City of London, Liveryman Worshipful Co of Clockmakers; Cross of Merit Gold Class Poland; *Clubs* Royal Air Force; *Style—* Peter Richard, Esq, DFC; 2 Leeside Crescent, London NW11 0DB (☎ 081 455 2905)

RICHARD, Ralph Henry; s of Dr Kurt Simon Richard (d 1958), and Emmy Rose, *née* Levi; *b* 24 Dec 1912; *Educ* Bryanston Sch; *m* 1, 21 May 1964 (m dis 1972), Vivienne Elspeth, da of the late Harold Bradley; 2 s (Daniel b 1968, Simon b 1968), 1 da (Debbie b 1966); m 2, 4 Sept 1975, Erica Robyn, *née* Greet; 2 s (Timothy b 1982, Zacharias b 1983); *Career* vice chm: Cereal Industries Ltd, Allied Mills Ltd; dir: ABR Foods Ltd 1984-, Bakery Exhibitors Ltd 1988- (chm 1990); md Westmill Foods 1988; Freeman: City of London, Worshipful Co of Bakers (1982); Tradesman City of Glasgow (1988); *Style—* Ralph H Richard, Esq; 31 Grand Ave, Muswell Hill, London N10 3BD (☎ 081 883 1295); Cereal Industries Ltd, Kingsgate, 1 King Edward Rd, Brentwood, Essex CM14 4HG (☎ 0277 262525, fax 0277 200320, telex 996500 AMLA)

RICHARD, Wendy (Mrs Paul Glorney); s of Henry William Emerton (d 1954), of Streatham, and Beatrice Reay, *née* Cutter (d 1972); *Educ* Royal Masonic Sch Rickmansworth, Italia Conti Drama Sch; *m* 17 March 1990, Paul Peter Anthony Glorney; *Career* actress; TV appearances incl: West One, Arthur Haynes Show, Dixon of Dock Green, Dad's Army, Z Cars, West Country Tales, various TV plays, Are You Being Served?, Up Pompeii, Spooner's Patch, Little and Large, Blankety Blank, Punchlines, Pyramid Game, Not on Your Nellie, On the Buses, Fenn Street Gang, Please Sir, Hugh and I, Hogg's Back, Rainbow, No Hiding Place, Both Ends Meet, Newcomers, Give us a Clue, Celebrity Squares, We Love TV, All Star Secrets, Crackerjack, Secrets Out, Music Game, Zodiac Game, Wogan, 3-2-1, TV AM, Breakfast TV, Nationwide, Thank Your Lucky Stars, Dad You're A Square, Vintage Quiz, Kelly Monteith, Dick Emery, Telly Addicts, Eastenders, Danger Man; theatre: Blithe Spirit, Cinderella, No Sex Please We're British, Are You Being Served?, Let's Go Camping; radio: Just a Minute, The Law Game; films: Bless This House, No Blade of Grass, Carry on Matron, Carry on Girls, Are You Being Served?, Gumshoe, Don't I Look Like the Lord's Son, Doctor in Clover; Northern TV Personality of the Year 1989; *Recreations* embroidery work, gardening, cooking; *Style—* Ms Wendy Richard; BBC TV, Elstree (☎ 071 724 7388)

RICHARDS, (Joseph) Alan; s of Albert John Knight-Richards (d 1967), of Whites Drive, Sedgley, Dudley, Worcs, and Sarah, *née* Jones (d 1968); *b* 23 March 1930; *Educ* Dudley GS, Birmingham Sch of Architecture (Dip Arch); *m* 20 Dec 1952, Tess, da of Frederic Dutton Griffiths (d 1981), of The Quadrant, Sedgley, Dudley, Worcs; 2 da (Julia, Wendy); *Career* princ asst architect Co Borough of Wolverhampton 1952-58, co fndr and jt sr ptnr Mason Richards Partnership 1958- (fndr consultancy serv for expert witness 1977-); Freeman City of London 1983; Liveryman: Worshipful Co of Arbitrators 1983, Worshipful Co of Architects 1988; memb RIBA 1952, FCIArb 1979, fell Br Acad of Experts 1989; *Recreations* power boating, cruising, travel; *Clubs* City Livery, RYA; *Style—* J Alan Richards, Esq; Salisbury House, Tettenhall Rd, Wolverhampton WV 4SG (☎ 0902 771331, fax 0902 21914)

RICHARDS, Sir (Francis) Brooks; KCMG (1976, CMG 1963), DSC and bar (1943); s of Francis Bartlett Richards (d 1955), of Little Court, Cobham, Surrey, and Mary Bertha, *née* Street (d 1974); *b* 18 July 1918; *Educ* Stowe, Magdalene Coll Cambridge (MA); *m* 1941, Hazel Myfanwy, da of Lt-Col Stanley Price Williams, CIE, of London (d 1977); 1 s (Francis Neville, *qv*), 1 da; *Career* served WWII RN (Lt-Cdr RNVR), Br Embassy Paris 1944-48; entered Foreign Service 1946: German Political Dept FO 1948-52, first sec Athens 1952-54, Political Residency Bahrain 1954-57, asst private sec to Foreign Sec 1958-59, cnsllr Paris 1959-64, head of Info Policy Dept FCO/CRO 1964, seconded to Cabinet Office 1966, HM min Bonn 1969-71; ambass: to Vietnam 1972-74, to Greece 1974-78; dep sec Cabinet Office 1978-80, security co-ordinator N Ireland 1980-81; vice pres Friends of The Imperial War Museum, pres The Farnham Soc; chm: Ctee of Mgmnt Br Inst Paris 1979-88, CSM Parly Conslts 1983-, Anglo-Hellenic League, Gerry Holdsworth Special Forces Club Charitable Tst, Paintings in Hosps; Chevalier de la Légion d'Honneur, Croix de Guerre; *Recreations* gardening, drawing, collecting, sailing; *Clubs* Traveller's, Royal Ocean Racing, Special Forces (chm 1983-86, pres 1986-89); *Style—* Sir Brooks Richards, KCMG, DSC; The Ranger's House, Farnham, Surrey (☎ 0252 716764)

RICHARDS, Catherine Margaret; da of John Phillips Richards, of Walcot, 437A Caerleon Rd, Newport, Gwent, and Edna Vivian, *née* Thomas; *b* 12 May 1940; *Educ* Newport HS for Girls Gwent, Bedford Coll Univ of London (BSc); *Career* info offr British Oxygen Co 1962-63, chemistry teacher St Joseph's Convent GS Abbeywood 1963-65, asst ed Soc for Analytical Chemistry 1965-70, sec and registrar Inst of Maths and its Applications 1987- (dep sec 1970-87); FIMA; *Clubs* University Women's; *Style—* Miss Catherine Richards; Institute of Mathematics and its Applications, 16 Nelson St, Southend-on-Sea, Essex SS1 1EF (☎ 0702 354020, fax 0702 354111)

RICHARDS, Christopher John D'Arcy; s of Kenneth Richards, MBE, LDS, of Heswall, Wirral, and Winifred Enid; *b* 29 Aug 1946; *Educ* Oundle Sch, St Andrews Univ; *m* Ruth Irene, da of Alan Gilroy, JP, of Heswall, Wirral; 2 s (John, Nicholas), 2 da (Claire, Philippa); *Career* main bd dir Tysons plc (dep md of the gp); dir Dental Designs Ltd; sch govr; FCIOB (memb nat cncl, chm professional practice bd); *Recreations* sailing; *Clubs* Athenaeum; *Style—* Christopher J D Richards, Esq; Lingcroft, Tower Road North, Heswall, Wirral, Merseyside L60 6RS (☎ 051 342 2470)

RICHARDS, David Gordon; CBE (1989); s of Gordon Charles Richards (d 1956), and Vera Amy, *née* Barrow (d 1962); *b* 25 Aug 1928; *Educ* Highgate Sch; *m* 1960, Catherine Stephanie, da of Edward Gilbert Woodward (d 1949); 1 s (Edwin), 2 da (Victoria, Katharine); *Career* 8 RTR 1947-49; CA; ptnr: Harmood Banner & Co 1955-74, Deloitte Haskins & Sells 1974-84; non exec chm: Walker Greenbank plc, Discretionary Unit Fund Managers Ltd; ICEAW: cncl memb 1970-87, vice pres 1977-78, dep pres 1978-79, centenary pres 1979-80, memb Gen Purposes and Fin ctee 1977-83, chm Int Affrs Ctee 1980-83; chm Cncl of Accountancy Bodies 1979-80, dep chm Monopolies and Mergers Cmmn 1983-90; memb: Ctee of London Soc of CAs 1966-70 and 1981-82 (chm 1969-70), Ctees of Investigations under Agric Mktg Act 1972-88, Cncl for Securities Indust 1979-80, Panel on Take Overs and Mergers 1979-80, Review Body of Doctors' and Dentists' Remuneration 1984-90, UK and Ireland Rep Cncl Int Fedn of Accounts 1981-83, Disciplinary Bd Inst of Actuaries 1986-; chm Disciplinary Bd Br Psychological Soc 1988-; govr Highgate Sch 1982- (chm 1983-); tstee: Bob Champion Cancer Tst 1983-, Princes Youth Business Tst 1986-, Royal Acad of Music Fndn 1985-; jr Warden Worshipful Co of CAs 1984-85, (sr Warden 1985-86, Master 1986-87); ACA 1951, FCA; *Recreations* gardening, silviculture, tennis, golf, shooting; *Style—* David Richards, Esq, CBE; Eastleach House, Eastleach, Glos GL7 3NW (☎ 036 785 416)

RICHARDS, Derek James; s of William Richards, of Kenmore, Cricket Lane, Lichfield, Staffs, and Grace Winifred, *née* Funnell; *b* 12 Nov 1934; *Educ* King Edward VI Sch Lichfield, Jesus Coll Cambridge (BA, MA), Guy's Hosp Med Sch (MB BChir, LRCP); *m* 22 Sept 1962, Angela, da of William Hugh Maton, of 4 High View Ct, Silverdale Rd, Eastbourne; 2 s (Michael John b 29 July 1964, Simon William b 11 Jan 1969), 2 da (Elizabeth Jane b 21 April 1966, Alice Louise b 16 April 1978); *Career* house offr and registrar Guy's Hosp, sr house offr Bristol Royal Infirmary, sr registrar Univ Coll Hosp, conslt surgn Eastbourne Health Authy; memb Ctee of Mgmnt Horder Centre Crowborough E Sussex, pres League of Friends Uckfield Hosp Uckfield E Sussex; memb BMA, fell BOA, FRCS 1964 (and memb); *Recreations* golf, shooting, following Grand Prix racing; *Style—* Derek Richards, Esq; Clare Glen, High Hurstwood, nr Uckfield, East Sussex TN22 4BN (☎ 082 581 3306); 28 Lushington Rd, Eastbourne BN21 4LL (☎ 0323 34030)

RICHARDS, Francis Neville; o s of Sir (Francis) Brooks Richards, KCMG, DSC, *qv*; *b* 18 Dec 1945; *Educ* Eton, King's Coll Cambridge (MA); *m* 16 Jan 1971, Gillian Bruce, da of I S Nevill, MC (d 1948); 1 s (James b 1975), 1 da (Joanna b 1977); *Career* Royal Green Jackets 1967-69, invalided following accident; third sec to second sec Br Embassy Moscow 1971-73; second sec to first sec UK Delgn to MBFR talks Vienna 1973-76, FCO 1976-85, asst private sec to Sec of State 1980-82, cnsllr (econ and commercial) Br High Cmmn New Delhi 1985-88, head of S Asian Dept FCO 1988-90, Br high cmmr Windhoek 1990-; *Recreations* riding, walking, travel; *Clubs* Travellers', President's Estate Polo (New Delhi); *Style—* Francis Richards, Esq; c/o Foreign and Commonwealth Office, London SW1

RICHARDS, Brig (Leslie) Frederick; CBE (1971, OBE 1963, MBE 1959); s of Frederick William Richards (d 1960), of Essex, and Edith Anne, *née* Orme (d 1971); *b* 12 April 1915; *Educ* CFS London; *m* 15 June 1945, Winifred Marjorie, da of Thomas Hyde (d 1974), of Essex; 2 s (Frederick Thomas b 1948, Phillip James b 1951); *Career* Brig, formerly II Sikh Regt, Essex Regt and RMP, cmmnd Indian Army 1941; served: India, Iraq, Persia, Syria, Burma, Egypt, NW Europe; fndr memb Indian Parachute Bde 1942-47, Brig, Provost Marshal (Army) and inspr Mil Corrective Estabs 1968-71; *Recreations* field and mounted sports, sailing; *Clubs* Cwlth Tst; *Style—* Brig Frederick Richards, CBE; The Old Stables, Stratford Rd, Dedham, Essex, Colchester (☎ 0206 322211)

RICHARDS, Hon Mrs (Gillian Mary); da of Baron Hunt of Fawley, CBE (Life Peer); *b* 1951; *m* 1972, Paul Andrew Richards; 3 s, 1 da; *Style—* The Hon Mrs Richards; Arborfield, Belmont, Wantage, Oxon

RICHARDS, Gordon W; *b* 7 Sept 1930; *m* 18 June 1980, Joan Dacre, da of late Lt-Col Henry Anthony Camillo Howard, CMG, yst s of 1 Baron Howard of Penrith; 2 c from previous m (Nicholas Gordon, Joanna); *Career* national hunt trainer; first ride as jockey 1943, trainer 1964-; major races won: Grand Nat twice, Scot Nat twice, Great Yorks Chase, Makeson Gold Cup, A F Budge Gold Cup, Whitbread Gold Cup, King George VI Chase, Stones Ginger Wine Chase, Greenall Witney Gold Cup; horses trained incl: Playlord, Lucius, Sea Pigeon, Noddys Ryde, Hello Dandy, Dark Ivy, Little Bay; *Recreations* tennis, swimming; *Style—* Gordon Richards, Esq; The Castle Stables, Greystoke, Penrith, Cumbria

RICHARDS, Hywel Francis; JP (1989); s of Sylfanus Richards (d 1983), of Brynheulog, Llanbrynmair, Powys, and Gwladus Jane, *née* Brown (d 1989); *b* 18 April 1926; *Educ* Machylleth GS; *m* 17 April 1957, Elizabeth Ellen, da of Griffith Owen (d 1938), of Glanllynnan, Chwilog, Pwllheli; 2 da (Lowri-Ann b 1958, Morfudd b 1959); *Career* farmer; chm Farmers Trading Co; winner All Wales Grassland Farming Competition 1972; memb cncl: NFU, Royal Welsh Agric Soc; govr Glynllifon Agric Coll; High Sheriff Gwynedd 1989-90; FRAgS; *Recreations* fishing, shooting; *Style—* Hywel Richards, Esq, JP; Rowen, Criccieth, Gwynedd, Wales

RICHARDS, Hon Mrs (Irene Mary); *née* Leatherland; da of Baron Leatherland (Life

Peer); *b* 1923; *Educ* Brentwood Co HS; *m* 1961 (m dis 1977), Douglas Richards; 1 s (David), 1 da (Jennifer); *Career* conference offr; *Style—* The Hon Mrs Richards; 19 The Greens Close, Loughton, Essex IG10 1QE

RICHARDS, Prof Ivor James; s of Philip James Richards (d 1981), of Landwade Hall, Exning, Newmarket, Suffolk, and Ivy Gwenllian, *née* Kimber; *b* 1 May 1943; *Educ* Newmarket GS, Univ of Wales (MA); *m* 5 June 1976, Anne Rostas; 1 s (Owen James b 30 Dec 1984), 1 da (Sarah Elizabeth b 13 March 1983); *Career* assoc architect; Sir Leslie Martin Architects Cambridge 1969-87, works incl Faculty of Music Univ of Cambridge 1975-85, Royal Scottish Acad of Music and Drama Glasgow 1988, Centro de Arte Moderna Gulbenkian Fndn Lisbon 1983-84; ARCUK, ARIBA; *Recreations* writing, walking, cities and architecture; *Style—* Prof Ivor Richards; 10 The Fairway, Bar Hill, Cambridge CB3 8SR (☎ 0954 780857); Univ of Wales Coll of Cardiff, P O Box 25, Cardiff CF1 3XE (☎ 0222 874430 ext 5970, fax 874192)

RICHARDS, Sir James Maude; CBE (1959); s of Louis Saurin Richards (d 1935), and Lucy Denes Clarence (d 1955); *b* 13 Aug 1907; *Educ* Gresham's, Architectural Assoc Sch London (AADipl); *m* 1, 1936 (m dis 1948), Margaret, da of late David Angus; 1 s (decd), 1 da; m 2, 1954, Kathleen Margaret, da of Henry Godfrey-Faussett-Osborne, of Queendown Warren, Sittingbourne, Kent (d 1948); 1 s (decd); *Career* architectural writer, critic and historian; ed The Architectural Review 1937-71, dir of pubns Miny of Information (Middle East, Cairo) 1943-46, architectural corr The Times 1947-71, ed Euro Heritage 1973-75; author of numerous books on art, architecture and travel prof of architecture Univ of Leeds 1957-59; Bicentenary Medal RSA 1971; memb Royal Fine Art Cmmn 1951-66; hon fell American Inst of Architects 1963; ARIBA, FSA; Order of the White Rose Finland (Chevalier 1 Class 1959, promoted Cdr 1985), Gold Medal Mexican Inst of Architects 1963; kt 1972; *Recreations* travel; *Clubs* Athenaeum, Beefsteak; *Style—* Sir James Richards, CBE; 29 Fawcett St, London SW10 9AY (☎ 071 352 9874)

RICHARDS, Ven John; s of William Richards, of 14 Premier Place, Exeter, and Ethel Mary Coates (d 1966); *b* 4 Oct 1933; *Educ* Reading Sch, Wyggeston GS Leicester, Sidney Sussex Coll Cambridge (MA), Ely Theological Coll; *m* 2 Sept 1958, Ruth, da of Wilfred Haynes (d 1985), of Heavitree, Exeter; 2 s (Peter b 1961, David b 1968), 3 da (Elizabeth b 1962, Rachel b 1964, Bridget b 1968); *Career* asst curate St Thomas Exeter 1959-64; rector: Holsworthy with Hollacombe and Cookebury 1964-74, Heavitree Exeter 1974-81; archdeacon of Exeter and canon of Exeter Cathedral 1981-; church cmmr 1988-; *Recreations* gardening, walking, fishing; *Style—* The Ven the Archdeacon of Exeter; 12 The Close, Exeter EX1 1EZ (☎ 0392 75745)

RICHARDS, Lt-Gen Sir John Charles Chisholm; KCB (1980), KCVO (1991); s of Charles Richards, and Alice Milner; *b* 21 Feb 1927; *Educ* Worksop Coll Notts; *m* 1953, Audrey Hidson; 2 s, 1 da; *Career* joined RM 1945, Commander 3 Commando Brigade 1975-76, Cmdt Gen RM 1977-81; HM Marshal of the Dip Corps 1982-, Rep Col Cmdt RM 1989-90; Freeman City of London 1982; CBIM 1980; *Recreations* golf, gardening, swimming; *Clubs* Army and Navy; *Style—* Lt-Gen Sir John Richards, KCB, KCVO; St James's Palace, London SW1

RICHARDS, John Deacon; CBE (1978); s of William John Richards (d 1985), and Ethel, *née* Waggott (d 1971); *b* 7 May 1931; *Educ* Geelong GS Aust, Cranleigh Sch, Architectural Assoc Sch of Architecture (AA Diploma); *m* 1958, Margaret, da of William Brown (d 1983); 1 s (Alan), 3 da (Kathleen, Lucy, Jessica); *Career* architect; sr conslt Robert Matthew, Johnson-Marshall and Ptnrs (architect and planner of Univ of Stirling); bd memb and dep chm Scottish Homes 1988-; *Recreations* country life; *Clubs* Athenaeum, Scottish Arts; *Style—* John Richards, Esq; John Richards Associates, Lady's Field, Whitekirk, Dunbar, East Lothian (☎ 062 087 206)

RICHARDS, Martin Edgar; s of Edgar Lynton (Tony) Richards, CBE, MC, TD (d 1983), and Barbara, *née* Lebus; *b* 27 Feb 1943; *Educ* Harrow; *m* 30 Jan 1969, Caroline, da of Edwin Billing Lewis (d 1948); 1 s (Charles b 1975), 1 da (Catherine b 1972); *Career* admitted slr 1968; ptnr Clifford Chance (formerly Clifford-Turner) 1973-; *Style—* Martin E Richards, Esq; Royex House, Aldermanbury Sq, London EC2V 7LD (☎ 071 600 0808, fax 071 726 8561)

RICHARDS, Michael Anthony; s of Edward Albert Richards (d 1975), of Argentina and UK, and Clara Muriel, *née* Webb (d 1970); *b* 12 Oct 1926; *Educ* St Alban's Coll Argentina, St Georges Coll Argentina, J M Estrada Coll Argentina, Royal Vet Coll; *m* 14 April 1956, Sylvia Rosemary, da of Geoffrey Charles Pain, JP (d 1986); 2 da (Claire Penelope b 3 Nov 1957, Sally Veronica (Mrs Wilson) b 18 Jan 1961); *Career* Br Latin American Vol Scheme Br Army 1945, Sgt Intelligence Corps ME 1945-47; gen veterinary practice 1953-59; lectr: veterinary med Univ of London 1961-65, veterinary pathology Univ of Edinburgh 1967-69; author various scientific pubns on veterinary med and pathology; chief inspr: Cruelty to Animals Act (1987) 1982-86 (inspr 1969-82), Animals (Scientific Procedures) Act (1986) 1986-87; CBiol, FIBiol 1985, MRCVS; *Recreations* philately; *Clubs* RSM; *Style—* Michael Richards, Esq; Hill View, Back Row, Charleston, By Glamis, Forfar, Angus DD8 1UG (☎ 030 784 231)

RICHARDS, Hon Michael Hugh; s of 1 Baron Milverton, GCMG (d 1978); hp of bro, 2 Baron Milverton; *b* 1 Aug 1936; *Educ* Ridley Coll Ontario, Clifton; *m* 1960, Edna Leonie B, da of Col Leo Steveni, OBE, MC, IA (ret); 1 s; *Career* Capt (ret) Rifle Bde; Malaya 1957 (despatches); attached Royal Nigerian Army 1962, memb UN Congo Force, 1963-65; md Philip Morris Nigeria Ltd 1972-, dir Africa Carreras-Rothmans Ltd 1978-82, md Murray Son & Co, dir personnel Rothmans International Tobacco; *Clubs* Naval and Military; *Style—* The Hon Michael Richards; Lovelynch House, Middleton Stoney Rd, Bicester, Oxon

RICHARDS, Brig Nigel William Fairbairn; OBE (1987); s of Lt-Col William Fairbairn Richards, TD (d 1987), of Eastbourne, and Marjorie May, *née* Salter; *b* 15 Aug 1945; *Educ* Eastbourne Coll, Peterhouse Cambridge; *m* 27 July 1968, Christine Anne Helen, da of Maj-Gen Charles William Woods, CB, MBE, MC; 2 s (Charles b 1972, Peter b 1976), 1 da (Helen b 1971); *Career* cmmnd RA 1965, RN Staff Coll 1976, CO 7 Regt RHA 1983-86, Cdr 5 Airborne Bde 1989-90; *Recreations* tennis, cricket, skiing, music, history; *Clubs* Army and Navy; *Style—* Brig Nigel Richards, OBE

RICHARDS, Paul William; s of William Frederick Richards (d 1979), of Bristol, and Mary Elizabeth, *née* Goddard; *b* 7 May 1963; *Educ* Clifton, Connaught Coll; *Career* trainee then account exec Wells O'Brien & Co 1982, account exec Davidson Pearce 1983-84, account dir Saatchi & Saatchi Advertising 1984-89, dir Toys in the Attic 1989-; *Recreations* flying, hunting, shooting, fishing; *Clubs* 2 Brydges Place, Gloucester Flying Centre; *Style—* Paul Richards, Esq; Toys In The Attic, 10-11 Moor St, London W1V 5LJ (☎ 071 287 1165, fax 071 287 1739)

RICHARDS, Prof Peter; s of Dr William Richards (d 1981), and Barbara Ashton, *née* Taylor (d 1971); *b* 25 May 1936; *Educ* Monkton Combe Sch, Emmanuel Coll Cambridge (MA, MB BCh, MD), St George's Hosp Med Sch, RPMS London (PhD); *m* 1, 6 July 1959 (m dis 1986), Anne Marie, da of Svend Larsen (d 1964), of Odense, Denmark; 1 s (Allan), 3 da (Marianne, Annette, Christina); m 2, 26 July 1987, Dr Carol Anne, da of Dr Raymond Seymour, of Wendlebury; *Career* hon sr lectr St Marys Hosp Med Sch (lectr in med 1967-70) and conslt physician St Peters Hosp Chertsey 1970-73, sr lectr and conslt physician St Georges Hosp and Med Sch 1973-79, dean prof of med and hon conslt physician St Mary's Hosp Med Sch 1979-, pro rector med educn Imperial Coll of Sci Technol and Med 1988-; memb Cncl Anglo-Finnish Soc; Liveryman Worshipful Soc of Apothecaries 1984, Freeman City of London 1985; FRCP 1976; *Books* The Medieval Leper and His Northern Heirs (1977), Understanding Water, Electrolyte and Acid Base Metabolism (jtly, 1983), Wasser-und Elektrolythaushalt: Diagnostik und Therapie (jtly, 1985), Learning Medicine (6 edn, 1989), Living Medicine (1990); *Recreations* social history, walking, listening to music; *Clubs* Garrick; *Style—* Prof Peter Richards; St Mary's Hospital Medical School, Norfolk Place, London W2 1PG (☎ 071 723 1252 ext 5009, fax 071 724 7349)

RICHARDS, Gp Capt Peter Bruce Mansell; s of Frank Mansell Richards (ka 1943), and Eileen Elizabeth, *née* Shaw; *b* 27 April 1942; *Educ* St Columba's Coll Dublin, RAF Coll Cranwell; *m* 24 June 1967, Marion Lesley, da of Leslie William Bass, of Ninfield, Sussex; 1 s (Robin b 1 Oct 1971), 1 da (Emma b 6 Feb 1970); *Career* stock control offr RAF Honington 1964-66, air transportation offr RAF Wildenrath, West Germany 1966-69, systems analyst RAF Hendon 1969-73, supply advsr to chief scientist (RAF) MOD London 1973, movement planning HQ RAF Germany, Rheindahlen 1974-78 cmd Supply and Movements sqdn RAF Coningsby 1978-79, freight movement policy MOD London 1979-83, Armed Forces Staff Coll Norfolk Virginia 1983, plans and progs HQ USAF, Pentagon, Washington DC 1984-86, ground supply support HQ Strike Command High Wycombe 1986-87, dir of defence logistics (NATO, UK) MOD London 1987-90, dep dir supply policy (RAF) MOD London 1991-; cncl memb IMPACT (charity to combat disability); *Recreations* travelling, theatre, skiing, countryside; *Clubs* RAF; *Style—* Gp Capt Peter Richards; Ministry of Defence, London (☎ 071 218 4552)

RICHARDS, Philip Brian; s of Glyn Bevan Richards (d 1976), of Ynysybwl, and Nancy Gwenhwyfar, *née* Evans of Bargoed; *b* 3 Aug 1946; *Educ* Cardiff HS, Univ of Bristol (LLB); *m* 17 July 1971, (m dis 1988), Dorothy Louise, da of Victor George, of Ystrad Mynach; 2 da (Rhuanedd b 1974, Lowri b 1978); *Career* called to Bar Inner Temple 1969; in practice 1969-; pt/t chm Soc Sec Appeal Tbnl 1987-, Plaid Cymru Parly candidate 1974 and 1979; vice pres: Mountain Ash RFC, Neyland RFC; tstee Welsh Writers' Tst, memb Mgmnt Ctee Cynon-Taf Housing Assoc, chm: Governors, Ysgol Gyfun Rhydfelen 1988-; *Recreations* music, sport, literature, walking; *Clubs* Cardiff and County, Newport and County; *Style—* Philip Richards, Esq; Cwm Pandy, Llanwynno Road, Cwmaman, Aberdare, M Glam CF44 6PG (☎ 0685 870 864); 30 Park Place, Cardiff CF1 3BA (☎ 0222 398 421, fax 0222 398 725)

RICHARDS, Sir Rex Edward; s of late Harold William Richards, of Colyton, Devon; *b* 28 Oct 1922; *Educ* Colyton GS Devon, St John's Coll Oxford (DSc); *m* 1948, Eva Edith, da of Paul Vago, of London (d 1948); 2 da; *Career* Univ of Oxford: fell and tutor Lincoln Coll 1947-64, Dr Lee's prof of chemistry and fell Exeter Coll 1964-69, warden Merton Coll 1969-84, vice chllr 1977-81; dir Leverhulme Trust 1985-; non exec dir: IBM-UK 1978-83, Oxford Instruments Group 1982-; memb: Scientific Advsy Ctee Nat Gallery 1978-, Advsy Bd Research Cncls 1980-83, advsy cncl for Applied Res and Devpt 1984-87; tstee: CIBA Fndn 1978-, Nat Heritage Meml Fund 1980-84, Tate Gallery 1982-88, Nat Gallery 1982-89, Henry Moore Fndn 1990; pres RSC 1990-92, chm Br Postgrad Med Fedn 1986- Corday - Morgan medal (Chemical Soc 1954-89, Davy medal (Royal Soc) 1976, Royal medal (Royal Soc) 1986, medal of Honour Rheinische Friedrich Wilhelm Univ, Bonn 1983; Hon DSc: UEA, Univ of Exeter, Univ of Leicester, Univ of Salford, Univ of Edinburgh, Univ of Leeds, Kent; Hon ScD Univ of Cambridge, Hon LLD Univ of Dundee; hon FRCP, hon FBA, FRS, FRSC; kt 1977; *Recreations* twentieth century painting and sculpture; *Clubs* Royal Soc; *Style—* Sir Rex Richards, FRS

RICHARDS, Stephen Price; s of Richard Alun Richards, of Llandre, Aberystwyth, Dyfed, and Ann Elonwy Mary, *née* Price; *b* 8 Dec 1950; *Educ* King's Coll Wimbledon, St John's Coll Oxford (MA); *m* 29 May 1976, Lucy Elizabeth, da of Dr Frank Henry Stubbings, of Cambridge; 2 s (Matthew b 1979, Thomas b 1981), 1 da (Emily b 1984); *Career* called to Bar Gray's Inn 1975, standing counsel to Dir Gen of Fair Trading 1989- (second jr counsel 1987-89), jr counsel to The Crown (common law) 1990-; *Books* Chitty on Contracts (co ed 25 and 26 edns); *Recreations* the Welsh hills, tennis; *Clubs* Hurlingham; *Style—* Stephen Richards, Esq; 4 Raymond Buildings, Gray's Inn, London WC1R 5BP (☎ 071 405 7211, fax 071 405 2084)

RICHARDS, Hon Susan Mary; da of 2nd Baron Milverton; *b* 1962; *Style—* The Hon Susan Richards

RICHARDS, Prof Thomas Harford Evans; s of (David) Brinley Richards, MBE, BEM, of Cwmbran, Gwent, and (Lizzie) Mary Evans (d 1988); *b* 21 Feb 1931; *Educ* Jones West Monmouth Sch, Univ of Birmingham (BSc, MSc), Univ of Aston (DSc); *m* 20 April 1957, Frances Jean, da of George Ewart Holden (d 1982); 2 s (Mark b 1959, David b 1968), 1 da (Louise b 1961); *Career* lectr in civil engrg Univ of Birmingham 1957-62, mechanical design conslt Lucas Gte Ltd 1961-62, sr lectr Birmingham CAT 1962-66; Univ of Aston: sr lectr 1966-78, reader 1978-89, head Mechanical Engrg Div 1983-86, sub dean of engrg 1984-86, dean of engrg 1986-90, prof of mechanical engrg 1989-, sr pro-vice chllr 1990-; former chm Stress Analysis Gp Inst of Physics; FIMEchE 1979, FIMA 1978; *Books* Stress, Vibration and Noise Analysis in Vehicles (with H G Gibbs, 1975), Energy Methods in Stress Analysis (1977), Stability Problems in Engineering Structures (with P Stanley, 1979); *Recreations* gardening, DIY, school governor; *Style—* Prof T H E Richards; Aston University, Aston Triangle, Birmingham B4 7ET (☎ 021 359 3611, fax 021 359 6470, telex 336997 UNIAST G)

RICHARDS, (David) Wyn; s of Evan Gwylfa Richards (d 1987), of Llanelli, and Florence Margretta, *née* Evans (d 1988); *b* 22 Sept 1943; *Educ* Gwendraeth GS, Llanelli GS, Trinity Hall Cambridge; *m* 23 Dec 1972, Thelma Frances, *née* Hall; 5 s (Mark b 1974, Cennydd b 1976, Hywel b 1977, Daniel Owen b 1981, Aled Wyn b 1988); *Career* called to the Bar Inner Temple 1968, rec 1985; *Style—* Wyn Richards, Esq; 2 Queens Rd, Sketty, Swansea, W Glamorgan SA2 0SD (☎ 0792 202 462); Iscoed Chambers, 86 St Helen's Rd, Swansea, W Glamorgan SA1 4BQ (☎ 0792 6529 88, fax 0792 458 089)

RICHARDSON; *see*: Stewart-Richardson

RICHARDSON, Prof Andrew; s of Andrew Phillips Harley Richardson (d 1977), and Williamina, *née* Mitchell; *b* 23 Jan 1933; *Educ* Grove Acad Broughty Ferry, Univ of St Andrews; *m* Margaret Elizabeth, da of George Dean Sweeney (d 1987), of Brazeel, Barnetts Rd, Belfast; 1 s (Mark Andrew b 1967, d 1985), 1 da (Lindsay Jane b 1966); *Career* Lt RADC 1956, Capt RWAFF 1956-59; Queen's Univ Belfast 1961-: tutor, registrar 1961-64, lectr, sr house dental offr 1964-68, sr lectr, conslt 1968-73, reader, conslt 1973-85, prof, conslt 1985-; pres: Br Dental Students Assoc 1955-56, Br Dental Assoc NI Branch 1982; memb: BDA, BSSO; *Books* Interceptive Orthodontics in General Dental Practice (1984), Interceptive Orthodontics (1989); *Recreations* restoration of classic cars; *Style—* Prof Andrew Richardson; 33 Cherryvalley Park, Belfast, N Ireland BT5 6PN (☎ 0232 796548); The Cottage, Dooey, Glencolumcille, Eire; Orthodontic Dept, School of Dentistry, Royal Victoria Hospital, Belfast BT12 6BP (☎ 0232 240503, fax 0232 438861)

RICHARDSON, (Henry) Anthony; s of Thomas Ewan Richardson (d 1974), of Batley, W Yorks, and Jessie, *née* Preston (d 1986); *b* 28 Dec 1925; *Educ* Giggleswick Sch, Univ of Leeds (LLB 1950, LLM 1956); *m* 8 May 1954, Georgina, *née* Lawford, step da of Gp Capt George Richard Bedford, RAF (ret), of Wetherby, W Yorks; *Career* called to the Bar Lincoln's Inn 1951; NE Circuit: dep circuit judge 1972-78, rec of the

Crown Ct 1978-; dep traffic cmmr and dep licensing authy N-Eastern Traffic Area 1989-; *Recreations* walking, gardening, listening to music; *Style—* Anthony Richardson, Esq; Grey Thatch, Wetherby Rd, Scarcroft, Leeds LS14 3BB (☎ 0532 892555); 38 Park Square, Leeds LS1 2PA (☎ 0532 439422)

RICHARDSON, Sir Anthony Lewis; 3 Bt (UK 1924); s of Sir Leslie Lewis Richardson, 2 Bt (d 1985), of Constantia Village, Cape Town, SA, and Joy Patricia, *née* Rillstone; *b* 5 Aug 1950; *Educ* Diocesan Coll Cape Town SA; *m* 1985, Honor Gillian, da of Robert Anthony Dauney, of Paddington, Sydney, Australia; 1 da (Honor Olivia Phoebe b 9 Sept 1990); *Heir* br, Charles John Richardson b 1955, *qv*; *Career* dir S G Warburg Securities, London; memb London Stock Exchange; *Recreations* various sports, photography; *Clubs* Boodle's, Hurlingham, Annabel's; *Style—* Sir Anthony Richardson, Bt; 7 Westover Rd, London SW18 2RE (☎ 081 870 8532); c/o S G Warburg Securities, 1 Finsbury Ave, London EC2 (☎ 071 606 1066)

RICHARDSON, Dr Arthur Tom (Tony); s of Arthur Whittaker Richardson, OBE (d 1985), of New Malden, Surrey, and Dora May, *née* Tattersall (d 1975); *b* 28 April 1923; *Educ* Caterham Sch, St Thomas Hosp Sch Univ of London (MB BS) DPhys Med (RCP); *m* 1, 2 March 1946 (m dis 1964), Doreen Marie Jackson; 2 s (Raymond b 1947, Desmond b 1952); m 2, 10 July 1964, Janet Elizabeth, da of Donald MacPherson, CIE, of Cannon Hill, London NW6; 2 da (Catriona b 1965, Kirsty b 1968); *Career* Flt Lt (Med) RAF 1947-49; conslt rheumatologist: Royal Free Hosp 1953-88, Royal Masonic Hosp 1970-; hon memb American Acad of Physical Med and Rehabilitation 1953-; memb: bd of govrs Royal Free Hosp 1965-72, sch cncl Royal Free Hosp Med Sch 1967-71, NW Thames Regnl Hosp Bd 1972-76, Cncl of Professions Supplementary to Med 1976-; pres Br Assoc for Rheumatology and Rehabilitation 1976-77; Freeman City of London 1952, Liveryman Worshipful Co of Apothecaries 1952; FRSM 1946, MRCS 1946, LRCP 1946, MRCP 1953, FRCP 1965; *Recreations* sailing; *Clubs* Savage, RAC, Royal Harwich Yacht; *Style—* Dr Tony Richardson; 8 Clifton Hill, London NW8 OQG (☎ 071 328 2665)

RICHARDSON, Hon Mrs (Averil Diana); *née* Betterton; da of 1 Baron Rushcliffe; *b* 1914; *m* 1, 1939, Maj Richard Wyndham-Quin Going, KOSB (ka 1944); 1 s, 1 da; m 2, 1946, Col Charles Walter Philipps Richardson, DSO and bar, KOSB (b 8 Jan 1905, educ RNCs Osborne and Dartmouth and RMC Sandhurst, served NW Europe WWII and enjoys fishing); 2 s; *Style—* The Hon Mrs Richardson; Quintans, Steventon, Hants (☎ 0256 473)

RICHARDSON, Charles John; s of Sir Leslie Lewis Richardson, 2 Bt (d 1985); hp of br, Sir Anthony Lewis Richardson, 3 Bt, *qv*; *b* 8 Dec 1955; *Educ* Diocesan Coll, Cape Town; *m* 6 June 1987, Gigi D M, da of late Lt-Col R R Morris, of Huish Farm, Sydling St Nicholas, Dorset; *Style—* Charles Richardson Esq; 9 Eglantine Road, London SW18

RICHARDSON, Gen Sir Charles Leslie; GCB (1967, KCB 1962, CB 1957), CBE (1945), DSO (1943); s of Lt-Col Charles William Richardson, OBE, of Springfield, Lurgan, Co Down, and Evaline Adah, *née* Wingrove; *b* 11 Aug 1908; *Educ* St Ronans, Wellington, RMA Woolwich, Clare Coll Cambridge (BA); *m* 1947, Audrey Elizabeth, da of Capt C R E Jörgensen, of Bushby Ruff House, nr Dover; 1 s (and 1 s decd), 1 da, 1 step da; *Career* 2 Lt RE 1928, served India 1931-38, served WWII France, Belgium, Dunkirk, UK, Palestine, Africa, Sicily, Italy, NW Europe, Actg Brig 1943-47, Brig Gen Staff (Ops) Eighth Army 1943, dep COS Fifth US Army 1944, BGS (Plans) 21 Army Gp 1944, chief of Mil Div Br Control Cmmn Berlin 1945-46, Lt-Col Co Engr Regt BAOR 1947-48, staff appts UK and Egypt 1949-52, cdr Inf Bde 1953-54, Maj-Gen Cmdt RMCS 1955-58, GOC Singapore District 1958-60, dir Combat Devpt WO 1960-61, dir gen Mil Trg WO 1961-63, GOC-in-C Northern Cmd 1963-64, QMG MOD 1965-66, Gen 1965, Master-Gen of the Ordnance 1966-71, ADC Gen to HM The Queen 1967-70, Col Cmdt RAOC 1967-71, Chief Royal Engr 1972-77; conslt and dir of various cos 1971-76, treas Kitchener Nat Memorial Fund 1971-76; chm: Gordon Boys Sch 1977-87, Combined Servs Winter Sports Assoc 1969-70; Legion of Merit USA 1944; *Books* Flashback (1985), Send for Freddie (1987); *Recreations* skiing, gardening, tennis; *Clubs* Army and Navy; *Style—* Gen Sir Charles Richardson, GCB, CBE, DSO; The Stables, Sandy Lane, Betchworth, Surrey RH3 7AA

RICHARDSON, David; s of Harold George Richardson (d 1986), of Ewell, Surrey, and Madeleine Raphaële, *née* Lebret; *b* 24 April 1928; *Educ* Wimbledon Coll, King's Coll London (BA); *m* 14 Feb 1951, (Frances) Jean, da of Ernest Pendrell Pring (d 1971), of Looe, Cornwall; 3 s (Stephen Michael b Dec 1951, Nicholas Henry b April 1954, Benedict Hugh b Sept 1965), 1 da (Catherine Anne b March 1957); *Career* RAF 1949-51: PO 1949, Flying Offr 1950; RAF Res 1951-56; HM Inspr of Taxes 1953-55; Miny of Lab (later Dept of Employment) 1956-82: chief exec Construction Indust Trg Bd 1964-66, chm Central Youth Employment Exec 1969-71, under sec industl rels 1972-75, dir of safety policy Health and Safety Exec 1975-77, dir ACAS 1977-82; dir: ILO (London) 1982-, Tablet Publishing Co Ltd 1985-, Industrial Training Service Ltd 1986-, govr Br Inst of Human Rights 1987; FIPM; *Recreations* music, landscape gardening; *Clubs* RAF; *Style—* David Richardson, Esq; 183 Banstead Rd, Carshalton, Surrey SM5 4DP (☎ 081 642 1052); International Labour Office, Vincent House, Vincent Square, London SW1P 2NB (☎ 071 828 6401, telex 886836 INTLAB G)

RICHARDSON, Sir Egerton Rudolf; CMG (1959); s of James Neil Richardson; *b* 15 Aug 1912; *Educ* Calabar HS Kingston Jamaica, Oxford Univ; *Career* entered Jamaican Civil Service 1933, clerk to Treasury 1939-43, sr clerk 1943-44, asst sec 1947-50, permanent sec 1953-55, financial sec Jamaica 1956-62, ambass and permanent rep to UN 1962-67; Jamaican ambass to: USA 1967-72, Mexico 1967-75; permanent sec Miny of Public Service 1973-75, permanent rep of Jamaica to UN in NY 1981-; kt 1968; *Style—* Sir Egerton Richardson, CMG; 215E 68th St, New York, NY 10021, USA

RICHARDSON, Sir (John) Eric; CBE (1962); s of William Richardson, of Birkenhead (d 1952); *b* 30 June 1905; *Educ* Higher Elementary Sch Birkenhead, Univ of Liverpool (BEng, PhD); *m* 1941, Alice May, da of Hugh Munro Wilson, of Hull (d 1979); 1 s, 2 da (and 1 da decd); *Career* engr and educationalist; head of Engrg Dept Hull Municipal Tech Coll 1937; princ: Oldham Municipal Tech Coll 1942, Royal Tech Coll Salford 1944, Northampton Poly (now City Univ London) 1947; dir Poly of Central London 1957-70; Hon DSc City Univ London; FIEE, MIMechE, FBHI, FBOA, FPS, FRSA, FCGI; kt 1967; *Recreations* photography, gardening; *Style—* Sir Eric Richardson, CBE; 73 Delamere Rd, Ealing, London W5 3JP (☎ 081 567 1588)

RICHARDSON, Frank Anthony; s of Albert Edward Richardson, and Eileen, *née* Roberts; *b* 20 March 1933; *Educ* Leeds Central HS; *m* 6 Sept 1958, Patricia Elsie, da of Robert Stevenson Taylor; *Career* agent and organiser Cons party 1956-73, sec Nat Union of Cons Agents 1971-73; assoc dir: John Addey Assocs 1973-77, Charles Barker Watney & Powell 1978-83; dir: Charles Barker Watney & Powell 1988, Shandwick Public Affairs 1990-; admin sec: Parly Info Tech Ctee 1985-, Parly Space Ctee 1989-, Parly Roads Study Gp 1987-; memb Yorks Athletics team 1958; MIPR; *Recreations* tennis, swimming, travel; *Style—* Frank Richardson, Esq; 22 Gloucester Place Mews, London W1 (☎ 071 487 4872); Shandwick Public Affairs, 49 Whitehall, London SW1 (☎ 071 839 7198, fax 071 930 1823)

RICHARDSON, Gp Capt Frederick Charles; CBE (1958); s of Frederick Haigh Richardson (d 1947), of Kingston upon Thames, and Edith Mary, *née* Tyrrell (d 1959); *b* 24 Jan 1912; *Educ* St Joseph's Coll Beulah Hill, Univ of London (BCom, Dip Business Admin, Sculling champion); *m* 21 June 1937, Mary Baird Flora Hathorn, da of Richard Hathorn Greaves (d 1955), of Cairo; 2 s (Richard b 7 May 1942, John b 25 Aug 1944 d 1972), 1 da (Ann (Mrs Wheadon) b 16 Oct 1939); *Career* cmmnd pilot RAF 1933, served Egypt 4 FTS and No 216 (BT) Sqdn 1933-37, qualified navigation specialist 1938, Flt Lt instr Sch of Air Navigation 1938-40, Sqdn Ldr Air Miny 1940-41, Wing Cdr OC No 502 (Ulster) Sqdn 1941-42, Gp Capt chief navigation offr HQ Coastal Cmd 1942-44, dir of studies and dep cmdt Empire Air Naval Sch Shawbury 1944-45, PSA Bracknell RAF Staff Coll 1946, sr offr admin RAF E Africa 1946-48, RN Staff Coll Greenwich 1948-49, Gp Capt DD Navigation Air Miny 1949-52, OC No 3 Air Navigation Sch Bishops Court Co Down 1952-54, DD Manning (plans) Air Miny 1954-56, offr i/c Navigation and Trg HQ Coastal Cmd 1956-58; controller of servs Univ of London Senate House 1958-77; chm RAF Rowing 1956-57; memb: Cncl Royal Inst of Navigation 1950-52, Br Univs Sports Fedn 1962, Cncl Aries Assoc 1960-90; fndr and hon sec Univ of London Boat Club Assoc 1962-87; FRIN 1953; *Books* RAF Manual of Air Navigation vol 1 (1941), author of various Navigation articles in jls; *Recreations* gardening, swimming, lazing; *Clubs* RAF; *Style—* Gp Capt Frederick Richardson, CBE

RICHARDSON, Dr George Barclay; CBE (1978); s of George Richardson (d 1970), and Christina Richardson (d 1975); *b* 19 Sept 1924; *Educ* Aberdeen Central Secdy Sch, Univ of Aberdeen (BSc), Univ of Oxford (MA); *m* 21 Sept 1957, Isabel Alison, da of Laurence Chalk (d 1979); 2 s (Graham b 25 April 1960, Andrew b 25 July 1962); *Career* Lt RNVR 1945-46; third sec Dip Serv 1949-50, fell St John's Coll Oxford 1951-88, reader in econs Oxford 1959-74, chief exec and sec to the delegates OUP 1974-88, pro vice chllr Univ of Oxford 1988-89, vice pres Oxford Univ Appeal Campaign 1988-; warden Keble Coll Oxford 1989-, econ advsr UK AEA 1968-74; memb: Econ Devpt Ctee For Electrical Engrg Ctee 1964-73, Monopolies Cmmn 1969-74, Royal Cmmn on Enviromental Pollution 1973-74; hon fell CCC Oxford 1987, Hon DCL Oxford 1988, hon fell St John's Coll Oxford 1989; *Books* Information and Investment (1960), Economic Theory (1964); *Recreations* reading, music, swimming; *Clubs* Oxford and Cambridge United Univ; *Style—* Dr George Richardson, CBE; Wardens Lodgings, Keble College, Oxford

RICHARDSON, Ian William; CBE (1989); s of John Richardson, and Margaret, *née* Drummond; *b* 7 April 1934; *Educ* Heriot's Sch Edinburgh, Tynecastle Edinburgh, Royal Scottish Acad of Music and Drama; *m* 2 Feb 1961, Maroussia, da of Alexei Simeonitch Frank (d 1967); 2 s (Jeremy b 24 Dec 1961, Miles b 15 July 1963); *Career* actor; joined Birmingham Repertory Co 1958, Hamlet 1959; RSC 1960-75: Arragon in Merchant of Venice, Malateste in Duchess of Malfi 1960, Oberon in a Midsummer Night's Dream 1961, Edmund in King Lear 1964, Herald and Merat in Marat/Sade 1964-65, Vendice in Revenger's Tragedy 1965 and 1969, Coriolanus 1966, Bertram in All's Well That Ends Well 1966, Cassius in Julius Caesar 1968, Pericles 1969, Angelo in Measure For Measure 1970, Prospero in The Tempest 1970, Richard II and Bolingbroke 1973, Berowne in Love's Labours Lost 1973, Ford in The Merry Wives of Windsor 1975, Richard III 1975; Professor Higgins in My Fair Lady New York 1976-77 (Drama Desk Award), Man and Superman Shaw Festival Ontario 1977, Lolita (Broadway) 1981; Films incl: Man of La Mancha 1972, The Sign of Four and The Hound of the Baskervilles (as Sherlock Holmes) 1982, Brazil 1984, Whoops Apocalypse 1987, Rosencrantz and Guildenstern Are Dead 1990, The Fourth Protocol 1987; TV series incl: Tinker Tailor Soldier Spy 1979, Private Schulz 1981, The Woman in White 1982, The Master of Ballantrae 1984, Mistral's Daughter 1985, Porterhouse Blue 1987, Troubles 1988, The Gravy Train 1989, House of Cards 1990; TV plays incl: Danton's Death 1978, Monsignor Quixote 1985, Blunt 1987; RTS Award 1982, American Arts Club Gold medal 1988; FRSAMD 1971; Publications: prefaces to Cymbeline (Folio Soc), Richard II (BBC Publications), Merry Wives of Windsor (Doubleday); *Recreations* history, music, reading; *Clubs* Garrick; *Style—* Ian Richardson, Esq, CBE; c/o London Mgmnt, 235-241 Regent St, London W1 (☎ 071 493 1610)

RICHARDSON, Rev Canon James John (Jim); s of James John Richardson (d 1957), of London, and Gladys May, *née* Evans; *b* 28 March 1941; *Educ* Catford Sch London, Univ of Hull (BA), Univ of Sheffield (DipEd), Cuddesdon Coll Oxford; *m* 30 July 1966, Janet Rosemary, da of Harold Welstand; 2 s (Mark b 1968, Ben b 1974), 1 da (Anna b 1970); *Career* asst master Westfield Comp Sch Sheffield 1964-66, curate St Peter's Collegiate Church Wolverhampton 1969-72, priest i/c All Saints Hanley Stoke-on-Trent 1972-75, rector Nantwich 1975-82, vicar Leeds 1982-88, hon canon Ripon Cathedral 1982-88 (canon emeritus 1988-); exec dir The Cncl of Christians and Jews 1988-; town cncllr Nantwich 1977-79; chm Racial Harrassment Cmmn Leeds 1986-87, N of Eng vice pres UN Year of Peace 1986-87, memb Court Univ of Leeds 1986-88; chm of Govrs: Leeds GS 1983-88, Abbey Grange HS Leeds 1982-86; govr Leeds Girl's HS 1982-88; contrib to: Yorkshire Post 1982-89, Four Score Years Lord Coggans 80th Birthday Tribute by his Friends; author of articles on interfaith subjects; *Recreations* leading pilgrimages, biography (especially life and times of Rupert Brooke); *Style—* The Rev Canon Jim Richardson; 27 Strawberry Hill, Wellingborough Rd, Northampton NN3 5HL (☎ 0604 405183); Council of Christians and Jews, 1 Dennington Park Rd, London NW6 1AX (☎ 071 794 8178, fax 071 431 3500)

RICHARDSON, Jeremy Francis; s of Robert Francis Richardson, and Maureen Anne Richardson (d 1986); *b* 7 Sept 1963; *Educ* Edinburgh Acad, Heriot-Watt Univ (BA); *Career* Rugby Union lock forward Edinburgh Academicals RFC and Scotland; Scottish Schs tour to Zimbabwe 1981 (4 caps); debut Edinburgh Academicals 1982; rep: Edinburgh (20 appearances), Scot U21, Scot B (capt v Ireland 1990, 6 caps); Scotland: memb World Cup Squad 1987, toured Zimbabwe 1988, toured NZ 1990; stockbroker Greig Middleton & Co Ltd; *Recreations* golf, squash, cinema; *Style—* Jeremy Richardson, Esq; c/o Edinburgh Academical Football Club, Raeburn Place, Stockbridge, Edinburgh EH14 1HQ (☎ 031 332 1070)

RICHARDSON, Jeremy William; s of Thomas William Sydney Raymond Richardson, of Retford, Nottinghamshire, and Jean Mary, *née* Revill; *b* 3 April 1958; *Educ* Forest Sch, QMC (LLB); *Career* called to the Bar Inner Temple 1980; memb North Eastern Circuit 1982-; cncllr Sheffield City Cncl 1983-87; *Recreations* amateaur theatre, badminton (badly); *Style—* Jeremy Richardson, Esq; 11 Kings Bench Walk, Temple, London EC4Y 7EQ (☎ 071 353 3337, fax 071 583 2190, car 0860 650371)

RICHARDSON, Joanna; da of Capt Frederick Richardson, Intelligence Corps (d 1978), and Charlotte Elsa, *née* Benjamin (d 1978); *Educ* The Downs Sch Seaford, St Anne's Coll Oxford (MA); *Career* memb Cncl RSL 1961-86; FRSL 1959; Chev de l'Ordre des Arts et des Lettres (France) 1987; *Books* Fanny Brawne: A Biography (1952), Théophile Gautier: His Life and Times (1958), Edward FitzGerald (1960), FitzGerald: Selected Works (ed, 1962), The Pre-Eminent Victorian: A Study of Tennyson (1962), The Everlasting Spell: A Study of Keats and His Friends (1963), Essays by Divers Hands (ed, 1963), Edward Lear (1965), George IV: A Portrait (1966), Creevey and Greville (1967), Princess Mathilde (1969), Verlaine (1971), Enid Starkie (1973), Verlaine, Poems (ed and translator, 1974), Stendhal: A Critical Biography (1974), Baudelaire, Poems (ed and translator, 1975), Victor Hugo (1976), Zola (1978), Keats and His Circle: An Album of Portraits (1980), Gautier, Mademoiselle de Maupin (translator, 1981), The Life and Letters of John Keats (1981), Letters From Lambeth: the Correspondence of the Reynolds Family with John Freeman Milward Dovaston 1808-1815 (1981), Colette (1983), Judith Gautier (1986, French edn 1989, awarded

Prix Goncourt de la biographie, first time to a non-French writer), Portrait of a Bonaparte: the Life and Times of Joseph-Napoleon Primoli 1851-1927 (1987); *Style—* Miss Joanna Richardson; c/o Curtis Brown Ltd, 162-168 Regent St, London W1R 5TB (☎ 071 872 0331)

RICHARDSON, John David Benbow; MC (and bar 1942), CBE (1988); s of His Hon Judge Richardson, OBE (d 1956); *b* 6 April 1919; *Educ* Harrow, Clare Coll Cambridge; *m* 1946, Kathleen Mildred, da of Dudley Charles Turner, CMG (d 1958); 4 s (Thomas, Hugo, Christopher, Vivian); *Career* Capt 1 Kings Dragoon Gds; barr, dep chm Durham Co Quarter Sessions 1964-71, rec 1972-73, pres North Rent Assessment Panel 1979-; *Recreations* fishing, gardening, golf; *Clubs* MCC, York County Stand, Northern Counties; *Style—* John Richardson Esq, MC, CBE; The Old Vicarage, Nine Banks, Whitfield, Hexham, Northumberland NE47 8DB (☎ 0434 345 217)

RICHARDSON, John Francis; s of Francis Richardson (d 1957); *b* 16 June 1934; *Educ* Scarborough Coll, Wadham Coll Oxford; *m* 1960, Jacqueline Mary; 2 c; *Career* joined Burnley Bldg Soc 1959, asst gen mangr Burnley Bldg Soc 1972-76, dep gen mangr Burnley Bldg Soc 1976-80, chief gen mangr Burnley Bldg Soc 1980-; *Recreations* golf; *Clubs* Clitheroe Golf; *Style—* John Richardson Esq; 'Hammerton', Old Rd, Chatburn, Clitheroe, Lancs

RICHARDSON, Baron (Life Peer UK 1979), of Lee, Co Devon; Sir John Samuel Richardson; 1 Bt (UK 1963), LVO (1943); s of Maj John Watson Richardson (ka 1917, formerly solicitor), of Sheffield, and Elizabeth Blakeney, da of Rt Hon Sir Samuel Roberts, 1 Bt, JP, DL; *b* 16 June 1910; *Educ* Charterhouse, Trinity Coll Cambridge (MA, MD); *m* 6 June 1933, Sybil Angela Stephanie (d 1991), 3 da of Arthur Ronald Trist (d 1971), of Stanmore; 2 da (Hon Elizabeth-Ann (Hon Mrs Stafford) b 1937, Hon Susan Clare (Hon Mrs Wales) b 1940); *Heir* to Btcy, none; *Career* sits as Independent peer in House of Lords; medical specialist RAMC 1939-45, Lt-Col; conslt physician St Thomas's Hosp 1947-75 and to Metropolitan Police 1957-80; hon conslt physician to Army 1963-75, emeritus 1976-; pres: Royal Soc of Med 1969-71, BMA 1970-71, Gen Medical Cncl 1973-80; FRCP; Hon FRCPE, G&I; Hon DSc: Nat University of Ireland 1975, Hull 1981; Hon DCL Newcastle 1980; Hon LLD: Nottingham 1981, Liverpool 1983; hon fell Trinity Coll Cambridge 1979; Hon FRCS, FRCPy, FRCGP, FFCM, FPS, hon bencher Gray's Inn; CStJ; kt 1960; *Style—* The Rt Hon the Lord Richardson, LVO; Windcutter, Lee, Ilfracombe, Devon (☎ 0271 63198)

RICHARDSON, Rev Prof John Stuart; s of Ronald Hugo Richardson (d 1975), and Enid Stuart, *née* Stephens (d 1980); *b* 4 Feb 1946; *Educ* Berkhamsted Sch, Trinity Coll Oxford (MA, DPhil); *m* 12 April 1969, Patricia Helen, da of Ralph Edward Robotham; 2 s (Thomas b 1971, Martin b 1974); *Career* lectr in ancient history: Exeter Coll Oxford 1969-72, Univ of St Andrews 1972-87; prof of classics Univ of Edinburgh 1987-; ordained deacon Scot Episcopal Church 1979, priest 1980, Anglican chaplain Univ of St Andrews 1980-87; *Books* Roman Provincial Administration (1976), Hispaniae (1986); *Recreations* choral singing; *Style—* The Rev Prof John Richardson; 29 Merchiston Ave, Edinburgh EH10 4PH (☎ 031 228 3094); Dept of Classics, Univ of Edinburgh, David Hume Tower, George Square, Edinburgh EH8 9JX (☎ 031 667 1011)

RICHARDSON, Josephine (Jo); MP (Lab) Barking Feb 1974-; *b* 28 Aug 1923; *Career* memb Lab NEC 1979-, vice pres CND 1975-; memb: PLP Civil Liberties Gp 1979- (chair person 1975-79), chair person Lab Pty Women's Ctee 1981-82 and 1988-89, memb Shadow Cabinet and spokesperson on women's rights 1983-; *Style—* Jo Richardson, MP; House of Commons, London SW1A 0AA (☎ 071 219 5028)

RICHARDSON, Joy, Lady Joy Patricia; *née* Rillstone; da of John Percival Rillstone, of Johannesburg, S Africa; *m* 1946, Sir Leslie Lewis Richardson, 2 Bt (d 1985); 2 s (Sir Anthony Lewis, 3 Bt, Charles John, *qqvv*), 1 da (Jennifer b 1947, m 1984, Richard Michael Fearon Gold); *Style—* Joy, Lady Richardson; Old Vineyard, Constantia, Cape Town, S Africa

RICHARDSON, Karen; *Educ* Somerville Coll Oxford (MA); *Career* admitted slr 1978, ptnr Travers Smith Braithwaite; memb Ctee City of London Law Soc, immediate past chm Assoc Women Slrs; Liveryman City of London Slrs Co; memb Law Soc; *Style—* Miss Karen Richardson; c/o Travers Smith Braithwaite, 10 Snow Hill, London EC1A 2AL

RICHARDSON, (William) Kenneth; s of James McNaughton Richardson, of Stirling, and Jane Ann McKay, *née* Monteith; *b* 16 Nov 1956; *Educ* High Sch of Stirling, Univ of St Andrews (MA); *Career* mgmnt trainee: United Biscuits, Sue Ryder Fndn; planning asst Scot Opera 1983-87, gen mangr Royal Opera 1990- (co mangr 1987-90), admin Royal Opera House Garden Venture 1987-, artistic dir Dublin Grand Opera Soc 1990-; *Style—* Kenneth Richardson, Esq; 58 Steele Rd, London E11 3JA (☎ 081 555 9532); Royal Opera House, Covent Garden, London WC2E 9DD (☎ 071 240 1200, fax 071 836 1762, telex 27988)

RICHARDSON, Mark Rushcliffe; s of Brig Charles Walter Philipps Richardson, DSO, of Quintans, Steventon, Basingstoke, Hampshire, and Hon Averil Diana Richardson *qv*; *b* 17 Sept 1947; *Educ* Wellington, Ch Ch Oxford (BA); *m* 28 Sept 1983, Cherry Victoria, da of Sidney Wallace Smart, of Oak Ash, Chaddleworth, Newbury, Berks; 1 s (Hugo b 24 Nov 1981), 2 da (Melanie b 13 Nov 1974, Davina b 19 Jan 1976); *Career* dir Lazard Bros & Co Ltd 1986-90, hon treas Riding for the Disabled Assoc, memb fin ctee Br Red Cross Soc; *Recreations* country pursuits, skiing; *Clubs* Boodles; *Style—* Mark Richardson, Esq; Priors Court, West Hanney, Wantage, Oxon (☎ 0235 868210)

RICHARDSON, Michael John; s of George Frederick Richardson (d 1979), and Mabel Alice, *née* Cox; *b* 28 March 1935; *Educ* Epsom Coll; *m* 22 Aug 1959, Helen Patricia, da of Percival Bluett Bray (d 1942); 1 s (David b 16 Jan 1962), 1 da (Susan b 2 Jan 1965); *Career* CA; FW Smith Riches 1952-60, Price Waterhouse 1960-63, dir 3i Group (3i Corporate Finance Ltd) 1963-80, fin dir Shandwick Group 1980-81, dir Chartered WestLB Ltd (formerly Standard Chartered Merchant Bank Ltd) 1986- (joined 1981); circuit steward Sevenoaks Methodist Church; Freeman City of London, Liveryman Worshipful Co of CAs; FCA; *Books* Going Public (1973); *Recreations* singing, swimming, gardening; *Style—* Michael Richardson, Esq; 19 Mount Harry Rd, Sevenoaks, Kent TN13 3JJ (☎ 0732 453839); Chartered WestLB Ltd, 33-36 Gracechurch St, London EC3V 0AX (☎ 071 623 8711, fax 071 626 1610, telex 884689)

RICHARDSON, Sir Michael John de Rougemont; s of Arthur Wray Richardson, of Hove, Sussex; *b* 9 April 1925; *Educ* Harrow, RMC Sandhurst; *m* 16 July 1949, Octavia, yr da of Arthur Joyce Mayhew (Capt Denbighshire Hussars); 1 s, 2 da; *Career* Capt Irish Gds 1943-49; Drayton Group 1949-52; ptnr: Panmure Gordon & Co 1952-71, Cazenove & Co 1971-81; vice chm: N M Rothschild & Sons Ltd 1990- (md 1981-90), Derby Trust Ltd, Brycourt Unit Trust Management Ltd; chm: Smith New Court plc 1990-, Drayton Far Eastern Trust plc, English & International Trust plc, Anglo-Scottish Amalgamated Corporation Ltd, The Savoy Hotel plc, Shield Trust Ltd, Hyde Park Finance Ltd, Hyde Park Financial (Holdings) Ltd, Drayton Far Eastern Trust (Finance) Ltd, The Rank Foundation, Sedgwick Group plc, Rothschild North America NMR International NV; kt 1990; *Recreations* sailing, foxhunting; *Style—* Sir Michael Richardson; Smith New Court plc, 20 Farringdon Road, London EC1M 3NH (☎ 071 772 1000)

RICHARDSON, Michael Norman; s of Norman Richardson (d 1965), and Ethel, *née* Spittle (d 1978); *b* 23 Feb 1935; *Educ* Dulwich; *m* 13 April 1976, Rosemarie Christina, da of Emmerich von Moers (d 1946); 4 da (Penelope, Theresa, Christina, Alexandra); *Career* RAF 1958-60, PO and Flying Offr in Directorate of Legal Servs Far E Air Force; admitted slr 1958; asst slr Coward Chance & Co 1960-63; ptnr: Jaques & Co 1963-73, Richardson & Oakley 1977-85, Lawrence Graham (specialising Int Corporte Fin) 1985-; dep chm Henry Ansbacher & Co Ltd 1970-77; memb Law Soc 1958, FInstD 1987; *Recreations* all sports, gardening, art; *Clubs* Oriental, MCC; *Style—* Michael Richardson, Esq; Fernhill Cottage, Hatchet Lane, Windsor Forest, Berks SL4 2DZ (☎ 0344 882 635); 190 Strand, London WC2R 1JN (☎ 071 379 0000, fax 071 379 6854, telex 22673)

RICHARDSON, (William) Norman Ballantyne; DL (Greater London 1985); s of Robert Richardson (d 1974), of Wishaw, Lanarkshire, and Sarah Maddick, *née* Shields; *b* 8 Oct 1947; *Educ* King Edward VI GS Birmingham, Goldsmiths' Coll London (CertEd); *Career* dep head Emmanuel C of E Sch London NW6 1979-81; headmaster: All Saints' C of E Sch London SW6 1981-85, Christ Church C of E Sch London SW3 1985-; chm: ILEA Divnl Consultative Ctee of Headteachers 1985-86 and 1989-, Local Advsy Ctee on Primary/Secondary Transfer 1987-88, ILEA Central Consultative Ctee of Headteachers 1989-90, Consultative Ctee of Heads and Deputies in the Royal Borough of Kensington and Chelsea 1989-90, London Headteachers' Assoc (Kensington and Chelsea) 1990-91, London Diocesan Headteachers' Cncl 1991-; memb: Colne/East Gade Advsy Ctee on Educn 1977-81, 90, Royal Borough of Kensington and Chelsea Standing Advsy Cncl on Religions Educn 1989-; govr: Leavesden Green Infant Sch 1977-81, Leavesden Green Junior Sch 1977-81, London Diocesan Headteachers' Cncl 1984-, ILEA Standing Advsy Ctee on Religious Educn 1985-; chm: London (South) Ctee Royal Jubilee and Prince's Tsts 1984-90, London (South) Ctee The Prince's Tst 1990-; sec: London Youth Involvement Ctee Queen's Silver Jubilee Tst 1981-83, Greater London Ctee Royal Jubilee and Prince's Tsts 1983-84; FRGS 1969, FRSA 1974, MCollP 1985, MBIM 1986, FCollP 1989, MInstAM 1990, MIIM 1990, MISM 1990, MInstFM 1990; *Recreations* reading biographies, watching tv and generally recharging the batteries; *Clubs* Royal Cwlth Soc, The Pilgrims, RSA; *Style—* Norman Richardson, Esq, DL; 12c Treport St, London SW18 2BP; Christ Church School, 1 Robinson St, London SW3 4AR

RICHARDSON, Paul Michael; JP (Nottingham 1978); JP (co of Nottingham, 1978); s of George Herbert Richardson, of Ravenshead, Nottingham, and Evelyn, *née* O'Neil; *b* 4 Jan 1941; *Educ* West Bridgford HS, Alfreton HS; *m* 14 Nov 1970, Jacqueline Margaret, da of John Sydney Edwards, of Aspley, Nottingham; 2 s (Michael b 10 Nov 1972, William b 22 July 1975), 1 da (Joanne b 16 Aug 1971); *Career* md FW Buck and Sons Ltd 1977-, dir Long Eaton Advertiser Co Ltd 1980-, head weekly publications T Bailey Forman Ltd 1982-; memb Rotary Club Sutton-in-Ashfield 1977-; Lib cncllr Sutton-in-Ashfield urban 1967-70; *Recreations* sports enthusiast; *Style—* Paul Richardson, Esq, JP; Long Eaton Advertiser Co Ltd, Newspaper Buildings, West Gate, Long Eaton, Nottingham, NG10 1EH

RICHARDSON, Paul Thomas; s of Thomas Alfred Richardson (d 1981), and Muriel Isabel, *née* Hart (d 1979); *b* 26 Sept 1939; *Educ* Sherborne, Clare Coll Cambridge (MA); *m* 29 Dec 1964, Sylvia Ruth; 1 s (Mark Nathaniel b 10 Aug 1977); *Career* history teacher Manchester GS 1964-67; Heinemann Educnl Books: ed and ed dir 1967-77, mktg dir 1977-79; sales and mktg dir Macmillan London Ltd 1979-81, md Reference and Professional Div Collins Publishers 1981-85, dir of publishing devpt Octopus Publishing Group 1986-, publishing conslt 1989-; *Books* Britain, Europe and the Modern World (1968); *Clubs* Athenaeum; *Style—* Paul Richardson, Esq; Harratom House, Church Lane, Exning, Suffolk

RICHARDSON, Philip Edward; s of Wilfrid Laurence Richardson (d 1983), of Solihull, and Nellie Elizabeth, *née* Hands (d 1966); *b* 6 Oct 1945; *Educ* Tudor Grange GS, Solihull, Coll of Law; *m* 26 May 1969, Corrinne Mary, da of John Woodall (d 1983), of Flyford Flavell; 2 s (Toby b 1972, Tom b 1977), 2 da (Polly b 1975, Prue b 1980); *Career* slr; ptnr Dawkins and Grey 1971-, dir English String Orch Ltd 1984-; (jt hon sec 1980-89, PR offr 1987), chm of govrs Pershore HS 1988-, pres Birmingham Consular Assoc 1987-89, vice chm Hill and Moor plc 1987-89, Hon Consul: The Netherlands 1982-, Belgium 1984-; memb: Law Soc 1970, Birmingham Law Soc 1970 (jt hon sec 1980-89, PR offr 1987, vice pres 1989-90, pres 1990-91); *Recreations* music, railways; *Clubs* The Birmingham; *Style—* Philip Richardson, Esq; Bluebell Cottage, Hill, Pershore, Worcs (☎ 0386 860664); 40 Great Charles St, Queensway, Birmingham (☎ 021 233 1021, fax 021 200 1548, car 0860 202994)

RICHARDSON, Lt-Gen Sir Robert Francis; KCB (1982), CVO (1978), CBE (1975, OBE 1971, MBE 1965); s of Robert Buchan Richardson; *b* 2 March 1929; *Educ* George Heriot's Sch Edinburgh, RMA Sandhurst; *m* 1, 1956, Maureen Robinson (d 1986); 3 s, 1 da; m 2, 7 May 1988, Mrs Alexandra Inglis, *née* Bomford; *Career* Bde Maj Aden Bde 1967 (despatches), GSO 2 asst chief Def Staff Ops MOD 1968-69, CO 1 Bn Royal Scots 1969-71, Col Gen Staff Staff Coll Camberley 1971-74, Cdr 39 Inf Bde NI 1974-75, Dep Adj-Gen HQ BAOR 1975-78, GOC Berlin 1978-80, V-Adj Gen/Dir Manning (Army) MOD 1980-82, Col The Royal Scots (The Royal Regt) 1980-90 (cmmnd 1949), GOC NI 1982-85, Lt-Gen 1982-85; admin The MacRobert Tsts 1985-; *Recreations* golf, outdoor sports, gardening; *Clubs* Caledonian, Royal Scots, Hon Co of Edinburgh Golfers (Muirfield); *Style—* Lt-Gen Sir Robert Richardson, KCB, CVO, CBE; c/o Lloyds Bank plc, Cox's & King's Branch, 6 Pall Mall, London SW1

RICHARDSON, Roger Hart; RD (1965); s of Justin Richardson, of Headley, Surrey (d 1975), and Margery, *née* Wolfe; *b* 13 Aug 1931; *Educ* Rugby, Christ's Coll Cambridge (MA); *m* 25 Oct 1967, Evelyn Louise, da of Dr Paul Kane, MD, of 24 Montagu Sq, London W1; 1 s (Matthew b 1967), 1 da (Lydia b 1970); *Career* Lt Cdr RNR 1949-70; chm and md Beaver & Tapley Ltd (furniture mfrs) Southall Middx 1975-; Master Worshipful Co of Furniture Makers 1988 (Liveryman 1961, memb Ct of Assts 1974, jr warden 1987, sr warden 1987); *Recreations* sailing, music, bird-watching, wine; *Clubs* RNSA; *Style—* Roger Richardson, Esq, RD; 11 Broom Water, Teddington, Middx (☎ 081 977 7921, 081 574 4311); Beaver & Tapley Ltd, Scotts Rd, Southall, Middx

RICHARDSON, Hon Mrs (Sarah Amy); da of 13 Baron Clifford of Chudleigh, OBE; *b* 22 June 1956; *Educ* Convent of the Sacred Heart Woldingham; *m* 25 April 1981, Robert Carwithen Richardson, s of C C Richardson; 2 da (Amy Natasha b 1984, Jessie Katharine b 1987); *Style—* The Hon Mrs Richardson; Greatcombe, Holne, Devon TQ13 7SP

RICHARDSON, Maj-Gen Thomas Anthony (Tony); CB (1974), MBE (1960); s of Maj Gen Thomas William Richardson, OBE, of Norfolk (d 1968), and Josephine Mary Herbert Wickham Clarke (d 1973); *b* 9 Aug 1922; *Educ* Wellington, Military Coll of Science; *m* 1, 1945, Katharine Joanna Ruxton (d 1988), da of Maj Charles Minto Roberts (d 1956), of Somerset; 1 s (Christopher), 1 da (Charlotte); m 2, Anthea Rachel, da of Prof Dennis Butler Fry (d 1973), of Wimbledon; *Career* CO 7 RHA 1964-67, Cdr RA 2 Div (Brig) 1967-69, Dir Operational Requirements (Brig) 1970-71, Dir Army Aviation (Maj Gen) 1971-74, Head Br Defence Liaison Staff India (Maj Gen) 1974-77; sec: Timbers Growers Eng and Wales 1978-84, Br Christmas Tree Growers Assoc; chm: Tree Cncl 1986, Army Aviation Assoc, Army Gliding Assoc, RA Rugby Club, Rhine Army Free Fall Parachute Club, 2nd Div Ski Ctee; Cdre Army Sailing Assoc, vice cdre: RA Yacht Club, (and chm) RAYC Germany; hon sec RA Garrison

Shoot Larkhill; *Recreations* fishing, skiing, sailing, travelling; *Clubs* Army and Navy; *Style—* Maj-Gen Tony Richardson, CB, MBE; 12 Lauriston Rd, Wimbledon, London SW19 4TQ (☎ 081 946 2695)

RICHARDSON, Thomas Legh; CMG (1991); s of Arthur Legh Turnour Richardson (d 1984), and Penelope Margaret, *née* Waithman; *b* 6 Feb 1941; *Educ* Westminster, Ch Ch Oxford (MA); *m* 10 Feb 1979, Alexandra Frazier, da of John D Ratcliff (d 1974), of New York; *Career* joined FCO 1962; serv in: Accra, Dar Es Salaam, Milan, New York, Rome; at present dep perm rep UK Mission to UN with personal rank of Ambass; *Recreations* reading, walking, music; *Clubs* United Oxford and Cambridge; *Style—* Thomas Richardson, Esq, CMG; c/o FCO, Whitehall, London

RICHARDSON, Tony; s of Clarence Albert Richardson (d 1969), and Elsie Evans Richardson (d 1974); *b* 5 July 1928; *Educ* Ashville Coll Harrogate, Wadham Coll Oxford; *m* 1962 (m dis 1967), Vanessa Redgrave (*qv*), da of Sir Michael Redgrave (d 1985); 3 da (Natasha, Joely, Katharine); *Career* artistic dir English Stage Co Royal Ct Theatre 1956-65, dir Woodfall Film Prodns 1958-; prods incl: Look Back in Anger, The Entertainer, Luther, The Seagull, Pericles and Othello (Stratford), Taste of Honey; films incl: Taste of Honey, The Loneliness of the Long Distance Runner, Tom Jones (20 Oscars), The Charge of the Light Brigade, The Border, The Hotel New Hampshire; *Recreations* tennis, travel, bird collecting; *Style—* Tony Richardson, Esq; 1478 N Kings Rd, Los Angeles, CA 90069 (☎ 0101 213 656 5314)

RICHARDSON, Hon Mrs (Valentine Ellen MacDermott); *née* Crittall; da of 1 Baron Braintree (d 1961); *b* 1918; *m* 1939, Karl Stewart Richardson; 2 s; *Style—* The Hon Mrs Richardson; Hungry Hall, Witham, Essex

RICHARDSON, William; CBE (1981), DL (Cumbria 1982); s of Edwin Richardson; *b* 15 Aug 1916; *Educ* Jr Tech Coll, Tech Colls Barrow-in-Furness; *m* 1941, Beatrice Marjorie Iliffe; 1 s, 1 da; *Career* chm: Vickers Shipbuilding & Engineering 1976-83 (md 1969-76), Vosper Thornycroft UK 1978-83, Barclay Curle 1978-83, Brooke Marine 1981-83; dep chm British Shipbuilders 1981-83 (memb Bd 1977-83); dir Vickers Cockatoo Dockyard Pty (Australia) 1977-84, Vosper Shiprepairers 1979-82; memb Res Cncl and office bearer Br Ship Res Assoc 1976-78, chm Mgmnt Bd Shipbuilders and Repairers Nat Assoc 1976-78 (memb Exec Cncl 1969-77), pres Br Productivity Cncl Area Assoc 1969-72, shipbuilding indust rep on Def Industs Quality Assur Panel 1972-82; memb: Shipbuilding Indust Trg Bd 1979-82, NE Coast Inst of Engrs and Shipbuilders 1967-; author of papers on various aspects of UK shipbuilding indust, contrib to tech journals; Silver Jubilee medal (1977); Liveryman Worshipful Co of Shipwrights 1978; CEng, FRINA 1970 (assoc memb 1950, memb 1955), FInstD, CBIM (fell 1977); *Recreations* sailing, small-bore shooting, golf, fishing; *Clubs* Grange-over-Sands Golf, National Small-Bore Rifle Assoc; *Style—* William Richardson, Esq, CBE, DL; Sequoia, Sunbrick Lane, Baycliff, Ulverston, Cumbria LA12 9RQ (☎ 0229 869434)

RICHARDSON, Air Marshal Sir (David) William; KBE (1986); *b* 10 Feb 1932; *Educ* Univ of Birmingham, Cranfield Inst of Technol (MSc); *m* 1954, Mary Winifred, *née* Parker; 2 s (b 1956 and 1958), 1 da (b 1960); *Career* RAF 1953, AOC Maintenance Gp HQ RAF Support Cmd 1981-83, Air Offr Engrg RAF Strike Cmd 1983-86, RAF Chief Eng 1986, ret 1988; dir Aero & Industrial Technology Ltd; tstee MONITOR (charity investigating motor neurone disease); CEng, FIMechE, FRAeS; *Clubs* RAF; *Style—* Air Marshal Sir William Richardson, KBE; c/o Lloyds Bank, Southborough

RICHARDSON-BUNBURY, Lt Cdr Sir (Richard David) Michael; 5 Bt (I 1787), of Augher, Co Tyrone; s of Richard Richardson-Bunbury (d 1951; gggs of Sir James Richardson-Bunbury, 2 Bt), and Florence Margaret Gordon, da of Col Roger Gordon Thomson; suc kinsman, Sir Mervyn Richardson-Bunbury, 4 Bt (d 1953); *b* 27 Oct 1927; *Educ* RNC Dartmouth; *m* 15 July 1961, Jane Louise, da of Col Alfred William Pulverman, IA (d 1938); 2 s (Roger Michael b 1962, Thomas William b 1965); *Heir* s, Roger Richardson-Bunbury; *Career* Midshipman RN (S) 1945, Sub Lt (S) 1947, Lt (S) 1948, Lt Cdr 1956, sec to Head of UK Serv Liaison Staff Australia 1956-58, RN Staff Coll, Greenwich 1960-61, Capt's sec HMS Ark Royal 1961-64, sec to Flag Offr Naval Flying Trg 1964-67, ret 1967; entered computer servs indust 1967, ret 1987; dir Sandy Laird Ltd 1988; *Recreations* woodwork, gardening, reading, travel; *Style—* Lt Cdr Sir Michael Richardson-Bunbury, Bt, RN; Woodlands, Mays Hill, Worplesdon, Guildford, Surrey GU3 3RJ (☎ 0483 232034)

RICHARDSON-BUNBURY, Roger Michael; s and h of Lt Cdr Sir Michael Richardson-Bunbury, 5 Bt, RN; *b* 2 Nov 1962; *Educ* Sherborne, Manchester Univ (BA); *Style—* Roger Richardson-Bunbury, Esq

RICHARDSON OF DUNTISBOURNE, Baron (Life Peer UK 1983), of Duntisbourne in the Co of Gloucestershire; Sir Gordon William Humphreys Richardson; KG (1983), PC (1976), MBE (1944), TD (1979); s of John Robert and Nellie Richardson; *b* 25 Nov 1915; *Educ* Nottingham HS, Gonville and Caius Coll Cambridge (BA, LLB); *m* 1941, Margaret Alison, er da of late Very Rev Hugh Richard Lawrie Sheppard, Canon and Precentor of St Paul's Cathedral; 1 s (Hon Simon Bruce Sheppard b 1944), 1 da (Hon Sarah (Hon Lady Riddell) b 1942); *Career* govr Bank of England 1973-83 (memb Ct 1967-83), serv WWII S Notts Hussars Yeo and Staff Coll Camberley; barr 1946-55, memb Bar Cncl 1951-55; wih ICFC 1955-57; former chm: J Henry Schroder Wagg, Schroders Ltd, Schroders Inc; former chm Industl Devpt Advsy Bd, former chm Ctee on Turnover Taxation 1963-64; memb NEDC 1980-83 (and 1971-73); one of HM Lts City of London 1974-; former memb Ct London Univ, former tstee Nat Gallery, dep high steward Cambridge Univ 1982-; dir: Glyndeboure Arts Tst 1980-88, Royal Opera House 1983-88; *Clubs* Athenaeum, Brooks's; *Style—* The Rt Hon the Lord Richardson of Duntisbourne, KG, MBE, TD; c/o Morgan Stanley International, Kingsley House, 1A Wimpole Street, London W1M 7AA

RICHES, Sir Derek Martin Hurry; KCMG (1963, CMG 1958); s of Claude W H Riches, of Cardiff (d 1947), and bro of Gen Sir Ian Riches, *qv*; *b* 26 July 1912; *Educ* Univ Coll Sch, Univ Coll London; *m* 1942, Helen (d 1989), da of George Washburn Hayes, of Poughkeepsie, NY, USA; 1 da; *Career* entered Foreign Service 1934, chargé d'affaires Jedda 1952, cnsllr and head of Eastern Dept Foreign Office 1955-59; ambass to: Libya 1959-61, Republic of Congo 1961-63, Lebanon 1963-67, ret; *Style—* Sir Derek Riches, KCMG; 48 The Ave, Kew Gardens, Surrey

RICHES, George James; s of George James Riches (d 1980), and Katherine, *née* Herbert (d 1982); *b* 1 Jan 1934; *Educ* Minchenden Sch; *m* 2 March 1957, Ann Pauline, *née* Carritt; 2 s (Hugh b 1967, Guy b 1970, Neil b 1971); *Career* Nat Serv, cmmnd Middx Regt, served Aust 1952-54, Parachute Regt TA 1954-57; md: Benson Int 1968-77, C J Lytle 1968-77, Pemberton Gp 1968-77, Kimper Ltd 1968-77, Phaidon Press 1977-81; currently chm and md Musterlin Gp; chm constituency Cons Patrons Club; FBIM 1988; *Recreations* sailing, golf, international affairs; *Clubs* Oriental; *Style—* George Riches, Esq; Copse Side, Lincombe Lane, Boars Hill, Oxford, Oxon (☎ 0865 735157); Musterlin Group plc, Musterlin House, Jordan Hill Rd, Oxford OX2 8DP (☎ 0865 310661, fax 0865 310662, telex 83307)

RICHES, Gen Sir Ian Hurry; KCB (1969, CB 1959), DSO (1945); s of Claud W H Riches (d 1947), and Flora Martin (d 1962); bro of Sir Derek Riches, *qv*; *b* 27 Sept 1908; *Educ* Univ Coll Sch; *m* 1936, Winifred Eleanor, da of Adm Sir Geoffrey Layton, GBE, KCMG, KCB, DSO (d 1964); 2 s (Jeremy, Jonathan); *Career* joined RM 1927, serv 1939-45 in Italy, Yugoslavia and India, Maj 1946, Lt-Col 1949, Col 1953, cmd 3 Commando Bde RM (Actg Brig) 1954-55, cmd Inf Trg Centre RM 1955-57, Maj-Gen RM Portsmouth 1957-59, Cmdt-Gen RM 1959-62, Gen 1961, regnl dir of Civil Def 1964-68; Rep Col Cmdt RM 1967-68; *Clubs* Hampshire, Royal Naval and Royal Albert Yacht; *Style—* Gen Sir Ian H Riches, KCB, DSO; 34 Cheriton Rd, Winchester, Hants (☎ 0962 854067)

RICHES, Roger John; s of Harry Watson Riches, of Burnham on Sea Somerset, and Joan, *née* Ratcliffe; *b* 12 March 1945; *Educ* Kettering Secdy Sch, Kettering Tech Coll, Sheffield Poly (Dip Mgmnt Studies); *m* 12 March 1974, Heather, da of Harvey Watson Tolley; 1 s (Mark b 1979), 1 da (Sarah b 1985); *Career* dist mangr Yorks Building Society: Wakefield 1972-73, Leeds 1973-74, Doncaster 1975-78, trg mangr 1978-83, regnl exec Yorks 1983-89, div mangr 1989-; chm Yorks Gp CBSI 1989-90 (educn liaison offr 1982-, vice chm 1988-89), visiting lectr CBSI; FCBSI; *Recreations* sport, music, theatre; *Clubs* Grange Burley in Wharfedale; *Style—* Roger Riches, Esq; 27 Stirling Rd, Burley in Wharfedale, Ilkley, W Yorks LS29 7LH (☎ 0943 864 588); Yorkshire Building Society Divisional Office, Yorkshire House, Westgate, Bradford, West Yorks (☎ 0274 734822)

RICHMOND, Archdeacon of; *see*: McDermid, The Ven Norman

RICHMOND, Sir Alan James; *b* 12 Oct 1919; *Educ* Les Rayons Switzerland, Univ of London (BSc, PhD); *m* 1951, Sally; 1 step s, 1 step da; *Career* chartered mech engr; lectr Battersea Poly 1946-55, head Dept of Mech Engrg Welsh Coll of Advanced Technol 1955-58, princ Lanchester Coll of Technol Coventry 1958-70, dir Lanchester Poly Coventry 1970-72, princ Strode Coll Street Somerset 1972-81, conslt expert witness and commercial arbitrator 1982-; Hon DSc CNAA; CEng, FIMechE, FCIArb; kt 1969; *Recreations* law, gardening, reading; *Clubs* Royal Cwlth Soc; *Style—* Sir Alan Richmond; 5 The Orchard, Westfield Park South, Bath, Avon BA1 3HT (☎ 0225 333393)

RICHMOND, Rear-Adm Andrew John; ADC (1984) CB (1987); s of Albert George Richmond (d 1976), and Emily Margaret, *née* Denbee; *b* 5 Nov 1931; *Educ* Kings Sch Bruton, Pangbourne Coll; *m* 1 June 1957, Jane Annette (Toni), da of Lionel Ley, of New Zealand; 1 s (Julian Andrew b 28 Nov 1958), 2 da (Alison Anna Claire b 18 Sept 1960, Carolyn Jane Louise b 21 Feb 1962); *Career* RN: joined 1950, staff of C-in-C East Indies 1953, flying training 1955, Cyprus 847 Sqdn 1956, HMS Victorious 824 Sqdn 1958, staff of Flying Offr Arabian Sea 1960, BRNC Dartsmouth 1963, sec to Flying Offr Carriers and Amphilbious Ships 1968, supply sch HMS Pembroke 1970, Fleet Supply Offr 1974, asst dir Naval Manpower 1976, sec to C-in-C Naval Home Command 1977, Capt HMS Cochrane 1979, dir Naval Logistic Planning 1982, ACDS (Logistics) 1985, Chief Naval Supply & Secretariat Offr 1986; chief exec RSPSA 1987-; *Recreations* golf, gardening, countryside; *Clubs* Royal Overseas League, Goodwood Golf; *Style—* Rear-Adm Andrew Richmond, ADC, CB; RSPCA, The Causeway, Horsham, West Sussex RH12 1HG (☎ 0403 64181, fax 0403 41048)

RICHMOND, Anthony John (Tony); s of Arthur Geoffrey Richmond (d 1981), of Parkstone, Poole, Dorset, and Hilda Mary, *née* Pumphrey (d 1986); *b* 11 April 1938; *Educ* Wychwood Sch Bournemouth, Leighton Park Sch Reading, Brasenose Coll Oxford; *m* 1, 1965 (m dis), Elizabeth Ann, da of Peter Marshall; 2 s (Mark Benjamin b 1968, Peter Spencer b 1971); m 2, 1983, Julia Ruth, da of Donald Diggles; *Career* articled clerk Edwin G Pulsford & Co Chartered Accountants Poole Dorset 1961-65; KPMG Peat Marwick McLintock (formerly Peat Marwick Mitchell & Co): joined 1965, ptnr Sheffield 1971, NE Region Corp Recovery ptnr Leeds 1980, provisional liquidator Middlesbrough FC 1986, first High Court admin Charnley Davies Group 1987, jt admin James Ferguson Holdings plc 1988, receiver Burrells Wharf Development Kentish Homes Ltd 1989, jt admin receiver Capital Airlines Ltd 1990-; memb Insolvency Courses Ctee ICAEW 1973-79; FCA (ACA 1965); memb: Insolvency Practitioners Assoc 1977, Soc of Insolvency Practitioners 1990; Dorset Co Golf Champion 1962 and 1964; *Recreations* golf, windsurfing, skiing; *Clubs* Lindrick Golf, Oxford & Cambridge Golfing Soc; *Style—* Tony Richmond, Esq; KPMG Peat Marwick McLintock, 1 The Embankment, Neville St, Leeds LS1 4DW (☎ 0532 313000, fax 0532 313200)

RICHMOND, Dr David Hugh; s of John Richmond, of Edinburgh, and Jenny McMillan McKinnon, *née* Nicol; *b* 4 March 1953; *Educ* George Watson's Coll, Univ of Edinburgh (BSc, MB ChB, MD); *m* 8 July 1977, Maureen Shannon, da of Kenneth Philpot Walker, of Kilmacolm, Scotland; 2 s (Michael Walker b 15 Aug 1983, Stuart David b 19 May 1986), 1 da (Nicola Kathryn b 30 Nov 1981); *Career* visiting fell Queen Elizabeth Hosp Adelaide Australia 1987-88, sr lectr in obstetrics and gynaecology Univ of Liverpool 1988- (lectr 1983-88), main interests incl gynaecological urology and infertility; MRCOG 1982, Int Continence Soc; *Recreations* golf, skiing, walking; *Clubs* Royal Liverpool Golf; *Style—* Dr David Richmond; 20 Kirby Park, West Kirby, Wirral (☎ 051 625 6966); Dept of Obstetrics and Gynaecology, Liverpool University, Liverpool (☎ 051 709 0141, fax 051 708 6502, telex 627095 UNIPLG)

RICHMOND, Dr David John Hamilton; s of Dr Jack Hamilton Richmond (Maj RAMC, d 1969), and Gwendoline Mabel, *née* Thompson; *b* 18 Oct 1936; *Educ* Leighton Park Sch Reading, Pembroke Coll Cambridge, Guy's Hosp (MA, MB BChir, DObst RCOG, FFARCS); *m* 14 Feb 1975, Susan Elizabeth Helen, da of Charles W Malcolm, of 249 Kepa Rd, Auckland, New Zealand; 1 s (William b 11 March 1979), 2 da (Felicity b 4 Oct 1977, Amanda b 11 Feb 1982); *Career* Nat Serv, PO navigator RAF 1955-57; former: registrar St George's Hosp, registrar Bart's, sr registrar Queen Elizabeth Hosp Birmingham; conslt anaesthetist Wolverhampton Gp of Hosps 1971-; memb: Obstetric Anaesthetist Assoc, Assoc of Anaesthetists of GB; *Recreations* golf, tennis, bridge; *Clubs* South Staffordshire Golf, Wolverhampton Lawn Tennis & Squash; *Style—* Dr David Richmond; Greenways, Stockwell End, Tettenhall, Wolverhampton WV6 9PH (☎ 0902 751448); New Cross Hospital, Wolverhampton WV10 0QP (☎ 0902 732255)

RICHMOND, Prof John; s of Hugh Richmond (d 1952), and Janet Hyslop, *née* Brown (d 1985); *b* 30 May 1926; *Educ* Doncaster GS, Univ of Edinburgh (MB ChB, MD); *m* 29 Sept 1951, Jenny, da of Thomas Nicol (d 1977); 2 s (David b 1953, Michael b 1956), 1 da (Virginia b 1961); *Career* RAMC 1949-50; served: Ethiopia, Kenya, N Rhodesia (MO 1 Bn KAR); jr hosp appts Edinburgh 1948-49, GP Galloway 1950-52, hosp appts Northants 1952-54, res fell N Gen Hosp Edinburgh 1955, lectr (later sr lectr and reader) Univ of Edinburgh 1956-73 (secondments: res fell Meml Sloan Kettering Cancer Center NY 1958-59, Makerere Univ Med Sch Uganda 1965); prof of med Univ of Sheffield 1973-89 (dean Med Sch 1985-88); pres RCPEd 1988-, chm MRCP Examining Bd 1985-88, sr censor and sr vice pres RCP London 1984-85; memb: Sheffield Health Authy 1981-84, High Constables of Edinburgh 1962-71, Bd of advsrs Univ of London 1984-, Cncl of Mgmnt Yorks Cancer Res Campaign; external advsr Chinese Univ Hong Kong 1982-; memb: Assoc Physicians GBI, Med Res Soc; *Style—* Prof John Richmond; 15 Church Hill, Edinburgh EH10 4BG (☎ 081 447 2760); Royal Coll of Physicians, 9 Queen St, Edinburgh EH2 1JQ (☎ 031 225 7324)

RICHMOND, Sir Mark Henry; s of Harold Sylvestor Richmond (d 1952), and Dorothy Plaistowe (d 1976); *b* 1 Feb 1931; *Educ* Epsom Coll, Clare Coll Cambridge (BA, PhD, ScD); *m* 1958, Shirley Jean, da of Dr Vincent Townrow (d 1982); 1 s (Paul b 1964), 2 da (Clare b 1959, Jane b 1962, d 1987); *Career* scientific staff Med Res Cncl 1958-65; reader in molecular biology Univ of Edinburgh 1965-68, prof of bacteriology Univ of

Bristol 1968-81, vice chllr Univ of Manchester 1981-90, chm SERC 1990-; chm Ctee of Vice Chllrs of Princs 1987-89; FRS 1980; kt 1986; *Recreations* walking, gardening; *Clubs* Athenaeum; *Style*— Sir Mark Richmond; Science and Engineering Reseach Council, Polaris House, North Star Avenue, Swindon SN2 1ET

RICHMOND, Timothy Stewart (Tim); MBE (1985), TD (1982), DL (Notts 1990); s of Stewart McKenzie Sylvestor Richmond (1970), and Nancie Barber; *b* 17 Nov 1947; *Educ* Birkdale Sch Sheffield, Nottingham HS; *m* 4 Sept 1974, Susan Carol, *née* Spencer; 2 s (William Stewart b 15 Dec 1976, Thomas Bruce b 22 April 1982), 1 da (Holly Victoria (twin) b 22 April 1982); *Career* Pannell Kerr Forster: articled clerk Nottingham Office 1966-70, mangr Audit and Tax Depts Nottingham Office 1970-74, ptnr 1974, gen practice ptnr and staff ptnr Nottingham Office 1974-81, managing ptnr Nottingham Office 1981-85; memb Nat Firm's Strategic Planning Gp 1984-85, nat managing ptnr 1985-; memb Nat Bd of Mgmnt 1985-, memb Euro Policy Bd memb Int Cncl; govr and dep chm Nottingham Poly 1988-, memb Nottingham Health Authy 1989-, TA: memb 1970-, cmmn Royal Regt of Artillery, cmd S Notts Hussars Yeomanry 1982-85, Lt Col cmd E Midlands Univs OTC 1989-91; Freeman City of London, memb Worshipful Co of CAs; FCA (ACA 1970), FBIM, assoc memb IOD; *Recreations* sailing and gardening; *Clubs* Cavalry and Gds; *Style*— Tim Richmond, Esq, MBE, TD, DL; Pannell Kerr Forster, 78 Hatton Garden, London EC1N 8JA (☎ 072 831 7393, fax 071 405 6736); Pelham Rd, Nottingham (☎ 0602 606260, fax 0602 622229)

RICHMOND, William John (Bill); s of Alfred Richmond, of Derby, and Muriel Harland, *née* Woodruff (d 1984); *b* 2 Aug 1947; *Educ* Bemrose GS, Derby Poly; *m* 21 Aug 1970, Ann, da of Bert Collis; 1 s (Andrew Peter b 7 Feb 1978), 1 da (Jill Laura b 23 May 1981); *Career* photographer's asst 1967-71 (Zoe Dominic theatrical work, Norman Gold advertising work), photographer Advertising and Design Dept Wiggins Teape Paper 1971-73, ind photographer 1973- (latterly specialising in still life, food and roomset work), proprietor studio practice 1977; external assessor and moderator: CNAA degree course Manchester Poly (former memb Validation Panel), BTech course Gloucester and Derby Colls until 1989; FBIPP 1974 (former memb Admissions Panel); *Recreations* 400 and 800 metre track athletics; *Clubs* Thames Valley Harriers Athletic; *Style*— William Richmond, Esq; 38 Normandy Ave, Barnet, Herts EN5 2JA (☎ 081 440 0822); BMR Studios, 51-55 Stirling Rd, London W3 8DJ (☎ 081 993 5545, fax 081 993 7589, mobile 0836 674730)

RICHMOND AND GORDON, 10 (and 5 respectively) Duke of (E 1675, UK 1876); Charles Henry Gordon Lennox; also Earl of March, Baron of Settrington (both E 1675), Duke of Lennox, Earl of Darnley, Lord Torbolton (all S 1675), Duc d'Aubigny (Fr 1684), Earl of Kinrara (UK 1876), and Hereditary Constable of Inverness Castle; s of 9 Duke of Richmond and (4 of) Gordon (d 1989); descended from King Charles II and Louise Renée de Penançoët de Kérouaille, who was cr Baroness Petersfield, Countess of Fareham and Duchess of Portsmouth for life by King Charles II and Duchesse d'Aubigny by King Louis XIV of France; *b* 19 Sept 1929; *Educ* Eton, William Temple Coll Rugby; *m* 26 May 1951, Susan Monica, o da of Col Cecil Everard Grenville-Grey, CBE, of Hall Barn, Blewbury, Berks, by his w, Louise Monica, eldest da of Lt-Col Ernest Fitzroy Morrison-Bell, OBE, JP, DL; 1 s (Earl of March and Kinrara), 2 da (Lady Ellinor Caroline b 1952, Lady Louisa Elizabeth b 1967), and 2 adopted da (Maria b 1959, Naomi b 1962); *Heir* s, Earl of March and Kinrara, *qv*; *Career* late 2 Lt KRRC; chartered accountant 1956-; chm Goodwood Group of Cos 1969-, vice chm John Wiley & Sons Ltd 1985-; memb: House of Laity Gen Synod 1960-80, Central and Exec Ctee World Cncl Churches 1968-75; church cmmr 1962-75; chm: Bd for Mission and Unity Gen Synod 1968-77; House of Laity Chichester Diocese 1976-79, Chichester Cathedral Tst 1985-; pres: Voluntary & Christian Serv 1982-; vice-chm Archbishops' Cmmn on Church and State 1966-70, memb W Midlands Regnl Econ Planning Cncl 1965-68, chm tstees Sussex Heritage Tst 1978-; pres: Sussex Rural Community Cncl 1973-; SE England Tourist Bd 1990- (vice pres 1974-90), Sussex CCC 1991-; chm: Rugby Cncl of Social Serv 1961-68, Dunford Coll (YMCA) 1969-82; treas Sussex Univ 1979-82, chllr 1985-; Lord Lt of West Sussex 1990- (DL 1975-90); hon treas and dep pres Historic Houses Assoc 1975-86; chm: Christian Organisations Research and Advisory Tst (CORAT) 1970-87, Special Gifts Gp Church Urban Fund 1990-; pres S of England Agric Soc 1981-82; chm Assoc of Int Dressage Event Organisers 1987-, pres Br Horse Soc 1976-78, dir Country Gentlemen's Association Ltd 1975-89; Hon LLD Sussex 1987; Medal of Honour Br Equestrian Fedn 1983; CBIM 1982; *Style*— His Grace the Duke of Richmond and Gordon; Goodwood House, Chichester, W Sussex PO18 OPY (☎ 0243 774760; office: 774107)

RICHMOND AND GORDON, Elizabeth, Duchess of; Elizabeth Grace; yst da of late Rev Thomas William Hudson, sometime Vicar of Wendover, Bucks; *m* 15 Dec 1927, 9 Duke of Richmond and (4 Duke of) Gordon (d 1989); 2 s (10 and 5 Duke, Lord Nicholas Gordon Lennox, *qqv*); *Style*— Her Grace Elizabeth, Duchess of Richmond and Gordon; Carne's Seat, Goodwood, Chichester, West Sussex

RICHMOND-WATSON, Anthony Euan; s of Euan Owens Richmond-Watson (d 1954), and Hon Gladys Gordon, *née* Catto (d 1967); *b* 8 April 1941; *Educ* Westminster, Edinburgh Univ (BCom); *m* 1, 1966, Angela, da of John Broadley, of Somerset (d 1979); 1 s (Luke b 1971), 1 da (Tamsin b 1967); *m* 2, 1976, Geraldine Ruth Helen, da of Charles Barrington, of Cornwall (d 1966); 1 da (Alice b 1976); *Career* merchant banker; dir Morgan Grenfell & Co Ltd 1975 (joined 1968), dir and dep chm Morgan Grenfell Gp plc 1989, non-exec dir Yule Catto and Co plc 1978, chm Norfolk Capital Gp plc 1986-90 (dir 1985-90); MICAS; *Style*— Anthony Richmond-Watson, Esq; 23 Great Winchester St, London EC2P 2AX (☎ 071 588 4545)

RICHTERICH, Pierre Albert Henri; s of Albert Richterich (d 1986), of Bingley, W Yorks, and Marguerite Anne, *née* Hoffmann; *b* 24 March 1934; *Educ* Bradford GS, Bradford Coll; *m* 26 Aug 1961, Patricia; 2 da (Carla b 1965, Annick b 1968); *Career* Nat Serv 1953-54: Intelligence Corps, RASC, posted to SHAPE HQ Paris; fndr chm and md PA Richterich & Co Ltd 1959-; former pres: Airedale Agricultural Soc, Rotary Club Bradford Blaize; formerly: chm and pres Bingley RT, chm Area 32, memb Nat Exec RTBI 1972-74; *Recreations* skiing, fellwalking, golf, windsurfing; *Clubs* Bradford, RAC, E India; *Style*— Pierre Richterich, Esq; P A Richterich Intl Ltd, Northvale Mills, Singleton St, Bradford BD1 4RF (☎ 0274 735 821, fax 0274 391 480, telex 51366)

RICKARD, Dr John Hellyar; s of Peter John Rickard, of Devon, and Irene Eleanor, *née* Hales; *b* 27 Jan 1940; *Educ* Ilford Co HS, Univ of Oxford (MA, DPhil), Univ of Aston (MSc); *m* 6 April 1963, Christine Dorothy, da of Claude Hudson (d 1963), of Essex; 1 s (Robin b 1965), 2 da (Rosemary b 1964, Wendy b 1967); *Career* former res fell Univ of Oxford; sr econ advsr: Dept of Prices and Consumer Protection 1976-78, central policy review staff Cabinet Office 1978-82, HM Treasy 1982-84; the econ advsr State of Bahrain 1984-87, chief econ advsr Dept of Tport 1987; *Books* Macro-Economics (with D Aston, 1970); *Recreations* sailing, music; *Clubs* Civil Service Sailing; *Style*— Dr John Rickard; The Department of Transport, 2 Marsham St, London SW1P 3EB (☎ 071 276 5299)

RICKARD, Stephen Leslie; s of late Aubrey Rickard, of Ventnor, IOW, and (Evelyn) Gladys, *née* Naylor; *b* 9 May 1917; *Educ* Berkhamstead Sch Herts, Kingston on Thames Art Sch, Royal Acad Schs (dip and gold medal in sculpture); *m* 4 May 1940, Evelyn Norman, da of late Maj Norman Loring, of Hove, Sussex; 2 s (Jeremy b 1942, Simon b 1946), 2 da (Harriet b 1952, Judith b 1955); *Career* WWII, served E Surrey Regt 1940, 2 Lt King's Own Royal Regt NI, transferred Indian Army 1942 (Capt and actg Maj), demob 1946; sculptor and glass engraver; sculptures incl three dimensional portrait heads of: Lord Fairhaven (Anglesey Abbey Cambs), Dr Margaret Murray (Univ Coll Library London), Prof J D Bernal (Sci Museum Library London); glass engravings: Princess Alexandra's 21st Birthday, Princess Margaret's Wedding, Winston Churchill's 80th Birthday, gifts to HM the Queen and HRH The Prince of Wales, many gifts from FO to int heads of state, innumerable retirement presents etc; memb Civic Tst, speaker on glass engraving to local gps; FRBS 1956 (ret), FSDC 1966 (ret), FGE 1979; *Recreations* none to speak of - art and life being inseparable; *Clubs* Savage; *Style*— Stephen Rickard, Esq; 33 Winchilsea Ave, Newark, Notts NG24 4AD (☎ 0636 71674)

RICKARDS, John Ayscough; s of George Ayscough Rickards, MC, and Barbara Ramsey, *née* Smyth; *b* 7 July 1939; *Educ* Harrow, Univ of Cambridge; *m* 1976, Joanna R R Roberts; 3 da (Anna b 1967, Clare b 1968, Harriet b 1983), 1 s (William b 1982); *Career* Greenwell & Co 1963-87, Samuel Montagu & Co 1987-88, Cazenove & Co 1989; *Clubs* Whites, City of London; *Style*— John A Rickards, Esq; West Stratton House, West Stratton, Michledever, Hants (☎ 096 289 266)

RICKARDS, Maurice George; s of Capt Eric Mansbridge (d 1969), of London, and Rosa Dolores, *née* Bernstein (who remarried George Somers Rikards) (d 1976), of Torquay; *b* 11 Aug 1919; *Educ* St Marylebone GS, Westminster Sch of Art; *m* 11 Aug 1945 (m dis 1981), Yolanda Maria Clementina, da of Alfredo Martelli (d 1963); *Career* civilian social relief 1940-44; freelance graphic designer, photographer and writer 1945-; work on children's tv progs Alexandra Place and Lime Grove; numerous long term graphic design and campaign conslts incl: Christian Aid (originator of name and logo), Keep Br Tidy, PO/Br Telecom, Procter & Gamble, BP, Pye Ltd, Unilever, Royal Soc for Prevention of Accidents (indust, home and road safety campaigns); chm publicity design gp Soc of Industl Artists 1960-64; former external examiner and conslt: Br Assoc of Industl Eds, Inst of PR, Central London Poly, Soc of Industl Artists; fndr and chm ephemera Soc (now vice pres) 1975, ed The Ephemerist 1975-, exec sec fndn for Ephemera Studies 1983, curator Rickards Collection of Printed Ephemera 1985; fndr memb: Ephemera Soc of America 1980, Ephemera Soc of Australia 1987, Ephemera Soc of Canada 1988; sec gen Int Ephemera Cncl 1988; FCSD, fell Inst of Br Photographers; *Publications* The Lovely Awful Thing (1959), Posters of the 1920s, Banned Posters (1969), The Rise and Fall of the Poster, The Public Notice - An Illustrated History (1973), This is Ephemera (1976), Collecting Printed Ephemera (1988); *Recreations* linguistics, phonetics, contemporary social history; *Clubs* Arts Club, London; *Style*— Maurice Rickards, Esq; 12 Fitzroy Square, London W1P 5HQ (☎ 071 387 7723)

RICKAYZEN, Prof Gerald; s of Solomon Rickayzen (d 1969), of London, and Jane Culank (d 1975); *b* 16 Oct 1929; *Educ* Teignmouth GS, Central Fndn Boys' Sch, QMC London (BSc), Christ's Coll Cambridge (PhD); *m* 20 Dec 1953, Gillian Thelma, da of Maurice Lewin (d 1972), of Dunstable, Beds; 3 s (Alan Michael b 15 Jan 1957, (Martin) Asher b 28 Dec 1960, Benjamin David b 1 June 1963), 1 da (Sonia Ruth (Mrs Joseph) b 29 Nov 1958); *Career* jr res fell Services Electronics Research Laboratory Baldock Herts 1954-57, res assoc Univ of Illinois USA 1957-59, lectr in physics Univ of Liverpool 1959-65, reader in theoretical physics Univ of Kent 1965-66; Univ of Kent: prof of theoretical physics 1966-, dean of Faculty of Natural Sciences 1977-82, pro vice-chllr 1982-, dep vice-chllr 1984-90; chm of Govrs Simon Langton Girls Sch Canterbury; govr: Simon Langton Boys' Sch, Christ Church Coll Canterbury; memb American Physical Soc 1958, fell Former Physical Soc 1957, FInstP 1982, CPhys 1985; *Books* Theory of Superconductivity (1965), Green's Functions and Condensed Matter (1980, reprinted in paperback 1984); *Recreations* playing the 'cello, tennis; *Style*— Prof Gerald Rickayzen; The Physics Laboratory, The University, Canterbury, Kent CT2 7NR (☎ 0227 764000, fax 0227 762616, telex 965449)

RICKETT, Sir Denis Hubert Fletcher; KCMG (1956, CMG 1947), CB (1951); s of Hubert Cecil Rickett, OBE, JP (d 1950), and Mabel Fletcher (d 1969); *b* 27 July 1907; *Educ* Rugby, Balliol Coll Oxford (scholar, Jenkyns exhibitioner, BA); *m* 1946, Ruth Pauline, da of late William Anderson Armstrong, JP; 2 s, 1 da; *Career* fell All Souls Coll Oxford 1929-49, joined staff of Economic Advsy Cncl 1931, Offices of War Cabinet 1939, PPS to Rt Hon Oliver Lyttelton, DSO, MC, MP (Min of Prodn, later Viscount Chandos) 1943-45, PA (for work on Atomic Energy) to Rt Hon Sir John Anderson, MP (Chllr of the Exchequer) 1945, transferred to Treasy 1947, PPS to Rt Hon Clement Atlee, OM, CH (PM) 1950-51, Economic Min Br Embassy Washington and head of UK Treasy and Supply Delegation 1951-54, third sec HM Treasy 1955-60 (second sec 1960-68); vice pres World Bank 1968-74; dir: Schroder Int 1974-79, De La Rue Co 1974-77; advsr J Henry Schroder Wagg & Co 1974-79; *Recreations* music, travel; *Clubs* Brooks's, Athenaeum; *Style*— Sir Denis Rickett, KCMG, CB; 9 The Close, Salisbury, Wiltshire SP1 2EB

RICKETT, Brig Johnny Francis; CBE (1990, OBE 1982, MBE 1967); s of Francis William Rickett (d 1981), and Lettice Anne, *née* Elliot (d 1984); *b* 7 Sept 1939; *Educ* Eton, Indian Staff Coll, Royal Coll of Defence Studies; *m* June 1964, Frances Seton (Fanny), da of Charles Seton De Winton, OBE, of Burford, Oxon; 1 s (Charles Edward Francis (Charlie) b 1975), 2 da (Sophy Frances b 1965 d 1970, Emily Frances b 1974); *Career* cmmnd Welsh Guards Nat Serv Offr 1959, 1st Bn UK and BAOR, seconded for loan serv Fed Reg Army S Arab Emirates 1963-65; 1st Bn Welsh Guards: Aden 1965-67 (Political Offr for some of period), Adj 1968-70, served Hong Kong Kenya, Germany, USA, NI, MOD 1977-80, CO 1980-82 (incl Falklands conflict); leader Falklands Presentation Team 1982, MOD 1983, cmd 19 Inf Brigade Colchester 1984-86, Dep Cdr and Chief of Staff HQ SE Dist Aldershot 1987-90, Regtl Lt-Col Welsh Guards 1989-; Queen Commendation for Brave Conduct 1964, mentioned in despatches 1974, author of articles in def magazines; govr boys prep sch, memb Parodial Church Cncl, pres Welsh Guards Regtl Assoc; FBIM 1990; Chevalier of the Order of Dannebrog Denmark 1975; *Recreations* country sports, riding, polo, rowing, running; *Clubs* Army and Navy; *Style*— Brig Johnny Rickett, CBE; c/o RHQ Welsh Guards, Wellington Barracks, Birdcage Walk, London SW1E 6HQ (☎ 071 414 3237, fax 071 414 3447)

RICKETT, Sir Raymond Mildmay Wilson; CBE (1984); s of Mildmay Louis Rickett (d 1967), and Winifred Georgina Ann, *née* Hazel (d 1974); *b* 17 March 1927; *Educ* Faversham GS, Medway Coll of Technol (BSc), Illinois Inst of Technol (PhD); *m* 1 Feb 1958, Naomi, da of Jitsuo Nishida (d 1984), of Parlier, California USA; 1 s (Guy b 1961), 2 da (Kimiyo b 1960, Vanessa b 1963); *Career* RN 1946-48; lectr Liverpool Coll Technol 1960-62, sr and princ lectr West Ham Coll Technol 1962-64, head dept Wolverhampton Coll Technol 1965-66, vice princ Sir John Cass Coll 1967-69, vice provost City of London Poly 1969-72, dir Middx Poly 1972-; chm: Ctee Dirs of Polys 1980-82 and 1986-88, UK Nat Cmmn UNESCO Educnl Advsy Ctee 1983-85, UK Erasmus (EEC) Student Grants Cncl; memb: Oakes Ctee 1977-78, Higher Educn Review Gp NI 1978-82, IUPC 1981-, NAB Bd 1981-87, Ctee Int Co-op in Higher Educn 1981- (vice chm 1986-89, chm 1989-), Open Univ Cncl 1983-, Cncl Indust and Higher Educn 1985-; hon fell: Ealing Coll, Newcastle Poly; FRSC; Officer's Cross of the Order of Merit Federal Republic of Germany 1988; kt 1990; *Books* Experiments in Physical Chemistry (jtly, 1961), Use of Chemical Literature (jtly, 1962); *Recreations* cricket, theatre going, opera; *Clubs* Athenaeum, English Speaking Union; *Style—* Sir Raymond Rickett, CBE; Principal's Lodge Park, Cockfosters Rd, Barnet, Herts EN4 0PS (☎ 081 449 9012); Middlesex Poly, Bramley Rd, Oakwood, London N14 4XS (☎ 081 368 1299, fax 081 449 0798, telex 8954762)

RICKETTS, Prof Peter Thomas; s of Thomas Edward Ricketts (d 1977), of Birmingham, and Rose Ellen, *née* Pennell (d 1988); *b* 14 Dec 1933; *Educ* King Edward VI GS Birmingham, Univ of Birmingham (BA, PhD); *m* 23 July 1960, Monica Ann, da of Frederick George Bishop (d 1977), of Broadstairs; 1 s (David), 1 da (Jane); *Career* Nat Serv Sgt Instr RAEC 1959-61; asst d'anglais Lycée des Garçons Nimes France 1954-55, lecteur d'anglais Université de Montpellier 1957-58; dept of French Victoria Coll Univ of Toronto: temp lectr 1958-59, lectr and asst prof 1961-64; Univ of Birmingham: lectr in romance philology Dept of Latin 1964-68, sr lectr in romance philology 1968-78, reader in romance linguistics 1978-80; visiting prof Dept of French Univ of Br Columbia Vancouver Canada 1967-68, James Barrow prof of French Univ of Liverpool 1980-83, prof of romance philology Queen Mary and Westfield Coll Univ of London (formerly Westfield Coll) 1983-, dean Westfield Coll Univ of London 1986-89 (dep dean 1984-86), dep dean Queen Mary and Westfield Coll 1989-; author of numerous articles in learned jls; memb Advsy Ctee Br Branch Int Courtly Lit Soc; Association Internationale d'Etudes Occitanes: fndr pres 1981-90, gen ed 1981-90; created Sòci of the Felibrige 1982, memb Comité d'honneur Revue des Langues Romanes 1982; *Books* incl: Introduction à l'étude de l'Ancien Provençal (with F Hamlin and J Hathaway, 1967), Fouke le Fitz Waryn (with J Hathaway C Robson and A Wilshere, 1976), Proceedings of the First Conference on Medieval Occitan Language and Literature (ed, 1979), Actes du premier congrès international de l'Association Internationale d'Etudes Occitanes (ed 1987), Le Breviari d'Amor de Matfre Ermengaud, tome II (1989); *Recreations* theatre; *Style—* Prof Peter Ricketts; Dept of French, Queen Mary & Westfield Coll, Hampstead Campus, Kidderpore Ave, London NW3 7ST (☎ 071 435 7141, fax 071 794 2173)

RICKETTS, Sir Robert Cornwallis Gerald St Leger; 7 Bt (UK 1828), of The Elms, Gloucestershire, and Beaumont Leys, Leicestershire; s of Sir Claude Ricketts, 6 Bt (d 1937); *b* 8 Nov 1917; *Educ* Haileybury, Magdalene Coll Cambridge; *m* 1945, (Anne) Theresa, *qv*; 2 s, 2 da (*see* His Hon Judge Mason); *Heir* s, Tristram Ricketts; *Career* slr 1949, formerly ptnr Wellington and Clifford; pa to COS Gibraltar 1942-45 and ADC to Lt-Govr of Jersey 1945-46; hon citizen of Mobile Alabama USA; FRSA; *Recreations* books, history; *Style—* Sir Robert Ricketts, Bt; Forwood House, Minchinhampton, Stroud, Glos GL6 9AB (☎ 0453 882160)

RICKETTS, Lady; (Anne) Theresa; CBE (1983); da of late Rt Hon Sir Stafford Cripps, CH, PC, QC (chllr of the Exchequer in Attlee's Govt and 4 s of Baron Parmoor, KCVO, PC, JP); *b* 12 April 1919; *m* 1945, Sir Robert Ricketts, 7 Bt, *qv*; 2 s, 2 da; *Career* chm Nat Assoc of Citizens' Advice Bureaux 1979-84; memb Electricity Consumers Cncl 1978-90; memb Direct Mail Services Standards Bd 1985-; *Style—* Lady Ricketts, CBE; Forwood House, Minchinhampton, Stroud, Glos (☎ 0453 882160)

RICKETTS, (Robert) Tristram; s and h of Sir Robert Ricketts, 7 Bt, of Forwood House, Minchinhampton, Glos, and Anne Theresa, *née* Cripps; *b* 17 April 1946; *Educ* Winchester, Magdalene Coll Cambridge (MA); *m* 1969, Ann, yr da of Eric William Charles Lewis, CB (d 1981), of 31 Deena Close, Queen's Drive, London; 1 s, 1 da; *Career* chief exec Horserace Betting Levy Bd 1980-; *Clubs* Athenaeum; *Style—* Tristram Ricketts, Esq; 47 Lancaster Ave, London SE27 9EL (☎ 081 670 8422); office: 52 Grosvenor Gardens, London SW1W OAU (☎ 071 730 4540)

RICKFORD, Christopher Richard Keevil; s of Richard Braithwaite Keevil Rickford (d 1990), of Dartmouth, Devon, and Dorothy Margaret Hart, *née* Latham; *b* 16 Feb 1942; *Educ* Sherborne, Univ of Cambridge (MA, MB BChir); *m* 2 April 1966, Maureen, da of Ronald Bell Jones, MBE (D 1985); 1 s (Nicholas b 22 July 1974), 2 da (Clare b 16 Dec 1967, Caroline b 24 May 1970); *Career* sr surgical registrar St Thomas' Hosp, conslt surgn Cornwall and Isles of Scilly AHA 1979-; memb: BMA, RSM; FRCS; *Recreations* sailing, photography; *Clubs* RSM; *Style—* Christopher Rickford, Esq; The Royal Cornwall Hospital, Treliske, Truro, Cornwall TR1 3LJ (☎ 0872 74242)

RICKFORD, (William) Jeremy Keevil

RICKFORD, Jonathan Braithwaite Keevil; s of Richard Braithwaite Keevil Rickford (d 1990), and Dorothy Margaret, *née* Latham; *b* 7 Dec 1944; *Educ* Sherborne, Magdalen Coll Oxford (BA, BCL, Gibbs prize in law); *m* 20 July 1968, Dora Rose, da of Rt Rev Norman Sargant (d 1985); 1 s (Richard b 7 July 1971), 2 da (Margaret b 10 Dec 1973, Alice b 24 March 1975); *Career* barr 1970-85, slr 1985-, teaching assoc in law Univ of California Sch of Law 1968-69, lectr in law LSE 1969-72, sr legal asst Dept of Trade 1974 (asst 1972), Law Offrs Dept AG's Chambers 1976-79; DTI (formerly Dept of Trade): asst slr (co law) 1979-82, under sec (legal) 1982-84, The Slr 1984-87; dir of govt rels British Telecommunications plc 1989- (slr and chief legal offr 1987-89); *Recreations* sailing; *Clubs* Reform, Royal Dart Yacht; *Style—* Jonathan Rickford, Esq; A806, BT Centre, 81 Newgate St, London EC1A 7AJ (☎ 071 356 5100)

RICKMAN, Prof Geoffrey Edwin; *b* 9 Oct 1932; *Educ* Peter Symonds Sch Winchester, Brasenose Coll Oxford (MA, DPhil); *m* 18 April 1959, Anna Rosemary, *née* Wilson; 1 s (David Edwin b 1964), 1 da (Elizabeth Jane b 1962); *Career* jr res fell The Queen's Coll Oxford 1959-62; Univ of St Andrews: lectr in ancient history 1962-, sr lectr 1968-, prof 1981-; FSA 1963, FBA 1989; *Books* Roman Granaries and Storebuildings (1971), The Corn Supply of Ancient Rome (1980); *Recreations* swimming, listening to opera; *Style—* Prof Geoffrey Rickman, FSA; 56 Hepburn Gardens, St Andrews, Fife, Scotland KY16 9DG (☎ 0334 72063); Department of Ancient History, St Salvator's College, The University, St Andrews, Fife, Scotland (☎ 0334 76161)

RICKMAN, John Eric Carter; s of Maj Eric Roper Rickman (d 1976), of 40 Cumberland Terrace, Regents Park, London, and Catherine Mary, *née* Carter (d 1964); *b* 28 May 1913; *Educ* Feltonfleet, Haileybury, Fleet St, Army; *m* 29 April 1939, Margaret Wood, da of Robert Oswald Law (d 1954), of 7 Princes Gate, London SW7; 1 s (Robin b 1942), 2 da (Jill b 1940, Rosemary b 1945); *Career* serv TA Cmmn, Glos and Reconaissance Regts 1931-46, serv WWII in NW Europe, 1 Canadian Air Staff, 84 Gp TAF (Maj) 1945; reporter: Bristol Evening World 1931, Glos Echo 1932, Daily Mail 1934 (reporter and zoo correspondent), succeeded from Robin Goodfellow, chief Daily Mail Horse Racing corr 1949, Gimcrack, Daily Sketch 1961-71, ITV horse racing commentator 1955-78 (front man famous for hat raising welcome to viewers); winner of showing awards with home bred Welsh Cobs and Faverolles poultry; *Books* Homes of Sport: Horse Racing (1952), Eight Flat Racing Stables (1979), Old Tom and Young John (1990); *Recreations* golf, writing, Euro travel, sailing, country pursuits; *Clubs* Kennel, Derby, Twelve, Liphook GC; *Style—* John Rickman, Esq; Pheasants Walk, Copyhold Lane, Fernhurst, Haslemere, Surrey GU27 3DZ (☎ 0428 643197)

RICKS, David Trulock; OBE (1981); s of Percival Trulock Ricks (d 1983), of Bromham, Beds, and Annetta Helen, *née* Hood (d 1967); *b* 28 June 1936; *Educ* Kilburn GS, RAM, Merton Coll Oxford (MA), Univ of London Inst of Educn, Univ of Lille (Licence-en-Lettres); *m* 1 Aug 1960, Nicole Estelle Aimée, da of André Armand Chupeau (d 1973), of Marans, France; 2 s (Ralph Antoine b 1964, Quentin Nicholas b 1969); *Career* teacher and lectr in London 1960-67; Br Cncl 1967-: dir of studies Morocco 1967-70, Univ of Essex 1970-71, dir State Inst of Language Studies Jaipur India 1971-74, dep dir Tanzania 1974-76, dep dir Iran 1976-79, dir Iran and cultural attaché HM Embassy Tehran 1979-80, dir Serv Conditions Dept London 1980-85, dir Italy and cultural cnsllr HM Embassy Rome 1985-90, govr Br Inst of Florence 1985-90, cultural cnsllr HM Embassy Paris 1990-; memb Rome Ctee Keats-Shelley Meml House Rome 1985-90; FRSA 1989; *Books* Penguin French Reader (jt ed, 1967); *Recreations* playing the piano, music, skiing; *Clubs* United Oxford and Cambridge; *Style—* David Ricks, Esq, OBE; c/o The British Council, 10 Spring Gdns, London SW1A 2BN (☎ 071 930 8466)

RICKS, Sir John Plowman; s of James Young Ricks (d 1949); *b* 3 April 1910; *Educ* Christ's Hosp, Jesus Coll Oxford (MA); *m* 1, 1936, May Celia (d 1975), da of late Robert William Chubb; 3 s; m 2, 1976, Doreen Ada, widow of Arthur Forbes Ilsley; *Career* slr PO 1953-72 (joined PO Slr's Dept PO 1935); kt 1964; *Style—* Sir John Ricks; 8 Sunset View, Barnet, Herts EN5 4LB (☎ 081 449 6114)

RICKS, Robert Neville; s of Sir John Plowman Ricks, of Sunset View, Barnet, Herts, and May Celia, *née* Chubb (1975); *b* 29 June 1942; *Educ* Highgate Sch, Worcester Coll Oxford (MA); *Career* admitted slr 1967; Treasy Slrs Dept: legal asst 1969-73, sr legal 1973-81, asst slr 1981-86, prihc asst slr 1986; legal advsr Dept of Education and Science 1990-; memb Gen Synod C of E 1980-85; *Recreations* wine, collecting original cartoons; *Clubs* United Oxford and Cambridge; *Style—* Robert Ricks, Esq; 2 Eaton Terrace, Aberavon Rd, London E3 5AJ (☎ 071 981 3722); Treasury Solicitors Dept, 28 Broadway SW1 (☎ 071 210 3140)

RIDD, Prof John Howard; s of Herbert William Ridd (d 1971), of 80 Chaffers Mead, Ashtead, Surrey, and Emma Roadley, *née* Elmes (d 1977); *b* 7 Oct 1927; *Educ* Epsom GS, UCL (BSc, PhD); *m* 31 Dec 1955, Freda Marie, da of Harold George Williams (d 1965), of 33 Bailey St, Mountain Ash, Glamorgan; 1 s (David b 1957), 1 da (Margaret b 1959); *Career* res fell Harvard Univ 1951-52, prof of chemistry UCL 1971- (asst lectr 1952-55, lectr 1955-65, reader 1965-71); chm Bd of Studies in Chemistry Univ of London 1983-85; awards: Ramsay medal 1950, Organic Reaction Mechanisms Royal Soc of Chemistry 1984; FRSC 1971; *Books* Aromatic Substitution (with P B D De La Mare, 1959); *Recreations* photography; *Style—* Prof John Ridd; Chemistry Dept, Univ College, 20 Gordon St, London WC1H 0AJ (☎ 071 387 7050 ext 4706, fax 071 380 7463)

RIDDELL, (William) James; MBE (1944); s of Col Archibald Riddell, DSO (d 1970), of Surrey, and Edith Mary, *née* Lawrie (d 1947); descended from Sir Walter Riddell, 2 Bt; *b* 27 Dec 1909; *Educ* Harrow, Clare Coll Cambridge; *m* 1, 1 Dec 1959, Jeannette Anne Oddie (d 1972), da of late Edward Kessler, of Manchester; m 2, 1972, Alison, da of Arthur Newton Jackson (d 1961), of Wilmslow; 1 da (Jemma Jeannette b 1976); *Career* WW II ADC to High Cmmr of Palestine and Trans-Jordan 1939-41, political offr (Capt): Syria and Lebanon, Beirut, Homs, Damascus, frequently with French Foreign Legion 1941; started up, organised and ran (as Maj) ME Mountain Warfare Ski Sch at Cedars of Lebanon 1941-44; led WO team of 15 observers on exercise 'Polar Bear' crossing the coastal range of British Columbia, subsequently coordinated WO trg pamphlets 1-5 on snow and mountain warfare; author of 27 books, some self illustrated; has worked freelance with Baynard Press, Selfridges, de Havilland Aircraft and others 1930-37; skiing - first season 1920 (Mürren), subsequently memb Br Ski Team 1929-36, winner of 1929 'Inferno', winner of combined Anglo-Swiss 1931, Br ski champion 1934, vice capt Br Olympic ski team 1936, awarded Pery medal 1962, Arnold Lunn medal 1979; *Books* Inside Britain, Outside Britain, Animal Lore and Disorder, In the Forests of the Night, Flight of Fancy, Dog in the Snow, The Holy Land, Ski Runs of Switzerland; *Recreations* landscape gardening, watercolours, anglo/swiss relationship; *Clubs* White's, Ski Club of GB, Kandahar Ski, Alpine Ski, DHO, Eagles, Martini Int, Swiss Academic Ski; *Style—* James Riddell, Esq, MBE; Foresters, Hightown Hill, Ringwood, Hants (☎ 04254 3593); 17 Hyde Park Gardens Mews, London W2 (☎ 071 723 2802)

RIDDELL, Sir John Charles Buchanan; 13 Bt (NS 1628), of Riddell, Roxburghshire, DL (Northumberland 1990); s of Sir Walter Riddell, 12 Bt (d 1934), and Hon Rachel Lyttelton, JP (d 1965) (yst da of 8 Viscount Cobham, JP, DL, and Hon Mary Cavendish, da of 2 Baron Chesham); *b* 3 Jan 1934; *Educ* Eton, Ch Ch Oxford (BA, MA); *m* 1969, Hon Sarah, da of Baron Richardson of Duntisbourne, KG, MBE, PC, *qv*, sometime govr of Bank of England; 3 s (Walter b 1974, Hugh b 1976, Robert b 1982); *Heir* s, Walter John Riddell b 10 June 1974; *Career* 2 Lt 2KRRC; CA; banker; contested (C) Durham NW Feb 1974, Sunderland S Oct 1974; dir: UK Provident 1975-85, First Boston (Europe) Ltd 1975-78, dep chm IBA 1981-85, dir: Northern Rock Bldg Soc 1981-85, Credit Suisse First Boston 1978-85; private sec and treas to TRH The Prince and Princess of Wales 1985-; memb Prince's Cncl; FRSA 1989; *Clubs* Garrick, Northern Countries; *Style—* Sir John Riddell, Bt, DL; Hepple, Morpeth, Northumberland; Wien House, Kensington Palace, London W8 4PL

RIDDELL, Norman Malcolm Marshall; *b* 30 June 1947; *m* ; 3 s; *Career* Royal Bank of Scotland plc 1965-79: commercial banking 1965-69, res analyst 1969-73, investmt analyst 1973-74, head of Investmt Res Dept and i/c of holdings in US 1974-79; dir Britannia Group of Unit Trusts Ltd 1980-85 (sr investmt mangr 1979-80), md Britannia Unit Trust Managers Ltd 1985-86, chief investmt dir then md Britannia Group of Investment Companies 1982-86, chief exec Capital House Investment Management Ltd 1986-; AIB (Scot) 1969, ASIA 1974; *Recreations* sports, travel, plate collecting; *Clubs* Hanbury Manor, Sloane; *Style—* Norman Riddell, Esq; Capital House Investment Management Ltd, 24 Chiswell Street, London EC1Y 4SP (☎ 071 638 2288)

RIDDELL-CARRE, Ralph John; s of Gervase Robert Riddell-Carre (d 1989), and Eileen Inez, *née* Tweedie; *b* 8 Oct 1941; *Educ* Harrow; *m* 1972, Valerie Caroline, da of late Walter Thomas Wells Tickler; 3 s (John Timothy b 1976, Peter Thomas b 1979, David Alexander b 1983); *Career* Lindsay Jamieson & Haldane Edinburgh 1960-65, Ernst & Young (formerly Arthur Young, Arthur Young McClelland Moores & Co, McClelland Moores & Co) 1965- (ptnr 1974-); MICAS 1965; *Recreations* golf; *Style—* Ralph Riddell-Carre, Esq; Ernst & Young, Becket House, 1 Lambeth Palace Rd, London SE1 7EU (☎ 071 928 2000, fax 071 928 1345)

RIDDELL-WEBSTER, John Alexander; MC (1943); s of Gen Sir Thomas Sheridan Riddell-Webster, GCB, DSO, DL (d 1974), of Lintrose, Coupar Angus, and Harriet Hill, *née* Sprot (d 1977); *b* 17 July 1921; *Educ* Harrow, Pembroke Coll Cambridge; *m* 16 Jan 1960, Ruth, da of (Samuel Plenderleith) Laurence Lithgow (d 1972), of The Old House, Great Barton, Suffolk; 2 s (Michael b 1960, Thomas b 1962), 1 da (Caroline b 1964); *Career* served Seaforth Highlanders 1940-46: UK, Madagascar, India, Paiforce, Syria, Sicily (wounded, MC), WO 1944-45, Staff Capt and DAQMG, BAOR 1945-46; Anglo-Iranian Oil Co (later BP): joined 1946, served Iran, Iraq, Bahrain and London 1946-54, Aden and Basrah 1954-55, London 1954-56, Canada 1956-63 (vice pres mktg BP Canada 1959-63), London 1963-80 (dir Shell Mex and BP 1965, md mktg 1971-75, md mktg BP Oil Ltd 1976-80), ret 1980; dir of Scot affairs BP Edinburgh 1980-82; farmer 1982-; memb Cncl: Incorporated Soc of Br Advertisers 1967-80, Advtg Assoc

1973-80, British Roads Fedn 1975-80, Royal Warrant Holders Assoc 1967 (pres 1980); memb Automobile Assoc Ctee 1980-90, pres Oil Industries Club 1977-78, chm Transport Action Scotland 1982; elected regnl cncllr Tayside 1986; CBIM, FInstPet; *Recreations* shooting, fishing, gardening; *Clubs* New (Edinburgh), Royal Perth Golfing Soc; *Style—* John Riddell-Webster, Esq; Lintrose, Coupar Angus, Perthshire PH13 9JQ (☎ 0828 27472)

RIDDELSDELL, Dame Mildred; DCB (1972), CBE (1958); da of Rev H J Riddelsdell; *b* 1 Dec 1913; *Educ* St Mary's Hall Brighton, Bedford Coll London; *Career* asst sec Min of Nat Insur 1945, under sec 1950, loaned to UN 1953-56, sec Nat Incomes Cmmn 1962-65, second perm sec DHSS 1971-73, chm CS Retirement Fellowship 1974-77; *Style—* Dame Mildred Riddelsdell, DCB, CBE; 26A New Yatt Rd, Witney, Oxon

RIDDICK, Graham Edward Galloway; MP (C) Colne Valley 1987-; s of John Julian Riddick, of Coldstream House, Shipton-under-Wychwood, Oxford, and Cecilia Margaret, da of Sir Edward Ruggles-Brise, 1 Bt, MC, TD, MP for Maldon (Essex) 1922-42; *b* 26 Aug 1955; *Educ* Stowe, Univ of Warwick; *m* 1988, Sarah Northcroft; 1 s (George James Galloway b 5 Jan 1991); *Career* PPS to Hon Francis Maude, MP (fin sec to the Treasy) 1990-; former chm Angola Study Gp, former vice chm Cons Back Bench Employment Ctee; former sec: All Pty Wool Textile Parly Gp, Cons Back Bench Trade and Industry Cte; chm N Yorks Freedom Assoc (memb Nat Cncl); *Recreations* shooting, fishing, tennis, squash, bridge; *Clubs* Carlton, Yorks Cricket; *Style—* Graham Riddick, Esq, MP; c/o House of Commons, Westminster, London SW1A 0AA (☎ 071 219 4215)

RIDDICK, Stewart Keith; s of Walter Claude Riddick, of Swindon, Wilts, and Margaret, *née* Lowman; *b* 17 Sept 1944; *Educ* Warneford Sch Highworth; *m* 2 Sept 1973, Victoria, da of Max Heliczer (d 1972), 2 s (Simon b 11 Oct 1979, Jonathan b 24 Sept 1983); *Career* chm SKR Group; memb: Fin Ctee Dacorum Volunteer Bureau, advsr Douglas Bader Fndn, Br Paraplegic Sports Assoc; Freeman City of London, Liveryman Worshipful Co of Joiners and Ceilers; FInstD; *Recreations* sailing, golf, shooting; *Style—* Stewart Riddick, Esq; Stewart House, 930 High Rd, London N12 9RT (☎ 081 446 4131, fax 081 291 801, car 0836 212 022, telex 24108 JAYBEE)

RIDDLE, Howard Charles Frazer; s of Cecil Riddle (d 1987), of Sevenoaks, Kent, and Eithne, *née* McKenna; *b* 13 Aug 1947; *Educ* Judd Sch Tonbridge, LSE (LLB); *m* 31 Aug 1974, (Susan) Hilary, da of Dr André Hurst, of Ottawa, Canada; 2 da (Stephanie b 1979, Poppy b 1984); *Career* SSRC Canada 1971-76, sr ptnr Edward Fail Bradshaw & Waterson 1985-; memb Law Soc 1978 (London Area Ctee 1986); *Recreations* rugby football; *Style—* Howard Riddle, Esq; Norton Cottage, Bethersden, Kent; Edward Fail Bradshaw & Waterson, 402 Commercial Rd, Stepney, London E1 0LG (☎ 071 790 4032, fax 071 790 2739)

RIDDLE, Brig Robert William; OBE (1974); s of Harold Riddle (d 1963), of Galashiels, and Clare, *née* Powell (d 1972); *b* 19 Jan 1933; *Educ* Stonyhurst, RMA Sandhurst; *m* 4 April 1959, Ann Mary Munro, da of John Grant Munro Millar (d 1987), of West Linton; 3 da (Frances b 23 Jan 1961, Fiona b 16 July 1963, Kirsty b 5 Feb 1966); *Career* 2 Lt KOSB 1953, Staff Coll Camberley 1961, CO 1 Bn KOSB 1971, mil sec C in C BAOR 1974, Col A/Q 3 Armoured Div 1977, Brig Scot Div 1980 (ret), Col KOSB 1985, Hon Col 2/52 Lowland Vols 1990; gen sec: Royal Br Legion Scot, The Earl Haig Fund Scot, The Offrs Assoc Scot 1983; memb Queens Bodyguard for Scot (Royal Co of Archers); *Recreations* field sports, golf; *Clubs* New (Edinburgh); *Style—* Brig Robert Riddle, OBE; Old Harestanes, Blyth Bridge, West Linton, Peebleshire EH46 7AH (☎ 0721 52255), New Haig House, Logie Green Rd, Edinburgh EH7 4HR (☎ 031 5572782, fax 031 5575819)

RIDDY, John Charles Philip; s of Prof Donald C Riddy, CBE (d 1979), and Kathleen Constance (d 1985); *b* 21 June 1934; *Educ* St Paul's, Hertford Coll Oxford (MA); *m* 2 Sept 1963, Felicity Jacqueline, da of Dr Kenneth John Maidment; 1 s (Gerson b 1964), 2 da (Francesca b 1966, Myrianthe b 1976); *Career* Flt Offr RAF 1955; Stirling Univ: business mangr 1969-89, conslt on conf matters 1989-; pres Assoc of Self-Catering Op Scotland; co-fndr British Univ Accommodation Consortium (BUAC) 1970, fndr Open Univ Hosts Club; FPWI (1974), MHCIMA (1978); Hon MUniv Open Univ; *Books* Hodson of Hodson's Horse (biog), Gen Sir John Cotton (biog), J G Farrell (study of writings), European Settlement in India 1780-1870, Warren Hasting's Scottish Supporters; *Recreations* cricket, swimming, snooker; *Style—* John Riddy, Esq; 3 Main St, Wilberfoss, York YO4 5NP (☎ 075 95 632); work (☎ 0786 73171)

RIDEL, David William; s of Maurice William Ridel, of 5 Noon Hill Drive, Verwood, Wimborne, Dorset, and Violet Georgina, *née* Tull (d 1983); *b* 20 Dec 1947; *Educ* Forest GS Wokingham Berks, Univ of Bristol (BA, B'Arch); *m* 23 Nov 1971, Felicity Laura, da of Rev Thomas Herbert Lewis; 2 s (Thomas William b 6 Jan 1976, Jack William b 7 Feb 1983), 1 da (Gemma Laura b 31 July 1977); *Career* architectural asst Marshall Macklin Monaghan Toronto Canada 1969-70, assoc architect Richard Lee Architect Bristol 1972-75, chief architect Community Housing Architects Team London 1975-79, chief exec Community Housing Assoc London 1979, sr architect YRM Architects London 1979-86; Building Design Partnership: sr architect 1986-, assoc 1987, ptnr 1989; corp memb RIBA 1974; *Recreations* skiing, jogging, windsurfing, ballet, opera, theatre; *Style—* David Ridel, Esq; Building Design Partnership, PO Box 4WD, 16 Gresse St, London W1A 4WD (☎ 071 631 4733)

RIDEOUT, Paul David; s of David Julian Rideout, of Swindon, Wilts, and Glenys, *née* Jefferies; *b* 14 Aug 1964; *Educ* Kingsdown Sch Swindon; *m* 15 July 1988, Carolyn, da of Raymond Edward Whatley; 1 s (Benjamin Paul b 19 Oct 1988); *Career* professional footballer; Swindon Town 1981-83 (95 appearances), Aston Villa 1983-85 960 appearances), Bari Italy 1985-88 (120 appearances), Southampton 1988- (over 80 appearances); England: 14 schoolboy under 15 caps (scored on each appearance at Wembley incl hat-trick v Scotland), 12 youth caps, 6 under 21 caps; *Recreations* golf, snooker, tennis; *Style—* Paul Rideout, Esq; John Mac, 1st Floor, Keystone, 60 London Rd, St Albans, Herts AL1 1NG (☎ 0727 48564); Southampton FC, The Dell, Milton Rd, Southampton S09 4XX (☎ 0703 220505)

RIDEOUT, Prof Roger William; s of Sidney Rideout (d 1949), of Bromham, Bedfordshire, and Hilda Rose, *née* Davies (d 1985); *b* 9 Jan 1935; *Educ* UCL (LLB, PhD); *m* 1, 30 July 1960 (m dis 1978), Marjorie Roberts, da of Albert Roberts of Bedford; 1 da (Tania Mary b 1965); m 2, 24 Aug 1978, Gillian Margaret, *née* Lynch; *Career* Nat Serv Lt RAEC 1958-60; lectr: Univ of Sheffield 1960-63, Univ of Bristol 1963-64; called to the Bar Gray's Inn 1964; prof of lab law UCL 1973- (reader in Eng law 1965-73, sr lectr 1964-65); vice dean and dep head Dept of Law UCL 1982-89 (dean of faculty 1975-77); memb Phelps-Brown Ctee 1967-68, chm Industl Law Soc 1977-80 (vice pres 1983-), pt/t chm Indust Tbnls 1983-, dep chm Central Arbitration Ctee 1978-; *Clubs* MCC; *Style—* Prof Roger Rideout; 255 Chipstead Way, Woodmansterne, Surrey SM7 3JW (☎ 073 7552033); Faculty of Laws University College London, Bentham House, Endsleigh Gardens, London WC1H OEG (☎ 071 380 7022, 071 387 7050 ext 2113)

RIDGEON, David Cyril Elliot; s of Cyril Elliot Ridgeon (d 1973), and Kathleen Joan, *née* Miller; *b* 6 May 1935; *Educ* Monkton Combe Sch Bath; *m* 30 Sept 1961, Jill Elizabeth, da of Lewis Starling (d 1966); 2 da (Rachel b 1962, Anne b 1966); *Career* builders merchant and timber importer; dir: Cyril Ridgeen and Son Ltd 1960-, Ridgeons (Saffron Warden) Ltd (previously Saffron Walden Building Material Supply Co Ltd) 1986- (joined 1960), CRS (wholesale) Ltd 1976-, National Home Improvements Cncl 1991; pres Builders Merchant Fedn 1989-90; Liveryman Worshipful Co of Builders Merchants; *Recreations* tennis; *Clubs* Rotary; *Style—* David Ridgeon, Esq; Rectory Farm, Madingley Rd, Coton, Cambridge CB3 7PG; Tenison Rd, Cambridge (☎ 0223 61177)

RIDGEON, Jonathan Peter; s of Peter James Ridgeon, of 60 Spring Close, Burwell, Cambridge, and Margaret Jane, *née* Allum; *b* 14 Feb 1967; *Educ* Newmarket Upper Sch, Magdalene Coll Cambridge; *Career* 110m hurdler, Euro jr champion 1985, second World Jr Championships 1986, second World Championships 1987 (Br record time), AAA champion 1987, World Student Games champion 1987, fifth Olympic Games Seoul 1988; *Recreations* tennis; *Clubs* Hawks, Achilles Athletics; *Style—* Jonathan Ridgeon, Esq; 60 Spring Close, Burwell, Cambridge

RIDGES, Martin John; s of John Rendel Ridges (d 1979), of New Earswick, York, and Muriel Iredale, *née* Walker; *b* 14 March 1926; *Educ* Bootham Sch York, Univ of Manchester (BA); *m* 16 July 1955, (Amy) Pauline Ridges, da of Edgar Percy Dale (d 1961), of Christchurch, Hants; 2 s (Peter b 1962, David b 1965); *Career* CA; ptnr Hodgson Morris & Co 1963-68, mgmnt accountant Morison Pollexfen & Blair Ltd 1971-74, sr internal auditor Ocean Transport & Trading plc 1981-88, co sec The Clinical Pathology Laboratories Ltd 1988-; hon auditor: Liverpool Branch Chartered Secs and Admin, Dalton Hall Centenary Fund; ACIS 1956, FCA 1960, MIIA 1983; *Recreations* walking, gardening, photography, travel; *Clubs* Rucksack; *Style—* Martin Ridges, Esq; Coneacres, Grammar School Lane, Wirral, Merseyside L48 8AY (☎ 051 625 5610); Les Emeraudes, 83420 La Croix Valmer, Var, France; The Clinical Pathology Laboratories Limited, 27 Rodney St, Liverpool L1 9EH (☎ 051 708 6767)

RIDGEWAY, Lt Cdr Thomas Graeme; s of Charles Lennox Ridgeway (d 1957), and Dorothy Sydney, *née* Wasbrough (d 1989); *b* 29 Dec 1918; *Educ* RNC Dartmouth; *m* 17 July 1948 (m dis 1957), Jane, da of late Adm Sir Lewis Clinton-Baker, KCB, KCVO, CBE, of Bayfordbury, Herts; 1 s (Rupert b 18 Dec 1950); *Career* RN 1932-59; WWII submarines 1940-47, cmd HMS Templar 1944-46; post-war cmd: HMS Fame, HMS Ulysses, HMS Carisbrooke Castle; Admty 1957-59, ret 1959; fenced and shot for both the Navy and Devon; master mariner 1970-82; Hereditary Freeman City of Exeter; *Recreations* hunting, fishing, shooting, sailing; *Clubs* Royal Naval; *Style—* Lt Cdr Thomas Ridgeway; Higher Hill, Hittesleigh, nr Exeter (☎ 064 723 348)

RIDGWAY, George; s of John George Ridgway (d 1988), of Leicester, and Constance Winifred, *née* Bruce (d 1980); *b* 16 Oct 1945; *Educ* Wyggeston Sch, Leicester Poly; *m* 20 June 1970, Mary Chamberlain, da of John Chamberlain; 2 c (Imogen Kate b 6 Nov 1973, Julian George b 14 March 1978); *Career* sr ptnr: Austin & Co Leicester 1976-86 (articled clerk 1965-72), Pole Arnold (following merger) 1986- (mangr 1972-76); fin dir and co sec Ridgway & Co (Leicester) Ltd 1985- (dir 1985-); memb Small Practioners Ctee ICAEW 1980-88, memb Ctee Leics and Northants Soc of CAs 1980- (pres 1990); former chm: Young Farmers Leics, Young Cons Leics; memb Leics RU Colts 1963, (selector 1980-85); trialist Midlands 1963; Aylestone St James RFC: 503 first XV appearances, capt 1972-74, pres 1982-84, chm 1984-86; chm Leics RU Colts 1986-88 (sec 1983-86), sec Midlands RU Colts 1984-88 (selector 1987-88); FCA (ACA 1972), FInstD 1980; *Recreations* Rugby Union, flying, engineering and aeronautical history; *Clubs* Leicestershire Aero, Aylestone St James RFC; *Style—* George Ridgway, Esq; 449 London Road, Leicester LE2 3JW (☎ 0533 705203); Pole Arnold, Chartered Accountants, Stoughton House, Harborough Rd, Oadby, Leicester LE2 4LP (☎ 0533 717551, fax 0533 710597)

RIDGWAY, (Charles) Ian; s of Harry Ridgway (d 1972),m of Hawthorn Cottage, Sandal, Wakefield, Yorks, and Eva, *née* Whitehead (d 1973); *b* 6 Jan 1934; *Educ* Queen Elizabeth GS Wakefield, Wakefield Tech Coll; *m* 22 Sept 1960, (Margaret) Heather, da of Reginald Arthur Wilkinson, of Pontefract, Yorks; 1 s (Mark b 1962), 1 da (Jacqui b 1964); *Career* Nat Serv 1951-53; tool engr Slater and Crabtree Ltd 1956-57, sales dir Rhodes Cowlishaw Sales Co Ltd 1972-78, md Rhodes Interform Ltd 1978-84, md Joseph Rhodes Ltd 1989- (mgmnt apprentice 1954, commercial dir 1967-72, jt md 1984); chm: Wakefield and Dist Engrs Employers Fedn 1965-69, Wakefield Sr C of C 1970-71, Ecclesiastical Tst Wakefield Cathedral 1969-, Metalforming Machinery Mfrs Assoc 1976-80, Europ Power Pres Mfrs Panel 1977-81; FBIM 1969; *Recreations* restoration of vintage cars; *Style—* Ian Ridgway, Esq; Hawthorn Cottage, Sandal Ave, Wakefield, Yorks WF2 7LD (☎ 0924 255119); Joseph Rhodes Ltd, Belle Vue, Wakefield, Yorks WF1 5EQ (☎ 0924 371161, fax 0924 370928, car 0836 316695, telex 55339)

RIDGWAY, Judith Anne (Judy); da of Dr Leslie Randal Ridgway, of Eastbourne, and Lavinia, *née* Bottomley; *Educ* St Christopher Sch Letchworth Garden City, Univ of Keele; *Career* former assoc dir Welbeck PR; cookery ed Woman's World Magazine 1984-90; freelance writer on: food, wine, cookery, catering, travel; memb: Guild of Food Writers, Circle of Wine Writers (prog sec), Soc of Authors; companion Guide de Fromagers, Confrerie de St Uguzon 1990; *Cookery Books (adult)*: The Vegetarian Gourmet (1979), Salad Days (1979), Home Preserving (1980), The Seafood Kithen (1980), The Colour Book of Chocolate Cookery (1981), Mixer, Blender, Processor Cookery (1981), The Breville Book of Toasted Sandwiches (1982), Waitrose Book of Pasta, Rice and Pulses (1982), Making the Most of: Rice, Pasta, Potatoes, Bread, Cheese, Eggs (1983), The Little Lemon Book, The Little Rice Book, The Little Bean Book (1983), Barbecues (1983), Cooking with German Food (1983), Frying Tonight (1984), Sprouting Beans and Seeds (1984), Man in the Kitchen (jtly, 1984), Nuts and Cereals (1985), The Vegetable Year (1985), Winning and Dinning at Home (1985), Wheat and Gluten-Free Cookery (1986), Vegetarian Wok Cookery (1986), Cheese and Cheese Cookery (1986), 101 Ways with Chicken Pieces (1987), Pocket Book of Oils, Vinegars and Seasonings (jtly, 1989), Carr's Connoisserus Cheese Guide (1989); The Vitimin and Mineral Diet Cookbook (1990); *Wine*: The Wine Lover's Record Book (1988), The Little Red Wine Book (1989), The Little White Wine Book (1989); *Cookery Children*: 101 Fun Foods to Make (1982), Cooking Round the World (1983), Festive Occasions (1986), Food and Cooking Round the World (jtly, 1986); *How to Books*: Home Cooking for Money (1983), Running Your Own Wine Bar (1984), Successful Media Relations (1984); *Recreations* opera, bridge, walking, cycling; *Style—* Ms Judy Ridgway; 124 Queens Court, Queensway, London W2 4QS (☎ 071 727 5050)

RIDGWAY, Laurence Victor; s of Hugh Bernard Ridgway (d 1956), of Spencer Rd, Harrow Weald, Middx, and Leonora, *née* Herger (d 1962); *b* 18 Dec 1915; *Educ* Harrow Business Coll; *m* 9 Aug 1941, Marie, da of Franz Breier (d 1927), of Ybbs an der Donau, Austria; 1 da (Heather-Ann (Mrs Clint) b 22 Feb 1944); *Career* cmmnd 2 Bn The Hampshire Regt 1942, Liaison Offr 209 Bde HQ 1942 (camp cmdt 1943), Staff Capt Allied Cmmn for Austria 1944, Maj and dep dir Army Welfare Servs BTA HQ Vienna; advertisement dir Tobacco magazine 1947-62, dir Trade Pubns Ltd 1962, md Int Trade Pubns Ltd 1963-80 (launched series of int business magazines, World Tobacco, International Tax Free Trader, Tableware International, Coffee International, Marine Stores International, Midle East Education), dir Industl Newspapers Ltd 1980 (sub-ed 1934-39), owner of the Ridgway Press 1980-; Freeman City of London 1966, Liveryman Worshipful Co of Tobacco Pipe Makers and Tobacco Blenders 1969; *Books* Stories of The Operas (co-ed, 1946); *Clubs* MCC; *Style—* Laurence Ridgway, Esq;

Sunrise House, Midford Lane, Limpley Stoke, Bath BA3 6JR (☎ 0225 723502)

RIDGWELL, Patrick John; s of Joseph Thomas Ridgwell (d 1969), and Ida May Mann (d 1988); *b* 15 March 1930; *Educ* St David's Coll Lampeter, Corpus Christi Coll Cambridge (MA); *m* 1965, Maryla, da of Capt Maximillian Statter (d 1947); 1 s (Jolyon b 1967), 1 da (Caroline b 1965); *Career* md Anthony Wieler & Co Ltd 1972-89; dir: Anthony Wieler Unit Tst Mgmnt 1973-89, Arbuthnot Unit Tst Mgmnt 1989-; chm The Assoc of Ind Investmt Mangrs 1976-88, pres Exec Int Investors 1978-83; *Recreations* choral singing, mountain walking, architecture; *Clubs* United Oxford and Cambridge Univ; *Style—* Patrick Ridgwell, Esq; Hambutts House, Painswick, Glos GL6 6UP; 131 Finsbury Pavement, London EC2A 1AY (☎ 071 628 9876, fax 071 280 8603, telex 885970)

RIDING, Peter Anthony; s of William Riding (d 1990), and Ina, *née* Bunnell; *b* 3 Nov 1941; *Educ* St Paul's Sch Sao Paulo Brazil, Rossall Sch, Imperial Coll London (BSc); *m* (m dis); 1 s (Dominic William b 27 Nov 1972); m2, 27 July 1990, Marylyn Susan (Lyn); *Career* BBC TV: researcher 1966-67, prodn asst 1967-68, asst prodr 1969-70, prodr 1970-74, sr prodr 1974-79, exec prodr 1980-; dep head Continuing Educn and Training Television 1991-; ARCS; *Recreations* tennis, photography, yoga, DIY; *Style—* Peter Riding, Esq; BBC Television, Villers House, The Broadway, London W5 2PA (☎ 081 991 8007, fax 081 567 9356)

RIDING, Robert Furniss; s of William Furniss Riding (d 1985), of Manchester, and Winifred, *née* Coupe; *b* 5 May 1940; *Educ* Stockport GS, Ch Ch Oxford (MA); *Career* dir and later chm Nat Commercial Devpt Capital Ltd 1980-85, gen mangr Williams & Glyn's Bank plc 1982-85, treas and gen mangr The Royal Bank of Scot plc 1985-86, dep chm and chief exec RoyScot Fin Group plc 1986-90; chm: RoyScot Tst plc 1986-90, Royal Bank Leasing Ltd 1986-90, RoyScot Vehicle Contracts Ltd 1986-90, RoyScot Factors Ltd 1986-90, RoyScot Fin Servs Ltd 1988-90; dir: Int Commodities Clearing House Ltd 1985-86, Royal Bank of Scot AG (Switzerland) 1985-86, Royal Bank of Scot Group Insurance Co Ltd 1986-88, Royal Bank Gp Servs Ltd 1987-90, Mays Group plc 1988-90; tstee and former chm Assoc of Sea Trg Orgns, memb cncl and chm trg The Royal Yachting Assoc 1984-89; tstee Seamanship Foundation 1990-; *Recreations* sailing; *Clubs* Island Cruising (vice pres, cdre 1988-90); *Style—* Robert Riding, Esq; Blandford House, Blandford Close, Maybury, Woking, Surrey GU22 7EJ (☎ 0483 770376); Middlewood, Old Banwell Road, Locking, Avon BS24 8BT (☎ 0934 822587); 2 Garden Close, Salcombe, S Devon TQ8 8DR

RIDLER, Anne Barbara; da of Henry Christopher Bradby (d 1947), and Violet Alice, *née* Milford (d 1956); *b* 30 July 1912; *Educ* Downe House Sch, Kings Coll London; *m* 2 July, 1938, Vivian Hughes Ridler, s of Bertram Hughes Ridler (d 1934); 2 s (Benedict b 1947, Colin b 1952), 2 da (Jane b 1941, Kate b 1943); *Career* sec and asst ed to T S Eliot Faber and Faber (publishers of The Criterion quarterly); memb Literary Panel for New English Bible Old Testament; *Books* New and Selected Poems (1988); verse plays incl: The Trial of Thomas Cranmer (1956), The Jesse Tree (1972); ed: Image of the City (1958), Poems of James Thomson (1963), Poems of Thomas Traherne (1966), Poems of George Darley (1979), A Victorian Family Postbag (1988); *Style—* Mrs Anne Ridler

RIDLEY, (Hon) (Helen Laura) Cressida; *née* Bonham Carter; da of Baroness Asquith of Yarnbury (Life Peer, d 1969); *b* 1917; *m* does not use courtesy title; 1939, Jasper Alexander Maurice Ridley, Lt KRRC (d on active service 1943); 1 s; *Style—* Mrs Ridley; Keeper's Cottage, Great Bottom, Stockton, Warminster, Wilts

RIDLEY, Sir Adam Nicholas; s of Jasper Ridley (s of Maj Hon Sir Jasper Ridley, KCVO, OBE, 2 s of 1 Viscount Ridley, by the Maj's w Countess Nathalie, da of Count Benckendorff, sometime Russian ambass in London) and Cressida Bonham Carter (da of Baroness Asquith of Yarnbury and gda of H H Asquith the Lib PM); nephew by marriage of Baron Grimond, TD, PC, of Firth, Co Orkney; *b* 14 May 1942; *Educ* Eton, Balliol Coll Oxford, Univ of California Berkeley; *m* 1, 1970 (m dis), Lady Katharine Rose Celestine Asquith, 2 da of 2 Earl of Oxford and Asquith; m 2, 1981, Margaret Anne (Biddy), da of Frederic Passmore, of Virginia Water, Surrey; 3 s (Jasper b 29 May 1987, Luke (twin) b 29 May 1987, Jo b 16 Aug 1988); *Career* Dep of Economic Affairs 1965-69, HM Treasy 1970-71, Central Policy Review Staff 1971-74; former econ advsr and asst dir CRD, dir CRD 1979 election campaign; special advsr: to the Chllr of the Exechequer 1979-84, to Chllr of the Duchy of Lancaster; min in charge of the office of Arts and Libraries (also mangr Personnel Office) 1985; appts dir Hambro's Bank & Hambro's plc 1985, dir Strauss Turnbull 1986, dep chm SGST Securities 1988, Sunday Correspondent 1988; kt 1985; *Style—* Sir Adam Ridley

RIDLEY, Hon Mrs (Annabel); da of 9 Baron Hawke (1985); *b* 27 Aug 1940; *Educ* Hatherop Castle Sch; *m* 1961, Nicholas Adam Ridley, s of Rev Michael Ridley (d 1953); 1 s, 2 da; *Career* artist, glass engraver; *Recreations* singing, tennis; *Style—* The Hon Mrs Ridley; 29 Richmond Hill, Richmond, Surrey (☎ 081 940 1732)

RIDLEY, Viscountess; Lady Anne Katharine; *née* Lumley; da of late 11 Earl of Scarbrough, KG, GCSI, GCIE, GCVO, TD, PC, and Katharine, *née* McEwen, DCVO; *b* 16 Nov 1928; *m* 3 Jan 1953, 4 Viscount Ridley, *qv*; *Style—* The Rt Hon The Viscountess Ridley; Blagdon, Seaton Burn, Northumberland

RIDLEY, Dame (Mildred) Betty; DBE (1975); da of Rt Rev Henry Mosley (d 1948), sometime Bishop of Southwell, and Mildred, *née* Willis (d 1963); *b* 10 Sept 1909; *Educ* North London Collegiate Sch, Cheltenham Ladies' Coll; *m* 3 Sept 1929, Rev Michael Ridley (d 1953), Rector of Finchley, s of Samuel Forde Ridley (d 1942); 3 s (Simon b 1933, Adam b 1937, Giles b 1946), 1 da (Clare (Mrs West) b 1930); *Career* vice pres Br Cncl of Churches 1954-56, church cmmr 1958-81, memb Gen Synod of C of E 1970-81, Third Church Estates cmmr 1972-81; govr: King Alfred's Coll Winchester, St Gabriel's Sch Newbury; MA Lambeth 1958; *Recreations* making and listening to music; *Clubs* Reform; *Style—* Dame Betty Ridley, DBE; 6 Lions Hall, St Swithun St, Winchester SO23 9HW (☎ 0962 55009)

RIDLEY, Lt Cdr (Charles) David Matthew; s of Arthur Hilton Ridley, CBE (d 1974), of Park End, Simonburn, Hexham, and Kathleen Thelma (d 1982); *b* 27 June 1928; *Educ* RNC Dartmouth; *m* 1960, Alison Hay (d 1989), da of Major David Hay Thorburn (d 1963), of Burnside, Fairlie, Ayrshire; 1 s; *Career* Lt Cdr RN on staff of SNO W Indies 1958-60, FOST 1960-62, HMS Ganges 1962-64, CINC S Atlantic 1964-66; farmer 1966-; chm Hexham Constituency Cons Assoc 1985-88 (pres 1988-91); High Sheriff Northumberland 1981; *Recreations* gardening, shooting; *Style—* Lt Cdr David Ridley; Little Park End, Simonburn, Hexham, Northumberland NE48 3AE (☎ 0434 681497)

RIDLEY, (Nicholas) Harold Lloyd; s of late N C Ridley, RN of Leicester; *b* 10 July 1906; *Educ* Charterhouse, Pembroke Coll Cambridge (MA, MD), St Thomas' Hosp London; *m* 1941, Elisabeth Jane, da of late H B Wetherill, CIE; 2 s, 1 da; *Career* Temp Maj RAMC; originator of intraocular implants 1949, former hon ophthalmic surgn Royal Buckinghamshire Hosp, hon consIt in ophthalmology MOD (Army) 1964-71; hon consIt surgn: Moorfields Eye Hosp 1938-48 and 1971 (surgn 1938-71 consIt surgn 1948-71) Ophthalmic Dep St Thomas' Hosp 1971 (ophthalmic surgn 1946-71); numerous contribs in textbooks and med jls on intraocular implant surgery, tropical ophthalmology and other subjects; hon memb Oxford Ophthalmological Congress, former vice pres Ophthalmological Soc UK, hon fell Int Coll of Surgns Chicago 1952; hon memb: Peruvian Ophthalmic Soc 1957, Ophthalmological Soc Aust 1963, Aust Coll of Ophthalmologist; memb Advsy Panel Parasitology WHO 1966-71, life pres Int Intraocular Implant Club 1972; memb: Irish Ophthalmological Soc, American Soc of Cataract and Refractive Surgery (formerly American Intraocular Implants Soc) 1974-, Euro Intraocular Implantlens Cncl 1983, Opthalmological Soc UK 1984; Hon LHD Med Univ of S Carolina 1989, Hon DSc City Univ 1990; Galen Medal Apothecaries Soc 1986, Lord Crook Gold Medal Spectacle Makers Co 1987; medals: Euro Implanthens Cncl 1979, UK Intraocular Lens Soc 1984, Swedish Med Assoc 1989, Congress d'Association Francaise des Implants Intraoculan 1979; FRCS 1932, hon FRCS 1986, FRS 1986, FCOphth 1988, Hon FCOphth 1990; *Books* Monograph on Ocular Onchocerciasis; *Recreations* fly-fishing; *Clubs* Flyfishers; *Style—* Harold Ridley, Esq, FRS; Keeper's Cottage, Stapleford, Salisbury, Wilts SP3 4LT (☎ 0722 790209)

RIDLEY, Ian Robert; s of Robert Edwin Ridley, of Weymouth, Dorset, and Barbara, *née* Fullbrook; *b* 23 Jan 1955; *Educ* Hardye's Sch Dorchester Dorset, Bedford Coll London (BA); *m* 22 Oct 1977, Josephine Anne, da of Gerland Leighton; 1 s (Jack William b 6 April 1990), 1 da (Alexandra Judith b 12 Feb 1986); *Career* editorial asst Building Magazine 1976, sports ed Worksop Gaurdian 1977-79, sports sub ed and reporter Evening Post Echo Hemel Hempstead 1979-80; The Guardian: sports sub ed 1980-85, asst sports ed 1985-87, dep sports ed 1987-88, sports writer 1988-90; sports feature writer The Daily Telegraph 1990-; memb: NUJ, Football Writers' Assoc, SWA, Assoc Internationale de Presse Sportive; *Style—* Ian Ridley, Esq; The daily Telegraph, Peterborough Court at South Quay, 181 Marsh Wall, South Quay, London E14 9SR (☎ 0800 289 251, 071 538 5000)

RIDLEY, Jasper Godwin; s of Geoffrey William Ridley, OBE (d 1957), of The Manor House, W Hoathly, E Grinstead, Sussex, and Ursula Mary, *née* King; *b* 25 May 1920; *Educ* Felcourt Sch E Grinstead, Sorbonne, Magdalen Coll Oxford; *m* 1 Oct 1949, Vera, da of Emil Pollak (d 1974), of Malostranské, Nabrezí I, Prague, Czechoslovakia; 2 s (Benjamin b 1952, John b 1956), 1 da (Barbara b 1950); *Career* called to the Bar Inner Temple 1945, in practice 1946-52; cncllr St Pancras Borough Cncl 1945-49; vice chm Tunbridge Wells and Dist Writers' Circle, chm Tunbridge Wells Gp of The Ramblers Assoc; Master Worshipful Co of Carpenters 1988 and 1990 (Liveryman 1943, Warden 1985); FRSL 1963, vice pres English section of Int PEN 1985; *Books* Nicholas Ridley (1957), The Law of Carriage of Goods (1957), Thomas Cranmer (1962), John Knox (1968), Lord Palmerston (James Tait Black Memorial Prize 1970), Mary Tudor (1973), Garibaldi (1974), The Roundheads (1976), Napoleon III and Eugenie (1979), The History of England (1981), The Statesman and the Fanatic (1982), Henry VIII (1984), Elizabeth I (1987), The Tudor Age (1988), The Love Letters of Henry VIII (1989); *Recreations* chess, walking; *Style—* Jasper Ridley, Esq; 6 Oakdale Rd, Tunbridge Wells, Kent (☎ 0892 22460)

RIDLEY, Hon Mrs (Julia Harriet); *née* McLaren; er da of 3 Baron Aberconway by his 1 w; *b* 22 Sept 1942; *Educ* Grenoble Univ; *m* Charles Walter Hayes Ridley; 1 s (Casper Charles b 1977), 2 da (Emma Jane b 1970, Harriet Deirdre b 1971); *Style—* The Hon Mrs Ridley; c/o UPI, Rome, Italy

RIDLEY, Malcolm James; s of Eric Malcolm Thomas Ridley (d 1972), and Pauline Esther, (d 1972); *b* 10 March 1941; *Educ* Trinity Sch Croydon, Univ of Bristol (LLB); *m* 1, 14 July 1962 (m dis 1976), Joan Margaret, da of Stanley Charles Martin, of Alfriston, Sussex; 2 da (Camilla b 1970, Estelle b 1972); m 2, 9 April 1977, Bridget Mina, da of Charles Edward O'Keeffe (d 1963); 1 s (John b 1979), 1 da (Susannah b 1977); *Career* CA; Price Waterhouse Vancouver 1962-68, commerc Price Waterhouse London 1974-79, ptnr Coopers & Lybrand Deloitte London 1981- (joined 1979); Price Waterhouse London 1974-79, ptnr Coopers & Lybrand Deloitte London 1981- (joined 1979); memb Worshipful Co of Founders 1981; CA Canada 1966, FCA 1980, ATII 1974; *Recreations* tennis, bridge, theatre, opera; *Clubs* RAC, MCC; *Style—* Malcolm Ridley, Esq; Moor Lodge, South Holmwood, Dorking, Surrey RH5 4NA (☎ 0306 889 594); Hillgate House, 26 Old Bailey, London EC4M 7PL (☎ 071 248 3913)

RIDLEY, Mark; s of Francis Rex Ridley, of Thorpeness, Suffolk, and Ann, *née* Garrod; *b* 8 Sept 1956; *Educ* Stowe, New Coll Oxford (MA, DPhil); *Career* EPA Cephalosporin res scholar Linacre Coll Oxford 1978-81, Hayward res fell Oriel Coll Oxford 1981-83, Astor fell New Coll Oxford 1983-86, res fell St Catharine's Coll Cambridge 1986-; Gibbs Prize (Oxford, 1978), Singer Prize (Br Soc for History of Sci, 1980), Rolleston Memorial Prize (Oxford, 1982); FLS; *Books* The Explanation of Organic Diversity (1983), The Problems of Evolution (1985), Evolution and Classification (1986), Animal Behaviour (1986), The Essential Darwin (ed, 1987); *Style—* Mark Ridley, Esq; St Catharine's College, Cambridge (☎ 0223 338353); Dept of Zoology, Downing St, Cambridge CB2 3EJ (☎ 0223 336610, fax 0223 336676)

RIDLEY, Hon Matthew White; s and h of 4 Viscount Ridley, TD, JP, DL; *b* 7 Feb 1958; *Educ* Eton, Magdalen Coll, Oxford (DPhil); *m* 16 Dec 1989, Anya Christine, da of Dr Robert Hurlbert, of Houston, Texas, USA; *Career* journalist; The Economist: sci ed 1984-87, Washington corr 1987-89, American ed 1990-; winner Glaxo Sci Journalism Award 1983; *Style—* The Hon Matthew Ridley; Blagdon, Seaton Burn, Newcastle upon Tyne NE13 6DD

RIDLEY, 4 Viscount (UK 1900); Sir Matthew White Ridley; 8 Bt (GB 1756), TD, JP (1957); also Baron Wensleydale (UK 1900); s of 3 Viscount Ridley, CBE (d 1964), and Ursula, OBE, 2 da of Sir Edwin Lutyens, OM, KCIE, the architect, by Sir Edwin's w Lady Emily Lytton (da of 1 Earl of Lytton, GCB, GCSI, CIE, PC, sometime Viceroy of India and s of the novelist Bulwer Lytton, cr Baron Lytton); *b* 29 July 1925; *Educ* Eton, Balliol Coll Oxford (BA); *m* 3 Jan 1953, Lady Anne Lumley, da of 11 Earl of Scarbrough, KG, GCSI, GCIE, GCVO, PC; 1 s, 3 da; *Heir* s, Hon Matthew Ridley; *Career* served Coldstream Gds NW Euro 1943-46, Lt-Col TA, Bt-Col, Hon Col Northumberland Hussars Sqdn Queen's Own Yeo RAC TA, Col Cmdt Yeo RAC TA 1982-86; chm Northumberland CC 1967-79, pres Assoc of CCs 1979-84, chllr Newcastle Univ 1989; Lord Steward of HM's Household 1989-; chm: Northern Rock Building Society, College Valley Estates, Samares Investments; dir MMI Group Ltd; Lord-Lt for Northumberland 1984- (DL 1968); chm N of England TA&VRA 1980-84; pres Cncl of TAVRAS 1984-; Hon DCL Newcastle 1989; hon fell ARICS; OM (W Germany); *Recreations* dendrology, shooting, fishing; *Clubs* Boodle's, Pratt's; *Style—* Col the Rt Hon the Viscount Ridley; Blagdon, Seaton Burn, Newcastle on Tyne NE13 6DD (☎ 0789 236)

RIDLEY, Michael Kershaw; s of George K Ridley, of Eccleston, Chester, and Mary Partington; *b* 7 Dec 1937; *Educ* Stowe, Magdalene Coll Cambridge (MA); *m* 1968, Diana Loraine, da of Roy A McLernon, of Knowlton PQ, Canada; *Career* Grosvenor Estate Canada and US 1965-68 (London 1969-72), property mangr British and Commonwealth Shipping Co 1972-81, clerk of the Cncl Duchy of Lancaster 1981-; memb Advsy Panel Greenwich Hosp 1978-; FRICS; *Recreations* reading, golf, walking; *Clubs* Royal Mid-Surrey (Golf); *Style—* Michael K Ridley, Esq; 37 Chester Row, London SW1

RIDLEY, Rt Hon Nicholas; PC (1982), MP (C) Cirencester and Tewkesbury 1959-; s of 3 Viscount Ridley, CBE; *b* 17 Feb 1929; *Educ* Eton, Balliol Coll Oxford; *m* 1, 1950 (m dis 1974), Hon Clayre Campbell, *see* Lady Richard Percy; 3 da; m 2, 1979, Judy, da of Dr E Kendall; *Career* formerly civil engrg contractor and dir various cos; contested (C) Blyth 1955, PPS to Min Educn 1962-64, delegate to Cncl Europe and WEU 1962-66, Parly sec Miny Technology 1970, Parly under sec DTI 1970, memb Royal

Commission Historical Manuscripts 1967-79, min state FCO 1979-81, financial sec to Treasury 1981-Oct 1983, sec state Transport Oct 1983-86, sec of state for the Environment 1986-July 1989, sec of state for Trade and Indust July 1989-July 1990; *Style*— The Rt Hon Nicholas Ridley, MP; Old Rectory, Naunton, Cheltenham, Glos; 50 Warwick Sq, London SW1

RIDLEY, Brig Nicholas John; OBE (1983, MBE 1979); s of Col C W Ridley, OBE, DL, of The Glebe House, Shrawadine, nr Shrewsbury, and late Heather Cameron, *née* Christison; *b* 25 March 1941; *Educ* Shrewsbury, RMA Sandhurst; *m* 25 June 1966, (Isabel) Susan, da of (Robert) Frank Spencer-Nairn, of Castle Carey, Guernsey, Channel Islands; 1 s (Nicholas Charles Philip Christion), 2 da (Alexia Kathleen, Susan Mary); *Career* enlisted Queen's Own Cameron Highlanders 1959; Queen's Own Highlanders: 2 Lt 1962, Lt-Col 1980, CO 1 Bn 1982-84, Col 1984; mil dir of studies RMCS Shrivenham 1984-87, procurement exec project mangr 1987-88, Brig and Cdr 54 Inf Bde 1988; *Recreations* field sports, music and cabinet making; *Clubs* New (Edinburgh); *Style*— Brig Nicholas Ridley, OBE; Headquarters 54 Infantry Brigade, Prince William of Gloucester Barracks, Grantham, Lincs (☎ 0476 67413 ext 3292, fax 0476 674136 ext 3197, car 0860 368890)

RIDLEY, Capt Peter William Wake; s of Rear Adm William Terence Colbourne Ridley, CB, OBE, of Bath, and Barbara Ridley; *b* 27 Nov 1939; *Educ* Marlborough, RNC Dartmouth, RNEC Manadon (BSc London); *m* 14 Aug 1965, Jenifer Gaye, da of Capt William Jaspar MacDonald Teale, of Chicester; 2 s (Timothy b 1967, Nicolas b 1971); *Career* RNC Dartmouth 1958, HMS Belfast 1960, RNEC Manadon 1961, HMS Ark Royal 1965, RNC Greenwich 1968, HMS Andromeda 1969, Aux Machinery Engrg Estab Hasler 1970, marine engrg offr HMS Ashanti 1973, dir gen ships in Forward Design Gp 1975, MEO during building of HMS Invincible 1978, dir gen ships as asst dir marine gas turbines 1981, CO Naval Party 2010 1985, head of prog co-ordination in Chief Strategic Systems Exec 1986; MIMechE 1970; *Recreations* music (esp opera), theatre, cricket, golf; *Style*— Capt Peter Ridley, RN; National Westminster plc, 17 The Hard, Portsmouth, Hants PO1 3DU

RIDLEY, Philip Waller; CB (1978), CBE (1969); s of Lt-Col Basil White Ridley, DSO, MC (d 1969), and Frida, *née* Gutknedt (d 1956); *b* 25 March 1921; *Educ* Lewes Co Sch for Boys, Trinity Coll Cambridge (BA); *m* 1942, Mary Foye, da of E K Robins; 2 s (Timothy, Mark), 2 da (Diana) (and 1 da Helen, decd); *Career* Army 1941-46 W Africa and NW Europe, Maj Int Corps; cnsllr Br Embassy Washington 1966-70, under sec 1971-75, dep sec Dept of Trade Indust 1975-80, Civil Serv 1948-80; dir: Avon Rubber plc 1980-89, Fingerscan Development Ltd 1987-; independant industl conslt; *Recreations* country pursuits, music, skiing; *Style*— Philip Ridley, Esq; Old Chimneys, Plumpton Green, Lewes, E Sussex BN8 4EN (☎ 0273 890342)

RIDLEY, Sir Sidney; s of John William Ridley, of Lancaster; *b* 26 March 1902; *Educ* Lancaster Royal GS, Sidney Sussex Coll Cambridge (MA); *m* 1929, Dorothy, da of Oswald Hoole, of Prestwich (d 1987); 3 da; *Career* entered ICS 1926, fin sec Govt of Sind 1936, sec to Agent Gen for India in SA 1936-40, chief sec to Govt of Sind 1945, cmmr Ahmedabad 1946, cmmr Poona 1947, revenue cmmr Sind 1947-54; rep in Ghana of the W Africa Ctee 1957-60; fell and domestic bursar St John's Coll Oxford 1960-68 (emeritus fell 1969); kt 1953; *Style*— Sir Sidney Ridley; Lambrook Cottage, Waytown, Bridport, Dorset DT6 5LF (☎ 030 888 337)

RIDLEY, Rear Adm (William) Terence Colborne; CB (1968), OBE (1954); s of late W H W Ridley; *b* 9 March 1915; *Educ* RNC Dartmouth, RNEC Keyham; *m* 1938, Barbara (d 1989), da of R L Allen; 1 s; *Career* serv RN: Atlantic, Mediterranean and Pacific, Capt RNEC 1962-64, Rear Adm 1966, Adm Superintendent HM Dockyard Rosyth 1966-71, Port Adm Rosyth 1971-72; chm Ex Serv Mental Welfare Soc 1973-83; *Recreations* gardening; *Style*— Rear Adm Terence Ridley, CB, OBE; 12 New King St, Bath, Avon BA1 2BL (☎ 0225 318371)

RIDLEY, Prof Tony Melville; CBE (1986); s of John Edward Ridley (d 1982), and Olive, *née* Armstrong; *b* 10 Nov 1933; *Educ* Durham Sch, King's Coll Univ of Durham (BSc), Northwestern Univ Illinois (MS), Univ of California Berkeley (PhD); *m* 20 June 1959, Jane, da of John William Dickinson (d 1984); 2 s (Jonathan b 1963, Michael b 1966), 1 da (Sarah b 1962); *Career* Nuclear Power Gp 1957-62; GLC 1965-69; DG Tyne & Wear Passenger Tport Exec 1969-75; md Hong Kong Mass Transit Railway Corporation 1975-80; memb Bd London Regnl Tport (formerly London Tport Exec) 1980-88 (md Railways 1980-85); chm London Underground Ltd 1985-88; dir: Docklands Light Railway 1982-88 (chm 1987-88), London Transport International 1981-88 (chm 1982-87); md Eurotunnel 1989-90 (non-exec dir 1987-90), dir Halcrow Fox & Associates 1980-; Rees Jeffreys prof of tport engrg Imperial Coll London 1991-; first recipient of Highways award of Inst of Highways and Transportation 1988; Freeman City of London 1982, Liveryman Worshipful Co of Carmen 1982; FCIT, FICE, Fell Hong Kong Inst of Engineers, Memb Inst of Transportation Engrs, FRSA; *Publications* articles in transport, engineering and other journals; *Recreations* theatre, music, international affairs, rejuvenation of Britain; *Clubs* IOD, Hong Kong, Hong Kong Jockey; *Style*— Prof Tony M Ridley, CBE; 77 Church Rd, Richmond, Surrey TW10 6LX (☎ 081 948 3898); Imperial College, Dept of Civil Engineering, Transport Section, Imperial College Rd, London SW7 2BU (☎ 071 5111 ext 4715, fax 071 823 8525, telex 918351)

RIDLEY, William Patrick (Bill); s of Lt-Col J E Ridley, of Mill Moorings, Felsted, Essex, and Edith Maude, *née* Tilley; *b* 22 March 1935; *Educ* Wellington, Lincoln Coll Oxford; *m* 1, 11 July 1964 (m dis 1985), Regine Elizabeth Margarete, da of Dr Hans Doelle; 2 da (Stephanie b 16 May 1965, Kirstin b 10 Dec 1966); *m* 2, 26 March 1986, Elizabeth Marie, da of Jan Chorosz; *Career* 2 Lt bomb disposal RE 1953-55, Capt RE Res 1955-65; CA; Res Dept Bank of London and of America 1962-65, sec and accountant to Development Company subsid of Cwlth Devpt Corpn 1965-68; ptnr: Merrett Cyriax Associated Management Consultants 1968-73, Wood Mackenzie and Co 1973-86; dir: Gower Press 1970-73, Hill Samuel and Co 1986-88, County Natwest 1988-89; econ/fin conslt 1989-91; memb: Watt Ctee, Quality of Markets Ctee; ACA 1962, FCA 1973; memb Stock Exchange 1974; *Books* Company Administration Handbook (contrib, 1970), Finance and International Economy (contrib, 1987), Making Use of Economics Statistics (1986); *Recreations* travel, archaeology; *Style*— Bill Ridley, Esq; 15 John Spencer Square, London N1 (☎ 071 354 1828)

RIDLEY-THOMAS, Roger; s of John Montague Ridley-Thomas (d 1973), of Norwich, and Christina Anne, *née* Seex (d 1976); *b* 14 July 1939; *Educ* Greshams Sch; *m* 1962, Sandra Grace McBeth, da of William Morrison Young, OBE, of Gt Glen, Leics; 2 s (Christopher b 1964, Simon b 1966), 2 da (Philippa b 1970, Sarah b 1972); *Career* Royal Norfolk Regt 1958-60; newspaper publishing; Eastern Counties Newspapers Ltd 1960-65; advertisement mgmnt: Middlesbrough Evening Gazette 1965-67, Western Mail and Echo Ltd 1968-70, Newcastle Chronicle and Journal Ltd 1970-72; asst md The Scotsman Publications Ltd 1972-80, md Aberdeen Journals Ltd 1980-84, md The Scotsman Publns Ltd 1984-89, md Thomson Regnl Newspapers Ltd 1989-, chm Thomson Free Newspapers Ltd 1989-; dir: Radio Forth Ltd 1978-81, Aberdeen Journals Ltd 1980-84, 1990-, Aberdeen C of C 1981-84, Scottish Business in the Community 1984-90, The Scotsman Publications Ltd 1984-, The Scotsman Communications Ltd 1984-, Thomson Regional Newspapers Ltd 1985-, Scottish Business Achievement Award Tst Ltd 1985-, Edinburgh C of C and Mfrs 1985-88, Thomson Free Newspapers Ltd 1989-, Regnl Daily Advertising Cncl 1989-, Belfast Telegraph Newspapers Ltd 1990-, Western Mail & Echo Ltd 1990-, Chester Chronicle Ltd 1990-, Newcastle Chronicle & Journal Ltd 1990-, Thames Valley Newspapers Ltd 1990-; pres Scottish Daily Newspaper Soc 1983-85; cncl memb CBI 1983-86; Scottish Wildlife Appeal Ctee 1985-88; *Recreations* vegetable growing, shooting, fishing, golf, tennis, travel; *Clubs* New (Edinburgh), Caledonian; *Style*— Roger Ridley-Thomas, Esq; Copse Hill House, Flaunden Lane, nr Bovingdon, Herts HP3 0PA (☎ 0442 834052); Thomson Regional Newspapers Ltd, Hannay House, 39 Clarendon Rd, Watford, Herts WD1 1JA (☎ 0923 55588)

RIDOUT, Dr Alan John; s of George Alfred Ridout (d 1958), and Dorothy Evelyn, *née* Gardner (d 1985); *b* 9 Dec 1934; *Educ* Haberdashers' Aske's, Guildhall Sch of Music, RCM; *Career* composer; works incl: operas, ballets, orchestral works, choral works, chamber music, instrumental music, liturgical music; teacher: Univ of Birmingham, Univ of London, Univ of Cambridge, Oxford Univ: prof RCM 1962-82; John Collard fell Worshipful Co of Musicians 1968-71; DMus Central Sch of Religion 1980; FRCM 1981; *Books* Background to Music (1982), Background to Musical Form (1964), The Music of Howard Ferguson (1989); *Style*— Dr Alan Ridout

RIDSDALE, Sir Julian Errington; CBE (1977), MP (C) Harwich Div of Essex 1954-; s of Julian Ridsdale, of Rottingdean, Sussex; *b* 8 June 1915; *Educ* Tonbridge, RMC Sandhurst; *m* 1942, Victoire Evelyn Patricia, DBE (1991), da of Col J Bennett, of Kensington; 1 da; *Career* serv WWII Royal Norfolk Regt, Royal Scots and Somerset LI, ret as Maj 1946; contested (C): SW Islington 1949, Paddington 1951; Parly under sec state for Air and vice-pres Air Cncl 1962-64, Parly under sec RAF MOD 1964, chm Br Japanese Parly Gp 1961-, vice chm UN Parly Assoc 1966-82, ldr Parly Delgns to Japan 1973, 1975 and 1977-83; memb Trilateral Cmmn EEC, USA and Japan 1973-; memb N Atlantic Assembly 1979-; dep chm Int Triangle USA, Japan and Europe 1981-86; vice pres Political Ctee N Atlantic Assembly 1983-87; chm All Party Gp Engrg Devpt 1985-; Br Cmmr Gen Expo 90 Osaka Japan 1990; Gd Cordon Order of the Sacred Treasure (Japan) 1990; kt 1981; *Style*— Sir Julian Ridsdale, CBE, MP; 12 The Boltons, London SW10 (☎ 071 373 6159)

RIEDL, Martin Paul; s of Kurt Riedl, and Ruth, *née* Schechner; *b* 12 Sept 1949; *Educ* Rokeby Sch, Sutton Valence Sch, Ealing Sch of Photography (Dip in Photography); *m* 18 April 1980 (m dis 1990), Patricia Kilbourn, *née* Dumond; 2 s (Alexander David b 17 Nov 1981, Arthur Jonathan b 15 June 1983); partner, Annie Bronwen, da of Edward Augustus Williams; 1 s (Harry Edward b 11 Sept 1990); *Career* photographer; asst to: Robert Dowling 1973-75, Derek Coutts 1975-77, freelance photographer 1978-, opened own studio 1979-; awarded two merits and two silvers Assoc of Photographers, D & AD silver nomination; memb Assoc of Photographers 1976; *Recreations* sculpture, skiing, badminton, tennis; *Clubs* Chelsea Arts Club; *Style*— Martin Riedl, Esq; Martin Riedl Studio, 16/19 Powis Mews, London W11 1JN (☎ 071 727 4006, fax 071 221 9541, car 0836 233 630)

RIFKIND, Rt Hon Malcolm Leslie; PC (1986), QC (1985), MP (C) Edinburgh Pentlands Feb 1974-; s of Elijah Rifkind, of Edinburgh; *b* 21 June 1946; *Educ* George Watson's Coll Edinburgh, Univ of Edinburgh (LLB, MSc); *m* 1970, Edith Amalia, *née* Steinberg; 1 s, 1 da; *Career* fought Edinburgh Central 1970, memb Select Ctee Euro Secdy Legislation 1975-76, oppn front bench spokesman Scottish Affrs 1975-76, jt sec Cons Foreign and Cwlth Affrs Ctee 1978, memb Select Ctee on Overseas Devpt 1978-79; parly under-sec state: Scottish Office 1979-82, FCO 1982-83; min of state FCO 1983-86; sec of state for Scotland 1986-90; sec of state for Transport 1990-; *Recreations* walking, reading, shooting; *Style*— Rt Hon Malcolm Rifkind, QC, MP; The House of Commons, London SW1

RIGBY, Alfred; s of Robert Marsden Rigby (d 1984), of Freckleton, Lancs, and Betsy Alice, *née* Bownass (d 1980); *b* 18 June 1934; *Educ* Kirkham GS Manchester, Univ of Manchester (BA, MA, DipTP), British Sch Rome; *m* 4 Sept 1958, Ann Patricia, da of Maj George Flynn, MBE, MC (d 1978), of Berkhamsted, Bucks; 1 s (Christopher Simon b 1961), 1 da (Susan Elizabeth b 1964); *Career* dep regnl architect NW Manchester RHB 1960-64, chief architect City of Westminister 1964-73 (2 civic tst awards), dir architecture London Borough of Camden 1973-79 (3 civic tst awards), sr ptnr John R Harris Ptnrship (conversion of Dorchester Hotel) 1986-; memb Cons Pty; FRIBA, FBIM, FRSA, RS (Rome Scholar), RTPI; *Books* Sir Banister Fletcher: A History of Architecture on the Comparative Method (contrib 1963 edn); *Recreations* painting, cricket, rugby, opera, theatre; *Clubs* MCC, Athenaeum; *Style*— Alfred Rigby, Esq; Meadlands, 3 Pickwick, Corsham, Wilts (☎ 0249 713 228); Flat 2, 23 Devonshire Place, London W1N 2BX; Chestnut Cottage, Carperby, Aysgarth, N Yorks; John R Harris Ptnrship, 24 Devonshire Place, London W1N 2BX (☎ 071 935 9353, telex 21353 JRH LDN G)

RIGBY, Anthony John; s and h of Sir John Rigby, 2nd Bt, ERD; *b* 3 Oct 1946; *Educ* Rugby; *m* 1978, Mary, da of Robert Oliver, of Cheshire; 3 s, 1 da; *Career* sch teacher; *Style*— Anthony Rigby, Esq; Honeysuckle Cottage, Haughton, West Felton, Oswestry (☎ 069 188 573)

RIGBY, Bryan; s of William George Rigby (d 1971), and Lily; *b* 9 Jan 1933; *Educ* Wigan GS, King's Coll London (BSc DipChemEng); *m* 1978, Marian Rosamund, da of David Ellis (d 1980); 1 s, 1 da; 1 step s, 1 step da; *Career* UKAEA Industl Gp (Capenhurst) 1955-60, Beecham Gp London and Amsterdam 1960-64, mktg dir Laporte Industs 1964-78, dep dir gen CBI 1978-Jan 1984, md BASF UK Ltd 1984-86; Regnl MD BASF AG Jan 1987-, CEng, FIChemE, FRSA, CBIM, MInstM; *Recreations* music, golf, gardening; *Clubs* Reform; *Style*— Bryan Rigby, Esq; Cluny, 61 Penn Rd, Beaconsfield, Bucks (☎ 049 46 3206); BASF plc, BASF House, 151 Wembley Park Drive, Wembley, Middx HAP 8JG (☎ 081 908 3188)

RIGBY, Jean Prescott; da of Thomas Boulton Rigby (d 1987), and Margaret Annie, *née* Whiteside; *Educ* Elmslie Girls' Sch Blackpool, Birmingham Sch of Music, RAM, RSA (prodr Peter Stuyvesant scholarships), Nat Opera Studio (Leverhulme & Munster scholar); *m* 21 Nov 1987, Jamie Hayes; 2 s (Daniel Thomas b 7 March 1989, Oliver James b 27 Nov 1990); *Career* opera singer (mezzo-soprano); princ mezzo-soprano ENO 1982-90; debut: Royal Opera House 1983, Glyndebourne 1984; roles incl: Carmen, Lucretia, Octavian, Penelope, Marina, Magdalena, Maddalena, Dorabella; numerous TV appearances and recordings; winner: Principal's prize RAM, bursary Royal Opera House, Royal Overseas League competition, ENO Young Artists competition, Silver medal Worshipful Co of Musicians; Hon ARAM 1984, Hon FRAM 1989, ARCM, ABSM; *Recreations* sport, cooking, British heritage; *Style*— Ms Jean Rigby; John Coast Personal Management, Manfield House, 376-379 The Strand, London WC2R 0LR

RIGBY, Lt-Col Sir (Hugh) John Macbeth; 2 Bt (UK 1929), of Long Durford, Rogate, Co Sussex; ERD and two clasps; s of Sir Hugh Rigby, 1 Bt, KCVO (d 1944); *b* 1 Sept 1914; *Educ* Rugby, Magdalene Coll Cambridge; *m* 1946, Mary (d 1988), da of Edmund Erskine Leacock; 4 s; *Heir* s, Anthony Rigby; *Career* Lt-Col (ret) RCT, serv UK and SEAC; dir Executors of James Mills Ltd to 1977; *Style*— Lt-Col Sir John Rigby, Bt, ERD and two clasps; Casa das Palmeiras, Armação de P^era, Algarve, Portugal (☎ 082 312548); 5 Park St, Macclesfield, Cheshire (☎ 0625 613959)

RIGBY, Dr Michael Laurence; s of Thomas Rigby, of 12 Fairways Drive, Glenview, Burnley and Kathleen, *née* Barker; *b* 19 March 1947; *Educ* Colne GS, Univ of Leeds

Med Sch (MB ChB, MRCP, MD); *m* 1976, Joanne, da of Roland Ireland; 3 da (Jessica Clair Louise b 27 March 1981, Olivia Jane b 21 Oct 1982, Claudia Anne b 19 April 1985); *Career* registrar Gen Infirmary Leeds 1974-75, res registrar Children's Hosp Birmingham 1975-77, Canadian Heart fndn fell Hosp for Sick Children Toronto Canada 1978-79, conslt paediatic cardiologist Brompton Hosp london 1983-90 (sr registrar 1979-83), dir Paediatrics and conslt paediatric cardiologist Royal Brompton and Nat Heart Hosp London 1990-, sr lectr in paediatics Nat Heart and Lung Inst London 1990-; memb: Paediatric Res Soc 1978, Br Paediatric Assoc 1983, Br Cardiac Soc 1990; FRCP 1988; *Books* The Morphology of Congenital Heart Disease (1983), The Diagnosis of Congenital Heart Disease (1986); *Recreations* Athletics, the study of terrapins; *Style—* Dr Michael Rigby; Royal Brompton and National Heart Hosp, Sydney St, London SW3 6NP (☎ 071 351 8542/352 8121, fax 071 352 7378); 35 Wimpole St, London W1M 7AE (☎ 071 224 1445, fax 071 224 6831)

RIGBY, Peter Philip; CBE (1990), JP; s of Philip James Rigby (d 1985), of Kingston ,and Edith, *née* O'Donoghue (d 1969); *b* 12 Aug 1929; *Educ* Ampleforth; *m* 3 April 1959, Jean Rosalie, da of Capt James Wilson Wilson (d 1958), of London; 3 s (Philip James Luke b 26 Feb 1960, Robert Charles b 19 April 1961, Richard Peter b April 1965); *Career* chm and md Philip Rigby and Sons Ltd; cncllr Middx CC 1961, mayor Hornsey Borough Cncl 1963 (elected 1953), fndr and chm Hornsey Centre for Handicapped Children 1963-, ldr London Borough of Haringey 1968-71 (elected 1964); memb BBFC 1975-, Spastics Soc Exec 1975-83, EITB 1976-84; chm Policy and Resources Ctee Ct of Common Cncl 1984-91 (elected 1972), chm Habinteg Housing Assoc 1989-91 (fndr 1969); Liveryman Worshipful Co of Fletchers (Master 1989-90); FRSA 1979; Knight Cdr of the Holy Sepulchre 1964, KSG 1973; *Recreations* golf, reading; *Clubs* Royal Overseas League, City Livery; *Style—* Peter Rigby, Esq, CBE, JP; 14 Creighton Avenue, Muswell Hill, London N10 1NU (☎ 081 883 3703, fax 081 444 3620)

RIGBY, Peter Stephen; *b* 30 July 1955; *Educ* King George V GS Southport, Univ of Manchester (BA); *m* 25 Aug 1979, Stasia Teresa; 1 s (Nicholas Ian b 1981); *Career* asst factory accountant Metal Box 1978-80 (trainee accountant 1976-78), fin accountant Book Club Assoc 1980-83; IBC (Holdings) plc (formerly Stonehart Publications): joined 1984, jt md 1985, gp accountant, fin dir 1987, dep chief exec 1988, chief exec 1989; formerly dir: Teacher Marks Deal Hldgs plc resigned 1989, Nicholas Stracey (UK) Ltd resigned 1989, RST Printers Ltd resigned 1987, Stonehart Leisure Magazines Ltd resigned 1986; chief exec International Business Communications (Holdings) plc 1989-; currently dir: Barham Group plc, A L Bawtree Limited, Barham Limited, Cocks Williamson Associates Limited, Fleet Street Publications Limited, IBC Magazines Limited, The New Law Publishing Company Limited; ACMA 1980; *Recreations* golfing, jogging, squash, weight training, soccer, rugby, reading; *Style—* Peter Rigby, Esq; 57/61 Mortimer St, London W1N 7TD (☎ 071 637 4383, fax 071 631 3214, telex 8956007)

RIGBY, Maj Reginald Francis; TD (1950 and clasp 1952); s of Reginald Rigby (d 1958), of Rudyard, Staffs, and Beatrice Mary, *née* Green (d 1934); *b* 22 June 1919; *Educ* Manchester GS; *m* 1949, Joan Edwina, da of Samuel E M Simpson, of Mayfield, Newcastle-under-Lyme; 1 s (and 1 s decd 1983); *Career* serv WWII Far E, Maj Staffs Yeo; admitted slr; rec Crown Ct 1977-83; *Recreations* fishing; *Clubs* Army and Navy, Flyfishers; *Style—* Maj Reginald Rigby, TD; The Rookery, Woore, Shropshire CW3 9RG (☎ 063 081414)

RILEY, Dr Alan John; s of Arthur Joseph Riley, of Chestfield, Kent, and Edith Ada, *née* Rashbrook; *b* 16 July 1943; *Educ* Bexley GS, Univ of London, Charing Cross Hosp Med Sch London Univ (MB BS), Univ of Manchester (MSc); *m* 1, 14 Nov 1964 (m dis 1976), Pamela Margaret, da of Leonard George Allum, of London; 1 s (John b 1971), 1 da (Veronica b 1968), 2 adopted s (Grant b 1968, Robert b 1970); m 2, 11 Dec 1976, Elizabeth Jane, da of Capt Arthur Norman Robertson (d 1959); *Career* GP Bideford Devon 1970-76, specialist in sexual med 1972-, med dir Advanced Clinical Res Ltd, dir Colgate Medical 1990-, ptnr: Greycoat Publishing 1991-, SMC Developments 1986-, SMC Research 1985-; ed: British Journal of Sexual Medicine 1983-, Sexual and Marital Therapy 1986-; author of over 100 pubns on aspects of sexual and reproductive med; dep co surgn St John Ambulance Bde (ret 1988); LRCP 1967, MRCS 1967, FZS 1977, MFPM, RCP 1989; memb: Assoc Sexual and Marital Therapists 1979, Endocrine Soc 1980; OStJ 1983; *Recreations* woodwork, photography, natural history; *Clubs* RSM, BMA; *Style—* Dr Alan Riley; Field Place, Dunsmore, Bucks HP22 6QH (☎ 0296 622070, car 0836 213469)

RILEY, Barry John; s of Peter Riley (d 1978), and Barbara, *née* Pitt; *b* 13 July 1942; *Educ* Jesus Coll Cambridge (BA); *m* 16 Aug 1969, Anne Geraldine; 2 s (Paul b 20 April 1971, Timothy b 16 April 1976), 1 da (Martha b 4 Nov 1972); *Career* ed asst Investors Chronicle 1964, dep city ed Morning Telegraph Sheffield 1966; Financial Times 1967-: ed Lex column 1978 (asst 1968, jt ed 1974), fin ed 1981, investmt ed and columnist 1987; memb Domestic Promotions Ctee Br Invisible Exports Cncl; *Style—* Barry Riley, Esq; 17 Mount Pleasant Rd, London W5 1SG (☎ 081 998 5829); The Financial Times, 1 Southwark Bridge, London SE1 9HL (☎ 071 873 3000)

RILEY, Bridget; CBE (1972); da of John Fisher Riley, of Cornwall and, Bessie Louise, *née* Gladstone (d 1975); *b* 1935; *Educ* Cheltenham Ladies Coll, Goldsmith's Coll of Art, RCA; *Career* AICA Critics Prize 1963, John Moores Exhibition Prize Liverpool 1963, Peter Stuyvesant Fndn travel bursary to USA 1964, Int Prize for Painting XXXIV Venice Biennale 1968, Ohara Museum 8 Int Print Biennale Tokyo 1972, two int retrospective museum touring exhibitions Arts Cncl 1970-71 and Br Cncl 1978-81; colour projects for: Royal Liverpool Hosp 1980-83, St Mary's Hosp Paddington 1987-88; designed Colour Moves for Ballet Rambert 1983; tstee Nat Gallery 1981-88, represented in major museums and art collections; Hon DLitt: Univ of Manchester 1976, Univ of Ulster 1986; *Style—* Miss Bridget Riley, CBE; 7 Royal Crescent, London W11 (☎ 071 603 4469); Mayor Rowan Gallery, 31a Bruton Place, London W1X 7AB (☎ 071 499 3011, fax 071 494 1377)

RILEY, Prof Christopher; s of Samuel Riley, MM (d 1978), of Pickmere, Church Rd, St Annes, and Mary Charlotte, *née* Barber (d 1981); *b* 6 Oct 1927; *Educ* King Edward VII Sch, Univ of Liverpool Sch Architecture (BArch, Master of Civic Design); *m* 14 Jan 1956, Elizabeth Mary, da of Joseph Norman Williams (d 1962), of Ivy Mount, Frodsham, Cheshire; 1 s (Simon b 2 March 1957), 1 da (Sarah (Mrs Hutchison) b 1 Mar 1957); *Career* apprentice bricklayer 1943-47, Tom Mellor & Ptnrs Architects 1953-56, chief architect Norwest Construction Group 1957-62; in practice: Christopher Riley Partnership, Plastic Design Consultants 1962-74; lectr Univ of Liverpool 1962-74 (previously 1956-57); Univ of Nottingham: prof of architecture 1974-89, Co of Designers res prof 1989-; princ Nat Hist Building Crafts Inst Lincoln 1989-; ARIBA, ARCUK, FRSA; *Recreations* vintage and historic racing car restoration and driving, wine, model railways; *Clubs* HLR; *Style—* Prof Christopher Riley; The School of Architecture, Dept of Architecture and Planning, University of Nottingham (☎ 0602 484848)

RILEY, (John) Derek; s of Alan Stanley Riley, of Northwood, Middx, and Joan Marjorie *née* Page; *b* 24 Jan 1950; *Educ* Henry Mellish GS, John Wilmott GS, Salford Coll of Technol; *m* 1 (m dis 1985) Elizabeth; 1 s (James Derek b 22 Nov 1980), 1 step s (James Lloyd Wooller b 8 Nov 1981); m 2, 28 June 1985, Deborah Louise, da of Warrant PO Howard Martin Lloyd Jones (d 1987); 1 s (Alexander Thomas b 5 feb 1988), 1 da (Sasha Louise b 22 Feb 1986); *Career* area dir Hambro Life (Allied Dunbar) 1981, regnl dir Allied Hambro (Allied Dunbar) 1985, exec dir sales Allied Dunbar Gp 1987; FLIA 1978; *Recreations* tennis, music; *Clubs* Bath Rugby Football; *Style—* Derek Riley, Esq; Allied Dunbar Assur Plc, Allied Dunbar Centre, Station Road Swindon Station Wiltshire SN1 1EL (☎ 0793 28291, fax 0793 512371, car 0836 617117)

RILEY, Prof Edward Calverley; s of Herbert Raby Riley (d 1966), and Dulcie, *née* Jones (d 1971); *b* 5 Oct 1923; *Educ* Clifton, The Queens Coll Oxford (MA); *m* 27 March 1971, Judith Mary, da of Horace Bull; 1 s (Nicholas b 1972), 1 da (Hannah b 1974); *Career* Trinity Coll Dublin: lectr 1949, head of dept 1954, fell 1957, prof Spanish 1966-70; prof Hispanic Studies Univ of Edinburgh 1970-89, ret 1989; visiting prof: Dartmouth Coll, Univ of Michigan, Ohio State Univ, Univ of Virginia, Northwestern Univ; memb: Anglo - Irish Assoc, Modern Humanities Res Assoc, Cervantes Soc of America, Asociacion de Cervantistas; *Books* Cervantes' Theory of the Novel (1962), Suma Cervantina (ed with JB Avalle-Arce, 1973), Don Quixote (1986); *Recreations* walking, cinema; *Style—* Prof Edward Riley; Westholme, Pencaitland, East Lothian EH34 5DP

RILEY, (Christopher) John; s of Bernard Francis Riley (d 1981), of Notts, and Phyllis Wigley (d 1954); *b* 20 Jan 1947; *Educ* Ratcliffe Coll, Wadham Coll Oxford (MA), Univ of East Anglia (MA); *m* 24 Sept 1982, Helen Marion, da of Ernest Amos Arthur Mynett, of Sidcup, Kent; 2 s (Timothy James b 1983, Mark Edward b 1985); *Career* HM Treasury: econ asst 1969-72, sr econ asst 1972-74, econ advsr 1974-79, sr econ advsr 1979-88, under sec 1988-; Gwilym Gibbon res fell Nuffield Coll Oxford 1977-78; *Recreations* music, especially choral singing; *Style—* C J Riley, Esq; c/o HM Treasury, 1 Parliament St, London SW1P 3AG (☎ 071 270 4439, fax 071 270 5653)

RILEY, Prof John Price; s of Capt Norman Riley (d 1958), of Southport, and Edith Elizabeth, *née* Price (d 1981); *Educ* Winterdyne Sch Southport, Dean Close Sch Cheltenham, Univ of Liverpool (BSc, PhD, DSc); *m* 1, 20 Dec 1964 (m dis), Elizabeth Anne, da of Stanley Powney (d 1983), of South Lopham; 1 da (Sarah Jane b 1966); m 2, 26 Nov 1985, Mary Denise Hayes, *née* Edwards; *Career* Univ of Liverpool: lectr oceanography 1949, sr lectr 1959, reader oceanography, personal chair oceanography 1972, head Oceanography Dept 1980-87, prof oceanography 1986-89; chm Standing Ctee Analysis DOE; FRSC, FRIC 1947; *Books* Introduction of Marine Chemistry (1970), Chemical Oceanography Vols 1 and 2 (1965), Chemical Oceanography Vols 1-10 (2 edn, 1975-89); *Recreations* riding, gardening; *Style—* Prof John Riley; Edgcott Farm Cottage, Exford, Minehead, Somerset TA24 7QG (☎ 064 383439)

RILEY, Maj John Roland Christopher; s of Lt-Col Christopher John Molesworth Riley, MC (d 1958), of Trinity Manor, Jersey, and Betty Maisie, *née* Hanbury (d 1928); *b* 4 July 1925; *Educ* Winchester; *m* 14 April 1956, Penelope Ann (d 1978), da of late Lt-Col J F Harrison, of Kings Walden Bury, Hitchin, Herts; 2 da (Bridget b 1958, Anna b 1962); *Career* cmmnd Coldstream Gds 1944; serv: NW Europe, Palestine, Malaya; Instr Army Staff Coll 1960-62; dep States of Jersey 1963, senator 1975, retired from govt 1981; dir: Air UK 1963-, chm Channel TV 1983-; dep chm: Jersey Gas Co 1970-, Servisair Jersey 1976-, Fuel Supplies CI 1976-, Royal Tst Fund Mgmnt CI 1987-, Royal Tst Asset Mgmnt CI 1987-; vice pres Royal Jersey Agric & Hort Soc 1986-88, Master Jersey Drag Hunt 1962-; Seigneur de la Trinité; landowner; FInstD; *Recreations* riding, yachting; *Clubs* Cavalry and Guards', Royal Yacht Sqdn; *Style—* Maj John Riley; Trinity Manor, Jersey, CI (☎ 0534 61026)

RILEY, (John) Martin; s of Rev Lambert Riley (d 1948), of Roehampton, London, and Marjorie Grace, *née* Maton (d 1973); *b* 15 Nov 1931; *Educ* Bradfield, Queens' Coll Cambridge (MA); *m* 5 Oct 1963, Alison Rosemary, da of Col Gordon Dewar, CBE (d 1985), of Frensham, Surrey; 2 s (Charles b 1965, Hugh b 1968), 1 da (Philippa b 1970); *Career* admitted slr 1963, sr ptnr Mercers of Henley-on-Thames 1977-(ptnr 1964-);chm Turners Ct Boys Home 1976-; cncllr Oxfordshire CC 1970-81; *Style—* Martin Riley, Esq

RILEY, Norman; s of Herman Riley (d 1975), and Ada Riley (d 1986); *b* 1 May 1926; *Educ* Univ of Sheffield (DipArch); *m* 31 July 1954, Madeleine, da of James Smith; 4 s (Andrew b 1955, Michael b 1958, Duncan b 1960, Lawrence b 1962), 1 da (Catherine b 1956); *Career* dep surveyor Univ of Oxford 1955-63, estates bursar Univ of Warwick 1963-67, dep divisional architect GLC 1970-75, official architect to the Church Commissioners 1976-81, conservation architect and expert witness Bickerdike Allen Partners 1981-87, Brock Riley Partners Architects 1987-; assessor for Civic Tst 1966-75, pres Ecclesiastical Architects' and Surveyors' Assoc 1985, ed Advsy Ctee Church Building 1986-, memb Advsy Ctee St Albans Diocese 1989-90; memb RIBA 1954; *Recreations* foreign travel; *Style—* Norman Riley, Esq; The Manor House, Wolston, Warwickshire CV8 3HH; Brock Riley Partners, Architects, 10 Albert St, London NW1 7NZ (☎ 071 3872077)

RILEY, Prof Norman; s of Willie Riley, of Hebden Bridge, West Yorkshire, and Minnie, *née* Parker; *Educ* Calder HS West Yorks, Univ of Manchester (BSc, PhD); *m* 5 Sept 1959, Mary Ann, da of Michael Mansfield, of Manchester; 1 s (Stephen b 1961), 1 da (Susan b 1964); *Career* asst lectr mathematics Univ of Manchester 1959-60, lectr mathematics Univ of Durham 1960-64; UEA: sr lectr mathematics 1964-66, reader mathematics 1966-71, prof applied mathematics 1971-; FIMA 1964; *Recreations* music, photography, travel; *Style—* Prof Norman Riley; School of Mathematics, Univ of East Anglia, Norwich Norfolk NR4 7TJ (☎ 0603 592586)

RILEY, Norman Robinson; s of James Herbert Riley (d 1979); *b* 20 July 1925; *Educ* Bury HS, QMC London, Oxford Univ; *m* 1956, Inger Clara, nee Linde; 1 da; *Career* legal adviser The Distillers Co Ltd 1955-62, legal advisor Kellogg Int Corpn 1962-65, legal dir STC plc 1965-85; *Recreations* tennis, golf, wines; *Style—* Norman Riley, Esq; 1 Macartney House, Chesterfield Walk, SE10

RILEY, Prof Patrick Anthony; s of Bertram Hurrell Riley (d 1961), and Olive, *née* Stephenson (d 1987); *b* 22 March 1935; *Educ* Manegg Sch Zurich, King Edward VII Sch King's Lynn, UCL, UCH Med Sch London (MB BS, PhD, DSc); *m* 5 July 1958, Christine Elizabeth, da of Dr Islwyn Morris (d 1972), of Treorchy, Rhondda, Glam; 1 s (Benjamin b 20 Feb 1968), 2 da (Sian b 12 Feb 1962, Caroline b 25 June 1963); *Career* Rockefeller res scholar 1962-63, MRC jr clinical res fell 1963-66, Beit Meml res fell 1966-68, Wellcome res fell 1968-70, sr lectr in biochemical pathology UCH Med Sch 1974-76 (lectr 1970-73), prof of cell pathology UCL 1984- (reader 1976-84); sec and treas Euro Soc Pigment Cell Res, vice pres Int Fedn of Pigment Cell Socs, treas NCUP; FIBiol 1976, FRCPath 1985; *Books* Faber Pocket Medical Dictionary (with PJ Cunningham, first edn 1966), Hydroxyanisole: Recent Advances in Anti-Melanoma Therapy (1984); *Recreations* music, stereo photography; *Style—* Prof Patrick Riley; 15 Laurel Way, London N20 8HS (☎ 081 445 5687); Department of Chemical Pathology, University College and Middlesex School of Medicine, London W1P 6DB (☎ 071 636 8333 ext 3384)

RILEY, Peter Lawrence; s of Lawrence Joseph Riley (d 1957), and Freda, *née* Cronshaw (d 1985); *b* 10 May 1947; *Educ* St Joseph's GS Blackpool; *m* 16 Oct 1971, Sandra Carol, da of Tom Gartside (d 1974); 1 s (Mark b 2 July 1974), 1 da (Caroline Louise b 6 June 1977); *Career* CA; ptnr Condy & Co 1973-80, dir numerous Cos 1974-87, dir Plymouth Argyle Football Co Ltd 1977-81, sr ptnr Peter Riley & co

1981-; FCA 1970; *Recreations* yachting, squash; *Clubs* Royal Western YC, St Mellion Golf And Country; *Style—* Peter Riley, Esq; 5 The Orchard, Yealmpton, Devon; Britannic House, 51 North Hill, Plymouth PL4 8HZ (☎ 0752 260451)

RILEY, Sir Ralph; s of late Ralph Riley, and late Clara Riley; *b* 23 Oct 1924; *Educ* Audenshaw GS, Univ of Sheffield (BSc, PhD, DSc); *m* 1949, Joan Elizabeth Norrington; 2 da (Susan, Jennifer); *Career* serv WWII Capt 6 KOSB and 1 S Lancs Regt 1943-47, W Europe and Palestine; Cambridge Plant Breeding Inst: res worker 1952-78, head of Cytogenetics Dept 1954-72 (dir 1971-78); dep chm and sec Agric and Food Res Cncl 1978-85, chm Rothamsted Experimental Station 1990-; fell Wolfson Coll Cambridge; Royal Soc Royal medal 1981, Wolf prize in Agric 1986, William Bate Hardy prize; foreign memb: Indian Nat Sci Acad, Nat Sci Acad USA, Acad Agric France; Hon DSc: Edinburgh 1976, Hull 1982, Cranfield 1985; Hon LLD Sheffield 1984; Hon FRASE 1980; FRS 1967; kt 1984; *Clubs* Athenaeum; *Style—* Sir Ralph Riley, FRS; 16 Gog Magog Way, Stapleford, Cambridge CB2 5BQ (☎ 0223 843845, fax 0223 845825)

RILEY, Hon Mrs (Ruth Margaret); da of 1 Baron Hives, CH, MBE (d 1965); *b* 1922; *m* 1941, Joseph Graham Riley; 3 s; *Style—* The Hon Mrs Riley; 7 Avenue Rd, Duffield, Derbys

RILEY, Simon James Blair; s of James Riley (d 1985), and Joanna, *née* Walker; *b* 27 Feb 1946; *Educ* Gordonstoun; *m* 1, 7 April 1973 (m dis 1984), Jacqueline Lila (Jackie), da of Col Henry Lancelot Gullidge (Harry), of Taunton, Somerset; 2 da (Claire-Louise b 6 Sept 1975, Victoria b 19 Aug 1980); m 2, 29 Oct 1988, Estaire Joyce Danielle, da of Prof Johan De Vree; *Career* surveyor; Kirk & Kirk 1964-67, Grant Wilkinson & Co 1967-73 (dir 1970), dir James Riley & Associates 1973-83, conslt in Spain 1983-88, specialist with Secure Storage 1989-; memb Ctee Br Automobile Racing Club; MNAEA 1965; *Recreations* racing motor cars, reading, collecting; *Clubs* Lighthouse, British Automobile Racing; *Style—* Simon Riley, Esq; 23 Rossetti Garden Mansions, Flood Street, Chelsea, London SW3 5QX (☎ 071 3510248), Secure Storage Ltd, Brent Rd, Southall, Middlesex UB2 5LE (☎ 081 574 6514, fax 081 574 0557, car 0836 317800)

RILEY, Major Timothy Richard; DL (Cumbria); s of Lt-Col Hamlet Lewthwaite Riley, DSO, OBE (d 1932), of Ennim, Penrith, Cumberland, and Joyce Nancy, da of Lt-Col Timothy Fetherstonhaugh, DSO, JP, DL; *b* 11 Dec 1928; *Educ* Shrewsbury, RMA Sandhurst; *m* 11 April 1955, Ankaret Tarn, da of Sir William Jackson, 7 Bt (d 1985), and Lady (Ankaret) Jackson; 2 da (Nicola Ankaret Katharine b 1959, Antonia Elizabeth Tarn b 1962); *Career* joined reg army 1946, cmmnd Rifle Bde 1948, served Germany, Middle East & UK, ret 1966; joined The Earl of Lonsdale's Estates 1966; dir: Lowther Wildlife Country Park Ltd 1969-79, Lowther Caravan Park Ltd 1970-, Lakeland Investments Ltd 1972-82; show dir Lowther Horse Driving Trials 1973-, jt organiser Brougham Horse Trials 1974-80, dir Border Museum of Rural Life 1975-81, chm Skelton Horticultural & Agric Soc 1979-82; memb: Penrith Rural District Cncl 1967-70, Cumberland CC 1969-74, Cumbria CC 1977-89; chm Cumbria Police Authy 1984-89; memb: ACC Police Ctee 1987-89, NW Eng & Isle of Man TA 1971-, County Employers' Liaison Team; chm: Ullswater Sch (Penrith) 1978-85; clerk of the Course Cartmel 1978- (dir sec & gen mangr 1985-), clerk the Course Carlisle 1986-; memb HARP (Jump) 1986-, point to point course inspector 1969-; High Sheriff of Cumbria 1989-90; *Recreations* shooting, racing, travel; *Clubs* Naval and Military; *Style—* Major Timothy Riley, DL; Burbank House, Blencowe, Penrith, Cumbria CA11 0DB (☎ 08533 246); Lowther Estate Office, Penrith, Cumbria CA10 2HG (☎ 09312 392)

RILEY-SMITH, Prof Jonathan Simon Christopher; s of Maj (William Henry) Douglas Riley-Smith (d 1981), of Toulston Grange, Tadcaster, N Yorks and Brewhurst, Loxwood, W Sussex, and Elspeth Agnes Mary, *née* Craik Henderson (d 1990); *b* 27 June 1938; *Educ* Eton, Trinity Coll Cambridge (BA, MA, PhD); *m* 27 July 1968, Marie-Louise Jeannetta, da of Wilfred John Sutcliffe Field, of Chapel Field House, Norwich, Norfolk; 1 s (Tobias Augustine William b 19 Oct 1969), 2 da (Tamsin Elspeth Hermione b 10 Sept 1971, Hippolyta Clemency Magdalen b 10 Nov 1975); *Career* lectr in mediaeval history Univ of St Andrews 1966-72 (asst lectr 1964-65); Univ of Cambridge: asst lectr 1972-75, lectr 1975-78, fell Queen's Coll Cambridge 1972-78, dir of studies in history 1972-78, praelector 1973-75, librarian 1973 and 1977-78; head of Dept of History Royal Holloway and Bedford New Coll Univ of London 1984-90 (prof of history 1978-); librarian Priory of Scotland Most Ven Order of St John 1966-78 (Grand Priory 1982-); KStJ 1969, CStJ 1966; FRHistS 1971; Knight of Magistral Grace SMOM 1971 (Officer of Merit Pro Merito Melitensi 1985); *Books* The Knights of St John in Jerusalem and Cyprus (1967), Ayyubids, Mamlukes and Crusaders (with U and M C Lyons, 1971), The Feudal Nobility and The Kingdom of Jerusalem (1973), What Were The Crusades? (1977), The Crusades Idea and Reality (with L Riley-Smith, 1981), The First Crusade and The Idea of Crusading (1986), The Crusades: A Short History (1987), Les Croisades (translation, 1990), The Atlas of the Crusades (ed, 1991); *Recreations* the past and present of own family; *Style—* Prof Jonathan Riley-Smith; Dept of History, Royal Holloway and Bedford New College, Egham Hill, Egham, Surrey TW20 0EX (☎ 0784 34455)

RIMBAULT, Brig Geoffrey Acworth; CBE (1954), DSO (1944), MC (1936), DL (Surrey 1971); s of Arthur Henry Rimbault (d 1926), of London, and Sarah Elizabeth, *née* Wilson (d 1945); *b* 17 April 1908; *Educ* Dulwich; *m* 9 Sept 1933, Joan Vera, da of Thomas Hallett-Fry (d 1912), of Beckenham, Kent; 1 s (Greville Hallett Lynden b 30 June 1935); *Career* cmmnd Loyal Regt N Lancs 1930, serv India Waziristan 1931-36, Palestine 1937, Staff Coll Camberley 1940, OC 1 Loyals Anzio Italy 1944 and Palestine 1945-46, chief instr RMA Sandhurst 1950-51, chief of staff E Africa 1952-54, cmd 131 Inf Bde 1955-57, cmd Aldershot Garrison 1958-61, Col Loyal Regt 1959 (until amalgamation 1970); life vice pres Surrey CCC (pres 1982-83); Freeman City of London, Master Worshipful Co of Mercers' 1970-71 (Liveryman 1961); *Recreations* cricket; *Clubs* MCC, Free Foresters; *Style—* Brig Geoffrey Rimbault, CBE, DSO, MC, DL; 10 Clarke Place, Elmbridge, Cranleigh, Surrey GU6 8TH (☎ 0483 271207)

RIMELL, Mercy; *née* Cockburn; da of Samuel Crosby Cockburn (d 1967), of Budbrook Lodge, Warwick, and Elsie, *née* Simkin; *b* 27 June 1919; *Educ* privately; *m* 23 June 1937, Thomas Frederick (Fred) Rimell (race horse trainer), s of Thomas Devereux Rimell (d 1976), of Windsor Lodge, Lambourn; 1 s (Guy b 1938), 1 da (Scarlet b 1943); *Career* ret race horse trainer, farmer; trained champion hurdle winner Gaye Brief 1983; *Recreations* racing; *Clubs* Turf; *Style—* Mrs Fred Rimell; The Hill, Upton-upon-Severn, Worcestershire (☎ 06846 2623)

RIMER, Colin Percy Farquharson; QC (1988); s of Kenneth Rowland Rimer, of Beckenham, Kent, and Maria Eugenia, *née* Farquharson; *b* 30 Jan 1944; *Educ* Dulwich, Trinity Hall Cambridge (MA, LLB); *m* 3 Jan 1970, Penelope Ann, da of late Alfred William Gibbs, of Beckenham, Kent; 2 s (David b 1972, Michael b 1974), 1 da (Catherine b 1971); *Career* res asst Inst of Comparative Law Paris 1967-68, called to the Bar Lincoln's Inn 1968, practising since 1969; *Recreations* music, photography, novels, walking; *Style—* Colin Rimer, Esq, QC; 13 Old Square, Lincoln's Inn, London WC2A 3UA (☎ 071 404 4800)

RIMINGTON, John David; CB (1987); s of John William Rimington, MBE, of Eastbourne, and Mabel, *née* Dorrington; *b* 27 June 1935; *Educ* Nottingham HS, Jesus Coll Cambridge (MA); *m* 16 March 1963, Stella, da of David Whitehouse, of Newstead; 2 da (Sophie b 30 Dec 1970, Harriet b 22 Nov 1974); *Career* Nat Serv Lt RA (TA) 1954-59; asst princ Bd of Trade and Treasy 1959-63, princ Tariff Div BOT 1963, first sec (econ) New Delhi 1965, asst sec (unemployment) Dept of Employment 1972, cnsllr UK representation to the EC Brussels 1974, under sec Trg Div MSC 1977, dir gen HSE 1984 (dir safety policy 1981); memb RIPA, FRSA; *Recreations* cricket, walking; *Style—* John Rimington, Esq, CB; Baynards House, Chepstow Place, London W2 (☎ 071 226 3456)

RIMINGTON, Richard John; *Career* chm: Hollis Bros & ESA (timber importers and woodworkers) 1981-, AND Engrg, Data Dynamics Gp, Torkmatic, Torkmatic UK (Sales), West Mills Light Engrg, Young and Marten, Zenith Electric Co; dep chm James Clark & Eaton Ltd; dir: A W Metal Works, Eastern Tractors Hldgs, Middlesex Machine Tool, Nash & Hodge Engrs, Suter Electrical, W H Welding Equipment, Weyside Engrg (1926) Ltd; memb IOD; FCA; *Style—* Richard Rimington, Esq; c/o Dixon Wilson & Co, Gillett House, 55 Basinghall St, London EC2Y 5EA (☎ 071 628 7251/4321)

RIMMER, Kenneth Archibald; s of Archibald Rimmer (d 1988), of Woodford Green, Essex, and Eliza Rhoda, *née* Roe; *b* 30 Jan 1940; *Educ* Buckhurst Hill County HS Essex; *m* 7 May 1966, Janice Lynne, da of Frederick Thomas Pigrome, of Leigh-on-Sea, Essex; 1 s (Matthew b 1970), 1 da (Helen b 1972); *Career* Australia and New Zealand Bank 1956-69, Bank Julius Baer 1969-73; vice pres and mangr The Bank of California 1980- (joined 1973); ACIB 1972; *Recreations* piano, bowls, snooker; *Style—* Kenneth Rimmer, Esq; The Bank of California, 18 Finsbury Circus, London EC2M 7BP (☎ 071 628 1883, fax 071 628 1864, telex 8814323)

RIMMER, Malcolm Thomas; s of Lt Samuel Robb McIntyre Rimmer (d 1961), and Edna Evelyn, *née* Emery (d 1981); *b* 11 June 1930; *Educ* Quarry Bank HS Liverpool, Colwyn Bay GS, Caer Rhun Hall Conway; *m* 23 June 1956, Jean, da of Frederick Holloway (d 1964); 1 s (Gary Julian b 18 March 1964); *Career* Pilot Offr RAF 1951; fin dir: Limocoat Ltd 1977-, Famous Army Stores Ltd 1977-, FAS Group plc 1988-; athlete (represented GB v USSR 1954 in triple jump); involved RSPCA fund raising; FICA; *Recreations* vintage motoring, photography, tennis; *Clubs* Maserati Owners, Vintage Sports Car, Brooklands Soc; *Style—* Malcolm Rimmer, Esq; Sunbeam House, Woolton Rd, Liverpool L19 5PH (☎ 051 427 5151, fax 051 427 3918)

RING, Malcolm Spencer Humbert; TD; s of Gp Capt Spencer Leonard Ring, CBE, DFC (d 1980), and Jessie Margaret Ring; *b* 25 Feb 1944; *Educ* Haileybury; *m* 17 Aug 1978, Elizabeth Anne Ring, da of Michael Henman; 3 s (Jonathan b 1980, Charles b 1982, Thomas b 1985), 1 da (Emma b 1987); *Career* Regtl Col TA HAC 1989-90 (joined 1969, CO Lt-Col 1986-88); admitted slr 1969; ptnr: Taylor & Humbert 1973-82, Taylor Garrett (now Taylor Joynson Garrett) 1982- (managing ptnr 1989-90); memb Law Soc; *Recreations* fishing, cricket, hockey, gardening; *Clubs* Oriental, HAC; *Style—* Malcolm Ring, Esq, TD; 180 Fleet St, London EC4A 2NT (☎ 071 430 1122, fax 071 528 7145, telex 25516)

RINGADOO, Hon Sir Veerasamy; s of Nagaya Ringadoo; *b* 1920; *Educ* Port Louis G S Mauritius, LSE (LLB, hon fellow 1976); *m* 1954, Lydie Vadamootoo; 1 s, 1 da; *Career* called to the Bar 1949; MLC for Moka-Flacq 1951-67, min Labour and Social Security 1959-64, min Educn 1964-67, first MLA (Lab) for Quartier Militaire and Moka 1967-, min Natural Resources 1967-68, min Fin 1968-82; govr IMF; Hon LLD (Mauritius) 1975, Hon DLitt (Andhra) 1978; kt 1975; *Style—* Hon Sir Veerasamy Ringadoo; Port Louis, Mauritius

RINK, Anthony Arnold (Tony); s of Paul Loather Max Rink (d 1978), and Mary Ida McCall, *née* McFarlane; *b* 3 Sept 1942; *Educ* Sedbergh, LSE (BSc); *m* 28 Aug 1965, Vivien, da of William Appleyard, OBE, of Adlington, Lancs; 1 s (Andrew b 25 Nov 1966); *Career* qualified ACA Peat Marwick Mitchell 1963-66, Lazard Brothers and Co Ltd (Corporate Finance) 1966-71, fin dir Wolstenholme Bronze Powders 1971-75, jt md Wolstenholme Rink plc 1975-; chm: Lancs Assoc of Boys Clubs 1982-87, Bolton Ind Hosp plc 1984-87; FCA 1967, fell Royal Soc for the Encouragement of Arts Manufactures and Commerce 1976; *Recreations* golf, rugby, music; *Clubs* Bolton Golf; *Style—* Tony Rink, Esq; Bhandar, 20 Regent Rd, Lostock, Bolton, Lancs BL6 4DJ (☎ 0204 46507); Wolstenholme Rink plc, Springfield House, Darwen BB3 0RP (☎ 0254 873888, fax 0254 703430, telex 63251)

RINK, Paul James Ernest; s of Paul Lothar Max Rink (d 1978), and Mary Ida McCall, *née* Moore; *b* 18 Dec 1940; *Educ* Sedbergh; *m* 26 July 1969, Marlene Ann, da of Maurice Hughes, of Lostock, Lancs; 1 s (Nicholas b 1971), 1 da (Sally b 1973); *Career* jt md Wolstenholme Rink plc 1978-; Wolstenholme Bronze Powders Ltd: sales dir 1967-73, jt md 1973-78, chm and md 1978-; chm and md Makin Metal Powders Ltd 1985-; chm Blackburn Groundwork Tst 1990-; *Recreations* golf, rugby, football, cricket; *Clubs* Bolton Golf, MCC; *Style—* Paul Rink, Esq; Wolstenholme Rink plc, Springfield House, Darwen, Lancs BB3 0RP (☎ 0254 873888, telex 63251)

RIPLEY, Sir Hugh; 4 Bt (UK 1880), of Rawdon, Yorks; s of Sir Henry Ripley, 3 Bt, JP (d 1956), and Dorothy, *née* Harley (d 1964); *b* 26 May 1916; *Educ* Eton; *m* 1, 1946 (m dis 1971), Dorothy Mary Dunlop, yr da of John Cumming Bruce-Jones, and Dorothy Euphemia Mitchell, da of Sir Thomas Dunlop, 1 Bt, GBE, JP, DL; 1 s, 1 da; m 2, 1972, Susan, da of William Parker, of Keythorpe Grange, E Norton, Leics; 1 da; *Heir* s, William, b 13 April 1950; *Career* former Maj King's Shropshire LI, served WW II N Africa, Italy; dir John Walker & Sons 1956-81; *Recreations* fishing, shooting; *Clubs* Boodle's; *Style—* Sir Hugh Ripley, Bt; The Oak, Bedstone, Bucknell, Shrops; 20 Abingdon Villas, London W8

RIPLEY, William Hugh; s and h of Sir Hugh Ripley, 4 Bt; *b* 13 April 1950; *Educ* Eton, McGill Univ Canada; *Recreations* fishing, writing; *Style—* William Ripley, Esq; Dove Cottage, Bedstone, Bucknell, Salop

RIPON, 11 Bishop of 1977-; Rt Rev David Nigel de Lorentz Young; see founded AD 678 but merged in York till reconstituted 1836; patron of 38 livings and 20 alternately with others, all the Canonries in the Cathedral, the Archdeaconries of Richmond and Leeds and the chancellorship of the diocese; s of Brig Keith Young, CIE, MC, and Ada Lilian, *née* Tollinton; *b* 2 Sept 1931; *Educ* Wellington, Balliol Coll Oxford (MA); *m* 1, 1962, Rachel (d 1966), da of Jack Lewis, of Liverpool; 1 s (Mark b 1965), 1 da (Kate b 1963); m 2, 17 June 1967, Jane, da of Lewis Herbert Collison, TD, JP (d 1988); 3 s (James b 1968, Peter b 1968, Thomas b 1981); *Career* RE 1950-51, 2 Lt Troop Cdr Sch of Mil Survey 1951; research mathematician Plessey Co 1955-59; ordained: deacon 1959, priest 1960; curate All Hallows Allerton Liverpool 1959-62, Church Missionary Soc missionary Sri Lanka 1962-67, lectr in buddhist studies Univ of Manchester 1967-70, vicar Burwell Cambridge 1970-75, archdeacon Huntingdon and hon canon Ely Cathedral 1975-77; chm: Governing Body SPCK 1978-87, Partnership World Mission 1978-85; memb Doctrine Cmmn 1978-81; *Recreations* fell walking, sailing; *Clubs* Royal Commonwealth Soc; *Style—* The Rt Rev the Bishop of Ripon; Bishop Mount, Ripon, N Yorks HG4 5DP (☎ 0765 2045)

RIPPENGAL, Derek; CB (1982), QC (1980); s of William Thomas Rippengal (d 1972), of Middlesex, and Margaret Mary, *née* Parry (d 1982); *b* 8 Sept 1928; *Educ* Hampton GS, St Catharine's Coll Cambridge (MA); *m* 1963, Elizabeth (d 1973), da of Charles Gordon Melrose (d 1985), of East Lothian; 1 s (Robert b 1966), 1 da (Emma b 1970); *Career* called to the Bar Middle Temple 1953; Chancery Bar and univ posts 1953-58, Treasy Slrs Office 1958-72 (princ asst treasy slr 1971), slr and legal advsr to DTI 1972-73, dep Parly counsel Law Cmmn 1973-74, Parly counsel 1974-76, counsel to chm of Ctees of House of Lords 1977-; *Recreations* music, fishing; *Clubs* Athenaeum; *Style—* Derek Rippengal, Esq, CB, QC; Wychwood, Bell Lane, Little Chalfont, Bucks HP6 6PF (☎ 02404 76 2350); House of Lords (☎ 071 219 3211)

RIPPON OF HEXHAM, Baron (Life Peer UK 1987), of Hesleyside, Co Northumberland; (Aubrey) Geoffrey Frederick Rippon; PC (1962), QC (1964); o s of Arthur Ernest Sydney Rippon (d 1966), of Surbiton, Surrey; *b* 28 May 1924; *Educ* King's Coll Taunton, BNC Oxford (MA); *m* 1946, Ann Leyland, OBE, da of Donald Yorke, MC, of Birkenhead; 1 s (Hon Anthony Simon Yorke b 4 Oct 1959), 3 da (Hon Fiona Carolyn b 28 June 1947, Hon Sarah Lovell (*see* Hon Mrs Taylor), Hon Penelope Ann (*see* Hon Mrs Rae)); *Career* Parly candidate (C): Shoreditch 1950, Finsbury 1951; MP (C): Norwich S 1955-64, Hexham 1966-87; PPS to: Min Housing and Local Govt 1956-57, min Def 1957-59; Parly sec Miny Aviation 1959-61, jt Parly sec Miny Housing and Local Govt 1961-62, min Public Bldgs and Works 1962-64 (with seat in Cabinet 1963-64); chief oppn spokesman: Housing, Local Govt and Land 1966-68, Def 1968-70; min Technol 1970, chllr Duchy of Lancaster 1970-72, sec state for Environment 1972-74; chief oppn spokesman Foreign and Cwlth Affrs 1974-75, chm Cons Foreign Affrs Ctee 1970-81; ldr: Cons Delgn to Cncl Europe and WEU 1967-70, Cons Gp Euro Parl 1977-79; called to the Bar 1948; Mayor of Surbiton 1951-52, ldr Cons Gp LCC 1957-59 (memb LCC (Chelsea) 1952-61); memb Ct Univ of London 1958-; chm: Dun & Bradstreet 1976-, Britannia Arrow Holdings (now Invesco/MIM plc) 1977-89 (pres 1989-), Robert Fraser Group 1985-, Michael Page Group 1989-; dir: Maxwell Communication Corporation, Groupe Bruxelles Lambert 1983-90; formerly dir: Fairey Co, Bristol Aeroplane Co, Hotung Estates; former chm: Holland Hanner & Cubitts, Singer & Friedlander; chm Br Section European League for Economic Cooperation; pres: Assoc of Dist Cncls 1987-, Town & Country Planning Assoc 1988-; hon fell BNC Oxford, Hon LLD London Univ; Grand Cross Order of Merit (Liechtenstein) 1967, Kt Grand Cross Royal Order of North Star (Sweden) 1982; *Clubs* White's, Pratt's, MCC; *Style—* The Rt Hon the Lord Rippon of Hexham, PC, QC; The Old Vicarage, Broomfield, Bridgwater, Somerset; 2 Paper Buildings, Temple, London EC4 (☎ 071 353 5835)

RISDON, Prof (Rupert) Anthony; s of Capt Dennis Stanley Risdon (d 1986), and Olga Caris Argent, *née* Davis; *b* 5 March 1939; *Educ* Charing Cross Hosp Med Sch (MB BS, MD); *m* 15 April 1961, Phyllis Mary, da of Frederick Hough, of IOM; 2 s ((James) Mark b 1964, Simon Paul b 1967); *Career* lectr in histopathology Charing Cross Hosp Med Sch 1966-68, conslt pathologist Addenbrookes Hosp Cambridge 1975-76, reader in morbid anatomy London Hosp Med Coll 1976-85; memb: Pathology Soc GB and I, Int Acad Pathology, Assoc Clinical Pathologists; FRCPath; *Recreations* walking, swimming; *Style—* Prof Anthony Risdon; The Hosp for Sick Children, Dept Histopathology, Gt Ormond St, London WC1N 3JH (☎ 071 409 9200 ext 5463)

RISK, Douglas James; s of James Risk (slr), of Glasgow, and Isobel Katherine Taylor, *née* Dow; *b* 23 Jan 1941; *Educ* Glasgow Acad, Gonville and Caius Coll Cambridge (BA, MA), Univ of Glasgow (LLB); *m* 4 Aug 1967, Jennifer Hood, da of John Howat Davidson (d 1985, schoolmaster), of Glasgow; 3 s (Kenneth b 1968, Malcolm b 1972, Colin b 1974), 1 da (Helen b 1970); *Career* admitted to Faculty of Advocates 1966; standing jr counsel Scottish Educn Dept 1975; Sheriff of: Lothian and Borders at Edinburgh 1977-79, Grampian Highland and Islands at Aberdeen 1979-; hon lectr Faculty of Law Univ of Aberdeen 1980-; *Clubs* Royal Northern and Univ (Aberdeen); *Style—* Douglas J Risk, Esq; Sheriffs Chambers, Sheriff Court House, Exchequer Row, Aberdeen AB9 1AP

RISK, Sir Thomas Neilson; s of late Ralph Risk, CBE, MC; *b* 13 Sept 1922; *Educ* Kelvinside Acad, Univ of Glasgow (BL, LLD); *m* 1949, Suzanne Eiloart; 4 s; *Career* served WWII RAF, RAFVR 1946-53; ptnr Murray & Spens slrs 1950-81, MSA (Britain) Ltd 1958-, chm Standard Life Assurance Co 1969-77 (dir 1965-88), Howden Group 1971-87, Merchants Trust plc 1973-; govr: British Linen Bank 1977-86, Bank of Scotland 1981- (dir 1971-, dep govr 1977-81); dir: Shell UK 1982-, Barclays Bank 1983-85, Bank of Wales 1986-; memb: Scottish Industl Devpt Bd 1972-75, Scottish Econ Cncl 1983-, NEDC 1987-; kt 1984; *Style—* Sir Thomas Risk; Bank of Scotland, The Mound, Edinburgh EH1 1YZ (☎ 031 243 5511)

RISLEY, George Francis; s of Thomas Risley (d 1971); *b* 23 Dec 1929; *Educ* Doncaster GS, Coll of Technol Liverpool, IMEDE Lausanne Switzerland; *m* 1; 2 s, 1 da; m 2, 1975, Rosemary Wendy Pamela, da of Cecil Lionel Bell; 1 s, 1 da; *Career* formerly sales and marketing dir Findus Ltd; dir: Hazlewood Foods plc, Hazlewood Intenational BV, Sandyford Meats Ltd, California Car Care Ltd, Wendy Jane Ltd; exec memb Cncl of Inst of Grocery Distribution; dir Campsie Springs (Scotland) Ltd; *Recreations* golf; *Clubs* RAC, Breadsill Priory Golf; *Style—* George Risley, Esq; Hazlewood Foods plc, Rowditch, Derby (☎ 0332 295295, fax 0332 292300, telex 377872)

RISNESS, Dr Eric John; CBE (1982); s of Kristen Riisnaes (sic) (d 1981), and Ethel Agnes, *née* Weeks, of 64 Leasway, Bedford; *b* 27 July 1927; *Educ* Stratford GS, Univ of Cambridge (MA, PhD); *m* 26 July 1952, Colleen Edwina, da of Reginald Edwin Armstrong (d 1975); 2 s (Michael b 1958, Stephen b 1972), 2 da (Susan b 1953, Julia b 1968); *Career* joined MOD 1954; various posts in res and devpt of naval equipment incl: dir of res Undersea Warfare 1975-76, project mangr Sting Ray torpedo 1976-78, dir Naval Analysis 1982-83, DG Surface Weapons 1983-84, dep dir and md Admty Res Estab Portland 1984-87; md STC Technology Ltd 1987-90; chm Shalford Choral Soc; FIEE 1963, FEng 1990; *Recreations* genealogy, music, golf; *Clubs* Bramley Golf; *Style—* Dr Eric Risness, CBE; 8 Orchard Rd, Shalford, Guildford, Surrey GU4 8ER (☎ 0483 34581)

RIST, Prof John Michael; s of Robert Ward Rist (d 1984), of Southend, and Phoebe May, *née* Mansfield (d 1984); *b* 6 July 1936; *Educ* Brentwood Sch, Trinity Coll Cambridge (MA); *m* 30 July 1960, Anna Thérèse, da of Sidney Vogler (d 1982); 2 s (Peter John Robert b 1964, Thomas Charles Kenelm b 1971), 2 da (Alice Mary Anna b 1966, Rebecca Agnes Clare b 1975); *Career* Nat Serv 1954-56; Univ of Toronto: lectr in Greek 1959-63, asst prof 1963-65, assoc prof 1965-69, prof of classics 1969- (and philosophy 1983-), Regius prof of classics Univ of Aberdeen 1980-83; past pres Campaign Life (Canada); past memb Bd: Oxfam (Canada), Canairelief; FRSC 1976-; *Books* Eros and Psyche (1964), Plotinus (1967), Stoic Philosophy (1969), Epicurus (1972, Italian translation 1978), The Stoics (ed 1978), On The Independence of Matthew and Mark (1978), Human Value (1982), Platonism and Its Christian Heritage (1985), The Mind of Aristotle (1989); *Recreations* travel, walking, swimming; *Style—* John Rist, Esq; Department of Classics, University of Toronto, Toronto M5S 1A1 (☎ 0101 416 978 5514)

RITBLAT, Jillian Rosemary (Jill); da of Max Leonard Slotover, FRCS, of Monte Carlo, Monaco, and Peggy Cherna, *née* Cohen; *b* 14 Dec 1942; *Educ* Newcastle upon Tyne Church HS, Roedean, Univ of London (BA); *m* 1, 21 April 1966, Elie A Zilkha, s of Abdulla K Zilkha, of Switzerland; 1 s (David b 1968), 1 da (Elaine b 1971); m 2, 27 Feb 1986, John Ritblat, s of Montie Ritblat, LDS (d 1984); *Career* called to the Bar 1963; alternative delegate UN Geneva for Int Cncl of Jewish Women 1977-79; events organiser Patrons of New Art Tate Gallery 1984-87 (chm 1987-90), memb: Advsy Cncl Friends of the Tate Gallery 1990-, Assoc of Museum of Modern Art Oxford 1986-; *Recreations* people, travel, skiing; *Style—* Mrs John Ritblat; 10 Cornwall Terrace, London NW1 4QP (☎ 071 486 4466)

RITBLAT, John Henry; s of Montie Ritblat (d 1984), and Muriel, *née* Glaskie; *b* 3 Oct 1935; *Educ* Dulwich, Univ of London, Coll of Estate Management; *m* 1, 1960, Isabel Paja Steinberg (d 1979); 2 s (Nicholas b 9 Aug 1961, James b 18 Feb 1967), 1 da (Suzanne b 15 Sept 1962); m 2, 27 Feb 1986, Jill Zilkha, *née* Slotover; *Career* articles West End firm of surveyors and valuers 1952-58, fndr ptnr Conrad Ritblat and Co (conslt surveyors and valuers) 1958, md Union Property Holdings (London) Ltd 1969, chm and md The British Land Company Plc 1970-; cmmr Crown Estate Paving Cmmn 1969, memb Exec Ctee Weizmann Inst 1970, sole sponsor Br Nat Ski Championships 1978-90, hon surveyor King George's Fund for Sailors 1979, memb Cncl RGS 1984 (life memb 1982), vice pres Br Ski Fedn 1984-89, tstee Zoological Soc of London Devpt Tst 1986; memb: Prince of Wales' Royal Parks Tree Appeal Ctee, Fin Devpt Bd NSPCC; dep chm and govr Hall Sch, govr London Business Sch; FSVA 1968, FBIM; *Recreations* antiquarian books & libraries, old buildings, squash, golf, skiing; *Clubs* RAC, MCC, Bath Racquets, Cresta (St Moritz); *Style—* John Ritblat, Esq; 10 Cornwall Terrace, Regent's Park, London NW1 4QP (☎ 071 486 4466, telex 28411 BLUK G, fax 071 935 5552)

RITCHIE, Dr Anthony Elliot; CBE (1978); s of Prof James Ritchie, CBE (d 1958), and Jessie Jane, *née* Elliot (d 1933); *b* 30 March 1915; *Educ* Edinburgh Acad, Univ of Aberdeen (MA, BSc), Univ of Edinburgh (MB ChB, MD); *m* 18 July 1941, Elizabeth Lambie, da of John Knox (d 1956), of Dunfermline; 1 s (James Knox b 1949), 3 da (Innes Elizabeth b 1945, Margaret b 1950, Alison b 1958); *Career* Carnegie res scholar and lectr Physiology Dept Univ of Edinburgh 1941-48, prof physiology Univ of St Andrews 1948-69, sec and treas Carnegie Tst for Univs of Scotland 1969-86; chm numerous govt educn and sci ctees, memb Advsy Ctee Med Res 1960-69, sci advsr civil defence 1961-80, memb Br Library Bd 1973-80; tstee: Nat Lib of Scotland 1975-, Carnegie Tst 1986-; Hon DSc St Andrews 1972, Hon LLD Strathclyde 1985; Hon FCSP 1970, Hon FRCPEd 1986, FRSE 1951 (memb Cncl 1957-80, gen sec 1966-76, bicentenary gold medal 1983); *Books* Clinical Electromyography (with Dr Jar Lenman, 4 edn 1986); *Recreations* reading, hill-walking, motor cars, electronics; *Clubs* New (Edinburgh), Caledonian; *Style—* Dr Anthony Ritchie, CBE, FRSE; 12 Ravelston Park, Edinburgh EH4 3DX (☎ 031 332 6560)

RITCHIE, Hon Charles Rupert Rendall; s and h of 5 Baron Ritchie of Dundee; *b* 15 March 1958; *m* 1984, Tara, da of Howard J Koch, Jr, of USA; *Style—* The Hon Charles Ritchie

RITCHIE, Prof Donald Andrew; s of Andrew Ritchie (d 1985), of Falkirk, and Winifred Laura, *née* Parkinson; *b* 9 July 1938; *Educ* Latymer's Sch Edmonton, Univ of Leicester (BSc), Postgrad Med Sch Univ of London (PhD); *m* 22 Aug 1962, (Margaret) Jeanne, da of Henry Eden Collister, of Port St Mary, IOM; 1 s (Charles b 1969), 1 da (Sarah b 1967); *Career* res assoc Biophysics Dept John Hopkins Univ Baltimore 1964-66, sr lectr Dept of Virology Univ of Glasgow 1972-78 (lectr 1966-72), prof of genetics and head Dept of Genetics and Microbiology Univ of Liverpool 1988- (prof of genetics and head Dept of Genetics 1978-88); published articles in scientific jls; memb: Sci Bd and chm Educn and Trg Panel Sci and Engrg Res Cncl, Biotechnol Jt Advsy Bd, Terrestrial Life Scis Ctee NERC; memb: Br Legion, Liverpool City Club; FIBiol 1978, FRSE 1979, FRSA 1983, CBiol 1985; *Books* Molecular Virology (with T H P Ennington, 1975), Introduction to Virology (with K M Smith, 1980); *Recreations* painting, gardening, walking; *Style—* Prof Donald Ritchie; Glenfinnan, 19 Bertram Drive, Meols, Wirral L47 OLG (☎ 051 632 1985); Univ of Liverpool, Dept of Genetics and Microbiology, Donnan Laboratories, Liverpool L69 3BX (☎ 051 794 3624, fax 051 708 6502, telex 627095)

RITCHIE, Douglas Malcolm; s of Ian David Ritchie, of Montreal, Canada, and Helen Mary, *née* Jamieson; *b* 8 Jan 1941; *Educ* McGill Univ Canada (BSc, MBA); *m* 11 Sept 1965, Cydney Ann, da of Raymond Brown, of Montreal, Canada; 3 s (Campbell, Raymond, Neill); *Career* exec vice pres Alcan Canada Prods Toronto 1975-78 (vice pres 1973-75), corporate vice pres Aluminium Co of Canada Ltd Montreal 1978-80, pres and chief exec Alcan Smelters & Chemicals Ltd 1982-86 (exec vice pres 1980-82), md and chief exec offr Br Alcan Aluminium plc 1986-; non-exec dir: The Laurentian Group Corp Montreal, Laurentian Life plc (UK) 1989-, Laurentian Financial Group plc (UK) 1989-; memb Fndn for Canadian Studies in the UK; *Recreations* shooting, fishing, golf; *Style—* Douglas Ritchie, Esq; Chalfont Park, Gerrards Cross, Bucks SL9 0QB (☎ 0753 887373, fax 0753 889667, telex 847343)

RITCHIE, Graham; *b* 13 July 1948; *Educ* Jesus Coll Cambridge (MA); *m* 6 Feb 1971, Jacqueline Mary; 1 s, 3 da; *Career* slr; sr ptnr Ritchie and Co Cambridge; dir Br Inst of Securities Law, exec sec Centre for Int Documentation on Organised and Economic Crime; articles and reports: International Child Kidnapping (1979), Domestic Violence and Women's Refuges (1979), report to Cwlth Law Mins Meeting 1983 on International Aspects of Child Abuse; *Recreations* sailing, swimming, cycling, literature; *Style—* Graham Ritchie, Esq; 10 Milton Rd, Cambridge (☎ 0223 355440, fax 0223 358865)

RITCHIE, Hamish Martin Johnston; s of James Martin Ritchie, of Beaconsfield, Bucks, and Noreen Mary Louise, *née* Johnston; *b* 22 Feb 1942; *Educ* Loretto, ChCh Oxford (MA); *m* 20 Sept 1967, (Judith) Carol, da of Frank Knight Young, of Bearsden, Scotland; 1 s (Stuart b 1970), 1 da (Susan b 1972); *Career* md Hogg Robinson UK Ltd 1980-81 (dir 1974-80); chm: Bowring London Ltd 1981-, CT Bowring & Co Ltd 1983-, CT Bowring (Charities Fund) Ltd 1983-; chm and chief exec Bowring UK Ltd 1985-; non-exec dir: RAC Insurance Brokers Ltd 1985-, RICS Insurance Services Ltd 1989-; non-exec dep chm British Insurance & Investment Brokers Association 1987-, dir The Royal Automobile Club 1990-; chm govrs Caldicott Sch, govr Loretto Sch; CBIM; *Recreations* music and all sport (especially golf); *Clubs* MCC, RAC, R & A, Denham Golf; *Style—* Hamish Ritchie, Esq; Oldhurst, Bulstrode Way, Gerrards Cross, Bucks SL9 7QT (☎ 0753 883262); The Bowring Building, Tower Place, London EC3P 3BE (☎ 071 357 1000, fax 071 929 2705, telex 882191)

RITCHIE, Ian Carl; s of Christopher Charles Ritchie (d 1959), and Mabel Berenice, *née* Long (d 1981); *b* 24 June 1947; *Educ* Varndean-Brighton Liverpool, Sch of Architecture Central London Poly (Dip Arch); *m* Jocelyne Van den Bossche; 1 s (Inti b 1983); *Career* architect; princ Ian Ritchie Architects 1981-, ptnr Chrysalis Architects 1979-81, dir Rice Francis Ritchie (RFR) Paris (engrg design) 1981-86 (now conslt); designs exhibited at: ICA, Biennale de Paris, Centre Pompidou Paris; RIBA: external examiner 1983-, pres medal assessor 1987, nat chm awards 1988; work published in architectural books and magazines in UK, Europe, USA, Asia 1976-; taught at: Oita Univ Japan 1970, Planning Sch PCL London 1972, Architectural Assoc 1979-82; visiting critic Univ of Sheffield 1985-87; Tableau de L'Ordre des Architectes Francais 1982, Silver medal Architectural Design 1982 (for Eagle Rock House); FRIBA, MCSD; *Recreations* art, swimming, reading, writing, film making, lecturing on concept design; *Clubs* Architecture; *Style—* Ian C Ritchie, Esq

RITCHIE, Ian Russell; s of Hugh Russell Ritchie (d 1985), of 11 Marsden Ave, Beeston, Leeds, and Sheelah, *née* Matthews; *b* 27 Nov 1953; *Educ* Leeds GS, Trinity Coll Oxford (MA); *m* 12 June 1982, Jill Evelyn, da of Douglas Middleton-Walker, of Thorpe Arch, Boston Spa, W Yorkshire; 1 s (Andrew Russell b 13 Jan 1987); *Career* called to the Bar Middle Temple 1976 (in practice 1976-78), industl rels advsr Engrg

Employers Assoc Yorks 1978-80, Granada TV Manchester 1980-88 (ultimately head of prodn servs), dir resources Tyne Tees TV 1988-; Newcastle exec memb The Common Purpose; *Recreations* golf, tennis, theatre, television; *Clubs* Vincents (Oxford); *Style*— Ian Ritchie, Esq; Tyne Tees TV, City Rd, Newcastle upon Tyne (☎ 091 261 0181)

RITCHIE, Sir James Edward Thomson; 2 Bt (UK 1918), of Highlands; TD (1943) and two clasps; s of Sir James William Ritchie, MBE, 1 Bt (d 1937), and Ada, da of Edward Bevan; *b* 16 June 1902; *Educ* Rugby, Queen's Coll Oxford; *m* 1, 1928 (m dis 1936), Esme (d 1939), only da of late James Montague Oldham, of Ormidale, Ascot; m 2, 1936, Rosemary, yr da of late Col Henry Sidney John Streatfeild, DSO, TD; 2 da; *Career* served WWII, various staff and regimental appts (Central Med Force 1944-45); chm M W Hardy & Co Ltd 1948-78, dir William Ritchie & Son (Textiles) Ltd, patron of Ashford and Dist Caledonian Soc, memb Court of Assts Merchant Taylors' Co (master 1963-64), Hon Lt-Col late Inns of Court Regt RAC (TA), a selected mil memb Kent T&AFA 1953-68, pres Ashford Branch Royal Br Legion 1951-75, jt hon treas and chm Fin and Gen Purposes Ctee London Sch of Hygiene and Tropical Med Univ of London 1951-61 (memb Fin and Gen Purposes Ctee and a co-opted memb Bd of Mgmnt 1964-65); FRSA; *Style*— Sir James Ritchie, Bt, TD; 3 Farquhar Street, Bengeo, Hertford SG14 3BN

RITCHIE, James Walter; MC; s of Sir Adam Ritchie (d 1957), and Vivienne, *née* Lentaigne; *b* 12 Jan 1920; *Educ* Ampleforth, Clare Coll Cambridge; *m* 10 March 1951, Penelope June, da of late Thomas Lawrence Forbes, of Chilbolton; 2 s (Michael b 3 Aug 1953, Peter b 21 Sept 1958), 2 da (Jennifer (Mrs Corry) b 3 March 1952, Vivienne (Mrs Brann) b 20 Sept 1956); *Career* 2 Lt to Capt (Res) Adj 5/7 and 1 Bn Gordon Highlanders 1942-46; Smith Mackenzie & Co Ltd: Tanzania Uganda Kenya 1946-61, chm Nairobi 1970; md Inchcape plc 1976-84; jt master Tedworth Hunt 1986-90; *Recreations* hunting, fishing, golf; *Clubs* Oriental; *Style*— James Ritchie, Esq, MC; Lockeridge Down, Marlborough, Wilts SN8 4EL (☎ 0672 86244)

RITCHIE, Hon Mrs (Jean Davina); *née* Stuart; da of 1 Viscount Stuart of Findhorn, PC, CH, MVO, MC (d 1971); *b* 7 Jan 1932; *m* 1, 1951, John Reedham Erskine Berney, Lt Royal Norfolk Regt (ka Korea 1952), s of late Maj Sir Thomas Reedham Berney, 10 Bt, MC; 1 s; m 2, 1954, Percy William Jesson, s of Lt-Col Harold Jesson; 2 s, 1 da; m 3, 1985, Michael Denison Ritchie, s of Maj-Gen W H D Ritchie, CB, CBE; *Style*— The Hon Mrs Ritchie; Ballindarroch, Scaniport, Inverness

RITCHIE, Dr John Hindle; MBE (1985); s of Charles Ritchie, of Wylam, Northumberland (d 1983), and Bertha, *née* Hindle (d 1972); *b* 4 June 1937; *Educ* Royal GS Newcastle upon Tyne, Univ of Liverpool (BArch), Univ of Sheffield (PhD); *m* 24 August 1963, Anne, da of John Leyland, of Upton Wirral; 2 da (Jane b 1968, Nicola b 1971); *Career* SRC 1963-66, Liverpool City Cncl 1966-69, Rowntree Housing Trust 1969-72, Cheshire CC 1972-74, Merseyside CC 1974-80, chief exec and memb Bd Merseyside Development Corporation 1985- (dir of devpt 1980-85); chm Merseyside Education and Training Enterprise Ltd; *Style*— Dr John Ritchie, MBE; Merseyside Development Corporation, Royal Liver Building, Pierhead, Liverpool L3 1JH (☎ 051 236 6090)

RITCHIE, John Vivian; s of Maj John Stewart Ritchie (ka 1940), and Doris Ritchie (d 1934); *b* 30 Oct 1928; *Educ* Clifton Coll Bristol, RMA Sandhurst; *m* 1 (m dis); 1 s (Guy b 1968), 1 da (Tabitha b 1966); m 2, Shireen, *née* Folkard; 1 step s (Oliver Williams b 1979); *Career* Army: private Seaforth Highlanders 1947-48, cadet RMA Sandhurst 1948-50, offr Seaforth Highlanders served Malaya 1950-53 and Germany 1953-56 (ret as Capt); advtg exec C J Lytle Advertising 1956-60, account exec Smith Warden 1960-62, TV prodr Grants Advertising 1962-63, Collett Dickenson Pearce 1963-64, mktg mangr John Player & Sons 1965-68; Collett Dickenson Pearce: account dir 1968-79, dep chm 1979-; accounts worked on incl: Harveys Bristol Cream, Cockburns Port, Chunky Dog Food, Benson & Hedges, Hamlet Cigars; MInstM, fell IPA; *Recreations* tennis, golf, sailing; *Style*— John Ritchie, Esq; 47 Oakley Gardens, London SW3 5QQ (☎ 071 376 8051); Collett Dickenson Pearce & Partners, 110 Euston Rd, London NW1 2DQ (☎ 071 288 2424)

RITCHIE, Margaret Claire; da of Roderick Macintosh Ritchie (d 1975), of Edinburgh, and Ida, *née* Neal; *b* 18 Sept 1937; *Educ* Central Newcastle HS, Leeds Girls' HS, Univ of Leeds (BSc), Univ of London (PGCE); *Career* asst sci teacher St Leonard's Sch St Andrews 1960-64, head of sci dept Wycombe Abbey Sch 1964-71, headmistress Queenswood Sch Hatfield 1971-81, headmistress Queen Mary Sch Lytham 1981-; memb Soroptimist Int; memb: SHA, GSA; *Style*— Miss Margaret Ritchie; Queen Mary School, Lytham, Lancs FY8 1DS (☎ 0253 723246)

RITCHIE, Hon Philippa Jane; da of 5 Baron of Ritchie of Dundee; *b* 14 Aug 1954; *Educ* St Mary's Convent Baldslow, UCL (BA); *Career* actress; *Style*— The Hon Philippa Ritchie; 12 Oxford Gdns, London W4

RITCHIE, Richard Bulkeley; s of William Charles Hamilton Bryan Ritchie (d 1984), of Hy-Brasail, Baily, Dublin, Eire, and Ruth Mary, *née* Bulkeley; *b* 6 Sept 1952; *Educ* Shrewsbury, St Catherine's Coll Oxford (BA); *m* 28 Sept 1985, Dr Susan Rosemary Foister, da of Walter Philip Chatby Foister, of 65 St Helen's Park Rd, Hastings, E Sussex; 1 s (Felix b 1986), 1 da (Isabella b 1988); *Career* called to the Bar Middle Temple 1978, standing counsel to the DTI in insolvency matters 1989; *Style*— Richard Ritchie, Esq; 24 Old Buildings, Lincoln's Inn, London WC2 (☎ 071 404 0946, fax 071 405 1360)

RITCHIE, Shirley Anne; QC (1979); da of James Ritchie, of Johannesburg, SA, and Helen Sutherland, *née* Peters; *b* 10 Dec 1940; *Educ* St Mary's Diocesan Sch Pretoria, Rhodes Univ (BA, LLB); *m* 23 May 1969, Robin Hamilton Corson Anwyl, s of Douglas Fraser Corson (d 1978); 2 s (Jonathan b 1973, James b 1975); *Career* called to S African Bar 1963 and Inner Temple 1966; rec of the Crown Ct 1981-; memb: Senate of Inns of Court and Bar 1978-81, Gen Cncl of the Bar 1987, Criminal Injuries Compensation Bd 1980-, Mental Health Review Tbnl 1983-; chm Barristers Benevolent Assoc 1989-; Master of the Bench of the Inner Temple 1985; FRSA; *Recreations* theatre, music, sailing; *Clubs* The Acad; *Style*— Shirley A Ritchie, QC; c/o 4 Paper Buildings, Temple, London EC4Y 7EX (☎ 071 353 1131, fax 071 353 4979)

RITCHIE, Prof William; s of Alexander Ritchie, and Rebecca Smith, *née* Caldwell; *b* 22 March 1940; *Educ* Wishaw High Sr Secdy Sch, Univ of Glasgow (BSc, PhD); *m* 29 March 1965, Elizabeth Armstrong Bell; 2 s (Derek Alexander b 26 June 1967, Craig William b 11 Dec 1968), 1 da (Lynne Elspeth b 10 Feb 1978); *Career* res asst Univ of Glasgow 1963; Univ of Aberdeen 1964-: asst lectr 1964-66, lectr 1966-72, sr lectr 1972-79, prof 1979-, dean of Faculty of Arts and Social Sciences 1988-89, vice princ 1990- ; visiting prof Louisiana State Univ; sometime memb: Scot Examination Bd, Scot Univs Cncl of Entrance, Nature Conservancy Cncl (Scot); formerly recorder and pres Section E Br Assoc for Advancement of Sci, cncl memb RSE; currently: vice chm Sullom Voe Oil Terminal Environmental Advsy Gp, chm St Fergus Dunes Tech Mgmnt Ctee, convenor SCOVACT, memb Environmental Ctee American Assoc of Petroleum Geologists; FRSGS 1980, FRSE 1982, FRICS 1989; *Books* Mapping for Field Scientists (1977), Beaches of Highlands and Islands of Scotland (1978), Beaches of Scotland (1984), Surveying and Mapping for Field Scientists (1988), The Coastal Sand Dunes of Louisiana (Volume 1 Isles Dernieres (1989), Volume 2 Plaquemines (1990), Volume 3 Chandeleurs (1991)); *Style*— Prof William Ritchie, FRSE; Department of Geography, The University, Old Aberdeen (☎ 0224 272328, fax 0224 487048, telex 73458 UNIABN G)

RITCHIE-CALDER, Baroness; Mabel Jane Forbes; yr da of David McKail, MD, DPH, FRCPG, of Glasgow; *m* 11 Oct 1927, Baron Ritchie-Calder, CBE, journalist and author; sometime chm Metrication Bd and prof of int rels Univ of Edinburgh (d 1982); 3 s, 2 da; *Style*— The Rt Hon Lady Ritchie-Calder; 4/57 Gillsland Road, Edinburgh EH10 5BW (☎ 031 229 7653)

RITCHIE OF DUNDEE, 5 Baron (UK 1905); (Harold) Malcolm Ritchie; s of 2 Baron Ritchie of Dundee (d 1948), and Sarah Ruth, da of Louis Jennings MP; suc bro, 4 Baron 1978; *b* 29 Aug 1919; *Educ* Stowe, Trinity Coll Oxford (MA); *m* 1948, Anne, da of Col Charles Johnstone, MC, of Durban; 1 s (Rupert), 1 da (Philippa); *Heir* s, Hon (Charles) Rupert Rendall Ritchie; *Career* served WWII as Capt KRRC, Middle East, Greece and Italy; headmaster Brickwall House Sch 1965-72; currently educn spokesman in Lords for Lib Democrat Peers; *Recreations* the arts, gardening, walking; *Style*— Rt Hon Lord Ritchie of Dundee; The Roundel, Springsteps, Winchelsea, E Sussex (☎ 0797 226440)

RITCHLEY, Martin Howard; s of Robert William Ritchley (d 1964), of Orpington, Kent, and Bertha Amy, *née* Jones; *b* 1 July 1946; *Educ* City of London Sch; *m* 3 July 1970, (Mary) Elizabeth, da of Albert William Burns (d 1969), of Stevenage; 1 s (David b 1975), 2 da (Catherine b 1971, Anna b 1980); *Career* articled to Barton Mayhew & Co CAs 1964-70; Coventry Econ Bldg Soc: chief accountant 1970-76, sec 1976-83; Coventry Bldg Soc: sec 1983-89, dir 1985, dep chief exec 1989-90, chief exec 1990-; FCA 1979; *Recreations* golf; *Clubs* Coventry GC; *Style*— Martin Ritchley, Esq; 6 Cannon Hill Rd, Coventry CV4 7AZ (☎ 0203 418 148); Coventry Building Society, Economic House, PO Box 9, High St, Coventry CV1 5QN (☎ 0203 555 255, fax 0203 226 469)

RITSON, Dr (Edward) Bruce; s of Maj Harold Ritson (d 1979), of Edinburgh, and Ivy, *née* Catherall (d 1972); *b* 20 March 1937; *Educ* Edinburgh Acad, Univ of Edinburgh, Harvard Univ (MD, MB ChB, DPM); *m* 25 Sept 1965, Eileen Teresa, da of Leonard Carey, of Dublin; 1 s (Gavin b 1970), 1 da (Fenella b 1968); *Career* dir Sheffield Region Addiction Unit 1968-71, conslt Royal Edinburgh Hosp 1971-, sr lectr in psychiatry Univ of Edinburgh 1971-, advsr WHO 1977-, conslt W Australia Alcohol and Driving Authy 1983; chm: Howard League (Scotland), Exec Med Cncl on Alcoholism, Professional Advsy Ctee Scottish on Alcohol; alcohol gp advsr Health and Safety Exec EEC; FRCPsych 1979, FRCP (Edinburgh) 1987; *Books* The management of Alcoholism (with C Hassall, 1970), Alcohol: The Prevention Debate (with M Grant, 1983), Alcohol Our Favourite Drug (1986); *Recreations* theatre, travel, squash; *Clubs* Edinburgh Univ; *Style*— Dr Bruce Ritson; 4 McLaren Rd, Edinburgh, Scotland EH9 2BH (☎ 031 667 1735); Royal Edinburgh Hospital, Morningside Park, Edinburgh (☎ 031 447 2011)

RITTNER, Luke Philip Hardwick; *b* 24 May 1947; *Educ* Blackfriars Sch Northants, City of Bath Tech Coll, Dartington Coll of Arts, LAMDA; *m* 1974, Corinna Frances Edholm; 1 da; *Career* asst administrator Bath Festival 1968, admin dir Bath Festival 1974, dir and founder Association for Business Sponsorship of the Arts 1976, sec-gen Arts Council 1983-90, chm English Shakespeare Co, Br Cultural dir Expo '92 Seville; *Style*— Luke Rittner, Esq; 29 Kelso Place, London W8 5QG (☎ 071 938 3164)

RIVERDALE, 2 Baron (UK 1935); Sir Robert Arthur Balfour; 2 Bt (UK 1929), DL (S Yorks 1959); s of 1 Baron Riverdale, GBE (d 1957); *b* 1 Sept 1901; *Educ* Oundle; *m* 1, 1926, Nancy, da of Engr Rear-Adm Mark Rundle, DSO; 1 s; m 2, 1933, Christian, da of Maj Rowland Hill (ka 1915, ggggs of Sir Rowland Hill, 1 Bt); 1 s, 1 da; *Heir* s, Hon Mark Balfour; *Career* former co dir; pres Br Assoc Chambers Commerce; chevalier Crown of Belgium, Order of Leopold Medaille Civique; *Recreations* yachting, shooting, stalking, fishing; *Clubs* Sheffield; *Style*— Rt Hon Lord Riverdale, DL; Ropes, Grindleford, via Sheffield SB0 1HX (☎ 0433 30408)

RIVETT, Dr Geoffrey Christopher; s of Frank Andrew James Rivett (d 1970), of Salford, Lancs, and Catherine Mary, *née* Barlow (d 1973); *b* 11 Aug 1932; *Educ* Manchester GS, Brasenose Coll Oxford (MA), UCH Med Sch (BM BCh, DObstRCOG); *m* 1, March 1958 (m dis 1976), Joan Dorothy, *née* Peacock; 2 s (John Graham b 1960, Barry Mark b 1963); m 2, 17 April 1976, (Elizabeth) Barbara, da of Maj William Alfred Hartman (d 1968), of Uckfield, Sussex; *Career* Nat Serv Capt RAMC 1958-60; GP Bletchley Bucks 1960-72, Dept of Health 1972- (currently sr princ med offr); Freeman City of London 1981; memb: Worshipful Co of Apothecaries 1981 (Liveryman 1985), Worshipful Co of Barbers 1989; ARPS 1970, FRCGP 1987; *Books* The Development of the London Hospital System 1823-1982 (1986); *Recreations* house conversion, photography; *Clubs* RSM; *Style*— Dr Geoffrey Rivett; 50 Andrews House, Barbican, London EC2Y 8AX (☎ 071 628 5682); Shilling Orchard, Shilling St, Lavenham, Suffolk CO10 9RH (☎ 0787 247 808)

RIVETT-CARNAC, Cdr Miles James; s of Vice Adm James Rivett-Carnac (d 1970), and Isla Nesta, *née* Blackwood (d 1973); hp of bro, Rev Sir Nicholas Rivett-Carnac, 8 Bt; *b* 7 Feb 1933; *Educ* RNC Dartmouth; *m* 11 Oct 1958, April Sally, da of Maj Arthur Andrew Sidney Villar (d 1966), of 48 Lowndes Square, London SW1; 2 s (Jonathan b 1962, Simon b 1966), 1 da (Lucinda b 1960); *Career* Cdr RN 1965, cmd HMS Woolaston 1963-65 (despatches), Armed Forces Staff Coll Norfolk Virginia USA 1965, cmd HMS Dainty 1966-68, MOD 1968-70, ret 1970; joined Baring Bros & Co Ltd 1970 (dir 1975), md Outwich Ltd Johannesburg 1976-78, pres Baring Bros Inc 1978-81; memb Exec Ctee Baring Bros & Co 1981, dir Barings plc 1986-, chief exec Baring Asset Management Ltd 1986-, chm Tribune Investment Trust 1985-; chm Hampshire and IOW Boys' Clubs, memb Exec Ctee King Edward VII Hosp, memb Cncl King George V Fund for Sailors; *Recreations* golf, tennis, stamps, racing; *Clubs* White's, Links (NY); *Style*— Cdr Miles Rivett-Carnac, RN; Martyr Worthy Manor, nr Winchester, Hants SO12 1DY (☎ 096 278 311); Baring Bros & Co Ltd, 8 Bishopsgate, London EC2 (☎ 071 283 8833)

RIVETT-CARNAC, Rev Canon Sir (Thomas) Nicholas; 8 Bt (UK 1836); s of Vice Adm James William Rivett-Carnac, CB, CBE, DSC (d 1970; 2 s of 6 Bt), and Isla Nesta, *née* Blackwood (d 1974); suc unc 1972; *b* 3 June 1927; *Educ* Marlborough; *m* 1977, Susan Marigold MacTier, yr da of late C Harold Copeland; *Heir* bro, Miles James Rivett-Carnac; *Career* served Scots Guards 1945-55; ordained 1962, curate Holy Trinity Brompton 1968-72, priest-in-charge St Mark's Kennington Oval 1972-89, rural dean of Lambeth 1978-82, hon canon Southwark Cathedral 1980-; memb London Probation Service 1958-60, pastor Kingdom Faith Ministries Roffey Place Horsham W Sussex 1989-; *Style*— The Rev Canon Sir Nicholas Rivett-Carnac, Bt; 23 Heather Close, Horsham, West Sussex RH12 4XD

RIVETT-DRAKE, Brig Dame Jean Elizabeth Rivett; DBE (1964, MBE 1947), JP (1965), DL (E Sussex 1983); da of Cdr Bertram Gregory Drake, and Dora Rivett-Drake; *b* 13 July 1909; *Educ* St Mary's Hall Brighton, Paris, RAM (LRAM piano); *Career* served WWII (despatches 1946), driver 1 London Motor Transport Co, Women's Tport Serv (FANY) 1940, cmmnd ATS 1942, served with Br Liberation Army 1945-47, Lt-Col WRAC 1948-56, dep pres Regular Cmmns Bd 1948-49, London Dist 1952-54, asst dep dir FARELF 1954-56, dep dir War Office 1957-60, Eastern Cmd 1960-61, Col 1957-61, Brig 1961-64, ADC (Hon) to HM The Queen 1961-64; memb Hove Borough Cncl 1966-83, lay memb Press Cncl 1973-78, memb E Sussex

CC 1973-77, mayor of Hove 1977-78; *Clubs* English Speaking Union; *Style—* Brig Dame Jean Rivett-Drake, DBE, JP, DL; c/o Barclays Bank, Town Hall Branch, 92 Church Rd, Hove, E Sussex

RIX, Bernard Anthony; QC (1981); s of Otto Rix (d 1982), of London, and Sadie, *née* Silverberg; *b* 8 Dec 1944; *Educ* St Paul's, New Coll Oxford (MA), Harvard Law Sch (Kennedy Scholar, LLM); *m* 1983, Hon Karen, da of Baron Young of Graffham, PC; 2 s, 1 da; *Career* called to the Bar Inner Temple 1970, memb Senate of the Inns of Ct and Bar 1981-83; bencher Inner Temple 1990, rec 1990; dir London Philharmonic Orch 1986-; chm British Friends of Bar Ilan Univ 1987-, memb Bd of Tstees of Bar Ilan Univ 1988-; *Recreations* music, opera, Italy; *Style—* Bernard Rix, Esq, QC; 3 Essex Court, London EC4 (☎ 071 583 9294)

RIX, Sir Brian Norman Roger; CBE (1977), DL (Greater London 1987); s of Herbert Dobson Rix (d 1966), of E Yorks, and Fanny, *née* Nicholson (d 1976); *b* 27 Jan 1924; *Educ* Bootham Sch York; *m* 1949, Elspet Jeans MacGregor, da of James MacGregor (d 1954), of Surrey; 2 s (Jamie, Jonathan), 2 da (Shelley, Louisa); *Career* WWII RAF and Bevin Boy; actor-manager 1948-77; ran repertory cos at Ilkley, Bridlington and Margate 1948-50, toured Reluctant Heroes and brought to Whitehall Theatre 1950-54, Dry Rot 1954-58, Simple Spymen 1958-61, One for the Pot 1961-64, Chase Me Comrade 1964-66, Stand By Your Bedouin, Uproar in the House and Let Sleeping Wives Lie Garrick Theatre 1967-69, She's Done It Again 1969-70, Don't Just Lie There, Say Something! 1971-73 (filmed 1973), Robinson Crusoe 1973, A Bit Between the Teeth 1974-75, Fringe Benefits 1976-77; entered films 1951 and subsequently made 13 films incl Reluctant Heroes 1951 and Dry Rot 1956; BBC TV contract to present farces on TV 1956-72, first ITV series Men of Affairs 1973, A Roof Over My Head 1977; presenter: Let's Go BBC TV series (first ever for people with a mental handicap) 1978-83, BBC Radio 2 Series 1978-80; dir and theatre controller Cooney-Marsh Group 1977-80, sec gen MENCAP 1980-87 (chm 1988-); memb: Arts Cncl,; Friends of Normansfield Drama Panel, Arts and Disabled People 1986-, Libertas 1987; tstee Theatre of Comedy 1983-, chm Ind Devpt Cncl for People with Mental Handicap 1981-88, hon vice pres Radio Soc of GB; Hon MA: Hull 1981, Open Univ 1983; Hon DSc Nottingham, Hon DUniv Essex 1984-, Hon LLD Manchester 1986; Vice Lord-Lt (Greater London 1988-); kt 1986; *Books* My Farce from My Elbow (autobiography, 1975), Farce about Face - a further autobiography (1989); *Recreations* cricket, gardening, amateur radio; *Clubs* Garrick, MCC, Lord's Taverners (past pres); *Style—* Sir Brian Rix, CBE, DL; 3 St Mary's Grove, Barnes Common, London SW13

RIX, Sir John; MBE (1955), DL (Hants 1985); s of Reginald Arthur Rix (d 1948), of Burnham, Bucks; *b* 30 Jan 1917; *Educ* ISC Haileybury, Univ of Southampton; *m* 1953, Sylvia Gene, da of Capt Cecil Lewis Howe (d 1979); 2 s, 1 da; *Career* Vosper plc: joined 1937, gen mangr 1955, dir 1958, md 1963-78, chm and chief exec 1978-82, chm 1982-85, dir Vosper Private Ltd 1966-85, chm and chief exec Vosper Thornycroft (UK) Ltd 1970-77 (md 1966-70), Charismarine Ltd 1976-88; chm: Vosper Ship Repairs Ltd 1977-78, Vosper Hovermarine Ltd 1980-85, Mainwork Ltd 1980-85, Southampton Cable Ltd 1985-87, Chilworth Centre Ltd 1985-, Seahorse Int Ltd 1986-90; dep chm Victorian Cruise Line Ltd 1988-; kt 1977; *Recreations* sailing, tennis, walking, golf; *Clubs* Royal Thames Yacht; *Style—* Sir John Rix, MBE, DL; Lower Baybridge House, Owslebury, Winchester, Hants (☎ 096 274 306

RIX, Hon Mrs (Karen Debra); *née* Young; er da of Baron Young of Graffham (Life Peer); *b* 1957; *m* 1983, Bernard Anthony Rix, *qv*; *Style—* The Hon Mrs Rix

RIX, Dr Keith John Barkclay; s of Sgt Kenneth Benjamin Rix, of Wisbech, and Phyllis Irene, *née* Cousins (d 1985); *b* 21 April 1950; *Educ* Wisbech GS, Univ of Aberdeen (B Med Biol, MB ChB, MD), Univ of Edinburgh (MPhil); *m* 30 Jan 1976, Elizabeth Murray, da of Robert Lumsden, of Tullibody, Clackmannshire; 3 da (Virginia b 1977, Marianne b 1981, Rowena b 1982); *Career* res fell Dept of Physiology Univ of Aberdeen 1975-76, registrar in psychiatry Royal Edinburgh Hosp 1976-79, lectr in psychiatry Univ of Manchester 1979-83, sr lectr in psychiatry Univ of Leeds 1983-, conslt psychiatrist St James's Univ Hosp Leeds, visiting conslt psychiatrist HM Prison Leeds; fndr Aberdeen Cncl on Alcohol Problems, fndr memb Scottish Cncl on Alcohol Problems; MRCPsych 1979, MIBiol Chartered Biologist 1985, memb RSM; *Books* Alcohol and Alcoholism (1977), Alcohol Problems (with Elizabeth Lumsden Rix 1983), A Handbook for Trainee Psychiatrists (1987); *Recreations* bird watching, jazz, theatre; *Style—* Dr Keith Rix; St James's University Hospital, Department of Psychiatry, Roundhay Wing, Leeds LS9 7TF (☎ 0532 433144 ext 5501, fax 0532 426496)

RIX, Timothy John; s of Howard Terrell Rix (d 1979), and Marguerite Selman, *née* Helps; *b* 4 Jan 1934; *Career* Sub Lt RNVR 1952-54; Mellon Fell Yale 1957-58; Longmans Green & Co Ltd: joined 1958, overseas educnl publisher 1958-61, publishing mangr Far E and SE Asia 1961-63, head of English language teaching publishing 1964-68, divnl md 1968-72, jt md 1972-76, chief exec 1976, chm 1984; chm and chief exec: Longman Group Ltd 1984-90, Addison-Wesley-Longman Group Ltd 1988-89; dir: Pearson Longman Ltd 1979-83, Goldcrest TV 1982-83, Yale University Press 1984-, ECIC (Management) Ltd 1990-, Blackie and Son Ltd 1990-; chm Book Marketing Ltd 1990-, sr conslt The Pofcher Co 1990-; pres Publishers Assoc 1982-84, dep chm Nat Book League 1985-86, govr Bell Educnl Tst 1990-; chm: Book Tst 1986-88, Book House Training Centre 1986-89, Br Library Centre for the Book 1990-, Soc of Bookmen 1990-; memb: Br Cncl Publisher Advsy Panel 1978-, Br Cncl Bd 1988-, Arts Cncl Lit Panel 1983-87, Br Library Advsy Cncl 1982-86, Br Library Bd 1986-; CBIM, FRSA; *Recreations* reading, landscape, wine; *Clubs* Garrick; *Style—* Timothy Rix, Esq; 27 Wolseley Rd, London N8 8RS (☎ 081 348 4143)

RIXSON, Air Cdre Denis Fenn; CVO (1986), OBE (1944), DFC (1941), AFC (1960); s of George Herbert Rixson (d 1954), of Westminster, and Anne, *née* Fenn (d 1958); *b* 12 Dec 1918; *Educ* Christs Hosp; *m* 7 Sept 1946, (Elizabeth) Hope (wid of Maj R H Northcott), da of George Douglas Budge (d 1957), of Monmouthshire and Fife; 2 s (Roderick George John b 26 Jan 1948 d Jan 1953, Robert Denis James b 14 March 1952), 1 da (Elizabeth Ann Mary b 12 Dec 1953); *Career* cmmnd RAF 1936, WWII serv ME and Europe 1939-45; serv: Rhodesia, India, UK 1946-60; Gp Capt dep dir operational requirements Air Miny 1960, Cdr RAF Geilenkirchen Germany 1962-63, Air Cdre Asst COS Intelligence AFCENT 1963-65, Air Offr i/c admin HQ Fighter Cmd Bentley Priory 1965-67, Cmdt ROC 1967-69; dir appeals and publicity Royal Hosp and Home for Incurables 1970-83, vice chm and trustee of Devpt Tst for the Young Disabled 1983-, tstee Amberley Chalk Pits Heritage Museum Tst 1983-, vice pres Throgmorton Euro Med Gp 1985-, conslt Home For Disbabled Ex-Servicemen Eastbourne 1987-, tstee Compaid Tst 1988-; *Recreations* swimming, gardening, fishing, cricket; *Clubs* RAF, MCC, Pratts; *Style—* Air Cdre Denis Rixson, CVO, OBE, DFC, AFC; Hesworth, Close Walks Wood, Midhurst, W Sussex GU29 OET (☎ 0730 084940)

RIZK, Dr Waheeb; CBE (1984, OBE 1977); s of Dr I Rizk, MD (d 1963), and Emily, *née* Elias (d 1935); *b* 11 Nov 1921; *Educ* EMC Cairo Egypt, Emmanuel Coll Cambridge (MA, PhD); *m* 5 April 1952, Vivien, da of Samuel Henry Leonard Moyle (d 1972), of Norwich, Norfolk; 1 s (Martin b 1959), 2 da (Imogen b 1953 d 1982, Meri b 1955); *Career* English Electric Research Laboratories: dept head 1954, chief engr Gas Turbine Dept 1957, gen mangr Gas and Industl Steam Turbine Div 1967; chm: Gas Turbines Ltd 1983-86 (md 1971), Ruston Diesels Ltd 1983-86; sr conslt W R Associates 1986-; winner American Soc Mech Engrs RT Sawyer award 1974, CIMAC Gold medal 1983; pres: Int Cncl of Combustion Engines CIMAC 1973-77, IMechE 1984-85 (memb Cncl 1978-89), dep pres BSI 1985- (chm Bd 1982-85), memb Cncl Cranfield Inst of Technol, memb Ct Brunel Univ; Freeman City of London 1983, Liveryman Worshipful Co of Engrg 1983 (memb Ct of Assts); FIMechE 1973, FEng 1979; *Clubs* Athenaeum; *Style—* Dr Waheeb Rizk, CBE; WR Associates, 20 Regent Place, Rugby, Warwickshire CV21 2PN (☎ 0788 567931, fax 0788 546449)

RIZZA, George Joseph; s of James Rizza (d 1974), and Emily Neri (d 1943); *b* 5 Nov 1925; *Educ* Gordons Sch Huntly, Royal Scottish Acad of Music; *m* 25 March 1969, Margaret, da of Harvey Gibson (d 1947); 1 da (Jane Diane b 1971); *Career* Novello & Co Ltd 1973-90, Laurel Music 1970-88, Cinderella 1978-88, Lorna Music 1978-88, Woodside Music 1978-82, Mayheu Music 1978-82, Fairfield 1975-88, Goodwin & Tabb 1975-88, Elkin 1975-88, Mercury Music 1973-88, Paxton 1976-88, Performing Right Society 1973, Jazz Journal 1973-83, Austria Travel 1986, Park Lane Gp 1964-80, J W Chester Ltd 1962-72; ARCM; *Style—* George Rizza, Esq; 14 Vine Avenue, Sevenoaks, Kent (☎ 0732 452429); Novello & Co Ltd, 8-10 Lower James St, London W1R 3PL (☎ 071 287 5060, fax 071 284 0816)

RIZZELLO, Michael Gaspard; OBE (1977); *b* 1926; *Educ* RCA (scholar, Drawing prize, maj travelling scholarship); *Career* sculptor; served WWII cmmnd Royal Fus, seconded 8 Punjab Regt India and Far East 1944-47; sculpture work incl: portrait busts of monarchs, rulers and heads of state and coin designs for 100 countries; most recent work incl: eleven foot statue for New Brunswick Canada, portrait bust of Lord Stevens of Ludgate at Ludgate House, over-lifesize bust of James Walker (civil engr) at Brunswick Quay Docklands, portrait of Nelson Mandela (exhibited Royal Acad 1990 and currently on perm exhibition at three locations incl Tanzania and TUC HQ); pres Royal Soc of Br Sculptors 1976 and 1981-86 (vice pres 1964-69, fell 1961), pres Soc of Portrait Sculptors 1968-73, chm Constance Fund 1990; *awards* Prix de Rome for Sculpture 1951, Sir Otto Beit Silver Medal for Sculpture 1961, Queen's Silver Jubilee Medal 1977; *Style—* Michael Rizzello, Esq, OBE; Melrose Studio, 7 Melrose Road, London SW18 1ND (☎ 081 870 8561, fax 081 877 9842)

RIZZI, Carlo; *Educ* Milan Conservatoire (studied with Maestro Rosada), Bologna (studied with Vladinir Delman), Academia Chigiana (studied with Franco Ferrara, awarded Dip of Merit); *Career* conductor; debut 1982 conducting Donizetti's L'Aio nell'imbarrazzo (Angelicum, Milan); work in Italian opera houses 1985-90 incl: Bologna, Palermo, Turin, Genoa, Bari, Lucca, Bergamo, Milan, Savona, Sassari, Treviso; works conducted incl: Rigoletto, La Traviata, Tancredi (Rossini), Torquato Tasso (Donizetti), Batrice de Tenda (Bellini), La Voix Humaine (Poulenc), Don Giovanni, L'Italiana in Algeri, Falstaff (Salieri's as well as Verdi's); other works conducted incl: all Tchaikovsky symphonies, several symphonies by Haydn, Mozart, Beethoven, Chausson, Saint-Saens, Franck and Roussel with orchestras in Milan, Bologna, Lucca, Piacenza, Treviso, San Remo and Holland; reg guest conductor with orchestras of the Hague, Arnhem and Haarlem 1985-, Br debut Torquato Tasso at Buxtom Festival 1988, conducted five different orchestras in tour of Japan 1989, conducted Fra Diavolo and Norma in Palermo 1989; debut with: Royal Philharmonic Orchestra in Barbican Hall London 1989, Australian Opera Co in Sydney (Il Barbiere di Siviglia) 1989, Netherlands Opera Amsterdam (Don Pasquale) 1989, Royal Opera House Covent Garden (La Cenerentola) 1990; recent work incl: Il Barbiere di Siviglia for WNO 1990, Tosca for Opera North 1990, seven concert tour of GB with London Philharmonic Orchestra conducting Schubert's Unfinished Symphony and Mahler's Symphony No 4; recordings incl: L'Italiana in Londra (Cimarosa), Il Furioso sull'Isola di San Domingo (Donizetti), Ciro in Babilonia (Rossini), La Scuffiara (Paisiello), La Pescatrice (Piccinni); *awards* second prize winner Besancon Conductor's Competition 1983, first prize winner Toscanini Conductors' Competition in Parma 1985, winner Italian Critics' prize (for L'Italiana in Londra); *Style—* Carlo Rizzi, Esq; Allied Artists, 42 Montpelier Square, London SW7 1JZ (☎ 071 589 6243, fax 071 581 6269, telex 9312100438 AA G)

ROACH, Prof Gary Francis; s of John Francis Roach (d 1982), and Bertha Mary Ann, *née* Walters (d 1975); *b* 8 Oct 1933; *Educ* Univ Coll of S Wales and Monmouthshire (BSc), Univ of London (MSc), Univ of Manchester (PhD); *m* 3 Sept 1960, Isabella Grace Willins Nicol; *Career* Flying Offr Educn Branch RAF 1955-58; res Mathmatician BP 1958-61, lectr UMIST 1961-66, visiting prof Univ of Br Columbia 1966-67; Univ of Strathclyde: lectr 1967-70, sr lectr 1970-71, reader 1971-79, prof 1979-, dean Faculty of Sci 1982-85; Incorporation of Bonnetmakers & Dyers Glasgow 1981; FRAS 1964, FIMA 1967, FRSE 1975; *Books* Green's Functions (second edn, 1982); *Recreations* mountaineering, photography, philately, gardening, music; *Style—* Prof Gary Roach, FRSE; 11 Menzies Ave, Fintry, Glasgow G63 0YE (☎ 036 086 335); Dept of Mathematics, Univ of Strathclyde, Livingstone Tower, 26 Richmond St, Glasgow G1 1XH (☎ 041 552 4400, ext 3800)

ROACH, Jill; da of Peter Roach, of the Cottage, Winthorpe, Notts, and Joan Catherine Roach; *b* 4 Sept 1946; *Educ* East Haddon Hall Sch Northants, Queen Mary Coll London (BA); *m* 1974 (separated), Robert Hedley Llewellyn Watkins, s of Arthur Goronwy Watkins, CBE; 2 s; *Career* former sr producer BBC TV (former ed John Craven's Newsround), head prodn Blackrod (ind TV prodn subsid of TVS), md Roach & Partners (ind prodn co); *Recreations* the children; *Style—* Miss Jill Roach; Roach and Partners, 2 Goldhawk Mews, London W12 9PA (☎ 081 746 2000)

ROACHE, Linus William; s of William Patrick Roache, of Manchester, and Anna, *née* Cropper; *b* 1 Feb 1964; *Educ* Bishop Luffa Comp Sch Chichester, Rydal Sch N Wales, Central Sch of Speech and Drama; *Career* actor; *roles incl* Clive in Five Finger Exercise (Cambridge Theatre Co), Pavel in the Mother (Contact Theatre Manchester), Billy in a Colder Climate (Royal Court), Geoff in A Taste of Honey (Theatre Royal Nottingham), Tom in Keeping Tom Nice (Almeida Theatre), Eric Blair in Divine Gossip; RSC Stratford/Barbican season 1987-88: Martius in Titus Andronicus, William in Indigo, Sacha in A Question of Geography, Mark Antony in Julius Caesar; Johnny Boyle in Juno and the Paycock (Royal Nat Theatre), Tom in The Glass Menagerie (Royal Exchange Manchester); RSC season 1990-91: Aumerle in Richard II, Edgar in King Lear, Don Juan in The Last Days of Don Juan; TV work incl: Peter Davison in A Sort of Innocence (BBC) 1986, Danny in Saracen (Central TV) 1989, Vincent in Vincent Van Gogh (Omnibus, BBC) 1990, Tom in Keeping Tom Nice (BBC) 1990; Manchester Evening News Awards nominations: Best Supporting Actor (for Pavel in The Mother) 1986, Best Actor (for Tom in The Glass Menagerie) 1990; *Recreations* golf, walking and exploring Great Britain; *Style—* Linus Roache, Esq; Kate Feast, 43a Princess Rd, Regents Park, London NW1 8JS (☎ 071 586 5502, fax 071 586 9817)

ROACHE, William; s of Dr William Vincent Roache (d 1982), and Hester Vera, *née* Waddicor; *b* 25 April 1932; *Educ* Rydal Sch Colwyn Bay N Wales; *m* 2, Sara McEwan, da of Sidney Mottram; 1 s (William James), 1 da (Verity Elizabeth b 1981); *Career* army serv: joined RWF 1951, cmmnd 1952, served W Indies and Germany, seconded Trucial Oman Scouts, Capt Gulf 1955-56; actor in repertory film and TV; role of Ken Barlow in Coronation St 1960-; dir: Lancashire Cable TV, Wigan Cable, Oyston Cable Communications; vice pres E Cheshire Hospice; *Recreations* golf, riding, tennis; *Clubs* Wilmslow Golf; *Style—* William Roache, Esq; Granada TV, Quay St, Manchester M60

9EA (☎ 061 832 7211)

ROAD, Christopher John; s of Alfred Sinclair Road, OBE, and Eve Helen, *née* Adlerova; *b* 7 May 1948; *Educ* St Paul's, Trinity Hall Cambrige (MA); *m* 5 June 1971, Zofia Alicja, da of Piotr Jan Pialucha (d 1972); 1 s (Thomas b 1980), 1 da (Katharine b 1974); *Career* gen serv offr Br Cncl 1971-78, ptnr Macfarlanes Slrs 1983- (joined 1979); memb: City of London Slrs Co, Law Soc; *Style*— Christopher Road, Esq; 50 Coalecroft Rd, London SW15 6LP (☎ 081 788 5601); 10 Norwich St, London EC4A 1BD (☎ 071 831 9222, fax 071 831 9607, telex 296381 MACFAR G)

ROADS, Dr Christopher Herbert; s of Herbert Clifford Roads (d 1963), of Kneesworth, Cambs, and Vera Iris, *née* Clark (d 1986); *b* 3 Jan 1934; *Educ* Cambridge & County Sch, Trinity Hall Cambridge (BA, MA, PhD); *m* 24 April 1976, Charlotte Alicia Dorothy Mary, da of Neil Lothian, of Mintern House, Minterne Magna, Dorchester, Dorset; 1 da (Cecilia Iris Muriel Lothian b 1981); *Career* Lt RA Egypt 1952-54, advsr to War Office on Disposal of Amnesty Arms 1961-62; keeper Dept of Records Imperial War Museum 1962-70 (dep DG 1964-79); fndr and dir: Cambridge Coral Starfish Res Gp 1968-, Duxford Aviation Museum (IWM) 1971-79; tstee later dir HMS Belfast Pool of London 1970-79; dir: Nat Sound Archive 1983-, Museums and Archives Devpt Associates Ltd 1977-85, Historic Cable Ship John W Mackay 1986-, Nat Discography Ltd 1986-, Cedar Audio Ltd, AVT Communications Ltd; UNESCO conslt in design and operation of audiovisual archives and museums in general 1976-; hon sec Cambridge Univ Long Range Rifle Club 1979; vice pres: World Expeditionary Soc 1971-, Duxford Aviation Soc 1974-, English Eight 1980-, Cambridge Univ Rifle Assoc 1987-; pres: Archive and Cataloguing Commission of Int Film and TV Cncl 1970-, Historical Breech Loading Small Arms Assoc 1973-, Int Film and TV Cncl 1990-, Cambridge Numismatic Soc 1964-66; memb: Cncl of Scientific Exploration Soc 1971-82, Cambridge Univ Rifle Assoc 1955-87; FRGS; Churchill Fellowship 1971; visiting fell Centre of Int Studies Univ of Cambridge 1983-84; Order of Independence 2 class (Jordan) 1977; *Recreations* rifle shooting (winner of various competitions), flying, marine & submarine exploration, wind surfing, cine & still photography; *Clubs* Hawks (Cambridge), United Oxford and Cambridge Univ; *Style*— Dr Christopher Roads; The White House, 90 High Street, Melbourn, nr Royston, Herts SG8 6AL; National Sound Archive, 29 Exhibition Road, London SW7

ROAKE, John; s of the late Joseph Henry Roake, and the late Muriel Mary, *née* Edgson; *b* 20 Dec 1923; *Educ* Leighton Park Sch Reading, Poly N London (Dip Arch); *m* 6 Nov 1948, Bertha, da of Louis Press (d 1987); 2 s (Matthew b 4 Feb 1955, Adam b 21 May 1958), 1 da (Dinah b 16 Jan 1961); *Career* chartered architect; ptnr WS Hattrell & Ptnrs 1961-88 (conslt 1988-); FRIBA; Membre de l'Ordre des Architectes Francais; *Recreations* swimming, walking, reading, theatre, travel; *Clubs* Reform; *Style*— John Roake, Esq; 22 St John's Rd, Bathwick, Bath, Avon BA2 6PX (☎ 0225 462726)

ROBARDS, Prof Anthony William; s of Albert Charles Robards, of Little Bayham, Lamberhurst, Tunbridge Wells, and Kathleen Emily Robards; *b* 9 April 1940; *Educ* The Skinners' Sch, UCL (BSc, PhD, DSc); *m* 1, 1962 (m dis 1985), Ruth, *née* Bulpett; 1 s (Martin David b 1967), 1 da (Helen Elizabeth b 1970); m 2, 30 March 1987, Eva Christina, da of Bo Knutson-Ek, of Lidingo, Sweden; *Career* prof and dir Inst for Applied Biology and Industl Devpt Univ of York; visiting res fell: Australian Nat Univ 1975, Univ of Stockholm 1986; pres Royal Microscopical Soc 1982-84, memb Rotary Club of York Ainsty; FIBiol, DipRMS; *Books* Low Temperature Methods in Biological Electron Microscopy (with U B Sleytr, 1985); *Recreations* horse-riding, horology; *Style*— Prof Anthony Robards; Shrubbery Cottage, Nun Monkton, York YO5 8EW (☎ 0423 331023); Inst for Applied Biology, Univ of York, York YO1 5DD (☎ 0904 432915, fax 0904 432917, telex 57933)

ROBARTS, (Anthony) Julian; s of Lt-Col Anthony Vere Cyprian Robarts (d 1982); *b* 6 May 1937; *Educ* Eton; *m* 1961, Edwina Beryl, da of the Rt Hon John Gardiner Sumner Hobson, OBE, TD, QC, MP (d 1967); 2 s, 1 da; *Career* banker; dir then md Coutts & Co 1963-, dir Coutts Fin Co, regnl dir NatWest Bank; dir: The Int Fund for Insts Inc (USA), The F Bolton Group Ltd; *Recreations* shooting, gardening, opera; *Clubs* MCC; *Style*— Julian Robarts, Esq; c/o Coutts & Co, 440 Strand, London WC2 (☎ 071 753 1000)

ROBB, Prof Alan MacFarlane; s of Alexander Robb (d 1982), of Aberdeen, and Jane Margaret; *b* 24 Feb 1946; *Educ* Robert Gordon's Coll Aberdeen, Gray's Sch of Art, RCA (MA); *m* 1969, Cynthia Jane, da of John Neilson, of Glasgow; 1 s (Daniel Alexander John b 1971), 1 da (Annabel Ellen Jane b 1974); *Career* artist; solo exhibitions incl: The New 57 Gallery Edinburgh 1972, Yarrow Gallery Oundle Sch 1973, E Midlands Tour of Nottingham Library Galleries 1974, Cork Art Soc 1976, Scot Arts Cncl touring exhibition 1978-79, Triskel Art Centre Cork 1979, Peacock Printmakers touring exhibition The Art of Thinking 1985, Gallery 22 Cupar 1986; gp exhibitions incl: Scot Young Contemporaries 1967-68, Univ of York 1970, RCA 1971, Architectural Assoc 1971, Napier Ct Trinity Coll Cambridge 1971, Eduardo Palozzi's choice of the London postgrad sch shows 1972, Royal Acad 1972, E Midlands Arts 1973, EVA Limerick 1977-81, Clare Morris Open 1980 and 1982, Cork Art Soc 1978 and 1980; exhibited regularly 1968- at: Aberdeen Artists, Scot Soc of Artists, Royal Scot Acad; work in various private and pub collections; *Awards* first prize painting Arbroath Open 1968, second prize painting Irish Open Exhibition of Visual Art Limerick 1977, first prize painting Clare Morris Open 1982, commended Aberdeen Artists 1989; art master Oundle Sch Peterborough 1972-75; Crawford Sch of Art Cork Ireland: lectr in painting 1975-78, head of painting and two-dimensional studies 1978-80, head of fine art 1980-82; head of fine art Duncan of Jordanstone Coll of Art 1953-; speaker on educnl dimension of pub art Int Pub Art Symposium Birmingham 1980, chief examiner in fine art Nat Cncl for Educn Awards 1980-82; CNAA: memb Fine Art Bd 1986-87, specialist advsr in fine art 1987-; external examiner in painting and printmaking Sheffield Poly 1987-90; memb Steering Gp Nat Assoc for Fine Art Educn 1988-; dir: Art in Partnership 1986-, Workshop and Studio Provision for Artists Scotland (WASPS) 1984-, Br Health Care Arts 1989-; *Style*— Prof Alan Robb; Duncan of Jordanstone College of Art, Perth Rd, Dundee (☎ 0382 23261, fax 0382 27304)

ROBB, Andrew MacKenzie; s of William MacKenzie Robb (d 1983), and Kathleen Rhona Harvey, *née* Gibbs (d 1990); *b* 2 Sept 1942; *Educ* Rugby; *m* 19 June 1965, Barbara Karin Erika, da of Ronald Hamm, of Cheltenham; 2 da (Fiona b 1967, Erica b 1969); *Career* accountant T Wall & Sons Ltd 1961-69, gp accountant Hoskyns Gp Ltd 1969-71; gp fin dir: P & O 1983-89 (fin controller Bulk Shipping Div 1971-75, gp fin controller 1975-83), Pilkington plc 1989-; J Dip MA 1973; memb 100 Gp; FCMA 1968; *Recreations* golf, gardening, bridge, reading; *Clubs* RAC; *Style*— Andrew Robb, Esq; Pilkington plc, Prescot Rd, St Helens WA10 3TT (☎ 0744 692786, fax 0744 30577, telex 627441)

ROBB, Lady (Violet) Cynthia Lilah; *née* Butler; da of 7 Marquess of Ormonde, MBE; *b* 31 Aug 1946; *m* 1971, Donald Leroy Robb; *Style*— The Lady Cynthia Robb; 2734 N Racine, Chicago, Ill, USA

ROBB, George Alan; WS (1968); s of George Robb (d 1969), of Inverdee, Cults, Aberdeen, and Phyllis Mary, *née* Allan (d 1966); *b* 20 May 1942; *Educ* Aberdeen GS 1946-60, Univ of Aberdeen (MA), Univ of Edinburgh (LLB); *m* 3 Aug 1973, Moira Ann, da of Sidney Milne Clark, of 12 Earlswells Drive, Bieldside, Aberdeen; 2 s (Andrew George b 19 Oct 1976, Michael Nicholas b 22 Dec 1984), 1 da (Judith Olivia b 30 May 1978); *Career* law apprentice Davidson and Syme WS Edinburgh 1966-68; asst: Davidson and Syme WS 1968-69, Edmonds and Ledingham Aberdeen 1969-71, Brander and Cruickshank Advocates Aberdeen 1971-73 (ptnr 1973-83); dir: Aberdeen Trust Holdings PLC 1983-91, Aberdeen Petroleum plc 1982, Abtrust Scotland Investment Co plc 1986, Radiotrust plc 1989, Abtrust New European Investment Trust plc 1990; memb: Law Soc of Scot 1966, WS Soc 1968, IOD 1984 (memb Aberdeen Ctee 1984-88); FInst Pet 1983; *Recreations* riding, shooting, gardening; *Clubs* Aberdeen Petroleum, Aberdeen; *Style*— George A Robb, Esq, WS; Birchwood, 6 Hillhead Rd, Bieldside, Aberdeen AB1 9EJ (☎ 0224 868358); Prince Arthur House, 10 Queen's Terrace, Aberdeen AB9 1QJ (☎ 0224 631999, telex 73683)

ROBBINS, Baroness; Iris Elizabeth; da of A G Gardiner, of The Spinney, Whiteleaf, Bucks; *m* 1924, Baron Robbins, CH, CB (d 1984, economist, Prof of Economics LSE 1929-61, chm Financial Times 1961-70), s of late Rowland Richard Robbins, CBE, of Hollycroft, Sipson, Middx; 1 s (Hon Richard), 1 da (Hon Mrs (Anne) Johnson), *qqv*; *Style*— The Rt Hon the Lady Robbins; 10 Southwood Hall, London N6 5UF

ROBBINS, John; s of Frederick Ernest Robbins, of Denham Gardens, Wolverhampton, and Dora Elizabeth Crump (d 1985); *b* 5 May 1933; *Educ* Wolverhampton GS, Univ of Birmingham (LLB); *m* 4 Sept 1963, Maria Krystina, da of Frank Grzymek, of Wolverhampton; 1 s (Robert b 1966), 2 da (Lucy b 1970, Annalisa b 1975); *Career* admitted slr 1957; sr ptnr Woolley Beavon Slrs Wolverhampton; govr Wolverhampton GS, pres Wolverhampton Law Soc 1985; memb Law Soc; *Recreations* cricket, music, local history; *Clubs* Wig and Pen, Old Wulfrunians; *Style*— John Robbins, Esq; George House, St John's Sq, Wolverhampton, West Midlands WV2 4BZ (☎ 0902 25733, fax 0902 311886)

ROBBINS, Prof Keith Gilbert; s of Gilbert Henry John Robbins, and Edith Mary, *née* Carpenter; *b* 9 April 1940; *Educ* Bristol GS, Magdalen and St Antony's Colls Oxford (MA, DPhil), Univ of Glasgow (DLitt); *m* 24 Aug 1963, Janet Carey, da of John Thomson, of Fulbrook, Oxon; 3 s (Paul b 1965, Daniel b 1967, Adam b 1972), 1 da (Lucy b 1970); *Career* lectr Univ of York 1963-71, dean of Faculty of Arts UCNW Bangor 1977-79 (prof of history 1971-79), prof of modern history Univ of Glasgow 1980-; vice pres RHS 1984-88; pres: Historical Assoc 1988-91, Ecclesiastical History Soc 1980-81; Raleigh lectr Br Acad 1984, Ford lectr Oxford 1987, ed History 1977-86; FRHistS 1970; FRSE 1991; Winston Churchill travelling fell 1990; *Books* Munich 1938 (1968), Sir Edward Grey (1971), The Abolition of War (1976), John Bright (1979), The Eclipse of a Great Power: Modern Britain 1870-1975 (1983), The First World War (1984), Nineteenth Century Britain: Integration and Diversity (1988), Appeasement (1988); *Recreations* music; *Style*— Prof Keith Robbins; 15 Hamilton Drive, Glasgow G12 8DN (☎ 041 339 7766); Dept of Modern History, University of Glasgow, Glasgow G12 8QQ (☎ 041 339 8855)

ROBBINS, Dr (Raymond Frank) Michael; CBE (1987); s of Harold Robbins (d 1982), of Wrexham, Clwyd, and Elsie, *née* Croft (d 1975); *b* 15 Feb 1928; *Educ* Grove Park GS, Univ of Wales Aberystwyth (BSc, PhD, Monsanto fell); *m* Ann Eirian Meredith, da of John Meredith Edwards (d 1970), of Bow-St, Dyfed; 2 da (Rhian Mair b 1960, Sian Eryl b 1964); *Career* RAF 1946-48; res chemist Monsanto Chemicals 1954-55, Med Res Cncl fell Univ of Exeter 1955-56, lectr in organic chemistry Nottingham Poly 1956-59, head Chemistry and Biology Dept Hatfield Poly 1961-70 (sr lectr in organic chemistry 1960), dir Poly South West (formerly Plymouth Poly) 1974-89 (dep dir 1970-74); chm Sci Prog Advsy Gp Poly & Colleges Funding Cncl; memb BAAS, FRIC 1962, hon fell Poly South West 1989; *Recreations* hill walking, gardening; *Style*— Dr Michael Robbins, CBE; British Association, Polytechnic South West, Drake Circus, Plymouth, PL4 8AA (☎ 0752 232090, fax 0752 232091)

ROBBINS, Dr (Richard) Michael; CBE (1976); s of (Alfred) Gordon Robbins (d 1944), of Cherry Wood, Woldingham, Surrey, and Josephine, *née* Capell (d 1987); *b* 7 Sept 1915; *Educ* Westminster, Ch Ch Oxford (MA), Univ of Vienna; *m* 21 Oct 1939, (Rose Margaret) Elspeth, da of Sir Robert Reid Bannatyne, CB (d 1956), of White Gates, Lindfield, Sussex; 1 s ((Michael) James Gordon b 19 Jan 1954), 2 da ((Helen) Caroline (Mrs Shaw) b 10 Feb 1941, Celia Margaret (Mrs Morley) b 2 April 1948); *Career* RE (Transportation) 1939-46, 2 Lt 1940, Capt 1942, Maj 1944; memb London Tport Bd/London Tport Exec 1965-80 (joined 1939, rejoined 1946, sec to Exec 1950, sec and chief PR offr 1955, chief commercial and PR offr 1960, md railways 1971-78); chm Museum of London 1979-90; hon DLitt City Univ 1989; FCIT 1954 (pres 1975-76), FRSA 1976, FSA 1957 (treas 1971-87, pres 1987-91); *Books* The North London Railway (1937), 190 in Persia (1951), The Isle of Wight Railways (1953), Middlesex (1953), Middlesex Parish Churches (ed, 1955), The Railway Age (1962), History of London Transport (with T C Barker, vol I 1963, vol II 1974), George and Robert Stephenson (1966), Points and Signals (1967), A Public Transport Century (1985), Journal of Transport History (jt ed, 1953-65); *Style*— Dr Michael Robbins, CBE, FSA; 7 Courthope Villas, London SW19 4EH (☎ 081 946 7308)

ROBBINS, Hon Richard; s of Baron Robbins, CH, CB (Life Peer, d 1984), and Baroness Robbins, *qv*; *b* 12 July 1927; *Educ* Dauntsey's Sch, New Coll Oxford; *m* 1, 1952 (m dis 1961), Wendy, da of Brig Nithsdale Dobbs; 2 s; m 2, 1961, Brenda, former w of A Rooker Roberts, and da of Douglas Edward Clark (d 1966), of Hong Kong; *Career* artist, teacher, painter, sculptor; princ lectr Middx Poly; *Recreations* golf; *Clubs* Hampstead Golf, Lyme Regis Golf; *Style*— The Hon Richard Robbins; 20 Muswell Ave, London N10 2E9 (☎ 081 442 0106); Fine Art Dept, Middlesex Polytechnic, Quicksilver Place, Western Rd, Wood Green, London N22

ROBBINS, Stephen Dennis; s of Lt-Col J Dennis Robbins, OBE, TD (d 1986), of Inworth Hall, Essex, and Joan, *née* Mason; *b* 11 Jan 1948; *Educ* Marlborough, Coll of Europe Bruges; *m* 28 Sept 1974, Amanda Robbins, JP, da of J Michael Smith, of Foden Bank Farm, Macclesfield, Cheshire; 3 da (Harriet b 1976, Victoria b 1979, Camilla (twin) b 1979); *Career* called to the Bar Gray's Inn 1969; practice SE Circuit 1972-, Recorder Crown Courts 1987-; London Common Law Bar Assoc and Senate Overseas Rels, chm Disciplinary Ctee Potato Mktg Bd 1988-; *Recreations* Scottish hill walking, fishing, swimming, shooting, cross country skiing, music, collecting ephemera; *Style*— Stephen Robbins, Esq; Hillcrest Farm, Sevington, nr Ashford, Kent (☎ 0233 629732); The Studios, Edge St, London W8 (☎ 071 727 7216); 1 Harcourt Buildings, Temple, London EC4 (☎ 071 353 9421)

ROBENS OF WOLDINGHAM, Baron (Life Peer UK 1961), of Woldingham, Co Surrey; Alfred Robens; PC (1951); s of George Robens, of Manchester, and Edith Robens, of Manchester; *b* 18 Dec 1910; *Educ* Manchester Secdy Sch, DCL, LLD; *m* 1937, Eva, da of Fred Powell, of Manchester; 1 adopted s; *Career* MP (Lab): Northumberland Wansbeck 1945-50, Blyth 1950-60; min Labour and Nat Service 1951; chm: NCB 1960-71, MLH Consultants 1971-83, Johnson Matthey & Co (precious metal refiners, traders and bankers) 1971-85, St Regis Newspapers Bolton 1975-80, St Regis International 1976-80, Snamprogetti 1980-; dir: Bank of England 1966-80, Times Newspapers Holdings 1980-83, British Fuel Co 1967-85, AAH 1971-88, St Regis Paper Co (NY) 1976-80, THF 1971-86, AMI Europe Ltd 1980-89; chm: Engrg Industs Cncl 1976-80, Guy's Hosp Med and Dental Sch 1974-; *Style*— The Rt Hon the Lord Robens of Woldingham, PC; Salcombe Court, Cliff Road, Salcombe, Devon TQ8 8JG

ROBERSON, Sidney (Sid); s of Percy Harold Roberson, of Worthing Sussex, and Ivy

Ethel Hannah, *née* Holliwell (d 1970); *b* 15 March 1937; *Educ* Enfield GS; *m* 1, 1961, Brenda, da of Harold Milverton; 1 da (Hannah b 1967); m 2, 1990, Susie Staniland; 1 s (Charlie b 1984), 1 da (Florence Ivy b 1988); *Career* runner in art studio, lived in USA 1961-64, art dir various advtg agencies then copywriter, int photographer 1968-, commercial dir 1971-, began own co 1973, freelance dir; films incl: Sweeney, Robin of Sherwood, Lab Pty Political Broadcasts 1988 and 1989; *awards* over fifty int awards for commercials incl: two Gold Lions at Cannes, two Gold Arrows Br TV Advtg awards, Silver award D & ADA 3rd place Mr Universe; *Recreations* gym, tennis, children, travel; *Style*— Sid Roberson, Esq; Sid Roberson and Partners, 11/29 Smiths Court, Great Windmill St, London W1 (☎ 071 437 9324, fax 071 734 4825, car 0860 599 508)

ROBERTON OF LAUCHOPE, Dr Norman Reid Clifford; s of Norman McCulloch Roberton of Lauchope (d 1981), of Hillcourt, Lockerbie, Dunfriesshire, and Nora Helen McCulloch, *née* Holden; *b* 3 Sept 1939; *Educ* Accrington GS, Downing Coll Cambridge (BA, MB BChir, MA, MRCP), UCH; *m* 1, 6 Sept 1964 (m dis 1978), Mary, da of Frank Lloyd, of 20 Gogarth Ave, Penmaenmawr, Dyfed; 2 s (David Hugh Gershom b 7 Sept 1966, Gareth Iain McCulloch b 4 Oct 1970), 1 da (Fiona Mairi b 6 July 1972); m 2, 26 Jan 1980, Patricia Marshall, da of Thos Alfred Parker, of 133 Lode Rd, Bottisham, Cambs; *Career* clinical reader paediatrics Univ of Oxford 1973-74, conslt paediatrician Cambridge Health Authy 1974-, head paediatrics Riyadh Armed Forces Hosp Saudi Arabia 1987-89; Fitzwilliam Coll Cambridge: fell 1979, dean 1980-87, dir studies in med 1983-, graduate tutor 1989-; memb Ctee paediatric section RSM 1980-87 and 1990- (sec 1982-84, pres 1991-); memb: Neonatal Soc 1968 (memb Ctee 1974-78, sec 1983-87) Br Assoc Perinatal Med 1976 (pres 1985-87), Sci and Pathology Advsy Ctee RCOG 1978-81, Paediatric Ctee RCP 1980-87, Res Advsy Ctee Birthright 1980-83, Cncl Baby Life Support Systems 1983, Br Paediatric Assoc, Euro Soc of Paediatric Res; Freeman City of London 1968, Liveryman Worshipful Soc of Apothecaries 1970 (memb Livery Ctee 1983-85); FRCP 1979; *Books* Separation and Special Care Baby Units (1978), Manual of Neonatal Intensive Care (1981, 2 edn 1986), Paediatrics (1981), Parent Baby Attachment in Premature Infants (1983), Textbook of Neonatology (1986), Lecture Notes in Neonatology (1987), Manual of Normal Neonatal Care (1988); *Recreations* cricket, Scottish history and archeology, nature conservation; *Style*— Dr Norman Roberton of Lauchope; 20 Great Lane, Reach, Cambridgeshire CB5 0JF (☎ 0638 741516); Department of Paediatrics, Addenbrookes Hospital, Hills Rd, Cambridge CB2 2QQ (☎ 0223 245151)

ROBERTS *see also*: Goronwy-Roberts, Hardy-Roberts

ROBERTS, Prof (Edward) Adam; s of Michael Roberts (d 1948), of London, and Janet, *née* Adam-Smith; *b* 29 Aug 1940; *Educ* Westminster, Magdalen Coll Oxford (BA); *m* 16 Sept 1966, Frances Primrose, da of Raymond Horace Albany Dunn (d 1951), of Ludham, Norfolk; 1 s (Bayard b 1972), 1 da (Hannah b 1970); *Career* asst ed Peace News 1962-65, lectr int rels LSE 1968-81 (Noel Buxton student 1965-68); Oxford Univ: Alastair Buchan reader int rels 1981-86, prof fell St Antonys Coll 1981-86, Montague Burton prof int rels 1986-, fell Balliol Coll 1986-; chm govrs William Tyndale Sch 1976-78; FBA 1990; *Books* The Strategy of Civilian Defence: Non-violent Resistance to Aggression (ed, 1967), Nations in Arms: The Theory and Practice of Territorial Defence (second edn, 1986), Documents on the Laws of War (with Richard Guelff second edn, 1989), United Nations, Divided World: The UN's Roles in International Relations (ed with Benedict Kingsbury, 1988), Hugo Grotius and International Relations (ed with Hedley Bull and Benedict Kingsbury, 1990); *Recreations* rock-climbing, mountaineering, running; *Clubs* Alpine; *Style*— Prof Adam Roberts; Balliol College, Oxford OX1 3BJ (☎ 0865 277777)

ROBERTS, Hon Mrs David; Aileen Mary; da of late Charles Burrow; *m* 1936, Hon David Stowell Roberts (d 1956); 2 s, 1 da; *Style*— The Hon Mrs David Roberts; Box Cottage, Box, Stroud, Glos

ROBERTS, Allan Deverell; s of Irfon Roberts, of Priory Wall House, Lewes, E Sussex, and Patricia Mary, *née* Allan; *b* 14 July 1950; *Educ* Eton, Magdalen Coll Oxford (MA); *Career* slr in private practice 1974-76; govt legal serv: legal asst 1976-78, sr legal asst 1978-84, asst slr 1984-89, under sec 1989-; memb Law Soc; *Recreations* walking, music, football; *Style*— Allan Roberts, Esq; Solicitors Office, Depts of Health and Social Security, New Court, Carey St, London WC2 (☎ 071 972 1465)

ROBERTS, Alwyn; s of Rev Howell Roberts and Buddug, *née* Jones; *b* 26 Aug 1933; *Educ* Penygroes GS, Univ Coll of Wales Aberystwyth (LLB), Univ Coll of North Wales Bangor (BA), Univ of Cambridge (MA); *m* 28 July 1960, Mair Rowlands, da of W R Williams; 1 s (Hywel Glyn b 9 June 1962); *Career* princ PM Govt Coll Aizawl Assam India 1960-67, lectr Univ Coll Swansea 1967-70; Univ Coll North Wales Bangor: lectr and sr lectr 1970-79, dir Extra Mural Studies 1979-, vice princ 1985; memb: Gwynedd CC 1973-81, Gwynedd Health Authy 1973-80, Royal Cmmn on Legal Servs 1976-79, Welsh Fourth Channel Authy 1981-86, Parole Bd 1987-90; Welsh Nat govr of BBC 1979-86, chm Royal Nat Eisteddfod of Wales 1989-; *Style*— Alwyn Roberts, Esq; Brithdir, 43 Talycae, Tregarth, Gwynedd (☎ 0248 600007); Univ Coll of North Wales, Bangor, Gwynedd (☎ 0248 351151)

ROBERTS, Andrew Denby; s of Sir James Roberts, OBE, 2 Bt (d 1973), and hp of bro, Sir William Roberts, 3 Bt; *b* 21 May 1938; *Educ* Rugby, Christ Church Oxford; *Style*— Andrew Roberts, Esq

ROBERTS, Air Vice-Marshal Andrew Lyle; CBE (1983), AFC (1969); s of Ronald Lyle Roberts, Ferndown, Wimborne, Dorset, and Nora, *née* Poole; *b* 19 May 1938; *Educ* Cranbook Sch, RAF Coll Cranwell; *m* 18 Aug 1962, Marcia Isabella, da of Lt-Col Christopher Lane Cecil Ward, of Bridge House, Buckland Newton, Dorchester, Dorset; 3 da (Katherine Lucy b 1963, Penelope Susan b 1965, Sarah Jane b 1968); *Career* RAF Coll Cranwell 1956-58, PO 1958, 38 Sqdn RAF Luqa Malta 1959-61, Flying Offr 1960, Flt Lt 1961, Instr RAF Coll Cranwell 1962-64, ADC AOC 18 Gp RAF Pitreavie Castle 1965-66, Flt Cdr 201 Sqdn 1967-68, Sqdn Ldr 1967, student RN Staff Coll 1969, personal air sec to Under Sec of State RAF 1970-71, Wing Cdr OC 236 Operational Conversion Unit RAF St Mawgan 1972-73, US Armed Forces Staff Coll 1974, HQ SACLANT 1975-77, Gp Capt Station Cdr RAF Kinloss 1977-79, Gp Capt Ops HQ Strike Cmd 1980-82, student Royal Coll of Def Studies 1983, Air Cdre Dir Air Force Plans and Progs MOD 1984-86, Air Vice-Marshal COS HQ 18 Gp 1987-89, ACDS (concepts) MOD 1989-; MBIM 1969-; *Recreations* walking, natural history, music (church organ and choral singing) off-shore sailing; *Clubs* RAF; *Style*— Air Vice-Marshal Andrew Roberts, CBE, AFC; c/o Midland Bank, 61 High St, Staines, Middx TW18 4QW

ROBERTS, Anne Clark; da of William Cunningham (d 1972), of Scotland, and Ann Simpson Lyon, *née* Clark; *b* 11 Jan 1961; *Educ* Larbert HS, Univ of Aberdeen (MA); *m* 13 Aug 1988, Thomas John Blackburn Roberts, s of Thomas Blackburn Roberts, CBE, TD, DL (d 1979), of Waterwynch, Park Drive, Blundellsands, Liverpool; *Career* Next plc 1984-88: personnel and training mangr, ops mangr jewellery; md Nat Tst (Enterprises) Ltd 1988-; winner: Nat Training Award 1987, Cosmopolitan Woman of Tomorrow Award (Indust and Commerce) 1989; *Recreations* antique collecting, interior decoration; *Style*— Mrs Anne C Roberts; The Lymes, Willoughby, Waterleys, S Leics; Nat Tst (Enterprises) Ltd, The Stableblock, Heywood House, Westbury, Wilts BA13 4NA (☎ 0373 858787, fax 0373 827575)

ROBERTS, Anthony Charles; s of Charles M Roberts, of Langford, and Kathleen, *née* Hind (d 1986); *b* 9 Sept 1934; *Educ* Monmouth; *m* 7 Sept 1957, Morwenna, da of Dr Allan Dewar (d 1958); 1 s (William), 2 da (Jennifer, Sarah); *Career* admitted slr 1957; ptnr Lester Aldridge; pres Old Monmothian Club 1976, chm Bournemouth Branch Missions to Seamen 1978-88, hon sec Dorset Family Concilation Serv 1983-, pres Bournemouth Rotary Club 1989-, currently tstee and bd memb Bournemouth YMCA (chm 1974-85), chm Poole Hospice 1988-, memb Soc of Provincial Notaries; memb Law Soc; *Recreations* squash, running; *Style*— Anthony Roberts, Esq; Messrs Lester Aldridge Solicitors, Westover Chambers, Hinton Rd, Bournemouth BH1 2EQ (☎ 0202 23663, fax 0202 298476, telex 417196, car 0836 554342)

ROBERTS, Antony Mabon (Tony); s of Lt Hylton Mabon Roberts (d 1987), and Phyllis Mary, *née* Dickinson; *b* 9 July 1939; *Educ* Birkenhead Sch, Univ of Hamburg, Univ of Cambridge (MA), Yale Univ (MA); *m* 7 Aug 1965, Angela Dale, da of Maj Eric William Huggins, of 18 Chester Rd, Southwold, Suffolk; 1 s (Benjamin Mabon b 1969), 1 da (Clare Joy b 1972); *Career* sr prodr BBC TV 1976-; prodns incl: English Law 1968, Avventura 1971, Ensemble 1975, The Living City 1977, Wainwright's Law 1980, Whatever Happened to Britain 1982, Honourable Members 1983, Politics of Pressure 1985, Téléjournal 1983, Heute Direkt 1984, Issues of Law 1986, Person to Person 1988, Give and Take 1989, When In Germany 1991; ptnr Gratus and Roberts Productions 1991-; memb HAC; *Recreations* cricket, tennis, golf; *Clubs* MCC, Birkenhead Constitutional; *Style*— Tony Roberts, Esq; 59 Breamwater Gardens, Ham, Richmond, Surrey (☎ 081 940 9631)

ROBERTS, Bernard; s of William Wright Roberts (d 1960), and Elsie Alberta, *née* Ingham (d 1976); *b* 23 July 1933; *Educ* William Hulme's GS Manchester, RCM (scholar); *m* 1955 (m dis 1987), Patricia May, da of Victor George Russell (d 1987); 2 s (Andrew John b 1958, Nicholas Keith b 1960); *Career* solo pianist; début Wigmore Hall 1957, numerous solo performances nationally and internationally, Henry Wood Promenade Concerts 1979, prof RCM 1962-80, played in numerous chamber groups (including Parikian Fleming Roberts Trio) 1975-84; Nimbus Records 1982-85: Complete Beethoven Piano Sonatas, Eroica and Diabelli Variations; Hon DUniv Brunel 1989; FRCM 1981; *Recreations* reading, philosophy, religion, model railway; *Style*— Bernard Roberts, Esq; Caroline Ireland Management, Uwchlaw'r Coed, Llanbedr, Gwynedd LL45 2NA (☎ and fax : 034 123 532)

ROBERTS, Bertie; s of Thomas Roberts (d 1947), of Blaengarw, S Wales, and Louisa Elizabeth Georgina, *née* Moore (d 1950); *b* 4 June 1919; *Educ* Garw GS S Wales; *m* 1, Aug 1946 (m dis 1961), Peggy Joan, da of George Clark (d 1971), of New Milton, Hants; 1 s (Andrew Mark); m 2, Feb 1962, Catherine Watson, da of William Allardyce Matthew (d 1966), of Montrose, Scotland; *Career* Capt RAOC 1944-46, Civil Serv 1936-79; Miny of Public Bldg & Works: ldr Study Gp on Feasibility of Using Computers 1958, comptroller of accounts 1963, dir of computer servs 1967; head of orgn and methods DOE 1969; dir of estate mgmnt overseas FCO 1971, regnl dir (Maj-Gen) Br Forces Germany 1976-79; memb: Community Health Cncl Hastings DHA, St Leonards-on-Sea Rotary Club; *Recreations* travel, music; *Clubs* Civil Serv, Dickens Pickwick; *Style*— Bertie Roberts, Esq; Fairmount, 41 Hollington Park Rd, St Leonards-on-Sea, E Sussex TN38 0SE (☎ 0424 714 177)

ROBERTS, Brian Reginald; *b* 3 Jan 1927; *Educ* Royal Liberty Sch Romford, Pembroke Coll Cambridge (MA); *Career* sr ptnr R A Coleman & Co; memb: Stock Exchange 1965, Cncl of Stock Exchange, Cncl's Info Servs Ctee; *Clubs* Royal Anglesey Yacht; *Style*— Brian Roberts, Esq; Walnut Cottage, Llandegai, Nr Bangor, Gwynedd; R A Coleman & Co, 204 High St, Bangor, Gwynedd LL57 1NY (☎ 0248 353242)

ROBERTS, Bruce; s of Arthur William Roberts, of Blackfordby, Burton-on-Trent, and Sara Ann, *née* Wood; *b* 30 May 1962; *Educ* Prince Edward Sch Zimbabwe, Peterhouse, Zimbabwe; *m* 12 Dec 1987, Ingrid Marie, da of Prof Victor Julius Bredenkamp; *Career* professional cricketer; Derbyshire CCC 1984- (awarded county cap 1986), Transvaal (B&A) SA 1985-89; SA Schs 1978, Rhodesian Schs 1978-79; jt proprietor family sports shop; *Recreations* squash, stamps, theatre, computers; *Style*— Bruce Roberts, Esq; Ashby de la Zouch, Leics

ROBERTS, Sir Bryan Clieve; KCMG (1973, CMG 1964), QC (1961), JP (Inner London 1975); s of Herbert Roberts, and Doris Evelyn Clieve; *b* 22 March 1923; *Educ* Whitgift, Magdalen Coll Oxford; *m* 1, 1958 (m dis), Pamela Campbell; m 2, 1976 (m dis), Brigitte Reilly-Morrison; m 3, 1985, Barbara Forter; *Career* WWII served RA and RHA; called to the Bar Gray's Inn 1950; dir of public prosecutions N Rhodesia 1959-61 (crown counsel 1953-59); Nyasaland: MLC 1961-63, slr gen 1961-64, min of justice 1962-63; attorney gen Malawi 1964-72, under sec Lord Chllr's Office 1977-82 (joined 1973); chm: Army Cncl 1965-72, Nat Security and Intelligence Cncl 1965-72, Nat Econ Planning Cncl 1965-72, Cwlth Magistrates and Judges Assoc 1979-; Metropolitan stipendiary magistrate 1982-; *Style*— Sir Bryan Roberts, KCMG, QC, JP; 3 Caroline Place, London W2

ROBERTS, Dr Bryon Edward; s of Albert Roberts, JP, DL (former MP Normanton), of 14 Aberford Rd, Oulton, nr Leeds, and Alice Ashton; *b* 17 Feb 1933; *Educ* Rothwell GS, Univ of Leeds (MB ChB, MD); *m* 17 Aug 1957, Audrey Jeanette, da of Herbert Knee (d 1964); 1 s (David b 27 Sept 1958); *Career* registrar Royal Postgrad Med Sch 1962-63, lectr Dept of Pathology Univ of Leeds 1963-70, conslt haematologist Leeds Western Health Authy 1970-; hon sec Br Soc for Haematology, regnl advsr RCPath; FRCPath 1965, FRCPE 1990; *Recreations* gardening, running, watching football; *Style*— Dr Bryon Roberts; 9 Ladywood Mead, Leeds LS8 2LZ (☎ 0532 659751); Dept of Haematology, Leeds General Infirmary, Leeds LS1 3EX (☎ 0532 432799)

ROBERTS, Christopher Keepfer; s of John Anthony Roberts, and Pauline Isobel, *née* Keepfer; *b* 26 March 1956; *Educ* Denbigh HS, Jesus Coll Cambridge (MA); *Career* ptnr slr 1980, Allen & Overy 1985- (asst 1978-85); memb Law Soc; *Recreations* sailing, squash; *Style*— Christopher Roberts, Esq; Allen & Overy, 9 Cheapside, London, EC2V 6AD (☎ 071 248 9898, fax 071 236 2192)

ROBERTS, Dr Clive John Charlton; s of Capt John Charlton Roberts (d 1982), of Taunton, and Monica, *née* Cousins; *b* 27 May 1946; *Educ* Taunton Sch, Kings Coll Med Sch London (MB BS), Univ of Bristol (MD); *m* 6 April 1968, Ruth Diane, da of Charles Henry Sandham, of Wigan; 2 s (Daniel John Charlton b 1975, Samuel James b 1982), 2 da (Sally Kathryn b 1973, Rebecca b and d 1972); *Career* registrar in med Plymouth Gen Hosp 1972-74, conslt sr lectr in clinical pharmacology and med Bristol Royal Infirmary and Univ of Bristol 1981-; author of papers and ed of books on clinical pharmacology; local cncllr Backwell Parish, memb Acad Med Gp at RCP; chm: Standing Ctee Membs of RCP 1986, Backwell Residents Assoc 1990-91; FRCP 1987; *Books* Treatment in Clinical Medicine, Gastro Intestinal Disease (1983); *Recreations* local and family history, cycling, running; *Style*— Dr Clive Roberts; 52 Church Lane, Backwell, Bristol BS19 3PQ (☎ 0275 463100); Bristol Royal Infirmary, Dept of Medicine, Bristol BS2 8HW (☎ 0272 230 000)

ROBERTS, Dr Colin Norman; s of late Norman Summerson Roberts, and late Agnes Fanny Smith; *b* 9 Jan 1936; *Educ* Chelsea Coll London (BPharm), Univ Coll Hosp Univ of London, Med Sch Birmingham Univ, Royal Veterinary Coll Univ of London (PhD); *m* 1972, Ann, *née* Blucher; 2 s (Alexander b 1977, Guy b 1981), 1 da (Jessica b 1978);

Career sr scientific cncllr Biosafety Res Centre, Foods, Drugs and Pesticides, Fukude Japan 1979-, expert agrée French Govt Toxicology Pharmacology 1983-, export dir Life Science Res Ltd 1978- (subsid of APBI, NY); contract res and consultancy for medical pharmaceutical agrochemical and food industs (Queen's Award for Export 1982) dep md 1987-; fell Pharmaceutical Soc of GB 1982; FRSM; fell Br Inst for Regulatory Affrs; scientific fell Zoological Soc; Liveryman Soc of Apothecaries; *Recreations* swimming, reading, music, history of medicine and pharmacy (esp toxicology); *Clubs* Athenaeum; *Style—* Dr C N Roberts; Life Science Research Ltd, Eye, Suffolk IP23 7PX (☎ 0379 4122, telex 975389 LIFSCI G, Fax 037971 427)

ROBERTS, David Edward Glyn; s of David Emlyn Roberts (d 1975), and Henrietta Liston, *née* Griffiths; *b* 29 Feb 1932; *Educ* Calday Grange GS; *m* 1, 13 Oct 1955, Beryl Shelia Price (d 1968); 3 da (Deborah Mary, Angela Margeret, Ruth Alexandra); m 2, 11 Aug 1972, Elizabeth Mary, *née* Grimwade; 2 step s (Adrian Edward Ainsworth Thorn, Richard Charles Ainsworth), 1 da (Patricia); *Career* Nat Serv 2 Lt RA 1955-57; actuary Royal Insur Co 1949-61, stockbroker Tilney and Co 1961-74, Roberts and Huish 1974-85; Ashton Tod McLaren 1985-, md: Quilter Goodison 1988-; Freeman Worshipful Co of Actuaries; FIA 1955, FCII 1959, memb Stock Exchange; *Style—* Glyn Roberts, Esq; Quilter Goodison & Co, 1 Undershaft, St Helen's, London EC3 (071 600 4177)

ROBERTS, His Hon Judge David Ewart; s of John Hobson Roberts (d 1969), of Birmingham, and Dorothy, *née* Rolason (d 1979); *b* 18 Feb 1921; *Educ* Abingdon Sch, St John's Coll Cambridge (MA, LLB); *Career* Nat Serv WWII 1941-46, cmmnd RA; serv: Egypt, N Africa, Italy, Yugoslavia, Germany; called to the Bar Middle Temple; practised Midland circuit 1948, asst rec Coventry QS 1966-71, rec Crown Ct Midland & Oxford circuit 1978-82, circuit judge 1982-; *Recreations* photography, skiing; *Style—* His Hon Judge David Roberts; 4 Greville Dr, Birmingham B15 2UU (☎ 021 440 3231)

ROBERTS, David Francis; s of Arthur Roberts; of Plealey, Shropshire, and Mary Kathleen, *née* Maddox; *b* 28 Aug 1941; *Educ* Priory GS Shrewsbury, Worcester Coll Oxford (MA); *m* 3 July 1974, Astrid Suhr, da of Ernest Suhr Henriksen, of Vancouver, Canada; 2 s (Peter b 21 July 1978, Mark b 24 July 1981), 1 da (Rachel b 1 July 1975); *Career* asst princ MAFF 1964, private sec to Parly Sec (John Mackie, MP) 1967-69, princ MAFF 1969, head of Branch Tropical Foods Div 1969-70, first sec (Agric) FCO Copenhagen 1971-74, private sec to Min of Agric (Fred Peart, MP) 1975-76, asst sec Head of Euro Community Div MAFF 1976; head of: Agric Div HM Treasy 1979-80, Sugar Oils and Fats Div MAFF 1980-84; under sec min (Agric) UK Representation to Euro Community 1985-90, dep dir gen DG VI in Euro Commision 1990; *Recreations* squash, sailing; *Style—* David Roberts, Esq; Commission of the European Communities, Rue de la Loi 120, 1040 Brussels

ROBERTS, Maj-Gen David Michael; s of James Henry (d 1983), of London, and Agnes Louise; *b* 9 Sept 1931; *Educ* Emanuel Sch, Royal Free Hosp Sch of Medicine (MB, BSc, MD); *m* 1964, Angela Louise, da of Capt James Henry Squire, of Herefordshire; 1 s (Justin b 1965), 2 da (Katie b 1966, Eleanor b 1970); *Career* dir of Army Med and conslt physician to the Army 1984-; jt prof of mil med Royal Army Med Coll and Royal Coll of Physicians 1975-81; Queen's hon physician 1984; examiner in tropical med RCP; published many papers in gastroenterology; Jubilee Medal; FRCP, FRCPE; *Recreations* squash, mixing concrete and making things; *Style—* Maj Gen David Roberts; Elmgrove, Normandy, Surrey GU3 2AS; Defence Medical Services Directorate, First Avenue House, High Holborn, London WC1V 6HE (☎ 071 430 5693)

ROBERTS, Denis Edwin; CBE (1974, MBE (Mil) 1945); s of Edwin Roberts (d 1964), of Bromley, Kent, and Alice Gertrude, *née* West (d 1982); *b* 6 Jan 1917; *Educ* Holgate GS Barnsley; *m* 19 Oct 1940, Edith, da of Harry Whitehead (d 1946), of Barnsley Yorks; 2 s (David Harry b 1947, Andrew John b 1950); *Career* Nat Serv WWII Royal Signals 1939-46: France, N Africa, Italy, Austria; PO 1933-80, numerous appts incl: dir ops 1971-75, sr dir Postal Servs 1975-77, md posts 1977-80; chm Br Philatelic Tst 1981-85, memb Industl Tbnl 1982-86; Freeman City of London 1978, Liveryman Worshipful Co of Gardeners; *Clubs* City of London, City Livery; *Style—* Denis E Roberts, Esq, CBE; 302 Gilbert House, Barbican, London EC2Y 8BD (☎ 071 638 0881)

ROBERTS, Hon Mr Justice; Hon Sir Denys Tudor Emil; KBE (1975, CBE 1970, OBE 1960); s of William David Roberts (d 1954), of St Albans; *b* 19 Jan 1923; *Educ* Aldenham, Wadham Coll Oxford (MA, BCL); *m* 1949 (m dis 1973), Brenda Dorothy, da of L Marsh; 1 s, 1 da; m 2, 1985, Anna Fiona Dollar, da of N G A Alexander; 1 s; *Career* WWII serv RA; called to the Bar Lincoln's Inn 1950; barr London 1950-53, crown counsel Nyasaland 1953-59, QC Gibralter 1960, attorney-gen Gibraltèr 1960-62, slr-gen Hong Kong 1962-66, QC Hong Kong 1964, attorney-gen Hong Kong 1966-73, chief sec Hong Kong 1973-78; chief justice: Hong Kong 1979-88, Brunei 1979-; memb Ct of Appeal for Bermuda 1988-; hon bencher Lincoln's Inn 1978, hon fell Wadham Coll 1984; SPMB (Brunei) 1984; *Books* Smuggler's Circuit (1954), Beds and Roses (1956), The Elwood Wager (1958), The Bones of the Wajingas (1960), How to Dispense with Lawyers (1964); *Recreations* cricket, tennis, writing, walking; *Clubs* MCC, Hong Kong, Royal Commonwealth Soc; *Style—* The Hon Mr Justice Roberts, KBE; PO Box 338, Paphos, Cyprus; The Supreme Court, Bandar, Seri Begawan, Brunei, Darussalam

ROBERTS, Prof Derek Frank Bruce; s of Lt-Col Percy Frank Roberts, of St Margarets at Cliffe, and Winifred Caroline, *née* Bromwich; *b* 20 July 1925; *Educ* St Catharine's Coll Cambridge (MA, Dip), Worcester Coll Oxford (DPhil); *m* Mary Josephine; 4 s (Ralph b 1951, Malcolm b 1954, Vaughan b 1958, Clive b 1961), 2 da (Honor b 1956, Caroline b 1963); *Career* Cmmnd Lincolnshire Regt 1943-46; demonstrator Dept of Human Anatomy Oxford 1949-63, Prof Univ of Washington Seattle 1963-64, MRC Population Genetics Unit Oxford 1964-65, prof Univ of Newcastle upon Tyne 1965-90 (emeritus prof 1990-); hon sec Galton Inst, hon treas Int Union of Biological Scis; FRSE; *Books* Genetic Variation in Britain (1973), Biology of Human Fetal Growth (1976), Climate and Human Variability (1978), Changing Patterns of Conception and Fertility (1981), Genetic Variation and its Maintenance (1986); *Recreations* travel, walking; *Style—* Prof Derek Roberts, FRSE; University of Newcastle upon Tyne, Department of Human Genetics, 19 Claremont Place, Newcastle upon Tyne NE2 4AA (☎ 091 2226000, fax 091 2227143)

ROBERTS, Derek Franklyn; s of Frank Roberts, MBE (d 1981), of Wirral, Cheshire, and May Evelyn Roberts; *b* 16 Oct 1942; *Educ* Park High GS Birkenhead, Liverpool Coll of Commerce, Harvard Business Sch (AMP); *m* 6 Sept 1969, Jacqueline, da of Sylvio Velho; 2 s (Maxwell Franklyn b 9 March 1971, Daniel Downes b 29 Dec 1972), 1 da (Katy Jane b 3 Sept 1976); *Career* chief exec and dir Yorkshire Bldg Soc 1987, dir BWD Securities plc 1988, chm Yorkshire Bldg Soc Est Agents Ltd 1988; pres Huddersfield Dist Centre Chartered Bldg Socs Inst; FCII, FCBSI; *Recreations* golf, gardening, walking; *Clubs* Huddersfield GC, Huddersfield RUFC; *Style—* Derek Roberts, Esq; Lower Snow Lea Farm, Lamb Hall Rd, Longwood, Huddersfield HD3 3TH; Yorkshire Bldg Soc, Yorkshire House, Westgate, Bradford, West Yorks (☎ 0274 734 822, fax 0274 726366)

ROBERTS, Dr Derek Harry; CBE (1983); s of Harry Roberts (d 1963), of Manchester, and Alice, *née* Storey (d 1973); *b* 28 March 1932; *Educ* Manchester Central HS, Univ of Manchester (BSc); *m* 2 Aug 1958, Winifred, da of James Short (d 1954), of Sheffield; 1 s (Simon b 1964), 1 da (Helen b 1966); *Career* various posts: Plessey Co plc 1953-79, Gen Electric Co plc; provost UCL 1989-; Freeman Worshipful Co of Goldsmiths 1983; HODSc: Univ of Bath 1982, Open Univ 1984, Loughborough Univ of Technol 1984, City Univ 1984, Univ of Lancaster 1986, Univ of Manchester 1987, Univ of Salford 1988, Univ of Essex 1988, Univ of London 1988; FRS 1980, FEng 1980; *Style—* Dr Derek Roberts, CBE, FRS; The Provost, University College London, Gower St, London WC1E 6BT (☎ 071 380 7234, fax 071 387 8057)

ROBERTS, Dorothy Elizabeth (Mrs Glen-Doepel); da of Noel Lee Roberts (d 1969), of Sydney, and Myrtle Winifred, *née* Reid (d 1969); *Educ* Methodist Ladies Coll Sydney, Sydney Conservatorium; *m* 1957 (m dis 1969), William Glen-Doepel, s of Otto Glen-Doepel; 1 s (Peter Lee b 1969); *Career* concert pianist; appeared: Royal Albert Hall, Hallé Orchestra, Northern Sinfonia Orchestra; recitals in London and provinces known as performer of Clara Schumann tradition; protogée of: Sir John Barbirolli, Sir Malcolm Sargent, Sir Eugene Goossens, Adelina de Lara, OBE; last surviving pupil of Clara Schumann; sold own paintings as professional painter to London, NY and provincial galleries; Hon: AMusA 1945, LMus 1947; *Recreations* travel, reading; *Clubs* The Royal Over-Seas League; *Style—* Ms Dorothy Roberts; Alveley House, 17 Lindum Rd, Lincoln LN2 1NS (☎ 0522 520942); Lincoln Fine Art, 33 The Strait, Lincoln LN2 1JD (☎ 0522 533029)

ROBERTS, His Hon Judge (Hugh) Eifion Pritchard; QC (1971), DL (Clwyd 1988); s of Rev Evan Pritchard Roberts, of Anglesey, and Margaret Ann, *née* Jones; *b* 22 Nov 1927; *Educ* Beaumaris GS, UCW Aberystwyth (LLB), Exeter Coll Oxford (BCL); *m* 14 Aug 1958, Buddug, da of Griffith John William; 1 s (Huw b 5 May 1971), 2 da (Siân b 13 March 1967, Rhian b 18 Aug 1969); *Career* flying Offr RAF 1948-50; called to the Bar Gray's Inn 1953, jr barr on Wales and Chester Circuit practising from Chester 1953-71, circuit judge 1977, liaison judge for Clwyd; asst Parly boundary cmmnr for Wales 1967-68, memb Crawford Ctee on Broadcasting Coverage 1973-74; *Recreations* gardening, cycling, walking; *Style—* His Hon Judge Eifion Roberts, QC, DL; Maes-y-Rhedyn, Gresford Rd, Llay, Wrexham, Clwyd (☎ 097 885 2292)

ROBERTS, Elizabeth Jane (Liz); da of Martin Gwylfa Roberts, of Timperly, Cheshire, and Hilda Elizabeth, *née* Gilbert; *b* 10 June 1960; *Educ* Sale GS for Girls, Univ of Sussex; *Career* waitress My Old Dutch Pancake Restaurant 1982, ed asst Phaidon Press 1982-83, Building Magazine 1984-86 (sub editor, chief sub editor); Media Week: broadcast reporter 1986-87, broadcast ed 1987-88, news ed 1988-89, dep ed 1989-90, ed 1990-; contrib LBC Radio; *Recreations* rock climbing, walking, travel, cinema, literature, drinking; *Style—* Ms Liz Roberts; Media Week Ltd, City Cloisters, 188-196 Old Street, London EC1V 9BP (☎ 071 490 5500, fax 071 490 0957)

ROBERTS, Prof Eric Hywel; s of John Hywel Roberts (d 1942), and Elizabeth Mildred, *née* Ryle; *b* 27 Jan 1930; *Educ* Lucton Sch Herefords, Univ of Manchester (BSc, PhD, DSc), Univ of Cambridge; *m* Dorothy Laura, *née* Mollart; 2 s (Peter b 15 March 1961, Ian b 9 Dec 1963); *Career* sr scientific offr W African Rice Res Station Sierra Leone 1955-63, lectr in horticulture Univ of Manchester 1963-68; Univ of Reading: prof of crop prodn 1968-, head Dept of Agric 1971-75, dean Faculty of Agric and Food 1989- (1977-80), pro vice chllr 1982-86; author of numerous scientific papers on seeds and plant physiology; FIBiol 1973, FIHort 1987; *Books* Viability of Seeds (1972), Food Production and Consumption (with A N Duckham and J G W Jones, 1976), Recalcitrant Crop Seeds (with H F Chin, 1980), Grain legume crops (with R J Summerfield, 1985); *Recreations* sailing; *Style—* Prof Eric Roberts; Department of Agriculture, University of Reading, PO Box 236, Earley Gate, Reading RG6 2AT (☎ 0734 318475, telex 847813)

ROBERTS, Ernest Alfred Cecil; MP (Lab) Hackney North and Stoke Newington 1979-; s of Alfred and Florence Roberts; *b* 20 April 1912; *m* 1953, Joyce Longley; *Career* former engineer, asst gen sec AUEW 1957-77; awarded Tom Mann Gold Medal for Trade Union Activity 1943; *Style—* Ernest Roberts Esq, MP; House of Commons, London SW1 (☎ 071 219 5066, 071 219 4609)

ROBERTS, Sir Frank Kenyon; GCMG (1963, KCMG 1953, CMG 1946), GCVO (1965); s of Henry George Roberts, of Preston, and Gertrude, *née* Kenyon; *b* 27 Oct 1907,(in Buenos Aires); *Educ* Bedales, Rugby, Trinity Coll Cambridge; *m* 1937, Celeste Leila (Celia) Beatrix (d 1990), da of Sir Said Shoucair Pasha, of Cairo, sometime financial advsr to Sudan Govt; *Career* entered FO 1930, serv Paris, Cairo, and as Br min Moscow 1945-47, princ private sec to Foreign Sec 1947-49, dep high cmmr India 1949-51, dep under sec state FO 1951-54, ambass Yugoslavia 1954-57, UK perm rep N Atlantic Cncl 1957-60; ambass: USSR 1960-62, W Germany 1963-68; dir: Hoechst UK, Mercedes-Benz, Amalgamated Metal Corp until 1990; vice pres Br-Atlantic Ctee (pres 1968-81), vice pres Euro-Atlantic Group (formerly presidential chm), patron Atlantic Treaty Assoc (pres 1969-73), pres Anglo-German Assoc; vice pres: UK-USSR Assoc, German Chamber of Commerce UK (former pres); German Order of Merit (1965); *Clubs* Brooks', RAC; *Style—* Sir Frank Roberts, GCMG, GCVO, KCMG; 25 Kensington Court Gardens, London W8 5QF (☎ 071 937 1140)

ROBERTS, Air Vice-Marshal (John) Frederick; CB (1967), CBE (1960); s of William John Roberts (d 1925), of Vine Villa, Brecon Road, Pontardawe, Swansea, and Catherine, *née* Hopkin (d 1959); *b* 24 Feb 1913; *Educ* Ponterdawe GS; *m* 1, Feb 1940, Mary Winifred (d 1968), da of late JE Newns; 1 s ((David) John b 1947); m 2, Dec 1976, Pamela Joy Roberts, da of Arthur Stiles, of Domewood, Copthorne, West Sussex; 2 step da (Gillian, Bryony); *Career* joined RAF 1938, ME 1942-45 (despatches), Staff Coll 1950, memb Directing Staff Staff Coll 1954-56, sr air staff offr Record Offr 1958-60, dep comptroller Allied Air Forces Central Europe 1960-62, station cdr RAF Uxbridge 1963, dir personnel servs MOD (Air) 1964-65, dir gen RAF Ground Trg (RAF) 1966-68, ret 1968; articled clerk 1931-36, qualified FCA 1936, Deloitte & Co Swansea 1937; played in various matches for Glamorgan CCC, played for RAF, 1939-48 and for Combined Servs 1946-47; involved with RAF Benevolent Fund 1968-87; *Recreations* cricket, golf; *Clubs* MCC, Pontardawe Golf (pres), RAF; *Style—* Air Vice-Marshal Frederick Roberts, CB, CBE; 1 Lon Cadog, Sketty, Swansea SA2 DTS (☎ 0792 203763)

ROBERTS, Prof Gareth Gwyn; s of Edwin Roberts (d 1974), of Penmaenmawr, N Wales, and Meri, *née* Jones (d 1959); *b* 16 May 1940; *Educ* John Bright GS Llandudno, Univ Coll of N Wales Bangor (BSc, PhD, DSc); *m* 15 Aug 1962, Charlotte, da of Albert William Standen, of Bournemouth; 2 s (Peris, Daron), 1 da (Bronwen); *Career* lectr Univ Coll of N Wales 1963-66, res scientist Xerox Corp Rochester NY 1966-68, prof of physics New Univ of Ulster Coleraine 1968-76, prof of applied physics Univ of Durham 1976-85, prof of electronic engrg Univ of Oxford 1985-, dir of res Thorn Emi plc 1985-, vice chancellor Univ of Sheffield 1991-; Holweck Gold Medal and Prize 1986, Royal Inst BBC christmas lectrs 1988; author of 200 articles and patents; ed Jl of Molecular Electronics; cncl memb Inst of Physics, physics pres Br Assoc for the Advancement of Sci; memb: Univ Grants Ctee, newly founded Univ Funding Cncl, SERC Ctees, Royal Soc Ctees; Hon MA Oxford 1987, Hon LLD Univ of Wales 1990; FRS 1984, FInstP 1972, FIEE 1974; *Books* Langmuir - Blodgett Films (1990); *Recreations* soccer, duplicate bridge, classical music; *Style—* Prof Gareth Roberts, FRS; The Croft, Snaithing Lane, Sheffield S10 3LS; The University of Sheffield, PO

Box 594, Firth Court, Western Bank, Sheffield S10 2UH (☎ 0742 768555, fax 0742 727407)

ROBERTS, Prof Geoffrey Frank Ingleson; CBE (1978); s of Arthur Reginald Wilfred Roberts (d 1959), of Venns Lane, Hereford, and Laura, *née* Ingleson (d 1971); *b* 9 May 1926; *Educ* Hereford Cathedral Sch, HS for Boys Hereford, Univ of Leeds (BSc); *m* 14 Sept 1949, Veronica, da of Capt John Busby, MN (d 1952); 2 da (Lesley Jane b 1952, Ellice Catherine b 1955); *Career* dep dir (ops) Gas Cncl 1968-71, full time memb Gas Cncl and Br Gas Corpn: prodn and supply 1972-78, external affrs 1979-81, ret 1988; chm Br Pipe Coaters; conslt prof of gas engrg Univ of Salford 1983-; *Recreations* reading, DIY, gardening, caravan touring; *Clubs* RAC; *Style—* Prof Geoffrey Roberts, CBE; Ranmoor, St Nicholas Rd, Ilkley, W Yorks LS29 0AN (☎ 0943 608915); Department of Chemical and Gas Engineering, University of Salford, Salford M5 4WT (☎ 061 745 5000)

ROBERTS, Sir Gilbert Howland Rookehurst; 7 Bt (UK 1809), of Glassenbury, Kent, of Brightfieldstown, co Cork and of the City of Cork; s of Sir Thomas Langdon Howland Roberts, CBE, 6 Bt (d 1979); *b* 31 May 1934; *Educ* Rugby, Gonville and Caius Coll Cambridge; *m* 1958, Ines Eleonore, da of late A Labunski; 1 s, 1 da; *Heir* s, Howland Langdon Roberts; *Career* serv Kenya with RE (E African GS medal); MIMechE; *Style—* Sir Gilbert Roberts, Bt; 3340 Cliff Drive, Santa Barbara, Calif 93109, USA

ROBERTS, Sir Gordon James; CBE (1975), JP (Northants 1952), DL (Northants 1984); s of Archie Roberts (d 1963), of Deanshanger, Milton Keynes, and Lily, *née* Maycock (d 1979); *b* 30 Jan 1921; *Educ* Deanshanger Sch Northants; *m* 1944, Barbara, da of Geoffrey Leach (d 1961), of Haversham, Milton Keynes; 1 s (Adrian), 1 da (Diane); *Career* ldr Northants CC 1974-77, dep chm Cmmn for the New Towns 1978-82; chm: Northants AHA 1973-78, Oxford RHA 1978-90, Computer Policy Ctee NHS 1981-84, Supervisory Bd Mgmnt Advsy Serv NHS 1982-86; High Sheriff Northamptonshire 1989-90, pres Br Red Cross (Northants branch) 1990; FRSA; kt 1984; *Recreations* local history, reading, walking; *Style—* Sir Gordon Roberts, CBE, JP, DL; 114 Ridgmont, Deanshanger, Milton Keynes, Bucks MK19 6JG (☎ 0988 562605); Oxford Regional Health Authority, Old Road, Headington, Oxford OX3 7LF (☎ 0865 64861)

ROBERTS, (David) Gwilym Morris; CBE (1987); s of Edward Humphrey Roberts (d 1949), of Crosby, Merseyside, and Edith, *née* Roberts (d 1983); *b* 24 July 1925; *Educ* Merchant Taylors', Sidney Sussex Coll Cambridge (BA, MA); *m* 1, 16 Oct 1960, Rosemary Elizabeth Emily (d 1973), da of John Edmund Giles (d 1971), of Tavistock, Devon; 1 s ((Edward) Matthew Giles b 1963), 1 da (Annabel Elizabeth Giles b 1967); m 2, 14 Oct 1978, Wendy Ann, da of Dr John King Moore (d 1975), of Beckenham, Kent; *Career* Lt Cdr RNR, ret 1961; chartered civil engr; sr ptnr John Taylor and Sons 1981- (ptnr 1956-), dir Thomas Telford Ltd 1983-89; chm: Acer Gp Ltd 1987-, Prog Bd BGS 1989-, Football Stadia Advsy Design Cncl 1990-; visiting prof Loughborough Univ of Technol 1991-; pres ICE 1986-87, cncl memb NERC 1987-; govr: Chailey Sch 1987-, Roedean Sch 1987-; FEng 1986; *Recreations* tennis, walking, local history, engrg archaeology of the ME; *Clubs* St Stephen's Constitutional, Utd Oxford and Cambridge, MCC; *Style—* Gwilym Roberts, Esq, CBE; North America Farm, Hundred Acre Lane, Westmeston, Hassocks, Sussex BN6 8SH (☎ 0273 890010); Acer Group Ltd, Acer House, Medawar Rd, Surrey Research Park, Guildford GU2 5AR (☎ 0483 35000, fax 0483 302961)

ROBERTS, (Hywel) Heulyn; s of John Roberts (d 1949), of Aigburth, Liverpool, and Lily, *née* Jones (d 1955); *b* 16 March 1919; *Educ* Liverpool Inst; *m* 29 July 1944, Margaret Eluned, da of Griffith Llewelyn Davies (d 1940), of Llanarth, Cardiganshire; 1 s (Glyn Heulyn b 1961), 3 da (Meinir Heulyn b 1948, Rhian Heulyn b 1950, Mair Heulyn b 1956); *Career* memb Cardiganshire CC 1952-74 (chm 1971-72) positions held incl: chm Superannuation Investmt Panel 1964-74, memb Nat Museum Ct 1961-74 (cncl 1964-74), memb SW Wales HMC 1961-73; memb Dyfed CC 1973-89 positions held incl: chm 1973-76, ldr Ind Gp ACC 1973-89, chm Superannuation Investmt Panel 1974-89, vice chm ACC 1985-89; other appointments incl: memb Bd Welsh Theatre Co 1961-69, memb Welsh Tourist Bd 1961-72, memb Bd Cwmni Theatr Cymru 1961-84, memb Welsh Counties Ctee 1964-89 (chm 1972-74), memb Dyfed-Powys Police Authy 1967-89 (chm 1980-82), chm Welsh Folk Museum St Fagans 1971-74, memb Sports Cncl for Wales 1972-84 (chm Facilities 1978-81, chm Grants 1981-84), tstee SW Wales Tstee Savings Bank 1973-80, memb Police Cncl & PNB (UK) 1974-89, chm JNC Coroners (Wales and Eng) 1974-88, memb Exec Bd WNO 1974-88; High Sheriff of Dyfed 1982-83, admitted Druidic Order Gorsedd of Bards 1976, memb Univ of Wales Ct and Cncl 1974-, memb Land Authy for Wales 1975-86; *Recreations* walking, reading; *Clubs* Farmers'; *Style—* H Heulyn Roberts, Esq; Synod Parc, Synod, Llandysul, Dyfed SA44 6JE (☎ 0545 580274)

ROBERTS, Hilary Llewelyn Arthur; s of Michael Hilary Roberts, MP (d 1983), of Cardiff, and Eileen Jean, *née* Billing; *b* 30 Sept 1953; *Educ* Whitchurch GS, Univ Coll of Wales Aberystwyth; *m* 5 Sept 1986, Shirley, da of Bryn Lewis, of Port Talbot; 1 s (Tom b 1986); *Career* barr 1978, head of chambers Newport 1985-; *Recreations* rugby; *Clubs* United Services Mess (Cardiff); *Style—* Hilary Roberts, Esq; 70 Brynteg, Rhiwbina, Cardiff (☎ 0222 610814); 12 Clytha Park Road, Newport (☎ 0222 67403)

ROBERTS, Dr Howard Frederick; s of William Frederick John Roberts (d 1985), of Wallington, Surrey, and Hilda Gertrude, *née* Ward; *b* 7 Jan 1937; *Educ* Univ of London (MB BS, MPhil, MRCP); *m* 22 Aug 1981, Judith Margaret, da of William Bertram Wilson, of Rowledge, Surrey; 3 da (Henrietta b 1983, Lucinda b 1985, Georgina b 1987); *Career* conslt psychiatrist St Thomas, Hosp; assoc memb Br Psycho Analytical Soc 1985; MRCPsych 1974; *Style—* Dr Howard Roberts; 73 Onslow Gardens, London N10 3JY (☎ 081 883 7473); St Thomas' Hospital, London SE1 (☎ 071 928 9292 ext 2195)

ROBERTS, Howland Langdon; s and h of Sir Gilbert Roberts, 7 Bt; *b* 19 Aug 1961; *Style—* Howland Roberts Esq

ROBERTS, Hugh Ashley; s of Rt Rev Dr Edward Roberts, *qv*, and Dorothy Frances, *née* Bowser (d 1982); *b* 20 April 1948; *Educ* Winchester, Corpus Christi Coll Cambridge (MA); *m* 13 Dec 1975, (Priscilla) Jane Stephanie, *qv*, er da of the Rt Hon The Lord Aldington, *qv*; 2 da (Sophie b 1978, Amelia b 1982); *Career* Christie Manson & Woods Ltd 1970-87 (dir 1978-87); dep surveyor of The Queen's Works of Art 1988-; *Recreations* gardening; *Clubs* Brooks's; *Style—* Hugh Roberts, Esq; Salisbury Tower, Windsor Castle, Berkshire (☎ 0753 855581)

ROBERTS, Humphrey Richard Medwyn; s of Hugh Medwyn Roberts (d 1961), of Southport, Lancs, and Enid Marjorie, *née* Pochin (d 1987); *b* 29 May 1931; *Educ* Leas Sch Hoylake, Aldenham Sch, King's Coll Cambridge (BA, MA), Westminster Med Sch (MB BChir, Bulkeley medal, Arthur Evans prize); *m* 21 March 1964, Pamela Ruth, da of Robert Barker; 1 s (James Hugh Medwyn b 28 June 1969), 2 da (Caroline Jane Medwyn b 1 Aug 1965, Katharine Lucy Medwyn b 29 June 1967); *Career* sr house offr Chelsea Hosp for Women 1963-64, res obstetrician Queen Charlotte's Hosp 1966-67, conslt obstetrician and gynaecologist Queen Mary's Hosp Roehampton 1968-79; Westminster Hosp: house surgn 1957-58, res obstetric asst 1958, registrar in obstetrics and gynaecology 1964-66, conslt obstetrician and gynaecologist 1968-91; hon conslt gynaecologist: Hosp of St John and Elizabeth 1971-80, St Lukes Hosp for Clergy 1986-; examiner: obstetrics and gynaecology Univs of Cambridge and London, diploma and membership RCOG, Central Midwives Bd; memb: BMA 1957, Medical Def Union 1957, Hospital Conslt and Staff Assoc 1982, Chelsea Clinical Soc 1982; FRCS (Eng) 1961, MRCOG 1965, FRCOG 1978; *Recreations* Sherlock Holmes, birdwatching, gardening; *Style—* Humphrey Roberts, Esq; 64 Chartfield Avenue, London SW15 6HQ (☎ 081 789 1758); Consulting Rooms, 40 Harley St, London W1N 1AB (☎ 071 580 7400)

ROBERTS, Ian; s of James William Roberts; *b* 23 March 1940; *Educ* Huddersfield Coll, Sheffield Univ; *m* 1966, Hilda Carole, *née* Bramwall; 2 s, 1 da; *Career* chm Wultex Machine Co Ltd 1978 (md 1974), dir Hampton Gold Mining Areas Ltd 1978; *Recreations* walking, music, English history; *Clubs* Marsden & Longwood Cons; *Style—* Ian Roberts Esq; 2 The Crescent, Filey, N Yorks

ROBERTS, (Thomas) Ian; s of Thomas Ormerod Roberts, of Settle, N Yorks, and Joan, *née* Bilsborough; *b* 8 Nov 1956; *Educ* Giggleswick, The Queen's Coll Oxford (BA, MA); *Career* admitted slr 1982; ptnr Booth & Co 1988 (joined 1982, assoc 1986); sec: Yorkshire Glass Manufacturers Assoc 1983-88, Yorkshire Young Slrs Gp 1982-88 (memb Ctee 1985-88); memb: Law Soc, Leeds Law Soc; *Books* A Walk Round Stackhouse (1979); *Recreations* genealogy, local history, long case clocks, fives; *Clubs* Jesters, Rugby Fives Association, Manchester Racquets & Tennis; *Style—* Ian Roberts, Esq; Booth & Co, PO Box 8, Sovereign House, South Parade, Leeds LS1 1HQ (☎ 0532 832000, fax 0532 832060, telex 557439)

ROBERTS, Ivor Anthony; s of Capt Leonard Moore Roberts (d 1981), and Rosa Maria, *née* Fusco; *b* 24 Sept 1946; *Educ* St Mary's Coll Crosby, Keble Coll Oxford (Gomm scholar, BA, MA); *m* 4 May 1974, Elizabeth Bray, da of Norman Douglas Bernard Smith, of Stanstead Hall, Halstead, Essex; 2 s (Huw Benedict Bernard b 1976, David Daniel Rowland b 1979), 1 da (Hannah Rebecca Louise b 1982); *Career* HM Dip Serv: joined 1968, ME Centre for Arabic Studies 1969, third then second sec Paris 1970-73, second then first sec FCO 1973-78, first sec Canberra 1978-82, dep head News Dept FCO 1982-86, head Security Co-ordination Dept FCO 1986-88, Minister Br Embassy Madrid 1989-; memb Inst of Linguists; *Recreations* opera, skiing, squash, golf; *Clubs* United Oxford & Cambridge University, Downhill Only, Club Wengen, Real Club de Puerta de Hierro; *Style—* Ivor Roberts, Esq; c/o British Embassy, Madrid (☎ 319 0200); c/o Foreign & Commonwealth Office, King Charles Street, London SW1A 2AH (☎ 071 270 2063, fax 071 839 2417)

ROBERTS, Dame Jean; DBE (1963), JP, DL; *Educ* Albert Sch, Whitehill Sch; *m* 1922, Cameron Roberts (decd); 1 da; *Career* taught handicapped children; rep of Kingston Ward in Corps of City of Glasgow 1929-1966; JP 1934, DL 1964, lord provost of the City of Glasgow and Lord-Lt of the Co of the City of Glasgow 1960-63; memb Scottish Arts Cncl 1963, memb Arts Cncl of Gt Britain 1965-68, chm Scottish Nat Orch Soc 1970-75; Hon LLD Glasgow 1977, Order of St Olav 1962; *Style—* Dame Jean Roberts, DBE, JP, DL; 35 Beechwood Drive, Glasgow, G11 7ET (☎ 041 334 1930)

ROBERTS, Jeremy Michael Graham; QC (1982); s of Lt-Col John Michael Harold Roberts (d 1954), and Eileen Dora, (*née* Chaplin); *b* 26 April 1941; *Educ* Winchester, Brasenose Coll Oxford (BA); *m* 25 July 1964, Sally Priscilla, da of Col Frederick Peter Johnson, OBE, of Centre Cottage, Eversley Centre, Hants; *Career* barr Inner Temple 1965; rec 1981; QC 1982; *Recreations* theatre, opera, reading, horse and dog racing, canals; *Style—* Jeremy Roberts, Esq, QC; 2 Dr Johnsons Buildings, Temple, London EC4 7AY (☎ 071 353 5371)

ROBERTS, (Anthony) John; s of Leonard Douglas Treeweek Roberts, of Tavistock, Devon, and Margaret, *née* Long; *b* 26 Aug 1944; *Educ* Hampton Sch, Univ of Exeter (BA); *m* 3 Oct 1970, Diana June, da of Norman George Lamdin, of Bexhill-on-Sea, Sussex; 2 s (Ian, Neil); *Career* GPO: various posts incl PA to chief exec 1967-74, regnl memb Bd for Personnel & Fin 1974-76, dir chms office 1976-80, sec of the PO 1980-82, dir Counter Servs 1982-85, md PO Counters Ltd 1985-, chm South Thames Trg and Enterprise Cncl 1989; Freeman City of London 1982, Liveryman Worshipful Co of Gardeners 1988; CBIM 1986; *Recreations* watching rugby, squash, reading, music; *Clubs* Betchworth Park Golf, Oxshott Squash; *Style—* John Roberts, Esq; Post Office Counters Ltd, Drury House, Blackfriars Rd, London SE1 9UA (☎ 071 922 1101)

ROBERTS, John Anthony; s of Walter Ben Roberts (d 1978), of Kirk Hammerton, Yorks, and Betty Joyce, *née* England; *b* 3 Dec 1940; *Educ* Harrow; *m* 9 Sept 1972, Margaret Mary, da of Maurice Houdmont, of Sheffied; 1 s (Piers b 1980), 2 da (Tabitha b 1973, Alexandra b 1975); *Career* HAC 1961-64; CA; articled clerk Mellors Basden & Co 1959-64; ptnr Coopers & Lybrand 1964-, memb: Trent Bus Sch Advsy Ctee, Bd Prince's Youth Bus Tst (Nottingham area); pres: Notts Soc CA, Farnsfield Horticultural Soc 1987-88; FCA 1964; *Recreations* wine, food, travel, music; *Clubs* Nottinghamshire United Services; *Style—* John Roberts, Esq; The Old Vicarage, Farnsfield, Nottinghamshire (☎ 0623 882 835); Coopers & Lybrand Deloitte, Cumberland House, 35 Park Row Nottingham NG1 6FY (☎ 0602 419066, fax 0602 470862)

ROBERTS, John Charles Quentin; s of Hubert C Roberts, of Bognor Regis, and Emilie, *née* Warden; *b* 4 April 1933; *Educ* King Coll Taunton, Univ of London (CSC Interpretership), Merton Coll Oxford (MA); *m* 1, 1959 (m dis 1979), Dinah, da of Maj Trevor Webster-Williams, TD (d 1987), of Cheltenham; 1 da (Gwen b 1960), 1 s (Stephen b 1963) 1960); m 2, 1982, Elizabeth, *née* Gough-Cooper; *Career* Nat Serv Intelligence Offr RAF 1951-53; Shell International Petroleum Co (various mgmnt posts in Europe and Africa 1956-61), asst master Marlborough 1963-73, dir The Great Britain-USSR Assoc 1974-; memb: Cncl Sch of Slavonic and E Euro Studies Univ of London, Inst of Linguists 1970, Ctee Int State Library of Foreign Lit Moscow 1991; *Recreations* music, family, skiing; *Clubs* Athenaeum, Special Forces; *Style—* John Roberts, Esq; 52 Paultons Square, London SW3 5DT (☎ 071 352 3882, fax 071 352 7108); The Great Britain-USSR Association, 14 Grosvenor Place, London SW1X 7HW (☎ 071 235 2116, fax 071 259 6254)

ROBERTS, John Frederick; *b* 30 March 1946; *Educ* Bristol GS, Univ of Bristol (BDS), Eastman Dental Center Rochester NY (Cert in Paedodontics); *m* Gabriele Elizabeth; 2 s (Alexander John b 14 Oct 1979, Sebastian Frederick b 24 March 1983); *Career* house offr Bristol Dental Hosp 1971, assoc gen dental practice Bristol 1972-74, princ gen dental practice Johannesburg 1974-76, ptnr private paedodontic practice London 1978-, sr demonstrator Dept of Orthodontics and Dentistry for Children UMDS Guy's Hosp 1989- (demonstrator 1979-89), hon lectr Dept of Child Dental Health London Hosp Med Coll 1986-88, visiting lectr Dept of Children's Dentistry Univ of Leeds Dental Sch 1986-, recognized teacher status in paediatrics Univ of London Faculty of Med and Dentistry 1990-; numerous invited lectures and courses UK and abroad; memb: BDA, Br Paedodontic Soc (hon treas and memb Ctee 1980), American Acad of Paedodontics, American Soc of Dentistry for Children, American Denta Soc of London (hon treas and memb Ctee 1986-89), Gen Dental Cncl, S African Med and Dental Cncl, American Bd of Paedodontics (bd-eligible), American Dental Assoc (Nat Bd Examinations 1 & 2 1978); *publications:* author of various articles in Br Dental Jl; *Style—* John Roberts, Esq; 74 Bois Lane, Amersham, Bucks (☎ 0494 725685); 33 Weymouth St, London W1N 3FL (☎ 071 580 5370)

ROBERTS, John Griffith; s of Griffith Roberts (d 1950), and Mary Ann Roberts (d 1942); *b* 10 June 1912; *Educ* Penygroes Co Sch; *m* 3 Nov 1948, Betty, da of David Thomas (d 1963), of Maesyrhedyn, Pontardawe, Swansea; 1 da (Rhiannon b 1960); *Career* admitted slr 1934, in private practice 1935-, chm Rent Tbnl for N W Wales until ret 1982; memb: Caernarvonshire CC 1946-74 (chm 1965-66), Gwynedd CC 1974-89, Pwllheli Town Cncl 1974- (former Mayor Pwllheli); former memb: Assoc of CCs and of Welsh Cos Ctee, Ct and Cncl of Univ of Wales, Ct and Cncl of UCNW; former chm: Gwynedd Educn Ctee, Policy and Resources Ctee Gwynedd CC; chm: Govrs Pwllheli Primary Sch and Pwllheli Youth and Community Centre; former memb Wales Advsy Body for local authy higher educn; memb Law Soc 1955; *Recreations* motoring, travel, billiards, bowls; *Clubs* Snooker Pwllheli, Clwb y Bont Literary Pwllheli; *Style*— John Roberts, Esq; Maesywern, Ffordd Talcymerau, Pwllheli, Gwynedd LL53 5PU (☎ 612 364); 26 Stryd Penlan, Pwllheli, Gwynedd (☎ 612 362)

ROBERTS, John Harvey Polmear; s of George Edward Polmear Roberts (d 1973), of Polmear, Illogan, Redruth, Cornwall, and Mary Harvey, *née* Sara (d 1975); *b* 11 June 1935; *Educ* Blundells, Coll of Law; *m* 14 Jan 1961, (Mary) Patricia, da of Dr Richard Raphael Gamble (d 1955), of Elm Tree House, Penkhull, Stoke on Trent, Staffs; 2 s (Hugh b 1962, Paul b 1963), 2 da (Emma b 1965, Louise b 1971); *Career* admitted slr 1957; HM Coroner for S Bucks 1980-, regnl chm Mental Health Review Tbnls for Oxford and Wessex Regions 1981-, recorder; managing ptnr Messrs Winter-Taylors 1984-; former pres and media spokesman Berks, Bucks and Oxon Inc Law Soc, memb Law Soc Negligence Panel; chm: Bucks Housing Assoc Ltd, Governing Cncl Pipers Corner Sch Ltd; dir: Wycombe Wanderers FC Ltd, Ercol Furniture Ltd, Ercol Holdings Ltd; hon slr and tstee local St John Ambulance Bde, hon slr Welfare Offrs and local Royal Br Legion Branches and Clubs, legal cncllr Middle Thames Marriage Guidance Cncl; Freeman City of London, Liveryman and memb of Ct of Assts Worshipful Co of Feltmakers, Liveryman Worshipful Co of Coopers; memb: Law Soc, Coroners Soc of England and Wales, Medico-Legal Soc, Br Acad of Forensic Scis; ACIArb; SBStJ; *Recreations* golf, hill walking, reading; *Clubs* Oriental, Wig and Pen; *Style*— John Roberts, Esq; Badgers Hill, Speen, Aylesbury, Bucks HP17 0SP (☎ 0494 488289); Messrs Winter-Taylors, Park House, London Rd, High Wycombe, Bucks HP11 1BZ (☎ 0494 450 171 , fax 0494 441 815, telex 937217)

ROBERTS, John Herbert; s of John Emanuel Roberts (d 1970), and Hilda Mary, *née* Webb (d 1981); *b* 18 Aug 1933; *Educ* LSE (BSc (Econ), Univ of London; *m* 1965, Patricia Iris, da of John Duck (d 1977); 1 s (Matthew b 1974), 3 da (Catherine b 1966, Jessica b 1968, Emma b 1972); *Career* cmmnd RASC, serv Suez and Cyprus 1955-56; tax inspr Inland Revenue 1957-81, under sec Dir of Ops Inland Revenue 1981-85; dir: Tech Div 2 Inland Revenue 1985-88, Compliance & Collection Div Inland Revenue 1988-; *Style*— John Roberts, Esq; New Wing, Somerset House, Strand, London WC2R 1LB (☎ 071 438 7649)

ROBERTS, John Houghton; s of John Noel Roberts, and Ida, *née* Houghton; *b* 14 Dec 1947; *Educ* Calday Grange GS, Trinity Hall Cambridge (MA); *m* 7 Oct 1972 (m dis 1990), Anna Elizabeth, da of Peter Tooke Sheppard, of Essex; 3 s (James b 1974, Edward b 1976, William b 1978); *Career* called to the Bar Middle Temple 1970; recorder of the Crown Ct 1988; *Recreations* golf, rugby football, music; *Clubs* Athenaeum (Liverpool), Heswall Golf, Birkenhead Park FC; *Style*— John Roberts, Esq; Refuge Assurance House, Derby Square, Liverpool (☎ 051 709 4222)

ROBERTS, John Leonard; s of Maj Robert Edward Roberts, and Dorothea, *née* Goodchild; *b* 19 Jan 1939; *m* 22 Oct 1963, Gillian Lesley, da of Leslie Low; 1 s (Alexander b 12 Dec 1972); *Career* reporter; sub ed and dir City Press 1957-63, fin ed Thomson Newspapers 1963-67, exec Minster Tst 1967-68, asst ed Investors' Chronicle 1968-73, City ed Daily Express 1974-76, freelance business journalist and broadcaster BBC Radio 4 and World Serv 1976-; award for business journalism for Men in the Middle 1977; *Books* Megalomania, Managers and Mergers (1987); *Recreations* beekeeping, gardening, standing on rainswept pitch watching son play rugby; *Style*— John Roberts, Esq

ROBERTS, John Lewis; CMG (1987); s of Thomas Hubert Roberts (d 1971), of Danygraig, Ynysmeudwy, Pontardawe, Swansea, and Hannah Meudwen, *née* Lewis (d 1968); *b* 21 April 1928; *Educ* Pontardawe GS, Trinity Hall Cambridge (BA); *m* 5 Dec 1952, Maureen Jocelyn, da of Lt-Col Denis Moriarty, IA (d 1985), of Eastbourne, Sussex; 2 s (Patrick Gereint b 4 Sept 1954, David Gareth b 31 Oct 1957); *Career* 2 Lt RA 1948-50; joined Miny of Civil Aviation 1950, private sec to Parly sec Civil Aviation 1954-56, civil air attaché British Embassy Bonn 1959-62, Def Supply cncllr Br Embassy Paris 1966-69; asst under sec of state: Def Sales 1975-77, Air Dept (Personnel) 1977-79, Industl and Int Policy 1982-88; memb Electronics Indust NEDC 1982-84; FRSA 1988; *Recreations* sailing, fly fishing, gardening; *Clubs* Piscatorial Soc; *Style*— John Roberts, Esq, CMG

ROBERTS, Dr John Morris; s of Edward Henry Roberts (d 1969), and Dorothy Julia Roberts (d 1963); *b* 14 April 1928; *Educ* Taunton Sch, Keble Coll Oxford (BA, MA, DPhil); *m* 29 Aug 1964, Judith Cecilia Mary, da of late Rev James Armitage; 1 s (Mark b 1967), 2 da (Susannah b 1969, Jessica b 1971); *Career* Nat Serv 67 Trg Regt RA 1949, Intelligence Corps 1949-50; prize fell Magdalen Coll Oxford 1951-53, Cwlth Fund fell Princeton and Yale 1953-54, ed Eng Hist Rev 1967-77, vice chllr Univ of Southampton 1979-85, warden Merton Coll Oxford 1984- (fell and tutor 1953-79, hon fell 1980-84), presenter TV Series The Triumph of The West 1985, govr BBC 1988-; sec Harmsworth Tst 1962-68, memb Gen Ctee Royal Literary Fund 1975-, cncl pres Taunton Sch 1978-88, cncl memb Euro Univ Inst 1980-88, memb US and UK Educn Cmmn 1981-88, tstee Nat Portrait Gallery 1984-, Rhodes tstee 1988-, memb Bd of Br Cncl 1991-; Hon D Litt Southampton 1987; FRHistS; *Books* French Revolution Documents (1966), Europe 1880-1945 (1967), The Mythology of the Secret Societies (1972), The Paris Commune from the Right (1974), The Age of Revolution and Improvement (1975), History of the World (1976), The French Revolution (1978), Illustrated History of the World (1980), The Triumph of the West (1985); numerous articles in academic jls; *Recreations* music; *Clubs* Utd Oxford and Cambridge Univ, Groucho; *Style*— Dr John Roberts, Merton College, Oxford (☎ 0865 276352 fax 0865 276361)

ROBERTS, Lady; Joya Mary Segar; da of Eric Scorer, OBE, and Maud Segar; *b* 27 July 1921; *Educ* St Marys Sch, Wantage Oxfordshire; *m* 1955, as his 2 w, Gen Sir Ouvry Lindfield Roberts, GCB, KBE, DSO (d 1986); *Recreations* portrait artist (sketching animals), breeding Shetland Sheep dogs, Br white and blue pedigree cats, organic gardening; *Style*— Lady Roberts; Upper Field House, 105 Church Way, Iffley, Oxford (☎ 0865 779 351)

ROBERTS, (Richard) Julian; s of Albert Reginald Roberts (d 1970), of Birmingham, and Kate Marjorie Scudamore-Roberts (d 1976); *b* 18 May 1930; *Educ* King Edward's Sch Birmingham, Magdalen Coll Oxford (MA); *m* 27 April 1957, Anne, da of Henry Bedford Ducé (d 1968), of Cardiff; 1 s (Alun b 1965), 1 da (Hilary b 1962); *Career* asst keeper Br Museum 1958-74, dep librarian Bodleian Library Oxford 1985- (keeper of printed books 1974-); fell Wolfson Coll Oxford 1975 (vice gerent 1983-85), Regents' prof Univ of Calif Los Angeles 1991; pres Bibliographical Soc 1986-88 (sec 1961-81), associate of Library Assoc; FSA; *Books* Beauty in Raggs: Poems by Cardell Goodman (ed, 1958), John Dee's Library Catalogue (with A G Watson, 1990); *Recreations* antiquarianism, natural history, fell walking; *Style*— Julian Roberts, Esq, FSA; St John's Farm House, Tackley, Oxford OX5 3AT (☎ 0865 277021, fax 0865 277182)

ROBERTS, Hon Mrs (Juliana Eveline); *née* Curzon; da of late 2 Viscount Scarsdale; *b* 1928; *Educ* Heathfield School Ascot; *m* 1, 1948 (m dis 1952), George Derek Stanley Smith (d 1963); 1 s, 1 da; m 2, 1953 (m dis 1956), Frederick Nettlefold; 1 da (Viscountess Windsor); m 3, 1956 (m dis 1962), as his 2 w, Sir Dudley Herbert Cunliffe-Owen, 2 Bt (d 1983); 1 da; m 4, 1962 (m dis 1972), as his 2 w, John Roberts; 1 s, 1 da; *Career* hotel mgmnt; *Recreations* sailing, fishing, gourment eating; *Clubs* LDYC (Ireland); *Style*— The Hon Mrs Roberts; Tomona, Bally Common, Nenagh, Co Tipperary; The Stables, Oakley Park, Ludlow, Shropshire

ROBERTS, Keith John Kingston; *b* 20 Sept 1935; *Educ* Kettering GS, Northampton Sch of Art (NOD); *Career* writer; gen work in advtg 1960-64, freelance assoc with Science Fantasy Magazine 1964-66, asst ed then gen ed SF Impluse 1966; books: The Chalk Giants (1974), Molly Zero (1980), Kiteworld (1985), Kaeti & Company (1985, best short story Br Sci Fiction Assoc 1986, year's best artwork BSFA 1986), Grainne (1987, year's best novel BSFA), The Road to Paradise, Winterwood and Other Hauntings; *Style*— Keith Roberts, Esq; 25 Essex Square, West Harnham, Salisbury, Wiltshire SP2 8JA (☎ 0722 324134); Uwe Luserke/Agentur Luserke, Brunnenstrasse 7/4, D 7259, Friolzheim, W Germany (☎ 010 497044/42291)

ROBERTS, Prof Kenneth; s of Ernest William Roberts, and Nancy, *née* Williams; *b* 24 Sept 1940; *Educ* Stockport Sch, LSE (MSc, BSc); *m* 8 Aug 1964, Patricia, da of Frank Newton, of Macclesfield; 1 s (Gavin Paul b 19 Feb 1968), 2 da (Susan Alexis b 18 Dec 1970, Vanessa Jane (twin) b 19 Dec 1970); *Career* Univ of Liverpool: asst lectr, sr lectr, reader, prof 1966-; memb: Br Sociological Assoc, Int Sociological Assoc; *Books* Youth and Leisure (1983), The Changing Structure of Youth Labour Markets (1987); *Style*— Prof Kenneth Roberts; 2 County Rd, Ormskirk, Lancs L39 1QQ (☎ 0695 574962); Sociology Dept, Univ of Liverpool, PO Box 147, Liverpool L79 3BX (☎ 051 794 2971)

ROBERTS, Malcolm John Binyon; s of Sqdn Ldr Kenneth Arthur Norman Roberts (d 1973), and Greta Kathleen, *née* Cooper; *b* 3 July 1951; *Educ* St Edmund's Sch Canterbury; *m* 28 April 1984, Caroline Mary, da of John Harry Scrutton; 1 s (Frederick), 1 da (Iona); *Career* ptnr Montagu Loebl Stanley 1979-86, dir Fleming Private Asset Management 1986-; memb Stock Exchange 1978; govr Granville Sch Sevenoaks; Freeman Worshipful Co of Barbers; Bewley Lane House, Plaxtol, Kent TN15 OPS; 31 Sun St, London EC2 (☎ 071 377 9242)

ROBERTS, Dr Marguerite Morrell; da of Dr Walter Morrell Roberts (d 1978), of Manchester, and Mildred Jane, *née* Leech (d 1988); *b* 4 Oct 1939; *Educ* Ackworth Sch Yorks, Victoria Univ of Manchester (MB ChB); *m* 4 July 1981, Anthony Donald Hill, s of Samuel Hill (d 1988), of Bromsgrove, Worcs; 1 da (Jennifer b 1982), 1 step s (Christopher b 1972), 1 step da (Lucy b 1968); *Career* lectr in dermatology Leeds Gen Infirmary 1971-75, conslt dermatologist Salford AHA and NW RHA 1975-; memb: Br Assoc of Dermatologists, Br Soc of Mycopathology, English Folk Dance and Song Soc; fell Manchester Med Soc; *Recreations* music, piano, violin, English concertina, swimming, fell walking, folk dance, solo clog dance; *Style*— Dr Marguerite Roberts; The Skin Hospital, Chapel St, Salford, Manchester M60 9EP (☎ 061 789 7373)

ROBERTS, Martin John Dickin; s of John Kenneth Dickin Roberts (d 1990), of Chester, and Iris Ruth, *née* Bond (d 1970); *Educ* Shrewsbury, Trinity Hall Cambridge (MA); *m* 26 Sept 1970, Ruth, da of Frank Packard (d 1982); 3 da (Anne b 1972, Sarah b 1975, Catheryn b 1985); *Career* admitted slr 1969; ptnr Slaughter & May 1975-; Freeman Worshipful Co of Slrs; memb Law Soc; *Recreations* spectator sports, boating, reading; *Clubs* RAC; *Style*— Martin Roberts, Esq; Arbourne, Copsem Lane, Esher, Surrey KT10 9HE (☎ 0372 465252)

ROBERTS, Michael Curig; s of Thomas Curig Roberts, of 11 The Green, Caldy, Wirral, and Violet Evelyn Roberts; *b* 2 June 1938; *Educ* Shrewsbury; *m* 10 June 1967, Tessa Mary, da of Guy Hughes, of Yew Tree Plat, Winchelsea; 1 s (William Thomas Curig b 1971), 2 da (Phillippa Jill b 1969, Elizabeth Mary b 1974); *Career* ptnr Coopers Lybrand Deloitte CAs; chm Abbots Hill Sch Ltd, dep chm London Pension Funds Authy, dir St James Malvern Ltd, memb London Residuary Body, treas Gt Gaddesden PCC; Freeman City of London, asst Worshipful Co of Gold and Silver Wyre Drawers; FCA; *Recreations* golf, tennis, reading, walking; *Clubs* Royal Liverpool Golf, Ashridge Golf, Gresham, RAC; *Style*— Michael Roberts, Esq; Lovatts Cottage, Gaddesden Row, Hemel Hempstead, Herts HP2 6HX; Coopers & Lybrand Deloitte, 128 Queen Victoria St, London EC4V 4DE (☎ 071 248 3913, fax 07 248 4897, telex 894941)

ROBERTS, Michael Victor; s of Ernest Alfred Roberts (d 1990), of Waltham Abbey, Essex, and Lilian May, *née* Piper (d 1979); *b* 23 Sept 1941; *Educ* Cheshunt GS, Clare Coll Cambridge (BA, MA), Loughborough Tech Coll; *m* 6 July 1972, Jane Margaret (d 1991), da of Francis Huddleston (d 1986); 1 s (Alfred b 1973), 1 da (Mary b 1975); *Career* asst librarian Loughborough Tech Coll 1964-66, asst cataloguer Leeds City Libraries 1966-68, dep bibliographical servs librarian City of London Libraries 1968-70; Guildhall Library: princ cataloguer 1970-73, keeper of Enquiry Servs 1973-82; dep dir City of London Libraries & Art Galleries 1982-, chm Library Assoc Local Studies Gp London & Home Counties Branch, ctee memb Library Assoc London & Home Counties branch, memb Br Records Assoc Cncl, assoc Library Assoc 1967; Freeman City of London 1983, Liveryman Worshipful Co of Fletchers 1984; *Books* ed Guildhall Studies in London History 1973-81; *Recreations* fishing, walking, local history; *Clubs* Harwich and Dovercourt Sailing; *Style*— Michael Roberts, Esq; Queenscliffe Cottage, Queenscliffe Rd, Ipswich; Guildhall Library, London EC2P 2EJ (☎ 071 260 1852)

ROBERTS, Michéle Brigitte; da of Reginald George Roberts, of Felton, nr Bristol, and Monique Pauline Joseph, *née* Caulle; *b* 20 May 1949; *Educ* St Mary's Abbey London, St Michael's Convent London, Univ of Oxford (BA); *Career* author; British Council Librarian Bangkok (responsible for S Vietnam and Cambodia) 1972-73; previous work incl: p/t journalist, p/t teacher, pregancy tester, cnsllr, res asst, book reviewer; poetry ed: Spare Rib 1974-76, City Limits 1981-83; various Arts Council fellowships, writer in residence Univ of Essex 1987-88; *Publications* Novels: A Piece of the Night (1978), The Visitation (1983), The Wild Girl (1984), The Book of Mrs Noah (1987), In The Red Kitchen (1990); Poetry: The Mirror of the Mother (1986), Psyche And the Hurricane (1991); contrib numerous stories and essays to anthologies, co-author numerous books of poetry and short stories, premier of play The Journeywoman Colchester 1988, recent film script The Heavenly Twins French TV and Channel 4; awarded: Gay News Literary award 1978, Arts Council Grant 1978; involved in int Women's Liberation Movement 1970-, ALA 1972; *Recreations* food, sex, foreign travel, reading; *Style*— Ms Michele Roberts; c/o Caroline Dawnay, Peters Fraser & Dunlop, 5th Floor, The Chambers, Chelsea Harbour, Lots Rd, London SW10 0XF (☎ 071 376 7676)

ROBERTS, Norman Stafford; s of Walter Stafford Roberts (d 1973), and Florence Ethel Roberts (d 1974); *b* 15 Feb 1926; *Educ* Quarry Bank HS Liverpool, Hertford Coll Oxford (MA, Dip Pub Admin); *m* 5 April 1965, Beatrice (Bea), da of George Best (d 1968); 1 s (Peter b 1969), 2 da (Patricia b 1967, Judith b 1971); *Career* cmmnd RA 1945: served with 6 field Regt RA in Palestine, Egypt, Libya 1945-47; commanding offr Monkton Combe Sch CCF 1959-65, Hon Maj; history and house master Berkhamsted Sch 1951-59, head of history and housemater Monkton Combe Sch

1959-65, headmaster Taunton 1970-87 (Sexey's Sch Bruton 1965-70), educn conslt 1987-; pres Taunton Rotary Club, chm of govrs St Audries Sch W Quantockshead; govr: King Edward's Sch Witley, WyCliffe Coll; Schoolmaster; fell Merton Coll 1964; *Recreations* sport, travel, bridge; *Clubs* Commonwealth; *Style*— Norman Roberts, Esq; Chestnut House, 23 Mount St, Taunton, Somerset TA1 3QF (☎ 0823 331 623)

ROBERTS, Paul Bartholemew; s of Joseph Roberts (d 1984), of London, and Angela, *née* Coletta; *b* 4 Sept 1941; *Educ* St Michael's Convent Finchley, St Aloyius Coll Highgate; *m* 1, 15 July 1972, Clare Celia Fay, da of Cochrane H Campbell, CBE, of Helensborough, Scotland; m 2, 10 Dec 1983 (m dis 1988), Nicola Anne, da of Dr Peter Stuart; 1 da (Lucy b 22 June 1984); *Career* dir John Rigby and Co Gunmakers 1984, chm Gun Trade Assoc 1986; memb Home Office Firearms Consultative Ctee 1989; Freeman: Worshipful Co of Gunmakers 1980, City of London 1980; *Recreations* shooting, big game hunting, polo; *Clubs* Cowdray Park Polo, Shikar; *Style*— Paul Roberts, Esq; Beeches, Loxwood, W Sussex; 66 Great Suffolk St London SE1 OBU (☎ 071 620 0690, fax 071 928 9205)

ROBERTS, Prof Paul Harry; s of Percy Harry Roberts (d 1969), and Ethel Francis, *née* Mann; *b* 13 Sept 1929; *Educ* Ardwyn Sch Aberystwyth, UCW Aberystwyth (David Davies scholar), Gonville & Caius Coll Cambridge (minor scholar, BA, MA, PhD, ScD, Smith Prize); *m* 15 Dec 1989, Mary Francis, *née* Tabrett; *Career* res assoc Univ of Chicago 1954-55, scientific offr AWRE Aldermaston 1955-56; ICI fell Univ of Durham 1956-59, lectr in physics King's Coll Univ of Durham 1959-61, assoc prof Yerkes Observatory Univ of Chicago 1961-63, prof of applied mathematics Univ of Newcastle upon Tyne 1963-86, prof of mathematics and geophysical sciences UCLA Los Angeles 1986-; FRAS 1955, FRS 1979; *Recreations* chess, playing bassoon; *Style*— Prof Paul Roberts, FRS; Dept of Mathematics, UCLA, Los Angeles, CA 90024, USA (☎ 213 206 2707, fax 213 206 6673, telex 3716012)

ROBERTS, Peter David Thatcher; s of Leonard Charles Roberts (d 1978); *b* 1 March 1934; *Educ* Alleyns Sch Dulwich, Sir John Cass Coll Univ of London; *m* 1959, Elizabeth June Dodds; 1 s, 2 da; *Career* MN 1951-59, Lt RNR; Leinster/Hispania Maritime Ltd: Joined 1960, dir 1963, md 1965; dir Hays plc 1983- (joined 1969); chm: Hays Marine Services Ltd, Hays Commercial Services Ltd, Hays Personnel Servs Ltd; vice chm: Shipowners P & I Assoc Ltd, dir Minories Holdings Ltd; memb Gen Ctee Lloyds Register of Shipping; Jr Warden The Co of Watermen and Lightermen of River Thames, Liveryman Worshipful Co of Shipwrights; MICS 1962, FBIM 1981; *Recreations* offshore sailing, golf; *Clubs* Royal Ocean Racing, RAC, Wildernesse Golf; *Style*— Peter Roberts, Esq; Callenders Cottage, Bidborough, nr Tunbridge Wells, Kent (☎ 0892 29053, office 0483 302203)

ROBERTS, Philip Bedlington; s of Richard John Samuel Roberts (d 1931), and Annie Mary, *née* Phillips (d 1959); *b* 15 Dec 1921; *Educ* Dawson Court, St Matthews London; *m* 22 July 1944, (Olive) Margaret, da of Edwin Randolph Payne, of Chipstead, Surrey (d 1960); 1 s (Andrew Philip Bedlington b 3 Jan 1953), 1 da (Jennifer Jane (Mrs Bergerhoff-Mulder) b 21 Dec 1949); *Career* RAFVR 1941-46 (flight mechanic 12 Sqdn Bomber Cmd 1941, Flt-Lt 1944); admitted slr 1949, ptnr Scholfield Roberts & Hill, hon county slr Br Legion, chm Nat Insur Tribunal, chm Compensation Appeal Tribunals, occasional dep circuit judge 1973, rec Crown Ct 1982, regnl chm Industl Tribunals (pt/t chm 1968, chm 1975); memb Law Soc; *Recreations* pottering in the garden, fox hunting; *Clubs* RAF; *Style*— Philip Roberts, Esq; Charlynch House, Spaxton, Bridgwater, Somerset TA5 1BY (☎ 0278 67 356)

ROBERTS, Dr Philippa Mary Elizabeth; da of Dr James Roberts, of Manchester, and Dr Raine Emily Ireland Roberts; *b* 11 April 1960; *Educ* Withington Girls Sch Manchester, Charing Cross Hosp Med (MB BS); *Career* joined Br waterskiing team 1974, nat champion 1985-90 (1977, 1982), Euro overall champion 1986-90, world games champion 1989; res fell Nat Heart and Lung Inst; *Recreations* waterskiing; *Clubs* Princes; *Style*— Dr Philippa Roberts; 20 Gregory Drive, Old Windsor, Berkshire SL4 2RG

ROBERTS, Hon Mrs (Priscilla Jane Stephanie); *née* Low; MVO (1985); da of 1 Baron Aldington, KCMG, CBE, DSO, TD, PC, DL; *b* 4 Sept 1949; *Educ* Cranborne Chase, Westfield Coll and Courtauld Inst of Art Univ of London; *m* 1975, Hugh Roberts, s of Rt Rev Edward Roberts, sometime Bishop of Ely; 2 da (Sophie Jane Cecilia b 28 March 1978, Amelia Frances Albinia b 8 Feb 1982); *Career* curator of the Print Room Royal Library Windsor Castle 1975-; *Style*— The Hon Mrs Roberts, MVO; Salisbury Tower, Windsor Castle, Berks (☎ 0753 855581)

ROBERTS, Ven Raymond Harcourt; CB (1984), QHC (1980); s of Thomas Roberts (d 1981), and Caroline Maud, *née* Braine; *b* 14 April 1931; *Educ* Pontywaun GS Gwent, St Edmund Hall Oxford (BA MA); *Career* clerk in Holy Orders, ordained Diocese of Monmouth, deacon 1956, priest 1957, curate of Bassaleg 1956-59, chaplain RNVR 1958-59, chaplain RN 1959-84; chaplain of the Fleet and archdeacon RN 1980-84; Hon Chaplain to The Queen 1980-84; hon canon of Gibraltar 1980-84; archdeacon emeritus 1985; gen sec Jerusalem and Middle East Church Assoc 1985-89; chm Customer Service Ctee Office of Water Services Wales 1990-; *Style*— The Venerable Raymond H Roberts, CB; 12 High Cross Lane, Newport, Gwent NP1 9AA

ROBERTS, Richard David Hallam; s of Arthur Hallam Roberts, and Ruvé Constance Jessie Roberts; *b* 27 July 1931; *m* 1960, Wendy Ewen Mount; 3 s; *Career* cmmnd 6 Field Regt RA 1952; King's Sch Canterbury: asst master 1956-57, housemaster 1957-61, head Dept Modern Languages 1961-65, sr housemaster 1965-67; headmaster: Wycliffe Coll Stonehouse 1967-80, King Edward's Sch Witley 1980-85; freelance academic and writer, yachtmaster, bookbinder's mate, semi-trained househusband, gardener, woodman, antiquarian cyclist; *Clubs* Orford Sailing; *Style*— Richard Roberts, Esq

ROBERTS, Roger Hugh; JP; s of Norman Puleston Roberts, JP (d 1973), of Montmillan, Knowles Hill, Newton Abbot, Devon, and Marion Emily Louisa, *née* Crocker (d 1973); *b* 28 May 1934; *Educ* Kelly Coll, Guildford Law Coll; *m* 21 March 1959, Joan, da of Walter Blakeney Spencer; 1 s (Phillip b 1961), 4 da (Louise b 1960, Kathryn b 1963, Sally b 1967, Caroline b 1971); *Career* slr; chm Bd of Govrs Stover Sch; pres Newton Abbot YMCA; tstee Bearnes Charity; *Recreations* riding, skiing, boating; *Clubs* Rotary, SW Water Sports; *Style*— Roger H Roberts, Esq, JP; Vikings, 22 Seymour Rd, Newton Abbot, Devon (☎ 0626 52359); Pidsley & Roberts, Slrs, 22 Union St, Newton Abbot, Devon (☎ 0626 54455)

ROBERTS, Roy Ernest James; CBE; *b* 14 Dec 1928; *Career* GKN Screws & Fasteners Ltd 1951-56, dir and gen mangr C & B Smith Ltd 1966-70 (joined 1956); md: GKN Cwmbran Ltd 1970-72, GKN Engineering Ltd 1972-73, Guest Keen & Nettlefolds Ltd 1980-87 (appointed to Main Bd 1975); chm GKN Engineering Ltd and GKN Building Suppliers and Services Ltd 1974-77, dep chm GKN plc 1987-88, currently chm Simon Engineering plc, dep chm Dowty Group plc; chm Standing Conference on School's Sci and Technol 1988, pres Inst of Mech Engrs 1989-90, vice pres Engrg Employers' Fedn 1988-; FEng, FIMechE, FIProdE, AMIBE, FInstM; *Style*— Roy Roberts, Esq; Simon Engineering plc, Buchanan House, 3 St James's Square, London SW1Y 4JU (☎ 071 925 0666)

ROBERTS, Sir Samuel; 4 Bt (UK 1919); s of Sir Peter Roberts, 3 Bt (d 1985), and Judith Randall, *née* Hempson; *b* 16 April 1948; *Educ* Harrow, Univ of Sheffield (LLB), Manchester Business Sch (MBA); *m* 1977, Georgina Ann, da of David Cory, of Bluetts, Peterston-super-Ely, nr Cardiff, S Glam; 1 s (Samuel b 1989), 3 da (Eleanor b 1979, Olivia b 1982, Amelia b 1985); *Heir* s, Samuel Roberts b 1989; *Career* called to the Bar Inner Temple 1972; chm Curzon Steels Ltd 1980-84, dir Cleyfield Properties Ltd, Wiltshire & Co Ltd (insurance brokers); *Style*— Sir Samuel Roberts, Bt; 42 Markham Square, London SW3 4XA (☎ 071 589 3332)

ROBERTS, Col Samuel John (Sam); s of late Capt George Roberts, of Amesbury, Wilts, and Mabel Grace, *née* White; *b* 29 Nov 1936; *Educ* Brighton Coll, Welbeck Coll, RMA Sandhurst, RMCS Shrivenham (BSc), Army Staff Coll; *m* 22 July 1961, Pauline Rosamunde (Paula), da of Maj Alan Edward Neville Ward, of Seaview, IOW; 3 da (Juliet b 1962, Nicola b 1966, Kathryn b 1971); *Career* cmmnd REME 1957, 4 ARMD Wksp REME 1962-63, 49 Regt RA 1964-66, 7 ARMD Wksp REME 1971-73, BDLS Ottawa 1973-75, AQMG EMAN 2/LOG SEC 2 1975-77, CREME 4 ARMD Div 1978-80, Col EME 1 1980-83, Cmdt Princess Marina Coll 1983-85, Col EME 10 1985-87, ret as Col 1987; head of tech trg IBA 1987-90, quality mangr National Transcommunications Limited 1991-; Andover rep Basingstoke Branch BIM; memb: Advsy Panel Andover Consortium TVEI, NW Hants TEC Advsy Bd, NW Hants Trg Consortium, Continuing Professional Devpt Ctee IEEIE; CEng, FIMechE, FIEE, FBIM, memb IQA; *Recreations* philately, vehicle restoration; *Clubs* GBPS, Ford Y and C Model Register (chm); *Style*— Col Sam Roberts; 16 Croye Close, Andover, Hants SP10 3AF (☎ 0264 65662); National Transcommunications Limited, Crawley Court, Winchester, Hants SO21 2QA (☎ 0962 822201, fax 0962 822378, telex 477211)

ROBERTS, Dame Shelagh Marjorie; DBE (1981); da of Ivor Glyn Roberts (d 1937), of Ystalyfera, and Cecelia May Roberts (d 1963), of Liverpool; *b* 13 Oct 1924; *Career* memb: GLC 1970-81, Race Relations Bd 1973-78, Occupational Pensions Bd 1973-79, Port of London Authy 1975-79; chm: London Tourist Bd 1989-, Payroll Giving Assoc 1989-; MEP (EDG) London SW by-election Sept 1979-July 1989; *Recreations* swimming, skiing; *Clubs* Hurlingham, St Stephen's; *Style*— Dame Shelagh Roberts, DBE; 47 Shrewsbury House, Cheyne Walk, London SW3 5LW (☎ 071 352 3711)

ROBERTS, Sir Stephen James Leake; s of Frank Roberts (d 1964), of Sandford Ave, Church Stretton, Shropshire, and Annie Leake (d 1933); *b* 13 April 1915; *Educ* Wellington GS; *m* 1940, Muriel, da of James Hobbins, of Rosedene, Lawley Bank, Shropshire; 2 s, 2 da; *Career* chm: Milk Marketing Board 1977-87 (W Midland regnl memb 1966-), Littleworth Enterprises Ltd; farmer (Salop delegate to NFU Cncl 1962-70); kt 1980; *Recreations* football; *Clubs* Farmers; *Style*— Sir Stephen Roberts; Little Worth, Little Wenlock, Telford, Shropshire TF6 5AX (☎ 0952 504569); Littleworth Enterprises Ltd, Little Wenlock, Shropshire TF6 5AX (☎ 0952 504569)

ROBERTS, Stephen Pritchard; s of Edward Henry Roberts (d 1987), and Violet, *née* Pritchard; *b* 8 Feb 1949; *Educ* RCM (ARCM 1969, GRSM 1971); *Career* professional singer (concert, oratorio and opera), baritone; regular performances Europe, tours to Far E, USA, Canada, S America, BBC recordings for radio and TV (Prom appearances); commercial recordings (Decca, EMI, Virgin) incl: St Matthew Passion, Carmina Burana, Sea Symphony; opera repertoire incl: Marriage of Figaro and Die Fledermaus (Opera North), Gluck's Armide, Ravel's L'Heure Espagnol; opera recordings incl: Tippett's King Priam and Birtwistle's Punch and Judy; *Style*— Stephen Roberts, Esq; 144 Gleneagle Rd, London SW16 6BA (☎ 081 769 1512, fax 081 769 1512)

ROBERTS, Tony Mark; s of Edward Rees Roberts, and Ruth Olive, *née* Simms; *b* 4 Aug 1969; *Educ* Holyhead Co Secdy Sch, Coleg Pencraig Llangefni; *Career* professional footballer Queens Park Rangers, 22 appearances; Wales: 6 youth caps (+ 1 sub), 2 under 21 caps (+ 1 sub); *Recreations* swimming, snooker; *Style*— Tony Roberts, Esq; QPR FC, Loftus Rd, Shepherds Bush, London W12 7PA (☎ 081 743 0262)

ROBERTS, Trevor John; s of Howard William Roberts (d 1982), of Wolverhampton, and Melba Lewis, *née* Bushell; *b* 22 April 1940; *Educ* King Edward GS Stafford, Wolverhampton Poly; *m* 30 March 1970, Judith, da of William Samuel Wiggin, of Cannock, Staffs; 1 s (James b 1980), 1 da (Andrea b 1978); *Career* mangr of manufacturing depts Charles Richards & Sons Ltd 1969-74, tech mktg mangr Charles Richards Fasteners Ltd 1978-80 (prodn mangr 1974-78); jt owner and md: Doran Engineering Co Ltd 1982- (manufacturing dir 1980-82), Doran Engineering Holdings Ltd 1983-; Village Engineering Co Ltd 1983-, dir Petrospec Bolting Ltd 1990; Inst of Industl Mangrs: former memb Nat Cncl, former memb Nat Membership Exec, former chm and pres Wolverhampton branch; vice pres Willenhall Rotary Club; CEng, FBIM 1987, FIIM 1987, FIProdE 1988; *Recreations* swimming, reading, photography; *Style*— Trevor Roberts, Esq; Ashley Croft, Church Eaton, Stafford ST20 0BJ (☎ 0785 823624); Doran Engineering (Holdings) Ltd, Planetary Rd, Willenhall, W Midlands WV13 3XW (☎ 0902 732691, fax 0902 864663, telex 339160)

ROBERTS, Sir William James Denby; 3 Bt (UK 1909), of Milner Field, Bingley, WR of Yorkshire; s of Sir James Denby Roberts, OBE, 2 Bt (d 1973); *b* 10 Aug 1936; *Educ* Rugby, RAC Cirencester; *Heir* bro, Andrew Roberts; *Career* collector of vintage aircraft; fndr and former owner Strathallan Aircraft Collection; *Style*— Sir William Roberts, Bt; Strathallan Castle, Auchterarder, Perthshire; Combwell Priory, Flimwell, Wadhurst, Sussex

ROBERTS, William Morys; s of Gwilym James Roberts, MD (Maj Royal Army Med Corps 1945-46) (d 1990), of Penarth, South Glamorgan, and Eileen Burford *née* Chivers; *b* 8 Dec 1934; *Educ* Kingswood Sch Bath Avon, Gonville and Caius Coll Cambs (BA, MA); *m* 29 July 1967, Patricia Anne, da of John Stratford Bettinson, of Ickleton, Cambridgeshire; 1 s (Simon b 1972), 2 da (Sarah b 1969, Alice b 1974); *Career* RA 1953-54, Intelligence Corps 1954-55, 2 Lt (later Lt RARO) 1955-67; Turquand, Youngs and Co 1958-61; dir: WM Brandt's Sons & Co Ltd 1971 (chief accountant 1965, sec 1970), Edward Bates and Sons Ltd 1973-75; ptnr Ernst & Young 1976 (head of London Insolvency Servs 1987-89, head of London Corp Advsy Servs 1989-); churchwarden All Saint's Church Great Chesterford 1976-, memb Insolvency Rules Advsy Ctee 1984-; ACA 1961, FCA 1971; *Books* Insolvency Law and Practice (with J S H Gillies, 1988); *Recreations* gardening; *Clubs* IOD; *Style*— W M Roberts, Esq; Brock House, Great Chesterford, Saffron Walden, Essex CB10 1PJ (☎ 0799 30470); 1 Elgin House, Ryde Rd, Seaview, IOW; Ernst & Young, Becket House, 1 Lambeth Palace Road, London SE1 7EU (☎ 071 928 2000, fax 071 928 1345, telex 885234)

ROBERTS, Prof (Meirion) Wyn; s of Tom Roberts, OBE (d 1979), of Ammaford, Dyfed, and Mary, *née* Williams (d 1968); *b* 1 Feb 1931; *Educ* Amman Valley GS Ammanford, Univ of Swansea, Univ of Wales (BSc, PhD, DSc); *m* 23 March 1957, Catherine Angharad, da of John Lewis, of Ammanford, Dyfed; 1 s (Mark b 6 March 1964), 1 da (Karen b 26 May 1961); *Career* Imp Coll of Sci London 1955-57, sr scientific offr Nat Chem Laboratory 1957-59, lectr Queen's Univ of Belfast 1959-66, chair of physical chem Univ of Bradford 1966-79, head Dept of Physical Chem Univ Coll Cardiff 1986-88 (chair 1978-86), dep princ Univ of Wales Coll of Cardiff 1989- (head of Sch of Chem 1988-); visiting prof: Univ of Xiamen China 1985-, Univ of California Berkeley 1984; centenary lectr Indian Acad of Sciences 1984; chm Tstees of the Wool Fndn 1981-; memb: SERC Chem Ctee 1972-78, Univ Grants Physical Scis Ctee 1982-88, Ctee for Nat Academic awards 1989; hon fell Univ Coll of Swansea 1987, Tilden medal and prize Royal Soc of Chem 1976, Royal Soc of Chem award in

Surface Chem 1987; FRSC 1966; *Books* Reactivity of Solids (ed, 1972), The Chemical Physics of Solids and their Surfaces (Chemical Soc Reports, 1972-79), Chemistry of the Metal Gas Interface (jtly, 1978); *Recreations* rugby football; *Style*— Prof Wyn Roberts; 37 Heol-Y-Delyn, Lisvane, Cardiff CF4 5SR (☎ 0222 752452); University of Wales College of Cardiff, School of Chemistry and Applied Chemistry, PO Box 912, Cardiff CF1 3TB (☎ 0222 874805, fax 0222 874030, telex 498635)

ROBERTS, Sir (Ieuan) Wyn Pritchard; MP (C) Conwy 1970-; s of Rev E P Roberts, of Anglesey; *b* 10 July 1930; *Educ* Harrow, Univ of Oxford; *m* 1956, Enid Grace, da of W Williams, of Anglesey; 3 s; *Career* formerly journalist with The Liverpool Post and news asst with the BBC, Welsh controller and exec prodr TWW 1959-68, programme exec Harlech TV 1969; PPS to Sec of State for Wales 1970-74, oppn front bench spokesman on Welsh Affrs 1974-79, Parly under sec Welsh Office 1979-87, min of state for Wales 1987-; memb Court of Govrs Nat Museum and Nat Library Wales; Gorsedd Royal National Elsteddfod (1966); kt 1990; *Style*— Sir Wyn Roberts, MP; Tan y Gwalia, Conway, Gwynedd

ROBERTS, Yvonne; da of John Trevor Ellis Roberts, of Southsea, Hants, and Annie, *née* Oakford; *b* 24 Aug 1948; *Educ* Univ of Warwick (BA); 1 da (Zoe Claire Roberts Pilger b 7 Sept 1984); partner, Stephen Scott; *Career* journalist; indentured Northampton Chronicle & Echos 1970-72; reporter: Weekend World 1972-77, The London Programme 1978-80; freelance journalist 1973-80 (The Sunday Times, New Statesman, New Society, Evening News, Evening Standard, The Times, The Telegraph Magazine), assoc features ed London Daily News 1987; reporter on: Man Alive 1980, Watch the Woman (Channel 4), This Week 1987-89, Family Matters (BBC 1) 1989-90, Business Matters (BBC 2) 1989-90; journalist for The Observer 1989-; winner Young Journalist of the Year award 1971-72; *Books* Man Enough (1984); *Recreations* squash, running, films, friends, family, reading, travel, doing nothing; *Clubs* South Bank, Squash & Fitness Club; *Style*— Ms Yvonne Roberts; The Observer, Chelsea Bridge House, Queenstown Rd, London SW8 4NW (☎ 071 350 3339)

ROBERTS-JONES, Ivor; CBE (1975); *b* 2 Nov 1913; *Educ* Oswestry GS, Worksop Coll, Goldsmith Coll Art Sch, Royal Acad Schs (Landseer Silver Medal); *m* May 1940, Monica Florence, da of James Booth (d 1918), of St John's Wood; 1 s (Mervyn b 1941 d 1962), 1 da (Corinne b 1944); *Career* WWII RA 1939-46 active serv Arakan Burma; sculptor; solo exhibitions: Beaux Arts Gallery 1957; Oriel Welsh Arts Cncl Gallery Cardiff 1978, Eisteddford 1983; works purchased by: Tate Gallery, Nat Portrait Gallery, Arts Cncl of GB, Welsh Arts Cncl, Beaverbrook Fndn New Brunswick, Nat Museum of Wales; public commissions incl: Augustus John meml Fordingbridge 1967, Winston Churchill (Parliament Sq 1973, Oslo 1975, New Orleans 1977), Earl Attler House of Commons 1979, Janus Rider Equestrian Gp Harlech 1983, Rupert Brooke Rugby 1985, Field Marshall Lord Slim Whitehall 1990; maj portraits incl: Paul Claudel, Somerset Maughan, Yehudi Menuhin, Augustus John, George Thomas, Duke of Edinburgh, Prince Charles, Lord Edmund Davies, Lord Callaghan, Geraint Evans; Hon LLD Univ of Wales 1983; FRBS 1972, RA 1973; *Recreations* sailing, rugby; *Style*— Ivor Roberts-Jones, Esq, CBE, RA; The Bridles, Hill Lane, Shimpling, nr Diss, Norfolk IP21 4UH (☎ 0379 740 204); 31 St James's Gdns, London W11

ROBERTS-WRAY, Lady; Mary Howard; da of late Frank Howard Smith; *m* 1, 1935, Sir Ernest Hillas Williams, JP (d 1965); 1 da; m 2, 1965, as his 2 w, Sir Kenneth Roberts-Wray, GCMG, QC (d 1983); *Style*— Lady Roberts-Wray; The Old Golf House, Forest Row, Sussex

ROBERTSHAW, John Desmond; s of late Horace Robertshaw, and Elsie Robertshaw; *b* 19 Dec 1928; *Educ* Bembridge Sch, Oxford Univ; *m* 1961, Lesley Lynette, da of Harry Carter; 1 s, 2 da; *Career* York Tst Ltd, chm Utd Scientific Hldgs plc; dir: Kode Int plc 1979-, Rights and Issues Investmt Tst Ltd 1962-, Safe Computing Ltd 1982-, Shorco Gp Hldgs plc, Assoc Farmers plc; alternate memb Panel on Take-overs and Mergers; FCA, FIMBRA (dep chm); *Recreations* golf; *Clubs* MCC; *Style*— John Robertshaw, Esq; Birches Farm, Isfield, Sussex (☎ 082 575 304); York Trust, Dauntsey House, Frederick Place, Old Jewry, London EC2R 8HN (☎ 071 606 2167, telex 889341)

ROBERTSON, Dr Alan; CBE; s of late William Arthur Robertson, and late Clarice Firby Robertson; *b* 15 Aug 1920; *Educ* Middlesbrough HS, Univ Coll Durham, Balliol Coll Oxford (BSc, PhD); *m* 1948, Dorothy Eileen, da of late Frank Freeman; 2 s, 1 da; *Career* indust chemist; dir ICI 1975-82; chm: Br Nutrition Fndn 1981-, AGC (Agricultural Genetics Company) 1983-90; dir First Step Housing Co Ltd 1990-; vice chm Br Waterways Bd 1983-90, chm Mgmnt Ctee Nat Waterways Museum, govr Lister Inst of Preventive Med 1985-; Chemical Industl medal Royal Soc 1982; memb Cncl China Soc; FRSC, CChem; *Recreations* all sports, gardening, biographical history; *Clubs* Farmers', Oriental; *Style*— Dr Alan Robertson, CBE; Woodlands, Tennysons Lane, Haslemere, Surrey GU27 3AF (☎ 0428 4196)

ROBERTSON, Alastair Macdonald; s of John Robertson (d 1980), and Elizabeth Watt Robertson; *b* 4 Nov 1930; *Educ* George Heriot's Sch, Univ of Edinburgh (MA, BSc); *m* 1969, Avril Margaret, *née* Willison; *Career* gen mangr and dir Scottish Equitable Life Assurance Soc, ret 1982; chief exec and dir City of Edinburgh Life (formerly Stevenston Life) 1983-87 (ret); non exec dir Edinburgh Money Mgmnt Ltd; FFA; *Recreations* golf, skiing, sailing (yacht 'Semlas' regd Leith); *Clubs* New (Edinburgh), Gullane Golf; *Style*— Alastair M Robertson, Esq; 13 Cumlodden Ave, Edinburgh (☎ 031 337 4264); 41A Charlotte Sq, Edinburgh EH2 4HQ

ROBERTSON, Alexander Hughes; s of Alexander Buchanan Robertson (d 1971), of Co Durham, and Anne, *née* Hughes (d 1977); *b* 20 Jan 1929; *Educ* Newcastle Royal GS, Durham Univ, Kings Coll (Dip Arch); *m* 17 Dec 1955, Pamela, da of James Foster Charlton, of Greasby, Wirral; 2 da (Sarah b 1957, Hilary b 1960), 1 s (Alexander b 1965); *Career* conslt architect; architect The Singapore Improvement Tst, sr ptnr The Alexander Robertson Ptnrship; Freeman City of London 1981, Liveryman Worshipful Co of Arbitrators 1982; FRIBA, FCIArb; *Recreations* study of historical buildings, golf; *Clubs* Caledonian, Caldy Golf, Old Novocastrian Soc; *Style*— Alexander Robertson, Esq; 30 Darmonds Green, W Kirby, Wirral L48 5DU (☎ 051 625 5655); The Alexander Robertson Partnership, The Oaks, Village Rd, W Kirby, Wirral (☎ 051 625 9256)

ROBERTSON, Anderson Bain; s of Mungo Manderson Robertson (d 1932), of Bristol, and Minnie McAllister Bain, *née* Anderson (d 1987); *b* 22 Oct 1929; *Educ* Ardrossan Acad Ayrshire, Gray's Sch of Art, Aberdeen and Glasgow Sch of Art (DA, BA); *m* 13 July 1955, Mary Margaret Moffat, da of Alexander Stewart Christie (d 1979), of Wishaw; 2 s (Maxwell Stewart b 1959, Paul Noel b 1961); *Career* RAOC 1948-50; head Dept of Art Nicolson Inst Stornoway 1969-79, govr Aberdeen Coll of Educn 1974-78, convener Central Advsy Ctee of Art EIS 1977-81, assessor Certificate of Sixth Year Studies in art and Design 1977-89; artist; exhibitions at: Royal Scot Acad, Royal Glasgow Inst of Fine Arts, Royal Scot Soc of Painters in Water Colours, Royal Soc of Portrait Painters, Scot Artists and Artist Craftsmen; private collections in GB and USA; *Recreations* sailing; *Clubs* Glasgow Art; *Style*— Anderson Robertson, Esq; The Coppice, 2 College Park, Barassie, Troon, Ayrshire, Scotland (☎ 0292 316003)

ROBERTSON, Andrew John; s of John Hector Robertson, and Jennifer Mary, *née* Cullen; *b* 17 Nov 1960; *Educ* Michaelhouse Balgowan Natal SA, City Univ (BSc); *m* 13 Feb 1987, Susan Louise, da of Michael John Bayliss; 1 da (Amy Louise b 13 Aug 1988); *Career* Ogilvy & Mather: trainee media planner 1982, account dir 1986, memb Bd of Dirs 1987, mgmnt supervisor and new business dir 1988-89; gp dir J Walter Thompson Co 1989, chief exec WCRS 1990-; IPA 1987; *Recreations* tennis, squash, opera, ballet; *Style*— Andrew Robertson, Esq; WCRS, 40-44 Great Queen St, London WC2B 5AR (☎ 071 244422800, fax 071 831 4126, mobile 0860 503291)

ROBERTSON, Angus Frederick; s of Eric Desmond Robertson, OBE (d 1987), and Aileen Margaret, *née* Broadhead; *b* 4 Nov 1954; *Educ* Westminster, Univ of Stirling (BA); *m* Frances Ellen, da of Patrick Carroll Macnamara, of Ardgay Sutherland; *Career* called to the Bar Middle Temple 1978; *Style*— Angus Robertson, Esq; 44 Rawlings St, London SW3 2LS (☎ 071 581 2719); 10 King's Bench Walk, Temple, London EC4Y 7EB (☎ 071 353 7742, fax 071 583 0579, telex 8811 61210 KBW G)

ROBERTSON, B A; *Educ* Allen Glen's Sch, RSAMD; *m* Karen, *née* Manners; 1 s (Rory b 1986), 1 da (Poppy b 1989); *Career* composer, lyricist, performer; writer/performer of records incl: *LPs* Wringing Applause (Ardent) 1974, Shadow of A Thin Man (Arista) 1976, Initial Success (Asylum) 1980, Bully for You (Asylum) 1981, R & BA (Asylum) 1982; *Singles* Bang Bang, Flight 19, Hold Me (with Maggie Bell) 1982, Knocked It Off, Kool in The Kaftan, Time (with Frida of Abba) 1984, To Be or Not To Be; writer of many hit records for artists incl: Cliff Richard, Mike and The Mechanics; music for TV incl: 1986 Commonwealth Games (BBC), Saturday Superstore (BBC), Swap Shop (BBC), Wogan (BBC); music for films incl: The Lost Boys, Heavenly Pursuits, Sweet Revenge, White Nights; performances in film, TV, theatre incl: BA in Music (BBC series), Dear Heart (BBC, Drama), The End of the Line (BBC, drama), Living Apart Together (film), The Monster Club (film), Scots and Their Pop Music (documentary, BBC, writer and presenter); guest bdcaster BBC Radio and TV 1980-84; awards incl: more than 40 Silver Gold and Platinum Record awards, Ivor Novello award, Br Music Indust award; memb: Assoc of Professional Composers, Nat Acad of Popular Music, Nat Acad of Recording Arts and Scis, Nat Acad of Songwriters, Soc of Distinguished Songwriters; *Style*— B A Robertson, Esq

ROBERTSON, (George) Brian; s of Henry Grieve Robertson, of Tillicoultry, and Margaret, *née* Cooper; *b* 9 Aug 1959; *Educ* Alva Acad, Falkirk Coll of Technol; *m* 18th July 1990, Morag, *née* Wilson; *Career* Rugby Union tight-head forward Stirling County RFC; joined Stirling County RFC 1981 (220 appearances); rep: Glasgow 1986- (won Inter-Dist Championship 1990, toured Holland and Belgium 1985 and Ireland 1989, 30 appearances), Scot B (debut v Ireland 1990); memb Scotland squad 1991; farm foreman, self-employed potato merchant 1986-; *Style*— Brian Robertson, Esq; 23 Harviestoun Grove, Tillicoultry FK13 6QS (☎ 0259 50315); Stirling County RFC, Bridge Haugh, Stirling, Scotland (☎ 0786 74827)

ROBERTSON, (James) Campbell; s of Surgn Lt James Robertson (ka 1942), of Edinburgh, and Mathilda Mary, *née* Campbell; *b* 15 Oct 1941; *Educ* Epsom Coll, Univ of London (MB BS); *m* 2 May 1970, Dr Margaret Elizabeth Robertson, da of Charles Edwin Kirkwood, of 9 Church Rd, Laverstock, Salisbury, Wilts; 3 s (Charles James b 1971, Andrew b 1973, Alastair b 1974); *Career* currently conslt physician in rheumatology and rehabilitation, Salisbury DHA and Southampton DHA, dir Wessex Regnl Rehabilitation Unit; fndr ed Care Science and Practice; papers incl: neck and back pain, measurement of physical signs, bandaging and interface pressure mgmnt, burns scarring; fndr memb Soc for Tissue Viability, memb Cncl Wessex Rehabilitation Soc; memb: Br Soc Rheumatology, Back Pain Soc, BMB, Soc for Res in Rehabilitation; LRCP, FRCP, MRCS; *Books* Blueprint for a Clinical Grip Strength Monitor and Limb Strength Measurement System (1986); *Recreations* windsurfing, sailing, DIY, medical journalism; *Clubs* S Wales and S W Wessex Rheumatology; *Style*— Dr James Robertson; Wessex Regional Rehabilitation Unit, Odstock Hospital, Salisbury, Wilts (☎ 0722 336262)

ROBERTSON, Carol Anne; *née* Moseley; da of Kenneth Marsingall Moseley, of Northampton, and Agnes Beryl, *née* Pegler (d 1983); *b* 2 Sept 1935; *Educ* Northampton HS for Girls, Univ of Southampton (BSc); *m* 31 Aug 1961, John Corbett, s of John Corbett Robertson; 1 s (Jack b 1964), 2 da (Sophie b 1969, Bernadette b 1969); *Career* registered nurse Barts Hosp London 1959, registered midwife Radcliffe & Churchill Hosps Oxford 1959, registered health visitor Liverpool 1962, community health nurse tutor RCN London 1979, health visiting lectr South Bank Poly 1979-82; health visitor: Bootle Liverpool 1962-63, Ilford Essex 1963-64, Portsmouth 1977-78; dir and co sec Raoul Ltd; memb Ctee West Sussex HPR Trg Gp; memb: Warsash Theatre Gp, Warsash and Dist Art Gp, Portsmouth and SE Hants Health Authy 1983-86; *Books* Health Visiting in Practice (1987, 2 edn 1991); *Recreations* walking, dog training; *Style*— Mrs Carol Robertson; 14 Solent Drive, Hook Park, Warsash, Southampton SO3 9HB (☎ 0489 584788)

ROBERTSON, Rev Charles; JP (City of Edinburgh 1980); s of Thomas Robertson (d 1941), of Glasgow, and Elizabeth, *née* Halley (d 1942); *b* 22 Oct 1940; *Educ* Camphill Sch Paisley, Univ of Edinburgh, New Coll Edinburgh; *m* 30 July 1965, Alison Margaret, da of the Rev John Strachan Malloch, MBE, of Aberdeen; 1 s (Duncan b 6 June 1967), 2 da (Mary b 29 Dec 1968, Margaret b 5 Feb 1976); *Career* asst minister N Morningside Church Edinburgh 1964-65; parish minister: Kiltearn Ross-shire 1965-78, Canongate Kirk (The Kirk of Holyroodhouse) Edinburgh 1978-; sec Gen Assembly's Panel on Worship 1982-, Church of Scotland rep Jt Liturgical Gp 1984-, tstee Church Hymnary Tst 1987-, pres Church Service Soc 1988-; chaplain: Clan Donnachaidh Soc 1981-, Elsie Inglis Maternity Hosp 1982-87, New Club Edinburgh 1986-, Moray House Coll of Educn 1986-, No 2 (City of Edinburgh) Maritime HQ Unit RAAF 1987-; lectr in Church Praise St Colm's Coll Edinburgh 1980-; tstee Edinburgh Old Town Tst 1987-, govr St Columba's Hospice 1986-; Queensberry House Hosp: dir 1978-, vice chm 1985-89, chm 1989-;memb: Exec Ctee Scot Veteran's Residences 1978-, Bdcasting Standards Cncl 1988-, Historic Bldgs Cncl for Scot 1990-; chaplain to the Lord High Cmmr to the General Assembly of the Church of Scotland 1990-91; *Books* Singing the Faith (ed, 1990); *Recreations* Scottish and Edinburgh history, hymnody, collecting Canongate miscellanea; *Clubs* Athenaeum, New (Edinburgh); *Style*— The Rev Charles Robertson, JP; Manse of Canongate, Edinburgh EH8 8BR (☎ 031 556 3515)

ROBERTSON, Brig Clive Henderson; DL (Dorset 1984); s of Lt-Col William Henderson Robertson, MC (d 1976), and Alice Maud, *née* Jackaman (d 1974); *b* 21 Aug 1927; *Educ* Radley; *m* 5 Sept 1959, Fiona Ann, da of Col Ronald Scott-Dempster; 1 s (Andrew b 19 May 1962), 1 da (Caroline b 22 June 1960); *Career* cmmnd 11 Hussars (PAO) 1947, ADC to GOC 7 Armd Div 1952-53 (despatches Malaya 1955 and 1956), Staff Coll Camberley 1960, JSSC 1964, CO 11 Hussars 1968-69, CO Royal Hussars (PWO) 1969-71, mil asst to Mil Sec 1971-72, Col Gen Staff MOD 1972-74, Cmdt RAC Gunnery Sch 1974-75, Cdr RAC Centre Bovington 1975-78, vice pres Reg Cmmns Bd 1978-80; asst private sec to HRH The Duke of Edinburgh 1984-; chm: Govrs Hardy's Sch 1982-83, Army Benevolent Fund Dorset 1983-; *Recreations* skiing, gardening, theatre; *Clubs* Cavalry & Guards; *Style*— Brig Clive Robertson, DL

ROBERTSON, Sheriff Daphne Jean Black; WS; da of Rev Robert Black Kincaid (d 1980), and Ann Parker Collins; *b* 31 March 1937; *Educ* Hillhead HS, Greenock Acad, Univ of Edinburgh (MA), Univ of Glasgow (LLB); *m* 1965, Donald Buchanan, s of

Donald Robertson (d 1948), of Argyll; *Career* admitted slr 1961; Sheriff of Glasgow and Strathkelvin 1979; *Style—* Sheriff Daphne Robertson, WS; Sheriff Court House, Glasgow (☎ 041 429 8888)

ROBERTSON, Douglas Laurence; s of Ronald John Robertson, of Milton Keynes, and Agnes McKay (Nanette), *née* Reid; *b* 12 June 1952; *Educ* Dalkeith HS, Langley Park Sch for Boys, St Edmund Hall Oxford (MA); *m* 1 Nov 1975, Susan Winifred, da of John Clair (d 1989), of Marden, Herefordshire; 1 s (Iain b 1979), 1 da (Carolyn b 1982); *Career* admitted slr 1977; ptnr: Kenneth Brown Baker Baker 1981, Turner Kenneth Brown 1983; memb Steering Ctee Professional Firms Gp Business in the Community; Freeman: City of London 1986, Worshipful Co of Slrs 1986; memb Law Soc 1977; *Recreations* rugby and football, reading; *Clubs* Vincents, Utd Oxford and Cambridge Univ; *Style—* Douglas L Robertson, Esq; Farleigh Cottage, Ricketts Hill Rd, Tatsfield, Westerham, Kent TN16 2NA (☎ 0959 77283); Turner Kenneth Brown, 100 Fetter Lane, London EC4A 1DD (☎ 071 242 6006, fax 071 242 3003)

ROBERTSON, (James) Douglas Moir; DL (Surrey 1988); s of George Robertson (d 1984), and Jessie Barrie, *née* Brough; *b* 15 Nov 1938; *Educ* Trinity Acad Edinburgh, Heriot Watt Univ Edinburgh; *m* 29 June 1963, Caroline Blanche, da of David Stephen Adams, of Edinburgh; 2 s (Graham b 1965, Brian b 1977), 1 da (Alison b 1970); *Career* princ Surveyors Collaborative 1969; exec dir: Building Cost Info Serv RICS 1962-, Building Maintenance Information Ltd 1970-; chm Building Data Banks Ltd 1985-; chm: Surrey CC 1987-90, Airports Policy Consortium 1984-; memb Cncl Univ of Surrey; memb ACC 1980- (chm Environment Ctee 1990-); FRICS 1969, FBIM 1971, FRSA 1989; *Recreations* golf; *Clubs* RAC; *Style—* Douglas Robertson, Esq, DL; 85/87 Clarence St, Kingston upon Thames, Surrey KT1 1RB (☎ 081 549 0102, fax 081 547 1238)

ROBERTSON, Hon Mrs (Elizabeth Anne); *née* Bourne; o da of Gen Baron Bourne, GCB, KBE, CMG (Life Peer, d 1982), and Agnes Evelyn, *née* Thompson (d 1990); *b* 1931; *m* 1952, Ian McKay Robertson (d 1984); children; *Style—* The Hon Mrs Robertson; Belmont House, Donhead St Mary, Shaftesbury, Dorset

ROBERTSON, Dr Elizabeth Margaret; da of Alastair Robertson, of Aberdeen, and Dorothy Elizabeth, *née* Barron; *b* 7 Oct 1951; *Educ* St Margaret's Sch for Girls Aberdeen, Univ of Aberdeen (MB ChB, DMRD); *Career* conslt radiologist Grampian Health Bd, hon clinical sr lectr in radiology Univ of Aberdeen; memb: BMA, BIR, RSM; FRCR; *Style—* Dr Elizabeth Robertson; 7 Queen's Ave, Aberdeen AB1 6WA (☎ 0224 316552); In Patient X-ray Dept, Aberdeen Royal Infirmary, Foresterhill, Aberdeen (☎ 0224 681818 ext 53446)

ROBERTSON, Frank; s of Francis Alexander Robertson (d 1977), of Aberdeen, and Margaret Daniel, *née* Glennie; *b* 25 Feb 1944; *Educ* Robert Gordon's Coll Aberdeen, Scott Sutherland Sch of Architecture Aberdeen (Dip Arch); *m* 23 June 1967, Aileen Hamilton, da of William Mathie, of Scone, Perthshire; 1 s (Neil b 1973), 2 da (Beverley b 1967, Lynn b 1970); *Career* Scot cricket international with 45 caps, registered first class with Worcs 1981; fndr ctee memb Aberdeen Sports Cncl; ARIAS 1968, RIBA 1968; *Recreations* cricket, snooker, swimming, golf, photography; *Clubs* Aberdeenshire Cricket, Aberdeen Sportsman's (hon memb), Aboyne Golf, The Seafield, Gordonians Cricket; *Style—* Frank Robertson, Esq; 110 Hammerfield Ave, Aberdeen AB1 6LB (☎ 0224 321305); Thomson Craig & Donald, 4 Carden Terrace, Aberdeen AB1 1US (☎ 0224 644461, fax 0224 646435)

ROBERTSON, Geoffrey Ronald; QC (1988); s of Francis Albert Robertson, of 20 Lucretia Ave, Longueville, Sydney, Australia, and Bernice Joy, *née* Beattie; *b* 30 Sept 1946; *Educ* Epping Boys HS, Sydney Univ (BA, LLB), Univ of Oxford (BCL); *m* Kathy Lette; 1 s (Julius Blake); *Career* called to the Bar Middle Temple 1973, head of Chambers 1990-; visiting fell: Univ of NSW Australia 1977, Univ of Warwick 1980-81; memb Exec Cncl ICA, exec memb Freedom of Info Campaign; tstee Parents For Safe Food; *Books* Reluctant Judas (1976), Obscenity (1979), People Against the Press (1983), Media Law (1984, 2 edn 1990), Hypotheticals (1986), Does Dracula Have Aids? (1987), Freedom The Individual and the Law (1989); *Recreations* tennis, opera, fishing; *Style—* Geoffrey Robertson, Esq, QC; 14 Thornhill Crescent, London N1 (☎ 071 609 0554); 11 Doughty Street, London WC1N 2PG (☎ 071 404 1313, fax 071 404 2283)

ROBERTSON, George Islay MacNeill; MP (Lab) Hamilton 1978-; s of George and Marion Robertson; *b* 12 April 1946; *Educ* Dunoon GS, Univ of Dundee (MA Econ); *m* 1970, Sandra Wallace; 2 s (Malcolm b 1972, Martin b 1975), 1 da (Rachael b 1980); *Career* res asst Econs Gp Tayside Study 1968-69, Scottish organiser GMWU (now GMB) 1969-78; elected to Parl 1978, PPS to Sec of State for Social Servs 1979; oppn spokesman on: Scotland 1979-80, Defence 1980-88, Foreign and Cwlth Affrs 1981-; princ spokesman on Europe 1986- (dep spokesman 1983-); memb Steering Ctee: Konigswinter (Br-German) Conf 1983-, Atlantic Conf 1988-; vice chm Br-German Parly Gp 1983-, co-chm Br Parly Lighting Gp 1983-, chm Scottish Lab Pty 1977-78; memb: Lab Pty Scottish Exec 1974-79, Britain in the World Policy Review Gp of Lab Pty, Int Ctee of Lab Pty; vice chm: Bd of Br Cncl 1986, Advsy Bd Know How Funds for Eastern Europe 1989-, GB/Eastern Europe Centre 1990-; memb: Exec and Cncl Scottish Business Sch 1973-78, Scottish Tourist Bd 1974-76, Bd Scottish Devpt Agency 1975-78, Bd of Govrs Scottish Police Coll 1975-78, Police Advsy Bd for Scotland 1975-78, Cncl Nat Tst for Scotland 1974-76 and 1978-80; memb Advsy Bd: European Business Journal (House Magazine), Br American Successor Generation Conf, 21st Century Tst; govr and memb Progs Ctee Ditchley Fndn 1988-, hon vice pres Operation Raleigh, vice chm Prince of Wales Blantyre Community Venture 1990-; *Style—* George Robertson, Esq, MP; 3 Argyle Park, Dunblane, Perths; c/o House of Commons, London SW1A 0AA

ROBERTSON, Dr George Slessor; s of John Bruce Robertson (d 1971), of Aberdeenshire, and Alice Jane Slessor Clyne (d 1980), of Aberdeenshire; *b* 30 Dec 1933; *Educ* Peterhead Acad, Univ of Aberdeen (MB ChB, MD); *m* 21 Sept 1960, Audrey Esslemont, da of Hector McDonald (d 1955), of Aberdeen; 1 s (Neil b 1961), 2 da (Denise b 1963, Judith b 1966); *Career* res asst anaesthetics Aberdeen Royal Infirmary 1964-65, asst anaesthetist Winnipeg Gen Hosp Canada 1967-68, conslt anaesthetist Aberdeen Royal Infirmary 1969-, hon sr lectr anaesthetics Univ of Aberdeen 1969-; SB St J 1985; memb: Scottish Soc of Anaesthetics, NE of Scotland Soc of Anaesthetics (pres 1973-74); FFARCS 1964; *Books* The Living Will (1988), author of numerous scientific and medical ethics papers incl jt author The Appleton Concensus on Decisions to Forgo Medical Treatment; *Recreations* golf, hill-walking, painting; *Style—* Dr George Robertson; Hazelwood, 12 Queen's Den, Woodend, Aberdeen AB1 8BW (☎ 0224 311903); Department of anaesthetics, Aberdeen Royal Infirmary, Foresterhill, Aberdeen AB9 2ZB

ROBERTSON, Dr (Andrew) Gerard; s of Henry Robertson, OBE, (d 1970), of Lagos Nigeria and Edinburgh, and Helen, *née* Flynn; *b* 14 Jan 1945; *Educ* St Josephs Coll Dumfries, Univ of Glasgow (BSc, PhD, MB ChB); *m* 2 April 1970, Margaret Mary Dorothy, da of John Joseph McKee, KSG, of Glasgow; 5 s (John b 1977, Andrew b 1980, Francis b 1984, Gregory b 1986, Bernard b 1986); *Career* sr registrar in radiotherapy and oncology Christie Hosp Manchester 1981, conslt in radiotherapy and oncology Western Infirmary Glasgow 1982- (formerly registrar); treas Assoc of Head and Neck Oncologists of GB, memb Catholic Union of GB, FRCR 1980, FRCR Glasgow 1988; *Recreations* golf; *Clubs* East Renfrewshire Golf; *Style—* Dr Gerard Robertson; Western Infirmary, Beatson Oncology Centre, Glasgow, Scotland, G11 6NT (☎ 041 339 8822)

ROBERTSON, Ian; s of Sqdn Ldr John Robertson (d 1982), and Alice, *née* Spero; *b* 17 Jan 1945; *Educ* George Watsons Coll Edinburgh, Univ of Aberdeen (MA), Christs Coll Cambridge (BEd); *m* 10 Dec 1975, Sonia Margaret, da of William Preston, of 85 Severn Drive, Wellington, Shropshire; 1 s (Duncan b 1978), 1 da (Clare b 1981); *Career* rugby corr: Sunday Times 1980-83, BBC 1983- (1972-80); rugby player; 8 int caps for Scotland 1968-70, coach Univ of Cambridge 1972-85, former player for The Barbarians; author and co-author of 15 books; *Recreations* golf, theatre; *Style—* Ian Robertson, Esq; 37 Cholmeley Park, Highgate, London N6 5EL (☎ 081 348 5119); BBC, Broadcasting House, Portland Place, London W1A 1AA (☎ 071 927 4293, fax 071 580 5780, car 0860 212527)

ROBERTSON, Maj-Gen Ian Argyll; CB (1968), MBE (1947); s of John Argyll Robertson (d 1943), and Sarah Lilian Pitt Healing (d 1962); *b* 17 July 1913; *Educ* Winchester, Trinity Coll Oxford; *m* 1939, Marjorie Violet Isobel, da of Maj Malcolm Bedford Duncan (d 1956); 2 da; *Career* cmmnd Seaforth Highlanders 1934-, cmd 1 Bn Seaforth Highlanders 1954-57, cmd Sch Inf 1963-64, cmmd 51 Inf Div 1964-66 (ret 1968); DL (Nairn 1973-88); HM Vice Lord Lt Highland Region 1973-88; *Recreations* gardening, golf; *Clubs* Army and Navy, MCC, Vincent's (Oxford); *Style—* Maj-Gen Ian Robertson, CB, MBE; Brackla House, Nairn (☎ 066 77 220)

ROBERTSON, Ian James; s of James Robertson (d 1986), of Drumfin, Killearn, Stirlingshire, and Mary Young Brown Steele; *b* 21 June 1937; *Educ* Merchiston Castle Sch, Edinburgh, Glasgow Univ (BA); *m* 14 Sept 1963, Fiona Elizabeth, da of Robert Bruce Mackinnon, of Bearsoen, Glasgow; 1 s (J I David), 2 da (Virginia, Victoria); *Career* dep chm Whatlings plc 1970-84; devpts dir: Whatlings, Alfred McAlpine Scotland 1984; dir Scottish Opera Theatre Royal Ltd; memb East End Exec Glasgow, Incorporation of Wrights of Glasgow; FBIM 1984; *Recreations* opera, golf, fishing; *Clubs* Buchanan Castle, RSAC; *Style—* Ian Robertson, Esq; Whatlings plc, North Claremont St, Glasgow G3 7LF (☎ 041 331 2151)

ROBERTSON, Dr Ian Macbeth; CB (1976), LVO (1956); s of Sheriff J A T Robertson (d 1942), of Edinburgh, and Brenda, *née* Lewis (d 1943); *b* 1 Feb 1918; *Educ* Melville Coll, Univ of Edinburgh (MA); *m* 1947, Anne Stewart, da of John McMillan Marshall, CBE (d 1949); *Career* civil servant; private sec to: Min of State Scottish Office 1951-52, Sec of State for Scotland 1952-55; under sec Scottish Office 1963-78, sec of cmmns for Scotland 1978-83; JP Edinburgh 1978; memb Williams Ctee on Nat Museums and Galleries in Scotland 1979-81; chm Bd of Govrs Edinburgh Coll of Art 1981-88; Hon DLitt Heriot Watt Univ 1988; HRSA 1987; *Clubs* New (Edinburgh); *Style—* Dr Ian Robertson, CB, LVO; Napier House, 8 Colinton Rd, Edinburgh EH10 5DS

ROBERTSON, Isabella (Belle); MBE (1973); da of Hugh McCorkindale (d 1966), of Eden Farm, Southend, Kintyre, Argyll, and Isabella MacNaughton, *née* Smith (d 1983); *b* 11 April 1936; *Educ* Southend Pub Sch, Campbeltown GS; *m* 17 Sept 1960, Ian Crombie Robertson, s of Peter Crombie Robertson (d 1943), of Clydebank, Glasgow; *Career* golfer; represented: Scotland 24 times, GB 19 times; memb of first GB team to win Curtis Cup in USA 1986; Frank Moran Trophy 1972, Woman Golfer of the Year 1985 (also 1971 and 1981), Scottish Sportswoman of the Year 4 times, McRobert Thistle Award Nat Playing Assoc of Scotland 1987; NPFA (Scotland); *Books* The Woman Golfer-A Lifetime of Golfing Success (with Lewine Mair, 1986); *Recreations* gardening, cookery, country pursuits; *Style—* Ms Belle Robertson, MBE; 25 Beechwood Court, Bearsden, Glasgow G61 2RY (☎ 041 942 2003)

ROBERTSON, James Ian Alexander (Nander); s of Capt Ian Greig Robertson, DSO, DSC (d 1987), of Mallorca, and Elizabeth Marion, *née* Aitken (d 1982); *b* 7 Feb 1943; *Educ* Ampleforth; *m* 1, 9 Sept 1966, Lucy (d 1987), da of The Rt Hon Lord Maclay, *qv*; 3 s (Hugh Sebastion b 4 Sept 1967, David Ian b 31 Dec 1969, Dominic James b 25 June 1973), 1 da (Anna Marcecle b 23 March 1971); m 2, 31 Aug 1990, Fiona, da of Jack Arnott Hunter, wid of Prof Patrick Hamilton (d 1988); 1 step s (John Paul b 16 June 1973), 1 step da (Elizabeth Lilias b 4 Jan 1977); *Career* shipping Glasgow 1961-68, forestry engr 1968-82, organic fertiliser 1982-, organic farmer 1968-; chm Organic Farmers and Growers Scot, memb Bd UK Register of Organic Food Stuffs, vice chm Scot Organic Prodrs Assoc; FICS 1965; *Recreations* shooting, sailing, planting, trees; *Clubs* Lansdowne; *Style—* Nander Robertson, Esq

ROBERTSON, Maj James Pearce; s of Capt Ronald Douglas Robertson (d 1968), and Mary Pearce, *née* Wills (d 1963); *b* 7 July 1920; *Educ* Stowe, Univ of St Andrew's, King Alfred's Coll Winchester; *m* 20 July 1957, June Mary O'Carroll, da of Maj-Gen Anthony Gerald O'Carroll Scott, CB, CBE, DL (d 1980); *Career* WWII cmmnd RA 1939; served: Western Desert (invalided UK) 1941, NW Europe (wounded Holland) 1944, Liberation Norway 1945, Palestine 1946, Malta 1955, Cyprus 1959, Aden 1961, ret 1964; schoolmaster 1966-85; head Dept of History and cncl head of House in Hants Comprehensive Schs; vice chm Parish Cncl 1971-78, memb PCC 1978-83, fund raising Save the Children Fund 1978-91, organiser Sealed Knot Soc, lectr Womens' Inst; *Recreations* whipping-in to hounds, polo, all team games (regimental rugger player), historical research, carpentry, restoring old houses, gardening, photography, writing; *Style—* Major James P Robertson; Rose Cottage, Penton Mewsey, nr Andover, Hampshire (☎ 026 477 2772)

ROBERTSON, Jean; CBE (1986); da of Alexander Robertson (d 1967), and Jean Turner, *née* McCartney (d 1987); *b* 21 Sept 1928; *Educ* Mary Erskine Sch for Girls; *Career* Queen Alexandra's Naval Nursing Serv: RN Hosp Chatham 1955, HMNAS Sanderline 1957, RN Hosp Haslar 1968 (1958, 1963), RN Hosp Hong Kong 1959, RN Hosp Plymouth 1959, HMS Terror Singapore 1961, RN Hosp Malta 1966, RN Hosp Gibraltar 1972, MOD (N) Empress State London 1974, RN Hosp Mauritius 1975, Matron RN Hosp Plymouth 1976, MOD (N) Matron-in-Chief's Dept 1979, Surg-Rear Adml Naval Hosp 1981, Matron-in-chief 1983-86; involved with Queen Elizabeth Fndn for the Disabled; *Recreations* swimming, gardening, lace making; *Style—* Miss Jean Robertson, CBE; 14 The Haven, Gosport, Hants PO12 2BD (☎ 0705 582301)

ROBERTSON, Lady Joan Patricia Quirk; *née* Wavell; da of Field Marshal 1 Earl Wavell, GCB, GCSI, GCIE, CMG, MC, PC (d 1950), and Eugénie Marie, CI, DStJ, *née* Quirk (d 1987); *b* 23 April 1923; *m* 1, 27 Jan 1943, Maj Hon Simon Nevil Astley (d 1946), yr s of 21 Baron Hastings and Lady Marguerite Nevill (da of 3 Marq of Abergavenny); 1 da; m 2, 19 June 1948, Maj Harry Alastair Gordon, MC (d 1965); 2 da; m 3, 1973, Maj Donald Struan Robertson, Scots Gds, s of Rt Hon Sir Malcolm Robertson, GCMG, KBE (d 1951); *Style—* The Lady Joan Robertson; Winkfield Plain Farm, Winkfield, Windsor, Berks SL4 4QU (☎ 0344 885360)

ROBERTSON, Maj-Gen John Carnegie; s of Sir William Charles Fleming Robertson, KCMG (d 1937), and Elizabeth Dora, *née* Whelan (d 1978); *b* 24 Nov 1917; *Educ* Cheltenham, Sandhurst; *m* 5 July 1961, Teresa Mary Louise (Tessa), da of Cecil Theodore Porter, of Heather Cottage, Sunningdale, Berks; *Career* cmmnd Glos Regt 1938, 2 Glos 1938-39, BEF 1940 (captured before Dunkirk, POW 1940-45), Staff Capt NI 1947-48, Co Cdr 1 Wilts, Staff Capt 29 Bde 1948 (attached JAG Dept), Staff Capt Dir Army Legal Servs Egypt 1949-52, Maj Dep Asst Dir Army Legal Servs Kenya, London and Hong Kong 1952-58, asst dir Army Legal Servs HQ BAOR 1958-60, Lt-

Col 1958, OC Army Legal Aid (Civil UK) 1960-62, Col Asst Dir Army Legal Servs Kenya 1962-64, Col Legal Staff Dir Army Legal Servs HQ BAOR 1965-66, Dep Dir Army Legal Servs HQ FARELF 1966-69, Col Dep Dir Army Legal Servs Stanmore 1969-71, Col Legal Staff Dir Army Legal Servs HQ BAOR 1971-73, dir Army Legal Servs 1973-76; called to the Bar Gray's Inn 1949; *Clubs* Huntercombe Golf; *Style—* Maj-Gen John Robertson; Berry House, Nuffield, Nr Henley-on-Thames, Oxon RG9 5SS (☎ 0491 641 740)

ROBERTSON, John Davie Manson; OBE (1978); s of John Robertson (d 1972), and Margaret Gibson Wright (d 1987); *b* 6 Nov 1929; *Educ* Kirkwall GS, Univ of Edinburgh (BL); *m* 25 Feb 1959, Elizabeth Amelia, da of Donald William Macpherson (d 1987); 2 s (John b 1961, Sinclair b 1967), 2 da (Susan b 1959, Fiona b 1965); *Career* Anglo Iranian Oil Co (later BP) UK and ME 1953, Robertson Group 1958- (chm 1980-), dir Stanley Services Ltd 1987-; hon vice consul Denmark 1972-, hon consul W Germany 1976-, Hon Sheriff Grampian Highland and Islands 1977-; chm Orkney Health Bd 1983-91 (memb 1974, vice chm 1979-83), Scot Health Mgmnt Efficiency Group 1985-, Highland Health Bd 1991-; memb Bd Highlands and Islands Enterprise 1990-; memb: Highlands and Islands Devpt Consultative Cncl 1988-91, Bd of Mgmnt Orkney Hosps 1970-74; chm: Orkney Savings Ctee 1974-78, Highland and Islands Savings Ctee 1975-78; memb Nat Savings Ctee for Scot 1975-78, chm Childrens Panel Orkney 1971-76 (chm Advsy Ctee 1977-82); Royal Order of Knight of Dannebrog Denmark 1982, The Cavalier's Cross of the Order of Merit W Germany 1986; *Books* Uppies & Doonies (1967); *Recreations* rough shooting, fishing; *Clubs* New Edinburgh; *Style—* John D M Robertson, Esq, OBE; Spinningdale House, Sutherland (☎ 0862 88223); S & J D Robertson Grp Ltd, Shore St, Kirkwall, Orkney, (☎ 0856 2961, fax 0856 5043, telex 75498)

ROBERTSON, John Trevelyan; s of Lt-Col Colin John Trevelyan Robertson, OBE, MC (d 1959), of Frinton-on-Sea, Essex, and Agnes Muriel, *née* Dolphin (d 1969); *b* 15 Sept 1926; *Educ* Imp Serv Coll Windsor, Univ of Cambridge (MA), Univ of Edinburgh; *m* 8 Sept 1951, (Katherine) Elizabeth, da of John Lennox Scott, Bridge of Allan, Stirling; 2 s (Andrew b 1955, James b 1958), 1 da (Katherine b 1952); *Career* RA and Royal Indian Artillery (Mountain) 1944-48; Br Oxygen Co 1951-60: dir and gen mangr Oxhycarbon Co Ltd 1958, dist sales mangr 1959; dir and gen mangr Kompass Register Ltd 1962-64 (sales mangr 1960-62), sales dir John G Stein and Co Ltd and GR-Stein Refractories Ltd 1964-73; dir: Stein and Robertson Ltd 1974-81, John Robertson (sales) Ltd 1981-; memb Bridge of Allan Community Cncl; memb Inst of Refractories Engrs 1965; *Recreations* sailing, tennis, golf, swimming, gardening; *Clubs* Aberdour Boat; *Style—* John Robertson, Esq; The Old Smithy, Cuthill, Dornoch, Sutherland IV25 3RW (☎ 086288); Flat 2L Buccleuch Court, Dunblane, Perthshire FK15 OAR (☎ 0786 825411); John Robertson (Sales) Ltd, PO Box 1, Crieff, Perthshire PH7 3YD (☎ 0764 4084, fax 0324 713027, telex 778583 CHACOM G)

ROBERTSON, John William; s of Ian Middleton Strachen Robertson, of Greenwood, 3 Castleroy Rd, Broughty Ferry, Dundee, and Agnes Ramsey Seaton, *née* Findlay; *b* 27 Aug 1956; *Educ* The HS of Dundee, Univ of Dundee (BSc, Zinn Hunter award, Henry Dickson prize, Gordon Mathewson award), Univ of Liverpool (BArch); *m* 27 July 1984, Judy Ann, da of Thomas Gordon John Peacock; 1 s (Edward James b 4 June 1990), 2 da (Charlotte Elizabeth b 21 April 1986, Georgina Emily b 10 Feb 1988); *Career* architect; Fitzroy Robinson Partnership: employed during intercalary year of training 1976-77 and 1979-80, qualified architect 1980, assoc 1983, ptnr 1985, currently specialises in interior architectural projects and the design and construction of well known architectural projects in the Cities of London and Westminster; commendation for high standard of design achieved in the Structural Steel Awards for Aviation House Gatwick Airport 1989; Freeman City of London 1986; RIBA 1981; *Recreations* golf, sailing, skiing; *Clubs* The Berkshire Golf (Ascot), RAC, Blairgowrie Golf (Rosemount Scotland); *Style—* John Robertson, Esq; The Fitzroy Robinson Partnership, 77 Portland Place, London W1N 4EP (☎ 071 636 8033)

ROBERTSON, John Windeler; s of Maj John Bruce Robertson (d 1973); *b* 9 May 1934; *Educ* Winchester; *m* 1959 (m dis 1984), Jennifer-Ann, da of Gontran Gourdou, of Switzerland; 1 s, 1 da; m 2, 1987, Rosemary Helen Jane Banks; *Career* dep chm Stock Exchange 1976-79 (memb 1956-89, memb Cncl 1966-86), sr ptnr Wedd Durlacher Mordaunt & Co 1979-86, dep chm Barclays de Zoete Wedd Securities Ltd (BZW) 1986-88; dir The Securities Assoc 1986-88; *Recreations* deer stalking, golf, powerboating; *Clubs* City of London; *Style—* John Robertson, Esq; Eckensfield Barn, Compton, nr Chichester, West Sussex PO18 9NT (☎ 070563 1239)

ROBERTSON, Julia Anne; da of Alan James Robertson, of Welwyn, Herts, and Pearl Anita, *née* Perrett; *b* 14 Feb 1970; *Educ* The Sir Frederic Osborn Sch Welwyn Garden City, Hatfield Poly; *Career* hockey player; Welwyn Garden City Ladies Hockey Club 1985-90, Ealing Ladies Hockey Club 1990-; England: under 18 debut 1988 (7 caps), under 21 debut 1989 (18 outdoor and 3 indoor caps), sr debut 1990 (4 caps); Silver medal Euro Indoor Under 21 Championships Vienna 1991, GB students debut 1990 (5 caps); also long jumper: represented GB jrs 1987, English Schs Athletics Championships 1984-88; *Recreations* jigsaw puzzles, theatre, reading; *Style—* Miss Julia Robertson; c/o All England Women's Hockey Association, 51 High St, Shrewsbury, Shropshire SY1 1ST (☎ 0743 233572)

ROBERTSON, Sir Lewis; CBE (1969); s of John Robertson (d 1976); *b* 28 Nov 1922; *Educ* Trinity Coll Glenalmond; *m* 1950, Elspeth, *née* Badenoch; 3 s, 1 da; *Career* served RAF; industrialist, administrator, accountant; dir Scottish & Newcastle Breweries 1975-87; dep chm and chief exec: Grampian Holdings Ltd 1971-76, Scottish Devpt Agency 1976-81; chm: F H Lloyd Holding 1982-87, Triplex Foundries Group 1983-90 (now Triplex Lloyd plc), Girobank Scotland 1984-90, Borthwicks 1985-89, Lilley plc 1986-, Havelock Europa plc 1989-90; dir Whitman Int SA Geneva 1987-; chm: Carnegie Tst for Univs of Scotland 1990- (tstee and memb Exec Ctee 1963-), Stakis plc 1991-; memb: Monopolies Cmmn 1969-76, Restrictive Practices Court 1983-; FRSE; kt 1991; *Recreations* work, reading, classical music, things Italian, listmaking; *Clubs* Athenaeum, New (Edinburgh); *Style—* Sir Lewis Robertson, CBE, FRSE; 32 Saxe-Coburg Place, Edinburgh EH3 5BP (☎ 031 332 5221)

ROBERTSON, Lady; Nancy; da of H S Walker, of Huddersfield; *m* 1926, Sir James Wilson Robertson, KT, GCMG, GCVO, KBE (d 1983, Govr-Gen and C-in-C Federation of Nigeria 1955-60); 1 s, 1 da; *Style—* Lady Robertson; The Old Bakehouse, Cholsey, nr Wallingford, Oxon

ROBERTSON, Cmdt Dame Nancy Margaret; DBE (1957, CBE 1953, OBE 1946); da of Rev William Cowper Robertson, and Jessie, *née* McGregor; *b* 1 March 1909; *Educ* Esdaile Sch Edinburgh, Paris; *Career* secretarial work in London and Paris 1928-39; WRNS 1939, dir of WRNS 1954-58, now retired; *Recreations* needlework, gardening; *Style—* Cmdt Dame Nancy Robertson, DBE; 14 Osborne Way, Tring, Herts (☎ 044 282 2560)

ROBERTSON, Neil; JP; s of Ian Stephen Robertson (d 1956); *b* 13 March 1921; *Educ* Cargilfield Sch, Loretto Sch; *m* 1948, Marie Forbes, da of Maj Robert Young (d 1957); 1 s, 4 da; *Career* farmer, co dir, cncllr 1955-75, regnl cncllr 1974-86, convener of Moray Co 1971-75; past pres: Elgin Branch NFU, Moray Area NFU; former memb Scottish Agric Advsy Ctee, former dir RHASS; past chm: Banff Moray & Nairn River Bd, Northeast River Purificationn Bd; chm Grampian Manpower Ctee 1974-82, memb of Cncl on Tbnls 1981-87; DL 1970-91; *Recreations* shooting, golf; *Style—* Neil Robertson, Esq, JP; Millburn, Linkwood, Elgin, Moray (☎ 0343 2139, office 0343 2355)

ROBERTSON, Prof Norman Robert Ean; s of Robert Robertson (d 1980), and Jean Thompson Robertson; *b* 13 March 1931; *Educ* Hamilton Acad, Univ of Glasgow (BDS), Univ of Manchester (MDS, DDS); *m* 14 Aug 1954, Morag Wyllie, da of George McNicol (d 1936); 3 s (Stephen b 1955, Peter b 1960, Nigel b 1963), 2 da (Lois b 1958, Mary b 1966); *Career* Nat Serv RAF 1954-56; sr lectr orthodontics Univ of Manchester 1963-70; hon conslt orthodontics: United Manchester Hosps, Manchester Regnl Hosp Bd 1965-70; prof and head of Dept Orthodontics Univ Wales Coll Med 1970-85, hon conslt in orthodontics S Glamorgan and Gwent Health Authy 1970-, prof and head Dept Child Dental Health 1985-, dean of Dental Sch 1985-; memb: UGC Dental Review Working Pty (co-author of its report 1988), S Glamorgan Health Authy 1976-, Gen Dental Cncl and Dental Educn Advsy Cncl 1985-, Cncl Univ of Wales Coll Med 1985-, Conslt Orthodontists Gp 1988-, Standing Dental Advsy Ctee 1989-, Welsh Cncl Postgrad Med and Dental Educn 1989-; memb: BDA, COG, BSSO, BAO; *Books* Oral Orthopaedics and Orthodontics for Cleft Lip and Palate. A Structured Approach (1983); *Recreations* sailing; *Clubs* RYA, Cruising Assoc; *Style—* Prof Norman Robertson; University of Wales College of Medicine, Dental School, Heath Park, Cardiff CF4 4XY (☎ 0222 755944 ext 2470, fax 0222 766343)

ROBERTSON, Peter Duncan Neil; s of Laurence Neil Robertson, Flt Lt RAF (despatches, d 1961), and Edith Pamela, *née* Moorhouse; *b* 23 May 1940; *Educ* Sandroyd Sch Harrow; *m* 13 July 1962, Diana Helen, da of Dr R C Barbor (d 1989), of Rosefield Peldon, nr Colchester, Essex; 1 s (Toby Neil b 1970), 1 da (Tania Gay b 1967); *Career* trainee R C Greig and Co 1958-61, Philip Hill Higginson Private Client and Pension Fund Management 1961-64; dir: M&G Investment Management Ltd 1965-, External Investment Trust, Drayton Far East Trust; fund mangr and investmt dir M & G Investment Management 1971-, investmt dir Japanese Dept and Pacific Basin; *Recreations* shooting, golf, tennis, cooking, racing; *Clubs* Turf; *Style—* Peter Robertson, Esq; 31 Dancer Road, London SW6 4DU (☎ 071 731 7118); M & G Investment Management Ltd, Three Quays, Tower Hill, London EC3 6BQ (car ☎ 0860 525 553, office 071 626 4588, fax 071 623 8615, telex 887196)

ROBERTSON, Peter McKellar; OBE (1988), JP (Ayrshire 1976), DL (1960); s of John McKellar Robertson, CBE (d 1939); *b* 5 June 1923; *Educ* Marlborough, Royal Tech Coll Glasgow (BSc); *m* 1951, Elspeth Marion, da of late James Charles Hunter, of Glentyan, Kilbarchan, Renfrewshire; 1 s (John), 2 da (Jane, Angela); *Career* RN VR 1944-46; landowner; memb: Ayrshire CC 1949-75, Local Authy Accounts Cmmn Scotland 1974-87 (vice chm 1983-87); pres Assoc of CCs in Scotland 1974-75; *Recreations* music; *Clubs* Western (Glasgow), Prestwick Golf; *Style—* Peter M Robertson, Esq, OBE, JP, DL; Noddsdale, Largs, Ayrshire (☎ 0475 672382)

ROBERTSON, (David) Ranald Craig; s of David Stanley Robertson (d 1989), and Olive Mary, *née* Svendsen; *b* 23 April 1948; *Educ* Pukekohe HS NZ, Univ of Auckland (LLB); *m* 10 Sept 1977, Gillian Susan, da of Reginald Berwick; 1 s (Andrew), 1 da (Rhiannon); *Career* Lt 4 Medium Battery Royal NZ Artillery 1971-76, attachment to 200 Sussex Yeomanry Medium Battery RA(V) 1974-76; admitted barrister and slr of Supreme Court of NZ 1973; EMI Music London 1974-80: business affrs exec, business affrs mangr (also of Liberty United Records); legal servs mangr CAP Gp plc 1980-87, admitted slr of supreme court of England 1980, ptnr and head of Information Technol Gp Stephenson Harwood 1987-, fndr chm Legal Affrs Gp Computing Servs Assoc 1982-87, chm Fedn Against Software Theft 1985-86 (fndr and dir); memb: Worshipful Co of Information Technologists, City of London Solicitors Co; memb Law Soc; *Books* Legal Protection of Computer Software, Encyclopaedia of Information Technology (contrib); *Style—* Ranald Robertson, Esq; Stephenson Harwood, One St Paul's Churchyard, London EC4M 8SH (☎ 071 329 4422, fax 071 606 0822)

ROBERTSON, Robert; CBE (1967), JP (1958); s of Rev Wlliam Robertson, HCF (d 1950), and Jessie Douglas (d 1961, authoress of Patchwork Quilt); *b* 15 Aug 1909; *Educ* Forres Acad, Royal Tech Coll Glasgow, Univ of Strathclyde; *m* 1938, Jean, da of James Moffatt (d 1931), of Glasgow; 1 s (Struan), 1 da (Margaret); *Career* Nat Serv WWII with jt responsibility for safe passage of special trains for important persons such as Churchill (code Rapier), Eisenhower (code Cutlass), Royalty (code Grove); ambulance trains for D day landings; civil engr; govr Jordanhill Coll of Educn 1960-83; memb: Scot Cncl for Res in Educn, Scot Cncl for Commercial Admin and Professional Educn 1962-68; chm: Renfrewshire Educn Ctee 1960-72, Sec of State for Scotland's Standing Ctee on Supply and Trg of Teachers for Further Educn 1963-72, Nat Ctee for In-service Trg of Teachers (Scotland) 1966-70, Renfrewshire CC 1972-75; govr Jordanhill Sch of Further Educn 1968-83, chm E Renfrewshire Cons Assoc 1971-74; memb Strathclyde Regnl Cncl 1974-86; memb Cncl: Glasgow Coll of Bldg and Printing, Langside Coll, Reid Kerr Coll 1974-86; FEIS Univ of Stirling 1973-; *Publications* Robertson Report on Supply and Training of Teachers in Scotland (HMSO, 1965); *Recreations* painting, fishing; *Style—* Robert Robertson, Esq, CBE, JP; 24 Broadwood Park, Alloway, Ayrshire (☎ 0292 43820); Castlehill, nr Maybole, Ayrshire (☎ 029 250 337)

ROBERTSON, Brigadier Sidney Park; MBE (1962), TD (1967), JP (1968), DL; s of John Davie Manson Robertson (d 1934), and Elizabeth Park, *née* Sinclair; *b* 12 March 1914; *Educ* Kirkwall GS, Univ of Edinburgh (BCom); *m* 1940, Elsa Miller, da of James Miller Croy (d 1943); 1 s, 1 da; *Career* served WWII cmmnd RA 1940 (despatches NW Europe 1945); Maj cmdg 861 (independent) Light Anti-Aircraft Battery RA (Orkney and Zetland) TA 1956-61, Lt-Col cmd Lovat Scouts TA 1962-65, Brig CRA 51 Div TA 1966-67, Hon Col 102 (Ulster and Scot) Light Air Def Regt RA (TA) 1975-80, Hon Col Cmdt RA 1977-80; managerial posts: Anglo-Iranian Oil Co ME 1946-51, mangr operations/sales Southern Div Shell-Max and BP 1951-54, fndr Robertson firm 1954; chm Orkney Hosps Bd of Mgmnt and Orkney Health Bd 1965-79; chm RA Cncl of Scotland 1980-84; Hon Sheriff Grampian Highlands and Islands 1969-; hon area vice pres Royal Br Legion (Orkney) 1975-, vice pres Nat Artillery Assoc 1977-, hon pres Orkney Bn Boys' Brigade, vice pres RNLI Inst 1985-; DL 1968; Vice Lord-Lt for the Islands Area of Orkney 1987-90; MIBS 1936; *Recreations* travel, angling; *Clubs* Army and Navy, Caledonian, New (Edinburgh); *Style—* Brig Sidney Robertson, MBE, TD, JP, DL; Daisybank, Kirkwall, Orkney KW15 1LX (☎ 0856 2085)

ROBERTSON, Simon Manwaring; s of David Lars Manwaring Robertson, of Ketches, Newick, Sussex, and Pamela Lauderdale Manwaring, *née* Meares; *b* 4 March 1941; *Educ* Cothill Sch, Eton; *m* 26 June 1965, Virginia Stewart Manwaring, da of Mark Richard Norman, of Garden House, Much Hadham, Herts; 1 s (Edward Manwaring b 1968), 2 da (Selina Manwaring b 1969, Lorna Manwaring b 1973); *Career* dir: Kleinwort Benson Ltd 1976, Mowlem Gp plc 1987, Kleinwort Benson Gp plc 1988; pres Mutual Life Assurance Association 1989; *Recreations* being in the Prättigau, tennis; *Clubs* Boodle's, Racquet (New York); *Style—* Simon Robertson, Esq; Kleinwort Benson Ltd, 20 Fenchurch St, London EC2 (☎ 071 623 8000)

ROBERTSON, (Charles) Speirs; s of Capt Charles Robertson, MC, CA (d 1952), of Hyndland, Glasgow, and Marion, *née* Sutter (d 1971); *b* 30 June 1924; *Educ* Glasgow Acad, Glasgow Univ (BSc); *m* 28 March 1953, Nora Beatrice, da of George Arthur

Kearle (d 1978), of Hoole Chester; 2 s (Morven b 1954, Graham b 1959), 1 da (Lynne b 1962); *Career* chm Speirs Robertson & Co Ltd 1967-; MIMC, CEng, FIEE, FBIM; *Recreations* music, reading, photography; *Style*— Speirs Robertson, Esq; Moliver House, Oakley Road, Bromham, Bedford (☎ 02302 3410)

ROBERTSON, Prof Stephen Edward; s of Prof Charles Martin Robertson, and Theodosia Cecil, *née* Spring Rice (d 1984); *b* 4 April 1946; *Educ* Westminster, Trinity Coll Cambridge (BA, MA), City Univ (MSc), UCL (PhD); *m* 25 June 1966, Judith Anne, da of Edwin Donald Kirk (d 1943); 1 s (Colin b 1979), 1 da (Magdalene b 1977); *Career* Royal Soc Scientific Info Res Fell UCL 1973-78, prof of info systems City Univ 1988-; memb Local Ctee Nat Schizophrenia Fellowship; fell Inst of Info Sci, MBCS; *Style*— Prof Stephen Robertson; Dept of Information Science, City University, Northampton Square, London EC1V OHB (☎ 071 253 4399, fax 071 250 0837)

ROBERTSON, Timothy Kenneth Hickman; s of Roy Hickman Robertson (d 1981), of Standish, Glos, and Kathleen Hilda Alice, *née* Barford (d 1988); *b* 10 Feb 1937; *Educ* Shrewsbury, Trinity Hall Cambridge (BA); *m* 5 Sept 1969, Bridget Sara, da of Edward Noel Riddihough Hewitt (d 1974), of Addingham, W Yorks; 2 s (James b 1972, Mark b 1974); *Career* Nat Serv; admitted slr 1963; ptnr Rubinstein Callingham Polden and Gale 1968-; tstee The Buttle Tst for Children; memb Law Soc; *Style*— Timothy Robertson, Esq; Little Manor, Hertingfordbury, Hertford (☎ 0992 584022); 2 Raymond Buildings, Gray's Inn, London WC1 (☎ 071 242 8404)

ROBERTSON, Timothy Patrick Vyvyan (Tim); s of George Ernest James Robertson; *b* 7 Nov 1943; *Educ* Winchester, Trinity Coll Cambridge (MA), Cranfield Inst of Technol (MBA); *m* 22 March 1969, Anna C, da of Thomas Edward Ray Moore, DSC, of Thruxton, Hants; 1 s (Hugo Sam Moore b 1982), 2 da (Chloe Mary Jean b 1971, Gemma Frances Ray b 1974); *Career* dir: WBB & Co plc, WBB GmbH, WBB de France SA, WBB Clay Sales Ltd, WBB Mineral Services Ltd, Pacific Clay Sales Ltd, Teignbridge Enterprise Agency; chief exec Cerapasta Ltda Portugal; cmmr Teignmouth Harbour; *Recreations* sailing, golf, skiing; *Clubs* Bembridge Sailing, Wykehamist Golfing Soc, DHO; *Style*— Tim Robertson, Esq; Mapstone, Lustleigh, S Devon TQ13 9SE; Park House, Courtenay Park, Newton Abbot TQ12 4PS (telex 42824 WBBG, fax 0626 332344)

ROBERTSON, (Sholto David Maurice) Toby; OBE (1978); s of late Cdr David Lambert Robertson, RN, and Felicity Douglas, *née* Tomlin; *b* 29 Nov 1928; *Educ* Stowe, Trinity Coll Cambridge (BA, MA); *m* 1963 (m dis 1981), (Teresa) Jane, *née* McCulloch; 2 s (Sebastian James Lambert b 1964, Joshua David Nathaniel b 1969) 2 da (Francesca Kate Tomlin b 1965, Sasha Corinna Jane b 1967); *Career* dir first professional prodn The Iceman Cometh (New Shakespeare, Liverpool) 1958, dir TV plays ITV/BBC 1959-63; dir of over 40 prodns Prospect Theatre Co incl: The Soldier's Fortune (1964), The Confederacy (1964), The Importance of Being Earnest (1964), The Man of Mode (1965), Macbeth (1966), The Tempest (1966), A Murder of No Importance (1967), A Room with a View (1967), Twelfth Night (1968, 1973-78), No Man's Land (1968), The Beggar's Opera (1968, also for Phoenix Opera 1972), The Servant of Two Masters (1968), Edward II (1969), Boswell's Life of Johnson (1969), King Lear (1971, 1978), Loves Labour's Lost (1971), Richard III (1972), Ivanov (1972, 1978), Pencles Royal Hour of the Sun (1973), The Pilgrims Progress (1974, 1977), Hamlet (1974, 1979), War Music (1974), Anthony and Cleopatra (1974), Smith of Smiths (1974, 1978, 1979), Buster (1974), The Lunatic (1978), The Lover and the Poet (1978, 1979), Romeo and Juliet (1979), The Government Inspector (1979), Next Time I'll Sing to You (1980), Pericles (1980, NY, OBIE Award for outstanding dir 1981), Measure for Measure (1981, Peoples Arts Theatre, Peking), The Revenger's Tragedy (1981, NY, Villager award for outstanding treatment of classical text 1982), York Cycle of Mystery Plays (York Fest, 1984), Midsummer Nights Dream (1985), Medea (1986), Taming of the Shrew (1986), You Never Can Tell (1987), Captain Canrallo (1988), The Glorious Years (1988), Richard II (Washington DC, 1988), Kingsley Amis The Old Devils (adapted Robin Hawdon, 1989), Othello (1989), Barnaby and the Old Boys; opera incl: Marriage of Figaro (1977), Elisir d'Amore Opera Co of Philadelphia, Oedipus Rex (1982), Dido and Aeneas; asst dir Lord of the Flies (film, 1961); dir of over 25 TV prodns; dir: Old Vic Theatre 1977-80, Old Vic Co 1979-80; currently artistic dir Theatre Clwyd; *Recreations* painting, sailing; *Clubs* Garrick; *Style*— Toby Robertson, Esq; 210 Brixton Rd, London SW9; Theatre Clwyd, Mold, Clwyd, North Wales CH7 1YA (☎ 0352 56331)

ROBERTSON, Vernon Colin; OBE (1977); s of Lt Col Colin John Trevelyan Robertson, OBE, DSO (d 1959), and Agnes Muriel, *née* Dolphin (d 1968); *b* 19 July 1922; *Educ* ISC (now Haileybury), Univ of Edinburgh (BSc), Univ of Cambridge (Dip Agric, MA); *Career* enlisted RA 1941, cmmnd 1942, serv 12 (HAC) Regt RHA N Africa, Italy and Austria 1942-45, Adj 1 Regt RHA (T/Capt) 1945 (despatches) demobbed 1946; memb HAC 1942-; univ demonstrator Sch of Agric Univ of Cambridge 1950-53; Hunting Aerosurveys Ltd: ecologist 1953, md New Consulting Div (Hunting Technical Services Ltd) until 1977, dir until 1977, environmental conslt 1988-; Groundwater Conslt (Int) Ltd Cambridge 1975-85; memb Bd Cwlth Devpt Corp 1982, 1985 and 1988; chm: Tropical Agric Assoc (UK) 1981-85, Frinton Arts & Music Soc 1983-86; Freeman City of London 1977, Liveryman Worshipful Co of Painters Stainers 1977; *Recreations* sailing, natural history, photography, music, gardening; *Clubs* Farmers; *Style*— Vernon Robertson, Esq, OBE; The Saltings, Manor Road, Great Holland, Frinton-on-Sea, Essex CO13 0JT (☎ 0255 674 585)

ROBERTSON, William Stewart; OBE (1983); s of William Robertson (d 1946), and Charlotte Ann, *née* Nairn; *b* 23 Feb 1902; *Educ* HS Pert, Glasgow Univ (BSc); *m* 6 Feb 1950, Phyllis Emily, da of John Henry Gaydon; 1 s (Martin); *Career* Sgt Inst Motor Transport RE 1944-47; Singer MFG Co Ltd: engr 1947-58, dir 1958, asst md 1962-66; tech dir Reid Gear Co 1966-69; Rediffusion Simulation: plant mangr 1969, md 1972, chm 1977; additional chm Rediffusion: Computers, Radio Systems, Television (Jersey), Simulation (FortWorth USA); external dir Evans & Sutherland Computers Utah USA; MIPE; memb: IOD, CBI; *Recreations* golf, model engineering, DIY, gardening; *Clubs* Athenaeum, Inst of Directors, Les Amassadors; *Style*— William Robertson, Esq, OBE; Flat 24, 39 Queensgate SW7; Roborough, Wyndhamlea, West Chiltington, Pulborough, Sussex (☎ 079 833 3085)

ROBERTSON-GLASGOW, Robert Foxcroft; s of Robert Wilson Robertson-Glasgow (d 1976), of Hinton House, Hinton Charterhouse, Bath, and Phyllis Mary Helen (d 1971), whose ggf Thomas Jones (d 1848) suc to Hinton in 1846 and was s of Thomas Jones, of Stapleton House, Glos, and Frances Foxcroft (*see* Burke's Landed Gentry, 18 ed, vol II, 1969); *b* 11 Sept 1935; *Educ* Radley, Lincoln Coll Oxford, RAC Cirencester; *m* 10 Sept 1983, Patricia Coleridge, da of Thomas Patrick Shevlin (d 1950), of Wallsend on Tyne; *Career* 2 Lt The Royal Scots (The Royal Regt) 1955-56; farmer; memb: Som CC, London Delgn of Som and S Avon branch Nat Farmers' Union; gen cmmr of taxes; High Sheriff of Avon 1990-91; *Recreations* shooting, gardening, art history; *Clubs* Army & Navy; *Style*— R F Robertson-Glasgow, Esq; Hinton House, Hinton Charterhouse, Bath, Avon (☎ 0225 722254)

ROBERTSON OF OAKRIDGE, 2 Baron (UK 1961); Sir William Ronald Robertson; 3 Bt (UK 1919); s of Gen 1 Baron Robertson of Oakridge, GCB, GBE, KCMG, KCVO, DSO, MC (d 1974); *b* 8 Dec 1930; *Educ* Charterhouse; *m* 1972, Celia, da of William Elworthy; 1 s; *Heir* s, Hon William Brian Elworthy Robertson b 15 Nov 1975; *Career* sits as Independent peer in House of Lords; memb London Stock Exchange 1973-, late Maj Royal Scots Greys; memb Worshipful Co of Salters (master 1985-86); *Style*— Lord Robertson of Oakridge; House of Lords, London SW1A 0PW

ROBERTSON-PEARCE, Anthony Brian; s of John Gilbert Robertson-Pearce (d 1967), of Testwood House, Lynhurst, Hants, and Damaris Aubrey, *née* Wilce (d 1946); *b* 3 April 1932; *Educ* Chideock Manor Sch, Christ's Coll Cambridge (BA), Univ of Stockhom (Dip Archaeological Photography), Alliance Francaise Paris (Dip in French); *m* 1, 18 May 1956 (m dis 1973), (Ingrid) Christina, da of Erik Nystrom (d 1957), of Holo, Sweden; 1 s (Michael b 3 Aug 1960), 2 da (Pamela b 22 April 1957, Penelope b 3 Oct 1965); m 2, 7 June 1974 (m dis 1980), Catharina Carlsdotter, da of Capt Soldan Carl Fredrik Henningsson Ridderstad (d 1973), of Linkoping, Sweden; *Career* supervisor and photographer excavations Motya Sicily 1965, Br Sch of Archaeology Baghdad 1966, supervisor and MO Tell-A-Rimah N Iraq 1967, photographer and MO Br Excavations Tawilan Jordan 1968; Central Bd of Nat Antiquities (Riksantikvarieambetet) Stockholm: field archaeological photographer 1969, Publishing Dept 1972, head of publishing; Swedish TV film debut The Inquiry 1990 as Cdr in Royal Swedish Navy; Duine Hasal of the Clan Dhonnachaidh (Scotland); dep govr Bd of Govrs American Biographical Inst Res Assoc, dep dir gen (Europe) Int Biographical Centre Cambridge, memb Swedish Nat Ctee ICOMOS; PRO Sollentuna Kommun Stockholm 1983-; FRAI, FIBA; *Books* Dr James Robertson 1566-1652 (1972), The Prehistoric Enclosure of Ekornavallen Sweden (1974), The Ruins of Kromoberg Castle (1974), Kaseberg Ship-setting (1975), The Battle of Rotebro 1497 (1986); *Recreations* riding, golf; *Clubs* Naval, Sallskapet Stockholm; *Style*— Anthony Robertson-Pearce, Esq; Nybrogatan 54, S-11440, Stockholm, Sweden (☎ 08 661 0268); SFP & Co, Banergatan 55, 11526 Stockholm, Sweden (☎ 08 663 0555, fax 660 3817)

ROBEY, Ian Crake; OBE (1985), JP (1979); s of Lt-Col A E L Robey, OBE (d 1973); *b* 4 July 1927; *Educ* Felsted; *m* 1, 1953 (m dis 1977), Pamela, *née* Elbourne; 2 s, 2 da; m 2, 1981, Sandra, *née* Levitt; *Career* builders' merchant; chm Cakebread Robey & Co plc 1965-90, dir Assoc Builders' Merchants Ltd 1964-87; chm: National Home Improvement Cncl 1982-83 (vice chm), Neighbourhood Revitalisation Services 1984-86; pres Builders Merchants Fedn 1979-81; FInstBM (1972); *Recreations* food, music, theatre; *Style*— Ian Robey, Esq, OBE, JP; The Willows, High St, Watton-at-Stone, Herts (☎ 0920 830 076)

ROBIN, Ian Gibson; s of Dr Arthur Robin (d 1956), of 8 Napier Rd, Edinburgh, and Elizabeth Parker, *née* Arnold (d 1953); *b* 22 May 1909; *Educ* Merchiston Castle Sch Edinburgh, Clare Coll Cambridge (MA, MB BCh); *m* 19 July 1939, Shelagh Marian, da of Cyril Merton Croft (d 1951), of 19 Marryat Road, Wimbledon; 1 s (Graham Luke), 2 da (Shirley, Wendy); *Career* RNVR 1939 (invalided out); registrar and chief clinical asst Guy's Hosp 1935-36, private practice Harley St 1937-, conslt ENT surgn Royal Northern Hosp 1937-74, surgn EMS Sector 3 London Area 1939-45; conslt ENT surgn: St Mary's Hosp 1948-74, Princess Louise Hosp for Children 1948-68, Paddington Green Children's Hosp 1968-74; formerly: vice chm Nat Inst for the Deaf, pres Br Assoc of Otolaryngologists, pres Laryngology Section and vice pres Otological Section RSM, memb Cncl Nat Deaf Children's Soc; memb: Med Soc of London 1947-67, Hunterian Soc 1948-; FRCS 1935; *Books* Diseases of Ear Nose and Throat (2 edn, 1961); *Recreations* golf, gardening, sketching; *Clubs* Hawks (Cambridge), Achilles, Hampstead Golf; *Style*— Ian Robin, Esq; Stowe House, 3 North End, Hampstead, London NW3 7HH (☎ 081 458 2292); 86 Harley Street, London W1N 1AE (☎ 071 580 3625)

ROBINS, (Robert Victor) Charles; s of (Robert) Walter Vivian Robins (d 1968), of London, and (Alice) Kathleen, *née* Knight (d 1979); *b* 13 March 1935; *Educ* Eton; *m* 6 Nov 1962 (m dis 1985), Vivian Mary, da of Alan Vivian Mackay, of Brazil; 3 s (Timothy b 1963, William b 1965, Archie b 1972); *Career* underwriting memb Lloyd's 1956, chm Lloyd's Brokers; former cricketer Middx (memb Ctee 1963-); former memb Ctee MCC 1973-79 and Cricket Cncl 1976-79, neutral observer Pakistan v West Indies Test Karachi 1981, memb Organising Ctee World Cup Cricket India and Pakistan 1987; Liveryman Worshipful Co of Glovers; *Recreations* golf; *Clubs* MCC, City of London; *Style*— Charles Robins, Esq; St Didier, Taggs Island, Hampton, Middx (☎ 081 941 0270); c/o Stafford Knight & Co Ltd, 4/5 London Wall Bldgs, London EC2M 5NR (☎ 071 628 3135, fax 071 638 2510)

ROBINS, Hon Mrs (Elizabeth Mary Gerran); *née* Lloyd; JP (SW London 1989); er da of Baron Lloyd of Kilgerran, CBE, QC, JP (Life Peer, d 1991), and Phyllis Mary, *née* Shepherd; *b* 1944; *m* 25 May 1968, Daniel Gerard Robins, QC (d 1989), s of William Albert Robins, of Malaga, Spain; 3 da (Charlotte b 1971, Sophie b 1974, Anneli b 1976); *Style*— The Hon Mrs Robins, JP; 66 Church Rd, Wimbledon, SW19

ROBINS, John Elgar; s of Herbert William Henry Robins (d 1951), of Bromley, and Anna Marie Angela, *née* Foley (d 1948); *b* 18 July 1926; *Educ* Hurstpierpoint Coll Sussex, St John's Coll Oxford (MA); *m* 4 Aug 1956, Hazel Margaret Rachel, da of John Archibald Robert Snape (d 1962), of 77 Cowbridge Rd, Bridgend, Glamorgan; 1 s (Timothy John b 1 Sept 1965), 1 da (Carol Hazel b 19 Aug 1958); *Career* RAF 1945-48; admitted slr 1953; conslt Trowers and Hamlins 1989- (slr 1953-58, ptnr 1958-89); former memb Legal Aid: Certifying Ctee, Area Ctee, panel chm Gen Ctee; memb Law Soc; *Recreations* travel and military history; *Style*— John Robins, Esq; Elmroyd, 60 Widmore Rd, Bromley BR1 3BD (☎ 081 460 2107); 6 New Square, Lincoln's Inn, London WC2A 3RP (☎ 071 831 6292, fax 071 831 8700, telex 21422)

ROBINS, John Vernon Harry; s of Col W V H Robins, DSO (d 1990), and Charlotte Mary, *née* Grier (d 1979); *b* 21 Feb 1939; *Educ* Winchester, Stanford Univ USA (SEP); *m* 11 Aug 1962, Elizabeth Mary, da of Alex Banister, OBE, of Sussex; 2 s (Nicholas Vivian James b 1963, Michael Victor Andrew b 1973), 1 da (Tessa Vivienne Mary b 1965); *Career* Nat Serv 2 Lt 2/10 PMO Gurkha Rifles 1959-61; md SNS Communications Ltd 1966-74, chief exec Bally Gp (UK) Ltd 1974-79, gp fin dir Fitch Lovell plc 1979-84, dir fin and mgmnt servs Willis Faber plc 1984-89, gp fin dir Willis Corroon plc 1990-; formerly chm Assoc Corporate Treasurers; Warden Worshipful Co of Glovers; FCT 1979; *Recreations* clocks, music; *Clubs* Brooks's; *Style*— John Robins, Esq; 56 Duncan Terrace, London N1 8AG; Willis Corroon plc, 10 Trinity Square, London EC3P 3AX (☎ 071 488 8578)

ROBINS, Gp Capt Leonard Edward; CBE (1979), AE (1958, clasps 1968, and 1978), DL (Gtr London 1978, rep for Wandsworth 1979-); s of Joseph Robins (d 1957), of Mitcham, Surrey, and Louisa Josephine, *née* Kent (d 1963); *b* 2 Nov 1921; *Educ* Singlegate Mitcham Surrey, City Day Continuation Sch London; *m* 6 Aug 1949, Jean Ethelwynne (d 1985), da of Roy Augustus Searle (d 1970), of Ryde, IOW; *Career* WWII RAF served: UK, Ceylon, India, SEAC; Airman (Co of London) Radar Reporting Unit RAuxAF 1950, cmmnd 1953, Pilot Offr, transferred to 1 (Co of Hertford) Maritime HQ Unit RAuxAF 1960, Flying Offr 1955, Flt Lt 1963, Sqdn Ldr 1968, Wing Cdr 1969, OC 1 MHU 1969-73, Gp Capt and Inspr RAuxAF MOD 1973-83, ret; ADC to HM the Queen 1974-83; civil servant: GPO 1936-48, Minys of Health, Housing, Planning, Local Govt and DOE 1948-80, ret; personal staff Lord Mayor of London: 1977-78, 1980-81, 1982-83, 1986-87, 1987-88, 1988-89, 1990-91; selected memb: Gtr London TAVRA 1973-83, City of London TAVRA 1980-84; pres Wandsworth Victim Support 1980-86, tstee Royal Fndn of Greycoat Hosp 1983-88; Freeman City of London 1976; Offr of Merit with Swords SMOM 1986; Coronation

Medal 1953, Jubilee Medal 1977; FBIM 1977; *Recreations* military history, book hunting, kipping, speech writing; *Clubs* RAF; *Style*— Gp Capt Leonard Robins, CBE, AE, DL; 16 Summit Way, Upper Norwood, London SE19 2PU (☎ 081 653 3173); Higher Bosigran, Pendeen, Penzance, Cornwall TR20 8YX (☎ 0736 796884)

ROBINS, Mark Gordon; s of Robert Gordon Robins, of Chadderton, and Marilyn, *née* Clarke; *b* 22 Dec 1969; *Educ* North Chadderton Comp Sch, Isdall Comp Sch Shifnal Shropshire; *Career* professional football player; Lilleshall Sch of Excellence 1984-86; England: 9 under 15 and under 16 caps, 6 under 21 caps (7 goals); Manchester United FC: apprentice 1986, signed professional Dec 1986, debut vs Wimbledon 1988; Young Player of the Year Manchester Utd 1989 and 1990; *Recreations* golf, reading, listening to music; *Style*— Mark Robins, Esq; c/o Ray Whelan, Bobby Charlton Enterprises, Daisy Mill, Stockport Rd, Longsight, Manchester (☎ 061 273 3113)

ROBINS, Peter Marshall; OBE (1981); s of Henry Joseph Robins (d 1951), of Newent, and Maudie Theresa, *née* White; *b* 3 July 1952; *Educ* Newent GS; *m* 20 Sept 1958, Iona Naomi Irene Juliana, da of Edwin Jack Hill (d 1987); 2 s (Adrian Peter b 1963, Arlene b 1966); *Career* slr; dir Bentham Properties Ltd 1966; farmer; Mayor City of Gloucester 1975-76, memb Gloucester City Cncl 1974-82 (chm 1973-74, ldr 1973-82), dep Mayor 1976-82; memb: Gloucester Co Borough Cncl 1965-74, Gloucester CC 1973-85; *Recreations* golf; *Style*— Peter Robins, Esq, OBE; Robins Farm, Matson Lane, Gloucester GL4 9DZ (☎ 0452 29681); Rowan House, Barnett Way, Gloucester GL4 7RT (☎ 0452 612345, fax 0452 611922)

ROBINS, Sir Ralph Harry; s of Leonard Haddon Robins, and Maud Lillian Robins; *b* 16 June 1932; *Educ* Imperial Coll, Univ of London (BSc, ACEI); *m* 1962, Patricia Maureen, *née* Grimes; 2 da; *Career* devpt engr Rolls-Royce Derby 1955-56, exec vice pres Rolls-Royce Inc 1971, md RR Indust & Marine Div 1973, chm International Aero Engines AG 1983-84; Rolls-Royce plc: md 1984, dep chm 1989, chief exec 1991; chm Defence Industries Cncl 1986-, dep pres Soc of Br Aerospace Cos 1987 (pres 1986-87); FEng, MIMechE; *Style*— Sir Ralph Robins; Rolls Royce plc, 65 Buckingham Gate, London SW1E 6AT (☎ 071 222 9020)

ROBINS, Prof Robert Henry; s of Dr J N Robins (d 1958), of Folkestone, Kent, and Muriel Winifred, *née* Porter (d 1960); *b* 1 July 1921; *Educ* Tonbridge, New Coll Oxford (BA, MA); *m* 29 Aug 1953, Sheila Marie (d 1983), da of Arthur Fynn (d 1944), of Norwood; *Career* WWII Flt Lt RAFVR 1942-45; lectr in linguistics Sch of Oriental and African Studies Univ of London 1948-55, prof of gen linguistics Univ of London 1966-86 (reader 1955-65), emeritus prof 1987-; pres: Int Ctee of Linguists 1977-, Philological Soc 1988; DLit Univ of London; FBA; hon memb Linguistic Soc of America, memb Academia European 1991; *Books* Ancient and Medieval Grammatical Theory in Europe (1951), The Yurok Language (1958), General Linguistics: an Introductory Survey (1964, 1989), A Short History of Linguistics (1967, 1990); *Recreations* gardening, travel; *Clubs* Royal Cwlth Soc, Athenaeum; *Style*— Prof Robert Robins; 65 Dome Hill, Caterham, Surrey CR3 6EF (☎ 0883 343778); School of Oriental and African Studies, Univ of London, London WC1H 0XG (☎ 071 637 2388)

ROBINSON; *see*: Lynch-Robinson

ROBINSON, (George) Adrian; s of Thomas Gerard Robinson, BEM, of Preston, Lancs, and Elizabeth, *née* Gillow; *b* 3 Nov 1949; *Educ* Preston Catholic Coll, Pembroke Coll Oxford (MA); *m* 6 April 1974, Susan Margaret, da of James Hopwood Edmondson, of Accrington, Lancs; 2 s (Philip Adrian b 9 Sept 1984, Andrew James b 3 May 1987); *Career* various appts Midland Bank Ltd 1971-80; Airbus Industrie: sales fin mangr 1980-82, dep sales fin dir 1982-84, sales fin dir 1984; corporate fin dir Midland Bank plc 1985; md special fin gp Chemical Bank 1987-89 (dir Aerospace 1986-87), dep gen mangr The Nippon Credit Bank 1990; ACIB 1973; *Recreations* golf, tennis, shooting; *Style*— Adrian Robinson, Esq; City Tower (10th Floor), 40 Basinghall St, London EC2V 5DE (☎ 071 638 6411, fax 071 920 0901, telex 893 273)

ROBINSON, (Francis) Alastair Lavie; s of Stephen Francis Thomas Lavie Robinson, of 9 Millington Rd, Cambridge, and Patricia Mavis, *née* Brett Plummer; *b* 19 Sept 1937; *Educ* Eton; *m* 29 April 1961, Lavinia Elizabeth Napier, da of late Cdr Trevylyan Napier, DSC, (d 1940), of Stokehill Wood, Buckland Monachorum, South Devon; 2 da (Camilla b 1967, Zoe b 1970); *Career* 2 Lt 4/7 Royal Dragoon Guards 1956-68; dir Mercantile Credit Co Ltd 1978-81 (joined 1959, gen mangr 1971-78), chief exec pres Barclays American Corpn NC USA 1981-84, regnl gen mangr Barclays Bank International 1984-87, dir personnel Barclays Bank plc 1987-90, exec dir Barclays plc 1990; tst govr London House for Overseas Students; *Recreations* music, fishing, shooting, gardening, golf; *Clubs* Cavalry and Guards, City of London; *Style*— Alastair Robinson, Esq; Easby House, Great Chesterford, Saffron Walden, Essex (☎ 0799 30473); 24 Clarendon St, London SW1; Barclays Bank plc, 4 Royal Mint Court, London EC3N 4HJ (☎ 071 626 1567)

ROBINSON, Alwyn Arnold; *b* 15 Nov 1929; *Educ* Queen Elizabeth Sch Darlington; *m* 1953, Dorothy Heslop; 2 s, 1 da; *Career* md Daily Mail 1975- (joined 1951, features ed 1966, asst ed 1969, managing ed 1971, gen mangr 1972, exec dir 1974); dir: Associated Newpapers Holdings plc, Mail Newspapers plc, Daily Mail Ltd, The Mail on Sunday Ltd, Harmsworth Publishing Ltd; jt vice-chm Press Cncl 1982-83 (memb 1977-); *Style*— Alwyn Robinson, Esq; c/o The Daily Mail, New Carmelite House, London EC4 (☎ 071 353 6000)

ROBINSON, Andrew William Stafford; s of Joseph William Cyril Maitland-Robinson, MBE, of Jersey, and Hilda, *née* Powell; *b* 20 Oct 1946; *Educ* Dragon Sch, Radley, Downing Coll Cambridge (MA), Univ of Exeter; *m* 2, Patricia Margaret, da of David Quigg (d 1976), of Corby, Northants; 2 da (Daisy b 1980, Frideswide b 1984), 1 s (Samuel b 1990); 2 da by earlier m (Caroline b 1973, Miria b 1974); *Career* admitted slr 1974, NP 1977, sole practitioner in Penzance 1982-; memb Child Care Panel Law Soc, treas Penwith Youth for Christ, tstee Duchy Addiction Rehabilitation Tst; fndr Lawyers Support Gp 1983; memb: Law Soc, Notaries Soc, Alcohol Concern; *Style*— Andrew Robinson, Esq; 5 Princes St, Penzance, Cornwall (☎ 0736 68369)

ROBINSON, Anne; da of Bernard Robinson, and late Anne, *née* Wilson; *b* 26 Sept 1944; *Educ* Fanborough Hill Covent, Les Ambassadrices Paris XVI; 1 da (Emma Alexander Wilson b 18 July 1970); *Career* columnist and presenter; Daily Mail 1966-67, Sunday Times 1968-77, Daily Mirror 1980-; presenter: Points of View BBC TV, The Anne Robinson Show BBC Radio 2, TVS Presents Questions; *Recreations* reading, television, dogs, riding; *Clubs* Bibury Cricket (vice pres); *Style*— Ms Anne Robinson; c/o International Management Group, 23 Eyot Gardens, London W6 9TN (☎ 081 846 8070)

ROBINSON, Anthony; s of Eric Frances Robinson (d 1984), of Wolverhampton, and Theresa May, *née* Lane; *b* 30 June 1940; *Educ* Wolverhampton GS, Univ of London (MD, DCH); *m* Mary Judith Lloyd, da of Oswald Merton Lloyd (d 1983), of Bristol; 1 s (Geir Patrick b 1968), 2 da (Rebecca Lynn b 1970, Kerry Abigail b 1971); *Career* med sr house offr The Royal Free Hosp London (former student locum sr house offr), surgical sr house offr Chase Form Hosp London, sr house offr Queen Elizabeth Hosp Hackney 1965-66, med registrar King George V Hosp Ilford, sr registrar paediatrics Univ Hosp of W Indies Kingston Jamaica, res fell Hosp for Sick Children Toronto Canada 1969-71, sr registrar paediatrics Great Ormond St 1971-75, conslt paediatrician Manchester S Dist 1975-, hon lectr Univ of Manchester; tstee: Allan Graham Tst, Ryecroft Childrens Fund; memb: Br Paediatric Assoc, Bowdon Conservation Gp; FRCP; *Books* contrib: Active Renal Water Excretion (jt 1967), Post Alcohlic Hypoglycaemia in a Child (jt 1976), An Unusual Neurological Disorder of Copper Metabolism Clinically Resembling Wilsons Disease but Biochemically a Distinct Entity (jtly 1977), Chronic Pancreatitis in Childhood Casualty of Heightened but Unmitigated Oxidative Detoxification Reactions (jt 1987); *Recreations* piano playing, opera, photography, skiing, foreign travel; *Style*— Anthony Robinson, Esq; The Downs Cottage, Woodville Road, Altrincham, Cheshire WA14 2AN (☎ 061 928 4946); Paediatric Department, Wythenshawe Hospital, Southmoor Road, Manchester M23 9LT (☎ 061 998 7070)

ROBINSON, Anthony Edward (Tony); s of Flt Lt Robbie Robinson, of St Albans, and Margaret Susan, *née* Harris; *b* 4 Oct 1943; *Educ* St Albans Sch, UCL, Univ of London (BSc); *m* 12 Aug 1969, Margaret Janet (d 1983), da of Alexander Buchanan (d 1967); 1 s (James Alexander b 26 March 1975); *Career* product mangr May & Baker Ltd 1969-73, dir ADA-P 1973-77; md: Pharmatek 1977-82, The PTK partnership 1983-; vice-pres OARFC; MRSC 1975, MInstM 1975; *Clubs* Old Albanian; *Style*— Tony Robinson, Esq; 23 Beech Way, Blackmore End, Wheathampstead, St Albans AL4 8LY (☎ 0438 832006); The PTK Partnership, 81 Gower St, London WC1E 6HJ (☎ 071 636 7436, fax 071 255 3132)

ROBINSON, Arthur Geoffrey; CBE (1978); s of Arthur Robinson (d 1987), and Frances May Mason (d 1970); *b* 22 Aug 1917; *Educ* Lincoln Sch, Jesus Coll Cambridge (MA), SOAS Univ of London; *m* 1, 1943, Patricia (d 1971), da of William MacAllister (d 1922), of Wetherby; 3 s (Matthew b 1944, Thomas b 1950, George b 1961), 1 da (Sophy b 1955); m 2, 1973, Gai Rencie, wid of Martin Treves and da of Baron Salmon of Sandwich; *Career* served RA 1939-46; admitted slr 1948; Treasy Slrs Dept 1954-62, PLA 1962-66, md Tees and Hartlepool Port Authy 1966-77; chm: English Industl Estates Corp 1974-84, Medway Ports 1978-87; memb Nat Ports Cncl 1980-81, chm Br Ports Assoc 1983-85; *Books* Hedingham Harvest (1977); *Recreations* music; *Clubs* United Oxford and Cambridge Univ; *Style*— A G Robinson, Esq, CBE; Salts End, Gosshall Lane, Ash, Canterbury CT3 2AN (☎ 0304 812366); La Baume, Uzes 30700, Gard, France (☎ 010 33 66 22 55 44)

ROBINSON, Dr Bill; s of Harold Desmond Robinson (d 1988), and Joyce Grover, *née* Liddington; *b* 6 Jan 1943; *Educ* Bryanston, Univ of Oxford (BA), Univ of Sussex (DPhil), LSE (MSc); *m* 19 Aug 1966, Heather Mary, da of James Albert Jackson; 2 s (Nicholas, Matthew), 1 da (Rosemary); *Career* systems analyst IBM 1968-69, econ asst Cabinet Office 1969-70, econ advsr HM Treasy 1971-74, head div Euro Cmmn 1974-78, ed Econ Outlook London Business Sch 1978-86, dir Inst Fiscal Studies 1986-90; advsr Treasy Ctee House of Commons 1981-86, memb Retail Prices Advsy Ctee 1988-; econ columnist The Independent 1989-91; Special advsr to Chllr of Exchequer 1991-; *Books* Medium Term Exchange Rate Guidelines for Business Planning (1983); *Recreations* the bassoon, skiing, opera, sailboarding; *Style*— Dr Bill Robinson; 7 Ridgmount St, London WC1E 7AE (☎ 071 636 3784)

ROBINSON, Gp Capt (Donald) Brian; s of Maj Dudley Clare Robinson, MC (d 1970), of Balvonie, 1 Shimna Park, Newcastle, Co Down, NI, and Margaret, *née* Moore; *b* 26 July 1927; *Educ* Wellington, Univ of Oxford, RAF Coll Cranwell, Royal Canadian Air Force Staff Coll, Jt Servs Staff Coll; *m* 9 Oct 1957, Rosabelle Ileene Zahra, da of Maj Edward Archibald Theodore Bayly, DSO (d 1959), of Ballyarthur, Woodenbridge, Co Wicklow, Ireland; 2 s (Colan b 1958, Tim b 1965), 1 da (Judy b 1962); *Career* RAF 1949-82; served: Malayan Emergency and Korean War on Sunderland Flying Boats (despatches 1954), NATO staff SACLANT 1966-69, directing staff RAF Staff Coll Bracknell 1969-72, HQ Strike Cmd High Wycombe 1972-76, AHQ Cyprus 1976-79, NATO staff AIRSOUTH 1979-82, ret Gp Capt 1982; memb design staff Ferranti Computer Systems Ltd Gwent 1983-87; official helper RAF Benevolent Fund Gwent; memb: Gwent Nat Tst Assoc, Chepstow Soc, Shirenewton Village Produce Assoc (chm 1986-90); *Recreations* walking, horticulture, the countryside; *Clubs* RAF; *Style*— Gp Capt Brian Robinson; Green Acres, Shirenewton, Chepstow, Gwent NP6 6BU (☎ 02917 539)

ROBINSON, Air Vice-Marshal Brian Lewis (Boz); s of Frederick Lewis Robinson, of Newton Abbott, and Ida, *née* Croft (d 1984); *b* 2 July 1936; *Educ* Bradford GS; *m* 21 April 1961, Ann, da of Albert Thomas Faithfull (d 1956), of Bristol; 1 s (Symon Andrew b 1964), 1 da (Sarah Ann b 1962); *Career* RAF: No 74 (Trinidad) Sqdn 1956-59, Oxford Univ Air Sqdn 1959-62, No 73 Sqdn 1963-65, Canberra Trials and Taceval Unit 1966, Directorate of Flight Safety 1967-69, 60 Course RAF Staff Coll Bracknell 1970, OC 1 Sqdn 4 Flying Training Sch 1971-73, S0 Second Allied Tactical Air Force 1973-74, memb Directing Staff Canadian Forces command and Staff College Toronto 1974-76, chief instr 4 Flying Training Sch 1976-78, OC RAF Valley 1978-80, memb Int Military Staff NATO Brussels 1980-82, defence and air attaché Moscow 1983-86, dir orgn MOD 1986-88, Air OC Directly Administered Units and Air Offr i/c admin Strike Command 1989-91, ret 1991; qualified flying instructor 1959, pilot attack instructor 1962; memb: RAF Bobsleigh Team 1965-74, Br Bobsleigh Team 1967, 1969 and 1972; Freeman Guild of Air Pilots and Air Navigators; *Recreations* travel, beekeeping, viticulture; *Style*— Air Vice-Marshal Boz Robinson

ROBINSON, Maj (Alfred) Christopher; s of Col Annesley Robinson, DSO (d 1976), of Long Melford, Suffolk, and Doris Lilian, *née* Barrett (d 1988); *b* 18 Nov 1930; *Educ* Wellington, RMA Sandhurst; *m* 1, 17 Aug 1957 (m dis 1961), Caroline Stafford, da of Maj Christopher Scott-Nicholson (ka 1945), of Ruthwell, Dumfriesshire; m 2, 31 March 1962 (m dis 1978), Amanda, da of Paul Boggis-Rolfe (d 1988), of Bampton, Oxon; 2 s (Charles b 1964, Barnaby b 1970), 2 da (Nicola b 1963, Polly b 1964); *Career* 16/5 The Queen's Royal Lancers 1951-65; Trade Imdemnity Co Ltd 1966-70, Glanvill Enthoven & Co Ltd 1970-73, The Spastics Soc 1973-; tstee The Little Fndn; chm Ferriers Barn Disabled Centre; memb: Ctee Colne Stour Countryside Assoc, Sudbury Deanery Synod; memb ICFM 1986; *Recreations* country pursuits, travel, wine appreciation; *Clubs* Essex; *Style*— Maj Christopher Robinson; Water Lane Cottage, Bures, Suffolk CO8 5DE (☎ 0787 227179); The Spastics Society, 12 Park Crescent, London W1N 4EQ (☎ 071 636 5020, fax 071 436 2601)

ROBINSON, Christopher John; LVO (1986); s of Rev Preb John Robinson (d 1974), of 40 Mathon Rd, West Malvern, and Esther Hilda, *née* Lane (d 1983); *b* 20 April 1936; *Educ* Rugby, ChCh Oxford (MA, BMus), Univ of Birmingham (Cert Ed); *m* 6 Aug 1962, Shirley Ann, da of Harry Frederick Churchman, of 36 Mill Lane, Sawston, Cambridge; 1 s (Nicholas b 3 June 1970), 1 da (Elizabeth b 27 Sept 1968); *Career* asst organist: ChCh Oxford 1955-58, New Coll Oxford 1957-58; music master Oundle Sch 1959-62; organist: Worcester Cathedral 1963-74 (asst organist 1962-63), St George's Chapel Windsor Castle 1975-91; organist and dir of Music St John's Coll Cambridge 1991-; conductor: City of Birmingham Choir 1964- (princ conductor Three Choirs Festivals 1966, 1969 and 1972), Leith Hill Festival 1977-80, Oxford Bach Choir 1977-; pres RCO 1982-84, chm Elgar Soc 1988-; hon memb: RAM 1980, MMus Univ of Birmingham 1987; hon fell Birmingham Poly 1990; FRCO 1954; *Recreations* cricket, foreign travel; *Clubs* MCC; *Style*— Christopher Robinson, Esq, LVO; 25 The Cloisters, Windsor Castle, Berks SL4 1NJ (☎ 0753 864529)

ROBINSON, Christopher Philipse; s of late Christopher Robinson, QC; hp of kinsman, Sir John Robinson, 7 Bt; *b* 10 Nov 1938; *m* 1962, Barbara Judith, da of Richard Duncan, of Ottawa; 2 s; *Style*— Christopher Robinson Esq; 5 Bedford

Crescent, Ottawa, Ontario, Canada

ROBINSON, Hon Mrs (Claire Elizabeth); *née* Portman; da of 9 Viscount Portman and Rosemary Joy (Farris) Maitland; *b* 1 Oct 1959; *Educ* St Mary's Wantage, Winkfield Place, Marlborough Secretarial Coll Oxford; *m* 1983, Anthony Henry Robinson, only s of Anthony Leonard á Court Robinson, of Blagdon, Avon; 3 s (Anthony b 1984, James b 1985, Patrick b 1987); *Style—* The Hon Mrs Robinson; Boxford House, Boxford, nr Newbury, Berkshire RG16 8DP (☎ 048838 434)

ROBINSON, Clifton Eugene Bancroft; CBE (1985, OBE 1973), JP (1973); s of Theodore Emanuel Robinson (d 1950), and Lafrance Steel Robinson (d 1970); *b* 5 Oct 1926; *Educ* Kingston Tech Coll Jamaica, Univ of Birmingham (BA), Univ of Leicester (Dip Ed); *n* 1 (m dis 1976), Elizabeth Ball, *née* McLean; 1 s (Barrie b 22 Dec 1947), 3 da (Sandra b 30 Jan 1950, Denise b 4 July 1953, Yvonne 21 Feb 1959); m 2, 10 Sept 1987, Margaret Ann, da of Lenoard Ennever (d 1979); *Career* RAF 1944-49; sr master: Kingston Sr Sch Jamaica 1950, Mellor Sch Leicester 1951-61; dep head Charnwood Sch Leicester 1964-68; head teacher: St Peter's Sch Leicester 1968-70 (i/c Special Educn Unit 1961-64), Uplands Sch Leicester 1970-77; dep chm Cmmn for Racial Equality 1977-85; vice pres Int Friendship League; pres: Roots Coll, Assoc of Jamaicans, Urban Tst, Community Indust, AIMS, LUCA; *Recreations* listening to music (mainly classical), walking, gardening, archaeology, reading; *Style—* Clifton Robinson, Esq, CBE, JP

ROBINSON, Prof Colin; s of James Robinson (d 1937), of Stretford, Lancs, and Elsie, *née* Brownhill (d 1959); *b* 7 Sept 1932; *Educ* Stretford GS, Univ of Manchester (BA); *m* 1, 13 July 1957 (m dis 1983), Olga, da of Harry West; 4 s (Julian b 1961, Stewart b 1964, Richard b 1966, Christopher b 1971), 2 da (Louise b 1967, Elaine b 1969); m 2, 18 June 1983, Eileen Catherine, *née* Marshall; *Career* RAF 1950-53; head Econs Div Corp Planning Dept Esso Petroleum 1960-66, econ advsr natural gas Esso Euro 1966-68, prof of econs Univ of Surrey 1968; memb Advsy Cncls Inst of Econ Affairs and Centre for Policy Studies; FSS 1969, FInstPet 1979; *Books* Business Forecasting (1970), North Sea Oil in the Future (1977), The Economics of Energy Self Sufficiency (1984), Can Coal Be Saved (1985); *Recreations* walking, music, home improvements; *Style—* Prof Colin Robinson; Department of Economics, University of Surrey, Guildford, Surrey GU2 5XH (☎ 0483 509171, car 0860 734479)

ROBINSON, David Foster; s of Arthur Robinson, of New Milton, Hants, and Ellen Robinson, *née* Jackson (d 1989); *b* 29 May 1936; *Educ* King's Sch Macclesfield, Univ of Manchester (BA); *m* 5 Nov 1966, Hannah, da of Roger Alan Watson (d 1979), of Edinburgh; 2 s (William b 1968, Edward b 1970), 1 da (Caroline b 1971); *Career* Nat Serv 2 Lt RAPC 1960-62; ptnr Spicer & Oppenheim 1974- (formerly Spicer & Pegler, joined 1962); dir: Spicer's Consulting Gp 1969- (formerly Spicer & Pegler Assocs), Sulaiman Assocs 1979- (formerly Egunjobi & Sulaiman Conslts (Nigeria) Ltd), Spicer's Exec Selection 1989-, Spicer's Centre for Europe 1990-; memb Langford & Ulting PC 1978-; FCA, FIMC; *Books* Human Asset Accounting (1972), Key Definitions in Finance (1980), Managing People (1984), Getting the Best out of People (1988); *Recreations* gardening, walking, tennis; *Clubs* City of London; *Style—* David Robinson, Esq; Luards, Langford, Maldon, Essex (☎ 0621 54242); 35 Taeping St London E14; Spicer & Oppenheim Friary Ct, 65 Crutched Friars EC3N 2NP (☎ 071 480 7766, fax 071 480 6958, telex 884257 ESAND G)

ROBINSON, Prof David Julien; s of Edward Robinson (d 1973), of Lincoln, and Dorothy Evelyn, *née* Overton (d 1979); *b* 6 Aug 1930; *Educ* Lincoln Sch, King's Coll Cambridge (BA); *Career* assoc ed Sight and Sound 1956-58, ed Monthly Film Bulletin 1956-58, programme dir Nat Film Theatre and London Film Festival 1959, ed Contrast 1962-63; film critic: The Financial Times 1959-74, The Times 1974-; prodr and dir films: Hetty King - Performer 1969, Keeping Love Alive 1987 (co-dir Stephen Garrett), Sophisticated Lady 1989 (co-dir David Mingay); memb: Williams Ctee on Obscenity and Film Censorship, numerous film festival juries incl Cannes, Berlin and Venice; visiting prof Westfield Coll London; *Books* Hollywood in the Twenties (1969), Buster Keaton (1969), The Great Funnies (1972) World Cinema (1973, 1980), Chaplin, The Mirror of Opinion (1983), Chaplin His Life and Art (1985); *Recreations* collecting, music hall, prehistory of cinema; *Style—* Prof David Robinson; 96-100 New Cavendish St, London WIM 7FA (☎ 071 580 4959); The Times, 1 Virginia St, London E19XN (☎ 071 782 5000, fax 071 583 9519, telex)

ROBINSON, Ven (William) David; s of William Robinson (d 1969), of Blackburn, and Margaret, *née* Bolton (d 1982); *b* 15 March 1931; *Educ* Queen Elizabeth GS Blackburn, Univ of Durham (BA, Dip Theol, MA); *m* 30 Jul 1955, Carol Averil Roma, da of Norman William Edward Hamm, of Blackburn; 1 s (Christopher b 1986), 1 da (Catherine b 1960); *Career* pilot offr RAF 1949-51; curate St Wilfrid Standish 1958-61, sr curate Lancaster Priory (priest i/c St George) 1961-63, vicar St James Blackburn 1963-73, diocesan stewardship advsr and priest i/c St James Shireshead 1973-86, hon canon Blackburn Cathedral 1975-86, vicar of Balderstone 1986-87, archdeacon of Blackburn 1986-; *Recreations* fell walking; *Style—* The Ven the Archdeacon of Blackburn; 7 Billinge Close, Blackburn, Lancs BB2 6SB (☎ 0254 53442)

ROBINSON, Derek; s of Alexander Smith Robinson (d 1957), of Bristol, and Margaret Low, *née* MacAskill; *b* 12 April 1932; *Educ* Cotham GS Bristol, Downing Coll Cambridge (MA); *m* 1968, Sheila, *née* Collins; *Career* copywriter: McCann Erickson Advertising London 1956-60, BBDO Advertising NY 1960-66; author and freelance writer; novels: Goshawk Squadron (1971, short-listed Booker prize), Rotten with Honour 1973, Kramer's War 1977, The Eldorado Network 1979, Piece of Cake (1983, televised, Book of the Month Club Choice), War Story 1987, Artillery of Lies 1991; non-fiction: Rugby: Success Starts Here 1969, Just Testing 1985, Run With The Ball! 1984; author of several books on the dialect of Bristol; memb The Authors Guild Inc USA 1977; *Recreations* squash, rugby union referee, dinghy sailing; *Style—* Derek Robinson, Esq; Shapland House, Somerset St, Kingsdown, Bristol BS2 8LZ (☎ 0272 241057); John Farquharson, 162-168 Regent St, London W1R 5TB (☎ 071 872 0331)

ROBINSON, Derek Hugh; s of Cyril Thomas John Robinson (d 1967), of Derby, and Doris Isabel, *née* Garrett (d 1960); *b* 5 June 1929; *Educ* Bemrose Sch Derby, Tech Coll Derby, Univ of Southampton, UCL (BSc); *m* 15 Dec 1958, Heather Margaret Anne, da of Reginald Walter Merrick (d 1962), of Midsomer Norton, Somerset; 2 s (Ian, Edward), 1 da (Fiona); *Career* offr US Army Corps of Engrs Labrador 1954; engr: John Laing & Son Ltd 1950-52, Ontario Dept of Highways Toronto 1952-54, Turriff Construction Corporation Warwick 1954-55, E W H Gifford & Partners Southampton 1957-63; consulting engr: D H Robinson Associatiates Winchester 1963-87, Allott & Lomax Winchester 1987-; CEng, FICE, FIStructE, MConsE; *Recreations* walking, photography, nature study, family life, motoring, travel; *Style—* Derek H Robinson, Esq; 6 Palmerston Court, Barnes Close, Winchester, Hants (☎ 0962 854905); Haven Lights, Castle Rd, Dartmouth, S Devon (☎ 0803 834382); Bridge House, East Hill, Winchester, Hants (☎ 0962 861077, fax 0962 861655)

ROBINSON, Prof Donald Sewart; s of Arthur Inman Robinson (d 1963), and Elizabeth Annie, *née* Sewart (d 1984); *b* 3 Oct 1927; *Educ* Queen Elizabeth GS Kirkby Lonsdale, Univ of Cambridge (BA, MA, PhD); *m* 6 Aug 1953, Marjorie Agnes Robinson; 2 s (Mark b 1958, Paul b 1960); *Career* res fell Sir William Dunn Sch of Pathology Univ of Oxford 1952-63, res fell Med Res Cncl Cell Metabolism Res Unit Dept of Biochemistry Univ of Oxford 1963-71, head of Dept of Biochemistry Univ of Leeds 1973-84 (prof 1971-); numerous articles in jls; FIBiol 1979; *Recreations* gardening, mountain walking; *Style—* Prof Donald Robinson; Department of Biochemistry, University of Leeds, Leeds LS2 9JT (☎ 0532 333122)

ROBINSON, Prof Duncan (David); s of Tom Robinson (ka 1944), and Ann Elizabeth, *née* Clarke; *b* 27 June 1943; *Educ* King Edward VI Sch Macclesfield, Clare Coll Cambridge (Scholar, BA, MA), Yale Univ (Mellon fellowship, MA); *m* 7 Jan 1967, Elizabeth Anne (Lisa), da of Frederick Totten Sutton (d 1979), of Fairfield, Conn, USA; 1 s (Thomas Edward b 1975), 2 da (Amanda Jane b 1971, Charlotte Elizabeth b 1989); *Career* keeper of paintings and drawings Fitzwilliam Museum Cambridge 1976-81 (asst keeper 1970-76), fell and coll lectr Clare Coll Univ of Cambridge 1975-81; dir of studies in history of art Univ of Cambridge until 1981: Churchill, Clare, Lucy Cavendish, Queens' and Sidney Sussex Colls and New Hall; currently dir Yale Center for British Art New Haven, chief exec offr Paul Mellon Centre for Studies in British Art London, adj prof of history of art Yale Univ 1981-; fell Berkeley Coll Yale Univ; memb: Ctee of Management and chm Exhibitions Ctee Kettle's Yard Univ of Cambridge 1970-81, Ct RCA 1975-78, Art Advsy Panel Arts Council of GB 1978-81 (memb Exhibitions Sub Ctee 1978-79, memb Art Fin Ctee 1979-80, memb Cncl and vice-chm Art Panel 1981), Assoc of Art Museum Dirs 1983-88; elector to Slade Professorship of Fine Art Univ of Cambridge 1978-81, govr Yale Univ Press 1987-; public, visiting and pt/t lectr UK and USA; FRSA 1990, memb Con Acad of Arts & Scis 1991; *Publications* numerous catalogues, articles and reviews; author of: A Companion Volume to the Kelmscott Chaucer (1975, re-issued as Morris, Burne-Jones and the Kelmscott Chaucer, 1982), Stanley Spencer (1979, revised edn 1990); *Clubs* Atheneum (London), Century (New York), Yale (New York); *Style—* Prof Duncan Robinson; 142 Huntington Street, New Haven, Conn 06511, USA; Hall's Farm, South Windham, Vermont 05359, USA; Yale Center For British Art, Box 2120 Yale Station, New Haven, Conn 06520

ROBINSON, Eric Embleton; s of Cyril Robinson, and late Florence Mary, *née* Embleton; *b* 12 March 1927; *Educ* Nelson GS Lancs; Univ of London: Kings Coll, Birkbeck Coll, Inst of Educn (BSc, MSc); *Career* lectr: Acton Tech Coll 1949-56, Brunel Coll Acton 1956-62; head Dept Faculty Enfield Coll 1962-70, dep dir NE London Poly 1970-73, princ Bradford Coll 1973-82, rector Lancashire Polytechnic 1982-90; vice pres Socialist Educn Assoc; Hon DEd 1990; *Books* The New Polytechnics (1968); *Clubs* Savile; *Style—* Eric Robinson, Esq; 5 Millfield Rd, Chorley, Lancs PR7 1RF (☎ 02572 62213)

ROBINSON, Hon Mrs (Gai Rencie); da (by 1 m) of Baron Salmon (Life Peer); *b* 1933; *m* 1, 1955, Martin Treves (d 1970); 3 s, 1 da; m 2, 1973, Geoffrey Robinson, CBE, *qv*; *Style—* The Hon Mrs Robinson; 19 Millers Court, Chiswick Mall, London W4 (☎ 081 748 2997); Salts End, Ash, nr Canterbury, Kent (☎ 0304 812366)

ROBINSON, Geoffrey; MP (Lab) Coventry NW 1976-; s of Robert Robinson; *b* 25 May 1938; *Educ* Emanuel Sch, Cambridge Univ, Yale Univ; *m* 1967, Marie Elena Giorgio; 1 s, 1 da; *Career* Lab Pty res asst 1965-68, sr exec Industl Reorganisation Corpn 1968-70, fin controller BL 1971-72, md Leyland Innocenti Milan 1972-73; chief exec: Jaguar Motor Cars Coventry 1973-75, Meriden Co-Op 1979-80; oppn spokesman: Regnl Affairs 1983-84, Indust 1984-86; *Style—* Geoffrey Robinson, Esq, MP; House of Commons, London SW1A 0AA

ROBINSON, Hilary Frances; da of Ivor Robinson, of Oxford, and Olive, *née* Trask; *b* 25 June 1956; *Educ* John Mason HS Abingdon Oxon, Univ of Newcastle upon Tyne (BA), RCA (MA, Allen Lane/Penguin Books award); *Career* painted and exhibited 1979-85, freelance writing tutor Glasgow Sch of Art 1987-, ed Alba (Scot visual art magazine) 1990-; memb Assoc of Art Historians 1988-; *Books* Visibly Female (ed, 1987); *Recreations* good food, good drink, good dancing, saunas; *Style—* Ms Hilary Robinson; Alba, Talbot Rice, Art Centre, Old College, South Bridge, Edinburgh EH8 (☎ 031 667 7875)

ROBINSON, Ian; s of Thomas Mottram Robinson (d 1972), and Eva Iris, *née* Bird (d 1984); *b* 3 May 1942; *Educ* Univ of Leeds (BSc), Harvard (SMP); *m* 28 Oct 1967, Kathleen Crawford, da of James Leay, of Edinburgh; 1 s (Andrew John b 1977), 1 da (Caroline Anne b 1973); *Career* Ralph M Parsons Co Ltd: dir of ops 1979, vice pres (USA) 1983, md 1985; md John Brown Engineering Constructors Ltd 1986-, chief exec John Brown Engineers & Constructors 1990-; dir: John Brown plc 1990-, Sofresid 1990-; FIChE, CEng; *Recreations* gardening, tennis, golf; *Clubs* Les Ambassadeurs, RAC; *Style—* Ian Robinson, Esq; John Brown Engineers & Constructors Ltd, 20 Eastbourne Terrace, London W2 6LE (☎ 071 262 8080)

ROBINSON, James Milner; s of Valentine Charles Robinson (d 1945), and Ruth Milner, *née* Brown (d 1987); *b* 2 Aug 1937; *Educ* Epsom Coll, Univ of London (MB, BS); *m* 1 May 1965, Diana Mary, da of Alexander Alfred Cross, MBE, of Wittonditch, nr Ramsbury, Wilts; 2 da (Lucy Anne b 1969, Ruth Kathryn b 1971); *Career* surgical registrar Royal Nat Throat Nose and Ear Hosp 1972-73, sr surgical registrar and lectr ENT Dept Bristol Royal Infirmary 1973-75, conslt ENT surgn Gloucester Royal Hospital 1975-; pubns on ear disease in jls; memb Faculty: Combined Univs Advanced Otology Course, J Causse et Institut D'Otologie Beziers France; pres Gloucester Branch Nat Deaf Childrens Soc, chm HEAR Tst (a local body supporting res and educn in ear disease); FRCS 1973, memb RSM; *Style—* James Robinson, Esq; High Meadows, Yartleton Lane, May Hill, Longhope, Gloucester GL17 0RF

ROBINSON, Jancis Mary (Mrs N L Lander); da of Thomas Edward Robinson, of Eden House, Kirkandrews-on-Eden, Cumbria, and Ann, *née* Conacher; *b* 22 April 1950; *Educ* Carlisle HS, St Annes Coll Oxford (MA); *m* 22 Oct 1981, Nicholas Laurence Lander, s of Israel Lennard Lander; 1 s (William Isaac b 5 Sept 1984), 1 da (Julia Margaux b 10 July 1982); *Career* mktg and producing skiing holidays Thomson Holidays 1971-74, odd jobs while writing for Good Food Guide 1975, ed (formerly asst ed) Wine and Spirit 1975-80, fndr Drinker's Digest (1977) (became Which? Wine Monthly 1980), ed Which? Wine Monthly and Which? Wine Annual Guide 1980-82; Sunday Times: wine corr, food corr, gen features 1980-86; wine corr: The Evening Standard 1987-88, Financial Times 1989-; bdcasting: presenter and writer The Wine Programme (1983, 1985, 1987), presenter Jancis Robinson's Christmas Wine List 1985, commentary writer and narrator 40 Minutes (Nuclear Dumps) 1986, presenter BBC Design Awards 1986-87, narrator Design Classics 1987; presenter and writer: Jancis Robinson Meets 1987, Matters of Taste 1989 and 1991; lectures incl: Christie's and Sotheby's wine courses, Gleneagles Wine Weekend; wine judging Britain and abroad; Glenfiddich Award: Best Book on Wine (The Great Wine Book) 1983, Wine and Food Writer/Broadcaster of the Year 1984, Wine Writer 1986, Food Writer 1986; winner: Marques de Caceres Award 1985, Wine Guild of UK Premier Award 1986, André Simon Meml Award 1987, Wine Guild Award for Reference Book 1987, Clicquot Book of the Year (Vines, Grapes and Wines) 1987, Silver Medal German Academy of Gastronomy 1988; memb Inst of Masters of Wine 1984; Jurade de St Emilion, Commanderie de Bontemps de Médoc et Graves; *Books* The Wine Book (1979), The Great Wine Book (1982), Masterglass (1983), How to Choose and Enjoy Wine (1984), Vines, Grapes and Wines (1986), Jancis Robinson's Food and Wine Adventures (1987), Jancis Robinson on The Demon Drink (1988), Vintage Timecharts (1989); *Style—* Ms Jancis Robinson

ROBINSON, Prof John; s of William Clifford Robinson (d 1982), and Annie, *née*

Banks; *b* 11 July 1933; *Educ* Little Lever Secondary Sch, Radcliffe Jr Tech Coll, Salford Tech Coll (HND), Cranfield Inst of Tech (MSc), Inst of Sound and Vibration Res Univ of Southampton (PhD); *m* 1, 3 Aug 1957 (m dis 1980), Cynthia, da of late Eric Nicholls; 2 s (Gary Edward b 16 Aug 1958, Lee John b 16 May 1961); m 2, 12 Sept 1984, Shirley Ann, da of Roland Walter Bradley, of Bidford-on-Avon, Warwicks; *Career* Br and USA Aerospace Indust 1949-71, head Robinson and Assocs 1971-; conslt organiser World Congress and Exhibition on Finite Element Methods 1975- (ed and publisher World Congress Proceedings 1975-), ed and publisher Finite Element News 1976-, lectr of worldwide courses on Understanding Finite Element Stress Analysis 1980-, fndr and memb Steering Ctee Nat Agency for Finite Element Methods and Standards 1983-, dir Robinson FEMInst 1986-, industl res prof Univ of Exeter 1986-; MRAeS 1962, MIMechE 1964, CEng; *Books* Structural Matrix Analysis for the Engineer (1966), Integrated Theory of Finite Element Methods (1973), Understanding Finite Element Stress Analysis (1981), Early FEM Pioneers (1985), articles; *Style*— Prof John Robinson; Great Bidlake Manor, Bridestowe, Okehampton, Devon EX20 4NT (☎ 083 786 220)

ROBINSON, John Barrie; s of Reginald Thomas Robinson (d 1987), of 197 Carleton Rd, Pontefract, W Yorks, and Constance Helen, *née* Sykes; *b* 15 Oct 1934; *Educ* Normanton GS; *m* 11 June 1960, (Margaret) Jill, da of Robert Victor Fisher (d 1976), of 7 Mount St, Walsall; 2 s (Andrew b 1961, Jonathan b 1964), 1 da (Helen b 1968); *Career* Nat Serv 1953-55; Parker Pen Co UK Ltd: sales mangr 1968-79, sales and mktg dir 1979-83, gen mangr 1983-; area dir (Europe, Africa, Middle East) Parker Pen plc 1986-89, ret; FInstD; *Recreations* golf; *Clubs* Royal Eastbourne Golf; *Style*— J Barrie Robinson, Esq; 2 Summerdown Close, Eastbourne, E Sussex BN20 8DW (☎ 0323 30693); Parker Pen plc, Parker House, Newhaven, E Sussex BN9 0AU (☎ 0273 513 233, ext 268)

ROBINSON, Sir John James Michael Laud; 11 Bt (E 1660), of London, DL (Northants); s of Michael Frederick Laud-Robinson (d 1971), and Elisabeth Bridge (d 1977); suc gf, Maj Sir Frederick Robinson, 10 Bt, MC (d 1975, descended from Sir John Robinson, 1 Bt, Lord Mayor of London 1662-63 and s of Ven William Robinson, sometime Archdeacon of Nottingham and half-bro of Archbishop Laud); *b* 19 Jan 1943; *Educ* Eton, Trinity Coll Dublin (MA); *m* 1968, (Kathryn) Gayle Elizabeth, da of Stuart Nelson Keyes, of Orillia, Ontario; 2 s, 1 da; *Heir* s, Mark Christopher Michael Villiers Robinson b 23 April 1972; *Career* chartered fin analyst; landowner; chm St Andrew's Hosp Northampton; *Style*— Sir John Robinson, Bt, DL; Cranford Hall, Cranford, Kettering, Northants NN14 4AD (☎ 053 678 248)

ROBINSON, John Martin; s of John Cotton Robinson, of Hill Top Farm South, Whittle-le-Woods, Lancs, and Ellen Anne Cecilia, eld da of George Adams, of Cape Town, S Africa; *b* 10 Sept 1948; *Educ* Fort Augustus Abbey, St Andrews, Oriel Coll Oxford (MA, DPhil); *Career* librarian to Duke of Norfolk 1978-; ptnr Historic Bldgs Conslts; memb: Exec Ctee Georgian Gp, Exec Ctee Abbot Hall Art Gallery Kendal, Donat of SMO Malta, Cncl Soc of Antiquaries 1990-, Maltravers Herald of Arms Extraordinary 1989-; FSA; *Books* The Wyatts (1980), Royal Residences (1982), Dukes of Norfolk (1983), Georgian Model Farms (1983), Latest Country Houses (1984), Architecture of Northern England (1986), Cardinal Consalvi (1987), English Country Estate (1988), Guide to Heraldry (jtly with Thomas Woodcock, 1988), Country House at War (1989), Temples of Delight (1990); *Clubs* Travellers', Atheneaum; *Style*— John Robinson, Esq, Maltravers Herald; Beckside House, Barbon, Via Carnforth, Lancs (Barbon 300); 8 Doughty Mews, London WC1 (☎ 071 405 2856, fax 071 831 8831)

ROBINSON, Rev Canon Joseph; s of Thomas Robinson (d 1967), of Wigan Lancs, and Maggie, *née* Wright (d 1981); *b* 23 Feb 1927; *Educ* Upholland GS, King's Coll London (BD, MTh); *m* 5 Sept 1953, Anne, da of James Antrobus (d 1978), of Wigan, Lancs; 2 s (Michael Francis b 1954, Christopher John b 1959), 2 da (Gillian Elizabeth b 1956, Katherine Mary b 1961); *Career* ordained: deacon 1952, priest 1953; curate Tottenham 1952-55, minor canon St Paul's Cathedral 1955-68, lectr in Old Testament studies King's Coll London 1959-68, canon of Canterbury 1968-80, master of the Temple 1980-; govr: Sons of the Clergy, Queen's Coll Harley St; fell Woodward Fndn; Liveryman Worshipful Co of Wax Chandlers, Chaplain Worshipful Co of Cutlers, former Master Worshipful Co of Parish Clerks; Hon LLD Simon Greenleafe Law Sch Anaheim California; FKC; *Books* Cambridge Bible Commentary on 1 Kings (1972), Cambridge Bible Commentary on 2 Kings (1976); *Recreations* reading, gardening; *Clubs* Athenaeum; *Style*— The Rev Canon Joseph Robinson; The Master's House, Temple, London EC4Y 7BB (☎ 071 353 8559)

ROBINSON, Keith; s of Wilfrid Robinson, of Acklam, Middlesbrough, and Florence Marshall, *née* Gray; *b* 8 Dec 1947; *Educ* Acklam Hall GS, Univ of London (BA); *m* 8 Sept 1979, Janet Wilson, da of Archibald Black, of Yarm, Cleveland; 2 s (William James b 1982, Richard Alexander b 1985); *Career* CA; dir York Planetarium Co Ltd 1983-; *Recreations* travel, eating out; *Style*— Keith Robinson, Esq; 54 Mount Leven Rd, Yarm, Cleveland TS15 9RJ (☎ 0642 785628); Keith Robinson & Co, 4 Woodlands Rd, Middlesbrough, Cleveland TS1 3BE (☎ 0642 225325)

ROBINSON, (Leonard) Keith; CBE (1981), DL (Hampshire 1985); s of Cuthbert Lawrence Robinson and Hilda Robinson; *b* 2 July 1920; *Educ* Queen Elizabeth's GS Blackburn, Victoria Univ Manchester (LLB); *m* 1948, Susan May, da of the late Vice-Adm W Tomkinson; 2 s, 2 da; *Career* WWII RAFVR Sqdn Ldr Coastal Cmd 1940-46; slr Bristol 1948-55; dep town clerk Birkenhead Co Borough Cncl 1955-65, town clerk Stoke on Trent City Cncl 1966-73, co chief exec Hants CC 1973-85; chm Assoc of Co Chief Execs 1975-77, a princ advsr to Assoc of CCs 1974-85, memb W Midlands Econ Planning Cncl 1967-73, former memb Central Ctee for Reclamation of Derelict Land, memb Advsy Cncl for Energy Conservation 1982-84; mgmnt conslt 1985-87; dir Salisbury Playhouse Bd 1978-; vice chm: Nuffield Theatre 1985-, Southern Arts Man Cncl 1985-; asst cmmr Local Govt Boundary Cmmn 1987-; pres: The Castle CC Winchester 1977-, Winchester Dramatic Soc; memb Mgmnt Ctee: Hillier Arboretum 1985-, Hants Devpt Assoc 1985-, Hants Gdn Tst 1984-; *Recreations* theatre, fly fishing, gardening, cricket; *Clubs* MCC; *Style*— Keith Robinson Esq, CBE, DL; Bransbury Mill Cottage, Bransbury, Barton Stacey, Winchester, Hants S021 3QJ (☎ 0962 760124)

ROBINSON, Keith Thomas; s of Leslie Robinson (d 1986), of Brook House, North End, Great Dunmow, Essex, and Dorothy Elizabeth, *née* Gregson; *b* 27 Feb 1944; *Educ* Tonbridge, Royal Agric Coll Cirencester (Dip Estate Mgmnt); *m* 4 Oct 1969, Penelope Jane, da of Norman Eustace Scott Miller, OBE; 1 s (Thomas), 3 da (Joanna, Catherine, Georgina); *Career* chartered surveyor; Bidwells of Cambridge 1965-67, ptnr Gunton & Gunton (architect and surveyors) 1967-81, chm and md of family property cos and farming co; pres High Easter CC; memb Worshipful Co of Glaziers; ARICS, Assoc Chartered Land Agents Soc; *Recreations* sailing, golf, tennis, fell walking, swimming; *Clubs* Farmers, Windermere Golf, Royal Windermere Yacht; *Style*— Keith Robinson, Esq; Spriggs, Ecclerigg, Windermere, Cumbria LA23 1LJ (☎ 0245 31291)

ROBINSON, Prof Kenneth; s of James Robinson (d 1977), of Liverpool, and Ethel, *née* Allen; *b* 4 March 1950; *Educ* Liverpool Collegiate GS, Wade Deacon GS, Bretton Hall Coll, Univ of Leeds (BED), Univ of London (PhD); *m* 30 Jan 1982, Marie-Thérèse, da of Frederick George Watts, of Leamington Spa; 1 s (James b 11 Oct 1984), 1 da (Katherine Marie b 4 May 1989); *Career* educationist: dir Nat Curriculum Cncl Arts in Schools project 1985-89, chm Artswork 1987-, prof arts educn Univ of Warwick 1989-; FRSA; *Books* Learning Through Drama (1977), Exploring Theatre and Education (ed 1980), The Arts in Schools (princ author, 1982), The Arts and Higher Education (ed 1983), The Arts 5-16 (1990); *Recreations* theatre, music, cinema; *Style*— Prof Ken Robinson; Univ of Warwick, Westwood, Coventry CV4 7AL (☎ 0203 524152)

ROBINSON, Rt Hon Sir Kenneth; PC (1964); s of Dr Clarence Robinson (d 1923); *b* 19 March 1911; *Educ* Oundle; *m* 1941, Helen Elizabeth Edwards; 1 da (Hester b 1955); *Career* served WWII Lt-Cdr RNVR; MP (Lab) St Pancras N 1949-70, asst whip 1950-51, oppn whip 1951-54, min of Health 1964-68, min for Planning and Land (min of Housing and Local Govt) 1968-69; md personnel BSC 1972-74; former Lloyd's insur broker; chm: LTE 1975-78, ENO 1972-77, Arts Cncl of Gt Britain 1977-82, Young Concert Artists Tst 1983-90; Hon DLitt Liverpool; FCIT, Hon FRCGP, Hon MRCP 1989; kt 1983; *Books* Wilkie Collins: a Biography (1951, republished 1974); *Recreations* music, visual arts, reading, playgoing; *Clubs* Arts; *Style*— The Rt Hon Sir Kenneth Robinson; 12 Grove Terrace, London NW5 (☎ 071 267 0880)

ROBINSON, Prof Kenneth Ernest; CBE (1971); s of Ernest Robinson (d 1917), of Plumstead, Kent, and Isabel May, *née* Chalk (d 1954); *b* 9 March 1914; *Educ* Sir George Monoux GS London, Hertford Coll Oxford (BA, MA), LSE; *m* 4 Nov 1938, Stephanie Christine Sara, da of William Wilson (d 1951), of Westminster; 1 s (Julian b 1944), 1 da (Miranda b 1947); *Career* Home Civil Serv Admin Class: asst princ Colonial Office 1936, princ 1942, asst sec 1946, resigned 1948; official fell Nuffield Coll Oxford 1948-57 (hon fell 1984), reader in cwlth govt Univ of Oxford 1948-57; Univ of London: dir of Inst of Cwlth Studies, prof of cwlth affrs 1957-65 (hon life memb 1979-); Reid lectr Acadia Univ Canada 1963, vice-chllr Univ of Hong Kong 1965-72, Hallsworth fell Univ of Manchester 1972-74, Callander lectr Univ of Aberdeen 1979; vice-pres Royal Cwlth Soc, pres Royal African Soc; govr LSE 1959-65; JP Hong Kong 1967-72; Hon LLD Chinese Univ of Hong Kong 1968, Hon DLitt Univ of Hong Kong 1972, Hon Dr Open Univ 1978, corresponding memb Academie des Sciences D'Outre-Mer Paris 1959-; FRHistS 1959; *Books* Five Elections in Africa (with WJM McKenzie, 1960), Essays in Imperial Government (with A F Madden, 1963), The Dilemmas of Trusteeship (1965); *Clubs* United Oxford and Cambridge University, Lansdowne, Hong Kong; *Style*— Prof Kenneth Robinson, CBE; The Old Rectory, Church Westcote, Oxford OX7 6SF (☎ 0993 830 586)

ROBINSON, Kent Seafield; s of Maj Geoffrey Seafield Robinson, (d 1974), of E Grinstead, Sussex, and Irene Marian, *née* Valpy; *b* 1 May 1938; *Educ* Kings Sch Canterbury, RMA Sandhurst; *m* 1, 12 March 1960 (m dis 1985), Cicelie Amanda Stewart, da of Sqdn Ldr Ronald Ernest Cheesman, of Hartley Wintney, Hants; 2 s (Mark b 1961, Andrew b 1963); m 2, 20 June 1985, Carol Patricia Palmer, da of Eric Dean, CB, CBE, of Hove, Sussex; *Career* RASC 1958-65; Army Cross Country Driving Champion Team 1963, Far E Army Rally Champion 1964, medically ret 1965; int money broker 1969-79; opened offs: Jersey 1972, Kuwait 1976, Tokyo 1978; currently chm Lionel Robinson & Co (electrical wholesalers and distributors), chm Basingstoke IOD 1985-87, pres Electrical Wholesalers Fedn 1989; FInstD 1974; *Recreations* squash, vintage motor cars, continental tours; *Style*— Kent Robinson, Esq; Wedmans Farm, Rotherwick, Basingstoke, Hants RG27 9BX; Lionel Robinson & Co Ltd, 163 Eldon St, Preston, Lancs PR2 2AD (☎ 0772 57975, fax 0772 204168, telex 67442)

ROBINSON, (Thomas) Lloyd; TD (1945); s of Thomas Rosser Robinson (d 1927), of Swansea, and Rebe Francis-Watkins (d 1962); *b* 21 Dec 1912; *Educ* Wycliffe Coll Glos; *m* 1939, Pamela Rosemary, da of William Henry Foster (d 1960), of Four Oaks, Warwicks; 1 s (Anthony), 2 da (Angela, Juliet); *Career* Maj Royal Warwickshire Regt 1939-45, 61 Divn PSC Staff Coll Camberley 1943, SHAEF; dir E S & A Robinson Ltd 1952-66; Dickinson Robinson plc: dir 1966, dep chm 1968, chm 1974-77, hon vice pres 1978-88, hon pres 1988-; dir: Legal & General Group 1970-83 (vice chm 1978-83), Van Leer Group Holland 1977-81, Bristol Waterworks Co 1978-84; chm: Legal and General Western Advsy Bd 1972-84, Cncl of Govrs Wycliffe Coll 1970-83 (pres 1988-), Cncl Bristol Univ 1977- (pro-chllr 1984-); LLD 1985; High Sheriff Avon 1978-79; Master Soc of Merchant Venturers 1977-78; pres: Gloucestershire CCC 1980-83, Warwicks Old County Cricketers Assoc 1988; *Recreations* music, golf; *Clubs* Army and Navy, Marylebone Cricket, R and A Clifton (Bristol); *Style*— Lloyd Robinson, Esq; Lechlade, Stoke Bishop, Bristol BS9 1DB (☎ 0272 681957)

ROBINSON, Gp-Capt Marcus; CB (1956), AFC (1941, and Bar 1944), AE (1942), DL (1953); s of Wilson Robinson (d 1953), of Glasgow, and Eileen Charlotte, *née* Colvil (d 1959); *b* 27 May 1912; *Educ* Rossall; *m* 1, 4 April 1941 (m dis 1950), Mary Playfair; 1 s (Ainslie b 18 April 1942), 1 da (Elaine b 26 Nov 1944); m 2, 25 Sept 1953, Joan Elizabeth Weatherlake, da of O C Carter (d 1964), of Bournemouth; *Career* cmmnd 602 Sqdn Aux Air Force 1934, Flt Cdr 1938-40, Sqdn Ldr i/c 616 Sqdn 1940, Sqdn Ldr flying instr 1940, Wing Cdr 1942, chief instr 15 Pilot Advanced Flying Unit, Gp Capt 1945, i/c 20 and 21 Flying Trg Schs 1945, Sr Air SO 23 Gp RAF, demob 1946, reformed 602 City of Glasgow Fighter Sqdn 1946-51; memb Air Advsy Cncl Air Min 1952-56, chm Glasgow Territorial and Aux Forces Assoc 1952-56; Robinson Dunn & Co Ltd: dir 1939-66, chm and md 1966-77, ret 1977; chm: Glasgow Rating and Valuation Appeals Ctee 1963-77 (dep chm 1958-63), Earl Haig Fund Scotland 1974-78 (vice pres 1978); awarded Silver Jubilee medal 1977; *Recreations* skiing, sailing, golf; *Clubs* Western, Royal Northern and Clyde Yacht; *Style*— Gp-Capt Marcus Robinson, CB, AFC, AE, DL; Rockfort, Helensburgh G8A 7BA (☎ 0436 72097)

ROBINSON, Mark Nicholas; s of Eric Robinson, of Leigh on Sea Essex, and Kate Emily Robinson; *b* 24 Jan 1952; *Educ* Westcliff GS for Boys, Univ of Dundee (MA, vice pres Students' Union); *m* 4 June 1976, Patricia Margaret, da of John Malone; 2 s (Matthew John b 31 July 1981, Rory Patrick b 20 Aug 1985), 1 da (Chloe Margaret b 16 Nov 1983); *Career* salesman Thomson Regional Newspapers 1975-76, Allardyce Advertising 1976-77, account exec Manton Woodyer Ketley 1977-78, account dir CDP/Aspect Advertising 1981-85 (account mangr 1978-81), dir Ted Bates 1985-87; business devpt dir: Dorland Advertising 1987-88, Horner Collis & Kirvan 1988-; IPA: chm IPA Soc 1987-88, chm courses III and IV, memb various ctees incl Effectiveness Awards Ctee; MIPA 1986; *Recreations* Glasgow, advertising, tennis, swimming, cycling; *Style*— Mark Robinson, Esq; Horner Collis & Kirvan, 11 Great Newport St, London WC2H 7JA (☎ 071 379 0631, fax 071 465 0552)

ROBINSON, Mark Noel Foster; s of John Foster Robinson, CBE, DL (d 1988), and Margaret Eva Hannah, *née* Paterson (d 1977); *b* 26 Dec 1946; *Educ* Harrow, ChCh Oxford (MA); *m* 1982, Vivien Radclyffe, da of Alan Roger Douglas Pilkington (d 1968); 1 s (James b 1986), 1 da (Alice b 1983); *Career* barr Middle Temple; UN Office 1972-77, exec office of UN Sec Gen as second offr 1975-77, asst dir Dip Staff Cwlth Secretariat 1977-83, MP (C) Newport W 1983-87, PPS to Rt Hon Nicholas Edwards, MP (Welsh sec) 1984-85, Parly under sec of state Welsh Office 1985-87; dir Leopold Joseph & Sons Ltd 1988-, memb Bd Cwlth Devpt Corp 1988-; fell Indust and Parl Tst; memb: RIIA, RUSI; FBIM, FRSA; *Recreations* fishing, country pursuits; *Clubs* Travellers'; *Style*— Mark Robinson, Esq; 33 Clarendon Rd, London, W11 4JB

ROBINSON, Air Vice-Marshal Michael Maurice Jeffries; CB (1982); s of Dr Maurice Robinson (d 1983), and Muriel Maud, *née* Jeffries (d 1981); *b* 11 Feb 1927;

Educ Kings Sch Bruton, Queen's Coll Oxford, RAF Coll Cranwell; *m* 19 April 1952, Drusilla Dallas, da of Dr Harry Julius Bush (d 1962); 1 s (Ian), 2 da (Jennie, Sarah); *Career* Cdr RAF Lossiemouth 1972-74, Asst Cmdt RAF Coll Cranwell 1974-77, sr air SO HQ No 1 Gp 1977-79, dir gen Orgn (RAF) MOD (Air) 1979-82; chm Housing Assoc for Offrs' Families; govr: King's Sch Bruton, Duke of Kent Sch (RAF Benevolent Fund) Ewhurst, Gordons Sch Woking; *Recreations* golf, gardening, going to the opera; *Clubs* RAF; *Style—* Air Vice-Marshal Michael Robinson, CB

ROBINSON, Michael Perkin; OBE (1984), TD (1948), DL (1971); s of Cecil Hall Robinson (d 1949), and Doris Mary Robinson (d 1973); *b* 12 April 1919; *Educ* Stowe; *m* 22 June 1946, Barbara Helen, da of Dr Cecil Ernest Clay (d 1962); 3 da (Shirley Rozanne (Mrs Stephen), Jennifer Jane Brionry (Mrs Hill), Alexandra Clare); *Career* Col, Dep Bde Cdr 146 Bde TA; pres Newspaper Soc 1968-69, chm Yorkshire Weekly Newspaper Group Ltd; Hon Col 5 LI 1982-85; *Recreations* golf, fishing, photography; *Style—* Michael Robinson, Esq, OBE, TD, DL; Carleton Lodge, Carleton, Pontefract, W Yorks (☎ 0977 703 818)

ROBINSON, Ven Neil; s of James Neesom Robinson (d 1972), and Alice Carter, *née* Harness (d 1976); *b* 28 Feb 1929; *Educ* Penistone GS, St John's Coll Durham (BA, Dip Theol); *m* 3 April 1956, Kathlyn, da of Thomas Williams (d 1951); 2 s (Peter b 1957, John b 1965), 2 da (Anne b 1958, Susan b 1962); *Career* Nat Serv RA 1947-49; curate and precentor of Holy Trinity Hull 1954- 58, vicar of Glen Parva with S Wigston Leicester 1958-69, hon canon of Leicester Cathedral 1968-83, rector and rural dean Market Bosworth 1969-83, residentiary canon of Worcester Cathedral 1983-87, archdeacon of Suffolk 1987-; chaplain of Hereford and Worcester CC; chm: Worcester Trg Centre, Suffolk Clergy Charity, Church Men in the Midlands; *Recreations* hill walking; *Style—* The Ven the Archdeacon of Suffolk; 38 Saxmundham Rd, Aldeburgh, Suffolk OP15 5JE

ROBINSON, Nicholas Ambrose Eldred; s of late Gerard Robinson; *b* 26 July 1941; *Educ* Birkenhead Sch; *m* 1977, Annie Georgette Gabrielle, *née* Barada; 2 s, 2 da; *Career* chartered surveyor; ptnr Eddisons (Leeds), dir Bradford Property Trust plc; FRICS, ACIArb; *Recreations* sailing; *Clubs* Bradford; *Style—* Nicholas Robinson, Esq; 6 Strayside Mews, 2 Leeds Rd, Harrogate HG2 8AA; (☎ 0423 502 530)

ROBINSON, Nicholas Ridley; s of Capt Leslie Jack Robinson, JP, of 15 Gainsborough Court, College Rd, Dulwich, and Eileen Mary, *née* Phillips; *b* 2 Sept 1952; *Educ* Dulwich; *m* 1, 26 May 1976 (m dis 1980), Vivienna; m 2, Joanna Mary, da of Wilford Henry Gibson, CBE, of 3 Blenheim Gardens, Sanderstead, Surrey; 2 s (Stuart Lawrence Ridley b 9 May 1984, Duncan Henry b 18 Aug 1987), 1 da (Felicity Mary b 1 April 1990); *Career* admitted slr 1977; sr ptnr Sandoms 1988 (ptnr 1978); hon sec Vauxhall League; co sec The Isthmian Football League Ltd; dir Dulwich Coll Mission; Freeman: City of London, Worshipful Co of Slrs, Worshipful Co of Farriers; memb Law Soc 1977; *Recreations* horse racing, football; *Clubs* RAC; *Style—* Nicholas Robinson, Esq; 226 Rye Lane, Peckham, London SE15 4NL (☎ 071 639 5726, fax 071 358 1108, home fax 071 653 4344 car 0836 241666)

ROBINSON, Nick; s of John Robinson, and Barbara Robinson; *b* 7 April 1947; *Educ* Wadham Coll Oxford (open scholar, MA); *m* 1986, Janice; 1 da (Elizabeth b 23 Nov 1989); *Career* dir Hicks Oubridge Public Affairs Ltd 1970-72, PR mangr Cooperative Wholesale Society 1972-74, PR mangr Manpower Ltd 1974-79, chm Datanews Ltd 1979-90, chm The Marketing Guild 1990-; hon ed Strategic Marketing magazine, fndr faculty dir in PR Inst of Mktg 1982-84; memb Br Assoc of Industl Editors 1976, MIPR 1984; *Books* The Marketing Toolkit (1988), Persuasive Business Presentations (1989), Strategic Customer Care (1991); *Style—* Nick Robinson, Esq; The Marketing Guild Ltd, Exchange House, 494 Midsummer Boulevard, Milton Keynes MK9 2EA (☎ 0908 672087, fax 0582 864913)

ROBINSON, Col Nigel George Douglass; MBE (1980); s of Maj G W Robinson (d 1988), of 1 Roseworth Terrace, Gosforth, Tyne and Wear, and Margaret, *née* Douglass; *b* 7 March 1940; *Educ* Newcastle Royal GS; *m* 28 July 1967, Patricia Greta, *née* Jackson; 1 s (Andrew Mark Edward b 26 Jan 1969), 1 da (Helen Victoria b 5 May 1971); *Career* cmmnd Royal Northumberland Fusiliers 1961, CO 1 Bn The Royal Regt of Fusiliers 1980-82, COS Army Staff Coll Camberley 1983-85 (DS 1983-85), Col PB2 MOD 1988-; FBIM 1988; *Recreations* rugby football, reading, walking; *Clubs* Army and Navy; *Style—* Col Nigel Robinson; MOD PB2, Government Buildings, Stanmore, Middlesex (☎ 081 958 6377 ext 3201)

ROBINSON, HE Paul Heron; Jr; s of Paul Heron Robinson, of Hinsdale, Illinois; *b* 22 June 1930 *Educ* Univ of Illinois Coll of Commerce and Business Admin (BD); *m* 1953, Martha Courtney, da of Edgar Merritt Bidwell (d 1967); 1 da; *Career* serv 1953-55 Korea as Lt USNR, Active Naval Res 1955-61; fndr and pres Robinson Inc 1960, Robinson Admin Servs Inc 1971, Robinson Coulter (London) 1972, Robinson Thomson (NZ) 1980, Robinson Thomson (Aust) 1980; US ambass to Canada 1981-; *Recreations* ranching, riding, sailing, history; *Clubs* Chicago, Shoreacres (Illinois), Capitol Hill, Army-Navy (both Washington DC), Mount Royal (Montreal); *Style—* HE Mr Paul Heron Robinson, Jr; US Embassy, 100 Wellington St, Ottawa, Ontario, Canada K1P 5T1 (☎ 613 238 5335)

ROBINSON, (Kenneth) Paul; s of John Robert Robinson (d 1965), of Skegness, Lincs, and Gertrude, *née* Major (d 1972); *b* 5 Feb 1925; *Educ* Skegness GS, Univ of Durham (BSc); *m* 30 June 1951, Helen Elizabeth, da of George McKissock (d 1980); 5 s (Ian Paul b 1957, Douglas Stewart b 1959, Nicholas Duncan b 1962, Andrew Simon b 1965, Robin Neil b 1966); *Career* GEC England: joined 1950, divnl mangr of Applied Electronics Laboratories 1960, gen mangr GEC Road Signals 1964; Plessey 1966, gen mangr Plessey Controls, Marconi Space and Def Systems 1973, gen mangr Frimley Unit 1974-81; md: Marconi Communications Systems Ltd 1984, Marconi Command and Control Systems Ltd 1984-; asst md: GEC Marconi Co 1986-89, GEC Marconi (Projects) 1989-; CEng, FIEE, FInstP; *Recreations* golf, swimming, DIY; *Clubs* Inst of Directors, Royal Cwlth Soc; *Style—* Paul Robinson, Esq; Frenchmans, 33 High St, Odiham, Basingstoke, Hants

ROBINSON, Peter Damian; CB (1983); s of John Robinson (d 1957), and Florence Eleanor, *née* Easten (later Mrs Clegg, d 1972); *b* 11 July 1926; *Educ* Corby Sch Sunderland, Lincoln Coll Oxford (MA); *m* 1, 1956, Mary Katinka (d 1978), da of Dr William Percy Bonner (d 1960), of Peterborough; 2 da; m 2, 1985, Sheila Suzanne Gibbins, da of Charles Gorguet Guille (d 1966), of Finchley, London; *Career* RM Commandos 1944-46; barr Middle Temple 1951, Common Law Bar 1952-59, clerk of Assize NE circuit 1959-70, admin NE circuit 1970-74, SE circuit 1974-80, dep sec Lord Chllr's Dept 1980-, dep clerk of the Crown in Chancery 1982-86, int consIt in judicial admin 1987-; *Recreations* books, walking, theatre, music, travel; *Clubs* Athenaeum; *Style—* Peter Robinson, Esq, CB; 6 Morpeth Mansions, Morpeth Terr, London SW1

ROBINSON, Peter David; MP (UDUP) Belfast E 1979-; s of David and Sheliah Robinson; *b* 29 Dec 1948; *Educ* Annadale GS, Castlereagh Coll of Further Educn; *m* 1979, Iris Collins; 2 s, 1 da; *Career* gen sec UDUP 1975-79 (dep ldr 1980-); memb NI Assembly 1982-; alderman Castlereagh Boro Cncl 1977-; *Style—* Peter Robinson Esq, MP; 51 Gransha Rd, Dundonald, Belfast (☎ 0232 56418)

ROBINSON, Peter Frank; s and h of Sir Wilfred Robinson, 3rd Bt, *qv*; *b* 23 June 1949; *Style—* Peter Robinson, Esq; 9 Bingham St, London N1

ROBINSON, Prof Peter Michael; s of Maurice Allan Robinson, and Brenda Margaret, *née* Ponsford; *b* 20 April 1947; *Educ* Brockenhurst GS, UCL (BSc), LSE (MSc), Australian Nat Univ (PhD); *m* 27 Feb 1981, Wendy Rhea, da of Morris Brandmark; 1 da; *Career* lectr LSE 1969-70; assoc prof: Harvard Univ 1977-79 (asst prof 1973-77), Univ of Br Columbia 1979-80; prof Univ of Surrey 1980-84, prof of econometrics LSE 1984-; author of numerous articles in learned jls and books, memb editorial bds of various jls; jt ed: Econometric Theory 1989-91, Econometrica 1991-; fell Econometric Soc; *Books* Econometric Theory 1989-91 (co ed), Econometrica (co ed, 1991); *Recreations* walking; *Style—* Prof Peter M Robinson; Dept of Economics, London Sch of Economics, Houghton St, London WC2A 2AE (☎ 071 955 7516)

ROBINSON, Prof (William) Peter; s of John Robinson (d 1955), of Chichester, Sussex, and Winifred Jenny, *née* Napper (d 1975); *b* 8 May 1933; *Educ* Christs Hosp, BNC Oxford (MA, DPhil); *m* 21 Sept 1973, Elizabeth Joan, da of Peter Peill (d 1973), of Duffield, Derbyshire; 2 da (Katherine b 1975, Clare b 1977); *Career* Intelligence Corps 1 Lt 1952-54; lectr in psychology Univ of Hull 1961-65, sr res offr Inst of Educn London 1965-66, reader in psychology Univ of Southampton 1966-73, prof of educn Macquarie Univ Aust 1974-77, prof of social psychology Univ of Bristol 1988- (prof of educn, dir Overseas Studies Centre, and dean of faculty 1977-88); memb: Econ and Social Res Cncl, Psychology Ctee Educn and Human Devpt Ctee; tstee Coll of St Paul and St Mary Cheltenham, govr Redmaids Sch Bristol, chm Deaf Studies Tst Bristol; hon prof Inst Superior de Psicologia Aplicada Lisbon; FBPsS; *Books* Language and Social Behaviour (1972), A Question of Answers (1972), Language Management in Education (1978), Communication in Development (1981), Handbook of Language and Social Psychology (1990); *Recreations* squash, badminton, travel; *Style—* Prof Peter Robinson; Dept of Psychology, University of Bristol, Bristol BS8 1HH (☎ 0272 303030, telex 445938, fax 0272 251537)

ROBINSON, (Henry) Richard Gwynne; s of Dr Henry Robinson, JP, DL (d 1960), and Margaret, *née* Barnes (d 1963); *b* 25 Oct 1916; *Educ* Radley; *m* 10 Jan 1959, Rose Mary, da of Col Leslie Herbert Queripel, CMG, DSO (d 1962), of Tunbridge Wells; 2 s (David b 1964, Philip b 1965); *Career* Gunner HAC TA 1939, HAC and RA 1939-46, Maj 1945, instr in gunnery; Prudential Assurance Co Ltd 1934-67; Lawn Tennis Assoc: cncl memb 1954, chm 1973, vice-pres 1974, hon life vice-pres 1987; Sports Cncl: memb 1979-88, memb governing bodies of sport consultative gp 1989-; Central Cncl of Physical Recreation: rep memb 1973, memb exec ctee 1979-, chm major spectator sports div 1983-; ctee memb: Wimbledon Championships 1972-87, Wimbledon Lawn Tennis Museum 1975-; Kent Co Lawn Tennis Assoc: memb cncl 1950, hon sec 1953, jt hon sec 1967, vice pres 1977-89, life vice pres 1990-; ctee memb: Tunbridge Wells Lawn Tennis Club 1947-65 (chm 1962-65), Tunbridge Wells Lawn Tennis Tournament 1948-85 (chm 1956-59 and 1967-85); memb HAC 1939, Freeman City of London 1946, Liveryman Worshipful Co of Skinners 1946; FCII 1950; *Recreations* lawn tennis, squash rackets, shooting, sports administration; *Clubs* All England Lawn Tennis & Croquet; *Style—* Richard Robinson, Esq; Long View, Limes Lane, Buxted, nr Uckfield, E Sussex TN22 4PB (☎ 082581 2551)

ROBINSON, Robert Henry; s of Ernest Redfern Robinson (d 1962), and Johanna Hogan (d 1978); *b* 17 Dec 1927; *Educ* Raynes Park GS, Exeter Coll Oxford (MA); *m* 1958, Josephine Mary, da of Paul Richard; 1 s (Nicholas), 2 da (Lucy, Suzy); *Career* writer and broadcaster; *Books* Landscape with Dead Dons (1956), Inside Robert Robinson (1965), The Conspiracy (1968), The Dog Chairman (1982), The Everyman Book of Light Verse (1984), Bad Dreams (1989), Prescriptions of a Pox Doctor's Clerk (1990); *Clubs* Garrick; *Style—* Robert Robinson, Esq; 16 Cheyne Row, London SW3; Laurel Cottage, Buckland St Mary, Somerset

ROBINSON, Prof Roger James; s of Albert Edward Robinson, of Axmouth, Devon, and Leonora Sarah, *née* Potts; *b* 17 May 1932; *Educ* Poole GS, Balliol Coll Oxford (BA, MA, DPhil, BM, BCh); *m* 1962, Jane Hippisley, da of John Douglas Packham (d 1941); 2 s (Andrew b 1964, James b 1971), 1 da (Sarah b 1965); *Career* lectr ChCh Oxford 1953-56; med appts 1960-67: Radcliffe Infirmary, Hammersmith Hosp, Nat Hosp Queen Square; sr lectr Inst Child Health 1967-71, conslt paediatrician Guy's Hosp 1971-75, Ferdinand James de Rothschild prof of paediatrics Guy's Hosp Med Sch (now Guy's and St Thomas's) 1975-90, emeritus prof of paediatrics Univ of London 1990-; FRCP 1975; *Books* Medical Care of Newborn Babies (jtly, 1972); *Recreations* walking, canoeing, literature; *Clubs* RSM; *Style—* Prof Roger Robinson; Guy's Hospital, London SE1 9RT (☎ 071 955 4019)

ROBINSON, Prof Ronald Edward; CBE (1971), DFC (1944); s of William Edward Robinson (d 1969), and Ada Teresa, *née* Goldsmith; *b* 3 Sept 1920; *Educ* Battersea GS, St John's Coll Cambridge (BA, MA, PhD); *m* 14 Aug 1948, Alice Josephine, da of Ludwell Howard Denny (d 1976), of Washington DC; 2 s (Peter Denny b 1950, Mark David Ludwell b 1958), 2 da (Alice Star Teresa b 1951, Kristin Day b 1954); *Career* res offr African Div Colonial Office 1947-49, fell St John's Coll Cambridge 1948-71 (res fell 1948-51); Cambridge Univ: lectr hist 1951-66, Smuts reader Cwlth Studies 1966-71; visiting fell Inst Advanced Studies Princeton 1959-61, Beit prof hist of Br Empire and Cwlth Oxford Univ 1971-87, emeritus prof and fell Balliol Coll 1987, visiting Cline prof of Br history Texas 1990; FRCSoc; *Books* Developing The Third World (1971), Africa and The Victorians (2 edn 1981) Bismarck, Europe and Africa (1988), Railway Imperialism (1991); *Recreations* room cricket; *Clubs* Hawks, Gridiron; *Style—* Prof Ronald Robinson, CBE, DFC; 79 Mill Rd, Cambridge (☎ 0223 357 063); Balliol College, Oxford

ROBINSON, Sheriff Stanley Scott; MBE (1944), TD (1953); s of William Scott Robinson (d 1962), of Edinburgh, and Christina Douglas, *née* Wallace (d 1989); *b* 27 March 1913; *Educ* Boroughmuir Sch Edinburgh, Univ of Edinburgh (BL); *m* 14 April 1937, Helen Annan, da of late John Hardie, of Edinburgh; 3 s (Derek John Scott b 1938, Alastair Stanley Scott b 1942, Ian George Scott b 1951); *Career* RA (TA): cmmnd 2 Lt 1935, Lt-Col 1945, ret 1953; served WWII in France 1939-40, France and Germany 1944-45 (despatches twice); admitted slr 1935, slr Supreme Cts 1962; Sheriff of Grampian Highlands and Is 1972 (ret 1985), Hon Sheriff of Inverness 1985-; Hon Sheriff of Forfarshire, vice-pres Law Soc Scot 1969-72, former dean Faculty of Slrs Slrs of Forfarshire (now Angus), govr Eden Ct Theatre Inverness; chm: Highland Club Inverness, formerly chm Regnl Advsy Ctee Forestry Cmmn (Highland); memb Soc of Slrs in Supreme Ct 1962; *Books* The Law of Interdict in Scotland (1987), Stair Encyclopedia of Laws of Scotland (contrib on law of crofting, law of railways and canals, law of game, 1987), Law of Game, Salmon and Freshwater Fishing (1990); *Recreations* bowling, caravanning; *Clubs* Highland (Inverness); *Style—* Sheriff Stanley Scott Robinson, MBE, TD; Drumalin House, 16 Drummond Rd, Inverness IV2 4NB (☎ 0463 233488)

ROBINSON, Hon Mrs (Stella Hope); 2 da of Hon Claude Hope-Morley (d 1968), and sis of 3 Baron Hollenden; raised to the rank of a Baron's da; *b* 15 April 1919; *m* 21 Oct 1950, Neville Whiteoak Robinson, yr s of late David Whiteoak; 2 s, 1 da; *Career* 1939-45 WWII as 2 Offr WRNS; *Style—* The Hon Mrs Robinson; 107 Old Church St, Chelsea, London SW3 6DX

ROBINSON, Stephen Joseph; OBE (1971); s of Joseph Alan Robinson, of Leicester, and Ethel Bunting (d 1962); *b* 6 Aug 1931; *Educ* Sebright Sch, Univ of Cambridge (MA), Harvard Business Sch; *m* 13 April 1957, Monica Mabs, da of John Scott (d

1986); 1 da (Marion Jean b 1961), 1 s (Peter Joseph b 1962); *Career* Pilot Offr RAF 1950; Mullard Research Lab 1954-71, MEL Equipment Ltd 1971-79, product dir MEL Bd 1973, md Pye TVT Ltd 1980-84, dir Royal Signals and Radar Establishment MOD 1989-; S G Brown Medal 1972; FRS, FEng, FIEE; *Recreations* saling, skiing, walking; *Style*— Stephen Robinson, Esq, OBE, FRS; Royal Signals and Radar Establishment, St Andrews Rd, Great Malvern (☎ 0684 894 345)

ROBINSON, Rev Thomas Hugh (Tom); CBE (1989); s of Lt Col James Arthur Robinson, OBE (d 1944), and Maud Loney, *née* Trayer (d 1980); *b* 11 June 1934; *Educ* Bishop Foy Sch Waterford, Trinity Coll Dublin (BA, MA); *m* 9 July 1959, Mary Elizabeth Doreen, da of Richard Edmund Clingan (d 1988), of Portadown; 2 s (Peter b 1962, Keith b 1964), 1 da (Kathryn b 1967); *Career* cmmnd Royal Army Chaplains' Dept 1966, dep asst chaplain gen 2 Armd Div 1977-80, chaplain RMCS 1980-82; sr chaplain: Eastern Dist 1982-84, 1 Br Corps 1984-85, BAOR 1985-86; dep chaplain gen 1986-89, team rector Cleethorpes 1990-; ordained: deacon 1957, priest 1958; curate asst St Clements Belfast 1957-60, chaplain Missions to Seamen Mombasa 1961-64, rector St Mary's Youghal Co Cork 1964-66; *Recreations* winemaking, social golf; *Style*— The Rev Tom Robinson, CBE; St Peters Rectory, 42 Queens Parade, Cleethorpes, S Humberside DN35 0DG (☎ 0472 693234)

ROBINSON, (Robert) Timothy (Tim); s of Eddy Robinson and Christine Verley; *b* 21 Nov 1958; *Educ* Dunstable GS, High Pavement Coll, Univ of Sheffield (BA); *Career* professional cricketer; memb: England Team, Nottinghamshire CCC (Capt), Mike Gatting's team to SA; *Style*— Tim Robinson, Esq; Nottinghamshire CCC, County Ground, Trent Bridge, Nottingham

ROBINSON, Timothy Morgan; s of Kenneth Hubert Robinson (d 1983), of Porthcawl, S Wales, and Winfred Glenice Mary, *née* Rees; *b* 17 May 1944; *Educ* Taunton Sch; *m* 8 May 1982, (Caroline Jane) Binna, da of Alexander Nicol, of Badgeworth, Glos; 4 s (Tom b 1977, Toby b 1978, Edward b 1986, Charlie b 1989), 1 da (Holly b 1984); *Career* admitted slr 1968; sr lectr in law Gloucester Coll 1971-72, pt/t immigration act judge 1973-76, sr ptnr Robinsons (criminal law specialists) 1976-; chief exec: Robinsons Law Servs 1980, Bristol Law Servs Ltd 1985; memb: Cheltenham Round Table 1978-, Glos and Dist Rugby Referees Soc; co rugby referee, Wales schs rugby cap; memb Law Soc 1968; *Recreations* rugby football, making money, family life; *Style*— Timothy Robinson, Esq; The Old Vicarage, Badgeworth, Glos (☎ 0452 712 660); Hesters Chambers, Edinburgh Place, Cheltenham Spa, Glos (☎ 0242 520530, fax 0242 222247, car 0860 742478)

ROBINSON, (Walter) Trevor; TD (1956); s of Joseph Robinson (d 1969), of Sheffield, and Nellie, *née* Briggs (d 1977); *b* 2 Sept 1925; *Educ* City GS Sheffield; *m* 6 Sept 1947, Olive, da of Frederick Richer (d 1942), of Sheffield; 2 s (Michael b 1950, Anthony b 1954); *Career* Capt York and Lancaster Regt 1943-47; gen mangr Nat West Bank (formerly Westminster Bank) 1969-73 (joined 1941), chief exec Texas Commerce Bank Int 1973-75, gen mangr Midland and Int Banks Ltd 1975-78, exec vice pres Manufacturers Hanover Tst Co 1978-86, dir TSB Bank plc 1986-90; chm Five Oaks Investments plc; dir: Nat Grid Co plc, Republic Nat Bank of NY (UK) Ltd; Freeman City of London 1974; FCIB; *Recreations* banking; *Style*— Trevor Robinson, Esq, TD; 30 Monument Street, London EC3R 8NB (☎ 071 409 2426, fax 071 623 2866, telex 889 217, car 0860 344218)

ROBINSON, Dr Trevor Walter Ernest; s of Sir Harold Ernest Robinson (d 1979), of Trinidad, W Indies, and Lady Clarice Graeme Robinson, *née* Yearwood (d 1989); *b* 9 Jan 1932; *Educ* Lodge Sch Barbados, Stowe, Univ of Cambridge (MA, MB BChir, MRCP); *m* 1, 27 April 1963 (m dis 1975), Jean Ewen, da of George Barbour, of India; 1 da (Karen b 19 Aug 1967); m 2, Angela Judith Keeble, *née* Hole; 1 da (Kate b 25 Feb 1985); *Career* RMO and SHO Inst of Dermatology London 1960-61, sr dermatological registrar St Bartholomew's Hosp 1962-67 (registrar), res fell in dermatology Scripps Clinic and Res Fndn La Jolla California USA 1968-69, conslt dermatologist UCH 1969-(lectr 1969-), conslt Middx Hosp 1986- (Edgware Hosp 1971-); memb Dowling Club, fell and pres St John's Dermatological Soc 1988-89, memb Nat Health and Med Res Cncl of Aust Panel of Independent Assessors for Project Grants; FRSM, FRCP 1975; *Books* Virus Diseases and the Skin (1983), Herpes Simplex in Practical Management of the Dermatologic Patient (1986); *Recreations* gardening, deep sea fishing, poetry, painting; *Clubs* RSM; *Style*— Dr Trevor Robinson; 18 Upper Wimpole St, London W1M 7TB (☎ 071 387 2160, 071 487 3393)

ROBINSON, Victor Philip; s of Francis Herbert Robinson (d 1962), and Constance Harriet, *née* Phillips (d 1975); *b* 26 Nov 1943; *Educ* Cranleigh Sch Surrey, St Mary's Hosp Med Sch (MB, BS); *m* 30 Oct 1965, Elizabeth Margaret, da of Lt Cdr Kenneth Thomas Basset, of Hareston Manor, Brixton, Devon (d 1989); 4 da ((Anne) Michelle b 30 Aug 1966, Louise Frances b 27 Aug 1969, Charlotte Faye b 31 Jan 1972, Victoria Jane b 29 Aug 1974); *Career* conslt obstetrician and gynaecologist: Queen Charlotte's Maternity Hosp, St George's Hosp Med Sch, Hillingdon and Mount Vernon Hosps, Hillingdon Health Authy, Harefield Hosp 1982-; obstetrician reponsible for the care of known pregnancies following heart and lung transplantations (presentation to World Congress); memb Sailing Tst; memb: RSM, BMA, BfS, RCOG; *Clubs* Ocean Youth; *Style*— Victor Robinson, Esq; Hillingdon Hospital, Uxbridge, Middx UB8 3NN

ROBINSON, Vivian; QC (1986); s of William Robinson (d 1986), of Wakefield, and Ann, *née* Kidd; *b* 29 July 1944; *Educ* Queen Elizabeth GS Wakefield, The Leys Sch Cambridge, Sidney Sussex Coll Cambridge (BA); *m* 19 April 1975, (Nora) Louise, da of Maj Peter Duncan Marriner, TD (d 1988), of Rayleigh; 1 s (Edward Duncan b 30 Jan 1980), 2 da (Katherine Anne b 12 Sept 1977, Anna Ruth b 12 July 1981); *Career* called to the Bar Inner Temple 1967; rec Crown Court 1986-; Liveryman and memb Court Assistants Worshipful Co of Gardeners; *Recreations* gardening, reading; *Style*— Vivian Robinson, Esq, QC; Queen Elizabeth Building, Temple, London EC4Y 9BS (☎ 071 583 5766, fax 071 353 0339)

ROBINSON, Hon Mrs Richard; Wendy Patricia; da of James Cecil Blagden (d 1973), of Bapchild Court, nr Sittingbourne, Kent, and Audrey Cecily Yeatman, *née* Small; *b* 3 Feb 1939; *m* 1959, Hon Richard Anthony Gasque Robinson (d 1979), s of 1 Baron Martonmere, GBE, KCMG, PC; 2 s (2 Baron Martonmere, *qv*, David Alan b 1965), 1 da (Carolyn Elizabeth b 1969); *Career* dir Heart and Stroke Fndn of Ontario, several private Corpns and Cos; *Style*— The Hon Mrs Richard Robinson; 382 Russell Hill Rd, Toronto, Ontario, Canada M4V 2V2 (☎ 416 485 3077)

ROBINSON, Sir Wilfred Henry Frederick; 3 Bt (UK 1908), of Hawthornden, Wynberg, Cape Province, S Africa, and Dudley House, City of Westminster; s of late Wilfred Henry Robinson (3 s of 1 Bt), and late Eileen, *née* St Leger; suc unc, Sir Joseph Benjamin Robinson 1954; *b* 24 Dec 1917; *Educ* Diocesan Coll Rondesbosch, St John's Coll Cambridge; *m* 1946, Margaret Alison Kathleen, da of late Frank Mellish, MC, of Rondebosch, Cape, S Africa; 1 s, 2 da; *Heir* s, Peter Robinson; *Career* former Maj Para Regt; vice-princ of Diocesan Coll Sch Rondebosch Cape S Africa; fin offr Soc of Genealogists; *Style*— Sir Wilfred Robinson, Bt; Society of Genealogists, 14 Charterhouse Bldgs, London EC1M 7BA; 24 Ennismore Gdns, London SW7 1AB

ROBJANT, Peter; s of Roland Walter Donald Robjant (d 1961), and Kathleen Elizabeth Florence, *née* Hagger; *b* 31 May 1942; *Educ* Buckhurst Hill Co HS, St Catherines Coll Cambridge (MA, LLM); *m* 14 Aug 1971, Jean Sheila, da of Maj Allan Forbes Malcolmson (d 1985); 1 s (David Allan b 1973), 1 da (Mary b 1975); *Career* articled clerk Church Adams Tatham & Co 1966-68, asst slr Wild Hewitson & Shaw 1968-71, ptnr Sylvester & Mackett 1972- (asst slr 1971-72), chm W Wilts CAB 1983-88 (memb Legal Servs Gp NACAB); memb Law Soc; *Recreations* walking; *Style*— Peter Robjant, Esq; 32 Hilperton Rd, Trowbridge, Wilts; 39 Castle St, Nether Stowey, Bridgwater, Somerset (☎ 0225 765 903); Sylvester & Mackett, Castle House, Trowbridge, Wilts BA14 8AX (☎ 0225 755 621, fax 0225 769 055, telex 444 258)

ROBOROUGH, 2 Baron (UK 1938); Sir Massey Henry Edgcumbe Lopes; 5 Bt (UK 1905), JP (Devon 1951); s of 1 Baron Roborough (d 1938), and Lady Albertha Edgcumbe, da of 4 Earl of Mount Edgcumbe, GCVO, PC, JP, DL, by his w Lady Katherine Hamilton, da of 1 Duke of Abercorn, KG; *b* 4 Oct 1903; *Educ* Eton, Ch Ch Oxford; *m* 1936, Helen, da of Lt-Col Edward Dawson, JP; 2 s (and 1 da decd); *Heir* s, Hon Henry Lopes; *Career* served Royal Scots Greys 1925-38 and 1939-45; DL Devon 1946, Vice Lieut 1951-58, Lord Lieut 1958-78, high steward Barnstaple, county alderman Devon 1956-74; chm: SW Devon Div Educn Exec 1952-74, Dartmoor Nat Park 1965-74, Devon Outward Bound Sch; ADC to Earl of Clarendon as Govr-Gen Union of S Africa 1936-37; memb Duchy of Cornwall Cncl 1958-68; Hon Col Devon Army Cadet Force 1967-78; KStJ; *Style*— The Rt Hon the Lord Roborough, JP; Seat: Maristow, Roborough, S Devon; Residence: Bickham Barton, Roborough, S Devon (☎ Yelverton 2478)

ROBOTHAM, (John) Michael; s of Alpheus John Robotham, OBE, JP, DL, of Quarndon, Derby, and Gwendolyn Constance, *née* Bromet; *b* 27 March 1933; *Educ* Clifton; *m* 29 June 1963 (m dis 1989), Diana Elizabeth, da of Alfred Thomas Webb (d 1967); 2 s (Guy Thomas Blews b 1967, Adam John Blews b 1971 d 1982); m 2 1990, Victoria Mary Cronje, da of Victor St Claus Yates; *Career* 2 Lt 12 Royal Lancers 1957-59; memb Stock Exchange 1963; dir: Western Selection plc 1969-, The Kwahu Co plc 1970-, Creston plc 1976-, NMC Investment Group 1976-, Afex Corporation plc 1983-, London Finance & Investment Co plc 1983-; chm Inst of Advanced Motorists 1989, chm Mile-Posts Publications 1975-; FCA, FIMBRA; *Recreations* tennis, shooting, skiing; *Clubs* Cavalry and Guards', HAC, City of London; *Style*— Michael Robotham, Esq; Brickwall Farm House, Clophill, Bedford MK45 4DA (☎ 0525 61333); J M Finn & Co, Salisbury House, London Wall, London EC2M 5TA (☎ 071 628 9688, fax 071 628 7314); City Group Ltd, 25 City Rd, London EC1X 1BQ (☎ 071 628 9371, fax 071 633 9426, car ☎ 0836 726960)

ROBOZ, Zsuzsi; da of Imre Roboz (d 1945), and Edith, *née* Grosz (d 1976); *b* 15 Aug 1939; *Educ* Royal Acad of Arts London; *m* 22 Jan 1964, (Alfred) Teddy Smith; *Career* solo exhibitions incl: Hong Kong Arts Festival 1976, Revudeville at the V&A 1978, Drawn to Ballet at the Royal Festival Hall 1983, Budapest Spring Festival 1985 and 1988, Music Makers at the Royal Festival Hall 1987, Lincoln Center New York 1989; protraits incl: Lord Olivier in the Theatre Museum, Dame Ninette de Valois in Nat Portrait Museum, Sir George Solti, Sir John Gielgud, Prince William of Gloucester in Barnwell Church; permanent collections incl: Tate Gallery London, Theatre Museum, V&A, Museum of Fine Arts Budapest, Pablo Casals Museum Puerto Rico, St John's Coll Cambridge, Royal Festival Hall London; memb Pastel Soc, FRSA; *Books* Women & Men's Daughters (1970), Chichester Ten, Portrait of a Decade (1975), British Ballet To-day (1980); *Recreations* music, swimming, reading; *Style*— Ms Zsuzsi Roboz; The Studio, 76 Eccleston Square Mews, London SW1 (☎ 071 834 4617)

ROBSON, Andrew Maxwell; s of Harry Robson (d 1977), and Maria Jenny Robson; *b* 11 April 1942; *Educ* St Peter's Sch York, Univ of Leeds (BSc); *m* 1 April 1967, Susan Jennifer, da of Guy Garside Davies, of Wybunbury, Nantwich, Cheshire; 2 s (Michael J b 1969, Guy A b 1972); *Career* Taylor Woodrow construction 1964-67, Ove Arup & Ptnrs (conslts) 1967-69, Dow Mac Concrete (precast concrete) 1969-72, chief engr Crendon Structures 1972-76, md and chm Turner Wright & Ptnrs (UK) Ltd 1988- (chief designer 1976-81, assoc ptnr 1981-87, dir 1987-88); memb Soc of American Mil Engrs 1981-, MInst D 1984- (branch sec 1982-84); MICE 1973; *Recreations* golf, bridge; *Clubs* IOD (Pall Mall), Henley Golf; *Style*— Andrew Robson, Esq; Turner Wright & Partners (UK) Ltd, Midland House, Buckingham St, Aylesbury, Bucks HP20 2LJ (☎ 0296 84151, fax 0296 84614)

ROBSON, Brian; s of Gilbert Brown Robson (d 1972), of Hexham, Northumberland, and Lily, *née* Robinson; *b* 3 Feb 1936; *Educ* Hexham Queen Elizabeth GS; *m* 1, Aug 1959 (m dis 1980), Christine Angela; 1 s (Dean Anthony b 5 April 1965), 1 da (Penelope Ann b 13 Jan 1963); m 2, Dec 1981, Esther; *Career* cricketer administrator; sec Nottinghamshire CCC 1982- (asst sec 1979-82); *Recreations* gardening, golf, squash; *Style*— Brian Robson, Esq; 18 Marl Rd, Radcliffe-on-Trent, Nottingham (☎ 0602 335807); Nottinghamshire CCC, Trent Bridge, Nottingham (☎ 0602 821525)

ROBSON, Prof Brian Turnbull; s of Oswell Robson (d 1973), and Doris Lowes, *née* Ayre (d 1984); *b* 23 Feb 1939; *Educ* RGS Newcastle, St Catharine's Coll Cambridge (MA, PhD); *m* 21 Dec 1973, Glenna, da of Jack Leslie Ransom, MBE, DCM, Croix de Guerre (d 1974); *Career* lectr Univ Coll of Wales Aberystwyth 1964-67, Harkness fellowship Univ of Chicago 1967-68, lectr Univ of Cambridge 1968-77, fell Fitzwilliam Coll Cambridge 1968-77, dean Faculty of Arts Univ of Manchester 1988- (prof of geography 1977-); chm Manchester Cncl for Voluntary Servs, vice pres Inst Br Geographers, memb Cncl Town and Country Planning Assoc; FRGS 1973; *Books* Urban Analysis (1969), Urban Growth (1973), Urban Social Areas (1975), Managing The City (1987), Those Inner Cities (1988); *Recreations* watercolour painting, gardening; *Style*— Prof Brian Robson; 32 Oaker Avenue, West Didsbury, Manchester M20 8XH (☎ 061 445 2036); La Ratiere, 82110 Lauzerte, Tarn et Garonne, France; Dept of Geography, University of Manchester, Manchester M13 9PL (☎ 061 275 3639, telex 666517 UNIMAN, fax 061 273 4407)

ROBSON, Bryan; OBE; s of Brian Jackson Robson, of 13 Pelaw Rd, S Pelaw, Chester-Le-Street, Co Durham, and Maureen, *née* Lowther; *b* 11 Jan 1957; *Educ* Birtley Lord Lawson Comp; *m* 2 June 1979, Denise Kathleen, da of George Brindley, of 18A Pages Lane, Gt Barr, Birmingham; 1 s (Ben b 2 Sept 1988), 2 da (Claire b 17 Sept 1980, Charlotte b 17 June 1982); *Career* footballer; 88 England caps (currently capt); Manchester United: FA Cup winners 1983, 1985 and 1990, Charity Shield winners 1983, currently capt; charity work with Wallness Hurdles and Adventure Farm; *Books* United I Stand (1984); *Style*— Bryan Robson, Esq, OBE

ROBSON, Christopher William; s of Leonard Robson (d 1970), of Egglescliffe, Cleveland, and Irene Beatrice, *née* Punch (d 1984); *b* 13 Aug 1936; *Educ* Rugby; *m* 17 July 1965, Susan Jane, da of Maj John Davey Cooke-Hurle (d 1979), of Startforth Hall, Barnard Castle, Co Durham; 1 s (Andrew Leonard Feilding b 1973), 2 da (Sarah Louise b 1966, Lydia Katharine b 1969); *Career* Nat Serv Lt RASC 1955-57; admitted slr 1962, sr ptnr Punch Robson Gilchrist Smith (formerly JWR Punch and Robson) 1971- (joined 1962); fell Woodard Schs (Northern Div) Ltd 1974-85, govr Aysgarth Sch N Yorks; memb: Law Soc, Br Astronomical Soc; *Recreations* astronomy, skiing, shooting, walking; *Style*— Christopher Robson, Esq; Rudd Hall, E Appleton, Richmond, N Yorks DL10 7QD (☎ 0748 811 339); 35 Albert Rd, Middlesbrough, Cleveland TS1 1NU (☎ 0642 230 700, fax 0642 218 923)

ROBSON, David Ernest Henry; QC (1980); s of Joseph Robson (d 1979), and Caroline, *née* Bowmaker; *b* 1 March 1940; *Educ* Robert Richardson GS Ryhope, ChCh Oxford (MA); *Career* called to the Bar Inner Temple 1965, memb NE circuit 1965, rec of the Crown Ct (NE circuit) 1979-, bencher Inner Temple 1988; pres Herrington Burn (Sunderland) YMCA 1986-, artistic dir Royalty Studio Theatre Sunderland 1986-88; *Recreations* acting, Italy; *Clubs* County Durham; *Style*— David Robson, Esq, QC; Whitton Grange, Rothbury, Northumberland NE65 7RL (☎ 0669 209 29); 3 Broad Chare, Quayside, Newcastle-upon-Tyne NE1 3DQ (☎ 091 232 2392)

ROBSON, Dr David John; s of Alan Victor Robson, TD, LDS, RCS (Edin), and Joan Dales, *née* Hawkins; *b* 23 Feb 1944; *Educ* Repton Sch, Middx Hosp Univ of London (MB BS); *Career* conslt physician Greenwich Health Authy 1978-; FRCP 1986; *Style*— Dr David Robson; Greenwich District Hospital, Vanbrugh Hill, London SE10 9HE (☎ 081 858 8141, fax 081 293 4030)

ROBSON, (William) David; s of (William) Michael Robson, of Hales Place, Tenterden, Kent, and Audrey Isobel Wales, *née* Dick (d 1964); *b* 28 Jan 1944; *Educ* Eton; *m* 27 Sept 1975, (Anne) Helen, da of Cecil Seymour Gosling (d 1974); 1 s ((William) Henry b 1979), 1 da (Emma Lucy b 1977); *Career* Lloyd's managing agent; dir Merrett Hldgs plc 1985-; Freeman of City of London, Liveryman Worshipful Co of Vintners; *Recreations* golf, opera; *Clubs* White's, Pratt's; *Style*— David Robson, Esq; The Woods, Hatfield Broad Oak, Bishops Stortford, Herts CM22 7BU (☎ 027970 452); Arthur Castle House, 33 Creechurch Lane, London EC3A 5AJ (☎ 071 283 3434)

ROBSON, Edward Stephen; s of John Arthur Robson (d 1931); *b* 15 July 1923; *Educ* Pitmans Coll Putney; *m* 1948, Joan Barbara; 1 s, 1 da; *Career* Warrant Offr RAF; md: Nickerson Fuel Oils Ltd, Nickerson Lubricants Ltd; dir: Nickerson Investments Ltd, Nickerson Transport Ltd 1971-; *Recreations* golf, cricket; *Clubs* Pathfinder, Albany Halifax, Sicklehome GC; *Style*— Edward Robson, Esq; Barnbrook, Hope, via Sheffield S30 2RA

ROBSON, Hon Mrs (Elizabeth); *née* Atkin; da of Baron Atkin Lord of Appeal (d 1944); *m* 1, 1932, John Kennedy Cockburn Millar (d 1952); m 2, 1960, His Hon Judge Denis Hicks Robson, QC (d 1983); *Career* called to the Bar Gray's Inn 1955; *Style*— The Hon Mrs Robson; Woodford, Dreemskerry, Isle of Man

ROBSON, Col Felix Guy; s of Guy Coburn Robson (d 1945), and Beryl Sinclair, *née* Nicholson; *b* 20 July 1921; *Educ* Merchant Taylors'; *m* 10 Aug 1954, Elizabeth Winifred, da of Cdr William Trinick, OBE, RD, RNR (d 1957); 2 s (Rupert b 1959, Angus b 1961); *Career* 2 Lt RA field branch 1941, Capt and Air Observer Pilot Italy 1944-46, 3 RHA 1947, Staff Coll Camberley PSC 1951, Mil Asst on Montgomery's Personal Staff Paris 1956, GSO2 Allied Forces Fontainebleau 1957-59, War Office 1961-62, Lt-Col Mil Attaché Br Embassy Cambodia 1964-66; Col Gen Staff: HQ BAOR 1970-73, HQ Allied Forces Central Euro 1973-76; ret 1976; corps secretary HQ Intelligence Corps 1978-86; village and church affrs, tstee of two local museums; memb RUSI 1962, MBIM 1973; *Books* Short History & Guide To Church Of St Mary Westwell (1988); *Recreations* country pursuits, military and local history; *Clubs* Naval; *Style*— Col Felix Robson; Dunn St Cottage, Pilgrims Way, Westwell, Ashford, Kent TN25 4NJ (☎ 023371 2521)

ROBSON, Dr Frank Elms; OBE (1991); s of Joseph Aisbitt Robson (d 1961), of Newbiggin-by-the-Sea, Northumberland, and Barbara, *née* Waters; *b* 14 Dec 1931; *Educ* King Edward VI GS Morpeth, Selwyn Coll Cambridge (MA), DCL (Lambeth) 1991; *m* 25 July 1958, Helen, da of Edward Challoner Jackson (d 1950), of Morpeth, Northumberland; 4 s (Aidan b 1960, Martin b 1963, Stephen b 1965, Jonathan b 1967), 1 da (Lorna b 1959); *Career* ptnr Winckworth & Pemberton 1960- (sr ptnr 1990-); registrar: Diocese of Oxford 1970, Province of Canterbury 1982; memb: Church Assembly 1960-70, Gen Synod 1970-75; *Recreations* supporting Oxford United, walking; *Style*— Dr Frank Robson, OBE; 2 Simms Close, Stanton St John, Oxford OX9 1HB (☎ 0865 735 393); 16 Beaumont St, Oxford (☎ 0865 241974)

ROBSON, (William) Frank; s of John William Robson (d 1956), and Mary, *née* Bradley (d 1981); *b* 27 Oct 1928; *Educ* St Aloysius Sch Newcastle upon Tyne; *m* 21 Sept 1957, Barbara Mary Hallwood; 3 da (Angela Mary b 28 July 1960, Susan Jennifer (twin) b 28 July 1960, Julia Charlotte b 19 June 1964); *Career* Nat Serv, able seaman RN 1947-49; journalist; reporter: Morpeth Herald 1949-51, and sub-ed Newcastle Evening Chronicle and Jl 1951-54, Sunderland Echo 1954-56; air corr Daily Express 1973-86 (joined 1956, dep def corr 1968-86), estab Aeronews London 1986, corr covering flight-testing of Concorde 001 prototype 1971, only newsman to accompany 002 prototype on world premiere demonstration tour 1972, author of Sunday Express Red Arrows special souvenir edn 1989; ARAeS 1986; *Clubs* Canterbury RFC; *Style*— Frank Robson, Esq; 12 Birchmead Avenue, Pinner, Middlesex HA5 2BG (☎ 081 866 4930, telex 94018381 AERO G)

ROBSON, Prof Sir (James) Gordon; CBE (1977); s of James Robson; *b* 18 March 1921; *Educ* Stirling HS, Univ of Glasgow; *m* 1, 1945, Dr Martha Kennedy (d 1975); 1 s; m 2, 1984, Jennifer Kilpatrick; *Career* prof of anaesthetics Royal Postgrad Med Sch Univ of London 1964-86, ret; hon conslt Hammersmith Hosp 1964-86, conslt advsr anaesthetics DHSS 1975-84; hon memb USA Assoc Univ Anaesthetists; memb: Physiological Soc, Cncl Assoc Anaesthetists of GB and Ireland 1973-84, Editorial Bd and consulting ed British Journal of Anaesthesia 1965-85; hon sec Conf of Med Royal Colls and Their Faculties in UK 1976-82; master Hunterian Inst RCS 1982-88, hon conslt in Anaesthetics to the Army 1983-87, chm Advsy Ctee on Distinction Awards 1984-; pres: Scottish Soc of Anaesthetists 1985-86, Royal Soc of Medicine 1986-88; memb Ctee of Automobile Assoc 1979-90; RNLI: memb Ctee of Mgmnt 1988-, chm Med and Survial Ctee 1988- (memb 1981); MB ChB, FRCS, FRSM, DSc McGill, FFARCS, Hon FFARACS, Hon FFARCSI, Hon FDSRCS; hon fell: Royal Coll of Physicians and Surgeons of Canada 1987, Royal Med Soc (Edinburgh) 1987; kt 1982; *Recreations* golf, wet fly fishing; *Clubs* Denham Golf, Council of Royal College of Surgeons; *Style*— Prof Sir Gordon Robson, CBE; Brendon, Lyndale, London NW2 2NY

ROBSON, Prof James Scott; s of William Scott Robson (d 1950), of Hawick, and Elizabeth Hannah, *née* Watt (d 1974); *b* 19 May 1921; *Educ* Hawick HS, Univ of Edinburgh (MB ChB, MD), New York Univ; *m* 2 March 1948, Mary Kynoch, da of Alexander Knight MacDonald (d 1960), of Perth; 2 s (Michael Knight b 1952, Christopher James b 1957); *Career* RAMC: Lt India 1945, Capt Palestine 1946, Egypt 1947-48, MO i/c Med Div BMH Suez; Rockefeller studentship NY 1942-44, Rockefeller res fell Harvard 1949-50; Univ of Edinburgh: sr lectr therapeutics 1959-60, reader therapeutics 1959-60 and 1961-68, reader med 1968-76, prof med 1977-86; contrib to numerous medical pubns; hon assoc prof med Harvard Univ 1962, visiting prof Merck Sharp & Dome Australia 1968; pres Renal Assoc London 1977-80, memb Biomedical Res Ctee SH & H Dept, chm Nat Med Consultative Ctee in Med, memb Ed Bd and dep ed chm Clinical Science; FRCPE 1948, hon memb Australasian Renal Assoc 1969, FRCP 1977; *Books* Companion to Medical Studies (co-ed, 1968-88); *Recreations* gardening, theatre, travel, reading; *Clubs* New (Edinburgh); *Style*— Prof James Robson; 1 Grant Ave, Edinburgh EH13 0DS (☎ 031 441 3508)

ROBSON, John Malcolm; s of Edward Stephen Robson (d 1989), and Joan Barbara, *née* Burchett; *b* 16 March 1952; *Educ* King's Coll Sch Wimbledon, Univ of London (LLB); *m* 22 July 1982, Jennifer Lillias, da of Bernard Seed, of Sutton, Surrey; 2 s (David, Aidan), 1 da (Lillias); *Career* called to the Bar Inner Temple 1974; *Recreations* swimming, ceramics, wines; *Style*— John Robson, Esq; 265 Fir Tree Rd, Epsom Downs, Surrey (☎ 0737 353834); 2 Gray's Inn Square, Gray's Inn, London WC1R 5AA (☎ 071 405 1317, fax 071 405 3082)

ROBSON, Rev John Phillips; s of Thomas Herbert Robson (d 1965), of Shenfield, Essex, and Nellie Julia, *née* Hilling (d 1984); *b* 22 July 1932; *Educ* Hele's Sch Exeter, Brentwood Sch Essex, St Edmund Hall Oxford (Liddon exhibitioner), King's Coll London (AKC); *Career* Nat Serv Br Mil Hosp Münster 1952-54; laboratory technician and med student Guy's Hosp London 1949-52; ordained priest Wakefield Cathedral 1960 (ordained deacon 1959), curate Huddersfield Parish Church 1959-62, asst chaplain and jr housemaster Christ's Hosp Horsham Sussex 1962-65 (sr chaplain, head of divinity and biology teacher 1965-80), sr chaplain Wellington Coll Berkshire 1980-89; chaplain: Queen's Chapel of the Savoy 1989-, Royal Victorian Order 1989-, Instn of Electrical Engineers, The Savoy Hotel, Actor's Church Union Vaudeville Theatre; memb West End/Central Police Community Consultative Group; *Recreations* golf, theatre, cinema, reading; *Clubs* Liphook Golf; *Style*— The Rev John Robson; The Queen's Chapel of the Savoy, Savoy Hill, Strand, London WC2R 0DA (☎ 071 379 8088)

ROBSON, John Robert; s of Maj William Michael Robson, of Hales Place, Tenterden, Kent, and Audrey Isabel, *née* Dick (d 1962); *b* 12 Jan 1947; *Educ* Eton; *m* 21 Jan 1969, Tessa Diana, da of Capt William J Straker-Smith, of Carham, Cornhill on Tweed, Northumberland; 1 s (James b 30 Oct 1975), 1 da (Claire b 2 Jan 1972); *Career* dir Merrett Holdings plc; chm: Merrett Syndicates Ltd, Anton Underwriting Agencies Ltd; underwriting memb Lloyds 1969, govr Wellesley House and St Peters Ct Sch; Freeman City of London 1977, Liveryman Worshipful Co of Vintners 1982; MRPS; *Recreations* sailing, golf, Zululand, philately; *Clubs* Pratts, Honourable Company Edinburgh Golfers, Rye Golf, Bembridge Sailing; *Style*— John Robson, Esq; Arthur Castle House, 33 Creechurch Lane, London EC3 5AJ (☎ 071 283 3434, fax 071 929 3995, car 0831 474 023, telex 885986)

ROBSON, Hon (Erik) Maurice William; s of Sir Lawrence William Robson (d 1982), and Baroness Robson of Kiddington (Life Peeress) (*qv*); *b* 1943; *Educ* Eton, Ch Ch Oxford; *m* 7 Sept 1985, Chloë Annabel, elder da of Richard Arthur Edwards, and Eileen Daphne, *née* Joliffe (ggd of 1 Baron Hylton); 1 s (James (Jamie) Patrick b 27 Sept 1990); *Career* CA, ptnr Robson Rhodes 1974-89, chm Prackley Sawmills Ltd; treas Highland Soc of London and Anglo-Swedish Soc; farmer and landowner; memb: Cncl CLA, Lloyds; dir Nat Liberal Club Ltd; FCA; *Recreations* sailing, skiing, stalking, fishing, shooting, hunting; *Clubs* Leander, Boodle's, National Liberal, Royal Lymington Yacht, etc; *Style*— The Hon Maurice Robson; Kiddington Hall, Woodstock, Oxon OX7 1BX (☎ 0608 677565)

ROBSON, Michael Anthony; s of Thomas Chester Robson, MM, CDM (d 1984), of Sunderland, and Gertrude Edith, *née* Thomas (d 1975); *b* 29 Nov 1931; *Educ* W Hartlepool GS, St Edmund Hall Oxford (MA); *m* 1, 6 Dec 1952, Cicely, da of James Frederick Bray (d 1934), of Hull; 1 s (Jake b 1957), 1 da (Zuleika b 1953); m 2, 11 Feb 1977, Judith, da of James Francis Smithies (d 1979), of Woolpit, Suffolk; *Career* RAF 1950-51; writer and film dir: Anglia TV 1963-69, BBC2 1970; freelance; radio plays incl: Landscape with Lies (1974), Weekend at Montacute (1976), Welcome, These Pleasant Days! (1981), Intent to Deceive (1988); TV plays incl: An Adventure in Bed (1975), No Name, No Packdrill (1977), Heart to Heart (1979), Swallows and Amazons Forever! (1984), This Lightning Strikes Twice (1985), Hannay (series 1988-89), Handles (1989), An Ideal Husband (1990); feature films incl: Got it Made (1974), The Water Babies (1978), Holocaust 2000 (jtly, 1978), The Thirty-Nine Steps (1979), The Ballad of the Lost Valley (1990), Intimate Details (jtly, 1991), In Silver Mist (1991); *Books incl* The Beargarden (1958), Time After Rain (1962), On Giant's Shoulders (jtly, 1976); *Recreations* riding, reading; *Clubs* Oxford and Cambridge; *Style*— Michael Robson, Esq; Coombe House, Ansty, Salisbury, Wiltshire SP3 5PX (☎ 0747 828467)

ROBSON, Nigel John; s of Col Hon Harold Burge Robson TD, JP, DL (d 1964, s of Baron Robson, Life Peer, who d 1918), and Iris Emmeline, *née* Abel Smith (d 1984); *b* 25 Dec 1926; *Educ* Eton; *m* 28 Sept 1957, Anne, da of Stephen Deiniol Gladstone (d 1965), of Lewins, Crockham Hill, Edenbridge, Kent; 3 s (Andrew b 27 Nov 1958, William b 3 Jan 1960, Hugo b 20 June 1962); *Career* served Grenadier Gds 1945-48, Lt Palestine 1946-47; banker, joined Arbuthnot Latham & Co Ltd 1949 (dir 1953, chm 1969-75); dir: Grindlays Bank plc (vice chm 1970, dep chm 1975, chm 1977-83), Ottoman Bank 1959- (dep chm 1983-, chm 1987-), British Sugar plc 1982-86, Royal Trust Co Ltd (Canada) 1985-89, TSB Group plc 1985-, TSB Bank plc 1984 (dep chm 1989-90), Bank of Tokyo International Ltd 1987-; London advsr The Bank of Tokyo Ltd 1984-; chm: Royal Trust Bank 1984-89, TSB England & Wales plc 1986-89; memb: Bd of Banking Supervision 1986-, Cncl Br Heart Fndn 1984-(chm F&GPC 1984-89, treas 1986-89); treas: AA 1986-89 (vice chm 1990-), Univ of Surrey 1986-; govr: St Aubyns School Trust Ltd, King Edward's Sch Witley; FCIB 1980 (vice pres 1980-83); *Recreations* music, tennis, walking; *Clubs* Brooks's, City of London; *Style*— Nigel Robson, Esq; Pinewood Hill, Wormley, Godalming, Surrey GU8 5UD; Ottoman Bank, King William House, 2A Eastcheap, LondonEC3M 1AA (☎ 071 623 3224, fax 071 626 2337)

ROBSON, Lady (Jane) Penelope Justice; *née* Shirley; da of 12 Earl Ferrers (d 1954); *b* 1925; *m* 1944, Rev Canon John Maurice Robson, TD (d 1989), Canon Emeritus of Derby Cathedral; 1 s, 1 da; *Style*— The Lady Penelope Robson; Bristow's Close, Southrop, Lechlade, Glos GL7 3QA

ROBSON, Peter; s of Tom Baker Robson (d 1979), of Redcar, Cleveland, and Elizabeth (d 1949), *née* Ord; *b* 6 July 1926; *Educ* St Peter's Sch York, Brasenose Coll Oxford (MA); *m* 1, 21 June 1952, Kari, da of Dialmar Petersen (d 1968), of Norway; 1 s (Eirik b 1958), 1 da (Annelise b 1960); m 2, 11 Feb 1984, Betty Mildred, da of John Sydney Hurford (d 1948), of St Leonards-on-Sea; *Career* slr, sr ptnr Maxwell Batley 1970-85, currently conslt; *Recreations* golf, cricket administration; *Clubs* Oriental; *Style*— Peter Robson, Esq; 14 Rochester Gardens, Hove, E Sussex

ROBSON, Peter Gordon; s of Donald Robson (d 1981), and Lette, *née* Brewer; *b* 5 Nov 1937; *Educ* Scarborough HS; *Career* asst master Marton Hall Bridlington 1962-70, head of maths Cundall Manor York 1972-89 (sr master 1973-76), fndr Newby Books publishers 1990; *Books* Between the Laughing Fields (poems, 1968), Maths Dictionary (1979), Maths for Practice and Revision (5 vols, 1982-90), Fountains Abbey, a Cistercian Monastery (1983), The Fishing Robsons (1991); *Recreations* music, genealogy, photography; *Style*— P G Robson, Esq; 31 Red Scar Lane, Scarborough, N Yorks YO12 5RH; Cundall Manor, Helperby, York YO6 2RW

ROBSON, Prof Peter Neville; OBE (1983); s of Thomas Murton Robson (d 1956), of Bolton, Lancs, and Edith, *née* Gresty (d 1980); *b* 23 Nov 1930; *Educ* Bolton Sch, Univ of Cambridge (BA), Univ of Sheffield (PhD); *m* 4 May 1957, Anne Ross, da of William Semple (d 1964), of Glasgow; 1 da (Fiona Susan b 1963); *Career* res engr Metropolitan Vickers Electrical Co Ltd Manchester 1954-57, reader (lectr, sr lectr) Univ of Sheffield 1957-68 (prof of electronic and electrical engrg 1968-); FIEE, FEng 1983, FRS 1987; *Style*— Prof P N Robson, OBE, FRS; 46 Canterbury Ave, Sheffield S10 3RU, S Yorks; Dept of Electronic and Electrical Engineering, Univ of Sheffield, Sheffield S1 3JD (☎ 0742 768555 ext 5131, telex 547216 UGSHEF G)

ROBSON, Richard Arnold; s of Sydney Arnold Robson, of York and Laura, *née* Patterson (d 1972); *b* 4 Aug 1946; *Educ* Wennington Sch, York Coll of Art, Guildhall

Sch of Music and Drama; *Career* teacher Suffolk 1966-67, curator of Costume Galleries Castle Howard York 1974- (asst curator 1967-74), furnishing offr Archdiocese of York 1978-81; reader parishes in Diocese of York: Stonegrave, Harome, Nunnington, Pockley; lectr and exhibitions in: UK, Japan, USA, Sweden; subjects incl: Castle Howard, social history, costume and textiles, vestments in the western church, christian art, the Crown Jewels; prog coordinator Costume Soc 1988 (memb Ctee 1980, memb Prog Sub Ctee 1981, chm Prog Sub Ctee 1985), chm Northern Soc of Costume and Textiles 1988 (fndr chm 1977 and former Ctee memb); BD St Justins' Theological Seminary California USA; Vigneron D'Honneur de Saint Emilion 1987; *Recreations* wine, food, travel, ecclesiology; *Style*— Richard A Robson, Esq; Castle Howard, York YO6 7BY (☎ 065 384 350); The Costume Galleries, Castle Howard, York YO6 7BA (☎ 065 384 444, fax 065 384 462)

ROBSON, Air Vice-Marshal Robert Michael (Bobby); OBE (1971); s of Dr John Alexander Robson, of Dorset, and Edith, *née* Knape; *b* 22 April 1935; *Educ* Sherborne, RMA Sandhurst; *m* 4 April 1959, Brenda Margaret, da of Leslie Clifford Croysdill, MBE (d 1970), of Dorset; *Career* cmmnd 1955, RAF Regt 1958, navigator trg 1959, strike sqdns 1965, sqdn cdr RAF Coll 1968, def advsr Br High Cmmr Sri Lanka 1972, Nat Def Coll 1973, CO 27 Sqdn 1974-75, staff duties MOD 1978, CO RAF Gatow 1978-80, RCDS 1981, dir of initial offr trg RAF Coll 1982-84, dir of PR (RAF) 1985-87, head of study into offrs' terms of service 1987; ADC to the Queen 1979-80; ret 1987; sheep farmer, freelance journalist 1987-; chm Aerotech Alloys Ltd 1990-; *Recreations* reading, opera, fishing; *Clubs* RAF; *Style*— Air Vice-Marshal Bobby Robson, OBE; Long Row Cottage, N Rauceby, Sleaford, Lincolnshire NG34 8QP (☎ 0529 98631)

ROBSON, Robert William (Bobby); s of Philip Robson, of Langley Park, Co Durham, and Lilian, *née* Watt; *b* 18 Feb 1933; *Educ* Waterhouses Secdy Modern Sch Co Durham; *m* 25 June 1955, Elsie Mary, da of Jack Wilfred Gray (d 1980); 3 s (Paul Martin b 24 June 1957, Andrew Peter b 28 March 1959, Robert Mark b 9 April 1963); *Career* professional footballer: Fulham FC 1950-56, transferred to West Bromwich Albion FC 1956-62, transferred to Fulham FC 1962-67; England international 1957-62: 20 full caps, under 23 and B caps, appeared in World Cup Sweden (1958) and Chile (1962); mangr: Vancover Royals 1967-68 (also coach), Fulham FC Jan 1968- Nov 1968, Ipswich Town FC 1969-82, England Football Team 1982-90, PSV Eindhoven 1990-; *Books* Time on the Grass (autobiography, 1982), So Near Yet So Far: Bobby Robson World Cup Diary (with Bob Harris, 1986), Against the Odds (1990); *Recreations* golf, squash, gardening, skiing, reading, music; *Style*— Bobby Robson, Esq; PSV Football Club, 10a Frederiklaon, Philips Stadium, Eindhoven, Nederlands

ROBSON, Stephen Arthur; s of Arthur Cyril Robson, ISO, of Scruton, N Yorks, and Lilian Marianne, *née* Peabody (d 1972); *b* 30 Sept 1943; *Educ* Pocklington Sch Yorks, St Johns Coll Cambridge (BA, MA, PhD), Stanford Univ California (MA); *m* 14 Dec 1974, Meredith Hilary, da of Ernest Lancashire (d 1982); 2 s (David Robert b 1 March 1978, Andrew Luke b 8 Sept 1979); *Career* under sec HM Treasy; *Recreations* sailing; *Clubs* Bosham SC; *Style*— Stephen Robson, Esq; H M Treasury, Parliament St, London SW1 (☎ 071 270 4440)

ROBSON, Sir Thomas Buston; MBE (1919); s of Thomas Robson (d 1928); *b* 4 Jan 1896; *Educ* Rutherford Coll Newcastle, Armstrong Coll Univ of Durham (MA); *m* 1936, Roberta Cecilia Helen (d 1980), da of late Rev Archibald Fleming; 2 da; *Career* WWI RGA Capt 1918 (despatches); ptnr Price Waterhouse & Co 1934-66, chm Renold Ltd 1967-72; memb: Cncl Inst of CA's 1941-66 (pres 1952-53), Central Valuation Bd for Coal Indust 1947, Accountancy Advsy Ctee Bd of Trade 1948 (chm 1955-68), MOT Advsy Ctee on Replacement of 'Queen' Ships 1959, Tport Tbnl 1963-69; chm EDO Ctee on Paper and Board Indust 1964-67; vice pres Gtr London Central Scout Cncl; ACA 1923, FCA 1939; kt 1954; *Style*— Sir Thomas Robson, MBE; 3 Gonville House, Manor Fields, London SW15 3NH (☎ 081 789 0597)

ROBSON, Prof (William) Wallace; s of Wilfrid Robson (d 1935), of London, and Kathleen, *née* Ryan (d 1961); *b* 20 June 1923; *Educ* New Coll Oxford (BA, MA); *m* 18 Aug 1962, Anne Varna, da of Capt Robert Moses, MC, of Stockton-on-Tees; 1 s (Hugh Wallace b 1965), 1 adopted s (Robert b 1959); *Career* asst lectr Kings Coll London 1946-48, fell Lincoln Coll Oxford 1948-70, prof of English lit Univ of Sussex 1970-72, Masson prof of English lit Univ of Edinburgh 1970, ret 1989-; FRSE 1987-; *Books* Critical Essays (1966), The Signs Among Us (poems 1968), Modern English Literature (1972), The Definition of Literature (1982), A Prologue to English Literature (1986); *Style*— Prof Wallace Robson, FRSE; Dept of English Literature, Univ of Edinburgh, David Hume Tower, George Sq, Edinburgh EH8 9JX (☎ 031 667 1011)

ROBSON OF KIDDINGTON, Baroness (Life Peeress UK 1974), of Kiddington in Oxfordshire; Inga-Stina Robson; JP (Oxon 1955); da of Erik R Arvidsson, of Stockholm; *b* 20 Aug 1919; *Educ* Stockholm; *m* 1940, Sir Lawrence William Robson (d 1982), sometime sr ptnr Robson Rhodes & Co (accountants); 1 s (Hon (Erik) Maurice William b 1943), 2 da (Hon Kristina Elizabeth (Hon Mrs Mason) b 1946, Hon Vanessa Jane (Hon Mrs Potter) b 1949); *Career* sits as Lib in House of Lords; chm: SW Thames RHA 1974-82, Bd Govrs Queen Charlotte's and Chelsea Hosps 1970-84, Midwife Teachers Training Coll; Swedish Foreign Office 1939-40, min of Info 1942-43; Party candidate (Lib): Eye 1955 and 59, Gloucester 1964 and 1966; pres Lib Pty Orgn 1970-71; chm: Anglo-Swedish Soc 1982, Nat Assoc of Leagues of Hosp Friends 1986; *Recreations* skiing, sailing, fishing; *Clubs* Nat Lib, Boodle's; *Style*— The Rt Hon the Lady Robson of Kiddington, JP; Kiddington Hall, Woodstock, Oxon (☎ 060 872 398)

ROCH, The Hon Mr Justice John Ormond; QC (1976); s of Frederick Ormond Roch (d 1973), and Vera Elizabeth Roch, *née* Chamberlain; *b* 19 April 1934; *Educ* Wrekin Coll, Clare Coll Cambridge (BA, LLB); *m* 1967, Anne Elizabeth, da of Dr Willoughby Hugh Greany; 3 da (Joanna b 1968, Lucinda b 1970, Charlotte b 1972); *Career* rec 1968-85, high ct judge Queens Bench Div, treas Wales and Chester Circuit 1980-84; *Recreations* music, reading, sailing (Cantabile of Dale); *Clubs* Dale Yacht; *Style*— The Hon Mr Justice Roch; Royal Cts of Justice, The Strand, London

ROCHDALE, Archdeacon of; see: Bonser, The Ven David

ROCHDALE, Archdeacon of; *see*: Bonser, Ven David

ROCHDALE, 1 Viscount (UK 1960); John Durival Kemp; OBE (1945), TD (1943), DL (Cumbria 1948); also Baron Rochdale (UK 1913); s of 1 Baron Rochdale, CB (d 1945), and Lady Beatrice Egerton, MBE, da of 3 Earl of Ellesmere, JP, DL (by his w Lady Katherine Phipps, 2 da of 2 Marquess of Normanby); *b* 5 June 1906; *Educ* Eton, Trinity Coll Cambridge; *m* 1931, Elinor, CBE, JP, da of Capt Ernest Pease, of Darlington; 1 s (and 1 da decd); *Heir* s, Hon St John Kemp; *Career* served 1939-45, Europe, UK, Pacific, India, Brig (despatches), Hon Col 251 Westmoreland and Cumberland Yeo, Field Regt RA (TA), later 651 Battery RA (TA) 1959-67; joined Kelsall & Kemp Ltd Rochdale woollen mfrs 1928 (chm 1952-71); dir: Consett Iron Co Ltd 1956-67, Geigy (Hldgs) Ltd 1959-64, Williams Deacon's Bank Ltd 1960-70, Williams & Glyn's Bank 1970-77 (dep chm 1973-77); dep chm W Riding Worsted & Woollen Mills Ltd 1969-72, chm Harland & Wolff Ltd Belfast 1971-75, dir Nat & Commercial Banking Group 1971-77, dep chm Williams & Glyn's Bank Ltd 1973-77; memb Central Tport Consultative Ctee for GB 1952-57, pres Nat Union of Mfrs 1953-56; memb: Dollar Exports Cncl 1953-60, Western Hemisphere Exports Cncl 1960-64; govr BBC 1954-59, vice pres Br Productivity Cncl 1955-56, pres NW Area Br Legion 1955-60; chm: Cotton Bd 1957-62, Ctee of Inquiry into Major Ports of GB 1961; memb Textile Inst 1962; chm Nat Ports Cncl 1963-67; pres Econ League 1964-67; chm Ctee of Inquiry into Shipping Ind 1967-70; pres NW Industl Devpt Assoc 1974-84; dir Cumbria Rural Enterprise 1986-91; memb European Select Ctee House of Lords (chm sub-ctee B) 1981-86; Textile Inst Medal 1986; upper bailiff Worshipful Co of Weavers 1956-57; MInstT; *Recreations* forestry, gardening, music; *Clubs* Lansdowne; *Style*— The Rt Hon Viscount Rochdale, OBE, TD, DL; Lingholm, Keswick, Cumbria CA12 5UA (☎ 07687 72003)

ROCHE, Hon Lady ((Helen) Alexandra Briscoe); *née* Gully; JP (1984); da of 3 Viscount Selby; *b* 1934; *Educ* Paris; *m* 1, 1952 (m dis 1965), Roger Moreton Frewen (d 1972); 3 s, 2 da; m 2, 1971, Sir David O'Grady Roche, 5 Bt, *qv*; *Career* Justice of the Peace 1984-; *Recreations* sailing, gardening; *Clubs* RYS; *Style*— The Hon Lady Roche, JP; Bridge House, Starbotton, Skipton, N Yorks BD23 5HY

ROCHE, Sir David O'Grady; 5 Bt (UK 1838), of Carass, Co Limerick; s of Lt-Cdr Sir Standish O'Grady Roche, 4 Bt, DSO, RN, (d 1977), and Evelyn Laura, only da of late Maj William Andon, of Jersey; *b* 21 Sept 1947; *Educ* Wellington, Trinity Coll Dublin; *m* 1971, Hon (Helen) Alexandra Briscoe Gully, JP, da of late 3 Viscount Selby (*see* Hon Lady Roche), and formerly w of late Roger Moreton Frewen; 2 s (David b 1976, 1 s decd), 1 da (Cecilia b 1979); *Heir* s, David Alexander O'Grady Roche b 28 Jan 1976; *Career* CA; formerly with Peat Marwick Mitchell & Co; mangr Samuel Montagu Ltd; chm: Carlton Real Estates plc 1978-82, Roche & Co Ltd, Carass Property Ltd, Echo Hotel plc; *Recreations* shooting, sailing (yacht Lady Nicola); *Clubs* Bucks, Kildare St, University (Dublin), Royal Yacht Squadron; *Style*— Sir David Roche, Bt; Norris Castle Farm, IOW PO32 6AZ (☎ 0983 299126); Bridge House, Starbotton, Skipton, N Yorks (☎ 075 676 863); 36 Coniger Rd, London SW6 (☎ 071 736 0382)

ROCHE, Dr Denis Arthur; s of Dr Augustine Kevin Roche (d 1929), and Dorothy Mabel, *née* Colmer; *b* 3 April 1929; *Educ* Epsom Coll; *m* 27 Sept 1958, Ann Denise, da of John Rupert Wilson; 4 da (Sarah b 21 July 1959, Elaine (Mrs Evans) b 3 Nov 1960, Jeanette (Mrs Happ) b 5 March 1962, Patsy (Mrs Greenslade) b 7 Nov 1964); *Career* Nat Serv Capt RAMC 1952-54; med supt United Mission Hosp Bhaktapur and Tansen Hosp Nepal 1960-78, occupational physician Worcester and Dist Health Authy 1979-90; memb: Droitwich and Dist Cncl of Churches, Hereford and Worcester Probation Serv; *Style*— Dr Denis Roche; 44 Corbett Avenue, Droitwich, Worcestershire WR9 7BE (☎ 0905 773956)

ROCHE, Prof Laurence Anthony; s of William Roche (d 1963), of Wexford, Ireland, and Brigitte, *née* Banville, of Wexford, Ireland; *b* 20 Oct 1927; *Educ* CBS Wexford Ireland, Trinity Coll Dublin (B Agric, MA), Univ of Br Columbia (MF, PhD); *m* 20 Oct 1962, Felicity Eleanor Anne, da of F A Bawtree, of Madaboy, Murroe, Co Limerick, Ireland; 1 s (Christopher b 5 June 1967), 2 da (Nicola b 4 Aug 1963, Patricia b 15 June 1968); *Career* res offr Br Columbia Forest Serv 1961-66, res scientist and res mangr Canadian Forestry Serv 1966-72, prof of forestry Univ of Ibadan Nigeria 1972-75, head Sch of Forest Scis Univ of Wales Bangor 1987-90 (head Dept of Forestry and Wood Scis 1975-87, prof of forestry 1975-); pres Int Union of Forestry Socs 1979-84, vice chm Bd of Tstees Int Cncl for Res in Agroforestry 1983-87, fndr and ed Int Jl of Forest Ecology and Mgmnt, memb Ctee for Int Cooperation in Higher Educn Br Cncl; memb: Univ Funding Agric Panel, Governing Cncl Cwlth Forestry Assoc; fell Inst Chartered Foresters; *Books* The Genetics of Forest Ecosystems (jtly, 1976); *Recreations* reading, sailing, fishing; *Clubs* Kildare Street Univ; *Style*— Prof Laurence Roche; 62 Upper Garth Road, Bangor, Gwynedd LL57 2SS (☎ 0248 362980); Madaboy, Murrow, Co Limerick, Ireland; School of Agricultural & Forest Sciences, University College of North Wales, Bangor, Gwynedd LL57 2UW (☎ 0248 351151 ext 2439)

ROCHE, Hon Thomas Gabriel; QC (1955); s of Baron Roche, PC (Life Peer, d 1956); *b* 1909; *Educ* Rugby, Wadham Coll Oxford; *Career* WW II as Lt-Col RA; barr 1932, rec Worcester 1959-71; church cmmr 1961-65; *Style*— The Hon Thomas Roche, QC; Ashcroft House, Chadlington, Oxford (☎ 060 876 421)

ROCHE-GORDON, Delphine Mary; da of Thomas William Edgar Roche (d 1972), of Cambridge, and Henrietta Laure Lea, *née* Bopp; *b* 2 April 1945; *Educ* Dover GS, Slough HS, Ealing Sch of Art (Dip); *m* 1, 27 Feb 1967 (m dis 1972), Norman Wynne Griffith; m 2, 28 Oct 1972, Campbell Munro Gordon, s of Murdoch Campbell Gordon (d 1973); 2 s (Christopher, Nicholas), 1 da (Amy); *Career* owner of and designer for The Bunny Shop Eton Bucks 1967, BBC TV costume asst on The First Churchills 1968; BBC costume designer 1969-; programmes incl: Black and White Minstrels, Val Doonican series, Harry Secombe series, Shirley Bassey special, Perry Como special, Royal Command Performance with Dad's Army, Weir of Hermiston, Secret Servant, All Creatures Great and Small 1985, Tutti Frutti (BAFTA nomination) 1986-87, The Dark Room 1987, Dunroamin' Rising, The Justice Game, The Shawl 1988, The Justice Game II; involved with: Gartmore Conservation Soc, The Princess of Wales Hospice; *Recreations* cycling, horse riding, sewing, reading, animals; *Style*— Mrs Delphine Roche-Gordon; Drummit Ho, Gartmore, Stirling, Scotland (☎ 08772 456); BBC TV Broadcasting House, Queen Margaret Drive, Glasgow (☎ 041 330 27209)

ROCHESTER, Prof Colin Herbert; s of Herbert Rochester (d 1973), and Doris, *née* Wilson; *b* 20 March 1937; *Educ* Hymers Coll Hull, Royal Liberty Sch Romford, King's Coll Univ of London (BSc, PhD, DSc); *m* 24 Oct 1959, Jennifer Mary, da of Capt William Orrell (d 1982); 2 s (Christopher b 1960, John b 1963), 2 da (Elizabeth b 1965, Lynda b 1968); *Career* reader in chemistry Univ of Nottingham 1973-80 (lectr 1962-73), Baxter prof of Chemistry Univ of Dundee 1980-; author of 198 scientific papers; FRSC 1973, FRSE 1985; *Books* Acidity Functions (1970); *Recreations* fossil collecting, swimming; *Style*— Prof Colin Rochester, FRSE; 18 Graystane Road, Invergowrie, Dundee DD2 5JQ (☎ 0382 562614); Department of Chemistry, The University, Dundee DD1 4HN (☎ 0382 23181)

ROCHESTER, David John; s of Edward Rochester (d 1983), and Anne Edna, *née* Raine; *b* 29 Oct 1939; *Educ* The GS Reigate, The Sorbonne Paris; *m* 1, 2 Sept 1961 (m dis 1977), Anne, da of Joseph Ganter, of Morden, Surrey; 2 da (Lisa b 1966, Susan b 1968); m 2, 31 Dec 1977, Shannon Marie, da of Joseph Clements, of Twin Falls, Idaho, USA; 2 da (Raine b 1981, Harley b 1984); *Career* ptnr Cazenove & Co 1961-81, pres Wedd Durlacher Mordaunt Inc 1981-83, md Merrill Lynch Ltd 1983-89, dir Private Fund Mangrs Ltd 1990-, non-exec dir Sevaine Adeney Ltd; *Recreations* shooting, tennis, golf; *Style*— David Rochester, Esq; 61 St George's Drive, London SW1; Blue Doors, South Stoke, Arundel, W Sussex; Private Fund Managers Ltd, 17 Sun Street, London EC2M 2PU

ROCHESTER, 2 Baron (UK 1931); Foster Charles Lowry Lamb; s of 1 Baron Rochester, CMG, JP, sometime MP Rochester and paymaster-gen in 1931 Nat Govt (d 1955); *b* 7 June 1916; *Educ* Mill Hill, Jesus Coll Cambridge (MA); *m* 12 Dec 1942, Mary, da of Thomas Benjamin Wheeler, CBE (d 1981); 2 s, 1 da (and 1 da decd); *Heir* s, Hon David Lamb; *Career* sits as Social and Lib Democrat in House of Lords; former Capt 23 Hussars WWII; personnel mangr Mond ICI; pro-chllr Univ of Keele; DL (Cheshire) 1979; Hon D Univ Keele 1986; *Clubs* Reform; *Style*— The Lord Rochester; The Hollies, Hartford, Cheshire (☎ 0606 74733)

ROCHESTER, 105 Bishop of 1988-; Rt Rev (Anthony) Michael Arnold

Turnbull; patron of seventy-six livings, of the Archdeaconries of Rochester, Tonbridge and Bromley, two Residentiary Canonries, and of all the Honorary Canonries; s of George Ernest Turnbull (d 1954), and Adeline Turnbull; *b* 27 Dec 1935; *Educ* Ilkley GS, Keble Coll Oxford (MA), St John's Coll Durham (DipTh); *m* 25 May 1963, Brenda, JP, da of Leslie James Merchant; 1 s (Mark b 1966), 2 da (Rachel (Mrs Michael Duff) b 1964, Rebecca b 1970); *Career* curate Middleton and Luton 1960-65; chaplain: Archbishop of York 1965-69, Univ of York; rector of Heslington 1969-76, chief sec Church Army 1976-84, archdeacon of Rochester and canon residentiary Rochester Cathedral 1984-88; memb Bd of Govrs Church Cmmrs, vice chm Central Bd of Fin C of E, chm Bible Reading Fellowship, religious advsr to TVS; patron: Dartford Almshouses Centenary Appeal, Medway Towns Spastic Soc, Kenward Tst, Lions Hospice Gravesend, Kent Assoc of Victim Support Schemes, Medway and Gillingham Community Rels Cncl, The Friends of Kent Churches; vice pres Royal London Soc for the Blind, pres Medway Towns Parkinsons Disease Soc; *Books* God's Front Line (1978), Parish Evangelism (1980); *Recreations* cricket, books, walking; *Clubs* Athenaeum, MCC; *Style—* The Rt Rev the Bishop of Rochester; Bishopscourt, Rochester, Kent ME1 1TS (☎ 0634 842721)

ROCK, Alan George; s of Ian George Rock, of Bicester, Oxon, and Anne Elizabeth, *née* Lyons; *b* 15 April 1959; *Career* electronic design engr rising to engrg mangr Golden River Ltd 1979-84, fndr dir and shareholder Stack Ltd 1984- (mfr of electronic equipment incl in-car instrumentation for motorsport); *award* winner Br Design Award 1990 (for Intelligent Tachometer); *Style—* Alan Rock, Esq; Stack Ltd, Wedgwood Road, Bicester, Oxon OX6 7UL (☎ 0869 240404, fax 0869 245500)

ROCK, Angus James; s of Ian George Rock, and Anne Elizabeth, *née* Lyons; *b* 16 Sept 1964; *Educ* Cooper Sch Bicester Oxfordshire, Gosford Hill Sch Kidlington Oxfordshire; *Career* designer Cherwell Laboratories 1983-86, proprietor A J R Marketing (design and mktg an electronic instrumentation range for motorsport) 1986-88, sales and mktg mangr Stack Ltd 1988-; winner Br Design award 1990; *Recreations* squash, tennis, skiing, music; *Style—* Angus Rock, Esq; 78 Isis Ave, Bicester, Oxfordshire (☎ 0869 246111); Stack Ltd, Wedgwood Rd, Bicester, Oxfordshire (☎ 0869 240404, fax 0869 245500)

ROCK, David Annison; FSA; s of Thomas Henry Rock (d 1964), of Sunderland, Co Durham, and Muriel Rock, *née* Barton (d 1964); *b* 27 May 1929; *Educ* Bede GS Sunderland, Univ of Durham (B Arch); *m* 18 Dec 1954 (m dis 1985), Daphne Elizabeth Richards; 3 s (Adam b 1960, Jacob b 1961, Mark b 1963), 2 da (Felicity b 1957, Alice b 1963); m 2, 1989, Lesley Patricia, *née* Murray; *Career* 2 Lt BAOR RE 1953-55; sr architect Sir Basil Spence 1952-53 and 1955-58, ptnr and fndr London Gp Bldg Design Ptnrship 1959-71, fndr ptnr and chm Rock Townsend 1971, co fndr Workspace Business Centre Concept in UK 1971, fndr dir Barley Mow Workspace 1974-; fndr chm Dryden Street Collective 1971-78; vice-pres RIBA 1987-88 (memb cncl 1970-76 and 1986-88), chm Soc of Architect Artists 1986-; Graham Willis visiting prof Univ of Sheffield 1990-; memb CNAA; personal awards: Soane Medallion, Owen Jones Studentship, H B Saint Award, RIBA Bldg Indust Tst Fellship, Crown Prize, Glover Medal; FRIBA, 1953, FCSD; *Books* Vivat Ware! Strategies to Enhance an Historic Town (1974), The Grassroot Developers (1980); *Recreations* painting, illustration, work; *Style—* David Rock, Esq, FSA; 27 Roupell St, London SE1 8TB (☎ 071 928 8738); Rock Townsend, 35 Alfred Place, WC1 (☎ 071 637 5300, fax 071 580 6080)

ROCK, Michael John; s of Arthur Edward Rock (d 1984), of Worcestershire, and Edna Davis; *b* 18 May 1942; *Educ* Halesowen GS, Birmingham Poly, Cologne Univ, Univ of London (BA, DipM); *m* 1, 11 Sept 1971 (m dis 1978), Zofia Kamilla, da of Rev Frederick Arlt, of Birmingham; m 2, 1 June 1979 (m dis 1983), Margaret; *Career* student apprentice Rheinisch Stahlwerke AG 1960-65, prod mgmnt Baker Perkins Int Germany 1965-66, (Austria 1966-70), commercial dir G D Peters Ltd 1970-73; dir: ITS Ltd 1973, Riehle-Iwa Ltd 1985; memb: Nat Cncl IMRA (Industrial Market Research Assoc) 1983-86, BIM Cncl Slough 1985-; Farnham Royal Parish cncllr 1987-; Freeman City of London 1986, Liveryman Worshipful Co of Marketers; FInstM, FIEx, FBIM, MIM, MIMC, FRSA, FRGS; *Recreations* walking, languages, music, books, painting, travel, geography, ind archaeology, following rugby; *Clubs* RAC, Directors, Stoke Poges Golf; *Style—* Michael Rock, Esq; 7 Sospel Court, Farnham Royal, Bucks SL2 3BT; ITS Ltd, PO Box 331, Slough SL2 3DQ (fax 02814 6461, telex 848314)

ROCK, Prof Paul Elliot; s of Ashley Rock, of 12 West Hill Court, Millfield Lane, London, and Charlotte, *née* Dickson (d 1969); *b* 4 Aug 1943; *Educ* William Ellis GS, LSE (BSc), Nuffield Coll Oxford (D Phil); *m* 25 Sept 1965, Barbara, da of Hayman Ravid (d 1989); 2 s (Matthew Charles b 1970, Oliver James b 1974); *Career* visiting prof Princeton Univ USA 1974-75, visiting scholar Miny of the Slr Gen of Canada, prof of sociology LSE 1986- (asst lectr 1967-70, lectr 1970-76); memb: Sociology and Social Admin Ctee SSRC 1976-80, Exec Ctee Br Sociological Assoc 1978-79, Parole Bd 1986-89; *Books* Making People Pay (1973), The Making of Symbolic Interactionism (1979), Understanding Deviance (jtly, 1982-1988), A View From The Shadows (1987), Helping Victims of Crime (1990); *Style—* Prof Paul Rock; London School of Economics, Houghton St, Aldwych, London WC2A 2AE (☎ 071 405 7086, fax 071 242 0392)

ROCK, Stuart Peter; s of Peter Illsley Rock, of 10 Marlborough Place, Wimborne Minster, Dorset, and Wendy Julie, *née* Ives; *b* 23 Sept 1960; *Educ* Malvern, Magdalen Coll Oxford (BA); *Career* pr exec Sabatini Taylor & Associates 1983-85, freelance writer 1985-87, ed Director Publications 1989- (joined 1987); *Books* Family Firms (1991); *Recreations* architecture, photography, beer, reading, would like to improve cooking; *Style—* Stuart Rock, Esq; Director Publications Ltd, Mountbarrow House, 12-20 Elizabeth St, London SW1W 9RB (☎ 071 730 6060, fax 071 235 5627)

ROCKER, David; s of Richard Frederick Rocker (d 1984), of Hatfield Peverel, Essex, and Elizabeth Ellen, *née* Lewis; *b* 9 June 1944; *Educ* King Edward VI Sch Chelmsford; *m* 1972, Jacolyn Jane, da of John Geoffry Matthews, of Finchingfield, Essex; *Career* admitted slr; ptnr Leonard Gray & Co 1968-71; legal advsr: Hawker Siddeley Gp Ltd 1971-73, Trident TV 1973-79; dir legal affrs Guinness plc 1982-86; chm: Guinness Superlatives Ltd 1984-85, Guinness Overseas Ltd 1985-86, Rocker Ltd 1989-, Toleman Holding Company Ltd; princ David Rocker & Co 1986-; *Recreations* motor-racing, riding; *Style—* David Rocker, Esq; The Maltings, 21 The Green, Writtle, Essex (☎ 0245 420141)

ROCKER, Israel; s of Baruch Rocker (d 1971), of London, and Rose, *née* Wiesenfied (d 1939); *b* 15 Sept 1926; *Educ* Guy's Hosp Univ of London (MD); *m* 19 June 1956, Thelma Ruth, da of David Fay; 2 s (Simon b 7 Dec 1957, Michael b 19 Dec 1961); *Career* Nat Serv civil def ambulance 1941-43; currently obstetrician and gynaecologist Royal Gwent Hosp Newport; examiner RCOG 1974-88 (postgrad advsr 1978-84); pres: Gwent Med Soc 1974-75, Welsh Obstetric and Gynaecological Soc 1982-83; memb: Rotary Club, Br Gynaecological Cancer Soc; FRCOG; *Books* Fetoscopy (ed, 1981), Pelvic Pain in Women (ed, 1990); *Style—* Israel Rocker, Esq; Lawnside, Stow Park Circle, Newport, Gwent NP9 4HE (☎ 0633 266362); Royal Gwent Hospital, Newport, Gwent (☎ 0633 252244)

ROCKLEY, 3 Baron (UK 1934); James Hugh Cecil; s of 2 Baron Rockley (d 1976, whose f, 1 Baron, was er s of Lord Eustace Cecil, 3 s of 2 Marquess of Salisbury by his 1 w, Frances, the Gascoyne heiress), and Anne, da of Adm Hon Sir Herbert Meade-Fetherstonhaugh, GCVO, CB, DSO, yr bro of 5 Earl of Clanwilliam; *b* 5 April 1934; *Educ* Eton, New Coll Oxford; *m* 1958, Lady Sarah Primrose Cadogan, eldest da of 7 Earl Cadogan, MC, DL; 1 s, 2 da; *Heir* s, Hon Anthony Robert Cecil b 29 July 1961; *Career* vice-chm Kleinwort Benson Gp; dir: Kleinwort Benson Ltd 1970-, Equity & Law plc 1980-, Christies International plc 1989-, F R Group 1989-; Abbey National plc 1990-, Kleinwort Development Fund plc 1990-, The Foreign and Colonial Investment Trust plc 1991; chm Dartford River Crossing 1988-; tstee Nat Portrait Gallery 1981-88; chm Issuing Houses Assoc 1987-89; memb Design Cncl 1988-; *Style—* The Rt Hon the Lord Rockley; Lytchett Heath, Poole, Dorset (☎ 0202 622228)

ROCKLEY, Baroness; Lady Sarah Primrose Beatrix; da (by 1 w) of 7 Earl Cadogan; *b* 1938; *m* 1958, 3 Baron Rockley; 1 s, 2 da; *Style—* The Rt Hon the Lady Rockley; Lytchett Heath, Poole, Dorset

RODBER, Timothy Andrew Keith (Tim); s of Keith Rodber, of Arlesford, Hampshire, and Sue, *née* Bates; *b* 12 July 1969; *Educ* Churchers Coll Petersfield Hants, Oxford Poly; *Career* Rugby Union No 8 Northampton FC and Army; clubs: Petersfield RFC 1987, Oxford Old Boys RFC 1987-88, Oxford Poly RFC 1988-, Northampton RFC 1989-, Army RFC 1989; rep: Eng U18 trialist 1986 and 1987, Oxfordshire RFC 1988, Br Polys 1988, Combined Servs RFC 1989, Midlands Div 1989; Eng U21 1989 (v Romania), Eng B (debut v France) 1990; England: tour Argentina 1990; Army Cadet 1988-; *Recreations* music, films, exercise (gen sport); *Style—* Tim Rodber, Esq; Chalton House, Love Lane, Petersfield, Hampshire (☎ 0730 63487); c/o Northampton FC, Franklin Gardens, Weedon Rd, Northampton (☎ 0604 751543)

RODD, Michael Philip; s of Howard Philip Rodd, of San Jose, Ibiza, and Jean Dunn, *née* Allon; *b* 29 Nov 1943; *Educ* Trinity Coll Glenalmond, Univ of Newcastle upon Tyne (LLB); *m* 1966, Nita Elizabeth, da of Dr Donald Robert Cubey, of Whitley Bay, Tyne and Wear; 3 s (Benjamin b 1968, Jonathan b 1971, Owen b 1978); *Career* broadcaster, TV prodr Border TV 1965-67, BBC Newcastle 1967-71, BBC London 1971-81; presenter BBC TV's Tomorrow's World and The Risk Business; Industrial Broadcaster of Year (Br Inst of Mngmt 1980); co-fndr (with Michael Blakstad) and exec dir of Blackrod (industl TV prodn subsid of Chrysalis plc) 1980, specialists in developing use of TV by business and indust; *Recreations* music, home decorating; *Style—* Michael Rodd, Esq; Blackrod, The Chrysalis Building, Bramley Rd, London W10 6SP (☎ 071 221 2213, fax 071 221 6337)

RODDAN, Ronald; s of Sidney Roddan (d 1976), of Crewe, Cheshire, and Constance Ada, *née* Cooke (d 1982); *b* 8 May 1931; *Educ* Acton Wells Sch, Acton Central Sch; *Career* joined Thames Valley Harriers 1947, competed until 1962-63 season first as 800-1500m runner, then as sprinter, finally as 400m runner (best time 50.3 s); engineer; BANC Coach of Year 1989, Barclaycard Coach of Year 1989, Nat Mastercoach 1990; coach to GB sprinters: L Christie, A Mafe, R Kinch, S Jacobs, K Bentham; *Recreations* coaching athletics; *Style—* Ronald Roddan, Esq; 6B Victoria Terrace, London NW10 6EG (☎ 081 961 3967); Thames Valley Harriers, West London Stadium, off Ducane Rd, Hammersmith, London

RODDICK, Anita Lucia; OBE (1988); da of Henry Perilli (d 1952), and Gilda, *née* de Vita; *b* 23 Oct 1942; *Educ* Worthing HS for Girls, Bath Coll of Educn; *m* 1970, Thomas Gordon Roddick; 2 da (Justine b 1969, Samantha b 1971); *Career* teacher of Eng and history 1962, Cuttings Dept New York Herald Tribune UN Geneva, Women's Dept ILO Geneva, owner and mangr of restaurant and hotel, opened first Body Shop in Brighton Eng 1976, floated The Body Shop International PLC 1984 (md 1976); tstee Healthcare Fndn; Hon Degrees: Univ of Sussex 1988, Univ of Nottingham 1990; *Style—* Anita Roddick, OBE; The Body Shop plc, Hawthorn Road, Wick, Littlehampton, West Sussex BN17 7LR (☎ 0903 717107, fax 0903 726250, telex 877055)

RODDICK, (George) Winston; QC (1986); s of William Daniel Roddick (d 1977), of Caernarfon, and Aelwen, *née* Hughes; *b* 2 Oct 1940; *Educ* Caernarfon GS, Tal-Handak Malta, UCL; *m* 24 Sept 1966, Cennin, da of James Parry, BEM (d 1986), of Caernarfon; 1 s (Daniel b 1977), 1 da (Helen b 1979); *Career* called to the Bar Gray's Inn 1968, rec 1986; memb Welsh Language Bd, dir Welsh Diabetes Res Tst; *Recreations* walking the countryside; *Clubs* Cardiff & County, Caernarfon Sailing; *Style—* Winston Roddick, Esq, QC; 17 Llandennis Avenue, Cyncoed, Cardiff CF2 6JD (☎ 0222 759376); 1 Harcourt Buildings (3rd Floor), Temple, London EC4Y 9DA (☎ 071 353 2214)

RODDIE, Prof Ian Campbell; CBE (1987), TD (1967); s of Rev John Richard Wesley Roddie (d 1953), of Belfast, NI, and Mary Hill, *née* Wilson (d 1973); *b* 1 Dec 1928; *Educ* Methodist Coll Belfast, Queen's Univ of Belfast (MB BCh, BAO, MD, DSc); *m* 1, 15 Feb 1958, Elizabeth (Betty) Ann Gillon (d 1974), da of Thomas Honeyman, of Cheltenham, Glos; 1 s (Patrick b 1965), 3 da (Mary b 1960, Catherine b 1963, Sarah b 1964); m 2, 29 Nov 1974 (m dis 1983), Katherine Anne, da of Edward O'Hara, of Belfast, NI; 1 s (David b 1977), 1 da (Claire b 1975); m 3, 14 Nov 1987, Janet Doreen, da of Thomas Russell Lennon (d 1978), of Larne, NI; *Career* RAMC and T and AVR 1951-68 Queen's Univ Belfast OC med subunit, ret Maj 1968; res med offr Royal Victoria Hosp Belfast 1953-54; Queen's Univ Belfast: reader (lectr and sr lectr) in physiology 1954-64, Dunville prof of physiology 1964-87, dean of the med faculty 1976-81, pro-vice chllr 1984-87, prof emeritus 1988-; Harkness fell Univ of Washington Seattle USA, staff conslt Asian Devpt Bank Manila 1978-; visiting prof Univ of NSW Sydney Aust 1983-84, The Chinese Univ of Hong Kong 1988-90; conslt physiologist Eastern Health and Social Servs Bd NI 1957-88 (bd memb 1976-81), med dir and head of med educn King Khalid Nat Gd Hosp Jeddah Saudi Arabia (1990-); memb: NI Postgraduate Med Cncl 1976-81, Home Def Scientific Advsy Ctee (chief-regnl scientific advsr) 1977-88, Gen Dental Cncl 1978-81, Royal Irish Acad 1978-, GMC 1979-81; pres Royal Acad of Medicine in Ireland 1985-87, chm of ctee The Physiological Soc (UK) 1986-88; memb Physiological Soc 1956, MRCPI 1957, FRCPI 1965, MRIA 1978; *Books* Physiology for Practitioners (1971), The Physiology of Disease (1975); *Recreations* reading, travel, work; *Clubs* Royal Cwlth Soc; *Style—* Prof Ian Roddie, CBE, TD; King Khalid National Guard Hospital, PO Box 9515, Jeddah 21423, Kingdom of Saudi Arabia; (☎ 010 966 6656200, fax 010 966 665 3031, telex 605422 HOSN 6J SJ)

RODDIE, Dr (Thomas) Wilson; s of Rev John Richard Wesley Roddie (d 1953), and Mary Hill, *née* Wilson (d 1974); *b* 19 Aug 1921; *Educ* The Methodist Coll Belfast, Queen's Univ Belfast (MB BCh, BAO); *m* 21 April 1949, Alix Pauline Mary, da of Rev Canon Frank Hurst (d 1973); 2 da (Elisabeth Margaret Anne (Mrs Nicholls) b 13 April 1950, Alexandra Frances Mary b 24 Sept 1953); *Career* RNVR; Surgn Lt: Ulster Div 1951-55, Malayan Div Singapore 1955-59; Surgn Lt Cdr Ulster Div 1959-72; res obstetrical offr Princess Mary Maternity Hosp Newcastle upon Tyne 1947, SHO Jessop Hosp for Women Sheffield 1948, sr registrar Royal Maternity and Royal Victoria Hosps Belfast 1950-55; conslt obstetrician and gynaecologist: Kandang Kerbau Hosp Singapore (and sr lectr Univ of Malaya) 1955-59, Eastern Health and Social Servs Bd Belfast 1959-86 (ret); civilian conslt gynaecologist UKLF (NI) 1969-86, examiner Royal Coll of Midwives 1959-86; fell: Ulster Med Soc, Ulster Obstetrical and Gynaecological Soc (pres) 1969; memb North of England Obstetrical and

Gynaecological Soc; BMA, FRCOG 1961 (memb 1949); *Recreations* travel; *Clubs* RNR; *Style—* Dr Wilson Roddie; Lodge Farm, Kirkby Fleetham, North Yorks DL7 0SN (☎ 0609 748673)

RODDIS, Judith Helen Anne (Judy); da of William Herbert (d 1964), of Northampton, and Nellie, *née* Brice (d 1985); *b* 26 Aug 1946; *Educ* Welford Rd Northampton Sch for Girls; 3 da; Sarah b 19 Jan 1965, Johanna Claire b 22 July 1967, Petra Lucy Anne b 12 Oct 1970; *Career* marketing and PR; pres St Ives Business and Professional Womens Club (memb 1981-87); chm: Burglary Ctee Crime Prevention Panel Cambridgeshire, Quality Assurance Panel, Dental Conciliation Bd; memb: FPC 1984-89, Family Health Servs Authy 1989-, Panel of Gen Med Servs (serious patient/doctor disputes); conciliator Cambridgeshire Patients' Complaints; *Recreations* bridge, tap dancing, walking; *Style—* Ms Judy Roddis; 39 Silver St, Buckden, Huntingdon, Cambridgeshire PE18 9TR (☎ 0480 810785); PRP Public Relations, Foundry Walk, Market Hill, St Ives, Huntingdon, Cambs PE17 4AL (☎ 0480 495495, fax 0480 492157)

RODDIS, Peter; s of John Roddis (d 1964), of Northampton, and Kathleen Maude, *née* Foster (d 1980); *b* 10 Dec 1937; *Educ* Kettering GS; *m* 6 May 1964, Judith Helen Ann, da of William Herbert (d 1964), of Northampton; 3 da (Sarah b 1965, Johanna b 1967, Petra b 1970); *Career* RAF 1956-59, PO 1958; chm PRP Communication Gp, md Cinesound Int Gp, dir MCA Records, dir artistes and repertoire RCA Records; chm: BBC local radio advsy cncl Cambridge, BBC TV E Advsy Ctee; vice chm BBC S and E regnl advsy cncl; ed Brooklands Soc Gazette 1978-82; MIPR 1985, FInstSMM 1986; *Books* Brooklands The 40 Acres (1978); *Style—* Peter Roddis, Esq; 15 Hawkes Lane, Neddingworth, Huntingdon, Cambridgeshire (☎ 0480 63932); Cody, Ferry View, Horning, Norfolk; PRP Public Relations, Foundry Walk, Market Hill, St Ives, Huntingdon (☎ 0480 495495, fax 0480 492157)

RODEN, 9 Earl of (I 1771); Sir Robert William Jocelyn; 13 Bt (E 1665); also Baron Newport (I 1743) and Viscount Jocelyn (I 1755); s of 8 Earl of Roden, DL (d 1956), and Elinor Jessie, da of Joseph Charlton Parr, JP, DL of Grappenhall Heyes, Cheshire; *b* 4 Dec 1909; *Educ* RNC Dartmouth; *m* 1937, Clodagh Rose (d 1989), da of Edward Kennedy (gs of Sir John Kennedy, 1 Bt); 3 s; *Heir* s, Viscount Jocelyn; *Career* served WWII (despatches three times) 1939-45, Capt RN, ret; *Style—* Capt The Earl of Roden, RN; 75 Bryansford Village, Newcastle, Co Down, N I BT33 0PT (☎ 23469)

RODGER, Alan Ferguson; QC (1985); s of Prof Thomas Ferguson Rodger, CBE (d 1978), of Glasgow, and Jean Margaret Smith, *née* Chalmers (d 1981); *b* 18 Sept 1944; *Educ* Kelvinside Acad Glasgow, Univ of Glasgow (MA, LLB), New Coll Oxford (DCL, MA, DPhil); *Career* jr res fell Balliol Coll 1969-70, fell and tutor in law New Coll Oxford 1970-72, memb Faculty of Advocates 1974 (clerk 1976-79), standing jr counsel (Scotland) to Dept of Trade 1979, advocate depute 1985-88, home advocate depute 1986-88, SG Scotland 1989-; memb Mental Welfare Cmmn for Scotland 1982-85; *Books* Owners and Neighbours in Roman Law (1972), Introduction to the Law of Scotland (asst ed, ninth edn, 1987); *Recreations* writing, walking; *Clubs* Athenaeum; *Style—* Alan Rodger, Esq, QC; The Crown Office, Regent Rd, Edinburgh, Lothian (☎ 031 557 3800)

RODGER, George William Adam; s of George F Eck Rodger (d 1956), and Hilda Seebohm Rodger (d 1961); *b* 19 March 1908; *Educ* Privately, St Bees Coll; *m* 1, 1942, late Cicely Joane Hussey-Freke; m 2, 1953, Lois Witherspoon; 2 s (Jonathan George b 1962, Peter Anthony b 1965), 1 da (Jennifer b 1959); *Career* war corr Life magazine 1940-45; service incl: W Africa (Free French), Eritrea (Foreign Legion), Ethiopia (Indian Army), Italy (American Army); photographer BBC 1936-39, staff photographer Life 1940-47, fndr memb Magnum Photos Inc 1947; in 1948 started 2 yr Cape-Cairo expedition resulting in the famous pictures of Kordofan; 1 man exhibitions incl: Photographers Gallery London 1974 1979 and 1987, S Africa 1978, Grenoble 1982, Marseilles 1984, Gerona 1986, Cyprus 1987, Founders Exhibition In Centre of Photography NY 1989, Musée d'Elysées Lausanne 1990, Musée de la Photographie Charleroi Belgium 1990, Le Blitz Paris 1990, The Blitz Nineteen Forty 1990 (London in July, Washington in Sept, Bradford Oct-Dec); won first prize Peace to the World Exhibition Moscow 1985; *Books* Red Moon Rising (1943), Desert Journey (1943), Far on the Ringing Plains (1943), Les Villages des Noubas (1955), World of the Horse (1977), George Rodger en Afrique text by Carole Naggar (1984), George Rodger - Magnum Opus (1987), The Blitz: Photographs by George Rodger (1990); *Style—* George Rodger, Esq; Waterside House, Smarden, Kent (☎ 023 377 322, fax 023 377 791)

RODGER, Nicholas Andrew Martin; s of Lt-Cdr Ian Alexander Rodger RN, of Arundel, Sussex, and Sara Mary, *née* Perceval; *b* 12 Nov 1949; *Educ* Ampleforth, Univ Coll Oxford (BA, MA, DPhil); *m* 28 Aug 1982, Susan Eleanor, da of Henry Meigs Farwell, of Ickenham, Middx; 2 s (Christopher b 1987, Alexander b 1989), 1 da (Ellen b 1984); *Career* asst keeper of Public Records 1974-; hon sec Navy Records Soc 1976-90; *Books* The Admiralty (1979), The Wooden World, An Anatomy of the Georgian Navy (1986); *Recreations* hill walking, hagiology, music, history of weights and measures; *Style—* Nicholas Rodger, Esq; Public Record Office, Chancery Lane, London WC2A 1LR

RODGER, Rt Rev Patrick Campbell; s of Patrick Wylie Rodger; *b* 28 Nov 1920; *Educ* Rugby, Ch Ch Oxford; *m* 1952, Margaret, da of Dr William Menzies Menzies, of Edinburgh (d 1989); 1 s (and 1 s decd); *Career* served WWII; ordained 1949, rector St Fillan's Kilmacolm with St Mary's Bridge of Weir 1958-61, exec sec Faith and Order in World Cncl of Churches 1961-66, provost St Mary's Cathedral Edinburgh 1967-70 (vice provost 1966-67); 8 bishop of Manchester 1970-78, 40 bishop of Oxford 1978-86; asst bishop, Diocese of Edinburgh 1986-; memb: House of Lords 1974-86, Praesidium Conf of Euro Churches 1974-86; *Style—* The Rt Rev Patrick Rodger; 12 Warrender Park Terrace, Edinburgh EH9 1EG (☎ 031 229 5075)

RODGERS, David Ernest; s of late Ernest Rodgers, of Sutton, nr Peterborough, and Pamela Anne, *née* Wilkins; *b* 1 Feb 1942; *Educ* King Edward VII Sch Sheffield, St John's Coll Cambridge (BA, MA); *Career* art asst York City Art Gallery 1963-65, dep dir Sheffield City Art Galleries 1965-68; curator: Old Battersea House 1968-69, Wolverhampton Art Gallery and Museums 1969-81; dir: Exeter Museums 1981-86, Geffrye Museum 1986-90; tutor Open Univ 1976-78, external assessor in history of art NCAA 1977-79, curator William Morris Soc 1990-; memb Bd of Mgmnt Ikon Gallery Birmingham 1976-81 (vice chm 1979-81), govr Wolverhampton Poly 1978-81, hon sec Exeter Festival Ctee 1981-86, served on Arts Cncl Panels and working parties; *Books* Coronation Souvenirs and Commemoratives (1976), A Victorian Schoolboy in London (ed, 1989); author of articles for Burlington Magazine, Apollo, Antique Collector; *Recreations* collecting, cooking, gardening, theatre; *Style—* David Rodgers, Esq; Clevedon Lodge, 15C Stockwell Park Rd, London SW9 0AP; William Morris Society, Kelmscott House, 27 Upper Mall, London W6

RODGERS, George; s of George Rodgers (d 1956), and Leticia Georgina, *née* Spriggs; *b* 7 Nov 1925; *Educ* Longview School Huyton; *m* 30 Aug 1952, Joan, da of James Patrick Graham (d 1984); 1 s (Ian b 1957), 2 da (Julie b 1956, Christine b 1961); *Career* Communications Branch Wireless Telegraphy RN (France Germany Star 1939-46 war medal); Co-operative Soc Whiston Lancs 1939-43; engr 1946-74 (Eaves Blackpool Civil Engineers, Whites Railway Engineers Widnes, British Insulated Callender Cables, Dyson's Engineers Liverpool); MP (Lab) Chorley 1974-79; chm Cncl Huyton Local Authy 1973-74 (chm Educn Ctee 1962-74), chm Huyton Constituency Lab Pty 1965-73, memb Liverpool Regnl Hosp Bd 1968-72; memb Amalgamated Engrg Union; *Books* A Life To Live (jt author with Ivor Clemitson, 1982); *Recreations* travel, swimming, walking; *Clubs* Huyton Labour; *Style—* George Rodgers, Esq; 32 Willoughby Road, Bowring Park, Liverpool L14 6XB (☎ 051 489 1913)

RODGERS, Ian Louis; s of Charles Augustus Rodgers (d 1942), and Doris, *née* Hanneman; *b* 12 Jan 1943; *Educ* Christ's Hospital; *m* 3 June 1967, Susanna, da of Rev Stanley James Pert (d 1974); 2 s (Mark b 1969, Paul b 1971); *Career* with Laurence Kenn & Gardner 1959-71, ptnr Laurence Prust 1977-86 (joined 1971); dir: Framlington Investment Mgmnt Ltd 1986-89, Framlington Investment Tst Services 1986-89; appeal dir Christ's Hosp 1989-; dir and memb gen cncl S American Missionary Soc, memb investment ctee The Girls Bde, donation govr Christ's Hosp; Freeman City of London 1978, Liveryman Worshipful Co of Poulters 1979; memb: Stock Exchange 1973-86, IOD 1989, ICFM 1989; *Recreations* fly fishing, music, theatre, photography; *Clubs* City Livery; *Style—* Ian Rodgers, Esq

RODGERS, Joan; da of Thomas Rodgers (d 1971), and Julia Rodgers; *b* 4 Nov 1956; *Educ* Whitehaven GS, Univ of Liverpool (BA), RNCM Manchester; *m* Paul Daniel; 1 da (Eleanor b 4 Sept 1990); *Career* opera singer; debut Pamina in Die Zaubekflote (Aix-en-Provence Festival), Zgrlina and Pamina Royal Opera House, Pamina Gilda and Nanngtta ENO, Susanna in La Nozze di Figaro (Glyndebourne), Susanna Despina Zerlina Pamina (with Daniel Bareriboim and Jean Pierre Ponnelle) Pans; venues incl: Opera Bastille Paris, Zurich, Amsterdam, Munich, has sung at concerts in : London, Vienna, Madrid, Copenhagen, Salzburg, Paris, Lisbon; has worked with: Colin Davis, Sir George Solti, Andrew Davis, Daniel Barenboim, Jeffrey Tate, Simon Rattle, Zubin Mghta; recordings incl: Mozart Mass with Harnoncourt (Toldec), Berlin Philharmonic with Barenboim (Erato), Sea Symphony (Vaughan Williams) Vernon Handleyand The RLPO (EMI Eminence), Beethoven 9th with Charles Mackerass and The RLPO (EMI Eminence), Messiah with Richard Hickbos (Chandos); winner Kathleen Ferrier Memb Scholarship 1981; *Recreations* walking, cooking; *Style—* Ms Joan Rodgers; Ingpen & Williams Ltd, 14 Kensington Court, London W8 5ND (☎ 071 937 5158)

RODGERS, Sir John Charles; DL (Kent 1973); 1 Bt (UK 1964), of Groombridge, Kent; s of late Charles Rodgers, of York, and late Maud Mary, *née* Hodgson; *b* 5 Oct 1906; *Educ* St Peter's Sch York, Ecole des Roches France, Keble Coll Oxford (MA); *m* 23 Dec 1930, Betsy Rodgers, JP, da of Francis Aikin-Sneath, JP (d 1939), of Burleigh Court, Glos; 2 s (Tobias, Piers b 1944); *Heir* s, Tobias Rodgers b 2 July 1940; *Career* FO WWII; J Walter Thompson Co: joined 1931, dir 1936-60, dep chm 1960-70; MP (C) Sevenoaks 1950-79, PPS to Rt Hon Viscount Eccles at Minys of Works Educn and BOT 1951-57, parly sec BOT and min Regnl Devpt and Employment 1958-60, memb Cncl of Europe and Western European Union; chm Radio Luxenbourg (London) 1979-84, vice chm Cocoa Merchants Ltd 1980; memb: BBC Gen Advsy Cncl 1946-52, Exec Cncl Fndn for Mgmnt Educn 1959-, Cncl Nat Tst 1978-; govr BFI 1958, fndr govr Admin Staff Coll; chm: Br Market Res Bureau, New Eng Library; Freeman City of London 1947, Master Worshipful Co of Masons 1968-69, memb Merchant Adventurers of York; CBIM, FSS, FIS, FRSA; awarded high hons: Spain, Portugal, Belgium, Taiwan, Sweden, Finland, Luxembourg, Liechtenstein; Cncl of Europe Medal of Merit; *Books* The Old Public Schools of England (1938), The English Woodland (1941), English Rivers (1948), One Nation (jtly, 1950), York (1951), Thomas Gray (ed, 1953); *Recreations* travel, theatre; *Clubs* Brooks's, Pratt's, Royal Thames Yacht; *Style—* Sir John Rodgers, Bt, DL; The Dower House, Groombridge, Kent (☎ 089 276 213)

RODGERS, (Doris) June (Mrs Roger Evans); da of James Alfred Rodgers, JP, of Craigavad, Co Down, Northern Ireland, and Margaret Doris, *née* Press; *b* 10 June 1945; *Educ* Victoria Coll Belfast, Trinity Coll Dublin (MA), Lady Margaret Hall Oxford (MA); *m* 6 Oct 1973, Roger Kenneth Evans, *qv*, s of Gerald Raymond Evans of Mere, Wilts; 2 s (Edward Arthur b 13 May 1981, Henry William b 8 Feb 1983); *Career* called to Bar Middle Temple 1971; chllr of the Dio of Gloucester 1990-; memb Ct Common Cncl City of London Ward Farringdon without 1975-, former memb City & East London Area Health Authy; Freeman City of London 1975; memb: Hon Soc Middle Temple, Ecclesiastical Law Soc; *Books* Financing Strikes (jtly); *Recreations* architectural history, Anglo-Normandy; *Clubs* United Oxford & Cambridge Universities; *Style—* The Worshipful Miss June Rodgers; 2 Harcourt Buildings, The Temple, London EC4 (☎ 071 353 6961, fax 071 353 6968)

RODGERS, Patricia Elaine Joan; da of Kenneth Vane Arnim Rodgers, OBE (d 1977), and Anatol Carridad, *née* Reeves, MBE (d 1985); *b* 13 July 1948; *Educ* St Hildas DHS Jamaica, Sch of St Helen and St Katherine Abingdon, Univ of Aberdeen (MA), Univ of The WI Trinidad (Dip in Rels), Graduate Inst of Int Rels Geneva (Doctorat es Sciences Politiques); *Career* Bahamas high cmmr to UK 1988- (Canada 1986-88); non res ambass to: Fed Repub of Germany and Kingdom of Belgium 1988-, Repub of France 1989-, to Head of Mission to EEC 1989-; perm rep to The IMO 1991-; memb: Bahamas Drama Circle, Bahamas Hist Soc, Friends of the Archives; *Books* Midocean Archipelagos and International Law: A Study in the Progressive Development of International Law (1981); *Recreations* painting, music, theatre, gourmet cooking, tennis; *Style—* Miss Patricia Rodgers; Bahamas High Commission, 10 Chesterfield St, London W1X 8AH (☎ 071 408 4488, fax 071 499 9937, telex 892617 BAHREG G, car 0836 623 557)

RODGERS, Peter David; s of Francis Norman Rodgers, of Glemsford, Suffolk, and Margaret Elizabeth, *née* Harte; *b* 8 Oct 1943; *Educ* Finchley Catholic GS, Trinity Coll Cambridge (MA); *m* 14 Sept 1968, Christine Mary Agnes, da of Dr Duncan Primrose Wilkie, OBE, of Epping, Essex; 2 s (Benedict b 3 Nov 1980, William b 18 Jan 1982), 2 da (Susannah b 29 May 1974, Georgia b 17 Oct 1985); *Career* trainee Oxford Mail 1966-67, features ed Industry Week 1967-69, industl corr The Guardian 1970-76, energy ed The Sunday Times 1976-81; The Guardian: fin corr 1981-84, city ed 1984-90; fin ed The Independent 1990-; *Recreations* offshore cruising and racing, fell walking, reading, music, rebuilding old houses; *Style—* Peter Rodgers, Esq; 163 Liverpool Rd, Islington, London N1 (☎ 071 278 5628); The Independent, 40 City Rd, London EC1Y 2DB (☎ 071 253 1222, fax 071 608 1552)

RODGERS, (Andrew) Piers Wingate; yr s of Sir John Charles Rodgers, 1 Bt, DL, *qv*; *b* 24 Oct 1944; *Educ* Eton, Merton Coll Oxford (BA); *m* 9 Sept 1979, Marie-Agathe, da of Charles-Albert Houette, Croix de Guerre (d 1989), of Langeais, France; 2 s (Thomas b 1979, Augustus b 1983); *Career* with J Henry Schroder Wagg & Co Ltd 1967-73 (PA to chm 1970-73), dir Int Cncl on Monuments & Sites Paris 1973-79, UNESCO Expert (Implementation of World Cultural Heritage Convention) 1979-80, sec of Royal Academy London (also sec of Chantrey Bequest and British Inst Fund) 1981-; Freeman of City of London, Hon Court Memb Worshipful Co of Masons; memb Co of Merchant Adventurers of City of York; FRSA; Chevalier Ordre des Arts et des Lettres (France); *Clubs* Brooks's, Pratt's, MCC; *Style—* Piers Rodgers, Esq; Peverell House, Bradford Peverell, Dorset; 18 Hertford Street, London W1; Royal Academy of Arts, Piccadilly, London W1

RODGERS, (John Fairlie) Tobias; s and h of Sir John Rodgers, 1 Bt, DL; *b* 2 July 1940; *Educ* Eton, Worcester Coll Oxford; *Career* bookseller and publisher; *Clubs*

Brooks's, Garrick, Pratt's; *Style*— Tobias Rodgers Esq; 34 Warwick Ave, W9

RODGERS, Walter Shaw; s of Booth Rodgers, JP (d 1961), of Netherthong, Yorks, and Beatrice, *née* Lockwood (d 1948); *b* 20 Jan 1922; *Educ* Holme Valley GS, Univ of Leeds (BCom); *m* 31 Aug 1957, Phyllis, da of Ernest Kenworthy (d 1971), of Totties, Holmfirth; 1 s (Martin Lockwood b 14 Jan 1959, Philip Nicholas (twin) b 14 Jan 1959), 1 da (Janet Christine b 20 March 1962); *Career* WWII 1942-47 flt sgt radar operator, edn instr SEAAF; cost accountant dyestuffs div ICI 1952-64, mgmnt accountant organics div ICI 1964-76; dir ICI subsidiaries: Armalux Flooring Ltd 1969-76, Bibby Chemicals Ltd 1971; business controller Vulnax International Group St Cloud Paris 1976-79, fin controller and company sec Pennine Fibres GP (now British Vita plc) 1979-87; dir: Pennine Fibre Inds Ltd, Package Recovery Servs Ltd 1987-; visiting lectr Ind Organisation and Mgmnt Huddersfield Poly 1951-60, reas New Mill Probus Club 1988-, ctee memb Huddersfield Family History Soc; ACCA 1957, FCCA 1964, memb Royal Economic Soc; *Recreations* travel, art & architecture, history, photography, swimming, gardening; *Clubs* ICI Woodlands, Manchester; *Style*— Walter Rodgers, Esq; Shaldon, 80 Marsh Lane, Shepley, Huddersfield HD8 8AS (☎ 0484 602945)

RODGERS, Rt Hon William Thomas; PC (1975); s of William Rodgers by his w Gertrude Helen; *b* 28 Oct 1928; *Educ* Quarry Bank HS Liverpool, Magdalen Coll Oxford; *m* 1955, Silvia, da of Hirsch Szulman; 3 da; *Career* MP (L to 1981, thereafter SDP) Teesside Stockton 1962-79, Stockton N 1979-83; fought Bristol W March 1957; in Lab Govts: parly under sec DEA 1964-67, FO 1967-68, BOT 1968-69, min state Treasy 1969-70, MOD 1974-76, tport sec 1976-79;' gen sec Fabian Soc 1953-60 (remained memb till 1981), ldr UK Delegn Cncl Europe & WEU 1967-68, chm Expenditure Ctee Trade & Industry 1971-74; dir gen RIBA 1987-; *Books* Hugh Gaitskell (1963), The People into Parliament (1966), The Politics of Change (1982), Government and Industry (1986); *Style*— The Rt Hon William Rodgers; 48 Patshull Rd, London NW5 2LD (☎ 071 485 9997)

RODIN, Jack; s of Mark Rodin (d 1966), of London, and Sarah, *née* Zeff (d 1960); *b* 2 Feb 1926; *Educ* Raines Fndn London, Univ of London (BSc); *m* 14 Feb 1964, (Marie) Elizabeth, da of Charles Paddison, of Newtown, Llantwit, S Glam; 1 s (Jonathan), 2 da (Penelope, Sarah); *Career* engr; Sir Alexander Gibb and Ptnrs Consulting Engrs 1947-54, sr engr specialist conslts (chief engr, dir) 1954-60, jt fndr Lowe and Rodin Consulting Engrs 1960 (merged with Bldg Design Ptnrship 1970), currently conslt Bldg Design Partnership (former chief exec); pres Concrete Soc 1988-; MConsE 1964, FICE 1968, FIStructE 1974; *Recreations* music, tennis; *Clubs* Arts; *Style*— Jack Rodin, Esq; 109 Blackheath Pk, Blackheath, London SE3 OEY (☎ 081 852 8048); Bldg Design Ptnrship, 16 Gresse St, London W1A 4WD (☎ 071 631 4733, fax 071 631 0393, telex 25322)

RODNEY, Hon Anne; da of 9 Baron Rodney *qv*; *b* 27 June 1955; *Educ* Lycée Français de Londres, Convent of the Sacred Heart, Woldingham, King's Coll London Univ; *Career* snr account exec Hill & Knowlton (UK) Ltd; *Style*— The Hon Anne Rodney

RODNEY, Hon Diana Rosemary; da of 8 Baron Rodney; *b* 19 April 1924; *Educ* McGill Univ; *Career* serv WWII WRCNS; agricultural writer, info office Alberta Agriculture Edmonton Alberta; *Style*— The Hon Diana Rodney; 5222 Sark Rd, Victoria, British Columbia V8Y 2M3, Canada

RODNEY, Hon George Brydges; s and h of 9 Baron Rodney; *b* 3 Jan 1953; *Educ* Eton; *Style*— The Hon George Rodney; 23 Hornton St, London W8

RODNEY, 9 Baron (GB 1782); Sir John Francis Rodney; 9 Bt (GB 1764); s of 8 Baron Rodney (d 1973; descended from the celebrated Admiral who won the decisive victory over the French in the Battle of the Saints 1782; the Admiral's gggf, Sir John Rodney, m Jane Seymour, niece of the Queen of the same name and 1 cous of King Edward VI), and Lady Marjorie Lowther (d 1968), da of 6 Earl of Lonsdale, OBE; *b* 28 June 1920; *Educ* Stowe, McGill Univ Montreal; *m* 3 Nov 1951, Régine Elisabeth Lucienne Jeanne Thérèse Marie Ghislaine, yr da of late Chevalier Robert Egide Marie Ghislain Pangaert d'Opdorp, of Château Rullingen, Looz, Belgium; 1 s, 1 da; *Heir* s, Hon George Brydges Rodney; *Career* sits as Cons in House of Lords (maiden speech 1982); serv WWII as Lt Commandos (despatches); formerly with Rootes and the Portals Gp of cos; chm Printers Educnl Equipment Tst, chm Standing Conference on Drug Abuse, chm FAIR (concerned with pseudo religious cults), sec All Party Ctee on Drug Abuse, chm All Party Ctee on Cults, memb House of Lords Select Ctee and Sub-Ctee on Energy, Transport & Technol; delegate to Cncl of Europe and Western European Union (memb of Sci & Technol and Agric Ctees); *Recreations* sailing, shooting, gardening; *Clubs* White's, Royal Yacht Sqdn; *Style*— The Rt Hon the Lord Rodney; 38 Pembroke Rd, London W8 6NU (☎ 071 602 4391)

RODNEY, Hon Michael Christopher; s of 8 Baron Rodney; *b* 26 June 1926; *Educ* McGill Univ; *m* 1, 1953 (m dis 1973), Anne, da of David Yuile, of Montreal; 3 da; m 2, 1974, Penelope, da of the late Capt E S Garner (ret), of Easton-on-the-Hill, Northamptonshire; *Career* serv WWII RCN; barr Canada 1950; *Style*— The Hon Michael Rodney; 11683-72 Ave, Edmonton, Alberta, Canada

RODNEY BENNETT; *see*: Bennett

RODRIGUE, Claude; s of Ezra Rodrigue (d 1946), of Cairo, and Bella, *née* Semah; *b* 17 April 1930; *Educ* English Sch Cairo, Imperial Coll London (SIMechE); *m* 17 Oct 1958, Ann, da of Lt-Col Sir John Rhodes, Bt, DSO (d 1954), of Westminster Gardens; 2 s (Philip b 24 March 1960, Michael b 16 Oct 1966), 1 da (Carolyn b 10 Oct 1962); *Career* memb: London Stock Exchange 1966, Dunkley Marshall and Co 1960-81 (ptnr 1975-81), Strauss Turnbull and Co Ltd 1981-88, Jacobson Townsley and Co Ltd 1988-; memb Br Bridge Team 1960-82, Euro Champion 1960, World Olympic par point Champion, 3 Olympic Championship 1976, multi-winner Camrose Trophy; invited commentator to first bridge match between nationalist and socialist China (Hong Kong) 1982; Freeman of the City of London 1977; memb IBPA; *Recreations* good food and wine, bridge, opera; *Clubs* St James' Bridge, Stock Exchange Bridge (pres); *Style*— Claude Rodrigue, Esq; Flat 1, 18 Hyde Park Gate, London SW7 5DH (☎ 071 225 2252); 44 Worship St, London WC2A 2JT (☎ 071 377 6161, fax 071 375 1380, telex 888 948)

RODRIGUES, Sir Alberto Maria; CBE (1964, OBE 1960, MBE 1948), ED; s of late Luiz Gonzaga Rodrigues; *b* 5 Nov 1911; *Educ* St Joseph's Coll, Univ of Hong Kong (MB BS); *m* 1940, Cynthia Maria de Silva; 1 s, 2 da; *Career* Med Offr Hong Kong Defence Force (POW 1940-45); general medical practitioner 1953-; MLC Hong Kong 1953-60, MEC Hong Kong 1960-74 (sr unofficial memb 1964-74); pro-chancellor Hong Kong Univ 1968-; dir: Jardine Securities 1969-, Hong Kong & Shanghai Hotels 1969-, Lap Heng Co 1970-, Peak Tramways Co 1971-, Computer Data (Hill) 1973-, Hong Kong Commercial Broadcasting Co 1974-, Jardine Strategic Hldgs 1987, Li & Fung Co Ltd 1970; kt 1966; *Style*— Sir Alberto Rodrigues, CBE, ED; St Paul's Hospital Annexe, Causeway Bay, Hong Kong (☎ 760017)

RODWAY, Simon Richard Noel; s of Flt Lt Ernest Allan Rodway, of Fordcombe, Kent, and Emily Alice, *née* Nutt; *b* 14 July 1932; *Educ* Westminster, Keble Coll Oxford, LSE (Dip in Social Science and Public Admin, Dip in Mental Health, Certificate in Child Care); *Career* sr house master The Caldecott Community 1958-63 (1951-56), sr child care offr The Royal Borough of Kensington and Chelsea 1964-68, lectr in child care The N W Poly 1968-70, asst dir of social servs London Borough of Barnet 1971-76 (dep childrens offr 1970-71), dir of social servs London Borough of Merton 1976-85, chief social servs advsr Br Red Cross 1986-, memb Inquiry Panel into Nye Bevan Lodge London Borough of Southwark 1986-87; dep chm: Caldecott Community Ashford Kent, Intermediate Treatment Fund; tstee: Disabled Living Fndn, John Hunt Tst; vice chm Assoc Workers with Maladjusted Children; chm: Charterhouse Gp of Therapeutic Communites, Tylehurst Sch Tst; memb Br Assoc Psychotherapists 1977, dep pres Merton Voluntary Assoc for Welfare of the Blind 1985, fell Royal Inst of Public Health and Hygiene 1988; *Recreations* theatre, travelling, walking, swimming; *Style*— Simon Rodway, Esq; 6 Cornwall Grove, London W4 2LB (☎ 081 994 7461); British Red Cross, 9 Grosvener Cresent, London SW1X 7EJ (☎ 071 235 5454)

RODWELL, Andrew John Hunter; er s of Col Evelyn John Clive Hunter Rodwell, MC, TD, JP (d 1981), of Woodlands, Holbrook, Suffolk, and Martha, *née* Girdlestone; the Rodwells have lived in Suffolk since the early 18 century and acquired Woodlands in 1840 (*see* Burke's Landed Gentry, 18 edn, vol II, 1969); *b* 23 Dec 1938; *Educ* Eton; *m* 20 July 1963, Susan Eleanor, da of Peter Comley Pitt, of Frensham Manor, Rolvenden, Cranbrook, Kent; 3 da (Camilla Eleanor Hunter b 21 July 1964, Miranda Harriet Hunter b 29 May 1967, Patricia Louise Hunter b 17 May 1971); *Career* short service cmmn with RWAFF 1957-60; farmer; md SCH (Supplies) Ltd; *Recreations* country pursuits, photography; *Style*— Andrew Rodwell, Esq; Woodlands, Holbrook, Suffolk (☎ 0473 328800/328272)

RODWELL, Hon Mrs (Christine Maralyn); *née* Woolley; da of Baron Woolley, CBE, DL (Life Peer); *b* 1946; *m* 1, 1970 (m dis 1980), Dr Barrie Scott Morgan; m 2, 1984, Cdr David Rodwell, RN; *Style*— The Hon Mrs Rodwell; 35 Northumberland Avenue, Wanstead, London E12

RODWELL, His Hon Judge Daniel Alfred Hunter; QC (1982); s of Brig Reginald Mandeville Rodwell, AFC (d 1974), and Nellie Barbara, *née* D'Costa (d 1967); *b* 3 Jan 1936; *Educ* Munro Coll Jamaica, Univ of Oxford (BA); *m* 1967, Veronica Frances Ann, da of Robin Cecil, CMG, of Hants; 2 s (William b 1967, Thomas b 1970), 1 da (Lucy b 1974); *Career* Nat Serv in W Yorks Regt, 2 Lt, TA (Capt); barr, rec Crown Ct 1980, circuit judge 1986; *Recreations* hunting, sailing (Emrys), gardening; *Clubs* Pegasus, Bar Yacht; *Style*— His Hon Judge Rodwell, QC; St Albans Crown Court, The Civil Centre, St Albans, Herts AL1 3XE

RODWELL, Dennis Graham; s of Albert James Rodwell, MBE, and Constance Edith Rodwell, *née* Scaddan, of Hampshire; *b* 24 Jan 1948; *Educ* Kingswood Sch Bath, Clare Coll Cambridge (MA, Dip Arch); *m* 10 May 1975, Rosemary Ann, da of Donald Ramsey Rimmer, of Somerset; 2 s (Nicholas b 1978, Christopher b 1979), 1 da (Melanie b 1982); *Career* architect 1973-; own practice 1975; architectural works include an extensive variety and scale of conversion, rehabilitation and restoration projects in housing and commercial uses in Edinburgh, Glasgow, Dundee and the Scottish Borders; projects include restorations of: The Signal Tower Leith, parts of St Mary's Street Edinburgh (commendation 1987 from Edinburgh Architectural Assoc), Greenside Park, St Boswells (commendation 1985 from Assoc for Protection of Rural Scotland), Melrose Station and its mgmnt as the Scottish Borders Crafts Centre 1986 (commendation from RICS/The Times Conservation Awards, first class award from The Ian Allen Railway Heritage Awards 1989, The Sunday Times Scotland/Morton Fraser Milligan Heritage award 1990); occasional lecturing: conservation and restoration subjects; *published articles include*: historical, travel and architectural conservation subjects in The Daily Telegraph, European Heritage, Architectural Conservation in Europe, Country Life, Scottish Field, Prospect, Craftwork, The Scotsman, Context, Civilising the City; chm The Trimontium Tst 1988-90, memb The Edinburgh New Town Conservation Ctee 1981-84 and 1987-90; served ctees: The Scottish Georgian Soc, The Borders Architects Gp, The Cncls of the Royal Incorpn of Architects in Scotland, The Edinburgh Architectural Assoc; RIBA 1973, FRIAS 1982, FSA Scot 1990; *Recreations* travel, walking, reading, photography; *Style*— Dennis Rodwell, Esq; Greenside Park, St Boswells, Melrose, Roxburghshire TD6 0AH (☎ 0835 23289); 8 Dundas St, Edinburgh EH3 6HZ (☎ 031 556 6710)

ROE, Dr Anthony Maitland; s of Percy Alex Roe (d 1953), and Flora Sara, *née* Kisch (d 1984); *b* 13 Dec 1929; *Educ* Harrow, Oriel Coll Oxford (BA, MA, DPhil); *m* 2 Nov 1958, Maureen, da of William James Curtayne (d 1950); 2 s (Adam William Maitland b 18 Dec 1963, Michael Felix Edward b 6 Feb 1966), 1 da ((Miriam) Lucy b 21 July 1969); *Career* Nat Serv Intelligence Corps (cmmnd 1956, Capt 1957); Univ of Rochester NY 1957-59, Smith Kline and French Res Inst 1959-86, dir chemistry Smith Kline and French Res Ltd 1978-86, exec Sec CSTI 1987-; author of various res papers patents and reviews in field of organic and medicinal chemistry; Royal Soc Chemistry: memb Cncl 1982-85 and 1987-, chm Heterocyclic Gp 1986-88, vice-chm Perkin Div 1986-88; chm Chemistry in Britain Mgmnt Ctee 1987-, fndr ctee memb Soc Drug Res 1966-77, memb Sci Bd Business and Technician Educn Cncl 1985-88; ARIC 1955, FRSC, CChem 1976; *Recreations* walking, listening to music, enjoying good food and wine; *Style*— Dr Anthony Roe; 10 Lodge Drive, Hatfield, Herts AL9 5HN; Council of Science and Technology Institutes, 20 Queensberry Place, London SW7 2DZ (☎ 071 581 8333, fax 071 823 9409)

ROE, (Colin) Graeme (Algernon Maitland); s of late Colin Drummond Roe, and late Irene Jesse; *b* 15 Aug 1935; *Educ* Hampton GS, Univ of Nottingham; *m* 15 Sept 1967, Jean, da of John Mcgregor (d 1987), of Minchinhampton, Glos; 1 da (Jessica b 29 May 1969); *Career* Nat Serv; Flt Lt RAF 1956-58; account dir Garland Compton 1958-61, Euro marketing dir Alberto-Culver 1961-63, marketing dir Philip Morris and Ever-Ready Personna 1963-68, chm Roe Downton and dir Saatchi and Saatchi 1968-78, vice-chm McCann Erickson 1978-82; chm: Roe Byfield 1982-, Greenaway Burdett Martin 1987-89; as racehorse trainer winners incl: All Bright, Dom Perignon, Nippy Chippy, We're in the Money, Kitty Wren, Le Grand Maitre; English Amateur Athletic Assoc 440 yards hurdles, amateur steeplechase jockey 1975-85; FIPA 1977; *Books* Profitable Marketing for the Smaller Company (1969), Changing Role of the Chief Executive (1977); *Recreations* reading, theatre, writing; *Clubs* Turf, RAF, American; *Style*— Graeme Roe, Esq; Hyde Park Farm, Lower Hyde, Chalford, nr Stroud, Gloucestershire (☎ 0453 885487, fax 0453 885204, telex 437105, car 0836 771822)

ROE, James Kenneth; s of Kenneth Alfred Roe (d 1988), of Spain, and Zirphie Norah, *née* Luke (d 1940); *b* 28 Feb 1935; *Educ* King's Sch Bruton; *m* 15 March 1958, Marion Audrey, *qv*, (MP for Broxbourne and parly under sec of state for DOE 1987-88), da of William Keyte (d 1977), of Chagford, Devon; 1 s (William b 1969), 2 da (Philippa b 1962, Jane b 1965); *Career* Nat Serv cmmnd RN; banker; dir: NM Rothschild & Sons Ltd 1970, Rothschild Tst Corp 1970, Tokyo Pacific Holdings NV 1969-; chm: Equity Consort Investment Trust plc 1973- (dir 1967-), N M Rothschild & Sons (CI) Ltd 1981-; dir: Kleeneze Holdings plc 1985-, Jupiter European Investment Trust plc 1990-; AMSIA, FRSA; *Clubs* Carlton, MCC; *Style*— James Roe Esq; Petleys, Downe, Kent BR6 7JS (☎ 0689 54901); New Court, St Swithin's Lane, London EC4P 4DU (☎ 071 280 5000)

ROE, Marion Audrey; MP (C) Broxbourne 1983-; da of William Keyte (d 1977), and Grace Mary, *née* Bocking (d 1983); *b* 15 July 1936; *Educ* Bromley HS, Croydon HS (both GPDST), English Sch of Languages Vevey, Switzerland; *m* 1958, James Roe, *qv*, s of Kenneth Roe; 1 s (William b 1969), 2 da (Philippa b 1962, Jane b 1965); *Career* PPS to: Under Secs of State for Tport 1985-86, Min of State for Tport 1986, Sec of

State for Tport 1986-87; Parly under sec of state DOE 1987-88; chm Cons backbench Horticulture and Markets Sub Ctee 1989- (sec 1983-85); memb Select Ctee: Agric 1983-85, Social Servs 1988-89, Procedure 1990-; chm Cons Parly Social Security Ctee 1990- (vice chm 1988-89), succeeded in bringing into law the private membs Act "Prohibition of Female Circumcision" 1985; cncllr London Borough of Bromley 1975-78, GLC memb for Ilford North 1977-86, Cons dep chief whip GLC 1978-82, leading Cons spokesman GLC Police Ctee 1982-83; contested Barking 1979 general election; vice pres Women's Nat Cancer Control Campaign 1985-87 and 1988, govr Research into Ageing Tst 1988-; govr St Olaves GS for Boys Orpington 1975-80, memb SE Thames RHA 1978-84, patron UK Nat Ctee for the UN Devpt Fund for Women 1985-87; Freeman City of London; *Books* The Labour Left in London - A Blueprint for a Socialist Britain (1985); *Recreations* opera, ballet, theatre; *Clubs* Carlton (lady assoc memb); *Style—* Mrs Marion Roe, MP; House of Commons, London SW1A 0AA (☎ 071 219 3464)

ROE, Mark Adrian; s of Gordon Arthur Roe, and Phyllis, *née* Flowers; *b* 20 Feb 1963; *Educ* Henry Fanshaw GS; *m* 12 Nov 1988, Jane Patricia, da of Kenneth Gill; *Career* former springboard and highboard diving champion of Derbyshire, junior int golfer GB & I and Eng 1980, professional golfer 1981-, joined EuroTour 1985, Catalan Open Champion 1989, represented Eng at World Cup 1989; *Recreations* snooker, history of golf, antiques; *Clubs* The Hallowes Golf; *Style—* Mark Roe, Esq; PGA European Tour, The Wentworth Club, Wentworth Drive, Virginia Water, Surrey (☎ 09904 2881)

ROE, Dr Peter Frank; s of Harry Frank Roe (d 1979), and Ruth Isabel Sadler (d 1976); *b* 17 Jan 1931; *Educ* Taunton Sch, St John's Coll Cambridge (MA), Univ of Edinburgh (MD); *m* 9 Aug 1956, Margaret, da of Edward Henry Sapp (d 1974), 1 s (Andrew b 1957), 1 da (Helen b 1962); *Career* conslt physician: Ugandan Govt 1966-67, geriatric med Somerset Health Authy 1970-; reader C of E 1970; FRCPG 1981; *Recreations* music, heraldic painting, walking; *Style—* Dr Peter Roe; Kirkmead, Staplegrove, Taunton, Somerset TA2 6AP (☎ 0823 284568); Musgrove Park Hospital, Taunton, Somerset (☎ 0823 333444)

ROE, Dame Raigh; DBE (1980, CBE 1975), JP (1966); da of A C Kurts (decd); *b* 12 Dec 1922; *Educ* Perth Girls' Sch; *m* 1941, James Arthur Roe; 3 s; *Career* world pres Assoc Country Women of the World 1977-80 (hon life memb 1972); Australian of the Year 1977; dir: ABC 1978-, Queen Elizabeth II Silver Jubilee Tst for Young Australians 1978, Airlines of WA 1981-, Hosp Benefits Fund of WA 1982-; memb Honour Deutscher Landfrauenverband 1980; *Style—* Dame Raigh Roe, DBE, JP; 76 Regency Drive, Crestwood, Thornlie, W Australia 6108 (☎ 459 8765)

ROE, Air Chief Marshal Sir Rex David; GCB (1981), KCB (1977, CB 1974, AFC); *b* 1925; *Educ* City of London Sch, London Univ; *m* 1948, Helen, *née* Nairn (d 1981); 1 s, 2 da; *Career* Air Memb Supply & Orgn 1978-81, when ret; AOC-in-C: Support Cmmd 1977-78, Trg Cmmd 1976-77; SASO HQ Near East AF 1972-76; RCDS 1971, commanded RNZAF Centl Flying Sch 1956-58, joined RAF 1943; *Style—* Air Chief Marshal Sir Rex Roe, GCB, KCB, CB, AFC; c/o Lloyds Bank, 6 Pall Mall, SW1

ROE, Hon Mrs (Susan); only da of Baron Lewin, GCB, MVO, DSC; *b* 1949; *m* 1969, Peter Roe; *Style—* The Hon Mrs Roe; c/o Adm of the Fleet The Rt Hon The Lord Lewin, KG, GCB, MVO, DSC, House of Lords, London SW1

ROEBUCK, Christina Rowena Margaret; da of Rev Eric Stopford, of Pewsey, Wiltshire, and Christina Heather Liddle, *née* Muir; *b* 28 Feb 1943; *Educ* Orme Girls' GS Staffs, Harper & Adams Agric Coll (Nat Dip in Poultry Husbandry); *m* 1, 1968 (m dis 1985), Ian Patrick, s of late Edward Caudwell, of Culter, Kincardineshire; 2 da (Charlotte b 1971, Rosalind b 1973); m 2, 1986, Simon John, s of John Frederick Roebuck, of Walton, Derbys; 1 s (Harry b 1987); *Career* farmer; agric advsr Br Egg Mktg Bd 1962-68; memb Judges' Panel Arab Horse Soc; co-ordinator World Arabian Horse Orgn Conf London 1988; *Recreations* breeding arabian horses, shooting; *Style—* Mrs Christina R M Roebuck; Lendrum Farm, Turriff, Aberdeenshire AB53 8HA (☎ 08883 285)

ROEBUCK, Dr Eric James; s of Wilfred Roebuck (d 1988), of Farnborough, Hants, and Ellen Hannah, *née* Welch (d 1988); *b* 3 March 1928; *Educ* Woodhouse Grove Sch, Charing Cross Hosp Med Sch (MB BS), Guy's Hosp (DMRD); *m* 13 Feb 1958, Rose Josephine, da of Owen Woods (d 1968), of Castle Blaney, Eire; 1 s (Jeremy b 25 Nov 1958), 1 da (Claire b 30 May 1961); *Career* RN 1946-48; house offr King Edward VII Hosp Windsor 1954, registrar Heatherwood Hosp Ascot 1956, sr registrar Guy's Hosp London 1958, conslt radiologist Univ Hosp Nottingham 1965-, clinical teacher Univ of Nottingham 1965-; visiting prof: Univ of Zaira Nigeria 1972, Kuala Lumpur Malaysia 1989; numerous pubns and lectures on: radiology, magnetic resonance imaging, breast cancer detection; memb: Nottinghamshire AHA, Forrest Ctee on Breast Cancer Screening, Euro GP for Breast Cancer Screening; RCR: officer, registrar, memb Bd and Cncl, examiner; FFR 1964, FRCR 1976; *Books* Positioning in Radiography (1986), Building and Extending a Radiology Department (1988), Clinical Radiology of the Breast (1990); *Recreations* shooting, fishing, swimming, music, travel; *Style—* Dr Eric Roebuck; Earleydene, 45 Private Rd, Sherwood, Nottingham NG5 4DD (☎ 0602 609547); University Hospital, Nottingham (☎ 0602 691689); 10 Regent St, Nottingham (☎ 0602 474835)

ROEBUCK, Roy Delville; *b* 25 Sept 1929; *m* 27 March 1957, Dr Mary Ogilvy, *née* Adams; 1 s (Gavin Macgregor b 1957); *Career* Nat Serv FEAF 1947-50; journalist: Stockport Advertiser, Northern Daily Telegraph, Yorkshire Evening News, News Chronicle, Daily Express, Manchester Evening Chronicle, Daily Herald 1950-66; contested (Lab) Altrincham and Sale gen election 1964 and by-election 1965, MP (Lab) Harrow E 1966-70, contested (Lab) Leek gen election 1974; called to the Bar Gray's Inn 1974; govr Moorfields Eye Hosp 1984-88, memb Islington Community Health Cncl 1988-; *Recreations* reading Hansard, music, tennis, walking; *Clubs* RAC; *Style—* Roy Roebuck, Esq; 12 Brooksby St, London N1 1HA (☎ 071 607 7057); Bell Yard Chambers, 16 Bell Yard, London WC2 2JR (☎ 071 306 9292, fax 071 404 5143)

ROEDY, William H; *b* 13 June 1948; *Educ* West Point, Univ of Harvard (MBA); *Career* Nat Serv 10 years W Point, mil serv incl pilot Vietnam; formerly mangr Nat Accounts LA; Home Box Office Cable TV: launched with Cinemax 1979, mktg 1979-89, recently vice pres affiliate operations; mgmnt conslt for TV stations Boston Mass USA; memb CCTA; *Style—* William Roedy, Esq; MTV Europe, Centro House, 20-23 Mandela Street, London NW1 0DU (☎ 071 383 4250, fax 071 388 2064, telex 929580 MTV G)

ROEG, Nicolas Jack; s of Jack Nicolas Roeg (d 1952), and Mabel Gertrude Silk (d 1985); *b* 15 Aug 1928; *Educ* Mercers Sch; *m* 1, 1957, Susan Rennie, da of Maj F W Stephen MC; 4 s (Joscelin, Nicolas, Lucien, Sholto); m 2, 1986, Theresa Russell; 2 s (Statten Jack, Maxmilian Nicolas Sextus); *Career* film dir: Performance, Walkabout, Don't Look Now, The Man Who Fell to Earth, Bad Timing, Eureka, Insignificance, Castaway, Track 29; *Style—* Mr Nicolas Roeg

ROFE, Brian Henry; s of Henry Alexander Rofe (d 1979), and Marguerite, *née* Browne; *b* 7 Jan 1934; *Educ* Shrewsbury, St John's Coll Cambridge (BA 1957, MA 1962); *m* 26 May 1962, (Margaret) Anne, da of Rev Phillip R Shepherd; 2 s (Christopher Henry b 16 Jan 1965, Andrew John b 1 April 1968), 1 da (Katharine (Mrs Johns) b 1 July 1963); *Career* Nat Serv RA 1952-54, 2 Lt 1953, Actg Lt TA 1955; chartered engr, asst civil engr John Laing Construction 1957-63, asst/sr engr Rofe and Raffety 1963-69, res engr Draycote Reservoir 1967-69; ptnr Rofe Kennard and Lapworth 1970- (consulting water engrs); contracts incl: Thames Groundwater Scheme 1971-76, Iraq Rural Water Supply 1975-77, Sherbourne and Wyre Flood Schemes, Blashford Lakes Scheme; memb Church Cncl St Marys Walton on Thames, Guildford Diocesan Steward ship Advsy Ctee; Freeman: City of London, Worshipful Co of Grocers; FIWES (vice-pres 1986-87), FIWEM (vice-pres 1988-89), FICE 1972, FGS, MConsE 1972; *Books* Kempe's Engineers Year Book (Water Supply Chapter 1970-), Civil Engineering Reference Book (Water Supply Section); *Recreations* bridge, sailing, painting; *Clubs* Royal Cwlth Soc; *Style—* Brian Rofe, Esq; Laleham Cottage, 40 Churchfield Rd, Walton-on-Thames, Surrey KT12 2SY (☎ 0932 223147); Raffety House, 2 Sutton Ct Rd, Sutton SM1 4SS (☎ 081 643 8201, fax 081 642 8469, telex 946688 ARKELL G)

ROFFE, Clive Brian; JP (1987); s of Philip Roffe (d 1961); *b* 4 June 1935; *Educ* Brighton Coll; *m* 1966, Jacqueline Carole, *née* Branston; 2 da (Danielle Philippa Geraldine b 1970, Natasha Nicole b 1974); *Career* Lloyd's underwriter 1966, fin conslt; chm: Melbo Petroleum Ltd 1970, Edinburgh Insur Servs 1971, Offshire Investmts Ltd 1968; co dir; Freeman City of London; *Recreations* organ, philately, jogging; *Clubs* MCC, Guards Polo, Hurlingham, City Livery, Lloyd's Yacht; *Style—* Clive Roffe, Esq, JP; 50 Kingsway Court, Hove, Sussex (☎ 0273 737 044)

ROFFE-SILVESTER, John Charles; s of Michael Raoul Rolfe-Silvester, and Brigid Mary Teresa, *née* Wicksteed; *b* 22 Aug 1951; *Educ* Downside, RAC; *Career* currently farmer and timber contractor; MFH 1978-; Master of Taunton Vale Harriers 1986-; *Style—* John Roffe-Silvester, Esq; Reapmay, West Buckland, Wellington, Somerset TA21 9LX (☎ 0823 662631)

ROGAN, Anthony Gerard Patrick (Anton); s of Sean Rogan, of Belfast, and Patricia Rogan; *b* 25 March 1966; partner, Clare Doran; *Career* professional footballer; Distillery NI 1984-86, over 160 appearances Celtic 1986- (debut v Hamilton Academical 1987); 17 full caps NI 1988-; honours with Celtic: Scot Cup 1988 and 1989 (runners up 1990), Scot League Championship 1988; *Recreations* hunting, golf, fishing; *Style—* Anton Rogan, Esq; Celtic FC, 95 Kerrydale St, Glasgow G40 3RE (☎ 041 556 2611)

ROGAN, Very Rev Canon John; s of William Rogan (d 1983), and Jane, *née* Whatmough (d 1985); *b* 20 May 1928; *Educ* Manchester Central HS, Univ of Durham, St John's Coll (BA, MA, DipTheol), Open Univ (BPhil); *m* 6 April 1953, (Dorothy) Margaret, da of George F C Williams (d 1982); 1 s (Peter Mark b 1956), 1 da (Ruth b 1955); *Career* RAF educn offr 1949-52; curate Ashton under Lyne 1954, chaplain Sheffield Industl Mission 1957-61, sec C of E Industl Ctee 1957-61, sec C of E Industl Ctee 1961-66, asst sec C of E Bd for Social Responsibility 192-66, vicar of Leigh Lancs 1966-78 (rural dean 1971-78), sec Manchester Bd for Social Responsibility 1967-74 (chm 1974-78), provost St Paul's Cathedral Dundee 1978-83, canon residentiary Bristol Cath 1983-, dir Bristol Bd for Social Responsibility 1983-; memb Bristol Drugs Project; memb: Ecclesiastical Soc, Roman Soc; *Books* Principles of Church Reform (ed with M J Jackson, 1962); *Recreations* walking, history; *Style—* The Very Rev Canon John Rogan; Bristol Cathedral, College Green, Bristol BS1 5JT (☎ 0272 264879)

ROGER, Alan Stuart; MBE (Mil) 1943; s of Sir Alexander Forbes Proctor Roger, KCIE (d 1961), and Helen Stuart, *née* Clark; *b* 27 April 1909; *Educ* Loretto, Trinity Coll Oxford (BA); *Career* war serv in France, India, Iraq, Persia, Hong Kong; chm of Bonsaikai of London 1964, memb of Cncl of Contemporary Art Soc 1980, Floral Ctee B of RHS, Scotlands Gdns Ctee; vice-pres Nat Tst for Scotland (1983-), tstee Nat Galleries of Scotland 1967-82, author Wisley Handbook on Bonsai; *Recreations* gardening; *Style—* Alan S Roger, Esq, MBE; Dundonnell, by Garve, Koss & Cromarty IV23 2QW; 81 Elms Road, London

ROGER, David Bernard; s of John Grant Roger, of Newstead, Scotland, and Margaret Jean, *née* Dymock; *b* 23 Feb 1951; *Educ* Melville Coll Edinburgh, Univ of Newcastle upon Tyne (BA), Univ of Bristol (MA), Univ of Paris (Scenographic Diploma), ENO theatre design course; *Career* theatre designer; designs incl: La Mort de Zarathustra (Lucernaire Paris) 1979-80, The Mission (Soho Poly) 1982, The Knot Garden (Opera Factory) 1984, Akhnaten (ENO) 1985, La Boheme (Opera North) 1986, Temptation (RSC The Other Place) 1987, Faust pts 1 and 2 (Lyric Hammersmith) 1988, Simplicius Simplicissimus 1989, Cosi Fan Tutte (TV version C4) 1989, Figaro (Opera Factory Zurich) 1990, Morte d'Arthur (Lyric Hammersmith) 1990, Manon Lescaut (Opera Comique Paris) 1990, Don Giovanni (TV version C4) 1990; memb Soc Br Theatre Designers; *Clubs* 2 Brydges Place; *Style—* David Roger, Esq; Garricks Managment, 7 Garrick St, London WC2E 9AR (☎ 071 240 0660)

ROGER, Peter Charles Marshall; s of Matthew McCargo Roger (d 1977), and Muriel Ethel, *née* Morrison; *b* 11 April 1942; *Educ* Glasgow HS; *m* 21 April 1972, Fiona Ann, da of James Murray (d 1986); 2 s (Kenneth b 1975, Andrew b 1979), 1 da (Alison b 1982); *Career* CA, Thompson McLintock & Co 1964-71, Speirs & Jeffrey 1971-, chm Stock Exchange Scot Unit; MICAS 1964; *Recreations* golf; *Clubs* Prestwick, Pollok, Boat of Garten; *Style—* Peter Roger, Esq; 36 Renfield St, Glasgow G2 1NA (☎ 041 248 4311, fax 041 221 4764, telex 777 902)

ROGERS, (David) Alan; s of Frederick George Rogers (d 1944), and Kathleen, *née* Fowler (d 1989); *b* 18 Aug 1940; *Educ* Univ Coll Hosp London (MB BS); *m* 1984, Katie, da of Tony Giovanni; 3 s (James b 1966, Owen b 1971, Thomas b 1989), 1 da (Megan b 1986); *Career* in gen practice 1964-66, Gynaecological Unit Princess Margaret Hosp Nassau 1966-70, gynaecologist Whittington Hosp London 1970-72, private practice in gynaecology 1972-, med dir Parkview Clinic London 1983-; helped establish day care female sterilisation programme Marie Stopes House and female sterilisation clinic in Kildare Ireland; trained medical staff in Italy and Rumania; MRCOG; *Style—* Dr Alan Rogers; 46 Harley St, London W1N 1AD (☎ 071 580 4918)

ROGERS, Dr Alan Rowland; s of George William Rogers (d 1983), and Rhoda, *née* Sutton (d 1982); *b* 6 Oct 1929; *Educ* Skinner's Sch Tunbridge Wells, Brighton Tech Coll, Univ of London (BPharm, BSc, PhD); *m* 31 Dec 1955, Joy Elizabeth, da of John William Henry Brace, of Hertford; 2 s (Adam b 1971, Duncan b 1974); *Career* physical chemist Allen and Hanburys Ltd 1953-55; Brighton Tech Coll: lectr 1957-60, sr lectr 1960-66; Heriot-Watt Univ: prof of pharmacy 1966-84; sec and scientific dir Br Pharmacopoeia Cmmn 1988-; FRPharms 1954, FRSC 1963; *Style—* Dr Alan Rogers; British Pharmacopoeia Commission, Market Towers, 1 Nine Elms Lane, London SW8 5NQ (☎ 071 720 9844, fax 071 720 5647)

ROGERS, Allan Ralph; MP (Lab) Rhondda 1983-, MEP; s of John and Madeleine Rogers; *b* 24 Oct 1932; *Educ* University Coll of Swansea; *m* 1955, Ceridwen James; 1 s, 3 d; *Career* sometime geologist, teacher; MEP (Lab) SE Wales 1979-84; *Style—* Allan Rogers Esq, MP, MEP; 70 Cemetery Road, Porth, Rhondda, Mid-Glamorgan

ROGERS, Prof (Claude) Ambrose; s of Sir Leonard Rogers, KCSI, CIE, FRS (d 1962), and Una Elsie North (d 1951); *b* 1 Nov 1920; *Educ* Berkhamsted Sch, UCL, Birkbeck Coll London (BSc, PhD, DSc); *m* 1952, Joan Marian, wid of W G Gordon and da of F North; 2 da; *Career* experimental offr Miny of Supply 1940-45; lect and reader UCL 1946-54, prof of pure mathematics Univ of Birmingham 1954-58, Astor prof of mathematics UCL 1958-86; pres London Mathematical Soc 1970-72; chm Jt

Mathematical Cncl 1981-84; prof emeritus Univ of London 1986; FRS; *Books* Packing and Covering (1964), Hausdorff Measures (1970), Analytic Sets (1980); *Style*— Prof Ambrose Rogers, FRS; 8 Grey Close, London NW11 6QG (☎ 081 455 8027); Department of Statistical Science, University College, London WC1E 6BT (☎ 071 387 7050)

ROGERS, Anthony Crawford Nugent; s of (Sidney) Crawford Rogers (d 1964), of Bardowie, and Joan Diane, *née* Nugent; *b* 22 July 1938; *Educ* Larchfield Sch Helensburgh, Second Glasgow Acad, Univ of Glasgow (MB ChB); *m* 4 June 1964, Teresa Rhind (Terri), da of Lt Cdr Eric Patrick (d 1944), of Glasgow; 3 da (Sarah Jane b 1965, Jennifer Diane b 1966, Gillian Victoria b 1970); *Career* registrar in surgery Glasgow 1966-68, registrar in urology Newcastle upon Tyne 1968-72, sr registrar urology Aberdeen 1972-76, conslt Stirling and Falkirk 976-; gp coach SAAJCC; memb BMA, FRCS, FRCSP; *Recreations* athletics coaching; *Clubs* Central Region Athletic; *Style*— Anthony Rogers, Esq; 5 Abercromby Place, Stirling FK8 2QP (☎ 0786 73948); Royal Infir mary, Livilands, Stirling FK8 2AU (☎ 0786 73151)

ROGERS, Ms Barbara; *b* 21 Sept 1945; *Educ* Univ of Sussex (BA); *Career* writer, researcher, journalist, ed Everywoman Magazine 1985-; cncllr London Borough of Islington 1982-86; *Recreations* gardening, music; *Style*— Ms Barbara Rogers; Everywoman Magazine, 34 Islington Green, London N1 8DU (☎ 071 359 5496)

ROGERS, Lady; Brenda Mary; CBE (1964); da of late Ernest Thompson Sharp; *m* 1939, Sir Philip James Rogers, CBE, *qv*; *Career* joined British Red Cross Somerset 1936, former cmdt First Lagos (Nigeria) Detachment, pres Nairobi Div 1953, dep pres Kenya Branch British Red Cross 1956, Red Cross rep Mauritius Hurricane Disaster Relief Ctee 1960, Red Cross organiser of refugees from Belgian Congo 1960, dep pres Sussex Counties Branch British Red Cross 1968-, memb Nat Exec Ctee BRCS 1964-67 and 1969-73 (hon vice pres 1980-); govr Delamere Girls Sch Kenya 1960-62; *Clubs* New Cavendish; *Style*— Lady Rogers, CBE; Church Close, Newick, Sussex (☎ 082 572 2210)

ROGERS, Christopher John (Chris); s of Robert William Rogers, of Old Martson, Oxford, and Mary Dolores, *née* Morant; *b* 1 April 1950; *Educ* Salesian Coll Cowly, Univ of Hull, Lanchester Poly (BSc); *m* 1, 2 Aug 1975, Irene Ann, da of William Mallis (d 1986), of Glasgow; m 2, 23 April 1988, Jane, da of Owen Elliott, of Loddiswell, Kingsbridge, Devon; *Career* prodr and presenter BBC Radio Carlisle 1973-79, continuity announcer BBC TV London 1976-77, presenter and reporter Border TV Carlisle 1979-81, presenter and political ed TV South West 1982-; progs presented incl ITV's 12 Summer Days 1988; memb Royal Photographic Soc; *Recreations* motoring, writing, photography, classical music, motorcycling, camping, hill-walking; *Clubs* BMW; *Style*— Chris Rogers, Esq; 7 Oakwood Park, Loddiswell, Kingsbridge, Devon TQ7 4SE (☎ 0548 550746); Television South West, Derrys Cross, Plymouth PL1 2SP (☎ 0752 663322, fax 0752 671970, car 0836 785039)

ROGERS, Prof Colin; s of William Joseph Rogers (d 1952), and Margaret Anne Gwendoline, *née* Goodgame (d 1971); *b* 1 Dec 1940; *Educ* Magdalen Coll Sch Oxford, Univ of Oxford (BA), Univ of Toronto (MEd), Univ of Toronto (MEd), Univ of Nottingham (MSc, PhD); *Career* lectr Univ of Nottingham 1969-71; assoc prof: Old Dominion Univ Virginia USA 1973-74, Univ of W Ontario Canada 1974-78 (asst prof 1971-73); visiting prof Univ of Adelaide Aust 1975, sr visitor Dept of Applied Mathematics and Theoretical Physics Univ of Cambridge 1979, prof Univ of Waterloo Canada 1981-88 (assoc prof 1978-81), visiting prof Georgia Inst of Technol USA 1982 and 1984, chair mathematical engrg Loughborough Univ of Technology 1988, adjunt princ res scientist Georgia Inst Technol 1989; FIMA 1977, FInst; *Books* Bäcklund Transformations and Their Applications (with W F Shadwick, 1982), Nonlinear Boundary Value Problems in Science and Engineering (with W F Ames, 1989), Wave Phenomena: Modern Theory and Applications (with T B Moodie, 1989); *Recreations* Welsh Studies; *Style*— Prof Colin Rogers; 32 Church Street, Shepsted, Leics (☎ 0509 503182); Dept of Mathematical Sciences, Loughborough University of Technology, Leics (☎ 0509 222785, fax 0509 231983, telex 34319)

ROGERS, Ven David Arthur; s of Rev Canon Thomas Godfrey Rogers (d 1974), and Doris Mary Cleaver, *née* Steele (d 1977); *b* 12 March 1921; *Educ* St Edward's Sch Oxford, Christ's Coll Cambridge (MA), Ridley Hall Cambridge; *m* 1951, Joan, da of Philip Malkin (d 1956); 1 s (Jeremy Peter b 1952), 3 da (Janet Elizabeth b 1954, Katharine Rosemary b 1956, Anne Sarah b 1960); *Career* Lt Green Howards and Royal Armd Corps, NW Europe 1945; rector St Peter Levenshulme 1953-59, vicar of Sedbergh, Cautley and Garsdale 1959-79, rural dean of Sedbergh and then Ewecross 1959-77, archdeacon of Craven 1977-86, archdeacon Emeritus 1986-; *Style*— The Venerable D A Rogers; Borrens, Leck, Carnforth, Lancs LA6 2JG (☎ 05242 71616)

ROGERS, David Bryan; CB (1984); s of Frank and Louisa Rogers; *b* 8 Sept 1929; *Educ* Grove Park Wrexham, UCL (BA); *m* 1955, Marjory Geraldine Gilmour *née* Horribine; 1 s, 2 da; *Career* inspr of taxes 1953, principal inspr 1968, sr princ inspr 1976, under sec and dir of Operations Bd of Inland Revenue 1978-81, dep sec and DG Bd Inland Revenue 1981-89; memb Cncl UCL 1983-; *Recreations* piano, organ, singing; *Style*— Bryan Rogers, Esq, CB

ROGERS, David Owen; s of Alan Edgar Rogers (d 1983), of Haslemere, Surrey, and Joan Grace, *née* Thornhill; *b* 5 May 1952; *Educ* Royal GS Guildford Surrey, Kingston-Upon-Hull Coll of Commerce (HND Business Studies); *m* 21 Aug 1982, Deborah June, da of Brian Geoffrey Sharp, of Godalming Surrey; 3 da (Jennifer Clare b 1984, Josephine Kate b 1986, Caroline Mary b 1990); *Career* Rank Leisure Servs Ltd 1973-77, EMI Records Ltd 1978-79, Office of Population Censuses and Surveys 1980-84, house husband 1984-; longstanding memb Lib Party, fndr memb Social and Lib Democrats; first elected to East Sussex CC 1977; memb for: Brighton (St Nicholas) 1977-85, Brighton (Seven Dials) 1985-89, Newhaven 1989-; ldr Lib Democrat Gp (and its precursors: Lib, Alliance, Democrat) E Sussex CC 1977-, elected to Brighton Borough Cncl as memb for St Nicholas Ward 1979-83 and Seven Dials Ward 1983-91, elected to Newhaven Town Cncl 1989, chair Lewes Constituency Lib Democrats 1989-; ASLDC (formerly ALC) 1977-; *Style*— David Rogers, Esq; 74 Fort Rd, Newhaven, East Sussex BN9 9EJ (☎ 0273 512 172)

ROGERS, Dr Eric William Evan; s of William Percy Rogers (d 1978), of Southgate, London, and Margaret, *née* Evans (d 1988); *b* 12 April 1925; *Educ* Southgate Co Sch, Imperial Coll London (DIC, BSc, MSc, DSc); *m* 1 April 1950, (Dorothy) Joyce, da of Alan Charles Loveless (d 1973), of Tankerton, Whitstable, Kent; 2 s (Christopher b 1958, Andrew b 1965), 1 da (Margaret b 1960); *Career* with Aerodynamics Div Nat Physical Lab 1945-70, dep dir (aircraft) Royal Aircraft Estab Farnborough 1978-85 (joined 1970, head of Aerodynamics Dept 1972-74), aeronautical res conslt 1985-; CEng 1970, FRAeS 1960, FCGI 1976; *Recreations* music, history; *Style*— Dr Eric Rogers; 64 Thetford Rd, New Malden, Surrey KT3 5DT (☎ 081 942 7452)

ROGERS, Sir Frank Jarvis; s of Percy Rogers (d 1960); *b* 24 Feb 1920; *Educ* Wolstanton GS; *m* 1949, Esma Sophia, *née* Holland; 2 da; *Career* military serv 1940-46; journalist 1937-49; gen mangr Nigerian Daily Times 1949-52, mangr Argus Melbourne 1952-55, md Overseas Newspapers 1958-60, dir Daily Mirror 1960-65, md IPC 1965-70, chm Nat Newspaper Steering Gp 1970-72, dir Newspaper Publishers Assoc 1971-73; chm: British Exec Ctee Int Press Inst 1978-88, Exec Ctee Industrial Soc 1976-79, EMAP plc (formerly East Midlands Allied Press Ltd) 1973-90; dir Plessey New Jersey Inc, advsr Corp Affrs Plessey Co Ltd 1973-81, chm Ansafone Ltd 1981-85, dep chm The Daily Telegraph plc 1986-; kt 1988; *Recreations* golf, travel; *Clubs* Moor Park Golf; *Style*— Sir Frank Rogers; Greensleeves, Loudwater Drive, Loudwater, Rickmansworth, Herts; c/o The Daily Telegraph, 181 Marsh Wall, London E14 9SR

ROGERS, Geoffrey; s of Arthur Frank Rogers (d 1967), and Florence Annie Rogers (d 1980); *b* 24 Nov 1946; *Educ* Bideford GS; *m* 19 April 1969, Janet Anne, da of Cyril John Langman; 1 s (Timothy b 1979), 2 da (Rebecca b 1973, Nicola b 1974); *Career* CA; sr ptnr Atkey Goodman Accountants taxation and mgmnt conslts Plymouth 1975-, ptnr Barretts Restaurants Plymouth 1988-; sec IOD Plymouth Centre 1981-89, memb Devon and Cornwall Branch Ctee IOD 1983-, non-exec memb Plymouth Health Authy 1990-; FInstD, MBIM, FCA, FCCA; *Recreations* yachting; *Clubs* Royal Western YC of England; *Style*— Geoffrey Rogers, Esq; The Manor House, Chapel Street, Devonport, Plymouth PL1 4DS (☎ 0752 558141)

ROGERS, (Leonard) John; OBE (1979); s of Leonard Samuel Rogers, JP (d 1964) of Croydon, Surrey, and Amy Mary, *née* Martlew (d 1958); *b* 30 Oct 1931; *Educ* Whitgift Sch Croydon, Städtisches und Staatliches Gymnasium Neuss am Rhein, Trinity Coll Cambridge (MA); *m* 16 July 1955, Avery Janet, da of Hugh Griffith Ernest Morgan (d 1968), of Croydon, Surrey; 4 s (Paul b 1956, Nicholas b 1958, Jonathan b 1962, Crispin b 1966); *Career* Nat Serv, E Surrey Regt 1950, Eaton Hall OCS 1951, Lt Intelligence Corps BAOR 1951-52; export contracts administrator (Guided Weapons) Bristol Aircraft Ltd 1958-60, asst sec Bristol Aeroplane Plastics Ltd 1960-62, export contracts mangr (Comm Aircraft Div) Br Aircraft Corp 1965-73, business dir BAC Commercial Acft Div 1973 (mktg dir 1977), divnl mktg dir British Aerospace 1978-79, aviation conslt Roconsult AG Zug Schweiz 1980-84; dir: AIM Gp plc 1984-, AIM Aviation Ltd 1984-; md AIM Aviation (Henshalls) Ltd; Methodist Church: Dorking and Horsham circuit steward 1977-82, memb Euro Affairs Ctee 1980-86 and 1989-, sec Connexional 1988 Steering Ctee 1986-89, led Wesley 250th Anniversary Pilgrimage to Moravian Church in Herrnhut GDR 1988; memb: Gen Purposes Ctee London Voluntary Serv Cncl 1980-83, Romanian Trade Ctee London C of C 1975-83; Freeman Freeman City of London 1979, Liveryman Worshipful Co of Coachmakers and Coach Harness Makers 1979; FIOD 1978, ARAeS 1989; *Recreations* European languages, opera, roses, mountain-walking; *Clubs* IOD; *Style*— John Rogers, Esq; Willow Pool, Effingham, Surrey KT24 5JG (☎ 0372 583 59); AIM Aviation (Henshalls) Ltd, Abbot Close, Oyster Lane, Byfleet, Surrey KT14 7JT (☎ 09323 510 11, fax 09323 527 92, telex 928460 WHS G)

ROGERS, John Michael Thomas; QC (1979); s of Harold Stuart Rogers, and Sarah Joan Thomas, *née* Bibby; *b* 13 May 1938; *Educ* Rydal Sch, Birkenhead Sch, Fitzwilliam House Cambridge (MA, LLB); *m* 1971, Jennifer Ruth; 1 da (Caitlin Sarah b 1981); *Career* called to Bar Gray's Inn 1963, rec 1976, ldr Wales and Chester Circuit 1990-; pres Mental Health Review Tribunal 1983-, chancellor Diocese of St Asaph 1983-; *Clubs* Reform, Pragmatists, Bristol Channel, Yacht; *Style*— John Rogers, Esq, QC; 2 Dr Johnson's Building, Temple, London EC4Y 7AY (☎ 071 353 5371)

ROGERS, Air Chief Marshal Sir John Robson; KCB (1981), CBE (1971); s of B Rogers; *b* 11 Jan 1928; *Educ* Brentwood Sch, RAF Coll Cranwell; *m* 1955, Gytha, *née* Campbell; 2 s, 2 da; *Career* dir-gen Orgn RAF 1977-79, Air Vice-Marshal 1977, AOC Trg Units HQ RAF Support Cmd 1979-81, Air Marshal 1981, Air Memb Supply and Orgn 1981-83, Controller Aircraft 1983-, Air Chief Marshal 1984; dir First Technology Gp; vice chm RAC, chm RAC Motor Sports Assoc; FRAeS, CBIM; *Recreations* motor sport; *Clubs* RAF, RAC; *Style*— Air Chief Marshal Sir John Rogers, KCB, CBE; c/o Lloyds Bank, 27 High St, Colchester, Essex

ROGERS, John Willis; QC (1975); s of Reginald John Rogers (d 1940); *b* 7 Nov 1929; *Educ* Sevenoaks Sch, Fitzwilliam Coll Cambridge; *m* 1952, Sheila Elizabeth, *née* Cann; 1 s, 1 da; *Career* called to the Bar Lincoln's Inn 1955, first prosecuting cncl to Inland Revenue S Eastern Circuit 1969-75, rec 1974-, hon rec for City of Canterbury 1985-; *Recreations* cricket, gardening, music, change ringing; *Clubs* Garrick, MCC, Band of Brothers; *Style*— John W Rogers, Esq, QC; 3 Serjeants' Inn, London, EC4Y 1BQ (☎ 071 353 5537)

ROGERS, Hon Mrs (Loretta Anne); *née* Robinson; da of 1 Baron Martonmere, GBE, KCMG, PC (d May 1989), and Maysie, *née* Gasque (d Sept 1989); *b* 1939; *m* 1963, Edward Samuel Rogers; 1 s (Edward Samuel b 1969), 3 da (Lisa Anne b 1967, Melinda Mary b 1971, Martha Loretta b 1972); *Style*— The Hon Mrs Rogers; 3 Frybrook Rd, Toronto, Ontario, Canada M4V 1Y7

ROGERS, Malcolm Austin; s of James Eric Rogers, and Frances Anne, *née* Elsey; *b* 3 Oct 1948; *Educ* Oakham Sch Rutland, Magdalen Coll Oxford, ChCh Oxford (MA, DPhil); *Career* dep dir Nat Portrait Gallery 1983- (asst keeper 1974-83, keeper 1985-); FSA 1986; *Books* Dictionary of British Portraiture 4 Vols (jt ed, 1979-81), Museums and Galleries of London Blue Guide (1983, 3 edn 1991), William Dobson (1983), John and John Baptist Closterman: A Catalogue of their Works (1983), Elizabeth II: Portraits of Sixty Years (1986), Camera Portraits (1989), Montacute House (1991), Champion Guide to London (ed with Sir David Piper, 1991); *Recreations* food, wine, opera, travel; *Clubs* Beefsteak; *Style*— Malcolm Rogers, Esq, FSA; 76A Ashley Gardens, Thirleby Rd, London SW1P 1HG (☎ 071 828 5304); National Portarait Gallery, St Martin's Place, London WC2H 0HE (☎ 071 306 0055, fax 071 306 0056)

ROGERS, Martin John Wyndham; s of John Frederick Rogers (d 1985), of Oxshott, Surrey, and Grace Mary, *née* Stride (d 1971); *b* 9 April 1931; *Educ* Oundle, Heidelberg Univ, Trinity Hall Cambridge (MA); *m* 31 August 1957, Jane, da of Harold Alfred Cook (d 1978), of Cobham, Surrey; 2 s (Mark Wyndham Edward b 31 May 1959, Stephen James Wyndham b 17 June 1961), 1 da (Sarah Lucy b 24 June 1966); *Career* Henry Wiggin & Co 1953-55; under master and master of The Queen's Scholars Westminster Sch 1967-71 (asst master 1955-60, sr chem master 1960-64, housemaster 1964-66), head master Malvern Coll 1971-82, chief master King Edwards Sch Birmingham and head master of the Schs of King Edward VI in Birmingham 1982-91; dir Farmington Inst for Christian Studies Oxford 1991-, fell Manchester Coll Oxford; seconded as Nuffield res fell (O level chem project) 1962-64, Salters Co fell Dept of Chem Engrg and Chem Technol Imperial Coll London 1969; chm: Curriculum Ctees of HMC, GSA and IAPS 1979-86, HMC 1987; memb Cncl Univ of Birmingham 1985-, govr Oundle Sch 1988-; *Books* John Dalton and the Atomic Theory (1965), Chemistry and Energy (1968),Foreground Chemistry Series (ed 1968), Gas Syringe Experiments (1970), Facts, Patterns and Principles (jtly, 1970), Francis Bacon and the Birth of Modern Science (1981); *Recreations* family life, history of science in 16th and 17th centuries; *Clubs* East India; *Style*— Martin Rogers, Esq; Vince House, 341 Bristol Road, Birmingham B5 7SW (☎ 021 472 0652); King Edward's Sch, Edgbaston Park Road, Birmingham B15 2UA (☎ 021 472 1672)

ROGERS, (John) Michael; s of John Patrick Rogers (d 1961), of 6 Market Place, Dalton-in-Furness, Lancs, and Constance Mary, *née* Fisher; *b* 25 Jan 1935; *Educ* Ulverston GS, CCC Oxford (BA, MA), Oriel Coll Oxford (BPhil), Pembroke Coll Oxford (DPhil); *Career* Nat Serv RA 1953-55, later Capt Intelligence Corsp TA; res fell Oriel Coll Oxford 1958-61, philosophy tutor Pembroke and Wadham Coll Oxford 1961-65, asst then assoc prof American Univ in Cairo 1965-77, asst then dep keeper Dept Oriental Antiquities Br Museum 1977-; advsr NACF, memb ed ctee Burlington

Magazine; FSA 1974, FBA 1988; Order Egyptian Republic Class II 1969; *Books* The Spread of Islam (1976), Islamic Art and Design 1500-1700 (1983), Suleyman the Magnificent (with R M Warde, 1980), numerous articles on arts and architecture of Islam; *Recreations* music, mountains, botany, slight mischief; *Clubs* Beefsteak; *Style—* Michael Rogers, Esq; Department of Oriental Antiquities, British Museum, London WC1 (☎ 071 323 8416, fax 071 323 8480, telex 94013362 BMUSG)

ROGERS, Nicholas Emerson (Nick); s of Reginald Emerson Rogers (d 1983), of 3 Fairfield Rd, Petts Wood, Kent, and Doreen, *née* Burbidge; *b* 15 March 1946; *Educ* Charterhouse, Orpington Secdy Sch; *m* 26 Oct 1973, Linda Jane, da of Reginald Douglas Bracey, of Little Tubbs, 19 Gifford Close, Thordun Park, Chard, Somerset; *Career* photographer The Sunday Independent Plymouth 1968-70 and The Evening Post Reading 1970-72, staff photographer The Daily Mail 1973-78, dep picture ed The Observer 1984-86; feature photographer: The Times 1986, The European 1990, The Sunday Telegraph 1990; Kodak Industl and Commercial Photographer of the Year 1987, Feature Photographer of the Year Br Press Awards 1988; memb: RPS, NUJ, BPPA; *Recreations* photography, sailing, walking, travel; *Style—* Nick Rogers, Esq; The Pound House, Wadstray, Blackawton, South Devon TQ9 7DE (☎ 080421 421, car 0860 380 347); The Sunday Telegraph, Peterborough Court, South Quay, 181 Marsh Wall, London E14 9SR (☎ 071 538 7373)

ROGERS, Nigel David; s of Thomas Rogers (d 1980), of Wellington, Shropshire, and Winifred May, *née* Roberts; *b* 21 March 1935; *Educ* Wellington GS, King's Coll Cambridge (BA, MA), Hochschule für Musik Munich; *m* 14 Oct 1961 (m dis 1974), Frederica Bement, da of Edmund Parker Lord (d 1985), of Framingham, Mass,USA; 1 da (Lucasta Julia Webster b 26 May 1970); *Career* singer and conductor; début Studio der Frühen Musik, Munich 1961, specialised as leading exponent of baroque style of singing 1964-; performances of baroque operas in England, Germany, Holland, Poland, Switzerland and Austria, world-wide concerts and recitals; numerous recordings incl: Monteverdi 1610 Vespers, Monteverdi "Orfeo", songs of John Dowland, Schütz, Christmas Story; Schubert, Die Schöne Müllerin; 17 C Airs de Cour etc; founder: Chiaroscuro Vocal Ensemble 1979, Chiaroscuro Baroque Orch 1987; conducted baroque orchs in Milan, Venice, Padua; teacher Schola Cantorum Basiliensis Bâle 1972-76, prof of singing RCM London 1979-; Hon FRCM 1981; *Books* Everyman's Companion to Baroque Music (Chapter on Voice, 1991); *Recreations* country life, walking, wine, travel; *Style—* Nigel Rogers, Esq; Chestnut Cottage, East End, near Newbury, Berks RG15 0AF (☎ 0635 253 319); Royal College of Music, Prince Consort Rd, London SW7

ROGERS, Nigel Harold John; s of Harold Rogers, of Prittlewell, Essex, and Lorna Mildred Rogers; *b* 18 Sept 1949; *Educ* Southend HS; *m* 1, 1 Oct 1977 (m dis April 1988), Linda Elizabeth Hardy; m 2, 29 Sept 1989, Julia Kim Rogers; *Career* CA; md Octavian Gp Ltd 1980-; memb Lloyds; FCA; *Recreations* skiing, riding, shooting; *Style—* Nigel Rogers, Esq; Octavian Group Limited, 84 Fenchurch St, London EC3M 4BY (☎ 071 265 0071, fax 071 481 1631, telex 895 1200, car 0836 576671)

ROGERS, (Thomas Gordon) Parry; s of Victor Frank Rogers (d 1947), of Harrow, Middx, and Ella Mary Rogers; *b* 7 Aug 1924; *Educ* West Hartlepool GS, St Edmund Hall Oxford (MA); *m* 1, 9 April 1947 (m dis 1973), Pamela Mary, da of J Leslie Greene (d 1950); 1 s (Michael b 1951), 7 da (Mary b 1948, Natalie b 1949, Patricia b 1955, Barbara b 1957, Bernadette b 1957, Frances b 1962, Philippa b 1964); m 2, 15 Sept 1973, (Patricia) Juliet, da of Richard D Curtis (d 1986); 1 s (Benedict b 1974), 1 da (Ruth b 1979); *Career* Nat Serv WWII 1944-47 RAC and RAEC; personnel mangr Procter & Gamble 1948-54, chief personnel offr Mars 1954-56, personnel dir Hardy Spicer 1956-61, dir of external affrs IBM (UK) 1971-74 (personnel dir 1961-71); Plessey: personnel dir 1974-78, dir personnel and Europe 1978-86, chm Plessey Pension Tst 1978-86; chm: Percam Ltd, Prima Europe Ltd, Future Perfect Ltd; dir: Hobsons Publishing plc, Ocean Gp plc, Butler Cox plc, Norman Broadbent Int; chm: Salisbury Health Authy 1985-, Business and Technician Educn Cncl 1986-, SW London Coll HEC 1988-; memb: Clegg Cmmn, Butcher Ctee, DHSS Review, Employment Apppeal Tbnl; Freeman City of London 1987, memb Worshipful Co of Information Technologists; CBIM 1980, CIPM 1980, FRSA 1978; *Books* Recruitment and Training of Graduates (1967); *Recreations* golf, tennis, birdwatching, music; *Clubs* Savile, Royal Wimbledon Golf, Sherborne Golf; *Style—* Parry Rogers, Esq; St Edward's Chantry, Bimport, Shaftesbury, Dorset (☎ 0747 2789); 32 Romulus Court, Justin Close, Brentford, Middx (☎ 081 568 6060)

ROGERS, Rev Percival Hallewell (Val); MBE (1945); s of Percy Charles Rogers (d 1956), of Brentwood, Essex, and Olivia Jane, *née* Horne (d 1970); *b* 13 Sept 1912; *Educ* Brentwood Sch, St Edmund Hall Oxford (MA, DipEd), Bishops' Coll Cheshunt, Int Acad for Continuous Educn Sherborne; *m* 1 Jan 1940, (Annie) Mary Stuart, da of Lt-Col James Morwood, IMS (d 1946), of 4 Malone Park, Belfast; 2 s (Julian Hallewell James b 1941, Bruce Henry Arthur b 1946, (k Alpine climbing 1969)), 1 da (Olivia Mary b 1948); *Career* Nat Serv TA 1939, RA 1940, cmmnd 1941 2 Lt RA 1941, War Substantive Lt 1942, Actg Capt 1943, Temp Capt 1944, Actg Maj DAA and QMG Milan 1945, War Substantive Capt and temp Maj 1945 (despatches twice), Maj, released 1946; head of english dept Haileybury Coll 1936-54, ordained priest St Albans 1948, chaplain Haileybury Coll 1948-54, headmaster Portora Royal Sch Enniskillen 1954-73, chaplain Gresham's Sch Holt 1974-75, dean Int Acad Sherborne 1975-76, asst priest Trinity Church New Orleans 1976-80, dir of ordinands and lay readers Diocese of Clogher 1980-84, priest i/c St Andrew's Sandford on Thames 1985-87; memb: Exec Ctee C of I Bd of Educn 1956-73, Alliance Party for Reconciliation NI 1970-84 (chm Fermanagh Assoc 1983-84); chm Student Christian Movement in Schs Ireland 1956-64, sec UNICEF Co Fermanagh 1982-84, schools lectr for UNICEF Oxford 1987-; memb HMC 1954-73; *Books* A Guide to Divinity Teaching (1962), The Needs of the Whole Man (1971); *Recreations* sailing, boating, chess, music; *Clubs* East India Public Schools and Sports, Union Soc (Oxford); *Style—* The Rev P H Rogers, MBE; 7 Eyot Place, Oxford OX4 1SA (☎ 0865 244 976)

ROGERS, Sir Philip James; CBE (1952); s of late James Henry Rogers; *b* 19 Sept 1908; *Educ* Blundells; *m* 1939, Brenda Mary, CBE, *qv*; *Career* Capt Royal West African Frontier Force; MLC Nigeria 1947-51, Kenya 1957-62; chm: E African Tobacco Co Ltd 1951-63, Rift Valley Cigarette Co Ltd 1956-63; memb E A Industl Cncl 1954-63; chm: Kenya Ctee on Trg and Study in USA 1958-63, African Teachers Serv Bd 1956-63; chm of Govrs Univ of Kenya 1958-63, tstee Outward Bound Tst of Kenya 1959-63, memb E A Air Cncl 1958-63, chm Bd of Govrs Coll of Social Studies 1960-63, chm Kenya Special Loan Cncl 1960-63, rep for Kenya E A Central Legislative Assembly 1962-63, chm Tobacco Res Cncl 1963-71, govr Plumpton Agric Coll 1967-72, chm Fedn of Sussex Countryside Preservation Socs 1968-80, memb E Sussex Co Cncl Educn Ctee 1967-77; kt 1961; *Style—* Sir Philip Rogers, CBE; Church Close, Newick, Sussex (☎ 082 572 2210)

ROGERS, Stuart Peter; s of Alfred Rogers, and Hannah, *née* Glicksman; *b* 12 March 1947; *Educ* Latymer Upper Sch; *m* 18 Sept 1979, Judith Frances, da of Harry Jacobs; 1 s (Nicholas Charles b 26 Sept 1983), 1 da (Sophie Esther b 12 June 1985); *Career* md: Contract Mail Ltd 1972-85, CM Direct Ltd 1985-88, dir CM Direct a div of The Hilton Taylor Partnership Ltd 1988-; co chm Variety Club of GB Sandown Park Brochure Ctee, memb mktg ctee Variety Club of GB; *Recreations* theatre, golf; *Style—* Stuart Rogers, Esq; 13 Dorset Dr, Edgware, Middx HA8 7NT (☎ 081 952 6354); 1 Livonia St, London WIV 3PG (☎ 071 734 1640, fax 071 434 4284)

ROGERS, Victor Alfred Baden; CBE (1986); s of Henry George Rogers (d 1963), of Norwood Green, Southall, Middx, and Louisa May, *née* Hall (d 1983); *b* 8 March 1926; *Educ* Cranfield Inst of Technol (MSc); *m* 1 April 1950, Jean Valentine, da of Joseph Franklin Stokes (d 1969); 2 s (David Edward b 1954, Peter John b 1962); *Career* Westland Helicopters Ltd: chief designer 1966-72 (Lynx Helicopter 1969-72), tech dir 1972-81 (RAeS Silver medal 1979), dir 1981-84; gp dir and tech dir Westland plc Helicopter and Hovercraft Gp 1984-86; ret 1988; former chm: SBAC (Tech Bd), AECMA (CTI) Europe; local pres RAeS (Yeovil Branch); FRAeS 1963, FIMechE 1972, FEng 1979; *Recreations* music, computers, golf; *Style—* Victor Rogers, Esq, CBE; Wrenfield, Bradford Rd, Sherborne, Dorset DT9 6BW (☎ 0935 81 2007)

ROGERS-COLTMAN, Charles Hugh; s of Lt Cdr Julian Rogers-Coltman, OBE (d 1944); *b* 25 April 1930; *Educ* Radley, Selwyn Coll Cambridge; *m* 1955, Olive Teresa Margaret, da of Lt-Col W H Bamfield; 1 s, 3 da; *Career* land agent, farmer, co dir; High Sheriff of Shropshire 1964; govr Wrekin Coll; *Recreations* shooting, fishing, skiing; *Clubs* Turf, MCC; *Style—* Charles Rogers-Coltman, Esq; The Home, Bishop's Castle, Shropshire (☎ 058 861 233)

ROGERSON, Michael Anthony; s of Peter Anthony Rogerson (d 1984), of Virginia Water, Surrey, and Yvonne Marie, *née* Kennedy; *b* 19 Feb 1941; *Educ* Harrow; *m* 27 Sept 1969, Margaret Jane, da of Keith Gordon Blake, CBE (d 1982), of Guildford; 1 s (Richard Pierce Gordon b 1974), 1 da (Belinda Jane b 1971); *Career* Spicer and Pegler: UK 1960-65, Aust 1965-67; Ernst Whinney 1967-73, ptnr Grant Thorton 1973-, non-exec chm Tech PR Ltd; CBI: past chm London Region (chm Urban Regeneration Task Force), memb cncl; chm Catholic Marriage Advsy Cncl, exec memb Sheriff and Recorders Fund, memb Advsry Cncl Catholic Soc Serv for Prisoners; memb Worshipful Co of Skinners 1971; FCA 1965, FBIM 1982; *Recreations* golf, bridge, gardening, racing; *Clubs* Boodles, Worplesdon Golf, Trevose Golf; *Style—* Michael Rogerson, Esq; Millcroft, Mill Lane, Pirbright, Surrey GU24 0BN (☎ 0486 781426); Grant Thornton House, Euston Square, London NW1 2EP (☎ 071 383 5100, fax 071 383 4715, telex 28984)

ROGERSON, Michael Cunliffe; TD (1966); s of Gordon Cunliffe Rogerson (d 1981), and Nora Margaret Stewart, *née* Boot (d 1984); *b* 30 March 1933; *Educ* Magdalen Coll Sch Brackley; *m* 4 April 1959, Sheila, da of Sidney Hugh Hyndman (d 1982), of Lichfield; 2 da (Catherine b 1962, Louise b 1964); *Career* Mil Serv Seaforth Highlanders 1951-54, Argyll & Sutherland Highlanders TA 1954-67; various mgmnt appts Clarks Ltd Somerset 1954-78, dir various cos 1978-; *Recreations* local politics, golf; *Style—* Michael C Rogerson, Esq, TD; Coopers, Coopers Hill, Eversley, Hampshire (☎ 0252 873583); SP Ltd, Fawley, Henley on Thames, Oxfordshire (☎ 0491 638810, fax 0491 63799)

ROGERSON, Philip Graham; s of Henry Rogerson, and Florence, *née* Dalton; *b* 1 Jan 1945; *Educ* William Hulmes GS Manchester; *m* 21 Dec 1968, Susan Janet, da of Jack Kershaw, of 12 Brampton Ave, Cleveleys, nr Blackpool, Lancs; 1 s (Simon Andrew b 19 July 1974); 2 da (Penelope Rose b 2 Dec 1971, Hannah Rosemary b 7 April 1988); *Career* various appts with the ICI Group 1978-, gen mangr fin ICI plc 1989-; FCA, MCT; *Recreations* golf, tennis, theatre; *Style—* Philip Rogerson, Esq; Baywood, 4 New Beacon Bungalows, Brittains Lane, Sevenoaks, Kent TN13 2ND (☎ 0732 461 402); Imperial Chemical Industries plc, 9 Millbank, London SW1P 3JF (☎ 071 834 4444, fax 071 834 2042, telex 21324)

ROHATGI, Pradip Krishna (Roy); s of Binay Krishna Rohatgi (d 1961), of Calcutta, India, and Shakuntala Rohatgi; *b* 10 Nov 1939; *Educ* St Xavier's Coll Calcutta, Univ of Calcutta (BCom), Univ of London (BSc); *m* 13 July 1974, Pauline Mary, da of Mervyn Harrold; *Career* sr econ and statistician in industl market res London 1963-66, articled Mann Judd & Co 1966-69; Arthur Andersen & Co: joined 1970, mangr 1973, ptnr 1980, i/c accounting and audit Dubai Office 1980-84, establish and ran Indian firm as managing ptnr 1984-89, returned to London as sr ptnr 1989-; written articles on various business and professional issues; memb: Direct and Indirect Tax Ctee Assoc of C of C in India, Exec Ctee Bombay Mgmnt Assoc, Appeals Ctee for Asian Piazza Appeal (Shakespeare's Globe Theatre); chm Econ Affrs Ctee Indo-American C of C 1986-89; ATII 1967, FCA 1969, MBCS 1976, fell Inst of CA's in India 1980; *Recreations* classical guitar, music, fine arts, travel, golf, sailing; *Clubs* Oriental, Rotary, Durbar; *Style—* Roy Rohatgi, Esq; 43 Great Brownings, College Road, London SE21 7HP (☎ 081 670 3512); Arthur Andersen & Co, 1 Surrey St, London WC2 (☎ 071 438 3612 or 071 438 3000 ext 3612, fax 071 831 1133)

RÓHL, Prof John Charles Gerald; s of Dr Hans-Gerhard Róhl (d 1976), of Frankfurt-am-Main, W Germany, and Freda Kingsford, *née* Woulfe-Brenan; *b* 31 May 1938; *Educ* Stretford GS, Corpus Christi Coll Cambridge (MA, PhD); *m* 7 Aug 1964, Rosemarie Elfriede, da of Johann Werner von Berg (d 1946), of Hamburg, W Germany; 2 s (Nicholas John b 1967, Christoph Andreas (twin) b 1967), 1 da (Stephanie Angela b 1965); *Career* RAF 1956-58; prof of history Univ of Sussex 1979- (lectr 1964-73, reader 1973-79); visiting prof of history: Univ of Hamburg 1974, Univ of Freiburg 1977-78; fell: Alexander von Humboldt Fndn 1970-71, Historisches Kolleg Munich 1986-87, Woodrow Wilson Int Center for Scholars Washington DC 1989-90; *Books* Germany Without Bismarck: The Crisis of Government in the Second Reich 1890-1900 (1967), From Bismarck to Hitler: The Problem of Continuity in German History (1970), 1914 - Delusion or Design? The Testimony of Two German Diplomats (1973), Philipp Eulenburgs Politische Korrespondenz (3 vols, 1976-83), Kaiser Willhelm II - New Interpretations (ed with N Sombart, 1982), Kaiser, Hof und Staat - Wilhelm II und die Deutsche Politik (1987); *Recreations* jazz, classical music, walking, running, bird watching; *Style—* Prof John C G Róhl; 11 Monckton Way, Kingston near Lewes, Sussex BN7 3LD (☎ 0273 472778), School of European Studies, University of Sussex, Brighton BN1 9QM (☎ 0273 678005)

ROKEBY-JOHNSON, (Henry) Ralph; s of Henry Spencer Rokeby-Johnson (d 1977); *b* 2 April 1931; *Educ* Eton, Brasenose Coll Oxford; *m* 1, 1958, Rosemary Ann, *née* Halford; m 2, 1965, Billinda Jessie Forster, *née* Pharazyn; 1 s (Rupert b 1966); m 3, 1979, Cecilia Bridget, *née* Cavendish; 1 s (Henry b 1979); *Career* non-marine underwriter R W Sturge & Co 1974-, dir A L Sturge (Mgmnt) Ltd 1966-, ptnr R W Sturge & Co 1968-88, dir A L Sturge (Hldgs) Ltd 1971-88; *Recreations* motoring, golf; *Clubs* City of London, Mark's, Sunningdale; *Style—* Ralph Rokeby-Johnson, Esq; Arthingworth, P O Box 1513, Rancho Santa Fe, Calfornia 92067

ROLES, Michael Bernard; s of Raymond William Rodes, and Lotte Johanna Katerina, *née* Hartmann; *b* 17 June 1948; *Educ* King Edward VII GS Southampton, Southampton Coll of Art, Univ of Newcastle (BA); *m* 18 March 1978, Amanda Corinne, da of Sqdn-ldr Doyne Garnet Thornton Rutter Hayes, DFC; *Career* asst prodr BBC TV 1974-80; BBC Enterprises: sales exec 1980-82, sales mangr Sydney office 1983-87; head of acquisitions and programming Super Channel 1987-; memb Old Edwardians; *Style—* Michael Roles, Esq; 10 Trevanion Road, West Kensington, London W14 9BJ (☎ 071 603 5371); Super Channel, 19-21 Rathbone Place, London W1 (☎ 071 631 5050, fax 071 631 5255)

ROLF, Percy Henry; s of Percy Algernon Rolf, of Ryde, IOW, and Lydia Kate, *née* Arnold; *b* 25 Dec 1915; *Educ* Sandown GS, Univ of London (LLB); *m* 28 Sept 1939,

Cecilia Florence, da of Frederick Thomas Cooper (d 1960), of Fishbourne, IOW; 1 s (Clive Frederick b 1940), 1 da (Mary Cecilia b 1947); *Career* Wing Cdr RAF, sr air traffic control office, tport cmd; admitted slr 1948; rec of Crown Ct 1978-87; *Recreations* golf, gardening; *Style—* Percy Rolf, Esq; Ashlake Water, Fishbourne, Isle of Wight PO33 4EY (☎ 0983 882513)

ROLFE, Christopher John; s of Frank Vere Rolfe, and Nesta Margaret, *née* Smith; *b* 16 Aug 1937; *Educ* Truro Cathedral Sch, Humphry Davy Sch, Royal West of Eng Acad Sch of Architecture (Dip Arch), Univ of Edinburgh (Dip CD, Dip TP); *m* 3 Oct 1964, Phyllis Roseline, da of Thomas Henry Harry (d 1972), of Newlyn; 1 s (David Jon Vere b 27 Nov 1971), 2 da (Kerstin Jane b 17 Feb 1967, Kerry Anne b 15 May 1969); *Career* architect; sr ptnr Christopher Rolfe & Assoc 1964-85, architect and planning conslt to the Bolitho Estates & Tst 1975-, chartered architect and conslt 1985-, chartered architect and conslt 1985-; chm and area rep Penzance Round Table 1968-74, chm St Clare Assoc 1981-82, local advsr to the Royal Mission of Deep Sea Fisherman 1984-, clerk to Madron Parish Cncl 1984-, tstee to the Garliana Almshouse 1986-; memb RIBA 1964; *Books* The Tourist & Leisure Industry (1966); *Recreations* badminton, tennis, photography; *Clubs* Mounts Bay, Penwith Lodge; *Style—* Christopher Rolfe, Esq; Polteggan Farm, Tremethick Cross, Penzance, Cornwall (☎ 0736 62167)

ROLFE, Hon Mrs (Louise Jane Denholm); da of Baron William Denholm Barnetson (d 1981), and Joan Fairley Barnetson, *née* Davidson; *b* 24 Dec 1952; *Educ* Eothen Sch for Girls Caterham; *m* 1982, Bernard Rolfe; 1 s (Guy b 1983), 1 da (Florence b 1985); *Career* PR conslt; *Style—* The Hon Mrs Rolfe; 5 St Ann's Crescent, London SW18 2ND

ROLFE, William David Ian; s of late William Ambrose Rolfe, and Greta Olwen Jones; *b* 24 Jan 1936; *Educ* Royal Liberty GS Romford, Univ of Birmingham (BSc, MSc, PhD); *m* 1960, Julia Mary Margaret, da of late Capt G H G S Rayer, OBE; 2 c; *Career* demonstrator in geology Univ Coll of N Staffs 1960, Fulbright scholar and asst curator Museum of Comparative Zoology Harvard Coll Cambridge Mass 1961-62; Univ of Glasgow: geological curator, lectr rising to sr lectr in geology Hunterian Museum 1962-81 (dep dir 1981-86); memb Museum Mgmnt Ctee and dep convener 1974-77, Faculty Library Ctee 1971-74; visiting scientist Museum of Nat History Chicago 1981, keeper of geology Nat Nuseums of Scotland (Edinburgh) 1986-; editorial chm of Geological Soc 1973-76, chm Conservation Ctee Geological Soc 1980-85, pres Edinburgh Geological Soc 1989-; Geological Soc of Glasgow: pres 1973-76, vice pres 1969-72 and 1976, sec 1972-73, cncllr 1964-67, convener Library Improvement Ctee 1966-69; ed: Proceedings of the Geological Soc of Glasgow 1965-68, Scottish Jl of Geology 1967-72; Museums Assoc: diploma tutor 1970-80, fellowship assessor 1975-; Palaeontological Assoc: vice pres 1974-76, sec and circular ed 1969-74, asst sec 1968-69, cncllr 1965-76; cncllr: Scottish Fedn of Museums 1962-65, 1967-70, 1975-78, Geological Curators Gp 1967-79; advsr for Treatise on Invertebrate Palaeontology Geological Soc of America and pres Univ of Kansas 1972-74; memb: Br Nat Ctee for Geology 1976-81, Touring Exhibitions Panel Cncl for Museums and Art Galleries in Scotland 1980-85, Museum Professionals Gp, Geological Sci Training Awards Ctee NERC 1980-83, Palaeontographical Soc, Scottish Museum Assts Gp (pres 1971-73), Soc History of Natural History (vice pres 1983-85); FGS 1960, FMA 1977, FRSE 1983, FRSA 1985; *Books* Phylogeny and Evolution of Crustacea (ed 1963), Treatise on Invertebrate Paleontology part R (1969), Geological Howlers (1980), papers on Fossil phyllocarid crustaceans and palaeontology and history of 18th century natural sci illustration; *Recreations* visual arts, walking, swimming, music; *Clubs* Geological, University Staff Edinburgh; *Style—* Dr W D Ian Rolfe, FRSE; 4A Randolph Crescent, Edinburgh EH3 7TH (☎ 031 226 2094)

ROLL, Rev Sir James William Cecil; 4 Bt (UK 1921), of The Chestnuts, Wanstead, Essex; s of Sir Cecil Ernest Roll, 3 Bt (d 1938), and Mildred Kate (d 1926), da of William Wells, of Snaresbrook, Essex; *b* 1 June 1912; *Educ* Chigwell Sch, Pembroke Coll Oxford, Chichester Theol Coll; *Heir* none; *Career* curate: St James the Great Bethnal Green 1937-39, St Matthews Custom House 1940-44; hon curate East Ham Parish Church 1944-58, vicar of St John The Divine Becontree from 1958-83 (ret); *Style—* The Rev Sir James Roll, Bt; 82 Leighcliff Rd, Leigh on Sea, Essex

ROLL, Michael; *m* Juliana Marloova; 1 s (Maximillian); *Career* musician; debut aged twelve Royal Festival Hall playing Schumann's Concerto under Sir Malcolm Sargent, winner Leeds Int Pianoforte competition aged seventeen; travelled extensively appearing with conductors such as: Boulez, Giulini, Leinsdorf, Masur, Previn, Sanderling; festivals incl: Aldeburgh, Bath, Edinburgh, Granada, Hong Kong, Vienna; frequent performer BBC Promenade Concertos London, American debut with Boston Symphony Orchestra 1974, reg appearances with major UK orchestras; recent recitals: Milan, East Berlin, Dresden, Leipzig, London; concerto appearances with: Kurt Masur in Leipzig and London, Valery Gergiev in Leningrad and UK; *Style—* Michael Roll, Esq; c/o Harold Holt Ltd, 31 Sinclair Rd, London W14 ONS (☎ 071 603 4600, fax 071 603 0019, telex 22339 Hunter)

ROLL OF IPSDEN, Baron (Life Peer UK 1977), of Ipsden, Co Oxford; Eric Roll; KCMG (1962, CMG 1949), CB (1956); yr s of Mathias Roll and Fany Roll; *b* 1 Dec 1907; *Educ* Birmingham Univ (PhD); *m* 1934, Winifred, o da of Elliott Taylor; 2 da (Hon Joanna b 1944, Hon Elizabeth (Hon Mrs Foldes) b 1946); *Career* sits as Independent peer in House of Lords; prof econs and commerce Univ Coll Hull 1935-46, under-sec Treasy 1948, dep sec MAFF 1959-61; dep head UK Delgn negotiating EEC entry 1961-63, UK Delgn NATO Paris 1952; exec dir UK IMF and IBRD 1963-64; hon chm Book Devpt Cncl 1967-; dir Bank of Eng 1968-77; chm: S G Warburg & Co 1974-84 (jt chm 1983-87), Mercury Securities 1974-84; currently pres S G Warburg Gp plc; dir Times Newspapers Hldgs 1966-83; appeal chm Loan Fund for Musical Instruments; chllr Southampton Univ 1974-84; Grosses Goldene Ehrenzeichen mit Stern Austria, Cdr 1 Class Order of the Dannebrog (Denmark), Offr Legion of Honour; *Style—* The Rt Hon the Lord Roll of Ipsden, KCMG, CB; 2 Finsbury Ave, London EC2M 2PA

ROLL PICKERING, John Anthony; s of Lt Cdr Thomas George Pickering, RN ret, of Pentland Newtake, 24 Frogston Rd West, Edinburgh, and Nora, *née* Roll; *b* 1 Nov 1949; *Educ* Edinburgh Acad, Trinity Coll Glenalmond; *m* 28 April 1973, Rosemary Anne, da of Maj Kenneth Aubrey Hearson, of Hordlea, Wigmore Lane, Halfway House, nr Shrewsbury, Shropshire; 1 s (Timothy b 1980), 1 da (Amanda b 1977); *Career* joined Queen's Own Lowland Yeo 1968, cmmnd 1970, transferred London Scot/51 Highland Vols 1972, RARO 1976; trainee Bell Lawrie Robertson & Co stock brokers Edinburgh 1968-72, with various firms London Stock Exchange 1972-82, exec Hill Samuel Investmt Servs 1982-85, sr conslt C Howard & Ptnrs 1986-88, conslt James Capel Fin Servs 1988-; dir Highland Soc of London 1984-, memb cncl Br Deer Soc 1981-88 (hon treas 1984-88); contested (Con) Epsom and Ewell Borough Cncl 1976 and 1979; Freeman City of London 1978, Liveryman Worshipful Co of Horners (1978); ALIA 1986; *Recreations* shooting, photography, deer; *Clubs* Cavalry & Guards; *Style—* John Roll Pickering, Esq; Waldhaus, 79 College Rd, Epsom, Surrey KT17 4HH (☎ 0372 725099)

ROLLAND, Lawrence Anderson Lyon; s of Lawrence Anderson Rolland (d 1959), of Leven, and Winifred Anne, *née* Lyon (d 1978); *b* 6 Nov 1937; *Educ* George Watsons Coll Edinburgh, Duncan of Jordanstone Coll of Art Dundee (Dip Arch); *m* 30 April 1960, Mairi, da of John McIntyre Melville (d 1980), of Kirkcaldy; 2 s (Michael b 1963, Douglas b 1966), 2 da (Gillian b 1961, Katie b 1967); *Career* sole ptnr L A Rolland 1960, jt sr ptnr Robert Hurd 1965, ptnr L A Rolland & Ptnr 1965, sr ptnr Hurd Rolland Ptnrship; awards and commendations incl: Saltire Soc Civic Tst, RIBA, Europa Nostra, Times Conservation, Stone Fedn; pres: RIAS 1979-81, RIBA 1985-87; fndr memb Scottish Construction Indust Gp 1980; memb: E Neuk of Fife Preservation Tst, N E Fife Preservation Soc; sec Kinghorn Singers, er Largo Parish Church, govr Duncan of Jordonstone Coll of Art Dundee, convenor advsy ctee for artistic matters for Church of Scotland 1975-80, gen tstee Church of Scotland 1979-; Hon Fell Bulgarian Inst of Architects 1987; memb: RIAS RIBA 1960; FRS 1988, FRSE 1989; *Recreations* music, fishing, shooting and more architecture; *Clubs* Reform, Commonwealth; *Style—* Lawrence Rolland, Esq; School House, Newburn, Upper Largo, Fife (☎ 03333 6383); Rossend Castle, Burntisland, Fife (☎ 031 226 6555); 25A Fitzroy Sq, London W1 (☎ 071 387 9565, fax 071 388 1848)

ROLLES, Keith; s of Trevor Rolles, of Port Talbot, W Glamorgan, and Betty, *née* Hopkins; *b* 25 Oct 1947; *Educ* Quakers Yard GS Mid Glamorgan, The Lonodn Hosp Med Coll (BSc, MB BS, MS); *m* 22 Aug 1970, Sharon, da of Thomas McGrath (d 1979); 2 s (David b 1981, Thomas b 1984); *Career* lectr in surgery and hon conslt surgn Univ of Cambridge and Addenbrookes Hosp 1984-88, conslt surgn and dir of liver transplant unit The Royal Free Hosp 1988-; Hon MA Univ of Cambrige 1983; Hon MS Univ of London 1985; FRCS 1976; *Recreations* squash, tennis, skiing; *Style—* Keith Rolles, Esq; Academic Dept of Surgery, The Royal Free Hosp and Sch of Medicine, Pons St, Hampstead, London NW3 2QG (☎ 071 435 6121)

ROLLETT, David Ian; s of Cyril Wells Rollett (d 1978), and Mildred Ada, *née* Moss; *b* 17 May 1924; *Educ* Lincoln GS, Magdalen Coll Cambridge (MA); *m* 7 Feb 1948, Patricia Diana, da of Charles Hubert Walters (d 1982), of Tollerton, Nottingham; 1 da (Anthea b 1948); *Career* WWII REME 1943-47, Capt served England and India; divnl and regnl mangr Anglia Water Authy 1974-83; FICE, FIWEM; *Recreations* photography, walking, DIY; *Clubs* Rotary Huntingdon (Rotary dist govr Dist 107 1988-89); *Style—* David Rollett, Esq; 11 Beech Ave, Great Stukeley, Huntingdon, Cambridgeshire PE17 5AX (☎ 0480 455820)

ROLLIN, Charles Austin Noble; s of Philip Talbot Noble Rollin (d 1985), of Val Plaisant, Jersey, CI, and Edith May, *née* Austin; *b* 14 Jan 1943; *Educ* St Edwards Sch Oxford; *m* 12 Oct 1963 (m dis 1977), Catherine, da of John William Nash; 3 da (Jeannette b 1967, Anne b 1970, Pamela b 1972); *Career* CA; proprietor Greenhow & Co; *Recreations* music, theatre, squash; *Style—* Charles Rollin, Esq; Greenhow & Co, 71 St Peters Rd, Reading RG6 1PD (☎ 0734 664 020)

ROLLIN, Dr Henry Rapoport; s of Aaron Rapoport Rollin (d 1973), of 35 Heathfield Gardens, London, and Rebecca, *née* Sorkin (d 1975); *b* 17 Nov 1911; *Educ* Central HS Leeds, Univ of Leeds (MB ChB, MD); *m* 27 July 1973, Dr (Anna) Maria Rollin, da of George Tihanyi, of 21 St Agnes Close, London; 1 s (Aron David Rapoport b 1976), 1 da (Rebecca Ilona b 1979); *Career* Wing-Cdr and sr neuropsychiatric specialist RAFVR 1942-47; Fulbright fell Temple Univ Hosp Philadelphia USA 1953-54, Gwilyn Gibbon res fell Nuffield Coll Oxford 1963-64, emeritus conslt psychiatrist Horton Hosp Epsom Surrey 1977 (conslt psychiatrist 1948-77), conslt forensic psychiatrist Home Office 1977-86; hon librarian RCPsych 1975-85, hon conslt psychiatrist Queen Elizabeth Fndn for the Disabled, hon med advsr Nat Schizophrenia Fellowship; memb: Mental Health Review Tbnls 1960-83, Parole Bd 1970-73; pres: Oser Club of London 1974-76, Section of History of Medicine RSM 1990-91; FRSM 1943, FRCPsych 1971, MRCP 1975, Hon FRCPsych 1989; *Books* The Mentally Abnormal Offender and the Law (1969), Coping with Schizophrenia (1980), Festina Lente: A Psychiatric Odyssey (1990); *Recreations* music, history of medicine, theatre; *Style—* Dr Henry Rollin; 101 College Rd, Epsom, Surrey KT17 4HY (☎ 0372 24772)

ROLLIN, Peter Hamilton; s of Lawrence Hamilton Rollin, of Hamilton House, Diss, Norfolk, and Hedy, *née* Gutgiser; *b* 13 Nov 1942; *Educ* Bedford Mod Sch; *m* 6 April 1976, Elizabeth Mary, da of Maj John Kellock Corbitt, of 8 Frenze Rd, Diss, Norfolk; 1 s (Matthew b 1977), 1 da (Rachael b 1974); *Career* admitted slr 1969; dep registrar Co Ct 1986, dep dist judge 1991-, former pres Diss Chamber of Trade and Commerce; memb Diss Urban Dist Town Cncl 1971-77, ldr Norfolk CC 1987-89 (memb 1973-); memb Law Soc 1970; *Recreations* choral singing, philately; *Style—* Peter Rollin, Esq; Jacques, Back St, Garboldisham, Diss, Norfolk (☎ 095381 362); Park House, Mere St, Diss, Norfolk IP22 3JY (☎ 0379 643 555, fax 0379 652 221)

ROLLO, Hon Mrs William; Diana Joan; da of Edward Castell Bourchier Wrey, 7 s of Sir Henry Wrey, 10 Bt, and bro of 11, 12 and 13 Bts; sis of Sir Bourchier Wrey, 14 Bt; *m* 1, 1932 (m dis 1946), Jocelyn Abel Smith (d 1966, of the Abel Smiths of Woodhill); 2 s; *m* 2, 1946, as his 2 w, Hon William Hereward Charles Rollo, MC (k out hunting 1962), bro of 12 Lord Rollo; *Style—* The Hon Mrs William Rollo; Barleythorpe, Oakham, Rutland LE15 7EQ

ROLLO, 13 Lord (S 1651); Eric John Stapylton Rollo; JP (Perthshire 1962); also Baron Dunning (UK 1869); s of Maj 12 Lord Rollo (d 1947), and his 1 w, Helen, da of Frederick Chetwynd-Stapylton (ggs of 4 Viscount Chetwynd); *b* 3 Dec 1915; *Educ* Eton; *m* 1938, Suzanne, da of W H B Hatton, of Broome House, Broome, Worcs; 2 s, 1 da; *Heir* s, Master of Rollo; *Career* Capt late Gren Guards 1939-45 War; farmer; *Style—* The Rt Hon the Lord Rollo, JP; Pitcairns, Dunning, Perthshire

ROLLO, Hon James Malcolm; 2 s of 13 Lord Rollo, JP; *b* 25 Sept 1946; *Educ* Eton, Christ Church Oxford; *m* 14 Sept 1968, Henrietta Elizabeth Flora, da of Maj Alasdair Boyle; 1 s (Malcolm b 1981), 1 da (Helen b 1985); *Style—* The Hon James Rollo

ROLLO, Hon Simon David Paul; s of 12 Lord Rollo (d 1947) by his 3 w Lily, nee Seiflow; half-bro of 13 Lord Rollo and Hon David (decd) and Hon John Rollo; *b* 4 Oct 1939; *Educ* Eton; *m* 1964, Valerie Ernestine, yr da of Robert William Gaspard Willis, of Sudbury; 2 da; *Style—* The Hon Simon Rollo; Biffens Boatyard, Staines, Middx

ROLLS, Peter John; s of Hector Lionel Rolls (d 1980), and Florence Susie Rolls (d 1989); *b* 7 May 1930; *Educ* Slough GS, Regent St Poly, Harrow Coll of HE, Univ of Surrey (Cert in Scientific Photography, BA, MSc); *m* 7 July 1956, Helen Jane, da of William Kirby; 3 s (Timothy John b 18 June 1957, Christopher Peter b 2 July 1959, Jeremy David b 23 June 1962), 1 da (Alison Jane b 28 Sept 1970); *Career* Nat Serv 1948-50; photographer Miny of Supply 1950-59, sr photographer Miny of Aviation 1959-66, chief photographer Miny of Defence 1966-67, head of printing RAE Farnborough 1967-90, head of profession for MOD(PE) photographers 1989-90, ret 1990; Inst of Incorporated Photographers: chief examiner 1970-74, chm of educn 1976-80; moderator of BTEC in Photography 1983-91, govr Berkshire Coll of Art 1990-91; President's award Inst of Incorporated Photographers 1975; FBIPP 1972; *Books* Applied Photography (jtly, 1971), Proceedings of 7 International High-Speed Congress (ed, 1975), Microform Systems and Reprography (1980); *Recreations* writing, photography; *Style—* Peter Rolls

ROLT, David Anthony; Dr Frederick Henry Rolt, OBE (d 1973), and Florence Mary, *née* Edwards (d 1968); *b* 30 Jan 1926; *Educ* Kingston GS, Imperial Coll of Sci and Technol; *m* 30 April 1949, Nettie Winifred, da of Herbert Charles Kinns (d 1953); 2 s (Anthony b 1951, Timothy b 1953); *Career* Royal Norfolk Regt 1945-46, cmmnd 2 Lt RE 1947, demob 1948; former dir construction bd Sir Robert McAlpine and Sons Ltd until 1989 (joined 1948); FCIOB 1973; *Recreations* boating; *Clubs* Royal Dorset YC (formerly Commodore of the Assoc of Dunkirk Little SMPS); *Style—* David Rolt, Esq; Hartlebury Cottage, 1 Trinity Terrace, Weymouth, Dorset DT4 8JW (☎ 0305 777 786); 40 Bernard St, London WC1N 1LG (☎ 071 837 3377, fax 071 833 4102)

ROMAIN, Richard David Anidjah; s of Philip Isaac Anidjah Romain, of Stanmore, Middx, and Joan, *née* Rose; *b* 10 Aug 1958; *Educ* City of London Sch, Loughborough Univ of Technol (BSc); *m* 12 March 1989, Juliet Barbara, da of Gerald Michael Raeburn, of Edgware, Middx; 2 da (Victoria Hannah b 19 Nov 1990, Alexandra Esther b (twin) 19 Nov 1990); *Career* md John Morley Presentations Ltd 1985 (dir 1983), main bd dir John Morley Jewellery Gp 1987; cncllr London Borough of Harrow 1982-; memb: Main Bd West London Waste Authy, Lord-Lt's Ctee Harrow, nat exec Aid for Addicts and Family, Nat Assoc of Goldsmiths; chm Ed Bd The Harrow Magazine; Freeman City of London 1981, Liveryman Worshipful Co of Bakers; *Recreations* snooker, swimming, motor cruising; *Style—* Richard Romain, Esq; 106/108 High St, Watford, Herts WD1 2BW (☎ 0923 226 883, fax 0923 39213, car 0836 223 637)

ROMAINES, Paul William; s of George Gelson Romaines, of Shildon, Co Durham, and Freda Mary, *née* Murray; *b* 25 Dec 1955; *Educ* Leeholme Sch, Bishop Auckland, Co Durham; *m* Julie Anne, da of Joseph William Warburton; 1 da (Clair Louise b 3 July 1987); *Career* cricketer, Northamptonshire CCC 1973-76 (debut Northamptonshire v Yorkshire 1975), Gloucestershire CCC 1981; highest innings 186 v Warwickshire; Benefit Year 1991; *Recreations* golf, squash, wine, food; *Style—* Paul Romaines, Esq; c/o Gloucestershire County Cricket Club, Phoenix County Ground, Nevil Rd, Bristol BS7 9EJ (☎ 0272 245216)

ROMANES, (Constance) Margaret; OBE (1981), JP (1965), DL (Dorset 1989); da of Claud Valentine Gee (d 1951), and Hilda, *née* Bentham (d 1968); *b* 9 Aug 1920; *Educ* St Leonard's Sch, Girton Coll Cambridge; *m* 29 June 1943, Giles John Romanes, s of Capt Francis John Romanes (d 1944); 1 s (Julian b 1951), 2 da (Jane b 1946, Rosalind b 1947); *Career* dep chm Magistrates Assoc 1981-87 (vice pres 1990); chm: Dorset branch Magistrates' Assoc 1981-89, Weymouth and Portland Bench 1985-91; contrib to various jls and reader of Papers at various int confs; memb: James Ctee (an Interdepartmental Ctee on Distribution of Criminal Business), Portland Borstal YCC Bd of Visitors 1971-86 (chm 1976-81), Salisbury Dio Synod 1976-84, Local Parole Review Ctee 1984-86, various govt working parties; Bishop's selector for ACCM 1976-83, chm Dorset Care Tst 1984-, Lord Chllr's nominee on Legal Aid Duty Slr Ctee 1986-; *Recreations* music (active memb of orchestras and chamber groups), gardening; *Clubs* RSM; *Style—* Mrs Margaret Romanes, OBE, JP, DL; Portesham House, nr Weymouth, Dorset (☎ 0305 871300)

ROME, Alan Mackenzie; s of John Mackenzie Rome (d 1969), and Evelyn Anne, *née* Rae (d 1978); *b* 24 Oct 1930; *Educ* Kings Sch Bruton, Royal W of Engl Acad Sch of Architecture (Dip Arch); *m* 8 Sept 1956, Mary Lilyan, da of Thomas William Barnard (d 1984); 1 s (Timothy b 1961), 1 da (Judith b 1963); *Career* Nat Serv RE 1949-50; in office of Sir George Oatley, FRIBA 1947-49, asst to architect Westminster Abbey 1955-60; own practice (initially with Michael Torrens, FRIBA, and Rolfe & Crozier-Cole) 1960-; cathedral architect to Dean and Chapter of: Bristol, Salisbury, Wells; architect to Bath and Glastonbury Abbeys and St Mary Redcliffe; memb: Cncl for the Care of Churches, Redundant Churches Fund, Bath and Wells Diocesan Advsy Ctee, SPAB; occasional lectr Univ of Bristol; FRIBA, FSA; *Recreations* walking, sketching; *Style—* Alan Rome, Esq; 11 Mayfair Ave, Nailsea, Bristol BS19 2LR (☎ 0272 853215)

ROME, Derek Patrick; s of Patrick Leslie Rome, MC, of Wiltshire, and Clare Pauline, *née* de Stacpoole; *b* 15 Nov 1949; *Educ* Worth Abbey Sch; *m* 23 Feb 1974 Penelope Jane, *née* Allen; 1 s (James Patrick b 1 Sept 1984), 2 da (Polyanna Clare b 8 March 1977, Lucinda Catherine b 8 April 1978); *Career* The Royal Hussars PWO 1971-1977; Financial Times 1978-83; Executrade Centres 1983-84, Grandfield Rork Collins 1984- (assoc dir 1987-88, dir 1988-) memb: Investor Relations Soc, Nat Investor Relations Inst; *Recreations* country sports; *Clubs* Cavalry; *Style—* Derek Rome, Esq; Coombe Bissett,Wiltshire; Grandfield Rork Collins, Prestige House, 14/18 Holborn, London EC1N 2LE (☎ 071 242 2002)

ROMER, Ian Lebeau Ritchie; s of Rt Hon Sir Charles Robert Ritchie Romer (d 1969), of Littlestone, Kent, and Frances Evelyn Lebeau, *née* Kemp (d 1989); previous 3 direct generations (and present) were all educated at Trinity Hall, went to the Chancery Bar and were benchers of Lincoln's Inn; *b* 26 Dec 1929; *Educ* Bryanston, Trinity Hall Cambridge (BA); *m* 1, 1952, Elizabeth, da of James Dales, of Vancouver; 1 s (James b 1955 decd), 1 da (Jane b 1956); m 2, 1960, Mary Rose, da of Col W H Crichton (d 1984), of Polstead, Suffolk; 1 s (Caspar b 1970), 1 da (Emma b 1961); *Career* called to the Bar Gray's Inn 1953, bencher Lincoln's Inn 1981; *Clubs* Garrick; *Style—* Ian L R Romer, Esq; The Old Rectory, Cadeleigh, Devon EX16 8HW (☎ 08845 200); 17 Old Buildings, Lincolns Inn, London WC2 (☎ 071 405 9653)

ROMER, Mark Lemon Robert; eld s of Sir Charles Robert Ritchie Romer (d 1969, Lord Justice of Appeal), of Littlestone, and Frances Evelyn Lebeau, *née* Kemp (d 1989); f, gf and ggf all members of Court of Appeal, gf going on to House of Lords where he sat with two brothers-in-law (Viscount Maugham, Lord Russell of Killowen); *b* 12 July 1927; *Educ* Bryanston, Trinity Hall Cambridge (MA, LLM); *m* 1953 (m dis 1991), Philippa Maynard, da of Maj Maynard Tomson, MC (d 1984) of Hitchin; 1 s (Stephen b 1957), 2 da (Caroline b 1955, Eugénie b 1961); *Career* served KRRC UK 1945-48; barr 1952; met stipendiary magistrate 1972-; *Recreations* bird-watching, travel, looking at pictures, painting watercolours; *Style—* Mark Romer, Esq; Gillings Hill, Arkesden Rd, Clavering, Essex CB11 4QU; Clerkenwell Magistrates Court, Kings Cross Rd, London WC1

ROMER, Cdr (Robert) Mark; s of Robert Parbury Romer (d 1927), and Evelyn Margaret Wall (d 1986); ggf Sir Robert Romer, Lord Justice of Appeal, gggf Mark Lemon first ed of Punch; *b* 31 July 1924; *Educ* Sherborne, Corpus Christi Coll Cambridge (BA); *m* 31 March 1948, Fay Patricia Wade, da of Maj Patrick Wade Gard'ner, MC (d 1970), of 32 Connaught Square, London; 3 da (Sally-Fay b 1957, Caroline b 1960, Melanie b 1963); *Career* RN 1944-74, serv WWII, Korean War 1950, Malaya 1964; MOD 1974-84, asst dir Standardization (Navy); consulting engr 1984-; FIEE; *Recreations* gardening, music, reading; *Style—* Cdr Mark Romer, RN; Sion Lodge, 34 Sion Hill, Bath BA1 2UW (☎ 0225 422430)

ROMER-LEE, Robin Knyvett; s of Knyvett Romer-Lee, OBE, of Green Farm, Hickling, Norfolk, and Jeanne Pamela, *née* Shaw (d 1982); *b* 27 Oct 1942; *Educ* Eton; *m* 30 March 1968, Annette Millet, da of George Henry Brocklehurst (d 1972); 2 s (Benjamin b 1971, Edward b 1973); *Career* insur broker and memb of Lloyds; dir Sedgwick Broking Servs Ltd, chm Sedgwick Non-Marine Ltd 1989; *Recreations* sailing, fishing, gardening; *Style—* Robin Romer-Lee, Esq; The Old Rectory, Groton, nr Colchester CO6 5EE (☎ 0787 210710); Sedgwick House, Sedgwick Centre, London E1 8DX

ROMNEY, 7 Earl of (UK 1801); Sir Michael Henry Marsham; 13 Bt (E 1663); also Baron of Romney (GB 1716) and Viscount Marsham (UK 1801); s of Lt-Col Hon Reginald Marsham, OBE (2 s of 4 Earl of Romney), and Dora, 4 da of Charles North, JP, DL (5 in descent from Hon Roger North, the memoirist and 6 s of 4 Baron North); suc first cous, 6 Earl, 1975; *b* 22 Nov 1910; *Educ* Sherborne; *m* 28 June 1939, Aileen, o da of Lt-Col James Russell Landale; *Heir* first cous once removed, Julian Marsham; *Career* late Maj RA, served WWII; *Recreations* foxhunting; *Style—* The Rt Hon the Earl of Romney; Wensum Farm, W Rudham, King's Lynn, Norfolk (☎ 048 522 249)

ROMSEY, Lord; Norton Louis Philip Knatchbull; s and h of Countess Mountbatten of Burma and of 7 Baron Brabourne; *b* 8 Oct 1947; *Educ* Gordonstoun, Univ of Kent; *m* 1979, Penelope Meredith, only da of Reginald and Marian Eastwood of Palma de Mallorca, Spain; 1 s, (Hon Nicholas b 1981), 2 da (Hon Alexandra b 1982, Hon Leonora b 1986); *Heir* s, Hon Nicholas Louis Charles Norton Knatchbull b 15 May 1981; *Career* film and TV prodr 1971-80; dir: Crown Communications Gp plc, Southern Radio plc, Ocean Sound Ltd, Southern Sound plc, Radio Mercury plc; chm: Britt Allcroft Gp Ltd (Thomas the Tank Engine and Friends), Friday Productions Ltd; High Steward Romsey 1980; Vice Adm Royal Motor YC 1985, vice pres Mary Rose Tst; memb Ct Univ of Southampton; *Clubs* Royal Motor Yacht; *Style—* Lord Romsey; Broadlands, Romsey, Hants SO51 9ZD (☎ (0794) 517888)

ROMYN, Conrad; MC (1946); s of Conrad Richardson (d 1936), and Anne Elizabeth Romyn (d 1918); *b* 18 Nov 1915; *Educ* St Lawrence Coll Geneva Univ Vienna; *m* Ann Dorothea, da of the late Isak Bergson; 1 da (Jenny Ann); *Career* Maj IA Regt attached to D Force Burma, on loan to 20 Indian Div 1939-46; author illustrated book on St Lucia (cmmnd by St Lucian Govt), Timothy Bhalu-Children's Book; painter; exhibitions in: RA London, Ecole de Paris, Salons de la Societé Francaise Paris, Prix Othon Friels Paris, Salon des Surindepandts Paris, Nyköping Museum Sweden; works purchased by: Museum of Modern Art Stockholm, Swedish Banks, Leicester Yorks and Surrey Depts of Educn; in private collections in: England, France, Holland, Sweden, Norway, Denmark, Canada, USA; *Recreations* music, visiting museums, antique books and maps, travel; *Style—* Conrad Romyn, Esq, MC; 1 North Cottage, Hampton Court, Surrey (☎ 081 977 5890); Royal Bank of Scotland, Kingston upon Thames

RONSON, Gerald Maurice; *b* 27 May 1939; *m* Gail, *née* Cohen; 4 da; *Career* chm and chief exec Heron Int plc; tstee Ronson Fndn (and fndr), Br Museum (Natural Hist) 1987-; a vice pres NSPCC 1985-; memb: Governing Cncl Business in the Community, Cncl Prince's Youth Tst; CBIM 1982; *Recreations* yachting, shooting; *Clubs* Royal Southern YC, One Per Cent; *Style—* Gerald Ronson, Esq; c/o Heron International plc, Heron House, 19 Marylebone Rd, London NW1 (☎ 071 486 4477)

RONEY, Richard Esmond Barham; s of Esmond Richard Roney (d 1979), of London NW6, and Muriel, *née* Barham; gs of Sir Ernest Roney, on mother's side descended from Fitzurse (first knight to kill Thomas A Becket) Admiral Lord Barham and Rev Richard Harris Barham (Thomas Ingoldsby); *b* 17 April 1943; *Educ* St Paul's; *m* 1, 28 Nov 1964, Georgina, da of Richard Wykes Stephens, of Henley-on-Thames; 1 s (Esmond b 1969), 1 da (Charlotte b 1972); m 2, 1 June 1981, Danielle, da of Marcel Bloch (d 1985); 1 step da (Karen); *Career* slr; dir: Denison Mines (North Sea) Ltd, LL & E (UK) Inc, Oranje Nassau (UK) Ltd, Pennozil Ltd; *Recreations* skiing, golf, theatre, music, reading, good food and wine, cinema, sightseeing; *Clubs* Boodles, Wentworth; *Style—* Richard Roney, Esq; 15 Queens Gate Gardens, London SW7 (☎ 071 584 6076); 84 Brook St, London W1Y 1YG (☎ 071 629 2382, fax 071 629 0027)

ROOKE, Sir Denis Eric; CBE (1970); s of F G Rooke; *b* 2 April 1924; *Educ* Westminster City Sch, Addey and Stanhope Sch UCL, (BSc); *m* 1949, Elizabeth Brenda, *née* Evans; 1 da; *Career* Maj REME 1944-49; joined S Eastern Gas Bd 1949 (devpt engr 1959); memb: Advsy Cncl for R&D 1972-77, Advsy Cncl for Energy Conservation 1974-77, Offshore Energy Tech Bd 1975-78, British National Oil Corporation (pt/t) 1976-82, NEDC 1976-80, Energy Cmmn 1977-79; pres IGasE 1975, chm Br Gas plc 1986-89 (chm British Gas Corporation 1976-86, dep chm 1972-76); pres: Welding Inst 1981-83, Pipeline Industs Guild 1981-83, chm CNAA 1978-83, tstee Sci Museum 1984-, cmmr Royal Cmmn for the Exhibition of 1851 1984-, chllr Loughborough Univ of Technol 1989; Hon DSc: Univ of Salford 1978, Univ of Leeds 1980, The City Univ 1985, Univ of Durham 1986, Cranfield Inst of Technol 1987; Hon DTech CNAA 1986, Hon LLD Univ of Bath 1987, Hon DEng Univ of Bradford, Hon DUniv Surrey; FRS 1978, FEng 1977 (pres 1986-91); kt 1977; *Recreations* listening to music, photography; *Clubs* Athenaeum, English-Speaking Union; *Style—* Sir Denis Rooke, CBE, FRS; 23 Hardy Rd, Blackheath, SE3 7NS (☎ 081 858 6710); 1 Great Cumberland Place, Marble Arch, London W1P 9LN (☎ 071 821 1444 ext 2233)

ROOKE, His Hon Judge; Giles Hugh; TD (1963), QC (1979); s of Charles Eustace Rooke, CMG (d 1947), and Irene Phyllis (d 1969), da of Thomas Main Patterson; *b* 28 Oct 1930; *Educ* Stowe, Exeter Coll Oxford; *m* 1968, Anne Bernadette Seymour, da of His Hon John Perrett; 4 s (Alexander b 1969, Nicholas b 1970, George b 1979, Charles b 1989), 1 da (Elizabeth b 1972); *Career* Maj (TA) Kent Yeo 1951-61, KCLY 1961-65; barr 1957; chm Kent Bar Mess 1975-79, rec Crown Ct 1975-81, judge SE Circuit (practised as barr from 1957) 1981-; hon of Margate 1980-; *Recreations* cultivant son jardin; *Style—* His Hon Judge Rooke, QC, TD; The Sessions House, Longport, Canterbury

ROOKER, Jeffrey William; MP (Lab) Birmingham, Perry Barr Feb 1974-; *b* 5 June 1941; *Educ* Handsworth Tech Sch, Handsworth Tech Coll, Warwick Univ (MA), Aston Univ (BScEng); *m* 1972, Angela; *Career* oppn front bench spokesman: social security 1981-Nov 1983, Treasy and Econ Affrs Nov 1983-; *Style—* Jeffrey Rooker Esq, MP; House of Commons, London SW1

ROOKLEDGE, Gordon Charles; s of Charles Harcourt Rookledge Collett (d 1954), of Johanesburg, SA, and Elsie Alicia, *née* Goodwin (d 1976); *b* 3 Dec 1933; *Educ* Stanley Park Secdy Sch; *m* 1 April 1960, Jennifer Mary, da of Robert Dampier Lush, of Carshalton, Surrey; 1 s (Gavin Alistair b 1964), 2 da (Sarah Louise b 1962, Emma Constance b 1966); *Career* Nat Serv RA 1952-54; sales rep: Austin Miles Ltd 1954-58, Eros Engraving Ltd 1958-64; sales mangr Westerham Press 1964-68; chm and md: Gavin Martin Ltd 1968-91 (fndr 1968), Sarema Press (Publishers) Ltd (fndr 1973), KGM (Offset) Ltd (fndr 1983); pt/t tutor RCA 1974-84, visiting lectr E Ham Coll of Technol and Middx Poly, proprietor Design Brief magazine 1985-86; chm Carshalton Soc; memb: Friends of the Earth, Media Natura; *Books* Rookledge's International Typefinder (ed), Rookledge's Handbook of Type Designers (A Biographical Directory from the 15th Century to the present, ed, 1990); *Recreations* film and video, collecting print ephemera, paintings, swimming, squash; *Clubs* Groucho, Chelsea Arts, Wynkyn De Worde Soc, Galley; *Style—* Gordon Rookledge, Esq; Sarema Press (Publishers) Ltd, 15 Beeches Walk, Carshalton Beeches, Surrey SM5 4JS (☎ 081 770 1953, fax 081 770 1957)

ROOLEY, Anthony; s of Henry Rooley, and Madge Rooley; *b* 10 June 1944; *Educ* Royal Acad of Music (LRAM); *m* 1967, Carla; 3 da, 1 s (by Emma Kirkby); *Career* lutenist, dir writers; concerts in: Europe, USA, Middle E, Japan, S America, NZ, Aust, numerous radio and TV broadcasts in UK and Europe; numerous recordings Decca, DHM, Virgin Classics; music admin: Eng Summer Schs 1973-79, The Future of Early Music in Br Conf 1977; fndr Early Music Centre 1976; teacher: RAM 1968, Guildhall Sch of Music and Drama 1971-74, RNCM 1975-76, Univ of Leicester 1976-79, Early Music Centre 1976-80, Schola Cantorum Basel 1985-, Japanese gashkus 1986-, Dartington Int Summer Sch 1986-; music theatre: Cupid and Death 1984, The Marriage of Pantalone 1985, Cupid and Psyche 1987, Venus and Adonis 1988, The Revels of Siena 1988, The Judgement of Paris 1989, Monteverdi's Balli 1990; dir The Consort of Musicke 1969-; FRAM (1990); *Books* Penguin Book of Early Music (1982), Performance: revealing the Orpheus within (1990); author of various articles: Guitar

Magazine 1976, Lute Soc Jls, Lute Soc Jl of America, Early Music Magazine, Temenos; *Recreations* food, wine, sculpture, gardening, philosophy; *Style*— Anthony Rooley, Esq; 54A Leamington Road Villas, London W11

ROOLEY, George Arthur; CBE (1972); s of Richard Arthur Rooley (d 1932), of Leicester, and Edith Mary Rooley (d 1931); *b* 16 Feb 1911; *Educ* Leicester Coll Art and Technol, Univ of Bath (MSc); *m* 1 June 1935, Valeria, da of Herbert Green (d 1966), of Leicester; 1 s (Richard Herbert b April 1940); *Career* chartered engr; fndr ptnr D Smith Seymour & Rooley Consulting Engrs 1945; chm Assoc of Conslt Engrs 1970-71, pres Int Fedn of Hosp Engrg 1972-74, sr ptnr DSSR 1981 (retd); Freeman: City of London 1977, Worshipful of Co of Engineers 1984, Worshipful Co of Constructors 1977; FICE, FIMechE, MConsE, Hon FCIBSE, SFInstE; *Recreations* golf, gardening; *Clubs* Stoke Poges Golf (former capt and pres), Royal Overseas, City Livery; *Style*— George Rooley, Esq, CBE; Greenways, Church Lane, Stoke Poges, Bucks SL2 4PB (☎ 0753 643339)

ROOLEY, Richard Hebert; s of George Arthur Rooley, CBE, *qv*, of Stoke Poges, Bucks, and Valeria Rooley; *b* 24 April 1940; *Educ* Glasgow Acad, Morrisons Acad, Trinity Coll Dublin (BA, BAI); *m* 25 July 1964, (Ismena) Ruth, da of George Young (d 1956), of Carlow, Eire; 1 s (George b 1966), 1 da (Ismena b 1968); *Career* Donald Smith & Rooley conslt engrs 1964-: assoc 1968-, ptnr 1971-; ptnr Project Mgmnt Ptnrship 1978-; memb cncl CIBSE 1972-81 and 1989-, chm Bldg Servs Res and Info Assoc 1984-86; churchwarden Stokes Poges 1980-86, lay chm Burnham Deanery Synod 1985-86; Liveryman Worshipful Co of Engrs (memb ct of Assts 1989), Renter Warden Worshipful Co of Constructors 1988; FEng, FICE, FIMechE, FCIBSE, MConsE, Fell American Soc of Heating Refrigerating and Air Conditioning Engrs (memb bd of dir 1980-83); *Recreations* golf; *Clubs* RAC; *Style*— Richard Rooley, Esq; 8 Cambridge Square, London W2 2PS (☎ 071 402 2488); Park House, 111 Uxbridge Rd, Ealing, London W5 3TE (☎ 081 567 1846, fax 081 566 2216)

ROOM, Adrian Richard West; s of Richard Geoffrey Room, of Littleton Danell, Devizes, Wilts, and Cynthia Ida, *née* West; *b* 27 Sept 1933; *Educ* Dauntsey's Scha, Exeter Coll Oxford (MA); *Career* teacher of English and modern languages 1958; lectr in: English and modern languages 1969, Russian 1974 (sr lectr 1980-84); full-time writer 1984-; memb: English Place Name Soc 1980, American Name Soc 1976; FRGS 1976; *Books* Great Britain: A Background Studies Dictionary (English-Russian 1978), Place-Name Changes since 1900 (1980), Naming Names (1981), A Concise Dictionary of Modern Place-Names in Great Britain and Ireland (1983), Dictionary of Translated Names and Titles (1985), Dictionary of Britain (1986), Dictionary of Place-Names in the British Isles (1988), Dictionary of Dedications (1990); *Style*— Adrian Room, Esq; 12 High St, St Martins, Stamford, Lincs PE9 2LF (☎ 0780 52097)

ROOME, Capt David Gordon; LVO (1962); s of Maj-Gen Sir Horace Eckford Roome, KCIE, CB, CBE, MC, DL, late RE (d 1964), late of IOW, and Helen Isabel Roome, *née* Walford (d 1970); *b* 8 Feb 1923; *Educ* Wellington; *m* 25 Jan 1949, Anne Patricia, da of Rear Adm Humfrey John Bradley Moore, CBE (d 1985), of Kent; 2 s (Geoffrey b 1951, Rowland b 1956), 1 da (Julia b 1950); *Career* RN 1940-72; WWII served: N Atlantic, Med, Far East; Royal Yacht 1960-62, IDC 1963, sr Naval Offr W Indies 1970-72 (as Cdre), ret as Capt RN; ADC to HM The Queen 1971; Civil Serv 1972-87; *Recreations* sailing, cider making, walking; *Clubs* Civil Serv; *Style*— Capt David Roome, LVO, RN; East Hall, Boughton Monchelsea, Maidstone, Kent ME17 4JX (☎ 0622 743410)

ROOME, John Walford; s of Maj-Gen Sir Horace Eckford Roome, KCIE, CB, CBE, MC, DL, (d 1964), and Helen Isabel, *née* Walford (d 1970); *b* 19 Feb 1928; *Educ* Wellington, Clare Coll Cambridge (MA, LLM); *m* 2 July 1955, (Mary) Katherine, da of James Douglas (d 1958); 1 s (James Henry b 7 Oct 1958), 3 da (Christian b 19 Feb 1957, Frances b 3 July 1960, Annabel b 3 Sept 1964); *Career* RN 1946-48; slr Withers 1953- (sr ptnr 1986-90); memb slrs Disciplinary Tbnl 1987-; Cdre: Royal Yacht Sqdn 1986-, Royal Ocean Racing Club 1976-78; chm Offshore Racing Cncl 1978-87, Younger Brother Trinity House 1984; Portsmouth Naval Base Property tstee 1986-, hon memb US Yacht Racing Union; *Recreations* sailing (yacht 'Flycatcher'); *Clubs* Royal Yacht Sqdn, Royal Cruising, Royal Ocean Racing, Royal Lymington Yacht, Island Sailing; *Style*— John Roome, Esq; Riversdale House, Boldre, Lymington, Hants

ROOME, Maj-Gen Oliver McCrea; CBE (1973), DL (Isle of Wight, 1981); s of Maj-Gen Sir Horace Roome, KCIE, CB, CBE, MC, DL, late RE (d 1964), and Helen Isabel, *née* Walford (d 1970); *b* 9 March 1921; *Educ* Wellington; *m* 1947, Isobel Anstis, da of Rev A B Jordan (d 1981), of Nottingham; 2 s (Peter b 1951, Harry b 1954), 1 da (Melanie b 1960); *Career* cmmnd RE 1940; WWII served: UK, Western Desert, Sicily, Italy; various appts 1946-68 in UK, Far East, ME and Berlin; IDC 1969, dir of army recruiting 1970-73, chief Jt Servs Liaison Orgn Bonn 1973-76, ret; Col Cmdt RE 1979-84; Co cmmr Scouts IOW 1977-85; High Sheriff IOW 1983-84; Vice Lord-Lt IOW 1987-; *Recreations* sailing (yacht 'Morning Sky'), youth activities; *Clubs* Army and Navy, Royal Yacht Sqdn, Royal Cruising, Royal Ocean Racing; *Style*— Maj-Gen Oliver Roome, CBE, DL; c/o Lloyds Bank, Cox's & King's, 7 Pall Mall, London SW1

ROONEY, Denis Michael Hall; CBE (1977); s of Frederick Joseph Rooney (d 1955), of Calcutta and Bognor Regis, and Ivy Anne, *née* Hall (d 1985); *b* 9 Aug 1919; *Educ* Stonyhurst, Downing Coll Cambridge (BA, MA); *m* 1, 29 Aug 1942, (Ruby) Teresa (d 1984), da of Thomas Frederick Lamb (d 1946), of Plymouth; 3 s (Nicholas b 30 Nov 1950, Simon b 15 May 1958, Damian b 20 Jan 1963), 3 da (Caroline b 25 Jan 1945, Alison 9 Nov 1947, Amanda 23 Nov 1959); *m* 2, 7 April 1986, Muriel Edith, wid of Bernard Franklin; 1 step da (Tilly b 2 Feb 1972); *Career* Lt (E) RN 1941-46, served maj war vessels and latterly staff engr offr to Adm German Minesweeping Admin Hamburg; apprentice Met Vickers 1937-38; regnl export mangr BICC Ltd 1955-57, exec dir and chief exec BICC Construction Ltd 1958-72 (engr and contract mangr 1946-54), regnl export mangr BICC Ltd 1955-57, chm Balfour Beatty Ltd 1975-80 (md 1973-77), dep chm BICC plc 1978-80, chm BICC Int Ltd 1978-80; Nat Nuclear Corpn: chm 1980-81, industl conslt and non-exec dir 1981-86; chm SE Asia Trade Advsy Gp BOTB 1975-79; memb: BOTB and BOTAC 1976-80, Cncl Christian Assoc of Business Execs, W London Ctee for Protection of Children (hon treas), Inst of Business Ethics; Freeman of City of London 1974, Liveryman of Worshipful Co of Turners 1974; FEng 1979, FIMechE 1960, FIEE 1965, CBIM 1978; USSR Jubilee Medal 1988; *Books* IEE Journal Railway Electrification in Brazil (1953); *Recreations* golf, visiting historic buildings; *Clubs* Roehampton, IOD; *Style*— Denis Rooney, Esq, CBE; 36 Edwardes Sq, London W8 6HH (☎ 071 603 9971)

ROOSE, Christopher Sturt (Chris); s of Arnold Roose, and Olive Lesley, *née* Sturt (d 1969); *b* 22 April 1946; *Educ* Univ Coll Sch Hampstead, St John's Coll Cambridge (MA); *m* 1, 10 Aug 1968 (m dis 1976), Judith Ann Muriel Blackett; partner, Ann Patricia (Mel) Churcher; 1 s (Ben b 1979); *Career* exec gp head Lintas 1969-73, sr writer Saatchi & Saatchi Garland Compton 1973-75, creative dir and head TV D'Arcy MacManus & Masius 1976-81, creative ptnr Thorne Roose Georgiades 1981-82, creative dir Broadbents 1982-; author: Gentlemen and Players (TV 1988), The Big Hand (short story 1988); *Recreations* opera, music, theatre; *Style*— Christopher Roose, Esq

ROOSE-EVANS, James Humphrey; s of Jack Roose-Evans, and Catharina Primrose, *née* Morgan; *b* 11 Nov 1927; *Educ* Crypt GS Gloucester, St Benet's Hall Oxford (MA); *Career* theatre director and author; plays: Cider with Rosie (adapted from Laurie Lee's novel) 1962, 84 Charing Cross Rd 1981, Re Joyce! 1988; prodns in West End incl: An Ideal Husband, The Happy Apple, Private Lives, Cider with Rosie, Under Milk Wood, Mate!, The Seven Year Itch, A Personal Affair, The Best of Friends, Vaclav Havel's Temptation 1990; dir: Chester Mystery Plays Chester Festival 1973, French prodn The Best of Friends Paris 1989; winner 7 awards incl Best Dir and Best Author (84 Charing Cross Rd); fndr: Hampstead Theatre 1959, Bleddfa Trust-Centre for Caring and the Arts 1974; former memb: Drama Panel Welsh Arts Cncl, SE Wales Arts Assoc; has taught regularly at: RADA, Julliard Sch of Music New York, Homerton Coll Cambridge; ordained non-stipendiary Anglican priest 1981 (first Br theatre dir to be also ordained priest); *Books* Directing a Play (1968), Experimental Theatre (4 edn, 1988), London Theatre (1977), The Adventures of Odd and Elsewhere (new edn, 1988), The Secret of the Seven Bright Shiners (new edn, 1989), Odd and the Great Bear (1973), Elsewhere and the Gathering of the Clowns (1974), The Return of the Great Bear (1975), The Secret of Tippity Witchit (1976), The Lost Treasure of Wales (1977), Inner Journey, Outer Journey (1987, published in America as The Inner Stage), Darling Ma (letters of Joyce Grenfell to her mother, ed 1988), The Time of My Life ENSA (memoirs of Joyce Grenfell, ed 1989); *Clubs* Garrick, Dramatists'; *Style*— James Roose-Evans, Esq; c/o David Higham Assoc, 5-8 Lower John St, Golden Square, London W1 (☎ 071 437 7888)

ROOT, Alan George; s of George Root, of Holyport, Berks (d 1966), and Lottie, *née* Singleton-Hayes (d 1975); *b* 16 Nov 1923; *Educ* Maidenhead Sch and privately; *m* 11 June 1949, Margaret Dorothy, da of Sidney Kentish (d 1981), of Holmer Green, Bucks; 4 da (Amanda b 1958, Sarah b 1959, Penelope b 1964, Emma b 1966); *Career* RAF 1941-45, 29 Sqdn Mosquito Night Intruders; gen mangr Newsweek int edns 1953-67, dir Life Magazine, int edns 1967-71; free house owner 1971-78; md Penthouse Gp of Cos 1978-80, dir Publishing Conslt Co 1981-82; antiques and art collator for Trusthouse Forte plc 1983-; *Recreations* cricket, gardening, cooking and wine, photography, antiques; *Clubs* Carlton, MCC; *Style*— Alan Root, Esq; Thornwell Cottage, Thornwell Lane, Wincanton, Somerset BA9 9DY (☎ 0963 34211); Trusthouse Forte plc, 166 High Holborn, London WC1V 6TT (☎ 071 836 7744)

ROOT, Hilary Margaret; da of Frederick James Root (d 1982), and Margaret Eleanor Root; *b* 7 July 1945; *Educ* Sherborne Sch for Girls, Trinity Coll Dublin (BA); *Career* fund mangr Sheppards stockbrokers until 1989, dir Jungle Bound 1990-; *Recreations* travel, tennis, entertaining; *Style*— Miss Hilary Root; 18 Bywater St, London SW3 4XD (☎ 071 584 3810, fax 071 225 3788)

ROOT, Neville Douglas; s of Neville Ernest Arthur Root, and Ada Jackson, *née* Shipley; *b* 17 March 1939; *Educ* Pinner GS; *m* 15 July 1961, Betty Vivienne, da of Rowland Twine (d 1983); 2 s (Neville b 1963, David b 1967), 1 da (Sally b 1964); *Career* dir: Black Clawson Int Ltd 1975-86, Greenbank Gp plc 1984-86; former dir Walker Greenbank plc 1986; dir NW Electricty Bd 1984-; *Recreations* sailing, golf; *Clubs* St James (Manchester); *Style*— Neville Root, Esq; 16 South Downs Road, Hale, Altrincham, Cheshire (☎ 061 928 2496)

ROOTES, 2 Baron (UK 1959); (William) Geoffrey Rootes; s of 1 Baron Rootes (d 1964), and his 1 w, Nora (d 1964), da of Horace Press; *b* 14 June 1917; *Educ* Harrow, Christ Church Oxford; *m* 1946, Marian, da of Lt-Col Herbert Roche Hayter, DSO, of Newbury, Berks, and wid of Wing Cdr James Hogarth Slater, AFC; 1 s, 1 da; *Heir* s, Hon Nicholas Rootes; *Career* served WWII RASC; sits as Cons in House of Lords; chm Chrysler UK (formerly Rootes Motors) 1967-73; dir: Rank Hovis McDougall 1973-84, Joseph Lucas Industries 1973-86; late memb NEDC for Motor Mfrg Indust, memb Cncl IOD 1953-78; vice-pres: Br Field Sports Soc 1978-, Game Conservancy 1979-; county pres Berks St John Ambulance (ret 1988); FBIM, FRSA; KStJ 1988 (CStJ 1983); *Recreations* shooting, fishing; *Clubs* Buck's, Flyfishers'; *Style*— The Rt Hon the Lord Rootes; North Standen House, Hungerford, Berks RG17 0QZ (☎ 0488 82441)

ROOTES, Hon Nicholas Geoffrey; s and h of 2 Baron Rootes; gf founded Rootes Motors; *b* 12 July 1951; *Educ* Harrow; *m* 1976, Mrs Dorothy Anne Burn-Forti, da of Cyril Walter James Wood (d 1979), of Swansea; 1 step s (Dante Burn-Forti b 1965), 1 step da (Lucinda Burn-Forti b 1963); *Career* writer; *Recreations* flyfishing, skiing, tennis; *Style*— The Hon Nicholas Rootes

ROOTHAM, Col Jasper St John; s of Dr Cyril Bradley Rootham (d 1938); *b* 21 Nov 1910; *Educ* Tonbridge, St John's Coll Cambridge; *m* 1944, Joan, *née* McClelland; 1 s, 1 da; *Career* WWII 1941-45 served: ME, Yugoslavia, France, Germany (despatches 1944); Civil Serv 1933-41: Miny of Agric, Colonial Office, Treasy, 10 Downing St; Bank of England 1946-67: asst chief cashier, advsr to govr, asst to govr; sr banking dir Lazard Bros & Co Ltd 1967-75; poet and prose writer; *Publications* Miss Fire, Demi-Paradise, Verses 1928-72, The Celestial City and Other Poems, Stand Fixed in Steadfast Gaze, Affirmation, Lament for a Dead Sculptor and other Poems (1985); *Recreations* music, country life; *Clubs* United Oxford & Cambridge; *Style*— Col Jasper Rootham; 30 West St, Wimborne Minster, Dorset

ROOTS, Guy Robert Godfrey; QC (1989); s of William Lloyd Roots, TD, QC, MP (d 1971) of London, and Elizabeth Colquhoun Gow, *née* Gray; *b* 26 Aug 1946; *Educ* Winchester, BNC Oxford (MA); *m* 17 May 1975, Caroline, da of (Alfred Saxon) Godfrey Clarkson (d 1970), of Herts; 3 s (William b 1978, Hamish b 1979, Sam b 1986); *Career* called to the Bar Middle Temple 1969; Harmsworth scholar 1969; Liveryman Worshipful Co of Drapers 1972; *Recreations* sailing, fishing, skiing, photography, woodworking; *Clubs* Itchenor Sailing; *Style*— Guy Roots, Esq, QC; 2 Mitre Court Buildings, Temple, London EC4Y 7BX (☎ 071 583 1380, fax 071 353 7772)

ROPER, Brian Arnold; s of Arnold Roper (d 1959), of Chesterfield, and Nora, *née* Tuxford (d 1948); *b* 1 Jan 1933; *Educ* Chesterfield Sch, The Queen's Coll Oxford (MA, BM BCh), UCH Med Sch; *m* 3 Aug 1957, Gillian Frances, da of John Michael (d 1971), of Bromsgrove; 1 s (Jonathan Christopher b 20 June 1967), 3 da (Karen Patricia b 8 Aug 1958, Shân Caroline b 8 May 1964, Tamsin Alexandra b 29 Nov 1965); *Career* Capt short serv cmmn RAMC 1958-61; hon conslt orthopaedic surgn Hosp for Sick Children Gt Ormond St London 1971-84; conslt orthopaedic surgn: The Royal London Hosp Whitechapel 1971, King Edward VII Hosp for Offrs Beaumount St London 1975; hon surgn West Ham Utd FC; chapters in med textbooks; Freeman City of London 1984, Liveryman Worshipful Soc of Apothecaries 1987; fell: Br Orthopaedic Assoc, Br Soc Surgery of Hand; FRCS; *Recreations* football, sailing; *Clubs* Crouch Yacht, Burnham Sailing; *Style*— Brian Roper, Esq; 96 Harley St, London W1N 1AF (☎ 071 935 0865)

ROPER, Jeremy James; s of Robert Burnell Roper, CB, of Lindfield, W Sussex, and Mary, *née* Pettit; *b* 13 June 1954; *Educ* Kings Coll Sch Wimbledon, Univ of Birmingham (LLB); *m* 20 Sept 1980, Alison Mary, da of Bryan Peter Studwell Cleal, of Wotton-u-Edge, Gloucestershire; 1 s (Richard James b 1987), 1 da (Katharine Mary b 1984); *Career* admitted slr 1979; ptnr Needham and James slrs 1983; memb Law Soc 1977; *Recreations* sport, vegetable gardening, theatre; *Style*— Jeremy Roper, Esq; Windsor House, Temple Row, Birmingham B2 5LF (☎ 021 2001188, fax 021 2369228, telex 338460)

ROPER, John Francis Hodgess; s of Rev Frederick Mabor Hodgess Roper, by his w

Ellen Frances, *née* Brockway; *b* 10 Sept 1935; *Educ* William Hulme's GS Manchester, Reading Sch, Magdalen Coll Oxford, Univ of Chicago; *m* 1959, Valerie, da of Rt Hon John Edwards, OBE, sometime MP; 1 da; *Career* former econs lectr Manchester Univ; Parly candidate: (Lab) Derbyshire High Peak 1964, (SDP) Worsley 1983; MP (Lab and Co-op 1970-81, SDP 1981-83) Farnworth 1970-83; PPS to Min of State for Indust 1978-79, Lab oppn spokesman Def (front bench), SDP chief whip 1981-; sec Anglo-Benelux Parly Gp 1974-; vice-chm: GB East Europe Centre 1974-, Anglo-German Parly Gp 1974-; memb WEU 1973-, hon treas Fabian Soc 1976-; memb: Gen Advsy Cncl IBA 1974-, Cncl Inst Fiscal Studies 1975-; res fell and ed Int Affrs Royal Inst of Int Affrs 1983-; vice-pres Manchester Statistical Soc 1971-, tstee History of Parliament Tst 1974-; *Style—* John Roper, Esq; House of Commons, London SW1

ROPER, Mark; s of Geoffrey Desmond Roper (d 1982), of Forde Abbey, and Diana Charlotte, *née* King (d 1988); *b* 27 June 1935; *Educ* Bradfield, Magdalene Coll Cambridge (MA); *m* 30 Sept 1967, Elizabeth Dorothy, da of (Oliver) Robin Bagot, of Levens Brow, Kendal, Cumbria; 3 da (Alice b 1 Aug 1968, Victoria b 9 Feb 1970, Lucinda b 29 Aug 1972); *Career* Nat Serv 2 Lt Rifle Bde 1954-56; farmer Forde Abbey and lands (specialising in forest nursery and fruit growing); chm Dorset Country Landowners 1985-88, memb Regnl Advsy Ctee The Forestry Cmmn 1972-88; High Sheriff Dorset 1984; *Style—* Mark Roper, Esq; Forde Abbey, Chard, Somerset

ROPER, (Mervyn Edward) Patrick; s of Capt Nigel Edward Godfrey Roper, DSO, RN (d 1983), and Marjorie Pamela, *née* Wrench; *b* 5 Oct 1954; *Educ* Marlborough, Coll of Law Surrey; *m* 17 Sept 1977, Sarah-Rose Mary, da of Dr D C Wilkins, CBE, TD; 2 s (Francis b 23 March 1987, Charles b 31 May 1989); *Career* mangr corp servs Turner Kenneth Brown Slrs London; Liveryman Worshipful Co of Drapers 1980; *Recreations* gardening, cooking; *Clubs* Naval and Mil; *Style—* Patrick Roper, Esq; 19 Criffel Ave, London SW2 4AY (☎ 081 674 4541); 100 Fetter Lane, London EC4A 1DD (☎ 071 242 6006, fax 071 242 3003, telex 29796 TKBLAW G)

ROPER, Hon Mrs (Sarah-Jane Leathes); *née* Prior; o da of Baron Prior, PC (Life Peer), *qv*; *b* 5 Sept 1959; *m* 4 Sept 1982, David Alexander Roper; 3 da (Lucy Victoria b 10 March 1987, Alexandra Florence (twin) b 10 March 1987, Rosanna Jane b 16 Jan 1989); *Style—* The Hon Mrs Roper; 122 Lower Ham Road, Ham, Kingston, Surrey KT2 5BD

ROPER, Stephen John; s of Stanley Dunham Roper, of Lucy's Mill, Mill Lane, Stratford-on-Avon, Warwicks, and Kathleen Nora Theresa, *née* Barry; *b* 14 April 1943; *Educ* Wimbledon Coll, Univ of Durham (BA); *m* 4 May 1969, Sophie Jaqueline, da of Georges Alex, Cmdt (ret) French Army; 2 da (Stephanie b 1970, Joanna b 1971), 1 s (Tristan b 1977); *Career* CA; Pannell Fitzpatrick & Co Kingston Jamaica WI 1971-75, ptnr Eacott Worrall & Co (Wokingham, Maidenhead, Burnham) 1975-; *Recreations* reading, squash; *Clubs* Royal Ascot Squash; *Style—* Stephen Roper, Esq; Lavendale House, Broomfield Park, Sunningdale, Berkshire SL5 0JS (☎ 0344 24032); Lisa House, 11-15 Peach St, Wokingham, Berks (☎ 0734 781714)

ROPER-CURZON, Hon David John Henry Ingham; s and h of 20 Baron Teynham; *b* 5 Oct 1965; *Educ* Radley; *m* 1985, Lucinda Airy, da of Maj-Gen Sir Christopher Airy; 2 s (Henry Christopher John Ingham b 5 Feb 1986, Jack b 24 Oct 1990 d 1990), 1 da (Elizabeth Poppy b 23 May 1989); *Style—* The Hon David Roper-Curzon

ROPER-CURZON, Hon Henrietta Margaret Fleur; da of 19 Baron Teynham, DSO, DSC (d 1972), and his 2 w, Anne, *née* Curzon-Howe; *b* 25 Aug 1955; *Educ* Warwick Univ; *Career* TV prodr, memb Bd of Govrs Blue Cross; *Style—* The Hon Henrietta Roper-Curzon; Inwood House, Holly Hill Lane, Sarisbury Green, Hants

ROPER-CURZON, Hon Holly Anne-Marie; da of 19 Baron Teynham, DSO, DSC (d 1972), and his 2 w, Anne, *née* Curzon-Howe; *b* 1963; *Educ* Nottingham Univ; *Career* slr; *Style—* The Hon Holly Roper-Curzon; Inwood House, Holly Lane, Sarisbury Green, Hants

ROPER-CURZON, Hon Michael Henry; s of 19 Baron Teynham, DSO, DSC (d 1972); *b* 1931; *m* 1964 (m dis 1967), Maria, da of late Maj R V Taylor, 16/5 Queen's Royal Lancers; *Career* Lt (ret) RN; OStJ; *Style—* The Hon Michael Roper-Curzon; 75 Eccleston Sq Mews, London SW1 (☎ 071 828 9559)

ROPNER, (William Guy) David; s of Sir William Guy Ropner, JP (d 1971), and Margarita (d 1973), da of Sir William Cresswell Gray, 1 Bt; *b* 3 April 1924; *Educ* Harrow; *m* 1, 10 Sept 1955, (Mildred) Malise Hare, da of Lt-Col George Armitage, MC, TD (d 1977); 3 s (Guy b 1959, Roderick b 1962, Peter b 1964), 1 da (Lucy (Mrs C Goelet) b 1957); m 2, 1985, Hon Charlotte Mary Piercy, da of 2 Baron Piercy (d 1981), and formerly w of Paolo Emilio Taddei; 1 s (Nicholas b 1986); *Career* WWII 2 Lt RA, Capt 3 Regt RHA Europe and UK 1942-47; joined Sir R Ropner & Co Ltd 1947, dir Ropner PLC (formerly Ropner Holdings Ltd) 1953- (chm 1973-84); dir: Mainsforth Investmts Ltd 1952-, Airvert Ltd 1975-, Cleveland Leasing Ltd 1982-, Guidehouse Expansion Mgmnt Ltd 1984-, Harcourt Devpts Ltd 1986-; memb Gen Ctee Lloyd's Register of Shipping 1961-; GCBS: vice pres 1978-79, pres 1979-80, chm Lights Advsy Ctee 1978-88, chm Tstees Retirement Benefits Plan 1986-; port and shipping controller designate Home Def 6 Region 1980-; chm: MN Welfare Board 1980-, Cleveland and Durham Industl Cncl 1980-; memb Lloyd's; *Clubs* St Moritz Tobogganing; *Style—* David Ropner, Esq; 1 Sunningdale Gardens, Stratford Rd, London W8 6PX

ROPNER, Jeremy Vyvyan; s of John Raymond Ropner (s of William Ropner (d 1947), who was 3 s of Sir Robert Ropner, 1 Bt), and Joan, *née* Redhead; *b* 3 May 1932; *Educ* Harrow, RNC Dartmouth; *m* 1955, Sally, da of Maj George Talbot Willcox, MC, and Constance (da of William Ropner *ante*); 1 s (and 1 s decd), 2 da; *Career* shipowner; chm: Ropner plc, National Westminster Bank (N Regnl Bd), Hartlepools Water Co, Ropner Shipping Co Ltd, Ropner plc; *Recreations* forestry, golf; *Clubs* Brooks's; *Style—* Jeremy Ropner, Esq; Firby Hall, Bedale, N Yorks (☎ 0677 22345)

ROPNER, Sir John Bruce Woollacott; 2 Bt (UK 1952), of Thorp Perrow, N Riding of Yorks; s of Sir Leonard Ropner, 1 Bt, MC, TD (d 1977). Sir Leonard's f, William, was 3 s of Sir Robert Ropner, JP, DL, cr a Bt 1904 (*see* Ropner, Bt, Sir Robert); *b* 16 April 1937; *Educ* Eton, St Paul's Sch USA; *m* 1, 1961 (m dis 1970), Anne Melicent, da of late Sir Ralph Delmé-Radcliffe; 2 da (Jenny b 1963, Katherine b 1964); m 2 , 1970, Auriol Veronica, da of Capt Graham Lawrie Mackeson-Sandbach, of Caerllo, Llangernyw, Abergele, Denbighshire; 1 s (Henry), 2 da (Carolyn b 1971, Annabel b 1974); *Heir* s, Henry John William Ropner, b 24 Oct 1981 (godparents include Earl of Shelburne, Count Colloredo-Mansfeld, Countess Peel); *Career* dir Ropner plc; *Clubs* Brooks's; *Style—* Sir John Ropner, Bt; Thorp Perrow, Bedale, Yorks

ROPNER, John Raymond (Jock); s of William Ropner, and Sarah, *née* Woolacott; *b* 8 May 1903; *Educ* Harrow, Univ of Cambridge (BA); *m* 28 July 1928, Joan Irene Dorothea (Jill), da of William Redhead; 2 s (William b June 1929, Jeremy b May 1931), 1 da (Susan b Sept 1935); *Career* dir National Provincial Bank; chm: Ropner plc, Hartlepools Water Co; chm: Tport Users NE area, Northern Gas Bd; memb: Chamber of Shipping, Shipping Fedn; Orange Nassau Holland; *Recreations* fishing, golf, gardening; *Clubs* Conservation, Bath; *Style—* Jock Ropner, Esq; The Limes, Dalton, Richmond, North Yorkshire (☎ 0833 21447); Ropner plc, 140 Coniscliffe Rd, Darlington (fax 0325 9462811)

ROPNER, Robert Clinton; s and h of Sir Robert Ropner, 4 Bt; *b* 6 Feb 1949; *Educ* Harrow; *Style—* Robert Ropner, Esq

ROPNER, Sir Robert Douglas; 4 Bt (UK 1904), of Preston Hall, Stockton-on-Tees, Co Palatine of Durham, and Skutterskelfe Hall, Hutton Rudby, North Riding of Yorks; s of Sir (Emil Hugo Oscar) Robert Ropner, 3 Bt (d 1962); *b* 1 Dec 1921; *Educ* Harrow; *m* 1943, Patricia Kathleen, da of William Edward Scofield, of West Malling, Kent; 1 s, 1 da; *Heir* s, Robert Clinton Ropner; *Career* formerly Capt RA; *Style—* Sir Robert Ropner, Bt

ROSCOE, (John) Gareth; s of late John Roscoe, and Ann, *née* Jones; *b* 28 Jan 1948; *Educ* Manchester Warehouseman and Clerks Orphan Sch (now Cheadle Hulme Sch), Stretford Tech Coll, LSE (LLB); *m* 1, 29 Aug 1970 (m dis 1979), Helen Jane, da of Geoffrey Duke Taylor, of Barn Garth, Litton, Skipton, N Yorks; 1 da (Kate b 26 July 1974); m 2, 29 Aug 1980, Alexis Fayrer, da of Raymond Arthur Brett-Holt, of New Rd, Esher, Surrey; 1 s (Jonathan Hugh b 1 Aug 1983), 1 da (Philippa Claire b 8 Feb 1982); *Career* called to the Bar Grays Inn 1972; in practice 1972-75; Law Offrs Dept Attorney Gens Chambers 1979-83, dep slr DOE 1987-89 (legal asst 1975-79, sr legal asst 1979, asst slr 1983-87), legal advsr to BBC and dir of BBC Enterprises 1989-; memb Bar Cncl 1979 (Race Rels Ctee and Law Reform Ctee); *Recreations* radio and television, music, horology, motorcycling; *Style—* Gareth Roscoe, Esq; British Broadcasting Corporation, Broadcasting House, London W1A 1AA (☎ 071 580 4425, fax 071 580 0199, telex 265781)

ROSE, Anthony John Wynyard; s of John Donald Rose, FRS (d 1976), and Yvonne Valerie, *née* Evans; *b* 22 Jan 1946; *Educ* Oundle; *m* 9 Dec 1972, Angela Katherine, da of Wing Cdr Thomas Kenneth Waite (d 1987), of Cheltenham, Glos; 3 s (Dominic John Wynyard b 4 Nov 1984, Alexander Richard Thomas (twin) b 4 Nov 1984, Oliver Louis Christopher b 2 Dec 1986), 1 da (Katherine Lucy b 19 March 1980); *Career* Hon Artillery Co 1970-75; admitted slr 1970; slr Slaughter & May 1970-72 and ICI Ltd 1972-77, ed Aerostat 1975-82, slr then ptnr Charles Russell & Co 1978-; author of various articles on euro competition law and hot air ballooning, awarded Aerostat medal; memb: Cranham Feast Ctee, St Barbara Ballon Gp; hon legal advsr Game Farmers Assoc; Freeman Worshipful Co of Salters 1975, Freeman City of London 1975; memb Law Soc; *Recreations* ballooning, shooting, fishing, reading, dogs; *Clubs* Hon Artillery; *Style—* Anthony Rose, Esq; Killowen House, Bayshill Rd, Cheltenham, Glos GL50 3AW; Hale Court, Lincoln's Inn, London WC2A 3UL (☎ 071 242 1031, fax 071 831 0872, telex 43682, car 0836 234662)

ROSE, Barry; MBE (1981); s of William George Rose, of Essex, and Beatrice Mary, *née* Castle; *b* 17 July 1923; *m* 18 May 1963, (Dorothy) Jean Colthrup, da of Lt-Col Walter Reginald Bowden; 1 da (Diana b 1964); *Career* ed and publisher; chm own gp of cos 1970-; ed: Justice of the Peace 1944-74, Local Government Review, Family Law and others; memb: Chichester RDC 1951-61, Pagham Parish Cncl 1951-62, W Sussex CC 1952-73 (ldr Cons Gp 1967-72, alderman 1972), Bognor Regis UDC 1964-68; RDCA 1960-63, CCA 1968-72; various offices held in Cons Pty 1945-74 incl: chm SE Area Cons Local Govt Advsy Ctee 1969-73, pres Chichester Young Cons 1959-69, chm Chichester Constituency Assoc 1961-69; fndr Assoc of Cncllrs 1960 (pres 1975-86); memb Medico Legal Soc, Br Soc of Criminology, Soc of Cons Lawyers, Royal Soc of Lit; hon life memb Justices' Clerks Soc 1985, hon memb American Soc of Criminology; Liveryman Worshipful Co of Stationers and Newspapermakers; FRSA; *Books* A Councillor's Work (1971), England Looks at Maud (1972); plays: Change of Fortune (1950), Funny Business (1951); *Recreations* talking politics; *Clubs* Athenaeum, Garrick, United Oxford and Cambridge Univ, West Sussex County, MCC; *Style—* Barry Rose, Esq, MBE; Courtney Lodge, Sylvan Way, Bognor Regis, West Sussex (☎ 0243 829902)

ROSE, Brian; s of Edwin Rose George (d 1984), and Emily (d 1967); *b* 26 Jan 1952; *Educ* Canford; *m* 4 Oct 1952, Audrey, da of Henry Barnes (d 1966); 1 da (Fiona Jane b 19 Dec 1965); *Career* Intelligence Corps 1948-50; Miny of Food 1950-54, CRO 1954; Dip Serv: Peshawar 1955-56, Ottawa 1958-61, Kingston Jamaica 1962-65, Rome 1966, Zagreb 1966-68, Zomba and Malawi 1968-71, FCO 1971-74, Dusseldorf 1974-77, E Berlin 1977-78, Zurich 1978-82, consul gen Stuttgart 1982-85, cnsllr Br Embassy Helsinki 1985-88; MIL; *Recreations* squash, tennis, music, reading; *Clubs* Travellers'; *Style—* Brian Rose, Esq; c/o Travellers Club, Pall Mall, London

ROSE, Hon Mr Justice; Sir Christopher Dudley Roger; s of Roger Rose (d 1987), of Morecambe, and Hilda, *née* Thickett (d 1986); *b* 10 Feb 1937; *Educ* Morecambe GS, Repton, Univ of Leeds (LLB), Wadham Coll Oxford (BCL); *m* 5 Aug 1964, Judith, *née* Brand; 1 s (Daniel b 1967), 1 da (Hilary b 1970); *Career* lectr in law Wadham Coll Oxford 1959-60, Bigelow teaching fell Law Sch Univ of Chicago 1960-61, barr 1960, QC 1974, rec Crown Ct 1978-85, bencher Middle Temple 1983, judge High Ct Queen's Bench Div 1985-, presiding judge Northern Circuit 1987-90 (practised 1961-85); govr Pownall Hall Sch 1977-89; memb senate Inns of Ct and Bar 1983-85; kt 1985; *Style—* Hon Mr Justice Rose; Royal Cts of Justice, Strand, London WC2A 2LL

ROSE, Dr (Frank) Clifford; s of James Rose (d 1958), and Clare Rose (d 1960); *b* 29 Aug 1926; *Educ* King's Coll London, Westminster Med Sch (MB BS); *m* 16 Sept 1963, Angela Juliet, da of Eric Halsted (d 1979); 3 s (Sebastian b 1964, Jolyon b 1966, Fabian b 1968); *Career* conslt neurologist Charing Cross Hosp 1965-91, physician i/c Dept of Neurology Regnl Neurosciences Centre 1978-91, dir Academic Neuroscience Unit Charing Cross and Westminster Med Sch 1985-89; hon dir Princess Margaret Migraine Clinic; prof assoc in human sciences Brunel Univ; sec-treas gen World Fedn of Neurology, ed World Neurology; chm: Headache and Migraine Res Gp World Fedn of Neurology, scientific advsy ctee Motor Neurone Disease Assoc, Action Res into Multiple Sclerosis (ARMS); pres Section of Neurology RSM, former pres Med Soc of London; *Books* author and ed of over 50 books on neurology incl: Advances in Stroke Research (1985), Advances in Headache Research (1987), James Parkinson: His Life and Times (1989); *Recreations* travelling; *Style—* Dr Clifford Rose; London Neurological Centre, 110 Harley St, London W1N 1DG (☎ 071 935 3546)

ROSE, Sir Clive Martin; GCMG (1981, KCMG 1976, CMG 1967); s of Rt Rev Alfred Rose (d 1971, sometime Suffragan Bishop of Dover), and Lois, *née* Garton (d 1978); *b* 15 Sept 1921; *Educ* Marlborough, Ch Ch Oxford; *m* 1946, Elisabeth Mackenzie, da of Rev Cyril Lewis; 2 s, 3 da; *Career* Rifle Bde (Maj) 1941-46; served: UK, Europe, India, Iraq; Dip Serv 1948: served India, Germany, France, US, Uruguay; head UK Delgn Negotiations on Mutual Reduction of Forces and Armaments 1973-76, dep sec Cabinet Office 1976-79, ambass and UK perm rep The N Atlantic Cncl 1979-82, ret 1982; conslt Control Risks 1983-, memb RCDS Advsy Bd 1985-, dir Control Risks Info Servs Ltd 1986-; vice pres Royal Utd Servs Inst 1986- (chm Cncl 1983-86), pres Assoc of Civil Def and Emergency Planning Offrs 1987-, vice pres Suffolk Preservation Soc 1988-91 (chm 1985-88); Hon FICD, FRSA; *Publications* Campaigns against Western Defence: NATO's Adversaries and Critics (1985), The Soviet Propaganda Network: a Directory of Organisations Serving Soviet Foreign Policy (1988); *Clubs* Army & Navy; *Style—* Sir Clive Rose, GCMG; Chimney House, Lavenham, Suffolk CO10 9QT

ROSE, David Leslie Whitfield; s of Leslie Rose (d 1980), of Leeds, and Joyce, *née* Whitfield (d 1981); *b* 27 Feb 1954; *Educ* Roundhay Sch Leeds, Downing Coll Cambridge, Inns of Ct Sch of Law (MA, LLB); *m* 14 April 1982, Genevieve Mary, da of Thomas Vernon Twigge, of Burley-in-Wharfedale, W Yorks; 1 s (Matthew b 1986), 1 da (Alice b 1989); *Career* called to the Bar 1977, memb NE Circuit and Northern

Chancery Bar Assoc; treas Leeds N Ward Cons Assoc 1988-89 (chm 1989), dep chm Leeds NE Cons Assoc 1990-; memb Hon Soc of Middle Temple; *Recreations* golf, philately; *Style*— David Rose, Esq; Atlow, 130 Wigton Lane, Leeds LS17 8RZ (☎ 0532 682459); 6 Park Square East, Leeds LS1 2LW (☎ 0532 45763, fax 0532 424395)

ROSE, Eda Mary Bernice; da of John Daniel Thomas (d 1983), of Merthyr Tydfil, and Llywela Mair, *née* Jones (d 1988); *b* 22 July 1941; *Educ* Cyfarthfa Castle GS, Goldsmiths' Coll Sch of Art, Int House London (NDD, RSA, TEFL); *m* 25 Aug 1968 (m dis 1976), Peter Christian Rose; *Career* exclusive bespoke hat designer and manfacturer; fndr Eda Millinery; fashion corr for press, radio and TV; regular radio and TV fashion reporter at Ascot, Henley and other social events; *Clubs* Royal Over-Seas League; *Style*— Mrs Eda Rose; 3 Upton Close, Henley-on-Thames, Oxon RG9 1BT (☎ 0491 573660)

ROSE, Eliot Joseph Benn (Jim); CBE (1979); s of Col Ernest Albert Rose, CBE (d 1976), of Old Kiln, Churt, Surrey, and Julia, *née* Levy (d 1969); *b* 7 June 1909; *Educ* Rugby, New Coll Oxford; *m* 1, 1940 (m dis 1945), Mollie Lipscombe; m 2, 14 Feb 1946, Susan Pamela, da of Thornely Carbutt Gibson; 1 s (Alan b 1949), 1 da (Harriet b 1950); *Career* WWII 1939-45: RAF 1939-41, Govt CCs Bletchley 1941-44, Wing Cdr Dep Dir Intelligence Air Miny 1945; sec Lord Baldwin's Fund for German Refugees 1938-39, literary ed The Observer 1948-51, first dir Int Press Inst 1951-62, dir Nuffield Survey of Race Relations in Br 1963-69, ed dir Westminster Press 1970-73, chm and chief exec Penguin Books 1974-80; fndr 33 Club for German Jewish Refugees 1933-39, co-fndr and tstee The Runnymede Tst, chm Inter-Action Tst 1968-84, memb Rampton Ctee of Enquiry into Educn of Ethnic Minority Children 1979-81, tstee Writers and Scholars Educnl Tst, conslt UNICEF; US Legion of Merit 1945; *Books* Colour and Citzenship (1969); *Recreations* music and walking; *Clubs* Garrick; *Style*— Jim Rose, Esq, CBE; 37 Pembroke Square, London W8 (☎ 071 937 3772); Rocks Farm, Groombridge, Kent (☎ 0892 864 223)

ROSE, Gregory; s of Bernard William George Rose, OBE, and Molly Daphne Rose, OBE, DL, JP, *née* Marshall; *b* 18 April 1948; *Educ* Magdalen Coll Oxford (BA); *Career* conductor; appts incl: princ conductor London Jupiter Orch, Singcirle, Circle, London Concert Choir; guest appts incl: BBC Singers, London Brass, Netherland Radio Chamber Orch, Nederland Kamerkoor, Groupe Vocal de France, Westdeutscher Rundfunk Chor, Steve Reich Ensemble, Netherlands Wind Ensemble; series dir Almeida Festival (Cage at 70 1982, Reich at 50 1986); festivals have included BBC Proms 1978 and 1989, many TV and radio recordings thoughout Europe, many compositions published, fndr ctee memb Assoc of Br Choral Dirs, exec ctee memb Soc for Promotion of New Music; *Recreations* walking, listening to music; *Style*— Gregory Rose, Esq; 57 White Horse Rd, London E1 0ND (☎ 071 790 5883, fax 071 265 9170)

ROSE, Lt-Col Hugh Vincent; s of Col Hugh Rose (d 1957), and Emma Maria, *née* Knowles (d 1951); *b* 11 April 1905; *Educ* Belgrave House Sch, Aldenham, RMC Sandhurst (Army Crammer, Carlisle and Gregson); *m* 1, 1937 (m dis), Barbara Alleard; m 2, 6 Jan 1954, Susan Muriel, da of Capt Guy Sclater, RN (killed 1914 when cmdg HMS Bulwark); 2 s (Hugh Michael b 1940, Philip Timothy b 1960), 1 da (Elizabeth b 1938); *Career* cmmnd offr Indian Army 1924, seconded Foreign and Political Serv Govt of India 1930, Staff Coll Quetta 1939, served NW Frontier M East, CO 3 Gurkhas in 1947 Calcutta riots, cmd 33 Bde Malaya, dep dir ops Eritrea 1950, Cdr Perak Home Gd 1952, colonial serv rep on jt intelligence ctee Far East 1954; asst def sec North Borneo 1956, dir Indr Hugh Rose Properties Ltd; first European to climb Kuh-i-Taftan an active volcano in Persian Baluchistan 1933, discovered unknown pass from Hoti area into Tibet in Himalayas; FRGS; chev Order of Menelik II; *Recreations* formerly polo, pig sticking, squash, writing, skiing and sailing; *Clubs* The Kandahar Ski, Naval & Military; *Style*— Lt-Col Hugh Rose; 7 Harbour Way, Emsworth, Hants PO10 7BE (☎ 0243 373907)

ROSE, Hon Mrs (Irene Phyllis); *née* Hirst; CBE (1961); da of 1 Baron Hirst of Witton (d 1943, title extinct); *b* 1901; *m* 1922, Gp Capt Trevor Felix David Rose, RAFVR, and late Maj RFA and RHA (d 1946); 2 da; *Career* admin WVS 1940-46; memb LCC 1952-58 and 1961-65 (North Lewisham constituency); chm Greater London area and London area of Cons Women's Nat Advsy Ctees 1954-57 and 1959-62, memb Cons Nat Exec Ctee 1959-62; *Style*— The Hon Mrs Rose, CBE; The Old Rectory, Ewhurst, Cranleigh, Surrey GU6 7PX (☎ 0483 267195)

ROSE, Lady Jean; *née* Ramsay; da of late 14 Earl of Dalhousie; *b* 1909; *m* 1945, Lt-Col David McNeil Campbell Rose, DSO, Black Watch; 1 s, 1 da; *Style*— The Lady Jean Rose; Trian, Glenartney, Comrie, Perthshire

ROSE, Jeffery Samuel; s of Stanley Rose (d 1983), of London, and Esther, *née* Israel (d 1986); *b* 22 Dec 1924; *Educ* Haberdashers' Aske's, Hampstead Sch, Guys Hosp Univ of London (BDs, FDSRCS, DOrthRCS); *m* 19 Dec 1949, Joyce Rose, da of Julius Bernstein (d 1987), of London; 1 s (Simon b 3 June 1960), 1 da (Ruth b 21 Oct 1956); *Career* Nat Serv Flt Lt RAF 1946-49; sr lectr in orthodontics The London Hosp Dental Sch 1957-67, dental surgn and conslt orthdontist The London Hosp 1967-90; staff examiner in orthodontics Univ of London 1972-76; memb: Academic Bd London Hosp Med Coll 1975-78, N E Metroplitan Regnl Dental Advsy Ctee, Tower Hamlets Dist Mgmnt Ctee 1976-79, Sub-Ctee in Orthodontics & Paedodontics Univ of London (vice chm 1981-84, chm 1984-87); pres London Hosp Dental Club 1977-78 (hon treas 1978-87); Br Soc for the Study of Orthodontics 1946-: Cncl memb 1961-74, hon treas 1962-70, pres 1972-73, sr vice pres 1976-78, Cncl chm 1980-83, special merit award 1986; Br Paedodontic Soc 1953-: hon sec and treas 1958-61, pres 1964-65; Euro Orthodontic Soc 1954-: hon auditor 1956-70, hon treas 1986-; memb: BDA 1946, Royal Soc of Med 1947-83, Br Assoc of Orthodontists 1967-, Int Assoc of Dentistry for Children 1969-, American Assoc of Orthodontists 1973-89; vice pres: North Western Reform Synagogue 1982-84 (chm 1966-68), Reform Synagogue of GB 1980-86 (chm 1976-79); chm: Leo Baek Coll 1985-88, Euro Bd of The World Union for Progressive Judaism 1990-; *Publications* Orthodontic Teaching Models (1954), Atypical Paths of Eruption - Some Causes and Effects (1958), Cases treated with Extractions of Permanent Canines (jtly, 1960), A Survey of Congenitally Missing Teeth, excluding Third Molars in 6,000 Orthodontic Patients (1966), Early Loss of Teeth in Children (1966), Simple Methods of Retracting Canine Teeth (jtly, 1967), 1,000 Consecutively treated Orthodontic Cases - a Survey (1977), Choice of Appliances in relation to demand for Orthodontic Treatment (1982); *Recreations* communal work, canal boating; *Style*— Jeffery Rose, Esq; 9 Meadway Close, London NW11 7BA (☎ 081 455 5771), 30 Wimpole St, London W1M 7AE (☎ 071 935 8867)

ROSE, Dr John Luke; s of Dr Howard Farnham Rose (d 1949), of Harley St, London, and Elizabeth Gwyneth, *née* Willcox (d 1989); *b* 19 July 1933; *Educ* Chislehurst GS, Trinity Coll of Music London (BMus, PhD, LMus TCL); *Career* Nat Serv as registered conscientious objector (food distribution) 1952-54; adult educn lectr Univ of Oxford 1958-66, pt/t lectr WEA 1959, examiner Trinity Coll of Music 1960 (pt/t lectr and teacher 1958); pt/t teacher of English, music and art: LCC Sch 1959-63, St Marylebone GS 1963-66; staff tutor Univ of London Senate House 1966-84; full-time composer, writer, pianist, poet and painter 1984-; Royal Philharmonic Soc prizewinner for first and second Symphonies; lectr and organiser WEA Kent and Surrey 1959-; lectr and examiner Trinity Coll of Music (UK Canada, Newfoundland, USA, Fiji, NZ, Aust, India), presenter BBC progs on music and art; lectr: V&A, ENO, various univs UK, Canada, USA, NZ, India; dir of studies Proms Summer Sch 1980; memb: TCM Guild (chm 1961), Union of Grads in Music Cncl, SPNM 1962, Assoc of Univ Teachers 1966-, Adult Educn Ctees 1966-, Composer's Guild 1967; hon fell Trinity Coll Univ of London 1961; piano recitals UK and abroad 1959; *compositions* Symphony No 1 The Mystic (BBC premiere), Symphonic Dances (Hallé), Piano Concerto (BBC), Overture Macbeth (BBC), Symphony No 2 Violin Concerto (BBC), Hymnos I-IV The Pleasures of Youth (Cantata for school choir and orch), String Quartet, Violin Sonata, Blake's Song of Innocence, Te Deum (for organ), Capriccio, Elegy and Scherzetto (for bassoon and piano); piano works incl: Toccata, Ariel, Night Music, 2 Sonatas, Landscapes (for young players), Dance Suite, Apocalyptic visions; St Francis (musical), Odysseus (opera), numerous songs, hymns and anthems; *Publications* Wagner's Musical Language (1963), Ludwig, Wagner and the Romantic View (1978), Wagner's Tristan und Isolde, a Landmark in Musical History (1980), Wagner's Music Dramas (a chronological study of his musical works, 1984), Some Basic Facts About Alcohol (1985, 2 edn 1988); *Recreations* reading, gardening, walking, golf, tennis, films, photography, activist, lifelong vegetarian, teetotaller, non-smoker, writing poetry, mystical philosophy and meditation; *Clubs* Foxhills Country; *Style*— Dr John Luke Rose; Kalon, Farnham Road, Guildford GU2 5PF

ROSE, John Raymond; s of Arthur Raymond Rose, MC (d 1961), and Edith Mary, *née* Snow (d 1990); *b* 22 April 1934; *Educ* Marlborough, Trinity Hall Cambridge (maj scholar, BA); *m* 1, 30 Dec 1961 (m dis 1990), (Vivienne) Jane, da of Charles Dillon Seabrooke (d 1975); 1 s (Mark Edward b 1966), 1 da (Deborah Jane b 1964); m 2, Betty Webb; *Career* Mil Serv 2 Lieut DCLI (Belize and Jamaica); House of Commons: asst clerk 1958, sr clerk 1962, dep princ clerk 1976, clerk of Standing Ctees 1987, ret 1991; Freeman City of London 1959, Liveryman Worshipful Co of Salters 1959, fell Indust and Parliament Tst 1987; *Style*— John Rose, Esq; 220 Woodcrest Rd, Raleigh, North Carolina 27605, USA (☎ 919 783 9424)

ROSE, Joyce Dora Hester; CBE (1981), JP (Herts 1963), DL (Herts 1990); da of Abraham (Arthur) Woolf, of Hampstead, London (d 1972), and Rebecca, *née* Simpson (d 1985); *b* 14 Aug 1929; *Educ* King Alfred Sch London, Queen's Coll London; *m* 6 Oct 1953, Cyril, s of Benjamin Rose, of Bedford (d 1971); 1 da (Gillian b 1955); 2 s (Stephen b 1957, Andrew b 1959); *Career* chm Watford Adult Ct 1990- and dep chm Juvenile and Domestic Panels; memb of Herts: Magistrates Ct Ctee, Probation Ctee; chm Cncl Magistrates Assoc 1990-; chm Nat Exec Magistrates Assoc 1990- (chm Herts Branch 1985-90); Lib Pty: pres 1979-80, chm 1982-83, chm Womens Fedn 1987-88 (pres 1972 and 1973), former memb: Women's Nat Cmmn, Nat Exec UK Ctee of UNICEF (vice chm 1968-70); *Clubs* Nat Lib; *Style*— Mrs Joyce Rose, CBE, JP, DL; 38 Main Avenue, Moor Park, Northwood, Middx HA6 2LQ (☎ 09274 21385)

ROSE, Sir Julian Day; 4 Bt (UK 1909), of Hardwick House, Whitchurch, Oxon and 5 Bt (UK 1872), of Montreal, Dominion of Canada; s of Sir Charles Henry Rose, 3 Bt (d 1966), by his w, Hon Phoebe Margaret Dorothy Phillimore, da of 2 Baron Phillimore; also suc kinsman, Sir Francis Rose, 4 Bt 1979; *b* 3 March 1947; *Educ* Stanbridge Earls Sch Romsey; *m* 1976, Elizabeth Goode Johnson, of Columbus Ohio, USA; 1 s (Lawrence Michael b 6 Oct 1986), 1 da (Miriam Margaret b 1984); *Heir* s, Lawrence Rose; *Career* co fndr and asst dir Inst for Creative Devpt Antwerp; commenced organic farming enterprise Hardwick Estate 1983; memb: Soil Assoc Cncl 1984, Bd UK Register of Organic Food Standards; agric correspondent Environment Now 1989; co-fndr The Assoc of Unpasteurised Milk Producers and Consumers 1989; memb BBC Rural and Agric Affrs Advsy Ctee 1991-; *Style*— Sir Julian Rose, Bt; Hardwick House, Whitchurch, Oxon

ROSE, Martin John; s of John Ewert Rose, of Chandlers Ford, Hants, and Margaret Mary, *née* Eames; *b* 21 March 1956; *Educ* St Mary's Coll Southampton, Univ of Warwick (LLB); *m* 7 May 1988, Emma Margaret Havilland, da of Robert Bernard Hutchinson, of Wimborne, Dorset; *Career* called to the Bar Middle Temple 1979, practising barr Western circuit 1980-86, legal conslt The Stock Exchange 1986, sr legal advsr The Securities Assoc 1986-89, sr asst slr Linklaters and Paines 1990, dir Kensquare Ltd; memb: Law Reform Ctee, Bar Assoc for Commerce, Fin and Indust; *Recreations* riding, cooking, mil history; *Style*— Martin Rose, Esq; Linklaters and Paines, Barrington House, 59-67 Gresham St, London EC2V 7JA (☎ 071 606 7080)

ROSE, Paul Bernard; s of Arthur Rose (d 1974), and Norah, *née* Helman; *b* 26 Dec 1935; *Educ* Bury GS, Univ of Manchester (LLB), Inst of Advanced Legal Studies, Sorbonne; *m* 13 Sept 1957, Eve Marie Thérèse, da of Jean Lapu, of 8 rue Boucry, Paris; 2 s (Howard Imre b 25 Jan 1961, Daniel Sean b 18 Oct 1970), 1 da (Michelle Alison b 11 Oct 1964); *Career* called to the Bar Gray's Inn 1958; legal advsr Cooperative Union Ltd 1958-61; lectr Univ of Salford 1961-63; MP (Lab) Manchester Blackley 1964-79, PPS for Tport 1966-68, memb SDP, frontbencher, asst recorder 1975-88, pt/t immigration adjudicator 1987-, HM Coroner Gtr London Southern Dist 1988-; chm NW Sports Cncl 1966-68; patron St Lucia Soc; memb: Cncl of Europe 1968-70, fndr Inst of Linguists, Coroner's Soc, Medico-legal Soc; *Recreations* sport, the arts, computers, writing, travel; *Style*— Paul B Rose, Esq; 47 Lindsay Drive, Kenton, Harrow, Middlesex HA3 0TA (☎ 081 204 3076); Coroner's Office, The Law Courts, Barclay Road, Croydon CR9 3NE (☎ 081 681 5019)

ROSE, Paul Michael Anthony; s of Sidney Samuel Rose, of 135 Palatine Rd, Didsbury, Manchester, and Golda, *née* Cohen; *b* 30 July 1948; *Educ* Manchester GS, St Edmund Hall Oxford (BA, MA); *m* 25 June 1973, Helen Louise, da of Harold Shapiro; 2 s (Jonathan Samuel b 29 April 1977, Nicholas Simon b 20 Oct 1980); *Career* slr; partner: Maurice Rubin & Co Solicitors Manchester 1975-85 (articled clerk 1970-72), Halliwell Landau 1985-; memb Law Soc, jt chm Greater Manchester Youth Assoc 1989-; *Clubs* Durham Forest Golf and Country; *Style*— Paul Rose, Esq; 63 Moss Lane, Sale, Cheshire M33 5AP (☎ 061 973 9910); Halliwell Landau, St James's Court, Brown St, Manchester (☎ 061 835 3003, fax 061 835 2994, car 0836 752 015)

ROSE, Hon Lady (Phoebe Margaret Dorothy); *née* Phillimore; da of 2 Baron Phillimore, MC (d 1947), and (1 w) Dorothy Barbara (d 1915), er da of Lt-Col Arthur Balfour Haig, CVO, CMG, JP; *b* 29 Feb 1912; *m* 1937, Sir Charles Henry Rose, 3 Bt (d 1966); 1 s (and 1 decd), 2 da; *Style*— The Hon Lady Rose; Hardwick House, Whitchurch, Reading, Oxon RG8 7RB (☎ 0734 842955)

ROSE, Prof Richard; s of Charles Imse, of St Louis, Missouri, USA, and late Mary Conely Rose; *b* 9 April 1933; *Educ* Clayton HS Missouri USA, John Hopkins Univ (BA), LSE, Univ of Oxford (DPhil); *m* 1956, Rosemary, da of late James Kenny, of Whitstable, Kent; 2 s, 1 da; *Career* political PR Mississippi River Road 1954-55, reporter St Louis Post - Dispatch 1955-57, lectr in govt Univ of Manchester 1961-67; Univ of Strathclyde: prof of politics 1966-81, dir Centre for the Study of Public Policy 1976-, prof of public policy 1982-; Ransome lectr Alabama 1990; fndr memb Exec Ctee Euro Consortium for Political Res 1970, US Ambassador's appointee US - UK Fulbright Educnl Cmmn 1970-75, sec Res Ctee on Political Sociology Int Political Sci Assoc and Int Sociological Assoc 1970-85, fndr memb Exec Ctee Br Politics Gp in the US 1974-; memb: Steering Ctee Choice in Social Welfare Policy Cncl of Euro Studies 1974-77, Home Office Working Pty on the Electoral Register 1975-77; convenor Work Gp on UK Politics Political Studies Assoc 1976-88, conslt and chm N Ireland Constitutional Convention 1976, memb Cncl Int Political Sci Assoc 1976-82, co-dir 1982 World Congress Programme Rio de Janeiro, conslt OECD 1980-, ed Journal of

Public Policy 1985- (chm Bd 1981-84), memb Cncl British Irish Studies Assoc 1987-, guest prof Wissenschaftszentrum Berlin 1988-90, founding fell Conf on Socio Economics 1989-, UN conslt Pres of Colombia 1990; fell: American SSRC Stanford Univ 1967, Woodrow Wilson Int Centre Washington DC 1974; Guggenheim fellowship 1973-74, foreign memb Finnish Acad of Sci and Letters 1985, hon vice pres UK Political Studies Assoc 1986; *Books* Governing without Perspective: an Irish Perspective (1971), Electoral Behavior (1974), Presidents and Prime Ministers (ed with E Suleiman, 1980), Do Parties Make a Difference? (2 edn, 1984), Understanding Big Government (1984), Ordinary People in Public Policy (1989), Politics in England (5 edition, 1989) Loyalties of Voters (with Ian McAllister, 1990), International Almanac of Electoral History (with T T Mackie, 3 edn, 1991), The Postmodern President: the White House Meets the World (2 edn, 1991); *Recreations* historical Britain, modern America, music, writing; *Clubs* Reform, Cosmos (Washington DC); *Style*— Prof Richard Rose; Bonnchy, 1 East Abercromby Street, Helensburgh, Dunbartonshire G84 7SP (☎ 0436 72164); Centre for the Study of Public Policy, Livingstone Tower, 26 Richmond St, Glasgow G1 1XH (☎ 041 552 4400, fax 041 552 4711)

ROSE, Dr Stephen John; s of Bernard Rose (d 1967), of London, and Grace Alberta, *née* Hefford; *b* 20 March 1951; *Educ* Highgate Public Sch, Univ of Cambridge, Guy's Hosp London (BA, MA, MB BChir, MD); *m* 29 Jan 1983, Beatriz; 2 da (Sybilla Alessandra b 1985, Eilidh Veronica b 1986); *Career* jr dr Guy's, registrar Westminster Hosp Med Sch London, lectr Univ of Aberdeen, currently conslt and hon sr lectr Dept of Child Health Univ of Birmingham; memb Nat Exec Jr Hosp Drs; MRCP 1979; *Books* Case Histories in Paediatrics (1984), Early Recognition of Child Abuse (1984), Textbook of Medicine for Medical Students (1986); *Recreations* squash; *Clubs* Univ of Cambridge Union; *Style*— Dr Stephen Rose; University Dept of Paediatrics, East Birmingham Hospital, Bordesley Green East, Birmingham B9 5ST (☎ 021 766 6611, fax 021 773 6736)

ROSE, Hon Mrs (Susan Jane); *née* James; da of 4 Baron Northbourne; *b* 1936; *m* 1961, Michael Hugh Rose, s of late Rt Rev Alfred Carey Wollaston Rose, formerly Bishop of Dover; 1 s, 3 da; *Style*— The Hon Mrs Rose; Le Sirondole, Panzano-in-Chianti, Florence, Italy

ROSE-INNES, Prof (Alistair) Christopher; s of John Francis Rose-Innes (d 1953), of London, and Audrey Henriette, *née* Lowenstam (d 1979); *b* 4 Dec 1926; *Educ* Rydal Sch, Univ of Oxford (MA, DPhil), Univ of Manchester (DSc); *m* 1956, Barbara Ellen, da of Frank William Nicholls (d 1978), of Shrewsbury; 2 s (Nicholas b 1957, Alexander b 1959), 2 da (Elizabeth b 1962, Jessica b 1964); *Career* Radar Instr RN 1944-47, princ scientific offr RN Scientific Serv 1954-64; Harkness fell Cwlth Fund and visiting fell Rutgers Univ 1960-61; UMIST: prof of physics and electrical engrg 1968-89, emeritus prof of physics and electrical engrg 1989-; memb of many nat and int ctees on low temperature and solid state physics; FInstP 1961, FIEE 1981, CEng 1981; *Books* Semiconducting III-V Compounds (1961), Low Temperature Laboratory Techniques (1973), Introduction to Superconductivity (1978); *Recreations* drawing and sculpture, growing cacti; *Clubs* Athenaeum; *Style*— Prof Christopher Rose-Innes; University of Manchester, Institute of Science and Technology, Sackville St, Manchester M60 1QD (☎ 061 200 4756, telex 666094)

ROSE OF KILRAVOCK, (Anna) Elizabeth Guillemard; 25 of Kilravock and Chief of Clan Rose; da of Lt-Col Hugh Rose of Kilravock, CMG, JP, DL (d 1946), and Ruth Antoinette, *née* Guillemard; suc f 1946; *b* 28 May 1924; *Educ* St Leonard's Sch; *Career* served with WRNS 1944-46; *Style*— Miss Elizabeth Rose of Kilravock; Kilravock Castle, Croy, by Inverness

ROSE PRICE, Hon Mrs (Maureen Maude Tower); *née* Butler; da of late 27 Baron Dunboyne; *b* 1919; *m* 1946, Lt-Col Robert Caradoc Rose Price, DSO, OBE, late Welsh Gds (d 1988); 1 s, 1 da; *Clubs* The Arts; *Style*— The Hon Mrs Rose Price; 98 Old Church St, London SW3 6EP

ROSEBERY, 7 Earl of (S 1703); Sir Neil Archibald Primrose; 9 Bt (S 1651), DL (Midlothian 1960); also Viscount of Rosebery, Lord Primrose and Dalmeny (both S 1700), Viscount of Inverkeithing, Lord Dalmeny and Primrose (both S 1703), Baron Rosebery (UK 1828), Earl of Midlothian, Viscount Mentmore, and Baron Epsom (all UK 1911); s of 6 Earl of Rosebery, KT, DSO, MC, PC (d 1974, the celebrated race horse owner and s of the Lib PM and Hannah, da of Baron Meyer de Rothschild, through whom Mentmore came into the family), by his 2 w, Hon Dame Eva, *née* Bruce, DBE, JP (da of 2 Baron Aberdare and former w of 3 Baron Belper); *b* 11 Feb 1929; *Educ* Stowe, New Coll Oxford; *m* 1955, (Alison Mary) Deirdre, da of Ronald William Reid, MS, FRCS; 1 s, 4 da; *Heir* s, Lord Dalmeny; *Style*— The Rt Hon The Earl of Rosebery, DL; Dalmeny House, South Queensferry, West Lothian (☎ 031 331 1784/1785)

ROSEDALE, Dr Neville; s of Arthur Rosedale (d 1982), of London, and Betty (d 1987); *b* 7 Nov 1923; *Educ* City of London Sch, Bart's London; *m* 1, 1948, Marian, *née* James (d 1955); m 2, 5 Feb 1958, Patricia Mary, da of Frederick Barnes (d 1957); *Career* RAF Med Branch: Nat Serv 1946-48, perm cmmn 1950-52; conslt venereologist W Middx and Hillingdon Hosps 1962-, civil conslt in Venereology to RAF 1982-89; MRCS, LRCP, FRCPE, Med Soc for Study of Venereal Diseases; *Books* The First Report (1970); *Clubs* RAF; *Style*— Dr Neville Rosedale; 46 Hatherley Court, Westbourne Grove, London W2 5RE (☎ 071 727 9639); 23 Peveril Heights, Sentry Rd, Swanage, Dorset BH19 2AZ (☎ 0929 423649); Hillingdon Hospital, Uxbridge, Middx UB8 3NN (☎ 0895 79537)

ROSEHILL, Lord; David John MacRae Carnegie; s and h of 13 Earl of Northesk; *b* 3 Nov 1954; *Educ* Eton; *m* 1979, Jacqueline, da of David Reid, by his w Elizabeth, of Sarasota, Florida; 1 s, 2 da (Hon Sarah Louise Mary b 29 Oct 1982, Hon Fiona Jean Elizabeth b 24 March 1987); *Heir* s, Hon Alexander Robert MacRae Carnegie b 16 Nov 1980; *Career* farmer and company dir; *Recreations* shooting; *Clubs* Kennel Club; *Style*— Lord Rosehill; Fair Oak, Rogate, Petersfield, Hants (☎ 073 080 508)

ROSEMONT, David John; s of Leslie Rosemont (d 1964), of Oxted, Surrey, and Elizabeth, *née* Williams (who m 2, 1974, Air Cdre Philip E Warcup); *Educ* Lancing, Architectural Assoc Sch of Architecture; *m* 8 Aug 1975, Elizabeth Abbott (Abbey), da of Frederick Milne Booth Duncan, of Ayr, Scot; 2 s (Hugo David b 3 March 1979, Jonathan Duncan b 22 Dec 1980); *Career* architect 1971; assoc: Fairhursts Manchester 1975-77, SKP Architects London 1977-81, commenced private practice David Rosemont Assocs 1981; chm and md: Rosemont Holdings Ltd 1989-, Rosemont Assocs Ltd 1989-; chm and dir: Rosemont Building Surveying Ltd 1989-, Alan Rigby Associates Ltd 1989-; memb Br Acad of Experts 1988, co chm Inner Cities Ctee Assoc of Ind Businesses 1988; memb AA, RIBA; *Recreations* opera, photography, gastronomy, classic cars, places; *Clubs* Carlton; *Style*— David Rosemont, Esq; 7 Trinity Crescent, London SW17 7AG (☎ 081 672 7117); Rosemont Holdings Ltd Group of Companies, 212 St Ann's Hill, London SW18 2RU (☎ 081 870 8622, 081 870 9824, fax 081 870 9885)

ROSEN, Albert; s of Dr Lazar Rosen (d 1951), and Terezie, *née* Ruzickova (d 1971); *b* 14 Feb 1924; *Educ* Vienna Gymnasium, Bratislava Gymnasium, Vienna Music Acad, Prague Conservatory; *m* 1, 1955 (m dis 1961), Anna, *née* Hartlová; 1 s (Alexander b 1956); m 2, 1962 (m dis 1975), Blahoslava, *née* Markvartova; 1 da (Susana b 1964); *Career* conductor: State Opera Pilsen 1949, Prague Nat Opera 1959; chief conductor: Prague Smetana Theatre 1965, Radio TV Symphony Orchestra Dublin 1969, Perth Aust 1981, Adelaide Aust 1986; Wexford Festival Opera 1965-88, San Francisco Opera 1980, Opera du Rhin Strasburg 1982, ENO 1987/88/89, Prague Nat Opera 1989; *Recreations* travel; *Style*— Albert Rosen, Esq; 70 Haddingon Rd, Dublin 4, Ireland (☎ 0001 687876); Prague 6, Glinkova 14, Czechoslovakia (☎ 010 42 2 3120775)

ROSEN, Anthony; s of Maurice Rosen (d 1971); *b* 19 Dec 1930; *Educ* Framlingham Coll; *m* 1954, Hilary June, da of Comins Mansfield (d 1983), of Paignton, Devon; 2 s (Andrew b 1956, Howard b 1958), 1 da (Philippa b 1965); *Career* Capt RA (Air Ops) 1950-52; chm Fordson Estates Ltd, chief exec Feenix Farming, ptnr Second Opinion Assocs and Green Eagle Golf, Rosen and Luckin Assocs, memb Agric Forum and 75 Club, political and econ columnist Farming News; *Books* Englands Pleasant Land - Vision and Reality, Farming and the Nation; *Recreations* work, photography, travel; *Clubs* Farmers'; *Style*— Anthony Rosen, Esq; Rosehill, Arford, Headley, Hants GU35 8DF (☎ 0428 717540, fax 0428 717540)

ROSEN, Cecil Kullman; s of Harris Lewis Rosen (d 1932), and Fanny Hetty (d 1943); *b* 1 Aug 1918; *Educ* Highbury Sr Boys Sch London; *m* 17 March 1951, Dorice; 1 da (Lisa Fiona (Mrs Voice) b 18 June 1953); *Career* WWII, MAP 1939-44; surveyor 1938-90; chm: Jewish Blind and Physically Handicapped Soc, Cavendish Housing Tst Ltd, Investment & Securities Trust Ltd, Central Town Properties Ltd; fndr and tstee: Heart Disease and Diabetes Res Tst, Nat Soc for Res into Mental Health (Queen Charlotte's Hosp); pres Jewish Youth Orch; Freeman City of London 1960, memb Guild of Freeman City of London 1961; *Style*— Cecil K Rosen, Esq; 118 Seymour Place, London W1H 5DJ (☎ 071 262 2003/5, fax 071 262 8185)

ROSEN, Emanuel; s of Capt Lionel Rosen, OBE (d 1977), of Hull, and Leah, *née* Levy, of Hull; *b* 23 Sept 1936; *Educ* Hull GS, Univ of Manchester (MD, BSc); *m* 9 Sept 1962, The Hon June Lever, da of Lord Lever of Ardwick (d 1976); 2 s (William David, Edward Leon), 1 da (Caroline Alexandra); *Career* med dir Manchester Cataract Centre, conslt ophthalmic surgn North West Regional Authy, lectr in ophthalmology Univ of Manchester, visiting prof Dept of Visual Sciences Univ of Manchester; pres: UK Intraocular Lens Implant Soc, Euro Intraocular Lens Implant Cncl; memb Cncl Coll of Ophthalmologists; FCOphth, FRCSE, FRPS; *Books* Fluorescence Photography of the Eye (1969), Basic Ophthalmoscopy (1972), Intraocular Lens Implantation (1983), Hazards of Light (1986), Visco-elastic Materials (1988), Intercapsular Surgery (1989), Quality of Cataract Surgery (1990); *Recreations* golf, photography; *Clubs* Athenaeum; *Style*— Emanuel Rosen, Esq; 10 St John St, Manchester M3 4DY (☎ 061 832 8778, fax 061 832 1486)

ROSEN, Rabbi Jeremy; s of Rabbi Dr Kopul Rosen (d 1962), and Bella, *née* Censor; *b* 11 Sept 1942; *Educ* Carmel Coll, Pembroke Coll Cambridge (MA), Mir Acad Jerusalem; *m* 1, 14 June 1971 (m dis 1987), Vera, *née* Zippel; 2 s (Jacky b 7 June 1976, Avichai b 23 Aug 1982), 2 da (Anushka Tanya b 23 Sept 1974, Natalia Ruth b 16 July 1979); m 2, 19 May 1988, Suzanne, *née* Kaszirer; *Career* rabbi Giffnock Hebrew Congregation Glasgow 1968-71, headmaster Carmel Coll 1971-84, rabbi Western Synagogue London 1985-, Chief Rabbi's rep on Interfaith 1986-90, dir Kaszirer Fndn 1990-; *Style*— Rabbi Jeremy Rosen; 37 Brendon St, London W1H 5DH (☎ 071 723 9333); 20 Bryanston Mansions, York St, London W1H 1DA (☎ 071 724 5494)

ROSEN, Hon Mrs (June Avis); *née* Lever; da of Baron Lever (Life Peer, d 1977); *b* 4 June 1940; *Educ* Cheltenham Ladies' Coll, Sch of Physiotherapy, Ancoats Hosp Manchester; *m* 1962, Emanuel Rosen, s of Lionel Rosen, MBE, of Hull; 3 children; *Career* physiotherapist; *Recreations* family, choral singing, politics, reading, ctee work; *Style*— The Hon Mrs Rosen; 18a Torkington Rd, Wilmslow, Cheshire (☎ 0625 522768)

ROSEN, Prof Michael; s of Israel Rosen (d 1969), of Dundee, and Lily Rosen, *née* Hyman; *b* 17 Oct 1927; *Educ* Dundee HS, Univ of St Andrews (MB ChB); *m* 17 Oct 1955, Sally Barbara, da of Leslie Israel Cohen (d 1960); 2 s (Timothy b 1956, Mark b 1962), 1 da (Amanda (Mrs Kirby) b 1959); *Career* Nat Serv RAMC Capt served UK, Egypt and Cyprus 1952-54; sr registrar Cardiff 1957, conslt anaesthetist Cardiff Teaching Hosp 1961-, hon prof in anaesthetics Univ of Wales 1984-8l, fell of Western Reserve Cleveland USA 1960-61; dean Faculty of Anaesthetists RCS 1988, pres Coll of Anaesthetists 1988-, hon memb Japanese Soc of Anaesthesiologists 1989 (Aust 1974, French 1978), pres Assoc of Anaesthetists of GB and I 1986-88, hon memb Univ Anaesthetists USA 1989, memb Acad of Med Malaysia 1989; Hon FFARCS I 1990, FRCOG 1989; *Books* Handbook of Percutaneous Central Venous Catheterisation (with I P Latto and W S Ng, 1981), Obstetric Anaesthesia and Analgesia: Safe Practice (contrib, 1982), Intubation: Practice and Problems (with I P Latto, K Murrin, W S Ng, R S Vaughan and W K Saunders, 1985), Difficulties in Tracheal Intubation (with I P Latto and B Tindall, 1985), Patient-Control Analgesia (with M Harmer and M D Vickers, 1985), Consiousness Awareness and Pain in General Anaesthesia (with J N Lunn, 1987); *Style*— Prof Michael Rosen; 45 Hollybush Rd, Cardiff CF2 6SZ (☎ 0222 753893); Dept of Anaesthetics, University Hospital of Wales, Heath Park, Cardiff CF4 4XW (☎ 0222 755944, fax 0222 747203)

ROSEN, Mikel; s of Philip Rosen (d 1973), and Sonia Rosen; *b* 14 Oct 1953; *Educ* North Manchester GS, Hornsey Sch of Art, St Martin's Sch of Art (BA); *Career* fashion designer and illustrator 1977, estab Mikal Rosen Productions Limited (fashion show prodn and design consultancy) 1984-; launched Mikel Rosen Promotions Limited (PR serv for the fashion indust) 1986-; lectr in fashion design Middlesex Poly 1979-84; *Books* contrib chapter Runaway by Rosen to Fashion Year Book (1985); *Recreations* walking the dog; *Style*— Mikel Rosen, Esq; Mikel Rosen Ltd, 23/29 Emerald St, London WC1N 3QL (☎ 071 831 2774, fax 071 831 7610)

ROSENBERG, Jenifer Bernice; OBE (1989); da of Philip Levene (d 1966), of London, and Jane-Sarah, *née* Kent (d 1982); *b* 1 Oct 1942; *Educ* Our Lady of Zion GS; *m* 1, 1 Aug 1975, Jack Goldstein (d 1975); m 2, 8 Feb 1982, Ian David Rosenberg, s of Alfred Rosenberg (d 1984), of London; *Career* sr buyer Marks and Spencer plc 1960-74, fndr and md J and J Fashions Ltd 1974-; memb: Clothing and Allied Products Trg Bd Design 2000 Ctee, CNAA, govr London Inst; hon conslt to Bournemouth and Poole Coll of Art and Design, organiser Woman of Distinction Luncheon for the Jewish Blind Soc, fndr and former chm JIA Woman in Business Ctee; memb: Dr Barnardo's Ball Ctee, Ctee for Ravenswood Village Home for the Mentally Handicapped, Advsy Ctee on Women's Employment, Advsy Panel on Deregulation Advsy Ctee DTI; dir City and Inner London North Trg and Enterprise Cncl (CILN TEC), patron Friends of Bar Ilan Univ Women's Gp; Award from Tyne and Wear Cncl for Industl and Commercial Enterprise (twice), Veuve Clicquot/IOD Business Woman of the Year Award 1986; CBIM, fell Royal Soc for the Encouragement of Arts Manufacture and Commerce; *Recreations* theatre, photography, music, travelling, bridge; *Style*— Mrs Jenifer Rosenberg, OBE; J and J Fashions Ltd, 260 York Way, London N7 9PQ (☎ 071 609 6261, fax 01 609 9845)

ROSENBLOOM, Prof Richard Selig; s of Iraving J Rosenbloom (d 1980), and Lillian S Rosenbloom (d 1972); *b* 16 Jan 1933; *Educ* Harvard Univ (AB, MBA, DBA); *m* 14 Oct 1956, Ruth Miriam, *née* Friedlander; 2 s (Joshua b 13 Aug 1958, Daniel b 27 Oct 1963), 1 da (Rachel b 13 Aug 1968); *Career* prof of business admin Harvard Univ 1960-; non-exec dir Lex Service plc, dir General Instrument Corporation; *Style*— Prof Richard Rosenbloom; Lex Services plc, Lex House, 17 Connaught Place, London W2

2EL (☎ 071 723 1212)

ROSENHEAD, Martin David; s of Louis Rosenhead, CBE (d 1984), of Liverpool, and Esther, *née* Brostoff, JP; *b* 19 May 1935; *Educ* Quarry Bank HS Liverpool, St John's Coll Cambridge (MA, pres Union Soc); *m* 20 Jan 1961, Lindsay Margaret, da of Stanislas Eugene Meunier, of Epping, Essex; 1 da (Annabel b 26 Jan 1967); *Career* various mgmnt appts ICI 1956-68, business devpt dir construction sector Foseco-Minsep plc 1969-70, dir Redland plc 1970-74, non exec dir Royal Brierley Crystal Ltd 1974-84, business devpt dir Wallpaper Manufacturers Ltd 1974-79, dir Arthur Sanderson and Sons Ltd 1974-79, chm Thomson Shepherd Ltd 1976-78, md Bradfield Brett Holdings Ltd 1978-79; chm: Royal Stafford China Ltd 1980-83, Spartan Holdings Ltd 1980-84, Teakspire Ltd 1980-86; non exec dir Cowan De Groot plc 1983-84, dir Profile Consulting Ltd 1988-90; dir Home Office supervisory Bd Sci and Technol Gp Directorate of Telecommunications 1986-, chm and chief exec Response Accessories Ltd 1989-90; dir: Instrop (Decormetall) Ltd 1989-90, Euro Assocs Ltd 1990-, Cytotechnics Ltd (non-exec) 1990-; chm Nicola Martin Tapes Ltd 1990-, business advsr Suffolk Water Co plc 1990-; former Parly candidate (Lib); FIOD 1970, FBIM 1980; *Recreations* music, walking, skiing, Europe, hypnosis; *Style*— Martin Rosenhead, Esq; 6A St Peters Rd, St Margarets-on-Thames, Twickenham, Middx TW1 1QX, (☎ 081 744 2530, fax 081 891 3242); 12 Latham Rd, Twickenham, Middx TW1 1BN, (☎ 081 891 3705, fax 081 892 4493, car 0860 396 388)

ROSENTHAL, Erwin Isak Jacob; s of late Moses Rosenthal, and late Amelie Rosenthal; *b* 18 Sept 1904; *Educ* Heilbronn, Univ of Heidelberg, Univ of Munich, Univ of Berlin (DPhil), Cambridge (MA, LittD); *m* 1933, Elizabeth Charlotte, *née* Marx; 1 s, 1 da; *Career* Nat Serv, RASC 1944-45; head of Dept of Hebrew UCL 1933-36 (former Goldsmid lectr in hebrew, lectr in north-semitic epigraphy), special lectr semitic languages and literatures Univ of Manchester 1936-44; lectr Central Advsy Cncl for Educn HM Forces 1940-44; attached to PID of FO 1945: German section 1946-48; tutor adult educn Univ Tutorial Class WEA London 1946-48, reader in oriental studies Univ of Cambridge 1959-71 (lectr in hebrew 1948-59), fell of Pembroke Coll Cambridge 1962-71 (emeritus 1971); visiting prof: Univ of Columbia 1967-68, El Colegio de Mexico 1968; Leverhulme emeritus fell 1974-75, pres Br Assoc for Jewish Studies 1977, corr fell American Acad for Jewish res 1984, corr memb Rhenish-Westphalian Acad of the Scis 1986; *Books* Ibn Khaldûns Gedanken über den Staat (1932), Law and Religion vol 3 Judaism and Christianity (1938), Saadya Studies (ed and contrib, 1943), Averrores' Commentary on Plato's Republic (ed and trans, 1956, 3 edn 1969), Political Thought in Medieval Islam (1958, 3 edn 1968), Griechisches Erbe in der Jüdischen Religionsphilosophie des Mittelalters (1960), Judaism and Islam (1961), Islam in the Modern National State (1965), Religion in the Middle East (ed Judaism section, 1969), Studia Semitica I Jewish Themes, II Islamic Themes (1971); *Recreations* music, walking, travelling; *Style*— Erwin Rosenthal, Esq; 199 Chesterton Rd, Cambridge CB4 1AH (☎ 0223 357648); Pembroke College, Cambridge

ROSENTHAL, Jack Morris; s of Samuel Rosenthal (d 1964), of Manchester and Blackpool, and Leah, *née* Miller (d 1977); *b* 8 Sept 1931; *Educ* Colne GS, Univ of Sheffield (BA); *m* 18 Feb 1973, Maureen, da of Maurice Julius Lipman (d 1999), of Hull; 1 s (Adam b 3 Oct 1976), 1 da (Amy b 7 June 1974); *Career* dramatist; 30 original TV films and over 300 TV dramas and comedies; winner BAFTA and Int Best Play awards for: The Evacuees, Bar Mitzvah Boy, Spend Spend Spend; winner Int awards for: Ready When You Are Mr McGill, Day To Remember; Nat and Int nominations for; The Knowledge, P'Tang Yang Kipperbang, London's Burning; feature films incl: Yentl (co-written with Barbra Streisand), The Chain; theatre work incl: Smash!, Dear Anyone; winner of The Br Acad Writer's award and The Royal TV Soc Writer's award; *Books* author five books of original TV screenplays; *Recreations* listing biographical data for publications such as this; *Clubs* Dramatists', The Academy; *Style*— Jack Rosenthal, Esq; c/o Margaret Ramsay Ltd, 14A Goodwin's Court, St Martin's Lane, London WC2N 4LL (☎ 071 240 0691)

ROSENTHAL, Thomas Gabriel (Tom); s of Dr Erwin Isak Jacob Rosenthal, and Elizabeth Charlotte, *née* Marx; *b* 16 July 1935; *Educ* Perse Sch Cambridge, Pembroke Coll Cambridge (MA); *m* Ann Judith Warnford-Davis; 2 s (Adam, Daniel); *Career* 2 Lt RA 1954-56, Lt Cambridgeshire Regt TA 1956-80; md: Thames and Hudson Int 1966 (joined Thames and Hudson 1959), Martin Secker and Warburg Ltd 1971 (chm 1980); chm William Heinemann 1980-84, chm and md various subsid cos 1980-84, chm and md Andre Deutsch Ltd (joined 1984); chm Soc of Young Publishers 1961-62; memb: Cambridge Univ Appts Bd 1967-71, exec ctee Nat Book League 1971-74, ctee of mgmnt and tstee Amateur Dramatic Club Cambridge, cncl RCA 1982-87, exec cncl ICA 1987-; *Books* A Reader's Guide to Modern European Art History (1962), A Reader's Guide to Modern American Fiction (1963), Monograph on Jack B Yeats (1964), Monograph on Ivon Hitchens (with Alan Bowness, 1973), Monograph on Arthur Boyd (with Ursula Hoff, 1986); introductions to: The Financier, The Titan, Jennie Gerhardt (Theodore Dreiser); articles in: The Times, The Guardian, TLS, London Magazine, Encounter, New Statesman, Spectator, Jnl of Br Assoc for American Studies, Studio International, Dictionary of National Biography, Nature, The Bookseller; *Recreations* bibliomania, opera, looking at pictures, reading other publishers' books, watching cricket; *Clubs* Garrick, MCC; *Style*— Tom Rosenthal, Esq; c/o Andre Deutsch Ltd, 105-106 Great Russell St, London WC1B 3LJ (☎ 071 580 2746, fax 071 631 3253, telex 261026 ADLIB G)

ROSEWELL, Michael John (Mike); s of Frederick Jack Rosewell (d 1974), of Walton-on-Thames, Surrey, and Anne Emma, *née* Helps (d 1984); *b* 22 Jan 1937; *Educ* Woking GS, LSE (BSc), Westminster Coll (PGCE); *m* 1961, Jill Drusilla, da of Stanley William Orriss; 1 s (Daniel James b 1966), 2 da (Anna-Marie b 1964, Michelle Jane b 1969); *Career* economics master and rowing coach: Ealing GS 1959-64, Gt Georges Coll Weybridge 1964-76, St Edwards Sch Oxford 1976-; rowing journalist and writer: Surrey Herald 1963-76, Surrey Comet 1967-76, Evening Mail 1968-77, Oxford Times 1976-; feature writer Rowing Magazine 1968-, features writer and tech ed Regatta 1987-, rowing corr The Times 1989-; memb Amateur Rowing Assoc Cncl 1968- (chm Publicity Ctee, chm Jr Rowing Ctee, asst ed Br Rowing Almanack, Eng Rowing Team mangr, memb Exec Ctee, GB Jr Team delegate, GB Jr Crew coach); chief coach: Christ Church 1978-, Oxford Womens Boat Race Crew 1979-87; memb: Sports Writers Assoc of GB 1990, Br Assoc of Rowing Journalists 1990; *Books* Beginners Guide to Rowing (1970); *Recreations* boating, angling, gardening; *Clubs* Walton Rowing, Leander; *Style*— Mike Rosewell, Esq; St Edwards School, Woodstock Rd, Oxford OX2 7NN (☎ 0865 59529)

ROSHIER, Christopher Edward; s of Edward Cecil Roshier (d 1974), of Exeter, and Muriel Gertrude, *née* Stratford (d 1978); *b* 30 March 1946; *Educ* Heles Sch Exeter, Fitzwilliam House Cambridge (MA); *m* 20 Sept 1969, Adrienne Mary, da of Harry James Langdon, of Richmond; 1 s (Giles b 1974), 2 da (Annabel b 1971, Holly b 1978); *Career* merchant banker; dir: Hill Samuel & Co Ltd 1977-87, Sharpe & Fisher plc (non-exec) 1986-, St Modwen Properties plc (non-exec) 1987-; md: Drexel Burnham Lambert 1987-90, European Capital Company Ltd (non-exec and Conslt); FCA; *Recreations* bridge, walking; *Style*— Christopher Roshier; 120 Strawberry Vale, Twickenham TW1 4SH (☎ 081 892 5376)

ROSIER, (Frederick) David Stewart; s of Air Chief Marshal Sir Frederick Rosier, GCB, CBE, DSO, *qv*, and Hettie Denise, *née* Blackwell; *b* 10 April 1951; *Educ* Winchester, Keble Coll Oxford (BA, MA), RMA Sandhurst; *m* 27 Sept 1975, Julia Elizabeth, da of David Leslie Gomme; 1 s (Charles Frederick James b 8 Dec 1990); *Career* cmmnd 1st The Queens Dragoon Gds 1973-78 served Germany NI, UK (Troop Ldr, Intelligence Offr, sqdn 2 i/c; resigned Capt 1978); exec dir S G Warburg & Co Ltd 1984 (joined 1978); dir: Warburg Investmt Mgmnt Ltd 1982, Mercury Asset Mgmnt Gp plc 1987, Bank SG Warburg Soditic AG 1990-; vice chm Mercury Asset Mgmnt plc 1989-; cncllr Wandsworth Borough Cncl 1982-86; Liveryman Worshipful Co of Coachmakers; *Recreations* squash, cricket, golf, skiing, shooting; *Clubs* Cavalry & Guards, Hurlingham, Fantasians; *Style*— David Rosier, Esq; 99 Thurleigh, London SW12 8TY (☎ 081 637 6077); 33 King William St London EC4R 9AS (☎ 071 280 2800, fax 071 280 2515, car 0831 134165)

ROSIER, Air Chief Marshal Sir Frederick Ernest; GCB (1972, KCB 1966, CB 1961), CBE (1955, OBE 1943), DSO 1942; s of Ernest George Rosier (d 1942), and Frances Elisabeth, *née* Morris (d 1934); *b* 13 Oct 1915; *Educ* Grove Park Sch Wrexham; *m* 30 Sept 1939, Hettie Denise, da of William Herbert Blackwell (d 1965); 3 s (David b 1951, Nicholas b 1953, John b 1961), 1 da (Elisabeth b 1943); *Career* cmmnd RAF 1935, 43 (F) Sqdn 1936-39, served UK, Western Desert and Europe 1939-45, OC Horsham St Faith 1947, exchange duties with USAF 1948-50, DSD Jt Servs Staff Coll 1950-52, Gp Capt Ops Central Fighter Estab 1952-54, Gp Capt Plans Fighter Cmd 1955-56, IDC 1957, dir Jt Plans Air Miny 1958, chm Jt Planning Staff 1959-61, AOC Air Forces Middle East 1961-63, SASO Tport Cmd 1964-66, AOC in C Fighter Cmd 1966-68, perm mil dep CENTO 1968-70, dep C in C AFCENT 1970-73, ADC to HM The Queen 1956-58, Air ADC to HM The Queen 1972-73; mil advsr and dir BAC 1973-77, dir i/c BAC Saudi Arabia 1977-80; vice pres 8 Army Veterans 1977-, chm of appeals Polish Air Force Benevolent Fund 1975-; Liveryman Worshipful Co of Coachmakers and Harnessmakers 1976, Freeman City of London 1976; Order of Orange Nassau Netherlands 1946, Order of Polonia Restituta Poland 1987; *Clubs* RAF; *Style*— Air Chief Marshal Sir Frederick Rosier, GCB, CBE, DSO; 286 Latymer Court, London W6 7LD (☎ 081 741 0765); Ty Haul, Llangollen, Clwyd (☎ 0978 861 068)

ROSKILL, Sir Ashton Wentworth; QC (1949); el s of John Roskill, KC (d 1940), and bro of Baron Roskill, *qv*, and Sybil Mary Wentworth Dilke; mother's f Ashton Dilke, MP, bro of Rt. Hon Sir Charles Dilke Bt, MP; *b* 1 Jan 1902; *Educ* Winchester Coll, Exeter Coll Oxford (MA); *m* 1, 1932, Violet Willoughby (d 1964), da of Lt-Col Charles W Waddington CIE, MVO (d 1946), 1 s (John), 1 da (Susannah, m Mr Justice Hobhouse, *qv*); m 2, 1965, Phyllis (d 1990), yr da of Sydney Burney, CBE; *Career* Cert of Hon Cncl of Legal Educ 1925; attached WO (Mil Intelligence) 1940-45; KC then QC 1949; barr Inner Temple 1925, bencher 1958, treas 1980; chm MMC 1965-75; hon bencher Middle Temple 1980; kt 1967; *Clubs* Reform; *Style*— Sir Ashton Roskill, QC; Heath Cottage, Newtown, Newbury, Berks, RG15 9DA (☎ 0635 40328)

ROSKILL, Baron (Life Peer UK 1980), of Newtown in Co of Hampshire; Eustace Wentworth Roskill; PC (1971), JP (1950), DL (Hants 1972); yst s of John Roskill, KC, and Sybil Mary Wentworth, *née* Dilke (niece of Sir Charles Dilke, 2 Bt); bro of Sir Ashton Roskill, QC, *qv*; *b* 6 Feb 1911; *Educ* Winchester, Exeter Coll Oxford (MA); *m* 1947, Elisabeth Wallace, 3 da of late Thomas Frame Jackson; 1 s (Hon Julian Wentworth b 1950), 2 da (Hon Jane Elisabeth Sybil (Hon Mrs Roberts) b 1948, Hon Katharine Lucy (Hon Mrs Williams) b 1953); *Career* called to the Bar Middle Temple 1933, bencher 1961, reader 1978, dep treas 1979, treas 1980; hon bencher Inner Temple 1980; with ministries of shipping and war tport 1939-45; QC 1953, chm Hants QS 1960-71 (dep chm 1951-60), cmmr of Assize Birmingham 1961, judge of High Court Queen's Bench Divn 1962-71, Lord Justice of Appeal 1971-80, a Lord of Appeal in Ordinary 1980-86; vice chm Parole Bd 1967-69, chm Cmmn on Third London Airport 1968-70, pres Senate of Four Inns of Court 1972-74 (hon memb 1974); life memb Canadian Bar Assoc 1974; chm: London Int Arbitration Tst 1981-, Fraud Trials Ctee 1983-85, Appeal Ctee of Panel on Take-overs and Mergers 1987-; hon fell Exeter Coll Oxford 1963; fell Winchester Coll 1981-86; kt 1962; *Style*— The Rt Hon the Lord Roskill, PC, JP, DL; New Court, Temple, EC4 Y9BE (☎ 071 353 8870); Heatherfield, Newtown, Newbury, Berks RG15 9DB (☎ 0635 40606)

ROSKILL, (Ann) Julia Scott; JP (Inner London 1978); da of Harold Edward Cooke (d 1968), and Dorothy Margaret, *née* Key (d 1987); *b* 24 Oct 1933; *Educ* Christ's Hosp HS Lincoln, Girton Coll Cambridge (MA); *m* 10 April 1965, Nicholas Wentworth Roskill, er s of Capt Stephen Wentworth Roskill, CBE, DSC, RN; 1 s (Edward Stephen Wentworth b 1968), 1 da (Sybil Margaret Julia b 1971); *Career* Queen's Coll Harley St London W1: tutor in history 1964-67, co-librarian 1974-86; memb Cncl Fairbridge-Drake Soc (formerly Fairbridge Soc) 1969- (chm: Future Policy Ctee 1983-86 and Housing Ctee 1986-), memb at large Nat Cncl for Eng and Wales ESU 1983-90, memb Educn Advsy Cncl Queen's Coll 1987-; *Recreations* music, gardening; *Clubs* ESU; *Style*— Mrs Julia Roskill, JP

ROSKILL, Hon Julian Wentworth; s of Baron Roskill, PC, QC, JP, DL (Life Peer), and Elisabeth Wallace, *née* Jackson; *b* 22 July 1950; *Educ* Horris Hill, Winchester Coll; *m* 1975, Catherine Elizabeth, 2 da of Maj William Francis Garnett, of Quernmore Park, Lancaster; 2 s (Matthew b 1979, Oliver b 1981); *Career* slr 1974, ptnr Rowe & Maw 1988; *Recreations* photography, music, theatre, squash, swimming; *Style*— The Hon Julian W Roskill; 8 Leigh Road, London N5 1SS (☎ 071 359 0628)

ROSLING, Derek Norman; CBE (1988); s of Norman Rosling (d 1984), and Jean, *née* Allen (d 1957); *b* 21 Nov 1930; *Educ* Shrewsbury; *m* (m dis); 2 s (Alan b 1962, John b 1964), 1 da (Jean b 1961); *Career* vice chm Hanson plc 1973-; FCA; *Recreations* sailing, golf, theatre; *Clubs* Royal Channel Island Yacht, Royal Guernsey Golf, Royal Southampton Yacht, Palm Valley Country; *Style*— Derek N Rosling, Esq, CBE; 388 Via Las Palmas, Palm Springs, California 92262, USA

ROSOMAN, Leonard Henry; OBE (1981); s of Henry Edward Rosoman (d 1979), of Cambridge Drive, Lee, London, and Lillian Blanch, *née* Spencer (d 1954); *b* 27 Oct 1913; *Educ* Deacons Sch Peterborough, Univ of Durham, Royal Acad Schs, Central Sch of Arts & Crafts; *m* 21 June 1963 (m dis 1969), Jocelyn, da of late Bertie Rickards, of Melbourne, Aust; *Career* Aux Fire Serv 1939-43, Home Office 1943-45, official War artist Admty 1945-46; artist; lectr: Reimann Sch London 1937-39, Camberwell Sch of Art 1946-47, Edinburgh Coll of Art 1948-56, Chelsea Sch of Art 1956-57; tutor RCA 1957-78; exhibitions in London incl: St Georges Gallery 1949, Roland Browse & Delbanco Gallery 1954, 1957, 1959, 1965, 1969, The Fine Art Soc 1974, 1978, 1983, Oldham Art Gallery 1977; exhibitions in USA incl: Lincoln Centre NY 1968, State Univ of NY at Albany 1971, Touchstone Gallery NY 1975; major murals incl: Festival of Britain 1951, Diaghilev Exhibition 1954, Brussels World Fair 1958, Shakespeare Exhibition 1964, Royal Acad of Arts 1986, vaulted ceiling Lambeth Palace Chapel 1988; Winston Churchill fell 1966; FRSA 1968, memb RA 1969, Hon ARCA 1978, Hon RSWS 1979, Hon RWA 1984; *Books* Painters on Painting, Bruegel's Mad Meg (1969); *Recreations* travelling and painting as much as possible; *Clubs* Arts, Chelsea Arts; *Style*— Leonard Rosoman, Esq, OBE; 7 Pembroke Studios, Pembroke Gardens, London W8 6HX (☎ 071 603 3638)

ROSPIGLIOSI, Hon Francesco; Prince Francesco Rospigliosi; 2 s of 11 Earl of Newburgh; *b* 1947; *m* 1974, Countess Clothilde, da of Count Henri Rival de Rouville ;

1 s (Prince Alessandro b 1978); *Style*— Prince Francesco Rospigliosi; via Modestino 3, 20 144, Milano, Italy

ROSPIGLIOSI, Princess Helen; Hon Helen Mary Grace; *née* Lyon-Dalberg-Acton; da of 2 Baron Acton, KCVO (d 1924); *b* 21 May 1910; *m* 1933 (m dis 1958) Prince Guglielmo Rospigliosi (s of Prince Ludovico Rospigliosi, 4 s of Princess Elena Giustiniani-Bandini, da of Sigismund Prince Giustiniani-Bandini who was also 8 Earl of Newburgh, by her husb Camillo Prince Rospigliosi); 2 s, 1 da; *Style*— Princess Helen Rospigliosi; 602 Park West, London W2

ROSPIGLIOSI, Princess Margherita Maria Francesca; da of late Prince Giambattista Pia Sigismondo Francesco Rospigliosi (s of Lady Elena Maria Concetta Isabella Gioacchina Giuseppa Giustiniani-Bandini *Princess Camillo Rospigliosi* 3 da of late 8 Earl of Newburgh) and sis of 11 Earl of Newburgh; *b* 1909; *Style*— Princess Margherita Rospigliosi

ROSS, Alan; CBE (1982); s of John Brackenridge Ross, CBE (d 1958), and Clare Margaret Fitzpatrick (d 1979); *b* 6 May 1922; *Educ* Haileybury, St John's Coll Oxford; *m* 1949 (m dis 1985), Jennifer, da of Sir Geoffrey Fry, KCB, CVO (d 1959), of Wiltshire; 1 s (Jonathan Timothy de Beaurepaire b 1953; *Career* RN 1942-47; asst staff offr Intelligence 16 Destroyer Flotilla 1944, on staff of Flag Offr W Germay 1945, interpreter Br Naval C in C Germay 1946; Br Cncl 1947-50; staff memb The Observer 1952-72, ed London Magazine 1961-, md London Magazine Edns 1961-; Atlantic Award for Literature 1946; FRSL; *Books* Open Sea (1975), Death Valley (1980), Colours of War (1983), Ranji (1983), Blindfold Games (1986), The Emissary (1986), Coastwise Lights (1988); *Recreations* the turf; *Clubs* Vincents (Oxford), MCC; *Style*— Alan Ross, Esq, CBE; 30 Thurloe Place, London SW7

ROSS, Alastair Robertson; s of Alexander James Ross (d 1985), and Margaret Elizabeth McInnes, *née* Robertson (d 1983); *b* 8 Aug 1941; *Educ* McLaren HS Callander Perthshire, Duncan of Jordanstone Coll of Art Dundee (Dip Art); *m* 12 April 1975, Kathryn Margaret Greig, da of late John Ferrier Greig Wilson, of Birmingham; 1 da (Alexandra b 1981); *Career* artist; lectr Duncan of Jordanstone Coll of Art 1969- (pt/t 1966-69), hon lectr Univ of Dundee 1969-; recent works incl: bronze for Blackness devpt project Dundee, portrait in bronze of Sir Iain Moncreiffe of that Ilk at HM New Register House Edinburgh 1988 (awarded Sir Otto Beit Medal of Royal Soc Br Sculptors 1988), cmmn for new Rank Xerox HQ Marlow Bucks 1988-89; awarded: Dickson Prize for Sculpture 1962, Holo-Krome (Dundee) Sculpture Prize and Cmmn 1962, Scottish Educn Dept Travelling Scholarship 1963, Royal Scottish Acad Chalmers Bursary 1964, Royal Scottish Acad Carnegie Travelling Scholarship 1965, Duncan of Drumfork Scholarship 1965, award winner in sculpture Paris Salon Exhibition 1967, awarded medailles de bronze 1968 and d'argent 1970 Societe des Artistes Francais (elected membre associé 1970), Sir William Gillies Bequest Fund Award RSA 1989; memb Exec Ctee Fife Branch St John Assoc 1979-; memb Soc Portrait Sculptors 1966; SBStJ 1979, OStJ 1984; Freeman City of London 1989; FRSA 1966, ARBS 1968 (vice pres 1988-90, Scottish rep on cncl 1972-), professional memb SSA 1969 (cncl memb 1972-75), FSA Scot 1971, FRBS 1975, ARSA 1980, MBIM 1989; *Recreations* heraldry, genealogy, Scottish history; *Clubs* St Johns House, Royal Perth; *Style*— Alastair Ross, Esq; Ravenscourt, 28 Albany Terrace, Dundee DD3 6HS (☎ 0382 24 235)

ROSS, Sir Alexander; s of William Alexander Ross (d 1947), and Kathleen Ross (d 1974); *b* 2 Sept 1907; *Educ* Mt Albert GS NZ, Auckland Univ (Dip Banking); *m* 1, 1933, Nora Bethia Burgess (d 1974); 2 s, 2 da; m 2, 1975, Cynthia Alice, da of Arthur Francis Barton (d 1946); *Career* dep govr Res Bank of NZ 1948-55 (joined 1934), mangr NZ team to Empire Games Vancouver 1954, selector for NZ rowing team Empire and Olympic Games; chm Utd Dominions Trust Ltd 1963-74, memb Br Nat Export Cncl 1965-69, memb NRDC 1966-74, chm East Euro Trade Cncl 1967-69, vice pres Br Export Houses Assoc 1968-71, chm Br Cwlth Games Fedn 1968-82, life vice pres Cwlth Games Fedn, chm ANZ Banking Gp 1970-75, dep chm Eagle Star Insur Co (ret from Bd Eagle Star Insurance Co and Eagle Star Holdings 1983), dir Drayton East Investmt Tst 1975-82, dir Power Components 1976-82; dep chm Royal Overseas League (life vice pres), dir Whitbread Investmt Tst, tstee Aust Musical Fndn Queensland, pres St John Ambulance Bde; chm Queensland Community Fndn, patron Gold Coast Rolo Club; *Recreations* walking; *Style*— Sir Alexander Ross; 20 Compass Way, Tweed Heads West, NSW 2485, Australia

ROSS, Alexander (Sandy); s of Alexander Coutts Ross (d 1978), and Charlotte Edwards, *née* Robertson (d 1978); *b* 17 April 1948; *Educ* Grangemouth HS, Univ of Edinburgh (LLB); *m* Alison Joyce, *née* Fraser; 2 s (Andrew b 1 Sept 1983, Francis b 29 May 1986); *Career* slr (former apprentice slr) Edinburgh 1971-74, lectr Paisley Coll of Technol 1974-76, prodr Granada TV Manchester 1978-86, controller of arts and entertainment Scot TV 1986-; cncllr: Edinburgh Town Cncl 1971-75, Edinburgh Dist Cncl 1974-78; *Recreations* reading, golf, music, watching football; *Style*— Sandy Ross, Esq; 7 Murrayfield Ave, Edinburgh EA12 6AU (☎ 031 337 3679); Scottish Television, Cowcaddens, Glasgow (☎ 041 332 9999, fax 041 332 6892)

ROSS, Alexander Patrick Joseph (Paddy); s of Dr Alexander Edward Ross (d 1977), and Josephine Bridget, *née* O'Connor (d 1988); *b* 15 April 1935; *Educ* Ampleforth, Bart's (MB BS, MS); *m* 1, Nov 1962 (m dis 1978), Anne Sinclair, da of Dr David Briggs (d 1980); 2 da (Caroline Joanna b 1966, Charlotte Anne b 1970); m 2, 26 May 1978, Margaret Elizabeth Stevenson; *Career* Nat Serv, 2 Lt RA 1953-55; fell Lahey Clinic Boston 1972-, conslt surgn Royal Hampshire Hosp 1974-; numerous pubns on med and medicopolitical subjects; chm Jt Conslts Ctee, memb GMC; FRCS 1966; *Recreations* travel, gardening, golf; *Clubs* Army and Navy; *Style*— Paddy Ross, Esq; 25 Canon St, Winchester, Hampshire SO23 9JJ (☎ 0962 869757); Royal Hampshire County Hospital, Romsey Rd, Winchester (☎ 0962 863535)

ROSS, Alistair Charles; s of Alan Alistair Ross, OBE (d 1984), and Marjorie Evelyn, *née* Catch; *b* 29 Nov 1951; *Educ* Westminster, Charing Cross Hosp Med Sch (MB BS); *m* 19 Nov 1977, Alexandra Jane Elaine, da of Samuel Philippe Alexandre Holland; 1 s (James Alistair George MacKenzie b 1984), 2 da (Katherine Alexandra MacKenzie b 1980, Victoria Isobel MacKenzie b 1982); *Career* surgical registrar The London Hosp 1979-82, sr orthopaedic registrar St Marys Hosp London 1982-88, conslt orthopaedic surgn Royal Utd Hosp and Royal Nat Hosp for Rheumatic Diseases Bath 1988-, dir Bath and Wessex Orthopaedic Res Unit 1988-; Euro Travelling Scholar Br Orthopaedic Assoc 1987; Freeman City of London 1977, Liveryman Worshipful Soc of Apothecaries 1989; LRCP, MRCS 1976, FRCS 1980, FRSM 1982, fell Br Orthopaedic Assoc 1988; *Recreations* music; *Clubs* Leander (Henley-on-Thames); *Style*— Alistair Ross, Esq; The Bath Clinic, Claverton Down Rd, Bath, Avon BA2 7BR (☎ 0225 835555)

ROSS, Anthony Lee (Tony); s of Eric Turle Lee Ross (d 1982), and Effie, *née* Griffiths (d 1981); *b* 10 Aug 1938; *Educ* Helsby Co GS, Liverpool Regnl Coll of Art (NND); *m* 1, 16 Sept 1961 (m dis 1971), Carole Dawn, *née* D'Arcy; 1 da (Alexandra Ruth b 10 Aug 1971); m 2, 1971 (m dis 1976), Joan Lillian, *née* Allerton; m 3, 30 June 1979, Zoë, da of Cyril Albert Goodwin, of Cuffley, Hertfordshire; 1 da (Katherine Lee b 12 April 1980); *Career* drawings in magazines incl Punch, Time and Tide, Town 1962-75, sr lectr Manchester Poly 1965-86, first book published 1973; exhibitions: London, Holland, Germany, Japan, USA, France; awards: USA, Holland, Japan, Belgium, E Germany, W Germany; 26 TV films made with King Rollo Films 1983; illustrator for over 200 childrens books incl: Fantastique Maitre Renard by Roald Dahl (1981), The Reluctant Vampire by Eric Morecombe (1982), Limericks by Michael Palin (1985); patron Malcolm Sargent Cancer Fund for Children Readathon; *Books* author of 40 children's books incl: The Enchanted Pig (1982), Stone Soup (1987), I Want my Potty (1986); *Recreations* sailing; *Clubs* Chelsea Arts; *Style*— Tony Ross, Esq; Anderson Press, 20 Vauxhall Bridge Rd, London SW1V 2SA

ROSS, Sir Archibald David Manisty; KCMG (1961, CMG 1953); s of John Archibald Ross, ICS; *b* 12 Oct 1911; *Educ* Winchester, New Coll Oxford; *m* 1939, Mary Melville, da of Melville Macfadyen; 1 s (and 1 s decd), 1 da; *Career* HM Dip Serv 1936-71: Berlin, Stockholm, Tehran, min in Rome 1953-56, asst under sec of state for Foreign Affrs 1956-60; ambass: Portugal 1961-66, Sweden 1966-71; chm: Alfa-Laval 1972-1982, Saab (GB) 1972-82, Scania (GB) 1972-82, Datasaab (later Ericsson Information Systems) 1976-86; memb Cncl RASE 1980-85; *Clubs* Travellers', Leander, Lansdowne; *Style*— Sir Archibald Ross, KCMG; 17 Ennismore Gdns, London SW7

ROSS, Barry Alan; *b* 11 Oct 1934; *Educ* Cheltenham, Guy's Hosp Med Sch (MB BS, LRCP); *m* 1 April 1967, P Jane M Burridge; 3 da (Joanna b 5 July 1968, Nicola b 6 May 1970, Tessa b 28 March 1972); *Career* Lt-Col RAMC (V) OC Surgical Div 257 (S) Gen Hosp (U); thoracic house surgn Guy's Hosp 1960 (house offr 1958-59), jr lectr physiology Guy's Hosp Med Sch; registrar surgery: Ipswich Hosp 1963, Guy's Hosp 1964-67; sr registrar cardiothoracic surgery: Guy's Hosp 1967-71, St Thomas' Hosp 1971-72; conslt thoracic surgn E Anglian RHA 1973-; post graduate dean Soc Cardiothoracic Surgns, sec Intercollegiate Examinations Bd Cardiothoracic Surgery; numerous pubns on cardiothoracic surgery in various jls; memb: Soc Cardiothoracic Surgns, Br Thoracic Soc; MRCS, FRCS; *Recreations* golf, gardening, politics, music (Wagner); *Style*— Barry Ross, Esq; Norfolk & Norwich Hospital, Brunswick Rd, Norwich NR1 3SR (☎ 0603 628377)

ROSS, Carl Philip Hartley; s of John Carl Ross (fndr Ross Foods Ltd); *b* 3 May 1943; *Educ* Shrewsbury; *m* 1, 1968, Pamela Jean, *née* Dixon; 3 da (Rachel b 1969, Kathryn b 1971, Amanda b 1975); m 2, 1985 Joanna Louise, *née* Norton; 2 s (Thomas b 1989, Samuel b 1991); *Career* CA; Peat Marwick Mitchell & Co, Forrester Boyd & Co; dir Cosalt Ltd 1971-75, md Orbit Holdings Ltd 1972-75, chm Bristol & West Cold Stores Ltd 1974-83, Philip Ross & Co CAs 1982-; FCA; *Recreations* foxhunting, golf; *Style*— Philip Ross, Esq; 42 Crabtree Lane, Sutton-on-Sea, Lincolnshire LN12 2RT (☎ 0507 441811, fax 0507 443033)

ROSS, Lt-Col (Charles) Christopher Gordon; s of Maj Charles Gordon Ross, MC (d 1964), of Moor Park, Herts, and Iris Jefford, *née* Fowler (d 1976); *b* 8 July 1931; *Educ* Marlborough, RMA Sandhurst; *m* 27 April 1963, Fiona Mary Ghislaine, da of Gp-Capt Albert Peter Vincent Daly, AFC (d 1985), of Garryannagh, Urra, Nenagh, Co Tipperary, Ireland; 1 s (Alastair Charles Gordon b 24 Jan 1964), 1 da (Geraldine Catherine Ghislaine b 7 April 1965); *Career* cmmnd 14/20 King's Hussars 1951, Troop Ldr ADC, Capt 1956, Adj Sqdn 2 i/c, Maj 1963, Sqdn Ldr, Staff Offr, Regt 2 i/c, Lt-Col GSO 1 UKLF 1974, GSO 1 DRAC 1976, resigned 1979; diocesan sec Salisbury Diocese 1979-; vice pres 14/20 Regt Assoc 1991- (vice chm 1982-85, chm 1986-91); churchwarden, tres Royal Br Legion Branch; FBIM 1981; *Recreations* shooting, gardening, reading; *Clubs* Army and Navy, St Moritz Tobogganing; *Style*— Lt-Col Christopher Ross; Wishford House, nr Salisbury, Wiltshire SP2 0PQ (☎ 0722 790486); Church House, Crane St, Salisbury SP1 2QB (☎ 0722 411922, fax 0722 411990)

ROSS, David Thomas Mcleod; s of David Ross, and Margert, *née* Mcleod; *b* 3 June 1949; *Educ* Boroughmuir Secdy Sch Edinburgh; *m* 25 Aug 1973, Margaret Gordon Sharpe Ross, da of Robert Charters Russell, of Loanhead; 3 da (Lindsay b 1976, Louise b 1978, Heather b 1984); *Career* CA 1976; md Ivory and Sime plc 1988-90 (dir 1982, joined 1968), ptnr Aberforth Ptnrs 1990-, non-exec dir Aberforth Smaller Companies Tst plc; memb Co of Merchants of the City of Edinburgh; FCCA; *Recreations* shooting; *Style*— David Ross, Esq; The Avenue, 40 Greenhill Gardens, Edinburgh, EH10 4BJ (☎ 031 447 4970); Aberforth Partners, 16 Chester Street, Edinburgh EH3 7RA (☎ 031 220 0733, fax 031 220 0735)

ROSS, Donald Campbell Mackay; s of Donald Campbell Ross, of Cromarty, Ross & Cromary (provost of Ross and Cromarty 1966-72 as was gf 1947-48), and Elizabeth, *née* Macleod; *b* 19 Aug 1941; *Educ* Fortrose Acad Ross & Cromarty, Heriot Watt Univ Edinburgh (B Arch); *m* 1 Jan 1968, Hilary, da of Frederick William Boulton, of Wigan, Lancashire (d 1959); 2 da (Zoe Karen b 1970, Sasha Victoria b 1976); *Career* architect, princ of Campbell Ross, chartered architect Inverness, 1971-; *Recreations* windsurfing, sailing, painting; *Clubs* Rotary of Inverness, The Highland; *Style*— Donald Ross, Esq; 20 Church St, Inverness IV1 1EB (☎ 0463 236903)

ROSS, The Rt Hon Lord; Donald MacArthur Ross; PC (1985); s of John Ross, slr; *b* 29 March 1927; *Educ* Dundee HS, Univ of Edinburgh; *m* 1958, Dorothy, *née* Annand; 2 da; *Career* dean Faculty of Advocates 1973-76, senator Coll of Justice Scotland (Lord of Session) 1977-85, Lord Justice Clerk of Scotland 1985-; QC Scotland 1964, Sheriff Princ Ayr & Bute 1972-73; dep chm Scottish Boundary Cmmn 1977-85, chm of Court Heriot-Watt Univ 1984-90; Lord High Cmmr to Gen Assembly of the Church of Scotland 1990 and 1991; Hon LLD Edinburgh 1987, Hon DUniv Heriot-Watt 1988; FRSE; *Recreations* gardening, walking; *Clubs* New; *Style*— The Rt Hon the Lord Ross, FRSE; 33 Lauder Rd, Edinburgh (☎ 031 667 5731)

ROSS, Donald Nixon; s of Donald Ross (d 1942), of Kimberley, SA, and late Jessie Ross; *b* 4 Oct 1922; *Educ* Kimberley HS SA, Univ of Capetown (BSc, MB ChB), RCS London; *m* 5 Feb 1953, Dorothy Maud, da of late James Curtis, of Chepstow; 1 da (Janet Susan b 1958); *Career* res fell Guy's Hosp 1953-58; conslt surgn: Guy's Hosp 1958-63, Nat Heart Hosp 1963-68, Middx Hosp 1968-70; sr surgn Inst of Cardiology 1970-; Freeman Worshipful Soc Apothecaries London 1968; hon: FACS 1976, FACC 1973, FRCS (Thailand) 1987, FRCS Ireland 1984, DSC CNAA 1982; FRSM, FRCS 1949, MInstD; memb Order Cedars of Lebanon 1975, Offrs Cross Order Merit FRG 1981; *Publications* Hypothermia (1960), Surgeons Guide To Card Diagnosis (1962), Surgical Cardiology (1969), Biological Tissue In Heart Valve Replacement (1972), Surgery And Your Heart (1982), contrib numerous scientific jls and books; *Recreations* horse riding, breeding Arabian horses; *Clubs* Kimberley (SA), Garrick; *Style*— Donald Ross, Esq; 69 Gloucester Crescent, London NW1 (☎ 071 482 0322); Rumbolds, Flanders Green, Cottered, Herts (☎ 076 381 474); 25 Upper Wimpole St, London WIM 7TA (☎ 071 935 8805, fax 071 935 9190, telex 2179249 mono Ref 916)

ROSS, Duncan Alexander; s of William Duncan Ross (d 1982), and Mary, *née* Maciver (d 1985); *b* 25 Sept 1928; *Educ* Dingwall Acad, Univ of Glasgow (BSc); *m* 17 May 1958, Mamie Buchanan Clark, da of Harold Parsons (d 1978); 1 s (Alastair b 1962), 1 da (Deborah b 1959); *Career* various engrg posts S Scotland Electricity Bd 1952-57, engrg commercial and mgmnt posts Midlands Electricity Bd 1957-77, (dep chm South Wales Electricity Bd 1977-81 (chm 1981-84), chm Southern Electricity Bd 1984-90, chm Southern Electric plc 1990-; FIEE, CBIM; *Recreations* golf, skiing, bridge; *Style*— Duncan Ross, Esq; Holly House, Canon Hill Way, Bray, Berkshire SL6 2EX (☎ 0628 782753); Southern Electricity plc, Littlewick Green, Maidenhead, Berks SL6 3QB (☎ 0682 82 2166)

ROSS, Ernest (Ernie); MP (Lab) Dundee West 1979-; *b* 1942; *Educ* St Johns Jr Secdy

Sch; *m* ; 2 s, 1 da; *Career* quality control engr Timex Ltd; joined Lab Pty 1973, chair of PLP Foreign Affrs Ctee; memb: MSF, Employment Select Ctee; *Style—* Ernie Ross, Esq, MP; House of Commons, London SW1

ROSS, Prof Euan Macdonald; s of Dr James Stirling Ross, of Redbourn, Herts, and Frances, *née* Blaze; *b* 13 Dec 1937; *Educ* Aldenham, Univ of Bristol (MD, DCH); *m* 11 June 1966, Jean Mary, da of George Palmer (d 1984); 2 s (Matthew b 1967, James b 1972); *Career* house physician Bristol Royal Infirmary 1962-63, sr house offr Aberdeen and Dundee Teaching Hosps 1963-64, registrar in paediatrics Dundee Teaching Hosps 1964-69, lectr in paediatrics Univ of Bristol 1969-74, sr lectr Middx and St Mary's Med Schs Univ of London 1974-84, conslt paediatrician Central Middx Hosp London 1974-84 and Charing Cross Hosp London 1984-89, prof of community paediatrics King's Coll Univ of London 1989; memb: delegacy King's Coll, Br Paediatric Surveillance Unit; chm Nat Child Health Computing Ctee NHS, chm elect Scientific Ctee; FRCP 1980; *Books* Paediatric Perspectives on Epilepsy (1985), Epilepsy in Young People (1987); *Recreations* Scottish matters, design, art and photography; *Clubs* Athenaeum; *Style—* Prof Euan Ross; Linklater House, Mount Park Rd, Harrow Hill HA1 3JZ (☎ 081 864 4746); Department of Community Paediatrics, King's College at St Giles Hospital, London SE5 7RN (☎ 071 708 0963, fax 071 701 9625)

ROSS, Harry Edward Thomas; TD (1945); s of Harry Ross (d 1958), and Rhoda, *née* Smith (d 1941), of Beckenham, Kent; *b* 3 June 1903; *Educ* St Dunstans Coll; *m* 16 Sept 1937, Vera Elizabeth, da of James Robert Davis, of Lahloo Hayes, Kent; 2 s (Robert b 1941, Timothy b 1948), 1 da (Elizabeth b 1953); *Career* ret md Port Line (Cunard); former dir: Montreal Australian New Zealand Line, London Steam-Ship Owners Mutual Insurance Association Ltd, Port of London Authy, Cunard House Ltd; shipowners rep on Pilotage Ctee of Trinity House, chm London Gen Shipowners Soc 1964-65; memb: London Shipowners Dock Labour Ctee, Lloyds Register of Shipping Gen Ctee, Chamber of Shipping; *Recreations* gardening, philately, rugby football; *Style—* Harry Ross, Esq, TD; 12 Kirk Court, Sevenoaks TN13 3JW (☎ 0732 454 724)

ROSS, Harvey Burton; RD; s of Sir James Paterson Ross, 1 Bt, KCVO, *qv* (d 1980), and Marjorie Burton, *née* Townsend (d 1978); *b* 1 Oct 1928; *Educ* St Pauls, Univ of London, Bart's Med Coll (MB BS, ChM); *m* 1, (m dis), Nancy Joan; 2 s (Edward Paterson b 13 Nov 1963, James Hilliam b 12 Feb 1972), 1 da (Imogen Mary b 17 June 1970); m 2, 8 July 1988, Susan Christine, da of Peter Maret Blandy, MBE, of Barn Cottage, Exlade St, Woodcote, Berks; *Career* Nat Serv Surgn Lt RNVR 1953-55 (pt/t Surgn Lt Cdr RNR); conslt surgn: Bart's 1968, Royal Berkshire Hosp Reading 1972; FRCS 1957, MS 1966; *Style—* Harvey Ross, Esq, RD; Springvale, Brewery Common, Mortimer, Reading, Berks RG7 3JE (☎ 0734 332374); The Royal Berkshire Hospital, London Rd, Reading, Berks (☎ 0734 584711, fax 0734 503847); Cons Rooms, 13 Bath Rd, Reading, Berks

ROSS, Howard David; s of Bernard Ross, and Esther, *née* Weitz; *b* 12 Aug 1945; *Educ* Owens GS, LSE (LLB); *m* 12 March 1972, Jennifer Susan; 3 da (Philippa Adine b 30 Aug 1975, Gemma Miri b 30 March 1977, Emily Yael b 30 June 1981); *Career* admitted slr 1970; called to the Israel Bar 1973; Legal Dept Bank Leumi 1974; Tax Dept Slaughter and May 1976 (articled clerk 1968), ptnr Clifford Turner (now Clifford Chance) 1981- (Tax Dept 1978); memb: Law Soc, Petroleum Revenue Ctee 1986; *Books* Doing Business in the UK (contrib 1986), Structuring Buy Out and other Investment Funds (1989); *Recreations* jogging, cycling, theatre; *Clubs* Reform; *Style—* Howard D Ross; Clifford Chance, St Peters House, 130 Wood St, London EC2V 6QQ (☎ 071 600 0808, fax 071 956 0156)

ROSS, Ian Henry; s of Maj Cecil Henry Ross (d 1986), of Edinburgh, and Margaret Elliot, *née* Armour; *b* 13 Oct 1942; *Educ* Merchiston Castle Sch Edinburgh; *m* 12 May 1973, Patricia Mary (Trishia), da of Col Peter Tooley Willcocks, MBE, MC (d 1967); 2 s (Alastair b 1977, Neil b 1980), 1 da (Nicola b 1984); *Career* sr export dir White Horse Distillers Ltd 1976-82 (joined 1960, dir 1972-76), md MacDonald Greenlees Ltd 1982-86, memb Cncl Scotch Whisky Assoc 1983-, chm John Walker & Sons Ltd 1988- (md John Walker & Sons Ltd 1986-87), memb Cncl Royal Warrant Holders Assoc 1988-; *Recreations* sailing, fishing; *Clubs* New (Edinburgh), Royal Highland Yacht; *Style—* Ian Ross, Esq; Woodhill, Tilford, nr Farnham, Surrey GU10 2BW (☎ 025 18 2431); Landmark House, Hammersmith, London (☎ 081 748 5041)

ROSS, Ian Malcolm MacLean; s of Murdo MacDonald Ross (d 1975), of Flodigarry, Isle of Skye, and Isabel Campbell MacDonald, *née* McCord; *b* 21 Oct 1945; *Educ* Rothesay Acad Isle of Bute, Univ of Glasgow (BSc); *m* 26 Oct 1968, Margaret Eleanor, da of Roelofvinus Johannes van Bogerijen; 1 s (Murdo Roel b 31 March 1975), 1 da (Eleanor Isabel b 14 Nov 1972); *Career* res British Steel Corporation 1968-70, mill mangr Culter Guard Bridge Holdings 1970-75, gen mangr then vice pres Avery-Dennison 1975-86, chief exec and dir M Harland & Son Ltd 1986-; Freeman City of London, memb Worshipful Co of Marketors; FInstD 1988, FCIM 1989; *Recreations* music, sailing, theatre, rugby; *Clubs* RAC, RNCYC, Rockcliff RFC; *Style—* Ian Ross, Esq; M Harland & Son Ltd, Land of Green Ginger House, Anlaby, Hull HU10 6RN (☎ 0482 56116, fax 0482 53240, car 0831 148671)

ROSS, His Hon James; QC (1966); s of John Stuart Ross (d 1943), and Maude Mary, *née* Cox (d 1966); *b* 22 March 1913; *Educ* Glenalmond, Exeter Coll Oxford (BA); *m* 16 Sept 1939, Clare Margaret, da of Alderman Robert Cort-Cox, of Stratford-upon-Avon; 1 da (Heather); *Career* admitted slr 1938; asst prosecuting slr Birmingham 1941-45, called to the Bar Grays Inn 1945, legal memb Mental Health Review Tbnl (Birmingham) 1962; dep chm: Agric Land Tbnl (E Midlands) 1963, Lincs (Lindsay) Quarter Sessions 1967-71; rec Coventry 1968-71, judge Co Ct 1971, circuit judge 1972, memb Parole Bd 1974-77, hon rec of Coventry 1979-85, sr circuit judge and rec order Birmingham 1985-87; *Recreations* sailing, walking; *Style—* His Hon James Ross, QC; 45 Avenue Rd, Dorridge, Solihull, W Midlands; 2 Dr Johnsons Bldgs, Temple, London

ROSS, James McConville; s of Dr David Sloan Ross, of Elderslie, Renfrewshire, and Maureen, *née* McConville (d 1979); *b* 29 Sept 1960; *Educ* Glasgow HS, Univ of St Andrews (MA); *Career* business ed Reid Business Publishing 1984-85; sr electronics analyst: James Capel & Co 1987-90 (analyst 1986-87), Hoare Govett 1991-; *Recreations* skiing, windsurfing, reading, theatre; *Style—* James Ross, Esq; 47/8 Cleveland Square, London W2; Hoare Govett, 4 Broadgate, London EC2M 7LE (☎ 071 601 0101)

ROSS, John Eugene; *b* 7 June 1933; *Educ* St Joseph's Coll Beulah Hill London, London Sch of Printing and Graphic Arts; *m* 27 June 1964, Joanna Nicola, da of S A Cloudesley Seddon; 4 s (Christopher John b 16 June 1965, Mark Eugene (twin) b 16 June 1965, Philip Howard b 15 Nov 1966, Henry William b 14 July 1968); *Career* photographer; Zoltan Glass 1952-54, fndr mangr of photographic studio for Colman Prentis and Varley 1964-67, freelance photographer 1967-; memb: NUJ 1963, AFAEP 1971; chm Ealing Arts Cncl 1988-91; *Recreations* the arts - organisation and managment, singing - Scuola di Chiesa, other voluntary work embracing photography the arts and cultural relations; *Style—* John Ross, Esq; John Ross Photography, 62 Tottenham Court Road, London W1P 9RH (☎ 071 323 4831)

ROSS, John Gordon; JP (1966), DL (1986); s of Maj William Gordon Ross (d 1953), of Two Shires Yew, Chinnor Hill, Oxon, and Louisa, *née* Horn (d 1948); *b* 2 Feb 1921; *Educ* Bedford Sch, Imperial Coll of Sci and Technol (BSc, DIC); *m* 1, 20 Dec 1951, Cynthia Abel (d 1987), da of Reginald Macauley Abel Smith, MC, JP, DL, sometime High Sheriff of Hertfordshire; 1 s (Christopher Lumsden Gordon b 22 Oct 1952, d 1974), 2 da (Jennifer Louisa b 2 Feb 1954, Mary Elizabeth b 17 Sept 1958); m 2, 23 Jan 1989, Veronica June, da of Sqdn Ldr Bernard Dudley Fletcher Austen; *Career* sci offr Royal Aircraft Estab Farnborough 1941-48; lectr and examiner UCL 1948-52, asst dir RA Lister & Co Ltd Dursley Glos 1959-64, conslt engr and poultry farmer 1963-77, asst gen mangr overseas ops RA Lister & Co Ltd 1977-84; diocesan lay reader 1964-; former memb: Bishop of Gloucester's Cncl, Horsley PCC (churchwarden); Glos lay rep on the Gen Synod of the C of E 1970-76, added memb Glos CC Educn Ctee, chm Forest Dean Devpt Assoc; govr: Dursley Tech Coll, Forest of Dean Tech Coll; mangr Horsley Aided Primary Sch, chm Horsley Sch Tstees, fndr chm Yercombe Tst; Dursley Bench 1966 (former dep chm, chm of the Juvenile & Domestic Benches 1977-85); chm Glos Magistrates' Cts Ctee 1985-89; Glos rep: Central Cncl of Probation & After-Care Ctees 1973-76, Central Cncl of Magistrates Cts Ctee 1986-90; memb Glos Police Ctee 1972-77, gen cmmr of Income Tax Berkley Upper Div 1967-, chm Whitstone Div of the Gen Cmmn of Income Tax 1989-; CEng, MAReS 1946, FIMechE 1963; *Recreations* music, photography, gardening; *Clubs* Naval & Army; *Style—* J G Ross, Esq, JP, DL; Marsh Mill House, Shadwell, Uley, Dursley, Glos GL11 5BW (☎ 0453 860 0044)

ROSS, John Malcolm Thomas; s of John Carl Ross; *b* 7 Oct 1934; *Educ* Shrewsbury, Clare Coll Cambridge; *m* 1, 1958, Gillian Mary Hampton; 1 s, 1 da; m 2, 1964, Linda Susan Thomas; 1 s, 2 da; m 3, 1981, Jennifer Mary Fawcett, née Clark; *Career* chartered accountant Peat Marwick Mitchell & Co, dir Ross Gp Ltd 1964-68; Cosalt Ltd: md 1968-73, chm and chief exec 1973-85, dep chief and chief exec 1985-86, FCA; *Recreations* golf, gardening; *Style—* John M T Ross, Esq; Five Gables, 27 Ferriby Lane, Grimsby, South Humberside DN33 3NS

ROSS, Sir (James) Keith; 2 Bt (UK 1960), of Whetstone, Middx; RD (1967); s of Sir James Paterson Ross, 1 Bt, KCVO, FRCS (d 1980; Surgn to HM 1952-64), and Marjorie Burton, *née* Townsend (d 1978); *b* 9 May 1927; *Educ* St Paul's, Middx Hosp Med Sch London (MB BS, MS); *m* 24 Nov 1956, Jacqueline Annella, da of Francis William Clarke (d 1971); 1 s, 3 da (Susan Wendy b 28 Feb 1958, Janet Mary b 20 Nov 1960, Anne Townsend b 10 Sept 1962); *Heir* s, Andrew Charles Paterson Ross b 18 June 1966; *Career* Surgn Lt RNVR 1952-54, Surgn Lt Cdr RNR 1954-72; conslt cardio thoracic surg Harefield Hosp 1964-67; conslt cardiac surgn: Nat Heart Hosp London 1967-72, Wessex regn Southampton 1972-90, King Edward VII Hosp Midhurst 1979-90; pres Soc of Cardiothoracic Surgns 1987-88; memb Cncl RCS 1986-; FRCS 1956, FRCSEd 1989, FRSM; *Recreations* fly-fishing, sailing, painting, shooting; *Clubs* MCC, Army and Navy, Royal Lymington Yacht; *Style—* Sir Keith Ross, Bt, RD; Moonhills Gate, Hilltop, Beaulieu, Hants SO42 7YS (☎ 0590 612104)

ROSS, Lt-Col (Walter Hugh) Malcolm; OBE (1988); s of Col Walter John Macdonald Ross, CB, OBE, MC, TD, JP, DL (d 1982), of Netherhall, Bridge-of-Dee, Castle-Douglas, Kirkcudbrightshire, and Josephine May, *née* Cross (d 1982); *b* 27 Oct 1943; *Educ* Eton, RMA Sandhurst; *m* 31 Jan 1969, Susan (Susie) Jane, da of Gen Sir Michael Gow, GCB; 1 s (Hector b 1983), 2 da (Tabitha b 1970, Flora b 1974); *Career* Scots Gds 1964-87; asst comptroller Lord Chamberlain's Office 1987-90, comptroller 1991-, mgmnt auditor The Royal Household 1987-89, Extra Equerry to HM The Queen 1988-, sec Central Chancery of The Orders of Knighthood 1989-90; memb Queen's Body Gd for Scotland (Royal Co of Archers) 1981-; *Clubs* Pratt's, New (Edinburgh); *Style—* Lt-Col Malcolm Ross, OBE

ROSS, Hon Mrs Charles; Mary Margaret; da of late Thomas Graham and late Margaret Graham, of Swan Park, Monaghan, Republic of Ireland; *m* 1953, as his 2 w, Hon Charles Dudley Anthony Ross (d 1976), yr s of Una Mary, Baroness de Ros; 1 s; *Style—* The Hon Mrs Charles Ross; 67 Seafield Rd, Southbourne, Bournemouth, Dorset (☎ 0202 428149)

ROSS, (Alexander) Michael Murray; s of Donald Ross (d 1982), and Margaret Grant Murray, of Newbury, Berks; *b* 10 Oct 1938; *Educ* Charterhouse; *m* 1962, Jessamine Barbara, da of Jack Desmond Willson; 2 da (Corina Katherine b 1965, Stephanie Tanya b 1966); *Career* Clark Battams CAs London 1957-63, Alexander Grant & Co LA Calif 1963-65, Finnie & Co 1965- (London 1965-85, Newbury 1985-); appointed by Miny of Agriculture to Exec Ctee of Land Settlement Assoc 1970-78; chm: Educn Ctee of London Soc of CAs 1983-85, Newbury Gp of CAs 1989-; memb Insolvency Practitioners Assoc, FCA; *Recreations* bridge, tennis, golf; *Clubs* Caledonian; *Style—* Michael Ross, Esq; Garvards Cottage, Woolton Hill, Newbury, Berks RG15 9TY (☎ 0635 253 056); Finnie & Co, 12/20 Oxford St, Newbury, Berks RG13 15B (☎ 0635 49699)

ROSS, Michael Stephen; s of Sims Ross (d 1972), and Rose Ross; *b* 17 Aug 1938; *Educ* Leeds GS; *m* 29 July 1969 (m dis); 2 s (Jeremy b 5 Jan 1974, Daniel b 16 June 1976), 1 da (Simone b 20 Oct 1972); *Career* dir S Ross & Co Ltd (later Lowland Drapery Holdings Ltd) 1960, chm LDH Group plc 1981, dir Porter Chadburn plc (acquired LDH Group plc) 1988-; *Recreations* tennis, cricket; *Style—* Michael Ross, Esq; Porter Chadburn plc, Battlehouse, 1 East Barnet Rd, New Barnet, Barnet, Herts EN4 8RR; LDH Group plc, Hales Rd, Lower Wortley Rd, Leeds, W Yorks LS12 4PL (☎ 0532 793531, fax 0532 310390)

ROSS, Nicholas David (Nick); s of John Caryl Ross, of Surrey, and Joy Dorothy, *née* Richmond; paternal gf Pinhas Rosen was signatory to Israel's Declaration of Independence and first Min of Justice; *b* 7 Aug 1947; *Educ* Wallington Co GS Surrey, Queen's Univ Belfast (BA); *m* 1 March 1985, Sarah Patricia Ann, da of Dr Max Caplin OBE, of London; 3 s (Adam Michael b 1985, Samuel Max b 1987, Jack Felix b 1988); *Career* BBC freelance reporter and presenter N Ireland 1971-72; presenter radio: Newsdesk, The World Tonight 1972-74, World at One 1972-75 and 1984, Call Nick Ross 1987-; presenter TV: Man Alive, Out of Court, Fair Comment 1975-83; prodr and dir documentaries The Fix and The Biggest Epidemic of Our Times 1981; fndr presenter BBC Breakfast TV, Sixty Minutes 1983-84, Watchdog, Star Memories, Drugwatch 1985-86, Crimewatch UK 1984-, A Week in Politics (Channel 4) 1986-88, Death on the Rock: the Inquiry (ITV) 1989; occasional BBC radio presenter incl: World at One, You the Jury, Any Questions, narrator and reporter for radio and TV documentaries, presenter company videos, chm corporate conf; *Recreations* scuba diving, skiing; *Style—* Nick Ross, Esq; c/o Jon Roseman Associates, 103 Charing Cross Rd, London WC2H 0DT (☎ 071 439 8245)

ROSS, Peter Angus; s of Maj John Milner Ross (d 1979), and Evangeline Joyce, *née* Robertson (d 1982); *b* 25 Feb 1936; *Educ* Glasgow Acad; *m* 16 Aug 1962, Elliot Wallace, da of James Allan Baillie Montgomery (d 1982), of Glasgow; *Career* Nat Serv RA 1954-56; managed farm 1956-58, asst tea taster and rep Wm Wright & Co (Pekoe) Ltd 1958-63; chm: Burnthills Gp Ltd (fndr dir Burnthills (Contractors) Ltd, first memb of the gp 1963), Bowfield Leisure Servs Ltd; chm: Goldenbolt Int Ltd and assoc cos, Huewind Ltd and assoc cos, Stonefield Castle Hotel Ltd, Corporate Capital Ltd, Covenanters Inn Ltd, Mull & West Highland Narrow Gauge Rlwy Co Ltd, Bute Newspapers Ltd; farms as Ladyland Estates and Grangehill Estates; underwriting memb Lloyds 1976-; fndr memb and past pres Johnstone Rotary Club 1975-; received Aims of Industry Award for Scotland 1982; *Style—* P A Ross, Esq; Grangehill, Beith,

Ayrshire, Scotland; 84 High St, Johnstone, Renfrewshire (☎ 0505 24461)

ROSS, Maj-Gen Robert Jeremy; OBE (1978); s of Lt Col Gerald Ross (d 1988), and Margaret Ross-Bell; *b* 28 Nov 1939; *Educ* Wellington, CCC Cambridge (MPhil); *m* 15 May 1965, Sara, da of Col W P S Curtis, OBE (d 1965); 1 s (Edward b 1966), 1 da (Annabel b 1968); *Career* entered RM 1957, commando and sea serv 1959-69, Army Staff Coll 1970, staff and commando serv 1971-86, RCDS 1983, Cdr 3 Commando Bde 1986-88, Maj Gen Trg Reserve and Special Forces 1988-90, Commando Forces 1990-; *Recreations* skiing, fishing, shooting, walking; *Clubs* United Oxford and Cambridge Univs; *Style—* Maj-Gen Robert Ross, OBE; Barclays Bank plc, 50 Jewry St, Winchester, Hampshire SO23 8RG

ROSS, Hon Mrs (Roxana Rose Catherine Naila); *née* Lampson; da of 1 Baron Killearn, GCMG, CB, MVO, PC (d 1964); *b* 1945; *m* 1966, Ian Cowper Ross; 2 s, 2 da; *Style—* The Hon Mrs Ross

ROSS, (Alexander) Sandy; s of Alexander Coutts Ross (d 1977), and Charlotte Edwardes, *née* Robertson (d 1977); *b* 17 April 1948; *Educ* Grangemouth HS, Univ of Edinburgh (LLB), Moray House Coll Edinburgh; *m* Alison, *née* Fraser; 1 s (Andrew b 1983), 1 da (Frances b 1986); *Career* slr 1970-75; prodr Granada TV 1977-86, controller of entertainment Scot TV 1986-; memb: Edinburgh Town Cncl 1971-74, Edinburgh DC 1973-76; memb BAFTA; *Recreations* golf, music, reading; *Style—* Sandy Ross, Esq; 7 Murrayfield Ave, Edinburgh EH12 6AU (☎ 031 337 3679); Scottish Television, Cowcaddens, Glasgow G2 3PR (☎ 041 332 9999, fax 041 332 6982)

ROSS, Stephen Lawrence; s of Julian Ross (d 1988), of London, and Miriam, *née* Gimmack; *b* 11 Dec 1950; *Educ* Woodhouse GS; *m* (m dis); 1 s (Daniel Paul b 20 Feb 1979), 1 da (Nicola Jane b 2 Oct 1981); *Career* CA 1974; audit mangr Deloitte Haskin & Sells (London) 1976, ptnr Keane Shaw & Co (London) 1978, sr ptnr Ross Bennet-Smith (London) 1983; FCA; *Recreations* tennis, horse racing, bridge; *Style—* Stephen L Ross, Esq; 46/47 Upper Berkeley St, London W1 (☎ 071 724 7724, fax 071 724 7070)

ROSS, Thomas Mackenzie; s of Duncan C Ross, of Muir of Ord, Rossshire, Scotland, and Elsie, *née* Mackenzie; *b* 4 May 1944; *Educ* Dingwall Acad, Univ of Edinburgh (BSc); *m* Oct 1967, Margaret, da of Robert Dewar; 1 s (Steven Graeme b 1970), 1 da (Elaine Caroline b 1968); *Career* trainee actuary Scottish Life Assurance Co Edinburgh 1966-70, consulting actuary and later vice pres Charles A Kench & Associates Vancouver Canada 1971-76, ptnr Clay & Partners Consulting Actuaries 1976-; memb Cncl: Faculty of Actuaries 1984-88, Nat Assoc of Pension Funds 1989-; memb: CBI Pensions Panel 1983-; fell: Faculty of Actuaries 1970, Canadian Inst of Actuaries 1971, Pensions Management Inst 1987; ASA 1971; *Recreations* horse racing, golf, gardening, hill walking; *Clubs* Naval, Racehorse Owners Assoc, Country Gentlemen's Assoc; *Style—* Thomas Ross, Esq; Clay & Partners, 61 Brook Street, London W1Y 2HN (☎ 071 408 1600, fax 071 493 0711)

ROSS, William; MP (UU) Londonderry East Feb 1974-; s of Leslie Alexander Ross (d 1973); *b* 4 Feb 1936; *m* 1974; 3 s, 1 da; *Recreations* shooting, fishing; *Clubs* Northern Counties, Londonderry; *Style—* William Ross, Esq, MP; Hillquarter, Turmeel, Dungiven, N Ireland (☎ 050 47 41428); House of Commons, London SW1 (☎ 071 219 3571)

ROSS, William Mackie; CBE (1987), TD (1970), DL (1971-); s of Harry Caithness Ross (d 1965), and Catherine, *née* Mackie; *b* 14 Dec 1922; *Educ* Johnston Sch, Univ of Durham (MB BS, MD); *m* 17 April 1948, Mary, da of Hedworth Burt, OBE (d 1972); 1 s (Duncan b 1959), 2 da (Heather b 1950, Hilary b 1955); *Career* TA 1951-70, Col RAMC (TA); conslt radiotherapist N Region 1953-87, lectr radiotherapy Univ of Newcastle 1963-87; pres: Br Inst Radiology 1978-79, RCR 1983-86; FRCS 1956, FRCR 1961, fell American Coll Radiology 1986; *Style—* William Ross, Esq, CBE, TD, DL

ROSS COLLINS, Michael Stewart; s of Leslie Ross Collins (d 1984), and Stella Mabel, *née* Stewart; *b* 21 June 1938; *Educ* Harrow; *m* 1972 (m dis 1976), Janette Mary, *née* Bryan; *Career* Lt 1 Bn Royal Fusiliers; chm Ross Collins Ltd Lloyds insur brokers 1969-81, dir Colne Valley Water Co plc 1975-90; dep chm Sedgwick UK Ltd 1987 (dir 1981-88), dep chm Rickmansworth Water Co plc 1988-90 (dir 1976-90), dir Three Valley Water Services plc 1990-, chm Sedgwick Risk Management Services 1988-, dir Sedgwick Europe 1988- and NGM Restaurants Ltd 1989; chm Totteridge branch NSPCC, underwriting memb of Lloyds 1965-; tstee: Sir Halley Stewart Tst, Sir Malcolm Stewart Tst, Fan Museum Tst; Freeman City of London 1961, Master Worshipful Co of Fanmakers 1985-86, Liveryman Worshipful Co of Insurers; FInstD; *Recreations* golf, food, wine, travel, gardening, collecting antique furniture, fans; *Clubs* Royal & Ancient, Royal Cinque Ports, Royal St Georges, Hadley Wood Golf, Hatfield House Tennis, City Livery; *Style—* Michael S Ross Collins, Esq; Southenhay, Totteridge, London N20 (☎ 081 446 2219); Sedgwick Group plc, The Sedgwick Centre, London E1 (☎ 071 481 5526, fax 071 377 3199, telex 882131)

ROSS MARTYN, John Greaves; s of Dr William Ross Martyn, of Wilmslow, Cheshire, and Ida Mary Martyn, *née* Greaves; *b* 23 Jan 1944; *Educ* Repton, Univ of Cambridge (BA, LLM); *m* 4 Aug 1973, Pauline, da of Ronald Jennings (d 1979), of Morley, Yorks; 1 s (Philip b 1978), 1 da (Elizabeth b 1975); *Career* asst lectr Birmingham Coll of Commerce 1966-68, called to the Bar Middle Temple 1969, in practice at Chancery Bar 1970-, asst rec 1988, SE Circuit; memb Chancery Bar Assoc; *Books* Williams, Mortimer and Sunnucks on Executors, Administrators and Probate (jt ed, 1982), Family Provision: Law and Practice (1985); *Recreations* gardening, skiing; *Style—* John Ross Martyn, Esq; 5 New Square, Lincoln's Inn, London WC2A 3RJ (☎ 071 404 0404, fax 071 831 6016)

ROSS-MUNRO, (William) Colin Gordon; QC (1972); *b* 12 Feb 1928; *Educ* Harrow, Lycee France de Londres, Univ of Cambridge (BA); *m* 22 Jan 1958, Janice Jill, *née* Brown; *Career* Army Educn Corp Scots Gds 1946-48; called to the Bar Middle Temple 1951; bencher Middle Temple 1983; *Recreations* tennis, travel; *Clubs* Hurlingham, Queens; *Style—* Colin Ross-Munro, Esq, QC; 36 Roland Way, London SW7 (☎ 071 370 0852); 2 Hare Ct, Middle Temple, London EC4 (☎ 071 583 1770, fax Gps 11 & 111, 071 583 9269, telex 27139 LINLAW)

ROSS OF NEWPORT, Baron (Life Peer UK 1987), of Newport, Co Isle of Wight; Stephen Sherlock Ross; s of Reginald Sherlock Ross and Florence Beryl, *née* Weston; *b* 6 July 1926; *Educ* Holmwood Sch Finchley, Bedford Sch; *m* 8 Oct 1949, Brenda Marie, da of Arthur Ivor Hughes, of Stanmore, Middx; 2 s (Hon James Gibb b 1 March 1956, Hon Huw Weston b 15 June 1960), 2 da (Hon Lesley Priscilla (Hon Mrs O'Sullivan) b 2 Oct 1950, Hon Judith Caroline (Hon Mrs Kiendl) b 1 Oct 1952); *Career* WWII 1939-45, RN 1944-48; asst Nock & Joseland Kidderminster 1948-53; ptnr Sir Francis Pittis & Son, Newport, IOW 1958-73 (joined 1953) conslt Fox & Sons Newport IOW 1987-89; memb IOW CC 1967-74 and 1981-85 (leader 1981-83), chm Policy and Resources Ctee 1973-74 and 1981-83; MP (L) IOW 1974-87; FRICS; *Recreations* cricket, collecting ceramics; *Style—* The Rt Hon Lord Ross of Newport

ROSS OF THAT ILK, David Campbell; s of Sheriff Charles Campbell Ross of Shandwick, QC; suc kinswoman Miss Rosa Ross Williamson Ross of that Ilk and Pitcalnie in 1968 as Chief of Clan Ross; *b* 1934; *m* 1958, Eileen, da of Lawrence Cassidy; *Heir* s, Hugh Andrew Campbell (b 1961); *Style—* David Ross of that Ilk; Old School House, Fettercairn, Laurencekirk AB3 1DL

ROSS RUSSELL, Graham; *b* 3 Jan 1933; *Educ* Loretto, Trinity Hall Cambridge, Harvard Business Sch; *m* 1963, Jean Margaret, da of the late Col K M Symington; 4 children; *Career* chm EMAP plc, pres CCF Holdings Ltd, dir CCF Laurence Prust Ltd; memb: Stock Exchange 1965-, Stock Exchange Cncl 1973-; dep chm Stock Exchange 1984-88, cmmr of Public Works Loan Bd 1981-, dir of Securities and Investmts Bd 1989-; *Style—* Graham Ross Russell, Esq; 30 Ladbroke Sq, London W11; EMAP plc, Scriptor Court, 155 Farringdon Rd, London EC1R 3AD

ROSS RUSSELL, Dr Ralph William; s of Robert Ross Russell, and Elizabeth, *née* Hendry; *b* 22 April 1928; *Educ* Edinburgh Acad, Loretto Sch, Univ of Cambridge (MA, MD); *m* 8 June 1957, Flora Mary, da of John Robert Dale (d 1967), of Auldhame, North Berwick, E Lothian; 2 s (Jock b 1964, Rory b 1965), 3 da (Clare b 1958, Fiona b 1959, Alison b 1961); *Career* capt RAMC 1954-56; physician: Nat Hosp Queen Square London 1963, St Thomas' Hosp 1964, Moorfields Eye Hosp 1966; FRCP 1969, FRCPE 1979; *Books* Vascular Disease of Central Nervous System (1984); *Recreations* country pursuits, golf; *Style—* Dr Ralph Ross Russell; 5 Roedean Crescent, London SW15 5JX; St Thomas' Hospital, London SE1 (☎ 071 928 9292)

ROSS SKINNER, Harry John Crawley; VRD; s of Lt Col Harry Crawley Ross Skinner, DSO, MC (d 1972), of Warmwell House, Dorchester, Dorset, and Joan, *née* Crawley; *b* 6 Feb 1932; *Educ* Eton, RAC Cirencester; *m* 1, 21 May 1955, Rosemary, da of Anthony Freestone-Barnes, of Winchester; 4 s (Andrew Harry b 1956, Sambrooke Anthony b 1958, Paul Stuart b 1960, Simon Francis b 1963); m 2, 13 Sept 1971, Venetia Caroline *née* Maynard, *qv*; 4 step children; *Career* Lt Cdr RN (Res); farmer; dir: Winchmore plc, Blaircourt Investmts Ltd, Woodstock Estates Ltd; *Recreations* sailing, skiing, shooting; *Clubs* Royal Cruising; *Style—* Harry J C Ross Skinner, Esq, VRD; Warmwell House, Dorchester DT2 8HQ

ROSS SKINNER, Venetia Caroline; *née* Maynard; da of Lt-Col Alister Cecil Maynard, MBE (d 1975), descended from a collateral branch of the Viscounts Maynard (ext 1865), and Muriel Violet, *née* Wingfield (d 1986); *b* 22 March 1936; *Educ* Queen's Coll Harley St; *m* 1, 21 June 1957 (m dis 1969), John Howard Cordle; 1 s (Rupert b 1959), 3 da (Sophie b 1958, Marina b 1960 m Hon Michael Pearson *qv*, Rachel b 1963); m 2, 13 Sept 1971, Harry John Crawley Ross Skinner *qv*; *Career* Welsh pony breeder; building co dir; *Recreations* yachting; *Style—* Mrs Venetia C Ross Skinner; Warmwell House, nr Dorchester, Dorset (☎ 0305 852269, fax 0305 852389, car 0863 245687)

ROSS STEWART, David Andrew; OBE (1985); s of Maj-Gen W Ross Stewart CB, CIE (d 1966), of Blakehope, Caddonfoot, Galashiels, Scotland, and Margaret Jean Denholm, *née* Fraser; *b* 30 Nov 1930; *Educ* Rugby, Clare Coll Cambridge (BA); *m* 23 May 1959, Susan Olive, da of Lt Col W H F Routh (d 1964), of Hillside, Kingston St Mary, Taunton, Somerset; 2 s (James b 20 Sept 1961, Charles b 15 May 1964); *Career* mgmnt trainee Alex Cowan & Sons Ltd 1952-55, asst to gen mangr Alex Cowan & Son (NZ) Ltd 1959-62; gen mangr: Alex Cowan & Sons (Stationery) Ltd London 1962-66, Spicers (Stationery) Ltd Sawston 1966-68; md John Bartholomew & Son Ltd Edinburgh 1968-89; chm: Scottish Provident Institute, St Andrews Trust plc, West Lothian Enterprise Ltd; dir East of Scotland Industrial Investments plc; memb Scot Advsy Bd Abbey National plc; convenor Univ of Edinburgh Advsy Ctee on Business Studies; fell Scot Cncl Devpt and Indust; *Recreations* fishing, gardening, golf; *Clubs* New (Edinburgh), Hon Co of Edinburgh Golfers, Muirfield GC; *Style—* David Ross Stewart, Esq, OBE; 13 Blacket Place, Edinburgh EH9 1RN (☎ 031 667 3221); Scottish Provident Institution, 6 St Andrew Square, Edinburgh EH2 2YA (☎ 031 556 9181, fax 031 558 2486)

ROSSBERG, Sara Jutta Maria; da of Manfred Rossberg, of Darmstadt, Germany, and Josefine, *née* Kamps (d 1978); *b* 14 Oct 1952; *Educ* Viktoria Sch Darmstadt Germany, Acad of Fine Art Frankfurt/Milan, Camberwell Sch of Art and Crafts; *Career* painter (based London 1978-); travelling scholar: German Nat Fndn 1976-77, Daad 1977-78; solo exhibitions: Acad of Fine Art Frankfurt/ Main 1973, Int Art Fair Basle 1986, Kunstkeller Bern 1987, Treadwell Gallery 1987, Thumb Gallery London 1988, Don't I Know You? (retrospective touring show) 1989, Rosenberg & Stiebel Inc NY 1990, Louis Newman Galleries LA 1990; group exhibitions incl: Summer Show (Royal Acad) 1978, Chelsea Art Soc 1978, Treadwell Gallery 1982, various int art fairs UK & abroad 1982-, Art by Woman (Wolverhampton Art Gallery) 1988, Nat Portrait Gallery 1989 and 1990, Drawing Show (Thumb Gallery) 1988 and 1990, European Artists Works on Paper (Kunstkeller Bern) 1990; Crown award 1978, prizewinner 16th John Moore's Liverpool Exhibition 1989, commendation BP awards Nat Portrait Gallery 1990; *Recreations* music, running; *Style—* Ms Sara Rossberg; Thumb Gallery, 38 Lexington St, London W1 (☎ 071 439 7343, fax 071 287 0478)

ROSSDALE, Fleur Viola; da of John Spencer Rossdale, and Lucie Marcelle Louise, *née* Bourcier; *b* 20 March 1957; *Educ* Francis Holland Sch, Florence Univ (Dip); *m* 11 Dec 1982, Fletcher Freeland Robinson, s of Patrick William Robinson, of London; 2 s (George b 1984, William b 1986); *Career* originator of The Br Interior Design Exhibition, co-originator with Weidenfeld and Nicolson of The Interior Design Yearbook, co-founder with Robin Guild of The Design & Decoration Building; *Recreations* walking, gardening, painting; *Style—* Miss Fleur Rossdale; 3 Pembroke Square, London W8 6PA (☎ 071 937 7045)

ROSSE, Anne, Countess of; Anne; da of Lt-Col Leonard Messel, OBE, TD (s of Ludwig Messel, of Nymans, Handcross, Sussex and 3 Hyde Park Gdns, London W2, s of Simon Messel of Darmstadt and gs of Simon Lindheim, private sec to the Grand Duke of Hesse and sec of the WO in Darmstadt), and of Maud Frances, MBE (da of (Edward) Linley Sambourne, the Punch cartoonist, of 18 Stafford Terrace, London W8, s of Francis Linley, of the Linleys of Bath); sis of late Linley Francis Messel and of late Oliver Messel, the portraitist and set designer; *m* 1, 1925 (m dis 1934), Ronald, s of Sir Robert Armstrong-Jones, CBE, of Plas Dinas, Caernarvonshire; 1 s (Earl of Snowdon, *qv*), 1 da (Viscountess de Vesci, *qv*); m 2, 1935, 6 Earl of Rosse, KBE (d 1979); 2 s (7 Earl and Hon Desmond Parsons, *qqv*); *Career* dir for the Nat Tst of Nymans Gardens; founder of The Victorian Soc at 18 Stafford Terrace; *Style—* The Rt Hon Anne, Countess of Rosse; Nymans, Handcross, Sussex; Womersley Park, Doncaster, Yorks; Birr Castle, Co Offaly, Republic of Ireland; 18 Stafford Terrace, London W8

ROSSE, 7 Earl of (I 1806); Sir William Brendan Parsons; 10 Bt (I 1677); also Baron Oxmantown (I 1795), Lord of the Manors of Towton and Womersley; s of 6 Earl of Rosse, KBE (d 1979), and Anne, Countess of Rosse, *qv*; *b* 21 Oct 1936; *Educ* Eton, Grenoble Univ, Ch Ch Oxford; *m* 1966, Alison, da of Maj John Cooke-Hurle, of Startforth Hall, Barnard Castle; 2 s (Lord Oxmantown b 1969, Hon Michael b 1981), 1 da (Lady Alicia b 1971); *Heir* s, Lord Oxmantown; *Career* late 2 Lt Irish Gds; UN official: Ghana, Dahomey, Mid-W Africa, Iran, Bangladesh, Algeria 1963-80; dir: Agency for Personal Services Overseas 1981-89, Sch of Int Educn Univ of Limerick, The IAM Group, the Historic Irish Tourist Houses and Gardens Assoc, Br Scientific Heritage Fndn; memb of Irish Govt's Advsy Cncl on Devpt Co-operation 1983-88; patron Halley's Comet Soc; tstee Edward de Bono Fndn; *Clubs* The International; *Style—* The Rt Hon the Earl of Rosse; Birr Castle, Co Offaly, Republic of Ireland (☎ 353 509 20023)

ROSSEN, Stig; s of Carlo Rossen, of Kolding, Denmark, and Lone, *née* Kruse; *b* 14 June 1962; *Educ* Kolding Gymnasium Denmark, Guildhall Sch of Music and Drama; *m* 27 Oct 1990, Rike-Yvonne da of Dr Karl-Albert Schetter, of Munich; 1 da (Josephine Annie b 27 Dec 1990); *Career* musical actor; role of Jean Valjean Les Miserables (Palace) 1990-; theatre in Denmark incl: Count Danilo in the Merry Widow, Russian tenor in Fiddler on the Roof, Henrik in Henrik and Pernille, Domingo in Farinelli, Bierbaum in Champagne galoppen; solo album Kerlighed Og Alt Det Der released in Denmark 1988; *Recreations* golf, tennis, backgammon, reading; *Style—* Stig Rossen, Esq; Caroline De Wolfe, Manfield House, 376-378 The Strand, London WC2R 0LR (☎ 071 379 5767, fax 071 836 0337)

ROSSER, Colin Richard; s of Edwin William Rosser (d 1988), and Edna Kestine Joan Rosser; *b* 18 Oct 1940; *Educ* Southfield GS, Oxford Coll of Technol, Univ of Southampton (BSc); *m* 27 Nov 1965, Susan, *née* Kilby; 1 s (Richard Charles b 18 March 1968), 1 da (Deborah Anne b 18 May 1966); *Career* dir AER Rosser Ltd 1964-73, chm and md Goodhead Press Ltd 1975-85 (md 1973-75), chm and chief exec Goodhead Group plc 1985-; chm: Assoc of Free Newspaper 1989-90 (vice chm 1988), Oxfordshire Regnl Ctee Nat Childrens Home 1987; govr Penhurst Sch Chipping Norton 1988; memb Advocacy Ctee Nat Children's Home 1989; *Recreations* golf, squash, swimming; *Style—* Colin Rosser, Esq; Goodhead Group plc, Unit 6, Chaucer International Estate, Launton Rd, Bicester, Oxon OX6 7QZ (☎ 0869 253322, fax 0869 244981)

ROSSER, Sir Melvyn Wynne; DL (West Glam 1986); s of David John Rosser, of Swansea, and Anita, *née* Rosser; *b* 11 Nov 1926; *Educ* Glanmor Sch Swansea, Bishop Gore GS Swansea; *m* 16 April 1959, (Mary) Margaret; 1 s (Neil), 2 da (Betsan, Mari); *Career* ptnr Deloitte Haskins & Sells: Swansea 1961-66, Cardiff 1966-79, London 1979-80; memb: Land Cmmn 1965-69, Welsh Econ Cncl 1964-72; chm Welsh Cncl 1972-80; dir: Nat Bus Co 1969-72, Wales Telecommunications Bd 1970-80, Br Steel Corp 1972-80, Nat Coal Bd 1980-; chm Manpower Services Ctee for Wales 1980-; memb: Royal Cmmn on Standards of Conduct in Public Life 1974, and Cmmn 1970-73, PM's Advsy Ctee on Outside Business Appts 1976-83; pres Univ Coll of Wales Aberystwyth 1985- (vice pres 1977-85); memb: Cncl and Ct of Univ of Wales, memb Gorsedd of Bards; Hon LLD Univ of Wales, hon fell Polytechnic of Wales; FCA; kt 1974; *Recreations* music, gardening, golf; *Clubs* RAC, Cardiff and County, Bristol Channel Yacht (Swansea); *Style—* Sir Melvyn Rosser, DL; Corlan, 53 Birchgrove Road, Lonlas, Swansea, W Glamorgan SA7 9JR (☎ 0792 812286); HTV Gp plc, Culverhouse Cross, Cardiff CF5 6XJ (☎ 0222 590590, fax 0222 592134, car 0860 810968)

ROSSER, Prof Rachel Mary; da of John Rosser (d 1983), and Madge; *Educ* Kings HS Warwick, Newham Coll Cambridge (BA), St Thomas' Hosp Med Sch (MB BChir), Charing Cross and Westminster Med Sch (PhD); *m* 17 June 1967, Vincent Challacombe Watts, s of Geoffrey Watts (d 1987), of Low Hall, Kirkbymoorside, N Yorks; 1 s (Benjamin b 1977), 1 da (Hannah b 1981); *Career* house offr St Thomas' Hosp 1966-67; house offr and sr house offr 1967-69: Hackney Hosp, Brook Gen Hosp, Regnl Neurosurgical Unit, Central Middx Hosp; res asst and hon registrar Guy's Hosp Med Sch 1969-71, registrar Bethlem Royal and Maudsley Hosps 1971-74; sr registrar 1974-76: Hammersmith Hosp, Kings Coll Dulwich, Maudsley Hosp; reader Charing Cross Med Sch 1983-84 (sr lectr and hon conslt 1976-82), prof and head of psychiatry UCL 1984-; author of scientific papers on: quality of life, psychotherapy res, psychosomatic med, post traumatic stress disorder; treas Int Coll of Psychosomatic Med 1983-, pres Soc for Psychosomatic Med 1984-86, vice pres psychiatry section RSM, memb UK and Euro Gps for res on quality of life and disasters; MRCP 1971, MRCPsych 1973, FRCPsych 1983, FRCP 1984; *Books* Health Care: Priorities and Management (jtly, 1980), Mind Made Disease: A Clinicians Guide to Psychosomatic Research (jtly, 1988), Quality of Life: Assessment and Application (with S R Walker, 1988); *Clubs* United Oxford and Cambridge Univ; *Style—* Prof Rachel Rosser; Department of Psychiatry, University College & Middx Sch of Medicine, Mortimer St, London W1 8AA (☎ 071 380 9468, fax 071 323 1459)

ROSSER, Richard Andrew; JP (1978); s of Gordon William Rosser (d 1985), and Kathleen Mary, *née* Moon (d 1985); *b* 5 Oct 1944; *Educ* St Nicholas GS Northwood, Univ of London (BSc); *m* 17 Nov 1973, Sheena Margaret, da of Iain Denoon; 2 s (Keith Malcolm b 1976, Colin Michael b 1977), 1 da (Rachel Anne b 1980); *Career* Transport Salaried Staff Assoc: res offr 1968-76, fin offr 1976-77, sec London Midland Regn 1977-82, asst gen sec 1982-89, gen sec 1989-; cncllr London Borough of Hillingdon 1971-78 (chm Fin Ctee 1974-78), Parly candidate (Lab) Croydon Central Feb 1974, memb Lab Pty Nat Exec Ctee 1988-; MCIT 1968; *Style—* Richard Rosser, Esq, JP; Transport Salaried Staffs' Association, Walkden House, 10 Melton Street, London NW1 2EJ (☎ 071 387 2101, fax 071 383 0656)

ROSSI, Francis Dominic Nicholas Michael; s of Dominic Rossi, of Kent, and Anne, *née* Traynor; *b* 29 May 1949; partners: m, 12 June 1967, Jean, *née* Smith; 3 s, (Simon b 1967, Nicholas b 1972, Kieran b 1979); Elizabeth Gurnan; 1 child; Eileen, da of Michael Quinn; 2 s (Patrick b 1988, Fynn b 1990); *Career* Status Quo (orignally known as Spectres formed 1962): co-fndr 1967, continual world touring 1967-, Gold and Silver discs every year since 1971; Silver Clef award 1982, Ivor Novello award (for outstanding servs to music indust) 1984; played at: Launch of Princes Tst 1983, Live Aid 1985, Knebworth 1990; *Recreations* collectiong Koi Carp fish, clay pidgeon shooting; *Style—* Francis Rossi, Esq; The Handle Group of Companies, 20 Woods Mews, London W1Y 3AH

ROSSI, Sir Hugh Alexis Louis; MP (C) Hornsey and Wood Green 1983-; *b* 21 June 1927; *Educ* Finchley Catholic GS, King's Coll London (LLB); *m* 1955, (Philomena) Elizabeth, da of Patrick Jennings (d 1951); 1 s, 4 da; *Career* slr 1950, MP (C) Hornsey 1966-1983; govt whip 1970-72, lord cmmr treasy 1972-74, Parly under-sec Enviroment Jan-March 1974, oppn spokesman Housing and Land 1974-79, min of state NI Office 1979-81, min of state for Social Security and the Disabled DHSS 1981-83, chm Enviroment Select Ctee 1983-; memb UK Delgn to Cncl of Europe and WEU 1970-73 (dep ldr 1972-73, Euro whip 1971-73); former memb Hornsey 7 Haringey Cncl and Middx CC; kt of Holy Sepulchre (1966 Papal), KCSG (1985 Papal); FKC (1986); kt 1983; *Style—* Sir Hugh Rossi, MP; House of Commons, London SW1 (☎ 071 219 5195)

ROSSI, Mario; s of Carlo Rossi, of Glasgow, and Vitoria, *née* Bertoncini; *b* 11 Feb 1958; *Educ* Glasgow Sch of Art (BA) Royal Coll of Art (MA); *Partner* Lindsay Alker; *Career* artist; lectr Goldsmiths' Coll London 1985-90; *solo exhibitions*: The Archaeologist (Demarco Gallery, City Arts Centre) 1984, Interim Art 1985, Cleveland Gallery Middlesbrough 1987, Atelier 1 Hamburg 1987, Anderson O'Day Gallery London 1988 and 1990, Ozones (wren Library, Trinity Coll Cambridge) 1989, Spacex Gallery Exeter 1990; *group exhibitions incl*: Cross Currents (Third Eye Centre Glasgow) 1979, Scottish Young Contemporaries (Travelling Exhibition) 1981, Expressive Images (New 57 Gallery Edinburgh) 1982, 12 Artisti Britannici A Roma (Palazzo Barberini Rome) 1983, Five Painter (Riverside Studios) 1985, New Image Glasgow (Third Eye Centre Glasgow) 1985, New Art-New World (Sothebys London and NY) 1986, Contemporary British Woodcuts (Worcester Museum) 1986, The Vigorous Imagination-New Scottish Art (Scottish Nat Gallery of Modern Art Edinburgh and touring) 1987, Glasgow Garden Festival 1988, Fire and Metal (Goldsmiths Gallery) 1988, Whitechapel Open (Whitechapel Gallery) 1988, John Moores 16 (Walker Art Gallery Liverpool) 1989, Scottish Art Since 1900 (Scottish Nat Gallery of Modern Art Edinburgh and The Barbican) 1989-90, Real Life Stories-The Cleveland Collection (Spacex Gallery Exeter) 1990, Post Morality (Kettle's Yard Cambridge) 1990; *work in the collections of*: Contemporary Arts Soc, Victoria & Albert Museum, Gallery of Modern Art Edinburgh, Cleveland Art Gallery Middlesbrough, Unilever, Nordstern Cologne; Gulbenkian Rome scholar Br Sch at Rome 1982-83, fellowship in creative arts Trinity Coll Cambridge 1987-89, Coopers & Lybrand under 35 award Whitechapel Open 1988; *Clubs* Chelsea Arts; *Style—* Mario Rossi, Esq; Anderson O'Day Gallery, 255 Portobello Rd, London W11 1LR (☎ 071 221 7592, fax 081 960 3641)

ROSSITER, Prof Charles Edward; s of Percy Rowland Rossiter (d 1948), of Peru, and Gertrude, *née* Smith (d 1976), of Melbourne, Aust; *b* 5 Dec 1935; *Educ* Framlingham Coll Suffolk, St John's Coll Oxford (BA, MA); *m* 1, 20 May 1961 (m dis), Averil Elizabeth Margaret Tucker; 1 s (Martin b 1970), 2 da (Jane b 1965, Ann b 1966), m 2, 14 Oct 1988, Jane Elizabeth, da of Joseph Wallace Hughes (d 1963); *Career* assoc prof McGill Univ Montreal 1966-68, head div of computing and statistics clinical res centre MRC 1979-84 (statistician pneumoconiosis unit 1959-79), prof of occupational health and dir TUC Centenary Inst of Occupational Health LSHTM 1984-88, emeritus prof of occupational health Univ of London 1988; Freeman: Worshipful Soc of Apothecaries 1984, City of London 1988; hon fell faculty of occupational med 1984, Hon DSc (med) Univ of London 1990; *Recreations* computing, food, gardening; *Style—* Prof Charles Rossiter; 10 Mynchen Rd, Knotty Green, Beaconsfield, Bucks HP9 2AS (☎ 0494 670677, fax 0494 670678)

ROSSITER, Rt Rev (Anthony) Francis; s of Leslie Anthony Rossiter (d 1952), and Winifred Mary, *née* Poppitt; *b* 26 April 1931; *Educ* St Benedict's Ealing, Sant Anselmo (LCL) Rome, Lateran Univ; *Career* ordained priest 1955, dep head St Benedict's Sch 1960-67; abbot of Ealing 1967-; pres Conf of Major Religious Superiors of Eng and Wales 1970-74, vicar Religious Archdiocese of Westminster 1969-89, abbot pres Eng Benedictine Congregation 1985- (second asst 1976-85); Hon DD St Vincent Coll Pensylvania 1988; *Style—* The Rt Rev the Abbot of Ealing; Ealing Abbey, London W5 2DY (☎ 081 998 2158)

ROSSITER, Nicholas Jeremy; s of Anthony Rossiter, of Litton, Somerset, and Anneka, *née* Hooving; *b* 17 July 1961; *Educ* Downside, Oxford Univ (MA); *Career* journalist; gen trainee BBC TV 1986, film dir BBC TV music and arts 1988, contrib to The Listener and other periodicals 1987, dir HRH The Prince of Wales film A Vision of Britain 1988; other films incl: The Great Picture Chase (with David Puttnam), Monsieur Eiffels Tower; nomination for best arts film BAFTA; *Books* Ram Ram India (1989); *Recreations* travel; *Style—* Nicholas Rossiter, Esq; 19 Woodlawn Rd, Fulham, London SW6 (☎ 071 385 6949); BBC TV, Kensington House, Richmond Way, London W14 0AX (☎ 071 895 6611)

ROSSITER, Richard Wellsted; s of William Rossiter (d 1959), of Bristol, and Christabel Ida, Rossiter, JP; *b* 30 Oct 1934; *Educ* Bristol GS; *m* 30 Sept 1966, Susan Jennifer, da of Reginald Brookes; 2 da (Emily, Charlotte); *Career* Nat Serv Sub Lt RN 1957-59, chm: Fromedale Estates Ltd, Westgate Discounts; past capt and chm Clifton RFC; played cricket for: RN, MCC, Free Foresters, Glos CCC (chm 1990-); former chm Clifton LTC; vice chm Bristol Cncl Disabled Adults; FCA 1957; *Recreations* cricket, tennis, sport generally, skiing; *Clubs* Clifton, Lansdowne, MCC, Free Foresters; *Style—* Richard Rossiter, Esq; Longwood, Tickenham, Avon BS21 6SW (☎ 0272 854616); 69 Whiteladies Rd, Bristol BS8 2NT (☎ 0272 237013)

ROSSLYN, 7 Earl of (UK 1801); Sir Peter St Clair-Erskine; 10 Bt (S 1666); also Baron Loughborough (GB 1780); s of 6 Earl of Rosslyn (d 1977), and Comtesse Athenaïs de Rochechouart-Mortemart; *b* 31 March 1958; *Educ* Eton, Bristol Univ; *m* 1986, Helen, el da C R Watters of Sussex; 1 s (Lord Loughborough), 1 da (Lady Alice b 14 June 1988); *Heir* s, Hon Jamie William St Clair-Erskine, Lord Loughborough, b 28 May 1986; *Career* tstee Dunimarle Museum, Metropolitan Police 1980-; *Clubs* Whites; *Style—* The Rt Hon the Earl of Rosslyn

ROSSMORE, 7 Baron (I 1796 & UK 1838) William Warner Westenra; s of 6 Baron Rossmore (d 1958); *b* 14 Feb 1931; *Educ* Eton, Trinity Cambridge; *m* 1982, Valerie Marion, da of Brian Tobin, of Riverstown, Birr, Ireland; 1 s, 1 step da; *Heir* s, Hon Benedict William Westenra, b 6 March 1983; *Career* 2 Lt Somerset LI; co-fndr Coolemine Therapeutic Community Dublin (Psychotherapeutic Counselling); *Recreations* drawing and painting; *Clubs* Kildare St & Univ Dublin; *Style—* The Rt Hon Lord Rossmore; c/o Lloyds Bank plc, 6 Pall Mall, London SW1

ROSSWICK, (Robert) Paul; s of John Rosswick (d 1959), and Phoebe, *née* Fagin (d 1982); *b* 1 June 1932; *Educ* Malvern Coll, London Hosp Med Coll (MB BS); *m* 25 March 1962, Elizabeth Rita, da of Horace Cooper; 1 s (Jonathan b 1965), 1 da (Sarah b 1966); *Career* conslt surgn St George's Hosp London 1970, hon sr lectr in surgery, St George's Hosp Med Sch, surgn Royal Masonic Hosp London 1977, prev first asst in surgery St Georges Hosp, Robertson Exchange fellow in surgery Presbyterian-St Lukes Hosp Chicago 1962-63, ed Proceedings of Med Soc London 1984-89, (pres 1990-91); Freeman City of London 1979, Liveryman Worshipful Soc of Apothecaries 1983; *Recreations* music, photography; *Clubs* Savage, RSM; *Style—* Paul Rosswick, Esq; 79 Harley St, London W1N 1DE (☎ 071 935 3046)

ROST, Peter Lewis; MP (C) Erewash 1983-; s of Frederick Rost, formerly Rosenstiel (d 1971), of NY, and Elisabeth Merz; *b* 19 Sept 1930; *Educ* Aylesbury GS, Univ of Birmingham (BA); *m* 1961, Hilary, da of Arthur Mayo (d 1971), of Boxmoor, Herts; 2 s, 2 da; *Career* RAF 1948-50; stockbroker, investment analyst and fin journalist; MP (C) Derbyshire S E 1970-1983; Grand Cross Order of Merit Germany 1979; *Style—* Peter Rost, Esq, MP; Norcott Court, Berkhamsted, Herts (☎ 044 27 6123)

ROSTEN, Leonard; *b* 5 Jan 1929; *Educ* Regent St Poly London, Northampton Engrg Coll, Univ of London (BSc); *m* 5 June 1956, Jeanette, *née* Jacobs, 2 da (Susan b 1959, Deborah b 1963); *Career* Sr Scientific Intelligence Offr CD Corps 1962-68; assoc W V Zinn and Assocs 1968-70 (engr 1955-68), fndr ptnr Cooper Macdonald and Ptnrs 1970-90, chm ACE Midland Gp 1981-82 (tres 1984); FIStructE 1973, FICE 1986, MConsE, FRSA; papers: Detailing by Computer (with W V Zinn), Civil Engineering (1971); *Recreations* music, ancient history; *Clubs* RAC; *Style—* Eur Ing Leonard Rosten; 23 Poolfield Drive, Solihull, Midlands B91 1SH (☎ 021 705 9620); Cooper Macdonald Plc, Bank House, Cherry St, Birmingham B2 5SF (☎ 021 643 7891)

ROSTON, Michael; s of Emanuel Rosenberg (d 1963), of London, and Hetty Rosenberg (d 1975); *b* 2 Aug 1935; *Educ* Wykeham Tech Sch Neasden; *m* Marlene Suzanne, da of Anthony Spears, of London; 2 s (Robert, Paul), 1 da (Caroline); *Career* dir Windsor Hosiery Co 1970-73; sales exec: Condax Agenices Ltd 1966-70, Gt Universal Stores Ltd 1960-66; sales/gen mangr Menwear Gp 1950-60; current chm and md: Unidoor Ltd, Dominex Ltd, David James Int, Uniport Shipping, Uniwell Knitwear Mfrg Co Ltd; *Recreations* golf, tennis; *Clubs* Hartsbourne Country; *Style—* Michael Roston, Esq; The Ferns, Shepherd's Walk, Hartsbourne Rd, Bushey Heath, Herts WD2 1LZ; Unidoor Hse, 137-139 Essex Rd, Islington N1 2XT (☎ 01 359 8261, fax 01 354 3595, car 0860 324 259, telex 265980 UNIDOR G)

ROSTRON, Chad Kenneth; s of Kenneth William Briggs Rostron, and Rosemary, *née* Arkwright; *b* 6 May 1951; *Educ* Sherborne, Univ of Newcastle (MB BS); *m* Josephine

Rose; *Career* conslt ophthalmologist St George's Hosp 1988, hon sr lectr Univ of London 1988; author of numerous pubns on corneal and kerato-refractive surgery; UK rep of the Euro Refractive Surgical Soc; DO 1979, FRCS 1983, FCOpth 1989, memb RSM; *Clubs* Royal Soc of Med; *Style—* Chad Rostron, Esq; 100 Harley St, London W1N 1AF (☎ 071 486 2135)

ROSTRON, Sir Frank; MBE (1954); s of late Samuel Ernest Rostron, of Oldham, and late Martha *née* Jagger; *b* 11 Sept 1900; *Educ* Oldham HS, Manchester Coll Science and Technol (HNC Elec Eng); *m* 1929, Helen Jodrell (d 1984), da of late Thomas Owen, of Manchester; 1 s (David), 1 da (Barbara); *Career* RAF 1941-45, electrical engr offr (Bomber Cmd) Eng, Pilot Offr to Sqdn Ldr (despatches); chartered electrical engr; pres Manchester C of C 1955-56; Ferranti Ltd 1917-70 (dir 1958-70), dir: Nat and Vulcan Boiler and Gen Insur Co Ltd 1958-70, McKechnie Bros Ltd 1966-71; chm: Cotton Bd 1963-68, Cotton and Allied Textiles Indust Trg Bd 1966-68 (fndr); CEng, FIEE; kt 1967; *Recreations* reading, walking, gardening; *Style—* Sir Frank Rostron, MBE

ROSTRON, Philip; s of Raymond Hugh Riley Rostron (d 1976), and Lilian, *née* Hewson; *b* 9 Sept 1951; *Educ* Chadderton GS for Boys; *m* 3 Sept 1977, Caroline Lorraine, da of Rowland Edmunds; 1 s (Gary Paul b 16 Dec 1980), 1 da (Joanna Marie b 25 Oct 1979); *Career* journalist; Oldham Evening Chronicle 1967-68, Oldham Press Agency 1968-69, Rochdale Observer 1969-71, Daily Telegraph Sydney Aust 1971-73, West Lancashire Evening Gazette Blackpool 1973-78, Daily Star 1978-, sports ed 1989; *Books* On The Level (ghosted autobiography of champion racehorse trainer Henry Cecil, 1986); *Recreations* lifelong fan of Oldham Athletic FC, music (favourite singer Scott Walker); *Style—* Philip Rostron, Esq; Daily Star, 245 Blackfriars Road, London SE1 9UX (☎ 071 922 7427)

ROSTRON, Timothy Peter (Tim); s of Frank Rostron, of Newbury, Berks, and Mildred Joan, *née* Scull; *b* 1 Oct 1955; *Educ* St Bartholomew's GS Newbury, Winchester Sch of Art (BA); *m* 1987, Elizabeth, da of Philip Arnold Draper; *Career* freelance textile designer 1978-79, counterhand ice cream parlour Harrods 1979-80, trainee Doctor newspaper 1980-83, chief sub ed She Magazine 1983-86, features ed Elle Magazine 1987-88; Daily Telegraph: rock critic and feature writer 1986-, asst arts ed 1988-90, ed Weekend section 1990-; *Recreations* buying books and records, reading and listening to some of them, dinner; *Clubs* Academy; *Style—* Tim Rostron, Esq; The Daily Telegraph, 181 Marsh Wall, London E14 9SR (☎ 071 538 5000, fax 071 538 3810)

ROTBLAT, Prof Joseph; CBE (1965); s of late Zygmunt Rotblat, and late Sonia Rotblat; *b* 4 Nov 1908; *Educ* Free Univ of Poland (MA), Univ of Warsaw (DPhys), Univ of Liverpool (PhD), Univ of London (DSc); *Career* res fell Radiological Laboratory Warsaw 1933-39, asst dir Atomic Physics Inst Warsaw 1937-39, Oliver Lodge fell Univ of Liverpool 1939-40, lectr (later sr lectr) Univ of Liverpool 1940-49; worked on atom bomb Liverpool and Los Alamos New Mexico 1939-45; dir of nuclear physics res Univ of Liverpool 1945-49, prof Univ of London and chief physicist St Bart's Hosp 1950-76, vice dean Faculty of Sci Univ of London 1974-76, treas St Bart's Med Coll 1973-76; ed in chief Physics in Medicine and Biology 1960-72; govr: St Bart's Med Coll 1977-, St Bart's Hosp 1978-; pres: Hosp Physicists Assoc 1969-70, Br Inst of Radiology 1971-72, Youth Sci Fortnight 1972-74, Pugwash Confs on Sci and World Affrs 1988-; Hon DSc: Bradford 1973, Liverpool 1989; hon fell UMIST 1985, Dr Honoris Causa Lomonosov Univ Moscow 1988, Polish Acad of Sciences 1966, American Acad Arts and Sciences 1972, Czechoslovak Acad of Sciences 1988; Order of Merit Polish Peoples Republic 1987, Order of Cyril and Methodius (first class) Bulgaria 1988, Knight Cdr Order of Merit Federal Republic of Germany 1989; *Books* Atoms and The Universe (1956), Science and World Affairs (1962), Aspects of Medical Physics (1966), Scientists in the Quest for Peace (1972), Nuclear Reactors - To Breed or not to Breed (1977), Nuclear Radiation in Warfare (1981), Scientists, The Arms Race and Disarmament (1982), The Arms Race at a Time of Decision (1984), Nuclear Strategy and World Security (1985), Strategic Defence and the Future of the Arms Race (1987), Co-existence, Cooperation and Common Security (1988), Verification of Arms Reductions (1989), Nuclear Proliferaton: Technical and Economic Aspects (1990), Building Global Security through Cooperation (1990); *Recreations* walking, travel; *Clubs* Atheneaum; *Style—* Prof Joseph Rotblat, CBE; 8 Asmara Rd, West Hampstead, London NW2 3ST (☎ 071 435 1471); Flat A, Museum Mansions, 63A Great Russell St, London WC1B 3BJ (☎ 071 405 6661, fax 071 831 5651)

ROTH, Andrew; s of Emil Roth, (d 1963), of New York, and Bertha, *née* Rosenberg (d 1984); *b* 23 April 1919; *Educ* De Witt Clinton HS NY, Coll of City of New York (BSS), Columbia Univ (MA), Michigan Univ, Harvard Univ; *m* 1, 2 Nov 1941 (m dis 1949), Renee Louise, da of Otto Knitel (d 1962), of NY; m 2, 30 June 1949 (m dis 1984), Mathilda Anna, *née* Friederich; 1 s (Bradley Neil Adrian b 1950), 1 da (Susan Teresa (Terry) b 1953); *Career* USNR Intelligence 1941-45; sr Lt 1945; reader History Dept City Coll NY 1939-40, high school history teacher 1940-41; journalist, foreign corr, author 1945-; memb NUJ; *Books* Japan Strikes South (1941), French Interests and Policies in the Far East (1942), Dilemma in Japan (1945), The Business Background of MPs (1959-70), MP's Chart (1967-87), Enoch Powell Tory Tribune (1970), Can Parliament Decide? (1971), Heath and the Heathmen (1972), Lord on the Board (1972), The Prime Ministers Vol II (1975), Sir Harold Wilson, Yorkshire Walter Mitty (1977), Parliamentary Profiles (1984-85, 1988, 3 edn 1991); *Recreations* sketching, jazz dancing, toin chasing; *Style—* Andrew Roth, Esq; 34 Somali Rd, London NW2 3RL (☎ 071 435 6673); Trepwll, Cilreddin Bridge, Llanychaer, Pembrokeshire, Dyfed; 2 Queen Anne's Gate Buildings, Dartmouth St, London SW1H 9BP (☎ 071 222 5884, fax 071 222 5889)

ROTH, Prof Klaus Friedrich; s of Franz Roth (d 1937), and Mathilde, *née* Liebrecht; *b* 29 Oct 1925; *Educ* St Paul's, Peterhouse Cambridge (BA), UCL (MSc, PhD); *m* 29 July 1955, Melek, da of Mahmoud Khairy, Pasha (d 1954), of Sultana Melek Palace, Heliopolis, Cairo, Egypt; *Career* asst master Gordonstoun 1945-46, memb dept maths UCL 1948-66, prof Univ of London 1961-; Imperial Coll Univ of London: prof pure maths 1966-88, (prof emeritus and visiting prof 1988-); MIT: visiting lectr 1956-57, visiting prof 1965-66; Fields medal awarded at Int Congress Mathematicians 1958, hon memb American Acad Arts and Scis 1966, fell UCL 1979, hon fell Peterhouse Cambridge 1989; memb: London Math Soc 1951 (De Morgan Medal 1983), American Math Soc 1956; FRS 1960; *Books* Sequences (with H Halberstam, second edn 1983); *Recreations* chess, cinema, ballroom dancing; *Style—* Prof Klaus Roth, FRS; 24 Burnsall St, London SW3 3ST (☎ 071 352 1363); Dept of Mathematics, Imperial Coll, 180 Queen's Gate, London SW7 2BZ (☎ 071 589 5111)

ROTH, Prof Sir Martin; s of late Samuel Simon Roth, and Regina Roth; *b* 6 Nov 1917; *Educ* Univ of London, St Mary's Hosp (FRCP), MA Cantab; *m* 1945, Constance Heller; 3 da; *Career* formerly sr registrar Maida Vale and Maudsley Hosps, physician Crichton Royal Hosp Dumfries, dir of clinical res Graylingwell Hosp, conslt WHO Expert Ctee on Mental Health Problems of Ageing and the Aged 1958; prof of psychological med Univ of Newcastle upon Tyne 1956-77, emeritus prof Univ of Cambridge (prof of psychiatry 1977-85, fell Trinity Coll 1977-), visiting asst prof Dept of Psychiatry McGill Univ Montreal 1954, Mayne visiting prof Univ of Qld 1968, Albert Sterne visiting prof Univ of Indiana 1976, Andrew Woods visiting prof 1976; Adolf Meyer lectr APA 1971, Upjohn Lecture Univ of Salford 1974, Wade Fndn lectr Univ of Southampton 1975, Jacobson lectr Univ of Newcastle upon Tyne 1983, Linacre lectr St John's Coll cambridge 1984, Eastman Meml lectr Univ of Rochestter NY 1988; memb: Med Consit Ctee Nuffield Prov Hosp Tst 1962, Standing Med Advsy Ctee Central Health Servs Cncl, Standing Mental Health Advsy Ctee DHSS 1966-75, Scientific Advsy Ctee CIBA Fndn 1970-, Syndication of Cambridge Univ Press 1979-87, WHO Special Project for Res of the Aged 1988-; MRC: memb 1964-68, hon dir Gp for Study of Relationship Between Functional and Organic Mental Disorders 1962-68, Clinical Res Bd 1964-70; distinguished fell American Psychiatric Assoc 1972; hon fell: American Coll Neuropsychopharmacology, Aust and NZ Coll of Psychiatry, Canadian Psychiatric Assoc 1972, RCPSGlas; hon ScD Trinity Coll Dublin 1977 (Burlingame Prize); pres FRCPsych 1971-75 (Fndn fell, hon fell 1975); awarded many nat and int prizes; corresponding memb Deutsche Gessellschaft fur Psychiatrie and Nervenheilkunde, hon memb Societe Royale de Medicine Mentale de Belgique; MD, FRCPsych, DPM; kt 1972; *Publications* incl: British J of Psychiatry (co-ed, 1967), Psychiatric Developments (ed with Samuel Gaze 1983-), Handbook of Anxiety (ed with Graham Burrows and Russell Noyes 1988-), Clinical Psychiatry (with Mayer-Gross and Slater 1954, translated with Slater into Spanish, Italian, Portuguese, Chinese, 3 edn 1977), The Reality of Mental Illness (with Jerome Kroll, 1986), Cambridge Examination for Mental Disorders of the Elderly (1988); *Recreations* music, literature, conversation, travel; *Clubs* Athenaeum; *Style—* Prof Sir Martin Roth; Trinity Coll, Cambridge

ROTH, Stephen Jeffery; s of Moritz Roth (d 1936), and Regina, *née* Kirsch (d 1945); *b* 19 Nov 1915; *m* 27 June 1946, Eva Marta; 1 s (Peter b 19 Dec 1952); *Career* dir: Euro Section World Jewish Congress 1955-75, Inst of Jewish Affrs 1966-88; consit in int law 1989-; chm: Foreign Affrs Ctee Bd Of Deputies of Br Jews 1978-84, Zionist Fedn of GB and Ireland 1985-89; *Books* The Helsinki Final Act and Soviet Jewry (1976), The Impact of the Six Day Wars (ed, 1988); *Recreations* painting, bridge; *Clubs* Reform; *Style—* Dr Stephen Roth; 54 Elsworthy Rd, London NW3 3BU (☎ 071 722 3881)

ROTHENBERG, Helmut; OBE (1990); s of Isak Rothenberg, and Dora, *née* Moses; *b* 22 Jan 1915; *Educ* Musterschule Frankfurt; *m* 23 Aug 1945, Anna Amalia, da of Prof Walter Hannes; 3 s (David, John, Robert), 2 da (Eve, Judy); *Career* articled clerk F W Porritt (Chartered Accountant) London; fndr and sr ptnr Blick Rothenberg & Noble 1945-89; dir: James North & Sons Ltd 1961-70 (chm 1968-70), Peter Black Holdings plc 1972-87; consit Blick Rothenberg (Chartered Accountants) 1989-; govr Mencap City Fndn 1982-, memb Exec Ctee Assoc of Jewish Refugees 1984-88, vice pres Royal Soc of Mentally Handicapped Children and Adults 1991-; *Recreations* opera, theatre, family; *Clubs* Garrick; *Style—* Helmut Rothenberg, Esq, OBE; 49 Holne Chase, London N2 0QG (☎ 081 455 1515); 12 York Gate, London NW1 4QS (☎ 071 486 0111, fax 071 935 6852, telex 298982)

ROTHENBERG, Hon Mrs (Mary); *née* Sinclair; da of 2 and last Baron Pentland (d 1984) and Lucy Elizabeth, da of late Sir Henry Babington Smith; *b* 21 Nov 1942; *Educ* Mount Holyoke USA (BA); *m* 1976, Jon Anderson Rothenberg; 1 da (Laura); *Career* art director; *Style—* The Hon Mrs Rothenberg; 131 East 66 St, New York, NY 10021, USA

ROTHENBERG, Robert Michael; s of Helmut Rothenberg, OBE, and Anna Amalia, *née* Hannes; *b* 10 Aug 1950; *Educ* Highgate Sch, Univ of Exeter (BA); *m* 10 July 1981, Philippa Jane, da of Stephen Fraser White, of Gt Doddington; 1 s (Simon b 1983), 2 da (Katie b 1982, Joanna b 1987); *Career* CA 1975-; ptnr Blick Rothenberg Chartered Accountants 1979-, managing ptnr Gatton Consulting Gp Ltd 1989- (dir 1987-), lectr to professional audiences on taxation and co law 1981-; hon treas Camden CAB 1982-87; FCA, ATII; *Books* Understanding Company Accounts (1987), Mastering Business Information Technology (1989); *Recreations* travel, skiing, opera, theatre; *Clubs* Garrick, MCC; *Style—* Robert Rothenberg, Esq; 74 Hillway, Highgate, London N6 6DP (☎ 081 348 7771); Blick Rothenberg, 12 York Gate, London NW1 4QS (☎ 071 486 0111, fax 071 935 6852, telex 298982)

ROTHENSTEIN, Sir John Knewstub Maurice; CBE (1948); s of Sir William Rothenstein, and Alice Mary, *née* Knewstub; *b* 11 July 1901; *Educ* Bedales, Worcester Coll Oxford (MA), UCL (PhD); *m* Elizabeth Kennard Wittington, da of Charles Judson Smith; 1 da (Lucy Catherine Dynevor b 16 Oct 1934); *Career* dir Tate Gallery 1937-64; asst prof: art history Univ of Kentucky 1927-28, Dept of Fine Arts Univ of Pittsburgh 1928-29; dir: City Art Gallery Leeds 1932-34, City Art Galleries and Ruskin Museum Sheffield 1933-38; memb: Exec Ctee Contemporary Art Soc 1938-65, Br Cncl 1938-64, Art Panel Arts Cncl of GB 1943-56; rector Univ of St Andrews 1964-67, dir Tate Gallery 1938-64; visiting prof: Dept of Fine Arts Fordham Univ USA 1967-68, history of art Agnes Scott Coll USA 1967-68; distinquished prof City Univ of NY at Brooklyn Coll 1971 and 1972, Regents' lectr Univ of Calif at Irvine 1973, ed The Masters 1965-67; hon ed Museums Jl 1959-61; hon fell: Worcester Coll Oxford 1963, UCL 1976; memb: Architectural and Art Advsy Ctee Westminster Cathedral 1979- (memb Advsy Ctee on Decoration 1953-79), Cncl Friends of the Tate Gallery 1958-; pres: Friends of the Bradford City Art Gallery and Museums 1973-, Friends of the Stanley Spencer Gallery Cookham 1981-; KCStG 1977; Hon LLD: New Brunswick 1961, St Andrews 1964; Knight Commander Mexican Order of the Aztec Eagle 1953; kt 1952; *Books* An Introduction to English Painting (1934), Augustus John (1944), Modern English Painters: 3 vols (1952-74); *publications incl:* The Portrait Drawings of William Rothenstein 1889-1925 (1926), An Introduction to English Painting (1933), The Life and Death of Conder (1938), Turner (1949), The Tate Gallery (1958, new edn 1962), A Wood to Hockney (1973), Correspondence and Reminiscences (1979), John Nash (1984), Stanley Spencer (1989), Summer's Lease (1) (autobiog 1965); *Clubs* Athenaeum (hon memb), Chelsea Arts (hon memb); *Style—* Sir John Rothenstein, CBE; Beauforest House, Newington, Dorchester-on-Thames, Oxon OX9 8DG

ROTHENSTEIN, Michael; yr s of late Sir William Rothenstein; *b* 1908; *m* 1, 1936 (m dis 1957), Betty Desmond Fitz-Gerald; 1 s, 1 da; m 2, 1958, Diana, da of late Cdr H C Arnold-Forster, CMG; *Career* painter and printmaker; gp exhibitions incl: Ljublyana Biennale of Graphic Art Albertina Vienna, Tokyo Int Print Exhibition; solo exhibitions: The Early Years (Redfern Gallery) 1986, Prints of the '50's and '60's (Redfern Gallery) 1987, Angela Flowers Gallery 1988; retrospective exhibitions: Kunstnernes Hus Oslo 1969, Stoke-on-Trent 1989; pub collections: Museum of Modern Art, NY, Tate Gallery, Br Museum, V & A Museum; RA 1983 (ARA 1977); *Publications* Frontiers of Printmaking (1966), Relief Printing (1970), Suns and Moons (1972), Seven Colours (with Edward Lucie Smith, 1975), Song of Songs (folio, 1979); *Style—* Michael Rothenstein, Esq; Columbia House, Stisted, Braintree, Essex (☎ 0376 25444)

ROTHERA, Anthony Charles Graham; TD and Bar (1946); s of Wilfred Stewart Rothera (d 1951), and Dulcie Alice, *née* Lisser (d 1943); *b* 11 Feb 1913; *Educ* Nottingham HS, Canford; *m* 10 Sept 1947, Phyllis, da of Claude Chadburn (d 1977), of Nottinghamshire; 3 s (Ian b 1950, Michael b 1952, Shane b 1957); *Career* slr admitted 1935; HM coroner: Nottingham 1951-81, Notts 1981-83; pres: Notts C of C 1963-65, Notts Law Soc 1965, Coroners Soc of Eng and Wales 1966, Notts Medico Legal Soc 1989-90; hon coroner Nottingham 1983; chm Derbys Leics and Notts Agric Wages

Ctee; *Recreations* shooting, horticulture; *Clubs* Victory Services; *Style*— Anthony C G Rothera, Esq; Normanton Hall, Southwell, Notts NG25 0PS

ROTHERHAM, Miles Edward; s of Leonard Rotherham, CBE, of Horningsham, Wilts, and Nora Mary, *née* Thompson; *b* 23 Nov 1941; *Educ* Dulwich, Christ's Coll Cambridge (BA, MA); *m* 8 April 1972, Anne Jennifer, da of Maj Alan Holier James, TD, DL (d 1983), of Northlands, Winterton, South Humberside; 1 s (James b 1976), 1 da (Joanna b 1978); *Career* tech offr INCO 1964-68, sales mangr Int Nickel 1968-78; dir: Amari World Metals 1978-, Br Petroleum Metals Marketing 1979-89; Olympic Dam Marketing 1989-; friend of Battersea Park; Freeman City London 1978, Liveryman Worshipful Co of Goldsmith's 1981; CEng (1979), FIM (1979); *Recreations* antique collecting, boule; *Clubs* Athenaeum; *Style*— Miles Rotherham, Esq; 13 Soudan Road, London SW11 4HH

ROTHERMERE, Mary, Viscountess; Mary; da of Kenneth Murchison, of Dallas, Texas, and formerly w of Richard Ohrstrom, of The Plains, Virginia; *m* 1966, as his 3 w, 2 Viscount Rothermere (d 1978); 1 s (Hon Esmond b 18 June 1967); *Style*— The Rt Hon Mary, Viscountess Rothermere; c/o Withers, 20 Essex Street, London WC2R 3AL

ROTHERMERE, 3 Viscount (UK 1919); Sir Vere Harold Esmond Harmsworth; 3 Bt (UK 1910); also Baron Rothermere (UK 1914); patron of three livings; s of 2 Viscount Rothermere (d 1978), and his 1 w Margaret Hunam, *née* Redhead; gn of 1 and last Viscount Northcliffe (d 1922) who founded the Daily Mail 1896, and also gs of 1 Viscount Rothermere who was first Air Sec 1917 and gave the RAF its first twin engine monoplane 1935; *b* 27 Aug 1925; *Educ* Eton, Kent Sch Conn USA; *m* 1957, Patricia Evelyn Beverley, da of late John Matthews, FRCS, and former w of Capt Christopher Brooks (gs of 2 Baron Crawshaw); 1 s, 2 da, 1 step da; *Heir* s, Hon Jonathan Harmsworth b 1967; *Career* chm: Associated Newspapers plc 1970-, Daily Mail and General Tst 1978-; tstee Reuters Ltd; dir: Power Corporation (Canada), Whittle Communications (USA); pres Cwlth Press Union 1983-89; patron London Sch of Journalism; FRSA, FBIM; Cdr: Order of Merit (Italy) 1977, Order of Lion (Finland) 1978; *Recreations* reading, painting, walking; *Clubs* Royal Yacht Sqdn, Beefsteak, The Brook (NY), Boodle's, Travellers' (Paris); *Style*— The Rt Hon the Viscount Rothermere; 36 Rue du Sentier, Paris 75002, France (☎ 010 3314 508 4841); Daily Mail and General Tst plc, Northcliffe House, 2 Derry St, Kensington W8 5TT (☎ 071 938 6610, fax 071 937 0043)

ROTHERWICK, 2 Baron (UK 1939); Sir (Herbert) Robin Cayzer; 2 Bt (UK 1924); s of 1 Baron Rotherwick, JP, DL (d 1958 5 s of Sir Charles Cayzer 1 Bt, cr 1904) and Freda, da of Col William Rathborne, of Co Cavan; *b* 5 Dec 1912; *Educ* Eton, Ch Ch Oxford; *m* 1952, Sarah Jane (d 1978), da of Sir Michael Slade, 6 Bt; 3 s, 1 da; *Heir* s, Hon Herbert Cayzer; *Career* WW II Mid East 1939-45, late Maj The Greys (supp reserve); dep chm Br & Cwlth Shipping Co & Assoc Cos; *Recreations* racing, shooting; *Clubs* White's, Turf; *Style*— The Rt Hon Lord Rotherwick; Cornbury Park, Charlbury, Oxon (☎ 810311); 50 Eaton Mews North, SW1 (☎ 071 235 6314)

ROTHES, 21 Earl of (S before 1457); Ian Lionel Malcolm Leslie; also Lord Leslie and Ballenbreich; s of 20 Earl of Rothes (d 1975) and Beryl, Countess of Rothes, *qv*; 3 Earl k at Flodden 1513, 6 Earl one of first signatories of Nat Covenant 1638, 7 Earl was imprisoned during Cwlth for supporting the King but was rewarded with a Dukedom on the Restoration (regranted Earldom in default of male issue upon his eld da and her descendants male and female 1663) d 1681 when suc by his da, w of 5 Earl of Haddington, on her d in 1700 Rothes passed to her eld s and Haddington to 2 s; *b* 10 May 1932; *Educ* Eton; *m* 8 July 1955, Marigold, o da of Sir David Martyn Evans Bevan, 1 Bt; 2 s; *Heir* s, Lord Leslie; *Career* late Sub Lt RNVR; *Style*— The Rt Hon the Earl of Rothes; Tanglewood, W Tytherley, Salisbury, Wilts

ROTHMAN, Dr Martin Terry; s of Harry Rothman (d 1971), of London, and June Rothman, *née* Simmons; *b* 25 May 1948; *Educ* Streatham GS, Strand GS, Univ of Manchester (MB ChB, MRCP); *m* 13 Sept 1976, Florence, da of Albert Knox, of Warrington, Lancs; 1 s (Alexander Matthew b 31 Oct 1979), 1 da (Emma Rachel b 26 March 1981); *Career* travelling scholar of the MRC 1980-82, Fogarty int fell 1980-82; travelling fellowship: US Nat Inst of Health 1980-82, Faculty in Dept of Cardiology Stanford Univ Calif 1980-82; conslt cardiologist Royal Brompton Nat Heart and Royal London Hosps 1982-, interventional cardiologist 1982-; currently dir: Intravascular Res Ltd, Circulation Res Ltd, Heartplan Ltd and Cardiolink Ltd; author of numerous articles and chapters; co-inventor of an intravascular ultrasound device; memb: Br Cardiac Soc, Cncl of Br Cardiovascular Intervention Soc; FRCP 1991; *Recreations* sailing, walking; *Style*— Dr Martin T Rothman; 16 Pennant Mews, London W8 5JN (☎ 071 370 6841, fax 071 370 6623, telex 893589 CROHOS G, car 0860 377441)

ROTHNIE, Sir Alan Keir; KCVO (1980), CMG (1967); s of John Rothnie (d 1962), of Aberdeen, and Dora Rothnie; *b* 2 May 1920; *Educ* Montrose Acad, Univ of St Andrews; *m* 1953, Anne Cadogan, da of late Euan Cadogan Harris, 2 s, 1 da; *Career* WWII serv RN Atlantic and N Russia; joined FO 1945, 1 sec 1952; cnsllr: Baghdad 1963-64, Moscow 1965-68; consul-gen Chicago 1969-72; ambass to: Saudi Arabia 1972-76, Switzerland 1976-80; Hon LLD St Andrews 1981; *Clubs* White's, MCC, Royal and Ancient (St Andrews); *Style*— Sir Alan Rothnie, KCVO, CMG; Little Job's Cross, Rolvenden Layne, Kent TN17 4PP

ROTHSCHILD, Hon Amschel Mayor James; s of 3 Baron Rothschild, GBE, GM, FRS (d 1990), and his 2 w, Teresa Georgina, MBE, JP, *née* Mayor; *b* 18 April 1955; *Educ* Leys Sch Cambridge, City Univ London; *m* 1981, Anita Patience, 3 da of James Edward Alexander Rundel Guinness (s of Sir Arthur Guinness, KCMG, of the Irish brewing and banking family); 1 s (James Amschel Victor b 1985), 2 da (Kate Emma b 1982, Alice Miranda b 1983); *Style*— The Hon Amschel Rothschild; 11 Herschel Rd, Cambridge CB3 9AG (☎ 0223 350488)

ROTHSCHILD, Hon Emma Georgina; da of 3 Baron Rothschild, GBE, GM, FRS (d 1990), and his 2 w, Teresa Georgina, MBE, JP, *née* Mayor; *b* 16 May 1948; *Educ* Somerville Coll Oxford (MA), Massachusetts Inst of Technology; *Career* sr res fell King's Coll Cambridge 1988-; *Style*— The Hon Emma Rothschild; King's College, Cambridge CB2 1ST

ROTHSCHILD, 4 Baron (UK 1885); Sir (Nathaniel Charles) Jacob Rothschild; 5 Bt (UK 1847); also a Baron of the Austrian Empire (1822); s of 3 Baron Rothschild, GBE, GM, FRS (d 1990), and his 1 w, Barbara, o da of late St John Hutchinson, KC; *b* 29 April 1936; *Educ* Eton, Ch Ch Oxford; *m* 1961, Serena Mary, da of Sir Philip Dunn, 2 Bt, and Lady Mary St Clair-Erskine, da of 5 Earl of Rosslyn; 1 s (Hon Nathaniel Philip Victor James b 1971), 3 da (Hon Hannah Mary b 1962, Hon Beth Matilda b 1964, Hon Emily Magda b 1967); *Heir* s, Hon Nathaniel Philip Victor James Rothschild b 1971; *Career* chm J Rothschild Hldgs plc; chm bd of Tstees Nat Gallery; *Clubs* White's; *Style*— The Rt Hon the Lord Rothschild; Stowell Park, Marlborough, Wilts; 14 St James's Place, London SW1A 1NP

ROTHSCHILD, Leopold David de; CBE (1985); 2 s of Maj Lionel de Rothschild, OBE (*see* Edmund de Rothschild); *b* 12 May 1927; *Educ* Harrow, Trinity Coll Cambridge; *Career* dir: Sun Alliance & London Insurance 1982-, N M Rothschild & Sons 1970-, Bank of England 1970-83; chm: English Chamber Orchestra and Music Soc Ltd, Bach Choir, Music Advsy Ctee Br Cncl 1986-; tstee: Glyndebourne Arts Tst, Nat Museum of Sci and Indust 1987-; memb Cncl Winston Churchill Meml Tst; FRCM; *Style*— Leopold de Rothschild Esq, CBE; New Court, St Swithin's Lane, London EC4P 4DU (☎ 071 280 5000, telex 888031)

ROTHSCHILD, Hon Miranda; da of 3 Baron Rothschild, GBE, GM, FRS (d 1990), and his 1 w, Barbara, *née* Hutchinson; *b* 25 Dec 1940; *Style*— The Hon Miranda Rothschild

ROTHSCHILD, Oliver; s of Herbert Rothschild (d 1975), and Mira, *née* Woznianski-Kliensmidt; *b* 24 April 1951; *Educ* Highgate Sch, Univ of Surrey (BSc); *m* May 1989, Marcelle, da of Chavelier Antony Casingena, of 38 Rousden St, London; *Career* former chm Grosvenor Travel Ltd; dir and vice pres: Bevington Lowndes Ltd, American Gen Investmt Corp; chm Duke Corp Ltd; former memb The Bow Gp, nat ctee memb of appeals Red Cross, life memb Nat Tst; MECI, HIMCA; *Recreations* bon vivant and gastronome, former participant of the Dangerous Sports Club, ie The Cresta Run, skiing, tennis, and when time permits benefactor of the arts; *Style*— Oliver Rothschild, Esq; 19 Princess Rd, Regents Park, London NW1 (fax 071 586 9388)

ROTHSCHILD, Hon Sarah; da of 3 Baron Rothschild, GBE, GM, FRS (d 1990), and his 1 w, Barbara, *née* Hutchinson; *b* 13 Sept 1934; *Educ* St Hilda's Oxford; *Style*— The Hon Sarah Rothschild

ROTHSCHILD, Teresa, Baroness; Teresa Georgina; JP; 2 da of Robert John Grote Mayor, CB (d 1947), and (Katharine) Beatrice, *née* Meinertzhagen; *Educ* Univ of Cambridge (MA); *m* 14 Aug 1946, as his 2 w, 3 Baron Rothschild, GBE, GM, FRS (d 1990); 1 s (Hon Amschel Mayor James, *qv*) (and 1 s decd), 2 da (Hon Emma Georgina b 1948, Hon Victoria Katherine b 1953); *Style*— The Rt Hon Teresa, Lady Rothschild, MBE, JP

ROTHSCHILD, Hon Victoria Katherine; da of 3 Baron Rothschild, GBE, GM, FRS (d 1990), and his 2 w, Teresa Georgina, MBE, JP, *née* Mayor; *b* 13 Aug 1953; *Educ* Bedford Coll London; *Style*— The Hon Victoria Rothschild

ROTHWELL, Margaret Irene; da of Prof Harry Rothwell (d 1980), and Martha Annabella, *née* Goedecke (d 1988); *b* 25 Aug 1938; *Educ* Southampton GS for Girls, Lady Margaret Hall Oxford (BA); *Career* FO: joined 1961, second sec UK Delgn to Cncl of Europe Strasbourg 1964-66, second (private) sec to UK Special Representative in Africa Nairobi 1966-68, first sec Washington 1968-72; FCO 1972-76, first sec and head of Chancery Helsinki 1976-79; FCO 1980-82, cncllr and head of Training Dept FCO 1982-84, cncllr and head of Chancery Jakarta 1984-87, cncllr Overseas Inspectorate FCO 1987-90; HM Ambass Abidjan 1990- (also accredited in Niger and Burkina Faso); *Style*— Miss Margaret I Rothwell; Foreign & Commonwealth Office, King Charles St, London SW1

ROUBANIS, Lady Sarah Consuelo; *née* Spencer-Churchill; da of 10 Duke of Marlborough (d 1972); *b* 1921; *m* 1, 1943 (m dis 1966), Lt Edwin F Russell, USA Navy; 4 da; m 2, 1966 (m dis 1967), Guy Burgos, of Santiago, Chile; m 3, 1967, Theodorous Roubanis; *Style*— The Lady Sarah Roubanis; 9454 Lloyd Crest Drive, Beverley Hills, Los Angeles, Calif 90210, USA

ROUECHÉ, Mossman (Jr); s of Col Mossman Roueché, of Sarasota, Florida, USA, and Elizabeth Molin, *née* Meier; *b* 14 Dec 1947; *Educ* Montgomery Blair HS Maryland USA, Kenyon Coll Ohio USA (BA), State Univ of NY at Buffalo (MA); *m* 29 July 1972, Charlotte Mary, da of Charles Percy Tunnard Wrinch, of Guernsey, CI; 1 s (Thomas b 1986), 1 da (Alice b 1979); *Career* trainee Standard Chartered Bank plc 1973-75, Samuel Montagu & Co Ltd 1975 (dir 1986-); memb PCC St Magnus the Martyr Church; *Recreations* archaeology; *Style*— Mossman Roueché, Esq; 19 Bartholomew Villas, London NW5 2LJ; Box Cottage, Fisher's Lane, Charlbury, Oxon; 10 Lower Thames St, London EC2 (☎ 071 260 9170)

ROUGIER, Maj-Gen (Charles) Jeremy; CB (1986); s of Lt Col C L Rougier, MC (d 1940), and Marjorie Alice, *née* Tanner (d 1981); *b* 23 Feb 1933; *Educ* Marlborough, Pembroke Coll Cambridge (MA); *m* 5 Dec 1964, Judith Cawood, da of Alan Wheen Ellis (d 1945); 3 s (Johnathan b 1966, Toby b 1967, Fergus b 1970); 1 da (Beth b 1971); *Career* Aden 1960, instr RMA Sandhurst 1961-62; psc 1963, MA to MGO 1964-66, Cdr 11 Engr Sqdn Cwlth Bde 1966-68, jssc 1968, Co Cdr RMA Sandhurst 1969-70, DSD Staff Coll Camberley 1970-72, CO 21 Engr Regt BAOR 1972-74, staff of CDS 1974-77, Cmd Royal Sch of Mil 1977-79, RCDS 1980, COS HQ N I 1981, ACGS (Trg) 1982-83, dir of Army Trg 1983-84, chm Review of Offr Trg and Educn Study 1985, Engr in Chief (Army) 1985-88, ret; dir RHS Garden Rosemoor 1988-; FICE (1986); *Recreations* squash, hill walking, DIY, gardening; *Clubs* Army and Navy; *Style*— Maj-Gen Jeremy Rougier, CB; RHS Garden Rosemoor, Great Torrington, Devon EX38 8PH

ROUGIER, Sir Richard George; s of G R Rougier, CBE, QC (d 1977), and Georgette, *née* Heyer (d 1974); *b* 12 Feb 1932; *Educ* Marlborough, Pembroke Coll Cambridge (BA); *m* 2 June 1962, Susanna Allen, da of Harvey Allen Whitworth, MC (d 1959); 1 s (Nicholas Julian b 23 Feb 1966); *Career* QC 1972, rec 1973, high Ct Judge 1986; kt 1986; *Recreations* fishing, bridge, golf; *Clubs* Garrick, Rye GC; *Style*— Sir Richard Rougier, KB; Royal Courts of Justice, Strand, London WC2

ROUMANIA, HRH The Princess Helen of; 2 da of HM King Michael of Roumania, GCVO, and HM Queen Anne of Roumania, *née* HRH Princess Anne of Bourbon-Parma; *b* 15 Nov 1950; *Educ* in Switzerland and England; *m* 24 Sept 1983, Dr (Leslie) Robin Medforth-Mills, *qv*; 1 s (Nicholas Michael de Roumanie Medforth-Mills b 1 April 1985), 1 da (Elisabetta Karina de Roumanie Medforth-Mills b 4 Jan 1989); *Style*— HRH The Princess Helen of Roumania, Mrs Robin Medforth-Mills; Flass Hall, Esh Winning, Durham DH7 9QD

ROUND, Ivan Frederick; s of Jame Round (d 1966), of 26 Newtown Lane, Cradley Heath, Warley, W Midlands, and Alice Beatrice, *née* Hickman (d 1960); *b* 9 Dec 1931; *Educ* King Edward VI GS Stourbridge; *m* 10 May 1951, Margaret (d 1974), da of Ernest David Willetts, of Rowley Regis Watley, W Midlands; 2 s (Gary b 5 Oct 1963, Nigel b 12 May 1967); *Career* chm: J Round & Sons (H/F) Ltd 1960-, Sades of Brown Ltd 1984-; hon memb Rotoract Club Halesowen; *Recreations* yachting, racket ball, badminton, tennis; *Clubs* The Carton Halesowen; *Style*— Ivan Round, Esq; 41 Bromsgrove Rd, Romsley, Halesowen, Worcs B62 0LE (☎ 0562 710 779); La Luna, 130 St Anthoney St, Bugibba, St Pauls Bay, Malta; 7/10 High St, Cradley Heath, Warley, W Midlands (☎ 0384 66301)

ROUND, Prof Nicholas Grenville; s of Isaac Eric Round, and Laura Christabel, *née* Poole; *b* 6 June 1938; *Educ* Launceston Coll Cornwall, Pembroke Coll Oxford (BA, MA, DPhil); *m* 2 April 1966, Ann, da of Louis Le Vin; 1 da (Grainne Ann b 1968); *Career* Queen's Univ Belfast: lectr in Spanish 1962-71, warden Alanbrooke Hall 1970-72, reader in Spanish 1971-72; Stevenson prof of hispanic studies Univ of Glasgow 1972-; exec memb: Clydebank/Milngavie Constituency Lab Pty (former vice chm), Strathclyde West Euro - Constituency Lab Pty, Strathclyde Regnl Lab Pty; memb: ALL, MHRA, SSMLL, AHGPI, AIH; *Books* Unamuno: Abel Sánchez (1974), The Greatest Man Uncrowned: A Study of the Fall of Don Alvaro de Luna (1986), Tirso de Molina: Damned for Despair (1986); *Recreations* music, reading, drawing, hill walking, politics, all aspects of Cornwall; *Clubs* Queen's Univ Belfast Student's Union (hon life memb); *Style*— Prof Nicholas Round; 11 Dougalston Ave, Milngavie, Glasgow G62 (☎ 041 956 2507); Dept of Hispanic Studies, Univ of Glasgow, Glasgow G12 8QL (☎ 041 339 8855, ext 8665)

ROUNDELL, James; s of Charles Wilbraham Roundell, and Ann, *née* Moore; *b* 23 Oct

1951; *Educ* Winchester, Magdalene Coll Cambridge (BA, Cricket blue); *m* 3 May 1975, Alexandra Jane, da of Sir Cyril Stanley Pickard; 1 s (Thomas b 1979), 1 da (Rebecca b 1982); *Career* Chrisites Fine Art Auctioneers 1973-: i/c of 18th and 19th Century English drawings and watercolours 1974-76, dir Old Master & Modern Prints 1976-86, dir Impressionist and Modern Pictures 1986- (during which time handled the sale of two of the three most expensive pictures ever sold); Liveryman Worshipful Co of Grocers 1981 (Freeman 1972); *Books* Thomas Shotter Boys (1975); *Recreations* cricket, opera; *Clubs* Hurlingham, MCC, Zingari various cricket clubs; *Style—* James Roundell, Esq; Christie's, 8 King St, St James's, London SW1 (☎ 071 839 9060)

ROUNTHWAITE, Francis Anthony; s of George William Rounthwaite (d 1963), and Eileen May, *née* Jones; *b* 3 Jan 1941; *Educ* Newcastle upon Tyne Royal GS, Univ of Durham (BA); *m* 19 March 1966, Shirley Mabel, da of Harold William Perkins, of Lanchester, Tyne & Wear; 1 s (Graham b 1969), 1 da (Julia); *Career* accountant Deloitte Haskins and Sells 1963-66, gen mangr for fin planning Euro operations Massey Ferguson (UK) 1967-70, memb Nat Mgmnt Bd Robson Rhodes (apptd mangng ptnr West Midlands 1987) 1970-; capt Berkswell Tennis Club; FCA 1966; *Recreations* tennis, skiing, gardening; *Clubs* Balsall Common Lions; *Style—* Francis Rounthwaite, Esq; 62 Kelsey Lane, Balsall Common, Coventry CV7 7GL (☎ 0676 32451); Robson Rhodes, Centre City Tower, 7 Hill St, Birmingham B5 4UU (☎ 021 643 5494, fax 021 643 7738, car 0860 373 043)

ROUNTREE, His Hon Judge Peter Charles Robert; s of Francis Robert George Rountree, MBE (d 1986), of Sark, C I, and Mary Felicity Patricia Rountree, MBE (d 1983); *b* 28 April 1936; *Educ* Uppingham, St John's Coll Cambridge (MA); *m* 20 Dec 1968, Nicola Mary, da of Nicholas Norman Norman-Butler, TD, DL (d 1971), of Leez Priory, Hartford End, Essex; 1 s (James Alexander Francis b 7 Dec 1975); *Career* called to the Bar 1961, recorder 1986; Circuit judge 1986-; Inner Temple; *Recreations* sailing, golf, tennis; *Clubs* RYS, Bar Yacht (Cdre), New Zealand Golf, Rye Coy, RAC; *Style—* His Hon Judge Peter Rountree

ROUS, Hon John; s of 5 Earl of Stradbroke (d 1983), and his 2 wife, Hon Mrs Keith Rous, *qv*; *b* 31 July 1950; *Educ* Gordonstoun, Univ of Kent at Canterbury; *m* 12 Nov 1984, Zeenat, da of Dr A Hameed (d 1976), of Lucknow; 2 da (Maha Magdalene b 1987, Zoya Constance b 1990); *Style—* The Hon John Rous; Clovelly Court, Bideford, Devon; 83 Flood St, London SW3

ROUS, Hon Mrs Keith; (April) Mary; does not use style of Mary, Countess of Stradbroke; da of Brig-Gen the Hon Arthur Melland Asquith, DSO (d 1939; s of 1 Earl of Oxford and Asquith, KG, PC), and Betty Constance (d 1962, da of Lord Manners); *b* 14 April 1919; *Educ* at home and in Paris, Vienna, Florence, St Thomas's Hosp (nursing trg); *m* 1943, as his 2 w, Hon (William) Keith Rous, 5 Earl of Stradbroke (d 1983, 4 days after succeeding his brother, 4 Earl); 1 s, 3 da (and 1 da decd); *Recreations* reading, gardening, cooking for guests; *Style—* The Hon Mrs Keith Rous; Clovelly Court, Bideford, N Devon (☎ 0237 73)

ROUS, Hon Peter James Mowbray; s of late 3 Earl of Stradbroke, KCMG, CB, CVO, CBE and Dame Helena, DBE, da of late Lt-Gen James Fraser, CMG; *b* 1914; *Educ* Harrow, Melbourne GS, Sandhurst; *m* 1942, Elizabeth Alice Mary (d 1968), da of late Maj the Hon Alastair Thomas Joseph Fraser, DSO, (s of 13 Lord Lovat), and Lady Sibyl, *née* Grimston, da of 3 Earl of Verulam; 6 s (and 2 s decd), 4 da; *Career* Maj (ret) 16/5 Lancers; *Style—* The Hon Peter Rous; c/o Drummond's Bank, 49 Charing Cross Rd, London SW1

ROUS, Lady Sophia Rayner; 2 da of 6 Earl of Stradbroke, *qv*, and his 1 w, Dawn Antoinette, *née* Beverley; *b* 27 Sept 1964; *Educ* New England Girls' Sch Armidale, Duval HS Armidale, Sydney Technical Coll Ultimo, Gymea Technical Coll Gymea; 1 da (Olivia Briarn Rous b 18 Aug 1990); *Style—* The Lady Sophia Rous; c/o Utilux Pty Ltd, Commercial Rd, Kingsgrove, NSW, Australia

ROUS, Maj-Gen Hon William Edward; OBE (mil 1980, MBE mil 1974); s of 5 Earl of Stradbroke (d 1983), by 1 w, Pamela Catherine Mabell (d 1972), da of Capt the Hon E J Kay-Shuttleworth; bro of 6 Earl of Stradbroke, *qv*; *b* 22 Feb 1939; *Educ* Harrow, RMA Sandhurst; *m* 1970, Judith Rosemary, da of Maj Jocelyn Arthur Persse, Rifle Bde (ka 1943); 2 s (James b 1972, Richard b 1975); *Career* cmmnd Coldstream Gds 1959, cmd 2 Bn 1979-81, Brig cmdg 1 Inf Bde 1983-84; dir PR (Army) 1985-87; GOC 4 Armd Div 1987-89; cmdt Staff Coll 1989-; *Style—* Maj-Gen the Hon William Rous, OBE; RHQ Goldstream Guards, Wellington Barracks, London SW1

ROUSE, Sir Anthony Gerald Roderick; KCMG (1969, CMG 1961), OBE (1945); s of Lt-Col Maxwell Emsley Rouse, JP, of Eastbourne, Sussex (d 1956), and Sybil Rose, *née* Thompson; *b* 1911; *Educ* Harrow; *m* 7 Sept 1935, Beatrice, da of Percival Ellis of Eastbourne (d 1962); *Career* HAC 1935, RA (TA) 1938, 2 Lt 1940 transferred Intelligence Corps served MEF and CMF on staff 3 Corps (commendation); Foreign Serv 1946, first sec (info) Athens 1946, transferred FO 1949, Br Embassy Moscow 1952-54, cnsllr 1955, off of UK high cmmr Canberra 1955-57, HM inspr Foreign Serv Estabs 1957-59, cnsllr (info) Br Embassy Bonn 1959-62, Br dep cmdt Berlin 1962-64, min Br Embassy Rome 1964-66, consul-gen NY 1966-71; *Style—* Sir Anthony Rouse, KCMG, OBE; St Ritas, Paradise Drive, Eastbourne, E Sussex

ROUSE, Lt Cdr (Derrick) Malcolm; MBE (1974); s of Claude Vernon Rouse, of Devon (d 1989), and Beatrice Ada Saxby, *née* Wellacott (d 1984); *b* 14 Feb 1922; *Educ* UC Sch; *m* 30 July 1952, Eileen Patricia, da of Maj Arthur Douglas Ingrams (d 1988) 2 s (Justin b 1958, Benedict b 1965); 4 da (Corinne b 1953, Deborah b 1955, Arabella b 1956, Josephine b 1960); *Career* with Br Aeroplane Co 1939-42; RN 1942-77, Fleet Air Arm, Flag Lt and personal pilot to Flag Offr Naval Air Cmd 1963-66, Flag Lt to Dep Supreme Allied Cdr Atlantic 1966-69, CO 781 Sqdn 1970-76, dep dir Fleet Air Arm Museum 1976-77, ret; staff mangr Saccone and Speed Ltd Wine Merchants 1977-82, with David Burns Wine Merchants IOW 1982-85, ptnr in own wine and delicatessen business 1985-; *Recreations* golf, fishing, sailing, theatre, photography; *Style—* Lt-Cdr Malcolm Rouse, MBE; The Dell, Bonchurch, IOW PO38 1NT (☎ 0983 852266); Benedict's, 28 Holyrood St, Newport, IOW PO30 5AU (☎ 0983 529596, fax 0983 822116)

ROUSE, Lt Cdr Peter James; s of Capt Norman S Rouse (d 1956), of Wilts, and Nancy A Campbell, *née* Johnston (d 1980); *b* 12 July 1922; *Educ* RNC Dartmouth; *m* 8 Sept 1951, Elizabeth Jeannette Stringer, da of P A S Stringer (d 1985), of Wilts; 1 s (Richard b 1956), 2 da (Nichola b 1953 (decd), Phillipa b 1954); *Career* ret RN 1954; Lloyd's underwriter 1951-; *Recreations* sailing, general country recreations; *Clubs* Royal Lymington Yacht; *Style—* Lt Cdr Peter J Rouse; Tarrant House, Tiptoe, Lymington, Hants (☎ 0590 682213)

ROUSE, Richard Meadows; s of Philip Graves Rouse, and Maud, *née* Ellis; *b* 20 July 1931; *Educ* Uppingham, Christ's Coll Cambridge (BA); *m* 29 May 1965, Susan, da of Sidney Thomas Croker, of 48 Brim Hill, London; 2 s (William b 26 July 1966, James b 21 May 1969); *Career* 2 Lt Army 1950-51; int tax ptnr Arthur Young 1966- (joined 1963); churchwarden St Peters Church St Albans; FCA 1958; *Books* UK Taxation of Offshore Oil and Gas (1980); *Recreations* sailing, stampcollecting; *Clubs* Reform; *Style—* Richard Rouse, Esq; Arthur Young, 7 Rolls Buildings, Fetter Lane, London EC4A 1NH (☎ 071 831 7130, fax 071 405 2147, telex 888604)

ROUSE-BOUGHTON, Lady; Elizabeth; *née* Hunter; da of late Ernest William Hathaway Hunter; *m* 1, 1933, Geoffrey Swaffer (d 1939); m 2, 1948, as his 2 wife, Maj Sir Edward Hotham Rouse-Boughton, 13 and last Bt (d 1963); *Style—* Lady Rouse-Boughton; Dickens Cottage, Seagrove Bay, Seaview, IOW

ROUSSEL, (Philip) Lyon; OBE (1974); s of Paul Marie Roussel (d 1958), and Lady Murray (Beatrice), *née* Cuthbert (d 1983); *b* 17 Oct 1923; *Educ* Hurstpierpoint Coll, St Edmund Hall Oxford (MA), Chelsea Sch of Art; *m* 18 July 1959, Elisabeth Mary, da of Kenneth Arnold Bennett (d 1988); 1 s (Edward b 1965), 1 da (Tanya b 1963); *Career* Nat Serv WWII Maj Indian Parachute Regt 1942-46, demob with hon rank of Maj; Parachute Regt TA 1946-50; Sudan political serv Kassala Upper Nile 1950-55, princ WO 1955-56, Assoc Newspapers 1956-57, Br Cncl 1960-83, India 1960-71 (regnl rep Western and Central India 1964-71), rep and cultural attaché Br Embassy Belgium and Luxembourg 1971-76, "Europalia" GB Festival Ctee 1973, cultural cnsllr and head Cultural Dept Br Embassy Washington 1976-79, controller arts div Br Cncl 1979-83, memb Festival of India Ctee 1981-88, memb Advsy Ctee Br Salutes NY 1981-83, sponsorship conslt Nat Theatre 1983-84, freelance artist 1984; memb: Br Legion Woodstock, Common Room Wolfson Coll Oxford (memb Arts Ctee); FRSA 1979, FRGS 1981; *Recreations* looking at and collecting pictures, travel, tennis; *Clubs* Athenaeum, Probus; *Style—* Lyon Roussel, Esq, OBE; 26 High St, Woodstock, Oxford OX7 1TG (☎ 0993 811 298); La Grange, Lacam, Loubressac, 46130, France

ROUSSOUNIS, Dr Socrates Hercules; s of Hecules Rossounis, and Mary, *née* Evagoras; *b* 30 Aug 1937; *Educ* Hawardian GS Cardiff, St Georges Hosp Univ of London (MB BS, DCH, DobstRCOG); *m* 22 Nov 1968, Loucia, da of Stephan Stephanou (d 1987); 3 s (Alexander b 24 Feb 1972, Eracles b 2 Sept 1975, Stephen b 1 Oct 1979); *Career* res fell in clinical neurophysicology Hosp for Sick Children Gt Ormond Street 1972-73, sr registrar in paediatrics and developmental medicine Charing Cross Hosp 1973-77, conslt paediatrician St James's Univ Hosp 1977, hon sr lectr in clinical paediatrics Univ of Leeds 1987, medico-legal claims assessor, conslt i/c Regnl Child Devpt Centre St James's Univ Hosp Leeds; FRCP 1989; *PS* author of various papers on aspects of paediatric neurology; *Recreations* photography; *Style—* Dr Socrates Roussounis; 1 Nichols Way, Wetherby, W Yorkshire L522 4AD (☎ 0937 64178); St James's University Hospital, Leeds (☎ 0532 433144)

ROUT, Owen Howard; s of Frederick Owen Rout (d 1983), and Marion, *née* Salter (d 1972); *b* 16 April 1930; *Educ* Grey HS Port Elizabeth SA; *m* 27 Feb 1954, Jean, da of Alfred Greetham (d 1961); 2 da (Gillian (Mrs Catchpole) b 16 June 1959, Jacqueline (Mrs Brabazon) b 26 Nov 1962); *Career* Barclays Bank: local dir York 1969-71, Chelmsford 1972-75, regnl gen mangr E Mids & E Anglia 1975-77, sr local dir Leeds Dist 1977-81, chm W Yorks Local Bd 1977-81, dir Barclays Bank UK Ltd 1977-87, gen mangr Barclays Bank plc and Barclays plc 1982-87 (exec dir UK ops 1987-90); chm: Barclays Insurance Services Co Ltd and Barclays Insurance Brokers International Ltd 1982-85, Barclays Financial Services Ltd 1988-90 (non-exec) Mercantile Gp plc 1989-; dir: Baric Ltd 1982-84, Spreadeagle Insurance Co Ltd 1983-85; memb Cncl Chartered Inst of Bankers 1985-90 (treas 1986-90), memb Supervisory Bd Banking World Magazine 1986-90, dir Bankers Books Ltd 1986-90; ACIS, FCIB; *Recreations* watching sport, playing golf, listening to music, gardening; *Clubs* Headingley Taverners (Leeds), Pannal Golf (Harrogate), Saffron Walden Golf; *Style—* Owen Rout, Esq; Pootings, Seven Devils Lane, Saffron Walden, Essex CB11 4BB

ROUTLEDGE, (Katherine) Patricia; da of Isaac Edgar Routledge (d 1985), of Birkenhead, Cheshire, and Catherine, *née* Perry (d 1957); *b* 17 Feb 1929; *Educ* Birkenhead HS, Univ of Liverpool (BA); *Career* actress and singer; trained Bristol Old Vic and with Walther Gruner Guildhall Sch of Music, first professional appearance as Hippolyta in A Midsummer Night's Dream (Liverpool Playhouse) 1952, first West End appearance in Sheridan's The Duenna (Westminster Theatre) 1954, first Broadway appearance in How's the World Treating You? (Music Box NY) 1966 (Whitbread Award), Darling of the Day (Broadway) 1968 (Antionette Perry Award), Love Match (Ahmanson Theatre Los Angeles) 1968-69, Cowardy Custard (Mermaid Theatre) 1972-73, Noises Off (Savoy Theatre) 1981, Queen Margaret in Richard III (RSC) 1984-85 (Laurence Olivier Award Nomination), The Old Lady in Candide (Old Vic) 1988-89 (Laurence Olivier Award), Come for the Ride (solo show) 1988; recent TV appearances incl: Sophia and Constance, A Woman of No Importance 1982 (Broadcasting Press Guild Critics Award), A Lady of Letters 1988 (BAFTA Nomination), First and Last Missing Persons; *Style—* Miss Patricia Routledge; Marmont Management Ltd, Langham House, 308 Regent St, London W1R 5AL (☎ 071 637 3183)

ROUTLEDGE, Paul; s of John James Routledge, of Surrey, and Barbara, *née* Saxton; *b* 23 Sept 1950; *Educ* E Grinstead GS; *m* 15 Aug 1979, Susan Jean, da of John Arthur Ashley, of Surrey; 1 s (James b 12 July 1988), 1 da (Gemma b 1982); *Career* CA 1975-; est own practice 1979; *Recreations* golf, boating; *Style—* Paul Routledge, Esq; The Owls, Cudworth Lane, Newdigate, Surrey; Abacus House, Wickhurst Lane Broadbridge Heath RH12 3LY (☎ 0403 210165, fax 0403 65886, car phone 0860 330612)

ROUTLY, (Ernest) John; s of Dr Ernest Sydney Routly (d 1931); *b* 4 Sept 1914; *Educ* Radley, Gonville and Caius Coll Cambridge; *m* 1939, Alice Janet Routly, JP, *née* Bailey; 2 da; *Career* RAFVR; slr; dir various cos incl: Rootes Gp, William Baird, Andrews Gp Hldgs; fin advsr Help the Aged and Action Aid; memb Bucks CC 1965-80 (vice chm 1977-79), High Sheriff of Bucks 1972-73; chm Festiniog Rly Co 1954-, dir Romney Hythe and Dimchurch Rly 1986-; tstee AIDS Caring Education and Training (ACET); *Recreations* railways; *Clubs* E India, RAF; *Style—* John Routly, Esq; Ormonde House, 18 St John's Hill, Shrewsbury SY1 1JJ (☎ 0743 231489)

ROUX, Michel André; s of Henri Roux (d 1983), and Germaine, *née* Triger; *b* 19 April 1941; *Educ* Ecole Primaire Saint St Mandé France, Brevet de Maitrise Patisserie; *m* 1 (m dis 1979), Françoise Marcelle, *née* Becquet; 1 s (Alain b 1968), 2 da (Christine b 1963, Francine b 1965); m 2, 21 May 1984, Robyn Margaret, *née* Joyce; *Career* French Mil Serv 1960-62; Versailles 1960, Colomb Bechar Algeria 1961-62, awarded the Medaille Commemorative des Operations de securité et de Maintien de L'Ordre en AFC avec Agiape Sahara BOPP no 42; commis patissier and cuisinier at Br Embassy Paris 1955-57, commis cook to Mlle Cecile de Rothschild Paris 1957-59 (chef 1962-67); restaurants opened in England: Le Gavroche 1967, Le Poulbot 1969, The Waterside Inn 1972, Gavvers 1981, Le Gavroche (moved to Mayfair) 1981, Roux Britannia 1986; awards: Silver medal des Cuisiniers Francais (Paris) 1963, Silver medal Ville de Paris 1966, Silver medal Sucre Tire et Souffle (London)1970, Prix International Taittinger (2nd, Paris) 1971, Gold medal Cuisiniers Francais (Paris) 1972, Meilleur Ouvrier de France en Patisserie (Paris) 1976, Vermeil medal du Prestige des Cuisiniers Francais (Paris) 1983, Laureat Best Menu of the Year prepared for a Private Function (Caterer and Hotel Keeper) 1984, Laureate Restaurateur of the Year (Caterer and Hotel Keeper) 1985, Laureat du Premier Hommage Veuve Cliquot aux Ambassadeurs de la Cuisine Francaise dans le Monde (Paris) 1985, Laureat Personality of the Year Gastronomie dans le Monde (Paris) 1985, Laureat Culinary Trophy Personality of the Year in Patisserie (Assoc of French Patissiers de la Saint-Michel) 1986, Chevalier de l'Ordre National du Merite 1987, Officier du Merite Agricole 1987, The Man of the Year award (RADAR) 1989, Chevalier de l'Ordre des Arts et des Lettres 1990 ; memb: l'Acamedie Culinaire de France (UK branch), Assoc Relais et Desserts, Assoc Relais et Chateaux; *Books* New Classic Cuisine (1983), Roux

Brothers on Patisserie (1986), At Home with the Roux Brothers (1987), French Traditional Country Cooking (1989), Cooking for Two (1991); *Recreations* shooting, walking, skiing; *Clubs* The Benedicts; *Style—* Michel Roux, Esq; The Waterside Inn, Ferry Rd, Bray, Berkshire SL6 2AT (☎ 0628 771966/20691, fax 0628 784710)

ROWALLAN, 3 Baron (UK 1911); Arthur Cameron Corbett; s of 2 Baron Rowallan, KT, KBE, MC, TD, DL (d 1977), and Gwyn, da of Joseph and sis of Rt Hon Lord Grimond, PC, *qv*; *b* 17 Dec 1919; *Educ* Eton, Balliol Coll Oxford; *m* 1, 1945 (m dis 1962), Eleanor, da of George Boyle (descent from David Boyle, Lord Justice Gen of Scotland, *see* Peerage, Earl of Glasgow, by Mary, 2 da of Sir Peter Mackie, 1 and last Bt; 1 s (Maj-Gen Hon William, OBE, *qv*), 3 da (Lady Christine Armstrong b 1946, Lady Henrietta b 1947, Lady Virginia Gibbs b 1954); m 2, 1963 (m annulled 1970), April Ashley; *Heir* s, Hon John Corbett; *Career* serv WWII, Capt Ayrshire Yeo; *Style—* The Rt Hon the Lord Rowallan; 22 Mediteranee, Torre de Marbella, Marbella, Spain

ROWAN, Alistair John; s of Francis Peter Rowan (d 1957), and Margaret Gemmell, *née* Scoular (d 1957); *b* 3 June 1938; *Educ* Campbell Coll Belfast, The Edinburgh Coll of Art (Dip Arch, Swimming blue), Magdalene Coll Cambridge (PhD), Univ of Padua; *m* 1968, Ann Martha, da of Charles Percy Tunnard Wrinch; 1 da (Harriet Grace b 1975); *Career* corr Country Life 1967-77 (architectural ed 1966-67), lectr in fine art Univ of Edinburgh 1967-77, prof of history of art Univ Coll Dublin 1977-90, Slade prof of fine art Univ of Oxford 1988, princ Edinburgh Coll of Art 1990-; major works incl: Mr David Bryce (Edinburgh Univ Exhibition) 1976, The Buildings of Ireland: North West Ulster 1979, Designs for Castles and Country Villas by Robert and James Adam 1985, catalogue of Robert Adam Drawings (V & A) 1988; *Awards* Silver medal RSA 1972, Cavaliere del Ordine al Merito 1983; chm: The Irish Architectural Archive 1982-87, Heritage Advsy Ctee Dept of the Taoiseach Dublin 1987; memb Historic Buildings Cncl for Scotland 1986-; *Recreations* gardening and broadcasting; *Style—* Alistair Rowan; The Edinburgh College of Art, Lauriston Place, Edinburgh EH3 9DF (☎ 031 229 9311, fax 031 229 0089)

ROWAN, Jack; s of Harry Rowan (d 1955), of Abbeydale Road, Sheffield, and Mary, *née* Allen (d 1952); *b* 10 Feb 1927; *Educ* Greystones Intermediate Sch, Sheffield Commercial Coll; *m* 10 Oct 1959, (Constance) Shirley, da of William Barraclough (d 1980), of Bradford; 1 s (Steven b 12 March 1962), 1 da (Lisa b 25 Oct 1965); *Career* RNAS 1946-48; CA, sr ptnr Barber Harrison & Platt (ptnr 1955), dir Sheffield Refreshment Houses Ltd 1975-82; memb Accreditation Bd Sheffield & Dist Soc of CAs, formerly area sec Round Tables of GB and Ireland, FCA 1950; *Recreations* golf, assisting daughter's equestrian activities; *Clubs* Sheffield, Abbeydale Golf; *Style—* Jack Rowan, Esq; 53 Heather Lea Ave, Dore, Sheffield (☎ 0742 366 050); Barber Harrison and Platt, 2 Rutland Park, Sheffield S10 2PD (☎ 0742 667 171, fax 0742 669 846)

ROWAN, Patricia Adrienne; da of Henry Matthew Talintyre (d 1962), and Gladys, *née* Gould; *Educ* Harrow County GS for Girls; *m* 1 April 1960, Ivan Settle Harris Rowan; 1 s (Matthew Settle Nicholas b 1960); *Career* journalist; Time and Tide 1952-56, Sunday Express 1956-57, Daily Sketch 1957-58, News Chronicle 1958-60, Granada TV 1961-62, Sunday Times 1962-66, ed Times Educational Supplement 1989- (staff reporter 1972-89); Hon FRSA 1989; *Books* What Sort of Life? (1980), Education - The Wasted Years? (contrib, 1988); *Recreations* gardening, cooking, reading; *Clubs* Reform; *Style—* Mrs Patricia Rowan; Times Supplements Ltd, Priory House, St John's Lane, London EC1M 4BX (☎ 071 253 300, fax 071 608 1599)

ROWAN, Robert; s of Joseph Rowan (d 1978), of Southend-on-Sea, and Anne, *née* Henderson; *b* 29 Nov 1934; *Educ* Westcliff-on-Sea HS, The Coll of Law; *m* 14 June 1958, Sandra Joyce, da of John Bertram Jackson (d 1974), of Ilford, Essex; 1 s (James Anthony Robert b 1965), 1 da (Claire b 1963); *Career* Nat Serv RAF 1953-55; inspr Guardian Royal Exchange Gp 1955-67, admitted slr 1970, sr ptnr Carter Faber 1970-; chm Writtle Cons Assoc 1982-86, memb Roxwell Essex 1974-79; hon slr The Cruising Assoc 1985-; Freeman City of London, memb Worshipful Co of Carmen; memb Law Soc, FCII; *Recreations* sailing, shooting; *Clubs* RAC, Royal Harwich Yacht; *Style—* Robert Rowan, Esq; Ratcliffes, The Green, Writtle, Essex (☎ 0245 420918); Flat 46, St Georges Wharf, Shad Thames, London SE1 (☎ 071 378 0161); Carter Faber, 10 Arthur St, London EC4R 9AY (☎ 071 929 5555, 071 929 3637, telex 887824)

ROWAN, Thomas Stanley; s of Thomas Rowan (d 1965); *b* 11 April 1935; *Educ* Wellington, Univ of Natal, Gonville and Caius Coll Cambridge (LLB); *m* 1964, Anne Strafford, *née* Sanderson; 1 s (Michael), 1 da (Vanessa); *Career* CA; dir Singer & Friedlander Ltd 1975-; FCA; *Recreations* golf; *Clubs* Leeds; *Style—* Thomas Rowan Esq; Strafford House, Fulwith Rd, Harrogate, N Yorkshire HG2 8HL (☎ 0423 873137 and 071 632 3000)

ROWAT, Lt-Col David Peter; OBE (1972), JP (1978); s of Ernest Ivimy Rowat (d 1972), of Roquebrune, France, and Phyllis Esdon, *née* Rowat (d 1979); *b* 24 Nov 1928; *Educ* Charterhouse, RMA Sandhurst, Staff Coll Camberley, JSSC Latimer; *m* 11 May 1968, Elizabeth, da of Cdr Richard Paston Mack, MVO (d 1974), of West House, Droxford, Hants; 1 s (Peter b 1970), 1 da (Sarah b 1969); *Career* enlisted 1947, cmmnd 5 Royal Inniskilling Dragoon Guards 1949; served: BAOR, Korea, Egypt, Aden, Bahrain, Cyprus; ADC to C in C MELF 1953-55, CO The Royal Yeomanry 1969-71; asst dir CLA Game Fair 1974-80; *Recreations* fishing, cricket, golf; *Clubs* MCC; *Style—* Lt-Col David Rowat, OBE, JP

ROWBOTHAM, Brian William; s of Laurence William Edward Rowbotham (d 1967), of Surbiton, and Florence Madge Rowbotham (d 1975); *b* 27 May 1931; *Educ* Oakham Sch; *m* 19 Sept 1959, Carol Ann, da of Henry Nordheim Webster (d 1966), of Wallasey; 3 s (Anthony Charles William, Nigel Henry, Jonathan Brian Nicholas); *Career* Nat Serv Lt RA 1955-57; chm and chief exec Morgan-Grampian plc 1969-86, fndr chm Br Business Press 1984-86, chm Periodical Publishers Assoc 1985-87, dep chm Adscene Group plc 1987-, chm London Newspaper Group 1988-; FCA; *Clubs* RAC; *Style—* Brian Rowbotham, Esq; Robins Mount, Alma Rd, Reigate, Surrey RH2 ODN (☎ 0737 244860); Newspaper House, Winslow Rd, London W6 9SF (☎ 081 741 1622, fax 081 741 1973)

ROWBOTHAM, Graham William Henry; s of Frederick Rowbotham, of Canterbury, Kent, and Gladys Emma Ellen, *née* Andrews; *b* 25 June 1948; *Educ* The King's Sch Canterbury, St John's Coll Oxford (MA); *m* 7 Oct 1977, Susan (Sue), da of Anthony Thomas Gordon Turner (d 1980); 3 da (Sophie b 1978, Natasha b 1979, Gemma b 1983); *Career* admitted slr 1973; Arthur Andersen & Co 1969, Slaughter & May 1970-79, Simmons & Simmons 1980- (ptnr 1981-, head of Banking and Capital Markets Gp 1985-); memb: editorial advsy bd Int Financial Law Review; memb Worshipful Co of Solicitors 1985; memb: Law Soc, Int Bar Assoc; *Recreations* lawn tennis, golf, real tennis, skiing, walking, reading; *Clubs* Roehampton, Royal Tennis Ct, Barbican; *Style—* Graham W H Rowbotham, Esq; Simmons & Simmons, 14 Dominion St, London, EC2M 2RJ (☎ 071 628 2020, fax 071 588 4129 and 071 588 9418, telex 888562 SIMMON G)

ROWBOTHAM, Dr Hugo Dalyson; s of George Frederick Rowbotham (d 1975), and Monica Dalyson, *née* Boyle, of Corduroys, Upton, nr Blewbury, Oxfordshire; *b* 30 March 1942; *Educ* Dragon Sch Oxford, Shrewsbury, King's Coll Durham (MB BS, Hockey colours); *m* 8 Sept 1973, Gloria Geraldine; 1 s (Richard b 23 Jan 1976), 2 da (Louisa b 12 Aug 1980, Emily b 23 Feb 1982); *Career* house surgn and physician Newcastle Gen Hosp 1965-66, ENT sr house offr Royal Victoria Infirmary 1966-67, surgical res asst Royal Marsden Hosp 1968-71, private GP 1971-; visiting med offr: King Edward VII Hosp 1975-, the London Clinic 1975-; memb: BMA, Soc of Occupational Med, Sloane Soc, Chelsea Clinical Soc; *Recreations* hockey; *Clubs* Surbiton Hockey, Llamas Hockey, English Nat Ballet Co (Gold Card memb); *Style—* Dr Hugo Rowbotham; 11 Cromwell Crescent, London SW5 9QW (☎ 071 603 6967); 147 Harley St, London W1N 1DL (☎ 071 935 4444, fax 071 486 3782)

ROWCLIFFE, (Sarah) Louise; da of Anthony Rowcliffe, of Milford on Sea, Hants, and Iris Florence Amy, *née* Bond; *b* 12 June 1962; *Educ* The Lady Eleanor Holles Sch Hampton Middx, St George's Sch Clarens Switzerland, Univ of Kent at Canterbury (BA); *Career* media exec CIA International Ltd 1984-86; MJP/Carat International: media exec MJP Ltd 1986-88, media gp head MJP Ltd 1988-89, media dir 1989-; memb IAA Assoc Ctee 1987-; *Style—* Miss Louise Rowcliffe; MJP/Carat International Ltd, Broadway House, 2-6 Fulham Broadway, London SW6 1AA (☎ 071 381 8010, fax 071 385 3233)

ROWCLIFFE, Hon Mrs (Una Mary); *née* Slim; da of late 1 Viscount Slim, KG, GCB, GCMG, GCVO, GBE, DSO, MC; *b* 1930; *m* 1, 1953 (m dis 1979), Maj Peter Nigel Stewart Frazer, Grenadier Gds; 3 da; m 2, 1980, Ronald Rowcliffe; *Style—* The Hon Mrs Rowcliffe; Bamson, Puddington, Tiverton, Devon

ROWDEN, Ray; s of William Charles Rowden (d 1987), of Kent, and Joyce Vera, *née* Wood (d 1983); *b* 11 July 1952; *Educ* Sir William Nottidge Sch Kent; *m* 15 Dec 1973 (m dis 1990), Linda Margaret; 2 da (Helen Louise Victoria b 12 Sept 1974, Elizabeth Christabel b 25 Sept 1980); *Career* trained as: registered mental nurse St Augustine's Hosp Kent 1970-73, SRN Kent and Canterbury Hosp 1976-78, oncology nurse Royal Marsden Hosp London and Surrey 1981; RCN: regnl N Wales 1978-79, sr offr Wales 1978-81, advsr in mgmnt London 1984-86; dir of nursing Royal Marsden Hosp Sutton 1981-84; unit gen mangr: Mental Health Servs W Lambeth 1986-89, Priority Servs W Lambeth DHA 1989-; assoc ed Nursing Times 1986-; memb: Lab Pty 1974-, Nat Exec RCN Assoc of Nursing Practice 1976-81, Ctee on Labour Relations RCN 1977-78, RCN Nat Cncl 1979-81, Vale of Glamorgan CHC 1979-81, Staffside Nurses and Midwives Whitley Cncl 1981-, Cncl for Music in Hosps 1985-; advsr Invitation to the Ballet project (Royal Ballet) 1982-, hon lectr Dept of Nursing Royal Marsden Hosp 1990, conslt in nursing and mgmnt to Govt of St Lucia, travel fellowship from King Edwards Hosp fund to examine health care in Canada 1984; MRCN 1970, memb Inst of Health Serv Mgmnt 1987; *Books* Managing Nursing (1984), How to Succeed in Nursing (with Alison Dunn, 1991); *Recreations* writing, ballet and other dance music, politics, collecting bronze sculpture and paintings; *Style—* Ray Rowden, Esq; Priority Service Unit, West Lambeth District Health Authority, Tooting BEC Hospital, Church Lane, London SW17 (☎ 081 672 9933, fax 081 767 4947)

ROWE, Prof Adrian Harold Redfern (Jack); s of Harold Ridges Rowe (d 1945) of Lymington, Hants and Emma Eliza, *née* Matthews (d 1979); *b* 30 Dec 1925; *Educ* King Edward VI GS Southampton, Guys Hosp Dental Sch (BDS, MDS, MCCD RCS); *m* 30 March 1951, Patricia Mary, da of Henry Roland Peter, *née* Flett (d 1969), of Forest Hill, London; 3 s (Paul Harold b 1952, Timothy David b 1954, Simon John b 1961); *Career* RADC Lt 1949, Capt 1950-51; head of Dept of Conservative Dental Surgery Guys Hosp Dental Sch 1967- (sr lectr 1963-67), dean of Dental Sch of UMDS 1985- (reader in conservative dental surgery 1967-71, prof 1971-); chief ed Companion to Dental Studies; memb: UGC Dental Sub Ctee 1974-83, Cncl Med Def Union 1977-, Bd of Faculty of Dental Surgery RCS 1980-; dir Med Sickness Soc 1987-; memb: BDA, FDI, IADR; BES, BSRD; FICD 1969, FDS; *Recreations* golf, DIY, gardening; *Style—* Prof A H R Rowe

ROWE, Andrew John Bernard; MP (C) Mid-Kent 1983-; s of John Douglas Rowe (d 1960), and Mary Katherine Storr; *b* 11 Sept 1935; *Educ* Eton, Merton Coll Oxford (MA); *m* 1, 1960 (m dis), Alison Boyd; 1 s (Nicholas); m 2, 1983, Sheila L Finkle; 2 step da; *Career* asst master Eton Coll 1959-62, princ Scot Office 1962-67, lectr Univ of Edinburgh 1967-74, dir community affrs CCO 1975-79, self employed 1979-83; tstee Community Serv Vols, fndr memb Kent Co Engrg Soc, chm Parly Panel for Personnel Social Servs All Pty Franchise Devpt Gp; *Clubs* Maidstone; *Style—* Andrew Rowe, Esq, MP; House of Commons, London SW1A 0AA (☎ 071 219 3000)

ROWE, Bridget; da of Peter Rowe, of Westerham Hill, Kent, and Myrtle, *née* Dodds; *b* 16 March 1950; *Educ* St Michael's Sch Limpsfield Surrey, Bromley Technical Coll (HND); partner, James Nolan; 1 s (Peter James b 8 July 1987); *Career* ed: Look Now 1971-76, Woman's World 1976-81; asst ed The Sun 1981-82; ed: Sunday Magazine 1982-86, Woman's Own 1986-90; memb: Br Soc of Magazine Editors 1971-, Editorial Steering Gp Ctee IPC Magazines Limited 1987-; *Recreations* talking, riding, sleeping; *Style—* Bridget Rowe; TV Times Magazine, Independent Television Publications Limited, 247 Tottenham Court Rd, London W1P 0AU (☎ 071 636 1109, fax 071 580 3986)

ROWE, Clive Jocelyn; s of Sqdn ldr Norman Francis Rowe (d 1990), and Suzanne Marian Townsend, *née* Richardson; *b* 1 Feb 1944; *Educ* Marlborough, Trinity Coll Dublin (LLB, MA); *m* 30 Sept 1972, Gillian Mary, da of Charles Edward Leigh Mather (d 1982); 1 s (Charles Edward Louis b 1 Sept 1979), 2 da (Anna Frances b 25 April 1974, Elizabeth Mary b 8 May 1976); *Career* admitted slr 1970; ptnr Barlow Lyde & Gilbert 1978-; memb Law Soc; *Recreations* gardening, family; *Style—* Clive Rowe, Esq; Beaufort House, 15 St Botolph St, London EC3A 7NJ (☎ 071 2472277, fax 071 7828500, telex 071 913281)

ROWE, Col David Christopher Lester; OBE (1986); s of Norman Lester Rowe, CBE, of Brackendale, Hollybank Rd, Hook Heath, Woking, Surrey, and Cynthia Mary, *née* Freeman; *b* 27 Dec 1939; *Educ* Malvern, Army Staff Coll Camberley, Royal Coll of Def Studies; *m* 1, 7 Aug 1962 (m dis 1975), Tessa Valerie, da of Gp Capt B J Crummy, CBE, of 100 Sea Rd, E Preston, W Sussex; 2 s (Simon b 17 Feb 1964, Nick b 18 April 1967); m 2, 21 Aug 1976, Susan Mary, da of Maj David Fantarrow, of Westafield Cottage, Seavington St Mary, Ilminster, Somerset; 2 s (Alexander b 30 March 1981, Jonathan (twin) b 30 March 1981), 1 da (Emma b 14 Sept 1977); *Career* cmmnd RM 1958, 42 Commando RM Plymouth Malta Libya Aden E Africa Singapore, short attachments to 2 (KEO) Gurkha Rifles and 1 Royal Aust Regt, completed basic flying and helicopter training, appointed to 845 Naval Air Sqdn (Wessex 1) 1962, Flt Cdr Far E 1962-64, conversion to Wessex V, Co Cdr 41 Commando RM Plymouth, House Offr RM Sch of Music Depot RM Deal 1965, Flt Cdr and Sqdn Staff Offr 845 Naval Air Sqdn HMS Bulwark Aden Persian Gulf Singapore Malaya Thailand Hong Kong Aust 1966-68, Dir Staff Offrs Sch Commando Trg Centre RM 1968, Royal Mil Coll of Sci 1971, Army Staff Coll Camberley 1972, GSO2 (Mountain and Arctic Warfare) HQ Commando Forces RM 1972, GSO2 (Plans) Dept of Cmdt Gen RM 1976, 2i/c 40 Commando RM NI 1978, GSO1 D Ops (ROW) ACDS (Ops) and project offr ind operation for S Rhodesia 1979, amphibious plans co-ordinator COMSTRIKFORSOUTH (NATO HQ US 6 Fleet) Naples 1982, Lt Col 1982, CO RM Poole 1984, Royal Coll of Def Studies 1986, Col 1986, Mil Sec to Cmdt Gen RM 1986, Chief of Staff Jt Warfare Attache and Asst Def Attache Br Def Staff Washington DC 1988; *Recreations* fishing, fly-tying, western riding, woodwork, gardening; *Clubs* Army and Navy, Washington DC; *Style—* Col David Rowe, OBE; Chief of Staff, British Defence Staff British Embassy, Washington DC, BFPO 2 (☎ 010 1 202 898 4415, fax 010 1 202 898 4255)

ROWE, David Gordon; s of Samuel Gordon Rowe, of Bowes, Co Durham, and Margaret Elizabeth, *née* Hammond; *b* 5 April 1963; *Educ* New Coll Huddersfield, Imperial Coll of Sci and Technol (BSc); *Career* ed Felix (weekly newspaper Imperial Coll of Sci and Technol) 1984-85, sub-ed Haymarket Publications 1985-86, news ed Chemistry in Britain (monthly magazine Royal Soc Chem) 1986, freelance journalist 1986-88, ed Decanter (int wine magazine) 1988-; assoc Royal Coll of Sci; *Recreations* listening to music, playing the piano; *Style*— David Rowe, Esq; 10 Kings Rd, Saint Margaret's, Middlesex TW1 2QS (☎ 081 892 8509); Decanter Magazine, Priory House, 8 Battersea Park Rd, London SW8 4BG (☎ 071 627 8181)

ROWE, Heather; da of Leonard Richard Rowe, of Welwyn, Herts, and Enid, *née* Livermore; *b* 16 Oct 1957; *Educ* Welwyn Garden City GS, Univ of Manchester (LLB); *Career* admitted slr 1981, articled clerk and slr Wilde Sapte 1979-83, S J Berwin & Co 1983-85, Durrant Piesse 1985-88, ptnr Lovell White Durrant 1988-; Freeman Worshipful Co of Slrs; memb Law Soc, FCI Arb; *Recreations* fishing, birdwatching, theatre, reading; *Clubs* Navy; *Style*— Miss Heather Rowe; 65 Holborn Viaduct, London EC1A 2DY (☎ 071 236 0066, telex 887122 LWD G, fax 071 248 4212)

ROWE, Sir Henry Peter; KCB (1978, CB 1971), QC (1978); 3 s of late Dr Richard, and Olga Röhr; *b* 18 Aug 1916; *Educ* Vienna, Gonville and Caius Coll Cambridge; *m* 1947, Patricia, da of R W King; 2 s, 1 da; *Career* first Parly counsel 1977-81; called to the Bar Gray's Inn 1947, Parly counsel offr 1947-, jt second Parly counsel 1973-76; *Style*— Sir Henry Rowe, KCB, QC; 19 Paxton Gardens, Woking, Surrey (☎ 0932 343816)

ROWE, Ian Alastair; s of Albert Rowe (d 1947), and Rose Marian, *née* Sheffield; *b* 23 June 1931; *Educ* Brentwood Sch; *m* 5 July 1971, Suzy Gay Denise, da of Howard Philip Baker (d 1984), of Knowle, Warwicks; 1 s (Alastair b 1975), 1 da (Samantha b 1972); *Career* Nat Serv 2 Lt Army 1949-51, Capt AVR; articles 1952-57; Mead Carney Int: euro fin controller 1959-64, euro treasy mangr 1965-69; Occidental Petroleum Corp; chm Meridian Deposit Brokers 1973-89; fin dir Donington Partners Ltd 1990-; ACA 1958-62, FCA 1963-; *Recreations* amateur motor racing, vintage, veteran car competitor; *Clubs* VSCC, VCC, RREC; *Style*— Ian A Rowe, Esq; Donington Partners Ltd, Park House, 16 Finsbury Circus, London EC2M 7DJ (☎ 081 549 9546)

ROWE, Sir Jeremy; CBE (1980); s of Col Charles William Dell Rowe, CB, MBE (d 1954); *b* 31 Oct 1928; *Educ* Uppingham, Trinity Coll Cambridge; *m* 1957, Susan Mary, da of Cdr Richard Noel Johnstone, RN; 4 da; *Career* dep chm Abbey Nat Building Soc 1978-89; chm: London Brick plc 1979-84, Peterborough Devpt Corp 1981-88, Occupational Pensions Bd 1987-, Family Assurance Soc 1986-; dir: Sun Alliance Insurance Gp W End Bd 1978-, John Maunders Gp plc 1984-, Telephone Rentals plc 1984-89; kt 1991; *Recreations* tennis, shooting, travel, music, history; *Clubs* All England Tennis, Buck's; *Style*— Sir Jeremy Rowe, CBE; Woodside, Peasmarsh, Rye, Sussex (☎ 079 721 335)

ROWE, John Richard; s of William Rowe (d 1990), of Hunter Court, Wanstead, London, and Anne, *née* Radley; *b* 1 Aug 1942; *Educ* St Barnabas Secdy Mod Sch; *m* 22 Oct 1966, Rosa Mary, da of Geoffrey Laurance Balls (d 1958), of Woodford Bridge, Essex; *Career* Sky TV: head of prodn res 1974-82, head of progs 1982-84, head of prodn 1984-; princ film researcher: The Life and Times of Lord Mountbatten 1966-68, The World at War 1972-74; prodr 1985: The Pet Show series, Live from the Escape, Live from Rotterdam; co-ordinating dir 1987 World Music Video Awards; prodr/dir: A Magical Disney Christmas, Ferry Aid Gala, Movietime 1987, Deadly Ernest Horror Show Series 1989-91; *Recreations* photograhy, cinema, walking, reading; *Style*— John Rowe, Esq; 63 Copthorne Avenue, Hainault, Ilford, Essex (☎ 081 500 9738), Sky Television, 6 Grant Way, Isleworth, Middx TW7 5QD (☎ 071 782 3000, 071 782 3115)

ROWE, Michael; *Educ* High Wycomb Coll of Art (DipAD), RCA (MA); *Career* in own silversmithing workshop 1972, sunglass designer Polaroid (UK) Ltd 1971-72; spectacle designer: Optica Info Cncl fashion promotion 1973, Merx International Optical Co 1974-76; visiting lectr: Bucks Coll of Higher Educn 1973-82, Camberwell Sch of Art and Crafts 1976-82; visiting lectr and tutor RCA 1978-84; researcher (with Richard Hughes) into : colouring, bronzing and patination of metals Camberwell Sch of Art and Crafts 1979-82 (work published as manual by Crafts Cncl 1982), ancient patinated surfaces British Museum 1984-87; course leader Dept of Metalwork and Jewellery RCA 1984-; guest lectr: colleges in Dusseldorf, Cologne, Schwabisch Gmund, Pforzheim and Munich 1983, Gerrit Rietreld Academic Amsterdam 1984, Oslo Statens Handverks-Og Kunstindustriskole Norway 1985, Bezaled Coll of Art Jerusalem Israel 1987; guest speaker: Soc of N American Goldsmiths Conf Toronto Canada 1985, Jewellers and Metalsmiths Gp of Aust Fourth Biennial Conf Perth Aust; *Group Exhibitions* incl: Europalia '73 Brussels 1973, Callab '74 (Br Design and Craft and Philadelphia and World Crafts Exhibition Toronto) 1974, Modern Silver (Lincolnshire and Humberside Arts Assoc) 1977, Southeby Contemporary British Crafts at Auction Munich and London 1980, Galerie Ra Amsterdam 1983, Our Domestic Landscape (one of five selector/writer/exhibitiors) London, Manchester and Aberystwyth 1986, Contemporary British Crafts (Br Cncl) 1988, Function Nonfunction (Rezac Gallery Chicago) 1989, New British Design Image and Object (Pompidou Centre Paris and Nat Museum of Modern Art Kyoto Japan) 1990; *Solo Exhibitions* Crafts Cncl Gallery London 1978, V & A Craft Show London 1985, Retrospective Exhibition (Princess of Museum Leeuwarden Holland) 1988, Contemporary Applied Arts London 1988; work in public collections: Birmingham City Museum and Art Galleries, Crafts Cncl London, Leeds City Art Gallery, V & A Museum London, Karlsruhe Museum W Germany, Art Gallery of Western Aust Perth, Shipley Art Gallery Gateshead; memb jury: Mecca Dante Stakes Trophy Competition 1981 and 1982, Perrier Trophy Competition 1982, Das Tablett (int silversmithing competition) 1983; *Awards* Frogmoor Fndn travelling scholarship 1967, dip World Crafts Cncl 1974, res award Camberwell Sch of Art and Crafts 1978, Sotheby Decorative Arts award 1988; Freeman: City of London 1983, Worshipful Co of Goldsmiths 1983; FRSA 1989; *Style*— Michael Rowe, Esq; David Taylor Design Consultants, 24-25 Princes St, London W1R 7RG

ROWE, Norman Lester; CBE (1976); s of Arthur William Rowe, OBE (d 1957), and Lucy Lester, *née* Adams (d 1980); *b* 15 Dec 1915; *Educ* Malvern, Guy's Hosp Univ of London; *m* 17 Sept 1938, Cynthia Mary, da of Augustus Morris Freeman (d 1948); 1 s (David b 1939), 1 da (Susan b 1941); *Career* WWII Capt RADC 1941-46 (France and Germany 1944-46); sr registrar Plastic and Jaw Injuries Unit Hill End Hosp St Albans 1947, conslt oral surgn Plastic and Oral Surgery Centre Rooksdown House Basingstoke and SW Met RHB 1948-59, conslt to RN 1955-80; conslt oral and maxillofacial surgery: Queen Mary's Hosp Roehampton 1959-80, Westminster Hosp 1961-80, Inst of Dental Surgery 1961-74, Eastman Dental Hosp London 1961-74; conslt to Army 1969-80, ret 1980, emeritus conslt to RN 1981; visiting prof Univ of: Seattle, Witswaterand, Hadesseh, Baghdad, Khartoum, Kuwait, Santiago, Montevideo; memb Bd of Faculty of Dental Surgery RCS 1956-74 (vice dean 1967), Webb-Johnson lectr 1967-69; former examiner RCS: England, Edinburgh, Glasgow, Ireland; sec gen Int Assoc of Oral and Maxillofacial Surgns 1968-71 (hon fell 1986), pres BAOMS 1969 (hon fell 1981), pres Euro Assoc for Craniomaxillofacial Surgery 1974-76 (hon memb 1980); Down's Surgical prize medal (BAOMS) 1976, Colyer Gold medal (RCS) 1981, Tomes' medal (BDA) 1985; memb numerous overseas socs; hon FDSRCS: Glasgow 1979, Edinburgh 1981; hon FRCS Edinburgh 1986, Hon FRACDS 1990; memb: BDA, BMA, BAOMS, IAOMS, EACMFS, OSC (GB); *Books* Fractures of the Facial Skeleton (2 edn, 1968), Maxillofacial Injuries (1985); *Recreations* music, photography; *Clubs* Royal Naval Medical; *Style*— Norman Rowe,Esq, CBE; Brackendale, Holly Bank Rd, Hook Heath, Woking, Surrey GU22 0JP (☎ 0483 760008)

ROWE, Richard; s of John James Rowe (d 1977), and Kathleen, *née* Guest; *b* 11 Nov 1959; *Educ* 29 June 1985, Yvonne Jane, da of Rex Norman Barford; 1 s (Richard James b 28 Nov 1986); *Career* Nat Hunt jockey; first jockey to J T Gifford 1982 (début as conditional jockey 1976-77); rider 500 winners from 2500 rides; memb GB Jump Jockeys Team: Belgium 1986, Australia 1988-89 (2 winners); winner Conditional Jockeys Championship 1978-79 season, 5th place Sr Jockeys Table 1978-79; winner: Mildway/Cazalet Chase (Modestry Forbids) 1979, Whitbread Gold Cup (Shady Deal) 1982, H & T Walker Gold Cup, SGB Chase (twice), Coral Golden Hurdle, Mildmay of Flere, Grand Annual Chase at Cheltenham, Mercedes Benz Chase (twice), The Free Handicap; 3 place Topham Trophy, 5 place Grand National (riding Earthstopper); proprieter successful equestrian establishment; *Recreations* football, squash, coursing, shooting, disco dancing, watching Prisoner Cell Block H and Blind Date!; *Style*— Richard Rowe, Esq; Ashleigh House, Sullington Lane, Storrington, West Sussex RH20 9BT (☎ 0903 742871)

ROWE, Richard Brian (Dick); s of Charles Albert Rowe (d 1967), of Perivale, Middx, and Mabel Florence, *née* Waller (d 1971); *b* 28 April 1933; *Educ* Greenford Co GS, King's Coll London (LLB); *m* 19 March 1959, Shirley Ann, da of William G Symons, of Bournemouth, Hants; 2 da (Melissa Jane b 1965, Hollie Ann b 1968); *Career* Nat Serv RAF 1952-54; Land Cmmn 1966-69, Lord Chllrs Offr House of Lords 1969-75, district judge (formerly registrar) Family Div High Ct 1979- (Probate Divorce and Admty Div 1954-66, sec Family Div 1975-79); *Books* Rayden on Divorce (ed, 1967), Tristram and Coote's Probate Practice (ed, 1978, 1983, 1989); *Recreations* most sports; *Clubs* MCC; *Style*— R B Rowe, Esq; Principal Registry Family Division (High Court), Somerset House, Strand, London WC2 1LP

ROWE, Robert Stewart; CBE (1969); s of James Stewart Rowe, MBE (d 1960), and Anna Gray Gillespie (d 1973); *b* 31 Dec 1920; *Educ* private tutors, Downing Coll Cambridge (MA); *m* 1953, Barbara Elizabeth Hamilton, da of Thomas Austin Hamilton Baynes, OBE (d 1973); 1 s, 2 da; *Career* RAF 1941-46; asst keeper of art Birmingham Art Gallery 1950-56, dep dir Manchester City Art Galleries 1956-58, dir Leeds City Art Gallery, Temple Newsam House and Lotherton Hall 1958-83; memb: Art Panel Arts Cncl of GB 1959-62 and 1969-74, Advsy Cncl V&A Museum 1969-74, Exec Cncl Yorks Arts Assoc 1973-84, Arts Cncl of GB 1981-86; pres Museum Assoc 1973-74, tstee Henry Moore Sculpture Tst 1983-, chm Bar Convent Museum York 1986-91; Hon DLitt Univ of Leeds; *Books* Adam Silver (1965); *Recreations* reading, writing, gardening; *Style*— Robert Rowe, Esq, CBE; Grove Lodge, Shadwell, Leeds LS17 8LB (☎ 0532 656365)

ROWE-HAM, Sir David Kenneth; s of Kenneth Henry Ham, and Muriel Phyllis Rowe; *b* 19 Dec 1935; *Educ* Dragon Sch, Charterhouse; *m* 1 (m dis 1980), Elizabeth, *née* Aston; 1 s (Adrian); m 2, 1980, Sandra Celia, widow of Ian Glover; 1 s (Mark b 1981), and 1 adopted step s (Gerald); *Career* CA since 1962; Lord Mayor of London 1986-87; conslt Touche Ross and Co 1984-; dir public and private cos including chm Asset Tst plc 1982-; cmmnd 3 King's own Hussars; sr ptnr Smith Keen Cutler 1972-82, dir The 1928 Investmt Tst 1984-86, regnl dir Lloyds Bank 1985-, dir W Canning plc 1981-86 (consultant 1986-); Savoy Theatre Ltd 1986; Advisory Panel Fund Mangrs Ltd 1986- (chm 1987); Alderman City of London Ward of Bridge and Bridge Without 1976-; Sheriff City of London 1984-85; chm: Birmingham Municipal Bank 1970-72, Political Cncl Jr Carlton Club 1977; dep chm Political Ctee Carlton Club 1977-79; Chief Magistrate of the City of London 1986-87; Adm of the Port of London 1986-87; memb: Soc of Investment Analysists, Stock Exchange 1964-84, memb Ct City Univ 1981-86 (Chllr 1986-87); memb: Worshipful Co of CA in England and Wales (Master 1985-86), Worshipful Co of Wheelwrights; hon memb Worshipful Co of Launderers, memb Ct HAC, memb Guild of Freeman; Princess Youth Tst 1986-87; Royal Shakespeare Theatre Tst; tstee Friends of D'oly Carte; memb: Lord's Taveners, United Wards Club Govr Hosp; JP City of London 1976; FCA Hon DLitt City Univ 1986; Cdr O of the Lion of Malawi 1985; Commandeur de l'Ordre Me'rite France 1984, Order of the Aztec Eagle (Cl II) Mexico 1987; holder of the Pedro Ernesto Medal (Rio de Janero) 1987; Order of Diego Losada of Caracas 1987; Her Majesty's Commn of Lieutenancy for City of London 1987; KJStJ 1986; *Recreations* theatre, shooting; *Clubs* Carlton, Guildhall, City Livery; *Style*— Sir David Rowe-Ham, Esq

ROWELL, Prof Neville Robinson; s of Thomas Rowell (d 1971), and Bertha, *née* Robinson (d 1981); *b* 3 Nov 1926; *Educ* Royal GS Newcastle upon Tyne, Univ of Durham (MB BS), Univ of Newcastle (MD), FRCP (London), DCH (England); *m* 5 Aug 1950, Elizabeth Rachel Martin, da of Dr Martin Edwards (d 1967); 3 s (Christopher b 1952, Martin b 1953, Marcus b 1962); *Career* MO RAF 1950-52; house physician, demonstrator in pathology and med registrar Royal Victoria Infirmary Newcastle upon Tyne 1949-58, conslt physician Dept of Dermatology Gen Infirmary Leeds and St James's Univ Hosp Leeds 1962-, conslt advsr in dermatology DHSS 1978-88, prof of dermatology Univ of Leeds 1988- (tutor 1958-62); examiner in med RCP 1980-; author over 250 articles on autoimmunity, connective tissue diseases and dermatology published in scientific jls; pres Br Med Students Assoc 1971-72; hon memb: Polish Med Soc 1974, Swedish Dermatological Soc 1975, French Dermatological Soc 1977, German Democratic Dermatological Soc 1987, Br Assoc of Dermatologists; memb: Med Appeals Tbnl DHSS, of Court Univ of Leeds 1987-89, Cncl of the Leeds Art Collection Fund 1984-87; vice chm Leeds Civic Tst 1969-, pres Br Assoc of Dermatologists 1986-87; memb BMA, FRSM, FRCP 1986; *Recreations* golf, opera, art and antiques; *Clubs* Alwoodley Golf; *Style*— Prof Neville Rowell; 16 Park Parade, Harrogate, North Yorkshire HG1 5AF (☎ 0423 566478), Univ Dept of Dermatology, The Leeds General Infirmary, Consulting Rooms, 20 Clarendon Rd, Leeds LS2 9PF (☎ 0532 432799/453395)

ROWLAND, (John) David; s of Cyril Arthur Rowland, and Eileen Mary Rowland; *b* 10 Aug 1933; *Educ* St Paul's, Trinity Coll Cambridge (MA); *m* 18 May 1957, Eileen Giulia, da of Trevor Powell; 1 s (Mark Trevor b 25 Dec 1959), 1 da (Belinda Jane b 25 Aug 1961); *Career* Mathews Wrightson & Co Ltd 1956-72 (dir 1965), dir Mathew Wrightson Hldgs 1972, chm Stewart Wrightson Hldgs plc 1981-87 (dep chm 1978-81), dir Royal London Mutual Insur Soc 1985-86, chm Westminster Insurance Agencies 1981-88, memb Cncl Lloyd's 1987-90, dep chm Willis Faber plc 1987-88, gp chief exec Sedgwick Gp plc 1988-89, dir Sedgwick Lloyd's Underwriting Agencies Ltd 1988-, chm Sedgwick Gp plc 1989; dir: Project Fullemploy 1973-88, Fullemploy Group 1989-91; vice pres Br Insurance and Investmt Brokers' Assoc 1980, memb Cncl Templeton Coll 1980 (chm 1985-), govr Coll of Insur 1983-85; memb: Cncl Industrial Soc 1983-88, Pres Ctee Business in the Community 1986-, Cncl for Indust & Higher Educn 1990-, Contemporary Applied Arts (formerly Br Crafts Centre) 1985-; memb Ct of Worshipful Co of Insurers; *Recreations* golf, running slowly; *Clubs* MCC, Royal & Ancient Golf, Royal St Georges (Sandwich), Royal Worlington & Newmarket, Sunningdale; *Style*— David Rowland, Esq; 6 Mountfort Crescent, London N1 1JW (☎ 071 609 2041);

Sedgwick Group plc, Sedgwick House, Sedgwick Centre, London E1 8DX (☎ 071 377 3456, fax 071 377 3199, telex 882131)

ROWLAND, Gilbert Raymond David; s of Capt Norman Denis Rowland, and Effy May, *née* McEwen; *b* 8 Oct 1946; *Educ* Catford Secdy Sch, RCM; *Career* harpsichordist; major performances include: Wigmore Hall 1973-75, Greenwich Festival 1975-84, Purcell Room 1979, 1983 and 1985, Berlin 1985, broadcasts for BBC Radio 3 1977, 1978, 1983, 1984, and 1985; various solo recordings for Nimbus Records and Scarlatti Sonatas for Keyboard Records; piano teacher Epsom Coll 1969-; ARCO 1967, ARCM; *Style—* Gilbert Rowland, Esq; 418 Brockley Road, London SE4 2DH (☎ 081 699 2549)

ROWLAND, John; s of Peter Rowland (d 1976), and Marion Agnes *née* Guppy; *b* 17 Jan 1952; *Educ* Aquinas Coll Perth W Aust, Univ of W Australia (BSc Econ), Univ of London (LLB); *m* 8 Dec 1979, Juliet Claire, da of Ernest John Hathaway, 3 s (Benjamin b 1985, Matthew b 1988, Luke b 1990); *Career* Pilot Offr RAAF 1971-72; tutor Kingswood Coll Univ of W Australia 1973-74; called to the Bar Middle Temple 1979, in practice 1979-; memb: Bar of England and Wales 1979, London Common Law Bar Assoc 1984, COMBAR; *Recreations* cricket, walking, skiing; *Style—* John Rowland, Esq; 4 Pump Court, Temple, London, EC4Y 7AN, (☎ 071 353 2656, fax 071 583 2036)

ROWLAND, Prof Malcolm; s of Stanley Rowland (d 1973); *b* 5 Aug 1939; *Educ* Univ of London (BPharm, PhD, DSc); *m* 5 Sept 1965, Dawn; 2 da (Lisa Claire b 21 Dec 1968, Michelle b 1 July 1970); *Career* assoc prof of pharmacy and pharmaceutical chemistry Univ of Calif San Francisco 1970-75 (asst prof 1967-71), head of Dept of Pharmacy Univ of Manchester 1988- (prof 1975-), chief exec Medeval Ltd 1983-; Hon DSc Univ of Poitiers France 1981, Hon DPh Univ of Uppsala Sweden 1989; fell: Inst of Mathematics and its Application 1978, Royal Pharmaceutical Soc of GB 1987 (memb 1965-), American Assoc of Pharmaceutical Scientists 1988; *Books* Clinical Pharmacokinetics: Concepts and Applications (with Dr T N Tozer, 2 edn 1989); *Style—* Prof Malcolm Rowland; Dept of Pharmacy, University of Manchester, Manchester M13 9PL (☎ 061 2752348, fax 061 2752396)

ROWLAND, Mark Robert; s of John Reginald Rowland, of Watersfield, Sussex, and Roberta Teresa, *née* Heather; *b* 7 March 1963; *Educ* Midhurst GS; *m* 3 Sept 1983, (Louisa) Stephanie, da of Maj Harry James Marshall Graham, TD; 1 s (Martyn b 1984), 1 da (Suzanne b 1982); *Career* long distance runner; UK 1500m champion 1985, 4 Euro (indoor) championship 1987, 4 World (indoor) championship 1987, 9 in World 1500m Rankings 1988, 3 in World 3000m Steeplechase Rankings 1988, champion AAA 3000m Steeplechase 1988, Olympic Bronze medal 3000m Steeplechase Seoul 1988, champion AAA 5000m 1989, Euro Silver medal 3000m Steeplechase 1990, 4th fastest in the world at 3000m Steeplechase 1990; *Clubs* Phoenix Athletic; *Style—* Mark Rowland, Esq; c/o British Olympic Assoc, 1 Wandsworth Plain, London SW18 1EH

ROWLAND, Peter Morton Bayard; s of Rev A Norman Rowland (d 1959), and Lydia Mary, *née* Strange (d 1952); *b* 25 Jan 1916; *Educ* Caterham Sch Surrey, Birkbeck Coll London (BA), King's Coll London (LLB); *m* 26 July 1969, (Ann) Clare Allingham, da of Sir Owen Arthur Aisher, *qv*; *Career* WWII T/Maj RASC 1939-46; with Farrow Bersey Gain Vincent CA 1933-40; called to the Bar Gray's Inn 1947; practised at bar 1947-72 and 1987-; chm: Rowland Debono Ltd 1972-, Project Fin Int Ltd 1984-, Kelvingate Int Ltd 1985-; vice chm Construction Indust Advsy Gp Ltd 1988-; dir: Anglo-Bahamian Bank Ltd 1965-, Exa Sarl 1985-, Manderstam Conslts Ltd 1986-, Just Unit Ltd 1988-, Associated Law Writers 1989-, Atlantic Bank of Commerce 1989; memb Exec Ctee: Economic Res Cncl 1949-58, European Atlantic Gp 1954-; pt/t memb VAT Tbnl 1985-; govr: Caterham Sch 1956-62, Hurlingham Sch 1958-73; memb Worshipful Co of Arbitrators 1985; FCA 1963, FCIArb 1978; *Books* Trust Accounts (1954, 1959, 1964), Corporation Tax (with John Talbot, 1965), Arbitration Law and Practice (1988); *Recreations* fishing, tennis, chess; *Clubs* City of London, Arts, Hurlingham; *Style—* Peter M B Rowland, Esq; 40 Green St, London W1Y 3FH (☎ 071 499 5904); 2 Temple Gardens, London EC4Y 9AY (☎ 071 353 4636, fax 071 583 3455)

ROWLAND, Richard Arthur Philip; s of William Barry Rowland, of Old Marston, Oxford, and Joyce Mary, *née* Cowdery; *b* 18 July 1944; *Educ* St Paul's Selwyn Coll Cambridge (MA, LLB); *m* 25 Sept 1971, Cherry Ann, da of Kenneth Alexander Adcock; 2 s (Ben Alexander b 20 Sept 1972, Philip Barry (twin) b 20 Sept 1972), 1 da (Tessa Martha b 11 June 1978); *Career* Allen & Overy: articled clerk 1967-69, asst slr 1969-74, ptnr 1974-; memb Co Law Sub Ctee City of London Law Soc; *Recreations* print making, music, vintage cars, travel; *Style—* Richard Rowland, Esq; Allen & Overy, 9 Cheapside, London EC2 6AD (☎ 071 248 9898, fax 071 236 2192)

ROWLAND PAYNE, Dr Christopher Melville Edwin; s of Maj Edwin Rowland Payne, and Rosemary Ann, *née* Bird; *b* 19 May 1955; *Educ* Clifton, Univ of London, St Bartholomew's Hosp (MB BS, MRCP); *Career* conslt dermatologist and landowner; house surgn St Bart's Hosp London 1978; house physician: Med Prof Unit Royal Infirmary Edinburgh 1978, Royal Marsden Hosp 1979; dermatological registrar St Thomas's Hosp London 1980-83, dermatological sr registrar Westminster Hosp 1983-89; professeur universitaire Faculté de Medicine de Paris 1985-86; conslt dermatologist: Kent and Canterbury Hosp, William Harvey Hosp Kent, Thanet Hosp Kent, Chaucer Hosp Kent, St Saviour's Hosp Kent, Lister Hosp London 1990-; clinical prof of dermatology Ross Univ NY 1990-; HAC 1975-76; memb: Societé Francaise de Dermatologie, Br Assoc Dermatologists; Liveryman Worshipful Soc of Apothecaries, Freeman City of London; Roxburgh prize 1977; Br Assoc Dermatologists awards: 1984, 1985, 1986, 1989; Dowling Club prizes: 1985, 1986, 1987, 1988; *Books* contrib: British Medical Journal, Journal Royal Soc Med and others; *Recreations* shooting, cycling, military history; *Style—* Dr Christopher Rowland Payne; High St, Elham, Kent (☎ 0303 840569); 29 Hans Place, London SW1 (☎ 071 584 7435)

ROWLANDS, Prof Brian James; *b* 18 March 1945; *Educ* Wirral GS Cheshire, Guy's Hosp Med Sch (MB BS); *m* 16 Oct 1971, Judith; 1 da (Rachel b 14 March 1975); *Career* lectr Dept of Surgery Univ of Sheffield 1974-77, fell surgical gastroenterology and nutrition Dept of Surgery Univ of Texas Med Sch Houston 1977-78; Univ of Texas Health Sci Centre Houston: instr surgery 1977-78, asst prof of surgery 1978-81, assoc prof of surgery 1981-86; prof and head Dept of Surgery Queen's Univ Belfast 1986-; memb Surgical Res Soc, sec Assoc of Profs Surgery; FRCS 1973, fell American Coll Surgns 1983; FRCSI 1988; *Books* The Physiological Basis of Modern Surgical Care (jt ed, 1988); *Style—* Prof Brian J Rowlands; Queen's Univ of Belfast, Dept of Surgery, Institute of Clinical Science, Grosvenor Rd, Belfast BT12 6BJ (☎ 0232 240503 ext 2558)

ROWLANDS, Edward (Ted); MP (Lab) Merthyr Tydfil and Rhymney 1983-; s of William Samuel Rowlands (d 1966), of Rhondda; *b* 23 Jan 1940; *Educ* Rhondda GS, Wirral GS, King's Coll London; *m* 1968, Janice Williams; 2 s, 1 da; *Career* res asst History of Parly Tst 1963-65, lectr in modern history and govr Welsh Coll of Advanced Technol 1965-66; MP (Lab): Cardiff N 1966-70, Merthyr Tydfil 1972-1983; parly under-sec of state: for Wales 1969-70 and 1974-75, FCO 1975-76; min of state FCO 1976-79; oppn front bench spokesman Energy 1981-87; memb: select ctee For Affrs 1987-, academic cncl Wilton Park, FCO, exec of Cwlth Inst; judge: Booker McConnell Novel of the Year Competition 1984, Manchester Oddfellows Social Award Book; *Style—* Edward Rowlands, Esq, MP; 5 Park Crescent, Thomastown, Merthyr Tydfil, Mid Glamorgan (☎ 0685 4912)

ROWLANDS, Rev Canon John Henry Lewis; s of William Lewis Rowlands (d 1986), and Elizabeth Mary, *née* Lewis (d 1973); *b* 16 Nov 1947; *Educ* Queen Elizabeth GS Carmarthen, Saint David's Univ Coll Lampeter (BA), Magdalene Coll Cambridge (MA), Univ of Durham (MLitt), Westcott House Cambridge; *m* 31 July 1976, Catryn Meryl Parry, da of the Reverend Canon Emrys Llewellyn Edwards, of Llys-y-Coed, New Quay, Dyfed; 1 s (William Parri Llywelyn b 6 Sept 1977), 2 da (Sara Kate Llea b 31 March 1979, Elena Angharad Lisa b 17 April 1981); *Career* diocesan youth chaplain Diocese of St David's 1976-79 (curate Rectorial Benefice of Aberystwyth 1972-76), chaplain Saint David's Univ Coll Lampeter 1976-79, lectr Faculty of Theology Univ Coll Cardiff (now Univ of Wales Coll of Cardiff) 1979-; Saint Michael and All Angels' Theological Coll Llandaff: dir of academic studies 1979-84, sub-warden 1984-88, warden 1988-; dean of divinity Univ of Wales 1991-; examining chaplain to Archbishop of Wales 1987-, pres Diwinyddiaeth (Guild of Theology Graduates of Univ of Wales) 1989-; hon canon Llandaff Cathedral 1990-; *Books* Essays on the Kingdom of God (ed, 1986), Church, State and Society - The Attitudes of John Keble, Richard Hurrell Froude and John Henry Newman 1827-1845 (1989); *Recreations* beachcombing, racket games, auctioneering, antique markets; *Style—* The Rev Canon John Rowlands; The Old Registry, Cardiff Rd, Llandaff, Cardiff CF5 2DQ (☎ 0222 563116); St Michael and All Angels' Theological College, Llandaff, Cardiff CF5 2YJ (☎ 0222 563379)

ROWLANDS, John Kendall; s of Arthur and Margaret Rowlands; *b* 18 Sept 1931; *Educ* Chester Cathedral Choir Sch, King's Sch Chester, Gonville and Caius Cambridge (BA, MA); *m* 1, 1957 (m dis 1981), Else A H Bachmann; 1 s, 2 da; m 2, 1982, Lorna Jane Lowe; 1 da; *Career* keeper Dept of Prints and Drawings Br Museum 1981 (dep keeper 1974-81); FSA 1976; *Books* The Paintings of Hans Holbein the Younger (1985), The Age of Dürer and Holbein (1988); *Recreations* organ and piano playing; *Clubs* Beefsteak; *Style—* John Rowlands, Esq, FSA; British Museum, Department of Prints and Drawings, Great Russell St, London WC1 (☎ 071 636 1555)

ROWLANDS, Air Marshal Sir John Samuel; GC (1943), KBE (1971, OBE 1954); s of Samuel Rowlands (d 1919), and Sarah Rowlands (d 1943), of Ewloe Green, Ewloe, Chester; *b* 23 Sept 1915; *Educ* Hawarden GS, UCNW Bangor; *m* 1942, Constance, da of Wing Cdr Harry R Wight, MC (d 1947), of Codshall, Staffs; 2 da; *Career* joined RAFVR 1939, Gp Capt 1958, Air Cdre 1963, dir-gen of trg (RAF) MOD 1968-70, Air Vice-Marshal 1968, AOC-in-C Maintenance Cmd 1970-73, Air Marshal 1970, ret 1973; asst princ Sheffield Poly 1974-80; *Recreations* photography; *Clubs* RAF; *Style—* Air Marshal Sir John Rowlands, GC, KBE

ROWLANDS, (John) Martin; CBE (1980); s of John Walter Rowlands (d 1936), and Mary Ace (Mrs Maitland), *née* Roberts; *b* 20 July 1925; *Educ* Charterhouse, Selwyn Coll Cambridge (MA); *m* 29 Oct 1956, Christiane Germaine Madeleine, da of Justin Lacheny (d 1984); 2 da (Diane Mary b 1957, Noelle Lucy b 1966); *Career* Capt RA serv India and SE Asia 1943-47; Overseas Civil Serv: admin offr Hong Kong 1952-85, sec for Hong Kong Civil Serv 1978-85, memb Hong Kong Legislative Cncl 1978-84, ret 1985; *Recreations* railways, birdwatching; *Clubs* Hong Kong, Royal Hong Kong Jockey; *Style—* Martin Rowlands, Esq, CBE; Flat 3, 15 Collingham Rd, London SW5 ONU

ROWLANDSON, Hon Mrs (Antonia Jane Hamilla); *née* Inskip; da of 2 Viscount Caldecote; *b* 1952; *m* 1972, Piers Rowlandson; 1 s (Titus b 1973); *Career* journalist; *Style—* The Hon Mrs Rowlandson; 83 Disraeli Road, London SW15

ROWLANDSON, Jack William Dunn; s of Brig George Dobbie Rowlandson, and Violet May, *née* Hatchard-Smith; *b* 24 Sept 1910; *Educ* Charterhouse; *m* 8 July 1939, Mary Elizabeth, da of Alfred Hobson (d 1953), of Epsom; 1 s (James b 3 Feb 1950), 1 da (Jillian b 3 Oct 1943); *Career* Air Miny 1936-37, airfield operator Whitney Straight 1937-39, Sqdn Ldr RAF 1940-47; trainee accountant Ware Ward & Co Exeter 1928-35, CA 1936, Moore Stephens 1947, chief accountant Bart's 1947-62, Newton Armstrong Management Consultants 1962-; hon sec Rahere Assoc 1950; FCA; *Recreations* sailing, gardening, swimming; *Clubs* Little Ship, Old Carthusian Yacht; *Style—* Jack Rowlandson, Esq; Peters Brae, Danehill, Sussex RH17 7EY (☎ 0825 790 212); 11/12 West Smithfield, London EC1A 9JR (☎ 071 489 8106)

ROWLATT, James Arthur; s of Arthur Rowlatt (d 1974), and Margaret Evangeline Rawlins (d 1977); *b* 27 June 1930; *Educ* Eton, Univ of Cambridge (BA); *m* 12 Sept 1968, Vita Marie Koefoed (d 1987), da of Jacob Nikolai Wichmann (d 1967), of Denmark; 2 da (Sophie b 1969, Kate b 1973); *Career* dir: Portfolio Management 1961-77, Parambe Ltd 1971-; chm Fleet Friendly Soc 1980-90; *Books* Pan Guide to Saving and Investment (1965); *Recreations* other people's gardens, science fiction; *Style—* James Rowlatt, Esq; 18 Holland St, Kensington, London W8 4LT (☎ 071 937 5929)

ROWLEY, Hon Lady (Celia Ella Vere); *née* Monckton; da of 8 Viscount Galway, GCMG, DSO, OBE, PC (d 1943), and Hon Lucia Emily Margaret, *née* White (d 1983), da of 3 Baron Annaly; *b* 1925; *m* 1959, Sir Joshua Francis Rowley, 7 Bt, *qv*; 1 da (Susan Emily Frances (Mrs Robert Holden) b 1965); *Style—* The Hon Lady Rowley; Holbecks, Hadleigh, Ipswich, Suffolk

ROWLEY, Sir Charles Robert; 7 Bt (UK 1836), of Hill House, Berkshire; s of Lt-Col Sir William Joshua Rowley, 6 Bt (d 1971); *b* 15 March 1926; *Educ* Wellington; *m* 1952, Astrid, da of late Sir Arthur Massey, CBE, MD; 1 s (Richard b 1959), 1 da (Mrs Edwin Phillipps de Lisle b 1955); *Heir* s; *Style—* Sir Charles Rowley, Bt; Naseby Hall, Northants; 21 Tedworth Sq, SW3

ROWLEY, (Joshua) Christopher; s of Lt-Col Sir William Joshua Rowley, Bt (d 1971), of Widdington Hse, nr Saffron Walden, Essex, and Beatrice, *née* Kirby (d 1978); *b* 10 Sept 1928; *Educ* Canford; *Career* currently interior designer; memb IDDA; *Recreations* tennis and gardening; *Style—* Christopher Rowley, Esq; The Hill Ct, Ross-on-Wye, Hereford (☎ 0989 62413); Christopher Rowley Int Dec Ltd, 69 Lower Sloane St, London SW1W 8DA (☎ 071 730 3500/3733)

ROWLEY, Christopher Owen Bergin; s of Owen Rowley (d 1987), and Sylvia Rowley; *b* 12 Aug 1938; *Educ* Rugby, Clare Coll Cambridge (MA); *m* 6 Aug 1964, Anna Mary, da of Roy Clarkson (d 1975), of Oxted, Surrey; 2 da (Katya b 1967, Juliet b 1969); *Career* drama coordinating offr ITV 1964-65, KYW-TV Philadelphia and Westinghouse Broadcasting USA 1965-66, prog planning exec Rediffusion TV 1966-67 (studio scheduling offr 1962-64); Thames TV: exec prodr In Sickness and In Health 1971 and Third World War 1972, prodr BAFTA award winning The Sun is God, dep controller factual prog to 1973; IBA TV scheduling offr 1974-84, head of planning TV 1984-90, md Five TV Network Ltd 1990-; fndr tstee One World Bdcasting Tst; pres Media Soc 1991; memb: RTS, Br Acad of Film and TV Arts, Soc of Int Devpt; *Style—* Christopher Rowley, Esq

ROWLEY, Prof David Ian; s of Sydney Garnett Rowley (d 1987), and Jessie, *née* Boot (d 1984); *b* 4 July 1951; *Educ* Wheelwright GS Dewsbury, Univ of Aberdeen (BMed Biol, MB ChB), Univ of Sheffield (MD); *m* 5 Aug 1975, Ingrid Ginette, da of K Mueller (d 1985); 1 s (Andrew Graham David b 1979), 1 da (Kristina Ann Ginette b 1976); *Career* lectr in orthopaedic surgery Univ of Sheffield 1981-85, sr lectr in orthopaedic surgery Univ of Manchester 1985-88, sr lectr in orthopaedic mechanics Univ of Salford 1986-88, prof of orthopaedic and trauma surgery Univ of Dundee 1988-; orthopaedic ed Jl of RCSEd; FRCS 1980; *Books* contribs incl: Yearbook of

Orthopaedics (1984), International Hospital Federation Yearbook (1986), Frontiers in Fracture Management (1989); *Style*— Prof David Rowley; Marclann Cottage, Kellie Castle, Arbirlot, Arbroath, Angus DD11 2PB (☎ 0241 76466), Univ Dept of Orthopaedic Surgery, Royal Infirmary, Dundee DD1 9ND (☎ 0382 22803, fax 0382 202460)

ROWLEY, Dr Donald; s of late Bertram Rowley; *b* 24 June 1926; *Educ* Selwyn Coll Cambridge; *m* 1950, Ruth Mary, *née* Dunkley; 1 s, 1 da; *Career* dir: BAC (Guided Weapons) Ltd 1967-77 (asst md 1975-77), Br Aerospace Dynamics Group 1977-85; md Naval Weapons Div Br Aerospace plc 1981-86; pres Electronic Engrg Assoc 1983-84; Hon DSc Univ of Bristol; British Silver medal for Aeronautics 1983; FEng; *Recreations* boating, gardening, music; *Style*— Donald Rowley, Esq; Manor Farm House, Northwick, Pilning, Bristol (☎ 04545 2327)

ROWLEY, John Howard; s of Capt Charles Donovan Rowley (d 1935), and Hon Irene Evelyn Beatrice, *née* Molesworth (d 1949); *b* 5 Nov 1931; *Educ* Gresham's Sch Holt, Univ of Reading (BSc); *m* 9 Feb 1963, (Aileen) Margery, da of Capt Robert Clifford Freeman, MC (d 1973); 1 s (Charles b 24 Jan 1969), 1 da (Irene b 18 Aug 1965); *Career* Lt RA 1950-52 (Capt CCF); entered educn Jamaica 1957; headmaster: de Carteret Prep Sch 1963, Gresham's Sch Holt 1975 (mathematics dept, i/c target rifle shooting); memb: Ctee BSSRA, Fullbore Ctee CCRS; Cmdt Cadet Competitors Bisley NRA, pres OGRE; *Recreations* fishing, gardening, walking; *Clubs* N London Rifle (Bisley); *Style*— John Rowley, Esq; Monk's Orchard, Blakeney, Holt, Norfolk (☎ 0263 740 488); Dalnabreac, Acharacle, Argyll (☎ 096 785 668); Gresham's Sch, Holt, Norfolk (☎ 0263 713271, fax 0263 712 028)

ROWLEY, John Stephen; s of John James Rowley, of Liverpool (d 1980), and Vera, *née* Hands; *b* 15 March 1948; *Educ* Liverpool Inst; *m* 3 June 1967, Linda, da of George Edward Kay, of Liverpool (d 1979); 2 s (John Stephen b 28 Nov 1967, Stuart Anthony b 18 July 1971); *Career* formerly: nat field sales mangr Colgate Palmolive Ltd, sales dir Playtex Ltd, gp sales and mktg dir Pretty Polly Ltd; currently chm and md: Focus on Legs Ltd, The Initiative Ltd; *Style*— John S Rowley, Esq; 17 Hays Mews, Mafair, London W1X 7RL (☎ 071 495 0515); The Cedars, Highgrove Gardens Edwalton Nottinghamshire NG12 4DF (☎ 0602 233549); The Initiative Ltd, 173 Wardour St, London W1; Focus on Legs Ltd, Sift House, Common Rd, Sutton in Ashfield (☎ 0623 551651, fax 0623 440760, telex 377302, car 0836 591911)

ROWLEY, Sir Joshua Francis; 7 Bt (GB 1786), of Tendring Hall, Suffolk; JP (Suffolk 1978); s of Col Sir Charles Samuel Rowley, OBE, TD, 6 Bt (d 1962); *b* 31 Dec 1920; *Educ* Eton, Trinity Coll Cambridge; *m* 1959, Hon Celia Ella Vere, *née* Monckton, da of 8 Viscount Galway (*see* Rowley, Hon Lady); 1 da; *Career* formerly Capt Gren Gds; dep sec Nat Trust 1952-55, chm W Suffolk CC 1971-74, Suffolk CC 1976-78, DL 1968, High Sheriff 1971, Vice Lord-Lt 1973-78, Lord-Lt 1978-; *Clubs* Boodle's, Pratt's, MCC; *Style*— Sir Joshua Rowley, Bt, JP; Holbecks, Hadleigh, Ipswich, Suffolk (☎ 0473 823211, 0206 262213)

ROWLEY, Keith Nigel; s of James Rowley, of 21 Blackwood Close, West Byfleet, Weybridge, Surrey KT14 6PP, and Eva, *née* Swales; *b* 20 Aug 1957; *Educ* Woking Co GS for Boys, King's Coll London (LLB), Cncl Educn; *m* 2 Aug 1986, Chantal Anna, da of Dewar Cameron Mackenzie, of Newton's Hill Cottages, Hartfield, East Sussex; *Career* barr Gray's Inn 1979; *Recreations* classical music, theatre, fishing, shooting, wine; *Style*— Keith Rowley, Esq; 12 Hestercombe Ave, London SW6 5LL; 11 Old Square, Lincoln's Inn, London WC2A 3TS (☎ 071 430 0341, fax 071 831 2469, telex 940 14894 JPAR G)

ROWLEY, Baroness; Mary Elizabeth; da of Ernest Verrall Barnes, of N Finchley; *m* 1, Harold Gliksten (decd), of Florida USA; m 2, 1958, Baron Rowley (Life Peer, d 1968); 2 husb Arthur Henderson, PC, QC, bro 1 Baron Henderson, cr Life Peer 1966; *Style*— The Rt Hon Lady Rowley; PO Box 5, Miami Shores, Florida 33153, USA

ROWLEY, Peter; MC (1944); s of Roland Rowley, MC, of Wembley, Middx (d 1955), and Catherine Isobel Whitticks (d 1944); *b* 12 July 1918; *Educ* Wembley Sch, Univ Coll Oxford (MA); *m* 19 Oct 1940, Ethnea Louis Florence Mary, da of John Howard-Kyan of Newell House, Grimston Ave, Folkestone, Kent (d 1958); 4 da (Rosemary b 1942, Anne b 1946, Carolyn b 1949, Julia b 1951); *Career* WWII Maj Sherwood Foresters; served ME, Italy, Germany; Bde Maj 13 Bde, GSO II 8 Corps; admitted slr 1950; sr ptnr Titmuss Sainer & Webb 1979-83; memb Land Law & Conveyancing Ctee Law Soc 1974-87; chm: Leonard Cheshire Fndn 1982-90, Euro Region Cheshire Homes 1990-; Liveryman Worshipful Co of Distillers'; *Recreations* opera, wine, carpentry; *Clubs* RAC; *Style*— Peter Rowley, Esq, MC; Underlea, 34 Radnor Cliff, Folkestone, Kent CT20 2JL (☎ 0303 48689); 26/29 Maunsel St, London SW1P 2QN (☎ 071 828 1822)

ROWLEY, (William) Philip; MBE (1945); s of Capt William Thomas John Rowley (d 1960), of London, and Gertrude Julia, *née* Hart (d 1967); *b* 3 April 1915; *Educ* Mil Coll of Sci; *m* 21 July 1939, Viva Maude, da of George Bartling (d 1960), of London; 1 s (Timothy b 1950); *Career* Nat Serv Signals Offr Reconaissance Bn 51 Highland Div 1941-42; Staff Offr radio to: Signal Offr-in-Chief GHQ Home Forces 1942, Signal Offr-in-Chief 21 Army Gp HQ (Field Marshall Montgomery's HQ) 1942-43, COS Supreme Army Cdr 1943, Signal Offr-in-Chief Supreme HQ AEF (Gen Eisenhower's HQ) 1943-46, sec Br Jt Communications Bd (Br Armed Forces) 1942-46, sec Combined Signal Bd (W Allied Armed Forces) 1943-46, Br jt sec Multipartite Signal Bd (W Allies and Russian Armed Forces) 1946; educn offr Radio and TV Retailers Assoc 1949-59, offr Sci Instrument Mfrs Assoc 1953-53, gen mgmnt appts various int electronic cos 1957-71, chm Telemotive UK Ltd 1971-87 (fndr chm and md 1971-80), conslt Satellite TV Engrg 1987-; memb Ctee Br Standards Instn; memb Br Inst Radio Engrs: Educn Ctee 1948-52, Membership Ctee 1953-56; memb Corpn King's Coll Sch Wimbledon; CEng, FIEE 1988, FIERE 1965, MBrit IRE 1945; author of numerous tv training courses (1949, further edns 1959); *Recreations* tennis, music, performing arts; *Clubs* Ballpark (Eastbourne); *Style*— Philip Rowley, Esq, MBE; 11 Clifton House, Pk Ave, Eastbourne, E Sussex BN22 9QN (☎ 0323 503252)

ROWLEY, Richard Charles; s and h of Sir Charles Rowley, 7 Bt; *b* 14 Aug 1959; *Style*— Richard Rowley, Esq

ROWLEY, Samuel Arthur; s of Joshua Ernest Rowley (d 1968), of West Hagley, Worcs, and Nora Rowley, *née* Cheshire (d 1967); *b* 12 June 1928; *Educ* Sebright Sch, Univ of Birmingham (LLM); *m* 25 May 1972, Brenda Maureen, da of Frank Lawson Musto, GSM, of Worthing; *Career* slr; memb Law Soc; *Recreations* gardening, travel, music, fine arts; *Style*— Samuel Rowley, Esq; Shannon Court, Corn St, Bristol BS99 7JZ (☎ 0272 294861, fax 0272 298313)

ROWLEY, Lady Sibell; *née* Lygon; 2 da of 7 Earl Beauchamp, KG, PC, KCMG (d 1938), and Lady Lettice Mary Elizabeth, *née* Grosvenor (d 1936), sis of 2 Duke of Westminster; *b* 10 Oct 1907; *m* 11 Feb 1939, Flt Lt Michael Richard Bernard Rowley, AuxAF (d 1952), s of George Francis Richard Rowley; *Style*— The Lady Sibell Rowley; 1 Stable Cottages, Barton House, Guiting Power, N Cheltenham, GL54 5UH

ROWLEY-CONWY, Hon John Seymour; s of 9 Baron Langford, OBE, DL; *b* 1955; *Educ* Marlborough, Magdalene Coll Cambridge (MA), Oriel Coll Oxford (MSc); *m* 1983, Emma Josephine, da of Maj Peter Brown, of Longworth, Oxon; 1 s (William Geoffrey Peter b 1988), 1 da (Katherine Grete Claire b 1985); *Style*— The Hon John Rowley-Conwy; 66 Fentiman Rd, London SW8

ROWLEY-CONWY, Hon Owain Grenville; s and h of 9 Baron Langford, OBE, DL; *b* 27 Dec 1958; *Educ* Marlborough, RAC Cirencester; *m* 3 May 1986, Joanna, da of Jack Featherstone, of Clwyd; 1 s (Thomas Alexander b 1987), 1 da (Magdalen Guinevere b 1988); *Style*— The Hon Owain Rowley-Conwy

ROWLEY-CONWY, Dr the Hon Peter Alexander; s of 9 Baron Langford, OBE; *b* 1951; *Educ* Marlborough, Magdalene Coll Cambridge (MA, PhD); *m* 1979, Deborah Jane, only da of Col J H G Stevens, of Betchworth, Surrey; 2 da (Gabrielle Catrin b 1984, Eleanor Marsli b 1986); *Books* Star Carr Revisited; a Re-Analysis of the Large Mammals (1987), Mesolithic Northwest Europe; Recent Developments (1987); *Style*— Dr The Hon Peter Rowley-Conwy; Department of Archaeology, University of Durham, 46 Saddler St, Durham

ROWLINSON, Prof John Shipley; s of Frank Rowlinson (d 1986), of Wilmslow, Cheshire, and Winifred, *née* Jones; *b* 12 May 1926; *Educ* Rossall Sch Fleetwood Lancs, Trinity Coll Oxford (BSc, MA, DPhil); *m* 2 Aug 1952, Nancy, da of Horace Gaskell (d 1970), of Walkden, Lancs; 1 s (Paul b 1954), 1 da (Stella (Mrs Barczak) b 1956); *Career* res assoc Univ of Wisconsin USA 1950-51, sr lectr in chem Univ of Manchester 1957-60 (res fell 1951-54, lectr 1954-57), prof of chem technol London Univ 1961-73, Dr Lee's prof of chem Oxford 1974-, fell Exeter Coll Oxford 1974-, A D White prof-at-large Cornell Univ USA 1990-; borough cncllr Sale 1956-59; hon fell City and Guilds Inst 1986; FRSC, FIChemE, FEng 1976, FRS 1970; *Books* Liquids and Liquid Mixtures (1959), The Perfect Gas (1963), Thermodynamics for Chemical Engineers (1975), Molecular Theory of Capillarity (1982), JD van der Waals, On the Continuity of the Gaseous and Liquid States (ed, 1988); *Recreations* mountaineering; *Clubs* Alpine; *Style*— Prof J S Rowlinson, FRS; 12 Pullen's Field, Oxford OX3 OBU (☎ 0865 67507); Physical Chemistry Laboratory, South Parks Road, Oxford OX1 3QZ (☎ 0865 275401)

ROWLINSON, Stephen Richard; s of Henry Robert Rowlinson (d 1988), of Godalming; *b* 25 Dec 1939; *Educ* Wanstead HS, Univ of Nottingham (BA); *m* 17 Aug 1967, Kathleen Ann (Kathy); 2 s (Benjamin Toby, Thomas Henry); 1 da (Emily Kate Louise); *Career* gen trainee Sullivan Stauffer Colwell Bayles Inc 1961-62, divnl gen mangr Harris Lebus Ltd 1962-67, conslt Mckinsey and Co Inc 1967-74; chm: TCK Gp Ltd 1974-77, Rowlinson Tomala and Assocs Ltd 1977-80, Bickerton Rowlinson Ltd 1980-84, Korn/Ferry Int Ltd 1985-89, Sanders & Sidney Plc 1989-; *Recreations* sailing, skiing, livery upholders; *Clubs* RAC, Harry's Bar; *Style*— Stephen Rowlinson, Esq; 16 Wallside, Barbican, London EC2Y 8BH; Sanders & Sidney Plc, Orion House, 5 Upper St Martin's Lane, London WC2H 9EA (☎ 071 413 0321, fax 07 497 0380)

ROWNTREE, Sir Norman Andrew Forster; s of Arthur Thomas Rowntree, of London; *b* 11 March 1912; *Educ* Tottenham Co Sch, London Univ; *m* 1939, Betty, da of William Thomas, of Stonehouse, Glos; 2 s, 1 da; *Career* consulting engr 1953-64, dir Water Resources Bd and visiting prof Resources Bd 1964-73, prof of civil engrg Manchester Univ Sci and Technol Ins 1975-79; CEng, FICE; kt 1970; *Style*— Sir Norman Rowntree; 97 Quarry Lane, Kelsall, Tarporley, Cheshire (☎ 0829 51195)

ROWORTH, Philip William; s of Leslie Norman Roworth (d 1964), and Marjorie Joan, *née* Wilcocks; *b* 16 Jan 1950; *Educ* Loughborough GS; *m* 1, 22 July 1972 (m dis 1985), Brenda, *née* Stekell; 1 s (Richard Alexander b 1977), 1 da (Deborah Louise b 1981); m 2, 5 April 1986, Laura Susan, da of Bernard Barker, of Woodthorpe, Nottingham; *Career* ptnr Rothmere & Co CAs 1982-; dir Dorson Financial Servs Ltd 1985-; ACA 1977, FCA 1983; *Recreations* swimming, sport and games in general; *Style*— Philip Roworth, Esq; 27 Nell Gwyn Crescent, Bestwood Lodge, Nottingham (☎ 0602 206036); 66 St James Street, Nottingham (☎ 0602 472949 or 412742 or 411101)

ROWSE, Hon Mrs (Rosemary Sybella Violet); er da of 1 Baron Grimston of Westbury (d 1979), and Sybil Rose (d 1977), da of Sir Sigmund Neumann, 1 Bt; *b* 4 March 1929; *m* 1, 10 Feb 1953 (m dis 1964), (Charles) Edward Underdown, o s of late Harry Charles Baillie Underdown, JP; m 2, 29 March 1984, Antony Herbert David Rowse, s of late Herbert James Rowse; *Career* interior designer; *Style*— The Hon Mrs Rowse; 75B Flood Street, London SW3

ROWSON, Peter Aston; s of Dr Lionel Edward Aston Rowson, OBE, FRS (d 1989); *b* 8 Oct 1942; *Educ* St Edmunds Coll Ware; *m* 1967, Jennifer Mary, *née* Smyth; 1 s, 2 da; *Career* accountant; fin dir and co sec: Panther Securities plc, Panther Devpts Ltd, Panther Shop Investmts Ltd, Neil Martin Ltd, Ingrams Opticians Ltd, Saxonbest Ltd, MRG Systems Ltd; co sec: Yardworth Ltd, Excelchoice Ltd, Snowbest Ltd, Christchurch Park Properties Ltd, Westmead Building Co Ltd, Multitrust plc, Multitrust Securities Ltd, Investment Trust Securities Ltd; *Style*— Peter Rowson, Esq; 38 Mount Pleasant, London WC1X 0AP (☎ 071 278 8011)

ROXBEE COX, Hon Christopher Withers; eld s of Baron Kings Norton (Life Peer), *qv*; *b* 31 Oct 1928; *Educ* Westminster; *m* 3 Sept 1955, Rosemary Joyce, da of late Frederick Day Ardagh; 2 s; *Career* dir Reed Taylor Mgmnt Consits 1981-89; *Style*— The Hon Christopher Roxbee Cox; 29 Pages Lane, Bexhill, East Sussex TN39 3RD (☎ 213151)

ROXBURGH, Dr Ian Archibald; s of Archibald Cathcart Roxburgh (d 1954), of London NW3, and Grace Mary Blanche, *née* Lambert (d 1967); *b* 30 Aug 1917; *Educ* Stowe, Trinity Coll Cambridge (BA, MB BChir), Univ of Edinburgh; *m* 1, 7 July 1951 (m dis 1985), Gillian Frances, da of Roger Edward Norton, CMG, OBE (d 1978), of London; 1 s (Alan b 1967), 1 da (Frances b 1955); m 2, 18 Oct 1985, Patricia Jean, da of James Alexander Stanley Wilson (d 1959), of Totteridge, Ifield, Sussex; *Career* Surgn-Lt RNVR, RN Barracks Portsmouth 1944; RN Hosp: Haslar 1944, Sydney 1944-46, Devonport 1946; St Bartholomew's Hosp: house physician Med Professorial Unit 1943, med registrar 1947; registrar Skin Dept Prince of Wales Gen Hosp Tottenham 1948-50, GP Chelsea 1951-, med advsr Cwlth Devpt Corp 1967-76, ret 1988; memb: Suffolk Wildlife Tst, Suffolk Naturalists' Soc, Suffolk Preservation Soc, Royal Br Legion; MRCS 1943, LRCP 1943, MRCGP 1953, memb BMA 1943, fell RSM 1948; *Recreations* natural history, travel; *Clubs* Royal Cwlth Soc; *Style*— Dr Ian Roxburgh; Brandon Lodge, Walberswick, Southwold, Suffolk (☎ 0502 724 741)

ROXBURGH, Prof Ian Walter; s of Walter McRonald Roxburgh, and Kathleen Joyce, *née* Prescott; *b* 31 Aug 1939; *Educ* King Edward VII GS Sheffield, Univ of Nottingham (BSc), Univ of Cambridge (PhD); *m* 1960, Diana Patricia, *née* Dunn; 2 s, 1 da; *Career* res fell Churchill Coll Cambridge 1963, lectr in maths Kings Coll London 1964-66 (asst lectr 1963-64), reader in astronomy Univ of Sussex 1966-67; Queen Mary College (now Queen Mary & Westfield Coll) London; prof of applied maths 1967-87, prof of maths and astronomy 1987-, pro princ 1987, currently head Sch of Mathematical Sciences and dir Astronomy Unit; conslt Euro Space Agency; chm Ctee of Heads of Univ Depts of Mathematics & Statistics 1988, senator for mathematics & statistics Univ of London; Parly candidate: (Liberal) Walthamstow West 1970, (SDP) Ilford North 1983; FInstP, FRAS, FRSA; memb: Euro Physical Soc, Br Soc Philosophy of Science, Royal Inst of Philosophy, Int Astronomical Union; *Style*— Prof Ian Roxburgh; 37 Leicester Road, Wanstead, London E11 2DW (☎ 081 989 7117)

ROXBURGH, Rt Rev James William; s of James Thomas Roxburgh, and Margaret Roxburgh; *b* 5 July 1921; *Educ* Whitgift, St Catharine's Coll Cambridge; *m* 1949, Marjorie Winifred, *née* Hipkiss; 1 s, 1 da; *Career* ordained priest 1945, vicar of Barking 1965-77, archdeacon of Colchester 1977-83, pro-prolocutor Convocation of Canterbury

1977-83, Bishop Suffragan of Barking 1983-90, asst Bishop of Liverpool 1991-; *Recreations* travel, philately; *Clubs* Rotary, Essex; *Style—* The Rt Rev James Roxburgh; 53 Preston Road, Southport, Merseyside PRG 9EE (☎ 0704 542927)

ROXBURGH, Vice Adm Sir John Charles Young; KCB (1972, CB 1969), CBE (1967), DSO (1943), DSC (1942, and bar 1945); s of Sir (Thomas) James Young Roxburgh (d 1974), and Mona Gladys Mabel, *née* Heymerdinguer (d 1982); *b* 29 June 1919; *Educ* RNC Dartmouth; *m* 1942, Philippa, 3 da of Major Charles Montague Hewlett, MC (d 1944); 1 s, 1 da; *Career* joined RN 1933 (psc 1955, idc 1962), joined Submarine Branch 1940; serv Norway, Bay of Biscay, Med 1940-42; cmd HMS Submarines H43, United and Tapir 1942-45 (Med, Norway), Br Jt Servs Mission Washington 1958-60, dep dir Def Plans (Navy) MOD 1963-65, cmd HMS Eagle 1965-67, flag offr Sea Trg 1967-69, Flag Offr Plymouth 1969, Flag Offr Submarines and NATO Cdr Subs E Atlantic 1969-72, Vice Adm 1970, ret 1972; chm Grovebell Gp Ltd 1972-75, co cncllr (Surrey) 1977-81, memb Cncl and Mgmnt Ctee of Freedom Assoc 1977-85, pres RN Benevolent Tst 1978-84; *Recreations* golf, sailing, walking, music; *Clubs* Army and Navy, Liphook Golf; *Style—* Vice Admiral Sir John Roxburgh, KCB, CBE, DSO, DSC; Oakdene, Wood Rd, Hindhead, Surrey GU26 6PT (☎ 042 860 5600)

ROXBURGH, Dr Ronald Cathcart; s of Dr Archibald Cathcart Roxburgh (d 1954), and Grace Mary Blanche, *née* Lambert (d 1967); descent from Dr John Grieve, body surgn to Empress Elizabeth of Russia; *b* 16 Aug 1920; *Educ* Stowe, Trinity Coll Cambridge (MA, MD); *m* 21 March 1952, Angela Mary Elisabeth, da of Brig William Edward Harvey Grylls, OBE, and sis of Michael Grylls, MP, *qv*; 2 s (Andrew Cathcart b 1958, Alistair Michael b 1962), 2 da (Fiona Elisabeth b 1954, Penelope Alexandra b 1956); *Career* temp Surgn Lt RNVR 1945-47, house surgn Barts 1944-45, conslt paediatrician E Anglian RHA 1960-82; conslt memb W Norfolk Dist Health Authy 1983-88; chm: Wiggenhall branch NW Norfolk Cons Assoc 1986-, Norfolk branch NSPCC 1988-; FRCP; *Recreations* shooting, fishing, gardening; *Style—* Dr Ronald Roxburgh; Wiggenhall House, Wiggenhall St Mary, King's Lynn, Norfolk PE34 3DN

ROXBURGH, Dr Stuart Thomas Dalrymple; s of Robert Roxburgh, and Helen Roxburgh; *b* 10 May 1950; *Educ* Camphill Sch, Univ of Glasgow (MB ChB); *m* 25 June 1975, Christine MacLeod Campbell, da of John Ramsay (d 1979); 1 s (Campbell b 27 March 1980), 1 da (Alison b 5 Oct 1982); *Career* conslt ophthalmologist Tayside Health Bd, hon sr lectr Univ of Dundee; chm Sub Ctee Optics and Refractions; FCOphth 1988 (examiner), FRCSEd 1979; *Recreations* golf, hill-walking, painting; *Style—* Dr Stuart Roxburgh; 4 Craigie Knowes Avenue, Perth, Scotland PH2 0DL (☎ 0738 34347), Ninewells Hosp and Medical Sch, Dundee (☎ 0382 60111)

ROXBURGHE, 10 Duke of (S 1707); Sir Guy David Innes-Ker; 11 Bt (Premier Bt of Scotland or Nova Scotia, S 1625); also Lord Roxburghe (S before 31 March 1600), Earl of Roxburghe, Lord Ker of Cessford and Cavertoun (both S 1616), Marquis of Bowmont and Cessford, Earl of Kelso, Viscount of Broxmouth (S, with the Dukedom the last Peerages cr in the Peerage of Scotland, 1707), and Earl Innes (UK 1837); s of 9 Duke of Roxburghe (d 1974) and his 2 w (late Mrs Jocelyn Hambro); 1 Earl obtained a charter in 1648 of succession to the honour, to his gs 4 s of his da Countess of Perth, and after him the 3 s successively of his gda Countess of Wigton; Dukedom in remainder to whoever succeeds to Earldom; *b* 18 Nov 1954; *Educ* Eton, Magdalene Coll Cambridge; *m* 1977 (m dis 1990), Lady Jane, *née* Grosvenor, da of 5 Duke of Westminster and Hon Viola Lyttelton, da of 9 Viscount Cobham; 2 s (Marquis of Bowmont and Cessford b 1981, Lord Edward b 1984), 1 da (Lady Rosanagh b 16 Jan 1979); *Heir* s, Marquis of Bowmont and Cessford; *Career* formerly Lt RHG/1 Dragoons; landowner, co dir; *Recreations* fishing, shooting, golf, cricket, skiing; *Clubs* White's, Turf; *Style—* His Grace the Duke of Roxburghe; Floors Castle, Kelso, Roxburghshire (☎ 0573 24288); Roxburghe Estate Office, Kelso, Roxburghshire, Scotland (☎ 0573 23333)

ROXBURGHE, Mary, Duchess of; Lady Mary Evelyn Hungerford; *née* Crewe-Milnes; da (by 2 m) of first and last Marquess of Crewe; 1 Baron Houghton m sis 3 and Last Baron Crewe (extinct 1894), their s 2 Baron cr Earl of Crewe 1895 and a Marquess 1911; *b* 1915; *m* 1935 (m dis 1953), 9 Duke of Roxburghe (d 1974); *Career* bore HM the Queen's Canopy at Coronation of King George VI; *Style—* Mary, Duchess of Roxburghe; 15 Hyde Park Gdns, London W2 2LU (☎ 071 262 3349); West Horsley Place, Leatherhead, Surrey

ROY, Allan; TD; s of Harold William Roy (d 1951), of Hawes House, Ainsdale, Southport, and Kathleen, *née* McLaren (d 1945); *b* 13 May 1911; *Educ* Fettes Coll, Sch of Architecture Liverpool Univ; *m* 3 June 1939, Margaret Helen Nicoll (Peggy), da of James Nicoll (d 1951), of The Woodlands, Harpenden; 1 s (Niall b 27 April 1949), 2 da (Kirsty (Mrs Gjertsen) b 7 Nov 1942, Jeannie (Mrs Galdstone) b 17 Dec 1946); *Career* 2 Lt Liverpool Scottish 1932, Capt 1 Bn Queen's Own Cameron Highlanders 1940, Maj 1942, serv India and Burma; released from Army 1945; chm Chisholm & Co (Holdings) Ltd 1951-; Scotland Rugby Int 1938-39; *Recreations* golf; *Clubs* Royal Ancient Golf, Formby Golf, Highland Brigade; *Style—* Allan Roy, Esq, TD; Hawes House, Ainsdale, Southport, Lancs PR8 2NZ (☎ 0704 77735); Chisholm & Co (Holdings) Ltd, 14/16 Derby Rd, Liverpool (☎ 051 207 6221, telex 629118 CHISOM)

ROY, Andrew Donald; s of Donald Whatley Roy (d 1960), of York, and Beatrice Anne, *née* Barstow (d 1968); *b* 28 June 1920; *Educ* Malvern, Sidney Sussex Coll Cambridge (BA, MA); *m* 22 Dec 1947, Katherine Juliet, da of James Herbert Grove-White (d 1979), of Cirencester and Perrots Brook; 1 s (Donald b 1948), 2 da (Juliet (Mrs Worboys) b 1950, Mary (Mrs Mitchell) b 1953; *Career* serv WWII RA 1939-46: 54 Heavy Regt UK 1940-41, 8 Medium Regt India and 14 Army 1941-44 (Adj 1942-44); Univ of Cambridge: econs lectr 1951-64, fell Sidney Sussex Coll 1951-64 (tutor 1953-56, sr tutor 1956- 62), Govt Econ Serv 1962-80; under sec (econ) 1969-80: Treasy 1969-72, DTI 1972-74, MOD 1974-76, chief econ advsr DHSS 1976-80; conslt NIESR 1981-83; memb: Royal Econ Soc, Royal Statistical Soc, Econometric Soc; *Books* British Economic Statistics (with CF Carter, now Sir Charles Carter, 1954); *Clubs* Utd Oxford and Cambridge Univ; *Style—* Andrew Roy, Esq; 15 Rusholme Rd, Putney, London SW15 3JX (☎ 081 789 3180)

ROY, Prof Donald Hubert; s of William Hadland Roy (d 1987), and Winifred Elizabeth Margaret, *née* Davies; *b* 5 April 1930; *Educ* Canton HS Cardiff, Univ of Wales (BA, MA, DipEd), Univ of Paris Sorbonne; *m* 1, 5 Aug 1955 (m dis 1959), Jane Elizabeth Ailwen (Sian); m 2, 25 Jan 1975, Arlette, da of James William Hopper, of 32 Rosehill Gardens, Sutton, Surrey; 1 s (Gareth b 1978), 1 da (Francesca b 1980); *Career* Nat Serv Cmmnd RAF 1954-56; asst lectr in French Univ of St Andrews 1958-59, lectr in French (former asst lectr) Univ of Glasgow 1959-63, dir and prof of drama (former lectr-i/c and sr lectr) Univ of Hull 1963-, visiting prof Univ of Delaware USA 1974, visiting dir Central Univ of Iowa USA 1987; memb: bd of dirs Hull Truck Theatre Co, Hull New Theatre consultative panel, Mgmnt Ctee Consortium for drama and media in Higher Educn; FRSA 1984; *Books* Molière: Five Plays (1982), Plays by James Robinson Planché (1986); *Recreations* reading, gardening, hill-walking; *Style—* Prof Donald Roy; Department of Drama, University of Hull, Hull, N Humberside HU6 7RX (☎ 0482 465615, fax 0482 466205, telex 592592 KHMAIL G)

ROY, Dr James Henry Barstow; s of Donald Whatley Roy (Surgn Lt RNVR, Capt RAMC d 1960), of London and Newbury, Berks, and Beatrice Anne, *née* Barstow (d 1968); *b* 17 July 1922; *Educ* Malvern, Sidney Sussex Coll Cambridge (BA, Dip Agric, MA), Univ of Reading (PhD, DSc); *m* Aug 1956, Irene Jill Ann, da of Edgar Frank Turner (d 1979), of Chichester, W Sussex; 1 s (Jonathan b 1964), 2 da (Caroline b 1957, Philippa b 1959); *Career* RR Artillery (field) NW Europe, ME: joined 1941, Cmmnd 1942, Capt 1944, Adj 1945-46; C in C certificate 1946; Nat Inst for Res in Dairying Shinfield Reading 1949-85: agric scientist, sr princ scientific offr, head Feeding and Metabolism Dept; contrib to various books on cattle, author of various scientific papers, reviews and popular articles, res award for animal nutrition Assoc of Fishmeal Mfrs 1959, res medal RASE 1971; memb: Mortimer and Burghfield Volunteer Bureau, Pangbourne Coll Choral Soc, Newbury Symphony Orch, Woodley String Orch; hon fell Univ of Reading 1985; memb: Nutrition Soc, Br Soc of Animal Prodn, Br Cattle Vet Assoc, Old Malvernian Soc; CBiol, FIBiol; *Books* The Calf (1 edn 1955, 5 edn volume 1 1990); *Recreations* squash, tennis, gardening, music; *Clubs* Henley Sailing, Vet Res; *Style—* Dr James Roy; Brunckettts, The Street, Mortimer, nr Reading, Berkshire RG7 3PE (☎ 0734 332478)

ROYCE, David Nowill; s of Bernard Royce (d 1977), and Christine Ida, *née* Nowill (d 1958); *b* 10 Sept 1920; *Educ* Reading Sch, Univ of Vienna; *m* 24 July 1942, Esther Syvia, da of Rev Thomas Francis Yule (d 1939); 2 s (Robert b 1944, George b 1952), 1 da (Jacqueline b 1946); *Career* serv WWII Army 1940-46, Maj GSO2 Int HQ Br Troops Berlin; asst princ German section FO 1948, second sec 1949, private sec to Parly Under Sec for Affrs 1950-51; first sec: Athens 1953-55, Saigon 1955-57, FO (asst head Econ Relations Dept) 1955-60; head Chancery Caracas 1960-62, commercial cnsllr Bonn 1963-66, commercial cnsllr and consul-gen Helsinki 1967-69, commercial inspector 1969-71, under sec DTI 1973-80 (asst sec DTI 1971-73); dir gen Inst Export 1980-85 (hon fell), export conslt 1985-; lay reader Chelsea Old Church 1976-; FIEX 1985; *Books* Successful Exporting for Small Businesses (1990); *Recreations* swimming; *Style—* David Royce, Esq; 5 Sprimont Place, London SW3 3HT (☎ 071 589 9148)

ROYCE, Norman Alexander; s of Joseph Samuel Royce (d 1960), of London, and Margaret, *née* Fraser (d 1954); *b* 4 Feb 1915; *Educ* Abbey Sch Beckenham, Bromley Coll of Art, Architectural Assoc (DipArch); *m* 10 Sept 1948, Molly Walden, da of late Alfred William Clarke, OBE; 3 s (Christopher b 1950, Darryl b 1952, Dominic b 1964), 1 da (Lesley b 1954); *Career* RAF 1940-46: Pilot Staff Offr 1945, Sqdn Ldr, served Europe and ME; pres CIArb 1942, vice pres RIBA 1968 (assoc 1940, fell 1960), pres Concrete Soc 1977; chm: Joint Contracts Tbnl 1978-83, London Ct Int Arbitration 1980, Biggin Hill Airport Consultative Ctee; memb: Ctee Royal London Soc for the Blind, vice pres Br Acad of Experts, vice chm Biggin Hill RAF Assoc; Freeman City of London 1952; Master: Worshipful Co of Gardeners 1973, Worshipful Co of Fanmakers 1979, Worshipful Guild of Air Pilots and Air Navigators 1981, Worshipful Co of Arbitrators 1983, Worshipful Co of Chartered Architects 1990; CIArb 1957 (former pres); *Recreations* flying, gardening, cricket; *Clubs* Carlton, RAF, City Livery, MCC; *Style—* Norman Royce, Esq; 4 Waldron Gardens, Shortlands, Bromley, Kent BR2 0JR (☎ 081 464 3256); 4 Verulam Buildings, Grays Inn, London (☎ 071 242 4381, fax 081 464 3256)

ROYCE, Roger John; QC (1987); s of John Roger Royce (d 1990), of Trig Rock, Cornwall, and Margaret, *née* Sibbald; *b* 27 Aug 1944; *Educ* The Leys Sch Cambridge, Trinity Hall Cambridge (BA); *m* 12 May 1979, Gillian Wendy, da of Geoffrey Guy Adderley, of High Trees, Whitedown Lane, Alton, Hants; 2 s (Andrew David Lyndon b 1986, David John Henry b 1989), 1 da (Joanna Katy Rachel b 1984); *Career* admitted slr 1969, called to the Bar Gray's Inn 1970, rec 1986; sport: Univ of Cambridge Hockey Blue 1965-66, East Hockey 1965-66, West Hockey 1972-73, capt Somerset Hockey 1976, qualified ski instr Austria 1969; *Recreations* skiing, cricket, golf, collecting corkscrews; *Clubs* Hawks, St Enodoc GC; *Style—* John Royce, Esq, QC; Guildhall Chambers, Broad St, Bristol (☎ 0272 273 366, fax 0272 298 941)

ROYDEN, Sir Christopher John; 5 Bt (UK 1905); s of Sir John Royden, 4 Bt (d 1976), of Netherfield Place, Battle, Sussex, and Dolores Catherine, da of Cecil Coward, of Lima; *b* 26 Feb 1937; *Educ* Winchester, ChCh Oxford (MA); *m* 1961, Diana Bridget, da of Lt-Col Joseph Henry Goodhart, MC (d 1975), of Keldholme Priory, Kirkbymoorside, York, by Evelyn, yst da of Henry Beaumont, JP, DL; 2 s (John b 1965, Richard b 1967), 1 da (Emma b 1971); *Heir* s, John Michael Joseph Royden, b 17 March 1965; *Career* Nat Serv 2 Lt 16/5 The Queen's Royal Lancers 1955-57; Duncan Fox & Co Ltd 1960-71, stockbroker Spencer Thornton & Co 1971-86, Gerrard Vivian Gray Ltd 1988-; *Recreations* shooting, fishing, gardening; *Clubs* Boodles; *Style—* Sir Christopher Royden, Bt; Bridge House, Ablington, Bibury, Glos

ROYDEN, Catherine, Lady (Dolores Catherine); da of Cecil Coward, of Lima; *m* 1936, Sir John Royden, 4 Bt (d 1976); 2 s, 2 da; *Style—* The Lady Catherine Roydon; Netherfield Place Farm, Battle, Sussex TN33 9PY

ROYDEN, John Michael Joseph; s and h of Sir Christopher John Royden, 5 Bt; *b* 17 March 1965; *Educ* Stowe, Univ of Reading (LLB); *Career* dir: EW Futures plc, ECU Group Ltd, ECU Holdings Ltd, Colour Counsellors Ltd; fin futures broker; memb Soc of Tech Analysts; *Recreations* shooting, fishing, backgammon, waterskiing, painting, bonking; *Style—* John Royden, Esq; Flat 2, 8 Nevern Sq, London SW5 9NW (☎ 071 370 2665)

ROYDON, Terry Rene; s of Leon Roydon, and Lyanne, *née* Hamoniere; *b* 23 Dec 1946; *Educ* Clifton Coll, Univ of London (BSc), Univ of Pittsburgh (MBA); *m* 29 Sept 1972, Carol Joycelyn, da of Stanley Norris; 1 da (Karen b 1977); *Career* md: Comben Group plc 1970-84, Prowting plc 1985-; memb Nat House Bldg Cncl 1981-, pres Housebuilder Fedn 1984, govr St Helen's Sch Northwood 1988-; *Style—* Terry Roydon, Esq; Breakspear Hse, Bury St, Ruislip, Middx HA4 7SY

ROYLANCE, Jayne Elizabeth; da of George Russell Spencer Ward (d 1990), of North Walsham, Norfolk, and Kathleen Mary, *née* Lock-Wood; *b* 8 Oct 1947; *Educ* Cromer HS; *m* 7 Oct 1967, John Michael Roylance, s of Robert James Roylance; 1 s (Paul Spencer b 3 Aug 1968), 3 da (Sara Jayne b 24 July 1970, Karen Elizabeth b 6 Aug 1973, Lisa Ann b 1 Jan 1976); *Career* bowls player; Cromer Marrams 1979-86, North Walsham 1986-, represented Norfolk 1980-; achievements incl: won all county honours, England debut 1986, Silver medal triples and fours World Bowls NZ 1988, Bronze medal pairs Cwlth Games NZ 1990; records: nat fours (skip) 1985, nat triples (skip) 1989, nat two wood singles 1989; also indoor bowls player: int badge holder, won nat honours mixed pairs and mixed fours; *Recreations* squash, working in family business; *Style—* Mrs Jayne Roylance; c/o North Walsham Bowls & Squash, Tungate Farm, North Walsham, Norfolk (☎ 0692 404966)

ROYLE, Carol Buchanan (Mrs Julian Spear); da of Derek Stanley Royle (d 1990), and Jane Irene, *née* Shortt; *b* 10 Feb 1954; *Educ* Streatham HS for Girls, Pitmans Wimbledon, Central Sch of Speech and Drama; *m* Julian David Barnaby Spear, s of Bernard Spear; 1 s (Taran Oliver Buchanan b 5 Nov 1983); *Career* actress; Harrogate Repertory Co 1976-77; RSC: Ophelia (Hamlet) and Cressida (Troilus and Cressida) 1980-82, Princess of France (Love's Labours Lost) 1990-91; Titania (Midsummer Night's Dream) 1988; TV incl: The Cedar Tree (ATV) 1977-79, Blakes 7 (BBC) 1979, The Professionals (ITV) 1980, Waxwork (ITV) 1980, Heartland (ITV) 1980, Girl Talk (ATV) 1980, Racing Game (YTV) 1980, Feet Foremost (Granada) 1982, Possibilities (BBC) 1982, The Outsider (YTV) 1983, Judgement Day (Thames) 1983, Bergerac (BBC) 1983, The Oxbridge Blues (BBC) 1984, A Still Small Shout (BBC) 1985, Ladies in Charge (Thames) 1985-86, Life Without George (BBC) 1987-89, Hedgehog Wedding (BBC) 1987, The London Embassy (Thames) 1987, Blackeyes (BBC 2) 1989, Casualty (BBC 1) 1990; films incl: Tuxedo Warrior 1982-83, When the Wall Comes Tumbling Down (EMI) 1984, Deadline (RSPCA) 1988; London Drama Critics award for Most Promising Actress (for Ophelia) 1980; *Style*— Ms Carol Royle; Hutton Management, 200 Fulham Rd, London SW10 9PN (☎ 071 352 4825)

ROYLE, Dr Edward; s of Fred Royle (d 1973), and Gladys Adelaide, *née* Lane; *b* 29 March 1944; *Educ* King James's GS Almondbury, Christ's Coll Cambridge (BA, MA, PhD); *m* 2 Aug 1968, Jennifer, da of Nicholaas du Plessis (d 1983); 1 da (Catherine Jane); *Career* fell Selwyn Coll Cambridge 1968-72, reader in history Univ of York 1989 (lectr 1972, sr lectr 1982, head of Dept of History 1988); local preacher Methodist Church 1965; FRHS 1975; *Books* Victorian Infidels (1974), Radicals, Secularists and Republicans (1980), Chartism (1980), Social History of Modern Britain 1750-1985 (1987); *Style*— Dr Edward Royle; Dept of History, University of York, Heslington, York YO1 5DD (☎ 0904 432974)

ROYLE, Joseph (Joe); s of Joseph Royle, of Maghull, Liverpool, and Irene May Royle; *b* 8 April 1949; *Educ* Quarry Bank HS; *m* 6 June 1970, Janet Lilian, da of late Henry Hughes; 3 s (Lee Joseph b 24 March 1971, Darren Henry b 7 March 1974, Mark b 21 March 1981); *Career* professional football manager; former player: Everton, Manchester City, Bristol City, Norwich City; England caps: youth, under 23, 6 full 1971-77, full debut v Malta 1970, 2 goals; mangr Oldham Athletic 1982-; honours as player: League Championship Everton 1970, League Cup Manchester City 1976; youngest player to to play in Div 1 for Everton on debut v Blackpool aged 16; *Style*— Joe Royle, Esq; Oldham Athletic FC, Boundary Park, Oldham, Lancashire OL1 2PA (☎ 061 624 4972)

ROYLE, Pauline Ann; da of William Royle, of Guildford, Surrey, and Jane Audrey Hedley, *née* Stewart; *b* 19 June 1959; *Educ* St Catherines Sch Bramley nr Guildford, Inchbald Sch of Design (Dip); *Career* jr designer Fitch & Co 1979-81; designer Conran Associates 1983-86, projects incl: offices, retail outlets, shopping centres; The Design Solution 1986-, clients incl: Littlewoods (design and implementation of new Corporate image), The Secret Garden (assoc ptnr 1989), Our Price Music (design of Video Shop Concept), M I Group and other slrs; also involved (with English Heritage) in refurbishment of 1900 Arts & Craft Building whilst at The Design Solution; *Recreations* swimming, tennis, skiing, windsurfing; *Style*— Ms Pauline Royle; The Design Solution, 20 Kingly Court, London W1R 5LE (☎ 071 434 0887, fax 071 434 0269)

ROYLE, Peter Richard; s of Eric Vernon Royle, and Marjorie Ethel, *née* Tomlin; *b* 28 Jan 1935; *Educ* Haileybury; *m* 1 (m dis), Vanessa Susan Colman; 4 da (Lucinda Mary b 1962, Bettina Jane b 1964, Melissa Gail b 1965, Amanda Claire b 1969); m 2, 7 July 1982, Margaret Helen Scatliff; *Career* chm and chief exec W R Royle Gp Ltd (and twelve operating susid cos); *Recreations* golf, photography; *Clubs* Reform, Royal Ashdown Golf, Piltdown Golf; *Style*— Peter Royle, Esq; W R Royle Gp Ltd, Wenlock Rd, London N1 7ST (☎ 071 253 7654)

ROYLE, Timothy Lancelot Fanshawe; s of Sir Lancelot Carrington Royle, KBE (d 1978); *b* 24 April 1931; *Educ* Harrow, Mons Mil Acad; *m* 1959, Margaret Jill, da of Sir Ivan Rice Stedeford, GBE; 2 s, 1 da; *Career* Church Cmmr 1967-83; chm: Lindley Lodge Educn Tst 1970-, Christian Weekly Newspapers 1976-; md: Hogg Robinson UK 1972-81, Hogg Robinson Ltd 1976-81, Hogg Robinson Gp 1980-81; chm: Control Risks Gp 1974-, Westminster Property Gp 1983-84, Fin Strategy 1983-84, Berry Palmer & Lyle 1984-; dir Wellmarine Reinsurance Brokers 1975-; memb General Synod of C of E 1985-; tstee: Wycliffe Coll Oxford, Ridley Coll Cambridge; CInstM, FBIBA; *Recreations* country pursuits, real tennis, skiing; *Clubs* Cavalry and Guards, MCC, St Moritz Toboganning; *Style*— Timothy Royle, Esq; c/o National Westminster Bank, 11 Leadenhall St EC3

ROZENBERG, Joshua Rufus; s of Zigmund Rozenberg (d 1982), and Beatrice Doris, *née* Davies; *b* 30 May 1950; *Educ* Latymer Upper Sch Hammersmith, Wadham Coll Oxford (MA); *m* 31 March 1974, Melanie, da of Alfred Phillips; 1 s, 1 da; *Career* trainee journalist BBC 1975, admitted slr 1976, legal affrs corr BBC radio news 1985, legal corr BBC TV news 1988; *Books* Your Rights and The Law (with N Watkins, 1986), The Case For The Crown (1987); *Style*— Joshua Rozenberg, Esq; BBC Television News, Television Centre, London W12 7RJ (☎ 081 576 1789, fax 081 749 9016, car 0860 370177)

ROZYCKI; *see*: Ross, Andrew

ROZZI, Prof Tullio; s of Rear Adm Francesco Rozzi, of 38 Via S Margherita, 60100 Ancona, Italy, and Leila, *née* Fusco; *b* 13 Sept 1941; *Educ* Univ of Pisa, Univ of Leeds (PhD), Univ of Bath (DSc); *m* 22 July 1967, (Ruth) Parween, da of Rev Ernest Tak, of Lahore, Pakistan; 2 da (Leila b 1 June 1972, Esther b 29 Oct 1977); *Career* Philips res labs Eindhoven Holland 1968-78, Dept of Electrical Engrg Univ of Liverpool 1978-81, Sch Electrial Engrg Univ of Bath 1981-; FIEE 1983, FIEEE 1990; *Style*— Prof Tullio Rozzi; School of Electrical Engineering, Univ of Bath, Bath BA2 7AY (☎ 0225 826615)

RUBASINGHAM, Arumugam Sinnathamby; s of Arumugam Sinnathamy, and Annaluxmi Kandiah; *b* 14 Nov 1937; *Educ* Sri Lanka (MB BS); *m* 24 March 1969, Parimala, da of Manickam V; 1 s (Lavan 18 Nov 1971), 1 da (Indhu 18 Feb 1980); *Career* sr house offr and sr registrar United Sheffield Hosp 1969-72; sr registrar: Singleton Hosp Swansea 1972-74, Sheffield Hosp 1974-76; conslt opthalmic surgn cntral Nottinghamshire Health Authy 1976-; first chm Fedn of tamil Assoc; FRCS, FRCOPhth, FRCSEd 1973; *Recreations* entertaining and being entertained; *Style*— Arumugam Rubasingham, Esq; 24 North Park, Mansfield, Nottinghamshire NG18 4PB (☎ 0623 614228), King's Mill Hosp, Mansfield Rd, Sutton-in-Ashfield, Notts NG17 4JL (☎ 0623 22515)

RUBENS, Col (Ralph) Alexander; s of Capt Joshua Ernest Rubens (d 1985), of Henley-in-Arden, Warwicks, and Anna Louba, *née* Markova Klionsky; *b* 5 Feb 1920; *Educ* King Edwards Sch, RMC Sandhurst, RAF Staff Coll Bracknell, Jt Servs Staff Coll; *m* 1, 21 Dec 1949, Lady Rosemary Alexandra, *née* Eliot (d 1963), da of 6 Earl of St Germans (d 1922); 1 da (Alexandra Louise (Mrs Peyronel) b 9 Oct 1951); m 2, 23 Oct 1967, Joan, da of Reginald Wilson Hawkes, of Shottery, Stratford upon Avon, Warwicks; *Career* cmmnd 1939, company cdr 2 Bn Sherwood Foresters served N Africa and Italy (Maj 1943), Anzio (wounded twice), staff appts attached RN and RAF, represented 3 Chiefs of Staff at 10 Downing St 1964-68 (Col), head of mgmnt info Army, ret 1974; clerk to Worshipful Co of Stationers and Newspaper Makers 1974-84, non-exec dir Graison (wine advsr) 1984-89, wine advsr Boddington Gp 1989-; vice chm Chelsea Soc; fndr memb Consultative Ctee of the Livery Corp of London; Freeman City of London 1976, Liveryman Worshipful Co of Stationers and Newspaper Makers 1976; *Recreations* wine, travel, theatre, reading, walking, swimming; *Clubs* Garrick, Saintsbury; *Style*— Col Alexander Rubens; 27 Gertrude St, Chelsea, London SW10 0JF; 45 Crag Path, Aldeburgh, Suffolk

RUBENS, Bernice Ruth; da of Eli Reubens (d 1958), of Cardiff, and Dorothy, *née* Cohen (d 1987); *b* 26 July 1928; *Educ* Cardiff HS for Girls, Univ Coll Cardiff (BA); *m* 29 Dec 1947 (m dis), Rudi Nassauer, s of Franz Nassauer; 2 da (Sharon b 1949, Rebecca b 1951); *Career* novelist; *Books* Set on Edge (1960), Madame Sousatzka (1962), Mate in Three (1965), The Elected Member (Booker prize 1970), Sunday Best (1972), Go Tell The Lemming (1974), I Sent a Leter to My Love (1976), The Ponsonby Post (1978), A Five Year Sentence (1979), Spring Sonata (1981), Birds of Passage (1982), Brothers (1983), Mr Wakefield's Crusade (1985), Our Father (1987), Kingdom Come (1990), A Solitary Grief (1991); documentary film maker; Hon Fell Univ of Wales 1984, Hon DLitt Univ of Wales; *Recreations* playing the cello; *Style*— Ms Bernice Rubens; 16A Belsize Park Gdns, London NW6 4LD (☎ 071 586 5365)

RUBENS, Robert David; s of Joel Rubens, of London, and Dinah, *née* Hasseck; *b* 11 June 1943; *Educ* Quintin GS, King's Coll London (BSc), St George's Hosp Med Sch (MB BS), Univ of London (MD); *m* 30 Oct 1970, Margaret, da of Alan Chamberlin, of Burncross, Yorks; 2 da (Abigail b 15 Nov 1971, Carolyn b 10 June 1974); *Career* house and registrar appts 1968-72: St George's, Brompton, Hammersmith & Royal Marsden Hosps; conslt physician Guy's Hosp 1975-; conslt med offr: Mercantile & General Reinsurance Co plc 1977- (chief med offr 1987-), Legal & General Assurance Society Ltd 1978-; dir of oncology servs Guy's Hosp 1985-90, prof of clinical oncology UMDS of Guy's and St Thomas's Hosps 1985-; Imp Cancer Res Fund: memb scientific staff 1972-85, dir Clinical Oncology Unit 1985-; memb Editorial Bd Cancer Treatment Reviews 1987-; examiner RCP 1987-, chm Div of Oncology UMDS of Guy's and St Thomas's Hosp 1989-; memb: Cncl Assur Med Soc 1982-90, SE Thames Regnl Cancer Ctee 1983-, Assoc of Cancer Physicians 1985; hon dir Inc Homes for Ladies with Limited Income 1983; memb: British Breast Gp 1976, American Assoc for Cancer Res 1977, American Soc of Clinical Oncology 1977; Freeman City of London 1979, Worshipful Soc of Apothecaries 1978- (Liveryman 1983-); memb BMA 1969, MRCP 1969, FRCP 1984; author of: A Short Textbook of Clinical Oncology (1980), pubns on experimental and clinical cancer therapy; *Recreations* golf, music, reading; *Clubs* Athenaeum, Royal Wimbledon Golf; *Style*— Prof Robert Rubens; 5 Currie Hill Close, Arthur Rd, Wimbledon, London SW19 7DX (☎ 081 946 0422); Guy's Hospital, London SE1 9RT (☎ 081 955 5000)

RUBIE, Hon Mrs (Jane Alice); *née* Liddell; da of 8 Baron Ravensworth and Wendy, adopted da of J Stuart Bell, of Cookham, Berks; *b* 1952; *m* 1984, Michael James Crowhurst Rubie; 3 da (Sophia Amy Elizabeth b 1986, Isabel Emma Mary b 1988, Francesca Louise b 1991); *Style*— THe Hon Mrs Rubie; Red Briars, 35 Drax Avenue, London SW20 0BQ

RUBIN, David (Antony); s of Leonard Rubin, and Sylvia Rubin (d 1987); *b* 11 Jan 1954; *Educ* Haberdashers Boys Sch; *m* 1 July 1982, Diana, da of Neville Curtis; 2 s (Guy Maurice b 1977, Scott James b 1987); *Career* CA; licenced insolvency practitioner and expert in insolvency matters; appointed in the High Ct in Insolvency matters, ACA; *Recreations* charity work, fund raising, golf, sport; *Clubs* Dyrham Park County; *Style*— David Rubin, Esq; Pearl Assurance House, 319 Ballards Lane N12 (☎ 081 446 8203, fax 081 446 2994)

RUBIN, Peter Charles; s of Woolf Rubin (d 1980), of Redruth, Cornwall, and Enis Muriel, *née* Cowling; *b* 21 Nov 1948; *Educ* Univ of Cambridge (MA), Univ of Oxford (DM); *m* 2 Oct 1976, Dr Fiona Anne, da of William Burns Logan (d 1967); 1 s (Jeffrey b 1984), 1 da (Victoria b 1979); *Career* American Heart Assoc Fell Stanford Med Center 1977-79, sr registrar in med and clinical pharmacology Glasgow 1979, Wellcome Tst sr fell Glasgow 1982, prof of therapeutics Univ of Nottingham Med Sch 1987-; FRCP 1989, memb Assoc of Physicians 1990; *Books* Lecture Notes on Clinical Pharmacology (edn 3, 1989), Prescribing in Pregnancy (1987), Hypertension in Pregnancy (1988); *Recreations* two young kids!; *Clubs* Oxford & Cambridge; *Style*— Prof Peter Rubin; 42 Richmond Drive, Mapperley Park, Nottingham NG3 5EL (☎ 0602 621441); Dept of Therapeutics, University Hospital, Nottingham NG7 2UH (☎ 0602 420820, fax 0602 422232, car 0860 284737)

RUBIN, Hon Mrs (Susan); *née* Rayne; da of Baron Rayne by his 1 w, Margaret; *b* 1945; *m* 1965, John Rubin; *Style*— The Hon Mrs Rubin

RUBINSTEIN, Hilary Harold; s of Harold Frederick Rubinstein (d 1974), of London, and Lena, *née* Lowy (d 1939); *b* 24 April 1926; *Educ* Cheltenham, Merton Coll Oxford (MA); *m* 6 Aug 1955, Helge, da of Gabriel Kitginger (d 1963), of Herts; 3 s (Jonathan Paul b 1956, Mark Gabriel b 1961, Ben Hilary b 1963), 1 da (Felicity Kate b 1958); *Career* trainee pilot RAF 1944-47, later Educn Corps and Vocational Advice Serv; ed dir Victor Gollancz 1952-63, special features ed The Observer Magazine 1964-65, md AP Watt Ltd Literary Agents 1965- (former ptnr, dir and chm); memb Cncl Inst of Contemporary Arts 1976-, tstee Open Coll of Arts; *Books* The Complete Insomniac (1974), The Good Hotel Guide (ed, 1978-), Hotels and Inns: An Anthology (ed, 1984); *Recreations* hotel watching, reading in bed; *Clubs* Garrick; *Style*— Hilary Rubinstein, Esq; AP Watt Ltd, 20 John St, London WC1N 2DR (☎ 071 405 6774, fax 071 831 2154)

RUBINSTEIN, Michael Bernard; s of late H F Rubinstein, and Lina, *née* Lowy; *b* 6 Nov 1920; *Educ* St Pauls; *m* 1955, Joy, *née* Douthwaite; 2 s, 2 da; *Career* served WWII RE TA 1939, Capt RA 1945; admitted slr 1948; Rubinstein Callingham Polden & Gale (formerly Rubinstein Nash & Co): sr ptnr 1976-86, conslt 1986-; memb Lord Chllr's Ctee on Defamation 1971-74, chm SPNM Tstees 1986- (tstee 1967-); *Books* Wicked, Wicked Libels (ed and contrib, 1972), Rembrandt and Angels (monograph, 1982), Malta's Ancient Temples and Ruts (incorporating The Cart-Ruts on Malta and Gozo (1984),with Roland Parker 1988), Music to my Ear (1985); *Clubs* Garrick, Groucho; *Style*— Michael Rubinstein, Esq; 2 Raymond Bldgs, Gray's Inn, London WC1R 5BZ (☎ 071 242 8408)

RUCK, Adam; s of Andrew Ruck, of Wrotham, and Patricia, *née* Creasey; *b* 9 Oct 1952; *Educ* Haileybury, New Coll Oxford, Courtauld Inst of Art (MA); *m* 1990, Jane Slade; *Career* travel writer/columnist, author; *Books* The Holiday Which? Guide to France (4 edn, 1989), The Holiday Which? Guide to Italy (jtly, 2 edn 1989), The Good Skiing Guide 1985 (co-ed, 5 edn 1990), The Holiday Which? Guide to Greece and the Greek Islands (jtly, 1989); *Recreations* tennis, skiing; *Clubs* Holland Park Lawn Tennis; *Style*— Adam Ruck, Esq; 29 Algarve Road, London SW18 (☎ 081 874 9491)

RUCK, Hon Mrs (Catherine Dorothy); *née* Neville; da of 7 Baron Braybrooke, JP, DL, by his 2 w, Dorothy, JP, da of late Sir George Lawson, KC; *b* 21 Jan 1922; *m* 1954, Gordon Alexander Egerton Ruck (d 1977); 1 da; *Style*— The Hon Mrs Ruck; Asherne, Strete, Dartmouth, Devon

RUCK KEENE, David Kenneth Lancelot; s of Thomas Ruck Keene, of Goulds Grove, Ewelme, Oxford, and Anne Coventry, *née* Greig; *b* 22 Sept 1948; *Educ* Eton; *m* 30 Oct 1976, Tania Caroline, da of William Anstey Preston Wild; 3 da (Katherine b 1981, Rosanna b 1983, Lucia b 1985); *Career* CA; Rowe & Pitman Stockbrokers 1977-82, (ptnr 1982-86), dir SG Warburg, Akroyd, Rowe & Pitman, Mullens Ltd 1986-; FCA 1974, memb Stock Exchange 1982; *Recreations* country pursuits, rackets, tennis, golf; *Clubs* White's, Queen's, MCC; *Style*— David Ruck Keene, Esq; Warburg Securities, 1 Finsbury Ave, London EC2M 2PA (☎ 071 606 1066, fax 071 382 4800)

RUCKER, Sir Arthur Nevil; KCMG (1942), CB (1941), CBE (1937); only s of Sir Arthur William Rucker (d 1915), and his 2 w Thereza, *née* Story-Maskelyne; *b* 20 June 1895; *Educ* Marlborough, Trinity Coll Cambridge; *m* 1922, Elsie Marion, da of late George Broadbent; 2 s, 2 da; *Career* serv WWI Lt Suffolk Regt; private sec to Min of Health 1928-35 (asst sec 1935-37); dir Estabs 1937-39, princ private sec to PM 1939-41, sec office of Min of State Cairo 1941-43, dep sec Miny of Health 1943-47, dep dir gen Int Refugee Orgn 1947, dep agent gen of UN for Korea 1951; chm Tithe Redemption Cmmn 1954, memb Cwlth War Graves Cmmn 1955-69; chm Stevenage

Devpt Corpn 1962-66 (vice chm 1956); Hon LLD (Wales); Korean Order of Diplomatic Merit (1974); *Clubs* Athenaeum; *Style—* Sir Arthur Rucker, KCMG, CB, CBE; Manor Farm House, Yattendon, nr Newbury, Berks (☎ 0635 201205)

RUCKER, Brig James William Frederick; s of Charles Edward Sigismund Rucker (d 1965), of South's Farm, Ashmore, Salisbury, Wilts, and Nancy Winifred, *née* Hodgson; *b* 3 May 1936; *Educ* Charterhouse; *m* 14 Sept 1963, Caroline Lloyd, da of Raymond Wilson Sturge (d 1984), of Lord's Mead, Ashmore, Salisbury, Wilts; 2 s (Rupert b 1967, Jeremy b 1970), 1 da (Sara b 1964); *Career* Col The QOH, Cdr RAC, BAOR, Brig; DOR MOD; md NAAFI 1987-; *Recreations* shooting, cricket, tennis, gardening; *Clubs* Cavalry and Guards, MCC; *Style—* Brig James Rucker; Manor Farmhouse, Ashmore, Salisbury, Wilts; 6 Beechmore Rd, London SW11; Imperial Ct, Kennington Lane, London SE11

RUCKER, His Hon Judge Jeffrey Hamilton; s of Charles Edward Sigismund Rucker, MC (d 1965), of Ashmore, nr Salisbury, Wilts, and Nancy Winifred, *née* Hodgson; *b* 19 Dec 1942; *Educ* Charterhouse, Univ of Heidelberg; *m* 15 May 1965, Caroline Mary, da of Col Philip Edward Salkeld (d 1975), of Stour House, Blandford, Dorset; 3 s (Simon b 3 Nov 1970, Nicholas b 26 Sept 1972, James b 3 Feb 1978); *Career* called to the Bar Middle Temple 1967, rec 1984, circuit judge 1988; *Recreations* sailing, skiing, music; *Style—* His Hon Judge Jeffrey Rucker; 36 Essex St, London WC2 3AS (☎ 071 413 0353)

RUCKMAN, Robert Julian Stanley; s of William James Ruckman (d 1962), late of Sycamore Rd, Chalfont, and Ida Marjorie, *née* Woodward (d 1989); *b* 11 May 1939; *Educ* Harrow Tech Coll, Cranfield Inst of Tech (MSc); *m* 16 Oct 1965, Josephine Margaret, da of Lieut RNVR George Colin Trentham, DSC (despatches) (d 1979); 1 s (Gordon b 1966), 1 da (Helen b 1973); *Career* chartered engr; systems analyst; memb tech staff Systems Sci Corp Virginia USA 1966, sr engr Kent Instruments 1968, civil servant (computer mangr) Dept of Tport 1970; author of pubns on digital systems; EurIng, CEng, MIEE, MBCS, MIEEE, MInstMC, MCIT, Comp IAP; *Recreations* hill walking, classical music, woodworking; *Clubs* CGA; *Style—* Eur Ing Robert Ruckman; Flamingo, 13 Alexander Ave, Droitwich, Worcs; Dept of Transport, Regnl Off, Room 105, 5 Broadway, Five Ways, Birmingham (☎ 021 631 8173)

RUDD, Hon Mrs (Fiona Catherine Ritchie); *née* Calder; da of Baron Ritchie-Calder, CBE; *b* 10 July 1929; *Educ* LSE; *m* 1949, Dr Ernest Rudd; 3 da; *Style—* The Hon Mrs Rudd; 19 South Parade, York YO2 2BA

RUDD, Hon Mrs (Hilary Aileen); *née* Peddie; da of Baron Peddie (Life Peer) (d 1978); *b* 1938; *m* 1959 (m dis), Christopher Geoffrey Rudd; 1 s, 1 da; *Style—* The Hon Mrs Rudd; 31 Nonsuch Court Ave, Ewell, Surrey

RUDD, Lewis Michael Cooper; MBE (1989); s of Dr A S Rudd, and Hannah, *née* Marcus (d 1983); *b* 16 Sept 1936; *Educ* Highgate, Magdalen Coll Oxford (MA); *m* 2 Dec 1964, Joan Muriel, da of R N Bower, of Osmanthorpe Manor, Kirklington, Notts; 2 s (Charles b 28 June 1967, Thomas b 2 May 1969), 1 da (Penelope b 4 April 1972); *Career* Nat Serv RASC 1954-56; head of children's programmes Rediffusion TV 1966-68, controller of children's programmes Thames TV 1968-72, asst controller of programmes Southern TV 1972-81, controller of young people's programmes Central TV 1981-, md FilmFair Ltd 1989-; *Style—* Lewis Rudd, Esq, MBE; FilmFair Animation, 1-4 Jacob's Well Mews, London W1H 5PD

RUDD, (Anthony) Nigel Russell; s of Samuel Rudd (d 1983), of West Bank Ave, Derby, and Eileen, *née* Pinder; *b* 31 Dec 1946; *Educ* Bemrose GS Derby; *m* 20 Sept 1969, Lesley Elizabeth, da of Bernard Thomas Hodgkinson (d 1990), of Rubha-Nan-Gall, Kilchoan, Acharacle, Scotland; 2 s (Timothy Nigel b 27 May 1971, Edward Thomas b 23 Sept 1973), 1 da (Jennifer Clare b 24 March 1978); *Career* exec chm Williams Holding plc 1982-; non-exec chm: Raine Industries plc 1986-, Pendragon plc 1989; memb: City and Industl Liaison Cncl, Round Table, Nuffield Nursing Home Appeal; FCA 1967; *Recreations* golf, squash, shooting, tennis; *Clubs* Duffield Squash, Chevin Golf, IOD; *Style—* Nigel Rudd, Esq; Pentagon House, Sir Frank Whittle Road, Derby, DE2 4EE (☎ 0332 364 257, fax 0332 384 402)

RUDD-JONES, Derek; CBE (1981); s of Walter Henry Jones (d 1966), of Betchworth, Surrey, and Doris Mary, *née* Dawes; *b* 13 April 1924; *Educ* Whitgift Sch Croydon, Repton, Emmanuel Coll Cambridge (BA, MA, PhD); *m* 4 Dec 1948, Joan Hancock, da of Edward Newhouse (d 1962), of Malvern, Worcs; 2 s (Julian b 1955, Nicholas b 1959), 1 da (Clare (Dr Symes) b 1951); *Career* HM Colonial Res Serv 1949-53; Agric Res Cncl postgrad studentship Botany Sch Univ of Cambridge 1945-48, sr scientific offr E African Agric and Forestry Res Orgn 1949-53, NRC postdoctoral fell Univ of Saskatchewan Saskatoon Canada 1952-53, ICI plc Akers Res Laboratories The Frythe Welwyn Herts 1954-56, Jealotts Hill Res Station Bracknell Berks 1956-59, scientific advsr Agric Res Cncl 1959-71 (memb Advsy Ctee on Pesticides 1960-70), fndn chm Br Crop Protection Cncl 1968-72, dir Glasshouse Crop Res Inst Littlehampton 1971-86, visiting fell Univ of Southampton 1975-86, conslt ed 1986-; author scientific papers in: Nature, Annals Applied Biology; govr W Sussex Inst of Higher Educn 1980-, memb Scientific Ctee RHS 1982-, tstee Thomas Phillips Price Tst 1988-; FIBiol 1965, FIHort 1986; *Books* Healthy Planting Material: Strategies and Technologies (1986); *Recreations* gardening, riding, fly fishing, arboriculture; *Clubs* Farmers; *Style—* Dr Derek Rudd-Jones, CBE

RUDDLE, Kenneth Anthony (Tony); s of Sir (George) Kenneth Fordham Ruddle (d 1979), of Islington Lodge, Langham, Oakham, Rutland, and Nancy Margaret, *née* Allen; gf, George Ruddle, bought family brewery in 1911; *b* 12 April 1936; *Educ* Repton; *m* 1, 20 Aug 1959 (div 1976), Elizabeth Margaret Duff Brown; 1 s (Guy Anthony b 1961), 1 da (Caroline b 1963); m 2, 20 Oct 1976, Fiona Eileen Morse; *Career* short service cmmn with 8 Hussars 1956-59; joined family co 1959, md 1968, chm 1973-; vice chm Rutland Branch Mental Health Foundation; jt MFH Cottesmore Hunt; Freeman of City of London, Liveryman of Worshipful Co of Brewers 1983; *Recreations* hunting, golf, skiing; *Style—* K A Ruddle, Esq; c/o Ruddles Brewery Ltd, Langham, Oakham, Leics LE15 7JD (☎ 0572 756911, telex 341648); Leesthorpe Hall, Melton Mowbray, Leics (☎ 066477 244)

RUDDLE, Peter; s of John Eric Ruddle, and Alice Emily, *née* Ambrose; *b* 16 May 1945; *m* 5 Oct 1968, Hazel Patricia, da of Sydney Robert Driscoll; 3 s (Simon Peter b 1970, Christopher John b 1972, William Edward b 1976); *Career* dir Senlac Consultants Ltd; *Recreations* swimming, gardening, DIY, bridge; *Clubs* Overseas Bankers; *Style—* Peter Ruddle, Esq; 3 Amherst Rd, Benhill-on-Sea, E Sussex (☎ 0424 214823, office 0424 730577, fax 0424 212944)

RUDDOCK, Joan; MP (Lewisham-Deptford 1987-); da of Kenneth Charles Anthony (d 1981), and Eileen Messenger; *b* 28 Dec 1943; *Educ* Pontypool GS for Girls, Imperial Coll London (BSc); *m* 1963, Keith, s of Charles Ruddock (d 1966), of Yorks; *Career* mangr Citizens Advice Bureau Reading (employment), chairperson CND 1981-85 (currently vice pres), shadow minister Transport 1989-; *Style—* Ms Joan Ruddock, MP; House of Commons, Westminster, London SW1

RUDDOCK, Neil; s of Edward Keith Ruddock, of 77 Sandyhurst Lane, Ashford, Kent, and Joyce Freida, *née* Valence; *b* 9 May 1968; *Educ* North Sch for Boys Ashford Kent; *m* 27 May 1989, Sarah-Jane Victoria, da of John Paul Michael Bennett; 1 s (Joshua Paul b 17 Feb 1990); *Career* professional footballer; apprentice Millwall FC, Tottenham Hotspur FC 1986, debut Southampton 1989 (78 games to date); rep: Eng Youth, Eng U19, Eng U20, Eng U21; Barclay's League Young Eagle award London and South 1989; *Recreations* golf, tennis, boxing; *Style—* Neil Ruddock, Esq; Southampton FC, The Dell, Milton Rd, Southampton, Hampshire (☎ 0703 220505)

RUDGE, Anthony John de Nouaille; s of John Edward Rudge (d 1970), and Beryl Florence Dovton, *née* Hamlyn (d 1985); *b* 17 Feb 1931; *Educ* Eton, Christ Church Oxford; *m* 1961, Kathleen Jill, da of George Craig Watson; 2 s (Anthony Alexander de Nouaille b 12 Feb 1963, Nicholas John de Nouaille b 15 July 1966); *Career* dir: Barclays Bank plc 1972-91 (chm Birmingham Region), Yorks Bank Ltd 1980-90, Mercia Sound Ltd 1989, W Midlands Devpt Agency, Task Undertakings Ltd; tstee Birmingham Hippodrome Theatre Devpt Tst, pres Evesham Rowing Club; *Recreations* travel, music, history; *Clubs* Travellers; *Style—* Anthony Rudge, Esq; Church Farm, Churchover, nr Rugby, Warwickshire

RUDGE, John Aulton; s of Kenneth James Rudge, of 8 Maidavale Crescent, Stivichall, Coventry, and Leigh, *née* Soames; *b* 29 Aug 1951; *Educ* Woodlands Sch Coventry, Sch of Architecture, Univ of Nottingham (BA, BArch); *m* 19 Aug 1973, Christine; da of William Hollowood (d 1956); 1 s (Robert Aulton b 7 May 1983), 2 da (Alexandra Jane b 25 Sept 1981, Sussanah Kate b 21 April 1987); *Career* architect: Erewash DC Derbyshire 1975-79, de Brant Joyce and Ptnrs London 1979-83; assoc Percy Thomas Partnership London 1983-86, ptnr Percy Thomas Partnership Bristol and London; most notable works incl: Kenstead Hall, London residence for HRH King Fah'D of Saudi Arabia, conversion of Grade 2 listed building (7 Albemarle St) into business and fine arts sch for Univ of Notre Dame, Royal Hosp Muscat, Armed Forces Hosp Muscat, Int Covention Centre and Symphony Hall Birmingham; RIBA 1976, ARCUK 1975; *Clubs* Midland Sporting Solihull; *Style—* John Rudge, Esq; Percy Thomas Partnership, 30 Eastbourne Terrace, Paddington, London W1 (☎ 071 262 3484, fax 071 724 0305, car 0836 731 789); Percy Thomas Partnership, 11 Whiteladies Road, Bristol BS8 1AX (☎ 0272 730316, fax 0272 733835)

RUDGE, John Robert; s of Frank Harold Rudge (d 1972), and Marie, *née* Baker; *b* 21 Oct 1944; *Educ* St Josephs Sch Wolverhampton, Huddersfield Coll, Carlisle Coll, Bournemouth Coll of Further Educn; *m* 2 April 1967, Dennice May, da of Leslie Brown Law Kelf; 2 da (Lisa Maria b 20 Dec 1968, Debbie Ann b 12 Nov 1971); *Career* professional football manager; former player: 5 appearances Huddersfield Town (debut 1962), 70 appearances Carlisle Utd, 120 appearances Torquay Utd, 90 appearances Bristol Rovers, 20 appearances Bournemouth; mangr Port Vale 1984-; FA full coaching licence; honours as mangr Port Vale: promotion to Div 3 1986, promotion to Div 2 1989, longest serving mangr for over 60 years; *Recreations* golf, tennis, family life; *Style—* John Rudge, Esq; Port Vale FC, Hamil Rd, Burstem, Stoke-on-Trent, Staffordshire ST6 1AW (☎ 0782 814134)

RUDGE, Peter John Harrington; s of William Charles Rudge London, and Edna May, *née* Brown; *b* 31 Jan 1934; *Educ* Lower Sch of John Lyon Harrow; *m* 1, 8 Aug 1961 (m dis 1980), Lisa Pauline Jean, da of John William Mackareth (d 1983), of Yorks; 1 s (Jeremy Charles Harrington b 9 Nov 1965); m 2, 14 July 1981, Tanis Shelmerdine, da of James Wells-Hunt; *Career* Nat Serv Sub Lt RN 1957-59 serv UK and Germany, Lt RNR 1959-62; CA; articled to Thornton and Thornton 1951-57, chief accoutant The Chequered Flag (SCS) Ltd 1959-65, fin dir London Lotus Centre Ltd 1965-, chm Professional Acceptances Ltd 1965-, EGO Computer Systems Ltd 1978-88; dir Forster and Hales Ltd 1980-, fin dir BA Peters PLC 1988-; chm W London Gp under Road Tport Indust Trg Bd, gen cmmr Income Tax; FCA; *Recreations* rugby, football, cricket, golf; *Clubs* MCC, Esher RFC, Richmond Golf; *Style—* Peter Rudge, Esq; London Lotus Centre Ltd, Ballards Mews, High Street, Edgware, Middlesex (☎ 081 952 6171, fax 071 951 5139)

RUDGE, Stanley Bickerton; s of Alfred Bickerton Rudge, OBE, and Dorothy, *née* Gardiner; *b* 28 Sept 1935; *m* 1962, Beryl Joyce; 2 s (James Edward Bickerton b 11 March 1971, William Bickerton b 16 Feb 1977); 1 da (Vanessa Louise b 12 April 1968; *Career* ptnr i/c Exec Office and memb Bd of Ptnrs Touche Ross & Co; FCA; *Style—* Stanley Rudge, Esq; Touche Ross & Co, 1 Little New St, London EC4A 3TR (☎ 071 936 3000, fax 071 353 8646)

RUDIN, Toni Richard Perrott; s of Richard William Rudin, and late Sarah Rowena Mary; *b* 13 Oct 1934; *Educ* Bootham Sch, Millfield, RMA Sandhurst, Army Staff Coll, Coll of Law Guildford; *m* Heather Jean, da of late Phillip Tom Farley; 1 s (Simeon b 24 April 1961), 3 da (Elizabeth b 28 Feb 1960, Jaqueline b 27 Dec 1963, Fenella b 13 March 1967); *Career* cmmd RA 1954, regtl duty 1955-60, long gunnery staff course 1960-61, instructor in gunery 1961-64, Adjutant City of London Field Regt RA (TA) 1964-65, MOD 1967-69, regtl duty 1969-72, Battery Commander then 2 i/c BAOR Field Regiment; articled clerk 1976-78, slr in private practice 1978-80, sr asst sec The Law Soc 1980-86, sec The Magistrates' Assoc 1986-; memb Law Soc 1978; *Recreations* riding, golf, reading; *Style—* Toni Rudin, Esq; Otterbank House, 60 Wedgwood Avenue, Blakelands, Milton Keynes MK14 5HX (☎ 0908 610965); The Magistrates Association, 28 Fitzroy Square, London W1P 6DD (☎ 071 387 2353)

RUDKIN, (James) David; s of David Jonathan Rudkin, of Westbourne, Emsworth, Sussex, and Anne Alice *née* Martin (d 1969); *b* 29 June 1936; *Educ* King Edward's Sch Birmingham, Univ of Oxford (MA); *m* 3 May 1967, (Alexandra) Sandra Margaret, da of Donald Thompson (d 1969); 2 s (Jamie b 1972, Tom (twin) b 1972), 2 da (Sophie b 1977, Jess b 1978); *Career* Nat Serv RCS 1955-57; playwright; Afore Night Come 1960 (staged 1962), The Sons of Light 1964 (staged 1974), Ashes 1972 (staged 1974), Cries from Casement as his Bones are Brought to Dublin 1972 (radio 1973), Penda's Fen (TV film) 1972 (shown 1974), The Triumph of Death 1976 (staged 1981), Hansel and Gretel 1979 (staged 1980), The Saxon Shore 1983 (staged 1986), Testimony film screenplay 1984 (released 1988), auth/dir White Lady (TV film) 1986, December Bride film screenplay 1988 (released 1990); translations: Hippolytus (Euripides) 1978, Peer Gynt (Ibsen) 1982, Rosmersholm (Ibsen) 1989 (broadcast 1990), When We Dead Waken (Ibsen) 1989 (staged 1990); *Recreations* bridge, languages, geology, music, the sea; *Style—* David Rudkin, Esq; Margaret Ramsay Ltd, 14a Goodwin's Court, London WC2N 4LL (☎ 071 240 0691, fax 071 836 6807)

RUDKIN, (Malcolm) Spencer; s of Edward Shaw Rudkin (d 1967), of 11 Dovedale Drive, Grimsby, and Alice Lilian (d 1966); *b* 24 July 1931; *Educ* Humberston Fndn Sch Cleethorpes, Grimsby Coll of Tech, Bradford Tech Coll; *m* 29 Sept 1955, Judith Mary (d 1989), da of William Humphrey (d 1965), of 95 Oxford St, Cleethorpes; 2 s (Malcolm Graham, Michael Charles), 2 da (Helen Judith, Karren Elizabeth); *Career* Nat Serv Royal Lincs Regt 1952-53, RMP 1953-54 served: Berlin, Border Detachment Helmstedt, Autobahn crossing point to Berlin corridor; Acting Sgt i/c Helmstedt Detachment 247 Berlin Provost Co; md: ES Rudkin Ltd (family firm) 1966-, A Sutton & Sons (Builders) Ltd 1971-; track and cross country running referee (Grade 1), referee English Cross-Country Union Championships Luton 1975; Grimsby Harriers & Athletic Club: treas 1961-68, tstee and vice pres 1975-; Lincolnshire AAA pres and chm 1968-74, life vice pres Eastern Countries Cross Country Assoc 1975- (chm 1969-72, pres 1973-74); hon memb English Cross Country Union; memb: Grimsby Borough Cncl 1968-79, Humberside CC 1974- (ldr 1979-81 and 1985-86, ldr opposition 1981-85 and 1986), Assoc of CC 1977-81 and 1985-89 (served on ctees inc social servs, policy, finance planning and transportation ctees, memb transportation sub-ctee); dep ldr cons gp 1978-79, cons gp spokesman planning and transportation 1987-89, vice chm planning and transportation ctee 1988-89; *Recreations* golf, swimming, athletics; *Clubs* Grimsby Cons, Grimsby GC; *Style—* Spencer Rudkin, Esq, DL; 5 East End Close, Scartho, Grimsby, South Humberside DN33 2HZ (☎ 0472 752192) E S Rudkin Ltd, 38-40 Louth Rd, Grimsby, South Humberside (☎ 0472 79102)

RUDKIN, Walter Charles; CBE (1981); s of Walter Rudkin (d 1970), of Sleaford, Lincs, and Bertha, *née* Charles (d 1985); *b* 22 Sept 1922; *Educ* Carres GS Lincs, Univ Coll Hull, Univ of London (BSc); *m* 8 April 1950, Hilda Mary, da of George Hope (d 1975) of Sunderland; 2 s (Alistair b 1951, Ian b 1957); *Career* WWII Navigator RAF 1942-46; lectr Univ of the Witwatersrand Johannesburg SA 1948-52; MOD: joined 1954, Hong Kong 1956-59, jr directing staff IDC 1962-64, Cabinet Office 1968-71, dir of economics Intelligence 1973-81, dir of economics and logistics Intelligence 1981-82; chm Bromley Police Community Consultative Gp 1986-88; *Recreations* fishing; *Clubs* Royal Cwlth Soc; *Style—* Walter Rudkin, Esq, CBE; 9 Speen Place, Speen, Newbury, Berks RG13 1RX (☎ 0635 49244)

RUDLAND, Malcolm; s of Harold William Rudland (d 1966), of Leeds, and Marika, *née* Széll (d 1943); *b* 17 Aug 1941; *Educ* Ashville Coll Harrogate, St Paul's Cheltenham, RAM (BMus); *Career* music teacher Cirencester Sch; conductor; works incl: Fiddler on the Roof, West Side Story, Peter Pan; pianist and organist; music critic for: Times, Opera, Musical Times; hon sec Peter Warlock Soc; FRCO; *Recreations* gliding, walking, reading; *Style—* Malcolm Rudland, Esq; 32A Chipperfield House, Cale St, London SW3 3SA (☎ 071 589 9595)

RUDLAND, Margaret Florence; da of Ernest George Rudland (d 1979), and Florence Hilda, *née* Davies; *b* 15 June 1945; *Educ* Sweyne Sch Rayleigh Essex, Bedford Coll Univ of London; *Career* asst mathematics mistress Godolphin and Latymer Sch 1967-70, VSO Ilorin Nigeria 1970-71, asst mathematics mistress Clapham Co Sch 1971-72, asst mathematics mistress and head of mathematics St Paul's Girls' Sch 1972-83, dep head mistress Norwich HS 1983-85, head mistress Godolphin and Latymer Sch 1986-; *Recreations* opera, travel, cinema; *Style—* Miss Margaret Rudland; The Godolphin and Latymer School, Iffley Rd, Hammersmith, London W6 0PG (081 741 1936)

RUDMAN, Michael Edward; s of Michael B Rudman, and Josephine, *née* Davis; *b* 14 Feb 1939; *Educ* St Mark's Sch Texas, Oberlin Coll (BA), St Edmund Hall Oxford (MA); *m* 1, 1963 (m dis 1981), Veronica Anne Bennett; 2 da; *Career* pres OUDS 1963-64, asst dir and assoc prod Nottingham Playhouse and Newcastle Playhouse 1964-68, asst dir RSC 1968; artistic dir: Traverse Theatre Club 1970-73, Hampstead Theatre 1973-78; dir Lyttelton Theatre 1979-81, assoc dir NT 1979-88, dir Chichester Festival Theatre 1989; *Plays* Nottingham Playhouse: Changing Gear, Measure for Measure, A Man for All Seasons, Julius Caesar, Death of a Salesman, Lily in Little India; The Fox and the Fly (RSC Theatregoround) 1968; Traverse Theatre: Curtains 1971, Straight Up 1971, Carravagro Buddy 1972, The Relapse 1972; Hampstead Theatre: Ride Across Lake Constance 1973, The Show-off 1974, Alphabetical Order 1975, Clouds 1977, Gloo Joo 1978; NT: For Services Rendered 1978, Death of a Salesman 1979, Measure for Measure 1980, The Second Mrs Tanquery 1981, Brighton Beach Memoirs 1986, Fathers and Sons 1987; West End: Donkeys Years 1976, Clouds 1978, Taking Steps 1980, The Dragon's Tail 1985, Brighton Beach Memoirs 1987; NY: The Changing Room 1973, Hamlet 1976, Death of a Salesman 1984; *Clubs* RAC, Dyrham Park Country, Cumberland LT, Royal Mid-Surrey Golf; *Style—* Michael Rudman, Esq; c/o Peter Murphy, Esq, Curtis Brown Group, 162-168 Regent St, London W1R 57A (☎ 071 872 0331)

RUDOFSKY, John Alec; s of Alexander Edward Rudofsky (d 1986), and Ethel, *née* Frost; *b* 13 Dec 1951; *Educ* St Clement Danes Sch, Selwyn Coll Cambridge (BA, MA); *m* 1978, Susan Judith, da of late James Ernest Riley; 3 s (James Alexander b 1980, Nicholas John b 1984, Joshua Lewis b 1987); *Career* fin journalist: City Press 1973-76, BBC radio 1973-76, Investors Chronicle 1976-79, Daily Telegraph 1979-86; asst dir and fin communications conslt Streets Communications 1987-88, fndr dir and communications conslt Citigate Communications 1988-; *Style—* John Rudofsky, Esq; Citigate Communications, 7 Birchin Lane, London EC3V 9BY (☎ 071 623 2737, 071 623 9050)

RUDOLF, Anthony; s of Henry Cyril Rudolf, (d 1986), of London, and Esther, *née* Rosenberg; *b* 6 Sept 1942; *Educ* City of London Sch, Institut Britannique Paris, Trinity Coll Cambridge; *m* (m dis); 1 s (Nathaniel b 1974), 1 da (Naomi b 1976); *Career* fndr and publisher The Menard Press 1969-; memb Gen Cncl Poetry Soc 1970-76, Adam lectr King's Coll London 1990, patron Safer World Fndn, juror Neustadt Int prize for Literature Oklahoma 1986; *Books* After the Dream: Poems (1980), Selected Poems of Yves Bonnefoy (1985), The Unknown Masterpiece: translation with essay of Balzac's Story (1988); *Recreations* talking, walking; *Style—* Anthony Rudolf, Esq; The Menard Press, 8 The Oaks, Woodside Ave, London N12 8AR (☎ 081 446 5571)

RUDOLF, Dr Noel de Montjoie; s of Dr Gerald RA de M Rudolf (d 1971), of Clevedon, Avon, and K Rosemary, *née* Fowles (d 1972); *Educ* Cheltenham, ChCh Oxford, King's Coll Hosp Med Sch (MA, BM BCh); *m* Claudie Lucienne Marcelle, da of M Roger Held, of Alpes-Maritimes; 1 s (Christopher); *Career* res asst info systems gp Wheatstone Physics Lab, demonstrator King's Coll Univ of London, house physician and surgn Plymouth Hosp, MRC res scholar and fell Univ of Keele, registrar Dept Applied Electrophysiology Nat Hosp London; conslt clincial neurophysiologist: Goodmayes Hosp, Oldchurch Hosp, St Margaret's Hosp, Charing Cross Hosp, Cheyne Centre London; memb Cncl C of E Children's Soc; *Recreations* boating, skiing, genealogy; *Style—* Dr Noel de M Rudolf; 22 Devonshire Place, London W1 (☎ 071 935 1825)

RUE, Dame (Elsie) Rosemary; DBE (1989, CBE 1977); da of Harry Laurence (d 1978), of Chorleywood, and Daisy Annie, *née* Sully (d 1976); *b* 14 June 1928; *Educ* Sydenham HS (GPDST), Univ of Oxford, Univ of London (MB BS); *m* 7 Jan 1950 (m dis 1960), Roger Harry Edward Rue, s of Harry Rue (d 1958), of London; 2 s (Randal b 1952, Rolf b 1955); *Career* clinical med in gen practice Public Health Serv 1952-65; Oxford RHA: SAMO 1971, RMO 1973, RGM/RMO 1984, ret 1988; secondment prof of community health LSHTM 1980-92; former pres: Med Womens Fedn, Faculty of Public Health Med RCP (fell 1972); pres BMA 1990-; Freedom City of London, Liveryman Worshipful Soc of Apothecaries 1976; Hon MA Univ of Oxford 1988; FRCP 1977, FRCPsych 1980- (hon fell 1990-), FRCGP, FRSM; *Books* The Oxford Companion to Medicine (contrib); *Style—* Dame Rosemary Rue, DBE; 2 Stanton St John, Oxford

RUFF, William Willis; CBE (1973), DL (Surrey 1964); s of William Ruff (d 1957); *b* 22 Sept 1914; *Educ* Durham Sch; *m* 1939, Agnes, *née* Nankivell; 2 s; *Career* serv Maj Royal Signal Corps (N Africa & India); slr; clerk Surrey Co Cncl 1952-74, chm Soc Clerks of Peace and Clerks of County Cncls 1969-72; memb Parly Boundary Cmmn for England 1974-83; *Recreations* music, watching cricket; *Style—* William Ruff Esq, CBE, DL; 3 Brympton Close, Ridgeway Rd, Dorking, Surrey (☎ 0306 882406)

RUFFER, Jonathan Garnier; s of Maj J E M Ruffer; *b* 17 Aug 1951; *Educ* Marlborough, Sidney Sussex Coll Cambridge; *m* 1982, Jane Mary, da of Dr P Sequeira; 1 da (Harriet b 16 Oct 1990); *Career* Myers and Co Stock Exchange; called to the Bar Middle Temple (jr Harmsworth exhibitioner); J Henry Schroder Wagg 1977-79, Dunbar Group Ltd 1980-85 (dir Dunbar Fund Management Ltd 198l-85), dir CFS (Investment Management) Ltd 1985-88, md Rathbone Investment Management 1988-; *Books* The Big Shots (1977); *Recreations* opera, name-dropping; *Clubs* Athenaeum; *Style—* Jonathan Ruffer, Esq; Harewood Cottage, Ugley Green, Bishops Stortford, Herts CM22 6HW (☎ 0279 813105)

RUFUS, Michael John; s of James Henry Rufus (d 1969), and Maisie Priscilla Rufus; *b* 10 Aug 1938; *Educ* King Edward VI Edgbaston Birmingham, Univ of Southampton (BSc, CBiol), Anglo European Coll of Chiropractice Bournemouth (DC); *m* 9 Sept 1989, Joanna Cynthia Marie, er da of Richard Emby; *Career* RN Aircrew (observer) 1958-71; served Antarctic and Arctic in HMS Endurance 1968-70, Far E in HMS Victorious 1961-62, HMS Hermes 1966-68; Zoologist at Freshwater Biological Assoc River Lab Wareham 1974-77; estab Sherborne Chiropractic Centre 1982; currently chm Dorset Working Spaniel Club (fndr memb Ctee, former sec/tres); organiser, judge and commentator of numerous gundog competitions and events in SW England; *Style—* Michael Rufus, Esq; Tilly Whim, Bradford-Peverell, Dorchester, Dorset DT2 9SJ (☎ 0305 264084); Sherborne Chiropractic Centre, Half Moon St, Sherborne (☎ 0935 815660)

RUFUS ISAACS, Lord Alexander Gerald; s of 3 Marquess of Reading, MBE, MC (d 1980); *b* 25 April 1957; *Educ* St Paul's, Oriel Coll Oxford (MA), City Univ London; *Career* barr Middle Temple 1982; *Clubs* Dangerous Sports; *Style—* The Lord Alexander Rufus Isaacs; 3 Tyrawley Rd, London SW6

RUFUS ISAACS, Lord Antony Michael; s of 3 Marquess of Reading, MBE, MC (d 1980); *b* 22 Sept 1943; *Educ* Gordonstoun; *m* 1, 1972 (m dis 1976), Anne Pugsley; m 2, 1983, Heide Lund, of Vancouver, BC; 2 da (Tallulah Elke Margot b 1987, Ruby Jacqueline Kirsten 1990); *Style—* The Lord Antony Rufus Isaacs; 9723 Oak Pass Rd, Beverly Hills, California 90210, USA

RUGBY, Margaret, Baroness; Margaret; da of Harold Bindley, of Burton-on-Trent; *m* 14 April 1947, 2 Baron Rugby (d 1990); 4 s (1 decd), 2 da; *Style—* The Rt Hon Margaret, Lady Rugby; Grove Farm, Frankton, Rugby, Warwicks

RUGBY, 3 Baron (UK 1947), of Rugby, Co Warwick; Robert Charles Maffey; 2 (but eldest surviving) s of 2 Baron Rugby (d 1990), and Margaret, *née* Bindley; *b* 4 May 1951; *m* 1974, Anne Penelope, yr da of David Hale, of Somerden, Chiddingstone, Kent; 2 s (Hon Timothy James Howard b 1975, Hon Philip Edward b 1976); *Heir* s, Hon Timothy James Howard Maffey b 23 July 1975; *Style—* The Rt Hon the Lord Rugby; Grove Farm Cottage, Frankton, Rugby

RUGGE-PRICE, Sir Charles Keith Napier; 9 Bt (UK 1804); s of Lt-Col Sir Charles James Napier Rugge-Price, 8 Bt (d 1966); *b* 7 Aug 1936; *Educ* Middleton Coll Ireland; *m* 1965, Jacqueline Mary, da of Maj Pierre Paul Loranger, MC, CD; 2 s (James b 1967, Andrew b 1970); *Heir* s, James Keith Peter Rugge-Price, b 8 April 1967; *Career* mangr Tomenson-Alexander Ltd Toronto 1971-76; supervisor Compensation City of Edmonton 1976-81; sr mgmnt consit City of Edmonton 1982-; *Style—* Sir Charles Rugge-Price, Bt; 23 Lambert Crescent, St Albert, Alberta T8N 1M1, Canada; City of Edmonton, 16156 Centennial Bldgs, 10015-103 Avenue, Edmonton Alberta T5J 0K1 (☎ 403 428 5909)

RUGGE-PRICE, Maeve, Lady; Maeve Marguerite; da of Edgar Stanley de la Peña, of Hythe, Kent; *m* 1935, Lt-Col Sir Charles James Napier Rugge-Price, 8 Bt (d 1966); *Style—* Maeve, Lady Rugge-Price

RUGGLES-BRISE, Guy Edward; TD, DL (Essex 1967); s of Col Sir Edward Ruggles-Brise, 1 Bt, MC, TD, sometime MP Maldon, JP, DL (d 1942), by his 1 w, Agatha, *née* Gurney, of the Norfolk family; hp to bro, Sir John Ruggles-Brise, 2 Bt, CB, OBE, TD; *b* 15 June 1914; *Educ* Eton; *m* 7 Dec 1940, Elizabeth (d 1988), da of James Knox, of Smithstone House, Kilwinning, Ayrshire; 3 s (Timothy Edward b 1945, James Rupert b 1947, Samuel Guy b 1956); *Career* 104 Essex Yeo 1934-38, 147 Essex Yeo 1938-40, Capt, No 7 Commando 1940, POW Bardia 1941, escaped from Italy 1944; sr ptnr Brewin Dolphin & Co (stockbrokers) 1973-79, ret; memb Stock Exchange 1946-88; pres Pony Riding for the Disabled Tst 1983-84 (chm Exec Ctee 1968-78); High Sheriff of Essex 1967-68; *Recreations* hunting, shooting, fishing; *Clubs* City of London; *Style—* Guy Ruggles-Brise, Esq, TD, DL; Ledgowan Lodge, Achnasheen, Ross (☎ 044 588 245); The Manor House, Housham Tye, Harlow, Essex (☎ 027 982 236)

RUGGLES-BRISE, Sir John Archibald; 2 Bt (UK 1935), of Spains Hall, Finchingfield, Essex, CB (1958), OBE (Mil 1945), TD, JP (Essex 1946); s of Col Sir Edward Ruggles-Brise, 1 Bt, MC, TD, MP (d 1942); *b* 13 June 1908; *Educ* Eton; *Heir* bro, Guy Ruggles-Brise, TD, DL; *Career* Lloyd's underwriter; pres CLA 1957-59 (sponsored first CLA Game Fair 1958); Ld-Lt of Essex 1958-78; chm: Essex Territorial Assoc 1950-58, Standing Cncl Baronetage 1958-63, Church cmmnr 1959-64; pro-chllr Essex Univ 1964-74; former govr: Felsted, Chigwell; hon DUniv Essex; hon Freeman of Chelmsford; *Clubs* Carlton; *Style—* Col Sir John Ruggles-Brise, Bt, CB OBE, TD, JP; Spains Hall, Finchingfield, Essex CM7 4PF (☎ 0371 810266)

RUGGLES-BRISE, Rosemary Elizabeth; *née* Craig; da of John Sommerville Craig, of 1 Buckland Court, 37 Belsize Park, London NW3, and Agnes Marchbank, *née* Marshall; *b* 23 Oct 1949; *Educ* St Leonards Sch St Andrews Fife; *m* 3 May 1975, Timothy Edward Ruggles-Brise, s of Capt Guy Edward Ruggles-Brise, of Housham Tye, Harlow, Essex; 3 s (Archie b 1979, Charlie b 1983, Iain b 1989), 2 da (Olivia b 1977, Felicity b 1984); *Career* Dip Serv 1971-75; ptnr Spains Hall Forest Tree Nursery 1979-; *Style—* Mrs Rosemary Ruggles-Brise; Spains Hall Farmhouse, Finchingfield, Essex CM7 4NJ (☎ 0371 810232)

RUIZ BARRERO, Lorenzo; s of Lorenzo Ruiz Jimenez, of Jorge Juan 55, 28001 Madrid, Spain, and Guadalupe Barrero Alonso (d 1979); *b* 20 March 1946; *Educ* Colegio Sagrados Corazones Madrid (Baccalaureate), Law Faculty Univ of Madrid (LLB); *m* 25 Oct 1978 (m dis 1985), Lady Katherine Lucy Lambart, da of Earl of Cavan (d 1988); 1 s (Lorenzo Cavan b 28 Aug 1980), 1 da (Natasha Pepa b 4 Dec 1982); *Career* slr; private practice Madrid Spain 1969-75, currently private practice messrs Amhurst Brown Colombotti; memb Working Ctee Slrs Euro Gp; memb: Madrid Bar Spain, Law Soc; *Books* contrib The Administration of Foreign Estates (1988); *Recreations* painting, swimming; *Clubs* RAC; *Style—* Lorenzo Ruiz Barrero, Esq; 2 Duke St, St James's, London SW1 (☎ 071 930 2366, fax 071 930 2250)

RULE, Brian Francis; s of Sydney John Rule, Pen-Y-FFordd, Chester, and Josephine, *née* Hegarty; *Educ* Ysgol Daniel Owen Mold, Loughborough Univ of Technol (BSc, MSc); *m* 30 Aug 1963, Kay M, da of Dr Neville Alexander Dyce-Sharp; *Career* res asst Loughborough Univ 1963-65, project mangr Glasgow Univ 1965-67, dir of computing Univ of Aberdeen 1974-77 (lectr 1967-71, sr lectr 1971-74); dir: Honeywell Info Systems Ltd London 1977-79, Sci Servs Natural Enviroment Res Cnsl 1979-85; dir gen info technol systems MOD 1985-; memb Antiquarian Horological Soc, dep chm City of Aberdeen Children's Panel 1971-74; *Recreations* antiquarian horology; *Clubs* Royal Cwlth Soc; *Style—* Brian Rule, Esq; c/o MOD, Whitehall, London (☎ 071 218 4828)

RULE, John Eric; s of Eric Houldsworth Rule, of Guildford, Surrey, and Alpha Rule (d 1988); *b* 15 Nov 1934; *Educ* John Bright GS Llandudno N Wales, Royal GS Guildford; *m* 5 Sept 1959, Georgina Frances, da of Frederick William Luck, of Guildford, Surrey; 1 s (Stephen b 1965), 1 da (Jane b 1961); *Career* Trooper 16/5 Queen's Royal Lancers 1957, cmmnd 2 Lt RAPC 1958, Capt 1958-59; articled clerk Wrigley Cregan Todd &

Co 1951-56; Arthur Andersen & Co: sr auditor 1960-63, audit mangr 1963-69, ptnr 1969-89, euro banking co-ordination ptnr 1975-83, euro fin servs co-ordinator 1984-86; ICAEW: former memb Banking Ctee, former chm Auditing Courses Ctee, former chm Auditing and Accounting Ed Ctee; chief exec fin servs dir Beresford Int plc; chm govrs Royal GS Guildford 1988-; ACA 1956, FCA 1966; *Recreations* gardening, golf, motor sailing; *Clubs* Naval and Military, City of London, Little Ship, NZ Golf; *Style*— John E Rule, Esq; Fairwinds, 29 Warren Rd, Guildford, Surrey GU1 2HG (☎ 0483 63828); Berisford International plc, Berisford Wing, 1 Prescot St, London E1 8AY

RULE, Hon Mrs (Miranda Jane Caroline); *née* Rhys; eldest da of 9 Baron Dynevor, *qv*; *b* 1960; *m* 1986, David Rule, 2 s of Ronald William Pritchard Rule, of Newcastle-under-Lyme, Staffs; 1 s (James Gareth b 1986), 1 da (Rhiannon b 1987); *Style*— The Hon Mrs Rule; c/o The Rt Hon Lord Dynevor, The Walk, Carmarthen Rd, Llandeilo, Dyfed

RUMBALL, Rev Frank Thomas; s of William Rumball (d 1979), of Shropshire, and Ethel Irine, *née* Peel; *b* 13 Jan 1943; *Educ* Ludlow GS, St Peter's Coll Saltley, Salisbury and Wells Theol Coll; *Career* head of music: Walsall-Wood Secdy Sch 1963-69 (head of religious educn 1966-69), Ludlow Sch 1969-72; deacon Hereford Cathedral 1974, priest 1975, asst curate Bromyard 1974-78, team vicar Ewyas Marold Team Miny 1978-81, Pastoral Care Minsterly 1982-82, priest i/c Eye, Lucton, Croft with Yarpole 1982-; organist; *Recreations* shooting, fencing, yachting, giving organ recitals for charity; *Style*— The Rev Frank T Rumball; The Smithy, Acton Scott, Church Stretton, Shropshire SY6 6QN (☎ 069 46 339); Eye Vicarage, Leominster, Herefordshire HR6 0DP (☎ 0568 5710)

RUMBELOW, (Howard) Clive; s of Leonard Douglas Rumbelow (d 1980), of Cardiff, and Phyllis Mary Rumbelow (d 1984); *b* 13 June 1933; *Educ* Cardiff HS, Univ of Cambridge (MA, LLM); *m* 29 June 1968, Carolyn Sandra, da of Dr Arthur Macdonald Macgregor (d 1963), of Epworth; 1 s (Michael b 1969), 2 da (Jane b 1970, Helen b 1972); *Career* RAF 1951-53; ptnr Slaughter and May 1968-89, dir The Law Debenture Corporation plc 1990-; *Recreations* golf, squash; *Clubs* RAF, Hurlingham, Royal Wimbledon GC; *Style*— Clive Rumbelow, Esq; 79 Princes Way, London SW19 6HY (☎ 081 789 4813)

RUMBELOW, (Roger) Martin; s of Leonard Douglas Rumbelow (d 1980), and Phyllis Mary, *née* Perkins (d 1984); *b* 3 June 1937; *Educ* Cardiff HS, Univ of Bristol (BSc), Cranfield Inst of Technol (MSc); *m* 24 July 1965 (Marjorie) Elizabeth, da of Charles Richard Glover, of 21 Harry Lawson Court, Brocklehurst Ave, Macclesfield, Cheshire; *Career* Nat Serv; RAF pilot and Flying Offr 1955-57; Concorde project mangr Br Aircraft Corp 1973-74 (tech sales 1960-67, dep prodn controller 1967-73), under-sec Mgmnt Servs and Manpower Div DTI 1987- (princ 1974-78, asst sec 1978-86); memb Royal Choral Soc; CEng, AFRAes; *Recreations* singing, theatre, electronics, computing; *Clubs* RAF; *Style*— Martin Rumbelow, Esq; 29 Bressenden Place, London SW1E 5DT (☎ 071 215 3609)

RUMBLE, Capt John Bertram; s of Maj Leslie Rumble, TD (d 1976), and Sybil Florence Leech-Porter (d 1988); *b* 30 Oct 1928; *Educ* Sherborne; *m* 26 Sept 1953, Jennifer, da of Col R H Wilson, CIE, MC (d 1971); 1 s (Peter b 1956); 3 da (Sally-Anne b 1956, Nicola b 1959, Fiona b 1963); *Career* entered RN 1946, Lt ADC to Govr of Malta 1952-53, specialised in communications 1954, Signal Offr HMS Ark Royal 1959-61, Cdr 1962, CO HMS Torquay 1964-66, staff communications offr to C-in-C Eastlant 1966-67, exec offr HMS Hermes 1967-69, Capt 1970, staff dir gen weapons 1970-71, CO HMS Fearless 1974-75, Cdre asst COS Communications C-in-C South 1976-77, MOD Intelligence 1977-79; dir gen Royal Overseas League 1979-; memb cncl Mayfair Picadilly and St James Assoc 1979 (chm 1989); FBIM, FIIM; *Recreations* fly fishing, shooting, goldleaf gilding, sailing; *Clubs* Farmers, Keyhaven Yacht, Milford-on-sea Tennis; *Style*— Capt John Rumble, RN; 88 Wroughton Rd, London SW11 6AT (☎ 071 223 9413); Royal Overseas League, Overseas House, Park Place, St James's St, SW1 (☎ 071 408 0214)

RUMBLE, Peter William; CB (1984); s of Arthur Victor Rumble and Dorothy Emily, *née* Sadler; *b* 28 April 1929; *Educ* Harwich Co HS, Oriel Coll Oxford (MA); *m* 1953, Joyce Audrey Stephenson; 1 s, 1 da; *Career* entered Civil Serv 1952, HM inspr of taxes 1952, princ Miny of Housing and Local Govt 1963; Dept of the Environment: asst sec 1972, under sec 1977; chief exec Historic Bldgs and Monuments Cmmn 1983-89, tstee American Friends of Eng Heritage 1988-, memb Cncl Architectural Heritage Fund 1988-, memb Ctee S Region Nat Tst 1990-, dir gen Euro Union of Historic Houses Assocs 1990-; *Recreations* working for MENCAP, music; *Style*— Peter Rumble, Esq, CB; 11 Hillside Road, Cheam, Surrey SM2 6ET (☎ 081 643 1752)

RUMBOLD, Sir (Horace) Algernon Fraser; KCMG (1960, CMG 1953), CIE (1947); s of Col William Rumbold, CMG, yr bro of Sir Horace Rumbold, 9 Bt; 1 cous of Sir Anthony Rumbold, 10 Bt (d 1983); hp of Sir Henry Rumbold, 11 Bt; *b* 27 Feb 1906; *Educ* Wellington, ChCh Oxford; *m* 1946, Margaret Adel, da of Arthur Hughes; 2 da; *Career* India Office 1929-47, CRO 1947-66 (dep high cmmr for UK Union of SA 1949-53, dep under sec of state 1958-66), advsr Welsh Office 1967; memb Governing Body SOAS 1965-80 (hon fell 1981), dep chm Air Tport Licensing Bd 1970-71; pres Tibet Soc of UK 1977-88; *Books* Watershed in India (1979); *Style*— Sir Algernon Rumbold, KCMG, CIE; Shortwoods, W Clandon, Surrey (☎ 0483 222757)

RUMBOLD, Rt Hon Angela Claire Rosemary; PC (1991), CBE (1981), MP (C) Mitcham and Morden 1982-; da of Prof Harry Jones (d 1986), and Frances Molly, Jones; *b* 11 Aug 1932; *Educ* Perse Sch Cambridge, Notting Hill and Ealing High Sch, King's Coll London; *m* 15 March 1958, John Marix Rumbold, s of Marix Henry Branscombe Rumbold (d 1980); 2 s (Philip b 15 Sept 1961, Matthew b 3 Dec 1966), 1 da (Polly-Ann (Mrs Postans) b 26 May 1964); *Career* former PA to Sir Horace Cutler (ldr Cons GLC, chm AHA Educn Ctee 1978-79); chm: Nat Assoc for Welfare of Children in Hosp 1974-77, Policy and Resources Ctee Kingston upon Thames Cncl 1979-83, chm of Local Educn Authorities 1979-80; PPS to Nicholas Ridley, MP 1983-85; Parly under sec of state on Environment 1985-86; min of state: DES 1986-90, Home Office 1990-; co chm Women's Nat Ctee 1986-90; Freeman City of London 1988; *Recreations* reading, swimming, music, gardening; *Style*— The Rt Hon Angela Rumbold, CBE, MP; House of Commons, London SW1

RUMBOLD, Sir Henry John Sebastian; 11 Bt (GB 1779), of Wood Hall, Watton, Herts; s of Sir (Horace) Anthony Claude Rumbold, 10 Bt, KCMG, KCVO, CB (d 1983, formerly an ambass to Thailand and Austria), by his 1 w, Felicity (d 1984), da of late Lt-Col Frederick Bailey and Lady Janet, *née* Mackay (da of 1 Earl of Inchcape); *b* 24 Dec 1947; *Educ* Eton, William & Mary Coll, Virginia, USA; *m* 1978, Frances Ann, da of Dr Albert Whitfield Hawkes (decd), and formerly w of Julian Berry; *Heir* Sir Algernon Rumbold (cous); *Career* solicitor-ptnr Stephenson Harwood; *Recreations* riding, shooting, reading; *Style*— Sir Henry Rumbold, Bt; 19 Hollywood Rd, London SW10 9HT; Hatch House, Tisbury, Salisbury, Wilts SP3 6PA; 1 St Paul's Churchyard, London EC4M 8SH (☎ 071 329 4422)

RUMBOLD, Sir Jack Seddon; QC (1963); s of William Alexander Rumbold, of Christchurch, NZ, and Jean Lindsay, *née* Mackay; *b* 5 March 1920; *Educ* St Andrew's Coll NZ, Univ of Canterbury NZ (LLB 1940), BNC Oxford (BCL); *m* 1, Helen Suzanne Davis; 2 da; m 2, Veronica Ellie Hurt, *née* Whigham; *Career* RN Lt RNVR (despatches) 1941-45; called to Bar Inner Temple 1948, private legal practice; Colonial Legal Serv Kenya 1957-62, AG Zanzibar 1963-64, QC 1963, legal advsr Kenya Govt 1964-66; academic dir British Campus of Stanford Univ USA 1966-1972; chm of Industl Tbnls 1967-1979, pres of Industl Tbnls England and Wales 1979-1984; *Recreations* books, music, formerly cricket (Oxford Blue 1946); *Clubs* Garrick, MCC; *Style*— Sir Jack Rumbold, QC

RUMBOLD, Pauline, Lady; Pauline Laetitia; da of late Hon David Francis Tennant, 3 s of 1 Baron Glenconner, and Hermione Youlanda Ruby Clinton (the actress Hermione Baddeley), da of late W H Clinton Baddeley, and Louise Bourdin; *b* 6 Feb 1929; *m* 1, 1946 (m dis 1953), Capt Julian Lane-Fox Pitt-Rivers; m 2, 1954, Euan Douglas Graham, yr s of Brig Lord Douglas Malise Graham, CB, DSO, MC, and n of 6 Duke of Montrose; m 3, 1974, (as his 2 w), Sir (Horace) Anthony Claude Rumbold, 10 Bt, KCMG, KCVO, CB (d 1983, former ambass to Thailand and Austria); *Style*— Pauline, Lady Rumbold; Hatch Cottage, Cokers Frome, Dorchester, Dorset

RUMGAY, Ian Charles; s of Alexander Edward Rumgay, and Violet Florence Emma, *née* Wright; *b* 26 May 1952; *Educ* Swanage GS; *Career* account mangr PR 1976-80, md Opinion PR 1980-82; dir: JPPR 1982-83, Shandwick PR Co 1983-; dept md: Sandwick Communications Ltd 1989-90, Gibson PR (Shandwick Hong Kong) 1990-; *Recreations* gardening, dining, tennis, salmon fishing; *Style*— Ian Rumgay, Esq; Gibson PR (HK) Ltd, 12/F Printing House, 6 Duddell St, Central, Hong Kong (☎ 5 241106/ 235164, fax 5 8680224, telex 66608 GPRHK HX)

RUMINS, John Sandford; *b* 16 Dec 1934; *Educ* Univ of Bristol (BA); *m* 13 Sept 1960, (Margaret) Ruth; 1 s (Christopher John b 9 Sept 1965), 2 da (Philippa Ann b 31 Dec 1961, Tanya Helen b 5 July 1969); *Career* RAF 1959-62, PO 1959-61, flying offr 1961-62; CA; qualified with Tansley Witt 1959, Cooper Brothers & Co (later Coopers & Lybrand) 1962-72, currently head of fin and resource planning div Bank of England (joined 1972); FCA 1959; *Recreations* tennis; *Style*— John Rumins, Esq

RUMSEY, (Raymond) Clive; s of Kenneth Walter Rumsey (d 1961), and Florence Alice, *née* Beveridge; *b* 21 March 1930; *Educ* Wimbledon Sch of Art (Nat Dip Design), RCA London (Graphic Design); *m* 4 Sept 1965, Lisa Anne, da of Patrick Vincent McGrath, of Chislehurst, Kent; 1 s (Julian St John b 17 Jan 1968); *Career* Nat Serv RCS 1949-51, NCO draughtsman Sch of Signals Catterick, HQ Southern Cmd Salisbury; Lintas Ltd London 1954-74: art dir, creative dir and head of Dept (seven yrs spent in Europe as agency creative dir); ind advertising conslt 1974-75; McCann-Erickson Advertising until 1988: joined 1975, set up Pan-Euro creative unit Euroteam, regnl creative dir (Europe, responsible for creative standards of 22 offices across Europe) 1981-87, dep mangr McCann Erickson Paris, conslt 1988-, lectr MIPA; *Recreations* travelling, collecting objets d'art; *Style*— Clive Rumsey, Esq; The Old Cottage, Mount Lane, Barford St Martin, Salisbury, Wilts SP3 4AF (☎ 0722 743 236); c/o McCann-Erickson Advertising Ltd, 36 Howland St, London W1A 1AT (☎ 071 580 6690)

RUMSEY, Stephen John Raymond; s of John William Raymond Rumsey, of Hampstead, and May, *née* Blemings; *b* 6 Nov 1950; *Educ* Windsor GS, LSE (BSc); *m* 3 June 1978, Anne Christine Elaine, da of Arnold Williamson (d 1988); 2 s (James b 1979, Edward b 1981); *Career* investmt mangr Postel Investmt 1977-85, ptnr de Zoete of Bevan 1985-86, md Fixed Div Barclays de Zoete Wedd 1986-; fndr Wetland Tst, Churchill fell 1970; cncllr Royal Borough of Kingston upon Thames 1978-82, dep chm Social Servs Ctee; memb Stock Exchange 1985; memb Cncl: RSPB, BTO; *Recreations* ornithology, agriculture, social servs; *Style*— Stephen Rumsey, Esq; Elms Farm, Pett Lane, Icklesham, Winchelsea, East Sussex, TN36 4AH (☎ 0797 226137) Barclays de Zoete Wedd Ltd, 2 Swan Lane, London EC4R 3TS (☎ 071 623 2323, fax 071 626 6106)

RUNCHORELAL, Sir Chinubhai Madhowlal; 2 Bt (UK 1913), of Shahpur, Ahmedabad, India; s of Sir Chinubhai Madhowlal Runchorelal, CIE (d 1916), whose name he then assumed in place of that of Girjaprasad; *b* 19 April 1906; *m* 1924, Tanumati Zaverilal Mehta, of Ahmedabad, India (d 1971); 3 s; *Style*— Sir Chinubhai Runchorelal, Bt; Shantikunj, Shahibag, Ahmedabad, India

RUNCHORELAL, Udayan Chinubhai Madhowlal; s and h of Sir Chinubhai Runchorelal, 2 Bt; *b* 25 July 1929; *m* 1953, Muneera Khodadad Foxdar, of Bombay; 1 s, 3 da; *Career* nat pres India Jr Chamber 1961-62, currently a Jaycee senator; represented Gujarat in Ranji Trophy in Cricket and played the combined Univ XI against Pakistan; represented India in int events in target shooting on 4 occasions; awarded Arjun award for target shooting 1972-73; *Recreations* cricket, target shooting; *Style*— Udayan Runchorelal Esq

RUNCIE, Baron (Life Peer UK 1991), of Cuddesdon in the County of Oxfordshire; Rt Rev the Rt Hon Robert Alexander Kennedy Runcie; MC (1945), PC (1980); s of Robert Dalziel Runcie (d 1945), of Crosby, Merseyside, and Ann Edna, *née* Benson (d 1949); *b* 2 Oct 1921; *Educ* Merchant Taylors' Crosby, BNC Oxford (MA), Westcott House Cambridge (Dip Theol); *m* 5 Sept 1957, (Angela) Rosalind, da of J W Cecil Turner, MC (d 1968), of Cambridge; 1 s (Hon James b 1959), 1 da (Hon Rebecca b 1961); *Career* served WWII Scots Gds, tank offr Normandy, Baltic, PA to Br Rep Italy/Yugoslavia Boundary Cmmn 1945-46; ordained 1949, curate All Saints Gosforth 1950-52, chaplain and vice princ Westcott House Cambridge 1953-56, dean Trinity Hall Cambridge 1956-60, princ Cuddesdon Theol Coll 1960-70, Bishop St Albans 1970-80; Archbishop of Canterbury 1980-91; Anglican chm Anglican-Orthodox Joint Doctrinal Cmmn 1973-80, Teape lectr Univ of Delhi 1962, Nobell lectr Harvard Univ 1987; Freeman City of: London, Canterbury, St Albans; Freeman: Worshipful Co of Merchant Taylors, Worshipful Co of Grocers, Worshipful Co of Butchers; Hon Bencher of Gray's Inn 1981; Hon DD: Univ of Oxford 1980, Univ of Cambridge 1981, Univ of the South Sewanee 1981, St Andrews Univ 1989, Univ of London 1990, King's Coll Toronto 1986, New Raday Coll Budapest 1987, Univ of South Carolina 1987, Yale Univ 1989; Hon DLitt: Univ of Keele 1981, Rikkyo Univ Tokyo 1987; Hon DCL Univ of Kent 1982, Hon LittD Univ of Liverpool 1983; Royal Victorian Chain 1991, Cross of the Order of the Holy Sepulchre 1986, Order of St Vladimir Class II 1975; *Books* Cathedral and City: St Albans Ancient and Modern (ed, 1978), Windows onto God (1983), Seasons of the Spirit (1983), One Light for One World (1988), Theology, University and the Modern World (1988), Authority in Crisis? (1988), The Unity We Seek (1989); *Recreations* opera, reading history and novels, owning Berkshire pigs; *Clubs* Athenaeum, Cavalry and Guards; *Style*— The Rt Rev the Rt Hon Lord Runcie, PC, MC; 26a Jennings Road, St Albans, Herts AL1 4PD (☎ 0727 48021)

RUNCIMAN, Hon Mrs (Anne Elizabeth); *née* Bewicke-Copley; da of 6 Baron Cromwell (d 1982); *b* 1955; *Educ* Oxford HS; *m* 1982, David James McNaught Runciman; 1 s (Findlay Redfers b 1990), 1 da (Ruth); *Career* television prodr; *Style*— The Hon Mrs Runciman

RUNCIMAN, Hugh Leishman Inglis (Peter); CBE (1989); s of Hugh Inglis Runciman (d 1950), of Aberdeen, and Gladys West, *née* Rowbotham (d 1986); *b* 9 Oct 1928; *Educ* St Alban's Coll Buenos Aires, King's Coll London (BSc); *m* 7 Aug 1957, Rosemary Janet, da of John Hadfield, of Sheffield; 3 da (Alison Jane b 1962, Rosemary Ann b 1964, Helen Mary b 1967); *Career* 2 Lt RE 1947-49; asst chief designer

Chloride Batteries Ltd 1953-60, md Derbyshire Stone Quarries Ltd 1961-68, dir Tarmac Roodstone Holdings Ltd 1969-79; chm: Shanks & McEwan Group plc 1980-, Scot Eastern Investment Trust plc 1989-; non exec dir: British Steel plc, Scottish Nat Tst plc; former pres Glasgow C of C; memb: Scottish Business Gp, Cncl Aims of Indust, Scottish Economic Cncl; Freeman City of Glasgow, memb Incorporation of Hammermen 1988; FIQ; *Recreations* fishing, shooting, gardening; *Clubs* Flyfishers', Western; *Style—* Peter Runciman, Esq, CBE; Shoreacres, Rhu, Dunbartonshire (☎ 0436 820445); Shanks & McEwan Group plc, 22 Woodside Place, Glasgow G3 7QY (☎ 041 331 2614, fax 041 331 2071)

RUNCIMAN, Hon Sir Steven (James Cochran Stevenson); CH (1984); 2 s of 1 Viscount Runciman of Doxford; *b* 7 July 1903; *Educ* Eton, Trinity Coll Cambridge; *Career* historian; prof of Byzantine history Istanbul Univ 1942-45, Br Cncl rep Greece 1945-47; recipient of Wolfson Literary award 1982; Kt Cdr Order of the Phoenix (Greece) 1961; FBA; kt 1958; *Books Incl:* A History of the Crusades (in 3 vols); *Clubs* Athenaeum; *Style—* The Hon Sir Steven Runciman, CH; Elshieshields, Lockerbie, Dumfriesshire (☎ 038 781 0280)

RUNCIMAN OF DOXFORD, Katherine, Viscountess; Katherine Schuyler Runciman; *née* Garrison; yst da of late William R Garrison, of New York, USA; *m* 11 April 1932, as his 2 w, 2 Viscount Runciman of Doxford, OBE, AFC, AE, DL (d 1989); 1 s (3 Viscount, *qv*); *Style—* The Rt Hon Katherine, Viscountess Runciman of Doxford; 46 Abbey Lodge, Park Road, London NW8 9AT (☎ 071 723 6882)

RUNCIMAN OF DOXFORD, 3 Viscount (UK 1937); Sir Walter Garrison (Garry) Runciman; 4 Bt (UK 1906), CBE (1987); also Baron Runciman (UK 1933); s of 2 Viscount Runciman of Doxford, OBE, AFC, AE, DL (d 1989), and his 2 wife, Katherine Schuyler, *née* Garrison; *b* 10 Nov 1934; *Educ* Eton, Trinity Coll Cambridge; *m* 17 April 1963, Ruth, da of Joseph Hellman, of Johannesburg; 1 s (Hon David Walter), 2 da (Hon Lisa b 18 Aug 1965, Hon Catherine b 18 July 1969); *Heir* s, Hon David Walter Runciman b 1 March 1967; *Career* fell Trinity Coll Cambridge 1959-63 and 1971-; chm: Andrew Weir and Co Ltd, Runciman Investments Ltd; jt dep chm Securities and Investments Bd; sociologist, former pt/t reader in sociology Univ of Sussex; treas Child Poverty Action Gp 1972-; pres Gen Cncl Br Shipping 1986-87 (vice-pres 1985-86); memb Securities and Investmts Bd 1986-; FBA 1975; *Books* Plato's Later Epistemology (1962), Social Science and Political Theory (1963), Relative Deprivation and Social Justice (1966), A Critique of Max Weber's Philosophy of Social Science (1972), A Treatise on Social Theory Vol I (1983), Vol II (1989); *Clubs* Brooks's; *Style—* The Rt Hon the Viscount Runciman of Doxford, CBE; 36 Carlton Hill, London NW8 (☎ 071 624 8419)

RUNCORN, Prof (Stanley) Keith; s of William Henry Runcorn (d 1966), of Southport, Lancs, and Lily Idina, *née* Roberts; *b* 19 Nov 1922; *Educ* King George V Sch Southport, Gonville and Caius Coll Cambridge (BA, MA, ScD), Manchester Univ (PhD); *Career* WWII serv experimental offr Miny of Supply Air Def (later known as Radar Res and Devpt Estab) 1943-46; lectr in physics Manchester Univ 1948-49 (asst lectr 1946-48), fell Gonville and Caius Coll Cambridge 1948-55, asst dir of res in geophysics Cambridge 1950-55; prof of physics and head of dept: King's Coll Univ of Durham 1956-63, Univ of Newcastle upon Tyne 1963-88; Royal Soc Rutherford Memorial lectr 1970, Halley lectr Univ of Oxford 1973, Sydney Chapman prof of physical sci Univ of Alaska 1988-, sr res fell Imperial Coll of Sci Technol and Med London 1988-; visiting prof: California Inst of Technol 1957, UCLA 1975, Univ of California (Hitchcock prof) 1982, Univ of Queensland 1981; J Ellerton Becker visiting fell Aust Acad of Sci 1963; memb Cncl Natural Environment Res Cncl 1965-69; Hon DSc: Utrecht 1969, Ghent 1971, Paris 1979, Bergen 1980; FRS 1965, FRAS, FInstP, hon memb EGS, fell AGU; memb: Pontifical Acad of Sci, Academia Euro; foreign memb: Royal Netherlands Acad of Arts and Sci 1970-, Royal Norwegian Acad of Sci and Letters 1985-, Bavarian Acad of Sci, Indian Nat Sci Acad; Vetlesen Prize Columbia Univ and Vetlesen Fndn NY 1971, John Adams Fleming Medal American Geophys Union 1983, Gold Medal RAS 1984, Wegener Medal Euro Union of Glosciences 1987; *Books* Dictionary of Geophysics (ed), Continental Drift (ed), Physics of the Earth and Planetary Interiors (ed, 1967); *Recreations* squash rackets, swimming, hiking, rugby; *Clubs* Athenaeum, Union Soc (Newcastle upon Tyne); *Style—* Prof Keith Runcorn; Blackett Laboratory, Imperial College, London SW7 2BZ (☎ 071 589 5111 ext 6752)

RUNDALL, Lady Rosalthé Frances; *née* Ryder; o da of 7 Earl of Harrowby, *qv*; *b* 1 May 1954; *Educ* Queensgate Sch London; *m* 1976, Francis Richard Seton Rundall, yr s of Frank Lionel Montagu Rundall, of Stoneleigh Hse, Loughborough, Glos; 3 s (Francis Thomas Mansell b 1981, Mark Dudley Ridgway b 1982, John William Nathaniel b 1987); *Style—* Lady Rosalthé Rundall; Greater Aston Farmhouse, Aston Subedge, Chipping Campden, Glos

RUNGE, Charles David; s of Sir Peter Runge (d 1970), of Lane End, High Wycombe, Bucks, and Hon Fiona Margaret Stewart, *née* Macpherson, da of 1 Baron Strathcarron; *b* 24 May 1944; *Educ* Eton, Christ Church Oxford (MA), Manchester Business Sch; *m* 1, 28 July 1969 (m dis 1979), Harriet, da of late John Bradshaw, of Inkpen, Berks; 1 s (Tom b 1971), 1 da (Louise b 1973); m 2, 9 April 1981, Jil, da of John Liddell (d 1987), of Greenock, Scotland; 1 da (Emma b 1986); *Career* Tate & Lyle: md tport 1977-79, chief exec refineries 1979-81, md agribusiness 1983-86, dir corporate affrs 1986-87; chief exec Milk Mktg Bd 1988-; *Recreations* music, walking, fishing; *Clubs* Boodle's; *Style—* Charles Runge, Esq; The Milk Marketing Bd, Thames Ditton, Kingston KT7 0EL (☎ 081 398 4101)

RUNGE, Hon Lady (Fiona Margaret); *née* Macpherson; er da of 1 Baron Strathcarron, KC, PC (d 1937), and Jill (d 1956), da of Sir George Wood Rhodes, 1 Bt, JP; *b* 9 Feb 1917; *m* 29 Oct 1935, Sir Peter Francis Runge (d 1970), 2 s of Julius Joseph Runge, of Sevenoaks, Kent; 3 s, 1 da; *Style—* The Hon Lady Runge; 4 Lammas Way, Lane End, High Wycombe, Bucks HP14 3EX

RUNKEL, Claus Dieter; s of Georg Runkel, of Ahornstrasse 20, D-2420 Eutin, and Inge Caroline Bull; *b* 28 March 1958; *Educ* Johann Heinrich Voss Gymnasium, Christie's Fine Art Course; *Career* apprenticeship at Buch und Grafik Hoffman Eutin 1977-80, head Dept of Art Books and Graphics Gustav Weiland Inc Lübeck 1980-81, freelance art conslt and curator Leinster Fine Art London 1984-86, opened CDR Fine Art Ltd (name later changed to Claus Runkel Fine Art Ltd) 1986, partnership with Michael Hue-Williams 1988, opened Runkel-Hue-Williams Gallery Bond St (Max Ernst Exhibition) 1988; author catalogue Will Maclean Sculptures and Box Constructions 1974-87 (1987); swimming champion: 25 medals and prizes won, represented Germany Int Relay Competition Nord-Cup (winner third prize) 1975; oboist; first oboe and soloist with Schleswig-Holstein Chamber Orch 1976-78; *Recreations* music, opera, reading, travelling; *Clubs* Patrons of New Art, Tate Gallery; *Style—* Claus Runkel, Esq; Runkel-Hue-Williams Ltd, 6/8 Old Bond St, London W1 (☎ 071 495 7017, fax 071 495 0179)

RUSBRIDGE, Brian John; CBE (1983); s of Arthur John Rusbridge (d 1974), of Appelton, Berks, and Leonora Rusbridge, *née* Hearn (d 1968); *b* 1 Sept 1922; *Educ* Willowfield Sch Eastbourne, Univ of Oxford (Dip Social Admin); *m* 21 July 1951, Joyce, da of Joseph Young Elliott (d 1953), of Darlington; 2 s (Michael John b 1955, Peter Graham b 1958); *Career* personnel mangr ICI Teeside 1949-63, dir industl rels BR Bd 1963-70, div mangr BR London 1970-73, sec, head of orgn and chief employers' negotiator for all local govt employers in UK LACSAB 1973-87, sr ptnr The Belgrave Conslts 1987-; ed The Municipal Year Book 1987-; dep chm of E Mosley Cons Assoc, chm The Beauchamp Gp; Freeman City of London 1976, memb Guild of Freeman 1977; MCIT 1964, CIPM 1975 (memb 1947); *Recreations* travel, walking, ancient civilisations, resisting developers; *Style—* Brian Rusbridge, Esq, CBE; 19 Beauchamp Rd, E Mosley, Surrey KT8 0PA (☎ 081 979 4952); The Belgrave Conslts, 32 Vauxhall Bridge Rd, London SW1V 2SS (☎ 071 973 6400, fax 071 233 5056)

RUSBRIDGER, Alan Charles; s of G H Rusbridger, of Guilford, Surrey, and Barbara, *née* Wickham; *b* 29 Dec 1953; *Educ* Cranleigh Sch, Magdalene Coll Cambridge (MA); *m* 1982, Lindsay, da of Lord Mackie of Benshie; *Career* reporter Cambridge Evening News 1976-79, reporter, columnist and feature writer The Guardian 1979-86, TV critic The Observer 1986-87, Washington corr London Daily News 1987, features ed The Guardian 1989- (feature writer and ed Weekend Guardian 1987-); commended Br Press Awards 1977 and 1978; memb NUJ; *Recreations* golf, cricket, music, family; *Style—* Alan Rusbridger, Esq; The Guardian, 119 Farringdon Rd, London EC1R 3ER (☎ 071 278 2332, fax 071 239 9935)

RUSBRIDGER, Hon Mrs (Lindsay Mary); *née* Mackie; da of Baron Mackie of Benshie (Life Peer); *b* 1945; *m* 1982, Alan Rusbridger, yr s of G H Rusbridger, of Warren Rd, Guildford, Surrey; *Style—* The Hon Mrs Rusbridger; c/o Ballinshoe, Kirriemuir, Angus DD8 5Q9

RUSBY, Vice Adm Sir Cameron; KCB (1979), LVO (1965); s of late Capt Victor Evelyn Rusby, CBE, RN, and late Irene Margaret, *née* Gunn; *b* 20 Feb 1926; *Educ* RNC Dartmouth; *m* 1948, Marion Bell; 2 da; *Career* Dep Supreme Allied Cdr Atlantic 1980-82, ret 1982; cmd offr HMS Ulster 1958-59, exec offr HM Yacht Britannia 1962-65, Dep Dir Naval Signals 1965-68, Cmd Offr HMS Tartar 1968-69, dep asst COS Plans and Policy on Staff of Allied C in C Southern Europe 1969-72, Sr Naval Offr West Indies 1972-74, Rear Adm 1974, Asst Chief Def Staff Ops 1974-77, Vice Adm 1977, Flag Offr Scotland and NI 1977-79; chief exec Scot Soc for the Prevention of Cruelty to Animals 1983-; *Style—* Vice Adm Sir Cameron Rusby, KCB, LVO; c/o Bank of Scotland, 70 High St, Peebles EH45 8AQ

RUSH, Michael Allen Frank; s of Colin Charles Rush (d 1968), of Richmond, Surrey, and Muriel Mary, *née* Hinds (d 1968); *b* 2 Jan 1933; *Educ* King's Coll Sch Wimbledon, King's Coll London (BSc); *m* 1, 26 July 1958 (m dis 1979), Janet Larema, da of Lt-Col David George Ogilvy Ayerst, of Burford, Oxon; 1 s (David b 1959), 2 da (Susan b 1961, Lindy b 1970); m 2, Linda Evelyn, da of Maurice Stratton Townsend, of High Wycombe; *Career* Flying Offr RAF 1954-56; mgmnt conslt A/C Inbucon 1961-65; WS Try Ltd: dir 1968, md 1972, chm of int subsid 1977, dep chm 1983; joined Michael Rush Assoc 1985, project mangr Daily Mail & Evening Standard New Devpt Printing Works 1985; MICE 1958, memb IOD 1975, FFB 1983; *Recreations* horse riding; *Clubs* RAF; *Style—* Michael A F Rush, Esq; Kingstreet End, Little Missenden, Amersham, Bucks HP7 ORA (☎ 02406 6864); PO Box 137, Amersham, Bucks HP7 0RS (☎ 02406 6214)

RUSH, Dr Michael David; s of Wilfrid George Rush (d 1983), of Richmond, Surrey, and Elizabeth May Winifred, *née* Gurney (d 1985); *b* 29 Oct 1937; *Educ* Shene GS Richmond Surrey, Univ of Sheffield (BA, PhD); *m* 25 July 1964, Jean Margaret, da of George Telford (d 1987), of Golcar, Huddersfield, Yorks; 2 s (Jonathan b 1968, Anthony b 1971); *Career* Nat Serv RASC 1957-59; head of Dept of Politics Univ of Exeter 1985- (asst lectr 1964-67, lectr 1967-81, sr lectr 1981-90, reader in Parliamentary Govt 1990-); visiting lectr Univ of Western Ontario 1967-68, visiting prof Univ of Arcadia Nova Scotia 1981, res fell Carleton Univ Ottawa 1975; chm Study of Parliament Gp 1990; RIPA; *Books* The Selection of Parliamentary Candidates (1969), The MP and his Information (jtly, 1970), An Introduction to Political Sociology (jtly, 1971), The House of Commons: Services and Facilities (co-ed, 1974), Parliamentary Government in Britain (1981), The Cabinet and Policy Formation (1984), The Parliament and the Public (1976 and 1986), Parliament and Pressure Politics (ed, 1990); *Recreations* listening to classical music, theatre, travel; *Style—* Dr Michael Rush; 2 St Loyes Rd, Heavitree, Exeter, Devon EX2 5HA (☎ 0392 54089); Dept of Politics, University of Exeter, Exeter, Devon EX4 4RJ (☎ 0392 263164)

RUSHDIE, (Ahmed) Salman; s of Anis Ahmed Rushdie (d 1987), and Negin, *née* Butt; *b* 19 June 1947, (Bombay); *Educ* Rugby, King's Coll Cambridge; *m* 1, 1976 (m dis 1987), Clarissa Luard; 1 s; m 2, 1988, Marianne Wiggins; *Career* former advertising copywriter; memb Gen Cncl Camden Ctee for Community Relations 1977-; novelist; *Books* Grimus (1975), Midnight's Children (winner of Booker Prize 1981), Shame (1983), The Jaguar Smile: a Nicaraguan Journey (1987), The Satanic Verses (1988); *Style—* Salman Rushdie, Esq; c/o Jonathan Cape Ltd, 30 Bedford Sq, WC1 (☎ 071 636 5674/9395)

RUSHFORD, Antony Redfern; CMG (1963); s of Stanley Rushford (d 1952), of New Milton, Hants, and Sarah Beatrice, *née* Gould (d 1979); *b* 9 Feb 1922; *Educ* Taunton Sch, Trinity Coll Cambridge (MA, LLM); *m* 1975, June Jeffery Wells, da of Charles Reginald Morrish, DSC, KPM (d 1952); 1 s (Simon), 1 da (Samantha), and stepchildren; *Career* RAFVR 1943-47, Sqdn Ldr 1946; called to the Bar Inner Temple, formerly admitted slr, asst slr EW Marshall Harvey & Dalton 1948, Home Civil Service Colonial Office 1949-68, joined HM Dip Serv Cwlth Office 1968 (later FCO), ret as dep legal advsr (asst under sec of State) 1982, Crown Counsel Uganda 1954-63, dir of studies Royal Inst of Public Admin 1982-86, princ legal advsr Br Indian Ocean Territory 1983, attorney gen Anguilla and St Helena 1983, legal advsr for Cwlth Sec Gen St Kitts' and Nevis' independence 1982-83, E Caribbean Cts 1983, maritime legislation for Jamaica Int Maritime Orgn 1983 and 1984, special legal advsr Govt of St Lucia 1982-, sec then pres IDB Inc 1985-86; has drafted many constitutions for UK dependencies and Cwlth countries attaining independence; presented paper on constitutional devpt to meeting of law offrs from smaller Cwlth jurisdictions IOM 1983; UK del and advsr at many constitutional conferences and discussions; co rep Inst of Advanced Legal Studies, lectr Overseas Legal Offrs Course, memb Editorial Bd Inst of Int Law and Econ Devpt Washington 1977-82, fndn memb Exec Cncl Royal Cwlth Soc for the Blind 1969-81 and 1983- (hon legal advsr 1984-); memb: Glyndebourne Festival, Saudi-Br Soc, Anglo-Arab Assoc, Cwlth Lawyers' Assoc, Cwlth Assoc of Legislative Counsel; govr Taunton Sch 1948, hon legal cnsllr 1978-; FRSA; CStJ; *Clubs* Royal Cwlth Soc; *Style—* Antony Rushford, Esq, CMG; The Penthouse, 63 Pont St, Knightsbridge SW1X 0BD

RUSHMAN, Dr Geoffrey Boswall; s of William John Rushman (d 1967), of Northampton, and Violet Helen Elizabeth, *née* Richards; *b* 20 Aug 1939; *Educ* Northampton GS, Univ of London, St Bartholomew's Hosp (MB BS); *m* 12 Oct 1963, Gillian Mary, da of Leslie George Rogers, of Alcester, Warks; 3 da (Alison b 1965, Ruth b 1967, Jacqueline b 1969); *Career* jr anaesthetist St Bartholomew's Hosp 1968-73, conslt anaesthetist Southend Hosp 1974-; Assoc of Anaesthetists prize for contribs to anaesthesia; memb Cncl Anaesthetics Section RSM 1985-88, lay reader Chelmsford Diocese; MRCS, LRCP, FFARCS 1970; *Books* Synopsis of Anaesthesia ed 8-10 (1977, 1982, 1987); *Recreations* skiing, preaching The Gospel, mountain marathons; *Clubs* RSM; *Style—* Dr Geoffrey Rushman; Department of Anaesthesia, Southend Hospital, Prittlewell Chase, Southend-on-Sea, Essex SSO ORY (☎ 0702 348911 ext 2319)

RUSHMAN, Nigel John; s of Maj Frederick William Edward Henry Rushman, of

Lancs, and Irene Vera, *née* Beer; *b* 25 May 1956; *Educ* Gillingham Tech HS, Gravesend GS, Thanet Tech Coll; *m* 1, 21 Sept 1980 (m dis), Deborah Sally, da of Kenneth William White, of London; 1 da (Louise Amanda b 1986); m 2, 28 July 1989, Nicola Susan, da of David Polding, of Cobham, Surrey; *Career* md CPMA Group; dir: Rushman Communications Ltd, The Moto Polo Assoc; MRSPHH, FInstSMM; *Recreations* motor polo, shooting, skiing, sailing; *Style*— Nigel Rushman, Esq; CPMA Group Ltd, Grove House, 45 Fernshaw Rd, London SW10 0TN (☎ 071 352 8888, fax 071 352 0997)

RUSHMORE, Brigadier Frederick Herbert Margetson; CBE (1962, OBE 1956, MBE 1951); s of Frederick Margetson Rushmore, master of St Catharine's Coll Cambridge (d 1933), and Millicent Sarah, *née* Beck (d 1965); *b* 19 May 1915; *Educ* King's Sch Bruton, Christ's Coll Cambridge (BA); *Career* served RA 1935-70 (Burma 1943-44, Korea 1952-53), Brig; dir Nat Assoc of Leagues of Hospital Friends 1970-80, chm General Cmmrs for Income Tax (Holborn Div) 1979-90; *Recreations* music, drama; *Clubs* London Rowing, Leander; *Style*— Brig Frederick Rushmore, CBE; 71 Lakeside House, Eaton Drive, Kingston upon Thames, Surrey (☎ 081 549 1877)

RUSHTON, Dr David Nigel; s of Dr Roland Rushton, of Bromley, and Pamela Anne, *née* Galzini; *b* 21 Dec 1944; *Educ* King's Sch Canterbury, Trinity Coll Cambridge (BA), King's Coll Hosp Med Sch (MB BChir), Univ of Cambridge (MD); *m* 30 March 1968, Anne, da of Leo Gallagher (d 1967), of Liverpool; 1 s (Samuel b 1982), 2 da (Nicola b 1970, Susannah b 1976); *Career* clinical scientific staff MRC Neurological Prostheses Unit 1971-, reader Dept of Neurology Inst of Psychiatry 1990; hon conslt Maudsley Hosp 1979-, hon conslt neurologist King's Coll Hosp 1984-; contrib scientific articles on neurology and neurological prostheses; memb: Assoc of Br Neurologists, Physiological Soc; Freeman Worshipful Co of Spectacle Makers 1979; FRCP 1989; *Books* Treatment in Clinical Medicine - neurological disorders; *Recreations* medieval house reconstruction, steam road vehicles; *Style*— Dr David Rushton

RUSHTON, Ian Lawton; *b* 8 Sept 1931; *Educ* Rock Ferry HS Birkenhead, King's Coll London (BSc); *m* 1, Julia, *née* Frankland (decd); 1 da (Jane b 1960); m 2, 1986, Anita, *née* Stevens; *Career* Mil Serv Flt Lt RAF 1953-56; Royal Insurance: joined 1956, dep gen mangr UK 1972, exec vice pres Royal USA NY 1980, md Royal Insurance (UK) Ltd 1983, dir and gen mangr Royal Insurance plc 1986, dep gp chief exec Royal Insurance Holdings plc 1988 (gp chief exec 1989-); dir Aachener und Münchener Beteiligungs AG (Germany) and Mutual & Federal Insurance Co Ltd (S Africa) 1989-; chm Fire Protection Assoc 1983-87, vice pres Inst of Actuaries 1986-89; memb: Cncl Assoc for Business Sponsorship of the Arts, Ct of Govrs RSC; Freeman: City of London, Worshipful Co of Actuaries, Worshipful Co of Insurers (court asst); FIA, FCII, FSS, FRS; *Style*— Ian L Rushton, Esq, FRS; Royal Insurance Holdings plc, 1 Cornhill, London EC3V 3QR (☎ 071 283 4300, fax 071 623 5282)

RUSHTON, James Edward; s of Edward Sydney Rushton (d 1983), of Wilmslow, Cheshire, and Stella Kathleen Joan Rushton; *b* 8 Aug 1936; *Educ* Repton; *m* 1, 6 June 1963, Fiona Patricia, da of George Stirling Tuite; 2 da (Emma b 1963, Sophie b 1965); m 2, 26 May 1972, Angela Christine, da of Harry Coupe Wrather; 1 s (Daniel b 1973); m 3, 24 June 1983, Marjorie Evelyn, da of James Eric Pickering (d 1958); *Career* chartered surveyor; ptnr Edward Rushton Son & Kenyon 1963 (sr ptnr 1978-); chm Gen Practice Div Educn Ctee 1980-83 (chm Gtr Manchester Branch 1987-88); MRICS Gen Practice Divnl Cncl 1976-84; memb Ctee Greater Manchester Branch IOD; *Recreations* golf, travel, photography; *Clubs* E India, St James's (Manchester); *Style*— James E Rushton, Esq; Legh House, Wilmslow Rd, Mottram St Andrew, Macclesfield, Cheshire (☎ 0625 828901); Edward Rushton Son & Kenyon, 1 St Ann Street, Manchester M2 7LG

RUSHTON, Dr Neil; s of John Allen Rushton, of Bridlington, Yorks, and Iris, *née* Street (d 1987); *b* 16 Dec 1945; *Educ* Oglethorpe Sch Tadcaster, The Middx Hosp London (MB BS), Univ of Cambridge (MD); *m* 12 June 1971, Sheila Margaret, da of Capt Geoffrey Greville Johnson, of Southwold, Suffolk; 2 s (Mark b 25 Sept 1973, Timothy b 24 Jan 1980), 1 da (Nicola b 15 Aug 1975); *Career* Univ of Cambridge: dir Orthopaedic Res Unit 1983, fell Magdalene Coll 1984, examiner Univs of Cambridge and London; Huntarian prof RCS, hon orthopaedic conslt Addenbrooke's Hosp; memb Br Assoc for the Surgery of the Knee, fndr memb Br Hip Soc, fell Br Orthopaedic Res Soc; Hon MA Univ of Cambridge 1979; LRCP, FRSM, FRCS, fell Br Orthopaedic Assoc; *Books* Colour Atlas of Surgical Exposures of the Limbs (1985), Orthopaedics: The Principles and Practice of Musculoskeletal Surgery (1987), Body Clock (contrib); *Recreations* dinghy sailing, snow skiing, wines, local radio; *Clubs* RSM, SCGB; *Style*— Dr Neil Rushton; 37 Bentley Road, Cambridge CB2 2AW (☎ 0223 353624); Orthopaedic Research Unit, University of Cambridge, Level E6, Addenbrooke's Hospital, Cambridge CB2 2QQ (☎ 0223 217551, fax 0223 214094)

RUSSELL; *see*: Hamilton-Russell

RUSSELL, Hon Mrs (Ann Bridget); *née* Parnell; 4 da of 6 Baron Congleton (d 1932); *b* 27 April 1927; *m* 5 Nov 1947 (m dis 1967), Major Derek Campbell Russell, RE; 3 children by adoption (2 s, 1 da); *Style*— The Hon Mrs Russell; Lyscombe Farm, Piddletrenthide, Dorset

RUSSELL, Rev Canon Anthony John; s of Michael John William Russell, and Beryl Margaret Russell; *b* 25 Jan 1943; *Educ* Uppingham, Univ of Durham (BA), Univ of Oxford (DPhil), Cuddesdon Theological Coll; *m* 1967, Sheila Alexandra, da of Alexander Scott; 2 s (Jonathan b 1971, Timothy b 1981), 2 da (Alexandra b 1969, Serena b 1975); *Career* formerly dir Arthur Rank Centre, chaplain to HM The Queen, canon theologian of Coventry Cathedral, examining chaplain to Bishop of Hereford; area bishop of Dorchester 1988-; also chaplain: Royal Agric Soc of England, Royal Agric Benevolent Inst; *Books* Groups and Teams in the Countryside (1975), The Clerical Profession (1980), The Country Parish (1986); *Style*— The Rt Rev Dr Anthony Russell; Holmby House, Sibford Ferris, Banbury, Oxfordshire OX15 5RG

RUSSELL, Hon Anthony John Mark; yst s of 4 Baron Ampthill; *b* 10 May 1952; *Educ* Stowe; *m* 22 June 1985, Christine L, er da of John O'Dell; 1 s (William Odo Alexander b 10 May 1986); *Style*— The Hon Anthony Russell; 6501 N Columbus Boulevard, Tucson, Arizona 85718, USA

RUSSELL, Anthony Patrick; s of Dr Michael Hibberd Russell (d 1987), of Little Sutton, S Wirral, and Pamela, *née* Eyre; *b* 11 April 1951; *Educ* The King's Sch Chester, Pembroke Coll Oxford (BA, MA); *Career* called to the Bar Middle Temple 1974, Northern Circuit 1974 (jr 1977, asst recorder 1989), sec Manchester Middle Temple Soc 1986-, memb Bar Cncl 1988-; memb Cncl Guild of Church Musicians 1985-, sec Fabric Ctee Manchester Cathedral 1987-; *Recreations* music, singing, sailing, reading; *Clubs* United Oxford and Cambridge Univ; *Style*— Anthony Russell, Esq; 37 Willow Park, Willow Bank, Fallowfield, Manchester M14 6XP (☎ 061 224 4413); Old Bank Chambers, 2 Old Bank St, Manchester M2 7PF (☎ 061 832 3791, fax 061 835 3054)

RUSSELL, Sir Archibald Edward; CBE (1955); s of Arthur Hallett Russell (d 1961); *b* 30 May 1904; *Educ* Fairfield GS, Bristol Univ (BSc); *m* 1929, Lorna Lillian, da of James J Mansfield (d 1932), of Newport; 1 s, 1 da; *Career* chief designer Bristol Aeroplane Co Ltd 1943 (tech dir 1952); Br Aircraft Corp: tech dir 1960-66, md 1966-67, chm (Filton Div) 1967-69, ret 1971; memb Cncl Air Registration 1961-71, FRS, RAeS Gold Medal 1955, Daniel Guggenheim Medal 1971; Elmer A Sperry Medal 1983; kt 1972; *Style*— Sir Archibald Russell, CBE, FRS; Glendower House, Clifton Park, Bristol 8 (☎ 0272 739208)

RUSSELL, Arthur Mervyn; s of Sir Arthur Russell, 6 Bt (d 1964), and hp of half-bro, Sir George Russell, 7 Bt; *b* 7 Feb 1923; *Style*— Arthur Russell, Esq

RUSSELL, Hon Mrs (Catherine Virginia); *née* Ponsonby; yst da of 2 Baron Ponsonby of Shulbrede (d 1976); *b* 21 July 1944; *m* 1972, Ian Macdonald Affleck Russell; 2 da; *Style*— The Hon Mrs Russell; Shulbrede Priory, Lynchmere, Haslemere, Surrey

RUSSELL, Charles Dominic; s and h of Sir Charles Russell, 3 Bt, *qv*; *b* 28 May 1956; *Educ* Worth Abbey Sch; *m* 24 May 1986, Sarah Jane Murray, da of Anthony Chandor, of Blackdown Border, Haslemere, Surrey; 1 s (Charles William b 1988); *Career* antiquarian book dealer; *Style*— Charles Russell, Esq; 3 Chartfield Sq, London SW15

RUSSELL, Sir Charles Ian; 3 Bt (UK 1916), of Littleworth Corner, Burnham, Co Buckingham; s of Capt Sir Alec Charles Russell, MC, 2 Bt (d 1938); *b* 13 March 1918; *Educ* Beaumont Coll, Univ Coll Oxford; *m* 18 Jan 1947, Rosemary, da of late Maj Sir John Theodore Prestige, of The Court House, Bishopsbourne, Canterbury; 1 s, 1 da; *Heir* s, Charles Dominic Russell; *Career* served WWII Capt RHA (despatches); slr 1947, former sr partner Charles Russell & Co, of Hale Court, Lincoln's Inn, WC2; *Clubs* Garrick, Army and Navy, Royal St George; *Style*— Sir Charles Russell, Bt; Hidden House, Strand St, Sandwich, Kent

RUSSELL, Christopher Garnet; s of George Percival Jewett (d 1948), of Michelgrove House, Michelgrove Rd, Boscombe, Hants, and Marjorie Alice Boddam-Whetham, *née* Keeling-Bloxam; *b* 6 April 1943; *Educ* Westminster, New Coll Oxford (MA); *m* 23 June 1973, Agatha Mary, da of Stephen Joseph Culkin (d 1984); 1 s (Charles b 1976), 2 da (Claire b 1974, Lucy b 1975); *Career* called to the Bar Middle Temple 1971, Lincoln's Inn 1985; *Style*— Christopher Russell, Esq; 11 Church St, Marcham, Oxon (☎ 0865 391 553); 86 Paramount Ct, University St, London WC1 (☎ 071 383 5943); 12 New Square, Lincoln's Inn, London WC2 (☎ 071 405 3808, fax 071 831 7376)

RUSSELL, 5 Earl (UK 1861); Conrad Sebastian Robert Russell; also Viscount Amberley (UK 1861); s of 3 Earl Russell, OM, FRS (d 1970, otherwise Bertrand Russell, the philosopher, writer and savant; ggs of Lord John Russell, of Great Reform Bill fame and twice PM, 3 s of 6 Duke of Bedford and later 1 Earl Russell), by his 3 w, Patricia Helen, *née* Spence; suc half-bro, 4 Earl (d 1987); *b* 15 April 1937; *Educ* Eton, Merton Coll Oxford (BA, MA); *m* 11 Aug 1962, Elizabeth Franklyn, da of Horace Sanders, of 43 Stockwood Rd, Chippenham, Wilts; 2 s (Nicholas Lyulph, Viscount Amberley b 1968, Hon John Francis b 1971); *Heir* s, Nicholas, Viscount Amberley b 1968; *Career* lectr in history Bedford Coll London 1960-74 (reader 1974-79); prof of history Yale Univ USA 1979-84, Astor Prof of British History UCL 1984-90, prof of history King's Coll London 1990-; memb Cncl Royal Historical Soc 1985 (vice-pres 1989); Hon MA Yale 1979; *Books* The Crisis of Parliaments: English History 1509-1660 (1971), The Origins of the English Civil War (ed, 1973), Parliaments and English Politics 1621-1629 (1979), The Causes of the English Civil War (Ford Lectures in the University of Oxford 1987-88) (1990); *Style*— The Rt Hon the Earl Russell; Department of History, King's College, Strand, London WC2 (☎ 071 836 5454)

RUSSELL, Cyril; s of Gerald Cyril Russell, MC (d 1962), of The Covert, Aldeburgh, Suffolk, and Barbara, *née* Reynolds; *b* 2 Oct 1924; *Educ* Beaumont Coll; *m* 30 June 1949, (Eileen Mary) Elizabeth, da of Maj William Douglas Grant Batten (d 1934); 3 s (Gerald b 1950, Patrick b 1952, Nicholas b 1958); *Career* cmmnd Irish Gds 1943; Serv 3 Bn: France, Belgium, Holland (wounded Sept 1944); admitted slr 1948; ptnr Charles Russell & Co 1951, conslt Charles Russell; memb Law Soc; *Recreations* golf, sailing; *Clubs* Boodle's, Swinley Forest Golf, MCC, Aldeburgh Yacht, Aldeburgh Golf; *Style*— Cyril Russell, Esq; The Covert, Aldeburgh, Suffolk; Hale Court, Lincoln's Inn, London, WC2 3UL (☎ 071 242 1031, fax 071 831 0872, telex 23521 LAWYER G)

RUSSELL, Hon (Francis) Damian; 2 s of Baron Russell of Killowen, PC (Life Peer, d 1986) and Joan (d 1976), only child of James Aubrey Torrens, of Wimpole St, London W1; *b* 8 June 1947; *Educ* Beaumont, Trinity Coll Dublin; *Recreations* art, books, skiing, shooting; *Style*— The Hon Damian Russell; 17 Lurline Gardens, London SW11 (☎ 071 622 6820)

RUSSELL, Hon Daniel Charles Edward; yst s of Capt the Hon Langley Gordon Haslingden Russell, MC (d 1981), o s of 2 Baron Russell of Liverpool, CBE, MC; bro of 3 Baron; granted rank of a Baron's s 1983; *b* 8 March 1962; *Style*— The Hon Daniel Russell

RUSSELL, Lady Daphne Crommelin; da of 12 Duke of Bedford (d 1953); *b* 2 Sept 1920; *Style*— The Lady Daphne Russell; Oak Cottage, Beckley, Rye, Sussex TN31 6TL

RUSSELL, David Francis Oliphant; CBE (1969), MC (1942), DL (1955); s of Sir David Russell, LLD (d 1956), of Silverburn, Leven, Fife, and Deborah Margaret Alison Russell (d 1958); *b* 9 Sept 1915; *Educ* Sedbergh; *m* 1945, Catherine Joan, *née* Robinson; 4 da (Margaret, Mary, Cecilia, Judy); *Career* serv WWII Maj: N Africa, Sicily, France; hon pres Tullis Russell Co Ltd (chm and md 1945-85), Chancellor's Assessor St Andrews Univ 1963-75 (remained Ct memb); memb: Royal Co of Archers (The Queen's Body Guard for Scotland) 1949, Bd of Tstees Nat Museum of Antiquities 1966-82; cncllr emeritus Nat Trust for Scotland 1976; Hon DSc Heriot Watt Univ, Hon LLD St Andrews Univ; FRSE; *Recreations* fishing, shooting; *Clubs* New (Edinburgh); *Style*— David Russell, Esq, CBE, MC, DL, FRSE; Rossie, Collessie, by Ladybank, Fife (☎ 0337 28 300)

RUSSELL, David Wallace; s of Charles Henry William Russell (d 1982), and Violet Lilian Vida, *née* David; *b* 2 July 1936; *Educ* Dulwich; *m* 1, 19 Sept 1959 (d 1967), Julia Eleanor, da of Raywood Ingham, of Eastbourne; 2 s (Simon b 1962, Timothy b 1963); m 2, 12 July 1969, Irene, da of Dirk Marinus Uijl (d 1965), of Rotterdam; 2 da (Christina b 1970, Rebecca b 1972); *Career* Nat Serv cmmnd RASC 1959-60; admitted slr 1958-; ptnr Blake Lapthorn Slrs 1962-, former chm Portsmouth Building Society (dir 1974-89), clerk to Gen Cmmrs of Income Tax Portsmouth and Havant Dists 1974-; chm of govrs Portsmouth GS (govr 1980-); memb Law Soc; *Recreations* squash, skiing, walking, caravanning; *Style*— David Russell, Esq; Montgomery House, 11 Montgomery Rd, Havant, Hants PO9 2RH; Blake Lapthorn, 8 Landport Terrace, Portsmouth PO1 2QW

RUSSELL, Hon David Whitney Erskine; s and h of 4 Baron Ampthill and his 1 w, Susan Mary, da of Hon Charles Winn (s of 2 Baron St Oswald, JP, DL); *b* 27 May 1947; *Educ* Stowe; *m* 15 Nov 1980, April McKenzie, yst da of Paul Arbon, of New York; 2 da (Christabel b 1981, Daisy b 1983); *Clubs* Turf, White's; *Style*— The Hon David Russell; 21 Albert Bridge Rd, London SW11 4PX (☎ 071 627 2080)

RUSSELL, Prof Donald Andrew Frank Moore; s of Samuel Charles Russell (d 1979), and Laura, *née* Moore (d 1966); *b* 13 Oct 1920; *Educ* King's Coll Sch Wimbledon, Balliol Coll Oxford (BA, MA, DLitt); *m* 22 July 1967, Joycelyne Gledhill Dickinson (Joy), da of Percy Parkin Dickinson (d 1972); *Career* served WWII: Royal Signals 1941-43, Intelligence Corps 1943-45; St John's Coll Oxford: fell 1948-88, univ lectr classical languages and lit 1957-58, reader classical lit 1978-85, prof of classical lit

1985-88; J H Gray Lectures Univ of Cambridge 1981; Paddison visiting prof: Univ of N Carolina 1985, Stanford Univ 1989-91; emeritus fell St John's Coll Oxford 1988-; FBA 1971; *Books* Longinus On the Sublime (1964), Plutarch (1972), Ancient Literary Criticism (with M Winterbottom, 1972), Criticism in Antiquity (1981), Menander Rhetor (with N G Wilson, 1981), Greek Declamation (1983), Anthology of Latin Prose (1990), Anthology of Greek Prose (1991); *Style*— Prof Donald Russell; 35 Belsyre Court, Oxford OX2 6HU (☎ 0865 56135); St John's Coll, Oxford OX1 3JP

RUSSELL, Edwin John Cumming; s of Edwin Russell (d 1962), and Mary Elizabeth, *née* Cumming (d 1969); *b* 4 May 1939; *Educ* Brighton GS, Brighton Sch of Art, Royal Acad Schs; *m* 7 Nov 1964, Lorne, da of Lt Cdr J A H McKean, RN (d 1981); 2 da (Rebecca b 21 Jan 1966, Tanya b 25 April 1968); *Career* sculpture for churches: Crucifix St Paul's Cathedral 1964, St Michael KCMG Chapel 1970, St Catherine Westminster Abbey 1966, Bishop Bubwith W Front Wells Cathedral; sundials incl: Jubilee Dolphin Dial Nat Maritime Museum Greenwich 1978, sundial Sultan Qaboos Univ Oman 1986, Botanical Armillary Sundial Kew Gardens 1987; forecourt sculpture Rank Xerox Int HQ 1989; shopping centre sculptures: Mad Hatters Tea Party Warrington 1984, Lion and Lamb Farnham 1987 (Best Shopping Centre Award); public works: Suffragette Meml London 1968, First Govr of Bahamas Sheraton Hotel Nassau 1968, Alice and the White Rabbit Guildford (Lewis Carroll commemorative sculpture) 1984, Panda World Wide Fund Int HQ 1988; private collections incl: Goodwood House, Arup Assocs, Trafalgar House plc, Cementation Int, John Mowlem & Co, City of London GS; FRBS 1970; *Recreations* practical philosophy; *Style*— Edwin Russell, Esq; Lethendry, Polecat Valley, Hindhead, Surrey GU26 6BE (☎ 042 860 5655)

RUSSELL, Hon Mrs; Hon Elizabeth Mary Gwenllian Lloyd; *née* Lloyd Mostyn; da of 4 Baron Mostyn (d 1965); *b* 18 Aug 1929; *m* 1, 14 Sept 1950 (m dis 1957), David Nicholas Goldsmith Duckham; 1 da; m 2, 25 May 1957, John Henry Russell; *Career* hotel proprietor; *Style*— The Hon Mrs Russell; Kings of Kinloch, Meigle, Perthshire

RUSSELL, Hon Lady ((Helen) Elizabeth); *née* Blades; da (twin) of 1 Baron Ebbisham, GBE (d 1953); *b* 27 July 1908; *m* 16 Feb 1939, Adm the Hon Sir Guy Herbrand Edward Russell, GBE, KCB, DSO (d 1977) s of late 2 Baron Ampthill, GCSI, GCIE, and Lady Margaret Lygon, CI, GCVO, GBE, da of 6 Earl Beauchamp; 2 s, 1 da; *Style*— The Hon Lady Russell; Flat 8, 89 Onslow Square, London SW7 3LT

RUSSELL, Hon Emma Kiloran; da of late Capt the Hon Langley Gordon Haslingden Russell, MC, only s of late 2 Baron Russell of Liverpool, CBE, MC; sis of 3 Baron; granted rank of a Baron's da 1983; *b* 15 June 1955; *Style*— The Hon Emma Russell

RUSSELL, Erica Rae; da of Innes Russell, of London, and Joan Rita, *née* Clare; *b* 14 June 1951; *Educ* Secdy Sch Johannesburg S Africa; *Partner* Adam Parker-Rhodes; 2 da (Ruby Russell b 2 Jan 1980, Bronwen Rhodes b 18 May 1982); *Career* freelance animator and film dir; worked in Art Dept Berman's Costumiers 1970, freelance model and prop maker 1972-74, painter and tracer at Richard Williams Studios, then asst to Art Babbit 1975; asst: animator Pink Floyd concert piece 1977, to Paul Vester Speedy Cartoons (film Sunbeam) 1978-80; animator and designer pop promotions and commercials Cucumber Studios 1983-85, fndr Eyeworks animation and design studio (dir Virgin Megastore commercial shown in BFI's Animation Syncopation and on BBC 2's Arts Review), made Feet of Song (winner BFI's Mari Kuttner award for Best Br Animated Film '89, shown at film festivals worldwide incl Modern Art Museum NY and Tate Gallery), guest artist Women Artists of the 20th Century exhibition Weisbarden 1990, lectr The Museum of the Moving Image and Nat Film Sch; memb ACTT, ASIFA; *Style*— Ms Erica Russell; 5 Muswell Hill Rd, London N10 3JB (☎ 081 883 9689)

RUSSELL, Sir Evelyn Charles Sackville; s of Henry Frederick Russell, of Brentwood, Essex; *b* 2 Dec 1912; *Educ* Douai, Château de Mesnières Seine Maritime France; *m* 1939, Joan (d 1990), da of Harold Edward Jocelyn Camps, of Coopersale, Epping; 1 da (Sarah); *Career* joined HAC 1938, serv WWII RA N Africa, Italy, Greece; called to the Bar Gray's Inn 1945, met stipendiary magistrate 1961-78, chief met stipendiary magistrate 1978-82; kt 1981; *Style*— Sir Evelyn Russell; The Gate House, Coopersale, Epping, Essex CM16 7QT (☎ 0378 72568)

RUSSELL, Hon Mrs (Frances Marian); da (by 1 m) of Lady Sempill, *qv*; *b* 1942; *m* 1976, David Ian Russell, s of Denis Russell, MBE, TD (unc of Sir Charles Russell, 3 Bt, *qv*); *Style*— The Hon Mrs Russell; 25 Eddiscombe Rd, London SW10

RUSSELL, Lord Francis Hastings; s (by 2 m) of 13 Duke of Bedford, of Les Ligures, Monte Carlo, and Lydia, Duchess of Bedford, *née* Yarde-Buller; *b* 27 Feb 1950; *Educ* Eton, NE London Poly (BSc); *m* 1971, Mrs (Faith Diane) Anak Carrington, da of late Dr S I M Ibrahim, of Singapore; 1 da (Czarina b 1976); *Career* chartered surveyor 1979; *Recreations* skiing; *Clubs* Buck's; *Style*— The Lord Francis Russell; 13 Tedworth Square, London SW3 4DU (☎ 071 351 1600/351 4363); 26A Cadogan Sq, London SW1X 0JP (☎ 071 225 3344)

RUSSELL, George; CBE (1985); s of William Henry Russell (d 1972), of Gateshead, Co Durham, and Frances Annie, *née* Atkinson (d 1973); *b* 25 Oct 1935; *Educ* Gateshead GS, Univ of Durham (BA); *m* 19 Dec 1959, Dorothy, da of Ernest Victor Brown (d 1969), of Gateshead, Co Durham; 3 da (Erica Frances b 1963, Livia Jane b 1966, Alison Victoria b 1969); *Career* vice pres and gen mangr: Welland Chemical Co of Canada 1968, St Clair Chemical Co Ltd 1968; chm: Luxfer Hldgs Ltd 1976, Alcan UK Ltd 1978, Basys Int Ltd 1987-88, IBA 1989-; md: Alcan Aluminium (UK) 1977-81, Alcan UK Ltd 1981-82 (asst md 1977-81); md and chief exec Br Alcan Aluminium 1982-86; dir: Alcan Aluminiumwerke GMBH Frankfurt 1982-86, Northern Rock Building Soc 1985-, Alcan Aluminium Ltd 1987- (joined World Bd 1987-); chm Marley plc 1989- (chief exec 1986-), dep chm Channel 4 TV Co Ltd 1987-88; chm: ITN 1988, IBA 1989-90, ITC 1991-; visiting prof Univ of Newcastle-upon-Tyne 1978-; memb: Bd Northern Sinfonia Orchestra 1977-80, Northern Industl Bd 1977-80, Washington Corp 1978-80, IBA 1979-86, Bd Civil Serv Pay Res Unit 1980-81, Megaw Inquiry into Civil Serv Pay 1981-82, CBI 1984-85, Widdicombe Ctee of Inquiry into Conduct of Local Authy Business 1985-86; tstee: Beamish Museum Tst 1985-89, Thomas Bewick Birthplace Tst 1986-89; FRSA, CBIM, fell Inst of Industl Mangrs; Hon DEng Newcastle-upon-Tyne 1985; *Recreations* tennis, badminton, bird watching; *Style*— George Russell, Esq, CBE; 46 Downshire Hill, Hampstead, London NW3 1NX; Marley plc, London Rd, Riverhead, Sevenoaks, Kent TN13 2DS (☎ 0732 455255, fax 0732 456585, telex 95231)

RUSSELL, Sir George Michael; 7 Bt (UK 1812), of Swallowfield, Berkshire; s of Sir Arthur Edward Ian Montagu Russell, 6 Bt (d 1964); *b* 30 Sept 1908; *Educ* Radley; *m* 1936, Joy Francis Bedford, da of late W Mitchell, of Irwin, W Australia; 2 da; *Heir* half-bro, Arthur Russell; *Style*— Sir George Russell, Bt

RUSSELL, Prof Gerald Francis Morris; s of Maj Daniel George Russell, MC (d 1958), of Ventnor, IOW, and Berthe Marie Mathilde Ghislaine, *née* De Boe (d 1981); *b* 12 Jan 1928; *Educ* George Watson's Coll Edinburgh, Univ of Edinburgh (MB ChB, MD); *m* 8 Sept 1950, Margaret Euphemia, da of John Taylor (d 1956), of Edinburgh; 3 s (Malcolm b 1951, Nigel b 1956, Graham b 1957); *Career* Capt RAMC 1951-53, regtl med offr Queen's Bays; dean Inst of Psychiatry Univ of London 1966-70, prof of psychiatry Royal Free Hosp Sch of Med Univ of London 1971-79, hon conslt psychiatrist Royal Free Hosp and Friern Hosp 1971-79, prof of psychiatry Inst of Psychiatry Univ of London 1979-, hon conslt psychiatrist Bethlem Royal and Maudsley Hosp 1979-; FRCP, FRCPEd, FRCPsych; *Books* The Neuroses and Personality Disorders, vol 4 of The Handbook of Psychiatry (jtly, 1983), Scientific and Clinical Articles on Eating Disorders; *Recreations* art galleries, photography, music; *Style*— Prof Gerald Russell; The Institute of Psychiatry, De Crespigny Park, London SE5 8AF (☎ 071 703 8408)

RUSSELL, Lord Hugh Hastings; yr s of 12 Duke of Bedford (d 1953), and Louisa Crommelin Roberta Jowitt, *née* Whitwell (d 1960); *b* 29 March 1923; *Educ* Christ's Coll Cambridge; *m* 7 Sept 1957, Rosemary, yr da of Keith Freeling Markby (d 1972), of Treworder, Blisland, Bodmin, Cornwall; 1 s, 1 da; *Career* ARICS; *Recreations* shooting, riding, ornithology; *Style*— Lord Hugh Russell; The Bell House, Dolau, Llandrindod Wells, Powys LD1 5UN

RUSSELL, Prof James Knox; s of James Knox Russell, and Jane Edgar, *née* Younger; *b* 5 Sept 1919; *Educ* Aberdeen GS, Univ of Aberdeen (BM ChB, MD); *m* 16 May 1964, Cecilia Valentine, MD, DCH, da of Patrick Urquhart (d 1956); 3 da (Janice Valentine b 1950, Hilary Margaret b 1951, Sarah Younger b 1956); *Career* serv WWII; MORAF 1954-56 serv Bomber Cmd in England and W Europe (particular interest in early diagnosis of stress in operational aircrew); trained as obstetrician and gynaecologist under Prof Sir Dugald Baird in Aberdeen 1946-50, chief asst to Prof Harvey Evers Newcastle upon Tyne 1950-58, prof obstetrics and gynaecology Univ of Newcastle upon Tyne 1958-82 (emeritus 1982-), dean post graduate medicine 1968-77, conslt in human reproduction WHO 1960-82; examiner obstetrics and gynaecology Univs of: London, Birmingham, Manchester, Aberdeen, Belfast, Liverpool, Tripoli, Kuala Lumpur 1980-82; visiting prof: NY 1967 and 1974, SA 1971 and 1978, Univ of Oviedo 1982; Graham Waite Meml lectr AM Coll Obstetrics and Gynaecology Dallas 1982; vice chm Mitford PC 1985-; FRCOG 1958 (memb 1949); *Books* Early Teenage Pregnancy (1982); *Recreations* curing & smoking: bacon, salmon, eels, rainbow trout, chicken; *Clubs* Royal Over-Seas League; *Style*— Prof J K Russell; Newlands, Tranwell Woods, Morpeth, Northumberland NE61 6AG (☎ 0670 515 666)

RUSSELL, John; s of Harold George Russell, of 44 Woodlands Park, Leigh-on-Sea, Essex, and Joyce Caroline, *née* Morris; *b* 1 June 1953; *Educ* Westcliff HS for Boys, Univ of Southampton (LLB); *m* 23 July 1977, (Ingegerd) Maria, da of Rolf Erik Norê; 2 da (Samantha b 2 June 1982, Emma b 5 April 1985); *Career* admitted slr 1977, Linklaters & Paines London and Hong Kong 1975-85, investmt banker Merrill Lynch International 1985-88, ptnr Simmons & Simmons 1988-; memb: Law Soc, Slrs Euro Gp, Young Slrs Gp; *Books* Mergers and Aquisitions in Europe (ed); *Recreations* skiing, walking, swimming, sailing; *Style*— John Russell, Esq; Simmons & Simmons, 14 Dominion St, London EC2M 2RJ (☎ 071 628 2020, fax 071 588 4129, telex 888562 SIMMON G)

RUSSELL, John Bayley; s of Frederick Charles Russell (d 1987), of Brisbane, Aust, and Clarice Emily Mander, *née* Jones (d 1959); *b* 22 Jan 1942; *Educ* C of E GS Brisbane Aust, Univ of Queensland (BComm); *m* 27 Sept 1968, Virginia, *née* Winsome; 1 s (Simon b 1972); *Career* Bain & Co Securities: ptnr 1972, ptnr i/c London Office 1980-84 and 1986-, ptnr i/c NY office 1984-86; memb Aust-Br C of C; FIOD; memb Aust Stock Exchange; *Recreations* golf, reading; *Clubs* Univ and Schs (Sydney); *Style*— John Russell, Esq; Bain & Co, 115 Houndsditch, London EC3A 7BU (☎ 071 283 9133, fax 071 626 7090)

RUSSELL, John Francis; s of Francis Frederick Russell (d 1987), and Barbara Mary, *née* Thornhill; *b* 12 Dec 1948; *Educ* Victoria Secdy Mod Sch, Bushey GS, Harrow Tech Coll and Sch of Art; *m* ;1 s (Drew Francis Robert b 1985), 1 da (Kelly Xenia b 1983); *Career* freelance fine art photographer and black and white printer; head: Audio Visual Serv, Bldg Res Estab; many exhibitions of fine art photography; BIPP Jubilee Fellowship award Gold medal, RIBA/BIPP Architectural Photographer of the Year, Ilford Photographer of the Year; FBIPP, FRPS; *Recreations* fine art photographer, sailing, golf, swimming, travelling; *Style*— John Russell, Esq; 25 How Wood, Park Street, St Albans AL2 2QY (☎ 0727 873989); Department of the Environment, Building Research Establishment, Garston, Watford WD2 7JR (☎ 0923 664354, fax 0923 664094)

RUSSELL, John Harry; s of Joseph Harry Russell (d 1983), and Nellie Annie Russell (d 1976); *b* 21 Feb 1926; *Educ* Halesowen GS; *m* 1951, Iris Mary, da of Thomas Cook, of 20 Olive Hill Road, Blackheath, Birmingham; 1 s (David John b 24 Jan 1953), 1 da (Susan Jane b 14 July 1959); *Career* served WWII RN; Joseph Lucas Ltd 1948-52, Vono Ltd (Duport Group) 1952-59, Standard Motors Ltd 1959-61; Duport Group 1961-86: md Foundries Engrg Div 1972-73, dep gp md 1973-75, gp md 1975-80, dep chm 1976-81, chm and chief exec 1981-86; dir Local Bd Barclays Bank Birmingham 1976-88; chm: Black Country Museum Tst Ltd, Camborne Industries plc; Liveryman Worshipful Co of Glaziers, Freeman City of London 1976; FCA, FBIM; *Recreations* reading, music, antiques; *Clubs* Annabel's, Mark's; *Style*— John H Russell, Esq; 442 Bromsgrove Rd, Hunnington, Halesowen, W Midlands B62 0JL

RUSSELL, Hon John Hugo Trenchard; s of 3 Baron Ampthill, CBE, by his 3 w, Adeline; *b* 13 Oct 1950; *Educ* Eton; *m* 1976, Susanna, da of Peter Merriam (s of Sir Laurence Merriam, MC, JP, DL, and Lady Marjory Kennedy, da of 3 Marquess of Ailsa); 2 s; *Career* dir Baring Brothers & Co Ltd; FCA; *Clubs* Turf; *Style*— The Hon John Russell; Ringstead Farm, Dorchester, Dorset DT2 8NF; 14 Brodrick Rd, London SW17 7DZ

RUSSELL, Hon Mrs Langley (Kiloran Margaret); *née* Howard; da of Hon Sir Arthur Howard, KBE, CVO (bro of 3 Baron Strathcona and Mount Royal), and Lady Lorna Baldwin, da of 1 Earl Baldwin of Bewdley, KG, PC (Stanley Baldwin, the PM); *b* 21 July 1926; *Educ* governess, Longstowe Hall, Cone Ripman Sch of Dancing; *m* 1951, Capt Hon Langley Russell, MC (d 1975), only s of 2 Baron Russell of Liverpool, CBE, MC; 3 s (3 Baron, Adam, Daniel), 3 da (Emma, Annabel, Lucy); *Career* served WWII WRNS 1944-45; temporary work in the theatre, and as a model, a shop assistant and a receptionist; memb Canadian Red Cross; *Recreations* theatre, travelling; *Style*— The Hon Mrs Langley Russell; Ash Farm, Stourpaine, Blandford, Dorset (☎ 0258 52177)

RUSSELL, Hon Lucy Catherine; da of late Capt the Hon Langley Gordon Haslingden Russell, MC, only s of late 2 Baron Russell of Liverpool, CBE, MC; sis of 3 Baron; granted rank of a Baron's da 1983; *b* 1968; *Style*— The Hon Lucy Russell

RUSSELL, Sir (Robert) Mark; KCMG (1985, CMG 1977); s of Sir Robert Russell CSI, CIE (d 1972), and Esther Rhona, *née* Murray (d 1983); *b* 3 Sept 1929; *Educ* Trinity Coll Glenalmond, Exeter Coll Oxford (MA); *m* 1954, Virginia Mary, da of George Swire de Moleyns Rogers (d 1957); 2 s (Neil, Alexander), 2 da (Claire, Lesley); *Career* 2 Lt RA 1952-54; joined Dip Serv 1954-, third sec FO 1954; second sec: Budapest 1956, Berne 1958; first sec: FO 1961, Kabul 1965 (and head of Chancery), FCO 1967 (cnsllr 1969); cnsllr: (commercial) Bucharest 1970, Washington 1974 (head of Chancery 1977); chief inspr and dep chief clerk FCO 1978, ambassador Ankara 1983, dep under sec of state (chief clerk) FCO 1986, ret 1989; chm Martin Currie European Investment Trust plc, special advsr Scottish Financial Enterprise; memb of Bd of Govrs The British Cncl; *Clubs* Royal Cwlth Soc, New (Edinburgh); *Style*— Sir Mark Russell, KCMG; c/o Foreign and Commonwealth Office, King Charles St, London SW1A 2AH

RUSSELL, Lady Mary Katherine; *née* Baillie-Hamilton; da of 12 Earl of Haddington, KT, MC, TD; *b* 13 Jan 1934; *m* 1, 21 July 1954 (m dis 1965), (John) Adrian Bailey; 2 s (William Anthony b 1957, Philip Graham b 1959), 1 da (Arabella Sarah Lucy b 1955, now Viscountess Chandos); m 2, 1 Oct 1965, David Russell, s of Brig Hugh Edward Russell, DSO; 1 s (Jason Dominic b 1966), 1 da (Mariana b 1968); *Style—* The Lady Mary Russell; 28 Northumberland Place, London W2; Combe Manor, nr Newbury, Berks

RUSSELL, Dr Michael Anthony Hamilton; s of James Hamilton Russell (d 1985), and Hon Kathleen Mary, *née* Gibson; *b* 9 March 1932; *Educ* Diocesan Coll Cape Town SA, Univ Coll Oxford (MA, BM BCh, DPM); *m* 27 Jan 1962, Audrey Anne, da of Archibald Timms (d 1940); 2 s (James Hamilton b 16 March 1974, Nicholas Hamilton b 3 Sept 1977); *Career* house physician and surgn Guy's Hosp London 1957-58, registrar in pathology and sr registrar med Groote Schuur Hosp Univ of Cape Town SA 1959-64, med registrar Ruttonjee Sanatorium Hong Kong 1964-65, registrar and sr registrar in psychiatry Maudsley Hosp London 1965-69, lectr in psychiatry Inst of Psychiatry London 1969-73, sr lectr and hon conslt Maudsley Hosp London 1973-, reader in addiction Univ of London Inst of Psychiatry 1985-, hon dir ICRF Health Behaviour Unit Maudsley Hosp London 1988-; numerous papers and articles on tobacco smoking in scientific jls; memb: Cncl Action on Smoking and Health (ASH), Br Assoc of Psychopharmacology; FRCP 1982, FRCPsych 1980, FRSH 1988; *Books* Nicotine Psychopharmacology (with S Wonnacott and I P Stolerman, 1990); *Recreations* reading, swimming, windsurfing, travel; *Style—* Dr Michael Russell; 14 Court Lane Gardens, Dulwich, London SE21 7DZ (☎ 081 693 3606); Institute of Psychiatry, The Maudsley Hospital, Denmark Hill, London SE5 8AF (☎ 071 703 6333, fax 071 703 6197)

RUSSELL, Sheriff (Albert) Muir Galloway; CBE (1989), QC (Scotland 1965); s of Hon Lord Russell (d 1975), Senator of the Coll of Justice, and Florence Muir, *née* Galloway (d 1983); *b* 26 Oct 1925; *Educ* Edinburgh Acad, Wellington, BNC Oxford (BA), Univ of Edinburgh (LLB); *m* 9 April 1954, Margaret Winifred, da of Thomas McWalter Millar (d 1970), of Edinburgh; 2 s (Douglas b 27 April 1958, Graham b 14 June 1962), 2 da (Anne b 1 Nov 1960, Jennifer b 22 Jan 1964); *Career* Lt Scots Gds 1944-47, served BLA and BAOR; memb Faculty of Advocates (Edinburgh) 1951, standing jr counsel to BOT, Dept of Agric and Forestry Cmmn; Sheriff of Grampian Highlands and Islands at Aberdeen 1971-; memb Sheriff Ct Rules Cncl 1977-86, vice chm Bd of Mgmnt Southern Gp of Hosps Edinburgh 1964, govr Moray House Coll of Educn 1966-70; *Recreations* golf, music; *Clubs* Royal Northern and Univ (Aberdeen); *Style—* Sheriff Muir Russell, QC; Easter Ord House, Skene, Aberdeenshire AB3 6SQ (☎ 0224 740228)

RUSSELL, Dr Nicholas John; s of Dr Michael Hibberd Russell (d 1987), of Little Sutton, Cheshire, and Pamela, *née* Eyre; *b* 23 Feb 1953; *Educ* The King's Sch Chester, Trinity Coll Cambridge (MA, MB BChir), Westminster Hosp Med Sch; *m* 17 Feb 1979, Christine Frances, da of Basil Ivor Lever, of Deanscales, Cockermouth; 2 s (Benjamin b 1979, Julian b 1981), 1 da (Eleanor b 1986); *Career* conslt physician in geriatric med W Cumberland Hosp 1988; MRCP 1980; *Recreations* tennis, fly fishing; *Clubs* Y; *Style—* Dr Nicholas Russell; West Cumberland Hospital, Whitehaven, Cumbria CA28 8JG (☎ 0946 693181)

RUSSELL, Hon Mrs (Nicole); *née* Yarde-Buller; da (by 1 m) of 4 Baron Churston; *b* 11 March 1936; *m* 1, 10 April 1958 (m dis 1962), Richard Wilfred Beavoir Berens; 1 s (Thomas), 1 da (Jessica); m 2, 6 Feb 1963, Michael Russell; 2 s (Francis, Alexander), 1 da (Lorna); *Style—* The Hon Mrs Russell; The Chantry House, Wilton, Salisbury, Wilts

RUSSELL, Lady; (Aliki) Olga; *née* Diplarakos; da of George Diplarakos, of Athens; *Educ* Lycee Victor-Duruy Paris, Piano Conservatoire; *m* 1, Cmdt Paul-Louis Weiller; 1 s (Paul-Annik b 1933, m 1965, Donna Olimpia Torlonia, gda of King Alfonso XIII of Spain and gggda of Queen Victoria); m 2, 1945, Sir John Wriothesley Russell, GCVO, CMG (d 1984); 1 s (Alexander b 1950, m 1986, Elizabeth Diana Manners), 1 da (Georgiana b 1947, m 1976 Brooke Boothby, *qv*); *Career* Order of Isabel la Catolica (Spain); *Recreations* sculpting, music; *Style—* Lady Russell; Flat 1, 48 Queen's Gate Gardens, London SW7 5ND; The Vine Farm, Northbourne, Deal, Kent (☎ 0304 374 794)

RUSSELL, Rt Hon Lord Justice; Rt Hon Sir (Thomas) Patrick; PC (1987); s of Sidney Russell (d 1953), and Elsie Russell (d 1948); *b* 30 July 1926; *Educ* Urmston GS, Univ of Manchester (LLB); *m* 1951, Doreen (Janie) Ireland; 2 da; *Career* called to the Bar Middle Temple 1949; prosecuting counsel to the Post Office Northern Circuit 1961-70, asst rec Bolton 1964-70, rec Barrow-in-Furness 1970-71, QC 1971, Crown Ct rec 1972-80, bencher 1978, ldr N Circuit 1978-80, High Ct judge (Queen's Bench) 1980-86, presiding judge N Circuit 1983-86, Lord Justice of Appeal 1987; Hon LLD Univ of Manchester 1988; kt 1980; *Style—* The Rt Hon Lord Justice Russell; Royal Courts of Justice, The Strand, London WC2

RUSSELL, Peter Jackson; s of Raymond John Russell (d 1986), of Chesterfield, Derbys, and Doris Sarah, *née* Jones (d 1990); *b* 17 Feb 1941; *Educ* Netherthorpe GS; *m* 11 April 1989, Gillian Isobel, da of Bernard Fenton; 1 da (Lucy Emma Victoria b 22 Nov 1989); *Career* res chemist H J Heinz 1959-60, prodn exec C Vernon & Sons 1960-64, mktg exec Young & Rubicam 1964-68, product devpt exec Maclaren Dunkley Friedlander 1968-72; account dir: Chetwynd Streets 1972-74, Phillips Russell 1974-; MIPA, MCIM; *Recreations* golf; *Clubs* Richmond Golf; *Style—* Peter Russell, Esq; 19 Hatch Place, Ham, Kingston-upon-Thames, London KT2 5NB (☎ 081 549 5906); Phillips Russell plc, 58 Wardour St, London W1V 3HN (☎ 071 439 0431, 071 734 7406)

RUSSELL, Peter John; s of Capt Raymond Colston Frederick Russell, of Bristol, and Marjorie Catherine, *née* Lock; *b* 14 Dec 1951; *Educ* Bedminster Down Sch Bristol, Univ of London (BA, LLM); *m* 7 April 1979, Dr Evelyn Mary, da of Sqdn Ldr Lorence Alan Scott, of Bridport, Dorset; 1 s (Timothy Paul b 1985), 1 da (Sarah Anne b 1982); *Career* barr Inner Temple 1975, Northern Circuit 1975-, lectr in law Univ of Manchester 1975-82; memb: Manchester Wine Soc, Manchester Medico-Legal Soc, Hon Soc of the Inner Temple; *Recreations* wine tasting; *Style—* Peter Russell, Esq; 18 Elm Rd, Didsbury, Manchester M20 0XD (☎ 061 434 4306); 5 John Dalton St, Manchester M2 6ET (☎ 061 6875, fax 061 834 8557)

RUSSELL, Dr Robin Irvine; s of John Russell (d 1952), and Mary Russell (d 1950); *b* 21 Dec 1936; *Educ* Univ of Glasgow (MD, PhD); *m* 18 Aug 1964, Ann, da of Andrew Wallace (d 1977), of Glasgow; 1 s (Bruce b 1965), 1 da (Kara b 1968); *Career* memb med and scientific staff MRC Gastroenterology Unit London 1966-68, lectr in med Univ of Glasgow 1968-70; memb: Assoc of Physicians 1976, Br Soc of Gastroenterology 1969; FRCPE, FRCP Glasgow; *Books* Investigative Tests and Techniques in Gastroenterology (1977), Elemental Diets (1981); *Recreations* golf, travel, literature, music; *Clubs* RSM; *Style—* Dr Robin Russell; Dept of Gastroenterology, Royal Infirmary, University of Glasgow, Glasgow (☎ 041 552 3535)

RUSSELL, Lord Rudolf; s (by 1 m) of 13 Duke of Bedford; *b* 7 March 1944; *Educ* Gordonstoun; *m* 2 June 1989, Farah, yr da of R Moghaddam; *Style—* The Lord Rudolf Russell; Charlton Park House, Malmesbury, Wiltshire SN16 9DG

RUSSELL, Rupert Edward Odo; s of David Hastings Gerald Russell (see Debrett's Peerage, Ampthill, B), of 88 Cambridge St, London SW1, and Hester Clere, *née* Parsons; *b* 5 Nov 1944; *Educ* Selwyn House Sch Montreal, Rannoch Sch Perthshire; *m* 9 Dec 1981, Catherine Jill, former Lady Brougham and Vaux, da of William Daniel Gulliver (d 1981); *Career* admitted slr 1973; ptnr: Blount Petre and Co 1979-81, Anhurst Brown Martin and Nicholson 1986-87, Payne Hicks Beach 1988-; vice pres Cities of London and Westminster Cons Assoc (former chm); memb Law Soc 1973; *Recreations* skiing, sailing, fishing, gardening; *Clubs* Buck's; *Style—* Rupert Russell, Esq; Highleaze, Oare, Marlborough, Wiltshire (☎ 0672 62487); 10 New Sq, Lincoln's Inn, London WC2A 3QG (☎ 071 242 6041, fax 071 405 0434, telex 24437 INNLAW G)

RUSSELL, Susan McCarrison; da of Dr Alfred MacCarrison Russell, of Dalisbury, Wiltshire, and Dr Dorothy Hazel, *née* Webster; *b* 6 Dec 1947; *Educ* Upper Chine Sch Sandown IOW, Coll of Law, Inns of Ct Sch of Law; *m* 22 May 1976, Capt Mark Richard Glasgow, s of Richard Edwin Glasgow, of Ipswich, Suffolk; 2 s (Edward McCarrison b 26 Jan 1979, Simon Markby b 9 July 1981); *Career* called to the Bar Middle Temple 1972, practising John Rankin QC's chambers 1973-; memb Hon Soc Middle Temple 1969-; Freeman City of London 1982; *Recreations* tennis; *Clubs* RAC, Hurlingham; *Style—* Miss Susan Russell

RUSSELL, Thomas; CMG (1980), CBE (1970, OBE 1963); s of late Thomas Russell OBE, MC; *b* 27 May 1920; *Educ* Hawick HS, St Andrews Univ, Peterhouse Cambridge; *m* 1951, Andrée Irma, *née* Desfosses (decd); 1 s; *Career* Capt Para Regt serv N Africa, Italy; Colonial Admin Serv Solomon Islands 1948, dist cmmmr 1948-49 and 1954-56, seconded Colonial Office 1956-57, fin sec 1965, chief sec 1970, govr Cayman Islands 1974-81, rep of Cayman Islands in UK 1982-; *Recreations* anthropology, archaeology; *Clubs* Caledonian, Royal Cwlth Soc; *Style—* Thomas Russell, Esq, CMG, CBE; 6 Eldon Drive, Farnham, Surrey GU10 3JE; office: Cayman Islands Govt Office, Trevor House, 100 Brompton Rd, London SW3 1EX (☎ 071 581 9418)

RUSSELL, Hon Mrs (Victoria Anne); da of 4 Baron Mottistone; *b* 23 Dec 1957; *m* 1984, Christopher Russell, s of late John Russell, and Lady Whitley, step s of Air Marshal Sir John Whitley; 1 da (Emily b 1985); 1 s (John Hugh b 1987); *Style—* The Hon Mrs Russell

RUSSELL, Prof William Clelland; s of Hugh McPherson Russell (d 1937), and Nora Catherine, *née* Peoples (d 1983); *b* 9 Aug 1930; *Educ* Allan Glens Sch Glasgow, Univ of Glasgow (BSc, PhD); *m* 1, 15 Oct 1962, Dorothy Ada, *née* Brown (d 1982); 1 s (Iain Andrew b 1967), 1 da (Lucy Anne b 1965); m 2, 31 March 1985, Reta, *née* Brown; *Career* chemist with Miny of Supply Royal Ordinance Factories Bishopton, Renfrewshire and Bridgewater Somerset 1955-56, res chemist J & P Coats Ltd Paisley Renfrewshire 1956-59, Lock res fell Royal Faculty of Physicians and Surgns of Glasgow at Dept of Virology Univ of Glasgow 1959-63, Eleanor Roosevelt Int Cancer fellowship Dept of Med Biophysics Univ of Toronto Canada 1963-64, head Div of Virology Nat Inst Med Res Mill Hill London 1973-84 (memb MRS res staf 1964-84), prof of biochemistry and head of Dept of Biochemistry and Microbiology Univ of St Andrews; ed Journal of General Virology 1972-77, memb Cncl Soc for Gen Microbiology 1988- (convener Virus Gp 1984-89); FRSE 1988; *Style—* Prof William Russell, FRSE; Netherburn, 2 Lade Braes, St Andrews, Fife KY16 9ET (☎ 0334 77705); Department of Biochemistry and Microbiology, University of St Andrews, Irvine Building, North St, St Andrews, Fife KY16 9AL (☎ 0334 76161, fax 0334 78721)

RUSSELL, Hon William Southwell; yr s (by his 1 w, Dorothy) of 26th Baron de Clifford, OBE, TD (d 1982); hp to bro, 27th Baron; *b* 26 Feb 1930; *Educ* Eton, King's Coll Cambridge, Princeton; *m* 1961, Jean Brodie, o da of Neil Brodie Henderson, and Conn, da of Adm of the Fleet Sir Charles Madden, 1st Bt, GCB, OM, GCVO, KCMG; 1 s (Miles Edward Southwell b 7 Aug 1966), 2 da (Mary-Jane Sophia b 13 March 1963, Joanna Clare b 23 Jan 1965); *Career* formerly with Tea Div of Tate & Lyle; md Avabe UK Ltd, chm MSS International Ltd; master of Science in Engineering (US); *Style—* The Hon William Russell; Five Chimneys, Hadlow Down, Uckfield, Sussex (☎ 082 581 3159)

RUSSELL BEALE, Simon; s of Maj-Gen PJ Beale, RAMC, and Dr Julia Beale, *née* Winter; *b* 12 Jan 1961; *Educ* St Paul's Cathedral Choir Sch, Clifton, Gonville & Caius Coll Cambridge, GSM; *Career* actor; Look to the Rainbow Apollo Theatre, Women Beware Women Royal Court Theatre, RSC A Winter's Tale, Everyman in His Humour, The Art of Success, The Fair Maid of the West, Speculators, The Storm, The Constant Couple, The Man of Mode, Restoration, Some Americans Abroad, Mary and Lizzie, Playing with Trains, Troilus and Cressida, Edward III, Love's Labour's Lost, The Seagull), Traverse Theatre (Die Hose, The Death of Elias Sawney, Sandra Manon), A Very Peculiar Practise BBC; *Style—* Simon Russell Beale, Esq; Richard Stone Partnership, 25 Whitehall, London SW1A 2BS (☎ 071 839 6421)

RUSSELL-COBB, Trevor; s of Herbert Edmund Cobb (d 1939), and Valerie Cecil Russell (d 1950); *b* 3 Feb 1918; *Educ* Wellington, Univ of London (BA, BSc); *m* 1, 8 May 1940, Suzanne, da of late Guy Chambers; 1 s (Rupert b 1943), 1 da (Theresa b 1947); m 2, 17 Dec 1952, Nan Piquet-Wicks, da of late John Stanley Hughes; 2 s (Piers b 1953, Fabian b 1955); *Career* Lt-Col Welsh Guards regtl and staff duty; chm and md Russell-Cobb Ltd (PR conslts) 1962-; dir: Campbell- Johnson Ltd (PR conslts) 1955-62, U N Fellowship Dept Br Cncl London 1946-51; tech asst UN (Geneva) 1952-54; dir English Chamber Orch and Music Soc 1963-78, memb Ctee Victorian Soc 1970-74, memb Cncl Tres Royal Soc of Arts 1972-83, sec Associates of the V & A 1978-82, tstee Sir John Soane's Museum 1978-, memb Policy Studies Inst Advsy Ctee The Economics of Historic Country Houses 1980-81, chm Fndn for Ephemera Studies 1984-; *Books* Paying the Piper (1968); *Recreations* playing the piano, walking, reading; *Style—* Trevor Russell-Cobb, Esq; 25 Alderney St, London SW1V 4ES (☎ 071 834 0605)

RUSSELL-HOBBS, Ronald Arthur; s of Samuel George Hobbs (d 1955), of Hounslow, and Kate, *née* Waghorn (d 1987); *b* 10 Nov 1940; *Educ* Duke of York's Royal Mil Sch Dover Kent; *m* 1 (m dis), Susan Frances, *née* Martin; 1 s (Andrew Martin b 1967), 2 da (Sarah Jane b 1966, Emma Louise b 1968); m 2, 27 March 1981, Joy, da of Noel Russell, of Dublin; 2 da (Lucy b 1979, Kate b 1981); *Career* divnl md Longman Gp Ltd 1969-81, jt md Pergamon Press Ltd 1981-83, dir Br Printing & Communications Corp plc 1981-83, md Millbank Publishing Gp Ltd 1983-87, gp chief exec Dunn & Wilson Gp ltd 1988; *Recreations* cricket, rugby, antiques; *Clubs* MCC, Leeds; *Style—* Ronald Russell-Hobbs, Esq; White Lodge, Tyringham, Rutland Drive, Harrogate, N Yorks HG1 2NX (☎ 0423 69183); Dunn & Wilson Ltd, Goodbard House, Infirmary St, Leeds LS1 2JS (☎ 0532 445 565)

RUSSELL JONES, Dr Robin David; s of John Lewis Russell Jones, JP (d 1970), of Bonvilles Court, Saundersfoot, Pembrokeshire, and Mary Elizabeth, *née* Ebsworth; *b* 5 March 1948; *Educ* Rugby, Peterhouse Cambridge (MA, MB BChir); *m* 1 Nov 1975, Ann Hilary Fair, da of Roger Brian Nixon (d 1988), of Coney Cree, Leckhampton Hill, Cheltenham; 1 s (Christopher b 1979), 1 da (Joy b 1976); *Career* conslt dermatologist 1983-: St John's Hosp for Diseases for the Skin, Ealing Hosp, Hammersmith Hosp; sr lectr Dept of Med Royal Post Graduate Med Sch London; chm: Friends of the Earth Pollution Advsy Ctee, Campaign for Lead Free Air 1984-89; FRCP 1990 (MRCP

1973); *Books* Lead Versus Health (1983), Radiation and Health (1987), Ozone Depletion (1989); *Recreations* skiing, sailing, squash; *Style*— Dr Robin Russell Jones; The Old Cottage, Wexham St, Stoke Poges, Bucks SL3 6NB

RUSSELL OF KILLOWEN, Baroness; Elizabeth; *née* Foster; da of Air Vice-Marshal W McNeece Foster, CB, CBE, DSO, DFC; *m* 1, 1952, Judge Edward Laughton-Scott, QC (d 1978); 2 s, 1 da; m 2, 1979, as his 2 w, Baron Russell of Killowen, PC (Life Peer UK 1975) (d 1986); *Style*— The Lady Russell of Killowen; 8 Daisy Lane, London SW6

RUSSELL OF LIVERPOOL, 3 Baron (UK 1919); Simon Gordon Jared Russell; s of Capt Hon Langley Russell, MC, s of 2 Baron Russell of Liverpool, CBE, MC, by his 1 w Constance, *née* Gordon; suc gf 1981; *b* 30 Aug 1952; *Educ* Charterhouse, Trinity Coll Cambridge, INSEAD; *m* 1984, Gilda F, yst da of F Albano, of Salerno, Italy; 2 s (Hon Edward Charles Stanley b 1985, Hon William Francis Langley b 1988), 1 da (Hon Leonora Maria Kiloran b 1987); *Heir* s, Hon Edward Charles Stanley; *Career* mgmnt conslt; *Style*— The Rt Hon Lord Russell of Liverpool; c/o House of Lords, London SW1A 0PW

RUSSELL-ROBERTS, Anthony de Villeneuve; s of Francis Douglas Russell-Roberts (d 1973), and Edith Margaret Gertrudis, *née* Ashton (d 1990); *b* 25 March 1944; *Educ* Eton, New Coll Oxford; *m* 1, 27 July 1966 (m dis 1974), Jenny, da of James Henry Lane Fox; m 2, 12 Dec 1975, Anne, *née* Dunhill; 1 step s (Ingo Ferruzzi b 10 Feb 1972), 1 step da (Anita Ferruzzi b 19 Dec 1973), 2 da (Tabitha b 10 March 1977, Juliet b 19 Dec 1979); *Career* VSO Br Honduras (now Belize) 1961-62; gen mgmnt trainee Watney Mann 1965-68, ptnr Lane Fox and Ptnrs 1971-76 (joined 1968), stage mangr Glyndebourne Festival Opera 1976, Kent Opera 1977, asst to Gen Dir Royal Opera House 1977-80, artistic admin Theatre Nationale de L'Opera de Paris 1981, admin dir Royal Ballet 1983-; *Recreations* gardening, golf; *Clubs* Garrick; *Style*— Anthony Russell-Roberts, Esq; 184 Ebury St, London SW1W 8UP (☎ 071 823 5405); Royal Opera House, Covent Garden, London WC2E 7QA (☎ 071 240 1200, fax 071 497 9220, telex 17988 COVGAR G)

RUSSELL VICK, His Hon Judge Arnold Oughtred; QC (1980); s of His Hon Judge Sir Godfrey Russell Vick, QC (d 1958), and Marjorie Hester Russell Vick, JP (d 1985), yst da of John A Compston, KC; *b* 14 Sept 1933; *Educ* The Leys Sch, Jesus Coll Cambridge (MA); *m* 5 Sept 1959, Zinnia Mary, da of Thomas Brown Yates (d 1968), of Godalming, Surrey; 2 s (Philip b 1960, Mark b 1964), 1 da (Tessa b 1963); *Career* serv RAF 1952-54, qualified pilot (Flying Off); called to the Bar Inner Temple 1958; memb of Bar Cncl 1964-68, dep rec Rochester City QS 1971, memb Lord Chllr's Co Court Rules Ctee 1972-80, rec of Crown Court 1972-82, circuit judge 1982-; princ co court judge Kent 1990-; govr New Beacon Sch Sevenoaks 1982-; Master Worshipful Co of Curriers 1976-77; *Books* A Hundred Years of Golf at Wildernesse (1990); *Recreations* golf, cricket, gardening, bridge; *Clubs* MCC, Hawks (Cambridge), Wildernesse Golf (capt 1978); *Style*— His Hon Judge Russell Vick, QC; Law Courts, Barker Rd, Maidstone, Kent (☎ 0622 754966)

RUSSELL VICK, Mary; OBE (1980); da of Pierre de Putron, OBE (d 1950), of La Bertozerie, Guernsey, CI, and Christobel, *née* Whitehead (d 1982); *b* 16 July 1922; *Educ* The Beehive Sch Bexhill-on-Sea, Somerville Coll Oxford (MA); *m* 2 Dec 1944, Clive Compston Russell Vick (d 1990), s of His Hon Judge Sir Godfrey Russell Vick, QC (d 1958); 3 da (Rosemary (Mrs Scott) b 21 Sept 1945, Susan (Mrs Clear) b 28 Feb 1950, Christabel b 1 Sept 1956); *Career* 3 Offr WRNS 1943-45; played hockey for Sussex and England 1947-49 and 1951-53, pres All England Women's Hockey Assoc 1976-86, chm GB Women's Hockey 1981-, chm GB Hockey Bd 1989; vice pres: Sevenoaks Hockey Assoc, Sussex Ladies Hockey Assoc, Southern Counties Women's Hockey Assoc; *Recreations* gardening, sport; *Style*— Mrs Clive Russell Vick, OBE; Ameroak, Seal, Sevenoaks, Kent TN15 0AG (☎ 0732 61154)

RUSSETT, Alan William Frank; s of William Frank Russett (d 1958), and Grace Undine, *née* Stokes (d 1978); *b* 21 July 1929; *Educ* Bristol GS, Univ of Oxford (MA); *m* 15 May 1954, Anne, da of Alexander Freyear Dickinson (d 1963), of Brazil; 1 da (Caroline); *Career* 2 Lt Somerset LI, King's African Rifles in E Africa; Regnl coordinator and gen mangr BP 1956-81, md Triton Europe plc 1983-87, chm AmBrit International plc 1989-; FRSA; *Recreations* yachting, history of art; *Clubs* Oriental, Royal Southern Yacht; *Style*— Alan W F Russett, Esq; 5 Hobury Street, London SN10 0JA (☎ 071 352 0451)

RUSSON, David; s of Thomas Charles Russon (d 1962), and Violet, *née* Jarvis; *b* 12 June 1944; *Educ* Wellington GS, UCL (BSc), Univ of York; *m* 29 July 1967, Kathleen Mary, da of Frederick Gregory, of Morecambe, Lancs; 1 s ((Charles) Benedict b 1975), 2 da (Katherine b 1971, Nicola b 1973); *Career* various appts DES 1969-74; Br Library: various appts 1974-85, dir Document Supply Centre 1985-88, dir gen for Sci Technol and Indust 1988-, Bd memb 1988-; dir AVT Communications Ltd 1989-; contrib to various learned journals; MIInfSc, FRSA; *Recreations* tennis, badminton, golf; *Clubs* National Liberal; *Style*— David Russon, Esq; March House, Tollerton, York YO6 2ET (☎ 034 73 253); British Library, Boston Spa, Wetherby, W Yorks LS23 7BQ (☎ 0937 546131, fax 0937 546185, telex 557381)

RUSTEM, Elvira Ada; da of Remo Brenna (d 1988), of Rome, and Maria Luisa, *née* Gazzan; *b* 16 Aug 1950; *Educ* Science Lycee; *m* 21 Feb 1976, Dr Berc Rustem, s of Kirkor Rustem (d 1955), of Istanbul; *Career* film maker, winner of Campoine Documentary Festival award 1968-71, interviewer Overseas Staff Agency 1971-72, translator and interpreter Italian Embassy London 1973-78, diplomatic corps Italian Embassy London 1978-, EEC CD Euro Parl Elections 1989; *Recreations* piano, painting, reading, languages, ski, swimming, travel; *Style*— Mrs Elvira Rustem

RUSTIN, Dr Gordon John Sampson; s of Maj Maurice Edward Rustin, MC (d 1972), of Hale, Cheshire, and (Barbara) Joan, *née* Goldstone; *Educ* Uppingham, Middx Hosp Med Sch (MB BS), Univ of London (MSc, MD); *m* 17 Feb 1977, Frances Phyllis, da of Lionel Rainsbury, of London; 1 s (Edward Samuel b 4 May 1981), 1 da (Jessica Leah b 3 Jan 1986); *Career* registrar Whittington Hosp and UCH 1974-76, res fell Hammersmith Hosp 1977-78, sr registrar Charing Cross Hosp 1978-84, sr lectr and hon conslt in med oncology Charing Cross Hosp and Mount Vernon Hosp 1984-; over 80 pubns on: tumour markers, germ cell, trophoblastic ovarian and cervical tumours; chm Tumour Marker Sub Ctee Gynaecological Working Pty MRC, pres Oncology Section RSM; memb: BMA 1971, RSM 1977, ACP 1985; MRCP 1974, BACR 1979; *Recreations* tennis, opera, skiing; *Style*— Dr Gordon Rustin; 15 Wellgarth Rd, London NW11 7HP (☎ 081 455 5943); Department of Medical Oncology, Charing Cross Hospital, London W6 8RF (☎ 081 846 1421, fax 081 748 5665)

RUSTON, (Edward) Harold; s of Major Allpress Harold Ruston, DSO (d 1970), of Huntingdon, and Edith Gertrude, *née* Francis (d 1983); *b* 2 July 1933; *Educ* Huntingdon GS, Worksop Coll Notts; *m* 29 April 1950, Patricia Frances, da of John Albert Norman Perkins (d 1973), of Cambs; 1 s (Nicholas John b 1957), 1 da (Anne Francis b 1953); *Career* served WWII RAF 1941-46: Flt Lt navigator 57 Sqdn, 5 Gp Bomber Cmd (POW Stalag Luft I 1944); chm Rustons Engineering Co Ltd 1970- (dir 1955-); dir: FT Ruston & Sons Ltd 1950-, Rustons Balsham Ltd 1975-, Ruston's Thrapston Ltd 1960-, Ruston's Ramsey Ltd 1950-, Ruston's Garden & Tool Hire Ltd; *Recreations* cricket, model engineering; *Clubs* MCC, Worcestershire CCC, Middlesex County Cricket; *Style*— Harold Ruston, Esq; Ruston's Engineering Co Ltd, Brampton Rd, Huntingdon, Cambs PE18 6BQ (☎ 0480 455151, fax 0480 52116)

RUTHERFORD, Prof Andrew; s of Thomas Armstrong Rutherford (d 1935), of Helmsdale, Sutherland, and Christian Proudfoot Russell, MBE, JP (d 1973); *b* 23 July 1929; *Educ* Helmsdale Sch Sutherland, George Watson's Boys' Coll Edinburgh, Univ of Edinburgh (MA), Merton Coll Oxford (BLitt); *m* 4 Sept 1953, Nancy Milroy, da of Dr Arthur Browning, (d 1962), of Bathgate, W Lothian; 2 s (Richard Browning, John Arthur Thomas), 1 da (Alison Jean); *Career* Nat Serv cmmnd 2 Lt Seaforth Highlanders 1951-53, serv Somaliland Scouts, Lt 11 Bn Seaforth Highlanders TA 1953-58; lectr Univ of Edinburgh 1956-65 (asst lectr 1955), visiting assoc prof Univ of Rochester NY 1963; Univ of Aberdeen: sr lectr 1964, second prof of English 1965-68, regius prof of English 1968-84, dean Faculty of Arts and Social Sci 1979-82, sr vice-princ 1982-84; warden Goldsmiths' Coll London 1984- (prof 1988-); chm of English Bd CNAA 1966-73, Br Cncl Lecture Tours 1973-89, pres Int Assoc of Univ Profs of English 1977-80, memb BBC Gen Advsy Cncl 1979-84, chm Literature Advsy Ctee British Cncl 1987-, memb various Scottish Educn Dept ctees on curriculum and examinations Hon DLitt State Univ of NY 1990; *Books* Byron: A Critical Study (1961), Kipling's Mind and Art (ed, 1964), Byron: The Critical Heritage (ed, 1970), The Literature of War (1979), Early Verse by Rudyard Kipling 1979-1989 (1986); *Recreations* shooting; *Clubs* Athenaeum, Royal Cwlth Soc; *Style*— Prof Andrew Rutherford; Goldsmiths' College, University of London, New Cross, London SE14 6NW (☎ 081 692 7171 ext 2001)

RUTHERFORD, David John Buckley; OBE (1987); s of Col Alexander John Buckley Rutherford, CVO, CBE (d 1979), of Assendon Lodge, Henley-on-Thames, Oxon, and Joan, *née* Begg (d 1979); *b* 27 July 1930; *Educ* Winchester, Trinity Coll Cambridge (MA); *m* 11 July 1959, Elisabeth Dagmar, da of Henri Thierry-Mieg (d 1938); 3 da (Virginia b 15 Aug 1960, Sophie b 19 Nov 1961, Alice b 21 Sept 1965); *Career* 2 Lt 9 Lancers 1949, City of London Yeo RR TA; chm Wine and Spirit Assoc GB 1974-76 and 1988-89; pres FIUS 1989-91; memb Ct Vintners Co; Ordre National De Mérite France 1976, Ordem do Infante Dom Henrique Portugal 1977, Ordine Al Merito Della Republica Italiana 1982; *Recreations* golf; *Style*— David Rutherford, Esq, OBE; Martini & Rossi Ltd, New Zealand House, 80 Haymarket, London SW1Y 4TG (☎ 071 930 3543)

RUTHERFORD, John Malcolm Chalmers; s of John Rutherford Rutherford (d 1957), and Doreen, *née* Hilton (d 1957); Sir John Rutherford (Baronet) was both MP and Mayor of Blackburn; He purchased the estate of Rutherford in 1923, the family name having been associated with the lands of Rutherford and others since the derivation of the place name in the twelfth century and as such the family claims to be the second oldest landed family in the Scottish borders; Sir John Rutherford had the good fortune to own Solario, winner of the St Ledger in 1925, the Ascot Gold Cup and The Epsom Coronation Cup in 1926; He left his estate to his g nephew on condition that he change his name from Chalmers to Rutherford; This he did by deed poll in 1933; John Rutherford Rutherford was MP for the Edmonton Constituency in London before serving in WWII; *b* 29 Sept 1938; *Educ* Repton, East of Scotland Coll of Agric; *m* 14 April 1962, Jean Gavin, da of Henry Ballantyne (d 1983); 3 s (Johnny b 1963, Guy b 1969, Alexander b 1973), 1 da (Sara Jane b 1966); *Career* Nat Serv 1957-59 in KOSB as 2nd Lt; farmer; dir Border Archery Ltd Mellerstain Kelso 1975-; chm Glenteviot Farmers Ltd 1971-76; memb Nat Playfields Assoc (Scotland) Ctee 1967-; *Recreations* shooting, fishing, cricket; *Clubs* Puffin's (Edinburgh); *Style*— John Rutherford, Esq; Rutherford Lodge, Kelso, Roxburghshire TD5 8NW

RUTHERFORD, (Gordon) Malcolm; s of Gordon Brown Rutherford (d 1988), of Newcastle upon Tyne, and Bertha, *née* Browne (d 1989); *b* 21 Aug 1939; *Educ* Newcastle Royal GS, Balliol Coll Oxford; *m* 1, 1965 (m dis 1969), Susan Margaret, *née* Tyler; m 2, 24 Feb 1970, Elizabeth Claude Rosemary Maitland, da of Pierre Pelen, of Paris; 3 da (Emma b 15 April 1973, Camilla b 10 Sept 1974, Laetitia b 6 July 1976); *Career* arts ed then foreign ed The Spectator 1962-65, fndr newsletter Latin America 1965; Financial Times: dip corr 1966-69, Bonn corr 1969-74, dep foreign ed 1974-77, chief political columnist and asst ed 1977-88, observer and asst ed 1988-, chief theatre critic and asst ed 1990-; *Books* Can We Save the Common Market (1981); *Recreations* tennis, theatre, reading; *Clubs* Travellers; *Style*— Malcolm Rutherford, Esq; 89 Bedford Gardens, London W8 (☎ 071 229 2063); Financial Times, London

RUTHERFORD, Michael John Cloette Crawford (Mike); s of Capt W H F C Rutherford (d 1986), of Surrey, and Annette, *née* Downing; *b* 2 Oct 1950; *Educ* Charterhouse; *m* 13 Nov 1976, Angela Mary, da of Harry Downing; 2 s (Tom Harry b 4 Oct 1980, Harry John Crawford b 19 Nov 1987), 1 da (Kate Elizabeth b 19 Oct 1977); *Career* fndr memb Genenis, first single released 1969, fifteenth album released 1991; fndr Mike and the Mechanics gp 1985; *Recreations* polo Cowdray Park; *Style*— Mike Rutherford, Esq

RUTHVEN OF CANBERRA, Viscount; Patrick Leo Brer Ruthven; o s and h of 2 Earl of Gowrie, PC, and his 1 w, Xandra, *née* Bingley; *b* 4 Feb 1964; *m* Feb 1990, Julie Goldsmith; 1 s (Heathcote Patrick Cornelius Hore b 28 May 1990); *Style*— Viscount Ruthven of Canberra

RUTHVEN-STUART, Dr Ian Alexander; s of Capt Alexander Whitewright Ruthven-Stuart, Gordon Highlanders and RFC (d 1974), and Stella Marion Grant Duff Ainslie (d 1979); *b* 5 July 1927; *Educ* Trinity Coll Glenalmond, Univ of Edinburgh (MB ChB); *m* 20 June 1953, Christina Adelaide, da of Capt Peter Tupper Carey (d 1976, RN); 3 s (Nicholas b 1955, David b 1961, Peter b 1967), 2 da (Sophie b 1967, Sarah b 1957); *Career* Surgn Lt RNVR 1952-54; med practioner; *Recreations* running, swimming, skiing, fishing, squash, tennis, golf, shooting, DIY, windsurfing, sailing; *Clubs* Naval; *Style*— Dr Ian Ruthven-Stuart; Hook Vinney, West St, Hambledon, Hants POT 4QL

RUTLAND, 10 Duke of (E 1703); Charles John Robert Manners; CBE (1962); also Earl of Rutland (E 1525), Baron Manners of Haddon (E 1679), Marquess of Granby (E 1703), and Baron Roos of Belvoir (UK 1896); s of 9 Duke of Rutland (d 1940), and Kathleen, *née* Tennant (d 1989); and fifteenth in descent from 1 Earl of Rutland's maternal grandmother Anne Plantagenet (sis of Edward IV); *b* 28 May 1919; *Educ* Eton, Trinity Coll Cambridge; *m* 1, 27 April 1946 (m dis 1956), Anne Bairstow, da of Maj William Cumming Bell, of Huddersfield; 1 da; m 2, 15 May 1958, Frances Helen, da of Charles Sweeny and Margaret Duchess of Argyll, *qv*; 2 s, 1 da (and 1 s decd); *Heir* s, Marquess of Granby; *Career* chm (4 yrs) Leics CC, DL and JP Leics; proprietor Rutland Hotels Ltd; proprietor of Belvoir Castle (rebuilt by Wyatt in 1800) and medieval Haddon Hall in Derbyshire; late Capt Gren Gds; patron of 11 livings, owner of 18,000 acres; *Style*— His Grace the Duke of Rutland, CBE; Belvoir Castle, Grantham, Lincs; Haddon Hall, Bakewell, Derbys

RUTLAND, Hon Mrs (Joan Claire Florence); *née* Milne; da of Field Marshal 1 Baron Milne, GCB, GCMG, DSO (d 1948); *b* 12 March 1907; *m* 16 March 1937, as his 2 w, James Hart Rutland (d 1954); *Style*— The Hon Mrs Rutland; Cromwell Cottage, Church St, Alresford, Hants

RUTMAN, Laurence David; s of Sidney Rutman, and Anne, *née* Smith; *b* 8 Oct 1937; *Educ* Hendon Co Sch, UCL (LLB), Yale Univ (LLM); *m* 26 July 1964, Sandra Christine, da of Philip Colvin; 2 s (Simon b 1966, Paul b 1970), 1 da (Laura b 1968); *Career* ptnr: Paisner & Co 1960-74, Ashurst Morris Crisp 1974-; *Recreations* music, literature, book collecting; *Style*— Laurence Rutman, Esq; Broadwalk House, 5 Appold

St, London EC2A 2HA (☎ 071 638 1111, fax 071 972 7990, telex 887067); Broxham House, Four Elms, Edenbridge, Kent; 38 Margaretta Terrace, London SW3

RUTT, Rt Rev (Cecil) Richard; CBE (1973); s of Cecil Rutt, and Mary Hare, *née* Turner; *b* 27 Aug 1925; *Educ* Kelham Theological Coll, Pembroke Coll Cambridge (MA); *m* 1969, Joan Mary Ford; *Career* served RNVR 1943-46; ordained priest 1952, rector St Michael's Seminary (Oryu Dong, Seoul, Korea) 1965-66, bishop of Taejon 1968-74 (asst bishop 1966-68), bishop suffragan of St Germans and hon canon St Mary's Cathedral Truro 1974-79, bishop of Leicester 1979-90; bard of Gorsedd of Cornwall Cornwhylen 1976; Hon DLitt Confucian Univ Seoul 1974; ChStJ 1978; Order of Civil Merit (Peony Class) Korea 1974; *Books* Korean Works and Days (1964), James Scarth Gale and his History of the Korean People (1972), An Anthology of Korean Sijo (1970), The Bamboo Grove (1971), Virtuous Women (translation, 1974), A History of Hand Knitting (1987); *Clubs* United Oxford and Cambridge; *Style*— The Rt Rev Richard Rutt, CBE; 3 Marlborough Court, Falmouth, Cornwall TR11 2QU (☎ 0326 312276)

RUTTEMAN, Paul Johannes; Johannes; CBE (1983); s of Cornelis Hendrikus Bernardus Rutteman, of Watford, Herts (d 1962), and Anna Smak; *b* 9 Nov 1938; *Educ* Merchant Taylors School, LSE (BSc); *m* 1, 1967, Annette Franklin (d 1978); 1 s (John b 2 June 1972), 1 da (Susan b 23 Nov 1970); m 2, 1981, Dorothy Louise, da of John Storie; 2 s (Thomas b 25 Dec 1981, Philip b 1 April 1983); *Career* articled clerk Broads Paterson 1960-64, chartered accountant 1964-, chm Fin Servs Arthur Young 1985-89 (sr tech ptnr 1970-85), ptnr Banking and Fin Servs Indust Gp Ernst & Young 1989-; memb Cncl ICAEW 1978-87 and 1989-, chm Ctee Inst Fin Reporting, pres Groupe d'Etudes des Exports Comptables Brussels 1985-87; FCA (ACA 1964); *Books* author various articles, contrib various books; *Recreations* walking, sailing, photography, family; *Style*— Paul Rutteman, Esq, CBE; Ernst & Young, Rolls House, Rolls Buildings, Fetter Lane, London EC4A 1NH (☎ 071 928 2000, 071 931 1156, fax 071 405 2147)

RUTTER, Rev Canon (Allen Edward Henry) Claude; s of Rev Norman Rutter (d 1967), and Hilda, *née* Mason (d 1979); *b* 24 Dec 1928; *Educ* Monkton Combe, Dauntsey's, Queens' Coll Cambridge (MA, DipAgric), Univ of Durham (DipTh); *m* 26 April 1960, Elizabeth Jane, da of Rt Rev Martin Patrick Grainge Leonard, DSO, MA (d 1963), Bishop of Thetford; 2 s (Christopher b 1962, Timothy b 1965), 2 da (Patricia b 1961, Miranda b 1976); *Career* scientific liaison offr E Malling Res Station Kent 1953-56; curate: Bath Abbey 1959-60, E Dereham Norfolk 1960-64; rector: Cawston Gp and Chap Cawston Coll Norfolk 1964-69, Gingindhlovu Zululand (and Agric Sec Helwel Diocese of Zululand) 1969-73, Queen Thorne Dorset 1973-; RD Sherborne Dorset 1976-; chm Salisbury Diocesan Lay Educnl and Trg Ctee 1984-, Canon and Preb Salisbury Cathedral 1986-, Diocesan co-ordinator Rural Miny Devpt 1987-, Diocesan Rural Link Offr 1989-, conslt Archbishops' Cmmn on Rural Areas 1989-; Co Cricket for: Univ of Cambridge 1953, Wilts CCC 1948-55, Norfolk CCC 1961-65 (the only clergyman to have played in the Gillette Cup); hockey for Camb Univ Wanderers Maidstone Clergy Golf Champ 1977; *Recreations* cricket, hockey, golf, farming, gardening, picture framing; *Clubs* Hawks' (Cambridge), MCC, Farmers'; *Style*— The Rev Canon Claude Rutter; Trent Rectory, Sherborne, Dorset DT9 4SL (☎ 0935 851049)

RUTTER, Hadyn Michael; s of Herbert Rutter (d 1985), of Winsford, Cheshire, and Mabel Rutter; *b* 29 Dec 1946; *Educ* Verdin GS Winsford, Lincoln Coll Oxford (BA); *m* 1 April 1970, Susan, da of Charles Robert Johnson, of Winsford; 3 da (Tanya b 1974, Amanda b 1977, Lisa b 1981); *Career* admitted slr 1971; Richards Butler & Co London 1969-72, sr ptnr Bruce Campbell & Co Cayman Islands 1977-80 (joined 1972), own practice 1980-; pres Cayman Islands Law Soc 1979 (sec 1975-79); dir: Golf Links Int Ltd, Golf Links Int Inc, Sun Centre Ltd; organiser World Pro-Am: Arizona, Acapulco, Hawaii; author Cayman Islands Handbook Tax Guide 1977; Duke of Edinburgh Award (Gold) 1965; *Recreations* cricket, golf, badminton, tennis; *Clubs* Utd Oxford and Cambridge; *Style*— Hadyn Rutter, Esq; The Mount, Cuddington Lane, Cuddington, Cheshire CW8 2SZ (☎ 0606 883070, fax 0606 889031)

RUTTER, James Edgar; s of Frederick Edgar Rutter (d 1951), of Shelton, Stoke on Trent, and Maggie, *née* Arthan (d 1956); *b* 23 July 1930; *Educ* Longton HS, LSE (BSc Econ); *m* 23 May 1953, Margaret Mary, eld da of Benjamin Brian, of Penkhull; 2 s (Mark b 14 Aug 1960, Richard b 13 Jan 1963), 1 da (Sally b 15 Oct 1967); *Career* Nat Serv 1953-55; articled clerk E Downward & Co Hanley 1947-53, accountant Rootes Ltd 1956-58, co sec Agricultural Finance 1958-61, md Peterborough Investment Co 1961-68, lectr Staffordshire Poly 1968-; pres: N Staffs Soc of Chartered Accountants 1981-82, Staffs Salop and Wolverhampton Soc of Chartered Accountants 1990-91; contrib articles in: Accountancy (1984), Public Finance and Accountancy (1984), International Accountant (1986); FCA 1964 (ACA 1954); *Recreations* walking, gardening; *Clubs* Trentham RUFC; *Style*— James Rutter, Esq; 35 Naples Drive, Westlands, Newcastle under Lyme, Staffs ST5 2QD (☎ 0782 632662); Business School, Staffordshire Polytechnic, Leek Road, Stoke on Trent, Staffs (☎ 0782 412515, fax 0782 744035)

RUTTER, His Hon Judge John Cleverdon; s of Edgar John Rutter (d 1971), of Cardiff, and Nellie, *née* Parker (d 1928); *b* 18 Sept 1919; *Educ* Cardiff HS for Boys, Univ Coll of the SW of Eng Exeter (LLB), Keble Coll Oxford (MA); *m* 4 Sept 1951, Jill, da of Maxwell Duncan McIntosh; 1 s (Jeremy b 1953), 1 da (Philippa (Mrs James) b 1955); *Career* serv WWII RA 1939-46, cmmnd 1941, serv overseas; called to the Bar Lincoln's Inn 1948; practising Wales and Chester circuit 1948-66; rec: Cardiff 1962-66, Merthyr Tydfil 1962-66, Swansea 1965-66; legal memb Mental Health Review Tbnl Wales 1962-66, Stipendiary Magistrate Cardiff 1966-71, dep chm Glamorgan Quarter Sessions 1969-71, circuit judge Cardiff Crown Ct 1972-90, sr Circuit Judge 1990-; *Recreations* golf, reading; *Style*— His Hon Judge Rutter; Law Courts, Cardiff

RUTTER, Prof Michael Llewellyn; s of Llewellyn Charles Rutter, and Winifred Olive, *née* Barber; *b* 15 Aug 1933; *Educ* Wolverhampton GS, Bootham Sch York, Univ of Birmingham Med Sch (MB ChB); *m* 28 December 1958, Marjorie, da of Richard Heys (d 1983); 1 s (Stephen b 5 April 1963), 2 da (Sheila b 22 April 1960, Christine b 18 Sept 1984); *Career* memb scientific staff MRC Social Psychiatry Res Unit 1962-65; Inst of Psychiatry Univ of London: sr lectr (later reader) 1966-73, prof of child psychiatry 1973-; hon dir MRC Child Psychiatry Unit Inst of Psychiatry 1984-; Hon Dr: Univ of Leiden 1985, Catholic Univ Leiden 1990; FRS 1987, foreign assoc memb Inst of Med US Nat Acad of Sciences 1988, foreign hon memb American Acad of Arts and Sciences 1989; *Books incl* A Neuropsychiatric Study in Childhood (with P Graham and W Yule, 1970), Maternal Deprivation Reassessed (1972, 2 edn 1981), The Child With Delayed Speech (ed with J A M Martin, 1972), Cycles of Disadvantage: A Review of Research (with N Madge, 1976), Changing Youth in a Changing Society: Patterns of Adolescent Development and Disorder (1979), Developmental Neuropsychiatry (ed 1983), Juvenile Delinquency: Trends and Perspectives (with H Giller, 1983), Language Development and Disorders (ed with W Yule, 1987), Straight and Devious Pathways from Childhood to Adulthood (ed with L Robins, 1990); *Recreations* grandchildren, fell walking, tennis, wine tasting, theatre; *Style*— Prof Michael Rutter, CBE, FRS; 190 Court Lane, Dulwich, London SE21 7ED; Inst of Psychiatry, De Crespigny Park, Denmark Hill, London SE5 8AF (☎ 071 703 5411, fax 071 708 5800)

RUTTER, Trevor John; CBE (1990, OBE 1976); s of Alfred Rutter (d 1974), of Gwent, and Agnes, *née* Purslow (d 1966); *b* 26 Jan 1934; *Educ* Monmouth Sch, BNC Oxford (BA); *m* 1959, Jo, da of David Barrs Henson (d 1980); 1 s (Orlando); *Career* Br Cncl Indonesia and W Germany (Munich) 1959-65, first sec FO 1967, Br Cncl 1968-, dir in Singapore 1968-71 and Bangkok 1971-75, HQ posts 1975-85 incl asst dir gen 1982-85, dir in Germany 1986-90, asst dir gen 1990-; *Style*— Trevor Rutter, Esq, CBE; West House, West St, Wivenhoe, Essex (☎ 0206 822562); The British Council, 10 Spring Gardens, London SW1A 2BN

RUTTLE, (Henry) Stephen Mayo; s of Henry Samuel Joseph Ruttle, and Joyce Mayo, *née* Moriarty (d 1968); *b* 6 Feb 1953; *Educ* Westminster, Queens' Coll Cambridge (BA); *m* 24 Aug 1985, Fiona Jane, da of William Mitchell-Innes; 1 s (James Patrick Mayo b 1990), 1 da (Emma Jane Mayo b 1988); *Career* called to the Bar Grays Inn 1976; *Clubs* Fly Fishers; *Style*— Stephen Ruttle, Esq; Brick Court Chambers, 15-19 Devereux Court, London WC2R 3JJ (☎ 071 583 0777, fax 071 583 9401 (Gp 3), telex 892687 1 BRICK G)

RYALL, David John; s of John Bertram Ryall (d 1978), of Shoreham-by-Sea, Sussex, and Gladys Lilian, *née* Bowles (d 1980); *b* 5 Jan 1936; *Educ* Shoreham GS, Wallington GS, RADA (scholar); *m* 1, 1964 (m dis 1984), Gillian, da of Rear Adm Eddison; 1 s (Jonathan Charles b 8 Feb 1966), 1 da (Imogen Victoria b 21 Sept 1967); m 2, 1985, Cathy, da of Benek Buchwald, of Poland; 1 da (Charlotte Maria Grace b 15 Oct 1986); *Career* actor; reportory at Salisbury Leicester Bristol and Birmingham incl: King Lear and The Masterbuilder; theatre appearances with NT at the Old Vic 1965-73: Armstrongs Last Goodnight, The Royal Hunt of the Sun, A Flea In Her Ear, The Idiot, Edward II, The Front Page; with Royal NT 1981-88: A Month In The Country, Guys and Dolls, Coriolanus (Clarence Dorwent award 1985), Animal Farm, A Chorus of Disapproval, Twelfth Night (Peter Hall Co, 1991); TV appearances incl: The Knowledge, The Singing Detective, The Paradise Club, The Saint, Saracen, Inspector Morse, The Men's Room, Minder, For the Greater Good, Shelley; film appearances incl: The Elephant Man, Empire of the Sun, Wilt, The Russia House, Shuttlecock; devised directed and performed Ego in the Cosmos (NT) 1989; *Style*— David Ryall, Esq; Scott Marshall Personal Management, 44 Perryn Rd, London W3 7NA (☎ 081 749 7692)

RYALL, Dr Roger Duncan Hall; s of Capt Sydney Kenneth Ryall (d 1947), of Shoreham-by-Sea, and Evelyn Elizabeth, *née* Wright (d 1989); *b* 9 March 1938; *Educ* Wellington, Middx Hosp Med Sch (MB BS, DMRT); *m* 15 June 1963, Rosemary Elizabeth, da of Kenneth David Brough, of Kenwood Gate, Hampstead Lane, London; 1 s (Edward b 1970), 1 da (Vanessa b 1967); *Career* conslt radiotherapy and oncology Wessex Radiotherapy Centre 1978-; pres Hosp Conslts and Specialists Assoc 1982-84 (hon vice pres 1988), memb Cncl Royal Coll of Radiologists 1989; memb Cruising Assoc; memb: RSM, Br Inst Radiology; FRCR; *Books* author of papers on various aspects of cancer res; *Recreations* sailing; *Style*— Dr Roger Ryall; Hampton House, Headbourne Worthy, Winchester, Hants SO23 7JH (☎ 0962 883270); Wessex Radiotherapy Centre, Royal Southants Hospital, Graham Rd, Southampton (☎ 0703 634288)

RYAN, David Edward; s of Thomas Ryan (d 1986), and Janet Stafford Ryan; *b* 17 May 1946; *Educ* Hyde GS; *m* 21 Dec 1968, Susan, da of John Cooper (d 1987); 2 s (Mark b 29 Sept 1969, Andrew b 30 July 1971), 1 da (Anna b 21 Nov 1981); *Career* articled Shuttleworth & Haworth, CA 1968, joined Webb Hanson Bullivant & Co 1969 (ptnr 1972); Neville Russell: ptnr 1986, sr ptnr Stockport office 1987-; dir Stockport Business Venture Ltd; bd memb Manchester City Mission, involved with Stockport C of C and Stockport Luncheon Club; *Recreations* walking, cycling, being out of doors, listening to music, theatre; *Style*— David Ryan, Esq; Neville Russell, Regent House, Heaton Lane, Stockport SK4 1BS (☎ 061 477 4750, fax 061 477 4750 ext 150)

RYAN, David Stuart; s of David Ryan, of Kingston-upon-Thames, and Eileen Inez, *née* Sullivan (d 1966); *b* 22 Oct 1943; *Educ* Wimbledon Coll, KCL (BA); *m* 16 June 1971, Jacqueline, da of Sydney Wills (d 1989), of Southfields, London; 1 da (Chloe Selena b 1972); *Career* author; pubns: John Lennon's Secret (1982), India A Guide to the Experience (1983), America A Guide to the Experience (1986), The Lost Journal of Robyn Hood - Outlaw (1989); memb: Br Direct Mktg Assoc (chm creative forum), IPG; *Recreations* photography, travel, poetry; *Clubs* Poetry Soc; *Style*— David Ryan, Esq; Kozmik Press Ltd, Kozmik Press Centre, 83 Gloucester Place, London W1H 3PG (☎ and fax 071 935 5913)

RYAN, Dr David William; s of Leslie Ryan (d 1989), and Fiona Ryan, *née* Gregson; *b* 2 May 1946; *Educ* Sheffield City GS, Univ of Sheffield (MB ChB); *m* 24 July 1969, Susan Margaret, da of James Edward Varley (d 1945); 2 s (James b 1973, Charles b 1976); *Career* conslt and hon lectr in anaesthesia Univ of Newcastle-upon-Tyne 1978, conslt Clinical Physiologist 1981, conslt in charge intensive therapy unit Freeman Hosp 1981; author of over 120 articles and res papers on intensive therapy, ed Care of The Critically Ill Journal; memb cncl: Intensive Care Soc 1983-89 (sec 1984-87), World Fedn of Intensive and Critical Care Med 1989-; memb: BMA 1970, Assoc of Anaesthetists 1972, Intensive Care Soc 1978; FFARCS; *Recreations* cricket, art; *Style*— Dr David Ryan; General Intensive Therapy Unit, Freeman Hospital, Newcastle upon Tyne NE7 7DN (☎ 091 2843111 3423, fax 091 2131968)

RYAN, Maj-Gen Denis Edgar; CB (1987); s of Reginald Arthur Ryan, of Westbury, Wilts, and Amelia, *née* Smith; *b* 18 June 1928; *Educ* Sir William Borlase, Marlow, Bucks, King's Coll London (LLB); *m* 6 Aug 1955, Jean Mary, da of Charles Waldemar Bentley (d 1963); 1 s (Mark b 1966), 1 da (Amanda b 1964); *Career* cmmnd RAEC 1950; instr: 3 HEC BAOR 1950-52, SO3 HQ BAOR 1952-54, RMA Sandhurst 1954-56; adj Army Sch of Educn 1956-59, Staff Coll 1960, DAQMG HQ Near E Land Forces (Cyprus) 1961-62, and SO2 Special Ops HQ E Africa (Kenya) 1962-64, SO2 AED 1 MOD 1964-66, GSO2 Intelligence Centre 1966-68, CAES HQ 4 Div BAOR 1968-70, GSO1 Cabinet Office 1970-72, trg devpt advsr Staff Coll 1972-75, Col GS DI4 MOD 1976-78, chief educn offr HQ SE Dist 1978-79, cdr educn HQ BAOR 1979-82 and UK 1982-84, dir of Army Educn MOD 1984-87, Col Cmdt RAEC 1990-; *Recreations* cricket, tennis, rugby, music, theatre; *Clubs* Army and Navy; *Style*— Maj Gen D E Ryan, CB; c/ Royal Bank of Scotland, Holt's Whitehall Branch, Kirkland House, Whitehall, London SW1A 2EB

RYAN, Sir Derek Gerald; 4 Bt (UK 1919), of Hintlesham, Suffolk; o s of Sir Derek Gerald Ryan, 3 Bt (d 1990), and his 1 w, Penelope Anne, *née* Hawkings; *b* 25 March 1954; *Educ* Univ of California at Berkeley (BA 1977); *m* (m dis 1990); *Heir* kinsman, Desmond Maurice Ryan b 1918; *Career* with Fowler Ferguson Kingston Ruben architects Salt Lake City Utah 1977-79, Atelier d'Urbanisme en Montagne architects/urban planners Chambery France June-Oct 1979; NBBJ architects/planners Seattle Washington 1980-; memb Nat Cncl of Architects Registration Bd (NCARB) 1984; *Recreations* skiing, guitar; *Style*— Sir Derek Ryan, Bt; 4618 South Austin Street, Seattle, WA 98118-3924, USA (☎ 206 723 6182); NBBJ, 111 South Jackson Street, Seattle, WA 98104, USA (☎ 206 223 5204, fax 206 621 2303, telex BURGESS SEA 329473)

RYAN, Dr Frank Patrick; s of Francis Ryan (d 1972), of Bolton, Lancs, and Mary

Alice, *née* Fitzpatrick; *b* 23 July 1944; *Educ* Thornleigh Coll, Univ of Sheffield Med Sch (MB ChB); *m* 14 Sept 1968, Barbara, da of Frank Horrocks, of Bolton; 1 s (John b 1973), 1 da (Catherine b 1972); *Career* conslt physician Northern Gen Hosp Sheffield; dir Bolton Fine Arts private gallery 1971-79; author of fiction incl: Sweet Summer (1987), Tiger Tiger (1988), The Eskimo Diet (1990), Goodbye Baby Blue (1990); author num med pubns; memb: Br Soc of Gastroenterology, Soc of Authors; FRCP 1985; *Recreations* football, walking, painting, appreciation of art; *Clubs* Univ of Sheffield Staff, Medico-Surgical Soc; *Style*— Dr Frank Ryan; Northern General Hospital, Herries Rd, Sheffield (☎ 0742 434343)

RYAN, Jennifer Mary; da of Arthur William Butterworth (d 1977), of Huddersfield, Yorks, and Elsie, *née* Morton; *b* 2 April 1947; *Educ* Holme Valley GS, LSE (BSc), Harvard (MBA); *m* 12 Aug 1978, John Ryan; *Career* fin mgmnt Ford Motor Co 1968-83, fin dir TI Raleigh Industries 1983-86, fin dir then distribution dir Ross Young's 1986-90, md Freezwest 1990-; treas UK Article Number Assoc; *Recreations* travel, sports; *Clubs* Harvard Business Sch (London); *Style*— Mrs Jennifer Ryan; Kenilworth House, Top Rd, Worlaby, Brigg, S Humberside DN20 0NE; Freezwest Ltd, Kenham House, Wilder Street, Bristol BS2 8NH (☎ 0272 421763, fax 0272 245356)

RYAN, John Gerald Christopher; s of Sir Andrew Ryan, KBE, CMG (d 1949), of E Bergholt, Suffolk, and Ruth Marguerite, *née* Van Millingen (d 1975); *b* 4 March 1921; *Educ* Ampleforth; *m* 3 Jan 1950, Priscilla Ann, da of Austin Blomfield (d 1968), of Chelsea; 1 s (Christopher b 1954), 2 da (Marianne b 1951, Isabel b 1957); *Career* war serv with The Lincolnshire Regt UK, India, Burma 1940-46, cmmnd 2 Lt 1941, demobilised Capt 1946; children's author, illustrator and cartoon film maker; cr Captain Pugwash, 35 pubns incl 16 Captian Pugwash titles 1955-, maker of BBC Captain Pugwash films and over 100 others incl Sir Prancelot and Mary Mungo & Midge 1956-80, cartoonist for the Catholic Herald 1981-; memb Soc of Authors; *Recreations* walking; *Style*— John Ryan, Esq; Gungarden Lodge, The Gungardens, Rye, East Sussex TN31 7HH (☎ 0797 222034)

RYAN, John James; s of Richard Joseph Ryan, and Catherine, *née* Kinsella; *b* 26 May 1949; *Educ* Oatlands Coll, Univ Coll Dublin (BA, MSc, MB BCh, BAO); *Career* fell in surgery: Memorial Sloan Kettering Cancer Centre 1985-86, The Mayo Clinic 1986-88, sr lectr in surgery Univ of Nottingham 1988; memb The Priestley Soc; FRSM, FRCS; *Books* Sympton Control (ed with T D Walsh, 1989); *Recreations* riding, painting, guitar, racing; *Clubs* Royal Soc of Med; *Style*— John Ryan, Esq; Long Cottage, Mansfield Rd, Farnsfield, Nottingham 22NG 8HG (☎ 0623 883233); 16 Pembroke Park, Ballsbridge, Dublin 4 Ireland; City Hospital, Hucknall Rd, Nottingham NG5 1PB (☎ 0602 691169)

RYAN, John Patrick; s of James Patrick Ryan (d 1960), of Rhos-on-Sea, N Wales, and Marie Elsie, *née* Gaines (d 1988); *b* 19 Aug 1943; *Educ* St Mary's Coll Rhos-on-Sea N Wales, Queen's Coll Cambridge (MA); *m* 8 Feb 1968, Verna Marguerite, da of Capt Charles Edward Henry Mytton, of Hampstead Garden Suburb; 2 s (Nicholas b 26 Feb 1972, Alastair b 13 Sept 1976), 1 da (Annabel b 22 March 1974); *Career* actuarial supt Guardian Royal Exchange 1968, ptnr James Capel & Co 1972-76, vice pres & princ Tillinghast 1976-(part of Towers Perrin Co); assoc Casualty Actuarial Soc USA 1979, memb American Acad of Actuaries USA 1979, fell Inst of Risk Mgmnt 1987, chm Futures Ctee Inst of Actuaries 1988- (memb cncl 1986-); Freeman: City of London, Liveryman Worshipful Co of Needlemakers; FIA 1968, AMSIA 1973; *Recreations* travel, walking, theatre, old buildings; *Style*— John Ryan, Esq; 15 Priory Gdns, Highgate, London N6 5QY (☎ 081 348 0195); Old Mill House, West Row Fen, Mildenhall, Suffolk; Tillinghast, Towers Perrin, Castlewood House, 77-91 New Oxford St, London WC1A 1PX (☎ 071 379 4000, fax 071 379 7478, telex 261 411)

RYAN, Katja, Lady; Katja; *née* Best; da of late Ernst Best, of Kassel, West Germany; *m* 1972, as his 2 w, Sir Derek Gerald Ryan, 3 Bt (d 1990); *Style*— Katja, Lady Ryan; Fuhrmannsbreite 11, 35 Kassel, West Germany

RYAN, Madge Winifred; da of Michael Edward Ryan (d 1955), of Bridge St, Epping, Aust, and Sarah Josephine, *née* Brady (d 1946); *b* 8 Jan 1919; *Educ* St Patrick's Coll; *m* 31 Jan 1939 (m dis), Milton Lynn Rumble, s of John Rumble; 1 da (Lynette Anne b 18 March 1940); *Career* actress, trained Independent Theatre Sydney Aust (appeared in various plays) 1941-57; theatre work (London) incl: Kath in original production of Entertaining Mr Sloane, Love for Love, Summer of the Seventeenth Doll, Mother Courage, Philadelphia Here I Come, Aren't We All, Juno and the Paycock, Aunt Eller in Oklahoma (1980 revival), Ring Round the Moon; film appearances incl: Pinter's Night Out, Tiara Tahiti, Summer Holiday, Someone Is Killing The Great Chefs, Frenzy, Clockwork Orange; TV appearances incl: Cymbeline, Heartattack Hotel, Say Goodnight to Grandma, A Horseman Riding By, London Belongs to Me, Flesh and Blood, Families; winner: Best Supporting Actress Summer of the Seventeenth Doll (Aust) 1956, Best Supporting Actress My Fair Lady (Aust) 1988; *Recreations* swimming, reading, cooking, bridge, scrabble; *Style*— Miss Madge Ryan; c/o Richard Hatton Ltd, 29 Roehampton Gate, London SW15 5JR (☎ 081 876 6699, fax 081 876 8278)

RYAN, (Christopher) Nigel John; CBE (1977); s of Brig C E Ryan, MC (d 1981), and Joy, *née* Dodgson; *b* 12 Dec 1929; *Educ* Ampleforth, Queen's Coll Oxford (MA); *Career* chief exec and ed Independent Television News 1969-77, vice pres NBC News (New York) 1977-80, dir of progs Thames Television 1980-82, non-exec dir TV-AM plc 1987-, chm TV-AM (News) 1987-; reg freelance writer for TV; *Books* A Hitch or Two in Afghanistan (1983), translations of George Simenon and others; *Clubs* Beefsteak; *Style*— Nigel Ryan, Esq, CBE; 45 Langton Street, London SW10 (☎ 071 351 6314)

RYAN, Peter Henry; s of John Ryan, CBE (d 1975), and Mabel Ryan; *b* 1 Oct 1930; *Educ* Harrow, Gonville and Caius Coll Cambridge (MA); *m* 1 (m dis 1980); 1 s (Mark b 1958), 2 da (Nicola b 1961, Jocelyn b 1965); m 2, 1986, Valerie Mary Bishop; 3 step s (Piers, Gavin, Warren); *Career* Nat Serv Flying Offr RAF; Peter Ryan Associates 1986-; dir: Thomas Tilling Ltd 1979-83, Central & Sherwood plc 1983-87, Stag Furniture Hldgs plc 1984-, M Y Hldgs plc 1984-, Norbain Electronics plc 1987-, Inoco plc 1988-, Lilleshall plc (non exec) 1989-; chm: Unistrut Europe plc 1988-, Elga Gp plc 1989-, Eagle Tst plc 1989-, Dan Air Services Ltd 1990-; dep chm Davies & Newman Holdings plc 1990-; memb Bd of Govrs Royal Marsden Hosp; CEng, MIMechE; *Recreations* golf, theatre, travel, DIY; *Clubs* RAF, MCC; *Style*— Peter Ryan, Esq; Park House, Queens Drive, Oxshott, Surrey KT22 0PF (☎ 0372 843 665)

RYAN, Richard Kevin de Burgo; s of Richard Jarlath de Burgo Ryan, and Ursula Clare, *née* Bradshaw; *b* 19 Oct 1957; *Educ* Bedford Sch, Univ of Leeds (BA), RMA Sandhurst; *Career* cmmnd 1 Bn Royal Green Jackets 1979-82, serv London and NI, Capt 1982, 4 Bn Royal Green Jackets (TA) 1983-, Maj; insurance broker with Willis Faber & Dumas 1982-87; stockbroker with Capel- Cure Myers 1987-88, Sheppards 1989-90, Panmure Gordon 1990-; *Recreations* shooting, fishing, music; *Clubs* Royal Green Jackets, Cavalry and Guards'; *Style*— Richard K de B Ryan, Esq; 87 Strathville Road, Earlsfield, London SW18 4QR (☎ 081 870 7754); Brookside, Cranbrook, Kent; 9 Moorfields Highwalk, London EC2Y 9DS (☎ 071 860 3584, fax 071 920 9305)

RYAN, Susan Frances (Mrs Alexander James); da of Maj Stephen Francis Ryan, of The Laurels, Shrewton, Salisbury, Wilts, and Shirley Anne, *née* Stafford; *b* 3 May 1961; *Educ* St Antony's Sherbourne Dorset, Westfield Coll London (BA), City Univ London (postgrad journalism course); *m* Alexander Michael Janes, s of Lt Col John Robert James Janes; *Career* nat PR mangr Arthur Young 1983; Shandwick Communications: account exec 1986, account mangr 1987, account dir 1988, assoc dir April 1989, Bd dir Sept 1989; *Recreations* theatre, cinema, entertaining, bargain hunting; *Style*— Ms Susan Ryan; Shandwick Communications, 114 Cromwell Rd, London SW7 (☎ 071 835 1001)

RYAN, William; s of Denis Ryan, of Great Chishill, Nr Royston, Herts, and Marshella Lavinia, *née* Stephenson; *b* 22 Dec 1964; *Educ* Melbourn Village Coll Comp; *m* 12 Nov 1988, Alison Louise, da of James Hall; 1 da (Sophie Louise b 11 May 1990); *Career* flat race jockey; apprenticed to Reg Hollinshead, Champion apprentice (with Gary Carter) 1986, rep GB Euro Apprentice Championship 1986; *Recreations* football (supporter of Arsenal), golf; *Style*— William Ryan, Esq; 18 The Green, Tuddenham, nr Bury St Edmunds, Suffolk IP28 5SD (☎ 0638 717236); c/o David Craig, 10 Mallinson Oval, Harrogate, N Yorks (☎ 0423 871624, car 0860 401683)

RYCROFT, Dr Charles; s of Sir Richard Rycroft, 5 Bt (d 1925), of Dummer House, Basingstoke, Hants, and Emily Mary, *née* Lowry-Corry (d 1982); *b* 9 Sept 1914; *Educ* Wellington, Trinity Coll Cambridge (Exhibitioner, BA), Univ Coll and Univ Coll Hosp London (MB BS, MRCS, LRCP); *m* 1, 1947 (m dis 1963), Chloë, da of late Edouard Majolier, 1 s (Francis Edward b 1950), 2 da (Alice Julia b 1947, Catherine Anne b 1949); m 2, 1978, Jenny, da of late William Pearson; *Career* house physician Maudsley Hosp 1946, private practice in psychotherapy and psychoanalysis 1956-, asst ed Int Jl of Psychoanalysis 1955-58, conslt in psychotherapy Tavistock Clinic 1956-68; book reviewer: Observer, New Society, New Statesman, Times Literary Supplement, NY Review of Books, Modern Painters 1959-; author; *Books* Imagination and Reality (1968), Anxiety and Neurosis (1968), Critical Dictionary of Psychonalysis (1968), Reich (1971), the Innocence of Dreams (1979), Psychoanalysis and Beyond (1985), contrib: Psychoanalysis Observed 1965; God I Want (1966), Symbols and Sentiments (1977), The Sources of Hope (1979); *Style*— Dr Charles Rycroft; 2 Modbury Gardens, London NW5 3QE (☎ 071 842 1817 (private), 071 482 6538 (professional)

RYCROFT, Sir Richard Newton; 7 Bt (GB 1784), of Calton, Yorks; s of Sir Nelson Edward Oliver Rycroft, 6 Bt (d 1958); *b* 23 Jan 1918; *Educ* Winchester, Christ Church Oxford; *m* 1947, Ann, da of late Hugh Bellingham Smith; 2 da (Susan b 1948, m 1974 Ian Martell, 1 s 1 da; Viscountess FitzHarris, *qv*); *Heir* unc, Henry Rycroft, OBE, DSC, RN; *Career* master New Forest Foxhounds; memb The Badger Protection Gp; serv WWII Maj (Beds and Herts Regt) on special work in Balkans (despatches); kt of Order of the Phoenix of Greece (with swords); patron of one living; *Style*— Sir Richard Rycroft, Bt; Winalls Wood House, Stuckton, Fordingbridge, Hants (☎ (0425) 2263)

RYDE, Hon Mrs (Mary Teresa); *née* Lister Robinson; da of 1 and last Baron Robinson, OBE (d 1952); *b* 1914; *m* 1, 1939 (m dis 1951), Wing Cdr Paul Richey, DFC; 2 s, 2 da; m 2, 1979, Peter Leighton Ryde; *Style*— The Hon Mrs Ryde; 4 Phene St, London SW3

RYDEN, Kenneth; MC (1944, and Bar 1944), DL (City of Edinburgh 1978); s of Walter Ryden (d 1947), of Blackburn, Lancs, and Elizabeth, *née* Culshaw (d 1966); *b* 15 Feb 1917; *Educ* Queen Elizabeth's GS Blackburn; *m* 27 July 1950, Catherine Kershaw, da of Herbert Wilkinson (d 1936), of Oswaldtwistle, Lancs; 2 s (Nicholas Charles b 20 March 1953, Peter Anthony b 16 Sept 1956); *Career* served WWII RA (V) 1939-45, cmmnd RE, attached Royal Bombay Sappers and Miners; served: India, Assam and Burma (despatches 1944), ret Capt RE 1946; articled and professional trg 1936-39, asst estate surveyor HM Office of Works Edinburgh 1939; Miny of Works: estate surveyor Glasgow and Edinburgh 1946-47 (attached to UK High Cmmn India and Pakistan 1947-50), sr estate surveyor Scotland 1950-59; fndr and sr ptnr Kenneth Ryden & Partners Edinburgh 1959-74, memb Bd Housing Corp 1971-77, chm Chartered Auctioneer and Estate Agents Inst Scotland 1960-61; memb: Lothian Regnl Valuation Appeal Panel 1965-75 and 1981-90 (chm 1987-90), Scottish Slrs Disciplinary Tbnl 1985-; Merchant Co of The City of Edinburgh: memb 1959, treas 1974-76, Master 1976-78; Liveryman Worshipful Co of Chartered Surveyors 1978; FRICS 1950, IRRV 1959, FRCPE 1983; *Recreations* golf, fishing, Scottish art; *Clubs* New (Edinburgh); *Style*— Kenneth Ryden, Esq, MC, DL; 19 Belgrave Crescent, Edinburgh EH4 3AJ (☎ 031 332 5893)

RYDER, Edward Alexander; s of Alexander Harry Ryder, of 47 The Grove, Halesroad, Cheltenham, and Gwendoline Gladys, *née* Morris (d 1979); *b* 9 Nov 1931; *Educ* Cheltenham GS, Univ of Bristol (BSc); *m* 24 March 1956, Janet, da of Alfred John Barribal (d 1973); 1 s (Clive b 1961), 1 da (Joanne (Mrs Rockley) b 1959); *Career* Nat Serv Flying Offr RAF 1953-55; civil servant; superintending inspr HM Nuclear Installations Inspectorate 1975-80, head Hazardous Installations Policy Branch Health and Safety Exec 1980-85, HM chief inspr of nuclear intallations 1985-; CPhys; FInstP; *Recreations* golf, concerts; *Style*— Edward Ryder, Esq; HM Nuclear Installations Inspectorate, 1 Chepstow Place, London W2 4TF (☎ 071 243 6000)

RYDER, Dr (Arthur) John; s of Charles Foster Ryder (d 1942), of Thurlow, Suffolk, and Mabel Elizabeth, *née* Sims (d 1974); *b* 17 April 1913; *Educ* Radley, Oriel Coll Oxford (MA), LSE (Ph D); *m* 9 April 1946, Krystyna Karolina, da of Henry Reicher; *Career* lectr Br Cncl 1939-45, educn offr Br Control Cmmn Germany 1946-56, memb Cons Res Dept 1958-62, lectr, sr lectr and reader St David's Univ Coll Wales 1962-80, freelance translator 1980-(co recipient The Schlegel-Tieck Prize for translation from German 1983); Parly candidate (C) Cardiganshire 1964; licensed reader C of E 1966; Freeman Worshipful Co of Salters 1934; *Books* The German Revolution of 1918 (1967), Twentieth Century Germany: From Bismarck to Brandt (1973), pamphlet published by the Historical Assoc; *Recreations* travel, antiques; *Style*— Dr John Ryder; 74 Clifton Hill, St John's Wood, London NW8 (☎ 071 624 8221)

RYDER, Hon John Stuart Terrick Dudley; s of 6 Earl of Harrowby (d 1987); *b* 1924; *Educ* Eton; *m* 1946, Dorothy Ethel, da of J T Swallow, of Mansfield; 2 s; *Career* serv WWII RAF pilot 1942-46; *Style*— The Hon John Ryder; Sandon Hall, Stafford

RYDER, Rt Hon Richard Andrew; PC (1990), OBE (1981), MP (C) Mid Norfolk 1983-; s of Richard Stephen Ryder, JP, DL, and Margaret MacKenzie; *b* 4 Feb 1949; *Educ* Radley, Magdalene Coll Cambridge (BA 1971); *m* 1981, Caroline, MBE, o da of Sir David Stephens, *qv*; 1 s (decd), 1 da; *Career* political sec to PM 1975-81; PPS to: fin sec Treasy 1984, sec of state foreign affrs 1984-86; chm Cons Foreign and Cwlth Cncl 1984-89; govt whip 1986-88; Parly sec MAFF 1988-89, econ sec Treasy 1989-90, paymaster gen 1990; chief whip 1990-; *Style*— The Rt Hon Richard Ryder, OBE, MP; The House of Commons, London SW1A 0AA

RYDER, Richard Hood Jack Dudley; s of Maj Dudley Claud Douglas Ryder, JP (d 1986), of Rempstone Hall, and Vera Mary, *née* Cook; *b* 3 July 1940; *Educ* Sherborne, Pembroke Coll Cambridge (MA), Columbia New York (res fell), Univ of Edinburgh (DCP); *m* 24 April 1974, Audrey Jane, da of Frank Rae Arthur Smith; 1 s (Henry Arthur Woden Calcraft Dudley b 1981), 1 da (Emily Nancy Charlotte b 1978); *Career* sr clinical psychologist Oxford 1968-83, princ clinical psychologist Portsmouth 1983-84; memb DHSS Health Advsy Serv 1976-78, chm Cncl RSPCA 1977-79 (vice chm 1990-), memb Cncl Lib Pty 1984-87 (contested Parly elections 1983 and 87), pres SLD Animal Protection Gp 1989-; chm: Teignbridge NSPCC, Teignbridge Home Start; dir Radon Control Ltd; fell Zoological Soc; AFBPsS; *Books* Victims of Science (1975, 2 edn 1983), Animal Revolution (1989), Animal Rights - A Symposium (ed, 1979);

Recreations rhododendroms; *Clubs* Nat Lib; *Style—* Richard D Ryder, Esq

RYDER, (Richard) Stephen; DL (1973); s of Charles Foster Ryder (d 1942), of Thurlow, Suffolk, and Mabel Elizabeth, *née* Sims (d 1974); *b* 6 Feb 1917; *Educ* Radley, Univ of Cambridge (MA); *m* 12 April 1947, Margaret, da of Neil MacKenzie; 2 s (Richard b 1949, *qv*, Charles b 1954); *Career* cmmnd KRRC 1940-46, serv UK and ME; farmer and landowner; former chm and pres Suffolk CLA, pres Suffolk Agric Soc 1971, chm exec ctee Suffolk Historic Churches Tst 1982-, pres S Suffolk Cons Assoc 1983-87, Lay Canon St Edmundsbury Cathedral 1984-, vice pres Suffolk Branch Magistrates Assoc (former cncl memb); JP 1956-87; vice chm: W Suffolk CC 1970-74, Suffolk CC 1978-81; High Sheriff Suffolk 1975-76; Freeman City of London 1959, memb Worshipful Co of Salters 1959; *Recreations* visiting old churches, travelling, shooting; *Clubs* Farmers', Lansdowne; *Style—* Stephen Ryder, Esq, DL; Great Bradley Hall, Newmarket, Suffolk, CB8 9LT (☎ 044083 294, 221)

RYDER, Dr Timothy Thomas Bennett; s of Thomas Alfred Ryder, MC (d 1956), and Enid Mary, *née* Sanger (d 1988); *b* 11 Jan 1930; *Educ* Eton, King's Coll Cambridge (BA, MA, PhD); *m* 12 April 1955, Jean (Jill), da of Capt Thomas Herbert Temple; 2 da (Penny (Mrs Burnham) b 1956, Pippa b 1962); *Career* Nat Serv RA 1948-49; Univ of Hull 1955-90: asst lectr in classics 1955-57, lectr 1957-66, sub-dean Faculty of Arts 1963-66, sr lectr 1966-71, reader 1971-90, dean Sch of Humanities 1987-90; visiting prof of history Michigan State Univ 1966-67 and 1981; reader in classics Univ of Reading 1990-; memb Cncl: Soc for Promotion of Hellenic Studies 1960-63 (also 1967-70 and 1975-78), Classical Assoc of GB 1967-70 and 1979-80; *Books* Koine Eirene: General Peace and Local Independence in Ancient Greece (1965), exec ed Ancient History and contrib of 200 articles to Dictionary of World History (1973); *Recreations* travel, squash rackets; *Style—* Dr Timothy Ryder; University of Reading, WhiteKnights, Reading RG6 2AA (☎ 0734 318420)

RYDER, William; s of Leonard Ryder (d 1948), and Bertha, *née* Barlow (d 1980); *b* 17 Oct 1933; *Educ* Batley GS Yorks, Univ of Edinburgh (MB ChB, DA), 1964; *m* 29 Aug 1956, Christine, da of Lawrence Wileman, of 21 Perrim Ave, Kidderminster, Worcs; 1 da (Karen b 16 Dec 1965); *Career* cmmnd RAF 1959-62; registrar Cardiff Royal Infirmary 1962-66, sr registrar Royal Victoria Infirmary Newcastle 1966-68, conslt Newcastle Health Authy 1968-, hon lectr Univ of Newcastle 1968-; sr fell Coll of Anaesthetists; memb: Assoc of Anaesthetists, Intensive Care Soc, Anaesthetic Res Soc; FFARCS; *Recreations* marathon running, swimming, dog training; *Clubs* Montagu Court Dining; *Style—* William Ryder, Esq; 16 Graham Park Rd, Gosforth, Newcastle upon Tyne; Royal Victoria Infirmary, Newcastle upon Tyne NE1 4LP (☎ 091 2325131)

RYDER OF EATON HASTINGS, Baron (Life Peer UK 1975), of Eaton Hastings, Oxon; Sydney Thomas (Don) Ryder; s of John Ryder; *b* 16 Sept 1916; *Educ* Ealing Co GS; *m* 1950, Eileen, da of William Dodds; 1 s (Hon Michael John b 1953), 1 da (Hon Jill Patricia b 1950); *Career* ed Stock Exchange Gazette 1950-60, jt md 1960-61 then sole md 1961-63 Kelly Iliffe Holdings and Assoc Iliffe Press Ltd, dir Int Publishing Corp 1963-70, md Reed Paper Group 1963-68, chm and chief exec Reed Int Ltd 1968-75, pres Nat Materials Handling Centre 1970-74, dir MEPC Ltd 1972-75; industl advsr to Govt 1974; memb Ct and Cncl Cranfield Inst of Technol 1970-74, vice pres ROSPA 1973-, chm NEB 1975-77; memb: Cncl and Bd Fells BIM 1970, Br Gas Corpn 1973-79, Cncl UK SA Trade Assoc 197, Reserve Pension Bd 1973-, Cncl Industl Soc 1971; kt 1972; *Style—* The Rt Hon Lord Ryder of Eaton Hastings; House of Lords, London SW1

RYDER OF WARSAW, Baroness (Life Peer UK 1978), of Warsaw in Poland and of Cavendish, Co Suffolk; (Margaret) Susan Cheshire; CMG (1976), OBE (1957); da of late Charles Ryder; *b* 3 July 1923; *Educ* Benenden; *m* 1959, Gp Capt (Geoffrey) Leonard Cheshire, VC, OM, DSO, DFC; 1 s (Jeremy Charles b 1960), 1 da (Elizabeth Diana b 1962); *Career* serv WWII SOE & FANY; social worker, fndr Sue Ryder Fndn for Sick and Disabled All Age Gps; tstee Cheshire Fndn, tstee and co-fndr Ryder-Cheshire Mission for the Relief of Suffering; Hon LLD: Liverpool 1973, Exeter 1980, London 1981, Leeds 1984, Cambridge 1989; Hon DLitt Reading 1982; Hon DCL Kent 1986; Pro Ecclesia et Pontifice award 1982; Offr's Cross Order of Polonia Restituta 1965, Medal of Yugoslav Flag with Gold Wreath and Diploma 1971, Golden Order of Merit (Poland) 1976, Order of Smile (Poland) 1981; *Books* And the Morrow is Theirs (autobiog 1975), Child of My Love (autobiog 1986), Remembrance (annual magazine of the Sue Ryder Foundation); *Clubs* SOE; *Style—* The Rt Hon Lady Ryder of Warsaw, CMG, OBE; Sue Ryder Home, Cavendish, Suffolk

RYDILL, Prof Louis Joseph; OBE (1962); s of Louis William Rydill (d 1975), and Queenie Elizabeth, *née* Gallagher (d 1974); *b* 16 Aug 1922; *Educ* Public Central Sch Plymouth, Dockyard Tech Coll Devonport, RNEC Keyham, RNC Greenwich; *m* 11 April 1949, Eva, da of Emanuel Newman (d 1961); 2 da (Sarah (Mrs Ash) b 1950, Jessica b 1959); *Career* asst constructor and constructor RCNC 1945-53, asst prof of naval architecture RNC Greenwich 1953-56, constructor then chief constructor on design of HMS Dreadnought 1956-62, chief constructor on design of aircraft carrier CVAOI 1962-67, prof of naval architecture RNC Greenwich and Univ Coll London 1967-72, asst and dep to dir of submarine project team, dir of warship design and engrg 1976-81, prof of naval architecture Univ Coll London 1981-85, visiting prof of naval architecture at US Naval Acad Annapolis 1985, conslt in ship and submarine design 1985-, hon res fell Univ Coll London 1985; memb DSAC; FRINA 1967, FEng 1982; *Recreations* music, books, plays; *Style—* Prof Louis Rydill, OBE; The Lodge, Entry Hill Drive, Bath BA1 5NJ (☎ 0225 427 888)

RYE, Renny Michael Douglas; s of Douglas Rye, of Union St, Maidstone, Kent, and Pamela, *née* Whitmore; *b* 2 Dec 1947; *Educ* Maidstone GS, St Catherine's Coll Oxford (BA); *m* 8 Aug 1970, Ann, da of (Andrew Frank) Peter Lynn, of Maidstone, Kent; 1 s (Thomas b 1977), 1 da (Helen b 1974); *Career* BBC: prodn ops asst BBC radio 1971-73, asst floor mangr TV plays dept 1973-79, prodr and asst ed Blue Peter 1979-81; freelance drama dir: The Box of Delights (BBC) 1983-84, The December Rose (BBC) 1985, Casualty (BBC) 1986, The Gemini Factor (Thames) 1987, All our Children (BBC) 1987-89, Agatha Christie's Poirot (LWT) 1988-91, TECX (Central TV) 1990, Paradise Club (Zenith/BBC) 1990; *Recreations* cricket, films, music; *Style—* Renny Rye, Esq; c/o Scott Marshall Personal Management, 44 Perryn Road, London W3 7NA (☎ 081 749 7692, 743 1669)

RYECART, Lady Marsha Mary Josephine; *née* Fitzalan Howard; known professionally as Marsha Fitzalan; da of 17 Duke of Norfolk, CB, CBE, MC; *b* 10 March 1953; *m* 1977, Patrick Geoffrey Ryecart, actor, s of Rev John Reginald Ryecart and Verena Maria Olga, da of Baron Hans Ludwig von Gablenz, of Schloss Weinberg, Austria; 1 s (Frederick b 1987) 2 da (Mariella b 1982, Jemima b 1984); *Career* actress; tv performances incl: Pride and Prejudice, Nancy Astor, Pygmalion, Anna Karenina, Paradise Postponed, Inside Story, Hedgehog Wedding, The New Statesman, Goldeneye, The Life of Ian Fleming; *Style—* The Lady Marsha Ryecart; Duncan Heath ICM, Paramount House, Wardour St, London W1

RYLANCE, John Randolph Trevor; s of Dr Ralph Curzon Rylance (d 1983), and Margaret Joan Clare, *née* Chambers; *b* 26 Feb 1944; *Educ* Shrewsbury; *m* 14 Dec 1974, Philippa Anne, da of Philip Sidney Bailey (d 1975); 2 da (Georgina b 1976, Charlotte b 1978); *Career* called to the Bar 1968, res asst to Sir Edward Gardner, QC, MP 1971-73, asst recorder 1989-; govr Fulham Cross Sch 1977-88, branch chm Fulham Cons Assoc 1983-89 (memb mgmnt ctee 1980-90), memb Exec Ctee Fulham Soc 1988-; *Clubs* Hurlingham; *Style—* John Rylance, Esq; 28 Doneraile St, Fulham, London SW6 6EN (☎ 071 731 1716); Francis Taylor Building, Temple, London EC4Y 7BY (☎ 071 353 7768, fax 071 353 0659)

RYLAND, David Stuart; s of Sir William Ryland, CB (d 1988), of Croydon, Surrey, and Lady Sybil Ryland; *b* 27 Oct 1953; *Educ* Dulwich, Exeter Coll Oxford; *m* 18 July 1986, Anne Helen, da of Kenneth Wright, of Benfleet, Essex; *Career* admitted slr 1981; Clifford Chance 1981-88, ptnr S J Berwin & Co 1988-; Freeman City of London; memb Law Soc; *Recreations* films, music, sport; *Style—* David Ryland, Esq; S J Berwin & Co, 236 Grays Inn Rd, London WC1X 8HB (☎ 071 278 0444, fax 071 833 2860, telex 8814928)

RYLAND, His Hon Judge Timothy Richard Godfrey Fetherstonhaugh; s of Richard Desmond Fetherstonhaugh Ryland (d 1983), and Frances Katharine Vernon, *née* Plummer (d 1990); *b* 13 June 1938; *Educ* St Andrew's Coll, Trinity Coll Dublin (BA, LLB); *Career* called to the Bar Gray's Inn 1961, dep circuit judge 1978, rec Crown Court 1983, circuit judge 1988; *Recreations* opera, wine; *Clubs* Kildare St and Univ Dublin; *Style—* His Hon Judge Ryland; Lamb Building, Temple, London EC4Y 7AS (☎ 071 353 0774)

RYLANDS, George Chapman; OBE (1976), TD (1959), DL (1975); s of Lt-Col Geoffrey Glazebrook Rylands JP (d 1957); *b* 16 Jan 1924; *Educ* Bromsgrove; *Career* JP 1959, CC 1969, chm Cheshire TA Assoc 1974, memb N W England and IOM TA & VR Assoc 1974, chm HM Prison Appleton Thorn Cheshire 1960, chm Cheshire Police Authy 1973, pres Runcorn Co Constituency Cons Assoc 1965-68; *Recreations* golf, reading; *Style—* George Rylands Esq, OBE, TD, DL; Woodstock, Tarporley Rd, Stretton, nr Warrington, Cheshire (☎ Norlott Brook 378)

RYLE, Alun; s of George Bodley Ryle, CBE (d 1978), and Margaret, *née* Bevan; *b* 10 June 1937; *Educ* Reigate GS, Britannia RNC Dartmouth, Emmanuel Coll Cambridge (BA, MA); *m* 23 Dec 1961, Carole Ann, da of Wing Cdr MF Clyne (d 1946); 1 s (James Bodley b 1969), 1 da (Susannah Caroline b 1964); *Career* weapon and electrical engr various ships and land estabs 1959-81 incl: HMS Mounts Bay, HMS Cavendish, HMS Hermes, HMS Mohawk, HMS Danae; Lt Cdr 1968, Cdr 1974, Capt 1981, dir NATO Maritime Electronic Warfare Support Group 1981-84, head Tech Naval Intelligence MOD 1984-87, Capt HMS Cochrane 1987-88, Royal Coll of Defence Studies 1989; facilities mangr Weatherall Green & Smith 1990-; dir Assoc of Old Crows 1981-87, chm RN & RM Amateur Rowing Assoc 1983-86; FIEE 1986; *Recreations* running, squash; *Style—* Capt Alun Ryle

RYLE, Lt-Col (Ian) Nigel; OBE (1961), MC (1945), DL (Kent 1976); s of Arthur John Ryle (d 1921); *b* 7 April 1914; *Educ* Epsom Coll; *m* 1, 1958 (m dis 1975), Jytte, da of Christian Skovby, of Denmark; 1 da (Jacqueline Lilian); m 2, 1976, Joanna, *née* Hawksworth (d 1977); *Career* cmmnd The Buffs (Royal East Kent Regt) 1940-46, American Bronze Star 1944, NW Europe 1944-45, RTR 1946, Staff Coll 1947, Lt-Col 1956, ret 1964; sec Worcs T&AFA 1965-68, sec SE Territorial & Aux Volunteer Res Assoc 1968-79; Freeman City of London 1984; *Recreations* foxhunting, shooting, fishing; *Style—* Lt-Col Nigel Ryle, OBE, MC, DL; 6 Ashlawn, The Green, Benenden, Cranbrook, Kent TN17 4DN (☎ 0580 240857)

RYLE, Sallie Elizabeth; da of Barry Eaton Smith, MBE, of Ilkley, Yorkshire, and Mary Elizabeth, *née* Priest; *b* 14 Nov 1950; *Educ* Ilkley GS; *m* 19 Sept 1981, Nicholas Peter Bodley Ryle, s of Michael Thomas Ryle, of Winsford, Exmoor; 1 s (George b 6 March 1987), 1 da (Vanessa Isabelle b 25 March 1990); *Career* Yorkshire TV: asst publicity offr 1982-84, head publicity 1984-87, head publicity and PR 1987-; memb Charity Ball Ctee Action Res for Crippled Child; memb RTS 1989; *Recreations* equestrian sports, tennis, travel; *Style—* Mrs Sallie Ryle; Yorkshire Television Ltd, The TV Centre, Leeds LS3 1JS (☎ 0532 438283, fax 0532 452106, telex 557232)

RYLE-HODGES, Carolyn; da of Harry Morton Neal, and Cecilia Elizabeth, *née* Crawford; *b* 10 June 1961; *Educ* Heathfield Sch Ascot, Courtauld Inst of Art Univ of London (BA); *m* 2 June 1988, Rupert, s of Edward Ryle-Hodges; *Career* sec and asst to dirs of Redfern Gallery London 1984-86, PA at Meltons Ltd Interior Decorators 1986-87, freelance writing 1987 (cmmnd to write novelization for LWT series Bust); fndr and ptnr Long & Ryle Art International 1988, clients incl: Morgan Grenfell, Société Générale, Mitsui Trust; memb Worshipful Co of Carpenters; memb: Friends of the Tate, Whitechapel Group, Friends of the Royal Acad; *Recreations* tennis, fishing, reading, visiting museums, opera, painting, drawing; *Style—* Mrs Carolyn Ryle-Hodges; 4 Redesdale St, London SW3; Long and Ryle Art International, 4 John Islip St, London SW1 P4RX (☎ 071 834 1434, fax 071 821 9409)

RYMAN, John; MP (Lab) Blyth Valley 1983-; *b* 7 Nov 1930; *Educ* Leighton Park, Pembroke Coll Oxford; *Career* barr Middle Temple, 1957; MP (Lab) Blyth Oct 1974-1983; *Style—* John Ryman, Esq, MP; Lowstead Wark, Hexham, Northumberland

RYMAN, Hon Shirley; *see*: Summerskill, Hon Shirley

RYRIE, Sir William Sinclair; KCB (1982, CB 1979); s of Rev Dr Frank Ryrie; *b* 10 Nov 1928; *Educ* Mount Hermon Sch Darjeeling, Heriot's Sch Edinburgh, Univ of Edinburgh; *m* 1, 1953 (m dis 1969), Dorrit Klein; 2 s, 1 da; m 2, 1969, Christine Gray Thomson; 1 s; *Career* Nat Serv Intelligence Corps Malaya; Colonial Office 1953-63; asst sec Int Monetary Affrs Treasy 1966-69, princ private sec to Chllr 1969-71, under sec Public Sector Gp 1971-75, econ min and head UK Treasy and Supply Delgn Washington and UK exec dir IMF and IBRD 1975-79, second perm sec (Domestic Economy) Treasy 1980-82, perm sec Overseas Devpt Admin 1982-84; exec vice pres and chief exec International Finance Corporation World Bank Washington 1984-; *Clubs* Reform; *Style—* Sir William Ryrie, KCB; 4840 Van Ness St, NW, Washington DC, 20016 USA (☎ 010 1 202 966 1139)

RYTON, Royce Thomas Carlisle; s of Reginald Thomas Ryton (d 1966), of Ferring, Sussex, and Olive Edwina (d 1963); *b* 16 Sept 1924; *Educ* Lancing, Webber Douglas Acad; *m* 6 Sept 1954, Morar Margaret, da of Capt Edward Coverley Kennedy, RN (ka 1939); 1 da (Charlotte Susan Teresa b 15 Oct 1955); *Career* serv WWII RN; actor-playwright: many years experience in rep tours all over the country incl Sheffield, Birmingham and Cambridge Theatre Cos; appeared in: West End as Bill in own play The Unvarnished Truth (Phoenix Theatre and long US tour) 1978, Terry in The Other Side of the Swamp (Phoenix) 1979 (also the author); toured UK and Hong Kong in Sir Anthony Quayle's Co in The Tempest and St Joan; author of; Crown Matrimonial (which ran for over 500 performances at the Haymarket London 1972-74 and was also performed on Broadway 1973 and on TV), Motherdear (Ambassadors), The Anastasia File (New York and London and two UK tours), The Royal Baccarat Scandal (Chichester Festival 1988 and Haymarket London 1989), the Little Father (BBC Radio Four, 1990); memb Br Actors Equity Assoc; *Books* Plays: Crown Matrimonial (1973), The Unvarnished Truth (1979), The Anastasia File (1986); *Recreations* genealogy, Victorian and Russian royalty; *Clubs* Dramatists; *Style—* Royce Ryton, Esq; 9 Cavendish House, Chertsey Rd, St Margarets, Twickenham, Middlesex TW1 1JD (☎ 081 891 6690)

S

SAATCHI, Charles; s of Nathan David Saatchi, and Daisy Saatchi, of London; *b* 9 June 1943; *Educ* Christ's Coll Finchley; *m* 1973, Doris Jean, da of Jack Lockhart of USA; *Career* dir Saatchi & Saatchi Co plc 1970-; *Style—* Charles Saatchi, Esq; Saatchi & Saatchi Co plc, Berkeley Square, London W1X 5DH (☎ 071 495 5000, telex 8950391)

SAATCHI, Maurice; s of Nathan David Saatchi, and Daisy Saatchi; *b* 21 June 1946; *Educ* LSE (BSc); *m* 1987, Josephine Hart; 1 s (Edward), 1 step s; *Career* chm Saatchi & Saatchi Co plc; *Style—* Maurice Saatchi, Esq; Saatchi & Saatchi Co plc, Berkeley Sq, London W1X 5DH (☎ 071 495 5000)

SABATINI, (Lawrence) John; s of Frederick Laurence Sabatini, and Elsie May, *née* Friggens; *b* 5 Dec 1919; *Educ* Watford GS; *m* 19 July 1947, Patricia, da of William Lawty Dyson; 1 s (Richard John Lawty b 1950), 1 da (Nicola Patricia Anne b 1954); *Career* Army 1940-46, cmmnd RTR 1943, serv 5 RTR NW Europe; HM Office of Works 1938, asst princ Miny of Works 1947 (asst private sec to min 1948-49, princ 1949), Jt Servs Staff Coll 1955, transferred MOD 1955, princ private sec to mins 1958-60, asst sec 1960, def cnsllr to UK Delegn to NATO on secondment to Dip Serv 1963-67, asst Undersec of State 1972-79; memb: RHS, RZS; *Recreations* travel, gardening, photography; *Clubs* MCC; *Style—* John Sabatini, Esq; 44A Batchworth Lane, Northwood, Middx HA6 3DT (☎ 09274 23249)

SABBEN-CLARE, Ernest Elwin; s of James W Sabben-Clare, DSO (d 1968), and Gladys, *née* Dickson (d 1961); *b* 11 Aug 1910; *Educ* Winchester, New Coll Oxford (BA, MA), Univ of London; *m* 9 Dec 1938, Rosamond Dorothy Mary, da of Lt Col H C Scott (d 1958); 2 s (Timothy b Dec 1939, James b Sept 1941, *qv*), 1 da (Penelope b June 1944); *Career* Colonial Serv Tanzania (formerly Tanganyika) 1935-40; Colonial Office: attache and cmmr Caribbean Cmmn, Br Embassy Washington 1940-50, Nigeria 1950-55; teaching 1955-70: under master (formerly asst master) Marlborough Coll 1955-60, headmaster Bishop Wordsworth Sch Salisbury 1960-63 and Leeds GS 1963-70; info offr Univ of Oxford 1970-77; treas Oxford branch CRUSE (nat orgn for widows and bereaved) 1979-87; chm of govrs:Bramcore Sch Scarborough 1970-80, Badminton Sch Bristol 1983-87; *Recreations* gardening, chess; *Clubs* Athenaeum; *Style—* Ernest Sabben-Clare, Esq; 4 Denham Close, Abbey Hill Rd, Winchester SO23 7BL (☎ 0962 55966)

SABBEN-CLARE, James Paley; s of Ernest Edwin Sabben-Clare, *qv*, of Winchester, and Rosamond Dorothy Mary, *née* Scott; *b* 9 Sept 1941; *Educ* Winchester, New Coll Oxford (BA, MA); *m* 30 Aug 1969, (Geraldine) Mary, da of (Henry) Stuart Borton (d 1985), of Blandford; 1 s (Matthew b 1973), 1 da (Rebecca b 1971); *Career* Flt Lt RAFVR 1965-81; asst master Marlborough Coll 1964-68, visiting fell All Souls' Coll Oxford 1967-68, headmaster Winchester Coll 1985-(second master 1979-85, head of classics dept 1969-79); patron Winchester Samaritans, vice pres Winchester Gp for the Disabled; govr: The Pilgrims' Sch, St Swithun's Sch, King Edward VI Sch Southampton, Northaw Sch, King Alfred's Coll; *Books* Caesar and Roman Politics (2 edn, 1981), Fables from Aesop (1976), The Culture of Athens (2 edn, 1980), Winchester Coll (2 edn, 1988), contrib to educnl and classical jls; *Recreations* games, theatre, furniture-making, hill-walking; *Clubs* Jesters; *Style—* James Sabben-Clare, Esq; Headmaster's House, Winchester Coll, Winchester, Hampshire SO23 9NA (☎ 0962 854328)

SABEY, Martin Alfred John; s of Norman Alfred Sabey, of Kingston Gorse, Rustington, Sussex, and Cecily Frances, *née* Martin; *b* 8 March 1944; *Educ* Brighton Coll; *m* 1970, Patricia Ann, da of Harold Street; 1 s (Andrew Martin b 5 Sept 1972, d Feb 1975), 2 da (Alexandra Ann b 26 June 1976, Charlotte Patricia b 3 Sept 1977); *Career* articled clerk Spofforth Hews & Burn Worthing 1962-68; Arthur Young McClelland Moore & Co: joined 1968, gp audit mangr 1975-78, ptnr i/c Audit Dept Jersey 1979-85, ptnr Offshore Cos & Trust Dept 1985; ptnr Ernst & Young (following merger) 1989-; FCA 1973 (ACA 1968); *Recreations* golf, squash (pres Jersey Squash Rackets Assoc 1988-), riding, snooker, real tennis; *Clubs* Royal Jersey Golf, Jersey Squash, Br Show Jumping Assoc, Hampton Court Tennis, United; *Style—* Martin Sabey, Esq; Montrose, Le Passage, St Lawrence, Jersey, Channel Islands (☎ 0534 63499); Ernst & Young, Le Gallais Chambers, 54 Bath St, St Helier, Jersey, Channel Islands (☎ 0534 33700)

SABIN, Paul Robert; s of Robert Reginald Sabin (d 1988), and Dorothy Maude, *née* Aston; *b* 29 March 1943; *Educ* Oldbury GS, Univ of Aston (DMS); *m* 19 June 1965, Vivien, da of Harry Furnival; 1 s (Martin Lawrence b 1969), 2 da (Ann Hazel b 1973, Caroline Jane b 1978); *Career* West Bromwich CBC 1961-69, chief fin offr Redditch Devpt Corp 1975-81 (joined 1969); City of Birmingham: joined 1981, city treas 1982-86, dep chief exec 1984-86; chief exec Kent CC 1986-; memb DTI/SERC Information Technology Advsy Bd (ITAB), dir Kent Economic Devpt Bd; bd memb: Kent Trg and Enterprise Cncl, Kent Trg Centres Ltd; Hon Citizen of the City of Baltimore USA 1985; DMS, IPFA 1966, FBIM, FRSA; *Recreations* antique maps and books, music; *Style—* Paul Sabin, Esq; Kent County Council, Chief Executive's Office, County Hall, Maidstone, Kent ME14 1XQ (☎ 0622 694001, fax 0622 681097)

SABINE, Dr Peter Aubrey; s of Bernard Robert Sabine (d 1970), and Edith Lucy, *née* Dew (d 1989); *b* 29 Dec 1924; *Educ* Brockley Co Sch, Chelsea Poly, Imperial Coll London (BSc, PhD, DSc); *m* 13 April 1946, Peggy Willis, da of Harry Augustus Lambert (d 1958); 1 s (Cedric Martin Peter b 1952); *Career* Geological Survey 1945-; Geological Museum 1945-50, i/c petrographical dept 1950-, chief petrographer 1959-70, asst dir field staff 1970, chief geochemist 1977, dep dir (chief sci offr and chief geologist) 1977-84, geological advsr 1984-; contrib to many professional jls and geological maps; chm Int Union Geological Sci Cmmn on Systematics in Petrology 1984- (memb sub cmmn Igneous Rocks 1969-, chief UK del 1980-84, cncl memb 1984-), chm Royal Soc sub-ctee on geochemistry 1977-86, visitor to Royal Inst 1979-82 (chm audit ctee 1989-90);memb: DTI chemical and minerals requirements bd 1973-82, Minerals Metals and Reclamation Ctee 1983-84, minerals and geochemistry ctees EEC 1975-84 (advsr 1985-86), ctee of dirs of W Euro Surveys 1978-84, Mineral Indust Res Orgn 1983-86, Mineral Soc of America 1953 (Fell 1959), Mineral Soc 1945 (cncl memb 1950-53), FGS 1944 Lyell Fund 1955- (cncl memb 1956-67, sec 1959-66, vice pres 1966-67 and 1982-84); FRSE 1964, FIMM 1965 (cncl 1976-80), CEng 1971, FRSA 1975; *Books* Gemstones (jtly 1983), Chemical Analyses of Igneous Rocks (jtly 1956), Petrography of British Igneous rocks (jtly 1982), Classification of Igneous Rocks (jtly 1989); *Recreations* gardening, genealogy, antique furniture restoration; *Clubs* Athenaeum, Geological Soc (hon memb); *Style—* Dr Peter Sabine; 19 Beaufort Rd, Ealing, London W5 3EB (☎ 081 997 2360)

SACH, Keith Howard; s of Cyril James Sach (d 1989), of Warwicks, and Jessie Annie, *née* Andlaw (d 1990); *b* 13 May 1948; *Educ* Strode's Sch, King George V Sch, St Peter's Coll Birmingham, Open Univ; *m* 14 July 1990, Elizabeth Anne (Mrs Brierley), da of Geoffrey Ball (d 1990); 1 step s (Jonathan b 1976), 2 step da (Alexis b 1973, Kathryn b 1979); *Career* asst master Solihull Sch 1970-79, dir RLSS UK 1979-88, (chief cwlth sec 1979-86, cwlth vice pres 1987), md S & P Safety 1988-90; Leisure safety conslt to: Sports Cncl, Amateur Swimming Assoc, IBRM, ILAM, Rank Organisation, Crossland Leisure, Biwater Filtration; broadcaster writer; memb Health and Safety Exec Working Pty, Br Insurance Law Assoc, Br Juvenile and Family Cts Soc; Civil Criminal and Coroners' Ct expert witness on swimming pool and leisure centre accidents; chm: Nat Water Safety Ctee 1980-83, Nat Rescue Trg Cncl 1981-88; Hon Constable St Helier Jersey 1984, Hon Citizen Burlington Ontario 1985; JP Warwickshire 1989; *Books* Safety in Swimming Pools (contrib, 1988); *Recreations* theatre, music, travel, swimming; *Clubs* New Cavendish, Ardencote (Warwickshire); *Style—* Keith Sach, Esq, JP; The Manor, Haseley, Warwickshire CV35 7LS (☎ 0203 537000/0831 608900, fax 0203 537028)

SACHAR, Jasbir Singh; s of Balwant Singh (decd), and Inder Kaur, *née* Phul; *b* 12 Dec 1936; *Educ* Punjab Univ Amritsar (BA, BT, MA), Univ of Agra India (LLB); *m* 8 Oct 1967, Kanwaljit, da of Avtar Singh Keer (decd), of India; 1 s (Navi b 22 April 1970), 1 da (Ruby b 26 Aug 1968); *Career* headmaster Govt Middle Sch Chamyari Dist Amvitsar India 1957-59, princ SGN Int Coll Bareilly India 1964-67; winner numerous prizes for literary and academic achievement; sec Headmasters Assoc India 1957-59, memb Allahabad Educn Bd India 1964-67, pres Asian Welfare and Cultural Assoc E London 1975 (gen sec 1974), PR offr Standing Conference of Asian Orgns in UK 1975-, dir publicity and PR First Int Convention of Overseas Indians (euro section) London 1989, fndr and UK delegate First Int Convention NY 1989; exec memb numerous other nat and int orgns; *Books* Asian Directory and Who's Who editions 1-5 (ed, 1974-89), Asian Observer (ed monthly); *Recreations* gardening, socialising; *Clubs* Rotary Int (Redbridge); *Style—* Jasbir Sachar, Esq; 47 Beattyville Gardens, Barkingside, Ilford, Essex IG6 1JW (☎ 081 550 3745, 081 551 0990)

SACHER, Hon Mrs (Rosalind Eleanor Cameron); *née* Corbett; da of 3 Baron Rowallan by his 1 w, Eleanor; *b* 2 Jan 1958; *m* 1977, Jeremy Sacher; 1 s (Harry b 1987), 2 da (Chloe b 1979, Charlotte b 1982); *Style—* The Hon Mrs Sacher; 30 Lansdown Crescent, London W11 2NT

SACHS, John Raymond; s of Andrew Sachs, of Cricklewood, London, and Adelaide Melody, *née* Good; *b* 3 May 1957; *Educ* Belmont Prep St Pauls; *m* 27 July 1985, Lisa Jayne, da of Brian James; 2 da (Kimberley b 29 Oct 1987, Charlotte Adelaide b 1 Jan 1990); *Career* radio personality; host morning show Capital FM, presenter Four Square (BBC), voice-over personality, TV programme creator (devised format for BBC's That's Rich and compiled questions for Channel 4's Music Matters); Personality of the Year: Variety Club of GB 1988 (vice pres 1991), NY Radio Festival World Awards 1988; barker: Variety Club of GB, Help A London Child, Children in Need; *Recreations* clay shooting, golf, watersports; *Clubs* RAC, Mossimans, Tramp; *Style—* John Sachs, Esq; Capital Radio plc, PO Box 95.8, London NW1 3DR (☎ 071 380 6188, fax 071 387 2345, car 0836 758418, telex 21365)

SACHS, Hon Lady ((Janet) Margaret); *née* Goddard; 2 da of Baron Goddard, GCB, PC, sometime Lord Chief Justice (Life Peer d 1971), and Mary Linda, da of Sir Felix Otto Schuster, 1 Bt; *b* 26 Oct 1909; *m* 12 May 1934, Rt Hon Sir Eric Sachs, MBE, TD, sometime Lord Justice of Appeal (d 1979); 1 s (Richard b 1935), 1 da (Katharine Frances b 1939, m 1, 1965, George Pulay, who d 1981; 2 da; m 2, 1987, Hon Mr Justice (Sir Jeremiah LeRoy) Harman, *qv*); *Style—* The Hon Lady Sachs; Antioch House West, Rotten Row, Lewes, E Sussex BN7 1TN

SACHS, His Honour Judge Michael Alexander Geddes; s of Dr Joseph Sachs (d 1954), of Penrith, Cumbria, and Ruby Mary, *née* Ross (d 1957); *b* 8 April 1932; *Educ* Sedbergh, Univ of Manchester (LLB); *m* 13 July 1957, Patricia Mary, da of James Conroy (d 1968), of Thrybergh, Yorks; 2 s (Hugh b 1964, Jeromy b 1966), 2 da (Madeleine (Mrs Morgan) b 1959, Elizabeth b 1962); *Career* admitted slr 1957; ptnr Slater Heelis Manchester 1962-84, rec Crown Ct 1980-84 circuit judge 1984-; memb No 7 (NW) Legal Aid Ctee 1966-80 (chm 1975-76), chm Greater Manchester Legal Servs Ctee 1977-81, pres Manchester Law Soc 1978-79; memb Ct Univ of Manchester 1977-84, memb Cncl Law Soc 1979-84 (chm Standing Ctee on Criminal Law); Knight of St Sylvester; *Style—* His Hon Judge Michael Sachs; c/o Circuit Administrator, Northern Circuit, Lord Chancellors Dept, Aldine House, New Bailey St, Salford M3 5EU (☎ 061 832 9571)

SACK, Barry Lawrence; s of Raphael Sack (d 1988), of Johannesburg, SA, and Daphne, *née* Shapiro (d 1980); *b* 3 Oct 1948; *Educ* Westminister City Univ of Witwatersrand SA (BCom); *m* (m dis); *Career* md Anglo Leasing 1973-78, fndr Aurit Serrs Ltd (a subsidiary of J Rothschilds Hldgs plc), md Target Unit Tsts 1980-; jt md: Comcap plc 1985, Summit Gp plc 1985; dir Atlantic Gp plc; *Recreations* music, art, sculpture; *Style—* Barry Sack, Esq; 49 Pall Mall, London SW1Y 5JG (☎ 930 7682)

SACK, Brian George; s of Thomas Jacob Sack (d 1972), of London, and Stella May, *née* Blake (d 1962); *b* 29 Jan 1923; *Educ* Hilldrop London, Northern Poly, Coll of Estate Mgmnt (ARICS), Westminster Coll (FHCIMA); business ptnr and co-ordinator of Sharrow Bay Country House Hotel, Francis Ernest Coulson; *Career* Serv WWII fighter pilot RAF; articled pupil to Potters Bar UDC Surveyor 1939-45, qualified as chartered surveyor, worked Miny of Works until 1951, trg in hotel keeping under Mrs Ashley Courtenay, joined Francis Coulson at Sharrow Bay 1952, became ptnr, changed hotel name to Sharrow Bay Country House Hotel 1956; *awards* memb Relais et Chateaux (second oldest memb UK), Egon Ronay's Restaurant of the Year 1975, Egon Ronay's Hotel of the Year 1980 (only hotel in UK to have received both Gold awards), Egon Ronay/Sunday Times Taste of England award 1983, RAC Blue Ribbon award for Excellence 1987-90, Catey Special Award 1988, Cumbria Tourist Bd 1988, AA Three Red Stars, AA Two Rosettes for Food, AA Care and Courtesy award 1990; ARICS 1951, FHCIMA 1955, memb Br Hotels and Restaurants Assoc 1960; *Recreations* music (especially opera), tennis (watching only), motoring, travelling; *Style*— Brian Sack, Esq; Sharrow Bay Country House Hotel, Ullswater, Penrith, Cumbria CA10 2LZ (☎ 07684 86301, fax 07684 86349, car 0831 403466)

SACKLOFF, Ms Gail Josephine; da of Myer Sackloff, of London, and Rachel, *née* Crivon; *b* 15 Dec 1944; *Educ* Norfolk Coll for Girls Dublin Ireland; *Career* Euro import co-ordinator for May Dept Stores USA Nigel French Fashion Consultancy 1970-78, merchandise mangr Batus Retail 1978-89, sr merchandiser Saks Fifth Ave Stores UDA 1989; memb Met Police Special Constabulary; *Recreations* theatre, weekends on my boat on the river Thames; *Clubs* Network; *Style*— Ms Gail Sackloff; Associated Merchandising Corporation, 78 St Martins Lane, London WC2 (☎ 01 486 4721)

SACKMAN, Simon Laurence; s of Bernard Sackman (d 1986), and Mamie, *née* Epstein; *b* 16 Jan 1951; *Educ* St Paul's, Pembroke Coll Oxford (BA, MA); *m* 7 Feb 1982, Donna, da of Solomon Seruya, of Gibraltar; 2 da (Sarah b 1984, Paloma b 1987); *Career* ptnr Norton Rose 1983- (articled clerk 1974-77, asst slr 1977-83); memb: City of London Slrs 1982, Law Soc 1977; *Recreations* theatre, music; *Style*— Simon Sackman, Esq; Norton Rose, Kempson House, Camomile St, London EC3A 7AN (☎ 071 283 2434, fax 071 588 1181, telex 883652)

SACKS, John Harvey; s of Joseph Gerald Sacks, of Dorset House, Gloucester Place, London NW1, and Yvonne, *née* Clayton; *b* 29 April 1946; *Educ* Perse Sch Cambridge, Univ of London (LLB); *m* 2 Dec 1969, Roberta Judith, da of Archy Arenson, of Regent's Park, London NW1; 1 s (David b 19 Jan 1981), 2 da (Deborah b 7 Oct 1972, Rachel b 1 March 1976); *Career* chief exec Arenson Group plc 1970-, chm and md Arenson International Ltd, memb Supervisory Bd Gispen Int BV, chm Office Furniture and Filing Div Electronic & Business Equipment Assoc; formerly chm London & SE Furniture Manufacturing Assoc; FCA, FCCA, FCT; *Recreations* bridge, law, tennis; *Style*— John Sacks, Esq; Barlogan, Priory Drive, Stanmore, Middx HA7 3HL; Arenson Group plc, Lincoln House, Colney St, St Albans, Herts AL2 2DX; (☎ 0923 857211, fax 0923 858387)

SACKS, Rabbi Dr Jonathan Henry; s of Louis David Sacks, of London, and Louisa, *née* Frumkin; *b* 8 March 1948; *Educ* Christ's Coll Finchley, Gonville and Caius Coll Cambridge (MA), New Coll Oxford, London (PhD), Jews' Coll London, Yeshivat Etz Hayyim London; *m* 14 July 1970, Elaine, da of Philip Taylor (d 1986); 1 s (Joshua b 1975), 2 da (Dina b 1977, Gila b 1982); *Career* lectr moral philosophy Middx Poly 1971-73; Jews' Coll London: lectr jewish philosophy 1973-76, lectr Talmud and jewish philosophy 1976-82, Chief Rabbi Lord Jakobovits prof (first incumbent) in modern jewish thought 1982-, dir rabbinic faculty 1983-90, princ 1984-90, Chief Rabbi elect of the Utd Hebrew Congregations of the Cwlth; Sherman lectr Univ of Manchester 1989 Reith Lecturer 1990, visiting prof of philosophy Univ of Essex 1989-90; rabbi: Golders Green Synagogue London 1978-82, Marble Arch Synagogue London 1983-90; editor L'Eylah, A Journal of Judaism Today 1985-90; memb CRAC; *Books* Torah Studies (1986), Tradition and Transition: Essays Presented to Chief Rabbi Sir Immanuel Jakobovits to Celebrate Twenty Years in Office (1986), Traditional Alternatives (1989), Tradition in an Untraditional Age (1990), The Reith Lectures 1990-, The Persistence of Faith (1991), Orthodoxy Confronts Modernity (ed, 1991); *Recreations* walking; *Style*— Rabbi Dr J Sacks; Office of the Chief Rabbi, Alder House, Tavistock Sq, London WC1H 9HN (☎ 071 387 1066, fax 071 383 4920)

SACKVILLE, Lady Arabella Avice Diana; *née* Sackville; da of 10 Earl De La Warr (d 1988); *b* 20 June 1958; *m* 1981 (m dis 1988), Conte Giovanni Emo Capodilista Maldura, s of Conte Gabriele Emo Capodilista Maldura (Austrian cr of 1829, Italian of 1917), a Patrician of Venice; has resumed her maiden name; *Style*— The Lady Arabella Sackville

SACKVILLE, 6 Baron (UK 1876); Lionel Bertrand Sackville-West; proprietor of Knole, one of the most spacious homes in private hands in the country, started, around 1456, by Thomas Bourchier, then Archbishop of Canterbury, and expanded in the early seventeenth century by Thomas Sackville, to whom it was made over by Elizabeth I; patron of eleven livings; s of late Hon Bertrand George Sackville-West (bro of 4 Baron and unc of Vita (Victoria) Sackville-West, w of Hon Sir Harold Nicolson, KCVO, CMG) and Eva, da of late Maj-Gen Inigo Richmond Jones, CB, CVO; suc cous 1965; *b* 30 May 1913; *Educ* Winchester, Magdalen Coll Oxford; *m* 1, 1953, Jacobine Napier (d 1971), da of J R Menzies-Wilson and widow of Capt John Hitchens, RA; 5 da; m 2, 1974 (m dis 1983), Arlie Roebuck, da of Charles Woodhead, of Romany Rye Brisbane Aust, widow of Maj Hugh Dalzell Stewart and formerly w of Maj-Gen Sir Francis Wilfred de Guingand, KBE, CB, DSO; m 3, Jean, JP, da of Arthur Stanley Garton (d 1963), and widow of Sir Edward Imbert-Terry, 3 Bt, MC (d 1978); *Heir* bro, Hugh Inigo Sackville-West; *Career* late Coldstream Gds, served WW II (POW); Lloyd's underwriter, ret; *Style*— The Rt Hon the Lord Sackville; Knole, Sevenoaks, Kent (☎ 0732 455694)

SACKVILLE, Hon Thomas Geoffrey; MP (C) Bolton W 1983-; yr s of 10 Earl De La Warr, DL (d 1988); *b* 26 Oct 1950; *Educ* Eton, Lincoln Coll Oxford (BA); *m* 1979, Catherine, da of late Brig James Windsor Lewis; 1 adopted s (Arthur Michael b 1983), 1 da (Savannah Elizabeth b 1986); *Career* formerly merchant banker; PPS to Min of State at the Treasy 1985-; govt whip 1988-; PPS Min of State for Social Security 1987-; *Style*— The Hon Thomas Sackville, MP; House of Commons, London SW1 (☎ 01 219 4050/3537)

SACKVILLE-WEST, Hon Catherine Jacobine; resumed use of maiden name 1984; da of 6 Baron Sackville, *qv*, and his 1 wife, Jacobine Napier (d 1971), da of J R Menzies-Wilson, of Fotheringhay Lodge, Nassington, Peterborough; *b* 10 March 1956; *Educ* Cranborne Chase Wilts, Queen's Coll London; *m* 1980 (m dis 1984), Stuart Cooper Bennett, er s of H M Bennett, of Pasadena, Calif, USA; *Style*— The Hon Catherine Sackville-West; 36 Iffley Rd, London W6 (☎ 01 748 1853)

SACKVILLE-WEST, Hugh Rosslyn Inigo; MC; s of late Hon Bertrand Sackville-West (bro of 4 Baron Sackville) and Eva, da of Maj-Gen Inigo Richmond Jones, CB, CVO; hp of bro, 6 Baron; *b* 1 Feb 1919; *Educ* Winchester, Magdalen Coll Oxford; *m* 1957, Bridget Eleanor, da of Capt Robert Lionel Brooke Cunliffe, CBE, RN (ggs of 3 Bt); 2 s, 3 da; *Career* Capt RTR, serv WWII (Croix de Guerre); admin offr N Nigeria 1946-59; ARICS; *Style*— Hugh Sackville-West, Esq; Knole, Sevenoaks, Kent

SADIE, Dr Stanley John; CBE (1982); s of David Sadie, of London (d 1966), and Deborah, *née* Simons (d 1988); *b* 30 Oct 1930; *Educ* St Paul's, Gonville and Caius Coll Cambridge (BA, MA, MusB, PhD); *m* 1, 10 Dec 1953, Adèle (d 1978), da of Henry Bloom (d 1974), of London; 2 s (Graham b 1956, Stephen b 1963), 1 da (Ursula b 1960); m 2, 18 July 1978, Julie Anne, da of Walter McCornack, of Eugene, Oregon; 1 s (Matthew b 1983), 1 da (Celia b 1979); *Career* prof Trinity Coll of Music 1957-65, music critic The Times 1964-81, ed The Musical Times 1967-87; ed: The New Grove Dictionary of Music and Musicians and assoc pubns 1970- (1980, 1984, 1986, etc), Master Musicians series (1976-); author of studies of: Handel (1962, 1972), Mozart (1966, 1983, 1986), Opera (1964, 1989) and others; *Recreations* watching cricket, reading, opera, canal boating; *Style*— Dr Stanley Sadie, CBE; 12 Lyndhurst Rd, Hampstead, London NW3 5NL (☎ 071 435 2482); c/o Macmillan, Stockton House, 1 Melbourne Place, London WC2B 4LF (☎ 071 836 6633, fax 071 379 4980, telex 914690)

SADLEIR, (Franc) Richard; s of Maj Franc Granby Sadleir (ka 1944), of Paignton, Devon, and Josephine Ruth, *née* Hepburn; *b* 27 Dec 1944; *Educ* Marlborough, New Coll Oxford (MA); *m* 25 July 1970, Frances Judith, da of Edward John Wilson (d 1986), of St Agnes, Cornwall; 1 s (Timothy b 1975), 1 da (Rebecca b 1972); *Career* Bank of London and S America Ltd 1967-70, J Henry Schroder Wagg and Co Ltd 1970-(dir 1984-); dir The Securities Association Ltd 1986-88; memb Chm's Ctee and chm Compliance Ctee Br Merchant Bankers Assoc 1991-; *Recreations* walking, reading, sailing; *Style*— Richard Sadleir, Esq; Fairwinds, Golden Ball Lane, Pinkneys Green, nr Maidenhead, Berks SL6 6NW (☎ 0628 31205); J Henry Schroder Wagg and Co Ltd, 120 Cheapside, London WC2V 6DS (☎ 071 382 6000, fax 071 382 3950, telex LONDON 885029)

SADLEIR, William Hugh Granby; s of Rev Ralph Edward Sadleir (d 1979), of The Chaplaincy, Goring Heath, Reading, and Pamela Sybil Campbell, *née* McTavish; *b* 16 Sept 1945; *Educ* Eton, LSE (BSc); *m* 1, 19 Dec 1970 (m dis 1985), Susan, da of George Kenneth Beaulah, of Oliver Lodge, Heads Lane, Hessle Humberside; m 2, 15 Feb 1986, (Vennor) Christina, da of John Callow Morris, of Middle Leys Cottage, Burmington, nr Shipston-on-Stour, Warwicks; 1 s (Hugh b 1979), 1 da (Harriet b 1984); *Career* Deloitte Plender Griffiths & Co 1966-70, Samuel Montagu & Co Ltd 1970-75 and 1978- (dir 1982); non-exec dir: Cedar Holdings Ltd 1976-78, Letinvest plc 1987; ACA 1970, FCA 1977; *Recreations* reading, walking, music; *Style*— William Sadleir, Esq; Lads House, Lynes Yard, Bishops Cannings, Devizes, Wilts SNL0 2LS (☎ 038 086 484); 10 Lower Thames St, London EC3R 6AE (☎ 071 260 9000, 071 488 1630, 887213)

SADLER, Brent Roderick; s of Philip Sadler (d 1957), and Ruth Sadler; *b* 29 Nov 1950; *Educ* Royal Masonic Sch Bushey; *m* 1986, Deborah, da of George Lockett; 1 da (Brooke Emma b 10 Oct 1988); *Career* news reporter; Harrow Observer, Reading Evening Post, Southern TV, Westward TV and HTV Bristol; ITN 1981-, sr reporter 1984-86, Middle East corr 1986-; assignments covered incl: the hunger strikes Maze Prison Belfast 1981, The Royal Wedding 1981, The Falklands War 1982, Lebanon, US invasion of Grenada, Middle East War 1982-84; winner: RTS Regional News award 1980, BAFTA award (with ITN team for quality of coverage from Lebanon); *Style*— Brent Sadler, Esq; ITN Ltd, 200 Gray's Inn Rd, London WC1X 8XZ (☎ 071 833 3000)

SADLER, (Arthur) Edward; s of Arthur William Sadler (d 1969), and Hilda, *née* Suckling (d 1984); *b* 27 Oct 1947; *Educ* Adams' GS Newport Shropshire, Univ Coll Oxford (MA), Coll of Law; *m* 1980, Patricia, da of Charles Cooper; 1 s (Matthew b 19 July 1981); *Career* articled clerk Farrer & Co 1971-73; ptnr: (specialising in corp tax) Clifford-Turner 1977 (joined Dept of Corp Tax 1973), Clifford Chance (following merger of Clifford-Turner and Coward Chance) 1987-; memb: Corp Tax Sub Ctee of Revenue Ctee Law Soc, Revenue Ctee City of London Solicitors' Co 1978-, Tax Ctee Int Bar Assoc 1980-; Freeman Worshipful Co of Haberdashers 1974; memb: City of London Solicitors' Co, Law Soc, Int Bar Assoc; *Books* Equipment Leasing (2 edn, with SC Reisbach and Marian Thomas); *Recreations* gardening, opera, hill walking, occasional sailing, christian activities, 20th Century history, son's homework; *Style*— Edward Sadler, Esq; Clifford Chance, Royex House, Aldermanbury Square, London EC2 (☎ 071 600 0808, fax 071 956 0156)

SADLER, John Stephen; CBE (1982); s of Bernard Eustace Sadler (d 1982), of Bromley, Kent, and Phyllis Dorothy Sadler, *née* Carey; *b* 6 May 1930; *Educ* Reading Sch, Corpus Christi Coll Oxford (BA, MA); *m* 1952, Ella, da of John McCleery, of Belfast; 3 s (Stephen, Hugh, Robert); *Career* Civil Serv 1952-66, princ BOT 1958, Br Trade Cmmr Lagos 1960-64, dep chm John Lewis Ptnrship plc 1984-89 (joined 1966, fin dir 1971-87); memb Monopolies and Mergers Cmmn 1973-85, tstee Br Telecommunications Staff Superannuation Scheme 1983-; dir: Investmt Mgmnt Regulatory Orgn Ltd 1987-, Debenham Tewson & Chinnocks Hldgs plc 1987-; chm: WRC plc 1989-, UK Bd Australian Mutual Provident Soc 1991-, Authorised Conveyancing Practitioners Bd 1991-; *Recreations* golf, rowing, walking; *Style*— John Stephen Sadler, Esq, CBE; Riverlea, The Warren, Mapledurham, Reading RG4 7TQ; 7 The Chilterns, 63 Chiltern St, London W1M 1HS (☎ 071 487 4452); WRC plc, PO Box 16, Marlow, Bucks SC7 2HD (☎ 01 0491 571531)

SADLER, Philip John; CBE (1986); s of Edward John Sadler (d 1977), and Adelaide Violet, *née* Parrish (d 1985); *b* 27 Jan 1930; *Educ* Enfield GS, LSE; *m* 11 July 1964, Teresa Jacqueline, da of Victor Coan (d 1949), of London; 2 s (Matthew John b 1965, Jonathan b 1968); *Career* princ scientific offr Civil Serv 1954-64, dir of res Ashridge Management Coll 1964-68 (princ 1969-87), regnl dir Lloyds Bank plc 1985-91, chief exec Ashridge Tst 1988-90 (vice pres 1990-); dir: Williams Lea Group Ltd 1983-, Broadway Lodge Ltd 1983-91; vice pres: Euro Fndn for Mgmnt Devpt 1981-88, Strategic Planning Soc 1984-, Assoc for Mgmnt Educn and Devpt 1988-; fell Int Acad of Mgmnt; CBIM, FIPM, FRSA, BIM Burnham Medal 1982; Hon DSc City Univ 1990; *Recreations* tennis, swimming, classical music; *Style*— Philip Sadler, Esq, CBE; Highfield, 115 Cross Oak Rd, Berkhamsted, Herts HP4 3HZ

SADOW, Geoffrey John; s of Alexander Sadow (d 1944), of London, and Anne, *née* Wildman (d 1987); *b* 22 Jan 1930; *Educ* St Paul's Sch London (MB BS); *m* 1, 3 March 1963 (m dis 1969), Janet Iris Forman; 1 da (Joanna Ruth b 1966); m 2, 18 Oct 1970, Daphne Treliving, *née* Wenzerul; *Career* formerly sr conslt orthopaedic surgn Kingston and Esher Health Auhty, currently conslt othopaedic surgn New Victoria Hosp Kingston and Parkside Hosp Wimbledon; fell: RSM, Br Orthopaedic Assoc; FRCS 1962; *Recreations* music, antique clocks, fine wine, horseracing; *Style*— Geoffrey Sadow, Esq; New Victoria Hospital, 184 Coombe Lane west, Kingston-upon-Thames

SAFFORD, John Francis; s of Sir Archibald Safford, MC, QC (d 1961), of Richmond, and Nora Iris Leighton (d 1949); *b* 2 Jan 1927; *Educ* Winchester, Trinity Coll Oxford (MA); *m* 15 Feb 1958, Nancy Helen Dorothy, da of Henry Marshall, MC (d 1981), of St Neots, Cambs; 2 s (Nicholas b 1962, Roger b 1967), 1 da (Judith b 1960); *Career* Nat Serv, Sgt Intelligence Corps Germany 1948-50; Bank of England 1951-52, asst to dep chm NCB (memb 1953-59), Guthrie & Co (UK) Ltd 1959-66, engrg dir Nat Econ Devpt Office 1974-76 (memb 1966-76), dir Br Iron and Steel Consumers Cncl 1977-; *Recreations* bird watching, gardening; *Style*— John Safford, Esq; 16 Berwyn Rd, Richmond, Surrey TW10 5BS (☎ 081 876 5179, 081 878 4898)

SAFINIA, Dr Khosrow; s of Gholam-Reza Safinia (d 1951), and Mehrvash, *née* Mostofi; *b* 18 April 1941; *Educ* Gosforth GS, Sutherland Dental Sch, King's Coll Durham (BDS, LDS RCS, DOrth RCS); *m* 9 April 1973, Dr Shirin, da of Mohammed-Ali Jafad-Shahidi; 2 s (Farhad b 25 July 1975, Bahram b 3 March 1977); *Career* dental surgn; house offr Middx Hosp 1967-68, sr house offr Royal Dental Hosp and St George's Hosp 1968-69, orthodontic course Eastman Dental Hosp Inst of Postgraduate Dental Surgery 1969-70, registrar in orthodontics Eastman Dental Hosp 1970-72, Tweed fndn course Tucson Arizona 1972; private practice: Tehran 1973-84, Harley St London 1984-; assoc prof Orthodontics Univ of Tehran 1973-79, sr dental offr Croydon Health Authy 1984-90, clinical lectr Eastman Dental Hosp Inst of Postgraduate Dental Surgery 1990-; memb: Br Soc for Study of Orthodontics 1970, American Assoc of Orthodontics 1971, Br Assoc of Orthodontists 1984; fndr memb Iranian Assoc of Orthodontics 1974; *Recreations* skiing, mountain hikes, classical music, photography; *Style*— Dr Khosrow Safinia; 97 Harley St, London W1N 1DF (☎ 071 935 8811)

SAGAR, Dr (Derrick) Alan; s of Derrick Leece Sagar, of New Parkside Farm, Caton,

Lancaster, and Mary Isobel, *née* Wilcock; *b* 3 Aug 1950; *Educ* Lancaster GS, Univ of Leeds (BSc, MB, ChB); *m* 29 Aug 1981, Elizabeth Morris, da of Francis Jordan, of 81 Biggar Rd, Cleland, Lanarkshire; 1 s (Alan Joseph Barney b 15 Feb 1983), 1 da (Fiona Mary Jordan b 29 June 1984); *Career* Med Res Cncl sponsored researcher dept anaesthesthesia Univ of Leeds 1981-83, sr registrar Yorkshire RHA 1984-87, conslt anaesthetist S Lincolnshire AHA 1987-, faculty tutor Coll of Anaethetists; chm Lincolnshire Ambulance Advsy Panel, sec Holland Div Br Med Assoc; involved advanced trg ambulance personnel, memb Lincolnshire Integrated Voluntary Emergency Serv; FFARCS 1981, memb Assoc Anaesthetists; *Style*— Dr Alan Sagar; Keys Toft House, Wainfleet, Lincolnshire PE24 4EX (☎ 0754 880885); Pilgrim Hospital, Boston, Lincolnshire (☎ 0205 64801)

SAGAR, Prof Geoffrey Roger; CBE (1990); s of Eric Sagar (d 1979), of Silverdale, Lancs, and Phyllis Margaret, *née* Rogers (d 1985); *b* 6 March 1933; *Educ* Kirkham GS, Univ of Oxford (MA DPhil); *m* 1 Oct 1955, Margaret Ann, da of William Herbert Beyer (d 1978), of Kennington, Oxford; 1 s (Stephen b 1959), 2 da (Jill b 1957, Helen b 1964); *Career* Nat Serv, RAF Flying Offr 1954-56; vice-princ Univ Coll N Wales Bangor 1981- (prof of agricultural botany 1977-, sr lectr 1965-77, lectr 1960-65); dept chm Advsy Ctee on Pesticides; *Recreations* gardening, music, books; *Clubs* Farmers; *Style*— Prof Geoffrey Sagar, CBE; Tan Y Graig, Llandegfan, Menai Bridge, Gwynedd (☎ 0248 713144); University of Wales, Bangor, Gwynedd (☎ 0248 351151, telex 61100, fax 0248 370451)

SAGE, Arthur Maxwell; s of Edward Frederick (d 1966), of Wembley, and Emily Mabel, *née* Bennett (d 1957); *b* 9 Jan 1922; *Educ* Kilburn GS, Univ of London (BSc, PhD); *m* 31 July 1948, Nerys Wyn, da of Herbert William Powell, of Bungay, Suffolk; 1 s (Richard Anthony b 1966), 2 da (Celia b 1950, Fiona b 1951); *Career* res metallurgist High Duty Alloys 1942-47, liaison offr Br Non Ferous Res Assoc 1947-49, res metallurgist and tech sec Br Iron and Steel Res Assoc 1949-56, devpt mangr Union Carbide 1956-63, sales mangr Woodall 1963-66, project mangr Atkins and Ptnrs 1966-67, dir R & D Highyield Steel and Vanadium corpn 1967-89; chm tech ctee Vanadium Int 1973-79; Freeman: City of London 1975, Worshipful Co of Blacksmiths 1975; *Style*— Dr Arthur Sage

SAGE, Melvyn (Mel); s of Harold Sage, of 25 Birch Grove, Hempstead, Gillingham, Kent, and Rita, *née* Dunning; *b* 24 March 1964; *Educ* Howard Sch Rainham Kent; *m* 18 June 1988, Joanne Lisa Eames, step da of Richard Tanner; 1 da (Louise Elizabeth b 5 Aug 1989); *Career* professional footballer; represented Kent Schs; Gillingham 1982-86: apprentice then professional, debut v Bristol City 1982, 132 league appearances, 5 goals; Derby County 1986-: joined for a fee of £60,000, over 100 appearances, 4 goals; Div 2 Championship Derby County 1987; *Recreations* golf, snooker; *Style*— Mel Sage, Esq; Derby County FC, Baseball Ground, Shaftesbury Crescent, Derby DE3 8NB (☎ 0332 40105)

SAGE, Morley William; OBE (1984); s of William George Sage (d 1968), of Worle, Weston Super Mare, and Grace Graves, *née* Smith (d 1977); *b* 15 Jan 1930; *Educ* Blundells, Emmanuel Coll Cambridge (MA); *m* 30 April 1955, Enid Muriel, da of Herbert Sim Hirst (d 1987); 1 s (Morley b 1962), 2 da (Caroline b 1957, Fiona b 1960); *Career* chartered electrical engr and conslt; lab and energy mangr Corporate Lab ICI plc 1962-75, dir computing serv Univ of Southampton 1975-88, princ conslt Systems Technol Conslt 1980-; visiting fell Clare Hall Cambridge 1967-69 (life fell 1986); memb: Br Computer Soc 1967, Univ Grants Technol Sub-Ctee 1974-79 (Computer Systems and Electronics Bd 1973-77), Inst of Measurement and Control 1977 (memb cncl 1967-71); chm: Data Communications Protocol Steering Ctee CSERB 1977-81, Inter Univ Ctee on Computing 1983-85, Integrated Prodn Systems SERC 1975-76, control engrg ctee SERC 1974-79 (memb computing sci ctee 1976-79); vice pres IEE 1984-88, dep chm resources and methods ctee ESRC 1982-85; FEng 1987, FIEE 1972, FBCS, FInstMC; *Recreations* reading, gardening, caravanning, DIY, model railways; *Clubs* Royal Cwlth Soc; *Style*— Morley Sage, Esq, OBE; Wiltown Place, Wiltown, Curry Rivel, Langport, Somerset TA10 0HZ, (☎ 0458 251407)

SAGGERS, Lady Kirstie; Cairistiona Anne; *née* Graham; 2 da of 7 Duke of Montrose (but er da by 2 w), of Dalgoram, Baynesfield, Natal, S Africa, and Susan Mary Jocelyn, *née* Semple; *b* 7 Jan 1955; *Educ* Salisbury Girls' HS Rhodesia, Ruskin Sch of Drawing and Fine Art (Dip AD), Oxford; *m* 8 May 1982, Philip Patrick Saggers, slr, yst s of Gordon Francis Saggers, of Narrandera Rd, Lockhart, NSW; 3 da (Susanna Mary b 1984, Marina Lilias b 1986, Georgina Frances b 1989); *Career* patron and chieftain of Clan Graham of Australia, patron of Scottish Australian Heritage Council; *Style*— Lady Kirstie Saggers; c/o 42 Cook St, Randwick 2031, Sydney, NSW, Australia

SAIDEMAN, Michael Allan; s of Morris Saideman, Bournemouth, Dorset (d 1983), and Rachel Saideman (d 1985); *b* 3 Feb 1935; *Educ* Barking Abbey; *m* 27 Aug 1961, Pamela, da of Nathan Bloom London W2; 1 s (Andrew b 1963), 1 da (Susan b 1965); *Career* CA; gp fin dir Campari International plc 1973-; *Recreations* golf, bowls; *Style*— Michael Saideman, Esq; International House, Priestley Way, London NW2 7AZ (☎ 081 450 661, telex 923396, fax 081 452 0443)

SAIDI, Samira Miriam (Sam); da of Hussein Ahmed Saidi, of Manchester, and Elizabeth Anne, *née* Bradshaw; *b* 8 July 1961; *Educ* Bush Davies Schs (ARAD), Royal Ballet Sch; *m* 28 Feb 1987, Alain Jacques Luis Dubreuil, s of Jacques E Dubreuil (d 1989), of Monaco; *Career* dancer Sadlers Wells Royal Ballet (now The Birmingham Royal Ballet) 1974- (currently first soloist); roles created incl: title role in David Bintley's The Snow Queen, Sybil Vane in The Picture of Dorian Gray, Giselle, Les Sylphides; active in educn work within co; *Recreations* theatre, interior design, antiques; *Style*— Miss Samira Saidi; Royal Opera House, Covent Garden, London WC2 (☎ 071 240 1200)

SAIN, Hon Mrs (Harriet Mary); *née* Lawson; 2 da of 5 Baron Burnham, *qv*; *b* 5 March 1954; *m* 1984, Marino Sain, o s of Silvano Sain, of Trieste, Italy; 1 s (Thomas Andrea b 1987); *Style*— The Hon Mrs Sain

SAINER, Leonard; s of Archer Sainer (d 1984), and Sarah Sainer (d 1971); *b* 12 Oct 1909; *Educ* Central Fndn Sch, UCL, LSE (LLB); *Career* slr; sr ptnr Titmuss Sainer & Webb 1938-79; life pres Sears plc (chm 1979-86); memb Law Soc; *Recreations* golf, horse racing; *Style*— Leonard Sainer, Esq; 8 Farm St, London W1X 7RE

SAINSBURY, Baron (Life Peer UK 1962), of Drury Lane, Borough of Holborn; Alan John Sainsbury; s of John Benjamin Sainsbury, and Mabel Miriam, *née* Van Den Bergh; *see also* Sainsbury, Sir Robert; *b* 13 Aug 1902; *Educ* Haileybury; *m* 1, 1925 (m dis 1939), Doreen Davan (d 1985), da of Leonard Adams; 3 s (Baron Sainsbury of Preston Candover, *qv*, Hon Simon David Davan b 1930, Hon Timothy Alan Davan b 1932); m 2, 1944, Anne Elizabeth (d 1988), da of Paul Lewy; 1 da (Hon Paulette Ann (Hon Mrs Anderson) b 1946); *Career* jt pres J Sainsbury Ltd 1967 (joined 1921, chm 1956-67), contested (Lib) Div of Suffolk Gen Elections 1929, 1931, 1935, subsequently joined Lab Pty and SDP in 1981; *Style*— The Rt Hon the Lord Sainsbury; J Sainsbury plc, Stamford House, Stamford St, SE1 (☎ 071 921 6000)

SAINSBURY, Jeffrey Paul; s of Walter Ronald Sainsbury, of Cardiff, and Joan Margaret, *née* Slamin (d 1974); *b* 27 June 1943; *Educ* Cardiff HS; *m* 1967, Janet Elizabeth; 1 s (Mark Christopher Paul b 1968), 1 da (Emma Louise b 1971); *Career* CA qualified 1966, ptnr in practice 1969- (now part of Pannell Kerr Forster); memb: Cardiff City Cncl 1969- (Dep Lord Mayor 1977-78), S Glam CC 1973-76, S Glam Health Authy 1988-90; chm Cardiff New Theatre 1984-89; *Recreations* theatre, music, sport; *Clubs* Cardiff and County; *Style*— Jeffrey Sainsbury, Esq; 34 Heol Iscoed, Rhiwbina, Cardiff CF4 6PA (☎ 0222 624489); Pannell Kerr Forster, 18 Park Place, Cardiff CF1 3PD (☎ 0222 378781, fax 0222 388455, car 0836 335879)

SAINSBURY, Sir Robert; s of late John Benjamin Sainsbury, and late Mabel Miriam, *née* Van Den Bergh; *see also* Baron Sainsbury; *b* 24 Oct 1906; *Educ* Haileybury, Pembroke Coll Cambridge; *m* 1937, Lisa Ingeborg, *née* Van Den Bergh (cousin); 1 s, 2 da (1 da decd); *Career* J Sainsbury: joined 1930, dir 1934, jt gen mangr 1938, dep chm 1956, chm 1967, jt pres 1969-; former tstee and chm Tate Gallery, memb Arts Panel Arts Cncl until 1974, memb Mgmnt Ctee Courtauld Inst of Art 1979-82, hon fell Pembroke Coll Cambridge 1983; Hon Dr RCA 1976, Hon LittD UEA 1977, Hon LLD Univ of Liverpool 1988; 1967; FCA, Hon FRIBA 1986; kt 1967; *Style*— Sir Robert Sainsbury

SAINSBURY, Roger Norman; s of Cecil Charles Sainsbury (d 1989), of Hitchin, Herts, and Ivy Evelyn, *née* Pettengell; *b* 11 June 1940; *Educ* Eton, Keble Coll Oxford (MA); *m* 16 May 1969, Susan Margaret, da of Henry William Higgs (d 1981); *Career* chartered engr; dir John Mowlem & Co plc 1982-; awarded Inst of Civil Engrs: George Stephenson medal, Reed and Mallik medal; FEng, FICE; *Recreations* gardening, theatre; *Style*— Roger N Sainsbury, Esq; 88 Dukes Ave, Muswell Hill, London N10 2QA; John Mowlem & Co plc, Lion Court, Swan St, Isleworth, Middx (☎ 081 568 9111)

SAINSBURY, Hon Timothy Alan Davan; MP (Cons Hove 1973-); yst s (by 1 m) of Baron Sainsbury; *b* 11 June 1932; *Educ* Eton, Worcester Coll Oxford (MA); *m* 26 April 1961, Susan Mary, da of Brig James Alastair Harry Mitchell, CBE, DSO; 2 s (Timothy b 1962, Alexander b 1968), 2 da (Camilla b 1962, Jessica b 1970); *Career* dir J Sainsbury plc 1962-83; PPS to: sec state Environment 1979-83, Sec State Def 1983; asst govt whip 1983-, Lord Cmmr (Govt Whip) 1985-87, Parly under sec of State for Def Procurement at MOD 1987-89; Parly under sec of state FCO 1989-90, Min for Trade 1990-; memb Cncl of RSA 1981-83; hon fell Worcester Coll Oxford 1982; *Style*— The Hon Timothy Sainsbury, MP; House of Commons, London SW1

SAINSBURY OF PRESTON CANDOVER, Baron (Life Peer UK 1989), of Preston Candover, Co Hants; Sir John Davan Sainsbury; eldest s (by 1 m) of Baron Sainsbury (Life Peer), *qv*, of Drury Lane; *b* 2 Nov 1927; *Educ* Stowe, Worcester Coll Oxford; *m* 8 March 1963, Anya (Anya Linden, the Royal Ballet ballerina), da of George Charles Eltenton; 2 s (Hon John Julian b 1966, Hon Mark Leonard b 1969), 1 da (Hon Sarah Jane b 1964); *Career* chm J Sainsbury plc 1969- (dir 1958-, vice chm 1967-69); chm Royal Opera House Covent Garden 1987- (dir 1969-85, tst dir 1974-84 and 1987-), cncl of Friends of Covent Garden 1969- (chm 1969-81); dir The Economist 1972-80; tstee: National Gallery 1976-83, Westminster Abbey Tst 1977-83, Tate Gallery 1982-83, Rhodes Tst 1984-; govr Royal Ballet Sch 1965-76 and 1987-; jt hon treas European Movement 1972-75 (a pres 1975-89); memb: Cncl Retail Consortium 1975-79, Nat Ctee for Electoral Reform 1976-85, President's Ctee CBI 1982-84; assoc V & A 1976-85; fell Inst of Grocery Distribution 1973-; vice pres Contemporary Arts Soc 1984-, chm Benesh Inst of Choreology 1986-87; hon fell Worcester Coll Oxford 1982, hon bencher Inner Temple 1985, Hon DSc Econ (London) 1985; Albert Medallist RSA 1989; kt 1980; *Clubs* Garrick, The Athenaeum; *Style*— The Rt Hon Lord Sainsbury of Preston Candover; J Sainsbury plc, Stamford House, Stamford St, SE1 (☎ 071 921 6000)

SAINT, Dora Jessie; JP; da of Arthur Gunnis Shafe (d 1970), and Grace Lilian, *née* Read (d 1936); *b* 17 April 1913; *Educ* Bromley County Girls' Sch, Homerton Coll Cambridge; *m* 26 July 1940, Douglas Edward John Saint, s of Edward Saint (d 1935); 1 da (Jill b 1941); *Career* author aka Miss Read: teacher in Middx 1933-40, over thirty novels; contrib: Punch, Times Educnl Supplement, BBC; Soc of Authors; *Books* novels: Village School (1955), Village Diary (1957), Storm in the Village (1958), Thrush Green (1959), Fresh from the Country (1960), Winter in Thrush Green (1961), Miss Clare Remembers (1962), Chronicles of Fairacre (1963), Over the Gate (1964), Market Square (1965), Village Christmas (1966), Fairacre Festival (1968), News from Thrush Green (1970), Tiggy (1971), Emily Davis (1971), Tyler's Row (1972), The Christmas Mouse (1973), Farther Afield (1974), Battles at Thrush Green (1975), No Holly for Miss Quinn (1976), Village Affairs (1977), Return to Thrush Green (1978), The White Robin (1979), Village Centenary (1980), Gossip from Thrush Green (1981), Affairs at Thrush Green (1983), Summer at Fairacre (1984), At Home in Thrush Green (1985), The School at Thrush Green (1987), Mrs Pringle (1989), Friends at Thrush Green (1990); for children: Hobby Horse Cottage (1958), Hob and the Horse Bat (1965), The Red Bus Series (1965); non-fiction: Country Bunch (1963), Miss Read's Country Cooking (1969); autobiography: A Fortunate Grandchild (1982), Time Remembered (1986); *Recreations* reading, theatre-going; *Style*— Mrs Dora Saint, JP; c/o Michael Joseph Ltd, 27 Wrights Lane, London W8 5TZ

SAINT, Lady (Josephine Sylvia) Rose; *née* Chetwynd-Talbot; da (by 1 m) of late 21 Earl of Shrewsbury and Waterford; *b* 23 May 1940; *m* 1965, (Stafford) Antony Saint, yr s of Stafford Eric Saint, CVO, FRCS, MRCP (d 1988); 1 s, 2 da; *Style*— The Lady Rose Saint

SAINT BRIDES, Baroness; Geneviève Christiane; da of Robert Henri Houdin (d 1960); *m* 1, Prof Reymond Sarasin (decd); m 2, 1968, as his 2 w, Baron Saint Brides, GCMG, CVO, MBE, PC (Life Peer, d 1989); *Style*— The Rt Hon the Lady Saint Brides; Cap Saint-Pierre, 83990 Saint-Tropez, France

ST ALBANS, Archdeacon of; *see*: Davies, Ven Philip Bertram

ST ALBANS, 8 Bishop of (cr 1877) 1980-; Rt Rev John Bernard Taylor; s of George Ernest Taylor and Gwendoline Irene Taylor; *b* 6 May 1929; *Educ* Watford GS, Christ's Coll Cambridge, Jesus Coll Cambridge (MA); *m* 1956, Linda Courtenay, da of Allan Dearden Barnes (d 1976); 1 s, 2 da; *Career* former examining chaplain to Bishop of Chelmsford, archdeacon of W Ham 1975-80, Lord High Almoner to HM the Queen 1988-, took seat House of Lords 1985; author; *Books* A Christian's Guide to the Old Testament, Tyndale Commentary on Ezekiel, Understanding the Old Testament: the Minor Prophets, Preaching through the Prophets; *Style*— The Rt Rev the Bishop of St Albans; Abbey Gate House, St Albans, Herts (☎ 0727 53305)

ST ALBANS, 14 Duke of (E 1684); Murray de Vere Beauclerk; also Baron Hedington and Earl of Burford (E 1676), Baron Vere of Hanworth (GB 1750); Hereditary Grand Falconer and Hereditary Registrar of Court of Chancery; s of 13 Duke of St Albans, OBE (d 1988), and his 1 w, Nathalie Chatham (d 1985), da of Percival Walker; gggggs of 1 Duke of St Albans, who was natural s of King Charles II and Eleanor (Nell) Gwynn; *b* 19 Jan 1939; *Educ* Tonbridge; *m* 1, 31 Jan 1963 (m dis 1974), Rosemary Frances, o da of Francis Harold Scoones, MRCS, LRCP, JP; 1 s (Earl of Burford), 1 da (Lady Emma Caroline de Vere b 22 July 1963); m 2, 1974, Cynthia Theresa Mary, da of late Lt-Col William James Holdsworth Howard, DSO, and former w of late Sir Anthony Robin Maurice Hooper, 2 Bt; *Heir* s, Earl of Burford, *qv*; *Career* Govr-Gen Royal Stuart Soc; Freeman of City of London, Liveryman of the Drapers' Co; FCA; *Clubs* Hurlingham; *Style*— His Grace the Duke of St Albans; 3 St George's Ct, Gloucester Rd, London SW7 (☎ 071 589 1771); Cranbourne Alley, Cranbourn St, London WC2 (☎ 071 287 6024)

ST ALBANS, Suzanne, Duchess of; Suzanne Marie Adèle; *née* Fesq; da of late Emile William Fesq, of Le Mas Mistral, Vence, France; *m* 19 March 1947, as his 2 w, 13 Duke of St Albans, OBE (d 1988); 3 s, 1 da (and 1 da decd); *Career* author and painter; *Style*— Her Grace Suzanne, Duchess of St Albans; 207 Park Palace, Monte Carlo, Monaco (☎ 93 50 87 39)

ST ALDWYN, 2 Earl (UK 1915); Sir Michael John Hicks Beach; 10 Bt (E 1619), PC (1959), GBE (1980, KBE 1964), TD (1949), JP (Glos 1952), DL (Glos 1950); also Viscount St Aldwyn (UK 1906), Viscount Quenington (UK 1915); s of Viscount Quenington (ka 1916, s of 1 Earl, Chllr of Exchequer 1885-86 and 1895-1902) by his w Marjorie, da of Henry Dent Brocklehurst, bro of 1 and last Baron Ranksborough; suc gf 1916; *b* 9 Oct 1912; *Educ* Eton, Ch Ch Oxford; *m* 1948, Diana Mary Christian, formerly w of Maj Richard Smyly and da of late Henry Mills (gs of 1 Baron Hillingdon); 3 s; *Heir* s, Viscount Quenington, *qv*; *Career* sits as Conservative peer in House of Lords; Parly sec Miny of Agric Fish and Food 1954-58; oppn chief whip House of Lords 1964-70 and 1974-78, govt chief whip 1958-64 and 1970-74; Capt Hon Corps of Gentlemen-at-Arms 1958-64 and 1970-74, Vice Lord Lieut of Glos 1981-87; GStJ (chllr 1978-87); *Recreations* shooting, fishing; *Clubs* Pratt's, Carlton, Royal Yacht Squadron; *Style*— The Rt Hon the Earl St Aldwyn, PC, GBE, TD, JP, DL; Williamstrip Park, Cirencester, Glos GL7 5AT (☎ 028 575 226); 13 Upper Belgrave St, London SW1X 8BA (☎ 071 235 8464)

ST ANDREWS, Earl of; George Philip Nicholas Windsor; er s and h of HRH The Duke of Kent, KG, GCMG, GCVO (*see Royal Family*); *b* 26 June 1962; *Educ* Eton, Downing Coll Camb; *m* 9 Jan 1988, Sylvana (b 28 May 1957), former w of John Paul Jones, and da of Max(imilian) Tomaselli and Josiane Preschez; 1 s; *Heir* s, Edward Edmund Maximilian George Windsor, Lord Downpatrick b 2 Dec 1988; *Style*— Earl of St Andrews

ST ANDREWS AND EDINBURGH, Archbishop of (RC) 1985-; Most Rev Keith (Michael) Patrick O'Brien; s of Mark Joseph O'Brien, DSM (d 1988), of Edinburgh, and Alice Mary, *née* Moriarty (d 1955); *b* 17 March 1938; *Educ* St Patrick's HS Dumbarton, Holy Cross Acad Edinburgh, Univ of Edinburgh (BSc), St Andrews Coll Drygrange, Moray House Coll of Educn (Dip Ed); *Career* Holy Cross Parish Edinburgh 1965-66, sch chaplain and teacher St Columba's Secdy Sch Dunfermline 1966-71; asst priest: St Patrick's Parish Kilsyth 1972-75, St Mary's Bathgate 1975-78; spiritual dir St Andrew's Coll Drygrange 1978-80, rector St Mary's Coll Blairs 1980-85; *Recreations* cycling, hill walking; *Clubs* New (Edinburgh); *Style*— The Most Rev the Archbishop of St Andrews and Edinburgh; St Bennet's, 42 Greenhill Gardens, Edinburgh EH10 4BJ (☎ 031 447 3337); Diocesan Centre, 106 Whitehouse Loan, Edinburgh EH9 1BD (☎ 031 452 8244)

ST ANDREWS, DUNKELD AND DUNBLANE, Bishop of 1969-; Rt Rev Michael Geoffrey Hare Duke; s of Arthur Robert Aubrey Hare Duke (d 1972), of United Service Club, Calcutta, India, and Dorothy Lee, *née* Holmes (d 1967); *b* 28 Nov 1925; *Educ* Bradfield Coll Berks, Trinity Coll Oxford, Westcott House Cambridge (MA); *m* 6 July 1949, Grace Lydia Frances McKean, da of Rev Walter Edward Fagan Dodd (d 1971); 1 s (Barnabas Martin b 1954), 3 da (Phillida Frances b 1950, Teresa Mary b 1956, Hilary Margaret b 1958); *Career* Sub Lt RNVR 1944-46; ordained: deacon 1952, priest 1953; curate St John's Wood Church 1952-56, vicar St Mark's Bury 1956-62, pastoral dir Clinical Theol Assoc 1962-64 (pastoral conslt 1964-69), vicar St Paul's Daybrook 1964-69, OCF E Midlands Dist HQ 1968-69; chm: Scottish Assoc for Mental Health 1978-85, Scottish Pastoral Assoc 1970-74; pres Br Region Christian Peace Conf 1982-, vice pres Scottish Inst of Human Relations 1974-76; *Books* The Caring Church (jtly, 1963), First Aid in Counselling (jtly, 1968), Understanding the Adolescent (1969), The Break of Glory (1970), Freud (1972), Good News (1976), Stories, Signs and Sacraments in the Emerging Church (1982); contrib to: Expository Times, Blackfriars, New Christian, Church Quarterly Review, Church Times, Contact; *Recreations* broadcasting, journalism, walking; *Style*— The Rt Rev the Bishop of St Andrews, Dunkeld and Dunblane; Bishop's House, Fairmount Road, Perth PH2 7AP (☎ 0738 21580)

ST AUBYN, Hon Giles Rowan; LVO (1977); yst s of 3 Baron St Levan (d 1978), and Hon Clementina Gwendolen Catharine, *née* Nicolson, da of 1 Baron Carnock; *b* 11 March 1925; *Educ* Wellington, Univ of Glasgow, Trinity Coll Oxford; *Career* author; FRSL; *Books* Macaulay (1952), A Victorian Eminence (1957), The Art of Argument (1957), The Royal George (1963), A World to Win (1968), Infamous Victorians (1971), William of Gloucester: Pioneer Prince (1977), Edward VII, Prince and King (1979), The Year of Three Kings (1983); *Clubs* Beefsteak, The Royal Over-Seas League; *Style*— The Hon Giles St Aubyn, LVO; Cornwall Lodge, Cambridge Park, St Peter Port, Guernsey CI (☎ 0481 724157)

ST AUBYN, Hon (Oliver) Piers; MC (1944); s of late 3 Baron St Levan and Hon Clementina, *née* Nicolson, da of 1 Baron Carnock and sis of Harold Nicolson, the writer (*see* Nigel Nicolson); hp of bro, 4 Baron St Levan, DSC; *b* 12 July 1920; *Educ* Wellington, St James's Sch Maryland USA; *m* 1948, Mary Bailey (d 1987), da of Bailey Southwell, of Olievenhoortpoort S Africa; 2 s (James b 1950, Nicholas b 1955) 1 da (Fiona); *Career* served WWII, Capt 60 Rifles and Parachute Regt (despatches); memb Stock Exchange 1949-; ptnr W Greenwell & Co 1957-78; High Sheriff E Sussex 1982-83; *Clubs* House of Lords Yacht, Brooks's; *Style*— The Hon Piers St Aubyn, MC; Hogus House, Ludgvan, Penzance, Cornwall TR20 8EZ (☎ 0736 740822)

ST AUBYN, Maj Thomas Edward; DL (1984); Maj; s of Capt The Hon Lionel St Aubyn, MVO (d 1964), and Lady Mary, *née* Parker (d 1932); *b* 13 June 1923; *Educ* Eton; *m* 21 Nov 1953 Henrietta Mary, da of Sir Henry Gray Studholme, 1 Bt, CVO (d 1987); 3 da (Sarah b 1955, Caroline b 1957, Clare b 1962); *Career* serv in KRRC 1941-62, Italian Campaign 1944-45, seconded to Sudan Def Force in rank of Bimbashi 1948-52, instr RMA Sandhurst 1955-56; ldr of Tibesti Mountain Expedition 1957 and other Sahara Expdn 1963-71; FRGS (1961), High Sheriff of Hants 1979-80, memb of HM Body Guard of the Hon Corps of Gentlemen at Arms 1973, Clerk of the Cheque and Adj 1986-, Lt 1990-; *Recreations* shooting, fishing, skiing, stalking, riding; *Clubs* Army and Navy; *Style*— Maj Thomas E St Aubyn; Dairy House Farm, Ashford Hill, Newbury, Berks RG15 8BL (☎ 0635 298493)

ST CLAIR, William; *b* 7 Dec 1937; *Educ* Edinburgh Acad, St John's Coll Oxford; 2 da (Anna b 1967, Elisabeth b 1970); *Career* under sec HM Treasy, served Admiralty and FCO, regular writer for Financial Times; writer; *Books* Lord Elgin and the Marbles (1967, 2 edn 1983), That Greece Might Still Be Free (1972), Trelawny (1978), Policy Evaluation: A Guide For Managers (1988), The Godwins and the Shelleys: The Biography of a Family (1989); memb Exec Ctee and chm Writers-in-Prison Ctee Eng Centre of Int PEN, chm (later vice pres) Byron Soc; fell All Souls Coll Oxford 1992- (visiting fell 1981-82), visiting fell Huntington Library Calif 1985; FRSL; *Awards* Heinemann prize for lit 1973, Time Life award for Br non-fiction 1990; *Recreations* old books, Scottish mountains; *Clubs* Athenaeum; *Style*— William St Clair; 52 Eaton Place, London SW1X 8AL (☎ 071 235 8329); Literary agent: Deborah Rogers, 20 Powis Mews, London W11

ST CLAIR-FORD, Capt Sir Aubrey; 6 Bt (GB 1793), DSO (and Bar 1942), RN; s of late Anson St Clair St Clair-Ford (s of late Capt St Clair St Clair-Ford, s of 2 Bt), and late Isabella Maria (Elsie), *née* Adams; suc kinsman, Sir (Francis Charles) Rupert Ford, 5 Bt, 1948; *b* 29 Feb 1904; *Educ* RNC Osborne, RNC Dartmouth; *m* 1945, Anne, da of Harold Cecil Christopherson; 1 s, 1 da; *Heir* s, James Anson St Clair-Ford; *Career* Cdr RN 1939, Capt HMS Kipling Ops Atlantic (despatches), Crete and Med 1942 (sunk by enemy action), Capt HMS Belfast during Korean War (despatches twice, offr American Legion of Merit) 1951-52, ret Capt 1955; Tarmac Civil Engineering Ltd 1955-69; *Style*— Capt Sir Aubrey St Clair-Ford, Bt, DSO, RN; Corner House, Sandle Copse, Fordingbridge, Hants (☎ 6523 28)

ST CLAIR-FORD, James Anson; s and h of Capt Sir Aubrey St Clair-Ford, 6 Bt, DSO, RN; *b* 16 March 1952; *Educ* Wellington, Univ of Bristol; *m* 1, 1977 (m dis 1985), Jennifer Margaret, da of Cdre J Robin Grindle, RN; m 2, 1987 Mary Anne, da of His Hon Judge Blaker, QC, DL; *Style*— James Anson St Clair-Ford, Esq; 161 Sheen Lane, London SW14

ST CLAIRE, Marian (Mrs Michael Beare); da of Matthew William Allsopp of 237 Leyland Lane, Leyland, Lancashire and Margaret Taylor; *b* 11 May 1946; *Educ* Wellfield Secdy Sch Leyland Lancs, Loretto Sch of Dance Southport Lancs, Ballet Rambert Sch London; *m* 2 Aug 1985, Michael Walter Beare, s of Douglas Charles Beare; *Career* ballet dancer; soloist: Ballet Rambert 1966-67 (former memb Corps de Ballet), The Cape Town Ballet Co S Africa 1967-69 (roles danced incl: Bluebird Pas de Deux, Peasant Pas de Trois and Neopolitan Danc (Swan Lake), The Misfit (leading role created by Gary Burn)); princ dancer The Scottish Ballet (formerly Western Ballet Co) 1969-75 (roles danced incl: Beauty (Beauty and the Beast), Giselle, Sugar Plum Fairy (The Nutcracker), The Sylph (La Sylphide), Antonia (Tales of Hoffman), Columbia (Le Carnival)); New London Ballet 1975-76 (roles danced incl: Desdemona (Othello), Elgie Pas de Deux, Faust Variations, Soft Blue Shadows); ballerina Dance Margot Fonteyn's Farewell tour of UK 1976-77, guest ballerina Nat Ballet of Rhodesia 1977, London Festival Ballet 1977-78 (roles danced incl: Bluebird Pas de Deux (Rudolf Nureyev's Sleeping Beauty), Pasant Pas de Deux (Giselle)); guest ballerina Northern Ballet 1978 (danced lead roles in Giselle, Les Sylphides and Cinderella), ballerina Harold King's Lunch Hour Ballet (Arts Theatre London) 1978, fndr, prima ballerina and asst artistic dir London City Ballet Co 1979- (leading roles danced incl: Carmen, Swan Lake, La Sylphide, Coppélia, Giselle, Cinderella); performed as guest artist in Canada, Tokyo, Zimbabwe, Stockholm and at Chicago, Cuba, Poland, Spain and Rumenia Dance Festivals; guest ballerina Wayne Sleep's Hot Shoe Show (London Palladium), Sleep with Friends, Bits and Pieces and World of Dance 1989; *Recreations* singing, cooking and entertaining, fashion, walking; *Style*— Ms Marian St Claire; The Garden Flat, 11A Inderwick Rd, Hornsey, London N8 9LB (☎ 081 341 1272); London City Ballet, London Studio Centre, 42-50 York Way, London N1 (☎ 071 837 3133, fax 071 837 3248)

ST CYRES, Viscount; John Stafford Northcote; s and h of 4 Earl of Iddesleigh; *b* 15 Feb 1957; *Educ* Downside, RAC Cirencester; *m* 14 May 1983, Fiona Caroline Elizabeth, da of Paul Alan Campbell Wakefield, of Barcelona, Spain; 1 s (Thomas Stafford b 1985), 1 da (Elizabeth Rose Adèle b 10 April 1989); *Heir* s, Hon Thomas Stafford Northcote, b 5 Aug 1985; *Career* farmer; *Recreations* shooting, sailing; *Style*— Viscount St Cyres; Lloyds Bank, 234 High St, Exeter, Devon

ST DAVIDS, 2 Viscount (UK 1918); Sir Jestyn Reginald Austen Plantagenet Philipps; 14 Bt (E 1621); also Baron Strange of Knokin (E 1299), Baron Hungerford (E 1426), Baron de Moleyns (E 1445); s of 1 Viscount (s of Rev Sir James Philipps, 12 Bt, and Hon Mary, da of Rev the Hon Samuel Best and sis of 5th Baron Wynford) and Baroness Strange of Knokin, Hungerford and de Moleyns in her own right, she being da of late Maj the Hon Paulyn Francis Cuthbert Rawdon-Hastings (bro of 11 Earl of Loudoun); suc to Viscountcy 1938, to mother's Baronies 1974; *b* 19 Feb 1917; *Educ* Eton, Trinity Cambridge; *m* 1, 1938 (m dis 1954), Doreen Guinness, *née* Jowett (d 1956); 1 s, 4 da; m 2, 1954 (m dis 1959), Elisabeth Joyce, *née* Woolf; m 3, 1959, Evelyn Marjorie, da of late Dr John Harris of Bray, Berks; *Heir* s, Hon Colwyn Philipps; *Career* sits as Independent in House of Lords; Lt RNVR; *Style*— The Rt Hon The Viscount St Davids; 15 St Mark's Crescent, Regent's Park, London NW1 (☎ 071 485 9953)

ST EDMUNDSBURY AND IPSWICH, Bishop of 1986-; Rt Rev John Dennis; patron of sixty-one livings, three Archdeaconries and twenty-four honorary Canonries; the See was founded 1914; s of Hubert Ronald Dennis (d 1990), of 4 Park Rd, Ipswich, and Evelyn Neville-Polley (d 1982); *b* 19 June 1931; *Educ* Rutlish Sch Merton, St Catharine's Coll Cambridge (MA); *m* 28 Aug 1956, Dorothy Mary, da of Godfrey Parker Hinnels (d 1975); 2 s (John David b 1959, Peter Hugh b 1962); *Career* RAF 1950-51; curate: St Bartholomew's Armley Leeds 1956-60, Kettering 1960-62; vicar: the Isle of Dogs 1962-71, John Keble Mill Hill 1971-79; area dean W Barnet 1979-86, prebendary St Paul's Cathedral 1977-79, bishop suffragan Knaresborough 1979-86; diocesan dir of Ordinands Diocese of Ripon 1980-86, episcopal guardian of Anglican Focolarini 1981-, chaplain Third Order of Soc of St Francis 1989-; co chm Anglican-Oriental Orthodox forum 1989-, english ctee Anglican-RC Relations 1989-; *Recreations* cycling, walking, gardening, wood carving, reading; *Clubs* RAF; *Style*— The Rt Rev the Bishop of St Edmundsbury and Ipswich; Bishop's House, 4 Park Rd, Ipswich IP1 3ST (☎ 0473 252829)

ST GEORGE, Charles Reginald; s of William Acheson St George, of Morecombe, Lancs, and Heather Atwood, *née* Brown (d 1978); *b* 20 April 1955; *Educ* Henley GS, Univ of Exeter (BA), Queens Univ Kingston Ontario Canada (MA); *m* 19 July 1980 (m dis 1989); 1 s (Michael John b 31 Dec 1985), 1 da (Imogen Margaret b 15 Jan 1984); *Career* CBI: sec Smaller Firms Cncl 1979-82, head of secretariat 1982-83, account mangr Ian Greer Assocs Ltd 1983-87, md Profile Political Relations Ltd 1989-90 (dir 1987-88), dir Political Planning Servs Ltd 1990; prospective Lib parly candidate Guildford 1980-82, Lib Alliance borough cncllr Guildford 1983-87; *Recreations* golf, tennis and skiing; *Style*— Charles St George, Esq; 107 Biggin Hill, Upper Norwood, London SE19 3HX (☎ 081 764 3155); Political Planning Services, Premier House, 10 Greycoat Place, London SW1 1SB (☎ 071 222 3599, fax 071 222 8051, car 0836 611504)

ST GEORGE, George Bligh; s of Sir Theophilus St George, 6, Bt; hp of bro, Rev Sir Denis Howard St George, 8 Bt; *b* 23 Sept 1908; *Educ* Univ of Natal (BA); *m* 1935, Mary Somerville, da of Francis John Sutcliffe; 2 s, 3 da; *Career* served WWII Lt Technical Services Corps; *Style*— George St George Esq; 4 Eastwood, 30 Springfield Cres, Durban 4001, Natal, S Africa

ST GEORGE, Lady Henrietta Fortune Doreen; *née* FitzRoy; da of 11 Duke of Grafton, KG; *b* 1949; *m* 1979, Edward G P St George; 1 s (Henry Edward Hugh b 1983); 1 da (Katherine Helen Cecilia b 1984); *Style*— The Lady Henrietta St George; 1 Chester Sq, London SW1; P O Box F2666, Grand Bahama Island, Bahamas

ST GERMANS, Bridget, Countess of; (Mary) Bridget; o child of Sir (Thomas) Shenton Whitelegge Thomas, GCMG, OBE (d 1962), and Lucy Marguerite, *née* Montgomery; *m* 1 (m dis), Lt-Col Jack Leslie Larry Lotinga, MC; m 2, 15 Nov 1965, as his 3 w, 9 Earl of St Germans (d 1988); *Style*— The Rt Hon Bridget, Countess of St Germans; Penmadown, St Clement, Truro, Cornwall TR1 1SZ

ST GERMANS, Jacquetta, Countess of; Hon Jacquetta Jean Fredricka; *née* Lampson; da of 1 Baron of Killearn, GCMG, CB, MVO, PC (d 1964); *m* 9 Oct 1964 (m dis 1990), 10 Earl of St Germans; 3 s; *Style*— Jacquetta, Countess of St Germans;

c/o Jacqueline, Lady Killearn, 23 Harley St, London W1

ST GERMANS, 10 Earl of (UK 1815); Peregrine Nicholas Eliot; also Baron Eliot (GB 1784); s of 9 Earl of St Germans (d 1988), by his 1 w Helen Mary (who d 1951, having m 2, 1947, Capt Ralph Benson, Coldstream Gds), da of Lt Charles Walters Villiers, CBE, DSO; *b* 2 Jan 1941; *Educ* Eton; *m* 9 Oct 1964 (m dis 1990), Hon Jacquetta Jean Fredricka Lampson, da of 1 Baron Killearn; 3 s (Lord Eliot, Hon Louis b 11 April 1968, Hon Francis b 16 Nov 1971); *Heir* s, Lord Eliot b 24 March 1966; *Career* landowner; patron of three livings; *Recreations* sitting still; *Clubs* Pratt's, The Cornish; *Style*— The Rt Hon the Earl of St Germans; Port Eliot, St Germans, Cornwall (☎ 0503 30211)

ST GERMANS, Bishop of 1985-; Rt Rev (John) Richard Allan Llewellin; s of John Clarence Llewellin, of Long Compton, Warwicks, and Margaret Gwenllian, *née* Low; *b* 30 Sept 1938; *Educ* Clifton Coll Bristol, Fitzwilliam Coll Cambridge (MA), Westcott House Theol Coll; *m* 24 July 1965, Jennifer Sally, da of Edward Terence House (d 1981), of Chard, Somerset; 1 s (David b 1966), 2 da (Sarah b 1968, Helen b 1970); *Career* slr 1960-61; curate Radlett 1964-68, asst priest Johannesburg Cathedral 1968-71, vicar Waltham Cross 1971-79, rector Harpenden 1979-85; *Recreations* sailing, DIY; *Style*— The Rt Rev the Bishop of St Germans; 32 Falmouth Rd, Truro, Cornwall TR1 2HX (☎ 0872 73190, fax 0872 77883)

ST HELENS, 2 Baron (UK 1964); Richard Francis Hughes-Young; s of 1 Baron, sometime Dep Govt Ch Whip (d 1980), and Elizabeth, da of late Capt Richard Blakiston-Houston (ggs of Sir Matthew Blakiston, 2 Bt); *b* 4 Nov 1945; *Educ* Nautical Coll Pangbourne; *m* 1983, Mrs Emma R Talbot-Smith; 1 s, 1 da (b 1987); *Heir* s, Hon Henry Thomas Hughes-Young, b 7 March 1986; *Style*— The Rt Hon the Lord St Helens; Marchfield House, Binfield, Berks

ST JOHN, Edmund Oliver; WS; s of late Col Edmund Farquhar St John, CMG, DSO, s of late Rev the Hon Edmund Tudor St John (s of 14 Baron St John of Bletso) and late Henrietta, da of late Col James Dalmahoy, MVO, WS; hp of cous, 21 Baron; *b* 13 Oct 1927; *Educ* Trinity Coll Glenalmond; *m* 1959, Elizabeth Frances, da of Lt-Col H R Nicholl, *qv*; 1 s (Charles b 1963), 2 da (Nicola b 1960, Emma b 1968); *Career* dir Beinn Bhuidhe Holdings Ltd; *Clubs* New (Edinburgh); *Style*— Edmund O St John, Esq, WS; Spittal, Biggar, Lanarkshire; 11 Atholl Crescent, Edinburgh EH3 8HE (☎ 031 229 1212)

ST JOHN, Hon Helen Evelyn; da (by 1 m) of late 18 Baron St John; *b* 1906; *Style*— The Hon Helen St John; c/o Balfour & Manson, Solicitors, 58 Frederick St, Edinburgh EH2 1LS

ST JOHN, Hon Henry Fitzroy; s (by 1 m) and h of 7 Viscount Bolingbroke and St John; *b* 18 May 1957; *Style*— The Hon Henry St John

ST JOHN, Cdr Michael Beauchamp; DSC (1943); s of Maj Beauchamp Tudor St John (d 1965), of Aberdeenshire, and Madeleine Ethel, *née* Goodbody (d 1982); *b* 13 May 1915; *Educ* RNC Dartmouth; *m* 7 Oct 1944, Pamela Patience, da of Sir Arthur Guinness, KCMG (d 1951), of Hants; 1 s (Andrew b 1945), 2 da (Clare b 1947, Hermione b 1951); *Career* joined RNC Dartmouth 1939, appt to Submarine Serv 1936, served throughout 1939-46 war (N Sea, Med, SE Asia, Far East), ret 1955; dir own private exempt co until 1962, staff mangr Nat Employers Mutual Assoc 1963-74; *Books* A Tale of Two Rivers (1989); *Recreations* shooting, walking, drinking in good company; *Style*— Cdr Michael St John, DSC; The Old Thatch, Heyshott, Midhurst, W Sussex GU29 0DJ (☎ 0730 813329)

ST JOHN, (Oliver) Peter; s of Lt-Col Frederick Oliver St John, DSO, MC (d 1977) and gs of late Sir Frederick Robert St John, KCMG (yst s of late Hon Ferdinand St John, 2 s of 3 Viscount Bolingbroke and St John); through Sir Frederick's w, Isabella Fitz-Maurice (gda of 5 Earl of Orkney), Peter is hp to his 2 cous once removed, 8 Earl of Orkney; *b* 27 Feb 1938; *m* 1, 1963 (m dis 1985), Mary Juliet, da of W G Scott-Brown; 1 s (Oliver Robert b 1969), 3 da (Juliet Elizabeth b 1964, Nicola Jane b 1966, Lucy Margaret b 1972); m 2, 1985, Barbara Huck; 1 step s (Anthony St John), 3 step da (Dawn Marie Huck, Caroline Jane Huck, Erin Katherine Huck); *Career* assoc prof of political sci Unvi of Manitoba; *Style*— Peter St John Esq; 200 Dromore Ave, Winnipeg, Manitoba, Canada R3M 0J3

ST JOHN, Hon Mrs (Sally Hayter); *née* Rootes; da of 2 Baron Rootes; *b* 12 Sept 1947; *m* 1968, Andrew St John, s of Cdr Michael St John, DSC, RN (ret), of Midhurst (gn of 15 and 16 Barons St John of Bletso) by Pamela, da of Sir Arthur Guinness, KCMG; *Style*— The Hon Mrs St John; Culnacloich, Glenalmond, Perth

ST JOHN, Hon Mrs (Vanessa Marguerite); *née* Palmer; da of 3 Baron Palmer, OBE, *qv*; *b* 15 Dec 1954; *m* 1977, Robert William St John, s of Lt-Col Carl St John, of Glebe Manor, Pook Lane, Havant, Hants; 1 s, 3 da; *Style*— The Hon Mrs St John; 20 Sudbrooke Rd, London SW12 8TG

ST JOHN-BROOKS, Maj Julian Gordon de Renzy; s of Ralph Terence St John-Brooks (d 1963), of Dublin, and Julia Margaret, *née* Gordon (d 1965); *b* 31 Aug 1919; *Educ* Cheam Sch, Harrow, RMA, Woolwich; *m* 5 Jan 1946, Diana, da of Maj Henry Wintersladen, TD (d 1959), of Marton-in-Cleveland; 1 s (Justin b 1960), 3 da (Caroline b 1947, Irena b 1949, Katharine b 1952); *Career* cmmnd RA 1939, WWII served M East and Italy 1941-45, WO 1945, Maj 1952, Staff Coll, Tech Staff Coll, Tech SO Min of Supply 1946-55, ret 1955; service mangr (Guided Weapons) Bristol Aeroplane Co 1955-60, poultry farmer 1960-65, restaurateur-cook 1965-90; CEng, MRAeS; *Recreations* gardening, reading; *Clubs* Gloucestershire CC; *Style*— Maj Julian St John-Brooks; The Manor House, Gaunts Earthcott, Almondsbury, Bristol BS12 4JR (☎ 0454 772225)

ST JOHN OF BLETSO, 21 Baron (E 1559); Sir Anthony Tudor St John; 18 Bt (E 1660); s of 20 Baron, TD (d 1978), and Katharine Emily, *née* von Berg; *b* 16 May 1957; *Educ* Diocesan Coll Cape Town, Cape Town Univ SA (BA, BSc, BProc), London Univ (LLM); *Heir* cous, Edmund St John; *Career* sits as Independent Peer in Lords (parly interests: foreign affairs, environment, financial and legal services), treas All Party Human Rights Gp; solicitor and stockbroker; conslt to Smith New Court plc London; *Recreations* tennis, golf, windsurfing, running; *Clubs* Western Province Sports, Royal Cape; *Style*— The Rt Hon The Lord St John of Bletso; By-the-Sea, Kalk Bay 7975, Cape Town South Africa

ST JOHN OF BLETSO, Baroness; Katharine; da of late Alfred von Berg; *m* 1955, 20 Baron St John of Bletso (d 1978); *Style*— The Rt Hon the Lady St John of Bletso; c/o Syfret's Trust Co Ltd, 24 Wale st, PO Box 206, Cape Town 8001, S Africa

ST JOHN OF FAWSLEY, Baron (Life Peer UK 1987), of Preston Capes, Co Northants; Norman Antony Francis St John-Stevas; PC (1979); s of late Stephen Stevas and Kitty St John O'Connor; *b* 18 May 1929; *Educ* Ratcliffe, Fitzwilliam Coll Cambridge, Christ Church Oxford; *Career* called to the Bar 1952; former jurisprudence tutor; political corr The Economist 1959; author; contested (C) Dagenham 1951, MP (C) Chelmsford 1964-87; under sec of state for Educn 1972-73, Min of State for Educn and Science with special responsibility for the Arts 1973-74, oppn spokesman the Arts 1974 and memb Shadow Cabinet 1974-79; Min Arts 1979, leader House of Commons and chllr of Duchy of Lancaster 1979-81; vice-pres Theatres Advsy Cncl 1983-; former pres Cambridge Union; OStJ 1980, Order of Merit (Italy) 1965, KSLJ 1963, FRSL 1966; *Clubs* White's, Garrick, Pratt's; *Style*— The Rt Hon the Lord St John of Fawsley, PC; 47 Ennismore Gardens, London SW7; The Old Rectory, Preston Capes, Daventry, Northamptonshire

ST JOHN PARKER, Michael; s of Rev Canon John William Parker, of Lincoln, and Doris Edna, *née* Nurse; *b* 21 July 1941; *Educ* Stamford Sch, King's Coll, Cambridge; *m* 5 Aug 1965, Annette Monica, da of Leonard Drake Ugle (d 1976), of West Wickham, Kent; 2 s (Sebastian b 1969, Dominic b 1972), 2 da (Arabella b 1966, Sophia b 1967); *Career* asst master: Sevenoaks Sch 1962-63, King's Sch Canterbury 1963-69, Winchester 1969-70; head history Winchester 1970-75, headmaster Abingdon Sch 1975- (schoolmaster student Ch Ch Oxford Trinity Term 1984); memb cncl Hansard Soc, chm Midland div HMC 1984, memb jt standing ctee Oxford and Cambridge Schs Examination Bd; govr: St Helen's Sch Abingdon 1975-83, Christ Church Cathedral Sch, Cokethorpe Sch, Joscas Prep Sch; *Books* The British Revolution - Social and Economic History 1750-1970 (co author 1972), Politics and Industry - the Great Mismatch (contrib 1979), author of numerous articles, pamphlets and reviews; *Recreations* mostly to do with buildings, books, music and gardens; *Clubs* East India, Leander; *Style*— Michael St John Parker, Esq; Lacies Court, Abingdon, Oxfordshire (☎ 0235 20 163); Abingdon School, Oxfordshire OX14 1DE (☎ 0235 21 563)

ST JOHN SUTTON, Dr Martin Graham; s of Dr John Sutton (d 1990), of Hertfordshire, and Phyllis Evelyn, *née* Fenner (d 1976); *b* 31 July 1945; *Educ* Highgate Sch London, Guy's Hosp London (MB BS); *m* (m dis), Dr Marianne Benichoux St John Sutton, da of Warren Shriver (d 1972); 2 da (Claire-Helene b 4 March 1983, Evelyn-Magali (twin)); *Career* clinical cardiology training Nat Heart Hosp and Brompton Hosp London 1972-76, res fell in physiology and biophysics Mayo Clinic Rochester Minnesota USA 1976-78, Univ of Pennsylvania Philedelphia USA 1979-84 (staff cardiologist, co-dir of non-invasive cardiac laboratories, asst prof of med), Brigham & Women's Hosp Harvard Med Sch Boston Mass USA 1984-90 (staff cardiologist, dir of non-invasive cardiology, assoc prof of med), conslt cardiologist Royal Brompton Nat Heart & Lung Hosp London 1990-; MRCP, FACC, memb American Heart Assoc; *Books* Textbook of Adult and Paediatric Echocardiography and Doppler (1989); author of numerous scientific articles; *Recreations* mountain walking, watercolours; *Style*— Dr Martin St John Sutton; 3A Neville St, London SW7 (☎ 071 581 1813); Royal Brompton, National Heart & Lung Hospital, Sydney St, London SW3 6HP (☎ 071 351 8609, fax 071 351 8637)

ST JOHNSTON, Andrew; s of Dr Adrian St Johnston (d 1955), and Eleanor Margaret, *née* Andrewes (d 1953); *b* 28 Aug 1922; *Educ* Charterhouse, Imperial Coll London (BSc); *m* 1, 1949 (m dis), Barbara, *née* Hemelryk; 2 da (Caroline b 1953, Harriet b 1955); m 2, 1958, Aldrina Nia (Dina), da of Clifford Vaughan (d 1985); *Career* WWII 1943-47 Lt Cdr RN served as radar offr; electronic engr Midgley Harmer Ltd 1947-49, Computing Div Elliott-Automation 1949-68 (project ldr for NRDC on 401 computer, the first plug-in unit machine), dir (formerly ptnr) Vaughan Systems & Programming Ltd 1968-; *Recreations* walking, countryside, food and drink, cooking; *Style*— Andrew St Johnston, Esq; Hedgegrove Farm, Pembridge Lane, Broxbourne, Herts EN10 7QR (☎ 0992 463054); Vaughan Systems & Programming Ltd, The Maltings, Hoe Lane, Ware, Herts SG12 9LR (☎ 0992 462282, telex 81516, fax 0992 460902)

ST JOHNSTON, Colin David; s of James Hallewell St Johnston, MC, TD, MA (d 1963), and Sheilagh Cassandra, *née* Davidson (d 1973); *b* 6 Sept 1934; *Educ* Shrewsbury, Lincoln Coll Oxford; *m* 1958, Valerie, da of John Thomas Gerald Paget (d 1969); 3 s, 1 da; *Career* Nat Serv N Staffs Regt 1953-55; md Ocean Cory Ltd 1976-85, dir Ocean Transport and Trading plc 1974-88 (dep chief exec 1985-88), non-exec dir FMC plc 1981-83, md Pro Ned Ltd 1989-; cncl memb: Royal Cwlth Soc for the Blind 1966-, Industl Soc 1981-; *Recreations* real tennis; *Clubs* MCC; *Style*— Colin St Johnston, Esq; 30 Fitzroy Rd, London NW1 8TY (☎ 071 722 5932); 1 Kingsway, London WC2B 6XF

ST JOHNSTON, Sir Kerry; s of George Eric St Johnston (d 1978), and Viola Rhona, *née* Moriarty; *b* 30 July 1931; *Educ* Eton, Worcester Coll Oxford (MA Jurisprudence); *m* 1, 25 Feb 1960, Judith Ann, da of Peter Nicholls (d 1972); 2 s (James b 1963, Rory Tilson b 1966), 1 da (Claire Marie b 1961); m 2, 1980, Charlotte Ann, da of John Scott Limnell Lyon (d 1942); *Career* mil serv XI Hussars (Lt) 1950-51; with Ocean Steamship Co 1955-76 (md 1963-68), fndr dir Overseas Containers 1965 (dep chm 1973-76), pres Private Investment Co for Asia Singapore 1977-81, chm P & O Containers Ltd (formerly Overseas Containers Ltd) 1982-89, md Diehl and St Johnston Ltd 1989-, chm Wilrig AS of Oslo 1989-; dir: Royal Inst 1972-76, Lloyds Bank Int 1983-86, P & O Steam Navigation Co 1986-89, Touche Remnant Investment Tst 1982-; kt 1988; *Recreations* fishing, racing, gardening; *Clubs* Boodles; *Style*— Sir Kerry St Johnston; 5/53 Drayton Gardens, London SW10; Beagle House, Braham St, London E1

ST LEVAN, Dowager Baroness; Hon Clementina Gwendolen Catharine; *née* Nicolson; da of 1 Baron Carnock (d 1928), and Catharine, *née* Hamilton (d 1951); sis of Sir Harold Nicolson (d 1968), the author; *b* 3 July 1896; *m* 6 Oct 1916, 3 Baron St Levan (d 1978); 3 s, 2 da; *Style*— The Rt Hon the Dowager Lady St Levan; Avallon, Green Lane, Marazion, Cornwall (☎ 0736 710 508)

ST LEVAN, 4 Baron (UK 1887); Sir John Francis Arthur St Aubyn; 5 Bt (UK 1866), DSC (1942), DL (Cornwall 1977); s of 3 Baron (d 1978), and Hon Clementina Gwendolen Catharine, *née* Nicolson, da of 1 Baron Carnock and sis of Harold Nicolson, the author; *b* 23 Feb 1919; *Educ* Eton, Trinity Coll Cambridge; *m* 1970, Susan, da of late Maj-Gen Sir John Noble Kennedy, GCMG, KCVO, KBE, CB, MC; *Heir* bro, Hon Piers St Aubyn, MC; *Career* slr 1948; Lt RNVR; landowner and farmer, co dir; High Sheriff of Cornwall 1974, fell of Royal Soc for Encouragement of Art; pres: London Cornish Assoc, St Ives Soc of Artists, YMCA Penzance, Friends of Plymouth Museum; vice pres: Royal Cornwall Agric Assoc, Royal Bath and West and Southern Counties Soc; *Clubs* Brooks's, Royal Yacht Squadron; *Style*— The Rt Hon the Lord St Levan, DSC, DL; St Michael's Mount, Marazion, Cornwall

ST MAUR, Edward Adolphus Ferdinand; s of Capt Frederick Percy St Maur (d 1975), and Hope Wilhelmina Albemarle, *née* Blakeney (d 1974); gggs of 12 Duke of Somerset and ggs of the Earl St Maur, he is a cousin of the present Duke of Somerset and the late Duke of Portland; *b* 26 May 1924; *Educ* Malvern, Sandhurst; *m* 11 March 1950, Sheila Matilda, da of Gen A V Hammond DSO (d 1980), of Ireland; 3 da (Caroline, Elizabeth, Philippa); *Career* Maj 17/21 Lancers 1941-59; past pres of Br Inst of Prof Photography; professional photographer; FBIPP, ARPS, MBKS, FRSA; *Recreations* travel, swimming, photography; *Clubs* Cavalry and Guards; *Style*— Edward St Maur, Esq; Flat 2, William IV Wing, Itton Court, Itton, Chepstow, Gwent (☎ 02912 79680); Town Gate House, Moor St, Chepstow, Gwent (☎ 0291 625329)

ST OSWALD, 5 Baron (UK 1885); Derek Edward Anthony Winn; DL; s of 3 Baron St Oswald (d 1956) and Eve Carew Green (d 1976); suc bro, 4 Baron, MC (d 1984); *b* 9 July 1919; *Educ* Stowe; *m* 1954, Charlotte Denise Eileen, da of Wilfrid Haig Loyd (d 1971), of Oakhill, Seaview, Isle of Wight; 1 s, 1 da; *Heir* s, Hon Charles Rowland Andrew Winn, *qv*; *Career* formerly Lt King's Royal Rifle Corps (Supp Reserve), Capt Parachute Regt (Regular Army Reserve) 1939-46; ADC to govr-gen of NZ 1943-45; substantive Capt Western Desert and N Africa (wounded); asst supt Malayan Police Force 1948-51; pres: S and W Yorks Br Legion, Wakefield Hospice Appeal Fund; *Books* I Served Caesar (1972); *Recreations* shooting, walking, horse racing; *Clubs* Lansdowne, Special Forces; *Style*— The Rt Hon Lord St Oswald, DL;

Nostell Priory, Wakefield, West Yorkshire; The Old Rectory, Bainton, Driffield, East Yorkshire YO25 9NG

ST PIERRE, Roger; s of Alexander Richard St Pierre, MBE, and Caroline Amelia Borrett (d 1985); *b* 8 Nov 1941; *Educ* Ilford County HS; *m* 10 Nov 1974, Lesley, da of Bernard Constantine, of Sheffield; 1 s (Richard b 1976), 2 da (Danielle b 1978, Nicole b 1979); *Career* author and journalist; editor: Disco International 1977-79, Voyager Magazine (British Midland in-flight Magazine); contrib to: Toyota Today, Motorway Express, London Evening Standard, The Dorchester Magazine, Travel GBI, Renaissance, The Times, Financial Weekly; PR mangr for: Diana Ross, Glen Campbell, Jerry Lee Lewis, Don Williams, Frankie Lane; author of nearly 1,000 record/album sleeve notes; broadcaster BBC and other broadcasting stations; cycle racer in many countries, mangr of int cycle teams; specialist writer on: travel, music, motoring, cycling and leisure; *Books incl:* Of The Bicycle (1973), The Rock Handbook (1986), Illustrated History of Black Music (1986), Marilyn Monroe (1987); *Recreations* cycling, music, travel; *Style—* Roger St Pierre, Esq; 24 Beauval Rd, Dulwich, London SE22 8UQ (☎ 081 693 6463, 081 299 0719)

ST VINCENT, 7 Viscount (UK 1801); Ronald George James Jervis; s of 6 Viscount (d 1940, himself ggs of 2 Viscount, who was in his turn n of 1 Viscount and Earl of St Vincent, whose title commemorated his victory over the Spaniards in 1797 despite being outnumbered 27 to 15 - the name title was chosen by George III himself; St Vincent, more modestly, had suggested Yarmouth and Orford, which did not call to mind his successful action) and Marion, *née* Broun; *b* 3 May 1905; *Educ* Sherborne; *m* 2 Oct 1945, Constance Phillida Anne, da of Lt-Col Robert Hector Logan, OBE, late Loyal Regt; 2 s, 1 da; *Heir* s, Hon Edward Jervis; *Career* served WW II, acting Lt-Cdr RNVR; *Style—* The Rt Hon the Viscount St Vincent; Les Charrieres, St Ouen, Jersey, CI

SAINTE CROIX, Geoffrey Ernest Maurice de; *b* 8 Feb 1910; *Educ* UCL (BA), Univ of Oxford (DLitt, MA); *m* 3 Sept 1959, Margaret, *née* Knight; 2 s; *Career* ancient historian: J H Gray Lectr Univ of Cambridge 1983, Gregynog Lectr Univ Coll of Wales Aberystwyth 1986, Townsend Lectr Cornell Univ USA 1988; contrib to numerous learned jls; fell: New Coll Oxford, UCL, memb Assoc of Univ Teachers, FBA; *Books* Studies in the History of Accounting (jtly, 1956), The Crucible of Christianity (jtly, 1969), The Origins of the Peloponnesian War (1972), Debts, Credits, Finance and Profits (jtly, 1974), Studies in Ancient Society (jtly, 1974), The Class Struggle in the Ancient Greek World, From the Archaic Age to the Arab Conquests (1981, revised edn 1983); *Style—* Geoffrey de Sainte Croix, Esq; Evenlode, Stonesfield Lane, Charlbury, Oxford OX7 3ER

SAINTY, John Christopher; KCB; s of Christopher Lawrence Sainty (d 1977), of Hassocks, Sussex, and Nancy Lee, *née* Miller (d 1945); *b* 31 Dec 1934; *Educ* Winchester, New Coll Oxford (MA); *m* 1965, (Elizabeth) Frances, da of Gp Capt Derek James Sherlock, OBE (d 1977); 3 s; *Career* clerk House of Lords 1959, private sec to ldr of House and chief whip 1963, clerk of journals 1965, research asst Inst of Historical Res 1970, reading clerk House of Lords 1974, clerk of the Parliaments 1983-; *Style—* Sir John Sainty, KCB; 22 Kelso Place, London W8 5QG; House of Lords, London SW1

SAKAKIBARA, Katsuro; s of Roichi Sakakibara (d 1953), and Kiku, *née* Oba (d 1939); *b* 30 Dec 1937; *Educ* Meiji Univ Tokyo (BA); *m* 11 March 1963, Kiyono, da of Masao Matsushita; 2 da (Sanae b 25 Jan 1965, Akiko b 26 Sept 1973); *Career* Matsushita Electrical Industrial Co Osaka Japan: joined 1960, rep Philippines 1964, sales dir Precision Electronics Corporation in Philippines 1967-71, exec advsr to Hagemeyer (Matsushita's distributor in Australia) 1971-76, gen mangr Asia/Oceania and E Asia Depts 1977-84; md Panasonic UK Ltd 1984-; *Recreations* golf, travelling, reading; *Style—* Katsuro Sakakibara, Esq; Panasonic UK Ltd, Panasonic House, Willoughby Rd, Bracknell, Berks RG12 4FP (☎ 0344 853104, fax 0344 861656, telex 847652)

SAKZEWSKI, Sir Albert; s of O T Sakzewski; *b* 12 Nov 1905; *Educ* Ipswich HS Qld; *m* 1935, Winifred May (d 1972), da of W P Reade; 2 s (Bryan Paul b 25 Feb 1939, Richard Anthony b 24 Feb 1941); *Career* CA, chm and govt nominee Totalisator Admin Bd Qld 1962-81, fndr Sir Albert Sakzewski Fndn; chm of dirs: Avanis Pty Ltd, Blend Investments Pty Ltd, Commercial Finance Pty Ltd, Queensland Securities Pty Ltd, Southern Cross Products Pty Ltd; tstee Tattersall's Club Brisbane; memb: Royal Cwlth Soc, Aust/Br Soc, Aust Ballet Fndn, Qd Art Gallery Fndn (fndr benefactor), fndr Sir Albert Sakzewski Fndn; FCA, FCPA; kt 1973; *Recreations* horse racing and breeding, golf, billiards (Aust Amateur Billards Champion 1932 with a then Aust record break of 206, Qld Amateur Billiards Champion 6 times), snooker (Qld Amateur Snooker Champion 8 times); *Clubs* Brisbane, Tattersall's (Brisbane, life memb), Queensland Turf, Tattersall's Racing (life memb), Brisbane Amateur Turf (life memb), Rockhampton Jockey (life memb), Southport Golf (life memb), Northcliffe Surf Life Saving Club (perpetual memb); *Style—* Sir Albert Sakzewski; Ilya Lodge, Rossiter Parade, Hamilton, Qld 4007, Australia; National Bank House, 255 Adelaide Street, Brisbane 4000

SALAKO, John Akin; s of Albert Akande Salako (d 1974), of Ilorin, Nigeria, and Jennifer Mary, *née* Fuller; *b* 11 Feb 1969; *Educ* Wildernesse Sch for Boys Sevenoaks; *Career* professional footballer; over 100 appearances Crystal Palace 1987- (debut v Barnsley 1987), 14 appearances on-loan Swansea City 1988; jr sport: Surrey football under 16, Kent cross country under 15, Kent CCC under 15; runners up FA Cup Crystal Palace 1990; *Recreations* golf, reading, cricket; *Style—* John Salako, Esq; Crystal Palace FC, Selhurst Park, London SE25 6PU (☎ 081 648 5893)

SALAM, Prof Abdus; Hon KBE (1989); *b* 29 Jan 1926; *Educ* Panjab Univ, St John's Coll Cambridge (BA Hons), Cavendish Lab Cambridge (PhD); *Career* prof physics Government Coll Lahore 1951-54, head dept mathematics Panjab Univ 1951-54, lectr Univ of Cambridge 1954-56, fndr and head dept theoretical physics Imperial Coll Univ of London 1957-, fndr and dir Int Centre for Theoretical Physics Trieste 1964-; scientific sec Geneva Conferences on Peaceful Uses of Atomic Energy 1955 and 1958; memb: bd govrs IAEA Vienna 1962-63, advsy ctee on science and technol UN 1971-72, UN panel and fndn ctee UN Univ 1970-73, advsy ctee UN Univ 1981-83, cncl Univ for Peace Costa Rica 1981-86; chm advsy panel on science technol and society UNESCO 1981; first pres: Third World Acad of Sciences (TWAS) 1983-, Third World Network of Scientific Orgns 1988-; memb: scientific cncl Stockholm Int Peace Res Inst (SIPRI) 1970-, scientific policy ctee CERN 1983-86, bd of dirs Beijir Inst Royal Swedish Acad of Sciences 1986-, South Cmmn 1987-; former vice pres IUPAP; received: seventeen awards in ten countries for contribs to physics 1958-83 (incl Nobel Prize for Physics 1979), seven medals for contribs towards peace and promotion of int scientific collaboration 1968-90, thirty eight Doctor Honoris Causa awards in twenty six countries; elected memb acads and socs in twenty three countries; published: 270 scientific papers on physics on elementary particles, numerous papers on scientific and educnl policies for developing countries; *Books* Symmetry Concepts in Modern Physics (1966), Aspects of Quantum Mechanics (1972), Science and Education in Pakistan (1987), A Man of Science (1987), Supergravity in Diverse Dimensions (1988), From a Life of Physics (1989), Unification of Fundamental Physics: The First of the 1988 Memorial Lectures (1990); *Style—* Prof Abdus Salam, KBE; Dept of Theoretical Physics, Imperial College of Science and Technol, University of London, London SW7; International Centre for Theoretical Physics, PO Box 586, 34100 Trieste, Italy

SALAMA, Nabil Youssef; s of Dr Youssef Salama (d 1985), and Malak Zaklama; *b* 5 Dec 1949; *Educ* Med Sch Univ of Cairo Egypt (MB BCh); *m* 30 Aug 1980, Susan Frances, da of James Willson Beale; 1 s (Adam b 5 Sept 1983), 2 da (Georgina b 8 March 1985, Helen Louise b 5 Sept 1990); *Career* conslt oto-laryngologist Lewisham and N Southwark and Greenwich Health Dists 1983-, private conslt Blackheath Hosp 1984-, surgical tutor Lewisham Hosp; author articles in various med jls; memb: BMA, RSM; BAOL, FRCS; *Style—* Nabil Salama, Esq; 7 Elm Rd, Beckenham, Kent BR3 4JB (☎ 081 658 3751); The Blackheath Hospital, 40-42 Lee Terrace, Blackheath, London SE3 9UD (☎ 081 318 7722, 081 852 8468, 267335 AMILDN G, 081 318 2542)

SALAMAN, Prof John Redcliffe; s of Arthur Gabriel Salaman, MB BCL, MRCS, LRCP (d 1964), and the Hon Nancy Adelaide, *née* Samuel; *b* 14 Oct 1937; *Educ* Bedales, Univ of Cambridge, The London Hosp (MA, MChir); *m* 4 Nov 1961, Patricia Faith, da of Edward George Burkett, of Antwerp, Belgium; 2 s (Robert Arthur b 1965, Paul William b 1971), 2 da (Janet Susan (Mrs Calladine) b 1967, Mary Elizabeth b 1969); *Career* surgical trainee Cambridge 1964-69, The London Hosp: lectr in surgery 1969-70, conslt surgn and sr lectr 1970-77, reader in transplantion surgery 1977-83, prof of transplantation surgery 1983-; past pres Br Transplantation Soc; FRCS; *Books* Clinical Immunosuppression (1980), Immunosuppressive Therapy (1981), Operative General Surgery (1988); *Recreations* family life, sailing, silversmithing; *Clubs* Royal Cwlth Soc; *Style—* Prof John Salaman; 25 Heol Don, Whitchurch, Cardiff CF4 2AR (☎ 0222 626539); Dept of Surgery, Royal Infirmary, Cardiff, S Glam CF2 1SZ (☎ 0222 492233)

SALAMAN, Hon Mrs (Nancy Adelaide); da of late 1 Viscount Samuel, GCB, OM, GBE, PC; *b* 1906; *Educ* Univ of Oxford; *m* 1935, Arthur Gabriel Salaman, MB BCh, MRCS, LRCP (d 1964); 2 s, 2 da; *Style—* The Hon Mrs Salaman; 5 Chestnut Court, Newport, Essex CB11 3QJ

SALAMAN, (Frederick) Nicholas Paul; s of Sebastian Max Alexander Clement Salaman (d 1976), and Joan Elisabeth; *b* 4 Feb 1936; *Educ* Radley, Trinity Coll Oxford (MA); *m* 1, 1960 (m dis 1974), Elisabeth Cecila, da of Francis Sclater, of Bunces Farm, Newick, nr Uckfield, Sussex; 2 da (Sophia, Charlotte); m 2, 1983, Lyndsay Margaret, da of James Meiklejohn, of Wise Lane, Mill Hill; 2 da (Rose Clementine b 1983, Phoebe Joy b 1987); *Career* writer; advtg and mktg; dir London Herb & Spice Co Ltd 1978-; *Books* The Frights, Dangerous Pursuits, Falling Apart, Mad Dog (play), Forces of Nature; *Recreations* harpsichords, tennis and unearthing old High Table recipes; *Clubs* Beefsteak, Chelsea Arts'; *Style—* Nicholas Salaman Esq; c/o Chelsea Arts Club, 143 Old Church St, London SW3

SALAMON, Julie Anne (Mrs Harrington); da of Jan Salamon, of Rickmansworth, Herts, and Jean Ada, *née* Dibbo; *b* 1 May 1960; *Educ* Rickmansworth GS, Casio Coll Watford; *m* 10 Aug 1985, Michael James Wiliam Harrington, s of Harold Harrington, of Residing, Otterbourne, Hants; *Career* sales exec: Daily Express 1980-82, Over 21 magazine 1982-84; dep advtg mangr Punch 1984-87, advertisement mangr World of Interiors 1987, publisher London Portrait magazine 1988-; *Style—* Miss Julie Salamon; Reed Publishing, London Portrait Magazine, 7-11 St Johns Hill, London SW11 1TE (☎ 01 924 3408)

SALE, Hon Mrs (Ismay Hilda Margaret); *née* FitzRoy; da of 4 Baron Southampton (d 1958), and Lady Hilda Mary Dundas (d 1957), da of 1 Marquess of Zetland; *b* 3 Dec 1908; *m* 8 Feb 1928, Brig Walter Morley Sale, CVO, OBE, late Royal Horse Guards (d 1976), 3 s of Charles Vincent Sale, of Aston Rowant House, Oxon; 1 s, 1 da; *Style—* The Hon Mrs Sale; 15 St Paul's Mews, Ramsey, IOM (☎ 0624 815408)

SALE, Robert John; s of Lt Col John Walker Sale, OBE (d 1974), of Ilderton Glebe, Wooperton, nr Alnwick, Northumberland, and Nancy Jaqueline Sale; *b* 24 Feb 1930; *Educ* RNC Dartmouth; *m* 14 Jan 1956, Susan, da of Richard Clement Parker (d 1955), of Redlands, nr Cambridge; 1 s (John Richard (Dick) b 1963), 1 da (Lynda Katherine b 1957); *Career* HMS Britannia 1943-47, Midshipman HMS Forth Med Fleet 1947-49, Sub Lt HMS Crispin Home Fleet 1949-50, Lt HMS Consort (served Far E Fleet and Korean War) 1950-53, HMS Diligence 1953-54, Flag Lt to Adm of the Fleet Sir George Creasy C-in-C Portsmouth 1972-77; Barclays Bank UK Ltd 1955-86: local dir 1962, gen mangr 1977, sr gen mangr 1985; dir: Halifax Building Soc, Ropner plc, Tees Towing Co Ltd, Whitehead Ltd, Newcastle Technology Centre, Command Credit Ltd; govr Aysgarth Sch, investmt advsr Dean and Chapter Durham Cathedral, chm NE Bd Prince's Youth Business Tst; FCIB; *Recreations* fishing, shooting, hill walking, tennis, gardening; *Clubs* Royal Ocean Racing; *Style—* Robert Sale, Esq; Eryholme Grange, nr Darlington, Co Durham (☎ 060 981 401)

SALEM, Daniel Laurent Manuel; s of Raphael Salem (d 1963), and Adriana Gentili di Giuseppe (d 1976); *b* 29 Jan 1925; *Educ* Harvard (BA, MA); *m* 1950, Marie-Pierre, da of Rene Arachtingi (d 1975); *Career* chm: Condé Nast Publications Ltd 1967-, Condé Nast International Inc 1970-, Mercury Selected Trust 1974-, Philharmonia Trust Ltd 1985-; dep chm Condé Nast Publications Inc 1987-; dir of various other cos; Chevalier de la Legion d'Honneur 1987, Commendatore dell' Ordine al Merito della Repubblica Italiana (1988); *Recreations* music, chess, bridge, backgammon, golf; *Clubs* White's, Portland, Harvard (NYC); *Style—* Daniel Salem, Esq; 3 Ennismore Gdns, London SW7 (☎ 071 584 0466); Condé Nast Publications Ltd; Vogue House, Hanover Sq, London W1 (☎ 071 499 9080)

SALES, Barry Edward; s of Lawrence Edward Sales, of Upwey, Dorset, and Doris May, *née* Heaton (d 1978); *b* 23 Oct 1933; *Educ* Sherborne and Corpus Christi Coll (MA); *m* 14 June 1958, Lois Marshall, da of Dr Roderick Marshall (d 1975), of New York; 2 da (Catherine b 1962, Elizabeth b 1967); *Career* Lt King's African Rifles (Africa Serv Medal 1954); dir: Murco Petroleum Ltd 1964-, Utd Refineries Ltd 1985-; *Recreations* piano, squash, antiquarian books; *Style—* Barry E Sales, Esq; The Croft, Chalfont Lane, Chorleywood, Herts WD3 5PP; Winston House, Dollis Park, London N3 1HZ (☎ 081 349 9191)

SALES, Christopher Hedley; s of Douglas William Sales (d 1988), and Marjorie Ethel, *née* Keast; *b* 24 Oct 1943; *Educ* City of London Sch; *m* 6 June 1970, Lynne Anne; 1 s (Philip b 21 March 1975), 1 da (Josephine b 29 Oct 1980); *Career* chartered accountant Ogden Hibberd Bull & Langton 1966-69 (articled clerk 1961-66), tax accountant British Steel Corporation 1969-73, Clark Battams 1973-82 (asst tax mangr, tax mangr, ptnr 1980), ptnr Clark Whitehill 1982-; UK Taxmaster 1984; Freeman City of London 1984; FCA (ACA 1967), ATII 1970; *Recreations* playing tennis, watching Chelsea FC and Middx CCC; *Style—* Christopher Sales, Esq; Clark Whitehill, 25 New Street Square, London EC4A 3LN (☎ 071 353 1577)

SALES, Harry Brimelow; MBE (1973); s of Harry Thomas Sales (d 1939), of Northenden, Manchester, and Mary, *née* Brimelow (d 1940); *b* 13 Sept 1918; *Educ* Stockport GS, Univ of Manchester (LLM); *m* 1 (m dis); 2 s (John Roger b 26 Sept 1944, Robert Anthony b 10 Oct 1949), 2 da (Janet Margaret (twin) b 26 Sept 1944, Rosemary Anne b 7 Oct 1947); m 2, Patricia Lois; *Career* slr 1940-74; prosecuting slr Manchester 1942-44; town clerk: Tottenham (acting dep) 1944-47, Guildford (dep) 1947-52, Aldershot 1952-74; called to the Bar Inner Temple 1975; memb Admin Law Ctee of Justice; chm Free Painters and Sculptors; *Books* Halsbury's Laws of England (ed, Housing vol and Public Health vol), Encyclopaedia of Rating and Local Taxation (ed); *Recreations* walking, climbing; *Clubs* Alpine, Climbers, Swiss Alpine; *Style*— Harry Sales, Esq, MBE; Little Yarrowfield, Guildford Rd, Mayford, Woking, Surrey (☎ 0483 770611); 2 Mitre Court Buildings, Temple, London EC4 (☎ 071 583 1380, fax 071 353 7772, telex 28916)

SALES, Hon Mrs (Isobel Caroline); *née* Irby; da of 7 Baron Boston (d 1958); *b* 1917; *m* 1, 1946 (m dis 1950), Maj Vernon Owain Roberts; m 2, 1950, Edward Horatio Sales (d 1988); 2 da (Christian b 1950, Alexandra b 1952); *Style*— The Hon Mrs Sales; 18 Fourth Avenue, Hove, E Sussex

SALFORD, Patrick Altham Kelly; s of John Kelly (d 1960), and Mary, *née* Altham (d 1989); *b* 23 Nov 1938; *Educ* Preston Catholic Coll, Venerable English Coll Rome Pontifical Gregorian Univ Rome (PhL, STL); *Career* curate Lancaster Cathedral 1964-66, rector St Mary's Coll Oscott Birmingham 1979-84 (prof of dogmatic theology 1966-79), memb clergy Archdiocese of Birmingham 1977, bishop of Salford 1984-; sec Hierarchy Theology Cmmn 1967, prelate of honour to HH the Pope 1980-; *Recreations* reading, music, opera; *Style*— The Rt Rev the Bishop of Salford; Wardley Hall, Worsley, Manchester M28 5ND (☎ 061 794 2825)

SALHA, Bushra; da of Amin Al-Hassan Al-Rasamny (d 1969), and Samia Younis (d 1960); *b* 25 March 1946; *Educ* American Girls' Sch, Univ Coll Beirut (BA), Christie's fine art course, Sotheby's styles in art course, modern art studies course ICA, The New Acad for Art Studies; *m* 3 Sept 1966, Mazen Najib Salha, s of Najib Salha; 4 c (Reem b 2 Oct 1967, Najib b 8 Dec 1968, Karim b 12 July 1972, Makram b 23 Sept 1973); *Career* conslt interior designer Hotel Vendôme Beirut Lebanon 1973-76, started own art consultancy London 1983, jtly organised exhibition Romantic Lebanon-The European View 1700-1900 (Leighton House Holland Park London) 1986, memb Exhibition Organising Ctee Lebanon-The Artist's View-Two Hundred Years of Lebanese Painting (Concourse Gallery Barbican London) 1989, memb Acquisitions Sub Ctee Patrons of New Art Tate Gallery London 1988-89; fund raiser for: The Lebanese Red Cross, The Br Lebanese Assoc, The Br Wildlife Appeal, The Gibran Khalil Gibran Chair Maryland Univ USA 1985-90; memb: Br Lebanese Assoc, Patrons of New Art Tate Gallery; *Publications* Auction Boom in the Art World (Ahlan Wasahlan Magazine, 1987), Exhibition Catalogue Lebanon The Artist's View - Two Hundred Years of Lebanese Painting (contrib, 1989); *Recreations* reading, opera, yoga, classical and pop music, theatre, tennis, swimming, cross country skiing; *Clubs* Queen's; *Style*— Mrs Bushra Salha

SALINGER, Pierre Emil George; s of Herbert Edgar Salinger (d 1940), and Jehanne, *née* Bietry; *b* 14 June 1925; *Educ* Univ of San Francisco (BS); *m* 1, 1 Jan 1947 (m dis 1956), Renee, *née* Laboure; 2 s (Marc Pierre b 30 Sept 1948 (d 1974), Stephen Richard b 6 Sept 1952), 1 da (Suzanne Renee b 3 Sept 1951); m 2, 1956 (m dis 1965), Nancy, *née* Joy; m 3, 1963 (m dis 1988), Nicole, *née* Gillman; 1 s (Gregory Edgar Jean b 25 March 1966); m 4, 17 June 1989, Nicole, da of Jean Beauvillain; *Career* sailor US Navy 1943-46, Cdr SC 1368 submarine chaser in Pacific War with Japan, ret as Lt; reporter and night city ed SF Chronicle 1942-43 and 1946-55, roving ed Colliers Magazine 1955-56, investigator and chief investigator US Senate Labour Rackets Ctee 1957-59, press sec to Senator John F Kennedy 1959-61, press sec to: Pres Kennedy 1961-63, Pres Lyndon Johnson 1963-64, US Senator California 1964; vice pres Int Affrs Continental Airways 1965-68, mangr of campaign of Senator Robert F Kennedy for Pres 1968, dir Gramco Ltd 1969-71, nat chm George McGovern for Pres 1972, roving ed l'Express Magazine Paris 1973-78, sr ed Euro and chief foreign correspondent ABC News (correspondent 1978, Paris Bureau chief 1979, Paris Bureau chief and chief foreign correspondent 1983); memb Nat Press Club Washington DC 1961; Chevalier of Legion of Honour France 1978, Offr of Legion of Honour France 1988; *Books* With Kennedy (1966), On instructions of my Government (1971), Je suis un Americain (1975), La France et le Nouveau Monde (1976), American Held Hostage (1981), The Dossier (with Leonard Gross, 1984), Above Paris (with Bob Cameron, 1985), Mortal Games (with Leonard Gross, 1988), La Guerre du Golfe - Le Dossier Secret (with Eric Laurent, 1990); *Recreations* tennis; *Style*— Pierre Salinger, Esq; c/o ABC NEWS, 8 Carburton St, London W1P 7DT (☎ 071 637 9222)

SALIS; *see*: de Salis

SALISBURY, 76 Bishop of 1982-; Rt Rev John Austin Baker; patron of 63 livings, and 45 shared, the Precentorship, Chancellorship, and Treasurership of his Cathedral and other Canonries and Archdeaconries of Dorset, Sarum, Wilts and Sherborne. The Bishopric was founded at Sherborne 705, Wells and Exeter were separated from it 905; in 1075 it was removed to Old Sarum, and in 1220 to Salisbury; s of George Austin Baker and Grace Edna; *b* 11 Jan 1928; *Educ* Marlborough, Oriel Coll Oxford; *m* 1974, Gillian Leach; *Career* ordained priest 1955, official fellow, chaplain and lectr in Divinity Corpus Christi Coll Oxford 1959-73, also lectr in theology Brasenose Coll Oxford and Lincoln Coll Oxford 1959-73, canon Westminster 1973-82, sub-dean and lector Theologiae 1978-82, rector St Margaret's Westminster and speaker's chaplain 1978-82; memb C of E Doctrine Cmmn 1967-87; *Books* The Foolishness of God (1970), Travels in Oudamovia (1976), The Whole Family of God (1981); *Clubs* Utd Oxford and Cambridge; *Style*— The Rt Rev the Bishop of Salisbury; South Canonry, The Close, Salisbury, Wilts SP1 2ER (☎ 0722 334031)

SALISBURY, Dr Jonathan Richard; s of George Richard Salisbury (d 1971), of Hereford, and Patricia Doreen, *née* Jones; *b* 25 July 1956; *Educ* Hereford HS, UCL (BSc), UCH Med Sch (MB BS); *m* 19 May 1984, Alyson Frances, da of Lister Wilfred Bumby; of Herne Bay, Kent; 1 da (Elizabeth b 1989); *Career* sr lectr morbid anatomy King's Coll Sch of Med London 1987-, hon conslt histopathologist King's Coll Hosp London 1987-; MRCPath 1986-; *Style*— Dr Jonathan Salisbury; 155 Abbeville Rd, London SW4 9JJ (☎ 071 622 2390) Dept of Morbid Anatomy, King's Coll Sch of Med, Bessemer Rd, London SE5 8RX (☎ 071 326 3093)

SALISBURY, Mark Pryce; s of Andrew Salisbury, of Llandudno, and Iris Helen Salisbury, *née* Roberts; *b* 15 Oct 1955; *Educ* Sir Hugh Owen GS Caernarfon, Liverpool Univ (LLB); *m* 12 Dec 1981, Christine Anne, da of Thomas Gordon Morris, of Gwynedd; 1 s (Adam b 1986); *Career* slr; sr ptnr Gamlin Kelly & Beattie Slrs Llandudno; *Recreations* shooting, golf, tennis, sailing; *Clubs* Maesdu Golf; *Style*— Mark P Salisbury, Esq; Bryn Teg, 23 Vicarage Road, Llandudno, Gwynedd (☎ 0492 870933); 14 Trinity Square, Llandudno, Gwynedd (☎ 0492 860 420, fax 0492 75296)

SALISBURY, 6 Marquess of (GB 1789); Robert Edward Peter Gascoyne-Cecil; DL (Dorset 1974); also Baron Cecil (E 1603), Viscount Cranborne (E 1604), Earl of Salisbury (E 1605); patron of seven livings; s of 5 Marquess of Salisbury, KG, PC, FRS (d 1972), sometime acting Foreign Sec, and Elizabeth Vere (d 1982), da of Rt Hon Lord Richard Cavendish, CB, CMG, PC, bro of 9 Duke of Devonshire; *b* 24 Oct 1916; *Educ* Eton; *m* 18 Dec 1945, Marjorie Olein, da of Capt the Hon Valentine Maurice Wyndham-Quin, RN (d 1983, s of 5 Earl of Dunraven and Mount-Earl); 4 s (and 1 s decd), 1 da; *Heir* s, Viscount Cranborne, *qv*; *Career* Capt Gren Gds; takes Cons whip in the House of Lords; memb editorial bd The Salisbury Review 1982-; pres Royal Assoc British Dairy Farmers; MP (C) W Bournemouth 1950-54; pres Monday Club 1974-81; high steward of Hertford 1972-; *Style*— The Most Hon the Marquess of Salisbury, DL; Hatfield House, Hatfield, Herts

SALISBURY-JONES, Raymond Arthur; s of Maj-Gen Sir Guy Salisbury-Jones GCVO, CMG, CBE, MC, DL, of Hambledon, Marshal of Dip Corps 1951-61, and Hilda Violet Helena, da of Sir Maurice de Bunsen, HBM Ambass to Madrid (1906-13) and Vienna (1913-14); *b* 31 July 1933; *Educ* Eton, Christ Church Oxford (MA); *Career* 2 Lt Coldstream Guards, serv Canal Zone 1951-53; export mktg mangr Rolls Royce Motors Ltd 1956-75; dir: Rolls Royce Motors International Ltd 1968-74, Daniel Thwaites plc, RSJ Aviation International Ltd; Liveryman Worshipful Co of Grocers; *Recreations* rowing, music, skiing; *Clubs* English Speaking Union, Pratt's; *Style*— R Salisbury-Jones, Esq; 4 Clifton Gardens, London W9 1DT (☎ 071 289 5169); The Glassmill, 1 Battersea Bridge Rd, London SW11 3BG (☎ 071 223 2111)

SALISSE, John; CBE (1986); s of Joseph Salisse (d 1966), of Bournemouth, and Ann, *née* Hull (d 1976); *b* 24 March 1926; *Educ* Portsmouth GS; *m* 7 July 1949, Margaret, da of James Horsfield (d 1950); 1 da (Caroline b 1960); *Career* Marks & Spencer plc 1944-85 (dir 1968-85); chm: CBI Distributive Trades Survey 1983-86 (memb Cncl 1984-89), St Enoch Management Centre Ltd 1986-, Jt London Tourism Forum 1986-, London Enterprise Agency 1983-88, Retail Consortium 1986-; dir: London Tourist Board 1984- (vice chm 1989-), Project Fullemploy 1984-86; vice pres Commerce and Distribution Ctee CECD 1986; memb: Cncl for Charitable Support 1984-89, CCD Ctee on Commerce and Distribution 1988; jt treas Euro Movement 1982-86, tstee Lenta Educn Trust 1987-; hon sec The Magic Circle 1965-86 (hon vice pres 1975-); memb Fin Ctee RCP 1986-; *Recreations* golf, theatre, history of magic; *Clubs* The Magic Circle, Highgate Golf, The Magic Castle (Los Angeles), IOD; *Style*— John Salisse, Esq, CBE; c/o Midland Bank, 90 Baker St, London W1M 2AX

SALLIS, Peter John; *b* 1 Feb 1921; *Educ* Minchenden GS Southgate London; *m* 9 Feb 1957, Elaine; 1 s (Crispian b 24 June 1959); *Career* prodr; W End prodns incl: Wait Until Dark, Cabaret, She Loves Me, Pride and Prejudice, Ivanof, Much Ado About Nothing, Moby Dick, The Matchmaker, Run for Your Wife, Look After Lulu 1959, Rhinoceros 1960, Cabaret 1968; TV prodns incl: The Diary of Samuel Pepys, Last of the Summer Wine, Strangers and Brothers, The Pallisers, Bel Ami, Come Home Charlie and Face Them, First of the Summer Wine, The New Statesman, The Bretts; writing incl an adaptation of Boucicaults' Old Heads and Young Hearts; *Clubs* Garrick; *Style*— Peter Sallis, Esq

SALLITT, Timothy William Baines; CBE (1991); s of Brig William Baines Sallitt, OBE (d 1979), and Mary Elaine, *née* Whincup; *b* 21 March 1934; *Educ* Rugby, Bradford Poly, Borough Poly, Georgia Tech Atlanta USA; *m* 14 June 1958, Angela Mary, da of Dr Brian Laidlaw Goodlet, OBE (d 1961); 1 s (Henry b 1962), 2 da (Amelia b 1960, Lucinda b 1965); *Career* Nat Serv 2 Lt RE Cyprus 1955-57; BP 1957-59; divnl mangr: Brush Electrical Engineering 1959-66, Plessey Co 1966-70; sub co md Hawker Siddeley Group 1970-77, gp dir Hawker Siddeley Group 1977-89; former memb Cncl Electrical Res Assoc, former pres BEAMA, dep chm Export Guarantees Advsy Cncl 1986-89; FIIM; *Recreations* sailing, gardening, Egyptology; *Clubs* Boodle's; *Style*— Timothy Sallitt, Esq, CBE; 61 Sinclair Rd, London W14 0NR (☎ 071 602 3204); Le Grè, 82110 Lauzerte, France (☎ 63 95 70 23)

SALMON, Rev Anthony James Heygate; s of Sir Eric Cecil Heygate Salmon, MC, DL (d 1946), of 115 Old Church St, London SW3, and (Hilda) Marion, *née* Welch (d 1990); *b* 20 Aug 1930; *Educ* Wellington, Corpus Christi Coll Oxford (MA, Dip Theol); *m* 18 Aug 1973, Anthea, da of Thomas Robert Calthorpe Blofeld, CBE, FSA, JP (d 1986), of Hoveton House, Wroxham, Norfolk; *Career* curate: St Mark's S Norwood Croydon 1956-59, Usuthu Mission Swaziland 1959-61; rector Gingindhlovu, Zululand 1961-69, chaplain Coll of the Ascension Selly Oak 1969-74, rector St John The Baptist Harrietsham 1974-85, vicar St Lawrence Chobham with St Saviour's Valley End 1985-; *Recreations* walking, gardening; *Style*— The Rev Anthony Salmon; The Vicarage, Bagshot Rd, Chobham, Surrey GU24 8BY (☎ 0276 858197)

SALMON, Baron (Life Peer UK 1972), of Sandwich, Co Kent; Cyril Barnet Salmon; PC (1964), JP (Kent 1949); s of late Montagu Salmon; *b* 28 Dec 1903; *Educ* Mill Hill, Pembroke Coll Cambridge (MA); *m* 1, 1929, Rencie (d 1942), da of late Sidney Gorton Vanderfelt, OBE; 1 s (Hon David Neville Cyril b 1935), 1 da (Hon Gai Rencie (Hon Mrs Robinson) b 1933); m 2, 1946, Jean Beatrice (d 1989), da of late Lt-Col David Edward Maitland-Makgill-Crichton and former w of 2 Baron Morris; *Career* barr 1925, QC 1945, judge High Ct of Justice, Queen's Bench Div 1957-64, a lord justice of appeal 1964-72, a lord of appeal in ordinary 1972-80; kt 1957; hon fell Pembroke Coll Cambridge, hon DCL Kent 1978, hon LLD Cambridge 1982; *Recreations* fishing, golf; *Style*— The Rt Hon Lord Salmon, PC, JP; Eldon House, 1 Dorset St, London W1H 3FB

SALMON, Hon David Neville Cyril; s (by 1 m) of Baron Salmon (Life Peer) *qv*; *b* 1935; *m* 1, 1958 (m dis 1972), Heather Turner-Laing; m 2, 1973, Sarah Harrison; *Style*— The Hon David Salmon; Holne Cott, Holne, nr Ashburton, Devon

SALMON, Jamie Lionel Broome; s of Gerald Mordaunt Groome Salmon, of Kent, and Margaret Ann, *née* Pike; *b* 16 Oct 1959; *Educ* Wellington; *m* Fiona Jane; 1 s (Michael Alan Broome b 16 May 1990); *Career* rugby player; 65 appearances Wellington Rugby Province 1978-83, 200 appearances Harlequins RFC 1982-90; 3 NZ All Black Caps 1981, 12 England Caps 1985-87; dir Pact Print & Design 1989-; contrib weekly rugby column Daily Telegraph 1989-; *Recreations* golf, cricket; *Style*— Jamie Salmon, Esq; 43 Gibbon Rd, Kingston, Surrey KT2 6AD

SALMON, Keith John; s of J W Salmon (d 1941), of Kent, and D B E Salmon (d 1990), *née* Evans; *b* 9 Sept 1937; *Educ* Chislehurst GS, Univ of London (BSc); *m* 12 Aug 1971, Denise; 2 da (Jessica Clare b 15 Dec 1972, Emma Louise b 23 July 1974); *Career* studio mangr BBC Radio Drama 1961-65, sound sequence composer BBC Radiophonic Workshop 1965-67, reporter BBC TV SW Plymouth 1967-68, prodr BBC Radio Nottingham 1968-70, prog organiser BBC Radio Oxford 1970-82, managing ed BBC Radio Norfolk 1982-; memb: Pub Ctee Norfolk Red Cross, Norwich Crime Prevention Panel; govr Heartsease Sch Norwich; *Recreations* sailing, travel; *Clubs* Strangers (Norwich); *Style*— Keith Salmon, Esq; 7 Eaton Rd, Norwich NR4 6PY (☎ 0603 51387); BBC Radio Norfolk, Norfolk Tower, Surrey St, Norwich NR1 3PA (☎ 0603 617411, telex 975515, fax 0603 622229)

SALMON, Col William Alexander; OBE (1956); s of Lt-Col William Harry Broome Salmon, Indian Army (d 1962), and Lillian Mabel (d 1963); *b* 16 Nov 1910; *Educ* Haileybury, RMC Sandhurst; *m* 1939, Jean Barbara (d 1982), da of late Rt Rev John Macmillan, OBE, DD (Bishop of Guildford 1935-49); 1 s, 2 da; *Career* cmmnd 2 Lt HLI 1930, ADC to govr of Sind 1936-38; serv WWII: France 1939, Middle E, Italy, Greece, Bde Maj 1942, GSO2 HQ Aegean Force 1943, CO 2 Beds and Herts Regt 1945-46, CO 2 Royal Irish Fus 1946-47, GSO1 (Trg) HQ Scottish Cmd 1947-49, COS to Lt Gen Glubb Pasha HQ Arab Legion 1950-53, CO 1 Bn HLI 1953-55, Col General Staff (O & T Div) SHAPE 1957-59, AQMG (QAE2) W O 1959-62, AAG (AG14) W O 1962-63, ret 1963; asst ecclesiastical sec to lord chllr and PM 1965-77; *Books* Churches and Royal Patronage (1983); *Recreations* shooting, fishing, writing; *Clubs* Army & Navy; *Style*— Col W A Salmon, OBE; c/o Mrs R N Young, Pembury Hall, Pembury, Kent TN2 4AT

SALMOND, Alexander Elliot Anderson; MP (SNP) Banff and Buchan 1987; s of Robert Fyfe Findlay Salmond, of 101 Preston Rd, Linlithgow, Scotland, and Mary Stewart Milen; *b* 31 Dec 1954; *Educ* Linlithgow Acad, Univ of St Andrews (MA); *m* 6 May 1981, Moira French McGlashan; *Career* asst economist Govt Econ Serv 1978-80, economist Royal Bank of Scotland 1980-87; Scottish Nat Pty: dep ldr 1987-90, ldr

1990-; *Publications* numerous articles and conference papers on oil and gas economics; *Recreations* reading, golf; *Style—* Alexander E A Salmond, Esq, MP; House of Commons, London (☎ 071 219 3494)

SALONGA, (Ma) Lea Carmen; da of Feliciano G Salonga, of the Philippines, and Ma Ligaya A Imutan; *b* 22 Feb 1971; *Educ* OB Montessori Center Inc, Ateneo de Manila Univ; *Career* actress; roles incl: title role in Annie (Philippines) 1980 and 1984, Lucy in The Goodbye Girl (Maverick Prodn) 1982, Rhoda in The Bad Seed (repertory Philippines) 1981, Addie in Paper Moon (SRO Philippines) 1983, Luisa in The Fantasticks (touring) 1988, Kim in Miss Saigon (London) 1989-90 (NY 1991-); *awards* Aliw award for Best Child Performer 1981, 1982 and 1983, Cecil award for Best Recording by a Child 1984, Tinig award for Outstanding Entertainer 1983, 1984 and 1990, Laurence Olivier award for Best Actress in a Musical 1990; *Recreations* reading, needlepoint, puzzles; *Style—* Ms Lea Salonga; Alan Wasser & Associates, 1650 Broadway Suite 800, New York, NY 10019, USA (☎ 212 307 0800 212 307 5936)

SALT, Anthony William David; s of late Lt-Col Sir Thomas Henry Salt, 3 Bt, JP, DL, and hp of bro, Sir Michael Salt, 4 Bt *qv*; *b* 5 Feb 1950; *Educ* Milton Abbey; *m* 1978, Olivia Anne, da of Martin Morgan Hudson; 1 s (Edward James Stevenson Salt, b 11 June 1981); *Career* bank official; *Recreations* veteran/vintage cars; *Clubs* Vintage Car of GB; *Style—* Anthony Salt Esq; 1 Titchwell Rd, SW18 (☎ 071 874 8888)

SALT, Julia Ann; da of Kenneth Gordon Richardson, and Nora, *née* McLachlan; *b* 4 May 1955; *Educ* St Mary's Senior HS Hull, St Hilda's Oxford (BA); *m* 29 March 1980, David Sidney Salt, s of John Frederick Salt (d 1987); 1 s (Frederick b 17 July 1985), 1 da (Freya b 12 Aug 1983); *Career* ptnr Allen & Overy 1985-; memb: City of London Solicitors Co 1985, The Law Soc 1977; *Recreations* sailing, birdwatching, opera, languages; *Clubs* Royal Yorks Yacht, Utd Oxford and Cambridge; *Style—* Mrs Julia A Salt; 32 Cromwell Tower, Barbican, London, EC2 (☎ 071 248 9898, fax 071 236 2192, telex 8812801)

SALT, Sir (Thomas) Michael John; 4 Bt (UK 1899) of Standon, and of Weeping Cross, Co Stafford; s of Lt-Col Sir Thomas Henry Salt, 3 Bt (d 1965); *b* 7 Nov 1946; *Educ* Eton; *m* 1971, Caroline, da of Henry Hildyard; 1 da (Henrietta Sophia b 1978); *Heir* bro, Anthony Salt *qv*; *Style—* Sir Michael Salt, Bt; Shillingstone House, Shillingstone, Dorset

SALT, Sir Patrick MacDonnell; 7 Bt (UK 1869), of Saltaire, Yorkshire; s of Cdr Sir John William Titus Salt, 4 Bt, RN (d 1952), and Stella Houlton, *née* Jackson (d 1974); suc bro, Sir Anthony Houlton Salt, 6 Bt, 1991; *b* 25 Sept 1932; *Educ* Stowe; *m* 1976, Ann Elizabeth Mary, da of late Dr Thomas Kay Maclachlan, and widow of Denys Kilham Roberts OBE; *Heir* kinsman, Daniel Alexander Salt b 1943; *Style—* Sir Patrick Salt, Bt; Hillwatering Farmhouse, Langham, Bury St Edmunds, Suffolk

SALT, (Douglas) Roy; OBE (1969); s of Capt James Salt MN (d 1969), of 65 West St, Polruan, Fowey, Cornwall, and Daisy Melita, *née* Rundle (d 1987); *b* 18 April 1918; *Educ* Fowey GS; *m* 1 June 1940, Edna May, da of John William Davies (d 1946), of Harrow Weald; 1 da (Heather Valerie (Mrs Milton)); *Career* serv WWII RE 1940, RAOC 1941, REME 1942-46; apprenticeship (later printing mangr) HMSO 1933-40 and 1946-51, asst gen mangr (later gen mangr) Gaskiya Corpn Zaria Nigeria 1951-60, McCorquodale Printers 1960-77; md: Caxton Press Co Ltd Ibadan Nigeria 1960-74; Benhams Colchester 1974-77; memb Western region C of C Nigeria, sec to Zaria Race Club Zaria Nigeria; fell Inst of Industl Mangrs; *Recreations* sailing, golf, swimming; *Style—* Roy Salt, Esq, OBE; 1 The Ridings, Leavenheath, Colchester, Essex (☎ 0787 210 684); Salts Cottage, 65 West St, Polruan, Fowey, Cornwall

SALTER, Rev (Arthur Thomas) John; TD (1988); er s of Arthur Salter (d 1982), of The Tong-Norton Farm, Tong, nr Shifnal, Shropshire, and Dora May, *née* Wright (d 1985); the Salter family has been seated in Shropshire since the reign of King John, when John de le Sel is mentioned in the records of Shrewsbury Abbey 1211 (*see* Burke's Landed Gentry, 18 edn, vol III, 1972); *b* 22 Nov 1934; *Educ* Wellington GS, King's Coll London (AKC 1960), St Boniface's Theological Coll Warminster; *Career* serv Intelligence Corps 1954-55, RAMC 1955-56; ordained deacon 1961, priest 1962; asst priest: St Peter's, Mount Park, Ealing 1961- 65, St Stephen with St Thomas the Apostle, Shepherd's Bush 1965-66, St Alban the Martyr, Holborn with St Peter, Saffron Hill 1966-70; vicar of St Silas with All Saints, Pentonville 1970-; priest-in-charge of St Clement, Barnsbury and St Michael the Archangel, Islington 1970-79; priest-in-charge of St Dunstan-in-the-West with St Thomas of Canterbury within the Liberty of the Rolls 1979-; chm The Anglican and Eastern Churches Assoc 1990- (gen sec 1975-), chaplain Law Courts Branch of Edward Bear Fndn for Muscular Dystrophy, chm Wynford Estate's Old Peoples Club, Royal Army Chaplains Dept 1975-, CF IV (Capt) 1975-81, CF III (Maj); chaplain: 36 Signal Regt 1975-80, 257 (S) Gen Hosp RAMC (V) Duke of York's HQ 1980-; memb Societas Sanctae Crucis (SSC); Hon Kt Order of St Michael of the Wing (Royal House of Braganza, Portugal) 1984, Companion of Honour Order of Orthodox Hospitallers (Cyprus) 1985, Hon Archimandrite's Cross of Byelo-Russian Autocephalic Orthodox Church-in-Exile 1979, Archpriest's Cross of Ethiopian Catholic Uniate Church (Eparchy of Asmara, Eritrea) 1980, Archpriest's Cross Exarchate of Pope Shenouda III (Coptic Orthodox Patriarchate of Alexandria) 1981; *Recreations* travelling in Eastern Europe, genealogy, reading; *Clubs* Army and Navy, City Livery, Polish Hearth; *Style—* The Rev John Salter, TD; St Silas and James Vicarage, 87 Richmond Ave, Islington, London N1 OLX (☎ 071 607 2865); St Dunstan-in-the-West Vestry, 184A Fleet Street, London EC4 (☎ 071 405 1929)

SALTER, John Rotherham; s of Herbert Salter (d 1978), of Cooden, Bexhill, and Nora, *née* Waters (d 1978); *b* 2 May 1932; *Educ* Queen Elizabeth's Sch, Ashridge Coll, Lincoln Coll Oxford (MA), King's Coll London; *m* 3 June 1961, Cynthia Rotherham, da of Frederick Brewer (d 1982), of Sevenoaks; 1 s (Jeremy b 1964), 2 da (Rachel b 1962, Christy b 1970); *Career* Nat Serv 2 Lt RA 65 Regt 1952, Lt RA 1953; slr; ptnr Denton Hall Burgin & Warrens 1961-; conslt UNIDO 1983-84; vice chm: Int Bar Assoc Ctee of Energy and Nat Resources Law 1976-79, Int Bar Assoc Ctee on Int Environmental Law 1979-82, ABA Ctee on Comparative Govt Law 1988-; chm: North Sea Gas Gathering Consortium 1979-80, Section on Business Law Int Bar Assoc 1986-88, SBL Ctee on Construction in the Oil Indust 1989-; tstee: Petroleum Law Educn Tst 1980-, Int Bar Assoc Educn Tst 1983-; treas Anglo-American Real Property Inst 1985-86; memb cncl: IBA 1982-90, SBL 1982-, Town and Country Planning Assoc 1984-88; govr: Lady Boswell's Sch 1980-, Copthorne Sch 1982-; memb: London and Middlesex Archaeological Soc, Soc for Promotion of Roman Studies, W Kent Branch Oxford Soc; Freeman: City of London 1984, City of Glasgow 1986; Liveryman: Incorporation of Hammermen 1988-, Worshipful Co of Slrs 1989-, Worshipful Co of Fanmakers 1990-; memb Law Soc 1959, FBIM 1984, FRSA 1984, FRGS 1987, ACIArb 1987; hon memb Bar of Madrid 1987; *Books* Planning Law for Industry (jt ed, 1981), UK Onshore Oil and Gas Law (1986), Oil and Gas Law (contrib, 1984), Halsbury's Laws of England (contrib, 1986), Law of the European Communities (contrib, 1986), Vaughan's Law of the European Communities Service (contrib, 1990), numerous articles for Int Bar Assoc; *Recreations* the arts, archaeology, sailing; *Clubs* Oxford and Cambridge; *Style—* John Salter, Esq; Five Chancery Lane, Clifford's Inn, London EC4 1BU (☎ 071 242 1212)

SALTER, Michael Anthony John; s of James Joseph Salter (d 1960), and Grace Elizabeth Salter (d 1978); *b* 21 May 1943; *Educ* Malvern; *m* 17 Aug 1968, Mary Elizabeth, da of Denis Oswald Feeny (d 1973); 1 s (Mark b 1969), 2 da (Helen b 1971, Jennifer b 1974); *Career* fin dir: Coral Racing Ltd 1980-85, Bass Wales and West Ltd 1985-90, Welsh Brewers Ltd 1985-90; md Crown Brewery plc 1990-; FCA; *Recreations* classical music, opera, tennis; *Clubs* Rugby; *Style—* Michael Salter, Esq; 6 The Paddock, Cherry Orchard Road, Lisvane, Cardiff CF4 5UE (☎ 0222 759519); Crown Brewery plc, Cowbridge Rd, Pontyclun, Mid Glamorgan CF7 9YG (☎ 0443 225433)

SALTER, Richard Stanley; s of Stanley James Salter (d 1980), and Betty Maud, *née* Topsom (d 1974); *b* 2 Oct 1951; *Educ* Harrow Co Sch, Balliol Coll Oxford (MA); *Career* called to Bar Inner Temple 1975, in practice 1975-, bencher 1991; arbitration sec and membership sec London Common Law and Commercial Bar Assoc 1986-; ACI Arb 1983; memb Cncl of Legal Educn 1990-; *Recreations* books, music, theatre; *Clubs* Savile; *Style—* Richard Salter, Esq; 14 Addison Cres, London W14 8JR; 3 Gray's Inn Place, Gray's Inn, London WC1R 5EA (☎ 071 831 8441, fax 071 831 8479, telex 295 119 LEXCOL G)

SALTER, Prof Stephen Hugh; s of Willoughby de Carle Salter, of Mansfield Notts, and Rachel, *née* Floyd (d 1984); *b* 7 Dec 1938; *Educ* Framlingham Coll, Sidney Sussex Coll Cambridge; *m* 24 April 1973, Prof Margaret Caldwell, da of James Donaldson (d 1947), of Aberfoyle, Perthshire; *Career* apprentice fitter tool maker Saunders Roe Ltd 1956-61, res asst Univ of Cambridge 1962-67, personal chair in engrg design Univ of Edinburgh 1986- (res fell 1967-71, lectr 1971-78, reader 1978-86); author of scientific papers on robotics, renewable energy and hydraulic machines; memb Scottish Exam Bd; *Recreations* photography, the invention of instruments and tools; *Style—* Prof Stephen Salter; Kings Buildings, Mayfield Rd, University of Edinburgh EH9 3JL (☎ 031 650 5703, fax 031 667 3677, telex 727442)

SALTHOUSE, Dr Edward Charles; s of Edward Salthouse, MBE (d 1965), of Belfast, and Winifred Charles, *née* Boyd (d 1977); *b* 27 Dec 1935; *Educ* Campbell Coll Belfast, Queen's Univ Belfast (BSc, PhD); *m* 1961, Denise Kathleen Margot, da of Dr Joseph Reid (d 1963), of Ballymena, N Ireland; 2 s (Michael, Kevin); *Career* lectr Univ of Bristol 1962-67; Univ of Durham: reader in electrical engrg sci 1962-79, master Univ Coll 1979-, dean Faculty of Sci 1982-85, pro-vice chllr 1985-88; FIEE 1980, FRSA (1986); *Recreations* photography, industl history; *Clubs* Royal Overseas League; *Style—* Dr Edward Salthouse; The Masters House, The Castle, Durham DH1 3RL; Shieldaig, Hume, Kelso TD5 7TR

SALTISSI, Dr Stephen; s of Victor Saltissi, of Leeds, and Betty, *née* Weinman; *b* 21 Sept 1950; *Educ* Roundhay Sch Leeds, King's Coll London (MB BS), Univ of London (MSc, MD); *m* 30 July 1972, Sandra Bernice, da of Maurice Aaron Bellman, of Leeds; 2 da (Nicola b 1978, Caroline b 1980); *Career* sr res fell St Thomas' Hosp 1979-80 (registrar 1977-78); sr registrar: N Tees 1981-82, Newcastle Upon Tyne 1982-84; conslt physician and cardiologist Royal Liverpool Hosp 1984-, hon lectr Univ of Liverpool 1984-, clinical sub dean Royal Liverpool Hosp, memb cncl Liverpool Med Inst, chm resuscitation ctee and physicians ctee Royal Liverpool Hosp; memb: Br Cardiac Soc 1985, Merseyside and N Wales Assoc Physicians 1984; MRCP 1975; *Recreations* tennis, supporter Liverpool FC, travel; *Style—* Dr Stephen Saltissi; Wansfell, 25 Hillside Drive, Woolton, Liverpool L25 5NR (☎ 051 428 2034); Royal Liverpool Hospital, Prescot St, Liverpool L7 8XP (☎ 051 706 2000 ext 3573 (sec), 051 706 3574 (direct line))

SALTONSTALL, James Edwin Rous; s of Peter Rous Saltonstall, (d 1984), of Bridlington, E Yorks, and Antonia, *née* Ernste; *b* 22 July 1947; *Educ* St George's Secdy Sch; *m* 26 June 1971, Christine Ann, da of Norman Woodhouse; 1 s (Jeremy Richard Rous b 11 Dec 1981); *Career* yacht racer and coach; yacht and dinghy racing commencing Royal Yorks Yacht Club 1952, RN dinghy team 1965-77 (capt 1974-76), sr nat racing coach RYA 1977-; attended over 100 int yacht and dinghy events (World, Euro, Olympic); achievements incl: runner-up J24 class World Championships Japan 1985, Euro champion J24 class Germany 1990, nat champion J24 class 1984-85; yachtsman of the year 1984; served RN 1962-77; *Books* RYA Race Training Manual (2 edns); *Recreations* sailing; *Style—* James Saltonstall, Esq; Royal Yachting Assoc, Romsey Rd, Eastleigh, Hants (☎ 0703 629962, fax 0703 629924)

SALTOUN, Lady (twentieth holder of title; S 1445); Flora Marjory; *née* Fraser; Chief of the Name of Fraser; family granted right to own Univ of Fraserburgh by King James VI; da of 19 Lord Saltoun, MC (d 1979), and Dorothy, da of Sir Charles Welby, 5 Bt, CB, by Maria, sis of 4 Marquess of Bristol; *b* 18 Oct 1930; *Educ* St Mary's Wantage; *m* 1956, Capt Alexander Ramsay of Mar, *qv*, *see* Peerage, Royal Family section; 3 da; *Heir* da, Hon Mrs Nicolson; *Career* sits as Independent in House of Lords; *Clubs* Turf; *Style—* The Rt Hon the Lady Saltoun; Cairnbulg Castle, Fraserburgh, Aberdeenshire AB43 5TN (☎ 0346 23149)

SALUSBURY-TRELAWNY, Sir John Barry; 13 Bt (E 1628), of Trelawny, Cornwall; s of Sir John William Robin Maurice Salusbury-Trelawny, 12 Bt (d 1956), by his 1 w, Glenys Mary, da of John Cameron Kynoch; *b* 4 Sept 1934; *Educ* HMS Worcester; *m* 1958, Carol Knox, yr da of C F K Watson, of The Field, Saltwood, Kent; 1 s, 3 da; *Heir* s, John Salusbury-Trelawny, *qv*; *Career* Nat Serv RNVR; dir: Martin Walter Group Ltd 1971-74, Korn/Ferry International 1977-83, Goddard Kay Rogers & Associates 1984- (mgmnt conslts); JP Kent 1973-78; FInstM; *Clubs* Army & Navy, Buck's, Royal Cinque Ports Yacht; *Style—* Sir John Salusbury-Trelawny, Bt; Beavers Hill, Saltwood, Hythe, Kent (☎ 0303 66476); 32 St James's Square, London SW1 (☎ 071 930 5100)

SALUSBURY-TRELAWNY, John William Richard; s and h of Sir John Salusbury-Trelawny, 13 Bt *qv*; *b* 30 March 1960; *m* 16 Aug 1980, Anita, yr da of Kenneth Snelgrove and Mrs L E Thorpe, of Iver Heath, Bucks; 1 s (Harry John b 10 Dec 1982), 1 da (Victoria Hayley b 1981); *Style—* John Salusbury-Trelawny Esq; 45 St Leonard's Rd, Hythe, Kent (☎ 0303 65571)

SALUSBURY-TRELAWNY, Col Jonathan William; OBE (1976); s of James Reginald Dorrington Salusbury-Trelawny (d 1980), and his 1 w, Muriel Mary, *née* Wrixon-Becher (d 1970); *b* 25 Feb 1934; *Educ* Charterhouse, RMA Sandhurst; *m* 1, 1959 (m dis 1969), Jill Rosamonde, da of Maj-Gen Cecil Benfield Fairbanks, CB, CBE; m 2, 1970 (m dis 197-), Gillian, o child of R J Ratcliff, of Fossebridge House, nr Cheltenham; 1 da (Katherine Sophie b 1972); *Career* cmmnd Coldstream Guards 1954, Army Staff Coll Camberley 1967, Armed Forces Staff Coll Norfolk Virginia USA 1974; cdr Frontier Force 1974-76, loan service with Sultan's Armed Forces 1976-79, Defence Advsr Brit High Cmmn Dacca and Defence Attaché Brit Embassy Rangoon 1979-80, asst sec NATO Mil Ctee 1980-83, cdr Dhekelia Garrison 1983-86, special project in Brunei 1987-88; sr Public Information Offr HQ London Dist 1989-; memb Gray's Inn; Order of the Crown of Belgium 1963, Sultan's Distinguished Service Medal (Oman) 1979; *Recreations* skiing; *Clubs* Cavalry and Guards'; *Style—* Col J W Salusbury-Trelawny, OBE; HQ London District, Horse Guards, Whitehall, London SW1A 2AX (☎ 071 873 6256, fax 071 873 6295)

SALUSBURY-TRELAWNY, Lt-Col Philip Michael; MC (1945), DL (Cornwall 1982); 2 s of Maj John Salusbury-Trelawny, MC (d 1954, himself ggs of Sir William Salusbury-Trelawny, 8 Bt), of Cotleigh House, Honiton, Devon, and Louisa Frederika, *née* Mainwaring (d 1985); *b* 11 Nov 1921; *Educ* Winchester; *m* 23 March 1946, Jean

Mary (sometime Flt Offr WAAF, d 1988), only da of Col Herbert Cecil Fraser, DSO, OBE, TD (d 1940), of Redlands, Ilkley, Yorks; 1 s (Simon Jonathan b 1948, m 1978 Marian MacAuley), 1 da (Diana Jane b 1947, m 1970 Robert Blake); *Career* cmmnd Indian Army 1941, Frontier Force Rifles 1941-47, Maj, N Africa and Italy (MC) 1942-45, Duke of Cornwall's LI 1947-75, Lt-Col 1964, Regtl Sec Light Inf in Cornwall 1979-84; *Recreations* shooting, gardening; *Clubs* Army and Navy; *Style*— Lt-Col Philip Salusbury-Trelawny, MC, DL; Colgare House, Lanhydrock, Bodmin, Cornwall PL30 4AE (☎ 0208 72887)

SALVESEN, Alastair Eric Hotson; s of Lt-Col Iver Ronald Stuart Salvesen (d 1957), and Marion Hamilton, *née* McClure; Christian Salvesen (fndr of family business) emigrated from Norway to Edinburgh 1836; bro Robin Salvesen, *qv*; *b* 28 July 1941; *Educ* Fettes, Cranfield (MBA); *m* 18 July 1979, Elizabeth Evelyn, da of Cdr Patrick Murray, RNVR, of Hawick, Roxburghshire; *Career* chm and md Dawnfresh Seafoods Ltd 1981-; chm Starfish Ltd 1986-; dir Mull of Kintyre Seafoods 1988-; memb The Queen's Body Guard for Scotland (The Royal Company of Archers); CA; MinstM; *Recreations* shooting, archery, farming and forestry; *Clubs* New (Edinburgh); *Style*— Alastair E H Salvesen, Esq; Rake Barn, Southwaite, Cockermouth, Cumbria (☎ 0900 824031); Westwater, Langholm, Dumfriesshire; Dawnfresh Seafoods Ltd, North Shore, Whitehaven, Cumbria CA28 7XQ (☎ 0946 61141, telex 64283, fax 0946 65027)

SALVESEN, Robin Somervell; s of Iver Ronald Stuart Salvesen (d 1957), and Marion Hamilton, *née* McClure; bro Alastair Salvesen *qv*; *b* 4 May 1935; *Educ* Cargilfield Sch Edinburgh, Fettes Coll Edinburgh, Univ Coll Oxford (Engrg), Hendon Tech Coll; *m* 6 Aug 1960, Sari Frances Judith *née* Clarke; 3 s (Francis b 26 Oct 1965, Thomas b 14 May 1967, Iver b 31 Jan 1969); 4 da (Ferelith b 3 May 1961, Alice b 25 Dec 1962, Tabitha b 13 Feb 1964, Emily b 22 June 1970); *Career* 5 bn QO Nigeria Reg 1955-56, Royal Scots TA 52 Lowland Volunteers 1957-69; chm: Lights Advsy Ctee, Br Shipowners' Assoc, Scot Cncl King George's Fund for Sailors; dep chm Queensberry House Hosp; dir: Christian Salvesen plc, The Murrayfield plc; memb: Ctee Scot Veterans Residences, Gen Ctee Lloyds Register of Shipping, Merchant Co of the City of Edinburgh; elder of St Mary's Church Haddington; Liveryman Worshipful Co of Shipwrights; Hon Danish Consul for E Scotland 1972-89; Silver Jubilee medal 1977; Royal Order of the Knights of Dannebrog (Denmark) 1981; *Recreations* shooting with long bow and shotgun; *Clubs* New (Edinburgh); *Style*— Robin S Salvesen, Esq; 50 East Fettes Ave, Edinburgh EH4 1EQ (☎ 031 552 7101, fax 031 552 5809)

SALZ, Anthony Michael Vaughan; s of Michael H Salz, of Yelverton, Devon, and Veronica, *née* Hall; *b* 30 June 1950; *Educ* Summerfields Sch, Radley, Univ of Exeter (LLB); *m* 17 May 1975, Sally Ruth, da of Harold J Hagger, of Broughton, Hants; 1 s (Christopher b 1978), 2 da (Emily b 1980, Rachel b 1982); *Career* admitted slr 1974; ptnr Freshfields 1980- (seconded to Davis Polk and Wardwell, NY 1977-78); memb Law Soc; contrib to various learned jls; *Recreations* fly fishing, tennis, golf and the family generally; *Style*— Anthony Salz, Esq; Whitefriars, 65 Fleet St, London EC4Y 1HT (☎ 071 936 4000)

SALZ, Michael; s of Michael Salz (d 1950), of London, and Tania, *née* Wagner (d 1955); *b* 1 May 1916; *Educ* Univ of Cambridge (MA); *m* 24 July 1948, Veronica Edith Dorothea Elizabeth, da of the late (Frank) Francis Vaughan Hall; 1 s (Anthony Michael Vaughan b 1950, *qv*), 1 da (Joanna Mary Vaughan (Mrs Leadbetter) b 1952); *Career* conslt orthopaedic surgn Cambridge and Middx Hosp; sec Br Rheumatoid Arthritis Surgical Soc, past pres Plymouth Med Soc; LRCP 1940, FRCS 1948, FRSM, fell Br Orthopaedic Assoc; *Recreations* flyfishing, skiing; *Clubs* Royal Western Yacht; *Style*— Michael Salz, Esq; Nuffield Hosp Plymouth (☎ 0752 790707), 144 Harley St, London W1 (☎ 071 935 0023, 0822 853633, 071 262 3860, 0841 520536)

SALZEDO, Leonard Lopes; s of Samuel Lopes Salzedo (d 1957), of 48 Darenth Rd, London N16, and Edna Gladys Gertrude, *née* Kilrow (d 1983); *b* 24 Sept 1921; *Educ* RCM; *m* Patricia Mary, da of Arthur James Clover (d 1972); 2 da (Susan b 21 March 1946, Caroline b 6 Dec 1952); *Career* composer of 17 ballet scores, 18 film scores and numerous orchestral and chamber works; has performed all over UK and in Holland, Germany and Austria; past conductor at Bath and Vienna Festivals, dir of recordings of own work by London Philharmonic and RPO; dir: Ballet Rambert 1966-72, London City Ballet 1982-86; ARCM; Commandeur dans le Conferie des Chevaliers du Sacavin d'Anjou, fell Int Inst of Arts and Letters (Genève et Zurich); *Recreations* photography, travelling, reading; *Clubs* Savage; *Style*— Leonard Salzedo, Esq; 363 Bideford Green, Leighton Buzzard, Beds LU7 7TX (☎ 0525 371126)

SAMAIN, Bryan Charles William; s of Charles William Samain (d 1930), of Chelmsford, and Ethel Mary Jane Witherow, *née* (d 1978), of Wimbledon; *b* 14 Jan 1925; *Educ* Royal Masonic Sch 1933-40; *m* 1 May 1948, Helen Pauline, da of Charles Maddison (d 1968), of Frinton; 2 s (Paul b 19 Sept 1949, Peter b 6 Feb 1953); *Career* WWII: RM 1942-46, Lt 45 and 46 Commandos Normandy, Holland, Germany, Far East; journalist; Daily Sketch and Sunday Graphic 1941-42, special corr Sydney Daily Mirror Hong Kong 1946; PR exec Richard Thomas and Baldwins Ltd 1950-58, chief publicity offr Cementation Gp 1958-60, mangr PR staffs UK Ford Motor Co 1960-62, head of PR Richard Thomas and Baldwins Ltd 1962-67, head of info servs Br Steel S Wales 1967-68, head of PR Costain Gp 1968-70, dir PR EMI Gp 1970-80, PR conslt and writer 1980-; former chm Publicity Ctee Save The Children Fund; *Books* Commando Men (1948, 3 edn 1988); *Recreations* theatre, swimming, walking; *Style*— Bryan Samain, Esq; 33 Warwick Gardens, Worthing, West Sussex BN11 1PF (☎ 0903 203877)

SAMARJI, William Norman; s of Elias Norman Samarji (d 1959), of Bombay, India, and Latifa Samarji (d 1967); *b* 15 March 1934; *Educ* Univ of Bombay (MS), Univ of London, Univ of Edinburgh; *m* 18 July 1964, Medha, da of Manmohandas Shah, of Bombay, India; 2 s (Richard Arun b 1965, Neal Elias b 1966), 1 da (Neena Latifa b 1968); *Career* sr Registrar gen surgery Manchester Royal Infirmary 1967-72, conslt surgn Tameside Gen Hosp 1972-, examiner primary FRCS RCS Edinburgh 1987-, surgical tutor RCS England 1988-; *Recreations* gardening, walking, travelling; *Style*— William Samarji, Esq; The Gerrards, Stockport Rd, Gee Cross, Hyde, Cheshire SK14 5ET (☎ 061 368 3464); Tameside Gen Hosp, Ashton-upon-Lyne, Lancs (☎ 061 330 8373)

SAMBAR, Dr David Habib; s of Habib David Sambar (d 1952), of Haifa, and Georgette, *née* El Khoury; *b* 19 Aug 1930; *Educ* Univ of London (BA), American Univ Beirut (MA), Doctorate magna cum laude Faculty Economics and Business Administration Lyons France; *m* 15 Oct 1966, Salma Renee Sambar, da of Labib Y Zacca, of Beirut (d 1982); 1 s (Habib David b 1968), 1 da (Syma Karine b 1970); *Career* Chase Bank Beirut 1955-73; asst auditor, auditor, asst mangr, mangr, vice pres; vice pres Chase NYC 1973-77, chm Sharjah Investment London 1977-81, Strategic Investmt Planning London 1982-85, chm Shambar International Investments Ltd 1984-, chm British American Properties NY 1990-, memb Lloyds of London 1984-; advsr to various companies, ed of articles and speeches for various US and Euro pubns and professional orgns; tstee Princeton in Asia 1965-, memb Stanford Res Inst 1979-, cnsllr in int affrs Peoples for UN NYC 1979-, tstee Woman's World Banking 1986-, memb Cons Pty; hon doctorate Mexican Acad of Int Law; *Recreations* tennis, skiing; *Clubs* Hurlingham, Institute of Directors, RAC; *Style*— Dr David Sambar; 11 Chelsea Square, London SW3 6LF (☎ 071 352 1713)

SAMBROOK, Prof (Arthur) James; s of Arthur Sambrook (d 1979) of Nuneaton, and Constance Elizabeth, *née* Gapper (d 1986); *b* 5 Sept 1931; *Educ* King Edward VI Sch Nuneaton, Univ of Oxford (MA), Univ of Nottingham (PhD); *m* 25 March 1961, Patience Ann, da of Sidney John Crawford (d 1973), of Finchingfield; 4 s (John b 1962, William b 1963, Robert b 1964, Thomas b 1969); *Career* RAF 1950-52; lectr English St David's Coll Lampeter 1957-64, prof English Univ of Southampton 1981- (lectr 1964-71, sr lectr 1971-75, reader 1975-81); *Books* A Poet Hidden, The Life of Richard Watson Dixon 1833-1900 (1962), William Cobbett, an Author Guide (1973), Pre-Raphaelistism (1976), English Pastoral Poetry (1983), The Eighteenth Century: The Intellectual and Cultural Context of English Literature 1700-89 (1986); editions: The Scriblerian, 1742 (1967), The Seasons and The Castle of Indolence by James Thomson (1972), The Seasons by James Thomson (1981), Liberty, The Castle of Indolence and Other Poems by James Thomson (1986), contributions to journals incl: Eighteenth Century Studies, English, English Miscellany, English Studies, The Library, Modern Language Review, Notes and Queries, Review of English Studies, Scriblerian, Times Higher Education Supplement, Times Literary Supplement, Victorian Studies, Yearbook of English Studies; *Recreations* squash, hill-walking; *Style*— Prof James Sambrook; Dept of English, Univ of Southampton, Southampton SO9 5NH (☎ 0703 593517)

SAMBROOKE-STURGESS, Gerald; OBE (1983); s of Frank Sturgess (d 1903), of Erdington Birmingham, and Marion Helen, *née* Taylor (d 1974); *b* 5 Dec 1901; *Educ* Edward VI Sch Norwich, Royal Dental Hosp, Middx Hosp; *m* 29 Sept 1933, Betty Muirhead, da of Aubrey Thorn Chittock, MBE (d 1953), of 12 Chapelfield North; 2 s (Peter b 1943, Anthony b 1944 (d 1965)), 3 da (Judy b 1936, Gillian b 1940, Katie b 1950); *Career* dental surgn Norwich 1925-71, inspector Norwich City Special Constabulary 1939-61; jt recipient Beppe Croce Trophy 1989; cdre: Yare and Bure Sailing Club 1936, Norfolk Punt Club 1939-45, Norfolk Broads Yacht Club 1948; memb: Int Yacht Racing Union, Royal Yachting Assoc; chm IYRU and RYA Racing Rules Ctee 1950-78, memb Olympic Jury for Yacht Racing Naples 1960, Tokyo 1964, Kiel 1972 and Ontario 1976; LDS, RCS 1925; *Books* Yacht Racing (3 edn 1947, 4 edn 1948, 5 edn 1957), Team Racing in Yachts (1959), IYRU Yacht Racing Rules (1959), Yacht Racing Management (1961), Yacht Racing for the Beginner (1962), The Rules in Action (1982); *Recreations* yacht racing; *Clubs* Royal Thames Yacht, Norfolk & Suffolk Yachting Assoc, Royal Norfolk and Suffolk Yacht, Norfolk County Miniature Rifle; *Style*— Gerald Sambrooke-Sturgess, Esq, OBE; Shepherd's Loke, Barton Turf, Norwich, Norfolk NR12 8BA (☎ 0692 60349)

SAMENGO-TURNER, Fabian Pius; s of late Joseph Frederick Samengo-Turner and Eva Turner; *b* 11 Feb 1931; *Educ* St Benedicts Sch, King's Coll London; *m* 1953, Maureen Ursula, *née* O'Connor; 3 s, 1 da; *Career* Lt Intelligence Corps; md: Laurentide Financial Trust 1962-67, Citibank Financial Trust 1968-72; chm Citibank Financial Trust 1973-74, exec dir Citicorp Investment Bank Ltd 1975-; *Recreations* squash, tennis, motor racing, sailing; *Clubs* RAC; *Style*— Fabian Samengo-Turner, Esq; Chapel Row Farm, Bucklebury, Reading, Berks RG7 6PB (☎ 0734 712 109); Citicorp Investment Bank Ltd, Cottons Centre, Hays Lane, London SE1 2QT (☎ 071 234 2151, telex 887094)

SAMMONS, Geoffrey Tait; s of Herbert Sammons, CBE (d 1967), and Elsie, *née* Kay (d 1951); *b* 3 July 1924; *Educ* Glenalmond, Univ Coll Oxford (MA); *m* 9 July 1949, Stephanie Anne, da of Stephen Hawley Clark (d 1961); 1 s (Timothy b 1956), 1 da (Anthea b 1952); *Career* RA 1943-45, Lt 8 Medium Regt RA Burma Campaign 1944-45; Allen & Overy Slrs London: joined 1946, ptnr 1953-86, sr ptnr 1981-86; cmmnr Bldg Socs Cmmn 1986-, non-exec dir Spirax Sarco Engineering plc; govr The Lister Inst of Preventative Med 1987-; memb Law Soc 1949; *Recreations* golf, gardening; *Clubs* Army & Navy; *Style*— Geoffrey Sammons, Esq

SAMPLES, Reginald McCartney (Mac); CMG (1970), OBE (1962), DSO (1942); s of William Samples, of N Wales, and Jessie, *née* McCartney (d 1980); *b* 11 Aug 1918; *Educ* Rhyl Co Sch, Univ of Liverpool (BCom); *m* 1947, Elsie Roberts Hide; 2 s (Graeme, William), 1 step da (Murcia); *Career* served WWII 1940-46 with RNAS (Fleet Air Arm), Lt (A) RNVR; COI 1946-48, CRO 1948-78 (ret); dir Br Info Servs in India Pakistan and Canada, asst under sec of state Cwlth Office London 1968, sr trade cmmr and Br consul-gen Toronto 1969; dir: National Ballet of Canada 1970-, Canadian Aldeburgh Fndn 1973-, Canadian/Scottish Philharmonic Fndn 1980-; asst dir Royal Ontario Museum 1978-83; *Recreations* tennis, watching ballet; *Clubs* Naval, RCS, York (Toronto), Queens (Toronto); *Style*— Mac Samples, Esq, CMG, OBE, DSO; Jackes Ave, Apt 1105, Toronto, Ontario M4T 1E5, Canada (☎ 010 1 416 962 1208)

SAMPSON, Colin; CBE (1988), QPM (1979); s of James Sampson, of Stanley, nr Wakefield, and Nellie; *b* 26 May 1929; *Educ* Stanley Sch, Univ of Leeds; *m* 1953, Kathleen Stones; 2 s; *Career* Nat Serv Duke of Wellington's Regt; West Riding Constabulary 1949-72 (CID, Fraud Squad, Special Branch), Cmdt Detective Trg Sch Wakefield 1971-72, operational asst Chief Constable W Yorks 1972-76; Dep Chief Constable: Notts 1976-80, W Yorks 1980-83; Chief Constable W Yorks 1983-89; HM Inspector of Constabulary: SE England 1989-90, NE England 1990-91, Scotland 1991-; chm Cncl of the Order of St John for W and S Yorks, pres Leeds Gilbert and Sullivan Soc, Barker Variety Club of GB; Hon DUniv Bradford 1988, Hon LLD Univ of Leeds 1990; *Recreations* music, reading, swimming, dog walking; *Style*— Colin Sampson, Esq, CBE, QPM; Kid Royd House, Shepley, W Yorkshire; HM Chief Inspector of Constabulary for Scotland, Scottish Office, St Andrews House, Edinburgh

SAMPSON, Ian Godfrey; JP (1975); s of Geoffrey Morgan Sampson (d 1978), of Peterborough, Cambs, and Dorothy Louise, *née* Dufty; *b* 29 May 1941; *Educ* Taunton Sch; *m* 11 July 1964, Gwendolen Celia Anne, da of Neil Cecil Alister Simon (d 1984), of Poole, Dorset; 2 da (Jacqueline b 1970, Philippa b 1972); *Career* HAC TA 1963 (ret 2 Lt); gen mangr Target Unit Trust Group 1975-80, md NM Schroder Unit Trust Group 1980-89, dir NM Schroder Life Assurance Co Ltd 1987-89, md Sun Life Trust Management 1989-, vice chm Painshill Park Trust Ltd; dir LAUTRO 1988-; borough cncllr 1974-76; *Recreations* restoration of Painshill Park, travel; *Clubs* HAC, United (Guernsey), City of London; *Style*— Ian Sampson, Esq, JP; 10 Crossway, Walton on Thames, Surrey KT12 3JA (☎ 0932 221 363); Granite House, 101 Cannon St, London EC4N 5AD (☎ 071 606 4044, fax 071 283 0715)

SAMPSON, Michael; s of William Thomas Sampson, of Horsham, Sussex, and Lilian Emma, *née* Edmonds; *b* 27 Sept 1942; *Educ* Collyers Sch Horsham, Univ of Southampton (BScEcon); *m* 7 June 1969, Elizabeth Victoria, da of Cdr Alfred Bryant Hilliar, of Bishops Caundle, Dorset; 2 da (Anna b 1978, Caroline 1980); *Career* res analyst Simon & Coates Stockbroker 1964-77, Lloyds investmt mangr 1977-85, md John Govett Pensions Ltd 1985-, dir John Govett & Co 1985-; *Recreations* tennis, skiing; *Style*— Michael Sampson, Esq; John Govett & Co, Shackleton House, 4 Battle Bridge Lane, London SE1 2HR (☎ 071 378 7979, fax 071 638 3468, telex 884266)

SAMPSON, Maj Richard Claude; s of Evelyn Sampson, eld s of Canon Gerald Sampson, of Moorhall, Ninfield, half bro of Stella Alleyne, cous of Sir John Alleyne Bt (d 1985), and Eva Bonham, cous of Sir George Bonham Bt, and sis of Elizabeth, Lady (Hugh) Clifford CBE, and Constance, the Hon Mrs Carteret Thynne; *b* 5 May 1916; *Educ* St Hugh's Prep Sch, privately, Exeter Coll Oxford; *m* 1947, Rosemary Anne, da of W B Collingridge, of Billing Manor and Mauritius; 1 s, 1 da (Mary, m Dan Shorland

Ball); *Career* cmmnd 2 Lt 1937 Wilts Regt (Duke of Edinburgh's) later Loyal Regt, served in WWII mostly with KAR (E Africa, Ethiopia, Madagascar and Europe), Br Military Mission to Ethiopia 1946-47, local Lt-Col (advsr to late Emperor Hailé Selassie on offr trg), personal staff offr and ADC to penultimate govr Nyasaland, rep Kenya on E Africa Security Conf, served as acting supt of Colonial Police and instr at Police Training Sch during Mau-Mau campaign in E Africa, ret 1969; formerly appeals dir with Richard Maurice Ltd, charities' conslt; former: pres Royal Br Legion N Norfolk, chm N Norfolk Army Benevolent Fund, vice pres Norfolk Red Cross, former memb Appeal Ctee Sue Ryder Fndn; *Recreations* shooting, gardening, history and labradors; *Clubs* Naval & Military, Norfolk; *Style—* Maj Richard Sampson; c/o National Westminster Bank, London St, Norwich

SAMSON, Greta Edith May; da of Charles Dudley Franks (d 1958), of Totnes, Devon, and Lilian Florence, *née* May (d 1974); *b* 3 July 1926; *m* 13 Sept 1952, John Louis Rumney Samson (d 1988), s of Air Cdre Charles Rumney Samson, CMG, DSO, AFC (d 1931), of Cholderton, Wilts; 2 da (Sally b 1954, Frances b 1955); *Career* dir Samson Books Ltd; *Recreations* gardening, walking, food, reading; *Style—* Mrs Greta Samson; Down House, Redlynch, Salisbury, Wilts SP5 2JP (☎ 0725 203 47)

SAMSON, Dr Thomas James (Jim); s of Edward Samson, of NI, and Matilda Jane, *née* Smyth; *b* 6 July 1946; *Educ* Queens Univ Belfast (BMus), Univ Coll Cardiff (MMus, PhD, LTCL); *Career* res fell in humanities Univ of Leicester 1972-73, reader in musicology Univ of Exeter 1987- (lectr in music 1973-87, head of dept 1986-); memb RMA; Order of Merit of the Polish Minstry of Culture 1989; *Books* Music in Transition: A Study in Tonal Expansion and Atonality (1977), Music of Szymanowski (1980), The Music of Chopin (1985), Chopin Studies (1988); *Recreations* walking, reading; *Style—* Dr Jim Samson; Music Department, University of Exeter, Knightley, Streatham Drive, Exeter EX4 4PD (☎ 0392 263810)

SAMUEL, Andrew William Dougall; s of Capt Andrew Samuel, RN (d 1952), and Letitia Shearer Samuel; *b* 12 July 1937; *Educ* Hutchesons' Boys GS, Glasgow; Glasgow Sch of Architecture; *m* 1, 20 Feb 1962 (m dis 1981), Sybille Marie Luise; 1 s (Craig Andrew Alexander Porter b 1966), 1 da (Katja b 1969); m 2, 2 Oct 1981, Mary Carswell, da of John Bisset (d 1978), of Homeglen, Carmunock, Glasgow; *Career* chartered architect; princ and dir Andrew Samuel & Co Ltd 1968; dir: Townhead Properties Ltd 1980, Gavin Watson Ltd 1983, Clouston Securities Ltd 1985; holder (with entry in Guinness Book of Records): World Canoeing Record Loch Ness 1975-85, World Canoeing Record English Channel 1976, World Canoeing K2 Doubles Record English Channel 1980-86; World Masters Games (with A Wilson) 1989: first K2 500m, first K2 5000m, third K2 Marathon; Scottish Nat Canoeing Racing Coach 1976-83; chm former E Central Tourist Assoc (Scotland), former chm Central Scotland Tourist Assoc, festival dir Trossachs Water Festival 1973-76, sec Trossachs Tourist Assoc 1969-76 (past pres); FRIAS, RIBA, FIPD, FFB; *Recreations* boating, travel, canoeing, photography; *Clubs* Trossachs Canoe and Boat, Bowfield Country; *Style—* Andrew Samuel, Esq; Woodside Farm, By Beith, Ayrshire, Scotland KA15 1JF

SAMUEL, Hon Anthony Gerald; s of 2 Viscount Bearsted, MC (d 1948), and Dorothea Montefiore, *née* Micholls (d 1949); *b* 18 Feb 1917; *Educ* Eton, New Coll Oxford; *m* 1, 1946 (m dis 1961), Mary Eve, da of late John Comyn Higgins, CIE, of Alford, Lincs; 2 da (Jacqueline Eve b 1948, Daphne Lavinia b 1951); m 2, 1962 (m dis 1966), Jenifer, da of Maj Kenneth Alfred Bridge Puckle, RM (ret), of Farnham; m 3, 1966, (Jean) Mercy, da of M C Haystead; *Career* Lt and Acting Capt Intelligence Corps WWII; co dir; ret; *Clubs* White's, Anglers' Club of NY, Flyfishers; *Style—* The Hon Anthony Samuel; 29 St Leonard's Terrace, London SW3 4QG (☎ 071 730 9089); Woodbury House, Longparish, Hampshire (☎ 026 472 409)

SAMUEL, Anthony John Fulton; s and h of Sir Jon Samuel, 5 Bt; *b* 13 Oct 1972; *Style—* Anthony Samuel Esq; c/o PO Box F 904, Freeport, Grand Bahama, Bahamas

SAMUEL, Hon Dan Judah; s of late 2 Viscount Samuel; hp of bro, 3 Viscount; *b* 25 March 1925; *Educ* Rugby, Balliol Coll Oxford, Sch of Advanced Int Studies (Johns Hopkins) Washington DC; *m* 1, 1957 (m dis 1977), Esther (Nonni), da of late Max Gordon of Johannesburg; 1 s (Jonathan b 1965), 2 da (Lia b 1961, Maia b 1963); m 2, 1981, Heather, da of Angus Cumming, of Haywards Heath; 1 s (Benjamin b 1983), 1 da (Sasha b 1982); *Career* late Maj Yorks Hussars; dir Shell Petroleum Co 1973-81, pres Scallop Corporation (NY) 1981-86, business conslt and co dir; tstee Asian Inst of Technol Bangkok, dir Br American Educnl Fndn; *Recreations* sailing (yacht 'Sanuk'); *Clubs* United Oxford and Cambridge Univ, Special Forces, Hurlingham, Chichester Yacht; *Style—* The Hon Dan Samuel; 154 Hillspoint Rd, Westport, Connecticut, USA

SAMUEL, 3 Viscount (UK 1937), of Mount Carmel, and Toxteth in the City of Liverpool; David Herbert Samuel; s of 2 Viscount, CMG (d 1978, gs of Edwin Samuel, whose yr bro Montagu cr Lord Swaythling), and Hadassah, Viscountess Samuel, *née* Goor-Grasovsky, *qv*; *b* 8 July 1922; *Educ* High Sch Jerusalem, Balliol Coll Oxford (MA), Hebrew Univ (PhD); *m* 1, 1950 (m dis 1957), Esther Berelowitz; 1 da (Hon Judith b 1951); m 2, 1960 (m dis 1978), Rinna Dafni, *née* Grossman; 1 da (Hon Naomi b 1962); m 3, 1980, Veronika Grimm, da of late Ernest Engelhardt, of 555 Sheppard Ave West, Downsview, Ontario; *Heir* bro, Hon Dan Samuel; *Career* Capt RA, served India, Burma, Sumatra 1942-45 (despatches); emeritus prof Weizmann Inst of Sci Israel 1949-; pres Shenkar Coll of Textile Technol and Fashion 1987- (memb Bd 1970-87, hon fell 1976); post-doctoral fell Chemistry Dept Univ Coll London 1956; research fell: Chemistry Dept Harvard Univ Cambridge Mass 1957-58, Lab of Chemical Biodynamics (Lawrence Radiation Lab) Univ of Calif Berkeley USA 1965-66; chm Bd of Studies on Chemistry at Feinberg Graduate Sch 1968-74, head Chemistry Gp Sci Teaching Dept 1967-84, visiting prof Sch of Molecular Sciences Univ of Warwick 1967; memb: Bd Bat-Sheva de Rothschild Fndn for Advancement of Sci in Israel 1970-84, Bd US-Israel Educnl (Fulbright) Fndn 1969-74 (chm 1974-75), Bd Israel Center for Scientific and Technol Info 1970-74, Scientific Advsy Ctee, Bd of Tstees Israel Center of Psychobiology 1973-; dean Faculty of Chemistry Weizmann Inst of Sci 1971-73; memb Ctee for Chemical Educn Int Union of Pure and Applied Chemistry (IUPAC) 1982-90 (nat rep 1973-82); visiting prof MRC Neuroimmunology Unit Zoology Dept UCL 1974-75, memb Acad Advsy Ctee Everyman's (Open) Univ 1976-84; memb: Israel Chem Soc (Cncl 1976-84), Int Brain Res Orgn (IBRO), head Centre for Neurosciences and Behavioural Res Weizmann Inst 1970-87, Israel Exec Ctee American-Israel Cultural Fndn 1975-87 (chm 1985-87), Bd of Govrs Tel Aviv Museum 1980-, visiting prof Pharmacology Dept Yale Sch of Med 1983-84; McLaughlin prof Sch of Med McMaster Univ (Canada) 1984; Anglo-Israel Assoc 1985-; Br Israel Arts Fndn 1986-; Bd of Govrs Bezalel Acad of Arts and Design 1977-; Bd Tstees Menninger Fndn (USA) 1989-, editorial bds Brain Behaviour and Immunity, Alzheimer Disease and Associated Disorders, Journal of Labelled Compounds and Radiopharmaceuticals; *Recreations* etching; *Style—* The Rt Hon the Viscount Samuel; Weizmann Institute of Science, Rehovot, Israel (☎ 8343115); 54 Rehov Hanasi Harishon, Rehovot, Israel (☎ 8468123)

SAMUEL, Edgar Roy; s of Lt Cdr Wilfred Sampson Samuel RNVR (d 1958), of London, and Viva Doreen, *née* Blashki (d 1977); *b* 13 Dec 1928; *Educ* Glebe Collegiate Ottawa, City of London Sch, Northampton Poly London (now City Univ), LSE (BA, MPhil); *m* 1956, Ruth Helena (d 1987), da of Joseph Cowen, CBE, of London; 1 s (Jonathan b 1959), 1 da (Deborah (Mrs Nevo) b 1957); *Career* asst steward Eastern Arctic Patrol 1945; optometrist 1950-71 and 1978-83, curator Jewish Museum 1988- (dir 1983); pres Jewish Hist Soc of E 1988-90; contrib to transactions of Jewish Hist Soc of E; FRHistS 1964, FBCO; *Recreations* sailing, historical reasearch; *Clubs* Reform; *Style—* Edgar Samuel, Esq; Jewish Museum, Woburn House, Tavistock Square, London WC1H 0EP (☎ 071 388 4525)

SAMUEL, John Graham; s of Geoffrey Graham Samuel (d 1985), and Cornelie Wilhelmina Petronella, *née* De Koning (d 1984); *b* 26 May 1941; *Educ* Felsted, Univ of Southampton (BSc); *m* 1989, Avril Elizabeth, da of John Erasmus, MBE; 1 s (Anthony Graham b 1973), 1 da (Abigail Lucy b 1971); *Career* chartered accountant; Andrew Barr & Co 1964-69, Harmood Banner & Co 1969-74; ptnr: Deloitte Haskins & Sells 1974-90, Coopers & Lybrand Deloitte 1990-; FCA 1968; *Recreations* walking, tennis, skiing, gardening; *Clubs* RAC; *Style—* John Samuel, Esq; 17 Billing St, London SW10 9UT (☎ 071 376 5195); Coopers & Lybrand Deloitte, 128 Queen Victoria St, London EC4P 4JX (☎ 071 583 5000, fax 071 248 3623)

SAMUEL, Sir John Michael Glen; 5 Bt (UK 1898), of Nevern Square, St Mary Abbots, Kensington; s of Sir John Oliver Cecil Samuel, 4 Bt (d 1962), and Charlotte Mary Desmond; *b* 25 Jan 1944; *Educ* Radley, London Univ; *m* 1, 24 Sept 1966, Antoinette Sandra, da of late Capt Anthony Hewitt, RE; 2 s (Anthony, Rupert); m 2, March 1982, Mrs Elizabeth Ann Molinari, yst da of Maj R G Curry, of Bournemouth; *Heir* s, Anthony Samuel; *Career* chm: Electric Auto Corporation (Detroit USA) 1978-82, Silver Volt Corpn (Freeport Bahamas) 1980-82, Whisper Electric Car A/S (Denmark) 1985-87, Synergy Research Ltd (UK) 1983-89, Clean Air Transport (Hldgs) Ltd 1989-; MIMechE, CEng; *Recreations* motor racing; *Style—* Sir John Samuel, Bt

SAMUEL, Hon Judith; da (by 1 m) of 3 Viscount Samuel; *b* 29 Jan 1951; *Educ* Technion-Israel Inst of Technol, Barch (Architectural Assoc London); *Career* Israel Defence Forces 1969-70; *Style—* The Hon Judith Samuel; 11 Lessin St, Tel Aviv, Israel; 5 Lipsky Street, Tel Aviv, Israel

SAMUEL, Hon Michael John; yr s of 4 Viscount Bearsted, MC, TD, *qv*; *b* 2 Nov 1952; *Educ* Eton; *m* 1980, Julia Aline, yst da of James Edward Alexander Rundell Guinness, *qv*; 1 s (Benjamin Marcus Peter b 1989), 3 da (Natasha Vivienne b 1981, Emily Elizabeth b 1983, Sophie Alexandra b 1986); *Recreations* shooting, fishing, riding, golf; *Clubs* White's; *Style—* The Hon Michael Samuel; 24 Hyde Park Gate, London SW7

SAMUEL, Hon Naomi Rachel; da (by 2 m) of 3 Viscount Samuel; *b* 27 May 1962; *Educ* Hebrew Univ, Jerusalem Sch of Law; *Career* Israel Defence Forces 1 Lt 1980-83; *Style—* The Hon Naomi Samuel; 15 Hanasi Harishon, Rehovot, Israel

SAMUEL, Hon Nicholas Alan; er s and h of 4 Viscount Bearsted, MC, TD, *qv*; *b* 22 Jan 1950; *Educ* Eton, New Coll Oxford; *m* 1975, Caroline Jane, da of Dr David Sacks; 1 s (Harry Richard b 23 May 1988), 4 da (Eugenie Sharon b 1977, Natalie Naomi b 1979, Zöe Elizabeth b 1982, Juliet Samantha b 1986)); *Style—* The Hon Nicholas Samuel; 9 Acacia Road, London NW8

SAMUEL, Hon Philip Ellis Herbert; s of late 1 Viscount Samuel, GCB, OM, GBE, PC (d 1963), and Beatrice Miriam (d 1959), yst da of Ellis Abraham Franklin; *b* 23 Dec 1900; *Educ* Westminster, Trinity Coll Cambridge; *Career* Hong Kong Vol Defence Corps (pow) 1939-45; office methods conslt; *Clubs* Royal Institution, Royal Overseas League, Victory Services; *Style—* The Hon Philip Samuel; c/o Royal Institution, 21 Albemarle St, London W1X 4BS

SAMUELS, Hon Mrs (Ann); eld da of Baron Bruce of Donington (Life Peer); *b* 1942; *m* T Samuels; *Style—* The Hon Mrs Samuels

SAMUELS, John Edward Anthony; QC (1981); s of Albert Edward Samuels (d 1982), of The Chantry, Reigate, Surrey; *b* 15 Aug 1940; *Educ* Charterhouse, Queens' Coll Cambridge (MA); *m* 1967, Maxine, da of Lt Col F D Robertson, MC, of Oakville, Ontario, Canada; 2 s (David b 1970, Adam b 1973); *Career* called to the Bar Lincoln's Inn 1964, rec Crown Ct 1985-, chm Jt Regulations Ctee of the Inns' Cncl and the Bar Cncl 1987-90, bencher Lincoln's Inn 1990; *Clubs* Athenaeum; *Style—* John Samuels, Esq, QC; Spring House, Sheen Road, Richmond, Surrey TW9 1AJ; 22 Old Buildings, Lincoln's Inn, London WC2A 3UJ (☎ 071 831 0222, fax 071 831 2239)

SAMUELS, Dr John Richard; s of Richard Arthur Samuels, of Istead-Rise, Kent, and Iris Molene Phylis, *née* Jenkins; *b* 13 Sept 1952; *Educ* Gravesend Tech HS, Univ Coll Cardiff (BA), Univ of Nottingham (PhD); *m* 1, 7 Sept 1979 (m dis 1985), (Frances) Naomi Field, da of Dr Gerard Field, of Dundas, Ontario, Canada; m 2, 10 Sept 1986, Harriet Annabel, da of Stephen Leslie Rickard, of Newark, Notts; 1 s (William b 1986), 1 da (Jenny b 1984); *Career* archaeologist, writer, lectr and publisher; archaeological field offr Humberside Archaeological Ctee 1975-76, res asst Dept of Archaeology Univ of Nottingham 1976-80, asst dir Rescue Archaeology Unit Univ of Liverpool 1980-81, tutor organiser for Notts in local history and archaeology Workers' Educnl Assoc 1981-, fndr The Cromwell Pres 1986-, ed East Midlands Archaeology (CBA Gp 14 Jl), ed Nottinghamshire Heritage Magazine 1990-; memb: Prehistoric Soc 1969-, Soc for Medieval Archaeology 1976-, N Lincs Archaeological Unit Ctee 1976-81, Tst for Lincs Archaeology 1982- (memb Exec Ctee 1984-87), Trent and Peak Archaeological Tst 1984-, Cncl for Br Archaeology (14 Exec Ctee) 1984-, Thoroton Soc 1987-; MIFA 1983; *Books* Figure Brasses in North Lincolnshire (1976), Aspects of Local History in Aslockton, Whatton and Scarrington Notts (1987), Excavation and Survey of Lydiate Hall, Merseyside (1982), Roman Pottery Production in the E Midlands (1983), Green Fields Beyond (1984), Life & Landscape in E Bridgford 1600-1900 (1985), Discovering Newark-on-Trent (1989), History Around Us (1989); *Recreations* squash, horse riding, walking dogs; *Clubs* Savages; *Style—* Dr John Samuels; 6 Old North Rd, Cromwell, Newark, Notts NG23 6JE (☎ 0636 821727)

SAMUELS, Prof Michael Louis; s of Harry Samuels, OBE (d 1976), of London, and Céline, *née* Aronowitz (d 1983); *b* 14 Sept 1920; *Educ* St Paul's, Balliol Coll Oxford (MA); *m* 21 Dec 1950, Hilary Miriam, da of Julius Marcus Samuel, of Glasgow (d 1942); 1 da (Vivien b 1953); *Career* lectr in English language Univ of Edinburgh 1949-59 (asst 1948-49), sr res fell in English language Univ of Glasgow 1989- (prof 1959-89); chm Scottish Studentships Selection Ctee Scottish Educn Dept 1975-88; FRSE 1989; *Books* Linguistic Evolution (1972), A Linguistic Atlas of Late Mediaeval English (jt ed 1986), The English of Chaucer (with J J Smith, 1988); *Style—* Prof Michael Samuels, FRSE; 4 Queen's Gate, Dowanhill, Glasgow G12 9DN (☎ 041 334 4999); Dept of English Language, The University, Glasgow G12 8QQ (☎ 041 339 8855, telex 777070 UNIGLA)

SAMUELSON, David Wylie; s of George Berthold Samuelson (d 1947), and Marjorie Emma Elizabeth, *née* Vint; bro of Michael Edward Wylie Samuelson, CBE; *m* 1, 1949 (m dis 1973), Joan, da of Philip Woolf; 2 s (Paul, Adam), 2 da (Gail, Zoe); m 2, 1978, Elaine Witz; *Career* served RAF 1944-47; with Br Movietone News 1941-60, fndr dir Samuelson Group plc 1958-84, dir Dsam Ltd 1984-, as cameraman filmed in over 40 countries and at 4 Olympic games; original inventions incl: through-the-lens video viewfinders for film cameras, Louma camera crane, Samcine inclining prism; winner of many awards incl: SMPTE Special Commendation award 1978, SMPTE Presidential Proclamation award 1984, AMPAS Scientific and Engrg award 1980, Acad Tech Achievement award 1987; govr London Int Film Sch 1981- (chm 1984-86), vice pres Int Union of Film Tech Assocs 1974-80; FRPS, FBKSTS (pres 1970-72, memb Cncl 1966-78 and 1984-), chm Br Bd of Film Classification 1972-89, memb Br Screen Advsy

Cncl 1985-, memb ACTT; *Books* Motion Picture Camera and Lighting Equipment, Motion Picture Camera Techiques, The Panaflex Users' Manual, The Cinematographers' Computer Calculator, Motion Picture Camera Data, The Samuelson Manual of Cinematography, American Cinematographer magazine (contrib ed, 1973-83); *Recreations* skiing, jogging, work; *Style*— D W Samuelson, Esq; 7 Montagu Mews West, London W1H 1TF, fax 071 724 4025

SAMUELSON, James Francis; s and h of Sir Michael Samuelson, 5 Bt; *b* 20 Dec 1956; *Educ* Hailsham; *Style*— James Samuelson Esq; c/o Hollingwood, Stunts Green, Herstmonceux, Hailsham, East Sussex

SAMUELSON, Michael Edward Wylie; CBE; s of George Berthold Samuelson (d 1947), pioneer film prodr making first film 1908, and Marjorie Emma Elizabeth, *née* Vint; bro of David Wylie Samuelson, *qv*; *b* 25 Jan 1931; *Educ* Shoreham GS; *m* Madeleine; 3 s (James b 1962, d 1970, Richard b 1964, Benjamin b 1972), 2 da (Louise b 1959, Emma b 1960, actress as Emma Samms); *Career* photographer RAF 1949-51, stage dir 1952-56, Br Movietone News cameraman 1957-61; Samuelson Gp plc 1957-88 (dep chm 1984-88), md Michael Samuelson Lighting Ltd 1989-; credits as dir or prodr or cinematographer on official films to Olympic Games 1968, 1972, 1974, 1976 and 1984 and World Cup Soccer 1966, 1970, 1974, 1982 and 1986; tstee Adopt-a-Student Scheme 1985-; exec crew Variety Club of GB 1967-74 (chief Barker 1974, memb Exec Bd 1974-); chm Sunshine Coach Scheme GB 1979-85, tstee Young Variety Club of GB 1980-; chm Worldwide Sunshine Coach 1983-87, memb Cncl Sick Childrens Tst 1983-, vice chm and tstee Hospital for Sick Children Great Ormond St redevelopment appeal 1984-, vice pres Nat Asson for Maternal and Child Welfare 1979, pres Variety Clubs International 1987-89, chm bd Variety Clubs Int 1989-; *Recreations* canal boating enthusiast, skiing, opera, shooting; *Clubs* MCC; *Style*— Michael Samuelson, Esq, CBE; 13 Phillimore Place, London W8 7BY (☎ 071 937 9711); Michael Samuelson Lighting Ltd, Pinewood Studios, Iver Heath, Bucks SLO ONH (☎ 0753 631133, fax 0753 630485)

SAMUELSON, Sir (Bernard) Michael Francis; 5 Bt (UK 1884), of Bodicote, Banbury, Oxfordshire; s of Sir Francis Samuelson, 4 Bt (d 1981), and Margaret (d 1980), da of H Kendal, of Barnes; *b* 17 Jan 1917; *Educ* Eton; *m* 1952, Janet Amy, da of Lt-Cdre Laurence Garrett Elkington; 2 s, 2 da; *Heir* s, James Francis Samuelson; *Career* Lt RA, Burma 1939-45 (despatches); *Style*— Sir Michael Samuelson, Bt; Hollingwood, Stunts Green, Herstmonceux, Hailsham, East Sussex

SAMWELL, Stanley David; s of David Arthur Samwell (d 1981), of Harrow, Middx, and Ergentine Ellen, *née* Evans (d 1981); *b* 12 June 1927; *Educ* Harrow Co GS; *m* 23 Aug 1974, Diana Mary, da of Capt Harry Lovibond Windsor (d 1946), of Johannesburg, SA; *Career* CA; ptnr Arthur Young (and predecessor firm) 1969-83; Dept of Trade inspr: affairs of Kuehne & Nagel Ltd 1974-75, Peachey Property Corpn 1977-78; pres Insolvency Practitioners Assoc 1980-81; memb Worshipful Co of CAs 1978; FCA 1954, MIPA 1970; *Books* Corporate Receiverships (second edn 1988); *Recreations* skiing, travel, theatre, photography; *Clubs* Ski Club of GB; *Style*— Stanley Samwell, Esq; 5 Old Manor Yard, London SW5 9AB (☎ 01 373 4067)

SAMWORTH, David Chetwode; CBE (1985), DL (1984); s of Frank Samworth; *b* 25 June 1935; *Educ* Uppingham; *m* 1969, Rosemary Grace, *née* Hobbs; 1 s (Mark b 1970), 3 da (Mary b 1972, Susannah b 1975, Victoria b 1977); *Career* Lt Sudan and Cyprus; chm: Pork Farms Ltd 1968-81, chm Meat and Livestock Cmmn 1980-84; dir Northern Foods Ltd 1978-81; vice chm Leics 33 Hosp Mgmnt Ctee 1970-74, memb Cncl of Univ of Nottingham 1975-76, vice chm governing body Uppingham Sch 1980-89; non exec dir: Imperial Gp 1983-85, Thorntons plc 1988-; chm Samworth Bro Ltd 1984, pres Br Meat Mfrs Assoc 1988-; *Recreations* tennis, hunting; *Style*— David Samworth Esq, CBE, DL; Markham House, Thorpe Satchville, Melton Mowbray, Leics

SANCROFT-BAKER, Raymond Samuel; s of Anthony Sancroft-Baker (d 1985), and Jean Norah, *née* Heron-Maxwell (d 1981); *b* 30 July 1950; *Educ* Bromsgrove Sch; *m* 29 Jan 1983, (Daphne) Caroline, da of Gp Capt Maurice Adams, OBE, AFC (d 1976); 2 s (Robert b 1985, Hugh b 1987); *Career* Christie's: head Coin and Metal Dept 1973, dir 1981, dir Jewellery Dept 1988; vice chm Bayswater Ward Conservatives; Freeman City of London 1972; Liveryman: Worshipful Co of Wax Chandlers 1973, Worshipful Co of Pattenmakers 1972 (asst 1987); FRNS 1971; *Recreations* tennis, squash, wood turning; *Clubs* RAC; *Style*— Raymond Sancroft-Baker, Esq; 4 Westbourne Park Rd, London W2 5PH (☎ 071 727 9600); Christie's, 8 King St, St James's, London SW1Y 6QT (☎ 071 839 9060)

SANCTUARY, Gerald Philip; s of John Cyril Tabor Sanctuary (d 1975), of Laleham-on-Thames, and Maisie Toppin, *née* Brooks; *b* 22 Nov 1930; *Educ* Bryanston, Law Soc Sch of Law; *m* 28 July 1956, Rosemary Patricia, da of Lt-Col Francis L'Estrange, of Dublin; 3 s (Nigel b 1960, Thomas b 1965, Charles b 1965), 2 da (Celia b 1958, Sophie b 1975); *Career* asst slr Sharrards Kingston on Thames 1955-57, ptnr Hasties Solicitors Lincoln's Inn Fields 1957-63, nat sec Nat Marriage Guidance Cncl 1965-68 (field sec 1963-65), exec dir Sex Info and Educn of USA 1969-71, sec professional and PR Law Soc 1971-78, exec dir Int Bar Assoc 1978-79, legal advsr and sr HQ Co-ordinator Regnl and Local Affrs MENCAP 1979-84, sec Provident Fund NUS 1984-; papers presented to confs in Europe, USA and Australasia; jt fndr Family Service Cncl Kenya, asst treas Guild of Air Pilots and Air Navigators City of London; memb Law Soc 1956-; *Books* Marriage Under Stress (1968), Divorce - And After (1970), Before You See a Solicitor (1973), After I'm Gone - What Will Happen to my Handicapped Child (1984), Running A Marriage Guidance Council, Local Society Handbook, It's Your Law - Law Soc Series (ed, 1973-78); *Recreations* amateur drama, travel, writing, organising murder mystery weekends, recording books for blind people; *Style*— Gerald Sanctuary, Esq; 6 Mercers Row, St Albans, Herts AL1 2QS (☎ 0727 42666); 314 Gray's Inn Rd, London WC1X 8DP (☎ 071 833 2766)

SANDALL, Robert Paul; s of Arthur Sandall, of 12 Wendover Close, Rippineale, Lincs, and Irene Norah, *née* Chard; *b* 9 June 1952; *Educ* Haberdashers' Aske's Elstree, Lincoln Coll Oxford (exhibitioner, BA), Cornell Univ NY USA; partner, Marina Salandy-Brown; *Career* freelance musican and composer 1976-84, writer critic and broadcaster 1985-; currently: pop/rock critic Sunday Times, presenter Mixing It BBC Radio 3; regular contrib to: Q, Rolling Stone, Kaleidoscope (Radio 4), Boy Office (Channel 4), Sky News; occasional feature writer and fiction reviewer Sunday Times; memb Performing Rights Soc 1984; Rolling Stones: Images of the World Tour 1989-90 (1991); *Recreations* skiing, tennis, scuba diving, fell walking; *Clubs* Embargo; *Style*— Robert Sandall, Esq; 51 Biscay Road, London W6 8JW (☎ 081 741 7576); Sunday Times, 1 Pennington St, London E1 5XN (☎ 071 782 5771, fax 081 746 3253)

SANDARS, Hon Mrs (Rowena Margaret); *née* Hawke; da of 9 Baron Hawke; *b* 1948; *Educ* Hatherop Castle Sch; *m* 1971, Philip William Leatham, *qv*; 2 s, 1 da; *Style*— The Hon Mrs Sandars; Hankerton Priory, nr Malmesbury, Wiltshire

SANDBACH, Richard Stainton Edward; s of Frank Stainton Sandbach (ka 1917), and Beatrice Emmeline, *née* Clifton (d 1963); *b* 13 June 1915; *Educ* Manchester GS, St John's Coll Cambridge (MA, LLM); *m* 10 Sept 1949, (Brenda Mary) Wendy, da of Charles Lionel Osborn Cleminson (d 1958), of the White House, Ickleford, Herts; 2 s (John Christopher Stainton b 1950, Richard Paul Stainton (Dickon) b 1956); *Career* Private VR Suffolk Reg 1939, OCTU 1940, 22 Cheshire Regt 1940-46, Maj Jr Staff Coll 1941, 1 Canadian Army 1943-44, Airborne Corps 1944-46, Lucknow Dist 1946; admitted slr 1946; sr ptnr Greenwoods Peterborough 1970-79 (ptnr 1951-79), clerk Huntingdon Freemen 1968-76; chm: DHSS Local Appeals Tbnl Peterborough 1980-88, Paten & Co Ltd 1988-, QCCC Ltd 1989-; past pres Peterborough & Dist Law Soc, fndr chm Minister Gen Housing Assoc Ltd; past chm: City & Cos Club Peterborough, Burgh Soc Peterborough; tstee: Peterborough Assoc of Boys' Clubs, Nat Deaf-Blind Helpers' League, Mark Masons' Fund of Benevolence; dir: FB Gibbons & Sons Wesby Ltd Arcade Properties (Peterborough) Ltd, Mark Catering Ltd; chm Peterborough Diocesan Bd of Fin 1974-84, provincial grand master for Northamptonshire & Huntingdonshire, Ancient Free & Accepted Masons of England 1984-90; memb Law Soc 1947; *Books* Introduction to The Book of the Lodge (G Oliver, 1986), Priest and Freemason (1988), Peterborough Booklets 1-3 (1990); *Recreations* hill walking, photography, historic research; *Clubs* United Oxford and Cambridge, City & Counties Peterborough; *Style*— Richard Sandbach, Esq; 91 Lincoln Rd, Peterborough PE1 2SH; (☎ 0733 343012); The Moorings, Fairbourne, Gwynedd; Drumnagarrachan, Kiltarlity, by Beauly, Inverness

SANDBERG, Alexander Christer Edward; s of Oscar Fridolf Alexander Sandberg, OBE (d 1942), and Audrey Maude, *née* Furber (d 1980); *b* 31 July 1923; *Educ* Charterhouse, City and Guilds Coll (BSc); *m* 19 Oct 1957, Aline Isobel, da of Brig W E Duncan, CVO, DSO, MC (d 1969); 3 s (Michael b 1959, Christopher b 1961, Neil b 1963); *Career* Lt RE 1942-45; sr ptnr Messrs Sandberg consulting engrs 1955-; former pres Br Section Sociètè des Ingenieurs et Scientifiques de France, sch govr, vice pres Old Centralians; FCGI, FEng, FICE, FIStructE, FIMechE, FIHT, FRSA; *Recreations* tennis, golf, sailing; *Clubs* Hurlingham, Anglo Belgian; *Style*— Alexander Sandberg, Esq; 32 Carlyle Square, London SW3 6HA (☎ 071 352 7210); Messr Sandberg, 40 Grovenor Gardens, London SW1W OLB (☎ 071 730 3461, fax 071 730 4972, telex 919518 SANDBER G)

SANDBERG, Sir Michael Graham Ruddock; CBE (1982, OBE 1977); s of Gerald Arthur Clifford and Ethel Marion Sandberg; *b* 31 May 1927; *Educ* St Edward's Sch Oxford; *m* 1954, Carmel Mary Roseleen, *née* Donnelly; 2 s, 2 da; *Career* served 6 Lancers (Indian Army) and King's Dragoon Gds 1945; Hong Kong and Shanghai Banking Corp: joined 1949, chm 1977-86; treas Univ of Hong Kong 1977-86, chm Br Bank of the Middle East 1980-86; dir: Marine Midland Bank 1980-87, The Interpublic Gp of Cos (USA) 1981, AmBase Corp, Int Totalizer Systems Inc, Global Yield Inc, New World Devpt Ltd, Winsor Ind Corp, Pioneer Int Ltd; memb exec cncl of Hong Kong 1978-86, chm bd of stewards Royal Hong Kong Jockey Club 1981-86 (Hon Steward 1986), pres Surrey CCC 1987-88; JP Hong Kong 1972-86; FCIB 1977 (vice-pres 1984-87), FRSA 1983; kt 1986; *Recreations* racing, horology, cricket, bridge; *Clubs* Cavalry and Guards', Carlton, MCC, Surrey CCC, Portland, Hong Kong; *Style*— Sir Michael Sandberg, CBE; 41 Montpelier Square, London SW7 1JZ (☎ 071 589 7606); Domaine de la Haut Germaine, 06510 Le Broc, Alpes Maritimes, France (☎ 010 33 93 290762)

SANDELL, Kenneth Edwin; s of Ernest Arthur Sandell (d 1980); *b* 28 April 1929; *Educ* Tollington Sch; *m* 1960, Lillian Rose, *née* Buckingham; 1 s (Mark b 1966), 1 da (Joanne b 1970); *Career* served Suez 1948-49; insur broker; dir: Fenchurch Marine Brokers Ltd 1971-85, Samson Menzies Ltd 1972-85, Well Marine Reinsurance Brokers Ltd 1985; memb Lloyds; *Recreations* reading, youth work; *Style*— Kenneth Sandell, Esq; 4 Cranley Rd, Westcliff-on-Sea, Essex (☎ 0702 342906)

SANDELL, Michael Charles Caines; s of Christopher Ernest Sandell (d 1974), of Amesbury, Wilts, and Doris Mary, *née* Waters; *b* 30 Sept 1933; *Educ* Cheltenham, Royal Agric Coll Cirencester (Dip in rural estate mgmnt); *m* 19 Sept 1959, (Janet) Heather, da of William Duncan Montgomery; 2 da (Camilla Gay b 3 March 1962), Georgina Caroline b 1 April 1964); *Career* Nat Serv Cmmnd RA served Gibraltar 1952-53; asst land agent Duke of Rutland's Belvoir Castle Estate 1957-59; Fisher & Co Market Harborough: asst land agent 1959-71, ptnr 1971-81, sr ptnr 1981-83; sr ptnr Fisher Hoggarth Chartered Surveyors Market Harborough 1983-; valuer Agricultural Mortgage Corporation plc 1976-; FRICA 1970; *Recreations* shooting, gardening, tennis; *Style*— Michael Sandell, Esq; Village Farm, Sutton Bassett, Market Harborough, Leicestershire LE16 8HP; Fisher Hoggarth, Chartered Surveyors, 40 High St, Market Harborough, Leicestershire LE16 7NX (☎ 0858 410200, fax 0858 410207)

SANDELSON, Bernice Helen; da of Maurice Wingate (d 1972), and Bella Davis; *b* 29 March 1937; *Educ* Queens Coll London; *m* 10 June 1958, Victor Sandelson; 2 s, 2 da; *Career* owner and md Cartoon Originals 1974-77, proprietor and md Montpelier Studio (gallery specialising in 20 C British Art) 1979-; *Recreations* gallery-crawling; *Clubs* Vanderbilt; *Style*— Mrs Bernice Sandelson; Montpelier Studio Ltd, 4 Montpelier St, London SW7 1EZ (☎ 071 584 0667

SANDELSON, Neville Devonshire; s of David Sandelson, OBE; *b* 27 Nov 1923; *Educ* Westminster, Trinity Coll Cambridge; *m* 1959, Nana Karlinski, of Neuilly sur Seine; 1 s, 2 da; *Career* barr Inner Temple 1946, MP (Lab) Hayes and Harlington 1971-74, Hillingdon, Hayes and Harlington (SDP 1981-84) 1974-83, having fought previous elections in other constituencies; fndr memb and treas Manifesto Gp 1975-80, fndr memb SDP 1981; former memb: European Cmmn Lab Ctee for Europe, European Cmmn Wider Share Ownership Cncl, National Ctee Electoral Reform Cncl; jt sec British-Greek Parly Gp, vice-chm SDP Friends of Israel (resigned over Israeli bombardment of Beirut 1982); SDP spokesman on NI and Arts to 1983; vice-chm Afghanistan Support Ctee; *Clubs* Reform; *Style*— Neville Sandelson Esq; 1 Hare Court, Temple, London EC4 (☎ 01 353 0691)

SANDEMAN, Gavin Fraser; s of Richard Fraser Sandeman, of The Moorings, Four Elms, Edenbridge, Kent, and Winifred Frances, *née* Richardson; *b* 30 May 1946; *Educ* Seaford Coll Sussex; *m* 1, (m dis); m 2, Josephine Anne, *née* Casey; 2 s (Hugh Philip Fraser b 1 May 1981, George Richard Fraser b 15 Aug 1986), 1 da (Claire Lucy Frances b 19 Dec 1983); *Career* dir Abbott & Nicol Advertising 1989-; *Style*— Gavin Sandeman, Esq; 37 Woodbury Ave, Petersfield, Hampshire (☎ 0730 63603); Abbott & Nicol Advertising, Linden House, Tork St, Alton, Hampshire (☎ 0420 86810)

SANDEMAN, John Charles; s of Ian Roberts Sandeman (d 1985), of Howick, SA; and Marie Jessie, *née* Hughes; *b* 10 Jan 1929; *Educ* Durban HS, Witwatersrand Univ (MB, Bch), Univ of Liverpool; *m* 16 Jan 1954, Dr (Eileen) Hilda Sandeman, da of Ven Cannon Redvers Percival Yates Rouse (d 1976); 2 s (Ian Peter b 1957, Derek David b 1958), 1 da (Jillian Joy b 1955); *Career* currently orthopaedic surgn; author of pubns on comparative anatomy and orthopaedics in med jls; memb various med and orthopaedics socs 1952-; FRCS, MChOrth, FCS (SA), FRCSEd; *Recreations* weight lifting, golf, wind surfing; *Style*— John Sandeman, Esq; 6 The Anchorage, Parkgate, Cheshire; 75 Rodney St, Liverpool (☎ 051 709 4511)

SANDEMAN, Hon Mrs (Sylvia Margaret); *née* Maclehose; yr da of Baron Maclehose of Beoch; *b* 29 July 1949; *Educ* Downe House; *m* 1970, Ronald Leighton Sandeman, s of Cargill Leighton Sandeman; 1 da (b 1975); *Career* chm Scottish Spinal Cord Injury Assoc; memb Scottish Cncl on Disability; *Recreations* sailing; *Clubs* Royal Northern and Clyde Yacht; *Style*— The Hon Mrs Sandeman; Rosgaradh, West Dhuhill Drive, Helensburgh G84 9AW (☎ 0436 75105)

SANDEMAN, Timothy Walter; s of Maj Patrick Walter Sandeman, MC (d 1959), and

Olive Eva, *née* Wootton; *b* 6 April 1928; *Educ* Eton; *m* 14 Dec 1951, Selma Anna Elizabeth, yst da of late Carl Dines Dreyer, of Copenhagen, Denmark; 2 s (John Carl Patrick b 1953, Michael Walter b 1962), 1 da (Susanne b 1956); *Career* chm Seagram UK Ltd Nov 1981-; *Style*— Timothy Sandeman Esq; c/o Seagram UK Ltd, Seagram Distillers House, Dacre St, London SW1 (☎ 071 222 4343)

SANDERCOCK, Dr Peter Andrew Gale; s of Capt Michael John Gale Sandercock, of Northwood, Midds, and Helen Betty, *née* Howland; *b* 16 April 1951; *Educ* Shrewsbury, New Coll Oxford (MA, BMB Ch, DM); *m* 10 Sept 1977, Janet Mary, da of Peter Searell Andrews, of Little Addington, Northants; 3 s (David, Robert, Andrew), 1 da (Eleanor); *Career* actg clinical lectr Univ of Oxford 1981-85, lectr Univ of Liverpool 1985-87, sr lectr Univ of Edinburgh 1988-; sec Br Stroke Res Gp; MRCP 1979; *Books* Stroke (1987); *Style*— Dr Peter Sandercock; Dept of Clinical Neuroscience, Western Gen Hosp, Crewe Rd, Edinburgh EH4 2XU (☎ 031 343 6639, fax 031 332 5150)

SANDERS, Brooke; da of Reginald Thomas Sanders, and Marjorie Dora, *née* Sims; *b* 3 May 1949; *Educ* Covent of the Scared Hearts; *Career* race horse trainer and amateur jockey; as a jockey: winner of 38 races flat and Nat Hunt, Lady Champion Jockey 1974, Malta champion 1975, winner Ladies Diamond Stakes Ascot 1976 (1974); as a trainer: winner Cesaerwitch with Double Dutch 1989; *Style*— Brooke Sanders; Chalk Pit Stables, Headley Road, Epsom, Surrey (☎ 03722 78453)

SANDERS, Prof Carol; da of Ronald Humphrey Sanders (d 1957), and Evelyn Maud, *née* Bradbury (now Mrs Payn); *b* 31 Dec 1944; *Educ* Univ of Cambridge (MA), Univ of London (PGCE), Univ of Paris (Doctorat de l'Université); *m* 29 July 1978, Peter Mary Eugene Figueroa, s of Rupert Aston (d 1969); 1 s (James Michael b 1986), 1 da (Emma Michelle b 1982); *Career* lectr in French: Univ of Reading 1969-72, Univ of W Indies 1972-76, Univ of Sussex 1977-84; reader then prof of French Australian Nat Univ Canberra 1984-88, prof of French Univ of Surrey 1988-; fndn pres Assoc for French Language Studies, memb Ctee Assoc Univ Professors of French, ed Journal of French Language Studies; FIL, memb Assoc for French Language Studies; Chevalier Des Palmes Académiques France 1983; *Books* F de Saussure: Cours De Linguistique Générale (1979), Cours De Français Contemporain (with M M Gervais, 1986), Lire Le Pacifique (with K Muller, 1989); *Recreations* travel, reading, writing; *Style*— Prof Carol Sanders; Dept of Linguistic & International Studies, University of Surrey, Guildford GU2 5XH (☎ 0483 571281, fax 0483 300803, telex 859331)

SANDERS, Colin Derek; s of Joseph Sanders (d 1988), and Josephine May, *née* Bryer; *b* 2 Jan 1944; *Educ* Cheltenham; *m* 7 Sept 1968, Marlene Elizabeth, da of Reginald Frank Webb; 2 s (Paul Edward, Timothy Colin), 1 da (Phillippa Jane); *Career* fndr and non-exec dir Brewmaker plc (formerly chm); *Recreations* travel, old cars, gardening; *Style*— Colin Sanders, Esq; Webb's Land, Wickham, Hants PO17 5N5 (fax 0329 832756)

SANDERS, (June) Deidre; da of Philip Ronald Heaton, of Scotland, and Audrey Minton, *née* Harvey (d 1972); *b* 9 June 1945; *Educ* Harrow County GS for Girls, Univ of Sheffield (BA); *m* 12 Dec 1969, Richard James, 2 da (Susan b 1976, Phoebe b 1988); *Career* journalist, author, broadcaster; problem-page ed The Sun; Jubilee Medal 1977; *Books* Kitchen Sink or Swim? (1982), Women and Depression (1984), Woman Book of Love and Sex (1985), Woman Report on Men (1987); *Style*— Mrs Deidre Sanders; PO Box 488, The Sun, Virginia Street, London E1 9BZ (☎ 071 481 4100, telex 925 088)

SANDERS, Donald Neil; CB (1983); s of Lorenzo George Sanders (d 1965), and Rosina May Marsh; *b* 21 June 1927; *Educ* Wollongong HS NSW Australia, Univ of Sydney (B Ec); *m* 1952, Betty Elaine, da of William Bertie Constance (d 1955); 4 s (Michael, Robert, Jonathan, Martin), 1 da (Jennifer); *Career* Cwlth Bank of Australia 1943-60, Aust Treasy 1956, Bank of England 1960; Reserve Bank of Australia 1960: supt credit policy, banking dept 1964-66, dep mangr banking dept 1966-67, dep mangr res dept 1967-70; Aust Embassy Washington 1968: chief mangr securities markets dept 1970-72, chief mangr banking & finance dept 1972-74 (advsr and chief mangr 1974-75); dep govr and dep chm Reserve Bank of Australia 1975-87; md Commonwealth Banking Corporation 1987-; *Recreations* opera, music, golf; *Clubs* Killara Golf; *Style*— D N Sanders, Esq, CB; Commonwealth Banking Corporation, Cnr Pitt St & Martin Place, Sydney NSW 2000

SANDERS, Dr Eric; s of Albert Sanders, and Caroline, *née* Johnson; *b* 22 Oct 1946; *Educ* Stanley GS Co Durham, Univ of Wales (BSc, MB); *m* 10 July 1971, Dianne Marilyn, da of David Denzil Harris Thomas, of St David's St, Carmarthen; 2 s (Gareth Wyn b 20 June 1974, Gethyn Huw b 21 Sept 1976), 1 da (Angharad Jane b 4 June 1980); *Career* pre-registration house offr Royal Infirmary Cardiff 1971, sr house offr Univ Hosp Wales 1972-74, res registrar and lectr Kruf Inst Renal Disease Royal Infirmary Cardiff 1974-80, conslt physician and dir dialysis servs W Wales Hosps Carmarthen 1980-; tstee and hon tres Kidney Res Unit Wales Fndn, memb cncl Wales Diabetes Res Tst, former pres and regnl offr Lions Int Dist 105W; memb Renal Assoc GB, EDTA, MRCP 1974, FRCP 1990; *Books* Nephrology Illustrated (1981); *Recreations* local community service, music; *Style*— Dr Eric Sanders; Dunelm, Ael-y-Bryn, Carmarthen, Dyfed SA31 2HB (☎ 0267 221528); W Wales Hosp, Carmarthen SA31 2AF (☎ 0267 235151)

SANDERS, Geoffrey (Geoff); MBE (1988); s of John Claridge Sanders (d 1979), and Elsie, *née* Boothby (d 1965); *b* 28 Feb 1928; *Educ* Hutton GS nr Preston Lancs, Hull Univ Coll, Univ of London (BA); *m* 16 Aug 1952, Nora Irene, da of Bertie Southgate (d 1965); 2 s (Paul b 24 Oct 1954, Mark b 25 Sept 1957); *Career* dep headmaster King Edward VI Camp Hill Sch for Boys Birmingham 1968-74 (joined 1952, sr history master 1953-68, sr house master 1956-58), headmaster King Edward VI Five Ways Sch Birmingham 1974-90; govr King Edward VI Schs Birmingham 1990-, tstee Ackers Tst Birmingham 1989-; C of E reader 1954-, fndr chm Br Schs Canoeing Assoc 1970-; chm: Cncl and Exec Br Canoe Union, Jubilee Canoeing Fndn 1988-, Nat Cncl for Schs Sports 1989- (1979); pres Solihull Canoe Club 1989-; memb SHA; *Books* BCU Coaching Handbook (1964-69), Canoeing for Schools and Youth Groups (1966-); *Recreations* canoeing, caravanning, swimming, industrial archeology; *Style*— Geoff Sanders, Esq, MBE; 4 Barston Lane, Solihull, W Midlands B91 2SS (☎ 021 705 2391)

SANDERS, Dr John Derek; s of Alderman John T Sanders, JP (d 1944), and Ethel Mary, *née* Trivett (d 1985); *b* 26 Nov 1933; *Educ* Felsted, Royal Coll of Music (major scholar, ARCM), Gonville & Caius Coll Cambridge (organ scholar, MA, MusB); *m* 22 July 1967, Janet Ann, da of Leonard Dawson (d 1976); 1 s (Jonathan Mark), 1 da (Anna Catharine); *Career* cmmnd offr RA 1956-58; dir of music King's Sch and asst organist Gloucester Cathedral 1958-63; organist and master of choristers: Chester Cathedral 1964-67, Gloucester Cathedral 1967-; dir of music Cheltenham Ladies' Coll 1968-; pres: Gloucestershire Organists Assoc, Cathedral Organists Assoc 1990-; conductor: Gloucestershire Symphony Orch, Gloucester Choral Soc, Gloucester Three Choirs Festival; Freeman City of London 1986, Liveryman Worshipful Co of Musicians 1987; Lambeth Degree Doctor of Music 1990; FRCO 1956; *Publications* Festival Te Deum (1962), Soliloquy for Organ (1977), Toccata For Organ (1979), Te Deum Laudamus (1985), Jubilate Deo (1986), Two Prayers (1989); *Recreations* gastronomy, travel, walking; *Style*— Dr John Sanders; 7 Miller's Green, Gloucester GL1 2BN (☎ 0452 24764)

SANDERS, Michael David; s of Norris Manley Sanders, of Priors Barn, Farringdon, Alton, Hants, and Gertrude Florence, *née* Hayley; *b* 19 Sept 1935; *Educ* Tonbridge, Guy's Hosp Med Sch (MB BS, DO); *m* 1 Nov 1969, Thalia Margaret, da of Thomas Garlick (d 1961), of The Bourne, Ashover, Derbyshire; 1 s (Rupert Miles, b 16 March 1971), 1 da (Melissa Tryce, b 25 May 1973); *Career* house surgn Guys Hosp 1959, res offr Moorfields Eye Hosp 1963-67, Alexander Piggot Werner Meml Fell Univ of California San Francisco 1967-68; conslt opthalmologist: Nat Hosp Nervous Diseases 1969, St Thomas' Hosp 1972; civil conslt opthalmology RAF 1972; distinguished lectures: Middlemore Lectre 1985, Percival Hay 1986, Sir Stewart Duke-Elder 1987, Ida Mann 1987, Lettsomian 1988; hon: memb Pacific Coast Oto-Opthalmological Soc, hon conslt Sydney Hosp Univ of Sydney; asst ed British Journal of Opthalmology, tstee Frost Fndn, med advsr Iris Fund for Prevention of Blindness, pres Int Neuro-Opthalmology Soc; FRCP, FRCS, FCOpth; *Books* Topics in Neuro-Ophthalmology (1979), Computerised Tomography in Neuro-Ophthalmology (1982); *Recreations* golf; *Clubs* Hurlingham, Hankley Cmmn; *Style*— Michael Sanders, Esq; 9 Alma Terrace, Allen St, London W8 6QY (☎ 071 937 7955); Ivy Cottage, Chawton, Alton, Hants (☎ 0420 86681); 8 Upper Wimpole St, London W1M 7TD (☎ 071 935 5038)

SANDERS, Michael John; s of Dr Laz Jacob Sanders (d 1975), and Sadie, *née* Ginsburg (d 1985); *b* 9 June 1938; *Educ* Grey HS Port Elizabeth, Univ of Witwatersrand Johannesburg; *m* 11 April 1965, Melanie Beil, da of Dr Maurice Peskin (d 1957); 2 s (Grant b 30 Oct 1968, David Lars b 9 Oct 1978), 1 da (Lisa Maree b 27 March 1967); *Career* med rep Merk Sharp & Dohme SA 1960-62, clinical trials mangr Warner Lambert SA 1962-64, institutional sales mangr Schering plough SA 1964-67; md: Panvet (Pty) Ltd SA 1967-75, Peter Hand Panvet (Pty) Ltd SA, Peter Hand GB 1975-80; chm and chief exec offr: Peter Hand Holdings Ltd, Peter Hand (GB) Ltd, PH Pharmaceutical Ltd, Nutrikem Ltd, Phenix Pharmaceuticals Antwerp; *Recreations* scuba diving, golf, sailing, skiing, tennis; *Clubs* RAC London, Dyrham Country Herts; *Style*— Michael Sanders, Esq; c/o Peter Hand, Peter Hand House, 15-19 Church Rd, Stanmore, Middx, England HA7 4AR (☎ 081 954 7422, fax 081 954 1897, telex 922029)

SANDERS, Paul David; s of David Melvyn Sanders, of Andover, Hants, and Pamela Margaret, *née* Freeth; *b* 11 Jan 1962; *Educ* Winton Comp Andover, Basingstoke Coll, Cricklade Coll Andover, Salisbury Tech Coll (dip in business studies); *m* 14 Nov 1987, Helen Claire, da of Alfred William Phillips (d 1980); 1 da (Amy Louise b 5 March 1990); *Career* athlete; has represented Eng and GB at 400m 1986-; 400m champion: Hampshire County 1985, 1986, 1987 and 1989 (200m champion 1990), Inter Counties 1986, UK 1989, London 1989; Gold medallist 4 x 400m relay Euro Athletics Championships 1990; represented sch and winner of Nat Schs Basketball Championships, played soccer for Eng Under 18 Boys Clubs; sales exec; GBE Legg Andover: former apprentice industl electrician then Spare Sales Dept then Contract Sales Dept; currently regnl sales exec in packaging machinery Padlocker Ltd; *Clubs* Team Solent Athletic (life memb); *Style*— Paul Sanders, Esq; 73 Watermills Close, Andover, Hants SP10 2ND (☎ 0264 333129); Padlocker Ltd, Unit 5, Brunel Gate, West Portway Industrial Estate, Andover, Hants (☎ 0264 57511, mobile 0831 448556)

SANDERS, Raymond Adrian; s of Leslie Harry Sanders, and Beatrice Sanders; *b* 13 May 1932; *Educ* Univ of Auckland NZ (LLB), LSE (LLB); *m* 1, 1961 (m dis), Anna Margaret Burton; 1 s; m 2, 1985, Virginia Varnell Dunn; 1 da; *Career* in practice as barr and slr NZ 1956-66, ptnr Jackson Russell and Co (barrs & slrs) Auckland NZ 1962-66, pt/t lectr Univ of Auckland 1960-66 (examiner 1961-66), slr Allen and Overy London 1967-71, in practise as barr 1971-73, DHSS 1973-74 and 1975-84, Law Offrs' Dept 1974-75, legal advsr to Warnock Inquiry (Human Fertilization and Embryology) 1982-84, regnl chm Social Security and Med Appeal Tbnls 1984-86, Social Security cmms 1986-; *Books* Credit Management (jtly, 1966), Building Contracts and Practice (1967); *Recreations* theatre, music, cycling, tennis; *Style*— Raymond Sanders, Esq; The Office of the Social Security Commissioners, Harp House, 83 Farringdon St, London EC4

SANDERS, Sir Robert Tait; KBE (1980), CMG (1974); s of Alexander Scott Wilson Sanders (d 1934), of Dunfermline, Fife, and Charlotte McCulloch; *b* 2 Feb 1925; *Educ* Canmore Public Sch Dunfermline, Dunfermline HS, Fettes, Pembroke Coll Cambridge (MA), LSE, SOAS; *m* 1951, Barbara, da of George Sutcliffe (d 1983); 3 s (1 decd); *Career* served Lt 1 Bn Royal Scots 1943-46; dist offr Fiji 1950, sec to Govt Tonga 1956-58, sec to Coconut Indust Inquiry 1963, MLC Fiji 1963-64, sec for Natural Resources 1965-67, actg sec Fijian Affrs 1967, actg chm Native Lands and Fisheries Cmmn 1967, MEC Fiji 1967, sec Chief Min and Cncl of Mins 1967-70; Cabinet 1970-79: Foreign Affrs 1970-74, Home Affrs 1972-74, Info 1975-76; treaties advsr to Govt of Fiji 1985-87; author of newspaper and magazine articles; Fiji Independence Medal 1970; *Books* Interlude in Fiji (1963), Fiji Treaties (1987); *Recreations* golf, music; *Clubs* Royal Scots (Edinburgh), Nausori Golf (Fiji); *Style*— Sir Robert Sanders, KBE, CMG; Greystones Lodge, Broich Terrace, Crieff

SANDERS, Ronald; *b* 26 Jan 1948; *Educ* Sacred Heart RC Sch Guyana, Westminster Sch (London), Boston Univ, Univ of Sussex; *m* 1975, Susan Ramphal; *Career* md Guyana Broadcasting Serv 1973-76, public affrs advsr to PM to Guyana 1973-76, lectr in communications Univ of Guyana 1975-76, pres Carribean Broadcasting Union 1975-76, memb bd of dirs Carribean News Agency 1976-77, conslt to pres Carribean Devpt Bank in Barbados 1977-78, special advsr to Min of Foreign Affrs of Antigua and Barbuda 1978-82, dep perm rep to UN in New York 1982-83, ambass extraordinary and plenipotentiary accredited to UNESCO 1983-87 (memb Bd UNESCO 1985-87), high cmmr to UK 1984-87, advsr on int affrs to Govt of Antigua and Barbuda 1990-; memb Bd of Dirs: Swiss American Bank and Swiss American Nat Bank of Antigua 1990-, Guyana Telephone and Telegraph Co 1991-; author of articles on int affrs; memb of delgn: Non Aligned Heads of Govt Conf 1976, Cwlth Heads of Govt 1975, 1983, 1985; fell Queen Elizabeth House Univ of Oxford 1988 and 1989; *Publications* Broadcasting in Guyana (1978), Antigua and Barbuda: Transition, Trial, Triumph (1984), Inseparable Humanity: An Anthology of Reflections of Shridath Ramphal (ed 1988); *Style*— Ronald Sanders, Esq; 24 Chelmsford Square, London NW10 3AR

SANDERS, Roy; s of Leslie John Sanders, and Marguerite Alice, *née* Knight; *b* 20 Aug 1937; *Educ* Hertford GS, Univ of London (BSc Hons, MB BS); *m* 1, 25 July 1961 (m dis 1977), Ann Ruth, da of William Costar; 2 s (Andrew St John William b 1965, Charles St John David b 1966), 1 da (Lyvia Ann b 1963); m 2, 6 Jan 1984, Fleur Annette, da of Brian Chandler, of St Gallen, Austria; *Career* HAC Gunner 1957-62, Regt MO 1963-75, HAC Co of Pikemen and Musketeers 1982-; conslt plastic surgn The Mount Vernon Centre for Plastic Maxillofacial and Oral Surgery; hon sr lectr Univ of London; sec: Br Assoc of Plastic Surgns 1986-88, Br Assoc of Aesthetic Plastic Surgns 1985-87; chm Medical Equestrian Assoc 1985-86, pres Plastic Surgery Section RSM of London 1989-90, memb Medical Artists' Assoc; Freeman City of London, Liveryman Soc of Apothecaries of London; LRCP, MRCS 1962, FRCS 1967; *Recreations* equestrian activities, painting in watercolour; *Clubs* Athenaeum; *Style*— Roy Sanders, Esq; 77 Harley St, London WIN 1DE (☎ 071 935 7417); Upper Rye Farm, Moreton in Marsh, Glos (☎ 0608 50542); Suite 1, 82 Portland Place, London W1 (☎ 071 580 3541, fax 071 436 2954)

SANDERS, Dr Samuel Chandrarajan; s of David Selvamanickam Sanders (d 1980), of Jaffna, Sri Lanka, and Harriet Chellammah, *née* Handy; *b* 1 July 1932; *Educ* Jaffna Coll Sri Lanka, Ceylon (MB BS), Univ Colombo; *m* 30 Jan 1960, Irene Mangaystkarasi, da of Sittampalam Saravanamuttu (d 1971), of Jaffna, Sri Lanka; 1 s (David b 27 Oct 1968), 2 da (Roshini b 15 Nov 1961, Sureshini b 12 Aug 1965); *Career* res house offr Ceylon 1957-58, varied experience in med surgery neurosurgery public health and forensic med Sri Lanka 1958-70, postgrad trg in forensic med and clinical therapeutics Univ of Glasgow, Guy's and Edinburgh Royal Infirmary 1971-72; registrar then sr registrar Glasgow Western Dist 1973-76, conslt physician Glasgow western Dist 1976-; author various papers on subjects incl cerebral abcesses and epilepsy in the elderly; hon clinical sr lectr Univ of Glasgow, hon lectr Scot Retirement Cncl; med advsr Social Serv Dept Glasgow NW dist; memb: Br Geriatrics Soc; BMA; FRCP; *Books* Advanced Geriatric Medicine (vol 4, contrib, 1984); *Recreations* sport, travel, reading, fishing; *Style—* Dr Samuel Sanders; 28 Hillfoot Drive, Bearsden, Glasgow G61 3QF (☎ 041 942 9388); Gartnavel General Hospital, 1053 Great Western Rd, Glasgow G12 OYN (☎ 041 334 8122)

SANDERS, Dr Stuart; s of David Sadofsky (d 1955), and Florence, *née* Rakusen; *b* 20 Nov 1934; *Educ* Hymers Coll Hull, Univ of Leeds Medical Sch (MB, ChB, MRCS, LRCP, DCH, DObst ROCG, James and Mabel Gaunt Prize in Paediatrics); *m* 15 March 1979, Kathryn, da of Rudolf Bleichroeder; 2 s (Jonathan b 25 Dec 1979, Jeremy b 16 June 1983); *Career* paediatric house physician Leeds Gen Infirmary 1958-59, obstetric house surgn Manygates Maternity Hosp Wakefield 1959, medical sr house offr Pinderfields Gen Hosp Wakefield 1960-61, res pathologist Royal Free Hosp 1961-62, GP NHS 1962-66, paediatric clinical asst Royal Free Hosp 1963-67, sr res fell Hosp for Sick Children Great Ormond St London 1966-74, private physician and princ medical advsr to Sears, Rosehaugh, Wickes, Chelsfield and other pub cos and doctor accredited to Swissair and Swiss Embassy 1962-; JP 1976-80; chm: St Marylebone Div BMA 1984-87, Ind Doctors Forum 1990-; Gold Medal Hunterian Soc 1963; Freeman City of London 1978; memb: Worshipful Soc of Apothecaries, RSM, Chelsea Clinical Soc, BMA; *Recreations* family, skiing, bridge, theatre, music; *Clubs* Annabel's, Mark's; *Style—* Dr Stuart Sanders; 22 Harmont House, 20 Harley Street, London W1 (☎ 071 935 5687, fax 071 436 4387, car 0836 625905)

SANDERS-CROOK, William Stanley; MBE (1972); s of William Charles Herbert Crook (d 1966), of Twickenham, Middx, and Mary Amelia, *née* Green (d 1986); *b* 2 Nov 1933; *Educ* Latymer Upper Sch, RMA Sandhurst; *m* 1, 5 May 1962; 1 s (William b 1963), 1 da (Deborah b 1972); m 2, 20 Dec 1982, Jean Rosemary, da of Eric Walker (d 1966), of Beaconside, Barnstaple, N Devon; *Career* Regular Army 1953-77; Maj BAOR; served: Suez, Malaya, Borneo, Singapore, Miny of Def, Brunei; equestrian journalist; dir: John Roberts Conslts 1977-79, Jean Kittermaster PR 1981; MBIM; *novels* Four Days (1979), Death Run (1980), Triple Seven (1981); *Recreations* journalism, travel, scuba diving (PADI instructor), riding (BHSAI), narrowboating, sport, racing canoeing, (Cross Channel record (Guinness Book of Records) 1961-80, Devizes to Westminster Record 1961), judo; *Style—* William Sanders-Crook, Esq, MBE; Jean Kittermaster Public Relations, 239 Kings Rd, London SW3 5EJ (☎ 01 352 6811, fax 01 351 9215)

SANDERSON, Dr Alan Lindsay; s (twin) of 1 Baron Sanderson of Ayot, MC (UK 1960); suc father 15 Aug 1971 and disclaimed his peerage for life 28 Sept 1971; *b* 12 Jan 1931; *Educ* Uppingham; *m* 1959, Gertrud, da of Herman Boschler; 1 s (Michael), 4 da (Evelyn, Frances, Andrea, Stephanie b 1970); *Career* conslt psychiatrist Luton and Dunstable Hosp; MB, BS London, MRCP London, MRCPsych; *Style—* Dr Alan Sanderson; 2 Caroline Close, W2 4RW (☎ 071 229 8533)

SANDERSON, Col (Thomas) Allan; s of James Brown Sanderson (d 1932), and Margaret Robertson, *née* Neil (d 1950); *b* 7 May 1927; *Educ* George Watson's Boys Coll, Univ of Edinburgh (MB, ChB); *m* 1 1954, (m dis) Winifred Brown; 2 da (Sarah b 1955, Janey b 1957); m 2, 2 Sept 1963, Anne Patricia, da of Walter Roland Haresign, of Durban; 1 da (Tracy b 1964); *Career* Col Cdr: Med Army in Scotland 1985, Med Br Forces Hong Kong 1982-85, Med Army in Scotland 1980-82; Maj 1 Bn 1 Kings African rifles Nyasaland 1962-64; *Recreations* golf, curling, reading; *Clubs* Murrayfield Golf Edinburgh; *Style—* Col Allan Sanderson; Kellerstain Lodge, By Gogar, Edinburgh EH12 9BS (☎ 031 339 5347); Army Headquarters, Scotland, Edinburgh EG1 2YX (☎ 031 336 1761)

SANDERSON, Annie Helena (Nan); *née* McDonagh; da of James McDonagh (d 1962), and Elizabeth, *née* McGeough (d 1935); *b* 8 Oct 1919; *Educ* St Clare's Convent and Sacred Heart Sch, Newry Co Down NI; *m* 1, 14 Feb 1942, Pilot Offr Edward Frederick Lloyd (ka 1942); m 2, 26 April 1947, Rupert Anthony Sanderson, s of late Herbert James Walter Sanderson; 2 s (Colin b 26 June 1948, Stephen b 5 Dec 1953); *Career* dir and co sec Sanderson Marine Craft Ltd Norwich; parish cncllr 1960-88, dist cncllr Blofield & Flegg RDC 1961-74, memb Broadland DC 1976-; memb: Gt Yarmouth and Waveney Co Health Cncl, Gt Yarmouth and Waveney DHA 1976-90, Norfolk Valuation Panel 1976-; *Recreations* sailing, reading, music; *Style—* Mrs Nan Sanderson; The Warren, Riverside, Reedham, Norwich NR13 3TE (☎ 0493 701 547)

SANDERSON, Sir (Frank Philip) Bryan; 2 Bt (UK 1920) of Malling Deanery, South Malling, Co Sussex; s of Sir Frank Bernard Sanderson, 1 Bt (d 1965); *b* 18 Feb 1910; *Educ* Stowe, Pembroke Coll Oxford; *m* 1933, Annette Irene Caroline (d 1967), da of late Col Korab Laskowski of Warsaw and gda of Gen Count Edouard de Castellaz; 2 s, 1 da; *Heir* s, Frank Sanderson; *Career* memb Lloyd's, chm Humber Fish Manure Co Ltd, Hull; *Style—* Sir Bryan Sanderson, Bt; Lychgate Cottage, Scaynes Hill, Haywards Heath, W Sussex

SANDERSON, Charles James; s of J C Sanderson, of 19 Ansell Terrace, London, and E K Sanderson; *b* 18 Aug 1949; *Educ* Millfield, Byam Shaw Sch of Drawing and Painting; *Career* painter; exhibited: Royal Academy, Paris Salon, Camden Arts Centre, Westminster Cathedral, New Arts Centre, John Neville Gallery Canterbury; *Recreations* jogging, music, gardening, cooking, travel; *Style—* Charles Sanderson, Esq; 7 Gordon Place, London W8 4JD (☎ 071 937 4922)

SANDERSON, Eric Fenton; s of Francis Kirton Sanderson, of Dundee, and Margarita Shand, *née* Fenton; *b* 14 Oct 1951; *Educ* Morgan Acad Dundee, Univ of Dundee (LlB, pres Students' Assoc) Harvard Business Sch (AMP); *m* 26 July 1975, Patricia Ann, da of Lt-Cdr Donald Brian Shaw; 3 da (Anna b 1 June 1979, Caroline b 30 June 1982, Emma b 12 April 1985); *Career* apprentice Touche Ross & Co Edinburgh, CA 1976; The British Linen Bank Ltd: joined 1976, dir and head corp fin 1984, chief exec 1989-; ACA 1976, memb IOD 1989; *Recreations* tennis, gardening, photography; *Clubs* New (Edinburgh); *Style—* Eric Sanderson, Esq; The British Linen Bank Ltd, 4 Melville St, Edinburgh EH3 7NZ (☎ 031 243 8301, fax 031 243 8393)

SANDERSON, Frank Linton; s and h of Sir Bryan Sanderson, 2 Bt, by Annette Irene Caroline (d 1967), da of late Col Korab Laskowski, of Warsaw, and gda of Gen Count Edouard de Castellaz; *b* 21 Nov 1933; *Educ* Stowe, Salamanca Univ; *m* 1961, Margaret Ann, da of John C Maxwell (d 1976), of New York USA; 2 s (David b 1962, Michael b 1965), 3 da (Caroline b 1966, Nina b 1968, Katherine b 1968 (twins)); *Career* RNVR 1950-65; *Style—* Frank Sanderson, Esq; Grandturzel Farm, Burwash, E Sussex

SANDERSON, Dr John Elsby; s of Arthur John Sanderson, of Rhoose Glamorgan, and Ruth Megan, *née* Griffiths; *b* 1 May 1949; *Educ* Blundell's, Cambridge (BA, MA, MD), St Bartholomews Hosp (MB BChir); *m* 1, 1972 (m dis 1977), Susanna Marion, da of Richard Tewson, of Hempstead Essex; m 2, 1980, Dr Julia Dorothy Billingham, da of David Billingham, of Crowhurst Sussex; 1 s (Henry John Elsby b 1981), 1 da (Vanessa Maureen b 1980); *Career* house physician and surgn St Bartholomew's Hosp London 1973-74, sr house physician Brompton and Hammersmith Hosps 1974-75, res registrar RPMS Hammersmith Hosp 1975-78, lectr in cardiovascular med Univ of Oxford and John Radcliffe Hosp 1978-81, Wellcome Tst lectr St Marys Hosp and hon conslt physician Kenyatta Hosp Nairobi 1981-83, conslt physician and cardiologist Taunton and Somerset Hosp and clinical tutor Univ of Bristol; memb: BMA, Br Cardiac Soc, Br Hypertension Soc, Euro Soc of Cardiology; MRCP, FRSTM & H; *Books* pubns & papers on cardiomyopathy, tropical heart disease, pacemakers and Ischaemic heart disease; *Recreations* family, music, reading novels, tennis and walking; *Clubs* Presidents; *Style—* Dr John Sanderson; Taunton and Somerset Hospital, Musgrove Park, Taunton, Somerset (☎ 0823 333444)

SANDERSON, Hon Murray Lee; s (twin) of 1 Baron Sanderson of Ayot, MC (d 1971), and bro of Dr Alan Sanderson, *qv*; *b* 1931; *Educ* Rugby, Trinity Coll Oxford, King's Cambridge; *m* 1, 1966 (m dis 1972), Muriel, da of late George Williams; m 2, 1973, Eva, da of Rev David Simfukwe; 1 s, 1 da; *Career* company dir; admin offr Kenya 1956-63; *Style—* The Hon Murray Sanderson; PO Box 2253, Kitwe, Zambia

SANDERSON, Very Rev Peter Oliver; s of Harold Beckwith Carling Sanderson (d 1978), and Doris Amelia, *née* Oliver (d 1981); *b* 26 Jan 1929; *Educ* South Shields HS, St Chad's Coll Durham Univ (BA, DipTh); *m* 4 April 1956, Doreen, da of Robert Kay Gibson (d 1968); 2 s (Michael b 1958, Richard b 1968, d 1985), 1 da (Jane b 1959); *Career* Nat Serv RAF 1947-49; ordained: deacon 1954, priest 1955; asst Curate Houghton-le-Spring Durham Diocese 1954-59, rector St Thomas-ye-Vale Diocese of Jamaica 1959-63, chaplains' branch RAF 1963-67; vicar: Winksley-cum-Grantley and Aldfield with Studley Ripon Diocese 1967-74, St Aidan's Leeds Diocese of Ripon 1974-84; provost St Paul's Cathedral Dundee Diocese of Brechin 1984-; *Recreations* reading, walking, listening to music; *Style—* The Very Rev the Provost of St Paul's Cathedral Dundee; Cathedral Rectory, 4 Richmond Terrace, Dundee DD2 1BQ (☎ 0382 68 548); Cathedral Office, Castlehill, Dundee DD1 1TD (☎ 0382 24 486)

SANDERSON, Dr Philip James; s of James Sanderson (d 1987), and Dorothy Mary Eustace Sanderson; *b* 13 Jan 1935; *Educ* Kings Sch Canterbury, Univ of London (MB BS, PhD), FRCPath; *m* 11 June 1960 (m dis 1983), Margaret Ayres; 1 s (James b 16 April 1966), 1 da (Sarah b 31 Oct 1963); *Career* trainee bacteriologist Central Public Health Laboratory 1961-64, St Mary's Hosp 1964-66, MRC 1966-70, currently conslt microbiologist Edgware Gen Hosp; memb: BMA 1960, Hosp Infection Soc 1972; FRCPath; *Books* Antibiotics for Surgical Infections (1983); *Style—* Dr Philip Sanderson; 26 Chalcot Rd, London NW1 (☎ 071 586 4442); Edgware Gen Hosp, Edgware, Middx HA8 0AD (☎ 081 952 2381 ext 6871)

SANDERSON, Roy; OBE (1983); s of George Sanderson (d 1938), and Lillian, *née* Charlesworth (d 1939); *b* 15 Feb 1931; *Educ* Leicester, King Richards Royal GS; *m* 25 Aug 1951, Jean Lillian, s of James Booth; 3 s (Roy James, Alan (d 1973), Kevin); *Career* Nat Serv Lance-Corpl REME 1949-51; convenor of shop stewards Lucas Aerospace Hemel Hempstead 1952-67, nat sec EETPU 1987- (asst educn offr 1967-69, nat offr 1969-87); non-exec dir UKAEA 1987-; memb: Exec Ctee The Industrial Soc, Armed Forces Pay Review Body, Exec Cncl Confedn of Shipbuilding and Engrg Unions, Econ and Social Ctee of Euro Communities; *Recreations* golf, snooker, supporter of Watford FC; *Clubs* Shendish (Hemel Hempstead); *Style—* Roy Sanderson, Esq, OBE; 162 Belswains Lane, Hemel Hempstead, Hertfordshire (☎ 0442 42033); Hayes Court, West Common Rd, Hayes, Bromley, Kent (☎ 081 462 7755)

SANDERSON, Theresa Ione (Tessa); MBE (1985); *b* 14 March 1956; *Educ* Wards Bridge Comp Wednesfield, Wolverhampton and Bilston Coll of Further Educn; *Career* athlete; represented GB 1974- (jr 1973-74); honours at javelin incl: English Schs champion twice, Gold medal Cwlth Games 1978, 1986, 1990, Silver medal Euro Championships 1978, Gold medal Olympic Games 1984 (Olympic record); records: UK javelin 1976 and 1983, UK heptathlon 1981; sports presenter Sky News 1989-; involved with numerous orgns and charities incl: Disabled Olympics (patron), Sickle Cell Anemia, Dance for Everyone, Br Inst for Brain Injured Children, Gt Ormond St, Variety Club, Save the Children; hon fell Wolverhampton Poly, Hon BSc Univ of Birmingham; memb Equity 1990; female athlete of the year Br Athletics Writers' Assoc 1977, 1978, 1984, sports personality of the year Midland Region Variety Club twice; Tessa - My Life in Athletics (Autobiography, 1985); *Recreations* cardiofunk, low impact aerobic exercise workout); *Clubs* Hounslow Athletics; *Style—* Miss Tessa Sanderson, MBE; Tee & Dee Promotions Ltd, Atlas Business Centre, Oxgate Lane, London NW2 7HU (☎ 081 450 9339, or 071 782 3213)

SANDERSON, Timothy William; s of Dr Michael William Bristowe Sanderson, and Mrs Kay Glendinning, *née* Holman; *b* 3 March 1958; *Educ* Uppingham, Univ Coll Oxford (MA); *m* 9 Oct 1987, Damaris Stella Lavinia Margot Muir, da of Armitage Clifford-Taylor (d 1967), of Hilden Hall, Penn, Bucks; 1 s (Hugh William Muir b 27 Nov 1990); *Career* Hill Samuel Investment Management Group 1979-90, dir Delaware International Advisers Ltd 1990-; tstee Dunhill Medical Tst; AMSIA; *Recreations* squash, walking, book collecting, literature, reading, theatre; *Clubs* Hurlingham; *Style—* Timothy Sanderson, Esq; Delaware International Advisers Ltd, 46 New Broad St, London EC2 M1JJ (☎ 071 638 2493, fax 071 638 2099)

SANDERSON OF AYOT, Barony of (UK 1960); *see*: Sanderson, Dr Alan

SANDERSON OF BOWDEN, Baron (Life Peer UK 1985), of Melrose in the District of Ettrick and Lauderdale; Sir (Charles) Russell Sanderson; DL (Roxburgh, Ettrick and Lauderdale 1990); s of Charles Plummer Sanderson (d 1976), of Melrose, Roxburghshire, and (Martha) Evelyn (d 1954), da of Joseph Gardiner, of Glasgow; *b* 30 April 1933; *Educ* St Mary's Sch Melrose, Trin Coll Glenalmond, Bradford Technical Coll, Scottish Coll of Textiles Galashiels; *m* 5 July 1958, (Frances) Elizabeth, da of Donald Alfred Ramsden Macaulay (d 1982), of Rylstone, Skipton, Yorks; 2 s (Hon (Charles) David Russell b 1960, Hon Andrew Bruce Plummer b 1968), 2 da (Hon (Evelyn) Claire (Hon Mrs Walker) b 1961, Hon (Frances) Georgina (Hon Mrs Riley) b 1963); *Career* cmmnd Royal Signals 1952, served 51 (Highland) Inf Div Signal Regt (TA) 1953-56, KOSB (TA) 1956-58; dir Illingworth Morris plc 1990-; chm Central & Southern Area, Scottish Cons Unionist Assoc, 1974-75 (vice pres 1975-77, pres 1977-79), ptnr Chas P Sanderson, Wool and Yarn Merchants Melrose 1978-87, vice chm Nat Union of Cons Assocs 1979-81 (memb Exec Ctee 1977-, chm 1981-86); govr: St Mary's Sch Melrose, Scottish Coll of Textiles 1980-87; memb Cncl Trin Coll Glenalmond 1982-; chm: Edinburgh Fin Tst 1983-87, Shires Investmt Tst 1984-87, Clydesdale Bank 1985-87; memb: Scottish Cncl Independent Schs 1984-87, Ctee Governing Bodies 1984-87; Minister of State Scottish Office 1987-, memb Scottish Conservative Pty 1990-; cmmr Gen Assembly Church of Scotland 1972; kt 1981; *Recreations* golf; *Clubs* Caledonian, Hon Co of Edinburgh Golfers; *Style—* The Rt Hon the Lord Sanderson of Bowden, DL; Becketts Field, Bowden, Melrose, Roxburgh TD6 0ST (☎ 0835 22736); Scottish Office, St Andrew's House, Edinburgh

SANDFORD, Arthur; DL; s of Arthur Sandford (d 1990), and Lilian Sandford; *b* 12 May 1941; *Educ* Queen Elizabeth's GS Blackburn, UCL (LLB); *m* 1963, Kathleen, da of James Entwistle (d 1976); 2 da (Allison b 1967, Janet b 1969); *Career* asst slr

Preston CBC 1965-66 (sr asst slr 1966-68), asst slr Hampshire CC 1969-70; Nottinghamshire CC: second asst clerk 1970-72, first asst clerk 1972-74, dep dir of admin 1974-75, dir of admin 1975-77, dep clerk of CC and co sec, clerk of the CC and chief exec 1978-90, chief exec The Football League 1990-; *Recreations* football, gardening; *Clubs* Royal Over seas League; *Style*— Arthur Sandford, Esq, DL; Fairford House, 66 Loughborough Road, Bunny, Nottingham NG11 6QD (☎ 0602 212440); The Football League, City House, Maid Marian Way, Nottingham (☎ 0602 508720, fax 0602 508621)

SANDFORD, Prof Cedric Thomas; s of Thomas Sandford (d 1951), of Bristol, and Louisa Kate, *née* Hodge (d 1971); *b* 21 Nov 1924; *Educ* Univ of Manchester (BA, MA), Univ of London (BA); *m* 1, 1 Dec 1945, Evelyn (d 1982), da of Horace Belch, of Leigh; 1 s (John b 1955) 1 da (Gillian b 1956); m 2, 21 July 1984, Christina Katarin Privett; *Career* WWII Pilot RAF 1943-46; Univ of Bath: prof political economy 1965-87, emeritus prof 1987-; consultancies incl: UN, World Bank, IMF, EEC, OECD, Irish Tax Cmmn; author of many pubns in field of pub fin; pres Econs Assoc 1983-86 (memb 1948); memb: Meade Ctee, SW Electricity consultative ctee; active in local and nat affrs of Methodist Church; memb: Bath DHA, Econs Assoc (1948); *Recreations* fishing, gardening, walking; *Style*— Prof Cedric Sandford; Old Coach House, Fersfield, Perrymead, Bath BA2 5AR (☎ 0225 832 683)

SANDFORD, Humphrey; o s of Maj Humphrey Sandford, TD (d 1988), and Marjory Travers, *née* Pickmere (d 1970); descended from Thomas de Saundford, a Norman recorded in Domesday Book as holding the manor of Sandford, Shropshire; Richard Sandford (d 1588) was the first to move to the Isle of Rossall, which has remained in the possession of the family ever since (*see* Burke's Landed Gentry, 18 edn, vol III, 1972); *b* 12 June 1922; *Educ* Shrewsbury, St John's Coll Cambridge (MA); *m* 1, 22 Aug 1953 (m dis 1975), Mary Evelyn (Eve), da of Maj William Blackwood Michael, of 6 Stormont Court, Belfast; m 2, Sheila Ann Tate (d 1987); m 3, 19 March 1988, Joan Margaret Michael; *Career* served WWII Maj 2/3 Gurkha Rifles; agricultural offr in HM Colonial Serv: Sarawak 1949-52, Tanganyika 1952-57; agronomist with Shell 1957-81; farmer and landowner; MFH South Shropshire Hounds; former pres Fertilizer Soc; *Recreations* hunting, fishing, golf; *Style*— Humphrey Sandford, Esq; The Isle, Bicton, Shrewsbury, Shropshire (☎ 0743 850912)

SANDFORD, (Christopher) Jeremy; s of Christopher Sandford (d 1985), of Eye Manor, Leominster, and Lettice Macintosh, *née* Rate; *Educ* Eton, Oxford (BA); *m* 1, 14 Feb 1956 (m dis 1978), Nell Dunn, da of Sir Phillip Dunn Bart (d 1978); 2 s (Roc b 1957, Ruben b 1963, Jem 1967); m 2, 1988, Philippa Sophia Finnis; *Career* writer; former works incl: talks and features writer BBC, writer and presenter ITV and BBC Radio, writer and presenter BBC TV womens progs, Thames TV religious broadcasting; wrote acclaimed BBC TV screenplays Cathy Come Home 1966 and Edna the Inebriate Woman 1971; BBC TV documentaries incl: Hotel de Luxe, Cathy Were Are You Now?; radio, stage and TV plays incl: Dreaming Bandsmen, Not Wishing to Return, It Is For Ever, Whelks and Chromium, The Fatted Calf, Death of a Teenager; books incl: Synthetic Fun, In Search of the Magic Mushroom, Smiling David, Tomorrow's People, Gypsies, Down and Out in Britain; newspaper series and enquiries incl: Families without a Home, The Dossers, Dark Side of Affluence, Reincarnation, The Other Health Service, The Age of Consent; poet and musician specialising in Spanish Gypsy and New Age music performing at festivals; memb Herefordshire Traveller Support Gp; former: dir Cyrenians and Simon Community, Nat Gypsy Cncl; patron of Shelter, currently running Green and New Age conference facility from Hatfield Court and teaching folk music at Oak Dragon and Rainbow Circle camps; *Recreations* riding, music, painting, mountain climbing; *Clubs* Chelsea Arts, Groucho; *Style*— Jeremy Sandford, Esq; Hatfield Court, Leominster HR6 0SD (☎ 056882 333)

SANDFORD, 2 Baron (UK 1945); Rev John Cyril Edmondson; DSC (1942); s of 1 Baron Sandford, DL, sometime MP Banbury, Lord Cmmr Treasy and Vice-Chamberlain HM's Household 1939-42 (d 1959), by his w Edith, *née* Freeman; *b* 22 Dec 1920; *Educ* Eton, RNC Dartmouth; *m* 4 Jan 1947, Catharine Mary, da of late Rev Oswald Andrew Hunt; 2 s, 2 da; *Heir* s, Hon James Edmondson; *Career* takes Cons Whip in House of Lords; RN: midshipman 1940, Med Fleet 1940-41, N African and Sicily Invasions 1942, Normandy Invasions 1944, Signal Offr 1945, House Offr RNC Dartmouth 1947, Flag Lt to Flag Offr cmdg 3 Aircraft Sqdn 1949, Flag Lt to flag offr air (Home) 1951, on Staff C-in-C Far East Station 1953, Cdr 1953, ret 1956; ordained 1958, curate Parish of St Nicholas Harpenden 1958-63, chm Herts Cncl Social Service 1966-69, exec chaplain to Bishop of St Albans 1965-68, chm bd of Church Army 1969-70; oppn whip House of Lords 1966-70, parly under-sec of state Dept of Environment 1970-73 and of Dept of Educn and Sci 1973-74; memb select ctee on European Community Directive 1978-88; bd memb Ecclesiastical Insurance Office 1978-89; pres: Anglo-Swiss Soc 1976-84, pres Assoc of Dist Cncls 1980-86; Church Cmmr chm Redundant Churches 1982-89; chm SE Regnl Planning Cncl (SERPLAN) 1981-89; Hon Fell Inst of Landscape Architects 1971; *Style*— The Rev the Rt Hon the Lord Sandford, DSC; 27 Ashley Gardens, Ambrosden Avenue, London SW1P 1QD (☎ 01 834 5722)

SANDFORD, Rear Adm Sefton Ronald; CB (1976); *b* 23 July 1925; *Educ* RNC Dartmouth; *m* 1, 1950, Mary Ann Prins (d 1972); 1 s; m 2, 1972, Jennifer Rachel Newell; 2 da; *Career* served WWII; cmd HMS Protector 1965-67, naval attaché Moscow 1968-70, cmd HMS Devonshire 1971-73, ADC to HM The Queen 1974, Flag Offr Gibraltar 1974-76; a yr bro Trinity House 1968; *Recreations* sailing, photography; *Clubs* Royal Yacht Sqdn, MCC; *Style*— Rear Adm Sefton Sandford, CB; Dolphins, Rue de St Jean, St Lawrence, Jersey, CI

SANDHURST, 5 Baron (UK 1871); (John Edward) Terence Mansfield; DFC (1944); s of 4 Baron, OBE (d 1964); *b* 4 Sept 1920; *Educ* Harrow; *m* 1, 1942 (m dis 1946), Priscilla Ann (d 1970), da of late J Fielder Johnson; m 2, 1947, Janet Mary, er da of late John Edward Lloyd, of Long Island, New York; 1 s, 1 da; *Heir* s, Hon Guy Mansfield; *Career* Nat Serv RAFVR WWII; md Leslie Rankin Ltd Jersey, Hon ADC to Lt-Govr of Jersey 1969-74; *Recreations* golf; *Clubs* RAF, MCC, United (Jersey); *Style*— The Rt Hon the Lord Sandhurst, DFC; c/o The Post Office, Jersey, CI

SANDILANDS, Sir Francis Edwin Prescott; CBE (1967); s of late Lt-Col Prescott Sandilands, DSO, and late Gladys Baird Murton; cadet branch of the Sandilands of Calder (Lords Torphichen, *see* 15 Lord Torphichen); *b* 11 Dec 1913; *Educ* Eton, Corpus Christi Coll Cambridge (MA); *m* 1939, (Susan) Gillian, da of Bramwell Jackson (d 1920), of Bury St Edmunds, Suffolk; 2 s; *Career* served WWII, Lt-Col Royal Scots Fus and Gen Staff (despatches); chm Commercial Union Assurance Co 1972-83 (dir 1965-83, vice chm 1968-72), chm: Royal Tst Co of Canada 1974-84; dir: Plessey Co, Lewis and Peat 1983-90; chm Ctee on Invisible Exports 1975-83, memb Royal Opera House Bd 1975-85, chm Royal Opera House Trust 1974-86, tstee British Museum 1977-85, memb Royal Fine Art Cmmn 1980-84; hon fell: Univ Coll London, Corpus Christi Coll Cambridge; Cdr Ordre de la Couronne (Belgium) 1974; kt 1976; *Recreations* music, mediaeval studies; *Style*— Sir Francis Sandilands, CBE; 53 Cadogan Square, London SW1X 0HY (☎ 071 235 6384)

SANDILANDS, James Sebastian; s of Sir Francis Sandilands, CBE, and Gill, *née* Jackson; *b* 15 Oct 1944; *m* 1 July 1972, Gabriele, *née* Mellich, da of Dr Theo Mellich, of Vienna Austria; 1 s (Christopher b 1980); *Career* ptnr: Sheppards and Chase 1966-76, Buckmaster & Moore 1976-85; md Fund Mgmnt Div Credit Suisse Buckmaster & Moore 1985-90; memb Soc Investmt Analysts asst md Quilter Goodison Co 1990-; *Recreations* reading, walking, skiing, opera, theatre; *Style*— James Sandilands, Esq; c/o Quilter Goodison Company Ltd, St Helen's, 1 Undershaft, London EC3A 8BB

SANDILANDS, Lt-Col Patrick Stanley; DSO (1945); s of Lt-Col Prescott Sandilands (d 1956), and Gladys Baird, *née* Murton (d 1964); family, Cadet Branch of the Sandilands of Calder (now Lords Torphichen); *b* 30 Nov 1911; *Educ* Wellington, RMC Sandhurst; *m* 12 March 1949, Madeleine Mary, o da of Lt-Col Sir Hugh Stephenson Turnbull, KCVO, KBE, of Moray; 1 s (Andrew b 1960), 1 da (Mary b 1956); *Career* cmmnd 1931 Royal Scots Fusiliers served: UK, Palestine, Egypt; 5 Bn Kings Africa Rifles Kenya 1935-38, BEF & Staff Coll 1939-40, Staff in UK & HQ 1 Army N Africa 1941-43, SA&SH Sicily, 2 RSF Italy & NW Europe 1943-45; CO 11 RSF, instr Sch of Inf; CO: 5 Scot Bn The Parachute Regt 1945-53, 15 Scot Bn The Parachute Regt TA 1953-56, HQ Allied Forces Central Europe 1956-59; ret 1959; landowner Lagganmore; memb of the Royal Co of Archers (Queen's Bodyguard for Scot) 1956; OStJ; elder of the Church of Scotland; *Recreations* fishing, gardening, family history; *Style*— Lt-Col Patrick S Sandilands, DSO; Lagganmore, Kilninver, by Oban, Argyll PA34 4UU

SANDISON, Francis Gunn; s of Capt Dr Andrew Tawse Sandison (d 1982), of Glasgow, and Dr Ann Brougham, *née* Austin; *b* 25 May 1949; *Educ* Glasgow Acad, Charterhouse, Magdalen Coll Oxford (BCL, MA); *m* 5 Sept 1981, Milva Lou, da of Prof John Emory McCaw, of Des Moines, Iowa; 1 s (Gavin b 1985); *Career* admitted slr 1974; ptnr Freshfields 1980- (asst slr 1974-80); memb: Law Soc 1974, City of London Law Soc 1980; *Books* Profit Sharing and Other Share Acquisition Schemes (1979), Whiteman on Income Tax (co-author 3 edn, 1988); *Recreations* fishing, wine, photography; *Style*— Francis Sandison, Esq; 2 The Chase, Churt, Farnham, Surrey GU10 2PU (☎ 025 125 2556); 3 Earl's Court Sq, London SW5 9BY (☎ 071 373 8811); Freshfields, Whitefriars, 65 Fleet St, London EC4Y 1HS (☎ 071 936 4000, fax 071 832 7001)

SANDLAND, Eric Michael (Mike); s of Eric Darnley Sandland (d 1989), and Mary Cairns, *née* Blyth (d 1956); *b* 29 April 1938; *Educ* Edinburgh Acad, Trinity Hall Cambridge (MA); *m* 1, 1961 (m dis 1965), Susan, *née* Wright; m 2, 15 Aug 1969, Jacqueline Marie-Therese (d 1990), da of Pierre Gauthier, of Broue, France; 3 s (James Alexander b 9 Jan 1980, Peter Michael (twin) b 9 Jan 1980, Thomas William 2 Feb 1982); *Career* Norwich Union Life Insur Soc: actuarial student 1961-64, actuarial asst 1964-66, asst sec for Fr (subsequently sec) 1966-69, gp statistician 1969-72, investmt mangr 1972-86, chief investmt mangr 1986; chief investmt mangr Norwich Union Fund Mangrs 1988; chm Investmt Ctee Assoc Br Insurers 1988-90; chm Institutional Shareholder's Ctee 1990-; FIA 1964, ASIA 1972; *Recreations* golf, DIY, snooker, bridge, music; *Style*— E M Sandland, Esq; 35 Mount Pleasant, Norwich, Norfolk NR2 2DH (☎ 0603 54212); Norwich Union Fund Managers Ltd, PO Box No 150, Sentinel House, 37 Surrey St, Norwich, Norfolk NR1 3UZ (☎ 0603 682226, fax 0603 681747, car 0860 347394, telex 97388)

SANDLE, Prof Michael Leonard; s of Charles Edward Sandle, and Dorothy Gwendoline Gladys, *née* Vernon; *b* 18 May 1936; *Educ* Douglas HS, Douglas Sch of Art and Technol Doughs, Slade Sch of Fine Art (AFA); *m* 1971 (m dis 1974), Cynthia Dora Koppel; m 2, 1988, Demelza Jane Spargo; *Career* various teaching posts in Britain 1961-64, lectr Coventry Coll of Art 1964-68, visiting prof Univ of Calgary Alberta 1970-71, assoc prof Univ of Victoria BC 1972-73, prof in sculpture Fachhochschule für Gestaltung Pforzheim W Germany 1977-80 (lectr 1973-77); has participated in exhibitions internationally 1957-: V Biennale Paris 1966, Documenta 1V Kassel W Germany 1968, Documenta V1 1977; works exhibited in pub collections including: Arts Cncl of GB, Tate Gallery, Australiam Nat Gall Canberra, Metropolitan Museum NY, Stziki Museum Lodz, Nat Gallery of Warsaw, Wilhelm Lehmbruck Museum Duisburg W Germany, Hakone Open Air Museum Japan; prof Akademie Fur Bildenden Kunste Germany 1980-; RA 1990 (elected ARA 1980); *Style*— Prof Michael Sandle, RA; Schloss Scheibenhardt, 7500 Karlsruhe, Germany (☎ 010 49 721 8686 33)

SANDLER, Prof Joseph John; s of Solomon Sandler (d 1964), of Cape Town, South Africa, and Leah, *née* Kussel (d 1977); *b* 10 Jan 1927; *Educ* Sea Point Boy's Sch Cape Town, Univ of Cape Town (BA, MA, DSc), Univ of London (PhD), Univ of Leiden (MD); *m* 1, 21 Nov 1949, Hannah Miriam (d 1955), da of Ernst Mayer (d 1967), of London; 1 da (Trudy Anne (Mrs McGuiness)b 31 Aug 1950); m 2, 21 Feb 1957, Anne-Marie, da of Col Otto Weil (d 1964), of Geneva, Switzerland; 1 s (Paul Gerard b 2 Dec 1962), 1 da (Catherine Judith b 18 June 1958); *Career* psychoanalyst British Psychoanalytical Soc 1952-, ed British Journal of Medical Psychology 1956-62 and 1968-74, ed International Journal of Psychoanalysis 1968-78, prof of psychoanalysis applied to med Univ of Leiden 1968-74, first Sigmund Freud prof of psychoanalysis Hebrew Univ of Jerusalem 1979-84, first holder Freud meml chair of psychoanalysis Univ of London 1984-, dir psychoanalysis unit UCL 1984-, pres Euro Psychoanalytical Fedn 1975-79, pres Int Psychoanalytical Assoc 1989-; sci chm Br Psychonalytical Soc 1986-; Hon FilDr Univ of Lund 1976, Hon LLD Clark Univ 1985; FBPsS 1957 (memb 1947); *Books* Psychosomatic Aspects of Paediatrics (with R MacKeith, 1961), The Patient and the Analyst (with C Dare and A Holder, 1973), The Technique of Child Psychoanalysis (with H Kennedy and R L Tyson, 1980), The Analysis of Defence (with Anna Freud, 1985), From Safety to Superego (1987), Projection Identificaiton Projective Identification (1987), Dimensions of Psychoanalysis (1989); *Recreations* reading, teaching, travelling; *Clubs* Reform; *Style*— Prof Joseph Sandler; Psychoanalysis Unit, University College London, 26 Bedford Way, London WC1H OAP (☎ 071 5806902)

SANDLER, Prof Merton; s of late Frank Sandler, of Salford, Lancs, and the late Edith, *née* Stein; *b* 28 March 1926; *Educ* Manchester GS, Univ of Manchester (MB ChB, MD); *m* 1961, Lorna Rosemary, da of late Ian Michael, of Colindale, London; 2 s, 2 da; *Career* Capt RAMC; jr specialist in pathology 1951-53, res fell in clinical pathology Brompton Hosp 1953-54, lectr in chem pathology Royal Free Hosp Sch of Med 1955-58; prof of chem pathology Royal Postgrad Med Sch Inst of Obstetrics and Gynaecology Univ of London 1973-, conslt chem pathologist Queen Charlotte's Maternity Hosp 1958-; visiting prof: Univ of New Mexico 1983, Chicago Med Sch 1984, Univ of S Florida 1988; recognised teacher in chem pathology 1960 (examiner various Br and foreign univs and Royal Colls); memb Standing Advsy Ctee Bd of Studies in Pathology Univ of London 1972-76 (Chem Pathology Sub Ctee 1973-); Inst of Obstetrics and Gynaecology: chm Academic Bd 1972-73, chm Bd of Mgmnt 1975-; govr: Br Postgrad Med Fedn 1976-78, Queen Charlotte's Hosp for Women; cncl memb and meetings sec Assoc of Clinical Pathologists 1959-70, cncl memb Collegium Int Neuro-Psychopharmacologicum 1982-, hon librarian RSM 1977-; pres: section Med Experimental Med and Therapeutics 1979-80, Br Assoc for Psychopharmacology 1980, Br Assoc for Postnatal Illness 1980-; chm tstees Nat Soc for Res into Mental Health 1983-; tstee (1987-) and memb: Med Advsy Cncls of Migraine Tst 1975-80 (chm Scientific Advsy Ctee 1985-); memb Schizophrenia Assoc of GB 1975-78, Parkinson's Disease Soc 1981; chm and sec Biol Cncl Symposium on Drug Action 1979, sec memb Bd of Mgmnt and chm Awards Sub Ctee Biol Cncl 1983; memb Exec Ctee: Marcé Soc

1983-86, Med Cncl on Alcoholism 1957-, sec and memb of Cncl Harveian Soc of London 1979-, memb of Cncl of Mgmnt and patron Helping Hand Organisation 1981-87, foreign corresponding memb American Coll of Neuropsychopharmacology 1975; hon memb: Indian Acad of Neurosciences 1982, Hungarian Pharmacological Soc 1985; jt ed: British Journal of Pharmacology 1974-80, Clinical Science 1975-77, Journal of Neural Transmission 1979-82; jt ed in chief Journal of Psychiatric Research 1982, present or past ed bd memb of 17 other sci jls; lectr to various learned socs incl: 1 Cummings Meml 1976, James E Beall II Meml 1980, Biol Cncl Lecture medal 1984; Anna Monika Int Prize for res on biological aspects of depression 1973, Gold medal Br Migraine Assoc 1974, Senator Dr Franz Burda Int Prize for res on Parkinsons disease 1988; FRCP, FRCPath, FRCPsych, CBiol, FIBiol; *Books* Mental Illness in Pregnancy and the Puerperium (1978), The Pschopharmacology of Aggression (1979), Enzyme Inhibitors as Drugs (1980), Amniotic Fluid and its Clinical Significance (1980), The Psychopharmacology of Alcohol (1980), The Psychopathology of Anticonvulsants (1981); jtly: The Adrenal Cortex (1961), The Thyroid Gland (1967), Advances in Pharmacology (1968), Monoamine Oxidases (1972), Serotonin - New Vistas (1974), Sexual Behaviour: Pharmacology and Biochemistry (1975), Trace Amines and the Brain (1976), Phenosulphotransferase in Mental Health Research (1981), Tetrahydroisoquinolines and B-Carbolines (1982), Progress towards a Male Contraceptive (1982), Neurobiology of the Trace Amines (1984), Psychopharmacology and Food (1985), Neurotransmitter Interactions (1986), Design of Enzyme Inhibitors as Drugs (1987), Progress in Catecholamine Research (1988), Migraine: A Spectrum of Ideas (1990); *Recreations* reading, listening to music, lying in the sun; *Clubs* Athenaeum; *Style—* Prof Merton Sandler; 27 St Peters Rd, Twickenham, Middx TW1 1QY (☎ 081 892 8433)

SANDLER, Michael Stephen; s of Carl Bernard Sandler, of Leeds and London, and Taube Irene Barash (d 1980); *b* 17 Oct 1947; *Educ* Leeds GS, Boston Univ (BA); *m* 1973, Gail Michele, da of Dr David Granet, JP, of Scotland; 2 s (Andrew b 1975, Jonathan b 1978); *Career* chartered surveyor, Conrad Ritblat & Co 1971-78, dir Streets Fin Ltd 1979-86, md Kingsway Fin Public Relations (Saatchi & Saatchi Co) 1986-88, md Hudson Sandler Ltd 1988-; ARICS; *Recreations* tennis, theatre, cinema, golf; *Style—* Michael Sandler, Esq; 2 Marston Close, London NW6 4EU (☎ 01 328 7510); Cap House, 9-12 Long Lane, London EC1A 9HD

SANDON, Viscount; (Dudley Adrian) Conroy Ryder; o s of 7 Earl of Harrowby, TD, *qv*; *b* 18 March 1951; *Educ* Eton, Univ of Newcastle upon Tyne, Magdalene Coll Cambridge (MA); *m* 1977, Sarah Nicola Hobhouse, o da of Capt Anthony Dennis Phillpotts Payne, of The Old Malt House, Marnhull, Dorset; 3 s (Hon Dudley Anthony Hugo Coventry b 5 Sept 1981, Hon Frederick Whitmore Dudley b 6 Feb 1984, Hon Henry Mansell Dudley b 13 July 1985); *Career* commercial property devpt; dir Compton St Securities Ltd 1988-; ARICS; *Style—* Viscount Sandon; c/o Sandon Estate Office, Sandon, Stafford ST18 ODA

SANDON, Raoul Peter Gauvain; s of Edward Gauvain Sandon (d 1961), of Bilbao Spain, and Jeanne Emilie, *née* Cottens (d 1979); *b* 2 May 1915; *Educ* Arcachon France, Kings Coll Hosp London Univ (MB BS); *m* 20 July 1940, Natalie Naomi (d 1988), da of Alfred Ewing (d 1950); 2 s (Peter b 1942, Ian b 1951); *Career* Capt RAMC 1942-46 (despatches), served Italy and Middle East; conslt plastic surgeon: Hosps for Sick Children London 1956-80, NE Thames Region 1958-80; hon civilian advsr British Army, past pres British Assoc of Plastic Surgeons (BAPS) (also elected to French, Belgian, Spanish and Italian assocs), UK rep and hon life pres Plastic Surgn Section Union Europ de Medecins Specialistes (UEMS); author of various chapters in surgical textbooks; MRCS, LRCP 1941, FRCS 1951; *Style—* Raoul P G Sandon, Esq; 17 Langley Ave, Surbiton, Surrey KT6 6QN (☎ 081 399 1487), 152 Harley St, London W1N 1HH (☎ 071 935 1858)

SANDS, Charles Francis; s of Arthur Langdale Sands (d 1954), and Margaret Soames (d 1978); *b* 3 March 1938; *Educ* Marlborough, Lincoln Coll Oxford (MA); *m* 19 Nov 1965, (m dis 1988), Carolyn Clare Barbadee; 2 s (Robert b 1970, David b 1973); *Career* Nat Serv 1956-58, 2 Lt 2 RTR; ptnr Herbert Smith (Slrs) 1972; memb: Law Soc, City of London Slrs Co; *Recreations* fishing, shooting, golf, tennis, riding; *Clubs* RAC; *Style—* Charles Sands, Esq; Forge House, 1c Ravensdon St, London SE11 4AQ (☎ 071 735 7010)

SANDS, Lawrence Alfred; s of Alfred Lawrence Sands (d 1971, of Weaverham, Cheshire, and Edith Carlihoe, *née* Wright (d 1972); *b* 21 March 1928; *Educ* Northwich Tech Coll, Mid Cheshire Coll of Art & Design; *m* 27 Feb 1953, Jean, da of Arnold Bebbington; 1 s (Stephen Duncan b 28 July 1967), 1 da (Jill Amanda b 28 Jan 1960); *Career* photographer; lectr in portraiture and wedding photography UK, Europe, USA and N Africa; *awards* Ilford award for Portraiture 1972, Ilford award for Wedding Photography 1974, BIPP Portrait award N W Region 1979, BIPP Wedding Photographer of the Year 1982, Craftsman Degree for services to photography Professional Photographers of America 1986, BIPP President's Award for services to photography 1988, Fuji Professional award for services to photographic educn 1990; BIPP: licentiate in wedding photography 1959, assoc in commercial photography 1969, N W regnl chm 1972-73, fell in portraiture 1979, chm of A & Q Bd Gen Practice 1989; FRSA 1961, ARPS 1978; *Recreations* aircraft & flying, old movies (Keystone, Chaplin, Laurel & Hardy, Harold Lloyd), gardening; *Style—* Lawrence Sands, Esq; Fairways, Malt Kiln Road, Plumley, Knutsford, Cheshire WA16 OTS (☎ 0565 722596); Lawrence Sands, Photographic Services, 8 Malt Rd, Plumley, Knutsford, Cheshire WA16 OTS

SANDS, Peter; s of John Sands, of Whitley Bay Tyne & Wear, and Jane Caroline, *née* Reay (d 1984); *b* 16 May 1955; *Educ* Whitley Bay GS, Huddersfield Poly (BA); *m* 29 March 1986, Pamela Jean, da of William Maurice Hutchinson; 2 s (Jack William b 1 March 1987, Daniel Peter b 12 July 1988); *Career* reporter Shields Weekly News (N Shields) 1977-79, sub ed The Northern Echo 1979-81, chief sub ed The Evening Despatch (Darlington) 1981-84; The Northern Echo: night ed 1984-86, asst ed 1986-89, dep ed 1989-90, ed 1990-; *Awards* (for The Northern Echo) Newspaper Design award for Provincial Morning Newspapers, Freedom of Information Newspaper award; memb Guild of Br Newspaper Eds 1990-; *Recreations* spending time with the family, Newcastle Utd FC, country pubs, newspapers, literature; *Clubs* Durham CCC (vice pres and co fndr); *Style—* Peter Sands, Esq; The Northern Echo, Priestgate, Darlington, Co Durham (☎ 0325 381313, fax 0325 380539)

SANDS, Roger Blakemore; s of Thomas Blakemore Sands (d 1980), and Edith Malyon, *née* Waldram (d 1986); *b* 6 May 1942; *Educ* Univ Coll Sch Hampstead, Oriel Coll Oxford (scholar, MA); *m* 24 Sept 1966, Jennifer Ann, da of Hugh T Cattell; 2 da (b 1972 and 1974); *Career* Clerks Dept House of Commons 1965-, sec to Chm of Ways and Means 1975-77, clerk to Select Ctee on Euro Legislation 1977-81, clerk to Scot Affrs Ctee 1981-84, sec to House of Commons Cmmn 1985-87, princ clerk of Overseas Office House of Commons 1987-; sec History of Parliament Tst 1974-80, memb Cncl RIPA 1989-, vice chm Study of Parliament Gp 1991- (memb 1970-); *Books* Official Guide to the Houses of Parliament (ed 13 edn, 1977); *Recreations* gardening, listening to music, occasional golf; *Style—* Roger Sands, Esq; Overseas Office, House of Commons, London SW1A 0AA (☎ 071 219 3314)

SANDWICH, Earldom of;; *see*: Montagu, (Alexander) Victor Edward

SANDY, Martyn Graeme; s of Albert Henry Sandy, and Victoria Margaret, *née* Squires; *b* 21 May 1949; *Educ* Plymouth Coll, North East London Poly (BA); *m* 23 Oct 1977, Gillian Evelyn, da of John Aird; 2 s (Daniel b 1982, James b 1984); *Career* dir Boase Massioni Pollitt Advertising 1982-; *Recreations* family, reading; *Style—* Martyn Sandy, Esq; 35 Wingston Lane, Teddington, Middx; Boase Massimi, Pollitt, 12 Bishopsbridge Rd, London W2 (☎ 071 258 3979)

SANDYS, Julian George Winston; QC (1983); s (by 1 m) of Baron Duncan-Sandys, CH, PC; does not use courtesy title of Hon; *b* 1936; *m* 1970, Elisabeth Jane, only da of John Besley Martin, CBE, of Kenton; 3 s, 1 da; *Career* called to the Bar Inner Temple 1959 and Gray's Inn 1970; dir Leisure Investmts plc 1989; *Recreations* flying small aeroplanes; *Style—* Julian Sandys, Esq, QC; Charnwood, Shackleford, Godalming, Surrey (☎ 04868 22167)

SANDYS, 7 Baron (UK 1802); Richard Michael Oliver Hill; DL (Worcs 1968); s of 6 Baron Sandys, DL (d 1961), and Cynthia Mary (d 1990), o da of Col Frederic Richard Thomas Trench-Gascoigne, DSO; *b* 21 July 1931; *Educ* RNC Dartmouth; *m* 1961, Patricia Simpson, da of late Capt Lionel Hall, MC; *Heir* cous, Marcus Hill; *Career* sits as a Cons peer in the House of Lords; late Lt Royal Scots Greys; patron of one living; a lord-in-waiting to HM Jan to March 1974, oppn whip House of Lords 1974-79, Capt HM Bodyguard of the Yeomen of the Guard (govt dep chief whip in House of Lords) 1979-82; FRGS; *Clubs* Cavalry & Guards; *Style—* The Lord Sandys, DL; Ombersley Court, Droitwich, Worcs (☎ 0905 620220)

SANDYS-LUMSDAINE OF THAT ILK AND BLANERNE, Patrick (Gillem); s of Colin Cren Sandys-Lumsdaine (d 1967), of Scotland, and Joyce Dorothy, *née* Leeson; *b* 15 Oct 1938; *Educ* Charterhouse; *m* 1966, Beverley June, da of Capt Ralph Ernest Shorter (d 1982); 2 s (Cren b 1968, Jas b 1976), 1 da (Amy b 1969); *Career* East India merchant; dir: George Williamson & Co Ltd 1977, George Williamson (Assam) Ltd 1978, Macneill & Magor Ltd 1982 Williamson Tea Holdings plc 1989; *Recreations* golf; *Clubs* Oriental, Tollygunge, Harewood Downs; *Style—* Lumsdaine of that Ilk and Blanerne; Kinderslegh, Bois Avenue, Chesham Bois, Amersham, Bucks HP6 5NS (☎ 0494 721466); George Williamson & Co Ltd, Sir John Lyon House, 5 High Timber St, London EC4V 3LD (☎ 071 248 0471, fax 071 248 3150, telex 887865)

SANDYS-RENTON, Maj James Stapleton Sandys; s of Maj Mervyn John Renton (d 1941), and Barbara Frances, *née* Sandys (d 1975); *b* 13 March 1926; *Educ* Sherborne, Queens Coll Oxford; *m* 24 April 1957, Elizabeth Anne, da of Major Astley Thomas Terry (d 1971); 2 s (Richard b 1959, William b 1964), 2 da (Jane b 1966, Lucia b 1967); *Career* cmmnd RA 1945, served Palestine 1946-48 (despatches), ret 1965 with rank of Maj; former memb Stock Exchange 1975, former ptnr Cawood Smithie & Co Harrogate 1980; *Recreations* conjuring; *Style—* Maj James Sandys-Renton; Laurel House, Dishfork, Thirsk, N Yorkshire YO7 3LP

SANFORD, Prof Anthony John; s of Edwin Sandford (d 1970), and Winnifred Olive, *née* Hrudman (d 1981); *b* 5 July 1944; *Educ* Waverly GS, Univ of Leeds (BSc), Pembroke Coll Cambridge (PhD); *m* 1, 3 Sept 1966 (m dis 1986), Valerie Ann, da of Frank Hines (d 1972); 1 da (Bridget Isobel b 27 March 1970); m 2 24, Jan 1987, Linda Mae, da of John Moxey; *Career* lectr in psychology Univ of Dundee 1971-74, head of Dept of Psychology Univ of Glasgow 1983-86 (sr lectr 1974-80, reader 1982-) Gillford lectr in natural theology 1983; AFBPS, chartered psychologist; *Books* Understanding Written Language (with S Garrod 1981), Models, Mind and Man (1983), Cognition and Cognitive Psychology (1985), The Mind of Man (1987); *Recreations* hill-walking, industrial archeology, music, cooking; *Style—* Prof Anthony Sanford; Dept of Psychology Univ of Glasgow G12 (☎ 041 3398855, fax 041 3304808)

SANFORD, Henry Ayshford; o s of Lt-Col Stephen Ayshford Sanford (d 1975), and Princess Olga Mickeladze (d 1955); *b* 26 May 1926; *Educ* Radley, Trinity Coll Cambridge (MA 1949), St Thomas's Hospital Medical Sch (MB BCh); *m* 1 16 June 1959, Marcelle Martha Maria, da of late Jean Louis Joseph Ghislain Van Caille, of Prevote St Christophe, Damme, Belgium; 1 s (Anthony Louis Ayshford b 21 March 1960); m 2, 1978, Akiko, da of Wakiji Nishida (d 1979), of Japan; 1 da (Marietta Sophia b 1981); *Career* Capt RAMC; assoc conslt Rheumatology Dept St Thomas's Hosp; chm and princ lecturer Cyriax Orgn; *Recreations* shooting, field sports; *Clubs* Savile; *Style—* Dr Henry A Sanford; Weatherham Farm, Brompton Regis, Somerset TA22 9LG; 59 Harley Street W1 N1AF (☎ 071 935 2414)

SANFORD, (Edward) William Ayshford; s of William Charles Ayshford Sanford (d 1974), of Chipley Park, Somerset, and his 1 w, Rosemary Jean Aileen (d 1968), yr da of Maj Hon Robert Hamilton Lindsay, Royal Scots Greys (s of 26 Earl of Crawford); descended from Henry Sanford (d 1644), of Nynehead, Somerset (of a family traceable since the reign of Richard II), who m Mary, da of Henry Ayshford, of Ayshford, Devon, where the Ayshfords had been seated since the reign of Henry III (*see* Burke's Landed Gentry, 18 edn, Vol III, 1972); *b* 3 June 1929; *Educ* Summer Fields Oxford, Geelong GS Aust; *m* 21 Jan 1977, Judy Ann, da of Samuel Anthony Parkington Vickery (d 1976), of The Quadrant, Glasgow; 1 s (Edward b 1978), 1 da (Susanna b 1980); *Career* served RHG 1947-49; in business 1950-60; govt service: Bahamas 1961-63, Central Office of Information 1964-85; hon treas Taunton Constituency Cons Assoc; Lord of the Manors of Nynehead and Burlescombe; *Recreations* travel, history, country pursuits; *Clubs* Lansdowne, Old Somerset Dining; *Style—* E W A Sanford, Esq; Chipley Park, Wellington, Somerset (☎ 0823 400 270)

SANGER, Dr Frederick; OM (1986), CH (1981), CBE (1963); s of Frederick Sanger, and Cicely, *née* Crewdson; *b* 13 Aug 1918; *Educ* Bryanston, St John's Coll Cambridge; *m* 1940, M Joan, da of Alfred Howe; 2 s, 1 da; *Career* res scientist Univ Biochemistry Laboratory and MRC Laboratory of Molecular Biol Cambridge 1951-83, ret; winner Nobel Prize for Chemisty 1958 (jt winner 1980); Hon DSc Cambridge 1983; FRS; *Style—* Dr Frederick Sanger, OM, CH, CBE, FRS; Far Leys, Fen Lane, Swaffham Bulbeck, Cambridge CB5 0NJ (☎ 0223 811610)

SANGER, James Gerald; s of Gerald Fountain Sanger, CBE, JP (d 1981), and Margaret Hope, *née* Munroe, MBE; *b* 29 April 1939; *Educ* Shrewsbury, Worcester Coll Oxford (MA), Harvard Business Sch (MBA); *m* 21 Sept 1968, Madeline Mary, da of George William Jack Collis (d 1986); 1 s (Christopher James b 1970), 1 da (Katherine Hope b 1972); *Career* CA; Farrow Bersey Gain Vincent & Co 1962-63 (articled 1957-59), asst to chm Assco Newspapers 1966-68 (joined 1963), md First Investors Ltd 1969-75, dir Henderson Admin 1974-75; fin dir: Blyth Greene Jourdain 1975-77, James Burrough plc 1977-84; exec dir: Tomkins plc 1985-88, Peek plc 1988-; govr: Benenden Sch, Shrewsbury Sch; ACA, FCA 1973; *Recreations* squash, tennis, travel, listening; *Clubs* Hurlingham, RAC; *Style—* James Sanger, Esq; Moreton House, Brightwell-cum-Sotwell, Oxon OX10 0PT (☎ 0491 33655); Peek plc, 207 Radley Rd, Abingdon, Oxon OX14 3XA (☎ 0235 528271, fax 0235 532836)

SANGER, Peter John; s of Percy James Sanger, of Eastcote, Pinner, Middx, and Maude Elizabeth, *née* Smith; *b* 18 Oct 1936; *Educ* Merchant Taylors', Open Univ (BA); *Career* Nat Serv 2 Lt RAOC 1957-59; asst then photographer Thomas Fall Studios 1954-57, lectr Sch of Photography Kodak Ltd 1959-62, lectr then sr lectr in photography Harrow Tech Coll 1962-72, princ lectr in photography Ealing Tech Coll 1972-74, head Dept of Audio-Visual Studies West Surrey Coll of Art and Design 1977-87 (head Dept of Photography 1974-77), asst dir and head Maidstone Coll Kent Inst of Art and Design 1988- (princ Maidstone Coll 1987-88), dir KIAD Enterprises

Ltd 1991; photographs published in many books and author numerous articles; exhibitions incl: Points of Contact (Royal Festival Hall) 1969, Images of Malta (Cwlth Inst) 1983, Visited Places (solo, touring); FBIPP 1969, FRPS 1975; *Recreations* travel, photography, classical music, opera; *Style—* Peter Sanger, Esq; Heddon's Gate, 67 Charlesford Avenue, Kingswood, Maidstone, Kent ME17 3PH (☎ 0622 842193); Kent Institute of Art and Design, Oakwood Park, Maidstone, Kent ME16 8AG (☎ 0622 757286, fax 0622 692003)

SANGSTER, Bruce; s of George Robertson Sangster, and Marie, *née* Davidson; *b* 12 March 1954; *Educ* Broxburn Acad Broxburn; *m* 22 Sept 1979, Jacqueline E R, da of John MacMillan Willison; 1 s (Jamie Sangster b 15 Aug 1982); *Career* commis chef then sr sous chef Old Course Hotel (British Transport Hotels) 1971-80, lectr Kingsway Tech Coll Dundee 1980-81; chef de cuisine: Kirroughtree Hotel Newton Stewart 1981-82, Rothley Court Hotel Rothley Leicestershire 1982-86, Balcraig House Hotel Scone Perthshire 1986-87; exec chef Murrayshall Country House Hotel Scone Perthshire 1987-; *awards* Silver Catch Fish Cookery award 1977, Gold medal Cold Fish Dish 1979, Bronze medal Fat Sculpture 1979, Gold medal Gourmet Entrée Dish 1981, semi finalist Br Chef of The Year 1982, finalist Br Chef of The Year 1984 and 1988, third prize Br Chef of The Year 1986 and 1990, AA rosette 1986-87, 1989 and 1990, Michelin Red M award 1987 and 1988, Taste of Scotland Restaurant of the Year 1988, Scottish Hotel Guide Restaurant of the Year 1989, Silver and Bronze award as memb Br Culinary Team at Food Asia '90 1990, winner Egon Ronay British Lamb Chef 1990, Hotel awarded Newcomer of The Year 1990, memb Culinary Olympic Team for Frankfurt 1990, entries in Good Food Guide and Egon Ronay 1981-; CFA 1975; memb: Master Chefs of GB 1985- (chm Scot Div 1989-), Craft Guild of Chefs 1990; *Style—* Bruce Sangster, Esq; Tir Nan Og, 1 Armadale Crescent, Balbeggie, Perthshire PH2 6HH (☎ 082 14 333); Murrayshall Country House Hotel & Golf Course, Scone, Perthshire PH2 7PH (☎ 0738 51171, fax 0738 52595)

SANGSTER, John Alexander; s of Alexander Findlay Sangster (d 1986), of Watton, Norfolk, and Doreen Magaret, *née* Bridgeford; *b* 4 July 1936; *Educ* Powis Sch Aberdeen, Twickenham Tech Coll; *m* 1, 1960 (m dis 1963), Violet Taylor; 1 da (Claire b 1961); m 2, 1964 (m dis 1975), Helen Swatman; 1 s (Alexander John b 1964), 1 da (Toni Allison b 1963); *Career* Pilot Offr Zambian Air Force 1967-69; structural engr designer AA Thornton Ltd 1953-58, design draughtsman Br Euro Airways 1958-61, sales exec Liebherr Tower Cranes Germany 1961-63, conslt and md family engrg co Scotland 1963-66, md Lonrho Cos Zambia 1966-72 (md/mangr 1972-84, sold 1984), md Silcom Ltd Export Buyers and Business Consultants 1984-; memb N London Rent Assessment Tbnl 1987; memb Rotary Club Lusaka Zambia 1966, currently vice pres Rotary Club Maidenhead; radio broadcaster Hosp Broadcasting Network 1981-; AMBIM 1970, FInstD 1971; *Recreations* gliding, sporting aircraft, collector and restorer of Rolls Royce vintage automobiles; *Clubs* Rolls Royce Enthusiasts, Bentley Drivers, Wig and Pen; *Style—* John Sangster, Esq; Bix House, Cannon Hill, Bray, Berkshire SL6 2EW (☎ 0628 26833); Silcom Limited, 1 Curfew Yard, Thames St, Windsor, Berkshire SL4 1SN (☎ 0753 855 553, fax 0753 831 320)

SANGSTER, Robert Edmund; s of Vernon Edmund Sangster (d 1988), and Margaret Martha Sangster; *b* 23 May 1936; *Educ* Repton; *m* 13 Aug 1985, Susan Mary, da of M Dean; 5 s (Guy, Ben, Adam, Sam, Max), 1 da (Kate); *Career* chm: Vernons Organisation 1976-88, Sangster Group Ltd 1988-91; dir Newmarket Thoroughbred Breeders plc 1985-; owner of: The Minstrel (won Derby 1977), Alleged (won Prix de l'Arc de Triomphe 1977 and 1978), Detroit (won Prix de l'Arc de Triomphe 1980) Beldare Ball (won Melbourne Cup 1980), Our Paddy Boy (won Australian Jockey Club Cup 1981), Golden Fleece (won Derby 1982) Assert (won Irish Sweeps Derby 1982), Lomond (won 2000 Guineas 1983), Caerleon (won French Derby 1983), El Gran Señor (won 2000 Guineas and Irish Sweeps Derby 1984), Sadler's Wells (won Irish 2000 Guineas 1984), Gildoran (won Ascot Gold Cup 1984 and 1985 and Goodwood Cup 1984), Committed (won Prix de l'Abbaye de Longchamp and was champion Euro sprinter and Royal Heroine champion of Grass Mare USA 1984), Marooned (won Sydney Cup 1986); owner of largest number of winning racehorses: 1977, 1978, 1982, 1983, 1984; *Recreations* golf; *Clubs* Jockey; *Style—* Robert Sangster, Esq; The Nunnery, Douglas, Isle of Man (☎ 0624 623351); Porte des Isles, Mougins, Cannes, France (☎ 33 93 900097); James Harbour, Sandy Lane, St James, Barbados (809 436 1241); Sangster Group Ltd, Wood Park, Neston, South Wirral L64 7TB (☎ 051 336 8898, fax 051 336 8517)

SANKEY, John Anthony; CMG (1983); o s of Henry and Ivy Sankey, of Plumstead Common; *b* 8 June 1930; *Educ* Cardinal Vaughan Sch, Peterhouse Cambridge (MA); *m* 1958, Gwendoline, da of Stanley and Winifred Putman, of Croxley Green; 2 s, 2 da; *Career* Lt RA served Singapore and Malaya 1951-53; FCO: UK Mission to UN New York 1961, dep high cmmr Guyana 1968, cnsllr Singapore 1971, NATO Def Coll Rome 1973, dep high cmmr Malta 1973-75, cnsllr The Hague 1975-79, special cnsllr African Affrs FCO 1979-82, high cmmr to Tanzania 1982-85; perm rep with personal rank of ambass 1985-90: UN, GATT, other int orgns at Geneva; sec gen Society of London Art Dealers 1991-; *Style—* John Sankey, Esq, CMG; United Kingdom Mission, 37/9 Rue de Vermont, Geneva; SLAD, 91A Jermyn St, London SW1Y 6JB SW1Y 6JB

SANT, William Howard; s of Stanley Sant (d 1967), of London, and Mary Sant (d 1976); *b* 22 March 1925; *Educ* BEC Secdy Sch, Regent St Poly Sch of Architecture (Dip Arch); *m* 1, 1950, Audrey Elizabeth (m dis 1972); 2 s (David b 1963, Paul b 1965), 3 da (Georgina b 1952, Claire b 1954, Louise b 1957); m 2 4 July 1974, Lesley Anne; 2 s (Dominich b 1976, Adam b 1978); *Career* architect and retail conslt; ptnr J P Bennet and Son 1957-69; sr ptnr Howard Saint Partnership 1969-85; md Saint Design 1985-; ptnr Saint Associates 1984-; princ Howard Sant 1987-; conslt Harrods Ltd 1984-86; ACIArb, FRSA, FCSD; *Recreations* walking, yachting; *Clubs* Royal Harwich Yacht; *Style—* Howard Sant, Esq; Royal House, Dedham, Essex CO7 6HD (☎ 0206 322107, fax 0206 322930)

SANT-CASSIA, Louis Joseph; s of Maj Henri Emmanuel Sant-Cassia, ED, of 450 St Paul's St Paul's Bay, Malta, and Anna, *née* De Piro Gourgion; *b* 19 Sept 1946; *Educ* Lyceum Malta Sch, Royal Univ of Malta (MD), Univ of Nottingham (DM); *m* 11 July 1974, Antoinette da of Gerald Ferro, MVO, MBE, of 81 Windsor Terrace, Sliema, Malta; 1 s (Henri b 1977), 1 da (Emma b 1980); *Career* cmmnd 1 Bn King's Own Malta Regt 1968-72; res fell Dept of Obstetrics and Gynaecology Nottingham 1981-83, conslt obstetrician and gynaecologist Coventry 1987-; Coventry Dist tutor RCOG 1988- (chm Div of Obstetrics and Gynaecology); memb Coventry Hosp Med Res and Ethical Ctee; goal-Keeper Malta water polo team Med Games 1967; MRCOG 1979; *Recreations* swimming, reading, melitensia; *Style—* Louis Joseph Sant-Cassia, Esq; Metchley Croft, 126 Metchley Lane, Harborne, Birmingham B17 0JA (☎ 021 4271502), 11 Dalton Rd, Earlsdon, Coventry CV5 6PB

SANTS, Hector William Hepburn; s of Hector John Sants, of Finlarig, Killin, Perthshire, and Elsie Ann Watt Hepburn; *b* 15 Dec 1955; *Educ* Clifton, Corpus Christi Coll Oxford (MA); *m* 21 Dec 1987, Caroline Jane, da of Kenneth Ord Mackenzie; 2 s (Hector Alexander b 9 Jan 1989, Edward Kenneth Richard b 16 Oct 1990); *Career* Phillips & Drew Stockbrokers: joined 1977, ptnr 1984; dir Phillips & Drew International 1984-86 (md and head NY office 1986-87), first vice pres and head int securities Union Bank of Switzerland Securities Inc NY 1987-88, head world wide broker res Union Bank of Switzerland 1988, head of equities and vice chm UBS Phillips & Drew 1988-; ASIA 1979; memb: Int Stock Exchange 1984, Stock Exchange Settlement Servs Bd 1990; *Recreations* gardening, stalking, shooting; *Style—* Hector Sants, Esq; Court Farm, Worminghall, nr Aylesbury, Buckinghamshire HP18 9LD; UBS Phillips & Drew Ltd, 100 Liverpool St, London EC2 2RH (☎ 071 901 3333)

SANTS, (Hector) John; s of Maj Edwin Hector Vincent Sants, MC (d 1954), of Norton St Philip, Som, and Gertrude Rose, *née* Collins (d 1975); descendant of Don Joseph Antonio Dos Santos, who sailed from Oporto to Gloucester in 1803 and founded clay-pipe factories in Gloucester and Bath; *b* 26 May 1923; *Educ* Haberdashers' Aske's, BNC Oxford (MA); *m* 1952, Elsie Ann, da of William Watt Hepburn (d 1953), of Aberdeen; 1 s (Hector b 1955), 1 da (Harriet b 1953); *Career* MN 1940-47 (ret as 2 Offr); educnl psychologist Kent and Birmingham LEAs 1952-60, lectr in educnl psychology Univ Coll of N Wales Bangor 1960-65, lectr and reader in developmental psychology Univ of Sussex 1965-86; *Books* Developmental Psychology: Selected Readings (co-ed with HJ Butcher, 1974), Developmental Psychology and Society (ed and contrib 1980); *Recreations* books, writing; *Style—* John Sants, Esq; Finlarig, Killin, Perthshire (☎ 056 72 259)

SAPHIR, Nicholas Peter George; s of Emanuel Saphir, MBE, and Anne Saphir; *b* 30 Nov 1944; *Educ* City of London, Univ of Manchester (LLB); *m* 1971, Ena, da of Raphael Bodin; 1 s; *Career* barr; chm Hunter Saphir plc; former: chm Food From Britain, memb Food & Drinks EDC; *Recreations* horses, modern art; *Clubs* Farmers'; *Style—* Nicholas Saphir, Esq; Hunter Saphir plc, Whitstable Rd, Faversham, Kent ME13 8BQ

SAPOCHNIK, Carlos Luis; s of Leon Sapochnik (d 1985), of Argentina, and Clara Aronovich; *b* 18 July 1944; *Educ* Buenos Aires Nat Univ, RCA (MA), City Univ; *m* 1966, Victoria, da of Vicente Rosenberg; 1 s (Miquel Vicente b 21 July 1974), 1 da (Manuela Maria b 8 Sept 1972); *Career* freelance graphic designer and illustrator 1970-; publishing clients incl: Methuen & Co, Tavistock Publications, Routledge & Kegan Paul and Hutchinson Educn; local govt: London Borough of Hackney, GLC; theatre clients incl: New London Arts Laboratory, Royal Court Theatre, Haymarket Leicester and Lyric Hammersmith; other clients incl: Midland Bank and CBS Records; art dir Free Assoc Books 1984-87, design conslt Burnett Assoc 1990- (creative dir 1988-90); pt/t lectr in graphic design: Chelsea Sch of Art 1981-84, Bath Acad of Art 1982-86; princ lectr B A graphic design course Middx Poly 1990-; solo exhibitions: Drawing & Pastels Vortex Gallery 1989, Drawing & Pastels Argile Gallery 1990; two-man exhibitions: Drawing & Pastels Boundary Gallery 1988; group exhibitions incl: Dublin Arts Festival 1975, Warsaw Poster Biennale 1976, 1978 and 1980, Lahti Poster Biennale Finland 1978, 1979 and 1983, Brno Graphic Design Biennale Czechoslovakia 1984, 1986 and 1988; memb CSD 1986 (fell 1991), memb Soc of Typographic Designers 1987; *Style—* Carlos Sapochnik, Esq; 6 Ridge Rd, London N8 9LG (☎ 081 340 4873)

SAPPER, Alan Louis Geoffrey; s of late Max Sapper, and Kate Sapper; *b* 18 March 1931; *Educ* Upper Latymer Sch, Univ of London, Royal Botanic Gardens Kew; *m* Dr Helen Sapper, *née* Rubens; 1 s (Simon), 1 da (Sarah); *Career* gen sec: Assoc of Cinematograph TV and Allied Technicians 1969-, Writers Guild of GB 1964-67, ACTT 1969-; memb Gen Cncl TUC 1970-84 (chm 1982); pres: Fedn of Entertainments Unions 1970-, Int Fedn of Audio-Visual Workers 1974-; govr: Hammersmith Hosp 1965-72, BFI 1974, Ealing Coll of Higher Educn 1976-78, Nat Film and TV Sch 1980-; chm League for Democracy in Greece 1970; *Publications* On Licence (stage play), Kith and Kin (stage play), The Return (TV play); articles, short stories; *Recreations* taxonomic botany, hill-walking, politics, human nature; *Style—* Alan Sapper, Esq; 19 Lavington Road, Ealing, London W13 9NN (☎ 081 567 4900); 111 Wardour St, London W1V 4AY (☎ 071 437 8506, fax 071 287 8984)

SAPSFORD, Danny Edwin; s of Donald Sapsford, and Olive, *née* Devonshire; *b* 3 April 1969; *Educ* St George's Coll, High Wycombe Royal GS; *Career* professional tennis player; began playing 1980, won first nat title (under 12) 1981, GB debut under 14 Germany 1982, memb LTA Tennis Sch 1985-87, turned professional 1987, memb LTA Laing squad 1988-90, memb Davis Cup squad 1988- (played at number two v Romania 1990); ranked 3 GB 1991 (ranked 1 under 18 1987); represented Surrey soccer 1981-82; *Recreations* cinema, reading; *Style—* Danny Sapsford, Esq; Walton-on-Thames Tennis Club, Walton-on-Thames, Surrey

SAPSTEAD, Gordon John; s of Herbert John Sapstead (d 1976), and Dora Lancaster, *née* Jemmett (d 1987); *b* 16 April 1923; *Educ* Hertford GS; *m* 1, 17 July 1947 (m dis); 2 s (Christopher Jolyon b and d 1948, Christopher Hugh b 17 July 1949), 1 da (Rosemary (Mrs Finch) b 12 July 1952); m 2, Jill, da of William Mcconnell, of Rhyl, N Wales; 1 s (Mark Richard b 28 Oct 1977), 2 da (Kathryn b 3 Feb 1973, Nicole b 18 April 1974); *Career* enlisted RAF Aircrew 1941, called up 1942, Pilot Offr 1943, Flying Offr 1944, Flt Lt 1945, Sqdn Ldr 1946; Westminster Bank 1939-42 and 1946-47, exec and managerial appts (India, Pakistan, Bahrain, Qatar) with Eastern Bank and Chartered Bank 1947-65; First Nat Bank of Chicago 1965-: mangr AVP London 1966, mangr VP London 1969, area head Asia Pacific (based Hong Kong) SVP 1975, head of treasy Chicago 1979, head int treasy Geneva 1981, seconded as md and chief exec offr Int Commercial Bank plc 1984; patron and memb Chicago Cncl For Relations; ACIB, MInstD; *Recreations* gardening, walking, golf; *Clubs* RAC, Overseas Bankers; *Style—* Gordon Sapstead, Esq

SARELL, Sir Roderick Francis Gisbert; KCMG (1968, CMG 1958), KCVO (1971); 2 s of Philip Sarell (d 1942), of Braeside, Ashurstwood, E Grinstead; *b* 23 Jan 1913; *Educ* Radley, Magdalen Coll Oxford; *m* 1946, Pamela Muriel, da of Vivian Crowther-Smith; 3 s; *Career* entered Consular Service 1936, cnsllr and consul gen Rangoon 1953-56, consul gen Algiers 1956-59, cnsllr FO 1960, ambass: Libya 1964-69, Turkey 1969-73; Coronation Medal 1953; *Clubs* Oriental, Leander; *Style—* Sir Roderick Sarell, KCMG, KCVO; The Litten, Hampstead Norreys, Newbury, Berks (☎ 0635 201274)

SARGAN, Prof John Denis; s of Harry Sargan (d 1981), of Humberston, S Humberside, and Gertrude Amy, *née* Porter (d 1984); *b* 23 Aug 1924; *Educ* Doncaster GS, Univ of Cambridge (BA); *m* 4 July 1953, Phyllis Mary, da of Walter Malcolm Millard (d 1969), of Pinner, Middx; 2 s (John b 1954, David b 1955), 1 da (Barbara b 1957); *Career* lectr of econs Univ of Leeds 1948-63; LSE: reader in econs 1963-64, prof of econs 1964-84, emeritus prof 1984, pres of Econometrics Soc 1979-80; FBA 1981, memb American Acad Arts and Sciences 1987; hon fell LSE 1990; *Books* contrib to: Econometrics Vols 1 and II (1988), Advanced Econometric Theory (1988); *Recreations* painting, bridge, playing the piano, gardening; *Style—* Prof John D Sargan; 49 Dukes Ave, Theydon Bois, Epping, Essex CM16 7HQ (☎ 037 881 2222)

SARGANT, Sir (Henry) Edmund; s of Rt Hon Sir Charles Sargant, Lord Justice of Appeal; *b* 24 May 1906; *Educ* Rugby, Trinity Coll Cambridge; *m* 1930, Mary Kathleen (d 1979), da of Tom Lemmey; 1 s; m 2, 1981, Evelyn Noel, *née* Arnold-Wallinger; *Career* served WWII RAF; slr 1930, ptnr Radcliffes & Co 1930-71; pres Law Soc 1968-69; *Style—* Sir Edmund Sargant; 902 Keyes House, Dolphin Square, London SW1V 3NB

SARGANT, Prof Naomi Ellen; *see*: McIntosh of Haringey, Baroness

SARGEANT, Col (William) Anthony Franks; TD (1965); s of Rev Preb William Sargeant (d 1969), of Lichfield, Staffs, and Gertrude Eveline, *née* Franks (d 1972); *b* 5

Oct 1929; *Educ* Lancing, Nat Foundry Coll (Dip); *m* 5 Sept 1953, Mary Elizabeth, da of Philip Burns Dumbell (d 1977), of Tettenhall, Wolverhampton; 1 s (Christopher Peter William b 1956), 1 da (Carolyn Mary b 1961); *Career* 2 Lt RA 1948-50, cmmnd Staffs Yeo 1953, Lt-Col cmdg offr 1968-69, appointed TA Col W Mid Dist 1971-73; dir Baelz Equipment Ltd 1966-75, chm (non-exec) Hope Works Ltd 1979-90, memb Farmer (breeding pedigree Hereford cattle) 1972-; memb Public Sch Exploring Soc 1947; asst ldr of Br Schs Exploring Soc 1952; Br Inst of Mgmnt Dip in Mgmnt Studies 1960, City & Guilds Cert Farm Business Mgmnt 1978 (Silver medal); DL Staffs 1973; High Sheriff Staffs 1980-81; *Recreations* skiing, sailing, nature conservation; *Style—* Col Anthony Sargeant; Bromesberrow Court, Bromesberrow, nr Ledbury, Herefordshire HR8 1RU (☎ 0531 650214)

SARGEAUNT, Lt-Col Henry Anthony (Tony); CB (1961), OBE (1948); s of Lt-Col Henry Sargeaunt (d 1951), and Nora Irene, *née* Carden Bart (d 1969); *b* 11 June 1907; *Educ* Clifton, Reading Univ, Emanuel Coll Cambridge (BA); *m* 13 July 1937, Winifred Doris, da of John Parkinson (d 1921); 2 s (Anthony John b 1941, David b 1942), 1 da (Julia b 1946); *Career* WWII Maj HQ 21 Army Gp 1941-47, Lt-Col Supt Army Operational Gp 1947-52, IDC 1952-53; scientific advsr: WO Army Cncl 1953-56, Defence Res Policy Ctee 1953-56, SHAPE and NATO 1959, Palais de Chaillot 1960; chief scientist Home Office 1960-67, ret 1967, conslt to UNO NY 1967-68; memb Operational Res Soc 1947, fndr memb Br Soc of the History of Sci; *Books* Grand Strategy (1941); *Recreations* fly fishing, horse racing, beagling, sailing, golf; *Clubs* Brokenhurst Fly Fishing, Bibury HR RLYC, Brockenhurst; *Style—* Lt-Col Tony Sargeaunt, CB, OBE; 7 Bond Close, Way, Lyminton, Hants (☎ 0590 683112)

SARGENT, Hon Dr (Caroline Mary); *née* McLaren; does not use husband's surname; yr da of 3 Baron Aberconway by his 1 w, Deirdre, *née* Knewstub; *b* 24 Oct 1944; *Educ* Imperial Coll London (BSc, DIC, PhD, FLS); *m* 1, 1962, Raimund Guernsey Sargent, of Massachusetts; 2 s (Dominic b 1963; Orlando b 1964); m 2, 1978, Graham Charles Steele; *Career* botanist, scientific Civil Service; dir forestry programme Int Inst for Environment and Development; holder of the Ness award for Exploration 1986 of the Royal Geographical Soc; *Style—* The Hon Dr Sargent; Beaulieu Hall, Hemington, Oundle, Northants; International Institute for Environment and Development, 3 Endsleigh St, London WC1H 0DD (☎ 071 388 2117)

SARGENT, John Richard (Dick); s of Sir John Philip Sargent, CIE (d 1972), and Ruth Taunton (d 1932); *b* 22 March 1925; *Educ* Dragon Sch, Rugby, ChCh Oxford (BA, MA); *m* 1, 16 July 1949 (m dis 1980), Anne Elizabeth, da of Lt-Col John F Haigh, MBE (d 1976); 1 s (Simon b 1953), 2 da (Sally b 1950, Vicky b 1957); m 2, Oct 1980, Hester Mary, wid of Dr J D E Campbell, 3 step s (Francis, Laurence, Nicholas); *Career* RN 1943-46, Sub Lt RNVR 1945; lectr in econs and fell Worcester Coll Oxford 1951-62, econ conslt HM Treasy 1963-65, prof and fndr memb Dept of Econs Univ of Warwick 1964-73 (pro vice-chllr 1970-72); gp econ advsr Midland Bank 1974-84 (ex-officio ed Midland Bank Review), economic advsr Miny of Technol 1969-71; memb: Doctors and Dentists Pay Review Body 1972-75, Armed Forces Pay Review Body 1972-86, Pharmacists Review Panel 1986-; Cncl Royal Econ Soc 1969-74; govr Nat Inst for Econ Res 1969-, pres Societé de Recherches Financiéres 1985-88 (memb Cncl 1976-); treas Comforts and Amenities Fund Burford Hosp 1986-, former memb Educn Ctee City of Oxford; author of numerous articles in econ jnls; *Books* British Transport Policy (1958); *Recreations* gardening; *Clubs* Reform; *Style—* Dick Sargent, Esq; Trentham House, Fulbrook, Burford, Oxon OX8 4BL (☎ 099 382 3525)

SARGENT, Peter Bertram James; s of Maj Bertram Sargent (d 1979), of 61 Maresfield Drive, Pevensey Bay, Sussex, and Hilda, *née* Rooms (d 1985); *b* 8 Nov 1932; *Educ* Sherwood Coll, Naini Tal UP India, The Stationers' Company's Sch London, LSE (BSc Econ); *m* Patricia Ann, da of Harry John William Mason (d 1984), of 33 Mapleton Crescent, Enfield, Middx; *Career* Nat Serv Flying Offr RAF 1957-59; gen mangr admin The Ever Ready Co GB Ltd 1967-69 (mgmnt accountant 1960-67), princ conslt Arthur Young Mgmnt Serv 1969-72, dep controller Barclays Bank Ltd 1972-78, gp planning mangr Grand Metropolitan plc 1978-83, asst corporate controller Europe Engelhard Corp 1983, md Sheffield Smelting Co Ltd, dep fin dir Europe Engelhard Corp 1983, Freeman: Worshipful Co of Stationers 1987, City of London 1987; FCA 1957; *Recreations* hockey, cricket, theatre, antiques; *Clubs* Marylebone Cricket, Tulse Hill Hockey (president), Apostles; *Style—* Peter Sargent, Esq; 13 East Ridgeway, Cuffley, Potters Bar, Herts EN6 4AW (☎ 0707 873754, fax 0707 872700), Engelhard Limited, Engelhard House, 8 Throgmorton Ave, London EC2N 2DL (☎ 071 588 4080, fax 071 374 4632, car 0860 829468, telex 496555)

SARGENT, Prof Roger William Herbert; s of Herbert Alfred Sargent (d 1959), and May Elizabeth, *née* Gill (d 1933); *b* 14 Oct 1926; *Educ* Bedford Sch, Imperial Coll London (BSc, PhD, DIC, DSc); *m* 11 Aug 1951, Shirley Jane Levesque, da of Archer Wilfrid Spooner (d 1973); 2 s (Philip Michael b 1 Aug 1954, Anthony John b 26 Dec 1955); *Career* Imperial Coll London: asst lectr 1950-51, sr lectr 1958-62, prof of chem engrg 1962-66, Courtaulds prof of chem engrg 1966-, dean City and Guilds Coll 1973-76, head Dept of Chem Engrg and Chem Technol 1975-88, dir Interdisciplinary Res Centre for Process Systems Engrg 1989-; ed of various learned jls and has made a prolific contrib to scientific literature; memb governing body Univ of London 1967-77 and 1979-87 (memb Bd of Studies Chem Engrg 1966-69); pres Inst of Chem Engrs 1973-74 (vice pres 1969-71 and 1972-73), chm chem engrg and technol ctee SRC 1971-73 (memb 1969-73), hon FCGI 1976, chm process plant ctee DTI 1981-87 (memb 1980-81), chm engrg and technol advsy ctee Br Cncl 1984-89 (memb 1976-89); memb: technol sub ctee UGC 1984-89, Br-French Mixed Cultural Cmmn 1985-, Br Nat Ctee for Int Engrg Affairs 1987-, ed advsy bd of Computers and Chem Engrg; Docteur Honoris Causa Institut National Polytechnique De Lorraine 1987; ACGI, FIChemE 1964, FIMA 1972, FEng 1976; *Style—* Prof Roger Sargent; Mulberry cottage, 291A Sheen Rd, Richmond upon Thames, Surrey TW10 5AW (☎ 081 876 9623); Imperial College, London SW7 2BY (☎ 071 589 5111 ext 4301, fax 071 584 1170, telex 929 484 IMPCOL G)

SARGENT, Wallace Leslie William; s of Leslie William Sargent (d 1979), and Eleanor, *née* Dennis (d 1964); *b* 15 Feb 1935; *m* 5 Aug 1964, Dr Anneila Sargent, da of Richard Cassells (d 1968), of Burntisland, Fife, Scotland; 2 da (Lindsay Eleanor b 8 July 1970, Alison Clare b 25 Jan 1972); *Career* res fell Caltech 1959-62, sr res fell Royal Greenwich Observatory 1962-64, asst prof of physics Univ of California San Diego 1964-66; Caltech: asst prof 1966-68, assoc prof 1968-71, prof 1971-81, exec offr for astronomy 1975-81, Ira S Bowen prof of astronomy 1981-; visiting fell: Mount Stromlo Observatory Aust Nat Univ 1965 and 1967, Inst of Theoretical Astronomy Univ of Cambridge 1968-72, 1974-75, 1979, 1982, 1987, Dept of Astrophysics Univ of Oxford 1973, Univ of Groningen 1978, Euro Southern Observatory 1980, 1982 and 1985, Univ of Florence 1981, Institut d'Astrophysique Paris 1984, Royal Observatory Edinburgh 1990; memb: N Hemisphere Review Ctee SRC 1968-69, Visiting Ctee Univ of Arizona 1970-73, Ctee on Space Astronomy and Astrophysics Nat Acad of Sciences 1975-78, Study Gp for Space Telescope Sci Inst Nat Acad of Sciences 1976, Harvard Coll Observatory Visiting Ctee 1979-86 (chm 1987-93), Ed Bd Annual Reviews of Astronomy and Astrophysics 1977-81, Bd Harvard-Smithsonlan Centre for Astrophysics 1983-, Sci Steering Ctee Keck Observatory 1985- (co-chm 1985-89 and 1990-); memb Visiting Ctee: in Astrophysics Stanford Univ 1986, Mount Wilson and Las Campanas Observatories 1987, Astronomy Prog State Univ of NY at Stony Brook 1987, Astronomy Dept U C Berkeley 1988, Space Telescope Sci Inst 1989-91; memb: Astronomy and Astrophysics Survey Ctee Nat Acad of Sciences 1989- (co-chm Optical/IR Panel), Space Telescope Advsy Ctee 1990-; Alfred P Sloane Fndn fell 1968-70, Helen B Warner prize American Astronomical Soc 1969, George Darwin lect RAS 1987, Dirs Distinguished lectr Lawrence Livermore Lab 1988, Dannie Heineman prize 1991; memb: American Astronomical Union, RAS, Int Astronomical Union; FAAAS 1977, FRS 1981; *Recreations* watching sports, oriental rugs, music, reading; *Clubs* Athenaeum (Pasadena, Ca); *Style—* Wallace Sargent, Esq, FRS; Astronomy Department, 105-24 California Institute of Technology, 1201 East California Boulevard, Pasadena, CA 91125, USA (☎ 818 356 4055, fax 818 568 1517)

SARGINSON, David Richard; s of Richard Herbert Sarginson (d 1984), and Ursula Rose, *née* Brown (d 1950); *b* 9 May 1936; *Educ* Wrekin Coll Shropshire; *m* 28 Sept 1961, Pamela Ann, da of Stephen James Clifford (d 1967); 1 s (Mark Richard b 1964); 1 da (Jane Elizabeth b 1962); *Career* slr; HM coroner for City of Coventry 1985; fndr of Sarginson & Co Slrs in Coventry and Leamington Spa; chm West Midlands Rent Assessment Panel 1985; chm and md Sarginson Bros Ltd; manufacturers of foundry equipment and aluminium fndrs automotive industry; *Recreations* france, its life and good food, music; *Clubs* Drapers (Coventry); *Style—* David Sarginson, Esq; Abbeyfield Lodge, Castle Road, Kenilworth, Warwickshire (☎ 0926 55272); 11 Warwick Row Coventry (☎ 0203 553181, fax 0203 58573)

SARKANY, Imrich; s of Dr Edmund Sarkany (d 1938), and Maria *née* Pollitzer; *b* 7 Jan 1923; *Educ* St Thomas' Hosp Med Sch; *m* 12 Dec 1956, Helen Ruth Veronica, da of Israel Pomerance, of St Albans; 2 s (Robert b 1962, Andrew b 1965), 1 da (Elizabeth b 1960); *Career* physician (diseases of the skin); conslt dermatologist Royal Free Hosp 1960-89; pres: Br Assoc of Dermatologists 1987-88, Dermatology Section RSM 1981-82, Monosection for Dermato-Venereology of Euro Union of Med Specialists 1987-, St Johns' Dermatological Soc 1976-77, Dermatological Dowling Club; memb: Bd of Govrs Royal Free Hosp, cncl RSM; fndr chm Br Soc for Investigative Dermatology; *Style—* Imrich Sarkany, Esq; 2 Romney Close, London NW11 7JD; 132 Harley St, London W1 (☎ 071 935 3678)

SARNE, Michael; s of Alfred Scheuer (d 1976), and Agathe, *née* Reiche; *b* 6 Aug 1940; *Educ* BEC Sch, Sch of Slavonic & European Studies (BA); *m* 15 Jan 1969 (m dis 1982), Tanya, da of John Gordon; 1 s (William Mordechai b 30 May 1972), 3 da (Claudia Aviva b 17 Jan 1970, Emma Miriam b 17 Dec 1986, Abigail Leah b 8 Nov 1989); *Career* actor and singer; records incl: Come Outside, Will I What?, Just for Kicks; films incl: Every Days a Holiday, A Place to Go; TV work incl: War and Remembrance, Minder; dir films of incl: Road to St Trope (writer) 1965, Joanna 1968, Myra Breckinridge 1970, Intimidade 1973; screenplays incl: Moonlighting, The Lightship, Ferdy durke; chm Celebrities Guild of GB, memb Bd of Mgmnt New West End Synagogue; ACTT, AIP; memb: Dirs Guild, Writers Guild, Equity; *Books* 3 Lives of Nigel Kelland (1965), Joanna (1968); *Recreations* tennis, bridge, poetry, painting; *Style—* Michael Sarne, Esq; 61 Campden Hill Towers, London W11 3QP (☎ 071 221 7185)

SAROOP, Narindar; CBE (1982); s of Chief Ram Saroop (d 1988), of Lahore and Chandigarh, and Shyam, *née* Devi (d 1981); *b* 14 Aug 1929; *Educ* Aitchison Coll for Punjab Chiefs Lahore, Indian Mil Acad Dehra Dun India; *m* 1, Oct 1952 (m dis 1967), Ravi Gill, da of the Sardar of Premgarh (d 1968), of Goodwood, Simla, Punjab, India; 1 s (Vijayendra b 1953, d 1983), 2 da (Vaneeta b 1954, Kavita b 1961); m 2, Feb 1968, Stephanie Denise, da of Alexander Panyotis Cronopulo (d 1977), of Zakynthos, Greece; *Career* 2 Royal Lancers (Gardner's Horse), Queen Victoria's Own The Poona Horse; served as: Sqdn Offr, Regtl Signals Offr, Regtl Gunnery Offr, Actg Sqdn Ldr; mgmnt trainee Yule Catto & Co Ltd 1954-55, sr exec Andrew Yule & Co Ltd 1955-61; subsidiary Bd dir: Davy Ashmore Group 1961-64, Turner & Newall Group 1965-71, mgmnt consultancy 1972-76; devpt advsr H Clarkson Group 1976-87, conslt Banque Belge 1987-91; pres India Welfare Soc 1984-91; memb Cncl: The Freedom Assoc 1980-88, IOD 1983-; memb: BBC Advsy Panel 1977-80, Charity Review Royal Borough of Kensington and Chelsea 1974-; Parly Candidate (Cons) Greenwich General Election 1979 (first Asian Tory Party candidate this century), cncllr Royal Borough of Kensington and Chelsea 1974-82, vice chm Cons Pty Int Office 1990-; fndr and chm: Anglo-Asian Cons Soc 1976-79 and 1985-86, The Durbar Club 1981-; *Books* In Defence of Freedom (jtly, 1978), A Squire of Hindoostan (1985); *Style—* Narindar Saroop, Esq, CBE; 25 de Vere Gdns, London W8

SARSON, Hon Mrs (Gillian Isolda Josephine); *née* Pollock; o da of 2 Viscount Hanworth; *b* 1 April 1944; *m* 24 Aug 1963, Timothy von Weber Sarson; 2 s, 2 da; *Style—* The Hon Mrs Sarson; 8 Gatcombe Rd, N19

SARTIN, John Henry; s of Arthur Henry Sartin (d 1989), of Hertford, and Mona, *née* Weston; *b* 2 March 1945; *Educ* Hertford GS; *m* 7 Sept 1974, Mary Stewart, da of George Newlands (d 1986), of Welwyn Garden City; 1 s (David b 1978), 1 da (Jane b 1976); *Career* self employed shopkeeper; Cons memb Hertford Borough Cncl 1970-73, ldr East Herts DC 1986- (memb 1973), chm Herts Assoc DCs 1986-87, chaired various ctees incl housing 1979-81; memb Hertford CAB mgmt cmmn, govr Richard Hale Sch Hertford; *Recreations* family, some DIY, the countryside; *Clubs* Hertford; *Style—* John Sartin, Esq; 2 Park Rd, Hertford (☎ 0992 553 335); 15 Market Place, Hertford (☎ 0992 584 889)

SARUM, Archdeacon of; *see*: Hopkinson, Ven Barnabas John (Barney)

SAS, Tadeusz Robert; JP (Inner London 1977); s of Tadeusz Julian Sas, of London (d 1974), and Zofia T Sas; *b* 13 Dec 1941; *Educ* Harrow; *m* 1967, Irena Eugenia; 2 s, 2 da; *Career* chm and md: Sas Gp of Cos Ltd, Sas Admin Services Ltd, Sas Devpts Ltd, Sas Chemicals Ltd, Sas Pharmaceuticals Ltd, Sas R & D Services Ltd, Sas of America Inc, Sas (Jersey) Ltd, Elektromodul Ltd, Varimex Ltd; vice chm Anglo Polish Conservative Assoc (APCS) 1967; memb Westminster City Council 1964-71 (also served on various ctees); ctee memb Assoc of Br Chemical Manufacturers 1972-75; ctee memb Defence Manufacturers Assoc 1978-82; memb Int Assoc of Bomb Technicians and Investigators 1974-; FBIM, FInstM, MNDEA; kt Cdr Order of Polonia Restituta 1980; *Recreations* sleeping, work; *Clubs* Carlton, Surf (Miami), Les Ambassadeurs (London); *Style—* Tadeusz Sas, Esq, JP; Craven House, Hamstead Marshall, Newbury, Berks RG15 0JG (radiophone 0039 222521); 10350 Old Cutler Road, South Miami, Florida 33156, USA (☎ 010 1 305 667 8494); Villa Annabell, Atalaya Park, Estepona, Malaga, Spain (☎ 78 13 98)

SASAKAWA, Yohei; s of Ryoichi Sasakawa, and Shizue Sasakawa; *b* 8 Jan 1939; *Educ* sch of politics-economics Meiji Univ (BA); *m* 28 Feb 1973, Kazuyo Sasakawa; 1 s (Takao), 3 da (Junpei, Kohei, Shohei); *Career* dir mgmnt cncl: Life Planning Centre 1974, US-Japan Fndn 1981, Scandinavia-Japan Sasakawa Fndn 1984, GB Sasakawa Fndn 1984, Sasakawa Peace Fndn 1986; pres Japan Shipbuilding Indust Fndn 1986- (dir mgmnt cncl 1981); *Recreations* reading, golf, tennis; *Style—* Yohei Sasakawa, Esq; 6-9-25 Matsubara, Setagaya-ku, Tokyo 156 Japan; President, Japan Shipbuilding Industry Foundation, The Great Britain Sasakawa Foundation, The Sasakawa Hall 8th Floor, 3-12-12 Mita, Minato-ku, Tokyo 108 (☎ 010 813 798 5971, fax 010 813 798 5973, telex 2423746 GBSFJA)

SASDY, Peter George; s of Ernst Sömjén (d 1973), and Magdolna, *née* Révész (d

1985); *b* 27 May 1935; *Educ* Univ of Budapest (BA), Univ of Bristol; *m* Mia Myrtill, da of Ferenc Nadasi; 2 da (Anita Judit b 1970, Carola Marian b 1979); *Career* trainee dir BBC TV, drama dir ATV Network, freelance drama prodr and dir of single plays, drama serials and series; feature films and US mini-series for: BBC TV, LWT, Thames TV, Universal MCA, Warner Brothers, Rank Films, NBC TV, Anglia TV, ABC TV, EMI Films, 20th Century Fox; recent film credits incl: Wuthering Heights (BBC), If Winter Comes (with Paul Scofield, BBC), Minder (pilot for Euston Films), Imaginary Friends, The Secret Diary of Adrian Mole aged 13 3/4, Ending Up; int Emmy Awards nominations 1986 and 1990; memb: Br Film Acad & TV Arts, Directors Guild of America, Directers Guild of GB; *Books* Four Black Cars (co-author, 1958); *Recreations* travel, swimming; *Style—* Peter Sasdy, Esq; Peter Sasdy Productions Ltd, c/o Robert John Specterman, Princess House, 50-60 Eastcastle Street, London W1N 7AP (☎ 071 323 3444, fax 071 323 1005)

SASSOON, Adrian David; s of Hugh Meyer Sassoon, of London, and Marion Julia, *née* Schiff; *b* 1 Feb 1961; *Educ* Eton, Inchbald Sch of Design, Christies Fine Arts Course; *Career* asst curator Dept of Decorative Arts J Paul Getty Museum Calif 1982-84 (curatorial asst 1980-82), dir Alexander & Berendt Ltd London 1990- (asst to md 1987-89); lectr on and dealer in French decorative arts and eighteenth century Sévres porcelain; patron of New Art Tate Gallery 1987, treas and memb Ctee French Porcelain Soc 1989 (joined as memb 1985), memb Ctee The Attingham Tst for the Study of the Country House 1990; memb: ICA, Nat Tst (life), Kenwood House (life) Contemporary Art Soc, Bowes Museum (life), Furniture History Soc; friend V&A, Nat Libraries (life), Lambeth Palace Library (Life); articles on French eighteenth Century Decorative Arts in the J Paul Getty Museum Jls 1981-85; *Books* Decorative Arts: A Handbook of the J Paul Getty Museum (1986), Catalogue of Vincennes and Serres Porcelain in the J Paul Getty Museum (1991); *Clubs* Lyford Cay, Nassau, Bahamas; *Style—* Adrian Sassoon, Esq

SASSOON, David; s of George Sassoon, and Victoria, *née* Gurgi; *b* 5 Oct 1932; *Educ* Chelsea Coll of Art, RCA; *Career* fashion designer, joined Belinda Belville 1958, first Ready to Wear Collection 1963, dir 1964, co became Belville Sassoon 1970, sole shareholder 1983; licencee: Vogue Butterick USA 1966, Japan 1988; *Recreations* theatre, ballet; *Style—* David Sassoon, Esq; Bellville Sassoon, 73 Pavilion Rd, London SW1 (☎ 071 235 3087)

SASSOON, James Meyer; s of Hugh Meyer Sassoon, of London, and Marion Julia, *née* Schiff; *b* 11 Sept 1955; *Educ* Eton, ChCh Oxford (Exhibitioner, MA, Gibbs book prize); *m* 23 Oct 1981, Sarah Caroline Ray, da of Sir(Ernest) John Ward Barnes; 1 s (Frederick b 1 April 1987), 1 da (Alexandra b 6 Nov 1990); *Career* Thomson McLintock & Co 1977-86, asst dir S G Warburg & Co Ltd 1987-; contrib of articles to art and fin jls; memb Tate Gallery Patrons of New Art (Acquistion Ctee 1986); FCA (1991, ACA 1980); *Recreations* dabbler in the arts (visual, musical, horticultural and oenological); *Style—* James Sassoon, Esq; S G Warburg & Co Ltd, 2 Finsbury Ave, London EC2M 2PA (☎ 071 860 1090, fax 071 860 0901)

SATCHELL, Keith; s of Dennis Joseph Satchell, of Hemel Hempstead, and Joan Betty, *née* Elms; *b* 3 June 1951; *Educ* Hemel Hempstead GS, Aston Univ (BSc); *m* 1 July 1972, Hazel Dorothy, da of Douglas Burston, of Birmingham; 2 s (Paul b 1978, Richard b 1980), 1 da (Olivia b 1984); *Career* gen mangr (Products) Friends Provident Life Office 1987-; govr Middle Sch Verwood; FIA 1976; *Recreations* sport, reading; *Style—* Keith Satchell, Esq; Oakfield, 63 Moorlands Road, Verwood, Dorset BH21 6PD (☎ 0202 824 118); Friends Provident, 72-122 Castle St, Salisbury, Wilts (☎ 0722 413366)

SATTERTHWAITE, Christopher James; s of Col R G Satterthwaite, LVO, OBE, of Meadow Cottage, East Harting, Petersfield, W Sussex, and Rosemary, *née* Messervy; *b* 21 May 1956; *Educ* Ampleforth, Lincoln Coll Oxford (MA); *m* 30 Jan 1988, Teresa Mary, da of Cdr L Bailey; 2 s (James Richard b 29 Oct 1988, Henry Frank b 8 Nov 1989); *Career* graduate trainee H J Heinz Ltd 1979-81; IMP Ltd: joined 1981, bd dir 1985, md 1987-; *Recreations* fly fishing, golf, motorbikes; *Clubs* Vincent's; *Style—* Christopher Satterthwaite, Esq; IMP Ltd, 197 Knightsbridge, London SW7 1RP (☎ 071 581 7666. fax 071 589 3903)

SATTERTHWAITE, Rt Rev John Richard; *see*: Gibraltar in Europe, Bishop of

SAUGMAN, Per Gotfred; OBE (1990); s of Emanuel A G Saugman (d 1962), and Esther, *née* Lehmann (d 1986); *b* 26 June 1925; *Educ* Gentofte GS, Commercial Coll Copenhagen; *m* 28 Dec 1950, Patricia, da of William Henry Fulford (d 1982); 3 s (Peter b 1951, Philip b 1955), and 1 s decd, 1 da (Penelope b 1959); *Career* bookselling and publishing in Denmark, Switzerland, England 1941-49; Blackwell Scientific Pubns Ltd: sales mangr 1952, md 1954-87, chm 1972-90; dir Univ Bookshops (Oxford) Ltd 1963; chm: Wm George's Sons Ltd 1965-87, Blackwell N America Inc 1973-90, Einar Munksgaard Publishers Copenhagen 1967, Kooyker Boehandel Leiden 1973; memb: Int Publishers Assoc 1976-79, Publishers Assoc of GB and Ireland 1977-82; hon memb Br Ecological Soc 1960-; govr: Oxford Poly 1972-82, Dragon Sch 1975; Hon MA Univ of Oxford 1978, hon fell Green Coll Oxford 1981, fell St Cross Coll Oxford 1980; kt Order of Dannebrog 1972, Chevalier Order of Icelandic Falcon 1984; *Books* From the First Fifty Years (1989); *Recreations* reading, art, English, watercolours, golf; *Clubs* Athenaeum, RAC, Frilford Golf (Oxford); *Style—* Per Saugman, Esq, OBE; Sunningwood House, Lincombe Lane, Boars Hill, Oxford OX1 5DZ (☎ 0865 735503); Blackwell Scientific Publications Ltd, Osney Mead, Oxford OX2 0EL (☎ 0865 240201, telex 83355 MEDBOK G, fax 0865 721205)

SAUL, Philip Bycroft; s of Maj John Bycroft Saul, MC (d 1946), and Juliana Margaret, *née* Watson (d 1987); *b* 19 Feb 1933; *Educ* Dover Coll, St Edmund Hall Oxford (MA); *m* 31 July 1956, Jane, da of Maj Gerald William Gostwyck May (d 1963); 2 s (George, Thomas), 3 da (Dorothy, Frances, Lucy); *Career* slr 1959, sr ptnr Stringer Saul; cncl memb NRA; *Recreations* match rifle shooting (for England 9 Occasions 1956-89), skiing; *Style—* Philip Saul, Esq; 6 Wyndham Mews, London W1 (☎ 071 262 4013); Valbonne, Alpes-Maritimes, France; Marcol House, 293 Regent St, London W1 (☎ 071 631 4048, fax 071 636 2306, telex 267427)

SAUL, Roger John; s of (Frederick) Michael Saul, of Chilcompton, Somerset, and Joan *née* Legg; *b* 25 July 1950; *Educ* Kingswood Sch Bath, Westminster Coll London; *m* 23 July 1977, Marion Joan, da of Clifford Cameron; 3 s (William Michael, Cameron Robert, Frederick Jakes); *Career* fndr, creator, designer and md of Mulberry Co 1971-, awarded Queen's Award for Export 1979, 1989; BKCEC Exporter of the Year 1987-88, brand label in Br contemporary classic fashion worldwide; memb Bd BKCEC; *Recreations* tennis, historic car racing, skiing, shooting, garden design; *Style—* Roger Saul, Esq; Mulberry Co, Chilcompton, Bath, Somerset (☎ 0761 232855, fax 0761 232876, telex 444305)

SAUMAREZ; *see*: de Saumarez

SAUNDERS, Dr Ann Loreille; da of George Cox-Johnson (d 1941), of 10 Manor Hall Ave, and Joan Loreille, *née* Clowser (d 1980); *b* 23 May 1930; *Educ* Henrietta Barnet Sch, Queen's Coll Harley St, UCL (BA), Univ of Leicester (PhD); *m* 4 June 1960, Bruce Kemp Saunders, s of Kemp Alexander Saunders (d 1973), of The Croft, The Ridgeway, East Grinstead; 1 s (Matthew Kemp b 1964), 1 da (Katherine Sophia Loreille b 1967 d 1984); *Career* dep librarian Lambeth Palace Library 1952-55, asst keeper Br Museum 1955-56, borough archivist St Marylebone Public Library 1956-63, asst to hon editor of Journal of the British Archaelogical Assoc 1963-75, hon ed Costume Soc 1967-, hon ed London Topographical Soc 1975-; pt/t lectr: Richmond Coll Kensington 1979-, City Univ 1981-; contrib to various jls incl Geographical Magazine, Burlington Magazine and The London Journal; FSA, FRSA; *Books* Regent's Park: A Study of the Development of the Area from 1066 to the Present Day (1969), London North of the Thames (revised 1972), London: The City and Westminster (revised 1975), Regent's Park (1981), The Regent's Park Villas (1981), The Art and Architecture of London: An Illustrated Guide (won London Tourist Bd award for specialist guidebook of the year 1984, 2 edn 1988), St Martin in the Fields: A Short History and Guide (1989); *Recreations* reading, embroidery, cooking, walking, studying London, going to exhibitions and the theatre and to churches; *Style—* Dr Ann Saunders, FSA; 3 Meadway Gate, London NW11 7LA

SAUNDERS, Dr (William) Anthony; s of Robert Valentine Saunders, of 5 Rockleaze, Sneyd Park, Bristol 9, and Mary Isabel, *née* Kerr; *b* 24 June 1940; *Educ* Clifton, Trinity Coll Cambridge (MA, MB BChir, FRCPsych, DPM, DCH); *m* 11 Feb 1967, Angela Pauline, da of Charles Alan Rapson (d 1971), of Pillifants, Lower Shapter St, Topsham, Exeter, Devon; 1 s (Jonathan b 7 May 1970), 2 da (Emma b 13 March 1968, Annabel b 29 July 1972); *Career* conslt in child and adolescent pyschiatry Wessex RHA 1973-, hon clinical lectr Univ of Southampton 1973-, psychiatric advsr Centro Studi Psico Sociali Rome 1987-; chm Wessex Child Psychiatrists, past nat chm Ctee of Mgmnt Assoc for Psychiatric Study of Adolescent; *Style—* Dr Anthony Saunders; Meadow Cottage, Otterbourne, Nr Winchester, Hampshire SO21 2EQ (☎ 0962 713129); Leigh House Hospital, Cuckoo Bushes Lane, Chandler's Ford, Hants (☎ 0703 252418)

SAUNDERS, Basil; s of Cdr John Edward Saunders, RN (missing presumed dead 1941), and Marjorie, *née* Purdon (d 1983); *b* 12 Aug 1925; *Educ* Merchant Taylors', Wadham Coll Oxford (MA); *m* 1957, Betty, da of Victor Smith (d 1957); 2 s (William, Edward), 4 da (Kate, Louisa, Etta, Charlotte); *Career* Sub Lt RNVR 1943-46; asst D'Anglais College De Tarascon 1951-52, writer General Electric (USA) 1953-54, PR offr BIM 1954-57, conslt Pritchard Wood (later Infoplan) 1958-63, head of PR The Wellcome Fndn 1963-78, dir gen ASLIB 1978-80, conslt Traverse-Healy Ltd 1981-84; dir: Traverse-Healy & Regester Ltd 1984-87, Charles Barker Traverse-Healy 1987-90; freelance PR conslt 1990-; FIPR; *Books* Crackle of Thorns (1968); *Clubs* Savile; *Style—* Basil Saunders, Esq; 18 Dartmouth Park Ave, London NW5 1JN (☎ 071 485 4672); Charles Barker Traverse-Healy Ltd, 30 Farringdon St, London EC4A 4EA (☎ 071 634 1000)

SAUNDERS, Christopher John; s of Rupert Henry Saunders (d 1977), of Guildford, Surrey, and Gladys Susan, *née* Harris (d 1975); *b* 7 May 1940; *Educ* Lancing, Fitwilliam Coll Cambridge (MA), Wadham Coll Oxford (Cert Ed); *m* 27 Oct 1973, Cynthia Elizabeth Saunders, JP, da of Harold Deverel Stiles, TD, JP, of Hove, Sussex; 1 s (Jonathan Mark Christopher b 31 March 1975), 1 da (Lucy Kathryn b 29 Aug 1976); *Career* housemaster Bradfield 1972-80 (asst master 1964-80), headmaster Eastbourne Coll 1981-; memb MCC cricket tour 1967, chm Independent Sch FA 1981-; govr: St Andrews Sch Eastbourne E Sussex, Ashdown House Forest Row E Sussex, Stoke Brunswick Sch Ashurst Wood E Sussex, Holmewood House Langton Green Kent, Horris Hill Newbury Berks; memb FA 1982-; *Recreations* music, theatre, gardening, soccer, cricket; *Clubs* Hawks (Cambridge), MCC; *Style—* Christopher Saunders, Esq; Headmaster's House, Eastbourne College, Old Wish Rd, Eastbourne, E Sussex BN21 4JX (☎ 0323 37655)

SAUNDERS, Christopher Thomas; CMG (1953); s of Thomas Beckenn Avening Saunders (d 1950), and Mary Theodora Slater (d 1928); *b* 5 Nov 1907; *Educ* St Edwards Oxford, Ch Ch Oxford (MA); *m* 1947, Cornelia Jacomijntje, da of Tjisse Gielstra (d 1957), of The Netherlands; 1 s (John); *Career* economist Univs of Liverpool and Manchester 1930-35; memb Jt Ctee Cotton Trade 1935-40, govr Cotton Control 1940-45; civil servant Miny of Labour and Central Statistical Office 1945-57, dir Nat Inst for Econ and Social Res London 1957-65, res dir UN Econ Cmmn for Europe Geneva 1965-73, prof Sussex Euro Res Centre Univ of Sussex 1973-84, visiting fell (pt/t) Science Policy Research Unit Univ of Sussex 1984-; *Books* Seasonal Variations in Employment (1936), Pay Inequalities in EEC (1981), many anonymous contribs to official nat and int reports, numerous journal articles and editing of conference transactions; *Recreations* walking, travel, painting; *Clubs* Reform; *Style—* Christopher Thomas Saunders, Esq, CMG; 73 Wick Hall, Furze Hill, Hove, E Sussex BN3 1NG (☎ 0273 24219)

SAUNDERS, Dame Cicely Mary Strode; OM (1989), DBE (1980, OBE 1967); da of Philip Gordon Saunders (d 1961), of The Chase, Hadley Common, Barnet, and Mary Christian Knight (d 1968); *b* 22 June 1918; *Educ* Roedean, St Anne's Coll Oxford, St Thomas's Hosp Med Sch; *m* 1980, Prof Marian Bohusz-Szyszko, s of Antoni Bohusz-Szyszko, of Wilno, Poland; *Career* fndr and medical dir St Christopher's Hospice London; dep chm Attendance Allowance Bd; Hon DSc Yale 1969, DUniv Open Univ 1978, DHL Jewish Theol Seminary of America 1982, Hon LLD Leicester 1983, Hon DUniv Essex 1983, Hon DSc London 1983, Hon LLD Oxford 1986, Hon LLD Cambridge 1986; Gold medal Soc of Apothecaries of London 1979, Templeton Fndn Award 1981, awarded British Medical Assoc gold medal 1987; *Recreations* home; *Style—* Dame Cicely Saunders, OM, DBE; St Christopher's Hospice, 51-59 Lawrie Park Rd, Sydenham SE26 6DZ (☎ 081 778 9252); 50 Lawrie Park Gardens, Sydenham SE26 (☎ 081 778 9252)

SAUNDERS, Cynthia Anne; *née* Llewellyn; da of Frank Horace Llewellyn (d 1961), of Walsall, and Ivy Evelyn, *née* Gwinnutt (d 1968); *b* 27 June 1939; *Educ* Joseph Leckie Comprehensive, Walsall Coll of Technol, Wenesbury Coll of Commerce; *m* 17 Sept 1960, Kenneth Thomas Saunders, s of Thomas Samuel Spencer Saunders, of Willenhall; 2 s (Mark Ryan b 1964, Jared Llewellyn b 1967); *Career* gp co sec Blue Ribbon Equestrian Group 1972-79, co sec and dir Qualis Group of Companies 1979-; Girl Guide Assoc: PR advsr Midlands, PR advsr W Mercia County; pres Soroptimist Int (Walsall Club) 1989-90 (sr vice pres 1988-89); FFA 1976; *Recreations* swimming, reading; *Style—* Mrs Kenneth Saunders; 16 Riding Way, Huntlands, Willenhall, West Midlands WV12 5PH (☎ 0922 476 058); Qualis Group, Noose Lane, Willenhall, West Midland WV13 3LW (☎ 0902 366 789, fax 0902 368 844)

SAUNDERS, David Martin St George; s of Hilary Aidan St George Saunders, CBE, MC, of Broadway, Sussex (d 1951), and Helen Foley (d 1937); f was a professional author (under the pseudonyms of Francis Beeding and David Pilgrim), offical historial for the RAF in WWII, and librarian of the House of Commons for some years; *b* 23 July 1930; *Educ* Marlborough, RMA Sandhurst, Staff Coll Quetta Pakistan; *m* 23 July 1960, Patricia Sybil, da of J H Methold, CBE (d 1984); 1 s (Rupert b 1965), 1 da (Camilla b 1968); *Career* cmmnd Welsh Gds 1950, Staff Capt 1 Gds Bde Egypt 1954-56, Asst Adj RMA Sandhurst 1956-58; Adj 1 Battalion Welsh Gds Pirbright 1958-60; GSO III The War Office 1960-62, Staff Coll Quetta 1963, Co Cdr 1 Bn Welsh Gds 1964, GSO II Br Def Liaison Staff, Canberra 1965-67, Co Cdr Gds Depot Pirbright 1967-68; joined the Foreign & Cwlth Office 1968, FCO London 1968-70, consul econ Johannesburg 1970-72; first sec: FCO London 1973-74, Dakar 1974-76, FCO 1976-77, Pretoria 1977-79, The Hague 1979-83; cncllr FCO London 1983-; *Recreations* cinema, skiing, military history, wines of Burgundy, shooting; *Style—* David M Saunders, Esq;

c/o National Westminster Bank, 246 Westminster Bridge Rd, London SE7

SAUNDERS, Brigadier (Arthur) David Rich; MBE (1947); s of Maj Harold Cecil Rich Saunders, DSO (ka 1918); and Dorothy May, *née* Triscott (d 1974); *b* 5 July 1917; *Educ* Clifton, RMC Sandhurst; *m* 3 July 1948, Margaret Mitchell, da of Robert Bell (ka 1914), of Dumfrieshire; 1 step s (Christopher b 10 October 1940); *Career* cmmnd 2 Lt E Yorks Regt 1937, Dunkirk evacuation 1940, Staff Coll Camberly 1941, Bde Maj 198 Inf Bde 1942, GS02 WO (SD) 1942, Bde Maj 197 Inf Bde NW Europe 1944-45, RAF Staff Coll 1945, Bde Maj 161 Ind Inf Bde 1945-46 Burma (Burma Star 1945), Netherlands, E Indies, India (despatches 1946); GS02 WO 1947-48, seconded to Jamaica Regt 1948-51, dep asst mil sec WO 1952-54, OC E York Regtl Depot 1955-56, 2 Cmmd 1 Bn E York Regt BAOR 1957-58, Lt-Col GS01 Allied Forces S Europe Naples 1958, OC 1 Bn Yorks & Lancs Regt Berlin BAOR 1959-62, Col (Mil Trg) WO 1963, Cdr (Brig) 47 Inf Bde TA 1964-66, Brig i/c Admin HQ Southern Cmmd and later HQ Army Strategic Cmmd 1966-68, ret 1968; sr inspr: DoE 1974 (main grade housing and planning inspr DoE 1969), Welsh Office 1975, ret 1986; hon sec (planning) Cncl for Protection of Rural Wales (Pembrokeshire Branch) 1988-90; *Recreations* gardening, walking; *Clubs* Army and Navy; *Style—* Brig David Saunders, MBE; Castle House, Castlefield, Narberth, Pembrokeshire, Dyfed SA67 8SW (☎ 0834 860979)

SAUNDERS, David William; CB (1989); s of William Ernest Saunders, of 5 Ernest Rd, Horchurch, Essex, and Lilian Grace, *née* Ward (d 1987); *b* 4 Nov 1936; *Educ* Hornchurch GS, Worcester Coll Oxford (BA, MA); *m* 15 April 1963, Margaret Susan Rose, da of William Colin Bartholomew (d 1980), of 7C Friese Greene House, Chelsea Manor St, London; *Career* Nat Serv RAF 1955-57 (Russian Linguist), articled clerk later slr private practice 1960-69; Parly Counsel: asst counsel 1970-75, on loan to Law Cmmn 1972-74, sr asst counsel 1975-78, dep counsel 1978-80, counsel 1980-, on loan to Law Cmmn as sr draftsman 1986-87; memb Law Soc 1964-; *Recreations* bridge, golf; *Style—* David Saunders, Esq, CB; 104A Belgrave Rd, London SW1V 2BJ (☎ 071 834 4403); Office of the Parliamentary Counsel, 36 Whitehall, London SW1 (☎ 071 210 6602)

SAUNDERS, Denis; s of James Edward Saunders (d 1966), and Maud, *née* Jefferson; *b* 15 April 1934; *Educ* Royal Belfast Academical Inst, Sale GS, Trinity Coll Cambridge (MA, LLM); *m* 17 Aug 1963, Julia Margaret Bragg; 2 s (Mark b 1965, Edward b 1968); *Career* called to the Bar Grays Inn 1958; dir TI Group plc 1990- (co sec 1975-); *Recreations* golf, gardening, bridge; *Style—* Denis Saunders, Esq; TI Group plc, 50 Curzon St, London W1Y 7PN (☎ 071 499 9131, fax 071 493 6533, telex 263740 TIGRUP G)

SAUNDERS, Air Vice-Marshal Derek Arthur (Dusty); CBE; s of Arthur William Edwin Chaplin Saunders (d 1970) and Dorothy May Helen, *née* Ives (d 1985); *b* 14 Nov 1933; *Educ* s of Dorking County GS, Kings Coll London, Coll of Aeronautics Cranfield; *m* 27 April 1957, (Ada) Margaret, da of John Robert Foster (d 1977); 2 s (Andrew b 1959, Mark b 1962), 1 da (Ailsa b 1964); *Career* RAF 1956-90; CEng FIEE 1982 (MIEE 1967); *Recreations* caravanning, church music, rural history; *Clubs* Royal Air Force; *Style—* Air Vice-Marshall D A Saunders, CBE; Ministry of Defence, Main Building, Whitehall, London (☎ 071 218 7445)

SAUNDERS, Emma Elizabeth (Mrs Peter Earl); da of Peter Saunders, of London, and Patricia Mabel, *née* Annesley; *b* 14 May 1955; *Educ* Godolphin and Latymer, Univ of Oxford (BA, MA); *m* 19 Jan 1980, Peter Richard Stephen Earl, s of Peter Richard Walter Earl; 1 s (Richard b 10 March 1987), 1 da (Amelia-Rose b 8 July 1985); *Career* Lazard Bros & Co Ltd 1977-80, vice pres Bear Stearns Int 1980-84, dir and fndr memb Tranwood Earl 1985-, chm and fndr memb Analysis Corp plc 1988-; FIMBRA; *Recreations* riding, skiing, picture restoration and framing; *Style—* Ms Emma Saunders; Shipton Lodge, Shipton Under Wychwood, Oxfordshire; Tranwood Earl & Company Ltd, 123 Sloane St, London SW1 9BW (☎ 071 730 3412, fax 071 730 5770, telex 932016 SLOANE G)

SAUNDERS, Prof George Albert; s of Barnett Stanley Saunders (d 1977), and Lilian Gladys Saunders (d 1976); *b* 4 Jan 1936; *Educ* Caterham Sch, Univ of London (BSc, PhD); *m* 16 April 1960, Linda Mary, da of Peter Butt; 2 s (Barnett Edward, Edward Alan); *Career* res fell Univ of California 1962-64, sr lectr (former lectr) Univ of Durham 1964-75, prof of physics Univ of Bath 1975-; FInstP 1970, CPhys 1980; *Recreations* mountaineering, ornithology; *Style—* Prof George Saunders; School of Physics, University of Bath, Claverton Down, Bath (☎ 0225 826441, telex 449097)

SAUNDERS, Howard William; s of Margaret Ellen Green; *b* 29 June 1939; *Educ* Alleyns Sch Dulwich; *m* 29 Oct 1960, Rita Doris, da of Thomas William Hardaway (d 1979); 2 s (Jeremy Howard b 31 March 1965, Jonathan James Howard b 29 July 1972); *Career* Nat Serv RAPC 1960-62; jt sr ptnr Keith, Bayley, Rogers & Co (formerly Keith Bayley & Rigg) (joined 1955, ptnr 1970); memb The Stock Exchange 1970; *Recreations* skiing, tennis, reading news and encyclopedias; *Style—* Howard Saunders, Esq; White Lodge, One The Chenies, Petts Wood, Kent BR6 OED (☎ 0689 821998); Keith, Bayley, Rogers & Co, Ebbark House, 93-95 Borough High St, London SE1 1NL (☎ 071 378 0657, fax 071 378 1795)

SAUNDERS, Iain Ogilvy Swain; s of Leslie Swain Saunders (d 1988), and Elizabeth, *née* Culme Seymour (d 1963); *b* 7 Nov 1947; *Educ* Radley, Univ of Bristol (BSc); *m* 1976, Roberta Ann, da of David Allen Phoenix; 1 da (Christina Ann Swain b 1983); *Career* Arbuthnot Latham 1968-71; Robert Fleming: joined 1971, Jardine Fleming Hong Kong 1976-78, gen mangr Jardine Fleming Tokyo 1978-84, dir Robert Fleming Holdings 1984-, pres and chief exec offr NY office 1985-89, chm Fleming Investment Management London 1990-; *Recreations* sailing, gardening; *Style—* Iain Saunders, Esq; Robert Fleming Holdings Ltd, 25 Copthall Ave, London EC2R 7DR (☎ 071 628 5858)

SAUNDERS, Jeremy Martin; s of Lt-Col John Grant Saunders (d 1973), of New Barn Farm, Seer Green, Beaconsfield, Bucks, and Helen, *née* McNeill; *b* 7 May 1933; *Educ* Repton; *m* 4 April 1959 (m dis 1968), Alaine Caroline Winnifred, da of Alan Paul Joell; *Career* Nat Serv Lt 16/5 Queen's Royal Lancers 1951-53, Capt Staff Yeo (TA) 1954-62; film and TV prodr 1956-; asst dir and film ed for Br and American Corps, recent work incl exec prodr The Shooting Party; currently md Motion Pictures Guarantors Ltd; memb: Br Acad Film and TV Arts, Br Film and TV Prodrs Assoc; *Recreations* off shore sailing, travel, the media; *Clubs* Garrick; *Style—* Jeremy Saunders, Esq; 4 Embankment Gdns, London SW3 4LJ (☎ 071 352 1683)

SAUNDERS, Joanna Christina; da of Col John Offley Crewe-Read, OBE, of Aston Tirrold, Didcot, Oxon, and Hon Diana Mary, *née* Robins; *b* 13 Dec 1941; *Educ* Rye St Anthony, Oxford; *m* 1, 28 April 1962 (m dis 1969), late Capt John A F Morton, late RHA; m 2, 1 March 1974, Alasdair James Hew Saunders, s of late Capt L S Saunders, RN, DSO, of Rockingham, Market Harborough, Leics; 2 s (Dominic b 1964, Tom b 1977), 2 da (Serena b 1966, Alice b 1975); *Career* interior designer; prev PA to: Lady Antonia Pinter, Kenneth Tynan; worked in theatre, reader to literary agents; design works incl: American banks, city offices, co flats, houses for prominent Greek families, many private houses in London, etc; *Recreations* books, opera, music, art, travel; *Clubs* Hurlingham; *Style—* Mrs Alasdair Saunders; 17 The Little Boltons, London SW10 9LJ; Pastures House, Rockingham, Leics (☎ 071 373 5314)

SAUNDERS, Prof John; s of John Saunders, and Queeni, *née* Thomas; *b* 27 Aug 1946; *Educ* Hatfield Secdy Mod Sch, Doncaster Tech Coll Univ of Loughborough (BTech), Cranfield Inst of Technol (MBA), Univ of Bradford (DPhil); *m* 7 Aug 1981, Veronica Wai Yoke, da of Wong Peng Chow; 1 s (Paul), 1 da (Carolyne); *Career* sales and marketing Hawker Siddeley Aviation; lectr: Univ of Bradford Mgmnt Centre, Univ of Warwick Business Sch; prof of marketing Univ of Loughborough; coordinator of the ESRC Marketing Initiative, memb of Parochial Church Cncl; FCIM, FRSA; *Books* Enterprise (1977), Practical Business Forecasting (1987), The Specification of Aggregate Marketing Phenomina (1987), The Best of Companies (1989); *Recreations* my family, travel, rock, literature, history, science and technology, exercise, DIY and gardening; *Style—* Prof John Saunders; 36 Sunnyhill, Burbage, Leicestershire LE10 2SB (☎ 0509 223111)

SAUNDERS, Sir John Anthony Holt; CBE (1970), DSO (1945), MC (1944); s of E B Saunders, of Kidderminster; *b* 29 July 1917; *Educ* Bromsgrove Sch; *m* 1942, Enid Mary Durant, da of C D Cassidy, of London; 2 da; *Career* former chm International Commercial Bank London, chm Hong Kong and Shanghai Banking Corp and of London Ctee 1964-72; JP 1955-72; Hong Kong MEC 1966-72; kt 1972; *Style—* Sir John Saunders, CBE, DSO, MC; The Dairy House, Maresfield Park, Uckfield, East Sussex

SAUNDERS, Michael Lawrence; CB (1990); s of Dr Samuel Rueben Saunders (d 1981), and Doris, *née* Brand; *b* 13 April 1944; *Educ* Clifton, Univ of Birmingham (LLB), Jesus Coll Cambridge (LLB); *m* 28 June 1970, Anna, da of Dr James Melven Stobo (d 1979); 1 s (Jocelyn b 19 Dec 1974), 1 da (Penelope b 19 March 1971); *Career* called to Bar Grays Inn 1970; legal sec Hague Conf on Private Int Law 1966-72; sr legal asst: Dept of Energy 1973-76, Law Offrs Dept 1976-79; asst legal advsr Cabinet Office Euro Secretariat 1979-83, legal sec Law Offrs of the Crown 1986-89 (asst legal sec 1983-86), the slr H M Customs and Excise 1989-; *Recreations* cricket, squash; *Style—* Michael Saunders, Esq, CB; H M Customs & Excise, New King's Beam House, 22 Upper Ground, London SE1 9PJ (☎ 071 865 5121)

SAUNDERS, Prof Sir Owen Alfred; s of Alfred George Saunders, and Margaret Ellen Jones; *b* 24 Sept 1904; *Educ* Emanuel Sch, Birkbeck Coll London, Trinity Coll Cambridge (MA, DSc); *m* 1, 1935, Marion McKechney (d 1981); 1 s, 2 da; m 2, 1981, Mrs Daphne Holmes; *Career* emeritus prof mechanical engrg Imperial Coll London (acting rector 1966-67, pro-rector 1964-67, head dept 1946-65, prof 1946), vice-chllr London Univ 1967-69; past pres IMechE, pres Br Flame Research Ctee, chm cncl Royal Holloway Coll 1971-; hon memb: Yugoslav Acad 1959-, Japan Soc Mech Engrs 1960-, Mark Twain Soc 1976-; Hon FIMechE, Hon FCGI, Hon DSc Strathclyde; FRS, FEng, FInstP, FInstF, FRAeS, life memb ASME; kt 1965; *Clubs* Athenaeum; *Style—* Prof Sir Owen Saunders, FRS; Oak Bank, 19 Sea Lane, Middleton-on-Sea, West Sussex PO22 7RX (☎ 0243 692966)

SAUNDERS, Sir Peter; s of Ernest Saunders, and Aletta Saunders; *b* 23 Nov 1911; *Educ* Oundle, Lausanne; *m* 1, 1959, Ann Stewart (d 1976); m 2, 1979, Catherine Imperiali di Francavilla (Katie Boyle, *qv*); *Career* impresario, prodns incl Agatha Christie's The Mousetrap; chm and md: Peter Saunders Ltd, Peter Saunders Group Ltd, Volcano Prodns; dir: Theatre Investment Fund Ltd, Theatre Investmt Fin Ltd, West End Theatre Mangrs Ltd, Duke of York's Theatre Ltd; former film dir and journalist; former dir Yorkshire TV; vice pres Actors' Benevolent Fund, memb Exec Cncl Soc of West End Theatre (pres 1961-62 and 1967-69); kt 1981; *Style—* Sir Peter Saunders; Vaudeville Theatre Offices, 10 Maiden Lane, London WC2E 7NA (☎ 071 240 3177)

SAUNDERS, Prof Peter Robert; s of Albert Edward Saunders, of Orpington, Kent, and Joan Kathleen, *née* Swan; *b* 30 Aug 1950; *Educ* Selhurst GS Croydon, Univ of Kent (BA), Univ of London (PhD); *m* 15 April 1971 (m dis 1990), Susan Elisabeth, da of Dr Frank Ellis, of Redhill, Surrey; 1 s (Michael b 1971), 1 da (Claire Louise b 1973); *Career* res offr Univ of Essex 1973-76, prof of sociology Univ of Sussex 1988- (lectr 1976-84, reader 1984-88); FRSA 1987; *Books* Urban Politics: A Sociological Interpretation (1979), Social Theory and the Urban Question (1981 and 1986), An Introduction to British Politics (1984), Social Class and Stratification (1989), A Nation of Home Owners (1990); *Style—* Prof Peter Saunders; School of Social Sciences, Univ of Sussex, Falmer, Brighton BN1 9QN (☎ 0273 606755, fax 0273 678335)

SAUNDERS, Richard; s of Edward Ernest Saunders (d 1971), of Henley-on-Thames, and Betty, *née* Belsey; *b* 4 July 1937; *Educ* St Edmund's Sch Hindhead, Uppingham; *m* 1, 21 Sept 1961, Suzannah, da of Thomas Rhodes-Cooke (d 1985), of Chiswick; 1 s (Andrew b 1964); m 2, 12 June 1970, Alison, da of Maj J A Fiddes (d 1964), of Wimbledon; *Career* 2 Lt LG 1958-60, served in Germany; govr Royal Star and Garter Home 1984-; chartered surveyor; chm Baker Harris Saunders Gp plc 1986-; dir: Baker Harris Saunders Ltd, Br Property Fedn 1974-90, St Edmunds Sch Tst Ltd, Star and Garter Trading and Promotions Ltd; chm: City Branch RICS 1979-80, Metropolitan Public Gdns Assoc 1984-91; dep for Ward of Candlewick 1983-; Sheriff City of London 1987-88; bd Gen Practice Finance Corp 1985-89, govr and almoner Christ's Hosp 1980-, govr Bridewell Royal Hosp and King Edward's Sch Witley 1976-; memb: Cncl Br Property Fedn 1974-90 (hon treas 1974-85), Ct of Common Cncl Corp of London 1975-; pres Associated Owners of City Properties 1984-86; Liveryman Worshipful Co of: Clothworkers' 1960 (Warden 1989), Chartered Surveyors 1979; FRICS; *Recreations* golf, tennis (lawn and real), music; *Clubs* Cavalry and Guards, MCC, City Livery; *Style—* Richard Saunders, Esq; 13 Caroline Place, London W2 4AW (☎ 071 727 1630); The Old Rectory, Bagendon, Cirencester (028 583 352); Saddlers House, Gutter Lane London EC2 (☎ 071 796 4000, fax 071 726 4122, telex 8953966)

SAUNDERS, Sandy - David Michael; RD; s of Aubrey Saunders, of High Mount, London, and Rosie Leonie Finestone; *b* 23 June 1935; *Educ* Highgate Sch, Stafford Coll of Technology; *m* 1958, Rosemary Ann, da of Trevor Smith, of Surrey Rd, Bournemouth; 4 da; *Career* Lt Cdr RNR; chm: Howmac plc, Sunleigh plc; dep chm Evered plc; *Recreations* squash, sailing, bridge; *Clubs* RNVR; *Style—* Sandy Saunders, Esq, RD; 11 Dorset Square, London NW1 6QB

SAUNDERS, Prof Trevor John; s of William John Saunders (d 1976), of Melksham, Wilts, and Phyllis Margaret, *née* Escott (d 1990); *b* 12 July 1934; *Educ* Chippenham GS, UCL (BA), Emmanuel Coll Cambridge (PhD); *m* 5 Sept 1959, Teresa Mary Louisa, da of Albert John Schmitz, of Felixstowe, Suffolk; 2 da (Clare b 14 April 1963, Angela b 7 June 1965); *Career* lectr 1959-72: Bedford Coll London, Univ of Hull, Univ of Newcastle upon Tyne; Univ of Newcastle upon Tyne: sr lectr in classics 1972-78, reader in greek philosophy 1978, prof of greek 1978-, memb Senate 1977-80, 1982-85 and 1988-, Dean of Faculty Arts 1982-85, memb Cncl 1984-87 and 1989-; memb cncl Univ of Durham 1987-; visiting memb Inst Advanced Study Princeton NJ USA 1971-72 and 1986, res fell humanities res centre ANU Canberra 1986; memb Cncl: Soc Promotion of Hellenic Studies 1968-71 and 1984-87, Classical Assoc 1974-79 (pres Northumberland and Durham branch 1974-76); chm Cncl Univ Classics Dept 1981-84; *Books* 3 Penguin Classics: Plato, The Laws (1970), Aristotle, The Politics (revised, 1981), Plato, Early Socratic Dialogues (contrib ed, 1987); Notes on the Laws of Plato (1972), Bibliography on the Laws of Plato (1976), Platos Penal Code (1991); *Recreations* railway history, cinema; *Style—* Prof Trevor Saunders; 27 Moorside South, Newcastle upon Tyne, NE4 9BD (☎ 091 273 7586); Dept of Classics, The Univ, Newcastle upon Tyne, NE1 7RU (☎ 091 222 6000 ext 7977, fax 091 261 1182, telex 53654)

SAUNDERS, Prof Wilfred Leonard; CBE (1982); s of Leonard Saunders (d 1962), of

Birmingham, and Annie, *née* Vine (d 1973); *b* 18 April 1920; *Educ* King Edward's GS Camp Hill Birmingham, Fitzwilliam House Cambridge (BA, MA); *m* 15 June 1946, Joan Mary, da of Maj W E Rider, TD (d 1949), of Birmingham; 2 s (John b 11 Jan 1948, Peter b 24 Nov 1952); *Career* enlisted Signalman 48 Div Signals TA; served BEF France and Belgium 1940 (evacuated Dunkirk), cmmnd RCS 1942, 1 Army N Africa 1942-43, CMF Italy 1943-46, Capt and Adj 1945, Staff Capt Q at GHQ Caserta 1945-46; dep librarian Inst of Bankers 1948-49, founding librarian Univ of Birmingham Inst of Educn 1949-56, dep librarian Univ of Sheffield 1956-63, seconded UNESCO Uganda 1962, founding dir Postgrad Sch of Librarianship (now Dept of Info Studies) Univ of Sheffield 1963, prof of librarianship and info sci Univ of Sheffield 1968-82 (dean Faculty of Educn Studies 1974-77, emeritus prof 1982-); pres Library Assoc 1980, library and info advsy work and consultancy UNESCO, Br Cncl and others 1981-, chm Library and Info Servs Cncl 1981-84, visiting prof Univ of California Los Angeles 1985; chm Br Cncl's Libraries Advsy Panel 1975-81 (memb 1970-87), memb Lord Chllr's Advsy Cncl on Public Records; author of numerous pubns on librarianship and info work; Hon LittD Univ of Sheffield 1989; FLA 1952, Hon FIInfSci 1977, Hon FCP 1983; *Recreations* gardening, listening to music, book collecting, walking, dancing; *Clubs* Royal Cwlth Soc; *Style—* Prof Wilfred Saunders, CBE; 15 Princess Drive, Sawston, Cambridge CB2 4DL

SAUNDERS WATSON, Cdr (Leslie) Michael Macdonald; DL (Northants 1979); s of Capt Leslie Swain Saunders, DSO, JP, RN, and Elizabeth, da of Vice Adm Sir Michael Culme-Seymour, 4 Bt, KCB, MVO; *b* 9 Oct 1934; *Educ* Eton, RNC Dartmouth; *m* 1958, Georgina Elizabeth Laetitia, da of Adm Sir William Davis, GCB, DSO, *qv*; 2 s, 1 da; *Career* served RN 1951-71 (Cdr 1969); High Sheriff Northants 1978-79; vice chm Northants Small Industs Ctee 1974-79; chm: Northants Assoc Youth Clubs 1977-, Heritage Educn Year 1977, Corby Community Advsy Gp 1979-86, Ironstone Royalty Owners Assoc 1979 Northants Tourism Advsy Panel 1986-91; memb: taxation and legal ctees CLA 1975-89, exec ctees CLA 1975-80 and 1987-, British Heritage Ctee 1978-88, chm Northants Branch CLA 1981-84 (memb 1974-); dir: Lamport Hall Preservation Tst 1978-91, English Sinfonia 1980-, Northants Enterprise Agency 1986-91; chm Govrs Lodge Park Comprehensive 1977-83, tstee Oakham Sch 1975-77 (dep pres 1978-82, chm tax and parly ctee 1975-82), pres Historic Houses Assoc 1982-88; tstee: Royal Botanic Gardens Kew 1983-, Nat Heritage Meml Fund 1987-; chm: Nat Curriculum History Working Gp 1989-90, Heritage Educn Tst 1989-, Bd Br Library Bd 1990-; *Recreations* sailing, music, gardening; *Clubs* Brooks's; *Style—* Cdr L M M Saunders Watson, DL, RN; Rockingham Castle, Market Harborough, Leics LE16 8TH (☎ 0536 770326, office 770240)

SAUNDERSON, (Edward) John Hardress; DSO (1944), DFC (1944); s of Capt John Vernon Saunderson, RFA (d 1960), and Hon Eva Norah, *née* Mulholland (d 1972), da of 2 Baron Dunleath; *b* 10 April 1918; *Educ* Eton; *m* 1, 30 June 1954, Diana Elizabeth, da of Maj Thomas Sydney d'Arcy Hankey (d 1977); 3 s (David John b 1956, Richard Michael b 1957, Thomas Alexander b 1961), 1 da (Joan Angela b 1958); m 2, 25 July 1980, Elisabeth Adelheid Rita Ingeborg Clara, da of Baron Philip von Behr, Cdr German Navy (d 1986), of Göttingen, Germany; *Career* RAF GD Branch 1938-45, Bomber Cmd 1940-44 (despatches twice), CO ME Flight Harwell 1943, tactics SO 91 Gp 1944, Empire Test Pilots Sch 1945, Sqdn Ldr, Test Pilot Percival Aircraft 1946-47; formed engrg co 1948; chm and md: Farrow Engineering Ltd 1956, Crotall Engineering Ltd 1959, Saunderson & Costin (cemented carbides) Ltd 1965-; MRAeS; *Recreations* gliding, music, gardening; *Style—* John Saunderson, Esq, DSO, DFC; Honeybottom, Newbury, Berks RG16 8AL (☎ 0635 43754)

SAUZIER, Sir (André) Guy; CBE (1959), ED; s of J Adrian Sauzier, of Mauritius; *b* 20 Oct 1910; *Educ* Royal Coll Mauritius; *m* 1936, Thérèse, da of Henri Mallac; 6 s, 2 da; *Career* served WW II Maj Mauritius TF; MLC Mauritius 1949-57, Mauritius rep at Coronation 1953, memb Mauritius political delgn to UK 1955, min Works and Communications 1957-59, gen overseas rep Mauritius Chamber of Agric 1959-79, min plen to EEC 1972-79; FRSA; kt 1973; *Clubs* Athenaeum, Cercle Royal Gaulois (Brussels); *Style—* Sir Guy Sauzier, CBE, ED; 15 Marloes Rd, London W8 6LQ

SAVAGE, David Jack; s of Arthur Jack Savage (d 1953), of Farnborough, and Sylvia Maude, *née* Bacon (descendant of Sir Nicholas Bacon Lord Keeper of the Great Seal to Queen Elizabeth I); *b* 7 Aug 1939; *Educ* Hurstpierpoint Coll, Univ of London (LLB), Coll of Law; *m* 16 May 1981, Elizabeth Mary, da of late Dr Edmond Louis Ives; 2 s (Nicholas David St John b 1982, Louis Arthur Ives b 1983); *Career* admitted slr 1963-; ptnr Foster, Savage & Gordon of Farnborough (sr ptnr 1984-), Notary Public 1988, numerous contribs to legal pubns; pres Hampshire Inc Law Soc 1983-84, dir Slrs Benevolent Assoc 1984-; cmmr of income tax 1969-, memb N Hants Local Valuation Tribunal 1976- (vice chm 1984-); chm of Govrs Farnborough GS 1970-72, dir Aldershot FC 1971; cncllr: Farnborough UDC 1964-73 (vice chm 1972-73), Rushmoor Borough Cncl 1973-80; Parly candidate (Cons): Birmingham Sparkbrook 1974, Birmingham Smallheath 1979; govr Swinton Cons Coll 1971-74, chm Aldershot Divnl Cons Assoc 1969-73 (vice pres 1973-); memb: No 3 Southern Area Legal Aid Ctee 1989-, Cncl Law Soc 1990- (memb Criminal Law Ctee 1988-); Liveryman: Worshipful Co of Arbitrators 1989, Worshipful Co of Scriveners 1990, Worshipful Co of Woolmen 1991, Freeman City of London 1989; Assoc Inst of Arbitrators 1988; *Recreations* travel (preferably by train), browsing, bricklaying; *Clubs* Royal Aldershot Offrs, Law Soc; *Style—* David Savage, Esq; Ridgeway, 16 Clockhouse Rd, Farnborough, Hants; Phillack, Hayle, Cornwall; 269 Farnborough Rd, Farnborough, Hants (☎ 0252 54140, fax 0252 373428, telex 858770 FOSTER G)

SAVAGE, Donald William John; s of George William Savage (d 1980), of the Firs, Mattishall, Norfolk, and Kate Ethel, *née* Logsdaile (d 1978); *b* 20 Aug 1922; *Educ* Grove Sch London, Regent St Poly, Battersea Poly (BSc); *m* 15 June 1962, Dorothy Clarissa, da of Stanley J Titterton (d 1977) of Gymea, NSW, Aust; 1 s (Adrian b 1963), 1 da (Lisa b 1965); *Career* WWII RAFVR 1941-46, cmmnd 1943 Capt flying boats 1943-46; coastal cmd: 204 Sqdn W Africa, 209 Sqdn E Africa, SEAC Ceylon, Hong Kong, Seletar, Singapore; demob Flt Lt 1946; pupil civil engr 1938-41, asst engr and agent for contractors Concrete Piling Ltd (London and Belfast) 1946-50; Gammon Pakistan Ltd (Karachi) 1950-58: civil engr, agent, divnl engr, chief engr, dir; res dir Gammon Pakistan Ltd Bahrain, md Gammon Gulf Ltd Bahrain 1958-62; Tilbury Contracting Group 1962-79: gp asst md, gp md, gp dep chm; non-exec dir various cos; hon sec and memb ctee Radlett Soc; memb: Green Belt Assoc, Probus Club of Radlett; Freeman Worshipful Co of Paviors 1967; FICE; *Recreations* travel, game shooting, walking, gardening; *Style—* Donald Savage, Esq

SAVAGE, Sir Ernest Walter; s of late Walter Edwin Savage; *b* 24 Aug 1912; *Educ* Brisbane GS, Scots Coll Warwick Queensland; *m* 1938, Dorothy Winifred, da of A W Nicholls; 1 s, 1 da; *Career* CA in public practice 1940-76, hon consul for Norway in Brisbane 1950-76; memb: bd of govrs Cromwell Univ 1950-77, Queensland State Cncl of CA 1951-76 (chm 1958-60 and 1966); chm Bank of Queensland 1960; Knight (1 class) of Order of St Olaf; FCA; kt 1979; *Style—* Sir Ernest Savage; 12 Mount Ommaney Drive, Jindalee, Brisbane, Qld 4074, Australia

SAVAGE, Paul Stephen Gladstone; s of Edward Stephen Savage (d 1980), of Southwick, Sussex, and Gladys Vera, *née* Turrell (d 1934); *b* 21 Jan 1934; *Educ* Steyning GS Sussex; *m* 16 March 1957, Patricia Polly, da of Alan Spencer Gill (d 1966), of Brighton; 1 da (Susan Carol (Mrs Pearson) b 1960); *Career* sr ptnr Hilton Sharp & Clarke; FCA 1957; *Recreations* wine, theatre, walking; *Style—* Paul Savage, Esq; 3 Lesser Foxholes, Shoreham-by-Sea, W Sussex BN43 5NT (☎ 0273 464246); 30 New Road, Brighton, E Sussex BN1 1BN (☎ 0273 24163, fax 0273 23983)

SAVAGE, Peter Edmund Annesley; s of Gordon Annesley (d 1988), and Margaret Emma, *née* Hyson; *b* 25 Nov 1935; *Educ* Welwyn Garden City GS, St Mary's Hosp Med Sch; *m* 1, 2 Sept 1961 (m dis 1973), Margaret Ann, da of late John Sweetman; 1 s (Michael b 1964), 1 da (Elizabeth b 1965); m 2, 12 Jan 1974, Anne Lowden (d 1989), da of late James Robertson; 2 s (James b 1975, Robert 1976); *Career* conslt surgn Queen Mary's Hosp Sidcup 1974; *Recreations* hill walking; *Style—* Peter Savage, Esq; 52 Grosvenor Rd, Petts Wood, Orpington, Kent BR5 1QU (☎ 0689 25053)

SAVAGE, Prof Robert Joseph Gay; s of Joseph Patrick Savage, MBE (d 1970), of Belfast, and Kate Edith Olive, *née* Beale (d 1971); *b* 2 July 1927; *Educ* Methodist Coll Belfast, Wesley Coll Dublin, Queen's Univ Belfast (BSc), Univ of London (PhD); *m* 4 Jan 1969, Shirley Cameron Coryndon, da of (Charles) Paul Wilson, CVO (d 1970), of Much Hadham; 2 step da (Anna b 1952, Virginia b 1955); *Career* asst lectr Queen's Univ Belfast 1952-54, prof Univ of Bristol 1981- (lectr 1954-66, reader 1966-81); chm: Bristol Centre Nat Tst, Avon Gardens Tst; memb Cncl Nat Tst; FLS, FGS, FZS; *Books* Teritary Faunas (1975), Geological Excursions in the Bristol District (1977), Mammal Evolution (1986); *Recreations* country walking, garden history; *Clubs* Geological, Linnean; *Style—* Prof Robert Savage; Dept of Geology, Univ of Bristol, Bristol BS8 1RJ (☎ 0272 303773, fax 0272 253385, telex 445938)

SAVAGE, Wendy Diane; da of William George Edwards (d 1984), and Anne, *née* Smith (d 1943); *b* 12 April 1935; *Educ* Croydon HS, Girton Coll Cambridge (BA), London Hosp Med Coll (MB BCh); *m* 27 July 1960 (m dis 1973), Miguel Babatunde Richard Savage (Mike), s of Richard Gabriel Akiwande Savage, of 35 Moray Place, Edinburgh; 2 s (Nicholas Richard b 10 June 1964, Jonathan Chukuma b 18 April 1969), 2 da (Yewande Patricia b 9 April 1961, Wendy Claire b 28 May 1962); *Career* res fell Harvard Univ 1962-64, md Awo-omama and Enugu Nigeria 1964 -67; registrar: Kenyatta Hosp Nairobi 1967-69, Royal Free Hosp London 1969-71, various posts Tower Hamlets, Islington Borough and Pregnancy Advsy Serv 1971-73, specialist in obstetrics Cook Hosp NZ 1973-76, lectr London Hosp 1976-77, sr lectr in obstetrics and gynaecology London Hosp Med Coll and hon conslt London Hosp 1977-; PR Doctors For Women's Choice on Abortion; tstee: Pregnancy Advsy Serv Simon Population Tst, Birth Control Campaign; advsr Maternity Alliance; fndr memb: Women in Medicine, Women in Gynaecology and Obstetrics; chair Forum on Maternity and the Newborn RSM 1987-89, elected GMC 1989; MRCOG 1971 FRCOG 1985; *Books* Hysterectomy (1982), Coping with Caesarian Section and Other Difficult Births (with Fran Reader 1983), A Savage Enquiry (1986); *Recreations* reading novels, playing piano duets, travel; *Style—* Mrs Wendy Savage; 19 Vincent Terrace, London N1 8HN (☎ 071 837 7635); Royal London Hospital, Whitechapel, London E1 1BB (☎ 071 377 7240)

SAVERNAKE, Viscount; Thomas James Brudenell-Bruce; only s, and h of Earl of Cardigan; gs of 8 Marquess of Ailesbury; *b* 11 Feb 1982; *Style—* Viscount Savernake

SAVIDGE, Dr Geoffrey Francis; *b* 16 Dec 1940; *Educ* Univ of Cambridge (MB BChir, MA), Karolinska Inst Stockholm Sweden (MD); *m* Paula Margaretha; 2 s (Tor b 1964, Kevin b 1975), 1 da (Kim b 1966); *Career* lectr: Dept of Neurology Karolinska Hosp Stockholm 1969-71, Dept of Pathology and Clinical Chemistry St Gorans Hosp Stockholm 1974-77 (Dept of Med 1971-74); res assoc Inst Coagulation Res Karolinska Inst Stockholm 1976-79, physician Dept of Coagulation Disorders Karolinska Hosp Stockholm 1977-79; St Thomas' Hosp London: dir Haemophilia Reference Centre 1979-, sr lectr and hon conslt 1979, dir coagulation res Rayne Inst 1988-; memb: Br Soc of Thrombosis and Haemostasis 1983, American Soc of Haematology 1988, Am Heart Assoc 1989; memb: NY Acad of Sci 1986; *Books* Factor VIII-von Willebrand Factor (2 vols, 1989); *Recreations* music, reading, sport; *Clubs* United Oxford & Cambridge Univs; *Style—* Dr Geoffrey Savidge; Haemophilia Centre, St Thomas' Hospital, Lambeth Palace Rd, London SE1 7EH (☎ 071 620 0378, fax 071 401 3125)

SAVILE, Hon Charles Anthony; yr s of 7 Earl of Mexborough (d 1980); *b* 28 June 1934; *Educ* Eton; *m* 5 Nov 1966, Zita Loretta, da of Leslie White; 2 s (Henry b 1970, Andrew b 1973); *Career* Lt Grenadier Guards; *Style—* The Hon Charles Savile; Youngsbury, Ware, Herts

SAVILE, 3 Baron (UK 1888); George Halifax Lumley-Savile; JP (Borough of Dewsbury 1955), DL (W Yorks 1954); patron of two livings; s of 2 Baron (d 1931), of Rufford Abbey, Ollerton, Notts, and Esmé Grace Virginia (d 1958), da of John Wolton; *b* 24 Jan 1919; *Educ* Eton; *Heir* bro, Hon Henry Lumley-Savile; *Career* formerly Capt Duke of Wellington's Regt, attached 1 Bn Lincs Regt, Burma 1943-44; chm St John Cncl S and W Yorks 1980, landowner (18,000 acres); CStJ 1983; *Recreations* shooting, listening to classical music; *Clubs* Brooks's, Huddersfield, Sloane; *Style—* The Rt Hon the Lord Savile, JP, DL; Gryce Hall, Shelley, Huddersfield, W Yorks (☎ 0484 602774); Savile Estate Office, Thornhill, Dewsbury, W Yorks (☎ 0924 462341)

SAVILE, Sir James Wilson Vincent (Jimmy); OBE (1971); s of Vincent Savile, and Agnes, *née* Kelly; *b* 31 Oct 1926; *Educ* St Annes Elementary Sch Leeds; *Career* 'Bevin Boy' Coal Mines 1942-48; TV and radio personality; presenter: Radio 1 Show, Jim'll Fix it, Mind How You Go, Top of The Pops; voluntary helper: Leeds Infirmary, Stoke Mendeville Hosp, Broadmoor Hosp; major fundraiser for various national charities; Hon LLD Univ of Leeds 1986; memb MENSA; KCSG (Holy See) 1982; kt 1990; *Books* As It Happens/Love is an Uphill Thing (autobiog 1975), God'll Fix It (1979); *Recreations* running, cycling, wrestling; *Clubs* Athenaeum; *Style—* Sir Jimmy Savile, OBE; National Spinal Injuries Centre, Stoke Mandeville Hospital, Aylesbury, Bucks

SAVILL, Timothy Lydall; s of Edwin Lydall Savill (d 1940), (gs of Alfred Savill, fndr Alfred Savill & Sons, Chartered Surveyors, in 1859) and Margaret H K Thorne (d 1976); uncle Sir Eric Savill, KCVO, MBE, MC, FRICS, fndr the Savill Gardens in Windsor Great Park when dep ranger, also chm Royal Forests, and Keeper of Gardens at Windsor; *b* 25 March 1940; *Educ* Haileybury and Imperial Services Coll Windsor, Radley, Coll of Estate Mgmnt Univ of London; *m* 1, 14 June 1963 (m dis 1973), Sonia Mary Barradale; 1 s (Nicholas b 1966), 1 da (Caroline b 1968); m 2, 1 June 1982 (m dis 1986), Ann Rosemary Stone; *Career* chartered surveyor; fndr dir Timothy Savill & Co; Freeman: City of London, Worshipful Co of Skinners; FRICS, IRRV; *Recreations* fly-fishing, shooting, gardening, swimming; *Clubs* RAC, Pall Mall London; *Style—* Timothy L Savill, Esq; Pikes Farm House, Forest Road, Bill Hill, Wokingham, Berkshire RG11 5QR (☎ 0734 783280); PO Box 7, Forest Rd, Bill Hill, Wokingham, Berkshire RG11 5NZ (☎ 0734 783280, fax 0734 794357)

SAVILLE, Clive Howard; *b* 7 July 1943; *Educ* Bishop Gore GS Swansea, Univ Coll Swansea (BA); *m* 1967, (Camille) Kathleen, da of Edmund St C Burke (d 1979); *Career* under sec for Teacher Training and Supply and Int Rels DES 1987- (joined 1965); *Style—* Clive Saville, Esq; Dept of Education and Science, Elizabeth House, York Rd, London SE1 7PH (☎ 071 934 9000)

SAVILLE, John David; JP; s of Bertie Edward Saville, of Barrie, and Catherine, *née* Taysum (d 1965); *b* 5 Jan 1932; *Educ* Aston Commercial Coll; *m* 1; 1 s (David John b

4 April 1964), 2 da (Sharon Ann (Mrs Wilson-Gunn) b 15 Jan 1958, Amanda Theresa (Mrs Cazalet) b 17 Feb 1960); m 2, 20 Dec 1989, Josephine Margaaret, da of John Whelan; *Career* Nat Serv Royal Warwicks 1950-52; chm and md J Saville Gordon Gp plc 1955-; dir: Industrial Metal Services Ltd, Wolverhampton Racecourse plc 1983-, Dunstall Park Securities Ltd, Leigh Interests plc 1989-; memb Ctee Solihull Inst for Med Trg and Res; scout co pres Birmingham; chm The Stonehouse Gang; dir: Birmingham Gang Show Ltd, Silhill Tst Ltd; *Recreations* horse riding, skiing, tennis, swimming, walking, light aircraft; *Clubs* Midlands Sporting; *Style*— John Saville, Esq, JP; Barrells Park, Ullenhall, Nr Henley in Arden, Warwicks B95 5NQ; J Saville Gordon Group plc, Savill Gordon House, 4 Wharfdale Rd, Tyselsey, Birmingham B11 2SB (☎ 021 707 3530, fax 021 707 5903, telex 339184)

SAVILLE, Hon Mrs (Yvonne Catherine); yr da of Baron Schon (Life Peer); *b* 12 June 1944; *Educ* Badminton Sch Bristol, St Godric's Secretarial Coll, Montessori Coll London Dyslexia Institute; *m* 1979, Norman Saville, s of Mark Saville, of Hampstead; 1 s (Daniel), 2 step s; *Career* Montessori teacher 1970-72, dyslexia teacher 1987-; *Recreations* theatre, tennis, music, cooking; *Style*— The Hon Mrs Saville; 21 Hillview Road, Mill Hill Village, London NW7

SAVIN, Dr John Andrew; s of Lewis Herbert Savin (d 1983), and Mary Helen, *née* Griffith (d 1983); *b* 10 Jan 1935; *Educ* Epsom Coll, Trinity Hall Cambridge (MD), St Thomas' Hosp London (DIH); *m* 31 Oct 1959, Patricia Margaret, da of Cdr Hugh Patrick De Crecy Steel, of St Ann's, York Rd, Berwick, Lothian; 2 s (William b 1963, Charles b 1968), 2 da (Penelope b 1960, Rosemary b 1964); *Career* RN Surgn Lt 1960-64; registrar Skin Dept St George's Hosp London 1966-68, sr registrar St Johns Hosp for Diseases of the Skin 1968-70, conslt dermatologist Royal Infirmary Edinburgh 1971-, sr lectr Dept of Dermatology Univ of Edinburgh 1971-; former sec Scottish Dermatological Soc, pres Dermatology Section RSM, memb Med Appeal Tbnl 1975; memb RSM, FRCP; *Books* Recent Advances in Dermatology (1980), Common Diseases of the Skin (1983), Common Skin Problems (1988), Clinical Dermatology (1989); *Recreations* golf, reading, painting; *Clubs* Hon Co of Edinburgh Golfers; *Style*— Dr John Savin; 86 Murrayfield Gardens, Edinburgh EH12 6DQ (☎ 031 337 7768); Dermatology Dept, The Royal Infirmary, Edinburgh (☎ 031 229 2477)

SAVLA, Dr Navin Chandra; s of Bhimsee Dungersee, and Valbai Saula (d 1947); *b* 25 Dec 1943; *Educ* Osmania Univ Hyderabad India (MB BS) Univ of London (DPM); *m* 8 May 1966, Dr Devyani Savla, da of Dr BK Naik; 2 s (Sandeep b 20 July 1970, Siddharth b 26 Nov 1976); *Career* sr registrar in psychiatry Oxford RHA 1972; conslt psychiatrist: St John's Hosp Lincoln 1972-74, India 1974-76; conslt psychiatrist and clinical tutor: Cherry Knowle Hosp Sunderland 1976-82, Claybury Hosp Essex 1982-; clinical tutor Br Postgrad Med Fedn 1986, hon sr lectr UCL Med Sch; chm Waltham Forest & Redbridge Div Overseas Doctors Assoc, memb World Psychiatrist Assoc; FRCPsych (MRCPsych 1972); *Books* pubns and papers incl Homicide Behaviour in the Elderly, Depression & Physical Disability in Waltham Forest, Depression & Schizophrenia; *Style*— Dr Navin Savla; 80 Overton Drive, Wanstead, London E11 (☎ 081 989 0859); Claybury Hospital, Woodford Bridge, Woodford Green, Essex 1G8 8BY (☎ 081 505 7171/3360, fax 505 6756)

SAVORY, James Howard; s of Peter Savory, and Rosemary, *née* Blake; *b* 5 May 1953; *Educ* Winchester, Queens' Coll Cambridge (MA); *m* 15 July 1978, Diana Mary, da of Richard Wackerbarth; 2 s (Tom b 1984, Oliver b 1988), 1 da (Rebecca b 1982); *Career* admitted slr 1978; ptnr Slaughter and May 1985-; ATII 1979; *Style*— James Savory, Esq; 35 Basinghall St, London EC2V 5DB (☎ 071 600 1200, fax 071 726 0039, 071 600 0289, telex 883486/888926)

SAVOURS; *see*: Campbell-Savours

SAWARD, Michael John; s of Donald Saward, and Lily, *née* Kendall; *b* 14 May 1932; *Educ* Eltham Coll London, Univ of Bristol (BA), Tyndale Hall Bristol; *m* 3 April 1956, Jackie, da of Col John Atkinson, DSO, OBE, TD; 1 s (Jonathan b 1961), 3 da (Rachel b 1960, Jill b 1965, Susan (twin) b 1965); *Career* asst curate: Christ Church Croydon 1956-59, Edgware Parish Church 1959-64; warden Holy Trinity Inter-Church Centre Liverpool 1964-67, sec Liverpool Cncl of Churches 1964-67, C of E radio and TV offr 1967-72, hon curate St John Beckenham 1969-72; vicar: St Matthew Fulham 1972-78, Ealing 1978-91; priest i/c St Paul Northfields Ealing 1986-89, preb Caddington Major in St Paul's Cathedral 1985-91, canon treas St Paul's Cathedral 1991; London Diocesan Synod 1973-: memb Bishop's Cncl 1989-, memb Vacancy-in-See Ctee 1975-, memb Pastoral Ctee 1989, memb fin Ctee 1989-; memb: Gen Synod 1975-, C of E Evangelical Cncl 1976-, Ealing East Deanery Synod 1978-91, Bowman Charitable Tst 1978-91, Willesden Area Synod 1980-91, Anglican Evangelical Assembly 1983-; tstee Church Urban Fund (memb Grants Ctee) 1989-90, Church Cmmr for Eng 1978- (memb Bd of Govrs 1986-, memb Pastoral Ctee 1988-), dir Jubilate Hymns Ltd 1980-, chm Bowman Ecclesiastical Tstees 1978-91, hon chaplain Royal British Legion Ealing 1979-90; *Recreations* hymn-writing, reading (esp military history), music, cricket, travel, food and drink; *Clubs* Athenaeum; *Style*— Canon Michael Saward; The Chapter House, St Paul's Churchyard, London EC4M 8AD

SAWBRIDGE, Edward Henry Ewen; s of Henry Raywood Sawbridge, CBE (d 1990), of The Moorings, Kingsgate, Kent, and Lilian, *née* Wood (d 1991); *b* 14 Aug 1953; *Educ* Radley, Balliol Coll Oxford (MA); *m* 23 July 1983, Angela Rose Louisa, da of Maj Anthony James MacDonald Watt, of Longwood, Sunning Hill, Berks; 2 s (Jack William Hugo b 1986, Hugh Anthony b 1988); *Career* Peat Marwick Mitchell & Co 1976-83, ACLI Metals (London) Ltd 1983- 85, fin dir Shearson Lehman Hutton Commodities Ltd 1985; *Recreations* bridge, fishing, cooking; *Clubs* United Oxford & Cambridge; *Style*— Edward Sawbridge, Esq; 1 Broadgate, London EC2 M7HA (☎ 071 260 2177, fax 071 260 2516, telex 917273 SLMETLG)

SAWCZUK, Basil; s of Petro Sawczuk, of Brockworth, Glos, and Maria, *née* Perik; *b* 22 May 1954; *Educ* Chosen Hill GS Churchdown, Leicester Poly (Dip Arch), Open Univ, CEM Univ of Reading; *m* 19 May 1979, Sonia Elizabeth, da Stefan Szewczuk (d 1987), of Leicester; 1 s (Luke Sebastian b 24 Oct 1988); *Career* project architect Harper Fairley ptnrs Birmingham 1979-80, assoc Malcolm Payne and Assoc Birmingham 1980-83, exec DGI Int plc 1991- (joined 1983, dir 1986-91); responsible for computer centre GDS Swindon and HQ SWEB Bristol, memb Main Ctee Birmingham AA 1980-83 (ed BAA gazette 1982-83); memb: Ctee Housing Centre Tst 1980, Birmingham and Sutton Coldfield Crime Prevention Panel 1981-82, Ctee of Midland Study Centre 1984, RIBA party action lobby; chm Midland Jr Liaison Organisation 1984, memb Br Acad of Experts 1990; Freeman: City of London 1983, Workshipful Co of Arbitrators 1983; memb: RIBA 1979, IOD 1988; FCIArb 1989, Br Acad of Experts 1990; *Recreations* photography, gardening, ornithology; *Clubs* City Livery; *Style*— Basil Sawczuk, Esq; Woodlands Cottage, North Littleton, Worcester WR11 5QP (☎ 0386 830782); DGI International plc, Talisman House, Talisman Sq, Kenilworth CV8 1JB (☎ 0926 57474, fax 0929 50857, telex 311133 DGIKEN)

SAWDY, Peter Bryan; s of Alfred Eustace Leon Sawdy (d 1972), Beatrice Sawdy (d 1984); *b* 17 Sept 1931; *Educ* Ampleforth, Regent St Poly, LSE; *m* 1, 1955 (m dis 1985), Anne, *née* Stonor; 2 da (Caroline Ann b 1957, Susan Angela b 1962); m 2, 1985, Judith Mary, da of Thomas Bowen (d 1989); *Career* Brooke Bond Group 1952-85 (trainee, commodity trader), chm Brook Bond Ceylon Ltd 1963-65; Brooke Bond plc: dir Bd 1965, jt md 1975, gp chief exec 1977, gp dep chm and chief exec 1981, currently chm Peter Sawdy Assocs; dir: Costain Group PLC 1978 (chm 1990), Griffin International 1984, Hogg Group PLC 1985 (dep chm 1989), Laing Properties 1989-90, Yule Catto PLC 1991; chm Taylor Chess Ltd 1989-91; capt Ceylon Nat Rugby team 1960-64; *Recreations* golf, music, collecting modern first editions; *Clubs* Naval and Military, Royal Ashdown Golf, Royal Mid Surrey Golf; *Style*— Peter Sawdy, Esq; Peter Sawdy Assoc, 13 Clarendon St, London SW3 VEW (☎ 071 834 2303, fax 071 630 0467)

SAWKO, Prof Felicjan; s of Czeslaw Sawko (d 1985), and Franciszka, *née* Nawrot; *b* 17 May 1937; *Educ* Lilford Hall, Univ of Leeds (BSc, MSc); *m* 18 April 1960, Genowefa Stefania, da of Wladyslaw Bak (d 1973); 4 s (Andrew Martin b 1961, Peter Ian b 1963, Richard Felicjan b 1965, Paul b 1968), 1 da (Barbara Maria b 1962); *Career* asst engr Rendel Palmer & Tritton 1959-62, reader in civil engrg Univ of Leeds 1967 (lectr 1962-67), prof Univ of Liverpool 1967-1988, prof of civil engrg Sultan Qaboos Univ 1986-; Hon DSc Univ of Leeds 1973; FICE 1986, FIStructE 1986, FASCE 1986; *Books* Developments in Prestressed Concrete (1982), Computer Methods for Civil Engineers (1984); *Recreations* bridge, numismatics, travel; *Style*— Prof Felicjan Sawko; 9 Harthill Road, Liverpool L18 6HU (☎ 051 724 2726)

SAWREY-COOKSON, Maj (John) Henry Crackanthorpe; s of John Clement Basil Sawrey-Cookson (d 1987), of Ashbrook, Winsford, nr Minehead, Somerset, and Joan, *née* Luxmoore; *b* 17 Sept 1913; *Educ* Uppingham, Royal Agric Coll Cirencester; *m* 16 Dec 1967, Merrilyn Patricia, da of Maj R Thomas (ka 1944); 1 s (Rawlinson b 1977), 1 da (Emma b 1973); *Career* Nat Serv 1959, cmmnd Lifeguards attended MONS OCS; cmmnd RA: 8/60 short-serv cmmn Royal West African Frontier Force, 2/66 reg cmmn; served: Sierra Leonean Army 1960-63, Nigerian & Army UN Congo 1961-62, 18/39 Regt RA BAOR Hong Kong and NI, ldr Overland Expedition Germany-Oman, US 8 Army S Korea 1966, Canadian Army 1969, Sultan's Forces Oman Dhofur War 1972, Nat Army Zimbabwe 1981-83; OC light gun roles USA 1985, ldr Op Raleigh Expedition Patagonia, Chile 1988; Lord of Manor: Newbiggin and Hale, Ousby and Bank; patron of living parishes Newbiggin, Kirby Thore, Temple Sowerby; MRAC, FRGS; *Recreations* game shooting, gardening, exploration; *Style*— Maj Henry Sawrey-Cookson

SAWTELL, Jeffrey James (Jeff); s of Ivor Charles Sawtell, (d 1979), of Ellesmere Port, and Anne, *née* Morris, (d 1984); *b* 29 Jan 1946; *Educ* John St Secdy Modern Ellesmere Port, Chester Sch of Art, London Coll of Printing, St Martins Sch of Art (Dip AD) RCA (MA); *m* 1969 (m dis), Trudi Gurling; 1 da (Hannah Rebecca b 1971); *Career* ed Artery 1971-84, artist, writer and pt/t lectr 1972-87; lectr: Wimbledon Sch of Art, Chelsea Coll of Art, Slade Sch, Coventry Poly, London Coll of Furniture, Goldsmith's Coll, Univ of Bremen, Univ of Humboldt; made documentaries in: Portugal, NI, USA, Panama, Guatemala, Jamaica, UK 1972-87; exhibitions incl: Pentonville Gallery (solo) 1981 and 1984, Camden Open 1989, Bookplumbing 1967, Minatures and Inferences (St Martins) 1969, Three Schools Exhibition (Royal Acad) 1970, History up to Date (RCA) 1972, The Shrewsbury Affair (TUC Conf, PCL Gallery, Parliament) 1975, Art for Society (Whitechapel Gallery London) 1978, Wildcat Theatre Gallery Edinburgh 1982, New Beginnings (Pentonville Gallery) 1983; full- time art feature writer for The Morning Star and writer of film, visual art, tv and cultural features 1987-; memb Critics Circle 1988; *Style*— Jeff Sawtell, Esq; 19 Lyme St, London NW1 0EH (☎ 071 267 5803); Morning Star, 1-3 Ardleigh Rd, London N1 4HS (☎ 071 254 0033 ext 251, fax 071 254 5950)

SAWYER, Gp Capt James Nankivell (Jim); CBE (1985); s of Harry Nankivell Sawyer, of Grange Lodge, Wroxham, Norwich, Norfolk, and Barbara Laidlaw, *née* Hope (d 1990); *b* 29 Oct 1934; *Educ* Langley Sch Loddon Norfolk, RAF Coll Cranwell, RAF Staff Coll Bracknell, Nat Def Coll Latimer; *m* 8 April 1961, Maureen Winifred (Mo), da of Patrick Joseph Tansey (d 1965); 2 s (Richard, Guy), 1 da (Lucy); *Career* cmmnd 1955; pilot on fighter sqdns based in Middle East, exchange posting as pilot US Marines in US and Japan 1963-65, instr and devpt pilot with Central Fighter Estab RAF, Wing Cdr RAF Coningsby 1977-79, then HQ 11 Gp short tour Germany, promotion to Gp Capt 1983, cmd Northern UK Air Def Sector; served in Falklands and CTTO; worked for rehabilitation of alcoholics Scotland 1983-85, associated with Marie Curie Meml Fndn; currently mangr nat census operation in E Norfolk; *Recreations* reading and writing poetry, walking, cycling, occasional amateur acting, dancing; *Clubs* RAF Assoc; *Style*— Gp Capt Jim Sawyer, CBE; The Shielings, 18a Ditchingham Dam, Bungay, Suffolk NR35 2JQ (☎ 0986 2128)

SAWYER, Dr Roger Martyn; s of Charles Frederick Sawyer (d 1961), of Badgeworth, Gloucestershire, and Winifred Alice, *née* Martin (d 1962); *b* 15 Dec 1931; *Educ* Wycliffe Coll, Univ of Wales (BA, DipEd), Univ of Southampton (PhD); *m* 30 Aug 1952, Margaret Frances Mulvagh (Diana), da of Thomas (d 1964), of Dromore West, Co Sligo; 2 s (Charles, Rupert); *Career* asst master Forton House Prep Sch 1950-52, housemaster The Blue Coat Sch Edgbaston 1958-60, headmaster Bembridge Prep Sch 1977-83 (dep head 1960-77, ret 1983); Airey Neave award for Res into Freedom under Nat Laws 1985; asst chief examiner for GCE Eng Univ of London 1987 (examiner in written and spoken Eng 1966-); memb: Governing Body Anti-Slavery Soc, Inc Assoc of Prep Schs, Govrs Wycliffe Coll, Isle of Wight Youth Tst; former chm RLSS Isle of Wight; *Books* Casement The Flawed Hero (1984), Slavery in the Twentieth Century (1986), Children Enslaved (1988), The Island From Within (ed, 1990); *Recreations* collecting rare books especially about Ireland and slavery, walking by the sea; *Clubs* Bembridge Sailing; *Style*— Dr Roger Sawyer; Ducie House, Darts Lane, Bembridge, Isle of Wight PO35 5YH (☎ 0983 873384)

SAX, George Hans; s of Oscar Sax (d 1974), of 37 Manor Way, Beckenham, Kent, and Margaret, *née* Bohm (d 1977); *b* 11 Feb 1913; *Educ* Dulwich, Univ of Leeds, Imperial Coll of Sci & Technol; *m* 19 Feb 1938, Yvonne Anna Marcelle, da of Leopold Joseph Trausel (d 1971), of IOW; 2 s (Richard Noel b 26 Dec 1938, John Paul b 3 Aug 1944); *Career* Territorial Serv Sharpshooters 3 Co of London Yeo 1932-37, cmmnd RASC 1939 served in France 1940, transferred RAOC served in France, Belgium, Germany 1944-46, GSO1 HQ 21 Army Gp Lt-Col 1944, demobbed 1946; md Martin Rice Ltd, dir GR Holdings, underwriter Lloyds 1965; pres Br Fur Trade Assoc; hon local rep Offrs Assoc Br Legion 1968-; Freeman City of London 1937, Liveryman Worshipful Co of Skinners 1937; *Recreations* travel, fly-fishing, gardening; *Style*— George Sax, Esq

SAX, Richard Noel; s of Lt-Col George Hans Sax, of Leeford Oaks, Whatlington, nr Battle, E Sussex, and Yvonne Anna Marcelle Sax; *b* 26 Dec 1938; *Educ* Tonbridge, St John's Coll Oxford (MA); *m* 8 April 1967, Margaret, da of Ronald Frank Penny (d 1988); 3 da (Catherine b 1968, Josephine b 1971, Charlotte b 1974); *Career* Nat Serv cmmnd 2 Lt RASC 1957, attatched 1 Gds Bde Irish Gds Cyprus (GSM Cyprus Clasp), Lt 1959; admitted slr 1967; managing ptnr Rubinstein Callingham 1984- (equity ptnr 1968-84); memb Law Cmmns Working Pty on Family Property 1974, former chm Slrs Family Law Assoc 1987-, memb Law Soc's Family Law Ctee 1990-, dep district judge Princ Registry Family Div; Liveryman Worshipful Co of Skinners; memb Law Soc 1967; *Recreations* current affairs, gardening, history and archaeology, travel, art; *Clubs* MCC; *Style*— Richard Sax, Esq; 29 Kelsey Way, Beckenham, Kent BR3 3LP; 2 Raymond Buildings, Grays Inn, London WC1R 5BZ (☎ 081 650 8272, fax 071 831 7413, telex 894 100 RUBCAL G)

SAXBY, Graham; s of Flinton Saxby (d 1972), of Seaton, Devon, and Eleanor Cora, *née* Pratt (d 1985); *b* 4 Nov 1925; *Educ* West Buckland Sch, Univ Coll of S W (now Univ of Exeter), Univ of London (BSc), Univ of Manchester (PGCE), Open Univ (BA); *m* Christine Mary, da of Ernest Smalley (d 1980); 1 step da; *Career* RAF: joined as photographer 1947, served Singapore, Hong Kong, Bahrain and Germany, latterly chief technician, cmmnd educn offr (technical) 1966, OC Photographic Science Flight Joint Sch of Photography until ret as Sqdn Ldr 1974; Wolverhampton Tech Teachers Coll (later part of Wolverhampton Poly): lectr in educnl technol 1974-90, estab Holography Unit 1986, hon res fell in holography 1990-; BIPP professional liaison visitor Nottingham Poly, tech advsr and visiting lectr Holography Dept RCA, contrib ed Holosphere, memb Distinctions Panel RPS and BIPP, exhibitions judge BIPP; *awards* Technical Writers awards (Specialist Division) 1981, second prize Diplome de la Musée de la Photographie (Prix Louis-Phillipe Clerc) 1983, nominee King Feisal award for science writing 1988, City and Guilds Insignia award (photographic technol)1970; RPS: memb 1946, fell 1981, hon fell 1988; FBIPP 1988 (memb 1956); *Books* The Focal Guide to Slides (1979), Holograms: How to Make and Display Them (1980), Newnes Book of Photography (contrib, 1983), Practical Holography (1988), Manual of Practical Holography (1991), author of numerous technical articles in professional jls; *Recreations* photography, music, vegetable gardening; *Style*— Graham Saxby, Esq; 3 Honor Ave, Goldthorn Park, Wolverhampton, West Midlands WV4 5HF (☎ 0902 341291); Holography Unit, Wolverhampton Polytechnic, Art & Design Building, Molineux St, Wolverhampton WV1 1SB (☎ 0902 321993, fax 0902 710171)

SAXBY, John; s of George Saxby, and Veronica, *née* Flynn; *b* 29 Sept 1949; *Educ* St Mary's Coll Crosby Liverpool, Kings Coll London (BA, MPhil), Univ of Cologne; *m* 15 Nov 1986, Janet Adelyne, da of Harold Livesey; 1 da (Emily-Jane Christine b 7 Nov 1989); *Career* overseas insur underwriter Legal and General Insurance Company 1972-74; admin asst: Westminster Hosp London 1974-75, St Francis and Dulwich Hosps London 1975-77; dep admin: Univ Coll Hosp London 1974-75, Hammersmith Hosp London 1980-83; Unit admin Southmead Hosp Bristol 1983-85, gen mangr Royal Cornwall Hosp Treliske Truro 1985-; AHSM 1983; *Recreations* marathon running, board sailing; *Style*— John Saxby, Esq; Royal Cornwall Hospital (Treliske), Truro, Cornwall TR1 3LJ (☎ 0872 74242)

SAXBY, John Christopher Leslie; s of Leslie Eric Saxby (d 1958), and Florence Mildred, *née* Gallimore (d 1983); *b* 2 April 1933; *Educ* Caterham Sch; *m* 19 Oct 1968, Heather Peel, da of Eric Peel Yates (d 1987); 1 s (Robin b 1975), 1 da (Fiona b 1972); *Career* chartered accountant, articled West Wake Price and Co 1951-58, qualified clerk Coopers and Lybrand 1959-65, chief accountant London Merchant Securities plc 1965-70 (gp accountant), co sec Carlton Industs plc 1970-81, sr ptnr Saxby and Sinden (previously Saxby and Marner) 1981-; FCA 1957; *Recreations* golf; *Clubs* Worlebury Golf, Winscombe Cricket (pres); *Style*— John Saxby, Esq; Orchard House, Main Road Cleeve, Bristol BS19 4PN (☎ 0934 832 262); 61 Park St, Bristol BS1 5NU (☎ 0272 221 751); 18 High St, Budleigh, Salterton, Devon EX9 6LQ (☎ 09354 3766)

SAXBY, John James; s of James Samuel Saxby (d 1967, Sqdn Ldr RAuxAf 1938-45), of Ovingdean, Sussex, and Florence Evelyn, *née* Wilson (d 1965); *b* 16 June 1925; *Educ* Bradfield, Magdalene Coll Cambridge; 1, 1952 (m dis 1964), Thelma Winifred Whitehouse; 1 s (Peter b 1955), 1 da (Judith b 1954); m 2, 1984, Susan Josephine Gabriel Scott, *née* White; *Career* RAFVR 1943-47, cmmnd Pilot Offr (as pilot) 1944, physical trg instr and staff parachute instr RAF Upper Heyford 1945, OC ME Parachute Sch (Aqir, Palestine) 1946-47, parachute advsr to OC 6 Airborne Div 1946-47 (Flt-Lt); Hecht Levis & Khan Group: China, Hong Kong, Singapore, Dutch East Indies, London 1947-54; md main commodity subsid of Wm Brandts Sons & Co Ltd 1954-64; called to the Bar Gray's Inn 1962; legal advsr Revertex Ltd 1964-72, UK legal advsr Int Mktg Div Kuwait National Petroleum Co (later Kuwait Petroleum Corporation) 1972-84; formerly: cncllr Met Borough Cncl Paddington South, adopted for LCC by Hackney S, gen cmmr Inland Revenue, memb Arbitration Panel Rubber Trade Assoc of London; panels chm Diary Produce Quota Tbnls 1984-85; Freeman Worshipful Co of Fruiterers 1973; FCIArb; *Recreations* fly fishing, falconry, fencing, oil painting; *Clubs* Flyfishers, Carlton, Br Falconers; *Style*— John Saxby, Esq; Freshfields, Whitefriars, 65 Fleet St, London EC4Y 1HT (☎ 071 936 4000)

SAXENA, Dr Sideshwar Raj; s of late Rai Bhim Raj Saxena, and late Mrs Gunna Bee Bee; *b* 6 Feb 1933; *Educ* (MB BS, MD, DCH); *m* 8 May 1960, Prahba Devi Saxena, da of late Rai Jadubans Chandra; *Career* formerly asst prof paediatrics Niloufer Hosp, Nuffield Fndn fell and hon sr registrar at Queen Elizabeth Hosp for Children; presently principal in gen practice, hon tutor and clinical asst Kings Coll Hosp, conslt Harley St; past pres Indian Med Assoc, ed Mediscene (journal for overseas doctors in UK), memb Euro assoc of Sci Eds, panel doctor of Indian High Cmmn; FRSM; *Books* Life of Ghandi 'Bapu' (1948), Jokes Jokes Jokes (1986), A Prescription for Laughter (1988); *Style*— Dr Sidehwar Raj Saxena; Prasidh, 12 A Alleyn Rd, W Dulwich SE21 8AL; 142 Harley St, London W1 (☎ 071 935 5790)

SAXON, Richard Gilbert; s of Rev Canon Eric Saxon, QHC, of 27 Padstow Drive, Stockport, and Ruth, *née* Higginbottom; *b* 14 April 1942; *Educ* Manchester GS, Univ of Liverpool (BArch, MCD); *m* 14 Sept 1968, (Elizabeth) Anne, da of Samuel Shaw Tatton, of 1 Richmondfield Way, Barwick in Elmet, Leeds; *Career* ptnr Bldg Design Ptnrship 1977- (assoc 1970-77), exec ptnr Practice Devpt 1984-86; design ptnr: J P Morgan HQ London 1986-, Paddington Basin Redevelopment 1989-; awards incl: RIBA Halifax Bldg Soc HQ 1975, Europa Nostra medal and Civic Tst Durham Milburngate Centre 1978, Civic Tst Commendation Merseyside Maritime Museum Masterplan 1981; advsr Bldg EDC 1984-86, memb Bldg Sub Ctee Sci and Engrg Res Cncl 1987-90, fndr memb and chm Tech Ctee Br Cncl for Office 1990-; Freeman City of London 1988, Liveryman Worshipful Co of Chartered Architects 1989; memb RIBA 1968, MBIM 1986, FRSA 1987, MInstD; *Books* Atrium Buildings, Development and Design: Architectural Press (1983 and 1986), Moscow (1987), Kajima Press Japan (1988); chapter Atrium Buildings Wiley/AIA Encyclopedia of Architecture (1988), The Trade Report BDP (1988), The Atrium Comes of Age (1991); *Recreations* travel, photography, music, theatre, film, writing; *Style*— Richard Saxon, Esq; Building Design Partnership, 16 Gresse Street, PO Box 4WD, London W1A 4WD (☎ 071 631 4733, fax 071 631 0393, telex 25322)

SAXTON, Patrick Vincent; s of Patrick Cyril Saxton (d 1979), and Zara Pearl, *née* Moore; *b* 6 Sept 1929; *Educ* High Oakham Sch Mansfield; *m* 19 July 1980, Vera (Vee) Margaret, da of Alexander John Temple (d 1958), of Sanderstead, Surrey; *Career* Nat Serv RA; Willis Faber and Dumas 1950-53, clerk to agency supt Caledonian Insurance Co 1953-63; Chartered Insurance Institute: careers advsy office 1964-, asst sec 1965-, admin sec 1979-, sec gen 1983-89, euro conslt 1990-; lay asst St Georges Church Beckenham; sec Insur Indust Trg Cncl 1972-80; chm: Br Insur Law Assoc 1981-83, Insur Trg Ctee of Comité Européen des Assurances, All Saints Educational Tst, Inst Trg and Devpt 1984-86; memb London Univ Careers Advsy Bd; Freeman City of London 1973; Liveryman: Worshipful Co of Gold and Silver Wyre Drawers 1973, Worshipful Co of Insurers 1984; assoc memb Inst of Insur Sci for services to Anglo-German insur educn, Hon FICO 1977; FCII 1956, FITD 1978, FBIM 1982; *Books* Allured to Adventure (1974); *Recreations* chess, music, photography, watching sport; *Clubs* MCC, Cripplegate Ward; *Style*— Patrick Saxton, Esq; 24 Lakeside, Wickham Road, Beckenham, Kent (☎ 081 658 6298); Chartered Insurance Institute, 20 Aldermanbury, London EC2V 7HY (☎ 071 606 3835, fax 071 726 0131, telex 957017)

SAXTON, Robert Louis Alfred; s of Capt Ian Sanders Saxton, of London, and Jean Augusta, *née* Infield; *b* 8 Oct 1953; *Educ* Bryanston, St Catharine's Coll Cambridge (MA), Worcester Coll Oxford (BMUS); *Career* visiting tutor Univ of Oxford 1980-82, lectr Univ of Bristol 1984-85, visiting fell Princeton Univ 1986, composer in residence City Univ 1987-89, head of Composition Dept GSM 1990- (composition tutor 1979-84 and 1986-90); composer of over 30 published works; contrib to various music jls; several radio and TV appearances; memb: Cncl SPNM 1978-90 (memb Exec Ctee 1979-82), BBC Advsy Music Panel 1988, Arts Cncl of GB Music Advsy Panel 1989-; artistic bd memb Blackheath Concert Halls 1987-; PRS 1976, FGSM 1986, MCPS 1990; *Recreations* theatre, cinema, watching cricket, reading biography and history; *Style*— Robert Saxton, Esq; c/o Chester Music, 8/9 Frith St, London W1V 5TZ (☎ 071 434 0066, fax 071 439 2848)

SAXTON, Robert Michael; s of Arthur Colin, and Joyce, *née* Dulson; *b* 12 Aug 1952; *Educ* Magdalen Coll Oxford (MA); *Career* publisher; Studio Vista 1975-80, exec ed Mitchel Beazley 1980- (responsible for lists on gardening, design, architecture, design, photography); titles commissioned incl: Vertical Gardening, The Small Garden Planner; *Recreations* squash, hillwalking, ornithology, modern jazz; *Style*— Robert Saxton, Esq; Mitchell Beazley International Ltd, Artists House, 14-15 Manette St, London W1V 5LB (☎ 071 439 7211, telex G24892 MB BOOK, fax 081 734 0389)

SAY, Rt Rev Dr (Richard) David; KCVO (1988); s of Cdr Richard Say, OBE, RNVR (d 1958), of London, and Kathleen Mary, *née* Wildy; *b* 4 Oct 1914; *Educ* Univ Coll Sch, Christ's Coll Cambridge (BA, MA), Ridley Hall Cambridge; *m* 16 Oct 1943, Irene Frances Say, OBE, JP, da of Seaburne Rayner (d 1952), of Exeter; 2 s (Richard William Gurney b and d 1950, William David b 1952), 2 da (Mary Penelope (Mrs Thompson) b 1945, Anne Caroline (Mrs Langley) b 1948); *Career* ordained Canterbury Cathedral: deacon 1939, priest 1940, bishop 1961; curate: Croydon Parish Church 1939-43, St Martin-in-the-Fields 1943-50; gen sec: C of E Youth Cncl 1944-47, Br Cncl of Churches 1947-55; rector of Hatfield Herts and chaplain to 5th Marquess of Salisbury 1955-61, hon canon St Albans 1957-61, 104th Bishop of Rochester 1961-88, chaplain to Pilgrims of GB 1968-, Lord High Almoner to HM The Queen 1970-88, asst Bishop of Canterbury 1988-; C of E del to World Cncl of Churches 1948 1954 and 1961; select preacher: Univ of Cambridge 1954, Univ of Oxford 1963; chaplain and sub-prelate OStJ 1961, memb House of Lords 1969-88, chm Ctee on State Aid for Churches in Use 1971-90, pro-chllr Univ of Kent 1983- (dep pro-chllr 1977-83), memb Court of Ecclesiastical Causes Reserved 1984-; vice-pres: UN Assoc of GB 1986, Age Concern England 1990- (chm 1986-89); pres Friends of Kent Churches 1988-; hon memb Inst of RE 1987; Freeman City of London 1953; Hon Freeman: Borough of Tonbridge and Malling 1987, City of Rochester upon Medway 1988; DD Lambeth 1961; Hon DCL Univ of Kent at Canterbury 1987; *Recreations* walking, travel; *Clubs* United Oxford and Cambridge Univ; *Style*— The Rt Rev Dr David Say, KCVO; 23 Chequers Park, Wye, Ashford, Kent TN25 5BB (☎ 0233 812720)

SAYE AND SELE, 21 Baron (E 1447 and 1603); Nathaniel Thomas Allen Fiennes; DL (Oxon 1979); s of 20 Baron, OBE, MC (Ivo Murray Twisleton-Wykeham-Fiennes, d 1968), and Hersey, da of late Capt Sir Thomas Dacres Butler, KCVO; relinquished by deed poll 1965 the additional surnames of Twisleton and Wykeham; *b* 22 Sept 1920; *Educ* Eton, New Coll Oxford; *m* 1958, Mariette Helena, da of Maj-Gen Sir (Arthur) Guy Salisbury-Jones, GCVO, CMG, CBE, MC (d 1985), and Hilda, da of Rt Hon Sir Maurice de Bunsen, 1 and last Bt, GCMG, GCVO, CB; 3 s, 1 da; *Heir* s, Hon Richard Fiennes; *Career* Rifle Bde (despatches twice) 1939-45; chartered surveyor; *Style*— The Rt Hon the Lord Saye and Sele, DL; Broughton Castle, Banbury, Oxon (☎ 0295 262624)

SAYED, Dr (Zulfiquar) Aly; s of Dr Niwazish Aly Sayed (d 1978), of Civil Lines, Khanewal, and Zubeba, *née* Mumtaz; *b* 23 May 1932; *Educ* Punjab Univ (MB BS), Univ of Edinburgh (MSc, Dip Psych); *m* 12 Oct 1966, (Elva) Arline, da of Joseph Gwilym Jones (d 1979), of St Helens, Lancs; 1 s (Shaun b 1969), 2 da (Zara b 1975, Michelle b 1977); *Career* registrar United Birmingham, Hosps Nat Hosp Queen Square London, res fell Univ of Edinburgh, sr registrar United Liverpool Hosps, conslt psychiatrist N Western RHA 1970-; memb BMA, MBIM, FRCPsych; *Recreations* good food, travel, reading; *Clubs* Consultants; *Style*— Dr Aly Sayed; 3 Healey Close, Salford, Greater Manchester M7 0PQ (☎ 061 792 3930); Tameside General Hospital, Ashton under Lyne, Gtr Manchester (☎ 061 330 8373)

SAYEED, Dr (Abul Fatah) Akram; OBE (1976); s of Mokhles Ahmed (d 1967), of Pirwalistan, Jessore, Bangladesh, and Noor Jehan Begum, *née* Munshi (d 1987); *b* 23 Nov 1935; *Educ* St Joseph's Sch Khulna, Univ of Dhaka (MB BS); *m* 11 Oct 1959, Hosen-ara, da of Al-Haj M Sabet Ali; 2 s (Rana Ahmed b 10 March 1967, Reza Abu b 15 April 1972), 1 da (Dina Jesmin b 17 June 1963); *Career* sr house offr in ophthalmology Dhaka Univ Hosp 1959-60 (house offr 1958-59), rotating internship Monmouth Med Centre Long Branch New Jersey 1960-61, GP 1964- (asst in practice 1963), pt/t MO Leicester Royal Infirmary (sr house offr in ophthalmology 1961-63); author of numerous articles on medico-politics; writer, lectr and broadcaster on med educn and trg in Bangladesh; memb: Leicester Cncl for Community Rels 1965- (fndr memb), CRC 1968-77, BBC Asian Programme Advsy Ctee 1972-77, Bangladesh Med Assoc UK 1972- (CEC memb 1982-),BMA Leics and Rutland Div 1975- (EC memb), Leics Med Ctee 1977, Leics Family Practitioners Ctee 1977, Univ Mgmnt Team 1977, Home Sec's Advsy Cncl on Community Rels 1983, DHSS Working Gps (Asian health, treatment of overseas visitors), Ophthalmic Soc of Bangladesh (life memb); advsr NCCI 1965-68; chm: Stop Rickets Campaign Leics, Standing Conf of Asian Orgns in UK 1973-77 (vice chm 1970-73); Overseas Dr's Assoc: fndr chm 1975, gen sec 1975-77, vice pres 1979-84, chm S Trent Div 1981, vice chm 1984, fell 1985, chm Annual Representative Meeting 1990; UK del First World Conf on Muslim Educn King Abdul Aziz Univ Mecca 1977, vice pres Fedn of Bangladeshi Orgns in UK and Europe 1984, sec Inst of Transcultural Health Care 1985; memb Editorial Bd: ODA News Review, Asian Who's Who (6 edn, 1990-91); co-ordinator and fecilitator in UK for Bangladesh Coll of Physicians and Surgeons 1990-; hon advsr Miny of Health Govt of Bangladesh 1991; memb: BMA 1961, MJA; FRSM 1981; *Books* Bangladesh Medical Directory (ed 3 edns), Caring for Asians in General Practice (contrib, 1989); *Recreations* reading, oriental music, photography, gardening; *Clubs* Rotary (Leicester City), Royal Overseas League (London and Edinburgh); *Style*— Dr Akram Sayeed, OBE; RAMNA, 2 Mickelton Drive, Leicester LE5 6GD (☎ 0533 416703); 352 East Park Rd, Leicester LE5 5AY (☎ 0533 737569/ 730388)

SAYEED, Jonathan; MP (C) Bristol East 1983-; *b* 20 March 1948; *Educ* RNC Dartmouth, RN Engrg Coll; *Career* RN then shipping conslt, chm insur serv co; defeated Rt Hon Tony Benn in 1983 election, and Ron Thomas in 1987 election; memb Select Ctee: on Environment 1987, on Defence 1987-; vice chm Shipping and Shipbuilding Ctee; dep chm Maritime Ctee; *Style*— Jonathan Sayeed, Esq, MP; House of Commons, London SW1A 0AA (☎ 071 219 6389)

SAYER, Maj Douglas James William; MBE (1941), TD; Lord of the Manor of Sparham; er s of Capt James Arthur Sayer, JP (d 1960), of Sparham Hall, Norfolk, and Georganna Margaret, *née* Garrod (d 1951); descends from John Sawyer, of

Cambrydges in Swanton Morley, Norfolk assessed there for subsidy 1543 (*see* Burke's Landed Gentry, 18 edn, Vol II, 1969); *b* 8 May 1906; *Educ* Aldenham; *m* 24 April 1946, Mary Elisabeth, 4 da and co-heiress of Rev Edward Croxton Weddall, MA (d 1961, formerly rector of Lyng, Norfolk) and gda of Rev William Charles Weddall, rector of Linby, Notts, by his w Susan, da of James Sutton, JP, DL, of Shardlow Hall, Derbys; 2 s (Michael *qv*, Charles); *Career* Lt Reserve of Offrs King's African Rifles 1934, Capt 5 Bn (TA) Royal Norfolk Regt 1937, served 1939-45, Maj 1941; cmmr of Taxes (Norfolk) 1945-81; JP Norfolk 1945-81; lord of manor of Sparham; *Recreations* arboriculture; *Clubs* Naval & Military, Norfolk (Norwich); *Style*— Maj Douglas Sayer, MBE, TD; Sparham Hall, Norwich, Norfolk NR9 5QY (☎ 0603 872226)

SAYER, Michael John; s of Maj Douglas James William Sayer, MBE, TD *qv*, of Sparham Hall, Norfolk, and Mary Elizabeth, *née* Weddall; *b* 11 Oct 1947; *Educ* Repton, Pembroke Coll Oxford (BA, MA, BLitt); *Career* landowner, author; chm: Norfolk Churches Tst 1984-86, Country Landowners' Assoc (memb: Norfolk Branch Ctee 1972, Water Sub Ctee 1980-84, Tax Sub Ctee 1989-); memb: Norwich Diocesan Synod 1973-82 (Pastoral Ctee 1974-82), Tax Ctee Historic Houses Assoc 1990-; tax cmmr 1979- (chm St Faith's and Aylsham Div 1988-); FSA 1982; *Books* English Nobility: The Gentry, The Heralds and The Continental Context (1979), Norfolk section of Burke's and Savill's Guide to Country Houses, vol III, East Anglia (1981); *Recreations* history, architecture, shooting; *Clubs* Norfolk; *Style*— Michael J Sayer, Esq, FSA; Sparham House, Norwich NR9 5PJ (☎ 0603 872268)

SAYER, Paul Anthony; s of John Sayer, of 9 Grove Crescent, South Milford, nr Leeds, and Adelaide, *née* Lambert (d 1985); *b* 4 Oct 1955; *Educ* Tadcaster GS; *m* 31 Jan 1981, Anne, da of James Bell; 1 s (Simon b 19 Dec 1984); *Career* author; shop asst 1973-76, RMN 1979, psychiatric nurse 1976-81 and 1986-89, shop keeper 1981-84, storeman 1984-85, author 1989-; *Publications* The Comforts of Madness (1988), Howling at the Moon (1990); *Awards* Constable Trophy for Fiction 1988, Whitbread First Novel award 1988, Whitbread Book of the Year award 1988; memb: Soc of Authors 1988, Yorkshire Arts 1988; *Recreations* lifelong supporter of York City FC, horse racing, gardening, walking; *Style*— Paul Sayer, Esq; c/o Carol Smith, 25 Hornton Court, Kensington High St, London W8 7RT (☎ 071 937 4874, fax 071 938 5323)

SAYER, Philip William; s of Edward George Poulton Sayer, of Basingstoke, Hants, and Jean, *née* Kennedy; *b* 7 Jan 1947; *Educ* Queen Mary's GS Basingstoke Hants; *m* Dec 1984, Joan Katherine, da of Ronald Frederick Taylor; 1 da (Rosie b Sept 1985); *Career* photographer; asst to Maurice Broomfield, photographer Butlins Holiday Camp Bogner 1965-67, photographic printer Derek Robinson Partnership 1967-70, freelance editorial photographer 1970-; currently contrib to various magazines incl: Management Today, Crafts, Blueprint, World of Interiors, GQ (USA), Travel & Leisure (USA), ES, The Times - Saturday Review; currently photographer numerous design gps Euro and USA, solo exhibitions: Portraits For Print Norwich Sch of Art 1983, The Face of Craft Br Crafts Centre 1984, Portraits Impressions Gallery York 1985, perm exhibition of portraits The Blueprint Café Design Museum London 1989; FCSD 1983; *Recreations* painting, cycling, music (jazz, country and western), reading; *Style*— Phillip Sayer, Esq; Philip Sayer Partnership, Hope House, 12A Perseverance Works, 38 Kingsland Rd, London E2 8DD (☎ 071 729 3566, fax 071 729 3591)

SAYER, Stephen Thomas; s of Charles Martin Sayer, of Epping, Essex, and Justina, *née* Marsden Jones; *b* 8 July 1945; *Educ* Framlingham Coll Suffolk, Coll of Law; *m* 1, 20 July 1968 (m dis 1987), Gillian Susan, da of John Talbot Warwick, of Rustington, Sussex; 2 s (Edward b 1971, Timothy b and d 1973), 1 da (Harriet b 1976); m 2, 30 Jan 1988, Aileen, da of Roy Victor Wegener, of Toowoomba, Queensland, Australia; *Career* admitted slr 1968; Richards Butler Slrs: asst slr 1968, ptnr 1974; Freeman City of London 1978, Liveryman Worshipful Co of Slrs 1975; memb: Law Soc 1968, Lawyers Club 1980; *Books* contrib to: Longmans Practical Commercial Precedents (1987), International Joint Ventures (1989); *Recreations* real tennis, rackets, theatre, reading; *Clubs* Reform, City of London, Queens; *Style*— Stephen Sayer, Esq; 21 Beltran Rd, Fulham, London SW6 3AL (☎ 071 736 9655); Beaufort House, 15 St Botolph St, London EC3A 7EE (☎ 071 247 6555, fax 071 247 5091, telex 949494 RBLAW G)

SAYERS, Arnold Lewis; CBE (1986), DL; s of Maj Lorne Douglas Watson Sayers (d 1940), of Alston Hall, Holbeton, Plymouth, and Dame Lucile Newell, JP, *née* Schiff (d 1959); *b* 28 April 1923; *Educ* Wellington Coll, CCC Cambridge (BA); *m* 10 July 1954, Sylvia Penelope, da of late Brig Gen Spencer Vaughan Percy Weston, DSO, MC, of Sevenoaks, Kent; 1 s (Geoffrey b 1965), 3 da (Charlotte b 1956, Priscilla b 1958, Catherine b 1961); *Career* farmer; ldr Devon CC 1981-85, govr Seale-Hayne Coll, memb Cncl Univ of Exeter; chm: Assoc CC Planning and Transportation Ctee 1981-84, Dartington Cattle Breeding Centre 1986-; *Recreations* walking, music; *Clubs* Farmers; *Style*— Arnold L Sayers, Esq, CBE, DL; Carswell, Holbeton, nr Plymouth (☎ 075 530 282)

SAYERS, Prof Bruce McArthur; s of John William McArthur Sayers (d 1980), of Melbourne, Aust, and Mabel Florence, *née* Howe (d 1980); *b* 6 Feb 1928; *Educ* Melbourne HS Aust, Univ of Melbourne (BSc MSc), Univ of London (PhD, DIC, DSc); *Career* professional biophysicist Baker Med Res Inst and Alfred Hosp Melbourne 1949-54; Imperial Coll London: res asst 1954-56, Philips electrical res fell 1956-58, lectr in electrical engrg 1958-62, sr lectr in med electronics 1963-65, reader 1965-68, prof of electrical engrg applied to med 1968-84, head Dept of Electrical Engrg 1979-84, prof of computing applied to med 1984-90, head Dept of Computing 1984-89, Kobler prof of the mgmnt of info technol 1990-; dean City & Guilds Coll 1984-88, dir Centre for Cognitive Systems 1989-, hon conslt Royal Nat Throat Nose and Ear Hosp 1974-; univ visiting prof: McGill, Melbourne, Rio de Janiero, Toronto; travelling lectr Nuffield Fndn and Nat Res Cncl Canada 1971; advsr: Advent Eurofund Ltd 1981-, Shinan Investment Service SA 1984-87, Advent Capital Ltd 1985-, Neuroscience Ltd 1985-, Transatlantic Capital (BioSci) Fund Ltd 1985-; dir: Imperial Software Technology Ltd 1984-90, Imperial Information Technology Ltd 1986-90; pres Section of Measurement in Med Royal Soc of Med 1971-72, memb Global Advsy Ctee on Health Res WHO Geneva 1988- (vice chm 1990-); Freeman City of London 1986, Liveryman Worshipful Co of Scientific Instrument Makers' 1985; hon foreign memb Societa Medica Chirurgica di Bologna 1965; hon memb: Med Soc WHO 1974, Eta Kappa Nu 1980; FRSA 1975, FIEE 1980, FCGI 1983, FEng 1990; *Recreations* composing comic doggerel, pottering around France and Switzerland; *Clubs* Athenaeum; *Style*— Prof Bruce Sayers; 40 Queen's Gate, London SW7 5HR (☎ 071 589 7953); Lots Cottage, Compton Abbas, Dorset; Centre for Cognitive Systems, Imperial College, London SW7 2AZ (☎ 071 225 8930, fax 071 589 7127)

SAYERS, Michael Bernard; s of Joseph David Sayers (d 1981), of London, and Miriam May, *née* Konskier (d 1989); *b* 23 April 1934; *Educ* Winchester, Magdalen Coll Oxford (MA); *m* 17 Dec 1958, Peta Ann, da of David Levi, of London; 1 s (Nicholas b 1959), 2 da (Catherine b 1961, Ruth b 1963); *Career* Nat Serv 1952-54: Midshipman 1953, Sub Lt 1954; slr 1960, asst slr 1960-62 Macfarlanes (articled clerk 1957-60), ptnr Norton Rose 1965- (asst slr 1962-64); *Style*— Michael Sayers, Esq; 9 Burgess Hill, London NW2 2BY (☎ 071 435 4348); The Old School House, Holwell, nr Burford, Oxfordshire OX8 4JS (☎ 099 382 3084); Norton Rose, Kempson House, PO Box 570, Camomile St, London EC3A 7AN (☎ 071 283 2434, fax 071 588 1181, telex 883652)

SAYERS, Michael Patrick; QC (1988); s of Maj (Herbert James) Michael Sayers, RA (ka 1943), and Sheilah De Courcy Holroyd, *née* Stephenson (d 1969); *b* 28 March 1940; *Educ* Harrow, Fitzwilliam Coll Cambridge (MA); *m* 12 Mar 1976, Moussie Brougham, *née* Hallstrom; 1 s (Frederick b 3 Dec 1981), 1 da (Nicola b 27 Dec 1980), 1 step s (Henry Brougham b 12 Nov 1971); *Career* called to the Bar Inner Temple 1970; recorder of the Crown Ct 1986-; *Recreations* shooting, stalking, theatre, Sweden; *Clubs* Garrick, Pratts, Queen's, Swinley Forest Golf; *Style*— Michael Sayers, Esq, QC; 2 Harcourt Buildings, Temple, London, EC4Y 9DB (☎ 071 353 2112, fax 071 353 8339)

SAYLE, Alexei David; s of Joseph Henry Sayle (d 1983), of Liverpool and Malka, *née* Mendelson; *b* 7 Aug 1952; *Educ* Alsop HS Liverpool, Southport Art Sch Lancs, Chelsea Sch of Art (DipAD), Garnet Coll Roehampton London (CertEd); *m* Linda Eleanor, da of Noel Rawsthorn; *Career* comedian actor and writer; master of ceremonies: Comedy Store Club 1979-80, Comic Strip Club 1980-81; various solo tours as stand-up comedian; TV work incl: The Young Ones 1982-85, The Strike 1987, Alexei Sayle's Stuff 1988-91, Night Voice 1990, Itch 1991, Selling Hitler 1991: films: Gorky Park 1983, Supergrass 1985, Siesta 1986, Indiana Jones and the Last Crusade 1989; single released Ullo John! Gotta New Motor? 1984; columnist: Time Out, Sunday Mirror; Best Comedy awards: Pye Radio 1981, RTS 1988, Broadcast Press Guild 1988, International Emmy 1988; *Books* Train to Hell (1982), Geoffrey the Tube Train and the Fat Comedian (1987), Great Bus Journeys of the World (1988); *Recreations* cycling, shooting, re-using envelopes; *Clubs* The Fridge; *Style*— Alexei Sayle, Esq; c/o Mayer Management, 2-3 Golden Square, London W1 (☎ 071 434 1242)

SAYWELL, (John Anthony) Telfer; JP (Richmond 1985); s of Maj John Rupert Saywell (d 1948), of Kensington, London, and Winifred, *née* Green (d 1980); *b* 19 Aug 1939; *Educ* Abingdon Sch, Open Univ (BA); *m* 8 June 1968, June Mary, da of Maurice Thomas Hunnable (d 1972), of Rivenhall, Essex; 2 s (Thomas b 1971, Henry b 1977), 1 da (Polly b 1969); *Career* CA; Fincham Vallance & Co 1958-63, Tansley Witt & Co 1963-69; Layton Fern & Co Ltd (coffee and tea specialists): joined 1969, md 1970, chm 1975-; underwriting memb of Lloyds 1983-; pres UK Coffee Trade Benevolent Soc 1985-86, govr RSC 1982-; treas: Harlequin FC 1971-78, Union Soc City of Westminster 1985-, St Lukes Educnl Centre 1989-; hon auditor Richmond Upon Thames Disabled Assoc 1973-, master Billingsgate Ward Club 1987-88; Freeman City of London 1981, memb Ct Assts Worshipful Co of Carmen 1986; FCA 1964; *Recreations* sailing, studying, skiing; *Clubs* Harlequin FC, Leander, Br Sportsman's, Surrey RFU; *Style*— Telfer Saywell, Esq, JP; 2 Cumberland Rd, Kew Gardens, Richmond, Surrey TW9 3HQ (☎ 081 940 0298); Layton Fern & Co Ltd, 27 Rathbone Place, London WIP 2EP (☎ 071 636 2237, fax 071 580 2869)

SCADDING, Prof John Guyett (Guy); s of John William Scadding (d 1960), of London, and Jessima Alice, *née* Guyett (d 1959); *b* 30 Aug 1907; *Educ* Mercers' Sch, Middx Hosp Med Sch Univ of London (MB BS, MD); *m* 30 Aug 1940, Mabel, da of John Pennington (d 1962), of Cheshire; 1 s (John b 1948), 2 da (Jane (Mrs Jarvis) b 1949, Sarah (Mrs Fielder) b 1950); *Career* WWII served in RAMC 1940-45: M East 1941-45, Maj 1940, Lt-Col 1942; hon conslt in diseases of the chest Army 1952-72 (awarded Guthrie medal 1973); jr hosp appts 1930-33, res med offr Brompton Hosp 1931-35; Royal (formerly Br) Postgrad Med Sch and Hammersmith Hosp: first asst Dept of Med 1935-45, sr lectr 1945-62; hon conslt physician Hammersmith Hosp 1935-, conslt physician Brompton Hosp 1939-; Inst for Diseases of the Chest Univ of London: dean 1946-60, dir of studies 1950-62, prof of med 1962-72 (emeritus 1972-); Royal College of Physicians: censor 1968-69, second vice pres 1971, Moxon medal 1974; visiting prof: Stanford Univ of Univ of Colorado 1965, McMaster Univ 1973, Univ of Manitoba 1974, Chicago 1976, Dalhousie Univ 1977; pres: Br TB Assoc 1959-61, Med Section RSM 1969-71, Thoracic Soc 1970-71, ed Thorax 1946-60; memb Standing Med Advsy Ctee and Central Health Servs Cncl Miny of Health 1954-66 (chm Standing TB Advsy Ctee), conslt advsr in diseases of the chest DHSS 1960-72, memb Clinical Res Bd MRC 1969-65, chm Industl Med Panel NCB 1962-72; hon memb: Société Francaise de la Tuberculose et des Maladies Respiratoires, Sociedad Espanola de Anatomia Patologica, Canadian Thoracic Soc; Freeman City of London 1950, Liveryman Worshipful Soc of Apothecaries 1950; Doctor Honoris Causa Univ Reims 1978; FRCP; *Books* Sarcoidosis (first edn 1967, second edn 1985); *Recreations* music, walking (preferably in hills); *Clubs* Athenaeum; *Style*— Prof Guy Scadding; 18 Seagrave Rd, Beaconsfield, Bucks HP9 1SU (☎ 0494 676033)

SCALES, Prof John Tracey; OBE (1986); s of Walter Laurence Scales (d 1972), of Heathfield, Wierfields, Totnes, and Ethel Margaret, *née* Tracey (d 1949); *b* 2 July 1920; *Educ* Haberdashers' Aske's, King's Coll London, Charing Cross Hosp Med Sch; *m* 22 May 1945, Cecilia May, da of Albert Wesley Sparrow (d 1960), of 67 Newport Rd, Barnstaple, Devon; 2 da (Sally (Mrs Miller) b 1949, Helen (Mrs Hargreaves) b 1955); *Career* Capt RAMC 1945-47; casualty and res anaesthetist Charing Cross Hosp 1944, Royal Nat Orthopaedic Hosp 1947-87 (hon conslt 1958-); Inst of Orthopaedics Univ of London 1951-87 (prof biomedical engrg 1974-87); hon conslt: Mt Vernon Hosp 1969-85, Royal Orthopaedic Hosp Birmingham 1978-87; emeritus prof Univ of London 1985-; hon conslt and hon dir RAFT Dept of Res in Plastic Surgery Mt Vernon Hosp 1988-; memb: Cncl Friends of the RNO Hosp, Action Ctee RNOH; tstee Restoration of Appearance and Function Tst Mt Vernon Hosp, memb advsy panel on med engrg Action Res, fndr memb Euro Soc of Biomechanics; MRCS, LRCP (1944), FRCS (1969), CIMechE (1966); memb: RSM, BSI, ISO; *Recreations* walking dogs, collecting Goss china; *Style*— Prof John Scales, OBE; 17 Brockley Avenue, Stanmore, Middx HA7 4LX (☎ 081 958 8773); RAFT Dept of Research in Plastic Surgery, Mount Vernon Hospital, Northwood, Middx HA6 2RN (☎ 0895 783 50, fax 0895 78031)

SCALES, Prunella Margaret Rumney; *née* Illingworth; da of John Richardson Illingworth (d 1977), and Catherine, *née* Scales (d 1982); *Educ* Moira House Eastbourne, Old Vic Theatre Sch London; *m* 1963, Timothy Lancaster West, s of H Lockwood West, of Brighton, Sussex; 2 s (Samuel b 1966, Joseph b 1969); *Career* actress, dir and teacher; seasons at Stratford-on-Avon and Chichester Festival Theatre 1967-68; plays on London stage include: The Promise 1967, Hay Fever 1968, It's a Two-Foot-Six-Inches-Above-The-Ground-World 1970, The Wolf 1975, Breezeblock Park 1978, Make and Break (Haymarket) 1980, An Evening with Queen Victoria 1980, The Merchant of Venice 1981, Quartermaine's Terms (Queen's) 1981, When We Are Married (Whitehall), Single Spies 1989, School for Scandal (NT) 1990; television: Fawlty Towers 1975-79, Doris and Doreen, A Wife like the Moon, Grand Duo, The Merry Wives of Windsor 1982, Outside Edge, Mapp and Lucia 1985, After Henry 1990; films include: The Lonely Passion of Judith Hearne (1989), A Chorus of Disapproval (1989); frequent broadcasts, readings, poetry recitals and fringe productions, has directed plays at: Bristol Old Vic, Arts Theatre Cambridge, Billingham Forum, Almost Free Theatre London, Nottingham Playhouse, Nat Theatre of WA Perth; taught at several drama schools; *Recreations* gardening, canal boat; *Clubs* BBC; *Style*— Prunella Scales; c/o Jeremy Conway Ltd, 109 Jermyn Street, London W1 (☎ 071 287 0077)

SCAMELL, Ernest Harold; s of Capt Ernest Harold Scamell (d 1981), and Lilian Kate, *née* Hall; *b* 9 March 1928; *Educ* Frays Coll Uxbridge, King's Coll London (LLB, LLM, AKC); *m* 1, 22 Aug 1952 (*m* dis), Patricia Annie, da of Percy Bullock (d 1979); 2 s (Grant b 11 Nov 1956, Adrian b 9 July 1958), 2 da (Joanna b 9 May 1960, Amanda b 19 Oct 1963); m 2, 11 Sept 1977, Ragnhild Bennedsen, da of Viggo Holdt, of Nyborg, Denmark; 1 step child (Cleere b 16 Nov 1967); *Career* called to the Bar Lincoln's Inn 1949; prof English law Univ of London 1966-90 (reader 1960-66), head of Chambers Lincoln's Inn 1971-, vice provost UCL 1978-84, prof emeritus of Eng law Univ of London 1990-; memb Bar Cncl; *Books* Precedents for the Conveyancer (1970-77), Lindley on Partnership (co ed, 1984), Butterworths Property Law Handbook (2 edn, 1989); *Recreations* flying, model building; *Clubs* Holy Trinity Meccano, Air Touring Flying; *Style—* Ernest Scamell, Esq; Oak Farm, Kennington, Ashford, Kent TN24 9BH (☎ 0233 628453); 5 New Sq, Lincoln's Inn, London WC2A 3RJ (☎ 071 405 6171/4797)

SCAMPTON, Ann Barbara; da of John Ewart March, MC (d 1984), and Laura Vera, *née* Vale (d 1981); *b* 2 Feb 1933; *Educ* Cathedral Sch for Girls Shanghai, Lunghwa Acad, Clifton HS for Girls, Royal West of England Acad Sch of Architecture; *m* 7 Aug 1954, Peter Gregory Scampton, s of Gregory Oliver Scampton (d 1970), of Bristol; 3 da (Gillian b 12 June 1959, Sarah b 15 Feb 1961, Katie b 15 Feb 1961 (twin)); *Career* architect; founded own practice 1965, amalgamated with Moxley Jenner and Ptnrs 1972, co-fndr dir and co sec Moxley Jenner and Ptnrs (London) Ltd 1986-; pres Bristol Soc of Architects, govr Clifton HS for Girls Bristol; FRIBA, RWA; *Recreations* painting, sailing; *Clubs* Crusing Assoc; *Style—* Ms Ann Scampton; Moxley Jenner & Partners (London) Ltd, 1 Hobhouse Court, Suffolk St, London SW1

SCANLAN, Charles Denis; s of late Francis Joseph Winsloe Scanlan, and late Eileen, *née* Terry; *b* 23 Dec 1944; *Educ* St Benedict's Sch Ealing, Balliol College Oxford (BA); *m* 11 Sept 1971, Dorothy, da of Frederick Albert Quick, of Laleston, Mid Glam; 2 s (Christopher b 1977, Stephen b 1980); *Career* admitted slr 1970; Simmons & Simmons: articled clerk 1967-70, asst slr 1970-73, ptnr 1973-; Freeman City Slrs Co; memb Law Soc; *Books* Know Your Rights (jtly, 1975); *Style—* Charles Scanlan, Esq; Simmons & Simmons, 14 Dominion St, London EC2M 2RJ (☎ 071 628 2020, fax 071 588 4129, telex 888562)

SCANLAN, Charles John; s of Michael Herbert Scanlan (d 1963), of London, and Mary Ann, *née* Inglis (d 1963); *b* 4 Sept 1920; *Educ* Robert Browning Sch, Archbishop Tenison's Sch; *m* 1, 24 Dec 1949 (m dis 1973), Doris Elsie, 2 s (Phillip b 4 Feb 1951, Michael b 1 Dec 1960), 1 da (Christine b 6 Jan 1954); m 2, 1973, Jennifer Jane, da of Dr Thomas; 1 da (Camilla b 13 Nov 1976); *Career* Essex Regt 1939-41, Middx Regt 1941-47: 2 Lt 1941, Lt 1943, Capt 1943, Maj 1944, Lt Col 1947; demob 1947; export mangr Coty Ltd 1948-69, export dir and gen sales mangr Fizer Ltd 1948-69, chief exec Revlon Ltd 1976 (gen sales dir 1969, gen mangr 1973), exec vice pres Revlon Int 1979, chief exec Revlon UK 1986-; dir: Vagabond Ltd 1987, Austin Morgan Ltd, chm Browns of Melbourne Ltd; memb ctee friends of Perse School (Cambridge); MIEX 1970, FBIM 1980, FInstD 1986; *Clubs* Les Ambassadors, Henry's Bar; *Style—* Charles Scanlan, Esq; Wheel Hall, Cole End Lane, Sewards End, Saffron Walden, Essex (☎ 0799 27477); 86 Brook St, London W1 (☎ 01 629 7400)

SCANLON, Baron (Life Peer UK 1979), of Davyhulme, Co Greater Manchester; Hugh Parr Scanlon; s of Hugh Scanlon; *b* 26 Oct 1913, in Australia; *Educ* Stretford Elementary Sch, Nat Council of Labour Colls; *m* 1943, Nora, da of James Markey; 2 da; *Career* apprentice instrument maker; chm Engrg Industry Training Bd until 1982; memb British Gas Corp 1976-, pres AEUW 1968-78 (formerly div organiser and memb London Exec Cncl); Hon DCL Kent 1988; *Style—* The Rt Hon the Lord Scanlon; 23 Seven Stones Drive, Broadstairs, Kent

SCANNELL, Vernon; *b* 23 Jan 1922; *Educ* Univ of Leeds; *m* 1 Oct 1954, Josephine, da of Lt-Col Claude Higson, of Edenbridge, Kent; 3 s (Toby b 1959, John b 1961, Jacob b 1967), 2 da (Jane b 1955, Nancy b 1957); *Career* 70 Bn Argyll & Sutherland Highlanders 1940-42, 5/7 Bn Gordon Highlanders 1942-45; poet in res: Berinsfield Oxfordshire 1975-76, King's Sch Canterbury 1979, Wakefield Dist Coll 1987, Mount Sch York 1987; awards: Heinemann Award for Lit 1961, Cholmondeley Poetry Prize 1974, Travelling Scholarship Soc of Authors 1987; FRSL 1961; *Books* A Sense of Danger (1962), Walking Wounded (1965), Epithets of War (1968), New and Collected Poems (1980), The Tiger and the Rose, An Autobiography (1971), Argument of Kings (1987); *Style—* Vernon Scannell, Esq; 51 North Street, Otley, W Yorks LSL2 1AH (☎ 0943 467 176)

SCARBOROUGH, Ian Patrick; s of HA Scarborough (d 1968), of Taplow, and Mrs DA Scarborough, *née* Wayne (d 1971); *b* 8 Feb 1932; *Educ* The Leys Sch, Univ of Nottingham (Dip) Univ of Bath (MSc); *m* 20 Sept 1958, B Ann, da of F L Huxtable (d 1978), of Pulborough; 2 s (Alistair b 5 Sept 1960, Matthew b 25 Dec 1962), 1 da (Vanessa b 14 Dec 1961); *Career* Nat Serv; asst asst dir Tea Res Fndn CA 1954-84; gen mangr Bandange Ltd Malawi 1989- (asst gen mangr 1984-89); tstee and branch chm Wildlife Soc of Malawi; *Style—* Ian Scarborough, Esq; P/Bag 2, Bvumbwe, Malawi (☎ 010 265 662434)

SCARBROUGH, Countess of; Lady Elizabeth; *née* Ramsay; da of 16 Earl of Dalhousie, KT, GCVO, GBE, MC; *b* 16 Sept 1941; *m* 1970, 12 Earl of Scarbrough, *qv*; *Style—* The Countess of Scarbrough; Sandbeck Park, Maltby, Rotherham, Yorks

SCARBROUGH, 12 Earl of (E 1690); Richard Aldred Lumley; DL (S Yorks 1974); also Viscount Lumley of Waterford (I 1628), Baron Lumley of Lumley Castle (E 1681), and Viscount Lumley of Lumley Castle (E 1690); s of 11 Earl, KG, GCSI, GCIE, GCVO (d 1969); *b* 5 Dec 1932; *Educ* Eton, Magdalen Coll Oxford; *m* 1970, Lady Elizabeth, *née* Ramsay, da of 16 Earl of Dalhousie, KT, GCVO, GBE, MC; 2 s (Richard Osbert b 18 May 1973, Thomas Henry b 6 Feb 1980), 1 da (Rose Frederica Lily b 31 Aug 1981); *Heir* s, Viscount Lumley; *Career* Lt Queen's Own Yorks Dragoons and 2 Lt 11 Hussars, ADC to Govr and C in C Cyprus 1956, Hon Col 1 Bn Yorks Volunteers 1975-88; pres N Area Royal Br Legion 1984; *Style—* The Rt Hon the Earl of Scarbrough, DL; Sandbeck Park, Maltby, Rotherham, S Yorks (☎ Doncaster 742210)

SCARFE, Gerald Anthony; s of Reginald Thomas Scarfe, and Dorothy Edna, *née* Garuner; *b* 1 June 1936; *m* Jane, da of Dr Richard Asher (d 1968), of 57 Wimpole St, London; 2 s (Alexander David b 16 Dec 1981, Rory Christopher b 10 Dec 1983), 1 da (Katie Geraldine b 11 April 1974); *Career* political cartoonist of the Sunday Times 1967-88; designer of theatre scenery and costumes: Orpheus in the Underworld (London Coliseum), What a Lucky Boy (Manchester Royal Exchange), Ubu Roi (Traverse Theatre), and many others; designer and dir of animation Pink Floyd the Wall MGM; dir of films for the BBC: Hogarth 1970, Scarfe by Scarfe 1986, Scarfes Follies 1987, I Like The Girls Who Do 1988, Scarfe on --- 1989; *Books* Scarfe by Scarfe (1986), Scarfes Seaven Deadly Sins (1987), Scarfes Line of Attack (1988), Scarfeland (1989); *Recreations* skiing; *Clubs* Brooks's; *Style—* Gerald Scarfe, Esq

SCARFFE, Dr John Howard; s of late Andrew Ernest, of Douglas, IOM, and Nancy May, *née* Fargher; *b* 11 March 1947; *Educ* King Williams Coll IOM, St Bartholomews Hosp Med Coll Univ of London (MB BS, MD); *m* 8 Jan 1972, Sheila Elizabeth, da of Alfred Coyte, of Broadstairs, Kent; 1 s (Christopher), 1 da (Elizabeth); *Career* house surgn Addenbrooks Hosp Cambridge 1971-72, sr house offr gen med Barts Hosp 1972-74 (house physician 1971), sr lectr and hon conslt Univ of Manchester 1980- (lectr and hon sr registrar 1976-80, lectr and hon registrar 1974-76), dir Regnl Acute Leukaemia and Bone Marrow Transplant Unit Christie Hosp Manchester and Hope Hosp Salford; publications chapters in a number of oncological textbooks; memb: Teaching Faculty Int Union Against Cancer 1980, S Manchester Health Authy 1983-89, NW Regnl Advsy Ctee for Oncology Services 1985-; MRCS 1970, FRCP 1986 (MRCP 1973, LRCP 1970); *Recreations* rugby, walking, reading; *Clubs* Lymm Rugby Football; *Style—* Dr J Howard Scarffe; Four Winds, Cinder Lane, Thelwall, Cheshire WA4 3JL (☎ 0925 63549); Cancer Research Campaign, Department of Medical Oncology, Univeristy of Manchester, Christie Hospital, Wilmslow Rd, Manchester M20 9BX (☎ 061 445 8123, fax 061 434 7728)

SCARISBRICK, Diana; da of Charles Wood, of Stoke Gabriel, Devon, and Genevieve, *née* Sutherland; *b* 8 Oct 1928; *Educ* Christ's Hosp, St Hugh's College Oxford (MA); *m* 5 July 1955, Peter Ewald Scarisbrick, s of Charles Ewald Scarisbrick (d 1966); 1 da (Sophie Hastings-Bass b 15 May 1956); *Career* freelance lectr and writer on jewellery and engraved gems; jewellery ed Harpers and Queen Magazine 1990-; contrib to: Burlington Magazine, Apollo Magazine, Country Life Magazine, Il Giornale Dell'Arte, exhibition and museum catalogues in Britain Germany and USA; memb: Soc of Antiquaries, Soc of Jewellery Historians; *Books* The Ralph Harari Collection of Finger Rings (with Prof John Boardman, 1977), Jewellery (1984), Il Valore Dei Gioielli e Degli Orologi da Collezione (1984 and 1987), 2500 Years of Rings (1988), Ancestral Jewels (1989); *Recreations* walking, sight-seeing; *Clubs* Lansdowne; *Style—* Mrs Diana Scarisbrick; 11 Chester Terrace, London NW1 4ND (☎ 071 935 9928)

SCARLETT, Albert James Morton; s of Albert James Scarlett (d 1975), of Fife, and Janet Dall, *née* Venters; *b* 25 Aug 1946; *Educ* The Royal HS Edinburgh, Edinburgh Sch of Architecture, Heriot Watt Univ (BArch); *m* 24 Aug 1968, Jean Bell, da of James Stenhouse (d 1969); 1 s (Euan b 1972), 1 da (Victoria b 1975); *Career* architect; City of Dundee DC 1972-79, area tech offr The Housing Corp (Glasgow) 1979-82, chartered architect in private practice 1982; MRIBA; ARIAS; *Recreations* reading, social and charitable activities, bowls, building; *Style—* Albert J M Scarlett, Esq; Strathyre Cottage, Longcroft by Bonnybridge, Stirlingshire (☎ 0324 841331); Morton Scarlett Associates, Chartered Architects, 91 Townhead, Kirkintilloch, Glasgow G66 1NX (☎ 041 776 0731)

SCARLETT, Hon James Harry; s and h of 8 Baron Abinger, DL, *qv*; *b* 28 May 1959; *Style—* The Hon James Scarlett

SCARLETT, His Hon James Harvey Anglin; s of Lt-Col James Alexander Scarlett, DSO (d 1925), and Muriel Blease (d 1945); *b* 27 Jan 1924; *Educ* Shrewsbury, ChCh Oxford (MA); *Career* Lt RA 1944-47; called to the Bar Inner Temple 1950, Malayan Civil Serv 1955-58, rec of the Crown Court 1972-74, circuit judge 1974-89; *Recreations* walking; *Clubs* Athenaeum; *Style—* His Hon James Scarlett; Chilmington Green, Great Chart, nr Ashford, Kent

SCARLETT, The Hon John Leopold Campbell; CBE (1973); s of 7 Baron Abinger, DSO (d 1943); *b* 18 Dec 1916; *Educ* Eton, Magdalene Coll Cambridge; *m* 26 April 1947, Bridget, da of late H B Crook, of Kensington; 2 s, 1 da; *Career* formerly Maj RA; *Style—* The Hon John Scarlett, CBE; Bramblewood, Castle Walk, Wadhurst, Sussex TN5 6DB

SCARLETT-STREATFEILD, Cdr Norman John; DSC (1940); s of Air Vice-Marshal Francis Rowland Scarlett, CB, DSO (d 1934 (*see* Burke's LG 18th Edn, vol ii), and yr bro of AVM James Rowland Scarlett-Streatfeild, CBE (d 1945), who assumed the latter surname upon inheriting the The Rocks, Uckfield, Sussex (sold 1979); and Dora, *née* Blakiston-Houston (d 1954) (*see* Burke's Irish family Records, 1976); *b* 4 Aug 1910; *Educ* RNC Dartmouth; *m* 14 Dec 1938, Pamela Susan (d 1990), da of Lt Col Richard Oakley, DSO, JP; 1 s (John b 1949), 4 da (Sarah Penelope b 1940, Anne b 1946, Rosemary b 1951 d 1952, Caroline b 1953); *Career* Naval Offr WWII; served: HMS Glorious 1938-40, HMS Illustrious 1940; took part in Fleet Air Arm attack on Taranto 1940 (POW 1940-45) (despatches 1945), various naval appts until ret 1958; *Recreations* sailing, fishing, gardening; *Clubs* The Farmers, Whitehall; *Style—* Cdr Norman J Scarlett-Streatfeild, DSC; The Field House, East Tytherton, nr Chippenham, Wilts (☎ 024 974 268)

SCARMAN, Baron (Life Peer UK 1977), of Quatt, Co Shropshire; Leslie George Scarman; OBE (1944), PC (1972); s of late George Charles Scarman; *b* 29 July 1911; *Educ* Radley, BNC Oxford (MA); *m* 1947, Ruth Clement, da of late Clement Wright; 1 adopted s (John Clement b 1946); *Career* sits as Ind peer in House of Lords; called to the Bar Middle Temple 1936; QC 1957, judge of the High Court 1961-72, Lord Justice of Appeal 1972-77, Lord of Appeal in Ordinary 1977-86; chm: Law Cmmn 1965-72, Tbnl Inquiry NI 1969-72; author of report into Brixton riots 1981; chllr Univ of Warwick 1977-89, visitor St Hilda's Coll Oxford, pres RIPA 1981-87, former memb Arts Cncl, pres Thanet Archaeological Soc; hon memb American Philosophical Soc; hon fell BNC Oxford, LSE; Hon DCL Univ of Oxford 1982; Hon MD: Univ of Glasgow, Univ of Kent, Univ of Dundee, Univ of London, Univ of Warwick, Univ of Wales, Queen's Univ Belfast, Univ of Freiburg, Univ of Keele, Univ of Exeter; kt 1961; *Style—* The Rt Hon the Lord Scarman, OBE, PC; House of Lords, London SW1

SCARPELLO, Dr John Hugh; s of William John Scarpello, of Sheffield, and Pauline Francis, *née* Berney; *b* 23 July 1947; *Educ* Haberdashers Askes, Welsh Nat Sch of Med Cardiff (MB, BCh, MD); *m* 20 April 1974, Barbara Jean, da of William John Erasmus; 1 s (Robert John b 27 April 1981), 2 da (Kay Elizabeth b 11 July 1975, Tracey Jane b 30 July 1977); *Career* house offr Univ Hosp of Wales 1971-72, sr house offr Nottingham Gen Hosp 1972-74, med registrar Royal Hosp Sheffield 1974-76, sr registrar Royal Hallamshire Hosp 1976-81, hon clinical tutor Univ of Sheffield 1976-81, conslt physician N Staffs Royal Infirmary 1981-, sr res fell Univ of Keele 1981-; divnl surgn St Johns Ambulance Stoke div; memb: scientific section Br Diabetic Assoc, Med Res Soc; FRCP 1989 (MRCP 1974); *Recreations* squash, swimming, walking; *Style—* Dr John Scarpello; Newlyn, Seabridge Lane, Newcastle, Staffs ST5 3LS (☎ 0782 613682); Department of Endocrinology and Diabetes, North Staffs Royal Infirmary, Princes Rd, Hartshill, Stoke on Trent ST4 7LN (☎ 0782 49144)

SCARR, Lady Davina Jane; 2 da of 6 Earl of Erne; *b* 25 June 1961; *m* 12 May 1990, Nicholas J R Scarr, er s of late Peter R R Scarr; *Style—* Lady Davina Scarr

SCARSDALE, 3 Viscount (UK 1911); Sir Francis John Nathaniel Curzon; 11 Bt (S 1636) and 11 Bt (E 1641); also 7 Baron Scarsdale (GB 1761); 30 Lord (territorial lordship) of Kedleston; s of late Hon Francis Nathaniel Curzon (yr bro of 1 & and last Marquess Curzon of Kedleston and s of 4 Baron Scarsdale), and Phyllis, da of Capt Christian Combe, by his w, Lady Jane Seymour, da of 3 Marquess Conyngham; *b* 28 July 1924; *Educ* Eton; *m* 1, 1948 (m dis 1967), Solange Yvonne Palmyre Ghislaine (d 1974), da of late Oscar Hanse, of Mont-sur-Marchienne, Belgium; 2 s, 1 da; m 2, 1968, Helene Gladys Frances, da of late Maj William Ferguson Thomson, of Kinellar, Aberdeenshire; 2 s; *Heir* s, Hon Peter Curzon; *Career* late Capt Scots Gds; *Recreations* piping, photography, shooting; *Clubs* County, Derby; *Style—* The Rt Hon the Viscount Scarsdale; Kedleston Hall, Derby (☎ 0332 840386)

SCARSDALE, Ottilie, Viscountess; Ottilie Margarete Julie; da of late Charles Pretzlik, of Lowfield Park, Crawley, and Ottilie Hennig; *b* 19 Nov 1905; *Educ* North

Foreland Lodge, Finishing School Berchtesgarden Bavaria and Munich; *m* 1, 1925, James Henry Harris; 2 s; m 2, 1946, as his 2 w, 2 Viscount Scarsdale (d 1977); *Career* Ensign FANY; *Recreations* fishing, gardening, travel; *Style—* The Rt Hon Ottilie, Viscountess Scarsdale; The Dower House, Rowler Manor, Croughton, Brackley, Northants (☎ 0869 810438)

SCHAEFER, Prof Stephen Martin; s of Gerhardt Martin Schaefer, OBE (d 1986), of Bramhall, Cheshire, and Helga Maria Schaefer; *b* 18 Nov 1946; *Educ* Manchester GS, Univ of Cambridge (BA, MA), Univ of London (PhD); *m* 26 July 1969, Teresa Evelyn; 2 s (Maximilian b 1974, Joshua b 1977); *Career* London Business Sch: res offr, sr res offr, lectr 1970-79; Stanford Univ asst prof 1979-80; visting asst prof: Univ of Chicago, Univ of California (Berkeley) 1977; sr res fell Prof of Finance London Business Sch 1981-; dir: Lawtex plc 1974-, The Securities Assoc 1990-; memb American Fin Assoc; *Style—* Prof Stephen Schaefer; London Business Sch, Sussex Place, Regents Park, London NW1 4SA (☎ 01 262 5050)

SCHAFFER, Louis Isaac; s of Harry Schaffer (d 1963), and Harriet, *née* Burman (d 1965); *b* 22 April 1930; *Educ* Luton GS, Trinity Coll Cambridge (MA, LLB); *m* 1 Jan 1961, Nina Valerie, da of Raymond Richard Thomas; 2 s (Daniel) b 13 Oct 1963, Benjamim b 5 May 1965), 1 da (Rachel b 8 April 1967); *Career* RAOC: 1949-62, Capt 1954; called to the Bar Middle Temple 1955; memb Brent Police Liason Gp 1985-, Bd of Deps of Br Jews 1985-; *Recreations* walking the dog; *Style—* Louis Schaffer, Esq; 3 Barn Rise, Wembley Park, Middlesex HA9 9NA; 10 King's Bench Walk, Temple, London EC4Y 7EB (☎ 071 353 2501)

SCHANSCHIEFF, Simon George; JP (1971-); s of Brian Alexander Schanschieff, and Nina, *née* Robinson (d 1990); *b* 22 Oct 1938; *Educ* Oakham Sch Rutland; *m* 27 June 1964, Arman Philippa (Pip), da of Charles Henry Arman (d 1970); 3 s (Guy b 1966, Christopher b 1968, Nicholas b 1978); *Career* qualified CA 1961; ptnr Grant Thornton Northampton 1966- (regnl managing ptnr 1989), chm Northampton Health Authy 1978-; chm tstees Oakham Sch 1980-, memb Ctee Northants CCC 1969-; FCA 1971; *Style—* Simon Schanschieff, Esq, JP; Old Rectory, Great Billing, Northampton (☎ 0604 407842); Elgin House, Billing Rd, Northampton (☎ 0604 27811)

SCHAUFUSS, Peter; *b* 26 April 1950; *Educ* Royal Danish Ballet Sch; *Career* apprenticeship Royal Danish Ballet Co 1965 and soloist 1969-70; Soloist Nat Ballet of Canada 1967-68, princ London Festival Ballet 1970-74, New York City Ballet 1974-77, National Ballet of Canada 1977-83; numerous guest appearances incl: Royal Ballet, Nat Ballet of Canada, Ballet of Canada, Ballet National de Marseille, La Scala Milan, Vienna State Opera, Tokyo Ballet Co, American Ballet Theatre, Royal Danish Ballet, Deutsche Oper Berlin, Scottish Ballet, Bavarian State Opera, Paris Opera, Teatro dell'Opera (Rome), Teatro Comunale (Florence); prodns incl: La Sylphide London Festival Ballet 1979, Ballet National de Marseille 1980, Deutsche Oper Berlin 1982, Stuttgart Ballet 1982, Teatro Comunale Firenze 1983, Vienna State Opera 1990, Operuhaus Zurich 1990, Napoli Nat Ballet of Canada 1981, Teatro San Carlo 1988, English National Ballet 1989, Folktale Deutsche Oper Berlin 1983, Dances from Napoli London Festival Ballet 1983, Bournonville Aterballetto 1984, The Nutcracker London Festival Ballet 1986; cr roles: George Balanchine The Steadfast Tin Soldier 1975, Rhapsodie Espagnole 1975, Roland Petit Phantom of the Opera 1980, Sir Kenneth MacMillan Verdi Variations 1982, Orpheus 1982; BBC TV ballet series: Dancer 1984, Phantom of the Opera 1980, documentary Great Dancers of the World French TV; present profession: dancer, choreographer, producer; artistic dir London Festival Ballet (now English National Ballet) 1984-90, ballet dir Deutsche Oper Berlin 1990-; Solo award 2nd Int Ballet Competition Moscow 1973, Stern des jahres (Star of the year) Fed Rep of Germany 1979, Soc of W End Theatres award for ballet 1979, Evening Standard award for most outstanding achievement in dance 1979, Manchester Evening News Theatre Awards-Dance 1986; created Knight of the Dannebrog 1988; *Recreations* boxing; *Style—* Peter Schaufuss, Esq; c/o Papoutsis Representation Ltd, 18 Sundial Ave, London SE25 4BX

SCHEER, Cherrill Sheila; *née* Hille; da of Maurice Hille (d 1968), and Ray Hille (d 1986); *b* 29 March 1939; *Educ* Copthall Co GS, Architectural Assoc London, Architectural Dept Kingston Sch of Art; *m* 3 Dec 1961, Ian Scheer, s of Oscar Scheer (d 1988); 1 s (TIvan), 1 da (Danielle Ann (Mrs Benson)); *Career* mktg dir Hille International Ltd 1970-83 (mktg mangr 1961-70); dir: Print Forum Ltd 1965-, S Hille & Co (Holdings) Ltd 1970; dir gp mktg: Hille Ergonom plc 1983-89, Scott Howard Furniture Ltd 1989-; vice pres Design & Indust Assoc (chm 1976-78); memb: Advsy Bd Sir John Cass Faculty of Arts Design and Manufacture City Poly, cncl Electronic Engrg and Business Equipment Assoc (chm Furniture Div); fell: Chartered Soc of Designers, Inst of Sales and Mktg Mgmnt; *Style—* Mrs Ian Scheer; 16 Kerry Ave, Stanmore, Middx HA7 4NN (☎ 081 954 3839); Scott Howard Furniture Ltd, Grimaldi Park, 154a Pentonville Rd, London N1 9JE (☎ 071 278 0440, fax 071 278 0448)

SCHEFFERS, Peter Anthony; s of Jean Maurice Scheffers (d 1950), and Vera Veronica Whately (d 1949); *b* 9 June 1924; *Educ* Downside, St Georges, ChCh Oxford (BSc); *m* 17 Dec 1954, Josephine Jean, da of Charles Johnson (d 1965), of Weybridge; 1 da (Sally Louise b 1960); *Career* Capt cmmnd RCS 1942; served Cairo joined SOE, captured in Yugoslavia 1944 (POW in Germany), invalided out of army 1945; joined father's textile importing business (took control 1950), ret; farmer of 128 acres; Freeman City of London 1954, memb Worshipful Co of Horners (memb Court of Assistants 1977-87); Goldene Ehrenzeichen (Austria) 1984; *Clubs* Special Forces (fndr memb 1945-46); *Style—* Peter A Scheffers, Esq; Punch Bowl Farm, Thursley, Godalming, Surrey GU8 6QJ

SCHER, Anna Valerie; da of Dr Eric Asher Scher (d 1982) and Constance, *née* Hurwitz (d 1984); *b* 26 Dec 1944; *Educ* St Angela's Coll Cork Eire, Hove Co GS Sussex, Trent Park Coll Cockfosters (Gen Teachers Cert), Brighton Sch Music and Drama (dip Drama); *m* 1976, Charles Verrall; 1 s (John Benedict b 1980); *Career* fndr and princ Anna Scher Theatre 1968-; drama workshops at: Round House, Sadler's Wells, Unicorn, Young Vic, numerous schs, hosps, libraries; TV: First Act (LWT) 1975, The Kids Are United (Man Alive Special, BBC2) 1982, Ain't Many Angels (BBC2) 1980, Acting with Anna (C4) 1983, Anna Scher on Acting (Danish TV) 1985, Desperate to Act (BBC) 1988, Drama with Anna 1988, When will I be Famous? (ITV) 1988; contribs to: Aquarius, Good Afternoon, Kaleidoscope, Tonight, Woman's Hour, TV-am; assoc RADA 1983; memb: Jury BAFTA 1984, Jury Sony Awards 1987; Community Award Irish Post 1983, Woman of Distinction Award 1988, nominated Woman of Europe 1990; *Books* 100+ Ideas for Drama (with Charles Verrall 1975), First Act Drama Kit (1976), Another 100+ Ideas for Drama (1987); Desperate to Act (1988); *Recreations* theatre-going, books, restaurants; *Style—* Ms Anna Scher; The Anna Scher Theatre, 70-72 Barnsbury Rd, London N1 OES (☎ 071 278 2101, fax 071 833 9467)

SCHIEMANN, Hon Mr Justice; Hon Sir Konrad Hermann Theodor; s of Helmuth Schiemann (d 1945), and Beate Schiemann, *née* von Simson (d 1946); *b* 15 Sept 1937; *Educ* King Edwards Sch Birmingham, Pembroke Coll Cambridge (MA, LLB); *m* 1965, Elisabeth Hanna Eleonore, da of late John Holroyd-Reece; 1 da (Juliet b 1966); *Career* jr counsel to the Crown (Common Law) 1978-80; QC 1980, rec Crown Court 1985, bencher Inner Temple 1985, High Court judge (Queen's Bench Div) 1986-; memb: Cncl St John's Smith Square 1984- (tstee 1990) Parole Bd 1990-; Kt 1986; *Recreations* music, reading, walking; *Style—* Hon Mr Justice Schiemann; Royal Courts of Justice, Strand, London WC2

SCHIFF, Andras; s of Odon Schiff, and Klara, *née* Osengeri; *b* 21 Dec 1953; *Educ* Franz Liszt Acad of Music Budapest, private study with George Malcolm; *m* Oct 1987, Yuuko, *née* Shikawa; *Career* concert pianist; regular orchestral engagements: NY Philharmonic, Chicago Symphony, Vienna Philharmonic, Concertgebown Orchestra, Paris Philharmonic, London Philharmonic, London Symphony, Royal Philharmonic, Israel Philharmonic, Washington Nat Symphony; festivals incl: Salzburg, Edinburgh, Aldeburgh, Tanglewood; *Recreations* literature, languages, soccer; *Style—* Andras Schiff, Esq; Terry Harrison Artists Mgmnt, 9A Penzance Place, London W11 4PE (☎ 01 221 7741, fax 01 221 2610, telex 25872)

SCHILD, Geoffrey Christopher; s of Christopher Schild (d 1963), of Sheffield, and Georgina Schild (d 1970); *b* 28 Nov 1935; *Educ* High Storrs GS Sheffield, Univ of Reading (BSc), Univ of Sheffield (PhD); *m* 1 Aug 1961, Tora, da of Rev Canon Peter Madland (d 1977), of Bergen, Norway; 2 s (Øystein Christopher b 1962, Peter Geoffrey b 1969), 1 da (Ingrid b 1965); *Career* lectr in virology Univ of Sheffield 1963-67; dir: World Influenza Centre at MRC Nat Inst for Med Res 1969-75 (memb scientific staff MRC 1967-75), Nat Inst for Biological Standards and Control 1985- (head Div of Virology 1975-85), MRC Prog of AIDS Res 1987-; memb: Ctee on Safety of Medicines, Dept of Health jt Ctee on Vaccination and Immunisation, chm MRC Working Gp on Hepatitis Vaccines; chm WHO Steering Ctee on AIDS Res 1989-; Freeman City of London 1988; FIBiol 1977; *Recreations* ornithology, music; *Style—* Geoffrey C Schild; National Institute for Biological Standards & Control, Blanche Lane, Potters Bar, Hertfordshire EN6 3QG (☎ 0707 46846/54753, fax 0707 46854)

SCHILIZZI, Lady (Gabrielle) Sophia Annette; Waldegrave; da of 11 Earl Waldegrave (d 1936); *b* 7 June 1908; *m* 20 Dec 1935, Maj John Stephen Schilizzi (d 1985), s of Stephen Schilizzi; 1 s, 2 da; *Style—* The Lady Sophia Schilizzi; The Old Vicarage, Chacombe, nr Banbury, Oxon

SCHLESINGER, Theodore; s of Angel Schlesinger (d 1956), and Areti, *née* Cokino (d 1975); *b* 21 April 1931; *Educ* St Joseph Public Sch Cairo, Univ of London (BSc); *m* 1, (m dis 1973), Patricia, *née* Turley; m 2, 3 Nov 1973, Ann, da of TM Jackson, of The Old Hall Cottage, Cheveley, Newmarket, Suffolk; *Career* mktg mangr American Cyanamid 1954-55, dir of subsid co Gallup Poll 1955-60, chm ERC Statistics Int Ltd 1979 (formed co in 1961); involved in charitable work in Egypt; *Recreations* opera, new fiction, gardening, philosophy; *Style—* Theodore Schlesinger, Esq; The Old Hall, Cheveley, Newmarket, Suffolk (☎ 0638 730334); ERC Statistics International Ltd, 5-11 Shorts Gardens, Covent Garden, London WC2H 9AT (☎ 071 497 2312, fax 071 497 2313, telex 926510 ERCG)

SCHNAPKA, Hon Mrs (Sarah Ann Vivien de la Poer); eld da of 6 Baron Decies (by 2 w); *b* 23 June 1949; *m* 1975 (m dis 1982), Joerg Schnapka; 1 s (Roland b 1976); *Style—* The Hon Mrs Schnapka; c/o Coutts and Co, 1 Old Park Lane, London W1Y 4BS

SCHOFIELD, Alfred; *b* 18 Feb 1913; *Educ* Queen Elizabeth GS Wakefield; *m* 5 April 1939, *née* Risingham; 1 da (Carolyn Ann); *Career* Nat Serv RAF 1940-46; Leeds Building Soc: chief exec 1969-73, dir 1970-86, pres 1975-77; dir Leeds Bd Royal Insurance Co 1969-83, dir Homeowner's Friendly Soc 1984-; Tstee Sutton Housing Tst 1969-83, gen cmmr of Income Tax 1970-80; FCBSI 1965; *Recreations* orchid growing; *Style—* Alfred Schofield, Esq; The Cottage, Rudding Lane, Harrogate, North Yorks (☎ 0423 872037); Homeowners Friendly Society, Springfield Ave, Harrogate HG1 2HM (☎ 0423 567355, fax 0423 501460)

SCHOFIELD, Andrew Noel; s of Rev John Nöel Schofield (d 1986), of Fleet, Hants, and Winifred Jane Mary, *née* Eyles; *b* 1 Nov 1930; *Educ* Mill Hill Sch, Christs Coll Cambridge (MA, PhD); *m* 17 June 1961, Margaret Eileen, da of Oswald Green (d 1983), of Cambridge; 2 s (Ben b 1963, Matthew b 1965), 2 da (Polly b 1962, Tiffany b 1967); *Career* asst engr Scott Wilson Kirkpatrick & Ptnrs (Malawi) 1951-54, lectr Cambridge Univ 1959-68 (res student and demonstrator 1954-59), res fell California Inst of Technol 1963-64, prof of civil engrg Univ of Manchester Inst of Sci and Technol 1968-74, prof of engrg Cambridge Univ 1974-; chm: Andrew N Schofield & Assocs Ltd (ANSA) 1984, Centrifuge Instrumentation and Equipment Ltd (CIEL) 1987-; FEng 1986, FICE 1972; *Books* Critical State Soil Mechanics (with C P Wroth 1968), Land Disposal of Hazardous Waste (with J R Gronog and R K Jain 1988), Centrifuges in Soil Mechanics (with W H Craig and R G James 1988); *Style—* Prof Andrew Schofield; 9 Little Saint Mary's Lane, Cambridge CB2 1RR (☎ 0223 314536); Cambridge University Engineering Department, Trumpington Street, Cambridge CB2 1PZ (☎ 0223 332717/460555, fax 0223 460777, telex 81239)

SCHOFIELD, Jack William Lionel; s of Capt Leslie Schofield (d 1971), and Edna Morris (d 1975), da of Ethel Lumley, undefeated Lady Champion Puntist on the Thames; *b* 29 April 1927; *Educ* Merchant Taylor's, Imperial Coll London; *m* 12 Sept 1954, Sonia Fay, da of Dr E G Copeland (d 1977); 1 s (Colin b 1960), 1 da (Rosalyn b 1956); *Career* Nat Serv RE 1946-48, Germany, N Italy (Trieste); ret; *Recreations* golf, tennis, rugby football; *Clubs* IOD, Finchley Golf, OMT Rugby; *Style—* Jack Schofield, Esq; Willowmead, Oakleigh Park North, London N20 9AU (☎ 081 445 8255)

SCHOFIELD, Dr Jennifer Anne; da of Stanley Stephen Goy (d 1979), and Mary Catherine, *née* Jones; *b* 12 July 1946; *Educ* Rosebery GS Epsom Surrey, Middlesex Hospital Med Sch (MB BS); *m* 1 Oct 1977, Neil McCallum, s of Fred Schofield; 2 s (Guy b 11 May 1980, Stuart b 25 Oct 1981), 1 da (Olivia b 13 March 1983); *Career* ships surgn MN P&O Shipping Co 1973-74; anaesthetist Duchess of Kent Children's Hosp Hong Kong 1975-76, sr registrar anaesthetics Hosp for Sick Children Gt Ormand St London 1977, med offr Grendon Underwood Prison Aylesbury 1979-81, conslt anaesthetist Stoke Mandeville Hosp Aylesbury 1981-; chm Oxford Regnl Anaesthetic Sub Ctee; FFARCS 1975; *Recreations* needlework, skiing, family life; *Style—* Dr Jennifer Schofield; Manor Barn, Bilwell, Long Crendon, Aylesbury Bucks HP18 9AD (☎ 0844 201585); Anaesthetic Dept (Dr Goy), Stoke Mandeville Hospital, Aylesbury, Bucks HP21 8AL (☎ 0296 84111 ext 3376)

SCHOFIELD, John McMichael; s of James William Schofield (d 1982), and Donaldina McKay McMichael; *b* 11 April 1926; *Educ* St Georges Sch Harpenden, Middx Hosp Med Sch and Univ of London (MB BS); *m* 3 June 1952, Arlette Marie-Elvire Julie, da of Francois van Calck; 2 s (Philip, James), 1 da (Olivia (Mrs Walker)); *Career* Surgn Lt RNVR 1950-53; conslt ENT surgn Warwick Hosp 1962-90; gen sec Br Academic Conf in Otology 1979-83 (chm 1983- 87); pres: Section of Laryngology RSM 1986-87, pres Midland Inst of Otology 1989; UK rep Euro Fedn of Otological Surgns; parish cncllr Kineton Parish Cncl; FRCS (Ed), FRCS; *Recreations* golf, real tennis, reading, travel; *Clubs* MCC, Anglo - Belgian; *Style—* John Schofield, Esq; Brookhampton Farm, Kineton, Warwick (☎ 0926 640 330); Warwick Hospital, Wakin Rd, Warwick

SCHOFIELD, Kenneth Douglas; s of Douglas Joseph Schofield (d 1978), and Jessie, *née* Gray; *b* 3 Feb 1946; *Educ* Auchterarder Sec Sch; *m* 12 June 1968, Evelyn May, da of Arthur Gordon Sharp (d 1973); 2 da (Susan b 28 Jan 1971, Evonne b 13 Nov 1973); *Career* mangr Dunblane branch Perth Tstee Savings Bank 1969-71 (joined 1962), George Simms Orgn 1971-74, exec dir and co sec The PGA Euro Tour 1984- (dep to Press and PR Offr 1971-74, first sec 1975); memb Cncl Jr Golf Fndn, memb Sparks Charity; Assoc Savings Bank Inst 1966-71; *Books* Pro Golf (1972-75), John

Player Golf Yearbook (1973-75); *Recreations* golf, squash, badminton; *Clubs* Wentworth Club, Crieff Golf, Foxhills County; *Style—* Kennneth D Schofield, Esq; Riding Cottage, 2 The Riding, Woodham, Woking, Surrey GU21 5TA (☎ 0483 714984); PGA European Tour, Wentworth Club, Virginia Water, Surrey GU25 4LS (☎ 0344 84 2881, fax 0344 84 2929, telex 848626 PGA ET G, car 0836 260 672)

SCHOFIELD, Leslie James; s of Frank Schofield, of Royton, Oldham, Lancs, and Alice, *née* Wardrop (d 1986); *Educ* Thames Rd Secdy Modern Blackpool, Tech Sch Rochester Kent; *m* 31 March 1967, Daphne Elizabeth Helen; 2 da (Anna b 27 May 1971, Louise b 15 Nov 1974); *Career* served in Fleet Air Arm for 10 years; actor; TV work incl: Oliver Twist, Fifteen Streets, Gentlemen & Players, Spoils of War, The Fall and Rise of Reginald Perrin, Johny Briggs, Night on the Tyne, Sherlock Holmes Tricky Business; film work incl: Villain, Star Wars, The Eagle has Landed, Force 10 in Navarone, The Wild Geese; stage work incl: Auturo UI (Queen's Theatre), The Last Meeting of the Knights of the White Magnolia (Hampstead Theatre), Rumblings (Bush Theatre); *Recreations* golf, enjoying warm weather (Florida); *Clubs* Leatherhead Golf; *Style—* Leslie Schofield, Esq; c/o Evans & Reiss, 221 New Kings Rd, London SW6 4XE (☎ 071 384 1843)

SCHOFIELD, Michael George; s of Snowden Schofield, JP (d 1949), and Ella, *née* Dawson (d 1968); *b* 24 June 1919; *Educ* Clare Coll Cambridge, Harvard; *Career* social res conslt; res dir: Central Cncl for Health Educn London 1961-65, Govt Advsy Ctee on Drug Dependence 1967, Wootton Ctee on Cannabis 1969, Police Powers of Arrest and Search 1970; many TV and radio programmes, ret; *Books* The Sexual Behaviour of Young People (1965), The Sociological Aspects of Homosexuality (1965), Society and the Young School Leaver (1967), Drugs and Civil Liberties (1968), The Strange Case of Pot (1971), The Sexual Behaviour of Young Adults (1973), Promiscuity (1976), The Sexual Containment Act (1978); *Recreations* arts, civil rights, environment; *Style—* Michael Schofield, Esq; 28 Lyndhurst Gardens, London NW3 5NW (☎ 071 794 5125)

SCHOFIELD, Phillip Bryan; s of Brian Homer Schofield, and Patricia, *née* Parry; *b* 1 April 1962; *Educ* Newquay GS; *Career* first in vision anchorman BBC Childrens TV 1985-87, main presenter BBC TV's marathon magazine programme Going Live, Schofield's Europe 1990-; voted Top Man on TV 1987-88, voted no 1 TV personality in all maj teenage magazines 1987-88; involved in: Children's Royal Variety Performance 1987-88, Stars Orgn for Spastics, NSPCC, Br Heart Fndn; *Style—* Phillip Schofield, Esq; James Grant Management, The Courtyard, 42 Colwith Road, London W6 9EY (☎ 081 741 4484, fax 081 741 8615)

SCHOFIELD, Dr Roger Snowden; s of Ronald Snowden Schofield (d 1970), of Leeds, and Muriel Grace, *née* Braime (d 1972); *b* 26 Aug 1937; *Educ* Leighton Park Sch Reading, Clare Coll Cambridge (BA, PhD); *m* 3 Sept 1961, Elizabeth Mary, da of Prof Anthony Clegg Cunliffe, of London; 1 da (Melanie b 1972); *Career* fell Clare Coll Cambridge 1969- (res fell 1962-65), sr res offr Cambridge Gp 1966-73, memb Ctee SSRC Computing Panel 1970-75, vice chm Statistics Ctee SSRC 1976-78 (memb 1974-78), dir SSRC Cambridge Gp for the History of Population and Social Structure 1974-, Software Provision Ctee UK Computer Bd 1977-79, ed Population Studies 1979- (ed Local Population Studies 1968-), pres Br Soc for Population Studies 1985-87 (memb Cncl 1979-87, treas 1981-85), treas Population Investigation Ctee 1987- (memb 1976-), chm Historical Demography Ctee Int Union for the Scientific Study of Population 1987- (memb 1983-); fell: Royal Historical Soc 1970, RSS 1987; FBA 1988; *Publications* The Decline of Mortality in Europe (with David Reher and Alain Bideau, 1991), Famine, Disease and Crisis Mortality in Early Modern Society (contrib with J Walter, 1989), The State of Population Theory: forward from Malthus (contrib, 1986), The Population History of England 1541-1871: a reconstruction (with E A Wrigley, 1981, 2 edn 1989), English Marriage Patterns Revisited (Journal of Family History, 1985), Crisis Mortality (Local Population Studies, 1972), various articles on historical demography and research methods; *Style—* Dr Roger Schofield; 27 Trumpington St, Cambridge CB2 1QA; Clare College, Cambridge CB2 1TL

SCHOLAR, Dr Michael Charles; s of Richard Herbert Scholar, of Truro, Cornwall, and Mary Blodwen, *née* Jones (d 1985); *b* 3 Jan 1942; *Educ* St Olave's and St Saviour's GS, St John's Coll Cambridge (MA, PhD), Univ of California at Berkeley, Harvard; *m* 26 Aug 1984, Angela Mary, da of William Whinfield Sweet (d 1984), of Wylam, Northumberland; 3 s (Thomas b 1968, Richard b 1973, John b 1980), 1 da (Jane b 1976, d 1977); *Career* asst lectr in philosophy Univ of Leicester 1968, fell St Johns Coll Cambridge 1969, asst princ HM Treasy 1970, private sec to Chief Sec HM Treasy 1974-76, sr int mangr Barclays Bank plc 1979-81, private sec to PM 1981-83, dep sec HM Treasy 1987 (under sec 1983); ARCO 1965; *Recreations* music, opera, walking, gardening; *Style—* Dr Michael Scholar; HM Treasy, Parliament St, London SW1 (☎ 071 270 4389)

SCHOLES, Alwyn Denton; s of Denton Scholes (d 1928), of Bournemouth, and Violet Penelope Hill, *née* Birch (d 1970); *b* 16 Dec 1910; *Educ* Cheltenham, Univ of Cambridge (MA); *m* 16 Dec 1939, Juliet Angela Ierne, da of Maj Frederick Sparke Pyne, DSO, RA; 1 s (Richard), 4 da (Sarah, Juliet, Petrina, Jill); *Career* Gold Coast Voluntary Army Force 1939-45, Hong Kong RNVR 1950-58; called to the Bar Inner Temple 1934, practised London and Midlands circuit 1934-38, appt dist magistrate Gold Coast 1938 (actg crown counsel and slr gen 1941), magistrate Hong Kong 1948; first magistrate: Kowloon 1949, Hong Kong 1949; dist judge Hong Kong 1953, puisne judge Hong Kong 1958, cmmr Supreme Ct of Brunei 1964-67 and 1968-71, pres memb Hong Kong Full Ct of Appeal 1949-71, sr puisne judge Hong Kong 1970, actg chief justice of Hong Kong 1970, ret 1971; memb: Sidmouth PCC 1972-82, Ottery Deanery Synod 1973-82; govr St Nicholas Sch Sidmouth 1984-89; *Recreations* walking, gardening; *Clubs* Royal Cwlth Soc (life memb); *Style—* Alwyn Scholes, Esq; West Hayes, Convent Rd, Sidmouth, Devon EX10 8RL (☎ 0395 512 970)

SCHOLES, Bryan Richard; s of Richard Scholes (d 1968), and Ellen Maud, *née* Heywood (d 1958); *b* 8 July 1914; *Educ* Ackworth Sch; *m* 29 April 1939, Joan Hilda Reeve; 4 da; *Career* chm W H Heywood & Co Ltd 1955-76 (joined 1930, dir 1947, md 1950); chm: W M Oddy & Co Ltd 1955-60, Neaversons Ltd 1940-87; former pres Huddersfield C of C, vice-pres Assoc Br C of C, past chm NE BIM; fndr pres: Aluminium Window Assoc, Suspended Ceilings Assoc; former pres Fedn of Euro Metal Window Mfrs Assocs, fndr tstee Huddersfield Common Good Tst; *Recreations* farming, walking, gardening, beagling; *Clubs* Huddersfield, RAC, Farmers, IOD; *Style—* Bryan Scholes, Esq; Folly Hall, Thornthwaite, Harrogate HG3 2QU (☎ 0423 780228)

SCHOLES, John Francis Millar; s of Frank Victor Gordon Scholes, CMG (d 1954), and Annie (Nancie) Noble, *née* Millar (d 1958); *b* 7 April 1919; *Educ* Scotch Coll Melbourne, Melbourne Univ (BEng Sc), Sydney Univ (BE); *m* 1947, Joyce Bartlett, da of Sidney Frank Henry Laws (d 1973), of Sydney; *Career* engr: Aeronautical Res Laboratory Melbourne 1943-49, Royal Aircraft Establishment 1950-58, Int Computers and Tabulators Ltd 1958-65, National Research Devpt Corp 1965-81 (memb and chief exec engrg 1977-81); Hon FInst MC (pres 1966-67); CEng, FIEE, MRAeS, MIEAust; *Recreations* genealogy, stamp collecting; *Style—* John Scholes, Esq; 22 Outlook Drive, Burwood, Victoria 3125, Australia (☎ 03 889 1923)

SCHOLES, Rodney James; QC (1987); s of Henry Scholes (d 1971), of Widnes, and Margaret Bower, *née* Aldred; *b* 26 Sept 1945; *Educ* Wade Deacon GS Widnes, St Catherinés Coll Oxford (BA, BCL); *m* 13 Aug 1977, Katherin Elizabeth (Kate), da of Dermot Keogh (d 1988), of Heaton Mersey; 3 s (Michael b 7 June 1978, Jonathan b 7 Oct 1980, Nicholas b 15 Dec 1982); *Career* called to the Bar Lincoln's Inn 1968, memb Northern circuit 1968-, rec Crown Ct 1986-; *Recreations* watching rugby league football; *Style—* Rodney Scholes, Esq, QC; 5 Essex Ct, Temple, London EC4Y 9AH (☎ 071 353 4363, fax 071 583 1491); 25 Byrom St, Manchester M3 4PF (☎ 061 834 5238, fax 061 834 0394)

SCHOLEY, Sir David Gerald; CBE; s of Dudley and Lois Scholey; *b* 28 June 1935; *Educ* Wellington, ChCh Oxford; *m* 1960, Alexandra Beatrix, da of Hon George Drew, of Canada; 1 s, 1 da; *Career* joined S G Warburg & Co Ltd 1965 (dir 1967, dep chm 1977), chm S G Warburg Group plc 1984 (jt chm 1980-84); dir: Mercury Securities plc 1969 (chm 1984-86), Orion Insurance Co Ltd 1963-87, Stewart Wrightson Holdings Ltd 1972-81, Union Discount Co of London Ltd 1976-87, British Telecom plc 1985-; memb Export Guarantees Advsy Cncl 1970-75 (dep chm 1974-75), chm Construction Exports Advsy Bd 1975-78, memb Ctee on Finance for Industry NEDO 1980-87, hon treas IISS 1984-, memb Gen Motors Euro Advsy Cncl 1988-, chm Business in the Community Target Team on Fiance Enterprise 1988-; memb: UK Advsy Bd INSEAD 1989-, Indust and Commerce Gp The Save the Children Fund 1989-; tstee Glyndebourne Arts Tst 1989-; govr Wellington Coll 1977-89; memb NIESR 1984-; FRSA 1987; kt 1987; *Style—* Sir David Scholey, CBE; c/o S G Warburg Group plc, 1 Finsbury Ave, London EC2M 2PA (☎ 071 606 1066)

SCHOLEY, Sir Robert; CBE (1982); *b* 8 Oct 1921; *Educ* King Edward VII Sch Sheffield, Univ of Sheffield; *m* ; 2 da; *Career* served REME 1943-47; engr Steel Peech & Tozer Rotherham 1947, formerley of United Steel Companies Ltd (head office 1972, md Strip Mills Div 1972); Br Steel Corp: memb Bd dirs 1973, dep chm and chief exec 1976, chm 1986-; pres Pipeline Industs Guild 1987-89, dir Eurotunnel Bd 1987-, pres Inst of Metals 1989-90, non-exec dir Nat Health Serv Policy Bd 1989-, vice pres Eurofer 1990- (pres 1985-90), vice chm Int Iron and Steel Inst 1990- (chm 1989-90), chm Ironbridge Gorge Museum Devpt Tst, memb ECSC Consultative Ctee; winner: Bessemer Gold medal Inst of Metals 1988, Gold medal BIM 1988; Hon PhD Engrg Univ of Sheffield 1987; FEng 1990, fell Inst of Metals 1990; kt 1987; *Style—* Sir Robert Scholey, CBE; British Steel plc, 9 Albert Embankment, London SE1 7SN (☎ 071 735 7654, fax 071 587 1142)

SCHOLTENS, Sir James Henry; KCVO (1977, CVO 1963); s of late Theo F J Scholtens; *b* 12 June 1920; *Educ* St Patrick's Marist Brothers' Coll, Sale, Victoria, Aust; *m* 1945, Mary, da of late C D Maguire; 1 s, 5 da; *Career* dir Office of Govt Ceremonial Hospitality Dept of PM and Cabinet 1973-80; dir of Visits to Australia by HM The Queen, HRH The Duke of Edinburgh and members of The Royal Family, Heads of State, Monarchs and Presidents; extra gentleman usher to HM The Queen 1981-; *see Debrett's Handbook of Australia and New Zealand for further details*; *Style—* Sir James Scholtens, KCVO; 74 Boldrewood St, Turner, Canberra, ACT 2601, Australia (☎ 06 248 6639)

SCHOLTZ, Dr Carl Ludwig; s of Carl Ludwig Scholtz (d 1977), of Tiuna Grove, Elwood, Melbourne, Aust, and Julia Ellen, *née* Ryan (d 1974); *b* 18 April 1939; *Educ* St Columba's, Christian Brothers Coll St Kilda, Univ of Melbourne (MB, BS), Univ of Manchester (MSc), Univ of London (PhD, DipEC); *m* 30 May 1970, (Catherine) Geraldine, da of Dennis Griffin, of Hillingdon, Middx; 1 s ((Carl) Lewis b 1977), 1 da (Laura Ellen b 1975); *Career* MO Alfred Hosp Melbourne 1965-67, registrar Prince Henry's Hosp Sydney 1968-71, lectr Univ of Manchester 1972-76, sr lectr in neuropathology and consIt neuropathologist The London Hosp 1977-; chm: Aust and NZ Med and Dental Assoc, Help in Need Assoc; memb Br Neuropathological Soc; Yeoman Worshipful Soc of Apothecaries 1982; memb RSM 1978; *Books* Clinical Neurpathology (1979); *Recreations* swimming, walking; *Style—* Dr Carl Scholtz; The Institute of Pathology, The London Hospital, Whitechapel, London E1 1BB (☎ 071 377 7437)

SCHON, Baron (Life Peer UK 1976), of Whitehaven, Co Cumbria; Frank Schon; s of late Dr Frederick Schon, of Vienna, and Henriette, *née* Nettel; *b* 18 May 1912; *Educ* Rainer Gymnasium Vienna, Prague Univ, Vienna Univ; *m* 1936, Gertrude, da of late Abraham Secher; 2 da (Hon Susan Henriette (Hon Mrs Keller) b 1941, Hon Yvonne Catherine (Hon Mrs Saville) b 1944); *Career* co-fndr Marchon Products Ltd 1939, Solway Chemicals Ltd 1943, chm and md of both until 1967; chm National Research Devpt Corpn 1969-79 (memb 1967-79), dir Blue Circle Industries 1967-82; memb cncl King's Coll Durham 1959-63; Univ of Newcastle upon Tyne: memb Cncl 1963-66, memb Court 1963-78; chm Cumberland Devpt Cncl 1964-68; memb: Northern Economic Planning Cncl 1965-68, Industrial Reorganisation Corp 1966-71, Advsy Cncl of Technology 1968-70; pt/t memb Northern Gas Bd 1963-66; Hon Freeman of Whitehaven 1961; Hon DCL Durham 1961; kt 1966; *Recreations* golf, reading; *Style—* The Rt Hon the Lord Schon; Flat 82, Prince Albert Court, 33 Prince Albert Rd, London NW8 7LU (☎ 071 586 1461)

SCHOUVALOFF, Alexander; s of Count Paul Schouvaloff (d 1961), and Anna, *née* Raievsky, MBE; *b* 4 May 1934; *Educ* Harrow, Jesus Coll Oxford (MA); *m* 1, 18 Feb 1959 (m dis), Gillian Baker; 1 s (Alexander b 1959); m 2, 18 Nov 1971, Daria Antonia Maria, da of late Marquis de Mérindol, and formerly wife of Hon (Geoffrey) Patrick Hopkinson Chorley; *Career* Nat Serv 2 Lt RMP SHAPE Paris 1957-59, Award of Merit Eaton Hall OCS; asst dir Edinburgh Festival 1965-67; dir: NW Arts Assoc 1967-74, Rochdale Festival 1971, Chester Festival 1973; curator Theatre Museum 1974-89; radio plays Radio Four: Summer of the Bullshine Boys 1981, No Saleable Value 1982; tstee London Archives of the Dance; Polonia Restituta Poland 1971; *Books* Summer of the Bullshine Boys (1979), Stravinsky on Stage (with Victor Borovsky, 1982), Catalogue of Set and Costume Designs in Thyssen-Bornemisza Collection (1987), The Theatre Museum (1987), Theatre on Paper (1990); *Clubs* Garrick; *Style—* Alexander Schouvaloff, Esq; 10 Avondale Park Gardens, London W11 4PR (☎ 071 727 7543)

SCHRADER, Richard Mietek Barclay; s of 2 Lt John Richard Schrader (d 1970), and Rosina Ellen, *née* Price; *b* 26 Aug 1945; *Educ* Sedgehill Comp Sch; *m* 1, 16 April 1966 (m dis 1984), Rebecca Ann, da of William Horsey; 1 s (Colin Mietek b 1966), 1 da (Candice Oriana b 1970); m 2, 25 June 1988, Kerry Yvonne, da of Karl Gale; 1 s (Lawrence John b 7 Nov 1990); *Career* md: Sloangate Ltd 1981, Sloangate Recruitment Advertising Ltd 1983, Tavnerstar Ltd 1983, JAB Executive Search Ltd 1984, Sir Silk Ltd 1984, Wisefile Ltd 1989; *Recreations* gourmet, travel; *Style—* Richard Schrader, Esq; 21 Cromford Way, New Malden, Surrey KT3 3BB (☎ 081 942 3946); Dominic House, 171-177 London Rd, Kingston upon Thames, Surrey KT2 6RA (☎ 071 549 9236, fax 071 546 5222, telex 918417)

SCHREIBER, Gaby; da of Gunther George Peter Wolff; *Educ* Baccalaureat, Art, stage and interior design in Vienna Florence, Berlin and Paris; *m* Leopold Schreiber; *Career* gen consIt Designer for Indust, chm Gaby Schreiber & Associates; interior design consIt: William Clark & Sons Ltd NI 1981-84, Nat West Bank Ltd, Westminster Foreign Bank Brussels 1972-73, Chm's Office GHP Group Ltd 1974, Pres Office Gulf Oil-Eastern Hemisphere 1973-74, Lythe Hill Hotel Surrey, Anglo - Continental Investment & Finance Co and Continental Bankers Agents London, Myers and Co, Peter Robinson Ltd, David Morgan Cardiff, West Cumberland Hosp, Newcastle Regnl Hosp Bd, Fine Fare Ltd (Queensway Store Crawley); gen consIt and designer: Cunard

Steamship Co Ltd (QE2), Zarach Ltd, Marquess of Londonderry, Cram Agents, Allen and Hanbury (Surgical Engrg) Limited, BOAC (whole fleet of aeroplanes 1957-63), Divs of Dunlop Rubber Group, Bartrer Group of Cos, Queen's Flight and RAF Hawker Siddeley Aviation Ltd, Rank Organisation Ltd; plastics design conslt Marks & Spencer Ltd; yachts: Sir Gerard d' Erlanger, Whitney Straight; designed exhibition stands Britain, Europe and USA; memb Co Interior Designers 1960-62 (memb Design Awards Ctee 1961), judge on Ind Panel Duke of Edinburgh prize for Elegant Design 1960 and 1961, MSIAD, fell and former chm Consultant Designers Gp and Int Rels Ctee; memb: UK delgn Gen Assembly of Int Cncl of Society of industl Design Venice 1961, Judges Panel for numerous newspaper and magazine Indust design competitions, advsr on purchases of works of art; FCSD; *Books* numerous articles in international jls and books on design; *Recreations* gardening, farming, arts and crafts; *Style—* Mrs Gaby Schreiber; 26 Kylestrome House, Cundy St, London SW1W 9JT (☎ 071 235 4656)

SCHREIBER, Mark Shuldham; s of John Shuldham Schreiber (d 1968), of Marlesford Hall, Woodbridge, Suffolk, and Constance Maureen Schreiber (d 1980); *b* 11 Sept 1931; *Educ* Eton, Trinity Coll Cambridge (MA); *m* 1969, Gabriella Federica, da of Conte Teodoro Veglio Di Castelletto Uzonne; 2 da (Nicola Charlotte b 1971, Sophie Louisa b 1973); *Career* Nat Serv Coldstream Gds, 2 Lt; Fisons Ltd 1957-63, Conservative Res Dept 1963-67, dir Conservative Party Public Sector Research Unit 1967-70, special advsr HM Govt 1970-74, special advsr to leader of the Opposition 1974-75, editorial conslt The Economist 1974- (Parly lobby correspondent); dir: Eastern Electricity plc 1989-, Financial Insurance Group 1989-; memb: Countryside Cmmn 1980-, Rural Devpt Cmmn 1985-; *Clubs* Pratt's; *Style—* Mark Schreiber, Esq; Marlesford Hall, Woodbridge, Suffolk; 5 Kersley St, London SW11; The Economist, 25 St James's St, London SW1 (☎ 071 839 7000)

SCHRODER, Baron Bruno Lionel; s of Baron Helmut William Bruno Schroder (d 1969) s of Baron Bruno Schroder or von Schröder, sr ptnr the London branch of the Banking House of J Henry Schroder & Co, cr Freiherr by Kaiser Wilhelm II aboard the yacht 'Hohenzollern' on 27 July 1904; the Baron's er bro Rudolph was cr Freiherr eight months later), and Margaret Eleanor Phyllis, eld da of Sir Lionel Darell, 6 Bt, DSO, JP, DL; *b* 17 Jan 1933; *Educ* Eton, Univ Coll Oxford (MA), Harvard Business School (MBA); *m* 30 May 1969, Patricia Leonie Mary (Piffa), da of Maj Adrian Holt (d 1984); 1 da (Leonie b 1974); *Career* 2 Lt The Life Gds 1951-53; dir: Schroders plc 1963-, J Henry Schroder Wagg & Co Ltd 1966-, Schroders Inc 1984-; memb exec ctee The Air Sqdn; memb ct of assts The Goldsmiths' Co; has Queen Beatrix of the Netherlands Wedding Medal; *Recreations* shooting, stalking, flying; *Clubs* Brooks's; *Style—* Baron Schroder; 42 Lansdowne Rd, London W11 4LU (☎ 071 229 1433); 120 Cheapside, London EC2V 6DS (☎ 071 382 6000, fax 071 382 6878, telex 885029)

SCHROEDER, Hon Mrs (Sheila Kathleen); *née* Atkins; eldest da of Baron Colnbrook, KCMG, PC (Life Peer), *qv*; *b* 26 Oct 1944; *m* 1, 15 Feb 1964 (m dis 1974), Peter Thornycroft Romer-Lee, er s of Charles Romer-Lee; 2 s (Richard Peter b 1965, Anthony James b 1967); m 2, 1975 (m dis 1978), Keith Allen Manners; m 3, 1982, Royston Joseph Schroeder; *Style—* The Hon Mrs Schroeder; Ellimore Farm, Lustleigh, Devon

SCHÜFFEL, Hon Mrs (Shân); da of Baron Edmund-Davies, PC (Life Peer); *b* 1940; *m* 1964, Wolfram Schüffel, MD; *Style—* The Hon Mrs Schüffel; 3550 Marburg/Lahn, Kaffweg 17A, W Germany

SCHUIL-BREWER, Graham; s of Lt A E Schuil (d 1943), and M E Brewer, *née* Hepple; *b* 20 Feb 1942; *Educ* Harrow; *m* 22 June 1968, Josephine Diana, da of David L Ellis (d 1969); 1 s (Justin b 6 June 1971), 1 da (Sophie b 28 April 1976); *Career* corporate fin controller Br Shipbuilders 1982-85; non-exec dir: Scott Lithgow Ltd 1982-85, Br Shipbuilders Offshore Div 1982-85; dir: Austin and Pickersgill Ltd 1985-87, Sunderland Shipbuilders Ltd 1986-87, NE Shipbuilders Ltd 1986-87, Courtaulds Engrg Ltd 1988-; *Recreations* golf, squash, rugby union football; *Style—* Graham Schuil-Brewer, Esq; 65 Newbold Road, Barlestone, nr Nuneaton, Warwickshire CV13 0DY (☎ 0455 290 412); P O Box 11, Foleshill Road, Coventry CV6 5AB (☎ 0203 688 771, fax 0203 687 325, telex 312 171)

SCHUSTER, Sir (Felix) James Moncrieff; 3 Bt (UK 1906), of Collingham Rd, Royal Borough of Kensington, OBE (Mil 1955), TD; s of Sir (Felix) Victor Schuster, 2 Bt (d 1962); *b* 8 Jan 1913; *Educ* Winchester; *m* 1937, Ragna, da of late Direktor Sundøoe of Copenhagen; 2 da; *Heir* none; *Career* served WWII with The Rifle Bde in Middle East and Combined Operations attaining rank of Maj 1939-45; Hon Col 5 Bn Royal Green Jackets T & AVR 1970-75; *Clubs* Naval and Military, Lansdowne; *Style—* Sir James Schuster, Bt, OBE, TD; Piltdown Cottage, Piltdown, Uckfield, E Sussex TN22 3XB

SCHUSTER, Hon Mrs (Lorna Frances); *née* Hermon-Hodge; da of 2 Baron Wyfold, DSO, MVO; *b* 25 Feb 1911; *m* 1941, John Schuster, TD, DL, eld s of Sir George Schuster, KCSI, KCMG, CBE, MC; 2 s, 1 da (all adopted); *Style—* The Hon Mrs Schuster; The Manor Farm, Nether Worton, Oxon (☎ 060883 254)

SCHUTZ, Prof Bernard Frederick; s of Bernard Frederick Schutz, of 12 Keswick Lane, Plainview, NY, and Virginia M, *née* Lefebure (d 1986); *b* 11 Aug 1946; *Educ* Bethpage HS NY, Clarkson Coll of Technol NY (BSc), California Inst of Technol (PhD); *m* 1, 13 Aug 1968 (m dis 1973), Joan Catherine, *née* Rankie; m 2, 16 Sept 1977 (m dis 1981), Susan, *née* Whitelegg; m 3, 22 Dec 1985, Sian Lynette, da of John Alexander Easton Pouncy, of 16 Cimla Crescent, Neath, W Glamorgan; 3 da (Rachel b 1984, Catherine b 1986, Annalie b 1989); *Career* postdoctoral res fell Univ of Cambridge 1971-72, instructor in physics Univ of Yale 1973-74 (postdoctoral res fell 1972-73), prof Univ Coll Cardiff 1984- (lectr 1974-76, reader 1976-84); memb Theory and Computation Panel and Educn Tr and Fellowships Panel Astronomy and Planetary Sci Div SERC; FRAS, FInstP; memb: American Physical Soc, Soc of Sigma XI; *Books* Geometrical Methods of Mathematical Physics (1980), A First Course in General Relativity (1985), Gravitational Wave Data Analysis (1989); *Recreations* singing, skiing; *Style—* Prof Bernard Schutz; Dept of Physics, University of Wales College of Cardiff, PO Box 913, Cardiff CF1 3TH (☎ 0222 874203, telex 498635, fax 0222 874058)

SCHWAB, Germain Eric; s of Eric Herbert Schwab (d 1967), of Champ Faudin 12, 2740 Moutier, Switzerland, and Therese Marie Anne, *née* Unternahrer; *b* 5 Dec 1950; *Educ* Ecole Chantemerle Moutier Suisse, Ecole D'Aptitude Professionnelle Delémont Suisse, Ecole De Formaiton professionnelle de Cuisiner Bienne Suisse, Diplome De Fin D'Apprentis Palais Des Congres Bienne; *m* 31 Oct 1977, Ann Dorothy, da of William Henry Clovis; *Career* chef; Hotel Central Tavanne Switzerland 1970, La Grenette Fribourg Switzerland 1970, Gstaad Palace Gstaad Switzerland 1970, Portledge Hotel Bideford England 1971, Frederick Restaurant Camden London 1971, Chesterfield Hotel Mayfair London 1971, Dorchester Hotel London 1972, St Moritz Club Wardour St London 1973, Seiler Haus Mount Cervin Zermatt Switzerland 1974, Le Mirabeau Hotel Zermatt 1975, Le Bristol Hotel Zermatt 1977, Beck Farm Restaurant Wilberfoss England 1980, Winteringham Fields Winteringham 1988; County restaurant of the Year: Good Food Guide 1990, La Ina 1990; Restaurant of the Year (The Independent) 1990, English Estates Humberside Rural Employment award 1990, English Estates Humerside County Winner (Tourism) 1990; Societie Master Chefs (UK) Feb 1983 Cercle Epicurien Mondial, Diplome D Honneur 1987, Euro Toque 1990; *Recreations* sketching; *Style—* Germain Schwab, Esq; Winteringham Fields, Winteringham, South Humberside DN15 9PF (☎ 0724 733096, fax 0724 733898)

SCHWABE, Prof Walter Wolfgang; s of Dr Walter Schwabe (d 1962), of Wimbledon, and Anne, *née* Lagershausen (d 1954); *b* 1 June 1920; *Educ* Regent St Poly, Imperial Coll London (BSc, ARCS, PhD, DIC, DSc, DAgric); *m* 15 Nov 1958 (m dis); 1 s (John b 1965), 2 da (Fiona b 1960, Ruth b 1962); *Career* princ scientific offr ARC 1958-65, plant physiologist and prof of horticulture Univ of London and Wye Coll 1965-85; former memb Governing Body Exec Ctee E Malling Res Station; memb: Nat Vegetable Res Station, Glasshouse Crops Res Station; ed in chief Jl of Experimental Botany; currently assoc ed: Jl Hort Sci Physiologia Plantarum (Scandinavia), Elais (Malaysia); *Recreations* hill walking, skiing; *Style—* Prof Walter W Schwabe; Audlea, Bilting, nr Ashford, Kent (☎ 0233 812 482); Department of Horticulture, Wye College, University of London, Wye, nr Ashford, Kent (☎ 0233 812 401)

SCHWARZ, Jonathan Simon; s of Harry Heinz Schwarz, of SA, and Annette Louise, *née* Rudolph; *b* 20 June 1953; *Educ* Univ of Witwatersrand SA (BA, LLB), Univ of California Berkeley (LLM); *m* 19 Jan 1986, Dr Denise Sheer Schwarz; 2 s (Benjamin b 1987, Daniel b 1989); *Career* advocate supreme of SA 1977-78, High Ct Repub of Botswana 1978-81; barr and slr Province of Alberta 1981-, int tax ptnr Stephenson Harwood 1988-; memb Exec Ctee Assoc Internationale des Jennes Avocats; ed Financial Times World Tst Report; Freeman Worshipful Co of Slrs 1989; memb: Law Soc, Int Bar Assoc, Int Fiscal Assoc, Canadian Bar Assoc, Canadian Tax Fndn; *Style—* Jonathan Schwarz, Esq; Stephenson Harwood, 1 St Paul Churchyard, London EC4M 8SH (☎ 071 329 4422, fax 071 606 0822, telex 886789)

SCHWARZ, Prof Kurt Karl; s of Benno Schwarz (d 1965), of Norwich, Norfolk, and Margaretha Emilia Julia, *née* Petz (d 1985); *b* 24 May 1926; *Educ* Leys Sch Cambridge, Univ of Cambridge (MA); *m* 6 Aug 1949, Brenda Patricia, da of Fred Pilling, CBE, of Lytham St Annes; 1 s (David Roger Charles b 31 May 1950), 2 da (Jennifer Patricia (Mrs Orton) b 15 Sept 1952, Mary Brenda Margaret b 7 May 1958); *Career* dir Laurence Scott and Electromotors Ltd 1968-86 (tech dir 1965-86), visiting indust prof Univ of Southampton 1987; memb Norfolk Engrg Soc, Norfolk and Norwich Music Club; memb: ctee BSI, BEAMA, EIC; MInstMC 1957, BNES 1960, FIEE 1961, FIMechE 1961; *Books* Design and Wealth Creation (1990); *Recreations* music, walking, swimming, gardening; *Style—* Prof Kurt Schwarz; Threshfield, Bullockshed Lane, Bramerton, Norwich NR14 7HG (☎ 050 88 446)

SCIAMA, Prof Dennis William; s of Abraham Sciama (d 1969), and Nellie, *née* Ades (1974); *b* 18 Nov 1926; *Educ* Malvern, Trinity Coll Cambridge (BA, PhD); *m* 26 Nov 1959, Lidia, da of Guido Dina (d 1975), of Venice; 2 da (Susan b 26 Oct 1962, Sonia b 30 Oct 1964); *Career* Private REME 1947-49; jr res fell Trinity Coll Cambridge 1952-56, lectr mathematics Univ of Cambridge 1961-70, sr res fell All Souls Coll Oxford 1970-85, prof astrophysics Int Sch Advanced Studies Trieste 1983-; foreign memb: American Philosophical Soc 1982, American Acad Arts and Scis 1983, Accademia Dei Lincei 1984; FRS 1983; *Books* The Unity of the Universe (1959), The Physical Foundations of General Relativity (1969), Modern Cosmology (1971); *Style—* Prof Dennis Sciama, FRS; 7 Park Town, Oxford (☎ 0865 59441); Sissa, Strada Costiera 11, 34014, Trieste, Italy (☎ 040 3787 475)

SCICLUNA, Martin Anthony; s of William L Scicluna, of Malta, and Miriam, *née* Gouder; *b* 20 Nov 1950; *Educ* Berkhamstead Sch Herts, Univ of Leeds (BCom); *m* 28 July 1979, (Katharine) Fenella, da of Rev Canon Norman Haddock, of Cheltenham, Glos; 2 s (Mark William b 26 April 1984, Edward James b 2 February 1989), 1 da (Claire Alexandra b 11 Aug 1987); *Career* CA; ptnr i/c London Audit Dept Touche Ross & Co 1982- (articled 1973-76); chm London Soc of CAs ICEAW 1988-89 (memb Cncl ICEAW 1990-); ACA 1976, FCA 1980, MBIM 1976; *Books* Money for Microchips (1983), High on Tech/Low on Cash (1986); *Recreations* tennis, gardening, wine appreciation; *Style—* Martin A Scicluna, Esq; Carnforth, The Warren, Radlett, Herts, WD7 7DU (☎ 0923 857390); Touche Ross & Co, Hill House, 1 Little New St, London, EC4A 3TR (☎ 071 936 3000, fax 071 583 8517, telex 884739)

SCLATER, Prof John George; s of John George Sclater, and Margaret Bennet Glen; *b* 17 June 1940; *Educ* Stonyhurst, Univ of Edinburgh (BSc), Univ of Cambridge (PhD); *m* 1, 1968, Fredrica Rose Feleyn; 2 s, (Iain, Stuart); m 2, 1985, Paula Anne Edwards; *Career* asst res geophysicist Scripps Insitution of Oceanography 1967-72 (postgrad res asst 1965-67), prof MIT 1977-83 (asst prof 1972-77), dir Joint Program in Oceanography and Ocean Engineering (with Woods Hole Oceanographic Institution) MIT 1981-83, The Institution for Geophysics Univ of Texas of Austin 1983- (assoc dir, sr res scientist, Shell Distinguished prof in geophysics); assoc ed Jl of Geophysical Res 1971-74; memb: Ocean Scis Ctee US Nat Acad of Sciences 1972-76, Nat Sci Review Ctee on Oceanography 1974-77, Review Ctee IDOE Nat Sci Fndn 1974, Heat Flow Panel JOIDES 1968-74, Sci Fndn 1974, Indian Ocean Panel JOIDES 1968-74, Ocean Cnist Panel IPOD 1974-76, Indian Ocean Panel Ocean Drilling Prog 1985-88 (Lithesphere panel 1984-86), Ocean Studies Bd/Naval Panel 1985-; chm Ocean Studies Bd US Nat Acad of Scis 1988- (memb 1985-88); FRS; fell: Geological Soc of America, American Geophysical Union; memb: AAPG, Nat Acad of Scis; Rosenstiel Award 1979, Bucher Medal AGU 1985; *Publications* numerous contribs to Jl of Geophysical Res, Bulletin Earthquake Res, Earth and Planetary Sci Letters, Geophysical Jl RAS, Tectonophysics, and other learned jls; *Style—* Prof John Sclater, FRS; Institute of Geophysics, The University of Texas at Austin, 8701 Mopac Boulevard, Austin, Texas 78759-8345 (☎ 512 471 6156, telex 910 874 1380 UTIGAUS)

SCLATER, John Richard; s of Arthur William Sclater, and Alice, *née* Collett; *b* 14 July 1940; *Educ* Charterhouse, Gonville and Caius Coll Cambridge, Yale, Harvard; *m* 1, 23 Aug 1968 (m dis), Nicola Mary Gloria, o da of late Anthony Charles Cropper, TD, DL, JP, of Tolson Hall, Kendal; 1 s (James Arthur b 17 April 1970), 1 da (Emma Mary b 18 Jan 1972); m 2, 25 April 1985, Grizel Elizabeth Catherine, o da of Lt-Col Herbrand Vavasour Dawson, of Weston Hall, Otley, Yorks; *Career* chm: Foreign & Colonial Investment Trust PLC, Berisford International PLC, Foreign & Colonial Enterprise Trust PLC; vice chm Hill Samuel Bank Ltd; dep chm: The Union Discount Co of London PLC, Yamaichi International (Europe) Ltd; dir: Economic Insurance Co Ltd, James Cropper PLC, Hafnia Holdings (UK) Ltd, The Equitable Life Assurance Society, Grosvenor Estate Holdings, Wilrig AS; tstee The Grosvenor Estate; memb: Cncl of The Duchy of Lancaster, CBI City Advsy Gp; *Recreations* country pursuits; *Clubs* Brooks's, Pratt's, Univ Pitt (Cambridge); *Style—* John Sclater, Esq; Sutton Hall, Barcombe, nr Lewes, E Sussex (☎ 0273 400450, fax 0273 401086); 117 Eaton Square, London SW1W 9AA (☎ 071 235 0446, fax 071 235 1228); office: Hill Samuel Bank Ltd, 100 Wood St, London EC2P 2AJ (☎ 071 628 8011, fax 071 606 9583)

SCLATER, Patrick Henry; s of Henry Nicolai Sclater, of Stockbridge, Hants, and Suzanna Mary, *née* Agnew; *b* 9 Jan 1944; *Educ* Charterhouse, RAC Cirencester; *m* 8 July 1968, Rosalyn Heather, da of Urban George Eric Stephenson, of Frith House, Stalbridge, Dorset; 3 s (William b 1969, Alastair b 1971, Peter b 1976), 1 da (Heather b 1978); *Career* estate agent; sole princ Sclater Real Estate Dorchester 1974-83, Symonds Sampson & Sclater 1983-87, local dir Fulljames & Still Dorchester 1987, relocation agent and princ Sclater Property Search 1988-; *Recreations* shooting, sailing, walking, gardening, reading, travel; *Style—* Patrick H Sclater, Esq; Old Farmhouse, Frith, Stalbridge, Sturminster Newton, Dorset (☎ 0963 251363)

SCOBIE, Kenneth Charles; s of Charles Smith Scobie (d 1965), and Shena Bertram, *née* Melrose (d 1990); *Educ* Daniel Stewart's Coll, Univ of Edinburgh (BA); *m* 29 Sept 1973, (Adela) Jane, da of Keith Somers Hollebone, of Brook House, Bridge St, Bampton Castle, Oxfordshire; 1 s (Charles b 11 Oct 1976), 1 da (Deborah b 19 May 1975); *Career* CA; profit planning BMC (Scotland) Ltd 1961-63, dep fin dir Motor Car Div Rolls Royce 1963-66, sr mgmnt conslt and ptnr Robson Morrow & Co 1966-70, memb Main Bd and Exec Ctee Black and Decker Euro Gp 1971-72, md Vavasseur SA Ltd 1972-76, chief exec and dir Vernon Orgn 1977, md H C Sleigh UK Ltd 1979-82, gp md Blackwood Hodge plc 1984-90, non-exec dir Albrighton plc 1990; CA 1961, CBIM 1987; *Recreations* rugby, golf, tennis, cricket; *Clubs* Stewart's Melville London Scottish RFC, Hunterscombe Golf; *Style—* Kenneth Scobie, Esq

SCOBLE, Christopher Lawrence (Chris); s of Victor Arthur Oliphant Scoble, of Looe, Cornwall, and Mabel, *née* Crouch; *b* 21 Nov 1943; *Educ* Kent Coll Canterbury, Corpus Christi Coll Oxford (BA); *m* 18 Nov 1972, Rosemary, da of Thomas Henry Hunter (d 1985), of Hamble, Hampshire; 1 s (Sampson b 6 Aug 1973); *Career* asst princ Home Office 1965-69, private sec to Min of State Welsh Office 1969-70; Home Office: princ 1970-78, sec to Advsy Cncl on Penal System 1976-78, asst sec 1978-88, vice chm Media Policy Ctee Cncl of Europe 1985-87; CS (Nuffield and Leverhulme) Travelling fellowship 1987-88; asst under-sec of state Broadcasting and Miscellaneous Dept Home Office 1988; *Style—* Chris Scoble, Esq; Home Office, 50 Queen Anne's Gate, London SW1H 9AT (☎ 071 273 3211)

SCOBLE, Peter Ernest Walter; er s of Walter George Scoble (d 1984), and Muriel Phyllis Mary, *née* Buckley; *b* 8 March 1938; *Educ* Malvern; *m* 1, 29 June 1963, (Marjorie) Lesley (d 1988), yr da of James Durban Wilkinson; 1 s (Mark Walter James b 7 Sept 1972), 2 da (Karen Lesley b 20 Oct 1967, Anna Jill b 2 July 1969); m 2, 3 Nov 1990, Carolyn Antonia Pilmore-Bedford, *née* Newnham; *Career* slr; articled clerk Joynson-Hicks & Co, admitted slr 1962, ptnr Boodle Hatfield & Co 1964- (joined 1962); past pres City of Westminster Law Soc, memb Cncl Law Soc 1986-; *Recreations* tennis, golf, music, philately; *Clubs* MCC, Lowtonian Soc; *Style—* Peter Scoble, Esq; Boodle Hatfield, 43 Brook Street, London W1Y 2BL (☎ 071 629 7411, fax 071 629 2621)

SCOFFHAM, (Roland) Brian; s of Rowland Albert Scoffham (d 1981), of Birmingham, and Janet Sutton (d 1983); *b* 29 April 1925; *Educ* King Edwards Sch Birmingham; *m* 5 Sept 1956, Thalia Monica, da of Robert Bernard Barnicle (d 1976), of Sutton Coldfield; 1 da (Lucinda b 1962); *Career* WWII Royal Signals 1943-47, served Italy with Eighth Army; chartered builder (ret); water ski judge: appointed int judge 1972, chief judge World Games 1985 and World Championships 1989; chm tech ctee Br Water Ski Fedn (hon memb 1975), sec euro tournament cncl and memb world tournament cncl Int Water Ski Fedn; fndr memb Dudley Water Ski Club 1963; MCIOB 1969; *Recreations* water skiing; *Style—* Brian Scoffham, Esq; 66 Anstruther Road, Edgbaston, Birmingham B15 3NP (☎ 021 454 8462)

SCOFIELD, (David) Paul; CBE (1956); s of Edward Henry Scofield (d 1976), of Hurstpierpoint, Sussex, and Mary, *née* Wild; *b* 21 Jan 1922; *Educ* Hurstpierpoint, Varndean Sch for Boys Brighton; *m* 15 May 1943, Joy Mary, da of Edward Henry Parker (d 1947); 1 s (Martin Paul b 6 March 1945); 1 da (Sarah b 22 Aug 1951); *Career* actor; Birmingham Repertory Theatre 1942-45; Stratford-upon-Avon 1946, 1947, 1948; London theatres: Adventure Story and The Seagull (St James's) 1949, Ring Round the Moon (Globe) 1950-52, Much Ado About Nothing (Phoenix) 1952, The River Line (Edinburgh Festival, Lyric (Hammersmith), Strand) 1952, Richard II, The Way of the World, Venice Preserved (Lyric (Hammersmith)) 1952-53; A Question of Fact (Piccadilly) 1953-54, Time Remembered (New Theatre) 1954-55, Hamlet (Moscow) 1955; Paul Scofield-Peter Brook Season 1956, The Power and the Glory, Hamlet and Family Reunion (Phoenix), A Dead Secret (Piccadilly) 1957, Expresso Bongo (Saville) 1958, The Complaisant Lover (Globe) 1959, A Man for All Seasons (Globe 1960, and Anta Theatre New York 1961-62), Coriolanus, Love's Labours Lost (Shakespeare Festival Theatre Stratford, Ontario), King Lear (Stratford on Avon, Aldwych 1962-63, and Moscow, W Berlin, Prague, Warsaw, Budapest, Bucharest, Belgrade and New York 1964), Timon of Athens (Stratford on Avon) 1965, The Government Inspector, Staircase (Aldwych) 1966, Macbeth (Stratford on Avon, Russia, Finland) 1967, A Hotel in Amsterdam (Royal Court and New) 1968, Uncle Vanya (Royal Court) 1970, Savages (Royal Court and Comedy) 1973; The Tempest (Wyndham's) 1975; National Theatre: Captain of Köpenick, The Rules of the Game, Volpone, Amadeus, Othello, Don Quixote, 1971-83; I'm Not Rappaport (Apollo) 1986-87; *Films* That Lady, Carve Her Name with Pride, The Train, A Man for All Seasons, Bartleby, King Lear, Scorpio, A Delicate Balance, Anna Karenina, Nineteen Nineteen, The Attic, When the Whales Came, Henry V and numerous television plays *Awards* Evening Standard 1956 and 1963, New York Tony 1962, Oscar and Br Film Academy 1966, Danish Film Academy 1971, Hamburg Shakespeare Prize 1972; Hon LLD Glasgow 1968; Variety Club 1956, 1963 and 1987; Hon DLitt: Kent 1973, Sussex 1985; *Recreations* walking, reading; *Clubs* Athenaeum; *Style—* Paul Scofield, Esq, CBE

SCOON, HE Sir Paul; GCMG (1979), GCVO (1985), OBE (1970); *b* 1935; *Career* taught in Grenada 1953-67, former Cabinet sec, govr-gen Grenada 1978-; *Style—* HE Sir Paul Scoon, GCMG, GCVO, OBE, Governor-General of Grenada; Governor-General's House, St George's, Grenada (☎ 440 2401)

SCOONES, Maj-Gen Sir Reginald Laurence; KBE (1955, OBE 1941), CB (1951), DSO (1945); s of late Maj Fitzmaurice Scoones, Royal Fusiliers; *b* 18 Dec 1900; *Educ* Wellington, RMA Sandhurst; *m* 1933, Isabella Bowie, da of John Nisbet, of Cumbrae Isles, Scotland; 1 da; *Career* late RAC; 2 Lt Royal Fusiliers 1920, transferred RTC 1923, attached Sudan Def Force 1926-34, 1939-45 War ME and Burma; Lt-Col 1941, Brig 1942, Asst Cmdt Sudan 1947, Maj-Gen 1950, Maj-Gen Cmdg Br Troops Sudan and Cmdt Sudan Def Force 1950-54; dir The Brewers' Soc 1957-69; *Style—* Maj-Gen Sir Reginald Scoones, KBE, CB, DSO; Flat 51, 50 Sloane St, London SW1X 9SN (☎ 071 235 4680)

SCOPES, Prof Jon Wilfred; s of Rev Wilfred Scopes (d 1986), missionary in India, and Edith Annie, *née* Hacker (d 1947); *b* 20 Nov 1930; *Educ* Eltham Coll, St Mary's Hosp Sch, Univ of London (MB BS, PhD, MRCS, LRCP, MRCP); *m* 5 Sept 1959, Evelyn Kathleen, da of Cdr Frederick Gordon Wynne, MBE, RN (d 1971), of Lymington, Hants (d 1971); 2 da (Heather b 1960, Jennifer b 1963); *Career* jr med posts 1953-60: St Mary's Ealing Hosp, ships surgn Orient Line, Rochford Hosp, Gt Ormond St, Guys; Nuffield res fell Oxford 1960-61, lectr in paediatrics Royal Postgrad Med Sch (RPMS) Hammersmith, visiting lectr Columbia Univ NY USA 1965-66; RPMS: sr lectr in paediatrics 1966-70, hon conslt paediatrician 1966-70, reader 1970-73; visiting lectr Makere Univ Uganda 1970; St Thomas' Hosp Med Sch: reader in paediatrics 1973-76, prof in paediatrics 1976-90, ret, prof emeritus 1990-; memb: BMA 1953, BPA 1966; Freeman City of London, Liveryman Worshipful Soc of Apothecaries; hon memb Burmese Med Assoc 1988, examiner in med finals (paediatrics) Nigeria and Burma; FRCP 1971, FRSM 1960 (pres paediatrics section 1988); *Books* Medical Care of Newborn Babies (co author, 1972); *Recreations* gardening, walking, DIY, former pres St Thomas' Hosp rugby football club; *Clubs* Savile; *Style—* Prof Jon Scopes; 3 Chestnut Ave, Hampton, Middx (☎ 081 979 6933); Department of Paediatrics, St Thomas' Hospital, London SE1 7EH

SCOPES, Sir Leonard Arthur; KCVO (1961), CMG (1957), OBE (1946); s of late Arthur Edward Scopes (d 1968), of Monifieth, Angus, by his w Jessie Russell Hendry; *b* 19 March 1912; *Educ* St Dunstan's Coll, Gonville and Caius Coll Cambridge; *m* 21 Dec 1938, Brunhilde Slater, da of late Victor Emmanuel Rolfe, of Worthing; 2 s, 2 da; *Career* memb Br Consular Foreign and Dip Servs 1933-67; vice consul: Antwerp 1933, Saigon 1935, Canton 1937; acting consul Surabaya 1941, vice consul Lourenço Marques 1942, consul Skoplje and Ljubljana 1945, commercial sec Bogota 1947, asst in UN (Econ and Social) Dept of Foreign Office 1950, cnsllr Djakarta 1952, FO inspr 1954; ambass: Nepal 1957-62, Paraguay 1962-67; memb Jt Inspection Unit of UN and Specialised Agencies 1968-71; *Style—* Sir Leonard Scopes, KCVO, CMG, OBE; 2 Whaddon Hall Mews, Whaddon, Bucks

SCOPES, Richard Henry; s of Eric Henry Scopes, of Funtington, W Sussex, and Ida Lucy Mary, *née* Hare; *b* 6 June 1944; *Educ* Univ Coll Sch, Magdalene Coll Cambridge (LLB); *m* 29 March 1969, Jacqueline Elizabeth Mary, da of Maj Ronald Walter Monk (d 1973), of Blackheath; 1 da (Katie b 1972); *Career* admitted slr 1969; Ashurst Morris Crisp & Co 1963-69, dir Scopes & Sons 1970-75, ptnr Wilde Sapte 1980- (joined 1976); memb City of London Slrs Co 1981; memb Law Soc; *Recreations* gardening, painting; *Clubs* Queenhithe Ward; *Style—* Richard Scopes, Esq; Westfield House, River Hill, Flamstead, Herts AL3 8DA; Wilde Sapte, Queensbridge House, 60 Upper Thames St, London EC4V 3BD (☎ 071 236 3050, fax 071 236 9624, telex 887793)

SCORER, Philip Segar; s of Eric West Scorer, OBE (d 1966), of Lincoln, and Maud, *née* Segar (d 1971); *b* 11 March 1916; *Educ* Repton School; *m* 23 Sept 1950, Monica, da of Rev Stanley Thomas Smith (d 1955), of Cambridge; 1 s (James b 1961), 3 da (Julia b 1951, Rachel b 1953, Sarah b 1956); *Career* RASC 1940-41, capt RCS 1943 (Cmmnd 1941), War Office 1941-43, Supreme HQ Allied Expeditionary Force 1944-45, Br Army Staff Paris 1945-46 (despatches 1945); admitted slr 1938, London Co Cncl 1938-46, Met Police 1947-57, ptnr Burton and Co Lincoln 1952-, clerk of the peace City of Lincoln 1952-71, asst dep coroner North Kesteven 1952-70, under sheriff of Lincs 1954-, chm Mil Serv Hardship Ctee 1954-60, dep chm Agricultural Land Tbnl 1974-84, crown ct rec 1976-83; pres: Soc of City and Borough Clerks of the Peace 1968-71, Lincs Law Soc 1966-67, Under Sheriffs Assoc of England and Wales 1978-84 (memb ctee 1955-72, vice pres 1972-78); memb Law Soc 1938-; *Recreations* swimming, reading dictionaries; *Clubs* National Liberal; *Style—* Philip S Scorer, Esq; 25 Eastgate, Lincoln LN2 4AA (☎ 0522 26800); Stonebow, Lincoln LN2 1DA (☎ 0522 523215)

SCORER, Timothy Rowland; s of Derek Rowland Scorer, TD, of Tallulah Falls, Georgia, USA, and Margaret Shirley, *née* Staveacre; *b* 25 June 1941; *Educ* Repton; *m* 1, 10 Oct 1965 (m dis 1981), Wendy Ann, da of Edward Thomas Glazier (d 1978), of San Antonio, Ibiza; 2 s (Craig b 29 Jan 1967, Jamie b 2 July 1969); m 2, 25 Sept 1982 (m dis 1989), Julia Jane, da of Jeremy John Booth; 1 da (Lucinda b 29 Oct 1987); *Career* admitted slr 1965; ptnr Josselyn & Sons Ipswich 1967, asst sec Law Soc 1976, ptnr Barlow Lyde & Gilbert London 1980; chm and fndr Lawyers Flying Assoc, int vice pres Lawyer Pilots Bar Assoc USA; hon slr: Helicopter Club GB, Euro Gen Aviation Safety Fndn, Guild of Air Pilots and Air Navigators, Jt Servs Parachuting Assoc; Freeman City of London 1987, Liveryman Guild of Air Pilots and Air Navigators 1988 (Freeman 1985); memb Law Soc 1966; *Recreations* flying, photography, travel; *Style—* Timothy Rowland, Esq; Harvest Farm, Milden, Ipswich, Suffolk IP7 7AN (☎ 0787 247 327); Flat 5, 11 Gloucester Square, London E2 8RS (☎ 071 256 0280); Beaufort House, 15 St Botolph St, London EC3A 7NJ (☎ 071 247 2277, telex 913281, fax 071 782 8505, car 0860 5577 66)

SCOREY, Dr John; s of Edward William Scorey (d 1976), of New Zealand, and Nancy Houston, *née* Glasgow; *b* 5 Aug 1928; *Educ* Portsmouth, Guy's Hosp Univ of London (MB BS); *m* 11 May 1955, (Julia) Diana, da of John Morris Wolley (d 1950), of Rowton Grange, Aston on Clun, Craven Arms, Shropshire; 1 s (Jeremy b 1957), 1 da (Phillipa b 1959); *Career* RAMC Capt Surgical Dept Cambridge Mil Hosp Aldershot 1952-54; princ Gen Practice 1956-86, hosp practitioner in surgery 1966-86 (tresmo 1958-86); MO: Equity & Law Life Assurance Society 1970-86, Wiggins Teape Ltd 1978-86; underwriter at Lloyd's of London 1985-; fund raising for London Fedn of Boys Clubs; Freeman City of London 1970, Master Worshipful Co of Woolmen 1989-90 (Liveryman 1970, asst 1983); *Recreations* fly fishing, walking, gardening; *Clubs* City Livery, Royal Soc of St George, Sloane; *Style—* Dr John Scorey; Griffin Cottage, Woodrow, nr Amersham, Bucks HP7 0QQ (☎ 0494 725 851)

SCOTT; *see*: Maxwell-Scott, Montagu Douglas Scott, Morrison-Scott

SCOTT, Rev Adam; TD (1978); s of Brig Fraser Scott, of Wonersh, and Bridget Penelope, *née* Williams; *b* 6 May 1947; *Educ* Marlborough, Ch Ch Oxford (BA, MA), City Univ Business Sch (MSc); *m* 30 Sept 1978, Oona MacDonald, da of Prof R J D Graham, (d 1950), of St Andrews; *Career* OUOTC 1965-68, CVHQ RA, 94 Locating Regt 1968-81, cmd Reserve Meteorologists, Capt 1968-81, ret 1981; reader Oxford 1970-75; ordained: deacon 1975, priest 1976 in Southwark; asst curate St Michael and All Angels Blackheath Park London SE3 1975-; dean: Ministers in Secular Employment, Woolwich Episcopal Area; trained as intellectual property lawyer 1970-74; called to the Bar Inner Temple 1972; with: ITT 1974-77, PO 1977-81; British Telecom: corporate planner 1981-86, dir office of Iain Vallance (chm of British Telecom) 1986-88; dir Int Affairs British Telecom 1988-; CEng, MIEE 1981; *Recreations* gardening, walking; *Style—* The Rev Adam Scott, TD; British Telecom, 918 Holborn Centre, 120 Holborn, London EC1N 2TE (☎ 071 492 2060, fax 071 492 3001, telex 21601 BTI G)

SCOTT, Dr (Christine) Angela; da of William Hurst Roy Grundy, of 187 The Close, Salisbury, Wilts, and Margaret, *née* Drury; *b* 19 June 1946; *Educ* Harrogate Coll, Kings Coll Med Sch London (MB, BS); *m* 7 June 1969, (John) Nigel (David), s of Lt-Col George William Inglis Scott, RA, DSO (d 1976); 3 s (Andrew b 1974, Robin b 1976, Alan b 1980); *Career* conslt histopathologist and cytologist to Salisbury District Health Authy 1981-, med dir pathology 1989-; FRCPath 1988; *Recreations* squash, gardening; *Style—* Dr Angela Scott; Pathology Dept, Salisbury Gen Infirmary, Fisherton St, Salisbury, Wilts (☎ 0722 336212 ext 658)

SCOTT, Hon Lady (Anna Drusilla); *née* Lindsay; da of 1 Baron Lindsay of Birker, CBE (d 1952); *b* 1911; *Educ* Somerville Coll Oxford (DipEd); *m* 1937, Sir Ian Dixon Scott, KCMG, KCVO, CIE; 1 s, 4 da; *Books* A D Lindsay, a Biography (1971), Everyman Revived: the Common Sense of Michael Polanyi (1985), Mary English: A Friend of Bolivar (1991); *Style—* The Hon Lady Scott; Ash House, Alde Lane, Aldeburgh, Suffolk

SCOTT, Anthony Douglas; TD (1972); s of late Douglas Ernest Scott; *b* 6 Nov 1933; *Educ* Gateshead GS; *m* 1962, Irene, *née* Robson; 1 s, 1 da; *Career* Maj TA; chartered accountant; in practice 1989-; chief exec and dir Cncl for Small Industries in Rural Areas 1981-88, dir Consumer Credit Office of Fair Trading 1975-80, dir gen Internal Audit MOD 1972-74; *Recreations* antique collecting, mountaineering; *Clubs* Army and Navy; *Style—* Anthony Scott, Esq, TD; 33 Barlings Rd, Harpenden, Herts (☎ 0582 763067)

SCOTT, Sir Anthony Percy; 3 Bt (UK 1913) of Witley, Surrey; s of Col Sir Douglas Scott, 2 Bt (d 1984), and Elizabeth Joyce, née Glanley (d 1983); *b* 1 May 1937; *Educ* Harrow, Ch Ch Oxford; *m* 1962, Caroline Teresa Anne, da of Edward Bacon; 2 s, (Henry Douglas, Simon b 1965), 1 da (Miranda b 1968); *Heir* Henry Douglas Edward, *qv*; *Career* barr 1960; ptnr in stockbroking firm Laurie Milbank & Co 1974-; chm and md LM (Moneybrokers) Ltd 1986-; *Style*— Sir Anthony Scott, Bt; North Park Farm, Fernhurst, Haslemere, Surrey (☎ 0428 52826, office 071 929 3171)

SCOTT, Bill; s of George Barclay Scott (d 1975), of Moniave, Dumfriesshire, and Jeanie Stuart, *née* Waugh (d 1962); *b* 16 Aug 1935; *Educ* Morton Acad, Dumfries Acad, Edinburgh Coll of Art (Dip, postgrad Dip), Ecole des Beaux Arts Paris (travel scholar, Clason Harvie Bequest prize); *m* 25 March 1961, Phyllis Owen, da of William Lauderdale Fisher; 1 s (Ian Alexander b 1 Jan 1962), 2 da (Phyllis Elizabeth b 7 July 1962, Jeanie May b 27 July 1971); *Career* sculptor; temp teacher Fife 1960-61; pt/t teacher Edinburgh Coll of Art 1961-63; Sculpture Sch Edinburgh Coll of Art: lectr 1963-76, sr lectr 1976-90, acting head 1990-; solo exhibitions: Compass Gallery Glasgow 1972, Stirling Gallery 1974, New 57 Gallery Edinburgh 1979, Artspace Art Gallery Aberdeen 1980, Kirkcaldy Museum and Gallery 1985; gp exhibitions: 11 Scottish Sculptors (Fruit Market Gallery, Edinburgh) 1975, Small Sculptures (Scottish Arts Cncl, Edinburgh) 1978, British Art Show (Mappin Gallery Edinburgh, Hatton Gallery and Arnolfini) 1979-80, V Int Exhibition of Small Sculpture Budapest 1981, Built in Scotland (Third Eye Centre Glasgow, City Arts Centre Edinburgh, Camden Art Centre London) 1982-83, One Cubic Foot Exhibition (Aberdeen & Glasgow) 1986; cmmns: New Byre Theatre St Andrews 1969, Cumbernauld Shopping Centre 1980, Kentigern House Glasgow 1985; memb: Cncl Soc of Scottish Artists 1970-73, Bd Fruit Market Gallery 1983-91, Selection Ctee for Sculpture Br Sch at Rome 1986-91; chm Awards Panel Arts Ctee Scottish Arts Cncl 1990- (memb Art Ctee 1989-); *Style*— Bill Scott, Esq

SCOTT, (John) Brough; s of Mason Hogarth Scott (d 1971), of Buckland Manor, Broadway, Worcs, and Irene Florence, *née* Seely (d 1976); *b* 12 Dec 1942; *Educ* Radley, CCC Oxford; *m* 3 Nov 1973, Susan Eleanor, da of Ronald Grant Macinnes, of Mark Ash Cottage, Abinger Common, Surrey; 2 s (Charles Ronald Brough b 21 Jan 1976, James Seely b 14 Feb 1979), 2 da (Sophie Diana b 20 July 1974, Tessa Irene b 3 Nov 1984); *Career* amateur and professional Jump Jockey (100 winners incl Imperial Cup and Mandarin Chase) 1962-70; TV journalist: ITV 1971-84 (chief racing presenter 1979-), Channel 4 1985-; sports journalist; columnist Evening Standard 1972-74, racing correspondent Sunday Times 1974-90, Independant on Sunday 1990-; dir Racing Post 1985- (ed dir 1988-); Lord Derby Award (racing journalist of the year) 1980, Clive Graham Trophy (services to racing) 1982, Sports Journalist of the Year 1983, Sports Feature Writer of the Year 1985; vice pres Jockeys Assoc 1969-71; trustee: Injured Jockeys Fund, Racing Welfare, Professional Riders Insurance Scheme; *Books* World of Flat Racing (1983), On And Off The Rails (1984); *Recreations* riding, making bonfires; *Style*— Brough Scott, Esq; Racing Post, 120 Coombe Lane, Raynes Park, London SW20 0BA (☎ 081 879 3377, fax 081 879 3722, car 0860 334357)

SCOTT, Hon Mrs (Cecilia Anne); *née* Hawke; da of 9 Baron Hawke (d 1985); *b* 1943; *m* 1, 1963 (m dis 1971), Peter Hannay Bailey Tapsell, MP (later Sir Peter Tapsell); 1 s (James Hawke b 1966, d 1985); m 2, 1979, as his 2 w, Nicholas Paul Scott, MBE, JP, MP, *qv*; 1 s (Patrick Martin Iain b 1982), 1 da (Amber Teresa b 1987); *Recreations* tennis, golf; *Clubs* Hurlingham, Royal Mid Surrey Golf; *Style*— The Hon Mrs Scott

SCOTT, Charles Clive; s of Lt-Col Sir James Walter Scott, 2 Bt, *qv*, of Rotherfield Park, Alton, Hants, and Anne Constantia, *née* Austin; *b* 31 July 1954; *Educ* Eton, Trinity Coll Cambridge (MA), INSEAD (MBA); *m* 6 Oct 1979, Caroline Frances, da of (Hugh Graham) Jago; 3 da (Eleanor, Rose, Alice); *Career* dir de Zoete & Bevan Ltd 1988; memb The Stock Exchange; Freeman City of London 1977, Liveryman Worshipful Co of Mercers 1980; memb Law Soc; *Recreations* usual fun and games; *Clubs* Leander; *Style*— Charles Scott, Esq; Ebbgate Hse, 2 Swan Lane, London EC4 (☎ 071 623 2323)

SCOTT, Charles Thomas; *b* 22 Feb 1949; *Career* accountant; Binder Hamlyn 1967-72, Itel Corporation 1972-77, IMS International Inc 1978-90, Saatchi & Saatchi Co plc 1990-; FCA 1979 (ACA 1972); *Style*— Charles Scott, Esq; Saatchi & Saatchi Co plc, Berkeley Square, London W1X 5DH (☎ 071 495 5000)

SCOTT, Christopher James Anderson; s and h of Sir Oliver Scott, 3 Bt; *b* 16 Jan 1955; *Educ* Bryanston, Trinity Coll Cambridge, INSEAD; *m* 23 July 1988, Emma Jane, o da of Michael John Boxhall, of Islington, London N1; 1 s (Edward James Saim b 25 Oct 1990); *Clubs* Brooks's; *Style*— Christopher Scott, Esq

SCOTT, Christopher Wilmot; s of Kenneth Wilmot Scott, of Thorpe on the Hill, Lincolnshire, and Kathleen, *née* Bacon; *b* 23 Jan 1964; *Educ* Robert Pattinson Comp Sch North Hykham Lincolnshire; *m* 18 March 1989, Jacqueline, da of Roger Arthur Crane; *Career* wicketkeeper and batsman Nottinghamshire CCC 1981- (debut Notts v Essex 1981), approximately 65 Championship appearances plus several other First Class and One Day games; County Cap 1988; *Recreations* skiing, rugby, football, current affairs, music; *Style*— Christopher Scott, Esq; Nottinghamshire County Cricket Club, Trent Bridge, Nottingham, NG2 6AG (☎ 0602 821525)

SCOTT, Sir David Aubrey; GCMG (1979, KCMG 1974, CMG 1966); s of Hugh Sumner Scott (d 1959), and Barbara Easton Scott, JP; *b* 3 Aug 1919; *Educ* Charterhouse, Univ of Birmingham; *m* 1941, Vera Kathleen, da of Maj G H Ibbitson, MBE, RA (d 1958); 1 da, 2 s; *Career* served WWII RA (Maj); Foreign Serv: high cmmr Uganda and ambass Rwanda 1967-70, asst under sec of state FCO 1970-72, high cmmr NZ and govr Pitcairn Is 1973-75, ambass S Africa 1976-79; chm: Ellerman Lines 1982-83 (vice chm 1981), Royal Overseas League 1981-86, Nuclear Resources Ltd 1984-88; dir: Barclays Bank International 1979-85, Mitchell Cotts Group 1980-86, Bradbury-Wilkinson plc 1984-86; vice pres UK-South Africa Trade Assoc 1981-85, govr Saddlers Wells Tst 1984-89, memb Manchester Olympic Bid Ctee; *Books* Ambassador in Black and White (1981); *Recreations* music, birdwatching; *Clubs* Royal Overseas League; *Style*— Sir David Scott, GCMG; Wayside, Moushill Lane, Milford, Surrey GU8 5BQ (☎ 0483 421935)

SCOTT, David Gidley; s of Bernard Wardlaw Habershon Scott (d 1978), of Little Almshoe, St Ippolyts, Hitchin, Herts, and Florence May, *née* Wheeler; *b* 3 Jan 1924; *Educ* Sutton Valence, St John's Coll Cambridge (MA, LLM); *m* 10 April 1948, (Elinor) Anne, da of Maj Alan Garthwaite, DSO, MC (d 1964), of Penny Bridge, Ulverston; 2 s (Antony b 1956, Robin b 1959), 2 da (Judith b 1952, Dinah b 1961); *Career* WWII RE 1942-47, cmmnd 1944, Trp Cdr assault sqdn (wounded Rhine Crossing 1945), Temp Capt (later Actg Maj) cmdg 4 BESD Haifa 1947; called to the Bar Middle Temple 1951, practised Chancery Bar 1952-84, registrar in bankruptcy High Ct 1984-; vice chm Parish Cncl, former churchwarden and memb PCC; *Recreations* sailing, choral singing; *Clubs* Bar Yacht, Parkstone Yacht; *Style*— David Scott, Esq; Little Almshoe House, St Ippolyt's, Hitchin, Herts (☎ 0462 434391); Thomas More Building, Royal Courts of Justice, Strand, London WC2

SCOTT, David Griffiths; s of Wilfred Emberton Scott (d 1967), and Gwenith, *née* Griffiths; *b* 15 Feb 1942; *Educ* Adams GS Newport Shropshire, Christs Coll Cambridge (MA), London Business School (MSc); *m* 1969, Alison Jane Fraser; 1 s (James b 1974), 2 da (Helen b 1971, Katherine b 1976); *Career* md: ISC Alloy Ltd 1975-84, Impalloy Ltd 1978-84, Kleen-e-ze Hldgs plc 1984-88, Yale Security Prods Ltd 1989-; *Recreations* golf, sailing, cricket; *Style*— David Scott, Esq; The Barn, Main St, Wick, nr Pershore, Worcs WR10 3NZ (☎ 0386 554185); Yale Security Products Ltd, Wood St, Willenhall, W Midlands WV13 1LA (☎ 0902 366911)

SCOTT, Dr David Henry Thomson; *b* 19 Feb 1949; *Educ* George Watsons Coll Edinburgh, Univ of Edinburgh (BSc, MB ChB); *m* 22 July 1972, Dr Mary Scott; 1 s (Angus b 1976), 2 da (Glenda b 1978, b Diana 1980); *Career* intern: Western Memorial Hosp Corner Brook Newfoundland Canada 1972, Charles A Janeway Hosp St John's Newfoundland Canada 1972, house offr Western Gen Hosp Edinburgh 1972-74; registrar Edinburgh Anaesthetic Trg Scheme 1974-76, Astra clinical res fell 1977, lectr Univ of Edinburgh 1978, conslt anaesthetist Royal Infirmary Edinburgh 1979-; Lasarettet i Ljungby Sweden 1978-83; memb: EESSA 1973, AAGBI 1974, SSA 1976, FFARCS 1976, memb SREEC 1979; *Recreations* electro-mechanical wizardry, skiing, hill walking, malt whisky, fishing; *Clubs* Watsonian, EUS; *Style*— Dr David Scott; Department of Cardiothoracic Surgery, Royal Infirmary of Edinburgh, Laurieston Place, Edinburgh EH3 9YW (☎ 031 229 2477 ext 2073, fax 031 229 337, car 0860 810997)

SCOTT, David Morris Fitzgerald; s of Rev Canon William Morris Fitzgerald Scott (d 1959), of St Aidan's Coll, Birkenhead, Cheshire, and Nora Compigne, *née* Shaw; *b* 7 June 1946; *Educ* St Lawrence Coll Ramsgate, The Hotchkiss Sch Lakeville Connecticut USA, Corpus Christi Coll Oxford (MA); *m* 10 June 1972, Jacqueline Mary, da of Kenneth Percy Pool; 1 s (Michael b 1981), 2 da (Elizabeth b 1976, Sarah b 1978); *Career* ptnr Kitcat & Aitken 1974-80 (investmt analyst 1967-74), vice pres Bank of NY 1980-83; dir: Warburg Investment Managment International 1983-85, Mercury Warburg Investment Managment 1985-87, Mercury Rowan Mullens 1987-89, Mercury Asset Managment Private Investors Group 1990-; Freeman City of London, Liveryman Worshipful Co Scriveners; FInstPet 1974, Assoc Soc of Investmt Analysts; *Recreations* reading; *Clubs* Brooks's, Turf, City of London; *Style*— David Scott, Esq; Windmill House, Windmill Lane, Wadhurst, East Sussex TN5 6HX (☎ 089 288 2683), Mercury Asset Management, 33 King William St, London EC4 (☎ 071 280 2800, fax 071 280 2820, telex 888478)

SCOTT, David Richard Alexander; s of Lt Cdr Robert Irwin Maddin Scott, OBE (d 1968), of Lyddington, Rutland, and (Margaret Sylvia) Daphne, *née* Alexander; *b* 25 Aug 1954; *Educ* Wellington; *m* 1 Aug 1981, Moy, da of Air Chief Marshal Sir John Barraclough, KCB, CBE, DFC, AFC, of Bath; 1 s (Alexander b 8 Aug 1982), 1 da (Arabella b 11 Jan 1985); *Career* CA; Peat Marwick Mitchell & Co Blackfriars London 1972-81, dir fin and co sec Channel Four TV Co Ltd 1988- (controller of fin and co sec 1981-88); FCA 1976; *Recreations* opera, theatre, ballet, bridge, sailing, country pursuits; *Clubs* Guards' Polo; *Style*— David Scott, Esq; Channel Four TV Co Ltd, 60 Charlotte St, London W1P 2AX (☎ 071 631 4444, fax 071 255 1616, telex 892355)

SCOTT, Rear Adm Sir (William) David Stewart; KBE (1977), CB (1974); yst s of Brig Henry St George Stewart Scott, CB, DSO (d 1940), and Ida Christabel Trower, *née* Hogg; *b* 5 April 1921; *Educ* Tonbridge; *m* 1952, Pamela Dorothy Whitlock; 1 s, 2 da; *Career* Capt RN 1962, Rear Adm 1971, Cdr British Naval Staff and Br Naval Attache Washington 1971-73, dep controller Polaris 1973, chief Polaris Exec 1976-80; *Style*— Rear Adm Sir David Scott, KBE, CB; c/o Lloyds Bank, 6 Pall Mall, London SW1

SCOTT, Donald Dundas; JP (1967), DL (1972); s of James Douglas Scott (d 1973), of Harsfold Farm House, Wisborough Green, W Sussex, and Bridget Violet Penfold-Wyatt (d 1968); *b* 1 June 1924; *Educ* Winchester, Ch Ch Oxford (BA); *m* 3 Oct 1953, Fiona Mary, da of The Hon Angus Dudley Campbell, CBE, JP, of Doddington Cottage, Nantwich, Cheshire; 2 s (Roderick b 16 Feb 1958, Angus b 15 Feb 1964), 2 da (Henrietta (Mrs Drake) b 18 Jan 1957, Rosanna b 23 Feb 1962); *Career* Capt Scots Gds 1944-47; underwriter Lloyds, ret 1972; dep chm King Edward VII Hosp Midhurst, lay chm Deanery Synod; ctee memb: Chichester Diocesan Housing Assoc, CLA; gen cmmr of revenue; High Sheriff 1975; *Recreations* shooting, gardening, music; *Clubs* Pratts; *Style*— Donald Scott, Esq, JP, DL; Harsfold Manor, Wisborough Green, Billingshurst, W Sussex (☎ 0403 700285)

SCOTT, Dr Donald Fletcher; s of Alexander Scott (d 1976), of Melton Lodge, Holt Road, Cromer, Norfolk, and Jean Scott (d 1976); *b* 29 Nov 1930; *Educ* Thetford GS, Univ of Edinburgh (MB ChB), Univ of London (DPM); *m* 2 Sept 1967, Adrienne, da of Dr A A Moffett (d 1984), of 9 Droxford, 34 Kitchener Rd, Pietermaritzberg, Natal, SA; 1 s (James b 1974), 1 da (Caroline b 1971); *Career* Nat Serv RAMC 1949-51; conslt clinical neurophysiologist London Hosp 1967-; sec EEG Soc Meetings, memb Br Epilepsy Assoc; FRCP 1977; *Books* Neurological and Neurosurgical Nursing (1966), About Epilepsy (1969), Psychology of Work (1970), Fire and Fire Raisers (1974), Understanding EEG (1975), An EEG Data and Retrieval System (1981), Coping with Suicide (1989), Beating Job Burnout (1989); *Recreations* gardening, writing, swimming; *Style*— Dr Donald Scott; 25 Park Gate, Blackheath, London SE3 9XF (☎ 081 852 5267); Flat 4I, Fase 2, Europlaya Calle Corbetta, Calpe, Allicante, Spain; Clinical Neurophysiological Dept, London Hospital, London E1 1BB (☎ 071 377 7239)

SCOTT, Douglas Gordon; s of Herbert Scott (d 1956), of Liverpool, and Emily, *née* Smith (d 1955); *b* 23 Dec 1928; *Educ* Liverpool Collegiate Sch; *m* 12 June 1948, Barbara Joyce, da of Reginald Arthur Cyril Rayner (d 1960), of Coulsdon, Surrey; 1 s (Ian Gordon); *Career* Scots Gds 1946-48; asst accountant Hambros Bank Gp 1950-53, area mangr Lombard Banking 1953-67; dir: Lyon Gp 1970-74, John Finlan 1974-77, Trust Securities 1977-80; chm Urban & City Properties 1980-; chm Purley Sports Club, sec Purley Bowls Club; Freeman City of London, Liveryman Worshipful Co of Carmen 1984; *Recreations* cricket; *Clubs* KMCC, Forty; *Style*— Douglas Scott, Esq; Caprice, Hillcroft Ave, Purley, Surrey; Appt Phenicia, Passeig Maritim, L'Escala, Costa Brava, Spain; Greenfield House, 69-73, Manor Rd, Wallington, Surrey (☎ 081 773 1429, fax 081 647 0321)

SCOTT, Douglas Keith (Doug); s of George Douglas Scott, of Nottingham, and Edith Joyce Scott; *b* 29 May 1941; *Educ* Cottesmore Secdy Modern Sch, Mundella GS Nottingham, Loughborough Teachers' Trg Coll (Cert); *m* 1962 (m dis 1988), Janice Elaine, da of Thomas Arthur Brook, of Notts; 1 s (Michael b 1963), 2 da (Martha b 1973, Rosie b 1978); *Career* began climbing 12 years old, visited Alps 17 years old and every year thereafter; first ascents: Tarso Teiroko Tibest Mountains Sahara 1965, Cilo Dag Mountains SE Turkey 1966, S face Koh-i-Bandaka (22500 feet) Hindu Kush Afghanistan 1967; first Br ascent Salathé Wall El Capitain Yosemite 1971; memb: Euro Mt Everest Expedition to SW face 1972; first ascent E pillar of Mt Asgard Baffin Island Expedition 1972, Br Mt Everest Expedition to SW face 1972 (autumn), first ascent SE spur Pic Lenin (7189m) 1974, Br Mt Everest Expedition (reached summit with Dougal Haston, via SW face, first Britons on summit) 1975, first alpine ascent of S face via new route Mt McKinley (6226m, with Dougal Haston) 1976; first ascents incl: E face direct Mt Kenya 1976, Orge (7330m) Karakoram Mountains 1977, N Ridge route Kangchenjunga 1977 (and without oxygen 1979), N summit Kussum Kangguru 1979, N face Nuptse 1979, alpine style Kangchungtse (7640m) 1980, Shivling E pillar 1981, Pungpa Ri (7445m) 1982, Shishapangma S face (8046m) 1982, Labsang Spire (Karakoram) 1983, Broad Peak (8047m) 1983, E summit Mt Chamlang (7287m) 1984, Diran (7260m) 1985, S face Mt Jitchu Drake (6793m) Bhutan 1988; pres Alpine Climbing Gp; *Publications* Big Wall Climbing (1974), Shishapangma Tibet (1984); contributor to Alpine Journal, American Alpine Journal and Mountain Magazine; *Recreations* rock climbing, photography, organic gardening; *Clubs* Alpine, Nottingham Climbers, Alpine Climbing Gp; *Style*— Doug Scott, Esq; Slate Cottage, Bewcastle,

Cumbria CA6 6PX

SCOTT, Lady Elizabeth Louise Margaret; *née* Meade; da of 5 Earl of Clanwilliam; *b* 18 April 1911; *m* 1933, Lt-Col Charles Rankin Scott, KRRC (d 1965); 2 s; *Style*— The Lady Elizabeth Scott; Culkerton, Tetbury, Glos

SCOTT, Esme; *née* Burnett; CBE (1985); da of David Burnett (d 1968), and Jane, *née* Thornton (d 1967); *b* 1 Jan 1932; *Educ* St George's Sch for Girls Edinburgh, Univ of Edinburgh (MA, LLB); *m* 1, 17 March 1956, Ian Macfarlane Walker (d 1988), s of James Walker (d 1950); 1 s (Angus David Macfarlane b 9 Aug 1960); m 2, 5 Jan 1990, Sir Kenneth Scott, KCVO, CMG, s of Adam Scott; *Career* lectr Queen Margaret Coll Edinburgh 1977-83; chm: Scottish Consumer Cncl 1981-85, Scottish Assoc of CAB 1986-88, Volunteer Devpt Scotland 1989-; vice chm Nat Consumer Cncl 1984-87, cmmnr Equal Opportunities Cmmn 1986-; tstee John Watson's Tst; memb: Scottish Consumer Cncl 1980-81, Scottish Ctee of the Cncl on Tbnls 1986-, Cncl St George's Sch for Girls, Social Security Advsy Ctee 1990-, Direct Mail Services Standards Bd 1990-, Ct Univ of Edinburgh 1989-; FRSA 1987, memb Law Soc of Scotland 1974; *Recreations* crosswords; *Clubs* New (Edinburgh); *Style*— Lady Scott, CBE; 13 Clinton Rd, Edinburgh (☎ 031 447 5191); Barrelfield, Waterfoot, by Carradale, Kintyre

SCOTT, (John) Fenwick Easton; JP; s of Dr (John) Alwyn Easton Scott (d 1955), of Midhurst, and Eveleen Dorothy, *née* Purcell (d 1984); *b* 30 May 1942; *Educ* Cranleigh; *m* 9 Sept 1966, Jayne Anne, da of Douglas Craven Hodgson, of Lincs; 1 s (Simon b 11 Oct 1969), 2 da (Clarissa b 24 Nov 1971, Kirstie b 7 July 1974); *Career* dir Nationwide Anglia Estate Agencies, chm and md King & Chasemore, gen cmmr for tax; Freeman City of London, Liveryman Worshipful Co of Armourers and Brasiers; FRICS; *Recreations* golf; *Clubs* W Sussex Golf; *Style*— Fenwick Scott, Esq, JP; Amblehurst Manor Farm, Wisborough Green, Billinghurst, W Sussex RH14 OEP (☎ 0403 700231); Richmond House, Carfax, Horsham, W Sussex RH12 1AQ (☎ 0403 64441)

SCOTT, (Celia) Gay; da of Ivor Norman Bailey (d 1986), and Enid Alice, *née* Sherwood; *b* 25 March 1944; *Educ* St Angela's Providence Convent London, NW London Poly, Brighton Coll of Librarianship; *m* 18 May 1967, Michael James Frederick Scott, s of Capt John Bristol Irwin Scott, of 20 De Parys Ave, Bedford; 1 s (Charles b 1982); *Career* membs' info serv House of Commons 1973-74, head of Euro Unit Greater London Cncl 1976-80, fndr and dir European Information Ltd (acquired by Eurofi 1982) 1980-, dir Eurofi 1982-; assoc Library Assoc 1967, MIInfSc 1977; *Books* The European Economic Community (1979), A Guide to European Community Grants and Loans (annual, 1980-), Money for Research and Development (jtly, 1986), Eurobrief (monthly, 1981-83); *Recreations* riding, walking, cookery, skiing, theatre going, gardening; *Style*— Mrs Michael Scott; The Old Rectory, Northill, Beds SG18 9AH (☎ 076727 680, fax 076727 580); Guildgate House, Pelican Lane, Newbury, Berks (☎ 0635 31900, fax 0635 37370)

SCOTT, Prof Gerald; *b* 28 July 1927; *Educ* Balliol Coll Oxford (MA, MSc, DSc); *Career* Dyestuffs Div ICI Ltd Blackley Manchester, mangr Polymer Auxiliaries Res 1959-65, head works Res and Devpt Dept 1965-67, prof of polymer sci Aston Univ 1967-79, prof emeritus 1979-; hon fell Materials Life Soc Japan 1988, academician Acad of Creators USSR; FRSC, FPRI; *Books* Atmospheric Oxidation and Antioxidants (1965), Developments in Polymer Stabilisation (vol 1 to 8, 1979), Polymer Degradation and Stabilisation (with N Grassie, 1984), Mechanisms of Polymer Degradation and Stabilisation (1991); *Recreations* photography, hill walking; *Style*— Prof Gerald Scott; Dept of Chemical Engineering and Applied Chemistry, Aston University, Aston Triangle, Birmingham B4 7ET (☎ 021 359 3611, fax 021 359 7358, telex 336997 UNIAST G)

SCOTT, Graham Robert; s of Robert Alexander Scott, of Alness, Ross-shire, and Helen, *née* Tawse (d 1987); *b* 8 Dec 1944; *Educ* Bryanston Sch, Nottingham Univ (BSc); *m* 19 Aug 1967, Wendy Jean, da of Harry Mumford (d 1983); 1 s (Andrew), 1 da (Harriet); *Career* gen mangr Unitrition Int Ltd 1984-86, md BP Nutrition (UK) Ltd 1987-, chm BP Nutrition (Ireland) Ltd 1988-; CEng 1971, MIChemE 1971; *Style*— Graham Scott, Esq; BP Nutrition (UK) Ltd, Wincham, Northwich, Ches (☎ 0606 41133, fax 0606 41963, telex 668994)

SCOTT, Guy Baliol; s of Reginald Benjamin Scott (d 1950), of Alan Rd, Wimbledon, and Eileen Ann, *née* Brownlow (d 1978); *b* 26 July 1919; *Educ* Charterhouse; *m* 1, 17 July 1948, Elizabeth Winifred (d 1982), da of Charles Hendry (d 1952), of Parkside, Wimbledon; m 2, Gale Stirling, da of James Athelstane Stedman (d 1985), of Boxford, Suffolk; 1 s (Benjamin Brownlow b 15 Sept 1984); *Career* RA: enlisted 1939, cmmnd 2 Lt 1940, Lt 1941, Capt 1943; attached Indian Artillery 1940, Maharajah Rao Scindia Field Battery 1943, demobbed Larkhill 1946; sr ptnr Benjamin J Scott & Co 1951, jt sr ptnr Penney Easton & Co 1985; memb London Stock Exchange 1946; *Recreations* shooting, fishing, historical reading, travel; *Clubs* Army & Navy; *Style*— Guy B Scott, Esq

SCOTT, Henry Douglas Edward; s and h of Sir Anthony Percy Scott, 3 Bt, and Caroline Teresa Anne, er da of (William Charles) Edward Bacon; *b* 26 March 1964; *Educ* Harrow; *Career* Anglo Chemical Commodities, a div of Philipp Brothers Ltd; *Style*— Henry Scott, Esq

SCOTT, Sir (Charles) Hilary; s of Lt-Col Charles Edward Scott (ka 1916), of Heaton, Bradford, Yorks, and Margaret Elizabeth Mary Ackroyd (d 1972); *b* 27 March 1906; *Educ* Sedbergh; *m* 16 July 1932, Beatrice Margery, da of late Rev Canon Robert Garrad, of Bentham, Yorks; 1 s, 2 da; *Career* articled Wade & Co Bradford Slr 1930; ptnr Slaughter and May 1937-74, RNVR 1940-45; memb: Cncl of Law Soc 1948-71 (vice-pres 1965-66, pres 1966-67), Nat Film Finance Corp 1948-70 (chm 1964-70), Jenkins Ctee on Co Law 1959-62; trustee Glyndebourne Arts Trust 1963-76; dir: Tarmac Ltd 1968-76, Equity and Law Life Assurance Soc Ltd 1955-82; chm Ctee on Property Bonds and Equity Linked Life Assurance 1971-73; memb: London Local Bd of Bank of Scotland 1966-76, Panel of Judges of the Accounts Awards for Company Accounts 1961-69, London Advsy Bd of Salvation Army 1966-81, Cncl of Royal Sch of Church Music 1975-85, Noise Advsy Cncl 1971-74; FRSA; kt 1967; *Style*— Sir Hilary Scott; Knowle House, Bishop's Walk, Addington, Surrey CR0 5BA (☎ 071 654 3638)

SCOTT, Hugh Johnstone; s of Hugh Johnstone Scott (d 1983), and Agnes Alison Leckie, *née* Storie; *Educ* Paisley GS, Glasgow Sch of Art (DA), Jordanhill Coll (Cert Ed); *m* 23 Dec 1960, Mary Smith Craig, da of James Hamilton; 1 s (David b 7 Oct 1961), 1 da (Caroline b 18 Sept 1963); *Career* Nat Serv 1958-60; art teacher various schs 1971-84 (latterly head of art Lomond Sch Helensburgh); full time author 1984-; books incl: The Shaman's Stone (1988), The Plant That Ate The World (1989), Why Weeps The Brogan? (1989), Freddie and the Enormouse, The Haunted Sand, The Camera Obscura, The Summertime Santa, Something Watching; writer in residence City of Aberdeen 1991 (Scottish Arts Cncl bursary), pt/t lectr in creative writing Adult and Continuing Educn Dept Univ of Glasgow 1988-; won Woman's Realm Children's Story Competition 1982, Scottish Arts Cncl bursary 1988-89, Whitbread Children's Category Book of the Year 1989; memb Soc of Authors 1988-; *Recreations* swimming, weight training, reading, exploring England; *Style*— Hugh Scott, Esq; Helensburgh; Walker Books Ltd, 87 Vauxhall Walk, London SE11 5HJ (☎ 071 793 0909, fax 071 587 1123)

SCOTT, Iain William St Clair; s of Lt-Col Joseph William St Clair Scott, and Margaret Brown, *née* Rodger (d 1977); *b* 14 May 1946; *Educ* George Watsons Coll Edinburgh; *m* 1 Oct 1971, Noelle Margaret Gilmour (Jill), da of Archibald Gilmour Young (d 1989), of 61 Newhailes Cresent, Musselburgh, Edinburgh; 1 s (Ruaridh b 1976), 1 da (Susan b 1973); *Career* CA 1970; Bank of Scot: cost accountant 1973, asst chief accountant 1981, mangr corp planning 1983, asst gen mangr corporate planning 1985, div gen mangr accounting and fin 1986-, gen mangr mgmnt servs; memb Scot Consultative Ctee on the Curriculum; AIB (Scot) 1988; *Recreations* golf, curling, squash; *Clubs* Hon Co of Edinburgh Golfers, Bruntsfield Links GS; *Style*— Iain Scott, Esq; 22 Bramdean Rise, Edinburgh EH10 6JR (☎ 031 447 2453); 13 Woodlands Road, Lundin Links, Fife; Bank of Scotland, Management Servs, Sighthill Centre, PO Box 403, 2 Bankhead Crossway North, Edinburgh EH11 4EF (☎ 031 243 7711, fax 031 442 7441, telex 72396)

SCOTT, Sir Ian Dixon; KCMG (1962, CMG 1959), KCVO (1965), CIE (1947); s of Thomas Henderson Scott, OBE, of Selkirk, and Mary Agnes, *née* Dixon; *b* 6 March 1909; *Educ* Queen's Royal Coll Trinidad, Balliol Coll Oxford, LSE; *m* 1937, Hon Anna Drusilla, o da of 1 Baron Lindsay of Birker, CBE (d 1952); 1 s, 4 da; *Career* entered ICS 1932, transferred Political Service 1935, dep private sec to Viceroy 1945-47, first sec UK High Cmmr's Office Pakistan 1947-48, dep dir personnel John Lewis & Co Ltd London 1948-50, entered FO 1950; first sec: British Legation Helsinki 1952-53, British Embassy Beirut 1954; cnsllr 1956-58, IDC 1959, consul gen Leopoldville 1960; ambass: Republic of Congo 1960-61, Sudan 1961-65, Norway 1965-68; dir Clarkson's Holidays Ltd 1969-72 (chm 1972-73); chm Suffolk Area Health Authy 1973-77; memb Cncl Dr Barnardo's 1970-84 (chm 1972-78); memb Bd of Govrs Felixstowe Coll 1971-84 (chm 1972-80); pres Indian Civil Service (ret) Association 1977-; *Books* Tumbled House, The Congo At Independence; *Recreations* yachting; *Style*— Sir Ian Scott, KCMG, KCVO, CIE; Ash House, Alde Lane, Aldeburgh, Suffolk

SCOTT, Prof Ian Richard; s of Ernest Richard Scott (d 1971), of Geelong, Aust, and Edith Miriam Scott (d 1976); *b* 8 Jan 1940; *Educ* Geelong Coll, Queen's Coll, Univ of Melbourne (LLB), King's Coll London (PhD); *m* 31 Oct 1971, Ecce Scott, da of Prof Boris Norman Cole, of Leeds; 2 da (Anneke b 1 Jan 1978, Kaatye b 3 Jan 1981); *Career* barr and slr Supreme Ct of Victoria 1964-, reader judicial admin Univ of Birmingham 1976-78, dir Inst of Judicial Admin Univ of Birmingham 1976-82, visiting res prof Whittier Coll California 1978-79, Barber prof of law Univ of Birmingham 1978-, exec dir Victoria Law Fndn 1982-84, dean Faculty of Law Univ of Birmingham 1985-, memb Lord Chllrs Review Body on Civil Justice 1985-88, chm Home Sec's N Yorkshire Magistrates' Courts Inquiry 1989; hon master of the Bench Gray's Inn 1988; *Books* The Crown Court (1971), English Criminal Justice (with E C Friesen, 1976); *Style*— Prof I R Scott; Faculty of Law, University of Birmingham, Birmingham B15 2TT (☎ 021 414 6291)

SCOTT, Ian Russell; s of William Russell Scott (d 1974), of Weymouth, and Winifred Mabel, *née* Morgan; *b* 12 Sept 1942; *Educ* Sherborne, Univ of London (LLB); *m* 3 May 1969, Mary Peverell, da of Robert Riggs Wright, TD, of Piddletrenthide, Dorchester, Dorset; 1 s (William b 1975), 2 da (Katharine b 1971, Louise b 1973); *Career* asst slr: Sharpe Pritchard & Co 1967-68, Ashurst Morris Crisp 1968-72 (ptnr 1972-); memb Law Soc 1965; *Recreations* theatre, tennis, hockey, golf, sailing; *Clubs* City of London, Roehampton; *Style*— Ian Scott, Esq; 15 Briar Walk, London SW15; Moonfleet, Ringstead Bay, Dorchester (☎ 081 788 1588); Ashurst Morris Crisp, Broadwalk Hse, 5 Appold St, London EC2A 2HA (☎ 071 638 1111, fax 071 972 7990, telex 887067)

SCOTT, James Alexander; OBE (1987); s of Douglas McPherson Scott (d 1971), and Mabel Mary, *née* Skepper (d 1962); *b* 30 April 1940; *Educ* Uppingham, Magdalene Coll Cambridge (scholar, MA), London Business Sch (MSc); *m* 24 April 1965, Annette, *née* Goslett; 3 s (David b 8 Jan 1967, Charles b 10 Dec 1971, Alastair b 2 May 1973), 2 da (Joanna b 1 May 1968, Catriona b 20 Oct 1979); *Career* BDO Binder Hamlyn (formerly Binder Hamlyn & Co): articled clerk 1961-64, ptnr 1969, managing ptnr London 1980, nat managing ptnr 1988; sec Review Bd for Govt Contracts 1969-; memb: Agric Wages Bd for Eng and Wales 1971-86, Pharmacists Remuneration Review Panel 1983; DTI inspr Atlantic Computers plc 1990; FCA (ACA 1964); *Recreations* walking, golf, tennis, skiing; *Clubs* Berkshire Golf, St Enodoc Golf; *Style*— James Scott, Esq, OBE; Southbrook, Shrubbs Hill, Chobham, Surrey GU24 8ST (☎ 0276 858431); BDO Binder Hamlyn, 20 Old Bailey, London EC4M 7BH (☎ 071 489 9000, fax 071 489 6283)

SCOTT, Prof James Alexander; CBE (1985); s of Thomas Scott (d 1976), of Doncaster, and Margaret Lilian, *née* Woodhouse (d 1976); *b* 3 July 1957; *Educ* Doncaster GS, Trinity Coll Dublin (BA, MB, BCh, BAO, MA, MD); *m* 13 July 1957, Margaret Olive, da of Charles Edward Slinger, of Harrogate (d 1976); 1 s (Julian b 1958), 2 da (Kathleen b 1959, Alexandra b 1961); *Career* sr admin med offr Sheffield Regnl Hosp Bd 1971-73, regnl med offr Trent Regnl Health Authy 1973-88, special prof of health care planning Univ of Nottingham 1974-, prof assoc health serv planning Univ of Sheffield 1988-; fell faculty of public health med, chm bd of govrs Mid Trent Coll of Nursing and Midwifery 1989-; hon LLD Univ of Sheffield 1987; FRCP; *Style*— Prof James Scott; 5 Slayleigh Lane, Sheffield S10 3RE (☎ 0742 302238)

SCOTT, James Archibald; CB (1988), LVO (1961); s of James Scott, MBE (d 1983), of Beechhurst, Hawick, Roxburghshire, and Agnes Bone, *née* Howie (d 1985); *b* 5 March 1932; *Educ* Dollar Acad, Univ of St Andrews, Queen's Univ of Ontario (MA); *m* 27 Aug 1957, Elizabeth Agnes Joyce, da of John Trant Buchan-Hepburn (d 1953), of Chagford, St Andrews, Fife; 3 s (Buchan b 1962, Robert b 1964, Hector b 1969), 1 da (Frances (Mrs Rive) b 1960); *Career* RAF Aircrew 1954-56, Flying Offr XI Sqdn 1956; joined CRO 1956; first sec: UK High Cmmn New Delhi 1958-62, UK Mission to UN NY 1962-65; transferred SO 1965, PPS to Sec of State for Scot 1969-71, asst sec Scot Devpt Dept 1971; sec: Scot Educn Dept 1984-87, Indust Dept for Scot 1987-90 (under sec 1976-84); chief exec Scot Devpt Agency 1990-; *Recreations* music, golf; *Clubs* Travellers'; *Style*— James Scott, Esq, CB, LVO; Scottish Development Agency, 120 Bothwell St, Glasgow G2 7JP (☎ 041 248 2700)

SCOTT, James Jervoise; s and h of Sir James Scott, 2 Bt, DL; *b* 12 Oct 1952; *m* 13 Oct 1982, Judy Evelyn, da of Brian Trafford, of Tismans, Rudgwick, Sussex; 1 s (Arthur Jervoise Trafford b 1984); *Style*— James Scott, Esq; 36 Endlesham Rd, London SW12 8JU

SCOTT, James Michael; s of the late William George Scott, CBE, of Bennets Hill Farm, Coleford, Bath, and Hilda Mary, *née* Lucas; *b* 9 July 1941; *Educ* Bryanston, Sorbonne Paris, UCL, Slade Sch of Art London; *m* 19 Feb 1966 (m dis 1977), Anna Katherine; 1 s (Alexander Ivan b 10 Sept 1967), 1 da (Rosie Beth b 5 Sept 1971); *Career* film dir; short films: The Rocking Horse 1962, In Separation 1965, A Shocking Accident 1982 (Oscar winner 1983), Crime in The City 1987, People are The Same The Universe Over; pop video Saxon 1983; documentaries: Love's Presentation 1966, RB Kitaj 1967, Richard Hamilton 1969, The Great Ice Cream Robbery 1971, Night Cleaners 1974, '36 to'77 1978, Chance History Art 1979 (Silver prize Melbourne); features: Adult Fun 1972, Coilin and Platonida 1976, Loser Takes All 1989; TV: Every Picture Tells a Story 1984, Getting Even - A Wimp's Revenge 1985, Inspector Morse 1989; memb: Dirs Guild of Br and USA, Br Film Acad, American Acad of Motion Picture Art; *Recreations* reading, painting; *Style*— James Scott, Esq; Richard Hatton Ltd (☎ 081 876 6999, fax 081 876 8278)

SCOTT, Sir James Walter; 2 Bt (UK 1962), of Rotherfield Park, Alton, Hants; s of Col Sir Jervoise Bolitho Scott, 1 Bt (d 1965); *b* 26 Oct 1924; *Educ* Eton; *m* 8 Dec 1951, Anne Constantia, da of late Lt-Col Clive Grantham Austin, DL, and Lady Lilian Mary Theodora Lumley, sis of 11 Earl of Scarbrough; 3 s, 1 da; *Heir* s, James Jervoise Scott; *Career* Lt-Col (ret) Life Gds formerly Grenadier Gds; served WWII, NW Europe 1944-45, Palestine 1945-46; ADC to viceroy and govr-gen of India 1946-48, Malaya 1948-49, Cyprus 1958, 1960 and 1964, Malaysia 1966, ret 1969; memb Lloyd's; Master of Mercers' Co 1976; HM Body Guard of Hon Corps of Gentlemen-at-Arms 1977-; High Sheriff Hants 1981-82, Lord-Lieut of Hants 1982- (DL 1978-82); JP 1982; hon Col 2 Bn The Wessex Regt; KStJ 1984; *Recreations* countryside activities; *Clubs* Cavalry and Guards', Farmers, IOD; *Style*— Sir James Scott, Bt; Rotherfield Park, Alton, Hants (☎ 042058 204)

SCOTT, John Gavin; s of Douglas Gavin Scott, and Hetty, *née* Murphy; *b* 18 June 1956; *Educ* Queen Elizabeth GS Wakefield, St John's Coll Cambridge (organ scholar, MA, MusB); *m* 28 July 1979, Carolyn Jane, da of David James Lumsden; 1 s (Alexander Gavin b 29 Oct 1987), 1 da (Emma Jane b 27 Dec 1984); *Career* asst organist: Wakefield Cathedral 1970-74, St Paul's and Southwark Cathedrals 1978-84; organist and dir of music St Paul's Cathedral 1990- (sub-organist 1984-90); debut Henry Wood Promenade Concerts 1977, Royal Festival Hall Debut March 1979; frequent solo tours, dir of St Paul's Cathedral Choir in numerous concerts, tours and recordings; as a Soloist: Ad nos, ad Salutarem undam by Liszt 1984, Organ Music by Marcel Dupré 1986, Organ Music by Maurice Duruflé 1989, Organ Music by Mendelssohn, Janacek Glagolitic Mass 1990; recordings as Conductor with St Paul's Choir: Christmas Music 1986, My Soul doth Magnify the Lord 1987, Herbert Howell's Church Music 1987, My Spirit hath Rejoiced 1988, Praise to the Lord 1989, The English Anthem 1989, Stainer: Crucifixion 1990; awarded first prize: Manchester International Organ Competition 1978, Leipzig J S Bach Competition 1984; Hon RAM 1990; *Recreations* reading, travel; *Style*— John Scott, Esq; 4 Amen Court, London EC4M 7BU (☎ 071 248 6868, fax 071 248 3104); Magenta Music Int Ltd, 64 Highgate High St, London N6 5HX (☎ 081 340 8321)

SCOTT, Dr John Graham; s of Walter Francis Scott (d 1985), of Beckenham, Kent, and Sybil, *née* Doré (d 1975); *b* 14 Feb 1938; *Educ* St Pauls, St Mary's Hosp Univ of London (MB BS); *m* 9 July 1970, Christina Sui-Lin, da of FS Lian (d 1987), of Kuala Lumpur, Malaysia; 1 s (William Francis b 10 Aug 1973); *Career* sr house offr in anaesthetics Edgeware 1963; registrar in anaesthetics: Portsmouth 1964, Royal Free Hosp 1965; sr registrar in anaesthetics E Grinstead 1966, visiting fell in Anaesthesiology N Western Univ of Chicago 1968; conslt anaesthetist: Nigerian Armed Forces Med Serv 1969, Bromley Health Dist 1970-; memb: Assoc of Anaesthetists, BMA; FFARCS 1966; *Recreations* skiing, golf; *Clubs* Old Pauline; *Style*— Dr John Scott; 8 Regents Drive, Keston, Kent BR2 6BU (☎ 0689 851542); Dept of Anaesthesia, Bromley Hospital, Cromwell Rd, Bromley, Kent (☎ 081 460 9933)

SCOTT, Dr John James; s of Lt-Col John Creagh Scott, DSO, OBE, of Langhill, Moretonhampstead, Devon (d 1959), and Mary Elizabeth Marjory, *née* Murray of Polmaise (d 1981), da of Maj Alastair Bruce Murray 13th of Touchadam and Polmaise, Co Stirling (d 1924) (*see* Burke's LG 19379 edn); *b* 4 Sept 1924; *Educ* Radley, Corpus Christi Coll Cambridge (BA, MA), Univ of London (PhD); *m* 1, 1948, Katherine Mary, da of Robert Bruce, of London (d 1955); 2 da (Caroline b 1950, Katherine b 1950 (twins)); m 2, 1956, Heather Marguerite, da of Lt-Col Ivor Douglas-Browne, of Vence, Alpes Maritimes, France (d 1948); m 3, 1963, June Rose, da of Arthur Ernest Mackie, of London; 2 s (James b 1966, John b 1966 (twins)); *Career* Capt Argyll & Sutherland Highlanders 1944-47, Palestine; Staff of Nat Inst for Med Res 1950-55, sr lectr Chemical Pathology St Mary's Hosp 1955-61, Editorial Bd Biochemical Journal 1956-61; memb Ctee Biochemical Soc 1961; visiting scientist Nat Insts of Health Bethesda Md 1961; entered Dip Serv 1961; Office of Cmmr Gen for SE Asia Singapore 1962; Office of Political Advsr to C-in-C Far East 1963; FO 1966; cncllr Rio de Janeiro and Brasilia 1971; seconded to NI Office as asst sec Stormont 1974; asst under sec of state FCO 1978-80; commercial dir Industl Engines (Sales) Ltd, Elbar Group 1980; fin planning conslt and md Dudmass Ltd 1983-; Francis Bacon prize Cambridge 1950; *Publications* in Biochem Jl, Proceedings Royal Soc and other learned jls 1951-61; rowed for Cambridge in Oxford Cambridge Boat Race 1944; *Recreations* botany, music, wine; *Clubs* Inst of Dirs, Leander, Hawks, Ski (of GB); *Style*— Dr John J Scott; The Cottage, South Rauceby, Sleaford, Lincs NG34 7QG (☎ 05298 254)

SCOTT, John Newton; OBE (1971), TD (1945); s of Newton Livingstone Scott (d 1955), of Bournemouth, and Dora, *née* Greenhill (d 1965); *b* 26 June 1917; *Educ* Marlborough; *m* 22 Dec 1949, Suzanne Louise, da of Frederick George Deane (d 1960), of Sydney, Aust; 2 s (James Antony b 1950, David b 1961), 1 da (Sarah Jane b 1954); *Career* WWII Capt Hampshire Regt, Maj RWAFF 1942; admitted slr 1947, sr ptnr Scott Bailey & Co Lymington 1950-82, dir Dukes Hotel London 1976-89; clerk to New Forest Ct of Verderers 1955-73, vice pres New Forest 9 Centenary Tst; memb Law Soc; *Recreations* boating, fishing, unskilled carpentry; *Clubs* Lymington Town Sailing; *Style*— John Scott, Esq, OBE, TD; The Old School House, Melbury Abbas, Shaftsbury, Dorset (☎ 0747 53408)

SCOTT, John Philip Henry Schomberg; s of Christopher Bartle Hugh Scott, of Hollybush, Galashiels, Scotland, and Anne Margaret D'Arcy, *née* Kerr; *b* 20 July 1952; *Educ* Eton, Magdalene Coll Cambridge (MA), INSEAD Fontainebleau France (MBA); *m* 6 Dec 1977, Jacqueline Dawn, da of Maj Colin George Champion Rae, MC, of Little Weston House, Little Weston, Somerset; 2 s (Alexander Hugh Frere b 8 Dec 1982, James Julian Frere b 1 April 1985); *Career* Jardine Matheson & Co Ltd Hong Kong 1974-80, dir Lazard Brothers & Co Ltd London 1988- (joined 1981-); memb Queens Body Guard for Scotland (Royal Co of Archers); Freeman: City of London 1981, Worshipful Co of Grocers 1981; FCII 1980; *Recreations* outdoor sports; *Style*— John Scott, Esq; Lazard Brothers & Co Ltd, 21 Moorfields, London EC2P 2HT (☎ 071 5882721, fax 071 6282485, telex 886438)

SCOTT, (Walter) John; s and h of Maj Sir Walter Scott, 4 Bt, JP, DL; *b* 24 Feb 1948; *Educ* privately; *m* 1, 5 July 1969 (m dis 1971), Lowell Patria, da of late Gp Capt Pat Vaughan Goddard, of Auckland, NZ; 1 da (Rebecca b 1970); m 2, 24 June 1977, Mary Gavin Anderson, 1 s (Walter Samuel b 1984), 1 da (Diana Helen Rose b 1977); *Career* farmer; *Recreations* field sports; *Style*— John Scott, Esq

SCOTT, John William; s of Donald Alan Scott (d 1960), and Minnie Gertrude, *née* Watts (d 1968); *b* 6 April 1930; *Educ* Marlborough, Worcester Coll Oxford (MA); *m* 1957, Rhoda Janet, da of Robert Cecil Mayall, CMG, DSO, MC (d 1962); 3 s; *Career* Nat and TA Serv, Mddx Regt, Capt; slr; ptnr Clifford-Turner 1961-86, conslt Clifford Chance 1987-90; *Books* Legibus, a history of Clifford-Turner, Caught in Court (legal cases with cricket connections); *Recreations* cricket, golf, family history; *Clubs* City Univ, MCC, Lord's Taverners; *Style*— John Scott, Esq; Bemerton, Lingfield Rd, East Grinstead, West Sussex RH19 2EJ; Clifford Chance, Blackfriars House, New Bridge St, London EC4V 6BY (☎ 071 353 0211, telex 887847)

SCOTT, (Ian) Jonathan; s of Col Alexander Brassey Jonathan Scott, DSO, MC (d 1978), of Lasborough, Tetbury, and Rhona Margaret, *née* Stewart; *b* 7 Feb 1940; *Educ* Harrow, Balliol Coll Oxford (BA); *m* 12 June 1965, Annabella Constance, JP, da of Francis William Hope Loudon (d 1985), of Olantigh, Kent, and his w Lady Prudence, *née* Jellicoe, da of 1 Earl Jellicoe; 2 s (Alexander b 1966, Justin b 1970), 1 da (Julia b 1969); *Career* dir: Charterhouse Japhet Ltd 1973-80, Barclays Merchant Bank Ltd 1980-85, Barclays de Zoete Wedd Ltd 1985-; chm Reviewing Ctee on the Export of Works of Art 1985-; tstee Imp War Museum 1984-; FSA 1980; *Books* Piranesi (1975); *Clubs* Brooks's; *Style*— Jonathan Scott, Esq, FSA; Lasborough Manor, Tetbury, Glos; 18 Abingdon Villas, London W8; Barclays de Zoete Wedd Ltd, Ebbgate House, Swan Lane, London EC4

SCOTT, (Norman) Keith; CBE (1989); s of Norman Scott (d 1986), and Dora Scott (d 1979); *b* 10 Feb 1927; *Educ* Preston GS, Univ of Liverpool Sch of Architecture (BArch, MA), Univ of Liverpool Sch of Planning (DipCD), Massachusetts Inst of Technol Boston USA (MArch); *m* 19 Jan 1952, Dorothy Anne, da of Frederick Walker (d 1958); 2 s (Quentin Nicholas b 3 Sept 1959, (Timothy) Tarquin b 7 March 1964), 2 da (Louise Amanda b 22 Nov 1953, Hilary Jane b 7 June 1956); *Career* architect to Dean and Chapter Liverpool Cathedral 1979-; chm: Awards Panel RIBA 1982-84, BDP 1984 (ptnr 1983-); memb Bd Lake Dist Summer Music Festival 1984- (chm 1990-); govr Lancs Poly 1988-; life memb Victorian Soc; chm: N Lancs Soc of Architects 1966-67, BDP Music Soc 1968-; FRIBA, MRTPI; *Books* Shopping Centre Design (1989); *Recreations* music, fell walking, sketching; *Clubs* Oriental; *Style*— Keith Scott, Esq, CBE; Overleigh House, East Cliff, Preston PR1 3JE (☎ 0772 53545); Building Design Partnership, Vernon St, Moor Lane, Preston PR1 3PQ (☎ 0772 59383, fax 0772 555845, telex 667160, car 0836 601170)

SCOTT, Laurence Keith; s of Dr Edward Keith Scott, of Beacon Ridge, Portscatho, Truro, Cornwall, and Mary, *née* Bond (d 1977); *b* 7 Nov 1947; *Educ* Downside; *m* 22 Aug 1981, Lucinda Jane, da of Lt Cdr HV Bruce, RN, JP, DL; 4 s (Edward b 1982, Toby b 1984, Oliver b 1987, Barnaby b 1989); *Career* RAF (pilot) 1967-72; commercial pilot 1972-73; with Lloyds 1973-88; chm Grimston Scott Ltd 1988-; dir: Heath Carroll Ltd 1988-, The Wilcox Gp (USA) 1988-, The Life Assur Redemption Corp; *Recreations* fishing, shooting, sailing, gardening, philately; *Clubs* MCC; *Style*— Laurence Scott, Esq; Roe Green, Martyr Worthy, Winchester, Hampshire (☎ 096 278 278)

SCOTT, Dame (Catherine) Margaret Mary (Mrs Denton); DBE (1981, OBE 1977); da of John Douglas Scott (d 1985), of Swaziland, and Marjorie Heath, *née* Bagley; *b* 26 April 1922; *Educ* Parktown Convent Johannesburg S Africa; *m* 1953, Prof Derek Ashworth Denton; 2 s (Matthew, Angus); *Career* founding dir Australian Ballet Sch 1962-90; awarded DBE for service to ballet; hon LLD Melbourne Univ 1989, hon life membership The Aust Ballet Fndn 1989; *Recreations* theatre, music, swimming, walking, garden; *Clubs* Alexander, Melbourne; *Style*— Dame Margaret Scott, DBE; 816 Orrong Rd, Toorak, Melbourne, Vic 3142, Australia (☎ 03 827 2640); Aust Ballet Centre, 2 Kauanagh St, S Melbourne, Vic 3205, Australia (☎ 03 649 8600)

SCOTT, Margaretta (Mrs John Wooldridge); da of Hugh Arther Scott (d 1950), of London, and Bertha Eugene, *née* Casano (d 1964); *b* 13 Feb 1912; *Educ* Convent of the Holy Child Cavendish Square London, RADA; *m* 14 Sept 1948, John De Lacy Wooldridge, DSO, DFC (d 1958), s of Gilbert De Lacy Wooldridge; 1 s (Hugh De Lacy b 1952), 1 da (Susan Margot b 1950); *Career* actress: various theatre film and TV productions 1928-; memb Ctee: The Theatrical Ladies Guild, The Actors Charitable Tst, The Stars Orgn for Spastics; *Recreations* my family; *Style*— Miss Margaretta Scott

SCOTT, Maurice FitzGerald; s of Col Gerald Chaplin Scott, OBE (d 1953), of Ramsey, Isle of Man, and Harriet Mary Geraldine, *née* FitzGerald (d 1983); *b* 6 Dec 1924; *Educ* Campbell Coll Belfast, Wadham Coll Oxford (BA, MA), Nuffield Coll Oxford (BLitt); *m* 30 March 1953, Eleanor Warren (d 1989), da of Norman Dawson (d 1971), of Cults, Aberdeen; 3 da (Alison b 1955, Sheila b 1957, Jean b 1960); *Career* RE 1943-46 (Temp Capt); OEEC Paris 1949-51, PM's Statistical Section under Lord Cherwell 1951-53, Econ Section Cabinet Office 1953-54, NIESR 1954-57, tutor in econs ChCh Oxford (fell) 1957-68, NEDO 1962-63, Devpt Centre of OECD Paris 1967-68, official fell in econs Nuffield Coll Oxford 1968-; FREconS 1950, FBA 1990; *Books* A Study of UK Imports (1963), Industry and Trade in some Developing Countries (with I M D Little and T Scitovsky, 1970), Induction, Growth and Trade: Essays in Honour of Sir Roy Harrod (ed with W A Eltis and J N Wolfe, 1970), Using Shadow Prices (ed with I M D Little, 1976), Project Appraisal in Practice: the Little-Mirlees Method Applied in Kenya (with J D MacArthur and D M G Newbery, 1976), Can We Get Back to Full Employment? (with R A Laslett, 1978), Economic Theory and Hicksian Themes (ed with D Collard, D Helm and A K Sen, 1984), A New View of Economic Growth (1989), Public Policy and Economic Development: Essays in Honour of Ian Little (ed with D K Lal, 1990); *Recreations* walking; *Clubs* Political Economy (Oxford); *Style*— Maurice Scott, Esq; 11 Blandford Ave, Oxford, OX2 8EA (☎ 0865 59115); Nuffield College, Oxford OX1 1NF (☎ 0865 278566, fax 0865 278621)

SCOTT, Sir Michael; KCVO (1979, MVO 1961), CMG (1977); s of John Scott (d 1957), and Kathleen Scott (d 1983), of Newcastle upon Tyne; *b* 19 May 1923; *Educ* Dame Allan's Sch, Univ of Durham; *m* 1, 1944 (m dis 1967), Vivienne Sylvia Vincent-Barwood (d 1985); 3 s; m 2, 1971, Jennifer Cameron Smith; *Career* served 1942-47 with 1 Gurkha Rifles; 1949-57 Colonial Office; Dip Serv: dep high cmmr Peshawar, Pakistan 1959-62, cnsllr British High Cmmn New Delhi 1963-65, dep high cmmr Nicosia 1968-72, RCDS 1973, ambass to Nepal 1974-77, high cmmr Malawi 1977-79, Bangladesh 1980-81, ret; sec-gen Royal Cwlth Soc 1983-88, cncl Overseas Devpt Inst 1983-; dir Tiger Mountaim Gp 1984-; tstee: Drive for Youth Charity 1987-, Int Agric Trg Prog 1988-, King Mahendra Tst for Nature Conservation 1989-; *Clubs* Oriental; Royal Cwlth Soc; *Style*— Sir Michael Scott, KCVO, CMG; 87A Cornwall Gdns, London SW7 4AY (☎ 071 589 6794)

SCOTT, Michael James; *b* 7 Dec 1942; *Educ* Sutton Valence, Univ of Edinburgh (MA); *m* 10 May 1969, Suzette; 1 s (Edward James b 6 Sept 1980), 1 da (Polly Elizabeth b 2 Sept 1971); *Career* CA 1968; Arthur Andersen 1970-72, ptnr Grant Thornton 1975- (joined 1972, formerly Thornton Baker); *Recreations* skiing, tennis, France; *Clubs* SCGB, Grasshoppers; *Style*— Michael Scott, Esq; Grant Thornton, 49 Mill St, Bedford MK40 3LB (☎ 0234 211521, fax 0234 325717)

SCOTT, Michael Sigsworth; s of Claude Moody Scott (d 1987), of Hull, N Humberside, and Sheila, *née* Sigsworth; *b* 19 Aug 1935; *Educ* Hymers Coll Hull, Hull Coll of Technol; *m* 2 Sept 1961, Norma; 2 da (Alison Jane b 8 April 1966, Jessica Claire Scott b 29 Dec 1968); *Career* res chemist Reckitt and Colman Hull 1956-60, asst works mangr Humber Fertilisers 1960-66, asst mangr Int Bulk Liquids 1966-71, md Tees Storage Co Middlesbrough 1977- (asst gen mangr 1971-73, gen mangr 1973-75, dir and gen mangr 1975-77); chm: Tees Wharf Operators Assoc 1985-87 (memb 1975-), Ind Tank Storage Assoc 1989- (memb Cncl 1977-); MIIM, MBIM; *Recreations* rugby football, sailing own yacht in Clyde, fell walking; *Clubs* Old Hymerians Rugby, Stockton Rugby; *Style*— Michael Scott, Esq; 23 Spring Hill, Welbury, Northallerton, North Yorkshire DL6 2SQ (☎ 060 982 291); Tees Storage Company Ltd, Erimus House, Queens Square, Middlesbrough, Cleveland TS2 1QX (☎ 0642 230000, fax 0642 230107, telex 58477)

SCOTT, Nicholas Paul; MBE (1964), PC (1989), MP (C) Chelsea 1974-; s of Percival John Scott; *b* 5 Aug 1933; *Educ* Clapham Coll, City of London Coll; *m* 1, 1964 (m dis 1976), Elizabeth, da of Robert Robinson, of Thornborough, Bucks; 1 s, 2 da; m 2,

1979, Hon Mrs Tapsell (Hon Cecilia, *qv*, da of 9 Baron Hawke); 1 s, 1 da; *Career* Parly candidate Islington (C) SW 1959 and 1964; MP (C): Paddington S 1966-Feb 1974, Chelsea 1974-; PPS to Rt Hon Iain Macleod as Chllr Exchequer 1970 and to Rt Hon Robert Carr as Home Sec 1972-74, Parly under sec Dept of Employment 1974, oppn spokesman Housing 1974-75; exec memb 1922 Ctee 1978-81; Parly under sec NI Office Sept 1981-86 (min of State 1986-87), min of State for Social Security and Disabled People 1987-; dir: A S Kerswill 1970-81, Eastbourne Printers 1970-81, Juniper Studios 1970-81, Bonusbond Hldgs 1980-81, Bonusplan Ltd 1977-81, Cleveland Offshore Fund Inc 1970-81, Learplan 1978-81; conslt Hill & Knowlton UK Ltd 1981; former chm Creative Conslts, former md E Allom & Co; govr Br Inst Human Rights, memb Cncl Community Serv Volunteers, dep chm Br Caribbean Assoc, nat pres Tory Reform Gp, former chm Conservative Parly Employment Ctee, nat chm Young Cons 1963, dir London Office Euro Cons Gp in Euro Parl 1974; JP London 1961, Liveryman Worshipful Co of Air Pilots & Air Navigators; *Clubs* Buck's, Pratt's, MCC; *Style—* Rt Hon Nicholas Scott Esq, MBE, MP; House of Commons, SW1A 0AA

SCOTT, Sir Oliver Christopher Anderson; 3 Bt (UK 1909) of Yews, Undermilbeck, Westmoreland; Sir Samuel Haslam Scott, 2 Bt (d 1960), and his 2 wife, Nancy Lilian, *née* Anderson (d 1935); *b* 6 Nov 1922; *Educ* Charterhouse, King's Coll Cambridge; *m* 1951, Phoebe Anne, er da of Desmond O'Neill Tolhurst; 1 s, 2 da; *Heir* s, Christopher James Scott b 16 Jan 1955; *Career* High Sheriff of Westmorland 1966; dir Res Unit of Radiobiology British Empire Cancer Campaign 1966-69, conslt Inst of Cancer Res 1974-82, radiobiologist St Thomas' Hosp London 1982-88; *Clubs* Brooks's; *Style—* Sir Oliver Scott, Bt; 31 Kensington Square, London W8

SCOTT, Dr Oliver Lester Schreiner; s of Ralph Lester Scott (d 1952), of Cape Town, and Ursula Hester (d 1965); *b* 16 June 1919; *Educ* Diocesan Coll Cape Town, Trinity Coll Cambridge (MA, MB), St Thomas's Hosp London; *m* 17 July 1943, Katherine Ogle, da of Hugh Shimwell Branfoot (d 1945); 2 da (Oenone b 1945, Lyndall b 1948); *Career* Sqdn Ldr Med Branch RAFVR, served NW Europe; conslt dermatologist: physician i/c Skin Dept Charing Cross Hosp and Med Sch 1956-84, St Luke's Hosp and Royal Surrey Co Hosp Guildford 1953-84; hon conslt: dermatologist L'Hôpital Française et Dispensaire Français 1960-88, King Edward VII Hospital 1977-85; hon memb and former pres (1982) British Assoc of Dermatologists, hon treas Royal Med Fndn Epsom Coll, former dir Medical Insurance Agency; author of articles on dermatology in med jls; FRCP; Chevalier de l'Ordre Merité (France) 1979; *Recreations* gardening, fishing; *Style—* Dr Oliver Scott; South Lodge, South Side, Wimbledon Common, London SW19 4TL

SCOTT, Patricia Mary; da of Gordon James Rouse (d 1978), and Hilda May, *née* Marchant; *b* 28 Nov 1954; *Educ* Hreod Burna Sr HS, Portsmouth Poly; *m* 1 Aug 1975, Anthony Vincent Scott, s of Thomas Arthur David Scott; *Career* various appts Thorn Television Rentals Ltd and Thorn EMI plc 1974-85, accountant Burmah Oil Exploration Ltd April-Sept 1985; Thorn EMI plc: mangr int tax and VAT 1985-86, gp tax mangr 1986-89, dir Taxation and Treasury 1989-; hon treas St Augustine's Church 1985-; fell Chartered Assoc of Certified Accountants 1989 (memb 1984), memb Assoc of Corporate Treasurers 1990; *Recreations* gardening, poultry keeping, reading; *Style—* Mrs Patricia Scott; The Annexe, Downend, Chieveley, Berkshire RG16 8TL (☎ 0635 248376); Thorn EMI plc, Westmount Centre, Uxbridge Rd, Hayes, Middlesex UB4 0HP (☎ 081 848 0011, fax 081 561 9211)

SCOTT, (Arthur) Peter Bedingfeld; DL (Wiltshire 1987); s of Capt Arthur Geoffrey Scott (d 1924), of Picket Piece, Andover, Hants, and Caroline Blanche, *née* Curry (d 1964); *b* 11 Oct 1923; *Educ* Wellington; *m* 24 June 1948, Anne Margaret, da of Stanly Gordon Hillyer, OBE (d 1962); 3 s (David Bedingfeld b 1950, Andrew Hillyer b 1952, Charles Geoffrey Gordon b 1955); *Career* RM 1941-49; T H White Ltd: md 1954-, chm 1983-; High Sheriff Wilts 1986-87; pres Br Agric Machinery Assoc 1960-62; *Recreations* fishing, gardening; *Style—* Peter Scott, Esq, DL; Grange Farm, Marden, Devizes, Wiltshire SN10 3RQ (☎ 0380 840204); T H White Ltd, Nursteed Rd, Devizes, Wiltshire SN10 3EA (☎ 0380 722381)

SCOTT, Sir (Charles) Peter; KBE (1978, OBE 1948), CMG (1964); s of Rev John Joseph Scott (d 1947), and Hannah Dorothea, *née* Senior (d 1953); *b* 30 Dec 1917; *Educ* Weymouth Coll, Pembroke Coll Cambridge; *m* 1954, Rachael, yr da of late Cyril Walter Lloyd-Jones, CIE, of Guildford; 1 s (Harry), 2 da (Katherine, Maria); *Career* ICS 1940-47, entered FO 1947, 1 sec Toyko 1949 (2 sec 1948), FO 1950-52, private sec to Gen Lord Ismay at NATO Paris 1952-54; 1 sec: Vienna 1954, British Info Services (NY) 1956; cnsllr and consular-gen Washington 1959-61, IDC 1962, head of UK perm mission to Euro Office of UN Geneva 1963-66, min Rome 1966-69, seconded to Centre for Contemporary Euro Studies Univ of Sussex 1969, asst under-sec of state FCO 1970-75, ambass Norway 1975-77; private sec to HRH Prince Michael of Kent 1978-79 (treas 1979-81); *Recreations* walking, skiing; *Clubs* United Oxford and Cambridge Univ, Norfolk (Norwich); *Style—* Sir Peter Scott, KBE, CMG; Bisley Farmhouse, Irstead, nr Norwich, Norfolk NR12 8XT (☎ 0692 630413)

SCOTT, Peter Denys John; QC (1978); s of John Ernest Dudley Scott, and Joan Steinberg, *née* Clayton-Cooper; *b* 19 April 1935; *Educ* Monroe HS Rochester New York USA, Balliol Coll Oxford (MA); *Career* Nat Serv Lt RHA; barr; chm Gen Cncl of the Bar 1987 (vice chm 1985-86); *Style—* Peter Scott, Esq, QC; 4 Eldon Rd, London W8 5PU (☎ 071 937 3301, fax 071 376 1169); Fountain Court, Temple, London EC4 9DH (☎ 071 583 3335, fax 071 353 0329, telex 8813408 FON LEG G)

SCOTT, Philip Edward Hannay; s of Edward Beattie Scott, MBE, and Mary, *née* Potter; *b* 6 April 1957; *Educ* Millfield, Cricklade Coll Andover; *m* 23 Sept 1989, Victoria, *née* Byles; *Career* formerly in films indust Tor Films Ltd (Tarka the Otter), paralysed in motor racing accident 1977, illustrator 1978-; work incl Poly series of childrens books; freelance journalist and broadcaster (BBC) 1979-: Radio 4, World series, Local Radio; work with the disabled to encourage movement tran res into the community 1979-; achievements incl: fndr memb Project 81, fndr memb Hampshire Centre for Ind Living 1982, became one of first people to be completely supported in the community by a health authy; promotor of interests of the disabled through aviation achievements incl: fndr Operation Ability Ltd 1984, first tetraplegic to pass a Civil Aviation Authy med to gain private pilots' licence, involved first G tests for tetraplegic person 1985; "Man of the Year" award for serv to disabled community 1988; Freeman: City of London, Worshipful Co of Haberdashers 1978; AMRAeS 1985; *Recreations* art, engineering, travel, chess, calligraphy, aviation; *Style—* Philip Scott, Esq; The Meadows, Firgrove Rd, Whitehill, Nr Bordon, Hampshire GU35 9DY (☎ 042 03 5062)

SCOTT, Sheriff Richard John Dinwoodie; s of Prof Richard Scott (d 1983), and Mary Ellen Maclachlan (d 1987); *b* 28 May 1939; *Educ* Edinburgh Acad, Univ of Edinburgh (MA, LLB); *m* 1969, Josephine Moretta, da of Allan Holland Blake, (d 1954), of Edinburgh; 2 da (Victoria b 1970, Joanna b 1972); *Career* advocate 1965, called to the Bar Scotland 1965, in practice 1965-77, Sheriff of Grampian Highland and Is at Aberdeen and Stonehaven 1977-86; *Style—* Sheriff Richard Scott; Sheriff's Chambers, Edinburgh EH1 2NS

SCOTT, Richard Norman; s of William Scott (d 1960), of Moat Hill, Marthall, Knutsford, Cheshire and Beatrice Mary, *née* Lewis; *b* 7 July 1936; *Educ* Whitegate Hall Northwich Cheshire; *m* 10 March 1961, Janet Mabel (d 1976), da of Granville Bradshaw (d 1983); 3 s (Richard b 25 July 1961, Adam b 31 Jan 1963, Giles b 16 Jan 1967), 3 da (Rebecca b 16 March 1964, Rachael b 18 Aug 1965, Sarah b 25 May 1975); *Career* took over late Father's country estate 1960, Lord of the Manor Betton in Hales; Marthall parish cncllr 1971-74, Parly candidate (Lib) for Wythenshawe Manchester 1974; *Recreations* flying (holds PPL); *Style—* Richard Scott, Esq, Lord of the Manor Betton in Hales; Moat Hall, Marthall, Knutsford, Cheshire WA16 8SU (☎ 0625 861 214); Marthall Mill, Marthall, Knutsford, Cheshire (☎ 0625 861272, fax 0625 861136)

SCOTT, Hon Mr Justice; Richard Rashleigh Folliott Scott; *Career* called to the Bar Inner Temple 1959; QC 1975, attorney-gen Duchy of Lancaster 1980-83, bencher 1981, High Court judge 1983-; vice chllr Co Palatine and Duchy of Lancaster 1987; *Style—* The Hon Mr Justice Scott; Royal Courts of Justice, The Strand, London, WC2

SCOTT, Hon Mrs (Rita); *née* Blyton; yst da of Baron Blyton (Life Peer; d 1987); *b* 1930; *m* 1954, Andrew Scott; has issue; *Style—* The Hon Mrs Scott; 67 Australia Grove, S Shields, Tyne & Wear

SCOTT, Simon Angus; s of John Moffat Hewitt Scott, of 32 Anne Street, Edinburgh, and Lora, *née* Rutherford (d 1976); *b* 31 May 1956; *Educ* Fettes, RMA Sandhurst (scholarship), Univ of Sussex (BA), Univ of Washington St Louis Missouri USA; *m* 9 June 1984, da of Norman Starrett (d 1987); 1 s (Thomas Starrett 6 18 June 1989); *Career* Boys Athletic League NY 1975; Bell Lawrie MacGregor Stockbrokers 1980-81, ptnr Maclean Dubois (Literary Agents) 1981-84; sr copywriter: Marr Associates (Advertising) 1984-86, Hall Advertising 1986-88; creative dir Faulds Advertising 1988-; awarded: Design and Art Direction Silver award 1986 Design and Direction awards 1983, 1984, 1985 and 1986, Independent Local Radio Gold award 1987, 5 Gold Clio awards, 10 Roses Gold awards, 12 Silver Roses awards, 26 Scotmedia awards; *Books* Hercules the Bear (1981), The Forth Bridge (1983), Forests of Northern England (1983), Coast of Echoes (1984), Prodigal Gun (1984), Startex Assignment (1984); *Recreations* breeding; *Style—* Simon Scott, Esq; 22 Danube St, Edinburgh, Lothian (☎ 031 332 8820); Faulds Advertising, Sutherland House, 108 Dundas Street, Edinburgh, Lothian EH3 5DQ (☎ 031 557 6003)

SCOTT, Hon Simon Peter; 2 s of 4 Earl of Eldon, GCVO (d 1976); *b* 13 Sept 1939; *Educ* Ampleforth, Salamanca and Madrid Univs, Sorbonne; *m* 28 Oct 1966, Mary Isabel, 2 da of late Andrew Ramon Dalzell de Bertodano; 3 s, 1 da; *Career* page of honour to HM The Queen 1953-56; Lt Scots Gds Army Emergency Reserve; *Clubs* White's; *Style—* The Hon Simon Scott; Frogden, Kelso, Roxburghshire TD5 8AB

SCOTT, Dr (James) Thomas; s of James Basil Spence Scott (d 1937), of London, and Alice Fawsitt, *née* Taylor (d 1987); *b* 11 Nov 1926; *Educ* Univ Coll Sch, St Mary's Hosp Univ of London (MB BS, MD); *m* 29 Oct 1956, Faith Margaret, da of William Ernest Smith (d 1944), of Fishguard, Pembs; 3 s (Humphrey, Matthew, Richard); *Career* RAMC 1952-54; conslt physician: Postgrad Med Sch 1962-65, Hammersmith Hosp 1962-65, Charing Cross Hosp 1966-; hon physician Kennedy Inst of Rheumatology 1966-, conslt physician in rheumatology Royal Navy 1970-; pres Med Soc of London, memb Fin and Exec Ctee Arthritis and Rheumatism Cncl; MRCP 1952, FRSM 1960, memb Assoc of Physicians 1964, FRCP 1968; hon memb: Australasian Assoc of Rheumatology 1983, American Coll of Rheumatology 1984; *Books* Copeman's Textbook of the Rheumatic Diseases (ed, 5 edn 1978, 6 edn 1986), Arthritis and Rheumatism: The Facts (1980); *Recreations* fly fishing, numismatics; *Style—* Dr Thomas Scott; 4 Northumberland Place, Richmond, Surrey TW10 6TS (☎ 081 940 4368); Charing Cross Hospital, Fulham Palace Rd, London W6 8RF (☎ 081 846 1234)

SCOTT, Sir Walter; 4 Bt (UK 1907), of Beauclere, Bywell St Andrews, Co Northumberland; DL (E Sussex 1975); s of Sir Walter Scott, 3 Bt (d 1967), and his 1 w, Nancy Margaret (Margot), *née* March (d 1944); *b* 29 July 1918; *Educ* Eton, Jesus Coll Cambridge; *m* 15 Jan 1944, Diana Mary, da of James Owen; 1 s, 1 da (Sarah Jane, now Duchess of Hamilton and Brandon); *Heir* s, (Walter) John Scott; *Career* Maj 1 Royal Dragoons; JP (E Sussex 1963); *Style—* Sir Walter Scott, Bt, DL; Newhouse Farm, Chalvington, Hailsham, Sussex

SCOTT, Walter Grant; s of Thomas Scott (d 1979), and Marion Urie Roberts; *b* 13 May 1947; *Educ* Eastwood HS, Univ of Edinburgh (BSc), Trinity Hall Cambridge (PhD); *m* 1973, Rosemary Ann Clark, da of Alfred W C Lobban, of Bedfordshire; 1 s (Matthew), 2 da (Rachel, Diana); *Career* dir Ivory & Sime Ltd 1972-82, Ind Investment Co nominee dir Systems Designers Int 1981-, dir Integrated Micro Applications Ltd 1981-, sr ptnr Walter Scott & Ptnrs 1982- (portfolio mgmnt (circa 500m)), chm Walter Scott Int 1983-; *Recreations* rowing, running, gardening; *Clubs* Leander, New (Edinburgh); *Style—* Walter Scott, Esq; Hillwood, Loanhead, Midlothian EH20 9SF (☎ 031 440 0587); Millburn Tower, Gogar, Edinburgh

SCOTT, William Joseph (Bill); s of Kenneth John Scott, of London, and Georgina Hilda, *née* Grisley; *b* 3 March 1961; *Educ* Forest Sch, UEA (BSc Econ); *Career* articled clerk Gerald Edelman & Co 1982-86, Investigations Dept Stoy Hayward 1986-87, fin controller (later asst gp fin controller) Leisure Investments plc 1987-89, fin dir Senior King Ltd 1989-; ACA 1986; *Recreations* reading, music, computing, military history; *Clubs* East India, Devonshire, Sports and Public Schs; *Style—* Bill Scott, Esq; Senior King Ltd, 14-15 Carlisle St, London W1V 5RE (☎ 071 734 5855 and 071 439 3049 and 071 437 1908)

SCOTT, Hon Lady; Winifred Kathleen; *née* Brodrick; *m* 1941, Hon Sir Ernest Stowell Scott, KCMG, MVO (s of 3 Earl of Eldon and who d 1953); 1 da; *Style—* The Hon Lady Scott; The Manor House, Bradford, Peverell, Dorchester, Dorset

SCOTT-BARRETT, Lt-Gen Sir David William; KBE (1976, MBE 1956), MC (1945); s of late Brig Rev H Scott-Barrett, CB, CBE; *b* 16 Dec 1922; *Educ* Westminster Sch; *m* 1948, Marie Elise, *née* Morris (d 1985); 3 s; *Career* cmmnd Scots Guard 1942, served NW Europe WWII, GOC Eastern Dist 1971-73, GOC Berlin 1973-75, Col Cmdt Scottish Div and GOC Scotland 1976-79, govr Edinburgh Castle 1976-79; former dir Arbuthnot Securities; chm Army Cadet Force Assoc 1981-, dir Haven Project for Mental Health Provision 1983-84; *Style—* Lt-Gen Sir David Scott-Barrett, KBE, MC; Hall House, Kersey, Ipswich, Suffolk IP7 6DZ (☎ 0473 822 365)

SCOTT-DEMPSTER, Lt-Col Ronald; WS (1923); s of Thomas Dempster, DL (d 1937), Lord Provost of Perth, and Constance Elizabeth Georgina, *née* Greig (d 1954); *b* 8 May 1898; *Educ* Perth Acad, Univ of Edinburgh (BL); *m* 5 Sept 1933, Ann, da of Rt Rev Edward Thomas Scott Reid, DD (d 1938), Bishop of St Andrew's, Dunkeld and Dunblane; 1 s (Colin b 1937), 2 da (Fiona b 1935, Jane b 1950); *Career* Lt RFA 1916-19, wounded Paschendale 1917, Lt-Col Army Welfare Offr Perthshire 1943-50; ptnr Robertson Dempster & Co WS Perth 1924-74, conslt Condie MacKenzie & Co WS Perth 1974-91; sec TA Assoc 1939-48; directorships incl: General Accident Assurance 1948-74, Grampian Properties Ltd 1967-77, English Life Assurance Co plc 1962-77; tstee Scottish Episcopal Church 1960-87 (convenor Exec Ctee 1959-67), jt legal advsr Br Deer Soc 1968-72, chllr Diocese of St Andrews Dunkeld and Dunblane 1974-86 (registrar 1928-74), deer conslt Grampian Properties 1977-83; *Recreations* golf, tennis, deer stalking, piping, gardening; *Clubs* Lansdowne, Royal Perth Golfing and County; *Style—* Lt-Col Ronald Scott-Dempster, WS; Tayhill, Brae St, Dunkeld, Perthshire PH8 0BA (☎ 03502 277); 2 Tay St, Perth (☎ 0738 33171, fax 0738 43425, telex 76557 PERSOL G)

SCOTT-HARDEN, Anthony Walter; s of Dr Walter Geoffrey Scott-Harden (d 1984), of Orchard House, Scotby, Carlisle, and Charmian Mary, *née* Connell; *b* 4 July 1940; *Educ* St Edwards Oxford, Cumberland Westmorland Farm Sch Newton Rigg Penrith (DipAgric); *m* July 1965, Daphne Elizabeth, da of Maj Laurence Wilfred Anrett (d 1966), of Pond House, Hurworth on Tees, Darlington; 1 s (James b 1969), 1 da (Lucy b 1966); *Career* Lt Cumberland and Westmorland Yeo (TA) 1960-66; dir: Lowther Scott-Harden Ltd (chm) chartered surveyors, New Cavendish Estates plc (property investmt and devpt), Metrorural Properties Ltd, West Hall Youngstock plc (bloodstock dealing), Simonside Farms Ltd (farming and consulting); FRICS 1963; *Recreations* shooting, foxhunting, scubadiving, travel, horse racing; *Clubs* Turf, Farmers, Northern Counties; *Style—* Anthony Scott-Harden, Esq; West Hall, Middleton Tyas, Richmond, N Yorks (☎ 0325 3772 65); Monkend Estate Office, Croft, Darlington, Co Durham (☎ 0325 720 614, fax 0325 377012, car 0860 814 517, telex 58657 ANSHG)

SCOTT-HOPKINS, Maj Sir James Sidney Rawdon; MEP (EDG) Herefordshire, Worcs and W Glos 1979-; s of Lt-Col Rawdon Scott-Hopkins, DSO, MC (d 1974), of Phyllis Court Club, Henley-on-Thames, formerly of Wadeford House, Chard, Somerset; *b* 29 Nov 1921; *Educ* Eton, Univ of Oxford, Univ of Cambridge; *m* 1946, Geraldine Elizabeth Hargreaves, CBE, o da of Lt-Col John Carne Hargreaves, of Drinkstone Park, Suffolk, by his former w Hon Angela, *née* Goschen (sis of 3 Viscount Goschen); 3 s, 1 da (*see* Timothy Smith, MP); *Career* served King's Own Yorks, Lt QAO Gurkha Rifles 1939-50; farmer and memb NFU 1950-59; MP (C) Cornwall N 1959-66, W Derbyshire 1967-79; PPS to: Jt Parly Sec State CRO 1961-62, Jt Parly Sec Min Agric Fish & Food 1962-64; dep ldr Cons Gp & spokesman Agric 1973-79 (vice-pres 1976-79); nominated MEP 1973-79; chm Euro Democratic Gp 1979-82; *Style—* Maj Sir James Scott-Hopkins, MEP; 602 Nelson House, Dolphin Sq, London SW1V 3NZ; Bicknor House, English Bicknor, W Glos GL16 7PF

SCOTT-JOYNT, Rt Rev Michael Charles; *see*: Stafford, Bishop of

SCOTT-MANDERSON, Marcus Charles William; s of Dr William Scott-Manderson, and Pamela, *née* Welch; *b* 10 Feb 1956; *Educ* Harrow, ChCh Oxford (BA, BCL), Univ of Glasgow, The Hague Acad of Int Law The Netherlands 1980; *Career* called to the Bar Lincoln's Inn 1980; sec Family Law Bar Assoc Conciliation Bd; memb: Br Acad of Forensic Sci, Forensisch Medisch Genootschap The Netherlands; *Recreations* ancient history, archaeology, fencing, travel; *Clubs* Lansdowne; *Style—* Marcus Scott-Manderson, Esq; 24 Burlington Rd, London SW6 (☎ 071 731 1476); Park House, The Strand, Ashton-in-Makerfield, nr Wigan, Lancs; 4 Paper Buildings, Temple, London EC4Y 7EX (☎ 071 353 3420, fax 071 353 4979)

SCOTT McIVER, Fiona; da of Major Dougal Campbell McIver, and Jessica Smith, *née* Castellano; *b* 13 Sept 1944; *Educ* St Martin's Convent; *Career* proprietor Images Health Studio; dir: Corporate Images Ltd, Outlines Ltd, Silhouettes Ltd, Profiles Ltd; features ed The Marylebone Times; chm ASTO; *Recreations* tennis, squash; *Style—* Miss Fiona Scott McIver; 19 Paddington St, London W1 (☎ 071 935 3166, fax 071 935 4131, telex 94012662 IMAG G)

SCOTT-MILLER, Melissa Emma; da of Jeremy David Scott-Miller, of Norfolk, and Elspeth Balfour, *née* Anderson; *b* 17 July 1959; *Educ* Queen's Coll London, Slade Sch of Fine Art UCL (BA, Lord Leighton prize, Andrey Wykeham prize); *Career* artist; solo exhibition The Albemarle Gallery 1989; gp exhibitions: Royal Soc of Portrait Painters 1981, Stowells Trophy, (Royal Acad) 1981, Hayward Annual Drawing Exhibition 1982, The Space Gallery 1981 and 1983, Three English Artists (Acquauelca Gallery, NY) 1983, South Bank Piture Show (Royal Festival Hall) 1987, 1989 and 1990, Summer Show (Royal Acad); awards, Rodney Byrne scholar 1981, Elizabeth Green Fndn scholar 1985, second prize South Bank Picture Show 1989; *Style—* Ms Melissa Scott-Miller; Albemarle Gallery, 18 Albemarle St, London W1X 3HA

SCOTT-NOBLE, Lt-Col James Robert; MC (1940), TD (1943), JP (Roxburghshire 1961), DL (1962); s of Robert Scott-Noble (d 1968), of Hawick, and Edith Alice Hutton (d 1978); *b* 23 Feb 1915; *Educ* Loretto, Musselburgh; *m* 18 June 1941, Diana Mabean, da of Lt-Col William Geddes Borran Dickson (d 1945); 1 s (Anthony William b 1952), 2 da (Sarnia Anne b 1942, Diana Vanessa b 1945); *Career* Lt-Col France 1942, Egypt, Italy 1943-44, instr Staff Coll 1945; woollen manufacturer 1934-65, farmer 1965-81 (ret); *Recreations* shooting, walking; *Style—* Lt-Col James Scott-Noble, MC, TD, JP, DL; Ravenslea, Hawick TD9 7HS (☎ 0450 72175)

SCOTT PLUMMER, (Patrick) Joseph; s of Charles Humphrey Scott Plummer, of Mainhouse, Kelso, Roxburghshire, and The Hon Pamela Lilias, *née* Balfour; *b* 24 Aug 1943; *Educ* Radley, Magdalene Coll Cambridge (MA); *m* 1, 12 March 1970 (m dis 1977), Elizabeth-Anne, da of Col Anthony Way, MC, of Kincairney, Murthly, Perthshire; 1 s (Charles b 18 Aug 1971), 1 da (Annabel b 26 June 1973); m 2, 15 Sept 1977, Christine Hermione Roberts, da of The Hon Anthony Gerard Bampfylde (d 1968), of Boyton Ho, Woodbridge, Suffolk; 1 s (Guy b 13 Aug 1978); *Career* ptnr Cazenove and Co 1974-80; dir: Martin Currie Ltd 1981-, Candover Invs plc 1987-, Life Assoc of Scotland 1988-; FCA 1967; *Recreations* foxhunting, tennis; *Clubs* New (Edinburgh), Pratt's; *Style—* Joseph Scott Plummer, Esq; Mainhouse, Kelso, Roxburghshire (☎ 0573 23 327); 20 Keith Row, Edinburgh; Martin Currie Ltd, 29 Charlotte Sq, Edinburgh (☎ 031 225 3811)

SCOTT-SMITH, Catharine Mary; da of Edward Montagu Scott-Smith (d 1951), and Catharine Lorance, *née* Garland (d 1949); *b* 4 April 1912; *Educ* Wycombe Abbey Sch High Wycombe Bucks, Girton Coll Cambridge (BA, MA); *Career* asst mistress: St Katharine's Sch Wantage 1933-37, Godolphin Sch Salisbury 1937-41; Headington Sch Oxford 1941-47: house mistress, sr mistress; sr mistress Wycombe Abbey Sch Bucks 1951-54 (house mistress 1947-55), headmistress Weston Birt Sch Gloucs 1955-65, princ Beachlawn Tutorial Coll Oxford 1966-71; AAM 1933-55, AHMBS 1955-65 (memb Ctee); *Recreations* gardening, travel, reading, crosswords; *Clubs* University Women's; *Style—* Miss Catharine Scott-Smith

SCOTT WARREN, Dr David Noël Martin; s of Rev Percival Scott Warren (d 1949), and Ione Mason (d 1941), da of Sir Joseph Wilkinson (d 1902); *b* 8 Jan 1924; *Educ* St John's Sch Leatherhead, London Hosp Med Coll; *m* 8 Jan 1949, June Mary, da of Howard Raymond John Feeny (d 1978), of The Little House, Feckenham, Worcs; 3 s (Anthony David b 1949, Jonathan Michael b 1952, Timothy Nicholas b 1954), 2 da (Amanda Frances Ione b 1957, Fiona Mary b 1959); *Career* med practitioner; CStJ; memb BMA Jersey Med Soc, MRCS, LRCP; *Recreations* motoring, photography; *Clubs* Jersey Old Motor, London Hosp Med, Jersey Motor Cycle & Light Car; *Style—* Dr D N M Scott Warren; Mont du Ouaisne, St Brelade, Jersey CI (☎ 0534 42939 43590); 41 David Place, St Helier, Jersey CI (☎ 0534 23318)

SCOTT-WHITE, Raymond; s of Lawson Scott-White, OBE (d 1967), and Muriel Annie, *née* Ward (d 1990); *b* 22 Aug 1934; *Educ* Whitgift Sch Croydon, Imperial Coll London (BSc, ACGI); *m* 6 July 1957, Patricia Anne, da of Ronald John Elmes (d 1981), of Hayes, Kent; 1 s (David Andrew b 9 Nov 1958, d 11 June 1976), 1 da (Sally Anne b 2 Nov 1959); *Career* fndr Scott-White & Hookins conslt engrs 1963; memb Croydon 41 Club, chm Croydon Round Table 1973; Freeman City of London, former Master Worshipful Co of Fan Makers; CEng, FIStructE, MICE, MIHT, MConsE; *Recreations* golf; *Clubs* Livery, Kingswood Golf; *Style—* Raymond Scott-White, Esq; London House, 42 West St, Carshalton, Surrey SM5 2PU (☎ 081 773 3131, fax 081 773 2605)

SCOTT-WILSON, John Beaumont; OBE (1987); s of Dr Hew William Scott-Wilson (d 1972), and Beatrice Mary, *née* Jackson (d 1977); *b* 18 Dec 1927; *Educ* Sutton Valence Sch, Downing Coll Cambridge (MA); *m* 2 June 1951, Elizabeth Madeline, da of Capt John Charles Grant-Ives (d 1959); 4 s (Timothy b 1952, Christopher b 1954, Peter b 1956, Rhodcrick b 1958); *Career* sci offr MOS 1950-56, engr AV Roe and Co, dir Hawker Siddeley Aviation Manchester 1972-77; div dir British Aerospace: Manchester 1977-84, Weybridge 1984-86, Civil Aircraft 1986-88; tech dir British Aerospace Commercial Aircraft Ltd 1989; chm UK Nat Del to NATO Advsy Gp for Aerospace Res and Devpt 1990-, memb CAA Airworthness Requirements Bd; FRAeS 1977, FEng 1985; *Recreations* sailing; *Clubs* Royal Anglesey Yacht; *Style—* John Scott-Wilson, Esq, OBE; Tor Top, Cobden Edge, Mellor, Stockport, Cheshire SK6 5NL (☎ 061 427 2170); British Aerospace Commercial Aircraft Ltd, Hatfield, Herts AL10 9TL (☎ 07072 62345, telex 22411, fax 07072 73078)

SCOUGALL, Capt Alexander Cuthbert (Alex); s of James Scougall (d 1968), of Dunning, Perthshire, and Margaret Baldwin Drury Spence, *née* Cuthbert (d 1969); *b* 8 Aug 1939; *Educ* Auchterarder, BRNC Dartmouth, RNEC, Univ of Glasgow (MEng, MLitt); *m* 19 Dec 1964, Gillian (Jill), da of Richard Park (d 1966), of Totnes, Devon; 2 da (Sasha b 1967, Kyla b 1972); *Career* HMDYO Rosyth 1978-81, staff of 10 Submarine Sqdn 1981-84, HMS Intrepid 1984-86, flag offr submarines 1986-87; MOD: Bath 1987-89, London 1989-; MIMechE 1973; *Recreations* riding; *Style—* Capt Alex Scougall; Ministry of Defence, Whitehall, London

SCOULLER, (John) Alan; s of Charles James Scouller (d 1974), of Banstead, Surrey, and Mary Helena, *née* Pyne (d 1972); *b* 23 Sept 1929; *Educ* John Fisher Sch Purley Surrey; *m* 29 May 1954, Angela Geneste, da of Harry Ambrose (d 1937), of Maidstone, Kent; 2 s (James Paul b 1955, Edward John b 1964), 5 da (Catherine Mary b 1956, Frances Elizabeth b 1958, Sarah Margaret b 1961, Helen Louise b 1966, Joanna Clare b 1968); *Career* Nat Serv 1948, cmmnd 2 Lt Queen's Own Royal West Kent Regt 1949, reg cmmn Lt 1951, 1 Bn Malaya 1953-54, Germany 1954, Capt Instructor Sch of Inf (Signals) 1955-56, 1 Bn Cyprus 1957-58, resigned cmmn 1958; Unilever Ltd: personnel mangr Walls Ice Cream Gloucester 1958-62, asst to trg mangr Rotterdam 1962, personnel mangr Domestos Ltd Newcastle Upon Tyne 1962-66, personnel mangr Commercial Plastics & Holpak 1966-69; head industl rels Midland Bank Group 1975-88, visiting prof in industl rels Kingston Poly 1988-, hon sr fell City Univ Business Sch 1989-; chm of govrs John Henry Newman Sch Stevenage Herts; cmmr Cmmn on Industl Rels 1973 (1969-74), pt/t memb Employment Appeal Tbnl 1976-; FIPM; *Recreations* music, reading, walking, travel, studying employment law; *Style—* Alan Scouller, Esq; 32 Sollershott West, Letchworth, Herts SG6 3PX (☎ 0462 682781)

SCOULLER, Anthony James; s of Charles James Scouller (d 1976), and Mary Helen, *née* Pyne; *b* 13 Sept 1936; *Educ* John Fisher Sch Purley; *m* 16 May 1964, Barbara Joy, da of Edward John Lawrence; 1 s (Matthew Edward John), 1 da (Susanna Barbara); *Career* 2 Lt Queens Own Royal West Kent Regt, active service Cyprus; Beecham Group Marketing 1960-66; J Walter Thompson Inc: London office 1966-69, NY 1969-72, dept mangr Caracas 1972-74, dir London 1975-83; mktg dir: International Distillers and Vinters UK 1983-89, Wyvern Internatoinal IDV 1989-; *Recreations* bridge, horse racing; *Clubs* RAC, Marketing Soc; *Style—* Anthony Scouller, Esq; 151 Marylebone Rd, London NW1 5QE (☎ 071 487 3412, fax 071 258 5151, telex 262548 SPIRIT G)

SCOWEN, Prof Sir Eric Frank; s of Frank Edward Scowen; *b* 1910; *Educ* City of London Sch, St Bartholomew's Hosp Med Coll Univ of London (MA, MD, DSc); *Career* physician St Bartholomew's Hosp 1946-75, dir Med Professorial Unit 1955-75, prof of med Univ of London 1961-75 (emeritus prof of med 1975), chm British Pharmacopoeia Cmmn 1963-69; chm: Cncl of Imperial Cancer Research Fund 1967-82 (vice-pres 1982), Ctee on Safety of Medicines 1970-81, Ctee on Review of Medicines 1975-78, Poisons Bd 1976-83, Cncl Sch of Pharmacy Univ of London 1979-88, Clinical Trials Ethical Ctee Royal Coll of Gen Practitioners 1981-88; FRCP, FRCS, FRCPE, FRCPath, FRCGP 1988; Hon LLD Univ of Nottingham, Hon Fell Royal Pharmeceutical Soc, Hon Fell Sch of Pharmacy 1986; kt 1973; *Clubs* Athenaeum; *Style—* Prof Sir Eric Scowen; Flat 77, 6/9 Charterhouse Sq, London EC1M 6EX (☎ 071 251 3212)

SCREECH, Dr Michael Andrew; s of Richard John Screech, MM (d 1986), of Pomphlet, Plymstock, Plymouth, and Nellie Ernestine, *née* Maunder (d 1977); *b* 2 May 1926; *Educ* Sutton HS Plymouth, UCL (BA); *m* 4 April 1956, (Ursula) Anne Grace, da of John William Reeve (d 1960), of Byfleet; 3 s (Matthew Erasmus John b 30 Jan 1960, Timothy Benjamin Mark b 28 Sept 1961, Toby Daniel Luke b 3 Oct 1963); *Career* Intelligence Corps Far East 1944-48; asst lectr (later lectr and sr lectr) Univ of Birmingham 1951-61, reader then prof of French UCL 1961-71, Fielden prof of French language and lit 1971-84, Johnson prof Inst for Res in the Humanities Madison Wisconsin 1978, Campion lectr Regina Saskatchewan 1983, Dorothy Ford Wiley prof of renaissance culture N Carolina 1986, Zaharoff lectr Oxford 1988, sr res fell All Soul's Coll Oxford 1984-, visiting prof Collège de France 1989, La Sorbonne 1990; memb comité d'Humanisme et Renaissance 1958-; formerly: memb Whitchurch Parish Cncl, memb Whitchurch St Mary's PCC, chm of Mangrs Whitchurch Primary Sch; Freeman Ville de Tours 1984; fell UCL 1982; Hon DLitt: Birmingham 1958, London 1982, Oxford 1990; FBA 1981, FRSL 1989; Chevalier dans l'Ordre National du Mérite France 1983; *Books* The Rabelaisian Marriage (1958), L'Evangélisme de Rabelais (1959), Marot Evangélique (1967); Rabelais edns: Tiers Livre (1964), Gargantua (1970), Prognostication (1975); Regrets (by Dubellay, ed 1964), Rabelais (1979), Ecstasy and the Praise of Folly (1980), Montaigne and Melancholy (1983), Apology for Raymond Sebond (by Montaigne, trans 1987), A New Rabelais Bibliography (1988); *Recreations* walking; *Style—* Dr M A Screech; 5 Swanston Field, Whitchurch, Reading RG8 7HP; All Souls College, Oxford OX1 4AL (☎ 0865 279379, fax 0865 279299)

SCRIMGEOUR, Angus Muir Edington; s of Dr David Muir Scrimgeour (d 1977), and May Burton Clair, *née* Edington (d 1988); *b* 19 Feb 1945; *Educ* Westminster, New Coll Oxford (MA), UCL (MSc); *m* 21 Dec 1968, Clare Christian Gauvain, da of Dr Ronald Ormiston Murray, MBE; 1 s (Alexander b 1971); *Career* vice pres Citibank NA 1974-84; dep chm: Edington plc merchant bank and chief exec 1986-90) 1990-, Henry Cooke Gp (jt chief exec 1988-90) 1990-; *Recreations* farming, design, chess, music; *Clubs* IOD, Berkshire Golf, Manchester Racquet; *Style—* Angus Scrimgeour, Esq; 29 Eaton Mews South, London SW1W 9HR; Paddock House Farm, Alstonefield, Nr Ashbourne, Derbyshire DE6 2FT (☎ and fax 03357 284)

SCRIMGEOUR, Dr John Beocher; s of William Stevenson Scrimgeour (d 1980), of Kelso, Scotland, and Ellen Fernie, *née* Beocher (d 1990); *b* 22 Jan 1939; *Educ* Hawick HS, Univ of Edinburgh Med Sch (MB ChB); *m* 22 Sept 1962, (Margaret) Joyce McDougall, da of Thomas Morrin, of Edinburgh; 1 s (Michael b 1966), 1 da (Jill b 1965); *Career* GP Edinburgh 1963-65, hon sr lectr Dept of Obstetrics and Gynaecology Univ of Edinburgh and conslt in obstetrics and gynaecology Western Gen Hosp Edinburgh 1973-; memb The Gynaecological Visiting Soc of GB and Ireland; FRCS 1987, FRCOG; *Books* Towards the Prevention of Foetal Malformation (1978); *Recreations* golf, tennis and gardening; *Style—* Dr John Scrimgeour; 4 Kinellan Rd, Edinburgh EH12 6ES, Scotland (☎ 031 337 6027); Department of Obstetrics and Gynaecology, Western General Hospital, Crewe Rd, Edinburgh EH4 2XU, Scotland

(☎ 031 332 2525, fax 031 332 7728)

SCRIVEN, Peter John Keith; s of Sydney Verdun Scriven, of Dudley, W Midlands, and Mona Patricia, *née* Gaston (d 1974); *b* 25 July 1956; *Educ* Alexandra GS Midlands, UCW Aberystwyth (BScEcon), Leicester Poly (DMS); *m* ; 1 s (Thomas Edward b Feb 1990); *Career* UK mktg mangr Barclays Bank 1977-83, investmt mktg mangr Charterhouse Merchant Bank 1983-84, strategic planning mangr Citicorp UK 1984-86, euro business planning mangr Chase Manhattan Bank 1986-87, gp head of business devpt National and Provincial Building Society 1987-90, sr offr UK and I Visa International Service Association 1990-; memb Nat Soc for Cancer Relief, MInstM; underwriting memb Lloyd's; *Recreations* flying, skiing, foreign travel, charity work; *Clubs* Lloyd's, BMAA; *Style—* Peter Scriven, Esq; 96 Talbot Road, Highgate, London N6 4RA

SCRIVEN, Richard Gordon; JP (W Sussex 1963); s of Charles Douglas Scriven (d 1966), of The Dower House, Walberton, Arundel, Sussex, and Jane Sheila, *née* Gordon (d 1985); *b* 6 June 1928; *Educ* Winchester; *m* 5 April 1954, Gillian Elizabeth, da of Llewelyn Wynn Riley, of Hollycrift, Hebers Ghyll Drive, Ilkley, W Yorks; 1 s (David John Gordon b 1960), 2 da (Hilary Elizabeth b 1955, Clare Jane b 1958); *Career* Mil Service, regular cmmn in Scots Gds Lt; merchant banker; dir: Morgan Grenfell Finance Ltd, Morgan Grenfell (Local Authy Services) Ltd, Morgan Grenfell (Local Authy Finance) Ltd (ret 1984); conslt to Phillips and Drew on local authy finance 1985-87, dir London Court of Int Arbitration Ltd, fin dir Citicare St Clements Ltd, chm Talbot Ct Design Ltd; Freeman City of London, past Master Worshipful Co of Slaters and memb of Court of Assistants 1982, Master Worshipful Co of Leather Sellers and memb Court of Assistants 1987-88; past chm Bd of Govrs of Queenswood Sch, vice-chm Bd of Govrs of Colfe's Sch; govr: Christs Hosp, City of London Freemans' Sch, Central Fndn Boys' Sch; tstee of Central Fndn Schs of London; gen cmmr of Income Tax; memb of Court of Common Cncl of Corp of London 1984 (elected for Ward of Candlewick); past chm E Grinstead UDC, ctee memb Friends of Ashdown Forset; MIEx; *Recreations* sailing, golf; *Clubs* Overseas Bankers, Third Guards, Guildhall, HAC; *Style—* Richard Scriven, Esq, JP; Shepherds Bank, Forset Row, E Sussex RH18 5BG (☎ 034282 4506)

SCRIVENER, Ronald Stratford; CMG (1965); s of Sir Patrick Stratford Scrivener, KCMG (d 1966), of Gt Bedwyn, Wiltshire, and Margaret Morris, *née* Dorling (d 1972); *b* 29 Dec 1919; *Educ* Westminster, St Catharine's Coll Cambridge; *m* 1, 1947 (m dis 1952), Elizabeth Drake-Brockman; m 2, 1962, Mary Alice Olga Sofia Jane, da of Robert Charlton Lane, and formerly w of Christopher Hohler; 2 step s, 2 step da; *Career* ambass to: Panama 1969-70, Czechoslovakia 1971-74; asst under-sec of State FCO 1974-76; *Recreations* travel, fishing; *Clubs* White's, Beefsteak; *Style—* Ronald Scrivener, Esq, CMG; 38 Lysia St, London SW6 6NG

SCRIVENOR, Sir Thomas Vaisey; CMG (1956); eld s of John Brooke Scrivenor, ISO (d 1950), of Horncastle, Lincs, and Violet, *née* Vaisey; *b* 28 Aug 1908; *Educ* King's Sch Canterbury, Oriel Coll Oxford (MA); *m* 4 June 1934, Mary Elizabeth, da of late Albert Augustine Neatby, of Court House, Chiselborough, Somerset; 1 s, 3 da; *Career* entered Colonial Office 1930, served in Tanganyika, Palestine and Malta; civil service cmmr Nigeria 1948-53, dep high cmmr Basutoland, Bechuanaland, and Swaziland 1953-60; sec Cwlth Agric Bureaux 1961-73; kt 1960; *Style—* Sir Thomas Scrivenor, CMG; Vine Cottage, Minster Lovell, Oxon

SCROPE, Philip Adrian; s of Ralph Scrope, and Lady Beatrice Scrope, *née* Savile; *b* 4 Jan 1943; *Educ* Ampleforth, RAC Cirencester; *m* 2 April 1975, Penelope Anne, da of Maj Eric Williams, of Lynturk, Alford, Aberdeenshire; 1 s (Richard b 20 Aug 1977), 1 da (Rosalind b 9 June 1979); *Career* ptnr Smiths Gore Chartered Surveyors and Land Agents; *Style—* Philip Scrope, Esq; Aydon House, nr Corbridge, Northumberland (☎ 0434 63 2096)

SCROPE, Simon Egerton; s of Richard Ladislas Scrope (d 1990), of Danby House, Middleham, N Yorks, and Lady Jane Egerton (d 1978), da of 4 Earl of Ellesmere; *b* 23 Dec 1934; *Educ* Ampleforth, Trinity Coll Cambridge; *m* 23 July 1970, (Jennifer) Jane, da of Sir Kenneth Wade Parkinson, DL (d 1981), of Aketon Close, Follifoot, Harrogate, N Yorks; 1 s (Simon Henry Richard b 3 Sept 1974), 1 da (Emily Katherine b 24 May 1972); *Career* Nat Serv 2 Lt Coldstream Guards 1953; insurance broker, memb Lloyd's 1956, chm Richards Longstaff Group 1974; farmer and landowner; *Recreations* shooting, fishing, gardening, racing; *Clubs* Brooks's; *Style—* Simon Scrope, Esq; Danby on Yore, Leyburn, N Yorks DL8 4PX (☎ 0969 23297); 6 Blomfield Rd, London W9 1AH (☎ 071 289 2457); Richards Longstaff (Insurance Holdings) Ltd, Battlebridge House, 97 Tooley St, London SE1 2RF (☎ 071 407 4466, fax 071 403 3610, telex 8888-93)

SCRUTON, Prof Roger Vernon; s of John Scruton, of High Wycombe, Bucks, and Beryl Clarys, *née* Haines (d 1967); *b* 27 Feb 1944; *Educ* Royal GS High Wycombe, Jesus Coll Cambridge (BA, MA, PhD); *m* 1975 (m dis 1979), (Marie Genevieve) Danielle, da of Robert Laffitte, of Orthez, France; *Career* called to the Bar Inner Temple 1974, fell Peterhouse Coll Cambridge 1969-71, prof of aesthetics Dept of Philosophy Birkbeck Coll London (formerly lectr and reader); ed Salisbury Review; *Books* Art and Imagination (1974), The Aesthetics of Architecture (1979), The Meaning of Conservatism (1980), Fortnight's Anger (1981), A Dictionary of Political Thought (1983), Sexual Desire (1986), Thinkers of the New Left (1986), A Land Held Hostage (1987), The Philosopher on Dover Beach (1990), Francesca (1991); *Recreations* music, hunting; *Clubs* Athenaeum; *Style—* Prof Roger Scruton; Department of Philosophy, Birkbeck College, Malet St, London WC1 (☎ 071 631 6549)

SCRYMGEOUR, Lord; Henry David; s and h of 12 Earl of Dundee; *b* 20 June 1982; *Style—* Lord Scrymgeour

SCUDAMORE, Paul Henry; s of James Henry Scudamore, JP (d 1973), of Ross-on-Wye, Herefords, and Mildred, *née* Davies; said to descend from a collateral branch of Lucas-Scudamore, of Kentchurch, Herefordshire; *b* 14 Nov 1941; *Educ* St Edward's Sch Oxford, Harper Adams Agric Coll; *m* 24 April 1965, Elizabeth Margaret, da of Capt Alfred Eric Crockatt, of Hereford; 1 s (Jeremy Paul Henry b 1969), 1 da (Nicola Jane Elizabeth b 1967); *Career* chm Farmplan gp of cos; dir: Farmplan Holdings, Farmplan Products, Farmplan Computer Systems, Farmplan Int 1972-, Aberfoyle Holdings plc 1984-; CMA Farm Mgmt Award; *Recreations* golf; *Clubs* BIM, Farmers, Ross-on-Wye Golf; *Style—* Paul H Scudamore, Esq; Brampton Lodge, Brampton Abbots, Ross-on-Wye, Herefords; Farmplan Gp, Farmplan House, Rank Xerox Business Park, Mitcheldean, Glos (☎ 0594 544 244, fax 0594 544 078)

SCUDAMORE, Peter Michael; MBE (1990); s of Michael John Scudamore (the former jockey), of Hoarwithy, Herefordshire, and Mary, *née* Duffield; *b* 13 June 1958; *Educ* Belmont Abbey Hereford; *m* 29 May 1980, Marilyn Linda, da of John Kington; 2 s (Thomas b 22 May 1982, Michael b 24 Feb 1984); *Career* national hunt jockey; former point-to-point and amateur rider, professional 1979-, first winner Devon & Exeter (Rolyat), first jockey to Fred Winter and Martin Pipe; major races won incl: Champion Hurdle 1988 (Celtic Shot), Hennessy Cognac Gold Cup 1989 (Strands of Gold), Edward Hanmer Memorial Chase 1989 (Beau Ranger), Mackeson Gold Cup 1989 (Pegwell Bay), Coral Welsh Nat 1990 (Bonanza Boy); has ridden for Br Jump Jockeys; has ridden winners in: Norway, Germany, Switzerland, Belgium, USA, NZ, Aust; champion jockey: 1981, 1982, 1986, 1987, 1989 and 1990; record for number of wins in a season (221) 1988-89 (158 trained by Martin Pipe), only nat hunt jockey to ride over 200 winners in a season, nat hunt record for career wins when reached 1,139 winners Nov 1989; farmer, jt fndr (with father) Bloodstock Co, dir and jt fndr (with Steve Smith Eccles) Chasing Promotions 1989-; jt pres Jockeys' Assoc 1989; *Books* A Share of Success: the Scudamore Family (with Alan Lee, 1983), Scudamore on Steeplechasing (with Alan Lee); *Recreations* cricket, music, watching sport; *Style—* Peter Scudamore, Esq, MBE; Chasing Promotions, Mucky Cottage, Grangehill, Naunton, nr Cheltenham, Gloucestershire GL54 3AY (☎ 0451 850741)

SCULLARD, (Rodney) Gordon Boyton; s of George Temple Boyton Scullard (d 1970), and Nellie, *née* Richards (d 1971); *b* 31 Jan 1934; *Educ* St Julians Sch, Ackhursts Sch, Cunninghams Sch; *m* 16 June 1956, Mildred Boyton, da of William Chadwick, of Ruskin Rd, Swalwell, Newcastle upon Tyne; 1 s (Howard Mark Boyton b 25 April 1962), 1 da (Helen Boyton b 25 Nov 1958); *Career* md Rodney Boyton Advertising Ltd 1971, chief exec Ross Woodroff Robertson & Scott Ltd 1981; chm and md: Rex Stewart (Newcastle) Ltd 1984, Alliance International (Newcastle) Ltd 1990-; chm Bd of Govrs Newcastle Coll; MIPA, MCIM; *Recreations* walking, gardening; *Clubs* Northern Constitutional; *Style—* Gordon Scullard, Esq; 25 Cornmoor Rd, Whickam, Newcastle upon Tyne NE16 4PU (☎ 091 488 1595); Alliance International (Newcastle) Ltd, 9 St James St, Newcastle upon Tyne NE1 4NF (☎ 091 261 2611, fax 091 232 9606, telex 537020 ROSWOD G)

SCULLY, (Marie Elizabeth) Ann; da of Charles Francis Lyons, and Mary Elizabeth, *née* Godfrey; *b* 21 Nov 1943; *Educ* Notre Dame HS Sheffield, Lanchester Coll Coventry, Univ of London; *m* 1965 (sep 1990), Michael Joseph Scully; 2 s (Nicholas Michael b 15 Sept 1972, Peter b 9 Jan 1983), 1 da (Clare b 16 April 1967); *Career* ptnr Regency Conslts Chester 1980-89; parish cncllr 1975-87, sch govr 1977-; memb: Nat Assoc of Citizens' Advice Bureaux Merseyside Area Ctee, Mgmnt Ctee Citizens' Advice Bureau Chester, European Coal and Steel Community Consultative Ctee Luxembourg 1990-; chm Domestic Coal Consumers Cncl London, vice chm Nat Consumer Cncl London; MBIM 1982, FICM 1986; *Recreations* membership Chester Music Soc Choir, badminton; *Style—* Mrs Ann Scully; Hockenhull House, Hockenhull Lane, Tarvin, Chester

SCULLY, Prof Crispian; s of Patrick Scully and Rosaleen, *née* Richardson; *b* 24 May 1945; *Educ* Univ of London (BDS, BSc, MB BS, PhD), Univ of Bristol (MD, MDS); *m* 5 Oct 1977, Zoë Boucoumani; 1 da (Frances b 31 Jan 1982); *Career* lectr: Univ of London (oral immunology) 1977-79, Univ of Glasgow (oral medicine and pathology) 1979-81; sr lectr Univ of Glasgow (oral medicine and pathology) 1981-82; prof of oral medicine, surgery and pathology Univ of Bristol 1982-; head of Sch Univ of Bristol Dental Sch 1986-90; chm Central Examining Bd for Dental Hygienists; immediate past pres British Soc for Oral Med, memb Health Ctee General Dental Cncl; *Books* incl: Medical Problems in Dentistry (with R A Cawson, 2 edn 1988), Multiple Choice Questions in Clinical Dentistry (with R A Cawson, 1985), Hospital Dental Surgeon's Guide (1985), Slide Interpretation in Oral Diseases and the Oral Manifestations of Systemic Disease (with J P Shepherd, 1986), Dental Surgery Assistant's Handbook (jtly, 1988), Colour Aids in Oral Medicine (with R A Cawson 1988), Dental Patient Care (1989), Atlas of Stomatology (with S Flint, 1989), Occupational Hazards to Dental Staff (1990); *Recreations* swimming, hill walking, skiing, travelling, music, windsurfing; *Style—* Prof Crispian Scully; Centre for the Study of Oral Disease, Univ Dept of Oral Medicine, Surgery and Pathology, Bristol Dental School, Lower Maudlin St, Bristol BS1 2LY (☎ 0272 276201, fax 0272 255738)

SCULLY, Sean; *b* 1945; *Educ* Croydon Coll of Art, Univ of Newcastle, Havard Univ; *Career* artist; lectr; Chelsea Sch of Art and Goldsmnith's Sch of Art 1973-75, Princeton Univ 1977-83; solo exhibitions incl: Rowan Gallery London 1973, 1975, 1977, 1979 and 1981, Tortue Gallery Santa Monica Calif 1975 and 1976, Duffy-Gibbs Gallery NY 1977, Nadin Gallery NY 1979, Susan Caldwell Gallery NY 1980, Museum fur (Sub-) Kultur Berlin 1981, Sean Scully: Paintings 1971-81 (Ikon Gallery Birmingham and touring) 1981, David McKee Gallery NY 1983, 1985 and 1986, Gallery S65 Aaslt Belgium 1984, Drawings (Barbara Krakow Gallery Boston Mass) 1985, Monotypes (Pamela Auchincloss Gallery Santa Barbara Calif, David McKee Gallery NY, Douglas Flanders Contemporary Art Minneapolis) 1987, Galerie Schmele Düsseldorf W Germany 1987, Art Inst of Chicago Illinois 1987, Fuji TV Gallery Tokyo 1988, David McKee Gallery NY 1989 and 1990, The Whitechapel Art Gallery London and tour 1989, Pastel Drawings (Grob Gallery London) 1989-90, Karsten Greve Gallery Cologne 1990, Galerie de France Paris 1990, Monotypes (Pamela Auchincloss Gallery NY) 1990; gp exhibitions incl: John Moore's Liverpool Exhibition 8 (prizewinner) 1972, La Peinture Anglaise Aujoud'hui (Museum of Modern Art, Paris) 1973, British Painting (Hayward Gallery London) 1974, Certain Traditions (travelling exhibition Canada) 1978, Aspects of All-Over (Harm Boukaert Gallery NY) 1982, Part 1: Twelve Abstract Painters (Siegel Contemporary Art, NY) 1984, Art on Paper (Weatherspoon Art Gallery, Greensboro, N Carolina) 1985, Structure/ Abstraction (Hill Gallery Birmingham Mississippi) 1986, Harvey Quaytman & Sean Scully (Helsinki Festival Island) 1987, Logical Foundations (Pfizer Inc NY) 1987-88, Drawings and Related Prints (Castelli Graphics NY) 1989, Drawing: Paul Beus, Paul Rotterdam, Sean Scully (Arnold Herstand & Co NY) 1990, Sean Scully/Donald Suton: Abstraction/ Representation (Stanford Art Gallery, Stanford Univ, Polo Alto, Calif) 1990; *awards* Guggenheim fellowship 1983, Artist's fellowship from the Nat Endowment for the Arts 1984; *Style—* Sean Scully

SCUPHAM, John Peter; s of John Scupham, OBE (d 1990), of Thorpe St Andrew, Norwich, Norfolk, and Dorothy Lacey, *née* Clark (d 1987); *b* 24 Feb 1933; *Educ* Perse Sch Cambridge, St Georges Harpenden, Emmanuel Coll Cambridge (BA); *m* 10 Aug 1957, Carola Nance, da of Hermann Justus Braunholtz, CBE (d 1963); 3 s (Christopher, Giles, Roger), 1 da (Kate); *Career* Nat Serv 1952-54; head of English St Christopher Sch Letchworth 1961-80, estab The Mandeville Press 1974; *Books* Prehistories (1975), The Hinterland (1977), Summer Palaces (1980), Winter Quarters (1983), Out Late (1986), The Air Show (1988), Watching the Perseids (1990), Selected Poems (1990); *Recreations* book-collecting; *Style—* Peter Scupham, Esq; The Mandeville Press, 2 Taylor's Hill, Hitchin, Hertfordshire SG4 9AD (☎ 0462 450796)

SCURFIELD, Hugh Hedley; s of William Russell Scurfield (d 1981), of Worcestershire, and Elizabeth, *née* Hedley; *b* 9 Dec 1935; *Educ* King's Sch Worcester, Hertford Coll Oxford (MA); *m* 1, 11 July 1959, Ann Beverley; 1 s (Bryan b 1960), 3 da (Jane b 1962, Mary b 1964, Clare b 1967); m 2, 8 Dec 1978, Gillian Myfanwy (Jill), da of Rt Rev Mervyn Charles-Edwards, Bishop of Worcester (d 1983); 1 step s (Timothy b 1956), 3 step da (Anne b 1955, Emma b 1958, Suki b 1973); *Career* gen mangr actuary and dir Norwich Union Insurance Group; FIA (pres 1990); rowing: winner at Henley Royal Regatta, rowed for GB and a national selector; *Recreations* large family, home, walking; *Style—* Hugh Scurfield, Esq; Norwich Union Life Insurance Society, Surrey St, Norwich, Norfolk NR1 3NG (☎ 0603 622200, telex 97388, fax 0603 685408)

SCURLOCK, Ralph Geoffrey; s of Walter Howard Scurlock, of Romsey, and Linda May, *née* James; *b* 21 Aug 1931; *Educ* Bishop Wordsworth Sch Salisbury, St Johns Coll Oxford (MA, DPhil); *m* 7 Aug 1956, Maureen Mary, da of Edwin Leonard Oliver,

MM (d 1933); 4 s (Jonathan b 1959, Robin b 1961, Timothy b 1964, Alexander b 1966); *Career* BOC prof of cryogenic engrg Univ of Southampton 1985- (lectr in physics 1959-66, sr lectr 1966-68, reader 1968-85, dir of Inst of Cryogenics 1979-); series ed OUP 1980-; chm Br Cryogenics Cncl 1979-82, vice-chm Int Cryogenic Engrg Ctee 1987-; FIOP 1971, FIMechE 1982, CEng 1982; *Books* Low Temperature Behaviour of Solids (1966); *Style—* Prof Ralph Scurlock; 22 Brookvale Rd, Highfield, Southampton SO2 1QP; Institute of Cryogenics, University of Southampton (☎ 0703 592046, fax 0703 593053, telex 47661)

SCURR, Dr Cyril Frederick; CBE (1979), LVO (1952); s of Cyril Albert Scurr (d 1961), of Barnet, and Mabel Rose, *née* Magrath; *b* 14 July 1920; *Educ* Kings Coll London (MB BS), Westminster Hosp (MRCS, LRCP); *m* 25 Aug 1947, Isabel Jean, da of Leonard Spiller (d 1973); 3 s (Martin John b 1950, David Antony b 1955, Andrew James b 1962), 1 da (Judith Ann b 1948); *Career* Maj (specialist anaesthetist) RAMC served N Africa, Italy, Greece 1942-47; conslt anaesthetist: Westminster Hosp 1949-85, Hosp of St John & St Elizabeth 1950-; dean faculty of anaesthetists 1970-73; pres Assoc of Anaesthetists 1973-76, memb Health Servs Bd 1976-79, Frederick Hewitt lectr RCS 1971; Dudley Buxton Prize 1977, Faculty Gold medal RCS 1983, John Snow Medal 1984, Magill Centenary Oration 1988; Hon FFARCSI 1977, FFARCS 1953, FRCS 1974, FRSM; *Books* Scientific Foundations of Anaesthesia, Drugs in Anaesthesia; *Recreations* photography, gardening; *Style—* Dr Cyril Scurr, CBE, LVO; 16 Grange Ave, Totteridge Common, London N20 8AD (☎ 081 445 7188)

SCURR, John Henry; s of Henry Scurr (d 1981), of Slough, and Joyce, *née* Standerwick; *b* 25 March 1947; *Educ* Langley GS, Middx Hosp Med Sch London Univ (BSc, MB BS); *m* 5 April 1986, Nicola Mary Alexandra, da of Ivor S Vincent, of London; 3 s (James b 1976, Edward b 1984, Thomas b 1990), 3 da (Ruth b 1971, Ingrid b 1972, Victoria b 1986); *Career* conslt surgn Middx Hosp and UCH, sr lectr in surgery Univ of London, hon conslt surgn St Lukes Hosp for the Clergy; hon sec Aeromedical Practitioners Assoc; Freeman Worshipful Soc of Apothecaries 1989; FRSM 1972, FRCS 1976; *Books* Microcomputer Applications in Medicine (1987); *Recreations* flying, walking; *Clubs* Royal Soc of Medicine; *Style—* John Scurr, Esq; 5 Balniel Gate, London SW1V 3SD (☎ 071 834 5578); Lister Hospital, London SW1 (☎ 071 730 9563, fax 071 834 6315, car 0836 311958)

SCUSE, Dennis George; MBE (1957), TD (1946); s of Charles Henry Scuse (d 1945), of Ilford, Essex, and Kate, *née* Hooder (d 1976, aged 98); *b* 19 May 1921; *Educ* Park Sch Ilford, Mercers' High Holborn London; *m* 23 April 1948, Joyce Evelyn, da of Frank Burt (d 1931), of Cheltenham, Glos; 1 s (Jeremy b 1953); *Career* WWII 1939-46, cmmnd RA (HAA) 1940, air def GB 1940-41, cmmd Entertainments Offr Ceylon 1941-42, served MELF and CMF 1942-44, Army Broadcasting Serv (Bari, Rome and Athens) 1945-46; BBC Overseas Serv (seconded WO for Forces Broadcasting Serv in Benghazi and Canal Zone) 1947, asst dir Br Forces Network Germany 1949-50, (dir 1950-57); introduced Two Way Family Favourites with Jean Metcalfe 1952-57, sr planning asst BBC TV 1958-59, chief asst light entertainment BBC TV 1960, chief asst (TV) BBC NY Office and BBC rep N America 1962; md: Trident TV Enterprises 1972-76, Dennis Scuse Ltd PR Radio and TV Conslts 1976-86; political and pr conslt Hanson plc 1984-89; contributed many articles to numerous pubns; *Recreations* writing, reading, watching television; *Clubs* Royal Green Jackets; *Style—* Dennis G Scuse, Esq, MBE, TD; 2 York House, Courtlands, Sheen Rd, Richmond, Surrey (☎ 081 948 4737); 1 Grosvenor Place, London SW1X 7JH (☎ 071 245 1245, telex 917698, fax 071 235 1270)

SCUTT, Robin Hugh (known professionally as Scott); CBE (1976); s of late Rev Arthur Octavius Scutt, MA, and Freda May, *née* Palmer; *b* 24 Oct 1920; *Educ* Bryanston, British Institute Paris, Jesus Coll Cambridge (MA); *m* 1, 16 Jan 1943 (m dis 1960), Judy, *née* Watson; 2 s (Mark Oliver b 9 June 1945, (John) Paul b 30 May 1947); m 2, 29 July 1961, Patricia Anne Marie, da of J Pilkington Smith; *Career* Intelligence Corps 1941-42; BBC radio prodr and exec (Euro Serv) 1942-54, BBC TV prodr 1955-58, BBC Paris rep 1958-62, BBC prodr 1963-66, controller BBC Radio 1 and 2 1967-68, BBC2 TV 1969-74, controller Devpt BBC TV 1974-77, dep md BBC TV 1977-80, exec prodr Nat Video Corp; chm United Media Ltd, memb Prog Advsy Bd London Weekend Television, fell and Gold medallist Royal TV Soc; Officier de la Légion d'Honneur 1983; FRSA 1985; *Recreations* gardening, theatre, travel; *Clubs* Garrick; *Style—* Robin Scott, Esq, CBE; The Abbey Cottage, Cockfield, nr Bury St Edmunds, Suffolk; United Media Ltd, 20 Wells Mews, London W1P 3FJ (☎ 071 580 5594, fax 071 323 0464)

SEABRIGHT, John Walter (Jack); s of Walter Alexander Seabright, of Henley-on-Thames, Oxon, and Emily Gladys, *née* Onion; *b* 2 May 1929; *Educ* Brentwood Sch Essex, Downing Coll Cambridge (MA); *m* 23 Oct 1954, Diana Bartlett, da of George Forrester Fairbairn (d 1966), of Torquay; 2 s (Paul b 1958, Alistair b 1961), 2 da (Theresa b 1960, Lucy b 1963); *Career* dir Coats Patons (UK) 1969-73, md MFI Furniture Group 1974-81, chief exec Henley Distance Learning Ltd 1981-85; dir: Church & Co plc 1982-, Clydesdale Group Ltd 1982-85, Thorntons plc 1988-; chm: Midlands Convenience Stores plc 1986-, Compular Ltd 1987-, Teamband Ltd 1981-; *Recreations* walking, travel; *Style—* John W Seabright, Esq; Wanwood, Park Corner, Nettlebed, Oxon (☎ 0491 641184); Teamband Ltd, Park Corner, Nettlebed, Oxon

SEABROOK, Air Vice-Marshal Geoffrey Leonard; CB (1965); s of Robert Leonard Seabrook (d 1946); *b* 25 Aug 1909; *Educ* King's Sch Canterbury; *m* 1949, Beryl Mary, *née* Hughes; 1 s, 1 da; *Career* CA 1931; RAF 1933 (Iraq & Far East), Air Vice-Marshal, dir of Personnel (G) Air Ministry 1961-63, AOA Tech Trg Cmd 1963-66 (ret); *Recreations* golf, sailing; *Clubs* RAF, Piltdown Golf; *Style—* Air Vice-Marshal Geoffrey Seabrook, CB; Long Pightle, Piltdown, Uckfield, Sussex (☎ 082 572 2322)

SEABROOK, Graeme; s of Norman Seabrook (d 1987), and Amy Winifred Seabrook; *b* 1 May 1939; *Educ* Box Hill Tech Sch Australia, Royal Melbourne Inst of Technol, Harvard Business Sch (AMP); *m* 18 Feb 1967, Lorraine Ellen, *née* Ludlow; 1 s (Mark Andrew b 6 Nov 1971), 1 da (Kym Michelle b 14 Jan 1970); *Career* Coles Myer Limited (formerly G J Coles & Company Limited) Australia: gp controller supermarket merchandise 1970-78, assoc dir gen merchandise 1978-82, dir and chief gen mangr 1982-85, gp md Discount Stores 1985-87, jt md Retail Servs 1987-88; joined Dairy Farm International 1988 and seconded to Kwik Save UK; Kwik Save Group plc: md 1988-89, md and chief exec 1989-; *Recreations* tennis, squash; *Style—* Graeme Seabrook, Esq; Kwik Save Group plc, Warren Drive, Prestatyn, Clwyd LL19 7HU (☎ 0745 887111, fax 0745 853733)

SEABROOK, Michael Richard; s of Robert Henry Seabrook (d 1983), of Solihull, and Clara, *née* Berry; *b* 24 March 1952; *Educ* King Edwards Sch Birmingham, Univ of Exeter (LLB); *m* 1 Sept 1979, Hilary Margaret, da of Anthony John Pettitt, of Bromley; 2 s (Nicholas b 1983, William b 1986); *Career* admitted slr 1976; articled clerk Lovell White & King 1974-76, asst slr Clifford-Turner 1976-79; ptnr: Needham & James 1981-86 (asst slr 1980), Evershed Wells & Hind 1986-; memb Law Soc 1976; *Recreations* sporting; *Clubs* (capt) Heath Golf, Warwicks Imps Pilgrims Cricket, Knowle & Dorridge Cricket, Warwicks Cricket, Bacchanalians Golf Soc; *Style—* Michael R Seabrook, Esq; 2 Granville Rd, Dorridge, Solihull, West Midlands, B93 8BY (☎ 0564 773732); Evershed Wells & Hind, 10 Newhall St, Birmingham, B3 3LX (☎ 021 233 2001, fax 021 236 1583, telex 336688)

SEABROOK, Peter John; s of Robert Henry Seabrook (d 1987), of Galleywood, Essex, and Emma Mary, *née* Cottey (d 1989); *b* 2 Nov 1935; *Educ* King Edward VI GS Chelmsford, Essex Inst of Agric Writtle (MHort, Dip Hort); *m* 14 May 1960, Margaret Ruth, da of Arthur Wilfred Risbey, of Churchdown, Glos (d 1990); 1 s (Roger b 9 Feb 1962), 1 da (Alison b 13 May 1964); *Career* Nat Serv RASC 1956-58; TV presenter; horticultural advsr and dir Cramphorn plc 1958-66, tech rep Bord na Mona 1966-70, horticultural conslt 1971; dir: William Strike Ltd 1972-, Roger Harvey Ltd 1981-; radio: In Your Garden 1965-70, Gardeners Question Time 1981-82; garden presenter: Pebble Mill at One BBC1 1975-86 (Gardeners Direct Line 1982-), WGBH TV Boston USA 1975-, Chelsea Flower Show 1976-89, Gardeners World BBC2 1976-81; gardening corr: The Sun 1977-, The Yorkshire Post 1981-; FIHort; *Books* Shrubs For Your Garden (1973), Complete Vegetable Gardener (1976), Book of the Garden (1979), Good Plant Guide (1981), Good Food Gardening (1983); *Recreations* gardening; *Style—* Peter Seabrook, Esq; 212A Baddow Rd, Chelmsford, Essex

SEABROOK, Robert John; QC (1983); s of Alan Thomas Pertwee Seabrook, MBE, of Hindhead, Surrey, and Mary, *née* Parker (d 1977); *b* 6 Oct 1941; *Educ* St George's Coll Salisbury Southern Rhodesia, UCL (LLB); *m* 19 Oct 1965, Liv Karin, da of Rev Bjarne Djupvik (d 1983), of Bergen, Norway; 2 s (Justin b 20 Dec 1969, Magnus b 23 April 1975), 1 da (Marianne b 23 Oct 1971); *Career* called to the Bar Middle Temple 1964, recorder 1984; memb of court Univ of Sussex 1988; Liveryman Worshipful Co of Curriers 1972; *Recreations* wine, listening to music, travel; *Style—* Robert Seabrook, Esq, QC; 41 Surrenden Rd, Brighton, E Sussex (☎ 0273 505491); 1 Crown Office Row, Temple, London EC4Y 7HH (☎ 071 353 1801, fax 071 583 1700, telex 24988 ICOR G)

SEABROOK, Timothy James; s of Frederick James Seabrook (d 1979), of The Walnuts, Ashton Keynes, Swindon, Wilts, and Ethel Mary Seabrook (d 1989); *b* 20 May 1940; *Educ* Wellington; *m* 1967, Catherine Marion-Jean, da of Cdr Herbert Geoffrey St John Bury (d 1989); 1 da; *Career* mangr Industl Subsids Div 3i Group plc 1975-82, dep chm Triangle International Ltd 1980-, dir: Dennis & Robinson 1982-, Wayne Kerr plc 1984-88; chm Dynamic Logic Ltd 1984-87, independent dir; FCA; *Recreations* golf, gardening; *Clubs* MCC; *Style—* Timothy Seabrook, Esq; Church Cottage, Greywell, Basingstoke, Hants RG25 1DA (☎ 0256 702108)

SEAFIELD, 13 Earl of (S 1701); Ian Derek Francis Ogilvie-Grant; Lord Ogilvy of Cullen and Viscount Seafield (S 1698), Lord Ogilvy of Deskford and Cullen and Viscount Reidhaven (S 1701); s of Countess of Seafield (12 in line, d 1969) and Derek Studley-Herbert (who assumed by deed poll 1939 the additional surnames of Ogilvie-Grant, the present Peer being recognised in those surnames by warrant of Lord Lyon 1971); *b* 20 March 1939; *Educ* Eton; *m* 1, 1960 (m dis 1971), Mary Dawn Mackenzie, da of Henry Illingworth; 2 s (Viscount Reidhaven b 1963, Hon Alexander b 1966); m 2, 1971, Leila, da of Mahmoud Refaat, of Cairo; *Heir* s, Viscount Reidhaven, *qv*; *Clubs* Whites; *Style—* The Rt Hon The Earl of Seafield; Old Cullen, Cullen, Banffshire

SEAGA, Rt Hon Edward Philip George; PC (1981); s of Philip Seaga; *b* 28 May 1930; *Educ* Wolmers Boys' Sch Kingston Jamaica, Harvard Univ; *m* 1965, Marie Elizabeth, *née* Constantine (Miss Jamaica 1964); 2 s, 1 da; *Career* MP Western Kingston (Jamaica) 1962-, leader Jamaican Labour Pty 1974- (asst sec 1960-62, sec 1962), oppn leader 1974-80, PM Jamaica 1980-; *Style—* The Rt Hon Edward Seaga; Vale Royal, Kingston, Jamaica (☎ 0101 809 927 7854)

SEAGER, Hon Douglas Leighton; s of 1 Baron Leighton of St Mellons, CBE (d 1963); *b* 1925; *m* 1960, Gillian Claire, da of Leonard Warwick Greenwood, of Pound Piece, Astley, Stourport, Worcs; 3 da; *Style—* The Hon Douglas Seager; Leighton House, 5929 Hudson St, Vancouver, British Columbia V6M 2Z4, Canada

SEAGER, Gerald Elliot; s of Capt John Elliot, MC (d 1955), and Dorothy Irene Seager, *née* Jones (d 1986); gs of Sir William Seager (d 1941) shipowner and MP (Lib) Cardiff East 1918-22; *b* 29 June 1924; *Educ* Charterhouse; *m* 17 April 1948, Margaret Elizabeth (d 1988), da of William Jones Morgan (d 1971), of Aberbran Fawr, Brecon; *Career* WWII Lt Welsh Gds 1943-46, served Italy, POW 1944; dir: Stalco Aden 1966-67, Newport Stevedoring Co Ltd and Newport Screw Towing Co Ltd 1967-69, Cory Bros Shipping Ltd 1968-77, Stephenson Clarke Shipping Ltd 1970-77, Newport Stevedoring Co Ltd 1970-77, Transcontinental Air Ltd, Powell Duffryn Shipping Services Ltd 1976-77; chief exec: Rais Hassan Saadi & Co Dubai (UAE) 1977-78, Rais Shipping Co Dubai (UAE) 1977-78; dir Thabet Int Ltd 1987- (chief exec 1978-86); vice chm Aden Shipping Conf 1967, life govr Royal Hosp and Home for Incurables Putney 1967; chm: Newport Shipowners Assoc 1972-77, Newport Harbour Cmmrs 1974-75, S Wales Coal Exporters Assoc 1970-71; memb Baltic Exchange 1964; *Recreations* antiques, football, Welsh affairs; *Style—* Gerald E Seager, Esq; Rudhall Barns, Rudhall, Ross-on-Wye, Herefordshire HR9 7TL

SEAL, Dr Barry Herbert; MEP (Lab) W Yorks 1979-; s of Herbert and Rose Ann Seal; *b* 28 Oct 1937; *Educ* Univ of Bradford, Harvard Business Sch; *m* 1963, Frances Catherine Wilkinson; 1 s (Robert), 1 da (Catherine); *Career* chem engr, control engr, univ lectr; former ldr Bradford Cncl Labour Gp; memb Economic and Monetary Ctee of Euro Parly; *Books* Dissertations on Computer Control; *Recreations* walking, reading, flying; *Clubs* Dudley Hill and Tong Socialist; *Style—* Dr Barry Seal, MEP; Brookfields Farm, Wyke, Bradford, W Yorks BD12 9LU

SEAL, David Herbert; s of Maj Jefferson Seal, TD (d 1977), and Florence Eileen, *née* Herbert (d 1980); *b* 7 April 1935; *Educ* Marlborough, Pembroke Coll Cambridge (MA); *m* 19 Nov 1958, Juliet Rose, da of John Perrot (ka Dunkirk 1940); 1 s (John Rupert Jefferson b 1964), 2 da (Kate b 1959, Sarah Juliet b 1962); *Career* ptnr: Jefferson Seal & Co 1956, Seal Arnold 1968, D Q Henriques Seal 1973, Charlton Seal 1976, Jefferson Seal Ltd 1986; memb: Conservative Assoc 1956-71, Stock Exchange 1956; *Recreations* horses, boats, vintage farming; *Clubs* St Helier Yacht, Jersey Riding (vice pres); *Style—* David Seal, Esq; Holmbury, Augres, Trinity, Jersey JE3 5DA (☎ 0534 61614); Channel House, Green St, St Helier, Jersey JE2 4UH (☎ 0534 25225, fax 0534 32786, telex 4192354)

SEAL, Julius Damien; s of Pulin Behari Seal (d 1982), and Julia Stuart, *née* Hogg; *b* 3 March 1945; *Educ* St Benedict's Sch; *m* 18 Feb 1970, Annie, da of Joseph Joseph, of Kuala Lumpur; 1 s (Giles b 1980), 3 da (Augusta b 1976, Harriet b 1978, Philippa b 1983); *Career* called to the Bar Lincoln's Inn 1967, memb of Inner Temple 1989; *Recreations* show jumping; *Style—* Julius Seal, Esq; 3 King's Bench Walk, Temple EC4

SEAL, Michael Jefferson; s of Jefferson Seal, and Florence Eileen, *née* Herbert; *b* 17 Oct 1936; *Educ* Marlborough; *m* 22 Sept 1962, Julia Mary Seton, da of late Malcolm Sinclair Gaskill, of Hale, Cheshire; 1 s (Jonathan Michael Jefferson), 2 da (Heather Caroline Seton, Rosanne Julia); *Career* Nat Serv 1955-57, TA 1957-68; The Carborundum Co Ltd 1957-59; ptnr: Jefferson Seal & Co 1961-68 (joined 1959), Seal Arnold & Co 1968-72, DQ Henriques Seal & Co 1972-75, Charlton Seal Dimmock & Co 1975-87, Charlton Seal Ltd 1987-88, Charlton Seal Schaverien Ltd 1988-90; dir 1990-: Wise Speke Ltd, Wise Speke Holdings Ltd, (non-exec) CST Emerging Asia Trust plc, (non-exec) Benchmark Group plc; memb: Manchester Fin and Professional Forum, Family Welfare Assoc Manchester, Humane Soc of Hundred Salford, Gtr Manchester Educnl Tst, Clonter Farm Music Tst; memb Int Stock Exchange (memb Ctee Northern Unit); *Recreations* outdoor; *Clubs* St James's (Manchester); *Style—* Michael Seal, Esq; The Dene House, Great Budworth, Northwich, Cheshire CW9

6HB (☎ 0606 891555); Charlton Seal a division of Wise Speke Ltd, PO Box 512, 76 Cross St, Manchester M60 2EP (☎ 061 953 9700, fax 061 832 9092, telex 666894, car tel 0860 710242)

SEAL, Raymond; s of Clifford Seal (d 1978), and Hannah, *née* Woodcock; *b* 23 Dec 1932; *Educ* Bingley GS; *m* 1, 14 Feb 1956, Mary; 2 s (Andrew David b 1957, Jeremy Charles b 1960); m 2, 10 May 1985, Gisela; *Career* textile speciality fibre specialist; md: Seal International Ltd, Morton Fibres Ltd, Bradford Mohair Ltd, Ladywell Fibres Ltd; *Recreations* golf, rugby, cricket; *Clubs* Shipley Golf, Yorkshire Cricket, Bingley Cricket, Headingley Taverners', Lloyds, Bradford; *Style—* Raymond Seal, Esq; East Beck Farm, Askwith, Otley, Yorkshire (☎ 0943 462635); Seal International Ltd, Ladywell Mills, Hall Lane, Bradford, Yorkshire (☎ 0274 726744, fax 0274 735522, telex 517471)

SEALE, Sir John Henry; 5 Bt (UK 1838), of Mount Boone, Devonshire; patron of one living; s of Sir John Carteret Hyde Seale, 4 Bt (d 1964); *b* 3 March 1921; *Educ* Eton, ChCh Oxford; *m* 1953, Ray Josephine, da of late R G Charters, MC, of Christchurch, New Zealand; 1 s, 1 da; *Heir* s, John Robert Charters Seale; *Career* Capt RA; architect; RIBA; *Style—* Sir John Seale, Bt; Slade, nr Kingsbridge, Devon

SEALE, John Robert Charters; s and h of Sir John Seale, 5 Bt; *b* 17 Aug 1954; *Style—* John Seale, Esq

SEALES, Peter Clinton; s of James M Seales (d 1940), of Dublin, and Angela, *née* O'Doherty; *b* 1 Nov 1929; *Educ* Dublin Univ; *m* May 1955, Bernadette Rogers; 1 da (Elizabeth Devereaux b 1962), and 1 da dec'd; *Career* called to the Bar 1953, chief exec Operation Raleigh 1984-; conslt to Saatchi & Saatchi Compton plc 1984-, commercial dir Wassen Int Ltd 1985-; hon cncl memb Operation Innovator 1987-; FInstD 1972; *Recreations* sailing, music; *Clubs* White Elephant, Wig and Pen, IOD, Real Tennis; *Style—* Peter Seales, Esq; 78 Northumberland Rd, Leamington Spa, Warwicks (☎ 0926 31562, office tel 0372 379828)

SEALEY, Barry Edward; CBE (1990); s of Edward Sealey, of Edinburgh, and Queenie Katherine, *née* Hill (d 1981); *b* 3 Feb 1936; *Educ* Dursley GS, St John's Coll Cambridge (BA); *m* 21 May 1960, Helen, da of Dr Frank Martyn (d 1979), of Grimsby; 1 s (Andrew b 1964), 1 da (Margaret (Mrs Cave) b 1962); *Career* Nat Serv RAF 1953-55; dep chm Christian Salvesen plc 1989 (trainee 1958, dir 1969, md 1981, md and dep chm 1987, ret 1990); directorships incl: S Equitable Life Assurance Soc, S American Investment Co, Northern Advsy Bd Nat West Bank, Albacom plc 1990-, Logitek plc 1990-, Warburton's Ltd 1990-, David A Hall Ltd 1990, The Caledonian Brewing Co Ltd 1990-; memb Cncl Industl Soc, govr Napier Poly of Edinburgh; CBIM; *Recreations* walking, music; *Clubs* New (Edinburgh); *Style—* Barry Sealey, Esq; 4 Castlelaw Rd, Edinburgh EH13 0DN (☎ 031 441 2801, fax 031 441 5576)

SEALY, Hon Mrs (Lavinia Caroline); 2 (twin) da of 2 Baron Piercy (d 1981); *b* 24 May 1947; *Educ* Badminton Sch, St Hugh's Coll Oxford (MA); *m* 1971, Nicholas John Elliot Sealy; 1 s, 1 da; *Style—* The Hon Mrs Sealy; Timber Hill, Chobham, Surrey (☎ 093 287 3875)

SEAMAN, Christopher Bertram; s of Albert Edward Seaman (d 1960), of Canterbury, Kent, and Ethel Margery, *née* Chambers (d 1985); *b* 7 March 1942; *Educ* Canterbury Cathedral Choir Sch, King's Sch Canterbury, King's Coll Cambridge Scholar MA); *Career* princ timpanist and memb Bd London Philharmonic Orch 1964-68; princ conductor: BBC Scot Symphony Orch 1971-77 (asst conductor 1968-70), Northern Sinfonia Orch 1974-79; chief guest conductor Utrecht Symphony Orch 1979-82, conductor in res Baltimore Symphony Orch 1987-; appears as guest conductor worldwide; FGSM 1972; *Recreations* people, reading, shopping, theology; *Style—* Christopher Seaman, Esq

SEAMAN, Sir Keith Douglas; KCVO (1981), OBE (1976); s of Eli Semmens Seaman (d 1955), and Ethel Maud Seaman (d 1930); *b* 11 June 1920; *Educ* Unley HS, Adelaide Univ (BA, LLB), Flinders Univ (MA, Dip Hum); *m* 1946, Joan Isabel, da of late Fred Birbeck; 1 s, 1 da; *Career* memb Exec World Assoc of Christian Broadcasting Cos 1960, chm 5KA, 5AU and 5RM Broadcasting Cos 1971-77 (dir 1960), memb Aust Govt Social Welfare Cmmn 1973-76, govr South Australia 1977-82; KStJ 1978; *see Debrett's Handbook of Australia and New Zealand for further details*; *Style—* Sir Keith Seaman, KCVO, OBE; 31 Heggerton St, Victor Harbor, South Australia 5211

SEAMAN, (Marvin) Roy; s of late Charles Seaman, of Harleston, Norfolk, and Mary Elizabeth, *née* Goldsmith; *b* 11 Sept 1945; *Educ* Stradbroke Secdy Sch, RAF Tech Trg Coll; *m* 19 Oct 1976, Judy, da of Joseph Ragobar, of Marabella, Trinidad; 2 s (Christian b 1978, Jonathan b 1982), 1 da (Michelle Anne b 1981); *Career* with RAF for 6 yrs; chm and md Franchise Devpt Services Ltd 1971-; visiting lectr seminars and colls on franchise and licensing laws; Int Licensing (servs to estab franchisors, prospective franchisors, franchise publications, public relations, seminars, exhibitions and marketing); memb CBI, FInstD, MCIM, MInstEx; *Recreations* running, hunting, climbing, fishing; *Clubs* IOD; *Style—* Roy Seaman, Esq; Cedar Lodge, Norwich Rd, Tasburgh, Norfolk (☎ 0508 470686); Franchise Development Services Ltd, Castle House, Norwich NR2 1PJ (☎ 0603 620301, fax 0603 630174)

SEARBY, Lt-Col Robin Vincent; s of Air Cdre John Henry Searby, DSO, DFC (d 1986), and Eva, *née* Rowland (d 1976); *b* 20 July 1947; *Educ* Leasam House Sch; *m* 8 May 1976, Caroline Angela, da of late Maj John Beamish, MC; 1 s (Henry b 6 June 1977), 2 da (Louisa b 19 Jan 1979, Alice b 31 March 1981); *Career* RMA Sandhurst 1966-68, 2 Lt 9/12 Royal Lancers (POW) 1968, regtl duty Berlin, BAOR, NI 1968-73, loan serv Dhofar (Sultanate of Oman) 1973-75, regtl duty NI and UK 1976-79, Maj 1979, Army Staff Coll Camberley 1980, GSO II Ops 2 Armd Div BAOR 1981-83, regtl duty 1983-85, Lt-Col dir staff Army Staff Coll 1985-87, CO 9/12 Royal Lancers 1987-89, COS to DRAC 1989-; Distinguished Service Medal (Gallantry) Sultanate of Oman 1975; *Recreations* reading, equitation; *Clubs* Cavalry; *Style—* Lt-Col Robin Searby; c/o HQ, Director Royal Armoured Corps, Bovington, Wareham, Dorset BH20 6JA

SEARLE, Geoffrey John; TD (1976); s of William Ernest Searle, of Cornwall, and Eileen Edith, *née* Girling; *b* 21 June 1945; *Educ* Bancroft's Sch Woodford Green Essex; *m* 25 Sept 1971, Nicole Nicette Suzanne, da of Gilbert Andre Paul Cochonneau, of Tours, France; 2 s (Dominic b 1973, Yann b 1976), 1 da (Olivia b 1984); *Career* TA RCS 1963-77, ret actg Maj; asst clerk of cncl Brentwood UDC 1969-73, managing ptnr Denton Hall Burgin & Warrens slrs 1988- (asst slr 1973-76, ptnr 1977-); memb: Ctee of Mgmnt Br Chapter of FIABCI; Int Bar Assoc; fndr memb UK Environmental Law Assoc, assoc memb American Bar Assoc; memb Law Soc; *Books* Development Land Tax (1985); *Recreations* family, reading, swimming, listening to pop music, conversing with young adults; *Style—* Geoffrey Searle, Esq, TD; Denton Hall Burgin & Warrens, Five Chancery Lane, Clifford's Inn, London EC4A 1BU (☎ 071 320 6165, fax 071 404 0087, telex 263567)

SEARLE, Geoffrey William; CBE (1972), DSC (1943); s of William Arthur Searle (d 1957); *b* 11 April 1914; *m* 1940, Constance, da of Charles Tyrrell; 1 s, 1 da; *Career* CA 1936; Lt Cdr RNVR; joined BP 1946: dir of fin & planning and chm of Exec Ctee BP Trading Ltd, ret 1974; chm: London & Scottish Marine Oil plc 1978-85 (md 1974-78, non-exec dir 1985-86), Assoc of British Independent Oil Exploration Cos (Brindex) 1982, Belden & Blake Int Ltd 1986-; *Recreations* tennis, golf, music, gardening; *Clubs* Naval, RAC, City of London; *Style—* Geoffrey Searle, Esq, CBE, DSC; 20 Beech Rd, Reigate, Surrey RH2 9LR (☎ 0737 245803); Belden & Blake International Ltd, 41 Cedar Avenue, Hamilton HM12, Bermuda

SEARLE, Graham William; s of Frederick William Searle (d 1969), and Margaret, *née* Hewitt (d 1961); *b* 26 Sept 1946; *Educ* Sir George Monoux GS Walthamstow, SW Essex Tech Coll, King's Coll London (BSc), Sir John Cass Coll London; *m* 4 Aug 1984, Francesca Vivica, *née* Parsons; 1 da (Rebecca b 7 March 1989); *Career* fndr and dir: Friends of the Earth Ltd London 1971, Earth Resources Research Ltd London 1973 (exec dir 1975); advsr Dept of Urban Affrs Fed Govt of Canada 1976, liaison offr Environmental Liaison Centre Nairobi Kenya 1977, prog offr UN Environmental Prog Nairobi 1978, ind environmental mgmnt conslt 1979-89; currently non-exec dir Rechem Environment Services plc; memb: Ind Cmmn on Tport Planning 1973, UK Standing Ctee on Nat Parks 1975, Standing Ctee of UK Waste Mgmnt Advsy Cncl 1975, Conservation Planning Ctee Suffolk Wildlife Tst, Rivers Advsy Ctee of Nat Rivers Authy (Anglia Region); Conservation Working GP, Broads Authy; FGS; *Books* Project Earth (1973), Rush to Destruction (1975), Energy (1977), Automatic Unemployment (co-author, 1979), The Habitat Handbook (1980), Major World Bank Projects (1987); *Recreations* fly-fishing, sea fishing, golf, spectator cricket and rugby; *Clubs* St Helena Golf (Halesworth); *Style—* Graham Searle, Esq; The Old Post Office, Huntingfield, Halesworth, Suffolk IP19 0PU (☎ 0986 798202, fax 0986 798 794); Rechem Environmental Services plc, Astor House, Station Rd, Bourne End, Bucks SL8 5YP (☎ 0628 810011, fax 0628 819059, telex 848079)

SEARLE, Norman Percy Walter; JP (Inner London); s of William Cecil Searle (d 1972), and Ada Gladys, *née* Page; *b* 7 June 1930; *Educ* Battersea GS, West Ham Coll of Technol; *m* 1, 1953 (m dis 1976), Dorothy Sylvia, da of Frederick Jackson; 1 s (Matthew b 1961), 2 da (Helen b 1959, Laura b 1966); m 2, 1977, Christine Joyce, da of Norman Frederick Jackson ; 1 s (Caspar b 1982), 1 da (Martha b 1978); *Career* Nat Serv RAMC 1948-49; md Mosford Joinery Ltd 1966, dir Eight Force Ltd 1982-; memb: Conservation Area Advsy Ctee City of London, Nat Cncl Prison Visitors; chm Wood St Crime Prevention Assoc, vice chm City Heritage Soc, chm West London Liquor Licencing Ctee; Freeman City of London, Liveryman Worshipful Co of Painter-Stainers, memb Worshipful Co of Parish Clerks; memb IWSc 1960; *Clubs* Royal Thames Yacht, Nat Lib; *Style—* Norman Searle, Esq, JP; 166 Defoe House, Barbican, London EC2Y 8DN (☎ 071 638 5233); 105 Mount Pleasant Rd, London NW10 4EH (☎ 081 459 6241, fax 081 451 1499, telex 888941 LCCI MOSFORD)

SEARLE, Ronald William Fordham; s of William James Searle (d 1967), and Nellie, *née* Hunt; *b* 3 March 1920; *Educ* Cambridge Sch of Art; *m* 1 (m dis 1967), Kaye Webb *qv*; 1 s (John b 1947), 1 da (Kate b 1947); m 2, 1967, Monica Ilse Koenig; *Career* Sapper 287 Field Co RE 1939-46 (Japanese POW, Siam and Malaya 1942-45, dept psychological warfare Allied Force HQ Port Said Ops 1956; contrib Punch 1947-61, special features artist Life Magazine 1955-62, contrib New Yorker Magazine 1966-, designer commemorative medals to the French Mint 1975- and BAMS 1984-; film designer: John Gilpin, On the Twelfth Day, Energetically Yours, Germany 1960, Toulouse-Lautrec, Dick Deadeye; designer of animation sequences: Those Magnificent Men in their Flying Machines 1965, Monte Carlo or Bust! 1969, Scrooge 1970; one-man exhibitions 1950-88 incl: Leicester Galleries London, Imperial War Museum, Kraushaar Gallery NY, Bianchini Gallery NY, Kunsthalle Bremen, Bibliotéque Nationale Paris, Munich, Neue Galerie Vienna; Awards: LA Art Dirs Club Medal 1959, Philadelphia Art Dirs Club Medal 1959, Nat Cartoonists Soc Award 1959 and 1960, Gold Medal III Biennale Tolentino Italy 1965, Prix de la Critique Belge 1968, Grand Prix de l'Humour Noir (France) 1971, Prix d'Humour Festival d'Avignon 1971, Medal of French Circus 1971, Prix Internationale 'Charles Huard' 1972, La Monnaie de Paris Medal 1974; RDI, AGI; *Books* Forty Drawings (1946), John Gilpin (1952), Souls in Torment (1953), Rake's Progress (1955), Merry England (1956), Paris Sketchbook (1957), The St Trinian's Story (with Kaye Webb 1959); with Alex Atkinson: The Big City (1958), USA for Beginners (1959), Russia for Beginners (1960); Refugees (1960), Which Way did He Go? (1961), Escape from the Amazon (1963), From Frozen North to Filthy Lucre (1964), Those Magnificent Men in their Flying Machines (1965), Haven't We Met Before Somewhere? (with Heinz Huber 1966), Searle's Cats (1967), The Square Egg (1968), Hello - Where did all the People Go? (1969), Secret Sketchbook (1970), The Second Coming of Toulouse - Lautrec (1970), The Addict (1971), More Cats (1975), Designs for Gilbert and Sullivan (1975), Paris! Paris! (with Irwin Shaw 1977), Searle's Zodiac (1977), Ronald Searle (monograph 1978), The King of Beasts (1980), The Big Fat Cat Book (1982), Illustrated Winespeak (1983), Ronald Searle in Perspective (monograph 1984), Ronald Searle's Golden Oldies 1941-1961 (1985), Something in the Cellar (1986), To the Kwai - and Back (1986), Ah Yes, I Remember It Well...: Paris 1961-75 (1987), Non-Sexist Dictionary (1988), Slightly Foxed - but still desirable (1989); *Clubs* Garrick; *Style—* Ronald Searle, Esq; c/o Tessa Sayle Agency, 11 Jubilee Place, Chelsea, London SW3 3TE (☎ 071 823 3883, fax 071 823 3363); John Locke Studios, 15 East 76th St, New York City, NY 10021 (☎ 0101 212 288 8010, fax 0101 212 288 8011)

SEARS, Dr Charles Alistair Newton; s of Dr Harold Trevor Newton Sears, *qv*, and Dr Janet Sorley, *née* Conn; *b* 30 Dec 1952; *Educ* Sandbach Sch, Middx Hosp Univ of London (MB BS); *m* 6 May 1978, Judith Lesley, da of Dr Leslie Victor Martin, of Oxbridge, Dorset; 3 s (James b 1979, Robert b 1982, Nicholas b 1986); *Career* house offr Middx Hosp 1978; sr house offr: neurosurgery Royal Free Hosp 1978-79, medicine Queen Elizabeth Hosp Birmingham 1979-82; ptnr in gen practice Salisbury 1983-, clinical asst Rheumatology Dept and Community Mental Handicap Unit Salisbury DHA; memb: Inst of Orthopaedic Med, Salisbury Med Educn and Med Audit Ctee, trainer in gen practice Salisbury Dist Vocational Trg Scheme; RCGP: Salisbury rep, memb faculty, Bd of Wessex Faculty; MRCGP 1988; *Clubs* Inst of Orthopoedic Medicine, RYA; *Style—* Dr Charles Sears; Close House, The Green, Pitton, Salisbury, Wilts SP5 1DZ (☎ 0722 72745); Grove House, 18 Wilton Rd, Salisbury, Wilts SP2 7EE (☎ 0722 333034)

SEARS, Dr (Harold) Trevor Newton; s of Dr Charles Newton Sears, MD (d 1944), of London, and Annie Florence, *née* Dew (d 1961); *b* 29 Dec 1919; *Educ* Westminster, Univ of London, St Thomas's Hosp London (MD); *m* 4 Sept 1948, Janet Sorley, da of Rev Dr James Charles Conn (d 1969), of Edinburgh; 2 s (Charles b 1952, Andrew b 1954), 1 da (Elizabeth b 1950); *Career* served RAMC in the CMF, RMO to the Kent Yeomanry and subsequently Maj med specialist 1944-47; sr med registrar Prince of Wales' Hosp Plymouth 1948-50, med registrar St Thomas's Hosp 1950-53 (house appts 1943-44), GP Holmes Chapel Cheshire 1954-82, clinical asst Professorial Unit Univ of Manchester, i/c the Hypertension Follow-Up Clinic at the Manchester Royal Infirmary 1954-79, Upjohn travelling fellowship 1960, Nuffield Fndn travelling fellowship 1962; MRCS, LRCP, FRCP; *Books* Hypertension, Encyclopaedia of General Practice (1960), Do Something About Those Arteries (1968 and 1969), Cardiovascular Disease: A Textbook of Medical Practice (1976); *Recreations* opera, photography, travel, gardening; *Clubs* British Med Assoc, Mid-Cheshire Pitt; *Style—* Dr Trevor Sears; 8 The Stables, Walpole Court, Puddletown, Dorset DT2 8TH (☎ 0305 848125)

SEARS, Victoria Jane; da of Philip John Morlock, of Court Lodge, West Farleigh, Maidstone, Kent, and Susan Mary, *née* Cotton; *b* 16 Oct 1960; *Educ* Roedean, Univ of Oxford (MA); *m* 14 July 1984, Robert David Murray Sears, s of Robert Murray Sears, of Haslemere, Surrey; *Career* ptnr Knight Frank and Rutley 1989- (assoc ptnr 1987-);

HMP Wandsworth: memb Bd of Visitors, memb Local Review Ctee; *Recreations* riding, hunting, gardening, travel; *Style*— Mrs Victoria Sears; Knight, Frank & Rutley, 20 Hanover Square, London W1R 0AH (☎ 071 629 8171, fax 071 493 4114, telex 265384)

SEATON, Prof Anthony; s of Dr Ronald Seaton (d 1986), and Julia, *née* Harrison; *b* 20 Aug 1938; *Educ* Rossall Sch, Kings Coll Cambridge (BA, MB, MD); *m* 4 April 1964, Jillian Margaret Duke; 2 s (Andrew b 1966, Jonathan b 1969); *Career* qualified in med 1962, asst prof of med Univ of W Virginia 1969-71, conslt chest physician Univ of Wales 1971-77, dir Inst of Occupational Med Edinburgh 1978-90, prof Univ of Aberdeen 1988-; author of numerous pubns in jls; memb: Br and American Thoracic Socs, Med Res Cncl Grants Ctee; MRCP 1964, FRCP 1977, FRCPE 1986, FFOM 1985; *Books* Occupational Lung Diseases (with W K C Morgan 1984), Respiratory Diseases (with D Seaton and A G Leitch, 1989), Thorax (ed, 1977-81); *Recreations* rowing, painting; *Clubs* Edinburgh Univ Staff, St Andrew Boat; *Style*— Prof Anthony Seaton; 8 Avon Grove, Barnton, Edinburgh EH4 6RF (☎ 031 336 5113); 71 Urquhart Rd, Aberdeen AB2 1NJ; Department of Environmental & Occupational Medicine, Medical School, University of Aberdeen, Foresterhill, Aberdeen AB9 2ZD (☎ 0224 681818)

SEATON, Colin Robert; s of Arthur William Robert Seaton (d 1959), and Helen Amelia, *née* Stone (d 1985); *b* 21 Nov 1928; *Educ* Wallington County GS, Worcester Coll Oxford (BA, MA); *m* 24 Dec 1952, Betty, da of James Oliver Gosling (d 1959); 2 s (Paul b 10 March 1961, David b 3 June 1966); *Career* RAF 1947-49, air wireless mechanic Berlin Airlift; schoolmaster with LCC 1953-57; called to the Bar Inner Temple 1956; entered govt legal serv 1957, served Minys of Health, Housing and Local Govt 1957-71; Master Nat Industl Rels Ct 1971-74; circuit admin Lord Chllr's Dept: N Circuit 1974-82, SE Circuit 1982-83; under sec Lord Chllr's Dept, head Legislation Gp 1983-88; sec: Lord Chllr's Law Reform Ctee 1983-88, Univ Cmmrs 1988-; pt/t chm Med Appeal Tbnls 1989-; *Books* Aspects of the National Health Service Acts (1966); *Recreations* golf, photography; *Clubs* Civil Serv; *Style*— Colin R Seaton, Esq; Treetops, The Drive, Coulsdon, Surrey CR5 2BL (☎ 081 668 5538); Office of The University Commissioners, 19-29 Woburn Place, London WC1 (☎ 071 278 4042)

SEATON, Dr Douglas; s of Dr Douglas Ronald Seaton (d 1986), of Ipswich, Suffolk, and Julia Seaton, *née* Harrison; *b* 5 Feb 1946; *Educ* Rossall Sch Lancashire, Univ of Liverpool (MB ChB, MD); *m* 1 Aug 1970, Anja Elisabeth, da of Fritz Conrad Neervoort, of Bussum, Netherlands; 3 s (Edward b 1972, Bart b 1974, Michael b 1978); *Career* sr med registrar United Liverpool Hosp 1976, instr in med W Virginia Univ USA 1977, conslt physician in gen and respiratory med The Ipswich Hosp 1979-, asst ed Thorax 1980-82; author of med papers on respiratory diseases, contrib chapters in med textbooks; memb Ctee Action on Smoking Health (ASH); MRCP, FRCP, LRCP; *Books* Crofton and Douglas's Respiratory Diseases (with A Seaton and A G Leitch, 1989); *Recreations* country walking, church architecture; *Style*— Dr Douglas Seaton; King's Field, 23 Park Rd, Ipswich, Suffolk IP1 3SX (☎ 0473 216671)

SEAWARD, Colin Hugh; CBE (1987); s of Sydney Widmer Seaward (d 1967), and Molly Wendela, *née* Darwen (d 1985); *b* 16 Sept 1926; *Educ* RNC Dartmouth, Univ of Cambridge; *m* 1, Jean, *née* Bugler (d 1971); 3 s (Jonathan Louis b 1952, Nicholas William b 1956, Thomas Edward b 1967), 1 da (Petronella Jane (Mrs Seccombe) b 1950); m 2, Judith Margaret, da of Canon W T Hinkley, of Alnwick, Northumberland; 2 da (Candida Harriet b 1974, Jessica Lucy b 1976); *Career* War Serv HMS Ajax 1944-45, served Far East 1946-48, Med 1951-52, Admty 1953-55, cmd HMS Aberford 1956-58, Asst Naval Attaché Moscow and Naval Attaché Warsaw 1958-60, HMS Centaur 1960-62, MOD 1962-64, ret; joined HM Dip Serv 1965, dep high cmmr The Gambia 1966-68, FCO 1968-71, Rio de Janeiro 1971, Prague 1972-73, FCO 1973-76; Sr Offrs War Course RNC Greenwich 1976, cnsllr (econ and commercial) Islamabad 1977-80, HM consul-gen Rio de Janeiro 1980-86, ret 1986, re-employed Protocol Dept FCO 1987-; hon sec Anglo-Brazilian Soc 1986; Freeman City of London 1987; Hon Citizen State of Rio de Janeiro 1985; *Recreations* country life; *Style*— Colin Seaward, Esq, CBE; Brasted House, Brasted, Westerham, Kent, TN16 1JA

SEAWARD, Prof Mark Richard David; *b* 10 Aug 1938; *Educ* City GS Lincoln, Univ of Birmingham (BSc, Dip Ed), Univ of Nottingham (MSc), Univ of Bradford (PhD, DSc); *Career* head of biology Brigg GS 1960-65, lectr Loughborough Trg Coll 1965-67, sr lectr Trinity and All Saints Colls 1967-73; Univ of Bradford: chm Post Grad Sch of Environmental Sci 1980-88, chm Bd of Studies and Higher Degrees Ctee 1981-84, Cncl and senate memb and prof environmental biology 1990-, ed The Naturalist; author of over 180 scientific papers; cncl memb: Linnean Soc, Br Lichen Soc, Brontë Soc; ed Brontë Soc Transactions, exec memb Yorkshire Naturalists Union; FIBiol, FLS; Nummo Aureo Univ of Wroclaw Poland; *Books* Lichen Ecology (1977), Lichenology in the British Isles 1568-1975 (1977), A Handbook for Naturalists (1980), Urban Ecology (1982), Atlas of the Lichens of the British Isles (1982); *Recreations* book-collecting, philately, postal history; *Clubs* Linnean; *Style*— Prof Mark Seaward; University of Bradford, Bradford BD7 1DP (☎ 0274 785775 ext 8540, fax 0274 305340, telex 51309 UNIBFD G)

SEBAG-MONTEFIORE, Charles Adam Laurie; s of Denzil Charles Sebag-Montefiore, of Highfield House, Fordcombe, Kent, and Ruth Emily, *née* Magnus; *b* 25 Oct 1949; *Educ* Eton, Univ of St Andrews (MA); *m* 5 Oct 1979, Pamela Mary Diana, da of Archibald Tennant (d 1955), of 12 Victoria Square, London SW1; 1 s (Archibald Edward Charles b 1987), 2 da (Elizabeth Anne b 1982, Laura Rose b 1984); *Career* Touche Ross & Co CAs, ptnr Grieveson Grant & Co 1981, dir Kleinwort Benson Securities Ltd 1986; chm projects ctee Nat Art Collections Fund 1977-86, tstee London Historic House Museums Tst 1987-; hon treas: of the Friends of the Nat Libraries 1990-, Friends of the British Library 1990-, Friends of Lambeth Palace Library 1990-; Liveryman Worshipful Co of Spectacle Makers 1973; FCA 1974, FRSA; *Recreations* visiting picture galleries, collecting books, opera; *Clubs* Brooks's; *Style*— Charles Sebag-Montefiore, Esq; 21 Hazlewell Rd, London SW15 6LT (☎ 081 789 5999), Kleinwort Benson Securities Ltd, 20 Fenchurch St, London EC3P 3DB (☎ 071 623 8000, fax 071 929 2657, telex 887348)

SEBAG-MONTEFIORE, Harold Henry; eldest s of late John Sebag-Montefiore (5 s of Arthur Sebag-Montefiore, himself s of Sir Joseph Sebag-Montefiore and gs of Sarah, sis of the philanthropist Sir Moses Montefiore, 1 and last Bt), and Violet Maud, *née* Solomon; *b* 5 Dec 1924; *Educ* Stowe, Lower Canada Coll Montreal, Pembroke Coll Cambridge; *m* 1968, Harriet, o da of Benjamin Harrison Paley, of New York; 1 step da (Jennifer Tess); *Career* served WW II with RAF; barr Lincoln's Inn 1951, dep circuit judge; contested (C) N Paddington 1959; tstee Royal National Theatre Fndn; Freeman City of London; Chevalier de la Legion d'Honneur 1973; *Recreations* theatre, broadcasting, polo; *Clubs* Carlton, Hurlingham, Garrick; *Style*— Harold Sebag-Montefiore Esq; 4 Bream's Buildings, Chancery Lane, London WC2 (☎ 071 353 5835)

SEBASTIAN, Timothy (Tim); s of Peter Sebastian, of Hove, E Sussex, and Pegitha, *née* Saunders; *b* 13 March 1952; *Educ* Westminster, New Coll Oxford (BA), Univ Coll Cardiff (DipJournalism); *m* 4 June 1977, Diane, da of John Buscombe, of Frensham, Surrey; 1 s (Peter b 1981), 2 da (Clare b 1983, Caroline b 1986); *Career* BBC TV: eastern Euro corr 1979-82, Moscow corr 1984-85, Washington corr 1986-89; *Books* Nice Promises (1984), I Spy in Russia (1985), The Spy in Question (1987), Spy Shadow (1989), Saviour's Gate (1990); *Style*— Tim Sebastian, Esq; c/o BBC, 2030 M St M W, Washington DC 20036, USA (☎ 0101 202 223 2050)

SEBLEY, (Frances) Rae; *née* Holt; da of Frederick Appleby Holt, OBE (d 1980), of The Red House, Muster Green, Haywards Heath, Sussex, and Rae Vera Franz, *née* Hutchinson; *b* 9 May 1921; *Educ* Oxford & Cambridge Jt Bd Sch; *m* 1, 28 Aug 1942 (m dis 1946), (Francis) Russel Jeffs, s of Harold Jeffs, of Twickenham, Middx; 1 da (Diane Rae b 8 Aug 1943); m 2, 5 June 1970, Peter Arnold Sebley; *Career* PA to Dir of Bombing Ops Air Miny Whitehall 1940-42; copywriter Lambe & Robinson 1949-50, advertising manager Hutchinson Assoc Cos 1950-57, publicity mangr Hutchinson Group 1957-62, freelance writer 1962-70; contrib: TLS, Encounter, Spectator and others; ed for Heron Books, advsr and participant in the film documentary, A Hungry Feeling: The Life and Death of Brendan Behan New York USA; memb Ctee Nat Whippet Assoc; involved with: Sussex Youth Assoc, Brighton Festival; hon memb: Mark Twain Soc, Soc of Authors; *Books* Brendan Behan: Man and Showman (1966), Brendan Behan's Island (with Brendan Behan, 1962), Brendan Behan's New York (1964), Confessions of an Irish Rebel (1965), Hold Your Hour and Have Another (ed, 1963), The Scarperer (ed, 1966); *Recreations* breeding and showing whippets, walking, needlepoint; *Style*— Mrs Peter Sebley; Rotherfield Farmhouse, Newick, Lewes, Sussex BN8 4JH (☎ 082572 2676)

SEBRIGHT, Sir Peter Giles Vivian; 15 Bt (E 1626) of Besford, Worcs; s of Sir Hugo Giles Edmund Sebright, 14 Bt (d 1984), and his 1 w, Deirdre Ann, née Slingsby Bethell, gggda of 1 Baron Westbury; *b* 2 Aug 1953; *m* 1977, Regina Maria, da of Francis Steven Clarebrough, of Melbourne, Australia; 1 s; *Heir* s, Rufus Hugo Giles Sebright b 1978; *Style*— Sir Peter Sebright, Bt

SECCOMBE, Hugh Digorie; CBE (1976); s of Lawrence Henry Seccombe, CBE (d 1954), and Norah, *née* Wood (d 1959); ggf Sir Thomas Lawrence Seccombe, GCSI, GCIE, was head of Fin Dept of E India Co and later Fin Sec for India; *b* 3 June 1917; *Educ* Stowe, Sidney Sussex Coll Cambridge Univ (MA); *m* 24 July 1947, Eirene Rosemary, da of Richard Whittow (d 1953), of Muryn, Brockenhurst, Hants, and wid of Lt P C McC Banister, DSC, RN; 1 s (Geoffrey b 1949), 1 da (Celia b 1948); *Career* served RN 1939-46; Lt Cdr RNVR Destroyers in Home Fleet and Med; chm Seccombe Marshall & Campion Ltd 1962-77 (dir 1947, ret 1977); chm YWCA Central Club 1971-86; *Recreations* gardening, fishing, study of wildlife; *Style*— Hugh Seccombe, Esq, CBE; Sparkes Place, Wonersh, Guildford, Surrey GU5 0PH (☎ 0483 893296); Benmore Lodge, Salen/Aros, Isle of Mull, Argyll PA71 6HU (☎ 0680 300351)

SECCOMBE, Baroness (Life Peer UK 1991), of Kineton in the County of Warwickshire; Dame Joan Anna Dalziel Seccombe; DBE (1984), JP (Solihull 1968); da of Robert John Owen (d 1941), of Solihull, W Midlands, and Olive Barlow; *b* 3 May 1930; *Educ* St Martin's Sch Solihull; *m* 1950, Henry Lawrence Seccombe, s of Herbert Stanley Seccombe (d 1951), of Lapworth, Warwickshire; 2 s (Hon Philip, Hon Murray); *Career* West Mids CC 1977-81, chm Trading Standards 1979-81, Mids Elec Consultative Cncl 1981-, magistrate 1968-; chm: Cons Womens Nat Ctee 1981-84, Nat Union of Cons & Unionists Assoc 1987- (vice-chm 1984-87); memb West Mids Police Ctee 1977-81 and 1985-; vice-chm Cons Party 1987-; govr Nuffield Hosps 1988-; *Recreations* skiing, golf; *Style*— The Rt Hon Lady Seccombe, DBE, JP; Trethias, Morton Grange, Little Kineton, Warwicks CV35 0DP (☎ 0926 640562)

SECCOMBE, Sir (William) Vernon Stephen; JP (Cornwall 1970); s of Stephen Seccombe (d 1964), and Edith-Violet, *née* Henbry-Smith (d 1980); *b* 14 Jan 1928; *Educ* Saltash GS, Plymouth and Devonport Tech Coll; *m* 2 Sept 1950, Margaret Vera, da of Joseph Edgar Profit (d 1988); 4 s (Michael b 1952, Paul b 1953, Tony b 1958, Patrick b 1960); *Career* Nat Serv XII Royal Lancers 1947-49; ret electrical engr; memb: Saltash Borough Cncl 1953-74, E Cornwall Water Co 1960-74, Caradon DC 1973-79; traffic cmmr Western Area 1977-81 (dep traffic cmmr 1970-77); chm: Cornwall and Isles of Scilly Health Authy 1981-83, South Western RHA 1983-90, Plymouth Health Authy; govr Saltash Comp Sch 1970-81; Defence Medal 1945, Queen's Silver Jubilee Medal 1977, Nat Assoc of Boys' Clubs Keystone Gold Award 1984; kt 1988; *Recreations* gardening, walking; *Style*— Sir Vernon Seccombe, JP; South Western Regional Health Authority, Chairman's Office, King Square House, 26/27 King Square, Bristol BS2 8EF (☎ 0272 423271, fax 0272 425398)

SECKER, Prof Philip Edward; s of Cyril Edward Secker (d 1980); *b* 28 April 1936; *Educ* Haberdashers' Aske's Hampstead Sch, Univ of London; *m* 1968, Judith Andrea, da of Douglas Eric Lee (d 1981); 2 s; *Career* chartered engr; lectr Univ of London 1961-64, visiting asst prof Massachusetts Inst of Tech 1964-65; Univ Coll of N Wales: lectr 1965-69, sr lectr 1969-73, reader 1973-75, prof 1975-80; md IDB (UCNW) Ltd 1971-80, engrg dir Royal Doulton Ltd 1980-, visiting prof Dept of Physics and Electronics Univ of Keele 1985-; dep chief exec IEE 1990-; *Recreations* flying light aircraft, gardening; *Style*— Prof Philip Secker; Gwel-Y-Don, Awel Menai, Beaumaris, Gwynedd (☎ 0248 810771)

SECKER-WALKER, Dr Jonathan; s of Geoffrey Secker-Walker (d 1968), of Farnborough, Hants, and Joan Alice, *née* Diplock; *b* 19 Oct 1942; *Educ* Sherborne, UCL (BSc), UCH Med Sch (MB BS); *m* 20 July 1968, Jan Lilian, da of Charles James Goodwin, of Ryde, Isle of Wight; 1 s (Thomas Adam b 30 April 1973), 1 da (Katherine Louise b 16 Aug 1971); *Career* registrar (anaesthetics): UCH 1970-72, Gt Ormond St 1972; sr registrar (anaesthetics) St Thomas' Hosp 1973, clinical asst Toronto Sick Children's Hospital 1974, conslt anaesthetist and sr lectr UCH 1975, sr lectr in clinical audit UCL 1988-; memb Charter 88; FFARCS 1972, FRSM; *Recreations* skiing, sailing, walking, theatre; *Style*— Dr Jonathan Secker-Walker; 40 Woodland Gardens, Highgate Wood, London N10 3UA ☎ 081 444 9426; Dept of Medical Audit, University College Hospital, Gower St, London WC1 (☎ 071 380 9590)

SECOMBE, Sir Harry Donald; CBE (1963); *b* 8 Sept 1921; *Educ* Dynevor Sch Swansea; *m* 1948, Myra Joan Atherton, of Swansea; 2 s, 2 da; *Career* entertainer, actor, singer, comedian, author; served WWII N Africa and Italy; films incl: Song of Norway, Oliver and others; radio: Educating Archie, The Goon Show; TV: numerous variety shows incl Highway; pres: Lord's Taverners 1980-81, Barker Variety Club of GB; former chm Stars Organisation for Spastics; pres: Panda (World Wildlife) Fund Club, Br Diabetic Assoc; kt 1981; *Books* Twice Brightly, Goon For Lunch, Katy and The Nurgla, Welsh Fargo, Goon Abroad, The Harry Secombe Diet Book, Harry Secombe's Highway, The Highway Companion, Arias & Raspberries (autobiog, vol 1); *Recreations* photography, cricket, golf; *Clubs* Savage, RAC; *Style*— Sir Harry Secombe, CBE; 46 St James's Place, London SW1

SECONDÉ, Sir Reginald Louis; KCMG (1981, CMG 1972), CVO (1968, MVO 1957); s of Lt-Col Emile Charles Secondé (d 1952); *b* 8 Feb 1991; *Educ* Beaumont, King's Coll Cambridge; *m* 1951, Catherine Penelope, da of Thomas Ralph Sneyd-Kynnersley, OBE, MC; 1 s, 2 da; *Career* Maj WWII Coldstream Gds in N Africa and Italy (despatches); served Dip Corps 1949-82: UK Delgn to United Nations and British Embassies in Portugal, Cambodia, Poland and Brazil 1949-69, head S European Dept FCO 1969-72, Royal Coll Def Studies 1972-73; ambassador: Chile 1973-76, Romania 1977-79, Venezuela 1979-82, ret 1982; *Recreations* gardening, shooting; *Clubs* Cavalry and Guards; *Style*— Sir Reginald Secondé, KCMG, CVO; Wamil Hall, nr Mildenhall,

Suffolk (☎ 0638 714160)

SECRETAN, Lance Hilary Kenyon; s of Kenyon Secretan, of Amersham, Bucks, and Marie-Therese, *née* Haffenden; *b* 1 Aug 1939; *Educ* St Peter's Bournemouth, Univ of Waterloo, Univ of Southern Calif (MA), LSE (PhD); *m* 1, 1961 (m dis 1985), Gloria Christina; 2 da (Natalie Marie, Sandre Lee McCallum); ptnr Tricia Sheppard; *Career* conslt, lectr, journalist, author; sales mangr J J Little and Ives Toronto 1959, analyst Toronto Stock Exchange 1960, sales mangr Office Overload Toronto 1960-67, md Manpower Ltd Group of Cos (UK, Ireland, ME, Africa) London 1967-81; fndr and pres: Thaler Corporation Inc 1972-, Thaler Resources Ltd 1981-; prof of Entrepreneurship McMaster Univ 1983-85, visiting prof York Univ; fndr The New Value Movement; memb: American Soc of Training and Devpt, Nat Speakers Assoc, The Int Inst of Small Business, The Inst of Employment Conslts, The Acad of Mgmnt, special goodwill ambass Canadian Assoc to UN Environment Prog 1990; FRSA; *Recreations* life, mother earth, the bottom line, skiing; *Clubs* MENSA, White Elephant, University (Toronto); *Style—* Lance Secretan, Esq; RR 2, Alton, Ontario, Canada, L0N 1A0

SEDCOLE, (Cecil) Frazer; *b* 15 March 1927; *Educ* Uppingham; *m* 1962, Jennifer B Riggall; 1 s, 1 da; *Career* RAF 1945-48; joined Unilever 1952; dir: Birds Eye Food Ltd 1960-66, Unilever plc and NV 1974 (vice chm Unilever plc 1982-85), Tate and Lyle 1982-90; dep chm Reed International 1985-87, vice chm Langnese-Iglo Germany 1966-67, chm UAC International 1976-79; memb: Overseas Ctee CBI 1979-86, Br Overseas Trade Bd 1982-86, Bd Commonwealth Development Corporation 1984-88; tstee Leverhulme Tst 1982-; *Recreations* golf; *Style—* Frazer Sedcole, Esq; Beeches, Tyrrells Wood, Leatherhead, Surrey KT22 8QH

SEDDON, Arthur William; s of William Seddon, MC (d 1946), of 274 Shobnall Rd, Burton-upon-Trent, Staffs, and Charlotte Annie, *née* Martin (d 1973); *b* 15 Dec 1934; *Educ* Denstone Coll, Manchester Coll of Tech; *m* 27 June 1959, Beryl, da of Arthur Bentley Crompton, of Robin Hill, Deganwy Rd, Llandudno; 2 da (Jane Helen (Mrs Woodward) b 21 May 1961, Anne Elizaeth b 30 July 1974); *Career* plant dir Bass Burton upon Trent 1967-74 (head brewer 1963-66, asst brewer 1956-62), md Bass Runcorn 1976-82 (plant dir 1975), regnl md Charrington & Co 1983-; memb Barton-under-Needwood Parish Cncl 1970-75; chm Burton upon Trent Jr C of C 1971-72, Halton C of C 1978-79; memb: Inst of Brewers, Inc Brewers Guild, Master Brewers of America; MBII; *Recreations* cricket, rugby, athletics, hockey, fly-fishing; *Style—* Arthur Seddon, Esq; Charrington West, Charrington & Co, 36-39 Cumberland Ave, Park Royal London NW10 7RF (☎ 081 965 0688, car 0860 419 530)

SEDDON, (Edward) Jeremy; s of Col Roland Nelson Seddon, OBE, of Stourton Caundle, Dorset, and Dorothy Ida Kathleen, *née* Canning (d 1982); *b* 14 April 1941; *Educ* Kings Sch Bruton, Univ of Southampton (BSc); *m* 20 Sept 1975, Prudence Mary, da of Arthur William George Clarke (d 1955); 1 s (Thomas b 1985), 2 da (Serena b 1979, Alexandra b 1980); *Career* Associated Electrical Industries Ltd 1958-68, Dalgety Ltd 1968-73, md Barclays de Zoete Wedd Ltd 1978- (head of Public Sector Unit), non exec dir Victaulic plc 1983-; Freeman City of London 1976; *Recreations* sailing, music, gardening; *Clubs* Royal Thames Yacht, Special Forces; *Style—* Jeremy Seddon, Esq; Jesters, Oak Lane, Sevenoaks, Kent TN13 1UF (☎ 0732 461 180); Barclays de Zoete Wedd Ltd, Ebbgate House, 2 Swan Lane, London EC4R 3TS (☎ 071 623 2323)

SEDDON, Dr John; s of Wilfrid Seddon (d 1968), of Lottie Burtonwood (d 1965); *b* 29 Sept 1915; *Educ* Leeds Modern Sch, Univ of Leeds (BSc, PhD), Univ of Bristol (DSc); *m* 30 Aug 1940, Barbara Mary, da of Gayland Mackintosh (d 1969); 1 s (Anthony b 1945), 2 da (Janet b 1942, Mary b 1949); *Career* scientific offr: RAE 1939-66, res directorate Miny of Technol 1939-68, MOD 1968-75; dir gen res (Air) MOD 1969-75, conslt Westland Helicopters Ltd 1976-83; Cwlth Fund fell Study Centre California Inst of Technol Pasadena, sr res fell Univ of Bristol 1976-84, visiting prof Nanjing Aeronautical Inst China 1980, 1984, visiting prof Middle East Tech Univ Ankara Turkey 1985-87; hon prof Nanjin Aeronautical Inst 1984; FRAes 1954, CEng 1954; *Books* Intake Aerodynamics (jtly, 1985), Basic Helicopter Aerodynamics (1990); *Recreations* music, gardening; *Style—* Dr John Seddon; 7 Vicarage Hill, Farnham, Surrey GU9 8HG (☎ 0252 723680)

SEDDON, Mark Richard Gwyn; s of John Seddon, of Liverpool, and Dorothy Margaret, *née* Handford; *b* 7 March 1959; *Educ* St Edwards Coll Liverpool, Univ of Liverpool (BA Hons); *Career* stockbroker; Charlton Seal Ltd Manchester 1981-83, Neilson Milnes Ltd Liverpool 1983-; local cnCllr Roby Ward Knowlsey 1984-, Parly candidate (Cons) Liverpool Broadgreen 1987; chm N West Young Cons 1981, fndr pres Huyton Rotaract Club 1983, memb Catholic Inst Edwardian Assoc 1989, press offr St Edwards Old Boys RUFC; memb Int Stock exchange 1985; *Recreations* photography, rugby union, amateur dramatics; *Style—* Mark Seddon, Esq; Da Pacem, 50 Acacia Ave, Huyton, Merseyside L36 5TP (☎ 051 489 7932); Neilson Milnes Ltd, 6th Floor Martins Building, 4 Water St, Liverpool L2 3LF (☎ 051 236 6666, fax 051 236 4996)

SEDDON, Nicholas Paul; s of Clive Seddon, of 40 Cross Lane, Congleton, Cheshire, and Alison Helen, *née* Dale; *b* 11 July 1960; *Educ* Sandbach GS, Univ of Birmingham (LLB); *m* 22 Oct 1988, Suzanne Elizabeth, da of John Clive Wilson; *Career* admitted slr 1984; ptnr Needham & James Birmingham 1988- (joined 1982); memb Birmingham Law Soc, memb Assoc Int des Jeunes Avocats; memb Law Soc; *Recreations* motor sport, cycling, photography, wine; *Style—* Nicholas Seddon, Esq; 5 Lower Farm, Hatton, Warwick CV35 7ED (☎ 0926 400815); Needham & James, Windsor House, Temple Row, Birmingham B2 5LF (☎ 021 200 1188, fax 021 236 9228, car 0836 679453)

SEDDON, Dr Richard Harding; s of Cyril Harding Seddon (d 1974), of Bury St Edmunds, and Mary Seddon, *née* Booth (d 1983); *b* 1 May 1915; *Educ* King Edward VII Sch Sheffield, Sheffield Coll of Arts & Crafts, Univ of Reading (PhD); *m* 1946, Audrey Madeline, da of Albert Edward Wareham (d 1973), of Sussex; *Career* Vol Lance-Corpl RAOC 1939-40 (invalided after Dunkirk, on pension; King's Badge 1940), Co Intelligence Offr Home Guard 1941-43, Instr (Lieut) Reading Univ Sr Training Corps 1943-45; staff tutor in fine art Univ of Birmingham 1947-47, dir Sheffield City Art Galleries 1948-64, head of art history & liberal studies Buckinghamshire Coll of Technol & Art 1964-80; co-fndr and pres Ludlow Art Soc 1948-64, pres Yorkshire Fedn of Museums of Art Galleries 1954-55, Nat Art Collections Fund rep for Yorkshire 1954-64, sec of Yorkshire Fact-Finding Ctee of Regionalisation of Art Galleries 1959, dep chm Sheffield Cncl for Gold, Silver and Jewellry Trades 1960 (also memb), memb BBC '51 Soc 1960; exhibitor at RA, RI and leading London Galleries 1947-; London art critic Yorkshire Post 1972-; hon memb Mark Twain Soc (USA) 1976, Ctee Royal Soc of Painters in Water Colours 1984-85 (memb 1972, treas 1974-84); ARCA 1939; Civic medal Neuchatel France 1978; *Books* A Hand Uplifted (1963), The Academic Technique of Painting (1960), Illustrated Dictionary of Art Terms (1984), The Artist's Studio Book (1983); *Recreations* gardening, photography; *Clubs* Royal Society of Painters in Water Colours; *Style—* Dr Richard Seddon; 6 Arlesey Close, London SW15 (☎ 081 788 5899)

SEDGEMORE, Brian Charles John; MP (Lab) Hackney South and Shoreditch 1983-; *b* 17 March 1937; *Educ* Heles Sch Exeter, Oxford Univ; *m* 1964, Mary Reece; 1 s; *Career* civil servant 1962-66, barr Middle Temple 1966; Wandsworth Boro cncllr 1971-74, MP (Lab) Luton West Feb 1974-79, PPS to Tony Benn 1977-78; researcher for Granada TV 1980-84; memb: NUJ, ACTT, Writers Guild of GB; *Style—* Brian Sedgemore, Esq, MP; c/o House of Commons, London SW1

SEDGHI, Bijan Martin; s of Mahmood Sedghi, of Sutton Coldfield, W Mids, and Jean, *née* Martin; *b* 3 Jan 1953; *Educ* King Edward VI Camp Hill Sch Birmingham, Univ of Durham (BA), Coll of Law Chester; *m* 18 Oct 1975, Carole Anne, da of Michael Ernest Colson, of Bispham, Blackpool, Lancashire; 3 s (Dominic Guy b 1980, Marcus Edward b 1982, James Jack b 1984); *Career* slr: Supreme Ct, Wragge and Co Birmingham 1977-78, Edge and Ellison 1978-81 (ptnr 1981-88, conslt 1988-); exec chm Bromsgrove Industries plc 1987-; memb Law Soc 1975; *Recreations* association football, rugby football, cricket, walking; *Clubs* The Priory (Edgbaston); *Style—* Bijan Sedghi, Esq; Harborne Court, 67-69 Harborne Rd, Birmingham, W Mids B15 3BU (☎ 021 456 1088, fax 021 456 1407)

SEDGWICK, Lady Henrietta Laura; *née* Phipps; 4 da of 4 Marquess of Normanby, KG, CBE, JP, DL; *b* 29 Nov 1962; *m* 1982, Adam C Sedgwick (d 1985), eldest s of John Sedgwick, *qv*, of 49 Novello St, London SW6; *Style—* The Lady Henrietta Sedgwick; Burtree House, York Rd, Hutton Sessay, Thirsk, N Yorks

SEDGWICK, John Humphrey Gerrie; s of Dr Charles Humphrey Sedgwick (d 1963), and Anne Jane, *née* Gerrie (d 1959); *b* 5 Jan 1923; *Educ* Eastbourne Coll, RMA Sandhurst; *m* 1 Jan 1949, Ursula Mary Thomason, da of Maj-Gen Clifford Thomason Beckett, CB, CBE, MC, DL (d 1972), of Templecombe, Somerset; 3 s (Adam Charles b 13 June 1952 d 1985, Toby John b 6 Dec 1954, Tom Oliver b 13 Aug 1956); *Career* Coldstream Gds 1942-46, serv N W Europe Campaign (Capt 1945); md: R E Thomas & Newman Ltd 1959-69, Wiltshire Contract Furnishing Ltd 1969-82, chm Bosham Yacht Service Ltd 1972-; *Recreations* sailing, painting, travel; *Clubs* Cavalry and Guards, Hurlingham, Household Div Yacht; *Style—* John Sedgwick, Esq; 49 Novello St, London SW6 4JB (☎ 071 736 7326); 21 Rue des Aires, La Garde-Freinet, 83310 Cogolin, France (☎ 010 33 94 43 65 50)

SEDGWICK, Dr John Philip; s of Philip Giles Sedgwick (d 1940), and Vera Constance, *née* Everard; *b* 6 Dec 1938; *Educ* Dean Close, Guy's, Univ of London (MB BS, DA); *m* 1, 23 March 1963 (m dis 1978), Judith Ann, da of Edgar Nelson, of Upper Shirley, Southhampton; 1 s (Philip Giles), 2 da (Nicola Jane, Helen Louise); m 2, 7 April 1982, Anne Louise Warren, da of Arthur Henry Dickinson, of Dinnington, nr Doncaster, Yorks; *Career* house surgn Guy's Hosp 1964, house physician Lewisham Hosp 1964-65, sr house offr Royal Sussex Co Hosp 1965-66; med advsr: John Wyeth 1966, Servier Laboratories 1967; GP 1968-75, private practitioner 1975-77, dir health servs Brunel Univ 1978, sr clincial occupational health physician Hillingdon Borough; MO: Pioneer, Milupa, Brunel Business Partnership, Brunel Science Park, Fujitsu, Nevil Long Gp, General Maintenance Services, Coca-cola; memb Worshipful Co of Feltmakers 1970; Hon Fell RSM; *Recreations* golf, riding; *Style—* Dr John Sedgwick; 13 The Pagoda, Boulters Lock, Maidenhead, Berks SL6 8EU (☎ 0628 328 13); The Medical Centre, Univ of Brunel, Uxbridge, Middx UB8 3P (☎ 0895 34 426)

SEDGWICK, (Ian) Peter; *b* 13 Oct 1935; *m* 6 Aug 1956, (Verna) Mary; 1 s (Paul b 17 March 1961), 1 da (Carey Anne b 30 Nov 1962); *Career* National Provincial Bank 1952-59, Ottoman Bank Africa and the ME 1959-69, J Henry Schroder Wagg & Co Limited 1969-90, chm Mediterranean Fund Limited 1989-; non-exec dir: Triplevest plc 1986-, Fundivest plc 1989-, City & Commercial Investment Trust 1989-; gp md Schroders plc 1987-; dir: Schroder Nominees Limited 1981-, Schroder Investment Management Limited (chief exec) 1985-, Schroder Unit Trusts Limited 1987-, Greece Fund Limited 1988-; *Recreations* golf; *Style—* Peter Sedgwick, Esq; 33 Gutter Lane, London EC2R 8BS (☎ 071 382 6476, fax 071 382 6965, telex 885029)

SEDGWICK, Peter Norman; s of Norman Victor Sedgwick, of 25 Allenview Rd, Wimborne, Dorset, and Lorna Clara, *née* Burton; *b* 4 Dec 1943; *Educ* Westminster Cathedral Choir Sch, Downside, Lincoln Coll Oxford (MA, BPhil); *m* 17 Feb 1984, Catherine Jane, da of Barry Donald Thomas Saunders, of Furnace Cottages, Forge Rd, Tintern, Gwent; 2 s (Richard b 30 Dec 1986, Christopher b 14 April 1988), 2 da (Victoria b 6 July 1989, Rebecca Elizabeth b 3 Dec 1990); *Career* HM Treasy: econ asst 1969, econ advsr 1971, sr econ advsr 1977, under sec 1984-; chm London Symphony Chorus 1979-84 (memb 1972); *Recreations* singing; *Style—* Peter Sedgwick, Esq; HM Treasury, Parliament St, London SW1 (☎ 071 270 4459)

SEEAR, Baroness (Life Peer UK 1971), of Paddington in the City of Westminster; Beatrice Nancy Seear; PC (1985); da of late Herbert Charles Seear, of Croydon; *b* 7 Aug 1913; *Educ* Croydon HS, Newnham Coll Cambridge, LSE; *Career* ldr of Liberal peers in House of Lords 1984-88, dep leader of Liberal Democrats 1988-; personnel mangr C J Clark Ltd 1936-46, reader in Personnel Mgmnt LSE 1946-78; pres Liberal Pty Orgn 1965-66; author of books on Women's Employment; Hon LLD Leeds 1979, Hon DLitt Bath 1982; *Recreations* gardening, reading, travelling; *Clubs* Royal Commonwealth Soc, Nat Lib; *Style—* The Rt Hon the Lady Seear, PC; 189b Kennington Rd, London SE11 6ST (☎ 071 587 0205)

SEEAR, Dr Michael Francis; s of Stephen James Seear (d 1959), of Leyton, London, and Norah Seear; *b* 23 Jan 1945; *Educ* UCL and Westminster Med Sch (MB BS, Charles Power essay prize); *m* 12 July 1983, Siok Kim Wee, da of Wee Hock Chye PJK; *Career* various house appts at Westminster, Guy's and Bart's; currently in gen practice in London (formerly in ME) and med offr to an alcohol rehabilitation centre; memb: Chelsea Clinical Soc, Assurance Med Soc; fell Med Soc of London (memb Cncl), MRCGP 1979, FRSTM & H; *Books* Guide To The Mammals of Essex (1963); *Recreations* birdwatching, antiques, dogs, admiring my wife's beauty; *Clubs* Great Eastern Railway Soc; *Style—* Dr Michael Seear; 86 Harley St, London W1N 1AE (☎ 071 580 3256)

SEEBOHM, Hon Richard Hugh; s of Frederic Baron Seebohm, TD (Life Peer, d 1990), of Hertford, and Evangeline, *née* Hurst (d 1990); *b* 1933; *m* 1966, Margaret Evelyne Hok; *Style—* The Hon Richard Seebohm; Stable Cottage, Flatford Lane, East Bergholt, Colchester, Essex CO7 6UN

SEEL, Derek; s of William Alfred Seel (d 1988) and Olive, *née* Greenwell (d 1989); *b* 2 April 1932; *Educ* Stockport Sch, Univ of Manchester (BDS, MOrth); *m* 27 Feb 1960, Gillian Mary, da of Roy Henderson (d 1966), of Bolton; 2 s (Richard Adrian, Ceri Dan); *Career* conslt orthodontist Univ Hosp Wales 1969-; memb cncl RCS 1987-, dean bd of faculty of dental surgeons RCS 1989- (memb 1979-); FDSRCS; *Recreations* music, photography, golf; *Style—* Derek Seel, Esq; 20 Blenheim Rd, Bristol BS6 7JP (☎ 0272 736635)

SEELY, Michael James; s of Frank James Wriothesly Seely (d 1956), and Vera Lilian, *née* Birkin (d 1970); *b* 20 Aug 1926; *Educ* Eton; *m* 1, 1952 (m dis 1964), Barbara Callahan; m 2, 1966, Patricia Ann Auchterlonie (d 1990), da of George Wright (d 1940); 1 da (Rachel b 1967); *Career* racing correspondant The Times 1975-; *Recreations* shooting, windsurfing; *Style—* Michael Seely, Esq; Ramsdale Farm, Arnold, Nottingham (☎ 0602 653872); The Times, 1 Pennington St, London E1 (☎ 071 481 4100)

SEELY, Sir Nigel Edward; 5 Bt (UK 1896) of Sherwood Lodge, Arnold, Notts and Brooke House, Brooke, Isle of Wight; s of Sir Victor Seely, 4 Bt (d 1980), by 1 w, Sybil Helen (now Baroness Paget of Northampton, *qv*), *née* Gibbons, widow of Sir John

Bridger Shiffner, 6 Bt; *b* 28 July 1923; *Educ* Stowe; *m* 1, 1949, Loraine, da of late Wilfred W Lindley-Travis; 3 da; m 2, 1984, Trudi, da of Sydney Pacter; *Heir* half-bro, Victor Seely; *Career* with Dorland International; *Clubs* Bucks, Royal Solent Yacht; *Style*— Sir Nigel Seely, Bt; 3 Craven Hill Mews, London W2

SEELY, Hon Patrick Michael; s of 4 Baron Mottistone; *b* 12 Oct 1960; *Educ* Harrow, Trinity Coll Cambridge; *m* 1984, Susannah Shelley, da of Cdr J C Q Johnson, RN (ret), of Bradfield, Berks; *Style*— The Hon Patrick Seely; 65 Castletown Road, London W14 9HG (☎ 071 385 7382)

SEELY, Hon Peter John Philip; s and h of 4 Baron Mottistone; *b* 29 Oct 1949; *Educ* Uppingham; *m* 1, 1972 (m dis 1975), Joyce, da of Mrs Ellen Cairns, of St Ninians, Stirling; 1 s (Christopher David Peter b 1 Oct 1974); m 2, 1982, Lynda, da of W Swain, of Judds Farm, Bulphan Fen, Upminster, Essex; 1 da (Penelope Jane b 1984); *Style*— The Hon Peter Seely; 99 Bow Lane, Finchley, London N12

SEELY, Maj Victor Ronald; s of late Sir Victor Seely, 4 Bt (d 1980), by his 3 w, Mary, da of late Ronald Collins; hp of half-bro, Sir Nigel Seely, 5 Bt; *b* 1 Aug 1941; *Educ* Eton, RMAS, Staff Coll Camberley; *m* 1972, Annette Bruce, da of late Lt-Col J A D McEwen; 1 s (William b 1983), 1 da (Natasha b 1979); *Career* Maj The Royal Hussars (PWO), served on attachment to US Army 1968, served on secondment to Sultan of Oman's Armed Forces 1970-71; dir of Devpt and Fund Raising The Spring Centre Gloucester; *Recreations* hunting, event riding; *Clubs* Army and Navy; *Style*— Maj Victor Seely; Church Farm, Siddington, Cirencester, Glos

SEENEY, Leslie Elon Sidney; OBE (1978); s of Sidney Leonard Seeney (d 1950), of Forest Hill, London SE23, and Daisy Florence Alice, *née* Norman (d 1975); *b* 19 Jan 1922; *Educ* St Matthews Camberwell, London Borough Poly (pre RAF Serv); *m* 4 Jan 1947, Marjory Doreen, da of Arthur William Greenwood (d 1946), of Spalding, Lincs; 1 s (Michael b 1951); *Career* RAF (Volunteer Reserve), War Serv, Flt Lt (pilot), coastal cmd; dir gen Nat Chamber of Trade 1971-87; dir: Retail Consortium (fndr dir) 1987, Assoc for Prevention of Theft in Shops 1987; memb: Home Sec Standing Conference on Crime Prevention 1971-86, Retail Prices Index Advsy Ctee 1984-; fell Soc of Assoc Executives 1976-86 (memb 1970-); *Recreations* reading, writing, travel, photography, grandchildren; *Style*— Leslie Seeney, Esq, OBE

SEFTON OF GARSTON, Baron (Life Peer UK 1978), of Garston, Co Merseyside; William Henry Sefton; s of George Sefton; *b* 5 Aug 1915; *Educ* Duncombe Rd Sch Liverpool; *m* 1940, Phyllis, *née* Kerr; *Career* sits as Labour peer in House of Lords; leader Liverpool CC 1964-78, oppn leader Merseyside CC 1977-79 (first chm 1973-77); chm: Runcorn Devpt Corpn 1974-81, North West Planning Corpn 1975-80; *Style*— The Rt Hon the Lord Sefton of Garston; c/o House of Lords

SEGAL, Prof Anthony Walter; s of Cyril Segal, and Doreen, *née* Hayden; *b* 24 Feb 1944; *Educ* Univ of Cape Town SA (MB ChB, MD), Univ of London (MSc, DSc, PhD); *m* 18 Dec 1966, Barbara Ann, da of Justice Solomon Miller (d 1987), of Durban SA; 3 da (Terry b 1969, Jessica b 1972, Penelope b 1975); *Career* Charles Dent Prof of Med Univ Coll and Middx Sch of Med 1986-; FRCP; *Recreations* squash, tennis, sailing, art, theatre; *Style*— Prof Anthony Segal; Dept of Medicine, University College London, University St, London WC1E 6JJ (☎ 071 380 9725, fax 071 380 7145)

SEGAL, Michael John; s of Abraham Charles Segal, of 18 Greenhill, London NW3 (d 1981), and Iris Muriel, *née* Parsons (d 1971); *b* 20 Sept 1937; *Educ* Strode's Sch Surrey; *m* 1 March 1963, Barbara Gina, da of Dr Joseph Leon Fluxman, of Johannesburg, S Africa (d 1954); 1 da (Leila b 10 Sept 1966); *Career* registrar family div High Court of Justice 1985, called to bar Middle Temple 1962, practised on Midland and Oxford circuit 1963-84; memb Queen's Bench Procedure Ctee 1975-80; dep stipendiary magistrate 1980-84; memb Medico - Legal Soc, fndr memb Trollope Soc; *Recreations* reading, music, watching cricket; *Style*— Michael Segal, Esq; 28 Grange Rd, London N6 (☎ 081 348 0680); Principal Registry, Family Division, Somerset House, London, WC2

SEGAL, Victor Maurice; s of John Segal, of London, and Theresa, *née* Nordman (d 1990); *b* 20 Oct 1940; *Educ* Clifton, The Queen's Coll Oxford (BA, MA); *m* 1, 21 Feb 1967 (m dis 1978), Rosemary, *née* Braunsberg; 1 s (Julian Daniel Joseph b 13 March 1971), 1 da (Alexandra Jane Natasha b 12 June 1969); m 2, 2 Dec 1979, Carol, *née* Norton; *Career* articled clerk Nicholson Graham & Jones 1962-65, admitted slr 1965, Bartlett & Gluckstein 1965-68, dir Singer & Friedlander Ltd 1976- (joined 1968); memb: Law Soc 1965, International bankers Club 1981; *Recreations* skiing, golf, tennis, bridge, music, watching Spurs; *Style*— Victor Segal, Esq; Director, Singer & Friedlander Ltd, 21 New St, Bishopsgate, London EC2M 4HR (☎ 071 623 3000, fax 071 623 2122)

SEGALL, Anne (Mrs David Evans); *b* 20 April 1948; *Educ* St Paul's Girls, St Hilda's Coll Oxford (BA); *m* David Howard Evans; 2 s (Oliver, Edward); *Career* economics and banking corr 1971-76, banking corr The Economist 1976-80, banking then economics corr Daily Telegraph 1980-; *Recreations* swimming, theatre, reading; *Style*— Ms Anne Segall; Daily Telegraph (City Office), Salters Hall, 4 Fore Street, London EC2Y 5DT (071 628 0343)

SEGAWA, Takao; s of Hideo Segawa, of Nara, Japan (d 1982), and Ayako, *née* Nishikawa; *b* 26 May 1948; *Educ* Unebi HS, Keio Univ (BA); *m* 1 Aug 1975, Chieko, da of Chikara Takiuchi, of Tokyo; 2 s (Hiroyoshi b 1976, Kohei b 1980), 1 da (Junko b 1978); *Career* Nomura Securities Co Tokyo 1971-73, asst sales mangr Nomura Int (HK) Ltd 1973-76, portfolio mangr Jardine Fleming Hong Kong 1976-77, asst mangr Nomura Securities Co Tokyo 1977-80, vice pres Nomura Securities Int Inc 1980-84, sr vice pres Singapore Nomura Merchant Banking Ltd 1984-87, dep gen mangr Nomura Bank Int Plc London 1987-; *Recreations* golf, tennis, swimming; *Style*— Takao Segawa, Esq; 3 Tilligham Way, London N12; Nomura Bank International plc, Nomura House, 24 Monument Street, London EC3 8AJ (☎ 071 929 2366, ext 2003, fax 071 626 0851, telex 9413062/4/5/6)

SEIFERT, John Michael; s of Lt-Col Richard Seifert, and Josephine Jeanette, *née* Harding; *b* 17 Feb 1949; *Educ* Mill Hill Sch, Bartlett Sch of Architecture, UCL (BSc, Dip Arch); *m* 1 Feb 1985, Johanna Marion, da of Elias Hofmann; 2 s (James, Edward), 1 da (Elizabeth), 1 step s (Marlon); *Career* architect, chm Seiferts Ltd; major projects incl: Cutlers Gardens 1983, Mermaid Theatre 1983, Bank of Chicago House 1984, Sheraton Hotel Lagos 1985, Bishopsbridge 1985, MISR Bank Tower 1986, South Quay Plaza 1987, Swiss Banking Corporation 1988, Hambros Bank 1988, Sceptre Court 1988, Greenwich View 1989, Glengall Bridge 1989; major competitions won: Surrey Docks Shopping Centre 1983, Limehouse Basin 1985, Heathrow Hotel 1988, Sandwell Mall 1988; Liveryman Worshipful Co of Glaziers and Painters of Glass 1967; RIBA 1976, CROAIF (France) 1981, NCARB (USA) 1983; *Recreations* painting, sculpture, numismatics; *Clubs* Carlton, Arts, Army and Navy; *Style*— John Seifert, Esq; 164 Shaftesbury Ave, London WC2 (☎ 071 242 1644)

SEIRADHAKIS, Hon Mrs (Mercy Burdett); *née* Money-Coutts; da of 6 Baron Money-Coutts, TD (d 1949); *b* 1910; *Educ* Lady Margaret Hall, Oxford (BA); *m* 1947, Michael Seiradhakis; 1 s, 1 da; *Career* served with British Red Cross Mission in Greece and Central Mediterranean and with UN Relief and Rehabilitation Administration in Crete; *Style*— The Hon Mrs Seiradhakis; 19 Odos Seirenon, Byrona, Athens

SEKACZ, Ilona Anna; da of Aleksander Sekacz, and Olive, *née* Swithenbank; *b* 6 April 1948; *Educ* Arnold HS Blackpool, Univ of Birmingham; *Career* composer of works for Royal Shakespeare Theatre: King Lear (1982), Twelfth Night (1983), Henry VIII (1983), Measure for Measure (1983) Les Liaisons Dangeureuses (1985), Cymbeline (1987), The Jew of Malta (1987), The Man of Mode (1988), Across Oka (1988), The Love of the Nightingale (1988), A Midsummer Night's Dream (1989), Dr Faustus (1989), Cymbeline (1989), As You Like It (1989), Much Ado About Nothing (1990), Edward II (1990); music composed for The Nat Theatre: Major Barbara (1982), The Cherry Orchard (1986), The Wandering Jew (1987), Countrymania (1987), Cat on a Hot Tin Roof (1987), The Secret Rapture (1988), Bartholomew Fair (1988); opera A Small Green Space ENO (1989); ballet The Queue English Dance Theatre 1989; many scores for TV and radio prodns 1982-; musical compositions for WWF for Nature: 25 anniversary celebration in Assisi 1986, harvest festival at Winchester Cathedral 1987 and advent serv at St George's Chapel Windsor 1988, multi- religious celebration at Canterbury Cathedral 1989; *Recreations* seeing friends, ecology, cinema; *Style*— Miss Ilona Sekacz; 40 Earlham St, London WC2H 9LA (☎ 071 240 9360)

SELBORNE, 4 Earl of (UK 1882); John Roundell Palmer; KBE (1987), DL (Hants 1982); also Baron Selborne (UK 1872), Viscount Wolmer (UK 1882); s of Viscount Wolmer (k on active service 1942; s of 3 Earl) and Priscilla (*see* Baron Newton); suc gf 1971. Lord Selborne's gggf, the 1 Earl, was Lord Chllr 1872-74 and 1880-85 and his ggf was First Lord of the Admiralty 1900-05 and helped establish the RNVR, the RFR, Osborne & Dartmouth Naval Colleges and the Designs Committee which resulted in the Royal Navy being equipped with Dreadnoughts; *b* 24 March 1940; *Educ* Eton, ChCh Oxford; *m* 1969, Joanna Van Antwerp, da of Evan James, of Upwood Park, Abingdon (and sis of Countess Baldwin of Bewdley); 3 s (Viscount Wolmer, Hon George b 1974, Hon Luke (twin) b 1974), 1 da (Lady Emily b 1978); *Heir* s, Viscount Wolmer; *Career* sits as Cons in House of Lords; chm Hops Marketing Bd 1978-82, former vice chm Apple and Pear Devpt Cncl, treas Bridewell Royal Hosp (King Edward's Sch Witley) 1972-83; memb Agric and Food Res Cncl 1975- (dep chm 1982, chm 1983-89); *Clubs* Brooks's, Farmers'; *Style*— The Rt Hon the Earl of Selborne, KBE, DL; Temple Manor, Selborne, Alton, Hants (☎ 042 47 3646)

SELBY, Harvey; s of Henry Mark Selby, of Hendon, London, and Jean Deborah, *née* Isaacs; *b* 13 April 1939; *Educ* Haberdashers' Aske's; *m* 20 Dec 1964, Jacqueline Linda, da of Nathan Gershinson, of Hampstead, London NW3; 2 s (Andrew Dean b 1966, Richard Grant b 1969); *Career* CA; articled clerk Rudolf Jeffries Marks London 1960-65, ptnr Lawrence S Fenton 1965-69, princ H Selby & Co 1969-73, chm and chief exec Audit & Gen plc and subsid cos 1974-; FCA; *Recreations* golf, reading; *Clubs* Hartsbourne Golf & Country (Herts), Las Brisas (Marbella Spain), IOD; *Style*— Harvey Selby, Esq; Summit House, 40 Highgate West Hill, Highgate, London N6 6LU (☎ 081 340 0231)

SELBY, Sir Kenneth; s of Thomas William Selby (d 1963), and Ruth Selby (d 1919); *b* 16 Feb 1914; *Educ* HS for Boys Worthing; *m* 1937, Elma Gertrude, da of Johnstone Sleator, of Roscrea, Co Tipperary; 2 s; *Career* chm: Bath & Portland Gp 1969-82 (pres 1982-), Air Travel Reserve Fund Agency 1975-86; pro-chllr Univ of Bath 1974-; kt 1970; *Clubs* Reform; *Style*— Sir Kenneth Selby

SELBY, Dr Leonard Milton; s of Israel Selby (d 1963), of Stellenbraak, Bird St, Stellenbosch, Cape Town, SA, and Rose, *née* Benjamin (d 1985); *b* 20 April 1925; *Educ* Paul Roos Gymnasium Stellenbosch, Univ of Cape Town (MB ChB, MRCGP); *m* 30 Jan 1974, Valerie, da of Harry Cope; 1 s (Mark b 7 Feb 1954); *Career* hon med offr Stellenbosch Hosp SA 1951-62, med advsr J Sainsbury plc 1968-; memb: BMA, RSM; *Style*— Dr Leonard Selby; 52 Harley St, London W1N 1AD (☎ 071 636 5250)

SELBY, 4 Viscount (UK 1905); Michael Guy John Gully; s of 3 Viscount (d 1959); *b* 15 Aug 1942; *Educ* Harrow; *m* 1965, Mary Theresa, da of Capt Thomas F Powell; 1 s, 1 da (Hon Catherine Mary Albinia b 1971); *Heir* s, Hon Edward Gully; *Career* chartered accountant; tribology consultant, fish farm advsr, banking systems computer conslt; FCA; *Recreations* shooting, sailing; *Style*— The Rt Hon the Viscount Selby; Ardfern House, by Lochgilphead, Argyll

SELBY, Prof Peter John; s of Joseph Selby, and Dorothy, *née* Cross; *b* 10 July 1950; *Educ* Lydney GS, Cambridge Univ (MA, MB, MB BChir, MD); *m* 8 July 1972, Catherine Elisabeth, da of Peter Thomas; 1 s (David b 1985), 1 da (Alexandra b 1980); *Career* conslt physician Royal Marsden Hosp London 1985-88, prof of cancer medicine and conslt physician, Univ of Leeds and St James's Univ Hosp Leeds 1988-, ed Br Jl Cancer; ctee memb: Cancer Res Campaign, Assoc Cancer Physicians, Br Assoc for Cancer Res, Br Oncological Assoc, Med Res Cncl, UK co-ordinator ctee Cancer Res and Euro Orgn for Res and Treatment of Cancer; FRCP; *Books* Hodgkin's Disease (1987); *Recreations* reading, music, sailing, running; *Clubs* RSM; *Style*— Prof Peter Selby; 17 Park Lane, Roundhay, Leeds LS8 (☎ 0532 663227); Institute for Cancer Studies, St James's University Hospital, Beckett St, Leeds LS9 7TF (☎ 0532 429883, fax 0532 429886)

SELBY, Ralph Walford; CMG (1961); s of Sir Walford Selby, KCMG, CB, CVO (d 1965), and Dorothy Orme, *née* Carter (d 1981); *b* 20 March 1915; *Educ* Eton, ChCh Oxford; *m* 8 Dec 1945, Julianna, da of Capt Ivan Edward Snell, MC (d 1958), and Marjorie Villiers (d 1981), gda of 4 Earl of Clarendon; 3 da (Virginia, Pamela, Cynthia); *Career* entered HM Dip Serv 1938, Capt Grenadier Gds 1939-45, served in Delhi, The Hague, FO, Tokyo, Copenhagen, Djakarta, Warsaw 1965-66; consul-gen Boston 1966, min Rome 1969, ambass Oslo 1972-75; *Recreations* sailing (yacht Jandar), mountain walking, beagling, lumberjack; *Clubs* Royal Yacht Squadron, MCC; *Style*— Ralph Selby, Esq, CMG; Mengeham House, Mengham Lane, Hayling Island, Hants PO11 9JX (☎ 0705 463833)

SELBY, Hon Mrs (Susan Lorna); *née* Pennock; er da of Baron Pennock (Life Peer), *qv*; *b* 1948; *m* 1970, David Frederick McLaren Selby; 2 s, 1 da; *Style*— The Hon Mrs Selby; Goodchilds Hill, Stratfield Saye, nr Reading, Berks

SELBY, Dowager Viscountess; Veronica Catherine Briscoe; da of late J George; *m* 1933, 3 Viscount Selby (d 1959); 2 s, 1 da; *Style*— The Rt Hon the Dowager Viscountess Selby; c/o The Rt Hon the Viscount Selby, Shuna Castle, Island of Shuna, Argyll

SELBY BENNETT, James Sebastian; TD (1987); s of Cdr Harry Selby Bennett RN, of Slepe Green, Slepe, nr Poole, Dorset, and Dolores, *née* Lees; *b* 14 June 1954; *Educ* Eton, Coll of Law; *m* 22 April 1978, Priscilla Mary, da of Charles Murray MacFarlane Barrow, of Mourne Cottage, Piddlehinton, Dorchester, Dorset; 2 s (Andrew b 1982, Nicholas b 1986); *Career* joined TA 1973; slr, farmer; Theodore Goddard & Co (London and Madrid), ptnr Humphries Kirk and Miller; slr Dorset Nat Farmers Union; The Law Soc; *Style*— James S Selby Bennett, Esq, TD; Slepe Farm, Slepe, nr Poole, Dorset (☎ 0202 622 737); Humphries Kirk, Glebe House, North St, Wareham, Dorset, BH20 4AN (☎ 09295 2141, fax 09295 6701)

SELDEN, Prof Raman; s of Atma Chuharmal Ramchandani (d 1978), and Phyllis Ruby, *née* Planten (d 1968); *b* 31 Dec 1937; *Educ* Battersea GS, UCL (BA), Birbeck Coll London (BA, PhD), Inst of Educn (PGCE); *m* 1, (m dis 1977) Monica Hollock; 3 s (Jan Dag Schroder b 16 Dec 1960, Paul Daniel Selden b 16 Sept 1965, William Matthew Selden b 25 May 1968), 1 da (Diana Vivien Schroder b 25 Dec 1962); m 2, 9 Sept 1978, (Margaret) Jane Vivien, da of James Brownbill Twemlow, MBE, of 22 Thornton Rd, Morecambe, Lancs; *Career* asst master Latymer Upper Sch 1961-64; lectr and sr lectr English: Portsmouth Poly 1965-71, Univ of Durham 1971-85, visiting prof Cornell Univ USA 1980 and 1982, prof English Univ of Lancaster 1986-89, Sunderland Poly 1990-; emeritus prof Univ of Lancaster 1989, dir Centre Seventeenth Century Studies Univ of Durham 1984-85; memb Exec Ctee: Wordsworth Centre, Centre for The study of Cultural Values; memb Planning Ctee Euro Soc Study of English; memb Assoc of Univ Teachers; *Books* English Verse Satire 1590-1765 (1978), Criticism and Objectivity (1984), A Readers Guide To Contemporary Literary Theory (1985), Dryden's Absalom and Architophel (1986), John Oldham: Poems (jt ed, 1987), The Theory of Criticism from Plato to the Present (1988), Practising Theory and Reading Literature: an Introduction (1989); *Style—* Prof Raman Selden; Sandyford, Farnley Mount, Durham City DH1 4DZ; School of Humanities, Sunderland Polytechnic, Chester Rd, Sunderland SR1 3SD (☎ 091 5152159)

SELF, Hugh Michael; QC (1973); s of Sir Henry Self, KCMG, KCB, KBE (d 1975), and Rosalind Audrey (d 1987); *b* 19 March 1921; *Educ* Lancing, Worcester Coll Oxford (BA); *m* 1950, Penelope Ann, da of John Drinkwater (d 1936, poet and playwright), and Daisy Kennedy (violinist); 2 da (Susannah, Melanie); *Career* served RN 1941-46, Lt RNVR 1946; called to the Bar Lincoln's Inn 1951, rec 1975, bencher 1980; *Recreations* golf, walking, wine; *Clubs* Savile; *Style—* Michael Self, Esq, QC; 59 Maresfield Gardens, Hampstead, London NW3 (☎ 071 435 8311); Christmas Cottage, Ingram's Green, Midhurst, Sussex

SELF, Hon Mrs (Ruth Kathleen); *née* Napier; twin da of 5 Baron Napier of Magdala, OBE; *b* 1947; *m* 1972, John Arthur Self, PhD; *Style—* The Hon Mrs Self; 70 Victoria Rd, Hawthorn East, Melbourne, Vic 3123, Australia

SELIGMAN, (Richard) Madron; MEP (EDG) W Sussex 1979-; 4 s of Dr Richard Joseph Simon Seligman, FCGI, FIM (d 1972), and Hilda Mary, *née* MacDowell (d 1966); bro of Sir Peter Seligman, *qv*; *b* 10 Nov 1918; *Educ* Harrow, Balliol Coll Oxford (MA), Sch of Slavonic Studies London Univ; *m* 1947, Nancy-Joan, da of Julian Marks (d 1950); 3 s, 1 da; *Career* Maj 1945, 6 Armd Divnl Signals, North Africa, Italy 1940-46; dir: ARV Holdings plc, Fluor GB 1966-83, St Regis Int 1983-85, chm Incinerator Co 1950-89; pres: Oxford Union Soc 1940, Oxford Univ Ski-Team 1938-39, Harrow cricket and rugby teams, EDG spokesman Ctee for Energy Res and Technol; *Recreations* skiing, tennis, travel, piano, gardening; *Clubs* Royal Thames Yacht, Royal Inst of International Affairs, MCC; *Style—* Madron Seligman, Esq, MEP; Micklepage House, Nuthurst, Horsham, West Sussex (☎ 0403 891533, fax 0403 891010)

SELIGMAN, Sir Peter Wendel; CBE (1969); s of Dr Richard Joseph Simon Seligman (d 1972), and Hilda Mary, *née* McDowell (d 1966); bro of Madron Seligman, *qv*; *b* 16 Jan 1913; *Educ* King's Coll Sch, Harrow, Kantonschule Zürich, Gonville and Caius Coll Cambridge (BA); *m* 1937, Elizabeth Lavinia Mary, da of Prof John Laviers Wheatley (d 1955); 2 s (John, Bruce), 4 da (Hildagrace, Lavinia, Johanna, Gabrielle); *Career* engineer; md APV Holdings Ltd 1942-65 (chm 1965-77), chm British Chemical Plant Manufacturers Assoc 1965-67; dir: St Regis International Ltd 1973-83, Eibis International Ltd 1980-90; chm: Kandahar Ski Club 1972-76, Nat Ski Fedn of GB 1977-81; FIMechE; kt 1978; *Recreations* carpentry, travel, boating (yacht 'Louise'); *Clubs* Hawks', Kandahar Ski (hon memb), Ski of Great Britain (hon life memb), Royal Lymington Yacht; *Style—* Sir Peter Seligman, CBE; King's Lea, King's Saltern Rd, Lymington, Hants SO41 9QF (☎ 0590 676569)

SELKIRK, Master of; Alasdair Malcolm Douglas-Hamilton; s of late Lord Malcolm Douglas-Hamilton, OBE, DFC (3 s of 13 Duke of Hamilton), and 1 w, (Clodagh) Pamela, da of late Lt-Col the Hon Malcolm Bowes-Lyon (s of 13 Earl of Strathmore); *b* 10 Sept 1939; *Educ* Gordonstoun, Univ of Edinburgh; *m* 1965, Angela Kathleen, da of John Molony Longley; 2 s, 2 da; *Career* with Morgan Guaranty Tst Co of New York 1964-68, Bank of Scotland 1969-; *Recreations* mountaineering, skiing, photography; *Clubs* New (Edinburgh); *Style—* The Master of Selkirk; Lessudden, St Boswells, Roxburghshire

SELKIRK, Hon Mrs (Nadia Mickey); *née* Lucas; er da of 1 Baron Lucas of Chilworth (d 1967); *b* 19 Jan 1923; *m* 4 March 1944 (m dis 1980), Flt Lt Hamish Rattray Selkirk, DFC, RAF, s of late James Logie Selkirk; 1 s (other twin s decd), 1 da; *Style—* The Hon Mrs Selkirk; Saffron Cottage, Northfield End, Henley-on-Thames, Oxon

SELKIRK, 10 Earl of (S 1646); (George) Nigel Douglas-Hamilton; KT (1976), GCMG (1959), GBE (1963, OBE 1941), AFC, AE, PC (1955), QC (Scot 1959); also Lord Daer and Shortcleuch (S 1646); s of 13 Duke of Hamilton (d 1940); yr bro of 14 Duke of Hamilton; suc to Earldom under terms of special remainder 1940, the Earldom having been held by the Duke of Hamilton in fiduciary fee until that date; *b* 4 Jan 1906; *Educ* Eton, Balliol Coll Oxford (MA), Edinburgh Univ (LLB); *m* 6 Aug 1949, Audrey Durell, da of late Maurice Drummond-Sale-Barker; *Heir* uncertain; *Career* takes Conservative whip in Lords; served AAF and RAF 1932-45, Gp Capt; cmd 603 City of Edinburgh Sqdn AAF 1934-38, cmmr for Special Areas Scot 1937-39; chm House of Lords Branch RAF Assoc; pres: Building Socs Assoc to 1982, Caledonian Club to 1986; advocate Scotland 1934, memb Royal Co of Archers (Queen's Body Guard for Scotland), Paymaster-Gen 1953-55, chllr Duchy of Lancaster 1955-57, First Lord of Admiralty 1957-59, UK cmmr for Singapore and cmmr-gen S E Asia 1959-63, Scottish rep peer 1945-63; hon chief Saulteaux Indians 1967, hon citizen of Winnipeg (Manitoba), Freeman of Hamilton; *Clubs* Athenaeum, New (Edinburgh), Caledonian; *Style—* The Rt Hon the Earl of Selkirk, KT, GCMG, GBE, AFC, AE, PC, QC; 60 Eaton Place, London SW1X 8AT (☎ 01 235 6926); Rose Lawn Coppice, Wimborne, Dorset BH21 3DB (☎ 0202 883160)

SELLAR, (Alexander) John Patrick; s of Lt-Col Thomas Byrne Sellar, CMG, DSO, KOSB (d 1924), and Evelyn, *née* Pugh (d 1952); *b* 16 April 1905; *Educ* Winchester, Balliol Coll Oxford (MA); *m* 20 Jan 1934, Mary Penelope, yr da of Ronald Collet Norman (d 1963), of Moor Place, Much Hadham, Herts, and Lady Florence Bridgeman, da of 5 Earl of Bradford; 2 da (Dione Isobel b 1935, Christina Mary b 1937); *Career* Res of Offrs 1938, KOSB 1939-45, Capt Intelligence Corps, serv 10 Army, Iran, 14 Army Far E, SEAC; sr ptnr Halsey Lightly & Co, chm Western Merthyr Tydfil Colliery, literary exec John Galsworthy Estate; legal advsr: King George's Tst, Arab Horse, Welsh Pony and Cob Soc; jt owner Lanhill Stud, winner, owner, rider point to point; memb: WWF, RSPB, RGS, Royal Soc Asian Affairs; *Recreations* ornithology, natural history, hunting, stalking, fishing, oriental travel, antarctica, mountaineering, photography, archaeology; *Clubs* United Univ, Lowtonian Soc, MCC (playing memb), Vincents; *Style—* John Sellar, Esq; Sparrow Farm, Lanhill, Chippenham, Wiltshire SN14 6LX

SELLARS, John Ernest; s of Ernest Buttle Sellars, of Grimsby, and Edna Grace Mordaunt; *b* 5 Feb 1936; *Educ* Wintringham GS Grimsby, Univ of Manchester (BSc, MSc); *m* 20 Dec 1958, Dorothy Beatrice, da of Maj Douglas Norman Morrison, of Humberston, Cleethorpes; 3 da (Karen b 1961, Fiona b 1962, Ann b 1964); *Career* res engr English Electric (GW) Ltd 1958-61; lectr Royal Coll of Advanced Technol (now Univ of Salford) 1961-67, head of Mathematics Lanchester Coll of Technol 1967-71, head of Computer Science Lanchester Poly 1971-74; chief offr Business Educn Cncl 1974-83, dir and chief exec Business and Technician Educn Cncl 1983-, dir City Technol Colls Tst 1989-; *Recreations* walking, aspiring broadcaster; *Clubs* Reform, IOD, Middlesex CCC; *Style—* John Sellars, Esq; 306 Cassiobury Drive, Watford, Herts WD1 3AW (☎ 0923 33055); BTEC Central House, Upper Woburn Place, London WC1H 0HH (☎ 071 431 8400)

SELLARS, Dr Leslie; s of Robert Norman Sellars (d 1980), of Flimby, Cumbria, and Hannah Elizabeth, *née* Pickering; *b* 14 Jan 1951; *Educ* Workington GS, Univ of Newcastle upon Tyne (MB BS, MD); *m* 29 June 1974, Joan, da of William Steele, of Maryport; 2 da (Kathryn Jane b 1978, Julia Anne b 1979); *Career* registrar in med Royal Victoria Infirmary Newcastle 1977-78, first asst in med (nephrology) Univ of Newcastle upon Tyne 1981-85, conslt physician and nephrologist Yorkshire RHA 1985; memb: Renal Assoc 1979, Br Hypertension Soc 1981, Euro Dialysis and Transplant Assoc; FRCP (Ed) 1988; *Recreations* fishing; *Clubs* Driffield Anglers; *Style—* Dr Leslie Sellars; 20 The Triangle, North Ferriby, North Humberside HU14 3AT (☎ 0482 631760); The Renal Unit, Princess Royal Hospital, Saltshouse Rd, Hull (☎ 0482 701151)

SELLERS, Geoffrey Bernard; s of Bernard Whittaker Sellers, of High Lane, Stockport, and Elsie, *née* Coop (d 1963); *b* 5 June 1947; *Educ* Manchester GS, Magdalen Coll Oxford (Mackinnon scholar, BCL, MA); *m* Susan Margaret, da of Arthur Donald Faulconbridge (d 1989); 2 s (Daniel b 1981, John b 1987), 2 da (Anna b 1984, Katherine b 1989); *Career* called to the Bar Gray's Inn 1971; legal asst Law Cmmn 1971, Cmmn on Industl Relations 1971-74, Office of Parly Counsel 1974, Law Cmmn 1982-85, Parly counsel 1987-; *Clubs* RAC; *Style—* Geoffrey Sellers, Esq; 36 Whitehall, London SW1A 2AY (☎ 071 210 6639)

SELLERS, His Hon Norman William Malin; VRD, DL (Lancs 1986); eld s of Rt Hon Sir Frederic Aked Sellers, Lord Justice of Appeal (d 1979), and Grace Lilian, *née* Malin (d 1987); *b* 29 Aug 1919; *Educ* Merchant Taylors', Silcoates Sch, Hertford Coll Oxford (MA); *m* 30 March 1946, Angela Laurie, da of Sydney Clapham Jukes; 4 da (Wendy b 1947, Elizabeth b 1950, Julia b 1952, Helena b 1956); *Career* Nat Serv RNVR 1940-65 (despatches HMS Nelson 1942), Lt Cdr 1953, cmd HMS Mersey; contested Liberal Crosby Div 1964; called to the Bar Grays Inn 1947; rec Crown Ct 1972, circuit judge Northern Circuit 1974-90; *Recreations* sailing, walking; *Clubs* Ribble Cruising, BHR Yacht; *Style—* His Hon Norman Sellers, VRD, DL; Hillside, Lower Road, Longridge, Preston PR3 2YN (☎ 0772 78 3222)

SELLERS, Dr Susan Mary; da of Geoffrey Noel Sellers, of Esher, Surrey, and Mary McNeil, *née* Boswell; *b* 13 Jan 1949; *Educ* Birkenhead HS, Univ of Manchester (MB ChB, MD); *m* 16 July 1983, Andrés, s of Andrés López Gil, of Murcia, Spain; 2 s (James b 3 Dec 1984, Teo b 11 Oct 1986), 1 da (Susannah b 24 May 1989); *Career* obstetrician and gynaecologist; registrar Southmead and Frenchay Hosps Bristol 1976-78; John Radcliffe Hosp Oxford: clinical lectr 1982-87, conslt 1988-; MRCOG 1977; *Recreations* music, family, cookery, travelling; *Style—* Dr Susan Sellers; John Radcliffe Maternity Hosp, Headington, Oxford OX3 9DU

SELLEY, Prof Richard Curtis; JP (1981); s of Harry Westcott Selley (d 1967), and Dorothy Joan, *née* Curtis; *b* 21 Sept 1939; *Educ* Eastbourne Coll, Univ of London (BSc, PhD), Imperial Coll London (DIC); *m* 15 May 1965, Pauline Selley, da of John Fletcher; 2 da (Helen b 24 Aug 1967, Andrea b 2 April 1969); *Career* Imperial Coll London: post doctoral res fell 1963-66, lectr in sedimentology 1966-69, reader petroleum geology 1974-89, head Dept of Geology 1988-, prof applied sedimentology 1989-; sr sedimentologist Oasis Oil Co of Libya 1969-71, sr geologist Conoco Europe Ltd 1971-74; FGS 1962, AAPG 1971, SPE 1981, PESGB 1971, memb Geologist's Assoc; *Books* Ancient Sedimentary Environments (1970), Introduction to Sedimentology (1975), Elements of Petroleum Geology (1985), Applied Sedimentology (1988); *Style—* Prof Richard Selley, JP; Dept of Geology, Royal School of Mines, Imperial College, Prince Consort Rd, London SW7 2BP (☎ 071 589 5111, fax 071 225 8544, telex 929484)

SELLIER, Robert Hugh; s of Maj Philip Joseph Sellier (d 1963), and Lorna Geraldine Luxton (d 1983); *b* 15 Nov 1933; *Educ* St Joseph's Coll Oxford, Kings Coll Durham (BSc); *m* 1, 16 Aug 1963, Cynthia Ann (decd), da of Lt-Col F W Dwelly (d 1984); 1 da (Nicola Jane b 1968); m 2, 15 April 1987, Gillian, da of late J Clark; *Career* md: New Ideal Houses 1972-74, Cementation Construction 1979-83; dep md Cementation International 1974-79, chm Cementation Group of Companies 1983-86, group md George Wimpey plc 1986-91, chief exec Y Y Lovell (Holdings) plc 1991-; *Recreations* skiing, squash; *Style—* Robert H Sellier, Esq; Heatherlands, Glenmore Rd, Crowborough, E Sussex TN6 1TN (☎ 0892 63413)

SELLS, (Edward) Andrew Perronet; s of Sir David Sells, of Guilder, Morden, Royston, Herts (*qv*); *b* 30 Nov 1948; *Educ* St Peters Seaford, Wellington, London Business Sch; *Career* chartered accountant 1971; J Henry Schroder Wagg & Co Ltd 1972-82, Thompson Clive & Partners 1982-87; md Nash Sells and Partners Ltd, dir Micrelec Group plc; *Recreations* reading, cricket, hunting; *Style—* Andrew Sells, Esq; 10 Kensington Place, London W8 7PT (☎ 071 727 5080); 25 Buckingham Gate, London SW1E 6LD (☎ 071 828 6944)

SELLS, David James Guthrie; s of Henry James Sells, of Birmingham (d 1967), and Anne Guthrie, *née* Milne (d 1990); *b* 21 Dec 1928; *Educ* King Edward's Sch Birmingham; Merchant Taylors, Lincoln Coll Oxford; *m* 17 Sept 1952 (m dis 1984), Pauline Alice, *née* Hill; 2 s (Adrian David Guthrie b 1957, Christopher James Guthrie b 1961); *Career* news correspondent; Reuters: Rome 1954-57, Warsaw 1957-60, Bonn 1960-64, Brussels mangr 1964-65; BBC TV: Beirut 1971-76, Newsday 1976-78, Assignment 1978-79, Newsnight 1980-; BBC Radio: World Tonight 1986-, World in Focus 1976; *Recreations* reading, swimming, travel; *Style—* David Sells Esq; Newsnight, BBC TV Centre, London W12 7RJ (☎ 081 743 8000); The World Tonight, BBC Broadcasting House, London W1A 1AA (☎ 071 580 4468)

SELLS, Sir David Perronet; s of late Edward Perronet Sells, and late Margaret Mary de Grave Sells; *b* 23 June 1918; *Educ* Repton, ChCh Oxford (MA); *m* 1948, Beryl Cecilia, da of late Cecil Ernest Wells Charrington, MC; 3 s (incl Andrew Sells, *qv*); *Career* chm Cons Central Cncl 1977-78, holder of numerous other offices in Nat Union of Cons and Unionist Assocs; kt 1980; *Recreations* fishing, shooting; *Clubs* Savile; *Style—* Sir David Sells; Garden House, Churdh St, Guilden Morden, Royston, Herts SG8 0JD (☎ 0763 853237)

SELLS, Oliver Matthew; s of Sir David Sells, of Royston, Herts, *qv*, and Lady Sells, *née* Charrington; *b* 29 Sept 1950; *Educ* Wellington Coll, The Coll of Law London; *m* 30 Aug 1986, Lucinda Jane, da of Gerard William Mackworth-Young (d 1984), of Fisherton de la Mere; 1 s (Hugo William b 17 June 1988); *Career* called to the Bar Inner Temple 1972; in practice SE Circuit, supplementary counsel to The Crown 1981-86, asst rec of The Crown Ct 1987-; dir Music for Charity; memb: Gen Cncl of the Bar 1985-89 (and 1977-80), Cwlth Law Assoc; hon memb American Bar Assoc; *Recreations* shooting, cricket, fishing; *Clubs* MCC; *Style—* Oliver Sells, Esq; 5 Paper Buildings, Temple, London EC4Y 7HB (☎ 071 583 6117, fax 071 353 0075)

SELLS, Robert Anthony; s of Rev William Blyth Sells (d 1977), of Portsmouth, and Eleanor Mary Sells; *b* 13 April 1938; *Educ* Christ's Hosp Sch, Univ of London Guys Hosp (MB BS); *m* 1, 1964 (m dis 1976), Elizabeth Lucy, *née* Schryver; 2 s (Rupert William Blyth b 1967, Henry Perronet b 1968), 1 da (Katherine b 1970); m 2, 10 May 1977, Dr Paula Gilchrist, da of Stephen Muir (d 1988), of Denbigh Clwyd; 2 s (Edward Anthony b 1981, Patrick David b 1982); *Career* lectr: Dept of Surgery Univ of London Guys Hosp 1967-68, Dept of Surgery Cambridge Univ 1968-70; MRC travelling scholar Peter Bent-Brigham Hosp Harvard Univ 1970-71, dir Regnl Transplant Unit;

conslt surgn: Royal Liverpool Hosps 1971-78, Liverpool Health Authy 1978-; vice pres The Transplantation Soc 1990- (cncllr 1982-88, pres 1983-86); MA Cambridge Univ; memb BMA 1962, FRCS, FRCSEd; *Books* Transplantation Today (1982), Organ Transplantation: Current Clinical and Immunological Concepts (1989); *Recreations* conductor, crosby symphony orchestra; *Clubs* Moynihan Chirurgial, The XX; *Style*— Robert Sells, Esq; 4 Marine Crescent, Waterloo, Liverpool 22 (☎ 051 928 3375); Link Unit 9C, Royal Liverpool Hospital, Prescot St, Liverpool L7 8XP (☎ 051 708 0163, fax 051 709 2247)

SELSDON, 3 Baron (UK 1932); Sir Malcolm McEacharn Mitchell-Thomson; 4th Bt (UK 1900); s of 2 Baron Selsdon, DSC (d 1963), and his 1 w, Phoebette Sitwell, da of Crossley Swithinbank; *b* 27 Oct 1937; *Educ* Winchester; *m* 1965, Patricia Anne, da of Donald Smith; 1 s; *Heir* s, Hon Callum Malcolm McEacharn Mitchell-Thomson b 7 Nov 1969; *Career* Sub Lt RNVR; banker with Midland Bank Gp, British del to Cncl of Europe and Western European Union 1972-78, chm Ctee of Middle East Trade (Comet) 1979-86, memb British Overseas Trade Bd 1983-86; chm: Greater London and S E Cncl for Sport and Recreation 1978-83, London Docklands Arena Tst 1984-; *Recreations* tennis, lawn tennis, skiing, sailing; *Clubs* MCC; *Style*— The Rt Hon the Lord Selsdon; Walker House, 87 Queen Victoria Street, London EC4V 4AP

SELVADURAI, Dr Leila Rachel Nevins; da of Ebenezer Devavarum Tambimuttu (d 1978), of Sri Lanka, and Florence Evangeline, *née* Samaraweera (d 1987); *b* 3 June 1937; *Educ* CMS Ladies' Coll Colombo Sri Lanka, Univ of Sri Lanka (MB BS); *m* 22 Jan 1970, Lt-Col Anton Jesuraj Nevins-Selvadurai, s of Dr David Durairaj Nevins-Selvadurai (d 1985), of USA; 1 s (Michael Vinodhkumar b 17 Dec 1972), 1 da (Harinee Rachel b 11 May 1971); *Career* posts in Sri Lanka 1964-77, registrar in radiology Bristol Royal Infirmary 1977-79, sr registrar N Staffs Hosp Centre 1979-83, conslt radiologist Leighton Hosp Crewe 1983-; fell faculty of radiology RCSI 1983; memb BMA 1983; *Recreations* swimming, table tennis; *Style*— Dr Leila Selvadurai; 8 Blenheim Court, Alsager, North Staffs ST7 2BY (☎ 0270 877500); Dept of Radiodiagnosis, Leighton Hospital, Crewe, Cheshire CW14 4QJ (☎ 0270 255141)

SELWOOD, Maj-Gen David Henry Deering; s of Cdr George Deering Selwood, RN (d 1972), and Enid Marguerite, *née* Rowlinson; *b* 27 June 1934; *Educ* Kelly Coll, Univ Coll of South-West, Law Soc's Sch of Law; *m* 1, 17 March 1962 (m dis), Joanne Christine, da of Capt R F Pink, of Saltash, Cornwall; 1 s (Stephen b 1963), 1 da (Suzanne b 1966); m 2, 3 Nov 1973, Barbara Dorothea, da of late Dr Kurt Franz Richard Hütter; 2 step-s (Andreas b 1967, Dominic b 1970); *Career* cmmnd (Nat Serv list) RASC 1958; TA (4 Devons) 1959-61, regular cmmn Army Legal Serv Staff List 1961; served on staff: of WO MOD, HQ BAOR, HQ MELF, HQ FARELF; admitted slr 1957; rec: SE Circuit 1985-90, W Circuit 1990-; dir Army Legal Servs 1990-; hon attorney and counsellor US Court of Mil Appeals; *Books* Criminal Law and Psychiatry (co-author, 1987); *Recreations* reading, writing, gardening; *Clubs* Lansdowne; *Style*— Maj-Gen David Selwood; c/o Barclays Bank plc, 7 North Street, Wilton, Salisbury SP2 0HA

SELWYN, Jeffrey Michael; s of Arthur Selwyn and Vera, *née* Schuchman (d 1984); *b* 2 Dec 1936; *Educ* Mill Hill; *m* 5 March 1961, June Margaret, da of Leonard Koetser (d 1979); 2 s (Richard Leonard b 17 Nov 1961, Anthony David b 14 May 1966), 1 da (Karina Margaret b 5 March 1964); *Career* chartered accountant; md Allied Dunbar Provident plc 1973-89, chm Assoc of Br Insur Housing Working Pty 1985-89; with HP Allsop Selwyn 1989-; FCA 1965; *Recreations* golf; *Style*— Jeffrey Selwyn, Esq; The Pines, Totteridge Village, London N20 (☎ 081 446 2206); 27 Soho Sq, London W1V 6AX (☎ 071 437 6977, fax 071 437 8984)

SELWYN, Maj John Jasper; MC (1942); s of Rev Stephen John Selwyn (d 1960), of Henley-on-Thames,and Phyllis Graeme, *née* Hickling (d 1967); *b* 11 Aug 1918; *Educ* Eton, Trinity Coll Cambridge (BA, MA); *m* 1, 1943, Margaret Evelyn Whittingham (d 1980), da of late George Gee, of Ely Grange, Frant, Sussex; 2 s (Nicholas Jasper b 1946, William Henry b 1947), 1 da (Albinia Victoria b 1950); m 2, 16 Mar 1983, Mary Mitchell, wid of Capt Michael Radcliffe (d 1975), and da of Leonard Brooke-Edwards (d 1988), of Philadelphia, USA; *Career* cmmnd 13/18 Queen Mary's Own Royal Hussars 1939; served: Dunkirk, Dieppe, D-Day (Normandy) 1940-44; cmd Sqdn in 6 Airborne RECCE in the Ardennes campaign 1944-45, Staff Coll Camberley 1948, cmd Sqdn 13/18 Hussars Malaya 1951-53 (despatches), Regtl 2 i/c 13/18 Hussars 1957-58, ret 1959; called to the Bar Lincolns Inn 1963; practised S E Circuit and Kent Sessions, dep circuit judge 1974/78, ret from practise 1978; memb Br Legion (formerly pres Cookham and Pinkneys Green Branch), Nat Tst, Museum Ctee 13/18 Hussars, Berks CC (C) 1962-68; *Recreations* field sports, sailing; *Clubs* Leander; *Style*— Maj John Selwyn, MC; The Orchards, Pinkneys Green, Maidenhead, Berks SL6 6PA (☎ 0628 30537)

SELWYN, Prof Sydney; s of Louis Selwyn, of Leeds, and Ruth, *née* Skibben; *b* 7 Nov 1934; *Educ* Leeds GS, Univ of Edinburgh (BSc, MB ChB, MD); *m* 14 July 1957, Flora Dagmar, da of Heinrich Schmerling (d 1962), of Vienna and London; 3 s (Alan b 1958, Barry b 1962, Jonathan b 1965), 1 da (Miriam b 1960); *Career* house physician Edinburgh City Hosp 1959-60, lectr in bacteriology Univ of Edinburgh Med Sch 1961-66, visiting prof WHO Baroda Univ India 1966-67, med conslt WHO SE Asia 1966-67; Westminster Med Sch: reader in medical microbiology 1967-79, conslt Westminster Hosp 1967-, prof 1979-; prof of med microbiology Charing Cross Hosp med sch 1983- (conslt 1983-); hon archivist RCPath; pres: Faculty of History and Philosophy of Medicine and Pharmacy, Med Sciences Historical Soc, Osler Club of London; vice pres: Pathology Section RSM, Harveian Soc; Freeman City of London 1974, Liveryman Worshipful Soc of Apothecaries 1974; memb BMA 1959, FRCPath 1967, FRSM 1969, FIBiol 1979; *Books* The Beta-Lactam Antibiotics: Penicillins and Cephalosporins in Perspective (1980); *Recreations* exotic travel, photography, music; *Clubs* Royal Over-seas League, RSM; *Style*— Prof Sydney Selwyn; Department of Medical Microbiology, Charing Cross & Westminster Medical School, St Dunstan's Rd, London W6 8RP (☎ 081 748 6923, fax 081 846 7261)

SELWYN GUMMER; *see*: Gummer

SEMKEN, John Douglas; CB (1980), MC (1944); s of William Richard Semken (d 1970), and Beatrice Rose, *née* Craymer (d 1964); *b* 9 Jan 1921; *Educ* St Albans Sch, Pembroke Coll Oxford (BCL, MA); *m* 4 Sept 1952, (Edna) Margaret, da of Thomas Robert Poole (d 1978); 3 s (Christopher b 1955, David b 1956, Robert b 1962); *Career* cmmnd Sherwood Rangers Yeo 1940, Lt 1941, Capt 1942, Maj 1944, tank cdr N Africa and NW Europe 1942-44; called to the Bar Lincolnshire 1949; barr at the Chancery Bar 1949-53, joined office of the Legal Advsr to the HO 1953, dep under sec of state and legal advsr to the HO 1977-83; Silver Star USA 1944; *Style*— John Semken, Esq, CB, MC; 2 The Ridgeway, London NW7 1RS (☎ 081 346 3092)

SEMMENCE, Dr Adrian Murdoch; CB (1986); s of Adrian George Semmence (d 1962), of Schoolhouse, Cults, Aberdeenshire, and Henrietta Scorgie, *née* Murdoch (d 1977); *b* 5 April 1926; *Educ* Robert Gordon's Coll, Univ of Aberdeen (MB ChB, MD), Univ of London (MSc); *m* 24 Sept 1949, Joan, da of Hugh McAskill Wood (d 1973), of Brighton Place, Aberdeen, 4 s (Adrian b 1950, Jonathan b 1953, Timothy b 1959, Peter b 1961), 1 da (Joanna b 1964); *Career* Pilot Observer trg FAA 1943-44, Able Seaman (torpedo man) RN 1944-47; house posts Aberdeen Royal Infirmary and Aberdeen Maternity Hosp 1953-54; gen practice: E Yorks 1954-60, Berks and Oxon 1961-76; princ med offr Civil Service Department 1976-79, med advsr Civil Service 1979-86, conslt Cabinet Office Office (Miny for Civil Service) 1987-; memb Oxford Med Soc 1961, FRSM 1976 (pres Occupational Med Section 1975-76); *Recreations* reading, gardening; *Clubs* Athenaeum, RSM; *Style*— Dr Adrian Semmence, CB; Stone Cottage, Steventon, Abingdon, Oxon OX13 6RZ (☎ 0235 831 527)

SEMPER, The Very Rev the Canon Colin Douglas; s of William Frederick Semper (d 1982), of Lincoln, and Dorothy Anne, *née* Baxter (d 1978), of Lincoln; *b* 5 Feb 1938; *Educ* Lincoln Sch, Keble Coll Oxford (BA), Westcott House Cambridge; *m* 7 July 1962, Janet Louise, da of Newlyn Harvard Greaves (d 1986), 2 s ((Andrew) Giles b 1963, Hugh Sebastian b 1965); *Career* asst curate Holy Trinity at St Mary Guildford 1963-67, sec Advsy Cncl The Church's Miny 1967-69, prodr BBC and head religious progs radio 1969-82, provost of Coventry 1982-87, canon of Westminster 1987-; chaplain Worshipful Co of Feltmakers; *Recreations* canals, reading modern novels; *Style*— The Very Rev the Canon of Westminster; 8 Little Cloister, Westminster Abbey, London SW1P 3PL (☎ 071 222 5791)

SEMPILL, Lady (20 in line, S 1489); Ann Moira Sempill; *née* Forbes-Sempill; da of Lord Sempill (19 in line, d 1965) by his 1 w, Eileen, da of Sir John Lavery, RA; niece of Hon Sir Ewan Forbes of Craigievar, 11th Bt, *qv*; half-sis of Hon Mrs Menuhin, *qv*; *b* 19 March 1920; *Educ* convents in Austria and Germany, Poles Convent Ware; *m* 1, 1942 (m dis 1945), Capt Eric Holt, Manchester Regt; 1 da; m 2, 1948, Lt-Col Stuart Whitemore Chant-Sempill, OBE, MC, late Gordon Highlanders (who assumed by decree of Lyon Court 1966 the additional name of Sempill); 2 s, 1 da; *Heir* s, Master of Sempill, *qv*; *Career* Petty Offr WRNS, ctee memb House of Lords, Cons Peer 1966-; *Style*— The Rt Hon the Lady Sempill; East Lodge, Druminnor, Rhynie, Aberdeenshire (☎ 046 46 663); 15 Onslow Ct, Drayton Gdns, London SW10

SEMPILL, Master of; Hon James William Stuart Whitemore Sempill; s (by 2 m) of Lady Sempill, *qv*; *b* 25 Feb 1949; *Educ* Oratory Sch, St Clare's Hall and Hertford Coll Oxford; *m* 1977, Josephine Ann Edith, da of Joseph Norman Rees, of Johannesburg; 1 s (Francis b 1979), 1 da (Cosima b 1983); *Career* with Argus of Ayr Ltd; *Style*— The Master of Sempill; Pibworth House, Aldworth, Berks (☎ 0635 202)

SEMPLE, Andrew Greenlees; s of William Hugh Semple (d 1981), of Manchester, and Hilda Madeline, *née* Wood (d 1978); *b* 16 Jan 1934; *Educ* Winchester, St John's Coll Cambridge (BA, MA); *m* 27 May 1961, Janet Elizabeth, da of Harold Richard Grant Whates (d 1961), of Ludlow; 1 s (Robert b 1965), 1 da (Susanna b 1969); *Career* Nat Serv RN 1952-54 (Russian interpreter), Actg Sub Lt (special) RNVR; princ Miny of Tport 1962-69 (joined 1957), asst sec 1969-75, princ private sec to Sec of State for the Environment 1972-75, under sec DOE 1976-83, sec Water Authy Assoc 1983-87, md Anglian Water 1987-89 (vice chm 1990-); hon memb AWO 1988; companion IWEM 1985; *Recreations* walking, travel, reading, gardening; *Style*— Andrew Semple, Esq; 83 Burbage Rd, London SE24 9HB (☎ 071 274 6550); 3 Church Lane, Covington, Cambs PE18 0RT (☎ 0480 860 497); Anglian Water plc, Ambury Rd, Huntingdon, Cambs PE18 6NZ (☎ 0480 44349)

SEMPLE, Dr Colin Gordon; s of Dr Thomas Semple, and Elspeth Roubaix, *née* Dewar; *Educ* Loretto, Brasenose Coll Oxford (BA, MA), Univ of Glasgow (MB ChB, MD); *m* 31 March 1979, Elaine Elizabeth, *née* Rankin; 1 s (Alan b 1981), 1 da (Gillian b 1983); *Career* conslt physician Southern Gen Hosp 1988-; author of various papers on diabetes and endocrinology; FRCP (Glasgow); *Recreations* golf, fishing, gardening; *Style*— Dr Colin Semple; 53 Tinto Rd, Newlands, Glasgow G43 2AH (☎ 041 637 3314); Consultant Physician, Medical Unit B, Southern General Hosptial, Glasgow G51 4TF (☎ 041 445 2466)

SEMPLE, (William) David Crowe; s of George Crowe Semple (d 1985), of 3 Athol Crescent, Laurieston, Falkirk, and Helen Davidson, *née* Paterson (d 1975); *b* 11 June 1933; *Educ* Grangemouth HS, Falkirk HS, Univ of Glasgow (BSc), Jordanhill Coll of Educn Univ of London (Dip Ed); *m* 9 July 1958, Margaret Bain, da of Andrew Kerr Donald (d 1972), of 2 Sharp Terrace, Grangemouth; 1 s (Richard b 1961), 1 da (Lynn b 1962); *Career* educn offr Northern Rhodesia 1958-61, educn offr and offr i/c educn TV Northern Rhodesia 1961-63, chief educn offr Zambia 1966-67 (dep chief educn offr 1964-66), actg dir of tech educn Zambia 1967-68, dep dir of educn Edinburgh 1972-74 (asst dir 1968-72), dir of educn Lothian Region 1974-; memb Edinburgh Rotary Club, gen sec Assoc of Dirs of Educn in Scotland 1985-; memb: UK Advsy Ctee on UNESCO 1981-86, UGC 1983-89, Sec of States Working Party on Educn Catering 1971-73, Scottish Cncl for Tertiary Educn 1979-83, STV Educn Ctee 1979-85 (chm 1979-85); FBIM 1985, ADES 1968; *Recreations* gardening, reading; *Style*— David Semple, Esq; 15 Essex Park, Edinburgh, Lothian (☎ 031 339 6157); Dept of Education, 40 Torphichen St, Edinburgh, Lothian EH3 8JJ (☎ 031 229 9166)

SEN, Srikumar; s of Sukumar Sen (d 1949), of Calcutta, India, and Elalata Mitra (d 1982); *b* 2 Oct 1931; *Educ* Highgate Sch Jesus Coll Oxford (Boxing blue, BA); *m* 15 April 1950, Eileen Fawcett, da of John Oldacre Hartwell; 3 c (Subir Stephen b 21 March 1957, Sarojini Ela Hardy b 29 Nov 1961, Mrinal Fawcett b 19 July 1966); *Career* trainee journalist London Express News and Feature Service 1953-54, trainee The Times 1954-55, managerial asst The Statesman Calcutta 1955-59, head of publicity and PR ICI (India) Ltd 1960-64; sub ed Sports Desk: The Guardian 1965-67, The Times 1967-78; boxing corr and sub ed The Times 1979-; *Recreations* tennis, squash; *Style*— Srikumar Sen, Esq; The Times Sports Desk, The Times, 1 Pennington St, London E1 (☎ 071 782 5960)

SENATOR, Dr Ronald Paul; s of Sydney Senator (d 1976), of London, and Catherine, *née* Franklin (d 1970); *b* 17 April 1926; *Educ* City of London Sch, Marlborough, Hertford Coll Oxford (PhD, BMus, FTCL); *m* 1, 15 July 1964, (Edith) Dita Branky (d 1981), da of Joseph Branky (d 1979); m 2, 17 Oct 1986, Miriam Brickman; *Career* sr lectr Univ of London 1963-79; ed Counterpoint Pubns 1946-56; musical compositions published by Boosey and Hawkes, Chesters, RSCM, St Martins, Lengwick, Stainer and Bell; dir SSRC prog 1969-75, Requiem for Terezin premiere Canterbury Cathedral 1986, Echoes City of London Festival 1986; recordings: Counterpoint, Musica Nova; exec Composers Guild, fndr memb Montserrat Sacred Music Assoc; dir: Liverpool Festival 1978, Nat Assoc Music Theatre; *Books* Musicolor; *Style*— Dr Ronald Senator; 20 Denbigh Gardens, Richmond, Surrey TW10 6EN (☎ 01 940 8831); 82 Hillcrest Ave, Yonkers, New York 10705, USA (☎ 914 476 1962)

SENINGTON, David James; s of Victor Samuel Colston Senington, of Bristol, and Ella Matilda, *née* Ridout; *b* 28 March 1947; *Educ* Queen Elizabeth's Hosp Bristol, Coll of Commerce Bristol; *m* 31 Aug 1974, Julie Elizabeth, da of Thomas Park Hill; 1 s (Richard James b 31 December 1980), 1 da (Helen Louisa b 21 June 1984); *Career* reporter New Observer Bristol 1966-67, news sub-ed then features sub-ed Western Daily Press Bristol 1969-70 (reporter 1967-69); travelling 1970-71: Europe, Middle East, India, Australia; Parly reporter The West Australian Perth Western Australia 1971; travelling 1971-72: Australia, New Zealand, Pacific, USA, Canada; news sub-ed: Western Daily Press 1972-73, Daily Telegraph London 1973, Daily Mail London 1973-74; travelling 1974-75: The Americas, West and North Africa; freelance sub-ed London 1975-76, contrib Sunday Express 1979- (Sunday Times 1977-78); Evening Standard: news sub-ed 1976-79, overnight dep chief sub-ed 1979-84, dep chief sub-ed 1984-85, chief sub-ed 1985-; memb: NUJ 1966, Soc of Genealogists 1982, Nat Trust 1988;

Recreations writing, genealogy, numismatics, travel, bricklaying, gardening, reading; *Style—* David Senington, Esq; Evening Standard, Northcliffe House, 2 Derry St, Kensington, London W8 5EE (☎ 071 938 7571)

SENIOR, Sir Edward Walters; CMG (1955); s of late Albert Senior, CBE, of Sheffield; *b* 29 March 1902; *Educ* Repton, Univ of Sheffield; *m* 1928, Stephanie Vera (d 1990), da of Basil M Heald, of Torquay; 1 s (John), 1 da (Jennifer); *Career* RA (TA) 1920-52, Maj 1938; JP Sheffield 1937-50; memb Iron and Steel Control 1940-44, controller of Ball and Roller Bearings 1944-45, DG British Iron and Steel Fedn 1962-66 (dir 1949-62); chm George Senior & Sons Ltd; kt 1970; *Clubs* Naval & Military; *Style—* Sir Edward Senior, CMG; Hollies, Church Close, Brenchley, Tonbridge, Kent (☎ 089 272 2359)

SENIOR, (Alan) Gordon; CBE (1981); s of Oscar Senior (d 1973), of Ash Vale, Surrey, and Helen, *née* Cooper (d 1964); *b* 1 Jan 1928; *Educ* Normanton GS, Univ of Leeds (BSc, MSc); *m* 1, Dec 1954 (m dis 1960), Sheila Mary, da of Ernest Lockyer (d 1959), of Normanton, Yorks; m 2, 29 Nov 1968 (m dis 1978), Lawmary Mitchell, da of Lawrence Champion (d 1981), of Cape Town, SA; 1 s (John b 12 Feb 1970); *Career* served UTC and TA 1945-49; engr; J B Edwards (Whyteleafe) Ltd 1949-51, Oscar Faber & Partners Consulting Engineers 1951-54, W S Atkins Group 1954-80 (tech dir 1967); md Atkins Research and Development 1971; dir: W S Atkins and Partners 1975, Atkins Franlab Ltd 1977; fndr Gordon Senior Associates Consulting Engineers 1980; dir: ANSEN Ltd 1981-83, McMillan Sloan and Partners 1981-83, Armstrong Technology Services Ltd 1986-87; chm: Surface Engineering and Inspection Ltd (subsid of Yarrow plc) 1983-86, Masta Corporation Ltd 1987-, Aptech Ltd 1988-89; FICE, FIStructE, FRICS, FSUT; *Books* Brittle Fracture of Steel Structures (co-author, 1970); author of various papers on welding, fatigue, brittle fracture and future devpts offshore and in the oceans; *Recreations* food, wine, travel, conversation, skiing; *Clubs* Athenaeum; *Style—* Gordon Senior, Esq, CBE; Deanlands, Normandy, Surrey GU3 2AR (☎ 0483 235 496/235 066)

SENIOR, Grahame; s of Raymond Senior, of Huddersfield, Yorks, and Evelyn, *née* Wood; *b* 21 Oct 1944; *Educ* King James Sch; *m* 10 July 1965, Prudence Elizabeth, da of William Holland; 1 s (Adam Michael b 3 June 1970), 2 da (Claire Elizabeth b 30 Oct 1967, Charlotte Elizabeth b 26 Sept 1980); *Career* mgmnt trainee then asst publicity exec Royal Insurance Group 1963-65, writer Radio Caroline 1965, copywriter Vernons 1965-66, devpt writer Royds 1966-67; Brunnings: copy chief 1967-69, creative dir 1969-73, md 1978-79; fndr Senior King Ltd 1980 (currently jt chm and chief exec), fndr MKA Films 1981, fndr Media Options Ltd (media independent) 1984; chm Northern Publicity Assoc, organiser Northern NABS fundraising initiatives, fndr Liverpool Gold medal awards for Man of the Year; ACII 1965, MIPA 1967, MInstM 1969; *Publications* author various articles and booklets on mktg, market targeting and tourism mktg 1973-87; *Recreations* dry fly-fishing, gardening, ballet, tennis, painting, reading, wine, cooking; *Clubs* RAC, IOD; *Style—* Grahame Senior, Esq; Greenways, Grove Rd, Tring, Herts HP23 5PD (☎ 044 282 2770); Senior King Ltd, 14-15 Carlisle St, London W1V 5RE (☎ 071 734 5855, fax 071 437 1908, mobile 0860 778475)

SENIOR, Michael; DL (Gwynedd 1989); s of Geoffrey Senior (d 1957), of Glan Conwy, N Wales, and Julia Elaine, *née* Cotterell (d 1984); *b* 14 April 1940; *Educ* Uppingham, Open Univ (BA); *Career* writer and farmer; radio play The Coffee Table (1964); *Books* Portrait of North Wales (1973), Portrait of South Wales (1974), Greece and its Myths (1978), Myths of Britain (1979), The Age of Myth and Legend in Heroes and Heroines (1980), Sir Thomas Malory's Tales of King Arthur (ed, 1980), The Life and Times of Richard II (1981), Who's Who in Mythology (1985), Conway, The Town's Story (1977), additional local history booklets; *Recreations* hill walking, painting, croquet; *Style—* Michael Senior, Esq, DL; Bryn Eisteddfod, Glan Conwy, Colwyn Bay, N Wales LL28 5LF; c/o David Higham Associates Ltd, 5-8 Lower John Street, London W1R 4HA

SENIOR, Hon Mrs (Rosemary); da of Baron Hunt of Fawley, CBE (Life Peer); *b* 1943; *Educ* St Andrews Univ (MA); *m* 1974, Dr Clive Malcolm Senior; 1 s, 1 da; *Style—* The Hon Mrs Senior; 20 Derby St, Swanbourne, Perth, W Australia

SENTANCE, David Geoffrey; *b* 17 Jan 1930; *Educ* Newark and Grantham Colls, Huddersfield Poly; *m* 1990, Ruth; 2 c; *Career* Son Ltd, dir Recticel Sutcliffe Ltd and Sutcliffe Impact Ltd; MIMechE, MIProdE, CDipAF, FIBC; *Recreations* music, gardening; *Style—* David Sentance Esq

SERBAN, Andrei; s of Gheorge Serban, and Elpis, *née* Lichiandopol; *b* 21 June 1943; *Educ* Theatre Inst Bucarest; *m* 26 oct 1985, Alexandra Gräfin, da of Graf Plettenberg; 2 s (Antony b 1986, Nicolas b 1987); *Career* Theatre and opera dir; prodns incl: Trojan Women, Medea and Electra la Mama Theatre NY 1972-75, Good woman of Setzuan La Mama Theatre NY 1975, Cherry Orchard, Agamemnon Lincoln Centre 1977, Carlo Gozzi Trilogy (King Stag, Serpent Woman, 3 Oranges) 1985-88, Turandot Covent Garden 1987, Twelfth Night American Rep Theatre Boston 1989, Onegin, Puritani WNO, Elektra Geneva Opera, Firey Angel Los Angeles, Magic Flute Paris, Prince Igor Covent Garden, Lucia di Lammamot Chicago Opera; dir Nat Theatre Bucharest 1990; *Style—* Andrei Serban, Esq; 19 Berkeley St, Cambridge Ma02138, USA ☎ 617 8763881; Royal Opera House, Covent Garden, London

SEREBRIAKOFF, Victor Vladimir; s of Vladimir Hesperovitch Serebriakoff (d 1958), and Ethel Lucy, *née* Graham (d 1972); *b* 17 Oct 1912; *Educ* Woolwich Poly; *m* 1, Gladys Mary (d 1952), da of Frank Ewart Whipp (d 1985); 1 s (Mark b 1959), 1 da (Judith b 1950); m 2, 5 Oct 1953, Winifred Ida Rouse, OBE, da of Jack Rouse (d 1955); *Career* Sgt Educn Corps 1945-47; Phoenix Timber Group 1947-80 (sawmill mangr and various higher posts), fndr and md MPC Ltd (pioneer of automatic quality control machines for timber), chm Timber Standards Ctee BSI 1960-80; parallel career as inventor, lectr and author; hon int pres Mensa 1969- (sec 1952, int gen sec 1953-69), fndr and chm Mensa Fndn for Gifted Children; Freedom of Hartford Connecticut USA; fell Inst of Wood Sci 1965; *Books* British Sawmilling Practice (1963), IQ A Mensa Analysis and History (1965), How Intelligent Are You? (1968), Metrication in the Timber and Allied Trades (1970), Brain (1976), Test Yours Child's IQ (1977), Hyperbolic Acid (1977), A Mensa Puzzle Book (1982), A Second Mensa Puzzle Book (1985), Mensa The Society for the Highly Intelligent (1985), The Future of Intelligence Biological and Artificial (1987), A Guide to Intelligence and Personality Testing (1988), Educating the Intelligent Child (1990), Test Your IQ (1990), My Alien Self (1990); *Recreations* meetings, theatres, dinner parties, reading; *Clubs* Savage; *Style—* Victor Serebriakoff, Esq; Flat 1, 6 The Paragon, Blackheath, London SE3 0NY (☎ 081 852 6754)

SERGEANT, Annette Lesley; da of John Richard Sergeant, of Scunthorpe, South Humberside, and Dorothy Ruth, *née* Sanderson; *b* 26 Nov 1953; *Educ* John Leggoth GS, Univ of Hull (BSc); *m* Sept 1983, Robert James Armstrong; *Career* trainee postgrad hosps 1976-77, asst admin Whipps Cross Hosp 1977-79, sector admin Barking Hosp 1979-82, unit admin small acute hosps Waltham Forest 1982-85, unit admin then dep gen mangr Whipps Cross Hosp 1985-87, High Fliers training scheme 1987-88, unit gen mangr acute servs Enfield Health Authy 1988-; winner Health Service Jl award 1989 (for work on quality); memb: assoc Inst Health Serv Mgmnt 1979; *Recreations* theatre, travel, playing pinball; *Style—* Ms Annette Sergeant; Chase Farm Hospital, The Ridgeway, Enfield, Middlesex (☎ 081 366 9101)

SERGEANT, Dr Howard Gordon Stanley; s of Stanley Victor Sergeant (d 1981), of Ryde, and Bertha Violet, *née* Buck; *b* 6 Feb 1932; *Educ* Cathedral Choir Sch Chester, Co GS Gravesend, Charing Cross Hosp Med Sch (MB BS, DPM); *m* 15 July 1961, Harriet Mary Courtenay, da of Francis Courtenay Mason (d 1953), of Hampstead; 3 da (Rosamond b 23 May 1963, Katharine b 13 Aug 1965, Briony b 15 Sept 1967); *Career* Nat Serv RA 1951-52; Maudsley Hosp 1962-70; conslt psychiatrist: Royal Northern Hosp 1970-74, Whittington Hosp 1970-74, Royal Free and Friern Hosp 1975; author of published articles on asthma, rehabilitation, employment and data protection; memb BMA; FRCPE 1976, FRCPsych 1978, FRSM; *Recreations* bridge, genealogy, opera, sailing, skiing; *Style—* Dr Howard Sergeant; 20 Well Walk, London NW3 1LD (☎ 071 435 2308); 2 Coach House Lane, Ryde, Isle of Wight PO33 3LU; 144 Harley St, London W1N 1AH (☎ 071 935 0023, fax 071 935 5972)

SERGEANT, Sir Patrick John Rushton; s of George and, Rene Sergeant; *b* 17 March 1924; *Educ* Beaumont Coll; *m* 1952, Gillian, *née* Wilks; 2 da (Harriet, Emma); *Career* Lt RNVR 1945; asst city ed News Chronicle 1948, city ed Daily Mail 1960-84 (dep city ed 1953), fndr and md Euromoney Publications 1969-85 (chm 1985-); dir: Assoc Newspapers Gp 1971-83, Daily Mail and Gen Tst 1983-; Winner Wincott award Financial Journalist of the Year 1979; fell Royal soc for the Encouragement of Arts Manufactures and Commerce; Freeman City of London; Domus fell St Catherine's Coll Oxford 1988; kt 1984; *Books* Another Road to Samarkand (1955), Money Matters (1967), Inflation Fighters Handbook (1976); *Recreations* tennis, skiing, swimming, talking; *Clubs* RAC, Annabel's, Mark's, Cumberland Lawn Tennis, All England Lawn Tennis and Croquet; *Style—* Sir Patrick Sergeant; No 1 The Grove, Highgate Village, London N6; Euromoney Publications plc, Nestor House, Playhouse Yard, London EC4V 5EX (☎ 071 779 8879)

SERGISON-BROOKE, Hon Mrs (Mary Anne); *née* Hare; er da of 1 Viscount Blakenham, OBE, PC (d 1982); *b* 9 April 1936; *m* 1964, Timothy Mark Sergison-Brooke, s late Gen Sir Bertram Norman Sergison-Brooke, KCB, KCVO, CMG, DSO; 1 s, 1 da; *Style—* The Hon Mrs Sergison-Brooke; Chipping Warden Manor, Banbury, Oxon

SERIES, Sir (Joseph Michel) Emile; CBE (1974); *b* 29 Sept 1918; *Career* chm and gen mangr Flacq United Estates Ltd 1968-; kt 1978; *Style—* Sir Emile Series, CBE; Flacq United Estates Ltd, Union Flacq, Mauritius

SERLE, Christopher Richard; s of Frank Raymond Serle (d 1988), of Bristol, and Winifred Mary, *née* Pugsley (d 1989); *b* 13 July 1943; *Educ* Clifton, Trinity Coll Dublin; *m* 22 Jan 1983, Anna Catharine, da of Stephen Readhead Southall, of Clifford, Hereford and Worcester; 2 s (Harry b 1983, Jack b 1987); *Career* actor 1964-68, prodr BBC radio and TV 1968-78, TV journalist and presenter; programmes incl: That's Life, In At The Deep End, People; *Recreations* gliding, jazz drumming; *Style—* Christopher Serle, Esq; c/o Curtis Brown, 162-168 Regent St, London W1R 5TB (☎ 071 872 0331)

SERMON, (Thomas) Richard; s of Eric Thomas Sermon (d 1978), of Nottingham, and Marjorie Hilda, *née* Parsons (d 1969); *b* 25 Feb 1947; *Educ* Nottingham HS; *m* 10 Oct 1970, Rosemary Diane, da of Thomas Smith (d 1971), of Sheffield; 1 s (Thomas Christopher b 1971), 1 da (Catherine Marjorie b 1975); *Career* co sec Crest Hotels Ltd 1969-74, dep chm Good Relations Gp Ltd 1974-79; md: Shandwick Conslts Ltd 1979-87, Shandwick Conslt Gp plc 1987-88; chief exec: Shandwick Europe plc 1988-90, Shandwick International plc 1990-; vice pres RADAR; Freeman City of London 1968; Liveryman Worshipful Co of: Wheelwrights 1968, Chartered Secs and Adminstrators 1974; FCIS 1972; *Clubs* City of London, City Livery, Marks; *Style—* Richard Sermon, Esq; 18 Dering St, London W1R 9AF (☎ 071 355 1908, fax 071 499 1926)

SEROCOLD, Lt-Col Walter Pearce; DSO (1945), TD and Bar 1945; s of Col Oswald Pearce Serocold, CMG, DL (d 1951), of Bucks, and Gwendolyn Pearce Serocold, *née* Combe (d 1966); *b* 11 Oct 1907; *Educ* Eton, Trinity Coll Cambridge; *m* 1, 1937, Ann, da of James Whitehouse; 1 s (Edward b 1938); m 2, 24 Oct 1957, Monica Elizabeth Gibbs, da of Sir Edmund Wyldbore-Smith (d 1938); *Career* Royal Berkshire Regt (TA) 1926-41, Reconnaissance Corps 1941-44, i/c 2 Derbyshire Yeomanry 1944-45 NW Europe; dir: Watney Combe Reid & Co Ltd 1937-59, Watney Mann Ltd 1959-68; master of the Brewers Co 1953, chm Governing Body Aldenham Sch 1964-68; *Recreations* fishing, gardening, travel; *Style—* Lt-Col Walter P Serocold, DSO, TD; Ridge House, Highclere, Newbury, Berks (☎ 0635 253 523)

SEROTA, Baroness (Life Peeress UK 1967), of Hampstead in Greater London; Beatrice Serota; JP (Inner London); da of Alexander Katz; *b* 15 Oct 1919; *Educ* LSE (BSc); *m* 1942, Stanley Serota, FICE; 1 s (Hon Nicholas Andrew b 1946), 1 da (Hon Judith Alexandra Anne (Hon Mrs Pugh) b 1948); *Career* fndr chm Cmmn for Local Administration 1974-82; memb: LCC 1954-65 (chm Children's Ctee 1958-65), GLC (Lambeth) 1964-67, Advsy Cncl in Child Care and Central Trg Cncl in Child Care 1958-68, min of state DHSS 1969-70, govr BBC 1977-82, dep speaker House of Lords 1985, princ dep chm Ctees and chm Select Ctee On The Euro Communities 1986-; pres Nat Cncl for Single Parent Families 1971-; *Style—* The Rt Hon the Baroness Serota, JP; The Coach House, 15 Lyndhurst Terrace, London NW3 5QA

SEROTA, (Hon) Nicholas Andrew; o s of Baroness Serota, *qv*; does not use courtesy prefix of Hon; *b* 27 April 1946; *Educ* Haberdashers' Aske's, Christ's Coll Cambridge (BA), Courtauld Inst (MA); *m* 1973, Angela Mary Beveridge; 2 da; *Career* regnl art offr and exhibition organizer Arts Council of GB 1970-73; dir: Museum of Modern Art Oxford 1973-76, Whitechapel Art Gallery 1976-88, The Tate Gallery 1988-; Dr hc City of London Polytechnic 1989, Hon DLitt City Univ 1990; hon fell Queen Mary College Univ of London; *Style—* Nicholas Serota, Esq; c/o The Tate Gallery, Millbank, London SW1P 4RG

SERPELL, Sir David Radford; KCB (1968, CB 1962), CMG (1952), OBE (1944); s of Charles Robert Serpell (d 1949), of Plymouth, and Elsie Leila Serpell (d 1958); *b* 10 Nov 1911; *Educ* Plymouth Coll, Exeter Coll Oxford, Toulouse Univ, Syracuse Univ NY, Fletcher Sch of Law and Diplomacy USA; *m* 1 (m dis), Ann Dooley; 3 s; m 2, Doris Farr; *Career* entered Civil Service 1939, Minys of Food, Fuel and Power; under-sec Treasy 1954-60, dep sec Miny of Tport 1960-63, second sec BOT 1963-66, second perm sec 1966-68, second sec Treas 1968, perm sec Miny of Tport 1968-70, perm sec Dept of Environment 1970-72; former chm: Nature Conservancy Cncl, Ordnance Survey Review Ctee; former memb Cncl Nat Tst; memb: British Railways Bd 1974-82, NERC 1973-76; chm of Independent Ctee to review BR's finances 1982; *Recreations* golf, walking; *Clubs* Utd Oxford and Cambridge Univ; *Style—* Sir David Serpell, KCB, CMG, OBE; 25 Crossparks, Dartmouth, Devon TQ6 9HP (☎ 0803 832073)

SERRELL-WATTS, D'Arcy John; s of John Serrell-Watts, CBE, JP (d 1975), of Marlow Place, Bucks, and Cynthia Mary, *née* Mason (d 1969); *b* 12 May 1939; *Educ* Harrow, Lincoln Coll Oxford; *m* 1, 1962 (m dis 1972), Lyn, *née* Tippetts; 1 s (Sebastian John b 1965), 1 da (Arabella Alice b 1968); m 2, 1977 (m dis), Linda, *née* Berry; m 3, 30 June 1987, Slyvaine, da of Comte Bernard de Robinet de Plas; *Career* md HTS Mgmnt Conslts Ltd 1964, vice pres Golightly Int NY 1974, md London Car Telephones Ltd 1982; underwriting memb of Lloyds 1977; Freeman City of London 1960, Warden Worshipful Co of Saddlers 1988; *Recreations* shooting, skiing, vegetable gardening; *Clubs* Turf; *Style*— D'Arcy Serrell-Watts, Esq; Bacons Farm, Bradwell-on-Sea, Essex; 9 Bedford Gardens House, London W8 7EE (☎ 071 727 2918, fax 071 221 5949)

SERVATIUS, Hon Mrs (Prunella Jane Alice); da of 9 Baron Hawke (d 1985); *b* 1951; *Educ* Heathfield Sch, Royal Acad of Fine Arts The Hague; *m* 1976, Albert Hendrik Servatius; 2 s (Timothy b 1979, Julian b 1982); *Style*— The Hon Mrs Servatius; Van Alkemadelaan 354, 2597 AS The Hague, Netherlands

SERVICE, Alastair Stanley Douglas; s of Lt Cdr Douglas Service (d 1976), and Evelyn Caroline, *née* Sharp (d 1986); *b* 8 May 1933; *Educ* Westminster, Queen's Coll Oxford; *m* 1959 (m dis 1984), Louisa Anne, *qv*, da of Lt-Col Henry Hemming; 1 s, 1 da; *Career* writer and publisher; chm: Birth Control Campaign 1970-74, Family Planning Assoc 1975-79, vice-chm Health Educn Cncl 1979-87, gen sec Family Planning Assoc 1980-89, dep chm Health Educn Authy 1987-89, memb Wessex Regnl Health Authy 1989-; *Books incl* A Birth Control Plan for Britain (jtly, 1972), Edwardian Architecture and its Origins (1975), The Architects of London, 1066-Today (1979), Lost Worlds (1981), A Guide to the Megaliths of Europe (1981), Anglo-Saxon and Norman Buildings of Britain (1982), Edwardian Interiors (1982), Victorian and Edwardian Hampstead (1989); *Recreations* cycling, opera, the pursuit of stone circles, mounds and historic buildings; *Clubs* Garrick; *Style*— Alastair Service Esq; Swan House, Avebury, Wilts SN8 1RA (☎ 06723 312)

SERVICE, Graham Andrew; s of Malcolm James Service, of Highcliffe, Dorset, and Janette Sophia, *née* McAdam; *b* 3 June 1947; *Educ* Kingston GS, Trinity Coll Oxford (BA); *m* 28 June 1974, Susan Elizabeth, da of John Ernest Brooke, of Woking, Surrey; 2 s (Timothy b 1980, Jonathan b 1984); *Career* CA Longcrofts 1969-73, dir corporate fin Hill Samuel Bank Ltd 1973-; FCA 1973; *Style*— Graham Service, Esq; Eagle Lodge, Mile Path, Hook Heath, Woking, Surrey GU22 0JX; 100 Wood St, London EC2P 2AJ (☎ 071 628 8011)

SERVICE, Hon Mrs (Helen); MBE, JP, DL; da of 2 Baron Loch, CB, CMG, MVO, DSO (d 1942); *b* 1919; *m* 1947, G Ronald Service (d 1961); 1 s; *Style*— The Hon Mrs Service, MBE, JP, DL; Kinfauns House, Kinfauns, by Perth

SERVICE, Louisa Anne; JP (1969); da of Lt-Col Henry Harold Hemming, OBE, MC (d 1976), of 35 Elsworthy Rd, London NW3, and Alice Louisa, *née* Weaver, OBE; *b* 13 Dec 1931; *Educ* schs in Canada, France, USA and UK, St Hilda's Coll Oxford (BA, MA); *m* 28 Feb 1959 (m dis 1984), Alastair Stanley Douglas Service (*qv*), s of Lt Cdr Douglas Service (d 1976), of 16 Reddington Rd, London NW3; 1 s (Nicholas Alastair McFee Douglas b 9 May 1961), 1 da (Sophia Alice Louisa Douglas b 20 April 1963); *Career* export dir Ladybird Electric 1955-59; jt chm: Municipal Group of Cos 1976- (fin dir 1966-76), Hemming Publishing 1985-; chm Glass's Guide Service Ltd 1981- (dir 1971-, dep chm 1976-81); memb Mgmnt Ctee Friends of Covent Garden 1982-, chm Mayer-Lismann Opera Workshop 1976-, chm Youth and Music 1990- (memb Cncl 1987-), memb Cncl Haydn/Mozart Soc 1990, hon sec Womans India Assoc 1967-74, dep chm Paddington Probation Hostel 1976-86; chm: Hackney Juvenile Ct 1975-82, Westminster Juvenile Ct 1982-88, Hammersmith and Fulham Juvenile Ct; memb: Dept of Trade's Consumer Credit Appeals Panel 1981-, FIMBRA Appeals Tribunal 1989-, Inner London Family Panel 1991; FRGS; *Recreations* music, travel, reading; *Clubs* Arts; *Style*— Ms Louisa A Service, JP; c/o Hemming Publishing Ltd, 32 Vauxhall Bridge Road, London SW1V 2SS (☎ 071 973 6404, fax 071 233 5049, telex 071 233 5082)

SESSFORD, George Minshull; *see*: Moray Ross and Caithness, Bishop of

SETCHELL, David Lloyd; s of Raymond Setchell (d 1967), and Phyllis Jane Setchell (d 1952); *b* 16 April 1937; *Educ* Woodhouse GS, Jesus Coll Cambridge (MA); *m* 11 Aug 1962, Muriel Mary, *née* Davies; 1 s (Andrew b 1970), 1 da (Justine b 1967); *Career* CA; Peat Marwick London 1960-64, Shawinigan Ltd 1964-71; mktg mangr Gulf Oil Chemicals (Europe) 1971-77 (vice-pres 1978-82), md Gulf Oil (GB) Ltd 1982-; dir UK Petroleum Industry Assoc; FCA; *Recreations* golf, tennis, theatre; *Clubs* Oriental, MCC, St George's Hill Golf, Cotswold Hills Golf; *Style*— David Setchell, Esq; South Hayes, Sandy Lane Rd, Cheltenham, Glos GL53 9DE (☎ 0242 571390); Gulf Oil (GB) Ltd, The Quadrangle, Imperial Square, Cheltenham GL50 1TF (☎ 0242 225300, fax 0242 225213, telex 43542)

SETCHELL, Marcus Edward; s of Eric Hedley Setchell (d 1980), of Cambridge, and Barbara Mary, *née* Whitworth; *b* 4 Oct 1943; *Educ* Felsted Sch, Univ of Cambridge, St Bartholomew's Hosp Med Coll (MA, MB BChir); *m* 1973, Sarah Loveday, da of Vernon Alfred Robert French (d 1967), of Middx; 2 s (Thomas b 1976, David b 1984), 2 da (Anna b 1974, Catherine b 1980); *Career* surgn and gynaecologist to The Queen; conslt gynaecologist and obstetrician: St Bartholomew's Hosp, King Edward VII Hosp for Offrs, St Luke's Hosp for the Clergy; dir Fertility Unit Portland Hosp; contributor: Ten Teachers Gynaecology (1990), Ten Teachers Obstetrics (1990), Progress in Obstetrics and Gynaecology (1987), General Surgical Operations (1982), Scientific Foundations of Obstetrics & Gynaecology (ed, 1991); FRCS, FRCSEd, FRCOG; *Recreations* tennis, skiing, travel, gardening; *Clubs* Royal Soc of Medicine (Cncl memb), Fountain, St Albans Medical; *Style*— Marcus Setchell, Esq; 64 Wood Vale, London N10 3DN (☎ 081 444 5266); 137 Harley Street, London W1 (☎ 071 935 6122)

SETCHELL, Michael Robert; s of George Robert Setchell (d 1989), of Bedford, and Violet, *née* Cooper; *b* 22 March 1944; *Educ* Bedford Modern Sch, Guy's Hosp Dental Sch, Univ of London (BDS, LDS, MRCS); *m* 5 Aug 1967, Mary, da of late Cecil Richardson; 1 s (Alexander Michael b 19 April 1976), 1 da (Joanne Mary b 26 May 1973); *Career* dental practitioner; Guy's Hosp: res house surgn 1966-67, registrar in dental conservation 1967-69, pt/t lectr (Dental Sch) in conservative dentistry 1969-72; pt/t gen practice with Mr C I Hagger Dulwich 1968-70, full time practitioner in Devonshire Place London 1972- (pt/t 1970-72); memb: BDA, The Dental Soc of London 1987 (currently treas); *Recreations* gardening, photography, hill walking; *Clubs* Rotary Int, Langley Park Rotary (past pres); *Style*— Michael Setchell, Esq; Glynn, Setchell & Allan, 35 Devonshire Place, London W1N 1PE (☎ 071 935 3342)

SETCHIM, Hon Mrs (Marjorie Elizabeth); *née* Yerburgh; da (by 1 m) of 1 Baron Alvingham (d 1955); *b* 1916; *m* 1, 1938, Abdul Hamid Mustafa Risk; 1 da; m 2, 1952, Leon Setchim; 2 s; *Style*— The Hon Mrs Setchim; 134 Lynton Rd, London W3

SETH-SMITH, Hon Mrs (Gabrielle Mary); *née* Sclater-Booth; yst da of 3 Baron Basing, TD (d 1969); *b* 18 Jan 1929; *m* 1953, Cdr Martin Parnell Seth-Smith, RN, s of Brig Hugh Garden Seth-Smith, DSO; 1 s (Nicholas John b 1961), 1 da (Imogen Gabrielle b 1963); *Career* LTCL; *Style*— The Hon Mrs Seth-Smith; The Triangle, Wildhern, Andover, Hants

SETH-SMITH, Hon Mrs (Moana Elizabeth Jean); *née* McGowan; da of 2 Baron McGowan (d 1966); *b* 1948; *m* 1978, John David Vaughan Seth-Smith; *Style*— The Hon Mrs Seth-Smith

SETHIA, Babulal; s of Babulal Sethia (d 1974), and Joan, *née* Gridley; *b* 9 Feb 1951; *Educ* Rugby, St Thomas' Hosp (BSc, MB BS); *m* 16 Dec 1978, Nicola Jane, da of Alan Thomas Austin, of Edgbaston, Birmingham; 1 s (Ashok James b 1990), 2 da (India Jane b 1984, Nalini Joanne b 1988); *Career* conslt cardiac surgn Birmingham Childrens Hosp and Queen Elizabeth Hosp 1987-, hon sr lectr Dept of Surgery Univ of Birmingham 1989-; pubns on aspects of acquired and congenital heart disease; FRCS 1981; memb: Soc of Thoracic and Cardiovascular Surgns 1983, Euro Assoc For Cardiothoracic Surgery 1988, Br Cardiac Soc 1989; *Recreations* music, reading, oenology; *Style*— Babulal Sethia, Esq; The Childrens Hosptital, Birmingham B16 8ET (☎ 021 454 4851); Dept Cardiac Surgery, Queen Elizabeth Hospital, Birmingham B15 2TH (☎ 021 472 1311)

SETON, Sir Iain Bruce; 13 Bt (NS 1663), of Abercorn, Linlithgowshire; s of Sir (Christopher) Bruce Seton, 12 Bt (d 1988); *b* 27 Aug 1942; *Educ* Colchester, Chadacre Agric Inst; *m* 1963, Margaret Ann, o da of Walter Charles Faulkner, of Barlee Road, W Australia: 1 s (Laurence Bruce), 1 da (Amanda Jane b 1971); *Heir* s, Laurence Bruce Seton b 1 July 1968; *Style*— Sir Iain Seton, Bt; PO Box 253, Bridgetown 6255, W Australia

SETON, James Christall; s of late Christall Seton, gs of 7 Bt; hp of kinsman, Sir Robert Seton, 11 Bt; *b* 21 Jan 1913; *m* 1939, Evelyn, da of Ray Hafer; *Career* Private US Army; *Style*— James Seton, Esq; 814 Buckeye St, Miamisburg, Ohio, USA

SETON, Joyce, Lady; Joyce Vivien; *née* Barnard; er da of late Oliver George Barnard, of Lockington House, Stowmarket, Suffolk; *m* 1939, Sir Christopher Bruce Seton, 12 Bt (d 1988); 2 s (Sir Iain Bruce, 13 Bt, *qv*, Michael Charles b 1944), 2 da (Sarah Ann (Mrs Good) (twin) b 1944, Joanna Mary (Mrs Gillespie) b 1946); *Style*— Joyce, Lady Seton; Flat 1B, Papillon House, Balkerne Gdns, Colchester CO1 1PR (☎ 0206 43364)

SETON, Lady; Julia; OBE; da of late Frank Clements; *m* 1962, as his 3 w, Sir Alexander Hay Seton, 10 Bt (d 1963); *Career* VMH; writer as Julia Clements; *Style*— Lady Seton, OBE; 122 Swan Court, Chelsea Manor St, London SW3 5RU

SETON, Sir Robert James; 11 Bt (NS 1683) of Pitmedden, Aberdeenshire; s of Capt Sir John Hastings Seton, 10 Bt (d 1956); *b* 20 April 1926; *Educ* HMS Worcester (Thames Nautical Training Coll) 1940-43; *Heir* kinsman, James Seton, *qv*; *Career* midshipman RNVR 1943-45; banker The Hong Kong and Shanghai Bank, ret 1961; *Recreations* philately; *Style*— Sir Robert Seton, Bt; 4B Morella Rd, Balham, London SW12 8UH

SEVERIN, Prof Dorothy Sherman; da of Wilbur B Sherman, of Dallas, USA, and Virginia, *née* Tucker; *b* 24 March 1942; *Educ* Harvard (AB, AM, PhD); *m* 24 March 1966 (m dis 1979), Giles Timothy Severin; 1 da (Ida); *Career* tutor Harvard Univ 1964-66, visiting lectr Univ of West Indies 1967-68, asst prof Vassar Coll NY 1968-69, lectr Westfield Coll London 1969-82, Gilmour prof of Spanish Univ of Liverpool 1982- (ed Bulletin of Hispanic Studies 1982-); visiting assoc prof: Harvard Univ 1982, Columbia Univ NY 1985, Yale Univ 1985; pro vice chllr Liverpool 1989-92; memb: Int Courtly Lit Soc (former pres Br branch), Ctee Modern Humanities Res Assoc, Assoc of Hispanists of GB and I; FSA; *Books* Memory in La Celestina (1970), Diego de San Pedro, La pasión trobada (1973), La Lengua de Erasmo romançada por muy elegante estilo (ed, 1975), Diego de San Pedro, Poesía (ed with Keith Whinnom, 1979), Cosas sacadas de la crónica del rey Juan II (ed with Angus Mackay, 1982), Celestina (edns 1969, 1987), Celestina with the Translation of James Mabbe 1631 (ed, 1987), Tragicomedy and Novelistic Discourse in Celestina (1989), Cancionero de Oñate-Castañeda (1990); *Style*— Prof Dorothy Severin, FSA; Department of Hispanic Studies, University of Liverpool, PO Box 147, Liverpool L69 3BX (☎ 051 794 2773, fax 051 708 6502, telex 627095 UNILPL G)

SEVERIN, Giles Timothy (Tim); s of Maurice Watkins, and Inge Severin; *b* 25 Sept 1940; *Educ* Tonbridge Sch, Keble Coll Oxford (MA, BLitt); *m* 1966 (m dis 1979), Dorothy Virginia Sherman; 1 da; *Career* author, film maker, historian, traveller; expeditions: led motorcycle team along Marco Polo route 1961, river Mississippi by canoe and launch 1965, Brendan Voyage from W Ireland to N America 1977, Sindbad voyage from Oman to China 1980-81, Jason Voyage from Iolkos to Colchis 1984, Ulysses Voyage from Troy to Ithaca 1985, First Crusade route by horse to Jerusalem 1987-88, travels on horseback in Mongolia 1990; films: The Brendan Voyage, The Sindbad Voyage, The Jason Voyage, Crusader, In Search of Genghis Khan; Founders medal RES, Livingstone medal RGS (Scotland), Sir Percy Sykes medal RSAA; *publications:* Tracking Marco Polo (1964), Explorers of the Mississippi (1967), The Golden Antilles (1970), Vanishing Primitive Man (1973), The African Adventure (1973), The Oriental Adventure (1978), The Brendan Voyage (1978), The Sindbad Voyage (1982), The Jason Voyage (1985), The Ulysses Voyage (1987), Crusader (1989); *Style*— Tim Severin, Esq; Courtmacsherry, Co Cork, Eire (☎ 010 353 23 46127)

SEVERIS, Nicolas Constantine; s of Constantine Demosthenes Severis (d 1991), of Nicosia, Cyprus, and Leto Severis; *b* 12 Oct 1943; *Educ* Giggleswick Sch, St John's Coll Cambridge (MA); *m* 1967, Michèle Louise, da of Frederick François, of Antwerp; 1 s (Constantine), 1 da (Alexia); *Career* banker; md Bank of Cyprus (London) Ltd 1969-75, gen mangr American Express Bank Belgium 1978-79, administratore delegato and direttore generale American Express Bank SPA 1979-81; gen mangr: Amex Bank Ltd 1981-82, FVP Europe, M East and Africa Private Banking 1982; central mangr Trade Devpt Bank Geneva, gen mangr Franck & Cie SA Bankers 1987; *Recreations* golf, tennis, squash; *Clubs* Travellers', RAC, Bonmont (Switzerland); *Style*— Nicolas Severis, Esq; 42 Rue De L'Athenee, 1206 Geneva

SEVERN, Prof Roy Thomas; s of Ernest Severn (d 1985), of Gt Yarmouth, Norfolk, and Muriel Breeta, *née* Woollatt (d 1978); *b* 6 Sept 1929; *Educ* Deacon's Sch Peterborough, Gt Yarmouth GS, Imperial Coll London (BSc, PhD, DSc); *m* 12 Sept 1957, Hilary Irene, da of Harold Batty Saxton, of Douglas, IOM; 2 da (Fiona Rae b 1960, Elizabeth Louise b 1962); *Career* 2 Lt RE (Survey) 1954-56; lectr Imperial Coll London 1952-54; Univ of Bristol: lectr 1956-65, reader 1965-68, prof 1968-, pro vice chllr 1981-84; memb: UGC Tech Sub Ctee 1982-89, Engrg Bd SERC 1986-90; pres Inst of Civil Engrs 1990-91; FICE, FEng 1982; *Books* Advances in Structural Engineering (1982); *Recreations* sailing, gardening, bee-keeping; *Style*— Prof Roy Severn; Department of Civil Engineering, University of Bristol, Bristol BS8 ITR (☎ 0272 303278, fax 0272 251154, telex 445938)

SEVERNE, Air Vice-Marshal Sir John de Milt; KCVO (1988, LVO 1961), OBE (1968), AFC (1955); s of Dr Alfred de Milt Severne (d 1967), and Joane Mary Margaret, *née* Haydon; *b* 15 Aug 1925; *Educ* Marlborough; *m* 1951, Katharine Veronica, da of Capt Vero Elliot Kemball, RN (d 1963); 3 da (Veronica, Amanda, Christina); *Career* joined RAF 1944, flying instr RAF Coll Cranwell 1948, staff instr Central Flying Sch 1950, Flt Cdr 98 Sqn 1954, Sqdn Cdr 26 Sqdn 1956, Air Miny 1958, Equerry to HRH The Duke of Edinburgh 1958, Staff Coll 1962, Chief Instr 226 OCU 1963, Jt Servs Staff Coll 1965, Jt HQ Middle East Cmd Aden and Air Advsr to S Arabian Govt 1966, directing staff Jt Servs Staff Coll 1968, Gp Capt ORG HQ STC 1968, Station cdr RAF Kinloss 1971, Royal Coll of Def Studies 1973, Cmdt CFS 1974, Air Cdre Flying Trg HQRAFSC 1976, Cdr Southern Maritime Air Region 1978, ret RAF 1980; Capt of The Queen's Flight 1982-89; ADC to HM The Queen 1972-73; pres SW Area RAFA 1981; Hon Air Cdre No 3 (County of Devon) Maritime Headquarters Unit RAuxAF 1990; won Kings Cup Air Race and Br Air Racing Champion 1960; pres RAF Equitation Assoc 1976-79 (chm 1973); *Style*— Air Vice-Marshal Sir John Severne, KCVO, OBE, AFC; c/o National Westminster Bank plc, 9 York Buildings, Cornhill, Bridgwater, Somerset TA6 3BA

SEVERNE, Michael Meysey Wigley; s of Capt Edmund Charles Wigley Severne (d

1935), of Thenford House, Banbury, Oxon, and Cecily Mary, *née* Burden-Muller (d 1981); *b* 15 Feb 1922; *Educ* Eton, Jesus Coll Cambridge; *m* 15 April 1952, (Giralda) Rachel, da of Desmond Fitz-Gerald, 28 Knight of Glin (d 1949), of Glin Castle, Co Limerick; 1 da (Amanda Caroline b 1954); *Career* RMA Sandhurst 1940-41, Capt Coldstream Guards 1942-47; dir Damancy Co Ltd (now Aspro Nicholas) 1948-65; md: Technacryl Ltd 1967-, Aluminium and Plastics Ltd 1967-, Argo Plastics Ltd 1980-; *Recreations* shooting, fishing; *Style—* Michael Severne, Esq; Shakenhurst Hall, Cleobury Mortimer, nr Kidderminster, Worcs (☎ 029922 300); 44 Cheyne Ct, Royal Hospital Rd, London SW3 5TS (☎ 071 352 1270, car 0836 260 953)

SEVITT, Dr Michael Andrew; s of Simon Sevitt (d 1988), of Birmingham, and Betty, *née* Woolf; *b* 13 Oct 1944; *Educ* King Edward's Sch Birmingham, Kings Coll Cambridge, UCH Med Sch London; *m* 12 Sept 1970, Dr Jennifer Margaret Duckham, da of William John Duckham, of London; 1 s (Timothy b 1974), 1 da (Deborah b 1976); *Career* lectr in psychiatry Univ of Southampton 1974-76, conslt in adolescent psychiatry SW Thames RHA 1978-; chm Assoc for Family Therapy; psychiatric advsr: Relate, Samaritans; MRCP 1971, MRCPsych 1974, MInstGPAnal 1979; *Recreations* theatre, music, gardening, supporting Wimbledon FC; *Style—* Dr Michael Sevitt; 7 Upper Park Rd, Kingston upon Thames, Surrey KT2 5LB (☎ 01 546 4173); Regional Adolescent Unit, Long Grove Hospital, Epsom, Surrey KT19 8PU (☎ 0372 729136)

SEWARD, David George; s of Arthur Ernest Seward, of Friern Barnet, London N11, and Vera Evelyn, *née* Todd (d 1989); *b* 23 Jan 1944; *Educ* Woodhouse GS Finchley, St Luke's Coll Exeter; *m* 13 Aug 1966, Barbara Louise, da of William Leslie Nichols (d 1959); 1 s (Jonathan David b 25 Jan 1970), 1 da (Joanna Louise b 4 April 1968); *Career* cricket administrator; playing career: Middlesex Grammar Schs 1959-61, Middlesex Young Amateurs 1960-61, Finchley 1959-66, St Luke's Coll Exeter 1962-65, Taunton 1967-72, Somerset CCC 2nd XI 1967; sec Somerset CCC 1980-82, mktg mangr Nottinghamshire CCC 1983-87, sec Surrey CCC 1987-; teacher: King's Coll Jr Sch Taunton 1966-69, Priory Jr Sch Taunton 1969-71; dep headteacher Holway Primary Sch Taunton 1971-73; headmaster: Warner C of E Primary Sch Loughborough 1973-76, Wilford C of E Primary Sch Nottingham 1976-80; LTCL; *Recreations* playing golf, piano and organ playing (organist St John the Evangelist Church Taunton and Loughborough Parish Church); *Style—* David Seward, Esq; Secretary, Surrey CCC, The Oval, Kennington, London SE11 5SS (☎ 071 582 6660, fax 071 735 7769)

SEWARD, Desmond; s of Maj W E L Seward, MC (d 1975); *b* 22 May 1935; *Educ* Ampleforth, St Catharine's Coll Cambridge (BA); *Career* author; Knight SMO Malta 1978; *Books* The First Bourbon (1971), The Monks of War (1972), Prince of the Renaissance (1973), The Bourbon Kings of France (1976), Eleanor of Aquitaine (1978), The Hundred Years War (1978), Monks and Wine (1979), Marie Antoinette (1981), Richard III (1983), Naples (1984), Italy's Knights of St George (1986), Napoleon's Family (1986), Henry V (1987), Napoleon and Hitler (1988), Byzantium (with Susan Mountgarret, 1988); *Recreations* walking, France, Italy; *Clubs* Brooks's, Pratt's, Puffin's (Edinburgh); *Style—* Desmond Seward, Esq; 53/54 Regency Square, Brighton, E Sussex BN1 2FF (☎ 0273 23914)

SEWARD, Lady; Ella Maud; da of Frederick L'Estrange Wallace by his w Gwendoline, *née* Gilling-Lax; *m* 1924, Sir Eric Seward, KBE, sometime chm British Chamber of Commerce in The Argentine (d 1981); 3 s; *Style—* Lady Seward; Dr G Rawson 2420, 1636 Olivos, Provincia de Buenos Aires, Argentina

SEWARD, Prof Gordon Robert; CBE (1990); s of Percy Robert Seward (d 1968), and Ruth Marie, *née* Mackenzie; *b* 18 Dec 1925; *Educ* Grocers Co Sch, Univ of London (MDS, MB BS); *m* 5 May 1962, Margaret Helen Elizabeth, da of John Hutton Mitchell (d 1970); 1 s (Colin Robert b 9 Sept 1966), 1 da (Pamela Elizabeth b 31 May 1964); *Career* Nat Serv Lt and Capt RADC 1949-50, Capt RADC (TA) 167 City of London Field Ambulance 1950-54; Dept of Oral and Maxillofacial Surgery The London Hosp Med Coll: sr lectr 1960-62, reader 1962-68, prof 1968-, dean of dental studies 1975-79; conslt advisor CMO and CDO 1980-86, dean Faculty of Dental Surgery RCS 1986-89; RCS: memb Bd of Faculty Dental Surgery 1977-, vice dean 1983, dean 1986-89, memb Cncl RCS 1985-84 and 1986-; memb: City and E London AHA 1976-80, Jt Conslts Ctee 1986-89, Conf Med Royal Colls 1986-89, Dental Educn Advsy Cncl 1975-79; emeritus prof or oral and maxillo-facial surgery; pres London Hosp Dental Club 1983-84; awarded Turner medal of BDA 1990; Hon FRCSEd 1986, Hon FRSC 1987, Hon FFARCS 1988; memb: BDA, RSM (vice pres section of odontology 1975-78, pres 1987-88), EACMFS, BAOMFS (pres 1981-82); FDS; *Books* Outline of Oral Surgery (jtly, 1971), Short Practice of Surgery (contrib, 1976), Surgery of the Mouth and Jaws (contrib, 1986); *Recreations* painting, walking, photography, woodwork; *Style—* Prof Gordon Seward, CBE; Dept Oral and Maxillo Facial Surgery, The London Hospital Medical College, Turner St, Whitechapel E1 2AD (☎ 071 377 7050)

SEWARD, John Richard Gowing; s of Henry Thomas Seward (d 1980), of Bramhall, and Helen Margaret, *née* Gowing (d 1974); *b* 6 Jan 1929; *Educ* Uppingham, Manchester Univ (Dip Arch); *m* 28 July 1955, (Anne) Hilary, da of George Reginald Davies (d 1978), of Marford; 1 s (Charles b 1963), 3 da (Nicola b 1961, Deborah b 1970, Anna b 1973); *Career* Nat Serv 2 Lt 7 Armd Div Engr Regt 1953-55; architect, sr ptnr Crickshank of Seward; princ buildings: HQ Royal London Mutual Insur Soc, Colchester Church and Chaplaincy Manchester Univ, Queen's Elms Halls of Residence Queen's Univ Belfast, Res and Devpt Bldgs ICL West Gorton; pres Manchester Soc Architects 1975-76; RIBA: chm Northwest Region 1977-78, chm Practice Ctee 1980-81, vice-pres 1980-81; pres: Manchester FC, Gentleman of Cheshire CC; tstee: Uppingham Sch, Broughton House Old Soldiers Home; dep chm of Cncl UMIST; FRIBA 1968, FRSA 1982; *Recreations* sport, painting; *Clubs* St James (Manchester), MCC, Free Foresters Cricket; *Style—* John Seward, Esq; The Garden Wood, Henshaw Lane, Siddington, Macclesfield, Cheshire SK11 9JW (☎ 02604 383); Cruickshank & Seward, Architects, Planners, Designers, Royal London Ho, 196 Deansgate, Manchester M3 3WP (☎ 061 832 6161, fax 061 832 0820)

SEWELL, Sir (John) Allan; ISO (1968); s of late George Allan Sewell; *b* 23 July 1915; *Educ* Enoggera State Sch, Brisbane GS; *m* 1939, Thelma (d 1965), da of H S Buchholz; 1 s, 1 da; *Career* dir local govt Qld 1948-61, under-treas of Qld 1961-69, former auditor-gen of Qld; chm State Electricty Cmmn; dir: Qld Alumina Ltd, Crusader Oil; dep chllr Griffiths Univ; AASA, ACIS, FIMA; kt 1977; *Style—* Sir Allan Sewell, ISO

SEWELL, (Edward Rainforth) Andrew; MC (1942); s of E O Sewell, OBE, MC (d 1979), and Lucy Theodora, *née* Walker (d 1934); *b* 23 Feb 1921; *Educ* Marlborough; *m* 11 Sept 1953, Ishbel, da of Dr J Milne, MC (d 1943); 1 s (John b 1958), 3 da (Anne b 1954, Rosemary b 1956 d 1982, Elspeth b 1961); *Career* Regular Army 1939-73; war serv Lanarkshire Yeo RA, Malaya; R & D MOD: HM Civil Serv 1973-81, princ DOE and Dept Tport, regnl offr Countryside Cmmn, chief admin offr Dept Tport SW Region; chm Wilts Archaeological and Natural History Soc 1987-90; *Recreations* archaeology, local history; *Style—* Andrew Sewell, Esq, MC; Bay House, Aldbourne, Wiltshire

SEWELL, Brian; *Career* art critic The Evening Standard; *Style—* Brian Sewell, Esq; The Evening Standard, Northcliffe House, 2 Derry Street, Kensington, London W8 5EE (☎ 071 938 6000, fax 071 937 3193)

SEWELL, Maj David Nigel Wynn; eld s of Maj Geoffrey Richard Michael Sewell (d 1983), of Tysoe Manor, Tysoe, Warwick, and Joan (d 1990), yst da of Sir Watkin Williams-Wynn, 8 Bt; *b* 4 April 1953; *Educ* Harrow; *m* 17 April 1982, Julia Anne; 2 s (Percy b 1984, Herbert b 1986); *Career* cmmnd Grenadier Gds 1974, served BAOR, N Ireland, Berlin, London; *Recreations* shooting, fishing, woodwork; *Style—* Maj David Sewell; Midland Bank plc, Shipston-on-Stour, Warwick; HQ London District, Horseguards, Whitehall, London SW1A 2AX

SEWELL, Prof John Isaac; s of Harry Sewell (d 1975), of Kirkby Stephen, Cumbria, and Dorothy, *née* Brunskill (d 1977); *b* 13 May 1942; *Educ* Kirkby Stephen GS, Univ of Durham (BSc), Univ of Newcastle upon Tyne (PhD); *m* 6 May 1989, Ruth Alexandra, da of Walter Baxter (d 1986), of Edinburgh; *Career* reader in integrated electronic systems Univ of Hull 1984-85 (lectr 1968-76, sr lectr 1976-84), prof of electronic systems Univ of Glasgow 1985- (dean of engrg 1989-); FIEE 1986 (sr memb IEE 1977); *Recreations* climbing, swimming; *Style—* Prof John Sewell; 62 St Germains, Drymen Rd, Bearsden, Glasgow G61 2RS (☎ 041 943 0729); Dept of Electronics and Electrical Engineering, University of Glasgow, Glasgow G12 8QQ (☎ 041 3398855, fax 041 3304907, telex 777070 UNIGLA G)

SEWELL, Col John Walter (Toby); s of Lt-Col Edward Owen Sewell, OBE, MC (d 1978), of Radlett, Herts, and Lucy Theodora, *née* Walker (d 1934); *b* 13 Jan 1923; *Educ* Marlborough; *m* 29 Jan 1948, Muriel Maureen, da of Leonard Hyde, of Lincoln; 1 s (Nicholas b 1951), 1 da (Sarah (Mrs Wadham) b 1949); *Career* enlisted Grenadier Gds 1941, cmmnd Queen's Royal Regt 1942, Italy 1943-45 (wounded, despatches twice), India 1946-47, seconded Para Regt 1947-53, Palestine 1948, Staff Coll Camberley 1954, Egypt 1955, Cyprus 1955-56, Aden and Hong Kong 1962-63, Borneo 1965, cmd 1 Bn Queens Royal Surrey Regt/Queen's Regt Germany and Bahrein 1965-68, Col 1969, sr army liaison offr RAF 1972-74, ret 1978; re-employed (RO 1) as schs liaison offr 1978-83; pres Queen's Royal Surrey Regt Assoc 1983-89, chm Diocesan Advsy Ctee Guildford Diocese 1987; Freeman: City of London 1953, Worshipful Co of Merchant Taylors 1953; FBIM 1979; *Clubs* Army & Navy; *Style—* Col J W Sewell; Uplands, Grayswood Road, Haslemere, Surrey GU27 2BS (☎ 0428 644543)

SEWELL, Nigel John; s of Charles John Sewell (d 1985), and Vera Kathleen, *née* Swann; *b* 27 April 1948; *Educ* Thames Poly, Int Mgmnt Centres (MBA); *m* 1972, Mary Ann, da of Alfred James Freeman; 2 da (Joy Rosemary b 13 May 1976, Eleanor Mary b 23 March 1979); *Career* legal and co secretarial asst J Lyons and Company Ltd 1967-71, mgmnt trainee SE Thames RHA 1971-73, dep hosp mangr Bromley AHA 1973-75, sector admin King's Health Dist 1975-80, gen mangr Acute Servs Unit Merton and Sutton Health Authy 1986-90 (sector admin 1980-86), chief exec St Helier NHS Tst 1990; FBIM 1990, fell Inst of Health Servs Mgmnt 1990; *Recreations* opera, swimming; *Style—* Nigel Sewell, Esq; 21 Wilmot Way, Banstead, Surrey SM7 2PZ (☎ 0737 355837); St Helier Hospital, Wrythe Lane, Carshalton, Surrey SM5 1AA (☎ 081 644 4343)

SEWELL, Robert Henry; s of Dr James Scott Sewell (d 1952), and Emily, *née* Patton (d 1960); *b* 21 Sept 1920; *Educ* Bolton Sch, Univ of Manchester, Manchester Royal Infirmary (BSc, MB ChB, MRCS, LRCP, ChM); *m* 20 July 1945, (Peggy) Joan Kearton, da of Albert Chandler (d 1970), of The Gables, Kingswood Way, Selsdon, Sanderstead, Surrey; 2 da (Gay Whittaker b 1949, Cherry Sewell b 1951); *Career* RAMC cmmnd Lt 1946, Capt 1947, surgn to N and S Caribbean Cmds 1946-48; house appts Manchester Royal Infirmary 1943-46, registrar and sr registrar Royal Nat Orthopaedic Hosp London 1948-52, conslt orthopaedic surgn Greenwich 1952-83; memb Greenwich DHA 1970; Freeman City of London, Liveryman Worshipful Soc of Apothecaries; FRCS (chm), FRCSEd; *Recreations* travel, gardening, bridge; *Style—* Robert Sewell, Esq; 4 Bayards, Warlingham, Surrey CR6 9BP (☎ 0883 624343)

SEWELL-RUTTER, John Stuart; s of Albert Alfred Sewell-Rutter (d 1983), and Edith, *née* Greeno; *b* 28 Aug 1943; *Educ* Harrow Co GS, London Poly Sch of Commerce, Brunel Univ (BSc, MTech); *m* 15 Sept 1973, Jean Joseanne, da of Ronald Norman Wood (d 1989), of Battenhall, Worcester; 1 s (Neil b 2 June 1976); *Career* market res asst Nabisco Ltd 1963-64, mktg servs mangr Leo Burnett Co Ltd 1964-68, brand mangr Cadbury-Schweppes Ltd 1968-71, mktg mangr Tower Housewares Ltd 1971-73; md: Whitecroft-Scovill Ltd 1982-87 (mktg dir 1973-82), J & J Cash Ltd 1987-; former chm: Tewkesbury Round Table (pres), Tewkesbury Carnival Ctee Tewkesbury 41 Club; fndr memb Bredon Hill Rotary Club, life memb Nat Tst, life fell Wild Fowl Tst; MBIM, MInstM; *Recreations* golf, donkeys, country life; *Clubs* Tewkesbury Park Golf and Country; *Style—* John Sewell-Rutter, Esq; J & J Cash Ltd, Torrington Ave, Coventry CV4 9UZ (☎ 0203 466 466, fax 0203 462 525, telex 31397 Cash CVG)

SEXTON, Maj-Gen Francis Michael; CB (1980), OBE (1966); s of Timothy Sexton, and Catherine Regan; *b* 15 July 1923; *Educ* Oxford Univ (MA); *m* 1947, Naomi, da of Bertram Alonzo Middleton; 1 s (Christopher), 1 da (Deborah); *Career* dir Military Survey 1980, inspr Panel of Independant Insprs 1980, bursar St Peters Coll Oxford 1980-85 (fell); *Clubs* MCC, Army and Navy, Geographical Soc; *Style—* Maj-Gen Michael Sexton, CB, OBE; Pipers Croft, Elsenwood Cres, Camberley, Surrey

SEXTON, Jean Margaret; da of Alistair George Charles Robertson (d 1959), of Barnes, and Eileen Margaret, *née* Henman (d 1973); *b* 1 May 1937; *Educ* Putney HS, Nat Coll of Domestic Subjects; *m* 2 Sept 1959, Reginald Clair Sexton, s of Reginald A W Sexton (d 1985); *Career* int lawn tennis referee (ITF), asst referee at Wimbledon Championships 1983-; memb Cncl Lawn Tennis Assoc, vice pres Br Womens Tennis Assoc, chm Nat Assoc for Gifted Children 1984-90; *Recreations* playing tennis, needlepoint; *Clubs* Sheen Lawn Tennis (chm), The All England; *Style—* Mrs Jean M Sexton; Parkview, 24 Fife Rd, East Sheen, London SW14 7EL (☎ 081 876 3695)

SEYMOUR, Lady Anne Frances Mary; only da of 18 Duke of Somerset, DL (d 1984); *b* 11 Nov 1954; *Style—* Lady Anne Seymour

SEYMOUR, Maj Conway John Edward; s of Maj John Edward Seymour (d 1972), of Upper Chilland House, Martyr Worthy, Winchester, Hants, and Elizabeth Norah, *née* Brand; *b* 13 May 1941; *Educ* Eton, RMA Sandhurst; *m* 1, 10 July 1969 (m dis 1979), Elizabeth, da of Maj Francis Holdsworth Hunt, of Inholmes Holt, Woodland St Mary, Hungerford, Berks; 1 s (Harry b 1971), 1 da (Arabella b 1974); m 2 Diana Elizabeth, da of Michael Edward Gibb (d 1972), of Forge House, Taynton, Oxon; 1 da (Emily b 1982); *Career* cmmnd Grenadier Gds 1961, served, UK, Germany, Cyprus, Sharjah (UAE), Hong Kong, N America, Regtl Adj Grenadier Gds 1985-90; *Recreations* country pursuits, sailing, music; *Clubs* Cavalry and Guards; *Style—* Maj Conway Seymour; Regimental Headquarters, Grenadier Guards, Wellington Barracks, Birdcage Walk, London SW1 (☎ 071 930 4466 ext 3280)

SEYMOUR, Lord Francis Charles Edward; yr s of 18 Duke of Somerset, DL (d 1984); bro of 19 Duke of Somerset, *qv*; *b* 10 Aug 1956; *Educ* Eton; *m* 1982, Paddy, yr da of Col Anthony John Irvine Poynder, MC, RE, of Gassons, Slindon, W Sussex; 1 s (Webb Edward Percy b 30 Aug 1990), 1 da (Poppy Hermione Alexandra b 25 Sept 1988); *Career* slr, memb HAC, dir Guinness Flight Global Asset Management; *Recreations* shooting, eating, collecting military vehicles; *Clubs* MCC; *Style—* The Lord Francis Seymour; 27 Palliser Road, London W14

SEYMOUR, George FitzRoy; JP (Nottinghamshire 1960-), DL (Nottinghamshire, 1973-); s of Richard Sturgis Seymour, MVO (d 1959, himself ggs of 1 Marquess of Hertford), of 108 Swan Court, Chelsea, and Lady Victoria Alexandrina Mabel FitzRoy (d 1969, sis of 10 Duke of Grafton); *b* 8 Feb 1923; *Educ* Winchester; *m* 1 June 1946, Hon Rosemary, *née* Scott-Ellis, *qv*, da of 8 Baron Howard de Walden, *qv*; 1 s (Thomas b 1952), 1 da (Miranda b 1948); *Career* War Serv 60th Rifles 1941-42 (invalided out); landowner; Lord of the Manor of Thrumpton (and Patron of the Living); High Sheriff of Nottinghamshire 1966; *Recreations* shooting, stalking; *Clubs* White's, Pratts', MCC; *Style—* George Seymour, Esq, JP, DL; Thrumpton Hall, Notts (☎ 0602 830333); 38 Molyneux St, London W1 (☎ 071 262 7684)

SEYMOUR, Jane; da of John Frankenberg, of Hillingdon, Middx, and Mieke, *née* van Tricht; *b* 15 Feb 1951; *Educ* Wimbledon HS, Arts Educnl Tst; *m* 1 (m dis), Michael Attenborough; m 2 (m dis), Geoffrey Planer; m 3, 18 July 1981, David Flynn, s of Lloyd Flynn, of Santa Barbara, California; 1 s (Sean Michael b 31 July 1985), 1 da (Katherine Jane b 7 Jan 1982); *Career* actress; films incl: Oh, What a Lovely War 1969, Sinbad and the Eye of the Tiger 1972, Young Winston 1973, Live and Let Die 1973, Four Feathers, Somewhere in Time 1980, Oh Heavenly Dog 1980, Lassiter 1984, Head Office 1986, The Tunnel 1987, Keys to Freedom 1989, Le Revolution Français 1899; theatre work incl: Amadeus (Broadway) 1981, Not Now Darling (Canterbury Repertory), Ophelia in Hamlet (Harrogate Repertory), Lady Macbeth in Macbeth, Nora in A Dolls House; TV work incl: The Onedin Line 1973, Seventh Avenue 1977, Awakening Land 1978, Battle Star Gallactica 1978, Dallas Cowboy Cheerleaders 1979, East of Eden 1981, The Scarlet Pimpernel 1982, The Haunting Passion 1983, The Phantom of the Opera 1983, The Sun Also Rises 1984, Dark Mirror 1984, The Leather Funnel 1984, Jamaica Inn 1985, The Hanged Man 1985, Obsessed with a Married Man 1985, The Woman He Loved (Golden Globe nomination) 1988, Onassis (Emmy Award) 1988, War and Remembrance (Emmy nomination) 1989, Jack the Ripper 1989, Angel of Death, Matters of the Heart; int ambassador Childhelp USA, nat chm Cityhearts, active involvement in CLIC UK, hon chm RP Fndn USA (fighting blindness), hon citizen Illinois USA 1977; *Books* Jane Seymour's Guide to Romantic Living (1987); *Style—* Miss Jane Seymour; c/o Jean Diamond, 235-241 Regent Street, London W1A 2JT (☎ 071 493 1610); CA, USA (☎ 213 659 6888)

SEYMOUR, Hon Mrs (Mary Quenelda); da of 1 Baron Ismay (d 1965); *b* 1929; *m* 1, 1952, Robert Mervyn Fitz Finnis (d 1955); 2 da; m 2, 1957, Maj George Raymond Seymour, CVO, *qv*; 1 da; *Style—* The Hon Mrs Seymour; The Old Vicarage, Bucklebury, Reading, Berks (☎ 0734 712504); Appletrees, Swains Rd, Bembridge, Isle of Wight (☎ 0983 872760)

SEYMOUR, Miranda; da of George Fitzroy Seymour, of Thrumpton Hall, Nottinghamshire, and Hon Rosemary Scott Ellis; *b* 8 Aug 1949; *Educ* private sch, Bedford Coll London (BA); *m* 1, 1972 (m dis 1981), Andrew Sinclair; 1 s (Merlin b 1973); m 2, Anthony Gottlieb b 1989); *Career* writer; children's books: Mumtaz the Magical Cat (1984), The Vampire of Verdonia (1986), Caspar and the Secret Kingdom (1986), Pierre and the Pamplemousse (1990); The Madonna of the Island: Tales of Corfu (short stories, 1980), A Ring of Conspirators: Henry James and his Literary Circle (biography, 1989); historical novels: The Stones of Maggiare (1974), Count Manfred (1976), Daughter of Darkness: Lucrezia Borgia (1977), The Goddess (1978), Medea (1981); modern novels: Carrying On (1984), The Reluctant Devil (1990); *Recreations* embroidery, walking, piano (jazz); *Clubs* Academy; *Style—* Ms Miranda Seymour; c/o David Higham Literary Agency, 5-8 Lower John St, London W1 (☎ 071 437 7888, fax 071 437 1072)

SEYMOUR, Prof Philip Herschel Kean; s of William Kean Seymour (d 1975), of Alresford, Hants, and Rosalind Herschel, *née* Wade, OBE (d 1989); *b* 9 March 1938; *Educ* Kelly Coll Tavistock Devon, Univ of Oxford (BA), Univ of St Andrews (MEd), Univ of Dundee (PhD); *m* 26 Jan 1962, Margaret Jean Dyson (Jane), da of Prof William Ian Clinch Morris, of Springfield, Fife; 2 s (Patrick b 1962, Dominic b 1975), 2 da (Emma b 1964, Mary Marcella b 1978); *Career* nat Serv RAEC 1957-59; prof Univ of Dundee 1988- (lectr and sr lectr 1966-82, reader 1982-88); chm Scot Dyslexia Assoc 1987; memb Br Psychological Soc; *Books* Human Visual Cognition (1979), Cognitive Analysis of Dyslexia (1986); *Recreations* gardening, fishing; *Style—* Prof Philip Seymour; Edenfield House, Springfield, by Cupar, Fife (☎ 0334 53177); Department of Psychology, The University, Dundee (☎ 0382 23181, fax 0382 29948, telex 76293 ULDUND)

SEYMOUR, Maj (George) Raymond; CVO (1990); s of Sir Reginald Seymour, KCVO (gs of Rt Hon Sir George Seymour, GCB, GCH, PC, and Hon Gertrude, da of 21 Baron Dacre; Sir George was gs of 1 Marquess of Hertford, KG); *b* 5 May 1923; *Educ* Eton; *m* 1957, Hon Mary Quenelda Stanley, *qv*, da of Gen 1 Baron Ismay (extinct 1965); 1 da, 2 step da; *Career* Maj KRRC, served Palestine, Germany; chm W H Brakspear & Sons; equerry to HM Queen Elizabeth, The Queen Mother 1955; *Recreations* sailing, fishing, shooting; *Clubs* Boodle's; *Style—* Maj Raymond Seymour, LVO; The Old Vicarage, Bucklebury, Reading, Berks (☎ 0734 712504) Appletrees, Swains Rd, Bembridge, Isle of Wight (☎ 0983 872760)

SEYMOUR, Hon Mrs (Rosemary Nest); *née* Scott-Ellis; da of 8 Baron Howard de Walden and 4 Baron Seaford (d 1946), and Margherita, CBE, er da of late Charles Van Raalte, JP; *b* 28 Oct 1922; *m* 1946, George FitzRoy Seymour, *qv*, yr s of Richard Sturgis Seymour, MVO (d 1959); 1 s, 1 da; *Style—* The Hon Mrs Seymour; Thrumpton Hall, Nottingham (☎ 0602 830333); 38 Molyneux St, London W1 (☎ 071 262 7684)

SEYMOUR, Lord; Sebastian Edward Seymour; s and h of 19 Duke of Somerset; *b* 3 Feb 1982; *Style—* Lord Seymour

SEYMOUR, Lady Susan Mary; da of late 17 Duke of Somerset, DSO, OBE; *b* 26 April 1913; *Career* Cmdt Wilts 36 Red Cross Detachment 1939-45, late Div Pres; Red Cross Long Service medal; *Style—* The Lady Susan Seymour; Sunnyside, Maiden Bradley, Wilts

SEYMOUR, Dr William Martin; s of Alexander William Charles Seymour, of Putney, and Eileen Patricia Olive, *née* Jameson (d 1971); *b* 28 Oct 1939; *Educ* Downside, London Hosp Med Sch Univ of London (MB BS, LRCP, MRCP); *m* 3 Dec 1966, (Penelope) Ann, da of Dr John Herbert Moseley, of Havant, Hampshire; 1 s (Carl b 1969), 2 da (Catherine b 1985, Charlotte b 1988); *Career* med registrar London Hosp 1968, res registrar Brompton Hosp 1970, conslt physician in gen and thoracic med Greenwich and Bexley AHA 1976-, sr lectr Guy'S 1976-85 (sr registrar 1974); chm SE Thames Thoracic Soc 1988; MRCS 1963, FRCP 1981; *Recreations* castle renovation, carpentry, music, gardening, photography; *Style—* Dr William Seymour; Vanbrugh Castle, Maze Hill, Greenwich, London SE10; Brook General Hospital, Shooters Hill Rd, London SE18 (☎ 081 856 5555)

SEYMOUR, Maj William Napier; s of Lt-Col Charles Hugh Napier Seymour, DSO (d 1933), and Mary Adelaide; *b* 8 Sept 1914; *Educ* Eton; *m* 28 April 1945, Rachel Mary, da of Angus Hambro (d 1957); 3 da (Carolyn b 1946, Sarah b 1947, Arabella b 1952); *Career* cmmnd Scots Gds 1934, served Palestine, Western Desert, Burma (despatches), Malaya (left Army 1949); land agent to Crichel Estate for 30 years; author of nine books incl Ordeal by Ambition, a biography of ancestor Edward Seymour, Duke of Somerset and Protector of the Realm; *Recreations* shooting, golf, racing; *Clubs* Army and Navy, Pratts; *Style—* Maj William Seymour; Park House, Shaftesbury, Dorset

SEYMOUR-NEWTON, Cyril Terence; s of Maj Cyril Frank Newton (d 1978), of Guernsey, and Mary Jane Frances Fermoix de Chantal Newton, *née* Gallagher (d 1976); *b* 8 Sept 1927; *Educ* Ampleforth, Trinity Coll Cambridge; *m* 31 Jan 1964, Carol, da of Lt-Col Ivor Watkins Birts (ka 1944); 1 s (Rupert Edward Cyril b 3 Nov 1968); *Career* elected underwriting memb Lloyd's 1954 (joined Lloyd's 1949); dir (at Lloyd's): Seymour-Newton Ltd 1964-89 (fndr and chm), Shead Gray Ltd 1966-72, Halford Shead Underwriting Agencies Ltd 1968-72, Hargreaves Reiss & Quinn Ltd 1979-87, Crump & Johnson Underwriting Agencies Ltd 1980-, Crump & Cackett Agencies Ltd 1983-, RK Harrison Underwriting Agencies Ltd 1986-89, Wendover Underwriting Agency Ltd 1987-; dir: London & Provincial Insurances Ltd 1962-72, Merritt Huthwaite Ltd 1962-64, Seton Wines Ltd 1964-72 (fndr and chm), Halford Shead Life & Pensions Ltd 1968-72; hon treas 1900 Club 1978- (memb Ctee 1970-, hon sec 1973-78), memb Cncl PDSA 1968-82 (dep chm 1971-82); Freeman City of London 1955, Liveryman Worshipful Co of Coachmakers and Coach Harness Makers 1955; *Recreations* reading, music, big game fishing; *Clubs* Brooks's, MCC, 1900; *Style—* C T Seymour-Newton, Esq; 34 Ennismore Gardens, London SW7 1AE (☎ 071 584 3143); Wendover Underwriting Agency Ltd, 3 St Helen's Place, London EC3A 6AU (☎ 071 628 1317, fax 071 628 1713)

SEYMOUR-SMITH, Martin; s of Frank Seymour-Smith (d 1972), and Marjorie, *née* Harris (d 1988); *b* 24 April 1928; *Educ* Highgate Sch, St Edmund Hall Oxford (MA); *m* 1952, Janet, da of Dr Lionel de Glanville; 2 da (Miranda b 1953, Charlotte b 1955); *Career* Sgt Br Army served ME 1946-48; schoolmaster 1954-60; freelance writer 1960-, gen ed Gollancz Classics 1967-69; books: Tea with Miss Stockport (1963), Shakespeare's Sonnets (ed, 1963), Bluff Your Way in Literature (1 edn, 1966, revised edn, 1972), Reminiscences of Norma (1971), Guide to Modern World Literature (1973, revised and rewritten as Macmillan Guide to World Literature, 1985), Robert Graves: His Life and Work (1982), Rudyard Kipling (1989); visiting prof and writer in residence Univ of Wisconsin-Parkside 1971-72; Southern Arts Prize for non-fiction 1982, Authors' Soc Travelling scholarship award 1985; memb Ctee Authors' Soc 1976-79; *Recreations* music, reading, travel, work, animals; *Style—* Martin Seymour-Smith, Esq; 36 Holliers Hill, Bexhill-on-Sea, East Sussex TN40 2DD (☎ 0424 215042); Sheil Land Associates, 43 Doughty St, London WC1N 2LF (☎ 071 405 9351, fax 071 831 2127)

SEYWRIGHT, Dr Morag Mathews; da of William Seywright, of Bearsden, Glasgow, and Flora McDonald, *née* Mathews; *b* 4 Feb 1958; *Educ* Bearsden Acad, Univ of Glasgow (MB ChB); *m* 30 Nov 1985, Alistair John Allan, s of David Allan, of Glasgow; *Career* sr registrar in histopathology Western Infirmary Glasgow 1986-87, conslt pathologist (dermatopathology) Western Infirmary Glasgow 1987-; memb Assoc of Clinical Pathologists, ctee memb Br Soc for Dermatopathology, past sec Scot Melanoma Gp; MRCPath 1986; *Recreations* golf, choral singing; *Style—* Dr Morag Seywright; Dept of Histopathology, Western Infirmary, Glasgow (☎ 041 339 8822)

SHACKLADY, Richard Linford; s of Richard Shacklady (d 1985), and Elsie, *née* Duxbury; *b* 31 Aug 1948; *Educ* Maghull GS, Kirkby Coll of Further Education, Univ of Aston; *m* 14 Feb 1972, Judith, da of George Boswell, of Herts; 1 s (Linford George b 5 June 1974); *Career* Inco Engineered Products Ltd dir subsids 1985-88: dir 1985-88: Doncasters Sheffield Ltd, Doncasters Moorside Ltd, Doncasters Blaenavon Ltd, Settas SA Belgium; Setlas SA Belgium 1985-88, md Philidas Ltd 1988-; dir Wakefield TEC (Trg and Enterprise Cncl); memb London Business Sch Assoc; *Recreations* tennis, gardening, North Norfolk; *Style—* Richard Shacklady, Esq; 43 Starkholmes Rd, Matlock, Derbyshire DE4 3DD (☎ 0629 56289); Philidas Ltd, Monkhill Lane, Pontefract, W Yorks WF8 1RL (☎ 0977 704141, fax 0977 790338, telex 55405, car 0860 48138)

SHACKLE, Prof George Lennox Sharman; s of Robert Walker Shackle (d 1934), and Fanny, *née* Sharman (d 1936); *b* 14 July 1903; *Educ* The Perse Sch Cambridge, Univ of London (BA), LSE (PhD), Univ of Oxford (DPhil); *m* 1, 1939, Gertrude Courtney Susan Rowe (d 1978); 2 s (Robert b 1941, Richard b 1945), 2 da (Frances b 1945 d 1947, Caroline b 1948); m 2, 30 Jan 1979, Catherine Squarey Gibb, *née* Weldsmith; *Career* Univ of Oxford Inst of Statistics 1937-39, asst Univ of St Andrews 1939, memb Winston Churchill's Statistical Branch Admty and Cabinet Office 1939-45, memb Economic Section Cabinet Secretariat 1945-50, reader in economic theory Univ of Leeds 1950-51, Brunner Prof of economic sci Univ of Liverpool 1951-69, (currently prof emeritus); F de Friès Lectr Amsterdam 1957; visiting prof: Univ of Columbia USA 1957-58, Univ of Pittsburg 1967; Keynes Lectr Br Acad 1976; memb Cncl Royal Economic Soc 1955-69, pres Section 7 BAAS 1966; New Univ of Ulster (Hon DSc), Univ of Birmingham (Hon DSocSci), Univ of Strathclyde (Hon DLitt); FBA 1967, distinguished fell American History of Economics Soc 1985, fell Econometric Soc 1960; *Books* Expectations Investment and Income (1938, 2 edn, 1968), Expectation in Economics (1949 and 1952), Mathematics at the Fireside (1952), Uncertainty in Economics and Other Reflections (1955, 2 edn, 1968), Time in Economics (1958, 2 edn, 1967), Economics for Pleasure (1959, 2 edn, 1968), Decision Order and Time in Human Affairs (1961, 2 edn, 1969), A Scheme of Economic Theory (1965), The Nature of Economic Thought (1966), The Years of High Theory (1967), Expectation Enterprise and Profit (1970), Epistemics and Economics (1972), An Economic Querist (1973), Keynsian Kaleidics (1974), Imagination and the Nature of Choice (1979), Business Time and Thought (1988), Time, Expectations and Uncertainty in Economics (1990); *Clubs* Utd Oxford and Cambridge; *Style—* Prof George Shackle; Rudloe, Alde House Drive, Aldeburgh, Suffolk IP15 5EE (☎ 0728 452227)

SHACKLES, (Derek George) Guy; s of Derek Holmes Shackles, CBE (d 1973), of Argyll, and Lella Dalglish Shackles (d 1980); *b* 19 Oct 1936; *Educ* Edinburgh Acad; *Career* slr, qualified 1959; clerk to Gen Cmmrs of Taxes, sr ptnr Shackles Slrs; *Recreations* yacht racing, yacht cruising, youth seamanship trg; *Clubs* Royal Ocean Racing, Royal Yorkshire Yacht; *Style—* Guy Shackles, Esq; Chequers, 64 A South Marine Drive, Bridlington, E Yorkshire (☎ 0262 676781); Merrs Shackles, 7 Land of Green Ginger, Hull, Humberside (☎ 0482 26404)

SHACKLETON, Lady Caroline Harriet; *née* Hastings; da of 15 Earl of Huntingdon (d 1990), and his 2 w, Margaret, *née* Lane; *b* 12 June 1946; *Educ* St Paul's Girls' Sch, Univ of Edinburgh (MA), Univ of Oxford (BA), Univ of London (MPhil, PhD); *m* 1970, Hon Charles Edward Ernest Shackleton (d 1979), s of Baron Shackleton, KG, OBE, PC (Life Peer); 2 c (Emma Jane Miranda b 26 Jan 1985, David Charles b 8 Feb 1986); *Career* lectr in clinical psychology Univ of London 1977-82; clinical and research psychologist 1982-; *Style—* The Lady Caroline Shackleton

SHACKLETON, Baron (Life Peer UK 1958), of Burley, Co Southampton; Edward Arthur Alexander Shackleton; KG (1974), AC (1990), OBE (1945), PC (1966); s of late Sir Ernest Henry Shackleton, CVO, OBE, the explorer of the Antarctic; *b* 15 July 1911; *Educ* Radley, Magdalen Coll Oxford (MA); *m* 1938, Betty Muriel Marguerite, da of Capt Charles E Homan, Elder Bro of Trinity House; (1 s decd), 1 da (Hon Alexandra Mary Swinford (Hon Mrs Bergel) b 1940); *Career* accompanied expeditions: Borneo and Sarawak 1932, Ellesmere Land 1934-35; author, lectr, broadcaster; lecture tours in Europe and America; served WWII RAF, Coastal Cmd, Naval and Military Intelligence Air Miny, Wing Cdr (despatches 2); MP (Lab) Preston 1946-50, Preston S 1950-55, min defence for RAF 1964-67, min without portfolio and dep leader House of Lords 1967-68, PMG 1968, Lord Privy Seal 1968-

70, leader House of Lords 1968-70, min in charge CSD 1968-70, oppn leader House of Lords 1970-74; chm: Advsy Cncl on Oil Pollution 1962-64, Political Honours Scrutiny Ctee 1976-, Economic Survey of Falkland Islands 1976 (updated 1982), report on Anti-Terrorist Legislation 1978, East European Trade Cncl 1977-86; chm Lords Select Ctee Sci and Technol; sr exec and dir J Lewis Partnership 1955-64, chm RTZ Devpt Enterprises 1973-83, dep chm RTZ Corp 1975-82 (exec dir 1973-82), chm Anglesey Aluminium Ltd 1981-85; pres: RGS 1971-74, Parly & Scientific Ctee 1976-80, Br Standards Inst 1977-80; elder brother Trinity House 1980, Hon LLD Newfoundland 1970, Hon DSc Univ of Warwick 1978, Hon DSc Univ of Southampton, Hon fell Magdalen Coll and St Hugh's Coll Oxford; Royal Scottish Geographical Soc medal 1990, Special Gold medal of Royal Geographical Soc 1990; Freedom of Stanley (Falkland Islands) 1988; Honorary Companion in the Order of Australia 1990; FRS 1989, FBIM; *Publications* Arctic Journeys, Nansen the Explorer, Borneo Jungle (jtly); *Clubs* Brooks; *Style—* The Rt Hon the Lord Shackleton, KG, AC, OBE, FRS; 11 Grosvenor Crescent, London SW1X 7EE (☎ 071 235 7096/071 245 6522)

SHACKLETON, Fiona Sara; da of Jonathan Philip Charkham,*qvqv*, of 22 Montpelier Place London, and Moira Elizabeth Frances, *née* Salmon; *b* 26 May 1956; *Educ* Benenden, Univ of Exeter (LLB); *m* 26 Sept 1985, Ian Ridgeway, s of Lt-Col Richard John Shackleton, MBE (d 1977); 2 da (Cordelia Molly Louise b 25 May 1988, Lydia Elizabeth Moira b 6 July 1989); *Career* slr; articled Clerk Herbert Smith & Co 1978-80, admitted 1980; ptnr: Brecher & Co 1981-84 (joined 1980), Farrer & Co 1986- (joined 1984); govr Benenden Sch; memb Law Soc Acad Matrimonial Lawyers; *Recreations* bridge, food and entertaining; *Style—* Mrs Fiona Shackleton; 66 Lincolns Inn Fields, London WC2A 3LH (☎ 071 242 2022, fax 071 405 2296, tlx 24318)

SHAFER, Prof Byron Edwin; *b* 8 Jan 1947; *Educ* Yale Univ (BA), Univ of Calif at Berkeley (PhD, Peter B Odegard prize); *m* ; 1 s; *Career* resident scholar Russell Sage Fndn 1977-84, assoc prof of political sci Florida State Univ 1984-85, Andrew W Mellon prof of American Govt Univ of Oxford 1985-; Univ of Oxford: Social Studies Bd 1989-, Modern History Bd 1989-, Bd of Electors Rhodes Professorship in American History 1989-, Bd of Electors Ford Lectureship in Int Rels 1988-89; editorial intern American Political Science Review 1970-74; memb American Political Sci Assoc Ctee on: Professional Devpt 1979-81, Publications 1983-86; memb: editorial Bd JL of American Studies 1986-, Screening Ctee American Cncl of learned Socs 1986-89; intermittent pub commentator for BBC World Serv and US Embassy London; current memb of: American Political Sci Assoc, American Hist Assoc, Political Studies Assoc UK, Br Assoc for American Studies, Nat Conf of Univ Profs; American Political Sci Assoc: E E Schattschneider award 1980, Franklin L Burdette Pi Sigma Alpha award 1990; Special Career Fellowship in Political Sci Univ of Calif at Berkeley; author of numerous pubns in learned professional jls: Hon MA Univ of Oxford 1985; *Style—* Prof Byron Shafer; Nuffield College, Oxford OX1 1NF (☎ 0865 278509, fax 0865 278621)

SHAFFER, Peter Levin; CBE (1987); s of Jack Shaffer (d 1987), of London, and Reka, *née* Fredman; *b* 15 May 1926; *Educ* St Pauls London, Trinity Coll Cambridge; *Career* playwright; Five Finger Exercise (1958), The Private Ear, The Public Eye (1961), The Royal Hunt of the Sun (1964), Black Comedy (1965), White Liars (1966), The Battle of Shrivings (1967), Equus (1973), Amadeus (1979), Yonadab (1986), Lettice and Lovage (1987); screeplays: Equus (1977), Amadeus (1984); radio play: Whom Do I Have The Honour of Addressing ?; *Recreations* walking; *Clubs* Garrick, Arts; *Style—* Peter L Shaffer, Esq, CBE; Lloyds Bank, Kensington, London

SHAFTO, Robert James; s of George Oliver Holt Shafto (d 1980), and Kathleen Mary, *née* Offer; *b* 4 Dec 1938; *Educ* Epsom Coll; *Career* audit ptnr Smith & Williamson 1969-81, sr ptnr Stainton & Shafto 1982-; dir Bavington Management Ltd 1983-; methodist local preacher 1980-; FCA 1961; *Books* Tax Aspects of Personal Investments (1984), Investments Other Than Land (1987); *Recreations* genealogy, mountain walking; *Style—* Robert Shafto, Esq; 7 Walkerscroft Mead, Dulwich, London SE21 8LJ (☎ 081 670 6350); 21 Wigmore St, London W1H 9LA (☎ 071 491 7355, fax 071 493 7177)

SHAH, Samir; s of Amrit Shah, of Bombay, India, and Uma, *née* Chaudhary (d 1973); *b* 29 Jan 1952; *Educ* Latymer Upper Sch London, Univ of Hull (BSc), St Catherine's Coll Oxford (DPhil); *m* 18 Dec 1983, Belkis Bhegani, da of Gan-Mohammed Hassan, of Kampala, Uganda; 1 s (Cimran Temur b 19 Oct 1986); *Career* memb Home Office 1978-79; LWT 1979-87: Skin, Weekend World, Eastern Eye, Credo, The London Programme; dep ed news and current affrs progs BBC TV 1987-89, ed weekly and special progs news and current affrs BBC 1990-; *Recreations* reading, music, sport; *Style—* Samir Shah, Esq; British Broadcasting Corporation, Lime Grove Studios, Shepherd's Bush, London W12 7RJ

SHAIL, Prof Ronald; s of Thomas Sidney Shail (d 1962), of Middlesbrough, Cleveland, and Leah, *née* Jones (d 1986); *b* 6 July 1935; *Educ* Middlesbrough Boys HS, Univ of London (BSc, PhD, DSc); *m* 3 Jan 1959, Jean Veronica, da of Leonard Page, of Saltburn-by-Sea; 1 s (John b 1959), 1 da (Helen b 1962); *Career* lectr Dept of Applied Mathematics Univ of Liverpool 1961-66 (asst lectr 1959-61); Univ of Surrey: reader in mathematics 1966-87, prof 1987-, head of Dept of Mathematics 1989-; some 60 pubns on applied mathematics in scientific jls; exec ed Quarterly Jl of Mechanics and Applied Mathematics 1969-89; FIMA; *Recreations* model construction, modern history; *Style—* Prof Ronald Shail; Department of Mathematics, University of Surrey, Guildford, Surrey GU2 5XH (☎ 0483 571281)

SHAKERLEY, Lady; Barbara Storrs; JP (Glos 1962); da of J Howard, JP, of Kidderminster; *m* 1932, Lt-Col Sir Geoffrey Shakerley, CBE, MC, TD (d 1982), sometime Vice-Lt Glos, chm Glos CC; 2 s, 2 da; *Style—* Lady Shakerley, JP; Carneggan Cottage, Lanteglos-by-Fowey, Cornwall PL23 1NW

SHAKERLEY, Charles Frederick Eardley; s of late Maj Sir Cyril Shakerley, 5 Bt and bro of Sir Geoffrey Shakerley, 6 Bt, *qv*; *b* 14 June 1934; *Educ* Harrow, Ch Ch Oxford, Univ of Pennsylvania; *m* 1962, Lucy Carolyn, da of Francis St G Fisher of Cragg, Cockermouth, Cumbria; 3 da; *Career* chm Provincial Insurance Co Ltd 1977-, dir Williams and Glyn's 1980-5, Royal Bank of Scotland Gp 1985; former memb Stock Exchange, sr ptnr Roger Mortimer & Co 1970-75; *Recreations* forestry, shooting, fishing; *Clubs* Brooks's; *Style—* Charles Shakerley, Esq; Cudworth Manor, Newdigate, Surrey (☎ 030 677 275)

SHAKERLEY, Lady Elizabeth Georgiana; *née* Anson; granted style, rank and precedence of an Earl's da 1961; da of Lt-Col Thomas William Arnold, Viscount Anson (d 1958), and late Princess Anne of Denmark, *née* Anne Bowes-Lyon; sis of 5 Earl of Lichfield; *b* 7 June 1941, (HM King George VI stood sponsor); *m* 1972, as his 2 wife, Sir Geoffrey Adam Shakerley, 6 Bt, *qv*; 1 da; *Career* proprietress Party Planners, dir Kanga, dir Mosimann's (a memb's only dining club); *Books* Lady Elizabeth Anson's Party Planners Book (1986); *Style—* The Lady Elizabeth Shakerley; 56 Ladbroke Grove, London W11 2PB

SHAKERLEY, Sir Geoffrey Adam; 6 Bt (UK 1838) of Somerford Park, Cheshire; s of Maj Sir Cyril Holland Shakerley, 5 Bt (d 1970), and Elizabeth Averil, MBE (d 1990), da of late Edward Gwynne Eardley-Wilmot, gggda of Sir John Eardley Eardley-Wilmot, 1 Bt; *b* 9 Dec 1932; *Educ* Harrow, Trinity Coll Oxford; *m* 1, 1962, Virginia Elizabeth (d 1968), da of W E Maskell; 2 s; m 2, 1972, Lady Elizabeth, *née* Anson, *qv*; 1 da; *Heir* s, Nicholas Shakerley; *Career* 2 Lt KRRC; dir Photographic Records Ltd 1970-; *Style—* Sir Geoffrey Shakerley, Bt; 57 Artesian Rd, London W2 5DB

SHAKERLEY, Nicholas Simon Adam; s (by 1 m) and h of Sir Geoffrey Shakerley, 6 Bt; *b* 20 Dec 1963; *Style—* Nicholas Shakerley, Esq; 57 Artesian Rd, London W2 5DB

SHAKESPEARE, Elizabeth, Lady; Elizabeth; da of Brig-Gen Robert William, CMG, DSO, DL (d 1953; great n of 2 Earl of Listowel), and Helen Mary, *née* Atkinson (d 1972); *b* 4 May 1914; *m* 29 Feb 1952, as his 2 w, Rt Hon Sir Geoffrey Shakespeare, 1 Bt, PC (d 1980); *Career* served WWII Section Offr WAAF (despatches); Bronze Star (USA); Freeman City of London 1974; *Recreations* gardening, travel; *Style—* Elizabeth, Lady Shakespeare; Flat 6, Great Ash, Lubbock Rd, Chislehurst, Kent BR7 5JZ

SHAKESPEARE, John William Richmond; CMG (1985), LVO (1968); s of Dr William Goodman Shakespeare (d 1975), and Ruth, *née* Potter; *b* 11 June 1930; *Educ* Winchester, Trinity Coll Oxford (MA); *m* 1955, Lalage Ann, da of S P B Mais (d 1975); 3 s, 1 da; *Career* served Irish Gds 1949-50, 2 Lt; lectr Ecole Normale Supérieure Paris 1953-54, on editorial staff The Times 1955-59; Dip Serv; FCO 1959, served Paris, Phnom Penh, Singapore, Rio de Janeiro, FCO 1969-73, cnsllr Buenos Aires 1973-75, chargé d'affaires Buenos Aires 1976-77, head Mexico and Caribbean Dept FCO 1977-79, cnsllr Lisbon 1979-83, ambass to Peru 1983-87, ambass to Morocco 1987-90; *Recreations* swimming, tennis, walking, gardening; *Style—* John Shakespeare, Esq, CMG, MVO; 10 South End Row, London W8

SHAKESPEARE, Nicholas William Richmond; s of John William Richmond Shakespeare, and Lalage Ann, *née* Mais; *b* 3 March 1957; *Educ* The Dragon Sch Oxford, Winchester, Magdalene Coll Cambridge (MA); *Career* asst prodr BBC TV 1980-84, dep arts/literacy ed The Times 1985-87; literary ed: London Daily News 1987-, Daily Telegraph 1988-; *Books* The Men Who Would Be King (1984), Londoners (1986), The Vision of Elena Silves (1989); *Recreations* travelling; *Clubs* Beeksteak, Groucho, Literary Soc; *Style—* Nicholas Shakespeare, Esq; Daily Telegraph, 181 Marsh Wall, London E14 (☎ 071 538 6132)

SHAKESPEARE, Sir William Geoffrey; 2 Bt (UK 1942) of Lakenham, City of Norwich; s of Rt Hon Sir Geoffrey Hithersay Shakespeare, 1 Bt, PC (d 1980), by his 1 w, Aimée (d 1950), da of Walter Loveridge, and widow of Cdr Sir Thomas Fisher, RN; half-bro of Sir Nigel Fisher, KCB, MC, *qv*; *b* 12 Oct 1927; *Educ* Radley, Clare Coll Cambridge (MA), St George's Hosp Cambridge (MB BChir, DCH); *m* 1964, Susan Mary, da of A Douglas Raffel (d 1965), of Colombo, Ceylon; 2 s; *Heir* s, Thomas William Shakespeare b 11 May 1966; *Career* GP 1968-87; clinical asst Manor House Hosp Aylesbury 1972-; registrar: St George's Hosp 1961-63, Stoke Mandeville Hosp 1964-66; memb Snowdon Working Party into Integration of Handicapped, medical advsr to Bucks Adoption Panel 1987-; vice-pres: Physically Handicapped and Able-Bodied 1977-, Restricted Growth Assoc (formerly Assoc for Res into Restricted Growth) 1982; *Recreations* gardening, reading; *Clubs* MCC, Leander, Stewards' Enclosure Henley Regatta; *Style—* Sir William Shakespeare, Bt

SHALE, Christopher Michael Henry; s of Michael Thomas Shale, of Edinburgh, and Norma Clementine, *née* Swan; *b* 23 Aug 1954; *Educ* Oakham Sch, RMA Sandhurst; *Career* cmmnd 17/21 Lancers 1975, ADC to Field Marshal Sir Richard Hull for Queens Silver Jubilee Parade 1977; dir: Bede Securities Ltd 1983-85, Holland Trust Ltd 1989-, Cleveland Capital Management Ltd 1989-; md SGL Ltd 1983-85; chm: SGL Communications plc 1985-, SGL Corporate Ltd 1985-, SGL Consumer Ltd 1986-, SGL Property Ltd 1987-, Kingsgate Communications Ltd 1987-, SGL Leisure Ltd 1988-, White Tie Ltd 1988-, SGL Defence Ltd 1989- SGL Presentations Ltd 1989-, Air Call Medical Services Ltd 1988-89; *Recreations* shooting, fishing; *Clubs* Cavalry and Guards, Annabels, Mark's, Harry's Bar; *Style—* Christopher Shale, Esq; 95 Eaton Terrace, London SW1W 8TW (☎ 071 823 6760); SGL Communications plc, Kingsgate House, 536 King's Rd, London SW10 0UH (☎ 071 973 8888, fax 071 351 4207)

SHALE, Dr Dennis John; s of Samuel Edward Shale, of Leicester, and Winifred Beatrice, *née* Newstead (d 1986); *b* 19 Feb 1948; *Educ* Charles Keene Coll, Univ of Newcastle upon Tyne (BSc, MB BS, MD); *m* 23 March 1970, Kathleen Patricia, da of Harry Clark, of Great Glen, Leicestershire; 1 s (Matthew b 1978), 1 da (Victoria b 1975); *Career* lectr in physiology Univ of Newcastle upon Tyne 1976-78, jr trg posts in med Newcastle upon Tyne and Oxford 1978-81, sr registrar in respiratory med Oxford 1981-84, sr lectr in respiratory med Univ of Nottingham 1985-, author of chapters in books on respiratory med and original articles in aspects of respiratory med incl shock lung and cystic fibrosis in int jls, contrib of editorials and reviews to med jls; assoc ed Thorax 1986; hon regnl advsr to Cystic Fibrosis Res Tst; MRCP 1980; memb: Br Thoracic Soc 1983, Med Res Soc 1984, Societas Euro Pneumonology 1985; *Recreations* gardening, archaeology, English and American literature, baroque music; *Style—* Dr Dennis Shale; Respiratory Medicine Unit, University of Nottingham, City Hospital, Hucknall Rd, Nottingham NG5 1PB (☎ 0602 691169)

SHALIT, Jonathan Sigmund; s of David Manuel Shalit, and Sophie Shalit, JP, *née* Gestetner; *b* 17 April 1962; *Educ* City of London; *Career* former exec and graduate trg scheme with Saatchi Group, chm F.A.B. 1987-; memb: The Princes Tst, Cancer Res Campaign; Freeman City of London, Liveryman Worshipful Co of Coachmakers and Harness Makers; memb Inst of Dirs; *Recreations* sailing, squash and skiing; *Clubs* Annabels, RAC, Inst of Directors, Tramp; *Style—* Jonathan Shalit, Esq; 2 Charleville Mansions, Charleville Road, London W14 9JB (☎ 071 385 3695); F.A.B., 191 Wardour St, London W1V 3FA (☎ 071 287 4363, fax 071 287 5117)

SHALLOW, Col (John) David; MC (1951); s of George Shallow (d 1971), of Wraxall, Somerset, and Phyllis Margaret, *née* Dawson (d 1988); *b* 4 June 1927; *Educ* Allhallows Sch Rousdon Devon; *m* 9 Sept 1952, Sally Robertson, da of Eric James Gordon Gibb, MC (d 1977), of S Africa; 2 s (Christopher Patrick b 9 Sept 1953, Andrew John Robertson b 7 May 1957), 1 da (Rosalind b 23 March 1961); *Career* RM; cmmnd 1945, HMS Leander 1946-47, 40 Commando 1948-51, RNC Dartmouth 1953-55, HMS Newfoundland 1958-59, mil asst to Cmdt Gen 1959-60, RAF Staff Coll 1961, 40 Commando 1963-65, Jt Servs Staff Coll 1967, asst sec Chiefs of Staff Ctee 1968-70, GSO1 HQ Commando Forces 1970-71, exchange appt US Marine Corps 1971-72, CO RM Eastney and CSO 1973-75, CO RM Deal and Cmdt Sch of Music 1976-77, ret 1978; entered Civil Serv; Civil Def Coll: tutor 1978, gp dir 1984, vice princ and dir of studies 1986, ret 1990; churchwarden; Freeman City of London 1976; FBIM 1977; *Style—* Col David Shallow, MC

SHAMMAS, Claude Jean; *b* 29 April 1941; *Educ* Seaford Coll, Loughborough Univ of Technol; *Career* md Plastic Prods Ltd; *Clubs* Roehampton; *Style—* Claude Shammas, Esq; 54 Murray Rd, London SW19 4PE; Plastic Products Ltd, Whitecliff House, 852 Brighton Rd, Purley, Surrey CR2 2UY (☎ 081 686 4411)

SHAMTALLY, Bhye Mahmood (Danny); s of Abdool Raffick Shamtally, of 18 Abbe Laval St, Eau Coulee, Mauritius, and Bibi Afroze, *née* Hisaindee; *b* 7 June 1951; *Educ* Mauritius Coll, Bhujoharry Coll; *m* 19 Sept 1973, Carmelia Panaligan, da of late Francisco Panaligan; 1 s (Reza b 2 Dec 1976), 1 da (Natasha b 17 Jan 1979); *Career* staff nurse Belmont Hosp 1974-76, offr-in-charge London Borough Sutton Social Serv 1977-85 (asst offr-in-charge 1976-77), princ ptnr Private Nursing Homes 1983-; memb: NSPCC, Nat Tst; MRIPHH 1974, FIWO 1985, FRSH 1985; *Recreations* country walks, antiques, collectors cars, poetry; *Clubs* Copthorne Country; *Style—* Danny Shamtally, Esq; Standish, Rockshaw Rd, Merstham, Surrey RH1 3BZ; Grennell Lodge

Nursing Home, 69 All Saints Rd, Sutton, Surrey SM1 3DJ (☎ 081 644 7567, car 0831 463941); Chaldon Rise Nursing Home, Rockshaw Rd, Merstham, Surrey RH1 3DE (☎ 0737 42281); Chipstead Lodge Rest Home, Hazelwood Lane, Chipstead, Surrey CR5 3QW (☎ 0737 553 552)

SHAND, Maj Bruce Middleton Hope; MC (1940, and bar 1942), DL (1962); s of Philip Morton Shand (d 1960); *b* 22 Jan 1917; *Educ* Rugby, RMC Sandhurst; *m* 1946, Hon Rosalind Maud Cubitt, *qv*; 1 s (Mark Roland b 1951), 2 da (Camilla Parker-Bowles, *qv*, Sonia Annabel (Mrs Elliot) b 1949); *Career* Maj 12 Royal Lancers, ret 1947; Clerk of the Cheque and Adj Queen's Body Guard of the Yeomen of the Guard 1985 (Ensign 1978, Exon 1971), ret 1987; Vice Lord Lt E Sussex 1974-; *Recreations* hunting, gardening; *Clubs* Cavalry and Guards; *Style—* Maj Bruce Shand, MC, DL; The Laines, Plumpton, nr Lewes, E Sussex (☎ 0273 890248)

SHAND, His Honour Judge; John Alexander Ogilvie Shand; s of Alexander Shand, MBE, QPM (d 1968), of West Bridgeford, Notts, and Marguerite Marie, *née* Farcy; *b* 6 Nov 1942; *Educ* Nottingham HS, Queens' Coll Cambridge (MA, LLB, Chancellor's Medal for Law 1965); *m* 18 Dec 1965 (m dis 1988), Patricia Margaret, da of Frederick of Toynbee, Nottingham (d 1958); 2 s (James b 1967, Simon b 1972), 1 da (Juliet b 1969); *Career* called to the Bar Middle Temple 1965; Midland and Oxford circuit 1965-70 and 1973-81, asst lectr fell and tutor Queens' Coll Cambridge 1970-73, chm Industl Tribunals 1981-88, recorder 1981-88; chllr Diocese of Southwell 1981-; chllr Diocese of Lichfield 1989-; circuit judge 1988; *Books* Legal Values in Western Society (1974, co-author); *Style—* His Honour Judge Shand; c/o Courts Administrator's Office, Greyfriars House, Greyfriars, Stafford ST16 2SE (☎ 0785 41643)

SHAND, Hon Mrs (Rosalind Maud); *née* Cubitt; only da of 3 Baron Ashcombe (d 1962); *b* 11 Aug 1921; *m* 1946, Maj Bruce Shand, MC, late 12 Royal Lancers; 1 s, 2 da; *Style—* The Hon Mrs Shand; The Laines, Plumpton, Lewes, E Sussex (☎ 0273 890248)

SHAND, Terence Richard; s of Terence James Shand, and Dorothy Joyce, *née* Shackell; *b* 27 Oct 1954; *Educ* Borehamwood GS; *m* 1 (m dis 1985) Maureen; 1 s (Elliot James b 1977); m 2, 22 March 1986, Arja, da of Paavo Saren; 1 s (Terence Elias b 1984), 1 da (Natalia Sirka b 1988); *Career* dir Stage One Records Ltd 1978-83, chm Castle Communications plc 1983-; *Recreations* tennis, shooting, skiing, reading; *Style—* Terence Shand, Esq; A29 Barwell Business Park, Leatherhead Rd, Chessington, Surrey KT9 2NY (☎ 081 974 1021, fax 081 974 2674)

SHAND, William Stewart; s of William Paterson Shand (d 1990), of Derby, and Annabella Kirkland Stewart, *née* Waddell (d 1952); *b* 12 Oct 1936; *Educ* Repton, St John's Coll Cambridge (MA, MB BChir, MD); *m* 26 Aug 1972, (Anne) Caroline Dashwood, da of Patrice Edouard Charvet, of Cheltenham; 2 s (Robert b 1974, James b 1976), 1 step s (Tom b 1967), 2 step da (Claire b 1964, Sophie b 1966); *Career* conslt surgn Bart's and Hackney and Homerton Hosps London 1973-, hon conslt surgn St Mark's Hosp for Diseases of the Colon and Rectum 1985-; Penrose-May teacher and memb Ct of Examiners RCS 1985-; memb: Worshipful Soc of Apothecaries 1974 (memb Ct of Assts), Worshipful Co of Barbers 1981; FRCS 1969, FRCS Ed 1970; *Books* The Art of Dying (jtly, 1989); *Recreations* painting, fishing, walking; *Style—* William Shand, Esq; 149 Harley St, London W1N 2DE (☎ 071 935 4444)

SHAND KYDD, Hon Mrs (Frances Ruth Burke); *née* Roche; yr da of 4 Baron Fermoy (d 1955), and Ruth, Lady Fermoy, DCVO, OBE, JP, *née* Gill; *b* 20 Jan 1936; *m* 1, 1 June 1954 (m dis 1969), 8 Earl Spencer, MVO, DL; 1 s (Viscount Althorp, and 1 s decd), 3 da (Lady Sarah McCorquodale, Lady Jane Fellowes, HRH The Princess of Wales); m 2, 2 May 1969, Peter Shand Kydd; *Style—* The Hon Mrs Shand Kydd; Ardencaple, Isle of Seil, by Oban, Argyll

SHANES, Eric; s of Mark Shanes of London, and Dinah, *née* Cohen (d 1977); *b* 21 Oct 1944; *Educ* Whittingehame Coll Brighton, Regent Street Poly Sch of Art, Chelsea Sch of Art (DipAD); *m* Jacky, da of Kenneth Darville (d 1969), of Windsor; 1 s (Mark b 1979), 1 da (Anna b 1976); *Career* author, journalist and artist; books: Turner's Picturesque Views in England and Wales 1979, Turner's Rivers Harbours and Coasts 1981, The Genius of the Royal Academy 1981, Hockney Posters 1987, Constantin Brancusi 1989, Turner's England 1990, Turner: The Masterworks 1990, Turner's Human Landscape 1990, Dali: The Masterworks 1990; journalist: classical music critic Daily Mail 1988-89, numerous contribs to Apollo and Modern Painters jls; artist: numerous studio shows of paintings and prints; photographic essay in Gustav Mahler: Songs and Symphonies of Death (Donald Mitchell, 1985); fndr ed: Turner Studies Art Book Review; guest exhibition curator: JMW Turner - the Foundations of Genius (Taft Museum Cincinnati) 1986, Masterpieces of English Watercolour from the Hickman Bacon Collection and the Fitzwilliam Museum Cambridge (touring Japan) 1990-91; lectr: Chelsea Sch of Art (pt/t) 1966-88, Dept of Art History Univ of Cambridge, Royal Coll of Music; lecture tours: N America 1982, 1983, 1984, 1986, Switzerland 1987, Malaysia 1988; Br Cncl Cultural Exchange award as official visitor: Romania 1982, Czechoslovakia 1984; Yorkshire Post Art Book award 1979; chm: Turner Soc 1988-, Save Acton Swimming Baths campaign (also fndr); *Recreations* music appreciation, swimming; *Style—* Eric Shanes, Esq; 7 Cumberland Rd, Acton, London W3 6EX (☎ 081 992 7985)

SHANIN, Prof Teodor; s of Meir Zajdsznur (d 1954), and Rebeka, *née* Jaszunski (d 1988); *b* 29 Oct 1930; *Educ* Univ of Jerusalem (BA), Univ of Birmingham (PhD), Univ of Manchester (MSc); *m* 1, (m dis 1962), Neomi; m 2, 1970, Dr Shulamith Ramon; 1 da (Aelita b 1976); *Career* 6 Regt of Commando (Palmakh) Israeli Army 1948-49; probation offr Miny of Welfare (former social worker Youth Care Servs) Tel Aviv 1952-56, dir Rehabilitation Centre (former rehabilitation offr for handicapped) Miny of Labour 1956-63, lectr in sociology Univ of Sheffield 1965-70 (on loan to Centre for Russian and E Euro Studies Univ of Birmingham 1968-70), assoc prof Haifa Univ Israel 1971-73 (sr lectr 1970-71), sr fell St Anthony's Coll Oxford 1973-74, head of Sociology Dept Univ of Manchester 1976- (prof 1974-); memb Br Sociological Assoc; *Books* Peasants and Peasant Societies (1971), The Awkward Class (1972), Russia as a 'Developing Society' (1985), Revolution as a Moment of Truth (1986), Defining Peasants (1990); *Recreations* fell walking, theatre; *Style—* Prof Teodor Shanin; Dept of Sociology, University of Manchester, Manchester M13 9PL (☎ 061 275 2503)

SHANK, Hon Mrs (Fiona Marilyn); *née* Monckton; 2 da of 12 Viscount Galway; *b* 1947; *m* 1974, Robert Wilford Shank; 1 s (Kevin William), 1 da (Adriane Leigh); *Style—* The Hon Mrs Shank; 9770 SW Buckskin Terrace, Beaverton, Oregon 97005, USA

SHANKS, Prof Ian Alexander; s of Alexander Shanks, of Maryville, 44 Victoria St, Dumbarton, Dunbartonshire, and Isabella Affleck, *née* Beaton; *b* 22 June 1948; *Educ* Dumbarton Acad, Glasgow Univ (BSc), CNAA (PhD); *m* 14 May 1971, Janice Smillie, da of J Coulter, of 3 Aitkenbar Circle, Bellsmyre, Dunbarton, Dunbartonshire; 1 da (Emma b 1977); *Career* projects mangr Scottish Colorfoto Labs Alexandria 1970-72, princ sci offr RSRE Malvern 1973-82, princ sci Unilever Res 1982-86, visiting prof of Electrical and Electronic Engrg Univ of Glasgow 1985-, chief sci Thorn EMI plc 1986-; memb: Optoelectronics Ctee The Rank Prize Funds 1985-, Steering Gp Sci and Engrg Policy Studies Unit 1988-90, Sci Consultative Gp BBC 1989-91, cncl and vice pres The Royal Soc 1989-; chm Inter-Agency Ctee on Marine Science and Technol 1991-; CEng, FIEE, FRS; *Recreations* music; *Style—* Prof Ian Shanks; Flintwood Cottage, Channer Drive, Penn, Bucks HP10 8HT (☎ 049 481 6941); Thorn EMI, Central Research Labs, Dawley Rd, Hayes, Middx UB3 1HH (☎ 081 848 6602)

SHANKS, Dr Jean Mary; da of Peter Martin Shanks (d 1960), and Gwendolen Margaret, *née* Thompson (d 1983); *b* 18 Nov 1925; *Educ* Badminton Sch Bristol, St Hugh's Coll Oxford (BA, BM BCh), Middlesex Hosp Med Sch; *m* 19 Nov 1976, Prince Yuri Nikolaivitch Galitzine, s of late Prince Nicolas Alexandrovitch Galitzine; *Career* house physician Princess Alice Hosp Eastbourne 1950-51, lectr Albany Med Sch 1951-52, house surgn Neurosurgical Dept Middlesex Hosp 1952-53, registrar in pathology West Middlesex Hosp, registrar and locum sr registrar in pathology Great Ormond St Hosp; fndr: Laboratory Harley St 1958 (became JS Pathology Servs Ltd 1977, now JS Pathology plc), Jean Shanks Fndn 1986-; memb Worshipful Soc of Apothecaries; memb: RSM, Hunterian Soc, Med Soc of London, Br Med Assoc, ACP, Soc of Occupational Med; *publications* Immune Aplastic Haemolytic Anaemia with Thrombocytopania (Br Med Jl, 1960), Haemoglobin Values in Business Executives (Br Jl Preventative and Social Med, 1967), Consequence of the provision of laboratory services for the National Health Service by commercial firms: a view from the private sector (1990); *Recreations* playing the piano, gardening, collecting antiques and paintings; *Style—* Dr Jean Shanks; 8 South Eaton Place, London SW1W 9JA (☎ 071 730 3175); Quaintree House, Braunston-in-Rutland LE15 8QS; JS Pathology plc, Bewlay House, 32 Jamestown Rd, London NW1 7BY (☎ 071 267 2672, fax 071 267 2551)

SHANKS, Rev Norman James; s of James Shanks, CBE, of Edinburgh (d 1990), and Marjory Kirkwood, *née* Hind (d 1967); *b* 15 July 1942; *Educ* Stirling HS, Univ of St Andrews (MA), Univ of Edinburgh (BD); *m* 29 July 1968, Ruth, da of Very Rev Dr Hugh Osborne Douglas, KCVO, CBE (former Dean of Chapel Royal in Scotland, d 1987); 2 s (Andrew b 1971, David b 1973), 1 da (Jane b 1969); *Career* civil servant Scottish Office 1964-79, private sec to Sec of State for Scotland 1977-79, chaplain Univ of Edinburgh 1985-88, lectr in theol and church history Univ of Glasgow 1988-; chm: Sec of States Advsy Ctee on Scotland's Travelling People 1986-88, Edinburgh Cncl of Social Serv 1986-88; convener Church of Scotland's Church and Nation Ctee 1988-, memb Bdcasting Cncl for Scotland 1988-; memb Iona Community 1980; *Style—* The Rev Norman Shanks; 1 Marchmont Terrace, Glasgow, Scotland G12 9LT (☎ 041 339 4421); Dept of Theology & Church History, The University, Glasgow G12 8QQ (☎ 041 339 8855)

SHANKS, Philip David; s of late Frank Ernest Shanks; *b* 6 Nov 1934; *Educ* Uppingham, Coventry Coll of Art; *m* 1, 1960 (m dis), Mary Christine, da of John Davis, of Stratford-on-Avon; 1 s (Jonathan David b 1961), 1 da (Katherine Mary b 1962); m 2, 1970 (m dis), Susan Elizabeth, da of late Walter Burnhill; 1 s (Hugo Christian b 1976); *Career* Nat Serv Lt RE 1953-55; design mangr Reckitt & Colman (Overseas) Ltd 1962-68, md Philip Shanks Associates Ltd 1968-75, ptnr Consortium Design 1968-72, dir Philip Shanks Design 1972-78, chief exec New Forest Show Soc 1978-, dir Agric Show Promotions 1985-86 (md 1986-); MSIAD; *Recreations* sailing, walking; *Clubs* Lymington Town Sailing; *Style—* Philip Shanks, Esq; 12 Carey's Cottages, Brockenhurst, Hants SO42 7TF (☎ 0590 23636)

SHANKS, Prof Robert Gray; s of Robert Shanks, and Mary, *née* Gray; *b* 4 April 1934; *Educ* Methodist Coll Belfast, The Queen's Univ of Belfast (MB, MD, BSc, DSc, MRCP); *m* 10 Dec 1960, Denise Isabel Sheila, da of (Victor) Cecil Woods (d 1971), of Bangor, NI; 4 da (Amanda b 1961, Melanie b 1962, Deborah b 1962, Rachel b 1968); *Career* head of cardiovascular pharmacology Pharmaceutical Div ICI Ltd 1962-66; Queen's Univ of Belfast: lectr and conslt in clinical pharmacology 1967-72, prof of clinical pharmacology 1972-77, Whitla prof and head Dept Therapeutics and Pharmacology 1977-, dean Faculty of Med 1986-; memb GMC; MRIA 1987; *Recreations* golf, gardening; *Style—* Prof Robert Shanks; Department of Therapeutics and Pharmacology, The Queen's University of Belfast, Whitla Medical Building, 97 Lisburn Rd, Belfast, Northern Ireland BT9 7BL (☎ 0232 329241 ext 2785, fax 0232 438346, telex 274895 QUBADM)

SHANNON, Dr (Michael) Colin; CBE (1988); s of Victor Charles Shannon, of Sandling House, Hollesley, Suffolk, and Ruth, *née* Fenton (d 1958); *b* 25 Dec 1929; *Educ* Whitgift Sch, Guys Hosp Univ of London (MB BS); *m* 31 Oct 1959, Patricia Anne, da of Rev Heber Goldsworthy (d 1938), of China; 2 s (Samuel Richard, George Russell), 2 da (Clare Margaret, Alexandra Jane); *Career* RAC 1948-50: 2 Lt 1949, Garrison Def Egypt Canal Zone 1949-50; GP Hollesley Suffolk 1959; MO 1966-: HMYCC Hollesley Bay, RAF Bawdsey; memb: Deben RDC 1964-74 (chm 1971-74), Suffolk Coastal DC 1973- (chm 1973-75, chm Policy Ctee 1979-89, ldr Cncl 1979-89), assoc DC 1977-, Health and Safety Cmmn 1981-; MRCGP 1966; *Style—* Dr Colin Shannon, CBE; Sandling House, Hollesley, Woodbridge, Suffolk (☎ 0394 411214)

SHANNON, John; s of John Shannon (d 1951), and Sarah, *née* McHenry (d 1968); *b* 29 March 1917; *Educ* Belfast Public Elementary Sch; *m* 15 June 1946, Isobel May Smith; 1 s (Thomas b 1957), 1 da (Moira b 1956); *Career* internal auditor Electricty Bd NI 1940-45, asst budget offr Fisons plc 1945-51, chief accountant Vitamins Ltd 1951-57, accounting mangr Du Pont UK 1959-62; dir and sec: Truscon Ltd 1964-74, Tileman Ltd 1975-82; ret 1982; active private investor 1982-; memb: Richmond and Barnes Cons Assoc, Investmt and Fin Servs Gp Inst of Chartered Secretaries; Freeman: City of London, Worshipful Co of Chartered Secretaries; FCIS 1945, FCMA 1950; *Clubs* City Livery, IOD; *Style—* John Shannon, Esq; Silver Birches, 2 Temple Sheen, E Sheen, London SW14 7RP (☎ 081 876 1701)

SHANNON, Michael Stuart (Mike); s of Dennis Shannon, of Newport Gwent, and Dorothy Shannon; *b* 28 June 1938; *Educ* Newport HS, UCW Aberystwyth (BSc, Dip Ed), Univ Coll of N Wales (M Ed), Univ of Nottingham, Open Univ Business Sch; *m* 9 Sept 1961 (m dis 1985), Jacky Townsend; 1 s (Alasdair), 1 da (Kirstie); *Career* tutor and cnsllr: Cyprus Forces Scheme 1972-74, Open Univ 1975-79; secdy teacher: St Saviour's Sch Poplar London 1961-62, Hartridge Comp 1962-63; RAF: educn offr RAF Hereford 1964-67 and RAF Valley Anglesey 1967-71, offr i/c Near East Air Force Mountain Rescue Team 1971-72, schs offr Limassol Cyprus 1972-74, sr educn and trg offr RAF Coningsby Lincolnshire 1974-77, head Instructional Techniques Dept RAF Sch of Educn RAF Newton 1978-80, staff offr Schs and Community Educn 1980-82; mangr Sir Isaac Pitman Ltd E Africa (Nairobi) 1982-83, md Pitman Central Coll 1983-85, unit gen mangr Acute and Gen Unit Warrington Health Authy 1988- (unit gen mangr Mental Illness Unit 1985-88); one time Welsh Int at basketball and athletics, Br Univs Br Jr Athletics champion, Combined Servs and RAF basketball rep; *Recreations* mountaineering, rock climbing, birdwatching, squash; *Clubs* mountain club of Kenya; *Style—* Mike Shannon, Esq; The General Manager, Warrington District, General Hospital, Loury Lane, Warrington WA5 1QG (☎ 0925 35911 ext 229, fax 0925 36789)

SHANNON, 9 Earl of (I 1756); Richard Bentinck Boyle; sits as Baron Carleton (GB 1786); also Viscount Boyle and Baron Castle-Martyr (both I 1756); s of 8 Earl (d 1963); *b* 23 Oct 1924; *Educ* Eton; *m* 1, 1947 (m dis 1955), Donna Catherine Irene Helen, da of Marchese Demetrio Imperiali di Francavilla (cr by King Victor Amadeus III of Sardinia 1779); m 2, 1957 (m dis 1979), Susan Margaret, da of late John Russell Hogg; 1 s, 2 da; *Heir* s, Viscount Boyle; *Career* Capt Irish Gds and RWAFF 1942-54; sec Fedn of Euro Indust Co-op Res Orgns 1975-86; chm: Fndn Sci and Technol 1977-83, Strategy Europe Ltd, Corporate Communications International Ltd, Community

Team Television Ltd (formerly Birmingham Team Television Ltd), Access Parly Public Affrs; dir Ctee Dirs Res Assoc 1969-85; vice pres Inland Waterways Assoc, dep speaker and dep chm Ctees House of Lords 1968-78; FRSA, FBIM, MBHI; *Recreations* horology, inland waterways; *Clubs* White's; *Style—* The Rt Hon the Earl of Shannon; Pimm's Cottage, Man's Hill, Burghfield Common, Berkshire RG7 3BD

SHANNON, Prof Richard Thomas; s of Edward Arthur Shannon (d 1958), of Auckland, New Zealand, and Grace, *née* McLeod (d 1985); *b* 10 June 1931; *Educ* Mt Albert GS Auckland, Univ of Auckland, Gonville and Caius Coll Cambridge; *Career* lectr in history Univ of Auckland 1961-62, reader in history UEA 1971-79 (lectr 1963-71), prof of modern history Univ Coll Swansea 1979- (head of dept 1982-88, dean Faculty of Arts 1985-88), visiting fell Peterhouse Cambridge 1988-89; FRHistS 1970; *Books* Gladstone and The Bulgarian Agitation 1876 (1963), The Crisis of Imperialism 1865-1915 (1974), Gladstone, Vol I: 1809-1865 (1982); *Recreations* travel, wine, gardens, books; *Clubs* Athenaeum; *Style—* Prof Richard Shannon; 33 Brynmill Terrace, Swansea SA2 0BA (☎ 0792 464 818); Dept of History, University College of Swansea, Singleton Park, Swansea SA2 8PP (☎ 0792 295225)

SHANNON, Dr Robert William Ernest; *b* 10 Oct 1937; *Educ* Belfast Tech HS, Belfast Coll of Technol (HNC, Inst Marine Engrs prize for Heat Engines, Belfast Assoc of Engrs prize for Best Student, Capt J S Davidson Meml prize for Best Student of the Year, Royal Aeronautical Soc (Belfast Branch) prize for Best Student in Aeronautics), Queen's Univ Belfast (BSc, PhD, Univ fndn scholarship); *m* Annabelle; 2 c; *Career* laboratory technician James Mackie & Sons Ltd Belfast 1954-55; Short Bro & Harland Ltd Belfast: aircraft engrg apprentice 1955-58, aerodynamicist Light Aircraft Div Design Office 1958-62 (pt/t 1959- 62), pt/t stressman 1962-63; The Queen's Univ of Belfast: asst lectr Dept of Aeronautical Engrg 1963-66, res fell Dept of Mechanical Engrg 1966-70 (lectr 1970); pt/t conslt 1966-70; Res and Devpt Div British Gas Corporation: specialist in fracture 1970-74 (seconded to Civil Engrg Dept The Queen's Univ of Belfast 1970-72), div mangr on-line inspection 1975-77 (asst div mangr 1974-75), chief project engr on-line inspection 1977-78, dir on-line inspection 1983-89 (asst dir 1978-83), HQ dir of engrg res 1989- (responsible for formation of a Tech Servs Div 1990-); memb Coquet HS TVEI Advsy Ctee 1988-, appointed to NE British Airways Consumer Cncl 1989, external examiner in BEng in engrg technol at Poly of Newcastle upon Tyne 1989-; memb Advsy Ctee for Dept of Mechanical Engrg Univ of Sheffield 1989, Poly and Colls Funding Cncl Res Ctee 1989-, Mgmnt Ctee Univ of Newcastle upon Tyne Design Centre 1990-; Inst of Mechanical Engrs: memb N Eastern Branch Mgmnt Ctee 1982, memb Cncl 1989-, memb Qualifications Bd 1989-, memb Cncl Exec Ctee 1989-; vice chm Communications Bd 1989-, chm N Eastern Branch 1989-; memb Cncl Inst of Gas Engrs 1990- (memb N Eastern Section Mgmnt Ctee 1985-88); author of numerous pubns concerned with gas pipelines; lectr President's Honour Lecture Br Inst of Non-Destructive Testing 1990; *Awards* Lee Guinness prize 1954, Inst of Marine Engrs prize 1957, Belfast Aeronautical Soc prize 1957, Royal Aeronautical Soc prize 1959, Belfast Assoc of Engrs prize 1962, Inst of Gas Engrs Gold Medal 1982, MacRobert Award 1989; FIMechE, FIGE fell Br Inst of Non-Destructive Testing, FEng, MRAes; *Style—* Dr Robert Shannon; Croft House, Beal Bank, Warkworth, Northumberland NE65 OTA (☎ 0665 711380); British Gas plc, Research & Technology Division, Engineering Research Station, Killingworth, Newcastle upon Tyne NE99 1LH (☎ 091 216 0202)

SHAPCOTT, Sidney Edward; s of Percy Thomas Shapcott (d 1966), of Torquay, and Beatrice, *née* Hobbs (d 1968); *b* 20 June 1920; *Educ* Hele's Sch Exeter, King's Coll London (BSc); *m* 4 Sept 1943, Betty Jean, *née* Richens; 2 s (Christopher b 1955, William b 1961), 1 da (Susan b 1951); *Career* Miny of Supply and Miny of Aviation 1941-65 (DCSO 1963), dir of projects Euro Space Res Orgn Delft Netherlands 1963-65, Navy Dept MOD 1965-75 (CSO 1968), dep dir Admty Surface Weapons Estab Portsmouth 1968-72, dir under water weapon projects Admty Under Water Weapons Estab Portland 1972-75, dir gen Airborne Weapons and Electronic Systems MOD Procurement Exec 1976-80; engrg conslt in private practice 1981-85; memb Devonshire Assoc; FInstP 1971, FIEE 1974; *Recreations* motoring, English churches; *Style—* Sidney Shapcott, Esq; 23 Upper Churston Rise, Seaton, Devon EX12 2HD (☎ 0297 21545)

SHAPER, Prof (Andrew) Gerald; s of Jack Shaper (d 1960), of Cape Town, SA, and Molly, *née* Harris (d 1980); *b* 9 Aug 1927; *Educ* Univ of Cape Town (MB ChB), Univ of Liverpool (DTMandH); *m* 5 July 1952, Lorna June, da of Lt-Col Cyril Ewart Clarke (d 1964), of Zimbabwe; 1 s (Nicholas b 1961); *Career* registrar Hammersmith Hosp and Postgrad Med Sch 1955-56, prof of cardiovascular res Makerere Univ Med Sch Kampala 1957-69 (former lectr, sr lectr, reader), memb scientific staff MRC Social Med Unit LSHTM 1970-75, hon conslt cardiologist UCH 1970-87, prof of clinical epidemiology Royal Free Hosp Med Sch 1975-; chm: MRC Health Serv Res Panel 1981-86, Heads of Academic Depts of Community Med 1987-90; memb: Harveian Soc London, Nat Forum for the Prevention of Coronary Heart Disease, Br Cardiac Soc, Atherosclerosis Discussion Gp, Soc for Social Med, Int Epidemiological Assoc; *Books* Medicine in a Tropical Environment (ed 1972), Cardiovascular Disease in the Tropics (ed 1974), Coronary Heart Disease: Risks and Reasons (1988); *Recreations* walking, second-hand and antiquarian books, theatre; *Style—* Prof Gerald Shaper; 8 Wentworth Hall, The Ridgeway, Mill Hill Village, London NW7 1RJ (☎ 081 959 8742); 2 Church Hill, Fremington, Barnstaple, North Devon; Dept of Public Health and Primary Care, Royal Free Hospital School of Medicine, Hampstead, London NW3 2PF (☎ 071 794 0500 ext 4293)

SHAPER, Hal; s of Jack Shaper (d 1961), of S Africa, and Malka Shaper (d 1981); *b* 18 July 1931; *Educ* Wunberg Boys HS S Africa, Univ of Capetown S Africa; *m* Philippa Marsh,; 1 da (Holly); *Career* writer, songwriter and lyricist; writer of book and lyrics for theatrical prodns incl: Jane Eyre (NY 1988), Treasure Island (Mermaid Theatre), Great Expectations (Australian Tour 1991), Cyrano 1991; writer of lyrics for over 100 films incl: Papillon, The Boys From Brazil, First Blood/Rambo; collaborator with: John Williams, Michel Legrand, Francis Lai, Gerry Goldsmith; works recorded by: Frank Sinatra, Barbara Streisand, Elvis Presley, Bing Crosby, Elton John and Grace Jones; songs incl over 400 versions of Softly, As I Leave You and many other hits; books incl Sinatra: The Man and The Music, chm Sparta Florida Music Group and Prestige Records; *awards* Br Acad awards for Treasure Island and Great Expectations as Best Musical of the Year and awards in Best Song Musically and Lyrically category; *Recreations* tennis, chess, collecting Faberg'e pieces; *Clubs* Queen's, Hurlingham, Chelsea Arts, The Manorial Assoc (Lord of Stoke Bruerne); *Style—* Hal Shaper, Esq

SHAPIRO, Erin Patria Margaret (aka Erin Pizzey); *née* Carney; da of Cyril Carney, MBE (d 1980), and Ruth Patricia Last; *b* 19 Feb 1939; *Educ* Leweston Manor Sherborne Dorset; *m* 1, 1961 (m dis 1979), John Leo Pizzey; 1 s (Amos b 1967), 1 da (Cleo b 1961); m 2, 1980, Jeffrey Scott Shapiro; 5 stepchildren (Francis, Trevor, Annie, Richard, Daren); *Career* author, journalist, social reformer; fndr Shelter Movement for Battered Men, Women and Children; Int Order of Volunteers for Peace Diploma of Honour 1981, Nancy Astor Award for Journalism 1983, Distinguished Leadership Award (World Congress of Victimology) 1987; *Books* Scream Quietly or the Neighbours Will Hear, Infernal Child, Sluts Cookbook, Erin Pizzey Collects, Prone To Violence, All In The Name of Love; fiction: The Watershed, In the Shadow of the Castle, The Pleasure Palace, First Lady, The Consul General's Daughter (1988), The Snow Leopard of Shanghai (1989), Other Lovers (1991), Pets (1991); short stories: The Man in the Blue Van, The Frangipani Tree, Addiction, Dancing; articles: Choosing a Non-Violent Relationship, Sexual Abuse Within the Family; has contributed to many leading newspapers and journals; TV documentaries incl: Scream Quietly (1975), Chiswick Womens Aid (1977), That Awful Woman (1987), Cutting Edge: Sanctuary (1991); *Recreations* reading, cooking, antiques, violin, wine, travel; *Style—* Mrs Shapiro; c/o Christoper Little, 49 Queen Victoria St, London EC4N 4SA (☎ 071 236 4881)

SHAPIRO, Dr Leonard Melvyn; s of Joseph Shapiro, of London, and Stella, *née* Solomon; *b* 9 March 1951; *Educ* Leyton County HS London, Univ of Manchester (BSc, MB ChB, MD); *m* 1978, Alison Patricia, da of Maj Frederick Howat; 1 s (Paul Richard Howat b 3 May 1984), 1 da (Laura Diana b 10 Sept 1980); *Career* sr registrar Nat Heart Hosp 1983-88, conslt cardiologist Papworth and Addenbrooke's Hosps Cambridge 1988-; special interests: echocardiography, athlete's heart, coronary artery disease, coronary balloon angioplasty; fndr chm Br Soc of Echocardiography; memb: Cardiac Soc, American Coll of Cardiology; MRCP (UK) 1978; *Books* A Colour Atlas of Hypertension (with K M Fox, 1985, 2 edn with M Bucalter, 1991), A Colour Atlas of Angina Pectoris (with K M Fox and C Warnes, 1986), A Colour Atlas of Heart Failure (with K M Fox, 1987), A Colour Atlas of Physical Signs in Cardiovascular Disease (with K M Fox, 1988), A Colour Atlas of Palpitations and Syncope (with K M Fox, 1989), A Colour Atlas of Congenital Heart Disease in the Adult (with K M Fox, 1989), A Colour Atlas of Coronary Artery Atherosclerosis (1990); *Style—* Dr Leonard Shapiro; Regional Cardiac Unit, Papworth Hospital, Papworth Everard, Cambridge CB3 8RE (☎ 0480 830541 ext 353, fax 0480 831083)

SHAPIRO, Hon Mrs (Virginia); *née* Makins; da of 1 Baron Sherfield, GCB, GCMG; *b* 1939; *Educ* LMH Oxford; *m* 1972, David Michael Shapiro; *Style—* The Hon Mrs Shapiro; 14 Woodstock Rd, London W4

SHAPLAND, Maj-Gen Peter Charles; CB (1977), MBE (1960); s of Frederick Charles Shapland (d 1960), of Merton Park, Surrey, and Annie Frances, *née* Carr (d 1970); *b* 14 July 1923; *Educ* Rutlish Sch Merton Park, St Catharine's Coll Cambridge (MA); *m* 1 April 1954, Joyce Barbara, da of Fraser Leopold Peradon (d 1973), of India, Jersey and Chichester; 2 s (Michael b 1958, Timothy b 1962); *Career* served WWII with RE in UK and India, Lt-Col 1965, Brig 1968, Cdr Engr Bde TA & VR 1968, RCDS 1971, dep cdr and COS HQ SE Dist 1972-74; dir volunteers territorials and cadets MOD 1974-78, Hon Col 73 Engr Regt TA 1979-89, sr planning inspr DOE 1980-, Col Cmdt RE 1981-86, pres inst RE 1982-87, chm Combined Cadet Force Assoc 1982-; Freeman City of London 1983, Liveryman Worshipful Co of Painter-Stainers 1983; *Clubs* Royal Ocean Racing, Royal Engr Yacht, Lansdowne; *Style—* Maj-Gen Peter Shapland, CB, MBE; c/o Holts Branch, Royal Bank of Scotland, Kirkland House, Whitehall, London SW1A 2EB

SHAPLAND, Sir William Arthur; s of Arthur Frederick Shapland and Alice Maud, *née* Jackson; *b* 20 Oct 1912; *Educ* Tollington Sch Muswell Hill; *m* 1943, Madeline Annie, da of James Amiss; 2 da (Janet, Anne); *Career* Allan Charlesworth & Co CAs: joined 1929, ptnr 1946-55; Blackwood Hodge plc: joined 1946, dir 1946-55, exec dir 1955-64, exec chm 1964-83; tstee dir Bernard Sunley Charitable Fndn 1960-; govr Utd World Coll of the Atlantic; tstee: Charing Cross Sunley Res Centre Tst, Monks Ferry Trg Tst; memb: Cncl Charing Cross Westminster Med Sch until 1990, Ct of Univ of Leicester; vice pres: London Fedn of Boys' Clubs, S London Scouts Cncl; Wayneflete Fell Magdalen Coll Oxford 1981; hon fell St Catherine's Coll Oxford 1982, Hon DSc Buckingham 1986, Hon DLitt Univ of Leicester 1983; memb Worshipful Co of Paviors (Master 1980-81); FCA 1936, Hon FRCS 1978; OStJ 1981, KStJ 1987; kt 1982; *Recreations* golf, fishing, travel; *Clubs* Garrick City Livery; *Style—* Sir William Shapland; 44 Beech Drive, London N2 9NY (☎ 081 883 5073); office: 50-51 Conduit St, London W1R 9FB (☎ 071 287 8333)

SHAREEF, Athar Ali; s of Safdar Ali Shareef (d 1985), of Karachi, Pakistan, and Khurshid, *née* Taki; *b* 27 Nov 1941; *Educ* Royal Coll Colombo Ceylon, Univ of Manchester (BSc); *m* 26 April 1962, Zujajeth (Zuju), da of Dr Hyder Ali Khan (d 1967), of Hyderabad, India; 2 da (Hinna b 1964, d 1978, Juhi b 1975); *Career* chm CMS Consits 1977-79, vice pres CACI Inc Int 1981-84, dir Inforem Ltd 1984-87, dep chm Inforem plc 1988-89 (dir 1987-); chm Shamley Green Village Soc; memb: Guildford Cons Assoc, Shamley Green Village CC; MIEE 1970, CEng 1970; *Recreations* reading, walking, cricket; *Style—* Athar Shareef, Esq; Pond Cottage, Shamley Green, Guildford, Surrey GU5 OUA (☎ 0483 893125); Inforem Plc, Inforem House, Weybridge Business Park, Weybridge, Surrey KT15 2UF (☎ 0932 859011, fax 0932 858310, car 0860 229205, telex 673761)

SHARKEY, Anna; da of William Sharkey, of Glasgow, and Catherine, *née* MacDonald; *Educ* St Catherine's Convent Edinburgh, Royal Acad of Dancing; *m* 1 (m dis 1974), Clive Benabou Cazes (d 1989); m 2, 3 Nov 1976, Jonathan Cecil, s of Professor Lord David Cecil, CH, of Red Lion House, Cranbourne, Dorset; *Career* actress, singer; theatre incl: Expresso Bongo 1958, World of Paul Slickey 1959, Divorce Me Darling 1964, Young Visitors 1969, Gigi 1976, Cowardy Custard 1972, Maggie 1977, Canterbury Tales 1979, The Little Night Music 1979, A Mummy's Tomb 1980, The Orchestra 1981, HMS Pinafore 1982, Ring Round the Moon 1985, Piaf 1985, Nunsense 1987, The Circle 1988; TV incl: Dr Finlay's Casebook, Mammon, Cilla Comedy Six 1974, Girls of Slender Means 1975, Freud Strauss, CQ, Rumpole of the Bailey (1990); opera incl: L'Elisir D'Amore 1970, Hansel and Gretel 1970, Zaza 1971, Poisoned Kiss 1972, La Vie Parisienne 1974; films incl: Oliver 1967, The Music Lovers 1968; radio incl: Morning Stories, Friday Night is Music Night, Among Your Souvenirs; SWET best actress in musical 1977; memb Catholic Stage Guild; *Recreations* cooking, gardening, French operetta; *Style—* Ms Anna Sharkey; c/o Patrick Freeman, 4 Cromwell Grove, London W6 7RG (☎ 071 602 4035)

SHARKEY, John; *b* 24 Sept 1947; *Educ* Univ of Manchester (BSc Maths); *m* 3 da; *Career* formerly with: Benton & Bowles, KMP; Saatchi & Saatchi: joined 1984, dep chm 1986, md 1987; chm: BDDP 1990-, Broad Street Group; fndr Bainsfair Sharkey Trott 1990 (jt chm and chief exec offr 1990-); *Style—* John Sharkey, Esq; BDDP Holdings (UK) Ltd, 4-6 Soho Square, London W1V 5DE (☎ 071 287 7778, fax 071 287 1635)

SHARLAND, Dr Desmond Edward; s of Edward Harry Sharland (d 1964), of London, and Beatrice, *née* Gleeson (d 1952); *b* 13 April 1929; *Educ* Gunnersbury Catholic GS, London Hosp Med Sch (BSc, MB BS, MD); *m* 1, 9 June 1956, Edna (d 1974), da of William Guscott (d 1953); 1 s (Stephen William *b* 3 April 1957), 1 da (Sarah Jane b 5 May 1961); m 2, 12 April 1986, Dulcie, *née* Newboult; *Career* conslt physician Whittington Hosp 1965-, hon sr lectr Univ Coll Hosp 1965-, sr lectr in anatomy Royal Free Hosp Sch of Med 1970-; memb Guild of Catholic Drs; FRSM 1960, FRCP 1975; *Books* Whittington Post-Graduate Medicine (jtly, 1974); *Recreations* cruising and dancing; *Style—* Dr Desmond Sharland; Fircroft, St Andrews Close, London N12 8BA (☎ 081 445 1214); Whittington Hospital, London N19 (☎ 071 288 5324)

SHARLAND, (Edward) John; s of William Rex Sharland (d 1987), and Phyllis Eileen, *née* Pitts (d 1990); *b* 25 Dec 1937; *Educ* Monmouth, Jesus Coll Oxford (BA, MA); *m*

14 Feb 1970, Susan Mary Rodway, da of Douglas Rodway Millard, of Mill Ford House, Long Melford, Sudbury, Suffolk; 4 da (Nicola b 1971, Sandy b 1972, Philippa b 1974, Rebecca b 1975); *Career* FCO: London 1961-62, second sec (commercial) Bangkok 1962-67, Far E Dept London 1967-69, first sec Vienna 1969-72, first sec and head of Chancery Bangkok 1972-75, first sec (commercial) and consul Montevideo 1976-79, asst Cultural Rels Dept London 1979-82; consul gen: Perth 1982-87, Cleveland 1987-89; high cmmr Port Moresby 1989-; *Recreations* tennis, bridge, gardening; *Style—* John Sharland, Esq; c/o FCO, King Charles St, London SW1A 2AH

SHARMA, Bhawani Persaud; s of Kedarnauth Maraj Sharma, and Sursatti Maraj; *b* 24 March 1930; *Educ* Queen's Coll Guyana, W London Coll, E London Coll, Inns of Court School of Law; *m* 7 Dec 1952 (m dis), Sabitri Persaud, da of Pandit Seepersand Tewarie; 4 da (Shree Viji Davi Persaud Sharma, Praimnauth Persaud Sharma, Roopnauth Persaud Sharma, Chumattie Persaud Sharma); *Career* certified accountants London C of C 1947-, memb Hon Soc of Inner Temple 1969-; FCIArb; *Style—* Bhawani Persaud Sharma, Esq; 2 Stone Buildings, Lincoln's Inn, London WC2 3TA (☎ 071 405 4232/3, fax 081 998 1806)

SHARMAN, Colin Morven; OBE (1980); *b* 19 Feb 1943; *m* Angela; 1 s (Richard b 1972), 1 da (Sarah b 1969); *Career* qualified Chartered Accountant WoolgarHennel & Co 1965; Peat Marwick McLintock (now KPMG Peat Marwick McLintock): joined 1966 audit and fin investigation London, mangr Frankfurt 1970-72, ptnr The Hague 1973 (joined 1972), estab Norwegian practice 1973, ptnr i/c The Hague 1975, expanded practice Benelux Scandinavia and the Netherlands 1977-81, large scale investmt London 1981-87, sr ptnr Nat Mktg and Indust Gps and chm KPMG Mktg Ctee 1987-90, sr mgmnt consultancy ptnr 1989-90, sr regnl ptnr for London and South East 1990-; past chm Bd of Govrs British Sch in the Netherlands, vice chm Cncl Br Ind Schs in the EC, memb Advsy Panel City Univ Business Sch, chm Bembridge Cadet Week; FCA (ACA 1965); *Recreations* outdoor and field sports, shooting, sailing; *Style—* Colin Sharman, Esq, OBE; Tytherton Lucas, nr Chippenham, Wiltshire

SHARMAN, Patrick George; s of Charles A Sharman (d 1988), of Peterborough, and Betty, *née* Roll; *b* 8 July 1939; *Educ* Marlborough, Pembroke Coll Cambridge (MA); *m* 1; 1 s (Robert b 2 April 1969), 1 da (Caroline b 21 Oct 1964); m 2, 26 July 1978, Wendy, *née* Read; 2 s (Timothy b 12 Oct 1978, Algernon b 19 Aug 1980); *Career* admitted slr 1965; articled clerk Theodore Goddard & Co, ptnr Bircham & Co 1968-73, dir and slr Sharman Newspapers Ltd 1973-89, chm Sharman & Co Ltd 1989-; dir: Anglia TV Group plc, Mid-Anglia Radio plc; Freeman: City of London, Worshipful Co of Slrs; memb Law Soc 1965; *Recreations* tennis; *Style—* Patrick Sharman, Esq; 5 Chaucer Road, Cambridge CB2 2EB (☎ 0223 356927); Sharman & Company Ltd, Newark Rd, Peterborough PE1 5TD (☎ 0733 555300, fax 0733 555400, car 0860 564216)

SHARMAN, Peter William; CBE (1984); s of William Charles Sharman (d 1971), and Olive Mabel, *née* Burl (d 1961); *b* 1 June 1924; *Educ* Northgate GS Ipswich, Univ of Edinburgh (MA); *m* 1946, Eileen Barbara, *née* Crix; 1 s, 2 da; *Career* chief gen mangr Norwich Union Insur Gp 1975-84 (dir 1974-); chm: Life Offices Assoc 1977-79, British Insur Assoc 1982-1983 (dep chm 1981-82); dir: Riggs A P Bank Ltd 1976-90, Norwich and Peterborough Bldg Soc 1985-, Jarrold & Sons Ltd 1987-; FIA; *Recreations* golf, tennis, badminton; *Style—* Peter Sharman, Esq, CBE; 28B Eaton Rd, Norwich NR4 6PZ; Norwich Union Insurance Group, P O Box 4, Norwich (☎ 0603 622200)

SHARMAN-RADFORD, Elizabeth St Clare; MBE (1990); da of Charles Eric Sharman, and Edith, *née* Ashbarry; *b* 8 Aug 1957; *Educ* Thurston Upper Sch Suffolk; *m* 12 July 1980, George Robert Radford 1 s (Jonathan George b 20 Nov 1990); *Career* canoeist; nat champion 1978-89, Euro champion 1986-88 (1982-84), world canoe slalom champion 1987-89 (1983-85), memb Olympic Team Seoul 1988, currently memb GB Canoe Slalom Squad; *Recreations* canoeing and general sports; *Clubs* Stafford and Stone Canoe, Bury St Edmunds Canoe, Nottingham Kayak; *Style—* Mrs Elizabeth Sharman-Radford MBE

SHARP, Sir Adrian; 4 Bt (UK 1922), of Warden Court, Maidstone, Kent; s of Sir Edward Herbert Sharp, 3 Bt (d 1985), and Beryl, Lady Sharp, *qv*; *b* 17 Sept 1951; *m* 1976, Hazel Patricia, only da of James Trevor Wallace, of Pietersburg, S Africa, and former w of William Ian Barrett Bothwell; *Heir* br, Owen Sharp, *qv*; *Career* exec sales mangr Ford Motor Co; *Style—* Sir Adrian Sharp, Bt; 119 Nirvana Road, Brighton Beach, Durban, S Africa

SHARP, His Hon Alastair George; MBE (1945), QC (1961), DL (1973); s of Alexander Sharp (d 1923), of Aberdeen, and Isabella, *née* Lyall, OBE (d 1962); *b* 25 May 1911; *Educ* Aberdeen GS, Fettes, Clare Coll Cambridge (BA); *m* 10 Sept 1940, Daphne Sybil, da of Maj Harold Smithers (ka 1916), of Plymouth; 1 s (Alastair b 13 April 1944), 2 da (Lindsay b 1 Oct 1942, Clare b 12 Jan 1950); *Career* cmmnd The Gordon Highlanders 1939, served 1939-45, 2 Bn The London Scottish 1943, WO Gen Staff 1944-45; called to the Bar Middle Temple 1935, in practice 1936-62, rec Rotherham 1960-62, county ct judge 1962-70, chm Durham County Quarter Sessions 1970-72, circuit judge 1972-84; chm Washington New Town Licenced Premises Ctee 1966-78, Faculty of Law Univ of Durham 1971-84, memb Ctee Durham County Magistrates Cts 1972-84, liaison judge Durham County Magistrates 1972-84, govr Sherburn Hosp 1978-81; *Recreations* golf, gardening, hillwalking, music, fishing; *Clubs* Durham County, Brancepeth Golf; *Style—* His Hon Alastair Sharp, MBE, QC, DL; High Point, Western Hill, Durham DH1 4RG; The Old Kennels, Tomintoul, Banffshire AB3 9EN

SHARP, Anthony Arthur Vivian; s of Vivian Arthur Sharp (d 1978), and Violet Elizabeth, *née* Johnson (d 1981); *b* 5 Nov 1938; *Educ* Repton; *m* 17 Sept 1966, Jill Treharne, da of Hugh Treharne Morgan, OBE, of Alchornes, Lordswell Lane, Crowborough, Sussex; 2 da (Antoinette b 1969, Fiona b 1970); *Career* Nat Serv 1957-59, cmmnd Midshipman 1958, RNR 1958-66, Sub Lt 1959, Lt 1962; dir: H Clarkson Ltd 1978-86 (asst dir 1975-78), Clarkson Puckle Ltd 1978-86, Horace Holman Ltd 1986-88, Nelson Hurst and Marsh Agencies Ltd 1988-90, Jardine Ltd (Lloyd's underwriting agents) 1990-; underwriting memb Lloyd's 1972; treas Wivelsfield Cons Assoc 1979-82 (memb Ctee 1978-82); memb: London Ctee Sail Trg Assoc 1968-81, Insur Brokers' Registration Cncl 1983-88; *Recreations* tennis, shooting, sailing, skiing; *Clubs* City Univ, Lloyd's Yacht, Lloyd's Lawn Tennis; *Style—* Anthony Sharp, Esq; Jardine (Lloyd's Underwriting Agents) Ltd., 6 Crutched Friars, London EC3N 2HT (☎ 071 528 4444, fax 071 528 4795, telex 8814844 JMIB)

SHARP, Beryl, Lady; Beryl Kathleen; *née* Simmons-Green; da of Leonard Simmons-Green, of 273 Langmore Road, Shirley, Warwickshire; *m* 1949, Sir Edward Herbert Sharp, 3 Bt (d 1985); 2 s, 1 da; *Style—* Beryl, Lady Sharp; 5 Raynham Gardens, 28 Howick Road, Pietermaritzburg 3201, Natal, S Africa

SHARP, (James) Christopher; s of Stanley Sharp (d 1962), of Stockport, Cheshire, and Annie, *née* Owrid; *b* 24 Dec 1939; *Educ* Stockport GS, Pembroke Coll Oxford (MA); *m* 20 July 1963, Mary, da of Roland Bromfield (d 1983), of Shrewsbury; 1 s (Jeremy b 1964), 2 da (Catherine b 1968, Rosemary b 1978); *Career* slrs articled clerk and asst slr Salop CC 1963-68, asst slr G H Morgan and Co Shrewsbury 1968-70, md Northern Rock Building Society; dir: Northern Rock Housing Trust Ltd, Northern Rock Property Services Ltd, Nat House Building Cncl, NHBC Building Control Services Ltd, North Housing Assoc Ltd, North Housing Ltd, North Housing Trust Ltd, Building Socs Ombudsman Co Ltd, Northern Rock Financial Services Ltd, Rock Asset Management Ltd, Rock Asset Management (Unit Trust) Ltd, Rock Asset Management (Nominees) Ltd, Homes Intown plc, The Newcastle Initiative, Durham Business Sch, Newcastle upon Tyne Poly, Tyneside Trg and Enterprise Cncl; dep chm The Building Societies Assoc; *Style—* Christopher Sharp, Esq; 5 Richmond Way, Ponteland, Newcastle upon Tyne NE20 9HU; Northern Rock Building Society, Northern Rock House, Gosforth, Newcastle upon Tyne NE3 4PL (☎ 091 285 7191)

SHARP, Dr David Henry; OBE (1982); s of Rev Douglas Simmonds Sharp (d 1938), and late Gwendoline Helen, *née* Roberts; *b* 24 Feb 1917; *Educ* Tynemouth HS, Queen Elizabeth's GS Blackburn, Univ Coll Southampton, Univ of London (BSc, PhD); *m* 18 July 1942, Enid Catherine, da of Rev Emlyn Maurice Williams (d 1953), of Caernarfon; 2 s (Roger b 28 Jan 1946, Richard b 24 Aug 1952), 1 da (Lalage b 11 Nov 1956); *Career* sci offr Chemical Def Res Dept 1937-44, head of res Sutcliffe Speakman & Co Ltd 1944-48, section head Bitish Ceramic Research Association 1948-51, works mangr asst to MD Fisons Ltd 1951-61; tech dir FBI and CBI 1961-67; gen sec: Inst Chemical Engrs, Soc of Chemical Indust 1967-82; assoc ed Ellis Horwood Ltd Chichester 1982-, served on various govt ctees including Key Ctee on Disposal of Solid Toxic Waste; active memb and office holder Methodist Church; FRSC 1943, FIChemE 1968, FRSH 1972; Das Grosse Verdienstkreuz, Federal Republic of Germany 1981; *Books* The Chemical Industry (jt ed, 1981), Bioprotein Manufacture (1989), Reclamation and Rehabilitation of Contaminated Land (jt ed, 1991); *Recreations* swimming, colour photography, model railways; *Clubs* Anglo-Belgian, Probus (Sevenoaks); *Style—* Dr David Sharp, OBE; Greenhill House, Shoreham Rd, Otford, Sevenoaks, Kent TN14 5RN (☎ 095 92 3332)

SHARP, David John; s of Norman Sharp, of Viggory Lodge, Horsell Common, Woking, Surrey, and Freda Madeleine, *née* Wakeford; *b* 15 April 1949; *Educ* Lancing, St Mary's Hosp Med Sch London (MB BS); *m* 7 Sept 1982, Marisa Nicole, da of John Parnes, of 58 Queen's Grove, St John's Wood, 2 s (Oliver b 1985, William b 1986), 1 da (Augusta b 1990); *Career* registrar on orthopaedic higher surgical trg scheme Royal Orthopaedic Hosp Birmingham 1981-83, sr registrar on orthopaedic higher surgical trg scheme Northampton and Royal Postgrad Med Sch London 1983-88, res fell Materials Dept QMC London 1986, conslt orthopaedic surgn The Ipswich Hosp 1988-; memb: Br Orthopaedic Res Soc, Clinical Advsy Bd of the Jl Clinical Materials; fell Br Orthopaedic Assoc, FRCS 1979; *Recreations* vintage car, drawing, squash, opera; *Style—* David Sharp, Esq; Orthopaedic Department, The Ipswich Hospital, Heath Rd, Ipswich, Suffolk IP4 5PD (☎ 0473 712233)

SHARP, David Stanley; s of Stanley Harold Sharp (d 1981), of Harrogate, Yorkshire, and Emeline Sharp, *née* Smith; *b* 9 July 1942; *Educ* Harrogate GS, St Marys Hosp Med Sch Univ of London (MB BS); *m* 3 Dec 1965, Margaret Irene, da of Dr John Sidney Johnston, of Bowdon, Cheshire; 1 s (Paul b 1969), 1 da (Jane b 1966); *Career* obstetrician and gynaecologist 1980-, assoc lectr Univ of Manchester Med Sch 1980-, chm Med Exec Ctee N Manchester Gen Hosp 1988-, clinical dir for obstetrics and gynaecology 1986-; memb Medico Legal Ctee of RCOG 1987-90 (memb Cncl 1986-88); memb BMA 1966, LRCP 1966, MRCS 1966, MRCOG 1972, FRCOG 1989; *Recreations* golf; *Clubs* Hale Golf, Manchester Golf; *Style—* David Sharp, Esq; Lyndhurst, 44 Ridgeway Rd, Higher Timperley, Altrincham, Cheshire WA15 7EZ (☎ 061 980 4984); North Manchester General Hospital, Delaunays Rd, Manchester M8 6RB (☎ 061 795 4567)

SHARP, Prof Dennis Charles; s of Walter Charles Henry Sharp (d 1976), of Bedford, and Elsie, *née* Evans; *Educ* Bedford Mod Sch, AA London (AADipl), Univ of Liverpool (MA); *m* 1, 1963 (m dis 1973), Joanna Leighton, da of William Scales (d 1986); 1 da (Melanie Clare); m 2, 8 Dec 1983, Yasmin, da of Amirali Shariff; 1 s (Deen b 1984); *Career* architect, writer; Dennis Sharp Architects London 1964-; lectr in architecture Univ of Manchester 1964-68, Leverhulme fell in architecture Univ of Liverpool 1960-63, sr lectr i/c history course AA Sch 1968-72 (sr tutor and lectr Gen Studies Unit 1973-81, gen ed AA 1968-82 (AA Quarterly, AA Papers), visiting prof Columbia Univ of NY 1981, distinguished visiting critic Finnish Assoc of Architects 1980-81, distinguished visiting scholar Univ of Adelaide SA 1984; visiting lectr: Imperial Coll Univ of London 1969-70, Royal Univ of Malta 1971, 1972 and 1974, PNL 1977-78, Univ of Sheffield 1988-89, UCL 1990-; Graham Lectures Chicago 1974 and 1986; John Player lectr on Film and Environment NFT 1977; external examiner: Bartlett Sch UCL 1971-78, Univs of Oxford, Sheffield, Bristol, Liverpool, Kingston Poly, Lanchester Poly, Trent Poly (CNAA); dir CICA 1979-; prof Int Acad of Architecture; exec ed World Architecture 1989-; ARIBA 1959; *Books* Modern Architecture & Expressionism (1966), Sources of Modern Architecture (1967, 1981), A Visual History of 20th Century Architecture (1972), The Picture Palace (1969), Glass Architecture (ed 1972), From Schinkel to the Bauhaus (1970), Van de Velde: Theatres 1904-14 (1974), The Rationalists (1978), Muthesius H: The English House (ed 1979 and 1987); *Recreations* photography, investigating towns and buildings; *Clubs* Arts; *Style—* Prof Dennis Sharp; Dennis Sharp Architects, 61-71 Collier St, London N1 9DF (☎ 0707 875253)

SHARP, (William) Drummond; s of William Sharp (d 1977), of Clackmannanshire, and Margaret, *née* Hutton; *b* 3 June 1932; *Educ* Dunfermline HS; *m* 1957, Kathleen Margaret Maxwell, da of Robert Alexander (d 1974), of Alloa; 2 da (Carol b 1961, Heather b 1964); *Career* merchant banker; dir Arbuthnot Latham Bank Ltd 1978-84, jt md Burns-Anderson plc 1982-87, alternate memb Bank of England Deposit Protection Bd 1986-87, chm Bushwing plc, non-exec dir Carbo plc; FIB (Scotland); *Recreations* golf; *Clubs* St James (Manchester), Hale Golf; *Style—* Drummond Sharp, Esq; Norwood, 12A Harrop Road, Hale, Altrincham WA15 9BX (☎ 061 941 2260); Bushwing plc, 10 Church View, Knutsford, Cheshire WA16 6DQ (☎ 0565 755213)

SHARP, Duncan McCallum; s of Duncan McCallum Sharp (Sr), of Wakefield, and Marjorie, *née* Lindley; *b* 29 April 1936; *Educ* Queen Elizabeth GS, Univ of Leeds (LLB); *m* 12 Sept 1959, Maureen, da of Percy William Kaye (d 1976); 2 s (Andrew b 1962, Iain b 1972), 3 da (Janet b 1960, Kathryn b 1965, Alison b 1968); *Career* admitted slr 1959; dep town clerk Bridlington Borough Cncl 1966-69, country prosecuting slr Cumbria CC 1979-86, chief crown prosecutor Cleveland and N Yorkshire 1986-; *Recreations* gardening, walking, reading, Victorian genealogy; *Style—* Duncan Sharp, Esq; 6th Floor, Ryedale Building, 60 Piccadilly, York YO1 1NS (☎ 0904 610726, fax 0904 610394)

SHARP, Sir George; OBE (1969), JP (Fife 1975), DL (Fife 1978); s of Angus Sharp and Mary, *née* McNee; *b* 8 April 1919; *m* 1948, Elsie May, da of David Porter Rodger; 1 s; *Career* vice-chm: Tay Road Bridge Joint Board 1942-48, Forth Bridge Ctee 1972-78; dir Grampian TV 1975-89; memb: Scottish Devpt Agency 1975-80, Royal Cmmn on Legal Services in Scotland 1978-80; chm: Forth River Purification Bd 1955-67 and 1975-78, Kirkcaldy Dist Cncl 1958-75, Scottish River Purification Advsy Ctee (and memb), Fife and Kinross Water Bd 1967-75, Fife CC (convenor) 1973-75 (memb 1945-75), Fife Regional Cncl 1974-78 (convenor), Glenrothes Development Corporation 1978-86 (memb 1973-86), Scottish Tourist Bd Consultative Cncl 1979-83; pres: Assoc of CCs 1971-73, Convention of Scottish Local Authys 1975-78; mangr tstee Municipal Mutual Insurance 1979-; memb: Nat Girobank (Scottish Bd) 1984-89, Ctee of Enquiry into Local Government Finance 1974-76, Ctee of Enquiry into Salmon and Trout Fishing; memb Econ and Social Ctee EEC 1982-86; kt 1976; *Style—* Sir George Sharp, OBE, JP, DL; Strathlea, 56 Station Rd, Thornton, Fife (☎ 0592 774347)

SHARP, Sir Kenneth Johnston; TD (1960); s of Johnston Sharp, and late Ann Sharp; *b* 29 Dec 1926; *Educ* Shrewsbury, St John's Coll Cambridge (MA); *m* 1955, Barbara Maud, *née* Keating; 1 s; *Career* Nat Serv Indian Army 1945-48, TA 251 (Westmorland and Cumberland Yeo) Field Regt RA; CA; ptnr: Armstrong Watson & Co 1955-75, Baker Tilly Chartered Accountants 1985-89; head Govt Accounting Serv DTI 1975-83; pres Inst of CAs 1974-75 (memb Cncl 1966-83); Master Worshipful Co of CAs 1979-80; FCA 1960 (assoc 1955); kt 1984; *Style—* Sir Kenneth Sharp, TD; Tavern Rocks, St Mawes, Cornwall TR2 5DR

SHARP, Kevin; s of Gordon Sharp, of Leeds, and Joyce, *née* Parker; *b* 6 April 1959; *Educ* Abbey Grange HS; *m* 1 Oct 1983, Karen, da of Edward Wrightson; 1 s (Nicholas Richard b 21 Oct 1989), 1 da (Amy Lauren b 28 Dec 1985); *Career* professional cricketer; Yorkshire CCC 1976-: awarded county cap 1982, 184 first class appearances, 199 one-day appearances; 17 appearances Griqualand West SA 1981-84; capt Young England v Aust and W Indies; honours with Yorkshire CCC: Benson & Hedges Cup 1987, John Player League 1983; sales mangr Credit Collections UK Ltd, Winston Churchill travelling fell Aust 1978; *Recreations* watching Leeds United, golf; *Style—* Kevin Sharp, Esq; 49 Durkar Low Lane, Durkar, Wakefield WF4 3BQ (☎ 0924 252774); Yorkshire CCC, Headingley Cricket Ground, Leeds (☎ 0532 787394, fax 0532 784099)

SHARP, Neil Muir; MBE (1976), TD (1966 and 2 bars); s of Col (John) Stuart Cadenhead Sharp, OBE, TD, DL (d 1986), of Bruce Court, Carnoustie, Angus, and Dorothy Kate, *née* Muir (d 1988); *b* 18 May 1934; *Educ* Trinity Coll Glenalmond; *m* 1, 1960 (m dis 1970), Jean Katherine, *née* Woodruffe; 2 da (Sarah b 1961, Heather 1963); m 2, 18 May 1974, Muriel Anne, da of Victor Slack, of Ormskirk, Lancs; 1 da (Sally b 1975); *Career* Nat Serv 2 Lt RA 1952-54, 2 Lt then Col RA TA 1954-82; CA 1954; ptnr: RC Thomson and Murdoch 1961-69 (student 1954-60), Ernst & Young 1969; chm, ctee memb and treas of a number of local charities; former chm Tayside Branch IOD; MIPA 1988; OStJ 1982; *Recreations* shooting, golf; *Clubs* R & A, Royal Northern & Univ (Aberdeen); *Style—* Neil Sharp, Esq, MBE, TD; Hilloch Wood, Letham Grange, By Arbroath, Angus (☎ 0241 89345); Ernst & Young, City House, 16 Overgate, Dundee (☎ 0382 202561, fax 0382 27177, telex 76356 AYDU)

SHARP, Owen; yr s of Sir Edward Herbert Sharp, 3 Bt (d 1985), and Beryl, Lady Sharp, *qv*; br and hp of Sir Adrian Sharp, 4 Bt; *b* 17 Sept 1956; *m* Caroline; 1 s (Declan b 1980); *Style—* Owen Sharp, Esq; c/o Beryl Lady Sharp, 5 Raynham Gardens, 28 Howick Road, Pietermaritzburg 3201, Natal, S Africa

SHARP, Peter John; s of John Frederick Sharp, of Plumstead, N Norfolk, and Joan Brimelow, *née* Hotchkiss; *b* 16 April 1956; *Educ* Berkhamsted, Univ of Oxford (BA); *m* 22 Dec 1984, Philippa Joanna, da of Sqdn Ldr William Ronald Stanley Body, of Drinkstone Green, Suffolk; 1 s (Samuel Frederick b 1985), 2 da (Holly Rose b and d 1987, Florence Emily b 1989); *Career* admitted slr 1982; ptnr Wilde Sapte 1984- (currently int commercial litigator); memb Law Soc; *Recreations* motor racing, cycling; *Style—* Peter Sharp, Esq; Wilde Sapte, Queensbridge House, 60 Upper Thames St, London EC4V 3BD (☎ 071 236 3050, fax 071 236 9624, telex 887793)

SHARP, Richard Adrian William; OBE (1986); s of Frederick George Sharp (d 1964), and Kathleen Muriel, *née* Chandler; *b* 9 Sept 1938; *Educ* Blundell's, Balliol Coll Oxford (MA); *m* 1963, Esther Marian, da of Sir Frederick Johnson Pedler, of Moor Park; 2 s (Quentin b 1965, Jeremy b 1967), 1 da (Rachel b 1970); *Career* Nat Serv 1957-59, 2 Lt RM Commandos; asst master Sherborne Sch 1963-68, joined English China Clays 1968 (distribution servs mangr 1986-), dir Treneglos Co Ltd 1977, tstee and treas Maitland Tst; pres Nanpean AFC 1969-90, chm SW Cncl for Sport and Recreation 1984-90 (vice chm 1982-84), rugby corr Sunday Telegraph 1976-85; played rugby for: Redruth, Wasps, Bristol, Barbarians, Oxford Univ 1959-62, Cornwall 1957-67 (Capt 1963-65), England 1960-67 (Capt 1963), Br Isles Touring Team 1962; played cricket for Cornwall 1956-69; FICDM 1981; *Recreations* golf, gardening, walking, bird watching; *Clubs* British Sportsman's; *Style—* Richard Sharp, Esq; Rosenannon, Carlyon Road, St Austell, Cornwall PL25 4LE; ECC International, John Keay House, St Austell, Cornwall PL25 4DJ

SHARP, Sir Richard Lyall; KCVO (1982), CB (1977); s of late Alexander Sharp, Advocate of Aberdeen, by his late w Isabella, OBE; bro of His Honour Alastair George Sharp, *qv*, and of late Lady Mackie of Benshie; *b* 27 March 1915; *Educ* Fettes, Univ of Aberdeen, Clare Coll Cambridge; *m* 1950, Jean Helen, eld da of Sir James Crombie, KCB, KBE, CMG; 2 s, 2 da (1 da decd); *Career* served WWII Royal Northumberland Fusiliers (POW Singapore and Siam); joined Treasy 1946, IDC 1961, under-sec Prices and Incomes Bd 1966-68, with Treasy 1968-77, ceremonial offr CSD 1977-82; *Style—* Sir Richard Sharp, KCVO, CB; Home Farm House, Briston, Norfolk NR24 2HN (☎ 0263 860445)

SHARP, Richard Simon; s of Sir Eric Sharp, CBE, of London, and Marion, *née* Freeman; *b* 8 Feb 1956; *Educ* Merchant Taylors', Christ Church Oxford (MA); *m* 29 Aug 1988, Victoria Susan, da of Lloyd Nelson Hull; *Career* Morgan Guaranty Tst Co 1978-84, exec dir investment banking dir Goldman Sachs Int Ltd 1984-; *Recreations* eating, tennis, reading; *Style—* Richard Sharp, Esq; 8-10 New Fetter Lane, London EC4A 1DB (☎ 071 459 5094, fax 071 459 5432)

SHARP, Thomas (Tom); CBE (1987); s of Margaret Tout, *née* Sharp (d 1986); *b* 19 June 1931; *Educ* Univ of Oxford; *m* 24 March 1962, Margaret Lucy, da of Sqdn Ldr Osmund Hailstone, AFC (d 1988), of Southborough, Kent; 2 da (Helen b 1965, Elizabeth b 1967); *Career* RAF 1949-51; civil servant (mainly with Bd of Trade and related depts) 1954-87, gen mangr Lloyd's of London 1987-91; memb Liberal Democrat Pty, co cncllr Surrey Co Cncl 1989-; *Recreations* walking, reading, music; *Style—* Tom Sharp, Esq, CBE; 96 London Rd, Guildford, Surrey GU1 1TH (☎ 0483 572669)

SHARP, William Johnstone; CB (1983); s of Frederick Matthew Sharp (d 1931), and Gladys Evelyn; *b* 30 May 1926; *Educ* Queen Elizabeth GS Hexham, Emmanuel Coll Cambridge (MA); *m* 1952, Joan Alice, MBE, da of Arnold Gardner Clark (d 1965); *Career* Capt Durham LI (Malaya); govt official; controller and chief exec Her Majesty's Stationery Office 1981-86; *Recreations* the turf; *Style—* William Sharp, Esq, CB; 43 Friars Quay, Norwich NR3 1ES (☎ 0603 624258)

SHARP OF GRIMSDYKE, Baron (Life Peer UK 1989), of Stanmore in the London Borough of Harrow; Sir Eric Sharp; CBE (1980); s of Isaac and Martha Sharp; *b* 17 Aug 1916; *Educ* LSE; *m* 1950, Marion, *née* Freedman; 1 s (Hon Richard Simon b 8 Feb 1956), 2 da (Nicola Rosemary b 10 March 1954 (decd), Hon Victoria Madeleine (Hon Mrs Chappatte) b (twin) 8 Feb 1956); *Career* chm Cable & Wireless 1981-, Monsanto 1975- (dep chm 1973-74), Polyamide Intermediates 1975-; memb Econ Devpt Ctee Chem Indust 1980-, CEGB 1980-; previously with Miny Fuel & Power; kt 1984; *Style—* The Rt Hon Lord Sharp of Grimsdyke, CBE

SHARPE, Andrew; s of late Frank Sharpe, of Glenfield, Leics, and Joyce Marjorie, *née* Slater; *b* 29 April 1949; *Educ* Ashby-De-La-Zouche Boys' GS; *m* 8 July 1972, Sybil Dorothea Sharpe, da of late Harold Myers, of Harborne, Birmingham; *Career* called to the Bar Gray's Inn 1972; practising barrister 1972-; lectr in law Univ of Reading 1971-73; *Recreations* sport, jazz, blues music; *Style—* Andrew Sharpe, Esq; Spon Chambers, 13 Spon St, Coventry, Warwickshire CV1 3BA (☎ 0203 632107)

SHARPE, David Thomas; OBE (1986); s of Albert Edward Sharpe, of 1 Alma Road, Swanscombe, Kent, and Grace Emily, *née* Large; *b* 14 Jan 1946; *Educ* GS for Boys Gravesend, Downing Coll Cambridge, Univ of Oxford Med Sch (MB BChir); *m* 23 Jan 1971, Patricia Lilian, da of Brinley Meredith (d 1965); 1 s (Timothy Richard Brinley b 4 Aug 1972), 2 da (Katherine Anna, b 24 June 1974, Caroline Louise b 2 Nov 1978); *Career* plastic surgeon; house surgeon Radcliffe Infirmary Oxford 1970-71, sr house offr Plastic Surgery Churchill Hosp Oxford 1971-72, Pathology Dept Radcliffe Infirmary 1972-73 (Accident Service 1972), gen surgery Royal United Hosp Bath 1973-75; registrar: Plastic Surgery Unit Chepstow 1976-78 (plastic surgeon 1976), Canniesburn Hosp Glasgow 1978-80; sr registrar Plastic Surgery Leeds and Bradford 1980-84, chm and md Plastech Research and Design Ltd 1984-, dir Plastic Surgery and Burns Research Unit Univ of Bradford 1986-, visiting conslt plastic surgeon 1985- (Yorkshire Clinic Bradford, BUPA Hosp Elland W Yorkshire, Cromwell Hosp London), conslt plastic surgeon 1985- (St Luke's Hosp Bradford, Bradford Royal Infirmary, Huddersfield Royal Infirmary); author of various chapters, leading articles and papers on Plastic Surgery topics, major burn disaster management, tissue expansion and breast reconstruction; memb Cncl British Assoc of Aesthetic Plastic Surgeons 1989-; FRCS 1975; *Recreations* painting, shooting, riding, flying (private pilot's licence); *Style—* David T Sharpe, Esq, OBE; Hazelbrae, Calverley, Leeds LS28 5QQ (☎ 0532 570027); The Yorkshire Clinic, Bradford Rd, Bingley, W Yorks (☎ 0274 560311, car 0836773239)

SHARPE, Hon Sir John Henry; CBE (1972), JP, MP (UBP) Warwick West Bermuda 1963-; s of late Harry Sharpe, and late Jessie, *née* White; *b* 8 Nov 1921; *Educ* Warwick Acad, Mount Allison Commercial Coll Canada; *m* 1948, Eileen Margaret Morrow, of Vancouver, Canada; 1 s (John), 1 da (Kathleen); *Career* served WWII Bermuda Rifles 1939-42, Royal Canadian AF 1942-45 (qualified as navigator in Canada, posted UK and served with RAF Bomber Cmd in ops over Europe); chm Purvis Ltd (joined 1938); elected Parl 1963, premier of Bermuda 1975-77 (dep premier 1972-75); min: fin 1968-75, tport 1980, marine and air servs 1980-81, lab and home affrs 1981-88, delegated and legislative affrs 1989, lab and home affrs 1990-; dir Bank of Bermuda Ltd 1978-87; hon vice patron RAF Assoc, hon life vice pres Bermuda Football Assoc; former: chm Bermuda Nat Olympic Cncl, former memb Synod C of E, church warden St Mary's Church Warwick; chm Bd of Inquiry into various Taxi matters 1980; kt 1977; *Recreations* reading, bridge, gardening, tennis, formerly soccer and rugby; *Clubs* Royal Hamilton Amateur Dinghy, Royal Bermuda Yacht, Coral Beach and Tennis; *Style—* The Hon Sir John Sharpe, CBE, JP, MP; Uplands, 26 Harbour Rd, Warwick West, Bermuda; Purvis Ltd, PO Box 461, Hamilton 5

SHARPE, Rev Canon Kenneth Henry; s of William Kenneth Sharpe (d 1962), of Portslade, Sussex, and Florence Annie, *née* Holmes (d 1964); *b* 29 March 1920; *Educ* Varndean Sch Brighton, Rochester Theol Coll; *m* 27 July 1957, Mary, *née* Swabey; 1 s (Simon b 1961), 1 da (Jacqueline b 1966); *Career* banker 1937-48, hon treas Cranleigh Village Hosp 1942-48, admin Dio of the Upper Nile 1949-54, sec and treas Mbale Cathedral Bldg Appeal 1949-60, diocesan sec and treas Diocese of the Upper Nile 1953-60, prov treas Church of Uganda Rwanda and Burundi 1962-69, chm Uganda Bookshop 1962-69; chm: Canon Law and Constitution Cmmn Church of Uganda 1965-69, Prov Liturgical Ctee Church of Uganda 1967-69; commissary to the Bishop of the Sudan 1963-69, hon corr for Uganda Royal Cwlth Soc 1962-69, vicar of the Mau Kenya 1969-78, canon of Nakuru Kenya 1973, canon emeritus 1978, hon treas of Diocese of Nakuru Kenya 1971-78, vicar of Coley Diocese of Wakefield 1978-89; AIB 1942; *Recreations* wine-making, dog walking; *Clubs* Alcuin, Anglican Soc, Uganda Kobs; *Style—* The Rev Canon Kenneth Sharpe; Mirembe, 54 Bradford Rd, Menston, W Yorks (☎ 0943 877710)

SHARPE, Sir Reginald Taaffe; QC; only s of Herbert Sharpe (d 1956), of Lindfield, Sussex; *b* 20 Nov 1898; *Educ* Westminster, accepted into Trinity Coll Cambridge but unable to attend due to WWI; *m* 1, 1922 (m dis 1929), Phyllis Maude, da of late Maj Edward Whinney, of Haywards Heath, 2 da; m 2, 1930, Eileen Kate (d 1946), yr da of Thomas Howarth Usherwood, of Christ's Hosp, Horsham; m 3, 1947, Vivien Travers (d 1971), da of late Rev Herbert Rowley, of Wretham, Norfolk; m 4, 1976, Mary Millicent, da of late Maj-Gen Patrick Barclay Sangster, CB, CMG, DSO, of Roehampton; *Career* 2 Lt Grenadier Gds 1917, Lt 1918, served with 2 Bn (wounded in France); called to the Bar Gray's Inn 1920, judge of High Court Rangoon 1937-48, dir of supply Burma (at Calcutta) 1942-44, JP Sussex 1949, dep chm E Sussex QS 1949-69, memb E Sussex Standing Jt Ctee 1958-65, chm Hailsham Petty Sessions 1957-58, asst chm W Sussex QS 1950-70, memb W Sussex Standing Jt Ctee 1953-65, dep chm W Kent QS 1949-62 and Kent 1962-69, asst chm Middlesex QS 1951-63, dep chm 1963-65 and Middx Area of Gtr London 1965-71; cmmr of assize 1949, 1950, 1952, 1954 and 1960; special divorce cmmr 1948-67, chm NHS Tbnl for Eng and Wales 1948-71, memb Nat Arbitration Tribunal and Industl Disputes Tbnl 1951, sole cmmr for Br Honduras Inquiry (at Belize) 1954, chm Departmental Ctee on Summary Trial of Minor Offences in Magistrates' Courts 1954-55; memb Governing Body Westminster Sch 1955-83; kt 1947; *Style—* Sir Reginald Sharpe, QC; The Old Post Office, Rushlake Green, Sussex

SHARPE, Hon Mrs (Sheena MacIntosh); *née* Carmichael; o da of Baron Carmichael of Kelvingrove (Life Peer), *qv*; *b* 1949; *m* 1974, Thomas Anthony Edward Sharpe, 1 s (Christopher b 1977), 1 da (Victoria b 1979); *Style—* The Hon Mrs Sharpe; 7 Lathbury Road, Oxford OX2 7AT

SHARPE, Thomas Ridley; s of Rev George Coverdale Sharpe (d 1944), and Grace Egerton, *née* Brown (d 1975); *b* 30 March 1928; *Educ* Lancing, Pembroke Coll Cambridge (MA); *m* 1969, Nancy Anne Looper; 3 da (Melanie, Grace, Jemima); *Career* RM 1946-48; social worker Johannesburg SA 1951-52, teacher Natal SA 1952-56, photographer SA 1956-61, deported from SA on political grounds 1961, teacher trg Cambridge 1962-63, lectr in history Cambridge Coll of Arts and Technology 1963-71, novelist 1971-; *Books* Riotous Assembly (1971), Indecent Exposure (1973), Porterhouse Blue (1974), Blott on the Landscape (1975), Wilt (1976), The Great Pursuit (1977), The Throwback (1978), The Wilt Alternative (1979), Ancestral Vices (1980), Vintage Stuff (1982), Wilt on High (1984); *Recreations* photography, old typewriters, gardening, reading, cats, talking; *Style—* Tom Sharpe, Esq; 38 Tunwells Lane, Great Shelford, Cambridge CB2 5LJ

SHARPE-NEWTON, Geraldine; da of late Jesse J Sharpe, of New York City, and Adrienne Rosaire; *Educ* Univ of Illinois (BA), Univ of Pittsburgh (MLS Hons); *m* June 1962 (m dis 1974), Thomas Alan Newton, s of Frank Newton, of Florida; 1 s (Matthew Ross b 1968), 1 da (Jennifer Jesse b 1965); *Career* assoc dir special projects Burson Marsteller PR 1974-77, vice pres Niki Singer Inc 1977-79, vice pres dir of PR Simon and Schuster 1979-80; dir Info Servs CBS News 1980-83, head of Press and Public Affrs ITN 1983-; *Recreations* reading, gardening, sailing, hiking, rock collecting; *Clubs* Reform, Groucho; *Style—* Mrs Geraldine Sharpe-Newton; 29 Albert Mansions, Albert Bridge Road, London SW11 (☎ 071 228 1151); ITN, 200 Gray's Inn Road, London WC1X 8XZ (☎ 071 833 3000)

SHARPEY-SCHAFER, Prof John Francis; s of Prof (Edward) Peter Sharpey-Schafer (d 1964), and Joyce Frances, *née* Adlard; *b* 29 Nov 1938; *Educ* Cheltenham GS, King's Coll Cambridge (BA), Univ of Liverpool (PhD); *m* 1, 14 June 1961 (m dis 1972), Susan Langdale, da of Dr Louis Fitch (d 1950); 2 s (Ben b 27 Feb 1962, Oliver b 16 Dec 1965), 1 da (Hannah b 23 Aug 1963); m 2, 11 Nov 1972, Sylvia Anne, da of Joseph Bosonnet, of Liverpool; 1 s (Kieren b 7 Oct 1982), 2 da (Siobhan b 6 Jan 1974, Barbra b 24 July 1976); *Career* Univ of Liverpool: ICI fell 1963-64, lectr in physics 1964-73, sr lectr 1973-78, reader 1978-88, prof of physics 1988-; sec and chm Edge Hill constituency Lab Pty 1974-80, memb Nuclear Physics Bd SERC 1986-89; FInstP 1974; *Recreations* pursuing beautiful ladies, preferably the wife; *Style—* Prof John Sharpey-Schafer; 8 Airdale Rd, Liverpool L15 5AR (☎ 051 733 5972); Oliver Lodge Laboratory, University of Liverpool, PO Box 147, Liverpool L69 3BX (☎ 051 794 3380, fax 051 794 3444, telex 627095 UNILPL G)

SHARPLES, Anthony Frederick Gillett; *b* 19 Jan 1936; *Educ* Ratcliffe Coll, Queens' Coll Cambridge; *m* 1969 (m dis), Anne Elizabeth, da of George Tallentire Blair; 1 da; *Career* md CTP Investments Ltd, chm CTP Group Ltd; *Recreations* sailing; *Style—* Anthony Sharples, Esq; Three Elms, Grosvenor Rd, Glos (☎ 0452 23077)

SHARPLES, Brian; s of Richard Sharples (d 1960), 211 Brownedge Rd, Bamber Bridge, Preston, and Mary Phyllis, *née* Carr (d 1987); *b* 18 Sept 1936; *Educ* Hutton GS, Harris Tech Coll Preston, Coll of Estate Mgmnt; *m* Annie, da of Joseph Marginson; 3 s (Ian Richard b 14 July 1963, Deryck Alan b 24 Dec 1964, Graeme Brian b 7 May 1966); *Career* quantity surveyor with BDP 1961-; work incl: Owens Park Devpt for Univ of Manchester and Edge Hill Coll Ormskirk (as sr quantity surveyor 1961-65), Northwich Town Centre Redevpt (as quantity surveyor 1966-67), Queens Med Centre and Teaching Hosp and Northgate Arena Leisure Centre (as assoc quantity surveyor 1966-76), study for proposed Design Test and Research Facility Leyland Cars Solihull (as coordinating assoc quantity surveyor 1976-77), St James Hosp Leeds Clinical Sciences Building (as assoc quantity surveyor 1977-80), Park Lane Fourth Special Hosp Liverpool (as project mangr 1980-84), Leeds Gen Infirmary Phase 1, Fermentation Pilot Plant Wilts, Birkenhead Town Centre Shopping Devpt, Canary Wharf London Shopping Devpt (as project mangr 1984-); currently mgmnt ptnr BDP Preston office and project ptnr BDP London office (for Morgan Bank's new HQ offices); FRICS, ACIArb, memb IQA; *Recreations* golf, general aviation pilot, property development; *Clubs* Ashton and Lea Golf (Preston); *Style—* Brian Sharples, Esq; Building Design Partnership, Vernon St, Moor Lane, Preston PR1 3PQ (☎ 0772 59383, fax 0772 201378)

SHARPLES, Hon Christopher John; s of Baroness Sharples, *qv*, and Sir Richard Sharples, KCMG, OBE, MC (d 1973); *b* 24 May 1947; *Educ* Eton, Business Sch of Neuchatel; *m* 1975, Sharon, da of late Robert Sweeny, DFC; 3 children; *Career* VSO India 1965-66; C Czarnikow Ltd (sugar brokers) 1968-72, co fndr and dir Inter Commodities Ltd (brokers in futures and options, renamed GNI Ltd in 1984 following partial acquisition by Gerrard & National plc) 1972-, chm IVC Information Systems Ltd (electronic publishers of int fin data) 1981-, dir Intercom Data Systems Ltd (software and systems house) 1982-90, vice chm International Petroleum Exchange (PR) 1986- (dir 1981-87, former memb Ctee); chm Assoc of Futures Brokers and Dealers (self-regulatory body designated under Fin Servs Act 1986) 1987-91 (former memb: Rules Ctee, Membership Ctee, Fin and Gen Purposes Ctee); served Ctees: London Commodity Exchange (PR), London International Financial Futures Exchange (Clearing), Br Fedn of Commodity Assocs (Taxation), London Commodity Exchange Regulatory Advsy Gp, Advsy Panel Securities and Investmts Bd (1986); dep chm Securities and Futures Authy 1991-; *Recreations* sailing; *Clubs* Royal Yacht Squadron, White's; *Style—* The Hon Christopher Sharples; 72 Elm Park Rd, London SW3 (☎ 071 352 3791, 071 378 7171)

SHARPLES, Clive Arthur; s of Arthur Sharples, of Bournemouth, and Winnifred May, *née* Wilmott; *b* 1 Sept 1947; *Educ* Univ of London (LLB); *m* 11 Sept 1973, Billie, da of Thomas Mitchell, of Bradford on Avon; 2 s (Thomas b 1978, Benjamin b 1987), 1 da (Rebecca b 1981); *Career* admitted slr 1974; currently head residential devpt dept Saunders Sobell Leigh and Dobin; memb: conveyancing ctee House Builders Fedn, Law Soc; *Recreations* riding, shooting; *Style—* Clive Sharples, Esq; The Sett, Ewshot, Farnham, Surrey; 20 Red Lion St, London WC1 (☎ 071 242 2525)

SHARPLES, Hon David Richard; s of Sir Richard Christopher Sharples, KCMG, OBE, MC (assass 1973), and Baroness Sharples, *qv*; *b* 14 April 1955; *Educ* Eton; *m* 1981, Annabel, da of Col Thomas Argyle Hall, OBE; *Career* company dir; *Recreations* skiing, sailing, surfing; *Clubs* Windermere Island; *Style—* The Hon David Sharples; 8721 Sunset Plaza Terrace, Los Angeles, CA 90069, USA (☎ 213 854 1819); office: 5818 W Third St, Los Angeles, CA 90036, USA (☎ 213 934 6000)

SHARPLES, Hon Fiona; *née* Sharples; da (by 1 m) of Baroness Sharples, *qv*; *b* 1949; *m* 1981 (m dis 1982), Alexander Paterson; resumed maiden name; 1 da (Natalie Louise Sharples b 23 Dec 1975); *Style—* The Hon Fiona Sharples; Poole Cottage, Station Rd, Over Wallop, Hants

SHARPLES, Baroness (Life Peer UK 1973), of Chawton in Hampshire; Pamela Swan; da of Lt Cdr Keith William Newall, RN (d 1937), and Violet Ruby, *née* Ashton (who m 2, Lord Claud Nigel Hamilton, GCVO, CMG, DSO, s of 2 Duke of Abercorn, and d 1986); *b* 11 Feb 1923; *Educ* Southover Manor Lewes, Florence Italy; *m* 1, 1946, Sir Richard Christopher Sharples, KCMG, OBE, MC, govr of Bermuda (assas in Bermuda 1973), s of Richard William Sharples, OBE; 2 s (Hon Christopher John b 1947, Hon David Richard b 1955), 2 da (Hon Fiona (Hon Mrs Paterson) b 1949, Hon Miranda (Hon Mrs Larkins) b 1951); m 2, 1977, Patrick David de Laszlo (d 1980); m 3, 1983, (Robert) Douglas Swan; *Career* served WAAF 1941-46, Armed Forces Pay Review Bd 1979-81; sits as Cons peer in House of Lords; chm TVS Tst 1981-; *Recreations* golf, tennis, gardening; *Clubs* R Cape Golf SA, Mid Ocean Bermuda, Mid Dorset Golf; *Style—* The Rt Hon the Lady Sharples; 60 Westminster Gdns, Marsham St, London SW1P 4JG (☎ 071 821 1875); Nunswell, Higher Coombe, Shaftesbury, Dorset SP7 9LR (☎ 0747 2971); TVS, 60 Buckingham Gate, London SW1 (☎ 071 828 9898)

SHARPLES, Robert William; s of William Arthur Sharples (d 1988), of Meopham, Kent, and Joan Catherine, *née* Affleck; *b* 28 May 1949; *Educ* Dulwich Trinity Coll Cambridge (MA, PhD); *m* 24 July 1976, Grace Elizabeth, da of William Nevard (d 1979), of Mill Hill, London; 1 da (Elizabeth b 1984); *Career* res fell Fitzwilliam Coll Cambridge 1972-73, lectr in Greek and Latin UCL 1973-; sec Cncl Univ Classical Depts 1983-87; *Books* Alexander of Aphrodisias on Fate (1983), Plato: Meno (1985), Alexander of Aphrodisias: Ethical Problems (1990); *Recreations* computing, model railways; *Style—* Robert Sharples, Esq; Department of Greek and Latin, University College London, Gower Street, London WC1E 6BT (☎ 071 387 7050 Ext 4577)

SHARPLEY, Mark Alistair; s of Dr John Edward Sharpley, of Field House, Fulbrook, Burford, Oxon, and Elizabeth; da of Maj-Gen Sir Colin Arthur Jardine, 3 Bt, CB, DSO, MC (d 1957); *b* 15 Aug 1947; *Educ* Marlborough; *m* 6 April 1974, Mhairi, da of Dr John Anderson, of Meikle Hill, Woodlands Ave, Kirkudbright; 1 s (James b 14 June 1976), 1 da (Clare b 3 Oct 1978); *Career* dir Amalgamated Metal Trading Ltd 1980-; *Recreations* fishing, rare pheasants, shooting; *Style—* Mark Sharpley, Esq; The Old Sun House, Pednor, Chesham, Bucks HP5 2SZ (☎ 0494 782870); Amalgamated Metal Trading Ltd, Ground Floor, Adelaide House, London EC4R 9DT (☎ 071 626 4521)

SHARPLEY, Ven Roger Ernest Dion; s of Frederick Charles Sharpley, OBE (d 1966), and Doris Irene, *née* Wills; *b* 19 Dec 1928; *Educ* Dulwich, ChCh Oxford (MA); *Career* vicar All Saints' Middlesbrough 1960-81, rural dean Middlesbrough 1970-81, canon York Minster 1974-81, archdeacon Hackney and vicar Guild Church of Saint Andrew Holborn 1981-; *Style—* The Ven the Archdeacon of Hackney; St Andrew's Vicarage, 5 St Andrew St, London EC4A 3AB (☎ 071 353 3544)

SHARRARD, Prof (William) John Wells; s of William Sharrard (d 1978), and Winifred Hannah, *née* Wells (d 1981); *b* 8 Nov 1921; *Educ* Westminster, Univ of Sheffield (MB ChB, MD, ChM); *m* 1, 17 March 1945, Ethel Margaret (d 1952), da of John Wilson Spedding (d 1956); 1 s (John b 1948), 1 da (Sally-Ann b 1947); m 2, 16 May 1953, Bessie Laura (Peta), da of Sqdn Ldr Frederick Petch, OBE (d 1974); 2 s (Michael b 1954, Mark b 1960); *Career* Sqdn Ldr RAFVR Med Serv 1945-48; emeritus prof of orthopaedic surgery Sheffield Royal Hallamshire Hosp and Sheffield Childrens Hosp (conslt orthopaedic surgn 1955-); over 200 pubns on orthopaedic surgery and res; pres: Monitoring Ctee on Orthopaedic Surgery EEC 1972-85, Br Orthopaedic Res Soc 1962-64, Br Orthopaedic Assoc 1978-79, Euro Paediatric Orthopaedic Soc 1982-84, Int Soc Orthopaedic Surgery 1984; rep for RCS on Central Manpower Ctee and Jt Conslt Ctee BMA; hon memb orthopaedic socs of: France, Germany, Italy, America, Japan, Hungary, Peru, Columbia; FRCS 1950, FRSM, memb Br Orthopaedic Assoc; *Books* Paediatric Orthopaedics and Fractures (1979); *Recreations* travel, music; *Style—* Prof John Sharrard; Uplands, 140 Manchester Rd, Sheffield S10 5DL (☎ 0742 664198)

SHARROCK, Ivan; s of William Arthur Sharrock, and Gladys Muriel, *née* Roberts; *b* 17 July 1941; *Educ* Newquay GS, Cornwall Tech Coll; *m* 5 Oct 1974, Suzanne Jacqueline Clare, da of Jack Cecil Edward Haig, of Sutton Coldfield; 1 s (Sky Kelly Ivan b 1975); *Career* joined BBC 1961, trained in film sound techniques at Ealing Film Studios 1961-64, outside broadcasts BBC TV 1964-65, freelance sound mixer with Alan King Assocs 1965-81; has recorded over 40 feature films including: The French Lieutenant's Woman 1981 (Br Acad award), Greystoke 1984 (Br Acad nomination), The Last Emperor 1987 (US Acad award); memb: Acad of Motion Picture Arts and Sciences, Cinema Audio Soc (USA), BAFTA, ACTT, BKSTS; *Recreations* sailing, skiing, windsurfing, music, reading; *Style—* Ivan Sharrock, Esq; 9 Burghley Road, London NW5 1UG (☎ 071 267 3170, 071 722 1572, car 0836 254983)

SHARWOOD-SMITH, Lady; (Winifred) Joan; da of late Thomas Mitchell; *Educ* Berkhamstead Sch; *m* 1939, as his 2 w, Sir Bryan Evers, KCMG, KCVO, KBE, ED (d 1983, govr Northern Nigeria 1954-57); 2 s, 1 da; *Clubs* RAF; *Style—* Lady Sharwood-Smith; 34 Redford Rd, Edinburgh EH13 0AA

SHATTOCK, David John; QPM (1985); s of Herbert John Shattock (d 1966), and Lucy Margaret, *née* Williams (d 1957); *b* 25 Jan 1936; *Educ* Huish's GS, RCDS; *m* 1, 1956 (m dis 1973); 3 s (Gerard David b 1959, Matthew John b 1962, Julian David William b 1972); m 2, 1 Nov 1973, Freda, da of late William Henry Thums; *Career* Nat serv RN 1954-56; joined Somerset Constabulary 1956, rising to asst chief constable Avon and Somerset Constabulary 1977; dep chief constable Wilts Constabulary 1983-86; chief constable: Dyfed-Powys Police 1988-89, Avon and Somerset Constabulary 1989-; memb: ACPO, St John Cncl Avon; dir The British Initiative; OStJ 1989; *Recreations* badminton, horse riding, tennis, antique restoration; *Clubs* Shakespeare (Bristol); *Style—* David Shattock, Esq, QPM; Police Headquarters, PO Box 188, Bristol BS99 7BH (☎ 0272 267201)

SHATTOCK, Sir Gordon; s of Frederick Thomas Shattock (d 1974), of Exeter, Devon, and Rose May Irene, *née* James (d 1988); *b* 12 May 1928; *Educ* Hele's Sch Exeter, RVC London; *m* 17 July 1952, Jeanne Mary (d 1984), da of Austin Edwin Watkins (d 1970), of Exeter; 1 s (Simon John b 1954), 1 da (Clare Lucinda b 1956); m 2, 17 Sept 1988, Mrs David Sale (wid); *Career* sr ptnr St David Veterinary Hosp Exeter 1951-84, dir and vice chm Veterinary Drug Co plc 1982-, divnl bursar Western Area Woodard Sch's 1988-; fndr chm (now pres) Devon Euro Constituency Cons Cncl, memb TV SW Political Advsy Bd, chm local Cancer Res Campaign 1972-88, fell Woodward Corp of Schs 1973-88, chm Grenville Coll and memb Sch Cncl 1973-88, pres Br Veterinary Hosps Assoc 1974, memb Exec Cncl Animal Health Tst 1974-, chm Western Area Cons Pty (Avon, Somerset, Devon, Cornwall) 1982-85, chm Exeter Cathedral Music Fndn 1985-, memb Exeter Health Authy 1985-, memb Exec Cncl Guide Dogs for the Blind; Freeman City of London 1978, Warden and Liveryman Worshipful Co of Farriers; MRCVS 1951; *Recreations* gardening, restoration of old houses; *Clubs* RSM; *Style—* Sir Gordon Shattock; Glasshayes, Higher Shapter St, Topsham, Exeter EX3 0AW (☎ 0392 877434)

SHAUGHNESSY, Alfred James; s of Capt the Hon Alfred T Shaughnessy (ka France 1916), of 905 Dorchester St, Montreal, and the late Sarah Polk, *née* Bradford (later Lady Legh), of Nashville, Tennessee; *b* 19 May 1916; *Educ* Eton, RMC Sandhurst; *m* 18 Sept 1948, Jean Margaret, da of George Lodge (d 1951), of Kirkella, Hull, Yorks; 2 s (Charles George Patrick b 9 Feb 1955, David James Bradford b 3 March 1957); *Career* WWII cmmnd Capt Grenadier Gds; served 1940-46: Normandy, Belgium, Holland, Germany, demob Maj 1946; playwright and screenwriter; author of 14 stage plays incl: Release, Holiday for Simon, Breaking Point, The Heat of the Moment, Old Herbaceous, Love Affair, Double Cut; author of numerous screenplays for films, TV plays, West End revues and radio plays; US Emmy nominee 1974 and 1975 (TV series Upstairs, Downstairs); memb Exec Cncl Writers Guild of GB 1982-88; *Books* Both Ends of the Candle (autobiography, 1978), Sarah, Letters and Diaries of a Courtier's Wife 1906-1936 (1989); *Recreations* music, golf, walking; *Clubs* Garrick; *Style—* Alfred Shaughnessy, Esq; The Grange, Yattendon, Newbury, Berks RG16 0UE (☎ 0635 201741)

SHAUGHNESSY, 3 Baron (UK 1916); William Graham Shaughnessy; CD; s of 2 Baron (d 1938); 1 Baron Shaughnessy was pres of Canadian Pacific Railway 1899-1918 and chm 1918-23; *b* 28 March 1922; *Educ* Bishop's Coll Sch, Bishop's Univ Lennoxville Canada (BA), Columbia Univ (MSc); *m* 1944, Mary, da of John Whitley (d 1953), of Letchworth, Herts; 1 s (and 1 s decd), 2 da; *Heir* s, Hon Michael Shaughnessy; *Career* WWII Canadian Grenadier Gds, Canadian Army 1941-46 served UK and NW Europe (despatches), ret Maj; co dir; exec asst Canadian Miny Fin 1945-51, dir Canada NW Energy Ltd 1955-83 (vice-pres 1969-82); dir: Arbor Capital Inc (Toronto), 1973-, Corona Corp (Toronto) 1987-; tstee Last Post Fund of Canada, pres Royal Cwlth Soc Montreal 1959-61; *Recreations* history, fishing; *Clubs* Cavalry & Guards', University (Montreal), Montreal Racket; *Style—* The Rt Hon the Lord Shaughnessy; House of Lords, London SW1

SHAVE, Prof Michael John Ramage; s of Leslie Herbert Shave (d 1982), of Stockport, and Edith Maud, *née* Ramage (d 1957); *b* 10 Aug 1934; *Educ* George Watsons Edinburgh, Hymers Coll Hull, Manchester GS, Wadham Coll Oxford (MA), Univ of Bristol (PhD); *m* 30 July 1959, Ann Morag, da of Donald Kirkpatrick (d 1975), of Manchester; 1 s (Peter Kirkpatrick b 1961), 1 da (Susan Elizabeth b 1964); *Career* asst master: St Edwards Sch Oxford 1957-59, Rugby Sch 1959-64; sr lectr Univ of Bristol 1978-82 (lectr 1964-78), prof of computer sci Univ of Liverpool 1983-; chm Merseyside branch BCS 1955-88; memb: Conf of Profs of Computer Sci, Joint Matriculation Bd; Royal Soc Euro fell Université de Grenoble 1978, MBCS 1967, FRSA 1985; *Books* Data Structures (1975), Computer Service Applied to Business Systems (1982); *Recreations* theatre, concerts, caravanning; *Style—* Prof Michael

Shave; Dept of Computer Science, University of Liverpool, PO Box 147, Liverpool L69 3BX (☎ 051 794 3667, fax 4451 708 6502, telex 627095 UNILPL G)

SHAW, Hon Alison Margaret; da of 3 Baron Craigmyle; *b* 8 Aug 1956; *Educ* Harvard Univ (BA 1979), Antioch Univ (MA 1991); *Career* counsellor/psychotherapist; *Clubs* Harvard (NYC); *Style—* The Hon Alison Shaw; 6/6 Collingham Gdns, London SW5 0HW

SHAW, Maj-Gen Anthony John (Tony); CB (1988), CBE (1985); s of Lt-Col William Arthur Shaw, MC (d 1962), and Ethel, *née* Malley (d 1980); *b* 13 July 1930; *Educ* Epsom Coll, Clare Coll Cambridge (MA, MB BChir), Westminster Hosp (MRCS, LRCP 1954); *m* 12 Aug 1961, Gillian, da of Dr Thomas Arthur Best (d 1974), of Ripley, Yorks; 1 s (David b 1965), 1 da (Fiona b 1963); *Career* cmmnd Lt RAMC 1956, Staff Coll Camberley 1963, served 1956-69 in BAOR, MOD, UK, Malta, Berlin, Malaya, Nepal, Penang, Cameron Highlands, CO Field Ambulance 1969-70, Chief instr RAMC Trg Centre 1970-72, NDC 1973, ADGAMS MOD 1973-76, CO Cambridge MH 1977-79, Cdr Med 2 Armd Div BAOR 1979-81 (SE Dist UK 1981), Brigadier Div of med supply MOD 1981-83, DDGAMS 1983-84, Cdr med UKLF (Maj-Gen) 1985-87, Dir Army Community and Occupational Med 1983-87; DG Army Med Servs 1988-90; DRCOG 1959, DTM & H 1961, FFCM (1983, MFCM 1973), FRCP 1989, CStJ (1989, OStJ 1975); *Recreations* sailing, gardening; *Clubs* Landsdowne; *Style—* Maj-Gen Tony Shaw, CB, CBE

SHAW, Sir (Charles) Barry; CB (1974), QC (1964), DL (Co Down 1990); *b* 12 April 1923; *Career* dir of Public Prosecutions for NI 1972-89; memb panel Chairmen of VAT Tbnls for NI 1991-; kt 1980; *Style—* Sir Barry Shaw, CB, QC, DL; Royal Courts of Justice, Belfast, Northern Ireland

SHAW, Prof Bernard Leslie; s of Tom Shaw (d 1971), and Vera (d 1989), *née* Dale; *b* 28 March 1930; *Educ* Hulme GS Oldham, Univ of Manchester (BSc, PhD); *m* 2 June 1951, Mary Elizabeth, da of William Birdsall Neild; 3 s (John Ewart Hardern b 1953, Andrew b and d 1956, Jonathan Bernard b 1960); *Career* sci offr Civil Serv 1953-56, res sci ICI 1956-61, prof Univ of Leeds 1971- (lectr 1962, reader 1966); FRS 1978; *Recreations* tennis, pottery; *Style—* Prof Bernard Shaw; 14 Monkbridge Rd, Leeds LS6 4DX (☎ 0532 755 895); School of Chemistry, Univ of Leeds, Leeds LS2 9JT (☎ 0532 336 401, fax 0532 336 565, telex 556473 UNILDS G)

SHAW, Sir Brian Piers; s of Percy Augustus Shaw; *b* 21 March 1933; *Educ* Wrekin Coll, CCC Cambridge; *m* 1962, Penelope Gay, *née* Reece; 3 s; *Career* chm Furness Withy & Co 1979-90 (md 1977-87), chm ANZ Grindlays Bank 1987-; chm Cncl of Euro and Japanese Nat Shipowners' Assocs 1979-84, pres Gen Cncl of Br Shipping 1985-86, chm Int Chamber of Shipping 1987-; kt 1986; *Recreations* golf, theatre, music; *Clubs* Brooks's, MCC, Denham Golf; *Style—* Sir Brian Shaw; 42 Norland Square, London W11 4PZ (☎ 071 221 4066)

SHAW, (Norman) Carey; s of Norman Henry Shaw, of Wrexham and Swansea, and Mair, *née* Jenkins; *b* 6 May 1940; *Educ* Grove Park GS, Wrexham, Charing Cross Hosp (MB BS); *m* 18 July 1964, Mary Fitzgerald, da of Harold Clarke, of Melton Constable; 3 s (Jeremy b 1968, Timothy b 1970, Jonathan b 1974); *Career* conslt orthopaedic surgn Kings Lynn 1974-; memb Central Ctee for Hosp Med Servs 1977-80, chm E Anglian Orthopaedic Advsy Ctee 1984-87, surgical tutor RCS Kings Lynn 1984-89, pres W Norfolk and Kings Lynn Div BMA 1988-89; FRCS 1970; *Recreations* flying (light aircraft), sailing, photography, computers; *Style—* Carey Shaw, Esq; Chestnut Byre, Manor Farm, Harpley, King's Lynn (☎ 0485 520646); Orthopaedic Dept, The Queen Elizabeth Hospital, Gayton Rd, King's Lynn PE30 4ET (☎ 0553 766266 ext 281)

SHAW, Maj Charles de Vere; s of late Capt John Frederick de Vere Shaw, yr s of 6 Bt; hp of unc, Sir Robert Shaw, 7 Bt; *b* 1 March 1957; *Educ* Michaelhouse S Africa; *m* 1985, Sonia, *née* Eden; 1 s (Robert b 1988), 1 da (Alexandra b 1986); *Career* co dir; associate memb Lloyd's; *Recreations* sport; *Style—* Maj Charles de Vere Shaw; West View, Nunnington, Hereford HR1 3NJ

SHAW, Prof Charles Thurstan; CBE (1972); s of Rev John Herbert Shaw, CF 1914-18 (d 1945), of Nethercott, Silverton, nr Exeter, Devon, and Grace Irene Woollatt (d 1964); *b* 27 June 1914; *Educ* Blundell's, Sidney Sussex Coll Cambridge (BA, MA, PhD), London Univ Inst of Educn (Post Grad Teachers Dip); *m* 21 Jan 1939, Gilian Ione Maud, da of Edward John Penberthy Magor (d 1941), of Lamellen, St Tudy, Bodmin, Cornwall; 2 s (Timothy, Jonathan), 3 da (Rosanne, Gilian, Joanna); *Career* Achimota College Gold Coast 1937-45, Cambridgeshire Educn Ctee 1945-51, Cambridge Inst of Educn 1951-63, prof of archaeology Univ of Ibadan Nigeria 1963-74, dir of studies in archaeology and anthropology Magdalene Coll Cambridge 1975-80; memb Cambridge Cncl for Racial Equality 1980-, fndr and chm Ichnield Way Assoc, pres Prehistoric Soc 1986-90; Hon DSc: Univ of Nigeria 1983, Univ of Ibadan 1989; FRAI, FSA; Onuna-Ekwulu Ora of Igbo-Ukwu Nigeria 1972, Enyofuonka of Igboland 1989, Onuna Ekwulu Nri 1989, Gold Medal Soc of Antiquaries 1990; *Books* Excavation at Dawu (1961), Archaeology and Nigeria (1963), Igbo-Ukwu: An Account of Archaeological Discoveries in Eastern Nigeria (2 Vols, 1970), Africa and The Origins of Man (1973), Why 'Darkest' Africa? (1975), Unearthing Igbo-Ukwu (1977), Nigeria: Its Archaeology and Early History (1978); *Recreations* walking; *Clubs* Athenaeum; *Style—* Prof Thurstan Shaw, CBE; 37 Hawthorne Rd, Stapleford, Cambridge CB2 5DU (☎ 0223 842283)

SHAW, Prof Charles Timothy (Tim); s of Charles John Shaw (d 1985), and Constance Olive, *née* Scotton (d 1961); *b* 10 Oct 1934; *Educ* Diocesan Coll Rondebosch Cape SA, Witwatersrand Univ (BSc), McGill Univ Montreal Canada (MSc); *m* 1 Sept 1962, Tuulike Raili, da of Dr Artur Aleksander Linari-Linholm (d 1984); 1 s (Jeffrey Charles b 15 Sept 1973), 2 da (Karen b 1 Sept 1963, Nicolette b 29 Jan 1966); *Career* Johannesburg Consolidated Investment Co Group: employed variously 1960-65, head of computing 1966-69, mangr 1969-71, consulting engr (Randfontein Estates, GM Co Ltd, Consolidated Murchison Ltd) 1971-73; consulting engr and dir Rustenburg Platinum Mines Ltd 1973-75, chief consulting engr and alternative dir JCI 1975-77, md Western Areas Gold Mining Co Ltd 1975-77; assoc prof Virginia Poly Inst and State Univ Blacksburg Virginia USA 1977-80, prof of mining Royal Sch of Mines Imperial Coll London 1980-; chm Special Sub Ctee on Engrg Qualifications Mining Qualifications Bd 1986-87, assessor for Inquiry Kinoulton Notts 1985, ed Mineral Resources Engineering 1988-; memb: Professional Engrs 1977, Scientific Ctee Inst for Archaeo-Metallurgical Studies 1982-, Safety in Mines Res Advsy Bd UK 1985-88, Res Advsy Ctee Mining Indust Res Orgn UK 1983-, Ctee of Mgmnt Inst of Archaeology 1985-87, Advsy Ctee Inst of Archaeology 1987-, Cncl Royal Sch of Mines Assoc 1982 (pres 1988-89); sec gen: Soc of Mining Profs, Societät der Bergbaukunde 1990; govr Camborne Sch of Mines 1982-90; fell: South African Inst of Mining and Metallurgy 1961, Inst of Mining and Metallurgy 1980 (memb Cncl 1981-88 and 1989-), Inst of Mining Engrs 1981 (memb Cncl 1988-, pres Southern Counties Branch 1988-89 and 1990-91), Inst of Quarrying 1981; CEng 1980; *Style—* Prof Tim Shaw; Imperial Coll of Science, Technology and Medicine, S Kensington, London SW7 (☎ 071 589 5111 ext 6401, fax 071 589 6806)

SHAW, Dr (James) Charlton Haliday; s of James Henry Shaw (d 1932), of Annamount, Kingstown, Co Dublin, and Eva Susanna, *née* Exshaw (d 1961); *b* 6 March 1921; *Educ* Kingstown Sch Dun Laoghaire Co Dublin, Trinity Coll Dublin (BA, MB BCh, BAO); *m* (Violet) Elizabeth, da of Ernest Joseph Cotter (d 1964); 1 s (Robert Charlton O'Molloy); *Career* Surgn Lt RNVR 1945-48, PMO 1 Submarine Flotilla Med Station, PMO 3 Destroyer Flotilla Palestine; sr ptnr Drs Shaw & Veale Fairford 1950-82; MO child welfare clinics: Cirencester, Fairford & Kempstord 1951-72; chm and fndr Fairford Preservaton Tst, hon sec Benevolent Ctee Royal Br Legion Fairford branch; DCH, RCPI and surgns; *Books* The Molloy Family of Kells (1961), The Waters of Waterstown Co Carlow (1965), The Charltons of Mount Charlton alias Curraghstown (1969); *Recreations* fishing, shooting, beagling, botany, fly tying, washing up; *Clubs* Naval and Military; *Style—* Dr Charlton Shaw; Waynes Cottage, Fairford, Glos (☎ 0285 712456)

SHAW, Colin Don; s of Rupert Morris Shaw (d 1980), and Enid Fryer, *née* Smith (d 1955); *b* 2 Nov 1928; *Educ* Liverpool Coll, St Peters Coll Oxford (BA, MA); *m* 1955, Elizabeth Ann, da of Paul Alan Bowker; 1 s (Giles), 2 da (Tessa, Susan); *Career* called to the Bar Inner Temple 1960; chief sec BBC 1972-76; dir: TV IBA 1977-83, Programme Planning Secretariat ITCA 1983-87, Broadcasting Standards Cncl 1988-; memb Arts Cncl 1977-80, govr ESU 1977-83; author of radio plays and a stage play for children; *Clubs* Reform; *Style—* Colin Shaw, Esq; Lesters, Little Ickford, Aylesbury, Bucks HP18 9HS (☎ 0844 339 225); Broadcasting Standards Council, 5-8 The Sanctuary, Westminster, London SW1P 3JS

SHAW, Prof David Aitken; CBE (1989); s of Col John James McIntosh Shaw, MC (d 1940), and Mina, *née* Draper (d 1979); *b* 11 April 1924; *Educ* Edinburgh Acad, Univ of Edinburgh (MB ChB); *m* 22 Oct 1960, Jill, da of Eric Parry, CBE, of Lydiate; 1 s (Andrew b 1965), 2 da (Alison b 1963, Katriona b 1969); *Career* WWII RNVR; Ordinary Seaman 1943, Sub Lt 1944, Lt 1946; lectr in clinical neurology Inst of Neurology Univ of London 1957; Univ of Newcastle upon Tyne: sr lectr in neurology 1964- 76, prof of clinical neurology 1976-89, dean of med 1981-89; FRCP 1976, FRCPE 1968, Hon FCST 1988; *Clubs* Athenaeum; *Style—* Prof David Shaw, CBE; The Coach House, Moor Rd North, Gosforth, Newcastle Upon Tyne NE3 1AB (☎ 091 285 2029)

SHAW, David Baxter; s of John Knowles Shaw (d 1967), of Sheffield, and Dorothy, *née* Baxter; *b* 6 Aug 1936; *Educ* Trent Coll; *m* 14 March 1964, Margaret Mary, da of Walter Edward Moore (d 1976), of Sheffield; 3 da (Katharine b 1964, Elizabeth b 1966, Victoria b 1968); *Career* Nat Serv Lt RA 1959-61; articled Jarvis Barber & Sons 1953-58; CA 1959; ptnr: Forsdike Paterson & Co 1962-67, Moore Fletcher Forsdike & Shaw 1968-75; sr ptnr Shaw Dunk Styring 1975-, chm The Manchester Hosiery Gp 1985-; pres Sheffield and Dist Soc of CAs 1976-77; memb: Investigation Ctee Inst of CAs 1986- (memb Trg Standards Bd 1986-90), IOD (memb Nat Cncl and chm Sheffield Branch 1985-89), S Yorks Ctee Prince's Youth Business Tst 1989; pres Rotary Club of Sheffield 1982-82; Freeman: The Co of Cutlers in Hallamshire 1974, City of London 1978; Master Worshipful Co of CAs in England and Wales 1989-90 (Liveryman 1978, memb ct 1979-); FCA 1959; *Recreations* the family, travel, motoring, swimming, photography; *Style—* David Shaw, Esq; Kireka House, 527 Fulwood Rd, Sheffield S10 3QB (☎ 0742 306431); Shaw, Dunk, Styring, 346 Glossop Rd, Sheffield S10 2HW (☎ 0742 738551, fax 0742 760934)

SHAW, David Lawrence; MP (C) Dover 1987-; *b* 14 Nov 1950; *Educ* King's Sch Wimbledon, City of London Poly; *m* 1986, Dr Lesley Christine Shaw, *née* Brown; 1 s (James b 1989); *Career* qualified CA 1974; Coopers & Lybrand 1971-79, County Bank 1979-83, fndr and md Sabrelance Ltd 1983-; dir: Invicta Sound plc, The Adscene Group plc, Hoskins Brewery plc, Palladian Estates plc; joined Cons Pty 1970, cncllr Royal Borough of Kingston upon Thames 1974-78, Parly Candidate (C) Leigh 1979, vice chm Kingston and Malden Cons Assoc 1979-86, chm Bow Gp 1983-84; sec Cons Pty: Fin Ctee, Smaller Business Ctee; co-chm All-Pty Dolphin Protection Gp; fndr Bow Gp/Ripon Soc Transatlantic Confs; ACA 1974, FCA; *Style—* David Shaw, Esq, MP; House of Commons, London SW1A 0AA

SHAW, Dr Dennis Frederick; CBE (1974); s of Albert Shaw (d 1957), of Kenton, Middx, and Lily Florence, *née* Hill (d 1968); *b* 20 April 1924; *Educ* Harrow Co Sch, ChCh Oxford, (BA, MA, DPhil); *m* 25 June 1949, Joan Irene, da of Sydney Chandler; 1 s (Peter James b 1951), 3 da (Margaret b 1953, Katherine b 1956, Deborah b 1959); *Career* memb Civil Def Corps 1942-45, jr sci offr MAP 1944-46; Univ of Oxford: demonstrator in physics 1946-49, res offr 1950-57, lectr in physics 1957-75, keeper of sci books 1975-, professorial fell Keble Coll 1977- (fell and tutor in physics 1957-75); visiting prof of physics Univ of S Tennessee USA 1974, pres Int Assoc of Technol Univ Libraries 1986-90, chm Sci and Technol Libraries Section IFLA 1987-; memb Oxford City Cncl 1963-67; Home Office: memb Sci Advsy Cncl 1966-78, chm Police Sci Devpt Ctee 1970-74, memb Def Sci Advsy Ctee 1968-; memb Hebdomadal Cncl Oxford Univ 1980-89; Almoner Christs Hosp 1980; memb: APS 1957, NYAS 1981; FZS 1970, FInstP 1971, CPhys 1984; *Books* Introduction to Electronics (2 edn, 1970), Oxford University Science Libraries (2 edn, 1981), Information Sources in Physics (1985); *Recreations* enjoying music; *Clubs* Utd Oxford and Cambridge Univ; *Style—* Dr Dennis Shaw, CBE; Keble Coll, Oxford (☎ 0865 272 768, fax 0865 272 821)

SHAW, Dr Donald George; s of George Shaw (d 1974), of Coventry, and Jane, *née* Humble (d 1955); *b* 21 June 1937; *Educ* Bablake Sch, Univ of Oxford, UCH (MA, MSc, BM BCh); *m* 8 Feb 1964, Anne Patricia, da of Gp Capt L Crocker, CBE, of London, and Lisbon; 2 da (Caroline b 1968, Katherine b 1971); *Career* conslt radiologist: UCH 1970-82, Hosps for Sick Children 1970-; ed British Journal of Radiology 1989- (dep ed 1985-89); examiner: RCR 1978-84, Univ of Malaysia 1989; memb: Faculty Bd RCR 1988, Br Inst of Radiology 1989; DMRD, FRCR, FRCP; *Recreations* gardening, music; *Style—* Dr Donald Shaw; 37 Sandy Lodge Rd, Moor Park, Rickmansworth WD3 1LP; 11 Wimpole St, London W1M (☎ 071 580 1660)

SHAW, Fiona Mary; da of Dr Denis Joseph Wilson, of Cork, Ireland, and Mary Teresa, *née* Flynn; *b* 10 July 1958; *Educ* Scoil Mhuire Cork, Univ Coll Cork, RADA; *Career* actress; Julia in the Rivals (Nat Theatre) 1983, Mary Shelley in Bloody Poetry (Leicester and Hampstead 1984); RSC 1985-88: Tatyana Vasilyevna in Philistines, Celia in As You Like It, Madame de Volange in Les Liasons Dangereuses, Erika Brückner in Mephisto, Beatrice in Much Ado About Nothing, Portia in The Merchant of Venice, Mistress Carol in Hyde Park, Katherine in The Taming of the Shrew, Lady Frampul in New Inn, title role in Electra; title role in Mary Stuart (Greenwich Theatre) 1988, Rosalind in As You Like It (Old Vic) 1989, Shen Te/Shui Ta in The Good Person of Sichuan (Nat Theatre) 1989, Elspeth in Fireworks for Elspeth (Granada TV) 1983; films: My Left Foot 1988, The Mountains of the Moon 1988, Three Men and a Little Lady 1990, London Kills Me 1991; winner: London Theatre Critics Award for Electra and Good Person of Sichuan 1990, Lawrence Olivier award 1990; *Books* Players of Shakespeare (1987), Clamerous Voices (contrib, 1988), Conversation with Actresses (1990); *Recreations* travel, hoping; *Style—* Miss Fiona Shaw; Eglantine, Montenotte, Cork, Ireland; c/o Jeremy Conway, Eagle House, 109 Jermyn St, London SW1 6HB

SHAW, Gavin Edmund; s of Alan Linsley Shaw, of Edinburgh, and Marjory Morton, *née* Brown; *b* 9 July 1946; *Educ* Altrincham GS, St John's Coll Cambridge (MA); *m* 19 Jan 1974, Gail, da of Ernest Thomas Inglis Wooderson, of Hertfordshire; 1 da (Georgina Kate b 1979); *Career* advertising mktg consultancy, video prodn; mktg dir Burton Menswear 1975-76, bd dir McCormicks Advertising Agency 1976-81, dir i/c J

Walter Thompson (London) 1981-85, dir of devpt and mktg Burger King Europe 1985; prodr dir and marketer of Transatlantic with Street (an instructional video for yachtsmen on ocean sailing) 1985-87, mktg conslt advertising agencies and retailers, proprietor Marine Marketing 1986-91; *Recreations* yachting, skiing, cycling; *Style*— Gavin Shaw, Esq; 54 Bolingbroke Grove, London SW11 6HR (☎ 071 223 7587); 47 Berners St, London W1 (☎ 071 436 3355, fax 071 637 1296)

SHAW, George Gavin; s of George Bernard James Shaw, and Audry June Rose, *née* Markwick; *b* 18 June 1957; *Educ* Sir Walter St Johns Sch, Univ of Bristol (BA); *Career* md: Joslin Shaw Ltd 1984, Shaw PR Co Ltd 1988; memb Ctee Sinjuns Club, Capt Old Sinjuns AFC; *Recreations* horse racing, shooting, fishing, assoc football, skiing; *Clubs* Whites', Sinjuns; *Style*— George Shaw, Esq; 241 Upper St, Islington, London N1 1RU (☎ 071 226 9177, fax 071 359 6351, car 0860 383 368)

SHAW, Sir (John) Giles Dunkerley; MP (C) Pudsey Feb 1974-; s of Hugh Dunkerley Shaw; *b* 16 Nov 1931; *Educ* Sedbergh, St John's Coll Cambridge; *m* 1962, Dione Patricia Crosthwaite, da of Prof Mervyn Ellison, of Dublin; 1 s, 2 da; *Career* former pres Cambridge Union; Parly candidate (C) Kingston-on-Hull W 1966, mktg dir Confectionary Div Rowntree Mackintosh Ltd 1969-74; Parly under sec state: NI Office 1979-81, DOE 1981-83, Energy 1983-84; min of state: Home Office 1984-86, Indust 1986-87; elected treas 1922 Ctee 1988, appointed to Speaker's Panel of Chairmen 1989; kt 1987; *Recreations* ornithology, fishing; *Style*— Sir Giles Shaw, MP; House of Commons, London SW1

SHAW, Prof Gordon; s of George Jessop Shaw (d 1959), of Halifax Yorkshire, and Alice May, *née* McComb (d 1983); *b* 19 Oct 1922; *Educ* Halifax Tech Coll (BSc London external), Imperial Coll Univ of London (BSc, ARCS, DIC, PhD), Univ of London (DSc); *m* 25 Oct 1947, Evelyn Shaw, da of Sydney Gerrard (d 1976), of Coventry Warwickshire; 1 s (Philip Gerard b 1965), 1 da (Helen Elizabeth Shaw b 1960); *Career* lectr and sr lectr in organic chemistry Univ of NSW Aust 1948-59, reader and prof of organic chemistry Univ of Bradford 1960-89; author of 300 scientific pubns incl books chapters; assoc memb Royal Soc of Chemistry; *Books* Origin and Development of Living Sytems (1972); *Recreations* philately, golf, gardening; *Style*— Prof Gordon Shaw; 7 Kirkfields, Shipley, W Yorks BD17 6HU (☎ 0274 581787); School of Chemistry & Chemical Technology, Univ of Bradford, Richmond Rd, Bradford, W Yorks BD7 1DP (☎ 0274 733466, fax 0274 305340, telex 51309 UNIBFD G)

SHAW, Henry Jagoe; VRD (1968); s of Dr Benjamin Henry Shaw (d 1955), and Adelaide Shaw, JP (d 1965); *b* 16 March 1922; *Educ* Eton, Univ of Oxford (BM BCh, MA), FRCS(Eng), NY Univ (MD); *m* 1, 10 March 1967 (m dis 1988), Susan Patricia, da of A D Ramsay (d 1952); m 2, 30 Dec 1988, Daphne Joan Hayes, da of H Charney (d 1978); *Career* conslt ENT surgn Royal Nat Throat Nose and Ear Hosp London, civilian conslt ENT surgn RN, conslt ENT surgn St Mary's Hosp Praed St London, conslt head and neck surgn Royal Marsden Hosp London, Hunterian prof RCS 1957, Semon lectr Univ of London 1984, Ernest Miles lectr Royal Marsden Hosp 1985; memb and former treas: Assoc of Head and Neck Surgns of GB, Br Assoc of Otolaryngologists, Br Assoc of Surgical Oncology; corresponding memb Assoc of Head and Neck Surgns of USA; hon memb: American Laryngological Assoc, Otolaryngological Assoc of Aust, Société Francaise d'Otorhinolaryngologie; *Publications incl*: Partial Laryngectomy after Irradiation (1978), Malignant Diseases of the Oropharynx (1980), Conservation and Repair in Cancer Surgery of the Head and Neck (1980), Head and Neck Oncology (jt ed 1987); *Recreations* walking, sailing, swimming; *Clubs* Hurlingham, Army and Navy, RSM; *Style*— Henry Shaw, Esq, VRD; Lislee House, Tredenham Rd, St Mawes, Cornwall TR2 5AN; 52 Winchester Court, London W8 4HL

SHAW, James Thomas Durrant; s of Lt-Col Geoffrey Devereux Shaw (d 1960); *b* 14 June 1927; *Educ* Eton, King's Coll Cambridge; *m* 1956, Jennifer June, da of the late Christopher Birkbeck, of Hevingham, Norfolk; 1 s, 1 da; *Career* chm and md Scottow Farms Ltd, dir Scottow Mgmnt Servs, chm of Sywell Airport & Sywell Motel Ltd; MFH North Norfolk Harriers 1973-78; *Recreations* hunting, shooting, horse breeding; *Clubs* RAC; *Style*— James Durrant Shaw Esq; Scottow Hall, Norwich, Norfolk (☎ 069 269 601)

SHAW, John Arthur (Jack); s of Arthur Shaw (d 1981), of Windridge, Guiseley, Leeds, and Genevieve, *née* Fattorini (d 1977); *b* 7 April 1925; *Educ* Stonyhurst, Univ of Leeds; *m* 1, 10 Dec 1948, Nan (d 1983), da of Herbert Armitage; 6 s (John b 1949, Michael b 1951, David b 1953, Brian b 1955, Richard b 1957, Patrick b 1961); m 2, Helgard Sofie Greth; *Career* RE 1944-47; Bradford Steel Pin Co Ltd: co sec 1948-60, dir 1960-67, asst md 1967-71, jt md 1971-74, md 1974-, chm 1978-; Cons Assoc: dep chm Pudsey constituency (chm, pres, election agent Aireborough Ward), former pres Rawdon Branch; jt winner Cons Nat Speaking Competition 1967; FBIM; *Recreations* pistol shooting, sea angling, trout fishing, photography; *Clubs* Shark Angling Club of GS, Irish Shark; *Style*— Jack Shaw, Esq; Larkfield Grange, Rawdon, Leeds LS19 6DZ (☎ 0532 506 128); Pinco (Bradford) Ltd, Dick Lane, Laisterdyke, Bradford BD4 8JE (☎ 0274 665 780, fax 0274 669 990, telex 51249)

SHAW, Prof John Calman (Jack); CBE (1989); s of Arthur John Shaw (d 1978), of Edinburgh, and Dorothy, *née* Turpie (d 1959); *b* 10 July 1932; *Educ* Strathallan Sch, Univ of Edinburgh (BL); *m* 2 Jan 1960, Shirley, da of James Botterill (d 1936), of Yedingham, Yorkshire; 3 da (Jane b 14 Jan 1961, Gillian b 31 Jan 1963, Catherine b 9 Oct 1966); *Career* local sr ptnr Deloitte Haskins & Sells Edinburgh 1980-86 (ptnr 1960-86), dir Scottish Financial Enterprise 1986-90; dir: Scottish Industl Devpt Advsy Bd 1987-, Financial Reporting Cncl 1990-, Scottish Enterprise 1990-; non-exec dir: Scottish Mortgage & Trust plc 1982-, Scottish American Investment Company plc 1986-, TR European Growth Trust plc 1990-, Bank of Scotland 1990-; ACA 1954 (pres 1983-84), FCMA 1958, MBCS 1975; *Books* The Audit Report (1980), Bogie Group Accounts (3 edn, 1973); *Recreations* walking, opera, foreign travel; *Clubs* New (Edinburgh), Western (Glasgow), Caldonian; *Style*— Prof Jack Shaw, Esq, CBE; Bank of Scotland, Head Office, The Mound, Edinburgh EH1 1YZ (☎ 031 243 5422, fax 031 243 5546, telex 72275)

SHAW, John Dennis; s of Frederick Shaw, of Willow Garth, 17 Park Avenue, Chapeltown, Sheffield, and Dorothy, *née* Wilson (d 1958); *b* 11 July 1938; *Educ* Ecclesfield GS, Univ of Sheffield Med Sch (MB ChB); *m* 5 Sept 1964, Margaret, da of William John Jones, of New Grange Villa, Dymock, Glos; 1 s (Simon b 1966), 1 da (Susan b 1965); *Career* rotating registrar United Sheffield Hosp 1965-67, sr registrar in otolaryngology Cardiff Royal Infirmary and Singleton Hosp Swansea 1967-70, res fell Wayne State Univ Detroit USA 1970, conslt ENT surgn Royal Hallamshire Hosp Sheffield 1971-; memb Cncl Sections of Otology and Laryngology RSM, regnl advsr in otolaryngology RCS Trent, memb Ct of Examiners RCS; FRCSEd 1967, FRCS 1969; *Books* Fibreoptic Endoscopy of the Upper Respiratory Tract; *Style*— John Shaw, Esq; The Gables, Sandygate Rd, Sheffield S10 5UE (☎ 0742 307784); The Royal Hallamshire Hospital, Glossop Rd, Sheffield (☎ 0742 766222)

SHAW, Josephine; da of James Henry Shaw, and Gwendoline Mabel, *née* Baker; *b* 15 Aug 1930; *Educ* Barr Hill GS Coventry, Birmingham Secretarial Coll; *Career* commercial trg advsr ILO Geneva 1965-76 (long-term assignments Sierra Leone and Ghana, short-term Africa), md Teaching Aids Ltd 1976- (chm 1988); MIPM, MInstAM, FBIM, FIOD; *Books* Teach Yourself Office Practice (1972), Essential Secretarial Studies (jtly, 1974), Secretarial Management, A Guide to the Effective Use of Staff (1977), Secretarial Work Experience (jtly, 1978), Office Organisation for Managers (1978), West African Office Practice (adaptation of Br edn, 1978), Office Management (5 edn, 1980), Administration in Business (1981), Caribbean Office Procedures (jtly, 1984), Word Processing and Computer Training Techniques (1988), Business Administration (1991); *Recreations* needlework, tapestry, photography, classical music; *Style*— Miss Josephine Shaw; Teaching Aids Ltd, Denestead House, Station Rd, New Milton, Hants BH25 6LD (☎ 0425 612 911, car 0836 589 629)

SHAW, Dr Kenneth Martin; s of Frank Shaw, of Norwich, Norfolk, and Gwendoline, *née* Mosson; *b* 20 April 1943; *Educ* City of Norwich Sch, Downing Coll Cambridge (MA, MD), UCH London; *m* 20 July 1968, Phyllis Margaret, da of George Dixon (d 1967), of Norwich; 2 s (Martin George b 17 June 1982, Edward Philip b 10 Feb 1984); *Career* conslt physician Portsmouth and SE Hants Health Authy 1978-, postgrad clinical tutor univ of Southampton 1982-, chm Wessex Diabetes and Endocrine Assoc 1989-, author of numerous articles on diabetes and Parkinson's disease; former memb: Med Advsy Ctee, Br Diabetic Assoc; dep ed Journal of Practical Diabetes; FRSM, FRCP, Scientific Fell Zoological Soc of London; *Recreations* golf, swimming, music, reading; *Clubs* RSM; *Style*— Dr Kenneth Shaw; Castle Acre, Hospital Lane, Portchester, Hants PO16 9QP; Queen Alexandra Hosp, Portsmouth, Hants (☎ 0705 379451)

SHAW, Dr Mark Robert; s of William Shaw, of Willowbeck, Drayton St Leonard, Oxon, and Mabel Courtenay, *née* Bower; *b* 11 May 1945; *Educ* Dartington Hall Sch, Oriel Coll Oxford (BA, MA, DPhil); *m* 11 July 1970, Francesca Dennis, da of Rev Dennis Wilkinson (d 1971); 2 da (Zerynthia b 23 Dec 1972, Melitaea b 19 April 1978); *Career* res asst Dept Zoology Univ of Manchester 1973-76, univ res fell Univ of Reading 1977-80; Nat Museums of Scotland (formerly Royal Scottish Museum): asst keeper Dept of Natural History 1980-83, keeper of natural history 1983-; frequent contrib to various pubns on entomology; FRES 1974; *Recreations* field entomology, family life; *Clubs* Univ of Edinburgh Staff; *Style*— Dr Mark R Shaw; Royal Museum of Scotland, Chambers St, Edinburgh EH1 1JF (☎ 031 225 7534, fax 031 220 4819)

SHAW, Martin; s of Albert Cyril Shaw (d 1967), of Leeds, and Letitia Whitehead (d 1978); *b* 31 Oct 1944; *Educ* Leeds GS, UCL (LLB); *m* 19 Aug 1967, Christine Helen, da of Maurice Grenville Whitwam (d 1986), of Leeds; 2 s (Simon b 17 March 1973, Jonathan b 4 Aug 1978), 1 da (Sarah b 25 Nov 1970); *Career* Simpson Curtis: articled clerk 1966-69, slr 1969-71, ptnr 1971-, head Corporate Dept 1980-88; chm: Minstergate plc 1985-89, ABI Caravans Ltd 1986-88, Legal Resources Gp 1988-, Minster Corp plc 1988-90; govr and chm Richmond House Sch, govr Gateways Sch; memb: Econ and Trade Ctee Leeds C of C and Indust, Yorks & Humberside Devpt Assoc, Leeds Business Venture (dir 1982); memb: Headingley Rotary Club, Variety Club of GB; memb: Slrs Euro Gp 1975, Law Soc 1969, Leeds Law Soc 1969, ABA 1985, IBA 1985; *Recreations* running, golf, squash, tennis; *Clubs* The Leeds, Alwoodley Golf, Chapel Allerton Lawn Tennis & Squash; *Style*— Martin Shaw, Esq; Sycamore Lodge, Harrowby Rd, West Park, Leeds LS16 5HN (☎ 0532 785350); Simpson Curtis, 41 Park Square, Leeds LS1 2NS (☎ 0532 433433, fax 0532 445598, telex 55376)

SHAW, Gp Capt Mary Michal; RRC (1982); da of late Ven Archdeacon Herbert Thorndike Shaw, and Violet Rosario, *née* Hobbs; *b* 7 April 1933; *Educ* Wokingham Co Girls Sch; *Career* SRN Royal Berks Hosp 1955, state registered midwife Battle Hosp Reading 1957, cmmr Princess Marys RAF Nursing Serv 1963-; sr matron RAF Hosp: Wegberg Germany 1981-83, Ely Cambs 1983-84; Gp Capt MOD 1984, appt Matron in Chief PMRAFNS, dir Nursing Serv RAF and dep dir Def Nursing Servs 1985-88, ret 1988; involved with St Edmundsbury Cathedral; OStJ 1975; *Recreations* gardening, cake decorating, handicrafts; *Clubs* RAF; *Style*— Gp Capt Mary Michal Shaw, RRC; 5 William Barnaby Yard, College St, Bury St Edmunds, Suffolk IP33 1PQ (☎ 0284 705 836)

SHAW, (Francis) Michael; s of Joseph Stanley Shaw (d 1959), of Yorks, and Irene Shaw, *née* Weldrake; *b* 12 Aug 1936; *Educ* Rotherham GS; *m* 1960, Margaret Elinor, da of Ralph William Russum (d 1986); 2 da (Caroline b 1963, Juliet b 1964); *Career* chief accountant: Eastern Counties Building Soc 1967-74, Britannia Building Soc 1974-75 (md 1985-); FICA; *Recreations* golf, photography, travel; *Clubs* Leek Golf, British Pottery Mfrs Fedn; *Style*— Michael Shaw, Esq; Rock House, Cheadle Road, Wetley Rocks, Stoke-on-Trent (☎ 0782 550655); Britannia Building Soc, Newton House, Leek, Staffs (☎ 0538 399399, fax 0538 399261)

SHAW, Hon Michael Frank; s of Baron Kilbrandon, PC (Life Peer; d 1989); *b* 1944; *m* 1978, Catherine Ballantine; 1 s (Torquil b 1981), 1 da (Tamara b 1980); *Career* md Portmor (Seil Island) Ltd; dir Argyll & The Islands Enterprise; chm Oban Mull and Dist Tourist Bd; memb: Easdale Sch Bd, Seil Community Cncl; *Recreations* sailing, shooting, skiing, fishing; *Clubs* New (Edinburgh), Royal Highland Yacht; *Style*— The Hon Michael Shaw; Kilbrandon House, Balvicar, By Oban, Argyll

SHAW, Michael Gordon (Mike); s of Leslie Shaw, of Buckhurst Hill, and Pauline, *née* Gordon (d 1971); *b* 8 July 1931; *Educ* Epsom Co GS; *m* 1, 23 Nov 1957 (m dis 1981), Ann, da of Henry Newbury; 3 s (Kevin b 1958, Simon b 1959, Adam b 1962), 2 da (Zoe b 1963, Melanie b 1969); m 2, 30 March 1989, Ann Hatton-James; *Career* Nat Serv RAF 1949-51; advtg copywriter and creative dir; Cunningham Hurst 1979, Progress Advertising 1981; author of three computer books; memb MENSA 1975; *Recreations* writing, computing, photography (video); *Style*— Mike Shaw, Esq; 45 Beechfield Rd, Bromley, Kent BR1 3BT (☎ 081 464 0853); No 2 Parkwest Place, Kendal Street, London W2 2QZ (☎ 071 402 9361)

SHAW, Michael Hewitt; CMG (1990); s of Donald Smethurst Shaw (d 1982), and Marian Clarissa, *née* Hewitt; *b* 5 Jan 1935; *Educ* Sedbergh, Clare Coll Cambridge (BA, MA); *m* 10 Aug 1963, Elizabeth Monica, da of Maj-Gen Sir Hubert Elvin Rance, GCB, GBE (d 1974); 4 da (Melanie b 1964, Sarah b 1968, Lucy b 1970, d 1973, Suzanna b 1973); *Career* Nat Serv 2 Lt RA 1953-55; dist offr and ADC to govr of Tanganyika HMOCS 1959-62; FCO 1963-: London 1963 and 1965, second sec The Hague 1964, second sec Vientiane 1966, first sec Valletta 1972, first sec and cnsllr Brussels 1982, cnsllr London 1987; *Recreations* cricket, theatre, walking; *Clubs* MCC, Army and Navy; *Style*— Michael Shaw, Esq, CMG; Foreign and Commonwealth Office, King Charles St, London SW1A 2AH

SHAW, Sir Michael Norman; JP (Dewsbury 1953), DL (W Yorks 1977), MP (C) Scarborough 1974-; eld s of late Norman Shaw; *b* 9 Oct 1920; *Educ* Sedbergh; *m* 1951, Joan Mary Louise, da of late Sir Alfred Mowat, 2 and last Bt, DSO, OBE, MC; 3 s; *Career* MP: (Lib and C) Brighouse and Spenborough 1960-64, (C) Scarborough and Whitby 1966-74; PPS: Min of Lab and Nat Serv 1962-63, sec of state DTI 1970-72; Chllr Duchy of Lancaster 1973-74; memb UK Delgn Euro Parl 1974-79; FCA; kt 1982; *Style*— Sir Michael Shaw, JP, DL, MP; Duxbury Hall, Liversedge, W Yorks WF15 7NR (☎ 0924 402270)

SHAW, (Robert) Michael; s of Sydney Ernest Shaw (d 1962), of Huddersfield, and Evelyn, *née* Bates (d 1968); *b* 21 July 1925; *Educ* Giggleswick Sch; *m* 12 July 1947, Margaret Sylvia, da of Sydney Osborne Hughes (d 1960), of Huddersfield; 1 s (Robert b 1958), 1 da (Nicola b 1950); *Career* REME 1945-48; various appts in Benjamin Shaw and Sons Ltd (family company) (chm 1968-), regnl dir Lloyds Bank plc; former pres:

Br Soft Drinks Assoc, Huddersfield and Spen Valley Inc Chamber of Commerce; FBIM, FCIM; *Style*— Michael Shaw, Esq; Benjamin Shaw and Sons Ltd, Willow Lane, Huddersfield HD1 5ED (☎ 0484 427427, fax 0484 435376)

SHAW, (Joseph) Neil; s of Maurice George Shaw (d 1982), of Summerhill, Prestbury, Cheshire, and Marjorie, *née* Whitehead (d 1981); *b* 30 Oct 1925; *Educ* Kings Sch Macclesfield, Univ of Leeds; *m* 11 Aug 1956, Lillian, da of Mark Mitchell; 2 da (Caroline Jane b 25 Feb 1960, Victoria Louise b 16 Sept 1961 d 11 March 1966); *Career* Army 1944-48; chm and md: John Reynolds & Co (Insurance) Ltd 1982-86 (dir 1952-88, dir of 4 subsids of The John Reynolds Gp Ltd), The John Reynolds Group Ltd 1986-, The MG Shaw Co Ltd 1988-; FCIB 1952-77, fell Br Insur & Investmt Brokers Assoc 1977 (memb UK Credit Insur Brokers Ctee), FRHS; *Recreations* horticulture; *Clubs* Nefyn Sailing; *Style*— J Neil Shaw, Esq; The John Reynolds Group Ltd, Byrom House, 21 Quay St, Manchester M3 3JA (☎ 061 832 9022, fax 061 832 3508)

SHAW, Hon Patrick James; s of Baron Kilbrandon, PC (Life Peer; d 1989); *b* 1938; *m* 1964, Elisabeth Campbell-Gibson; *Style*— The Hon Patrick Shaw; Highfield, Taynuilt, Argyll

SHAW, Capt Peter Jack; CBE (1990); s of Jack Shaw (d 1968), of London, and Gladys Elizabeth, *née* Knight (d 1981); *b* 27 Oct 1924; *Educ* Watford GS, RNC Dartmouth, RN Staff Coll Greenwich, NATO Def Coll Paris; *m* 18 Aug 1951, Pauline, da of Sir Frank William Madge, 2 Bt (d 1962); 1 s (Christopher John b 1957), 1 da (Carol Anne (Mrs Livett) b 1952); *Career* WWII 1942-45; served: Russian, Atlantic, Malta convoys, Normandy invasion (on HM Ships: Kenya, Quadrant, Resolution, London, Kelvin); cmd HM LCI (L) 377 1945, staff of Flag Offr Germany 1946-48 and 1951-53, HMS Corunna 1949-51, exec offr HMS Chevron and HMS Whirlwind 1953-55, naval instr RAF Coll Cranwell 1956-58, cmd HMS Venus and HMS Carron 1958, HMS Vigilant 1960, staff of C-in-C Portsmouth 1961-63, MOD 1963-65, SHAPE 1966-68, exec offr RN Coll Greenwich 1968-70, def and naval attache The Hague 1971-73; Capt of the Port and Queen's Harbourmaster: Plymouth 1973-76, Chatham; chief of staff to Flag Offr Medway 1976-79, gen sec Interparly Union (Br Gp) 1979-90; exec sec Br Delgn to Interparly Confs incl: Caracas 1979, E Berlin 1980, Manila 1981, Lagos 1982, Rome 1982, 1985, Seoul 1983, Geneva 1984, Ottowa 1985, Mexico City 1986, Bangkok 1987, Guatemala 1988; organiser IPU Centenary Conf London 1989; FIL 1956, MBIM 1975; *Recreations* international affairs, foreign languages, domestic pursuits; *Style*— Capt Peter Shaw, CBE, RN; Woodside Rogate, Petersfield, Hants, GU31 5DJ (☎ 0730 821 344); Interparliamentary Union, Palace of Westminster, London SW1 (☎ 071 219 3013)

SHAW, Richard John Gildroy; s of Edward Philip Shaw (d 1970), and Mary Elizabeth Shaw; *b* 7 June 1936; *Educ* The Dragon Sch, Eton; *m* 1973, Yvonne Kathleen, da of Henry Percival Maskell (d 1978); 1 s (Rupert Henry Gildroy b 1974); *Career* chm and chief exec Lowndes Lambert Group Ltd (insur brokers); *Recreations* golf, cricket, yachting (MY Moonmaiden II), reading, horseracing; *Clubs* Royal Thames Yacht, Sunningdale Golf, Portland, Clermont, Lloyd's Yacht; *Style*— Richard Shaw, Esq; 18 Phillimore Gdns, London W8 7QE (☎ 071 937 2942); Lowndes Lambert Group Ltd, Lowndes Lambert House, PO Box 431, 53 Eastcheap, London EC3P 3HL (☎ 071 283 2000, telex 8814631, fax 071 283 1970)

SHAW, Sir Robert; 7 Bt (UK 1821), of Bushy Park, Dublin; s of Lt-Col Sir Robert de Vere Shaw, 6 Bt, MC (d 1969); *b* 31 Jan 1925; *Educ* Harrow, Iklahome Univ, Missouri Univ; *m* 1954, Jocelyn Mary, da of Andrew McGuffie (decd), of Mbabane, Swaziland; 2 da; *Heir* n, Charles de Vere Shaw; *Career* Lt RN (ret); professional engr (Alberta); *Style*— Sir Robert Shaw, Bt; 234 40 Avenue SW, Calgary, Alberta, Canada

SHAW, Prof Robert Alfred; s of Walter Schlesinger (d 1964), and Lily Karoline, *née* Plahner (d 1954); *b* 2 Nov 1924; *Educ* Univ of London (BSc, PhD, DSc); *m* 23 Aug 1980, Dr Leylâ Süheylâ Shaw, da of Yusuf Gözen, of Tarsus, Turkey; 1 s (Robert b 28 March 1984), 1 da (Lily b 30 May 1989); *Career* WWII Royal Fusiliers and Queen's Royal Regt UK, India, SE Asia command 1944-47; Birkbeck Coll Univ of London: asst lectr 1953-56, lectr 1956-65, prof of chemistry 1965-90, prof emeritus 1990-; author of numerous articles dealing with chemistry educn, and third world countries; memb Academic Policy Ctee of the Inter-Univ Cncl for Higher Educn Overseas 1976-81, UNESCO conslt to Turkish Govt 1977, main speaker and memb Organising Ctee of Conf sponsored by Institut Mondial du Phosphate Rabat Morocco 1977, main speaker on Life-long Educn in Koblenz W Germany 1978, fndr memb and on steering ctee of Univ of the Third Age London; Dr hc Univ Paul Sabatier Toulouse 1978; memb Soc of Chemical Indust; CChem, FRSC; *Recreations* reading, music, gardening, travelling, skiing, fencing; *Style*— Prof Robert A Shaw; Brettargh Holt, Camden Way, Chislehurst, Kent BR7 5HT (☎ 081 467 5656); Department of Chemistry, Birkbeck College, University of London, Gordon House, 29 Gordon Square, London WC1H 0PP (☎ 071 380 7475, fax 071 380 7464)

SHAW, Robert Ian (Bob); s of Robert Shaw (d 1975), of Glasgow, and Lily Shaw (d 1990); *b* 2 Jan 1939; *Educ* Whitehill Sch Glasgow; *m* 19 Aug 1963, Doreen, da of Alexander Archibald; 2 s (Trevor John b 20 Feb 1967, Leonard b 21 Feb 1971); *Career* Peat Marwick McLintock Glasgow 1961-64, Brownlee plc Glasgow 1964-67, Swedish Match Corp (STAB) Glasgow and Surrey 1967-78, EFG plc Edinburgh and Oxford 1978-; MICAS; *Recreations* golf, gardening; *Style*— Bob Shaw, Esq; EFG plc, Great Haseley, Oxford OX9 7PG (☎ 0844 279571, fax 0844 279541, telex 837137)

SHAW, Sir Roy; s of late Frederick Shaw, and Elsie, *née* Odgen; *b* 8 July 1918; *Educ* Firth Park GS Sheffield, Univ of Manchester; *m* 1946, Gwenyth Baron; 5 s, 2 da; *Career* writer and lectr; lectr in adult educn Univ of Leeds, prof and dir of adult educn Univ of Keele 1962-75, sec gen Arts Cncl 1975-83; exec memb Action on Smoking and Health; Hon DLitt: City Univ, Univ of Southampton; Hon DUniv Open Univ; *Books* The Arts and the People (1987); *Recreations* arts, walking, swimming; *Clubs* Arts; *Style*— Sir Roy Shaw; 48 Farrer Rd, London N8 8LB (☎ 081 348 1857)

SHAW, Roy Edwin; OBE (1991); s of Edwin Victor Shaw (d 1938), and Edith Lily, *née* Clarke (d 1987); *b* 21 July 1925; *Educ* William Ellis Sch London; *Career* tank crew 5 RIDG 1943-45, CSM Intelligence Corps 1945-47; mktg conslt and lectr; memb: Hampstead Cncl 1956-62, St Pancras Cncl 1962-65; memb Camden Cncl 1964-: chm Planning Ctee 1967-68, memb Fin Ctee 1971-74, chief whip and dep ldr 1965-75, ldr 1975-82; vice chm Assoc of Met Authorities 1980-83, dep chm and ldr Lab Pty London Boroughs Assoc 1978-83; memb: Consultative Cncl of Local Govt Fin 1978-83, Advsy Ctee on Local Govt Audit 1979-82, Audit Cmmn for England and Wales 1983-, LEB (pt/t) 1977-83, Tport Users Consultative Ctee for London 1974-80; *Recreations* listening to music; *Style*— Roy Shaw, Esq, OBE; Town Hall, Euston Rd, London NW1 2RU (☎ 071 278 4444)

SHAW, Sebastian Lewis; s of Geoffrey Turton Shaw (d 1943), and Mary Grace Shaw (d 1954); *b* 29 May 1905; *Educ* Gresham's, Slade Sch of Fine Art, RADA; *m* 9 June 1929, Margaret Kate, *née* Wellesley-Lynn (decd); 1 da (Drusilla b 9 Sept 1932, m 1961, John Macleod of Macleod, 29th Chief); *Career* Nat Serv WWII RAF 1940-44; actor, author; first stage appearance as one of the Juvenile Band in Me Cockyolly Bird Court Theatre 1912; distinguished career in theatre, radio, films, TV 1925-; pre-war appearances 1926- incl: Meml Theatre Stratford on Avon, numerous West End prodns, contract to London Films (Men are not Gods, Spy in Black, Farewell Again); post-war career 1950-; His Excellency at the Princes and Piccadilly Theatres; TV work incl: 1 TV Hamlet (Claudius), 1 colour TV Shakespeare All's Well (The King); radio incl: Man and Superman (Tanner), 1 play on the Third Prog, The Small Back Room; repertory season Royal Ct Theatre 1969-; joined RSC 1971: assoc artist, numerous lead roles during 70s and 80s; films incl: It Happened Here, High Season; The Wizard of Oz performed for RSC and TV Chelworth; author of: poems, works for the theatre (The Cliff Walk, London Sketches, The Glass Maize, Take a Life); RSC tours: Russia, America, Finland, Germany, Switzerland; toured Norway and Holland with the Dublin Festival Co; lecture tours USA and elsewhere with RSC; *Books plays*: The Cliff Walk, Take a Life, The Glass Maze; *novel* The Christening (1975); *Recreations* chess, music; *Style*— Sebastian Shaw, Esq; c/o The Garrick Club, London

SHAW, Stephen; s of Ivan Shaw, and Phyllis, *née* Niechciki; *b* 20 Dec 1952; *Educ* Harrow Co GS, Univ of Birmingham (LLB); *m* 26 Sept 1978, Fabia Melanie, da of John Alexander; 2 s (Gideon David b 20 Sept 1982, Aaron Alexander b 7 Jan 1987), 1 da (Gabrielle Leah b 25 March 1984); *Career* called to the Bar Gray's Inn 1975; ACIArb; *Books* contrib New Law Journal and Estates Gazette on landlord and tenant matters; *Recreations* amateur magic, occasional sleep; *Style*— Stephen Shaw, Esq; Lamb Building, Temple, London EC4Y 7AS (☎ 071 353 6701, fax 071 353 4686, telex 261511 JURIST G)

SHAW, Hon Thomas Columba; s and h of 3 Baron Craigmyle; *b* 19 Oct 1960; *m* 25 April 1987, Alice, 2 da of David Floyd, of Combe Down, Bath; *Style*— The Hon Thomas Shaw; c/o Rt Hon Lord Craigmyle, 18 The Boltons, London, SW10 9SY

SHAW, Rev Prof (Douglas) William David; WS (1951); s of Capt William David Shaw, MC (d 1955), and Nansie, *née* Smart (d 1982); *b* 25 June 1928; *Educ* Loretto, Ashbury Coll Ottawa, Edinburgh Acad, Univ of Cambridge (BA, MA), Univ of Edinburgh (LLB, BD); *Career* ptnr Davidson & Syme WS Edinburgh 1953-57; ordained minister in Church of Scotland 1960; observer for World Alliance of Reformed Churches at II Vatican Cncl 1962; lectr in divinity New Coll Edinburgh 1963-79; dean Faculty of Divinity and princ New Coll Edinburgh 1974-78; prof of divinity Univ of St Andrews 1979-, princ St Mary's Coll St Andrews 1986-; *Books* Who is God? (1968), The Dissuaders (1978), In Divers Manners (ed, 1990); *Recreations* squash, golf, hill walking; *Clubs* Royal and Ancient, New (Edinburgh), Edinburgh Sports; *Style*— The Rev Prof William Shaw, WS; St Mary's College, University of St Andrews, St Andrews, Fife KY16 9JW (☎ 0334 76161)

SHAW OF TORDARROCH, John; 22 Chief of the Highland Clan of Shaw; s of late Maj Charles John Shaw of Tordarroch, MBE, TD, DL, JP; *b* 1937; *Educ* Eton, Magdalene Coll Cambridge (MA); *m* 1960, Silvia Margaret, da of late Rev David John Silian Jones; 1 s; *Heir* s, Iain b 1968; *Career* late 2 Lt Seaforth Highlanders 1955-57; memb Royal Co of Archers (Queen's Body Guard for Scotland); hon vice-pres Clan Chattan Assoc (UK); memb standing Cncl of Scottish Chiefs, Convenor of the Northern Meeting 1984-; *Books* A History of Clan Shaw (ed); *Clubs* New, Turf, Puffins; *Style*— John Shaw of Tordarroch; Tordarroch, Farr, Inverness IV1 2XF; Newhall, Balblair, by Dingwall, Ross-shire IV7 8IQ

SHAW-STEWART, Sir Houston Mark; 11 Bt (NS 1667) of Greenock and Blackhall, Renfrewshire, MC (1950), TD (1968); s of Lt-Col Sir (Walter) Guy Shaw-Stewart, 9 Bt, MC (d 1976); suc bro, Sir Euan Guy Shaw-Stewart, 10 Bt, 1980; *b* 24 April 1931; *Educ* Eton; *m* 1982, Lucinda Victoria, yr da of Alexander Fletcher, of The Old Vicarage, Wighill, nr Tadcaster; 1 s (Ludovic Houston); *Heir* s, Ludovic Houston b 1986; *Career* 2 Lt RUR Korea 1950, Ayrshire Yeo 1952, ret Maj 1969; jt MFH Lanarkshire and Renfrewshire 1974-78, Vice Lord-Lieut Strathclyde Region 1980-; memb Royal Co Archers; *Recreations* shooting and racing; *Clubs* White's, Turf, Pratt's; *Style*— Sir Houston Shaw-Stewart, Bt, MC, TD; Ardgowan, Inverkip, Renfrewshire (☎ 0475 521226)

SHAWCROSS, Brian Ellis; s of Ellis William Hope Shawcross (d 1981), and Gladys Lily, *née* Cartwright (d 1988); *b* 16 Aug 1938; *Educ* Radley, Sidney Sussex Coll Cambridge (MA); *m* 9 Sept 1961, Judy Gwynn, da of Cdr Hugh Vaughan Lavington (d 1957); 1 s (James William Ellis b 5 June 1971), 1 da (Annabel Mary b 9 March 1966); *Career* chm Hunkydory Designs 1970-; dir: Sir Joseph Causton plc 1980-84, Norton Opax plc 1985-86, Pavilion Productions 1990-; 2 Warden Worshipful Co of Haberdashers; FRSA 1989; *Recreations* reading, gardening, travel, music, theatre; *Style*— Brian Shawcross, Esq; Hunkydory Designs, Millboard Rd, Bourne End, Bucks SL8 5XD (☎ 06285 29621, fax 06285 29488, car 0836 340913)

SHAWCROSS, Baron (Life Peer UK 1959), of Friston, Co Sussex; Sir Hartley William Shawcross; GBE (1974), PC (1946), QC (KC 1939); s of John Shawcross (d 1968), and Hilda (d 1942); *b* 4 Feb 1902; *Educ* Dulwich, Univ of London, Univ of Geneva; *m* 1, 1924, Rosita Alberta (d 1943), da of William Shyvers (d 1944); m 2, 1945, Joan Winifred (d riding accident 1974), da of Hume Mather (d 1968), of Carlton Lodge, Tunbridge Wells; 2 s, 1 da; *Career* called to the Bar Gray's Inn 1925; chief UK prosecutor Nuremburg Trials, asst chm Sussex QS 1941; rec: Salford 1941-45, Kingston-upon-Thames 1946-61; JP Sussex 1948-61; former dir: EMI Ltd, Rank Hovis McDougall Ltd, Hawker Siddeley Gp, (and chm) Upjohn & Co Ltd, Times Newspapers, TVB (Hong Kong) Ltd, Shaw Bros (Hong Kong) Ltd; former chm Morgan Guaranty Tst Co's Int Advsy Cncl; MP (Lab) St Helens 1945-58, attorney-gen 1945-51, pres BOT 1951, princ delegate for UK to Assemblies of UN 1945-50, UK memb Perm Ct Arbitration The Hague 1950-67; chllr Sussex Univ 1965-86, chm Int C of C Cmmn on Unethical Practices 1976; dir: Caffyns Motors Ltd, Morgan et Cie SA, Observer Newspapers 1982-; a dir of public cos and a conslt on foreign business to Morgan Guaranty Trust of NY and other cos; Hon FRCS, Hon FRCOG; Kt Grand Cross of Imperial Iranian Order of Homayoon 1965; kt 1945; *Recreations* yachting (yacht, Talisker); *Clubs* Bucks, White's, Garrick, RAC, Royal Cornwall Yacht, Royal Yacht Squadron, New York Yacht, Travellers' (Paris); *Style*— The Rt Hon the Lord Shawcross, GBE, PC, QC; 12 Gray's Inn Sq, London WC1 (☎ 071 242 5500); Friston Place, Sussex BN20 0AH (☎ 032 342 2206); Anchorage, St Mawes, Cornwall; Morgan Bank, 1 Angel Court, London EC2 (☎ 071 325 5133); I-1 Albany, Piccadilly, London W1V 9RP (☎ 071 734 5494)

SHAWCROSS, Dr Hon Joanna (The Hon Mrs Peck); da (by 2 m) of Baron Shawcross (Life Peer); *b* 20 Sept 1948; *Educ* Benenden, Univ of London (MB BS); *m* 11 Oct 1986, Charles Russell Peck, s of Russell Hastings Peck, of Cambridge, Mass, USA; 1 s (Henry Russell Hartley b 6 Aug 1988), 1 da (Alice Joan b 19 Dec 1989); *Career* med practitioner; *Style*— Dr The Hon Joanna Shawcross; 105 Mayola Rd, London E5 0RG

SHAWCROSS, Roger Michael; s of Michael Campbell Shawcross (d 1945), of London, and Friedel Marie Partington, *née* Freund (d 1983); *b* 27 March 1941; *Educ* Radley, Christ Church Oxford (MA); *m* 15 Feb 1969, Sarah, da of Maurice Henry Peter Broom (d 1987), of Farnham, Surrey; 1 s (Philip b 1974), 1 da (Miranda b 1972); *Career* called to the Bar Grays Inn 1967, rec Western circuit 1985; *Recreations* tennis, music, literature, travel; *Style*— Roger Shawcross, Esq; Oakleigh, Sarum Road, Winchester; College Chambers, 2/3 College Place, Southampton (☎ 0703 230338)

SHAWCROSS, Hon William Hartley Hume; s (by 2 m) Baron Shawcross (Life Peer); *b* 28 May 1946; *Educ* Eton, Univ Coll Oxford; *m* 1, 1972, Marina Warner; m 2,

1981, Michal, da of late A J Levin by his w Leah; *Style*— The Hon William Shawcross; 40 Estelle Rd, London NW3 (☎ 071 267 1852)

SHAWE-TAYLOR, Desmond Christopher; CBE (1965); s of Francis Manley Shawe-Taylor (d 1920), of Moor Park, Athenry, Co Galway, by his w, Agnes Mary Eleanor (d 1939), elder da of Christopher Ussher, of Eastwell, Loughrea, Co Galway; *b* 29 May 1907; *Educ* Shrewsbury, Oriel Coll Oxford; *Career* WWII served Capt RA (AA); literary and occasional musical criticism New Statesman and Nation and Spectator until 1939, music critic New Statesman and Nation 1945-58, Sunday Times 1958-83 (on music staff 1983-), New Yorker (guest critic) 1973-74; *Books* Covent Garden (1948), The Record Guide (with Edward Sackville-West, later Lord Sackville, with supplements 1951-56); *Recreations* travel, croquet, gramophone; *Clubs* Brooks's; *Style*— Desmond Shawe-Taylor, Esq, CBE; Long Crichel House, Wimborne, Dorset BH21 5JU (☎ 0258 89250)

SHAWYER, Peter Michael; s of Edward William Francis Shawyer (d 1986), of Brookmans Park Herts, and Marjorie Josephine Shawyer; *b* 11 Sept 1950; *Educ* Enfield GS, Univ of Sheffield (BA); *m* 23 June 1979, Margot Anne, da of Wing Cdr Norman Edwin Bishop (d 1975), of Sidmouth, Devon; 1 s (Richard b 14 March 1984), 1 da (Emily b 3 Dec 1980); *Career* CA; joined Touche Ross & Co 1972 (ptnr 1982-), specialist in taxation and author of numerous tax articles in specialist journals; ACA 1975; *Recreations* golf, squash; *Clubs* Enfield Golf, Broxbourne Sports; *Style*— Peter Shawyer, Esq; Touche Ross & Co, Hill House, 1 Little New St, London EC4A 3TR (☎ 071 936 3000, fax 071 583 8517, telex 884739 TRLNDN G)

SHEA, Michael Sinclair MacAuslan; CVO (1987, LVO 1985); s of James Michael Shea, of Lenzie; *b* 10 May 1938; *Educ* Gordonstoun, Univ of Edinburgh (MA, PhD); *m* 1968, Mona Grec Stensen, da of Egil Stensen, of Oslo; 2 da; *Career* FO 1963, former 1 sec Bonn, head of chancery Bucharest 1973, DG Br Info Servs NY 1976, press sec to HM The Queen 1978-87; dir of pub affrs for Hanson plc 1987-; govr Gordonstoun Sch; author; *Books* Britain's Offshore Islands (1981), Tomorrow's Men (1982), Influence (1988), Leadership Rules (1990), and six novels under the name Michael Sinclair; *Recreations* writing, sailing; *Clubs* Garrick; *Style*— Michael Shea, Esq, CVO; c/o Hanson plc, 1 Grosvenor Place, London SW1X 7JH

SHEAR, Warren Ivor; s of Alec Shear, of 21 The Hollies, New Wanstead, and Edith Bessie, *née* Onnie (d 1989); *b* 8 Aug 1937; *Educ* East Ham GS, Univ of Sheffield, Royal Coll of Surgeons (LDS); *m* 1961, Marion, da of Aron Hollander; 1 s (Daniel Marc b 3 Dec 1968), 1 da (Sarah Jane b 20 Jan 1970); *Career* dentist; joined Prof H Singer's practice Holland Park 1964, own practice Wimpole St 1967-, pt/t clinical lectr in restorative dentistry Royal Dental Hosp London 1975, pt/t sr clinical lectr in restorative dentistry UCL 1982-; memb: RSM 1985, BDA 1962, London Dental Fellowship 1984, Soc for Advancement of Anaesthesia in Dentistry; *publications:* author of various articles published in dental jls; *Recreations* reading, walking, swimming, working for human rights; *Style*— Warren Shear, Esq; 19 Wimpole St, London W1M 7AD (☎ 071 580 3863)

SHEARD, (John) Neville; s of Edgar Sheard (d 1982), of Huddersfield, and Kathleen, *née* Frobisher; *b* 7 July 1935; *Educ* Rossall, Exeter Coll Oxford (MA); *m* 1, 26 Feb 1962, Glenys Mary (d 1970), da of Eric Jebson, of Huddersfield; 2 s (Charles b 1962, James b 1965); m 2, 20 July 1973, Elizabeth Mary, da of Eustace Lloyd Howell-Jones (d 1976), of Leamington Spa; 1 s (Jonathan b 1975); *Career* Nat Serv 2 Lt RCS TA; admitted slr 1962, sr ptnr Armitage Sykes & Hi Hinchcliffe Huddersfield 1980 (ptnr 1963-80); chm Kirkwood Hospice Huddersfield, tstee Huddersfield YMCA; memb Law Soc 1962-; *Recreations* cricket, fell walking; *Style*— Neville Sheard, Esq; 4 Butternab Rd, Beaumont Park, Huddersfield, W Yorks HD4 7AH (☎ 0484 652 996); 72 New North Rd, Huddersfield, W Yorks HD1 5NW (☎ 0484 538 121, fax 0484 518968, telex 518123 ASHUD G)

SHEARER, Alan; s of Alan Shearer, and Anne, *née* Collins; *b* 13 Aug 1970; *Educ* Gosforth HS Newcastle; *Career* professional footballer Southampton FC 1988- (over 50 appearances); England: 7 under 17 caps (scored on debut v Eire), 3 under 21 caps (scored twice on debut v Eire); represented Newcastle and Northumberland schoolboys; youngest player to score a hat-trick in Div 1 (on debut v Arsenal 9 April 1988 aged 17); *Recreations* walking my dog; *Style*— Alan Shearer, Esq; Southampton FC, The Dell, Milton Rd, Southampton, Hants S09 4XX (☎ 0703 220505)

SHEARER, Anthony Patrick (Tony); s of James Francis Shearer, of London, and Judith Margaret, *née* Bowman; *b* 24 Oct 1948; *Educ* Rugby; *m* 1 Dec 1972, Jennifer, da of Alfred Dixon (d 1981); 2 da (Juliet b 19 Aug 1980, Lauretta b 30 March 1982); *Career* ptnr Deloitte Haskins & Sells 1980-88 (joined 1967), dir M & Group plc 1988-; FCA; *Recreations* skiing, tennis, garden, family, rock 'n' roll; *Clubs* Brooks'; *Style*— Tony Shearer, Esq; Gaston House, East Bergholt, Suffolk (☎ 0206 298 525); Quarter, Denny, Stirlingshire (0324 822 271); Three Quays, Tower Hill, London EC3R 6BQ (☎ 071 626 4588, fax 071 623 8615, telex 887196)

SHEARER, John Charles Johnston; s of Brig Eric James Shearer, CB, CBE, MC (d 1980), and Phyllis Muriel, *née* Mules (d 1981); *b* 10 Nov 1924; *Educ* Eton, RMA Sandhurst; *m* 1, 1952 (m dis), Sylvia Elizabeth, da of Wilfrid F Coombs (d 1977), of Surrey; 2 s (Charles b 1952, d 1984, Michael b 1961); m 2, 10 April 1975, Ellen Ingeborg, da of Cdr Edward Nennecke, of Hamburg (d 1952); 2 s (Philip b 1974, Edward b 1976); *Career* served Scots Gds 1943-49: 2 Lt 1944, Lt 1944, Capt 1946 (despatches), 24 and 4 Gds Bde 1946-48, ret 1949; joined Thomas R Miller & Son 1952 (ptnr 1962-85), ptnr T R Miller & Son (Bermuda) 1968-87; dir: Turks Caicos Islands, Hanseatic Conslt Ltd 1974-, Blue Hills Aviation Ltd 1977-, Hanseatic Investmt 1977-, Pelican Hldgs 1985-, Grand Turk Petroleum Ltd 1987-; *Recreations* skiing, fishing, tennis, music, boating; *Clubs* MCC, Mid Ocean Bermuda, Royal Hamilton Amateur Dinghy; *Style*— John C Shearer, Esq; c/o S C Warburg & Co Ltd, 33 King William St, London EC4R 9AS; P O Box 665, Hamilton, Bermuda (☎ 809 292 4724, telex 3317 MUTUAL BA)

SHEARER, Capt Magnus Macdonald; JP (Shetland 1969); s of Col Magnus Shearer, OBE, TD, JP (d 1960), and Flora, *née* Stephen (d 1987); *b* 27 Feb 1924; *Educ* Anderson Educnl Inst Shetland, George Watson's Coll Edinburgh; *m* 1949, Martha Nicholson, da of John Henderson, DSM, Master Mariner (d 1957); 1 s; *Career* served RN 1942-46, 2 Lt RA (TA) 1949, Capt TARO 1959; md J & M Shearer Ltd 1960-85; hon consul in Shetland: Sweden 1958-, West Germany 1972-88; hon sec Lerwick Life Boat Station (RNLI) 1968-; DL (Shetland 1973), Lord-Lieut for Shetland 1982-; Kt first class Royal Order of Vasa (Sweden), Offr first class Order of Merit Federal Republic of Germany 1983, Offr first class Order of Polar Star Sweden 1983; *Recreations* reading, bird watching, ships; *Style*— Capt Magnus M Shearer, JP; Birka, Cruester, Bressay, Shetland ZE2 9EL (☎ 0595 82 363)

SHEARER, Robert John; s of Lewis George Shearer (d 1985), and Kathleen Mary Justina, *née* Humphreys; *b* 12 March 1939; *Educ* Wellington, Bart's Med Sch Univ of London (MB BS), FRCS 1967; *m* 6 April 1963, Shaune Vanessa, *née* Vance; 1 s (Paul b 23 Sept 1964), 1 da (Rebecca b 13 May 1970); *Career* conslt urologist: Royal Marsden Hosp, St George's Hosp; sr lectr Inst of Cancer Res; Liveryman Worshipful Co of Apothecaries, Freeman City of London; FRSM 1975; *Style*— Robert Shearer, Esq; St George's Hospital, Blackshaw Rd, London SW17 (☎ 081 672 1255)

SHEARER, Thomas Hamilton (Tom); CB (1974); s of Thomas Appleby Shearer, OBE (d 1972), and Isabella Fleming Hamilton (d 1969); *b* 7 Nov 1923; *Educ* Haberdashers' Aske's, Emmanuel Coll Cambridge (BA); *m* 1 June 1945, Sybil Mary; 1 s (Thomas (Thoss) b 1953), 1 da (Judith b 1946); *Career* RAF 1942-45; Air Miny 1948, dir of estabs Miny of Public Bldgs and Works 1967, dep chief exec PSA 1972-73; chm: Maplin Devpt Authy 1974-77, Br Channel Tunnel Co 1975-77, Location of Offices Bureau 1980; *Recreations* wine, music; *Style*— Tom Shearer, Esq, CB; 9 Denny Crescent, London SE11 4UY (☎ 071 587 0921)

SHEARLOCK, Very Rev David John; s of Arthur John Shearlock (d 1947), and Honora Frances Baker, *née* Hawkins; *b* 1 July 1932; *Educ* Surbiton Co GS, Univ of Birmingham (BA), Westcott House Cambridge; *m* 30 May 1959, Jean Margaret, da of John Marr, of Sandlands, Sidbury, Devon; 1 s (Timothy b 1963), 1 da (Ann b 1961); *Career* RA 1950-52, HAC 1952-56; curate: Guisborough Yorkshire 1957-60, Christchurch Priory Hants 1960-64; vicar: Kingsclere Hants 1964-71, Romsey Abbey Hants 1971-82; diocesan dir of ordinands Winchester 1977-82, hon canon of Winchester Cathedral 1978-82, Dean of Truro 1982-; Cornwall area chm Royal Sch of Church Music 1983-; chm Truro Victims Support Scheme 1985-; pres: Three Spires Festival, Truro Cancer Relief; vice pres Truro RA Assoc; *Books* The Practice of Preaching (1990); *Recreations* railways, music, walking, wine making; *Style*— The Very Rev the Dean of Truro; The Deanery, Lemon St, Truro TR1 2PE (☎ 0872 72661); Maxfield Cottage, Netherbury, Bridport, Dorset; Truro Cathedral Office, 21 Old Bridge St, Truro TR1 2AH (☎ 0872 76782)

SHEARMAN, Prof John Kinder Gowran; s of Brig CEG Shearman, CBE, DSO, MC (d 1968), and Evelyn, *née* White; *b* 24 June 1931; *Educ* Felsted, Courtauld Inst Univ of London (BA, PhD); *m* 1, Jane Dalrymple (d 1982), da of Charles C Smith; 1 s (Michael b 1968), 3 da (Juliet b 1961, Niccola b 1963, Sarah b 1967); m 2, 1983, Deirdre Roskill; *Career* Nat Serv 1949-50; Courtauld Inst Univ of London: asst lectr, lectr and sr lectr 1957-67, reader 1967-74, prof 1974-79, dep dir 1974-78; res fell Inst for Advanced Study 1964, chm Dept of Art and Archaeology Princeton Univ 1979-85 (prof 1979-87), chm Dept of Fine Arts Harvard Univ 1990- (prof 1987-); FBA 1976 (Serena medal 1979); Accademia del Disegno (Florence) 1979, Bronze medal Collège de France 1983; *Books* Andrea Del Sarto (1965), Mannerism (1967), Raphael's Cartoons (1972), Early Italian paintings in the collection of HM The Queen (1983), Funzione & Illusione (1983); *Recreations* music, sailing; *Clubs* Bembridge Sailing; *Style*— Prof John Shearman; 3 Clement Circle, Cambridge, Mass 02138, USA (☎ 617 876 9548); Department of Fine Arts, Harvard University, Cambridge, MA 021138 (☎ 617 495 2377, fax 617 4951769)

SHEASBY, (Herbert) Basil; OBE (1957, MBE 1947) JP (1948); s of Herbert James Sheasby (d 1957), and Kate Helen, *née* Worwood (d 1947); *b* 1 Aug 1905; *Educ* Lawrence Sheriff Sch, Rugby; *m* 5 Sept 1934, (Edith) Barbara, OBE (d 1989), da of William Norman Parker (d 1970), of Ecclesfield, Sheffield; 2 s (Michael b 1936, David b 1939), 1 da (Margaret b 1943); *Career* qualified CA 1929; in practice 1934-75; memb: Maidenhead and Dist Civic Soc, Ellington Lodge, Windsor and Maidenhead Cons Assoc; Freeman: City of London 1963, Worshipful Co of Tobacco Pipe Makers and Tobacco Blenders 1960; FCA 1929; *Books* Design of Accounts (1944); *Clubs* Royal Commonwealth Soc, Maidenhead Cons; *Style*— H Basil Sheasby, Esq, OBE, JP; 2 Clarefield Drive, Pinkneys Green, Maidenhead, Berks SL6 5DP (☎ 0628 20726)

SHEASBY, (John) Michael; s of Herbert Basil Sheasby, OBE, of Maidenhead, Berks, and Edith Barbara Sheasby, OBE (d 1989); *b* 31 May 1936; *Educ* Haileybury; *m* 3 June 1961, Juliet Sylvia Gillett; 1 s (Christopher Mark Andrew b 30 Nov 1966); *Career* qualified CA 1958; Arthur Young & Co UK and Italy 1953-63, fin dir then md Gp Admin RCA Ltd 1964-81, vice pres fin and planning Squibb Europe Inc 1982-88, fin ptnr Ernst & Young 1989-90, gp controller Glaxo Holdings plc 1990-; FCA 1958; *Recreations* rugby watching, sailing, skiing; *Clubs* Harlequin FC, Cambridge Univ RFC; *Style*— J Michael Sheasby, Esq; Glaxo Holdings plc, Lansdowne House, Berkeley Square, London W1X 6BP (☎ 071 493 4060, fax 071 408 0228)

SHEDDEN, Prof (William) Ian Hamilton; s of George Shedden (d 1966), of Bathgate, Scotland, and Agnes Hamilton, *née* Heigh (d 1979); *b* 21 March 1934; *Educ* The Acad Bathgate, Univ of Edinburgh (BSc, MB ChB, MRCP), Univ of Birmingham (MD), City Univ London (Dip Law); *m* 21 March 1960, Elma Joyce, da of Lewis M Jobson (d 1985), of Edinburgh; 3 s (Malcolm b 1960, Andrew b 1962, Colin b 1971), 1 da (Clare b 1968); *Career* cmmnd Capt RAMC 1961-67, regtl MO Hallamshire Bn York and Lancaster Regt 1961-67; lectr Univ of Sheffield 1960-64, sr res fell MRC 1964-67, dir R & D Lilly Industries Ltd 1968-77, vice pres Eli Lilly & Co USA 1977-83, prof of med Indiana Univ USA 1979-, md Glaxo Group Res Ltd 1983-86; underwriting memb Lloyds of London 1987-, md Porton Developments Ltd 1988-, vice pres Porton Development Corporation Inc 1989-; asst dep coroner St Pancras London 1987-; Freeman City of London 1975, Liveryman Worshipful Soc of Apothecaries 1974; FRCP 1983, FACP 1981, FFPM 1990; *Books* Vinca Alkaloids in the Chemotherapy of Malignant Disease (ed vol 1-3, 1968-70); *Style*— Prof Ian Shedden; Brook House, Park Rd, Stoke Poges, Bucks SL2 4PG (☎ 0753 645773); Porton International plc, 100 Piccadilly, London W1V 9EN (☎ 071 629 0200, fax 071 499 6486, telex 946162 HITECH G, car 0836 318910)

SHEDDEN, Hon Mrs (Joan Frances); MBE (1946); da of 2 Baron Vestey (d 1954); *b* 1914; *m* 1, 1934 (m dis 1944), Maj John Hammon Paine, formerly KRAC; 1 s; m 2, 1954, John Lindesay Compton Shedden; *Career* sometime Lt First Aid Nursing Yeo; *Style*— The Hon Mrs Shedden, MBE; The Manor, Fossebridge, Cheltenham, Glos

SHEEHAN, Sheriff Albert Vincent; s of Richard Greig Sheehan, of Bo'ness, and Mary, *née* Moffat; *b* 23 Aug 1936; *Educ* Bo'ness Acad, Univ of Edinburgh (MA, LLB); *m* 1965, Edna Georgina Scott, da of Andrew Hastings, of Coatbridge; 2 da (Wendy b 1968, Susan b 1971); *Career* Capt Royal Scots (The Royal Regt) 1959-61; slr; depute procurator fiscal 1961-71, Leverhulme fell 1971-72, dep crown agent for Scot 1974-79, Scot Law Cmmn 1979-81; sheriff: Edinburgh 1981, Falkirk 1983; *Recreations* curling, naval history, gardening; *Style*— Sheriff Albert Sheehan; 63 Murrayfield Gdns, Edinburgh EH12 6DL; Falkirk Sheriff Ct, Falkirk (☎ 0324 20822)

SHEEHY, Hon Mrs (Mary Ann); *née* Lyon-Dalberg-Acton; 5 da of 3 Baron Acton, CMG, MBE, TD (d 1989); *b* 30 March 1951; *m* 1972, Timothy John Sheehy; 2 da; *Style*— The Hon Mrs Sheehy; 8 St Margaret's Rd, Oxford

SHEEHY, Sir Patrick; s of Sir John Francis Sheehy, CSI, and Jean Newton Simpson; *b* 2 Sept 1930; *Educ* Australia, Ampleforth; *m* 1964, Jill Patricia Tindall; 1 s, 1 da; *Career* Nat Serv Irish Gds 1948-50 (2 Lt); British-American Tobacco Co: joined 1950, various appts Nigeria, Ghana, Ethiopia and West Indies, mktg advsr London 1962-67, gen mangr Holland 1967, memb Gp Bd 1970, memb Chm's Policy Ctee and chm Tobacco Div 1975; BAT Industries: dep chm 1976-81 (chm BATCo Bd), vice chm 1981-82, chm 1982-; non-exec dir British Petroleum Company plc 1984-, memb Cncl of Int Advsrs Swiss Bank Corporation 1985-, memb Bd The Spectator, chm South London Business Initiative Ltd; memb: Presidents' Ctee CBI, CBI Task Force on Wider Share Ownership, Internal Mkt Support Ctee of European Roundtable of Industrialists, Action Ctee for Europe, Cncl RIIA; kt 1991; *Recreations* golf, reading, skiing; *Style*— Sir Patrick Sheehy; BAT Industries plc, Windsor House, 50 Victoria Street, London SW1H 0NL (☎ 071 222 7979)

SHEEN, Hon Mr Justice; Hon Sir Barry Cross Sheen; s of Ronald Cross Sheen (d

1973), and Ethel May, *née* Powell (d 1980); *b* 31 Aug 1918; *Educ* Haileybury, Trinity Hall Cambridge (MA); *m* 1, 27 July 1946, Diane (d 1986), da of Cecil Lucas Donne (d 1957); 3 s (Christopher b 1948, Adrian b 1952, Roderick b 1959); m 2, 5 Nov 1988, Helen Ursula, *née* Woodmansey, wid of Philip Spink; *Career* RNVR 1939-46, CO HMS Kilkenzie 1943-45; called to the Bar Middle Temple 1947, wreck commr, Lloyd's arbitrator in salvage claims, memb Gen Cncl of the Bar 1960-64, jr counsel to Admty 1961-66, QC 1966, bencher 1971, rec of the Crown Ct 1971-78, judge of the High Ct of Justice Queen's Bench Div 1978-; pres Haileybury Soc 1982, chm Assoc of Average Adjusters 1986-87; Liveryman Worshipful Co of Shipwrights 1983; kt 1978; *Recreations* golf; *Clubs* Royal Wimbledon Golf, Hurlingham; *Style*— The Hon Mr Justice Sheen; Royal Courts of Justice, London WC2

SHEENE, Barry Stephen Frank; MBE (1978); s of Frank Sheene and Iris Sheene; *b* 11 Sept 1950; *Educ* St Martins in the Field; *m* 1984, Stephanie, da of Frederick Harrison; 1 da (Sidonie b 1984), 1 s (Freddie b Nov 1988); *Career* motor cycle racer 1969-84, World Champion 1976-77, more Int Race wins than any other UK rider 1974-84, winner Foreign Sportsman award Italy, Spain, France; dir: Spectra Automotive Products plc Ltd 1983, Barry Sheene Racing Ltd 1972; presenter ITV Just Amazing 1983-85; helicopter licence 1980, currently presenter Channel 9 TV; survived 2 accidents at high speed 1975 (175 mph), 1982 (165 mph), most satisfying achievement regaining 100 per cent fitness; landowner (22 acres); *Recreations* Hughes 500 Helicopter GSTEF; *Style*— Barry Sheene, MBE; The Manor House, 2 Riverbend Avenue, Carrara, Gold Coast, Queensland 4211, Australia

SHEEPSHANKS, David Richard; s of Capt Robin John Sheepshanks, CBE, DL, *qv*, of the Rookery, Eyke, Woodbridge, Suffolk, and Lilias, *née* Noble; *b* 30 Oct 1952; *Educ* Eton; *m* 26 Aug 1978, Mona Gunilla, da of Nils Rickard Ullbin, of Bragevagen 12, Stockholm, Sweden; 1 da (Sophie Anna Lisa Kirsty b 16 Feb 1987); *Career* mangr Arabian Fish and Canning Co 1974, md Interocean Seafoods Co Ltd 1975-79, fndr and md Starfish Ltd Ipswich 1980-89; co-fndr and chm Suffolk Foods Ltd 1988-; dir: Radio Orwell 1985-, Ipswich Town FC 1987-; memb of Shellfish Ctee Sea Fish Indust Authy; *Recreations* football, shooting, tennis, music, fishing, cricket; *Clubs* Turf; *Style*— David Sheepshanks, Esq; The White Lodge, Eyke, Woodbridge, Suffolk IP1Z 2RR (☎ 039 461 540); Suffolk Foods Ltd, Rendlesham Hall, Woodbridge Suffolk IP12 ZRS (☎ 0394 460816, fax : 039 4460716, ☎ car 0860 574319)

SHEEPSHANKS, Robin John; CBE (1990), DL (Suffolk 1979); s of Maj Richard Sheepshanks, DSO, MVO (d 1951), by his w Hon Bridget, *née* Thesiger (d 1983), da of 1 Viscount Chelmsford; *b* 4 Aug 1925; *Educ* Eton; *m* 1951, Lilias Mulgrave, da of Maj Sir Humphrey Noble, 4 Bt, MBE, MC (d 1968), of Walwick Hall; 4 s (David b 1952, Richard b 1955, Andrew b 1960, Christopher b 1964); *Career* Capt 1 King's Dragoon Gds 1943-52; farmer 1952-; chm ADFAM (Suffolk) 1987-, memb E Suffolk CC 1963-74, chm Suffolk CC 1982-84 (memb 1974-); High Sheriff Suffolk 1981; chm: Suffolk Police Authority, Standing Conference of E Anglian Local Authyoritys 1987-, Felix Cobbold Trust 1985-; dir East Coast Cable Ltd 1989-; *Recreations* shooting, golf, gardening; *Clubs* Cavalry and Guards', Pratt's; *Style*— Robin Sheepshanks, Esq, CBE, DL; The Rookery, Eyke, Woodbridge, Suffolk IP12 2RR (☎ 0394 460226)

SHEERIN, His Hon Judge John Declan; s of John Patrick Sheerin (d 1969), and Agnes Mary Josephine Sheerin, *née* Keane (d 1975); *b* 29 Nov 1932; *Educ* Wimbledon Coll, LSE (LLB); *m* 1958, Helen Suzanne, da of Philippus Lodewicus le Roux (d 1964); 2 s (Paul, James), 2 da (Sarah, Nicola); *Career* RAF 1958-60, MEAF Nicosia Flying Offr; slr 1957, ptnr Greene & Greene 1962, ret 1982; rec 1979, circuit judge 1982; *Recreations* Golf; *Clubs* Flempton Golf; *Style*— His Hon Judge Sheerin; c/o The County Ct, Arcade St, Ipswich

SHEERMAN, Barry John; MP (Lab) Huddersfield 1983-; s of Albert Sheerman; *b* 17 Aug 1940; *Educ* Hampton GS, Kingston Tech Coll, LSE, Univ of London; *m* 1965, Pamela Elizabeth, *née* Brenchley; 1 s, 3 da; *Career* former lectr; MP (Lab) Huddersfield E 1979-1983, memb Public Accounts Ctee 1980-83; chm: Parly Advsy Cncl for Tport Safety, Parly Lab Pty Trade Ctee 1981-83; oppn front bench spokesman on Employment and Educn with special responsibility for devpt of educn policy and trg for over-16s 1983-87, spokesman on employment 1987-, home affairs front bench spokesman on police, prisons, crime prevention, drugs, civil def, fire serv, dep to Rt Hon Roy Hattersley MP 1988-; *Style*— Barry Sheerman, Esq, MP; House of Commons, SW1A 0AA (☎ 071 219 5037, home 0484 710 687, office 0924 495277)

SHEFF, Sylvia Claire; JP (1976); da of Isaac Glickman (d 1981), of 2 Bristol Court, Bury Old Road, Prestwich, Manchester, and Rita, *née* Bor (d 1976); *b* 9 Nov 1935; *Educ* Stand GS for Girls, Univ of Manchester (BA); *m* 28 Dec 1958, Alan Frederick Sheff (d 1986), s of Lewis Sheff (d 1975), of 1 Stanley Rd, Broughton Park, Salford; 1 s (Marcus Jeremy b 1963), 1 da (Janine Rachel b 1960); *Career* teacher 1958-77; fndr and dir Friendship with Israel All Party Gp (in Euro Parl) 1979-, asst nat dir Cons Friends of Israel 1985-89 (nat projects dir 1974-85), assoc dir Manchester Jewish Cultural Centre 1990-, int co-ordinator Yeted Yafeh Fellowship of Children of Chernobyl Project 1990-, lectr Jewish Rep Cncl of Gtr Manchester, Bury Family Conciliation Serv Mgmnt Ctee 1985-87, Magistrates Assoc; pres Manchester 35 Gp Women's Campaign for Soviet Jewry 1980- (chm 1972-80), hon sec Nat Cncl for Soviet Jewry UK 1987-89 (memb Cncl 1975-87), del Bd of Deps of Br Jews 1987-; *Recreations* bridge, theatre, opera, travel, antiques; *Clubs* Last Drop; *Style*— Mrs Sylvia Sheff, JP; 6 The Meadows, Old Hall Lane, Whitefield, Manchester M25 7RZ (☎ 061 766 4391); Canada House, 6/2nd Floor, Chepstow St, Manchester M1 5FN (☎ 061 228 0495)

SHEFFIELD, Archdeacon of; *see*: Lowe, Ven Stephen Richard

SHEFFIELD, Bishop of (1980-); Rt Rev David Ramsay Lunn; the see was founded in 1914; *b* 1930; *Educ* King's Cambridge (MA), Cuddesdon Coll Oxford; *Career* deacon 1955, priest 1956; curate: Sugley 1955-59, N Gosforth 1959-63; chaplain Lincoln Theol Coll 1963-66, sub-warden 1966-70, vicar St George Cullercoats 1970-75, rector 1975-80 and rural dean of Tynemouth 1975-80; *Style*— The Rt Rev the Bishop of Sheffield; Bishopscroft, Snaithing Lane, Sheffield, S Yorks S10 3LG (☎ 0742 302170)

SHEFFIELD, John Vincent; CBE; s of late Sir Berkeley Sheffield, 6 Bt; *b* 11 Nov 1913; *Educ* Eton, Magdalene Coll Cambridge (MA); *m* 1, 1936, Anne Margaret (d 1969), da of Sir Lionel Lawson Faudel Faudel-Phillips, 3 Bt; 1 s, 3 da; m 2, 1971, Frances Mary Agnes, da of Brig-Gen Goland Clarke; *Career* former private sec Miny of Works, chm: Norcros Ltd 1956-81, Portals Hldgs 1968-78, Atlantic Assets Tst Ltd 1972-83, Business Educn Cncl 1980-83; High Sheriff Lincs 1944-45; OStJ; *Clubs* White's; *Style*— John Sheffield, Esq, CBE; New Barn House, Laverstoke, Whitchurch, Hants (☎ 0256 893187)

SHEFFIELD, (John) Julian Lionel George; s of John Vincent Sheffield, CBE (himself 4 s of Sir Berkeley Sheffield, 6 Bt, JP, DL), *qv*; *b* 28 Aug 1938; *Educ* Eton, Christ's Coll Cambridge Univ; *m* 1961, Carolyn Alexandra, er da of the late Brig Sir Alexander Abel Smith, TD, by his 1 w, Elizabeth (da of David B Morgan, of N Carolina); 3 s (John b 1963, Simon b 1964, Lionel b 1969), 1 da (Nicola b 1973); *Career* industrialist; chm: Portals Holdings plc (papermaking, Queen's Award for Export 1966, 1977, 1982), Norcros plc 1989- (joined 1974); dep chm Guardian Royal Exchange 1981-; dir: North Foreland Lodge Ltd 1987, Tex Holdings plc, Newbury Racecourse plc, Br Water and Effluent Treatment Assoc 1979-83 (chm 1981); chm Basingstoke Sports Tst 1975-84; *Recreations* outdoor sports, collecting; *Clubs* White's, MCC; *Style*— Julian Sheffield, Esq; Laverstoke House, Whitchurch, Basingstoke, Hants (☎ 0256 770 245); Portals Holdings plc, Laverstoke Mill House, Whitchurch, Hants RG28 7NR (☎ 0256 89 2360)

SHEFFIELD, Michael Joseph Forster; OBE, TD, DL (1975); s of Brig Thomas Tredwell Jackson Sheffield, CBE, TD, DL; *b* 11 April 1930; *Educ* Denstone College Staffs, Univ of London (LLB); *m* 1958, Joan Margaret, *née* Ridley; 2 children; *Career* slr; HM coroner Cleveland 1973-; chm Solicitors' Benevolent Assoc 1986- (dir 1973-86); chm Teesside Cheshire Home 1988 (sec 1973-81), chm Middlesbrough Rugby Club 1977-80 (vice pres 1961); Cmdt Durham and South Tyne Army Cadet Force 1977-87; chm: Med Appeal Tbnl 1986-, Social Security Appeal Tbnl 1985; govr Middlesbrough HS 1965-67, hon Col Durham Army Cadet Force 1988-; *Recreations* tennis, rugby, theatre, mil affairs, gardening; *Clubs* Lansdowne, Cleveland Middlesbrough; *Style*— Michael Sheffield Esq, OBE, TD, DL; Ayton House, Easby Lane, Great Ayton, N Yorks; 9-13 Bedford St, Middlesbrough, Cleveland (☎ 0642 241311)

SHEFFIELD, Sir Reginald Adrian Berkeley; 8 Bt (GB 1755), of Normanby, Lincolns; DL (Humberside); s of Maj Edmund Sheffield, JP, DL (d 1977), of Sutton Park, Sutton-on-the-Forest, York; (s of 6 Bt), and Nancie Miriel Denise, wid of Lt Cdr Glen Kidston, RN, and yst da of Edward Roland Soames, of Framland House, Melton Mowbray; suc unc, Sir Robert Sheffield, 7 Bt 1977; *b* 9 May 1946; *Educ* Eton; *m* 1, 1969 (m dis 1975), Annabel Lucy Veronica, da of late Timothy Angus Jones, and late Hon Mrs Pandora Astor; 2 da (Samantha b 1971, Emily b 1973); m 2, 1977, Victoria Penelope, da of late Ronald Walker, DFC; 1 s (Robert b 1984), 2 da (Alice b 1980, Lucy Mary b 1981); *Heir* s, Robert Charles Berkeley; *Career* chm: Aylesford Holdings Ltd, Normanby Estate Holdings and subsidiaries; memb Lloyd's, county cncllr Humberside, vice chm S Humberside Business Advice Centre Ltd, memb CLA taxation ctee; landowner (6,000 acres); pres: S Humberside CPRE, Scunthorpe FC Ltd; *Recreations* shooting, stalking; *Clubs* Whites; *Style*— Sir Reginald Sheffield, Bt, DL; Thealby Hall, Thealby, Scunthorpe, S Humberside DN15 9AB; Estate Office, Normanby, Scunthorpe, South Humberside DN15 9HS (☎ 0724 720618)

SHEGOG, Rev Eric Marshall; s of George Marshall Shegog, of Salford, and Helen, *née* Whitefoot; *b* 23 July 1937; *Educ* Leigh GS, Coll of St Mark and St John, Lichfield Theol Coll, City Univ London (CertEd, DipTheol, MA); *m* 5 Aug 1961, Anne, da of late Elfed Llewellyn Thomas; 2 s (Andrew b 20 May 1963, Simon b 30 May 1966), 1 da (Sarah b 28 July 1969); *Career* Nat Serv RAMC 1955-57, Sgt; asst master Holy Trinity Sch Wimbledon 1960-63, asst curate All Saints Benhilton 1965-68, youth advsr Diocese of Southwark 1968-70, vicar St Michael Abbey Wood 1970-76, chaplain Sunderland City Centre 1976-83, head of religious bdcasting IBA 1984-, dir of communications C of E 1990-; chm Age Concern Sunderland 1976-83, vice pres Euro Regn World Assoc of Christian Communications; *Books* Religious Television: Controversies and Conclusions (contrib, 1990); *Recreations* gardening, music, jogging; *Style*— The Rev Eric Shegog; Director of Communications, The Church of England, Church House, Great Smith St, London SW1 3N7 (☎ 071 222 9011, fax 071 799 2714)

SHELBOURNE, Sir Philip; s of late Leslie John Shelbourne; *b* 15 June 1924; *Educ* Radley Coll, CCC Oxford, Harvard Law Sch; *Career* barr Inner Temple, taxation barr 1951-62, ptnr N M Rothschild & Sons 1962-70, chief exec Drayton Corp 1971-72 (chm 1973-74), chm and chief exec Samuel Montagu & Co 1974-80, Br Nat Oil Corp 1980-(Britoil 1982-88), chm Henry Ansbacher Hldgs plc; kt 1984; *Recreations* music; *Clubs* Brooks's; *Style*— Sir Philip Shelbourne; One Mitre Square London EC3A 5AN

SHELBURNE, Earl of; Charles Maurice Petty-Fitzmaurice; DL (Wiltshire 1990); s (by 1 m) and h of 8 Marquess of Lansdowne, *qv*, and Barbara Stuart Chase (d 1965); *b* 21 Feb 1941; *Educ* Eton; *m* 1, 1965 (m dis 1987), Lady Frances Eliot, da of 9 Earl of St Germans; 2 s (Simon b 1970, William b 1973), 2 da (Arabella b 1966, Rachel b 1968); m 2, 1987, Fiona Mary, da of Donald Merritt; *Heir* s, Viscount Calne and Calstone, *qv*; *Career* page of honour to HM The Queen 1956-57; served: Kenya Regt 1960-61, Wiltshire Yeomanry (TA), amalgamated with Royal Yeomanry Regt 1963-73; pres Wilts Playing Fields Assoc 1965-75, Wilts Co cncllr 1970-85, memb SW Econ Planning Cncl 1972-77; chm: Working Ctee Population & Settlement Pattern (SWEPC) 1972-77, N Wilts DC 1973-76; memb: Calne and Chippenham RDC 1964-73, Historic Bldgs and Monuments Cmmn 1983-89; pres: Wilts Assoc of Boys' Clubs and Youth Clubs 1976-, NW Wilts Dist Scout Cncl 1977-88; Parly candidate (Cons) Coventry NE 1979; dep pres HHA 1986-88, pres 1988-; memb Cncl Duchy of Cornwall 1990-; *Clubs* Turf, Brooks; *Style*— Earl of Shelburne, DL; Bowood House, Calne, Wiltshire SN11 0LZ (☎ 0249 812102)

SHELBURNE, Countess of; Lady Frances Helen Mary; *née* Eliot; da (by 1 m) of 9 Earl of St Germans, *qv*; *b* 1943; *m* 1965 (m dis 1987), Earl of Shelburne, *qv*; *Style*— Francis Countess of Shelburne; 60 Abingdon Rd, London W8 6AP

SHELDON, Hon Sir (John) Gervase Kensington Sheldon; s of Dr John Henry Sheldon (d 1960), of Hopton, Churt, Surrey, and Dr Eleanor Gladys, *née* Kensington (d 1966); *b* 4 Oct 1913; *Educ* Winchester, Trinity Coll Cambridge (MA); *m* 1, 10 Jan 1940, Patricia Mary, da of Lt-Col Arthur Claude Mardon, DSO (d 1950), of Willingdon, Sussex; 1 s (Robin b 1942); m 2, 10 Aug 1960, Janet Marguerite, da of George Wilfrid Seager (d 1979), of Sevenoaks, Kent; 2 s (Jeremy b 1961, Timothy b 1962), 1 da (Sophie b 1964); *Career* served RA (TA) 1939-45 (despatches twice) Egypt, N Africa, Italy, Maj 1943; called to the Bar Lincoln's Inn 1939, co ct judge 1968-72, circuit judge 1972-78, bencher 1978, judge of High Court of Justice (Family Div) 1978-88, presiding judge Western circuit 1980-84; kt 1978; *Recreations* shooting, stalking, cricket; *Clubs* Oxford and Cambridge; *Style*— The Hon Sir Gervase Sheldon; Hopton, Churt, Surrey GU10 2LD (☎ 025 125 2035); Royal Courts of Justice, Strand, London WC2A 2LL

SHELDON, Mark Hebberton; s of George Hebberton Sheldon (d 1971), and Marie, *née* Hazlitt (d 1974); *b* 6 Feb 1931; *Educ* Stand GS, Wycliffe Coll, CCC Oxford (BA, MA); *m* 16 June 1971, Catherine Eve, da of Edwin Charles James Ashworth (d 1968), of USA; 1 s (Edward b 1976), 1 da (Alice b 1972); *Career* Nat Serv Lt Royal Signals 1949-50, TA 1950-54; admitted slr 1957; Linklaters & Paines: articled 1953-56, asst slr 1957-59, ptnr 1959-, resident ptnr New York 1972-74, sr ptnr 1988-; dep vice pres Law Soc 1990-91 (treas 1981-86, memb Cncl 1978), pres City of London Law Soc 1987-88, memb Cncl Corp of Lloyd's 1989-90, memb Financial Reporting Cncl 1990-; Freeman City of London Slrs Co (Master 1987-88); *Recreations* music, English watercolours, wine and food, swimming; *Clubs* Travellers, City of London; *Style*— Mark Sheldon, Esq; 5 St Albans Grove, London W8 5PN; Barrington House, 59-67 Gresham St, London EC2V 7JA (☎ 071 606 7080, fax 071 606 5113, telex 884349/ 888167)

SHELDON, Dr Peter John Schalscha; s of Otto Schalscha (d 1974), of Hadley, Shropshire, and Ilse, *née* Kunz; *b* 24 April 1940; *Educ* Wellington GS, Univ of Birmingham (MB ChB, MD); *m* 28 July 1973, Meera, da of Jyoti Sharma, of Nairobi, Kenya; 3 s (Nicholas, Matthew, Roland), 1 da (Eloise); *Career* house physician Dudley Rd Hosp 1964, med registrar Lister Hosp Hitchin 1968, sr registrar Middx Hosp 1970, memb scientific staff MRC Rheumatism Unit Taplow 1972, sr lectr in immunology Univ of Leicester 1975-, hon conslt rheumatology Leicester Royal Infirmary 1975-; MRCP 1969; *Recreations* squash, jogging, classic cars; *Clubs* Daimler and Lanchester Owners, Leicester Squash; *Style—* Dr Peter Sheldon; PO Box 138, Medical Sciences Building, University Rd, Leics LE1 9HN (☎ 0533 522953); Dept of Rheumatology, Royal Infirmary, Leics (☎ 0533 586473)

SHELDON, Rt Hon Robert Edward; PC (1977), MP (Lab Ashton-under-Lyne 1964-); *b* 13 Sept 1923; *m* 1, 1945, Eileen Shamash (d 1969); 1 s, 1 da; m 2, 1971, Mary Shield; *Career* trained as engr; Parly candidate (Lab) Manchester Withington 1959, dir Manchester C of C 1964-74 (DAD 1979); chm: Lab Parly econ affrs and fin gp 1967-68, NW Gp Lab MPs 1970-74; oppn spokesman Treasy matters, civil service and machinery of govt 1970-74, memb Public Expenditure Ctee 1972-74 (chm gen sub-ctee); min state: CSD 1974, Treasy 1974-75; fin sec to Treasy 1975-79, oppn front bench spokesman Treasy and econ affrs 1981-83, memb Select Ctee on Treasury and Civil Service until 1981 (and chm sub ctee), chm Public Accounts Ctee 1983- (memb 1965-70 and 1975-79); *Style—* The Rt Hon Robert Sheldon, PC, MP; 2 Ryder St, London SW1 (☎ 071 839 4533, fax 930 1528); 27 Darley Ave, Manchester M20 8ZD (☎ 061 445 3489)

SHELDON, Thomas Clifford; s of John Rodney Clifford Sheldon, and Pamela, *née* Watney, JP; *b* 6 Nov 1952; *Educ* Marlborough, Poly of Central London; *m* 20 Oct 1979, Julie Gay, da of Rev (Michael) David Mumford, of The Rectory, Ewhurst Green, Sussex; 2 da (Amelia b 1982, Georgina b 1985); *Career* assoc: Donaldsons 1979-81, Savills plc 1984-88; dir Sheldon Scammell (property devpt co) 1988-; Freeman City of London, Liveryman Worshipful Co of Mercers; ARICS 1978; *Recreations* sailing, skiing, walking, theatre; *Clubs* Medway Yacht; *Style—* Thomas Sheldon, Esq; 86 Kings Rd, Wimbledon, London SW19 8QW (☎ 081 542 8034); Hammond House, 117 Piccadilly, London W1V 9PJ (☎ 071 629 2484, fax 071 491 2367, telex 0836 723575)

SHELDON, Timothy James Ralph (Jamie); s of Anthony John Sheldon, and Elizabeth Mary, *née* Ferguson; *b* 9 July 1956; *Educ* Eton, Exeter Univ (BA); *m* 25 Feb 1984, Susan Jean (Susie), da of John Ridell Best; 1 s (Charles b 14 Oct 1985, Richard b 30 June 1990), 1 da (Sophie b 23 Nov 1987); *Career* CA; Armitage & Norton 1978-82, Robert Fleming & Co Ltd 1982-87, dir GNI Ltd 1987-, non-exec dir Harry Ferguson Ltd 1983-; memb ICAEW; *Recreations* sailing, skiing, farming, tennis, squash, piano; *Clubs* Royal Thames Yacht, Royal Yacht Squadron; *Style—* Jamie Sheldon, Esq; Colechurch House, 1 London Bridge Walk, London SE1 2SX (☎ 071 378 7171, fax 071 403 1635)

SHELDRICK, Dr (Evelyn) Carol; da of Clement Gordon Sheldrick (d 1979), and Doris Evelyn, *née* Sackett (d 1982); *b* 29 March 1942; *Educ* Woodford HS, Univ of Oxford (MA, BM BChir), Univ of London (MPhil); *m* 17 Dec 1983; *Career* Maudsley Hosp: res asst 1969-70, house offr 1970-71 (1968-69), sr house offr 1971, registrar, sr registrar 1978, conslt 1978-; author of articles and chapters on changing diagnosis in psychiatry, delinquency and sexual abuse; MRCP, FRCPsych 1989; *Recreations* music, theatre, gardening, walking; *Style—* Dr Carol Sheldrick; Maudsley Hospital, Denmark Hill, London SE5 (☎ 071 703 6333)

SHELFORD, William Thomas Cornelius (Bill); s of C W Shelford, DL, and Helen Beatrice Hilda, *née* Schuster; *b* 27 Jan 1943; *Educ* Eton, Ch Ch Oxford (MA); *m* 20 March 1971, Annette Betty, *née* Heap Holt; 2 s (Henry b 1973, Thomas b 1980), 1 da (Laura b 1975); *Career* admitted slr 1969; ptnr Cameron Markby Hewitt 1970- (sr ptnr 1990); *Recreations* skiing, gardening; *Clubs* Brooks's, City of London; *Style—* Bill Shelford, Esq; Chailey Place, Chailey Green, nr Lewes, Sussex BN8 4DA; Cameron Markby Hewitt, Sceptre Court, 40 Tower Hill, London EC3N 4BB (☎ 071 702 2345)

SHELLEY, Alan John; s of Stanley Arnold Shelley (d 1983), and Ivy May Shelley; *b* 7 Aug 1931; *Educ* People's Coll Nottingham; *m* 20 Sept 1958, Josephine Flintoft, da of James Flood (d 1981); 1 s (Matthew b 1965), 1 da (Joanna b 1962); *Career* sr ptnr: Knight Frank & Rutley 1983-, Knight Frank & Rutley (Nigeria) 1965-1979; dir John Holt Investment Co 1981-; chm W Africa Ctee 1985-, gen cmmr of Income Tax 1983-; govr RSC; *Recreations* squash, theatre; *Clubs* Oriental, MCC; *Style—* Alan Shelley, Esq; 20 Hanover Square, London W12 0AH (☎ 071 629 8171, fax 071 493 4114)

SHELLEY, Andrew Colin; s of Charles Andrew Shelley (Chief Inspr Essex Constabulary, d 1944), of Chelmsford, and Elizabeth Annie Constance, *née* Harper (d 1985); *b* 17 Jan 1937; *Educ* Royal Masonic Sch, Harvard Business Sch; *m* 22 Aug 1963, Susan, da of Jack Trevor Mills (d 1987); 2 s (Gerald Robin b 1964, Robert Andrew b 1967); *Career* CA; joined Crittall Manufacturing 1961, chief accountant Munton and Fison Ltd 1965 (co sec 1968), fin dir Munton and Fison plc 1972; dir: Munton and Fison (Holdings) plc 1979 (gp chief exec 1982), Edward Fison Ltd, Suffolk Trg Enterprise Cncl 1989-; chm: Eling Tport Ltd, Bridlington Farms Ltd, Munton and Fison (Exports) Ltd, Newnham Holdings (Beford) Ltd, Luzcampo Sociedade Agricola Intensiva do Algarve LDA (Portugal); ptnr Shelley and Co Chartered Accountants Stowmarket; pres: E Anglian Dist Soc of Chartered Accountants 1989-90, Ipswich and Colchester soc of CA's 1978-79; vice chm ICA's Industl and Commercial Membs Ctee 1982-84, chm CA's Working Party re Prevention of Fraud in Industry; memb: ICA's Res Bd 1982, CA's Tech Advsy Ctee E Anglia, CA's Nat TAC 1978-90, ICA's Parly and Law Ctee 1987, Cncl ICA 1981-84, Cncl CBI 1988-; treas Malsterers' Assoc of GB 1986-; examiner Suffolk Coll DMS 1983-88 (govr 1989-); memb Inst of Brewing 1983; FID 1982, FCA 1959, AMP Harvard 1981, FBIM 1982; *Recreations* gardening, swimming, estate maintenance; *Clubs* Harvard Club of London, Chartered Accountants Dining; *Style—* Andrew Shelley, Esq; Munton and Fison plc, Cedars Factory, Stowmarket, Suffolk IP14 2AG (☎ 0449 612401, fax 0449 677800, telex 98205)

SHELLEY, Howard Gordon; s of Frederick Gordon Shelley (d 1979), and Katharine Anne, *née* Taylor; *b* 9 March 1950; *Educ* scholar: Highgate Sch, RCM; *m* 7 June 1975, Hilary Mary Pauline, *née* Macnamara; 1 s (Alexander Gordon b 1979), 1 step s (Peter Cullivan b 1962); *Career* concert pianist and conductor; London debut Wigmore Hall 1971, Henry Wood Prom debut (TV) 1972, conducting debut London Symphony Orch Barbican 1985, solo career extends over five continents; piano concertos written for him by Cowie Chapple and Dickinson; performed first cycle of the complete solo piano works of Rachmaninov at Wigmore Hall 1983; recordings include: complete solo piano works and concertas of Rachmaninov, Mozart Piano Concertos, Chopin recital, Schumann recital, Piano Concertos by Vaughan Williams, Howard Ferguson and Peter Dickinson; assoc conductor London Mozart Players; memb Worshipful Co of Musicians; Chappell Gold medal 1971, Silver medal of Worshipful Co of Musicians, Dannreuther Concerto prize; ARCM, ARCO; *Style—* Howard Shelley, Esq; 38 Cholmeley Park, Highgate, London N6 5ER; c/o Intermusica Artists Management, 16 Duncan Terrace, London N1 8BZ (☎ 071 278 5455, fax 071 278 8434, telex 931 210 2058 sl g)

SHELLEY, James Edward; CBE (1991); s of Vice Adm Richard Benyon, CB, CBE, DL (d 1968), name changed by Deed Poll 1964, and Eve Alice, *née* Cecil; *b* 18 June 1932; *Educ* Eton, Univ Coll Oxford (MA); *m* 16 June 1956, Judith, da of George Grubb (d 1970); 2 s (Timothy b 1966, Philip b 1966), 2 da (Alison b 1959, Penelope b 1960); *Career* Church Cmmrs Staff: memb 1954-, under-sec gen 1976-81, assets sec 1981-85, sec 1985-; *Recreations* country pursuits; *Clubs* Naval and Military; *Style—* James Shelley, Esq, CBE; Mays Farm House, Ramsdell, Basingstoke, Hants RG26 5RE (☎ 0256 850 770); Church Commissioners, 1 Millbank, London SW1P 3JZ (☎ 071 222 7010, fax 071 233 0171)

SHELLEY, Dr (Sir) John Richard; 11 Bt (E 1611) of Michelgrove, Sussex; does not use title; s of John Shelley (d 1974); suc gf, Maj Sir John Frederick Shelley, 10 Bt (d 1976); *b* 18 Jan 1943; *Educ* King's Sch Bruton, Trinity Coll Cambridge (MA), St Mary's Hosp Univ of London (MB BChir); *m* 1965, Clare, da of Claud Bicknell, OBE; 2 da; *Heir* bro, Thomas Shelley; *Career* general practitioner; ptnr Drs Shelley, Doddington & Ayres (med practitioners); farmer; DObstRCOG, MRCGP; *Style—* Dr John Shelley; Shobrooke Park, Crediton, Devon EX17 1DG; Molford House, 27 South St, South Molton, Devon EX36 4AA (☎ 076 95 3101)

SHELLEY, Ruth (Mrs Michael Silverman); da of Jack Shelley, of London, and Mildred, *née* Schama, of London; *b* 19 July 1942; *Educ* S Hampstead HS for Girls; *m* 20 March 1966, Michael Anthony Silverman, s of Ernest Silverman, of London; 1 s (Paul Conrad Alexander b 1969), 1 da (Katie Mimi b 1971); *Career* accountant and prodn mangr Libertas Film Prodns Ltd 1960-63, accountant PA Mgmnt (conslts) SA 1963-65, gen mangr Drake Personnel Ltd 1965-66, fin dir and divnl dir Lloyds Gp of Co's 1966-75, fin dir Merton Transearch International 1976-; AMIPM 1971; *Recreations* tennis, swimming, yachting; *Clubs* Club Nautico (Santa Ponsa); *Style—* Miss Ruth Shelley; Merton House, 70 Grafton Way, London W1P 5LE (☎ 071 388 2051, fax 071 387 5324, telex 8953742 MERTON G)

SHELLEY, Thomas Henry; s of late John Shelley and hp of bro, Sir John Shelley, 11 Bt; *b* 3 Feb 1945; *Educ* King's Sch Bruton, Trinity Coll Cambridge; *m* 1970, Katharine Mary Holton; 3 da (Kirsten Rachel Irvine b 1973, Victoria Juliet b 1974, Benita Mary 1978); *Style—* Thomas Shelley, Esq

SHELTON, Graham John; s of Alfred Thomas Shelton (d 1987), of Derby, and Louisa Emily, *née* Clarke (d 1984); *b* 26 Oct 1950; *Educ* Bemrose GS for Boys Derby, Wolverhampton Poly (BA Econ), Univ of Birmingham (scholar, M Social Sci); *m* 15 Dec 1979, Noelle Margaret, da of James Minihan, of Limerick, Eire; 2 s (Matthew William Henry b 31 Dec 1982, James Eoin b 11 Oct 1984), 2 da (Lydia Louise b 9 April 1987, Naomi Marie b 18 July 1989); *Career* admin trainee Southern Derbys Health Authy 1970-72, regnl trainee Trent RHA Sheffield 1972-74, asst hosp sec New Cross Hosp Wolverhampton 1974-78, dep hosp sec The Royal Hosp Wolverhampton 1978-81, dep sector admin The Ipswich Hosp 1981-83, dep unit admin The Royal Hallamshire Hosp Sheffield 1983-85, unit admin Raigmore Hosp Inverness 1985-86, dir and unit gen mangr Mental Handicap & Psychiatric Servs Norwich Health Authy 1986- (acting dist gen mangr 1988-89); former pt/t lectr in health servs mgmnt Sheffield City Poly; hon pres Norfolk branch Chartered Soc of Physiotherapy 1989-; memb Norwich Medico-Legal Soc; Assoc of Inst of Health Servs Mgmnt 1976; *Recreations* my family, church, music, theatre, memb local branch of MIND, various sporting activities; *Clubs* United Norwich Hosp's Cricket (pres); *Style—* Graham Shelton, Esq; 187 Drayton High Rd, Drayton, Norwich, Norfolk NR8 6BN (☎ 0603 409685); Mental Handicap & Psychiatric Services, St Andrew's Hospital (South Side), Thorpe, Norwich, Norfolk NR7 0SS (☎ 0603 31122, fax 0603 700249)

SHELTON, Hon Mrs (Sarah); *née* Fellowes; da of 3 Baron De Ramsey, KBE; *b* 1938; *m* 1972, Peter Shelton; 1 s, 1 da; *Style—* The Hon Mrs Shelton; Es Moli Nou de Canet, Es Glayeta, Mallorca

SHELTON, Shirley Megan; da of Lt-Col T F Goodwin, DSO, TD (d 1965), of SA, and Lucia Vera May, *née* Pike (d 1983); *b* 8 March 1934; *m* 21 July 1960, (William) Timothy Shelton, s of Stephen Shelton (d 1956); 1 s (Edward b 1964), 2 da (Alice b 1961, Laura b 1965); *Career* journalist; ed: Woman and Home 1978-82, Home and Freezer Digest 1988-89; currently freelance; *Recreations* Open Univ, music; *Style—* Mrs Shirley Shelton

SHELTON, Sir William Jeremy Masefield; MP (C) Streatham 1974-; s of late Lt-Col Richard Charles Masefield Shelton, MBE, of St Saviour's, Guernsey, and (Ruth Evelyn) Penelope, *née* Coode; *b* 30 Oct 1929; *Educ* Radley, Tabor Acad (Mass), Worcester Coll Oxford (MA), Univ of Texas (Austin); *m* 24 Sept 1960, Anne Patricia, da of John Arthur Warder, CBE, of Guernsey; 1 s (Charles b 17 Dec 1972), 1 da (Victoria b 14 Dec 1968); *Career* with the advertising agency Colman Prentis & Varley 1952-55, Corpa (Caracas) 1955-60; md: CPV (International) Bogotà 1960-64, CPV (International) 1967-74, Grosvenor Advertising 1969-74; chm: Fletcher Shelton Delaney & Reynolds 1974-81, GGK London 1984-; memb Wandsworth GLC 1967-70, chief whip ILEA 1968-70; PPS to: Min of Posts and Telecommunications 1972-74, Rt Hon Margaret Thatcher 1975; Parly under sec DES 1981-83; memb Cncl of Europe and Western Euro Union 1987-; kt 1989; *Clubs* Carlton, Huntercombe Golf; *Style—* Sir William Shelton, MP; The Manor House, Long Crendon, Bucks (☎ 0844 208748); 27 Ponsonby Terrace, London SW1 (☎ 071 821 8204)

SHEMILT, Elaine Katherine Mary; da of Harold J Shemilt, of Lime Tree Farm, Bagnal, Stoke on Trent, Staffs, and Margarita Isabel Diaz Mediva; *b* 7 May 1954; *Educ* Bloomfield Collegiate Sch Belfast NI, Brighton Poly, Winchester Sch of Art (BA), RCA (MA); *m* 1, 1977 (m dis 1984) David A Duly, s of Frank Duly; 2 s (Benjamin b 1979, Emile Joseph b 1980); m 2, 1985, Dr T J C Murphy; 1 da (Genevieve Clare b 1988); *Career* artist; exhibitions incl: Bexley Heath Kent 1975, Serpentine Gallery London 1976, Guildhall Winchester 1976, Nat Gallery Singapore 1977, RCA London 1977, ICA London 1978, London Poly 1978, Hayward Annual London 1979, RCA London 1980, Ikon Gallery Birmingham 1980, Fylde Arts Assoc 1981, Arteder '82 Muestra International De Arte Grafico Bilbao Spain 1982, RCA 1983, The Nude Cheltenham 1983, The Winchester Gallery 1984, Plymouth Arts Centre 1984, Ferens Art Gallery Hull 1985, Compass Gallery 1985, Landesbank Stuttgart W Germany 1986, Hull Coll of Further Educn 1986, Royal Festival Hall London 1987, RSA Diploma Galleries 1987, Kingfisher Gallery Edinburgh 1987, Stamford Theatre and Arts Centre 1988, Gallerie Twerenbold Lucerne Switzerland 1988 and 1990, Andrew Jones Gallery 1988, Bellfrie Gallery Copenhagen Denmark 1988, Soc of Scottish Artists Edinburgh 1989, Paperworks (Seagate Gallery Dundee) 1989, Women's Photography Exhibition (The Small Mansion Arts Centre London) 1990, Kindred Spirits (Ancrum Gallery and Matthew Gallery Duncan of Jordanstone) 1990, Frameworks (BDP Exhibition Preston touring) 1990, 11th Int Bradford Print Biennale (touring) 1990, McManus Gallery group staff exhibition 1990, Lumley-Cazalet Gallery Kensington 1990; work in various pub and private collections; art teacher Winchester 1979-80, artist and printmaker in residence South Hill Park Arts Centre Berkshire 1980-82, fell in fine art and printmaking Winchester Sch of Art 1982-84, sr lectr Duncan of Jordanstone Coll of Art Dundee 1988- (lectr 1985-88), dir Dundee Printmakers Workshop 1989-; most important works incl: Ritual series 1980-90, woman soldiers film prints and installation South Hill Park Arts Centre 1981, Bell Jar series 1988, Tell Me My Name and Bony Mother....White flesh to the White bone....1990, Pierrot Lunaire 1991; *Style—* Ms Elaine Shemilt; 5 Home Terrace, 86 Dundee Rd, Broughty Rd, Dundee, Scotland DD5 1DW (☎ 0382 79851); 51 Warrender Park Rd, Edinburgh, Scotland EH9 1EU (☎ 031 229 8743); Director of Printmaking, Dept of Printmaking Fine Art, Duncan of Jordanstone, College of Art, 13 Perth Rd, Dundee

SHENKIN, Prof Alan; s of Louis Shenkin, of Glasgow, and Miriam Leah, *née* Epstein; *b* 3 Sept 1943; *Educ* Hutchesons' GS Glasgow, Univ of Glasgow (BSc, MB ChB, PhD, MRCP); *m* 27 June 1967, Leonna Estelle, da of Godfrey Jacob Delmonte (d 1978), of

Glasgow; 1 s (Stephen b 1975), 2 da (Susie b 1970, Trudi b 1971); *Career* lectr in biochemistry Univ of Glasgow 1970-74, Royal Soc Euro exchange fell Karolinska Inst Stockholm 1976-77; conslt in clinical biochemistry Glasgow Royal Infirmary 1978-90 (sr registrar 1974-78); prof of clinical chemistry Univ of Liverpool 1990-, author of various book chapters on nutritional support and micronutrients; treas Euro Soc of Parenteral and Enteral Nutrition, sec Clinical Metabolism and Nutritional Support Gp of The Nutrition Soc; FRCPath 1990; *Recreations* golf, word games, travel; *Style*— Prof Alan Shenkin; 10 Rockbourne Green, Woolton, Liverpool L25 4TH (☎ 051 428 9756); Dept of Chemical Pathology, University of Liverpool, PO Box 147, Liverpool L69 3BX (☎ 051 706 4232)

SHENNAN, Francis Gerard (Frank); s of Thomas Gerard Shennan, of Tadley, Hants, and Cecelia, *née* Strype; *b* 14 Sept 1949; *Educ* Preston Catholic Coll, St Joseph's Coll, Dumfries, Univ of Edinburgh (LLB); *Career* writer and journalist; news sub ed: Daily Mirror Manchester 1975-76, Scottish Daily Record 1976-88; recruitment columnist the Scotsman 1988-89, fndr Francis Shennan Agency 1988-, scot business ed The Sunday Times 1989-; law examiner for Scot Nat Cncl for the Trg of Journalists 1981-84, external examiner media law Napier Poly Edinburgh 1984-; guest lectr and speaker: Napier Poly, NW Writers Assoc, SE Writers Assoc; contrib to: Scottish Field, Woman, Woman's Own, Television Weekly; *Books* The Life, Passions, and Legacies of John Napier (1990); *Recreations* travelling, walking; *Clubs* Country Gentlemen's Assoc; *Style*— Frank Shennan, Esq; Francis Shennan Agency, 134 Wilton Street, Glasgow G20 6DG (☎ 041 946 9030)

SHENSTONE, Gerald Guy; TD (1946); s of Brig Gerald Shenstone, CBE, TD, JP, DL (d 1976), and Muriel Berna, *née* Johnson (d 1977); *b* 3 May 1918; *Educ* Tonbridge, Univ of Cambridge (MA); *m* 22 Nov 1947, Pamela Patricia, da of Reginald Hugh Poole (d 1949); 1 s (Simon), 1 da (Clare); *Career* chartered architect, conslt Gerald Shenstone & Partners; architect of Chelmsford Cathedral 1977-84 and numerous churches and historic buildings; AADipl, FRIBA, FCIArb; *Recreations* golf; *Clubs* Surveyors; *Style*— Gerald G Shenstone, Esq, TD; 25 Kings Court, Kings Road, Westcliff-on-Sea SS0 8LL (☎ 0702 352722); 26 Bloomsbury Square, London WC1A 2PN (☎ 071 636 8595)

SHENTON, David William; s of Sir William Leonard Shenton, KB (d 1967), and Erica Lucy, *née* Denison (d 1978); *b* 1 Dec 1924; *Educ* Westminster, Magdalen Coll Oxford (BA); *m* 1, 1972 (m dis 1987), Della, da of F G Marshall (d 1977), of Sutton, Surrey; m 2, 12 May 1988, Charmian Nancy, LVO, da of Christopher William Lacey (d 1966), of Walmer, Kent; *Career* WWII Lt Coldstream Gds 1943-46, served Italy (despatches); admitted slr 1951; ptnr Lovell White and King 1955, conslt Lovell White and Durrant 1988-89; int arbitrator; conslt Studio Legale Ardito 1990-; chm: Slrs Euro Gp of Law Soc 1980-81, Ctee D of Int Bar Assoc 1983-87 (chm emeritus 1987-); memb: Editorial Ctee International Business Lawyer 1986-88, Chms Advsy Ctee Int Bar Assoc 1988-90; Freeman City of London 1950; Liveryman: Worshipful Co of Grocers 1954, Worshipful Slrs Co 1970; FCIArb (memb Cncl 1990); *Recreations* sailing, visiting ancient sites and buildings, photography; *Clubs* RYS, Carlton; *Style*— David Shenton, Esq; 16 Eldon Grove, Hampstead, London NW3 5PT (☎ 071 794 8002); Moons Hill House, Moons Hill, Totland Bay, IoW PO39 0HS (☎ 0983 752255, fax 071 633 3245/ 0983 756027)

SHEPARD, Giles Richard Carless; s of Richard Stanley Howard Shepard, MC, TD, and Kathleen Carless (d 1977); *b* 1 April 1937; *Educ* Eton, Harvard Business Sch; *m* 1966, Peter Carolyn Fern, da of Geoffrey Keighley (d 1966); 1 s, 1 da; *Career* Coldstream Guards 1955-60; dir: Charrington & Co Ltd 1962-64, H P Bulmer & Co Ltd 1964-70; md: Westminster & Country Properties Ltd 1970-76, Savoy Hotel plc 1976-; govr Gresham's Sch Holt, memb: Exec Ctee Cystic Fibrosis Research Tst, Cncl of Hotel and Catering Benevolent Assoc; High Sheriff of Gtr London 1986-87; memb Exec Ctee of Royal Sch of Needlework; dep chm Bd of Mgmnt of the British Hotels Restaurants and Caterers Assoc; prime warden Worshipful Co of Fishmongers 1987-88; *Recreations* gardening, shooting, tennis; *Clubs* White's, Pratt's; *Style*— Giles Shepard, Esq; 1 Savoy Hill, London WC2R 0BP (☎ 071 836 1533)

SHEPHARD, Hon Mrs (Belinda Anne); *née* Renwick; da of 1 Baron Renwick, KBE, by his 1 w, Dorothy; *b* 6 March 1934; *m* 1959, John Horatio Gordon Shephard; 1 s, 1 da; *Style*— The Hon Mrs Shephard; The Barn, Elcot, nr Newbury, Berks, RG16 8NJ

SHEPHARD, Air Cdre Harold Montague; CBE (1974, OBE 1959); s of Rev Leonard Benjamin Shephard (d 1961), of Wareham, Dorset, and Lilian Shephard (d 1982); *b* 15 Aug 1918; *Educ* St John's Leatherhead; *m* 20 May 1939, Margaret Isobel, da of Frederick Girdlestone, of Ewell; 1 s (David Harold Andrew), 1 da (Angela Margaret (Mrs Colgate)); *Career* RAF 1941-74, Air Cdre, provost marshal and dir RAF Security 1971-74; Met Police (CID) 1937-41; MBIM 1970-74; *Recreations* sport, reading; *Clubs* RAF, Tenterden Golf, Tenterden Cricket (vice pres); *Style*— Air Cdre Harold Shephard, CBE; 6 Bennetts Mews, West Cross, Tenterden, Kent TN30 6JN (☎ 05806 4945)

SHEPHARD, Hon Mrs (Harriet Olivia); *née* Davies; da of Baron Davies of Leek, PC (Life Peer, d 1985); *b* 1930; *Educ* London (BSc); *m* 1950, Derek Shephard; 1 da (Sue); *Style*— The Hon Mrs Shephard; 36 Clevenden Mansions, Lissenden Gdns, NW5

SHEPHARD, (John) Horatio Gordon; s of Harold Shephard (d 1946), and Grace Winifred, *née* Birbeck (d 1942); *b* 12 Aug 1921; *Educ* Summer Fields Oxford, Eton, New Coll Oxford (BA); *m* 1, 29 June 1948 (m dis), Carola, da of Cdr Sir Geoffrey Congreve,DSO, 1 Bt (ka 1941); 2 s (Thomas b 1949, Henry b 1955); m 2, Belinda Anne, da of 1 Baron Renwick of Coombe, KBE, of Berks (d 1973); 1 s (William b 1962), 1 da (Sarah b 1959); *Career* Capt Grenadier Gds 1941-46, served in N Africa and Italy; ptnr Thicknesse and Hull Slrs Westminster 1951-80, sr ptnr Goddens and Thicknesse 1980-87; *Recreations* travelling, golf; *Clubs* Boodles, Swinley Forest Golf, Berkshire Golf, Inst of Directors; *Style*— Horatio Shephard, Esq; The Barn, Elcot Park, nr Newbury, Berks RG16 8NJ (☎ 0488 57049); William Sturges and Co, Alliance House, 12 Caxton St, SW1 (☎ 071 222 1391)

SHEPHARD, Hon Mrs (Mary Anna); *née* Shaw; 2nd da of Baron Kilbrandon, PC (Life Peer; d 1989); *b* 1946; *m* 1971, Thomas H C Shephard; 4 s (Samuel b 1973, Edward b 1975, Francis b 1977, Christian b 1985), 1 da (Josephine b 1981); *Style*— The Hon Mrs Shephard; The Keeper's Cottage, Dunvegan Castle, Isle of Skye

SHEPHARD, Prof Ronald William; s of William Joseph Shephard (d 1975), of Leicester, and Nellie, *née* Simmonds (d 1964); *b* 25 April 1923; *Educ* Manchester GS, Stockport Sch, Wyggeston Sch Leicester, Queens' Coll Cambridge (BA, MA); *m* 2 May 1949, Betty Mabel Shephard; 1 s (Michael Clive Anthony), 1 da (Gillian Elizabeth); *Career* operational res sci MOD Army Dept 1943-, supt weapons and tactics Army Operational Res Estab 1961-64, supt land ops Def Operational Analysis Estab 1964-68, prof operational res RMCS 1969-83, mil ops advsr Royal Ordnance plc 1983-; conslt: Centre for Operational Res and Def Analysis London, BDM International Mclean VA USA; memb: CNAA, NATO Advsy Panel on Operational Res, FOR 1970 (chm), Assoc Inner Magic Circle F; *Books* Applied Operations Research: Examples from Defense Assessment (jtly, 1988); *Recreations* magic, military archival research; *Clubs* Magic Circle; *Style*— Prof Ronald Shephard; Old Westmill Farmhouse, Watchfield, Swindon, Wilts SN6 8TH (☎ 0793 782 321); Royal Ordnance Future Systems Group, P O Box 243, Shrivenham, Swindon, Wilts SN6 8QD (☎ 0793 783 610, fax 0793 783 616, telex 444112)

SHEPHEARD, Sir Peter Faulkner; CBE (1972); s of Thomas Faulkner Shepheard; *b* 1913; *Educ* Birkenhead Sch, Liverpool Sch of Architecture; *m* 1943, Mary, da of Charles James Bailey; 1 s, 1 da; *Career* architect, town planner and landscape architect; ptnr Shepheard, Epstein & Hunter 1948-; dean Graduate Sch of Fine Arts Univ of Pennsylvania (USA) 1971-; kt 1980; *Clubs* Savile, Athenaeum; *Style*— Sir Peter Shepheard, CBE; 21 Well Rd, London NW3 1LH

SHEPHEARD-HEALEY, Michael Kingsley; s of Patrick Kingsley Shepheard, of London and Rio De Janeiro, and Vivienne, *née* Nathan; *b* 6 Dec 1951; *Educ* Keil Sch Dumbarton Scotland, Glasgow Sch of Art (BA, postgrad dip, Leverhulme travel scholar); *Career* designer: Pushpin Studios, J Walter Thompson NY, McCann Erickson Snazelle Films San Francisco 1976; sr designer J P Coats Glasgow (Jaeger products, Ladybird, Coats Patons) 1977, jr art dir J Walter Thompson Rio de Janeiro 1978-81, dir Rex Stewart and Assocs Glasgow 1981-84, head Dept of Graphic Design, Illustration and Photography Glasgow Sch of Art 1984-; freelance designer, many design and painting cmmns incl work for Euro Parliament 1989; work in several private collections; MInstM; *Recreations* drawing and painting, history, fly fishing, sailing; *Clubs* Glasgow Art; *Style*— Michael Shepheard-Healey, Esq

SHEPHERD, Colin Ryley; MP (C) Hereford Oct 1974-; *b* 13 Jan 1938; *Educ* Oundle, Caius Coll Cambridge, McGill Univ Montreal; *Career* mktg dir and Parly advsr Haigh Engineering Co Ltd 1963-; jt vice chm Cons Parly Ctee Agric 1979-87, memb Select Ctee House of Commons Serv 1979-, chm Library Sub Ctee 1983-, PPS to sec of State for Wales 1987-; fell Indust & Parliament Tst, memb Cncl RCVS 1983-, govr Cwlth Inst 1989-, memb Int Exec Ctee CPA 1989-; *Style*— Colin Shepherd Esq, MP; Manor House, Ganarew, Nr Monmouth, Gwent (☎ 0600 890220)

SHEPHERD, (Richard) David; OBE (1979); s of Raymond Oxley Shepherd (d 1960), and Margaret Joyce, *née* Williamson (d 1978); *b* 25 April 1931; *Educ* Stowe; *m* 2 Feb 1957, Avril Shirley, da of Hugh Dowling-Gaywood (d 1940); 4 da (Melinda b 1958, Mandy b 1960, Melanie b 1962, Wendy b 1964); *Career* trained under Robin Goodwin 1950-53, exhibited RA Summer Exhibition 1956, first one man exhibition 1962, painted religious painting of Christ for Army Garrison Church Bordon Hants 1964; one man shows: London 1966, 1978 and 1984, Johannesburg 1966, NY 1979; portraits: HE Dr K Kaunda Pres of Zambia 1967, HM The Queen Mother 1969, Sheikh Zaid of Abu Dhabi 1970; lifestory World About Us BBC TV 1971 (The Man Who Loves Giants), BBC documentary Last Train to Mulobezi 1974, series for Thames TV In Search of Wildlife 1988; memb of hon World Wide Fund for Nature, fndr David Shepherd Conservation Fndn for the Enviroment and Wildlife, fndr and chm E Somerset Railway; Hon Doctorate Pratt Inst of NY 1971, Hon DSc Hatfield Poly; FRSA 1987; FRGS 1989; Order of Distinguished Service First Div Rep of Zambia; *Books* An Artist in Africa (1967), The Man Who Loves Giants (autobiog, 1975), Paintings of Africa and India (1978), A Brush With Steam (1983), David Shepherd The Man and His Paintings (1986); *Recreations* raising funds for wildlife conservation and driving steam locomotives; *Style*— David Shepherd, Esq, OBE; Winkworth Farm, Hascombe, Godalming, Surrey GU8 4JW (☎ 048 632 220)

SHEPHERD, David Robert; s of Herbert Howell Shepherd (d 1962), of Instow, Bideford, Devon, and Doris Sarah, *née* Smallbridge (d 1990); *b* 27 Dec 1940; *Educ* Barnstaple GS, St Luke's Coll Exeter; *partner* Jennifer Margaret Hoare; *Career* cricket umpire; player: English Schs 1959, Devon 1959-64, Gloucestershire CCC 1965-79 (awarded county cap 1969), total 282 first class matches; scored 108 on debut Gloucs v Oxford Univ; appointed first class umpire 1981-: first match at Oxford, first one-day Int England v W Indies 1984, first Test Match England v Aust 1985; other matches umpired incl: World Cup England 1983, World Cup India and Pakistan 1987, MCC Bicentenary Lord's 1987, Asia Cup Sri Lanka, tournaments in Sharjah UAE, numerous domestic cup finals Lord's; *Recreations* all sports, stamp collecting; *Style*— David Shepherd, Esq; Test and County Cricket Board, Lords Cricket Ground, London NW8 8QN (☎ 071 286 4405)

SHEPHERD, Hon Douglas Newton; s of 2 Baron Shepherd, PC; *b* 1952; *Style*— The Hon Douglas Shepherd

SHEPHERD, Prof (William) Douglas; s of Capt William Davidson Shepherd, of Bournemouth, and Jessie, *née* Douglas (d 1988); *b* 14 Sept 1939; *Educ* Bournemouth Sch, Univ of London (BSc); *m* 30 Dec 1967, Eileen May, da of Harry Trafford Stott (d 1974), of Woking; 1 s (Harry b 1985); *Career* technologist BP Res Centre 1965-67, sr lectr Dept of Computer Sci Portsmouth Poly 1967-71, res fell computer laboratory Univ of Kent 1969-70, lectr Dept of Computer Sci Univ of Strathclyde 1971-83, sr visitor computer laboratory Univ of Cambridge 1980-81, visiting scientist IBM Euro Network Centre Heidelberg W Germany 1988-89, dean of Sch of Engrg Computing and Mathematical Scis 1989- (prof of computing and head of dept 1983-88); memb Advsy Panel on Strategy for Communications and Distributed Systems in Successor Prog to Alvey 1987-88, chm Communications and Distributed Systems Club IED 1989-; MBCS 1970, MIEEE 1988; *Books* Local Area Networks: An Advanced Course (1982), Object Oriented Languages (1991); *Recreations* squash, golf and hill walking; *Clubs* Royal Victoria YC, Lancaster Golf and Country; *Style*— Prof Douglas Shepherd; Univ of Lancaster, School of Engineering Computing and Mathematical Sciences, Lancaster LA1 4YR (☎ 0524 65201, fax 0524 381707, telex 65111 LANCUL G)

SHEPHERD, Freda Margaret; da of John Edward Gresley (d 1958), of 252 Calais Hill, Burton upon Trent, Staffs, and Sarah Margaret Gresley, *née* Harden (d 1979); *Educ* Burton upon Trent Girls' HS; *m* 31 Aug 1957, Richard John Shepherd, s of Arthur John Shepherd (d 1971), of 176 Rolleston Rd, Burton upon Trent, Staffs; *Career* audit clerk and PA Thomas Bourne & Co 1946-67, chief exec and sec Burton upon Trent & Dist C of C and Indust 1986- (co sec 1969); memb PCC St John's Horninglow, sec Burton upon Trent Girls' HS Assoc; memb Br C of C Execs; *Recreations* music, gardening, travel, cookery; *Style*— Mrs Richard Shepherd; 158 Derby St, Burton upon Trent, Staffs DE14 2NZ (☎ 0283 63761, fax 0283 510 753)

SHEPHERD, Hon Graeme George; s and h of 2 Baron Shepherd, PC; *b* 6 Jan 1949; *m* 1971, Eleanor; 1 s (Patrick Malcolm); *Style*— The Hon Graeme Shepherd; Suite 72, Wheelock House, 20 Pedder st C, Hong Kong

SHEPHERD, Lt Col Ian; s of Edward Basil Branch Shepherd (d 1980), and Una, *née* Sadler (d 1987); *b* 6 April 1939; *Educ* Queen's Coll of Br Guiana, Dollar Acad, RMA Sandhurst; *m* 19 June 1965, Belinda, da of Brig Archibald Ian Buchanan-Dunlop, CBE, DSO, of Broughton Place, Broughton, Peebles-shire; 2 s (Rupert Graham b 1968, Christian James b 1971), 1 da (Josephine Mary b 1975); *Career* cmmnd into Royal Highland Fusiliers 1960, Assist Mil Attaché (Tech) Moscow 1981-82; cmmdg offr: Scot Infantry Depot (Bridge of Don) 1984-86, Univ of Aberdeen OTC 1986-88; *Recreations* history, mil costume, photography, Russian-Soviet empire; *Clubs* Army and Navy; *Style*— Lt-Col Ian Shepherd; c/o Bank of Scotland, 426 Morningside Road, Edinburgh EH10 5QF

SHEPHERD, Prof James; s of James Bell Shepherd, of 46 Ardmory Rd, Ardberg, Bute, and Margaret McCrum, *née* Camick; *b* 8 April 1944; *Educ* Hamilton Acad, Univ of Glasgow (BSc, MB ChB, PhD, MRCP); *m* 5 July 1969, Jan Bulloch, da of William Bulloch Kelly, of 34 Wellview Drive, Motherwell; 1 s (Ewen James b 7 Feb 1974), 1 da (Fiona Elizabeth b 7 July 1976); *Career* lectr in biochemistry Univ of Glasgow 1969-72; Dept of Pathological Biochemistry Univ of Glasgow and Glasgow Royal Infirmary: lectr 1973-77, sr lectr and hon conslt 1977-84, prof and head of dept 1988-; asst prof of med Methodist Hosp Houston Texas 1976-77, visiting prof of med Cantonal Hosp Geneva 1984; memb: Coronary Prevention Gp, Int Atherosclerosis Soc, Euro Atherosclerosis Soc; MRCPath 1982, FRCP (Glasgow) 1990; *Books* incl: Lipoproteins in Coronary Heart Disease (jtly, 1986), Atherosclerosis: Developments, Complications and Treatment (jtly, 1987), Lipoprotein Metabolism (1987), Coronary Risks Revisited (ed jtly, 1989); *Style—* Prof James Shepherd; 17 Barriedale Ave, Hamilton ML3 9DB (☎ 0698 428259); Dept of Pathological Biochemistry, Royal Infirmary, Glasgow G4 0SF (☎ 041 552 3535 ext 5279, fax 041 553 1703, telex 779234 HLAGLA G)

SHEPHERD, John Dodson; CBE (1979); s of Norman Shepherd (d 1970), of Gawthwaite, nr Ulverston, and Elizabeth Ellen, *née* Dodson (d 1970); *b* 24 Dec 1920; *Educ* Barrow GS; *m* 21 Aug 1948, Marjorie, da of Albert James Nettleton (d 1983), of Barrow in Furness; 1 s (David b 1949), 2 da (Margaret (Mrs Chadwick) b 1952, Elizabeth (Mrs Adkinson) b 1952); *Career* WWII RAF 1940-46; sec Newcastle Gen Hosp 1958-62, gp sec E Cumberland Hosp Mgmnt Ctee 1962-67, sec Liverpool Regnl Hosp Bd 1967-74; regnl admin: Mersey RHA 1974-77, Yorks RHA 1977-82; tstee The Leonard Cheshire Fndn; pres: Rotary Club of Harrogate 1990-91, Inst of Health Serv Admins 1974-75; *Recreations* golf, caravanning, music; *Style—* John Shepherd, Esq, CBE; 14 Leconfield Garth, Follifoot, Harrogate, North Yorks HG3 1NF (☎ 0423 870520)

SHEPHERD, John H; s of Dr Henry Robert Shepherd, DSC, of Little Cheriton, 4 The Glade, Enfield, Middx, and Mimika, *née* Matarki; *b* 11 July 1948; *Educ* Blundell's, St Bartholomew's Hosp Med Coll (MB BS); *m* 27 May 1972, Alison Sheila, da of Capt Henry Stephen Brandram-Adams, MBE, of Wootton, IOW; 1 s (David b 1976), 2 da (Katy b 1978, Emily b 1985); *Career* conslt gynaecological surgn: St Bartholomew's Hosp 1981, Chelsea Hosp for Women 1983-84, Royal Marsden Hosp 1983-; author numerous chapters and scientific articles on med topics relating to cancer, gynaecology and obstetrics; memb: Cncl RCOG 1989- (1984-87), Working Pty in Gynaecological Oncology MRC; chm Ovarian Cancer Sub Ctee of UK Co-ordinating ctee for Cancer Res; memb Worshipful Soc of Apothecaries; memb: BMA 1971, RSM 1972; FRCS 1975, MRCOG 1978, FACOG 1981; fell: Belgian Royal Acad of Med 1986, Singaporian Acad of Sci 1987; *Books* Clinical Gynaecological Oncology (1985, 2 edn 1990); *Recreations* skiing, sailing, cricket, squash, classical music; *Style—* John Shepherd, Esq; Pickwick Cottage, 31 College Rd, Dulwich, London SE21 7BG (☎ 081 693 6342); 40 Harley St, London W1 1AB (☎ 071 935 7054, fax 071 323 3067, car 0836 219 806)

SHEPHERD, Lord Malcolm Newton Shepherd; PC (1965); 2 Baron (UK 1946); s of 1 Baron Shepherd, PC, sometime Chief Labour Whip Lords, Capt Yeomen of the Gd & Hon Corps Gentlemen at Arms, also Nat Agent Lab Pty (d 1954), and Ada, *née* Newton; *b* 27 Sept 1918; *Educ* Friends' Sch Saffron Walden; *m* 15 Nov 1941, Allison, The Lady Shepherd, JP, da of Patrick Redmond (d 1980); 2 s (Graeme George b 1951, Douglas Newton b 1954); *Heir* s, Hon Graeme Shepherd; *Career* chm: Mitchell Cotts & Co (FE) Ltd 1950-56, Fielding Brown & Finch (FE) Ltd 1951-62, National Bus Company 1980-85, Cheque Point International 1988-, Czech Banka Cheque joint Prague; dir: Sterling Group of Cos 1976-82, Sum Hung Kai Ltd 1980-85; chief whip House of Lords 1964-67 (oppn chief whip 1960-64), min of state FO 1967-70, lord privy seal and ldr House of Lords 1974-76; chm: MRC 1976-80, Civil Serv Pay Res Unit Bd 1976-81, Packaging Cncl; pres Inst Road Tport Engrs 1987-; *Recreations* golf; *Clubs* Tenterden Golf; *Style—* The Rt Hon the Lord Shepherd, PC; 29 Kennington Palace Court, Sancroft St, London SE11 (☎ 071 582 6772); Cheque Point International, Berkeley St, London W1 (☎ 071 409 0868)

SHEPHERD, Prof Michael; CBE (1989); s of Solomon Shepherd (d 1979), and Cissie, *née* Wayne (d 1973); *b* 30 July 1923; *Educ* Cardiff HS, Univ of Oxford (MA, DM), DPM; *m* 13 April 1947, Margaret, da of Lewis Rock (d 1944); 2 s (Simon b 1951, Daniel b 1962), 2 da (Catherine b 1949, Lucy b 1954); *Career* RAF 1949-51; prof of epidemiological psychiatry Inst of Psychiatry 1967-88 (reader in psychiatry 1960-67), emeritus prof of epidemiological psychiatry Univ of London 1988-; hon FRCPysch, FRCP; *Books* A Study of the Major Psychoses in an English County (1957), Psychiatric Illness in General Practice (1966), Psychotropic Drugs in Psychiatry (1981), Psychiatrists on Psychiatry (1983), Sherlock Holmes and The Case of Dr Freud (1985), Conceptual Issues in Psychological Medicine (1990); *Recreations* literature, chess, music, tennis; *Clubs* Athenaeum; *Style—* Prof Michael Shepherd, CBE; Institute of Psychiatry, De Crespigny Park, London SE5 8AF (☎ 071 703 5411)

SHEPHERD, Sir Peter; CBE (1967), DL (N Yorks 1982); s of Alderman Frederick Welton Shepherd, and Martha Eleanor; *b* 18 Oct 1916; *Educ* Nunthorpe GS York, Rossall; *m* 1940, Patricia Mary, da of Frank Edward Welton; 4 s; *Career* dir Shepherd Bldg Gp Ltd (chm 1958-86), chm Shepherd Construction Ltd; memb President's Consultative Ctee Bldg Employers Confedn 1956- (formerly Nat Fedn Bldg Trades Employers), pres Chartered Inst of Building 1964-65 (memb Nat Cncl 1956-87), chm Bd of Bldg Educn 1965-68 (memb 1957-75), cncl memb CBI 1976-; BIM: memb Nat Cncl 1965-71, memb Bd Fellows 1969-73, fndr chm Yorks and N Lincs Advsy Bd 1969-71; fndr memb Technician Educn Cncl 1973-79, vice-chm CIOB Professional Practice Bd 1975- (chm 1964-75), former chm Construction Indust Trg Bd and Wool Jute and Flax Indust Trg Bd, govr St Peter's Sch York; memb: Co of Merchant Adventurers of City of York (govr 1984-85), Court of the Univ of York; DSc Heriot Watt 1979, Hon DUniv York; Hon Life memb: BEC Yorkshire Region 1986, BEC York Assoc 1986; Hon Fellowship of Leeds Poly 1987; FCIOB (Hon Fell 1987-), CBIM, FInstD; kt 1976; *Recreations* sailing; *Clubs* Yorkshire; *Style—* Sir Peter Shepherd, CBE, DL; Galtres House, Rawcliffe Lane, York Y03 6NP (☎ 0904 24250); office: Blue Bridge Lane, York Y01 4AS (☎ 0904 53040, telex 57402)

SHEPHERD, Peter Geoffrey; CBE (1988); s of Raymond Oxley Shepherd (d 1960), of Farnham, Surrey, and Margaret Joyce, *née* Williamson (d 1977); *b* 13 April 1927; *Educ* Stowe, Trinity Coll Cambridge (BA); *m* 12 Jan 1951, da of Thomas Llewelyn Roberts (d 1948), of Hinderton Cheshire, High Sheriff of Merionmeth; 2 s (Robert b 1953, Jonathan b 1959); *Career* chm: Brighton & Storrington Investmts Ltd 1965-, Business Fin (Sussex) Ltd 1970-; memb: W Sussex CC 1969- (chm 1985-89), Assoc of CCs 1974-, Local Authorities Mgmnt Servs 1982- (chm 1986-88), Schools Cncl 1976-82; *Recreations* horse racing (steward at Fontwell, Plumpton, Brighton); *Style—* Peter Shepherd, Esq, CBE

SHEPHERD, Philip Alexander; s of Col John Ernest Shepherd, of Cobham, Surrey, and Eve, *née* Zacharious; *Educ* St Georges Coll Weybridge, LSE (BSc); *m* 17 March 1983, Amanda Robin, da of Gavin Clezy, OBE, of Milan, Italy; 2 s (Freddy b 12 Dec 1985, William b 28 Oct 1987); *Career* called to the Bar Gray's Inn 1975; *Recreations* walking, skiing, my boys; *Clubs* RAC; *Style—* Philip Shepherd, Esq; 1 Harcourt Buildings, Temple, London EC4 (☎ 071 353 9371, fax 071 586 1656)

SHEPHERD, Richard Charles Scrimgeour; MP (C) Aldridge-Brownhills 1979-; s of Alfred Shepherd; *b* 6 Dec 1942; *Educ* LSE, Johns Hopkins Univ; *Career* dir: Partridges of Sloane St Ltd, Shepherd Foods Ltd; memb SE Econ Planning Cncl 1970-74, contested (C) Nottingham E Feb 1974; Lloyds underwriting memb 1974-; memb Select Ctee on Treasy and CS 1979-, sec Euro Affairs and Indust C Ctees 1980-81; *Style—* Richard Shepherd Esq, MP; 14 Addison Rd, London W14 (☎ 071 603 7108)

SHEPHERD, Richard James; s of late William James Affleck Shepherd (d 1970), of Stratton End, Cirencester, Glos, and Katharine Flora, *née* MacAndrew; *b* 8 March 1947; *Educ* Marlborough, St Catherine's Coll Oxford (BA); *m* 10 January 1974, Clare Harriet Faviell, da of Sir Charles Ian Russell, of Hidden House, Sandwich, Kent; 3 s (Edward b 1977, Andrew b 1979, Thomas b 1982); *Career* CA, ptnr Shepherd Smail & Co Cirencester 1973-; amateur rider: winner 118 point to points and steeplechases; tstee Cirencester Benefit Soc; FCA 1979 (ACA 1971); *Recreations* hunting, racing; *Style—* Richard Shepherd, Esq; Stratton End, Cirencester, Glos (☎ 0285 653 686); Northway House, Cirencester, Glos (☎ 0285 655 955)

SHEPHERD, Dr Robert John; s of Reginald John Stuart Shepherd (d 1973), of Glos, and Ellen, *née* Pritchard; *b* 16 Jan 1946; *Educ* King's Sch Glos, Univ of Liverpool (MB ChB); *Career* med registrar Nat Heart Hosp London 1975, sr med registrar Radcliffe Infirmary Oxford 1976, conslt physician Dept of Med for the Elderly Leics DHA 1977-; contrib various articles to Postgraduate Medical Journal 1971-87; MRCP (UK); *Recreations* travel, photography, collecting antiques; *Style—* Dr RJ Shepherd; Leicester General Hospital, Gwendoline Rd, Leics (☎ 0533 490490)

SHEPHERD, Robert Priestley; JP (Lancs, 1979), DL (1989); s of Harry Priestley Shepherd (d 1956), of Rossendale, and Marion Scott, *née* Neill; *b* 1 Dec 1931; *Educ* Rossall Sch, Leicester Coll of Art and Technol; *m* 30 June 1954, Anne, da of Donald Robert Heyworth (d 1980), of Rossendale; 2 s (Philip b 22 June 1955, Henry b 3 Jan 1960), 1 da (Joy (Mrs Allsop) b 19 Nov 1956); *Career* dep chm Pentland Industries plc, chm Priestley Footwear Ltd; govr and tstee Rossall Sch, tstee Richard Whittaker Charity Tst, area dep chm Rossendale Br Heart Fndn; pres: Otters Swimming Assoc Lancs, Rossendale Museum; High Sheriff Lancs 1987-88; Freeman City of London, memb Worshipful Co of Patternmakers 1983; ACFI 1974, FInstD 1986, FRSA 1990; *Recreations* sailing, travel; *Clubs* Royal Windermere Yacht; *Style—* Robert Shepherd, Esq, JP, DL; Woodcliffe, Horncliffe, Rossendale, Lancs (☎ 0706 213096); Pentland Industries (Northern) plc, Albion Mill, Gt Harwood, Lancs (☎ 0254 886241)

SHEPHERD, Prof William; s of William Edward Shepherd, of Nottingham, and Mary Elizabeth, *née* Hurst; *b* 20 Oct 1928; *Educ* St John's Coll York, Imperial Coll London (BSc), Univ of Toronto Canada (MASc), Univ of London (PhD, DSc); *m* 28 July 1956, Elisabeth Mary, da of Hugh Leslie Gahan (d 1987), of Otford, Kent; 4 s (David William b 1959, Peter Gerald b 1961, Michael John b 1963, Andrew James b 1970 d 1972); *Career* Nat Serv Sergeant instr RAEC 1947-49; sch teacher in Nottingham 1951-52; asst prof Univ of Manitoba Canada 1959-62, princ lectr RMCS 1966-67 (sr lectr 1963-66), prof Univ of Bradford 1978-85 (reader 1967-78), Fulbright prof Univ of Wisconsin Madison USA 1985, pro vice chllr Univ of Bradford 1988- (dean of engrg 1985-88); cncl memb Institution of Electrical Engrs 1977-80; chm: Yorkshire Centre 1977-78, Scholarships Cte 1981-83; FIEE, FIEEE; *Books* Thyristor Control of AC Circuits (1975), Energy Flow and Power Factor in Nonsinusoidal Circuits (1979), Power Electronics and Motor Control (1987); *Recreations* music (especially church music), tennis, cricket, soccer, gardening (flowers and shrubs), reading detective stories and cricket books; *Style—* Prof William Shepherd; 5 Nab Wood Drive, Shipley, W Yorks BD18 4HP (☎ 0274 587153); Department of Electrical Engineering, University of Bradford, Bradford, W Yorks BD7 1DP (☎ 0274 733466 ext 232, fax 0274 305340, telex 51309 UNIBFD G)

SHEPHERD-BARRON, John Adrian; s of Wilfred Phillip Shepherd-Barron, MC, TD, LLD, (d 1979), and Dorothy Cunliffe Shepherd (d 1953), Wimbledon Ladies Doubles Champion (1931) and Wightman Cup Capt (1950-53); *b* 23 June 1925; *Educ* Stowe Cambridge; *m* 21 April 1954, Caroline, da of Sir Kenneth Murray, Kt (d 1979); 3 s (Nickolas b 1955, James b 1957, Andrew b 1959); *Career* Capt RA; served India, Egypt, Palestine 1945-47; chm: Security Express 1963-79, De La Rue Instruments 1967-79; regnl dir De La Rue Co plc 1979-85; chm Atlantic Freshwater plc 1987-; panel memb Scottish Ventures Fund; *Recreations* fishing, shooting, tennis; *Clubs* Army and Navy, All England LTC, New York Univ; *Style—* John A Shepherd-Barron, Esq; 14 Onslow Square, London SW7; Mains of Geanies, Fearn, Ross-shire (☎ 071 581 2491 and 086 287 443)

SHEPLEY, Richard Seymour Duart; s of Seymour Beadle Shepley (d 1987), and Marion Lea, *née* Jolly (d 1969); *b* 30 April 1950; *Educ* Oundle, Univ of Reading (BSc Agric); *m* 23 Sept 1978, Sarah Susan Raisbeck, da of Sqdn-Ldr Douglas Raisbeck Gelling, of Buxton; 2 s (Timothy b 1983, Nicholas b 1990), 1 da (Rosanna b 1981); *Career* estate mgmnt, farming and forestry; memb Historic Commercial Vehicle Soc; *Recreations* pressing of cider, restoration of a variety of human artefacts; *Style—* Richard Shepley, Esq; Woodthorpe Hall, Holmesfield, Sheffield (☎ 0742 360134)

SHEPPARD, Sir Allen John George; s of John Sheppard (d 1985), and Lily, *née* Palmer; *b* 25 Dec 1932; *Educ* Ilford Co HS, LSE (BSc); *m* 1, 1958 (m dis 1980) Damaris, da of David Jones (d 1964); m 2, 1980, Mary, da of Harry Stewart, of London; *Career* Ford UK and Ford Eur 1958-68, dir Rootes 1968-71, Br Leyland 1971-75, chief exec Watney Mann & Truman Brewers of Grand Met, gp md Grand Met 1982 (chief exec 1986, chm 1987), non exec dir and subsequently chm UBM 1981-85, non exec chm Mallinson Denny Gp Ltd 1985-87, non-exec dir Meyer International plc 1989-; pt/t memb Br Railways Bd 1985-90, vice pres Brewers Soc 1987-, govr and memb standing ctee LSE, dep chm Business in the community, chm Prince's Youth Business Tst 1990; kt 1990; *Recreations* gardens, reading, red-setter dogs; *Style—* Sir Allen Sheppard; 11-12 Hanover Square, London W1A 1DP (☎ 071 629 7488, telex 299606)

SHEPPARD, Hon Mrs (Angela); *née* Spring Rice; twin da of 6 Baron Monteagle of Brandon and Anne, *née* Browncow, The Lady Monteagle of Brandon; *b* 23 April 1950; *m* 1973 (m dis 1982), Christopher Richard Seton Sheppard; 1 da (Catherine b 1976); *Recreations* bridge, tennis, gardening; *Clubs* Hurlingham; *Style—* The Hon Mrs Sheppard

SHEPPARD, (Richard David) Anthony; s of Daniel Gurney Sheppard (d 1988), of Bennetts, Ashwell, Baldock, Herts, and Cinthia, *née* Hill; *b* 17 Feb 1950; *Educ* Milton Abbey, Royal Agric Coll Cirencester; *m* 27 Sept 1975 (m dis 1989), Angela Marion, da of Col Arther Clerke Brown, MBE; 1 s (Harry 8 Aug 1984), 1 da (Amanda b 16 June 1982); *Career* farmer; memb: Oxfordshire Ctee Co Landowners Assoc, Oxfordshire Ctee Game Conservancy; *Recreations* shooting, riding the cresta; *Clubs* Saint Moritz Toboggan, Raffles; *Style—* Anthony Sheppard, Esq; Red House Farm, Murcott, Islip, Oxon OX5 2BJ (☎ 0869 244 886, car 0860 824 563)

SHEPPARD, Rt Rev David Stuart; *see*: Liverpool, Bishop of

SHEPPERD, Sir Alfred Joseph; s of Alfred Charles Shepperd (d 1939), of London, and Mary Ann, *née* Williams (d 1975); *b* 19 June 1925; *Educ* Archbishop Tenison's Sch, UCL (BEcon); *m* 1950, Gabrielle Marie Yvette (Gay), da of late France Bouloux; 2 da (Sasha (Mrs Lancaster) b 1959, Rosemary b 1963); *Career* Sub-Lt (A) RNVR UK and Canada 1943-46; fin dir The Wellcome Fndn Ltd 1972-77 (chm and chief exec 1977-90), chm and chief exec Wellcome plc 1986-90; dir: Anglia Maltings (Holdings) Ltd 1972-, Mercury Asset Management Group plc 1987-, Zoo Operations Ltd 1988-,

The Oxford Instrument Group plc 1990-; memb Advsy Cncl on Sci and Indust (ACOST); Freeman City of London, Liveryman of the Worshipful Soc of Apothecaries 1987; FBIM 1977; Commandatore della Republica Italy 1983, Encomienda al Merito de Sanidad Spain 1988, Cdr Order of Leopold II Belgium 1989; kt 1989; *Clubs* Oriental; *Style—* Sir Alfred Shepperd

SHEPSTONE, Dr Basil John; s of James John Shepstone (d 1957), of Bloemfontein, SA, and Letitia Isabel, *née* Robinson (d 1984); *b* 4 Aug 1935; *Educ* Brebner HS Bloemfontein SA, Univ of the Orange Free State (BSc, MSc, DSc), Univ of SA (BA), Univ of Oxford (BM BCh, MA, DPhil), Capetown Univ (MD); *m* 23 Sept 1961, (Brenda) Victoria, da of James Dudley Alen, of Cambridge; 1 s (Jonathan James b 21 Nov 1962), 1 da (Charlotte Isabel b 8 Dec 1965); *Career* jr lectr in radiation physics Univ of The Orange Free State and hosp physicist Nat Prov Hosp Bloemfontein SA 1958-60, house offr in paediatrics and thoracic surgery United Oxford Hosps 1969, head of Dept of Nuclear Med Univ of Cape Town and Groote Shuur Hosp Cape Town 1972-78 (sr specialist Dept of Radiotherapy 1970-72), dean of degrees Wolfson Coll Oxford 1980-, Univ lectr and hon conslt in radiology Oxford Univ and Oxfordshire Health Authy 1981-, head of Dept of Radiology Oxford Univ 1984- (clinical lectr 1978-81), dir of clinical studies Oxford Univ Med Sch 1988- (dep dir 1985-88), contrib jls and books on solid state physics, radiobiology, radiotherapy, radiodiagnosis, nuclear med and med educn; memb: Br Inst of Radiology, Br Nuclear Med Soc; fell Wolfson Coll Oxford; FInstP, LRCP, MRCS, FRCR; *Recreations* art history, reading, travelling; *Style—* Dr Basil Shepstone; 464 Banbury Rd, Oxford OX2 7RG (☎ 0865 58889); Department of Radiology, University of Oxford, The Radcliffe Infirmary, Woodstock Rd, Oxford OX2 6HE (☎ 0865 249891)

SHER, Antony; s of Emanuel Sher, and Margery, *née* Abramowitz; *b* 14 June 1949; *Educ* Sea Point Boys HS Cape Town SA, Webber-Douglas Acad of Dramatic Art London, Post Grad drama course Manchester Univ Drama Dept and Manchester Poly Sch of Theatre; *Career* actor; roles incl: Howard Kirk in The History Man (BBC TV) 1980, Austin in True West (Nat Theatre) 1981; assoc artist RSC 1982-90; roles incl: Richard III (Drama magazine Best Actor award 1984, London Standard Best Actor Award 1985, Laurence Olivier Best Actor Award 1985), Shylock in Merchant of Venice, The Fool in King Lear, Vindice in The Revenger's Tragedy, Tartuffe, Johnnie in Hello and Goodbye, title role in Singer; Arnold in Torch Song Trilogy 1985 (Albery Theatre, Laurence Olivier Best Actor award 1985); *Books* Year of the King (actor's diary and sketchbook, 1985), Middlepost (1988), Characters (painting and drawings, 1989), The Indoor Boy (1991); *Style—* Antony Sher, Esq; c/o Hope & Lyne, 108 Leonard St, London EC2 4RT (☎ 01 739 6200)

SHER, Samuel Julius (Jules); QC (1981); s of Philip Sher (d 1985), and Isa Phyllis, *née* Hesselson; *b* 22 Oct 1941; *Educ* Athlone HS, Witwatersrand Univ SA (BCom, LLB), Oxford Univ (BCL); *m* 29 Aug 1965, Sandra, da of Michael Maris, of Johannesburg, SA; 1 s (Brian b 10 July 67), 2 da (Joanne b 8 Aug 69, Debby b 6 May 74); *Career* called to the Bar Inner Temple 1968, rec 1987, master of the bench of the Hon Soc of the Inner Temple 1988-; *Recreations* tennis; *Style—* Jules Sher, Esq, QC; 12 Constable Close, London NW11 (☎ 081 455 2753); 3 New Square, Lincoln's Inn, London WC2 (☎ 071 405 5296, fax 071 831 6803, telex 267 699 EQUITY)

SHERBORN, Derek Ronald; FSA (1960); s of Ronald Thorne Sherborn (d 1971), of Fawns Manor, Bedfont, Middx, and Evelyn May, *née* Allman (d 1982); *b* 7 May 1924; *Educ* Streatham GS, Streatham Hill Coll; *Career* investigator historic bldgs Miny of Town and Country Planning 1948, ret as princ inspr historic bldgs DOE and Historic Bldgs Cncl 1983; special interests: country houses and contents, historic parks and gdns, theatres, music halls, cinemas; various articles in Country Life and Architectural Review and elsewhere; memb: Ctee of Regency Soc of Brighton and Hove, Ctee of Friends of Brighton Pavilion; vice chm Conservation Areas Advsy Gp Brighton Cncl, pres Kingscliffe Soc, sr tstee Robert McKenzie Charitable Tst; FSA 1960; *Recreations* visiting country houses, churches, art exhibitions, auctions, theatre, opera, ballet; *Style—* Derek Sherborn, Esq, FSA; Bedfont House, 161 Marine Parade, Brighton, Sussex BN2 1EJ

SHERBORNE, Archdeacon of; *see*: Oliver, Ven John

SHERBORNE, Bishop of 1976-; Rt Rev John Dudley Galtrey Kirkham; s of Canon Charles Dudley Kirkham (d 1968), and late Doreen Betty, *née* Galtrey; *b* 20 Sept 1935; *Educ* Lancing, Trinity Coll Cambridge (BA, MA), Westcott House Theological Coll; *m* 1 Oct 1986, Hester Elizabeth Lockett Gregory, da of Reese Blake Lockett (d 1977), of Brenham, Texas, and wid of Thorne Gregory (d 1982); 1 step s (Thorne Gregory Jr), 3 step da (Hester Gregory Hodde, Wynne Gregory Dorsett, Anne Harrison Gregory); *Career* Cmmnd Royal Hampshire Regt 1954, Seconded to King's African Rifles 1955; asst curate St Mary le Tower Ipswich 1962-65, resident chaplain to Bishop of Norwich 1965-69, priest i/c Rockland St Mary With Hellington 1967-69, chaplain to Bishop of New Guinea 1967-70, asst priest St Martin in the Fields and St Margarets Westminster 1970-72, chaplain to Thames TV Euston Studios 1970-72, domestic chaplain to Archbishop of Canterbury 1972-76, Archbishop's advsr Headmasters' Conf; pres: Age Concern Dorset, Chaplains' Conf: memb Cncl: Wycombe Abbey Sch, St Luke's Hosp for the Clergy; govr: Canford Sch, Sherborne Sch for Girls; patron Dorset Assoc of Boys' Clubs; *Recreations* running, cross country skiing, woodwork; *Clubs* Army and Navy, Kandahar Ski; *Style—* The Rt Rev the Bishop of Sherborne; Little Bailie, Sturminster Marshall, Wimborne, Dorset BH21 4AD (☎ 0258 857659, fax 0258 857961)

SHEREK, Hon Mrs (Kathleen Pamela Mary Corona); *née* Boscawen; da of late 7 Viscount Falmouth, KCVO, CB; *b* 1902; *m* 1937, Maj Henry Sherek, Rifle Bde (d 1967); *Style—* The Hon Mrs Sherek; 89A Route de Florissant, 1206 Geneva, Switzerland

SHERFIELD, 1 Baron (UK 1964), of Sherfield-on-Loddon, Co Southampton; Roger Mellor Makins; GCB (1960, KCB 1953), GCMG (1955, KCMG 1949, CMG 1944), DL (Hants 1978); FRS (1986); s of Brig-Gen Sir Ernest Makins, KBE, CB, DSO (d 1959, n of Sir William Makins, 1 Bt), and Maria Florence, *née* Mellor; *b* 3 Feb 1904; *Educ* Winchester, Christ Church Oxford; *m* 30 April 1934, Alice (d 1985), da of Hon Dwight Filley Davis (d 1945), of Washington DC, USA; 2 s, 4 da; *Heir* s, Hon Christopher Makins; *Career* barr 1927; joined FO 1928, ambass to USA 1953-56, jt perm sec of Treasury 1956-60, chm UKAEA 1960-64, dir Times Newspapers Ltd 1964-67; sits as Ind peer in House of Lords; chm House of Lords Select Ctee on Sci and Technol 1984-87; memb Cncl Royal Albert Hall 1962-87; former chm: Industrial and Commercial Finance Corporation, Finance for Industry Ltd, Hill Samuel & Co Ltd, A C Cossor Ltd, Raytheon Europe International Co, Wells Fargo Ltd; fell: Winchester Coll 1962-79 (warden 1974-79) All Souls' Coll Oxford; chllr Reading Univ; hon student ChCh Oxford; chm Governing Body Imperial Coll of Science and Technol 1962-72; pres BSI 1970-73; Hon DCL Univ of Oxford, Hon LLD Univs of London and Sheffield, Hon DL Univ of Reading, Hon FICE; awarded RSA's Benjamin Franklin medal 1982; FRS 1986; *Clubs* Boodle's, Pratt's MCC; *Style—* The Rt Hon the Lord Sherfield, GCB, GCMG, DL, FRS; 81 Onslow Sq, London SW7 (☎ 071 589 6295); Ham Farm House, Ramsdell, nr Basingstoke, Hants RG2G 5SD (☎ 0734 813526)

SHERIDAN, Cecil Majella; CMG (1961); s of John Peter Sheridan (d 1959), of Liverpool, and Teresa, *née* Myerscough (d 1970); *b* 9 Dec 1911; *Educ* Ampleforth, Univ of Liverpool (Faculty of Law); *m* 19 Sept 1949, Monica, da of late Herbert Frank Ereaut, MBE, of St Helier, Jersey; 2 s (Richard b 1952, Michael b 1956), 1 da (Pauline b 1980); *Career* WWII: RAFVR 1940-41, cmmnd Pilot Offr 1941, instr Rhodesian Air Trg Gp 1941-42, RAF Tport Cmd 1943-45, Br Mil Admin Malaya 1945-46, demobbed Sqdn Ldr 1946; admitted slr 1934, slr in private practice 1934-40, attached to Colonial Office 1946, state legal advsr and dep public prosecutor Malayian Union and Fedn of Malaya 1946-55; Fedn of Malaya: legal draughtsman 1955-57, slr-gen 1957-59, attorney-gen 1959-63; attorney-gen Malaysia 1963, called to the Bar Inner Temple 1952, slr in private practice (assoc Stepherson Harwood) 1963-, dir Michael Sheridan & Co Ltd 1983-; chm: of traffic Cmmrs E Midlands 1965-81, Licensing Authy for Goods Vehicles E Midlands 1965-83; memb Nottingham Mechanics Inst; PMM Fedn of Malaya 1962; *Style—* C M Sheridan, Esq, CMG; 18 Private Rd, Sherwood, Nottingham NG5 4DB

SHERIDAN, Dinah Nadyejda (Mrs John Merivale); da of Fernard Archer Sheridan (d 1958), and Lisa Charlotte, *née* Everth (d 1966, both photographers by appt to HM The Queen and Queen Elizabeth The Queen Mother); *b* 17 Sept 1920; *Educ* Sherrards Wood Sch Welwyn Garden City, Italia Conti Stage Sch; *m* 1, 8 May 1942 (m dis 1952), Jimmy Hanley (d 1970); 1 s (Jeremy b 17 Nov 1945), 2 da (Carol Ann b and d June 1944, Jenny b 15 Aug 1947); m 2, 3 March 1954 (m dis 1965), Sir John Davis, *qv* ; m 3, 29 May 1986, John Herman Merivale, *qv*; *Career* actress; has made numerous stage, TV and film appearances; sister offr St John's Ambulance Bde; *Recreations* gardening, tapestry, cooking; *Style—* Miss Dinah Sheridan; 7A Berkeley Gardens, London W8

SHERIDAN, John Phillip; s of John David Hatton Sheridan (d 1987), of Beckenham, Kent, and Marjorie Eleanor, *née* Rich; *b* 18 Feb 1936; *Educ* Dulwich, Royal Veterinary Coll Univ of London (BVetMed); *m* 6 June 1960, Maureen Dorothy, da of William Alfred Sullivan (d 1984), of Hildenborough Kent; 1 s (Gavin b 1963), 2 da (Corinne b 1961, Bridie b 1966); *Career* gen vet practice: Fakenham Norfolk 1960-61, Reigate Surrey 1961-64, Southwick Sussex 1964; partnership then practice princ 1971-86, md Anicare Gp Servs (mgmnt servs to veterinary profession) 1976-; pres Br Small Animal Veterinary Assoc 1974-75, chm policy/resources W Sussex Co Cncl 1989-(memb 1976-, ldr 1984-89); memb: Sussex Police Authy 1985-, Arundel Castle Tstees 1988-; MRCVS 1960; *Recreations* skiing, sub aqua; *Style—* John Sheridan, Esq; High Banks, Bracken Lane, Storrington, Pulborough, W Sussex RH20 3HR (☎ 0903 745341); Anicare Group Services (Veterinary) Ltd, 23 Buckingham Rd, Shoreham by Sea, W Sussex BN4 5UA (☎ 0273 463 022, fax 0273 463 431)

SHERIDAN, Dr (Lionel Astor) Lee; s of Stanley Frederic Sheridan (d 1949), and Anne Agnes, *née* Quednau (d 1980); *b* 21 July 1927; *Educ* Whitgift Sch, Univ of London (LLB, LLD), Queens Univ Belfast (PhD); *m* 1 June 1948, Margaret Helen, da of Louis Charles Béghin (d 1961); 1 s (Peter b 1958), 1 da (Linda b 1955, d 1975); *Career* called to the Bar Lincoln's Inn 1948, prof of law Univ of Malaya Singapore 1956-63, prof of comparative law Queens Univ Belfast 1963-71, dep princ Univ Coll Cardiff 1977-80 (prof of law 1971-88, actg princ 1980 and 1987); chm NI Office of Law Reform Land Law Working Pty 1967-70; LLD Univ of Singapore 1963; *Books* Fraud in Equity (1957), Federation of Malaya Constitution (1961), Constitutional Protection: Expropriation and Restrictions on Property Rights (1963), The British Commonwealth: Malaya, Singapore, The Borneo Territories: The Development of their Laws and constitutions (1961), The Cy-Prés Doctrine (with V T H Delany, 1959), The Constitution of Malaysia (with H E Groves, 1987), Equity (with G W Keeton, 1987), The Modern Law of Charities (with G W Keeton, 1983), The Law of Trusts (1983), The Comparative Law of Trusts in the Commonwealth and the Irish Republic (1976), Digest of the English of Trusts (1979); *Recreations* walking, theatre going; *Clubs* Athenaeum; *Style—* Dr Lee Sheridan; Cherry Trees, Broadway Green, Vale of Glamorgan CF5 6SR (☎ 0446 760 403)

SHERIDAN, Paul Richard; TD 1982; s of Patrick William Sheridan, of Grimsby, and Claire Sheridan, JP, *née* Marklew (d 1990); *b* 19 July 1951; *Educ* Havelock Sch Grimsby, Grimsby Coll of Tech, Univ of Kent (BA); *m* 30 Jun 1985, Beverley, *née* Seagger; *Career* serves RCT TA, Maj 1985- (Cadet 1969, 2 Lt 1970, Lt 1972, Capt 1977); admitted slr 1979; ptnr Wilkin & Chapman 1982-, NP 1985; chm League of Friends of Grimsby Hosps 1985-88 (hon membership offr 1988-), Lord of the Manor of Aspenden Herts 1985; Freeman City of London 1985, Liveryman Worshipful Co of Carmen 1986; memb: Law Soc 1979 , Notaries Soc 1985; *Recreations* heraldry; *Clubs* Victory Services, London; *Style—* Paul R Sheridan, Esq, TD; 93 Scartho Rd, Grimsby, S Humberside DN33 2AE (☎ 0472 77 039); Wilkin & Chapman, The Hollies, 46 St Peter's Avenue, Cleethorpes, S Humberside DN35 8HR (☎ 0472 691 285, fax 0472 695 872)

SHERIDAN, Peter Warner Alexander; QC (1977); s of Hugo Sheridan (d 1973), of Park Rd, Regents Park, London, and Marie Sheridan (d 1927); *b* 29 May 1927; *Educ* Lincoln Coll Oxford (BA); *Career* called to the Bar Middle Temple 1954, Queen's Counsel 1977, master of the Bench 1988; *Recreations* sports cars, archery, radio, astronomy; *Style—* Peter Sheridan, Esq, QC; 17 Brompton Sq, London SW3 (☎ 071 584 7250); Pile Oak Lodge, Donhead-St-Andrew, Dorset; 2 Crown Office Row, The Temple, London EC4Y 7HJ (☎ 071 583 2681, fax 071 583 2850, telex 8955733 INLAWS)

SHERIDAN, Richard Jonathan; s of Dr Morris (Roger) Sheridan, of 15 The Brookdales, Bridge Lane, London NW11, and Yvonne, *née* Brook; *b* 20 Dec 1956; *Educ* City of London Sch, Guy's Hosp Med Sch Univ of London; *Career* Conslt obstetrician and gynaecologist Watford Gen Hosp; Freeman City of London, Liveryman Worshipful Soc of Apothecaries; MRCOG 1985, FRCS 1985; *Papers* Fertility in a Male with Trisomy 21 (1989); *Recreations* squash, skiing, riding; *Style—* Richard Sheridan, Esq; Christmas Cottage, Scatterdells Lane, Chipperfield, Hertfordshire WD4 9EZ (☎ 0923 264105); Watford General Hospital, Vicarage Rd, Watford (☎ 0923 244366)

SHERIDAN, Dr (Morris) Roger; JP; s of William Sheridan (d 1964), of London, and Rebecca Sheridan (d 1982); *b* 11 Nov 1923; *Educ* Central Fndn Sch, UCL, UCH Med Sch; *m* 3 July 1947, Yvonne Leila, da of Abraham Brook (d 1957), of London; 1 s (Richard Jonathan b 1956), 1 da (Amanda Jane b 1959); *Career* substantive Capt RAMC 1947-49, (ENT Surgn F East Land Forces, staff surgn Br Troops Austria); gen cmmr Taxes, dep chm Haringey Petty Sessional Area; divnl MO Br Boxing Bd of Control, former chm Local Med Ctee; former memb: Haringey DMT, NE Thames Med Advsy Ctee; Freeman City of London, Liveryman Worshipful Soc of Apothecaries of London; MRCS, LRCP, fell BMA, fell Hunterian and Harveian Soc; VMSP 1962; *Books* Really Nurse (1959), Wake up Nurse (1962); *Recreations* cricket, bridge; *Clubs* Bluc del Sol Calahonda; *Style—* Dr Roger Sheridan, JP; 15 The Brookdales, Bridge Lane, London NW11 9JU (☎ 081 455 8848)

SHERLAW-JOHNSON, Dr Robert; s of Robert Johnson (d 1980), and Helen Smith (d 1976); *b* 21 May 1932; *Educ* Gosforth GS Newcastle upon Tyne, Univ of Durham (BA, BMUS), Univ of Leeds (DMUS), Univ of Oxford (MA, DMUS); *m* 28 July 1959, Rachael Maria, da of Cyril Clarke (d 1974); 3 s (Christopher b 1962, Austin b 1964, Oliver b 1976), 2 da (Rebecca b 1960, Griselda b 1966); *Career* lectr in music Univ of Oxford; recordings (as pianist) of Catalogue D'Oiseaux, Br Messiaen (and other works), and later works by Liszt; composer of: 3 piano sonatas, piano concerto, clarinet concerto, Opera The Lambton Worm, Carmina Vernalia, 2 string quartets, various songs and other chamber works; *Books* Messiaen (1975, 2 edn 1989); *Recreations* collecting playing cards, croquet; *Style*— Dr Robert Sherlaw-Johnson; Malton Croft, Woodlands Rise, Stonesfield, Oxon (☎ 099 389 318); Worcester College, Oxford (☎ 0865 278342); Faculty of Music, St Aldates, Oxford (☎ 0865 276125)

SHERLOCK, Dr Alexander; CBE (1989); s of Thomas Sherlock, MM (d 1971), of Bognor Regis, Sussex, and Evelyn Mary, *née* Alexander (d 1990); *b* 14 Feb 1922; *Educ* Magdalen Coll Sch Oxford, Stowmarket GS, London Hosp (MB BS 1945); *m* 1, 24 March 1945, Clarice Constance (Peggy) (d 1975), da of Edward G Scarff (d 1976), of Stowmarket, Suffolk; 1 s (Jim b 18 Feb 1951), 2 da (Penny b 10 March 1946, Clare b 6 March 1960), 1 step da (Sandra b 18 Aug 1948); m 2, 1976, Eileen, da of Leslie Hall (d 1976), of Bawtry; *Career* Flt Lt RAF 1946-48; med practitioner and conslt 1948-79; called to the Bar Gray's Inn 1961; asst dep coroner St Pancras 1971-72; memb: Felixstone UDC 1960-74, E Suffolk CC 1966-74, Suffolk CC 1974-79; MEP (EDG) S W Essex 1979-89;; chm Fire and Public Protection Ctee 1977-79; vice-pres: Assoc of Dist Cncls, Inst of Environmental Health Offrs, Trading Standards Inst; OStJ 1974; FRSA 1987; *Recreations* walking, gardening; *Clubs* RAF, Royal Belgian Automobile; *Style*— Dr Alexander Sherlock, CBE; 58 Orwell Road, Felixstowe, Suffolk IP11 7PS (☎ 0394 284503)

SHERLOCK, (Edward) Barry Orton; CBE (1991); s of Victor Edward Sherlock (d 1973); *b* 10 Feb 1932; *Educ* Merchant Taylors', Pembroke Coll Cambridge (MA); *m* 1955, Lucy Trerice, da of Prof Basil Willey (d 1978); 2 da; *Career* dir, gen mangr and actuary The Equitable Life Assurance Society, chm Lautro 1986-; FIA; *Recreations* music; *Style*— Barry Sherlock, Esq, CBE; 63 Sunnyfield, London NW7 4RE (☎ 081 959 5193)

SHERLOCK, Nigel; s of Horace Sherlock (d 1967), and Dorothea, *née* Robinson (d 1980); *b* 12 Jan 1940; *Educ* Barnard Castle Sch, Univ of Nottingham (BA); *m* 3 Sept 1966, Helen Diana Frances, da of M Sigmund; 2 s (Andrew b July 1968, Mark b 7 July 1976), 1 da (Emma b 5 Sept 1970); *Career* stockbroker; dir Wise Speke Ltd; High Sheriff of Tyne and Wear 1990-91; memb: Cncl Univ of Newcastle, Cncl St John's Coll Univ of Durham, Bishops Cncl Dio of Newcastle; chm: Northern Sinfonia Orchestra, Northumberland Co Scout Assoc; Freeman City of Newcastle Upon Tyne; AMSIA 1972, FBIM 1985; *Recreations* the countryside; *Clubs* New (assoc memb, Edinburgh), Northern Counties (Newcastle); *Style*— Nigel Sherlock, Esq; 14 North Ave, Gosforth, Newcastle Upon Tyne NE3 4DS (☎ 091 2854379); Commercial Union House, 39 Pilgrim St, Newcastle Upon Tyne NE1 6RQ (☎ 091 2611266)

SHERLOCK, Prof Dame Sheila Patricia Violet; DBE (1978); da of Samuel Philip Sherlock (d 1979), and Violet Mary Catherine Beckett (d 1969); *b* 31 March 1918; *Educ* Folkestone Co Sch, Univ of Edinburgh (MD), Yale; *m* 1951, David Geraint James; 2 da (Amanda, Auriole); *Career* physician and lectr in med Postgrad Medical Sch of London 1948-59, prof of med Univ of London Royal Free Hosp Sch of Med 1959-83; Rockfeller fell Yale; memb Senate Univ of London 1976-81, sr censor and vice-pres Royal Coll of Physicians of London 1976-77; Hon MD: Lisbon, Oslo, Leuven 1985; Hon LLD Aberdeen 1982; Hon DSc: City Univ (NY), Yale 1983, Univ of Edinburgh 1985, Univ of London 1989; Hon FACP, Hon FRCP (C), Hon FRCP (I), Hon FRCP (Glasgow), Hon FRCS; FRCP, FRCPEd, FRACP; *Books* Diseases of the Liver and Biliary System (8 edn, 1985); *Recreations* cricket, travel; *Style*— Prof Dame Sheila Sherlock, DBE; 41 York Terrace East, London NW1 4PT (☎ 071 486 4560); Royal Free Hospital, London NW3 2QG (☎ 071 431 4589)

SHERMAN, Sir Alfred; s of Jacob Vladimir Sherman, and Eva, *née* Goldental; *b* 10 Nov 1919; *Educ* Hackney Downs Co Secdy Sch, LSE (BSc); *m* 1958, Zahava, *née* Levin; 1 s; *Career* journalist and public affrs advsr, leader writer Daily Telegraph, conslt; co fndr (with Sir Keith Joseph, MP, and Mrs Margaret Thatcher, MP) Centre For Policy Studies 1974, Speed writer and aide to Mrs Thatcher 1974-83; kt 1983; *Clubs* Reform, Hurlingham; *Style*— Sir Alfred Sherman; 10 Gerald Rd, London SW1 (☎ 071 730 2838)

SHERMAN, Sir Lou (Louis); OBE (1967), JP (Inner London); *m* Sally, CBE, JP; *Career* chm Housing Corpn 1977-80, dep chm Harlow Dvpt Corpn, initiator Lea Valley Regnl Park Authy; kt 1975; *Style*— Sir Lou Sherman, OBE, JP

SHERRARD, Michael David; QC (1968); s of Morris Sherrard (d 1965), and Ethel, *née* Werbner (d 1983); *b* 23 June 1928; *Educ* Kings Coll London (LLB); *m* 6 April 1952, Shirley, da of Maurice Bagrit (d 1973); 2 s (Nicholas b 9 June 1953, Jonathan b 5 Aug 1957); *Career* called to the Bar Middle Temple 1949, memb Winn Ctee on Personal Injury Litigation 1966-68, rec Crown Ct 1974-, master of the Bench Middle Temple 1977, bench rep on Senate 1978-80, inspr Dept of Trade under Companies Acts (London Capital Gp) 1975-77; chm Normansfield Hosp Public Inquiry 1977-78, memb Bar Assoc of City of NY; contrib British Accounting Standards - The First 10 years (1981); *Recreations* travel, listening to opera, oriental art; *Style*— Michael Sherrard Esq, QC; Flat 15, 55 Portland Place, London W1N 3AH (☎ 071 255 1513); Crooked Beams, 4 Church Road, Alderton, Glos; 2 Crown Office Row, Temple, London EC4Y 7HJ (☎ 071 583 2681, fax 071 583 2850)

SHERRARD, Simon Patrick; s of Patrick Sherrard, and Angela Beatrice, *née* Stacey (d 1988); *b* 22 Sept 1947; *Educ* Eton; *m* 23 Aug 1975, Sara Anne, da of Maj Peter Pain Stancliffe, MBE; 1 s (James b 19 Oct 1984), 3 da (Emma b 11 Jan 1977, Kate b 4 Aug 1978, Polly b 6 April 1983); *Career* Samuel Montagu & Co Ltd 1968-74, Jardine Matheson & Co Ltd Hong Kong 1974-84, md Bibby Line Group Ltd Liverpool 1985-; *Recreations* tennis, farming; *Clubs* White's, MCC, I Zingari; *Style*— Simon Sherrard, Esq; Bibby Line Group Ltd, Norwich House, Water Street, Liverpool L2 8VW (☎ 051 236 0492, fax 051 236 1163, telex 629241 PATROL G, car 0836 263156)

SHERRIN, Ned (Edward George); s of Thomas Adam Sherrin (d 1965), of Lower Farm, Kingweston, Somerset, and Dorothy Finch, *née* Drewett (d 1974); *b* 18 Feb 1931; *Educ* Sexey's Bruton, Exeter Coll Oxford (MA); *Career* 2 Lt Royal Corps of Signals 1949-51; called to the Bar Gray's Inn; prodr, dir, presenter and writer for film, theatre, radio and TV; ATV 1956-58, BBC 1958-65 (TW3, Tonight); films incl: The Virgin Soldiers (1967), The National Health (1972); theatre includes: Side by Side by Sondheim, Jeffrey Bernard is Unwell, The Mitford Girls, Sing a Rude Song, Mr and Mrs Nobody, Ratepayers Iolanthe, Metropolitan Mikado, Bookends, Victor Spinetti's Private Diary; radio: Loose Ends; *Books* Cindy Ella or I Gotta Shoe, Rappell 1910, Benbow Was His Name, A Small Thing Like an Earthquake (autobiography), Cutting Edge, Loose Neds; *Recreations* eating, theatre; *Clubs* Groucho; *Style*— Ned Sherrin, Esq

SHERRINGTON, Prof David; s of James Arthur Sherrington, KSG (d 1986), of Middlesborough, Cleveland, and Elfreda, *née* Cameron; *b* 29 Oct 1941; *Educ* St Mary's Coll Middlesbrough, Univ of Manchester (BSc, PhD); *m* 20 July 1966, Margaret, da of Richard Gee-Colough (d 1980), of Blackpool, Lancashire; 1 s (Andrew b 20 Feb 1967), 1 da (Lesley Jane b 14 Jan 1971); *Career* lectr in theoretical physics Univ of Manchester 1967-69 (asst lectr 1964-67), prof of physics Imperial Coll London 1983-89 (lectr in theoretical solid state physics 1969-74, reader 1974-83), Wykeham prof of physics Univ of Oxford 1989-; jls ed: Communications on Physics 1975-78, Advances in Physics 1984-, Journal of Physics A: Mathematical and General 1989-; contrib many articles in scientific jls; fell New Coll Oxford 1989-; hon MA Univ of Oxford 1989; FInstP 1974, fell American Physical Soc 1984; *Books* Phase Transitions in Soft Condensed Matter (co-ed, 1989); *Style*— Prof David Sherrington; Theoretical Physics, Univ of Oxford, 1 Keble Rd, Oxford OX1 3NP (☎ 0865 273952, fax 0865 273418, telex 83295 NUCLOX G)

SHERRY, Neil; s of Ronald Sherry (d 1966), and Sherry, *née* Warwick; *b* 7 May 1947; *m* 1967, Margaret Helen, da of Harry Wolfenden (d 1979); 1 s (Thomas b 1970), 2 da (Elizabeth b 1972, Helen b 1981); *Career* Crane Wood 1965-66, Farmers 1966-67, Brunning Group 1967-71, Stowe Bowden 1971-75, Brockie Haslam Ltd 1975-79, Ingham Middleton Dicks Maud Ltd 1979-81, Baglow Harris Sherry & Partners Ltd 1981-83, Baglow Sherry & Partners Ltd 1983-90, chm Crescent Advertising & Marketing Ltd; MIPA, FInstD; *Style*— Neil Sherry, Esq; Croft House, Weaverham Rd, Sandiway, Cheshire (☎ 0606 883151); 22-23 The Crescent, Salford, Manchester M5 4PF (☎ 061 736 9696)

SHERRY, Prof Norman; s of Michael Sherry, and Sarah, *née* Taylor; *b* 6 July 1935; *Educ* Univ of Durham (BA), Univ of Singapore (PhD); *m* June 1960, Dulcie Sylvia, da of Samuel William Brunt; *Career* lectr in English lit, Univ of Singapore 1961-66, lectr and sr lectr Univ of Liverpool 1966-70, prof of English Univ of Lancaster 1970-82, Mitchell Distinguished prof of literature Trinity Univ San Antonia Texas 1983-; fell Humanities Res Center N Carolina 1982; FRSL 1986; *Books* Conrad's Eastern World (1966), Jane Austen (1966), Charlotte and Emily Bronte (1969), Conrad's Western World (1971), Conrad and His World (1972), Conrad; The Critical Heritage (1973), Conrad in Conference (1976), The Life of Graham Green Vol One 1904-39 (1989); ed Conrad Edns: Lord Jim (1967, 1974), An Outpost of Progress, Heart of Darkness (1973), Nostromo (1974), The Secret Agent (1974), The Nigger of The Narcissus, Typhoon, Falk and Other Stories (1975); contrib: The Academic American Encyclopedia, Guardian, Daily Telegraph, Oxford Magazine, Modern Language Review, Review of English Studies, Notes and Queries; BBC book contrib: Kenneth Muir Festschrift (1987), Creativity (1989); TV and radios; Conrad and His Critics BBC Radio 3 1981, film on Graham Greene Arena BBC TV 1989; *Recreations* talking, writing, reading, public speaking, jogging, weight training, table tennis; *Clubs* Savile; *Style*— Prof Norman Sherry

SHERSBY, (Julian) Michael; MP (C) Uxbridge 1983-; s of William Henry, and Elinor Shersby; *b* 17 Feb 1933; *Educ* John Lyon Sch Harrow on the Hill; *m* 1958, Barbara Joan, da of John Henry Barrow; 1 s, 1 da; *Career* MP (C): Uxbridge 1972-; PPS to Min of State for Aerospace and Shipping 1973-74; jt sec Cons Party Indust Ctee 1973-74, chm Cons Party Trade Ctee 1974-76 (vice chm 1977-79), jt sec Parly and Scientific Ctee 1977-80 (vice pres 1981-83); vice chm: Cons Party Environment Ctee 1979-83, Cons Party Smaller Businesses Ctee 1979-80; chm Cons Party Food and Drink Industs Sub Ctee 1976-89; memb: CPA Delgn to Caribbean 1976, Br Parly Delgn to UN 1978, UK Delgn to Cwlth Parly Conf 1973, 1985 and 1990, Exec Ctee UK Branch CPA 1988-, Br American Parly Gp Delgn to Washington 1990, Speaker's Panel of Dep Chairmen of the House 1983-, Select Ctee of Public Accounts 1983-; Parly advsr to Police Fedn of Eng and Wales 1989-; memb: Paddington Borough Cncl 1959-64, Westminster City Cncl 1964-71 (chm children's ctee 1964-67); dir The Sugar Bureau 1966-67 (dir gen 1977-88), sec UK Sugar Indust Assoc 1978-88; memb Court Brunel Univ 1975-, pres London Green Belt Cncl 1989-, tstee Harefield Heart Transplant Tst 1989-; *Recreations* theatre, travel; *Clubs* Carlton, Conservative (Uxbridge); *Style*— Michael Shersby, Esq, MP; House of Commons, London SW1A 0AA (☎ 071 219 3000); constituency office: 36 Harefield Rd, Uxbridge, Middx (☎ 0895 39465)

SHERSTON-BAKER, Sir Robert George Humphrey; 7 Bt (GB 1796), of Dunstable House, Richmond, Surrey; o s of Sir Humphrey Dodington Benedict Sherston Sherston-Baker, 6 Bt (d 1990), and Margaret Alice, *née* Binns; *b* 3 April 1951; *Heir* kinsman, Maj Peter Baker, MC b 1918; *Style*— Sir Robert Sherston-Baker, Bt; 22 Frognal Court, London NW3

SHERWANI, Imran Ahmed Khan; s of Asrar Ahmed Khan Sherwani, and June, *née* Hassell; *b* 9 April 1962; *Educ* Edward Orme HS, Stoke-on-Trent Sixth Form Coll; *m* 22 Oct 1988, Louise Karen, da of Rex Nadine; 1 s (Aaron Imran Khan b 1 Sept 1990); *Career* hockey player; former memb N Staffs Hockey Club then Stone Hockey Club, currently Stourport Hockey Club; England and GB int (former schoolboy and jr int); honours: Silver medal World Cup 1986, Gold medal Olypic Games Seoul 1988; police constable 1981-85, newsagent 1985-, hockey specialist retailer 1990-; Access Men of the Year 1988; *Recreations* all sports; *Style*— Imran Sherwani, Esq; c/o The Hockey Association, 16 Northdown St, London N1 9BG

SHERWEN, J Timothy R; s of A R Sherwen, of Correnden, Dry Hill Park Rd, Tonbridge, Kent, and Catherine Joyce Sherwen (d 1982); *b* 21 Nov 1937; *Educ* Tonbridge, Selwyn Coll Cambridge (BA); *m* 1969, Mary Christiane, da of Gerald Charles Stokes (d 1980); 1 s; *Career* md: Thomas Nelson & Sons Ltd 1982, Linguaphone Gp 1986; dir Centaur Communications Ltd 1989, chm Linguaphone Inst Ltd 1990; Parly candidate Faversham 1979; *Recreations* sailing, music (eighteenth century wind music); *Style*— Timothy Sherwen, Esq; Linguaphone Institute Ltd, St Giles House, 50 Poland St, London W1V 4AX (☎ 071 439 4222, fax 071 734 0469, telex 261352)

SHERWOOD, Dr Anthea Joy; da of Antony Hugh William Sherwood (d 1963), and Gladys Lilian, *née* Spackman (d 1968); *b* 21 July 1949; *Educ* Crediton HS for Girls, Univ Coll London (BSc), Univ Coll Hosp Med Sch (MB BS); *m* 10 April 1979, Evan Richard Llewelyn Davies, s of David Ronald Davies, of Newland Farm, Withypool, Somerset; 2 s (Huw b 1982, Owen b 1985); *Career* John Marshall fell; lectr and registrar Inst of Child Health and GOS, lectr and sr registrar UCH 1978-79, registrar in histopathology Plymouth Hosp 1979-81, conslt histopathologist Torbay Hosp 1981-87, conslt histopathologist Derriford Hosp 1987-; hon conslt histopathologist to the RN; cncl memb Assoc Clinical Pathologists; memb: BMA Pathology Soc, IAP; MRCPath 1980; *Recreations* gardening, family life; *Clubs* Ivybridge Leisure Centre; *Style*— Dr Anthea Sherwood; The Department of Histopathology, Derriford Hospital, Derriford Rd, Plymouth (☎ 0752 792352)

SHERWOOD, (Robert) Antony Frank; CMG (1981); s of Frank Henry Sherwood (d 1964), and Mollie, *née* Moore (d 1952); *b* 29 May 1923; *Educ* Christs Hosp, St Johns Coll Oxford (MA); *m* 21 Nov 1953, Margaret Elizabeth, da of Frank Ratcliffe Simpson (d 1979); 2 s (Simon b 1956, Jeremy b 1957), 2 da (Deborah b 1954, Harriet b 1958); *Career* RAF 1942-46; Br Cncl 1949-81: serv Turkey, Nigeria (twice), Syria, Uganda, Somalia, UK, ret as asst dir gen 1981; Help The Aged: chm International Ctee 1988- (memb 1982-), tstee 1988; ed Directory of Statutory and Voluntary Health Social and Welfare Servs in Surrey 1986 and 87; memb Mgmnt Ctee and Fin Ctee Guildford Inst Univ of Surrey; *Recreations* reading, travel, genealogy; *Style*— Antony Sherwood, CMG; 18 Rivermount Gardens, Guildford, Surrey GU2 5DN (☎ 0483 38277)

SHERWOOD, The Bishop of, The Rt Rev Harold Richard Darby; s of William Darby (d 1978), and Miriam, *née* Jephcott (d 1936); *b* 28 Feb 1919; *Educ* Cathedral Sch Shanghai, St John's Coll Durham (BA); *m* 3 Sept 1949, Audrey Elizabeth Lesley, da of Charles Leslie (d 1968); 2 s (John b 1953, Mark b 1964), 3 da (Jane b 1950, Anne b 1955, Mary b 1959); *Career* WWII 1939-45 Army, serv Far East (POW)

1941-45; Thomson & Co chartered accountants Shanghai and Hong Kong 1936-39; Hong Kong Govt revenue dept 1939; deacon, priest 1951; curate of: Leyton 1950-52, Harlow 1952-53; vicar of: Shrub End Colchester 1953-59, Waltham Abbey Essex 1959-70, dean of Battle 1970-75, consecrated bishop of Sherwood in York Minster 1975; *Recreations* vintage motoring; *Style*— The Rt Rev Harold Sherwood; Applegarth, Halam, Newark, Notts NG22 8AN (☎ 0636 814041)

SHERWOOD, James Blair; s of William Earl, and Florence Balph Sherwood; *b* 8 Aug 1933; *Educ* Yale Univ (BA); *m* 31 Dec 1977, Shirley Angela, da of Geoffrey Masser Briggs, of The Garden House, Hinton Manor, Hinton Waldrist, Oxon; 2 step s (Charles Nigel Cross b 1959, Simon Michael Cross b 1960); *Career* Lt US Naval Reserve 1955-58; pres Sea Containers Ltd; chm Orient-Express Hotels Ltd; proprietor Illustrated London News; *Recreations* tennis, skiing, sailing; *Clubs* Pilgrims, Mory's, Hurlingham, Mark's; *Style*— James Sherwood, Esq; (☎ 071 928 6969)

SHERWOOD, John Herman Mulso; s of Rev Edward Charles Sherwood (d 1946), and Naomi Claire, *née* Flecker (d 1936); *Educ* Marlborough, Oriel Coll Oxford (open scholar, BA); *m* 1952, Joan Mary, *née* Yorke; 1 da (b 13 Oct 1954); *Career* Intelligence Corps 1940-45; control cmmn for Germany 1945-46, BBC 1946-73 (head of French Service 1963-73); author of 18 crime novels incl: A Botanist at Bay (1987), The Mantrap Garden (1986), Flowers of Evil (1987), Menacing Groves (1988), A Bouquet of Thorns (1989), The Sunflower Plot (1990); memb: Detection Club 1957, CWA 1960, Soc of Authors 1976; *Recreations* gardening, crime writing; *Clubs* Oriental; *Style*— John Sherwood, Esq; Northend Cottage, 36 The High St, Charing, Ashford, Kent TN27 0HX (☎ 023 371 3226)

SHERWOOD, Kenneth Alan; s of Frederick Sherwood (d 1950), of Pinner, and Winifred Edith Maud, *née* White (d 1987); *b* 20 May 1935; *Educ* Merchant Taylors'; *m* 18 Feb 1961, Jennifer Edith, da of Geoffrey Higginson Allard (d 1986), of Watford; 1 s (Graham b 1961), 2 da (Heather b 1964, Frances b 1966); *Career* ptnr Kidsons Impey (formerly Hodgson Impey & Co) chartered accountants 1968- (nat tech ptnr 1978-, dir of professional servs 1990-); memb Cncl ICAEW 1977-83, pres AAT 1988-89 (memb Cncl 1983-91), chm ICAEW Ctee on Housing Assocs 1976-, hon treas Notting Hill Housing Tst 1988-91, chm Hightown Housing Assoc 1990- (memb Ctee 1980-), vice chm Berkhamsted Town Hall Tst 1986-90, chm Berkhamsted Citizens Assoc 1974-76; *Recreations* gardening, walking, reading, theatre, local community gps; *Clubs* Chartered Accountant Dining, Old Merchant Taylors' Soc; *Style*— Kenneth Sherwood, Esq; Rhenigidale, Ivy House Lane, Berkhamsted, Herts HP4 2PP (☎ 0442 865158); Kidsons Impey, Spectrum House, 20-26 Cursitor Street, London EC4A 1HY (☎ 071 405 2088, fax 071 831 2206)

SHERWOOD, Hon Mrs (Lucy Jane); *née* Hamilton-Russell; da of 10 Viscount Boyne, JP, DL; *b* 13 Sept 1961; *m* 1, 1983 (m dis 1986), Patrick James Bailey, yst s of Sir Derrick Thomas Louis Bailey, 3 Bt, *qv*; m 2, 29 Sept 1989, Simon E H Sherwood, s of Nathaniel Edward Carwardine Sherwood, of Prested Hall, Kelvedon, Essex; *Style*— The Hon Mrs Sherwood; Summer Down, East Ilsley, nr Newbury, Berks

SHERWOOD, Oliver Martin Carwardine; s of Nathaniel Edward Carwardine Sherwood, of Easthorpe nr Colchester Essex, and Heather Patricia Motion, *née* Carolin; *b* 23 March 1955; *Educ* Radley; *m* 20 Oct 1981, M Denise Fiona, da of Fred T Winter; 1 s (Peter Frederick Carwardine b 27 Oct 1986), 1 da (Davina Ruth b 7 July 1984); *Career* racehorse trainer; asst trainer to: G Pritchard-Gordon Newmarket 1975-76, Arthur Moore Ireland 1976-79, Fred Winter Lambourn 1979-84; racehorse trainer Rhonehurst Upper Lambourn 1984-; trained 250 winners incl winners of: EBF Novice Hurdle Final Cheltenham 1986, Glenlivet Hurdle Liverpool 1987, Sun Alliance Novices Hurdle Cheltenham 1987 and 1988, Sun Alliance Novices Steeplechase Cheltenham 1988, Bic Razor Gold Cup Handicap Hurdle Lingfield 1989, Rapid Raceline Scottish Champion Hurdle Ayr 1989, Gerry Fielden Hurdle Newbury 1989, Charles Heidsieck Champagne Bula Hurdle Newbury 1989, New Year's Day Hurdle Windsor 1990, ASW Hurdle Ascot 1990, Ekbalco Handicap Hurdle Newcastle 1990, Hennessy Cognac Gold Cup Steeplechase Newbury 1990, Tingle Creek Handicap Chase Sandown 1990, Baring Securities Tolworth Hurdle Sandown 1990, First Nat Steeplechase Ascot 1990; champion amateur rider (ridden 95 winners incl 3 Nat Hunt Cheltenham Festival winners); *Recreations* shooting, cricket; *Style*— Oliver Sherwood, Esq; Rhonehurst, Upper Lambourn, nr Newbury, Berkshire RG16 7RG (☎ 0488 71411)

SHETH, Pranlal; s of Purashotam Virji Sheth (d 1936), and Sakarben Sheth (d 1985); *b* 20 Dec 1924; *m* 1951, Indumati, da of Dr Chaganlal Druva (d 1958); 1 s (Sunil), 1 da (Vandna); *Career* journalist Kenya 1943-52, chm Nyanza Farmers Co-op Soc 1954-60, called to the Bar Lincoln's Inn 1962; memb: Central Agric Bd Kenya 1963-66, Econ Planning and Devpt Cncl Kenya 1964-66; dep chm Asian Hosp Authy 1964-66; chief ed Gujararat Samacher Weekly 1972-73; dir: Abbey Life Assur Co Ltd 1974-88, Ambassador Life Assurance Co Ltd 1980-88, Abbey Life Assurance (Ireland) Ltd 1981-85; legal dir Hartford Europe Gp of cos 1977-86, gp sec ITT gp of cos in UK 1983-86, dep chm CRE 1977-80; sec Abbey Life Gp plc (dir 23 companies within the gp); chm Abbey Ethical Unit Tst Advsy Bd; vice pres UK Immigrants Advsy Serv 1986-; memb: N Metropolitan Conciliation Ctee Race Rels Bd 1973-77, BBC Consultative Gp on Industry and Business Affrs 1986-89, IBA 1990-, Independent TV Cmmn 1990-, shop and premises ctee Oxfam 1988-; tstee: Project Fullemploy (charitable tst) 1977-89, Sangam 1979-, Runnymede Tst 1987-, Urban Tst 1987-, Shelter 1989-90, Womankind Worldwide 1988-; Windsor Fellowship 1987-; dir: Roundhouse Arts Centre 1986-, Reed Executive plc 1990-; patron Int Centre for Child Studies, vice patron UK Assoc Int Year of the Child 1978-80; hon legal advsr and memb exec and gen cncls Nat Assoc of Victim Support Schemes 1988-; govr Poly of N London 1979-; FInstD, FBIM; *Recreations* music, theatre, sports, literature; *Clubs* Royal Over-Seas League, Scribes, Cwlth Tst; *Style*— P Sheth, Esq; 70 Howberry Rd, Edgware, Middx (☎ 081 952 2413)

SHEW, Edmund Jeffrey; s of Edmund Robert Shew (d 1952), of Herefordshire, and Dorothy May, *née* Teague (d 1988); *b* 23 Dec 1936; *Educ* Rossall Sch Fleetwood; *m* 1, 24 June 1960 (m dis); 1 s Michael b 14 June 1962), 1 da (Dorothy b 19 May 1966); m 2, 21 Nov 1987, Vivien Dawn, da of Meirion Jones; *Career* Nat Serv RAF 1960-62; articled clerk 1954-59, ptnr Stanley Marsh & Co CAs St Helens 1962-66, princ Edmund Shew & Co CA St Helens 1966-; pres Liverpool Soc of CAs 1983-84, memb Cncl ICAEW 1989-; memb Worshipful Co of CAs in Eng and Wales, Freeman City of London; FCA (ACA 1960), ATII 1963, FCCA 1983, FBIM 1986; *Recreations* St Helens & Dist Scout Assoc (sec), classical music, gardening, art, theatre, agriculture; *Style*— Edmund Shew, Esq; 46 Crank Rd, Billinge, nr Wigan, Lancs WN5 7EZ (☎ 0744 895361); 8 Le Golf, Gros Bissinges, 74500 Evian-les-Bains, France (☎ 50 75 27 91); Edmund Shew & Co, 35 Westfield St, St Helens, Merseyside WA10 1QD (☎ 0744 30888, fax 0744 451785)

SHEWEN, Lt-Col Antony Gordon Mansel; s of Lt-Col Douglas Gordon Mansel Shewen (d 1982), of Ipplepen, Devon, and Margaret Evelyn, *née* Walker (d 1979); *b* 7 Oct 1927; *Educ* Sherborne, Ch Ch Oxford, RMA Sandhurst; *m* 17 May 1958, Rosemary Margaret, da of Dudley Frederick Oliphant Dangar, of Dittisham; 1 s (Christopher b 1959), 2 da (Celia b 1963, Laura b 1967); *Career* serv in RHA The Queen's Bays, Queen's Dragoon Guards, Malaya 1964, Aden 1967 (despatches); seconded Cabinet Office 1969-71; memb Trg Ctee The Pony Club, Clerk of the Course Taunton; *Recreations* horses, hunting, racing, farming; *Style*— Lt-Col Antony G M Shewen; Myrtle Farm, Bickenhall, Taunton, Somerset (☎ 0823 480656); Taunton Racecourse (☎ 0823 337172)

SHIACH, Allan George; s of Maj Gordon Leslie Shiach, WS (d 1948), and Lucie Sybil, *née* de Freitas; *b* 16 Sept 1941; *Educ* Gordonstoun, McGill Univ (BA); *m* 12 Nov 1966, Kathleen Beaumont, da of Richard B Swarbreck (d 1977), of Rhodesia; 2 s (Dominic Leslie b 1967, Luke Allan b 1974), 1 da (Philippa Lucie b 1969); *Career* chm Macallan-Glenlivet plc 1980- (dep chm 1978-80); dir: Rafford Films Ltd 1984-, Whitegate Leisure plc 1988-; screenwriter/producer 1970-; writer/co-writer: Don't Look Now 1975, Castaway 1985, The Girl from Petrovka 1978, DARYL 1984, Tenebrae 1982, Joseph Andrews 1979, The Witches 1988, Cold Heaven 1990, and others; memb: BBC Broadcasting Cncl (Scotland), Cncl of Scotch Whisky Assoc; chm Writers Guild of GB; Freeman City of London 1988, Liveryman Worshipful Co of Distillers; BAFTA, WGA, AIP; *Clubs* Savile; *Style*— Allan Shiach, Esq; 1 Hereford Square, London SW7 4TT (☎ 071 370 2694, fax 071 373 4044)

SHIACH, Sheriff Gordon Iain Wilson; s of John Crawford Shiach (d 1978), and Florence Bygott, *née* Wilson; *b* 15 Oct 1935; *Educ* Gordonstoun, Univ of Edinburgh (MA, LLB); *m* 1962, Margaret Grant, da of Donald Duff Smith, of Grantown-on-Spey; 2 da (Katherine, Alison); *Career* advocate 1960-72 (Edinburgh); Sheriff: Fife and Kinross at Dunfermline 1972-79, Lothian and Borders at Linlithgow 1979-84, Lothian and Borders at Edinburgh 1984-; *Recreations* walking, swimming, music, art, theatre; *Clubs* New (Edinburgh); *Style*— Sheriff Gordon Shiach; Sheriffs' Chambers, Sheriff Ct House, Lawnmarket, Edinburgh EH1 2NS (☎ 031 226 7181)

SHIATIS, Michael; s of Avraam Constantine (d 1974), and Kalliopi Avraam; *b* 18 May 1934; *Educ* Pancyprian Gymneseum Cyprus, Inst of Chartered Accountants; *m* 31 March 1964, Helena Joyce, da of Symeon Michael Pittas, of London; 2 s (Constantine Michael b 1965, Andreas Michael b 1966), 1 da (Christina Helena b 1970); *Career* CA; dir: M A S Enterprises Ltd, Skilful Finance Ltd, Europafrica Ltd, Ion Finance (London) Ltd, Earnison Hldgs plc, Guestguard Ltd, Guestlock Ltd, Guestcare Ltd, Free Trade Warf Ltd, Feiser Ltd, Corintia Court Properties Ltd; FCA, ATII, AM, MBIM, MInstD; *Recreations* jogging, shooting, walking; *Style*— Michael Shiatis, Esq; 23 Craven Terrace, Lancaster Gate W2 3QH (☎ 071 262 9324); work: (☎ 071 402 2223, telex LONDON 22359)

SHIELD, Dr Michael James; s of Joseph Wishart Shield, DSC, and Phyllis Mabel Rosina Liffin, *née* Bullivant; *b* 17 Oct 1949; *Educ* Cheltenham, Univ of London, Middx Hosp Med Sch (MB BS, MRCPath); *m* 27 March 1976, Amelia Joan, da of Leyshon Edward Thomas (d 1952); 1 s (James b 1981), 1 da (Zabrina b 1983); *Career* sr lectr and hon conslt microbiologist St Mary's Hosp 1980-81, dir Med Dept UK and Republic of Ireland G D Searle & Co Ltd UK 1986-; *Recreations* golf, photography, travel, house renovation; *Style*— Dr Michael Shield, Esq; G D Searle & Co, PO Box 53, Lane End Rd, High Wycombe, Bucks HP12 4HL (☎ 0494 21124)

SHIELDS, Elizabeth Lois; da of Thomas Henry Teare (d 1977), and Dorothy Emma Elizabeth, *née* Roberts-Lawrence (d 1977); *b* 27 Feb 1928; *Educ* Whyteleafe Girls' GS Surrey, UCL (BA), Univ of York (MA); *m* 12 Aug 1961, David Cathro Shields, s of Arthur William Strachan Shields; *Career* teacher: classics at St Philomena's Carshalton, Jersey Coll for Girls, St Swithun's Winchester, Trowbridge HS, Queen Ethelburga', Harrogate, Malton Sch; lectr Hull Univ 1989-; memb Lib Dem, cncllr Ryedale DC May 1980, MP (SLDP) Ryedale May 1986-June 1987, re-selected prospective Parly candidate Ryedale; chm: Rydale Dist Cncl 1989-90, Rydale Housing Assoc 1990-, Malton Sch PTA, govrs Langton CP Sch; govrs memb Norton Sch, patron Malton and Norton Boys' Club; *Clubs* Nat Lib, Ryedale House; *Style*— Mrs Elizabeth Shields; Firby Hall, Kirkham Abbey, Westow, York TO6 7LH (☎ 0653 81 474)

SHIELDS, Frank Cox; s of Joseph F Shields (d 1973), of Dublin, and Alice, *née* Cox (d 1972); *b* 10 Sept 1944; *Educ* Harvard Coll (AB), Wharton Sch of Fin and Commerce (MBA); *m* 9 Oct 1971, Elizabeth Jean, da of John Blythe Kinross, CBE, of London; 2 s (Oliver b 1975, Alexander b 1980), 1 da (Henrietta b 1973); *Career* res staff LSE 1969-71; stockbroker: Cazenove & Co 1971-73, Grieveson Grant & Co 1973-78; exec dir: European Banking Co Ltd 1978-85, EBC AMRO Bank Ltd 1985-86; sr rep Maruman Securities Co Ltd London 1987, dir and gen mangr Maruman Securities (Europe) Ltd 1987-; *Recreations* architecture, reading, travel; *Clubs* Buck's; *Style*— Frank Shields, Esq; 24 Church Row, Hampstead, London NW3 6UP (☎ 071 435 1175); Maruman Securities (Europe) Ltd, 1 Liverpool St, London EC2M 7NH (☎ 071 374 4000, fax 071 382 9143, telex 929347 MSEL G)

SHIELDS, Sir Neil Stanley; MC (1946); s of Archie Shields (d 1958), and Hannah Shields (d 1976); *b* 7 Sept 1919; *m* 1970, (Gloria) Dawn, *née* Wilson; *Career* Maj NW Europe 1940 and 1944-46; dir Central and Sheerwood plc 1969-84; chm: Holcombe Hldgs plc 1978-84, Standard Catalogue Co Ltd 1976-84, Anglo Continental Investment & Finance Co Ltd 1965-74, Trianco Redfyre Ltd 1979-84; md Chesham Amalagamations & Investments Ltd 1968-78 (dir 1964-84), dep chm London Transport 1989- (chm 1988-89, memb 1986-, chm Property Bd 1986-); chm London Area Nat Union of Conservative and Unionist Assocs 1961-63; chm Cmmn for the New Towns 1982-; memb Cncl Aims of Indust 1975-; govr Bedford Coll 1983-85; kt 1964; *Recreations* reading, music, wining and dining; *Clubs* Carlton, HAC; *Style*— Sir Neil Shields, MC; 12 London House, Avenue Rd, London NW8; office: Glen House, Stag Place, London SW1 (☎ 071 828 7722)

SHIELDS, Prof Sir Robert; s of Robert Alexander Shields (d 1947), of Paisley, Scotland, and Isobel MacDougall, *née* Reid (d 1982); *b* 8 Nov 1930; *Educ* John Neilson Inst Paisley, Univ of Glasgow (MB ChB, MD); *m* 19 Jan 1957, (Grace) Marianne, da of George Swinburn (d 1953), of London; 1 s (Andrew Duncan Robert b 1966), 2 da (Gillian Elizabeth b 1959, Jennifer Anne b 1962); *Career* RAMC: Nat Serv 1954-56, Lt 1954, Capt 1955, Maj (TA) 1956-61; Regtl MO: 1 Bn Argyll and Sutherland Highlanders 1954-56, 7 Bn Argyll and Sutherland Highlanders (TA) 1965-61; Western Infirmary Glasgow: house offr 1953-54, sr house offr 1956-57, registrar in surgery 1958-59; Univ of Glasgow: Hall tutorial fell 1957-58, lectr in surgery 1959-62; res asst Dept of Surgical Res Mayo Clinic USA 1959-60, sr lectr then reader in surgery Welsh Nat Sch of Med 1962-69, prof of surgery Univ of Liverpool 1969-, hon conslt surgn Royal Liverpool Hosp and Broadgreen Hosp 1969-, dean Faculty of Med Univ of Liverpool 1982-85; memb Liverpool Health Authy 1974-78, chm Mil Educn Ctee Univ of Liverpool 1987-, vice chm Mersey RHA 1983-85 (memb Res Ctee 1976-), pres Liverpool Med Inst 1988, regnl advsr RCS 1986-; memb: GMC 1984-, MRC 1987-91, Cncl RCS Ed, Assoc of Surgns of GB and Ireland (pres 1986-87), Surgical Res Soc (pres 1983-85), Cncl Br Soc of Gastroenterology (pres 1990-91); hon fell American Coll of Surgns 1990; DSc Univ of Wales 1990; FRCS, FRCSEd; kt 1990; *Books* Surgical Emergencies II (1979), Surgical Management (1983); *Recreations* sailing, horse riding, reading; *Clubs* Army and Navy, Racquets (Liverpool); *Style*— Prof Sir Robert Shields; Strathmore, 81 Meols Drive, West Kirby, Wirral L48 5DF (☎ 051 632 3588); Dept of Surgery, Univ of Liverpool, P O Box 147, Liverpool L69 3BX (☎ 051 708 7139, fax 051 708 6502, telex 67095 UNILPL)

SHIELDS, Tom; s of Charles Shields (d 1982), of 36 Brockburn Rd, Glasgow, and Annie Shields (d 1988); *b* 8 Feb 1948; *Educ* St Bernard's Comprehensive Sch, Bellarmine Comprehensive Sch, Strathclyde Univ; *m* 21 June 1969, Mhairi Couper, da of Robert Graham; 1 s (Graham b 19 July 1971), 1 da (Anna b 1 Nov 1969); *Career* journalist; Sunday Post 1969-73, diary ed Glasgow Herald 1986- (reporter 1978-86, joined 1983), publisher and chm Culture City Magazine; *Books* Celtic/Rangers Joke Book (1976); *Recreations* culture, viniculture; *Clubs* Hamilton Accies Supporters; *Style*— Tom Shields, Esq; Torrance House, East Kilbride, Glasgow (☎ 03552 369 11); 195 Albion St, Glasgow (☎ 041 552 6255, fax 041 552 2288)

SHIER, Jonathan Fraser; s of Frank Eric Shier, of 25 Bede House, Manor Fields, Putney, London, and Margery Mary, *née* Dutton; *b* 18 Oct 1947; *Educ* Geelong C of E GS Aust, Monash Univ Melbourne (LLB, BEC); *Career* private sec to dep senate ldr and AG of Aust 1973-76, mktg controller and dir of sales and mktg Scottish TV 1977-85, dir of sales and mktg Thames TV plc 1985-, dep chief exec Thames TV plc 1990-; chm ITV Marketing Ctee 1989-; dir Broadcasters' Audience Res Bd Ltd 1989-; MInstM; *Recreations* travel, theatre, music, skiing, diving; *Clubs* East India, Annabels, Hurlingham, IOD; *Style*— Jonathan Shier, Esq; 14 Bowerdean St, Fulham, London SW6; Thames Television plc, 149 Tottenham Court Rd, London W1P 9LL (☎ 071 387 9494, fax 071 383 5534)

SHIERS, Harry Robert Beaumont Percival; s of Leslie Gordon Percival Shiers, and Elizabeth Anne, *née* Mathews; *b* 25 March 1963; *Educ* Chatham House, Univ Coll Hosp London (BDS, LDS RCS, MRCS); *Career* dental surgn The Harley Street Cosmetic Dental Surgery 1987-; int competitor Admirals Cup Fastnet 1987; memb: BDA 1984, RSM 1984, Med Protection Soc 1987; FRCS; *Recreations* offshore racing, marathon running, squash, swimming; *Clubs* Royal Temple Yacht, Lansdowne, Broadstairs Sailing; *Style*— H R B P Shiers, Esq; Harley Street Cosmetic Dental Surgery, 121 Harley St, London W1N 1DH (☎ 071 224 6196)

SHIFFNER, George Frederick; s of late Capt Edward Shiffner (gs of 4 Bt); hp of kinsman, Sir Henry Shiffner, 8 Bt; *b* 3 Aug 1936; *Educ* Wellington; *m* 1961, Dorothea Helena Cynthia, da of late T H McLean; 1 s, 1 da; *Career* photographer, ABIPP; *Style*— George Shiffner, Esq; 14 Coggeshall Rd, Braintree, Essex (☎ 0376 22524); Searles, Alderford Street, Sible Hedingham, Essex (☎ 0787 60486)

SHIFFNER, Sir Henry David; 8 Bt (UK 1818) of Coombe, Sussex; s of Maj Sir Henry Burrows Shiffner, 7 Bt, OBE (d 1941); *b* 2 Feb 1930; *Educ* Rugby, Trinity Hall Cambridge; *m* 1, 1951 (m dis 1956), Dorothy, da of W G Jackson; 1 da; m 2, 1957 (m dis 1970), Beryl, da of George Milburn; 1 da; m 3, 1971, Joaquina Ramos Lopez of Madrid; *Heir* kinsman, George Shiffner; *Career* company dir; *Style*— Sir Henry Shiffner, Bt

SHILLAKER, (George) Graham; s of George Edward Shillaker, and Kathleen Eva, *née* Pridgton; *b* 12 July 1939; *Educ* St Paul's; *m* 4 April 1973, Mary Jennifer, da of Tom Thomas (d 1964), of 22 Trafalgar Rd, Strawberry Hill, Middx; *Career* shipping accountant Matheson & Co Ltd 1961-64; dir: Howe Robinson & Co Ltd 1978 (shipbroker 1964-), Matheson (Chartering) Ltd 1979, Howe Robinson (Hldgs) Ltd 1984; md Howe Robinson Investmts Ltd 1988; memb Baltic Exchange 1964-; FCIS 1975; *Recreations* cricket, golf; *Clubs* MCC, Royal Mid-Surrey Golf; *Style*— Graham Shillaker, Esq; 130-138 Minories, London EC3N 1NS (☎ 071 488 3444, fax 071 488 4679, car 0860 306095, telex 8811461)

SHILLING, David; s of Ronald Shilling, and Gertrude Shilling; *b* 27 June 1953; *Educ* Colet Ct, St Paul's London; *Career* designer; important shows incl Ulster Museum Exhibition The Hats' exhibited: at Worthing, Plymouth, Salisbury, Durham, Leeds and Exeter museums 1981-; other exhibitions incl: Angela Flowers London, Tino Ghelfi Vicenza Italy, Rendezvous Gallery Aberdeen, Phillip Francis Sheffield; in other museum collections: V & A London, Met NY, Los Angeles County, Mappin Gallery Sheffield, Musée de l'Art Décoratif Paris; designs include: menswear, womens wear, lingerie, furs, jewellry, fine china limited edn pieces ceramic tiles, wallpapers, upholstery fabrics and designs for film and theatre; *Books* Thinking Rich (1986); *Recreations* listening and/or looking, swimming, jet-skiing, driving, antique collecting; *Style*— David Shilling, Esq; 5 Homer St, London W1H 1HN (☎ 071 935 8473)

SHILLINGFORD, James Hugh; *b* 18 Aug 1953; *Educ* Westminster, Christ Church Oxford (MA), London Business Sch (MSc); *Career* Coopers & Lybrand 1975-79, md M & G Investmt Mgmnt Ltd 1987-, dir M & G Gp plc 1988-; ACA; *Style*— James Shillingford, Esq; Three Quays, Tower Hill, London EC3

SHILLINGTON, Sir (Robert Edward) Graham; CBE (1970, OBE 1959, MBE 1951), DL (Co Down 1975); s of Maj D Graham Shillington, DL, MP (d 1944); *b* 2 April 1911; *Educ* Sedbergh, Clare Coll Cambridge; *m* 1935, Mary E R Bulloch (d 1977); 2 s, 1 da; *Career* dep chief constable RUC (chief constable 1970-73); kt 1972; *Recreations* golf, gardening; *Clubs* Royal Over-Seas, Royal Co Down Golf; *Style*— Sir Graham Shillington, CBE, DL; Ardeevin, 184 Bangor Road, Holywood, Co Down, NI

SHILLITOE, Peter Christie Mauldon; LVO (1974), MBE (1954); s of Cyril Arthur Shillitoe (d 1931), and Margaret Anna Mauldon (d 1974); *b* 21 Oct 1917; *Educ* Dickson's Sch, BEC (Abbey) Sch; *m* 19 Jan 1945, Frederica Lilian, da of David Templeton (d 1942), of Oxford; *Career* trainee Imperial Airways Ltd 1937-40, various appts BOAC in M East, Africa and India 1940-46; BEA: ops mangr 1946-62, gen mangr (ops) and dep to Dir of Flight Operations 1962-66; dir: Cyprus Airways Ltd 1967-76, Gibraltar Airways Ltd 1972-76; freelance aviation conslt 1976-; chm Chawton Parish Cncl; Freeman Sudbury Suffolk 1955 (Freedom by Patrimony - Family Freemen for over 200 years); FCIT 1970; *Recreations* squash, gardening; *Clubs* Royal Aero, Royal Ascot Squash; *Style*— Peter Shillitoe, Esq, LVO, MBE; White Gates, Chawton, Alton, Hants (☎ 0420 82142); 227 Dedworth Road, Windsor (☎ 0753 855860)

SHINDLER, Alfred Burnett; s of Louis Shindler (d 1957), of London, and Celia, *née* Garfinkle (d 1940); *b* 31 Aug 1912; *Educ* Highbury Co Sch London, Law Soc Coll of Law; *m* 25 June 1939, Phyllis Netta, da of Louis Myers (d 1930), of London; 3 da (Hilary Louise, Karolyn Celia, Barbara Elise); *Career* WWII RAF; slr 1935; hon slr: The United Wards Club, Metro Parks and Gardens Assoc, The Hon Ir Soc, The Royal Soc of St George; chm London Ct of Int Arbitration Inc; Master Billingsgate Ward Club 1955, memb Ct of Common Cncl (London) 1966, dep for the Ward of Billingsgate 1982, life govr Imperial Cancer Res; memb: Hon Irish Soc (dep govr 1979), City Lands and Bridge House Estates, Establishment (chm 1984-87), Coal Corn and Rates Fin, Central Markets (chm 1974-78), Working Party concerned with the future of Central Markets; chm Gresham Ctee, memb Ctee of Mgmnt W Ham Park (chm 1972), former chm of the Med Servs Ctee of the FPC for City and E London Area Health Authy 1974-86; memb Ctee of Mgmnt Hampstead (Heath) Ctee; Freeman of the City of London 1947; memb Worshipful Co of: Slrs 1948-, Gardeners 1973-, Arbitrators 1976- (Master 1987-88); immediate past pres City Livery Club 1989; Order of the Ghurkas (Nepal 1979); *Recreations* gardening (past chm Orchid Soc of GB), skiing; *Clubs* Guildhall, City Livery (past pres), RAC, Billingsgate Ward, United Wards (life govr), Royal Soc of St George (vice pres City of London branch); *Style*— Alfred B Shindler, Esq; 10 North End Rd, London NW11 7PW; 37-39 Eastcheap, London EC3M 1AY (☎ 081 455 9925, 071 283 6376, fax 081 458 8523, telex 924404 SHNDLR G)

SHINDLER, Dr Colin; s of Israel Shindler, of Prestwich, Manchester, and Florence, *née* Weidberg; *b* 28 June 1949; *Educ* Bury GS Lancs, Gonville and Caius Coll Cambridge (BA, MA, PhD); *m* 23 Sept 1972, (Nancy) Lynn, da of Prof Robert Stephen White, of Riverside, Californa, USA; 1 s (David b 1977), 1 da (Amy b 1975); *Career* res fell American Film Inst Beverly Hills 1972; film and TV writer and prodr; prodr: Love Story series (BBC TV) 1981-, East Lynne (BBC TV) 1982-, The Worst Witch (Central TV, winner American Cable Emmy) 1985-, A Little Princess (LWT, BAFTA winner) 1986-; Wish Me Luck (LWT) 1987, 1914 All Out (Yorkshire TV, first prize Reims Int Film Festival) 1989; writer and prodr Young Charlie Chaplin (Thames TV & PBS, US Prime Time Emmy nomination); author screenplay Buster feature film 1988; memb BAFTA; *Books* Hollywood Goes to War (1979), Buster (1988); *Recreations* cricket, soccer, golf, tennis, badminton, theatre, music, fell walking in the Lake District; *Style*— Dr Colin Shindler; c/o Duncan Heath Associates Ltd, 162 Wardour St, London W1 (☎ 071 439 1471)

SHINDLER, Geoffrey Arnold; s of Israel Shindler, of Manchester, and Florence Shindler (d 1962); *b* 21 Oct 1942; *Educ* Bury GS, Gonville and Caius Coll (WM Tapp Scholar, MA, LIM); *m* 20 Feb 1966, Gay, da of late Harry Kenton; 3 da (Freya b 29 Dec 1966, Nicola b 8 Oct 1968, Caroline b 29 Jan 1971); *Career* ptnr March Pearson & Skelton 1971-86 (articled clerk 1966-68, asst slr 1968-71), ptnr Halliwell Landau Manchester 1986-; memb: Bd of Visitors HM Prison Manchester 1973-84, Salford FPC 1984-89, Exec Ctee N W Arts 1984-, chm Local Review Ctee (Parole) HM Prison Manchester 1979-84; hon assoc Centre For Law and Business Univ of Manchester 1990; memb: Law Soc, Inst for Fiscal Studies NW region; Law of Trusts (with K Hodkinson, 1984); *Recreations* Theatre, Opera, Books; *Clubs* St James's Club, Manchester Lancashire County Cricket Club; *Style*— Geoffrey Shindler, Esq; Hazelhurst, 54 Higher Lane, Whitefield, Manchester M25 7WE (☎ 061 766 3078); Halliwell Landau, St James Court, Brown St, Manchester M2 2JF (☎ 061 835 3003, fax 061 835 2994)

SHINDLER, His Hon Judge; George John; QC (1970); s of Bruno Schindler (d 1964), and Alma Schindler (d 1958); *b* 21 Oct 1922; *Educ* Regents Park Sch, Univ Coll Sch Hampstead; *m* 16 Oct 1955, Eva, da of Otto Muller (d 1961); 3 s (David b 1958, Daniel b 1961, William b 1969); *Career* served RTR NW Europe 1942-47; called to the Bar Inner Temple 1952, master of the bench Inner Temple 1978, circuit judge 1980; Mental Health Review Tbnls 1983-87; sr resident judge Inner London Crown Ct 1987-; *Recreations* theatre, music, watching cricket, football, reading, travel, swimming; *Clubs* MCC; *Style*— His Hon Judge George Shindler, QC; Inner London Sessions House, Newington Causeway SE1 (☎ 071 407 7111)

SHINER, Brendan Elias John; s of G L O Shiner (d 1969), and N K Shiner (d 1942); *b* 23 June 1928; *Educ* Stonyhurst, Pembroke Coll Oxford (MA); *m* 27 May 1954, Mary Gwyneth, da of J C T Thornton (d 1960); 3 s (Brendan Niall b 18 April 1959, Charles Graham b 7 Jan 1963, Timothy John b 30 Dec 1968), 1 da (Ceridwen Mary (Mrs Scott) b 24 Sept 1960); *Career* 2 Lt RTR 1948-49; called to the Bar Middle Temple 1955; ldr Cons gp Stroud DC 1983-88, vice chm planning ctee Lambeth Borough Cncl 1968-70 (vice chm highways ctee 1970-71); *Recreations* farming, racing; *Style*— Brendan Shiner, Esq; The Culver House, Culver Hill, Amberley, Glos GL5 5BA (☎ 045 387 3337); All Saints Chambers, Bristol (☎ 0272 211 966, fax 0272 276 493)

SHINGLES, Raymond Edward Laws; MBE (1945); s of Charles Edward Shingles (d 1948), and Lillie Waldock (d 1957); *b* 11 March 1913; *Educ* Cranleigh Sch; *m* 1952, Phyllis Willan, da of Lt-Col Charles Edward Jefferis, of Cookham House Hotel (d 1963); 2 s (Justin, Rupert); *Career* Lt-Col 9 JAT Regt Indian Army, served in forces 1939-46, passed Staff Coll Quetta, served in India; slr Supreme Ct, ptnr Linklaters & Paines 1950-74; dir: Air Products Ltd 1957-80, Brown Shipley Holdings plc 1969-74, Brown Shipley & Co Ltd 1969-74, Bowthorpe Holdings Ltd 1970-76, Hongkong & Shanghai Banking Corporation (Jersey) Ltd 1975-84, Fleming Albany American Fund Ltd 1978-, Brown Shipley (Jersey) Ltd 1977-87, Brown Shipley (Guernsey) Ltd 1977-87, Brown Shipley Sterling Bond Fund Ltd 1978-88, Brown Shipley International Currency Fund Ltd 1982-88, Brown Shipley International Bond Fund Ltd 1983-88, Brown Shipley Sterling Capital Fund Ltd 1979-88, Robert Fleming (Jersey) Ltd, Robert Fleming Investment Management (Jersey) Ltd 1985-, Decahedron Ltd, Property Security Investsment Trust (CI) Ltd; *Recreations* horse racing, golf; *Clubs* Victoria, Channel Islands Race and Hunt, La Moye Golf; *Style*— Raymond Shingles, Esq, MBE; La Sergenté, La Grande Route de Rozel, St Martin, Jersey, CI (☎ 0534 54967)

SHINGLETON, Andrew Philip; s of Wilfrid James Shingleton (d 1984), of Suffolk, and Grace Bernadina Shingleton, *née* Pole; m direct descendent of Cardinal Reginald Pole, Archbp of Canterbury under Tudors; *b* 28 June 1943; *Educ* Douai Sch; *m* 1, 1967, Vanessa Jane (d 1977), da of Capt John Liley, of Marbella; 3 s (Toby John-James b 1972, Alexander William (b 1975), Barnaby Andrew (twin) b 1975); m 2, 1982, Wendy Elizabeth, da of Alec Barnes, of S Lancing; *Career* advertising dir McCann Erickson 1987; MIPA 1972; memb CAM 1973; *Recreations* walking the Cornish cliffs, golf, 18 century French history; *Style*— Andrew P Shingleton, Esq; Bossiney, Orchehill Avenue, Gerrards Cross SL9 8QH (☎ 0753 887985); McCann Erickson Advertising, 36 Howland Street, London W1A 1AT (☎ 071 580 6690)

SHIPLEY, (Norman) Graham (de Mattos); s of Capt Norman Douglas Holbrook Shipley (d 1979), of Bromborough, Wirral, Merseyside, and Lesley Cynthia, *née* Stott; *b* 10 Jan 1948; *Educ* Kings Sch Chester, Trinity Coll Cambridge (BA, Dip Computer Sci, MA), Inns of Ct Sch of Law; *m* 11 Sept 1982, Helen Rhian, da of David Neville De Mattos, of Witchampton, Wimborne, Dorset; 2 da (Jemima, Kate); *Career* called to the Bar Lincoln's Inn 1973; currently specialising in: patent, copyright, trade mark law, confidential information, computer law, entertainment law; *Recreations* electronics, motor cycling, DIY, children, Japanese cookery; *Clubs* Wig & Pen; *Style*— Graham Shipley, Esq; New House Farm, Purton End, Debden, Saffron Walden, Essex CB11 3JT (☎ 0799 40565, fax 0799 41906); 3 Pump Court, Temple, London EC4Y 7AJ (☎ 071 583 5110, fax 071 583 1130)

SHIPMAN, John Jeffrey; s of late H Shipman, and late R Horwich; *b* 20 Sept 1917; *Educ* UCL, UCH (MB BS, MS); *m* 18 April 1942, Elizabeth Mary, da of late W R Corlett, of Cumberland; 1 s (Dr John Anthony b 1952); *Career* 2 Army 5 Bn DLI, RMO and Capt RAMC 1942-46, served Normandy, Caen, Seine, Somme, Ardennes, Norway; asst lectr Post-Grad Sch 1947-51, sr registrar St Mark's Hosp and Southend Gen Hosp 1951-52, surgn Lister Hosp 1952-83; memb Cncl Conslts and Specialist Ctee; chm: Hitchin Hosp, Med Staffing (HCSA); *Books* Operative Surgical Revision (4 edn, 1987), Mnemonics & Tactics in Surgery & Medicine (2 edn, 1987); MRCS 1941, FRCS 1947, LRCP 1941, Queen's Silver Jubilee Medal 1977; *Recreations* golf, game fishing, gardening; *Style*— John J Shipman, Esq; Conoleigh, 505 Broadway, Letchworth, Herts (☎ 0462 683248)

SHIPMAN, Stephen; s of William Arthur Shipman, of Southampton, and Dorothy, *née* Harrison; *b* 13 Oct 1957; *Educ* Reigate GS, London Coll of Printing (BA); *m* 1 Aug 1981, Amanda Jane, da of Clifford Bird; 1 da (Eleanor Rose b 10 Aug 1989); *Career* professional photographer; asst to Graham Hughes 1980-82, freelance photographer 1982-; memb Assoc of Photographers; *Recreations* photography, music, collecting antique glass, walking; *Style*— Stephen Shipman, Esq; Steve Shipman Photography, 12 Printing House Yard, 15 Hackney Rd, London E2 (☎ 071 739 5858, fax 071 739 1756, mobile 0831 355 966)

SHIPPEY, Prof Thomas Alan; s of Ernest Shippey (d 1962), and Christine Emily, *née* Kjelgaard; *b* 9 Sept 1943; *Educ* King Edward's Sch Birmingham, Queens' Coll

Cambridge (BA, MA, PhD); *m* 27 Dec 1966 (m dis 1983), Susan Margaret, da of John Veale, of Bingley, W Yorks; 1 s (John b 1973), 2 da (Louise b 1970, Gillian b 1972); *Career* lectr Univ of Birmingham 1965-72, fell St John's Coll Oxford 1972-79, prof of Eng language and medieval Eng lit Univ of Leeds 1979-; *Books* Old English Verse (1972), Poems of Wisdom and Learning in Old English (1976), Beowulf (1978), The Road to Middle-Earth (1982), Fictional Space (1991); *Recreations* walking, running, science fiction; *Style—* Prof Thomas Shippey; School of English, University of Leeds, Leeds LS2 9JT (☎ 0532 334737, fax 0532 336017, telex 556473 UNILDS G)

SHIPSTER, Col John Neville; CBE (1973), DSO (1944); s of Col G C Shipster, MC (d 1941); *b* 31 Jan 1922; *Educ* Marlborough; *m* 1948, Cornelia Margarethe, *née* Arends; 2 s, 1 da; *Career* WWII served 2 Punjab Regt Indian Army, CO 1 Bn Middlesex Regt 1965-67, Cdr British Forces Belize 1970-73, Cmdt Def NBC Sch 1974; Dep Col Queen's Regt 1975; *Recreations* golf, sailing; *Clubs* Army and Navy; *Style—* Col John Shipster, CBE, DSO; Deben House, 41 Cumberland St, Woodbridge, Suffolk (☎ 039 43 3957)

SHIPTON, (Lady) Janet Helen; *née* Attlee; da of late 1 Earl Attlee; does not use courtesy title; *b* 1923; *m* 1947, Harold William Shipton; 1 da; *Style—* Mrs Harold Shipton; 820 Woodside Drive, Iowa City, Iowa, USA

SHIPWAY, Frank; s of Alfred Edwin Shipway (d 1986), and Edith Doris Owen; *b* 9 July 1935; *Educ* RCM; *m* 17 July 1986, Imogen Vanessa (distinguished int oboeist), da of David Alan Triner; 1 da (Eugene); *Career* symphonic opera conductor; studied with: Igor Markevitch, Sir John Barbirolli, Herbert von Karajan; worked with: Eng Nat Opera, Glyndebourne Fest Opera, Deutche Opera Berlin (at personal invitation of Lorin Maazel; conducted orchestras in: Germany, Italy, France, Belgium, Denmark, Sweden, Norway, Iceland, Finland; in GB has given concerts for: BBC, Royal Philharmonic, London Philharmonic, Philharmonica, Royal Liverpool Philharmonic, City of Birmingham Symphony Orchestra; conducts works of: Strauss, Mahler, Rachmaninar, Wagner, Verdi; also worked in field of 20 century music; gave first Euro performance of Polish composer Andrzej Panufriks 8 Symphony, was first conductor Boulez' Livre pour Cordes; received Gold Disc for recordings with Royal Philharmonic Orchestra; *Recreations* antiques, gardening, riding, painting, vintage cars; *Style—* Frank Shipway, Esq; Corner Cottage, Friars, Stile Place, Richmond Hill, Richmond, Surrey TW10 6NL

SHIPWRIGHT, Adrian John; s of Jack Shipwright, and Jennie, *née* Eastman; *b* 2 July 1950; *Educ* King Edward VI Sch Southampton, ChCh Oxford (BA, BCL, MA); *m* 17 Aug 1974, Diana Evelyn, da of Percival Denys Treseder (d 1971); 1 s (Henry b 1983), 1 da (Fiona b 1985); *Career* asst slr Linklaters & Paines 1977, official student and tutor in law Christ Church Oxford 1977-82, ptnr Denton Hall Burgin & Warrens 1984-87 (asst slr 1982-84), hon lectr in laws Kings Coll London 1986-90, visiting prof in laws Kings Coll London; ptnr S J Berwin & Co 1987-; govr King Edward VI Sch Southampton; memb Law Soc; *Books* CCH British Tax Reporter Vol 5 (1986) Tax Planning and UK Land Development (1988, 2 edn 1990), Capital Gains Tax Strategies in the New Regime (1989), UK Tax and Intellectual Property (1990), VAT, Property and the New Rules (1990), Strategic Tax Planning (ed and contrib); *Recreations* music; *Style—* Adrian Shipwright, Esq; 55 Homlesdale Rd, Teddington, Middx TW11 9LJ; c/o S J Berwin & Co, 236 Grays Inn Rd, London WC1X 8HB (☎ 071 278 0444, fax 071 833 2860, telex 8814928 WINLAW G)

SHIRAISHI, Yuko; da of Masahiro Shinoda, of Tokyo, Japan, and Kazuko Shiraishi; *b* 6 March 1956; *Educ* Shinmei Jr Sch Tokyo, Myojyo HS Tokyo, Chelsea Sch of Art (Br Cncl scholar, BA, MA); *m* 1983, David Juda, *qv*; *Career* artist; solo exhibitions: Curwen Gallery 1984, Edward Totah Gallery 1988 and 1990, Tleerhuys Galerij Belgium 1989, Shigeru Yokota Gallery Tokyo 1989, Galerie Konstruktiv Tendens Stockholm 1990, Artsite Bath 1990; selected group exhibitions: New Contemporaries (ICA) 1980, Contemporary Japanese Prints (Royal Acad) 1981, Nantenshi Gallery Tokyo 1983, Int Euro Print Exhibition (Musée d'Art Moderne, Liège, Belgium) 1983, Abstraction in Japan (Warwick Arts Tst) 1984, Whitechapel Open Exhibition 1985, 1989 and 1990, Int Biennale of Graphic Art (Moderna Galeria, Ljubljana, Yugoslavia) 1985, The Print Show (Angela Flowers Gallery) 1986, Nancy Halfman Gallery NY 1988, The Presence of Painting: Aspects of British Abstraction 1957-88 (Arts Cncl Mappin Gallery Sheffield and touring) 1988, From Prism to Paintbox Colour Theory and Practice in Modern British Painting (Oriel Gallery Clwyd) 1989, Galerie Konstruktiv Tendens Stockholm 1989 and 1990, Kunstlerinnen des 20 Jahrhunderts (Museum Wiesbaden Germany) 1990; work in the collections of: Unilever, Br Museum, YKK Japan, IBM, Arthur Andersen collection, Seibu Japan, McCrory Corporations NY, London & Continental Bankers Ltd, Ove Arup, Arts Cncl of GB, Contemporary Art Soc; *Style—* Ms Yuko Shiraishi; Acme Studio, Studio F, 11-31 Orsman Rd, London N1 (☎ 071 739 8949); c/o Edward Totah Gallery, 13 Old Burlington St, London W1X 1LA (☎ 071 734 0343, fax 071 287 2186)

SHIRLEY, Agnes (Ness); *née* Kerr; da of William Shaw Kerr, of Ayrshire, Scotland, and Helen, *née* Collins; *b* 28 Sept 1934; *Educ* St Joseph's HS Kilmarnock, Int Graphoanalysis Soc Chicago (MGA); *m* 22 April 1957, Robert Gerald, s of Robert Shirley, of Normoss, Blackpool; 1 s (Martin b 1963), 2 da (Helen b 1958, Mairi b 1959); *Career* handwriting analyst and cnsllr; co fndr and dir Ross Shirley & Assocs 1972-76 (md Ross Int SA Brussels 1976-80), dir PACE Assessments Ltd 1982- (researcher on how to assess business women from significant traits in their handwriting), co fndr (with Prof Alice Coleman) PACE method distance learning course of graphology 1990; Cert Cnslling (RCA London); memb Exec Res Assoc; FInstD; *Books* Characteristics of High Achieving Business Women (1976, 1988), feature in Personnel Today (1988); *Recreations* swimming, golf, reading; *Clubs* RAC, Network; *Style—* Mrs Ness Shirley; 10 Groom Place, Belgravia, London SW1X 7BA; PACE Assessments Ltd, Collier House, 163/169 Brompton Road, London SW3 1HW (☎ 071 589 4567)

SHIRLEY, Hon Andrew John Carr Sewallis; yr s of 13 Earl Ferrers, PC, DL, *qv*; *b* 24 June 1965; *Educ* Ampleforth, RAC Cirencester; *Style—* The Hon Andrew Shirley; c/o Ditchingham Hall, Bungay, Suffolk NR35 2LE

SHIRLEY, Gerald Ferrers; MBE (Mil); s of John Lawrence Shirley (d 1932), and Ellen Mary, *née* Jefferis (d 1969); *b* 3 April 1911; *Educ* Dauntsey's Sch; *m* 14 July 1945, Evelyn Bridget, da of Murray Newton Phelps (d 1952); 1 s (Martin b 1946); *Career* CO RNVR Mine and Bomb Disposal Unit in Med and Black Sea 1941-46; dir: British Oil and Cake Mills Ltd 1960-70, Utd Agric Merchants 1965-70; pres Nat Seed Crushers of Scotland 1970; *Recreations* cricket, rugby, tennis; *Style—* Gerald Shirley, Esq, MBE; Knowle House, Knowle St Giles, Chard, Somerset

SHIRLEY, Maj John Evelyn; s of Lt-Col Evelyn Charles Shirley (d 1956), and Kathleen Mary, *née* Cardew (d 1977); *b* 11 Nov 1922; *Educ* Eton; *m* 17 Jan 1952, Judith Margaret, da of Sir William Francis Stratford Dugdale, 1 Bt, of Merevale Hall, Atherstone, Warwicks; 2 s (Philip Evelyn b 1955, Hugh Sewallis b 1961), 1 da (Emily Margaret b 1957); *Career* Army, served 60 Rifles 1941-55; landowner; *Recreations* field sports; *Clubs* Kildare Street (Dublin), Army and Navy; *Style—* Maj John Shirley; Ormly Hall, Ramsey, Isle of Man; Ettington Park, Stratford on Avon, Warwickshire; Lough Lea, Carrickmacross, Co Monaghan

SHIRLEY, Capt Malcolm Christopher; s of Lt Cdr Leonard Noel Shirley, RN (1988), of Burford, Oxon, and Edith Florence, *née* Bullen; *b* 10 April 1945; *Educ* Churchers Coll Petersfield, RN Engrg Coll (BSc); *m* 18 April 1970, Lucilla Rose Geary, da of Cdr Thomas Geary Dyer, RN, of Bradford-on-Avon; 3 s (Guy b 1 March 1975, Ben b 1 March 1977, Hugo b 2 Jan 1979); *Career* Midshipman 1964, Sub Lt 1965-69, Lt 1969, dep marine engr offr HMS Zulu 1970-73, trg offr HMS Eastbourne 1973-75, sr engr offr HM Yacht Britannia 1975-77, Lt Cdr 1976, RN Staff Coll 1977-78, Ship Design Authy MOD Bath 1978-79, marine engr off HMS Coventry 1980-81, asst naval attaché Paris (1982-84), manning and trg policy desk offr MOD Whitehall 1984-86, OC Machinery Trials Unit 1987-89, Capt 1989, asst dir MOD Bath 1989-; FIMarE, CEng; *Recreations* sailing, skiing, house restoration, wine; *Clubs* RNSA, Royal Naval and Royal Albert Yacht; *Style—* Capt Malcolm Shirley

SHIRLEY, Vera Stephanie (Steve); OBE (1980); da of Arnold Buchthal (d 1970), and Margaret, *née* Schick (d 1987); arrived in UK on Kindertransport as child refugee in 1939; f moved from being friendly enemy alien (one of the Dunera boys) prior to UK Army, to US Army (serving at Nuremberg trials) later German equivalent of High Ct Judge, changed name on naturalisation to Brook to honour Rupert Brooke; *b* 16 Sept 1933; *Educ* Sir John Cass Coll London (BSc); *m* 14 Nov 1959, Derek George Millington Shirley, s of George Millington Shirley (d 1970); 1 s (Giles Millington); *Career* PO Res Station Dollis Hill 1951-59; CDL 1959-62; fndr dir FI Group plc 1962; vice pres Br Computer Soc 1979-82; memb: Computer, Systems and Electronics Requirements Bd 1979-81, Electronics and Avionics Requirements Bd 1981-83; memb: Cncl Industl Soc 1984-90, Nat Cncl for Vocational Qualifications 1986-89; tstee Help The Aged 1987-, pres Br Computer Soc 1989-90; Freeman City of London 1987, jr warden Co of Info Technologists; hon fell: Manchester Poly 1989, CGIA 1989; patron Disablement Income Gp 1989; FBCS 1971, CBIM 1984; *Publications* articles in professional jls; *Recreations* sleep; *Clubs* Reform; *Style—* Mrs Steve Shirley, OBE; FI Group plc, Campus 300, Maylands Ave, Hemel Hempstead, Herts HP2 7EZ (☎ 0442 233339, telex 94016626)

SHIRLEY-BEAVAN, Mary Sevasty; *née* Hamilton; da of Capt George Hamilton, RD, RNR, and Lilian Ellen, *née* Jackson; *b* 19 Oct 1917; *Educ* Chelsea Poly, Hammersmith Sch of Art; *m* 17 June (m dis 1972), Michael Shirley-Beavan, s of Lt-Col FW Shirley-Beavan, DSO, DL; 4 s (David b 1951, Mark b 1952, Simon b 1954, Jack b 1956), 2 da (Boo b 1959, Buff b 1963); *Career* WWII CPO WRNS 1940-45; equine and wild life artist in oils and watercolours, painting under maiden name of Mary Hamilton; JP 1960-86; *Recreations* hunting, racing; *Style—* Mrs Mary Shirley-Beavan; Gardener's Cottage, North Moor, Dulverton, Somerset

SHIRLEY-QUIRK, John Stanton; CBE (1975); s of Joseph Stanley Shirley-Quirk, and Amelia Shirley-Quirk; *b* 28 Aug 1931; *Educ* Holt Sch Liverpool, Univ of Liverpool (BSc, DipEd); *m* 1, 1955, Patricia, *née* Hastie (d 1981); 1 s, 1 da; m 2, 1981, Sara V, *née* Watkins; 1 s, 2 da; *Career* Offr Educn Branch RAF 1953-57; asst lectr in chemistry Acton Tech Coll 1957-61, lay clerk St Paul's Cathedral 1961-62; professional singer 1961-: Elegy For Young Lovers (Glyndebourne Opera) 1961, Curlew River 1964, The Burning Fiery Furnace 1966, The Prodigal Son 1968, Owen Wingrave 1970, Death in Venice 1973, Confessions of a Justified Sinner 1976, The Ice Break 1977; world wide appearnces and tours incl: America 1966, Aust 1967, Metropolitan Opera NY 1974; numerous recordings: operas, songs, cantatas etc; memb Ct Brunel Univ 1977; Hon RAM 1972; Univ of Liverpool Chem Soc medal 1965, Sir Charles Santley Meml gift Worshipful Co of Musicians 1969; Hon D Mus Univ of Liverpool, Hon D Univ Brunel Univ; *Recreations* trees, canals, clocks; *Style—* John Shirley-Quirk, CBE; 51 Wellesley Road, Twickenham TW2 5RX (☎ 081 894 1714); 4246 South 35 St, Arlington, Virginia 22206 USA (☎ 703 998 5554)

SHIVAS, Mark; s of James Dallas Shivas (d 1986), of Banstead, Surrey, and Winifred Alice, *née* Lighton (d 1978); *b* 24 April 1938; *Educ* Whitgift Sch, Merton Coll Oxford (MA); *Career* asst ed Movie Magazine 1961-64, dir prodr and presenter Granada TV 1964-68; drama prodr BBC TV 1969-79; prodns incl: The Six Wives of Henry VIII, Casanova, To Encourage the Others, The Evacuees, 84 Charing Cross Road, Abide with Me, The Glittering Prizes, Rogue Male, She Fell Among Thieves, Professional Foul, On Giants Shoulders, Telford's Change; dir Southern Pictures 1979-81 (exec prodr Winston Churchill the Wilderness Years and Bad Blood); prodr Channel 4: The Price 1985, What if it's Raining? 1986, The Storyteller 1987; film prodr: Moonlighting 1982, A Private Function 1985, The Witches 1989; head of drama BBC TV 1988-; *Recreations* swimming, gardening, windsurfing; *Clubs* Groucho's; *Style—* Mark Shivas, Esq; BBC TV, Wood Lane, London W12 (☎ 081 743 8000)

SHIVELY, William Jerome (Jerry); s of Robert Shively; *b* 3 Jan 1929; *Educ* Hamilton HS NY, Deerfield Acad Mass, Colgate Univ Hamilton NY, Harvard Business Sch; *m* 1953, Eleanor, da of Dr William Jackson; 4 children; *Career* served USAF 2 Lt; advtg and mktg exec; chm and md McCann & Co London 1981-; regnl dir McCann-Erickson Int 1980-; formerly exec vice-pres Johnson Wax; exec vice-pres McCann-Erickson 1980-89, chm Shandwick Marketing Services 1990-; *Recreations* scuba diving, skiing, flying, ballooning, shooting, fishing; *Clubs* American, Philippics, Hindhead Golf; *Style—* Jerry Shively, Esq; 25 Elm Park Rd, London Sw3 6DH (☎ 071 352 4567); Avalon, Old Barn Lane, Churt, Surrey (☎ 042 876 4686)

SHNEERSON, Dr John Michael; s of Gregory Shneerson, of Orpington, Kent, and Alfreda, *née* Ledger (d 1980); *b* 27 Sept 1946; *Educ* St Pauls, St Edmund Hall Oxford (MA, DM), St Mary's Hosp London; *m* 15 March 1975, Dr Anne Shneerson, da of Dr Kenneth Maclean, of Oxted, Surrey; 1 s (Robert b 1983), 2 da (Joanna b 1979, Catherine b 1981); *Career* sr registrar Westminster & Brompton Hosps London 1978-80; conslt physician: Newmarket Gen Hosp 1980-, Papworth Hosp 1980-, Addenbrookes 1980-, W Suffolk Hosp 1980-; dir Assisted Ventilation Unit Newmarket Gen Hosp 1981-; FRCP 1986; *Recreations* squash, golf, fives, gardening; *Style—* Dr John Shneerson; Newmarket General Hospital, Exning Road, Newmarket, Suffolk CB8 7JG (☎ 0638 665111, fax 0638 665719)

SHODA, Toshio; s of Atsushi Shoda, of Japan and Ayako; *b* 12 March 1938; *Educ* Meiji Univ Tokyo Japan (BEcon); *m* 11 Nov 1964, Keiko da of Takeshi Abe, of Japan; 1 s (Ken-Ichi b 1966), 1 da (Kanako b 1972); *Career* Nikko Securities Co Ltd: chief rep Singapore Office 1979-84, jt gen mangr Int Fin Div 1984-85, jt gen mangr Int Underwriting Div 1985-87, md corporate fin Nikko Securities (Europe) Ltd 1987-; *Recreations* music, skiing; *Clubs* Tanglin; *Style—* Toshio Shoda, Esq; 55 Victoria St, London SW1H OEU (☎ 071 799 2222, fax 071 222 3642, telex 884717)

SHONE, Richard Noel; *b* 8 May 1949; *Educ* Wrekin Coll Shropshire, Clare Coll Cambridge (BA); *Career* writer; assoc ed The Burlington Magazine 1979; *Publications* Bloomsbury Portraits: Vanessa Bell, Duncan Grant and their circle (1976), The Century of Change: British Art Since 1900 (1977), Sisely (1979), Augustus John (1979), The Post Impressionists (1980), Walter Sickert (1988), Rodrigo Moynihan (1988); selected and catalogued: Portraits by Duncan Grant (1969), Portraits by Walter Sickert (1990); contrib numerous articles on modern Br art and Bloomsbury to: The Spectator, The Observer, Art in America, The Burlington Magazine; closely involved in restoration and opening of Charleston Farmhouse Sussex (home of Vanessa Bell and Duncan Grant) 1980-; memb: Jury Turner prize 1988, Advsy Ctee Govt Picture Collection 1990; *Style—* Richard Shone, Esq; The Burlington Magazine, 6 Bloomsbury Square, London WC1A 2LP

SHONE, Sir Robert Minshull; CBE (1949); s of Robert Harold Shone of Liverpool; *b* 1906; *Educ* Sedbergh, Liverpool Univ, Chicago Univ; *Career* Cwlth fell USA 1932-34, lectr LSE 1935-36, Br Iron and Steel Fedn 1936-39 and 1945-53 (dir 1950-53); dir Iron and Steel Control 1940-45, jt chm UK and Euro Coal and Steel Community Steel Ctee 1954-62, exec memb Iron and Steel Bd 1953-62, dir-gen of staff and memb NEDC 1962-66; dir: M & G Group Ltd 1966-84, Rank Organisation 1969-78, APV Holdings Ltd 1970-76; visiting prof City Univ London 1967-84, special prof Univ Nottingham 1972-74; kt 1955; *Style*— Sir Robert Shone, CBE; 7 Windmill Hill, London NW3 (☎ 071 435 1930)

SHOOSMITH, Brian Guy; s of Guy Tate Shoosmith, of Gangbridge House, St Marybourne, Andover, Hants, and Ethel Dulas Ann, *née* Grant; *b* 19 July 1941; *Educ* Oundle; *m* 1 (m dis 1974), Wendy Ann Rose; 2 s (Stephen b 1967, Duncan 1968); m 2, 14 June 1986, Elizabeth Susan, da of Kaye McCosh, of Coulter Allers, Biggar, Lanarkshire; *Career* int dir Hero SA Brasil 1974-78, md Hawker Siddeley Power Plant 1981-84 (prodn dir 1978-81), chm Crompton Parkinson Ltd 1988- (md 1984-); memb: Nat Tst; *Recreations* vintage Bentleys, good food and wine, travel; *Clubs* Bentley Drivers, Hellidon Tennis and Croquet; *Style*— Brian Shoosmith, Esq; Clare Cottage, Hellidon, Daventry, Norhants NN11 6LG (☎ 0327 60390); Snaip Farm, Coulter, Biggar, Lanarkshire ML12 6PZ; Hawker Siddeley Group plc, at Crompton Parkinson Ltd, Woodlands House, The Ave, Cliftonville, Northampton NN1 5BS (☎ 0604 30201, fax 0604 28769, car 0836 652306, telex 518333)

SHOOTER, Prof Reginald Arthur; CBE (1980); s of Rev Arthur Edwin Shooter, TD, and Mabel Kate, *née* Pinniger; *b* 4 April 1916; *Educ* Univ of Cambridge (MA, MD); *m* 4 Dec 1946, Jean, da of Prof T W Wallace, CBE, MC, of Long Ashton Res Station; 1 s (Adrian), 3 da (Joanna, Felicity, Anthea); *Career* Surgn Lt RNVR 1943-46; Rockefeller travelling fell 1950-51, prof of med microbiology Univ of London 1961-81, bacteriologist Bart's 1961-81, dean of Med Coll Bart's 1972-81; memb: Public Health Lab Servs Bd 1970-82, City and E London AHA 1974-81, Scientific Advsy Cncl Stress Fndn 1980-88, Gloucester Health Authy 1981-85; tstee: Mitchell City of London Tst 1958-82, Jenner Tst 1989-; chm Dangerous Pathogens Advsy Gp 1975-81; govr: Bart's 1972-74, Queen Mary Coll 1972-81; Pybus medal N of Eng Surgical Soc 1979; FRCP, FRCS, FRCPath; *Recreations* fishing, gardening; *Style*— Prof Reginald Shooter, CBE; Eastlea, Back Edge Lane, Edge, Stoud, Glos GL6 6PE (☎ 0452 812408)

SHORE, Andrew; s of Frank Shore (d 1969), of Oldham, Lancashire, and Edith, *née* Ashton (d 1963), of Oldham, Lancashire; *b* 30 Sept 1952; *Educ* Counthill GS Oldham, Univ of Bristol (BA), Royal Northern Coll of Music, London Opera Centre; *m* 1976, Fiona Mary, da of John Macdonald; 3 da (Sarah Jane b 12 Sept 1983, Emily Ann b 22 Sept 1985, Harriet Mary Edith b 16 March 1990); *Career* stage mangr and singer Opera for All tours (Frosch in Die Fledermaus, Fiorello in Barber of Seville, Giacomo in Fra Diavolo, Marquis in La Traviata) 1977-79; Kent Opera: joined chorus 1979, subsequent roles incl Antonio in Marriage of Figaro, Pasha Selim in Seraglio, Dr Bartolo in Barber of Seville, Papageno in Magic Flute, devisor and presenter educnl material; Opera North roles incl: debut as King Dodon in The Golden Cockerel 1985, Sacristan in Tosca, Leander in Love for Three Oranges, Varlaam in Boris Godunov, Don Inigo in L'heure Espagnole and Dr Bartolo, title roles in Don Pasquale, Gianni Schicchi and King Priam; Scottish Opera roles incl: debut as Mr Flint in Billy Budd 1987, Baron in La Vie Parisienne, Don Alfonso in Cosi Fan Tutte; English National Opera roles incl: debut as Cappadocian in Salome 1987, Doeg in Philips Glass's Planet 8, Don Alfonso, Falstaff, Papageno, Frank in Die Fledermaus, Dr Bartolo; Glyndebourne Festival roles incl: debut as Baron Douphol in La Traviata 1988, Vicar in Albert Herring, Falstaff, and Dr Bartolo and Don Alfonso with Glyndebourne Touring Opera; debut as Dr Bartolo: with Welsh Nat Opera 1990, in Vancouver and Ottawa 1991; prodr for various amateur and professional gps: Nabucco, Manon Lescaut, Carmen, Orpheus in the Underworld, Bastien and Bastienne, Der Freischütz, Hugh the Drover, La Traviata, Romeo & Juliet, Handel's Faramondo, Wolf-Ferrari's School for Fathers; winner Tim Brandt award in Opera Prodn 1977; recording of Nightingale by Charles Strouse released 1983; *Style*— Andrew Shore, Esq; Athole Still International Management, 113 Church Road, Crystal Palace, London SE19 2PR (☎ 081 653 9595, fax 081 771 8172)

SHORE, Darryl; *b* 30 Aug 1946; *Educ* De La Salle Coll Sheffield, Sheffield Univ Med Sch (MB ChB); *Career* house surgn Royal Infirmary Sheffield 1972 (house physician 1971-72), demonstrator in pathology Univ of Sheffield 1972-73, sr house offr orthopaedic surgery Royal Hosp Sheffield 1973, sr house offr in gen surgery Bristol Royal Infirmary 1974 (sr house offr in urology 1973-74), sr house offr in orthopaedic surgery Dept of Orthopaedics Bristol 1974-75, registrar in paediatric surgery Children's Hosp Sheffield 1975-76, registrar in gen and vascular surgery Royal Infirmary Sheffield 1976 (registrar in gen surgery 1975); registrar in cardiothoracic surgery: Royal Infirmary and Children's Hosp and Cardiothoracic Unit Northern Gen Hosp Sheffield 1976-78, Brompton Hosp London 1978; res fell in cardiothoracic surgery Albert Einstein Coll of Med NY USA 1979; sr registrar in cardiothoracic surgery: Brompton Hosp London 1980, Hosp for Sick Children Gt Ormond St London 1981, sr registrar in cardiac surgery Nat Heart Hosp London 1982, conslt in cardiac surgery to the Southampton and SW Hampshire Health Authy and clinical teacher Univ of Southampton 1982-87, conslt cardiac surgn in adult and paediatric cardiac surgery Nat Heart and Brompton Hosps 1987-; *Publications incl:* Urinary Lithiasis in Childhood in the Bristol Clinical Area (jtly in Br Jl of Urology, 1975), Results of Mitral Valvuloplasty with Suture Plication Technique (jtly in Jl of Thoracic and Cardiovascular Surgery, 1980), Atresia if Left Atrio-Ventricular Connection (jtly in Br Heart Jl, 1982), Oral Verapamil fails to Prevent Supraventricular Tachycardia following Coronary Artery Surgery (jtly in Int Jl of Cardiology, 1985), Thirteen Years evaluation of the Bjork-Shiley isolated mitral valve prosthesis (jtly in Jl of Cardiovascular Surgery, 1989), Surgical Treatment for infaret-related ventricular septal defects (jtly in Jl of Thoracic Surgery, 1990); *Style*— Darryl Shore, Esq; Brompton Hospital, Sydney St, London SW3 6NP (☎ 071 352 5541)

SHORE, David Teignmouth; OBE (1982); s of Geoffrey Teignmouth Shore (d 1963), of Morden, Surrey, and Cecilia Mary, *née* Proctor; *b* 15 Nov 1928; *Educ* Tiffin Boys' Sch, Imperial Coll of Sci London (BSc, MSc); *m* 15 April 1950, Pamela Rose, da of Arthur Henry Goodge (d 1964); 1 s (Timothy b 1954), 2 da (Hilary b 1956, Sarah b 1963); *Career* APV Co Ltd: process design engr 1950-52, chief process engr 1954-64, res dir 1964-77 (md 1977-82); heat transfer engr Foster Wheeler Ltd 1953-54; dir Food Div APV Hldgs plc 1982-84, tech dir APV plc 1984-88; chm: Food Res Assoc 1983-87, Engrg Bd SERC 1985-89; memb Ct and Cncl Univ of Reading; FIMechE 1967, FIChemE 1970, FIFST 1970, FCGI 1979, FEng 1979; *Recreations* walking, astronomy, wine making; *Clubs* Nat Lib; *Style*— David Shore, Esq, OBE; Hembury, Garratts Lane, Banstead, Surrey SM7 2BA (☎ 0737 353 721)

SHORE, Dr Elizabeth Catherine; *née* Wrong; CB (1978); da of Edward Murray Wrong (d 1928), and Rosalind Grace Smith (d 1983); *b* 19 Aug 1927; *Educ* Newnham Coll Cambridge, Bart's; *m* 1948, Peter David Shore, *qv*, s of Robert Norman Shore (d 1942); 2 s (Piers (d 1977), Crispin), 2 da (Thomasina, Tacy); *Career* dep chief MO DHSS, 1977-84, postgrad med dean NW Thames Region 1985-; Child Accident Prevention Tst: cncl chm 1985-88, chm of Professional Ctee 1988-90, tstee 1985-; pres Med Women's Fedn 1990-; memb GMC 1989; *Recreations* swimming, reading; *Style*— Dr Elizabeth Shore, CB; 23 Dryburgh Rd, London SW15 1BN; British Postgraduate Medical Federation, 33 Millman St, London WC1 (☎ 071 831 6222)

SHORE, Rt Hon Peter David; PC (1967), MP (Lab) Bethnal Green and Stepney 1983-; *b* 20 May 1924; *Educ* Quarry Bank HS Liverpool, King's Coll Cambridge; *m* 1948, Dr Elizabeth Catherine Shore, CB, *qv*, *née* Wrong (dep chief med offr DHSS 1977-); 1 s, 2 da (and 1 s decd); *Career* Parly candidate (Lab): St Ives (Cornwall) 1950, Halifax 1959; MP (Lab): Stepney 1964-74, Tower Hamlets, Stepney and Poplar 1974-83; head Lab Res Dept 1959-64; PPS to Harold Wilson as PM 1965-66; jt parly sec Miny Technol 1966-67 and Dept Econ Affrs 1967, sec state Econ Affrs 1967-69, min without portfolio and dep ldr House of Commons 1969-70, oppn spokesman on Europe 1971-74, trade sec 1974-76, environment sec 1976-79; memb Shadow Cabinet and chief oppn spokesman on: Foreign Affrs 1979-80, Treasy and Econ Affairs 1981-Nov 1983, Trade and Indust and shadow ldr of The House Nov 1983-, memb Select Ctee on Foreign Affrs 1970; *Recreations* swimming; *Style*— The Rt Hon Peter Shore, MP; 23 Dryburgh Rd, London SW15

SHORE, Sydney Frederick; s of Sydney George Gordon Shore (d 1951), and Beatrice Maud, *née* Turner; *b* 13 March 1933; *Educ* Wanstead Co HS; *m* 28 May 1955, Joyce Margaret Lucy, da of Albert Edward English (d 1983); 1 s (Graeme Edward b 1966), 1 da (Elizabeth Jane b 1963); *Career* Nat Serv RCS 1951-53; Lloyds Bank plc: branch mangrs appts City of London 1966-78, mangr Colmore Row Birmingham 1978-81, regnl dir and gen mangr West Midlands 1981-83, asst gen mangr Corporate Banking Div 1983-87, gen mangr Corporate Banking Div 1987-; elder and chm of Ctees Utd Reformed Church; FCIB, FRSA; *Recreations* theatre, opera, music; *Style*— Sydney Shore, Esq; 17 Robin Hill Drive, Camberley, Surrey GU15 1EC (☎ 0276 29830); Lloyd's Bank plc, St Georges House, 6-8 Eastcheap, London EC3M 1LL (☎ 071 418 3636, fax 071 418 3688)

SHORROCK, (John) Michael; QC (1988); s of James Godby Shorrock (d 1987), and Mary Patricia, *née* Lings; *b* 25 May 1943; *Educ* Clifton Coll, Pembroke Coll Cambridge (MA); *m* 25 Nov 1971, Marianne, da of Jack Mills (d 1983); 2 da (Amabel b 13 Dec 1971, Rose b 1 Sept 1974); *Career* called to the Bar 1965, rec Crown Ct 1982; *Style*— Michael Shorrock, Esq, QC; 2 Old Bank Street, Manchester (☎ 061 832 3791)

SHORT, (Charles) Alan; s of Charles Ronald Short, of Hillingdon, Middx, and Dorothea Henrietta Winterfeldt; *b* 23 March 1955; *Educ* Lower Sch of John Lyon Harrow, Trinity Coll Cambridge (MA), Harvard Univ Graduate Sch of Design; *m* 12 April 1985, The Noble Romina Scicluna Patrizia Corinne Desirée, da of Alan Edward Marshall (d 1983), and the Noble Mignon Scicluna-Marshall, sister of the Baron of Tabria and the Marquis Scicluna; *Career* architect; ptnr Edward Cullinan Architects 1981-86, founded Peake Short & Ptnrs 1986; visiting lectr and critic at Univ of Edinburgh, Leicester Poly, Univ of Manchester; visiting asst prof Washington Univ USA; fndr Int Summer Sch for Architects Malta (with UNESCO); Dip Arch RIBA; *Recreations* collecting drawings, restoration of family home (Palazzo Parisio Malta); *Clubs* Groucho; *Style*— Charles Short, Esq; 212 Old Brompton Rd, London SW5 (☎ 071 370 1759); Peake Short and Ptnrs, Prescott Studios, 15 Prescott Place, London SW4 (☎ 071 720 9994)

SHORT, Clare; MP (Lab) Birmingham Ladywood 1983-; da of Frank Short, and Joan Short; *b* 15 Feb 1946; *Educ* Univ of Keele, Univ of Leeds; *m* Alexander Lyon, former MP (Lab) York; *Career* dir Youthaid and the Unemployment Unit; *Style*— Clare Short, MP; House of Commons, London SW1

SHORT, (Bernard) David; s of Bernard Charles Short (d 1970), and Ethel Florence, *née* Matthews (d 1990); *b* 9 June 1935; *Educ* St Edmund Hall, Oxford (MA); *m* 3 Sept 1960, Susan Yvonne, da of Charles Henry Taylor; 2 s (Nicholas b 1970, Timothy b 1973), 1 da (Katharine b 1972); *Career* Royal Scots 1953-56, cmmnd 2 Lt 1954, Lt 1955; teacher Ingliz Erkek Lisesi Istanbul 1960-65, lectr Univ of Fukjova Kyushu Japan 1963-65, asst lectr Garretts Green Tech Coll Birmingham 1966-67, sr lectr Henley Coll of Further Educn Coventry 1971-73, head Dept Gen Studies Bournville Coll Further Educn Birmingham 1973-76 (lectr 1967-71); HM inspr schs 1976- (staff inspr 1984, chief inspr further educn 1986-); *Books* A Guide to Stress in English (1967), Humour (1971); *Recreations* music, boats, gardening; *Style*— David Short, Esq; Department of Education and Science, Elizabeth House, York Rd, London

SHORT, Dr David James; s of Jesse Short (d 1955), of Bolton Lancs, and Elaine Alice, *née* Lunn; *b* 11 Oct 1936; *Educ* Bolton Sch, Univ of Durham, Univ of Bristol, Univ of London; *m* 1, July 1961, Jennifer, da of Arthur Law (d 1982); 1 da (Gillian Andrea Claire b 28 Jan 1963); m 2, 31 May 1978, Sondra Nicholson Archer; 1 da (Elizabeth Francis Emily b 18 Nov 1983); *Career* offr and pilot RAF 1960-68: flying trg, sqdn pilot, duty combat survival intr; Sqdn Ldr RAuxAF; house and res positions Bristol Maternity Hosp 1973-74, GP trainee Cheddar Somerset 1975, MO Br Aerospace Riyadh 1975-76, flying doctor Australia (outback) 1976, hon clinical asst cardiology and respiratory physiology UCH London, princ gen practise Brixham 1977-80, hosp practitioner Brixham 1977-80, specialist advsr Bristol Airport Mgmnt Ctee 1981-85, princ gen practise Bristol 1981-85, regnl MO BR Western Regn (memb exec) 1985-; accredited specialist in occupational med Jt Ctee Higher Med Trg 1987; lectr and examiner Red Cross and St John's Ambulance Bde 1977-80, hon memb Torbay Hosps Dist Mgmnt Team 1978-80, Locum Physician Saudi Arabia Armed Forces 1981-, clinical teacher gen practise Univ of Bristol 1981-85, aviation med examiner CAA 1982-, lectr and examiner first aid at work (Health and Safety Exec) 1985-; numerous articles in learned jls; MRCS, LRCP, MFOM, MBIM; *Recreations* flying fast aerobatic light aircraft, outdoor pursuits, photography; *Clubs* RAF; *Style*— Dr David Short; 12 Whitesfield Rd, Nailsea, Bristol BS19 2DT (☎ 0272 855294); Medical Centre, Platform 3 British Rail Temple Meads Station, Bristol (☎ 0272 291001)

SHORT, (Andrew) Gregor; s of Dr Ian Alexander Short (d 1976), of Glasgow, and Dr Margaret Alberta Elder Smith; *b* 9 Nov 1955; *Educ* Glasgow Acad, Christ Church Oxford (MA); *m* 18 Aug 1984, Jane Anne, da of Robert Geoffrey Lunn, of Marbella, Spain; 1 s (Alexander McGregor b 23 Aug 1990); *Career* Citibank NA London: corp fin exec 1977, vice pres 1982; fndr new fin co Sleipner UK Ltd 1985-; *Recreations* downhill skiing, tennis, golf; *Style*— Gregor Short, Esq; Sleipner UK Ltd, 417 Finchley Rd, London NW3 6HL (☎ 071 431 4373, fax 071 435 3554)

SHORT, Hon Michael Christian; o s of Baron Glenamara, CH, PC (Life Peer), *qv*; *b* 1943; *Educ* Durham Sch, Durham Univ; *m* 1968, Ann, da of Joseph Gibbon, of Whickham, Tyne and Wear; *Career* slr; *Recreations* theatre; *Clubs* Reform; *Style*— The Hon Michael Short; Holly House, Whickham Park, Whickham, Newcastle upon Tyne (☎ 091 4887617)

SHORT, Michael Edward; s of Thomas Edward Short, of Blackheath, and Anne Elizabeth, *née* Roffe; *b* 16 Sept 1941; *Educ* Greenwich Boys Tech Coll; *m* 12 May 1962, Maureen, da of Christoher Thorington (d 1984); 1 s (Ian Michael Edward b 1973), 1 da (Joanne Maureen (twin) b 1973); *Career* gp md Pearce Group Holdings Ltd; chm: Pearce Maintenance Ltd, Pearce Southern Ltd, Pearce Northern Ltd, Pearce Gowshall Ltd, Davand Plastics Ltd; md Haaxman Lichtreclame BV; FIOD 1974; *Recreations* golf, badminton, music; *Clubs* RAC; *Style*— Michael Short, Esq; Rowans, High Halstow, Kent ME3 8SF; Pearce Group Holdings, Insignia House, New Cross, London SE14 6AB (☎ 081 692 6611, fax 081 692 1753/081 694 8015, car 0863

360309)

SHORT, (Orville) Peter; s of Francis Augustus Short (d 1970), and Lucy Minnie Edwards (d 1968); *b* 23 Nov 1927; *Educ* Priory Sch for Boys, Shrewsbury Sch of Architecture, Univ of Liverpool; *m* 2 April 1961, Fiona Mary, da of George Francis McConnell (d 1978); 1 s (Stephen b 1962), 1 da (Rachel b 1963); *Career* Nat Serv, KOYLI Berlin, DCLI Jamaica; chartered architect; Salop Co Architects, Sir Percy Thomas & Son, IDC & Turriff Tech Servs, sr ptnr Peter Short & Ptnrs (Architectural and Planning Conslts) 1971-87, princ Peter Short architect 1987-; memb Worcester Festival Choral Soc 1968- (memb ctee 1985-); memb church choirs: St Giles Shrewsbury 1939-45, Abbey Shrewsbury 1955-64, St Nicholas Alcester 1964-; memb Alcester: Town Hall Restoration Ctee, Civic Soc (public footpath sub ctee for Heart of England Way, produced footpath booklets), Rotary Club 1981-; ARIBA; *Recreations* tennis, badminton, walking, watching cricket, singing, water colour painting; *Clubs* Alcester Tennis, Alcester Unionist, Worcestershire CCC; *Style*— Peter Short, Esq; 46 Birmingham Road, Alcester, Warwickshire B49 5EP (☎ 0789 762731); Peter Short, Chartered Architect, 9c High Street, Alcester, Warwickshire B49 5AE (☎ 0789 764250)

SHORT, Philip; s of Wilfres Short (d 1976), and Marion, *née* Edgar; *b* 17 April 1945; *Educ* Sherborne, Queen's Coll Cambridge CMA); *m* 9 Aug 1968, Christine Victoria, da of (Francis) Donald Baring-Gould; 1 s (Sengan b 1 March 1971); *Career* correspondent BBC Moscow 1974-76, Peking 1977-81, Paris 1981-90, Tokyo 1990; *Books* Banda (1974), The Dragon and The Bear (1982); *Recreations* Chinese porcelain; *Style*— Philip Short, Esq; BBC, 4th Floor, NTV Yonbancho-Bakkan, 5-6 Yonbancho, Chiyoda-Ku, Tokyo 102, Japan (☎ 010 81 32880011, fax 010 81 32880010)

SHORT, Renee; *Educ* Univ of Manchester; *m* 2 da; *Career* freelance journalist; memb Watford RDC 1952-64, cncllr Herts CC 1952-67; contested St Albans 1955 and Watford 1959; MP (Lab) Wolverhampton NE 1964-87; chm (now vice pres) Parly and Scientific Ctee 1982-, chm Parly Select Ctee Social Servs 1979-87, memb Lab NEC 1970-81 and 1983-87; hon fell Wolverhampton Poly; memb MRC, Hon Fell RCPsych, Hon memb RCP; *Books* The Care of Long Term Prisoners (1979); *Recreations* theatre, music; *Style*— Mrs Renée Short; House of Commons, London SW1

SHORT, Rodney Neil Terry; s of Flt Lt Cyril Herbert Terry Short, AFC, of Edgarley, Allandale Rd, Burnham-on-Sea, Somerset, and Deborah Allen, *née* Hobbs; *b* 4 Aug 1946; *Educ* Sherborne, Coll of Law, INSEAD (MBA); *m* 16 April 1977, Penelope Anne, da of Capt Emile William Goodman, OBE; 1 s (Jonathan b 1980), 1 da (Anna b 1983); *Career* admitted slr 1970, asst slr Freshfields 1970-73 and 1974-77, Corp Fin Dept Kleinwort Benson 1974-75; Clifford Chance (formerly Coward Chance) 1977-: Dubai office 1978-81, Bahrain office 1981-83, ptnr 1982-; Freeman City of London Solicitors Co 1983; memb: Law Soc 1970, IBA 1982; *Recreations* tennis, golf, shooting, skiing; *Clubs* Roehampton; *Style*— Rodney Short, Esq; 18 Langside Ave, London SW15 (☎ 081 876 1859); Clifford Chance, Royex House, Aldermanbury Sq, London EC2V 7LD (☎ 071 600 0808, fax 071 726 8561, telex 8959991)

SHORT, Roger Guy; MVO (1971); s of Harold Short (d 1973), and Alice Ames Short; *b* 9 Dec 1944; *Educ* Malvern, Univ Coll Oxford (MA); *m* 19 June 1971, (Sally) Victoria, da of Bernard Thomas Taylor; 1 s (Thomas b 1988), 2 da (Katherine b 1978, Elizabeth b 1982); *Career* FCO 1967-, third and second sec Ankara 1969, FCO 1974, commercial consul Rio de Janeiro 1978, first sec and head of chancery Ankara 1981, cnsllr FCO 1984, head personnel Services Dept FCO 1990, head of chancery cnsllr and consul gen Oslo 1986; *Recreations* skating; *Style*— Roger Short, Esq, MVO

SHORTALL, Michael Patrick; Lord of Ballylorcan, Anglo-Norman Territorial Barony (Irish) dating from before 1208, although first authenticated use dates from 1408; s of John Shortall (d 1967), and Mary Shortall (d 1967); *b* 16 March 1934; *Educ* Medway Coll, RMA Sandhurst, Staff Coll Camberley; *m* 7 June 1969, Patricia Hastings, da of Cdr John Manwaring Parker, RN (d 1979); 1 d (Clare b 1979); *Career* Maj cmd Sqdn, Europe, N Ireland, ME, Far East; ADC to COS N Army Gp DAAO QMG; logistic opr MOD, ret 1972; fine art auctioneer and valuer; chm and md The Shortall Group of Companies, md Tunbridge Wells Auction Centre; FRICS, FSVA, FBIM; *Recreations* shooting, sailing, music; *Clubs* MCC; *Style*— Michael Shortall, Esq; The Tunbridge Wells Auction Centre, Western Road, Southborough, Tunbridge Wells TN4 0HQ (☎ and fax 0892 514100)

SHORTER, John Jeffery; s of Charles Jeffery Shorter (d 1968), of East Wittering, Sussex, and Adelaide, *née* Deacon; *b* 28 Sept 1936; *Educ* Reading Sch, Chichester HS, Brocklands Tech Coll (ONC Mech Eng) Kingston Tech Coll; *m* 1, 1961 (m dis 1968), Judith, da of James Shattock; m 2, 1968, Vera Threadgold, da of Cecil Triggs; 3 da (Joanne b 16 Sept 1971, Toni b 1 Feb 1973, Louise b 21 Sept 1975); *Career* Bengr apprentice Vickers Armstrong (Aircraft) Ltd Weybridge 1953-58 (design draughtsman in engine installations Vanguard VC 10), design draughtsman CF Taylor (Unity Designs) 1963-66; Chas A Blatchford & Sons Ltd: design draughtsman 1966-69, prodn mangr 1969-71, chief engr 1971-84, tech dir 1984-87, tech and mktg dir 1987-; memb Br design Awards Judging Panel 1990, del ISO Tech Ctee on Physical Testing of Prostheses, UK rep for Interbor, conslt to UNIDO (artificial limb mfr); *awards* Br Design Cncl award and Queen's award for Technol: (for Modular Assembly Prosthesis) 1976, (for Endolite System) 1990; memb: Instn of Engrg Designers 1969-, Inst of Industl Mangrs 1972-, MBIM 1979-, memb Inst D 1984-, memb Int Soc for Prosthetics and Orthotics; *Recreations* golf, off-shore sailing; *Clubs* Basingstoke Golf, Rotary (Basingstoke & Deane); *Style*— John Shorter, Esq; Chas A Blatchford & Sons Ltd, Research & Development Unit, Unit 6, Sherrington Way, Basingstoke, Hampshire (☎ 0256 465771, fax 0256 810450, car 0831 478293)

SHORTIS, Maj-Gen Colin; CB (1988), CBE (1980, OBE 1977, MBE 1972); *b* 18 Jan 1934; *Educ* Bedford Sch; *m* 1955, Sylvia Mary Jenkinson; 2 s, 2 da; *Career* Cdr 8 Inf Bde 1978-80, RCDS 1981, Cdr Br Mil Advsy and Trg Team Zimbabwe 1982-83, Dir of Inf 1983-86, GOC NW District 1986-89, Col Cmdt Prince of Wales Divn 1983-89, Col Devonshire and Dorset Regt 1984-90; *Recreations* sailing; *Clubs* Army and Navy; *Style*— Maj-Gen Colin Shortis, CB, CBE; c/o Bank of Scotland, 57/60 Haymarket, London SW1Y 4QY

SHOTTER, Very Rev Edward Frank; s of Frank Edward Shotter (d 1970), of Grimsby, and Minnetta, *née* Gaskill (d 1976); *b* 29 June 1933; *Educ* Humberstone Fndn Sch Clee, St David's Coll Lampeter, Univ of Wales (BA), St Stephen's House Oxford; *m* 9 Dec 1978, Dr Jane Edgcumbe, da of Dr John Oliver Pearce Edgcumbe; 2 s (James b 1982, Piers b 1984), 1 da (Emma b 1987); *Career* ordained: deacon 1960, priest 1961; asst curate St Peter's Plymouth 1960-62, intercollegiate sec Student Christian Movement London 1962-66; dir: London Medical Gp 1963-89, Inst of Medical Ethics 1974-89; chaplain Univ of London 1969-89, prebendary St Paul's Cathedral London 1977-89, dean of Rochester 1990-; memb: Editorial Bd Journal of Medical Ethics, working party on ethics of med involvement in torture, working party on ethics of prolonging life and assisting death; Inst of Med Ethics (Amulree fell 1991-); FRSM; Patriarchal Cross Romanian Orthodox Church 1975; *Books* Matters of Life and Death (ed, 1970), Life Before Birth (jt author, 1986); *Recreations* Romania, restoring country houses, hill walking; *Clubs* Reform, Castle (Rochester); *Style*— The Very Rev the Dean of Rochester; The Deanery, Rochester, Kent ME1 1TG (☎ 0634 844023); Northseat of Auchedly, Tarves, Aberdeen

SHOULER, Hon Mrs (Margaret Fiona); *née* Eden; er da of 9 Baron Auckland and Dorothy Margaret, JP, yr da of Henry Joseph Manser, of Beechwood, Friday St, Eastbourne, Sussex; *b* 12 Dec 1955; *m* 1979, Michael Shouler, yr s of J R Shouler, of Wollaton, Nottingham; 1 s (Benjamin b 1987), 3 da (Elizabeth b 1982, Katherine b 1983, Abigail b 1989); *Style*— The Hon Mrs Shouler; 137 Appledore Ave, Wollaton, Nottingham NG8 2RW

SHOVELTON, Prof David Scott; s of Leslie Shovelton (d 1967), of Kirkee, Croft Rd, Evesham, Worcs, and Marion, *née* de Winton Scott (d 1948); *b* 12 Sept 1925; *Educ* King's Sch Worcester, Univ of Birmingham (BSc, LDS, BDS, FDS, RCS); *m* 20 April 1949, (Dorothy) Pearl, da of Sam Herbert Holland (d 1955); 2 s (Christoher John b 1950, Michael Paul b 1956); *Career* RAF Dental Branch: Flying Offr 1951-52, Flt Lt 1952-53; lectr in operative dental surgery Univ of Birmingham 1953-60, visiting asst prof clinical dentistry Univ of Alabama 1959-60, sr lectr operative dental Surgery Univ of Birmingham 1960-64, conslt dental surgn Utd Birminghams Hosps (now Centl Birmingham Health Authy) 1960-89, dir of dental sch Univ of Birmingham 1974-78, emeritus prof of conservative dentistry Univ of Birmingham 1989- (prof 1964-89); pres Br Soc for Restorative Dentistry 1970-71, conslt Cmmn on Dental Practice Fedn Dentaire Int 1972-79; memb: Birmingham Area Health Authy (teaching) 1973-79, Gen Dental Cncl 1974-89, Jt Ctee for Higher Trg in Dentistry 1979-84, Standing Dental Advsy Ctee 1982-88, bd of faculty of Dental Surgery RCS 1983-91, ctee of Enquiry into Unnecessary Dental Treatment 1984-85, Jt Dental Ctee of MRC Health Depts and SERC 1984-87; conslt advsr in restorative dentistry DHSS 1983-89; memb: Br Dental Assoc, Br Soc for Restorative Dentistry; *Books* Inlays, Crowns and Bridges (jtly 1963, 4 ed 1985); *Recreations* gardening, caravanning, learning about wine; *Clubs* RAF; *Style*— Prof David Shovelton; 86 Broad Oaks Rd, Solihull, W Midlands B91 1HZ (☎ 021 705 3026)

SHOVELTON, Walter Patrick; CB (1976), CMG (1972); s of Sydney Taverner Shovelton, CBE (d 1968), and May Catherine Kelly (d 1958); *b* 18 Aug 1919; *Educ* Charterhouse, Keble Coll Oxford (MA); *m* 1968, Helena, da of Denis George Richards, OBE; *Career* WWII 1940-46, Maj; civil servant; dep sec 1946-78, dir gen GCBS 1978-85; dir: Br Airports Authy 1982-85, The Maersk Co Ltd 1985-87 (vice chm 1987-); chm Birmingham Euro Airways 1988-; advsr: House of Lords Ctee on Euro Communities 1985-86, House of Commons Select Ctee on Tport 1986; chm Maritime Ctee William & Mary Tercentenary Tst 1985-; *Recreations* golf; *Clubs* Brooks's, Royal Ashdown Forest Golf, Rye Golf, Hampstead Golf, Seniors Golf; *Style*— W P Shovelton, Esq, CB, CMG; 63 London Rd, Tunbridge Wells, Kent TN1 1DT (☎ 0892 27885)

SHRAGER, Robert Neil; s of Benjamin Shrager, of London, and Rose Ruth, *née* Kempner; *b* 21 May 1948; *Educ* Charterhouse, St John's Coll Oxford (MA), City Univ (MSc); *m* 1982, Elizabeth Fiona, da of Mortimer Stuart Bogod (d 1964); 2 s (James b 1985, Edward b 1987); *Career* dir: Morgan Grenfell & Co Ltd 1985-88, Dixons Group plc 1988-; *Recreations* family, golf, arts, walking; *Clubs* RAC; *Style*— Robert Shrager, Esq; Woodstock, 5 Hollycroft Avenue, London NW3 7QG (☎ 071 435 4367); Dixons Group plc, 29 Farm St, London W1X 7RD (☎ 071 499 3494)

SHRANK, Dr Alan Bruce; s of Philip Shrank, of 36 Hertford Ct, London, and Hetty, *née* Rosenberg; *b* 18 Aug 1932; *Educ* City of London Sch, Magdalen Coll Oxford, Middx Hosp London (MA, BM BCh); *m* 12 March 1960, Lucy Rose Désirée, da of Lt Chesley Gordon Murcell (d 1970); 1 s (Alexander b 9 Sept 1970), 1 da (Catherine b 23 March 1973); *Career* Corpl Air Trg Corps 1947-48; conslt dermatologist: Ibadan Univ 1962-63, Shropshire Health Authy 1967-; chm: Computer Gp Br Assoc of Dermatologists 1986-89 (memb 1970), Regnl Advsy Ctee of Dermatology 1989-; memb Med Appeal Tbnl 1989-; author of numerous articles on epidemiology of skin diseases; borough cncllr Shrewsbury and Atcham Borough Cncl 1970-83, memb TUC Health Servs Ctee 1979-84, pres Hosp Conslts and Specialists Assoc 1984-86, vice pres Nat Pure Water Assoc 1984-; memb RSM 1960, FRCP 1977; *Books* International Coding Index for Dermatology (jtly, 1978); *Recreations* furniture making, fell walking, fighting for lost causes; *Style*— Dr Alan Shrank; Salop Nuffield Hospital, Shrewsbury, Shropshire SY3 9DP (☎ 0743 353441)

SHREEVE, Ven David Herbert; s of Hubert Ernest Shreeve (d 1965), of Oxford, and Ivy Eleanor, *née* Whiting; *b* 18 Jan 1934; *Educ* Southfield Sch Oxford, St Peter's Coll Oxford (MA), Ridley Hall Cambridge; *m* 12 Dec 1957, Barbara, da of Arthur Thomas Fogden (d 1964), of Oxford; 1 da (Gillian Barbara b 1960), 1 s (Ian David b 1962); *Career* ordained deacon Exeter 1959, asst curate St Andrew's (Plymouth) 1959-64, priest 1960; vicar: St Anne (Bermondsey) 1964-71, St Luke (Eccleshill) 1971-84; rural dean Calverley 1978-84, hon canon Bradford Cathedral 1983-84, archdeacon Bradford 1984-; *Recreations* walking, camping, jogging, photography; *Style*— The Ven the Archdeacon of Bradford; Rowan House, 11 The Rowans, Baildon, Shipley, W Yorks BD17 5DB (☎ 0274 583735)

SHREWSBURY, Bishop Suffragan of, 1987-; Rt Rev John Dudley Davies; s of Charles Edward Steedman Davies (d 1960); *b* 12 Aug 1927; *Educ* Trinity Coll Cambridge (MA), Lincoln Theol Coll; *m* 1956, Shirley Dorothy, da of late Alfred Gough; 1 s, 2 da; *Career* ordained deacon 1953, priest 1954; curate: Halton Leeds 1953-56, Yeoville Johannesburg 1957; p-in-c Evander, Diocese of Johannesburg 1957-61, rector and dir of missions Empangeni Diocese of Zululand and Swaziland 1961-63, Anglican chaplain Univ of Witwatersrand and Johannesburg Coll of Educn 1963-70, sec for Chaplaincies of Higher Educn, C of E Bd of Educn 1970-74, vicar Keele and Anglican chaplain Univ of Keele 1974-76, princ Coll of Ascension Selly Oak 1976-81, preb of Sandiacre in Lichfield Cathedral 1976-87, diocesan missioner St Asaph 1982, canon residentiary and Hellins lectr, Diocese of St Asaph 1982-85; vicar and rector: Llanrhaeadr-ym-Mochnant, Llanarmon MM, Pennant, Hirnant and Llangynog 1985-87; *Books* Crisis, Free to Be, Beginning Now, Good News in Galatians, Creed and Conflict, The Faith Abroad, Seeing our Faith, His and Ours, Agenda for Apostles, Mark at Work; *Style*— The Rt Rev the Bishop of Shrewsbury; Athlone House, 68 London Road, Shrewsbury, Shropshire SY2 6PG (☎ 0743 235867)

SHREWSBURY, Bishop of (RC, cr 1851) 1980-; Rt Rev Joseph Gray; s of late Terence Gray, and Mary, *née* Alwill; *b* 20 Oct 1919; *Educ* St Patrick's Cavan, Oscott Coll Sutton Coldfield, Maynooth Coll, Pontifical Univ Rome (DCL); *Career* ordained priest 1943, vicar gen of Birmingham 1960-69, Aux Bishop of Liverpool 1969-80, Bishop of Shrewsbury (RC) 1980-; *Recreations* music, reading, travel; *Style*— The Rt Rev the Bishop of Shrewsbury; The Bishop's House, 99 Eleanor Rd, Birkenhead L43 7QW (☎ 051 653 3600)

SHREWSBURY, Nadine, Countess of; Nadine Muriel; da of late Brig-Gen Cyril Randell Crofton, CBE; *m* 1936 (m dis 1963), 21 Earl (d 1980); 2 s, 4 da; *Style*— The Rt Hon Nadine Countess of Shrewsbury; The Annexe, Upper Bolney, Henley-on-Thames, Oxon

SHREWSBURY AND WATERFORD, 22 Earl of (E 1442, I 1446 respectively); Charles Henry John Benedict Crofton Chetwynd Chetwynd-Talbot; Premier Earl (on the Roll) in peerages both of England and Ireland; Baron Talbot (GB 1723), Earl Talbot and Viscount Ingestre (GB 1784); Hereditary Lord High Steward of Ireland and Great Sencchal; patron of 11 lvings; s of 21 Earl (d 1980) by 1 w, Nadine, Countess of Shrewsbury, *qv*; *b* 18 Dec 1952; *Educ* Harrow; *m* 1974, Deborah Jane, da of Noel Staughton Hutchinson, of Ellerton House, Sambrook, Salop; 2 s (Viscount Ingestre b 11 Jan 1978, Hon Edward William Henry Alexander b 18 Sept 1981), 1 da (Lady Victoria Jane b 7 Sept 1975); *Heir* s, Viscount Ingestre; *Career* dep chm Britannia Building Soc; dir Richmount Enterprise Zone Managers Ltd; patron: St Giles Hospice, British Red Cross (Staffs County); hon pres SSAFA (Wolverhampton); pres: Shropshire Bldg Preservation Tst, Staffs Soc; vice pres: Midlands and West Assoc of Bldg Socs, Staffordshire Small-bone Rifle Assoc; chm: Stafford Hospital Scanner Appeal; *Recreations* all field sports; *Clubs* The Flyfishers; *Style—* The Rt Hon the Earl of Shrewsbury and Waterford; Wanfield Hall, Kingstone, Uttoxeter, Staffs ST14 8QT (☎ and fax 0889 500 275)

SHRIMPLIN, John Steven; s of John Reginald Shrimplin (d 1977), of Chelmsford, Essex, and Kathleen Mary, *née* Stevens; *b* 9 May 1934; *Educ* Colchester Royal GS, Kings Coll London (BSc); *m* 17 August 1957, Hazel, da of Frederick Baughen (d 1969), of Coventry, Warwickshire; 2 s (Peter b 1960, Russell b 1963); *Career* Guided Weapons Dept Royal Aircraft Estab Farnborough 1956-66, Def Operational Est W Byfleet 1966-71, attended JSSC 1971, Def Res and Devpt Staff Br Embassy Washington USA 1972-73, asst dir (Future Aircraft System) MOD Procurement Exec 1974-79, asst chief scientist RAF MOD 1979-83, Head of Weapons Dept Royal Aircraft Estab Farnborough 1983-85, minister/cncllr Def Equipment 1985-88, dep head Br Dep Staff Br Embassy Washington 1985-88, dir of Sci Studies MOD 1988-; *Recreations* walking, gardening, travel; *Style—* John Shrimplin, Esq; MOD, Whitehall, London (☎ 071 218 3534)

SHRIMPLIN, Roger Clifford; s of Clifford Walter Shrimplin (d 1987), and Grace Florence, *née* Davis; *b* 9 Sept 1948; *Educ* St Albans Sch, Jesus Coll Cambridge (MA, DipArch); *m* 21 Sept 1974, Catalina Maria Eugenia, da of L Alomar - Josa (d 1982); 3 s (Robert b 1977, Richard b 1980, Edward b 1985); *Career* architect; ptnr and princ CW & RC Shrimplin (Chartered Architects and Chartered Town Planners) 1975-; occasional lectr Univ of Cambridge Sch of Architecture; chm Tstees of Temple Island Henley; cncl memb ARCUK 1985-88, memb various ctees RIBA, ARCUK; Lord of the Manor Shimpling Norfolk 1987; Freeman and Liveryman: City of London, Worshipful Co of Glaziers Painters of Glass 1974 (steward 1990); hon repository admin The London Stained Glass Repository; RIBA 1974, FRTPI 1985, FCI Arb 1986, Arquitecto Colegiado (Baleares) 1990; *Style—* Roger Shrimplin, Esq; 11 Cardiff Road, Luton, Bedfordshire LU1 1PP

SHRIMPTON, David Everard; s of Col G H T Shrimpton, CBE, TD, of Dulwich, and Joyce Margaret, *née* Little; *b* 19 May 1943; *Educ* Dulwich; *m* 25 Oct 1969, Rosemary Sarah, da of Frank Victor Fone; 3 s (Matthew John b 3 Nov 1972, Benjamin James b 24 May 1975, Daniel Thomas b 11 April 1978); *Career* student trainee mangr Deloitte Haskins & Sells 1961-75, princ Industl Devpt Unit DTI 1975-77, corp fin exec Midland Bank plc 1977-79; Stoy Hayward: ptnr in charge corporate finance 1979-89, gen practice ptnr 1989-, memb Mgmnt Ctee; Freeman City of London; FCA 1967; *Recreations* tennis, rugby and Fulham FC; *Style—* David Shrimpton, Esq; Stoy Hayward, 8 Baker St, London W1M 1DA (☎ 071 486 5888, fax 071 487 3686)

SHRIMSLEY, Bernard; s of John Shrimsley (d 1975), and Alice Shrimsley (d 1942); *b* 13 Jan 1931; *Educ* Kilburn GS; *m* 1952, Norma Jessie Alexandra, da of Albert Porter (d 1959), of Southport; 1 da; *Career* RAF 1949-51; journalist and author; dep northern ed Sunday Express 1961, northern ed Daily Mirror 1964; ed: Liverpool Daily Post 1968-69, The Sun 1972-75, News of the World 1975-80, The Mail on Sunday 1982; dir News Group Newspapers Ltd 1975-80, dir (later vice chm) Mail on Sunday Ltd 1981-82; assoc ed Daily Express 1986-; memb Press Cncl 1989 (vice chm 1990), judge Br Press Awards 1988-; *Books* The Candidates (1968), Lion Rampant (1984); *Clubs* Garrick; *Style—* Bernard Shrimsley, Esq; 245 Blackfriars Rd, London SE1 9UX

SHRUBSALL, Brian Thomas Edward; s of Thomas Bertie Charles, and Eva Allen; *b* 23 Sept 1940; *Educ* Westlands Sch, Sittingbourne & Medway Coll; *m* 14 March 1964, Dawn, da of Norman Marcus Bassart Camp (d 1986), of Faversham, Kent; 2 s (Ian b 1967, David b 1970); *Career* vice chm Speyhawk PLC; chm: Tellings Limited, Speyhawk Development Management Limited, Carter Commercial Limited; other Gp directorships; FCIOB, FFB; *Recreations* golf, racehorse owner, sport, theatre; *Clubs* Wentworth; *Style—* Brian Shrubsall, Esq; Greenworth House, Lake Road, Virginia Water Surrey (☎ 0344 844708); Speyhawk PLC, Osprey House, Lower Square, Old Isleworth, Middlesex TW7 6BN (☎ 081 560 2161, fax 081 847 2704, telex 8954569, car 0836 290018)

SHRUBSOLE, Dr Alison Cheveley; CBE (1981); da of Rev Stanley Smith (d 1959), and Margaret Castelfranc Cheveley (d 1984); *b* 7 April 1925; *Educ* Milton Mount Coll, London Univ (BA), Cambridge Univ (MA), Open Univ (Hon Doctorate); *Career* posts held in schs and colls 1946-57; princ: Machakos Trg Coll Kenya 1957-63, Philippa Fawcett Coll London 1963-71, Homerton Coll Cambridge 1971-85; *Recreations* books, music, gardening, cooking, mountain walking; *Style—* Dr Alison Shrubsole, CBE; Cortijo Abulagar, Rubite, Granada, Spain

SHUBIK, Irene; da of Joseph Leib Meyerov Shubik (d 1958), of Vitebsk Russia, and Sara Soloweiczyk (d 1961); *Educ* Havergal Coll Toronto Canada, Univ Coll Toronto (BA, Epstein award for short story competition), UCL (MA); *Career* staff writer Encyclopaedia Britannica Films Inc Chicago USA 1958, story ed on Armchair Theatre and originator Sci Fiction series Out of This World in Drama Dept ABC TV 1960; story ed Story Parade BBC TV 1963; prodr BBC: Out of the Unknown 1966-67, Thirteen Against Fate 1966, Wednesday Play (subsequently Play For Today) 1967-72, Wessex Tales 1973, two stories by Isaac Bashevis Singer for playhouse 1974-75, Rumpole 1975 (Play For Today); wrote and directed Scrolls from The Son of A Star for BBC, Chronicle and Israel TV 1974-75; prodr: Rumpole Thames TV 1977-79, Staying On, Granada TV deviser and writer Jewel In The Crown 1979-82; freelance writer prodr 1982-; *Awards* BAFTA award for best single prodn (Edna The Inebriate Woman) 1971, critics circle award (Edna The Inebriate Woman) 1972, first prize Trieste Sci Fiction Festival (The Machine Stops) 1967, Jury award Jerusalem Film Festival (Scrolls From The Son of A Star) 1976, Gold drama award NY Festival and nominated Best Foreign Import of The Year NY Times (Staying On) 1981; *Books* Play For Today: The Evolution of TV Drama (1975), The War Guest (1986), The Mind Beyond (ed and contrib, 1976); *Recreations* learning Russian; *Clubs* BAFTA; *Style—* Ms Irene Shubik; 36 The Quadrangle, Cambridge Square, London W2 2RW (☎ 071 723 1557)

SHUBROOK, Brian Ralph; s of Ronald Kenneth Shubrook, of Barking, Essex, and Audrey Gwendoline, *née* Jones; *b* 22 July 1950; *m* 20 May 1972, Pauline, da of George Frederick Edgill, MBE, of Leigh-on-Sea, Essex; 2 da (Nicola Jane b 9 Aug 1974, Jessica Anne b 8 Jan 1979); *Career* sr foreign exchange dealer Lloyds Bank Int London 1968-74, foreign exchange mangr Banco de Santander London 1974-81, treas Bayerische Hypotheken und Wechsel Bank London 1981-86, first vice pres and treas Swiss Volskbank London 1986-; memb Foreign Exchange Ctee Foreign Banks Assoc London, tstee Br SLE Aid Gp charity; *Recreations* golf, squash, tennis; *Style—* Brian Shubrook, Esq; Starlings, 36A Monkhams Ave, Woodford Green, Essex IG8 0EY (☎ 081 505 6876); Swiss Volksbank, 48-54 Moorgate, London EC2R 6EL (☎ 071 628 7777, fax 071 628 2786, telex 937777, car 0860 835 006)

SHUCKBURGH, Sir (Charles Arthur) Evelyn; GCMG (1967, KCMG 1959, CMG 1949), CB (1954); eld s of Sir John Evelyn Shuckburgh, KCMG, CB (d 1953); *b* 1909; *Educ* Winchester, King's Coll Cambridge; *m* 1937, Hon Nancy Mildred Gladys Brett *qv*, 2 da of 3 Visc Esher, GBE (d 1963); 2 s, 1 da; *Career* cnsllr HM Diplomatic Service 1947, Buenos Aires 1942-45, Prague 1945-47, principal private sec to sec state Foreign Affrs 1951-54, asst under-sec state FO 1954-56, civilian instr IDC 1956-57, asst sec gen (political) NATO 1958-60, dep under-sec state FO 1960-62, perm UK rep NATO 1962-66, ambass Italy 1966-69; chm: exec ctee Br Red Cross Soc 1970-80, Standing Cmmn Int Red Cross 1976-80; *Style—* Sir Evelyn Shuckburgh, GCMG, CB; High Wood, Watlington, Oxon

SHUCKBURGH, Hon Lady; Hon (Nancy Mildred Gladys); *née* Brett; da of late 3 Viscount Esher, GBE; *b* 1918; *m* 1937, Sir (Charles Arthur) Evelyn Shuckburgh, GCMG, CB, *qv*; *Style—* The Hon Lady Shuckburgh; High Wood House, Watlington, Oxon

SHUCKBURGH, Sir Rupert Charles Gerald; 13 Bt (E 1660), of Shuckburgh, Warwickshire; s of Sir Charles Gerald Stewkley Shuckburgh, 12 Bt, TD, JP, DL (d 1988), and his 2 w Nancy Diana Mary, OBE (d 1984), da of late Capt R Egerton Lubbock, RN, bro of 1 Baron Avebury; *b* 12 Feb 1949; *Educ* Worksop Coll; *m* 1, 1976 (m dis 1987), Judith, da of late William Gordon Mackaness, of Paddock Lodge, Everdon, Daventry; 2 s (James Rupert Charles, Peter Gerald William b 1982); m 2, 5 Sept 1987, Margaret Ida, da of late William Evans, of Middleton, Derbyshire; *Heir* s, James Rupert Charles Shuckburgh b 4 Jan 1978; *Style—* Sir Rupert Shuckburgh

SHUFFREY, Ralph Frederick Dendy; CB (1983), CVO (1981); s of Frederick Arthur Shuffrey, MC (d 1982), of Windmill House, Uppingham, Rutland, and Mary, *née* Dendy (d 1951); *b* 9 Dec 1925; *Educ* Shrewsbury, Balliol Coll Oxford; *m* 1953, Sheila, da of Brig John Lingham, CB, DSO, MC (d 1976); 1 s, 1 da; *Career* served Army 1944-47, Capt (occupation of Greece); joined Home Office 1951, dep under-sec of state and princ estab offr 1980-84; hon sec Soc for Individual Freedom 1985-89; chm: The Canstoun Projects Ltd 1988-, Fire Serv Res and Trg Tst 1989-; *Recreations* riding, squash; *Clubs* Reform; *Style—* Ralph Shuffrey, Esq, CB, CVO; Bridge House, 21 Claremont Rd, Claygate, Surrey (☎ 0372 65123)

SHULMAN, Keith John; s of Leonard Shulman, of Northampton, and Sylvia, *née* Samuels; *b* 23 Feb 1944; *Educ* St Giles VP Sch, Trinity HS Northampton; *Career* fin dir co sec: The Equine and Livestock Insur Co Ltd 1979-88, Equine Underwriting Agencies Ltd 1976-88, Oriden Ltd 1983-88; conslt 1988-; FCA, FINSTD; *Recreations* bridge, reading; *Style—* Keith Shulman, Esq; 11 Harley Court, High Rd, Whetstone, London N20 0QD (☎ 081 446 4072)

SHULMAN, Milton; s of Samuel Shulman and Ethel Rice; *Educ* Univ of Toronto (BA), Osgood Hall Ontario Canada (barr); *m* 1956, Drusilla, da of Norman Beyfus; 1 s (Jason), 2 da (Alexandra, Nicola); *Career* Maj Canadian Armoured Corps 1940-46 (despatches); writer; Evening Standard: film critic 1948-53, theatre critic 1953, TV critic 1966-72; TV exec: Granada 1958-62, Rediffusion 1962-64; film critic Vogue 1975-87, political and social columnist Evening Standard and Daily Express 1973-89; regular memb Radio 4 Stop The Week 1972; memb Advsy Cncl Br Theatre Museum 1983-86; *Books* Defeat in West (1948), How to be a Celebrity (1950), Preep (1964), Preep in Paris (1967), Kill Three (1967), Preep and The Queen (1970), Ravenous Eye (1973), Least Worst Television in World (1973); *Clubs* Hurlingham, Garrick; *Style—* Milton Shulman, Esq; 51 Eaton Square, London SW1 (☎ 071 235 7162)

SHULMAN, Neville; OBE (1990); s of J W Shulman (d 1971), and A Shulman; *b* 2 Dec 1939; *m* 8 Jan 1970, Emma, *née* Broide; 2 s (Alan Hamilton b 9 Sept 1970, Lee Hamilton b 23 June 1973), 1 da (Lauren Hamilton b 8 Aug 1984); *Career* CA in private practice 1961-; ed magazine Industry 1967 and 1968; mangr actors and film dirs 1973-, prodr theatrical prodns, documentaries and short films; chm and dir Int Theatre Inst 1985-, Land and City Families Tst 1987-, Friends of Camden Arts Centre 1988-; sec Fedn of Industrial Devpt Assocs 1965-68, offr and memb Theatres Advsy Cncl 1985-; prison visitor Pentonville 1966; Hon Col Tennessee Army 1977-; memb NUJ 1967-; FCA 1961; *Books* Exit of a Dragonfly (1985), Blindly Runs The Minotaur (1990), Zen In the Art of Climbing Mont Blanc (1991); *Recreations* contemporary art, archaeology, theatre; *Style—* Neville Shulman, Esq, OBE; 4 St George's House, 15 Hanover Square, London W1R 9AJ (☎ 071 486 6363, fax 071 408 1388)

SHURMAN, Laurence Paul Lyons; s of Joseph Shurman (d 1964), and Sarah, *née* Lyons; *b* 25 Nov 1930; *Educ* Newcastle upon Tyne Royal GS, Magdalen Coll Oxford (MA); *m* 22 Nov 1963, Mary Seamans, da of the late Orin McMullan; 2 s (Daniel b 1965, Morley b 1966), 1 da (Ruth b 1970); *Career* admitted slr 1957; fndr: Shurman & Bindman 1961, Shurman & Co 1964 (amalgamated with Kingsley Napley 1967); managing ptnr Kingsley Napley 1975, Banking Ombudsman 1989; govr (vice chm) Channing Sch, legal memb Mental Health Review Tbnl 1976-, memb Cncl Justice 1973-, pres City of Westminster Law Soc 1980-81; memb Law Soc 1957; *Books* The Practical Skills of the Solicitor (1981, 1985), Atkins Encyclopaedia of Court Forms, Vol 26- (contrib mental health review tbnls); *Recreations* law reform, lit, fell walking, jogging, swimming; *Clubs* Leander; *Style—* Laurence Shurman, Esq; 14 Southwood Avenue, London N6 5RZ (☎ 081 348 5409); Citadel House, 5-11 Fetter Lane, London EC4A 1BR (☎ 071 583 1395, fax 071 583 5873)

SHUTE, Kenneth; s of Stanley Oswald Shute, of 3 South Close, Llanfrechfa, Gwent, and Elizabeth Hannah, *née* Davies; *b* 22 Dec 1945; *Educ* Jones West Monmouth Sch Pontypool, St Thomas' Hosp London (MB BS, MS); *m* 28 June 1975, Jennifer Catherine, da of Dr Robert William Burchfield, CBE, of The Barn, 14 The Green, Sutton Courtenay, Oxon; 1 s (Daniel b 2 Aug 1980), 1 da (Susannah b 13 July 1982); *Career* conslt surgn gen and vascular Royal Gwent Hosp 1982-; memb Vascular Surgical Soc of GB, patron Pontypool Rugby Club, hon surgn Monmouthshire Rugby Football Club; FRCS; *Recreations* skiing, squash, rugby; *Style—* Kenneth Shute, Esq; Llangybi House, Llaangybi, Gwent NP5 1NP (☎ 0633 49651); Royal Gwent Hospital, Newport, Gwent (☎ 0633 252244, car 0836 726609)

SHUTLER, Ronald Barry (Rex); s of Ronald Edgar Coggin Shutler, and Helen Emile, *née* Lawes; *b* 27 June 1933; *Educ* Hardye's Sch Dorchester; *m* 6 Dec 1958, Patricia Elizabeth, da of Henry George Longman; 2 s (Mark Richard Scott b 1962, Lee Howard Lawes b 1965); *Career* chartered surveyor HY Duke & Son Dorchester 1952-59; Inland Revenue valuation office 1959-: dist valuer Hereford 1972-75, superintending valuer Wales 1975-85, dep chief valuer 1985-88, chief valuer 1988-; FRICS 1975; *Recreations* golf, county pursuits; *Style—* Rex Shutler, Esq; Chief Valuers Office, New Court, Carey St, London WC2A 2JE (☎ 071 324 1155, fax 071 324 1190)

SHUTTLE, Penelope Diane; da of Jack Frederick Shuttle, of Middlesex, and Joan Shepherdess Lipscombe; *b* 12 May 1947; *m* Peter William Redgrove, s of G J Redgrove, of Hampstead; 1 da (Zoe b 1976); *Career* writer and poet; radio plays: The Girl who Lost her Glove 1975 (jt third prize winner Radio Times Drama Bursaries Competition 1974), The Dauntless Girl 1978; poetry recorded for Poetry Room Harvard; Arts Cncl Award 1969, 1972 and 1985, Greenwood Poetry Prize 1972, EC Gregory Award for Poetry 1974; *Books* novels: An Excusable Vengeance (1967), All the Usual Hours of Sleeping (1969), Wailing Monkey Embracing a Tree (1974), Rainsplitter in the Zodiac Garden (1976), Mirror of the Giant (1979); poetry: Nostalgia Neurosis (1968), Midwinter Mandala (1973), Photographs of Persephone (1973),

Autumn Piano (1973), Songbook of the Snow (1973), Webs on Fire (1977), The Orchard Upstairs (1981), The Child-Stealer (1983), The Lion from Rio (1986), Adventures with my Horse (PBS Recommendation 1988); with Peter Redgrove: The Hermaphrodite Album (poems, 1973), The Terrors of Dr Treviles (novel, 1974), The Wise Wound (psychology, 1978 re-issued 1986); *Recreations* gardening, walking, collecting first day covers; *Style—* Ms Penelope Shuttle; c/o David Higham Associates, 5-8 Lower John Street, Golden Sq, London W1R 4HA

SHUTTLEWORTH, Dowager Baroness; Anne Elizabeth; *née* Phillips; JP, DL; da of late Col Geoffrey Francis Phillips, CBE, DSO; *b* 17 March 1922; *m* 1947, 4 Baron (d 1975); 3 s, 1 da; *Style—* The Rt Hon The Dowager Lady Shuttleworth, JP, DL; Heber House, Leck, Carnforth, Lancs

SHUTTLEWORTH, 5 Baron (UK 1902); Sir Charles Geoffrey Nicholas Kay-Shuttleworth; 6 Bt (UK 1850), DL (Lancs); s of 4 Baron, MC (d 1975), and Anne, da of late Col Geoffrey Francis Phillips, CBE, DSO; *b* 2 Aug 1948; *Educ* Eton; *m* 1975, Ann Mary, da of James Whatman and former w of late Daniel Henry Barclay; 3 s; *Heir* s, Hon Thomas Kay-Shuttleworth; *Career* dir Burnley Building Society 1978-82, dir and dep chm National and Provincial Building Society 1983-; chartered surveyor; ptnr Burton Barnes and Vigers 1977-; memb Bd Skelmersdale Development Corporation 1982-85; govr Giggleswick Sch N Yorks 1982- (chm of Govrs 1984-), chm Rural Devpt Cmmn 1990-; FRICS; *Clubs* Brooks's; *Style—* The Rt Hon the Lord Shuttleworth, DL; Leck Hall, Carnforth, Lancs; 14 Sloane Ave, London SW3 (☎ 071 589 8374)

SHUTTLEWORTH, Hon Mrs (Idonea Mary Ellice); da of 2 Viscount Cross, of Eccle Riggs, Broughton-in-Furness (d 1932), and Maud Evelyn; da of late Maj Gen Inigo Richmund Jones, CVO, CB; *b* 30 Nov 1918; *m* 1946, Lt-Col William Preston Ashton Shuttleworth, RCT, late Royal Norfolk Regt (gggs of 1 Bt (Preston)); 2 s (Hugh Ashton John b 4 May 1948, William Richard Ashton b 1 March 1958), 2 da (Celia Mary Ashton b 16 Feb 1951, Rosamond Ashton b 30 Dec 1953); *Style—* The Hon Mrs Shuttleworth; Stoke Lodge, Clee Downton, Ludlow, Shropshire

SHUTTLEWORTH, Maj Noel Charles; s of Rev Richard Charles Shuttleworth (d 1955), and Doris Marian, *née* Sims (d 1978); *b* 4 Jan 1933; *Educ* Haileybury, ISC, RMA Sandhurst; *Career* Scots Guards 1953-63 served Germany, Canada, Kenya, UK, ret Maj 1963; winner: 4 Civic Tst Commendations, 6 Housing Design awards from DOE, RIBA, NHBC for excellence in housing design; dir Les Blancs Bois Ltd Guernsey 1987-; fndr and chm The English Courtyard Assoc 1979-; govr The Elderly Accomodation Cncl 1987-, vice pres Devizes Constituency Cons Assoc 1980- (chm 1977-80); *Recreations* cricket, tennis; *Clubs* Cavalry and Guards; *Style—* Maj Noel Shuttleworth; 38 St John's Rd, Hampton Wick, Middx; Crabtree, Savernake Forest, Marlborough, Wiltshire; The English Courtyard Assoc, 8 Holland St, London W8 4LT (☎ 071 937 4511, fax 071 937 3890)

SHUTTLEWORTH, Richard James Christopher; s of Donald Harrop Shuttleworth, and Barbara, *née* Whaley; *b* 22 June 1938; *Educ* Dragon Sch, Christ's Hosp, St John's Coll Oxford; *m* 1965, Sheila Joan; *Career* Freshfields: articled clerk 1961-64, asst slr 1964-69, ptnr 1969-; *Style—* Richard Shuttleworth, Esq; Freshfields, Whitefriars, 65 Fleet St, London EC1Y 1HS (☎ 071 736 4000)

SHUTZ, Roy Martin; s of Joseph Shutz (d 1969), of Birmingham, and Alice, *née* Susz (d 1989); *b* 23 Jan 1943; *Educ* King Edward's Five Ways Sch Birmingham, Univ of Birmingham (LLB), Coll of Law; *Career* teacher Longsands Sch Cambridge 1966-68, admin asst Univ of Warwick 1968-69, asst to Academic and Fin Secs LSE 1969-74, chm Romar Investments Ltd 1969-; barr 1974-90; London Borough of Barnet: cllr 1982-, chm Educn Ctee 1985-90; memb: Middex Area Probation Ctee, London NW Valuation and Community Charge Tribunal; Mayor of Barnet 1990-91; *Recreations* golf, rugby union, theatre; *Clubs* Aldenham Golf, Warwickshire Co Cricket; *Style—* Roy Shutz, Esq; 41 Denman Drive North, Hampstead Garden Suburb, London NW11 (☎ 081 455 2248)

SIAW, Jacob Aning Kwadwo; s of Kwasi Aning (d 1950), of Ghana, and Abenaa Aniniwaa; *b* 28 Sept 1933; *Educ* Presbyterian Schools Ghana, Teacher Trg Coll Ghana; *m* 1 (m dis), Comfort yaa Twumwaa; 1 s (Kwaku Aning b 10 July 1957), 1 da (Helen Somea b 22 May 1959); m 2, 27 July 1968, Mary Afua Kyeremaa, da of Kwaku Benne (d 1972); 2 s (Jacob Kofi Boadu b 29 Aug 1969, Benjamin K Osei b 2 May 1972), 1 da (Joyce Yaa Aniniwaa b 24 Jan 1980); *Career* teacher 1956-61; headteacher 1961-68; called to the Bar Lincoln's Inn 1976, practising 1981-; vice chm Pan African orgn 1982, cncllr London Borough of Hackney 1986-, chm Ghana Union London; memb Bar Cncl; *Style—* Jacob Siaw, Esq; 12 Old Square, Lincoln's Inn, London WC2A 3TX (☎ 071 404 0875)

SIBBALD, Maj-Gen Peter Frank Aubrey; CB (1982), OBE (1972); s of Maj F V Sibbald, MBE, MM, BEM (d 1957), and Alice Emma, *née* Hawking (d 1971); *b* 24 March 1928; *Educ* Haileybury; *m* 27 July 1957, (Margaret) Maureen (d 1990), da of W E Entwistle (d 1972); 1 s (Paul Edward b 9 Jan 1965), 1 da (Joanna Bonney b 23 Feb 1963); *Career* enlisted 1946, RMA Sandhurst 1947-48, cmmnd KOYLI 1948, Malayan Emergency (despatches) 1948-51, Capt Korea 1953-54, Kenya 1954-55, Staff Coll 1961, JSSC 1964, Aden 1965, Lt-Col Cmdg 1968-71, Col BAOR 1972, Brig Hong Kong 1972, Maj-Gen 1977, dir of info 1979-83, ret 1983; conslt to: def indust co's 1983-, Def Mfrs Assoc 1982-; FBIM 1973-84; *Recreations* shooting, fishing; *Clubs* Army and Navy; *Style—* Maj-Gen Peter Sibbald, CB, OBE; c/o Lloyds Bank plc, 8 Royal Parade, Plymouth PL1 1HB (☎ 0252 332 482)

SIBBERING, George Seymour Leslie Ewart; s of John Cyril Pritchard Sibbering (d 1983), of Charmouth, Dorset, and late Florence, *née* Ewart; *b* 13 Dec 1920; *Educ* Pangbourne Coll Berks; *m* 13 June 1942, Vivien, da of Sir Horace Perkins Hamilton, GCB (d 1971); 2 s (Michael John b 1945, Anthony Paul b 1947); *Career* RNVR 1940-45, Lt Coastal Forces Home Fleet; incorporated surveyor and estate agent; jt sr ptnr Hampton and Sons St James's 1964-69; dir: Whitbread Trafalgar Properties 1969-73, Trollope and Colls Devpts 1969-73; underwriting memb of Lloyds 1973-; Freeman City of London 1950, Liveryman Wordshipful Co of Horners 1950; FSVA; *Recreations* gardening, golf; *Clubs* The City Livery, Piltdown Golf; *Style—* George Sibbering, Esq; Oak Hatch, Cowbeech, Hailsham, E Sussex

SIBLEY, Antoinette; CBE (1973); da of Edward George Sibley, of Kent, and Winifred Maude, *née* Smith; *b* 27 Feb 1939; *Educ* Arts Educnl Sch Tring Herts, Royal Ballet Sch; *m* 1974, Richard Panton, s of William Corbett, of Salop; 1 s (Isambard b 1980), 1 da (Eloise b 1975); *Career* graduated into the Royal Ballet 1956, promoted to soloist 1959 and to princ dancer 1960, achieved outstanding success at Covent Garden when she took over the role of Odette/Odile in Swan Lake at short notice 1959; noted for interpretation of Aurora in Sleeping Beauty, the title role in Giselle, the title role in Ashton's Cinderella, and Juliet in Macmillan's Romeo & Juliet, Titania in Ashton's The Dream, Manon in the ballet of that name created for her by Macmillan, Dorabella created for her by Ashton for his Enigma Variations, Chloe in Ashton's Daphnis & Chloe, Ashtons A Month in the Country and many other roles; toured N and S America, USSR, Aust, Europe; prima ballerina role film Turning Point; vice pres Royal Acad of Dancing 1989-; *Publications* Sibley and Dowell (1976), Antoinette Sibley (1981), Antoinette Sibley - Reflections of a Ballerina (1986); *Recreations* opera going, reading, music; *Style—* Miss Antoinette Sibley, CBE; c/o The Royal Opera House, Covent Garden, London WC2

SIBLEY, Edward; s of William Sibley (d 1941), of Rhymney, Gwent, and Myfanny, *née* Williams (d 1987); *b* 21 July 1935; *Educ* Rhymney GS Gwent, UCW Aberystwyth (LLB, Samuel Evans Prize), Coll of Law; *m* 3 Aug 1957, Sonia, da of Harold Beynon; 2 s (Stephen b 6 Dec 1965, Neil Edward b 24 May 1970), 1 da (Deborah Jane b 1 Dec 1962); *Career* articled clerk Clifford Turner 1962-65, ptnr Berwin & Co 1967 (joined as asst slr 1965), fndr ptnr Berwin-Leighton 1970, qualified NY Bar USA 1985; memb Worshipful Co of Solicitors 1985; memb Law Soc; *Recreations* rugby, running, opera, theatre, literature; *Clubs* Reform; *Style—* Edward Sibley, Esq; Berwin Leighton, Adelaide House, London Bridge, London EC4R 9HA (☎ 071 623 3144, fax 071 623 4416)

SIBLEY, Richard Edmonde Miles Phillippe; s of William Alfred Sibley, JP, of Street Farm, Crowfield, Suffolk, and Florence May, *née* Marsh; *b* 23 May 1949; *Educ* Clark's Coll London, Anglican Regnl Coll; *m* 5 June 1976, Hannelore, da of Hans Njammasch, of W Germany; 1 s (Alexander b 21 March 1979); *Career* co sec Caldenwood Housing Association 1970-75, chief exec Ogilby Housing Society Ltd 1987-; dir: Sibley Property Co Ltd, Libra Finance Co Ltd (co sec 1971-80); dep chm NE London Valuation Ct (rating) 1981- (memb 1976); Rotarian 1982-; Freeman City of London 1980, Liveryman Worshipful Co of Coopers 1980 (sec Soc of the Livery 1986-90); *Recreations* painting, politics, English vinyard owner; *Style—* R E M P Sibley, Esq; 60 Parkstone Ave, Emerson Park, Hornchurch, Essex RM11 3LS (☎ 04024 71320); Ogilby Housing Society, Estate Office, Greenways Court, Butts Green Rd, Hornchurch, Essex RM11 2JL (☎ 04024 75 115/6)

SICH, Sir Rupert Leigh; CB (1953); s of Alexander Ernest Sich (d 1926); *b* 3 Aug 1908; *Educ* Radley, Merton Coll Oxford; *m* 1933, Elizabeth Mary, *née* Hutchison; 1 s, 2 da; *Career* barr 1930; Bd of Trade 1932-48, princ asst Treasy slr 1948-56, registrar Restrictive Trading Agreements 1956-73; kt 1968; *Recreations* music, gardening, golf; *Clubs* United Oxford and Cambridge, MCC; *Style—* Sir Rupert Sich, CB; Norfolk House, The Mall, Chiswick, London W4 (☎ 081 994 2133)

SICHEL, Ronald James; s of Walter Adolf Sichel (d 1989), Chalfont St Peter, Bucks, and Thea Anna, *née* Tuchler; *b* 22 May 1940; *Educ* Repton, L'Ecole Superieure, Neuchâtel, Switzerland; *m* 16 Jan 1965 (m dis 1979), Colette Jeannine, da of Dr Charles Stagnaro (d 1983), of St Raphael France; 1 s (Edward b 27 June 1973); *Career* wine shipper: H Sichel and Sons Ltd 1960, dir 1969-79, vice chm 1979-1988, chm 1988-; memb Worshipful Co of Founders 1963, Freeman City of London 1963; *Recreations* fly-fishing, competition pistol and rifle shooting, game shooting, skiing, painting, golf, photography; *Style—* Ronald Sichel, Esq; 53 Cadogan Square, London SW1 OHY (☎ 071 235 3321); H Sichel & Sons Ltd, 4 York Bldgs, Adelphi, London WC2N 6JP (☎ 071 930 9292, fax 071 930 1176, car 0860 258468)

SIDAWAY, Dr Muriel Elizabeth; da of Capt Frederick Emanuel Sidaway, MC (d 1953), of Halesowen, W Midlands, and Doris Muriel, *née* Jaquiss; *b* 22 June 1924; *Educ* Dudley Girls HS, Girton Coll Cambridge, Univ of Birmingham Med Sch (MB BChir, MA); *m* 21 Aug 1969, Cyril Henry Sheridan, s of Henry Sheridan (d 1956), of London; 1 da (Elizabeth Anne b 6 Dec 1969); *Career* house offr 1949-52: Birmingham United Hosp, London Chest Hosp, St James' Balham, Connaught Hosp; registrar Hackney Hosp and Edgware Gen 1952-56, trainee radiologist Bart's 1956-58, sr registrar UCH and Gt Ormond St 1958-64; conslt in radiology: Charing Cross Hosp 1964-90 (univ lectr), 70 Harley St; memb: Faculty of Radiologists 1958, London Wildlife Tst; FRCPEd 1971, MRCP 1956, FFR 1958, FRCR 1960; *Books* Renal Infection (contrib, 1967), Pelvic Malignancy (contrib, 1972); *Recreations* skiing, swimming, walking, wind surfing, gardening; *Clubs* Ski of GB, Friends of Royal Acad, RSPB, Nat Tst; *Style—* Dr Muriel Sidaway; 1 Stanhope Rd, Highgate, London N6 5NE (☎ 081 340 3773); 70 Harley St, London W1N 1AE (☎ 071 580 3383); Charing Cross Hospital, Fulham Palace Rd, London W6 8RF

SIDAWAY, Ronald; OBE; *b* 19 March 1916; *Educ* Wolverhampton GS; *m* 1969, Irene Mary Catherine; 1 s, 3 da; *Career* chm: Ironbridge Gorge Museum Devpt Trust, Advisory Ctee Wolverhampton Nuffield Hospital; *Recreations* golf, skiing, gardening, Wolverhampton Wanderers Football Club; *Style—* Ronald Sidaway Esq, OBE; Meadow House, Oldbury, Bridgnorth, Salop (☎ 074 62 3331)

SIDDALL, Sir Norman; CBE (1975), DL (Notts 1988); *b* 4 May 1918; *Educ* Univ of Sheffield (BEng); *m* 1943; 2 s, 1 da; *Career* National Coal Bd: chief mining engr 1966-67, dir-gen of prodn 1967-71, bd memb 1971-, dep chm 1973-82, chm 1982-83; Hon DSc Univ of Nottingham; CEng, FEng, FIMinE, CBIM; kt 1983; *Style—* Sir Norman Siddall, CBE, DL; Brentwood, High Oakham Rd, Mansfield, Notts NG18 5AJ

SIDDELEY, Hon Mrs Norman; Pamela; da of late G A Williams, of Gorey, Jersey; *m* 1953, as his 2 wife, Hon Norman Goodier Siddeley (d 1971), 3 s of 1 Baron Kenilworth; *Style—* The Hon Mrs Norman Siddeley; 1 Belle Vue Court, Longueville, St Saviour, Jersey, CI (☎ 0534 52031)

SIDDLE, Nicholas Charles; s of Stephen Geoffrey Siddle, of Chichester, and Penny, *née* Farthing; *b* 4 July 1949; *Educ* Lancaster Royal GS, Univ of Liverpool (MB ChB); *m* 1978, Johanna Elizabeth, da of Bartholomew Anthony Finn; 2 s (Benedict Daniel b 20 Jan 1982, Leo Dominic b 1 Oct 1984), 1 da (Chloe Anneliese b 22 June 1990); *Career* jr hosp posts in Liverpool Chester and Manchester 1972-77, tutor Univ Hosp S Manchester 1977-79; lectr: Kings Coll Hosp 1981-85 (res fell 1979-81), Chelsea Hosp for Women 1981-85; conslt and hon sr lectr Univ Coll Hosp and Middx Hosp 1985-; Regnl Cncls Gold medal RCOG 1977; memb Worshipful Soc of Apothecaries; MRCOG, MRSM; *Books* Managing the Menopause A Practical Guide (1991); *Recreations* food, music, skiing; *Clubs* Gynaecological Research Society; *Style—* Nicholas Siddle, Esq; 8 Devonshire Place, London W1N 1PB (☎ 071 935 2357); University College Hospital, Gower St, London W1 (☎ 071 387 9300)

SIDDONS, Peter Robert; s of (Arthur) Harold Makins Siddons, of Farnham, Surrey, and Joan Richardson, *née* McConnell (d 1949); *b* 25 June 1943; *Educ* Harrow, Jesus Coll Cambridge (MA); *m* 12 Oct 1974 Elvina Lucy, da of Maj Roger Alexander Howard; 3 c (Philippa Sarah b 7 March 1977, Alastair Mark b 29 July 1978, Melanie Sarah b 30 Aug 1980); *Career* Coopers & Lybrand Deloitte: articled clerk Cooper Brothers & Co 1965-68, ptnr 1974, seconded to HM Treasury 1978-79, ptnr-in-charge Litigation Support Unit 1985-87, ptnr-in-charge London Audit Div 1985-88, fin dir and memb Bd 1988-; FCA 1979 (ACA 1968); *Recreations* golf, theatrical art research; *Style—* Peter Siddons, Esq; Coopers & Lybrand Deloitte, Plumtree Court, London EC4A 4HT (☎ 071 822 4585, fax 071 822 4433)

SIDEBOTTOM, Arnold (Arnie); s of Jack Sidebottom, of Barnsley, Yorks, and Florence, *née* Litherland; *b* 1 April 1954; *Educ* Barnsley Broadway GS; *m* Gillian, da of James Terence Anderson, 2 s (Ryan Jay b 15 Jan 1978, Dale b 27 Nov 1980); *Career* professional cricketer Yorkshire CCC: debut 1973, awarded county cap 1980, benefit season 1988; Orange Free State SA 1981-84, 1 England test cap v Australia 1985; former professional footballer: Manchester Utd, Huddersfield Town, Halifax Town; *Recreations* horse racing, football, reading; *Style—* Arnie Sidebottom, Esq; c/o Yorkshire County Cricket Club, Headingley Cricket Ground, Leeds LS6 3BU (☎ 0532 787394)

SIDEY, Air Marshal Sir Ernest Shaw; KBE (1972), CB (1965); s of Thomas Sidey (d 1943), of Alyth, Perthshire; *b* 2 Jan 1913; *Educ* Morgan Acad Dundee, Univ of St Andrews; *m* 1946, Doreen Florence, da of Cecil Ronald Lurring, of Dublin, Eire; 1 da (and 1 da decd); *Career* RAF (UK and Burma) WWII, Air Cdre 1961, PMO Tport Cmd 1965-66, dep dir gen RAF Med Servs 1966-68, Air Vice-Marshal 1966-71, PMO Strike Cmd 1968-70, dir gen RAF Med Servs 1971-74 (ret), Air Marshal 1971; QHS 1966-74; dir gen Chest, Heart and Stroke Assoc 1974-85, govr Royal Star and Garter Home 1974-86; MD, FFCM, DPH; *Recreations* racing, golf, bridge; *Clubs* RAF; *Style*— Air Marshal Sir Ernest Sidey, KBE, CB; Callums, Tugwood Common, Cookham Dean, Berks SL6 9TU

SIDMOUTH, 7 Viscount; John Tonge Anthony Pellew Addington; s of 6 Viscount Sidmouth (d 1976, himself fourth in descent from 1 Viscount, PM 1801-04), and Gladys Mary Dever (d 1983); *b* 3 Oct 1914; *Educ* Downside, BNC Oxford; *m* 1940, Barbara Mary Angela (d 1989), da of Bernard Rochford, OBE; 2 s (1 decd), 5 da; *Heir* s, Hon Jeremy Addington; *Career* Colonial Serv E Africa 1938-54; md Joseph Rochford & Sons Ltd; memb Cncl and chm Glasshouse Ctee NFU 1962-69; memb: ARC 1964-74, Central Cncl for Agric Co-operation 1970-73, Lords Select Ctee on Euro Community 1984-87; pres Nat Cncl on Inland Tport 1978-84, tstee John Innes Fndn 1974-90, chm Governing Body Glasshouse Crop Res Inst 1981-84; St Gregory's Soc (old boys of Downside); kt of Malta 1962; *Style*— The Rt Hon the Viscount Sidmouth; 12 Brock Street, Bath, Avon BA1 2LW

SIDNEY, Elizabeth Anne; JP (1964); da of James Frank William Mudford (d 1954), and Charlotte Mary Henrietta, *née* Hawes (d 1975); *b* 14 June 1924; *Educ* Sherborne Sch for Girls, Univ of Oxford (BA), Univ of London (MA); *m* 1952 (m dis 1972), Deryck Malcolm Sidney, s of John Barham Sidney (d 1939); 1 s (David b 1956), 3 da (Francesca b 1954, Rebecca b 1959 (decd), Madeleine b 1962); *Career* ed Nat Inst of Industrial Psychology 1946-49, lectr Mgmnt Studies Poly of Central London 1949-55, psychologist (pt/t), Civil Service Cmmn 1957-72, trg dir (pt/t) Family Planning Assoc 1970-74, managing ptnr Mantra Consults and Trainers in Public & Private Sectors UK, Europe, USA, India, Far East; memb Kensington Chelsea and Westminster Area Health Authy 1972-80, pres Women's Lib Fedn 1982-84, chm Lib Pty Policy Panel on Employment 1980-83, dep chm Candidates Ctee Lib Pty 1986-87, pres Women Liberal Democrats 1988-, dep chm Liberal Democrats Working Pty on Industl Democracy 1990-, chm The Green Alliance 1984-89; *Books* The Skills of Interviewing (1961), Case Studies of Management Initiative (1967), The Industrial Society (1970), Skills with People: A Guide for Managers (1973), Future Woman: How to Survive Life (1982), ed Managing Recruitment (1989), One to One Management (1991); *Recreations* political work, environment, travel; *Clubs* Reform, RSA; *Style*— Ms Elizabeth Sidney; 25 Ellington Street, London N7 8PN (☎ 071 607 6592); Mantra Consultancy Group, United House, North Road, N7 9DP (☎ 071 609 9055, 609 1051)

SIDNEY, Maj Hon Philip John Algernon; MBE (1977); s and h of 1 Viscount De L'Isle, VC, KG, GCMG, GCVO, PC, *qv*, and his 1 w, Hon Jacqueline Corinne Yvonne, *née* Vereker (d 1962); *b* 21 April 1945; *Educ* Tabley House Cheshire; *m* 15 Nov 1980, Isobel Tresyllian, da of Sir Edmund Gerald Compton, GCB, KBE; 1 s (Philip William Edmund b 2 April 1985), 1 da (Sophia Jacqueline Mary b 25 March 1983); *Career* cmmnd Grenadier Gds 1966, served BAOR, NI, Belize, GSO3 Ops/SD HQ 3 Inf Bde NI 1974-76, ret 1979; farmer and landowner; dir and chm Wood Products of Westerham 1984-; memb: Ctee CLA Kent (chm 1983-85), Kent Archives Office Advsy Ctee; Freeman City of London, Liveryman Worshipful Co of Goldsmiths; *Clubs* White's, Pratt's, The Brook (NY); *Style*— Maj The Hon Philip Sidney, MBE; Estate Office, Penshurst Place, Penshurst, Tonbridge, Kent TN11 8DG (☎ 0892 870304)

SIDWELL, Prof (John William) Martindale; s of John William Sidwell, of Glastonbury, Somerset, and Mary, *née* Martindale; *b* 23 Feb 1916; *Educ* Wells Cathedral Sch; *m* 5 Sept 1944, Barbara Anne, da of Edwin Hill; 2 s (Peter, Timothy); *Career* N Somerset Yeo TA 1937, acting Lance Corpl 1939-42 (boarded out); sub organist Wells Cathedral, dir music Warwick Sch 1943-46, organist Holy Trinity Church Leamington Spa 1943-46; organist and dir of music: Hampstead Parish Church 1946, St Clement Danes Church (centl church of RAF) 1957; prof: Royal Sch of Church Music 1958-63, Trinity Coll of Music 1955-63, RAM 1963-82; fndr and conductor: Hampstead Choral Soc 1946-81, London Bach Orchestra 1967, Martindale Sidwell Choir 1954, St Clement Danes Music Soc, St Clement Danes Chorale; guest conductor: BBC Symphony Orchestra, BBC Singers, LSO; conductor for numerous broadcastings and recordings; winner Harriet Cohen Bach medal; FRAM, FRCO; *Clubs* Savage, Wig & Pen; *Style*— Prof Martindale Sidwell; 1 Frognal Gardens, Hampstead NW3 6UY (☎ 071 435 9210)

SIE *see also*: Tejan-Sie

SIEFF OF BRIMPTON, Lady; (Pauline) Lily; da of Frederick Spatz (d 1958), of Vienna Austria, and Hania, *née* Zimand (d 1975); *b* 16 July 1930; *Educ* Univ of Geneva (BA); *m* 1, 1954, Martin Morecki; m 2, 1963, Marcus Sieff, s of Israel Sieff; 1 da (Daniela b 13 Feb 1965); *Career* owner L S Graphics (arts consultancy business), memb Br Cncl of Rheumatism and Arthritis, tstee Israel Philharmonic Orch, chm Br Friends of the Art Museums of Israel, patron Br WIZO; *Style*— The Lady Sieff of Brimpton; Michael House, Baker Street, London W1 (☎ 071 935 4422)

SIEFF OF BRIMPTON, Baron (Life Peer UK 1980); Hon Sir Marcus Joseph Sieff; OBE (1944); 2 s of Baron Sieff (Life Peer, d 1972), and Rebecca Doro, *née* Marks, OBE (d 1966); *b* 2 July 1913; *Educ* Manchester GS, St Paul's, CCC Cambridge (MA); *m* 1, 1937 (m dis 1947), Rosalie Fromson; 1 s (Hon David Daniel b 1939); m 2, 1951 (m dis 1953), Elsie Florence Gosen; m 3, 1956 (m dis 1962), Brenda Mary Beith; 1 da (Hon Amanda Jane b 1958); m 4, 1963 (as her 2 husb), Mrs (Pauline) Lily Moretzki, da of Friedrich Spatz; 1 da (Hon Daniela Frederica b 1965); *Career* WWII 1939-45, Col RA; memb BNEC 1965-71; joined Marks & Spencer Ltd 1935 (pres 1984-85), hon pres Marks & Spencer 1985- (chm and jt md 1972-84, asst md 1963, vice-chm 1965, jt md 1967, dep chm 1971); chm First Inst Bank of Israel Financial Trust Ltd 1983, non-exec chm The Independent 1986-, non-exec dir Wickes plc 1986; hon pres Joint Israel Appeal 1984, vice-pres Policy Studies Inst Exec 1975; pres Anglo-Israel C of C 1975; tstee Nat Portrait Gallery 1986; Hon FRCS 1984, Hon LLD Univ of St Andrew's 1983, Hon Dr Babson Coll 1984, Hon DLitt Univ of Reading 1986; D Univ Stirling 1986; fell CCC Camb 1975; Hambro award Businessman of the Year 1977, Aims Nat Free Enterprise award 1978, B'nai B'rith Int Gold medal 1982, Retailer of the Year award USA 1982, BIM Gold medal 1983, Presidents medal 1982 (Ist Public Relations); kt 1971; *Books* Don't Ask the Price (1987); Marcus Sieff on Management (1990); *Style*— The Rt Hon The Lord Sieff of Brimpton, OBE; Michael House, Baker St, London W1 (☎ 071 935 4422)

SIEFKEN, Prof Hinrich Gerhard; s of Werner Johann Hinrich Siefken (d 1968), and Lisel, *née* Menne (d 1963); *b* 21 April 1939; *Educ* Carl Duisberg Gymnasium Leverkusen, Univ of Tubingen (Dr Phil), Univ of Nottingham (DLitt); *m* 1 August 1968, Marcia Corinne, da of Harry Birch (d 1989), of Sheffield; 1 s (Kristian Hinrich b 8 August 1973), 1 da (Brigitte Christiane 14 March 1970); *Career* tutor Univ of Tubingen 1962-65, lectr Univ Coll of N Wales Bangor 1965-66, wissenschaftlicher asst Univ of Tubingen 1966-67, sr lectr St Davids Univ Coll Lampeter 1973-79 (asst lectr 1967-68, lectr 1968-73), prof of German Univ of Nottingham 1979 (dem of Faculty of Arts 1988-); ed Trivium 1978-79 (subject ed 1974-79), gen ed Renaissance and Modern Studies 1986-88, memb Ed Bd New Manchester German Texts; memb: English Goethe Soc, Deutsche Thomas Mann Gesellschaft, Deutsche Schiller Gesellschaft; *Books* Kudrunepos (1967), Ungeduld und Lässigkeit-Kafka (1977), Thomas Mann-Goethe Ideal der Deutschheit (1981), Theodor Haecker (1989), Theodor Haecker, Tag- und Nachtbücher (ed, 1989), Die Weisse Rose, Student Resistance to National Socialism (ed, 1991); *Recreations* music, walking, gardening; *Style*— Prof Hinrich Siefken; 6 Mountsorrel Drive, Westbridgford, Nottingham NG2 6LJ (☎ 0602 811617); Department of German, University of Nottingham, University Park, Nottingham NG7 2RD (☎ 0602 484848 ext 2550, fax 0602 420825, telex 37346 UNINOT G)

SIEGEL, Jeffrey; s of Harold Siegel, and Ruth Berman (d 1972); *b* 18 Nov 1942; *Educ* Chicago Musical Coll, Royal Acad of Music London, Juilliard Sch of Music (Dr of Musical Arts 1971); *m* 20 May 1973, Laura, da of Edmund Mizel; 1 s (Noah b 1988), 1 da (Rachel b 1983); *Career* piano soloist with world's leading orchestra's including: LSO, London Philharmonic, Royal Philharmonic, Philharmonia, Hallé Orchestra, Birmingham Symphony, New York, Chicago, Boston, Philadelphia, Cleveland; solo concerts at: Carnegie Hall, Queen Elizabeth Hall, Festival Hall; *Style*— Jeffrey Siegel, Esq; Inspell and Williams Concert Agents, 14 Kensington Court, London W8 5DN; (☎ 071 937 5158)

SIEGER, Joshua; CBE (1981, OBE 1970); s of Maurice Sieger (d 1950); *b* 5 Jan 1907; *Educ* Latymer Sch, London Poly Sch Engrg; *m* 1935, Sylvia Doreen de Wilton, *née* Tabbernor; 2 da; *Career* tech staff: Amateur Wireless, Wireless Magazine 1920-29; chief engr Lotus Radio Liverpool 1929-30, design engr Scophony TV Ltd, responsible for large screen high definition TV pictures in London theatres 1930-40, princ tech offr TRE Malvern 1940-44, dir Hamworthy Engineering Ltd Poole 1944-46, engr Servo Corp Long Island USA 1946-47, vice pres and dir of engrg and res Freed Radio Corpn (NY) 1947-51, pres JH Bunnell & Co Ltd (NY) 1952-53, chm and md J & S Sieger Ltd 1954-80, dir Sieger Ltd 1980-, chm UK Export Clubs Steering Ctee 1980-85; FInstD (chm Wessex branch 1975-82), FRTS; *Recreations* yachting, motoring; *Clubs* Wessex Export (pres and chm 1968-85, pres 1985-); *Style*— Joshua Sieger Esq, CBE; Tinkers Revel, 8 Crichel Mount Rd, Parkstone, Poole, Dorset (☎ 0202 700353)

SIEGHART, Mary Ann Corinna Howard; da of Paul Sieghart (d 1988), and Felicity Ann, *née* Baer; *b* 6 Aug 1961; *Educ* Cobham Hall, Bedales, Wadham Coll Oxford (major scholarship, BA); *m* 17 June 1989, David Stephens Prichard, s of Maj Micheal Prichard; *Career* journalist Eye to Eye Publishing 1978-79, reporter Sunday Express 1979, arts ed rising to news ed Cherwell 1979-80, ldr and feature writer Daily Telegraph 1980-82, Eurobond corr rising to Lex Columnist Financial Times 1982-86, city ed Today 1986, political corr The Economist 1986-88, presenter The World This Week 1988; The Times: ops-ed and page ed 1988-, arts ed 1988-90, ed 1988-; runner up young journalist of the year Br Press Awards 1983, Harold Wincott prize for young financial journalist of the year 1983, winner Laurence Stern fellowship 1984 (worked for the Washington Post); *Recreations* tobogganing, trekking in remote places, doodling, reading novels on holiday, listening to music; *Style*— Ms Sieghart; The Times, 1 Pennington St, London E1 (☎ 071 782 5160, fax 071 782 5142)

SIEMENS, Herman Werner; s of Prof Dr Hermann Werner Siemens (d 1969), of Leiden, The Netherlands, and Berta Luise, *née* von Müller (d 1985); *b* 21 May 1925; *Educ* Leiden Gymnasium Sch, Delft Technol Univ (MSc), Universidad Del Valle (MBA); *m* 7 June 1955, Cornélie, da of Herman Constantyn, Count Schimmelpenninck (d 1948), of The Hague; 1 s (Herman Werner b 1963), 4 da (Louise b 1956 m Dr Ignazio Savona, Clara b 1957 m Richard Charles Furse, Sabine b 1959 m Maurits, Baron Van Hövell tot Westerflier, Julie b 1961); *Career* res engr Centre à l'Energie Atomique Paris 1953, former exec with aluminium companies in Colombia, Denmark, Nigeria and UK, pres and chief exec Aluminio Alcan de Colombia SA Cali Colombia 1961-69, md and chief exec Aluminord AS Copenhagen Denmark 1969-75, chm and chief exec Alcan Aluminum of Nigeria Ltd and Alcan Aluminum Products Ltd (both in Lagos) 1978-83, chm and chief exec Siemens Mgmnt Conslts Ltd London, sr conslt for ILO Geneva, memb Exec Ctee Westminster Christian Cncl; *Recreations* music, riding, sailing, squash; *Clubs* Lansdowne, Lagos Yacht, IOD, Metropolitan (Lagos); *Style*— Herman W Siemens, Esq; Kendal Lodge, 19 Garrad's Road, London SW16 1JX (☎ 081 677 2585); 108 Riouwstraat, The Hague, The Netherlands (☎ 070 350 4018); 3940 Côte-des-Neiges, appt 113, Montreal, Quebec H3H 1W2, Canada (☎ 010 1 514 486 6758)

SIGWART, Prof Ulrich; s of Dr August Robert Sigwart, and Elizabeth Augusta Sigwart; *b* 9 March 1941; *Educ* Univ of Basel, Univ of Munster Medical Sch Univ of Freiburg; *m* 2 Sept 1967, Christine Rosemary, da of Peter Sartorius; 2 s (Philip Martin Christopher b 10 Aug 1970, Jan Michael Pierre b 27 April 1973), 2 da (Anne Elizabeth b 27 Feb 1969, Catherine Isabel b 15 Oct 1976); *Career* intern Community Hosp Loerrach, res Framington Union Hosp 1968-71, chief of Cath Lab Gollwitzer Meier Inst Bad Oeynhause 1973-79, chief of Invasive Cardiology Univ Hosp Lausanne 1979-89, conslt cardiologist dir of Invasive Cardiology Royal Brompton Nat Heart Hosp London; academic career: prof of med Univ of Dusseldorf, assoc prof of Cardiology Univ of Lausanne; memb Editorial Bd: Clinical Cardiology, Herz & Gefaesse, Cardiac Imaging, Interventional Cardiology; memb: Br Cardiac Soc, American Heart Assoc; Swiss Soc of Cardiology, German Soc of Cardiology, chm: Working Gp on Myocardial Function, Working Gp on PTCA & Lysis SSC; FACC, fell Euro Soc of Cardiology; *Books* Automation in Cardiac Diagnosis (1978), Ventricular Wall Motion (1984), Coronary Stenting (1991); *Recreations* flying, sailing, music, skiing, photography; *Style*— Prof Ulrich Sigwart; 7 Sydney Place, London SW7 3NL (☎ 071 581 5991); Royal Brompton & National Heart Hospital, Sydney Street, London (☎ 071 351 8615 ext 44, fax 071 351 8614)

SIKORA, Prof Karol; s of Witold Karol Sikora (d 1966), and Thomasina Sikora; *b* 17 June 1948; *Educ* Dulwich, Univ of Cambridge (MA, PhD, MB BChir), Middx Hosp; *m* 6 Dec 1975, Alison Mary; 1 s (Simon b 1977), 2 da (Emma b 1980, Lucy b 1982); *Career* former dir Ludwig Inst for Cancer Res Cambridge, currently prof of clinical oncology Royal Postgrad Med Sch Hammersmith; FRCR 1980, FRCP 1987; *Books* Monoclonal Antibodies (1984), Treatment of Cancer (1989), Fight Cancer (1989); *Recreations* boating; *Clubs* Athenaeum; *Style*— Prof Karol Sikora; Dept of Clinical Oncology, Hammersmith Hospital, London W12 0HD (☎ 081 740 3060, fax 081 743 8766)

SILAS, Dr Aaron Michael; s of Rev Abraham Joshua Silas of London, and Sybil, *née* Lanyahdo (d 1986); *b* 26 April 1935; *Educ* St Xavier's Coll Calcutta, Calcutta Med Coll Hosp (MB BS); *m* 31 May 1959, Hannie, da of Samuel Albert Parry (d 1975), of London; 2 s (Adrian b 1961, Douglas b 1966); *Career* sr registrar in rheumatology UCH and Whittington Hosp London 1974-79, conslt rheumatologist Oldchurch Hosp Romford 1979-; memb: BARR 1974; MRCP 1977; *Recreations* music, swimming, motor maintenance, motor sport, photography; *Style*— Dr Aaron Silas; 7 St Mary's Ave, Wanstead, London E11 2NR (☎ 0708 746090); Oldchurch Hospital, Romford, Essex (☎ 0709 46090)

SILBER, (Rudolf) Martin; s of Paul Silber (d 1931), and Vally, *née* Schlochauer (d 1944); *b* 22 Sept 1918; *Educ* Univ of London, London Sch of Building (HND); *m* 1, 9 Jan 1938 (m dis 1948), Irene, da of Thomas Arnold White (d 1936), of Australia; 1 s (Paul Dorian b 1939); m 2, 10 Sept 1949, Ila MacNeill, da of Dr William Fraser (d 1971); 1 s (Andrew Ernest b 1954), 1 da (Lucy Anne b 1950); *Career* WWII cmmnd

RE 1940-46, serv Egypt, Persia and Iraq, SO WO Ctee (Fortification and Works Europe); dist surveyor: Lambeth (responsible for NT) 1965-75, City of London (responsible for Barbican Devpt and Nat West Tower) 1975-79; ptnr Silber & James 1979-; former pres: Dist Surveyors Assoc 1966, Assoc of Architects & Surveyors 1963, Faculty of Bldg 1970; Freeman City of London, Liveryman Worshipful Co of Fan Makers; CEng, FIStructE, FIAS, ACIArb; *Recreations* music theatre, gourmet; *Clubs* Royal Cwlth; *Style—* Martin Silber, Esq; Crittle's Ct, Wadhurst, East Sussex TN5 6BY (☎ 0892 88 3743)

SILBERSTON, Prof (Zangwill) Aubrey; CBE (1987); s of Louis Silberston (d 1975), of London, and Polly, *née* Kern (d 1976); *b* 26 Jan 1922; *Educ* Hackney Downs Sch London, Jesus Coll Cambridge (BA, MA), Univ of Oxford (MA); *m* 1, 1945 (m dis), Dorothy Marion, da of A S Nicholls (d 1965), of London; 1 s (Jeremy b 1950), 1 da (Katharine b 1948 d 1982); m 2, 1985, Michèle, da of Vitomir Ledić, of Zagreb; *Career* Royal Fusiliers 1942-45, served in: Iraq, Egypt, N Africa, Italy; economist Courtaulds Ltd 1946-50; Univ of Cambridge: res fell St Catharine's Coll 1950-53, lectr in econ 1951-71, fell St John's Coll 1958-71; official fell Nuffield Coll Oxford 1971-78, prof of econs Imperial Coll London 1978-87, prof emeritus of econs Univ of London 1987-, sr res fell Mgmnt Sch Imperial Coll 1987-; memb: MMC, Bd Br Steel Corpn, Royal Cmmn on Environmental Pollution, Royal Cmmn on Press, Restrictive Practices Ct; sec gen Royal Econ Soc 1979-(memb 1946), pres Confedn of Euro Econ Assocs 1988-90; *Books* The Motor Industry (jtly, 1959), Economic Impact of the Patent System (jtly, 1973), The Steel Industry (jtly, 1974), The Multi-Fibre Arangement and the UK Economy (1984), The Future of the Multi-Fibre Arrangement (1989); *Recreations* opera, ballet; *Clubs* Travellers; *Style—* Prof Aubrey Silberston, CBE; Imperial College, 53 Princes Gate, London SW7 2PG, (☎ 071 589 5111, fax 071 823 7685, telex 929484)

SILK; *see*: Kilroy-Silk

SILK, Dr David Baxter A; *b* 14 April 1944; *Educ* Univ of London (MB BS, LRCP, MRCP); *Career* lectr in med Dept of Med and Gastroenterology St Bart's Hosp London 1971-75, MRC Travelling fell and visiting assoc prof Univ of Calif San Francisco USA 1975-76, sr lectr and conslt Liver Unit King's Coll London 1976-78, conslt physician and co dir Dept of Gastroenterology and Nutrition Central Middx Hosp London 1978-; appointed to Editorial Bd: GUT 1978, Jl of Clinical Nutrition and Gastroenterology 1985, Gastroenterology in Practice 1987; Research medal The British Soc of Gastroenterology; memb Assoc of Physicians, MRCS 1968, MD 1974, FRCP 1983; *Books* Nutritional Support in Hospital Practice (1983), author of over 200 articles in learned jls; *Style—* Dr David Silk; Dept of Gastroenterology and Nutrition, Central Middx Hospital, Acton Lane, Park Royal, London NW10 7NS

SILK, Dennis Raoul Whitehall; JP (Oxon 1973); s of Rev Dr Claude Whitehall Silk (d 1974), and Louise Enicita, *née* Dumoret (d 1936); *b* 8 Oct 1931; *Educ* Christ's Hosp Horsham, Sidney Sussex Coll Cambridge (MA); *m* 6 April 1963, Diana Merilyn, da of William Frank Milton (d 1970), of Taunton, Somerset; 2 s (Thomas b 1967, William b 1969), 2 da (Katharine b 1964, Alexandra b 1966); *Career* housemaster Marlborough Coll 1957-68 (asst master 1955-68), warden of Radley Coll 1968-91; memb: Ctee MCC 1965-89, TCCB 1984-89; *Books* Cricket for Schools (1964), Attacking Cricket (1965), Blues in Cricket (1955), Rugby Football, Rugby Fives; *Recreations* gardening, reading; *Clubs* Hawks', E India Sports', Devonshire; *Style—* Warden Dennis Silk, JP; The Warden's House, Radley Coll, Abingdon, Oxon OX14 2HR (☎ 0235 520585)

SILK, Donald; s of Robert Silk, of London, and Polly, *née* Silk (d 1980); *b* 6 Sept 1928; *Educ* Magdalen Coll Sch Oxford, New Coll Oxford (BA, MA), Hague Acad of Int Law (Certificat d'Assiduité), London Graduate Sch of Business Studies; *m* 1, 8 Feb 1959 (m dis 1969), Angela Kate, da of Harry Buxton (d 1973), of London and Manchester; 2 s (Benjamin b 1960, Joseph b 1961); 1 da (Rebecca b 1966); m 2, 6 April 1983, Hilary Wells, da of George William Jackson (d 1985), of Chesterfield, Derbyshire; 1 s (James b 1984), 1 da (Polly Georgina Charlotte b 1986); *Career* Nat Serv Sgt instr RAEC 1947-49, memb HAC; dir Silk's Estates Investments Ltd 1949-69, slr and cmmr for oaths 1956-, underwriting memb Lloyds 1985-, chm Property Equity and Life Assur Co 1969-88; hon vice pres Zionist Fedn 1971- (chm 1967-71), former common councilman City of London, former memb Bd of Deps of Br Jews, tstee Chichester Festival Theatre; Freeman City of London, memb: City of London Slrs Co 1971, Worshipful Co of Arbitrators 1983-; SSC 1956, memb Law Soc; *Recreations* food and wine, theatre, opera, travel, yachting, watching polo; *Clubs* Reform, Royal Thames Yacht, City Livery; *Style—* Donald Silk, Esq; 69 Charlbury Rd, North Oxford OX2 6UX (☎ 0865 513881)

SILK, Dr Nicholas; s of Colin Edward Bailey Silk, of 13 Highdown Rd, Lewes, Sussex, and Beryl Mary, *née* Greenslade; *b* 26 May 1941; *Educ* Lewes Co GS, Merton Coll Oxford (MA, BSc, BM BCh), St Thomas' Hosp London (DObst, Dch); *m* 2 March 1968, Beverley-Anne, da of Norman James Bazell (d 1953); 3 s (William b 1973, Edward b 1977, Jonanthan b 1979), 1 da (Harriet b 1971); *Career* MO Bedales Sch 1972-84, sr ptnr Dr Silk & Ptnrs Petersfield; rugby football: capt Oxford Univ RFC 1963, Blue 1961-63, 4 England Caps against Wales, Ireland, France, Scotland, capt Br Univs 1966, Harlequins FC 1959-66, chm Petersfield Mini Jr Rugby 1988-89; Freeman City of London, memb Worshipful Soc of Apothecaries of London; MRCS, LRCP, RCOG; *Recreations* golf, tennis, bee-keeping; *Style—* Dr Nicholas Silk; Brownfields, Westmark, Petersfield, Hants GU31 5AT (☎ 0730 638 22); 18 Heath Rd, Petersfield, Hants GU31 4DU (☎ 0730 640 11)

SILK, The Ven Robert David; s of Robert Reeve Silk (d 1990), and Winifred Patience Silk (d 1985); *b* 23 Aug 1936; *Educ* Gillingham GS, Univ of Exeter (BA), St Stephen's House Oxford; *m* 21 Sept 1957, Joyce Irene, da of Richard Bracey (d 1981, Brig in the Salvation Army); 1 s (Richard b 1967), 1 da (Mary b 1970); *Career* deacon 1959, priest 1960; curate: St Barnabas Gillingham 1959-63, Holy Redeemer Lamorbey 1963-69; priest-in-charge of The Good Shepherd Blackfen 1967-69; rector: Swanscombe 1969-75, Beckenham St George 1975-80; proctor in Convocation 1970-, memb of the Liturgical Cmmn 1976-91, archdeacon of Leicester 1980-, prolocutor of the Convocation of Canterbury 1980-, team rector of the Holy Spirit Leicester 1982-88; chm Leicester Cncl of Faiths 1986-, moderator Ctee for Rels with People of Other Faith 1990-; *Publications* Prayers For Use At The Alternative Services (1980), Compline - An Alternative Order (1980), In Penitence and Faith (1988); *Recreations* tennis, Richard III; *Clubs* Athenaeum; *Style—* The Ven the Archdeacon of Leicester; 13 Stoneygate Avenue, Leicester LE2 3HE (☎ 0533 704441)

SILKIN, Hon Christopher Lewis; er s of Baron Silkin of Dulwich (Life Peer, d 1988); *b* 12 Sept 1947; *Educ* Dulwich, Mid-Essex Tech Coll (LLB); *Career* slr 1977; *Style—* The Hon Christopher Silkin

SILKIN, Jon; s of Joseph Silkin, and Doris, *née* Rubenstein; *b* 2 Dec 1930; *Educ* Wycliffe Coll, Dulwich; *m* 4 March 1974, Lorna, *née* Tracy; 3 s (Adam (decd), David, Richard), 1 da (Rachel); *Career* Nat Serv Sgt Instr Educn Corps 1948-50; journalist 1947-48, manual labourer 1950-56, teacher of english to foreign students in language sch 1956-58; poet: awarded Gregory Fellowship in Poetry Univ of Leeds 1958-60, undertook res on poets of WWI 1962, Beck visiting lectr Denison Univ Ohio 1965, teacher Writers Workshop Univ of Iowa 1968-69, visiting lectr Aust Arts Cncl and Univ of Sydney 1974-, C Day Lewis Fellowship London 1976-77, teacher creative writing Coll of Idaho 1978, visiting poet Mishkenot Sha'ananim Jerusalem 1980, Bingham poet Univ of Louisville 1981, Elliston poet Univ Cincinnati 1983, visiting poet at yearly fest of Univ of Notre Dame 1985, visiting poet Writers Conf of Univ of N Alabama, visiting poet The American Univ 1989; FRSL 1987; *Books* The Peacable Kingdom (1954), The Two Freedoms (1958), The Re- ordering of the Stones (1961), Nature with Man (1965), Poems New and Selected (1966), Amana Grass (1971), Out of Battle (Criticism of poets of WWI 1972/1987), Poetry of the Committed Individual (anthology of poetry from Stand, 1973), The Principle of Water (1974), The Little Time-keeper (1976), The Penguin Book of First World War Poetry (ed, 1979), The Psalms with their Spoils (1980), Selected Poems (1980, 1988), Gurney: A Play in Verse (1985), The War Poems of Wilfred Owen (ed, 1985), The Penguin Book of First World War Prose (ed with Jon Glover, 1989), The Ship's Pasture (poems 1986), The first twenty-four years (1987); *Style—* Jon Silkin, Esq; 19 Haldane Terrace, Newcastle on Tyne, Tyne and Wear NE2 3AN (☎ 091 281 2614)

SILKIN, Hon Patricia Jane; *née* Silkin (to which she has reverted); yr da of Baron Silkin of Dulwich (Life Peer, d 1988); *b* 12 Sept 1947, (twin); *Educ* James Allen's Girls' Sch, Sussex Univ (BA); *m* 1970, Michael Johnson, BA, PhD; *Style—* The Hon Patricia Silkin

SILKIN, Hon Peter David Arthur; yr s of Baron Silkin of Dulwich (Life Peer, d 1988); *b* 28 Dec 1952; *Educ* Dulwich, Sussex Univ (BA, MA); *m* 1974 (m dis 1982), Frances, da of Dr Patrick Kemp, of Woking; *Career* CIPFA; *Style—* The Hon Peter Silkin

SILLARS, Derek Gordon; TD (1961); s of Ralph Gordon Sillars (d 1959), of Middlesbrough, and (Nancy) Annie Clifford, *née* MacFarlane (d 1976); *b* 4 May 1918; *Educ* Oundle; *m* 22 June 1942, Patricia Dora, da of Henry Chandler Lovell (d 1953), of Middx; 4 s (Michael Gordon b 1943, Timothy John b 1945, Anthony Geoffrey b 1950, Duncan Henry Clifford b 1953); *Career* mil serv; TA cmmn 1939 (RA), France 1939-40, Brig Gunnery Offr UK 1941-42, Battery Cdr E Africa 1945-46, Maj; co dir; emigrated S Africa 1948; fndr and md Sillars Constructions (pty) Ltd Cape Town 1951, Sillars SW Pty Ltd Windoek SW Africa (now Namibia), dir and gen mangr Tarmac Roadstone Ltd N England 1961, fndr and md Sillars Road Construction Ltd 1965, dir Sillars Building and Civil Engrg Ltd 1981, chm and dir Sillars Hldgs Ltd 1981; *Recreations* fishing, shooting, tennis, golf, gardening; *Clubs* Kelvin Grove (Cape Town), Cleveland (Middlesbrough); *Style—* Derek G Sillars, Esq, TD; Greendales, Nether Silton, Thirsk, North Yorkshire YO7 2JZ (☎ 060983 355); Sillars Hldgs Ltd, Sillcon House, Graythorp Industrial Estate, Hartlepool, Cleveland TS25 2DJ (☎ 0429 268125)

SILLARS, Michael Gordon; s of Derek Gordon Sillars, of Greendales, Nether Silton, Thirsk, North Yorkshire, and Patricia Dora, *née* Lovell; *b* 2 Aug 1943; *Educ* Forres Sch Rondebosch Cape Town SA, Diocesan Coll Rondebosch Cape Town SA; *m* 16 June 1973, Lavinia Charlotte, da of Eric James Fletcher; 2 da (Amanda Louise b 16 July 1976, Emma Charlotte b 23 Nov 1979); *Career* Peat Marwick Mitchell & Co: articled clerk Middlesbrough 1963-69, qualified chartered accountant 1969, London 1970-71, Johannesburg SA 1971-73; Haggie Rand Ltd Johannesburg SA: chief accountant Haggie Rand Industrial Products Ltd 1973-74, fin accountant Haggie Steel Ropes Ltd 1974-75, project accountant Haggie Rand Wire Ltd 1975-77; ptnr H H Kilvington Chartered Accountants Hartlepool Cleveland 1978- (joined 1977), WT Walton & Son Hartlepool (following merger 1980), BDO Binder Hamlyn 1987- (following merger); chm Teeside Soc of Chartered Accountants 1989-90; FCA 1979 (ACA 1969); *Recreations* golf, tennis, music, photography; *Clubs* West Hartlepool; *Style—* Michael Sillars, Esq; Lorne Cottage, 16 East Green, Heighington, Darlington, Co Durham DL5 6PP (☎ 0325 313159); BDO Binder Hamlyn, 40 Victoria Rd, Hartlepool, Cleveland (☎ 0429 234414, fax 0429 231263)

SILLERY, William Moore; s of William Sillery, of Belfast, and Adeline, *née* Moore; *b* 14 March 1941; *Educ* Methodist Coll Belfast, St Catharine's Coll Cambridge (MA); *m* 19 Aug 1963, Elizabeth Margaret, da of James S Dunwoody, of Belfast; 2 da (Clare, Jane); *Career* Belfast Royal Acad: head modern languages 1968, vice princ 1974, dep headmaster 1976, headmaster 1980-; memb NI Ctee Univs Funding Cncl, educn advsr Ulster TV, memb Headmasters Conf; *Recreations* reading, golf, bridge; *Clubs* East India, Belvoir Park Belfast; *Style—* William Sillery, Esq; Ardmore, 15 Saintfield Rd, Belfast BT8 4AE (☎ 0232 645260); Belfast Royal Academy, Belfast BT14 6JL (☎ 0232 740423)

SILLEY, Jonathan Henry; s of Henry Arthur John Silley, CBE (d 1972), and Betty Stewart, *née* Cotton (d 1981); *b* 2 May 1937; *Educ* Winchester; *m* 17 June 1961, Alison Mary, da of Richard Kenneth May (d 1965), of Purley, Surrey; 3 da (Jennifer Mary b 1964, Jane Elizabeth b 1965, Nichola Anne b 1969); *Career* Nat Serv 1955-57, 2 Lt Queens Royal Regt; joined Samuel Hodge Gp 1959; dir: Surface Protection 1959-84 (chm 1971-84), E Wood Ltd 1963-84 (chm 1971-84), S Hodge Ltd 1965- (chm and md 1971-), Hodge Clemco Ltd 1965- (chm 1971-), Victor Pyrate Ltd 1965- (chm 1971-), Hodge Separators Ltd 1976- (chm), Stetfield Ltd 1987- (chm), Western Selection plc 1988-; memb HAC 1988; *Recreations* golf, tennis, racquets; *Clubs* City of London; *Style—* Jonathan Silley, Esq; Oudle House, Much Hadham, Herts SG10 6BT (☎ 027 984 2359); Samuel Hodge Ltd, Prince of Wales House, 3 Bluecoats Avenue, Hertford SG14 1PB (☎ 0992 558675)

SILLITOE, Alan; s of Christopher Archibald (d 1959), and Sylvina Burton (d 1986); *b* 4 March 1928; *Educ* Radford Boulevard Sch Nottingham; *m* 19 Nov 1959, Ruth, da of Leslie Alexander Jonas Fainlight, of Sussex; 1 s (David Nimrod b 1962), 1 da (Susan Dawn b 1961); *Career* air traffic control 1945-46, RAF wireless operator 1946-49; writer 1948-; Hon Degree: Manchester Poly 1976, Nottingham Poly 1990; *Books* Saturday Night and Sunday Morning (1958, Authors Club award 1958, film 1960, play 1964), The Loneliness of the Long Distance Runner (1959, Hawthornden prize film 1962), Key to the Door (1961), Raw Material (1972), The Widower's Son (1976), The Storyteller (1979), Her Victory (1982), The Lost Flying Boat (1983), The Open Door (1989), Last Love (1990); poetry collections incl: The Rats and Other Poems (1960), A Falling Out of Love (1964), Show on the North side of Lucifer (1979), Tides and Stone Walls (1986); Marmalade Jim City Adventures (1967), Marmalade Jim At The Farm (1980), Marmalade Jim And The Fox (1985); *Recreations* short wave world morse code listening, travel; *Clubs* Savage; *Style—* Alan Sillitoe, Esq; 14 Ladbroke Terrace, London W11

SILLITOE, David Nimrod; s of Alan Sillitoe, of London, and Ruth Esther, *née* Fainlight; *b* 30 March 1962; *Educ* City of London Sch, Kingsway Princeton Coll of Further Educn, Hammersmith and W London Coll, NE London Poly; *Partner* Helen Hirons; *Career* photographer; freelance: various London organisations (GLC, unions, magazines) 1986, Mail on Sunday 1986-87, with The Independent and The BBC Central Stills Library and contrib to Reflex 1987-88, The Guardian 1988; staff photographer The Guardian 1989-; memb NUJ; *Books* Alan Stillitoe's Nottinghamshire (photographs, 1987); *Recreations* motorcycle touring, recorded music and radio, photography; *Clubs* The BMW, Br Motorcyclists Fedn; *Style—* David Sillitoe, Esq; The Guardian, 119 Farringdon Rd, London EC1R 3ER (☎ 071 278 2332)

SILLITOE, Leslie Richard; OBE (1977), JP (1963); s of Leonard Richard Sillitoe (d 1926), and Ellen, *née* Sutton (d 1933); *b* 30 Aug 1915; *Educ* St George's, St Giles

Sch, Stoke-on-Trent Sch of Art, Stoke-on-Trent Tech Coll; *m* 1939, Lucy, da of Arthur Goulding (d 1923); 2 da (Christine, Margaret); *Career* Nat Serv WWII with N Staffs Regt, RE, and RA, served with Br Liberation Army and BAOR (Normandy to Hartz Mountains), Sr NCO 30 Corps (France, Belgium, Holland, Luxembourg and Germany, Territorial Efficient Serv medal 1945); modeller ceramics indust 1931-63, gen pres Ceramic and Allied Trade Union 1961-63 (organiser 1963-67, asst gen sec 1967-75, gen sec 1975-80), dep chm Ceramic Glass Mineral Prods Trg Bd 1977-83; chm: Nat Jt Cncl for Ceramic Indust 1975-80, N Staffs Manpower Ctee 1975-83; pres N Staffs Trades Cncl 1963-81, memb Stoke-on-Trent City Cncl 1953-83, hon memb N Staffs Med Inst, vice chm Museums Ctee; Lord Mayor Stoke-on-Trent 1981-82 (dep Lord Mayor 1982-83); memb: W Midland TAURA 1979-83, Ctee Staffs War Pensions 1980-, Cncl Univ of Keele 1989-; chm: Friends of the Staffs Regt 1982-, Stoke-on-Trent Branch Normandy Veterans 1986-; vice pres Pottery and Glass Benevolent Inst 1980-; re-elected to Stoke-on-Trent City Cncl 1986-; *Recreations* walking, photography, swimming, history; *Clubs* Gideons Int, Longton Rotary (pres 1987-88); *Style*— Leslie Sillitoe, Esq, OBE, JP; 19 Sillitoe Place, Penkhull, Stoke-on-Trent ST4 5DQ (☎ 0782 47866)

SILLS, Dr John Anthony; s of Oliver Anthony Sills, of Barton, Cambridge, and Joan, *née* Webster; *b* 7 Sept 1943; *Educ* Perse Sch Cambridge, Queens' Coll Cambridge, Bart's Med Sch (MA, MB BChir, DCH); *m* 24 June 1974, Hope Glen Milne, da of James Paterson Forsyth; 2 s (Benjamin b 29 Dec 1975, Daniel b 17 Dec 1979), 2 da (Laura b 9 Feb 1978, Emily b 16 May 1983); *Career* sr registrar Royal Hosp For Sick Children Edinburgh 1974-78, conslt paediatrician Royal Liverpool Childrens Hosp Alder Hey and Whiston Hosp Prescot 1978-; memb: Nat Tst Scotland, Br Paediatric Assoc, BAPSCAN; FRCP 1988; *Books* Surgical Management of Rheumatoid Arthritis (contrib), author of papers on paediatrics; *Recreations* classical music, jazz, films, Liverpool FC; *Style*— Dr John Sills; Royal Liverpool Childrens Hospital, Alder Hey, Eaton Rd, Liverpool L12 2AP (☎ 051 228 4811); Whiston Hospital, Prescot, Merseyside L35 1DR (☎ 051 426 1600, ext 1453)

SILSOE, 2 Baron (UK 1963); Sir David Malcom Trustram Eve; 2 Bt (UK 1943), QC (1972); s of late 1 Baron Silsoe, GBE, MC, TD, QC (d 1976), by 1 w, Marguerite, da of Sir Augustus Meredith Nanton; *b* 2 May 1930; *Educ* Winchester, Ch Ch Oxford; *m* 1963, Bridget Min, da of Sir Rupert Hart-Davis, *qv*; 1 s (Hon Simon Rupert), 1 da (Hon Amy Comfort b 13 June 1964); *Heir* s, Hon Simon Rupert Trustram Eve b 17 April 1966; *Career* barr 1955, bar auditor Inner Temple 1965-70, bencher 1970; *Style*— The Rt Hon The Lord Silsoe, QC; Neals Farm, Wyfold, Reading, Berks

SILVER, Prof Ian Adair; s of Capt George James Silver (d 1937), and Nora Adair, *née* Seckham (d 1979); *b* 28 Dec 1927; *Educ* Rugby, Corpus Christi Coll Cambridge (BA, MA), Royal Veterinary Coll London; *m* 30 June 1950, Marian, da of Dr Frederick John Scrase (d 1981); 2 s (Alastair b 1960, Angus b 1963), 2 da (Alison b 1956, m Andrew Hunter, *qv*, Fiona b 1959); *Career* RN 'Y' Scheme 1945, seconded Cambridge Univ, trans to Tech & Scientific Reg 1948; demonstrator in zoology Cambridge 1952-57 (lectr anatomy 1957-70), prof comparative pathology Bristol 1970-81, prof and chm Dept of Pathology Univ of Bristol 1981- (dean Faculty of Medicine 1987-); prof of neurology Univ of Pennsylvania USA 1977-, visiting prof Cayetana Heredia Univ Lima Peru 1976, Royal Soc prof Federal Univ Rio de Janeiro Brazil 1977, visiting prof Louisiana Tech Univ USA 1973; pres: RCVS 1985-86 and 1987, Int Soc for Study of O Transport to Tissue 1977 and 1986; fell and sr tutor Churchill Coll Cambridge 1965-70; memb research cncl ctees: MRC, SERC, AFRC, ARC; MRCVS; *Books* edited 6 scientific books, published over 200 learned papers; *Recreations* exploration, DIY, fishing; *Style*— Prof Ian Silver; c/o Dept of Pathology, Medical School, Bristol Univ, Bristol BS8 1TD (☎ 0272 303446)

SILVER, Leslie Howard; OBE (1982); s of Harry Silver, and Bessie, *née* Hoffman; *b* 22 Jan 1925; *m* 1, Anita (d 1983); 1 s (Mark b 1960), 2 da (Hilary b 1948, Jane b 1950); m 2, 29 April 1984, Sheila Estelle; *Career* WWII Warrant Offr RAF 1943-46; pres: Paintmakers Assoc of GB, Oil Colour Chemists Assoc, Paint Res Assoc, Paint Indust Club; chm Leeds Utd AFC; MBIM; *Style*— Leslie Silver, Esq, OBE

SILVER, Max Joseph; s of Benjamin Silver (d 1981), of Cardiff, and Rose, *née* Spira (d 1941); *b* 14 April 1925; *Educ* City of Cardiff HS, Univ of Wales (BSc), Croydon Poly (Dip Telecoms); *m* 4 Feb 1964, Muriel, da of Jack Grasin (d 1960), of Palmers Green, London; 1 s (Jonathan b 1970), 1 da (Rochelle b 1965); *Career* electronics res worker GEC Wembley 1947-50, res and prodn mgmnt with assoc co of GEC on airborne def projects 1950-59, with Elliot Automation and md Assoc Automation Ltd (later part of GEC) 1960-70, co doctor Philips Gp and Pye of Cambridge Sub Gp 1971-80, princ of consultancy on co-aquisitions and mergers with contracts to PA Conslts and M & A Int 1980-; advsr on educn ctee Brent Cncl, vice chm of Govrs Kilburn Poly 1982-86; CEng, FIEE, FIERE, FIProdE, FBIM, FSCA, FMS, FFA; *Recreations* reading, gardening, travel; *Style*— Max Silver, Esq; 34 Pangbourne Drive, Stanmore, Middx HA7 4QT (☎ 081 958 7885)

SILVER, Petronilla; da of Prof Peter Hele Spencer-Silver, of London, and Patricia Anne, *née* Cuffe; *b* 16 Sept 1950; *Educ* Godolphin and Latymer GS London, Redland Coll of Educn Bristol (DipEd); *Career* sec and sales asst Redfern Gallery London 1973-77, organising sec and exec dir The Contemporary Art Society 1981- (organising sec as asst 1977-81); memb: Construction History Soc, ICA, Friends of the Tate; *Recreations* travel, cooking, gardening, visiting exhibitions, walking, swimming, theatre; *Clubs* Cape Cornwall Golf and Country; *Style*— Ms Petronilla Silver; The Contemporary Art Society, 20 John Islip St, London SW1P 4LL (☎ 071 821 5323)

SILVER, Prof Robert Simpson; CBE (1967); s of Alexander Clark Silver (d 1962), of Montrose, Angus, and Isabella Simpson (d 1950); *b* 13 March 1913; *Educ* Montrose Acad, Univ of Glasgow (MA, DSc); *m* 1937, Jean McIntyre (d 1988), da of Alexander Bruce (d 1937), and Elizabeth, *née* Livingstone (d 1950); 2 s; *Career* engrg scientist, consultant, James Watt prof of mechanical engrg Univ of Glasgow 1967-79, prof emeritus 1979-, prof of mechanical engrg Heriot-Watt Coll Edinburgh 1962-66, dir G & J Weir Ltd 1958- (head of res 1939-46, chief of R & D 1956-62); UNESCO Sci Prize 1968, for assoc of US Acad of Engrg 1979; FInstP (1942), FIMechE (1953), FRSE (1963); Hon DSc Strathclyde 1948; *Books* Introduction to Thermodynamics (1971), The Bruce (A Play in 3 acts, 1986); *Recreations* fly-fishing, poetry; *Style*— Prof Robert Silver, CBE, FRSE; 5 Panmure St, Montrose, Angus, Scotland DD10 8EZ (☎ 0674 77793)

SILVERMAN, Prof Bernard Walter; s of Elias Silverman, of London, and Helen, *née* Korn (d 1989); *b* 22 Feb 1952; *Educ* City of London Sch, Univ of Cambridge (MA, PhD, ScD); *m* 9 March 1985, Dr Rowena Fowler; 1 s (Matthew b 1989); *Career* res fell Jesus Coll Cambridge 1975-77, devpt mangr Sinclair Radionics Ltd 1976-77, lectr Univ of Oxford 1977-78, head of Sch of Mathematical Sciences Univ of Bath 1988- (lectr 1978-80, reader 1981-84, prof of statistics 1984); over fifty papers in jls; hon sec Royal Statistical Soc 1984-90; fell Inst Mathematical Statistics USA 1986-; *Books* Density Estimation for Statistics and Data Analysis (1986); *Style*— Prof Bernard Silverman; Sch of Mathematical Sciences, University of Bath, Bath BA2 7AY (☎ 0225 826224)

SILVERMAN, Michael Anthony; s of Ernest Silverman, of London, and Anne, *née* Taylor; *b* 12 Aug 1940; *Educ* Dulwich; *m* 1966, Ruth, da of Jack Shelley, of London; 1 s (Paul b 1969), 1 da (Katie b 1971); *Career* chm and md: Merton Assoc (conslts) 1977-87, Lloyd Group of Cos 1968-76; pres Transearch Int 1981-; hon librarian Carlton Club 1979-; memb Cons Med Soc 1985-; Freeman and vice pres Ward of Cheap City of London, Freeman Worshipful Co of Marketors; FIMC, FIPM, MBIM, memb Market Research Soc; *Recreations* horse riding, sailing, rugby; *Clubs* Carlton, Nautico (Mallorca) Crouch Yacht; *Style*— Michael Silverman, Esq; 181 Adelaide Road, Hampstead, London NW3 3NN (☎ 071 722 7425); Merton House, 70 Grafton Way, London W1P 5LE (☎ 071 388 2051, fax 071 387 5324, telex 8953742)

SILVERMAN, Prof (Hugh) Richard; s of S G Silverman (d 1985), and N E, *née* Braley, of New South Wales; *b* 23 Sept 1940; *Educ* Brighton Coll of Art and Craft (Dip Arch), Univ of Edinburgh (MSc); *m* 24 Feb 1963, Aase Kay, da of Knud Sonderskov Madsen; 2 da (Jennifer Solvej b 24 April 1971, Sophie Annelise b 23 Nov 1974); *Career* dir Alec French Partnership (Architects) Bristol 1984-86, prof and head The Welsh Sch of Architecture Cardiff 1986-; memb: Bd Cardiff Bay Devpt Corp 1990- (chm Design and Architecture Review Panel), ARIBA 1965, FRSA 1989; *Style*— Prof Richard Silverman; 15 Clifton Vale, Bristol BS8 4PT (☎ 0272 292676); Welsh Sch of Architecture, Univ of Wales, PO Box 25, Cardiff CF1 3XE (☎ 0222 874431, fax 0222 371521, telex 0222 497368)

SILVESTER, Frederick John; s of William Silvester and Kathleen Gertrude, *née* Jones; *b* 20 Sept 1933; *Educ* Sir George Monoux GS, Sidney Sussex Coll Cambridge; *m* 1971, Victoria Ann, da of James Harold Lloyd Davies; 2 da; *Career* former teacher Wolstanton GS 1955-57; political educn offr Cons Political Centre 1957-60; memb Walthamstow Borough Cncl 1961-64; chm Walthamstow W Cons Assoc 1961-64; MP: Walthamstow W 1967-70, Manchester Withington 1974-87; oppn whip 1974-76, PPS to Sec State of Employment 1979-81; Sec of State NI 1981-83; memb: Public Accounts Ctee 1983-87, Procedure Ctee 1983-87; Exec 1922 Ctee 1985-87; vice-chm Cons Employment Ctee 1976-79; sr assoc dir J Walter Thompson; *Style*— Frederick Silvester, Esq; J Walter Thompson, Astley House, Quay St, Manchester M3 4AS

SILVESTER, Peter; s of Eric William James Silvester, and Dorothy May, *née* Collier; *b* 21 Jan 1936; *Educ* Godalming GS; *m* 8 Feb 1964, Christine Catherine; *Career* Nat Serv RAF sac; Friends Provident Life Office: asst gen mangr 1981-87, gen mangr (Investmt) 1987-88, dir and gen mangr Investmt 1988-; dir of various subsid cos; non-exec dir Presidio Oil Co, Esprit, Kairos Gen, Kairos Vida and Maindrive; former vice pres The Pensions Mgmnt Inst, pres Insur Lawn Tennis Assoc, memb RSPB; FIA 1971, FPMI 1979, MInstD; *Recreations* skiing, fishing, golf, tennis; *Style*— Peter Silvester, Esq; Friends Provident Life Off, Pixham End, Dorking, Surrey (☎ 071 329 4454)

SIM, John Mackay; MBE (Mil 1944); s of William Aberdeen Mackay Sim (d 1952), of Dunragit House, Dunragit, Wigtownshire, and Zoë, *née* Jenner (d 1973); *b* 4 Oct 1917; *Educ* Glenalmond, Pembroke Coll Cambridge (MA); *m* 1, 1944, Dora Cecilia Plumridge (d 1951), da of Sir Cecil Levita, KCVO, CBE; 2 da (Amanda Baird, Alexandra Baird); m 2, 1963, Muriel Harvard Harris; *Career* WWII RA 2 Lt 1941, Lt 1942, Capt 1943; dir Inchcape and Co Ltd, dep chm Inchcape plc; *Style*— John Sim, Esq, MBE; 6 Bryanston Mews West, London W1H 7FR (☎ 071 262 7673)

SIM, Peter Anderson; s of Stuart Anderson Sim (d 1970), and Bertha Roberts (d 1980); *b* 16 July 1939; *Educ* High Wycombe Royal GS, Coll of Estate Mgmnt; *m* 8 Oct 1966, Gillian Margaret Anne, da of Thomas Cedric Nicholson (d 1960); 2 s (Andrew b 1968, David b 1970), 1 da (Christina b 1976); *Career* dir Taylor Woodrow Property Co 1974, md Property Legal & Gen 1974-89; dir: Legal & Gen Investmt Mgmnt (Hldgs) Ltd, Legal & Gen Assur (Pensions Mgmnt) Ltd, Legal & Gen Property Ltd, Cavendish Land Co Ltd, Watling Street Properties Ltd, Paramount Reality Hldgs Ltd, Bridge End Properties Ltd, Glanfield Securities Ltd, Investmt Property Databank Ltd; chm and md Wildoak Properties Ltd 1989-; FRICS; *Recreations* gardening, swimming; *Style*— Peter Sim, Esq; Little Mount, Church Road, Cookham Dean, Berks SL6 9PR (☎ 0628 484196); Enterprise House, 370/386 Farnham Rd, Slough, Berkshire SL2 1JD (☎ 0753 34888)

SIMCOX, Richard Alfred; CBE (1975, MBE 1956); s of late Alfred William Simcox, and Alice Simcox; *b* 29 March 1915; *Educ* Wolverhampton, Gonville and Caius Coll Cambridge; *m* 1951, Patricia Elisabeth, *née* Gutteridge; 1 s, 2 da; *Career* Br Cncl 1943-75; rep: Jordan 1957-60; Libya 1960, cultural attaché Br Embassy Cairo 1968-71, rep Iran 1971-75, currently govr Gabbitas-Thring Educnl Tst; *Style*— Richard Simcox, Esq, CBE; Little Brockhurst, Lye Green Rd, Chesham, Bucks (☎ 0494 783797)

SIME, Peter Ernest Miller; s of Ian Falconer Sime, and Marjorie Joan Thompson, *née* Miller; *b* 18 Nov 1954; *Educ* Crewe Co GS, Jesus Coll Oxford (MA), Birbeck Coll London (MSc); *Career* CA; Deloitte Haskins & Sells 1976-83, fin dir and co sec Gardner Lohmann ltd 1983-85, head of enforcement Assoc of Futures Brokers & Dealers Ltd 1988-90 (compliance mangr 1985-88), head of market supervision London Int Fin Futures Exchange 1990; memb ICEAW 1979; *Recreations* flying, mountaineering; *Style*— Peter Sime, Esq; London International Financial Futures Exchange, Royal Exchange Buildings, London EC3U 3PJ (☎ 071 623 0444, fax 071 588 3624)

SIMEON, Sir John Edmund Barrington; 7 Bt (UK 1815) of Grazeley, Berks; s of Sir John Walter Barrington Simeon, 6 Bt (d 1957); 1 Bt m da and heir of Sir FitzWilliam Barrington 10 Bt, extinct 1833; *b* 1 March 1911; *Educ* Eton, ChCh Oxford; *m* 10 July 1937, Anne Robina Mary, er da of Hamilton Dean; 1 s, 2 da; *Heir* s, Richard Edmund Barrington Simeon, *qv*; *Career* served WWII RAF 1939-43, invalided rank of Flt Lt, emigrated to Canada 1951, civil servant Dept of Social Welfare Govt Br Columbia 1951-75; *Style*— Sir John Simeon, Bt; 987 Wavertree Rd, N Vancouver, BC V7R 1S6, Canada

SIMEON, Prof Richard Edmund Barrington; s and h of Sir John Simeon, 7 Bt, by his w, Anne Mary Dean; *b* 2 March 1943; *Educ* St George's Sch Vancouver, Br Columbia Univ (BA), Yale Univ (MA, PhD); *m* 6 Aug 1966, Agnes Joan, o da of George Frederick Weld; 1 s (Stephen b 1970), 1 da (Rachel b 1973); *Career* prof dept of political studies, Queen's Univ Kingston Canada; dir: Inst of Intergovernmental Relations Queen's Univ 1976-83, Sch of Pub Admin Queen's Univ Kingston 1986-; res co-ordinator (Royal Cmmn on the Economic Union and Canada's Dvpt Prospects Canada) 1983-85; *Books* Federal-Provincial Diplomacy (1972), Federalism and the Economic Union with K Novine and M Knosnick (1985), Federal Society, Federal State: A History with Ian Robinson (1987), Politics of Constitutional Change, ed with Keith Bonting (1984), and others; *Style*— Prof Richard Simeon; 95 Mack St, Kingston, Ontario, Canada (☎ 010 613 544 5667); Queen's Univ, Kingston, Ontario K7L 3N6, Canada (☎ 010 613 545 2159)

SIMEONE, Reginald Nicola (Reggie); CBE (1985); s of Nicola Francisco Simeone (d 1985), of Horsham, Sussex, and Phyllis Simeone, *née* Iles (d 1985); *b* 12 July 1927; *Educ* Raynes Park GS, St John's Coll Cambridge (MA); *m* 2 April 1954, Josephine Frances, da of Robert Hope (d 1979), of Beverley, Yorks; 2 s (Nigel b 1956, Robert b 1961); *Career* Nat Serv RN instr Lt (meterologist) 1947-50, Admty 1950-59; UKAEA 1959-90: Fin Branch 1959-61, Econs and Progs Branch 1961-65, chief personnel offr AWRE 1965-69, princ estab offr 1970-76, authy personnel offr 1976-84, comptroller of fin and admin 1984-87, memb Bd for Fin and Admin 1987-88, advsr to chm 1988-90;

exec vice pres Euro Atomic Energy Soc 1987-90; chm Police Ctee for AEA Constabulary 1986-90; advsr to chm Nuclear Electric plc 1990-; *Recreations* travel, music, theatre; *Clubs* United Oxford and Cambridge Univs; *Style*— Reginald N Simeone, Esq, CBE; Nuclear Electric plc, 123 Pall Mall, London SW1Y 5EA (☎ 071 389 3435)

SIMEONS, Charles Fitzmaurice Creighton; DL (Beds 1987); s of Charles Albert Simeons (d 1957), and Vera Hildegarde, *née* Creighton (d 1982); *b* 22 Sept 1921; *Educ* Oundle, Queens' Coll Cambridge (MA); *m* 10 March 1945, Rosemary Margaret, da of Ashley Tabrum, OBE; 1 s (Peter), 1 da (Jennifer (Mrs Bishop)); *Career* cmmnd RA 1942, 52 Field Regt, serv 8 Indian Div ME and Italy, Maj; md Br Gelatine Works 1957, Croda Gelatins 1968-70, environmental control conslt 1974-, health and safety advsr Control of Toxic Substances 1980-, int market res studies communication with govt covering Europe, Japan and the US; pres: Rotary Club Luton 1960-61, Luton and Dunstable C of C 1967-68; dist govr Rotary Int Dist 109 1967-68, chm: Luton Cons Assoc 1960-64, Ampthill Cheshire Home 1963-72, Cancer Res Campaign Luton 1963-80, Nat Childrens Home Luton 1976-; hon sec Union of Ind Companies 1978-80, memb: Customer Consultative Ctee Anglia and Thames Water 1984-89, Small Firms Panel ABCC 1985-, Anglian Customer Servs Ctee, Office of Water Servs 1990-; JP Luton 1959-74, MP Luton 1970-74, DL Beds 1987-; Freeman City of London 1969, Master Worshipful Co of Feltmakers 1987-88 (Liveryman 1969); FIIM 1975; *Books* Coal: Its Role in Tomorrows Technology (1978), Water As An Alternative Source of Energy (1980); *Recreations* charitable activities, watching most sports, walking; *Clubs* City Livery, Clover (8 Indian offrs, hon sec); *Style*— Charles Simeons, Esq, DL; 21 Ludlow Ave, Luton LU1 3RW (☎ 0582 30965)

SIMEY, Baroness; Margaret Bayne; *née* Todd; da of John Aiton Todd, sometime clerk of the Ct Gorbals, Glasgow; *m* 1935, Baron Simey (Life Peer, d 1969); 1 s (Hon Thomas b 1938); hus Thomas Simey cr Life peer 1965; *Career* Liverpool City Cncllr for Granby in Toxteth 1963-74, Merseyside Co Cncllr 1974-86; chm Merseyside Police Authy 1981-86; *Books* Government By Consent (1985), Democracy Rediscovered (1988), Active Citizens (1991); *Style*— The Rt Hon Lady Simey; 3 Blackburne Terrace, Blackburne Place, Liverpool 8

SIMISTER, Graham Richard; s of Andrew Gordon Simister MBE, of Manchester, and Winifred *née* Thompson; *b* 13 April 1956; *Educ* Trinity Coll Cambridge (BA, MA), Harvard Business Sch Boston Mass USA (MBA); *m* 26 May 1984, Ceiri, da of Norman Roberts, of New Brighton, Wirral; 1 s (Paul Richard b 1987); *Career* banker Citibank London 1977-82, Midland Bank London 1984-86 (head of foreign exchange, head of futures and options); gen mangr treasy dir Nomura Bank London 1986-; *Recreations* squash, travel, fine wine; *Clubs* Cottons, Mosimanns; *Style*— Graham Simister, Esq; Nomura Bank Int Ltd, 24 Monument St, London EC3R 8AJ (☎ 071 929 2366)

SIMKIN, (Richard) Graham; s of Frederick Simkin (d 1986), and Edna, *née* Turner; *b* 14 July 1952; *Educ* Univ of Leeds (LLB); *m* 6 July 1974, Susan Mary, da of Rev Keith Shackleton (d 1974); 1 s (Matthew b 1989), 3 da (Elizabeth b 1980, Sarah b 1981, Rachel b 1986); *Career* slr; ptnr Boodle Hatfield 1978-90, seconded to Directeur Jurdique Terre Armee Internationale SA 1980-83, head corp serv Boodle Hatfield 1988-90, dep chief exec Terre Armee Group 1990-, ptnr Girham Simkin & Co 1990-; Law Soc 1976; *Recreations* theatre, photography; *Clubs* RAC; *Style*— Graham Simkin, Esq; Buckland House, Dower Mews, Berkhamsted, Herts H34 2BL (☎ 0442 877306, fax 0442 877312)

SIMKISS, Prof Kenneth; s of Clifford Simkiss (d 1970), of Poulton-le-Fylde, Lancs, and Edith Howe (d 1978); *b* 4 July 1934; *Educ* Blackpool GS, Univ of London (BSc, Dsc), Univ of Reading (PhD); *m* 25 March 1961, Nancy Carolyn, da of Dr Travis Bain McGilvray, of Michigan, USA; 2 s (Douglas Eric b 1964, Gregory Daryl b 1970), 1 da (Gillian Varina b 1966); *Career* prof Dept of Zoology Queen Mary Coll Univ of London 1968-72 (lectr 1958-65), prof Dept of Zoology Univ of Reading 1972- (reader in physiology and biochemistry 1965-68); memb Cncl: Soc for Experimental Biology 1975-77, Zoological Soc 1978-80, Marine Biological Assoc 1979-82, 1983-86, 1987-, Freshwater Biological Assoc 1980-84; FIBiol 1973; *Books* Bird Flight (1963), Calcium in Reproductive Physiology (1967), Bone and Biomineralisation (1975), Biomineralisation (1989); *Recreations* music, art; *Style*— Prof Kenneth Simkiss; Foxhill, Foxhill Lane, Playhatch, Reading RG4 9QF (☎ 0734 473008); Pure & Applied Zoology, Animal & Microbiological Sciences, PO Box 228, University of Reading, Reading RG6 2AJ (☎ 0734 318463, fax 0734 310180, telex 847813 ROLIBG)

SIMMERS, Graeme Maxwell; OBE (1982); s of William Maxwell Simmers (the Scottish rugby int, d 1972), and Gwenyth Reinagle, *née* Sterry, tennis champion (Wightman Cup); gm Mrs C R Sterry, *née* Cooper (tennis champion, won Wimbledon 5 times); *b* 2 May 1935; *Educ* Glasgow Acad, Loretto; *m* 10 Sept 1966, Jennifer Margaret Hunter, da of William Roxburgh, OBE, of Fife; 2 s (Mark William b 1967, Peter Hunter Maxwell b 1973), 2 da (Corinne Charlotte b 1969, Kirstin Margaret b 1970); *Career* Nat Serv Lt RM 1959-61; CA 1959, ptnr Kidson Simmers 1959-88, chm Scottish Highland Gp Ltd 1972; memb: Hotel and Catering Benevolent Assoc Scotland 1984-87, Bd of Mgmnt Br Hotels Restaurants and Caterers Assoc 1987, Scottish Tourist Bd 1979-86; chm Champion Ctee Royal and Ancient Golf Club 1988; govr The Queen's Coll Glasgow, vice chm of govrs Loretto Sch, er and treas of Killearn Kirk; *Recreations* golf, tennis, skiing; *Clubs* R & A, All England Lawn Tennis; *Style*— Graeme M Simmers, Esq, OBE; Kincaple, Boquhan, Balfron, Glasgow G63 0RW (☎ 0360 40375); 98 West George Street, Glasgow G2 1PW (☎ 041 332 6538)

SIMMONDS, Lady Caroline; *née* Knox; o da of 6 Earl of Ranfurly, KCMG (d 1988); *b* 11 Dec 1948; *m* 1975, John Edward Simmonds; 3 da; *Style*— The Lady Caroline Simmonds; Great Pednor, Chesham, Bucks

SIMMONDS, David Anthony Kenward; JP (Hertfordshire 1980-); s of Maurice Alan Charles Simmonds (d 1983), and Florence Mary, *née* Kenward, of Orchard End, Nan Clarks Lane, Mill Hill, London NW7; *b* 8 Sept 1939; *Educ* Stowe, Univ of London (BSc); *m* 1, 23 Sept 1963 (m dis 1974), Carole Anne, da of Geoffrey Charles Thomas Parkes (d 1987); 2 da (Jane b 1965, Lucy b 1968); m 2, 27 March 1975, Valerie, da of John Barsley (d 1972); 2 s (Matthew b 1975, Mark b 1978); *Career* chartered surveyor Hendon; chm Hendon Round Table 1974-75; Barnet PSA: dep chm Juvenile Panel 1988-, chm Licensing Ctee 1990-; Freeman City of London 1963, Liveryman Worshipful Co of Tallow Chandlers 1963; ARICS 1963, FRICS 1972; *Recreations* travel, gardening, wine, philately, railways; *Clubs* MCC; *Style*— David Simmonds, Esq, JP; Little Orchard, Barnet Lane, Elstree, Herts WD6 3QX (☎ 081 207 1232); Burroughs House, The Burroughs, Hendon NW4 4AP (☎ 081 202 8181, fax 081 202 3383)

SIMMONDS, Jeremy Basil Canter; RD (1979); s of Reginald Arthur Canter Simmonds (d 1974), of Woodlands Farm, Cookham Dean, Berks, and Betty, *née* Cahusac; *b* 2 July 1941; *Educ* Trinity Coll Glenalmond, Keble Coll Oxford (BA); *m* 4 March 1967, Sally, da of John Bertrand Aust (Capt RA, d 1979), formerly of Tugwood, Cookham Dean; 2 s (Timothy b 1967, Michael b 1970), 2 da (Anne b 1973, Clare b 1973); *Career* Ordinary Seaman London Div RNR 1963, Actg Sub Lt 1965, Sub Lt 1966, Actg Lt 1968, Lt 1969, Lt Cdr 1976, ret 1982; Radcliffes & Co: articled 1965-67, admitted slr 1967, asst slr 1967-69, ptnr 1969-73; ptnr Glovers (formerly Glover & Co) 1973-; chm E Berks Branch Nat Asthma Campaign; Freeman City of London 1980, Liveryman Worshipful Co of Fishmongers 1980; memb Law Soc 1967; *Publications* Rebirth of the Floating Charge, Lenders and the Miscellaneous Problems Act, Collateral Warranties: Pass the Parcel (1990), Solicitors Journal (1990); *Recreations* walking, photography; *Clubs* Naval; *Style*— Jeremy Simmonds, Esq, RD; Woodmancutts, Church Rd, Cookham Dean, Maidenhead, Berks SL6 9PJ (☎ 0628 474991); Glovers, 115 Park St, London W1Y 4DY (☎ 071 629 5121, fax 071 491 0930, telex 261648 VERGLO G)

SIMMONDS, Jeremy Peter; s of late John Armstrong Simmonds, of 12 Chestnut Close, Uppingham, Rutland, and Elizabeth, *née* Buckley; *b* 3 June 1944; *Educ* Bolton Sch, Oakham Sch, Univ of Cambridge (MA); *m* 20 September 1969, Patricia Mary, da of George Charles Gray, of 5 Hannah's Field, Ridlington, Rutland; 1 s (Jeremy b 1972), 1 da (Lucy b 1975); *Career* admitted slr 1971, in private practice; *Recreations* cricket, golf, gardening, fell walking; *Clubs* MCC, Cambridge Univ Hawks, Gentlemen of Leics Cricket, Burghley Park Cricket, Luffenham Heath Golf, Achilles; *Style*— Jeremy Simmonds, Esq; The Old Hall, Morcott, nr Oakham, Rutland LE15 9DN (☎ 0572 87408); 4 Mill St, Oakham, Rutland LE15 6EA (☎ 0572 756866)

SIMMONDS, Prof Kenneth; s of Herbert Marshall Simmonds, and Margaret, *née* Trevurza; *b* 17 Feb 1935; *Educ* Univ of NZ (BCom, MCom), Harvard Univ (DBA), LSE (PhD), Univ of de Deusto Spain (MGCE, JDIP MA); *m* 19 June 1960, Nancy Miriam, *née* Bunai; 2 s (John, Peter), 1 da (Jane); *Career* clerk Guardian Trust Company Wellington NZ 1950-53, asst co sec Gordon & Gotch Ltd Wellington 1953-55, chief accountant William Cable Ltd Wellington 1955-59; conslt: Arthur D Little Inc Cambridge Mass 1959-60, Harbridge House Inc Boston 1962-64; sr lectr Cranfield Inst of Tech 1963-64, asst prof of int business Indiana Univ Bloomington 1964-66, prof of mktg Univ of Manchester 1966-69, Ford Fndn prof of int business Univ of Chicago 1974-75, prof of mktg and int business London Grad Sch of Business 1969-, mktg advsr International Publications Corporation 1967-78; dir: British Steel Corporation 1970-72, Redpath Dorman Long Ltd 1972-74, EMAP plc 1981-; chm Planners Collaborative 1985-88, MIL Research Group plc 1986-89; govr London Business Sch 1980-86, chm London Business Group 1988-, chief ed International Journal of Advertising 1982-; memb: Textile Cncl UK 1968-70, Ctee Social Science Res Cncl UK 1971-72, Ctee CBI 1971-74, Electrical Engrg Econ Devpt Ctee UK 1982-86; fell NZ Soc Accountants; memb: ICSA, Chartered Inst Cost and Mgmnt Accountants, Chartered Inst Mktg, Academy Int Business, NZ Inst Cost and Mgmnt Accountants; *Books* International Business and Multinational Enterprises (1973, 4 edn 1989), Case Problems in Marketing (1973), Strategy and Marketing (1982, 2 edn 1986), Short Cases in Marketing (1987); *Style*— Prof Kenneth Simmonds; London Business School, Regents Park, London SW1 4SA

SIMMONDS, Kenneth Willison; CMG (1956); s of William Henry Simmonds (d 1958), and Ida, *née* Willison (d 1956); *b* 13 May 1912; *Educ* Bedford Sch, Humberstone Sch, St Catharine's Coll Cambridge (MA); *m* 1, 1939 (m dis 1974), Ruth Constance, er da of Thomas Howard Sargant (d 1958), of Leatherhead; 2 s; m 2, 1974, Mrs Catherine Clare Lewis, yst da of Col Francis Brakenridge, CMG, RAMC (d 1955); *Career* Colonial Admin Serv (HMOCS): dist admin and secretariat Kenya 1935-48, dep fin sec Uganda 1948-51, fin sec Nyasaland (now Malawi) 1951-57, chief sec Aden 1957-63; painter, exhibited: RA, Royal W of England Acad, Southern Arts Open, Westward Open, Royal Bath & West, Bladon Andover (one-man); FRSA; *Recreations* angling, gardening; *Style*— Kenneth Simmonds, Esq, CMG; 1 Fons George Rd, Taunton, Somerset TA1 3JU (☎ 0823 333128)

SIMMONDS, Richard James; MEP (EDG) Wight and Hants E 1984- (Midlands West 1979-84); s of Reginald A C Simmonds, and Betty, *née* Cahusac; sis Posy Simmonds the illustrator and cartoonist; *b* 1944; *Career* vice chm Young Cons 1973-75, fndr chm Young Euro Democrats 1974; PA to Rt Hon Edward Heath, MBE, MP 1973-75, PPS to Sir James Scott-Hopkins ldr EDG 1979-82; spokesman: Youth and Educn 1982-84, Budget Control 1984-87; Br whip 1987-89; chm govrs Berks Coll of Agric 1979; *Publications* The Common Agricultural Policy, a sad misnomer (1979), A to Z of Myths and Misunderstandings of EEC (1981), European Parliament Report on Farm Animal Welfare (1985, 1987 and 1990); *Clubs* Carlton, Tamworth, Ancient Britons; *Style*— Richard Simmonds, Esq, MEP; Woodlands Farm, Cookham Dean, Berkshire

SIMMONDS, Lady; Sheila; *née* Kingham; *m* 1979, as his 2 w, Sir Oliver Edwin Simmonds (fndr Simmonds Aircraft Ltd and Simmonds Aerocessories Ltd, sometime MP (C) Duddleston Birmingham; d 1985), s of Rev F T Simmonds (decd); 1 step s, 2 step da; *Style*— Lady Simmonds; PO Box 1480, Nassau, Bahamas

SIMMONDS, Stefan Marshall; s of Paul Benjamin Simmonds, of Bradford, and Edna Margaret Simmonds; *b* 16 Aug 1945; *Educ* Bradford Tech Coll; *m* 1970, Shahnaz, da of late Col Ambass Sadeghian, of Tehran, Iran; 3 da (Shaeda, Samantha, Sara); *Career* chm: Drummond Gp plc, Tavirno Property Gp; *Style*— Stefan Simmonds, Esq; Drummond Group plc, Drummond House, PO Box 18, Lumb Lane Mills, Bradford, W Yorks BD8 7RP (☎ 0274 721435)

SIMMONS, His Honour Judge Alan Gerald; s of Maurice Simmons (d 1949), of Bedford, and Sophie, *née* Lasserson (d 1952); *b* 7 Sept 1936; *Educ* Bedford Modern and Quintin Sch; *m* 26 Nov 1961, Mia, da of Emanuel Rosenstein (d 1956); 1 s (Richard b 1964), 1 da (Joanne b 1966); *Career* Nat Serv RAF 1956-58; dir: Aslon Laboratories Ltd, Record Productions (Surrey) Ltd, Ashcourt Ltd; called to the Bar 1968, rec 1989 (asst rec 1985); circuit judge (South Eastern Circuit) 1990; memb: Bd of Deps of Br Jews 1982-88, Cncl of United Synagogues; *Recreations* music, reading, fencing; *Style*— His Honour Judge Simmons

SIMMONS, Andrew Douglas Henry; s of Flt Lt Ronald Herbert Simmons, of Louth, Lincolnshire, and Katherine Mary, *née* Fryer; *b* 13 Aug 1955; *Educ* Kingston Secdy Sch Stafford, Graham Balfour GS Stafford, Preston Poly; *m* 22 Aug 1981, Constance Ann, da of John Richard Chell (d 1969), of 17 Second Ave, Holmcroft, Stafford; 3 s (John Andrew b 28 Dec 1983, Richard James b 24 Dec 1985, Edward Ronald b 16 May 1988); *Career* reporter Staffordshire Newsletter 1972-76, sr reporter Shropshire Star 1976-77, reporter and newsreader Beacon Radio 1977-79, network news ed IRN 1982-83 (sr reporter 1979-82), reporter and presenter Central TV News 1983-85, reporter and newscaster TV-am 1985-86; ITN: reporter 1986-, Ireland corr 1989-; maj assignments: Israeli Invasion of Lebanon 1982, Gulf Crisis 1987, Zeebrugge Disaster 1987, Romanian Revolution 1989; received Royal TV Soc Home News Story Award 1988; *Recreations* motor sports (spectator), water sports, wildlife; *Style*— Andrew Simmons, Esq; Independant Television News, 48 Wells St, London W1P 4DE (☎ 071 637 2424)

SIMMONS, David; s of Charles Simmons, and Margaret Elizabeth, *née* Fixter; *b* 23 Dec 1937; *Educ* Haberdashers' Aske's; *m* 3 Jan 1963 (m dis), Christine, *née* Plowman; 1 s (Dale Stuart b 12 Jan 1964), 1 da (Lynn Michelle b 7 Aug 1967); *Career* Nat Serv RAF 1956-58; accounts supervisor Harris & Graham Ltd Lloyds brokers 1954-60, office mangr Leonard Davis Associates Washington DC 1961-64, vice pres admin International Group Plans Inc Washington DC 1964-72; fndr and md: Group Plans Marketing Ltd London 1972-78, Asien Dilect 1978-; registered insur broker; memb: Cncl Br Direct Mktg Assoc, Ctee Insur Direct Mktg Practitioners Gp; *Books* chapter on direct mktg in Insurance Markets (1987 and 1988); *Recreations* badminton, computers, skiing, theatre, music; *Style*— David Simmons, Esq; 13 Fielding Court, Earlham Street, Covent Garden, London WC2H; 2 Regents Place, Blackheath, London SE3 OLX (☎ 071 240 9499, 071 853 1525); Aspen Direct, 28-32 Shelton St, Covent Garden, London WC2H 9HP (☎ 071 836 0055, fax 071 379 5076)

SIMMONS, Frank Ronald; s of Ronald Simmons, of Ashtead (d 1974), and Florence Lilian, *née* Cummins (d 1964); *b* 8 May 1932; *Educ* Glyn GS Epsom, Poly of South Bank (Post Graduate Dip); *m* 11 Oct 1958, Mary Elizabeth, da of late Harry Barker, of Dorking, Surrey; 2 s (Howard b 1959, John b 1968), 2 da (Catherine b 1961, Louise b 1967); *Career* short serv cmmn RAF 1953-56; tech mangr Benham & Sons Ltd 1957-67, chief mechanical engr JE Firman & Associates 1967-70, sr ptnr Tilney Simmons & Partners 1976- (ptnr 1970), dir Technol Systems Engineers Ltd 1988-; chm CIBSE Task Gp on Fire Protection; FCIBSE 1971 (memb 1957-), ACE 1973; *Recreations* skiing, sailing, mountain walking; *Clubs* RAF, Royal Southampton Yacht; *Style*— Frank Simmons, Esq; White Acre, Pitton, Salisbury, Wilts (☎ 0772 72261); Tilney Simmons & Partners, Foresters House, 29/33 Shirley Rd, Southampton SO1 3EW (☎ 0703 227086, fax 0703 330536); Broadwall House, Broadwall, London SE1 9PL (☎ 071 261 1815)

SIMMONS, Prof Ian; s of Charles Frederick Simmons (d 1984), of Iver, Bucks, and Christina Mary, *née* Merrills; *b* 22 Jan 1937; *Educ* Slough GS, UCL (BSc, PhD); *m* 28 July 1962, Carol Mary, da of John Saunders (ka 1941), of Ealing, W London; 1 s (David b 1968), 1 da (Catherine b 1966); *Career* ACLS fell Univ of California Berkeley 1964-65, Churchill Meml fell 1971; prof: Univ of Bristol 1978-81, Univ of Durham 1981- (sr lectr 1970-76, reader 1976-78); memb: Peace Action Durham, Cncl for Nat Parks, Town and Gown Soc; FSA 1981; Bergwanden medal Kirchberg Austria 1988; *Books* incl: The Ecology of Natural Resources (2 edn 1981), Biogeographical Processes (1982), Changing the Face of the Earth (1989), Dartmoor Essays (ed, 1964), British Prehistory: the Environment (jt ed, 1981); *Recreations* all high culture except ballet; *Clubs* St Chad's and St Aidan's Coll SCR; *Style*— Prof Ian Simmons, FSA; Science Labs, South Rd, Durham DH1 3LE (☎ 091 374 2464, fax 091 374 2456, telex 537351 DURLIB G)

SIMMONS, Prof Jack; s of Seymour Francis Simmons, and Katharine Lillias, *née* Finch; *b* 30 Aug 1915; *Educ* Westminster, ChCh Oxford (BA, MA); *Career* Beit lectr in the history of Br empire Univ of Oxford 1943-47; Univ of Leicester: prof of history 1947-75, pro vice chllr 1960-63, public orator 1965-68, emeritus prof 1975-; chm Leicester Local Bdcasting Cncl 1967-70, pres Leics Archaeological and Hist Soc 1966-77, memb Advsy Cncl Sci Museum London 1969-84, chm Advsy Ctee Nat Railway Museum York 1981-84; FSA 1975; *Books* Southey (1945), Parish & Empire (1952), New University (1958), The Railways of Britain (1961, 3 edn 1986), Britain and the World (1965), St Pancras Station (1968), Transport Museums (1970), Leicester Past and Present (1974), The Railway in England and Wales 1830-1914 (1978), A Selective Guide to England (1979), The Railway in Town and Country (1986), The Victorian Railway (1991); *Clubs* United Oxford and Cambridge Univ; *Style*— Prof Jack Simmons, FSA; c/o Dept of History, The University, Leicester LE1 7RH

SIMMONS, Air Marshal Sir Michael George; KCB (1989, CB 1988), AFC (1976); s of George Martin Simmons (d 1990), and Thelma Alice Cecilia, *née* Howie (d 1975); *b* 8 May 1937; *Educ* Shrewsbury, RAF Coll Cranwell; *m* 23 May 1964, Jean, da of Arthur Aliwell (d 1990); 2 da (Susan Jean b 17 Nov 1965, Sally Ann b 22 March 1968); *Career* cmmnd 1958, 6 Sqdn Cyprus 1959-61, ADC to AOC-in-C FTC 1961-64, 39 Sqdn Malta 1964-67, 51 Sqdn Wyton 1967-69, RN Staff Coll 1970, MOD 1971-72, OC XV Sqdn Germany 1973-76, MOD 1976-79, OC RAF Cottesmore 1980-82, MOD 1982-84, SASO Headquarters Strike Cmd 1984-85, AOC 1 Gp RAF 1985-87, ACAS 1987-89, dep controller aircraft MOD 1989-; ADC to HM The Queen 1980-81; Upper Freeman Gapan 1989; *Recreations* golf, walking; *Clubs* RAF; *Style*— Air Marshal Sir Michael Simmons, KCB, AFC; c/o Royal Bank of Scotland, Holts Branch, Kirkland House, Whitehall, London SW1A 2EB

SIMMONS, Dr Paul Douglas; s of Gordon Edward Frank Simmons (d 1976), and Joan Madeline, *née* Eade; *b* 4 Oct 1947; *Educ* Felixstowe GS, Univ of Leeds (MB ChB); *m* 4 Sept 1982, Ruth Danae, da of Rev Gp Capt Kenneth James Holt; *Career* hon conslt physician St Paul's Hosp London 1980-; conslt physician: Leicester Royal Infirmary 1980-82, Bart's London 1982- (sr registrar 1976-80, hon lectr 1982-); hon conslt physician St Luke's Hosp for the Clergy 1986-; chm: Genito-urinary Regnl Advsy Ctee, NE Thames RHA; pres Soc of Health Advsrs in STD; Yeoman of Worshipful Soc of Apothecaries; MRCP 1976; *Recreations* gardening; *Style*— Dr Paul Simmons; St Bartholomew's Hospital, West Smithfield, London EC1A 7BE (☎ 071 606 3182)

SIMMONS, Peter Hamilton; s of Hamilton Webster Simmons (d 1963), of Saltdean, Brighton, Sussex, and Mabel, *née* Brazil (d 1977); *b* 2 Sept 1926; *Educ* Westminster, Univ of London (MB BS); *m* 29 Sept 1956, Elizabeth Coralie, da of Alfred Thomas Houghton; 2 s (Jonathan Mark b 13 May 1963 d 1965, Mark Christopher b 20 Dec 1968), 2 da (Rosemary Jane b 23 Sept 1959, Joanna Mary b 19 Sept 1965); *Career* Nat Serv RAMC Capt 1952-53; conslt anaesthetist: The N Middx Hosp Edmonton 1959-, The Royal Northern Hosp 1960-, The Royal Free Hosp 1986-; FFARCS 1954; *Books* Anaesthesia for Nurses (1966); *Recreations* gardening, walking; *Style*— Peter Simmons, Esq; Garden House, 3 Queens Rd, Barnet, Herts EN5 4DH (☎ 081 449 4130)

SIMMONS, Richard John; s of John Eric Simmons, and Joy Mary, *née* Foat; *b* 2 June 1947; *Educ* Moseley GS Birmingham, LSE (BSc), Univ of California Berkeley Business Sch; *m* 23 April 1983, Veronica, da of Richard Sinkins; 1 s, 1 da; *Career* CA, asst sec to IASC 1973-75, ptnr Arthur Andersen & Co 1979-; non-exec dir Cranfield Info Techno Inst 1987-89; memb: Advsy Bd Royal Acad of Arts, Political Ctee Carlton Club; chm Bow Gp 1980-81; FCA 1971; *Recreations* horse racing, tennis, gardening; *Style*— Richard Simmons, Esq; 1 Surrey St , London WC2R 2PS (☎ 071 438 3302)

SIMMS, Alan John Gordon; s of Edward Gordon Clark, formerly Januskiewiscz (d 1981), of 12 Lucan Rd, Aigburth, Liverpool, and Hilda Mary, *née* Gordon; *b* 3 April 1954; *Educ* Liverpool Collegiate GS, Univ of London (LLB); *m* 2 Aug 1980, Julia Jane, da of Paul Ferguson, of Leintwardine, Shropshire; *Career* called to the Bar Lincoln's Inn 1976; ad eundum Northern Circuit 1980-; sec Inst of Advanced Motorists 1986-88, chm ROSPA Chester (ROSPA Advanced Drivers Assoc Class One and Diploma holder); memb: Br Motor Racing Marshals Club, Br Automobile Racing Club (Oulton Park), Hon Soc of Lincoln's Inn 1976, Br Acad of Forensic Sci 1978, Bar Assoc of Commerce Fin and Indust 1980; *Recreations* reading, motor racing, motor racing marshalling, road safety, blues and jazz music, guitar playing, crime (theory only); *Style*— Alan Simms, Esq; Fruit Exchange, Victoria St, Liverpool (☎ 051 236 3778)

SIMMS, (Antony) Blake; s of Cdr Hugh Crofton Simms, DSO (ka 1942), of Bordon, Hampshire, and Joan Frances, *née* Partridge (d 1984); *b* 10 July 1939; *Educ* Shrewsbury, Battersea Coll, Univ of London (BSc); *m* 6 Nov 1976, Alexandra Sonia, da of Rear Adm Cecil Robert Peter Charles Branson; *Career* plant mangr and economics technologist Shell Refining Co Ltd Essex 1961-64, exec dir Chesham Amalgamations and Investments Ltd 1965-79, fndr and chief exec Select Amalgamations and Investments Ltd 1979, chm and md Evoyachts Ltd 1979; played squash for Hampshire 1969-72, sec Escorts Squash Rackets Club 1965-76, competed in 9 Fastnet races and numerous Cross Channel races; *Recreations* ocean racing, squash rackets, naval archives, marine paintings; *Clubs* Royal Ocean Racing, Island Sailing, Seaview Yacht, Escorts Squash Rackets; *Style*— Blake Simms, Esq; Gloucester Court, Kew Road, Kew, Surrey TW9 3DZ

SIMMS, Most Rev George Otto; 3 s of John Francis Arthur Simms (crown slr, d 1941), of Combermore, Lifford, Co Donegal, Ireland, and Ottilie Sophie Simms (d 1960); *b* 4 July 1910; *Educ* Cheltenham, Trinity Coll Dublin (BA, MA, BD, PhD, DD); *m* 1941, Mercy Felicia, da of Brian James Gwynn (d 1973), of Temple Hill, Terenure, Dublin; 3 s, 2 da; *Career* ordained: deacon 1935, priest 1936; curate asst St Bartholomew's Dublin 1935-38, chaplain and lectr Lincoln Theol Coll 1938-39, dean of residence and lectr Trinity Coll Dublin 1940-52, dean of Cork 1952, bishop of Cork, Cloyne and Ross 1952-56, archbishop of Dublin and primate of Ireland 1956-69, archbishop of Armagh and primate of All Ireland 1969-80; pres The Leprosy Mission 1964; hon fellow Trinity Coll Dublin 1977, Hon DD Huron Univ 1963, Hon DCL Univ of Kent 1978, Hon DLitt New Univ of Ulster 1981, hon life memb The Royal Dublin Soc 1984-; MRIA 1957; *Publications* Book of Kells (short description 1949), The Psalms in the Days of St Columba (1963), Christ within Me (1974), In My Understanding (1982); contrib to facsimile edns: The Book of Kells (1950), The Book of Durrow (1960); Irish Illuminated Manuscripts (1980), Tullow's Story (1983), Pioneers and Partners (with R G F Jenkins, 1985), contributor to Treasures of the Library of Trinity Coll Dublin (1986), Exploring The Book of Kells (1988), Angels and Saints (1988), Brendan The Navigator (1989); *Recreations* walking; *Clubs* Royal Irish Acad, Trinity Coll Common Room; *Style*— The Most Rev George Simms; 62 Cypress Grove Rd, Dublin 6, W Ireland (☎ 0001 905594)

SIMON, Hon Brian; 2 s of 1 Baron Simon of Wythenshawe (d 1960); *b* 1915; *Educ* Gresham's, Trinity Coll Cambridge; *m* 1941, Joan Home, da of late Capt Home Peel, DSO, MC, and Hon Mary Gwendolen, *née* Emmott, da of 1 and last Baron Emmott (extinct 1926); 2 s (Alan b 1943, Martin b 1944); *Style*— The Hon Brian Simon; 11 Pendene Rd, Leicester

SIMON, Hon (Dominic) Crispin Adam; s (by 2 m) of Baron Simon of Glaisdale (Life Peer); *b* 1958; *m* 1983, Georgina, da of R G Brown, of Albrighton, Shrops; *Style*— The Hon Crispin Simon

SIMON, David Alec Gwyn; CBE (1991); s of Roger Simon, and Barbara, *née* Hudd; *Educ* Christ's Hosp, Gonville and Caius Coll Cambridge (MA); *m* 1964 (sep 1987), Hann, *née* Mohn; 2 s; *Career* mktg dir BP Oil UK 1980-82, md BP Oil International 1982, md The BP Company plc 1986- (dep chm and chief operating offr 1990); non-exec dir Grand Metropolitan plc; memb: Int Cncl and UK Advsy Bd INSEAD, Sports Cncl; *Recreations* music, golf, reading, tennis; *Style*— David Simon, Esq, CBE; The British Petroleum Company plc, Britiannic House, 1 Finsbury Circus, London EC2M 7BA (☎ 071 496 4000)

SIMON, Hon Jan David; s and h of 2 Viscount Simon, CMG, *qv*, and Lady Simon; *b* 20 July 1940; *Educ* Westminster, Univ of Southampton, Sidney Tech Coll; *m* 28 April 1969, Mary Elizabeth, da of John Joseph Burns, of Sydney, NSW; 1 da (Fiona Elizabeth b 1971); *Career* MN 1958-68; nautical res 1968-70; co sec Shipbroker 1970-82; currently mgmnt and fin consit; former examiner Advanced Motorists Aust; ALIA (Dip) 1988; *Recreations* classical music, motor vehicles; *Clubs* Oriental; *Style*— The Hon J D Simon; Rose Cottage, Parsonage Lane, Barnston, Great Dunmow, Essex CM6 3PA (☎ 0371 821117)

SIMON, 2 Viscount (UK 1940); John Gilbert Simon; CMG (1947); s (by 1 m) of 1 Viscount, GCSI, GCVO, OBE, QC, PC (d 1954); *b* 2 Sept 1902; *Educ* Winchester, Balliol Coll Oxford; *m* 1930, Christie, da of William Stanley Hunt; 1 s, 1 da; *Heir* s, Hon Jan Simon, *qv*; *Career* with Miny of War Tport 1940-47, md P & O Steam Navigation Co 1947-58 (dep chm 1951-58), chm Port of London Authy 1958-71; pres: Chamber of Shipping UK 1957-58, Inst of Marine Engrs 1960-61, RINA 1961-71, Br Hydromechanics Res Assoc 1968-80; Offr Order of Orange Nassau; *Style*— The Rt Hon the Viscount Simon, CMG; 2 Church Cottages, Abbotskerswell, Newton Abbot, Devon TQ12 5NY (☎ 0626 65573)

SIMON, Hon (Benedict) Mark Leycester; s (by 2 m) of Baron Simon of Glaisdale (Life Peer); *b* 1953; *m* 1980, Patricia, da of Ricardo Hernandez y Perez, of Mexico City; 1 da; *Style*— The Hon Mark Simon

SIMON, Hon Matthew; s and h of 2 Baron Simon of Wythenshawe (who does not use his title, *see Roger Simon*); *b* 10 April 1955; *Educ* St Paul's; *Style*— The Hon Matthew Simon

SIMON, Hon Peregrine Charles Hugo; s (by 2 m) of Baron Simon of Glaisdale (Life Peer); *b* 1950; *Educ* Ashdown House; *m* Francesca, da of Maj T W E Fortescue Hitchins; 1 s (Alexander b 1986), 2 da (Polly b 1982, Lucy Persephone Frances b 1984); *Clubs* Coningsby; *Style*— The Hon Peregrine Simon

SIMON, Peter Walter; s of Prof Walter Simon (d 1981), and Kate, *née* Jungmann (d 1984); *b* 25 Nov 1929; *Educ* Thames Valley Sch, LSE (BSc, PhD); *m* 1960, Sheila Rose, da of James Brimacombe (d 1985); 1 s (Nicholas b 1961), 1 da (Susannah b 1964); *Career* dir: Legal and Gen Group plc and subsids, Lion Holdings 1974-87, Victory Insurance Holdings 1984-87, The British Land Co plc 1987-, Concord Financial Advsrs UK Ltd 1987-88; vice chm Export Fin Co Ltd 1984-89; chm: Cogent Ltd 1984-88, Conrad Ritblat Residential Properties Ltd 1989-; ACII; *Recreations* cricket, hockey, golf, bridge; *Clubs* MCC, East India Sports, Teddington Cricket, Teddington Hockey, Lord's Taverners; *Style*— Peter W Simon, Esq; 54 Ormond Ave, Hampton, Middlesex TW12 2RX (☎ 081 979 2538)

SIMON, Robin John Hughes; s of Most Rev William Glyn Hughes Simon, Archibishop of Wales (d 1972), and Sarah Ellen (Shelia), *née* Roberts (d 1963); *b* 23 July 1947; *Educ* Cardiff HS, Univ of Exeter (BA), Courtauld Inst of Art (MA); *m* 1, 1971, Margaret, *née* Brooke; m 2, 1979, Joanna, *née* Ross; 1 s (Benet Glyn Hughes b 1974), 1 da (Alice Emily Hughes b 1976); *Career* univ lectr in history of art and English 1972-78, hist bldgs rep The Nat Tst 1979-80, dir Inst of Euro Studies London 1980-90, art critic The Daily Mail 1990- (arts corr 1987-90), ed Apollo 1990-; visiting prof of history of art and architecture Westminster Coll 1989; *Books* The Art of Cricket (with Alastair Smart, 1983), The Portrait in Britain and America (1987); articles in various jls, papers and magazines; Delmas fndn fell Venice 1978; *Recreations* cricket (capt Poor Fred's XI), music; *Style*— Robin Simon, Esq; Apollo, 3 St James's Place, London SW1A 1NP (☎ 071 629 4331, fax 071 701 1682)

SIMON, Roger; 2 Baron Simon of Wythenshawe (UK 1947), but does not use title; s of 1 Baron (d 1960); *b* 16 Oct 1913; *Educ* Gresham's, Gonville and Caius Cambridge; *m* 1951, (Anthea) Daphne, da of Sidney May; 1 s, 1 da (Margaret); *Heir* s, Hon Matthew Simon, *qv*; *Style*— Roger Simon Esq; Oakhill, Chester Av, Richmond, Surrey

SIMON OF GLAISDALE, Baron (Life Peer UK 1971), of Glaisdale, in N Riding, Co York; Jocelyn Edward Salis Simon; PC (1961), DL (N Yorks 1973); s of Frank Cecil Simon, of 51 Belsize Park, London NW3; *b* 15 Jan 1911; *Educ* Gresham's Sch Holt, Trinity Hall Cambridge; *m* 1, 1934, Gwendolen Helen (d 1937), da of E J Evans; m 2, 1948, Fay Elizabeth Leicester, JP, da of Brig H Guy A Pearson, of Jersey; 3 s (Hon Peregrine Charles Hugo b 1950, Hon (Benedict) Mark Leicester b 1953, Hon (Dominic) Crispin Adam b 1958); *Career* called to the Bar 1934, KC 1951, MP (C) Middlesbrough W 1951-62, jt parly under sec of state Home Office 1957-58, fin sec to the Treasy 1958-59, slr-gen 1959-62, pres Probate Divorce and Admty Div

High Ct of Justice 1962-71, Lord of Appeal in Ordinary 1971-77, er bro Trinity House; kt 1959; *Style*— The Rt Hon The Lord Simon of Glaisdale, PC, DL; Midge Hall, Glaisdale Head, Whitby, N Yorks

SIMON OF WYTHENSHAWE, Barony of; *see* Roger Simon

SIMONDS-GOODING, Anthony James Joseph; s of Maj Hamilton Simonds-Gooding, of Buncar House, Dooks, Glenbeigh, Co Kerry, Eire, and Dorothy, *née* Reilly; *b* 10 Sept 1937; *Educ* Ampleforth and Britannia RNC Dartmouth; *m* 1, 1961, Fiona; 4 s (Rupert, Benedict, George, Harry), 2 da (Lucinda, Dominique); m 2, 8 July 1982, Marjorie Anne, da of William John Pennock (d 1987); 1 step s (Daniel Porter); *Career* RN 1953-59; Unilever 1960-73; Whitbread & Co plc 1973-85: mktg dir, md, gp md; chm and chief exec all communication and advertising companies worldwide for Saatchi & Saatchi plc 1985-87, chief exec Br Satellite Broadcasting 1987-90; *Recreations* family, opera, tennis, fishing, reading, painting, travelling, skiing; *Clubs* Queens, Hurlingham; *Style*— Anthony Simonds-Gooding, Esq

SIMONIAN, Lady (Imelda) Clare; *née* Feilding; da of late 10 Earl of Denbigh and Desmond; *b* 1941; *m* 1, 1966 (m dis 1979), David Rodney Doig; 1 s (Andrew b 1969), 2 da (Rowena b 1967, Zoe b 1971); m 2, 1984, Jack Levon Simonian, of Harrogate; *Style*— The Lady Clare Simonian; Grounds Farm, Monks Kirby, Rugby, Warwickshire CV23 ORH

SIMONIS, Peter George; *b* 3 June 1926; *Educ* Cranleigh Sch; *m* 1956, Erica, da of Eric Marsden; 1 s, 1 da; *Career* Lt RNVR; dir Burmah Oil Co Ltd 1970-79, chm Haden plc 1979-87; dir: Ellerman Lines Ltd 1979-83, The Morgan Crucible Co plc 1983-, Rowan Cos Inc (USA) 1985-, Gibraltar Shiprepair Ltd 1985-90, Haden MacLellan Holdings plc 1987-, Whessoe plc 1988-; chm: Br American Offshore Ltd, Beans Engineering Ltd, Teredo Petroleum Plc 1990-; *Clubs* Naval, Oriental; *Style*— Peter Simonis, Esq; British American Offshore Ltd, 79 Park Street, London W1Y 3HP

SIMONS, Allan Barry; s of late Douglas David Simons, and late Anne Bessie Simons; *b* 3 Jan 1936; *Educ* Univ of Manchester, Univ of London; *m* 1961, Shirley; 1 s (Keith Michael b 1968); *Career* admitted slr 1961; cmmr for Oaths; law tutor; former FBSC, life memb Slrs Benevolent Assoc, memb Law Soc; *Recreations* violin, involved in evangelistic & divine healing crusades; *Clubs* Gospel Businessmens Fellowship International; *Style*— Allan Simons, Esq; Solicitor, Cheadle, Cheshire

SIMONS, Barry; s of Maj Elkan Simons (d 1969), of London, and Sylvia, *née* Norris; *b* 18 Aug 1927; *Educ* Marlborough; *Career* Capt Rifle Bde 1943-47, seconded to Br Forces Network 1945-47; dir: Norris & Simons Ltd (theatrical agents) 1948-52, Barry Simons Agency Ltd (theatrical agents) 1948-69; motor racing driver 1952-54, motor sport commentator 1954-; chm and md: Elkan & Barry Simons (theatrical prodrs) Ltd 1958-69 (dir 1952-58), Elkan & Barry Simons (Insurance Brokers) Ltd 1969-88; bank exec Liberty Bank 1991-; elected underwriting memb of Lloyd's 1978; FBIM 1982, FInstIC 1983; *Recreations* motor racing, photography, sport commentator, wild animal training; *Style*— Barry Simons, Esq; 44 Glenn Drive, Tolland, Connecticut 06084, USA; 31 Shirehall Park, London NW4 2QN (☎ 081 202 9321)

SIMONS, Prof John Philip; s of Mark Isaac Simons (d 1973), of London, and Rose, *née* Pepper (d 1961); *b* 20 April 1934; *Educ* Haberdashers' Aske's, Sidney Sussex Coll Cambridge (BA, PhD, ScD); *m* 1 Dec 1956, Althea Mary (d 1989), da of Robert Douglas Screaton (d 1988), of Nottingham; 3 s (Thomas John b 1960, Joseph Robert b 1962, Benjamin David b 1965); *Career* Univ of Birmingham: ICI fell 1960, reader 1975, prof of photochemistry 1979-81; prof of physical chemistry Univ of Nottingham 1981-; memb: SERC Chemistry Laser Facility Ctees, NATO Sci Ctees; hon sec and vice pres Faraday Div Royal Soc Chemistry; CChem, FRSC 1979, FRS 1989; *Books* Photochemistry and Spectroscopy (1970); *Recreations* verse; *Style*— Prof John Simons, FRS; Chemistry Dept, University of Nottingham, Nottingham NG7 2RD (☎ 0602 484848, fax 0602 588138)

SIMONS, (Alfred) Murray; CMG (1983); s of Louis Simons (d 1950), and Fay Simons; *b* 9 Aug 1927; *Educ* City of London Sch, Magdalen Coll Oxford (MA), Columbia Univ (NY); *m* 1975, Patricia Jill, da of David Murray Barclay (d 1959); 2 s (Julian b 1977, Jonathan b 1978); *Career* HM Dip Serv 1951-85; first sec: Office of Commr-Gen for SE Asia and Singapore 1958-61, Br High Cmmn New Delhi 1964-68; head of SE Asia Dept FCO 1975-79, consul-gen Montreal 1980-82, ambass & head of UK Delgn (negotiations on mutual reduction of forces and armaments and assoc measures in Central Europe, at Vienna) 1982-85; memb Int Inst of Strategic Studies; Freeman City of London 1990; *Recreations* theatre, tennis; *Style*— Murray Simons, Esq, CMG; 128 Longland Drive, Totteridge, London N20 8HL (☎ 081 445 0896)

SIMONS, Paul; s of Francis Simons (d 1964), and Kathleen, *née* Ruddy (d 1983); *b* 11 March 1948; *Educ* Bridley Moor HS, Kingston Poly, Univ of Lancaster (MA); *m* 1, (m dis), Lesley Bailey; 2 s (Neil b 27 Dec 1968, Nicholas b 6 Sept 1971); m 2, Ann, da of William Perry, of Long Ashton, Bristol; 1 da (Kate b 7 Dec 1984); *Career* Cadbury Schweppes 1972-75 (asst product mangr, product mangr), gp product mangr Imperial Tobacco Foods 1975-76, mktg mangr United Biscuits 1976-78, Cogent Elliott 1978-84 (account dir, client serv dir); Gold Greenlees Trott 1984-88 (client serv dir, dep md, vice chm), chm and chief exec Simons Palmer Denton, Clemmow and Johnson Ltd 1988; rock musician (guitar) 1963-67, played with several bands (started first band with late John Bonham of Led Zeppelin), released various unsuccessful records; MIPA, fell IOD; author numerous articles; *Recreations* gym, sailing, concerts, travel; *Style*— Paul Simons, Esq; 3 The Gables, Vale of Health, Hampstead, London NW3 1AY (☎ 071 794 8822); Simons Palmer Denton Clemmow & Johnson Ltd, 19-20 Noel St, London W1V 3PD (☎ 071 287 4455)

SIMONS, Sidney; s of Woolf Simons (d 1967), of London N16, and Deborah, *née* Kosatsky; *b* 6 Dec 1930; *Educ* St Marylebone GS; *m* 1, 31 Aug 1958, Valerie Marion, da of Harry Davis (d 1961), of Ilford, Essex; 2 s (David Russell b 1963, Adrian Mark b 1966); m 2, 21 Aug 1971, Sophie Ann, da of Eliezar Isaac Reynolds Tomlinson (d 1986), of Ilford, Essex; *Career* Corpl RAPC Reading and Devizes; CA; divnl fin controller BP Nutrition (UK) Ltd 1980-82; dir: Kevin Mayhew Ltd 1982-88, Palm Tree Press Ltd 1982-88; accountant Moledene Group of Cos 1988-; *Recreations* reading newspapers, gardening; *Style*— Sidney Simons, Esq; 52 Leasway, Westcliff-on-Sea, Essex SSO 8PB (☎ 0702 78959); 54/56 Euston Street, London NW1 2ES (☎ 071 387 0155)

SIMONS, Susannah Catherine; da of Peter Simons, of Windsor, and Betty, *née* Edwards; *b* 19 April 1948; *Educ* Langley GS Berks, GSM; *m* 17 July 1976, Richard Percival Taylor, s of Percival Taylor; 1 s (Sebastian Richard b 29 Oct 1982), 1 da (Sarah Kate b 7 May 1980); *Career* television presenter; radio drama studio mangr BBC 1970-73 (BBC trainee 1969), prodr and presenter Capital Radio 1973; presenter: IRN 1975, Tonight (BBC) 1977, PM (BBC Radio) 1977, 1977-87 (The World at One, The World This Weekend, Radio 4 Budget Special, 1981 Royal Wedding, 1987 General Election, The Jimmy Young Show, The News Quiz), The Business Programme (Channel 4) 1986, Business Daily (Channel 4) 1987; dir Business Television 1990-; Variety Club Female Radio Personality of the Year 1984; *Recreations* theatre, opera, walking, skiing, cooking; *Style*— Ms Susannah Simons; Business Television, The Trocadero, 19 Rupert St, London W1 (☎ 071 287 4444)

SIMPKIN, Andrew Gordon; s of Ronald William Simpkin, of Menorca, and Garry, *née* Braidwood; *b* 31 March 1947; *Educ* Chethams Hosp Sch Manchester; *m* 9 Sept 1972, Gail Yvonne, da of John Hartley Turner, of Knutsford, Cheshire; 2 s (Robert Gordon b 1974, James William b 1976); *Career* slr; ptnr: Ogden & Simpkin 1973-78, Pannone March Pearson (formerly Pannone Blackburn) 1978-; non-exec dir Trafford Park Estates plc 1986-; memb of the Equal Opportunities Cmmn 1986-; memb young slrs gp Law Soc 1972-82; *Recreations* fell walking, sailing, gardening; *Clubs* Law Soc, St James's; *Style*— Andrew G Simpkin, Esq; Chapel Lane House, Mere, Cheshire WA16 6PP; 41 Spring Gardens, Manchester M2 2BB (☎ 061 832 3000, fax 061 834 2067, telex 66817 2)

SIMPKIN, Dr Paul; s of Leslie Simpkin (d 1968), and Cynthia, *née* Wardle; *b* 17 Aug 1945; *Educ* Queen Elizabeth GS Wakefield, St Thomas's Hosp Med Sch London (scholar, MB BS); *m* 1980, Marie-Louise, da of Dr Albert Edward Meechan Sieger; 2 da (Arabella Louise b 1981, Victoria Lucy b 1983); *Career* hon clinical asst Chest Dept St Thomas's Hosp 1975-80 (jr med appts 1970-75); conslt staff physician: GLC 1975-86, ILEA 1975-90; consulting occupational health physician 1980-, med advsr London Residuary Body 1986-, md Medicine At Work Ltd 1989-; med advsr to numerous cos, professional instns and local govt authorities; MRCP (UK) 1974, AFOM 1982; *Recreations* walking the Yorkshire Moors; *Style*— Dr Paul Simpkin; 2 Upper Wimpole Street, London W1M 7TD (☎ 071 935 5614)

SIMPKISS, Michael John; s of Percival Frederick Simpkiss (d 1985), of Stourbridge, Worcs, and Mary Adeline, *née* Jones; *b* 1 Oct 1924; *Educ* King Edward VI Sch Stourbridge, Univ of Birmingham (MB ChB); *m* 3 Feb 1949, Eileen Edna, da of Enoch Bartlett (d 1978), of Stourton, Worcs; 1 s (Jonathon b 1951), 1 da (Alison b 1954); *Career* Sqdn Ldr RAF Med Branch 1948-50, dep dir Med Servs 11 Gp Fighter Cmd; hon sr conslt paediatrician E Dorset (Wessex RHA), hon conslt paediatrician Hosp for Sick Children Gt Ormond St London; hon sr lectr Inst of Child Health Univ of London, hon clinical teacher Univ of Southampton, res asst physician The Hosp for Sick Children Gt Ormond St 1959-61; seconded Kampala Uganda 1956-58; memb Cncl Br Paediatric Assoc 1977-80; author of numerous papers on metabolic and genetic diseases of childhood; *Recreations* flyfishing, shooting, stalking, gardening, music; *Style*— Michael John Simpkiss, Esq; 41 Western Rd, Branksome Park, Poole, Dorset BH13 6EP (☎ 0202 765877)

SIMPSON, Alan; s of Alfred Robert Simpson (d 1945), and Mary Jane, *née* Wind; *b* 8 Feb 1935; *m* 1, 1957; 1 da (Catherine b 14 March 1959); m2, 6 Sept 1966, Anne, da of Francis James Ross; 2 da (Jacqueline Anne b 31 May 1969, Juliet Claire b 25 March 1973); *Career* RAF 1953-58 (Photographic Active Serv 1954-56); trainee engr Dorman Long Steel 1950-53, photographer rising to chief photographer (specialising in heavy indust advtg, aerial and architecutral photography) Head Wrightson (formerly subsid of and currently known as Davy Corporation) 1958-78, freelance photographer 1978-83, pt/t tutor in photography Cleveland Coll of Art and Design 1961-64 and 1978-83, lectr in photography Harrogate Coll of Art and Technol 1983-; FIBPP 1978; *Recreations* long distance walking; *Style*— Alan Simpson, Esq; Harrogate College of Arts & Technology, Hornbeam Park, Hookstone Rd, Harrogate, North Yorkshire HE12 8OT (☎ 0423 879466, fax 0423 879829)

SIMPSON, Alan Francis; s of Francis Simpson (d 1947), and Lilian, *née* Ellwood (d 1988); *b* 27 Nov 1929; *Educ* Mitcham GS; *m* 1958, Kathleen (d 1978), da of George Phillips (d 1975); *Career* author and scriptwriter 1951- (in collaboration with Ray Galton, *qv*); works incl: TV: Hancock's Half Hour (1954-61), Comedy Playhouse (1962-63), Steptoe and Son (1962-), Galton-Simpson Comedy (1969), Clochmerle (1971), Casanova (1974), Dawson's Weekly (1975), The Galton and Simpson Playhouse (1976); films: The Rebel (1960), The Bargee (1963), The Wrong Arm of the Law (1963), The Spy with a Cold Nose (1966), Loot (1969), Steptoe and Son (1971), Den Siste Fleksnes (Norway, 1974); theatre: Way out in Piccadilly (1966), The Wind in the Sassafras Trees (1968), Albert och Herbert (Sweden, 1981); radio with Ray Galton: Hancock's Half Hour 1954-59, Steptoe and Son 1966-73, The Frankie Howerd Show, Back with Braden; awards: Scriptwriters of the Year (Guild of TV Prodrs and Dirs) 1959, Best TV Comedy Series (Steptoe and Son, Screenwriters Guild) 1962/3/4/5, John Logie Baird Award 1964, Best Comedy Series (Steptoe and Son, Dutch TV) 1966, Best Comedy Screenplay (Screenwriters Guild) 1972; *Books* with Ray Galton: Hancock (1961), Steptoe and Son (1963), The Reunion and Other Plays (1966), Hancock Scripts (1974), The Best of Hancock (1986), Hancock - The Classic Years (1987), The Best of Steptoe and Son (1988); *Recreations* gastronomy, football, travelling, after dinner speaking; *Clubs* Hampton Football (pres); *Style*— Alan Simpson, Esq; c/o Tessa Le Bars Management, 18 Queen Anne Street, London W1 (☎ 071 636 3191)

SIMPSON, Alasdair John; s of James White Simpson (d 1987), and Joan Margaret, *née* Ebsworth; *b* 10 March 1943; *Educ* Queen Elizabeth GS Carmarthen, Univ of London (LLB); *m* 11 March 1966, (Judith) Jane, da of Sidney Zebulin Manches, of St John's Wood, London; 1 s (Thomas), 2 da (Emily, Sarah); *Career* admitted slr 1967; sr ptnr Manches & Co 1981- (asst slr 1967, ptnr 1968); govr Christ Church Sch Hampstead; memb The Law Soc 1967-; *Recreations* tennis, thoroughbreds, claret and Provence; *Clubs* RAC, Turf; *Style*— Alasdair Simpson, Esq; Cannon Hall, 14 Cannon Place, London NW3 1EJ (☎ 071 435 0763, 071 794 9053); Villa Chapman, 19 Chemin du Bois d'Opio, Residences du Golf, 06650, Le Rouret, South of France (☎ 010 33 93 774183); Messrs Manches & Co, Aldwych House, 71-91 Aldwych, London WC2B 4RP (☎ 071 404 4433, fax 071 430 1133, car 0836 271 586, telex 266174)

SIMPSON, Alastair Derek McLean; s of John McLean Simpson (d 1968), and Edith, *née* Alexander; *b* 25 March 1938; *m* 11 July 1963, Morag, da of William Frederick McDonald; 1 s (Gavin Alexander b 1972), 3 da (Elidh Jane b 1965, Morna Anne b 1968, Kirstine McDonald (twin) b 1972); *Career* architect and planning conslt, qualified 1966; work incl: housing for Univ of Zambia 1970-71, oil related offices, electronics factory, housing; *Recreations* swimming, shooting, travelling; *Clubs* Western Glasgow; *Style*— Alastair Simpson, Esq; Dunstan House, Buchltvie, by Stirling FK8 3LS (☎ 036 085 271); Simpson Associates, Chartered Architects, 2 Stewart St, Milngate

SIMPSON, Anthony Maurice Herbert; TD (1973), MEP (EDG) Northants and South Leics 1979-; s of Lt-Col M R Simpson, OBE, TD, DL (d 1981), and Renée Claire Lafitte (d 1973), of Leicester; *b* 28 Oct 1935; *Educ* Rugby, Magdalene Coll Cambridge (MA, LLM); *m* 1961, Penelope Gillian, da of Howard Dixon Spackman (d 1965), of Swindon; 1 s, 2 da; *Career* serv TA 1960-73, Maj 1968; called to the Bar Inner Temple 1961; memb Euro Cmmn Legal Serv 1975-79, quaestor of Euro Parl 1979-87 and 1989-; *Recreations* walking, travelling; *Clubs* Special Forces; *Style*— Anthony Simpson, Esq, TD, MEP; Bassets, Great Glen, Leics (☎ 053 759 2386); Avenue Michel-Ange 57, 1040 Brussels, Belgium (☎ 02 736 4219)

SIMPSON, Anthony Victor Joseph (Tony); s of Vincent Joseph Simpson (d 1972), of Doncaster, Yorks, and Lily Winifred, *née* Chantrey; *b* 6 May 1931; *Educ* Harrow Weald GS, Hendon Coll of Technol (Business Mgmnt Dip), St Albans Coll; *m* 15 March 1956, (Joan) Sheila, da of Horace James Broughton (d 1980); 2 s (Gary Keith b 31 Jan 1957, Dean Kevin b 19 Dec 1958), 1 da (Claire Karla b 11 March 1971); *Career* comptroller Frigidaire Divn G M Ltd 1966, controller Hoover Ltd 1967-73, divnl exec 1973-74, assoc dir admin 1974-81, dir operations Continental Europe 1979-86, main bd dir 1981-86; md Hoover Europe 1986-, pres Hoover Trading Co 1988-, jt md Hoover plc 1986-; chm: Hoover Apparete Switzerland, Hoover Oy Finland; pres Supervisory

Bd SA Hoover France, dir Hoover Etab Belgium; hon treas Middx Assoc of Boys' Clubs, chm Hoover Fndn (charitable tst); memb: RSA, French C of C in London; hon memb Helsinki Univ; FCMA, FBIM; *Recreations* golf, soccer supporter Watford AFC; *Clubs* Crockfords, Comandeur Confrerie Des Chevaliers Du Tastevin; *Style—* Tony Simpson, Esq; Rothlea Lodge, Flaunden Lane, Bovingdon, Herts (☎ 0442 833898); Hoover Trading Co, Hayes Gate House, 27 Uxbridge Rd, Hayes, Middx (☎ 081 848 8228, fax 081 848 1440, telex 915245 HOOVER G)

SIMPSON, Brian; MEP (Lab) Cheshire E 1989-; s of John Hartley Simpson, of Golborne, Lancashire, and Freda, *née* Mort; *b* 6 Feb 1953; *Educ* Golbourne Comp Sch Wigan, West Midlands Coll of Educn Walsall (CertEd); *m* 2 Aug 1975, Linda Jane, da of late Harold Gwynn; 1 s (Mark Bevan b 22 Dec 1981), 2 da (Rachael Anne b 21 July 1979, Bethan Victoria b 30 May 1989); *Career* memb Merseyside Police Authy 1981-86, dep chm Liverpool Airport 1981-86; rep: Liverpool Speke Ward Merseyside CC 1981-86, Penketh and Cuerdley Ward Warrington Borough Cncl 1987-89 (dep chm of fin 1987-89); memb: Br Yugoslav Soc, Gt Central Steam Railway Loughborough, Crewe Heritage Centre, League Against Cruel Sports; *Recreations* rugby league, cricket, steam railways; *Clubs* Golbourne Sports and Social (Golborne Wigan), Penketh Sports and Social (Penketh Warrington)

SIMPSON, Air Cdre Charles Hunting; CBE (1961); s of John Andrew Simpson (d 1936, Maj Calcutta Light Horse), of Elmdon, IOW, and Winifred Elizabeth Louise, *née* Hunting (d 1952); *b* 11 Feb 1915; *Educ* Oundle, Pembroke Coll Cambridge (MA); *m* 1945, Beatrice Gillian Patricia, da of Capt Arthur Noel Vernon Hill-Lowe (d 1964), of Court of Hill, Shrops; 2 da; *Career* joined RAF 1937, Bomber and Flying Trg Cmds 1939-45, Air Attaché Stockholm 1946-48, Cdr Univ of Cambridge Air Sqdn 1948-50, Staff Coll 1951, Air Staff Policy 1951-53, dep dir Air Intelligence 1953-54, Asst Cmdt RAF Staff Coll Andover 1954-58, Gp Capt 1954, Cdr RAF E Africa 1958-61, ret 1961 with rank of Air Cdre; memb Lloyd's; Freeman City of London, Liveryman Worshipful Co of Gunmakers; FRMets, FBIS; *Recreations* yachting, racing; *Clubs* Royal Yacht Squadron, Boodle's, RAF; *Style—* Air Cdre Charles Simpson, CBE; Fugelmere Grange, Fulmer, Bucks SL3 6HN (☎ 0753 662051)

SIMPSON, Christopher Robert; s of Lt-Col Maurice Rowton Simpson, OBE, TD, DL (d 1981), of Leics, and Renée Claire, *née* Laffitte (d 1973); *b* 7 Dec 1929; *Educ* Rugby, Magdalene Coll Cambridge (MA, LLM); *m* 2 July 1955, Jane (d 1990), da of Ernest Gustav Byng (d 1944), of Northants; 1 s (David b 1957), 1 da (Charlotte b 1959); *Career* Nat Serv RA 1955-57, TA 1957-61, Capt 1961, ret; admitted slr 1955; ptnr: Herbert Simpson Son & Bennett 1957-77, Stone & Simpson 1978-87; FAI Diamond Badge for Gliding, Royal Aero Club Silver Medal 1976, vice pres Br Gliding Assoc 1976- (chm 1972-76), chm IOD Leics branch 1977-79, vice chm E Midlands Regnl Cncl for Sport and Recreation 1981-, chm Royal Aero Club 1990- (vice chm 1988-90); *Recreations* gliding, mountaineering; *Clubs* Army & Navy, Alpine; *Style—* Christopher Simpson, Esq; The Clock House, Roman Rd, Birstall, Leics LE4 4BF (☎ 0533 674173)

SIMPSON, David; s of David Donald Simpson, of Dundee, and Elizabeth, *née* McGaw; *b* 9 Aug 1949; *Educ* Morgan Acad Dundee, Univ of Aderdeen; *Career* business mangr publication Univ of Aberdeen 1973-74, dep ed Accountancy Age 1974-76, journalist Sunday Express 1976-79, city correspondent The Guardian 1979-86 (also business correspondent), industl ed and dep ed business news The Observer 1986-88, dir Dewe Rogerson Ltd 1988-; *Style—* David Simpson, Esq; Dewe Rogerson Ltd, 3 1/2 London Wall Buildings, London Wall, London EC2 (☎ 071 638 9571, fax 071 374 6997)

SIMPSON, Prof David Ian Hewitt; s of Harold George Simpson, of 131 Ballylesson Rd, Belfast, and Helena, *née* Hewitt; *b* 4 Jan 1935; *Educ* Campbell Coll Belfast, The Queen's Univ of Belfast (MB BCh, BAO, MD); *m* 28 July 1960, Cintra Marguerite, da of Donald Sidney Caldwell (d 1970); 3 s (Andrew b 1962, Gawain b 1965, Jonathan b 1966), 1 da (Alexandra b 1964); *Career* med res offr: East African Virus Res Inst Entebbe Uganda 1962-65, Microbiological Res Estab 1966-71, MRC Laboratory Kisumu Kenya 1971-73; sr lectr and conslt London Sch of Hygiene and Tropical Medicine 1973-78, conslt and dir PHLS Special Pathogens Laboratory CAMR Porton 1978-83, prof of microbiology The Queen's Univ of Belfast 1983-; various govt and MRC Ctees; FRCPath 1983; contrib to various textbooks; *Style—* Prof David Simpson; Fallow Hill, 129 Ballylesson Rd, Belfast BT8 8JU (☎ 0232 826300); Department of Microbiology & Immunobiology, The Queen's University of Belfast, Grosvenor Rd, Belfast BT12 (☎ 0232 240503)

SIMPSON, David Macdonald; s of James Simpson (d 1990), of Perth, and Helen Macdonald, *née* Butters; *b* 25 May 1941; *Educ* Fettes, Univ of Oxford (MA); *m* Elizabeth Cochran, da of James Cochran Hamilton (d 1987), of Paisley; 1 s (Andrew b 1971), 1 da (Shona b 1974); *Career* gen mangr (investmt) and sec Standard Life 1988- (investmt mangr 1973-88); govr Fettes Coll; FFA 1966; *Recreations* golf, curling, hill walking, skiing; *Clubs* Elie Golf House, Bruntsfield Links GS, Honourable Company of Edinburgh Golfers; *Style—* David Simpson, Esq; The Standard Life Assurance Company, 3 George St, Edinburgh EH2 2XZ (☎ 031 225 2552, telex 72539)

SIMPSON, David Martin Wynn; s of William Wynn Simpson, OBE (d 1987), of Northwood, and Winifred Marjorie, *née* Povey, of Bristol; *b* 31 Jan 1938; *Educ* Queen's Coll Taunton, Christ's Coll Cambridge (MA); *m* 6 Dec 1968, Susan Katherine, da of Robert Windsor, of Steyning; 4 da (Amanda b 1964, Phillippa b 1966, Vanessa b 1970, Fiona b 1971); *Career* slr, ptnr Trump & Ptnrs 1968, chm Legal Aid Ctee 1987, pres Bristol Law Soc 1989, vice chm Govrs Queens Coll Taunton; chm Wrington Div Gen Cmmrs of Taxes 1986; MBIM, ACIArb, FFB; *Recreations* flying, gardening, swimming; *Style—* David Simpson, Esq; The Post House, Burrington, Bristol BS18 7AA (☎ 0761 62664); 34 Gt Nicholas St, Bristol BS1 1TS (☎ 0272 299901, fax 0272 298232)

SIMPSON, David Rae Fisher; s of David E Simpson (d 1986), and Roberta Muriel, *née* Wilson; *b* 29 Nov 1936; *Educ* Gordonstoun, Univ of Edinburgh (MA), Harvard (PhD); *m* 1 March 1980, Barbara Dianne Goalen, da of Norward James Inglis; 1 s (Fergus Rae Goalen b 1981), 1 step s (Donald Mclean b 1967), 1 step da (Jacqueline Barbara b 1966); *Career* instr in economics Harvard Univ 1963-64, assoc statistician UN Headquarters New York 1964-65, lectr in political economy UCL 1967-69, prof of economics Univ of Strathclyde 1975-89, dir The Fraser of Allander Inst Univ of Strathclyde 1975-80, economist Standard Life Assurance Co 1989-; *Books* Problems of Input-Output Tables and Analysis (1966), General Equilibrium Analysis (1975), The Political Economy of Growth (1983), The Challenge of New Technology (1988); *Recreations* reading, golf, swimming; *Style—* David Simpson, Esq; Standard Life, 3 George St, Edinburgh EH2 2XZ (☎ 031 245 0813, fax 031 245 6168)

SIMPSON, David Richard Salisbury; OBE (1989); s of Richard Salisbury Simpson, and Joan Margaret, *née* Braund; *b* 1 Oct 1945; *Educ* Merchiston Castle Sch Edinburgh; *Career* VSO teacher W Pakistan 1963-64; CA; joined Peat, Marwick, Mitchell & Co 1964-72, Scot dir Shelter Campaign for the Homeless 1972-74; dir: Amnesty Int (Br Section) 1974-79, Action on Smoking and Health 1979-90; fndr and dir International Agency on Tobacco and Health 1991-; conslt: Int Union against Cancer, Special Project on Smoking and Cancer (responsibility for Indian Sub-Continent) 1980-; sundry journalism, broadcasting and public lectures; hon MFCM (1991); *Recreations* reading, music, hill-walking, Orkney; *Style—* David Simpson, Esq, OBE; 5-11 Mortimer St, London W1 (☎ 071 637 9843)

SIMPSON, Douglas Arthur Reginald Norman; s of Joseph Norman Simpson (d 1932), of Gormyre, Kurunegala, Ceylon, and Alice Dorothy, *née* Peake (d 1966); *b* 28 Dec 1920; *Educ* Ashburton GS, Ellesmere Coll Shrops, Univ Coll Cardiff (BSc); *m* 9 Oct 1941, Tryfana Jenny, da of John Woodford-Williams (d 1941), of Park Grove, Cardiff; 1 s (James b 24 July 1959), 2 da (Mary b 28 May 1953, Angela b 18 June 1958); *Career* mangr Abercynon Colliery 1947-49, mangr (later agent) Nantgarw Colliery 1949-53, chief mining engr Abernant Colliery 1953-58, dep area prodn mangr NCB Area 3 (Rhondda) S Wales 1958-63; NCB London: head of mining (gen) Prodn Dept 1963-67, head of reconstruction and capital projects 1967-72, chief maj projects engr 1972-84, ret 1984; fell Univ Coll Cardiff 1983; pres: Nat Assoc of Colliery Mangrs S Wales 1961, S Wales Inst of Engrs 1966-67, Inst of Mining Engrs 1983-84; chm Nat Advsy Ctee on Mining City & Guilds of London Inst 1980-89; chm Meath Green Protection Soc Horley Surrey 1974-, vice chm Reigate & Dist Crime Prevention Panel 1986-89 (chm 1990-), memb Ctee Gatwick Area Conservation Campaign 1984-; chm Horley branch Cons Assoc 1976 and 1988 (chm Reigate 1989-); memb: Surrey CC 1987-, E Surrey Health Authy 1987-89; awarded Inst Medal by Inst Mining Engrs 1985; Freeman City of London 1984, Liveryman Worshipful Co of Engrs 1984; CEng, fell Inst of Mining Engrs; *Recreations* beekeeping, vintage cars; *Style—* Douglas Simpson, Esq; Meath Green House, Meath Green Lane, Horley, Surrey RH6 8HZ (☎ 0293 784 990)

SIMPSON, Air Vice-Marshal (Charles) Ednam; s of Charles Walker Clark Simpson (d 1970) , of Stirling, and Margaret Gourlay, *née* Doig (d 1970); *b* 24 Sept 1929; *Educ* Stirling HS, Falkirk HS, Univ of Glasgow (MB ChB), Univ of London (MSc); *m* 2 May 1955, Margaret Riddell, da of (Robert) Wallace Hunter (d 1981), of Glasgow; 2 s (David b 1956, Ian b 1957), 1 da (Fiona b 1960); *Career* joined RAF 1955, Staff Offr (aviation med) Br Def Staff Washington DC 1975, dep dir health and res RAF 1979; offr cmdg RAF hosps: Wegberg 1981, Princess Alexandra Hosp Wroughton 1982; dir health and res RAF 1984, asst surgn-gen (environmental health and res) 1985, princ MO RAF Strike Cmd 1986-88; currently dir RAF Benevolent Fund (Scotland); QHS 1984-89; MFCM, FFOM; *Recreations* golf, bird-watching; *Clubs* RAF; *Style—* Air Vice-Marshal Simpson; Am Bruach, Kippen, Stirling FK8 3DT (☎ 078687 281)

SIMPSON, Prof Edward Smethurst; s of George Edward Simpson (d 1955), and Betsy, *née* Smethurst; *b* 9 April 1926; *Educ* Royal GS Lancaster, Univ of Liverpool (BA, MA, PhD); *m* 1 Aug 1959, (Brenda) Christine, da of Alexander Anderson (d 1937); 3 da (Julia b 7 Sept 1960, Alison b 21 June 1962, Ruth Claire b 9 July 1965); *Career* WWII served RN 1944-47; asst lectr Univ of Hull 1951-54, lectr and sr lectr Univ of Liverpool 1954-70; on secondment Ahmadu Bello Univ of Nigeria 1965-67; prof of geography, dean of sci, co dir Rural Econ Res Unit; fndn prof of geography Univ of S Pacific, econ advsr govt of Fiji 1970-72, reader Univ of Hong Kong 1973-75, emeritus prof Univ of Newcastle upon Tyne 1989- (chair geography 1975-88); visiting prof: Univ of Nebraska 1958-59, Ahmadu Bello Univ 1972-73, Univ of Hong Kong 1981-82; conslt: Univ of Malawi 1981-83, Open Univ 1972; memb Inst Br Geographers; *Books* Coal and the Power Industries (1966), The Rural Agricultural Sector (ed, 1980), The Developing World (1987); *Recreations* music, painting, gardens, travel; *Style—* Prof Edward Simpson; The Univ of Newcastle upon Tyne, Newcastle upon Tyne NE1 7RU (☎ 091 222 6000, fax 091 261 1182, telex 53654)

SIMPSON, Ffreebairn Liddon; CMG (1967); s of James Liddon Simpson (d 1969), of Uckfield, Sussex; *b* 11 July 1916; *Educ* Westminster, Trinity Coll Cambridge (BA); *m* 1947, Dorina Laura Magda, da of Nencho Iiev (d 1944), of Sofia, Bulgaria; 1 s (Christopher Liddon b 5 Aug 1952); *Career* FO and Dip Serv Tokyo and Sofia 1939-48, Overseas Fin Div HM Treasy 1948-50, Colonial Serv Gold Coast 1950-55, dep colonial sec Mauritius 1955; perm sec: Miny of Works and Internal Communications Mauritius 1961-66, Premier's Office Mauritius 1966-68; sec Cncl of Ministers Mauritius 1967-68 (Mauritius became independent 1968), sec Cabinet and head Civil Serv Mauritius 1968-76, ret 1976; gen mangr Central Water Authy Mauritius 1976-78; *Recreations* reading, philately; *Clubs* United Oxford & Cambridge Univ; *Style—* Ffreebairn Simpson, Esq, CMG; c/o United Oxford & Cambridge University Club, 71 Pall Mall, London SW1Y 5HD

SIMPSON, George; s of William Simpson (d 1979), of Dundee, Scotland, and Eliza Jane, *née* Wilkie (d 1982); *b* 2 July 1942; *Educ* Morgan Acad Dundee, Dundee Inst of Technol (Dip in Business Admin); *m* 5 Sept 1963, Eva, da of William Chalmers, of Dundee; 1 s (George Anthony b 22 Feb 1965), 1 da (Gillian b 23 Oct 1966); *Career* sr accountant Scottish Gas 1964-68, sr fin position Br Leyland 1969-77, fin dir Leyland Truck & Bus Ltd 1978-79; md: Coventry Climax 1980-82, Freight Rover 1983-85, Rover Group Commercial Vehicles 1986-87; chief exec Leyland DAF 1987-88, md Rover Group 1989-; bd memb: DAF NV Supervisory Bd 1989-, NW Venture Capital Fund Ltd, Br Aerospace plc; memb DTI Ctee CVMAC, vice pres Inst of Motor Indust, exec ctee and cncl memb SMMT (also vice pres); FCCA, ACIS, FIMI; *Recreations* golf; *Clubs* Royal Birkdale Golf, Leamington and Co Golf; *Style—* George Simpson, Esq; Covert Hall, Woodloes Lane, Warwick, Warwickshire (☎ 0926 492190); Rover Group, Fletchampstead Highway, Coventry CV4 9DB (☎ 0203 674659, telex 31567, fax 0279 443431, car 0836 843315)

SIMPSON, Gordon Russell; DSO (1944 and Bar 1945), LVO (1979), TD (1945 and 2 bars), DL (Central Region - Stirling and Falkirk 1981); s of Alexander Russell Simpson, WS (d 1928); *b* 2 Jan 1917; *Educ* Rugby; *m* 1943, Marion Elizabeth, *née* King (d 1976); 2 s; *Career* 2 Lothians and Border Horse 1938-50, Col (TA) UK 1950; stockbroker 1938; sr ptnr Bell Cowan & Co (now Bell Lawrie) 1955-82, chm General Accident Fire & Life Assurance Co 1979-87 (dir 1967-87), former chm Edinburgh then Scottish Stock Exchange, former dep chm The Stock Exchange; Brig Royal Co of Archers (Queen's Body Guard for Scotland, treas 1959-79); cmmr Queen Victoria Sch, memb Ct Univ of Stirling 1980-88; *Recreations* skiing, archery, music; *Clubs* New (Edinburgh); *Style—* Gordon R Simpson, Esq, DSO, LVO, TD, DL; Arntomie, Port of Menteith, Perthshire FK8 3RD

SIMPSON, Dr Graeme Kenneth; s of Kenneth Caird Simpson, of 11 Fraser-Place, Grangemouth, Stirlingshire, and Edna Muriel, *née* Graham; *b* 25 Sept 1956; *Educ* Grangemouth HS, Univ of Edinburgh Med Sch (BSc, MB ChB); *m* 6 May 1978, Jacqueline Sara, da of Andrew Auchterlonie, of 1 Queens Walk, The Thistle Foundation, Edinburgh; 1 s (David Malcolm b 1978), 2 da (Elspeth Margaret b 1981, Patricia Hannah b 1984); *Career* sr house offr med renal unit Royal Infirmary Edinburgh 1981-82 and med unit Roodlands Hosp Haddington 1982-83 (house surgn 1981), registrar in med Eastern Gen Hosp Edinburgh 1983-86 (house physician 1980-81), sr registrar in gen and geriatric med Newcastle upon Tyne 1986-89, conslt physician in geriatric med Royal Alexandra Hosp Paisley 1989-; memb: Collegiate Membs Ctee RCP 1985-89 (chm and memb College Cncl 1988-89), Br Geriatric Soc; life memb Royal Med Soc; MRCP 1983; *Books* contrib Body Weight Control (1988); *Recreations* golf, swimming, carpet making; *Style—* Dr Graeme Simpson; Weybridge, 18 Stanely Drive, Paisley; Royal Alexandra Hosp, Paisley

SIMPSON, Graham; s of Geoffrey Albert Simpson, of Grays, Essex, and Sarah Elizabeth, *née* Thompson; *b* 5 Sept 1951; *Educ* Torells Boys Sch, Univ of S California, Arch Assoc Sch of Arch (AADip); *m* 16 Aug 1980 (m dis 1990), Elaine

Emily, da of Joseph Frederick Darby, of Stanford-Le-Hope, Essex; 1 s (Bertram Rupert Oscar), 1 da (Chloë March Louise); *Career* architect; Piers Gough 1987-90, responsible for The Circle London SE1 (apartments, houses, business units, shops and courtyards); MRIBA; *Recreations* cricket, skiing; *Style—* Graham Simpson, Esq; 45 Anstice Close, Chiswick, London W4 2RL (☎ 081 747 1720)

SIMPSON, Harry Arthur; AE; s of Cyril Simpson (d 1950), of Ferndown, Dorset, and Nellie, *née* Buckley (d 1967); *b* 16 Dec 1914; *Educ* Moseley GS Warwicks; *m* 1, 10 July 1943 (m dis 1983), Lilian Jackson, *née* Macdonald; 1 s (Roger Graham b 13 Feb 1948 d 1974), 2 da (Dianne Gail b 13 March 1945, Julie Jackson b 11 Dec 1956); m 2, 9 May 1984, Deborah Jane, da of Philip J Camp, of Bookham, Surrey; *Career* Nat Serv WWII RAF, specialist 'N' Symbol Award 1942, Pilot, Sqdn Ldr; chemist Bakelite Ltd 1936-39; Flexible Abrasives Ltd 1947-65, chm and chief exec Arrow Abrasives Ltd 1966-; FRMetS, FInstD; *Recreations* yachting, golf, fishing; *Clubs* Royal Thames Yacht, RAC, RAF; *Style—* Harry Simpson, Esq, AE; Little Langley Farm, Rake, nr Liss, Hampshire (☎ 0730 892 142); Arrow Abrasives Ltd, Rodney Rd, Portsmouth, Hampshire PO4 8TH (☎ 0705 750 836, fax 0705 826 323, car 0836 227 869, telex 86787 ARROWA G)

SIMPSON, Prof Hugh Walter; s of Rev Ian Simpson (d 1976), and Dr Elenora Simpson, *née* Howie (d 1989); *b* 4 April 1931; *Educ* Bryanston, Univ of Edinburgh (MB ChB, MD), Univ of Glasgow (PhD); *m* 21 March 1959, Myrtle Lilias, da of Maj H Emslie; 3 s (Maj Robin Gordon b 5 Jan 1960, Bruce Brian b 7 Feb 1961, Rory Drummond b 13 Jan 1968), 1 da (Rona O'Clanise b 17 June 1962); *Career* med offr Br Antarctic Survey Hope Bay 1955-58, leader of many scientific expeditions to polar regns, pathologist then prof and head of div Glasgow Royal Infirmary and Univ of Glasgow 1959-; inventor of Chronobra for detection of breast pre-cancer risk; over 150 scientific pubns; chm Ethical Ctee; FRCPath, FRCP; Polar medal 1964, Mungo Park medal 1970; *Recreations* skiing; *Style—* Prof Hugh Simpson; 7 Cleveden Crescent, Glasgow G12 0TQ (☎ 041 3571091); Farleitter, Kincraig, Inverness-shire PH21 1NU (☎ 05404 288); Pathology Dept, Glasgow Royal Infirmary, Glasgow G4 OSF (☎ 041 5523535 ext 5327, fax 041 3521524, telex 777 070 UNIGLA)

SIMPSON, Ian; s of Herbert William Simpson (d 1972), of Sunderland, Co Durham, and Elsie, *née* Jagger; *b* 12 Nov 1933; *Educ* Bede GS Sunderland, Sunderland Coll of Art, RCA; *m* 26 July 1958 (m dis 1982), Joan, da of Donald Charlton (d 1958), of Sunderland; 2 s (Robert b 2 Sept 1962, Howard b 13 Feb 1964), 1 da (Katharine b 8 March 1967); m 2, 26 March 1982, Birgitta, da of Yngve Brädde (d 1976), of Björketorp, Sweden; *Career* Nat Serv RAF 1953-55; head Dept of Co-ordinated Studies Hornsey Coll of Art 1969-72 (head Dept of Visual Res 1967-69), visiting prof Syracuse Univ NY 1977, head St Martin's Sch of Art 1986-88 (princ 1972-86), asst rector London Inst 1986-88, freelance artist and writer 1988-; one man exhibitions: Cambridge 1975, Durham 1977, Hambledon Gallery Blandford 1985; broadcast wrote and presented: Eyeline 1968, Picture Making 1973, Reading the Signs 1976; chm Fine Art Bd CNAA 1976-81 (memb Cncl 1974-80), conslt Leisure Study Gp 1986-87; ARCA 1958, FSAE 1976, FRSA 1983; *Books* Eyeline (1968), Drawing Seeing and Observation (1973), Picture Making (1973), Guide to Painting and Composition (1979), Painters Progress (1983), An Encyclopaedia of Drawing Techniques (1987), A Course in Painting (1988); *Recreations* reading, music; *Style—* Ian Simpson, Esq; Motts Farm House, Chilton St, Clare, Sudbury, Suffolk CO10 8QS (☎ 0787 277835)

SIMPSON, Sheriff Ian Christopher; s of Maj David Francis Simpson, of 17 Hallowhill, St Andrews, and Joss, *née* Dickie (d 1975); *b* 5 July 1949; *Educ* Trinity Coll Glenalmond, Univ of Edinburgh (LLB); *m* 7 Aug 1973, (Christine Margaret) Anne, da of Duncan D Strang, of 2 Dollerie Crescent, Crieff; 2 s (Richard David b 1977, Graham Mark b 1979); *Career* appointed Sheriff of S Strathclyde Dumfries and Galloway (floating) 1988; memb Faculty of Advocates 1974; *Recreations* golf; *Clubs* Royal and Ancient, Dunbar Golf; *Style—* Sheriff Ian Simpson; 30 Cluny Drive, Edinburgh, Scotland EH10 6DP (☎ 031 447 3363); Hamilton Sheriff Court, Sheriff Court House, Beckford St, Hamilton

SIMPSON, James; s of William Watson Simpson, of N Baddesley, Southampton, Hants, and Beatrice Hilda, *née* Dixon; *b* 16 April 1944; *Educ* Barton Peveril GS Eastleigh Hants, Univ of London (LLB); *m* 28 Dec 1968 (m dis 1982), Patricia Vivian (Tricia), da of Michael Joseph Sheridan, of Southampton; 1 s (Toby b 1973), 1 da (Charlotte b 1975); *Career* RNR 1965, cmmnd Sub Lt 1966, Lt 1969, resigned cmmn 1974; admitted slr 1969, asst litigation slr Coffin Mew & Clover Southampton 1969-70, prosecuting slr Hants CC Portsmouth 1970-72, asst slr Brutton & Co Fareham 1972-73 (ptnr 1973-87, sr ptnr 1987-89), dep High and Co Ct registrar 1978-89; called to the Bar Middle Temple 1990; hon sec Hants Inc Law Soc 1987-89; fndr chm Hamble Valley Round Table 1975-76 (chm Area I 1981-82); ward cncllr Fareham Borough Cncl 1978-82; *Recreations* foreign travel, photography, golf; *Clubs* Hamble Valley Stick, Meon Valley Golf, Grenelefe FL Golf; *Style—* James Simpson, Esq; Bell Yard Chambers, 16 Bell Yard, London WC2A 2JR (☎ 071 306 9292); 12 East St, Titchfield, Hants PO14 4AD (☎ 0329 46639)

SIMPSON, Cdr (Cortlandt) James Woore; CBE (1956), DSC (1945); s of Rear Adm C H Simpson, CBE (d 1943), of Old Vicarage House, Stoke-by-Nayland, Suffolk, and Edith Octavia, *née* Busby (d 1954); *b* 2 Sept 1911; *Educ* St Ronans Sch, RNC Dartmouth, Univ of London (BSc); *m* 1, Lettice Mary, *née* Johnstone; m 2, Ann Margaret, *née* Tooth; m 3, Joan Mary, *née* Cooke; 1 da (Bonella Mary b 1971); m 4, 13 April 1985, (Vanessa) Ann, *née* Heald; *Career* RN: Midshipman 1929, Lt 1934, WWII serv Home and Med Fleets, Cdr 1948, ret 1961; summer expeditions to Greenland 1950 and 1951, ldr Br N Greenland Expedition 1952-54; Polar Medal 1954, RGS Founder's Medal 1955; *Publications* Northice (1957); *Recreations* mountaineering, sailing, fishing; *Clubs* Alpine; *Style—* Cdr James Simpson, CBE, DSC; Lower Lambie, Luxborough, Watchet, Somerset

SIMPSON, Jeremy Miles; s of Gordon Simpson (d 1984), of Glastonbury, and Barbara, *née* Wilkes (d 1976); *b* 25 Nov 1933; *Educ* Malvern, Clare Coll Cambridge (MA); *m* 21 July 1956, Penelope Ann Mary, da of Harvey James (d 1979), of Hayle, Cornwall; 1 s (Mark b 1962), 4 da (Clare b 1957, Rebecca b 1961, Miranda b 1962, Catherine b 1964); *Career* Lt RN 1955-58; md Tan Sad Chair Co 1967-69, chm Giroflex Ltd 1972-86, md Papropack Ltd 1972-86, chm Gordon Russell plc, non-exec dir Havelock Europa plc 1989-; Freeman City of London 1988, memb Worshipful Co of Furniture Makers; Order of the Finnish Lion ((First Class) Finland) 1986; *Recreations* family, reading, walking, travel; *Clubs* United Oxford and Cambridge Univ; *Style—* Jeremy Simpson, Esq

SIMPSON, Prof John Alexander; s of Henry Keith Lindsay Simpson (d 1941), of Greenock, and Mrs Simpson (d 1972); *b* 30 March 1922; *Educ* Greenock Acad, Univ of Glasgow (MB ChB, MD); *m* 15 Dec 1951, Elizabeth Marguerite Hood, da of Dr James Hood Neill (d 1958), of Edinburgh; 2 s (Henry Keith Lindsay b 1952, Neill John b 1954), 1 da (Guendolen Hope b 1960); *Career* Surgn Lt RNVR 1945-48; MRC fell Nat Hosp for Nervous Diseases London 1953-55, conslt physician Western Infirmary Glasgow 1956, reader in neurology (formerly sr lectr) Univ of Edinburgh 1956-64; physician i/c: Regnl Neurological Unit Edinburgh 1956-64, Dept of Neurology Inst of Neurological Sciences Glasgow 1964-87; hon conslt neurologist to Br Army 1965-81, ed Jl of Neurology Neurosurgery and Psychiatry 1970-79, conslt neurologist to Civil Serv Cmmn 1974-87, emeritus prof of neurology Univ of Glasgow 1987- (lectr in med 1950-56, prof of neurology 1964-87); vice pres Myasthenia Gravis Assoc, former chm Scot Epilepsy Assoc and Glasgow Chamber Orch; FRCPE 1961, FRCP 1963, FRCPG 1964, FRSE 1969; Istiqlal Decoration (first class) Hashemite Kingdom of Jordan 1973; *Books* Applied Neurophysiology (with W Fitch, 1988); *Recreations* sailing, violin playing, painting; *Clubs* Clyde Cruising; *Style—* Dr John Simpson, FRSE; 87 Glencairn Drive, Glasgow G41 4LL (☎ 041 423 2863)

SIMPSON, John Andrew; s of Robert Morris Simpson, and Joan Margaret, *née* Sersale; *b* 13 Oct 1953; *Educ* Dean Close Sch Cheltenham, Univ of York (BA, univ colours in hockey), Univ of Reading (MA); *m* 25 Sept 1976, Dr Hilary Simpson, da of Edmund Wilfred Croxford; 2 da (Katharine Jane b 1982, Eleanor Grace b 1990); *Career* ed Concise Oxford Dictionary of Proverbs 1978-80, sr ed Supplement to the Oxford English Dictionary 1980-84 (asst ed 1976-78), co-ed Oxford English Dictionary 1986 - (ed new words 1984-85); *Recreations* cricket, computing; *Style—* John Simpson, Esq; 36 Kennett Road, Headington, Oxford OX3 7BJ (☎ 0865 68053); Oxford English Dictionaries, 37A St Giles', Oxford OX1 3LD (☎ 0865 56767, fax 0865 53106)

SIMPSON, Very Rev John Arthur; s of Arthur Simpson (d 1958), and Mary Esther, *née* Price (d 1982); *b* 7 June 1933; *Educ* Cathays HS Cardiff, Keble Coll Oxford (BA, MA), Clifton Theol Coll; *m* 15 Aug 1968, Ruth Marian, da of Leo Dibbens (d 1966); 1 s (Damian b 1972), 2 da (Rebecca b 1970, Helen b 1974); *Career* curate: Leyton 1958-59, Christ Church Oprington 1959-62; tutor Oak Hill Coll London 1962-72, vicar Ridge Herts 1972-79, dir Ordinands and Post-Ordination Trg Diocese of St Albans 1975-81, hon canon St Albans Cathedral 1977-79, residentiary canon St Albans and priest i/c of Ridge 1979-81, archdeacon of Canterbury and residentiary canon of Canterbury Cathedral 1981-86, dean of Canterbury 1986-; dir Ecclesiastical Insurance Group 1983-; chm: (Canterbury) Cathedral Gifts Ltd 1986-, The Canterbury Cathedral Co Ltd; chm Govrs Kings Sch Canterbury 1986-; *Recreations* travel, theatre, opera; *Clubs* Athenaeum; *Style—* The Very Rev the Dean of Canterbury; The Deanery, Canterbury, Kent CT1 2EP (☎ 0227 765983); Cathedral House, 11 The Precincts, Canterbury CT1 2EH (☎ 0227 762862)

SIMPSON, (Robert) John Blantyre; MBE (1954), TD (1947, and three clasps), WS; s of Alexander Russell Simpson, WS (d 1928), of Edinburgh, and Dorothy, *née* Lowe (d 1974); *b* 28 Aug 1914; *Educ* Rugby,Magdalen Coll Oxford (MA), Edinburgh Univ (LLB); *m* 1, 7 Oct 1939, Helen Mary Radmore, da of William Percival Miller (d 1966), of Warwicks; m 2, 2 April 1962, Barbara Helen, da of John MacRobert (d 1949), of Paisley; 1 s (Michael John Russell b 1941), 1 da (Elizabeth Mary Darley b 1948); *Career* Lt-Col Royal Scots (TA) 1935-60; writer to HM Signet (ret); sec Highlands and Islands Educn Tst 1958-90; sec Soc in Scotland for Propagating Christian Knowledge 1958; govr and hon sec St Columba's Hospice 1971, chm The Royal Scots Museum Tst 1959; dir The Royal Scots Regtl Shop, chm Scottish Veterans Garden City Assoc 1965; dir and hon sec Gem and Jar Ltd; Belgian Croix Militaire; *Recreations* fishing, reading, gardening; *Clubs* New (Edinburgh), The Royal Scots, Hon Co of Edinburgh Golfers; *Style—* R J B Simpson, Esq, MBE, TD, WS; 6 Belgrave Crescent, Edinburgh EH4 3AQ (☎ 031 332 5722); Reef, Glenfinnan, Invernesshire PH37 4LT (☎ 039 783 291)

SIMPSON, John Cody Fidler-; s of Roy Simpson Fidler-Simpson (d 1980), of Dunwich, Suffolk, and Joyce Leila Vivienne, *née* Cody (d 1983); *b* 9 Aug 1944; *Educ* St Paul's, Magdalene Coll Cambridge (MA); *m* 14 Aug 1965 (m dis 1990), Diane Jean, da of Dr Manville Petteys, of La Jolla, Calif, USA; 2 da (Julia Anne b 1969, Eleanor Mary b 1971); *partner*, Tira, da of Harry Shubart, of Evanston, Illinois, USA; *Career* with The BBC 1966-; sub ed Radio News 1966, corr Dublin 1972; foreign corr: Brussels 1975, Johannesburg 1977; diplomatic corr TV News 1978, political ed 1980, presenter Nine O'Clock News 1981, diplomatic ed 1982 (reporting assignments from numerous countries incl Afghanistan, Argentina, Lebanon, Libya, Iran, Nicaragua and USSR and interviews with various world leaders), foreign affairs ed 1988 (reporting on the Gulf War 1991); FRGS 1990; *Books* The Best of Granta (jt ed, 1966), Moscow Requiem (novel, 1980), A Fine and Private Place (novel, 1982), The Disappeared (1985), Behind Iranian Lines (1988), Despatches from the Barricades (1990); *Recreations* books, travelling, tennis; *Clubs* Athenaeum, Chelsea Arts, Queen's; *Style—* John Simpson, Esq; BBC Television Centre, Wood Lane, London W12 (☎ 081 743 8000)

SIMPSON, Prof John Harold; s of Frederick Harold Simpson (d 1990), of Clifton, York, and Margaret Morrison, *née* Lees-Wallace; *b* 21 May 1940; *Educ* Bootham Sch York, Exeter Coll Oxford (BA), Univ of Liverpool (PhD, DSc); *m* 31 Aug 1964, Frances Mary, da of Thomas Estell Peacock (d 1989); 3 da (Amanda b 1967, Rachel b 1968, Joanna b 1970); *Career* lectr in physical oceanography Univ of Wales Bangor 1965, res fell Nat Inst of Oceanography 1969-70, personal chair in physical oceanography 1982, visiting prof of physical oceangraphy Virginia Inst of Marine Sciences USA 1989; NERC: memb Ctee AAPS 1975-79, memb Cncl 1982-88, chm North Sea Project Scientific Steering Gp 1987-; memb Cncl Scottish Marine Biological Assoc, govr David Hughes Sch Menai Bridge; *Recreations* hill walking, windsurfing, gardening; *Style—* Prof John Simpson; Sch of Ocean Sciences, Univ of Wales, Bangor, Menai Bridge, Gwynedd LL59 5EY (☎ 0248 351151, telex 61100, fax 0248 716367)

SIMPSON, John Lindsay; s of Lindsay Athol Simpson, of Cockfield, Suffolk, and Mary Jacqueline, *née* Luke; *b* 15 Nov 1948; *Educ* UCL (LLB); *m* 25 Sept 1976, Catherine Marie, da of Vincent Paul Goethals, of Kortijk, Belgium; 3 s (Edward b 1979, Oliver b 1981, Alexander b 1984), 1 da (Isabelle b 1986); *Career* admitted slr 1974; Paris office Linklaters & Paines 1981-88 (articled clerk 1972, Brussels office 1975-79, ptnr 1981); Freeman Worshipful Co of Watermen and Lighterman; memb Law Soc; *Recreations* European travel, English watercolour paintings, gardening; *Style—* John Simpson, Esq; 29 Ellerker Gardens, Richmond, Surrey TW10 6AA (☎ 081 940 3464); Barrington House, 59/67 Gresham St, London EC2V 7JA (☎ 071 606 7080, fax 071 606 5113, telex 884349)

SIMPSON, Lt-Col John Rowton; TD (1963), DL (1972); s of Lt-Col Maurice Rowton Simpson, OBE, TD, DL (d 1981), of Leicester, and Renee Claire, *née* Lafitte; *b* 19 Sept 1926; *Educ* Rugby, Magdelene Coll Cambridge (MA, LLM); *m* 8 Oct 1959, Roxane Eveline, da of William Pickford (d 1984), of Leicester; 2 s (Jeremy b 17 Nov 1963, Matthew b 29 Sept 1966), 1 da (Lucy b 28 Dec 1970); *Career* Coldstream Gds 1944, cmmnd 2 Lt Gordon Highlanders 1945, Lt Sierra Leone Regt 1946 (Capt 1947), transfd to reserve 1948, Maj RA TA 1958 (Lt 1951, Capt 1954), RE TA 1961 (Lt-Col 1965), Sherwood Foresters 1966, reserve RE 1968; admitted slr 1953; ptnr Herbert Simpson & Co 1960; sr ptnr: Stone & Simpson 1978, Harvey Ingram Stone & Simpson 1988-91; memb TAVR Assoc E Midlands 1958-; hon sec Westleigh RFC 1954-59; capt Leicestershire GC 1972; vice chm Leicestershire Sports & Recreation Advsy Cncl 1976-; chm: City of Leicester Sport and Recreation Advsy Cncl 1976-88, Cadet Ctee TAVR Assoc 1985-89; pres: Leicestershire Rugby Union 1979, 1980 and 1985 (ctee memb 1959-), Rugby Football Union 1988 (ctee memb 1968-); Freeman City of London; memb: Worshipful Co of Framework Knitters, Law Soc; *Recreations* rugby football, golf; *Clubs* E India; *Style—* Lt-Col John R Simpson, TD, DL; 16 Knighton Grange Rd, Leicester LE2 2LE (☎ 0533 705753)

SIMPSON, Lady Juliet; da of late 4 Earl of Cranbrook by 2 w, Fidelity (*see Dowager Countess of Cranbrook*); *b* 1934; *m* 1958 (m dis 1970), Charles Colin Simpson, TD; 2 s

(Charles b 1962, Edward b 1965), 2 da (Fidelity b 1960, Amanda b 1964); *Style*— The Lady Juliet Simpson; The White House, Rooks Hill, Underriver, Sevenoaks, Kent

SIMPSON, Keppel Moore; *b* 10 Aug 1933; *Career* Sub Lt RN 1953-55; dir: Conf Européene des Postes et des Telecommunications 'Eurodata' Programme 1971-73, Intelsat Permanent Management Arrangements 1974-76, PA International Management Conslultants Ltd 1976-84, Sundridge Park Management Centre Ltd 1979-84, PA International Holdings Ltd 1982-84, Yeoward Bros Ltd 1983-, The Watts Group plc 1985-, CSL Group Ltd 1989-; chm PA International Management Consultants Inc 1980-84; prog dir UK Nat Microelectronics Awareness Prog 1978; fndr memb Workaid, chm Chesham Prep Sch Tst Ltd; CEng, MIEE, FIMC; *Clubs* Naval; *Style*— Keppel Simpson, Esq; Galloway House, High St, Amersham, Bucks HP7 0ED (☎ 0494 724984, office 0494 728659, fax 0494 721785)

SIMPSON, Rear Adm Michael Frank; CB (1985); s of Robert Michael Simpson, and Florence Mabel Simpson; *b* 27 Sept 1928; *Educ* King Edward VI Sch Bath, RNEC Manadon (CEng); *m* 1973, Sandra, *née* Cliff; 2 s, 1 da; *Career* joined RN 1944, Air Engr Offr 1956; served: FAA Sqdns, cruisers and carriers; US Navy 1964-66, Ark Royal 1970-72, supt RN Aircraft Yard Fleetlands 1978-80; Cdre RN Barracks Portsmouth 1981-83, dir-gen Aircraft (Navy) 1983-85, dir Field Aircraft of Croydon 1985-; md Field Airmotive Ltd 1988-, chm Somet Ltd 1988-, dir Field Aviation Ltd 1988-; *Style*— Rear Adm Michael F Simpson, CB; Keppel, Blackhills, Esher, Surrey KT10 9JW

SIMPSON, Norman; s of James Robert Simpson (d 1942), of Warsop, Notts, and Alice May Lody, *née* Eaton (d 1982); *b* 22 Sept 1933; *Educ* Warsop Infants and Secdy Sch, Mansfield Technical Sch, Mansfield Sch of Art, Nottingham Sch of Architecture, Nottingham Poly (Dip Landscape Design); *m* 2 Sept 1958, Margaret Audrey, da of Frederick Israel Woodhouse (d 1969), of Sutton in Ashfield, Notts; *Career* architect; has won several awards incl: for W Burton 'A' Power Station Civic Tst Award 1968 and Countryside Award 1970, for Nat Watersport Centre Holme Pierrepont Sports Cncl Mgmnt Award 1973 and 1978, for Altrincham Leisure Centre Bldg for Disabled Award 1976; assoc: Inst of Baths and Recreational Mgmnt 1972, Landscape Inst 1976; memb: The Assoc of Consulting Architects 1980, The Assoc for the Studies in Conservation of Hist Bldgs 1981; former chm East Midland Landscape Group; ARCUK 1964, ARIBA 1964, FRIBA 1968, FBIM 1982; *Recreations* photography, rotary club work; *Clubs* Rotary (Nottingham North, former pres); *Style*— Norman Simpson, Esq; 68A Front St, Arnold, Nottingham (☎ 0602 670107, fax 0602 671182)

SIMPSON, Peter; *Educ* Bournemouth and Poole Coll of Art; *m* Dec 1970, Jennifer Carol, *née* Johnson; 2 da (Rebecca Caroline b 21 Sept 1972, Naomi Rosalind Mary b 18 July 1975); *Career* ceramic designer; exhibitions incl: one-man exhibition (Pace Gallery and Design Centre London) 1970, Ceramics '71 (Bradford City Art Gallery and Design Centre London) 1971, More British Potters (Keetles Yard Cambridge) 1972, International Ceramics '72 (V & A) 1972, Craftsman's Art (V & A) 1973, Modern British Crafts (Royal Scottish Museum Edinburgh) 1973, Gordon Baldwin, Peter Simpson (British Crafts Centre London) 1974, Chunichi 3 Int Exhibition of Ceramic Art Tokyo 1975, 6 Studio Potters (V & A Museum) 1976, 2-man show (British Crafts Centre London) 1979, 4-man show (CPA London) 1980, Pottery Now (Sotheby's Gallery Belgravia London) 1985; numerous works in public collections incl Royal Scottish Museum (Edinburgh) and V & A Museum (London); visiting tutor and lectr in ceramics; memb Craftsmen Bursary Panel Southern Arts Assoc 1976-79 (memb Visual Arts Panel 1976-78), exhibition memb The Contemporary Applied Arts London; *Style*— Peter Simpson, Esq; Department of Ceramics, Camberwell College of Arts, Peckham Rd, London SE5 8UF

SIMPSON, His Hon Judge Peter Robert; s of Surgn Capt Donald Lee Simpson, RN (d 1985), of Erskine House, 1 Old Fold Close, Hadley Green, Barnet, Herts, and Margaret Olive, *née* Lathan; *b* 9 Feb 1936; *Educ* St John Coll Southsea Hants; *Career* admitted slr 1960; called to the Bar Inner Temple 1970, ad eundem Lincoln's Inn 1972, practised on the South Eastern Circuit then at Chancery Bar (mainly in property and conveyancing matters), rec 1987-89, appointed circuit judge 1989; *Recreations* reading legal and political biographies, listening to music, playing chess, dining out; *Style*— His Hon Judge P R Simpson; 12 New Square, Lincoln's Inn, London WC2A 3SW; Erskine House, 1 Old Fold Close, Hadley Green, Barnet, Herts

SIMPSON, Ven Rennie; LVO (1974); o s of Doctor Taylor Simpson (d 1966), and May Simpson (d 1962); *b* 13 Jan 1920; *Educ* Lambeth (MA), Kelham Theol Coll; *m* 30 April 1949, Margaret, da of Herbert Hardy (d 1957), of Yorks; 1 s (Jonathan Michael b 1961), 1 da (Katherine Mary b 1957); *Career* chaplain RNVR 1953-55; curate S Elmsall Yorks 1945-49; succentor: Blackburn Cathedral 1949-52, St Paul's Cathedral London (and sacrist) 1952-58 (jr cardinal 1954-55, sr 1955-58); vicar John Keble Church Mill Hill 1958-63, precentor Westminster Abbey 1963-74, vice dean Chester Cathedral 1974-78, archdeacon of Macclesfield and rector of Gawsworth 1978-85; dep priest to HM the Queen 1956-67, priest in ordinary to HM the Queen 1967-74, chaplain to HM the Queen 1982-90; life govr Imperial Cancer Res Fndn 1963; sub-prelate OStJ 1973-; Freeman City of London 1955, Liveryman Worshipful Co of Wax Chandlers; Hon Chaplain Worshipful Soc of Apothecaries 1984-85; jt hon treas Corpn of Sons of the Clergy 1967-74; *Style*— The Ven Rennie Simpson, LVO; Gawsworth Cottage, 18 Roseberry Green, North Stainley, nr Ripon, North Yorks HG4 3HZ (☎ 0765 85286)

SIMPSON, Dr Robert Wilfred Levick; s of Robert Warren Simpson, and Helena Hendrika, *née* Govaars; *b* 2 March 1921; *Educ* Westmister; *m* 1, 1946, Bessie Fraser (d 1981); m 2, 1982, Angela Mary Musgrave; *Career* BBC music prodr 1951-80; composer of 11 Symphonies, 14 String Quartets, many other chamber and orchestral works; memb: CND, Peace Pledge Union, Kerry Peace Gp, Musicians Against Nuclear Arms, Royal Astronomical Soc, Br Astronomical Assoc, Inc Soc of Musicians, Composer's Guild of GB, Assoc of Professional Composers; *Books* Carl Nielsen, Symphonist (1952 and 1979), The Essence of Bruckner (1966), The Symphony (ed, 1967), Beethoven's Symphonies (1970), The Proms and Natural Justice (1981); *Recreations* astronomy; *Style*— Dr Robert Simpson; Siochāin, Killelton, nr Camp, Tralee, County Kerry, Eire (☎ 010 3536630213)

SIMPSON, Robin Muschamp Garry; QC (1971); s of Ronald Simpson (d 1957), of Aldeburgh, Suffolk, and Lila, *née* Muschamp (d 1951); *b* 19 June 1927; *Educ* Charterhouse, Peterhouse Cambridge (MA); *m* 1, 13 Oct 1956 (m dis 1968), Avril Carolyn, da of Dr J E M Harrisson, of Bovey Tracey, S Devon; 1 s (Charles b 17 Oct 1961), 1 da (Anna b 13 Aug 1963); m 2, 23 March 1968, Faith Mary, da of Dr F G Laughton-Scott, of 25 Upper Wimpole St, London W1; 1 s (Hugo b 14 March 1972), 1 da (Kate b 14 Oct 1968); *Career* called to the Bar Middle Temple 1951; memb Central Criminal Ct Bar Mess, practising SE Circuit, rec Crown Ct 1976-86, Master of Bench Middle Temple 1979, appeal steward Br Boxing Bd of Control; *Recreations* real tennis, sailing; *Clubs* MCC, Garrick, Aldeburgh Yacht; *Style*— Robin Simpson, Esq, QC; 9 Drayton Gardens, London SW10 9RY (☎ 071 373 3284); 3 Raymond Bldgs, Grays Inn, London WC1 (☎ 071 831 3833)

SIMPSON, Dr Roderick Howard Wallace; s of Dr Robert Wallace Simpson, of Salisbury, and Betty Noreen, *née* Mollett; *b* 10 Jan 1951; *Educ* Kings Sch, Bruton Univ of St Andrews (BSc), Univ of Dundee (MB ChB), Univ of Stellenbosch (M Med); *m* 10 Nov 1979, (Alethea) Avrille, da of Cecil Alfred Milborrow, of Johannesburg, SA; 2 s (Andrew b 1980, Richard b 1983), 1 da (Eleanor b 1987); *Career* registrar in pathology Guys Hosp 1976-79, lectr in pathology Univ of Stellenbosch 1980-82, sr lectr in pathology and neuropathology Univ of the Witwatersrand SA 1982-85, conslt pathologist and sr lectr Univ of Exeter 1985-; author of various pubns in med jls on aspects of histopathology; MRCPath 1983; *Recreations* cricket, travel, dining well with good company, the past; *Clubs* East India; *Style*— Dr Roderick Simpson; Iron Pool, Dry Lane, Christow, nr Exeter, Devonshire EX6 7PF (☎ 0647 52034); Area Dept of Pathology, Church Lane, Heavitree, Exeter, Devonshire EX2 5DY (☎ 0392 402941)

SIMPSON, Roderick Wykeham; s of Dr John Emerson Simpson, of 23 Knebworth Rd, Bexhill-on-Sea, Sussex, and Margot Cobbett, *née* Hughes; *b* 3 Feb 1941; *Educ* The Edinburgh Acad; *m* 4 June 1966, Valerie Patricia Jean, da of Frederick John Taylor Huggett, of Shaftesbury, Dorset; 2 s (Jeremy John Cobbett b 1971, Michael Giles Cobbett b 1976); *Career* Peat Marwick Mitchell & Co London 1959-69, dir and vice pres Operations & Aviation Data Serv Inc Kansas USA 1969-71, asst md Gardner Merchant Ltd Surrey 1971-; dir: Kelvin International Services Ltd, SNSA France, Lockhart Catering Equipment Ltd, Servosnax Inc USA, CERES France, Interserve SA Belgium, Personal Restaurant Systeme GmbH Germany, Grooms Coffee House Ltd, Gardner Merchant Keyline Travel Ltd; princ ptnr Aeroplan Servs; MICAS 1965; *Books* The General Aviation Handbook (3 vols 1981, 1982, 1984), numerous papers published on aviation historical and tech subjects; *Recreations* photography, private flying, aviation historical res; *Style*— Roderick Simpson, Esq; The Haven, South Close Green, Merstham, Surrey RH1 3DU (☎ 0737 642 527); Kenley House, Kenley Lane, Kenley, Surrey CR2 5YR (☎ 081 763 1212, fax 081 763 1044)

SIMPSON, Prof Thomas James (Tom); s of Thomas Simpson (d 1989), of Dollar, Clackmannanshire, Scotland, and Hughina Ross, *née* Hay; *Educ* Univ of Edinburgh (BSc, DSc), Univ of Bristol (PhD); *m* 1, 30 July 1970 (m dis 1987), Elizabeth Crosthwaite, *née* Nattrass; 1 s (David Thomas b 19 Jan 1978), 1 da (Anna Mary b 1 March 1982); m 2, 14 April 1987, Dr Mary Norval, da of John Norval, of Lanark Rd, Edinburgh; *Career* res fell Australian Nat Univ 1974-76, res fell Univ of Liverpool 1977-78 (sr univ demonstrator 1973-74), lectr Univ of Edinburgh 1978-88; prof of organic chemistry Univ of Leicester 1988-89; memb: Ctees Royal Soc of Chemistry, Editorial Bd Natural Product Reports, SERC Ctees and panels; memb: Phytochemical Soc, Royal Soc of Chemistry; *Recreations* hill walking, squash, theatre, travel; *Style*— Prof Tom Simpson; University of Bristol, Department of Organic Chemistry, Cantock's Close, Bristol BS8 1TS (☎ 0272 303678, fax 0272 251295, telex 445938)

SIMPSON, Sir William James; s of William Simpson, and Margaret, *née* Nimmo; *b* 1920; *Educ* Victoria Sch, Falkirk Tech Sch; *m* 1942, Catherine McEwan Nichol; 1 s; *Career* WWII 1939-45, Sgt Argyll and Sutherland Highlanders; gen sec Foundry Section AUEW 1967-75, memb Race Relations Bd 1967-74, chm Lab Pty 1972-73, memb Flixborough Inquiry 1973-74, chm Advsy Ctee on Asbestos 1976-79, former chm Health and Safety Cmmn; kt 1984; *Books* Labour - The Unions and The Party (1973); *Style*— Sir William Simpson; 11 Strude Howe, Alva, Clacks, Scotland (☎ 0259 60859)

SIMPSON-ORLEBAR, HE Michael Keith Orlebar; CMG (1982); s of Aubrey Orlebar Simpson (d 1933), and Laura Violet, *née* Keith-Jones; *b* 5 Feb 1932; *Educ* Eton, ChCh Oxford (MA); *m* 19 April 1964, Rosita, da of Ignacio Duarte (d 1959); 2 s (Aubrey b 1965, Edward b 1966), 1 da (Charlotte b 1972); *Career* Nat Serv Lt KRRC 1950-51; Dip Serv 1954-: Tehran 1955-57, FO 1957- 62, Bogota 1962-65, FCO 1966-68, Paris 1969-72, Tehran 1972-76, FCO 1977-80, min Rome 1980-83, head Br Interest Section Tehran 1983-85; ambassador: Lisbon 1986-89, Mexico City 1989-; *Recreations* gardening, fishing; *Clubs* Travellers'; *Style*— HE Michael Simpson-Orlebar, CMG; British Embassy, Mexico City, Mexico (☎ 010 525 207 2089, 661191)

SIMS, Prof Andrew Charles Petter; s of Dr Charles Henry Sims, of Exeter, and Dr Norah Winnifred Kennan, *née* Petter; *b* 5 Nov 1938; *Educ* Monkton Combes Sch, Emmanuel Coll Cambridge, Westminster Med Sch London (MA, MB BChir, MD); *m* 25 April 1964, Ruth Marie, da of Dr John Cuthbert Harvey (d 1988), of Birmingham; 2 s (David b 1965, John b 1968), 2 da (Mary b 1966, Ann b 1970); *Career* house surgn Westminster Hosp 1963-64, registrar Manchester Royal Infirmary 1965-68, conslt psychiatrist All Saints Hosp Birmingham 1971-76, sr lectr and hon coslt psychiatrist Univ of Birmingham 1976-79, prof of psychiatry Univ of Leeds 1979-; pres RCPsych 1990- (dean 1987-90) FRCPsych 1979, RSM; *Books* Neurosis in Society (1983), Psychiatry CMT (1984), in Clinical Practice (1988); *Recreations* music, theatre, hill walking, gardening; *Clubs* Christian Medical Fellowship, RSM; *Style*— Prof Andrew Sims

SIMS, Bernard John; s of John Sims (d 1949), of London, and Minnie, *née* Everitt (d 1962); *b* 13 May 1915; *Educ* Wimbledon Coll London, LSE (LLB); *m* 27 April 1963, Elizabeth Margaret Eileen, da of Philip Edward Filbee (d 1960), of St Leonards on Sea, Sussex; *Career* WWII: RA 1940-42, RAOC 1942-45, SO HQ AA Cmd 1943-45, Capt 1944, SO Northumbrian Dist Northern Cmd 1945; slr 1938, lectr Law Soc's Sch of Law 1945-47, sr legal asst Bd of Inland Revenue 1947-53, legal advsr Indust and Commercial Fin Corp 1953-61, chief examiner and moderator Law Soc 1953-81; consult ed Encyclopaedia of Forms and Precedents 1965-; chm Editorial Bd: Simon's Taxes 1970-, Capital Taxes Encyclopeadia 1976-; Freeman: City of London 1951, Worshipful Co of Slrs; memb Law Soc 1938, FIT 1965; kt Cdr of the Equestrian Order of the Holy Sepulchre 1967; *Books* Controls on Company Finance (1958), Estate Duty Changes (1969), Capital Duty (1975), Halsbury's Laws of England (contrib, fourth edn 1983), UK Tax Guide 1990-91 (contrib ed chapter on stamp duties), and Sims on Stamp Duties (1988, and supplement 1990); *Recreations* music; *Clubs* City Livery, Lansdowne; *Style*— Bernard Sims, Esq; 89 Dovehouse St, Chelsea, London SW3 6JZ (☎ 071 352 1798)

SIMS, Frank; s of Frank Sims (d 1986), and Doris Elizabeth, *née* Hayes; *b* 21 July 1943; *Educ* Hitchin GS, Univ of Sheffield (BA); *m* 29 Oct 1966, Jean Caroline, da of Edward Francis Whitworth; 1 s (Richard b 1974), 1 da (Claire b 1972); *Career* CA BDO Binder Hamlyn; Freeman City of London 1977, memb Worshipful Co of Glovers; FCA 1970; *Recreations* golf, music, travel; *Clubs* Wig and Pen; *Style*— Frank Sims, Esq; 52 Russell Rd, Buckhurst Hill, Essex IG9 5QE (☎ 081 505 0019); BDO Binder Hamlyn, 20 Old Bailey, London EC4M 7BH (☎ 071 489 9000, fax 071 489 6060, telex 8812282)

SIMS, Frank Alexander; OBE (1986); s of Frank Howell Sims (d 1980), of Bognor Regis, and Mary, *née* Laidlaw; *b* 18 Jan 1932; *Educ* Chichester HS for Boys, Univ of Nottingham (BSc); *m* 11 June 1956, Kathleen Veronica, da of Rodney Vernon Fox-Kirk; 1 s (Anthony James Alexander b 15 Feb 1960), 1 da (Amanda Jane b 27 March 1957); *Career* Nat Serv 1955-57 sapper and OCTU trg 1955-56, Military garrison engr (West Kent Area) 1956-57; resident engr Corby Development Corporation 1954-55 (asst engr 1953-54), tech staff offr on attachment to Military experimental estab 1957; W Riding CC: asst bridge engr 1957-59, resident engr 1959-61, princ asst engr (Bridges) 1961-63, chief asst county engr (Bridges) 1963-68, superintending engr road construction sub-unit 1968-73; exec dir of engrg (chief offr) W Yorkshire Metropolitan CC 1973-86, chief exec Pell Frischmann Consultants Ltd 1986-; memb: Res Ctee on Bridges Road Research Laboratory, Bridge Design Ctee Miny of Transport, Computers in Construction Industry, Working Party Miny of Building and Public

Works, Reclamation and Waste Disposal Working Party Inst Municipal Engrs, Structural Codes Advsy Ctee IStructE, Advsy Ctee Dept of Civil & Structural Engrg Univ of Sheffield, Nat Steering Ctees & BSI Ctees on Eurocodes, Exec Ctee Inst of Highways and Transportation Yorkshire & Humberside; chm: BSI Steel Concrete Bridge Code Ctee, Structural Engrg Gp Bd; jt chm: Eurocode Advsy Panel ICE, Standing Ctee on Structural Safety; specialist advsr Assoc of Met Authorities, former chm Advsy Ctee Dept of Civil Engrg Univ of Leeds; Concrete Soc: fndr memb Yorkshire and Humberside Branch, former chm Prestressed Concrete Ctee, memb Int Panel, former memb Cncl, vice pres; winner Lewis Angell medal and prize Inst Municipal Engrs 1982; author of numerous technical papers concerning design construction and maintenance of highways & bridges, waste management and assoc subjects; FEng 1982, FICE, FIHT; fell: Inst of Municipal Engrs, Inst of Waste Mgmnt; *Recreations* gardening, DIY, music, walking, fishing, golf; *Style*— Frank Sims, Esq, OBE; Pell Frischmann Consultants Ltd, George House, George St, Wakefield, W Yorkshire WF1 1HL (☎ 0924 368145, fax 0924 376643)

SIMS, Prof Geoffrey Donald; OBE (1971); s of Albert Edward Hope Sims, and Jessie Elizabeth Sims; *b* 13 Dec 1926; *Educ* Wembley Co GS, Imperial Coll of Sci and Technol (BSc, MSc, PhD, DIC); *m* 9 April 1949, Pamela Audrey, da of Thomas Edwin Richings; 1 s (Graham b 12 Jan 1950), 2 da (Patricia b 7 Feb 1953, Anne b 16 Sept 1960); *Career* res physicist GEC Wembley 1948-54, seconded to work with Prof D Gabor (Nobel Laureate) Imperial Coll 1950-54, sr sci offr UKAEA Harwell, lectr (later sr lectr) Dept Electrical Engrg UCL 1956-63; Univ of Southampton: prof and head Dept Electronics 1963-74, dean Faculty of Engrg and Applied Sci 1967-70, sr dep vice chllr 1970-72; vice chllr Univ of Sheffield 1974-90; memb: Br Library Organising Ctee 1971-73, Annan Ctee on the Future of Broadcasting 1974-77; chm Engrg Advsy Ctee BBC 1981-90, vice chm Br Cncl Ctee Int Cooperation Higher Educn 1985- (memb 1981-), hon dep treas Assoc Commonwealth Univs 1983-90, memb Conf Euro Rectors Perm Ctee 1981-, pres Liaison Ctee Rectors Confs of Memb States of Euro Communities 1987-89; fell Midland Chapter Woodard Sch 1977-, Custos Worksop Coll 1984-, Guardian of the Standard of Wrought Plate within the Town of Sheffield 1984-, Capital Burgess Sheffield Church Burgesses Tst 1988-89 (memb 1984-); memb Royal Naval Engrg Coll Advsy Cncl 1988 (chm Res Ctee 1990-); Hon DSc Univ of Southampton 1980, Hon LLD Univ of Dundee 1987, Hon ScD Alleghany Coll 1989, Hon DSc Queens Univ Belfast 1990, Hon LLD Univ of Sheffield 1991; hon fell Sheffield City Poly 1990; Symons Medal ACU 1991; ARCS (physics) 1947, ARCS (mathematics) 1948, FIEE 1963, FEng 1980, FCGI 1980; *Books* Microwave Tubes and Semiconductor Devices (with I M Stephenson, 1963), Variational Techniques in Electromagnetism (1965); *Recreations* golf, travel, music; *Clubs* Athenaeum; *Style*— Prof Geoffrey Sims, OBE; North Leigh, 53 Sandygate Park Road, Sheffield S10 5TX (☎ 0742 303 113)

SIMS, George Frederick Robert; s of George Sims (d 1976), and Ada, *née* Harrison (d 1954); *b* 3 Aug 1923; *Educ* Lower Sch of John Lyon Harrow; *m* 7 Aug 1943, Beryl, *née* Simcock; 2 s (Christopher b 12 July 1944, Timothy b 25 June 1962), 1 da (Libda b 29 April 1947); *Career* Army Service Special Communications Unit No1 1942-47; author; jr reporter Press Association 1940-42, dealer in rare books 1947-87; books: The Terrible Door (1964), Sleep No More (1966), The Last Best Friend (1967), The Sand Dollar (1969), Deadhand (1971), Hunters Point (1973), The End of the Web (1976), Rex Mundi (1978), Who is Cato? (1981), The Keys of Death (1982), Coat of Arms (1984), The Rare Book Game (1985), More of the Rare Book Game (1988), Last of the Rare Book Game (1990); memb: Crime Writer's Assoc 1966, Detection Club 1989; *Recreations* swimming in warm seas, walking in the Hambleden Valley, watching people; *Style*— George Sims, Esq; Peacocks, Hurst, Berkshire RG10 0DR (☎ 0734 341030); c/o Giles Gordon, Anthony Sheil Ltd, 43 Doughty St, London WC1N 2LF

SIMS, Surgn Cdr Harrington; s of Enoch Sims (d 1940), and Mary Hannah, *née* Murphy (d 1963); *b* 13 April 1930; *Educ* Wath GS, Univ of Sheffield (MB ChB); *m* 4 July 1953, Joyce, da of Haydn Parkin (d 1987); 3 s (Christopher Martin, Andrew Jon, David Murray); *Career* permanent RN med serv 1955-74, advsr in genito-urinary med and dermatology to Dir Gen Naval Med Serv 1965-74; hon clinical lectr in genitourinary med Univ of Sheffield 1975-77, physician i/c Genito-Urinary Med Dept Norwich Health Authy 1977-; memb WM Navy Lodge London 1982-83, chm Norwich Conslt Staff 1988-89; FRCPE 1982; *Recreations* music (especially Elgar), history, gardening; *Clubs* Royal Overseas League; *Style*— Surgn Cdr Harrington Sims; Barleycorn, Old Brewery Lane, Reepham, Norwich NR10 4NE (☎ 0603 870722); N and N Hosp, Brunswick Rd, Norwich, Norfolk (☎ 0603 667369)

SIMS, John Haesaert Mancel; s of Capt Harold Mancel Sims (d 1958), of London, and Jeanie Emilie Anne, *née* Haesaert (d 1965); *b* 16 Dec 1929; *Educ* Highfield Sch Wandsworth, Brixton Sch of Bldg; *Career* Nat Serv RE 1948-50; various appts with quantity surveyors' firms in private practice 1950-73, sole princ in private practice as bldg contracts conslt; lectr writer and arbitrator 1973-, author of numerous articles on bldg contracts for Building 1975-89; Freeman City of London 1981, Liveryman Worshipful Co of Arbitrators 1982; ARICS 1954, FRICS 1967, FCIArb 1970; *Books* with Vincent Powell-Smith: Building Contract Claims (1983, 2 edn 1988), Contract Documentation for Contractors (1985, 2 edn 1990), Determination and Suspension of Construction Contracts (1985), The JCT Management Contract: A Practical Guide (1988), Construction Arbitrations (1989); *Recreations* classical music, choral singing, reading; *Clubs* Wig and Pen; *Style*— John H M Sims, Esq; 15 Cheyne Place, London SW3 4HH (☎ 071 353 0643); 7 Gray's Inn Square, London WC1R 5BG (☎ 071 242 0572, fax 071 404 0039)

SIMS, Monica Louie; OBE (1971); da of Albert Charles Sims (d 1959), of Gloucester, and Eva Elizabeth, *née* Preen; *Educ* Denmark Rd HS for Girls Gloucester, St Hugh's Coll Oxford (MA, LRAM, LGSM); *Career* tutor in English and drama Dept of Adult Educn Univ Coll of Hull 1947, educn tutor Nat Fedn of Women's Insts 1950; BBC: radio talks prodr 1953, TV prodr 1956, ed Women's Hour 1964, head of children's progs (TV) 1967, Controller Radio 4 1979, dir of progs (radio) 1983; dir of prodn Children's Film and Television Foundation 1985, vice pres Br Bd of Film Classification; memb Cncl Univ of Bristol; memb Building Socs Ombudsman Cncl; FRSA 1984; *Recreations* theatre, cinema, gardening; *Style*— Miss Monica Sims, OBE; 97 Gloucester Terrace, London W2 3HB (☎ 071 262 6291); Children's Film and Television Foundation, Goldcrest Elstree Studios, Boreham Wood, Herts WD6 1JG (☎ 081 953 0844, fax 081 207 0860, telex 922436 EFILMS G)

SIMS, Neville William; MBE (1974); s of William Ellis Sims (d 1954), of Whitchurch, Cardiff, and Ethel Stacey Colley, *née* Inman (d 1980); *b* 15 June 1933; *Educ* Penarth Co Sch; *m* 2 April 1964, Jennifer Ann, da of Horace George Warwick, of Rhiwbina, Cardiff; 2 s (Jeremy b 1971, Matthew b 1981), 2 da (Heather b 1973, Caroline b 1980); *Career* articles with T H Trump, qualified CA 1957; Ernst & Young: ptnr 1960-85, managing ptnr Cardiff Office 1974-84, ret 1985; conslt Watts Gregory & Daniel 1986-, dir Compact Cases Ltd Caerphilly 1986-89; chm: Wales Area Young Cons 1960-63, Barry Cons Assoc 1962-72, Govrs Howell's Sch Llandoff Cardiff 1981-; hon treas: YWCA Centre Cardiff 1963-70, Cardiff Central Cons Assoc 1987-; pres S Wales Soc of CAs 1977-78; memb Cncl: ICAEW 1981-, AAT 1989-; memb Welsh Regnl Bd Homeowners Friendly Soc 1984-88; FICA; *Recreations* theatre, music, gardening, walking; *Clubs* Cardiff Business, Cardiff and County; *Style*— Neville Sims, Esq, MBE; The Chimes, 15 Westminster Crescent, Cyncoed, Cardiff CF2 6SE (☎ 0222 753424, fax 0222 383022)

SIMS, Roger Edward; MP (C) Chislehurst 1974-; s of Herbert William Sims (d 1981), of Chislehurst, and Annie Amy, *née* Savidge (d 1987); *b* 27 Jan 1930; *Educ* City Boys' GS Leicester, St Olave's GS Tower Bridge London; *m* 15 June 1957, Angela, da of John Robert Mathews (d 1951), of Chislehurst; 2 s (Matthew Robert b 31 March 1962, Toby Edward b 27 July 1966), 1 da (Virginia Claire b 29 May 1959); *Career* Campbell Booker Carter Ltd 1953-62, advsr Dodwell & Co Ltd 1974-90 (dept mangr 1962-74), dir Inchcape International Ltd 1981-90; memb Chislehurst and Sidcup UDC 1956-62, JP Bromley 1960-72, chm Juvenile Court 1970-72, PPS to Home Sec 1979-83, vice chm Cons Health Ctee; chm 1912 Club; memb: Central Exec Ctee NSPCC 1980- (pres Bromley and Dist Branch), Gen Med Cncl 1989-; *Recreations* swimming, singing (Royal Choral Soc); *Clubs* Bromley Cons; *Style*— Roger Sims, Esq, MP; House of Commons, London SW1A 0AA (☎ 071 219 5000/4404)

SIMSON, Peregrine Anthony Litton; s of Brig Ernest Clive Litton Simson, of Aston Rowant, Oxon, and Daphne Camilla Marian, *née* Todhunter (d 1985); *b* 10 April 1944; *Educ* Charterhouse, Worcester Coll Oxford (BA); *m* 6 May 1967 (m dis 1979), Caroline Basina, da of Frank Hosier (d 1965), of Wexcombe Manor, Marlborough, Wilts; 1 s (Christian Edward Litton b 9 April 1970), 1 da (Camilla Basina Litton b 12 July 1972); *Career* slr; ptnr: Clifford-Turner 1972-87, Clifford Chance (merged firm of Clifford Turner and Coward Chance) 1987-; Liveryman Worshipful Co of Slrs 1974; memb Law Soc 1970; *Recreations* shooting, tennis, travel; *Clubs* City, Hurlingham, Annabel's; *Style*— Peregrine Simson, Esq; Corn Hall, Bures St Mary, Suffolk; 59 Waterford Rd, London SW6; Clifford Chance, Blackfriars House, 19 New Bridge St, London EC4V 6BY (☎ 071 353 0211)

SINCLAIR; *see*: Alexander-Sinclair

SINCLAIR, Lady (Margaret) Alison; raised to the rank of an Earl's da 1948; 3 da of Rev Canon the Hon Charles Augustus Sinclair (d 1944, s of 16 Earl of Caithness), and Mary Ann, *née* Harman (d 1938); *b* 29 Nov 1910; *Style*— The Lady Alison Sinclair; Wych Elm, Kennington, Oxford (☎ 0865 735856)

SINCLAIR, Dr Allan; s of Henry Williamson Sinclair (d 1988), of Glasgow, and Mary, *née* Turner (d 1955); *b* 9 Oct 1929; *Educ* Perth Academy, Hillhead HS Glasgow, Univ of Glasgow (MB ChB); *m* 4 Sept 1961, Isobel Alexander, da of John McCowan Stevenson (d 1987), of Hamilton; 3 s (John b 1962, Allan b 1965, Martin b 1968); *Career* Capt RAMC 1954-56; sr registrar and conslt in psychiatry St Andrews Hosp Northampton 1960-68, conslt in psychiatry Lanarkshire Health Bd 1968; former chm: Lanarkshire Div of Psychiatry, Med Staff Assoc Monklands Hosp; elder Hamilton Old Parish Church; FRCPGlas 1976, FRCPsych 1987; *Recreations* fishing, golf, classical literature; *Clubs* Hamilton Golf, New Club St Andrews, Bothwell & Blantyre Angling; *Style*— Dr Allan Sinclair; Monklands District General Hospital, Airdrie, Lanarkshire (☎ 0236 69344)

SINCLAIR, Dr Andrew Annandale; s of Stanley Charles Sinclair CBE, (d 1973), and Kathleen, *née* Nash-Webber; *b* 21 Jan 1935; *Educ* Eton, Trinity Coll Cambridge, Harvard Univ, Columbia Univ; *m* 1, (m dis 1971), Marianne Alexandre; 1 s (Timon Alexandre); m 2, (m dis 1984), Miranda Seymour; 1 s (Merlin George); m 3, 25 July 1984, Sonia, Lady Melchett; *Career* Ensign Coldstream Gds 1953-55; ed and publisher Lorrimer Publishing 1968-87, md Timon Films 1968-; FRSL 1970, FSAH 1970; *Books* novels: The Breaking of Bumbo (1957), My Friend Judas (1958), The Project (1960), The Hallelujah Bum (1963), The Raker (1964), Gog (1967), Magog (1972), A Patriot for Hire (1978), The Facts in the Case of E A Poe (1980), Beau Bumbo (1985), King Ludd (1988); non-fiction: Prohibition The Era of Excess (1962), The Available Man The Life Behind the Mask of Warren Gamaliel Harding (1965), The Better Half The Emancipation of the American Woman (1965), A Concise History of the United States (1967), The Last of the Best The Aristocracy of Europe in the Twentieth Century (1969), Che Guevara (1970), Dylan Thomas Poet of His People (1975), The Savage A History of Misunderstanding (1977), Jack A Biography of Jack London (1977), John Ford (1979), Corsair The Life of J Pierpont Morgan (1981), The Other Victoria The Princess Royal and the Great Game of Europe (1981), The Red and the Blue (1986), Speigel (1987), War Like a Wasp (1989), The War Decade (1989), The Need to Give the Patrons and the Arts (1990); *Recreations* visiting ruins; *Clubs* Groucho's; *Style*— Dr Andrew Sinclair; 16 Tite St, London SW3 4HZ (☎ 071 352 7645)

SINCLAIR, Hon Angus John; s of 1 Viscount Thurso, KT, CMG, PC (d 1970); *b* 1925; *Educ* Eton, New Coll Oxford; *m* 1, 1955 (m dis 1967), Pamela Karen, da of Dallas Bower; m 2, 1968, Judith Anne Percy; 1 s; *Career* WWII Lt Scots Gds 1944-47, NW Europe 1945; BBC 1950-54, Nigerian Bdcasting Corp 1954-58, Central Office of Info 1959-85, Br Cncl 1985-90, dir Universal Aunts Ltd 1990-; memb Brain Damage Res Tst 1990-; author: poetry, radio features; *Clubs* Pratt's; *Style*— The Hon Angus Sinclair; 19 The Chase, London SW4

SINCLAIR, Lady Bridget Ellinor; da (by 1 m) of late 6 Earl Fortescue; *b* 1927; *m* 1952, Wing Cdr Gordon Leonard Sinclair, DFC; 2 s (Alan b 1956, Robert b 1965), 2 da (Fiona (Mrs Julian Smith) b 1958, Joanna b 1963); *Style*— The Lady Bridget Sinclair; Fairwood House, Great Durnford, Salisbury, Wiltshire SP4 6BD (☎ 0980 623372)

SINCLAIR, Charles James Francis; s of Sir George Evelyn Sinclair, CMG, OBE, of Carlton Rookery, Saxmundham, Suffolk, and Katharine Jane, *née* Burdekin (d 1971); *b* 4 April 1948; *Educ* Winchester, Magdalen Coll Oxford (BA); *m* 1974, Nicola, da of Maj W R Bayliss, RM; 2 s (Jeremy b 1977, Robert b 1979); *Career* CA 1974; Dearden Farrow CAs London 1970-75, fin accountant Assoc Newspaper Gp 1975; Assoc Newspapers Hldgs plc: asst md 1986, dep md 1987, md 1988, md and gp chief exec Daily Mail and Gen Tst plc 1989; non-exec dir Schroders PLC 1990-; chm tstees Minack Theatre Tst (Porthcurno Cornwall); FCA 1980; *Recreations* opera, fishing, skiing; *Clubs* The Athenaeum, Vincents; *Style*— Charles Sinclair, Esq; Northcliffe House, 2 Derry St, London W8 5TT (☎ 071 938 6614, fax 071 938 3909)

SINCLAIR, 17 Lord (S *c* 1449, confirmed 1488-9); Charles Murray Kennedy St Clair; LVO (1953); s of 16 Lord Sinclair, MVO, JP (d 1957); 1 Lord resigned the Earldoms of Orkney and Caithness to the crown 1470, 10 Lord obtained Charter under Gt Seal 1677 confirming his honours with remainders to male heirs whatsoever; *b* 21 June 1914; *Educ* Eton, Magdalene Coll Cambridge; *m* 1968, Anne Lettice, da of Sir Richard Cotterell, 5 Bt, CBE, TD; 1 s, 2 da (Hon Laura b 1972, Hon Annabel b 1973); *Heir* s, Master of Sinclair b 9 Dec 1968; *Career* Maj Coldstream Gds; memb Queen's Body Guard for Scotland (Royal Co of Archers), Portcullis Pursuivant of Arms 1949-57, York Herald 1957-68, hon genealogist to Royal Victorian Order 1960-68, an extra equerry to HM Queen Elizabeth The Queen Mother 1953-; Lord-Lieut Dumfries and Galloway (Dist of Stewartry) 1982-89 (Vice Lord-Lieut 1977-82, DL Kirkcudbrights 1969), rep peer for Scotland 1959-63; *Clubs* New (Edinburgh); *Style*— The Rt Hon the Lord Sinclair, LVO; Knocknalling, St John's Town of Dalry, Castle Douglas, Kirkcudbrightshire DG7 3ST (☎ 064 43 221)

SINCLAIR, Sir Clive Marles; s of George William Carter Sinclair, and Thora Edith Ella, *née* Marles; *b* 30 July 1940; *Educ* Highgate Sch, St George's Coll Weybridge; *m*

1962 (m dis 1985), Ann, *née* Trevor Briscoe; 2 s, 1 da; *Career* ed Bernards (publishers) 1958-61, chm Sinclair Res Ltd 1979- (Sinclair Radionics 1962-79, produced pocket TV), fndr Sinclair Browne (publishers) 1981 (annual Sinclair Prize for fiction); visiting fell Robinson Coll Cambridge; chm: Br MENSA, Cambridge Computer Ltd 1986-; Hon DSc: Bath 1983, Warwick 1983, Heriot Watt 1983; hon fell: Imperial Coll of Sci and Technol 1984, UMIST 1984; Mullard award Royal Soc 1984; kt 1983; *Publications* Practical Transistor Receivers (1959), British Semiconductor Survey (1963); *Recreations* music, poetry, mathematics, science; *Clubs* Chelsea Arts; *Style*— Sir Clive Sinclair; 18 Shepherd House, 5 Shepherd St, London W1Y 7LD (☎ 071 408 0199)

SINCLAIR, David Grant; s of Leslie Sinclair (d 1978), of London, and Beatrice Zena, *née* Samuel (d 1979); *b* 12 Feb 1948; *Educ* Latymer Upper Sch; *m* 7 June 1970, Susan Carol, da of Alexander Merkin (d 1963), of London; 2 s (Alexander James b 1972, Julian Lloyd b 1974); 1 da (Olivia Lesley b 1982); *Career* fndr and sr ptnr Sinclair Roth 1972-, exec chm Summer International plc 1987-; non-exec chm Master Financial Services Ltd; recognised expert in forensic accounting; ACA 1972, FCA 1978; *Recreations* charity work; *Style*— David G Sinclair, Esq; Suite 15, Third Floor, Morley House, 320 Regent St, London W1R 5AE (☎ 071 636 8621 and 071 431 0911, fax 071 636 7236 and 071 794 3707, car 0836 261691)

SINCLAIR, Eldon McCuaig; s of Maj Charles Eldon Sinclair, MC (d 1956), of Toronto, Canada, and Margaret, *née* McCuaig (d 1929); *b* 13 March 1928; *Educ* Upper Canada Coll, Trinity Coll Sch, Univ of Toronto (BASC); *m* 13 Feb 1970, Judith Ellen, da of Albert Rule (d 1965), of Toronto, Canada; 1 s (Joseph McCuaig b 1974); *Career* Unilever: int mgmnt trainee UK and Canada 1950-52, brand mangr Canada 1952-54; Leo Burnett Co Inc (advtg): account exec Canada 1954-56, vice pres account supervisor USA 1956-58, pres in Canada 1958-65, chm and md UK 1965-70, exec vice pres int 1970-73; EM Sinclair Conslts Ltd 1974-86; chm and md UK Storwal Int Inc 1986-; memb Bd govrs: Lockers Park Sch Herts, Trinity Coll Sch; chm Dunford Novelists Assoc, memb Exec Ctee Southern Writers Assoc; *Recreations* field sports, writing; *Clubs* Denham GC; *Style*— Eldon Sinclair, Esq; 16 Chester St, London SW1 (☎ 071 235 4177); Storwal International Home Park, Kings Langley, Herts WD4 8LZ (☎ 092 326 0411, fax 092 326 7136, telex 923273 ELMAR G)

SINCLAIR, Sir George Evelyn; CMG (1956), OBE (1950); s of Francis Sinclair (d 1953), of Chynance, St Buryan, Cornwall; *b* 6 Nov 1912; *Educ* Abingdon Sch, Pembroke Coll Oxford (MA); *m* 1, 1941, Katharine Jane (d 1971), da of Beauford Burdekin (d 1963), of Sydney, NSW, and Mrs K P Burdekin (d 1964), of The Firs, Marlesford, Suffolk; 1 s, 3 da; m 2, 1972, Mary Violet, wid of G L Sawday; *Career* WWII RWAFF (W Africa) 1940-43, temp Maj; entered Colonial Serv 1936, Gold Coast 1936-40, Colonial Office 1943-45, sec Elliot Cmmn on Higher Educn in W Africa 1943-45, Gold Coast 1945-55, regnl offr Trans-Volta Togoland 1952-55, dep govr Cyprus 1955-60, ret 1961; political work in UK and overseas 1960-64; memb Wimbledon Borough Cncl 1962-65; MP (C) Dorking 1964-1979; dir Intermediate Technol Devpt Gp 1979-82 (vice pres 1966-79), fndr tstee Physically Handicapped & Able Bodied; fndr memb Human Rights Tst 1971-74, memb Bd Christian Aid 1973-78; memb Cncl: Oxford Soc 1982-, Overseas Servs Resettlement Bureau; memb Assoc of Governing Bodies of Public Schs (chm 1979-84); memb Bd of Govrs: Abingdon Sch 1971-88 (chm 1973-80), Felixstowe Coll 1980-87, Campian Sch Athens 1983-; chm Independent Schs Jt Cncl 1980-83, tstee Runnymede Trust 1969-75; conslt: UN Fund for Population Affrs, Int Planned Parenthood Fedn; special advsr Global Ctee of Parliamentarians on Population and Devpt; chm UK Consultative Ctee for Oxford Conf of Global Forum of Spiritual and Parly Ldrs on Human Survival 1988; hon fell Pembroke Coll Oxford; kt 1960; *Recreations* golf, fishing; *Clubs* Athenaeum, Royal Cwlth Soc; *Style*— Sir George Sinclair, CMG, OBE; Carlton Rookery, Saxmundham, Suffolk IP17 2NN (☎ 0728 602217)

SINCLAIR, Sir Ian McTaggart; KCMG (1977, CMG 1972), QC (1979); s of John Sinclair (d 1950), of Whitecraigs, Renfrewshire, and Margaret Wilson Gardner, *née* Love (d 1965); *b* 14 Jan 1926; *Educ* Merchiston Castle Sch, King's Coll Cambridge (BA, LLB); *m* 24 April 1954, Barbara Elizabeth, da of Stanley Lenton (d 1982), of Grimsby; 2 s (Andrew b 1958, Philip b 1962), 1 da (Jane b 1956); *Career* Intelligence Corps 1944-47; called to the Bar Middle Temple 1952 (bencher 1980); entered Dip Serv 1950; legal cnsllr: NY and Washington 1964-67, FCO 1967-71; dep legal advsr FCO 1971-72, second legal advsr 1973-75, legal advsr 1976-84; barr 1984-; memb Int Law Cmmn 1981-86; assoc memb Institut de Droit Int 1983-87 (memb 1987-); FRGS 1987; *Books* Vienna Convention on the Law of Treaties (1973, 2 edn 1984), International Law Commission (1987); *Recreations* golf, bird-watching, reading; *Clubs* Athenaeum; *Style*— Sir Ian Sinclair, KCMG, QC; 2 Hare Court, Temple, London EC4Y 7BH (☎ 071 583 1770, telex 27193 LINLAW)

SINCLAIR, Jeremy; s of Donald Alan Forrester Sinclair (d 1987), of London; *b* 4 Nov 1946; *m* Jan 1976, Jacqueline Margaret, da of Jack Metcalfe; 2 s (Leon b 21 Oct 1981, David b 13 March 1985), 1 da (Naomi b 26 Jan 1979); *Career* dir Saatchi and Saatchi 1970-; *Style*— Jeremy Sinclair, Esq; Saatchi & Saatchi, Berkeley Square, London W1A 4NX (☎ 071 495 5000, fax 071 495 4717)

SINCLAIR, Kenneth Brian; s of Joseph Frederick Sinclair, and May, *née* Haddon; *b* 14 March 1931; *Educ* Heath Clark Sch Croydon; *m* 5 Jan 1957, Yvonne Joan, da of Walter Henry Tucker; 1 s (Keith Andrew Brian b 1 May 1960); *Career* Eagle Star Insur 1949-54, investmt offr NCB 1954, managing ptnr David A Bevan Simpson 1960-70 (joined 1954), exec ptnr de Zoete and Bevan 1974 (ptnr 1963, managing ptnr 1969), chm Barclays de Zoete Wedd Securities Ltd 1988-, dir Barclays Bank plc 1988, vice chm BZW Hldgs Ltd 1990; *Recreations* bridge, chess, football; *Clubs* City of London, Gresham; *Style*— Kenneth Sinclair, Esq; Hedley, High Drive, Woldingham, Surrey (☎ 0883 6503240); Barclays de Zoete Wedd Ltd, Ebbgate House, 2 Swan Lane, London EC4R 3TS (☎ 071 623 2323, fax 071 895 1525, telex 917102 BZWGLT G)

SINCLAIR, Air Vice-Marshal Sir Laurence Frank; GC (1941), KCB (1957, CB 1946), CBE (1943), DSO (1940, bar 1943); s of late Frank Sinclair, Nigerian Political Serv; *b* 1908; *Educ* ISC, RAF Coll Cranwell; *m* 1941, Valerie (d 1990), da of Lt-Col Joseph Dalton White; 1 s (Mark), 1 da (Susan); *Career* Sqdn Ldr 1938, CO No 110 (Blenheim) Sqdn 1940, CO RAF Watton 1941, CO No 324 Wing N Africa 1943, Gp Capt 1943-44, ADC to the King 1943-49, AOC Tactical Bomber Force, MAAF, SASO, Balkan Air Force, 1944, AOC No 2 Gp BAFO 1949-50, asst cmdt RAF Staff Coll Bracknell 1950; cmdt: RAF Coll Cranwell 1950-52, Sch of Land-Air Warfare Old Sarum 1952-53; Air Vice-Marshal 1952, asst chief of air staff (ops) 1953-55, AOC Br Forces Arabian Peninsula 1955-57, cmdt Jt Servs Staff Coll 1958, ret 1960; controller: Ground Servs Miny Aviation 1960-61, Nat Air Traffic Control Servs 1962-66; Legion of Merit USA 1943, Légion d'Honneur France 1944, Partisan Star with gold leaves (Yugoslavia); *Recreations* fishing; *Clubs* RAF; *Style*— Air Vice-Marshal Sir Laurence Sinclair, GC, KCB, CBE, DSO; Haines Land, Great Brickhill, Bucks

SINCLAIR, Dr Leonard; s of Sidney Sinclair (d 1973), of London, and Blanche, *née* Appele (d 1988); *b* 23 Sept 1928; *Educ* Rochelle Sch, Raine's Fndn Sch, Middx Hosp Med Sch Univ of London (Neyerstein scholar, James McIntosh scholar, BSc, MB BS, Lyell Gold medal, Football colours); *m* 22 March 1959, Ann, da of Frederick Franks; 1 da (Judith b 19 Dec 1959), 3 s (Jonathan b 30 Oct 1962, David b 5 Feb 1964, Anthony b 27 Aug 1979); *Career* house surgn and house physician: Southend Gen Hosp 1954-56, Queen Elizabeth Hosp for Children 1956-57 (med registrar 1960-62); house physician Whittington Hosp 1957, jr lectr and hon registrar Guy's Hosp Med Sch 1957-60, sr paediatric registrar Westminster & Westminster Children's Hosp 1962-66, hon conslt paediatrician Hosp of St John & St Elizabeth 1965-; conslt paediatrician: St Stephen's Hosp 1966-88, Westminster Hosp 1973-, Royal Nat Throat Nose & Ear Hosp 1969-, Westminster Children's Hosp 1988-, Charing Cross Hosp 1988; New Heath Tst fell 1959-61; visiting prof: Mount Sinai Hosp 1969, St Sophia's Children's Hosp Univ of Rotterdam 1983, hon sr lectr Faculty of Med Univ Coll London 1984; dep pres Paediatric Section RSM 1974-75 (sec Paediatric Section 1971-73); DCH 1957, FRCP 1974 (MRCP 1960), FRSM 1966, memb BPA 1968, fell Soc for Endocrinology 1968, memb BMA 1969; *Books* Metabolic Disease in Childhood (1979), Enfermedades Metabolicas en la Infancia (1981), BMA Complete Family Health Encyclopedia (paediatric section, 1990); *Recreations* tennis, old books, other people's problems; *Style*— Dr Leonard Sinclair; 34 Armitage Rd, London NW11 8RD (☎ 081 458 6464); 152 Harley St, London W1 (☎ 071 935 3834); Westminster Children's Hosp, Vincent Square, London SW1P 2NS (☎ 081 746 8000); Charing Cross Hosp (☎ 081 846 1306)

SINCLAIR, Master of; Hon Matthew Murray Kennedy St Clair; s and h of 17 Lord Sinclair, MVO; *b* 9 Dec 1968; *Style*— The Master of Sinclair

SINCLAIR, Lady (Euphemia) Meredith; raised to the rank of an Earl's da 1948; da of Rev the Hon Charles Augustus Sinclair (d 1943; s of 16 Earl of Caithness), and Marianne Sinclair (d 1938); *b* 22 Oct 1915; *Career* SRN; *Style*— The Lady Meredith Sinclair; The Old Exchange, 13 Station Road, Wheatley, Oxon OX9 1ST (☎ 08677 3876)

SINCLAIR, Michael David Bradley; s of Francis Sinclair (d 1989), and Edna, *née* Bradley; *b* 16 April 1942; *Educ* Repton; *m* 24 April 1962, Judith Margaret, da of Graham Allen, of Chartley Manor, Stowe by Chartley, Staffordshire; 1 s (Adam), 2 da (Victoria, Jessica); *Career* Capt TA 1964-72; dir Mulberry Hall (fine china and crystal specialists) 1962-; chm York City FC 1979- (dir 1977-), chm 3 and 4 divs Football League 1989-, dir and memb Mgmnt Ctee Football League Ltd 1989-; memb Merchant Adventurers Co York; *Recreations* hill-walking; *Style*— Michael Sinclair, Esq; Mulberry Hall, Stonegate, York YO1 2AW (☎ 0904 620736, fax 0904 620251)

SINCLAIR, Hon Patrick James; s of 2 Viscount Thurso; *b* 1954; *m* 1974 (m dis), Carol North; 2 s; also has issue, 1 da (Celeste); *Style*— The Hon Patrick Sinclair; Archway Cottage, Thurso East, Thurso, Caithness KW14 8HW

SINCLAIR, Sir Patrick Robert Richard; 10 Bt (NS 1704), of Dunbeath, Caithness; s of Alexander Robert Sinclair (d 1972, bro of 8 Bt), and Mabel Vera, *née* Baxendale (d 1981); suc his cousin, Sir John Rollo Norman Blair Sinclair, 9 Bt (d 1990); *b* 21 May 1936; *Educ* Winchester, Oriel Coll Oxford (MA); *m* 1974, Susan Catherine Beresford, eldest da of Geoffrey Clive Davies, OBE, of Greenshaw Holbrook, Ipswich, Suffolk; 1 s (William Robert Francis b 1979), 1 da (Helen Margaret Gwendolen b 1984); *Heir* s, William Robert Francis Sinclair b 1979; *Career* RNVR; called to the Bar Lincoln's Inn 1961; *Style*— Sir Patrick Sinclair, Bt; 1 New Square, Lincoln's Inn, London WC2 (☎ 071 242 7427); 5 New Square, Lincoln's Inn, London WC2 (☎ 071 404 0404)

SINCLAIR, Roderick John (Rod); s of Maj-Gen Sir John Sinclair, KCMG, OBE (d 1977), and Lady Esme Beatrice, *née* Sopwith (d 1983); *b* 10 July 1944; *Educ* Gordonstoun; *m* 1, (m dis 1976), Lucinda Mary Martin-Smith; m 2, 15 May 1977, Sarah Margaret, da of Brig Harold Dolphin; 1 s (James Alexander b 1984), 1 da (Natasha Esme b 1982); *Career* short serv cmmn Scots Gds 1963-66; stockbroker L Messel & Co 1969-77, ptnr De Zoete & Bevan 1977-85, dir Barclays De Zoete Wedd Securities Ltd 1985-; chm: Brokerservices Ltd 1987-88, Thamesway Investment Services 1987-; memb Int Stock Exchange 1978; *Recreations* tennis, skiing; *Clubs* Boodles; *Style*— Rod Sinclair, Esq; Downgate Farm, Steep Marsh, Petersfield, Hants GU32 2BP (☎ 0730 63321); Thamesway Investment Service, 21 Garlick Hill, London EC4V 2AU (☎ 071 357 7621, fax 071 357 7750, telex 927491)

SINCLAIR, Ronald Iain; RD (1970); s of Alexander Sinclair (d 1974), of Hamilton, and Margaret Neto, *née* Bell; *b* 21 Dec 1936; *Educ* Hamilton Acad; *m* 7 June 1965, Dorothy Buckley, da of Rev Alexander Marshall (d 1984), of Motherwell; 3 s (Colin b 1966, Alistair b 1968, Stephen b 1971); *Career* Lt Cdr RNR, resigned 1981; co sec Marshall & Anderson Ltd Motherwell 1964-79, princ shareholder following mgmnt buyout Herd & Mackenzie 1985 (joined 1981); pres Moray Soc Elgin, sr vice pres Rotary Club Buckie, elder St Giles Parish Church Elgin; FSA Scotland 1978; *Recreations* sailing, local history, amateur dramatics, photography; *Style*— Ronald Sinclair, Esq, RD; Cora Linn, 8 Seafield Crescent, Elgin, Moray IV30 1RE (☎ 0542 31245, fax 0542 31825, telex 73684)

SINCLAIR, Sonia Elizabeth; *née* Graham; da of late Col Roland Harris Graham, RAMC (ret), and Kathleen Graham (d 1983), of the Lodge, Bridge, Kent; *m* 1, 1947, 3 Baron Melchett (d 1973); 1 s, 2 da; m 2, 1984, Dr Andrew Annandale Sinclair, historian and writer; 2 step s; *Career* novelist and travel writer; JP for 10 years; memb: exec NSPCC for 7 years, cncl Royal Court Theatre, Nat Theatre 1983-; *Recreations* travelling, reading; *Style*— Mrs Andrew Sinclair; 16 Tite St, Chelsea, London SW3 (☎ 071 352 7645)

SINCLAIR, Thomas Humphrey; s of William Sinclair Boston (d 1972), and Jean, *née* Matthews; *b* 17 Aug 1938; *Educ* Oundle, RAC Cirencester; *m* 1, (m dis 1970), Sheila Kyle, *née* Davies; m 2, 30 May 1970, Ann Pauline, da of Flt Lt Harold Rowson (d 1983); 2 s (Michael, John); *Career* Nat Serv 1958-60; chm William Sinclair Holdings plc 1984- (md 1978); FInstD, FNIAB; *Recreations* golf, tennis; *Style*— Thomas Sinclair, Esq; Wyberton, Boston, Lincs; Vale-Do-Lobo, Algarve, Portugal; WM Sinclair Holdings plc, Firth Rd, Lincoln (☎ 0522 537 561, fax 0522 513 609, telex 56367)

SINCLAIR, Walter Isaac; s of Leonard Sinclair, of London, and Hilda, *née* Rosen; *b* 29 May 1934; *Educ* Hendon County GS; *m* 1 Nov 1964, Margaret Susan, da of Robert Ernest Halle; 1 s (Julian Bernard b 8 May 1966), 2 da (Debra Eleanor b 17 July 1968, Emma Louise b 14 Aug 1971); *Career* articled clerk Bernard Philips & Co (later Newman Harris & Co) 1953-59, sr Fuller Wise Fisher & Co (later Fuller Jenks Beecroft & Co) 1960-66; ptnr: Blick Rothenberg 1967-76, Kidsons (later Kidsons Impey) 1976-90; numerous contribs to nat pubns; FCA; *Books* Allied Dunbar Tax Guide (19 edns), Allied Dunbar Capital Taxes and Estate Planning Guide (5 edns), Allied Dunbar Business Tax and Law Guide (2 edns); *Recreations* bridge, tennis, classical music, theatre; *Style*— Walter Sinclair, Esq; 81 Wembley Park Drive, Wembley Park, Middx HA9 8HE (☎ 081 902 2394, fax 081 903 7691)

SINCLAIR-LOCKHART, Sir Simon John Edward Francis; 15 Bt (NS 1636), of Murkle Co Caithness, and Stevenson, Co Haddington; s of Sir Muir Edward Sinclair-Lockhart, 14 Bt (d 1985); *b* 22 July 1941; *m* 1973, Felicity Edith, da of late Ivan Lachlan Campbell Stewart, of Havelock North, NZ; 2 s (Robert Muir b 1973, James Lachlan (twin) b 1973), 1 da (Fiona Mary b 1979); *Heir* s, Robert Muir Sinclair-Lockhart; *Style*— Sir Simon Sinclair-Lockhart, Bt; 54 Duart Rd, Havelock North, New Zealand

SINCLAIR-LOCKHART, Winifred, Lady; Winifred Ray (Graham); da of late Tom Ray Cavaghan, of Aglionby Grange, Carlisle; *m* 1949, Sir John Beresford Sinclair-

Lockhart, 13 Bt (d 1970); *Style*— Winifred, Lady Sinclair-Lockhart; 17 Chiltern Close, Crown Lane, Benson, Oxon

SINCLAIR OF CLEVE, 3 Baron (UK 1957); John Lawrence Robert Sinclair; o s of 2 Baron (d 1985), and Lady Sinclair of Cleve, *née* Patricia Hellyer; *b* 6 Jan 1953; *Educ* Winchester Coll, Bath Univ, Manchester Univ; *Heir* none; *Career* craft, design and technol; workshop technician in an Inner London Comprehensive Sch; teaching support staff rep on sch bd of govrs 1985-; *Recreations* mime, motorcycling, music; *Clubs* Scala Cinema; *Style*— Rt Hon Lord Sinclair of Cleve; c/o The Royal Bank of Scotland, Holt's Branch, Kirkland House, Whitehall, London SW1

SINCLAIR, YOUNGER OF ULBSTER, Hon John Archibald; s and h of 2 Viscount Thurso; *b* 10 Sept 1953; *Educ* Eton; *m* 1976, Marion Ticknor, da of Louis D Sage, of Connecticut, USA; 2 s (James Alexander Robin b 14 Jan 1984, George Henry MacDonald b 29 Oct 1989), 1 da (Louisa Ticknor Beaumont b 1980); *Career* mangr Lancaster Hotel (Paris, part of the Savoy Gp) 1981-85, dir SA Lancaster 1983-85, vice-chm Prestige Hotels 1984-89, gen mangr Cliveden Bucks for Blakeney Hotels 1985-; dir Cliveden House Ltd 1987-; *Style*— The Hon John Sinclair, younger of Ulbster; Cliveden, Taplow, Berks SL6 0JF

SINDEN, Donald Alfred; CBE (1979); s of Alfred Edward Sinden (d 1972), and Mabel Agnes, *née* Fuller (d 1959); *b* 9 Oct 1923; *Educ* Webber-Douglas Sch of Dramatic Art; *m* 3 May 1948, Diana, da of Daniel Mahony (d 1981); 2 s (Jeremy b 14 June 1950, Marcus b 9 May 1954); *Career* TV, film and stage actor; first stage performance 1942; Rank Orgn 1952-60 appearing in 23 films incl: Doctor in the House, The Cruel Sea; RSC 1963-, assoc artist RSC 1967-; TV series include: Two's Company, Never the Twain, Discovering English Churches; Drama Desk award (for London Assurance) 1974, Variety Club of GB Best Stage Actor 1976, Evening Standard Drama award 1977 (for King Lear); pres: Fedn of Playgoers Socs 1968-, Royal Theatrical Fund 1983-, Theatre Museum Assoc 1985-; tstee Br Actors Equity Assoc 1988-; FRSA; *Books* A Touch of the Memoirs (autobiog, 1982), Laughter in the Second Act (autobiog, 1985), The Everyman Book of Theatrical Anecdotes (ed, 1987), The English Country Church (1988); *Recreations* serendipity; *Clubs* Garrick (tstee), Beefsteak, MCC; *Style*— Donald Sinden, Esq, CBE; 60 Temple Fortune Lane, London NW11 7UE

SINDEN, Jeremy Mahony; s of Donald Sinden, CBE, of London, and Diana, *née* Mahony; *b* 14 June 1950; *Educ* Lancing, LAMDA; *m* 1 July 1978, Delia Ann Patricia, da of P A R Lindsay, of West Orchard, Dorset; 2 da (Kezia b 18 Dec 1979, Harriet b 1 July 1984); *Career* actor; TV incl: The Expert, Brideshead Revisited, Danger UXB, The Far Pavillions, Fairly Secret Army, Have His Carcase (Dorothy L Sayers), After The War, Square Deal, Fortunes of War, Virtuoso; theatre incl: RSC 1969-72, Lady Harry (Savoy Theatre), Spin of the Wheel (Comedy Theatre), Bless the Bride (Sadler's Wells Theatre), The Chiltern Hundreds (on tour), Conduct Unbecoming (on tour), French Without Tears (Greenwich Theatre and tour), The Winslow Boy (on tour as dir), The Jungle Book (Adelphi Theatre), The Philanthropist (Chichester), John Bull's Other Island (Cambridge Theatre Co, on tour), Mother Goose (Leatherhead), Semi Monde (Royalty Theatre), An Ideal Husband (Touor and West End - produced), Sunsets and Glories (West Yorkshire Playhouse); films incl: Star Wars, Chariots of Fire, Madame Sousatzka, Object of Beauty, Let Him Have It (1990); chm Catchfavour Ltd (prodn co); cncllr: Br Actors' Equity Assoc 1980-84, Actors Benevolent Fund 1984-; tstee Evelyn Norris Tst 1984-; Freeman City of London 1977, Liveryman Worshipful Co of Innholders; *Recreations* tree climbing, walking, photography, cinema, opera; *Clubs* Garrick; *Style*— Jeremy Sinden, Esq; C/O ICM, 388/396 Oxford St, London WC1 (☎ 071 629 8080)

SINDEN, Marcus Andrew (Marc); s of Donald Alfred Sinden, CBE, *qv*, of London, and Diana, *née* Mahony; *b* 9 May 1954; *Educ* Hall Sch Hampstead, Edgeborough Surrey, Stanbridge Earls Hants, Bristol Old Vic Theatre Sch; *m* 20 Aug 1977, Joanne Lesley, da of Geoffrey Gilbert, of Dorset; 1 s (Henry b 1980), 1 da (Bridie b 1990); *Career* jeweller and goldsmith H Knowles-Brown Ltd Hampstead 1973-78; actor 1978-; West End: Enjoy, Her Royal Highness, Underground, School for Scandal, Two into One, Ross, Over My Dead Body, The Beaux Stratagem, John Bulls Other Island (Dublin), Major Barbara (Chichester Festival Theatre); films: The Wicked Lady, Clash of Loyalties, White Nights, Manges D'Homme; TV: Crossroads, Home Front, Magnum PI, Country Boy; md Smallhythe Productions; Freeman City of London, Liveryman Worshipful Co of Innholders; FZS; *Recreations* theatrical history, zoology, ethology, cricket, motor racing, history of stunt-work; *Clubs* Garrick; *Style*— Marc Sinden, Esq; 1 Hogarth Hill, London NW11 6AY; Smallhythe Productions Ltd, 1 Hogarth Hill, London NW11 6AY (☎ 081 455 2323)

SINFIELD, Prof (Robert) Adrian; s of Robert Ernest Sinfield (d 1983), of Diss, Norfolk, and Agnes Joy, *née* Fouracre; *b* 3 Nov 1938; *Educ* Mercers Sch, Balliol Coll Oxford (BA), LSE (Dip); *m* 17 Sept 1964, Dorothy Anne, da of George Stanley Palmer, of Watford; 2 da (Beth b 1965, Laura b 1969); *Career* jr admin Lutheran World Service Hong Kong 1961-62, res asst LSE 1963-64, res assoc NY State Mental Health Res Unit Syracuse 1964-65, Univ of Essex 1965-79 (asst lectr, lectr, sr lectr, reader of sociology); prof of social policy Univ of Edinburgh 1979; visiting posts 1969: Graduate Sch of Social Work and Soc Res Bryn Mawr Coll Pa, NY Sch of Social Work Univ of Columbia; conslt: on long term unemployed OECD Paris 1965-68, on industl social welfare UN NY 1970-72, on income maintenance servs N Tyneside CDP 1975-78; exec Child Poverty Action Gp 1974-78, co-fndr and chm Mgmnt Ctee Unemployment Unit 1981-, chm Social Policy Assoc 1986-89; *Books* The Long-Term Unemployed (1968), Industrial Social Welfare (1971), What Unemployment Means (1981), The Workless State (co-ed With Brian Showler, 1981); *Recreations* reading, walking, travel; *Style*— Prof Adrian Sinfield; 12 Eden Lane, Edinburgh EH10 4SD (☎ 031 4472182); University of Edinburgh, Department of Social Policy and Social Work, Adam Ferguson Building, George Square, Edinburgh EH8 9LL (☎ 031 6503931, fax 031 6677938, telex 727442 UNIVED G)

SING, Prof Kenneth Stafford William; s of Reginald William Sing (d 1984), of Exeter, Devon, and Edith, *née* Popham (d 1983); *b* 25 Feb 1925; *Educ* Univ Coll Exeter (BSc, DSc), Univ of London (PhD); *m* 25 March 1950, Ruby, da of Leonard Corner; 1 s (Jonathan Millington b 15 Nov 1959), 3 da (Deborah Diane b 5 Sept 1951, Anne Millington b 27 April 1954, Margaret Claire b 2 March 1958); *Career* tech offr in Res Dept Billingham Div Imperial Chemical Industs Ltd 1948-49, lectr in physical chemistry Royal Tech Coll (now Univ of Salford) Salford 1949-55, head of Chemistry Dept Coll of Technol (now Liverpool Poly) Liverpool 1956-65, prof and head of Dept of Chemistry Brunel Univ 1965-84; memb Ctee: Soc of Chemical Indust, Royal Soc of Chemistry; memb: Soc of Chemical Indust, American Chemical Soc; *Books* Absorption, Surface Area and Porosity (with S J Gregg, 1984), ed various published proceedings; *Style*— Prof Kenneth Sing; Oak Grove, Coombe Lane, Hughenden Valley, High Wycombe, Bucks HP14 4NX (☎ 024 0242074), Dept of Chemistry, Brunel Univ, Uxbridge, Middx UB8 3PH (☎ 0895 74000 ext 2481, fax 0895 56844, telex 261173 G)

SINGER, Albert; s of Jacob Singer (Capt in Polish Army, d 1989), of Sydney, Aust, and Gertie, *née* Sadik (d 1986); *b* 4 Jan 1938; *Educ* Sydney GS, Univ of Sydney (MB BS, PhD), Univ of Oxford (DPhil); *m* 27 June 1976, Talya, da of Maurice Goodman; 3 da (Leora b 1978, Rebecca b 1980, Alexandra b 1983); *Career* Nat Serv Royal Aust Airforce 1956-57, Univ Sqdn Flt Lt 1960, active serv with RAAF Reserve in Vietnam 1968-69; Commonwealth fell Oxford 1970, visiting fell to Europe and USA 1968-69, pt/t consit WHO 1969-70, in res 1970-73, sr lectr then reader Univ of Sheffield 1973-80, conslt gynaecologist Royal Northern Hosp London 1980-; has published extensively on subject of gynaecological surgery and res into causes of female cancer; served on numerous govt panels and ctees primarily concerned with female cancer, memb Med Ctee of Women's Nat Cancer Control Campaign; memb RSM, FRCOG; *Books* The Cervix (with Dr Jordan), The Colour Atlas of Gynaecological Surgery (6 vols with David Lees); *Recreations* sport, especially tennis, swimming and sailing; *Clubs* Oxford and Cambridge; *Style*— Albert Singer, Esq; 37 Southway, London NW11 6RX (☎ 081 4585925), 148 Harley St, London W1N 1AH (☎ 071 9351900)

SINGER, Aubrey Edward; CBE (1984); s of Louis Henry Singer, and Elizabeth, *née* Walton; *b* 21 Jan 1927; *Educ* Bradford GS; *m* 1949, Cynthia Adams; 1 s, 3 da; *Career* BBC TV: joined 1949, asst head of outside broadcasts 1956-59, head of sci features 1959-61, head of Features Gp 1967-74, controller BBC2 1974-78, md BBC Radio 1978-82, dep dir gen BBC 1982-84, md BBC TV 1982-84; chm White City Films 1984-, dir Goldcrest Films and TV 1988-90; vice pres RTS 1982-88 (fell 1978), memb Ctee Nat Museum of Photography Film and TV Bradford 1985-, fell Royal Asiatic Soc; Hon DLitt Univ of Bradford 1984; *Recreations* walking; *Clubs* Savile; *Style*— Aubrey Singer, Esq, CBE; White City Films Ltd, 79 Sutton Court Rd, Chiswick, London W4 3EQ (☎ 081 994 6795, 081 994 4856, fax 081 995 9379, telex 9312102353 AS G)

SINGER, Hon Mrs (Evelyn Anne); da of Baron Kissin (Life Peer); *b* 1944; *Educ* BA; *m* 1972, Jack Donald Singer, MD, FAAPaed; 1 s (Jeremy b 1974), 1 da (Juliet b 1978); *Style*— The Hon Mrs Singer; 45 Campden Hill Court, Campden Hill Rd, London W8 (☎ 071 937 9406)

SINGER, His Hon Judge Harold Samuel; s of Ellis Singer, and Minnie, *née* Coffman (d 1964); *b* 17 July 1935; *Educ* Salford GS, Fitzwilliam House Cambridge (BA); *m* 1966, Adele Berenice, da of Julius Emanuel; 1 s (Andrew b 1967), 2 da (Rachel b 1970, Victoria b 1974); *Career* called to the Bar Gray's Inn 1957, rec Crown Court 1981-84, circuit judge 1984; *Recreations* golf, music, reading, painting, photography; *Style*— His Hon Judge Singer

SINGER, Dr Norbert; CBE (1990); s of Salomon Singer (d 1970), and Mina, *née* Korn (d 1976); *b* 3 May 1931; *Educ* Highbury Co Sch, QMC London (BSc, PhD); *m* 23 May 1980, Dr Brenda Margaret Walter, da of Richard Walter, of Tunbridge Wells; *Career* project ldr Morgan Crucible Co Ltd 1954-58; N London Poly 1958-70 (lectr, sr lectr, princ lectr, dep head of Dept of Chemistry), prof and head of Life Sci Dept Poly of Central London 1971-74, asst dir (later dept dir) Poly of N London 1974-78, dir Thames Poly 1978-; memb Cncl CNAA 1982-88; CChem, FRSC 1954; *Recreations* reading, walking; *Style*— Dr Norbert Singer, CBE; Croft Lodge, Bayhall Road, Tunbridge Wells, Kent TN2 4TD (☎ 0892 23821); Thames Polytechnic, Wellington St, Woolwich, London SE18 6PF (☎ 081 316 8000)

SINGER, (Jan) Peter; QC (1987); s of Dr Hanus Kurt Singer, and Anita, *née* Muller; *b* 10 Sept 1944; *Educ* King Edward's Sch, Birmingham, Selwyn Coll Cambridge; *m* 2 Jan 1970, Julia Mary, da of Norman Stewart Caney (d 1988); 1 s (Luke b 1985), 1 da (Laura b 1983); *Career* called to the Bar Inner Temple 1967, rec 1987 (asst rec 1983); Family Law Bar Assoc: sec 1980-83, treas 1983-90, chm 1990-; Bar nominee: Matrimonial Causes Rule Ctee 1981-85, Nat Legal Aid Ctee Law Soc 1984-89; memb: Senate of the Inns of Court and the Bar 1983-86, Fees and Legal Aid Ctee Bar Cncl 1986-; ex officio memb: Gen Cncl of the Bar 1990-; Bar Ctee Gen Cncl of the Bar 1990-; *Recreations* travel, walking, gardening; *Style*— Peter Singer, Esq, QC; 1 Mitre Court Buildings, Temple, London EC4Y 7BS (☎ 071 353 0434, fax 071 353 3988)

SINGER, Very Rev Samuel Stanfield; s of William Haus Singer (d 1944); *b* 2 May 1920; *Educ* Acad Baubridge Dublin, Trinity Coll Dublin (BA, MA); *m* 1942, Helen Audrey, *née* Naughton; 3 s, 1 da; *Career* vicar of Middleton-by-Wirksworth 1949-52, rector St George's Maryhill Glasgow 1952-62, rector All Saints' Glasgow 1962-75, synod clerk and canon St Mary's Cathedral Glasgow 1966-74, dean of Diocese of Glasgow and Galloway 1974-, rector Holy Trinity Ayr with St Oswald's Maybole 1975-87; *Recreations* fishing; *Style*— The Very Rev the Dean of Glasgow and Galloway; 12 Barns Terrace, Ayr, Scotland (☎ 0292 62382)

SINGH, Dr Ajeet; s or Wir Singh (d 1961), and Jachanan Kaur; *b* 6 June 1935; *Educ* King George Med Coll Lucknow India (MB BS), Univ of Bombay (DA); *m* 5 Aug 1962, Sharda, da of Mangesh Nadkarny, of Bankikiodla, India; 1 s (Bobby b 15 June 1963), 2 da (Aarti, Vineeta); *Career* Bombay 1964-67, sr registrar anaesthesia Liverpool 1969-72, conslt anaesthetist West Midland RHA 1972-; former dir Midland community Radio Coventry, chm Radio Harmony Coventry, fndr memb and vice pres Rotary Club of Coventry Jubilee; memb: Assoc of Anaesthestists GB and Ireland, Intractable Pain Soc, Midland Soc of Anaesthetists, Rugby Med Soc; former minute sec Obstetric Anaesthetist Soc; FFARCS; *Books* six papers in professional jls; *Recreations* music, photography, painting; *Clubs* Rotary (Coventry); *Style*— Dr Ajeet Singh; Walsgrave Hosp, Clifford Bridge Rd, Walsgrave, Coventry CV2 2DX (☎ 023 602020, ext 8580), Hosp of St Cross, Barby Rd, Rugby CV22 5PX (☎ 0788 572831, ext 2438)

SINGH, Prof Ghan Shyam; s of Thakur Kaloo Singh, and Gulab, *née* Kunwar; *b* 24 Jan 1929; *Career* Muslim Univ Aligarh India 1954-57, Bocconi Univ Milan Italy 1963-65, Queen's Univ Belfast 1965; *Books* Leopardi and the Theory of Poetry (1964), Le poesie di Kabir (ed with Ezra Pound 1966), Leopardi e L'Inghilterra (1968), Poesie di Thomas Hardy (ed 1968), Contemporary Italian Verse (1968), A Critical Study of Eugenio Montale's Poetry Prose and Criticism (1973), Ezra Pound (1979), T S Eliot Poeta Drammaturgo Critico (1985), Neanche un minuto (1986), The Circle and Other Poems: Olga and Pound (1988); *Recreations* reading, travelling; *Style*— Prof G Singh; Italian Department, The Queen's University of Belfast, 71 University Road, Belfast, Northern Ireland (☎ 0232 245133/3400, fax 0232 247895, telex QUBADM 74487)

SINGH, Harjit; s of Sewa Singh Alg (d 1965), of Tanzania, and Alg Waryam Kaur, *née* Oberoi; *b* 19 Feb 1934; *Educ* Magna Cum Laude (LLB), Univ of London (LLM); *m* 12 Nov 1969, Harsharan Bir Kaur, da of Maj Gurdial Singh (d 1970), of Chandigarh, Punjab, India; 2 s (Jasdeep b 21 June 1972, Dalbir b 25 April 1979), 1 da (Arshdeep b 15 Dec 1970); *Career* called to the Bar Lincoln's Inn 1956; practised at E African Bar 1957-71, memb SE Circuit 1975-; pres: Tanzania Table Tennis Assoc 1964-67, Tanzania Hockey Assoc 1967-70, Wandsworth Anglo-Asian Cons's 1979-82; currently pres Punjab Human Rights Orgn (UK); *Books* Tanganyika Law Society's Draft Constitution of Tanzania (1961); *Recreations* hockey, cricket, reading, political history and religion, chess; *Style*— Harjit Singh, Esq; 32 Malbrook Road, Putney, London SW15 6UF (☎ 081 7886328), 41-44 Temple Chambers, Temple Ave, London EC4Y OHP (☎ 071 3531356, 071 3531357, fax 071 583 4928)

SINGH, Prof Madan Gopal; s of Gurbachan Singh, of Chandigarh, India, and Pushpa, *née* Bawa; *b* 17 March 1946; *Educ* Univ of Exeter (BSc), Univ of Cambridge (PhD), France (Docteur Sciences), Univ of Manchester (MSc); *m* 1, 1 July 1969 (m dis 1979), Dr Christine Mary, *née* Carling; m 2, 24 Nov 1979, Dr Anne-Marie Claude Singh, da of Francis Bennavail, of Mont de Marsan, France; 2 s (Alexandre b 11 April 1980, Christophe b 9 June 1985); *Career* fell St Johns Coll Cambridge 1974-77, Maitre de Conferences Associe Univ of Toulouse 1976-78, charge de recherche au CNRS 1978-

79, prof of information engrg UMIST 1987- (prof of control engrg 1979-87, head of Control Systems Centre 1981-83 and 1985-87); vice chm SECOM IFAC 1981-84, chm IMACS Tech Ctee TC18 1987-, vice pres IEEE Systems Man and Cybernetics Soc 1990-; CEng, FIEE 1984, FIEEE 1989; *Books* Systems: Decomposition, Optimisation and Control (with A Titli, 1978), Applied Industrial Control - An Introduction (with J P Elloy, R Mezencev and N Munro, 1980), Large Scale Systems Modelling (with M S Mahmound, 1981), Large Scale Systems: Theory and Applications (ed with A Titli, 1981), Parallel Processing Techniques for Simulation (ed with A Y Allidiria and B K Daniels, 1987), Knowledge Based and Other Approaches to Reliability (ed with G Schmidt, S Tzafestas and K Hindi, 1987), Systems and Control Encyclopedia (ed, vols 1-8 1987, vol 9 1990); *Recreations* tennis, swimming, walking; *Style—* Prof Madan Singh; Computation Department, UMIST, Sackville St, Manchester M60 1QD (☎ 061 2003347, fax 061 2287386)

SINGH, Dr Manmeet; s of Dr Bakhtawar Singh (d 1986), of Kisumu, Kenya, and Sukhbir Kaur, *née* Soin; *b* 26 June 1935; *Educ* Kisumu HS Kenya, Univ of London (MB BS); *m* 11 Aug 1968, Seema Manmeet, da of Jabar Jang Singh (d 1985), of Toronto, Canada; 1 s (Sadmeet b 1970), 1 da (Aushima b 1973); *Career* sr lectr urology Univ of London Hosp Medical Coll 1973-75, conslt urological surgn Whipps Cross Hosp 1975-, hon sr clinical lectr UCL Inst of Urology 1986-; fell: Hunterian Soc, Societe Internationale d'Urologie; FRCS, FRSM; *Books* Urology (contrib, 1976), Current Operative Urology (contrib, 1984), Tropical Urology and Renal Disease (contrib, 1984); *Recreations* books, photography, african history, vintage cars; *Style—* Dr Manmeet Singh; 97 Hainault Rd, Chigwell, Essex 1G7 5DL (☎ 081 500 6137), Dept of Urology, Whipps Cross Hosp, Whipps Cross Rd, Leytonstone, London E11 (☎ 081 593 5522); 86 Harley St, London W1 1AE (☎ 071 637 2705)

SINGH, His Hon Judge; Mota; QC (1978); s of Dalip Singh, and Harnam Kaur; *b* 26 July 1930; *Educ* Duke of Gloucester Sch Nairobi; *m* 9 Nov 1950, Swaran, da of Gurcharan Singh Matharu, BEM (d 1987); 2 s (Satinder b 1956, Jaswinder b 1958), 1 da (Paramjeet b 1951); *Career* called to the Bar Lincoln's Inn 1956, rec 1979, circuit judge 1982; late city cncllr and alderman of Nairobi, sec Law Soc of Kenya, vice chm Kenya Justice, memb and chm London Rent Assessment Ctee, memb Race Rel Bd UK; Hon LLD Guru Nanak Dev Univ 1981; *Recreations* reading; *Clubs* MCC; *Style—* His Hon Judge Mota Singh; 3 Somerset Rd, Wimbledon, London SW19 5JU; (☎ office 071 403 4141 ext 279)

SINGH, Rameshwar (Ray); s of Brijmohan Singh (d 1960), and Ramkumari; *b* 13 Nov 1940; *Educ* Cncl of Legal Educn London; *m* 1 Sept 1968, Gwynneth Dorothy, da of David Llewllyn Jones, of Ty-Draw, Cilfrew, Neath; 3 s (David-Marc Ramesh b 20 Sept 1969, Rodric Andrew b 6 Nov 1971, Richard Owain b 16 March 1974); *Career* barr at law; local Bar jr Swansea; Wales and Chester circuit: dep jr 1989, jr 1990-; chm Indian Soc of W Wales, W Glamorgan Community Relations Cncl; memb: Bar Cncl, Hon Soc of Middle Temple, Family Law Bar Assoc; *Recreations* cooking, watching cricket, rugby; *Clubs* Glamorgan CCC (vice pres), Swansea Rugby (patron), Neath CC (vice pres); *Style—* Ray Singh, Esq; Maranatha, Cilfrew, Neath, West Glamorgan SA10 8NE (☎ 0639 635387), Angel Chambers, 94 Walter Rd, Swansea SA1 5QA (☎ 0792 46423)

SINGH, Sant Parkash; s of Shiv Singh (d 1975), and Rukman Devi, *née* Toor (d 1976); *b* 10 Oct 1931; *Educ* Univ of Agra India (MB BS); *m* 21 Jan 1961, Santosh Rani, da of Ram Nath Parmar (d 1970), of Jalandhar, India; 4 c (Kiran b 1968, Jyoti b 1969, Arpana b 1971, Anoop b 1972); *Career* house surgn Royal Infirmary Edinburgh 1958-59, sr registrar ENT Infirmary Liverpool 1964-65, sr lectr Univ of Ibadan Nigeria 1965-72, conslt surgn Northern RHA 1981; *Recreations* walking, bridge; *Style—* Sant Singh, Esq; 24 Oakdene Ave, Darlington, Co Durham DL3 7HS (☎ 0325 465159), ENT Dept, Memorial Hospital, Darlington, Co Durham DL3 6HX (☎ 0325 380100)

SINGH, Dr Shyam P; s of Capt G P Singh, and R Singh; *b* 4 April 1932; *Educ* Lucknow Univ (MB BS); *m* 1 (m dis 1980); 2 s (K S Herriotts b 2 Nov 1958, S P Herriotts b 29 Nov 1961), 1 da (Sheila H b 12 Oct 1973); *Career* med registrar United Birmingham Hosp 1960-62, clinical and res fell and asst tutor Univ of Harvard and Massachusetts Gen Hosp Boston 1962-63, sr registrar in cardiology and hon tutor United Birmingham Hosps 1964-67, conslt cardiologist and dir Cardiothoracic Unit Birmingham Children's Hosp 1968-83; FRCP; *Books* Coronary Artery Disease in Young Women (jlty, 1977); *Recreations* cricket, reading, visiting foreign countries; *Clubs* Rotary Club Birmingham; *Style—* Dr Shyam Singh; 101 Westfield Rd, Edgbaston, Birmingham B15 3JE 021 4545943), Consultant Cardiologist, Dudley Road Hospital, Dudley Rd, Birmingham 18

SINGH, Dr Waryam; s of the late L R Brara, and the late Karmawali; *Educ* (MB BS, DLO); *m* 30 Jan 1980, Maya Sudha; 1 s (Arjun); *Career* conslt otolaryngologist Lothian Health Bd and hon sr lectr in otolaryngology Univ of Edinburgh 1980-; hon prof USA and Germany; contrib clinical papers to numerous pubns and books, organiser and symposium dir of Int Voice Symposium 1987, inventor of the Speech Valve; pres Lothian BMA; pres elect: Union of Euro Phoniatricians, Assoc of Head and Neck Oncologists of GB; chm Scot Div Overseas Drs Assoc, liaison offr Bd of Union of Euro Phoniatricians for GB; memb: The Euro Acad of Facial Surgery, Int Assoc of Logopedics and Phoniatricians, The Scot Otolaryngologist Soc, Br Assoc of Otolaryngologists, The Overseas Drs Assoc, BMA, RSM; hon memb Hungarian Otolaryngology Soc; FRCS 1977; *Recreations* photography, travel and cricket; *Style—* Dr Waryam Singh; St John's Hospital, Livingston, W Lothian, Scotland (☎ 0506 419 666)

SINGLETON, Lady Amelia Myfanwy Polly; da of 7 Marquess of Anglesey, DL; *b* 12 Sept 1963; *m* 1984, Andrew Michael Singleton, 2 s of Sir Edward Henry Sibbald Singleton, *qv*; 1 da (Isabella Polly b 19 Aug 1990); *Style—* The Lady Amelia Singleton

SINGLETON, (Richard John) Basil; s of Richard Carl Thomas Singleton, of Crumlin, Co Antrim, and Marion Frances, *née* Campbell (d 1981); *b* 25 April 1935; *Educ* Foyle Coll Londonderry, Campbell Coll Belfast, Hong Kong Univ; *m* 14 Sept 1957, Florence Elizabeth, da of Albert McRoberts, of Dunmurry, Co Antrim (d 1981); 1 s (Richard David b 1961, d 1975), 1 da (Wendy Marion Jane b 1964); *Career* RA 1953-55; Ulster TV Ltd: mktg exec 1959-64, mktg mangr 1965-73; md AV Browne Advertising Ltd 1973-82, chm and chief exec Basil Singleton Ltd 1982-; dir: Brookville Ltd 1982-, Contractors Communications Ltd 1986-; Belfast Jr Chamber of Commerce 1961-75, chm Publicity Assoc of NI 1969-70, Ulster Branch Irish Hockey Union 1976-88; MCIM, MIPR; *Recreations* hockey, tennis; *Clubs* Ulster Reform; *Style—* Basil Singleton, Esq; Basil Singleton Ltd, 72 Circular Road, Belfast, County Antrim BT4 2GD (☎ 0232 768330)

SINGLETON, (William) Brian; CBE (1974); s of William Max Singleton (d 1977), and Blanche May Singleton (d 1975); *b* 23 Feb 1923; *Educ* Queen Elizabeth GS Darlington, Royal (Dick) Sch of Vet Med Univ of Edinburgh; *m* 1947, Hilda, da of Herbert A Stott (d 1974); 2 s (Neil, Mark), and 1 s decd, 1 da (Maxine); *Career* vet advsr IBA 1968-, pres RCVS 1969-70; served on Govt Ctee of Inquiry into the Future Role of the Vet Profession in GB (chm Sir Michael Swann) 1971-75, visiting prof of surgery Ontario Vet Coll Guelph Canada 1973-74, hon vet advsr Jockey Club 1977-88; pres: Br Small Animal Vet Assoc 1960-61, World Small Animal Vet Assoc 1975-77; dir Animal Health Tst 1977-88, pres Br Equine Vet Assoc 1987-88, memb UGC working Pty on Veterinary Educn into the 21 Century; FRCVS 1976; Diplomate American Coll of Vet Surgns 1972; Dalrymple Champney Br Vet Assoc highest honour for meritorius servs to the vet profession 1987; *Recreations* gardening, sailing, bird watching, horse riding; *Clubs* Farmers; *Style—* Brian Singleton, Esq, CBE; Vine Cottage, Blakeney, Norfolk, NR25 7BE (☎ 0263 740246)

SINGLETON, Sir Edward Henry Sibbald; s of William Parkinson Singleton, JP (d 1960), Florence Octavia, da of Sir Francis Sibbald-Scott, 5 Bt; *b* 7 April 1921; *Educ* Shrewsbury, BNC Oxford (MA); *m* 1943, Margaret Vere, *née* Hutton; 3 s (*see* Singleton, Lady Amelia), 1 da; *Career* Lt RNVR 1941-45, Pilot Fleet Air Arm; arbitrator and slr; former ptnr Macfarlanes (conslt 1977-86), dir Abbey National Building Society and various other cos 1980-89, chm Slrs' Law Stationery Soc plc 1980-85; tstee Fleet Air Arm Museum and Temple Bar Tst 1976-; memb Cncl: Securities Indust 1979-84, Law Soc 1961-80 (pres 1974); Companion Inst of Civil Engrs 1982; FCIArb; kt 1975; *Recreations* relaxing; *Clubs* I Zingari, Vincent's (Oxford); *Style—* Sir Edward Singleton; Flat 7, 62 Queen's Gate, London SW7 5JP (☎ office: 071 581 4151)

SINGLETON, Michael John Houghton; s of Clifford Houghton Singleton, OBE, of 55 Lammack Rd, Blackburn, Lancs, and Kathleen, *née* Slater; *b* 28 March 1951; *Educ* Baines GS Poulton-le-Flyde, Sheffield Univ (LLB); *m* 2 Oct 1976, Carolyn Anne, da of Geoffrey Ewart Lawrence, of 46A Wrottesley Rd, Tettenhall, Wolverhampton; 1 s (Matthew b 1983), 1 da (Jennifer b 1985); *Career* slr; ptnr Fieldings; *Style—* Michael Singleton, Esq; 34 Somerset Ave, Wilpshire, Blackburn, Lancs (☎ 0254 246191); 7 Richmond Terrace, Blackburn, Lancs (☎ 0254 679321)

SINGLETON, Roger; s of Malcolm Singleton (ka 1944), and Ethel, *née* Drew; *b* 6 Nov 1942; *Educ* City GS Sheffield, Univ of Durham (MA), Univ of Bath (MSc), Univ of London (Dip Soc Studies), Univ of Leeds (CertEd); *m* 30 July 1966, Ann, da of late Lawrence Edmond Hasler; 2 da (Jane b 1968, Katharine b 1969); *Career* various appts in care and educn of deprived and delinquent young people 1961-71, professional advsr to Children's Regnl Planning Ctee 1971-74, sr dir Barnardo's 1984- (dep dir 1974-84), contribs to various jls; chm Nat Cncl of Voluntary Child Care Organisations, memb Nat Youth Bureau Mgmnt Ctee; FBIM 1983; *Recreations* house and garden; *Clubs* Reform; *Style—* Roger Singleton, Esq; Barnardo's Tanners Lane, Barkingside, Ilford, Essex IG6 1QG (☎ 081 5508822, fax 081 5516870)

SINGLETON, Valerie; da of Wing Cdr Denis Gordon Singleton, OBE, and Catherine Eileen Singleton, LRAM; *Educ* Arts Educnl Sch London, RADA; *Career* Bromley Rep 1956-57, No 1 tours Cambridge Arts Theatre 1957-62, TV appearances in Compact and Emergency Ward 10, top voice over commentator for TV commercials 1957-62; BBC 1: continuity announcer 1962-64, Blue Peter 1962-72, Nationwide 1972-78, Val Meets the VIPs (3 series), Blue Peter Special Assignment (4 series), Blue Peter Royal Safari with HRH The Princess Anne, Tonight and Tonight in Town 1978-79, Blue Peter Special Assignments Rivers Yukon and Niagara (1980); BBC 2: Echoes of Holocaust 1979, The Migrant Workers of Europe 1980, The Money Programme 1980-88; PM Radio 4 1981-, several Midweeks; numerous appearances in TV advertising; memb: NUJ, Equity; *Recreations* travelling, photography, exploring London, sailing, walking, visiting salesrooms, museums; *Style—* Valerie Singleton; c/o Arlington Enterprises, 1-3 Charlotte St, London W1 (☎ 071 580 0702)

SINHA, Nirupama, Baroness; Nirupama; da of Rai Bahadur Lalit Mohan Chatterjee; *m* 1919, 2 Baron (d 1967); 2 s, 1 da; *Style—* The Rt Hon Nirupama, Lady Sinha; 7 Lord Sinha Rd, Calcutta, India

SINHA, 3 Baron (UK 1919); Sudhindro Prasanna Sinha; s (by 2 m) of 2 Baron Sinha (d 1967, s in his turn of 1 Baron, the first Indian raised to the Peerage and the first memb of the Viceroy's Exec Cncl in the wake of the Morley-Minto Reforms under the Raj); *b* 29 Oct 1920; *Educ* Bryanston; *m* 1945, Madhabi, da of late Monoranjan Chatterjee, of Calcutta; 1 s, 2 da; *Heir* s, Hon Susanta Prasanna Sinha *qv*; *Career* chm and md McNeill and Barry Ltd Calcutta; *Style—* The Rt Hon The Lord Sinha; 7 Lord Sinha Rd, Calcutta, India

SINHA, Hon Susanta Prasanna; only s and h of 3 Baron Sinha, *qv*; *b* 1953; *m* 1972, Patricia Orchard; 1 da (Caroline b 1973), 1 s and 1 da (decd); *Career* tea broker; *Style—* The Hon Susanta Sinha; 7 Lord Sinha Rd, Calcutta, India

SINKER, David Tennant; JP; s of Philip Tennant Sinker (d 1986), of Merton Cottage, Queens' Rd, Cambridge, and Mary Louisa, *née* Pearson; *b* 12 May 1938; *Educ* Winchester, Trinity Coll Cambridge (MA); *m* 6 Aug 1966, (Alice) Selina Marjorie, da of Charles Evelyn Townley (d 1983), of Fulbourn Manor, Cambridge; 1 s (Andrew b 9 July 1968); *Career* Nat Serv 1 Royal Dragoons 1957-58; 2 Lt Kent and London Yeo Sharpshooters TA 1961-64; articled clerk Peat Marwick Mitchell & Co 1961-64, chief economist Hunting Tech Servs Ltd 1969-71 (conslt economist 1964-69), dir Leach Gp 1971- (chm 1978-88), md Hunting Survey & Conslts 1978-86 (fin dir 1971-76, dep md 1976-78); dir: Hunting Survey & Photographic 1984-, City Technol 1988-; seconded to Nat Bd for Prices and Incomes 1967-69; memb: Ctee of Enquiry into Handling of Geographical Info 1985-87, Legal Aid Bd 1988-; Freeman City of London, Liveryman Worshipful Co of Broderers 1981; FCA 1964, FBIM 1987, FInstD 1987; *Recreations* gardening, walking, golf, tennis, skiing; *Clubs* IOD; *Style—* David Sinker, Esq, JP; Tare Close, Benington, Herts (☎ 0438 85 238, fax 0438 85 601)

SINKER, Patrick Andrew Charles Chisholm; s of Capt Leonard Chisholm Sinker, RN (d 1970), and Nancy, *née* Johnston (d 1990); *b* 14 Jan 1939; *Educ* Pangbourne Nautical Coll; *m* 3 April 1964, Letitia Ann, da of Robert King Anderson, of Whitstable, Kent; 2 da (Kate Letitia b 1967, Polly Anna b 1969); *Career* co dir; FCA; *Recreations* sailing, golf; *Clubs* Chestfield Golf; *Style—* Patrick Sinker, Esq; The Orchard, Alexandra Rd, Whitstable, Kent; Brent's Boatyard, Brents, Faversham, Kent (☎ 0795 537 809)

SINNATT, Maj-Gen Martin Henry; CB (1984); s of Dr Oliver Sturdy Sinnatt (d 1965), and Marjorie Helen, *née* Randall (d 1964); *b* 28 Jan 1928; *Educ* Hitchin GS, Hertford Coll Oxford, RMA Sandhurst; *m* 20 July 1957, Susan Rosemary, da of Capt Sydney Landor Clarke (d 1966); 4 da (Jacqueline Margaret b 22 April 1959, Katherine Susan b 30 March 1961, Nicola Jane b 16 Aug 1963, Victoria Helen b 1 Oct 1965); *Career* RTR 1948-; served: W Germany, Korea, Hong Kong, Aden, Norway; CO 4 RTR BAOR 1969-71, cdr RAC 1 Corps BAOR 1972-74, dir operational requirements MOD 1974-77, dir combat devpt 1979-81, COS and head UK Delgn 'Live Oak' SHAPE 1982-84; ret 1984; sr exec and sec Kennel Club 1984-; Freeman City of London 1981; *Recreations* golf, skiing, gardening, travel, medieval history; *Clubs* Army and Navy, Kennel; *Style—* Maj-Gen Martin Sinnatt, CB; c/o Barclays Bank, 92 Church Rd, Hove, E Sussex BN3 2ED

SINNOTT, Kevin Fergus; s of Myles Vincent Sinnott (d 1974), of Wales, and Honora, *née* Burke; *b* 4 Dec 1947; *Educ* St Roberts Aberkenfig, Cardiff Coll of Art (fndn course), Glos Coll of Art and Design (Dip AD), RCA (MA); *m* 30 Aug 1969, Susan Margaret, da of Lawrence Hadyn Forward; 3 s (Matthew b 22 Aug 1971, Gavin b 6 June 1975, Thomas b 4 March 1983), 1 da (Lucy Anne b 24 Aug 1984); *Career* artist; visiting lectr: Ruskin Sch of Drawing Oxford 1975-76, Canterbury Coll of Art 1981-88, Epsom Coll of Art 1981-88; pt/t teacher St Martin's Sch of Art London 1981-; solo exhbitions: House Gallery London 1980 and 1983, Ikon Gallery Birmingham 1980, Riverside Studios London 1981, Gallery Gwyn Hodges Oxford 1981, St Paul's Gallery

Leeds 1981, Blond Fine Art London 1982 and 1984, Chapter Arts Centre Cardiff 1984, Bernard Jacobson Gallery (London 1986, London and NY 1987, NY 1988, London 1990), Jan Turner Gallery LA 1987, Roger Ramsay Gallery Chicago 1988, Anne Berthoud Gallery London 1990; gp exhibitions incl: Whitechapel Open London 1978 and 1980, John Moores Liverpool 1978 and 1980, Ruskin Sch of Art Oxford 1981, Blond Fine Art London 1982-85, LA Louver Gallery California 1986, Bernard Jacobson Gallery London 1986, Lefevre Gallery London 1988, The Contemporary Arts Centre Cincinnati 1988; museum and public collections: Br Cncl, Arts Cncl of GB, RCA, Br Museum; *Style—* Kevin Sinnott, Esq; Bernard Jacobson Gallery, 14A Clifford St, London W1X 1RF (☎ 071 495 8575, fax 071 495 6210)

SIRA, Gurmit Singh; s of Nirmal Singh Sira (d 1982), and Bhagwanti Sira, *née* Paddi; *b* 19 July 1938; *Educ* Duke of Gloucester (Nairobi), Nairobi Univ (Kenya), Leeds Univ (BA); *m* 16 Sept 1972, Jaswant Kaur, da of Ronak Singh Sagoo, of Ealing; (2 da Amrita b 1982, Shateen b 1975), 1 s (Manoreet b 1974); *Career* slr and Notary Public; dir: Tanglewood Properties (Lichfield) Ltd, Masu Properties Ltd; *Recreations* walking, badminton, reading, theatre; *Style—* Gurmit S Sira, Esq; Permanent House, 6A Conduit St, Lichfield (☎ 254382/3, fax 253713)

SISLEY, Francis Barton; s of John Barton Sisley (d 1940), of SE London, and Elsie May, *née* Hawkins (d 1963); *b* 28 Nov 1921; *Educ* Woolwich Poly, Woolwich Poly Sch of Art; *m* 1, 29 Nov 1941 (m dis 1953), May Victoria, da of James Mortimer (d 1950); 1 da (Janet Irene b 23 Feb 1944); m 2, 24 Nov 1962, Joan Patricia, da of William Patrick Veness (d 1963); *Career* artist; group exhibitions incl: Young Contemporaries RBA Galleries, AIA Gallery London, Redfern Gallery, Havant Art Centre, Free Painters and Sculptors, Ford Exhibition Dearborn USA and Lisbon Portugal; one-man exhibitions incl: Loggia Galleries London 1974 (also 1976 and 1979), Assembly Rooms Chichester 1975, Gallery 20 Brighton 1977, Christ's Hosp Arts Fair 1977 and 1979, Bognor Regis Centre 1984 (twice); work in private collections in: USA, Canada, Australia, Spain, UK; large acrylic painting Celtic Cross acquired for Catholic Educn Centre Canterbury 1977; memb Free Painters and Sculptors 1963; *Recreations* chess, wine making, DIY, gardening, reading, walking, travel; *Style—* Francis Sisley, Esq; 7 James Rd, Dorchester, Dorset, DT1 2HB (☎ 0305 69246)

SISMEY, Lt-Col Oliver North Deane; DL (Hunts 1952-74, Cambs 1974); s of George Herbert Sismey (d 1958), of Offord Cluny Manor, Huntingdon, and Catherine Edith, *née* Buckmaster (d 1953); *b* 25 Oct 1900; *Educ* Cheam Sch, Eton, Sandhurst; *m* 1, 1931, Anne Laetitia, da of Brig-Gen Lewis Francis Philips, CB, CMG, CBE, DSO (d 1935); 1 da (Islay Anne); m 2, 1956, Pauline Vincent, *née* Turner (d 1980); *Career* cmmnd 2 Lt KRRC 1920, Adj 1 Bn KRRC 1926-29, instr RMC Sandhurst 1935-38, AMS to Govr and C-in-C Malta 1939-40, CO 2 Bn KRRC 1941 (with 1 Armd Div and 7 Armd Div in Middle East and took part in actions in Libya and Egypt 1941-42), GSO1 No 2 Dist 1942-45, Tripolitania, Sicily, Italy (despatches); dep pres Regular Cmmns Bd 1947, dep pres Sandhurst Selection Bd 1947, ret Lt-Col 1948; chm Police Authy 1954-64; County Alderman: Huntingdonshire 1960-65, Huntingdon and Peterborough 1965-74; *Recreations* formerly hunting, shooting, polo, rackets, now gardening; *Clubs* Naval and Military; *Style—* Lt-Col Oliver Sismey, DL; Offord Cluny Manor, nr Huntingdon, Cambridgeshire (☎ 0480 810 259)

SISSON, Brig Arthur Alexander; MBE (1968), CBE (1978); s of Prof Geoffrey Roy Sisson, OBE (d 1964), and Lucy Cameron, *née* Ward (d 1982); *b* 30 May 1924; *Educ* Highgate Sch, Univ of Edinburgh; *m* 1 Oct 1951, Pamela, da of Maj John Chadwick (d 1981); 2 s (Richard b 1957, Peter b 1962), 2 da (Jennifer b 1954, Sarah Jane b 1965); *Career* cmmnd RA 1945; serv: SE Asia, India, Palestine, Malaya, Cyprus, Aden; intro Army bulk refuelling system 1970-79, initiated DROPS (demountable rack system), dir logistic orgn and devpt MOD (Army) 1976-79; mgmnt and def conslt; FMS; *Reports* Logistic Concept 1985-2005 (1979), Vulnerability of the British LOC in Europe (1985); *Recreations* butterfly conservation, racehorse owner; *Clubs* Naval; *Style—* Brig Arthur Sisson, CBE; Ferranti International plc, Millbank Tower, London SW1P 4QS (☎ 071 834 6611)

SISSON, Dr Charles Hubert; s of Richard Percy Sisson (d 1958), and Ellen Minnie, *née* Worlock (d 1955); *b* 2 April 1914; *Educ* Fairfield Secdy Sch Bristol, Univ of Bristol (BA), Univs of Berlin and Freiburg, Sorbonne; *m* 19 Aug 1937, Nora, da of Anthony Huddleston Gilbertson (d 1954), of Bristol; 2 da (Janet, Hilary); *Career* WWII Sgt Intelligence Corps 1942-45 served India; Miny of Lab: asst princ 1936, under sec Dept of Employment 1962-72; Simon sr res fell Univ of Manchester 1956-57; Hon DLitt Bristol 1980; FRSL 1972; *Books* The Spirit of British Administration, with some European comparisons (1959), Christopher Homm (novel, 1965), English Poetry 1900-1950 (1971), In the Trojan Ditch (collected poems and selected translations, 1974), The Avoidance of Literature (1978), Collected Poems (1984), God Bless Karl Marx (poems, 1987), On the Look-out: A Partial Autobiography (1989), In Two Minds: Guesses at other Writers (1990), English Perspectives (1991); translations incl: Dante, Virgil, Lucretius; *Recreations* gardening, washing up; *Style—* Dr Charles Sisson; Moorfield Cottage, The Hill, Langport, Somerset TA10 9PU (☎ 0458 250845)

SISSON, Lady Emma Bridget; da of 12 Earl of Carlisle, MC, *qv*; *b* 20 July 1952; *m* 1, 1974 (m dis 1981), John Philip Charles Langton-Lockton; 1 s (Maximilian b 1980), 1 da (Tabitha b 1978); m 2, 1983 (m dis 1988), Robie Patrick Maxwell Uniacke, s of Capt Robie David Corbett Uniacke, of Challons Yarde, Midhurst, Sussex; 1 s (Robie Jonjo b 12 Oct 1984); m 3, 16 July 1988, Guy Mark Sisson, yst s of late John Hamilton Sisson; *Style—* The Lady Emma Sisson; c/o Rt Hon Earl of Carlisle, MC, Naworth Castle, Brampton, Cumbria

SISSON, Rosemary Anne; da of Prof Charles Jasper Sisson (d 1965), and Vera Kathleen Ginn; *b* 13 Oct 1923; *Educ* Cheltenham Ladies Coll, UCL (BA), Newnham Coll Cambridge (MLit); *Career* WWII with Royal Observer Corps 1943-45; lectr in english: Univ of Wisconsin 1949-50, UCL 1950-55, Univ of Birmingham 1956-58; co-chm The Writers Guild of GB 1979 and 1980; tstee Ray Cooney's Theatre of Comedy; stage plays incl: The Queen and the Welshman (1957), Fear Came to Supper (1958), The Splendid Outcasts (1958), Home and the Heart, The Royal Captivity (1960), Bitter Sanctuary (1963), I Married a Clever Girl, A Ghost on Tiptoe (with Robert Morley), The Dark Horse (1979); novels incl: The Exciseman (1972), The Killer of Horseman's Flats (1973), The Stratford Story (1975), The Queen and the Welshman (1979), Escape from the Dark (1976), The Manions of America (1981), Bury Love Deep (1985), Beneath the Visiting Moon (1986), The Bretts (1987, televised 1987), also six children's books; contrib to TV series: Upstairs, Downstairs, The Duchess of Duke Street, and adaptations for TV and radio; *Recreations* riding, travel; *Clubs* BAFTA; *Style—* Miss R A Sisson; Andrew Mann Ltd, 1 Old Compton St, W1 (☎ 071 734 4751)

SISSONS, Clifford Ernest; s of George Robert Percival Sissons (d 1964), and Elsie Emma, *née* Evans; *b* 26 Jan 1934; *Educ* Liverpool Inst HS for Boys, Univ of Liverpool University Med Sch (MB ChB); *m* 28 Dec 1956, Mary Beryl, da of James Davies (d 1941); 2 s (Mark Christopher John, Guy Richard James), 1 da (Amanda Jane Elizabeth); *Career* Nat Serv Capt RAMC 1959-61; house physician and house surgn Liverpool Stanley Hosp 1958-59; med registrar: Birkenhead Gen Hosp 1962-67, professional med unit Liverpool Royal Infirmary 1967; sr med registrar David Lewis Northern and Sefton Gen Hosp Liverpool 1969-72, conslt physician Wrexham War Memorial and Mealor Hosps 1972-; cncl memb RCP 1985-87 (regnl advsr 1982-87), FRCP 1977; *Recreations* languages, travel, reading, painting; *Style—* Dr Clifford Sissons; Wrexham Maelor Hosp, Crosenwydd Rd, Wrexham, Clwyd (☎ 0978 29110)

SISSONS, (Thomas) Michael Beswick; s of Capt T E B Sissons (ka 1940), and Marjorie, *née* Shepherd; *b* 13 Oct 1934; *Educ* Winchester, Exeter Coll Oxford (BA, MA); *m* 1, 1960 (m dis), Nicola Ann, *née* Fowler; 1 s, 1 da; m 2, 1974, Ilze, *née* Kadegis; 2 da; *Career* Nat Serv 2 Lt 13/18 Royal Hussars 1953-55; lectr in history Tulane Univ New Orleans 1958-59, freelance writer and journalist 1958-60. AD Peters & Co Ltd Literary Agency 1959- (dir 1965, chm and md 1973-88), jt chm and md The Peters Fraser & Dunlop Gp Ltd 1988-, dir London Broadcasting Co 1973-75; pres Assoc of Authors' Agents 1978-81, memb ctee MCC (chm arts and library sub-ctee 1985-); *Books* Age of Austerity (ed with Philip French 1963, 2 edn 1986); *Recreations* riding, gardening, cricket, music; *Clubs* Garrick, Groucho, MCC (memb ctee 1984-87, chm arts and library sub-ctee 1985); *Style—* Michael Sissons, Esq; Flinty, Clanville, Andover, Hants SP11 9HZ (☎ 026 477 2197); Peters Fraser & Dunlop, Fifth Floor, The Chambers, Chelsea Harbour, Lots Rd, London SW10 0XF (☎ 071 376 7676, fax 071 352 7356)

SISSONS, (Thomas) Michael Beswick; s of Capt T E B Sissons (KA 1940), and Marjorie, *née* Shepherd; *b* 13 Oct 1934; *Educ* Win chester, Exeter Coll Oxford (BA, MA); *m* 1, 1960, Nicola Ann Fowler; 1 s, 1 da; m 2, 1974, Ilse Kadegis; 2 da; *Career* Nat Serv 2 Lt 13/18 Royal Hussars 1953-55; lectr in history Tulane Univ New Orleans 1958-59, freelance writer and journalist 1958-60; AD Peters Literary Agency 1959-; dir 1965, chm and md 1973-88; chm and md The Peters Fraser and Dunlop Gp Ltd 1988-; dir LBC 1973-75; pres Assoc of Author's Agents 1978-81, memb cncl Consumers Assoc 1974-77; *Books* Age of Austerity (ed with Philip French 1963); *Recreations* riding, gardening, circket, music; *Clubs* Garrick, Groucho, MMC (memb ctee 1984-87, chm arts and lib sub-ctee 1985-); *Style—* Michael Sissons, Esq; Flinty, Clanville, Andover, Hants SP11 9HZ (☎ 026 4772197), Peters, Fraser & Dunlop, 5th Floor, The Chambers, Chelsea Harbour, Lots Rd, London SW10 0XF (☎ 01 3767676, fax 01 3527356)

SISSONS, (John Gerald) Patrick; s of Gerald William Sissons (d 1966), and Georgina Margaret, *née* Cockin (d 1960); *b* 28 June 1945; *Educ* Felsted, St Mary's Hosp Med Sch London (MB BS, MD); *m* April 1971 (m dis 1985), Jennifer Anne Scovell; 2 da (Sarah b 1973, Rebecca b 1974); *Career* registrar and hon lectr Royal Post Grad Med Sch London 1973-76, NIH Forgarty fell and asst memb Scripps Clinic San Diego USA 1977-80, reader in infectious diseases Royal Post Grad Med Sch 1987 (Welcome sr lectr 1980-86), prof of med Univ of Cambridge 1988; fell Darwin Coll Cambridge, Bd memb MRC; FRCP; *Recreations* travel; *Style—* Patrick Sissons, Esq; Dept of Medicine, Univ of Cambridge Clinical Sch, Hills Rd, Cambridge CB2 2QQ (☎ 0223 336849)

SISSONS, Peter George; s of George Robert Percival Sissons (d 1964), and Elsie Emma, *née* Evans; *b* 17 July 1942; *Educ* Liverpool Inst HS for Boys, Univ Coll Oxford (MA); *m* Sylvia; 2 s, 1 da; *Career* tv journalist and presenter; ITN 1964-78: gen trainee then script writer, gen reporter, foreign correspondent, news ed, indust correspondent, indust ed; presenter News at One 1978-82, presenter Channel Four News 1982-89, chm Question Time and presenter 6 O'Clock News BBC 1989-; Broadcasting Press Guild's Best Front of Camera Performer 1984, Royal TV Soc's Judges Award 1989; *Recreations* relaxing; *Style—* Peter Sissons, ESq; c/o BBC TV Centre, Wood Lane, London W12 7RJ (☎ 081 576 7776)

SITTAMPALAM, Dr Arumugam; s of Visuanather Arumugam, and Kanapathiyar, *née* Sinnappillai; *b* 30 Nov 1922; *Educ* St Patrick's Coll Jaffna Srilanka, Univ of Colombo, Univ of London (MB BS, DPM); *m* 2 Feb 1951, Puaneswary, da of Cajipillai Paramu; 5 s (Yogeiswaran, Jegatheswaran, Naguleswaran, Ganeshwaran, Ketheswaran), 1 da (Thayalini); *Career* psychiatric specialist Ceylon Health Serv, sr psychiatrist Union Hosp Moosejaw Sakatchuan Canada, med offr HM Prison Brixton; conslt forensic psychiatrist: Rampton Hosp Notts, Broadmoor Hosp; visiting psychiatrist Wormwood Scrubs Prison; FRCPE, FRCPsych, memb World Psychiatrist Assoc; *Recreations* gardening, travel, reading, detective fiction; *Style—* Dr Arumugam Sittampalam; 18 Wycherley Crescent, Barnet, Herts EN5 1AR (☎ 081 440 4537), 6 Wentworth Ave, North Ascot, Berks SL5 8HQ (☎ 0344 882585), Bradmoor Hosp, Crowthorne, Berks RG11 7EG (☎ 0344 773111)

SITWELL, Francis Trajan Sacheverell; yr s of Sir Sacheverell Sitwell, 6 Bt (d 1988); bro and h of Sir Reresby Sitwell, 7 Bt, *qv*; *b* 17 Sept 1935; *Educ* Eton; *m* 21 June 1966, Susanna Carolyn, 3 da of late Rt Hon Sir Ronald Hibbert Cross, 1 Bt, KCMG, KCVO; 2 s (George Reresby Sacheverell b 22 April 1967, William Ronald Sacheverell b 1969), 1 da (Henrietta Louise Vereker b 1973); *Career* late Sub Lt RN; assoc dir Charles Barker City Ltd 1969; memb Cncl London Philharmonic Orch 1965; MIPR 1969; *Clubs* Brooks's; *Style—* Francis Sitwell, Esq; 20 Ladbroke Grove, London W11

SITWELL, Sir (Sacheverell) Reresby; 7 Bt (UK 1808), of Renishaw, Derbyshire; DL (Derbyshire 1984); s of Sir Sacheverell Sitwell, 6 Bt (d 1988), by his w, Georgia Louise, *née* Doble (d 1980); *b* 15 April 1927; *Educ* Eton, King's Coll Cambridge; *m* 1952, Penelope, da of Col the Hon Donald Forbes, DSO, MVO (d 1938), s of 7 Earl of Granard; 1 da (Alexandra b 1958); *Heir* br, Francis Trajan Sacheverell Sitwell b 17 Sept 1935; *Career* former Lt 2 Bn Grenadier Gds, BAOR Germany 1946-48; advtg and PR exec 1948-60, vending machines operator 1960-70, wine merchant 1960-75; landowner 1965-; lord of the manors of Eckington and Barlborough in Derbyshire and of Whiston and Brampton-en-le-Morthen in South Yorks; High Sheriff Derbyshire 1983; Freeman of City of London 1984; *Recreations* travel, music, architecture, racing; *Clubs* White's, Brooks's, Pratt's, Pitt (Cambridge), Soc of Dilettanti; *Style—* Sir Reresby Sitwell, Bt, DL; Renishaw Hall, Renishaw, nr Sheffield S31 9WB (☎ 0246 432042); 4 Southwick Place, London W2 2TN (☎ 071 262 3939)

SIVEWRIGHT, Bt-Col (Robert) Charles Townsend; CB (1983), MC (1945), DL (Glos 1965); s of Capt R H V Sivewright DSC, RN (d 1981), and Sylvia Townsend, *née* Cobbold (d 1988); *b* 7 Sept 1923; *Educ* Repton, RAC Glos; *m* 1951, Pamela Molly, da of Dr J C Ryder-Richardson (d 1961), of Whitchurch, Bucks; 3 da (Pamela, Amanda, Sarah); *Career* Bt-Col, cmmnd 11 Hussars 1943, served Italy and NW Europe (despatches), CO Royal Gloucestershire Hussars TA 1964-67; jt princ Talland Sch of Equitation Glos; chm W Wessex TA & VRA 1980-83, vice-chm cncl TA & VRA 1970-83; High Sheriff Glos 1977; *Recreations* racing; *Style—* Bt-Col Robert Sivewright, CB, MC, DL; Talland House, Clark's Hay, South Cerney, Cirencester GL7 6HU (☎ 0285 860830)

SIZER, Prof John; CBE (1989); s of John Robert Sizer, and Mary Sizer; *b* 14 Sept 1938; *Educ* Univ of Nottingham (BA), Loughborough Univ of Technol (DLitt); *m* 1965, Valerie Davies; 3 s; *Career* accountancy asst Ross Group Ltd Grimsby 1954-57, sr cost clerk Eskimo Foods Ltd Cleethorpes 1957-58, asst accountant Clover Dairies Ltd Grimsby 1958-61, fin advsr Guest Keen & Nettlefolds Ltd 1964-65, Univ of Edinburgh 1965-68 (teaching fell, lectr), London Graduate Sch of Business Studies 1968-70 (sr lectr in accounting, asst academic dean); Loughborough Univ of Technol: prof of fin mgmnt 1970-, dean Sch of Human & Environmental Studies 1973-76, sr pro vice-chllr 1980-82, fndr and head Dept of Mgmnt Studies 1971-80, 1982-84 and 1990, dir

Business Sch 1991-; Nat Forum for Mgmnt Educn & Devpt 1987- (alternate memb UGC/UFC, memb Exec Ctee, chm Fin and Resourcing Ctee), advsr Business & Mgmnt Studies UFC 1989-; memb: Jt CVCP/UFC Steering Ctee on Performance Indicators 1989-, Research Performance Indicators Gp 1989-, UFC NI Ctee 1989-, DECD/IMHE Prog Int Expert Gp on Performance Indicators 1989-, Sub-Gp on Govt/ Funding Bodies-Institutional Relationships 1989-; memb: SSRC/ICAEW/CIMA Mgmnt Accounting Seminar Gp, Bd of Accreditation for Accounting Degree Courses 1989-; memb Editorial Bd: Journal of Industrial Affairs 1980-, Financial Accountability and Management 1985-, Higher Education 1990-; tech assessor ACME Directorate SERC 1987-, advsr Bertelsmann Fndn Germany; *Books* An Insight into Management Accounting (1969, 3 edn 1979), Case Studies in Management Accounting (1974), Perspectives in Management Accounting (1981), Resources and Higher Education (jt ed, 1983), A Casebook of British Management Accounting (jtly 1984, 1985), Institutional Responses to Financial Reductions in the University Sector (1987); *Recreations* table tennis, walking; *Style*— Prof John Sizer, CBE; 17 Maplewell Road, Woodhouse Eaves, nr Loughborough, Leicestershire LE12 8RG (☎ 0509 890927); Loughborough University Business School, Loughborough University of Technology, Loughborough, Leicestershire LE11 3TU (☎ 0509 223120, fax 0509 210232)

SKAE, John Robin; s of Reginald John Skae (d 1988), and Gwendoline Catharine Bleakley Skae (d 1981); *b* 11 July 1936; *Educ* Oundle; *m* 1 Sept 1961, Cynthia Fay, da of Norman Louis Forrest (d 1988), of Stoke-on-Trent; 1 s (Christopher b 13 Sept 1962), 2 da (Jennifer b 18 March 1965, Joanna b 16 Dec 1968); *Career* dir and co sec Bamfords Ltd Uttoxeter Staffs 1964-74, gp sec Dowty Group plc Cheltenham 1974-85, gp co sec Midland Bank plc London 1985-; FCA 1962; *Recreations* sport, music, countryside, gardening; *Clubs* RAC; *Style*— John Skae, Esq; Midland Bank Plc, Head Office, 27-32 Poultry, London EC2P 2BX (☎ 071 260 8180, fax 071 260 8463)

SKAN, Martin; s of Reginald Norman Skan (d 1985), of Worcester, and Millicent May, *née* Vaughan (d 1977); *b* 28 Dec 1934; *Educ* Haileybury, Harvard Sch California (exchange scholar); *m* 1, 1970 (m dis 1988), Sally Elizabeth Margaret, da of John Eric Wade; 2 da (Lara Julie b 1971, Tilly Matina b 1975); m 2, 1989, Brigitte Berta, da of Erwin Heinrich Joos; *Career* cmmnd Dorset Regt 1955-57; British Market Research Bureau Ltd (subsid of JWT Advertising) 1957-58, Kinloch (PM) Ltd 1958-89; dir: Skan Taylor & Co Ltd 1959-65, J A & P Holland Ltd 1962-65, Parkinsons (Doncaster) Ltd 1962-65, Holland Distributors Ltd 1962-65, Harper Paper Group (and subsid cos) 1962-65, LMS (Consultants) Ltd 1986-; chm Chewton Glen (Hotels) Ltd 1966-; for Chewton Glen Ho☎ Egon Ronay Hotel of The Year award 1976, Michelin Star 1981-, Times Hotel Restaurant of the Year 1990, Tourism Catey award 1990; Personality of the Year 1990; *Recreations* tennis, golf, cycling, skiing; *Clubs* IOD, Brockenhurst Golf, Royal Lymington Yacht, Mosimann's, Mark's, Harry's Bar, Annabel's; *Style*— Martin Skan, Esq; Chewton Glen Hotel, Christchurch Rd, New Milton, Hants BH25 6QS (☎ 0425 275341, fax 0425 272310)

SKEET, Muriel Hilda Henrietta; da of Col Frederick William Claude (d 1974), of Colchester, Essex, and Mabel Constance, *née* Pitt-King (d 1976); *b* 12 July 1926; *Educ* Endsleigh House, London Univ (MPH, DipH and TM), Yale Univ; *Career* trg Middx Hosp and London Sch of Hygiene and Tropical Med 1949-40 (SRN), ward and admin sister Middx Hosp 1949-60, field work organiser operational res unit Nuffield Provincial Hosps Tst 1961-64, res organiser Dan Mason Nursing Ctee of Nat Florence Nightingale Meml Ctee of GB and NI 1965-70, chief nursing offr and nursing advsr BRCS and St John of Jerusalem and BRCS Jt Ctee 1970-78, res conslt WHO SE Asia 1970, euro del and first chm bd of Cwlth Nurses' Fedn 1971, Leverhume Fellowship 1974-75, health servs advsr and conslt WHO and other int agencies and orgns 1978-; memb: Hosp and Med Servs Ctee 1970, Ex-Servs War Disabled Help Ctee 1970, Br Cwlth Nurses War Meml Fund 1970 ctee and cncl, Br Cwlth Nurses War Meml Fund 1970, mgmnt cncl Nat Florence Nightingale Meml Ctee 1970, cncl Queen's Inst of Dist Nursing 1970, cncl of nurses Royal Coll of Nursing; MRSH, FRSN, FRCN 1977, memb RSM 1980; *Books* Waiting in Outpatients Departments (1965), Marriage and Nursing (1968), Home from Hospital (1970), Home Nursing (1975), Health Needs Help (1977), Health Auxiliaries in the Health Team (jtly, 1978), Self Care for the People of Developing Countries (1979), Discharge Procedures (1980), Notes on Nursing 1860 and 1980 (1980), Emergency Procedures and First Aid for Nurses (1981), The Third Age (1982), Providing Continuing Care for Elderly People (1983), First Aid for Developing Countries (1983), various articles for professional jls; *Recreations* music, opera, painting, reading; *Clubs* Arts, Royal Overseas League; *Style*— Miss Muriel Skeet; World Health Organisation, Geneva, Switzerland

SKEET, Sir Trevor Herbert Harry; MP (C) N Bedfordshire 1983-; s of Harry May Skeet; *b* 28 Jan 1918; *Educ* King's Coll Auckland NZ, Univ of NZ (LLB); *m* 1, 1957, Elizabeth (decd), da of Montague Gilling, of Bedford; 2 s, 1 da; m 2, 1985, Valerie A E Benson; *Career* Lt RNZNVR; barr and slr NZ, barr UK; MP (C): Willesden E 1959-64, Bedford 1970-83; chm Parly and Scientific Ctee 1983-88; kt 1986; *Recreations* walking, travel, gardening; *Clubs* Royal Cwlth Soc, Army & Navy; *Style*— Sir Trevor Skeet, MP; The Gables, Milton Ernest, Beds MK44 1RS (☎ 02302 2307)

SKEFFINGTON, Hon John David Clotworthy Whyte-Melville Foster; s and h of 13 Viscount Massereene and Ferrard; *b* 3 June 1940; *Educ* Millfield, Inst Monte Rosa; *m* 1970, Anne Denise, da of Norman Rowlandson (d 1966); 2 s, 1 da; *Career* served Grenadier Gds 1959-61; dir: Shirlstar Container Tport Ltd, Wingspan Travel Ltd; chm: Atkin Grant & Lang (Gunmakers), Ambrit Industries; stockbroker with Dunbar Boyle & Kingsley Ltd; *Recreations* shooting, vintage cars; *Clubs* Turf, Pratt's; *Style*— The Hon John Skeffington; Scarisdale House, New Rd, Esher, Surrey (☎ office: 071 623 9898)

SKEGGS, Dr David Bartholomew Lyndon; s of Dr Basil Lyndon Skeggs (d 1956), of Herts, and Gladys Jessie, *née* Tucker (d 1978); *b* 26 Aug 1928; *Educ* Winchester Coll, Oriel Coll Oxford, St Bart's Hosp London; *m* 16 Nov 1957, Anita Violet, da of Horace Norman Hughes, of Worcs; 2 da (Lucinda b 1960, Imogen b 1963); *Career* RN 1954-56; Surgn Lt Cdr RNR 1956-70; dir of Radiotherapy Royal Free Hosp London 1966-86, hon conslt Royal N Hosp London and Lister Hosp Stevenage; chm bd of examiners Part 1 FRCR, sr examiner DMRI 1970-75; use of computerised radiotherapy and devpt of computerised 3 D radiotherapy treatment planning; memb bd of visitors for prisons; memb Cncl Wycombe Abbey Sch; *Books* contribs: Maingot's Textbook of Surgery, Shaw's Textbook of Gynaecology, Scott Brown's Textbook of ENT Surgery; *Recreations* gardening, music, travel, competitive games; *Style*— Dr David Skeggs; The Coach House, Barnes Common, London SW13 (☎ 081 876 7929); 152 Harley St, London W1N 1HH (☎ 071 935 0444)

SKELDING, Barry Howard; s of Denis Howard Skelding, of Finchley London, and Stella, *née* Scott Eliott; *b* 2 Jan 1945; *Educ* The Stationers' Co's Sch; *m* 27 Aug 1977, Margaret Marion, da of Gordon David Carnegie (d 1969); 2 da (Katie b 1981, Sarah b 1983); *Career* slr; assoc ptnr Gamlens 1970, gp property slr EMI Ltd 1970-80, ptnr Rowe and Maw 1980-; memb Law Soc 1970; *Recreations* lawn tennis, squash rackets, music; *Clubs* Cumberland, Marlborough; *Style*— Barry Skelding, Esq; 2 Folly Pathway, Radlett, Herts WD7 8DS (☎ 0923 855456); 20 Black Friars Lane, London EC4V 6HD (☎ 071 2484282, fax 071 2482009)

SKELLEY, Dr Eva; da of Dr Francis Kosek, of Brno, Czechoslovakia, and Blazena Koskova (d 1982); *b* 7 Oct 1932; *Educ* Charles Univ Prague Czechoslovakia (MA, PhD, Dip); *m* 26 July 1957, Jeff, s of Francis Skelley; 1 da (Danielle Barbara); *Career* Radio Prague: translator, reporter, broadcaster; md Collets Holdings 1981-; govr Brighton Poly 1991-; *Books* Soviet Satire (gen ed, 1968), Soviet Scene (co-ed 1987), Perestroika in Action (1988), One Way Ticket to Democracy (1989); *Recreations* skiing, gardening, music, travel; *Style*— Dr Eva Skelley; Collets Holdings, Denington Estate, Wellingborough, Northants (☎ 0933 22 4351, fax 0933 76402, telex 317 320 Collet G)

SKELMERSDALE, 7 Baron (UK 1828); Roger Bootle-Wilbraham; s of Brig 6 Baron Skelmersdale, DSO, MC (d 1973), and Ann (d 1974), da of Percy Quilter and gda of Sir Cuthbert Quilter, 1 Bt; *b* 2 April 1945; *Educ* Eton, Lord Wandsworth Coll; *m* 1972, Christine, da of Roy Morgan, of Hamel Evercreech Somerset; 1 s, 1 da (Hon Carolyn Ann b 1974); *Heir* s, Hon Andrew Bootle-Wilbraham b 9 Aug 1977; *Career* horticulturist; md Broadleigh Nurseries 1973-81; pres Somerset Tst for Nature Conservation 1980-, pres Br Naturalists Assoc 1980-; Lord in waiting to HM 1981-86; Parly under sec of state: DOE 1986-87, DHSS 1987-88, DSS 1988-89, NI Office (DHSS and Agric) 1989-90; *Recreations* gardening, reading, bridge; *Style*— The Lord Skelmersdale; c/o House of Lords

SKELTON, John Martin; s of Martin Oliver Skelton, and Marie Lillian, *née* Bartlett; *b* 22 May 1952; *Educ* Westminster, BNC Oxford (BA); *m* 3 Sept 1982, Clare Louise; 1 s (Simon Martin Sheridan), 1 da (Georgina Louise); *Career* admitted slr 1977, ptnr Withers 1980-87 (asst slr 1977-79), ptnr Macfarlanes 1987-; *Style*— John Skelton, Esq; 46 Blackheath Park, London SE3 9SJ (☎ 081 852 6077); 10 Norwich St, London EC4A 1BD (☎ 071 831 9222, fax 071 831 9607)

SKELTON, Joseph Osmotherley; s of Matthew Skelton; *b* 10 May 1929; *Educ* Cockermouth GS, Univ of Durham (BCom); *m* 1953, Sheila Daphne Trimble, da of Laurence Trimble Carruthers (d 1976); 2 s; *Career* md The Wagon Finance Corporation plc 1967-88, chm Fin Houses Assoc 1978-80, dir HP Information plc 1979-90, chm Frilford Heath G C Ltd 1987-; memb Cncl Euro Fedn of Fin Houses Assoc 1978-88; memb Bank of England Deposit Protection Bd 1982-87; ACA, FCA; *Recreations* golf, gardening, swimming; *Clubs* Frilford Heath GC; *Style*— Joseph Skelton, Esq; Kinloss, Woodside, Abingdon, Oxon (☎ 0865 390500)

SKELTON, Rt Rev Kenneth John Fraser; CBE (1972); s of Henry Edmund Skelton (d 1957); *b* 16 May 1918; *Educ* Dulwich, Corpus Christi Coll Cambridge; *m* 1945, Phyllis Barbara, da of James Emerton; 2 s, 1 da; *Career* ordained 1941, rector of Walton-on-the-Hill Liverpool 1955-62, bishop of Matabeleland 1962-70, asst bishop of Durham, rural dean of Wearmouth and rector of Bishopwearmouth 1970-75, ninety-sixth bishop of Lichfield 1975-84, asst bishop in Dios of Sheffield and Derby 1984-; *Books* Bishop in Smith's Rhodesia (1985); *Style*— The Rt Rev Kenneth Skelton, CBE; 65 Crescent Rd, Sheffield S7 1HN (☎ 0742 551260)

SKELTON, Nick David; s of David Frank Skelton, of Odnull Farm, Wase Lane, Berkswell, and Norma, *née* Brindley; *m* 25 Oct 1982, Sarah Sue Poile, da of Charles Edwin Edwards; 2 s (Daniel b 9 April 1985, Harry b 20 Sept 1989); *Career* showjumper; ridden 100 World Cup classes and 60 Nations Cup teams; jr Euro champion 1975, winner 10 classes Wembley 1981, 3 team Gold medals Euro Championships (individual Bronze), team Silver medal and 2 team Bronze medals World Championships (individual Bronze), winner Hickstead Derby 3 times (runner up twice); Grand Prix wins: Dublin 3 times, NY twice, Aachen Germany 3 times; GB high jump record Olympia 1975; *Recreations* skiing, farming; *Style*— Nick Skelton, Esq; c/o Annette Batchelor, British Show Jumping Association, British Equestrian Centre, Stoneleigh, Kenilworth, Warwickshire CV8 2LR

SKELTON, Robert William; OBE (1989); s of John William Skelton (d 1989), of South Holmwood, Surrey, and Rosa Ellen Victoria Ena, *née* Wright (d 1969); *b* 11 June 1929; *Educ* Tiffins Sch Kingston; *m* 31 July 1954, Frances, da of Lionel Aird (d 1990), of Clapham; 3 s (Oliver b 1957, Gregory b 1959, Nicholas b 1962); *Career* tstee Asia House Tst 1977-; memb cncl: Soc for S Asian Studies 1984-, Royal Asiatic Soc 1970-73, 1975-78 and 1988-; *Books* Indian Miniatures for The XVth to XIXth Centuries (1961), Rajasthani Temple Hangings of The Krishna Cult (1973), Indian Painting (jtly, 1978), Arts of Bengal (jtly, 1979); *Recreations* chamber music, walking; *Style*— Robert Skelton, Esq, OBE; 10 Spencer Rd, S Croydon, Surrey CR2 7EH (☎ 081 688 7187)

SKENE, Charles P; *b* 30 April 1935; *Educ* Loretto; *Career* gp chm and chief exec of The Skene Group of Companies; pres: Jr Chamber & Aberdeen 1967, Aberdeen C of C 1983-85, Assoc of Scot Chambers of Commerce 1985-86; nat sec Jr Chamber Scot 1970 (dir 1969), fndr Aberdeen Civic Soc 1968; chm: NE Branch of Lorettovian Soc 1976-86, Royal Northern and Univ Club 1981-82, Industry Year Grampian Area 1986, Industry Matters Grampian Area 1987-89; indust conslt Scot Educn Indust Ctee 1986-87, former memb Exec Ctee Scot Cncl Devpt and Indust, dir Aberdeen and NE Soc for the Deaf 1973-, assessor to Dean of Guild, govr Robert Gordons Inst of Tech 1985-; memb: Economic Affrs Ctee SCUA 1986-, Exec Ctee CBI (Scot), Oil Experience Steering Gp, Oil Experience Venture Gp, Grampian Initiative Tourism Task Force Ctee, Open Univ Enterprise in Higher Educn Advsy Ctee for Scot; chm: RGIT Enterprise Mgmnt Ctee, Scot Industrialists' Cncl Grampian Branch; donor of the annual Skene Aberdeen Festival award 1976; initiator: Skene Young Entrepreneurs award (organiser since 1987), Scotland Tomorrow (televised banquet); author of paper Educating Scotsmen and Women; MSC Fit for work awards Euro Year of the Enviroment: conservation award, design award commendation; FRSA, FBIPP; *Style*— Charles Skene, Esq; The Skene Group, 23 Rubislaw Den North, Aberdeen AB2 4AL

SKEPPER, (Herbert) Gordon; MBE (1962); s of Herbert Amos Skepper (d 1958), and Ethel, *née* Grundy (d 1982); *b* 2 May 1923; *Educ* UMIST (BSc); *m* 23 June 1951, Ann Rosemary, da of Arthur Gilbert Hewlett, MM (d 1968); 2 s (John Gordon b 1953, Michael David b 1955), 1 da (Helen Catherine b 1958); *Career* civil engr; Colonial Serv (later-HMOCS) asst dir public works Malaya 1953-65, conslt (former exec ptnr and regnl dir) Ove Arup & Partners 1966-; CEng, FICE, FIHT; *Recreations* music, reading, travel; *Style*— Gordon Skepper, Esq, MBE; 57 Bullimore Grove, Kenilworth, Warwickshire LV8 2QF (☎ 0926 53092); Ove Arup and Partners, The Oaks, Westwood Way, Conventry CV4 8JB (☎ 0203 474347, fax 0203 466690, telex 312635 OVARPART G)

SKEWIS, Dr (William) Iain; s of John Jamieson Skewis, and Margaret Jack; *b* 1 May 1936; *Educ* Hamilton Acad, Univ of Glasgow (BSc, PhD); *m* 1963, Jessie Frame, da of John Weir (d 1982); 2 s (Alan b 1971, Guy b 1980), 1 da (Jan b 1968); *Career* dir: of tourism Highlands and Islands Devpt Bd 1966-72, Industl Devpt and Mktg Highlands and Islands Devpt Bd 1966-72, Yorks and Humberside Devpt Assoc 1972-77, chief exec Mid Wales Devpt 1977-91; chm Regnl Studies Assoc; MCIT, FIT; *Recreations* assoc football; *Style*— Dr Iain Skewis; Rock House, The Square, Montgomery, Powys SY15 6RA (☎ 0686 81276); Ladywell House, Newtown, Powys SY16 1JB (☎ 0686 626965, telex 35387)

SKIDELSKY, Prof Robert Jacob Alexander; s of Boris J Skidelsky (d 1982), and Galia V, *née* Sapelkin (d 1987); *b* 25 April 1939; *Educ* Brighton Coll, Jesus Coll Oxford (BA, MA, DPhil); *m* 2 Sept 1970, Augusta Mary Clarissa, da of John Humphrey Hope (d 1974); 2 s (Edward b 1973, William b 1976), 1 da Juliet (b 1981); *Career* res fell Nuffield Coll Oxford 1965, assoc prof John Hopkins Univ USA 1970, prof int studies

Univ of Warwick 1978; memb: Lord Chllr's Advsy Cncl on Public Records, Bd of the Social Market Fndn and the Humanitas Tst; FRHistS 1973, FRSL 1978; *Books* Politicians and the Slump (1967), English Progressive Schools (1970), Oswald Mosley (1975), John Maynard Keynes (1983); *Recreations* tennis, opera; *Clubs* United Oxford and Cambridge; *Style*— Prof Robert Skidelsky; Tilton House, Firle, E Sussex BN8 6LL (☎ 032 183 570)

SKIDMORE, (Frederic) David; OBE (1984); s of Frederick Ernest Skidmore, of Bexhill on Sea (d 1984), and Mary Elizabeth Skidmore (d 1980); *b* 10 Dec 1939; *Educ* Gonville and Caius Coll Cambridge (MA, MB BChir, MD), Birmingham Med Sch; *m* 12 July 1966 (m dis 1983), Yvonne, da of John Steel (d 1979); 1 s (David James Benedict b 1970), 1 da (Rebecca Mary b 1969); m 2, 1983, Diana Sarah; *Career* Univ of Manchester; currently conslt surgn; chm Cons Pty Foreign Affrs forum; Freeman: City of London, Worshipful Co of Tylers and Bricklayers; memb: Royal Inst of Int Affrs, RSM, Br Assoc for Surgical Oncology; FRCSEd 1968, FRCS 1970; *Books* Studies on Development of the Heart and Great Vessels (1973); *Recreations* swimming, windsurfing, ornithology; *Clubs* Hawks, Otter, Carlton; *Style*— David Skidmore, Esq, OBE; 2025 Chadbourne Ave, Maidson, Wisconsin, 53705 USA

SKIDMORE, Hon Mrs (Felicity Margaret); *née* Hall; da of Baron Roberthall, KCMG, CB; *b* 30 June 1936; *Educ* Oxford HS for Girls, Lady Margaret Hall Oxford; *m* 1957, Thomas Skidmore; 3 s; *Style*— The Hon Mrs Skidmore; 3701 Connecticut Avenue, NW, Washington, DC, 20008, USA

SKILBECK, (Norman) Stewart; s of Neilson Skilbeck (d 1978), of Northallerton, and Alice, *née* Jamieson; *b* 8 Dec 1947; *Educ* Durham Cathedral Chorister Sch, Durham Sch; *m* 16 Aug 1975, Margaret Rosamund, da of Albert Alma Wilson (d 1978), of The Grange, Camblesforth, Selby; 2 s (John b 1977, William b 1980), 1 da (Jennifer b 1983); *Career* CA; in practice 1972-78, fin dir Grindlays Humberclyde 1979-84; dir Vintage Car Dept Sotheby's, 1990- (conslt 1984-89); memb Exec Ctee Veteran Car Club of GB; FCA 1971; *Recreations* music, travel, gardening; *Clubs* Veteran Car, Rolls-Royce Enthusiasts; *Style*— Stewart Skilbeck, Esq; The Villa, Main Street, Hemingbrough, Selby, North Yorkshire (☎ 0757 638312); Sotheby's, 34-35 New Bond St, London W1A 2AA (☎ 071 408 5441, fax 0757 630346, car 0860 367633)

SKILTON, Prof David John; s of Henry Charles Stanley Skilton, of London, and Iris Flora Marion, *née* Redfern (d 1975); *b* 10 July 1942; *Educ* Tollington GS London, King's Coll Cambridge (MA, MLitt), Univ of Copenhagen; *m* 1, 29 Oct 1976 (m dis 1981), Marvid Elaine Graham, da of David King Wilson (d 1976), of Glasgow; m 2, 12 April 1984, Joanne Vivien, da of Norman Louis Papworth, of Huntingdonshire; 1 s (Adam Jonathan b 1989), 1 da (Hannah Catherine b 1985); *Career* sr lectr Univ of Glasgow 1978-80 (lectr 1970-80), dean Faculty of Arts St Davids Univ Coll Lampeter 1983-86 (prof of English 1980-86), prof of English and head of Dept of English UWIST 1986-88, prof of English and head Sch of English Studies Journalism and Philosophy Univ of Wales Coll of Cardiff 1988-; memb nat curriculum English working gp 1988-89, literary advsr to Trollope Soc 1988; *Books* Anthony Trollope and his Contemporaries (1972), Defoe to the Victorians: Two Centuries of the English Novel (1978), The Complete Novels of Anthony Trollope (gen ed); *Recreations* music; *Style*— Prof David Skilton

SKINGSLEY, Air Chief Marshal Sir Anthony Gerald; KCB (1986, CB 1983); *b* 19 Oct 1933; *Educ* Univ of Cambridge (MA); *m* 1957 Lilwen Dixon; 2 s, 1 da; *Career* joined RAF 1955, HQ 2 ATAF (ACOS Offensive Ops) 1977-78, Hon ADC to HM The Queen 1976-77, RCDS course 1978, Dir Air Plans MOD 1979-80, ACOS Plans and Policy SHAPE 1980-83, Cmdt RAF Staff Coll Bracknell 1983-84, Asst Chief of Air Staff 1985-86, Air Memb for Personnel 1986-87, C-in-C RAF Germany, Cdr 2 Allied Tactical AF 1987-89, Dep C-in-C AFCENT 1989-; *Recreations* off-shore sailing, golf, travel; *Clubs* RAF; *Style*— Air Chief Marshal Sir Anthony Skingsley, KCB; c/o National Westminster Bank plc, 43 Swan St, West Malling, Kent ME19 6LE

SKINNER, Alan Kenneth; s of Kenneth Alfred Skinner of Hindhead, Surrey and Millicent Louise, *née* Chapman; *b* 27 Aug 1948; *Educ* Sutton Valence Sch; *m* 24 March 1973, Heather, da of Peter Campbell; 1 da (Hannah b 13 June 1978); *Career* Edward Moore & Sons (now Moores Rowland): articled clerk 1966-70, qualified 1970, ptnr 1975, sr ptnr Kingston upon Thames; chm Accreditation of Training Surrey Bd ICAEW, jt chm Kingston Practitioners Gp, chm SW London Dist soc 1981-82, external examiner Accountancy Fndn Course Kingston Poly 1986-, non-exec dir Kingston Hosp 1990-; FCA 1979 (ACA 1970); *Recreations* squash, DIY; *Style*— Alan Skinner, Esq; Forest Rd, Pyrford, Woking, Surrey GU22 8LU; Moores Rowland, Applemarket House, 17 Union St, Kingston upon Thames, Surrey KT1 1RP (☎ 081 549 6399, fax 081 549 6209)

SKINNER, Alexander Morrison (Sandy); s of Lt-Col James Beattie Skinner, OBE, TD, of 50 Liberton Dr, Edinburgh, and Gertrude, *née* Morrison; *b* 23 Sept 1942; *Educ* Daniel Stewart's Coll Edinburgh, Forres Acad, Univ of Aberdeen (MA); *m* 16 July 1966, Gay Henderson, da of William Brown (d 1979); 2 s (Alastair Neil b 16 Sept 1972, Ian Malcolm b 20 Feb 1975), 1 da (Alison Jane b 6 Feb 1970); *Career* Standard Life Assur Co: asst pensions actuary Head Office Edinburgh 1963-70, asst actuary Head Office Montreal 1970-72, Head Office Edinburgh 1972- (asst pensions mangr, pension sales mangr, asst gen mangr, dep gen mangr admin); FFA, FPMI; *Recreations* swimming, gardening, theatre, occasional golf; *Clubs* Royal Scots, Scottish Actuaries (hon sec), Univ of Edinburgh Staff, Mortonhall Golf; *Style*— Sandy Skinner, Esq; 20 Hallhead Rd, Edinburgh (☎ 031 667 6254); Standard Life Assurance Company, 3 George St, Edinburgh EH2 2XZ (☎ 031 225 2552)

SKINNER, Prof Andrew Stewart; s of Andrew Paterson Skinner (d 1975), of Cardross, Dunbartonshire, and Isabella Bateman, *née* Stewart (d 1986); *b* 11 Jan 1935; *Educ* Kiel Sch Dumbarton, Cornell Univ, Univ of Glasgow (MA, BLitt); *m* 29 Aug 1966, Margaret Mary Dorothy, da of William Robertson (d 1986), of Alloway, Ayrshire; *Career* Queens Univ Belfast 1960-62, Queens Coll Dundee 1962-64; Univ of Glasgow: lectr 1964, reader 1976, head Dept of Political Economy 1979-86, dean Faculty of Social Scis 1980-83, clerk of senate 1983-90, Daniel Jack chair of political economy 1985, vice princ (Arts) 1991-; govr: Mackinnon Macniel Tst 1976-86, Jordanhill Coll of Educn 1986-; FRSE 1988; *Books* Principles of Political Economy (ed Sir James Steuart, 1966), Adam Smith - The Wealth of Nations (ed with RH Campbell and WB Todd, 1976), A System of Social Science - papers relating to Adam Smith (1979); *Recreations* gardening; *Clubs* The University, Caledonian; *Style*— Prof Andrew Skinner; Glen House, Cardross, Dunbartonshire G82 5ES (☎ 038 9841 603); Senate Office, Univ of Glasgow, Glasgow G12 8QQ (☎ 041 339 8855 ext 4242, fax 041 330 4920, telex 777070 UNIGLA)

SKINNER, David Lennox; s of Lt-Gen Arthur Lennox Skinner (d 1946), of St Andrews, Fife, and Helen Russell, *née* Gilles (d 1981); *b* 20 Sept 1932; *Educ* Marlborough, Univ of Glasgow (CA); *m* 30 April 1960, Elspeth Agnes, da of William Blackmore Surrey, of West Ferry, Dundee; 2 s ((Colin) James Marshall b 11 Feb 1961, Donald William Lennox b 26 May 1962), 2 da (Judith Evelyn (twin) b 26 May 1962, Amanda Helen b 1 Feb 1965); *Career* CA 1965; ptnr Scott Moncrieff Thomson & Shiells CA 1962-68, mangr Securities Tst of Scotland plc 1968-72, ptnr Martin Currie & Co 1972-85, chm Martin Currie Ltd 1989- (chief exec 1985-89); *Recreations* golf, forestry, reading; *Clubs* Royal & Ancient, Honourable Co of Edinburgh Golfers, New Edinburgh; *Style*— David Skinner, Esq; Lathrisk House, Falkland, Cupar, Fife KY7 7HX (☎ 0337 57419), Martin Currie Ltd, 29 Charlotte Sq, Edinburgh EH2 4HA (☎ 031 2253811)

SKINNER, David Michael Benson; s of Michael Owen Skinner, of Chichester, W Sussex, and Patricia Alma, *née* Benson-Young; *b* 1 Feb 1942; *Educ* Rugby, Christ Coll Cambridge (MA); *m* 5 June 1965, Judith Diana, da of John Kennedy Cater, of Chichester, W Sussex; 1 da (Mary Diana b 1 May 1966); *Career* dir JT Davies and Sons Ltd 1968- (joined 1964); Freeman City of London, Liveryman Worshipful Co of Cordwainers; *Recreations* tennis, squash, gardening, golf; *Style*— David Skinner, Esq; 7 Aberdeen Rd, Croydon, Surrey CRO 1EQ (☎ 081 681 3222, fax 081 760 0390, telex Davson G 8955142)

SKINNER, Dennis Edward; MP (Lab) Bolsover 1970-; s of Edward Skinner; *b* 11 Feb 1932; *Educ* Tupton Hall GS, Ruskin Coll Oxford; *m* 12 March 1960, Mary, da of James Parker; 1 s, 2 da; *Career* former miner; joined Lab Pty 1950; NEC: memb lab Pty Home Policy Ctee 1978-, Lab Pty Orgn Policy Ctee 1978, Lab Pty chm 1988-89; memb: Campaign Gp Labour MPs 1982-, Lab Pty Youth Ctee until 1982, Tribune Gp until 1982; memb Clay Cross Cncl 1960-72, pres Derbyshire miners 1966-70; *Style*— Dennis Skinner, Esq, MP; House of Commons, London SW1

SKINNER, (Thomas) James Hewitt; s and h of Sir (Thomas) Keith Hewitt Skinner, 4 Bt, *qv*; *b* 10 Sept 1962; *Style*— James Skinner, Esq; Wood Farm, Reydon, nr Southwold IP18 6SL

SKINNER, Jennifer Dingley; da of John Corbett, and Hilary, *née* Dingley; *b* 12 June 1939; *Educ* Howells Sch, Birmingham Coll of Art (NDD); *m* 4 June 1966, Peter Girling Hewitt Skinner, s of Sir Thomas Gordon Hewitt Skinner, 2 Bt (d 1969); 2 s (Justin b 1968, Dominic b 1970), 1 da (Gemma b 1977); *Career* children's book illustrator (Alice Uttley) 1962-67; *Recreations* swimming, tennis; *Clubs* Chris Lane Tennis Centre; *Style*— Mrs Jennifer Skinner; Highway Farm, Downside, Cobham, Surrey

SKINNER, Jeremy John Banks; s of R Banks Skinner (d 1978), of Moor Park, Herts, and Betty, *née* Short; *b* 15 Nov 1936; *Educ* Rugby, Clare Coll Cambridge (BA); *m* 31 Aug 1963, Judith Anne, da of Jack William Austin (d 1986), of Letchworth, Herts; 1 s (Spencer b 13 July 1966), 2 da (Sophie (Mrs Payne) b 24 Nov 1964, Sasha b 9 July 1968); *Career* Nat Serv 2 Lt 16/5 The Queen's Royal Lancers 1956-57; ptnr Linklaters & Paines 1967-; memb: Cncl and Exec Ctee Inst of Fiscal Studies, Int Bar Assoc; memb Governing Body Rugby; sr warden Worshipful Co of Cordwainers; *Recreations* hunting; *Style*— Jeremy Skinner, Esq; Stocking Farm, Stocking Pelham, nr Buntingford, Herts (☎ 0279 777556); Barrington House, 59/67 Gresham St, London EC2 (☎ 071 606 7080)

SKINNER, Sir (Thomas) Keith Hewitt; 4 Bt (UK 1912) of Pont Street, Borough of Chelsea; s of Sir (Thomas) Gordon Skinner, 3 Bt (d 1972), and his 1 w, Mollie Barbara, *née* Girling (d 1965); *b* 6 Dec 1927; *Educ* Charterhouse; *m* 29 April 1959, Jill, da of late Cedric Ivor Tuckett, of Tonbridge, Kent; 2 s; *Heir* s, (Thomas) James Hewitt Skinner; *Career* chm and chief exec Reed Publishing, dir Reed Int; *Style*— Sir Keith Skinner, Bt; Wood Farm, Reydon, nr Southwold IP18 4SL

SKINNER, Michael Gordon (Mick); s of Geordie Skinner, of Newcastle upon Tyne, and Chrissie, *née* Jackson; *b* 26 Nov 1958; *Educ* Wallbottle GS; *partner*, Anna (Kipper) Palmer; *Career* Rugby Union flanker Harlequins FC and England (12 caps); clubs: Blaydon RFC 1974-79, Blackheath RFC 1979-84, Harlequins FC 1984-; rep: Blaydon Colts (winner Durham Co Colts Cup), Northumberland U21, Kent, London Div, England B (debut v France 1987); England debut v France 1988; freelance computer conslt; *Style*— Mick Skinner, Esq

SKINNER, Nicholas James Sylvester; s of Ian William Sylvester Skinner (d 1973), of Holt Lodge, Kintbury, Newbury, Berks, and Cecily Joan Burns, *née* Dumbell; *b* 9 Jan 1948; *Educ* Marlborough, RAC (MRAC); *m* 24 Nov 1984, Jacqueline Irene Kaye, da of Jack Woolly, of Rowan Dr, Wolverton, Milton Keynes; *Career* farmer and sport horse breeder; *Recreations* riding, travel; *Style*— Nicholas Skinner, Esq; Clere House, Ecchinswell, Newbury, Berks (☎ 0635 298 341)

SKINNER, Prof Quentin Robert Duthie; s of Alexander Skinner, CBE (d 1979), and Winifred Rose Margaret, *née* Duthie; *b* 26 Nov 1940; *Educ* Bedford Sch, Gonville and Caius Coll Cambridge (BA, MA); *m* 31 Aug 1979, Dr Susan Deborah Thorpe, da of Prof Derrick James, of London; 1 s (Marcus b 13 July 1982), 1 da (Olivia b 7 Dec 1979); *Career* Univ of Cambridge: fell Christ's Coll 1962-, prof of political sci 1978-; FRHS 1970, FBA 1980; *Books* The Foundations of Modern Political Thought (1978), Machiavelli (1981), Meaning & Context (1988); *Style*— Prof Quentin Skinner; Christ's College, Cambridge, Cambs, CB2 3BU

SKINNER, Robin Charles Owen; s of Michael Owen Skinner, of Meadow Cottage, Sandy Lane, East Ashling, Chichester, West Sussex, and Patricia Alma, *née* Benson-Young; *b* 20 Sept 1949; *Educ* Rugby, Fitzwilliam Coll Cambridge (MA), Coll of Law Guildford; *m* 21 July 1973, Jillian Mary, da of Benjamin Ian Gilmour Mantle, of 62 Storeys Way, Cambridge; 2 s (Charles b 30 May 1974, Toby b 24 June 1976), 1 da (Emily b 20 Oct 1982); *Career* articled Linklaters & Paines 1974; admitted slr 1975; sr ptnr Rawlinson & Butler 1984-; memb Worshipful Co of Cordwainers (Steward, Warden 1988); Rugby Blue 1970-71, Rugby Fives Blue 1971; *Recreations* squash, tennis, golf, family; *Clubs* Hawks, City Livery; *Style*— Robin Skinner, Esq; Beacon Platt, Dormansland, Lingfield, Surrey RH7 6RB; Rawlinson & Butler, Griffin House, 135 High St, Crawley, West Sussex RH10 1DQ (☎ 0293 527744, fax 0293 520202) RAWLEX)

SKINNER, Hon Mrs (Rose Marian); da of Maj Geoffrey Seymour Rowley-Conwy, and sis of 9 Baron Langford, OBE; *b* 6 June 1915; *m* 1938, Ralph Becher Skinner; 1 s, 2 da; *Career* raised to the rank of a Baron's da 1955; *Style*— The Hon Mrs Skinner; The Fold, Cwm, nr Rhyl, Clwyd

SKINNER, Thomas Monier; CMG (1956), MBE (1941); s of Lt-Col Thomas Burrell Skinner, of Devon, and Mona Isobel, *née* Brown (d 1967); ancestors founded: RE, 1 Newfoundland Fencibles, Skinner's Horse; *b* 2 Feb 1913; *Educ* Cheltenham, Lincoln Coll Oxford (MA); *m* 1935, Margaret Adeline (d 1969), da of Frederick Robert Pope (d 1934), of Sussex; 2 s (Anthony, Keith); m 2, 1981, Elizabeth Jane, da of Phillip Leicester Hardie (d 1977), of Cumbria; *Career* dist offr Tanganyika 1947 (asst dist offr (cadet) 1935, asst dist offr 1937), sr asst sec E Africa High Cmmn 1952, dir of estabs Kenya 1955-62, memb Civil Serv Cmmn E Caribbean Territories 1962-63, chm Nyasaland Local Civil Serv Cmmn 1963, salaries cmmr Basutoland The Bechuanaland Protectorate and Swaziland 1964; reports on: localisation of Civil Serv, Gilbert and Ellice Islands Colony, Br Nat Serv New Hebrides 1968; chm and md: Bear Securities Ltd 1962-73, Exeter Trust plc 1973-78; chm: The Glassmaster Co Ltd 1979-87, Edinburgh Bond and Mortgage Corporation 1988-; dir Business Mortgages Trust plc 1979-87; *Recreations* fishing; *Clubs* Army and Navy; *Style*— Thomas Skinner, Esq, CMG, MBE; Innerpeffray Lodge, by Crieff, Perthshire PH7 3QW

SKIPPER, David John; s of Herbert George Skipper (d 1962), and Edna Skipper; *b* 14 April 1931; *Educ* Watford GS, Univ of Oxford (MA); *m* 1955, Brenda Ann, da of late Alfred George Williams; 3 s, 1 da; *Career* served RAF 1954-57; asst master: Radley Coll 1957-63, Rugby Sch 1963-69; headmaster: Ellesmere Coll Salop 1969-81, Merchant Taylors' Sch 1981-; chm: special needs ctee ISJC, Soc of Sch Masters; *Recreations* golf, hill walking, painting, fungi, herbs; *Clubs* E India, Devonshire Pub

Schs; *Style—* David Skipper, Esq; Headmaster's House, Merchant Taylors' School, Northwood, Middx (☎ home 09274 27980, office 09274 21850)

SKIPWITH, Alexander Sebastian Grey d'Estoteville; s (by 1 m) and h of Sir Patrick Skipwith, 12 Bt; *b* 9 April 1969; *Educ* Harrow; *Style—* Sir Patrick Skipwith, Bt; 27H Bramham Gdns, London SW5

SKIPWITH, Sir Patrick Alexander d'Estoteville; 12 Bt (E 1622), of Prestwould, Leicestershire; s of Grey d'Estoteville Townsend Skipwith (ka 1942), and Sofka, da of Prince Peter Alexandrovitch Dolgorouky; suc gf, Sir Grey Humberston d'Estoteville Skipwith 1950; *b* 1 Sept 1938; *Educ* Harrow, Trinity Coll Dublin (MA), Imperial Coll London (PhD); *m* 1, 24 June 1964 (m dis 1970), Gillian Patricia, adopted da of late Charles Frederick Harwood; 1 s, 1 da; m 2, 1972 (separated 1986), Ashkhain, da of Bedros Atikian, of Calgary, Alberta, Canada; *Heir* s, Alexander Sebastian Grey d'Estoteville Skipwith b 9 April 1969; *Career* marine geologist: Ocean Mining Inc 1966-70, Directorate-Gen of Mineral Resources Jeddah 1970-73; geological ed Bureau de Recherches Géologiques et Minières Jeddah Saudi Arabia 1973-86, md Immel Publishing Ltd 1988-89; freelance editing, translating and public relations 1986-; *Recreations* riding, deep sea fishing, hill walking; *Clubs* Chelsea Arts; *Style—* Sir Patrick Skipwith, Bt; 1 rue Jean Hupeau, 45000 Orléans, France; c/o Lloyds Bank plc, 164 Kings Road, Chelsea, London SW3 4UR Chelsea, London SW3 4UR

SKIPWITH, Peyton Stephen; s of Sir Grey Humberston d'Estoteville Skipwith, 12 Bt (d 1949), and Cynthia, *née* Egerton Leigh; *b* 30 June 1939; *Educ* Canford; *m* 1 Oct 1971, Anne, da of Cecil England Barren, of Seasalter, Kent; 1 s (Grey b 1981), 2 da (Selina b 1972, Amber b 1974); *Career* dep md The Fine Art Soc; contrib to: The Connoisseur, Apollo, Burlington Magazine; *Style—* Peyton Skipwith, Esq; The Fine Art Society, 148 New Bond St, London W1Y 0JT (☎ 071 629 5116)

SKIRROW, Dr Martin Bingham; s of Geoffrey Howe Skirrow (d 1965), of The Chase, Upper Welland, Malvern, and Marjorie, *née* Vaughan (d 1979); *b* 2 May 1929; *Educ* Oundle, Univ of Birmingham (MB ChB), Univ of Liverpool (PhD, DTM & H); *m* 23 March 1957, Mary Ethel, da of late Frank Reginald White, of 52 Chantry Ave, Bexhill-on-Sea, Sussex; 1 s (Andrew b 1961), 1 da (Helen b 1959); *Career* Nat Serv RAF 1954-56 (MO ME cmd); lectr Liverpool Sch Tropical Med Liverpool and Nigeria 1957-64, sr registrar microbiology and haematology Birmingham Children's Hosp 1965-68, sr microbiologist Worcester Public Health Laboratory 1968-76, conslt med microbiologist Worcester Royal Infirmary 1976-90, hon emeritus conslt microbiologist to Public Health Laboratory Service Bd 1990-; co-discoverer of campylobacter enteritis; contrib major med textbooks, author of over 20 sci papers on campylobacter and related infections in med jls and pubns; former chm Eng branch Br Soc for Study of Infection; FRCPath 1979 (memb 1967); *Recreations* music, natural history, photography; *Style—* Dr Martin Skirrow; Public Health Laboratory, Gloucestershire Royal Hospital, Gloucester GL1 3NN (☎ 0452 305334, fax 0452 307 213)

SKLAR, Dr Jonathan; s of Vivian Sklar, of London, and Joyce, *née* Longworth; *b* 9 June 1949; *Educ* Latymer Upper Sch, Royal Free Hosp Univ of London, Inst of Psychoanalysis London, LRCP; *m* 25 March 1975, Rina, da of Anthony Herbert-Caesari, of London; 2 da (Clea b 1 Aug 1978, Livia b 31 Oct 1981); *Career* sr registrar in psychiatry Friern and Royal Free Hosps 1978-79, sr registrar in psychotherapy Tavistock Clinic 1979-83, conslt psychotherapist Cambridge Health Authy 1983-; regnl tutor in psychotherapy E Anglia, head of Dept of Psychotherapy Cambridge, visiting prof Arhus Univ and Psychiatric Hosp Denmark 1991-; chm Zeitlyn Psychotherapy Tst, sec psychotherapy exec of Joint Ctee of Higher Psychiatric Trg; Freedom City of Cusco Peru 1989; MRCS 1973, MB BS 1974, MRCPsych 1977, assoc memb Br Psychoanalytical Soc 1984 (memb 1991), Examination Notes for the MRC Psych Part 1 (with B Puri, 1989); *Recreations* reading, gardening; *Clubs* Mossiman's; *Style—* Dr Jonathan Sklar; Dept of Psychotheraphy, 2 Benet Place, Off Lensfield Rd, Cambridge CB2 1EL (☎ 0223 66461)

SKYNNER, Dr (Augustus Charles) Robin; s of Reginald Charles Augustus Skynner (d 1965), of Wainsford House, Two-Waters-Foot, nr Liskeard, Cornwall, and Mary Flemming, *née* Johns (d 1966); *b* 16 Aug 1922; *Educ* St Austell Co Sch Cornwall, Blundell's, Univ of London (MB BS, DPM); *m* 1, 12 July 1948 (m dis 29 April 1959), Geraldine Annella; m 2, 8 May 1959, Prudence Mary (d 1987), da of John Francis St Aubyn Fawcett (d 1954); 1 s (David b 1961), 1 da (Rosemary b 1963); *Career* WWII serv: RAF 1940, pilot trg cmmnd 1941, active serv pilot 21 Sqdn 2 Tactical Airforce, demobbed 1946; appts as conslt psychiatrist 1959-, physician i/c Dept Psychiatry Queen Elizabeth Hosp for Children 1965-70, sr tutor psychotherapy and hon conslt Bethlem Royal and Maudsley Hosp 1971-82; fndr memb: Group-Analytic Practice 1960-, fndr memb Inst of Gp Analysis 1968-; fndr memb and first chm Inst of Family Therapy 1976-78, memb Cncl Tavistock Inst of Med Psychology 1988-, regular columnist The Guardian 1989-; advsr London Diocese Pastoral Work Devpt Scheme, conslt Gp and Family Dynamics Exploring Parenthood; FRCPsych, fndr memb Assoc of Family Therapy, memb American Family Therapy Assoc, distinguished affiliate memb American Assoc of Family and Marital Therapists; *Books* One Flesh, Separate Persons: Principles of Family and Marital Psychotherapy (1976), Families and How to Survive Them (with John Cleese, 1983), Explorations with Families: Group Analysis and Family Therapy (1987), Institutes and How to Survive Them: Mental Health Training and Consultation (1989); *Recreations* country pursuits, windsurfing; *Style—* Dr Robin Skynner; 88 Montagu Mansions, London W1H 1LF (☎ 081 935 3103/3085)

SKYRME, Hon Mrs (Barbara Suzanne); *née* Lyle; da of 1 Baron Lyle of Westbourne (d 1954); *b* 1915; *m* 1938 (m dis 1953), William Thomas Charles Skyrme, KCVO, CB CBE, TD, JP, *qv*; 1 s, 2 da (*see* Sir Gerard Waterlow, Bt); *Style—* The Hon Mrs Skyrme; River House, Remenham, Henley-on-Thames, Oxon; 1 Sloane Court East, London SW3

SKYRME, Sir (William) Thomas Charles; KCVO (1974), CB (1966), CBE (1953), TD (1949), JP (Oxon 1948), DL (Glos 1983); s of C G Skyrme of Monmouth; *b* 1913; *Educ* Rugby, New Coll Oxford, Dresden Univ, Paris Univ; *m* 1, 1938 (m dis 1953), Hon Barbara Suzanne, *qv*, yr da of 1 Baron Lyle of Westbourne (d 1954); 1 s, 2 da (*see* Sir Gerard Waterlow, Bt); m 2, 1957, Mary, da of Dr R C Leaning; *Career* WWII RA (wounded twice), Lt-Col; called to the Bar Inner Temple 1935 (Master of the Bench 1988), in practice Western circuit, sec to Lord Chllr 1944-48, sec of Cmmns 1948-77; pres Cwlth Magistrates' and Judges' Assoc 1970-79, (life vice pres 1979), chm Magistrates' Assoc of Eng and Wales 1979-81 (vice pres 1981-), gen cmmr Income Tax 1977-88, cmmr Broadcasting Complaints Cmmn 1981-87 (chm 1985-87), memb Top Salaries Review Bd 1981-, chm Judicial Salaries Ctee 1984-90; Freeman City of London 1970, HM Lt City of London 1977-; FRGS; *Books* The Changing Image of the Magistracy (1979), History of the Justices of the Peace (1991); *Clubs* Army and Navy, Hurlingham; *Style—* Sir Thomas Skyrme, KCVO, CB, CBE, TD, JP, DL; Casa Larissa, Klosters, Switzerland; Elm Barns, Blockley, Moreton-in-Marsh, Glos

SLACK, His Hon Judge John Kenneth Edward; TD (1964); s of Ernest Edward Slack (d 1967), of Broadstairs, Kent, and Beatrice Mary, *née* Shorten (d 1972); *b* 23 Dec 1930; *Educ* Univ Coll Sch, St John's Coll Cambridge (MA, Cricket Blue 1954); *m* 4 April 1959, Patricia Helen, da of William Keith Metcalfe (d 1979), of Southport, Lancs; 2 s ((Mark) Christopher b 1960, Martin Andrew b 1962); *Career* Nat Serv Capt RAEC 1949-51, TA, RA Middx Regiment (DCO) 1951-64; slr 1957, ptnr Freeborough Slack & Co 1958-76, rec Crown Courts 1972-77, circuit judge 1977-; memb Cncl Univ Coll Sch 1974-90 (chm 1980-88); Club Cricket Conference: capt 1959-64, active vice pres 1969-77, pres 1978; capt Bucks CCC 1967-69, played rugby for Middlesex; *Recreations* golf; *Style—* His Hon Judge Slack, TD; c/o Crown Court, 38 Market Square, Aylesbury, Bucks (☎ 0296 434401, fax 0296 435665)

SLACK, Dr Richard Charles Bewick; s of Dr Horace George Bewick Slack (d 1966), of Bramhall, Cheshire, and Dorothy Edith, *née* Smith; *b* 4 March 1944; *Educ* Manchester GS, Jesus Coll Cambridge (MA, MB BChir); *m* 10 May 1969, Dr Patricia Mary Slack, da of Dr Arthur Hamilton Cheshire (d 1982), of Brewood, Staffs; 2 s (Benjamin b 1972, William b 1974), 2 da (Clare b 1976, Eleanor b 1981); *Career* house surgeon St Mary's Hosp London 1969-70; lectr: Middx Hosp Med Sch 1971-73, Univ of Nairobi 1973-77; sr lectr Univ of Nottingham 1978-, hon conslt PHLS and Nottingham Health Authy 1978-, temp conslt WHO Special Programme AIDS 1987-88; memb: cncl Br Soc Antimicrobial Chemotherapy, ctee Pathologic Soc GB and I, Assoc Med Biologists, Nottingham Medico-Chirugical Soc; MRCPath 1977; *Books* Antimicrobial Chemotherapy (1989); *Recreations* fell walking, skiing, political argument; *Style—* Dr Richard Slack; 5 Magdala Road, Mapperley Park, Nottingham, NG3 5DE (☎ 0602 605940), Dept of Micorbiology, Univ of Nottingham Medical Sch, Queen's Medical Centre, Nottingham NG7 2UH (☎ 0602 421421, fax 0602 422190)

SLACK, Timothy Willatt; s of Cecil Moorhouse Slack, MC (d 1986), and Dora, *née* Willatt (d 1978); *b* 18 April 1928; *Educ* Winchester, New Coll Oxford (MA); *m* 31 Aug 1957, Katharine, da of Norman Hughes (d 1982); 1 s (Henry b 1962), 3 da (Caroline b 1960, Louisa b 1966, Rebecca b 1969); *Career* Nat Serv RN; asst master: Lycée de Garcons Rennes France 1951-52, Schule Schloss Salem W Germany 1952-53, Repton Derbys 1953-59; headmaster: Kambawsa Coll Burma 1959-62, Bedales Sch Hants 1962-74, Hellenic Coll London 1983-84; dir FCO Wiston House Conf Centre 1977-83 (asst dir 1975-77); princ St Catharine's Fndn Cumberland Lodge Windsor 1985-; Parly candidate: (Lib) Petersfield Feb and Oct 1974, (Alliance) Enfield Southgate 1984, (Alliance) Fareham 1987; chm: Soc of Headmasters of Ind Schs 1965-67 (memb), of govrs Royal Sch Windsor Gt Park; *Style—* Timothy Slack, Esq; Hamlet House, Hambledon, Hants PO7 6RY (☎ 070132 358); Cumberland Lodge, The Great Park, Windsor, Berks SL4 2HP (☎ 0784 432316/434893, fax 0784 438507)

SLACK, Sir William Willatt; KCVO (1990); s of Cecil Moorhouse Slack, MC (d 1986), and Dora, *née* Willatt (d 1979); *b* 22 Feb 1925; *Educ* Winchester, New Coll Oxford (MA), Middx Hosp Med Sch (MCh MB); *m* 29 July 1951, Dr Joan Slack, da of Lt-Col Talbot H Wheelwright, OBE (d 1938); 2 s (Robert b 1953, Graham b 1955), 2 da (Diana b 1962, Clare b 1966); *Career* conslt surgn and sr lectr in Surgery Middx Hosp 1962-; surgn King Edward VII Hosp for Offrs 1975-; various surgical articles in med jls and textbooks; sergeant surgn to HM The Queen 1983-90; dean: Middx Hosp Med Sch 1983-87, Univ Coll and Middx Sch of Med 1987-90; memb: NE Thames RHA, Conf Met Deans, Conf Deans UK Med Schs; hon fell UCL; Upper Warden Worshipful Co of Barbers; FRCS, FRSM (pres coloproctology section 1980); *Recreations* skiing, gardening; *Style—* Sir William Slack, KCVO; 22 Platts Lane, London NW3 7NS (☎ 071 435 5887, 0278 722719)

SLADE, Adrian Carnegie; CBE (1988); s of George Penkivil Slade, KC (d 1942), and Mary Albinia Alice, *née* Carnegie (d 1988); *b* 25 May 1936; *Educ* Eton, Trinity Coll Cambridge (BA); *m* 22 June 1960, Susan Elizabeth, da of Edward Forsyth (d 1978); 1 s (Rupert b 15 Jan 1965), 1 da (Nicola b 28 March 1962); *Career* Nat Serv 9 Lancers 1955-56 (Emergency Res 1956-61); dir S H Benson (advertising) 1969-71, co fndr and chm Slade Hamilton Fenech 1986- (previously Slade Bluff & Bigg 1975-86, Slade Monico Bluff 1971-75); mgmnt Wandsworth Cncl for Community Rels 1967-81; dir: Orange Tree Theatre Ltd Richmond, Longslade Media Training Ltd; chm ONE plus ONE Marriage and Partnership Research; Parly Candidate: (Lib) Putney 1966 and 1974, Wimbledon (Alliance) 1987; memb GLC Richmond, ldr Alliance Gp 1981-86; pres Lib Pty 1987-88 (vice pres 1988-89), jt pres Lib Democrats 1988-; *Recreations* theatre, music, photography, piano playing; *Style—* Adrian Slade, Esq, CBE

SLADE, (Sir) (Julian) Benjamin Alfred; 7 Bt (UK 1831), of Maunsel House, Somerset; does not use title; s of Capt Sir Michael Niall Slade, 6 Bt (d 1962), and Angela (d 1959), da of Capt Orlando Chichester; *b* 22 May 1946; *Educ* Millfield; *m* 1977, Pauline Carol, da of Maj Claude Myburgh; *Career* chm and md Shirlstar Container Transport Ltd, dir Pyman Bell Ltd; Freeman City of London 1979, memb Worshipful Co of Ironmongers; *Recreations* hunting, shooting, racing, polo, bridge; *Clubs* Turf, Old Somerset Dining, Bucks; *Style—* Benjamin Slade, Esq; 164 Ashley Gdns, Emery Hill St, London SW1 (☎ 071 828 2809); Maunsel, North Newton, Bridgwater, Somerset (☎ 0278 663413; estate office ☎ 0278 663398); office: Shirlstar House, 37 St John's Road, Uxbridge, Middx (☎ 0895 72929, telex 885635)

SLADE, Brian John; s of Albert Edward Victor Slade, of Portsmouth, Hants, and Florence Elizabeth, *née* Eveleigh; *b* 28 April 1931; *Educ* Portsmouth Northern GS, Univ of London; *m* 5 March 1955, Grace, da of William McKerrow Murray (d 1943), of Ayr; 1 s (Ian Murray b 1962), 1 da (Maureen Grace b 1959); *Career* joined Miny of Supply 1951, private sec to perm sec Miny of Aviation 1962-64, head industl personnel branch Miny of Technol 1968-73; MOD: head of contracts policy branch 1978-82, princ dir of contracts (air) 1982-86, dir gen of def contracts 1986-; memb Synod London SW Dist Methodist Church 1981-, sec to church cncl Epsom Methodist Church 1981-; FInstPS 1986; *Recreations* downs walking, cricket; *Style—* Brian Slade, Esq; Doonbank, 16 Greenway, Gt Bookham, Surrey (☎ 0372 54359); St George's Ct, 14 New Oxford St, London WC1A 1EJ (☎ 071 632 3600)

SLADE, Rt Hon Sir Christopher John; PC (1982); s of George Penkivil Slade, KC (d 1942), and Mary Albinia Alice Slade; *b* 2 June 1927; *Educ* Eton, New Coll Oxford; *m* 1958, Jane Gwenllian Armstrong, da of Rt Hon Sir Denys Buckley, MBE; 1 s, 3 da; *Career* barr 1951, QC 1965, attorney-general Duchy of Lancaster 1972-75, bencher Lincoln's Inn 1973, judge High Ct of Justice (Chancery Div) 1975-82, judge Restrictive Practices Ct 1980-82 and pres 1981-82, Lord Justice of Appeal 1982-91; kt 1975; *Clubs* Garrick; *Style—* The Rt Hon Sir Christopher Slade; 12 Harley Gdns, London SW10 9SW (☎ 071 373 7695)

SLADE, Hon Mrs (Constance); *née* Montague; da of 2 Baron Amwell; *b* 2 March 1915; *Educ* N London Collegiate Sch; *m* 1938, Albert Slade; 1 s, 2 da; *Style—* The Hon Mrs Slade; 1 Park Rd, NW3

SLADE, Julian Penkivil; s of George Penkivil Slade, KC (d 1942), of London, and Mary Albina Alice, *née* Carnegie (d 1988); *b* 28 May 1930; *Educ* Eton, Trinity Coll Cambridge (BA); *Career* composer and author; musical plays incl: Bang Goes the Meringue! Lady May (1951), Christmas in King Street (with Dorothy Reynolds, 1952), The Duenna (1953), The Merry Gentleman (1953), Salad Days (1954-60), Free as Air (1957), Hooray for Daisy (1959), Follow that Girl (1960), Wildest Dreams (1961); other musicals incl: Vanity Fair (1962), Nutmeg and Ginger (1963), Sixty Thousand Nights (1966), The Pursuit of Love (1967), Winnie the Pooh (1970), Trelawny (1972), Out of Bounds (1975), Love in a Cold Climate (Thames TV, 1981), Now We Are Sixty (1986); published scripts incl: Salad Days, Free as Air, Follow that Girl, The Duenna, The Merry Gentleman, Trelawny; Nibble The Squirrel (1946); *Recreations* going to theatre and cinema, drawing, listening to music; *Style—* Julian Slade, Esq; 86 Beaufort Street, London SW3 6BU (☎ 071 376 4480)

SLADE, Dr Robert Rodney; s of William Alfred John Slade, of Swindon, Wists, and Mary, *née* Corbett; *b* 29 June 1947; *Educ* UCL (BSc), UCH (MB BS, MRCP); *m* 25 May 1974, Sarah Anne (Siân), da of Edwin Howell Morgan, of Lianelli, Wales; 2 s (Mathew Edward b 1975, William James b 1975); *Career* conslt haematologist SW RHA 1982, clinical dean Univ of Bristol Med Sch 1989 (clinical lectr in haematology 1983), conslt haematologist to BUPA Hosps Bristol 1989; fund raiser for Leukameia Res Fund 1981-, govr Marlwood Sch Bristol; MRCPath 1981; *Books* Blood Cell Labelling (1988), Haematological Maliganancy In Pregnancy (1989); *Recreations* cricket, squash, golf; *Clubs* Cotsworld Edge Golf; *Style*— Dr Robert Slade; Dept of Haematology, Southmead Hosp, Bristol (01 454505050)

SLADEN, Angus Murray; s of Sqdn Ldr Algernon Ivan Sladen, DSO (d 1976), and Dorviegelda Malvina, *née* MacGregor; *b* 17 Dec 1950; *Educ* Stowe, Univ of Texas; *m* 1989, Sarah, da of John William Hayter, DL, of Cagebrook Hereford; *Career* insur broker 1974-; dir: Wendover Underwriting Agency Ltd (Lloyd's underwriting agencies); *Recreations* shooting, stalking, fishing; *Clubs* Buck's, City of London; *Style*— Angus Sladen, Esq; Glencarron Lodge, Achnashellach, Ross-shire; 14 Shafto Mews, London SW1; 3 St Helens Place, Bishopsgate, London EC3 (☎ 071 628 1317)

SLANE, Viscount; Alexander Burton Conyngham; s and h of Earl of Mount Charles, *qv*; *b* 30 Jan 1975; *Style*— Viscount Slane

SLANEY, Prof Sir Geoffrey; KBE (1984); s of Richard Slaney, and Gladys Lois Slaney; *b* 19 Sept 1922; *Educ* Brewood GS, Univs of Birmingham, London and Illinois; *m* 1956, Josephine Mary Davy; 1 s, 2 da; *Career* Queen Elizabeth Hosp Birmingham: Barling prof and head Dept of Surgery 1971-87, currently prof of surgery emeritus; hon conslt surgn: Utd Birmingham Hosps and Regnl Hosp Bd 1959-87, Royal Prince Alfred Hosp Sydney 1981-; pres Royal Coll of Surgeons 1982-86; *Style*— Prof Sir Geoffrey Slaney, KBE; 23 Aston Bury, Edgbaston, Birmingham B15 3QB (☎ 021 454 0261)

SLAPAK, Maurice; s of Abraham Szlapak, of Fairview Hotel, Nairobi (d 1966), and Rachelle Szlapak; *b* 15 Feb 1930; *Educ* Prince of Wales Sch Nairobi, Millfield, Downing Coll Cambridge (MA, MB MChir); *m* 16 June 1960, Catherine Elisabeth, da of Arthur Ellis (d 1966), of 828 Echo Drive, Ottawa, Canada; 2 da (Gabrielle Isobel b 16 Jan 1964, Alexander Rachel b 10 Feb 1968); *Career* Capt RAMC: RMO i/c Household Cavalry Regt 1959, MO i/c SHAPE Paris; assoc prof of surgery Harvard Med Sch 1972, co chm first Int Symposium Organ Preservation 1973, sr asst surgn Univ of Cambridge 1972-75, conslt and co dir Transplant Unit St Mary's Hosp Portsmouth, Hunterian prof of surgery RCS, memb Editorial Advsy Bd Transplantation Proceedings; pres: Transplant, World Transplant Games; fndr and pres Transplant Olympic Games 1978, vice pres Euro Soc for Organ Transplantation; FRCS 1964, FRCS (Canada) 1967, FACS 1971; *Books* Experimental and Clinical Methods in Fulminant Liver Failure Support (1973), The Acute Abdomen (in Tice Sloane Practice of Medicine 1972); *Recreations* tennis, squash, windsurfing, reading; *Clubs* All England Lawn Tennins (Wimbledon), Queen's, Hurlingham; *Style*— Maurice Slapak, Esq; Abbey House, Itchen Abbas, Hants (☎ 0962 78233); 37 Rutland Gate, London SW5; Transplant Unit, St Mary's Hospital, Portsmouth, Hants (☎ 0705 818296, fax 0705 821231, car 0860 311406); 144 Harley St, London W1

SLATER, Dr Alan John; *b* 20 Oct 1948; *Educ* Univ of Birmingham (MB ChB), Open Univ (BA); *m* 30 June 1973, Jane Slater; 2 da (Jenny b 1976, Gill b 1978); *Career* res assoc in MRC leukaemia trials Welsh Nat Sch of Med Cardiff 1974-76, registrar in radiotherapy and oncology Velindre Hosp Cardiff 1976-79, resident res fell Princess Margaret Hosp Toronto 1979-81, clincial scientist MRC Addenbrookes Hosp Cambridge 1981-82; conslt in oncology and radiotherapy: Clatterbridge Hosp, BUPA Murrayfield Hosp, Ysbyty Glan Clwyd 1982-; author of numerous papers and chapters on oncology; memb: neutron therapy sub-gp MRC, Mersey Regnl Conslts and specialists Ctee; visiting conslt: Royal Liverpool Hosp, Countess of Chester Hosp, Grosvenor Nuffield Hosp; FRCR 1980; *Recreations* horticulture, steam railways, postal history; *Style*— Dr Alan Slater; 5 Burlingham Ave, West Kirby, Wirral, L48 8AJ (☎ 051 625 9868); Clatterbridge Hospital, Bebington, Wirral L63 4JY (☎ 051 334 4000, fax 051 346 1445)

SLATER, Hon Mrs (Alexandra Janet); eld da of Dr Geoffrey Tyndale Young, and Baroness Young (Life Peer); *b* 1951; *m* 1974, John Douglas Slater; 1 s, 1 da; *Style*— The Hon Mrs Slater; 12 Edgar Road, Winchester, Hants

SLATER, Arnold; s of Arnold Slater, of Holmfirth, Yorks, and Pauline Margaret, *née* Shaw-Parker; *b* 26 March 1948; *Educ* Hadham Hall Sch, Regent St Poly; *m* 21 Oct 1972, Judith Helen, da of Philip Ellison, of Bishops Stortford, Herts; 1 s (Ross Adrian b 24 Sept 1973), 1 da (Anthea Helen b 15 Feb 1978); *Career* chief photographer Herts and Essex Observer 1973-78; photographer: Press Assoc 1978-87, London Daily News Jan - June 1987, Sunday People 1987-88, Daily Mirror 1988-; winner: Simeon Edmunds award Best Young Press Photographer, Ilford Press Photographer of the Year 1987; *Recreations* squash, skiing, fly tying, fly fishing; *Style*— Arnold Slater, Esq; Shingle Sand, Copthall Lane, Thaxted, Essex, CM5 2LG (☎ 0371 830452); Mirror Group Newspapers, Holborn Circus, London, EC1P 1DQ (☎ 071 822 3851)

SLATER, Duncan; CMG (1982); *b* 15 July 1934; *m* 1972, Candida Coralie Anne Wheatley; 1 s, 2 da; *Career* joined FO 1958; served: Abu Dhabi, Islamabad, New Delhi; head of chancery Aden 1968-69, FO 1969, special asst to Sir William Luce 1970-71, first sec UK Representation to EEC Brussels 1973-75, UK rep to Int Atomic Energy Authy and UN Industl Devpt Orgn 1975-78, cnsllr and head of chancery Lagos 1978-81 and on staff of Govt House Salisbury 1979-80, ambass to Muscat 1981-86, asst reader Sec of State FCO 1986-; *Style*— Duncan Slater, Esq, CMG; c/o Foreign and Commonwealth Office, London SW1

SLATER, Prof (James) Howard; s of Arthur Robert Frank Slater, of Arundel, Sussex, and Mildred Dorothy, *née* White; *b* 16 Dec 1947; *Educ* Worthing Tech HS, UCL (BSc, PhD, DSc); *m* 13 Sept 1969, Georgette Eloise Edwina, da of Cecil Edwin Baldwin, of Worthing, Sussex; 2 da (Elisabeth b 15 Nov 1977, Catherine b 20 June 1979); *Career* lectr in microbiology Univ of Kent at Canterbury 1972-75, sr lectr in environmental sciences Univ of Warwick 1979-82 (lectr 1975-79), visiting prof in microbiology Univ of Connecticut 1982, prof of applied microbiology Univ of Wales Coll of Cardiff (formerly Univ of Wales Inst of Sci and Technol) 1982-, ed 5 books and author many scientific pubns and patents; sr res conslt BioTechnica Int Inc 1982-84, res dir Biotal Ltd 1984-88, dir Int Inst of Biotechnology 1990-; FIBiol 1984, fell Int Inst of Biotechnol 1988; *Recreations* photography, sailing, travelling, sports-watching; *Style*— Prof Howard Slater; School of Pure and Applied Biology, University of Wales College of Cardiff, PO Box 915, Cardiff CF1 3TL Wales (☎ 0222 874771, fax 0222 874305)

SLATER, James Derrick; s of Hubert Slater, and Jessica Slater; *b* 13 March 1929; *Educ* Preston Manor County Sch; *m* 1965, Helen Wyndham Goodwyn; 2 s, 2 da; *Career* articled clerk to chartered accountants 1946-53, accountant then gen mangr to a group of metal finishing cos 1953-55, sec Park Royal Vehicles Ltd 1955-58, dir AEC Ltd 1959, dep sales dir Leyland Motor Corporation 1963, chm Slater Walker Securities Ltd (formerly H Lotery & Co Ltd) 1964-75 (md 1964-72), dir British Leyland Motor Co 1969-75, chm Salar Properties Ltd 1983-; FCA 1963 (ACA 1953); *Books* Return to Go (autobiography, 1977); childrens books incl: Goldenrod, Goldenrod and the Kidnappers, Grasshopper and the Unwise Owl, Grasshopper and the Pickle Factory, The Boy who Saved Earth, A Mazing Monster Series, Roger the Robot Series; *Recreations* salmon fishing, bridge, chess, backgammon; *Style*— James Slater, Esq; Combe Court, Combe Lane, Chiddingfold, Surrey GU8 4XN

SLATER, Vice Adm Sir (John Cunningham Kirkwood) Jock; KCB (1988), LVO (1971); s of Dr James K Slater, OBE (d 1965), of Edinburgh, and Margaret Claire Byrom, *née* Bramwell; *b* 27 March 1938; *Educ* Edinburgh Acad, Sedbergh; *m* 1972, Ann Frances, da of late William Patrick Scott, OBE, DL, of Orkney Islands; 2 s (Charles b 1974, Rory b 1977); *Career* RN; Equerry to HM The Queen 1968-71; CO: HMS Jupiter (frigate) 1972-73, HMS Kent (guided missile destroyer) 1976-77; Royal Coll of Def Studies 1978; CO: HMS Illustrious (aircraft carrier) 1981-83, HMS Dryad & Capt Sch of Maritime Ops 1983-85; ACDS (Policy and Nuclear) 1985-87; Flag Offr Scotland and N Ireland, Naval Base Cdr Rosyth, NATO Cdr N sub area E Atlantic, Cdr Nore sub area Channel 1987-89, Chief of Fleet Support 1989-91, C-in-C Fleet, Allied C-in-C Channel and C-in-C Eastern Atlantic 1991-; *Recreations* outdoor; *Clubs* Army and Navy; *Style*— Vice Adm Sir Jock Slater, KCB, LVO; c/o Royal Bank of Scotland, West End Office, Princes St, Edinburgh; Office of CINCFlEET, Northwood, Middlesex HA6 3HP

SLATER, Kenneth Frederick; s of Charles Frederick Slater (d 1929), and Emily Gertrude, *née* Rodmell (d 1959); *b* 31 July 1925; *Educ* Hull GS, Manchester Univ (BSc); *m* 1965, Marjorie Gladys, da of Horace Beadsworth (d 1942); *Career* leader UK team of nat experts for definition of NATO Air Defence Ground Environment Malvern 1964, head of Ground Radar and Air Traffic Control Gp 1971, head of Applied Physics Dept and dep dir Royal Signals and Radar Estab (RSRE) Malvern 1976, head of Civil and Mil Systems Dept and dep dir RSRE 1977; dir: Admty Surface Weapons Estab Portsmouth 1978, engrg dir Marconi Underwater Systems Ltd Waterlooville 1984; engrg conslt 1988; FIEE, FEng; *Publications* articles for scientific jls and conferences incl articles in the Dictionary of Applied Physics and the Encyclopaedia Britannica; *Recreations* yacht ('Ripples'), music, photography, walking; *Clubs* RN Sailing Assoc; *Style*— Kenneth Slater, Esq; Valinor, Blackheath Way, W Malvern, Worcs (☎ 0684 567641)

SLATER, Marcia Astrid; da of Arthur Henry Simmons (d 1986), of Ashford House, 28 Slade Rd, Erdington, Birmingham, and Florence Irene, *née* Bayliss (d 1974); *b* 10 Oct 1945; *Educ* Erdington GS for Girls; *m* 5 Aug 1968, David William Slater, s of William James Slater (d 1976), of 53 Olton Rd, Shirley, Solihull, Warks; 1 s (Adrian David b 8 June 1974), 1 da (Tania Angelina b 27 July 1970); *Career* Gemma Burnett Beauty Products: fndr memb 1966, co re-named Midland Cosmetic Sales Ltd Inc 1978, listed as one of top 1000 fastest growing cos in country 1988, currently co sec; *Recreations* cycling, skiing, swimming; *Style*— Mrs Marcia Slater; Midland Cosmetic Sales Ltd, 15 Cato St, Nechells, Birmingham B7 4TS (☎ 021 359 0099, fax 021 359 0010, telex 335176 TFSTRS G)

SLATER, Peter; s of Harry Slater (d 1984), of Yorks, and Vivian, *née* Buckle (d 1987); *b* 22 Jan 1934; *Educ* Cockburn HS Leeds; *m* 1957, June Marlene; 1 da (Linda Anne b 1958); *Career* dir: IMI Valves International Ltd 1978, IMI Fluid Power International Ltd 1983, Norgren Martonair Hong Kong Ltd 1984, Shavo Norgren (India) Pvt Ltd 1986, IMI Control and Instrumentation Ltd 1988, CCI Ltd 1988, Norgren Martonair Pacific PTE Ltd (Singapore) 1990; fin dir IMI Fluid Control Group 1988; FCA (1972, ACA 1962); *Recreations* clay pigeon shooting, motoring, reading; *Style*— Peter Slater, Esq; Springfield, Appletree Lane, Inkberrow, Worcs (☎ 0386 792934); 21 Storry Hills Park, Limestone Rd, Burniston, nr Scarborough, Yorks; IMI plc, PO Box 216, Witton, Birmingham B6 7BA (☎ 021 356 4848)

SLATER, Richard; s of Dennis Slater (d 1979), and Freida, *née* Hodgson; *b* 18 Aug 1948; *Educ* UCS, Pembroke Coll Cambridge (MA); *m* Julie Norma, da of Gordon Jolley Ward; 2 s (Samuel Rupert b 1980, Frederick James b 1985), 1 da (Amy Louise b 1980); *Career* Slaughter and May: articled clerk 1970-72, asst slr 1972-79, ptnr 1979-, Hong Kong Office 1981-86; memb Law Soc 1972; *Recreations* tennis, real tennis, theatre, cinema, opera, travel, photography; *Clubs* Queen's, Riverside, Carlton Tennis, The Hong Kong, Ladies' Recreation (Hong Kong); *Style*— Richard Slater, Esq; Slaughter and May, 35 Basinghall Street, London EC2V 5DB (☎ 071 600 1200, fax 071 600 0289, car 0860 224334)

SLATER, Prof Trevor Frank; s of Samuel William Frank Slater, and Eliza Florence, *née* Lock; *b* 18 Feb 1931; *Educ* UCL (BSc, MSc, PhD, DSc); *m* 23 March 1961, Hazel, da of Adam King, of New Milton, Hants; 2 s (Andrew Frank Guiscard, David John Trevor); *Career* sr lectr in biochemical pathology Univ Coll Hosp Med Sch London 1967-70 (lectr in chemical pathology 1960-67); Brunel Univ 1970-: head Dept of Biochemistry 1971-84, head Sch of Biological Sci 1978-82, dean Faculty of Sci 1984-88, head Dept of Biology and Biochemistry 1987-, vice princ 1988-90; visiting prof Univ of Turin 1983-; numerous pubns in jls; memb: Biochemistry Soc Ctee 1973-76, Med Res Cncl Cancer Res Campaign Jt Ctee 1976-80, Expert Ctee MOD 1977-80; hon sec the Biology Cncl 1981-84; chm: UNESCO Expert Ctee for Biophysics for North America and Europe 1986-88 (memb 1982-88), Scientific Ctee Assoc of Int Cancer Res 1979-; memb Wellcome Tst Biology and Biochemistry Panel 1986-; MD med and surgery honoris causa Univ of Turin Italy 1980, memb honoris causa Academia di Medicina Torino 1974, memb honoris causa Academia Senensis Physiocriticorum Siena Italy 1980, Hon DUniv René Descartes Sorbonne 1980, assoc foreign memb Institut de Biologie Physico-Chimique Paris 1982, DUniv (honoris causa) Université René Descartes Sorbonne Paris 1990; CBiol 1967, Chem 1965, FIBiol 1967, FRSC 1965; *Recreations* music, cricket; *Style*— Prof Trevor Slater; Brunel University, Uxbridge, Middx UB8 3PH (☎ 0895 74000, telex 261173 G, fax 0895 74348, 0895 73545)

SLATER, William Bell; CBE (1982), VRD (1959); s of William Bell Slater (d 1985), of 15 King's Walk, W Kirby, Wirral, Cheshire, and May Slater; *b* 7 Jan 1925; *Educ* Lancaster Royal GS; *m* 1950, Jean Mary, da of George William Kiernan (d 1964); 2 s; *Career* War Serv RM Commando Capt Far East, RM Res 1949-63, Lt-Col and CO Mersyside Unit 1959-63, Hon Col 1986; chm: Thos & Jno Brocklebank 1972-85 (dir 1966-85, joined as trainee 1947), Cunard Brocklebank Ltd 1975-85 (dir 1967-85), Cunard Ship Mgmnt Servs Ltd 1970-85, Cunard Int Servs Ltd 1972-85, Albion & Overseas Shipping Agency Ltd 1972-85, Charles Howson & Co Ltd 1972-85, Moss Tankers Ltd 1972-85, Port Line Ltd 1975-85 (dir 1972-85), Cunard Shipping Servs Ltd 1972-85, Cunard Int Tech Servs Ltd 1974-85, Transworld Leasing Ltd 1977-85, Heavy Lift Cargo Airlines Ltd 1978-85; dir: Cunard Steam-Ship Co plc 1972-85 and 1986-88 (md Cargo Shipping and Aviation Div 1974-85), Cunard Gp Pension Tstees Ltd 1972-88, Osmarine Int Ltd 1972-85, Trafalgar House Tstees Ltd 1978-88 (Port Line Assoc cos), ACTA/ANL Assets Ltd 1975-85, ACT (A) Leasing Ltd 1975-85, Blueport ACT (NZ) Ltd 1976-85, Blue Star Port Lines Mgmnt 1974-85, ACT (A) Investmts (Aust) Ltd 1978-85; chm Assoc Container Tportation (Aust) Ltd 1982-85 (dir 1974-85); chm Cunard Assoc cos: Assoc Containers Tportation 1982-85 (dir 1974-85), Atlantic Container Line Ltd 1977-78 and 1983-84 (dir 1968-85), Mersey Docks & Harbour Co 1987- (dep chm 1985-87, dir 1980-); dir Trafalgar House plc 1975-88; gen cmmr of Income Tax 1987-; memb Gen Cncl of Br Shipping 1975-85, pres Br Int Freight Assoc (previously Inst of Freight Forwarders Ltd) 1987-88 (external dir 1989-), FCIT (vice-pres 1984-87), Order of El Istiglal (2nd Class) Jordan 1972; *Recreations* swimming, gardening, walking, (previously rugby, cricket); *Clubs* Naval; *Style*— William Slater, Esq, CBE, VRD; Gayton Court, 419 Woodham Lane, Woodham, Weybridge, Surrey KT15 3PP (☎ 09323 49389)

SLATTERY, David Antony Douglas; MBE (1958); s of Rear Adm Sir Matthew Sausse Slattery, KBE (d 1990), of Harveys Farm, Warninglid, Sussex, and Mica Mary, *née* Swain; *b* 28 Jan 1930; *Educ* Ampleforth, St Thomas' Hosp London (MB BS); *m* 1, 5 May 1954 (m dis 1973), Mary Winifred, da of Robert Miller (d 1942); 2 s (Nicholas b 1955, Simon b 1961), 2 da (Penelope b 1957, Jennifer b 1962); m 2, 22 Feb 1974, Claire Louise, da of Maj L B McGuinness (d 1972); 1 s (Benjamin b 1979); *Career* Capt RAMC 1954-58; MO E Midlands Gas Bd 1959-69, SMO Br Steel Corpn 1969-73, CMO Rolls-Royce plc 1973-; civilian advsr occupational med RAF, special lectr Univ of Nottingham, memb Advsy Bd Civil Serv Occupational Health Serv, dean Faculty of Occupational Med RCP, md advsr Derbyshire Branch BRCS; FRCP, FFOM; *Recreations* fishing, shooting, history; *Style*— David Slattery, Esq, MBE; The Croft, Aston Lane, Shardlow, Derby (☎ 0332 792738, fax 0332 792938); Rolls-Royce plc, PO Box 31, Derby (☎ 0332 249351)

SLATTERY, Peter Anthony; s of Rear Adm Sir Matthew Sausse Slattery, KBE, CB (d 1990), and Mica Mary, *née* Swain; *b* 21 March 1926; *Educ* Ampleforth; *m* 1, 1951 (m dis 1979), Joanella Elizabeth Agnes, *née* Scrymsour-Nichol; 1 s, 2 da; m 2, 1979, Judith Mary, *née* Gilbert; *Career* barr Middle Temple 1957; md: Hobbs Savill & Bradford Ltd 1967-71 (asst md 1961-67), H S Tstees Ltd 1961-71, Williams & Glyn's Insurance Conslts Ltd 1971-75; dep dir Williams & Glyn's Bank 1972-75, dir and gen mangr Marine and Gen Mutual Life Assurance Soc 1975-85 (non-exec dir 1985-86), chm and md MGM Unit Managers Ltd 1982-85 (non-exec chm 1985-86), chm MGM Assurance (Tstees) Ltd 1985-86 (dir 1976-85), dir Shield Assurance Ltd 1986-, dir and sec Unicorn Heritage plc 1987-90; *Recreations* photography, gardening; *Style*— Peter Slattery, Esq; 18 Holmwood Rd, Cheam, Sutton, Surrey (☎ 081 393 6018)

SLATTERY, Tony Deklan; s of Michael Slattery, and Margaret Slattery; *b* 9 Nov 1959; *Educ* London Catholic GS, Trinity Hall Cambridge (MA, pres Footlights); *Career* writer and performer; repertoire incl: drama, revue, comedy, soap opera, current affrs; tv incl: Whose Line is it Anyway (Channel 4), This is David Harper (Channel 4), writer and presenter Saturday Night at the Movies (ITV); theatre work incl: Edinburgh Fringe Festival, Me and My Girl (West End); *Recreations* musicals, white wine, Victoria Wood; *Style*— Tony Slattery, Esq; Duncan Heath Associations, London W1

SLAUGHTER, Giles David; s of Gerald Slaughter (d 1945), of Harpenden, Herts, and Enid Lilian, *née* Crane (d 1987); *b* 11 July 1937; *Educ* Royal Masonic Sch Bushey Herts, King's Coll Cambridge (BA, MA); *m* 14 Aug 1965, Gillian Rothwell, da of Philip Rothwell Shepherd (d 1981); 3 da (Miranda b 1966, Victoria b 1967, Imogen b 1976); *Career* Nat Serv 2 Lt 1 Bn Suffolk Regt 1955-57; housemaster Ormiston House Campbell Coll Belfast; headmaster: Solihull Sch West Midlands 1973-82, Univ Coll Sch Hampstead 1983-; memb HMC 1973-; tstee Assoc Prevention of Addiction; govr: Cobham Hall Sch, Godolphin and Latymer Sch; JP Solihull 1977-82; FRSA; *Recreations* theatre, gardening, cricket, golf; *Clubs* East India, Devonshire Sports, Public Schs; *Style*— Giles Slaughter, Esq; 5 Redington Rd, Hampstead, London NW3 7QX; 6 Church Lane, Lower Ufford, Woodbridge, Suffolk (☎ 0394 461 281); University College, Frognal, London NW3 6XH (☎ 071 435 2215)

SLAY, Prof Desmond; s of Wilfred Charles Slay (d 1986), of Oxford, and Doris Elizabeth, *née* Walker (d 1978); *b* 30 Dec 1927; *Educ* Lord William's GS Thame, Univ of Oxford (BA, MA); *m* 10 April 1958, Leontia Mary Cecilia, da of Bernard Patrick Alphonsus McCartan (d 1966), of Belfast; 4 s (Gregory b 1959, Benet b 1961, Jonathan b 1965, Matthew b 1965), 1 da (Deborah b 1960); *Career* Dept of English UCW: asst lectr 1948-50, lectr 1950-62, sr lectr 1962-72, reader 1972-78, acting head of dept 1976-78, Rendel Prof of English and head of dept 1978-90, res prof 1990-; former memb Aberystwyth Round Table, memb Viking Soc for Northern Res (pres 1970-72), fndr chm and memb 41 Club for former tablers 1972-, county sec N Ceredigion Scout Cncl 1990- (dist sec 1983-90); *Books* Codex Scardensis (1960), The Manuscripts of Hrólfs Saga Kraka (1960), Romances (1972), Proceedings of the First International Saga Conference (jtly 1973); *Recreations* supporting scouting; *Style*— Prof Desmond Slay; 52 Maeshendre, Waunfawr, Aberystwyth, Dyfed SY23 3PS (☎ 0970 623841); Department of English, University College of Wales, Aberystwyth (☎ 0970 622534, fax 0970 617172, telex 35181 ABY UCW G)

SLAYMAKER, Paul Ellis; s of Ellis Hamilton Slaymaker, of Surrey, and Barbara Joan, *née* Langfield; *b* 10 March 1945; *Educ* Sunbury GS (BA), Ealing Tech Coll; *m* 1968, Ann Elizabeth, da of Edward Michael Frederick Piercey (d 1982), of IOW; 1 s (Nicholas b 1978), 1 da (Emma b 1975); *Career* advertising; mgmnt conslt McKinsey & Co Inc 1975-76, head of mktg CPC (UK) Ltd 1977-80, dep md Leo Burnett Ltd 1980-86; md Delaney Fletcher Slaymaker Delaney 1986-; *Recreations* photography, badminton, running, shooting; *Style*— Paul Slaymaker, Esq; 10 Beaufort Close, Lynden Gate, London SW15 3TL (☎ 071 836 3474)

SLEDGE, The Ven Richard Kitson; s of Sidney Kitson Sledge (d 1968), and Mary Sylvia, *née* Harland, of Sandal, Wakefield; *b* 13 April 1930; *Educ* Epsom Coll, Peterhouse Cambridge (MA); *m* 12 April 1958, Patricia Henley, da of Gordon Sear (d 1985), of Dunstable; 2 s (Timothy b 1964, Nicholas (decd)), 2 da (Elizabeth b 1959, Hilary b 1966); *Career* ordained deacon 1954, priest 1955; curate of: Emmanuel Plymouth Devon 1954-57, St Martin, St Stephen and St Laurence Exeter 1957-63; rector of Dronfield Derbyshire 1963-78, rural dean of Chesterfield 1972-78, rector of Hemingford Abbots Cambs 1978-89; hon canon of Ely 1978-, archdeacon of Huntingdon 1978-; *Style*— The Ven R K Sledge; The Rectory, Hemingford Abbots, Huntingdon, Cambs PE18 9AN (☎ 0480 69856)

SLEE, William Robert; *b* 13 Jan 1941; *Educ* Holy Cross Coll Massachusetts (BSc); *m* 1981, Heidi, *née* Burklin; 2 s (Alexander, Maximilian); *Career* vice pres and Euro petroleum coordinator Citibank 1963-73, md and chief operating offr European Banking Co Ltd 1973-84; currently: gp md Schroders plc, dir J Henry Schroder Wagg & Co Ltd; *Recreations* sailing, tennis; *Clubs* Royal Ocean Racing, Royal Lymington Yacht; *Style*— William Slee, Esq; Schroders plc, 120 Cheapside, London EC2V 6DR (☎ 071 382 6000, fax 071 382 3950, telex 885029)

SLEEMAN, Prof Brian David; s of Richard Kinsman Sleeman, of Marnhull, Dorset, and Gertrude Cecilia, *née* Gamble; *b* 4 Aug 1939; *Educ* Canterbury Rd Sch Morden Surrey, Tiffin Boy's Sch Kingston Surrey, Battersea Coll of Technol (BSc), Univ of London (PhD), Univ of Dundee (DSc); *m* 7 Sept 1963, Juliet Mary, da of Frederick James John (d 1972); 2 s (Matthew b 19 Feb 1969, David b 12 June 1972), 1 da (Elizabeth b 15 Sept 1966); *Career* Univ of Dundee: asst lectr 1965-67, lectr 1967-71, reader 1971-78, prof 1978-, head Dept of Mathematics and Computer Sci; various hon visiting professorships at univs in: USA, Canada, Sweden, France, Chile, China; chm Scot Branch for Inst of Mathematics and its applications 1982-84, pres of Edinburgh Mathematical Soc 1988-89; FIMA 1972, FRSE 1976; *Books* Multiparameter Spectral Theory in Hilbert Space (1978), Differential Equations and Mathematical Biology (1983); *Recreations* choral music, hill walking; *Style*— Prof Brian Sleeman, FRSE; Department of Mathematics and Computer Science, University of Dundee, Dundee DD1 4HN (☎ 0382 23181 ext 4470, fax 0382 201604, telex 76293)

SLEEMAN, His Hon (Stuart) Colin; s of Stuart Bertram Sleeman (d 1970), of Alton, Parry's Lane, Bristol, and Phyllis Grace, *née* Pitt (d 1976); *b* 10 March 1914; *Educ* Clifton, Merton Coll Oxford (MA); *m* 1944, Margaret Emily, yst da of William Joseph Farmer (d 1939), of Minehead, Somerset; 2 s (Stuart, Jeremy), 1 da (Jenifer); *Career* WWII Lt-Col 16/5 Lancers; called to the Bar Gray's Inn 1938, Western Circuit 1938-49, admin offr Prize Dept Miny of Economic Warfare 1939-40, asst judge advocate-gen HQ Allied Land Forces SE Asia 1945-46, Midland Circuit 1949, London corr Scottish Law Review 1949-54, bencher Gray's Inn 1974, rec 1975, circuit judge 1976-86; *Books* The Trial of Gozawa Sadaichi and Nine Others (1948), The Double Tenth Trial (with S C Silkin, 1951); *Recreations* travel, genealogy; *Style*— His Hon Colin Sleeman; West Walls, Cotmandene, Dorking, Surrey RH4 2BL (☎ 0306 883616)

SLEEMAN, John Henry; s of Herbert Sleeman (d 1950); *b* 4 May 1922; *Educ* Thorpe Sch; *m* 1945, Elsie; 2 s; *Career* chartered sec; chm Charterhouse Japhet Bank & Tst Int Ltd (Nassau) until 1982, dir Charterhouse Japhet plc until 1982; chm: Industl Finance & Investmt Corpn plc, Personal Assurance plc; dir: Personal Assurance plc, Refuge Gp plc, Refuge Assurance plc, Canterbury Life Assurance Co Ltd, chm Nat Children's Charities Fund; *Style*— John Sleeman Esq; 1 Paternoster Row, St Paul's, London EC4M 7DH (☎ 071 248 3999)

SLEIGH, Prof (James) Douglas; s of Andrew Scott Sleigh (d 1958), of Glasgow, and Margaret Handbury Lennox, *née* Jefferson (d 1938); *b* 5 July 1930; *Educ* Glasgow Acad, Univ of Glasgow (MB ChB); *m* 4 Sept 1956, Rosemary Margaret, da of David Falconer Smith (d 1972); 2 s (Andrew Falconer b 1957, David Douglas b 1960); *Career* Nat Serv Lt RAMC 1954-55, Capt RAMC 1955-56, pathologist Mil Hosp Tidworth Hants; registrar Dept of Bacteriology Western Infirmary Glasgow 1956-58, lectr Dept of Bacteriology Univ of Edinburgh 1958- 65, conslt pathologist Dunbartonshire Area Laboratory 1965-69, prof Dept of Bacteriology Univ of Glasgow 1969- (sr lectr, reader), currently at Royal Infirmary Glasgow (formerly Western Infirmary Glasgow); author of numerous pubns in med lit and editorial contrib to the British Medical Journal and the Lancet; memb: Assoc of Clinical Pathologists, Assoc Med Microbiologists; FRCPath, FRCPG; *Books* Notes on Medical Bacteriology (with MC Timbury, 1981); *Recreations* bargain hunting, spending time on the Isle of Arran; *Clubs* Univ of Glasgow, Coll; *Style*— Prof Douglas Sleigh; Clynder, 5 Sutherland Ave, Glasgow G41 4JJ (☎ 041 427 1486); Department of Bacteriology, Royal Infirmary, Glasgow G4 OSF (☎ 041 552 3535, fax 041 552 1524)

SLEIGH, Prof Michael Alfred; s of Cyril Button Sleigh (d 1978), of Bath, and Ida Louisa, *née* Horstmann (d 1987); *b* 11 June 1932; *Educ* Taunton Sch, Bristol GS, Univ of Bristol (BSc, PhD, DSc); *m* 28 Dec 1957, Peggy, da of Maurice Arthur Mason (d 1982), of Calne, Wilts; 2 s (Roger b 1960, Peter b 1965), 1 da (Anne b 1962); *Career* Nat Serv Flying Offr RAF educn branch 1957-58; lectr in zoology Univ of Exeter 1958-63, lectr and reader in zoology Univ of Bristol 1963-74, prof of biology Univ of Southampton 1975-; sec Soc for Experimental Biology (Nat) 1965-69, vice pres Int Soc of Protozoologists 1987-88 (pres Br sec 1982-85); memb: Cncl Marine Biological Assoc of the UK, Freshwater Biological Assoc; FIBiol 1977; *Books* The Biology of Cilia and Flagella (1962), The Biology of Protozoa (1973), Cilia and Flagella (1974), Microbes in the Sea (1987), Protozoa and other Protists (1989); *Recreations* travel, gardening, microscopy, walking, photography, natural history; *Style*— Prof Michael Sleigh; Department of Biology, University of Southampton, Medical and Biological Sciences Building, Bassett Crescent East, Southampton SO9 3TU (☎ 0703 594397, telex 47661, fax 0703 594269)

SLEIGHT, Jacqueline, Lady; Jacqueline Margaret; eldest da of Maj H R Carter, of Brisbane, Queensland; *m* 1, Ronald Mundell (decd); 1 s (Anthony); m 2, 1942, Sir John Frederick Sleight, 3 Bt (d 1990); 1 s (Sir Richard, 4 Bt); *Style*— Jacqueline, Lady Sleight; 4 Plumosa Court, Broadbeach Waters, Queensland 4218, Australia

SLEIGHT, Michael Marcus; s of George Frederick Sleight (d 1954), 4 s of Sir George Frederick Sleight, Bt, of Binbrook Hall, Binbrook, Lincoln, and Edith Mary, *née* Brockway (d 1963); *b* 12 Aug 1924; *Educ* private tutor Cambridge; *Career* WWII ROC 1942-45; landowner; jt patron of 21 parishes, lord of 3 manors, churchwarden, memb Cncl Lincoln Record Soc; memb: Royal Archaeological Inst, Br Archaeological Assoc; *Recreations* visiting old churches; *Style*— Michael Sleight, Esq; Binbrook Hall, Binbrook, Lincoln LN3 6BW (☎ 047283 209)

SLEIGHT, Sir Richard; 4 Bt (UK 1920), of Weelsby Hall, Clee, Co Lincoln; s and h of Sir John Sleight, 3 Bt; *b* 27 May 1946; *m* 1978, Marie-Thérèse, da of O M Stepan, of Bromley, Kent; *Heir* s, James Alexander Seight, b 1981; *Style*— Sir Richard Sleight, Bt; c/o National Westminster Bank, 9 Hill Street, Richmond, Surrey TW9 15Y

SLESSOR, Gp Capt John Arthur Guinness; DL (Hants 1989); s of Marshal of the RAF Sir John Slessor, GCB, DSO, MC (d 1979), and Hermione Grace, *née* Guinness (d 1970); *b* 14 Aug 1925; *Educ* Eton, ChCh Oxford; *m* 6 Oct 1951, Ann Dorothea, da of late George Gibson; 1 s (Anthony b 1954), 1 da (Catherine b 1955); *Career* joined RAF 1943, served N France 1944, cmmnd 1945, various flying appts 1946-59 (inc Germany and Rhodesia), Staff Coll 1959-60, USAF Acad Colorado 1960-62, OC 83 Sqdn (V-Force) 1962-65, Jt Servs Staff Coll 1965, MOD 1966-68, Air Attaché Madrid 1968-70, OC RAF Odiham 1971-73, Chief Intelligence Offr RAF Germany 1973-75, MOD 1976-77, ret 1978; sec Overseas Rels HQ St John Ambulance 1978-89, pres Alton Div St John Ambulance 1988-; govr Alton Coll 1990-; Gentleman Usher to HM The Queen 1978-; CStJ 1990 (OStJ 1981); *Recreations* country pursuits; *Clubs* RAF; *Style*— Gp Capt J A G Slessor, DL; Honeywell, Burkham, Alton, Hants GU34 5RT (☎ 025 683 325)

SLEVIN, Brian Francis Patrick; CMG (1975), OBE (1973), QPM (1968), CPM (1965); s of Thomas Francis Slevin, and Helen, *née* Murray (d 1954); *b* 13 Aug 1926; *Educ* Blackrock Coll Ireland; *m* 15 July 1972, (Constance) Gay, da of Maj Ronald Moody (d 1988); 1 s (Simon b 1973); *Career* Palestine Police 1946-48; Royal Hong Kong Police 1949-79: ADC to HE Govr of Hong Kong 1952-53, directing staff overseas police courses Met Police Coll Hendon London 1955-57, dir Special Branch 1966-69, sr asst cmmr of police (cmdg Kowloon Dist) 1969-70, dir CID 1971, dep cmmr of police 1971, cmmr of police 1974-79; recently in Hong Kong: vice pres Hong Kong RFU, vice pres Hong Kong Boy Scouts Assoc, govr Hong Kong Life Gd Club; *Recreations* walking, golf, tennis, gardening, reading, painting; *Clubs* Royal Hong Kong Golf, Royal Hong Kong Jockey, The Hong Kong; *Style*— Brian Slevin, Esq, CMG, OBE, QPM, CPM; Lantau Lodge, 152 Coonanbarra Rd, Wahroonga, Sydney, NSW 2076, Australia (☎ 02 489 6671)

SLEVIN, Dr Maurice Louis; s of David Slevin, of 13 Gorleston Rd, Sea Point, Cape Town, South Africa, and Nita, *née* Rosenbaum; *b* 2 July 1949; *Educ* De La Salle Coll East London South Africa, Univ of Cape Town South Africa (MB ChB); *m* 5 Jan 1975 (m dis 1988), Cherry Lynn, 2 da (Lindi b 1978, Amy b 1981); *Career* med registrar Groote Schuur Hosp Cape Town South Africa 1977, registrar and sr registrar Dept of Med Oncology Bart's Hosp London 1978-82, conslt physician and med oncologist Depts of Med Oncology Bart's and Homerton Hosps London 1982-; chm Br Assoc Cancer United Patients MRCP 1978, MD 1984, FRCP 1989; *Books* Randomised Trials in Cancer: A Critical Review by Sites (jt ed, with Maurice Staquet); *Style*— Dr Maurice Slevin; Dept of Medical Oncology, St Bartholomew's Hospital, West

Smithfield, London EC1A 7BE (☎ 071 606 6662, fax 071 796 3979); 134 Harley St, London W1N 1AH (☎ 071 224 0685)

SLIGO, 10 Marquess of (I 1800); Denis Edward Browne; sits as Baron Monteagle (UK 1806); Baron Mount Eagle (I 1760), Viscount Westport (I 1768), Earl of Altamont (I 1771), Earl of Clanricarde (I 1543 and 1800, with special remainder); s of late Lt-Col Lord Alfred Eden Browne, DSO (s of 5 Marquess of Sligo); suc unc, 9 Marquess of Sligo 1952; *b* 13 Dec 1908; *Educ* Eton; *m* 1930, José Gauche; 1 s; *Heir* s, Earl of Altamont; *Style*— The Most Hon The Marquess of Sligo; c/o Messrs Trower, Still and Keeling, 5 New sq, Lincoln's Inn, London WC2

SLIM, Aileen, Viscountess; Aileen; da of Rev J A Robertson, of Edinburgh; *m* 1926, 1 Viscount Slim, KG, GCB, GCMG, GCVO, GBE, DSO, MC (d 1970); 1 s, 1 da; *Career* DStJ, has Kaisar-i-Hind Medal; *Style*— The Rt Hon Aileen, Viscountess Slim; 18 Stack House, Cundy St Flats, Ebury St, London SW1W 9JS

SLIM, Hon Hugo John Robertson; s of 2 Viscount Slim, OBE; *b* 1961; *Educ* Eton, Univ of Oxford (MA); *Career* field admin Save The Children Fund Morocco 1983, Sudan 1985, Ethiopia 1986; UN Ethiopia 1987-88, conslt 1989-; FRGS; *Clubs* Special Forces; *Style*— The Hon Hugo Slim

SLIM, 2 Viscount (UK 1960); John Douglas Slim; OBE (1973), DL (Greater London 1988); s of Field Marshal 1 Viscount (Sir William Joseph) Slim, KG, GCB, GCMG, GCVO, GBE, DSO, MC, sometime GOC Allied Land Forces SE Asia, govr-gen Aust and govr and constable Windsor Castle (d 1970); *b* 20 July 1927; *Educ* Prince of Wales Royal Indian Mil Coll Dehra Dun; *m* 1958, Elisabeth, da of Arthur Rawdon Spinney, CBE (decd); 2 s, 1 da; *Heir* s, Hon Mark Slim; *Career* cmmnd Indian Army 6 Gurkha Rifles 1945-48, Lt Argyll and Sutherland Highlanders 1948, Staff Coll 1961, Jt Serv Staff Coll 1964, Cdr 22 SAS Regt 1967-70, GSO1 (Special Forces) HQ UK Land Forces 1970-72, ret 1972; chm Peek plc; dir various other cos; pres Burma Star Assoc; vice-pres Br-Aust Soc; vice-chm Arab-Br C of C and Indust; FRGS 1983; *Clubs* White's, Special Forces; *Style*— The Rt Hon the Viscount Slim, OBE, DL; c/o Lloyds Bank plc, 6 Pall Mall, London SW1

SLIM, Hon Mark William Rawdon; s and h of 2 Viscount Slim, OBE; *b* 13 Feb 1960; *Career* mktg dir Stavling Projects Inc Dallas Texas USA; *Clubs* Bucks, Special Forces; *Style*— The Hon Mark Slim

SLIMMINGS, Sir William Kenneth MacLeod; CBE (1960); s of George Slimmings (d 1952), of Dunfermline, Fife; *b* 15 Dec 1912; *Educ* Dunfermline HS; *m* 1943, Lilian Ellen, da of Walter Edward Willis, of Hornchurch, Essex; 1 s, 1 da; *Career* CA; ptnr Thomson McLintock & Co 1946-78, chm Bd of Trade Advsy Ctee 1957-66; memb: Ctee of Inquiry on Cost of Housebuilding 1947-53, Ctee on Tax-paid Stocks 1952-53, Ctee on Cheque Endorsement 1955-56, Performing Right Tbnl 1963-72, Cncl Scottish Inst of CAs 1962-66 (pres 1969-70), Scottish Tourist Bd 1969-76, Review Body on Doctors and Dentists Remuneration 1976-83, Crown Agents' Tbnl 1978-82; chm Review Body for Govt Contracts 1971-81; kt 1966; *Style*— Sir William Slimmings, CBE; 62 The Avenue, Worcester Park, Surrey (☎ 081 337 2579)

SLINGER, Edward; s of Thomas Slinger (d 1957), of Lancs, and Rhoda, *née* Bradshaw (d 1987); *b* 2 Feb 1938; *Educ* Accrington GS, Balliol Coll Oxford (BA); *m* 31 July 1965, Rosalind Margaret, da of Stanley Albert Jewitt, of Chiddingfold, Surrey; 2 s (Giles b 1969, Fergus b 1975), 2 da (Nicola b 1967, Emma b 1971); *Career* admitted slr 1961; dep dist registrar High Ct 1981-88, asst rec Crown Ct 1988-; vice chm: Lancs CCC 1987-, TCCB Disciplinary Ctee 1989- (memb 1987-); *Clubs* Lancashire CCC, MCC; *Style*— Edward Slinger, Esq; 25/29 Victoria St, Blackburn, Lancs (☎ 0254 672222)

SLINGER, (Alexander) Michael Foulds; s of Milton Slinger (d 1957), of Colne, Lancs, and Edith, JP, *née* Foulds; *b* 8 Feb 1939; *Educ* Giggleswick, Clare Coll Cambridge (MA); *m* 15 April 1967, Felicity Margaret, da of Sir William Rowley, Bt (d 1971), of Widdington, Saffron Walden, Essex; 2 da (Arabella b 1972, Katharine b 1977); *Career* Nat Serv 2 Lt Loyals, Malaya 1959, Germany 1960; Allied Breweries 1964-73, sales dir Hatch Mansfield & Co 1970-73, nat accounts dir Saccone & Speed 1975-78, md John E Fells & Sons 1978-81; estab own businesses of fine wine merchants and shippers: Chesterford Vintners 1981, Tempest Slinger & Co 1981, Town & Country Vintners 1981; capt Cambridge Univ Ski Club 1962-63, memb Br Univs Ski Team 1963; Freeman City of London 1982, Liveryman Worshipful Co of Distillers 1982; *Recreations* travel, skiing, photography, wine, food, golf; *Clubs* Hawks, Pitt, Ski Club of GB, Kandahar Ski; *Style*— Michael Slinger, Esq; Slaters House, Widdington, Saffron Walden, Essex CB11 3SN (☎ 0799 40066); 34 Hornton St, London W8 7NR (☎ 071 937 0303); The Old Greyhound, Great Chesterford, Saffron Walden, Essex CB10 1NY (☎ 0799 30088)

SLIPMAN, Sue; da of Max Slipman (d 1971), of London, and Doris *née* Barham (d 1972); *b* 3 Aug 1949; *Educ* Stockwell Manor Sch, Univ of Wales (BA), Univ of London (PGCE); 1 s (Gideon Max b 1988); *Career* pres NUS 1977-78, vice chm Br Youth Cncl 1977-78, memb Cncl the Open Univ 1978-81, memb City and Guilds Numeracy Examination Bd 1984, chm Ctee of Mgmnt Workbase 1981-86; memb: Exec Ctee 300 Group 1985, Advsy Cncl for Adult and Continuing Educn 1978-, Nat Union of Public Employees 1970-85, memb EC Econ and Social Ctee 1990; dir: Nat Cncl for One Parent Families 1985-, London East TEC 1989; author of chapters in: The Re - Birth of Britain 1983, Public Issues, Private Pain 1988; *Books* Helping Ourselves to Power: A Training Manual for Women in Public Life Skills (1986), Helping One Parent Families to Work (1988), Maintainance: A System to Benefit Children (1989), Making Maintainance Pay (1990); *Recreations* swimming; *Style*— Ms Sue Slipman; National Council for One Parent Families, 255 Kentish Town Road, London, NW5 (☎ 071 267 1361, fax 071 482 4851)

SLIWERSKI, Trevor Zygmunt; s of Zdzislaw Andrzej Sliwerski, of Ben Rhydding, Ilkley, W Yorks, and Irene Sliwerski (d 1990); *b* 30 Dec 1950; *Educ* John Fisher Sch Purley Surrey; *m* Lynn, da of Leonard Arthur Francis, of Wallington, Surrey; 1 s (Jeremy Andrew Zbigniew b 1987), 1 da (Claire Louise b 1983); *Career* dealer: Savory Milln 1968-71, R Layton 1971-74, Nomura 1978-80; dir RBT Fleming 1980-85, dir i/c Japanese equity warrants Baring Securities 1985-; *Recreations* walking, flying; *Clubs* Surrey Walking, Stock Exchange Athletic; *Style*— Trevor Sliwerski, Esq; Baring Securities, Lloyds Chambers, 1 Portsoken St, London E1 8DF (☎ 071 621 1500, fax 071 623 1873)

SLOAM, Nigel Spencer; s of Maurice Sloam, of London, and Ruth, *née* Davis, of London; *b* 17 Dec 1950; *Educ* Haberdashers' Aske's, Corpus Christi Coll Oxford (BA, MA); *m* 3 Sept 1978, Elizabeth Augusta, da of Arnold Hertzberg; 1 s (Oliver Julian Richard b 1983), 1 da (Natalia Sylvia Caroline b 1979); *Career* trainee actuary Messrs Bacon & Woodrow 1972-76, actuary Sahar Insurance Co of Israel 1976-77, mangr Actuarial Dept Charterhouse Magna Assurance Co 1977-78, dir Messrs Bevington Lowndes Ltd 1978-79, princ and ptnr Nigel Sloam & Co 1979-; Freeman City of London, Liveryman Worshipful Co of Basketmakers; FIA 1977, AFIMA 1979, ASA 1987; *Clubs* Utd Oxford and Cambridge Univ, City Livery, PHIATUS, Goose and Beast (pres); *Style*— Nigel Sloam, Esq; Nigel Sloam & Co, Annandale, West Heath Ave, London NW11 7QU (☎ 081 209 1222, fax 081 455 3973, telex 261507 (ref 2921))

SLOAN, Sir Andrew Kirkpatrick; QPM; s of Andrew Kirkpatrick Sloan, of Kirkcudbright, and Amelia Sarah, *née* Vernon; *b* 27 Feb 1931; *Educ* Kirkcubright and Dumfries Acad, Open Univ (BA), Storvik; *m* 1953, Agnes Sofie, da of Nils Jaeger Aleksander, of Norway (d 1975); 3 da (Ann-Soffi, Dorothy, Janet); *Career* RN 1947-53, served in cruisers and submarines in Home Waters, Mediterranean and Caribbean, petty offr; West Yorks Police (reaching rank of Chief Supt) 1955-66, Asst Chief Constable Lincs Police 1976-79, nat co-ordinator Regnl Crime Squads England & Wales 1979-81, dep chief constable Lincs Police 1981-83; chief constable: Beds Police 1983-85, Strathclyde; kt 1991; *Recreations* walking, travel, conversation; *Style*— Sir Andrew Sloan, QPM; 173 Pitt St, Glasgow (☎ 041 204 2626); Strathclyde Police HQ, 173 Pitt St, Glasgow (☎ 041 204 2626)

SLOAN, Gordon McMillan; s of Samuel Sloan, of Muirkirk, Ayrshire, Scotland, and Christine McMillan, *née* Turner; *b* 30 Dec 1934; *Educ* Muirkirk Sch, Kilmarnock Acad, Glasgow Royal Tech Coll; *m* 5 Aug 1961, Patricia Mary, da of William Stewart McKim (d 1979); 1 s (John), 4 da (Christine, Elizabeth, Mary, Rachel); *Career* dir: Parsons Brown & Newton Consulting Engineers 1973-81, McMillan Sloan & Partners Consulting Engineers 1981-; notable works incl: studies, master plans, reports and detailed plans for major new ports at Dammam (Saudi Arabia), and Muara (Brunei), study and re-devpt plan with designs for Cardiff Port, design of floating port Aqaba (Jordan), detailed study of abandonment and removal of major N Sea prodn platform; Freeman City of London 1967, Liveryman Worshipful Co of Turners 1968 (memb Ct of Assts 1987); CEng 1967, FInstPet 1974, FIMechE 1978, MSocIS (France) 1978, FPWInst 1988, Eur Ing 1989; *Recreations* music appreciation, property renovation and restoration; *Style*— Gordon Sloan, Esq; 32 Murray Rd, Wimbledon, London SW19 4PE (☎ 081 947 0767, fax 081 947 7801)

SLOAN, Ronald Kenneth (Ronnie); *b* 21 July 1943; *Educ* Edinburgh Acad; *m* 29 May 1965, Sandra; 2 s (Elliot b 1969, Moray b 1971), 1 da (Hazel b 1978); *Career* Standard Life 1960-67, Friends Provident 1967-70; dir: Antony Gibbs Pensions Ltd 1971, Martin Paterson Assocs Ltd 1972-87; divnl dir and actuary Buck Paterson Conslts Ltd 1987-; vice-pres Edinburgh Academicals RFC 1990-92 (capt 1973-74); fund raiser for RSSPCC running 20 marathons dressed as Superman in Edinburgh, Glasgow, Aberdeen, Dundee, Dublin, London, NY, Boston, Athens, raising over £80,000 to date; govr Scottish Sports Aid Fndn; FFA 1967, FPMI 1977, FInstD 1980; *Recreations* tennis, rugby, marathons, Scottish country dancing; *Clubs* New (Edinburgh); *Style*— Ronnie Sloan, Esq; Buck Paterson Conslts, 12 Alva St, Edinburgh EH2 4QG (☎ 031 225 3324, fax 031 225 2192)

SLOANE, Prof Peter James; s of John Joseph Sloane, of Cheadle, Cheshire, and Elizabeth, *née* Clarke; *b* 6 Aug 1942; *Educ* Cheadle Hulme Sch, Univ of Sheffield (BA), Univ of Strathclyde (PhD); *m* 30 July 1969, Avril Mary, da of Kenneth Urquhart (d 1984), of Morayshire; 1 s (Christopher Peter b 1971); *Career* asst lectr and lectr in political economy Univ of Aberdeen 1966-69, lectr in industl econmics Univ of Nottingham 1969-75, econ advsr Unit for Manpower Studies Dept of Employment 1973-74, prof of econs and mgmnt Paisley Coll 1975-84, visiting prof McMaster Univ Hamilton Ontario Canada 1978 (Cwlth Fell), prof of political economics Univ of Aberdeen 1984- (Jaffrey prof of political economics 1985-); memb: Sec of State for Scotland's Panel of Econ Conslts 1981-, Cncl Scottish Econ Soc 1983-, ct Univ of Aberdeen 1987-, ESRC 1979-85; *Books* Changing Patterns of Working Hours (1975), Sex Discrimination in the Labour market (with B Chiplin, 1975), Sport in the Market? (1980), Women and Low Pay (ed 1980), The Earnings Gap Between Men and Women in Great Britain (1981), Equal Employment Issues (with H C Jain, 1981), Tackling Discrimination in the Workplace (with B Chiplin, 1982), Labour Economics (with D Carline, et al 1985), Sex at Work: Equal Pay and the Comparable Worth Controversy (1985); plus contributions to various academic jls; *Recreations* sport; *Clubs* Royal Cwlth Soc; *Style*— Prof Peter Sloane; Hillcrest, 45 Friars Feild Rd, Cults, Aberdeen AB1 9LB (☎ 0224 869412); Department of Economics, University of Aberdeen, Edward Wright Building, Dunbar St, Aberdeen AB7 2TY (☎ 0224 272166, fax 0224 487048, telex 73458 UNIABN G)

SLOCOCK, (David) Michael; s of Maj Arthur Anthony Slocock, of Budleigh Salterton, Devon and Elizabeth Anthea, *née* Sturdy; *b* 1 Feb 1945; *Educ* Radley, Lincoln Coll Oxford (BA); *m* 12 April 1969, Theresa Mary, da of Maj Anthony Clyde-Smith (d 1989), of Jersey CI; 2 s (Julian Mark Anthony b 1973, Mark David Philip b 1976), 1 da (Lucinda Sheila Mary b 1971); *Career* fin journalist The Sunday Telegraph 1967-69, with Hill Samuel & Co Ltd merchant bankers 1969-71, dir various cos including Normans Group plc, Empire Plantations & Investments, L K Industrial Investments 1971-79, chm and chief exec Normans Group plc 1973-90; *Recreations* sailing, gardening; *Clubs* IOD, Royal Southern Dorset Yacht; *Style*— Michael Slocock, Esq; Linkon Ltd, Southover House, Tolpuddle, Dorchester, Dorset DT2 7HF (☎ 0305 848220, fax 0305 848516)

SLOCOMBE, Sue; da of Capt Leonard William Ellis, MBE (d 1977), and Phyllis Muriel, *née* Chick (d 1984); *b* 8 June 1949; *Educ* Nailsea GS, Bedford Coll of Physical Educ, Univ of Bristol; *m* 5 Aug 1972, Martin Charles Slocombe, s of Charles Slocombe (d 1976); *Career* teacher Clifton HS for Girls 1970-74, lectr Coll of St Matthias 1974-76, Dept of Educn Bristol Poly 1976-90, currently princ lectr and dir of studies Bristol Poly; sportswoman; int hockey player: Outdoor World Cup 1979, Euro Bronze medallist 1985, indoor capt 1985-88; coach England Ladies Sr Hockey Team 1986-90 (Euro Silver medal 1987), asst coach GB Ladies Hockey Squad 1989-90; memb Coaches Advsy Panel Br Olympic Assoc, involved in hockey coaching to club and int standard (also childrens hockey coach); memb: BISC, PE Assoc of GB and NI, BAALPE; *Books* Indoor Hockey (1985), Make Hockey Fun-Hockey for 8-12 year olds (1985); *Style*— Mrs Sue Slocombe; Brackenwood, 2 Folleigh Close, Long Ashton, Bristol BS18 9HX (☎ 0275 394116); Principal Lecturer, Director of Studies (Initial Teacher Education), Department of Education, Redland Hill, Bristol BS6 6U2 (☎ 0272 741251, fax 0272 732251)

SLOGGETT, Jolyon Edward; s of Edward Cornelius Sloggett (d 1974), of Harrow, Middx, and Lena May, *née* Norton; *b* 30 May 1933; *Educ* John Lyon Sch, Univ of Glasgow (BSc); *m* 4 July 1970, Patricia Marjorie Iverson, da of Leonard Artemus Ward, of Steyning, W Sussex; 2 da (Alexandra, Clementine); *Career* joined RNVR 1955, Nat Serv 1957-58, cmmnd temporary Actg Sub Lt(E) 1957, RNEC 1957, HMS Camperdown 1958, sr engrg offr 51 minesweeping sqdn 1958, resigned as Lt(E) from RNR 1964; ship designer WM Denny & Bros Ltd 1956-57 and 1959-60; Houlder Bros & Co Ltd: naval architect 1965-68, mangr new projects 1968-72, exec dir fin and devpt 1972-78, exec dep chm Houlder Offshore; md Br Shipbuilders: mktg and product devpt 1978-79, offshore 1979-81; chm Vickers Offshore (P & D) Ltd 1979-80, conslt Jolyon Soggett Assocs 1981-86; vice pres Old Lyonian Assoc; Liveryman Worshipful Co of Shipwrights; FIMarE (sec 1986-), FRINA 1972, FICS 1967; *Books* Shipping Finance (1984); *Recreations* gardening, woodwork, sailing; *Style*— Jolyon Sloggett, Esq; Annington House, Steyning, W Sussex BN44 3WA (☎ 0903 812 259); Inst of Marine Engineers, 76 Mark Lane, London EC3R 7JN (☎ 071 481 8493, fax 071 488 1854, telex 886841)

SLOMAN, Prof Aaron; s of Reuben Sloman, and Hannah, *née* Rest; *b* 30 Oct 1936; *Educ* Cape Town Univ (BSc), Oxford Univ (DPhil); *m* 29 May 1965, Alison Mary, da of Wilfred Dresser; 2 s (Benjamin b 1967, Jonathan b 1973); *Career* Rhodes scholar

Univ of Oxford 1957-60, St Antony's scholar Univ of Oxford 1960-62; lectr in philosophy: Univ of Hull 1962-64, Univ of Sussex 1964-76; sr visiting fell Univ of Edinburgh 1972-73; Univ of Sussex: reader in philosophy & artificial intelligence 1976-84, professor of artificial intelligence & cognitive science 1984-91; prof of computor science Univ of Birmingham 1991-; *Books* The Computer Revolution in Philosophy (1978); *Style*— Prof Aaron Sloman; School of Computor Science, University of Birmingham, Edgbaston, Birmingham B15 2TT (☎ 021 414 4773, fax 021 414 3971)

SLOMAN, Sir Albert Edward; CBE (1980); s of Albert Sloman (d 1969), of Launceston, Cornwall, and Lillie Brewer (d 1973); *b* 14 Feb 1921; *Educ* Launceston Coll Cornwall, Wadham Coll Oxford (MA, DPhil); *m* 4 Aug 1948, Marie Bernadette, da of Leo Bergeron (d 1976); 3 da (Anne Veronique b 1949, Isabel Patricia b 1952, Bernadette Jeanne b 1955); *Career* WWII serv Flt Lt 1939-45: night-fighter pilot with 219 and 68 Sqdns, served UK, N Africa, Malta, Sicily (despatches); lectr in Spanish Univ of California Berkeley USA 1946-47, reader in Spanish Univ of Dublin 1947-53, fell Trinity Coll Dublin 1950-53, Gilmour Prof of Spanish Univ of Liverpool 1955-62, dean Faculty of Arts 1960-62, vice chllr Univ of Essex 1962-87; chm: Ctee of Vice Chllrs Princs 1981-83, Br Acad Studentship Ctee 1965-87, Bd of Govrs Centre for Info on Language Teaching in Res 1979-87, Overseas Res Students Fees Support Scheme 1980-87, Univs Cncl for Adult Continuing Educn 1984-87, Inter Univ and Polytechnic Cncl 1985-, Ctee for Int Coop in Higher Educn 1985-, Selection Ctee of Cwlth Scholarship Cmmn 1986-, Int Bd Utd World Coll 1988; vice chm Assoc of Cwlth Univs 1985-, vice pres Int Assoc of Univs 1970-75, memb Bd Br Cncl 1985; Reith lectr 1963, Guildhall Granada lectr 1969; kt 1987; *Recreations* travel; *Clubs* Savile; *Style*— Sir Albert E Sloman; 19 Inglis Rd, Colchester, Essex CO3 3HU (☎ 0206 47270)

SLOMAN, Kenneth Thomas; s of Arthur Thomas Sloman (d 1980), and Nina Elizabeth Emma, *née* Davis; *b* 3 June 1925; *Educ* Hillcroft Coll; *m* 10 Nov 1956, Eliane, da of Elie Jean Tournoud (d 1960); 1 s (Gregory Thomas Boyd b 26 May 1961), 1 da (Gillian Michele b 22 March 1966); *Career* WWII forces 1944-47; dir Starline Paints Ltd 1963-; chm: Logis Ltd 1955, Aviation Marine & Auto Ltd 1968, Starline Decorating Centres Ltd 1973-; Freeman City of London 1976, Liveryman Worshipful Co of Upholders 1976; *Recreations* yachting, shooting; *Clubs* Burnham Sailing, BASC; *Style*— Kenneth Sloman, Esq

SLOWEY, Brian Aodh; *b* 1933; *Educ* Castleknock Coll, Univ Coll Dublin; *m* Marie; 4 children; *Career* vice chm Guinness Brewing Worldwide Ltd London; chm: Guinness Ireland Ltd, Aer Lingus plc, Aerlinte Eireann plc; memb: Nat Exec Ctee and Cncl Confedn of Irish Indust, Irish Mgmnt Inst Cncl; fell Irish Mgmnt Inst; *Style*— Brian Slowey, Esq; Guinness Ireland Ltd, St James's Gate, Dublin 8, Eire (☎ 0001 753645)

SLYNN, Hon Mr Justice; Sir Gordon; s of John and Edith Slynn; *b* 17 Feb 1930; *Educ* Sandbach Sch, Goldsmiths' Coll, Trinity Coll Cambridge; *m* 1962, Odile Marie Henriette Boutin; *Career* called to the Bar Gray's Inn 1956; vice lectr 1987, lectr air law LSE 1958-61, jr counsel Miny of Labour 1967-68, jr counsel Treasy 1968-74, rec 1971 (hon rec Hereford 1972-76), QC 1974, leading counsel Treasy 1974-76, High Ct judge Queen's Bench 1976-81, judge Ct of Justice Euro Communities 1988- (advocate gen 1981-88); pres Employment Appeal Tbnl 1978-81; visiting prof of law: Univ of Durham 1981-88, Univ of Technol Sydney 1990-; chief steward Hereford 1978- (dep chief steward 1977-78); govr Int Students' Tst 1979-85; hon vice pres Union Internationale des Avocats 1976-, chm Exec Cncl Int Law Assoc 1988-; memb Ct Worshipful Co of Broderers; Hon Decanus Juris Mercer USA; hon fell Univ Coll Buckingham 1982; Hon LLD Univs of: Birmingham 1983, Buckingham 1983, Exeter 1985, Technol Sydney 1991; Hon DCL Univ of Durham 1989; Commandeur d'honneur de Bontemps de Medoz et des Graves; kt 1976; *Clubs* Beefsteak, Garrick, Athenaeum; *Style*— The Hon Mr Justice Slynn; Court of Justice, Kirchberg, Luxembourg

SMAIL, Col James Ingram Miles; QSO (1989), OBE (1963), MC (1944), TD (1962), DL (Northumberland 1971); s of James Ingram Smail (d 1947), of Christchurch, New Zealand, and Jane Louise (d 1974); seventh generation in family newspaper business, The Tweeddale Press Group, which produces six papers, including NZ, News UK; *b* 21 Aug 1921, New Zealand; *Educ* Christ's Coll NZ, Canterbury Univ New Zealand, Heriot Watt Coll Edinburgh; *m* 1948, Dorothy Margaret, da of Daniel Reese (d 1954), of Cashmere Hills, Christchurch, NZ; 2 s, 2 da; *Career* served WWII with 1 Canterbury Regt, then 2 NZEF in Africa, Tunisia and Italy, cmd 7 Bn RNF TA 1963, 149 Inf Bde TA 1967, Territorial Col 4 Bns 1968-69; newspaper proprietor; dir Border TV, chm Northumberland County Planning Ctee 1973-83; pres: Scottish Newspaper Proprietors' Assoc 1962-64, NZ Soc 1977; fndr chm Berwick-upon-Tweed Preservation Trust 1971, memb CPU Cncl 1977-; Berwick upon Tweed: memb Borough Cncl for 18 years, Sheriff 1964-65 and 1975-76, Mayor 1971, alderman 1983, alderman CC 1985; OStJ 1985; *Recreations* shooting, gardening; *Clubs* Northern Counties, Newcastle, Lansdowne, Press; *Style*— Col James Smail, QSO, OBE, MC, TD, DL; Kiwi Cottage, Scremerston, Berwick upon Tweed, Northumberland TD15 2RB (☎ 0289 306219); Tweeddale Press Group, 90 Marygate, Berwick upon Tweed, Northumberland TD15 1BW (☎ 0289 306677)

SMAIL, William Prophet; s of William Galbraith Smail (d 1962), and Jean Prophet Ramsay (d 1963); *b* 8 March 1925; *Educ* Perth Acad, Dundee Coll of Art (DipArch); *m* 4 Aug 1951, Joyce, da of Peter Scott Whyte (d 1955); 1 s (Roderick b 1960), 2 da (Deborah b 1954, Julie b 1957); *Career* War Serv RN 1943-46; chartered architect, ptnr Wilson Mason & Partners London and Middle East 1960-76, sr ptnr Wilson Mason & Partners 1976-87 (conslt 1987-91); ARIBA; *Recreations* shooting, gardening; *Clubs* Caledonian; *Style*— William Smail, Esq; Southend House, High Ham, Langport, Somerset (☎ 0458 250436); 30 Ashley Court, Morpeth Terrace, London (☎ 071 834 0809); II "Le Murier", 9 Ave Bosquet, Antibes, France; 3 Chandos Street, London W1 (☎ 071 637 1501, telex 262597, fax 071 631 0325)

SMALE-ADAMS, (Kenneth) Barry; s of Douglas William Smale-Adams; *b* 30 June 1932; *Educ* St John's Coll Johannesburg, Camborne Sch of Mines; *m* 1953, Marion June, *née* Hosken; 2 s (Mark, Jeremy), 1 da (Deborah); *Career* mining engr; Anglo American Corporation of SA 1953-59, gen mangr Associated Mines Malaysia Ltd 1960-65, res mining advsr Hellenic Industrial Development Bank Athens 1965-67, The Rio Tinto Zinc Corpn 1967-87 (exec dir Con Zinc Rio Tinto Malaysia Ltd and Rio Tinto Bethlehem Indonesia 1967-72), gen mangr and dir Rio Tinto Fin and Exploration Ltd 1973-80, md RTZ Deep Sea Mining Enterprises Ltd 1974-87, chm Riofinex Ltd 1976-83 (dep chm 1983-87), consulting engr to mining dir 1983-87; non-exec dir Robertson Gp plc, chm Robertson Mining Fin 1987-89, dir Anglesey Mining plc 1988-, chm Plateau Mining plc 1990-; pres Inst of Mining and Metallurgy 1983-84, chm Court of Govrs Camborne Sch of Mines 1984-; FIMM, Assoc Camborne Sch of Mines, FEng; *Recreations* fishing, reading, music, theatre, sports (generally now as spectator); *Clubs* RAC; *Style*— Barry Smale-Adams, Esq; 4 The Hermitage, Richmond, Surrey TW10 6SM (☎ 081 948 3439); Plateau Mining plc, 1 Castlefield Court, Church St, Reigate, Surrey RH2 0AH (☎ 0737 241224)

SMALL, David Purvis; CMG (1988), MBE (1966); s of Joseph Small (d 1958), of Wishaw, Scotland, and Ann Purvis (d 1985); *b* 17 Oct 1930; *Educ* Our Lady's HS Motherwell; *m* 12 Oct 1957, Patricia, da of John Kennedy (d 1980); 3 s (Joseph b 25 March 1959, John b 10 Aug 1960, David b 30 June 1965); *Career* Nat Serv RAF, serv Egypt Sudan Eritrea and Kenya 1949-51; clerical offr Admty (Civil Serv) 1953 (asst sec 1955-60), CRO 1961, Madras 1962-64, FCO Madras 1962-64, second sec Ibanian 1964-68, first sec Ecuador 1968-73 (former second sec), first sec FCO 1973-76, first sec and head of Chancery Dacca 1976-80, first sec Stockholm 1980-82, cnsllr commercial and econ Copenhagen 1982-87, high commr Georgetown Guyana and ambass Paramibo Surinam 1987-90; *Recreations* golf, soccer, gardening; *Clubs* Cowal Golf; *Style*— David Small, Esq, CMG, MBE; Ashbank, Strachur, Argyll, Scotland, (☎ 036986 282)

SMALL, Gladstone Cleophas; s of Chelston Cleophas Small, of Birmingham, and Gladys, *née* Carter; *b* 18 Oct 1961; *Educ* Combermere GS Barbados, Hall Green Tech Coll Birmingham; *m* 19 Sept 1987, Lois Christine, da of Peter Bernhardt Friedlander, of Mandurah, W Australia; 1 s (Zachary Peter b 13 June 1989); *Career* cricketer Warwickshire CCC 1979-; test debut v NZ 1986, career best 5 wickets for 42 runs v Australia 1986; supporter many charitable orgns; *Recreations* golf, tennis; *Clubs* Kings Norton Golf; *Style*— Gladstone Small, Esq; Warwickshire CCC, County Ground, Edgbaston, Birmingham B5 7QU (☎ 021 446 4422)

SMALL, Prof John Rankin; s of David Carmichael Small (d 1960), and Annie, *née* Stirling (d 1985); *b* 28 Feb 1933; *Educ* Univ of London (BSc Econ); *m* 17 Aug 1957, Rena, da of John Wood (d 1980); 1 s (John Rankin b 1962), 2 da (Karen Elaine b 1960, Mandy Jayne b 1965); *Career* accountant Dunlop Rubber Co 1956-60, lectr Univ of Edinburgh 1960-64, sr lectr Univ of Glasgow 1964-67, prof accountancy and fin Heriot Watt Univ 1967- (dep princ 1990-); chm: Accounts Cmmn Scot 1983-, Nat Appeal Panel for Entry to Pharmaceutical Lists Scot 1987-; dir: Orkney Water Test Centre Ltd, Edinburgh Instruments Ltd; FCCA 1958, FCMA 1960; *Books* Introduction to Managerial Economics (1967), Accounting (1991); *Style*— Prof John Small; 39 Caiystane Terrace, Edinburgh, Scotland EH10 6ST (☎ 031 445 2638); Heriot Watt University, Lord Balerno Building, Riccarton, Edinburgh EH14 4AS (☎ 031 449 5111, fax 031 449 5153)

SMALL, Dr Ramsay George; s of Robert Small (d 1974), of Dundee, and Ann Stewart, *née* Ramsay (d 1967); *b* 5 Feb 1930; *Educ* Harris Acad Dundee, Univ of St Andrew's (MB ChB, DPH); *m* 29 Sept 1951, Aileen Stiven, da of Anson Stiven Masterton (d 1959), of Dundee; 4 s (Ronald b 1954, Douglas b 1955, Kenneth b 1958, Iain b 1961); *Career* Nat Serv RAMC 1955-57, Lt 1955, Capt 1956, RAMC TA 1957-61; asst med offr of health Ayr CC 1958-61, princ med offr Corp of Dundee 1968-74 (sr med offr 1961-68), hon sr lectr Univ of Dundee 1974-89, chief admin med offr Tayside Health Bd 1986-89 (community med specialist 1974-86); memb Jt Ctee on Vaccination and Immunisation 1978-86, chm Eastern Regnl 1 Postgrad Med Educn Ctee 1980-83, convenor Scottish Affrs Ctee Faculty of Community Med 1983-86 (memb bd 1983-90), cncl memb RCPE 1987-90; sec Broughty Ferry Baptist Church 1969-, pres Baptist Union of Scotland 1972-73; FFCM 1978, FRCPE 1987; *Recreations* music, local history, bird watching; *Style*— Dr Ramsay Small; 46 Monifieth Rd, Broughty Ferry, Dundee DD5 2RX (☎ 0382 78408)

SMALLEY, Very Rev Dr Stephen Stewart; s of Arthur Thomas Smalley, OBE, of Banstead, Surrey (d 1975), and May Elizabeth Selina, *née* Kimm (d 1986); *b* 11 May 1931; *Educ* Battersea GS, Jesus Coll Cambridge (MA, PhD), Eden Theol Seminary USA (BD); *m* 13 July 1974, Susan Jane, da of Wing Cdr Arthur James Paterson, of Banstead, Surrey (d 1987); 1 s (Jovian b 1977), 1 da (Evelyn b 1983); *Career* asst curate St Paul's Church Portman Square 1958-60, chaplain Peterhouse Cambridge 1960-63, acting dean 1962-63; lectr and sr lectr: Univ of Ibadan Nigeria 1963-69, Univ of Manchester 1970-77; canon residentiary and precentor Coventry Cathedral 1977-86, vice provost 1986, dean of Chester Cathedral 1987-; *Books* Christ and Spirit in the New Testament (ed with B Lindars, 1973), John: Evangelist and Interpreter (1978), 1, 2, 3, John (1984); *Recreations* music, drama, literature, travel; *Style*— The Very Rev Dr Stephen S Smalley; The Deanery, 7 Abbey St, Chester CH1 2JF (☎ 0224 351380); Hadrians, Bourton-on-the-Hill, Moreton-in-Marsh, Glos GL56 9AE (☎ 0386 700564); Cathedral Office, 1 Abbey Square, Chester CH1 2HU (☎ 0224 324756)

SMALLMAN, Barry Granger; CMG (1976), CVO (1972); s of Charles Stanley Smallman, CBE, ARCM (d 1981), of Worthing, Sussex, and Ruby Marian, *née* Granger (d 1949); *b* 22 Feb 1924; *Educ* St Paul's, Trinity Coll Cambridge (MA); *m* 6 Sept 1952, Sheila Maxine, da of William Henry Knight, of Sissinghurst, Kent; 2 s (Mark b 1955, Robin b 1957), 1 da (Joy b 1953); *Career* served 1939-45, Lt Intelligence Corps; Br dep high cmmr Sierra Leone 1963-64 and NZ 1964-67, IDC 1968, consul-gen Br Embassy Thailand 1971-74, Br high cmmr Bangladesh 1975-78, Dip Serv resident chm Civil Service Selection Bd 1978-81, Br high cmmr Jamaica and ambass Haiti 1982-84; chm Cncl Benenden Sch 1986-; memb Cncl: St Lawrence Coll Ramsgate 1984-, The Leprosy Mission 1984-, The Soc for Promoting Christian Knowledge 1984-; fndr and dir Granger Consultancies 1984-; *Recreations* reading, writing, short stories and verse, singing, piano, bird watching, tennis, golf; *Clubs* Royal Cwlth Soc; *Style*— Barry Smallman, Esq, CMG, CVO; Beacon Shaw, Benenden, Kent TN17 4BU (☎ 0580 240 625)

SMALLMAN, Prof (Edward) Raymond; s of David Smallman, and Edith, *née* French; *b* 4 Aug 1929; *Educ* Rugeley GS, Univ of Birmingham (BSc, PhD, DSc); *m* 6 Sept 1952, Joan Doreen, da of George Faulkner, of Wolverhampton; 1 s (Robert Ian b 1959), 1 da (Lesley Ann (Mrs Grimer) b 1955); *Career* sr scientific offr AERE Harwell 1953-58; Univ of Birmingham: lectr Dept of Physical Metallurgy 1958-63 (sr lectr 1963-64), prof Physical Metallurgy 1964-69, head Physical Metallurgy and Sci of Materials 1969-81, head Dept Metallurgy and Materials 1981-88, dean Faculty of Sci and Engrg 1984-85, dean Faculty of Engrg 1985-87, vice princ 1987-; Sir George Beilby Gold medal 1969, Rosenhain medal 1972, Elegant Work prize 1979, Platinum medal 1989; pres Birmingham Metallurgical Assoc 1972, vice pres Metals Soc 1980-85; Hon DSc: Univ of Wales, Univ of Novi Sad Yugoslavia 1990; CEng, FIM 1965, FRS 1986; *Books* Modern Physical Metallurgy (1962, 4 edn 1985), Modern Metallography (1966), Structure of Metals and Alloys (1969), Defect Analysis in Electron Microscopy (1975), Vacancies '76 (1976); *Recreations* golf, bridge, travel; *Clubs* Athenaeum, South Staffs Golf; *Style*— Prof Raymond Smallman, FRS; 59 Woodthorne Rd Sth, Tettenhall, Wolverhampton WV6 8SN (☎ 021 414 5223, fax 021 414 5232, telex SPAPHYG 338938)

SMALLMAN, Timothy Gilpin; s of Stanley Cottrell Smallman (d 1965), of Sedgemere, Fen End, Kenilworth, Warwicks, and Grace Mary Louise, *née* Wilson (d 1990); *b* 6 Nov 1938; *Educ* Stowe; *m* 18 April 1964, Jane, da of Edward Holloway (d 1988), of Acocks Green, Birmingham; 2 s (Guy b 1965, Simon b 1967); *Career* chm: Smallman Lubricants (Hereford) Ltd 1972, WF Smallman and Son Ltd 1978 (md 1965); chm and md Smallman Lubricants Ltd 1978, chm Coronet Oil Refineries Ltd 1979, nat pres Br Lubricants Fedn Ltd 1983-85 (dir 1977-89), chm Needwood Oils and Solvents Ltd 1984; FInstD 1965, FInstPet 1968; *Recreations* golf, bridge, ornithology, nature and wildlife conservation; *Clubs* St James's, Copt Heath Golf, Rugby Club of London; *Style*— Timothy Smallman, Esq; Luddington Manor, nr Stratford-upon-Avon CV37 9SJ; W F Smallman & Son Ltd, 216 Great Bridge St, W Bromwich, W Midlands (☎ 021 557 3372)

SMALLPEICE, Sir Basil; KCVO (1961); s of Herbert Charles Smallpeice (d 1927), and Georgina Ruth, *née* Rust (d 1970); *b* 18 Sept 1906; *Educ* Shrewsbury; *m* 1, 1931,

Kathleen Ivey Singleton (d 1973), da of Edwin Singleton Brame; m 2, 1973, Rita, yr da of late Maj W Burns; *Career* CA 1930; Hoover Ltd 1930-37, chief accountant and then sec Doulton and Co Ltd 1937-48, dir of costs and statistics British Transport Commission 1948-50; BOAC: fin comptroller 1950, memb Bd 1953, dep chief exec 1954, md 1956-63; dir BOAC-Cunard Ltd 1962-63, admin advsr HM Household 1964-80; chm: Nat Jt Cncl for Civil Air Tport 1960-61, Cunard Steam-Ship Co Ltd 1965-71, Eng Speaking Union of the Cwlth 1965-68, Offshore Marine Ltd 1968-70, ACT(A) Australian Nat Line Co-ordinating Bd 1969-79, Cncl BIM 1970-72 (memb 1959-75, vice-pres 1972-), Associated Container Transportation (Australia) Ltd 1971-79, The Air League 1971-74 (vice-pres 1975), Cavendish Medical Centre Ltd 1973-79; dep chm Lonrho Ltd 1972-73; memb: Cncl Inst of Chartered Accountants 1948-57, Cncl Inst of Tport 1958-61, Ctee for Exports to USA 1964-66, Martins Bank 1965-69, Barclays Bank London Local Bd 1969-74; OStJ, Order of the Cedar Lebanon (1955); *Books* Of Comets and Queens (1981); *Clubs* Athenaeum, Boodle's, Melbourne (Australia); *Style*— Sir Basil Smallpeice, KCVO; Bridge House, 45 Leigh Hill Rd, Cobham, Surrey KT11 2HU (☎ 0932 65425)

SMALLPEICE, (Charles) Peter; s of (Herbert) Frank Smallpeice, of Cromer, Norfolk, and Cordula Caroline Marie Mau; *b* 25 Aug 1939; *Educ* Framlingham Coll; *m* 8 April 1967, Elisabetta Teresa Alda, da of Commandante Aldo Ferrari (Italian Navy ret); 1 da (Joanna Mary b 7 April 1969); *Career* articled clerk Bullimore & Co Norwich 1957-63, qualified chartered accountant 1963, sr mangr Deloitte Plender Griffiths Annan & Co Salisbury Rhodesia 1963-66; ptnr: Lovewell Blake & Co Norwich 1969-80 (mangr 1967-69), Coopers & Lybrand Norwich 1980-90, Coopers & Lybrand Deloitte (following merger) Norwich 1990; pres: Salisbury (Rhodesia) Jr C of C 1966, Norwich Jr C of C 1971, Norfolk & Norwich Soc of CAS 1983-84, East Anglian Soc of CAS 1990-91; chm Eastern Regional Gp Br Jr C of C 1973, senator Jr Chamber Int 1978; treas: Br Senate, Norfolk & Norwich Festival; tstee: H J Sexton Norwich Asts Tst, Norfolk Care Tst; FCA 1974 (ACA 1963); *Recreations* travel, the arts, food and wine, living in our flat in Venice; *Clubs* Norfolk (Norwich), Norwich Rotary; *Style*— Peter Smallpeice, Esq, JP; 33 Eaton Rd, Norwich NR4 6PR (☎ 0603 58975)

SMALLWOOD, Air Chief Marshal Sir Denis Graham; GBE (1975, CBE 1961, MBE 1951, KCB (1969, CB 1966), DSO (1944), DFC (1942); s of Frederick William Smallwood, of Moseley, Birmingham; *b* 13 Aug 1918; *Educ* King Edward's Sch Birmingham; *m* 1940, Frances Jeanne, da of Walter Needham, of Birmingham; 1 s, 1 da; *Career* RAF 1938; served WWII as fighter pilot Fighter Cmd nos: 605, 87, 247 Hurricane Sqdns 1939-42, ldr Spitfire Wing 1943-44; dir staff RAF Staff Coll Haifa 1945-46, asst sec Chiefs of Staff Ctee 1947-49, dir staff Jt Servs Staff Coll 1950-53, Cdr RAF Biggin Hill 1953-55, dir staff IDC 1955-56, Gp Capt Plans Air Task Force Suez Campaign 1956, Cdr RAF Guided Missiles Station Lincs 1959-61, AOC and Cmdt RAF Coll of Air Warfare, Manby 1961, Air Cdre 1961, asst chief of air staff (Ops) 1963-65, AOC 3 Gp Bomber Cmd 1965-67, SASO Bomber Cmd 1967-68, COS Strike Cmd 1969, Air Marshal 1969, Cdr Br Forces Near East and AOC-in-C NEAF and Admin of Sovereign Base Areas of Akrotiri and Dhekelia Cyprus 1969-70, Vice-Chief of air staff 1970-73, AOC-in-C Strike Cmd 1974, Air Chief Marshal 1973, C-in-C UK Air Forces 1975-76; ADC to HM The Queen 1954-59, mil advsr Br Aerospace 1977-83; chm/pres Air League 1977-84 (now life vice pres); Freeman City of London; Liveryman Guild of Air Pilots and Navigators; FRSA, FRAeS; *Books* RAF Biggin Hill; *Recreations* Equitation, gardening, swimming, wild life, hiking, antiques; *Clubs* RAF, Les Ambassadeurs; *Style*— Air Chief Marshal Sir Denis Smallwood, GBE, KCB, DSO, DFC; The Flint House, Owlswick, Aylesbury, Bucks HP17 9RH

SMALLWOOD, Hon Mrs (Kirsty Jane); *née* Aitken; da (by 2 w) of Sir Max Aitken, Bt (d 1985; 2 Baron Beaverbrook who disclaimed his title 1964), and Ursula Jane Kenyon-Slaney; *b* 22 June 1947; *m* 1, 1966 (m dis 1973), Jonathan Derek Morley, yr s of Brig Michael Frederick Morley, MBE; 2 s (Dominic b 1967, Sebastian b 1969); m 2, 1975, Christopher Marten Smallwood, s of Canon Graham Marten Smallwood; 1 da (Eleanor b 1982); *Style*— The Hon Mrs Smallwood; The Vineyard, Hurlingham Rd, London SW6 3NR (☎ 071 736 3240)

SMART, Adrian Michael Harwood; s of Harold Leslie Harwood Smart (d 1976), of Cuckfield, Sussex, and Moira, *née* Scanlon (d 1986); *b* 20 Nov 1935; *Educ* Eastbourne Coll; *m* 14 Sept 1963, Anne Sara, da of Richard Buxton Morrish; 1 s (Richard Anthony Harwood b 29 March 1967), 1 da (Amanda Hilary Harwood b 6 Oct 1964); *Career* Slaughter and May: articled clerk 1957-61, asst slr 1961-68, ptnr 1969; *Recreations* landscape gardening, oenology; *Clubs* Oriental, Hong Kong; *Style*— Adrian Smart, Esq; Slaughter and May, 35 Basinghall St, London EC2V 5DB (☎ 071 600 1200, fax 071 726 0038)

SMART, Clive Frederick; s of Charles Frederick Smart (d 1983), of Altrincham, Cheshire, and Gladys, *née* Morton; *b* 14 April 1932; *Educ* Manchester GS; *m* 22 June 1957, Audrey (d 1982), da of Stanley Walker Brown (d 1965), of Altrincham; 2 s (David b and d 1959, Philip b 1971), 4 da (Karen b 1958, Angela b 1960, Valerie b 1962, Nicola b 1966); *Career* CA; articled clerk Edwin Guthrie & Co CAs 1949, Peat Marwick 1954-58, gen mangr Halle Concerts Soc 1960-91 (co sec 1958-90); arts mgmnt conslt 1991-; dir Assoc of Br Orchestras; hon memb: Royal Northern Coll of Music, Inc Soc of Musicians; FCA 1954, FRSA 1987; Queen's Silver Jubilee medal; *Recreations* sailing, photography, gardening, music; *Clubs* Royal Over-Seas League; *Style*— Clive Smart, Esq; 297 Washway Rd, Sale, Cheshire (☎ 061 962 1707)

SMART, Geoffrey John Neville; s of John Frederick Smart (d 1979), of Lincoln, and Elsie, *née* Blunt; *b* 19 Sept 1946; *Educ* Lincoln Sch, Emmanuel Coll Cambridge (MA); *m* 5 Nov 1970, Karen Martha Margareta, da of Maj August Wilhelm Cordes; 3 da (Katherine b 1974, Harriet b 1976, Clare b 1978); *Career* analyst Mgmnt Dynamics Ltd 1967-70, ptnr Deloitte Haskins & Sells 1980 -89 (mgmnt conslt 1970-74, mangr 1974-80), ptnr Coopers & Lybrand Deloitte 1990-; *Recreations* golf, theatre, music; *Clubs* RAC; *Style*— Geoffrey Smart, Esq; Coopers & Lybrand Deloitte, 128 Queen Victoria St, London EC4P 4JX (☎ 071 248 3913, fax 071 248 3623, telex 894941)

SMART, Prof Sir George Algernon; s of Algernon Smart (d 1952), and Mary Ann Smart (d 1984); *b* 16 Dec 1913; *Educ* Uppingham, Univ of Durham (BSc, MD); *m* 1939, Monica Helen, da of Joseph Ernest Carrick; 2 s, 1 da; *Career* prof of med Univ of Durham and Newcastle upon Tyne 1956-72; dir British Postgraduate Medical Fedn and prof of med Univ of London 1971-78; vice-pres and sr censor RCP 1972; kt 1978; *Books* Fundamentals of Clinical Endocrinology (co-author); *Style*— Prof Sir George Smart; Taffrail, Crede Lane, Old Bosham, Chichester, Sussex PO18 8NX

SMART, Prof (Arthur David) Gerald; s of Arthur Herbert John Smart (d 1979), of Seaton, Devon, and Amelia Olwen Mona, *née* Evans (d 1967); *b* 19 March 1925; *Educ* Rugby, King's Coll Cambridge (MA), Regent St Poly (DipTP); *m* 18 June 1955, Anne Patience, da of Charles William Baxter, CMG, MC (d 1969), of Storrington, Sussex; 2 da (Amelia b 1 May 1959, Susan b 9 July 1960); *Career* planner in local govt 1950-75, co planning offr Hants CC 1963-75, head of Bartlett Sch of Architecture and Planning UCL 1975-80, prof of urban planning (later emeritus prof) Univ of London 1975-85; conslt Countryside Cmmn 1989-90; memb: Cncl Solent Protection Soc, Governing Body GB E Europe Centre, various govt ctees on planning 1963-77, Cncl RSPB 1985-90; chm: Milford on Sea Parish Cncl, Structure Plan Examinations in Pub DOE; ARICS 1953, FRTPI 1964; *Recreations* ornithology, sailing, walking, music; *Clubs* Royal Lymington Yacht; *Style*— Prof Gerald Smart; 10 Harewood Green, Keyhaven, Lymington, Hants SO41 0TZ (☎ 0590 645475)

SMART, Sir Jack; CBE (1976), JP (Castleford, 1960), DL (West Yorkshire, 1987); s of James William Smart (d 1968), and Emily, *née* Greenanay (d 1955); *b* 25 April 1920; *Educ* Altofts Colliery Sch; *m* 1941, Ethel, da of Henry King, (d 1963), of Cutsyke, Castleford; 1 da (Joan); *Career* miner 1934-59; mayor Castleford 1962-63; memb: Wakefield Metropolitan Dist Cncl 1973- (leader 1973-), Layfield Ctee of Inquiry on Local Govt Fin; chm Wakefield DHA 1977-, former chm Assoc of Met Authys, pres The Yorkshire Soc 1980; hon fell Bretton Coll; Hon Freeman City of Wakefield Met Dist Cncl 1985; FRSA; *Recreations* golf, swimming; *Style*— Sir Jack Smart, CBE, JP, DL; Churchside, Weetworth, Pontefract Rd, Castleford, W Yorks (☎ 0977 554880)

SMART, Prof (Roderick) Ninian; s of late Prof W M Smart, FRSE, and Isabel, *née* Carswell; *b* 6 May 1927; *Educ* Glasgow Acad, Queen's Coll Oxford (Major open scholar, BA, BPhil); *m* 1954, Libushka Baruffaldi; 4 c; *Career* 2 Lt, Capt Army Intelligence Corps 1945-48 (overseas service in Ceylon); lectr in philosophy UCW Aberystwyth 1952-56, lectr in history and philosophy of religion Univ of London 1956-61 (acting head of Dept 1959), H G Wood prof of theology Univ of Birmingham 1961-67; prof of religious studies: Univ of Lancaster 1967-82 (hon prof 1982-89, prof emeritus 1989, pro vice chllr 1969-72), Univ of Calif at Santa Barbara 1976- (J F Rowny Prof of Comparative Religions); author of numerous articles and reviews; visiting lectr in philosophy: Yale Univ 1955-56, Banaras Hindu Univ 1960; visiting prof: Univ of Wisconsin 1965, Princeton 1971, Univ of Otago NZ 1981, Univ of Queensland Aust 1980 and 1985, St Martin's Coll of Educn Lancaster 1980-89, Univ of Cape Town SA 1982, Harvard Univ 1983, United Theol Coll India 1984, Univ of Hong Kong 1989; dir Schools Cncl Projects on Secdy and Primary Religious Educn Univ of Lancaster 1969-79; memb: Archbishops' Cmmn of Christian Doctrine (C of E) 1966-70, Cncl American Soc for the Study of Religion 1979- (pres 1984-87); pres: Shap Working Party on World Religions in Educn 1977- (co chm 1968-77), Br Assoc for the History of Religions 1981-85, Oxford Soc of Historical Theology 1981-82; vice pres: World Congress of Faiths 1978-79, Inst of Religion and Theology of GB and Ireland 1978-82 (gen sec 1974-78); editorial conslt The Long Search BBC TV 1974-77, external examiner for numerous undergraduate and graduate degrees, numerous special lectures worldwide; Hon DHumane Letters Loyola Univ 1968, Hon DLitt Univ of Glasgow 1984, Hon DUniv Univ of Stirling 1986; hon prof of religious studies: Univ of Wales 1987-, Univ of Stirling 1988-; *Books* incl: Reasons and Faiths (1958), The Teacher and Christian Belief (1966), The Yogi and the Devotee (1968), The Message of the Buddha (1975), The Religious Experience (1979, 4 edn 1991), Religion and Politics in the Contemporary World (with Peter Merkl, 1983), Worldviews (1983), Religion and the Western Mind (1989); *Recreations* cricket, poetry, tennis; *Clubs* Athenaeum; *Style*— Prof Ninian Smart; Department of Religious Studies, University of California at Santa Barbara, CA 93106, USA

SMART, (Alexander Basil) Peter; s of (Henry) Prescott Smart (d 1981), of Houghton le Spring, Co Durham, and (Mary) Gertrude, *née* Todd; *b* 19 Feb 1932; *Educ* Ryhope GS, Co Durham; *m* 24 Sept 1955, Joan Mary, da of Alex Cumming (d 1973); 3 s (Peter b 1960, Michael (twin) b 1960, Jeremy b 1966); *Career* 2 Lt RAEC 1951-53, supervising offr for educn Gibraltar Cmd 1951-52; Foreign (later HM Dip) Serv 1953, Duala French Cameroons 1956, Cyprus 1956-59, Seoul Korea 1959-63, Rangoon Burma 1968-71, head communications tech servs dept FCO 1975-77, cnsllr later dep high cmmr Canberra 1977-82, dep head mission Prague 1983-86, Br high cmmr Seychelles 1986-89, Br ambass Fiji and Br high cmmr Tuvalu and Nauru 1989; FRSA; *Recreations* music and the arts, exploring little-used roads; *Style*— Peter Smart, Esq; c/o FCO (Suva, Fiji), King Charles St, London SW1A 2AH

SMART, Richard; s of Horace Alfred (David) Smart (d 1985), and Vera Mary Naomi, *née* Latham; *b* 9 Oct 1942; *Educ* The Sorbonne (Diplome d'Etudes), Univ of Bristol (BA), Univ of London (MA); *m* 21 Feb 1976, Margaret Mary, da of Richard Gregory, of 26 Kineton Road, Sutton Coldfield; *Career* cmmnd RAFVR (TR) 1966; headmaster Hampden House Sch 1978-80, princ Milestone Tutorial Coll 1981-, dir Milestone Search Ltd; chm Conf for Ind Further Educn 1983-85, memb Cncl Assoc of Tutors 1984-; Liveryman Worshipful Co of Bakers; FBIM, FCollP; *Recreations* chamber music, tennis, travel; *Clubs* Reform, Leander, Athenaeum; *Style*— Richard Smart, Esq; 170 Sloane Street, London SW1 (☎ 071 235 1736); Whistler Court, Preston Park Avenue, Brighton (☎ 0273 506 818); Milestone Tutorial College, 85 Cromwell Road, London SW7 (☎ 071 373 4956)

SMART, Richard Anthony; s of James Clifford Smart (d 1972) of Neath, West Glamorgan, and Rose Beryl, *née* Penn; *b* 8 March 1942; *Educ* Neath GS; *m* 1968, Gaynor, da of Oswald Isaac; 2 s (Matthew James b 4 Oct 1974, Jonathan Anthony (twin) b 4 Oct 1974); *Career* CA 1966; joined Deloitte Plender Griffiths & Co 1959, ptnr; Deloitte Haskins & Sells 1976-90, Coopers & Lybrand Deloitte 1990, Cork Gully 1990; memb: Insolvency Practitioners Assoc 1976, Inst of Credit Mgmnt 1988, Soc of Practioners of Insolvency; FCA 1977; *Recreations* sport and music; *Clubs* Cardiff and County; *Style*— Richard Smart, Esq; Coopers & Lybrand Deloitte, Churchill House, Churchill Way, Cardiff CF1 4XQ (☎ 0222 237000, fax 0222 237720)

SMEDLEY, His Hon Judge (Frank) Brian; QC (1977); s of Leslie Smedley (d 1970); *b* 28 Nov 1934; *Educ* West Bridgford GS, Univ of London (LLB); *Career* called to the Bar Gray's Inn 1960, rec Crown Court 1971-84, memb Senate of Inns of Court and the Bar 1973-77, circuit judge 1987-, Central Criminal Court 1987, sr judge Sovereign Base Areas Cyprus 1991; *Recreations* travel, gardening; *Clubs* Garrick; *Style*— His Hon Judge Brian Smedley, QC; c/o Central Criminal Court, Old Bailey, London EC4

SMEDLEY, (Roscoe Relph) George Boleyne; s of Lt Charles Boleyne Smedley (d 1920), and Aimie Blaine, *née* Relph (d 1948); *b* 3 Sept 1919; *Educ* King's Sch Ely, King's Coll London (LLB); *m* 1, 27 Sept 1947, Muriel Hallaway (d 1975), da of Arthur Stanley Murray (d 1945); 1 s (Robert Charles b 1948); m 2, 11 July 1979, Margaret Gerrard Gourlay, da of Augustus Thorburn Hallaway (d 1939), and wid of Dr John Stewart Gourlay; *Career* WWII Artists Rifles TA 1939-40, Lt S Lancs Lancs Regt 1940-42, Capt Indian Army 1942-46; FO 1937 and 1946; Dip Serv (formerly Foreign Serv): Rangoon 1947, Maymo 1950, Brussels 1952, Baghdad 1954, FO 1958, Beirut 1963, Kuwait 1965, FCO 1969, consul gen Lubumbashi 1972-74, Br Mil Govt Berlin 1974-76, FCO 1976, head Nationality and Treaty Dept 1977-79; pt/t appts since ret: legal memb Mental Health Review Tbnl, chm Rent Assessment Ctee, adjudicator under Immigration Act 1971, inspr planning inspectorate Depts of Environment and Tport, dep traffic cmmr NE Traffic Area, memb No 2 Dip Serv Appeal Bd; churchwarden; *Clubs* RAC, Royal Over-Seas League; *Style*— George Smedley, Esq; Garden House, Whorlton, Barnard Castle, Co Durham DL12 8XQ (☎ 0833 27 381)

SMEDLEY, Sir Harold; KCMG (1978, CMG 1965), MBE (1946); s of Ralph Davies Smedley (d 1954), of Worthing; *b* 19 June 1920; *Educ* Aldenham, Pembroke Coll Cambridge; *m* 1950, Beryl, da of Harold Brown, of Wellington, NZ; 2 s, 2 da; *Career* Nat Serv WWII RM served UK, Med, W Europe; entered Dominions Office 1946, private sec to Sec of State Cwlth Rels Office 1954-57, Br high cmmr Ghana 1964-67, ambass Laos 1968-70, asst under sec FCO 1970, sec gen Cmmn on Rhodesian Opinion 1971-72, high cmmr Republic of Sri Lanka and ambass to Maldives Republic 1973-75, high cmmr in NZ and govr of Pitcairn 1976-80; chm Bank of NZ (London) 1983-90 (dep chm 1981-83); pres Hakluyt Soc 1987-; vice chm Victoria League 1981-90; *Clubs* United Oxford and Cambridge Univ, Cwlth Tst; *Style*— Sir Harold Smedley, KCMG, MBE; 11A Beehive Lane, Ferring, West Sussex BN12 5NN

SMEDLEY, Peter Lawrence; s of Graham Powell Smedley (d 1983), of Carmichael's House, Carmichaels, Longforgan, Dundee, Tayside, and Jean Grace, *née* Ludlow; *b* 20 Jan 1939; *Educ* King's Sch Canterbury, RAC Cirencester; *m* 1977, Christine June, da of Donald William Howard; *Career* fndr light aircraft business in SA 1971-72; National Canning Company (family business) 1963-65, fndr own co Smedley Powell & Co (surveying and land agency) 1965, purchased Ston Easton Park 1977, undertook restoration 1977-82, opened as hotel 1982 (winner Egon Rony Gold Plate Hotel of the Year), dir (with estate mgmnt responsibilities) Family Farming Co Scotland 1985; awarded RAF Flying Scholarship; *Recreations* shooting, garden planning; *Style*— Peter Smedley, Esq; Ston Easton Park, Ston Easton, Bath, Somerset BA3 4DF (☎ 076 121 631, fax 076 121 377)

SMEDLEY, Roger William; MBE; s of Thomas Smedley (d 1947), and Marguerite Esther, *née* Taylor; *b* 21 April 1935; *Educ* Colston's Boys Sch Bristol; *m* 19 Aug 1961, Suzanne, da of Ian Murray Robertson; 2 s (Christopher b 1963, Tobias b 1965); *Career* chm Ricardo International plc 1961-; Eur Ing, CEng, FIMechE, FRAeS; *Recreations* motor cycling; *Clubs* Clifton (Bristol); *Style*— Roger Smedley, Esq, MBE; Savernake, 5 Stoke Paddock Rd, Stoke Bishop, Bristol BS9 2DJ (☎ 0272 683673); Ricardo International plc, Brunswick House, Upper York St, Bristol (☎ 0272 232162)

SMEE, Clive Harrod; s of Victor Woolley Smee, of Kingsbridge, Devon, and Leila Olive, *née* Harrod (d 1956); *b* 29 April 1942; *Educ* Royal GS Guildford, LSE (BEcon), Business Sch Indiana Univ (MBA), Inst of Cwlth Studies Oxford; *m* 5 April 1975, Denise Eileen, da of Edward Ernest Sell (d 1968), of Shafton, Yorks; 1 s (David b 1981), 2 da (Anna b 1978, Elizabeth b 1985); *Career* Br Cncl Nigeria 1966-68, econ advsr ODM 1969-75, sr econ advsr DHSS 1975-82, Nuffield and Leverhulme travelling fell USA and Canada 1978-79, advsr Central Policy Review Staff 1982-83, sr econ advsr HM Treasy 1983-84; chief econ advsr: DHSS 1984-89, Dept of Health 1989-; conslt NZ Treasy 1988; chm Social Policy working pty OECD 1987-89; *Recreations* running, gardening, family; *Style*— Clive Smee, Esq; c/o Dept of Health, Friars House, Blackfriars Rd, London SE1 (☎ 071 972 3080)

SMEE, John Michael Alan; s of Edward Albert Smee (d 1975), of Wentworth, Surrey, and Hilda Florence, *née* Smith; *b* 29 Dec 1927; *Educ* Ealing Coll, Taunton and Ealing Art Coll; *m* 12 July 1952, Daphne Violet Joan, da of Albert Edward Mallandain (d 1982); 1 s (Anthony Edward b 1954), 1 da (Susan Pamela b 1960); *Career* chm and md: Smee's Advertising Ltd 1975, Smee's Estates (London) Ltd 1975; chm Taylor Advertising Ltd 1975; *Recreations* rugby, golf; *Clubs* IOD, Wentworth; *Style*— John M A Smee, Esq; c/o Smee's Advertising Ltd, 3/5 Duke St, London W1 (fax 071 935 8588, telex 27719 SMET AY)

SMEE, Roger Guy; s of Donald Arthur Smee, and Valerie Patricia Smee; *b* 14 Aug 1948; *Educ* Forest GS, Inst of Building; *m* 24 Aug 1969 (m dis), (Rosamund) Bridget, da of Maj Eric Francis Hatch; 1 s (Alistair b 18 Jan 1974), 2 da (Victoria b 23 Oct 1970, Charlotte b 22 Dec 1981); *Career* fndr Rockfort Group 1976 (currently chm and md); former professional soccer player Chelsea FC and Reading FC; pres Berks Assoc of Young People, memb Exec Ctee W Berkshire Macmillan Cancer Care Fund, chm Dellwood Cancer Care Centre Appeal; *Recreations* all sport, principally running; *Style*— Roger Smee, Esq; Commercial House, 24/26 East St, Reading, Berks RG1 4QH (☎ 0734 509905, fax 0734 504433)

SMEETON, Vice Admiral Sir Richard Michael; KCB (1964, CB 1961), MBE (1942), DL (Surrey 1976); s of Edward Leaf Smeeton (d 1935), and Charlotte Mildred, *née* Leighton (s 1934), of Triangle, Halifax, Yorks; *b* 24 Sept 1912; *Educ* RNC Dartmouth; *m* 1940, Mary Elizabeth, da of Cecil Horlock Hawkins, of London; *Career* joined RN 1926; served in HMS: Ark Royal, Furious and Br Pacific Fleet WW II, Capt 1950, IDC 1955; dir of Plans, Admty 1957-59; Rear Adm 1959, Flag Offr Aircraft Carriers 1960-62, Vice Adm 1962, Dep Supreme Allied Cdr Atlantic 1962-64, Flag Offr Naval Air Cmd 1964-65, ret at own request 1965; dir and chief exec Soc of Br Aerospace Cos 1966-79, sec Def Industs Cncl 1970-79; *Clubs* Army and Navy; *Style*— Vice Admiral Sir Richard Smeeton, KCB, MBE, DL; St Mary's Cottage, Woodhill Lane, Shamley Green, Guildford, Surrey (☎ 0483 893478)

SMELLIE, Keith Graham; s of James Maclure Smellie (d 1961), and Hilda Kathleen, *née* Lamsdale; *b* 8 April 1934; *Educ* Repton; *m* 13 August 1960, Meriel Hill, da of George Benjamin Hill Parkes; 4 c (Tiona Jayne b 16 Feb 1962, Alastair James b 14 Nov 1963, Stuart Guy b 2 Feb 1967, Justin Charles b 1 May 1968); *Career* Nat Serv cmmnd RA 1953; articled clerk Impey Cudworth & Co Birmingham, qualified chartered accountant 1961, memb Birmingham Stock Exchange 1965, dir Albert E Sharp Holdings plc 1988- (ptnr Albert E Sharp & Co 1967-88), fndr dir NMW Computers plc 1972-; memb Stock Exchange Midlands & Western Unit Ctee Birmingham 1972-88; ACA 1961, memb Int Stock Exchange 1965, ASIA 1967; *Style*— Keith Smellie, Esq; South Lawn, Rowington, Warwick CV35 7AA (☎ 0926 843247); Albert E Sharp Holdings plc, Edmund House, 12 Newhall St, Birmingham B3 3ER (☎ 021 200 2244, fax 021 200 2245)

SMETHURST, John Michael; s of Albert Smethurst (d 1973), of 20 Cliffe Lane, Barrow-in-Furness, and Nelly, *née* Kitchin (d 1985); *b* 25 April 1934; *Educ* William Hulme's GS Manchester, Univ of Manchester (BA); *m* 2 Jan 1960, Mary, da of Ernest Edwin Clayworth (d 1986), of Manchester; 1 s (Matthew b 1966), 1 da (Laura b 1964); *Career* sch master 1956-60, lectr and coll librarian Lancaster Coll of Art 1960-63, tutor librarian Bede Coll Univ of Durham 1963-66, librarian Inst of Educn Univ of Newcastle 1966-69, dep librarian Univ of Glasgow 1969-72, univ librarian Univ of Aberdeen 1972-86, DG Humanities and Social Scis Br Library 1986-; former chm: Friends of Aberdeen Art Gallery, Aberdeen Maritime Museum Appeal; pres: Friends of Aberdeen Univ Library 1986-, Scottish Library Assoc 1983, Liber Ligue Int Des Bibliotheques Européens de Researches 1989-; chm: Standing Conf of Nat and Univ Libraries 1983-85 and 1989-90 (vice chm 1988-89, memb Cncl 1981-), Library and Info Servs Ctee Scotland 1980-86, Tstees of the Brotherton Collection Univ of Leeds 1987-; tstee Nat Library of Scotland 1975-86, memb Bd Br Library 1986-; ALA, FRSA; hon memb SLA, hon res fell UCL 1986-; *Books* various articles in professional jls and other pubns; *Recreations* music, gardening, art, travel; *Clubs* Athenaeum; *Style*— Michael Smethurst, Esq; Romney, 72 Grove Rd, Tring, Herts HP23 (☎ 044 282 5465); British Library, Gt Russell St, London WC1B 3DG (☎ 071 323 7530, telex 21462)

SMFRSON, Dr David John; s of Eric Pearson (d 1977), of Eccleston, Chester, and Winifed Mary Pearson (d 1988); *b* 29 Jan 1946; *Educ* Ampleforth, St Georges Hosp Med Sch London (MB BS), Univ of Manchester (PhD); *Career* house offr St Georges Hosp 1068, sr house offr Manchester Royal Infirmary 1970, visiting scientist US Pub Health Serv 1977, asst prof of med Univ of W Virginia 1977, sr lectr in med Univ of Manchester 1979- (res fell 1972, lectr in med 1976), hon conslt physician S Manchester DHA 1979-; author of numerous res papers on allergy, immunology, food and health; memb: BR Soc for Immunology, Br Soc for Allergy and Clinical Immunology, Soc for Free Radical Res; FRCP 1987; *Recreations* skiing, windsurfing, sailing; *Style*— Dr David Pearson; Department of Medicine, University Hospital of South Manchester, Nell Lane, Manchester M20 8LR (☎ 061 4473828)

SMIDDY, (Francis) Geoffrey; s of Francis William Smiddy (d 1953), and Anne Smiddy (d 1953); *b* 4 Jan 1922; *Educ* Leeds GS, Leeds Univ Med Sch (MCh, MD); *m* 16 Aug 1951, Thelma Vivienne, da of Harry Charles Penfold, of 11 Ashleigh Rd, Leeds; 1 s (Francis Paul b 13 Nov 1953), 1 da (Clare Elizabeth 6 Jan 1957); *Career* RAMC 1945-48; res fell surgery Harvard Univ 1958-59, sr lectr surgery Leeds Med Sch 1960-61, conslt surgn Gen Infirmary Leeds 1961-87; memb: Assoc Surgns 1948-85, Ct Examiners RCS; FRCS 1950; *Books* Medical Management of Surgical Patients (1978), Tutorials in Surgery Vols 1-V (1982); *Recreations* golf, writing; *Style*— Geoffrey Smiddy, Esq; 2A Harrowby Road, Leeds LS16 5HN (☎ 0532 757129)

SMIDDY, (Francis) Paul; s of Francis Geoffrey Smiddy, of Leeds, and Thelma Vivenne Smiddy, JP; *b* 13 Nov 1953; *Educ* Winchester, Univ of Manchester; *m* 2 Sept 1978, Katy, da of Stewart MacDougall Watson, Newport, Gwent; 2 s (Oliver b 1980, Alexander b 1982); *Career* mangr Price Waterhouse 1978-82, fin analyst J Sainsbury 1982-84, res analyst Capel-Cure Myers 1984-85, assoc dir Wood Mackenzie 1985-88, dir Retail Res Kleinwort Benson Securities 1988-; ACA 1978, FCA 1988; *Recreations* flying, motor sport, squash, theatre, walking; *Clubs* BARC; *Style*— Paul Smiddy, Esq; West Hall, 54 Wood Vale, London SE23 3ED (☎ 081 693 4927); Kleinwort Benson Securities Ltd, PO Box 560, 20 Fenchurch St, London EC3P 3DB (☎ 071 623 8000, fax 071 623 4572, telex 922241)

SMIETON, Dame Mary Guillan; DBE (1949); da of John Guillan Smieton, and Maria Judith, *née* Toop; *b* 5 Dec 1902; *Educ* Perse Sch Cambridge, Wimbledon HS, Bedford Coll London, Lady Margaret Hall Oxford (MA); *Career* asst keeper PRO 1925-28, Miny of Labour and Nat Serv 1928-59, gen sec Women's Vol Servs 1938-40, on loan to UN as dir of personnel 1946-48, perm sec Miny of Educn 1959-63, UK rep UNESCO Exec Bd 1962-68; hon fell: Lady Margaret Hall Oxford 1959, Bedford Coll 1971, Royal Holloway Bedford New Coll 1985; tstee Br Museum 1963-73, cncl chm Bedford Coll 1963-70; memb: Advsy Cncl on Public Records 1965-73, Standing Cmmn on Museums and Galleries 1970-73; vice pres Museums Assoc 1974-77; *Clubs* United Oxford and Cambridge University; *Style*— Dame Mary Smieton, DBE; 14 St George's Rd, St Margaret's on Thames, Middlesex TW1 1QR (☎ 081 892 9279)

SMILEY, Col David de Crespigny; LVO (1952), OBE (Mil, 1945), MC (1943, and bar 1944); s of Maj Sir John Smiley, 2 Bt (d 1930), and Valerie, *née* Champion de Crespigny (d 1978); *b* 11 April 1916; *Educ* Nautical Coll Pangbourne, RMC Sandhurst; *m* 28 April 1947, Moyra Eileen, da of Lt-Col Lord Francis George Montagu Douglas Scott, KCMG, DSO (d 1952; yst s of 6 Duke of Buccleuch), and widow of Maj Hugo Douglas Tweedie, Scots Gds (ka 1945); 2 s (Xan, *qv*, Philip b 1951); *Career* cmmnd Royal Horse Gds (The Blues) 1936; served WWII with 1 Household Cav Regt in M East (despatches) 1940-42, SOE 1943-45, in Balkans 1943-44, Far East 1945; Staff Coll 1946, asst mil attaché Warsaw 1947, cmd RHG 1952-54, mil attaché Stockholm 1955-58 (Kt Cdr of Order of Sword of Sweden 1957), Cdr Armed Forces of Sultan of Oman 1958-61, mil advsr to Imam of Yemen 1963-68; memb HM Bodyguard of Hon Corps of Gentlemen-at-Arms 1966-68; Order of Skanderbeg (Albania); *Books* Arabian Assignment (1975), Albanian Assignment (1984); *Recreations* shooting, cooking, gardening; *Clubs* White's, Special Forces, MCC; *Style*— Col David Smiley, LVO, OBE, MC; Well Farm, Lower Ansford, Castle Cary, Somerset BA7 7JZ (☎ 0963 50619)

SMILEY, Hon Mrs (Jane); *née* Lyon-Dalberg-Acton; 6 and yst da of 3 Baron Acton, CMG, MBE, TD (d 1989); *b* 25 Jan 1954; *m* 1, 1975 (m dis 1982), Charles Thomas Pugh (d 1989); 2 da (Charlotte b 1978, Rebecca b 1979); m 2, 1983, Xan Smiley, *qv*; 2 s (Ben b 1985, Adam b 1988); *Style*— The Hon Mrs Smiley; 4820 de Russey Parkway, Chevy Chase, MD 20815, USA (☎ 010 1 301 986 4815)

SMILEY, Lt-Col Sir John Philip; 4 Bt (UK 1903), of Drumalis, Larne, Co Antrim, and Gallowhill, Paisley, Co Renfrew; o s of Sir Hugh Houston Smiley, 3 Bt, JP, DL (d 1990), and Nancy Elizabeth Louise Hardy, *née* Beaton; *b* 24 Feb 1934; *Educ* Eton, RMA Sandhurst; *m* 2 Nov 1963, Davina Elizabeth, da of Denis Charles Griffiths (d 1949), of Orlingbury Hall, nr Kettering, Northants; 2 s (Christopher b 1968, William b 1972), 1 da (Melinda b 1965); *Heir* s, Christopher Hugh Charles Smiley b 1968; *Career* cmmnd Grenadier Guards 1954, served in BAOR Cyprus and Hong Kong, ADC to Govr of Bermuda 1961-62, Regtl Adj 1970-73, ret 1986; govr Oundle Sch 1987-; memb Ct of Assts Worshipful Co of Grocers 1987-; *Clubs* Army and Navy; *Style*— Lt-Col Sir John Smiley, Bt; Cornerway House, Chobham, nr Woking, Surrey GU24 8SW (☎ 0276 858992)

SMILEY, Xan de Crespigny; s of Col David Smiley, LVO, OBE, MC, *qv* (3 s of Sir John Smiley, 2 Bt), and Moyra, widow of Maj Hugo Tweedie, and da of Lt-Col Lord Francis Montagu Douglas Scott, KCMG, DSO (6 s of 6 Duke of Buccleuch); *b* 1 May 1949; *Educ* Eton, New Coll Oxford (MA); *m* 1983, Hon Jane, *qv*; 2 s (Ben Richard Philip de Crespigny b 1985, Adam David Emerich b 1988), 2 step da (Charlotte, Rebecca); *Career* journalist and broadcaster; commentator BBC Radio External Serv current affrs 1974-75, corr Spectator and Observer in Africa 1975-77, dir African Confidential Newsletter 1981- (ed 1977-81); Noel Buxton lectr in African politics 1980; ldr writer The Times 1982-83; The Economist 1983-86: foreign affrs, staff writer, Middle East ed; Moscow corr Daily Telegraph 1986-89, Washington corr The Sunday Telegraph 1990-, publisher The Soviet Analyst 1991-; *Recreations* food, sport (memb Br ski team 1969), travel, genealogy; *Clubs* White's, Beefsteak, Polish Hearth; *Style*— Xan Smiley, Esq; 4820 de Russey Parkway, Chevy Chase, MD 20815, USA (☎ 301 986 4815)

SMILLIE, James; s of Maj Robert Smillie (d 1977), of Stanmore, Middx, and Jean Young, *née* Burnside (d 1970); *b* 7 June 1929; *Educ* Merchant Taylors; *m* 1, 19 June 1949 (m dis 1978), Brenda, da of Herbert Lionel Kelsey, of Harrow, Middx; 4 da (Anne Patricia (Mrs Palmer) b 22 Jan 1958, Sheena Jane (Mrs Owen) b 26 July 1959, Elizabeth Dawn b 10 Dec 1963, Susan Carole b 14 Dec 1965); m 2, 7 March 1981, Chloë Ann, *née* Rich; *Career* Nat Serv 2 Lt/Actg Capt RASC 1953-55; CA; Ramsay Brown & Co 1947-53, Rootes Gp Coventry 1955-56; Stratstone Ltd (subsid Thomas Tilling Ltd) 1956-: co sec, dir, md (mgmnt buy-out 1982), chm and md 1982-90, exec chm 1991-; chm Stratsons Leasing Ltd 1982-, sr ptnr Rover Tport Co 1968-84, non exec dir Great Southern Gp plc 1987-(chm 1989), chm Jaguar Dealer Cncl 1982-89; pres Motor Agents Assoc 1988-89 (dep pres 1987-88), vice-pres Motor Trade Benevolent Soc 1988-89; memb: Stanmore (later Beaconsfield) Cons Assoc 1961-84, Chesham and Amersham Cons Assoc 1984-; life govr Imp Cancer Res Fund 1987-; Liveryman Worshipful Co of Coachmakers and Coach Harness Makers 1975 (memb Ct 1983); CA (Scot) 1953, FIMI 1978, FInstD; *Recreations* golf, theatre, Glyndebourne; *Clubs* Carlton, RAC, Denham Golf; *Style*— James Smillie, Esq; Whyteposts, 66 High St, Old Amersham, Bucks (☎ 0494 727181); Stratstone Ltd, 40 Berkeley St, London W1 (☎ 071 629 4404, telex 071 499 0881)

SMILLIE, (William) John Jones; s of John Smillie (d 1978), and Emily Mary Caroline, *née* Jones (d 1981); *b* 18 Feb 1940; *Educ* Lauriston Sch Falkirk, Territorial Sch Stirling, Stirling HS; *Career* House of Commons Catering Dept: personnel mangr 1967, asst to catering mangr 1970, gen mangr 1971, head of dept 1980-; fndr memb Wine Guild of UK 1984; memb: Br Inst of Cleaning Science 1976, Health Soc 1979, Restaurateurs Assoc of GB 1983, Br Epilepsy Assoc 1981, League Against Cruel

Sports 1983; FHCIMA 1979, ACF 1972, FCFA 1967; contrib articles to catering trade papers; *Recreations* theatre, ballet, music, piano, motoring, boating, disc jockey, travel, gourmandising, rock music, intervals at the opera; *Style—* John Smillie, Esq; House of Commons, London SW1

SMITH; *see*: Abel Smith, Alec-Smith, Austen-Smith, Babington Smith, Bracewell Smith, Buchanan-Smith, Harrison-Smith, Humphrey-Smith, Johnson Smith, Law-Smith, Montagu-Smith, Newson-Smith, Seth-Smith, Sharwood-Smith, Walker-Smith, Wyldbore-Smith

SMITH, Adrian Ewart; s of Frank Ewart Smith (d 1977), of Semley, Wilts, and Winnie Wilson (d 1967); *b* 10 Aug 1935; *Educ* Bournemouth Sch, LSE, Univ of Cambridge; *m* 29 July 1972, Hilary Kathryn, da of Kenneth Pearson (d 1985), of Doncaster, Yorks; 1 s (Kieron Alexander b 1977), 1 da (Claire Querida b 1975); *Career* RAF 1953-55; Shell Petroleum Co 1963-67, Miny of Tport 1967-68, Bd of Trade 1968-70, Dept of Employment 1970-73, Euro Cmmn Brussels 1978-81, FCO 1973- (PM's office 1982-83 and 1989); *Style—* Adrian Smith, Esq; Foreign & Commonwealth Office, London SW1, (☎ 071 270 2557)

SMITH, Agnes, Lady; Agnes; o da of Bernard Page, of Wellington, NZ; *m* 20 July 1935, Sir Thomas Turner Smith, 3 Bt (d 1961); 2 s, 2 da; *Style—* Agnes, Lady Smith; 118 Liverpool Street, Wanganui, New Zealand

SMITH, Sir Alan; CBE (1976), DFC (1941, and bar 1942), DL (Kinross 1967); s of Capt Alfred Smith, MN (d 1931), of Sunderland, and Lilian, *née* Robinson (d 1956); *b* 14 March 1917; *Educ* Bede Coll Sunderland; *m* 1, 10 July 1943, Margaret Stewart (d 1971), da of Herbert Charles Todd (d 1954), of St Ronans, Kinross; 3 s (Michael Charles b 1948, Bruce Alan b 1948, Stuart Duncan b 1956), 2 da (Susan Janet Anstead b 1945, Ailsa Hilda b 1959); m 2, 1977, Alice Elizabeth, da of Robert Stewart Moncur (d 1961); *Career* served WWII pilot RAF 1939-45; chief exec Todd & Duncan Ltd 1946-60, chm and chief exec Dawson International 1960-82 (life pres 1982-); chm: Quayle Munro Ltd 1983-90, Gleneagles Hotels 1982-84, Scottish Cashmere Association 1964-; dir Global Recovery Investment Trust 1981-86; memb Bd: Scottish Devpt Agency 1981-86, Scottish Tourist Bd 1982-85; cncllr Kinross Borough Cncl 1952-65, provost of Kinross 1959-65, cncllr Tayside Reg 1979-90; CTI; kt 1982; *Recreations* sailing, swimming; *Clubs* Lansdowne; *Style—* Sir Alan Smith, CBE, DFC, DL; Ardgairney House, Cleish, by Kinross (☎ 0577 5265); Dawson International plc, Lochleven Mills, Kinross, Scotland (☎ 0577 63521, telex 76168)

SMITH, Alan Christopher; s of Herbert Sidney Smith (d 1986), of Birmingham, and Elsie Blanche, *née* Ward (d 1989); *b* 25 Oct 1936; *Educ* King Edward's Sch Birmingham, Bransenose Coll Oxford (BA); *m* 12 Oct 1963, Anne Elizabeth, da of John Gill Boddy, of Braunston, nr Rugby; 1 s (Mark b 1965), 1 da (Lara b 1969); *Career* Nat Serv 2 Lt RCS 1956; capt Oxford Univ CC 1959-60, Warwicks CCC 1958-78 (capt 1968-74), 6 tests for England, England selector 1969-73 and 1982-86; England mangr: W Indies test 1981, NZ and Pakistan 1984; gen sec Warwicks CCC 1976-86, chief exec TCCB 1987-; dir: Aston Villa FC 1972-78, Royds Advtg and Mktg 1970-86; *Recreations* cricket, both football codes, golf, motoring, bridge; *Clubs* MCC, I Zingari, Vincents; *Style—* Alan Smith, Esq; The Bridge House, Oversley Green, Alcester, Warwicks B49 6LE (☎ 0789 762847); TCCB, Lord's Cricket Ground, London NW8 (☎ 071 286 4405, fax 071 289 5619, car 0831 515961, telex 24462 TCCB G)

SMITH, Alan Martin; s of Robert George Smith, of Birmingham, and Elsie, *née* Bailey; *b* 21 Nov 1962; *Educ* King's Norton GS, Conventry Poly; *m* 2 July 1988, Penny, da of Allan Schofield; 1 da (Jessica Ann b 22 Feb 1990); *Career* professional footballer; 191 league appearances Leicester City 1982-87 (73 goals); Arsenal: joined for a fee of £800,000 March 1987-, over 150 appearances, over 60 goals; England: 2 B caps, 4 full caps 1989 (v Saudi Arabia, Greece, Albania, Poland), only player to represent England at both semi professional and professional level; League Championship medal 1989, winner Golden Boot 1988-89; *Recreations* my family, music; *Style—* Alan Smith, Esq; c/o Jonathan Holmes, Benson McGarvey Murdoch, 6 George St, Nottingham NG1 3BE (☎ 0602 483206)

SMITH, Alec Quinton; JP (Herts); s of Thomas Quinton Smith (d 1953), of London Colney, Herts, and Irene Ethel, *née* Eames (d 1958); *b* 15 Dec 1927; *Educ* St Albans GS for Boys, Sch of Architecture and Surveying Northern London Poly, Brunel Univ (MA); *m* 19 July 1952, Monica Joan, da of Thomas William Hill (d 1965), of London Colney, Herts; 1 s (Graham b 1956), 1 da (Andrea b 1954); *Career* 5002 Sqdn RAF 1946-48; conslt V B Johnson and Partners (Chartered Surveyors); chm: Beds and Herts Chartered Surveyors 1973, Masterbill Micro Systems Ltd 1981-; dir Fencing Contractors Assoc 1983-; tstee Lucy Kemp-Welch Meml Tst; dep chm Watford Bench of Magistrates; Freeman City of London 1981, Liveryman Worshipful Co of Arbitrators 1981; FRICS 1960, FCIArb 1972 (panel memb 1972-), MScL 1987; *Recreations* photography, light gardening, after dinner speaking; *Style—* Alec Smith, Esq, JP; The Corners, 23 Finch Lane, Bushey, Herts (☎ 081 950 3811); St John's House, 23 St John's Rd, Watford, Herts WD1 1PY (☎ 0923 227236, fax 0923 31134)

SMITH, Sir Alexander (Alex) Mair; s of John Smith; *b* 15 Oct 1922; *Educ* Univ of Aberdeen (PhD); *m* 1, 1956, Doris, *née* Patrick (d 1980); 3 da; m 2, 1984, Jennifer, *née* Pearce; *Career* co dir, physicist with UKAEA 1952-56, dir and chief scientist Rolls Royce & Assocs Ltd 1967-69 (head of advanced res 1956-67), dir Manchester Poly 1969-81; chm: Ctee of Dirs of Polys 1974-76, Schs Cncls 1975-78; memb: Univ Grants Ctee 1974-76, BBC Gen Advsy Cncl 1978-81, RSA Cncl 1979-84; vice pres City & Guilds of London Inst 1981-; FInstP; kt 1975; *Recreations* golf; *Clubs* Athenaeum; *Style—* Sir Alex Smith; 33 Parkway, Wilmslow, Cheshire SK9 1LS (☎ 0625 522011)

SMITH, Dr (Edward) Alistair; CBE (1982); s of Archibald Smith (d 1977), of 14 Maryfield Crescent, Inverurie, Aberdeenshire, and Jean Milne, *née* Johnston; *b* 16 Jan 1939; *Educ* Aberdeen GS, Univ of Aberdeen (MA, PhD); *Career* lectr in geography 1963-1988; dir: Univ of Aberdeen Devpt Tst 1982-90, overseas office Univ of Aberdeen 1988-; memb: Grampian Health Bd 1983-, NE Cncl on Disability, Exec Ctee Grampian Ash; pres Scottish Cons and Unionist Assoc 1979-81, dep chm Scottish Cons Pty 1981-85, Scot Vocational Educn Cncl Bd 1989-, memb Ctee for Scotland Nature Conservancy Cncl 1989-; *Books* Europe: A Geographical Survey of the Continent (with REM Mellor, 1979); *Recreations* photography, travel, music; *Style—* Dr Alistair Smith, CBE; 68A Beaconsfield Place, Aberdeen AB2 4AJ (☎ 0224 642932); University of Aberdeen, Regent Walk, Aberdeen, AB9 1FX (☎ 0224 273503, fax 0224 488611, telex 73458 UNIABN G)

SMITH, Dr Alistair Fairley; s of Dr Arthur Fairley Smith (d 1972), and Jane Meikle Marshall Bird (d 1980); *b* 5 Oct 1935; *Educ* Bootham Sch York, Univ of Cambridge (MA, MD); *m* 13 Sept 1961, Carol Ann, da of Edmond Stephen Smith; 1 s (Charles b 1967), 1 da (Helena b 1964); *Career* house offr London Hosp 1960-61, jr asst pathologist Addenbrookes Hosp Cambridge 1962-65, lectr (later sr lectr) clinical chemistry Univ of Edinburgh 1965-, hon conslt Lothian Health Bd; FRCPE 1964, FRCPath 1967; *Books* Lecture Notes on Clinical Chemistry (jtly 4 edn, 1988), Multiple Choice Questions on Lecture Notes on Clinical Chemistry (1981); *Recreations* golf, bridge; *Clubs* Royal Burgess Golf, Bruntsfield Links Golf; *Style—* Dr Alistair Smith; 38 Cammo Rd, Edinburgh EH4 8AP (☎ 031 339 4931); Dept of Clinical Chemistry, The Royal Infirmary, Edinburgh EH3 9YW (☎ 031 229 2477)

SMITH, Allan Keppie; CBE; s of Allan Smith d(d 1977), of Kincardineshire, and Margaret Isobel, *née* Keppie; *b* 18 May 1932; *Educ* Univ of Aberdeen (BSc); *m* 2 Sept 1965; 1 s (Stephen Allan b 4 March 1971), 3 da (Valerie May b 18 May 1976, Fiona Margaret Keppie b 5 Dec 1981, Leanne Isabel b 20 May 1983); *Career* Nat Serv 1953-55, cmmnd REME 1954; Babcock and Wilcox: graduate trainee 1955-57, welding engr Metallurgical and Welding Dept 1957-62, facilities engr Indust Engrg Dept 1962-65 (indust engrg mangr 1965-74), production dir Renfrew Works 1974-76; md: Renfrew and Dumbarton Works 1976-86, Babcock Thorn Ltd 1986-, Rosyth Royal Dockyard plc 1986-; dir Babcock Int Gp PLC 1989-; former pres Scot Engrg Employers Assoc, past chm Cncl Welding Inst, memb Scot Indust Devpt Advsy Bd, fell Paisley Coll of Technol (chm Integrated Graduate Devpt Scheme Mgmnt Ctee); FEng, FIMechE, FWeldI; *Recreations* DIY, shootings, gardening; *Style—* Allan Smith, Esq, CBE; Rosyth Royal Dockyard, Rosyth, Fife KY11 2YD (☎ 0383 422001, fax 0383 417774, car 0836 730170)

SMITH, Allen Donald Warren; OBE (1984); s of Donald Charles Wesley Smith (d 1983), and Olive Kathleen Smith (d 1979); *b* 20 Oct 1922; *Educ* Ipswich Sch, Univ of London (BSc); *m* 12 Aug 1949, June Mary, da of Kenneth Pearce (d 1946); 3 s (Andrew b 1951, Christopher b 1953, Nicholas b 1958); *Career* RAF Airfield Construction Serv 1944-47, Flt Lt, serv France, Belgium, Holland, Germany and Singapore; various engrg appts 1948-62: E Suffolk CC, Surrey CC, W Riding of Yorks CC, Somerset CC, Sir Alexander Gibbs Partners (Conslt Engrs); dep county surveyor; E Sussex CC 1962-68, Kent CC 1968-71; county surveyor Kent 1972-84, conslt transportation planning and highways; pres County Surveyor's Soc 1978-79, parish cncllr Frittenden Kent, chm Engrg Cncl Regnl Orgn Kent and Sussex; Freeman City of London 1984, Liveryman Worshipful Co of Engrs 1984; FEng, FICE, FIHT, MIWM, FRSA; *Books* A History of the County Surveyors' Society 1885-1985 (1985); *Recreations* music, gardening, reading; *Clubs* RAC; *Style—* Allen Smith, Esq, OBE; Kippens, Frittenden, Cranbrook, Kent TN17 2DD (☎ 058 080 358)

SMITH, Prof (Ernest) Alwyn; CBE (1986); s of Ernest Smith (d 1976), and Constance Barbara, *née* Webster; *b* 9 Nov 1925; *Educ* Queen Mary's Sch Walsall, Univ of Birmingham (MB, ChB, PhD); *m* 6 May 1950, Doreen Florence, da of John Preston (d 1974); 1 s (Jeremy b 1954), 1 da (Wendy b 1960); *Career* RM Lt 1943-46; prof Univ of Manchester 1967-90, pres Faculty of Community Med RCP UK; Medaille D'Argent Nationale De Medecine France; *Books* The Science of Social Medicine (1968), Genetics In Medicine (1966), Recent Advances In Community Medicine (1982 and 85); *Recreations* sailing, birdwatching, walking; *Style—* Prof Alwyn Smith, CBE; Plum Tree Cottage, Arnside, Cumbria LA5 0AH (☎ 061 434 1395)

SMITH, Andrew David; MP (Lab) Oxford East 1987-; s of late David E C Smith, and Georgina H J Smith; *b* 1 Feb 1951; *Educ* Reading Sch, St John's Coll Oxford (MA, BPhil); *m* 26 March 1976, Valerie, da of William Labert; 1 s; *Career* Oxford City cncllr 1976-; chm: Recreation and Amenities Ctee 1980-83, Planning Ctee 1985-87, Race and Community Relations Ctee 1985-87; relations offr Oxford and Swindon Co-op Soc 1979-87; memb: Parly Panel Union of Shop Distributive and Allied Workers 1986, Social Servs Select Ctee 1988-89, Labour front bench educn spokesman (higher educn) 1988-; jt sec All Pty Gp for Overseas Devpt 1987- chm Govrs of Oxford Poly 1987-; *Clubs* Headington Labour, Blackbird Leys Community Assoc; *Style—* Andrew Smith, Esq, MP; 4 Flaxfield Rd, Blackbird Leys, Oxford OX4 5QD; Constituency (☎ 0865 772893); c/o House of Commons, London SW1 (☎ 071 219 5102)

SMITH, Andrew James; s of Clifford John Smith, of Leatherhead, Surrey, and Ella Smith; *b* 9 Oct 1958; *Educ* Malvern, Magdalene Coll Cambridge (MA); *Career* Peat Marwick McLintock 1980-88, fin controller Foreign & Colonial Ventures Ltd 1989-; ACA 1986; *Recreations* sailing, horseriding; *Clubs* RAC; *Style—* Andrew J Smith, Esq; 16 Claremont Rd, Highgate, London N6 (☎ 081 340 0063); 6 Laurence Pountney Hill, London EC4R 0BL (☎ 071 782 9829, fax 071 782 9834 telex 886197 Forcol G)

SMITH, Andrew Thomas; s and h of Sir Gilbert Smith, 4 Bt; *b* 17 Oct 1965; *Style—* Andrew Smith Esq

SMITH, Dame (Katharine) Annis Calder; DBE; *see*: Gillie, Dame A C

SMITH, Anthony David; CBE (1987); s of Henry Smith (d 1951), and Esther, *née* Berdiowsky (d 1967); *b* 14 March 1938; *Educ* Harrow Co Sch, Brasenose Coll Oxford (BA); *Career* current affrs prodr BBC TV 1960-71, fell St Antony's Coll Oxford 1971-76, dir BFI 1979-88, memb Bd Channel Four TV Co 1980-84, pres Magdalen Coll Oxford 1988-; memb: Acton Soc Trust 1978-, Writers and Scholars Educn Tst 1982-; *Books* The Shadow in the Cave: the broadcaster, the audience and the state (1973), British Broadcasting (1974), The British Press Since the War (1976) Subsidies and the Press in Europe (1977), The Politics of Information (1978), Television and Political Life (1979), The Newspaper: an international history (1979), Newspapers and Democracy (1980), Goodbye Gutenberg - the Newspaper revolution of the 1980's (1980), The Geopolitics of Information (1980); *Style—* Anthony Smith, Esq, CBE; 1 Albany, Piccadilly, London W1V 9RP (☎ 071 734 5494); Magdalen College, Oxford (☎ 0865 276101)

SMITH, Anthony Howard Leslie; s of Wing Cdr Arthur Leslie Smith (d 1983), of Thames Ditton, Surrey, and Marjorie Jean, *née* Dodridge; *b* 26 Nov 1943; *Educ* Allhallows Sch; *m* 1 (m dis), Rosemary Smith; m 2, 18 April 1981, Heather, da of John Beattie, of Harrow, Middx; 1 da (Lucy Jeannine Antonia); *Career* admitted slr 1967, memb Law Soc Child Care Panel; former chm and pres Brackhell Round Table; memb Law Soc; *Recreations* sailing and skiing; *Style—* Anthony Smith, Esq; 3 The Brambles, Crowthorne, Berks (☎ 0344 776352); Coppid Hall, Warfield Rd, Bracknell, Berks (☎ 0344 420555, fax 0344 860486)

SMITH, Anthony John Francis; s of Hubert J F Smith (d 1984), of Dorset, and Diana, *née* Watkin (d 1990); *b* 30 March 1926; *Educ* The Dragon Sch Oxford, Blundell's Sch Devon, Balliol Coll Oxford (MA); *m* 1, 1 Sept 1956 (m dis 1983), Barbara Dorothy, da of Maj-Gen Charles Richard Newman CB, CMG, DSO (d 1954), of Ottery St Mary, Devon; 1 s (Adam b 1963), 2 da (Polly b 1968, Laura b 1969); m 2, 1984, Margaret Ann (formerly Mrs Holloway), da of George Hounsom (d 1987); 1 s (Quintin b 1986); *Career* RAF 1944-48; reporter Manchester Guardian 1953-57, sci corr Daily Telegraph 1957-63; freelance: broadcaster, author, journalist 1964-; FRGS 1966, FZS 1969; *Books* Blind White Fish in Persia (1953), High Street Africa (1961), Throw Out Two Hands (1963), The Body (1968), The Dangerous Sort (1970), Mato Grosso (1971), The Human Pedigree (1975), Wilderness (1978), A Persian Quarter Century (1979), The Mind (1984), Smith & Son (1984), The Great Rift (1988), Explorers of the Amazon (1990); *Recreations* ballooning; *Clubs* Explorers (NY); *Style—* Anthony Smith, Esq; 10 Aldbourne Rd, London W12 (☎ 081 743 6935); St Aidan's, Bamburgh, Northumberland

SMITH, Antony Gervase; s of Gervase Gorst Smith, JP (d 1963), and Gladys Alford (d 1968); *b* 31 July 1927; *Educ* Haileybury; *m* 4 Nov 1955, Penelope Faux, da of Pearson Faux, of Durban Natal (d 1964); 1 s (Julian Gervase b 21 Feb 1958); 2 da (Miranda b 9 Mar 1962, Philippa b 30 Apr 1963); *Career* served KRRC 1945-48, Capt Queen Victoria's Rifles 1948-52; dir Long Till & Colvin 1960-68, md Astley & Pearce (Sterling) 1980, chm MH Cockell Ltd 1987; Liveryman Worshipful Co of Turners 1969; Belt of Honour at Rifles OCTU; *Recreations* shooting, walking a labrador; *Clubs* Army & Navy, Royal Green Jackets; *Style—* Antony Smith, Esq; Cozen's House, Ocheston, Salisbury, Wilts SP3 4RW (☎ 0980 620 257)

SMITH, Barrie Edwin; JP (Sheffield, 1979); *m* June; 2 da (Dawn, Helen); *Career* Nat Serv 1959-61; accountant; articled clerk JE Forsdike & Co 1953-58; Franklin Greening: audit mangr 1961, ptnr 1964, co merged with Pannell Kerr Forster 1971, taxation ptnr 1971, managing ptnr 1988-; directorships: Congregational & General Insurance plc, Congregational & General Charitable Trust, South Yorkshire Supertram Limited, Northern General Hosp Tst, Sheffield Chamber of Commerce & Manufacturers, Sheffield Chamber Training Limited, Sheffield Leisure and Recreation Limited, Sheffield Media & Exhibition Centre Limited, Sheffield Regeneration Limited, Knowle House (Services) Limited, Club 81 Ltd; Freeman of the City of London, memb Worshipful Co of CAs, pres Sheffield Chamber of Commerce (memb of Cncl, chm Econ and Industl Affairs Ctee), elder and treas Central United Reformed Church; past pres: Sheffield and District Soc of CA, Rotary Club of Abbeydale, life patron S Yorks Opera; memb IOD, FBIM; *Recreations* gardening, maintaining a Victorian house, keeping fit by running (completed the Sheffield Marathon 1990), badminton, walking, keen interest in soccer; *Style*— Barrie E Smith, Esq, JP; Pannell Kerr Forster, Knowle House, 4 Norfolk Park Road, Sheffield S23 QUE (☎ 0742 767991)

SMITH, Barry Andrew; s of Brian Walter Hellyar Smith, of 11 Evesham Rd, Lytham St Annes, Lancs, and Josephine Patricia, *née* Wrigley; *b* 4 Feb 1951; *Educ* Hutton Gs Hutton Lancs, Univ of Keele Staffs (BA), Univ of Madison Wisconsin USA (MA); *Career* teacher Heathmount Prep Sch 1971, writer prodr and presenter BBC Radio Stoke 1972-74, teacher of geography and art St Dunstans Prep Sch 1974-75, writer prodr and presenter WHA-TV Wisconsin USA 1975-76, teacher of sci and history Cundall Manor Prep Sch 1976-80, freelance composer Electron Studios 1978-80 (composed score for the BFI award-winning Pride of India 1979), teacher of English, computing and electronics Breckenbrough Sch 1980-87, founded Crakehill Press educnl publishers 1980-; awarded Rotary Int Acad scholarship to study USA 1975, Public Broadcasting Serv Nat TV Drama award In Quest of an Elephant 1976; *Books* incl: Hieros; a collection of academic essays (ed with V Trigg, 1974), Life and Living (1977-82), English through Practice (1981-84), The World and Man (1984-89), Fieldwork-Firsthand (1988), History by Question (series 1990), short stories for ME Magazine (1991); *Recreations* writing, computer generated sound and graphics (Mac), transcendental meditation, running, squash; *Style*— Barry Smith, Esq; 32 Kings Meadows, Sowerby, Thirsk, N Yorks YO7 1PA (☎ 0845 52660, fax 0485 526601)

SMITH, (Donald) Barry; *b* 22 May 1948; *m* 1 Nov 1975, Sophie Janina, *née* Pasko (Rachel b 1978, Claire b 1980, Alice b 1986); *Career* divnl fin accountant Showerings Vine Products & Whiteways Ltd 1971-78, accountant CH Beazer Holdings plc 1973-78, sr ptnr Rossiter Smith & Co Chartered Accountants 1978-; Dolphin Packaging plc: fin dir 1987-89, chm 1989-90, dep chm 1990-; FCA 1971, AT11 1972; *Style*— Barry Smith, Esq; Rossiter Smith & Co, 8-10 Whiteladies Rd, Clifton, Bristol BS8 1PD (☎ 0272 730863, fax 0272 237929)

SMITH, Barry Howard; *b* 8 Sept 1949; *Educ* QMC London (LLB); *Career* admitted slr 1974; media and entertainment ptnr Richards Butler 1980-; advsr to bd of Br American Arts Assoc; *Recreations* art, cinema, theatre; *Clubs* Reform; *Style*— Barry Smith, Esq; Richards Butler, Beaufort House, 15 St Botolph St, London EC3A 7EE (☎ 071 247 6555, telex 949494 RBLAW G, fax 071 247 5091)

SMITH, Bartholomew Evan Eric; s of Sir John Lindsay Eric Smith, CBE, and Christian Margaret, Lady Smith; *b* 1 Feb 1955; *Educ* Eton, New Coll Oxford; *m* 4 Dec 1987, Catherine Blanche Nicola, da of Gavin Rowan-Hamilton, of Stenton, East Lothian; 1 s (Matthew b 27 March 1988), 1 da (Emily b 17 Nov 1989); *Career* chm Cumulus Systems Ltd 1990- (dir 1985-), dir The Lundy Co Ltd 1985-; farmer Lour Angus Scotland; Freeman City of London 1989, Liveryman Worshipful Co of Fishmongers 1989; *Recreations* flying; *Style*— Bartholomew Smith, Esq; Garden House, Cornwall Gardens, London SW7 4BQ; 21 Dean's Yard, London SW1P 3PA (☎ 071 222 6581)

SMITH, Brian; OBE (1975); s of Charles Francis Smith (d 1966), and Grace Amelia, *née* Pope (d 1972); *b* 15 Sept 1935; *Educ* Hull GS; *m* 1955, Joan Patricia, da of Ernest John Rivers, of Bournemouth; 1 s, 2 da; *Career* Royal Army Pay Corps 1954-57; HM Dip Serv 1952-54 and 1957-: FO 1952, Bahrain 1957, Qatar 1959, vice consul Luxembourg 1960, Morocco 1962, Iran 1964, Switzerland 1967-69, FCO 1969, Uganda 1973, Iran 1975-77, FCO 1977, NY USA 1979, commercial cnsllr Bonn FDR 1982-86, overseas inspector FCO 1986, Br high cmmr Botswana 1989-; *Recreations* horse riding, reading, embroidery; *Style*— Brian Smith, Esq, OBE; British High Commission, Private Bag 0023, Gaborone, Botswana (☎ 352 841)

SMITH, Brian Anthony; s of (Gordon Ernest) Barry Smith, and Patricia Helen, *née* Loveday; *b* 9 Sept 1966; *Educ* Brisbane State HS, Brisbane Coll of Advanced Educn (dip teaching), Univ of Qld (BEd), Univ of Oxford (MA, Rugby blue); *Career* rugby football player; Qld XV and Aust under 21 teams 1985, Wallaby tour of NZ 1986; competed: World Cup 1987, Bicentennial Test 1988, (Aust test record 26 points), Five Nations Cup 1990 and 1991; int caps: 7 Aust, 6 Irish; 3 Hong Kong Sevens (winner Aust 1988), Aust club Wests (Aust champions 1985), current club Leicester; scored over 600 points in 1988 (including Eng and Aust seasons) first Aust and Irish dual International; *Recreations* films, sports, politics; *Style*— Brian Smith, Esq; Leicester RFC, Aylestone Rd, Leicester (☎ 0533 541607)

SMITH, Ven Brian Arthur; s of Arthur Smith, of 224 Telford Rd, Edinburgh, and Doris Marion, *née* Henderson; *b* 15 Aug 1943; *Educ* George Heriot's Sch Edinburgh, Univ of Edinburgh (MA), Univ of Cambridge (MA, MLitt); *m* 1 Aug 1970, Elizabeth Berring, da of Lt-Col Charles Francis Hutchinson (d 1980), of Moor Farm, Longframlington, Northumberland; 2 da (Tessa b 1974, Alice b 1978); *Career* ordained: deacon 1972, priest 1973; curate of Cuddesdon 1972-79, tutor in doctrine Cuddesdon Coll Oxford 1972-75; dir: of studies Ripon Coll Oxford 1975-78 (sr tutor 1978-79), of ministerial trg Diocese of Wakefield 1979-87; priest i/c Cragg Vale 1978-86, warden of readers Diocese of Wakefield 1981-87, hon canon of Wakefield Cathedral 1981-87, archdeacon of Craven 1987-; vice chm Northern Ordination Course 1986-; *Recreations* reading, music, walking, browsing in junk shops, short-wave radio listening; *Clubs* National Liberal; *Style*— The Ven the Archdeacon of Craven; Brooklands, Bridge End, Long Preston, Skipton, N Yorks BD23 4RA (☎ 07294 334)

SMITH, Prof Brian Clive; s of Cyril Ernest Smith, of Whiteknights, Barton-on-Sea, Hants, and Hilda Jane, *née* Padengtion; *b* 23 Jan 1938; *Educ* Colfe's GS, Univ of Exeter (BA PhD), McMaster Univ Ontario, Canada (MA); *m* 27 Aug 1960, Jean, da of Frank Baselow, of 4 Leyham Court, Norwich; 1s (David William b 22 Aug 1968), 1 da (Rebecca Jane b 23 Aug 1963); *Career* lectr politics Univ of Exeter 1963-70; Univ of Bath: sr lectr politics 1972-80, reader in politics 1980-89; memb: RIPA, Political Studies assoc; currently ed Public Administration and Devpt; *Books* Regionalism in England (1964), Field Administration. An Aspect of Decentralisation (1967), Advising Ministers (1969), Administering Britain (with J Stanyer 1976), Policy Making in British Government (1976), Government Departments. An Organisation Perspective (with DC Pitt 1980), The Computer Revolution in Public Administration (ed with DC Pitt 1984), Decentralisation. The Territorial Dimension of the State (1985), Bureaucracy and Political Power (1987); *Recreations* walking, travel; *Style*— Prof Brian Smith; Dept of Political Science and Social Policy, Universtiy of Dundee, Dundee DD1 4HN (☎ 0382 23181)

SMITH, Dr (Eric) Brian; s of Eric Smith, and Dilys Olwen, *née* Hughes; *b* 10 Oct 1933; *Educ* Mold Alun Sch, Wirral GS, Univ of Liverpool (BSc, PhD); *m* 1, 31 Aug 1957 (m dis 1977), Margaret; 2 s (Mark b 10 Sept 1961, Nicholas b 27 Jan 1965), 1 da (Caroline b 14 Jan 1960); m 2, 9 July 1983, Regina Arvidson Ball; *Career* master St Catherine's Coll Oxford; FRCS; *Books* Basic Chemical Thermodynamics (1973-1980), Intermolecular Forces (jtly, 1981), Forces Between Molecules (jtly, 1986); *Recreations* mountaineering; *Clubs* Alpine, Gorphwysfa; *Style*— Dr Brian Smith; Master's Lodgings, St Catherine's College, Oxford OX1 3UJ

SMITH, (John) Brian; s of Sydney John Smith (d 1979), of Beaconsfield, and Florence May Dean Smith; *b* 5 June 1928; *Educ* Bradford GS, Sidney Sussex Coll Cambridge (MA); *m* 23 July 1953, Joan Margaret, da of Horace Newton Jennings (d 1951), of Bradford; 2 s (Timothy b 1954, Nicholas b 1962), 2 da (Penelope b 1956, Joanna b 1963); *Career* dir: The Rank Orgn 1976-83, Eley & Warren Ltd 1984-89, Manganese Bronze Hldgs plc 1984-, Oxford Gobert Hldgs Ltd 1985-; chm: J B Smith Consits Ltd 1983, City Jeroboam plc 1988, Eagle Trust plc 1989-; business cncllr DTI 1985; memb: Bucks CC 1985-89, Exec Ctee Beaconsfield Constituency Cons Assoc; Freeman: City of London, Worshipful Co of Scientific Instrument Makers; FIOD, CBIM 1981; *Recreations* golf, tennis, bridge; *Style*— Brian Smith, Esq; Hebden House, Eghams Close, Beaconsfield, Bucks HP9 1XN (☎ 0494 673063, fax 0494 676212, car 0836 229819)

SMITH, Dr (Norman) Brian; CBE (1980); s of Vincent Smith (d 1963), and Louise, *née* Horsfield; *b* 10 Sept 1928; *Educ* Sir John Deane's GS Northwich, Univ of Manchester (BSc, MSc, PhD); *m* 2 April 1955, Phyllis, da of Edmund and Sarah Ellen Crossley; 2 s (Clive b 1959 d 1963, David b 1961), 1 da (Jane b 1962); *Career* tech off ICI Terylene Cncl 1954-; ICI Fibres Div: textiles devpt dir 1969, dep chm 1972, chm 1975-78; dir: Fiber Industries Inc 1972-83, ICI plc 1978-85, Canadian Industries Ltd 1981-85; chm: ICI Americas Inc 1981-85, MB Group plc (formerly Metal Box plc) 1986-89 (dep chm 1985); non-exec dir: Lister & Co plc 1985-90, dep chm 1990-; non-exec dir: Davy Corporation plc 1986-, Cable & Wireless plc 1988-, Yorkshire Chemicals plc 1990-; dir Oxford Diocesan Board of Finance 1990-; Berisford International plc 1990-; chm: Man-Made Fibres Producers Ctee 1976-78, Wool Textile EDC 1979-81, BOTB N American Advsy Gp 1983-87, Priorities Bd for Res and Devpt in Agric and Food 1987-; pres Br Textile Confederation 1977-79, memb BOTB 1980-81 and 1983-87; Freeman City of London 1986, Liveryman Worshipful Co of Glovers 1986; Hon DBA, IMC Buckingham 1990; FTI 1981, CBIM 1985, FCIM; *Recreations* sailing, tennis, gardening; *Clubs* Brooks's; *Style*— Dr Brian Smith, CBE

SMITH, Brian Roy; s of Arthur Roy Smith (d 1971), and Phyllis Edith Smith (d 1990); *b* 18 Aug 1937; *Educ* Sir George Monoux GS; *m* 4 July 1959, Barbara Gladys, da of James Richard Beasley (d 1980); 1 s (Stewart Spencer b 26 Jan 1963), 1 da (Justine Caroline b 10 April 1967); *Career* RAF 1956-58; English & American INSOE Co 1959-68, BR Smith and Others (Lloyds Syndicate) 1969-; dir: Garwyn Ltd 1972-, Bankside Syndicates Ltd 1985-, Bankside Members Agency Ltd 1985-, Bankside Underwriting Agencies Ltd 1985-, Cotesworth and Co Ltd 1985-, Reed Stenhouse Syndicates Ltd 1976-85; memb Lloyds 1972- (Non Marine Assoc Ctee 1985-); *Recreations* squash, tennis, theatre, opera, boating; *Clubs* Old Chigwellians; *Style*— Brian Smith, Esq; Bishops Hall, Lambourne End, Essex (☎ 081 500 6510); B R Smith and Others, 120 Middlesex St, London EC1 (☎ 071 247 0304)

SMITH, Brian Stanley; s of Ernest Stanley Smith (ka 1943), of Leeds, and Dorothy Maud Smith; *b* 15 May 1932; *Educ* Bloxham, Keble Coll Oxford (BA, MA); *m* 28 Sept 1963, Alison Margaret, da of Robert George Alexander Hemming, of Cardross, Dumbarton; 2 da (Frances b 1964, Jennifer b 1966); *Career* asst archivist: Worcs 1956-58, Essex 1958-60, Glos 1961-68 (co archivist 1968-79); pt/t ed Victoria Co Hist Glos 1968-70, sec Royal Cmmn Historical MSS 1982- (asst sec 1980-81), memb Ctee of Mgmnt Inst Hist Res Univ of London 1982-87, vice pres Bristol and Glos Archaeological Soc 1987- (ed 1971-79, pres 1986-87); lay memb Glos Diocesan Synod 1972-76; FSA 1972, FRHistS 1980, memb Soc of Archivists (chm 1979-80); *Books* History of Malvern (1964, second edn 1987), History of Bristol and Gloucestershire (1972, second edn 1982), The Cotswolds (1976), History of Bloxham School (1978); *Recreations* mountaineering, gardening; *Style*— Brian Smith, Esq, FSA; Midwoods, Shire Lane, Cholesbury, Tring, Herts HP23 6NA; Royal Commission on Historical Manuscripts, Quality House, Quality Court, Chancery Lane, London WC2A 1HP (☎ 071 242 1198)

SMITH, Hon Mrs (Bridget Mary); *née* Astor; eldest da of 2 Baron Astor of Hever (d 1984), and Dowager Baroness Astor of Hever, *qv*; *b* 16 Feb 1948; *m* 1, 31 Oct 1980, Count Arthur Tarnowski, s of Count Hieronym Tarnowski (a supposed Polish cr of Sigismund III has been claimed dated 1588; more tenable is that by Ferdinand III in his capacity as King of Hungary 1655 and subsequent recognition as an Austrian title by Emperor Joseph II 1785); 2 s (Sebastian b 1981, Lucian b 1984); m 2, 23 Dec 1989, Geofrey Richard Smith; *Career* photographer; freelance and with Harpers and Queen 1968-; author of children's book; *Books* Darling Dennis; *Style*— The Hon Mrs Smith

SMITH, Carl Bernard; s of Peter Smith, of 29 Mowbray Gardens, West Bridgford, Nottingham, and Ada Elizabeth, *née* Barclay (d 1990); *b* 1 Dec 1961; *Educ* West Bridgford Comp Sch, Basford Hall Coll (City & Guilds exam, ONC, HND), Trent Poly (BSc); *m* 1985, Rosalind Ann, da of Geoffrey Stanforth (d 1971); 1 s (Benjamin Carl b 29 Oct 1987), 1 da (Lydia Ann b 7 Sept 1989); *Career* rower; memb: Nottingham Boat Club, Nottingham County Rowing Assoc; 11 place Mens Quad Sculls Jr world championship (Moscow) 1979; World Championships (Men's Lightweights): 9 place Single Sculls (Munich) 1981, Silver medallist Coxless (IVs (Duisberg) 1983, Bronze medallist Coxless IVs (Montreal) 1984, 8 place Double IVs (Hazelwinkel) 1985 Gold medallist Double IVs (Nottingham) 1986, Bronze medallist Double IVs (Copenhagen) 1987, 8 place Single IVs (Milan) 1988, Bronze medallist VIIIs (Tasmania) 1990; Henley Royal Regatta: 1 place Wyfold Challenge Cup (Coxless IVs) 1982 and 1984, 1 place (record time) Ladies Challenge Plate (VIIIs) 1989, 1 place Times Challenge Cup (VIIIs) 1990; winner Grand Challenge cup (VIIIs) Japanese Henley Royal Henley Regatta (Tokyo) 1990; Cwlth Games Edinburgh 1986: Bronze medallist Men's Heavyweight Double Scull, Bronze medallist Men's Lightweight Single Scull; Nat Championships of GB: Gold medallist Jr Men's Quad Sculls 1979, Bronze medallist Men's Lightweight Double Sculls 1980, Mens Lightweight Single Sculls (Gold medallist 1981, Silver medallist 1982), Gold medallist Men's Lightweight Coxless IVs 1983 and 1984, Gold medallist Men's Heavyweight (and Men's Lightweights) Double Sculls 1985, Gold medallist Men's Heavyweight (and Men's Lightweights) VIIIs (record times) 1990; Head of the River Race for Scullers: Gold medallist Men's Lightweight Single Sculls 1982-86 and 1988-90 winner Heavyweight Div 1985; Head of the River Race for IVs: Gold medallist Men's Heavyweight Quad Sculls 1985-88 and 1990 Heavyweight Div 1985; Gold medallist Men's Heavyweight Quad Sculls Head of the River Race for Fours 1985-88 and 1990; Lucerne Int Regatta: Bronze medallist Men's Lightweight Coxless IVs 1983, Gold medallist Men's Lightweight Double Sculls 1986-1987 (7 place 1985), 5 place Men's Lightweight Single Sculls 1988, Silver medallist (world record in heat) Men's Lightweight VIIIs 1990 (4 place 1989); *Awards* Nottingham Boat Oarman of the Year 1986, Ted Moult Meml award for E Midland Sports Aid 1989; *Style*— Carl Smith, Esq; 33 Jumelles Drive, Calverton, Nottingham

NG13 6QD (☎ 0602 653 160); Nottinghamshire County Rowing Association, National Water Sports Centre, Holme Pierrepont, Nottingham; Mrs M Marshall, 60 Green Lane, Ockbrook, Derby DE7 3SE (☎ 0332 673619)

SMITH, Sheriff Charles; s of Charles Smith (d 1973), of Perth, and Mary Allan, *née* Hunter (d 1988); *b* 15 Aug 1930; *Educ* Kinnoull Sch, Perth Acad, Univ of St Andrews (MA, LLB); *m* 1959, Janet Elizabeth, da of James Hurst (d 1942); 1 s (Charles), 1 da (Jennifer); *Career* admitted slr 1956; princ Perth 1961-82 (in practice 1956-62); hon tutor Dept of Law Univ of Dundee; memb Perth Town Cncl 1966-68, temp Sheriff 1977-82, memb Cncl Law Soc of Scotland (convenor various ctees) 1977-82; Sheriff of: Glasgow and Strathkelvin 1982-86, Tayside Central and Fife at Perth 1986-; *Recreations* tennis, golf, croquet; *Style—* Sheriff Charles Smith; c/o Sheriff Court, Perth (☎ 0738 205416)

SMITH, Sir Charles Bracewell; *see*: Bracewell-Smith, Charles

SMITH, Charles John Wolstenholme; s of Dr Maurice Wolstenholme Smith, of Leamington Spa, Warks, and Winifred Daisy, *née* Parr; *b* 7 Dec 1940; *Educ* Uppingham; *m* 2 Nov 1968, Jennifer Ann, da of John Robinson Bennett; 2 s (Edward Charles Wolstenholme b 15 Dec 1970, Henry James Wolstenholme b 23 Dec 1973); *Career* articled Burgis & Bullock Leamington Spa 1959-64, joined Foster & Stephens 1964 (became Touche Ross & Co), specialist tax ptnr Touche Ross & Co 1972- (ptnr 1967); represented Warwicks and Midlands at Hockey 1960-68; ACA 1964; *Recreations* horse riding, golf, tennis; *Clubs* Birmingham, Chamber of Commerce, Olton Golf, Edgbaston Priory; *Style—* Charles Smith, Esq; Touche Ross & Co, Newater House, 11 Newhall St, Birmingham B3 3NY (☎ 021 631 2288, fax 021 236 1513)

SMITH, Dr Charles Stuart; s of Ebenezer Smith (d 1956), of Calcutta, and Mary, *née* Reid (d 1987); *b* 21 April 1936; *Educ* George Watsons Coll, Univ of Glasgow (BSc, PhD, DSc); *m* 9 Aug 1962, (Colette Marie) Claude, da of Gustav Paulicand (d 1983), of Grenoble, France; 1 s (Robin b 1965), 3 da (Caroline b 1968, Annabelle-Noelle b 1969, Catherine b 1971); *Career* Admty Res Estab: head Stress Analysis Section 1968, head dir Ship Structures 1974, head Structures Res 1981, dep chief scientific offr (IM) 1989-; memb Wave Power Steering Gp; FEng, FRINA, MISTRUCTEng; *Recreations* sailing, skiing, squash, hillwalking; *Style—* Dr Charles Smith; Admty Res Estab, St Leonards Hill, Dunfermline, Fife KY11 5PW (☎ 0383 721346)

SMITH, Christopher Gordon; s of Maj (Joseph) Gordon Smith, of St Aster, Duras 47120, France, and Sheila Mary, *née* Gleeson (d 1982); *b* 3 Sept 1952; *Educ* The Abbey Sch Fort Augustus; *m* 16 Aug 1980, Jean Helen, da of (James Craufuird) Roger Inglis, of Gifford, E Lothian, Scotland; 1 s (Jeremy b 14 June 1983), 1 da (Camilla b 4 June 1985); *Career* dir: C R McRitchie & Co Ltd (co sec 1977-84), Norloch Ltd (co sec 1977-84); asst dir Noble Grossart Ltd 1987 (dir 1989, treas 1985); *Recreations* squash, skiing, running; *Clubs* Edinburgh Sports; *Style—* Christopher G Smith, Esq; 1 Wester Coates Terrace, Edinburgh EH12 5LR; Noble Grossart Ltd, 48 Queen St, Edinburgh (☎ 031 226 7011, fax 031 226 6032)

SMITH, Rev Christopher Hughes; s of Rev Bernard Hughes Smith (d 1963), of Petts Wood, Orpington, Kent, and Dorothy Lucy, *née* Parker (d 1985); *b* 30 Nov 1929; *Educ* Bolton Sch, Emmanuel Coll and Wesley House Cambridge (BA, MA); *m* 28 July 1956, (Margaret) Jean, da of Frank Passmore Smith (d 1960), of Middlesbrough; 3 s (Jeremy b 1959, Philip b 1962, Robert b 1964), 1 foster s (Ernest b 1962); *Career* Nat Serv RAOC 1948-50, Sgt 1950; intercollegiate sec Student Christian Movement 1955-58, Leicester (S) Methodist Circuit 1958-65, Birmingham (SW) Methodist Circuit 1965-74, chm Birmingham Methodist Dist 1974-87, Lancaster Methodist Circuit 1987-88, gen sec Div of Educn and Youth 1988-, pres Methodist Conf 1985-86; jt pres Birmingham Cncl of Christian Churches 1976-87, govr Queen's Coll Birmingham; memb: governing bodies of Westhill Coll Birmingham, Westminster Coll Oxford, Southlands Coll Wimbledon, Roehampton Inst, Methodist Residential Schs (The Leys, Queenswood, Kingswood, Rydal, Ashville); Hon MA Univ of Birmingham 1985; *Recreations* walking, books, gardening; *Style—* The Rev Christopher Hughes Smith; 3 Hazlehyrst, 7 Colney Hatch Lane, Muswell Hill, London N10 1PN (☎ 081 883 1304); 2 Chester House, Pages Lane, Muswell Hill, London N10 1PR (☎ 081 444 9845)

SMITH, Christopher Robert (Chris); MP (Lab) Islington S and Finsbury 1983-; s of Colin Smith, and Gladys, *née* Luscombe; *b* 24 July 1951; *Educ* George Watson's Coll Edinburgh, Pembroke Coll Cambridge (PhD), Harvard (Kennedy scholar); *Career* cnclIr London Borough of Islington 1978-83, chief whip 1978-79, chm of housing 1981-83, Parly candidate (Lab) Epsom and Ewell 1979; ASTMS branch: sec 1978-80, chm 1980-83; memb Cncl for Nat Parks, housing devpt worker, memb of Environment Select Ctee 1983-87; chm: Tribune Group of MPs 1988-89 (sec 1984-88), of Lab Campaign for Criminal justice 1985-88; Labour spokesman on Treasy and Econ Affrs 1987-; chm Bd of Tribune Newspaper 1990-; memb: Bd of Shelter 1987-, Exec Ctee NCCL 1986-88, Bd Sadlers Wells Theatre 1986-, Exec Ctee Fabian Soc 1989-; *Recreations* lit, music, theatre, mountaineering; *Style—* Chris Smith, Esq, MP; House of Commons, London SW1 (☎ 071 219 5119)

SMITH, Sir Christopher Sydney Winwood; 5 Bt (UK 1809) of Eardiston, Worcestershire; s of Sir William Sydney Winwood Smith, 4 Bt (d 1953); *b* 20 Sept 1906; *m* 1932, Phyllis Berenice, da of late Thomas Robert O'Grady; 3 s, 2 da; *Heir* s, Robert Sydney Winwood Smith; *Style—* Sir Christopher Smith, Bt; Junction Rd, via Grafton, NSW, 2460, Australia

SMITH, Colin; s of Henry Edmund Smith (d 1976), and A Estelle, *née* Pearson (d 1979); *b* 4 July 1941; *Educ* Upton House Sch; *Career* sec gen Int Assoc Against Painful Experiments on Animals 1969-, dir American Fund for Alternatives to Animal Res 1977-, gen sec Nat Anti-Vivisection Soc 1971-81, ed Animals' Defender and Anti-Vivisection News 1982-86; *Style—* Colin Smith, Esq; PO Box 215, St Albans, Herts AL3 4RD

SMITH, Prof (Christopher) Colin; s of Alfred Edward Smith (d 1969), of Brighton, and Dorothy May, *née* Berry (d 1984); *b* 17 Sept 1927; *Educ* Varndean Sch for Boys Brighton, Univ of Cambridge (BA, MA, PhD, LittD); *m* 14 Aug 1954, Ruth Margaret, da of Harry James Barnes (d 1987), of Brighton; 1 s (Roderick b 1958 d 1960), 3 da (Jennifer b 1960, Rebecca b 1961, Jocelyn b 1964); *Career* asst lectr Dept of Spanish Univ of Leeds 1953-56 (lectr 1956-64, sr lectr 1964-68, sub dean of arts 1963-67), lectr in Spanish Univ of Cambridge 1968-75 (fell St Catharine's Coll Cambridge 1968-, prof of Spanish 1975-90) visiting prof Univ of Virginia USA 1981; memb Assoc of Hispanists of GB (pres 1977-79); comendador de numero de la Orden de Isabel la Catõlica (Spain) 1988; *Books* Spanish Ballads (1964), Collins English/Spanish, Spanish/English Dictionary (1971, 2 edn 1988), The Poema de mio Cid (1972, 2 edn 1985), Estudios Cidianos (1977), Place-names of Roman Britain (with A L F Rivet, 1979), The Making of the Poema de mio cid (1983), Christians and Moors in Spain (1989, 2 vols); *Recreations* natural history (especially entomology), archaeology, squash; *Style—* Prof Colin Smith; 56 Girton Rd, Cambridge CB3 0LL (☎ 0223 276 214); St Catharine's Coll, Cambridge CB2 1RL (☎ 0223 338 351)

SMITH, Colin Ferguson; s of Henry Ferguson Smith, of Silligrove Farm, Kinlet, Salop, and Barbara Catharine, *née* Tangye; *b* 12 Oct 1932; *Educ* Leighton Park Sch Reading, Gonville and Caius Coll Cambridge (MA, LLB); *Career* prodn controller Tangyes Ltd 1960-62 (chief buyer 1962-64, co sec and accounts mangr 1964-67), asst co sec Central Wagon Co Ltd 1967-69, dir Smith Keen Cutler Ltd 1986- (ptnr and res mangr 1971-86); memb Stock Exchange FCIS 1971; *Clubs* Carlton; *Style—* Colin Smith, Esq; 55 Warwick Crest, Arthur Road, Birmingham B15 2LH; The Clos Mill, St Clears, Dyfed, Wales (☎ 021 454 4698); Smith Keen Cutler Ltd, Exchange Buildings Stephenson Place, Birmingham, B2 4NN (☎ 021 643 9977, fax 021 643 0345, telex 336730)

SMITH, Colin Hilton; s of Reginald Walter Smith (d 1982), and Barbara, *née* Milligan; *b* 21 Feb 1953; *Educ* Falmouth Sch of Arts, RCA London (minor travelling scholarship); *m* 1, 1976 (m dis 1980), Barbara Ann, da of William Henry Spicer; m 2, 1983, Rosemary Victoria, da of Gerald Henry Dean; 1 s (William Lawrence Hilton b 1986); *Career* artist; solo exhibitions: Nicola Jacobs Gallery 1982, 1984, 1987 and 1989, Ruth Siegal NY 1986, Anderson O'Day Gallery London 1991, Kunstlandschaft Europa (Kunstverein Freiburg) 1991; gp exhibitions: Falmouth Sch of Art 1974-75, PCL Gallery London 1977, New 57 Gallery London 1977, The First Exhibition (Nicola Jacobs Gallery London) 1979, Sculpture and works on paper (Nicola Jacobs Gallery) 1980, Fourteenth Int Festival of Painting Cagnes-sur-Mer-France 1982, Tolly Cobbold Eastern Arts Fourth Nat Exhibition and tour 1983, The Figurative Exhibition II (Nicola Jacobs Gallery) 1983, New Talent (Hal Bromm NY) 1984, The Image as Catalyst (Ashmolean Museum) 1984, Royal Over-Seas League Annual Exhibition (jt first prize winner) 1987, Winter '88 (Nicola Jacobs Gallery) 1988, Academicians Choice (Mall Galleries London and The Eye Gallery Bristol) 1990, The London Group Exhibition (RCA) 1990; works in the collections of: Galerie de Beerenburght Holland, RCA, Unilever London, Arts Cncl of GB, Prudential Holborn, Pepsi Cola London; Great London Arts Assoc award 1982; Harkness fell and res assoc Faculty of Fine Art Yale Univ 1983-86; *Recreations* reading, films; *Clubs* Chelsea Arts; *Style—* Colin Smith, Esq; 59 Whipps Cross Rd, London E11 1NJ (☎ 081 989 6607); Anderson O'Day Fine Arts, 255 Portobello Rd, London W11 1LR (☎ 071 221 7592, fax 081 960 3641)

SMITH, Colin Milner; QC (1985); s of Alan Milner Smith, OBE, of Russets, Hillydeal Road, Otford, Kent, and Vera Ivy, *née* Cannon (d 1973); *b* 2 Nov 1936; *Educ* Tonbridge, BNC Oxford (MA), Univ of Chicago (JD); *m* 14 Dec 1979, Moira Soraya, da of Charles Reginald Braybrooke, (d 1989) of Crofts, Lower Layham, Suffolk; 1 s (Alexander b 1982), 1 da (Camilla b 1987); *Career* Nat Serv Lt RM (3 Commando Brig) 1955-57; called to the Bar Gray's Inn 1962, rec 1987-; *Recreations* cricket, skiing, reading; *Clubs* MCC; *Style—* Colin Smith, Esq, QC; 3 Gray's Inn Place, Gray's Inn, London WC1R 5EA (☎ 071 831 8441)

SMITH, Colin Roderick; CVO (1984), QPM (1987); s of Humphrey Montague Smith, OBE, of Bexhill, and Marie Louvsin, *née* Prior (d 1988); *b* 26 March 1941; *Educ* Dorking County GS, Bexhill GS, Univ of Birmingham (BSoc Sc); *m* 5 Aug 1961, Patricia Joan, da of Charles Coppin (d 1962); *Career* Lt 18 Co (Amph) RASC 1959-62; constable rising to chief supt East Sussex Constabulary (later Sussex Police) 1962-77, asst chief constable Thames Valley Police 1977-82, dep asst cmmr Metropolitan Police 1982-85 (fndr Royalty and Diplomatic Protection Dept), chief constable Thames Valley Police 1985-91, HM Inspector of Constabulary 1991-; ACPO 1990 (chm: SE Region, Gen Purposes Ctee, Negotiating Ctee), co-dir Extended Interview Board 1988-91; *Books* various professional papers on police related subjects; *Recreations* horse riding; *Clubs* Naval and Military; *Style—* Colin Smith, Esq, CVO, QPM; 10th Floor, Sheaf House, The Pennine Centre, Hawley Street, Sheffield S1 3GA (☎ 0742 701054, fax 0742 720313)

SMITH, Colin Roland Francis; s of Roland Alfred Smith, of 353 Monmouth Drive, Sutton Coldfield, and Anne, *née* Colley (d 1954); *b* 6 Sept 1944; *Educ* John Willmott GS; *m* 19 May 1966, Sylvia Arlene, da of Sidney Albert Skillett, of Guernsey; 1 s (Gavin Nigel b 7 April 1966), 1 da (Helena Anne b 22 Aug 1964); *Career* harbour corr Guernsey Evening Press 1962-63; reporter: Sutton Coldfield News 1963-64, Romford Recorder and Brentwood Review 1964-65, Kent and Sussex Courier 1966-67, Birmingham Post 1967, Daily Sketch 1968; The Observer: joined as home news reporter 1968, chief roving corr 1972-77, ME corr 1977-85, chief roving corr 1985-88, Asia ed based in Bangkok 1988-90, asst ed and def corr 1990; Int Reporter of the Year 1975 and 1985 (runner up 1983); *Books* Carlos: Portrait of a Terrorist (1976), Cut-Out (1980); *Recreations* tennis, walking, military history; *Clubs* Travellors', Pall Mall; *Style—* Colin Smith, Esq; The Observer, Chelsea Bridge House, Queenstown Rd, London SW8 4NN (☎ 071 627 0770/5570)

SMITH, Lady Corisande; *née* Bennet; da of 8 Earl of Tankerville (d 1971), and his 2 w, Violet, *qv*; *b* 1938; *m* 1963, Lt Cdr Timothy Bain Smith, RN; 2 s; *Style—* The Lady Corisande Smith; Wickens Manor, Charing, Kent

SMITH, Sir Cyril; MBE (1966), MP (Lib) Rochdale 1972-; *b* 28 June 1928; *Educ* Rochdale GS for Boys; *Career* cnclIr Rochdale 1952-66, Alderman 1966-74, Mayor of Rochdale 1966-67, memb Rochdale Metropolitan Dist Cncl 1974-75, chief Lib whip 1975-76; kt 1988; *Recreations* listening to music, reading, TV; *Clubs* National Liberal (chm 1987-88); *Style—* Sir Cyril Smith, MBE, MP; 14 Emma St, Rochdale, Lancs (☎ 0706 48840)

SMITH, Dr Cyril Stanley; CBE (1985); s of Walter Charles Smith (d 1932), of London, and Beatrice May Smith (d 1978); *b* 21 July 1925; *Educ* Plaistow Municipal Secdy Sch, LSE (MSc), Univ of London (PhD); *m* 1, 1949 (m dis 1968), Helena Ursula; 2 da (Vanessa (Mrs Hallam) b 1952, d 1989, Emma Josephine b 1956, d 1978); m 2, 8 May 1968, Eileen Cameron, da of Samuel Dentith (d 1976), of Salford; *Career* Dorset Regt 1943-47; dir Dept of Youth Work Univ of Manchester 1961-70, dir of social policy studies Civil Serv Coll 1971-75, sec SSRC 1975-85, md Restrat 1985-; chm Br Sociological Assoc 1972-74, memb Sec of State's Ctee on Inequalities in Health (DHSS) 1977-80; author of various books and articles on adolescence, leisure, social sciences; chm Br Assoc for Servs to the Elderly 1988-; *Books* Adolescence (1968), The Wincroft Youth Project (1972), Society of Leisure in Britain (jt ed, 1973); *Recreations* football; *Clubs* West Ham FC; *Style—* Dr Cyril Smith, CBE; Cornwall House, Cornwall Gardens, London SW7 4AE

SMITH, Dr Cyril William; s of Reginald William Smith (d 1971), of Gt Massingham, Norfolk, and Maud Evelyn Smith (d 1978); *b* 7 Jan 1930; *Educ* Douai Sch, Univ of Exeter (BSc), Univ of London (BSc, PhD); *m* 14 June 1958, Eileen Dorothy, da of Cyril Jackson (d 1955), of Norwich; 3 s (Andrew b 1959, Paul b 1960, Martin b 1962); *Career* asst exp offr TRE Malvern 1947-56, res fell Imperial Coll London 1956-59, physics master Downside Sch 1959-64, sr lectr Univ of Salford 1973-89 (lectr 1964-73), conslt 1989-; scientific advsr to Environmental Med Fndn; CEng, FIEE, CPhys, MInstP, SMIEEE, MBES; *Books* Electromagnetic Man (1989); *Recreations* walking, gardening, travel, cooking; *Style—* Dr Cyril Smith; Medical Instrumentation Division, Salford University Business Services Ltd, PO Box 50, Salford M6 6BY (☎ 061 736 8921/061 745 5000, telex 668680 SULIB, fax 061 737 0880)

SMITH, David; s of Walter Horace Smith (d 1960), and Annie, *née* Matthews (d 1971); *b* 18 July 1927; *Educ* Burton GS, Univ of Sheffield (BSc, PhD); *m* 1951, Nancy Elizabeth, da of Harold Hawley (d 1968); 2 s, 3 da; *Career* vice pres Exxon Chemical Co 1971-78, chm and md Esso Chemical Ltd 1979-86; petroleum and chemical conslt 1987-; memb Cncl Chemical Indust Assoc 1982-86, pres Southampton C of C 1990-91; *Recreations* golf, cricket; *Clubs* MCC, Royal Winchester GC; *Style—* David Smith, Esq; Meadowlands, Stockbridge Rd, Winchester, Hants (☎ 0962 64880)

SMITH, Prof (Anthony) David; s of Rev William Beddard Smith (d 1985), and Evelyn, *née* Eagle (d 1987); *b* 16 Sept 1938; *Educ* Kingswood Sch Bath, ChCh Oxford (Bostock exhibitioner, BA, MA, DPhil); *m* 1, 1962 (m dis 1974), Wendy Diana, *née* Lee; 1 s (Richard David b 1968), 1 da (Catherine Anne b 1965); m 2, 1975, Dr Ingegerd Östman; 1 s (Niklas Carl William b 1987); *Career* Royal Soc Stothert res fell Oxford 1966-70, res lectr Christ Church Oxford 1966-71, Wellcome res fell Oxford 1970-71, univ lectr in pharmacology and student of Christ Church 1971-84, prof and head Dept of Pharmacology Univ of Oxford 1984-, hon dir MRC Anatomical Neuropharmacology Unit Oxford 1985-, fell Lady Margaret Hall Oxford 1984-; ed and contrib articles in various jls; memb: Gen Bd of the Faculties Oxford 1980-84, Neurosciences Bd MRC 1983-85; seventh Gaddum meml prize Br Pharmacological Soc; memb: Physiological Soc, Pharmacological Soc; *Recreations* music, travel; *Style—* Prof David Smith; Department of Pharmacology, Mansfield Road, Oxford OX1 3QT (☎ 0865 271883, fax 0865 271882)

SMITH, Hon Judge David Arthur; QC (1982); s of Arthur Heber Smith (d 1983), of Kent, and Marjorie Edith Pounds, *née* Broome (d 1989); *b* 7 May 1938; *Educ* Lancing, Merton Coll Oxford (MA); *m* 1967, Clementine, da of William Taylor Gordon Urquhart (d 1977); 2 s (Rupert b 1969, Julian b 1970); *Career* official princ Archdeaconry of Hackney 1973-, rec Crown Ct 1978-86, circuit judge 1986-; wine treas Western Circuit 1980-86; sec Int Bee Res Assoc; *Style—* His Hon Judge David Smith, QC; Bristol Crown Court, The Guildhall, Bristol

SMITH, David Arthur George; JP (Bradford 1975); s of Stanley George Smith (d 1967), of Bath, and Winifred May Francis Smith (d 1985); *b* 17 Dec 1934; *Educ* City of Bath Boys' Sch, Balliol Coll Oxford (BA, Dip Ed, MA); *m* 31 Aug 1957, Jennifer, da of John Ronald Anning (d 1963), of Launceston; 1 s (John b 1962), 2 da (Sarah b 1961, Charlotte b 1967); *Career* asst master Manchester GS 1957-62, head of history Rossall Sch 1963-70; headmaster: Kings Sch Peterborough 1970-74, Bradford GS 1974-; JP: Peterborough 1972-74, West Yorkshire 1975-; chm HMC 1988; FRSA 1985; *Books* Left and Right in Twentieth Century Europe (1970), Russia of the Tsars (1970); *Recreations* walking, writing; *Clubs* Athenaeum (Bradford); *Style—* David Smith, Esq, JP; Bradford Grammar School, Bradford, W Yorks BD9 43P (☎ 0274 545 461)

SMITH, David Bruce Boyter; s of Bruce Aitken Smith, of Dunfermline, and Helen Brown, *née* Boyter; *b* 11 March 1942; *Educ* Dunfermline HS, Univ of Edinburgh (MA, LLB); *m* 7 Aug 1965, Christine Anne, da of Robert McKenzie (d 1972); 1 s (Andrew b 1 Aug 1969), 1 da (Caroline b 1 July 1974); *Career* admitted slr 1968, NP 1969, slr Standard Life Assur Co 1969-73; Dunfermline Bldg Soc: sec 1974, gen mangr 1981, dep chief exec 1986, chief exec 1987, dir 1987; former chm BSA Scottish Liaison Ctee 1988-90, cncl memb NHBC 1987-, vice chm Care and Repair Nat Ctee 1988-, dir South Fife Enterprise Tst 1988-, dir Fife Enterprise Ltd 1991-; dep chm Glenrothes New Town Devpt Corp 1990-, life tstee Carnegie Dumferline and Hero Fund Tsts, gen cmmr Inland Revenue 1975-; memb Law Soc of Scotland 1968-; *Recreations* golf, sailing, the arts; *Clubs* New (Edinburgh), Forth Cruising, Dunfermline Golf; *Style—* David Smith, Esq; 4 Garvock Hill, Dunfermline, Fife KY12 7TZ (☎ 0383 723863); Dunfermline Building Society, 12 East Port, Dunfermline, Fife KY12 7LD (☎ 0383 721621, fax 0383 738845, car 0836 707080)

SMITH, Sheriff David Buchanan; s of William Adam Smith (d 1955), of Elderslie, Renfrewshire, and Irene Mary Calderwood, *née* Hogarth (d 1976); *b* 31 Oct 1936; *Educ* Paisley GS, Univ of Glasgow (MA), Univ of Edinburgh (LLB); *m* 1 April 1961, Hazel Mary, da of James Alexander Walker Sinclair, MBE (d 1960), of Edinburgh; 2 s (David Ewan b 1962, d 1986, Patrick Sinclair b 1965), 1 da (Alison Mary b 1963); *Career* advocate 1961-75, standing jr counsel to Scottish Educn Dept 1968- 75; tutor Faculty of Law Univ of Edinburgh 1964-72; Sheriff of N Strathclyde at Kilmarnock 1975-; pres Kilmarnock & Dist History Gp, treas The Sheriffs' Assoc 1979-89 (archivist 1989-), tstee Scot Curling Museum Tst 1980-; FSA Scot; *Books* Curling: an Illustrated History (1981), The Roaring Game: Memories of Scottish Curling (1985), The Sheriff Court (in The Stair Memorial Encyclopedia of the Laws of Scotland vol 6, 1988), George Washington Wilson in Ayrshire (1991); *Recreations* history of the laws and institutions of Scotland, curling, collecting curliana, music, architecture; *Style—* Sheriff David B Smith; Sheriff Court House, Kilmarnock, Ayrshire KA1 1ED (☎ 0563 20211)

SMITH, Sir David Cecil; s of William John Smith, and Elva Emily, *née* Deeble; *b* 21 May 1930; *Educ* St Paul's, Queen's Coll Oxford (MA, DPhil); *m* 1965, Lesley Margaret, s of Henry John Mollison Mutch (d 1946); 2 s (Adam, Cameron), 1 da (Bryony); *Career* 2 Lt RA 1955-56; Swedish Inst scholar Uppsala Univ 1951-52, Brown res fell Queen's Coll Oxford 1956-59, Harkness fell Berkeley Univ California 1959-60, lectr Dept of Agric Oxford Univ 1960-74, tutorial fell and tutor for admissions Wadham Coll Oxford 1971-74 (Royal Soc res fell 1964-71), Melville Wills prof of botany Univ of Bristol 1974-80 (dir of biological studies 1977-80), Sibthorpian prof of rural economy Oxford Univ 1980-87, princ and vice chllr Univ of Edinburgh 1987-; Hon DSc: Liverpool 1986, Exeter 1986, Hull 1987, Aberdeen 1990; Hon DL: Pennsylvania 1990, Queen's (Ontario) 1991; FRS (1975); *Books* The Biology of Symbiosis (with A Douglas, 1987); *Clubs* Farmers' New; *Style—* Sir David Smith, FRS; 14 Heriot Row, Edinburgh EH3 6HP (tel and fax : 031 556 6959); University of Edinburgh, Old College, South Bridge, Edinburgh EH8 9YL (☎ 031 667 1011, fax 031 667 7938, telex 727442 UNIVED G)

SMITH, Rt Rev David James; *see*: Maidstone, Bishop of

SMITH, David John; s of John Burton Smith, of Shropham, Norfolk, and Margaret Cameron, *née* Rowan; *b* 18 July 1950; *Educ* Carlton-le-Willows GS, Trent Poly; *m* 29 Sept 1979, Carole Lynn, da of John Walters, of Nottingham; 1 s (Haydn) Rory b 1981); *Career* asst exec engr GPO 1970-72, sr devpt engr Chronos Richardson 1973-78, sr engr Babcock Jenkins 1978-80, devpt mangr Haden 1980-82, engrg mangr Richard Simon 1982-; radio communications office Br Hang gliding Assoc, sec Derby and Notts Microlight Aircraft Club; *Recreations* general aviation; *Style—* David Smith, Esq; 87 Bridle Rd, Burton Joyce, Nottingham NG14 5FS (☎ 0602 312254); Richard Simon & Sons Ltd, Park Lane, Basford, Nottingham NG6 ODT (☎ 0602 277721, fax 0602 763473, telex 37545)

SMITH, Dr David John Leslie; s of Arthur George Smith (d 1975), and Gertrude Mary Duce, *née* Buck; *b* 8 Oct 1938; *Educ* North Gloucs Tech Coll (HND), Coll of Aeronautics (MSc), Univ of London (PhD), RCDS; *m* 14 April 1962, Wendy Lavinia, da of Frederick James Smith (d 1955); 2 da (Andrea, Penelope); *Career* Nat Gas Turbine Estab: scientific offr 1961, head turbomachinery dept 1979; student RCDS, dir aircraft mechanical and electrical equipment controllerate of aircraft MOD (PE) 1980, head aerodynamics dept Royal Aircraft Estab 1981; dep dir: Marine Technol Admty Res Estab 1984, planning Admiralty Res Estab 1986; head of def res study team and asst under sec state civilian mgmnt specialists MOD 1988; CEng 1972, FRAes 1986; *Recreations* gardening; *Style—* Dr David Smith; MOD, Northumberland House, Northumberland Ave, London WC2N 5BP (☎ 071 218 5662)

SMITH, Very Rev Dr David Macintyure Bell Armour; s of Rev Frederick Smith (d 1977), and Matilda Shearer (d 1958); *b* 5 April 1923; *Educ* Monkton Combe, Peebles HS, Univ of St Andrews (MA, BD), Univ of Stirling (DUniv); *m* 1, 1951, Margaret (d 1958), da of Charles Alexander Piper and Margaret Harcus; 2 s (David, Donald); m 2, 1960, Mary Kulvear, da of William Baxter Cumming (d 1939); 1 s (Alasdair); *Career* min Logie Kirk Stirling 1965-89, moderator of the Gen Assembly of the Church of Scotland 1985-86; *Style—* The Very Rev Dr David Smith; 28 Millar Place, Stirling FK9 1XD

SMITH, David Mark; s of Dennis Henry Smith, of Southampton, Hants, and Tina, *née* Boland; *b* 9 Jan 1956; *Educ* Battersea GS; *m* 7 Jan 1977, Jacqui, da of Douglas Ward; 1 da (Sarah-Jane Louise b 4 April 1982); *Career* professional cricketer; Surrey CCC 1973-83 and 1987-88 (awarded county cap 1980), Worcestershire CCC 1984-86 (awarded county cap 1984), Sussex CCC 1989- (awarded county cap 1989); Sydney Univ CC 1979-82 (Whitbread scholar); England: 2 Test matches v W Indies Jamaica and Trinidad 1986, 2 one-day Ints v W Indies 1986 and 1990; Nat West Trophy winners Surrey 1982; represented London Schs football and cricket; off-seasons: Medical Sickness Life Assurance Society 1973-74, Harrods 1975-76, Capital Building and Decorations Ltd 1978- (dir 1987-), advsr Crest Sporting Enterprises; *Recreations* motor racing competitor, golf, cooking, anything on J F Kennedy; *Style—* David Smith, Esq; c/o Sussex CCC, County Ground, Eaton Rd, Hove BN3 3AN (☎ 0273 732161)

SMITH, Prof (Norman John) David; s of Norman Samson Smith, (d 1962), of Kensington, London, and Eileen Tatton, *née* Oakley (d 1971); *b* 2 Feb 1931; *Educ* King's Coll Sch, King's Coll Hosp Med Sch Univ of London (BDS, MPhil), Univ of London (KCHMS BDS), Royal Free Hosp Sch of Med (MSc); *m* 2 Oct 1954, 1, 2 Oct 1954 (m dis), Regina Eileen, da of Reginald Lugg (d 1961), of Highgate London; 1 s (Malcolm David Oakley b 1964); m 2, 21 Sept 1983, Mary Christine, da of Alfred Thomas Pocock (d 1977); 1 da (Clare Zillah Mary b 1983); *Career* serv MN, apprentice Pacific Steam Navigation Co 1948-52, offr serv Royal Mail Lines 1953-58, gen dental practice jr hosp experience 1964-73, head dept dental radiology King's Coll Sch of Med 1973-; memb: Southwark Cncl 1974-78, GLC 1977-86, Thames Water Authy 1977-83, South East Thames RHA 1978-86, Hon Co of Master Msariners; *Books* Simple Navigation by the Sun (1974), Dental Radiography (1980), Dental Radiography (2nd ed, 1988); *Recreations* nature, photography, walking; *Style—* Prof David Smith; Dept of Dental Radiology, King's Coll Sch of Medicine & Dentistry, Caldecot Rd, London SE5 9RW (☎ 071 274 6222 ext 2503)

SMITH, Denis; s of Harold Smith (d 1990), of Stoke-on-Trent, and Emily Anne, *née* Bullock (d 1975); *b* 19 Nov 1947; *Educ* Queensberry Road Secdy Sch; *m* 7 Oct 1967, Kathryn Elizabeth, da of Thomas Finney; 2 s (Paul Denis b 16 April 1969, Thomas James b 5 March 1978), 1 da (Rebecca Emily b 6 June 1971); *Career* professional football mangr; player Stoke City 1966-82: 407 league appearances, 34 League Cup appearances, 22 FA Cup appearances; player-mangr York City 1982-87: 37 league appearances, 2 League Cup appearances, 4 FA Cup appearances; mangr Sunderland 1987-; achievements as player: England Schs Trophy Stoke-on-Trent 1962-63, represented Football League v Irish League 1971, League Cup medal Stoke City 1972, FA Cup semi-finalist Stoke City 1971 and 1972; honours as mangr: Div 4 Championship York City 1984, promotion to Div 1 Sunderland 1990; full coaching licence FA 1979; *Recreations* reading, walking, watching, cricket and athletics; *Style—* Denis Smith, Esq; Sunderland AFC, Roker Park Ground, Sunderland SR6 9SW (☎ 091 5140332)

SMITH, Derek Randall; OBE (1989); s of Edgar Thomas Smith, and Winifred Mabel Smith; *b* 20 Jan 1928; *Educ* Swansea GS, Pembroke Coll Cambridge (MA); *m* 28 Aug 1954, Sonia Elizabeth, *née* Snow; 4 s (Richard Brian b 20 July 1956, David Alan b 23 Jan 1958, Philip Christopher b 3 Sept 1960, John Nicholas b 10 July 1968); *Career* Engr BTH Co Ltd 1950-54 (graduate apprentice 1948-50), tech dir NNC Ltd (formerly AEI John Thompson Nuclear Energy Co Ltd) 1984-91 (joined 1955); author of numerous papers articles and lectures; memb Radioactive Waste Mgmnt Advsy Ctee; FEng 1983, FIMechE, MIEE, CEng; *Recreations* church, gardening, walking, squash, sailing; *Style—* Derek Smith, Esq, OBE

SMITH, Maj-Gen (James) Desmond Blaise; CBE (1944, OBE 1943), DSO (1944), CD (1948); s of William George Smith, of Bronson Ave, Ottawa, Canada; *b* 7 Oct 1911; *Educ* Univ of Ottawa, RMC Canada, IDC London, Nat Def Coll Canada; *m* 1, 1937, Miriam Irene (d 1969), da of Walter Juxton Blackburn, of London, Ontario; 2 s; m 2, 1979, Dr Belle Shenkman, CM, of Ottawa; *Career* joined Canadian Army 1933, served WWII in Italy and NW Europe (despatches twice), mil sec Canadian Cabinet Def Ctee 1948-50, QMG Canadian Army 1951, chm Canadian Jt Staff London 1951-54, Cmdt Nat Def Coll of Canada 1954-58, Adj-Gen 1958-62, resigned 1962; Col HM Regt of Canadian Gds 1961-66; chm and chief exec Pillar Engrg Ltd 1964-82; chm 1970-90: Blaise Investments, Desmond Smith Investments, Dashabel Properties & Interiors Ltd; dir: RTZ Pillar 1970-82, Meco Holdings Hong Kong, Indal Technols Ltd Canada 1980-85; sec gen Canada Meml Fndn 1988-90, cmmr Cwlth War Graves Cmmn 1985-; Croix de Guerre 1944, Chevalier Legion of Honour 1944, Cdr Military Order of Italy 1944, Offr Legion of Merit USA 1944, Order of Valour of Greece 1945, KStJ 1961, CStJ, KLJ 1985; *Clubs* Annabels, Marks, Harry's Bar; *Style—* Maj-Gen Desmond Smith, CBE, DSO, CD; 50 Albert Court, Prince Consort Rd, London SW7 2BH (☎ 071 584 6817, fax 071 584 2104)

SMITH, Prof (Stanley) Desmond; s of Henry George Stanley Smith (d 1969), and Sarah Emily Ruth Weare; *b* 3 March 1931; *Educ* Cotham Bristol, Univ of Bristol (BSc, DSc), Univ of Reading (PhD); *m* 1 July 1956, Gillian Anne, da of Howard Stanley Parish; 1 s (David), 1 da (Nicola); *Career* SSO RAE Farnborough 1956-59; res asst Imperial Coll (Met Dept) 1959-60, reader Reading Univ 1966-70 (lectr 1960-66), prof of Physics and dept head Heriot-Watt Univ Edinburgh 1970-; chm and dir: Edinburgh Instruments Ltd 1971-, Edinburgh Sensors Ltd 1988; dir Edinburgh C of C 1981-84; memb: cabinet ACOST 1987-88 (formerly ACARD 1985-87), Def Sci Advsy Cncl MOD 1985-; Inst P, FRMetS 1962, FRS 1976, FRSE 1973; *Recreations* mountaineering, skiing, tennis, golf; *Clubs* Royal Soc; *Style—* Prof Desmond Smith, FRS, FRSE; Tree Tops, 29D Gillespie Rd, Colinton, Lothian EH13 0NW (☎ 031 441 7225); Physics Department, Heriot-Watt University, Riccarton, Edinburgh EH14 4AS (☎ 031 449 5542, fax 031 451 3088, telex 72553 EDINST G)

SMITH, Lady; Diana May Violet Peel; da of Warwick Goodchild; *m* 1, George Ian Young; m 2, 1958 (as his 2 w), Lt-Cdr Sir (William) Gordon Smith, 2 Bt, VRD (d 1983); 2 s; *Style—* Lady Smith; Crowmallie House, Pitcaple, Inverurie, Aberdeenshire AB51 9HR

SMITH, Ven Donald John; *b* 10 April 1926; *Educ* Clifton Theol Coll Bristol; *m* 1 Jan 1948, Violet Olive Goss; 2 s (Timothy b 1951, Michael b 1954), 1 da (Alison b 1956 d 1986); *Career* ordained St Paul's Cathedral 1953; asst curate: St Margaret's Edgeware 1953-56, St Margaret's Ipswich 1956-58; vicar St Mary's Hornsey Rise London 1958-62, rector Whitton Suffolk 1962-75, canon St Edmundsbury 1973-, rector Redgrave cum Botesdale and The Rickinghalls 1975-79, archdeacon of Suffolk 1975-84, archdeacon of Sudbury Suffolk 1984-; memb Nat Tst, tstee Pro-Corda Music Sch Leiston; *Books* A Confirmation Course (1974), Covenanting for Disunity (1981), Tourism and The Use of Church Buildings (ed 1983), Thank You Lord for Alison (1986), Straight forward and Simple - a handbook for churchwardens (1990); *Recreations* caravanning, foreign travel, dining out, collecting; *Style—* The Ven the Archdeacon of Sudbury; 84 Southgate St, Bury St Edmunds IP33 2BJ (☎ 0284 766796); St Peter's Cottage, Stretton-on-Fosse, Moreton-in-Marsh, Glos GL56 9SE

(☎ 0608 62790)

SMITH, Douglas; TD, DL (Tyne and Wear); s of Douglas Smith (d 1972), of Newcastle upon Tyne, and Maggie Annie Jane, *née* Symon (d 1956); *b* 23 Nov 1924; *Educ* Fettes; *m* 4 Aug 1949, Freda, da of George Frederick Thompson (d 1957), of Newcastle upon Tyne; 3 da (Christine b 19 Sept 1951, Julia b 15 April 1954, Fiona b 19 April 1958); *Career* Nat Serv WWII: 2 Lt Sandhurst 1943, 5 RTR 1944, demob 1947; 324 HAA Regt RA TA 1949, Lt-Col Cmd Offr; 101 Northumbria Field regt RA TA (Hon Col); chm (formerly dir) Ringtons Ltd 1953-; involved in Boy Scouts Newcastle and St John Ambulance; memb Worshipful Co of CA's in England and Wales; ACA 1951; *Recreations* golf, rugby; *Clubs* RA, Gosforth, Army and Navy; *Style—* Douglas Smith, Esq, TD, DL; Dene Grange, Lindisfarne Rd, Newcastle Upon Tyne NE2 2HE (☎ 091 281 5096); Ringtons, Algernon Rd, Newcastle Upon Tyne NE6 2YN (☎ 091 265 6181, fax 091 276 3500, tlx 53120)

SMITH, (Brian) Douglas; s of Henry Charles Smith (d 1958), of 41 Rosebery Gardens, Crouch End, London, and Ruby Constance, *née* Hall (d 1976); *b* 17 Aug 1935; *Educ* Stationers' Co Sch Hornsey, King's Coll London, LSE (BA, cricket purple); *m* 1, 1961, Verity Anne, da of late William Wright; 2 da (Tracy McClure b 1965, Francesca McClure b 1967); m 2, 1985, Mary Barbara, *née* Gillman; 1 da (Rebecca Barbara); *Career* London publicity offr Cons Party Central Office 1960-62, head of publicity Fire Protection Assoc 1962-64, sec Int Cooperation Year Ctee 1964-66, dir Intercapita Public Relations 1966-68, assoc dir Planned Public Relations 1968-71, dir MDA Public Relations 1971-85; chm: Parliamentary Monitoring Services Ltd 1985-, PMS Publications Ltd 1985-; chief exec Westminster Advisers Ltd 1985-, md PRCI Limited (later Countrywide Political Communications) 1987-90; cncllr Hornsey Borough Cncl 1961-65 (chm Housing Ctee 1963-65); Haringey Cncl: local cncllr 1964-86, dep ldr Cons Gp 1966-70, Dep Mayor 1968-69, chm Planning and Devpt Ctee 1968-70, chm Personnel Ctee 1969-71, ldr Cons Oppn 1980-84; chm PR Consltts Assoc 1984-85 (treas, vice chm), pres IPR 1990 (chm Govt Affrs Gp 1986-87), PR Week award for outstanding career achievement in PR 1990, hon PR advsr UK Scout Movement 1965-; MCAM; Lobbying the UK Parliament (with Arthur Butler, 1984); *Recreations* watching and talking cricket, visiting old pubs; *Clubs* Kent County Cricket, Foreign Press Assoc; *Style—* Douglas Smith, Esq; 11 Moreton Terrace, Pimlico, London SW1V 2NS (☎ 071 821 8774); Chequer Lodge, Ash, nr Sandwich, Kent CT3 2ET (☎ 0304 812 768); Parliamentary Monitoring Services, 19 Douglas St, Westminster SW1 (☎ 071 233 8283); Countrywide Political Communications, 29 Tufton St, Westminster SW1P 3QL (☎ 071 233 0588)

SMITH, (Fraser) Drew; s of Capt Frank Smith, and Beatrice, *née* Blank; *b* 30 March 1950; *Educ* Westminster; *m* 19 June 1987, Susan Mary, da of Liam Maloney; 1 s (Oliver b 1988), 1 da (Grace b 1989); *Career* IPC Magazines 1968-72, Westminster Press 1972-80; Consumers' Assoc 1981-90; Alfresco plc 1990-; chm Guild of Food Writers; *Books* Good Food Guide (1983-90), Good Food Directory (1986), Modern Cooking (1990); *Recreations* life; *Style—* Drew Smith, Esq; 35 Tadema Road, London SW10 (☎ 071 823 3115/3161, fax 071 351 7157)

SMITH, Sir Dudley Gordon; MP (C) Warwick and Leamington 1968-, DL (Warwickshire 1988-); s of Hugh William Smith (d 1977), of Cambridge, and Florence Elizabeth Smith (d 1967); *b* 14 Nov 1926; *Educ* Chichester HS; *m* 1, 1958 (m dis 1974); 1 s, 2 da; m 2, 1976, Catherine, o da of late Thomas Amos, of Liverpool; *Career* mgmnt consIt and former journalist; asst news editor Sunday Express 1953-59, divnl dir Beecham Gp 1966-70; contested (C) Peckham, Camberwell 1955, MP (C) Brentford and Chiswick 1959-66, oppn whip 1964-66; Parly under sec of state: Dept of Employment 1970-74, (Army) MOD 1974; vice chm Parly Select Ctee on Race Rels and Immigration 1974-79, UK del to Cncl of Europe and WEU 1979-, (sec gen European Democratic Gp 1983-), chm WEU DEF Ctee 1989-; United and Cecil Club 1975-80; Freeman City of London, memb Worshipful Co of Horners; kt 1983; *Books* Harold Wilson: A Critical Biography (1963); *Recreations* travel, books, music, preservation of wild life; *Style—* Sir Dudley Smith, DL, MP; Church Farm, Weston-under-Wetherley, nr Leamington Spa, Warwicks (☎ 0926 632352; House of Commons, Westminster, London SW1A 0AA (☎ 071 219 3445)

SMITH, (Wallace) Duncan; s of I Wallace Smith (d 1960), of Glencoe, Ontario, Canada and Augusta Elizabeth, *née* Hildebrand; *b* 5 May 1934; *Educ* Mount Douglas Sch Br Columbia Canada, Univ of Br Columbia Canada (BA); *m* 3 Sept, Marcia Annabel, da of Raymond Gregory (d 1969); 1 s (Paul b 2 March 1963), 2 da (Caroline b 28 March 1964, Michaela b 26 Jan 1973); *Career* Nesbitt Thomson & Co Ltd 1961-70: dir, vice pres, head of money mkt and banking dept, md Nesbitt Thomson Ltd London 1963-67; chm Wallace Smith Gp Ltd 1969; *Recreations* country pursuits, reading, travel; *Clubs* City of London (London), The Downtown Assoc (NY), The National (Toronto); *Style—* W Duncan Smith, Esq; Winchester House, 77 London Wall, London EC2N 1AB (☎ 071 638 6444, fax 071 588 1413)

SMITH, Edward Richard; s of Albert Edward Smith (d 1961), of Finchley, London, and Elsie Florence, *née* Turner; *b* 19 March 1936; *Educ* Highgate Sch; *m* 10 Sept 1960, Pamela Margaret, da of Alfred Montague Mundy (d 1977), of Gidea Park and Tunbridge Wells; 2 s (Donald Edward Philip b 1966, Philip Richard Jeremy b 1969); *Career* Nat Serv RAOC 1954-56; Martins Bank Ltd 1954-68; dir: Hill Samuel Bank Ltd 1974-90, Gross Hill Properties Ltd 1983-, Sydney and London Properties Ltd 1986-, Consolidated Land Properties Ltd, Control Securities plc 1988-, European Equity Corporation Ltd 1988-90, Waterglade International Holdings PLC 1990-; proprietor Felstead Books; Freeman City of London, Liveryman Worshipful Co of Pattenmakers; FCIB 1980; *Recreations* antiquarian books, gardening, travel; *Clubs* East India, RAC, MCC; *Style—* Edward R Smith, Esq; Phildon Lodge, Seal Hollow Rd, Sevenoaks, Kent TN13 3SL (☎ 0732 456928, fax 0732 740253)

SMITH, Hon Mrs (Elissa); *née* Haden-Guest; o da of 4 Baron Haden-Guest; *b* 10 Jan 1953; *m* 1981, Nicholas Carey Smith, s of Corlies Morgan Smith; 1 s (Nathanael Haden b 1988), 1 da (Gena Haden b 1984); *Style—* The Hon Mrs Smith; 824 Nowita Place, Los Angeles, California 90291, USA

SMITH, Elizabeth Jean; da of Lt-Gen Sir Robert Hay, KCIE (d 1980), of Denholm, Roxburghshire, and Mary Carnegie, *née* McAusland, MBE; *b* 15 Aug 1936; *Educ* St George's Sch Edinburgh, Univ of Edinburgh (MA); *m* 23 Feb 1960, Geoffrey Peter Smith, s of William Stanley Smith (d 1958), of 10 Oakland Vale, Wallasey, Cheshire; 1 s (Graham b 1968), 1 da (Catherine b 1965); *Career* BBC: studio mangr 1958-61, prodr radio news 1961-70, dep ed consumer affrs Radio 4 1970-78, prodr TV current affrs 1978-79, sr asst Secretariat 1979-81, Cwlth fellowship to study the impact of satellite TV on India 1984, asst head central talks and features World Service 1981-84, head current affrs World Service 1984-88, controller English servs World Service 1988-; monthly columnist for The Listener 1975-78; memb: Radio Acad, Royal Inst of Int Affrs; *Books* Healing Herbs (jtly 1978), Sambo Sahib (1981); *Style—* Mrs Elizabeth Smith; 12 Highbury Terrace, London N5 1UP (☎ 071 226 3519); BBC World Service, Bush House, Strand, London WC2B 4PH (☎ 071 257 2374, fax 071 379 6841, telex 265781)

SMITH, Brig Eric David; CBE (1975, MBE 1951), DSO (1945); s of Christopher Smith (d 1958), and Jessica Lucy, *née* Bartram (d 1965); *b* 19 Aug 1923; *Educ* Allhallows Sch Devon; *m* 5 Jan 1957, Jill Helene, da of Brig J C Way Cott, OBE (d 1981); 2 da (Joanna (Mrs Davis) b 1959, Beverly (Mrs Stark) b 1962); *Career* cmmnd 7 Gurkha Rifles 1942, active service Italy and Greece 1944-45 (wounded), operational serv Malaya 1950-54, student Staff Coll Camberley 1956, operational serv Borneo 1963-64 (badly injured in helicopter 1964), operational serv Sabah 1965, Co 1/2 Gurkha Rifles 1965-68, Col Bde of Gurkhas 1970-71, Brig cmdg Br Gurkhas Nepal 1971-74, Hon Col 7 Gurkha Rifles 1975-83, ret active list 1978; special advsr to Commons Def Ctee on Bde of Gurkhas Report 1988-89; author; chm Sidmouth Town Cncl 1988-90; *Books* Britain's Brigade of Gurkhas (1973), Battles For Cassino (1975), East of Kathmandu (1976), Even the Brave Falter (1978), Battle for Burma (1979), Malaya and Borneo (counter-insurgency) (1985), Johnny Gurkha Victory of a Sort (1988); *Recreations* keen on all sport until loss of right arm (now a spectator), walking; *Style—* Brig Eric Smith, CBE, DSO; 2 Balfour Mews, Sidmouth, Devon

SMITH, Hon Mrs (Margaret Bertha Meriel) ERIC; *née* Ward; da of late 6 Viscount Bangor, OBE, PC; *b* 1914; *m* 1, 1938, Maj Desmond Charles Forde, Coldstream Gds (m dis 1947), 1 s, 1 da; m 2, 1947 (m dis 1962), Gavin Robert Sligh; m 3, 1969, Maj Dennis Eric Smith; *Style—* The Hon Mrs Eric Smith; Flat 6, 17/21 Sloane Court West, London, SW3 4TD (☎ 071 730 4153)

SMITH, Sir (Frank) Ewart; s of Richard Sidney Smith (d 1938), and Laura, *née* East (d 1952); *b* 31 May 1897; *Educ* Christ's Hosp Sch, Univ of Cambridge (MA); *m* 1924, Kathleen Winifred (d 1978), da of Herbert Rudd Dawes (d 1950); 1 s (d 1976), 1 da; *Career* Lt RGA Flanders 1916-19; chartered engr; joined ICI Ltd 1923, dep chm 1954-59; past chm Br Productivity Cncl, chief engr and supt armament design dept Min of Supply 1942-45; former memb: Scientific Advsy Cncl Miny of Fuel and Power, Advsy Cncl of Scientific Policy; former chm Advsy Cncl for Mgnt Efficiency; hon fell Sidney Sussex Coll Cambridge; kt 1946; *Recreations* gardening, cabinet making; *Style—* Sir Ewart Smith; Park Hill Cottage, Sandy Lane, Watersfield, W Sussex RH20 1NF

SMITH, Fiona; da of Brian Elliott, of Woodham, Surrey, and Annette Barbara, *née* Mousley; *b* 13 Nov 1963; *Educ* France Hill Secdy Sch, Brooklands Tech Coll; *m* 13 Aug 1988, Peter Anthony Smith, s of Ian Edward Smith; *Career* badminton player; Wimbledon Squash and Badminton Club 1976-, represented Surrey at all jr levels then first team 1981-; England: under 16, under 18, over 50 sr caps; major achievements: Nat Singles champion 5 times, Nat Mixed champion, Euro Singles Silver medal 1990; Cwlth Games: Gold medal team event 1986, Silver medal singles and mixed 1986, Bronze medal doubles 1986, Gold medal singles 1990, Gold medal doubles 1990, Gold medal team event 1990; *Recreations* all sports, cooking, reading; *Style—* Mrs Fiona Smith; Wimbledon Squash & Badminton Club, Cranbrook Rd, Wimbledon, London SW19 (☎ 081 947 5806)

SMITH, Rev Francis Taylor (Frank); s of James William Smith (d 1977), of Aberdeen, and Jeannie Moir Catto, *née* Cockburn (d 1970); *b* 22 Jan 1933; *Educ* Aberdeen GS, Aberdeen Univ (MA), Christ's Coll Aberdeen; *m* 22 July 1957, Jean Millar, da of William Wallace (d 1973), of IOM; 3 s (Mark, Philip, Barry), 1 da (Naomi); *Career* sr asst minister Govan Old Parish Church Glasgow 1957-58; parish minister: Aberlour Banffshire 1958-64, St Paul's Dunfermline 1964-; chaplain Dunfermline and W Fife Maternity Hosps 1964-; cncllr Banff 1964, chm W Fife Local Health Cncl 1975-84, pres Assoc of Scottish Local Health Cncls 1979-81 (vice pres 1978), memb GMC 1979-; *Recreations* reading, fishing, music; *Clubs* Caledonian; *Style—* The Rev Frank T Smith; 6 Park Avenue, Dunfermline, Fife KY12 7HX (☎ 0383 721124)

SMITH, Dr Francis William; s of Capt William Smith, RAMC (d 1978) of Harare, Zimbabwe, and Frances Marrianne May, *née* Emslie; *b* 8 Jan 1943; *Educ* Prince Edward Sch Harare Zimbabwe, Univ of Aberdeen (MB ChB, DMRD, MD); *m* 5 Dec 1970, Pamela Anne, da of James Cox (d 1958) of Gateshead, Co-Durham; 1 s (James b 1976), 1 da (Jane b 1971); *Career* dir Clinical Magnetic Resonance Res Aberdeen Royal Infirmary 1980 (conslt in nuclear med 1979-), chief ed Magnetic Resonance Imaging 1985-91, club doctor Montrose Football Club 1990-; pres Soc for Magnetic Resonance Imaging 1983, pres Rotary Club of Aberdeen 1991-92; FFR, RCSI 1978; *Books* magnetic Resonance in Medicine and Biology (1984), Practical Nuclear Medicine (1989); *Recreations* swimming, walking, entomology, fly fishing, golf; *Style—* Dr Francis Smith; 7 Primrosehill Rd, Cults, Aberdeen, Scotland AB1 9ND (☎ 0224 868745); Dept of Nuclear Medicine, Aberdeen Royal Infirmary, Foresterhill, Aberdeen AB9 2ZB (☎ 0224 681818, fax 0224 662412)

SMITH, Frank Arthur; s of George Frederick Stanley Smith (d 1984), of Nottingham, and Doris Hannah, *née* Simcock (d 1984); *b* 18 Dec 1941; *Educ* King Edward VII Sch Sheffield, Trinity Coll Oxford (MA); *m* 14 Oct 1967, Eva June (d 1990), da of George Henry Larner, of Haverfordwest; 1 s (Thomas Louis b 19 March 1972), 1 da (Anna Margaret b 23 March 1969); *Career* nat tax ptnr Robson Rhodes 1983-; memb Tax Ctee ICAEW 1984-; tstee Geffrye Museum 1989-; FCA 1966, fell Inst of Taxation 1978; *Recreations* walking, reading, gardening, jazz, theatre; *Style—* Frank Smith, Esq; 77 Manor Way, Blackheath, London SE3 9XG (☎ 081 852 7137); Robson Rhodes, 186 City Rd, London EC1V 2NU (☎ 071 251 1644, fax 071 250 0801)

SMITH, Prof Frank Thomas; s of Leslie Maxwell Smith, of Havant, Hants, and Catherine Matilda, *née* Wilken; *b* 24 Feb 1948; *Educ* Kinson CP Sch, Bournemouth GS, Jesus Coll Oxford (BA, DPhil); *m* 16 Sept 1972, Valerie Sheila, da of Albert Alfred Hearn; 3 da (Helen b 1976, Natalie b 1978, Amy b 1987); *Career* res fell Theoretical Aerodynamics Unit Southampton 1972-73, lectr Imp Coll London 1973-78, visiting prof Univ of W Ontario 1978-79, reader and prof Imp Coll 1979-84, Goldsmid prof in applied maths UCL 1984-; FRS 1984; *Books* Boundary - Layer Separation (with Prof Susan Brown 1987); *Recreations* sports, reading, family; *Style—* Prof F T Smith, FRS; Mathematics Dept, Univ Coll, Gower St, London WC1E 6BT (☎ 071 387 7050 ext 2837)

SMITH, Gary Andrew; s of Walter Henry Smith (d 1984), and Claire Elizabeth, *née* Copps; *b* 13 Oct 1958; *Educ* Colfes GS; *m* 18 April 1990; 1 s (Darren Anthony b 13 Sept 1986), 2 step da (Kim Louise b 2 Nov 1984, Hannah Jayne b 17 Feb 1987); *Career* Barclays Bank 1976-; bowls player; E Int 1982-, E Indoor Pairs winner 1986, Br Isles Pairs winner 1987, World Indoor Pairs runner up 1987, UK Indoors singles champion 1988, E Indoor singles champion 1988, E Indoor Fours winner 1989, 1990 (1983, 84, 88), Br Isles Fours Pairs winner 1989 and 1990; ACIB; *Recreations* bowls; *Clubs* Cyphers; *Style—* Gary Smith, Esq; Barclays Bank plc,131 Eltham High St, Eltham, London SE9 1TJ (☎ 081 850 2245, fax 081 850 2245); 110 High St, Henlow, Beds SG16 6AE (☎ 0462 812512)

SMITH, Geoffrey Edwin; OBE (1981); s of Curtis Edwin Smith, of Hertford, Herts, and Mabel Alice, *née* Bacon (d 1971); *b* 9 Nov 1930; *Educ* Hertford GS; *m* 5 April 1958, (Jeanette) Jan Mary, da of Rex Saynor (d 1976), of Mirfield; 1 s (Jeremy Redington b 12 March 1969), 1 da (Charlotte Victoria b 2 Oct 1964); *Career* RAF 1949; sr asst co librarian Herts CC, dep co librarian Hants Co Library 1959-63, co librarian Leicestershire CC 1963-73, dir libraries and information serv Leicestershire CC 1973-90, dir T C Farries and Co 1990-, sr res fell Loughborough Univ of Technol 1987-; memb: Library Assoc Cncl 1962-79, Library Advsy Cncl 1972-78, Library and Information Servs Cncl 1985-88; Soc Co Librarians: memb Exec Ctee 1963-89, vice pres 1982-88, pres 1989; memb Management Ctee Royal Leicester Rutland and Wycliffe Soc for the Blind; FRSA, FBIM, FLA 1956; *Recreations* swimming, cinema;

Clubs Book Trust, Society of Bookmen; *Style*— Geoffrey Smith, Esq, OBE; 16 Soar Rd, Quorn, Loughborough, Leics LE12 8BW (☎ 0509 412 655); T C Farries and Co Ltd, Watling Drive, Sketchley Meadows Business Park, Hinckley LE10 3EY (☎ 0455 250077, fax 0455 233187)

SMITH, Prof Geoffrey Harry; s of Stanley James Smith (d 1956), and Barbara Preston (d 1988); *b* 11 Nov 1937; *Educ* Derby Sch, St, Mary's Hosp Med Sch; *m* 30 March 1960, Brenda, da of Edward Lawson (d 1983); 3 da (Analisa b 1962, Katy b 1964, Shan b 1965); *Career* conslt cardiothoracic surgn Northern Gen Hosp Sheffield 1969-88, prof of cardiac surgery Univ of Sheffield 1988-; FRCS; *Books* Complications of Cardiopulmonary Surgery (1984); *Recreations* golf, fell walking; *Style*— Prof Geoffrey Smith; Department of Cardiac Surgery, University of Sheffield, Northern General Hospital, Sheffield 10 (☎ 0742 434343)

SMITH, Wing Cdr Geoffrey Wilfred Tracey; s of Claude Smith (d 1974), of Upper Poppleton, York, and Doris Lilian Tracey Smith (d 1977); *b* 18 March 1927; *Educ* West Hartlepool GS, Downing Coll Cambridge (MA, MB BChir), St Bartholomews Hosp; *m* 22 Dec 1954 (m dis 1977), (Barbara) Megan, da of William Ashley, DSM (d 1946), of Cairo; 1 s (Nigel b 1963); m 2, 16 Feb 1978, Teresa Jeanne, da of Robert Audley Furtado, CB, of Langton Herring, Dorset; *Career* Lt HLI 1945-48, RAF 1959-75 (ret Wing Cdr); conslt ophthalmology RAF 1971-75, asst opthalmic surgn Guys Hosp 1976-78, sr conslt Miny of Public Health QATAR 1978-85; pty candidate (Lab) Fylde constituency 1987, Euro Parly candidate (Lab) Lancs Central 1989, chm Monks Orchard Branch (Croydon NE) Lab Pty; FRCSE 1971, FCOphth 1989; *Recreations* organist; *Clubs* The Golfers; *Style*— Wing Cdr Geoffrey Smith; 77 Groome Court, Regency Walk, Orchard Way, Shirley, Croydon, Surrey CR0 7UT (☎ 081 776 0553)

SMITH, Gerald Albert; s of Albert George Smith (d 1981), of Braxted, Essex, and Eliza Kate, *née* Cranmer; *b* 28 Aug 1935; *Educ* Colchester GS; *m* 1 Feb 1964, Pauline Mary, da of Herbert Charles Songer (d 1952), of Cockfosters, Middlesex; 1 s (Roland b 1965); *Career* dir County Bank Ltd 1970-80, dir and chm Cramphorn plc 1980-; Freeman: City of London 1977, Worshipful Co of Chartered Accountants 1978; FCA 1960, ATII 1963; *Recreations* breeding waterfowl; *Style*— Gerald Smith, Esq; Read's Hall, Mickfield, Stowmarket, Suffolk, IP14 5LU (☎ 0449 711663); Cramphorn plc, Cuton Mill, Springfield, Chelmsford, Essex, CM2 6PD (☎ 0245 466221, fax 0245 450298)

SMITH, Prof Gerald Stanton; s of Thomas Arthur Smith (d 1974), of Manchester, and Ruth Annie, *née* Stanton; *b* 17 April 1938; *Educ* Stretford GS, Sch of Slavonic and E Euro Studies Univ of London (BA, PhD); *m* 2 Aug 1961 (m dis 1981), Frances, da of Percy Wetherill, of Deganwy, N Wales; 1 s (Ian b 1964), 1 da (Gillian b 1963); m 2, 16 Feb 1982, Barbara, da of Maj John Henry Heldt (d 1986, US Army), of Sarasota, Florida; 1 step s (Gus b 1969), 1 step da (Elizabeth b 1971); *Career* RAF 1957-60, Cpl 1959 Jt Servs Sch for Linguists 1958, RAF Gatow, Berlin 1959-60; lectr in Russian: Univ of Nottingham 1964-71, Univ of Birmingham 1971-79; res fell Univ of Liverpool 1979-82; visiting prof: Indiana Univ 1984, Univ of California Berkeley 1984; private scholar Social Scis and Humanities Res Cncl of Canada 1985, John Simon Guggenheim Meml Fell 1986, prof of Russian and fell New Coll Oxford Univ 1986-; jazz musician London 1961-64; fndr Jazz Orchestra: Nottingham 1968, Birmingham 1970; memb: Br Assoc for Slavonic Soviet and E Euro Studies, American Assoc for Advancement of Slavic Studies; *Books* Songs to Seven Strings (1985); *Recreations* jazz music, watching water; *Style*— Prof Gerald Smith; Taylor Institution, Oxford University, St Giles, Oxford OX1 3NA (☎ 0865 270476)

SMITH, Sir (Thomas) Gilbert; 4 Bt (UK 1897) of Stratford Place, St Marylebone, Co London; s of Sir Thomas Turner, 3 Bt (1961); *b* 2 July 1937; *Educ* Huntley Sch, Nelson Coll; *m* 1962, Patricia Christine, da of David Cooper, of Paraparaumu, New Zealand; 2 s, 1 da; *Heir* s, Andrew Thomas Smith; *Career* engr; *Style*— Sir Gilbert Smith, Bt; PO Box 654, 50 Titoki St, Masterton, New Zealand

SMITH, Dr (Charles) Gordon; s (by 2 m) of Sir (William) Gordon Smith, 2 Bt, VRD (d 1983); hp of bro Sir Robert Hill Smith, 3 Bt; *b* 21 April 1959; *Educ* Merchant Taylors', St Andrew's Univ (BSc), Oregon Univ, Trinity Hall Cambridge (PhD); *Career* res sci; *Recreations* windsurfing, drinking; *Clubs* Grafham Water Sailing; *Style*— Dr Gordon Smith; c/o Cavendish Laboratory, Madingley Road, Cambridge

SMITH, Dr (Charles Edward) Gordon; CB (1970); s of John Alexander Smith (d 1966), of Fife, and Margaret Inglis, *née* Fletcher; *b* 12 May 1924; *Educ* Forfar Acad, Univ of St Andrew's (MD, DSc); *m* 1948, Elsie, da of Samuel Sydney McClellan (d 1971), of Cockermouth; 1 s (Alastair), 2 da (Elizabeth, Sally); *Career* HM Colonial Med Serv Malaysia 1948-57, sr lectr and reader LSHTM 1957-64, dir Microbiological Res Estab MOD 1964-70, dean LSHTM 1971-89, chm Public Health Lab Serv 1972-89, A Wellcome tstee 1972- (dep chm 1983-); Prime Warden Worshipful Co of Goldsmiths 1991-92 (warden 1988); *Recreations* golf, gardening; *Clubs* Savile, Bramshaw Golf, New Zealand Golf; *Style*— Dr Gordon Smith, CB; Flat A, Guilford Court, 51 Guilford St, London WC1; Wild Close, Woodgreen, Fordingbridge, Hants SP6 2QX; Wellcome Trust, 1 Park Square West, London NW1 4LJ (☎ 071 486 4902, fax 071 935 0359)

SMITH, Gordon Walkerley; JP (1977); s of George Arthur Smith (d 1976), and Elsie, *née* Johnson; *b* 20 March 1933; *Educ* St James Sch Grimsby, Hull Coll of Architecture; *m* 15 Sept 1956, Anne, da of George Adam Young (d 1978); 1 s (David b 1957), 1 da (Diane b 1961); *Career* architect; princ Sir Charles Nicholson Gp; diocesan surveyor: Lincoln 1970, Southwell 1974; fell Woodard Corpn 1976, Custos St James Sch Grimsby 1985; Liveryman Worshipful Co of Paviors; FRIBA; *Recreations* reading, gardening, walking, music; *Clubs* City Livery; *Style*— Gordon W Smith, JP; Walkerley House, Barnoldby le Beck, nr Grimsby DN37 0AS (☎ 0472 827665); The Old Rectory, Bargate, Grimsby DN3L 2AL (☎ 0472 355 288)

SMITH, Graham Frederick; s of Archibald Frederick Smith, of High Wycombe, Bucks, and Janet Mearing, *née* Hall; *b* 17 Feb 1943; *Educ* Royal GS High Wycombe; *m* 8 Oct 1966, Wendy Elizabeth, da of John Maltby (d 1982), of Oxford; 1 s (Andrew b 1968), 2 da (Lucy b 1972, Melanie b 1976); *Career* ptnr Ernst & Young (CAs) 1975-; former chm High Wycombe Lawn Tennis Club, Bucks County Tennis Colour 1967; FCA 1964; *Recreations* golf, garden, music; *Style*— Graham F Smith, Esq; Crabtrees, Nairdwood Lane, Prestwood, Great Missenden, Bucks HP16 0QH (☎ 02406 5128); Ernst & Young, Becket House, 1 Lambeth Palace Rd, London SE1 7EU (☎ 071 928 2000, fax 071 928 1345)

SMITH, Graham Paul; s of James Alfred Smith (d 1985), and Elsie Winifred, *née* Cleathero; *b* 25 Dec 1949; *Educ* Royal GS High Wycombe, Univ of Durham (BA), Osgoode Hall Law School Toronto (LLM); *Career* slr Supreme Ct 1975; ptnr: Clifford-Turner 1981-87, Clifford Chance 1987-; Memb Computer Law Assoc; Liveryman Worshipful Co of Slrs; memb Law Soc 1975; *Books* contrib chapters to: Computer Law (1990), The Encyclopaedia of Information Technology Law (1990); *Recreations* opera, cricket; *Clubs* MCC; *Style*— Graham Smith, Esq; Clifford Chance, Bow Bells House, Bread St, London EC4 (☎ 071 600 0808, fax 071 956 0199, telex 887847)

SMITH, Graham Richard Elliott; s of Donald Smith (d 1978), and Betty Lillian, *née* Elliott; *b* 24 Feb 1958; *Educ* Royal GS Guildford, Univ of Nottingham (BA); *m* 19 Sept 1987, Sharon Elizabeth Peterson, da of Aubrey Owen Mulroney, of Nortonbury, Morgans Rd, Hertford, Herts; *Career* admitted slr 1982; ptnr Wilde Sapte 1987-, (articled clerk 1980-82, slr 1982-87); Freeman Worshipful Co of Slrs 1986-; memb: Law Soc, Int Bar Assoc; *Recreations* skiing, fine wine, travel; *Style*— Graham Smith, Esq; Wilde Sapte, Queensbridge House, 60 Upper Thames St, London EC4V 3BD (☎ 071 236 3050, fax 071 236 9624, telex 887793)

SMITH, Guy Thornton; s of Charles William Smith (d 1957), and Beatrice Emeline, *née* Stratford (d 1981); *b* 21 July 1923; *Educ* Latymer Upper Sch London, Kings Coll and Imperial Coll Univ of London (BSc); *m* 1, 26 May 1962, Gwynneth (d 1973), da of Frank Fishlock (d 1940); 3 da (Sally-Anne b 17 March 1964, Catherine Julia b 26 Nov 1967, Bridget Louise b 1 Nov 1970); m 2, 17 Dec 1988, (Rhona) Charmian Whitby; *Career* Rolls Royce plc: chief engr new projects and mktg dir Bristol engine div, euro dir 1974-81, dir public affrs 1981-83; independent aviation conslt 1983; AKC Univ of London 1944; CEng, FRAeS; *Recreations* music, gardening; *Style*— Guy Smith, Esq; Chinnock House, Middle Chinnock, Somerset TA18 7PN (☎ 093 588 229)

SMITH, Prof Hamilton; s of Alexander Forrest Smith, of Kilsyth, and Elsie May Annie, *née* Dinnick (d 1988); *b* 27 April 1934; *Educ* Kilsyth Acad, Univ of Glasgow (BSc, PhD); *m* 14 May 1962, Jacqueline Ann, da of Robert Brechin Spittal (d 1983), of Maybole Univ of Glasgow; *Career* Univ of Glasgow: MRC fell 1960-63, special res fell 1963-64, lectr then sr lectr in forensic med 1964-84, reader in forensic med and sci 1984-87, titular prof of forensic med and toxicology 1987-; author of several scientific papers; FRSC 1973, FRCPath 1984; *Books* Glaister's Medical Jurisprudence and Toxicology (edn 13, 1973); *Recreations* golf, gardening; *Clubs* Royal Scottish Automobile, New (St Andrews), Crail Golfing Soc; *Style*— Prof Hamilton Smith; Department of Forensic Medicine and Science, University of Glasgow, Glasgow G12 8QQ (☎ 041 339 8855, fax 041 330 4602)

SMITH, Lady Helen; *née* Pleydell-Bouverie; OBE (1946), DL (Berkshire); 5 and youngest da of 6 Earl of Radnor; *b* 2 Jan 1908; *m* 1931, Lt-Col Hon David Smith, CBE, JP (d 1976), Lord Lt of Berks 1960-74, sometime chm W H Smith & Son Hldgs, 3 s of 2 Viscount Hambleden; 4 s (Julian b 1932, m 1966 Eleanor Blyth; 1 s, 1 da; Antony b 1937, m 1962 Alison Pyper; 2 s, 2 da; Peter b 1939, m 1967 Scilla Ann Bennett; 1 s, 2 da; David b 1947, m 1970 Caroline Ardill; 1 s, 1 da), 1 da (Esther Joanna b 1934); *Style*— The Lady Helen Smith, OBE, DL; King's Copse House, Bradfield-Southend, Reading, Berks RG7 6JR (☎ 0734 744366)

SMITH, Lady Helen Dorothy; *née* Primrose; da of 6 Earl of Rosebery, KT, DSO, MC, PC, by his 1 w, Lady Dorothy Grosvenor, sis of 3 Duke of Westminster; half-sis of 7 Earl of Rosebery; *b* 1913; *m* 1933, Hon Hugh Vivian Smith (d 1978), 3 s of 1 Baron Bicester; 1 s, 1 da; *Style*— The Lady Helen Smith; The Old Rectory, Souldern, Bicester, Oxon OX6 9HU

SMITH, Hon (William) Henry Bernard; s and h of 4 Viscount Hambleden; *b* 18 Nov 1955; *m* 1983, Sara, da of Joseph Anlauf, of Palos Verdes Estates, California; *Style*— The Hon Henry Smith; 109 Eccleston Mews, London SW1X 8AQ (☎ 071 235 4785)

SMITH, Prof Henry Sidney (Harry); s of Prof Sidney Smith (d 1979), of Barcombe Sussex; *b* 14 June 1928; *Educ* Merchant Taylors', Christ's Coll Cambridge (BA, MA); *m* 18 May 1981, Hazel, da of Francis Robert Flory (d 1929); *Career* Nat Serv RCS 1946-49; lectr in Egyptology Univ of Cambridge 1959-63 (asst lectr 1954-59), pt/t prof of Egyptology UCL 1986- (reader in Egyptian archaeology 1963-70, Edwards prof of Egyptology and head of dept 1970-86); field dir of Egypt Exploration Soc Nubian Survey 1961 (Kor 1965, N Saqquara 1971-81, Memphis 1981-88); fell Christ's Coll Cambridge 1955-63; FBA Hon DLit Univ of London; *Books* A Visit to Ancient Egypt: Life at Memphis and Saqqara, The Fortress of Buhen (vol 1, 1979, vol 2 1976), Saqqara Demotic papyri (with W J Tait, 1985), The Anubieion at Saqqara (vol 1 with D G Jeffreys, 1988); *Recreations* travel, fine art; *Style*— Prof H S Smith; Ailwyn House, High Street, Upwood, Huntingdon, Cambridgeshire PE17 1QE (☎ 0487 812196); Dept of Egyptology, University College London, Gower St, London WC1E 6BT (☎ 071 387 7050 ext 2885)

SMITH, Horace Anthony; s of Osbourne Smith (d 1975), and Gertrude Mabel, *née* Reason; *b* 17 Jan 1941; *Educ* De Aston Sch Market Rasen; *m* 1, 4 June 1959 (m dis 1981), Catherine Mary, da of Flt Lt J A Tindall, DFC, of E Yorks; 2 s (David b 1960, Richard b 1962); m 2, 30 Aug 1984, Imelda, da of Jesus Paez, of Manila; 2 da (Annalisa b 1985, Emma Jade b 1987); *Career* sr exec offr Dept of Employment 1965-73, overseas dir Professional and Exec Recruitment 1973-85; md: Int Trg and Recruitment Link 1985-, Coppas International Group Ltd 1989-; dir Associated Health Care Consultants Ltd 1990-; chm Wychling CC; MRGS 1974; *Books* Guide to Working Abroad (1983, 1985, 1986, 1987, 1988); *Recreations* cricket, horseracing, bridge, oriental studies; *Clubs* Lions Int; *Style*— Horace Smith, Esq; 21 Tilton Rd, Borough Green, Kent TN15 8RS; ITRL, 51A Bryanston St, London W1H 7DN (☎ 071 706 3646, fax 071 724 3948, telex 928079 TRL G)

SMITH, Sir Howard Frank Trayton; GCMG (1981, KCMG 1976, CMG 1966); s of Frank Howard Smith (d 1975), of Brighton; *b* 15 Oct 1919; *Educ* Sidney Sussex Coll Cambridge; *m* 1, 1943, Winifred Mary (d 1982), da of Edward Cropper, of London; 1 da; m 2, 1983, Mary Penney; *Career* HM Dip Serv: Washington 1950-53, Caracas 1953-56, FO 1956-61 and 1964-68, ambass to Czechoslovakia 1968-71, dep sec Cabinet Office (secondment) 1972-75, ambass to Moscow 1976-78 (cnsllr 1961-63), ret; *Style*— Sir Howard Smith, GCMG; Coromandel, Cross in Hand, Heathfield, E Sussex TN21 0TN (☎ 043 52 4420)

SMITH, Ian Newell; s of Harry Smith (d 1985), of Ashthorn, Southbank Rd, Kenilworth, and Edith Mary, *née* Newell; *b* 27 July 1933; *Educ* Malvern; *m* 3 Oct 1964 (José) Jillian, da of Flt Lt John Foster Drake, DFC, BEM (d 1959); 1 da (Anna Louise b 9 Sept 1965); *Career* Pilot Offr RAF 1958; admitted slr 1957, ptnr Seymour Smith Box & Sharpe Coventry 1960, dir Coventry Building Society 1973- (chm 1985-87 and 1991-); tstee: Edwards Charity 1962, Coventry Nursing Tst 1972- (chm 1984-), Helen Ley House 1975-, Warwicks Boys Tst 1977-, Samuel Smiths Charity 1987-; sec: Milverton Lawn Tennis 1960-62, Leamington and Dist Round Table (chm 1967-68); Freeman City of Coventry 1960, memb Drapers Guild (Coventry) 1986, clerk Broadweavers and Clothiers Co (Coventry) 1988; memb Law Soc 1957; *Recreations* golf, sailing, skiing, choral singing, gardening; *Clubs* Drapers (Coventry); *Style*— Ian Smith, Esq; Hexworthy, Birches Lane, Kenilworth (☎ 0926 53238); Queens House, Queens Rd, Coventry (☎ 0203 553961, fax 0203 251634)

SMITH, Ian William; s of John Douglas Smith (d 1986), and Pauline June, *née* Atkins; *b* 29 Sept 1949; *Educ* High Pavement GS, Nottingham, Trent Poly; *m* 14 Feb 1970 (m dis 1982), Alyson Mary, da of Sqdn Ldr Fred Kenny (d 1965); 2 s (James b 8 June 1970, Robert b 29 July 1973); *Career* chief engr KCH 1972-77, dir Motivair Compressors Gp 1977-80, md Hepaire Manufacturing 1980-81; chm: Frenger Holdings Ltd 1989-87 (md 1981-84), The Stewart Group Ltd 1987-88, Brunswick Industs plc 1988-; FIHospE, Memb Inst of Plant Engrs; *Style*— Ian Smith, Esq; Ventura House, 72-74 Station Rd, Hayes, Middx UB3 4DP (☎ 081 848 3969, fax 081 848 8405, telex 296514)

SMITH, Ivo; s of Guy Sydney Smith (d 1972), of Market Rasen, Lincs, and Florence Maud, *née* Titmarsh (d 1981); *b* 31 May 1931; *Educ* De Aston GS Market Rasen Lincs, Jesus Coll Cambridge (MA, MChir), Saint Mary's Hosp Med Sch Univ of

London; *m* 17 Feb 1962, Janet, da of George James Twyman (d 1936), of Deal, Kent; 2 s (Robin b 1966, Simon b 1969), 1 da (Mary b 1965); *Career* Nat Serv RAF (Educn Branch) 1950-51; consult surgn, lectr and author on surgery of the breast and the breast in art; Freeman City of London 1965, Liveryman Worshipful Soc of Apothecaries 1964; FRCS; *Recreations* my family, fishing, farming; *Style—* Ivo Smith, Esq; 100 Harley St, London W1N 1AF (☎ 071 935 0721)

SMITH, Prof Ivor Ramsay; s of Howard Smith (d 1966), of Birmingham, and Elsie Emily, *née* Underhill (d 1980); *b* 8 Oct 1929; *Educ* Univ of Bristol (BSc, PhD, DSc); *m* 3 Jan 1962, Pamela Mary, da of Alfred Voake (d 1976), of Birmingham; 3 s (Laurence David b 12 May 1963, Andrew Paul b 25 June 1965, Michael Jonathan b 8 Nov 1968); *Career* design and devpt engr GEC Birmingham 1956-59, reader (also lectr and sr lectr) Univ of Birmingham 1959-74; Loughborough Univ of Technol: prof of electrical power engrg 1974-, head Dept of Electronic and Electrical Power Engrg 1980-90, dean of engrg 1983-86, pro vice chllr 1987-; dir: Loughborough Consultants Ltd 1980-, E Midlands Regnl Technol Network (Qazar 7) 1989-; CEng 1974, FIEE 1974, FEng 1988; *Recreations* gardening, walking, reading; *Style—* Prof Ivor Smith; 83 Nanpantan Rd, Loughborough, Leics LE11 3ST; Department of Electronic & Electrical Engineering, University of Technology, Loughborough, Leics LE11 3TU (☎ 0509 222821, fax 0509 222854, telex 34319)

SMITH, Jack; s of John Edward Smith (d 1984), and Laura Amanda, *née* Booth (d 1949); *b* 18 June 1928; *Educ* Netheredge GS Sheffield, Sheffield Coll of Art, St Martins Sch of Art, RCA (ARCA); *m* 23 June 1956, Susan, da of Brig Gen Hugh Marjoribanks Craigie Halkett (d 1951); *Career* Nat Serv RAF 1946-48; artist; exhibitions: Beaux Arts Gallery London 1952-58, Catherine Viviano Gallery NY 1958, 1962 and 1963, Whitechapel Gallery 1959 and 1971, Matthiesen Gallery 1960 and 1963, Grosvenor Gallery 1965, Marlborough Fine Art 1968, Fischer Fine Art 1981, 1983, Angela Flowers Gallery 1990; work shown: Venice Biennale 1956, Br Painting Madrid 1983 et al; work in permanent collections incl: Tate Gallery, Arts Cncl, Contemporary Art Soc, Br Cncl; *Style—* Jack Smith, Esq; 29 Seafield Rd, Hove, Sussex BN23 2TP (☎ 0273 738 312)

SMITH, (John Herbert) Jack; CBE (1977); s of Thomas Arthur Smith (d 1979), of Shipley, West Yorks, and Pattie, *née* Lord (d 1962); *b* 30 April 1918; *Educ* Salt HS Shipley Yorks; *m* 22 Sept 1945, Phyllis (Mary), da of Jacob Baxter (d 1949), of Bradford, Yorks; 2 s (Robert b 1946, Nigel b 1952), 3 da (Helen b 1949, Rosamond b 1953, Alison b 1956); *Career* WWII, RAMC N Africa and Italy 1940-46; dept clerk and chief fin offr Littleborough Lancs 1946-48, various posts West Midlands Gas Bd 1949-61, chief accountant Southern Gas Bd 1961-65, dep chm E Midlands Gas Bd 1968-72 (dir of fin and admin 1965-68), dep chm and chief exec Br Gas Corp 1976-83 (memb for fin 1973-76), memb Mgmnt Ctee Lazard American Exempt Fund 1976-; chm: Moracrest Investmts 1977-85, Nationalised Industs Fin Panel 1978-83; dep chm Mgmnt Ctee Pension Fund Property Unit Tst 1984-89 (memb 1975), chm United Property Unit Tst 1986-89 (memb 1983); memb: Trilateral Cmmn 1976-85, Br American Property Unit Tst 1982, Cncl ICAEW 1977-81; FCA 1939, memb IPFA 1949, CGASE 1968, FRSA 1985; *Recreations* piano playing, walking; *Clubs* Royal Automobile; *Style—* Jack Smith, Esq, CBE; 81 Albany, Manor Rd, East Cliff, Bournemouth, Dorset BH1 3EJ

SMITH, Prof (Albert) James; s of William John Smith (d 1962), of Crosskeys, Gwent, and Annie Laura, *née* Davies (d 1960); *b* 5 Nov 1924; *Educ* Univ Coll of Wales Aberystwyth, Oriel Coll Oxford, Univ of Florence; *m* 12 April 1950, Gwyneth Margaret, da of John Henry Lane, of Newbridge, Gwent; 1 s (Geraint Owain b 2 June 1958); *Career* RAFVR 1943-47; Manchester GS 1956-59, lectr and sr lectr Univ Coll of Swansea 1959-71; prof of English: Univ of Keele 1971-74, Univ of Southampton 1974-90; *Books* John Donne: The Songs and Sonnets (1964), John Donne: The Complete English Poems (ed, 1971), John Donne: Essays in Celebration (1972), John Donne: The Critical Heritage (1975), Literary Love (1983), The Metaphysics of Love (1985), Metaphysical Wit (1991); *Recreations* theatre, walking, music; *Clubs* National Liberal; *Style—* Prof James Smith; Hafod, Romsey Rd, Whiteparish, Salisbury, Wilts SP5 2SD (☎ 0794 884620); Dept of English, Univ of Southampton, Highfield, Southampton SO9 5NH (☎ 0703 595000)

SMITH, Hon Sir James Alfred; CBE (1964), TD; s of late Charles Silas Smith; *b* 1913,May; *Career* serv WWII Maj (on staff of Supreme Allied Cdr SE Asia 1944-45); RA barr Lincoln's Inn 1949; entered Colonial Legal Service Nigeria 1946, Puisne judge 1955, Northern Nigeria: High Ct judge 1955, Sr Puisne High Ct judge 1960-65; Bahamas: Supreme Ct Puisne judge 1965-75, sr justice 1975-78, chief justice 1978-80, memb Ct of Appeal 1980- (and Cts of Appeal for Bahamas and Belize 1981-); kt 1979; *Style—* The Hon Sir James Smith, CBE, TD; Court of Appeal for the Bahamas, Nassau, Bahamas

SMITH, Dr James Andrew Buchan; CBE (1959); s of James Fleming Smith, JP (d 1919), of Whithorn, Scotland, and Emma Jane Adelaide Lawrence, *née* Buchan (d 1949); *b* 26 May 1906; *Educ* Leamington Coll, Univ of Birmingham (BSc, PhD), Univ of London (DSc); *m* 29 July 1933, (Elizabeth) Marion, da of James Kerr (d 1929), of Wallasey, Cheshire; 4 da (Margaret b 1936, Sheila b 1940, Alison b 1943, d 1966, Brenda b 1947); *Career* graduate res asst: UCL 1929-30, Imperial Coll London 1930-32; lectr Univ of Liverpool 1932-36, biochemist Hannah Res Inst Ayr 1936-46, lectr Univ of Glasgow 1946-47, dir Hannah Res Inst 1951-70 (acting dir 1948-51); pres: Soc of Dairy Technol 1951-52, Nutrition Soc 1968-71; treas Int Union of Nutritional Sciences 1969-75; FRSC, FRSE; memb: Biochemical Soc, Nutrition Soc; *Recreations* gardening, walking; *Clubs* Farmers'; *Style—* Dr James Smith, CBE, FRSE; Flaxton House, 1 St Leonard's Rd, Ayr KA7 2PR (☎ 0292 264 865)

SMITH, James Boyd; GM (1943); s of James Hughes Smith (d 1950); *b* 9 Feb 1920; *Educ* George Heriot's Sch Edinburgh, Univ of Edinburgh; *m* 1946, May, *née* Campbell; 1 s (Peter), 1 da (Pamela); *Career* served WWII Capt RE; chartered electrical engr; joined Ferranti plc 1947; dir of various subsidiary cos: Ferranti Offshore Systems 1974-85, Ferranti Cetec Graphics 1977-85, TRW Ferranti Subsea 1977-85, asst gen mangr Ferranti Edinburgh 1980-83, pt/t advsr 1983-85; dir Wolfson Microelectronics Ltd 1984-; memb Ct Univ of Edinburgh 1975-84; hon fell Univ of Edinburgh 1989; FRSE; *Recreations* organ playing, orchid growing, gardening; *Clubs* New (Edinburgh); *Style—* James Smith, Esq, GM, FRSE; 28 Murrayfield Road, Edinburgh EH12 6ER (☎ 031 346 8604)

SMITH, Dr James Cadzow; CBE; s of James Smith (d 1954), of Edinburgh, and Margaret Ann, *née* Cadzow (d 1982); *b* 28 Nov 1927; *Educ* Belle Vue Sch Edinburgh, Heriot-Watt Univ, Univ of Strathclyde (scholarship, post graduate dip nuclear engrg); *m* 1954, Moira Barrie, da of Joseph Watt Hogg; 1 s (Norman Barrie b 1955), 1 da (Elaine Margaret b 1958); *Career* NI Electricity Serv 1973-77 (dir of Engrg, dep chm and chief exec), chm E Midlands Electricity Bd 1977-82, chm Eastern Electricity Bd 1982-90, chm and chief exec Eastern Electricity plc; memb: Cncl of Indust Soc, Bd of Mgmnt Royal Greenwich Hosp Sch Holbrook, Bd of Tstees ATV Telethon; past chm BNCE, vice pres Int Union for Electro-heat 1985-88, visiting prof of electrical engrg Univ of Strathclyde (memb Advsy Panel on Info Tech); memb Worshipful Co of Engrs, Freeman City of London; Hon LLD Univ of Strathclyde; FIEE 1960 (pres 1989-90), fell Inst of Mechanical and Marine Engrs 1960, FRSE 1981, FEng 1984; *Recreations* mountaineering, skiing, music, theatre; *Clubs* Caledonian, Alpine; *Style—* Dr James Smith, CBE, FRSE; Eastern Electricity plc, Wherstead Park, PO Box 40, Wherstead, Ipswich, Suffolk 1P9 2AQ (☎ 0473 690596, fax 0473 680541, car 0836 206437)

SMITH, James Michael (Jim); s of James Smith (d 1965), of Sheffield, and Doris, *née* Rawson; *b* 17 Oct 1940; *Educ* Firth Park GS; *m* 29 July 1961, Yvonne, da of Richard Hammond; 3 da (Alison Jane b 11 Jan 1963, Suzanne Elizabeth b 5 July 1965, Fiona Yvonne b 25 Jan 1968); *Career* professional football mangr; former player: Sheffield Utd (no first team appearances), Aldershot (league debut 1961), Halifax Town, Lincoln City, Boston Utd, Colchester Utd; mangr: Boston Utd, Colchester Utd, Blackburn Rovers 1975-78, Birmingham City 1978-82, Oxford Utd 1982-85, Queens Park Rangers 1985-88, Newcastle Utd 1988-; honours as mangr: Eastern Floodlight League Boston Utd, promotion to Div 3 Colchester Utd 1974, promotion to Div 1 Birmingham City 1980, Div 3 Championship Oxford Utd 1984, Div 2 Championship Oxford Utd 1985, runners up League Cup Queens Park Rangers 1986; Bells Mangr of the Month award 15 times; *Books* Bald Eagle (1990); *Recreations* golfing, gardening; *Style—* Jim Smith, Esq; Newcastle United Football Club, St James Park, Newcastle Upon Tyne (☎ 091 232 8361)

SMITH, Jan Eileen; da of Harold Douglas Smith, of Morecambe, and Lena, *née* Barrett; *b* 5 April 1947; *Educ* Convent Sch Lusaka Zambia, Casterton Sch Kirkby Lonsdale Cumbria, Carlisle & County HS Carlisle Cumbria, Univ Coll of Rhodesia Salisbury Rhodesia (BA of Univ of London); *m* 28 April 1973, Ian Dudley Brawn, s of late John Dudley Brawn; *Career* Commercial Bank Zambia Ltd Lusaka Zambia 1965-66; Int Div Midland Bank plc London: graduate trainee 1970-72, area rep trade devpt 1972-76, asst mktg mangr Corp Devpt Area 1978-79; TSB England & Wales plc/TSB Group London: mangr product devpt Mktg Div 1983-86 (asst mangr 1980-83), mangr market devpt Mktg Div 1986; sr mangr market planning and devpt Mktg Dept Lloyds Bank plc London 1986-89, mktg dir Mktg/Business Devpt Div First Direct-Midland Group plc London 1989-90, dir network mktg TSB Bank plc 1990; product excellence award The Mktg Soc 1989; *Recreations* motor racing, Jaguar cars, reading, ballet, swimming; *Clubs* Local Hist Soc, Jaguar Drivers (Concours d'elegance 1978, 1979); *Style—* Miss Jan E Smith; TSB Bank plc, 60 Lombard St, London EC3 (☎ 071 623 6000 ext 5100, (office) 0860 641 960, 0836 232 834)

SMITH, Jane Caroline; da of Gordon John Smith, of Bickley, Kent, and Brenda Mary, *née* Hardy; *b* 5 April 1969; *Educ* Ravensbourne Sch for Girls; *Career* hockey player; Sevenoaks Hockey Club 1985-90, Chelmsford Ladies Hockey Club 1990-; England: capt under 18 outdoor 1985-87, under 21 outdoor 1988-90, sr outdoor 1990, sr indoor 1989-90; competed in Jr World Cup Ottawa 1989; bank clerk National Westminster Bank plc; *Recreations* all sports, dog showing, music; *Style—* Ms Jane Smith; 208 Southlands Rd, Bickley, Kent BR2 9RD (☎ 081 290 1573)

SMITH, Mrs Janet Hilary (Mrs R E A Mathieson); QC (1986); da of Alexander Roe Holt (d 1970), and Margaret Holt, *née* Birchall; *b* 29 Nov 1940; *Educ* Bolton Sch; *m* 1, 6 June 1959 (m dis 1982), J S (Edward) Stuart Smith, s of Edward Austin Carruthers Smith (d 1990); 2 s (Richard b 1959, Alasdair b 1963), 1 da (Rachel b 1962); m 2, 12 Oct 1984, Robin Edward Alexander Mathieson, s of Alexander John Mathieson, MC (d 1974), of Yoxall, Staffs; *Career* called to the Bar Lincoln's Inn 1972, rec Crown Ct 1988, memb Criminal Injuries Compensation Bd 1988; *Style—* Mrs J Smith, QC; 5 Essex Ct, Temple, London (☎ 071 353 4363, fax 071 583 1491); 25 Byrom St, Manchester (☎ 061 834 5238, fax 061 834 0394)

SMITH, Jennifer Evelyn; da of David Smith (d 1988), of Glasgow, and Doris Evelyn, *née* McMeekin; *b* 28 Sept 1961; *Educ* Fernhill Sch Letchworth Hertfordshire, Hertfordshire Coll of Art and Design St Alban's Herts (fndn course), Edinburgh Coll of Art (BA), Heriot Watt Univ (Andrew Grant scholar); *Career* graphic designer Ash Gupta Communications 1985-87, graphic designer then sr graphic designer Graphic Partners 1987-90, sr graphic designer Tayburn Design Ltd 1990-91, design dir The Foundry Creative Consultants Ltd 1991-; awards: Bronze Nat Graphic award 1988, CLIO finalist 1989, Roses commendation 1989; *Recreations* chess, gardening, hillwalking, jogging; *Style—* Ms Jennifer Smith; 2 Malta Terrace, Stockbridge, Edinburgh EH4 1HR; The Foundry Creative Consultants Ltd, 10 Commercial St, Leith, Edinburgh EH6 1BC (☎ 031 555 2882)

SMITH, Jeremy Fox Eric; DL; s of Capt Evan Cadogan Eric Smith, MC (d 1950), and Beatrice Helen , *née* Williams (d 1988); *b* 17 Nov 1928; *Educ* Eton, New Coll Oxford; *m* 1953, Julia Mary Rona, yr da of Sir Walter Burrell, 8 Bt, CBE, TD, DL (d 1985); 2 s (Julian b 1956, Hugo b 1957), 2 da (Dione (Countess of Verulam) b 1954, Sarah (Mrs Ashley Preston) b 1962); *Career* 2 Lt 9 QR Lancers; dir: Transparent Paper Ltd 1958-76 and 1980-83 (chm 1965-76), BARD Discount House Ltd 1959-86, Discount House of S Africa Ltd 1961-86, Tech Devpt Capital Ltd 1962-66, Ship Mortgage Fin Co 1963-78; chm Smith St Aubyn & Co Ltd 1973-86 (joined 1951, dir 1955); chm London Discount Market Assoc 1978-80 (dep chm 1976-78), tstee Henry Smith's Charity 1971-; *Recreations* hunting, shooting, stalking, skiing; *Clubs* Cavalry and Guards', Beefsteak, Leander; *Style—* Jeremy Smith, Esq, DL; Balcombe House, Balcombe, Sussex RH17 6PB (☎ 0444 811267); Flat 11 Tarnbrook Court, 9 Holbein Place SW1

SMITH, Joan Alison; da of Alan Smith (d 1985), and Ann Anita, *née* Coltman; *b* 27 Aug 1953; *Educ* Girls GS Stevenage, HS for Girls Basingstoke, Univ of Reading (BA); *partner*, 1984-, Francis Wheen, *qv*; *Career* journalist: Evening Gazette Blackpool 1976-78, Piccadilly Radio Manchester 1978-79, Sunday Times 1979-84; freelance writer 1984-; *Books* Clouds of Deceit (1985), A Masculine Ending (1987), Why Aren't They Screaming? (1988), Misogynies (1989), Don't Leave Me This Way (1990); *Recreations* photography, collecting antique clothes, travel; *Clubs* Academy; *Style—* Ms Joan Smith; A P Watt, 20 John St, London WC1N 2DR (☎ 071 405 6774, fax 071 831 2154)

SMITH, Rt Hon John; PC (1978), QC (Scot, 1983), MP (Lab) Monklands E 1983-; s of late Archibald Leitch Smith, of Dunoon, Argyll; *b* 13 Sept 1938; *Educ* Dunoon GS, Univ of Glasgow (MA, LLB); *m* 1967, Elizabeth Margaret, da of late Frederick William Moncrieff Bennett; 3 da; *Career* advocate 1967, MP (Lab) N Lanarkshire 1970-1983, Parly under sec of state Energy 1974-75, min of state Energy 1975-76, min of state Privy Cncl Office 1976-78, sec of state for Trade 1978-79; memb Shadow Cabinet and oppn front bench spokesman on: Trade, Prices and Consumer Protection 1979-82, Energy 1982-83, Employment 1983-84, Trade and Indust 1984-87, Treasy and Econ Affrs 1987-; *Recreations* opera, hill walking; *Style—* The Rt Hon John Smith, QC, MP; 21 Cluny Dr, Edinburgh EH10 6DW (☎ 031 447 3667)

SMITH, John Alfred; QPM (1986); s of Alfred Joseph Smith (d 1988), of Clacton, Essex, and Ruth Alice, *née* Thorpe; *b* 21 Sept 1938; *Educ* St Olave's and St Saviour's GS London SE, Police Staff Coll; *m* 28 May 1960, Joan Maria, da of James Noel Francis (d 1979); 1 s (Martin John b 1965), 1 da (Amanda Jayne (Mrs Hale) b 1962); *Career* joined Met Police 1962, foot beat duty Carter St 1962-66, special course Staff Coll 1966, Inspr Bow St and West End Central Stations 1968-73, Obscene Pubns Branch New Scotland Yard 1973-76, Lewisham Div 1976-77, head Central Drugs Squad 1977-79 (sr cmd course 1978), Cdr 1981, P Dist Bromley and Lewisham Police 1980-81, Dep Chief Constable Surrey Constabulary 1981-84, Met Police 1984-90, head Force Reorganisation Team and Force Inspectorate 1985-87, Asst Cmmr Mgmnt

Support Dept 1987-89, Asst Cmmr Specialist Ops Dept 1989-90; vice pres: Surrey Assoc of Youth Clubs, Surrey PHAB; Freeman City of London 1981; memb Assoc of Chief Police Offrs 1981; *Recreations* occasional golf, horse riding, gardening; *Clubs* Crystal Palace FC; *Style*— Her Majesty's Inspector of Constabulary; White Rose Court, Oriental Rd, Woking, Surrey GU22 7LG (☎ 0483 729337)

SMITH, John Allan Raymond; s of Alexander MacIntyre Smith (d 1979), of Edinburgh, and Evelyn Joyce, *née* Duthie (d 1988); *b* 24 Nov 1942; *Educ* Boroughmuir Sch Edinburgh, Univ of Edinburgh (MB, ChB), Univ of Aberdeen (PhD); 2 s (Richard b 1967, Michael b 1968), 3 da (Jane b 1966, Sheri b 1970, Sara b 1975); m 18 April 1979, Valerie, da of James Fullalove (d 1988), of Eaglecliffe; *Career* house offr Royal Infirmary Edinburgh 1966-67, dept of surgery Univ of Aberdeen 1974-76, sr surgical registrar Aberdeen Teaching Hosp 1976-78, sr lectr in surgery Univ of Sheffield and hon conslt surgn Royal Hallamshire Hosp 1978-85, conslt surgn Northern Gen Hosp Sheffield 1985-; contrib of numerous chapters in textbooks; memb Specialist Advsy Ctee in Gen Surgery, ed bd of Clinical Nutrition, Alimentary Pharmacology and Therapeutics; FRCS and FRSCEd 1972; *Style*— John Smith, Esq; 4 Endcliffe Grove Ave, Sheffield S10 3EJ (☎ 0742 683094); Northern General Hospital, Herries Rd, Sheffield S5 7AU (☎ 0742 434343)

SMITH, Dr John Derek; s of Richard Ernest Smith (d 1933), of Mayfield, Wetherby, Yorks, and Winifred Strickland, *née* Davis (d 1932); *b* 8 Dec 1924; *Educ* King James' GS Knaresborough, Clare Coll Cambridge (MA, PhD); *Career* scientific staff ARC Virus Res Unit Cambridge 1945-59, res fell Clare Coll Cambridge 1949-52, visiting scientist Inst Pasteur Paris 1952-53, Rockefeller Fndn fell Univ of California Berkeley 1955-57, sr res fell California Inst of Technol 1959-62, memb scientific staff MRC Laboratory of Molecular Biology Cambridge 1962-88, ret; Sherman Fairchild Distinguished Scholar California Inst of Technol 1974-75; FRS 1976; *Recreations* travel, cuisine; *Style*— Dr John Smith, FRS; 12 Stansgate Avenue, Cambridge CB2 2QZ (☎ 0223 247 841)

SMITH, (Edward Ernest) John; s of Ernest Frederick Smith, DCM, of Chiswick, London, and Elizabeth, *née* Reilly; *b* 13 Aug 1950; *Educ* Latymer Upper Sch London, Emmanuel Coll Cambridge (MA, MB BChir), St Thomas's Hosp Med Sch; *m* 23 April 1984, Muriel Susan, da of Daniel Shannon, of Ayr; 1 s (David b 1989), 2 da (Susan b 1985, Katherine b 1987); *Career* conslt cardiothoracic surgn St George's Hosp London and Royal Surrey Co Hosp Guildford; memb BMA 1974; FRCS 1978; *Recreations* opera, skiing; *Clubs* London Rowing; *Style*— John Smith, Esq; Homewood, 4A Drax Avenue, Wimbledon SW20 0EU (☎ 081 946 1893); 69 Harley St, London W1N 1DE (☎ 071 486 2090)

SMITH, John Ernest; s of Ernest Theodore Smith of Chigwell, and Sybil Margaret, *née* Jones; *b* 30 March 1949; *Educ* Chigwell Sch; *m* 2 Sep 1971, Jill Kathleen, da of Leonard Victor George Dennis, of Wanstead, London; 1 s (Richard b 1979), 1 da (Sarah); *Career* qualified CA 1971; regnl managing ptnr: Arthur Young 1986-89, Ernst and Young 1989-90 (nat dir Business Servs 1982-85, ptnr 1978-89); dir Security Design Associates Ltd 1990-; pres CA Students Soc London 1983-85, chm London Soc CA 1986-87, memb Cncl ICAEW 1987- (chm Res Bd 1988-90, chm Ethics Ctee 1989-90), Agric Trg Bd 1989-; ind memb Agric Wages Bd Eng and Wales 1987-89; FCA 1971; *Recreations* golf, cricket, football, food and drink; *Clubs* MCC, Wig and Pen; *Style*— John E Smith, Esq; 10 Bearswood End, Beaconsfield, Bucks HP9 2NR (☎ 0494 671275); Security Design Associates Ltd, Axis 7, Rhodes Way, Radlett Rd, Watford, Herts (☎ 0923 211550, fax 0923 211 590, telex 337904 AYBI)

SMITH, Prof John Harold; s of Reginald William Smith (d 1967), of Hythe, Kent, and Cicely Doreen, *née* Page (d 1984); *b* 21 April 1927; *Educ* Harvey GS Folkestone, LSE (BA); *m* 13 Jan 1951, Jean, da of Henry John Horton, BEM (d 1973), of Hythe, Kent; 2 s (Christopher b 1953, Nigel b 1954), 1 da (Rachel b 1964); *Career* RNVR 1944-48; res worker Acton Soc Tst 1950-52, lectr LSE 1952-64, curator and chm Hartley Library Univ of Southampton 1983-87 (prof of sociology 1964-, dean of Faculty of Social Scis 1967-70, dep vice-chllr 1974-78); contrib to numerous articles in scientific jls; memb: Cncl CNAA 1967, Educn Ctee King's Fund 1970-76, Cncl Central Cncl for Educn and Trg in Social Work 1971-78, DHSS Small Grants Ctee 1975-79, Mgmnt Cncl Southern Arts Assoc 1978-, Advsy Ctee Open Univ 1986-, Min for the Arts Advsy Ctee on the Arts and Heritage 1990-, Br Sociological Assoc 1952-; govr King Alfred's Coll Winchester 1976-89; FRSA 1978-; *Books* Management under Nationalization (1954), Industrial Sociology (1961), Married Women Working (1963), Manpower Policy and Employment Trends (1967), Select List of British Parliamentary Papers (1979); *Recreations* walking, photography; *Style*— Prof John Smith; Gable End, Timsbury Manor, Romsey, Hants SO51 0NE (☎ 0794 68730); Dept of Sociology and Social Policy, Univ of Southampton, Southampton SO9 5NH (☎ 0703 592636, fax 0703 593938, telex 47661)

SMITH, Sir John Lindsay Eric; CBE (1975), JP (1964, Berks), DL (1978); s of Capt E C E Smith, MC, of Ashfold, Handcross, Sussex; *b* 3 April 1923; *Educ* Eton, New Coll Oxford; *m* 1952, Christian, da of late Col Ughtred Elliott Carnegy, DSO, MC and bar, of Lour, Forfar, Angus; 2 s, 2 da (and 1 da decd 1983); *Career* served RNVR 1942-46; dir: Coutts & Co 1950-, Rolls Royce 1955-75, Financial Times 1959-68, Fleming American Tst plc, Greycoat Gp plc London, Gen Ctee Ottoman Bank; chm: Cumulus Systems Ltd, Manifold Tstee Co Ltd (and fndr); dep govr Royal Exchange Assurance 1961-66; MP (C) Cities of London and Westminster 1965-70; High Steward Maidenhead 1966-75; memb: Historic Buildings Cncl 1971-78, Redundant Churches Fund 1972-74, Nat Heritage Memorial Fund 1980-82; Lord-Lt Berks 1975-78, dep chm Nat Tst 1980-85 (memb Exec Ctee 1961-85); fell Eton 1974-89; hon fell New Coll Oxford 1979; Hon FRIBA; KStJ; kt 1988; *Style*— Sir John Smith, CBE, JP, DL; Shottesbrooke Park, Maidenhead, Berks; 21 Dean's Yard, Westminster, London SW1P 3PA (☎ 071 222 6581)

SMITH, John Patrick; s of Col Neville Frederick Smith (d 1979); *b* 25 Aug 1932; *Educ* St Edward's Sch, Brasenose Coll Oxford; *m* 1961, Ann Felicity, *née* Hawker; 2 s, 1 da; *Career* actuary; chief investmt mangr Equity and Law Life Assur Soc Ltd 1977- (dir 1984-); *Recreations* golf; *Clubs* Dale Hill Golf; *Style*— John Smith, Esq; Hadlow Lodge, Burgh Hill, Etchingham, Sussex (☎ 058 025 270)

SMITH, Sir John Wilson; CBE, JP, DL; s of Robert Henry Smith, JP (d 1956), and Edith, *née* Wilson; *b* 6 Nov 1920; *Educ* Oulton HS Liverpool; *m* 22 Nov 1946, Doris Mabel, da of Percy Albert Parfitt; 1 s (Colin Parfitt b 25 May 1951); *Career* serv WWII RAF 1940-46; chm Sports Cncl 1985-89; chm: Liverpool Football Club 1973-, BLESMA Merseyside 1975-80, Min's Enquiry into Lawn Tennis 1977-80, Appeals Ctee SSAFA 1980-86; Hon LLD; kt 1990; *Recreations* association football, golf; *Clubs* Reform; *Style*— Sir John Smith, CBE, JP, DL; Pine Close, Mill Lane, Gayton, Wirral, Merseyside (☎ 051 342 5362); Brunswick Business Park, 212 Tower St, Liverpool L3 4BS (☎ 051 709 3949, fax 051 709 3824)

SMITH, Dr Joseph William Grenville; s of Douglas Ralph Smith (d 1987), of Cardiff and Hannah Leticia Margaret, *née* Leonard (d 1968); *b* 14 Nov 1930; *Educ* Cathays HS for Boys Cardiff, Welsh Nat Sch of Med (MB BCh), Univ of London, Univ of Wales (MD); *m* 3 Aug 1954, Nira Jean, da of Oliver Davies (d 1964), of Burry Port Carms; 1 s (Jonathan b 1955); *Career* Nat Serv RAF 1954-56, Flying Offr Med Branch (later Flt Lt), MO RAF SYLT, 2 TAF BAOR; lectr (later sr lectr) bacteriology and immunology London Sch of Hygiene and Tropical Medicine 1960-65, conslt clinical bacteriologist Radcliffe Infirmary Oxford 1965-69, head of bacteriology Wellcome Res Laboratories 1969, princ in gen practice Islington 1970-71, dep dir epidemiological res lab Public Health Laboratory Serv 1971-76; dir: Nat Inst for Biological Standards and Control 1976-85, Public Health Laboratory Serv of England and Wales 1985-; memb Cncl RC Path 1988, memb MRC 1988; FRCPath 1975, FFCM 1976, FRCP 1987; *Books* Tetanus (jtly, 1969); *Style*— Dr Joseph Smith; Public Health Laboratory Service Board, 61 Colindale Ave, London NW9 (☎ 081 200 1295, fax 081 200 8130)

SMITH, Karl Wingett; s of Ernest Walter Smith (d 1979), of Wheathampstead, Herts, and Muriel Mary Wingett; *b* 16 Dec 1932; *Educ* Pontypridd Intermediate Sch S Wales, John Ruskin GS Croydon, Battersea Coll of Technol Univ of London; *m* 17 Sept 1962, Patricia Grace Smith (Pat), da of James David Franklin, of Plympton, Plymouth, Devon; 6 s (Andrew b 1965, Ian b 1969, Gavin b 1972, Neil b 1974, Alastair b 1975, Duncan b 1977); *Career* aircraft fluid systems design engr Handley Page Ltd 1952-60, design and devpt engr Hawker Aircraft Ltd 1960-62, liaison engr and asst tech sales mangr Teddington Aircraft Controls Ltd 1962-68, project mgmnt and tech sales Hawker Siddeley Dynamics Ltd 1968-72, airliner sales exec Hawker Siddeley Aviation Ltd 1974-75, aviation conslt 1975-78; lectr: RAF Halton 1978-82, RAF Coll Cranwell 1982-; research into and design of breathing apparatus (for aircraft passengers and others) and into fire resistance and breakdown emissions of composite materials; patents pending: Safebeek (safe breathing equipment of every kind), centrifugal pre-filter means of air cleaning; cncllr Wheathampstead Herts 1972-75; former Scout asst dist cmmr: S Croydon, Abergavenny; dist cmmr Sleaford 1985-87; CEng 1973, MRAes; *Recreations* aviation (private pilot); *Style*— Karl Smith, Esq; Heckington House, Heckington, Lincs NG34 9JD (☎ 0529 60502)

SMITH, Kate; da of Reginald Ernest Bayston, of Co Durham, and Mabel, *née* Jackson; *b* 8 May 1951; *Educ* Orpington Co Secdy Sch Kent, Wilby Carr HS Doncaster Yorkshire, Doncaster Coll of Technol, Univ of Leeds (BA), Wine & Spirit Educn Tst (higher cert in wines & spirits, instructors cert in wines & spirits Dip pt A&B); *m* 14 Oct 1973, Richard Francis Smith, s of late William Henry Bernard Smith; 1 s (Giles Edward b 25 April 1983); *Career* asst mangr restaurant and banqueting div Trust House Forte London 1974-75, lectr in food and beverages North Devon Coll 1976-77; Royal Garden Hotel London: project mangr Garden Cafe 1978, acting banqueting mangr 1978-80, promotions mangr 1980; sales and mktg dir Hyatt Carlton Tower London 1982, conslt Rank Hotels Ltd 1982-84, dir Smith Giddings Ltd (parent co of The Royal Oak Yattendon Berkshire and The Beetle & Wedge Hotel Moulsford-on-Thames Oxon); winner: Pub of the Year award The Royal Oak, Badoit Restaurant of the Year award Beetle & Wedge 1991; Master Innholder, memb Academie Culinaire de France; *Recreations* skiing, theatre, interior design, wine and food; *Style*— Mrs Kate Smith; The Beetle & Wedge Hotel, Moulsford-on-Thames, Oxford OX10 9JF (☎ 0491 651381, fax 0491 651376)

SMITH, Kay Edwina; da of George Edward Smith, and Myra Mae, *née* MacPhee; *b* 9 Oct 1958; *Educ* Church HS Newcastle, Newcastle upon Tyne Poly (BA); *m* 23 April 1987, John Slater, s of John Clifford Slater; *Career* Tayburn: joined 1980, dir 1985, design dir 1986-; work incl: Scottish Enterprise Corporate ID, Scottish Electricity Privatisation; lectr and course advsr Newcastle Coll of Art; *Awards* annual report prizes for Goldbergs and Grampian Holdings 1988 and 1990, Design Week Re-cycled Paper award 1990, Conservation Paper award 1990; *Recreations* riding, racehorses; *Style*— Ms Kay Smith; Tayburn, 15 Kittleyards, Causewayside, Edinburgh (☎ 031 662 0662, fax 031 662 0606)

SMITH, Prof Keith; s of Joseph Smith (d 1972), and Catherine Maria, *née* Carr (d 1985); *b* 9 Jan 1938; *Educ* Hyde County GS Cheshire, Univ of Hull (BA, PhD); *m* 29 July 1961, Muriel Doris, da of George Hyde (d 1988); 1 s (Matthew b 1968), 1 da (Fiona b 1966); *Career* tutor in geography Univ of Liverpool 1963-65, lectr in geography Univ of Durham 1965-70, prof of geography Univ of Strathclyde 1982-86 (sr lectr 1971-75, reader 1975-82), prof of environmental sci Univ of Stirling 1986-; FRSE 1988; *Books* Water in Britain (1972), Principles of Applied Climatology (1975), Human Adjustment to The Flood Hazard (1979); *Recreations* gardening, hill-walking; *Style*— Prof Keith Smith, FRSE; 11 Grinnan Rd, Braco, By Dunblane, Perthshire, Scotland FK15 9RF (☎ 0786 88359); Dept of Environmental Science, University of Stirling, Stirling, Scotland FK9 4LA (☎ 0786 73171, fax 0786 67843, telex 777557)

SMITH, Kenneth David; s of Percival Smith (d 1985), and Doris Lillian, *née* Townsend; *b* 27 Feb 1944; *Educ* Beckenham Tech Sch, Beckenham Art Sch, S E London Tech Coll; *m* 28 Aug 1964, Pamela Jean Smith; 1 s (Ivan David b 26 Feb 1969), 2 da (Julia Hazel b 4 Dec 1966, Michelle Christine b 18 Aug 1970); *Career* designer; Elsom Pack Roberts (chartered architects, and town planners) 1978-86, ptnr EPR Design Partnership 1985-89, md EPR Design Ltd 1988, Freeman: City of London 1981, Worshipful Co of Paviors (ctee memb 1988-); FCSD; *Recreations* art, theatre, music; *Clubs* Travellers'; *Style*— Kenneth Smith, Esq; Hartfield Cottage, 91 Harvest Bank Rd, West Wickham, Kent; 90 Meddon St, Bideford, North Devon, (☎ 081 462 1797); EPR Design Ltd, 56-62 Wilton Rd, London SW1V 1DE (☎ 081 834 2299, fax 081 834 7524, telex 917940 PRLON G)

SMITH, Lance, né Tchisic; s of Dragan Tchisic, of Yugoslavia, and Lilian May, *née* Smith (d 1990); *b* 8 Oct 1950; *Educ* Reed's Sch Cobham Surrey, Camberwell Sch of Arts and Crafts London, Royal Academy Schools London; *m* 1987, Putrisha, da of Soloman Fintan Lawlor (d 1975); *Career* artist; solo exhibitions Painting and Drawings (Fabian Carlsson Gallery London and Arnolfini Gallery Bristol, illustrated catalogue) 1986, Forum Int Kunstmesse Zurich 1987, Paintings and Drawings 1984-88 (Turnpike Gallery Leigh Gtr Manchester, South Hill Park Arts Centre Bracknell, The Minories Colchester, The Arts Cncl Gallery Belfast and Hendriks Gallery Dublin, illustrated catalogue) 1988, Fabian Carlsson Gallery (London) 1989, Blasón Gallery (London, illustrated catalogue) 1990; Group exhibitions incl: Nat Open Art Exhibition TSWA (Newlyn and Penwith Galleries, Cornwall and nat tour, illustrated catalogue) 1984, Second Int Contemporary Art Fair (London) 1985, Tolly Cobbold/ Eastern Arts Fifth Nat Exhibition (Fitzwilliam Museum, Cambridge and tour, illustrated catalogue) 1985, Contemporary Art Fair (Galleri Mustad Stockholm) 1986, Fabian Carlsson Gallery (London) 1986, New Year - New York (Fabian Carlsson Gallery London) 1987, The Romantic Tradition in Contemporary British Painting (Sala de Exposiciones Comunidad, Autónoma de la Region de Murcia, Circulo de Bellas Artes Madrid and Ikon Gallery Birmingham, illustrated catalogue) 1988, Landscape and Beyond (Cleveland Gallery Middlesbrough) 1988, Salama-Caro Gallery (London) 1988, Second Int Festival of Art (Baghdad) 1988, The Drawing Show (Thumb Gallery London) 1988 and 1990, Reflexions Abstraites (Galerie Faris Paris) 1989, Galeri B & W (St Galen Switzerland) 1990; work in public collections incl Fitzwilliam Museum Cambridge; work in private collections throughout Eng, Denmark, France, Ireland, Monaco, NZ, Spain, Sweden, Switzerland and USA, *Awards* Arts Cncl of GB award 1980; first prize: Tolly Cobbold/ Eastern Arts Fifth Nat Exhibition 1985, Second Int Festival of Art Baghdad 1988; *Style*— Lance Smith, Esq; 17 Reardon House, Reardon St, London E1 9QJ (☎ 071 481 4508); Carysfort Rd Studios, 53b Carysfort Rd, London N16 9AD (☎ 071 923 3346); c/o Iwan Wirth and Ursula Hauser, Felsegg 60, 9247 Henau, Switzerland

SMITH, Lawrence George Albert; s of Lawrence Cyril Smith (d 1966), of 150 St

John's Ave, Kidderminster, Worcs, and Ida Mildred Smith, *née* Moule (d 1970); *b* 17 Dec 1930; *Educ* King Charles I Sch Kidderminster, Univ of Birmingham (LLB); *m* 12 Nov 1955, Tess, da of Bertram Bishop (d 1957), of Worcs; 3 da (Sally b 1960, Rachel b 1963, Rebecca b 1968); *Career* Nat Serv Lt S Staffs Regt BAOR 1955; admitted slr 1954; ptnr Thursfields 1964-, NP 1977-, clerk Clare Witnell & Blount Charity 1973-91; dep chm Kidderminster Cons Assoc 1971-73, pres Kidderminster and Dist C of C 1984-86; *Recreations* rugby football, sailing, politics; *Style—* Lawrence Smith, Esq; Bracton House, 5 Westville Ave, Kidderminster, Worcs DY11 6BZ (☎ 0562 824806); Thursfields, 14 Church St, Kidderminster (☎ 0562 820575, fax 0562 66783, telex 337837)

SMITH, Sir Leslie Edward George; *b* 15 April 1919; *Educ* Christ's Hosp; *m* 1, 1943, Lorna Pickworth; 2 da; m 2, 1964, Cynthia Holmes; 1 s, 1 da; *Career* chm The BOC Group 1979- (chm and chief exec 1972-79, gp md 1969-72, joined 1956), dir Cadbury Schweppes 1977-; memb: Exec Ctee King Edward VII Hosp for Offrs 1978-, NEB 1979; part-time memb British Gas Corpn 1982-; FCA; kt 1977; *Style—* Sir Leslie Smith; Cookley House, Cookley Green, Swyncombe, Henley-on-Thames, Oxon (☎ 0491 641258); The BOC Group, Hammersmith House, London W6 9DX (☎ 081 748 2020)

SMITH, Hon Mrs (Lois Jean); da of Baron Pearson, CBE, PC (Life Peer) (d 1980); *b* 1938; *m* 1961, Rt Rev Robin Jonathan Norman Smith, Suffragan Bishop of Hertford; *Style—* The Hon Mrs Smith; Hertford House, Abbey Mill Lane, St Albans, Herts AL3 4HE

SMITH, Dame Margot; DBE (1974); da of Leonard Graham-Brown, MC (d 1950); *b* 5 Sept 1918; *Educ* Hilders Hindhead, Westonbirt Glos; *m* 1947, Roy Smith, MC, TD (d 1983); 2 s, 1 da; *Career* chm: Yorks Cons Women's Ctee 1963-66, Nat Cons Women's Ctee 1969-72, Nat Assoc of Cons & Unionist Assocs 1973-74; memb NSPCC Central Exec Ctee 1969-85; *Recreations* foxhunting, riding, gardening; *Style—* Dame Margot Smith, DBE; Howden Lodge, Spennithorne, Leyburn, N Yorks (☎ 0969 23621)

SMITH, Marisa; da of Robert Nish, of Macclesfield, Cheshire, and Eleanor Mary, *née* Laidlaw (d 1978); *b* 22 Feb 1954; *Educ* Christ's Hosp Lincoln, Macclesfield HS for Girls, Univ of Exeter (BA); *m* 1, 3 Feb 1979 (m dis 1986), Mark Stephen Horsley Heseltine; m 2, 13 Dec 1989, William Victor John Smith; *Career* called to the Bar Middle Temple 1981; practised western circuit 1982, Albion Chambers Bristol 1983-87, Crown Prosecution Serv Portsmouth 1987-88, Stanbrooke & Hooper Brussels 1988-; memb: RNW, Nat Tst, RSPB, Woodland Tst, Action Aid Oxfam; memb Family Law Bar Assoc 1984; *Recreations* sailing, music, reading, country life; *Style—* Mrs Marisa Smith; 5 Paper Buildings, Temple, London EC4Y 7HB (☎ 071 583 6117, fax 071 353 0075, telex 895631)

SMITH, Mark Aynsley; s of Frank Sidney Smith (d 1987), and Sheila Gertrude, *née* Cowin (d 1987); *b* 24 May 1939; *Educ* KCS Wimbledon; *m* 10 Oct 1964, Carol Ann, da of Harold Jones (d 1983); 1 s (Jeremy b 1973), 1 da (Melissa b 1975); *Career* CA, Peat Marwick Mitchell & Co London 1958-66, S G Warburg & Co Ltd 1966- (dir 1971, dep head of Corp Fin Div 1986); govr Milbourne Lodge Jr Sch Esher Surrey; ACA 1971, FCA 1976; *Recreations* tennis, walking, collecting; *Style—* Mark Smith, Esq; S G Warburg & Co Ltd, 2 Finsbury Avenue, London EC2M 2PA (☎ 071 860 1090, fax 071 860 0901, telex 920301)

SMITH, Mark Barnet; s of David Smith (d 1933), by his w, Sophie Abrahams (d 1960); *b* 11 Feb 1917; *Educ* Manchester GS, Sidney Sussex Coll Cambridge; *m* 1943, Edith Winifred, *née* Harrison; 2 da; *Career* serv WWII RA 1940-46, asst examiner HM Patent Off 1939, promoted to examiner 1944; barr Middle Temple 1948, temp rec of Folkestone 1971, rec 1972, circuit judge 1972-87; *Recreations* gardening, spectator sports; *Style—* His Hon Mark Smith; 6 Pump Court, Temple, London EC4

SMITH, Martin Gregory; s of Archibald Gregory Smith, OBE (d 1981), of St Albans, and Mary Eleanor Smith (d 1975); *Educ* St Albans Sch, St Edmund Hall Oxford (BA, MA), Stanford (MBA, AM); *m* 2 Oct 1971, Elise Becket, da of late George Campbell Becket, of Lakeville, Conn, USA; 1 s (Jeremy b 28 Jan 1974), 1 da (Katie b 5 Aug 1975); *Career* asst brewer Arthur Guinness Son and Co Dublin Ltd 1964-69, engagement mangr McKinsey and Co Inc 1971-74, vice pres and dir head of corp fin Citicorp Int Bank Ltd 1974-80, sr vice pres and chm Bankers Trust International Ltd 1980-85; dir: Phoenix Securities Ltd 1983-, River and Mercantile Extra Income Trust plc; chm Bd of Tstees and dir Orchestra of the Age of Enlightenment; *Recreations* hunting, sailing, skiing, tennis; *Clubs* Royal St George Yacht (Dublin), Vanderbilt Racquet; *Style—* Martin Smith, Esq; Phoenix Securities Ltd, 99 Bishopsgate, London EC2 (☎ 071 638 2191, fax 071 638 0707)

SMITH, Lt-Col (Henry) Martin Lockhart; s of Col Henry Brockton Lockhart Smith, MC, of Ellingham Hall, nr Bungay, Suffolk, and Dorothy Helen, *née* Douglas; *b* 23 Dec 1936; *Educ* Royal Nautical Coll Pangbourne, RMA Sandhurst, NDC Latimer; *m* 31 March 1962, Margaret Louise, da of Sydney Wilfred Eaton (d 1977); 2 s (Vaughan b 1963, Charles b 1965); *Career* joined Army 1955, cmmnd Grenadier Gds 1957, Staff Coll Camberley 1969, NDC Latimer 1978, cmd 2 Bn Grenadier Gds 1978-80; served: Cyprus, Malta, Ireland, Br Guiana, W Germany (despatches 1974), ret 1983; Corps of Queens Messengers 1984-90 (ret); *Recreations* shooting, skiing, conservation; *Style—* Lt-Col Martin Smith; Ellingham Hall, Bungay, Suffolk NR35 2EN (☎ 050845 314)

SMITH, (Isabel) Mary; MBE (1987); da of John George Nevin, MBE, JP (d 1969), of Parkside, Allendale, Northumberland, and Elizabeth Jane, *née* Renwick (d 1962); *b* 27 June 1924; *Educ* Queen Elizabeth GS for Girls Hexham, Univ of Durham (BSc, Dip Educn); *m* 1, 1 Sept 1951, Dr Claude Robson Clayburn, TD (d 1962); 3 s (Nigel Claude Nevin b 27 June 1952, Ridley Richard Robson b 2 July 1956, John Alwyn Palmer b 10 Sept 1957); m 2, 1964, Douglas Smith, OBE, JP (d 1974); *Career* Hexham Cons Constituency: over forty years serv, held almost every office from branch chm to patron, first woman chm; vice chm Northern Area Women's 1969-73, co cncllr Northumberland (vice chm 1988-89, actg chm 1989, elected for Plenmeller Div of ten parishes 1973); chm The Smith (Haitwhistle) Charitable Family Tst, memb PCC Beltingham and Henshaw, chm of govrs Haydon Bridge HS, pres Bardon Mill CC; *Recreations* gardening, walking, tennis and travelling to remoter countries abroad; *Style—* Mrs I Mary Smith, MBE; The Grange, Bardon Mill, Hexham, Northumberland (☎ 04343 344232)

SMITH, Maureen; *b* 30 July 1947; *m* 8 Nov 1978, Alan Lewis Sutherland; 1 da (Natasha b 1980); *Career* md: BBDO PR Ltd 1972 (dir 1971), Good Relations Ltd 1973; chief exec: Good Relations Group Ltd 1975, Good Relations Group plc; chm The Communication Group plc (PR consultancy); *Style—* Ms Maureen Smith; The Communication Group plc, 19 Buckingham plc, London SW1E 6LB (☎ 071 630 1411)

SMITH, Maurice Arthur; DFC 1941 (Bar 1942); s of Arthur Leonard Smith (d 1970), and Amy, *née* Parkinson (d 1976); *b* 10 March 1920; *Educ* Douai Sch Woolhampton Berks; *m* 24 May 1941, Mary Smith, da of Joseph Maurice Hurley (d 1926); 4 da (Elizabeth Mary (Mrs Mason) b 1942, Susan Mary (Mrs Carey) b 1944, Gillian Wendy (Mrs Garner) b 1946, Caroline Anne (Mrs Copping) b 1950); *Career* Sgt Pilot RAFVR 1938, mobilised 1939, cmmnd Pilot Offr 1941 (despatches 1944), demob as Sqdn Ldr 1946; co fndr and md Hampden Industl Filters Ltd (merged with Chapman & Smiths 1985), chm Chapman & Smith Ltd 1987 (fndr ptnr 1949, md 1969); co cnllr E Sussex 1967-70, chm Industrial Safety (Protective Equipment) Manufacturers Assoc 1976 (fndr memb and cnllr, chm 1975); Knight Cdr Equestrian Order Holy Sepulchure of Jerusalem 1982; *Recreations* gardening, bowls, philately; *Clubs* RAF, Piccadilly; *Style—* Maurice Smith, Esq, DFC; KCHS Chapman & Smith Ltd, Safir Works, E Hoathly, nr Lewes, E Sussex BN8 6EW (☎ 082 584 323, fax 082 584 827, telex 95263)

SMITH, Maxwell; TD (1967); *b* 19 Dec 1929; *Educ* Royal Liberty Sch Romford, Univ of London (BSc, DipEd); *m* 29 Sept 1956, Anne; 1 s (Duncan b 1970), 2 da (Helen b 1962, Isobel b 1965); *Career* RE 1951-67 (Maj i/c Essex Field Sqdn 54 Div Engrs 1964-67); South Bank Poly: head Dept of Estate Mgmnt 1970-77, dean of faculty 1972-77, asst dir 1977-86, co dir and mgmt conslt 1986-; chm CNAA Surveying Bd 1975-81, chm SERC Building Sub-Ctee 1980-86, memb Gen Cncl RICS 1975-86 (divnl pres 1977-78); memb Worshipful Co of Chartered Surveyors 1977; hon fell South Bank Poly 1988; ARICS 1951, FRICS 1965, MBIM 1969; *Books* Manual of British Standards in Building Construction & Specification (second edn, 1987); *Recreations* walking, music, painting; *Style—* Maxwell Smith, Esq, TD; 50 Pickwick Rd, Dulwich Village, London SE21 7JW (☎ 081 274 9041)

SMITH, Hon Mrs (Melanie Frances); yr da of 3 Baron Fairhaven, JP, DL (*qv*); *b* 23 Aug 1966; *m* 22 Nov 1989, Matthew E Smith, eldest s of Mark Smith, of Ballacurn, Ballaugh, Isle of Man; 1 s (Shamus Oliver b 1 June 1990); *Style—* The Hon Mrs Smith; c/o The Rt Hon the Lord Fairhaven, JP, DL, Anglesey Abbey, Cambridge

SMITH, Michael John; s of Jack Smith (d 1962) of London, and Ada, *née* Cotton; *b* 12 Feb 1933; *Educ* Aylesbury C of E Sch Highwood, Mill Hill Sch; *m* 1, 1959 (m dis 1974), Genifer, *née* Joseph; 2 s (Steven Alexander b 25 July 1963, Timothy Daniel b 7 June 1971); m 2, 6 Aug 1976, Lorna, da of Henry White, of Dublin; 1 step s (Stefan Prescott b 1967), 1 step da (Nadia Prescott b 1963); *Career* articled to Goodman & Mann Auctioneers Surveyors & Valuers 1950-54; valuer: Cecil Lewis 1954-56, Moss & Partners 1956-61; founding jt sr ptnr (with Harold Melzack) Smith Melzack & Company 1961-; Freeman: City of London 1987, Worshipful Co of Plumbers 1989; fell: Valuers Inst 1963 (memb 1958), Incorporated Soc of Valuers and Auctioneers 1968; assoc The Zoological Soc 1970, memb The Firemark Circle 1980, Lloyd's Underwriting memb 1973; *Recreations* golf, foreign travel; *Clubs* Arts, Lloyd's Yachting, Coombe Hill Golf (former membership chm); *Style—* Michael Smith, Esq; Smith Melzack, 17/18 Old Bond St, London W1 (☎ 071 493 1613, fax 071 493 5480); 109 Old Broad St, London EC2 (☎ 071 638 1856, fax 071 588 7256, car 0860 584136)

SMITH, Michael John; s of late Reginald Charles George Smith, of Ashford, Kent, and late Kate, *née* Godden; *b* 9 March 1943; *Educ* Ashford GS; *m* 15 Sept 1965 (m dis 1978), Anne; 1 s (Ian Michael Sommerfield b 1969), 1 da (Samantha Jane b 1967); *Career* joined CAP Group 1963 (md 1981-88), jt md Sema Group plc 1988-, chm and chief exec Thorn EMI Software 1989-; tstee Leadership Tst; memb Worshipful Co of Information Technologists 1988; FBIM 1986; Lord of the Manor Hawridge and Cholesbury 1987; *Style—* Michael Smith, Esq; Hawridge Court, Hawridge, Bucks HP5 2UG (☎ 024 029240); Thorn EMI Software, 79 Staines Rd West, Sunbury on Thames (☎ 0932 765 511)

SMITH, Michael John; s of John Edward Smith, and Dorothy, *née* Hall; *b* 23 Sept 1941; *Educ* Uppingham; *m* 1, 31 Aug 1963, Bridget Ann Smith (d 1986); 2 s (Charles b 1965, Anthony b 1967), 4 da (Anna b 1970, Lucy b 1973, Rachael b 1974, Joanna b 1977); m 2, 18 Sept 1987, Frances Isabel, da of Geoffrey Herbert Golden, of Towcester; *Career* dir: Drury Holdings Ltd 1969-72, Francis Parker plc 1972-81; chm: Wassall plc 1981-88, Benson Shoe Ltd 1980- (md 1980-89); memb Kibworth and Fleckney Rotary Club, treas Kibworth PCC; FCA; *Style—* Michael Smith, Esq; Benson Shoe Ltd, PO Box 134, Haramead Business Centre, Humberstone Rd, Leicester LE1 2LH (☎ 0533 654433, fax 0533 654422, car 0836 624471)

SMITH, Michael John; s of Frank Smith (d 1988), of Cowbridge, S Glam, and Marjory Smith (d 1987); *b* 23 Sept 1939; *Educ* City of London Sch; *m* 20 Aug 1966, Diane, *née* White; 2 s (Jeremy b 26 June 1970, Philip b 24 May 1972); *Career* journalist: Wilson Daily Times N Carolina USA 1960-62, Enfield Herald N London 1963-65; PR Bullock & Turner 1965-69, fndr and md Golley Slater PR Cardiff 1969-; chm Inst of PR Wales Gp 1987-; FIPR; *Style—* Michael Smith, Esq; Golley Slater Public Relations Ltd, 9-11 The Hayes, Cardiff, South Glamorgan CF1 1NU (☎ 0222 388621, fax 0222 238729, car 0836 587009)

SMITH, Michael Kendrick; s of William James Smith (d 1974), of Coverack, Helston, Cornwall, and Marjorie Louise Smith (d 1974); *b* 6 Sept 1930; *Educ* Malvern; *m* 20 April 1957, Susan Frances, da of Lt-Col John William Edward (Jack) Blanch, TD (d 1990), of Brockham Green, Betchworth, Surrey; 2 s (Thomas Alexander Kendrick b 1961, Martin Andrew Kendrick b 1964); *Career* Nat Serv Mandarin linguist RAF 1956-57; fin dir in various public cos 1958-75, dir maj London Housing Assoc 1975-87; treas West Kent Housing Assoc, pres Brockham Green Cricket Club; Freeman City of London; FCA; *Recreations* walking, cricket, aviation; *Style—* Michael Smith, Esq

SMITH, Michael Peter (Mike); s of Dr Peter Hubert Smith, of 1A Woodlands Way, Alkrington, Middleton, Manchester, and Gertrude Iris Watts, JP; *b* 10 Oct 1948; *Educ* Ellesmere Coll Sch Shropshire, City of London Coll; *m* 7 June 1986, Anne Carolyn, da of Maj Leonard Charles Bendall; 1 da (Fiona b 30 June 1989); *Career* Ciba Geigy 1970-72, team mangr Euro championships Brands Hatch 1972-76, PA to Richard Berry and Ptnrs 1976-79, fndr Pipeline Induction Heat Ltd 1979 (mktg dir 1980-85, md 1985-89, gp md 1989-); cncl memb Pipeline Indust Guild 1988-90, bd memb and UK dir Int Pipeline and Offshore Contractors Assoc 1987-90; memb Inst of Corrosion Sci and Technol; *Recreations* racing driver, golf, squash; *Clubs* British Racing Drivers, Bugatti Owners, RAC; *Style—* Mike Smith, Esq; Pipeline Induction Heat Ltd, The Pipeline Centre, Farrington Rd, Rossendale Rd Industrial Estate, Burnley, Lancs BB11 5SW (☎ 0282 415323, fax 0282 415326, telex 63366 PIHBY G, car 0836 286065)

SMITH, Mike; s of Reginald George Smith, (d 1976), of Chelsford, and Barbara, *née* Martin; *b* 23 April 1955; *Educ* King Edward VI Sch Chelmsford; *m* 21 June 1989, Sarah Greene, da of Harry Greene, of London NW5; *Career* broadcaster; Capital Radio 1978-82, BBC Radio 1 1982-84 and 1986-88, BBC TV Breakfast Time 1983-86, also ind TV and LBC Radio; cncl memb: various charity projects (incl Comic Relief) 1984-, The Royal Acad 1988-; involved with The Children's Soc; *Recreations* motor racing, flying; *Clubs* Royal Automobile; *Style—* Mike Smith, Esq; Bagenal Harvey Organisation, 141-143 Drury Lane, London WC2B 5TB (☎ 071 379 4625, fax 071 836 1735, telex 8814360)

SMITH, Dr The Hon Mildred Vivian; OBE (1962); da of late 1 Baron Bicester; *b* 1908; *Educ* Univ of London (BSc, BS, MD), Univ of Oxford (MA); *Career* MRCS, LRCP, MRCP, FRCP; *Style—* Dr the Hon M V Smith, OBE; Croft Lodge, Yarpole, Leominster, Herefordshire HR6 0BN

SMITH, (George) Neil; CMG (1987); s of George William Smith (d 1982), of Sheffield, and Ena Hill; *b* 12 July 1936; *Educ* King Edward VII Sch Sheffield; *m* 5 May 1956, Elvi Vappu, da of Johannes Hämäläinen, of Finland (d 1962); 1 s (Kim b 1959), 1 da (Helen b 1957); *Career* joined Dip Serv 1953, Nat Serv RAF 1954-56; commercial attaché Br Embassy Rangoon 1958-61; second sec (commercial) Br Embassy Berne 1961-65; Dip Serv Admin 1965-66, first sec Cwlth Office 1966-68, Br Mil Govt Berlin 1969-73, FCO (European Integration and N America Depts) 1973-77; cnsllr (commercial) Br Embassy Helsinki 1977-80, HM Consul Gen Zurich and Principality of Liechtenstein 1980-85, head of Trade Rels and Exports Dept FCO 1985-88, ambass to Republic of Finland 1989-; *Recreations* music; *Clubs* Travellers; *Style—* Neil Smith, Esq, CMG; Foreign and Commonwealth Office, Whitehall, London SW1 (☎ 071 270 2568)

SMITH, Prof Neilson Voyne (Neil); s of Voyne Smith, of Hewelsfield Lodge, Brockweir Rd, Hewelsfield, Glos, and Lilian Freda, *née* Rose (d 1973); *b* 21 June 1939; *Educ* Trinity Coll Cambridge (BA, MA), UCL (PhD); *m* 2 July 1966, Dr Saraswati Keskar, da of Dr Govind Raghunath (d 1963); 2 s (Amahl b 4 June 1967, Ivan b 13 July 1973); *Career* lectr linguistics and W African languages SOAS 1970-72 (lectr W African languages 1964-70), head Dept Phonetics and Linguistics SOAS 1983-90 (reader linguistics 1972-81, prof linguistics 1981-); memb: Linguistics Assoc GB (pres 1980-86), Philological Soc 1964- (sometime memb Cncl), SSRC 1973-89; *Books* An Outline Grammar of Nupe (1967), The Acquisition of Phonology (1973), Modern Linguistics (with Deirdre Wilson, 1979), Mutual Knowledge (ed, 1982), Speculative Linguistics (1983), The Twitter Machine (1989); *Recreations* travel, music, walking; *Style—* Prof Neil Smith; 32 Long Buftlers, Harpenden, Herts AL5 1JE (☎ 0582 761313); Dept of Phonetics and Linguistics, University College London, Gower St, London WC1E 6BT (☎ 071 380 7173)

SMITH, Norman Jack; s of Maurice Leslie Smith (d 1967), of Newton Abbot, Devon, and Ellen Dorothy, *née* Solly; *b* 14 April 1936; *Educ* Henley GS, Oriel Coll Oxford (MA), City Univ (MPhil); *m* 4 March 1967, Valerie Ann, da of Capt Arthur Ernest Frost (d 1978), of Ramsgate, Kent; 1 s (Malcolm b 1970); 1 da (Gail b 1974); *Career* market analyst Dexion Ltd 1957-60, comm evaluation mangr Vickers Ltd 1960-69, business devpt mangr Baring Bros and Co Ltd 1969-80; dir: Burntisland Engineers and Fabricators Ltd 1974-76, Zenith Reed Ltd 1975-76, International Economic Services Ltd 1975-76, SAI Tubular Services Ltd 1983-88, Atkins Oil and Gas Engineering Ltd 1984-86, Smith Rea Energy Analysts Ltd 1985-, Gas Transmission Ltd 1989-, Smith Rea Energy Aberdeen Ltd 1990-; dir gen Offshire Supplies Office 1978-80; chm: British Underwater Engineering Ltd 1981-83, Mentor Engineering Consultants Ltd 1988-; md Smith Rea Energy Assocs Ltd 1983-; *Recreations* archaeology, walking, swimming, gardening; *Clubs* United Oxford and Cambridge; *Style—* Norman Jack Smith, Esq; Smith Rea Energy Associates Ltd, Hunstead House, Nickle, Chartham, Canterbury, Kent CT4 7PL (☎ 0227 738822)

SMITH, Paul Andrew; s of Kenneth Desmond Smith, and Joy, *née* Moore; *b* 15 April 1964; *Educ* Heaton GS Newcastle upon Tyne; *m* 31 July 1987, Caroline Jayne, da of Stanley Terence Sowry; 1 s (Oliver James b 1988); *Career* professional cricketer; debut Warwickshire CCC 1982-, awarded county cap 1986; youth player: Northumberland CCC 1971-80, Northumberland under 13, under 15, under 19, N of Eng 1979, England under 19 v Young Aust; world record most consecutive partnership over 50 (11 with Andy Moles), youngest Warwicks player to score 1000 runs in a season 1984 and 1500 runs in a season 1986, 2 first class hat-tricks v Northants 1989 and Sussex 1990; honours with Warwickshire: Nat West Trophy 1989, runners up Benson & Hedges Cup 1984; all-rounder of the year Warwickshire 1986 and 1989; Advtg and PR Dept Birmingham Post and Mail Newspaper Group off-season 1986-88, classic car restorer Earlsway Classics Halesowen; *Recreations* restoration of classic cars; *Style—* Paul Smith, Esq; c/o Warwickshire County Cricket Club, County Ground, Edgbaston, Birmingham B5 7QU (☎ 021 446 4422)

SMITH, Paul David John; s of Ernest Smith, of Walton-on-the-Maze, Essex, and Margaret Gillian, *née* Taylor; *b* 12 June 1949; *Career* jr art dir Davis and Page 1968-70; art dir: Charles Barker Ltd 1970-72, Vernons 1972-73, Royds 1973, Collett Dickinson and Pearce 1973-75 (dir 1975-1987); creative dir Allen Brady and Marsh 1987-; many nat and int awards incl 4 D & ADA Silver awards; memb Cncl Creative Circle 1990-; *Recreations* tennis; *Style—* Paul Smith, Esq; Allen Brady & Marsh, Lynton House, 7-12 Tavistock Square, London WC1H 9SX (☎ 071 388 1100, fax 071 387 1155)

SMITH, Paul John; s of John Joseph Smith, of Sunderland, Tyne and Wear, and Mary Patricia, *née* Maher; *b* 25 July 1945; *Educ* Ampleforth,Univ of Newcastle (MB BS); *m* 14 July 1972, Anne Westmoreland Snowdon; 1 s (Mark b 1977), 3 da (Jaime b 1980, Victoria b 1982, Francesca b 1982); *Career* asst lectr in anatomy 1969-71, surgical registrar Glasgow Western Infirmary 1971-76, Wexham Park Hosp 1976-78; res asst Microsurgical Laboratory Univ of Louisville 1978; Christine Kleinert Fell in Hand Surgery Louisville 1978, resident and instructor in plastic surgery Duke Univ N Carolina 1979; conslt plastic surg: Mount Vernon Hosp 1982-, Gt Ormond St Hosp for Sick Children 1988-; memb: Cncl Brit Hand Soc 1988-90, Editorial Bd Journal of Hand Surgery; sec Plastic Surg Royal Soc of Med; FRCS Glasgow 1974; Hayward Foundation Scholar 1978, 1st prize American Assoc Hand Surgery Toronto 1979, Pulvertaft Prize British Hand Soc 1983; BMA, RSM, BSSM, BAPS, BAAPS; *Books* Principles of Hand Surgery (1990); *Recreations* skiing; *Style—* Paul Smith, Esq; Westmorelands, Collingwood Rd, Farnham Common, Bucks SL2 3LQ (☎ 0753 644369); Wellington Hospital, London W1 (☎ 0753 645551)

SMITH, Paul Ronald; s of Ronald Edward Smith (d 1980), of Bristol, and Doreen Alice, *née* Young; *b* 4 July 1948; *Educ* Glasgow Acad, Weston-Super-Mare Tech Coll; *m* 20 July 1974, Sarah, da of Horace William (Digger) Knight (d 1985), of Bristol; 1 s (Adam b 1981), 1 da (Georgina b 1979); *Career* CA; trainee W O & H O Wills 1967-69, asst chief accountant May & Hassell plc 1969-72, commercial dir Carlton JCB Ltd 1972-75, PA to sr ptnr Watkins Gray Woodgate Architects 1975-76; J A Devenish plc: admin dir gp mgmnt bd 1979, md Devenish Redruth Brewery Ltd 1985 (chief accountant 1976-79), gp md 1987; FCCA 1972; *Recreations* squash, sailing, rugby football; *Clubs* Redruth RC, Clifton RC; *Style—* Paul Smith, Esq; Carclew, Perranarworthal, Truro, Cornwall TR3 7PB (☎ 0872 865045); J A Devenish plc, Trinity House, 15 Trinity St, Weymouth, Dorset DT4 8TP (☎ 0305 761111, fax 0305 782397, car 0836 243683)

SMITH, Paul William Cliburn; s of Alfred Edward Smith (d 1985), professional golfer and world record holder, and Georgina, *née* Cliburn; *b* 28 Aug 1949; *Educ* St Lawrence Coll Ramsgate, Queen's Univ Belfast (BA); *m* 7 Sept 1974, Elizabeth Anne, da of William Arthur Smitton, of High Rigg, Heathwaite, Windermere, Cumbria; 2 da (Rebecca Emily Louise b 1979, Catherine Lauren Elizabeth b 1984); *Career* slr; ptnr Pearson & Pearson, chm Herdwick Historical Reprints (specialist book publishers) 1987-, dir Herdwick Investmts Ltd 1984-; *Recreations* local history, fell walking, golf; *Style—* Paul Smith, Esq; The Croft, 18 Kentrigg, Kendal, Cumbria (☎ 0539 28 763); Pearson & Pearson, 98A Stricklandgate, Kendal, Cumbria (☎ 0539 29 555)

SMITH, Canon (Anthony Michael) Percival; s of Canon Kenneth Percival Smith (d 1951), and Audrey Mary, *née* Clarke (d 1972); *b* 5 Sept 1924; *Educ* Shrewsbury, Gonville and Caius Coll Cambridge (MA), Westcott House Cambridge; *m* 16 July 1950, Mildred Elizabeth, da of William Brown, OBE (d 1978), of Covington, Huntingdon, Cambridgeshire; 2 da (Susan Percival b 1951, Claire Percival b 1954); *Career* Lt Rifle Bde 1943-46 N Euro; domestic chaplain to Archbishop of Canterbury 1953-58; vicar: All Saints' Upper Norwood S London 1958-66, Yeovil 1966-72; rural dean of Murston 1968-72, prebendary of Wells Cathedral 1970-72, vicar St Mildred's Addiscombe Croydon 1972-80, archdeacon of Maidstone 1980-90; diocesan dir Ordinands 1980-90, hon canon Canterbury Cathedral 1980; *Recreations* reading; *Style—* Canon A M P Smith

SMITH, Peter; s of Walter Smith (d 1984), of Brotton, Cleveland, and Mary Elizabeth, *née* Welham; *b* 14 March 1941; *Educ* St Mary's Coll Middlesbrough; *m* 20 Feb 1965, Maureen, da of Maurice O'Brien, (d 1957); 3 da (Katherine b 4 March 1966, Josephine b 16 Sept 1967, Clare b 31 Aug 1980); *Career* CA; sr ptnr Calvert Smith and Co 1969-; Chllr Worshipful Co of Merchant Taylors in the City of York, former pres and sec York Catenian Assoc, tres Lawrence Sterne Tst; Pro Ecclesia et Pontifice (Papal Decoration) 1983; FCA 1965; *Recreations* walking, cricket; *Style—* Peter Smith, Esq; The Hollies, Bonneycroft Lane, Easingwold, York YO6 3AR (☎ 0347 21570); Calvert Smith and Co, Chartered Accountants, 104-106 The Mount, York YO2 2AR (☎ 0904 655626)

SMITH, Peter; s of Laurence Willis Smith (d 1983), of Aberystwyth, and Hilda, *née* Halsted (d 1980); *b* 15 June 1926; *Educ* Peter Symonds' Sch Winchester, Oriel Coll Oxford, Lincoln Coll Oxford (BA), Hammersmith Sch of Building Arts and Crafts; *m* 30 March 1954, Joyce Evelyn, da of John William Abbot (d 1963), of Brynford, Clwyd; 2 s (Stephen Lloyd b 1955, Charles Kenyon b 1957), 1 da (Sarah Caroline b 1960); *Career* Royal Cmmn for Ancient Monuments of Wales: jr investigator 1949-54, sr investigator 1954-63, investigator i/c of Nat Monuments Record 1963-73, sec of the cmmn 1973-; pres: Cambrian Archaeological Assoc 1979, Vernacular Architecture Gp 1984-87; Alice Davis Hitchcock medallion (Soc of Architectural Historians) 1978; inter ARIBA 1950, FSA; *Books* Houses of the Welsh Countryside (2 edn, 1988), The Cambridge Agricultural History (contrib); *Recreations* reading, learning Welsh, sketching, bricklaying; *Style—* Peter Smith, Esq, FSA; Ty-coch, Lluest, Llanbadarn Fawr, Aberystwyth, Dyfed (☎ 0970 623556); RCAHM (Wales), Crown Building, Plas Crug, Aberystwyth, Dyfed (☎ 0970 624381)

SMITH, Peter; s of Ernest Sidney Smith (d 1950), of Yotes Cottage, St Mary's Platt, Sevenoaks, Kent, and Ellen Smith (d 1967); *Educ* Sevenoaks Sch; *m* 1 (m dis), Christina De Vries; m 2, 17 Oct 1953, Pamela Mary, da of Cyril Leigh Francis, MM (d 1972), of 33 Goldington Ave, Bedford; 1 s (Richard Peter b 26 May 1954), 3 da (Jane Alexander b 28 July 1945, Susan Christina b 27 Oct 1947, Sally Ann b 1 May 1956); *Career* 2 Lt Royal W Kent 1955; chm Borough Green Sawmills Ltd 1967-90 (md 1962); pres Full Gospel Business Men's Fellowship Maidstone Chapter 1989; memb: Boughton Monchelsea Parish Cncl 1972-90, Boughton Monchelsea PCC 1973-90, Rochester Deanery Synod 1982-87; church warden St Peter's Boughton Monchelsea; *Recreations* walking, racing; *Clubs* Lingfield Park, Folkestone Racing; *Style—* Peter Smith, Esq; The White House, Boughton Monchelsea, Maidstone, Kent (☎ 0622 743555); Borough Green Sawmills Ltd, Borough Green, Kent (☎ 0732 882012)

SMITH, Peter; s of Peter Smith (d 1971), of Grantown-on-Spey, Morayshire, and Lily Smith (d 1933); *b* 20 Feb 1925; *Educ* Grantown-on-Spey GS; *m* 21 March 1953, Joyce Mildred, da of Henry Stephen (d 1966), of Gants Hill, Ilford, Essex; 1 s (Stephen Peter b 9 April 1959), 2 da (Pamela Joyce b 27 Jan 1954, Janet Moira b 21 Feb 1957); *Career* writer RN 1943-46; internal auditor J & P Coats Ltd 1947-81; sec and treas Scottish Bowling Assoc 1982-90; hon memb Scottish Bowling Assoc; *Recreations* bowls, motoring, walking, reading; *Clubs* Shawlands Bowling; *Style—* Peter Smith, Esq; 113 Durward Ave, Glasgow G41 3SG (☎ 041 649 1960)

SMITH, Peter Alan; s of Dudley Vaughan Smith (d 1983), and Beatrice Ellen, *née* Sketcher; *b* 5 Aug 1946; *Educ* Mill Hill Sch, Univ of Southampton (BSc); *m* 2 Oct 1971, Cherry, da of Thomas A Blandford (d 1986); 2 s (Nicholas David b 1975, Richard James b 1977); *Career* RAFVR 1964-67, cmmnd actg PO 1967; Coopers & Lybrand Deloitte CAs 1967- (ptnr 1975-, managing partner London City Office 1989-, memb Ptnrship Bd 1990-), chm Int Banking Indust Ctee 1988-90; vice pres Beaconsfield Cons Assoc, former hon treas UK Housing Tst; FCA; *Books* Housing Association Accounts and their Audit (1980); *Recreations* golf, gardening; *Clubs* Carlton, Beaconsfield Golf; *Style—* Peter Smith, Esq; Littleworth House, Common Lane, Littleworth Common, Bucks (☎ 0628 605018); 208 Bunyan Court, Barbican, London EC2; Coopers & Lybrand Deloitte, Plumtree Court, London EC4A 4HT (☎ 071 822 4586, fax 071 822 4652, telex 884730)

SMITH, Peter Alexander Charles; OBE (1981); s of Alexander Smith, and Gwendoline, *née* Beer; *b* 18 Aug 1920; *Educ* St Paul's; *m* 1945, Marjorie May, *née* Humphrey (d 1983); 1 s; *Career* served WWII RA; admitted slr 1948; chm Securicor Gp plc 1974- (chief exec 1974-85), dir Fitch Lovell 1982-, non-exec chm Metal Closures Gp plc 1983-87 (dir 1972-87, dep chm 1981-83), chm Br Security Indust Assoc 1977-81; pres Royal Warrant Holders Assoc 1982-83 (memb cncl 1976-, vice-pres 1981-82); FRSA; CBIM; *Recreations* golf, music, photography; *Clubs* British Racing Drivers'; *Style—* Peter Smith, Esq, OBE; Securicor Gp plc, Sutton Park Hse, 15 Carshalton Rd, Sutton, Surrey SM1 4LE (☎ 081 770 7000)

SMITH, Peter Angus; s of Edward Angus Smith, JP (d 1970), of Southerndown, Highworth, Wilts and Mary Glenn, *née* Wallis; *b* 28 March 1936; *Educ* Winchester; *m* 30 May 1964, Bridget Rosemary, da of Maj Ernest Oscar Yates (d 1955), of Haywards, Woodmancote, nr Cheltenham; 2 da (Nicola b 8 Oct 1966, Annabel b 1 July 1969); *Career* Nat Serv 1954-56, cmmnd 15/19 Royal Hussars served Malaya; sales dir Wilts Carpets Ltd 1963-70, md Humphries & Taplings Ltd 1970-72; dir: Richard Bondy Ltd 1970-71, Dorville Fashions Ltd 1970; chm: Peter Smith Associates Ltd 1972-87, Threshold Floorings Ltd 1974-87; md Alvescot Int Ltd 1987-, ptnr Prime Designs 1987-; memb Bampton Parish Cncl 1970-73; pres: London Floorcovering Assoc 1980-, Bampton CC 1987-; *Recreations* cricket, tennis, fishing, shooting; *Clubs* Cavalry and Guards'; *Style—* Peter Smith, Esq; Churchgate House, Bampton, Oxford OX8 2LZ (☎ 0993 850 251)

SMITH, Dr Peter Arthur John; s of Arthur Critchley Smith (d 1956), of Orchards, Beckford, Glos, and Lysbeth Thomson, *née* Margach (d 1985); *b* 11 Aug 1919; *Educ* Tewkesbury GS, Guy's Hosp Univ of London (MB BS); *m* 8 Sept 1956, Elizabeth Mary Morris Evans; *Career* WWII Emergency Cmmn RAMC and 8 Army, El Alamein 1942, Salerno 1943, released with rank of Maj RAMC 1947; registrar Dermatology Dept Guy's Hosp 1949 (ex-serv registrar 1947), res in dermatology Univ Hosp Minneapolis (Fulbright Travel Grant) 1950-51, res fell in dermatology Massachusetts Gen Hosp Harvard Univ 1951-53, sr registrar in dermatology Univ Coll Hosp London 1953-55; conslt dermatologist: Queen Mary's Hosp Roehampton 1956, Worthing Hosp Gp 1956-82, Queen Victoria Hosp East Grinstead 1956-84; in private practice Harley Street 1955-; MRCS, FRCP, FRSM; memb: Br Assoc of Dermatologists, Int Dendrology Soc; *Recreations* gardening, hill-walking, wine; *Clubs* Brooks's, Army and Navy, Boodle's; *Style—* Dr Peter Smith; 82 Harley Street, London W1N 1AE (☎ 071 935 9727); 118 Heene Road, Worthing, West Sussex BN11 4PN (☎ 0903 205405)

SMITH, Peter James Mead; s of Douglas William Mead Smith (d 1985), of Port Talbot, and Doris Maud, *née* Duchien; *b* 25 Aug 1948; *Educ* St Clares Convent Porthcawl Mid Glam, Dyffryn GS Port Talbot, Coll of Law Guildford Surrey; *m* 3 Oct 1972, Sarah Madeline Anita, da of William Thomas Richards, of Swansea; 1 s (Richard b 1976); *Career* admitted slr 1972; sr ptnr Smith Llewelyn Partnership 1972; hon sec Aberavon Green Stars RFC, fndn govr St Josephs Primary Sch Neath W Glam 1985-89, memb Br Legal Assoc; *Recreations* rugby union and other sports, antique collecting; *Style—* Peter Smith, Esq; Hendre, 1 Westernmoor Rd, Neath, W Glam SA11 1BJ (☎ 0639 636635); 18 Princess Way, Swansea SA1 3LW (☎ 0792 464444, fax 0792 464726)

SMITH, Peter John; *b* 31 Dec 1936; *Educ* Rastrick GS Brighouse West Yorksire; *m* Marie Louise; 1 s, 1 da; *Career* local govt treas; trainee Huddersfield CBC 1953-59, accountant Bradford CBC 1959-61, asst chief accountant Chester CBC 1961-63, computer mangr Keighley Municipal Borough Cncl 1963-66, asst city treas Gloucester CBC 1966-69, dep borough treas Gateshead CBC 1969-73; Tyne and Wear CC: asst co treas 1973-74, dep co treas 1974-80, co treas (incl treas of Northumbria Police Authy, Northumbria Probation and After-Care Ctee, Newcastle Airport, Northumbria Tourist Bd) 1980-86, gen mangr Tyne and Wear Residuary Body 1985-88; freelance consultant 1988-89, exec dir Westgate Trust plc 1990-; memb: Bd of Tyne & Wear Passenger Tport Exec 1981-86, Ctee N American Property Unit Tst 1981-, Bd Northern Investors Co 1984-87; IPFA; *Style*— Peter Smith, Esq; Wheatsheaf House, Station Rd, Beamish, Co Durham DH9 0QU

SMITH, Peter Michael; s of Peter William Smith (d 1944), of Reading, and Margaret, *née* Gilchrist (d 1971), of St Georges College, Weybridge; *b* 10 Jan 1938; *m* 6 Dec 1975, Sarah Diana, da of John Seyfried; 2 s (Benjamin b 18 June 1977, Matthew b 17 Oct 1981); *Career* served BSA Police Rhodesia 1956-59; Barclays Bank plc 1955-56, Barclay's Bank International 1959-62; PR and marketing management: Total Oil Products Central Africa 1962-66, Gallaher plc 1966-69; PR advsr Booker McConnell plc (responsible for early development of Booker Prize for Fiction) 1970-78, public affrs mangr Powell Duffryn plc 1978-85, head of corporate relations Reed International plc 1985-87; currently: jt managing ptnr City and Corporate Counsel (co-fndr 1987), dir UK Radio Developments, tstee One World Broadcasting Trust; councillor London Borough of Camden 1968-71; Parly Candidate (C): Rowley Regis and Tipton 1970, West Bromwich West Feb 1974; joined SDP 1982, currently memb Social and Liberal Democratic Party; memb Nat Cncl and Exec Ctee Euro Movement in UK 1981-82; chm PR Educn and Res Tst 1984-89, memb Cncl Centre for World Development Educn; Royal Cwlth Soc: founder and chm Focus Gp 1975, pres Focus Gp 1978-83, dep chm 1980-83, currently vice pres; FIPR (chm City and Fin Gp 1981-82, pres 1984), memb Int PR Assoc; Investor Relations Soc: co-fndr 1980, memb Ctee 1980-, chm 1986-89, currently dep chm; FRSA FIOD; *Recreations* golf, reading, music; *Clubs* RAC, Royal Commonwealth Soc; *Style*— Peter Smith, Esq; 31 Camberwell Grove, London SE5 8JA (☎ 071 701 3636); City and Corporate Counsel Limited, 14 Soho Square, London W1V 5FB (☎ 071 287 6616, fax 071 724 7030)

SMITH, Peter Vivian Henworth; CB (1989); s of Vivian Smith (d 1973), of Craig, 22 Victoria Rd, Clacton-on-Sea, Essex, and Dorothea, *née* Ovenden (d 1941); *b* 5 Dec 1928; *Educ* Clacton Co HS, BNC Oxford (BA, BCL, MA); *m* 19 Feb 1955, Mary Marjorie, da of Frank John Willsher (d 1947), of Babbacombe, Holland Rd, Clacton-on-Sea; 5 da (Kathleen b 1955, Jacqueline b 1958, Susan b 1961, Linda b 1962, Johanna b 1967); *Career* RASC 1947-49, 2 Lt 1948, RARO 1949-70 (Lt); called to the Bar Lincoln's Inn 1953, practised at bar 1953-55; joined HM Overseas Legal Serv 1955; resident magistrate Nyasaland 1955-64, sr resident magistrate Malawi 1964-69, puisne judge Malawi 1969-70; HM Customs and Excise (England): legal asst 1970-72, sr legal asst 1972-76, asst slr 1976-82, princ asst slr 1982-86, slr 1986-89; legal advsr: Broadcasting Standards Cncl 1989-, Registry of Bldg Socs 1990-; chm Clacton-on-Sea Cncl of Churches; *Recreations* bridge, classical music, walking, computers; *Style*— Peter Smith, Esq, CB; Likabula, 14 St Albans Rd, Clacton-on-Sea, Essex CO15 6BA (☎ 0255 422053); Broadcasting Standards Council, 5-8 The Sanctuary, London SW1P 3JS (☎ 071 233 0544, fax 071 233 0397); Registry of Building Societies, 15 Great Malborough St, London W1V 2AX (☎ 071 494 6669)

SMITH, Philip Henry; s of Alfred Henry Smith (d 1977), of Leicester, and Georgina May, *née* Ives (d 1969); *b* 24 Nov 1946; *Educ* Loughborough Coll GS, Leicester Regnl Coll of Technol, Nottingham Poly; *m* 27 Dec 1968, Sonia Idena, da of Ivan Garnet Moody (d 1964), of Leicester; 2 s (Christian Philip b 13 June 1972, Philip Raoul b 28 Feb 1975), 1 da (Melissa b 21 June 1969); *Career* sr audit asst Leics CC 1964-69, gp accountant Lusaka City Cncl Zambia 1969-72, branch accountant Dairy Produce Bd Zambia 1972-74, divnl dir and sec Dorada Hldgs plc 1974-81, divnl fin dir Brook Tool Engrg Hldgs plc 1981-83, gp treas Asda Gp plc 1983-; chm Padbury Utd Football, life memb Clifton Rangers Youth Football; memb IPFA 1971, fell CIMA 1974, FBIM 1974, MCT 1988; *Recreations* sports, wine, gardening, political and economic affairs; *Style*— Philip Smith, Esq; The Old White Horse, Main St, Padbury, Buckingham, Bucks MK18 2AY (☎ 0280 814848); Asda Group plc, Asda House, Southbank Great Wilson St, Leeds, W Yorks (☎ 0532 418908, fax 0532 418018, telex 556623 ASDAHO G)

SMITH, Philip Henry; s of Reginald Smith, and Grace, *née* Howgate; *b* 14 July 1934; *Educ* Leeds GS, Univ of Leeds (MB ChB); *m* 13 Aug 1960, Margaret, da of Wilfred Glover (d 1967); 1 s (Richard b 1965 d 1988), 4 da (Alison (Mrs Dawson) b 1962, Catherine b 1964 d 1964, Anne b 1967, Rosemary b 1967); *Career* Nat Serv and OC FST Br Cameroons, OC Surgical Div Tidwork Mil Hosp; head Dept of Urology St James Hosp Leeds 1967-, urologist to Regnl Spinal Injuries Unit Pinderfields Hosp Wakefield 1967-; sec urology gp of European Orgn for Res on Treatment of Cancer 1979-82 (chm 1976-79); chm: Prostatic Cancer Sub Gp MRC 1965, Urology Working Party MRC 1968-; memb: RSM, BAUS, Spinal Injuries Assoc, Int Soc of Urology and of Paraplegia; FRCS 1960; *Books* Bladder Cancer (ed, 1984), Combination Therapy in Urological Malignancy (ed, 1988); *Recreations* grandchildren, gardening; *Style*— Philip Smith, Esq; Department of Urology, St James Hospital, Leeds LS9 7TF (☎ 0532 433144, fax 0532 426496)

SMITH, Philip John Mytton; s of Herbert George Smith (d 1988), of Northleach, Gloucs, and Margery Eleanor, *née* Haynes (d 1983); *b* 6 Jan 1936; *Educ* Uppingham, Aston Univ (BSc); *m* 1974, Sarah Anne Ruth, da of David Hugh Stafford Forsyth, of Stanton, Glos; 2 da (Heather b 1976, Philippa b 1978); *Career* General Electric Co plc 1954-64, Ian Heath Ltd Birmingham 1964-67, P-E Consulting Group 1968-72; dir Brass Turned Parts Ltd Birmingham 1972-; CEng, FIEE, MIMC; *Recreations* hunting; *Style*— Philip Smith, Esq; Garretts Farm, Buckland, Broadway, Worcs; Brass Turned Parts Ltd, Fallows Rd, Sparkbrook, Birmingham B11 1PL

SMITH, Sir Raymond Horace; KBE (1967, CBE 1960), AFC (1968); s of Horace P Smith (d 1965), of London, and Mabelle E, *née* Couzens (d 1960); *b* 18 March 1917; *Educ* Salesian Coll London, Barcelona Univ Spain; *m* 1943, Dorothy, da of Robert Cheney Hart (d 1946), of London; 3 s; *Career* serv WWII with Br Security Co-ordination W Hemisphere (USA, Canada, Caribbean and S America), civil attaché Br Embassy Caracas 1941, negotiator for sale of British owned railway cos to S American Govts 1946-53; pres British Cwlth Assoc of Venezuela 1955-57; consultant to: Rolls Royce, Fairey Engineering, Hawker Siddeley, Brackett; CRAeS; *Recreations* Cresta Run, tennis, skiing, water skiing; *Clubs* White's, Naval and Military, Country, Jockey (Caracas); *Style*— Sir Raymond Smith, KBE, AFC; Quinta San Antonio, Calla El Samancito, Caracas Country Club, Caracas, Venezuela (☎ 32 92 18/33 36 96); 37 Lowndes St, London SW1 (☎ 071 235 6249); Calle Real de Sabana Grande, Edificio Las Américas, Chacaîto, Caracas, Venezuela (☎ 71 40 18/ 72 92 29; telex 21644)

SMITH, Hon Richard Edward; s of 3 Viscount Hambleden (d 1948); *b* 1937; *m* 1973, Christine Hickey; 1 s; *Style*— The Hon Richard Smith; c/o 19 Warwick Square, London SW1

SMITH, Dr Robert Carr; CBE (1989); s of Mr Edward Albert Smith, of Herts, and Olive Winifred, *née* Carstairs; *b* 19 Nov 1935; *Educ* Queen Elizabeth's Sch Barnet, Univ of Southampton (BSc), Univ of London (PhD); *m* 1960, Rosalie Mary, da of Talbot Victor Spencer, of Sussex; 1 s (James b 1965), 1 da (Georgina b 1968); *Career* dir Kingston Poly 1982-, previously prof of physical electronics Univ of Southampton; chm Polys and Colls Employers Forum 1988-90; memb Cncl: for Industry and Higher Educn, Inst of Manpower Studies, Polys and Colls Funding; *Recreations* visual arts, collecting; *Style*— Dr Robert Smith, CBE; Maybury Cottage, Raleigh Drive, Claygate, Surrey KT10 9DE (☎ 0372 463352); Kingston Polytechnic, Penrhyn Road, Kingston upon Thames, Surrey KT1 2EE (☎ 081 549 1366 ext 2000)

SMITH, Sir Robert Courtney; CBE (1980); s of John Smith, JP, DL (d 1954), of Glasgow and Symington, and Agnes, *née* Brown (d 1969); *b* 10 Sept 1927; *Educ* Kelvinside Acad Glasgow, Sedbergh, Trinity Coll Cambridge (BA,MA); *m* 6 March 1954, Moira Rose, da of Wilfred Hugh Macdougall (d 1948), of Glasgow; 2 s (Nigel b 1956 d 1971, Christopher b 1958), 2 da (Lorna (Mrs Bromley-Martin) b 1958, Rosalind b 1964); *Career* RM 1945-47, RMFVR 1951-57; CA 1953; ptnr Arthur Young McClelland Moores 1957-78; chm: Alliance Tst plc, Second Alliance Tst plc; dir: Bank of Scotland, Br Alcan Aluminium plc, Edinburgh Investmt Tst plc, Sidlaw Gp plc, Standard Life Assur Co, Volvo Trucks (GB) Ltd; chllr's assessor Glasgow Univ, dir Merchants House of Glasgow, pres Business Archives Cncl Scotland, tstee Carnegie Tst for Univs of Scotland, memb Scottish Industs Devpt Bd 1972-88 (chm 1981-88); Hon LLD Glasgow 1978; FRSE 1988; kt 1987; *Recreations* gardening, racing; *Clubs* East India, Western (Glasgow), Hawks (Cambridge); *Style*— Sir Robert Smith, CBE, FRSE; North Lodge, Dunkeld, Perthshire PH8 0AR (☎ 035 02 574); 64 Reform Street, Dundee DD1 1JJ (☎ 0382 201700, fax 0382 25133, telex 76195)

SMITH, Sir Robert Hill; 3 Bt (UK 1945), of Crowmallie, Co Aberdeen; s (by 2 m) of Sir Gordon Smith, 2 Bt, VRD (d 1983); *b* 15 April 1958; *Educ* Merchant Taylors', Aberdeen Univ; *Heir* bro, Charles Gordon Smith, b 21 April 1959; *Recreations* sailing; *Clubs* Royal Thames Yacht; *Style*— Sir Robert Smith, Bt; Crowmallie, Pitcaple, Aberdeenshire

SMITH, Robert James; s of James Alexander Smith, of Crawley, Sussex, and Rita Mary, *née* Emmott; *b* 21 April 1959; *Educ* Notre Dame Middle Sch Crawley, St Wilfrids Comp Crawley; *m* 13 Aug 1988, Mary Theresa, da of John Richard Poole; *Career* pop singer, musician and song-writer; stage debut with Malice (school group) 1976, name changed to Easy Cure (debut concert 1977), band now called The Cure (debut concert 1978); first tours: Britain Feb-April 1979, Europe July 1979, USA April 1980, Antipodes July-Aug 1980, Japan Oct 1984; performer in over 1000 concerts worldwide; LPs (world sales figures in brackets): Three Imaginary Boys (US version Boys Don't Cry, 850,000) 1979, Seventeen Seconds (650,000) 1980, Faith (550,000) 1981, Pornography (800,000) 1982, Japanese Whispers (compilation, 1,100,000) 1983, The Top (1,200,000) 1984, Concert (Live, 850,000) 1984, The Head on the Door (1,700,000) 1985, Standing on a Beach (compilation, 2,300,000) 1986, Kiss Me Kiss Me Kiss Me (Double LP, 1,850,000) 1987, Disintegration (2,600,000) 1989, Mixed Up (compilation 1,600,0000) 1990; videos incl: Staring at the Sea (singles compilation) 1986, The Cure in Orange (concert) 1986; awards: BPI award Best Video 89 (for Lullaby), ASCAP award Best US Radio Song 89 (for Lovesong); other work incl: guitarist Siouxsie and the Banshees Sept-Oct 1979 and Oct 1982-May 1984, co-fndr The Glove (Studio Project - One Album) 1983; *publications* Ten Imaginary Years (offical Cure biography, jtly 1987), Songwords (co-author and ed, 1989); *Recreations* deep sea diving, hot air ballooning, reading, writing, looking into space; *Style*— Robert Smith, Esq; Fiction Records, 97 Charlotte St, London W1P 1LB (☎ 071 323 5555, fax 071 323 5323)

SMITH, Robert James; s of Mervyn Daniel Smith (d 1982), of Rangeworthy, Avon, and Marjorie Irene, *née* Griffin; *b* 22 July 1945; *Educ* King's Coll Taunton, Royal Holloway Coll Univ of London (BA); *m* 20 Aug 1970, Anne Rosemary, da of Brendan Fitzpatrick, of London; 1 s (Daniel b 1983), 1 da (Kate b 1979); *Career* managing ed: Gower Press Ltd Xerox Corp Inc 1971-75, Octopus Books Ltd 1975-78; ed dir Ebury Presss Nat Magazine Co Ltd 1979-85, publishing dir Sigwick and Jackson Ltd 1985-90, chm and md Smith Gryphon Ltd 1990-; treas Link Rd Action Gp; *Recreations* conservation, theatre, local history, collecting antiques and antiquarian books; *Clubs* Groucho; *Style*— Robert Smith, Esq; Smith Gryphon Ltd, Swallow House, 11-21 Northdown St, London N1 9BN (☎ 071 278 2444, fax 071 278 1677)

SMITH, Robert Sydney Winwood; s and h of Sir Christopher Smith, 5 Bt; *b* 1939; *Style*— Robert Smith, Esq

SMITH, Robert Walter; s of (Robert) Harvey Smith, and Irene, *née* Shuttleworth; *b* 6 May 1961; *Educ* Cavendish Sch, Cottingley Middle Sch, Beckfoot GS; *m* 2 April 1988, Leanne Carole, da of Leslie Noel Alston; *Career* professional horseman; Euro Bronze medallist 1977, Sunday Times cup Grand Prix of GB Rider of the Year award 1979, nat champion 1988, King George cup 1988 (1979), Cock of the North 1989 (1988), Nations Cup winner Aachen 1989 (Rome 1988), Dubai cup 1989, gentleman's champion 1989; memb Br teams in Nation's Cup for twelve years; *Recreations* tennis, boxing, skiing, golf, running; *Style*— Robert Smith, Esq

SMITH, Robert William; s of Harold Francis Smith (d 1981), of Burton-on-Trent, and Edith Ivy, *née* Dawson; *b* 11 Dec 1946; *Educ* Burton GS, Exeter Coll Oxford (MA); *m* 28 March 1970, Jennifer Lynn, JP, da of George William Roberts (d 1974), of Sydenham; *Career* admitted slr 1971; ptnr Macfarlanes 1977-; *Clubs* City of London; *Style*— Robert Smith, Esq; 10 Norwich St, London EC4A 1BD (☎ 071 831 9222, fax 071 831 9607, telex 296381)

SMITH, Robin Anthony; TD (1978, bar 1984); s of Tom Sumerfield Smith (d 1990), of Wetherby, and Mary, *née* Taylor; *b* 15 Feb 1943; *Educ* St Michael's Coll Leeds, Univ of Manchester (LLB); *m* 5 Oct 1967, Jennifer ELizabeth, da of Eric Anthony Roslington (d 1978), of Leeds; 1 s (Jonathan b 1969), 1 da (Sarah b 1972); *Career* cmmnd KOYLI 1966, 5Bn The Light Inf 1967-86, ret as Lt-Col 1986; admitted slr 1966, ptnr Dibb Lupton 1968; managing ptnr: Dibb Lupt Broomhead 1987-, Slrs Fin and Property Servs Ltd; memb Law Soc 1966- (memb Cncl 1982-); *Recreations* golf, tennis; *Clubs* Army and Navy, Leeds; *Style*— Robin Smith, Esq, TD; 117 The Headrow, Leeds LS1 5JX (☎ 0532 439301, fax 0532 452632, car 0836 719972, telex 557181)

SMITH, Robin Barker; s of Arthur Smith of Clandown, Somerset, and Mary, *née* Thompson; *b* 22 Aug 1946; *Educ* Ulverston GS, Univ of Leeds (MB, ChB, ChM), Univ of Oxford (MA), Univ of Chicago; *m* 4 Dec 1971 (m dis 1987), Judith Mary, da of Robert Walton Anderson (d 1986); 1 s (Matthew Robert b 18 Feb 1978), 1 da (Victoria Clare b 5 Feb 1975); m 2, 21 Sept 1990, Carol Jane, da of Joseph Peden; *Career* surgical tutor Radcliffe Infirmary Oxford 1975-81 (registrar 1973-75), res fell Univ of Chicago 1979-80; conslt surgeon Royal United Hosp Bath 1981-; FRCS (1975); *Books* chapters in various surgical texts 1980-88; *Recreations* skiing, tennis, music, reading; *Style*— Robin Barker Smith, Esq; Homefield, Widcombe Hill, Bath BA2 6EA (☎ 0225 64718); Longwood House, The Bath Clinic, Claverton Down Rd, Bath (☎ 0225 835 555)

SMITH, Baron (Life Peer UK 1978), of Marlow, Co Bucks; Sir (Edwin) Rodney Smith; KBE (1975); o s of Dr Edwin Smith; *b* 10 May 1914; *Educ* Westminster, London Univ (MS, BS, MRCS, LRCP, FRCS); *m* 1, 1938 (m dis 1971), Mary Rodwell; 3 s (Hon Martin Rodney b 1942, Hon Andrew Edward Rodney b 1948, Hon

Robert Aidan Rodney b 1956), 1 da (Hon Elinor b 1950); m 2, 1971, Susan, da of Dr Rowdon Marrian Fry; *Career* pres RSC 1973-77, chm Conference of Royal Colls (UK) 1976-78, pres Royal Soc of Med 1978; examiner in surgery London Univ; consulting surgn: St George's Hosp (surgn 1946), Wimbledon Hosp, Royal Prince Alfred Hosp Sydney NSW: memb House of Lords Bridge Team in match against Commons 1982; *Style*— The Rt Hon The Lord Smith, KBE; 135 Harley St, W1

SMITH, Dr Roger; s of Sylvanus Joseph Smith (d 1973), of Newcastle under Lyme, Staffs, and Winifred Beatrice, *née* Adams (d 1979); *b* 3 Feb 1930; *Educ* Newcastle under Lyme HS, Trinity Coll Cambridge (MA, MD), UCH London (PhD); *m* 25 June 1955, Barbara Ann, da of Harold Willatt (d 1987), of Newcastle under Lyme, Staffs; 1 s (Julian b 22 May 1960); 3 da (Philippa b 7 Dec 1956, Clare b 6 April 1962, Katharine b 3 April 1966); *Career* served: Rifle Bde 1948, Intelligence Corps 1949; Sr Wellcome res fell UCH London 1965-68, clinical reader Nuffield Depts Med and Orthopaedic Surgery Oxford 1969-77, fell Nuffield Coll Oxford 1971-77, conslt physician in metabolic med John Radcliffe Hosp and Nuffield Orthopaedic Centre Oxford 1977, fell Green Coll Oxford 1984-; memb Cncl RCP 1985-89 (regnl advsr 1981-85), chm Med Staff Cncl and Med Exec Ctee Oxford Hosps 1987-89; memb: Scientific Advsy Ctee Brittle Bone Soc, Soc for Relief of Paget's Disease, Cncl Nat Osteoporosis Soc; memb Assoc of Physicians, FRCP; *Books* Electrolyte Metabolism in Severe Infantile Malnutrition (1968), Biochemical Disorders of the Skeleton (1979), Osteoporosis 1990 (1990); *Recreations* badminton, tennis; *Style*— Dr Roger Smith; 6 Southcroft, Elsfield Rd, Old Marston, Oxford OX3 0PF; Nuffield Orthopaedic Centre Headington, Oxford OX3 7LD (☎ 0865 741155)

SMITH, Roland Hedley; s of Alan Hedley Smith, of Sheffield, and Elizabeth Louise, *née* Froggatt; *b* 11 April 1943; *Educ* King Edward VII Sch Sheffield, Keble Coll Oxford (BA, MA); *m* 27 Feb 1971, Katherine Jane, da of Philip Graham Lawrence (d 1975), of Brighton; 2 da (Rebecca b 1972, Ursula b 1975); *Career* HM Dip Serv: third sec FO 1967, second sec Moscow 1969, second later first sec UK Delegation to NATO Brussels 1971, first sec FCO 1974, first sec and cultural attaché Moscow 1978, FCO 1980, attached to Int Inst for Strategic Studies 1983, political advsr and head of Chancery Berlin 1984, Sci Energy and Nuclear Dept FCO 1988, head of Non Proliferation and Def Dept FCO 1990-; *Books* Soviet Policy Towards West Germany (1985); *Recreations* music, choral singing; *Clubs* Royal Cwlth Soc; *Style*— Roland Smith, Esq; c/o Foreign & Commonwealth Office, London SW1A 2AH (☎ 071 270 2258)

SMITH, Ronald Frederick; s of Norman Fred Smith (d 1959), and Alice Blanch, *née* Wright (d 1980); *b* 9 Aug 1930; *Educ* Sch of Architecture Birmingham, Tech Coll (Dip Arch); *m* 1, 1955, Joan Dorothy, da of Fred Snape (d 1970); 1 s (Martyn b 1965), 1 da (Tracy b 1961); m 2, Eunice Gillian, da of Walter Hooley; 1 s (Adam b 1975), 1 da (Claire b 1978); *Career* architect; The Ronald Smith Partnership: ptnr 1958-69, assoc 1969-79, ptnr 1979-; dir Fred Smith Walsall Ltd 1980-; *Recreations* classic cars, motor racing, photography; *Style*— Ronald Smith, Esq; 5 Heathfield Drive, Bloxwich, Walsall, W Midlands WS3 3NN (☎ 0922 475046)

SMITH, (George) Ronald; MBE (1984); s of George Cran Smith (d 1979), and Hilda Jane, *née* Jack; *b* 14 July 1939; *Educ* George Watson's Coll Edinburgh, Univ of Edinburgh (MA, LLB); *m* 1 April 1966, Frances Margaret, da of John Leete Paterson (d 1943); 1 s (Ronald Michael b 1968), 1 da (Susan Frances b 1970); *Career* ptnr Wallace & Somerville Edinburgh 1965-69 (merged with Whinney Murray & Co, now Ernst & Young); Ernst & Whinney (prior to merger with Arthur Young) 1969-86: ptnr UK firm 1969-71, ptnr in charge Hamburg, managing ptnr Netherlands, managing ptnr Scandinavia, chm and sr ptnr Continental firm, memb Int Exec Ctee; dir ops and dep chief exec Investment Management Regulatory Organisation (IMRO) Ltd 1990- (dir compliance 1987-90); govr The Br Sch in the Netherlands 1977-85; MInstCAs of Scotland 1965, MICAEW 1976; *Books* De Vierde Richtlijn - Kluwer - Deventer (contrib, 1978); *Recreations* gardening, fishing, occasional golf; *Style*— G Ronald Smith, Esq, MBE; IMRO, Broadwalk House, 5 Appold St, London EC2A 2LL (☎ 071 628 6022, fax 071 920 9285)

SMITH, Sheriff Ronald Good; s of Adam Smith (d 1961), and Selina Spence, *née* Wotherspoon (d 1969); *b* 24 July 1933; *Educ* King's Park Sr Secondary Sch, Glasgow Univ (BL); *m* 16 Feb 1962, Joan Robertson Beharrie (d 1984), of Perth (d 2 Oct 1984); 2 s (Douglas Adam b 1964, Andrew John b 1967); *Career* Nat Serv 1952-54, served in Korea and Keyna (Corpl); slr 1962-84; Sheriff 1984-85; *Style*— Sheriff Ronald Smith; 369 Mearns Rd, Newton Mearns, Glasgow G77 5LZ (☎ 041 639 3904); The Sheriff Court, St James St, Paisley, Strathclyde (☎ 041 887 5291)

SMITH, Rowland Austin; TD, JP (S Humberside); s of Frank Smith (d 1968), of Heck House, Grimsby, and late Florence Elizabeth, *née* Frusher; *b* 30 June 1914; *Educ* Worksop Coll; *m* 21 June 1946, Joan, da of late Hugh Halmshaw, of Riby Grove, Grimsby; *Career* Maj RA TA 1937; underwriting memb Lloyds 1983; Freeman Worshipful Co of Paviors 1985; FGS 1950; *Recreations* shooting, racing; *Style*— Rowland Smith, Esq, JP, TD; Old Rectory, Swinhope, Lincoln LN3 6HT (☎ 0472 83258)

SMITH, Maj Roy Alfred; s of Alfred Philip Smith (d 1962), of Dartford, and Jane Smith (d 1966); *b* 16 March 1919; *Educ* Dartford GS, King's Coll London; *m* 30 April 1948, Zeline Monrad, da of Wilhelm Frederik Holst (d 1981), of Oslo; 1 s (Paul b 1953), 1 da (Christine (Mrs Hunter) b 1949); *Career* cmmnd Middx Regt 1939, France and Belgium 1940, instr Machine Gun Trg Centre Middx Regt 1940-41, No 5 Army Air Support Control UK 1941, Iraq Lebanon and Western Desert 1942, GSO3 (Air) HQ Eighth Army 1942-43, HQ Fifth US Army for Salerno landings 1943, GSO2 Fifth US Army 1943, OC No 9 AASC 1944, dir of studies (Air) Tactical Sch Central Med Trg Centre 1944, GSO2 (Air) HQ Palestine & Trans-Jordan and OC 21 AASC 1945, dir of studies Sch of Land/Air Warfare UK 1946, ret 1946; Dunlop Rubber Co 1946-: Scandinavia and London Head Office 1948-63, gen mangr Euro Sales Div 1963, Euro coordinator 1968; dir of mktg coordination Dunlop European Tyre Group 1977, ret 1979; chm Overseas Trade Ctee Fndn of Br Rubber Mfrs Assocs 1968-72; memb: Business Advsy Gp Sch of Euro Studies Univ of Sussex 1970-79, Exec Ctee Int Road Fedn Geneva 1972-79; chm Abbeyfield Lingfield Soc 1986; *Books* Air Support in the Desert (1988); *Clubs* Army and Navy; *Style*— Maj Roy Smith

SMITH, Sally Lou; da of Arthur L Jones (d 1977), of Bradford, USA, and Agnes, *née* Atwood (d 1987); *b* 6 Aug 1925; *Educ* Wellesley Coll Wellesley Mass USA (BA), Camberwell Sch of Arts and Crafts; *m* 5 July 1952 (m dis 1962), Charles Ross Smith, s of Charles Ross Smith (d 1957), of Pa USA; *Career* bookbinder; work on flood-damaged books Biblioteca Nazionale Florence 1966-68, pres Designer Bookbinders 1979-81, solo bookbinding exhibition Wellesley Coll Mass USA 1982 (also at Centro Del Bellibro Ascona Switzerland 1974); work in pub collections: Br Library, V & A, Birmingham Reference Library, NY Pub Library, Rosenbach Collection USA, Lilley Library USA, Wellesley Coll Library USA, Univ of Texas Humanities Res Centre, Br Crafts Cncl, Royal Library The Hague, Eton Coll Library; Maj J R Abbey Award for Bookbinding 1965, Sunday Telegraph Br Crafts Award for Bookbinding 1977; fell Designer Bookbinders 1965, memb Art Workers Guild 1975; *Recreations* reading, walking, friends; *Style*— Mrs Sally Lou Smith; 6 Leighton Grove, London NW5 2RA (☎ 071 267 7516)

SMITH, Col Stanley Jackman; s of George Stanley Smith (d 1960), of Purley, Surrey, and Dorothy Ellen, *née* Jackman (d 1980); *b* 16 Sept 1921; *Educ* St Paul's, The Law Soc's Sch of Law; *m* 15 Feb 1958, Gisela, da of Kurt Flessa; 3 da (Karoline Susanne b 4 Feb 1959, Jennifer Christine b 9 June 1960, Helen Deborah b 20 April 1962); *Career* served Army 1942-75: RA 1942-43, Intelligence Corps 1943-46 (active serv Burma Campaign 1944-45), dep asst judge advocate gen (Indian Army) 1946-47, prosecuting offr Japanese & German War Crimes Trials (Singapore, Malaya, Burma, Borneo, Hong Kong, Germany) 1946-50, Mil Dept Office Judge Advocate Gen of the forces 1947-48, joined Directorate of Army Legal Services 1948, dep asst dir Army Legal Services 1951-60 (served BAOR, Korea (active serv), Middle East Land Forces, Kenya), promoted Maj, asst dir Army Legal Services as Lt Col 1960-67 (War Office, BAOR), promoted Col 1967, dep dir Army Legal Services (Far East Land Forces 1969-71, MOD 1971-73), CO Army Legal Aid Section, Germany 1973-75, Col RARO 1975-; decorations: 1939-45 Star, Burma Star, Defence medal 1939-45, War medal 1945, Queen's medal for Korea, UN medal for Korea 1953; articled clerk Evill & Coleman Solicitors London 1938-42, admitted slr 1944, prosecuting slr Hampshire Constabulary 1975-85; lay memb Investigation Ctee ICAEW 1988-, summary writer Criminal Appeal Office of Court of Appeal (Criminal Div) 1989-; memb Law Soc 1959-; *Recreations* reading history, gardening, walking, The USA; *Clubs* Army and Navy; *Style*— Col Stanley Smith; 5 St Lawrence Close, Stratford-Sub-Castle, Salisbury, Wiltshire SP1 3LW (☎ 0722 324173)

SMITH, Prof Stephen Kevin; s of Albert Smith, DFC, of 4 Wellington Court, Wellington Rd, Birkenhead, and Drusilla, *née* Hills; *b* 8 March 1951; *Educ* Birkenhead Sch, Univ of London (MB BS, MD); *m* 8 July 1978, Catriona MacLean, da of Alan Maclean Hobkirk, of 53 Netherby Rd, Edinburgh; 1 s (Richard Alan), 2 da (Lucinda Jane, Alice Charlotte); *Career* lectr Univ of Sheffield 1982-85, conslt in obstetrics and gynaecology MRC Reproductive Biology Unit and Lothian Health Bd 1985-88, prof of obstetrics and gynaecology Univ of Cambridge 1988-; author of various scientific and med pubns; MRCOG, MRCS, LRCP; *Recreations* cricket, football, politics, military history, music; *Style*— Prof Stephen Smith; Department of Obstetrics and Gynaecology, University of Cambridge Clinical School, The Rosie Maternity Hospital, Robinson Way, Cambridge (☎ 0223 336871, fax 0223 242474)

SMITH, Stewart Ranson; CBE (1987); s of John Smith (d 1980), of Ashington, Northumberland, and Elizabeth Atkinson, *née* Barnes; *b* 16 Feb 1931; *Educ* Bedlington GS, Univ of Nottingham (BA, MA), Yale Univ USA (MA); *m* 2 Jan 1960, (Lee) Tjam Mui Smith; *Career* Nat Serv RAEC 1955-57; Br Cncl: asst rep Singapore 1957-59, HQ London 1959-61, dir Br Inst Curitiba Brazil 1961-65, asst rep Sri Lanka 1965-69, seconded to ODA London 1970-73, rep Kenya 1973-76, controller overseas B HQ 1976-80, rep Spain 1980-87, controller Higher Educn Div 1988, controller Europe Div 1989-; *Recreations* cricket, music; *Style*— Stewart Smith, Esq, CBE; Br Cncl, 10 Spring Gardens, London SW1A 2BN (☎ 071 389 4310, telex 8952201 BRICON Cr)

SMITH, Stuart Crawford; s of David Norman Smith, of Spain, and Sheila Marie, *née* Hallowes; *b* 17 Sept 1953; *Educ* City of Bath Boy's Sch, Wadham Coll Oxford (major scholar, BA), Univ of Sussex (MA); *m* 23 Dec 1987, Hilary Joy Phillips; *Career* ed Marketing Week Magazine 1988 (joined as sub ed 1982); *Recreations* skiing, reading, swimming; *Style*— Stuart Smith, Esq; Centaur Publishing, St Giles House, 49-50 Poland St, London W1 (☎ 071 439 9429, fax 071 439 9669)

SMITH, Hon Mrs (Susanna Mary); *née* Arbuthnott; only da of 16 Viscount of Arbuthnott, DSC; *b* 1 May 1954; *Educ* Overstone Sch Northants, Dorset House Sch of Occupational Therapy; *m* 1978, Hugh T B Smith; 1 s (Andrew b 1981), 1 da (Emma b 1983); *Style*— The Hon Mrs Smith; 52 King's Rd, Wimbledon, London SW19 8QW

SMITH, Terence Charles (Terry); s of Ernest George Smith (d 1985), of London, and Eva Ada, *née* Bruce; *b* 15 May 1953; *Educ* Stratford GS, Univ Coll Cardiff (BA), Mgmnt Coll Henley (MBA); *m* 31 Aug 1974, Barbara Mary, da of Ivor Thomas George, of Ebbw Vale; 2 da (Katy b 1981, Emily b 1984); *Career* Barclays Bank 1974-83: mgmnt trainee, branch mangr, fin mangr; bank analyst W Greenwell and Co 1984-86; Barclays de Zoete Wedd 1986-88: dir, bank analyst, head of fin desk; bank analyst James Capel and Co 1989-90, dep md and head UK Co Res UBS Phillips & Drew; ACIB, memb Int Stock Exchange; *Recreations* riding, motorcycling, gliding; *Style*— Terry Smith, Esq; 9 Springfield Place, Springfield Green, Chelmsford, Essex CM1 5ZA (☎ 0245 268209); 64 Trafalgar Court, Glamis Rd, Wapping, London E1 9TF (☎ 071 488 3496); UBS Phillips & Drew, 100 Liverpool St, London EC2M 2RH (☎ 071 901 3524, fax 071 901 1905, car 0831 506054, telex 923333)

SMITH, Terence Denby (Terry); s of Sydney Smith (d 1986), of Wakefield, Yorkshire, and Florence Evelyn, *née* Lister; *b* 28 Jan 1934; *Educ* Wheelwright GS Dewsbury Yorks; *m* 1, 1957 (m dis 1980), Audrey Booth; 2 s (Howard Michael b 1965, David Mathew b 1968); m 2, 1983, Pamela Elaine Leather; *Career* professional journalist 1951-60, fndr Mercury Press Agency Ltd 1960, fndr and md Radio City plc 1973-, chm Broadcast Marketing Services Ltd 1982-; dir: Independent Radio News Ltd 1988-, Satellite Media Services Ltd 1988-, Liverpool Empire Theatre Trust Ltd 1980-; chm Assoc of Ind Radio Cos 1983-85; *Recreations* football, golf, winter sports; *Clubs* Royal Liverpool Golf, Liverpool Artists, Liverpool Raquet; *Style*— Terry Smith, Esq; Radio City plc, PO Box 194, Liverpool L69 1LD (☎ 051 227 5100, fax 051 227 3045, telex 628277)

SMITH, Thomas William David; s of George Ernest Smith, of Sheffield, and Dora Staniforth; *b* 4 Aug 1939; *Educ* Selwyn Coll Cambridge (MA, MB BChir), St Mary's Hosp Med Sch (FRCS, FRCSE); *m* 24 Nov 1967, Christina Mary, da of William O'Connor, of Dublin; 3 s (Nicholas William Patrick b 1968, Thomas Fitzgerald George b 1972, Hugh Francis Niall b 1974), 2 da (Gillian Mary b 1970, Alexandra Gwen b 1972); *Career* orthopaedic registrar Oxford 1968-70, sr orthopaedic registrar Sheffield 1970-73, lectr Univ Sheffield 1973-76, conslt orthopaedic surgn Sheffield 1976-; cncl memb Br Orthopaedic Assoc; *Recreations* fly fishing, skiing; *Style*— Thomas Smith, Esq; Cleveland House, 3 Whitworth Rd, Sheffield, South Yorkshire S10 3HD (☎ 0742 308398); Orthopaedic Department, Northern General Hospital, Herries Rd, Sheffield S5 7AU (☎ 0742 434343)

SMITH, Hon Timothy Hamilton; s of late 2 Baron Colwyn; *b* 1944; *Educ* Cheltenham, Oxford Univ (MA); *m* 1967, Carolyn, da of Bernulf Llewelyn Hodge, MRCS, LRCP, of The Old Cottage, Jac-na-Pare, Polperro, S Cornwall; 2 da; *Style*— The Hon Timothy Smith; 45 Third Ave, Claremont 7700, S Africa

SMITH, Timothy John; MP (C) Beaconsfield 1982-; s of late Capt Norman Wesley Smith, CBE (sometime Cdre Orient Steam Navigation Co), and late Nancy Phyllis, da of Engr Capt F J Pedrick, RN; *b* 5 Oct 1947; *Educ* Harrow, St Peter's Coll Oxford (MA); *m* 1980, Jennifer Jane, da of Maj Sir James Scott-Hopkins, MEP, *qv*; 2 s (Henry b 1982, Charles b 1984); *Career* articled Gibson Harris & Turnbull 1969-71, sr auditor Peat Marwick Mitchell 1971-73, co sec Coubro & Scrutton Holdings 1973-79, MP Ashfield 1977-79, PPS to Rt Hon Leon Brittan 1983-85; pres Univ of Oxford Cons Assoc 1968, sec Parly and Law Ctee Inst of CA's 1979-82, memb Public Accounts Ctee 1987-; FCA; *Style*— Timothy Smith, Esq, MP; 27 Rosenau Cres, London SW11; House of Commons, London SW1 (☎ 071 219 3000)

SMITH, Prof Trevor Arthur; s of Arthur James Smith, of Newnham-on-Severn, Gloucs, and Vera Gladys, *née* Cross; *b* 14 June 1937; *Educ* LSE (BSc); *m* 1, 14 Feb

1960 (m dis 1973), Brenda Susan, *née* Eustace; 2 s (Adam James William b 6 June 1964, Gideon Matthew Kingsley b 14 May 1966); m 2, 9 Aug 1979, Julia Donnithorne, *née* Bullock; 1 da (Naomi Thérése b 8 June 1981); *Career* schoolteacher LCC 1958-59, temp asst lectr Univ of Exeter 1959-60, res offr Acton Soc Tst 1960-62, lectr in politics Univ of Hull 1962-67 visiting assoc prof California State Univ Los Angeles 1969; QMC (later QMW) London: lectr (later sr lectr) in political studies 1967-83, head of dept 1972-85, dean of social studies 1979-82, prof 1983-, pro-princ 1985-87, sr pro-princ 1987-89, sr vice princ 1989-90; dir: Job Ownership Ltd 1978-85, New Society Ltd 1986-90, Statesman and Nation Publishing Co Ltd 1988-90, Gerald Duckworth & Co Ltd 1990-; chm: Joseph Rowntree Reform Trust Ltd 1987-, Political Studies Assoc of UK 1988-89 (vice pres 1989-); govr: Sir John Cass and Redcoats Sch 1979-84, Univ of Haifa 1985-, Bell Educn Tst 1988-; memb Tower Hamlets DHA 1987-91 (vice chm 1989-91), vice pres Patients Assoc 1988-; Parly candidate (Lib) Lewisham West 1959; FRHistS 1986; *Clubs* Reform; *Style—* Prof Trevor Smith; University of Ulster, Coleraine, Co Londonderry, Northern Ireland BT52 1SA (☎ 0265 44141, fax 0265 40902, telex 747597)

SMITH, Hon Mrs (Vera Lesley Meryl); *née* West; da of Baron Granville-West (Life Peer); *b* 1937; *m* 1959, William Smith; children; *Style—* The Hon Mrs Smith; Hollycroft, Sunnybank Rd, Griffithstown, Monmouthshire

SMITH, Dr William David; s of Kenneth Smith, of 27 Chesham Drive, New Longton, Preston, Lancs, and Gladys May, *née* Ward; *b* 29 July 1945; *Educ* Balshaw's GS Leyland Lancs, Univ of Liverpool (MB ChB); *m* 7 June 1967, Georgina, da of William Mole; 1 s (Paul David), 1 da (Rachel Ann); *Career* conslt anaesthetist Manchester Royal Infirmary 1976- (chm div of anaesthesia 1983-85), hon assoc lectr in anaesthesia Univ of Manchester 1985; memb: BMA 1968, Assoc of Anaesthetists GB and I 1972, Obstetric Anaesthetists Assocs 1972; fell Manchester Med Soc 1972 (memb section of anaesthetists), FFARCS 1972; *Books* Practical Anaesthesia for Surgical Emergencies (contrib 1985); *Recreations* walking in the Lake District, choral music; *Style—* Dr William Smith; 1 Vaudrey Drive, Cheadle Hulme, Cheshire SK8 5LR (☎ 061 485 6557); Department of Anaesthetics, Manchester Royal Infirmary, Oxford Rd, Manchester M13 9WL (☎ 061 276 4551)

SMITH, William Finch; s of William Frederich Smith (d 1968), of 50 Storey Lane, Winchester, Hants, and Mary Janet, *née* Melton (d 1971); *b* 16 April 1916; *Educ* Borough Poly, Croydon Poly; *m* 30 June 1941, Edith Theresa (d 1982), da of Charles Charlwood (d 1970), of Leeford Place, Whatlington, E Sussex; 2 s (Peter b 1946, Alan b 1950); *Career* WWII memb HG, res occupation instrument mfrs; ptnr (ret) F J Samuely 1956 (engr 1946-53, chief engr 1953-56); maj projects incl: Hatfield Tech Coll maj precast bldg, Slough Hosp, Battle Hosp, St Thomas' Stage 1 and residential blocks, Stage 2 library Trinity Coll Dublin, Kuwait housing, Newcastle Shopping Centre, Wakefield Shopping Centre, Banks for Saudi Arabian Monetary Banks of Damman Rehad and Jeddah; Fell Inst Welding 1959, FIStructE 1964, memb Assoc Conslt Engrs 1964, memb Civil Engrs 1968; *Style—* William Smith, Esq; Beech House, Stonestile Lane, Hastings, E Sussex (☎ 0424 752 168)

SMITH, William James; s of William Smith, and Alice, *née* Divers; *b* 2 Dec 1954; *Educ* St Alouysius Coll Glasgow, Heriot Watt Univ (BSc); *m* 3 July 1978, Marion Anne, da of Hugh Charles Slevin (d 1989); 1 s (Alastair b 1983), 2 da (Sarah b 1981, Hannah b 1985); *Career* asst investmt mangr Standard Life Assur Co 1977-84, jt md Prudential-Bache 1986-90, dir BZW Securities 1990-; FFA 1982; *Recreations* running; *Style—* William Smith, Esq; BZW Securities, Ebbgate House, 2 Swan Lane, London EC4R 3TS (☎ 071 956 4652, fax 071 956 3488)

SMITH, Dr William Leggat; CBE (1988), MC (1944), TD (1945); s of Rev Dr William James Smith (d 1953), and Isabella, *née* Leggat (d 1969); *b* 30 Jan 1918; *Educ* Glasgow Acad, Queen's Coll Oxford (BA), Univ of Glasgow (LLB); *m* 10 Oct 1941, Yvonne Menna, da of Arthur Williams, JP, High Sheriff of Carmarthenshire; 1 s (Lindsay), 2 da (Deborah (Mrs Walker), Alison (Mrs Ferguson)); *Career* WWII 1939-46, cmmnd TA The Cameronians served France, USA, Holland, Germany, demobbed as Maj 1946; admitted slr 1948, ptnr Carruthers Gemmill 1948-87; Dean Royal Faculty of Procurators 1977-79, Deacon Convenor Glasgow 1964-65; govr: Glasgow Acad War Memorial Tst 1962-80 (chm 1972-80), Glasgow Sch of Art 1967-88 (chm 1975-88); chm: Trades Hall of Glasgow Tst 1977-87, The Charles Rennie MacIntosh Soc, Cumbernauld New Town Licensing Planning Ctee 1979, Royal Soc for the Relief of Indigent Gentlewomen of Scotland; LLD Glasgow 1987; OStJ 1965; *Clubs* Western (Glasgow), RSAC; *Style—* Dr W Leggat Smith, CBE, MC, TD; Clachan of Campsie, Glasgow GL6 7AB

SMITH-BINGHAM, Col Jeremy David; s of Col Oswald Cyril Smith-Bingham (d 1979), of Glos, and Vera Mabel Johnson (d 1989); *b* 29 July 1939; *Educ* Eton, Sandhurst; *m* 22 July 1969, Priscilla Mary, da of Lt-Col Godfrey Sturdy Incledon-Webber TD (d 1986); 3 s (Richard David b 1970, Alexander John b 1973, Guy Jeremy b 1978); *Career* cmmnd Royal Horse Gds (The Blues) 1959, served England, Cyprus, N Ireland, Germany, CO The Blues and Royals 1982-85, Lt-Col cmdg Household Cavalry 1990-; *Recreations* skiing, tennis, squash, water sports, riding; *Clubs* Whites, Cavalry; *Style—* Col Jeremy Smith-Bingham; St Brannocks House, Braunton, Devon EX33 1HN (☎ 0271 812 270)

SMITH-CARINGTON, Wing Cdr John Hanbury; AFC (1953), DL (Leics 1972); s of Hamo Folville Smith-Carington (d 1946); *b* 26 Oct 1921; *Educ* Harrow, Oriel Coll Oxford; *m* 1951, Noreen, *née* Magee; 1 da; *Career* RAF 1941-71 (Queens Commendation for valuable serv in the air 1952), asst Air Attache Poland 1957-59, Mil and Air Attache Denmark 1965-68, Insp Serv Attaches 1970-71, ret as Wing Cdr; landowner Ashbey Folyille Estate 1946-; chm: Lord Carington Charity 1950-, Parish Cncl (and dist cncllr) 1972-; memb Borough Cncl 1972-79, dir Leics Red Cross 1972-86, E Leics Community Health Cncl 1973-79, High Sheriff Leics 1982-83, chm E Midlands Heraldic Soc 1982-, tstee Tobias Rustat Charity 1984-, pres Leics Assoc of of Parish Cncls 1985-, chm local Cons Branch 1985-, patron Leics History Soc 1985-, memb Central Cncl Leics Ctee Country Landowners 1985- (memb 1973-), vice pres Leics Record Office, memb Exec Ctee Leics Rural Community Cncl 1985-; *Recreations* country pursuits; *Clubs* RAF, Leics, Far and Near; *Style—* Wing Cdr John Smith-Carington, AFC, DL; Ashby Folyille Lodge, nr Melton Mowbray, Leics (☎ 066 64 840293)

SMITH-COX, (Sidney) Clifton; CBE (1963), TD (1947), JP (1955); s of Sidney Cox, JP (d 1949), of Bristol, and Ada Beatrice, *née* Smith (d 1939); *b* 8 Feb 1911; *Educ* Clifton; *m* 1, Margot, *née* Randal; 1 s (Geoffrey Randal b 7 April 1933); m 2, 10 May 1943, Marjorie Joyce, da of Frank Lawrence Payne (d 1976), of Newmarket; 1 s (Peter b 15 Aug 1947); *Career* WWII Lt-Col areas of operation Malaya and Normandy; CA; dir of co now subsidiary of Mount Charlotte Investmts plc 1944, dir of various other cos, chm Mount Charlotte Investmts plc and subsid cos (head office Leeds); former pres Bristol Zoological Soc, pres Dudley Zoological Soc; FCA, HCMIA, CBIM; *Recreations* swimming, walking, golf; *Clubs* Clevedon Golf, Clevedon Swimming; *Style—* Clifton Smith-Cox, Esq, CBE, TD, JP; Westward House, 27 Edgehill Rd, Walton St Mary, Clevedon BS21 7BZ (☎ 0272 872455); Mount Charlotte Investments plc, 2 The Calls, Leeds LS2 2JU (☎ 0532 439111, fax 0532 440238, telex 557934)

SMITH-DODSWORTH, David John; s and h of Sir John Smith-Dodsworth, 8 Bt; *b* 23 Oct 1963; *Educ* Ampleforth; *Career* farmer; *Style—* David Smith-Dodsworth, Esq; Thornton Watlass Hall, Ripon, Yorkshire

SMITH-DODSWORTH, Sir John Christopher; 8 Bt (GB 1784) of Newland Park, Yorks; s of Sir Claude Matthew Smith-Dodsworth, 7 Bt (d 1940); *b* 4 March 1935; *Educ* Ampleforth; *m* 1961, Margaret Anne, da of Alfred Jones, of Pludds, Glos; 1 s, 1 da; *Heir* s, David Smith-Dodsworth; *Style—* Sir John Smith-Dodsworth, Bt

SMITH ECCLES, Stephen; s of Stanley Smith Eccles, of 16 Hawthorne Road, Pinxton, Nottingham, and Joan Mary, *née* Ball; *b* 9 June 1955; *Educ* Swanick GS; *Career* Nat Hunt jockey 1984-; runner-up Nat Hunt Championship 1979-80 and 1982-83, 3 consecutive Champion Hurdles 1985-87, 2 Trumph Hurdle Winners; represented country in Aust, NZ, USA and Europe; fndr memb Br Jockeys team 1980; *Books* Turf Account (1985), Tails of the Turf (1987); *Recreations* reading, ornithology; *Style—* Stephen Smith Eccles, Esq; The Rectory, Snailwell, nr Newmarket, Suffolk (☎ 0638 77238)

SMITH-GORDON, Sir (Lionel) Eldred Peter; 5 Bt (UK 1838); s of Sir Lionel Eldred Pottinger Smith-Gordon, 4 Bt (d 1976); *b* 7 May 1935; *Educ* Eton, Trinity Coll Oxford; *m* 1962, Sandra Rosamund Ann, da of late Wing Cdr Walter Farley, DFC; 1 s, 1 da; *Heir* s, Lionel Smith-Gordon; *Style—* Sir Eldred Smith-Gordon, Bt; 13 Shalcomb St, London SW10 (☎ 071 352 8506)

SMITH-GORDON, Lionel George Eldred; s and h of Sir Eldred Smith-Gordon, 5 Bt; *b* 1 July 1964; *Educ* Eton, Westfield Coll and King's Coll Univ of London; *Career* with J P Morgan 1986-; *Clubs* Hurlingham; *Style—* Lionel Smith-Gordon, Esq; Flat 4, 48/50 Harrington Gardens, London SW7 4LT (☎ 071 373 6206)

SMITH-MARRIOTT, Sir Hugh Cavendish; 11 Bt (GB 1774), of Sydling, St Nicholas, Dorset; s (by 1 m) of Sir Ralph Smith-Marriott, 10 Bt; *b* 22 March 1925; *Educ* Bristol Cathedral Sch; *m* 1953, Pauline Anne (d 1985), da of Frank Fawcett Holt, of Bristol; 1 da (b 1958); *Heir* bro, Peter Francis b 1927; *Clubs* Gloucestershire CCC, MCC; *Style—* Sir Hugh Smith-Marriott, Bt; 26 Shipley Rd, Westbury-on-Trym, Bristol BS9 3HS

SMITH-MAXWELL, Archie Lonsdale Shipley; s of Lt Col John Douglas Hamilton Smith-Maxwell (d 1959), of Lemington Grange, Moreton-in-Marsh, Glos, and Winifred Joan, *née* Formby; *b* 6 March 1927; *Educ* Eton; *m* 28 Nov 1950, Patricia Mary, da of Maj Philip Wentworth Bell (d 1961), of The Old Rectory, Ilmington, Warwickshire; 2 s (Charles James Lonsdale b 1952, Philip John b 1953); *Career* served 1 The Royal Dragoons 1944-49; MFH The Ledbury 1966-76; livestock and bloodstock breeder (int judge); pres Irish Draught Horse Soc of GB; memb: S Worcs Cons Assoc, Br Legion; *Recreations* field sports; *Clubs* Cavalry and Guards'; *Style—* Archie Smith-Maxwell, Esq; Welland Lodge Farm, Upton-on-Severn, Worcestershire WR8 0SS (☎ 06846 2161)

SMITH-RYLAND, Hon Lady (Jeryl Marcia Sarah); *née* Gurdon; DL (1990); raised to rank of a Baron's da 1964; da of late Hon Robert Brampton Gurdon (s of 2 Baron Cranworth), and Hon Daisy, *née* Pearson, da of 2 Viscount Cowdray and subsequently w of (1) Lt-Col Alistair Gibb and (2) 1 Baron McCorquodale of Newton; sis of 3 Baron Cranworth; *b* 1932; *m* 1952, Sir Charles Mortimer Tollemache Smith-Ryland, KCVO, JP, Lord Lt for Warwicks (d 1989); 2 s (Robin, David), 3 da (Sarah, Joanna, Petra); *Career* DStJ 1990 (CStJ 1981); *Style—* The Hon Lady Smith-Ryland, DL; Sherbourne Park, Warwick CV35 8AP

SMITHERS, Prof Alan George; s of Alfred Edward (d 1976), of London, and Queenie Lilian, *née* Carmichael; *b* 20 May 1938; *Educ* Barking Abbey, King's Coll London (BSc, PhD), Univ of Bradford (MSc, PhD); *m* 27 Aug 1962, Angela Grace, da of David Wykes, of Exeter; 2 da (Vaila Helen b 1967, Rachel Hilary b 1969); *Career* lectr in botany Birkbeck 1964-67, sr lectr in educn Univ of Bradford 1967-75 (res fell 1967-69), prof of educn Univ of Manchester 1976-; fell Soc for Res in Higher Educn, chartered psychologist; *Books* Sandwich Courses: An Integrated Education (1976), The Progress of Mature Students (with A Griffin, 1986), The Growth of Mixed A Levels (with P Robinson, 1988), The Shortage of Mathematics and Physics Teachers (with P Robinson, 1988), Increasing Participation in Higher Education (with P Robinson, 1989), Graduates in the Police Service (with S Hill, 1990), Teacher Provision in the Sciences (with P Robinson, 1990), Gender, Primary Education and the National Curriculum (with P Zientek, 1991), The Vocational Route into Higher Education (1991); *Recreations* theatre, walking, swimming; *Style—* Prof Alan Smithers; School of Education, University of Manchester, Manchester M13 9PL (☎ 061 275 3446, fax 061 275 3519)

SMITHERS, Andrew Reeve Waldron; s of Prof Sir David Waldron Smithers, MD, FRCP, FRCS, FRCR, of Ringfield, Knockholt, Kent, and Gwladys Margaret, *née* Angel: gs of Sir Waldron Smithers, MP for 30 yrs Chiselhurst and Orpington; *b* 21 Sept 1937; *Educ* Winchester, Clare Coll Cambridge (MA); *m* 8 June 1963, (Amanda) Jill, da of Edward Gilbert Kennedy, of 23 The Street, Chirton, Devizes, Wilts; 2 s ((Matthew) Pelham b 10 Oct 1964, (Jonathan) Kit b 6 Dec 1967); *Career* chm: Whatman Reeve Angel plc 1969- (dir 1960-), Smithers & Co Ltd (Economic Consits) 1989-; dir: S G Warburg Securities 1967-89 (joined co 1962), Drayton Asia Trust plc 1989-, Mercury Selected Tst 1977-; memb Soc of Investment Analysts; *Recreations* conversation, reading, performing arts, cricket, tennis; *Clubs* Brooks's; *Style—* Andrew Smithers, Esq; Smithers & Co Ltd, Sedgwick House, The Sedgwick Centre, London E1 8DX (☎ 071 377 3765, fax 071 377 3292, telex 882131)

SMITHERS, Prof Sir David Waldron; s of Sir Waldron Smithers, JP, MP (d 1954); *b* 17 Jan 1908; *Educ* Charterhouse, Clare Coll Cambridge; *m* 1933, Gwladys Margaret, *née* Angel; 1 s, 1 da; *Career* frof of radiotherapy Inst of Cancer Res and Royal Marsden Hosp 1943-72; hon conslt radiotherapist: Brompton Hosp Diseases of the Chest, RN; kt Cdr SMOM 1972; kt 1969; *Books* Jane Austen in Kent (1982), Not a Moment to Lose Some Reminiscences (1989), This Idle Trade: on doctors who were writers (1989); *Recreations* book collecting, growing roses, arts; *Style—* Prof Sir David Smithers; Ringfield, Knockholt, Kent (☎ 0959 32122)

SMITHERS, Sir Peter Henry Berry Otway; VRD (and clasp); s of Lt-Col H O Smithers, JP, of Itchen Stoke House; *b* 9 Dec 1913; *Educ* Harrow, Magdalen Coll Oxford (MA, DPhil); *m* 1943, Dojean, da of T M Sayman of St Louis, USA; 2 da; *Career* WWII Lt Cdr RNVR, Naval staff France, Br Embassy Washington, Mexico, Central American Republics, Panama; called to the Bar Inner Temple 1946, memb Winchester RDC 1946-49; MP (C) Winchester 1950-64; PPS to: min state Colonial Affrs 1952, Sec State Colonies 1956-59, vice chm Cons Parly Foreign Affrs Ctee 1959-61, Parly Under Sec State FO 1962-64; del Consultative Assembly Cncl of Europe 1952-56, UK del to UN Gen Assembly 1960-62, sec gen Cncl of Europe 1964-69; Master Worshipful Co of Turners 1955; sr fell UN Inst for Trg and Res 1969-72; hon DJur Zurich 1969, Alexander von Humboldt Gold Medal 1970, chevalier de la Légion Honneur, Aguila Azteca Mexicana, medal of the Parly Assembly of the Cncl of Europe 1984, RHS Gold medal (4 times) and Grenfell medal for Photography; sixteen one man shows of photography in museums and galleries in the US and Europe; kt 1970; *Books* Life of Joseph Addison; *Recreations* gardening; *Clubs* Carlton, Everglades (Palm Beach), Bath & Tennis (Palm Beach); *Style—* Sir Peter Smithers, VRD; CH-6921, Vico Morcote, Switzerland

SMITHERS, Sir Reginald Allfree; s of F Smithers; *b* 3 Feb 1903; *Educ* Melbourne

GS, Melbourne Univ (LLB); *m* 1932, Dorothy, da of J Smalley; 2 s, 1 da; *Career* served RAAF Australia, New Guinea, Philippines 1942-45, Sqdn Ldr; liaison offr Gen MacArthur's Publicity Section; QC 1951, judge of Supreme Ct Papua New Guinea 1962-64, additional judge Supreme Ct of ACT and Supreme Ct of NT 1964-, judge Aust Indust Ct 1965-, dep pres Admin Appeals Tribunal 1977-80, judge of Fed Ct of Australia 1977-86; chm Victorian Bar Cncl 1959-60, pres Young Nationalists Orgn of Victoria 1959-, chllr La Trove Univ Melbourne 1972-80; kt 1980; *see Debrett's Handbook of Australia and New Zealand for further details*; *Style—* Sir Reginald Smithers; 11 Florence Ave, Kew, Vic 3101, Australia

SMITHSON, Peter Denham; s of William Blenkiron Smithson (d 1974), and Elizabeth, *née* Denham (d 1978); *b* 18 Sept 1923; *Educ* The GS Stockton-on-Tees, The Sch of Architecture Univ of Durham, Newcastle upon Tyne, Royal Acad Schs London; *m* 18 Aug 1949, Alison Margaret, da of Ernest Gill (d 1980); 1 s (Simon), 2 da (Samantha Target, Soraya Wilson); *Career* RE 1942-45; architect in private practice; maj projects incl: Hunstanton Secdy Modern Sch 1950-54, The Economist Bldg St James St 1959-64, Robin Hood Gdns Tower Hamlets 1963-72, Garden Bldg St Hildas Coll Oxford 1967-70, Second Arts Bldg 1978-81 and Amenity Bldg 1978-85, Univ of Bath, Sch of Architecture and Bldg Engrg Univ of Bath 1982-87, Arts Bath Auditorium Univ of Bath 1980-90; visiting prof: Delft, Munich, Harvard, Univ of Bath; memb The Boltons Assoc; *Books* The Shift (1982), The 30's (1985), Upper Lawn (1986); with Alison Smithson: Ordinariness and Light (1970), Without Rhetoric (1973); *Style—* Peter Smithson, Esq; The Limes, Off Priory Walk, London SW10 9SP; Cato Lodge, 24 Gilston Rd, London SW10 9SR (☎ 071 373 7423)

SMITHWICK, Michael Stewart; s of Everard Edward Smithwick (d 1976), of Talywain, Monmouthshire, and Eva, *née* Riddington (d 1980); *b* 6 July 1941; *Educ* Stationers' Co Sch, Univ of Leicester (BSc Econ), Univ of Lancaster (MSc); *m* 1 Aug 1964, Karen Dorothy, da of John Alfred Stevenson; 2 s (Marcus Jonathan Justin b 13 Feb 1968, Jason Michael Lance b 22 May 1969), 1 da (Sarah Annabel b 24 Jan 1971); *Career* Dexion Ltd 1959-64 (graduate trainee, distribution promotion offr, product mangr), agric mktg mangr Saville Tractors Ltd 1965-66, Massey Ferguson Ltd 1966-71 (regnl mangr south, Euro mktg mangr), Boc Group 1971-80 (mktg dir then dir and gen mangr Electric Welding, md Sparklets International Group), md Nicklin Advertising Ltd 1980-; non-exec dir: Edwards High Vacuum International Ltd 1975-7, TSL Group PLC 1988; MIPA 1982; *Recreations* reading, painting (appreciation rather than practice); *Style—* Michael Smithwick, Esq; Nicklin Advertising Ltd, 56 Marsh Wall, London E14 9UE (☎ 071 538 5521, fax 071 538 5704, car 0831 359 375)

SMITS, Benjamin Arthur; s of Arthur Charles Smits, of 5 Woodlands Way, St Ives, nr Ringwood, Hants, and Laurance Maria, *née* Panjoul; *b* 21 Sept 1934; *Educ* Watford GS, Watford Coll of Further Educn; *m* 1, 14 Feb 1958 (m dis 1986), Ann, *née* Jarvis; 2 s (David Charles b 30 June 1959, Jeremy Paul b 19 Nov 1960), 1 da (Joanna Louise b 3 July 1965); m 2, 16 April 1988, Monica Mary, da of Thomas Dempsey (d 1970), of Dublin; *Career* Nat Serv RAF 1952-54; sales and mktg dir Hosiery Div Courtaulds (Hinckley Group) 1964-73, sales dir Pretty Polly Ltd 1973-84, sales and mktg dir Great Marketing Ltd 1987-88 (md 1984-87), md Bear Brand Hosiery Ltd 1988-; represented Herts CC Athletics 1956-57; MInstM 1965; *Recreations* reading, gardening, music; *Style—* Benjamin Smits, Esq; 35 Pershore Grove, Ainsdale, Southport PR8 2SY; Bear Brand Hosiery Ltd, Allerton Rd, Woolton, Liverpool L25 7SF, (☎ 051 428 1291, fax 051 428 7320, telex 627209)

SMITS, Dr Bernard John; s of Johannes Petrus Smits (d 1951), of Hoddesdon, Herts, and Helena Catherina, *née* Sinnige (d 1985); *b* 3 Aug 1929; *Educ* St Ignatius Coll Stamford Hill London, Univ of London Charing Cross Hosp (MB BS); *m* 1, 29 May 1955 (m dis 1977), Norma Marie, *née* Douglas; 1 s (John Bernard Douglas b 1966), 1 da (Helen Anne Marie b 1965); m 2, 25 March 1978, Patricia Anne, da of Henry Bamford (d 1967), of Chorley, Lancs; 2 s (Benjamin Patrick Anh b 1974, James Bernard Leo b 1979), 1 da (Sophie Catherine Ava b 1985); *Career* Nat Serv Royal Hampshire Regt and RAMC 1947-50; sr med registrar and res fell Univ of Birmingham early 1960s, conslt physician and gastroenterologist Coventry and N Warwicks AHAs 1967-, currently in private med consultancy; numerous med pubns and med films; currently chm Coventry Consulting Rooms Ltd; dir: Allambie Ltd, Allanbie's Care-on-Wheels Ltd; memb: Br Soc of Gastroenterology, Midlands Soc of Gastroenterology, Br Pancreatic Soc, Euro Soc of Parental and Enteral Nutrition, Lourdes Med Assoc of GB, Int Med Cmmn of Lourdes, Dutch Swiss and Flemish Socs of Gastroenterology; memb: BMA, BSG; FRCPsych (London); Knight of the Order of St Gregory the Gt conferred by Pope Paul VI 1978; *Recreations* theatre, food and wine, reading; *Style—* Dr Bernard J Smits; Dept of Gastroenterology, Walsgrave Hospital, Coventry CV2 2DX (☎ 0203 602020 ext 8596); Consulting Rooms, 11 Dalton Rd, Coventry CV5 6PB (☎ 0203 677445)

SMOLLETT OF BONHILL; *see*: Telfer-Smollett of Bonhill

SMOUHA, Brian Andrew; s of Wing Cdr Edward Ralph Smouha, OBE, of Switzerland, and Yvonne Annie, *née* Ades; *b* 3 Sept 1938; *Educ* Harrow, Magdalene Coll Cambridge; *m* 28 Dec 1961, Hana Smouha, da of Simon Btesh (d 1974); 2 s (Joe b 21 Jan 1963, Stephen b 12 April 1965); *Career* CA; ptnr Touche Ross & Co 1970, seconded under-sec industl devpt unit Dept of Indust 1979-80; pres Cambridge Athletics Union 1961, rep UK at athletics; FCA 1973; *Recreations* skiing, tennis; *Style—* Brian Smouha, Esq; Touche Ross & Co, Hill Hse, 1 Little New St, London EC4A 3TR (☎ 071 936 3000, car 0860 336600, fax 071 583 8517, telex 884739 TRLUNDN G)

SMOUT, Prof (Thomas) Christopher; s of Arthur Smout (d 1961), of Sheriffs Lench, Evesham, Worcs, and Hilda, *née* Follows (d 1979); *b* 19 Dec 1933; *Educ* Leys Sch Cambridge, Clare Coll Cambridge (MA, PhD); *m* 15 Aug 1959, Anne-Marie, da of Alfred Schøning, of Charlottenlund, Denmark; 1 s (Andrew b 1963), 1 da (Pernille Anne b 1961); *Career* prof of econ history Univ of Edinburgh 1971 (asst lectr 1959), prof of Scottish history Univ of St Andrews 1980; memb: Royal Cmmn on Ancient and Historical Monuments (Scotland), Bd NCC (Scotland); FRSE 1978, FBA 1988; *Books* A History of the Scottish People (1969), A Century of the Scottish People (1986), Scottish Voices (with Sydney Wood, 1990); *Recreations* birds, butterflies, dragonflies and bees; *Style—* Prof Christopher Smout, FRSE; Chesterhill, Shore Rd, Anstruther, Fife KY10 3DZ (☎ 0333 310330); Department of Scottish History, University of St Andrews, St Andrews, Fife (☎ 0334 76161)

SMYLIE, Dr (Henry) Gordon; s of Roland Cecil Smylie (d 1967), of 14 Dunvegan Drive, Newton Mearns, Glasgow, and Margaret Beveridge, *née* Wardlaw (d 1966); *b* 31 July 1926; *Educ* Robert Gordon's Coll, Univ of Aberdeen (MB ChB, MD); *m* 4 Aug 1954, Evelyn Allan, da of Christopher Gray (d 1964), of Netherton Lodge, Bieldside, Aberdeen; 4 s (Alan b 5 May 1955, Graeme b 8 Jan 1957, Christopher b 25 March 1959, David b 1 March 1963); *Career* vol RN 1943 substantive rating Coder released to Reserve 1947 Class A; trainee jr sales mangr Bon-Accord Newspaper Aberdeen 1942, clerk to builders merchants J & W Henderson Ltd Aberdeen 1943, farming and forestry 1947-48, GP 1955, univ lectr 1956, sr lectr in bacteriology Univ of Aberdeen 1964, conslt to Grampian Health Bd 1964, visiting conslt to Min of Health Kuwait 1976-; govr Robert Gordons Coll Aberdeen, past pres Gordonian Assoc; Burgess City of Aberdeen 1985; FRCPath; *Books* Some Studies on the Control of Pyogenic Staphylococci in Hospital (1960); *Recreations* running, cycling, swimming, music and art; *Style—* Dr Gordon Smylie; Birken Lodge, Bieldside, Aberdeen AB1 9BQ (☎ 0224 861305); Dept of Microbiology, The Medical School, University of Aberdeen, Foresterhill, Aberdeen (☎ 0224 681818 ext 2446)

SMYLY, Hon Mrs (Harriet Lucy); *née* Beckett; da of 4 Baron Grimthorpe, OBE; *b* 18 Feb 1961; *Educ* Heathfield; *m* 1985, Capt Mark Smyly; *Career* interior decorator; *Recreations* skiing, racing; *Style—* The Hon Mrs Smyly; Snelsmore Farmhouse, Snelsmore, Newbury, Berkshire RG16 9BU

SMYTH, Christopher Jackson; s of Col Edward Hugh Jackson Smyth, of 29 Castle Street, Farnham, Surrey, and Ursula Helen Lucy, *née* Ross (d 1984); *b* 9 Aug 1946; *Educ* St Lawrence Coll, Trinity Hall Cambridge (MA); *m* 9 Dec 1972, Jane Elizabeth, da of Dr Robert Alexander Porter (d 1981); 3 da (Debbie b 1976, Sophie b 1979, Amanda b 1982); *Career* Lt RN 1966-76, Lt Cdr Sussex Div RNR 1978-82; called to the bar Inner Temple 1972, practice SE Circuit; *Recreations* sailing; *Clubs* Army and Navy; *Style—* Christopher Smyth, Esq; Ridge House, Kingston, Lewes, East Sussex BN7 3JX (☎ 0273 480 075); 1 Crown Office Row, Temple, London EC4Y 7HH (☎ 071 353 1801, fax 071 583 1700, telex 24988 ICOR G)

SMYTH, Des; s of Patrick Smyth, and Josephine, *née* Rock; *b* 12 Feb 1953; *Educ* Christian Brothers Sch Drogheda; *m* Vicki; 2 s (Gregory b 1984, Shane b 1988), 1 da (Karen b 1982); *Career* profesional golfer; former amateur int, turned professional 1974; tournament victories: Sun Alliance Euro Matchplay Championship 1979, Newcastle Brown 900 1980, Greater Manchester Open 1980, Coral Classic 1981, Sanyo Open 1983, BNP Jersey Open 1988; Winner Irish Championship 1979, 1985, 1986, 1990; team events: Ryder Cup 1979 and 1981, represented Ireland World Cup and Dunhill Cup (winners 1988); *Recreations* tennis, horse racing; *Style—* Des Smyth, Esq

SMYTH, Frances, Lady; Frances Mary Blair; da of Lt-Col Robert Alexander Chambers, OBE, IMS (decd), and Elsie Blair Saunders (decd); *b* 30 Jan 1908; *Educ* St Georges Harpenden; *m* 1, Lt-Col J E Read, IA (dec'd), 1 s (Charles), 1 da (Mary); m 2, 1940, as his 2 w, Brig Rt Hon Sir John George Smyth, Bt, VC, MC (d 1983); *Style—* Frances, Lady Smyth; 603 Grenville House, Dolphin Sq, London SW1V 3LR

SMYTH, John Clifford; TD; s of Harold Smyth, of Liverpool, and Alice, *née* Halsall; *b* 22 Aug 1920; *Educ* Liverpool Collegiate; *m* 29 Nov 1944, Norah Myfanwy, da of Percival J Powell, of Castle Donington, Leics; 1 s ((John) Rodney b 23 Aug 1953); *Career* RA (TA) 1939-56: 87 (1 West Lancs) FD Regt, 136 (1 West Lancs) FD Regt, 287 (1 West Lancs) Medium Regt (despatches 1946); admitted slr; ptnr: Weightman Pedder & Co 1949-70, Weightmans 1970-88, Weightman Rutherfords 1988-89 (conslt 1989-); chm Wirral UDC 1973-74 (councillor 1963-74), co councillor Merseyside CC 1976-86; pres and chm Royal Sch For Blind Liverpool 1955- (memb Ctee 1951-); former: chm Abbeyfield Heswall and vice pres Heswall Cncl Voluntary Serv; memb Ctee Heswall Soc 1960-; memb Law Soc; *Clubs* Racquet (Liverpool); *Style—* John Smyth, Esq, TD; Chestnut Cottage, 67 Thurstaton Rd, Heswall, Wirral, Merseyside L60 6SA (☎ 051 342 3475); Weightman Rutherfords, Richmond House, Rumford Place, Liverpool L3 9QW (☎ 051 227 2601, fax 051 227 3223, telex 627538)

SMYTH, Maj John Montagu (Monty); MBE (1983); s of Capt John Robert Henry Smyth (d 1938), of The Manor House, Fladbury, Pershore, Worcestershire, and Elizabeth, *née* Stone (d 1945); *b* 18 Feb 1905; *Educ* Charterhouse, RMC; *m* 22 April 1936, Rosamund May (d 1987), da of Maj William Harker (d 1950), of Blofield Hall, Norwich, Norfolk; 1 da (Margaret Ann (Mrs R A Humphries)); *Career* joined Norfolk Regt 1924, Adj Depot 1935-36, Adj and QM The Royal Militia Island of Jersey 1936-40, Maj 1941, POW Malaya 1942-45, ret 1946; vice-chm and vice pres S Worcs Cons Assoc 1946-; memb: Fladbury PC 1946-50 (and chm), Pershore RDC 1946-50 (vice-chm 1948-50), Hanley Castle PCC 1951-65, Upton on Severn RDC 1963-73, Worcs CC 1967-71, for Upton on Severn, Hereford and Worcester CC 1973-85 for Powick; govr of two schs, Guarlford PC 1963-90 (chm 1976-88), Lasletts tstee, memb CLA Co Ctee; High Sheriff Worcestershire 1966; memb Three Co's Agric Soc, life govr RASE; *Recreations* shooting, travel; *Clubs* Army and Navy; *Style—* Maj J M Smyth, MBE; 19 Upton Gdns, Upton on Severn, Worcester WR8 0NU (☎ 06846 4488)

SMYTH, Rev (William) Martin; MP (Ulster Unionist) Belfast South, March 1982-; s of James Smyth, JP, of 40 Ardenlee Ave, Belfast (d 1982), and Minnie Kane; *b* 15 June 1931; *Educ* Methodist Coll Belfast, Magee Univ Coll Londonderry, Trinity Coll Dublin (BA, BD), Presbyterian Coll Belfast; *m* 1957, Kathleen Jean, da of David Johnston (d 1978), of Ballymatoskerty, Toomebridge; 2 da (and 1 da decd); *Career* ordained Raffrey Presbyterian Church 1957, installed Alexandra (Belfast) 1963-82, minister without charge April 1982; grand master: Grand Orange Lodge of Ireland 1972-, World Orange Cncl 1973-82; hon dep grand master Orange Order: USA, NZ, NSW; hon past grand master Canada; elected NI Assembly Oct 1982-86, chm of assembly Health and Social Services Ctee; Ulster Unionist Pty spokesman on health and social servs; vice chm All Party Ctee on Soviet Jewry; memb: Br Exec IPU 1985-, Social Servs Select Ctee 1983-90, UK exec CPA 1989-, Health Select Ctee 1991-; vice chm Br-Brazilian Gp; treas: Br-Namibia Gp, Br-Morocco Gp; sec: Br-Israel Gp, Parly Social Servs Panel; *Recreations* reading, photography, travel; *Style—* The Rev Martin Smyth, MP; 6 Mornington, Annadale Ave, Belfast BT7 3JS, N Ireland; office: 117 Cregagh Rd, Belfast BT6 0LA, N Ireland (☎ 0232 457009); House of Commons, London SW1 (☎ 071 219 4198)

SMYTH, Hon Mrs (Patricia Margaret); da of Baron Black (Life Peer, d 1984), and his w Margaret Patricia (d 1976), da of James Dallas, of Dundee; *b* 26 June 1919; *m* 1942, Leslie John Smyth; 1 s (Timothy), 2 da (Tessa, Lesley-Anne); *Style—* The Hon Mrs Smyth; Goudie's Farm, Lower Hamswell, Bath, Avon BA1 9DE

SMYTH, His Hon Judge (James) Robert Staples; s of Maj Robert Smyth, of Gaybrook, Mullingar, Co Westmeath (d 1952), and Mabel Anne Georgiana, *née* MacGeough-Bond (d 1985); *b* 11 July 1926; *Educ* St Columba's Coll Dublin, Merton Coll Oxford (BA, MA); *m* 3 April 1971, Fenella Joan, da of Ian Blair Mowat, of Bridge of Weir, Renfrewshire; 1 s (Ralph b 1976); *Career* served WWII RAF; called to the Bar Inner Temple 1949; Magistrate Northern Rhodesia 1951-55, dep chm Agric Land Tbnl 1974, Stipendiary Magistrate West Midlands 1978, rec of the Crown Court 1983, circuit judge 1986-; *Recreations* shooting, fishing; *Style—* His Hon Judge Robert Smyth; Leys, Shelsley Beauchamp, Worcester WR6 6RB (☎ 088 65 291)

SMYTH, (John) Rodney; s of John Clifford Smyth, of Heswall, Merseyside, and Norah Myfanwy, *née* Powell; *b* 23 Aug 1953; *Educ* Shrewsbury, Magdalene Coll Cambridge (MA); *m* 20 July 1990, Sarah, *née* Johnson; *Career* barr 1975-79; admitted slr 1980; asst slr: Holman Fenwick & Willan 1980-82, Lovell White Durrant (formerly Durrant Piesse) 1982-85 (ptnr 1985-); memb Law Soc; *Recreations* birdwatching, paintings; *Style—* Rodney Smyth, Esq; Brickhouse Farm, Main Rd, St Mary Hoo, Rochester, Kent ME3 8RP (☎ 0634 270 326); Lovell White Durrant, 65 Holborn Viaduct, London EC1A 2DY (☎ 071 236 0066, fax 071 248 4212, telex 887122 LWD G)

SMYTH, Stephen Mark James Athelstan; s of Marcus Smyth (d 1965), of Walnut Tree Cottage, Ditchling, and Ann, *née* Symons; *b* 28 Dec 1946; *Educ* Hurstpierpoint Coll, Alliance Francaise; *m* 22 May 1981, Bridget Rosemary Diana, da of Maj (Arthur) Creagh Gibson (d 1970), of Glenburn Hall, Jedburgh; 2 da (Lalage Vivien b 5 Jan 1986, India b 24 May 1989); *Career* called to the Bar Inner Temple 1974; *Recreations* books, sailing; *Clubs* Bosham Sailing; *Style—* Stephen Smyth, Esq; 27 Cleaver Square, Kennington, London (☎ 071 735 5582); 2 Harcourt Buildings, Temple, London EC4 (☎ 071 353 2112, fax 071 353 8339)

SMYTH, Sir Timothy John; 2 Bt (UK 1956), of Teignmouth, Co Devon; s of Julian Smyth (d 1974, himself 2 s of Brig Rt Hon Sir John Smyth, 1 Bt, VC, MC, PC (d 1983)), and his 1 w Margaret; *b* 16 April 1953; *Educ* Univ of NSW (MB BS, LLB, MBA); *m* 1981, Bernadette Mary, da of Leo Askew; 2 s, 2 da; *Heir* s, Brendan Julian Smyth (b 1981); *Career* hosp mangr; *Style—* Dr Sir Timothy Smyth, Bt; 21 King St, Sydney, NSW 2031, Australia

SMYTHE, Clifford Anthony (Tony); s of Clifford John Smythe, and May Florence, *née* Howarth (d 1988); *b* 2 Aug 1938; *Educ* Univ Coll Sch, North West Poly; *m* Jeanne; 4 c (Quita b 1960, Petra b 1962, Nicole b 1963, Hansi b 1968); *Career* teacher Burgess Hill Sch London 1958-59, gen sec War Resisters International 1959-64, personnel mangr Scott Bader and Co 1965, gen sec NCCL 1966-72, nat field dir American Civil Union 1973, nat dir Nat Assoc for Mental Health 1974-82, conslt 1982 and 1988-89; dir: Assoc of Community Health Cncls for Eng and Wales 1983-86, Shelter Housing Aid Centre 1986-88, Med Campaign Against Nuclear Weapons 1989-; chm Nat Assoc of Voluntary Hostels 1991-, tstee Lansbury House Tst Fund; *Books* Conscription - A World Survey (1966), Privacy Under Attack (1973); *Recreations* travel, reading, bird watching; *Style—* Tony Smythe, Esq; 136 Stapleton Hall Road, London N4 4QB (☎ 081 348 2516); Medical Campaign Against Nuclear Weapons, 601 Holloway Rd, London N19 4DJ (☎ 071 272 2020, fax 071 281 5717)

SMYTHE, Colin Peter; s of Wing Cdr Cyril Richard Smythe (d 1985), and Jean Edith, *née* Murdoch (d 1949); *b* 2 March 1942; *Educ* Bradfield, Trinity Coll Univ of Dublin (BA, MA); *Career* md Colin Smythe Ltd 1966-, hon res assoc Royal Holloway and Bedford Coll Univ of London; OStJ 1987; memb Ed Bd Yeats Annual; vice chm Int Assoc of the Study of Anglo Irish Lit 1988-91 (memb Exec Ctee 1973-), chm Biographical Sub-Ctee 1973-79, academic advsr to the Princess Grace Irish Library Monaco; memb: Br Assoc for Irish Studies, Canadian Assoc for Irish Studies, American Conference for Irish Studies; visiting prof Universidade Moderna Lisbon, overseas corresponding academician Academia de Letras e Artes Portugal, charge d'affaires for GB of the Grand Chancery of the SM Constantinian Order of St Georege Naples; FRSA; Insigne Aeneum Concillium Ecumenicum Vaticanum II, Knight of the Order of Polonia Restituta, Knight Cdr of Grace with Star, Sacred and Military Constantinian Order of St George; *Books* The Coole Edition of Lady Gregory's Writings (gen ed 1970), Lady Gregory Seventy Years 1852-1922 (ed 1974), Robert Gregory 1881-1918 (ed 1981), A Guide to Coole Park Home of Lady Gregory (2 edn 1983), Lady Gregory, Fifty Years After (ed with A Saddlemeyer 1987); *Clubs* Athenaeum; *Style—* Colin Smythe, Esq; PO Box 6, Gerrards Cross, Bucks SL9 8XA (☎ 0753 886000, fax 0753 886469)

SNAGGE, Maj Carron Edward Mordaunt; s of Maj Ralph Mordaunt Snagge, MBE, TD, of Folly Hill, 10 Baring Rd, Cowes, IOW PO31 8DA, and Pamela Mordaunt, *née* Scrimgeour; *b* 23 June 1951; *Educ* Eton; *m* 15 Dec 1973, Jennifer Anne, da of (John) Dugald Thomson, of 11/107 Darling Point Rd, Darling Point, Sydney 2027, New South Wales, Australia; 1 s ((Thomas) Henry Dugald b 15 April 1984), 2 da (Emily Jane b 20 Aug 1977, Jemima Alice b 8 May 1979); *Career* Cadet Mons OCS 1970, 2 Lt 1 Bn Royal Creek Jackets (IRGJ) Germany and NI 1971, Platoon Cdr Jr Infantrymen's Bn Shorncliffe 1972, Lt Reg Careers Course Sandhurst 1974, Capt IRGJ Dover, NI, Cyprus, Hong Kong 1975, Adj Rifle Depot Winchester 1979, Maj Co Cdr Rifle Depot 1980, student Australian Cmd and Staff Coll 1983, Co Cdr IRGJ Falkland Islands Tidworth 1984, Co's Br Forces Belize 1986, 2 i/c IRGJ Germany; Freeman City of London 1972, Liveryman Worshipful Co of Skinners 1978; *Recreations* sailing, sub aqua diving, hill walking; *Clubs* Royal Yacht Sqdn, Pratt's, Army and Navy; *Style—* Maj Carron Snagge; 1 Bn Royal Green Jackets, Mercer Barracks, BFPO 36

SNAGGE, Air Cmdt Dame Nancy Marion; DBE (1955), OBE (1945); da of late Henry Thomas Salmon; *b* 2 May 1906; *Educ* Notting Hill High Sch; *m* 1962, Thomas Geoffrey Mordaunt Snagge, DSC (d 1984); *Career* joined WAAF 1939, offr in the WAAF and WRAF 1939-, ADC to HM King George VI 1950-52, ADC to HM The Queen 1952-56, dir WRAF 1950-56; *Style—* Air Cmdt Dame Nancy Snagge, DBE; Test Lodge, Longstock, Stockbridge, Hampshire (☎ 0264 810558)

SNAILHAM, (George) Richard; s of Capt William Rushton Snailham (d 1942), and Mabel, *née* Wilson (d 1989); *b* 18 May 1930; *Educ* Oakham Sch, Keble Coll Oxford; *m* 19 Jan 1990, Dr Christina March; *Career* Nat Serv 1948-50, Duke of Wellingtons Regt, Intelligence Corps MI8; schoolmaster: Alleyn Ct Sch Westcliff 1954-55, Clayesmore Sch Iwerne Minster Dorset 1955-57, Exeter Sch Devon 1957-65; sr lectr RMA Sandhurst 1965-90; semi finalist Mastermind 1973, semi finalist Brain of Britain 1976, twice winner Busman's Holiday 1987; fndr memb Scientific Exploration Soc 1969 (memb Cncl), pres Globetrotters Club 1977-90, sec Young Explorers Trust 1986-90 (memb Cncl), Winston Churchill Fellowship Surrey and West Sussex 1984-91 (chm); expeditions to Ethiopia: 1966, Blue Nile 1968, Dahlak Islands 1970-71, 1972; expeditions to: Zaire River 1974-75, Ecuador 1976, Kenya (Op Drake) 1980 and 1986, Kenya (Op Raleigh) 1988-89; Mrs Patrick Ness Award RGS 1980; FRGS 1973 (memb Cncl 1986-88), hon foreign sec 1990; *Books* The Blue Nile Revealed (1970), A Giant Among Rivers (1976), Sangay Survived. (1978), Normandy and Brittany (1986); *Recreations* reviewing books, giving travel and expedition talks; *Clubs* Globetrotters, Mastermind; *Style—* Richard Snailham, Esq; 13 Gloucester Place, Windsor, Berks

SNAITH, Prof Martin Somerville; s of Gp Capt Leonard Somerville Snaith, CB, AFC, DL (d 1985), and Joyce Edith, *née* Taylor; *b* 20 May 1945; *Educ* Bedford Sch, Trinity Coll Dublin (MA, BAI, MSc, ScD), Univ of Nottingham (PhD); *m* 15 June 1974, Jane Dorothy Elizabeth, da of Aubrey Alexander Maxwell Clark, of Ballyclough House, Ballyclough Rd, Bushmills, Co Antrim, NI; 1 s (Timothy James b 15 Nov 1982), 1 da (Lucinda Jane b 18 May 1979); *Career* materials engr Kenya Govt, post-doctoral res fell Trinity Coll Dublin, lectr Queens Univ Belfast, prof of highway engrg Univ of Birmingham (ODA sr lectr); memb: Br Nat Ctee of the Perm Int Assoc of Road Congresses, Gaffney Ctee (and author Snaith Report for NI), Construction Bd Inst of Highways and Transportation, SERC Environment Ctee; rep athletics Ireland 1969; Freeman City of London 1989, Liveryman Worshipful Co of Paviors; FICE 1986, FIHT 1987, FIEI 1987; *Recreations* shooting, skiing, fishing, coin collecting; *Clubs* Kildare Street and Univ (Dublin), Nairobi; *Style—* Prof Martin Snaith; 281 High St, Henley-in-Arden, Warwickshire B95 5BG (☎ 0564 793223); School of Civil Engineering, University of Birmingham, Edgbaston, Birmingham B15 2TT (☎ 021 414 5161, fax 021 414 5160, telex 333762 UOBHAM G)

SNAITH, Dr (Richard) Philip; s of Herbert Longridge Snaith (d 1960), of Darlington, and Katherine Elizabeth, *née* Smith (d 1958); *b* 1 May 1933; *Educ* Sedbergh, Guys Hosp Med Sch Univ of London (MD); *m* 21 April 1972, Joanna; 2 s (Douglas b 1959, Julian b 1961), 1 da (Polly b 1965); *Career* conslt psychiatrist Stanley Royal Hosp Wakefield 1967-77, sr lectr in psychiatry Univ of Leeds 1977-, hon conslt psychiatrist St James Univ Hosp Leeds 1977-; FRCPsych 1977; *Books* Clinical Neurosis (1981); *Recreations* fell walking; *Style—* Dr Philip Snaith; 30 Gledhow Wood Rd, Leeds LS8 4BZ; Dept of Psychiatry, Clinical Sciences Building, St James's Univ Hospital, Leeds LS9 7TF (☎ 0532 433144)

SNAPE, Peter Charles; MP (Lab) West Bromwich E Feb 1974-; s of Thomas & Kathleen Snape; *b* 12 Feb 1942; *Educ* St Joseph's Stockport, St Winifred's Stockport; *m* 1963, Winifred Grimshaw; 2 da; *Career* former railway signalman then guard, soldier (RE & RCT), British Rail clerk; memb Cncl Europe & WEU 1975, asst govt whip 1975-77, Lord Cmmr Treasury 1977-79; oppn front bench spokesman: Def and Disarmament 1981-82, Home Affrs 1982-83, Transport Nov 1983-; *Style—* Peter Snape, Esq, MP; Dane House, Buglawton, Congleton, Cheshire (☎ 026 02 3934)

SNAPE, (Thomas) Peter; OBE (1988); s of Charles Snape (d 1961), of Leeds, and Jane Middleton (d 1956); *b* 4 June 1925; *Educ* Cockburn Sch Leeds, Exeter Coll Oxford (MA); *m* 1951, Anne Christina, da of Dr H E McColl (d 1964), of Shropshire; 1 s (Adam), 3 da (Penelope, Sarah, Virginia); *Career* gen sec Secdy Heads Assoc and Headmasters Conf 1983-88; former headmaster: King Edward VI Sch Totnes Devon 1964-83, Settle HS Yorks 1960-64; Leverhulme res fell USA 1970, memb of Consultative Ctee of Assessment of Performance Unit 1975-83, chm Leechwell Press Ltd; FRSA 1989; *Style—* Peter Snape, Esq, OBE; 10 Chalcot Square, London NW1 8YB (☎ 071 722 9478)

SNAPE, Royden Eric (Roy); s of John Robert Snape (d 1961), and Gwladys Constance, *née* Jones (d 1971); *b* 20 April 1922; *Educ* Bromsgrove; *m* 4 June 1949, Unity Frances (Jo), da of George Chester Tancred Money (d 1938); 1 s (Peter b 1950); 1 da (Sarah b 1952); *Career* RA Field 1940-46: Adj 80 Field Regt 1945, Maj (DAAG); admitted slr 1949, rec 1979-; chm Med Appeal Tbnl 1985-; govr St Johns Sch Porthcawl 1971-88; *Recreations* golf, rugby union football, cricket, swimming; *Clubs* Royal Porthcawl Golf, Cardiff Athletic, Glamorgan CCC; *Style—* Roy Snape, Esq; West Winds, Llanblethian Cowbridge, S Glamorgan CF7 7JQ (☎ 0446 772362); Wyndham House, Bridgend, Mid Glamorgan (☎ 0656 661115)

SNAREY, Anthony John (Tony); s of George Norman Snarey, of Wilsford Cottage, Manthorpe, Grantham, Lincs, and Mary Isobel, *née* Craven (d 1974); *b* 24 March 1939; *Educ* Stamford Sch Stamford Lincs; *m* 23 May 1963, Wendy Jane, da of James Henry O'Hara; 2 da (Louise Jane b 27 March 1964, Helen Liza b 29 June 1966); *Career* Harrods Estate Office Knightsbridge London 1956-58, Mackinder Bennett Balderston chartered surveyors Boston Lincs 1958-63; William H Brown: mangr Grantham office 1963-66, local ptnr Grantham 1966-70, full ptnr 1970-76, jt sr ptnr 1976-86, chief exec 1986-88, chm and chief exec 1988-; underwriting memb of Lloyds 1979-; memb Worshipful Co of Chartered Surveyors; ACIArb, FRICS, FRVA; *Recreations* golf, cricket, rugby football; William H Brown, The Mill, Manthorpe, Granthorpe, Lincolnshire NG31 8NH (☎ 0476 60880, fax 0476 71805, car 0860 857956, home tel 0476 65244)

SNAYDON, Dr Roy William; s of Percy Frederick Snaydon (d 1989), and Ivy Lillian, *née* King; *b* 14 April 1933; *Educ* Yeovil Sch, Univ of Wales (BSc, PhD); *m* 3 April 1956, Rita Anne, da of Ronald Harries Maddox; 2 s (Geoffrey b 7 Aug 1957, Timothy b 18 Dec 1960), 1 da (Judith b 15 Oct 1962); *Career* Sgt Instructor RAEC 1955-57; lectr Univ of Reading 1960-64, res scientist CSIRO Canberra Australia 1964-67; Univ of Reading: lectr 1967-77, reader 1977-, head of agric botany dept 1982-87; hon memb treasy Br Ecological Soc 1968-74; *Books* Managed Grasslands (1987); *Recreations* choral singing, walking; *Style—* Dr Roy Snaydon; Tararua, Ryhill Way, Lower Earley, Reading, Berkshire RG6 4AZ (☎ 0734 872839); Agric Botany Department, University of Reading, Reading RG6 2AS (☎ 0734 318093, fax 0734 750630)

SNEATH, Christopher George; s of Arthur George Sneath (d 1972), and Dorothy Ada, *née* Knight (d 1989); *b* 27 June 1933; *Educ* Canford Sch Dorset; *m* 12 May 1962, Patricia Lesley, da of Anthony Spinks (d 1982); 1 s (James Rupert b 19 Jan 1966), 1 da (Deborah Jane b 16 July 1963); *Career* CA 1957; articled to Merrett Son & Street London EC2, sr ptnr specialising in int business matters KPMG Peat Marwick McLintock 1978- (sr mangr 1966, jt ptnr 1971), dep sec gen Peat Marwick Int 1978-80; chm: Br American C of C; memb Embethics Ctee Inst of CAs; receiver gen Order of St John; hon treas: Saracens RFC 1981-, Nightingale Ball (Charity); memb Bd of Govrs Queenswood Sch; FCA; *Books* Guide to Acquisitions in the US (1989); *Recreations* watching cricket and rugby football, maintaining motor cars (Lotus's); *Clubs* Carlton, Marylebone Cricket, Pilgrims; *Style—* Christopher Sneath, Esq; 109 High St, London N14 6BP (☎ 081 886 6990); 4 Chatsworth Gardens, Eastbourne, Sussex EN20 7SP (☎ 0323 25709); c/o KPMG Peat Marwick McLintock, 1 Puddle Dock, Blackfriars, London EC4V 3PD (☎ 071 236 8000, fax 071 832 8253, telex 881154)

SNEATH, Christopher Gilbert; s of Colin Frank Sneath, of Brookmans Park; *b* 25 June 1938; *Educ* Framlingham Coll Suffolk; *m* 25 May 1963, Elizabeth Mary, da of Bernard Stephen Copson, Little Heath, Potters Bar, Herts; 2 da (Lucy Jane b 1965, Julia Elizabeth b 1967); *Career* Nat Serv RCS 1957-59; gp md dir Barrett & Wright Group Ltd 1982- (md 1971-); pres Heating & Ventilating Contractors Assoc 1990-91, capt Brookmans Park Golf Club 1980-81, chm London Area Clubs Physically Handicapped Able Bodied 1987; companion memb Chartered Inst of Bldg Servs Engrs 1983; *Recreations* golf, marathon running; *Clubs* Brookmans Park Golf, RAC; *Style—* Christopher Sneath, Esq; 31 Brookmans Ave, Brookmans Pk, Hatfield, Herts AL9 7QH (☎ 0707 58709); Barrett & Wright Gp Ltd, 200 Hornsey Rd, London N7 7LG (☎ 071 607 6700, fax 071 700 4683)

SNEDDEN, David King; s of David Snedden; *b* 23 Feb 1933; *Educ* Daniel Stewart's Coll Edinburgh; *m* 1958, Jean, da of Edward Goldie Smith; 2 s (Keith b 1961, Stuart b 1963), 1 da (Ann); *Career* formerly: investmt advsr Guinness Mahon Ltd, dir Radio Forth Ltd, memb Press Cncl; md: Belfast Telegraph Newspapers 1966-70 (dir 1979-82), Scotsman Publications 1970-79; jt md Thomson Regnl Newspapers Ltd 1980-82 (dir 1974-, gp asst md 1979-80); md and chief exec Trinity International Holdings plc; chm Press Assoc; dir Reuters Holdings plc; *Recreations* golf, fishing; *Clubs* Caledonian, Bruntsfield Links Golfing Soc; *Style—* David Snedden, Esq; Apartment 223, The Colonnades, Albert Dock Village, Liverpool L3 4AA, Merseyside

SNEDDON, Hutchison Burt; CBE (1983, OBE 1968), JP (1964-), DL (Motherwell, E Kilbride, Monklands, Clydesdale and Hamilton 1989-); s of Robert Cleland Sneddon, of 261 Bonkle Road, Newmains, Wishaw, Lanarks, and Catherine McDade, *née* McComisky (d 1978); *b* 17 April 1929; *Educ* Wishaw HS, Burnbank Tech Coll; *m* 3 Oct 1960, Elizabeth Ross, da of Allan Jardine (d 1963); 1 s (Cleland b 1967), 2 da (Joanne b 1961, Irene b 1964); *Career* Nat Serv NCO RE 1950-52; served: Sch of Survey Newbury, II Armd Div HQ Herford W Germany 1951-52; air photo graphic interpreter; construction engr 1953-64; Br Gas: tech sales mangr 1964-71, area mangr 1971-79, sales mangr (special projects) 1983-89; memb: W Regnl Hosp Bd 1968-70, Motherwell and Wishaw Borough Cncl 1958-75 (provost 1971-75), Scottish Tourist Bd 1969-83, JP advsy ctee 1975-; chm Motherwell Dist Cncl 1974-77; Scottish chm: Nat Bldg Agency 1977-82 (dir 1974-82), Housing Corp 1980-83 (memb 1977-83); chm Cumbernauld Devpt Corpn 1979-83, vice pres Confedn of Scottish Local Authys 1974-76; sec Wishaw Branch Nat Bible Soc of Scotland 1986-, pres World Fedn of Burns Clubs 1989-90, chm Gas Higher Mangrs Assoc 1986-88 (asst gen Sec 1988-); City of Schweinfurt Gold Medal of Freedom 1975; *Recreations* watching football, philately; *Style—* Hutchison Sneddon, Esq, CBE; 36 Shand St, Wishaw M62 8HN (☎ 0698 73685)

SNELGROVE, Rt Rev Donald George; *see*: Hull, Bishop of

SNELL, John; s of Flt Lt Sydney Snell, and Grace, *née* Walker; *b* 23 Sept 1949; *Educ* Lincoln City GS, Univ of Hull (LLB); *Career* called to the Bar Inner Temple 1973; sometime lectr in law North Staffordshire Polytechnic; practised: Northern circuit 1975-77, South Eastern circuit 1987-89, Midland and Oxford circuit 1977-87 and 1989-; friend of Lincoln Cathedral; memb Criminal Bar Assoc; *Books* Modern Law Review (contrib); *Recreations* the Church, music, rural railways, idling; *Style*— John Snell, Esq; 16 Minster Yard, Lincoln; 24 Millstone Lane, Leicester LE1 5JN (☎ 0533 517176, fax 0533 536249)

SNELL, John Bernard; s of Harold Emley Snell (d 1966); *b* 28 March 1932; *Educ* Bryanston, Balliol Coll Oxford; *Career* author and barr Lincoln's Inn; md Romney Hythe and Dymchurch Railway Co 1972-; *Recreations* music, literature and photography; *Style*— John Snell, Esq; 15 Tudor Avenue, Dymchurch, Kent (☎ 0303 872789)

SNELLING, Sir Arthur Wendell; KCMG (1960, CMG 1954), KCVO (1962); s of Arthur Snelling; *b* 7 May 1914; *Educ* Ackworth Sch Yorks, UCL; *m* 1939, Frieda, da of Lt-Col F Barnes; 1 s; *Career* Royal Inst of Int Affrs 1934-36; entered Dominions Office 1936, jt sec to UK Delegn to Int Monetary Conf Bretton Woods USA 1944; UK dep high cmmr in: NZ 1947-50, S Africa 1953-55; asst under-sec CRO 1956-59, high cmmr Ghana 1959-61, dep under-sec state FCO 1961-69, ambass to S Africa 1970-72; dir Gordon & Gotch Holdings 1973-81; fellow UCL 1970 and memb Cncl 1976, vice-pres UK-South Africa Trade Assoc 1974-80, memb Ciskei Cmmn 1978-80; *Style*— Sir Arthur Snelling, KCMG, KCVO; 19 Albany Park Rd, Kingston-upon-Thames, Surrey KT2 5SW (☎ 081 549 4160)

SNELLING-COLYER, Nigel John; s of the late John Edward Snelling-Colyer, and Miriam Annette, *née* Edbrooke, of Wadhurst, Sussex; *b* 21 Sept 1954; *Educ* The Skinners' Sch Tunbridge Wells, RMA Sandhurst; *Career* Lt RE 1978-83, served UK, BAOR, Cyprus, Belize; asst to md Pauling plc 1983-85, London Residential Office of Chestertons 1985-86, Cluttons 1986-88; property devpt 1988-; *Recreations* riding, hunting, shooting, classic cars; *Clubs* Army and Navy; *Style*— Nigel Snelling-Colyer, Esq; Nat West Bank, 1 St James' Square, Wadhurst, Sussex

SNELSON, Sir Edward Alec Abbott; KBE (1954), OBE (1946); er s of Thomas Edward Snelson (d 1965), of Chester; *b* 1904; *Educ* St Olave's, Gonville and Caius Coll Cambridge, SOAS London; *m* 1956, Prof Jean Johnston, da of Donald Mackay, of Craigendoran; 2 s; *Career* called to the Bar Gray's Inn 1929, entered ICS 1929, dist judge Central Provinces 1936, legal sec 1946, jt sec Govt of India 1947, sec Pakistan Minys of Law and Parly Affrs 1951-61; Justice Supreme Restitution Court Herford (FDR) 1962-81, memb Arbitral Tbnl for Agreement on German External Debts and the Mixed Cmmn 1969-77; *Clubs* Utd Oxford and Cambridge; *Style*— Sir Edward Snelson, KBE; The Forge House, Binsted, Alton, Hants

SNOAD, Harold Edward; s of Sidney Edward Snoad, of Bankside, Silverdale Rd, Eastbourne, Sussex, and Irene Dora, *née* Janes; *b* 28 Aug 1935; *Educ* Eastbourne Coll; *m* 1, 21 Sept 1957 (m dis 18 June 1963) Anne Christine, *née* Cadwallader; m 2, 6 July 1963, Jean, da of James Green (d 1968), of 46 Pemberton Gardens, London; 2 da (Helen Julie b 1969, Jeanette Clare b 1975); *Career* Nat Serv RAF 1954-56; with BBC 1957-: prodr and dir 1970-83, exec prodr and dir 1983-; produced and directed many successful comedy series incl: The Dick Emery Show, Rings on their Fingers, The Further Adventures of Lucky Jim, Tears Before Bedtime, Hilary, Don't Wait Up, Ever Decreasing Circles, Brush Strokes, Keeping up Appearances; dir feature film Not Now Comrade, re-wrote Dad's Army for radio; scripted original comedy series: Share and Share Alike and It Sticks Out Half a Mile (radio), High and Dry (TV); *Books* Directing Situation Comedy (1988); *Recreations* swimming, gardening, theatre going, DIY, motoring; *Style*— Harold Snoad, Esq; Fir Tree Cottage, 43 Hawkewood Rd, Sunbury-on-Thames, Middx TW16 6HL (☎ 0932 785887); Room 4138 BBC Television Centre, Wood Lane London W12 7RJ (☎ 081 743 8000 exts 4816/1817/8490, telex 265 781)

SNODGRASS, John Michael Owen; CMG (1981); s of Maj William McElrea Snodgrass (d 1934), and Kathleen Mabel, *née* Owen (d 1988); *b* 12 Aug 1928; *Educ* Marlborough, Univ of Cambridge (MA); *m* 1957, Jennifer, da of Robert James (d 1970), of S Rhodesia; 3 s (Andrew, Peter, James); *Career* HM Dip Serv: consul gen Jerusalem 1970-74, cnsllr British Embassy S Africa 1974-77, head of S Pacific Dept FCO 1977-80; ambass to: Zaire 1980-83, Bulgaria 1983-86; ret; *Recreations* skiing, travel; *Style*— John Snodgrass, Esq, CMG; The Barn House, North Warnborough, Hants RG25 1ET (☎ 0256 702816)

SNOOK, Paul Robert; s of Gordon Robert Snook, of Sheffield, and Jean Rosemary, *née* Barber; *b* 6 April 1954; *Educ* Abbeydale Boy's GS, LSE (LLB); *m* 1, 24 April 1982 (m dis 1987), Judith Helen, *née* Laybourn; m 2, 8 Oct 1988, Victoria Marie, da of George Sadler, of Chesterfield, Derbyshire; 1 da (Gabriella Victoria b 29 Jan 1990); *Career* dir Bradway Machinery 1975-79, articled clerk Taylor Son & Co Solicitors 1979-81, Keeble Hawsons Solicitors 1981-84, sr mangr Cork Gully 1984-87, princ Touche Ross 1987-; Creditors' Rights in Insolvency (1988); *Recreations* enjoying life to the full; *Clubs* Annabel's; *Style*— Paul Snook, Esq; Friary Court, 65 Crutched Friars, London EC3N 2NP (☎ 071 480 7766, fax 071 480 6958, telex 884257, car 0836 539305, mobile 0831 577748)

SNOW, Adrian John; s of Edward Percy John Snow, of Middleton-on-Sea, W Sussex, and Marjory Ellen, *née* Nicholls; *b* 20 March 1939; *Educ* Hurstpierpoint Coll, Trinity Coll Dublin (BA, MA, H Dip Ed), Univ of Reading (M Ed); *m* 1963, (Alessina) Teresa, da of Charles Arthur Kilkelly, of Far Field, Killiney Hill Rd, Killiney, Co Dublin; 1 s (Robin Edward Charles b 1965), 1 da (Susan Alessina b 1963); *Career* PO RAF 1962; asst master: New Beacon Prep Sch 1958-59, Kings Sch Sherborne 1963-64, Dublin HS (pt/t) 1964-65, Brighton Coll 1965-66; The Oratory: head of econ and political studies 1966-73, head of history 1967-73, housemaster 1967-73, actg headmaster 1972-73, headmaster 1973-88; dir: Oratory Construction Ltd 1988-, Oratory Trading Ltd 1989-; govr: Prior Park Coll 1980-87, Moreton Hall 1984-, The Highlands Reading 1985- (chm), St Edwards Reading 1985- (chm), St Mary's Ascot 1986-; warden to the govrs The Oratory Sch Assoc 1989-, vice chm Berkshire Ctee The Princes Tst, hon treas Reading Amateur Regatta 1990-; *Recreations* bridge, farming, golf, real tennis; *Clubs* Leander, La Manga Golf; *Style*— Adrian Snow, Esq; Ward's Farmhouse, Greenmore, Woodcote, nr Reading

SNOW, Antony Edmund; s of Thomas Maitland Snow, CMG, of Montreux, Switzerland, and Phyllis Annette Hopkins, *née* Malcolmson; *b* 5 Dec 1932; *Educ* Sherborne, New Coll Oxford; *m* 31 March 1961, Caroline, da of Comar Wilson (d 1961), of Oakley Manor, nr Basingstoke, Hants (d 1961); 1 s (Lucian b 21 Aug 1965), 2 da (Arabella b 1 Feb 1964, Henrietta b 2 April 1970); *Career* 10 Royal Hussars, cmmnd 1952-53; dep chm Charles Barker & Sons 1971-76, vice pres Market Planning Stueben Glass NY 1976-78, dep dir Corning Museum of Glass USA 1978-79, dir Rockwell Museum USA 1979-83; dir: Charles Barker plc 1983- (chm and chief exec 1983-87), Hogg Robinson & Gardner Mountain plc 1988-; dep chm and chief exec Hill and Knowlton (UK) Ltd; tstee: Arnott Museum USA 1980-, Corning Museum of Glass USA 1983-; memb: Ctee of Mgmnt Courtauld Inst of Art 1985-89, Exec Ctee Nat Art Collections Fund 1985-; cncllr Design Cncl 1989-, tstee Monteverdi Choir 1988-, memb AMAC Ctee English Heritage 1989-; FRSA, FIPA, MIPR; *Recreations* English watercolours; *Clubs* Cavalry and Guards', City of London; *Style*— Antony Snow, Esq; 16 Rumbold Rd, London SW6 2JA (☎ 071 731 2881); Fyfield Hill Barn, Marlborough, Wilts (☎ 067 286 498)

SNOW, Hon Harriet Flavia Hazlitt; only child of Baron Burntwood (Life Peer d 1982); *b* 1950; *Educ* Lycèe Français de Londres, London Coll of Printing; *Career* Illustrator; *Style*— The Hon Harriet Snow; The Thatched Cottage, Walberswick, Southwold, Suffolk; Flat 2, 37 Chester Way, London SE11 (☎ 071 735 6770)

SNOW, Jonathan George (Jon); s of Rt Rev George D'Oyly Snow, Bishop of Whitby (d 1977), and Joan Monica, *née* Way; *b* 28 Sept 1947; *Educ* St Edward's Sch Oxford, Univ of Liverpool; 2 da (Leila Snow Colvin b 1982, Freya Snow Colvin b 1986); *Career* dir New Horrizon Youth Centre Covent Garden 1970-73; journalist: LBC and IRN 1973-76, ITN 1976- (Washington corr 1983-86, dep ed 1986-89); presenter Channel Four News 1989-; NUJ; *Books* Atlas of Today (1987); *Style*— Jon Snow, Esq; 9 Torriano Cottages, Torriano Ave, London NWS ZTA (☎ 071 485 3513); ITN, ITN House, 48 Wells St, London W1 (☎ 071 637 5454, fax 071 636 0349, telex 22101)

SNOW, Rear Adm Kenneth Arthur; CB (1987); s of Arthur Chandos Pole-Soppitt (d 1986, assumed the surname of Snow by deed pole), and Evelyn Dorothea, *née* Joyce (d 1957); *b* 14 April 1934; *Educ* St Andrews Coll Grahamstown, S African Nautical Coll; *m* 1956, Pamela Elizabeth Terry, da of Ald Frank Harold Ernest Sorrell, of Southsea, Hants; 1 s (Christopher b 1958), 2 da (Vanessa b 1960, Penelope b 1965); *Career* cadet RN 1952, cmd HMS Kirkliston 1962, 1st Lt HMY Britannia 1968-69, cmd HMS Llandaff 1970, HMS Arethusa 1979, HMS Hermes 1983, Rear Adm 1984; receiver gen and chapter clerk Westminster Abbey 1987-; *Recreations* painting, gardening; *Style*— Rear Adm Kenneth Snow; 2 The Cloister, Westminster Abbey, London SW1 3PA; The Chapter Office, 20 Deans Yard, Westminster Abbey, London SW1P 3PA

SNOW, Dr Percy John (Deryk); OBE (1989); s of Maj Percy John Snow (d 1965), of Kidsgrove, N Staffs, and Eileen Caroline, *née* Thompson (d 1975); *b* 23 May 1925; *Educ* Newcastle under Lyme HS, Univ of Manchester (MB ChB, MD); *m* 1, 19 April 1949 (m dis 1970), Marjorie, da of John Thomas Worrall (d 1960), of Kidsgrove, N Staffs; 2 da (Susan b 31 Oct 1950, Pamela b 8 May 1958); m 2, 16 Dec 1970, Jacqueline, da of George Albert Blackstock (d 1944), of Manchester; 1 s (Paul Jason b 17 Oct 1972); *Career* Sqdn Ldr RAF Med Branch 1953-55; conslt physician Bolton Hosps 1959-90, author of various papers and chapters on med topics incl ishaemic heart disease and hyper-tension; vice chm Bolton AHA 1972-75, regnl advsr RCP 1975-80, memb N Western RHA 1976-80; FRCP 1970; *Recreations* gardening, photography, walking; *Clubs* RAF; *Style*— Dr Deryk Snow, OBE

SNOW, Peter John; s of Brig John Fitzgerald Snow, Som LI (d 1973), and Peggy Mary, *née* Pringle (d 1970); *b* 20 April 1938; *Educ* Wellington Coll, Balliol Coll Oxford (BA); *m* 1, 30 Sept 1964 (m dis 1975), Alison Mary, da of late George Fairlie Carter, of Piltdown, Sussex; 1 s (Shane Fitzgerald b 1966), 1 da (Shuna Justine b 1968); m 2, 15 May 1976, Ann Elizabeth, da of Dr Robert Laidlaw MacMillan, of Toronto, Canada; 1 s (Daniel Robert b 1978), 2 da (Rebecca Olwen b 1980, Katherine Peggy b 1983); *Career* Nat Serv 2 Lt Somerset LI 1956-58; dep and def corr ITN 1966-79 (reporter and newscaster 1962-), presenter BBC TV Newsnight and election progs 1979-; *Books* Leila's Hijack War (1970), Hussein: A Biography (1972); *Recreations* tennis, sailing, skiing, model railways; *Style*— Peter Snow, Esq; c/o BBC TV, BBC TV Centre, Wood Lane, London W12 (☎ 071 749 7512)

SNOW, Philip Albert; OBE (1985, MBE 1979), JP (Warwicks 1967-76, W Sussex 1976-); s of William Edward Snow (d 1954), and Ada Sophia, *née* Robinson; bro of late Baron Snow, of Leicester, CBE (Life Peer, better known as C P Snow, the author); *b* 7 Aug 1915; *Educ* Alderman Newton's Sch Leicester, Christ's Coll Cambridge (MA); *m* 1940, (Mary) Anne, da of Henry Harris (d 1970), of Leicester; 1 da (Stefanie Dale Vivien Vuikaba (Mrs Peter Waine) b 1947); *Career* author, bibliographer, administrator; Colonial Admin Serv: admin offr, magistrate, provincial cmmr and asst colonial sec Fiji and Western Pacific 1937-52 (ADC to Govr and C-in-C Fiji 1939, liaison offr with US and NZ forces WWII); vice pres Fiji Soc 1944-52, fndr Fiji Cricket Assoc 1946 (vice patron 1952-), bursar governing body Rugby Sch 1952-76, memb Jt Ctee Governing Bodies of Schs Assoc 1959-64, chm Ind Schs Bursars' Assoc 1962-65 (vice chm 1959-62), Foreign specialist award USA 1964, perm Fiji rep on Int Cricket Conference and Cncl 1965-, memb first Cricket World Cup Ctee 1970-75, first chm Assoc Memb Countries of Int Cricket Conference 1982-86, first pres The Worthing Soc 1983- (vice chm 1977-83), literary executor and executor of Lord Snow; FRSA, FRAI; elected Special Hon Life Memb MCC for services to int cricket; *Books* Civil Defence Services, Fiji (1942), Cricket in the Fiji Islands (1949), Report on the Visit of Three Bursars to the United States of America in 1964 (1965); Best Stories of the South Seas (1967), Bibliography of Fiji, Tonga and Rotuma (1969), The People from the Horizon; an illustrated history of the Europeans among the South Sea Islanders (1979, with Stefanie Waine), Stranger and Brother: a Portrait of C P Snow (1982), numerous articles in jls and book introductions; *Recreations* formerly cricket (capt MCC teams 1951-65, capt Fiji Nat first class team touring NZ 1948), table tennis for Univ of Cambridge and Cambridgeshire, deck tennis, tennis; *Clubs* MCC, Hawks (Cambridge), Mastermind, Stragglers of Asia CC (hon memb); *Style*— Philip Snow, Esq, OBE, JP; Gables, Station Rd, Angmering, W Sussex BN16 4HY (☎ 0903 773594)

SNOW, Hon Philip Charles Hansford; s of Baron Snow, CBE (d 1980; C P Snow, the author and public servant), and Pamela Hansford Johnson, CBE (d 1981; novelist); *b* 26 Aug 1952; *Educ* Eton, Balliol Coll Oxford; *m* 19 Sept 1987, Amanda C, er da of Sir Clive Anthony Whitmore, *qv*; *Career* writer on China and int affairs; res assoc Oriental Inst Univ of Oxford; memb: Royal Inst of Int Affairs, GB-China Centre; cncl memb China Soc; *Books* The Star Raft: China's Encounter with Africa (1988); *Style*— The Hon Philip Snow; 39 Alderney St, London SW1V 4HH

SNOW, Surgn Rear Adm Ronald Edward; CB (1991), LVO (1972), OBE (1977), QHP (1984); s of Arthur Chandos Pole Snow (formerly Soppitt, name changed by deed poll, d 1984), of Cape Town, SA, and Evelyn Dorothea, *née* Joyce (d 1956); *b* 17 May 1933; *Educ* St Andrew's Coll Grahamstown S Africa, Trinity Coll Dublin (MA, MB BCh, BAO), RCS Ireland (DA), RCP Ireland (MFOM), LMCC; *m* 16 Dec 1959, Valerie Melian, da of Raymond Arthur French (d 1981), of Dublin, Ireland; 2 da (Suzanne Lynn, Nicola Jane); *Career* MO HMS Victorious 1966; MO Submarine Escape Trg Tank, HMS Dolphin 1967; princ MO HM Yacht Britannia 1970; asst to SMO (Admin) RN Hosp Haslar 1972; duties with MDG(N) as Naval Health 2 MOD (Navy) 1973; dir of Studies Inst Naval Med 1975; duties with MDG(N) as dep dir of med personnel (Naval) 1977; Staff MO to Surgn Rear Adm (Naval Hosps) 1980; Fleet MO to CINCFLEET and med advsr to CINCHAN and CINCEASTLANT 1982; MO i/c Inst of Naval Med 1984; Asst Surgn Gen (Serv Hosps) and Dep Med Dir-Gen (Naval) 1985; Surgn Rear Adm (Support Med Servs) 1987; Surgn Rear Adm (operational med servs) 1989; RSM (fell of Cncl of Utd Servs Section) 1987, memb Soc of Occupational Med 1977, OStJ 1986; *Recreations* Nat Hunt racing, cruising; *Clubs* Army & Navy, RN Sailing Assoc (Portsmouth); *Style*— Surgn Rear Adm Ronald Snow, CB, LVO, OBE, QHP; c/o Naval Secretary, Ministry of Defence, Ripley Block, Old Admiralty Building, Spring Gardens, London SW1A 2BE (☎ 071 218 7600)

SNOW, Terence Clive; s of Ernest William George Snow (d 1968), and Elsie May, *née* Baynes; *b* 18 Sept 1931; *Educ* Poly of N London Sch of Architecture; *m* 28 March 1953, Phyllis, da of Frank Mann (d 1971); 4 s (Graeme b 1956, David b 1958, Phillip b 1960, John b 1969), 1 da (Patricia b 1971); *Career* Nat Serv RAF 1956-58; dir Architects' Co Partnership 1973-, vice pres RIBA 1979-81 (memb Cncl 1979-86); chm: RIBA Services Ltd 1982-, Library Planning Conslt Ltd 1982-, National Building Specification Ltd 1982-; dir RIBA Cos Ltd 1986-, chm NBS Servs Ltd 1990-; FRIBA 1970 (ARIBA 1960); *Recreations* magic; *Clubs* The Magic Circle; *Style*— Terence Snow, Esq; Architects Co-Partnership, Northaw House, Potters Bar, Herts EN6 4PS (☎ 0707 51141, telex 27997 ACPSCP G, fax 0707 52600)

SNOWBALL, Hon Mrs (Clarinda Susan); da of 3 Viscount Knollys; *b* 1960; *m* 4 Feb 1988, Andrew M B Snowball, yr s of late Brig E J D Snowball, OBE, of Ballochneck, Thornhill, Perthshire; *Career* exhibition organiser Andrew Montgomery Ltd 1978-89; dir Scottish Industrial & Trade Exhibitions Ltd 1990-; *Style*— The Hon Mrs Snowball; Mill of Gask, Trinity Gask, Auchterarder, Perthshire PH3 1JA (☎ 073 873 238)

SNOWDEN, (Frederick) Alan; s of Frederick Albert Snowden (d 1963), and Verna Withers (d 1977); *b* 14 Dec 1920; *Educ* London Coll of Printing; *m* 18 July 1943, Kathleen Ellen, da of George Charles Baxter (d 1972); 1 s (Martin Alan), 1 da (Rosemary Kay); *Career* RAF 1941-46 SE Asia Cmd; Daily Sketch 1946-61, Daily Telegraph 1961-87, ed International magazine 1972-; memb Gen Cncl and Assoc RAC 1963-91, sec Nat Pres Auto Assoc, chm S Area Assoc of Br Motor Clubs, memb Burma Star Assoc, life memb United Wards Club of the City of London 1950, memb Inner Magic Circle 1976, hon vice pres The Magic Circle 1990; fell World Literary Assoc 1985; cmmnd Hon Col in the state of Kentucky USA 1988; *Recreations* travel, photography, antique automobiles, prestidigitation; *Clubs* United Ward Club of the City of London, Royal Automobile; *Style*— Alan Snowden, Esq; 5 Folkington Corner, Woodside Park, Finchley, London N12 7BH (☎ 081 445 7607)

SNOWDEN, Maj Peter Barry; s of Arthur Jackson Snowden (d 1956), of Seaview, IOW, and Dorothy Swift, *née* Hoyland (d 1948); *b* 20 Aug 1919; *Educ* Canford, Sandhurst, Staff Coll Quetta, RAF Staff Coll Bracknell; *Career* cmmnd Devonshire Regt 1939 served: Waziristan, India, Ceylon, Burma; ret 1956; Stone Platt Industries 1956-71; mangr Br Olympic Sailing Team Naples 1960, sec Cowes Combined Clubs 1971-90; memb Worshipful Co of Saddlers (Liveryman 1946, Asst 1979, Master 1982-83), Queens Coronation medal; *Recreations* sailing, skiing, hunting; *Clubs* Royal Yacht Squadron, Royal London Yacht, Royal Thames Yacht, Sea View Yacht, Societe Des Regates Du Havre, Royal Ocean Racing, Household Division Yacht; *Style*— Maj Peter Snowden; The Keep, Castle Hill, Cowes, Isle of Wight P031 7QU (☎ 0983 295300)

SNOWDON, 1 Earl of (UK 1961); Antony Charles Robert Armstrong-Jones; GCVO (1969); also Viscount Linley (UK 1961); s of Ronald Owen Lloyd Armstrong-Jones, MBE, QC, DL (d 1966), of Plas Dinas, Caernarfon, and Anne, Countess of Rosse, *qv*; *b* 7 March 1930; *Educ* Eton, Jesus Coll Cambridge; *m* 1, 6 May 1960 (m dis 1978), HRH The Princess Margaret Rose (*see* Royal Family), yr da of HM the late King George VI; 1 s, 1 da; m 2, 15 Dec 1978, Lucy Mary, da of Donald Brook Davies, of Hemingstone Hall, Ipswich, and formerly w of Michael Lindsay-Hogg (film dir, s of Edward Lindsay-Hogg, gs of Sir Lindsay Lindsay-Hogg, 1 Bt, JP); 1 da (Lady Frances b 17 July 1979); *Heir* s, Viscount Linley, *qv*; *Career* Constable of Caernarfon Castle 1963-; photographer; artistic advsr Sunday Times and Sunday Times Publications 1962-90, consultative advsr to Design Cncl London 1962-87, The Telegraph Magazine 1990-, ed advsr Design Magazine 1962-87; *Exhibitions* Photocall (London 1958), Assignments (Photokina 1972), London (1973), Brussels (1974), Los Angeles, St Louis, Kansas, New York, Tokyo (1975), Sydney and Melbourne (1976), Copenhagen (1976), Paris (1977), Amsterdam (1977); Seredipity exhibition: Brighton 1989, Bradford 1989, Bath 1990; *TV films* Don't Count the Candles (CBS 1968; 2 Hollywood Emmys, St George Prix, Venice Dip, Prague and Barcelona Film Festival award), Love of a Kind (BBC 1969), Born to be Small (ATV 1971, Chicago Hugo award), Happy being Happy (ATV 1973), Mary Kingsley (BBC 1975), Burke and Wills (1975), Peter, Tina and Steve (ATV 1977), Snowdon on Camera (BBC 1981); pres: Contemporary Art Soc for Wales, Civic Tst for Wales, Welsh Theatre Co, Gtr London Arts Assoc, Int Year of Disabled People England (1981); vice pres Bristol Univ Photographic Soc; memb: Cncl of Nat Fund for Research into Crippling Diseases, Faculty of Designers for Industry, The Prince of Wales Advsry Gp on Disability; patron: Metropolitan Union of YMCAs, British Water Ski Fedn, Welsh Nat Rowing Club, Physically Handicapped and Able-Bodied, Circle of Guide Dog Owners, Demand; designer: Snowdon Aviary for London Zoo 1965, electrically-powered wheelchair for disabled people (Chairmobile) 1972; fndr Snowdon award Scheme for Disabled Students 1980; Arts Dirs Club of NY Certificate of Merit 1969; Soc of Publication Designers: Cert of Merit 1970, Designers award of Excellence 1973; Wilson Hicks Cert of Merit for Photocommunication 1971, Design and Art Directors award 1978, Royal Photographic Soc Hood award 1979; RDI, FRSA, FSIAD, FRPS, sr fell Royal Coll of Arts 1986, fell Manchester Coll of Art and Design; Hon DUniv of Bradford 1989, Hon Dr of Law Univ of Bath 1989; *Publications* Malta (collaborated with Sacheverell Sitwell 1958), London (1958), Private View (collaborated with John Russell and Bryan Robertson 1965), Assignments (1972), A View of Venice (1972), The Sack of Bath (1972), Inchcape Review (1977), Pride of the Shire (collaborated with John Oaksey 1979), Personal View (1979), Tasmania Essay (1981), Sittings (1983), My Wales (collaborated with Lord Tony Pandy 1986), Israel: a first view (1986), Stills 1984-87 (1987); *Style*— The Rt Hon the Earl of Snowdon, GCVO; 22 Launceston Place, London W8 5LR (☎ 071 937 1524)

SNOWDON, Graham Richard; s of Thomas Richard Snowdon (d 1970), of Doncaster, and Edna Mary, *née* Storm; *b* 8 Feb 1944; *Educ* Doncaster GS; *m* 5 Aug 1967, Peta Dawn, da of Frederick Alfred Rawlings; 1 s (Frazer Richard b 6 March 1974), 1 da (Jessica Louise b 21 March 1972); *Career* jr reporter: Barnsley Chronicle 1960-61, Yorkshire Evening News 1961-63; family sports agency Doncaster 1963-64, competitions press offr RAC Motor Sport Div London 1964-66, northern press offr RAC Manchester 1966-70, freelance sports journalist 1970- (cycling corr The Guardian, Daily Telegraph (as Graham Richards) and Press Assoc), ptnr (with Peta Snowdon) Snowdon Sports Editorial 1970- (sports press agency and official collators of nat sporting leagues and competitions), conslt Guinness Book of Records 1971-; *Recreations* food and drink, walking, travel, motoring; *Style*— Graham Snowdon, Esq; 6 Hallam Grange Croft, Fulwood, Sheffield, S Yorks S10 4BP (☎ 0742 302233); Snowdon Sports Editorial, PO Box 154, Sheffield S10 4BW (☎ 0742 303093, fax 0742 302128, car 0836 381409)

SNOWMAN, Daniel; s of Arthur Mortimer Snowman (d 1982), and Bertha, *née* Lazarus; *b* 4 Nov 1938; *Educ* Jesus Coll Cambridge, Cornell Univ NY (MA); *m* 17 Dec 1975, Janet Linda, *née* Levison; 1 s (Benjamin b 1977), 1 da (Anna b 1978); *Career* lectr Univ of Sussex 1963-67; chief prodr features arts and education BBC Radio 1967; prodns incl: A World in Common, The Vatican, Reith Lectures, variety of historical and cultural programmes; *Books* America Since 1920 (1968), Eleanor Roosevelt (1970), Kissing Cousins: British and American Culture, 1945-75 (1977), If I Had Been ... Ten Historical Fantasies (1979), The Amadeus Quartet: The Men and the Music (1981), The World of Placido Domingo (1985), Beyond the Tunnel of History (1990); *Recreations* singing with London Philharmonic Choir (former chm); *Style*— Daniel Snowman, Esq; 47 Wood Lane, Highgate, London N6 5UD (☎ 081 340 2913); BBC, Broadcasting House, London W1A 1AA (☎ 071 927 4702)

SNOWMAN, (Michael) Nicholas; s of Kenneth Snowman and, Sallie, *née* Moghi-Levkine; *b* 18 March 1944; *Educ* Highgate Sch, Magdalene Coll Cambridge (BA); *m* 1983, Margo Michelle Rouard; 1 s; *Career* asst to Head of Music Staff Glyndebourne Festival Opera 1967-69, co-fndr and gen mangr London Sinfonietta 1968-72, admin Music Theatre Ensemble 1968-71, artistic dir Institut de Recherche et de Co-ordination Acoustique/Musique 1972-76, co-fndr and artistic advsr Ensemble Inter Contemporain 1975-, memb Music Ctee Venice Biennale 1979-86; Festival d'Automne de Paris: artistic dir Stravinsky 1980, Webern 1981, Boulez 1983; Officier de l'Ordre des Arts et des Lettres 1985, Polish Order of Cultural Merit 1990; *Books* The Best of Granta (co-ed 1967), The Contemporary Composers (series ed 1982-), Opera Now; *Recreations* films, eating, spy novels; *Clubs* Garrick; *Style*— Nicholas Snowman; South Bank Centre, Royal Festival Hall, London SE1 8XX (☎ 071 921 0600)

SNYDER, Michael John; s of Percy Elsworth Snyder (d 1953), and Pauline Edith, *née* Davenport; *b* 30 July 1950; *Educ* Brentwood Sch, City of London Coll; *m* 14 Dec 1974, Mary Barbara, da of Rev Wilfrid Edgar Dickinson; 2 da (Julia Caroline b 10 Nov 1976, Susanna Jane b 9 Sept 1978); *Career* CA; sr ptnr Kingston Smith 1990- (joined 1968, ptnr 1974, managing ptnr 1979-); chm: JR Gp plc, Gp Consultancy (Computer Servs) Ltd, Kingston Smith Fin Servs Ltd; dir: Jade Interiors Internaional Ltd, Cheviot Asset Mgmnt Ltd; ICAEW: chm City Dist Trg Bd, memb Business Law Ctee, fndr memb and sec Assoc of Practising Accountants, common councilman City of London; memb: Coal Corn and Rates Fin Ctee, Music Ctee, Port and City of London Health and Soc Servs Ctee, Bd of Govrs City of London Sch for Girls; hon treas Hoddeston Area Victims Support Scheme, asst The Hon The Irish Soc; Freeman City of London 1980, Liveryman Worshipful Co of Needlemakers, Freeman Worshipful Co of Tallow Chandlers; FCA 1978 (ACA 1973), FInstD; *Recreations* narrowboat and inland waterways, music, squash; *Clubs* City Livery, Cordwainer Ward, Bishopgate Ward; *Style*— Michael Snyder, Esq; Devonshire House, 146 Bishopsgate, London EC2H 4JX (☎ 071 377 8888, fax 071 247 7048, car 0836 733 761, telex 894477)

SOAMES, Hon Emma Mary; *née* Soames; da of Baron Soames, GCMG, GCVO, CH, CBE, PC (Life Peer; d 1987); *b* 6 Sept 1949; *m* 4 July 1981 (m dis 1989), James MacManus, features ed for The Sunday Telegraph, s of Dr Niall MacManus, of Warwick Sq, London SW1; 1 da (Emily Fiona b 1983); *Career* journalist Evening Standard, former ed Literary Review, features ed Vogue, ed Tatler; *Clubs* Groucho; *Style*— The Hon Emma Soames; Vogue House, Hanover Square, London W1R 0AD (☎ 071 499 9080)

SOAMES, Hon Jeremy Bernard; s of Baron Soames, GCMG, GCVO, CH, CBE, PC (d 1987); *b* 1952; *Educ* Eton; *m* 1978, Susanna, da of (James) David Agar Keith; 1 s (Archie Christopher Winston b 1988), 2 da (Gemma Mary b 1979, Flora Caroline b 1982); *Style*— The Hon Jeremy Soames; c/o West Barsham Hall, Fakenham, Norfolk

SOAMES, Baroness; Hon Mary; *née* Spencer Churchill; DBE (1980, MBE Mil 1945); da of late Rt Hon Sir Winston Leonard Spencer Churchill, KG, OM, CH, TD, PC, FRS (gs of 7 Duke of Marlborough and who d 1965), and Baroness Spencer Churchill (Dame Clementine Ogilvy, GBE, cr Life Peeress 1965, da of late Col Sir Henry Montague Hozier, KCB, bro of 1 Baron Newlands, and Lady (Henrietta) Blanche Ogilvy, da of 5 (10 but for attainder) Earl of Airlie, KT); *b* 1922; *m* 1947, Capt Christopher Soames (later Baron Soames, GCMG, GCVO, CH, CBE, PC, d 1987); 3 s, 2 da; *Career* formerly Jr Cdr ATS; memb Cncl Winston Churchill Memorial Tst 1978-, chm Royal Nat Theatre Bd 1989-; pres Nat Benevolent Fund for the Aged 1978-; govr Harrow Sch 1981-; Hon Fell Churchill College Cambridge; Hon DLitt Sussex 1989; *Books* Clementine Churchill by Her Daughter Mary Soames (1979), A Churchill Family Album (1982), The Profligate Duke: George Spencer Churchill, 5th Duke of Marlborough and his Duchess (1987), Winston Churchill: His Life as a Painter - A Memoir by his daughter Mary Soames (1990); *Style*— The Rt Hon the Lady Soames, DBE

SOAMES, Hon (Arthur) Nicholas Winston; MP (C) Crawley 1983-; s of Baron Soames, GCMG, GCVO, CH, CBE, PC (Life Peer; d 1987), and Hon Mary, DBE, *née* Spencer-Churchill, da of late Sir Winston Churchill and Baroness Spencer-Churchill; *b* 12 Feb 1948; *Educ* Eton; *m* 1981 (at which wedding HRH The Prince of Wales was best man), Catherine, da of Capt Tony Weatherall, of Dumfries; 1 s (Arthur Harry David b 1985); *Career* served 11 Hussars, extra equerry to HRH The Prince of Wales, Lloyd's insurance broker; *Clubs* White's, Turf, Carlton; *Style*— The Hon Nicholas Soames, MP; The House of Commons, London SW1 0AA

SOAMES, Hon Rupert Christopher; s of Baron Soames, GCMG, GCVO, CH, CBE, PC (Life Peer, d 1987), and Hon Mary, DBE, *née* Spencer-Churchill; *b* 18 May 1959; *Educ* Eton, Worcester Coll Oxford (BA); *m* 1988, Camilla Rose, eldest da of Thomas Raymond Dunne, of Gatley Park, Leominster, Herefordshire; 1 s (Arthur Christopher b 3 Feb 1990); *Career* pres The Oxford Union 1980; employed by GEC plc 1981-; *Clubs* Turf; *Style*— The Hon Rupert Soames

SOBELL, Sir Michael; s of Lewis Sobell (d 1945), and Esther Sobell (d 1952); *b* 1 Nov 1892; *Educ* Central London Fndn Sch; *m* 1917, Anne, da of Samuel Rakusen (d 1933), of London; 2 da; *Career* chm GEC (Radio and TV) Ltd, hon dir Technion Israel; hon doctorate Bar Ilan Univ Israel; hon fell: Jews Coll London, RCPath; kt 1972; *Recreations* racing (racehorse owner, Charity); *Clubs* Jockey (Newmarket); *Style*— Sir Michael Sobell; Bakeham House, Englefield Green, Surrey TW20 9TX

SOBER, Phillip; s of Abraham Sober, and Sandra Sober; *b* 1 April 1931; *Educ* Haberdasher's Aske's; *m* 20 Nov 1957, Vivien Louise, da of Frank Maurice Oppenheimer; 3 da (Belinda Clare b 1961, Juliet Anne b 1963, Georgina Jane b 1966); *Career* sr ptnr Stoy Hayward 1985-90 (ptnr 1958-), dir Transatlantic Holdings plc; memb: Gen Nursing Cncl 1978-80, UK Central Cncl for Nat Nurses Health Visitors and Midwives 1980-83; Crown Estate Cmmr 1983-, tstee Royal Opera House 1985-; Freeman City of London; fell Inst CA; *Recreations* opera, theatre, golf; *Clubs* Savile, RAC, Hurlingham, Roehampton; *Style*— Phillip Sober, Esq; Stoy Hayward, 8 Baker St, London W1M 1DA (☎ 071 486 5888, fax 071 487 3686, telex 267716 Horwat, car 0836 761 270)

SOBERS, Sir Garry (Garfield) St Auburn; *b* 28 July 1936,Bridgetown, Barbados; *Educ* Bay St Sch Barbados; *m* 1969, Prudence Kirby; 2 s, 1 da; *Career* cricketer; played in 93 test matches for WI (39 as capt) 1953-74, capt WI and Barbados teams 1964-74, capt Notts CCC 1968-74, ret; held world records in test cricket: 365 not out, 26 centuries, 235 wickets, 110 catches; memb Appeal Panel Immigrations Dept 1982; kt 1975; *Books* Cricket Advance (1965), Cricket Crusader (1966), Cricket in the Sun (1967); *Style*— Sir Garry Sobers; Melbourne, Victoria, Australia

SOBOLEWSKI, Dr Stanislaw; s of Kazimierz Sobolewski (d 1979), of Scunthorpe, and Bronislawa Sobolewska (d 1989); *b* 9 Feb 1943; *Educ* Bialystok GS Poland, med Acd of Bialystok Poland (MB BS), Univ of Bradford (PhD); *m* 1, 1968 (m dis 1976), Elizabeth, *née* Olszewska; 1 s (Edward b 1974), 2 da (Marta b 1970, Anastasia b 1972); m 2, Patricia, da of George Pearson (decd), of Rawmarsh, Rotherham, S Yorks; *Career* Grajewo Hosp Poland 1967, Olecko Hosp Poland 1968-70, sr house offr in rheumatology Harrogate 1971-72, registrar in pathology Seffield 1974-77 (registrar in clinical haematology 1972-74), sr registrar in haematology Leeds and Bradford, conslt haematologist Trent RHA S Lincs Dist Boston; regnl rep RCPath, rndr chm Trent Region Haematology Sub Ctee, chm Boston Leukaemia and Cancer Fund, memb Med Exec Ctee Pilgrim Hosp; ACP 1974, memb Br Soc of Haematologists 1976, MRCS 1976, LCRP 1976, MRCPath 1979; *Books* A New Function of Megakaryoctes in Malignancy (1986); *Recreations* classic cars restoration, swimming, football; *Clubs* Polish Social (Scunthorpe); *Style*— Dr Stanislaw Sobolewski; Pinewood, 32 Linden Way, Boston, Lincs PE21 9DS (☎ 0205 351655); Consultant Haematologist, Pilgrim Hospital, Sibsey Rd, Boston Lincs PE21 9QS (☎ 0205 64801)

SODOR AND MAN, Bishop of 1989-; Rt Rev Noel Debroy Jones; CB (1986); s of Brinley Jones, of Gwent, and Gwendoline Alice, *née* White (d 1988); *b* 25 Dec 1932; *Educ* West Monmouth Sch for Boys, St Davids Coll (BA), Wells Theol Coll; *m* 1969, Joyce Barbara Leelavathy, da of Arumugam Arulanandam (d 1979), of Singapore; 1 s (Benjamin b 1972), 1 da (Vanessa b 1970); *Career* clerk in Holy Orders 1955, Parishes Dio of Monmouth; vicar of Kano N Nigeria 1960, chaplain Royal Navy 1962, chaplain of the Fleet 1984-, Queens Hon Chaplain 1983; GSM; *Recreations* formerly rugby, squash, music, family; *Clubs* Sion Coll, Army and Navy; *Style*— The Rt Rev the Bishop of Sodor and Man; Bishop's House, Quarterbridge Road, Douglas, IOM

SOFER, Hon Mrs (Anne Hallowell); da of Baron Crowther (Life Peer, d 1972); *b* 1937; *Educ* St Paul's Sch, Swarthmore Coll USA, Somerville Coll Oxford (MA); *m* 1958, Jonathan Sofer, barrister-at-law; 2 s, 1 da; *Career* sec Nat Assoc of Govrs and Mangrs 1972-75, additional memb ILEA Educn Ctee 1974-77, chm ILEA Schs Sub Ctee 1978-81; dir Channel 4 1981-83; columnist The Times 1983-87; memb GLC St Pancreas N (Lab 1977-81, SDP 1981-86); *Books* The School Governors' Handbook (with Tyrrell Buyess, 1978 and 1986), The London Left Takeover (1987); *Style*— The Hon Mrs Sofer; 46 Regent's Park Rd, London NW1 (☎ 071 722 8970)

SOFIER, Jacob (Jack); s of Abraham Sofier (d 1986), of London, and Renee Sarah, *née* Shine (d 1983); *b* 2 July 1932; *Educ* Quintin Sch, Regent St Poly; *m* 3 July 1955, Maureen Barbara, da of Emanuel Lyttleston (d 1962), of London; 2 da (Rochelle Katrina (Shelley) b 2 Sept 1956, Hilary Deborah b 27 Oct 1958); *Career* S London rep Raelbrook Ltd 1955-68, sales dir Mr Harry Menswear 1968-70, ptnr Jacob Bernard 1970-73, fndr and chm Gabicci plc 1973-; chm business div JIA; *Recreations* golf, bridge and gin rummy; *Clubs* Potters Bar, Herts and Las Brisas Marbella Spain; *Style*— Jack Sofier, Esq; 54 Highpoint, North Hill, Highgate, London N6 4AZ (☎ 081 340 3491); 9B Molambo Residencia, Neuva Andalucia, Marbella, Malaga, Spain (☎ 52 81 15 84); Gabicci plc, Gabicci House, Humber Road, London NW2 6HN (☎ 081 208 1111, fax 081 208 2809, car 0860 626499, telex 299177)

SOKOLNICKI, Count Juliusz (Nowina-); s of Count Antoni (Nowina-)Sokolnicki (d 1946; proprietor of the manors of Siedlemin (district of Jarocin) and Izabelin (district of Biala Podlaska), Poland; descendant of old Polish nobility dating from 1284), and Irena, *née* Skirmunt (d 1981; heiress of Albrechtow, nr Pinsk; descendant of old Lithuanian nobility and niece of Constantin Skirmunt, Polish Ambass to London 1926-35); *b* 16 Dec 1920; *Educ* Joseph Pilsudski Coll Pinsk, Warsaw Univ; *m* 1, Elizabeth Mary Krokowski, *née* Mayal (d 1982); m 2, 29 July 1983, Margaret Thornburn, da of Francis Docherty (d 1947); *Career* Cadet Offr 84 Bn Polish Armed Forces during campaign in Poland Sept 1939, captured by Russians escaped, active Polish underground, arrested by Gestapo Aug 1940, released 1942 and rejoined underground in Lublin, Capt 1943, escaped to Italy after Warsaw Rising, Lt-Col 1945; active in Polish political organisations in Britain since 1947; chm Polish Nat Revival Movement 1954; memb Cncl of Republic of Poland in exile 1954-72 (vice-chm 1963-67); ed fortnightly 'Rzeczpospolita Polska' 1967-71; Min of Information Govt in Exile 1967-71, and Home Affairs 1970-71; Pres of the Republic of Poland in Exile 1972-; a fndr Central Euro Cncl New York 1986 (membership comprising seven govts or monarchs in exile: Albania, Bulgaria, Croatia, Czechoslovakia, Estonia, Poland and Roumania); vice-pres London Appreciation Soc 1981; memb: Royal Soc of St George, Club des Intellectuels Français 1979, Polish Nobility Assoc in USA 1982; delegtate for England of Inst Héraldique, Historique et Généalogique de France 1971; hon Life Memb Augustan Soc (USA) 1982; hon Citizen: State of Texas 1982, State of Nebraska 1982, city of Minneapolis 1982, city of Baltimore 1985; Hon Lt-Col State of Alabama Militia 1981; Recteur Hon de l'Institut de Documentation et d'Etudes Européannes Bruxelles 1981, Hon Prof of Political Science Institut St Irène France, Dr of Art and Philosophy Academia Int Americana Mexico 1981; Sen Int Parliament for Safety and Peace 1982; orders and decorations include: Order of Besa (Albania) 1988, Order of the White Eagle (Poland), Order of Polonia Restituta (Poland), Cdr Merito Commercial (Mexico) 1979, Order of Masaryk (Czechoslovakia) 1987, Gd Collar Equitem Crucis Hierosolimae (Patriarchate of Antioch) 1982, Gd Croix Etoile de la Paix (France) 1948, Etoile Civique Medaille d'Or (France) 1980, Gd Croix Encouragement Public (France) 1982, Medaille de Vermeil Grand Prix Humanitaire (France) 1980; *Recreations* travelling, painting; *Clubs* Special Forces; *Style*— Count Juliusz Sokolnicki; Oak Lodge, 42 Cornflower Close, Stanway, Colchester, Essex CO3 5SE (☎ 0206 41696)

SOLANDT, Jean Bernard; s of Alfred Ernest Solandt (d 1977), and Mathilde, *née* Braun; *b* 23 Dec 1936; *Educ* Lycee Pasteur Strasbourg France; *m* 6 Aug 1966, Sheila, da of Capt James William Hammill, OBE (d 1974); 1 s (Jean-Luc), 1 da (Nathalie Claire); *Career* dir Schroder plc 1982, jt vice-chm J Henry Schroder Wagg & Co Ltd 1984; md Treasy & Securities; chm Schroder Securities London, Hong Kong, Tokyo 1986; *Recreations* golf, skiing, reading, music; *Style*— Jean Solandt, Esq; 120 Cheapside, London EC 2 (☎ 071 382 6363)

SOLANKI, Ramniklal Chhaganlal; s of Chhaganlal Kalidas Solanki (d 1963), and Ichchhaben Chhaganlal Solanki; *b* 12 July 1931; *Educ* Irish Presbyterian Mission Sch Surat, MTB Coll Gujarat Univ (BA), Sarvajanik Law Coll Surat (LLB); *m* 16 June 1955, Parvatiben Ramniklal, da of Makanji Dullabhji Chavda (d 1979); 2 s (Kalpesh b 9 Nov 1960, Shailesh b 3 June 1964), 2 da (Sadhana (Mrs Ravindra Karia) b 18 May 1956, Smita (Mrs Mukesh Thakkar) b 5 July 1958); *Career* sub ed Nutan Bharat and Lok Vani Dailies Surat 1954-56, freelance columnist for several newspapers while serving State Govt in India 1956-63, London corr Gujarat Mitra Surat 1964-68, Euro corr Janmabhoomi Gp of Newspapers 1968-; ed and md: Garavi Gujarat Newspapers 1968-, Asian Trader 1985-; md Garavi Gujarat Property Ltd 1982; Reporter of the Year Award 1970; memb: Asian Advsy Ctee BBC 1976-80, Nat Centre for Indian Language Trg Steering Gp 1978, exec ctee Gujarati Arya Kshtriya Maha Sabha UK 1979-84, exec ctee Gujarati Arya Assoc 1974-84 (vice-pres 1980-83), CPU 1964-, Foreign Press Assoc 1984-, Parly Press Gallery House of Commons; sec Indian Journalists Assoc of Europe 1978-79; memb Guild Br Newspaper Eds 1976; *Recreations* reading, writing, meeting people, politics, travelling; *Style*— Ramniklal Solanki, Esq; 74 Harrowdene Rd, Wembley, Middlesex HA0 (☎ 081 902 2879/2586); Garavi Gujarat Publications, Garavi Gujarat House, 1 Silex St, London SE1 0DW (☎ 071 928 1234, fax 071 261 0055, telex 8955335 GUJARAT G)

SOLE, Brig Denis Story; CVO (1971), OBE (1964); s of Brig Denis Mavesyn Anslow Sole, DSO (d 1962), and Lilian May, *née* Story (d 1974); *b* 26 July 1917; *Educ* Cheltenham, Sandhurst Staff Coll Quetta; *m* 5 March 1957, Susan Margaret, da of Maj Cecil Arnold Williams (d 1951); 1 s (Simon John b 1960), 1 da (Sarah Elizabeth b 1958); *Career* served in The Border Regt 1937, Palestine 1937-39, India, Burma 1939-48, AAG Royal Nigerian Mil Forces 1959-62; def advsr to Br High Cmmn Zambia 1964-66, Def and Mil Attache Turkey 1968-72; *Recreations* sailing, shooting, fishing, tennis; *Clubs* Army and Navy; *Style*— Brig Denis S Sole, CVO, OBE

SOLÉ-ROMEO, HE Dr Luis Alberto; s of Luis Alberto Solé-Pons, and Julia, *née* Romeo-Podestá; *b* 31 Aug 1934; *Educ* Faculty of Law Montevideo (LLD); *m* 1, (m dis); 3 da (Silvia Solé-Cestau b 1 Feb 1963, Adriana Solé-Cestau b 1 Dec 1964, Telma Mariana Solé-Cestau b 19 Nov 1971); m 2, 28 June 1986, Mońica de Assumpçao; *Career* former lawyer and journalist; attorney cnsllr Govt Exchequer 1973-84, writer Opinar (weekly newspaper) 1980-81, co-dir Correo de los Viernes (weekly newspaper) 1981-85, co-ed El Día (nat daily newspaper) 1985-86, Uruguayan ambass to the Court of St James 1987-; former pres Nat Assoc of Broadcasting (Uruguay), memb Exec Ctee World Press Freedom Ctee; author numerous pubns on Uruguayan govt and broadcasting; *Recreations* tennis, shooting; *Clubs* Les Ambassadeurs, Atheneum, Travellers, Golf Club del Uruguay; *Style*— HE The Ambassador of Uruguay; 1 Campden Hill, London W8 (☎ 071 727 6557); Ituzaingó 1312 - Apto 505, Montevideo, Uruguay (☎ 010 598 2 95 72 30); 48 Lennox Gardens, London SW1X 0DL (☎ 071 589 8835, fax 071 581 9585, telex 264180)

SOLESBY, Tessa Audrey Hilda; CMG (1986); da of Charles Solesby (d 1982), and Hilda, *née* Willis (d 1981); *b* 5 April 1932; *Educ* Clifton HS, St Hugh's Coll Oxford (MA); *Career* Miny of Lab and Nat Serv 1954-55, Dip Serv 1956, FO 1956, Manilla 1957-59, Lisbon 1959-62, FO 1962-64, first sec UK Mission to UN Geneva 1964-68, FO 1968-70, FCO 1972-75, cnsllr 1975, seconded NATO Int Staff Brussels 1975-78, cnsllr E Berlin 1978-81, temp min UK Mission to UN NY 1981-82 (first sec 1970-72), head Central African Dept FCO 1982-86, min Pretoria 1986-87, ambass and ldr UK Delgn to Conf Disarmament Geneva 1987-; hon fell St Hugh's Coll Oxford 1988; *Recreations* hill walking, music; *Style*— Miss Tessa Solesby, CMG; Foreign and Commonwealth Office, King Charles St, London SW1

SOLEY, Clive Stafford; MP (Lab) Hammersmith 1983-; *b* 7 May 1939; *Educ* Downhill Secondary Modern, Newbattle Abbey Adult Educ Coll, Strathclyde Univ, Southampton Univ; *Career* probation offr 1970-75, sr probation offr 1975-79, MP (Lab) Hammersmith N 1979-83, oppn front bench spokesman: NI 1981-82 and Nov 1983-, NI 1983-84, Home Affrs 1984-87, Housing 1987-; *Style*— Clive Soley, Esq, MP; House of Commons, London SW1 (☎ 071 219 5118/5490, home: 071 740 7585)

SOLIMAN, Dr John Iskandar; s of Iskandar Soliman, and Ines, *née* Abdallah; *b* 24 Sept 1926; *Educ* Alexandria Univ (BSc, MSc), Univ of London (PhD); *m* 17 July 1953 (m dis 1981), Gabrielle, da of John Zammit; 1 s (Andre b 1955), 1 da (Monette b 1956); *Career* lectr Alexandria Univ Egypt 1948-61, sr sci offr Br Iron and Steel Res Assoc London 1961-62, lectr QMC 1962-87, chm Int Cmmns Europe, organizer Int Confs Europe, prof Univ of Rome 1981-, visiting prof to Univs in USA and Europe, conslt to multinational cos; numerous articles in jls; MIMechE; memb: Soc of Automotive Engrs USA, VDI Germany, AIA France, ATA Italy; *Clubs* Anglo Belgian, Annabel's; *Style*— Dr John Soliman; 42 Lloyd Park Avenue, Croydon, CR0 5SB (☎ 081 688 2719, fax 081 686 1490)

SOLMAN, Robert Frederick; s of Edward Vickery Solman (d 1977), of Spire House, Comberton, Kidderminster, and Marjorie Anne Watts, *née* Styles; *b* 27 Jan 1934; *Educ* Sebright Sch, Univ of Birmingham (LLB); *Career* called to the Bar Middle Temple 1958, Midlands and Oxford circuit, rec 1985; *Style*— Robert Solman, Esq; Roydfield, Blakedown, nr Kidderminster, Worcs (☎ 0562 700 275); 5 Fountain Court, Steelhouse Lane, Birmingham (☎ 021 236 5771)

SOLOMON, David; s of Leslie Ezekiel Solomon, of London, and Peggy, *née* Shatzman; *b* 6 Aug 1948; *Educ* Clarks Coll, City of London Coll; *m* 15 July 1973 (m dis 1986), Sarah-Lou Reekie; 1 s (Tony Daniel b 1980); *Career* began in advertising with Garland-Compton, fndr Pink-Soda Fashion Co 1983- (opened Euro Office in Paris 1988); winner Queen's Award for Export Achievement 1987, BKCEC Award for Export Achievement (awarded by The Princess Royal); MInstMSM; *Recreations* marathon, running, tennis; *Style*— David Solomon, Esq; 22 Eastcastle St, London W1N 7PA (☎ 071 636 9001, fax 071 637 1641, telex 22827 PK SODA G)

SOLOMON, David Joseph; s of Sydney Solomon (d 1963), of Bournemouth, Hants, and Rosie, *née* Joseph (d 1978); *b* 31 Dec 1930; *Educ* Torquay GS, Univ of Manchester (LLB); *m* 5 April 1959, Hazel, da of Joseph Boam, of London; 1 s (Jonathan b 1961), 2 da (Ruth b 1963, Joanne b 1966); *Career* Sgt Royal Hants Regt 1955-57; slr; ptnr Nabarro Nathanson 1961-68, head of Property Dept D J Freeman & Co 1976-90 (chief exec 1990-); memb Cncl Oriental Ceramic Soc; Freeman Worshipful Co Slrs; memb Law Soc; *Recreations* chinese ceramics, music, architecture, modern art, wine, tai chi; *Style*— David Solomon, Esq; Russell House, 9 South Grove, London N6 6BS (☎ 081 341 6151); Longecourt Les Culetre, 21230 Arnay le Duc, Cote d'Or, France; D J Freeman & Co, 43 Fetter Lane, London EC4A 1NA (☎ 071 583 4055, fax 071 353 7377)

SOLOMON, Gerald Oliver; s of Thomas Oliver Solomon (d 1987), of Barnard Castle, Co Durham, and Florence, *née* Towers (d 1978); *b* 18 June 1935; *Educ* King James I GS Bishop Auckland, UCL (LLB); *m* 4 May 1957, Norma, da of Harold Crofton Barron, BEM (d 1965), of Barnard Castle, Co Durham; 1 s (Jeremy b 1959 d 1981), 1 da (Amanda b 1963); *Career* Lloyds Bank 1958-: asst treas 1976-79, dep chief accountant 1979-80, regnl dir S Wales 1980-82, gen mangr UK Retail Banking 1982-; dir: Jt Credit Card Co Ltd (Access) 1984-90 Visa International (EMEA) 1989-; memb Cncl of Banking Ombudsman 1987-90; Freeman City of London 1970; FCIB 1983; *Recreations* golf, fell walking; *Clubs* Royal Overseas League, United (Jersey); *Style*— Gerald Solomon, Esq; Littlegarth, Churchfields Ave, Weybridge, Surrey KT13 9YA (☎ 0932 847 337); Lloyds Bank plc, 71 Lombard St, London EC3P 3BS (☎ 071 626 1500)

SOLOMON, Harry; s of Jacob Eli Solomon (d 1987), and Belle Brechner (d 1951); *b* 20 March 1937; *Educ* St Albans Sch, Law Society Sch of Law; *m* Judith Diana, da of Benjamin Manuel (d 1974); 1 s (Daniel Mark b 2 Sept 1965), 2 da (Louise Sara b 3 July 1964, Juliet Kate b 6 Aug 1969); *Career* admitted slr 1960, in private practice 1960-75; Hillsdown Holdings: md 1975-84, jt chm 1984-87, chm 1987-; chm RCP Help Medicine Appeal, dir Nat Heart Charity CORDA; *Recreations* jogging, cricket, tennis, collecting of historical Autographed Letters; *Style*— Harry Solomon, Esq; Hillsdown Holdings plc, Hillsdown House, 32 Hampstead High St, London NW3 1QD (☎ 071 794 0677, fax 071 435 1355, telex 297220)

SOLOMON, John William; s of George William Solomon (d 1957), of Roehampton, London, and Ivy Louie (Pat), *née* Castle; *b* 22 Nov 1931; *Educ* Charterhouse; *m* 1, 25 July 1953 (m dis 1972), Anne, da of (David) Robert Thomas Lewis (d 1979), of Carshalton, Surrey; 3 s (Andrew b 1954, John b 1956, Gregory b 1964); m 2, 5 Dec 1972, Barbara Arthur; *Career* md William P Solomon Ltd 1957-83 (joined 1951), md John Solomon Inc Ltd 1983-; Tobacco Trade Benevolent Assoc: hon treas 1970-76, vice chm 1976-82, chm 1982-86, vice pres 1980-; chm Imported Tobacco Prods Advsy Ctee 1984-86 (1976-80 and 1990-); The Croquet Assoc: chm 1962-64, vice pres 1975-83, pres 1983-; nat titles in assoc croquet: ten GB Open Championship, ten GB Mens Championship, ten GB Open Doubles Championship, one GB mixed Doubles Championship, nine times holder Presidents Cup, twice winner NZ Open Championship, twice winner NZ open Doubles Championship, four times winner

Championship of Champions; Worshipful Co of Tobacco Pipe Makers and Tobacco Blenders: Freeman 1960, Liveryman 1962, Court 1974, Master 1989-90; *Books* Croquet (1966); *Recreations* music, golf, acting, croquet; *Clubs* Hurlingham; *Style—* John Solomon, Esq; Pipersfield, Rusper Rd, Newdigate, Dorking, Surrey RH5 5BX (☎ 0293 871320); John Solomon Inc Ltd, 6 Edenbridge Trade Centre, Hever Rd, Edenbridge, Kent TN8 5EA (☎ 0732 864222, fax 0732 866727)

SOLOMON, Jonathan; s of Samuel Solomon, ICS (d 1988), of London, and Moselle Solomon; *b* 3 March 1939; *Educ* Clifton, King's Coll Cambridge (MA); *m* 6 Oct 1966, Hester Madeline, da of Orrin McFarland, of Florida, USA; 1 s (Gabriel b 27 April 1967); *Career* supervisor Sidney Sussex Coll Cambridge 1960-72, lectr Extra-Mural Dept Univ of London 1963-70; princ 1967-72: Bd of Trade (asst princ 1963-67), DTI, Treasy; asst sec 1973-80: Dept of Prices and Consumer Protection, Dept of Indust; under sec Dept of Indust 1980-85; Cable and Wireless plc: dir Special Projects 1985-87, dir Corp Strategy 1987-88; dir: Int Digital Communications 1987-, Corp Business Devpt 1988-, Tele 2 1990-; *Recreations* sport, research, futurology, writing; *Clubs* English Speaking Union; *Style—* Jonathan Solomon, Esq; 12 Kidderpore Gardens, London NW3 (☎ 071 794 6230); Mercury House, Theobalds Road, London WC1 (☎ 071 315 4611)

SOLOMON, Prof Louis; s of Samuel Solomon (d 1976), of Johnannesburg, and Ann, *née* Miller (d 1976); *b* 31 May 1928; *Educ* SA Coll Sch Cape Town, Univ of Cape Town (MB ChB, MD); *m* 1 July 1951, Joan Sarah, da of Philip Mendelsohn, of Johannesburg; 1 s (Ryan b 1956), 1 da (Caryn b 1953); *Career* prof of orthopaedic surgery: Univ of the Witwatersrand Johannesburg 1967-85, Univ of Bristol 1985-; memb: Br Soc of Rheumatology, Br Orthopaedic Assoc; *Books* with A G Apley: A System of Orthopaedics and Fractures (1982), A Concise System of Orthopaedics and Fractures (1988); *Recreations* cycling; *Style—* Prof Louis Solomon; Dept of Orthopaedic Surgery, Bristol Royal Infirmary, Bristol BS2 8HW (☎ 0727 213449, fax 0272 252736)

SOLOMON, Nathaniel; s of Leopold Solomon (d 1984), and Fanny, *née* Hartz; *b* 20 Nov 1925; *Educ* Owen's Sch London, Emmanuel Coll Cambridge (MA); *m* 24 Feb 1951, Patricia, da of Arthur Creak (d 1954); 2 s (Max b 1957, Justin b 1962), 1 da (Claire b 1959); *Career* Midshipman Fleet Air Arm 1944-47; dir: United Africa Co Ltd 1964-72 (joined 1949), William Baird PLC 1972-74; md Assoc Leisure PLC 1974-84, chm Pleasurama plc 1984-88, dir Bally Manufacturing Corp 1989-, dir Harrap Publishing Gp 1989-, chm Tottenham Hotspur plc 1991-; memb Nat Cncl Br Amusement Catering Trades Assoc; CBIM 1986; *Recreations* bridge, tennis, wine, opera, theatre, watching soccer especially Tottenham Hotspur; *Clubs* Reform, Harvard Business Sch, The Wimbledon; *Style—* Nathaniel Solomon, Esq; Tottenham Hotspur plc, 748 High Rd, Tottenham, London N17 OAP (☎ 081 808 8080, fax 081 885 1951, telex 295261)

SOLOMON, Stephen Edward; s of Maj William Edward Solomon (d 1977), and Winifred Constance, *née* Day; *b* 29 Nov 1947; *Educ* Royal GS Guildford Surrey, Univ of Manchester; *m* Maureen Diane, da of William Robert Wilkins, of Tenby, Dyfed; 2 s (Robert William Petrie b 1980, John Christopher Petrie b 1981); *Career* admitted slr 1973; ptnr: Crossman Block and Keith slrs 1978-87 (joined 1976), Withers Crossman Block 1988-89, Crossman Block 1989-; memb: Guildford Round Table 1979-89, Guildford XRT 1988-90; memb: City of Westminster Law Soc, Law Soc; *Recreations* golf, skiing, photography, astronomy, plumbing; *Clubs* Bramley Golf, Tenby Golf; *Style—* Stephen Solomon, Esq; Crossman Block, Aldwych House, Aldwych, London WC2B 4HN (☎ 071 836 2000, fax 071 240 2648, telex 21457)

SOLOMONS, Anthony Nathan; s of Lesly Emmanuel Solomons (d 1938), and Susy, *née* Schneiders; *b* 26 Jan 1930; *Educ* Oundle; *m* 16 Dec 1958, Jean, da of Dr Jack Joseph Golding; 2 da (Nicola Jane b 2 June 1960, Jennifer Anne b 30 June 1963); *Career* Nat Serv cmmnd Dorset Regt 1953-54; Singer & Friedlander Ltd: joined 1958, chief exec 1973, chm 1976-; dir Britannia Arrow Hldgs 1984-, chm Singer & Friedlander Gp plc 1987-; dir: Bullough plc, ACT plc, Milton Keynes Devpt Corp; FCA, FBIM; *Clubs* Carlton; *Style—* Anthony Solomons Esq; 10 Constable Close, London NW11 6TY (☎ 081 458 6716); 21 New St, London EC2M 4HR (☎ 071 623 3000, fax 071 623 2122, telex 886977)

SOLTI, Sir Georg; KBE (1971, Hon CBE 1968); *b* 21 Oct 1912, Budapest; *Educ* Budapest HS of Music; *m* 1, 1946, Hedwig Oeschli; m 2, 1967, Anne Valerie Pitts; 2 da (Gabrielle b 1970, Claudia b 1973); *Career* studied under Kodály, Bartók, Dohnányi; won First Prize as pianist Concours Int Geneva 1942; former conductor and pianist Budapest State Opera; musical dir: Bavarian State Opera 1946-52, Frankfurt Opera 1952-61, Covent Garden Opera 1961-71, Chicago Symphony Orchestra 1969-, Orchestre de Paris 1971-75; princ conductor and artistic dir LPO 1979-83 (conductor emeritus 1983-); Hon FRCM 1980; Hon DMus Univ of Leeds (1971), Oxford (1972), Yale (1974), De Paul (1975), Harvard (1979), Furman (1983), Surrey (1983) London (1986), Rochester (1987); prof (honoris causa) Baden-Württemberg (1985); Knight Commander's Cross with Badge and Star, Fed Republic of Germany (1986), 29 Grammy Awards (1987); adopted UK citizenship 1972; *Style—* Sir Georg Solti, KBE; Chalet Haut Pre, Villars sur Ollon, Vaud, Switzerland

SOLTMANN, Diana-Margaret; da of HE Dr Otto Soltmann, of 5411 Neuhausel Uber Koblenz, W Germany, and Ethel Margaret, *née* Oakleigh-Walker; *b* 29 Oct 1952; *Educ* Rosemead Sch Littlehampton, Univ of Keele (BA), LSE (Dip Personnel Mgmnt); *m* 16 June 1980, Timothy Congreve Stephenson, s of Augustus William Stephenson, of Saxbys Mead Cowden Kent; 3 s (Kit b 2 Feb 1983, William b 8 July 1985, James b 1 Dec 1989); *Career* dir: Good Relations Technol 1980-85, The Communication Gp 1985-89; head corp communications Blue Arrow plc 1988-89, md Royle Communications 1990-; AIPM, MIPR; *Recreations* reading, theatre, golf; *Style—* Miss Diana Soltmann; Royle Communications, Royle House, Wenlock Rd, London N1 7ST (☎ 071 608 2151, fax 071 251 1209, telex 894181 ROYLE G)

SOLYMAR, Dr Laszlo; *b* 24 Jan 1930; *Educ* Tech Univ of Budapest (Dip of Electrical Engrg, PhD); *m* 2 da (Gillian Kathy Solymar b 1963, Lucy Suzanne Solymar b 1970); *Career* lectr Tech Univ Budapest 1952-53; res engr: Res Inst for Telecommunications Budapest 1953-56, Standard Telecommunications Laboratories Ltd Harlow Essex 1956-66; Univ of Oxford: fell and tutor BNC 1966-86, lectr Dept of Engrg Sci 1971-86, Donald Pollock reader in engrg sci Dept of Engrg Sci 1986-, professorial fell Hertford Coll 1986-; visiting positions and consultancies: visiting prof Laboratoire de Physique Ecole Normale Superieure Univ of Paris 1965-66, visiting prof Tech Univ of Denmark 1972-73, conslt Tech Univ of Denmark 1973-76, visiting scientist Thompson-CSF Res Laboratories Orsay France 1984, conslt BT Res Laboratories 1986-88, conslt Hirst Res Laboratories GEC 1986-88, visiting prof Dept of Physics Univ of Osnabruck Germany 1987, visiting prof Optical Inst Tech Univ Berlin 1990, conslt Pilkington plc 1990; FIEE; *Books* Lectures on the Electrical Properties of Materials (with D Walsh, 1 edn 1970), Super Conductive Tunnelling and Applications (1972), A Review of the Principles of Electrical and Electronic Engineering (4 volumes, ed, 1974), Lectures on Electromagnetic Theory (1 edn, 1976), Holography and Volume Gratings (with D J Cooke, 1981), Solutions Manual to Accompany Lectures on the Electrical Properties of Materials (4 edn, 1988) Lectures on Fourier Series (1989); *Recreations* languages, twentieth century history particularly that of the Soviet Union, theatre, chess, skiing, swimming; *Style—* Dr Laszlo Solymar

SOMERLEYTON, 3 Baron (UK 1916); Sir Savile William Francis Crossley; 4 Bt (UK 1863), JP (Lowestoft), DL (Suffolk 1964); s of 2 Baron, MC, DL (d 1959), and Bridget, Baroness Somerleyton (d 1983); *b* 17 Sept 1928; *Educ* Eton; *m* 1963, Belinda Maris, da of late Vivian Loyd, of Kingsmoor, Ascot; 1 s (Hugh b 1971), 4 da (Isabel b 1964, Camilla b 1967, Alicia b 1969, Louisa b 1974); *Heir* s, Hon Hugh Francis Savile Crossley b 27 Sept 1971 (page of honour to HM The Queen 1983-84); *Career* cmmnd Coldstream Gds 1948, Capt 1956; former co cnclr E Suffolk, non-political lord-in-waiting to HM The Queen (permanent) 1978-; farmer; patron of one living; dir E Anglian Water Co; landowner (5000 acres); *Recreations* hunting, shooting; *Clubs* Pratt's, White's; *Style—* The Rt Hon the Lord Somerleyton, JP, DL; Somerleyton Hall, nr Lowestoft, Suffolk NR32 5QQ (☎ 0502 730308, 0502 730224)

SOMERS, 8 Baron (GB 1784); Sir John Patrick Somers Cocks; 8 Bt (GB 1772); s of 7 Baron Somers (d 1953, fifth in descent from the sis of the 1 and last Baron Somers of a previous creation. The latter was the celebrated Lord High Chllr, who was a memb of the Whig Junta in Queen Anne's reign and architect of the Union with Scotland); *b* 30 April 1907; *Educ* privately, RCM (BMus, ARCM); *m* 1, 15 Aug 1935, Barbara Marianne (d 1959), da of late Charles Henry Southall, of Norwich; m 2, 28 July 1961, Dora Helen, da of late John Mountfort, of Sydney, NSW; *Heir* kinsman, Philip Sebastian Somers Cocks b 4 Jan 1948; *Career* sits as independent in House of Lords; organist and professional musician; organist and choirmaster Westonbirt Sch 1935-38, dir of music Epsom Coll 1949-53, prof of theory and composition RCM 1967-77; *Recreations* carpentry; *Style—* The Rt Hon the Lord Somers; c/o Musicians Benevolent Fund, Dulas Court, nr Derbyshire, Herefordshire

SOMERS, Hon Mrs (Sara Margaret); *née* Byers; da of Baron Byers (Life Peer, d Feb 1984), and Baroness Byers, *qv*; *b* 1952; *m* 1979 (m dis), Simon John Somers; 2 da (Laura Sian b 1982, Amy Rowena b 1984); *Style—* The Hon Mrs Somers

SOMERS COCKS, Anna Gwenilian (Mrs J Hardy); da of John Sebastian Somers Cocks, CVO, CBE (d 1964), and Marjorie Olive, *née* Weller; *b* 18 April 1950; *Educ* Convent of the Sacred Heart Woldingham, St Anne's Coll Oxford (MA), Courtauld Inst Univ of London (MA); *m* 1, 1971 (m dis 1977), Martin Walker; m2, 1978 (m dis 1990), John Hardy; 1 s (Maximilian John Lee b 10 March 1980), 1 da (Katherine Isabella Eugenia b 15 March 1982); *Career* asst keeper: Dept of Metal Work V & A 1973-85, Dept of Ceramics V & A 1985-87; ed: Apollo 1987-90, The Art Newspaper 1990-; memb Cons Advsy Ctee on the Arts and Heritage; memb Worshipful Co of Goldsmiths 1989; FRBA; *Publications* The Victoria and Albert Museum: the making of the collection (1980), Princely Magnificence: court jewels of the Renaissance (ed and jt author, 1980), Renaissance Jewels, Gold Boxes and Objets de Vertu in the Vertu Thyssen Collection (1985); *Recreations* skiing, entertaining, travelling, walking; *Clubs* Arts; *Style—* Ms Anna Somers Cocks; c/o The Art Newspaper, Mitre House, 44-46 Fleet St, London EC4 (☎ 071 936 2886)

SOMERSET, Lady John; Lady Cosima Maria Gabriella; *née* Vane-Tempest-Stewart; yr da (by his 1 w) of 9 Marquess of Londonderry; *b* 25 Dec 1961; *Educ* St Paul's Girls' Sch; *m* 1, 1 Oct 1982 (m dis 1986), Cosmo Joseph Fry, s of Jeremy Fry, of 7 Royal Crescent, Bath; m 2, 18 Oct 1990, Lord John Robert Somerset, yst s of 11 Duke of Beaufort; *Style—* The Lady John Somerset

SOMERSET, David Henry FitzRoy; s of Brig Hon Nigel FitzRoy Somerset, CBE, DSO, MC (d 1990; s of 3 Baron Raglan), and Phyllis Marion Offley, *née* Irwin (d 1979); *b* 19 June 1930; *Educ* Wellington Coll, Peterhouse Cambridge (MA); *m* 1955, Ruth Ivy, da of Wilfred Robert Wildbur (d 1978), of King's Lynn, Norfolk; 1 s (Henry b 1961), 1 da (Louise b 1956); *Career* joined Bank of England 1952, personal asst to md of Int Monetary Fund Washington DC 1959-62, priv sec to Govr of Bank of England 1962-63, chief cashier and chief of Banking Dept Bank of England 1980-88 (ret 1988); dir: Prolific Group plc 1988-, Yamaichi Bank (UK) plc 1988-, Hafnia Holdings (UK) Ltd; Peterhouse Cambridge: memb Cncl of Friends 1981-, fell and fin advsr 1988-; chm Old Wellingtonian Soc 1988-, cmmr English Heritage 1988-, govr Wellington Coll 1989-; FCIB; *Recreations* gardening, shooting, racing; *Clubs* RAC; *Style—* D H F Somerset, Esq; White Wickets, Boars Head, Crowborough, Sussex TN6 3HE (☎ 0892 661111)

SOMERSET, Lord Edward Alexander; s of 11 Duke of Beaufort; *b* 1 May 1958; *m* 1982, Hon (Georgina) Caroline Davidson, *qv*, 2 da of 2 Viscount Davidson; 1 da (Francesca b 1984); *Style—* The Lord Edward Somerset

SOMERSET, Hon Geoffrey; 2 surv s of 4 Baron Raglan, JP (d 1964); bro and hp of 5 Baron Raglan, JP, DL; *b* 29 Aug 1932; *Educ* Westminster, RAC Cirencester; *m* 6 Oct 1956, Caroline Rachel, o da of Col Edward Roderick Hill, DSO, JP, DL, of Manor Farm Cottage, Stanford-in-the-Vale, Oxon; 1 s (Arthur b 27 April 1960), 2 da (Belinda (Mrs Nicholas Boyd) b 9 Feb 1958, Lucy b 8 Feb 1963); *Career* Nat Serv with Grenadier Gds 1952-54; instr Standard Motor Co Ltd Coventry 1956-60, gp marketing mangr Lambourn Engrg Gp 1960-71, dir Trenchermans Ltd 1971-79, underwriting memb of Lloyd's 1981; chm Stanford Area Branch Conservatives; memb: Berks CC 1966-75 (chm Children's Ctee and Mental Welfare Sub Ctee), Newbury Dist Cncl 1979-83 (chm Recreation and Amenities Ctee) Oxfordshire Valuation Court 1988-, Oxfordshire CC 1988-; Freeman City of London, Liveryman Worshipful Co of Skinners 1968; *Recreations* shooting, gardening, conservation; *Clubs* City Univ; *Style—* The Hon Geoffrey Somerset; Manor Farm, Stanford-in-the-Vale, Faringdon, Oxon SN7 8NN (☎ 036 77 558); 3 Market Place, Cirencester, Glos GL7 2PE (☎ 0285 657807)

SOMERSET, Jane, Duchess of; Gwendoline Collette (Jane); *née* Thomas; 2 da of late Maj John Cyril Collette Thomas, N Staffordshire Regt, of Burn Cottage, Bude, Cornwall; *m* 18 Dec 1951, 18 Duke of Somerset (d 1984); 2 s (19 Duke, Lord Francis Seymour), 1 da (Lady Anne Seymour); *Style—* Her Grace Jane, Duchess of Somerset; Bradley Cottage, Maiden Bradley, Warminster, Wilts

SOMERSET, Sir Henry Beaufort; CBE (1961); s of Henry St John Somerset (d 1952), and Jessie Bowie, *née* Wilson (d 1957); *b* 21 May 1906; *Educ* St Peter's Coll Adelaide, Melbourne Univ (BSc, MSc); *m* 1930, Patricia Agnes, da of Tom Percival Strickland (d 1955); 2 da (Susan, Diana); *Career* industrial chemist; company dir: Goliath Cement Hldgs Ltd 1948-82 (chm 1967-82), ICI Australia Ltd 1963-76; chllr Univ of Tasmania 1964-72; The Perpetual Executors & Tstees Assoc of Australia Ltd 1971-81 (chm 1973-81); pres Aust Inst of Mining and Metallurgy 1958 and 1966 (cnclr 1956-82), memb exec CSIRO 1965-74; chm: Australian Mineral Fndn 1970-83, Cncl Nat Museum 1968-78; dir: Nioxide Australia Pty 1949-82 (chm 1953-76), Humes Ltd 1957-82 (chm 1961-82), Assoc Pulp & Paper Mills Ltd 1945-81 (md 1948-69, dep chm 1969-81), EZ Industs Ltd 1953-78, Aust Fertilisers Ltd 1961-78, Central Norsemon Gold Ltd 1977-82; Hon DSc Univ of Tasmania 1973-; FRACI; FATS; kt 1966; *see Debrett's Handbook of Australia and New Zealand for further details*; *Clubs* Melbourne, Australian; *Style—* Sir Henry Somerset, CBE; Flat 10/1, 193 Domain Rd, South Yarra, Vic 3141, Australia; 360 Collins St, Melbourne, Vic 3000

SOMERSET, 19 Duke of (E 1547); Sir John Michael Edward Seymour; 17 Bt (E 1611); also Baron Seymour (E 1547); s of 18 Duke of Somerset, DL (d 1984), and Gwendoline Collette (Jane), née Thomas; *b* 30 Dec 1952; *Educ* Eton; *m* 20 May 1978, Judith-Rose, da of John Hull; 1 s, 2 da (Lady Sophia b 1987, Lady Henrietta Charlotte b 1989); *Heir* s, Sebastian Edward, Lord Seymour, b 3 Feb 1982; *Style—* His Grace the Duke of Somerset; c/o House of Lords, London SW1

SOMERSET, Lord John Robert; s of 11 Duke of Beaufort; *b* 5 Nov 1964; *m* 18 Oct 1990, Lady Cosima Maria Gabriella, da of 9 Marquess of Londonderry, and former w of Cosmo Joseph Fry; 1 s (b 16 Feb 1991); *Style*— The Lord John Somerset

SOMERSET FRY, Peter (George Robin) Plantagenet; s of Cdr (E) Peter Kenneth Llewellyn Fry, OBE, RN (d 1977), of Chagford Cross, Moretonhampstead, Devon, and Ruth Emily, *née* Marriott (d 1978); *b* 3 Jan 1931; *Educ* Lancing, St Thomas's Hosp Med Sch, Univ of London, St Catherine's Coll Oxford; *m* 1, 29 March 1952 (m dis 1957), Audrey Anne, *née* Russell; m 2, 29 May 1958, Daphne Diana Elizabeth Caroline (d 1961), o da of Lt-Col Frederick Reginald Yorke; m 3, 17 Nov 1961 (m dis 1973), Leri (d 1985), eldest da of Dr Gruffydd Llywelyn-Jones (d 1952), of Bryn Glas, Llangefni, Anglesey, and formerly w of Hon Pierce Alan Somerset David Butler, TD (s of 7 Earl of Carrick); m 4, 5 March 1974, Pamela Fiona Ileene, eld da of Col Henry Maurice Whitcombe, MBE (d 1984); *Career* asst master Wallop Preparatory Sch Weybridge Surrey 1952-54 and 1958-60; account exec TAF International Ltd (public relations conslts) 1960-63; dir and head of public relations Maxwell Public Relations 1963-64; information offr: Incorporated Assoc of Architects and Surveyors 1965-67, Miny of Public Building and Works 1967-70; head Information Cncl for Small Industs in Rural Areas (COSIRA) 1970-74; ed of books HMSO 1975-80; sr memb Wolfson Coll Cambridge 1980-; p/t mangr Eastern Region Charities Aid Fndn 1987-, parish councillor and clerk Little Bardfield Parish Cncl Essex 1973-74; fndr and hon sec: Little Bardfield Community Tst 1973, Burgh Soc Norfolk 1977-80; antique furniture conslt Christ Church Mansion (Ipswich Museums) Ipswich 1987-; FRSA 1966; *Books* include: The Cankered Rose (1959), Antique Furniture (1971), Children's History of the World (1972), Great Caesar (1974), 1000 Great Lives (1975), 2000 Years of British Life (1976), Chequers, the Country Home of Britain's Prime Ministers (1977), The Book of Castles (1980), Fountains Abbey (official guide, 1981), Revolt Against Rome (1982), A History of Scotland (with Fiona Somerset Fry, 1982); Battle Abbey (official guide, 1984), Roman Britain: History and Sites (1984), Rievaulx Abbey (official guide, 1986), A History of Ireland (with Fiona Somerset Fry, 1988), The Tower of London (1990), The Kings & Queens of England and Scotland (1990); *Recreations* visiting castles, studying 18th Century French furniture, campaigning for Freedom of Information; *Style*— Peter Plantagenet Somerset Fry, Esq; Wood Cottage, Wattisfield, Bury St Edmunds, Suffolk (☎ 0359 51324)

SOMERSET JONES, Eric; QC (1978); s of late Daniel Somerset Jones, and Florence Somerset Jones, of Birkenhead; *b* 21 Nov 1925; *Educ* Birkenhead Inst, Lincoln Coll Oxford (MA); *m* 1966, Brenda Marion, da of late Hedley Shimmin; 2 da (Wendy b 1967, Felicity b 1970); *Career* served RAF Coll Cranwell, link trainer instr SE Asia Cmd 1944-47; called to the Bar Middle Temple 1952, Bencher 1988; memb Lord Chllr's County Cts Rule Ctee 1975-78, rec Crown Ct 1975-; *Recreations* family pursuits, travel, listening to music, photography; *Clubs* Oxford and Cambridge, Royal Chester Rowing; *Style*— Eric Somerset Jones, Esq, QC; Goldsmith Building, Temple, London EC4Y 7BL (☎ 071 353 7881); Southmead, Mill Lane, Willaston Wirral, Cheshire L64 1RL (☎ 051 327 5138); Cloisters, 1 Pump Court, Middle Temple, London EC4Y 7AA (☎ 071 353 8461)

SOMERSET-WARD, Richard Adrian; s of Rev Canon A D Somerset-Ward (d 1976); *b* 29 May 1942; *Educ* Charterhouse, CCC Cambridge; *Career* joined BBC 1963, seconded to HM Diplomatic Service 1964-65, BBC dir in USA 1976-78, head of Music and Arts Programming BBC-TV 1981-; *Recreations* opera, music, tennis, golf; *Clubs* Savile; *Style*— Richard Somerset-Ward Esq; 47 Welsby Court, Eaton Rise, London W5 (☎ 081 998 5789)

SOMERTON, Viscount; James Shaun Christian Welbore Ellis Agar; s and h of 6 Earl of Normanton; *b* 7 Sept 1982; *Style*— Viscount Somerton

SOMERVILLE, (Irene) Dione; da of Willoughby Eric O'Connell Cole Powell (d 1954), of Nairobi, Kenya, and Dr Edna Grace, *née* Merrick; *b* 30 April 1945; *Educ* The Highlands Sch Eldoret Kenya, Trinity Coll Dublin (BA, MB BCh, BAO), Coll Surgns I (DA), Coll of Med SA (FFA(SA)); *m* 29 Aug 1970, Julian John Fitzgerald Somerville, s of Michael Fitzgerald Somerville, of Wantage, Oxfordshire; 1 s (Nigel John Powell b 12 May 1972), 1 da (Grainne Fitzgerald b 26 May 1975); *Career* intern Adelaide Hosp Dublin 1970-71, sr house offr in anaesthetics Dublin 1971-73; registrar in anaesthetics: King Edward VIII Hosp Durban SA, King George V Hosp Durban SA; clinical asst later sr registrar Yorkshire RHA 1981-87, conslt anaesthetist Hailfax Gen Hosp Royal Halifax Infirmary W Yorkshire 1988-; *Recreations* sailing, tennis, gardening; *Style*— Dr Dione Somerville; Department of Anaesthetics, Royal Halifax Infirmary, Free School Lane, Halifax (☎ 0422 357222)

SOMERVILLE, Ian Christopher; *b* 2 Oct 1948; *Educ* St Edwards Coll Liverpool, Imperial Coll London (BSc); *m* 11 July 1970, Felicity Ann; *Career* taxation mangr Arthur Andersen & Co (London and Manchester) 1976-82, VAT ptnr Coopers & Lybrand Deloitte 1985- (sr taxation mangr 1982-85); sometime chm Stockport Family Practitioner Ctee, memb Ctee Family Welfare Assoc Manchester 1980-85, chm N Cheshire Branch BIM 1984-85; ACA 1973, FCA 1978, FBIM 1984; *Books* Tolley's VAT Planning (contrib, 1986-90), ICAEW Taxation Service (contrib, 1988-90); *Recreations* music, gardening, cats; *Style*— Ian Somerville, Esq; Coopers & Lybrand Deloitte, Plumtree Court, London EC4A 4HT (☎ 071 583 5000, fax 071 828 4607, telex 887470)

SOMERVILLE, Dr Jane; da of Capt Bertram Platnauer, MC, of London, and Pearl Annie, *née* Backler (d 1969); *b* 24 Jan 1933; *Educ* Queens Coll London, Guys Hosp Univ of London (MB BS, MD); *m* 2 Feb 1957, Walter Somerville, s of Patrick Somerville (d 1954), of Dublin; 3 s (Lorne b 1963, Rowan b 1966, Crispin b 1972), 1 da (Kate b 1961); *Career* sr lectr Inst of Cardiology London 1964-74, hon conslt physician Hosp For Sick Children 1968-88; hon sr lectr: Nat Heart and Lung Inst Univ of London 1974-, Inst of Child Health to 1988; conslt physician Nat Heart Hosp 1974-, conslt cardiologist St Bartholomews Hosp 1988-; memb Ctee on Cardiology RCP 1985-90, advsr on congenital heart disease for The Sec of States Hon Med Advsy Panel On Driving And Disorders Of The Cardiovascular System 1986; memb: Cncl Stonham Meml, Bd of Govrs Queens Coll London; FACC 1972, FRCP 1973; *Recreations* collecting blue opaline and object d'art, studying Fabergé, growing orchids, roof gardening; *Style*— Dr Jane Somerville; 30 York House, Upper Montagu St, London W1H 1FR (☎ 071 262 2144); Royal Brompton National Heart and Lung Hospital, Sydney St, London SW3 6NP (☎ 071 351 8602/8600/8200, fax 071 351 8201)

SOMERVILLE, John Arthur Fownes; CB (1977), CBE (1964), DL (1985); s of Admiral of the Fleet Sir James Fownes Somerville, GCB, GBE, DSO (d 1949), and Mary Kerr, *née* Main (d 1945); *b* 5 Dec 1917; *Educ* RNC Dartmouth; *m* 16 June 1945, (Julia) Elizabeth, da of Vice Adm Christopher Russell Payne (d 1952); 1 s (Christopher b 1949), 2 da (Julia b 1947, Louisa b 1956); *Career* served RN 1931-50; GCHQ Cheltenham 1950-78 (ret as undersec); *Recreations* walking; *Clubs* Army & Navy; *Style*— JAF Somerville, Esq, CB, CBE, DL; The Old Rectory, Dinder, Wells, Somerset BA5 3PL (☎ 0749 74900)

SOMERVILLE, Julian John Fitzgerald; s of Michael Fitzgerald Somerville, of Alfredston Place, Wantage, Oxon, and Barbara, *née* Gregg (d 1982); *b* 21 June 1944; *Educ* Kings Sch Canterbury, Trinity Coll Dublin (BA, MB BCh, MA, MD RCSE (d) MD); *m* 29 Aug 1970, (Irene) Dione, da of Willoughby Eric O'Connell Cole Powell (d 1954); 1 s (Nigel John Powell b 12 May 1972), 1 da (Grainne b 26 May 1975); *Career* Maj RAMC TA (joined 1973); internship Sir Patrick Duns Hosp Dublin 1970-71, anatomy demonstrator Trinity Coll Dublin 1971-72, res fell Sir Patrick Duns Hosp Dublin 1972-73; surgical and urological registrar: King Edward VIII Hosp Durban SA 1973-76, King Edward VIII Hosp Durban SA 1976-81, Leeds Gen Infirmary Yorks 1981-85; conslt urologist Halifax Gen Hosp Yorks 1985-; memb: BMA, Br Assoc Urological Surgns 1982; FRCS Ed 1976; *Recreations* sailing; *Style*— Julian Somerville, Esq; White Chimneys, Rawson Ave, Halifax, West Yorkshire HX3 0LR (☎ 0422 341997); The BUPA Hospital, Elland, nr Halifax, W Yorkshire (☎ 0422 375577)

SOMERVILLE, Brig Sir (John) Nicholas; CBE (1978); e; yr s of Brig Desmond Henry Sykes Somerville, CBE, MC (d 1976), of Drishane House, Castletownshend, Skibbereen, Co Cork, and Moira Burke, *née* Roche (d 1976); *b* 16 Jan 1924; *Educ* Winchester; *m* 6 Aug 1951, Jenifer Dorothea, da of Capt W M Nash, OBE, of The Point House, Castletownshend, Skibbereen, Co Cork; 1 s (Robin b 1959), 2 da (Philippa b 1953, Penelope b 1954); *Career* enlisted 1942, cmmnd 2 Lt 24 Regt SWB 1943, active serv D Day to VE Day intelligence offr (later Adj and Co Cdr) 1944-45, signal offr (later Adj) 1 SWB Palestine and Cyprus 1945-48, instr RMA Sandhurst 1949-52, Staff Coll Camberley 1954, DA & QMG (ops and plans) BAOR 1955-57, Co Cdr 1 SWB Malayan Emergency 1958-59, Brevet Lt-Col 1963, JSSC 1963, GSO1 (plans) HQ FARELF 1964-66, CO 1 SWB Hong Kong and Aden 1966-68, instr Jt Servs Staff Coll 1969, cmdt Jr Div Staff Coll 1970-73, Brig dir army recruiting 1973-76, Regular Cmmns Bd 1976-79; devpt co-ordinator Royal Cwlth Soc 1980-81, md Saladin Security Ltd 1981-85, self-employed conslt personnel selection 1985-, voluntary conslt Parly Selection Bd on Procedure Cons Pty; kt 1985; *Recreations* sailing; *Clubs* Landsdowne; *Style*— Brig Sir Nicholas Somerville, CBE; Deptford Cottage, Greywell, Basingstoke, Hants RG25 1BS (☎ 0256 702796)

SOMERVILLE, Sir Robert; KCVO (1961, CVO 1953); s of Robert Somerville, of Dunfermline; *b* 5 June 1906; *Educ* Fettes, St John's Coll Cambridge, Univ of Edinburgh; *m* 1, 1932, Marie-Louise Cornelia (d 1976), da of Heinrich Bergené, of Aachen; 1 da; m 2, 1981, Mrs Jessie B Warburton, wid of Dr Colin Warburton, of Sydney; *Career* served in Miny of Shipping (later War Transport) 1940-44; entered Duchy of Lancaster Office 1930, chief clerk 1945, clerk of the Cncl 1952-70; memb: Advsy Cncl on Public Records 1959-64, Royal Cmmn on Historical Manuscripts 1966-88; Hon DLitt; FSA, FRHistS; *Style*— Sir Robert Somerville, KCVO, FSA; 3 Hunt's Close, Morden Rd, London SE3 0AH

SOMMERVILLE, Brian; s of Alfred Sommerville (d 1966), and Evelyn, *née* North (d 1957); *b* 30 May 1931; *Educ* Kayes Coll Huddersfield; *Career* served RN 1946-61; worked for The Daily Express 1961-62; music publicist 1963-74; clients incl: The Beatles, The Who, Manfred Mann, and others; music publisher and TV commercial music prodr; called to the Bar Middle Temple 1974; in practice Temple and NE Circuit; farmer Yorks; *Recreations* football; *Clubs* Naval and Military; *Style*— Brian Sommerville, Esq; 2 Harcourt Buildings, Temple, London EC4Y 9DB (☎ 071 353 1394); Toft Green, York YO1 1JT (☎ 0904 620048)

SOMMERVILLE, William; s of William Sommerville, of Bay Trees, Church St, Blagdon, nr Bristol, and Mary Salome, *née* Whiskard (d 1988); *b* 28 April 1939; *Educ* Marlborough, Clare Coll Cambridge (MA), Imperial Coll London (MSc); *m* 21 Nov 1964, Mary, da of James Westhead, of 27 Lyndrick Rd, Mannamead, Plymouth; 1 s (John b 12 Jan 1970), 2 da (Katherine (Kate) b 13 Aug 1965, Rachel b 12 Feb 1967); *Career* ptnr MRM Partnership (consulting engrs); FICE 1984, FIStructE 1990; *Style*— William Sommerville, Esq; Kilncroft, Limekiln Lane, Countess Wear, Exeter EX2 6LW (☎ 0392 52 301); MRM Partnership, 11-15 Dix's Field, Exeter EX1 1QA (☎ 0392 50 211)

SONDES, 5 Earl (UK 1880); Henry George Herbert Milles-Lade; also Baron Sondes (GB 1760) and Viscount Throwley (UK 1880); s of 4 Earl Sondes (d 1970, descended from 1 Baron Monson through the latter's 2 s, who was cr Baron Sondes), and Pamela, da of Lt-Col Herbert McDougall, of Cawston Manor, Norfolk; *b* 1 May 1940; *Educ* Eton; *m* 1, 1968 (m dis 1969), Primrose Anne, da of late Lawrence Stopford Llewellyn Cotter (s of 5 Bt); m 2 1976 (m dis 1981), Altgräfin Sissy, da of Altgraf Niklas zu Salm-Reifferscheidt-Raitz; *Heir* none; *Style*— The Rt Hon The Earl Sondes; Stringman's Farm, Faversham, Kent

SONDHEIMER, Prof Ernst Helmut; s of Max Sondheimer (d 1982), and Ida, *née* Oppenheimer; *b* 8 Sept 1923; *Educ* Univ Coll Sch, Trinity Coll Cambridge (MA, PhD, ScD); *m* 18 Aug 1950, Janet Harrington, da of Edgar Harrington Matthews (d 1968); 1 s (Julian b 1952), 1 da (Judith (Mrs Robertson) b 1956); *Career* WWII Cavendish Laboratory Cambridge 1944-45; fell Trinity Coll Cambridge 1948-52; Univ of London: lectr in mathematics Imperial Coll of Science and Technol 1951-54, reader in applied maths Queen Mary Coll 1954-60, prof of maths Westfield Coll 1960-82 (prof emeritus 1982-); ed Alpine Journal 1986-91; memb Highgate Literary and Sci Inst; fell: King's Coll London 1985-, Queen Mary and Westfield Coll London 1989-; memb London Mathematical Soc 1963-; *Books* Green's Functions for Solid State Physicists (with S Doniach, 1974), Numbers and Infinity (with A Rogerson, 1981), papers on the electron theory of metals; *Recreations* mountains, growing alpines, reading history; *Clubs* Alpine; *Style*— Prof Ernst Sondheimer; 51 Cholmeley Crescent, London N6 5EX (☎ 081 340 6607)

SOOKE, Thomas Peter; s of Dr Paul Sooke, of London, and Gertrude, *née* Klinger (d 1969); *b* 8 Jan 1945; *Educ* Westminster, Pembroke Coll Cambridge (MA), Columbia Univ New York (MBA); *m* 8 June 1975, Ceridwen Leeuwke, da of Derek Matthews; 1 s (Alastair b 1981), 1 da (Leonie b 1985); *Career* Price Waterhouse 1968-70, Wallace Bros Bank Ltd 1972-76, dir Granville & Co Ltd 1976-87 also Venture Funds, co fndr Br Venture Capital Assoc 1983, Franchise Investors Ltd 1985-, corp fin ptnr Touche Ross & Co 1988-; FCA 1979; *Recreations* tennis, golf, old watercolours; *Clubs* United Oxford and Cambridge, Isle of Purbeck Golf; *Style*— Thomas Sooke, Esq; Touche Ross & Co, Hill House, 1 Little New St, London EC4A 3TR (☎ 071 936 3000, fax 071 583 8517)

SOOLE, Michael Alexander; s of Brian Alfred Seymour Soole (d 1974), and Rosemary Una, *née* Salt; *b* 18 July 1954; *Educ* Berkhamsted Sch, Univ Coll Oxford (MA); *Career* called to Bar Inner Temple 1977, practising barr 1978-; Parly candidate Aylesbury (SDP/Liberal Alliance) general elections 1983 and 1987; pres Oxford Union 1974; *Recreations* conversation; *Clubs* National Liberal; *Style*— Michael Soole, Esq; 9 Charlton Place, London N1 8AQ (☎ 071 359 0759); 1 Harcourt Buildings, 3rd Floor, Temple, London EC4Y 9DA (☎ 071 353 2214, fax 071 583 1656)

SOPER, Baron (Life Peer UK 1965), of Kingsway, London Borough of Camden; Rev Donald Oliver Soper; s of Ernest Frankham Soper (d 1962), of Wallington, Surrey, and Caroline Amelia, *née* Pilcher; *b* 31 Jan 1903; *Educ* Haberdashers' Aske's St Catharine's Coll Cambridge, Wesley House Cambridge, LSE (PhD); *m* 3 Aug 1929, Marie Gertrude, da of late Arthur Dean, of Norbury; 4 da (Hon Ann Loveday Dean (Hon Mrs Horn) b 15 April 1931, Hon Bridget Mary Dean (Hon Mrs Kemmis) b 17 Dec 1933, Hon Judith Catharine Dean (Hon Mrs Jenkins) b 25 Oct 1942, Hon Caroline Susan Dean (Hon Mrs Blacker) b 11 Aug 1946); *Career* sits as Lab

Peer in House of Lords; min: South London Mission 1926-29, Central London Mission 1929-36; supt min W London Mission 1936-78, chm Shelter 1974-78; pres: League Against Cruel Sports, Christian Socialist Movement, Fellowship of Reconciliation, Methodist Conference (1953); World Methodist Peace prize 1982; open-air speaker Tower Hill every Wednesday for last 60 years, Hyde Park every Sunday; Hon DD Cambridge; *Books* Aflame with Faith, It is hard to work for God, The Advocacy of the Gospel, All His Grace, Christianity and Politics, Calling for Action (Autobiography); Practical Christianity Today, Will Christianity Work?; *Style—* The Rev the Rt Hon the Lord Soper; 19 Thayer Street, London W1M 5LJ

SOPER, Michael Henry Ray; OBE (1963); s of John Philpott Henry Soper (d 1946), of Woodlands, Theydon Bois, Essex, and Edith Munro (d 1942); *b* 30 Sept 1913; *Educ* Tonbridge, Pembroke Coll Cambridge (MA, Dip Agric); *Career* lectr in agric Univ of Reading 1936-38; inspr of agric Sudan Govt 1938-40, dep exec offr Surrey WAEC 1940-46; lectr in Agric Univ of Oxford 1946-81; dir Univ of Oxford Farm 1950-81, student ChCh (tutorial fell) Oxford 1976-81; chief assessor Nat Certificate in Agric Examinations Bd 1962-87, organiser Oxford Farming Conf 1950-80; chm: Assoc of Agric 1982-90, Oxfordshire Agric Soc Tst 1983-, City and Guilds Advsy Ctee for Agric 1963-76, Eng Panel Cncl for Awards of Royal Agric Soc 1984-87; FRAgS, Hon FCGI, hon fell City and Guilds of London Inst, MIBiol; *Books* Modern Farming and the Countryside (with E S Carter, 1985); *Recreations* golf, gardening; *Style—* Michael Soper, Esq, OBE; Larksmead, Brightwell cum Sotwell, Wallingford, Oxon OX10 0QF (☎ 0491 37416)

SOPHER, Ivan; s of James Joseph Sopher, of 22 Manor Hall Ave, London, and Sophie Sopher; *b* 27 Aug 1949; *m* 1973, Helen; 1 s, 2 da; *Career* sole proprietor Ivan Sopher & Co CAs, Ernst & Young Sopher (jt venture with Ernst & Young); dir: Professional Publications Ltd, Delta Financial Management Ltd; FCA, FCCA, ATII, MBIM; *Recreations* travel, sport; *Style—* Ivan Sopher, Esq; 5 Elstree Gate, Elstree Way, Borehamwood, Herts WD6 1JD

SOPWITH, Sir Charles Ronald; s of Alfred Sopwith (d 1946), of S Shields, Co Durham; *b* 12 Nov 1905; *Educ* S Shields HS; *m* 1946, Ivy Violet (d 1968), da of Frederick Leonard Yeates, of Gidea Park, Essex; *Career* CA 1928, slr 1938, asst dir Press Censorship 1943-45, princ asst slr Bd of Inland Revenue 1956-61, public tstee 1961-63, slr Inland Revenue 1963-70, dep sec Cabinet Office 1970-72, dir Royal Acad of Music 1973-87 (hon fell 1984), second counsel to chm of ctees House of Lords 1974-82; kt 1966; *Recreations* music; *Clubs* Reform; *Style—* Sir Charles Sopwith; 18 Moor Lane, Rickmansworth, Herts

SOREL-CAMERON, Air Cdre Robert; CBE (1945), AFC (1943); s of Lt-Col George Cecil Minett Sorel-Cameron, CBE (d 1947), and Marguerite Emily, er da of Hon Hamilton James Tollemache (4 s of 1 Baron Tollemache); *b* 27 Nov 1911; *Educ* Wellington, Univ of Edinburgh; *m* 1939, Henrietta Grace, *née* Radford-Norcop; 2 s, 1 da; *Career* joined RAF 1931 (served UK, Burma, India, Netherlands, East Indies), Air Cdre 1960, air attaché Athens 1960-62 (ret 1962); *Recreations* fishing, flat racing, wildlife; *Clubs* RAF; *Style—* Air Cdre Robert Sorel-Cameron, CBE, AFC; The White House, Whitwell, Norfolk NR10 4RF (☎ 0603 872394)

SORENSEN, (Nils Jorgen) Philip; s of Erik Philip Sorensen, consul-gen, of Lillon, Skane, Sweden, and Brita Hjordis Bendix, *née* Lundgren (d 1984); *b* 23 Sept 1938; *Educ* Herlufsholm Kostskole Naerstved Denmark, Niels Brock Commercial Sch Copenhagen; *m* 1962, Ingrid, da of Eigil Baltzer-Anderson (d 1965); 1 s (Mark b 13 March 1973), 3 da (Annette b 27 Aug 1963, Christina b 29 June 1965, Louisa b 18 Feb 1968); *Career* chm fndr Gp 4 Securitas cos: UK, Ireland, Belgium, Denmark, Luxembourg, Malta, Netherlands, Greece, Spain, Portugal; bd memb var security cos: Sweden, Norway, Australia, France, Japan, Thailand; pres Ligue Internationale des Societes de Surveillance, memb cncl Br Security Industl Assoc; owner of two small select hotels: Dormy House Hotel, Broadway and Strandhotellet, Skagen Denmark; Soldier of the Year Award Sweden; hon citizen Cork 1985; *Recreations* sailing (fishing vessel 'Oke'), photography, travelling, book collecting; *Clubs* Buck's, Eccentric, Hurlingham, Mosimanns; *Style—* Philip Sorensen, Esq; Prinsevinkenpark 2, PO Box 85911, 2508 Den Haag, The Netherlands (☎ 010 31 70 519191); Group 4 Securitas Ltd, Farncombe House, Broadway, Worcs WR12 7LJ (☎ 0386 858585, fax 0386 858254, telex 338571)

SORKIN, (Alexander) Michael; s of Joseph Sorkin, of London (d 1984), and Hilda Ruth, *née* Fiebusch; *b* 2 March 1943; *Educ* St Paul's Manchester Univ (BA); *m* 27 Nov 1977, Angela Lucille, da of Leon Berman (MC), of London; 1 s (Jacob b 1983), 2 da (Zoe b 1979, Kim b 1980); *Career* joined Hambro Bank 1968 (dir 1973, exec dir 1983, vice chm 1987); dir: Fleet Street Properties Ltd 1986, Hambros Bank Ltd (vice-chm) 1973-, Hambros plc 1986-, TNT (UK) Ltd 1979-, Hambro America Inc (USA) 1986-; *Recreations* opera, golf, tennis; *Style—* Michael Sorkin, Esq; 3 Robin Grove, London N6 (☎ 081 348 7111); Hambros Bank, 41 Tower Hill, London EC3 (☎ 071 480 5000)

SORLEY WALKER, Kathrine; da of James Sorley Walker, and Edith Jane, *née* Robertson; *Educ* St Margaret's Sch Aberdeen, Crouch End Coll London, King's Coll Univ of London, Besancon Univ France, Trinity Coll of Music; *Career* author; ed asst The Geographical Magazine (London), ballet dance and mime critic The Daily Telegraph 1969-; non-fiction works: Eyes on the Ballet (1963, revised edn 1965), Eyes on Mime (1969), Dance and its Creators (1972), Ballet for Boys and Girls (1980), The Royal Ballet: A Picture History (1981, revised edn 1986), De Basil's Ballets Russes (1982), Ninette de Valois: Idealist without Illusions (1987); verse: The Heart's Variety (1959), Emotion and Atmosphere (1975); editor of: Raymond Chandler Speaking (1962), Writings on Dance 1938-68 by AV Coton (1975); contrib to numerous periodicals incl: The Dancing Times, Dance and Dancers, Dance Chronicle (NY), Vandance (Vancouver), The World and I (Washington DC); also contrib to numerous encyclopedias; *Style—* Ms Sorley Walker

SORRELL, Alec Dudley Mott; JP (City of London 1969-); s of Dudley Sorrell (d 1972), of Theydon Bois, Essex, and Mary Dorothy Sybil, *née* Mott (d 1947); *b* 17 April 1925; *Educ* Forest Sch, Downing Coll Cambridge (MA, LLM); *m* 3 Feb 1951, Elisabeth ffolliot, da of Dr Albert Malcolm Barlow (d 1957), of Porthcurno, Cornwall; 2 s (Jeremy b 1951, Robin b 1955); *Career* Lt Royal Marines Far East and Malta 1943-47; sr ptnr Craigen Wilders & Sorrell slrs; clerk Parmiter's Govr's Fndn and Sch 1959-, Dr Spurstowe's Charity Tstee 1959-; dir: Queen Adelaide's Charity Tstees 1963-, other London charities; Royal Nat Throat Nose and Ear Hosp: govr 1972-74 and 1980-82, special tstee 1982-; govr Forest Sch 1985-; gen cmmr of Income Tax 1962; JP Inner London 1968-69; Liveryman Worshipful Co of Basketmakers 1954- (prime warden 1986-87); *Recreations* open air, walking; *Clubs* Naval, City Livery; *Style—* Alec D M Sorrell, Esq, JP; Clunes House, Toot Hill, nr Ongar, Essex CM5 9SF (☎ 037 882 2281); 81/83 High Road, London N22 6BE (☎ 081 888 2255, fax 081 881 5080)

SORRELL, John; *m* Frances Newell, *qv*; 3 c; *Career* fndr and co chm Newell & Sorrell Ltd (corporate identity consits) 1976-; clients incl: BAA, The Berol Corporation, The Body Shop International, Boots Company plc, British Rail, Charbonnel et Walker, InterCity; chm Design Business Assoc; CSD: a vice pres, memb Cncl, memb Design Mgmt Gp; memb Strategic Planning Soc; speaker and lectr on corporate identity: Mgmnt Res Gp BIM, Blueprint's Moving Up Workshops, Henley Mgmnt Coll, CBI Design or Decline Conference; awards incl: D&AD, Clio, Design Week, Design Effectiveness; FCSD; *Style—* John Sorrell; Newell & Sorrell Ltd, 4 Utopia Village, Chalcot Rd, London NW1 8LH (☎ 071 722 1113, fax 071 722 0259)

SORRELL, Martin Stuart; s of Jack Sorrell, of Mill Hill, London NW7; *b* 14 Feb 1945; *Educ* Haberdashers' Aske's, Christ's Coll Cambridge, Harvard Business Sch; *m* 1971, Sandra Carol Ann, *née* Finestone; 3 s; *Career* gp fin dir Saatchi & Saatchi Co plc (business serv) 1977-86, gp chief exec WPP Group plc (mktg servs) 1986-; *Recreations* skiing; *Clubs* Reform, Harvard; *Style—* Martin Sorrell, Esq; Courtlands, 3 Winnington Rd, London N2 OTP; WPP Group plc, 27 Farm St, London W1X 6RD (☎ 071 408 2204)

SORRIE, Dr George Strath; s of Alexander James Sorrie (d 1945), and Florence Edith, *née* Strath; *b* 19 May 1933; *Educ* Robert Gordon's Coll Aberdeen, Univs of (Aberdeen, London and Dundee (MB ChB, DPH, DIH, FFOM)); *m* 22 Sept 1959, Gabrielle Ann, da of late James Baird; 3 da (Rosalind b 1961, Ann b 1962, Catherine b 1977); *Career* Flt Lt Med Branch RAF 1958-61; lectr in epidemiology Univ of London 1965-67, GP Rhynie Aberdeen 1967-73, dep dir of med servs Health and Safety Exec 1980-87 (med advsr 1973-80), dir and med advsr Civil Serv Occupational Health Serv 1987-; FFOM, RCP; *Recreations* book-keeping, practising patience; *Clubs* Athenaeum; *Style—* Dr George Sorrie; 20 Hill St, Edinburgh (☎ 031 220 4177, fax 031 220 4183)

SOSKICE, Hon David William; s of Baron Stow Hill, PC, QC (Life Peer, d 1979), and Baroness Stow Hill, *qv*; *b* 1941; *Educ* Winchester, Trinity Oxford; *m* 1966, Alison, da of Walter Black, of Nateley Scures House, Hook, Hants; 1 s, 1 da; *Career* economist HM Treasury 1965-66, fell and praelector in economics Univ Coll Oxford 1966-; *Style—* The Hon David Soskice; 10 Staverton Rd, Oxford

SOSKICE, Hon Oliver Cloudesley Hunter; s of Baron Stow Hill (Life Peer, d 1979), and Baroness Stow Hill, *qv*; *b* 1947; *Educ* Winchester, Trinity Hall Cambridge; *m* 1982, Janet, eldest da of A M Martin, of St Louis, Mo; 2 da (Catherine b 1984, Isabelle b 1987); *Style—* The Hon Oliver Soskice

SOUBRY, Anna Mary (Mrs Gordon); da of David Stuart Soubry (d 1985), and Frances Margaret, *née* Coward; *b* 7 Dec 1956; *Educ* Hartland Comp Worksop Notts, Univ of Birmingham (LLB); *m* 29 Aug 1987, (John) Haig Gordon, s of John Irvine Haig Gordon; *Career* Grampian TV, Central TV; presenter: Central News, Central Weekend, This Morning, The Time The Place; exec NUS 1980, hon pres Univ of Stirling 1981; *Recreations* cycling, eating, football, music; *Style—* Miss Anna Soubry; Central Television, Lenton Lane, Nottingham (☎ 0602 863322)

SOUHAMI, Mark J; s of John F Souhami, and Freda Souhami; *b* 25 Sept 1935; *Educ* St Marylebone GS; *m* 1964, Margaret, da of Joseph Austin; 2 da (Emma b 1966, Charlotte b 1968); *Career* Dixons Gp plc: gp mktg dir 1970, md Retail Div 1973, chm and md Dixons Ltd 1976, dir 1978, md 1986; memb Cncl CBI, tstee Photographers Gallery; *Clubs* Savile, RAC; *Style—* Mark Souhami, Esq; Brewham House, Brewham, Somerset

SOUKOP, Wilhelm Joseph; s of Karl Soukop (d 1919), of Vienna, and Anna, *née* Vogel (d 1976); *b* 5 Jan 1907; *Educ* Staats Sch, Acad of Fine Art and Sculpture Vienna; *m* 1945, Simone, da of Marcel Moser, of Paris; 1 s (Michel b 15 April 1947), 1 da; *Career* freelance sculptor 1934-38; teacher: Dartington Art Sch 1938-40, Arts Dept Blundell's Sch until 1945; pt/t teacher of sculpture: Bromley Sch of Art Guildford, Guildford and Chelsea Sch of Art; exhibitions every year at RA Summer Show, i/c Sculpture Sch RA 1972-82, ret 1982; numerous works for schools, housing estates and museums in England and America; first prize Oxfam Int Competition For Sculpture for Oxford; judge: Prix de Rome, Sculpture Certificate in England and Scotland; ARA 1972 (electat 1969); *Recreations* gardening; *Style—* Wilhelm Soukop, Esq; 26 Greville Road, London NW6 5JA (☎ 071 624 5987)

SOUKUP, Lady (Constance) Ann; *née* Butler; da of 7 Marquess of Ormonde, MBE; *b* 13 Dec 1940; *m* 1965, Henry Lea Soukup; 1 s (Andrew), 1 da (Meghan); *Style—* The Lady Ann Soukup; 618 North Washington, Hinsdale, Illinois, USA

SOULBURY, 2 Viscount (UK 1954); James Herwald Ramsbotham; also Baron Soulbury (UK 1941); s of 1 Viscount, GCMG, GCVO, OBE, MC, PC (d 1971); *b* 21 March 1915; *Educ* Eton, Magdalen Oxford; *m* 1949, Anthea Margaret (d 1950), da of late David Wilton; *Heir* bro, Hon Sir Peter Edward Ramsbotham, GCMG, GCVO; *Style—* The Rt Hon the Viscount Soulbury; c/o The House of Lords, Westminster, London SW1

SOUNDY, Andrew John; s of Maj Harold Cecil Soundy, MBE, MC, TD (d 1969), and Adele Monica Templeton, *née* Westley; *b* 29 March 1940; *Educ* Boxgrove Sch Guildford, Shrewsbury, Trinity Coll Cambridge (BA, MA); *m* 12 Oct 1963, Jill Marion, da of Frank Nathaniel Steiner, of Gerrards Cross, Bucks; 1 s (Mark b 1964), 2 da (Emma b 1967, Victoria b 1969); *Career* admitted slr 1966; ptnr Ashurst Morris Crisp slrs, farmer and breeder of pedigree cattle; *Recreations* opera, tennis, good living; *Clubs* Cavalry and Guards; *Style—* Andrew J Soundy, Esq; Bartletts Farm, Mattingley, nr Basingstoke, Hampshire RG27 8JU (☎ 0734 326 279, fax 0734 326 335); Broadwalk House, 5 Appold St, London EC2A 2HA (☎ 071 638 1111, fax 071 972 7990, telex 887067)

SOUNESS, Graeme James; s of James Souness, and Elizabeth, *née* Ferguson (d 1984); *b* 6 May 1953; *Educ* Carrickvale Secdy Sch; *m* ; 2 s (Fraser b 29 May 1980, Jordan Cameron b 17 March 1985), 1 da (Chantelle Karen b 20 June 1975); *Career* professional football manager; player: Tottenham Hotspur 1969-73, Middlesbrough 1973-78, Liverpool 1978-84, Sampdoria Italy 1984-86, Scotland 1975-86 (54 full caps); mangr Glasgow Rangers 1986- (also player 1986-90); achievements as player for Liverpool incl: 3 Euro Cup Winners medals (v Bruges 1978, Real Madrid 1981, Roma 1984), 5 League Championship medals 1979-84, 4 League Cup Winner's medals 1981-84; achievements as mangr: Scot League Championship 1987, 1989, 1990, Skol Cup 1987, 1988, 1989, 1990; *Books* No Half Measurers (1984), A Manager's Diary (1990); *Recreations* gardening; *Style—* Graeme Souness, Esq; Rangers Football Club, Ibrox Stadium, Edmiston Drive, Glasgow G51 2XD (☎ 041 427 8500, fax 041 427 2676)

SOUSTER, Peter John Robertson; s of Eric George Souster (d 1987), and Lillian, *née* Robertson; *b* 22 March 1944; *Educ* Whitgift Sch, Queens' Coll Cambridge (Golf blue); *m* 1975, Anna Geraldine, da of Andrew Frederick Smith; 1 s (Timothy Michael Peter b 1978), 1 da (Rachel Catherine Anna b 1980); *Career* Peat Marwick Mitchell: articled clerk 1966-69, Hong Kong office 1973-75, London office 1974-78; ptnr Baker Tilly & Co (formerly Howard Tilly & Co) 1981- (joined 1978); *Books* The Responsible Director (1986) reprinted as Directors' Responsibilities and Liabilities (1990); *Recreations* golf, squash; *Clubs* Hawks, Chartered Accountants Golfing Soc (capt 1990-91); *Style—* Peter Souster, Esq; Baker Tilly, 2 Bloomsbury St, London WC1B 3ST (☎ 071 413 5100)

SOUTAR, Air Marshal Sir Charles John Williamson; KBE (1978, MBE 1958); s of Charles A Soutar, and Mary H Watson; *b* 1920 June; *Educ* Brentwood Sch, London Hosp; *m* 1944, Joy Dorée Upton; 1 s, 2 da; *Career* RAF 1946, QHS 1974-81, PMO Strike Cmd 1975-78, Dir-Gen RAF Med Servs 1978-81; CStJ 1972; *Clubs* RAF; *Style—* Air Marshal Sir Charles Soutar, KBE; Oak Cottage, High St, Aldeburgh, Suffolk

SOUTAR, (Samuel) Ian; s of James Soutar of Ballymena, NI, and Maud, *née* McNinch;

b 2 June 1945; *Educ* Ballymena Acad, Trinity Coll Dublin (BA); *m* 10 August 1968, Mary Isabella, da of William Boyle (d 1951), of Ballymena, NI; 1 s (Michael b 26 Dec 1971), 1 da (Kim b 16 July 1973); *Career* FCO 1968; second sec: UK delgn to EURO communities 1970-72 (formerly third sec), Br Embassy Saigon 1972-74; first sec: FCO 1974, Br Embassy washington 1977-80, FCO 1981-86; private sec to Parly Sec FCO Affrs 1976-77, dep high Cmmr Br High Cmmn Wellington 1986-91, Royal Coll of Defence Studies 1991-; *Recreations* walking, listening to music; *Style*— Ian Soutar, Esq; c/o Foreign & Commonwealth Office, London SW1A 2AH

SOUTER, Hon Amanda Elizabeth; da and co-heiress presumptive of 25 Baron Audley; *b* 5 May 1958; *Style*— The Hon Amanda Souter; c/o Friendly Green, Cowden, nr Edenbridge, Kent TN8 7DU

SOUTER, Christopher David William; s of David Cowley Souter, VRD, of Belford, Northumberland, and Joan Margaret, *née* Wear; *b* 9 March 1941; *Educ* Fettes; *m* 14 Nov 1964, Erica Sibbald, da of Geoffrey Balfour Stenhouse (d 1975); 2 s (Rory b 1967, Justin b 1970), 1 da (Zoë b 1965); *Career* dir WA Souter & Co Ltd Sheaf Steam Shipping Co Ltd 1970, owner Souter Ship Spares 1980; dir: James Marine Servs Ltd 1987-90, James Industl Servs Ltd, Brandling Lawn Tennis Club Hldgs Ltd; former chm N of Eng Shipowners Assoc 1974, Offr First Class Royal Order of Polar Star (Sweden) 1986, hon consul of Sweden Newcastle upon Tyne; MICS; *Recreations* tennis, ornithology, victorian art; *Style*— Christopher Souter, Esq; 30 Brandling Place South, Jesmond, Newcastle upon Tyne, NE2 4RU (☎ 091 281 7421)

SOUTER, David Cowley; VRD (1951); s of Sir William Alfred Souter (d 1968), and Madalene, *née* Robson (d 1972); *b* 13 April 1917; *Educ* Fettes; *m* 25 Nov 1939, Joan Margaret, da of Lt-Col Dr Arthur Taylor Wear (d 1932), of Newcastle Upon Tyne; 3 s (Christopher, Julian, Nigel), 1 d (Diana); *Career* RNVR Tyne Div HMS Calliope 1936, mobilised Munich Crisis, HMS Carlisle 1938, MTB 22 HMS Vernon 1939, HMS Hornet 1940, i/c MTB 100, 68 and 268 Br Waters and Med 1940-44, HMS Windsor, HMS Montrose Harwich, HMS Arbella 1945, ret RNVR Lt Cdr 1951; William Dickinson & Co Ltd Newcastle Upon Tyne 1934-39, WA Souter & Co Ltd 1945-80 (later years jt md and chm); chm: Sheaf Steam Shipping Co Ltd 1975, North of Eng Shipowners Assoc 1958; former pres: Gosforth Unit Sea Cadets, Northumberland Lawn Tennis Assoc, Mission to Seamen South Shields, Blyth Harbour Cmmn; gen cmmr of taxes 1953-, High Sheriff Tyne & Wear 1984-85, vice pres Royal Merchant Navy Sch; FICS, fell NE Coast Inst of Engrs and Shipbuilders; *Recreations* golf, tennis, bee-keeping, ornithology, shooting, forestry, gardening; *Clubs* Army & Navy; *Style*— David C Souter, Esq, VRD; Chatsworth, Moor Crescent, Gosforth, Newcastle Upon Tyne NE3 4AQ (☎ 091 2852412); Detchant Park, Belford, Northumberland NE70 7PQ (☎ 0668 213353)

SOUTER, William Alexander; s of William Souter (d 1951), and Jean Smith, *née* Troup (d 1975); *b* 11 May 1933; *Educ* George Watson's Boy's Coll Edinburgh, Univ of Edinburgh (MB ChB); *m* 12 Sept 1959, Kathleen Bruce, da of William Caird Taylor (d 1936); 1 s (Ewen b 1966), 2 da (Catriona b 1960, Lorna b 1962); *Career* sr registrar Orthopaedic Dept Edinburgh Royal Infirmary and Princess Margaret Rose Orthopaedic Hosp 1965-68, conslt orthopaedic surgn Princess Margaret Rose Orthopaedic Hosp Edinburgh 1968-, hon sr lectr Orthopaedic Dept Univ of Edinburgh, visiting prof Bioengineering Dept Univ of Strathclyde 1985-; fndr memb and first hon sec European Rheumatoid Arthritis Surgical Soc 1979-83, chm EULAR Standing Ctee on Surgery of Rheumatoid Disease 1987-, memb Cncl: British Soc for Surgery of the Hand 1976-78, Ed Bd Jl of Bone and Joint Surgery 1981-84, Cncl of British Orthopaedic Assoc 1986-88; first pres and memb Br Elbow and Shoulder Soc 1987-; memb: Cncl Royal Coll of Surgeons of Edinburgh 1988-, Br Ortho Assoc and Br Ortho Res Soc 1968, Rheumatoid Arthritis Surgical Soc 1974, European Surgical Soc 1978; FRCSEd 1960; *Recreations* gardening, photography, music, skiing, golf; *Style*— William Souter, Esq; Old Mauricewood Mains, Penicuik, Midlothian EH26 0NJ (☎ 0968 72609); Consultant Orthopaedic Surgeon, Surgical Arthritis Unit, Princess Margaret Rose Orthopaedic Hosp, Frogston Rd, Edinburgh EH10 7EH (☎ 031 445 4123 ext 265, fax 031 445 3440)

SOUTH, Sir Arthur; JP (Norwich 1949); s of Arthur South; *b* 29 Oct 1914; *Educ* City of Norwich Sch; *m* 1, 1937 (m dis 1976), May Adamson; 2 s; m 2, 1976, Mary June (d 1982), widow of Robert Carter, JP, DL; *Career* former Lord Mayor Norwich and former chm Norwich Lowestoft, and Gt Yarmouth Hosp Mgmnt Ctee, chm Norfolk AHA 1974-78 and E Anglian RHA 1978-87; former chm Labour Party Gp Norwich City Cncl; DCL; kt 1974; *Style*— Sir Arthur South, JP; The Lowlands, Drayton, Norfolk (☎ 0603 867 355)

SOUTHALL, Derek William; s of William Southall, and Esther Ann, *née* Stockton (d 1974); *b* 5 June 1930; *Educ* Coventry Coll of Art, Camberwell Sch of Art, Goldsmiths Coll London, Hochschule fur Bildende Kunste Berlin, Univ of Munich; *m* 30 March 1961, Jennifer Anne, da of John Henry Peter Wilson; 2 da (Justine b 4 Jan 1962, Rosanna b 11 Jan 1964); *Career* artist; cmmnd by DOE to make a mural for the main office of DHSS Newcastle upon Tyne 1972, subject of BBC 2 film (dir Barrie Gavin, 1972), artist in residence Univ of S Carolina and Yale Univ 1972-75, sr res fell fine art Cardiff 1980-83, artist in residence Nat Art Sch Sydney Aust 1984; collections incl: Tate Gallery, Arts Cncl of GB, Contemporary Arts Soc, Br Collection (Yale), various public and corp collections in Europe USA and Aust; *Recreations* walking, visiting churches; *Clubs* Royal Overseas League (hon memb); *Style*— Derek Southall, Esq; The Chapel, Heatherton Park, Bradford-on-Tone, Taunton, Somerset TA4 1EU (☎ 0823 461755)

SOUTHAM, Prof John Chambers; s of Frank Lloyd Southam (d 1975), of Leeds, and late Marjorie, *née* Chambers; *b* 3 Feb 1934; *Educ* Leeds GS, Cambridge Univ (MA, MD), Univ of Leeds; *m* 27 Aug 1960, Susan, da of Reginald Alfred Saxty Hill (d 1977), of Hereford; 2 s (Philip b 1963, Jeremy b 1966); *Career* lectr in oral pathology Univ of Sheffield 1963-70, dean of dental studies Univ of Edinburgh 1983-88 (sr lectr in dental surgery 1970-77, prof of oral med and pathology 1977-); memb gen Dental Cncl 1984-94; FDS, RCS Ed 1981, FRCPath 1983; *Books* Oral Pathology (with J V Soames, 1984); *Recreations* gardening, walking, travelling, scouting; *Clubs* Royal Society of Medicine; *Style*— Prof John Southam; 13 Corstorphine House Ave, Edinburgh EH12 7AD (☎ 031 334 3013); Dept of Oral Medicine and Pathology, Univ of Edinburgh (☎ 031 664 1011, fax 031 556 0544, telex 727442 UNIVED G)

SOUTHAM, Kenneth (Hubert); s of Hubert Basil Southam, MBE (d 1978), and Millicent Edith, *née* Johnson (d 1982); *b* 24 Feb 1927; *Educ* Harborne Collegiate Birmingham; *m* 29 Aug 1953, Marjorie, da of Herbert Lever (d 1985); *Career* served RA 1944-48; qualified CA 1955; chief accountant Atomic Power Constructions Ltd 1957-76, own practice Southam & Co 1977-; Freeman City of London, Liveryman Worshipful Co of Woolmen 1969-; *Recreations* photography, philately, reading, charitable work; *Clubs* City Livery; *Style*— Kenneth Southam, Esq; 23 Penshurst Rd, Potters Bar, Herts (☎ 0707 56129); Southam & Co, St George's House, 44 Hatton Garden, London EC1N 3ER (☎ 071 831 0401)

SOUTHAMPTON, Barony of (GB 1780); *see*: FitzRoy, Charles

SOUTHAMPTON, 6 Baron (GB 1780); Charles James FitzRoy; o s of Charles FitzRoy (d 1989), who suc as 5 Baron Southampton 1958, but disclaimed his peerage for life, and his 1 w, Margaret, *née* Drake (d 1931); *b* 12 Aug 1928; *Educ* Stowe; *m* 29 May 1951, Pamela Anne, da of Edward Percy Henniker, of Clematis, Yelverton, S Devon; 1 s (Hon Edward Charles b 1955), 1 da (Hon Geraldine Anne (Hon Mrs Fuller) 1951), and 1 s decd; *Heir* s, Hon Edward Charles FitzRoy, *qv*; *Style*— The Rt Hon the Lord Southampton; Stone Cross, Stone Lane, Chagford, Devon

SOUTHAN, His Hon Judge Robert Joseph; s of Thomas Southan (d 1962), of Warwicks, and Kathleen Annie, *née* Beck (d 1987); *b* 13 July 1928; *Educ* Rugby, St Edmund Hall Oxford (MA), UCL (LLM); *m* 1960, Elizabeth Andreas, da of Clive Raleigh Evatt, QC (d 1984), of Aust; 1 s (Richard b 1962, d 1984), 1 da (Anne b 1969); *Career* barr: England and Wales 1953, New South Wales 1974; rec Crown Ct 1982, circuit judge 1986; *Recreations* sailing, skiing, tennis, squash, theatre, opera; *Clubs* Royal Corinthian Yacht, Bar Yacht, Cumberland LT; *Style*— His Hon Judge Robert Southan; Snaresbrook Crown Court, Hollybush Hill, London E11 1QW (☎ 081 989 6666)

SOUTHBOROUGH, Audrey, Baroness; Audrey Evelyn Dorothy; yr da of Edgar George Money; *m* 1918, 3 Baron Southborough (d 1982), sometime md Shell Transport and Trading; 1 s (4 Baron), 1 da (Hon Mrs Rank); *Style*— The Rt Hon Audrey, Lady Southborough; The Dower House, Landhurst, Hartfield, E Sussex (☎ 0892 770835)

SOUTHBOROUGH, 4 Baron (UK 1917); (Francis) Michael Hopwood; only s of 3 Baron Southborough (d 1982), and Audrey, Baroness Southborough, *qv*; *b* 3 May 1922; *Educ* Wellington, Ch Ch Oxford; *m* 1945, Moyna Kemp (d 1987), da of Robert John Kemp Chattey; 1 da (Anne Mary b 29 March 1960); *Heir* none; *Career* serv Lt Rifle Bde WWII; Lloyd's underwriter 1949-; dir Glanvill Enthoven & Co Ltd 1954 (dep chm 1977-80); dir Robert Woodson Ltd 1950 and chm 1970-72; *Clubs* Brooks's, City of London; *Style*— The Rt Hon the Lord Southborough; 50a Eaton Sq, London SW1W 9BE (☎ 071 235 3181)

SOUTHBY, Iris, Lady; Iris Mackay; *née* Heriot; da of late Lt-Col Granville Mackay Heriot, DSO, RM, and Marta Luisa, da of William Paynter; *m* 1, Brig Ian Charles Alexander Robertson; m 2, 1979, as his 4 w, Lt-Col Sir (Archibald) Richard Charles Southby, 2 Bt, OBE (d 1988); *Style*— Lady Southby; Greystone House, Stone, Tenterden, Kent; No 7 Bolur Ave, Kenilworth 7700, Cape, S Africa

SOUTHBY, Sir John Richard Bilbe; 3 Bt (UK 1937), of Burford, Co Oxford; 3 Bt (UK 1937); s of Sir (Archibald) Richard Charles Southby, 2 Bt, OBE (d 1988) and his 2 w, Olive, da of late Sir Thomas Bilbe-Robinson, GBE, KCMG; *b* 2 April 1948; *Educ* Peterhouse Rhodesia, Loughborough Univ (BSc); *m* 1971, Victoria, da of John Wilfred Sturrock, of Tettenhall, Wolverhampton; 2 s (Peter John b 20 Aug 1973, James William b 1984), 1 da (Sarah Jane b 1975); *Heir* s, Peter John Southby b 20 Aug 1973; *Style*— Sir John Southby, Bt; 20 Harrowby Lane, Grantham, Lincs NG31 9HX

SOUTHBY, Noreen, Lady; Noreen Vera; da of late Bernard Compton Simm; *m* 28 March 1962, as his 2 w, Cdr Sir Archibald Richard James Southby, RN, 1 Bt (d 1969); *Style*— Noreen, Lady Southby; 18 Harbour View Rd, Parkstone, Poole, Dorset

SOUTHERN, (Guy) Hugo; s of Cdr John Dunlop (d 1972), and Gloria Millicent, *née* Usborne; *b* 12 Oct 1929; *Educ* Harrow; *m* 7 July 1958, Rosamund Antonia, da of Gerald Alexander McAndrew (d 1952); 1 s (Humphrey b 1960), 2 da (Augusta b 1959, Frances b 1964); *Career* admitted slr 1955; ptnr: Alfred Blundell 1957-58, Frere Cholmeley 1959-; slr to Duchy of Lancaster 1974-84; *Recreations* collecting; *Clubs* Beefsteak, Brooks's; *Style*— Hugo Southern, Esq; 28 Lincoln Inn Fields, London WC2 (☎ 071 405 7878, fax 071 405 9056, telex 27623 FRERES G)

SOUTHERN, Sir Richard William; s of Matthew Southern; *b* 8 Feb 1912; *Educ* Newcastle upon Tyne Royal GS, Balliol Coll Oxford; *m* 1944, Sheila, *née* Cobley, widow of Sqdn Ldr C Crichton-Miller; 2 s; *Career* served WWII: Oxford and Bucks LI, Durham LI, RAC, Political Intelligence Dept FO; historian: fell and tutor Balliol Coll Oxford 1937-61, jr proctor Univ of Oxford 1948-49, Birkbeck lectr Ecclesiastical History Trinity Coll Cambridge 1959-60, Chichele Prof Modern History Univ of Oxford 1961-69; pres: St John's Coll Oxford 1969-81 (hon fell 1981-), Royal Historical Soc 1968-72, Selden Soc 1973-76; FBA; hon fell: Sidney Sussex Coll Cambridge, Balliol Coll Oxford; Hon DLitt: Univ of Glasgow, Univ of Durham, Cantab, Univ of Bristol, Univ of Newcastle, Univ of Warwick; Hon LLD Harvard Univ; kt 1974; *Style*— Sir Richard Southern; 40 St John St, Oxford (☎ 0865 57778)

SOUTHERN, Sir Robert; CBE (1953); s of Job Southern of Parkview, Park Lane, Whitefield; *b* 17 March 1907; *Educ* Stand GS, Co-op Coll Univ of Manchester; *m* 1933, Lena, da of George Henry Chapman, of Whitefield; 1 s, 1 da; *Career* gen-sec Co-operative Union Ltd 1948-72; kt 1970; *Style*— Sir Robert Southern, CBE; 22 Glebelands Rd, Prestwich, nr Manchester (☎ 061 773 2699)

SOUTHESK, 11 Earl of (S 1633); Sir Charles Alexander Carnegie; 8 Bt (NS 1663), KCVO (1926), DL (Angus); also Lord Carnegie (S 1616), Baron Balinhard (UK 1869); s of 10 Earl (d 1941, whose f, the 9 Earl, was a poet, antiquary and author of Herminius, described as a romance) and Ethel, da of Sir Alexander Bannerman, 9 Bt; *b* 23 Sept 1893; *Educ* Eton; *m* 1, 1923, HH Princess (Alexandra Victoria Georgina Bertha) Maud (d 1945), yr da of HRH Princess Louise, Princess Royal and the 1 Duke of Fife; 1 s, 1 da; m 2, 1952, Evelyn Julia, da of Lt-Col Arthur Peere Williams-Freeman, DSO, OBE, and widow of Major Ion Edward FitzGerald Campbell, Duke of Cornwall's LI (gs of 2 Bt, cr UK 1815); *Heir* s, Duke of Fife; *Career* Maj (ret) Scots Gds; ADC to The Viceroy of India 1917-1919; *Style*— The Rt Hon the Earl of Southesk, KCVO, DL; Kinnaird Castle, Brechin, Angus (☎ 067 481 209)

SOUTHEY, Sir Robert John; CMG (1970); s of late Allen Hope Southey, and late Ethel Thorpe McComas, MBE; *b* 20 March 1922; *Educ* Geelong GS, Magdalen Coll Oxford (MA); *m* 1, 1946, Valerie Janet Cotton (d 1977), da of Hon Sir Francis Grenville Clarke, KBE, MLC (d 1955); 5 s; m 2, 1982, Marigold Merlyn Baillieu, da of Sidney Myer (d 1934) and Dame (Margery) Merlyn Myer, DBE (d 1982); *Career* WWII Coldstream Gds 1941-46, served N Africa and Italy, Capt 1944; dir: Buckley & Nunn 1958-78, BP Company of Australia Ltd 1965-91, International Computers (Australia) Pty Ltd 1977-90, NatWest Finance Australia Ltd 1983-85, NatWest Australia Bank Ltd 1985-87, General Accident Fire & Life Assurance Corporation plc 1968-89 (chm Aust Advsy Cncl), Wm Haughton & Co Ltd 1953-80, Kawasaki (Australia) Pty Ltd 1986-; chm NZI Insurance Australia Ltd 1989-; memb Fed Exec Lib Pty 1966-82, pres Lib Pty Victoria 1966-70, fed pres Lib Pty 1970-75; chm Aust Ballet Fndn 1980-90; kt 1976; *See Debrett's Handbook of Australia and New Zealand for further details*; *Recreations* music, fishing, golf; *Clubs* Cavalry and Guards, MCC, Leander, Melbourne and Australian (Melbourne), Union (Sydney); *Style*— Sir Robert Southey, CMG; 3 Denistoun Ave, Mt Eliza, Vic 3930, Australia

SOUTHGATE, Crispin John; s of Brig John Terence Southgate, OBE, and Stancia Lillian, *née* Collins; *b* 16 Feb 1955; *Educ* Christ's Hosp Horsham, Merton Coll Oxford (MA); *m* 15 Sept 1979, Joanna Mary, da of Gerald Norman Donaldson, TD; 2 s (William b 1987, Richard b 1990), 1 da (Eleanor b 1985); *Career* Price Waterhouse & Co 1977-82, dir Charterhouse Bank Ltd 1987- (joined 1982); treas Rainer Fndn 1984-; ACA 1980; *Style*— Crispin Southgate, Esq; Charterhouse Bank Ltd, 1 Paternoster Row, St Pauls London EC4M 7DH (☎ 071 248 4000, fax 071 248 6522, telex 884276)

SOUTHGATE, Very Rev John Eliot; s of Reginald Henry Southgate; *b* 2 Sept 1926; *Educ* City of Norwich, Univ of Durham; *m* 1958, Patricia Mary, *née* Plumb; 2 s, 1 da; *Career* ordained Leicester 1955, vicar of Plumstead Southwark 1962, rector of

Charlton Southwark 1966, dean of Greenwich 1968, archdeacon of Cleveland York 1974, dean of York 1984-; Hon D Univ York 1989; *Recreations* music; *Clubs* Yorkshire, Royal Commonwealth; *Style—* The Very Rev The Dean of York; The Deanery, York YO1 2JD

SOUTHWARD, Dr Nigel Ralph; LVO (1985); s of Sir Ralph Southward, KCVO, of 9 Devonshire Place, London W1N, and Evelyn, *née* Tassell; *b* 8 Feb 1941; *Educ* Rugby, Trinity Hall Cambridge (MA, MB BChir); *m* 24 July 1965, Annette, da of Johan Heinrich Hoffmann, of Strandvesen, Skodsborg, Denmark; 1 s (Nicholas b 1966), 2 da (Karen b 1968, Emma b 1970); *Career* apothecary to HM The Queen, apothecary to the household and to the households of: HM Queen Elizabeth the Queen Mother, the Princess Margaret Countess of Snowdon, Princess Alice Duchess of Gloucester, the Duke and Duchess of Gloucester and the Duke and Duchess of Kent 1975-; *Recreations* sailing, golf, skiing; *Clubs* RYS, RCC; *Style—* Dr Nigel R Southward, LVO; 56 Primrose Gardens, London NW3 4TP (☎ 071 935 8425); 9 Devonshire Place, London W1N 1PB (☎ 071 935 8425, car 0836 255 900)

SOUTHWARD, Sir Ralph; KCVO (1975); s of Henry Stalker Southward, of Cumberland; *b* 2 Jan 1908; *Educ* Glasgow HS, Univ of Glasgow (MB ChB), MRCP; *m* 1935, Evelyn, da of J G Tassell, of Harrogate; 4 s; *Career* med practitioner; Mil Serv RAMC, served N Africa, India, Ceylon 1940-45; apothecary to: Royal Household 1964-74, HM Queen Elizabeth the Queen Mother 1966-87, TRH the Duke and Duchess of Gloucester 1966-75, HM The Queen 1972-74; Hon Freeman Worshipful Soc of Apothecaries 1975; FRCP 1970; *Recreations* fishing (trout, salmon), golf, travel; *Style—* Sir Ralph Southward, KCVO; 9 Devonshire Place, London W1N 1PB (☎ 071 935 7969); Amerden Priory, Taplow, Maidenhead, Berks (☎ 0628 23525)

SOUTHWARK, Most Rev Archbishop and Metropolitan of Michael George Bowen; s of late Maj C L J Bowen, and Lady Makins; *b* 23 April 1930; *Educ* Downside, Trinity Coll Cambridge, Gregorian Univ Rome; *Career* 2 Lt Irish Gds 1948-49; wine trade 1951-52, English Coll Rome 1952-59, ordained 1958, curate Earlsfield and Walworth South London 1959-63, theology teacher Beda Coll Rome 1963-66, chllr Diocese of Arundel and Brighton 1966-70, bishop of Arundel and Brighton 1971-77 (coadjutor bishop 1970-71), archbishop of Southwark 1977-; Freeman City of London 1984; *Recreations* golf, tennis; *Style—* The Most Rev Archbishop of Southwark; Archbishop's House, St George's Road, Southwark, London SE1 6HX (☎ 071 928 2495/5592)

SOUTHWARK, 7 Bishop of 1980-; Rt Rev Ronald Oliver Bowlby; patron of one hundred and sixty-three livings, of the Archdeaconries of Southwark, Lewisham, Lambeth, Wandsworth, Croydon and Reigate, and of the Provostship and five Residentiary Canonries in Southwark Cathedral; the See was founded by Act of Parliament 1905; s of Oliver Bowlby; *b* 16 Aug 1926; *Educ* Eton, Trinity Coll Oxford, Westcott House Cambridge; *m* 1956, Elizabeth Trevelyan Monro; 3 s, 2 da; *Career* curate 1952-57, vicar of St Aidan Billingham 1957-66, vicar of Croydon 1966-72, bishop of Newcastle 1973-80; chm: Hosp Chaplaincies Cncl 1975-82, Soc Policy Ctee C of E Bd for Soc Responsibility 1985-89; memb: Anglican Consultative Cncl 1978-85, Duke of Edinburgh's Nat Housing Inquiry 1984-85; pres Nat Fedn of Housing Assocs 1989-; hon fell: Newcastle upon Tyne Poly 1980, Trinity Coll Oxford 1989; *Books* contrib to: Church without Walls (1969, 1 edn), Church and Politics Today (1985, 2 edn); *Recreations* gardening, walking, music, family history; *Style—* The Rt Rev the Bishop of Southwark; Bishop's House, 38 Tooting Bec Gardens, Streatham, London SW16 1QZ (☎ 081 769 3256)

SOUTHWELL, Hon Mrs John; Daphne Lewin; da of Sir Geoffrey Lewin Watson, 3 and last Bt (cr 1918, extinct 1959); *m* 1932, Lt-Cdr Hon John Michael Southwell, RN (ka 1944, 3 s of 5 Viscount Southwell); *Style—* The Hon Mrs John Southwell; Buckclose, Longparish, nr Andover, Hants

SOUTHWELL, Bishop of 1988-, Rt Rev Patrick Burnet Harris; s of Edward James Burnet Harris, and Astrid, *née* Kendall; *b* 30 Sept 1934; *Educ* St Albans Sch, Keble Coll Oxford (MA); *m* 1968, Valerie Margaret Pilbrow; 2 s, 1 da; *Career* asst curate St Ebbe's Oxford 1960-63, missionary with S American Missionary Soc 1963-73, archdeacon of Salta Argentina 1969-73, diocesan bishop Northern Argentina 1973-80, rector Kirkheaton and asst bishop Diocese of Wakefield 1981-85, sec Ptnrship for World Mission 1986-88, asst bishop Diocese of Oxford 1986-88; *Recreations* ornithology, S American Indian culture, music; *Style—* The Rt Rev the Bishop of Southwell; Bishop's Manor, Southwell, Notts NG25 0JR

SOUTHWELL, 7 Viscount (I 1776); Sir Pyers Anthony Joseph Southwell; 10 Bt (I 1662); also Baron Southwell (I 1717); s of late Hon Francis Joseph Southwell, 2 s of 5 Viscount; suc unc 1960; *b* 14 Sept 1930; *Educ* Beaumont Coll, RMA Sandhurst; *m* 1955, Barbara Jacqueline, da of A Raynes; 2 s; *Heir* s, Hon Richard Southwell; *Career* Capt (ret) 8 Hussars; company dir; *Clubs* MCC, Woburn Golf and Country, Diners; *Style—* The Rt Hon the Viscount Southwell; 4 Roseberry Av, Harpenden, Herts (☎ 05827 5831)

SOUTHWELL, Hon Richard Andrew Pyers; s and h of 7 Viscount Southwell; *b* 15 June 1956; *Style—* The Hon Richard Southwell

SOUTHWELL, Richard Charles; QC (1977); s of late Sir Philip Southwell, CBE, MC, and Mary, *née* Scarratt; *m* 1962, Belinda Mary, da of Col F H Pownall, MC; 2 s, 1 da; *Career* called to the Bar Inner Temple 1959; *Style—* Richard Southwell, Esq, QC; 1 Hare Court, Temple, London EC4 (☎ 071 353 3171)

SOUTHWICK, Douglas Arthur; OBE (1988); s of Norman Arthur Fitton, and Hilda, *née* Schofield (d 1988); *b* 2 Oct 1924; *Educ* Thirsk GS N Yorks; *m* 4 June 1949, Enid Lillian, da of William Howard Screeton (d 1959), of Willowfield House, Keyingham, N Humberside; *Career* NFS 1939-45; owner and occupier farmer Village Farm Skipsea Driffield N Humberside 1948-87, publican Board Inn Skipsea 1964-73, turf accountant Skipsea and other offices 1961-; memb: Bridlington RDC, Skipsea Parish Cncl, E Riding of Yorks CC (until reorganisation 1973); Humberside CC 1973-: chm and shadow chm Public Protection Ctee 1974-88, dep ldr 1979-81, chm 1988-89; 40 years serv to local Cons Pty; constituency chm: to Lord Holderness 1970-77, to John Townend MP Bridlington 1977-80; chm local Parish Cncl; memb Soc of Industl and Emergency Safety Officers; *Style—* Douglas A Southwick, Esq, OBE; The Finishing Post, Skipsea, Driffield, N Humberside YO25 8SW (☎ 026 286 217/367/607/716)

SOUTHWOOD, Prof Sir (Thomas) Richard Edmund; s of Edmund William Southwood (d 1984), of Parrock Manor, Gravesend, and Ada Mary (d 1949), da of Ven Archdeacon Thos R Regg, of Newcastle, NSW; *b* 20 June 1931; *Educ* Gravesend GS, Imperial Coll London (BSc, PhD, DSc), Univ of Oxford (MA, DSc); *m* 1955, Alison Langley, da of Arthur Langley Harden (d 1983), of Fallows Green, Harpenden, Herts; 2 s (Richard, Charles); *Career* prof of zoology and applied entomology Univ of London and head of Dept of Zoology Imperial Coll London 1967-79, Linacre prof of zoology and head of dept Univ of Oxford 1979-, vice chllr Univ of Oxford 1989-; fell Merton Coll Oxford 1979-, chm Bd of Tstees Br Museum (Nat Hist) 1980-84 (memb 1973), chm Royal Cmmn on Environmental Pollution 1981-86 (memb 1974-), vice pres Royal Soc of London 1982-84 (fell 1987), pres Royal Entomological Soc of London 1983-85, prof at large Cornell Univ USA 1985-, chm Nat Radiological Protection Bd 1985 (memb 1981-); memb Academia Europaea 1989; foreign memb: American Acad of Arts and Scis 1980, Norwegian Acad of Sci and Letters 1987, US Nat Acad of Scis 1988; Hon DSc: Griffith, East-Anglia, McGill, Warwick; Hon Doctorate Lund; Cavaliere Ufficiale Repubblica d' Italia 1991; kt 1984; *Books* Land and water Bugs of the British Isles (with D Leston, 1959), Life of the Wayside and Woodland (1963), Ecological Methods (1966, 2 ed 1978), Insects on Plants (jtly, 1984), Insects & The Plant Surface (jtly, 1986), Radiation and Health (jtly, 1987); *Recreations* reading, natural history; *Clubs* Athenaeum, Oxford and Cambridge; *Style—* Prof Sir Richard Southwood; Merton College, Oxford; Zoology Dept, South Parks Rd, Oxford (☎ 0865 271255); University Offices, Wellington Square, Oxford (☎ 0865 270242)

SOUTHWOOD, William Frederick Walter; s of Stuart Walter, Southwood, MC (d 1982), of London, and Mildred Mary, *née* Southwood (d 1988); *b* 8 June 1925; *Educ* Charterhouse, Cambridge (MB BChir, MA, MChir, MD); *m* 1 May 1965, Margaret Carleton, da of Sir Ernest William Holderness, 2 Bt, CBE (d 1968); 2 s (Robert b 1966, John b 1967); *Career* Nat Serv Capt RAMC 1949-51; conslt surgn Bath Health Dist 1966-, Hunterian prof RCS 1961, memb Professional and Linguistic Assessment Bd 1976-87 (chm 1984-87), visiting prof of surgery Univ of Cape Town 1987; memb Court Worshipful Soc of Apothecaries 1975-, (Liveryman 1953, Master 1986-87); FRSM 1952; *Books* Progress in Proctology (chapter on carcinoid tumours, 1969); *Recreations* fishing, shooting, snooker; *Clubs* East India, Bath and County; *Style—* William Southwood, Esq; Upton House, Bathwick Hill, Bath BA2 6EX (☎ 0225 465 152); The Bath Clinic, Claverton Down, Bath BA2 7BR (☎ 0225 835 555)

SOUTHWORTH, Ian Robert; s of Robert Southworth, and Margaret Elizabeth, *née* Illingworth; *b* 18 Dec 1961; *Educ* Scarisbrick Hall Lancs, Tuson Coll Preston; *m* 22 Sept 1989, Catherine Jane, da of Alan Carl Hamel, of 4 Syddal Crescent, Bramhall, Stockport, Cheshire; *Career* yachtsman 1974-; major races: Enterprise Jr Nat 1978-80, Enterprise Inland Championship 1981-84, Endeavour Trophy 1983-85 and 1988, GP14 Nat 1982, 1983, 1988, 1990, J24 Nat 1989-90, Lark Nat 1984 and 1989, GP14 World 1983, J24 Euro 1989, 420 Nat 1985, James Capel Nat Match Racing Championship 1990; memb Southern Cross Br Team 1985, hon memb Southport Sailing Club; sailmaker 1982-, currently dir Ullman Sails (UK) Ltd; *Recreations* squash, skiing, chess; *Style—* Ian Southworth, Esq; 5 Netley Lodge Close, Netley Abbey, Southampton, Hampshire SO3 5BT (☎ 0703 453232)

SOUTTER, Lucy Caroline; da of David Fraser Souttrer, of Stratton Firs, Cheltenham Rd, Glos, and Joyce Elizabeth Anne, *née* Smith; *b* 17 March 1967; *Educ* Charlton Park Convent for Girls Cheltenham Glos; *Career* squashplayer; Br number 1, world number 2 1987; represented England: under 16's 4 times (capt), under 19's 19 times, srs 27 times; Br under 16 Open champion 1983 (1981 and 1982), Br under 19 Open champion 1984 (1983), World Sr Masters Champion (invitation) 1984, world jr champion 1984, Br sr champion 1985, world sr team champion 1987 (1985), Br Open sr championships runner up 1987, Br under 23 Open champion 1988 (1987), Portugese Open champion 1988, Swiss Open champion 1988, Edmonton womens int champion; exec memb Womens Int Squash Players Assoc; *Recreations* health and fitness, sport, reading, music; *Clubs* Richmond Town Squash and Health, Cannons Sports; *Style—* Miss Lucy Soutter; 6 Manor Park, Richmond, Surrey TW9 1XZ (☎ 081 940 7402)

SOUTTER, William Patrick (Pat); s of William Paterson Soutter, of Glasgow, and Eleanore Louise, *née* Siekawitch; *b* 12 Jan 1944; *Educ* Glasgow HS, Univ of Glasgow (MB ChB, MD), Univ of Strathclyde (MSc); *m* 30 June 1973, Winifred Christine, da of William Hanworth, of Paisley; 2 da (Elizabeth b 1980, Eleanor b 1986); *Career* lectr in obstetrics and gynaecology Univ of Glasgow 1978-81, sr lectr in obstetrics and gynaecology Univ of Sheffield 1981-85, reader in gynaecological oncology Inst of Obstetrics and Gynaecology 1985-; hon sec for Br Gynaecological Cancer Soc, hon sec gynaecological sub ctee UK coordinating ctee for cancer res; FRCOG 1988; *Recreations* fishing, golf; *Style—* Pat Soutter, Esq; Inst of Obstetrics & Gynaecology, Royal Postgraduate Medical Sch, Hammersmith Hospital, Du Cane Rd, London W12 0HS (☎ 081 740 3267)

SOUYAVE, His Honour Judge; Sir (Louis) Georges Souyave; *b* 29 May 1926; *Educ* St Louis Coll Seychelles; *m* 1953, Mona de Chermont; 2 s, 4 da; *Career* barr Gray's Inn 1949; Seychelles: asst attorney-gen 1956-62, additional Judge Supreme Ct 1962-64, Puisne Judge 1964-70, chief justice 1970-76; High Ct res judge and Br judge of Supreme Ct of Condominium, New Hebrides 1976-80, district judge Hong Kong 1980-; kt 1971; *Style—* His Honour Judge Souyave; District Court, Victoria, Hong Kong

SOWANDE, Olatunji Eugene Olufemi; s of Rev Emanuel Josiah Sowande (d 1918), and Comfort Adeyola, *née* Taylor (d 1968); *b* 4 Oct 1912; *Educ* King's Coll and The Sch of Pharmacy Lagos Nigeria; *m* Clarice Yejide, da of Thomas Wright; 1 s (Babatunde b 6 May 1941), 1 da (Ayudele b 3 April 1939); *Career* pharmacist Nigeria 1935-45, called to the Bar Inner Temple 1956, dep circuit judge 1978-65, elected sr master of the bench of the Inner Temple 1986; *Recreations* music, reading, dancing; *Clubs* MCC; *Style—* Olatunji Sowande, Esq

SOWDEN, Harold Thomas (Harry); s of Frank Thomas Sowden (d 1982), of Minehead, Somerset, and Gladys Panton, *née* Harrison (d 1970); *b* 3 Jan 1924; *Educ* Kings Coll Sch Wimbledon, Merton Coll Oxford; *m* 25 May 1949, (Eiyred) Margaret, da of Rev Canon Frederick James Meyrick (d 1945), of Hove, Sussex; *Career* various appts Exchequer and Audit Dept (now Nat Audit Off) 1946-72, dir Office of Health Serv Cmmrs 1973-83; churchwarden St Michael's Church Mickleham Surrey 1976-82; memb RSM 1974-77; *Recreations* reading, writing, travel; *Style—* H T Sowden, Esq; Larch Cottage, Pilgrims' Close, Westhumble, Dorking, Surrey RH5 6AR

SOWDEN, John Percival; s of Percival Sowden (d 1956), of Todmorden, Yorks, and Gertrude, *née* Moss (d 1953); *b* 6 Jan 1917; *Educ* Hebden Bridge GS, Silcoates Sch Wakefield, Imperial Coll of Sci and Technol London (BSc (Eng), ACGI); *m* 1, 29 March 1940 (m dis 1969), Ruth Dorothy, da of Gustave Keane (d 1967), of Canon's Park, London; 1 s (Christopher b 26 Aug 1948); m 2, 11 July 1969, Joyce Diana Mary Timpson, da of Charalambos Hji-Ioannou (d 1947), of Nicosia, Cyprus; *Career* cmmnd RE 1939; served: UK, ME, Italy (despatches); demobolised with rank of Capt; joined Richard Costain Ltd 1947; site project mangr on various projects including: Festival of Britain, Apapa Wharf, Nigeria and Bridgetown Harbour, Barbados 1948-60; jt md Richard Costain (Associates) Ltd 1960-62, md Costain-Blankevoort International Dredging Co Ltd 1962-65, mangr Civil Engrg Div Richard Costain Ltd 1965-69 (memb Bd 1967), chief exec International Area Richard Costain Ltd 1969-70 (group chief exec 1970-75), chm Costain Group 1972-80; memb Governing Body Imperial Coll of Sci Technol and Med 1971; FCGI 1972, FIC 1979, FBIM 1972, FRSA 1983; *Recreations* reading, joinery, cabinet making; *Clubs* RAC; *Style—* John Sowden, Esq; Below Star Cottage, East Tytherley Road, Lockerley, Romsey, Hants (☎ 0794 41172)

SOWDEN, Terence Cubitt; QC (1989); s of late George Henry Sowden, RNR, and Margaret Duncan, *née* Cubitt; *b* 30 July 1929; *Educ* Victoria Coll, Overseas Nautical Training Coll, Hendon Tech Coll London, Univ of London; *m* 1955, Doreen Mary Lucas (d 1983); 1 s (Gary), 2 da (Sally Ann Dallimore, Jayne); *Career* called to the Bar Middle Temple 1951, advocate Royal Ct of Jersey 1951, private practice in Jersey, then States dep St Helier No 1 Dist 1961-64, currently conslt Crill Cubitt Sowden & Tomes Advocates and solicitors (sr ptnr 1962-83), HM Solicitor Gen for Jersey 1986-; former memb Bd Channel Television, dep chm Royal Bank of Scotland (Jersey) Ltd; memb Br swimming team: for tour to Denmark and Sweden 1949, holder of record for

Corbière to St Helier and Sark to Guernsey crossings; *Books* The Jersey Law of Trusts (with Paul Matthews, 1988); *Recreations* writing, walking the low tide; *Style—* Terence Sowden, Esq, QC

SOWERBUTTS, Rev Janet Elise; da of Francis Alfred Owen Sowerbutts (d 1964), and Esmeralda Helen, *née* Woodward (d 1967); *b* 17 Aug 1938; *Educ* Westcliff HS for Girls, Westminster Coll Cambridge; *Career* co dir Messrs James Brodie & Co (Export Ltd) 1962-69, atlantic sec Girls' Bde 1970-75, ordained minster Utd Reformed Church 1978, cheshunt chair Westminster Coll Cambridge 1985, provincial moderator Thames North Province 1990- (first woman to be appointed); *Style—* The Rev Janet Sowerbutts; Westminster College, Cambridge (☎ 0223 353997); Thames North Province, The City Temple, Holborn Viaduct, London EC1A 2DE (☎ 071 583 8701)

SOWERBY, Amanda Louise (*née* Smith); da of Geoffrey Norman Smith, of Dewsbury, West Yorkshire, and Kathleen, *née* Heaton; *b* 29 Jan 1963; *Educ* Westborough HS Dewsbury, Whitcliffe Mount Sixth Form Coll, Wheelwright Coll Dewsbury; *m* 7 May 1987, Mark Richard Sowerby, s of John William Sowerby; 1 s (Joseph Richard b 28 June 1989); *Career* hockey player; former clubs: Wakefield, Laund Hill Ladies; currently Doncaster; England cups: under 21, under 23, full debut 1987, over 23 caps; achievements incl: Silver medal Euro Cup London 1987, fourth place World Cup Sydney 1990, scored 2 goals v USA Wembley 1987 (player of match award); former employment: supervisor Dewsbury Sports Centre, residential child care offr Doncaster; *Recreations* most sports, walking, music, reading especially Ludlum or King; *Style—* Mrs Amanda Sowerby; 36 Westmorland Way, Sprotbrough, Doncaster, South Yorkshire DN5 7PW (☎ 0302 851406); c/o All England Womens Hockey Association, 51 High Street, Shrewsbury SY1 1ST

SOWREY, Air Marshal Sir Frederick Beresford; KCB (1978, CB 1968), CBE (1965), AFC (1954); s of Gp Capt F Sowrey, DSO, MC, AFC (d 1968), of Eastbourne, and Warsash; *b* 14 Sept 1922; *Educ* Charterhouse; *m* 1946, Anne Margaret, da of Capt C T A Bunbury, OBE, RN (d 1951), of Crowborough; 1 s, 1 da; *Career* RAF 1940, served WWII in Fighter Reconnaissance Units in Euro Theatre, Gp Capt 1962, Air Cdre 1965, SASO Air Forces, ME Aden, dir Overseas Def Policy MOD 1968-70, SASO RAF Trg Cmd with rank of Air Vice-Marshal 1970-72, Cmdt Nat Def Coll 1972-75, dir gen RAF Trg 1975-77, UK Rep Perm Mil Deputies Gp CENTO 1977-79; res fell Int Inst of Strategic Studies 1980-81; author of and contrib to articles and reviews in military and def jnls; pres Victory Servs Assoc 1989- (chm 1985-89), chm RAF Historical Society 1986-, memb Bd of Conservators of Ashdown Forest 1983-; *Recreations* early motoring, industrial archaeology; *Clubs* RAF; *Style—* Air Marshal Sir Frederick Sowrey, KCB, CBE, AFC; c/o National Westminster Bank, 67 High Street, Staines, MIddlesex

SOWTON, Dr (George) Edgar; s of George Sowton (d 1948), and May Amreta, *née* Stevens; *b* 1 Aug 1930; *Educ* Dulwich, Corpus Christi Coll Cambridge (BA, MA, MB BChir, MD); *m* 3 Aug 1957, Patricia Mary, da of Reginald Squires, of Doncaster; 2 s (Christopher John b 11 Aug 1960, Jonathon Paul b 18 July 1962), 2 da (Elizabeth Mary b 16 Dec 1958, Margareta Caroline b 12 July 1964); *Career* former: conslt cardiologist Nat Heart Hosp London, reader in cardiology Univ of London, asst dir Inst of Cardiology London; WHO and Wellcome fell Karolinska Hosp 1964, dir Cardiac Servs Guy's Hosp 1986-, pres British Cardiac Soc 1987-90 (sec 1972-74); bishop lectr American Coll of Cardiology; examiner Univs of: Cambridge, Oxford, London, Manchester, Belfast, Dublin, Durham, Bergen, Stockholm; ctee memb: DHSS, Euro Soc of Cardiology, Br Cardiac Soc, RCP; former bd memb Internat Soc of Cardiac Pacing, former pres Euro Working Gp on Cardiac Pacing, cncl memb Br Soc for Electrophysiology and Cardiac Pacing, memb of many Int Cardiac Socs; MRCP 1959, FRCP 1971, fell American Coll of Cardiology 1971, fndr fell Euro Soc of Cardiology 1989; Knight's Cross of the Order of the Icelandic Falcon 1986; *Books* Cardiac Pacemakers (with H Siddons), more then 600 articles on cardiac subjects in med jls; *Recreations* sailing, travel, music, cars; *Clubs* RYA; *Style—* Dr Edgar Sowton; 25 Upper Wimpole St, London W1 (☎ 071 935 5625, fax 071 224 6395 car 0836 616948); Cardiac Dept, Guy's Hospital, London Bridge, London SE1 9RT (☎ 071 955 5000; direct line 071 407 9800)

SPACIE, Maj-Gen Keith; CB (1987), OBE (1974); s of Frederick Percy Spacie (d 1981), and Kathleen, *née* Wrench (d 1989); *b* 21 June 1935; *m* 16 Sept 1961, Valerie Elise, da of Lt-Col Harry William Wallace Rich (d 1971); 1s (Dominic b 1964); *Career* RMA Sandhurst 1954-55, cmmnd Royal Lincolnshire Regt 1955, transferred Para Regt 1959, cdr Ind Para Co 1964-65, Army Staff Coll 1965-66, DAA & QMG Para Bde 1968-70 instr RMA Sandhurst 1970-72, Nat Def Coll 1972-73, cdr 3 Bn Para Regt 1973-75, NATO staff SHAPE, 1976-78, instr Nat Def Coll 178-79, cdr 7 Field Force 1979-81, RCDS 1982, Mil Cdr and Cdr Br Forces Falkland Islands 1983-84, dir Army Trg 1984-87; md Cranfield Edn and Trng Ltd 1987-89; dir Sudbury Conslts Ltd 1989-; MIOD; *Recreations* cross country running, military history, country pursuits; *Clubs* Army and Navy, Thames Hare and Hounds; *Style—* Maj-Gen Keith Spacie, CB, OBE; c/o Lloyds Bank, Obelisk Way, Camberley, Surrey; business address: 2 Park Chase, Guildford, Surrey GU1 1ES (☎ 0483 301736)

SPACKMAN, Brig John William Charles; s of Lt-Col Robert Thomas Spackman, MBE (d 1984), and Ann, *née* Rees (d 1984); *b* 12 May 1932; *Educ* Cyfarthfa Castle GS Merthyr Tydfil, Wellington GS, Royal Mil Coll of Sci, Univ of London (external BSc, PhD), UMIST (MSc); *m* 2 April 1955, Jeanette Vera, da of George Samuel (d 1956); 2 s (Michael b 1956, David b 1964), 1 da (Sarah b 1959); *Career* Nat Serv 1950-52; cmmnd RAOC 1952, regtl appts 1952-72, Lt-Col Project Wavell 1969-72, Lt-Col GSO1 RARDE 1972-75, Col sr mil offr Chemical Def and Microbiological Def Estab Porton Down 1975-78, branch chief Info Systems Div SHAPE 1978-80, Brig, dir Supply Computer Servs 1980-83, ret Brig 1983; dir (under sec) operational strategy DHSS 1983-87; dir: Computing and Info Servs Br Telecom UK 1987-90, Act Logsys 1990-, Intelligent Networks Ltd 1991, John Spackman Assocs 1990; Freeman City of London 1987, Asst to Ct of Info Technologists 1989, govr Int Cncl for Computer Communication 1989-; MBIM 1970, MIOD 1983, FBCS 1987, CEng 1990; *Recreations* gardening, tennis, hill walking, opera; *Clubs* Naval and Military; *Style—* Brig John Spackman; 4 The Green, Evenley, Brackley, Northants (☎ 0280 703317); John Spackman Associates, 3 Kennington Palace Court, Sancroft St, London SE11 (☎ 071 587 1909)

SPACKMAN, Michael John; s of Geoffrey Bertram Spackman (d 1976), and Audrey Ivy Elizabeth, *née* Morecombe; *b* 8 Oct 1936; *Educ* Malvern Coll, Clare Coll Cambridge (MA), Queen Mary Coll, London (MScEcon); *m* 27 Feb 1965, Judith Ann, da of Walter Henry Leathem (d 1966); 2 s (Sean Michael b 1968, Keir David b 1972), 2 da (Juliet Sarah Helen Christina b 1977, Helena Claire Nicola b 1982); *Career* Mil Serv 2 Lt RA 1955-57; physicist UKAEA Capenhurst 1960-69, sr physicist/engr The Nuclear Power Group Ltd 1969-71, princ scientific offr then econ advsr Dept of Energy 1971-77, dir econs and accountancy Civil Serv Coll 1979-80; HM Treas: econ advsr 1977-79, head Pub Servs Econs Div 1980-85, undersec and head Pub Expenditure Econs Gp 1985; *Recreations* walking, children; *Style—* Michael Spackman, Esq; 44 Gibson Square, Islington, London N1 0RA (☎ 081 359 1053); H M Treasury, Parliament St, London SW1P 3AG (☎ 071 270 5492)

SPACKMAN, Michael Kenneth Maurice; s of Harry Maurice Spackman (d 1984), of Godalming, and Mary Madeline (Molly) Pinson (d 1959); *b* 2 Feb 1926; *Educ* Marlborough; *m* 9 Jan 1960, Ann Veronica, da of Francis Mervyn Cook (d 1979), of Burford; 2 da (Henrietta b 1960, Catriona b 1962); *Career* Lt attached Indian RA; merchant banker; dir Singer & Friedlander Investment Management Ltd 1986, First Spanish Investment Trust 1987, Vallehermoso SA 1986-90; *Recreations* horse trials, tennis; *Style—* Michael Spackman, Esq; c/o Singer and Friedlander plc, 21 New Street, Bishopsgate, London EC2M 4HR (☎ 071 623 3000, telex 886977, fax CG37 623 2122)

SPACKMAN, Nigel James; s of George William Spackman, of Hampshire, and Sheila Irene, *née* Hook; *b* 2 Dec 1960; *Educ* Winton Comp Sch, Cricklade Coll; *m* 8 June 1985, Nicola Jane, da of Victor Stanley Groves; 1 da (Hannah Juliet b 10 March 1986); *Career* professional footballer; represnted Hants under 18 and under 19; 119 appearances Bournemouth 1980-83 (10 goals), 141 appearances Chelsea 1983-87 (12 goals), 51 appearances Liverpool 1987-89, 29 appearances Queens Park Rangers 1989 (1 goal), transferred for £500,000 to Glasgow Rangers 1989-; also represented Hants at cross country and 800m, played at All England Sch basketball finals; *Recreations* golf, swimming, listening to music, being with family; *Style—* Nigel Spackman, Esq; c/o Neil Ramsey, 45 Potterton Lane, Barwick in Elmet, Leeds (☎ 0532 813801); Glasgow Rangers FC, Ibrox Stadium, Glasgow (☎ 041 427 8500)

SPACKMAN, Susan Jane; da of William John Wotton, of Devon, and Dorothy Wotton, *née* Cooper; *b* 14 March 1947; *Educ* St Dunstan's Abbey Plymouth, Tavistock Comprehensive, Plymouth Poly Sch of Architecture (Dip Arch); *m* 28 Aug 1970, Richard Benjamin James, s of Arthur James Spackman, of Tavistock; 1 s (Edward b 1979), 1 da (Clair b 1974); *Career* chartered architect; principal Crookes & Spackman; ARIBA (chm Plymouth Branch 1987-89), nat jt vice pres The Assoc of Conslt Architects 1987-89 (representing the Assoc of Conslt Architects with The Campaign for the Bar, investigating Law Reform for all professionals with respect to liability); *Recreations* equestrianism; *Style—* Mrs Susan J Spackman; Briar House, 243 Whitchurch Road, Tavistock, Devon (☎ 0822 615221); Crookes & Spackman, The Old Stables, Paddons Row, Tavistock, Devon (☎ 0822 614222)

SPALDING, Prof (Dudley) Brian; s of Harold Andrew Spalding, and Kathleen Constance Spalding; *b* 9 Jan 1923; *Educ* Kings Coll Sch Wimbledon, Univ of Oxford (BA, MA), Univ of Cambridge (PhD, ScD); *m* 1, Eda Isle-Lotte Goericke; 2 s, 2 da; *m* 2, Colleen King; 2 s; *Career* prof of heat transfer Imperial Coll 1958-88 (emeritus prof 1988-); md Concentration Heat & Momentum Ltd (CHAM) 1970-, chm and dir CHAM of N America Inc 1977-; Reilly prof Purdue Univ Indiana 1978-79; awards incl; Medaille d'Or (Inst Francais de l'Energie) 1980, Bernard Lewis medal 1982, Luikov medal 1986; hon prof USTC Hefei China 1988; FRS (1989), FIMechE, FInstE, FIChemE, ASME, FEng 1989; *Books* incl: Some Fundamentals of Combustion (1955), Convective Mass Transfer (1963), Heat and Mass Transfer in Recirculating Flows (jtly, 1969), Engineering Thermodynamics (with Cole, 1974), Genmix (1978), Combustion and Mass Transfer (1974); *Recreations* computing, jogging; *Style—* Prof Brian Spalding, FRS; Concentration Heat and Momentum Ltd, Bakery House, 40 High St, London SW19 5AU (☎ 081 947 7651, fax 081 879 3497, telex 928517)

SPALDING, Frances; da of Hedley Stinston Crabtree (d 1985), and Margaret, *née* Holiday (d 1989); *b* 16 July 1950; *Educ* Farringtons Sch Chislehurst, Univ of Nottingham (BA, PhD); *m* 20 April 1984, Julian Spalding; 1 s (Daniel b 11 Aug 1983); *Career* art historian and biographer; lectr Sheffield City Polytechnic 1978-88, currently freelance; author of: Magnificent Dreams: Burne-Jones and the late Victorians (1978), Whistler (1979), Roger Fry: Art and Life (1980), Vanessa Bell (1983), British Art since 1900 (1986), Stevie Smith: A Critical Biography (1988), Twentieth Century Painters & Sculptors (Dictionary of British Art series, 1990), Dance till the Stars Come Down: A Biography of John Minton (1991); FRSL 1984; memb: Soc of Authors, PEN; *Recreations* music; *Style—* Frances Spalding; c/o Coleridge & Rogers, 20 Powis Mews, London W11

SPALDING, John Anthony (Tony); s of John Eber Spalding (d 1964), of Wrexham, Clwyd, and Katherine, *née* Davies; *b* 17 Feb 1938; *Educ* Wellington, Brasenose Coll Oxford; *m* (m dis), Joan Pauline, *née* Hanley; 2 da (Joanna b 19 Oct 1962, Deborah b 15 July 1964); *Career* journalist 1959-61, Public Affairs Dept Ford Motor Co 1961-64 and 1966-73, PR offr Vauxhall Motors Ltd Ellesmere Port 1964-66; dir of PR: British Leyland 1974-79 (car PR mangr 1973), Wilkinson Match 1979-80, Spillers 1980, Dalgety 1980-81; dir of Communications Sea Containers/Seaco 1981-84, dir external affairs Whitbread 1985-86; dir pub affairs: Battersea Leisure/Alton Towers 1984-85, Dalgety 1986-89, Vauxhall Motors Ltd 1989-; fell Inst of Pub Affairs 1988, FIMI 1989, FRSA 1988; *Style—* Tony Spalding, Esq; Vauxhall Motors Limited, Griffin House, PO Box 3, Luton, Bedford LU1 3TY (☎ 0582 427620, fax 0582 426926, car 0860 575572)

SPALDING, John Oliver; CBE (1988); s of John Spalding, OBE (d 1954), of Manchester, and Winifrid Ethel, *née* Trigger (d 1965); *b* 4 Aug 1924; *Educ* William Hulme's GS Manchester, Jesus Coll Cambridge (MA); *m* 20 Sept 1952, Mary Whitworth, da of James Birch Hull (d 1972), of Manchester and Eastbourne; 1 s (Simon John b 1960), 1 da (Sarah Mary (Mrs Parkes) b 1958); *Career* RA 1943-47, attached IA (5 Indian Field Regt and Mountain Artillery Trg Centre Ambla) Overseas Serv in Burma, Singapore, Jarva and India, Capt RA; admitted slr 1952; articled clerk to Sir Derek Hilton Manchester 1949-52, asst slr: Manchester Corp 1952-55, rising to sr slr Hampshire CC 1955-62; Halifax Building Soc: asst slr 1962-64, Head Office slr 1964-74, gen mangr 1970, dir 1975-88, dep chief gen mangr 1981, chief exec 1982-88; chm Nat House-Bldg Cncl 1988-; dir: NMW Computers plc 1989-, Morton Hodson & Co Ltd 1989-; chm: Future Constitution and Powers of Bldg Socs Working Pty (The Spalding Ctee) 1981-83, Calderdale Small Business Advice Centre 1983-88; memb: Cncl Bldg Socs Assoc 1981-88, Farrand Ctee on Conveyancing 1984, Nat House-Bldg Cncl 1985-; memb Law Soc; *Recreations* boating and bird watching; *Style—* John Spalding, Esq, CBE; Water's Edge, Springe Lane, Swanley, Nantwich, Cheshire CW5 8NR (☎ 0270 74 520); Nat House-Bldg Council, Chiltern Ave, Amersham, Bucks HP6 5AP (☎ 0494 434477, fax 0494 728521, car 0836 629006)

SPALDING, Julian; s of Eric Spalding, and Margaret Grace, *née* Savager; *b* 15 June 1947; *Educ* Chislehurst and Sidcup GS for Boys, Univ of Nottingham (BA, Dip Museums Assoc); *m* 1974, Frances; 1 s; *Career* art asst: Leicester Museum and Art Gallery 1970-71, Durham Light Infantry Museum and Arts Centre 1971-72; keeper Mappin Art Gallery 1972-76; dir: Sheffield City Cncl 1982-85 (dep dir 1976-82), Manchester City Art Galleries 1985-89, Glasgow Museums 1989-; acting dir Nat Museum of Labour History 1987-88, BBC Broadcaster (talks and reviews), Third Ear (BBC Radio Three) 1988; chm: Exhibitions Sub Ctee 1981-82 and 1986, Arts Cncl; memb: Art Panel 1978-82, Art Galleries Assoc 1987- (fndr and memb Ctee 1976-); dir Guild of St George John Ruskins Guild 1983- (companion 1978); Crafts Cncl: memb Projects and Orgn Ctee 1985-87, memb 1986-, memb Purchasing Ctee 1986, memb Exhibitions Ctee 1986-90; FMA 1983; *Books* L S Lowry (1979), Three Little Books on Painting (1984), Is There Life in Museums? (1990), exhibition catalogues incl: Modern British Painting (1975), Glasgow's Great British Art Exhibition (1990); contrib to: Burlington Magazine; *Style—* Julian Spalding, Esq; Art Gallery and Museum, Kelvingrove, Glasgow G3 8AG

SPALDING, Richard Lionel; s of Frederick Lionel (d 1966), of Worcester, and Ines

Sylvia, *née* Salkeld; *b* 21 May 1938; *Educ* Malvern; *m* 14 Sept 1963, Cicely Jane, da of late Philip Cecil King-Lewis; 1 s (William Joseph b 11 May 1973), 2 da (Henrietta Jane b 5 Nov 1966, Frederica Victoria b 7 Dec 1968); *Career* Hubert Leicester & Co CAs Worcester 1957-63, Peat Marwick Mitchell & Co London 1963-86, managing ptnr KPMG Peat Marwick McLintock Guildford 1986; ACA 1963; *Recreations* operas, gardens, cathedrals, Spain; *Clubs* Brooks's; *Style—* Richard Spalding, Esq; KPMG Peat Marwick McLintock, Eastgate Court, Guildford, Surrey GU1 3AE (☎ 0483 303000, fax 0483 68732)

SPALDING, Ruth Jeanie Lucile; da of late Henry Norman Spalding, of Oxford, and late Nellie Maud Emma, *née* Cayford; *Educ* Headington Sch for Girls Oxford, Somerville Coll Oxford (MA); *Career* author; formerly: stage actor and dir, typist, lectr and advsr in art and crafts and social studies, gen sec Assoc of Head Mistresses; author of: Play With This Sword (performed at Royal Festival Hall), The Word, Pleasure or Pain in Education, The Improbable Puritan, The Diary of Bulstrode Whitelocke 1605-1675 (ed), Contemporaries of Bulstrode Whitelocke 1605-1675 (1990), feature articles The Times, feature and documentary radio progs BBC; winner Whitbread Literary award for The Improbable Puritan 1975; FRHistS, FRSA, memb Soc of Authors, Br Actors Equity Assoc; *Recreations* walking, theatre, organic gardening; *Clubs* English-Speaking Union; *Style—* Ruth Spalding; 34 Reynards Rd, Welwyn, Herts AL6 9TP (☎ 043 871 4696)

SPALTON, David John; s of John Roland Spalton, of Duffield, Derbyshire, and Gertrude Edna, *née* Massey; *b* 2 March 1947; *Educ* Buxton Coll Derbyshire, Westminster Med Sch (MB BS); *m* 26 May 1979, Catherine, da of Donald George Bompas, CMG, of Petts Wood, Kent; 2 s (George b 1980, James b 1983); *Career* sr registrar Moorfields Eye Hosp 1976-77; conslt ophthalmic surgn: Charing Cross Hosp 1981-82, St Thomas' Hosp 1982; hon conslt ophthalmic surgn Royal Hosp Chelsea, hon sr lectr in clinical pharmacology UMDS; memb ed bd Br Jl of Ophthalmology; Freeman Worshipful Soc of Apothecaries; memb RSM, MRCP 1973, FRCS 1975, FCOphthal 1988, FRCP 1990; *Books* Atlas of Clinical Ophthalmology (1985); *Recreations* fly fishing; *Style—* David Spalton, Esq; 59 Harley St, London W1N 1DD (☎ 071 935 6174)

SPALVINS, (Janis Gunars) John; s of Peter Spalvins, and Hilda Blumentals, *née* Dritmanis; *b* 26 May 1936; *Educ* Concordia Coll Adelaide South Australia, Univ of Adelaid (BEc); *m* 16 Dec 1961, Cecily Westall, da of late Jack Rymill; 2 s (Ry b 1965, Richard b 1968); *Career* gp sec and dir Camelec Group 1955-73, Adelaide Steamship Co Ltd: asst gen mangr 1973-77, gen mangr 1977-79, chief gen mangr 1979, dir 1979, md 1981; chief exec David Jones Ltd 1980; David Jones Ltd Group, chm Industrial Equity Ltd, Macmahon Holdings Ltd, Kern Corporation Ltd, Pioneer Property Group ltd; chm: John Martin Retailers Ltd, Metro Meat Holdings Ltd, National Consolidated Ltd Group, Peterville Sleigh Ltd Group, Tooth and Co Ltd Group, Markheath Securities Plc UK; memb The Aust Inst of Co Dirs, Business Cncl of Aust; fell Aust Inst of Management; *Recreations* sailing, tennis, snow and water skiing; *Clubs* Ski Club of Victoria, Royal SA Yacht Squadron, The Cruising Yacht Club of SA; *Style—* John Spalvins, Esq; 2 Brookside Rd, Springfield SA 5062, Australia (☎ 010 61 8 3792965); 123 Greenhill Rd, Unley, South Australia (☎ 010 61 8 2723077, fax 010 61 8 3730940, telex 82133, car 010 61 18 821900)

SPANNER, John Hedley; TD (1981); s of Maj Sydney Spanner, of Gatcombe Cottage, Streatley-on-Thames, Berks, and Una, *née* Brown; *b* 21 Feb 1945; *Educ* Reading Sch; *m* 19 Aug 1967 (m dis 1984); 2 da (Annabel b 1968, Rebecca b 1970); m 2, 27 Oct 1989, Mary Elizabeth, *née* Carpenter; *Career* cmmnd Royal Berks Regt (TA) 1966, currently Co Cdr and PMC Offrs Mess 2 Wessex (V); support servs mangr Standard Chartered Bank, former chm Broad St Ward Club, common cncllr Ward of Broad St in City of London 1984-, govr City of London Sch, memb City of London TAVRA; Freeman City of London 1975, Liveryman Worshipful Co of Glovers; *Recreations* TA, art, gardening; *Clubs* Cavalry and Guard's; *Style—* John Spanner, Esq, TD; Weighbridge Cottage, Merstham, Surrey RH1 3BN (☎ 0737 642094); Standard Chartered Bank, Aldermanbury Square, London EC2Y 7SB (☎ 071 280 7411)

SPANTON, (Harry) Merrik; OBE (1975); s of Henry Broadley Spanton (d 1947), of Canterbury, and Edith Jane, *née* Castle; *b* 27 Nov 1924; *Educ* Eastbourne Coll, Royal Sch of Mines London (BSc); *m* 3 Feb 1945, Mary Margaret, da of George Westcombe Hawkins (d 1958), of Bournemouth; 1 s (Graham Leslie b 1949); *Career* colliery mangr 1950, agent 1954, gp mangr 1956, dep area prodn mangr 1958, dep prodn dir Yorkshire 1960, asst area gen mangr 1962, gen mangr Kent 1964, area dir N Notts 1967-80, memb NCB 1980-85; dir: J H Sankey & Son (chm 1982-83), British Mining Consultants 1980-87 (chm 1981-83), Compower 1981-85 (chm 1984-85), NCB (Coal Products) Ltd 1981-83, British Fuel Co Ltd 1983-87; chm Br Coal Enterprise Ltd 1984-; memb: W Euro Coal Prodrs Assoc 1980-85, CBI Overseas Ctee 1981-85; jt sec Coal Indust Social Welfare Orgn 1983-85, vice pres Coal Trade Benevolent Assoc 1979- (chm 1978); Hon FIMinE 1986; ARSM 1945, CEng, CBIM 1979; *Recreations* travel, shooting; *Style—* Merrik Spanton, Esq, OBE; 4 Roselands Gardens, Canterbury, Kent CT2 7LP (☎ 0227 769356); Hobart House, Grosvenor Place, London SW1X 7AE (☎ 071 630 5304)

SPARK, Muriel Sarah; OBE (1967); da of Bernard Camberg, and Sarah Elizabeth Maud, *née* Uezzell; *Educ* James Gillespie's Sch for Girls Edinburgh, Heriot Watt Coll Edinburgh; *m* 1937 (m dis), 1 s; *Career* gen sec The Poetry Soc, ed The Poetry Review 1947-49; Hon memb American Acad of Arts and Letters 1978, Hon D Litt Strathclyde 1971; Hon DLitt Edinburgh 1989; FRSL 1963; *Books* critical and biographical: Tribute to Wordsworth (ed jtly, 1950), Selected Poems of Emily Brontë (ed, 1952), Child of Light: Reassessment of Mary Shelley (1951, revised as Mary Shelley 1987), My Best Mary: The letters of Mary Shelley (ed jtly, 1953), John Masefield (1953), Emily Brontë: Her Life and Work (jtly, 1953), The Brontë Letters (ed, 1954), Letters of John Henry Newman (ed jtly, 1957), Mary Shelley (1987); poems: The Fanfarlo and other Verse (1952), Collected Poems 1 (1967), Going Up to Sotheby's and other Poems (1982); fiction: The Comforters (1957), Robinson (1958), The Go-Away Bird (1958), Memento Mori (1959 adapted for stage 1964), The Ballad of Peckham Rye (1960, Italia Prize for dramatic radio 1962), The Bachelors (1960), Voices at Play (1961), The Prime of Miss Jean Brodie (1961, adapted for stage 1966, filmed 1969, BBC TV 1978), Doctors of Philosophy (play 1963), The Girls of Slender Means (1963, adapted for radio 1964, BBC TV 1975), The Mandelbaum Gate (1965, James Tait Black Memorial Prize), Collected Stories 1 (1967), The Public Image (1968), The Very Fine Clock (for children, 1969), The Driver's Seat (1970, filmed 1974), Not to Disturb (1971), The Hothouse by the East River (1973), The Abbess of Crewe (1974, filmed 1977), The Takeover (1976), Territorial Rights (1979), Loitering with Intent (1981), Bang-Bang You're Dead and other Stories (1982), The Only Problem (1984), The Stories of Muriel Spark (1987), A Far Cry from Kensington (1988), Symposium (1990); *Recreations* reading, travel; *Style—* Mrs Muriel Spark, OBE; c/o David Higham Associated Ltd, 5-8 Lower John St, Golden Square, London W1R 4HA

SPARKES, Prof John Jackson; s of Malcolm Sparkes (d 1933), of Jordans Bucks, and Elizabeth, *née* Jackson (d 1968); *b* 4 Dec 1924; *Educ* Bootham Sch York, Univ of Manchester (BSc), Univ of Essex (PhD); *m* 30 Aug 1952, Sheila Margaret, da of late John Wells; 2 s (Julian Malcolm b 7 Nov 1956, Kevin John b 20 Jan 1958), 1 da (Camilla Jane Elizabeth b 25 Sept 1959); *Career* Admiralty Signal Estab Haslemere 1944-46; hosp physicist: Middlesex Hosp 1946-47, St Marys Hosp London 1948-49; sch teaching: Ardingly Coll Sussex 1949-51, Watford GS 1951-52; physicist British Telecommunications Research Taplow Bucks 1952-62, sr lectr Imperial Coll London 1962-67, reader in electronics Univ of Essex 1067-70; The Open Univ: prof of electronics 1970- (pt/t following early retirement 1986), pro vice chancellor 1972-74, dean of technology 1974-84; memb: Standing Ctee on Continuing Educn, Hong Kong Govt appointed Cncl for Academic Accreditation; MIEE 1957, SMIEEE (NY) 1960, FEng 1984; *Books* Junction Transistors, (1966), Transistor Switching and Sequential Circuits (1969), Semiconductor Devices (1987); *Recreations* philosophy of science, golf, tennis, mountaineering; *Style—* Prof John Sparkes; Long Gable, 40 Sheethanger Lane, Felden, Hemel Hempstead, Herts HP3 0BQ (☎ 0442 251388); Faculty of Technology, The Open University, Milton Keynes MK7 6AA (☎ 0908 652856)

SPARKES, Kenneth Henry Norman; s of Henry Arthur Sparkes (d 1963), of Ilford, Essex, and Hilda Agnes Sparkes; *b* 27 Nov 1932; *Educ* Bancroft's Sch Essex; *m* 1959, Pamela Jean, da of William Bernard Woods (d 1968), of Oxted, Surrey; 3 s, 1 da (decd); *Career* farmer; slr; sr ptnr Constant & Constant; *Recreations* sailing (yacht 'Keramos' Ocean 75) gardening, farming and forestry; *Clubs* RAC, Little Ship; *Style—* Kenneth Sparkes Esq; 2 Parkside, Henley on Thames, Oxfordshire, (☎ 0491 410580, fax 0491 410590)

SPARKES, Martin John Hughes; s of James Raymond Sparkes, and Peggy Christine, *née* Hughes; *b* 4 Feb 1953; *Educ* St John's Coll Southsea, UWIST Cardiff (LLB); *m* 27 Oct 1979, Jenny Elizabeth, da of (James) Michael Reeves, of Field Lodge, Shepton Mallet, Somerset; 1 da (Poppy Elizabeth b 29 Oct 1988); *Career* slr; sr ptnr Sparkes Corbin and Co; memb Law Soc; *Recreations* cycling, squash, fishing; *Clubs* Bordon Officers' Sports, Petersfield Squash; *Style—* Martin Sparkes, Esq; 1 Bell Hill Ridge, Petersfield, Hants (☎ 0730 61082); Sparkes Corbin & Co, 24-28 Forest Centre, Bordon, Hants GU35 0TW (☎ 0420 475356)

SPARKES, Sir Robert Lyndley; s of Sir James Sparkes (d 1974), and Alice, *née* Scott; *b* 30 May 1929; *Educ* Southport Sch; *m* 1953, June, da of Methuen Young Morgan (d 1969); 2 s; *Career* memb Wambo Shire Cncl 1952-55 and 1964-67 (chm 1967-); state pres Nat Party of Australia 1970-90; pastoralist; kt 1979; *Style—* Sir Robert Sparkes; Dundonald, PO Box 117, Jandowae, Qld 4410, Australia

SPARKS, Alexander Pratt; s of Cedric Harold Sparks (d 1973), of Surrey, and Lilian Margaret, *née* Johnson (d 1982); *b* 28 Jan 1931; *Educ* Repton, St John's Coll Cambridge (MA); *m* 2 July 1976, Serena Evelyn, da of Gavin Thomas Fairfax (d 1987), of Shurlock Row, Berks; 1 s (Hugo b 20 Feb 1981), 1 da (Emma b 1 Dec 1978); *Career* Bateson & Payne (Lloyd's insur brokers) 1953-56, James Howden 1956-60, Stewarts & Lloyd's 1960-63, Air Prods 1963-66, Coopers & Lybrand (mgmnt conslt) 1966-75, CT Bowring (Lloyds insur brokers) 1975; dir: Bowring UK, Bowring London, RICS Insurance Services, RAC Insurance Brokers; chm Bowring Financial Services Ltd; memb Cncl and Gen Purposes Ctee BIBA; memb Ct Worshipful Co of Grocers (Master 1985-86); *Recreations* tennis, horse racing, gardening, golf; *Style—* Alexander Sparks, Esq; 35 Cornwall Gdns, London SW7 4AP; CT Bowring, Tower Place, London EC3 (☎ 071 357 1000)

SPARKS, Ian Leslie; s of Ronald Leslie, of Southport, Merseyside, and Hilda, *née* Bullen; *b* 26 May 1943; *Educ* Holt HS Liverpool, Brunel Univ (MA); *m* 1 July 1967, Eunice Jean, da of Reginald Robinson (d 1983); 1 da (Clare b 1973); *Career* social worker Merseyside 1971, asst divisional dir Barnardos 1974, dir The Children's Soc 1986- (social work dir 1981); tstee Linkage Tst, chm Social Policy Ctee Child Care; memb Br Assoc of Social Workers; *Recreations* piano playing, gardening in miniature; *Style—* Ian Sparks, Esq; Edward Rudolf House, Margery St, London WC1X 0JL (☎ 071 837 4299, fax 071 837 0211)

SPARKS, Hon Mrs (Juliet Jane Margaretta); *née* Moynihan; da of 2 Baron Moynihan, OBE, TD (d 1965); *b* 1934; *m* 1, 1958, Thomas Edwin Bidwell Abraham (d 1976); 2 s; m 2, 1978, Harry Hougham Sparks; *Style—* The Hon Mrs Sparks; Uplands, Bonnington, W Ashford, Kent

SPARKS, Hon Mrs (Rosemary); *née* Monslow; da of Baron Monslow (Life Peer, d 1966) and Mary, *née* Rogers (d 1959); *b* 12 Oct 1921; *Educ* convent; *m* 1948, William Harold Sparks (d 1985); *Style—* The Hon Mrs Sparks; 41 Trinity St, Rhostyllen, Wrexham, Denbighshire

SPARKS, Prof (Robert) Stephen John; s of Kenneth Grenfell Sparks, and late Ruth Joan, *née* Rugman; *b* 15 May 1949; *Educ* Wellington, Bingley GS Yorks, Imp Coll London (BSc, PhD); *m* 19 June 1971, Ann Elizabeth, da of Frederick Currie Talbot (d 1986); 2 s (Andrew Robert James b 24 Aug 1978, Daniel Joseph b 1 May 1982); *Career* Royal Exhibition of 1951 fell Univ of Lancaster 1974-76, NATO fell Univ of Rhode Island 1976-78, lectr in geology Univ of Cambridge 1978-89, prof of geology Univ of Bristol 1989-; memb: Grants Ctee NERC 1985-88, various ctees Royal Soc; FRS 1988, FGS; Wager medal Int Assoc of Volcanology and Chemistry of the Earth's Interior, Bigsby medal Geological Soc London; *Books* Tephra Studies (co-ed with S Self, 1980), author of 110 published scientific papers; *Recreations* soccer, squash, tennis, cricket, music, theatre; *Style—* Prof Stephen Sparks, FRS; 28 Stonewell Drive, Congresbury, Avon BS19 5DW (☎ 0934 876414); Department of Geology, University of Bristol, Bristol BS8 1RJ (☎ 0272 303774)

SPARROW, Bryan; *b* 8 June 1933; *Educ* Hemel Hempstead GS, Pembroke Oxford; *m* 1958, Fiona Mylechreest; 1 s, 1 da; *Career* Dip Serv; served: Belgrade, Moscow, Tunis, Casablanca, Kinshasa, Prague, Belgrade; ambassador Cameroon 1981-84, non-res ambassador Central African Republic and Equatorial Guinea 1982-84, Canadian Nat Def Coll 1984-85, consul gen Toronto 1985; *Style—* Bryan Sparrow, Esq; British Consultate General, Suite 1910, College Park, 777 Bay St, Toronto, Ontario, Canada; Foreign and Commonwealth Office, King Charles St, London SW1

SPARROW, Derek Tuart; s of Sydney Sparrow (d 1976), of Lytham St Annes, Lancs, and Dagmar May, *née* Wisternoff (d 1976); *b* 11 April 1935; *Educ* Denstone Coll Uttoxeter Staffs, Keble Coll Oxford (MA); *m* 16 Aug 1958, Doreen Beryl, da of Frank Keener (d 1975), of Hove, E Sussex; 2 s (Simon Charles Tuart b 1964, Christopher b 1965), 1 da (Sarah May b 1963); *Career* Nat Serv 2 Lt RA 1953-55; admitted slr 1961; asst examiner accounts Law Soc 1966-88; dir: Regency & West of England Bldg Soc 1973-90, Old Ship Hotel (Brighton) Ltd 1977-, Downs Crematorium Ltd 1979-; pres Sussex Law Soc 1984; tstee and sec Brighton Festival Tst 1978-, vice pres Sussex Co Golf Union 1984-; Freeman: City of London 1968, Worshipful Co of Curriers (Master 1986); memb: Law Soc 1961-, IOD 1979-; *Books* Accounting for Solicitors (1965), Some Aspects of the Family Company (with M J Long, 1979); *Recreations* golf, reading, after dinner speaking; *Style—* Derek Sparrow, Esq; 12 Sackville Gardens, Hove, East Sussex BN3 4GH (☎ 0273 773988); Donne Mileham & Haddock, 42 Frederick Place, Brighton, E Sussex BN1 1AT (☎ 0273 29833, fax 0273 739764)

SPARROW, Sir John; s of Richard Albert Sparrow, and Winifred Sparrow; *b* 4 June 1933; *Educ* Stationers' Company's Sch, LSE (BSc Econ); *m* 1967, Cynthia Naomi Whitehouse; *Career* with Rawlinson & Hunter CAs 1954-59, Ford Motor Co 1960, AEI Hotpoint Ltd 1960-63, United Leasing Corporation 1963-64, Morgan Grenfell 1964-88; dir: Federated Chemicals (formerly Greeff Chemicals) 1969-78 (chm 1974-

78), Morgan Grenfell & Co Ltd 1970-82 and 1983-85, Harris Lebus 1973-79, United Gas Industries 1974-82 (dep chm 1981-82), Gas and Oil Acreage 1975-78, Tioxide Group 1977-78; chm: Wormald International Holdings (formerly Mather & Platt) 1979-81, Head of Central Policy Review Staff 1982-83; dir Morgan Grenfell Group plc (formerly Morgan Grenfell Holdings Ltd) 1971-82 and 1983-88; chm: Morgan Grenfell Asset Management Ltd 1985-88, Morgan Grenfell Laurie Holdings Ltd 1985-88; dir: Coalite Group plc 1974-82 and 1984-89, Short Bros plc 1984-89 (dep chm 1985-89), ASW Holdings plc 1987-, National & Provincial Building Society 1989- (memb London Advsy Bd 1986-89), Regalian Properties plc 1990-; Cons cncllr in Enfield 1961-62; memb: Peterborough Development Corporation 1981-88; chm: Process Plant EDC 1984-85, Ctee of Enquiry into the Future of the Nat Stud 1985, National Stud 1988-, Universities Superannuation Scheme Ltd 1988- Horserace Betting Levy Bd 1991-; vice chm Govrs LSE 1984-; hon fell Wolfson Coll Cambridge 1987; FCA 1957; kt 1984; *Recreations* reading, walking, racing, cricket, crosswords; *Clubs* MCC; *Style—* Sir John Sparrow; 48-50 Cannon St, London EC4N 6JJ

SPATHIS, Dr Gerassimos Spyros (Memos); s of Spyros Andrew Spathis (d 1975), of Cephalonia, Greece, and Olga, *née* Georgopoulos; *b* 20 April 1935; *Educ* The King's Sch Canterbury, Exeter Coll Oxford (MA, DM), Guy's Hosp London; *m* 3 June 1967, Maria, da of Demetrius Messinezy, of Tinos and Geveva; 2 da (Anna b 1969, Sonia b 1971); *Career* physician St Helier Hosp Carshalton 1972, hon physician Royal Marsden Hosp Sutton, hon sr lectr St George's Hosp Med Sch, sub dean St Helier Hosp; vice chm SW Thames RHA 1989- (memb 1984-), memb Cncl NAHA 1989-; FRCP 1977, DPMSA; *Recreations* hill walking, photography; *Style—* Dr Memos Spathis; St Anthony's Hospital, London Rd, N Cheam (☎ 081 337 6691)

SPAWFORTH, David Meredith; s of Lawrence Spawforth (d 1965), and Gwendoline, *née* Meredith; *b* 2 Jan 1938; *Educ* Silcoates Sch, Hertford Coll Oxford (MA); *m* 17 Aug 1963, Yvonne Mary, da of Roy Gude (d 1987); 1 s (Graham David b 22 Dec 1964), 1 da (Fiona Jane b 20 Sept 1968); *Career* asst master Winchester Coll 1961-64, house master Wellington Coll 1967-80 (asst master 1964-), headmaster Merchiston Castle Sch Edinburgh 1981-; govr of various schs, memb Br Atlantic Educn Ctee; memb HMC; *Recreations* walking, theatre, France; *Clubs* East India; *Style—* David Spawforth, Esq; Headmaster's House, Merchiston Castle Sch, Colimton, Edinburgh (☎ 031 441 3468, 031 441 1722)

SPEAIGHT, Anthony Hugh; s of George Victor Speaight, of Kew Gardens, Surrey, and Mary Olive, *née* Mudd; *b* 31 July 1948; *Educ* St Benedict's Sch Ealing, Lincoln Coll Oxford (MA); *Career* called to the Bar Middle Temple 1973; elected memb Gen Cncl of the Bar 1987-, memb Bar Cncl Working Pty on Televising Cts 1988-; nat chm Fedn of Cons Students 1972-73, chm Youth Bd of the Euro Movement (UK) 1974-75, dep chm Cons Gp for Europe 1977; Freeman City of London; Schuman Silver medal (awarded by FVS Fndn of the FDR 1976); *Books* The Law of Defective Premises (with G Stone, 1982), The Architects Journal Legal Handbook (jtly, 1985-90); *Recreations* fox-hunting, acting in and writing reviews; *Clubs* Carlton, Hurlingham; *Style—* Anthony Speaight, Esq; 83 Napier Court, Ranelagh Gardens, London SW6 (☎ 071 736 1842); Cliff Cottage, Gutch Common, Semley, Shaftesbury, Dorset; 12 King's Bench Walk, Temple, London EC4 (☎ 071 583 0811, fax 071 583 7228)

SPEAR, Prof Walter Eric; s of David Spear (d 1945), of London, and Eva, *née* Reineck (d 1978); *b* 20 Jan 1921; *Educ* Musterschule Frankfurt Main, Univ of London (BSc, PhD, DSc); *m* 15 Dec 1952, Hilda Doris, da of John Charles King (d 1985), of London; 2 da (Gillian b 1961, Kathryn b 1963); *Career* lectr in physics (later reader) Univ of Leicester 1953, Harris Prof of physics Univ of Dundee 1968-; author of numerous res papers on electronic and transport properties in crystalline solids, liquids and amorphous semi-conductors; Europhysics Prize of Euro Physical Soc 1977, Max Born Medal and Prize Inst of Physics and German Physical Soc 1977, Makdougall-Brisbane Medal of RSE 1981, Maxwell Premium of IEE 1981 and 1982, Rank Prize for Optoelectronics 1988; Mott Award 1989, Rumford Medal of RS 1990; FInstP 1962, FRSE 1972, FRS 1980; *Recreations* music, literature; *Style—* Prof Walter Spear, FRS, FRSE; 323 Blackness Rd, Dundee DD2 1SH (☎ 0382 67649); Carnegie Lab of Physics, The University of Dundee, Dundee DD1 4HN (☎ 0382 23181 ext 4563, fax 0382 201604, telex 76293 ULDUND G)

SPEARING, Prof Anthony Colin; s of Frederick Spearing, and Gertrude, *née* Calnin; *b* 31 Jan 1936; *Educ* Alleyn's Sch Dulwich, Jesus Coll Cambridge (BA, MA); *m* 1961, Elizabeth; 1 s, 1 da; *Career* res on Piers Plowman under supervision of CS Lewis and Elizabeth Salter 1957-60; Univ of Cambridge: WM Tapp fell Gonville & Caius Coll 1959-60, asst lectr in English 1960-64, supernumerary fell Gonville and Caius Coll 1960; Queens' Coll: official fell 1960-67, asst dir of studies in English 1960-67, lectr in English 1964-85, dir of studies in English 1967-85, sec Faculty of English 1970-71, chm Degree Ctee Faculty of English 1977-79, reader in Medieval English Lit 1985-87, chm Faculty of English 1986-87, life fell Queen's Coll 1987-; Univ of Virginia: visiting prof of English 1979-80 and 1984, Center for Advanced Studies 1987-89, prof of English 1987-89, William R Kenan prof of English 1989-; external examiner: Univ of Bristol 1974, MA in Medieval Studies Univ of York 1974-76; Studentship Selection Ctee UK Dept of Education and Science 1976-79, William Matthews lectr Birkbeck Coll Univ of London 1983-84; visiting lectr at numerous univs in Britain, Europe, Canada and USA; *Books* Criticism and Medieval Poetry (1964, 2 edn 1972), An Introduction to Chaucer (with Maurice Hussey and James Winny, 1965), The Gawain Poet: A Critical Study (1970), Chaucer: Troilus and Criseyde (1976), Medieval Dream-Poetry (1976), Medieval to Renaissance in English Poetry (1985), Readings in Medieval Poetry (1987); contrib to numerous learned jls; *Style—* Prof A C Spearing; Department of English, Wilson Hall, University of Virginia, Charlottesville, Va 22903, USA

SPEARING, (David) Nicholas; s of George David Spearing, of Caterham, Surrey, and Josephine Mary, *née* Newbould; *b* 4 May 1954; *Educ* Caterham Sch, Hertford Coll Oxford (BA, MA); *m* 20 Sept 1980, Annemarie, da of Ernest Thomas John Gatford (d 1989), of Smallfield, Surrey; 2 da (Laura b 1982, Elizabeth b 1987), 1 s (James b 1989); *Career* articled clerk Gordon Dadds & Co 1976-78, ptnr Freshfields 1984 (admitted slr 1978); chm Law Soc Slrs' Euro Gp; memb: Jt Law Soc, Bar Competition Law Working Pty; memb City of London Slrs Co; *Books* Encyclopedia of Forms and Precedents (1985), Articles in Professional Journals; *Recreations* reading, tennis, snooker; *Style—* Nicholas Spearing, Esq; The Coach House, St Mary's Abbey, Woolmer Hill, Haslemere, Surrey GU27 1QA (☎ 0428 653 210, fax 0428 661 570); Whitefriars, 65 Fleet Street, London EC4Y 1HS (☎ 071 936 4000, fax 071 248 3487/8/9)

SPEARING, Nigel John; MP (Lab) Newham S 1974-; s of T A E Spearing, of Hammersmith; *b* 8 Oct 1930; *Educ* Latymer Upper Sch, St Catharine's Coll Cambridge; *m* 1956, Wendy, da of Percy Newman, of Newport; 1 s, 2 da; *Career* Nat Serv RCS ranks and cmmn 1950-52; teacher Wandsworth Sch 1956-68, dir Thameside R & D Group 1968-69; housemaster Elliott Sch Putney 1969-70; Parly candidate (Lab) Warwick and Leamington 1964, co-opted GLC Planning Ctee, regained Acton for Lab 1970 (MP until 1974); pres Socialist Environment and Resources Assoc 1977-86, chm Anti-Common Market Campaign 1977-83; memb Select Ctees on: Procedure 1975-79, Overseas Devpt 1972-74 and 1977-79, Sound Bdcasting 1978-83, Foreign Affrs 1979-87, Euro Legislation 1979- (chm 1983-); memb Bd Christian Aid 1987-; *Style—* Nigel Spearing, Esq, MP; House of Commons, London SW1

SPEARING, Roger Edward; s of Edward George Spearing (d 1986), and Joan Audrey, *née* Greaves, of Court House, Park Rd, Aldeburgh, Suffolk; *b* 19 Feb 1946; *Educ* Felsted; *m* 24 July 1971, Lindy Frances, da of Walter Freeman (Mickie), of 56 The Bowls, Chigwell, Essex; 3 da (Emma b 1976, Charlotte (twin) b 1976, Victoria b 1982); *Career* CA; Chalmers Impey & Co 1964-72, qualified 1968, tech mangr Save & Prosper Group Ltd 1972-79, co fndr and dir Sun Life Unit Services Ltd 1980-89; FCA 1979 (ACA 1968); *Recreations* equestrian activities; *Style—* Roger Spearing, Esq; Hastingwood Farm, Hastingwood, Essex CM17 9JX (☎ 0279 22718); The Water Tower, Westgate, Thorpeness, nr Aldeburgh, Suffolk

SPEARMAN, Sir Alexander Young Richard Mainwaring Spearman; 5 Bt (UK 1840) of Hanwell, Middlesex; s of Sir Alexander Bowyer Spearman, 4 Bt (d 1977); *b* 3 Feb 1969; *Heir* unc, Dr Richard Spearman; *Style—* Sir Alexander Spearman, Bt; Windwards, Klein Constantia Rd, Constantia, Cape Town, 7800, S Africa

SPEARMAN, Lady (Diana Josephine); da of Col Sir (Albert) Lambert Ward, 1 Bt, CVO, DSO, TD (d 1956); *b* 1921; *m* 1951, as his 2 w, Sir Alexander Cadwaller Mainwaring Spearman (s of late Com Alexander Young Crawshay Mainwaring Spearman, RN, himself half-bro of 2 Bt; d 1982); 4 s, 1 da; *Style—* Lady Spearman; The Old Rectory, Sarratt, Herts

SPEARMAN, Richard; s of Clement Spearman, CBE, of 56 Riverview Gardens, Barnes, London, and Olwen Regina, *née* Morgan; *b* 19 Jan 1953; *Educ* Bedales Sch, King's Coll Cambridge (BA, MA), Coll of Law; *m* 30 April 1983, Alexandra Elizabeth, da of Bryan A Harris, of Churchills, Sidmouth, Devon; 2 da (Olivia b 6 July 1985, Annabel b 11 Oct 1987); *Career* called to the Bar Middle Temple 1977; *Books* Sale of Goods Litigation (with FA Philpott, 1983); *Recreations* tennis, skiing; *Clubs* Hurlingham; *Style—* Richard Spearman, Esq; 62 Clonmel Rd, London SW6 5BJ; 10 South Square, Gray's Inn, London WC1R 5EU (☎ 071 242 2902, fax 071 831 2686)

SPEARMAN, Dr Richard Ian Campbell; s of Sir Alexander Young Spearman, 3 Bt (d 1959), and Dorothy Catherine (d 1982); hp of nephew, Sir Alexander Spearman, 5 Bt; *b* 14 Aug 1926; *Educ* Clayesmore Sch, Birkbeck Coll London (BSc), UCL (PhD, DSc); *Career* biologist; MRC staff 1957-70, res conslt 1970-, hon sr lectr UCL 1970-; memb: Soc of Experimental Biology, Int Cmmn for Avian Anatomical Nomenclature 1971-; chm Integument Sub-Ctee 1985, fndr memb European Soc for Dermatological Res 1971-, memb Mgmnt Ctee London Skin Club 1977-81, pres Euro Soc for Comparative Skin Biology 1978-1982, chm Int Cmmn on Skin Biology of Int Union for Biological Sciences 1979-82, memb Mgmnt Ctee Biological Cncl 1980-, memb Royal Soc and Inst of Biology Jt Ctee on Biological Educn 1980-86, ed Biological Cncl Conference Guide 1981-89 (and Handbook 1989-); CBiol, FIBiol, scientific FZS, FLS (vice-pres 1977-79); author of over 80 research papers, reviews and books, mainly on cell biology, skin biology (especially keratinization) and ornithology; *Books* Birds Ecology and World Distribution, The Integument, Comparative Biology of Skin, The Skin of Vertebrates, The Biochemistry of Skin Disease; *Recreations* travel, appreciation of ballet, music; *Style—* Dr Richard Spearman; Oaks Bungalow, Oaks Avenue, London SE19 1QY (☎ 081 670 5488)

SPECTOR, Prof Roy Geoffrey; s of Paul Spector, and Esther, *née* Cohen; *b* 27 Aug 1931; *Educ* Univ of Leeds (MB ChB, MD), Univ of London (PhD, Dip Biochemistry); *m* 1960 (m dis 1979), Eva Freeman; 2 s (David Marshall b 1960, Colin Richard b 1964), 1 da (Gillian Sarah b 1962); *Career* sr lectr Paediatric Res Unit Guy's Hosp 1961-66 (former lectr), prof of applied pharmacology United Medical Schools of Guy's and St Thomas' Hosps 1967-89 (former reader, sub dean for admissions 1975-89), visiting prof of clinical pharmacology West China Med Univ Sichuan 1986-87, emeritus prof Univ of London 1989-; vice chm Br Univs' Film and Video Cncl 1976-87, memb Dartford and Gravesham Health Authy 1988-89; memb RSM; FRCP, FRCPath; *Books* Psychiatry - Common Drug Treatments (1984), The Nerve Cell (1986), Textbook of Clinical Pharmacology (1986), Aids to Clinical Pharmacology (1989), Drugs People Use (1989), Therapeutics In Dentistry (1989); *Recreations* music, walking; *Style—* Prof Roy Spector; 60 Crescent Drive, Petts Wood, Orpington, Kent BR5 1BD (☎ 0689 875885); Drug Research Unit, Guy's Hospital, Newcomen St, London SE1 1YR (☎ 071 403 3756/7, fax 071 403 4409)

SPECULAND, Bernard; s of Cyril Speculand (d 1953), and Hannah, *née* Shelower; *b* 26 Aug 1949; *Educ* City of Norwich GS, Univ of Bristol (BDS, MDS); *m* 19 Dec 1975, Christine, da of Alec Turner; 1 s (Alex b 1982), 2 da (Caroline b 1977, Mary b 1980); *Career* sr registrar: Royal Adelaide Hosp 1977, Bristol Royal Infirmary, Bristol Dental Hosp and Frenchay Hosp 1978-85; conslt oral and maxillo-facial surgn Dudley Rd Hosp Birmingham 1985; fell BAOMS, FRACDS 1977, FDSRCS 1975, FFDRCSI 1975; *Books* The Mouth and Peri-Oral Tissues in Health and Disease (contrib, 1989); *Recreations* squash, running, sailing; *Style—* Bernard Speculand, Esq; Dept of Oral Surgery & Orthodontics, Dudley Rd Hospital, Birmingham B18 7QH

SPEDDING, Charles; s of Joseph Bryce Spedding, of Durham, and Mabel, *née* Todd; *b* 19 May 1952; *Educ* Durham Sch, Sunderland Poly (BSc); *m* 9 Aug 1986, Jane Elizabeth, da of James Halliwell, of Orrell, Wigan; 1 s (Joseph James b 25 May 1988), 1 da (Catherine Victoria b 22 March 1990); *Career* athlete; winner London Marathon 1984, Bronze medallist Marathon Olympic Games 1984, sixth Marathon Olympic Games 1988, English record holder Marathon since 1985; life memb Gateshead Harriers, pres Valli Harriers; *Style—* Charles Spedding, Esq; Lowes Financial Management, Holmwood House, Newcastle NE2 1TL (☎ 091 281 8811)

SPEDDING, Prof Colin Raymond William; CBE (1988); s of late Rev Robert K Spedding, and Ilynn, *née* Bannister; *b* 22 March 1925; *Educ* Univ of London (BSc, MSc, PhD, DSc); *m* 6 Sept 1952, Betty Noreen (d 1988), da of the late A H George; 2 s (Peter George b 1954, d 1958, Geoffrey Robert b 1957), 1 da (Lucilla Mary (Mrs Weston) b 1960); *Career* Sub Lt RNVR 1943-46; Grassland Res Inst 1949-75 (dep dir 1972-75); Reading Univ: visiting prof then pt/t prof Dept of Agric and Hort 1970-75, prof of agric systems Dept of Agric 1970-90, head Dept of Agric and Hort 1975-83, dir Centre for Agric Strategy 1981-90, dean Faculty of Agric and Food 1983-86, pro vice chllr 1986-90, emeritus prof 1990-; dir and dep chm Lands Improvement Group Ltd; dir: Croxden Horticultural Products Ltd, Centre for Economic and Environmental Devpt; pres: Euro Assoc of Animal Prodn Study Cmmn on Sheep and Goat Prodn 1970-76, Br Soc of Animal Prodn 1979-80; ed Agricultural Systems 1976-88, vice chm Prog Ctee Int Livestock Centre for Africa Addis Ababa 1980-83 (memb 1976-80); chm: Bd of UK Register of Organic Food Standards 1982-, Farm Animal Welfare Cncl 1988-, Nat Resources Policy Gp Inst of Biology 1988-, Apple and Pear Res Cncl 1989-, Scientific Advsy Panel of World Soc for Protection of Animals 1989, Bd of Dirs Kintail Land Res Fndn 1990; vice pres Inst of Biology 1987-; memb: Governing Body Inst of Grassland and Environmental Res 1987, Food Safety Policy Gp Inst of Biology 1990; conslt dir Centre for Agric Strategy, patron Small Farmers' Assoc, vice patron Fruit Culture Tst; awards: Canadian Inst of Agric Recognition award 1971, George Hedley Meml award 1971, Wooldridge Meml lectr and medallist (BVA) 1982; FZS 1962, FIBiol 1967, CBiol 1984, FRASE 1984, FIHort 1986, FRAgS 1986, FRSA 1988; *Books* Sheep Production and Grazing Management (2 edn, 1970), Grassland Ecology (1971), Grasses and Legumes in British Agriculture (ed with E C Diekmahns, 1972)

The Biology of Agricultural Systems (1975), Vegetable Productivity (ed, 1981), Biological Efficiency in Agriculture (with J M Walsingham and A M Hoxey, 1981), Fream's Agriculture (ed, 1983), An Introduction to Agricultural Systems (2 edn, 1988); *Clubs* Athenaeum, Farmers'; *Style—* Prof Colin Spedding; Vine Cottage, Orchard Rd, Hurst, Berks, RG10 0SD (☎ 0734 341 771)

SPEDDING, David Rolland; CVO (1984), OBE (1980); s of Lt-Col Carlisle Montague Rodney Spedding, OBE, TD (d 1977), and Gwynfydd Joan Llewellyn; *b* 7 March 1943; *Educ* Sherborne, Hertford Coll Oxford (MA); *m* 7 March 1970, Gillian Leslie, da of Charles Blackadder Kinnear (d 1958); 2 s (Richard b 1971, Christopher b 1975); *Career* HM Diplomatic Service; third sec FO 1967; second sec 1969: Mecas 1968, Beirut 1970, Santiago 1972; first sec FCO 1974: Abu Dhabi 1978, FCO 1981; cnsllr: Amman 1983, FCO 1987-; *Recreations* golf, tennis, reading, walking; *Clubs* Huntercombe Golf; *Style—* David R Spedding, CVO, OBE; c/o FCO, King Charles Street, London SW1A 2AH

SPEED, Gary Andrew; s of Roger Speed, of 8 Courtland Drive, Aston Park, Deeside, Clwyd, and Carol, *née* Huxely; *b* 8 Sept 1969; *Educ* Deeside HS, Hawarden HS; *Career* professional football player (midfield); Leeds United FC: joined from school 1986, first team debut v Oldham Athletic 1989, 60 appearances (10 goals); 6 Welsh Youth Cups, 2 U-21 Cups, 4 full Internationals; *Recreations* golf, snooker, cricket, fishing, films, tv, fashion; *Style—* Gary Speed, Esq; Leeds United FC, Elland Road, Leeds, West Yorkshire LS11 OES (☎ 0532 716037)

SPEED, George Raymond (Mac); s of William George Hamilton Speed (d 1975), of Ravensdale, Long Eaton, Nottingham, and Dorothy Amelia, *née* Sutton (d 1964); *b* 15 April 1925; *Educ* Long Eaton County Secdy Sch, Univ of London; *m* 15 May 1954, Helena Christina (Helen), da of Joseph Fallowfield (d 1948), of 2 Bearton Rd, Hitchin, Herts; 1 s (Martin b 1958), 1 da (Madeleine b 1961); *Career* TA, REME 1943-47; Midland Bank Group 1941-85 (supervisory credit controller 1978-85); dir: Richmond Finance Ltd 1977-80, Tririding Finance Ltd 1977-80, Forward Trust Car Leasing Ltd 1977-84, Roadmaster Finance Ltd 1977-84; underwriting memb Lloyd's; district memb TOCH, auditor and memb Exec Ctee Int Camellia Soc, hon divnl sec SSAFA; chm Cyclamen Soc; memb: Cncl Royal Nat Rose Soc, Royal Soc of St George, Int Shakespeare Soc, RHS, Nat Tst for Scotland, Econ Res Cncl, CABE; involved locally with: Nat Tst, RSPB; Freeman City of London 1977, Liveryman Worshipful Co of Feltmakers 1977; MIL 1945, FBSC 1949, FCIB 1965, FBIM 1975, FLS 1984; *Recreations* horticulture, photography, music; *Style—* G R Speed, Esq; High Trees, Oldhill Wood, Studham, Bedfordshire (☎ 0582 872 293)

SPEED, Hugh David McConnachie; s of Hugh Neill Speed (d 1982), of Newcastle upon Tyne, and Mary Bell McConnachie (d 1975); *b* 28 Sept 1936; *Educ* George Watson's Boys Coll Edinburgh, Univ of Edinburgh (BSc), Univ of Glasgow (MEng); *m* 14 July 1960, Joan, da of Robert Walker Forsyth (d 1987), of Edinburgh; 3 s (Neil b 28 Sept 1963, Mark b 25 Aug 1965, Paul b 23 Dec 1969); *Career* RAF 1960-63: Flt Lt Airfield Construction Branch, serv Cyprus; sr engr (later assoc ptnr) Crouch & Hogg conslt engrs Glasgow 1963-71, md Newcastle & Gateshead Water Co 1986- (chief engr 1971-86); chm NSPCC Newcastle Branch 1986- (pres 1989-), memb Ctee CBI Northern Region; former chm: BIM Northumbria, BIM NE Branches Area Ctee; memb Cncl 'Water Aid', govr Newcastle Prep Sch; FICE 1972, FIWEM (vice pres IWEM), CBIM 1988; *Recreations* sailing, hill walking, gardening; *Clubs* Northern Counties, Northumberland Golf; *Style—* Hugh Speed, Esq; Montana, 86 Moorside North, Newcastle upon Tyne, NE4 9DU; Newcastle and Gateshead Water Company, PO Box 10, Allendale Road, Newcastle upon Tyne, NE6 2SW (☎ 091 265 4144, fax 091 276 6612, telex 537681/2 (NGWC)

SPEED, (Herbert) Keith; RD (1967), MP (C) Ashford 1974-; s of Herbert Victor Speed (d 1971), of Bletchley, Bucks, and Alice Dorothy Barbara, *née* Mumford; *b* 11 March 1934; *Educ* Bedford Modern, RNC Dartmouth, RNC Greenwich; *m* 14 Oct 1961, Peggy Voss, da of Cedric Cyril Clarke (d 1983); 3 s (Herbert Mark Jeffrey b 1963, Crispin Nicholas b 1965 d 1967, Nicholas William b 1968), 1 da (Emma Jane b 1970); *Career* offr RN (incl Korean War) 1947-57, Lt Cdr RNR; sales mangr Amos (Electronics) 1957-60, mktg mangr Plysu Products 1960-65, CRD 1965-68; MP (C) Meriden 1968-74, asst govt whip 1970-71, lord cmmr Treasy 1971-72; Parly under sec: Environment 1972-74, Def (RN) 1979-81; oppn spokesman: Environment 1975-77, Home Affrs 1977-79; Parly conslt to Professional Assoc Teachers 1982-, memb Parly Assembly Cncl of Euro and Western Euro Union 1987-; chm: Westminster Communications Gp 1983-, Machine Tool Trades Assoc 1984-; dir Folkestone Water Co 1986-; patron: E Ashford Rural Tst, Ashford Branch BDA; memb Governing Cncl and Exec Ctee SPCK; *Books* Blueprint for Britain (1964), Sea Change (1982); *Recreations* classical music, opera, reading; *Clubs* Garrick; *Style—* Keith Speed, Esq, RD, MP; House of Commons, London SW1 1AA (☎ 071 219 4516)

SPEED, Sir Robert William Arney; CB (1946), QC (1963); s of Sir Edwin Arney Speed (d 1941), of Remenham House, Henley-on-Thames, and Ada Frances, *née* Ross (d 1953); *b* 18 July 1905; *Educ* Rugby, Trinity Coll Cambridge (MA); *m* 25 April 1929, Phyllis, da of Rev Philip Armitage (d 1960), of Farne, Nettlebed, Oxon; 1 s (John b 30 March 1934), 1 da (Sarah b 5 April 1931, d 24 Aug 1976); *Career* called to the Bar Inner Temple 1928, princ asst slr to HM Procurator Gen and Treasy 1945-48, slr BOT 1948-60, bencher 1961, counsel to the Speaker 1960-80; kt 1954; *Recreations* golf; *Clubs* United Oxford and Cambridge, Hon Co of Edinburgh Golfers, Huntercombe Golf; *Style—* Sir Robert Speed, CB, QC; Upper Culham, Wargrave, Reading, Berks RG10 8NR (☎ 0491 574271)

SPEELMAN, Jonkheer Sir Cornelius Jacob; 8 Bt (E 1686); s of Jonkheer Sir Cornelius Speelman, 7 Bt (d 1949); *b* 17 March 1917; *Educ* Perth Univ Western Australia; *m* 1972, Julia Mona Le Besque (d 1978); *Heir* none; *Career* formerly in Education Dept Royal Dutch Army, former master of Geelong GS and Clifton Coll, tutor Exeter Tutorial Coll; British subject; *Style—* Jonkheer Sir Cornelius Speelman, Bt; The Nab House, Flat 5, Beach House Road, Bembridge, IOW

SPEIGHT, Stanley Lester; OBE (1976); s of Clifford Speight (d 1945), and Elizabeth Winifred, *née* Raynes (d 1974); *b* 20 Dec 1920; *Educ* Firth Park GS, Sheffield Tech Coll; *m* 7 June 1947, Barbara Joan, da of John Robert Alborough (d 1955); 1 s (Stephen Lester b 1955), 1 da (Elizabeth Anne b 1958); *Career* Capt RA, served Europe and SE Asia 1939-46; chm Neepsend plc (Engrg Gp) 1972-89; chm Sheffield Health Authy 1982-90; vice pres Assoc Br C of C; Master Worshipful Co of Cutlers in Hallamshire 1977-78, Freeman Sheffield and City of London, Liveryman Worshipful Co of Marketors; FIEx, FCIM, CBIM; *Recreations* golf; *Clubs* Army and Navy, Sickleholme Golf; *Style—* Stanley Speight, Esq, OBE; The Limes, Froggatt Lane, Froggatt, Derbys S30 1ZA (☎ 0433 31023); Neepsend plc, Lancaster St, Sheffield S3 8AQ (☎ 0742 723231, fax 0742 768628, telex 54140)

SPEIR, Sir Rupert Malise; 3 s of Lt-Col Guy Speir (whose mother was Hon Emily Gifford, 3 da of 2nd Baron Gifford), by his w Mary (6 da of John Fletcher of Saltoun, JP, DL, whose w Bertha was a member of the Talbot family of Lacock Abbey & hence a connection of William Henry Fox Talbot, the pioneer of photography); *b* 10 Sept 1910; *Educ* Eton, Pembroke Coll Cambridge; *Career* served WWII Intelligence Corps (Lt-Col 1945); chm: Matthew Hall & Co until 1982 (remains as non-exec dir), Common Bros; dir J Henry Schroder Wagg, Lloyds Bank N Regnl Bd; slr 1936; MP (C) Hexham 1951-66, PPS to: Min State FO & Parly Sec CRO 1956-59, Parly & Financial Sec Admiralty & Civil Lord of the Admiralty 1952-56; fought (C) Linlithgow 1945, Leek 1950; vice pres Keep Britain Tidy Gp; kt 1964; *Style—* Sir Rupert Speir; Birtley Hall, Hexham, Northumberland (☎ 0660 30275); 240 Cranmer Court, Sloane Ave, SW3 (☎ 071 589 2057)

SPEKE, (Ian) Benjamin; s of Col Neil Hanning Reed Speke, MC, TD, of Aydon White House, Corbridge, Northumberland, and Averil Allgood, *née* Straker; *b* 12 March 1950; *Educ* Eton; *m* 30 July 1983, Ailsa Elizabeth, da of Matthew Hall Fenwick, of New Onstead, Gt Bavingon, Capheaton, Newcastle upon Tyne; 1 s (Toby b 1989), 2 da (Zara b 1988, Thea b 1990); *Career* 9/12 Royal Lancers (Prince of Wales) 1968-72, Northumberland Hussars (Queen's Own Yeo) 1974-87; Pinchin Denny 1974-77, Hoare Govett Equity sales 1977-80, ptnr Wise Speke & Co 1980-87, dir Wise Speke Ltd 1987-; memb Int Stock Exchange 1980; *Recreations* field sports; *Clubs* Pratt's, Cavalry & Guards, Northern Cos; *Style—* Benjamin Speke, Esq; Thornbrough High House, Corbridge, Northumberland NE45 5PR (☎ 0434 633080); Wise Speke Ltd, Commercial Union House, 39 Pilgrim St, Newcastle upon Tyne NE1 6RQ (☎ 091 261 1266, telex 53429)

SPEKE, Lt-Col Neil Hanning Reed; MC (1942, Bar 1945), DL (Northumberland 1971); only s of Capt Herbert Speke, OBE, JP (himself n of John Speke, the African explorer, who discovered Lake Victoria and the source of the Nile and (with Sir Richard Burton) Lake Tanganyika); *b* 11 May 1917; *Educ* Eton, Magdalene Coll Cambridge; *m* 1948, Averil Allgood, da of Maj John Straker; 2 s (Ian b 1950, Charles b 1960), 2 da (Rosalind b 1951, Clayre b 1955); *Career* Nat Serv cmmnd into 12 Royal Lancers 1937; serv WWII: NW Europe, M East, N Africa, Italy; Maj 1942, resigned 1948, Northumberland Hussars 1950, Lt-Col 1955; one of HM's Body Guard of Hon Corps of Gentlemen-at-Arms 1967-87; High Sheriff Northumberland 1959; Hon Col Northumberland Hussars Sqdn Queen's Own Yeo 1974, Queen's Own Yeo 1975-79; *Style—* Lt-Col Neil Speke, MC, DL; Aydon White House, Corbridge, Northumberland (☎ 0434 632248)

SPELLER, Antony (Tony); MP (C) N Devon 1979-; s of late John and Ethel Speller; *b* 12 June 1929; *Educ* Exeter Sch, Univ of London (BSc), Univ of Exeter (BA); *m* 1960, Maureen R McLellan; 1 s, 1 da; *Career* Maj TA, Devonshire & Dorset Regt Regular Serv 1951-53; worked in Nigeria 1953-62; chm Copyshops of SW England 1963-; cncllr Exeter CC 1963-74, contested (C) N Devon Oct 1974, vice-chm E Devon Water Bd; memb Energy Select Ctee 1982-; chm: Parly Alternative Energy Liaison Ctee 1983-, West County Cons MP's 1983-87, Cons W Africa Ctee; chm Euro-Speedy Printing Centres (UK) Ltd 1990-; pres Catering Industs Liaison Ctee, fell Hotel Catering Institutional Mgmnt Assoc, hon fell Euro Catering Assoc; *Clubs* Carlton, North Devon Yacht; *Style—* Tony Speller Esq, MP; House of Commons, London SW1 0AA (☎ 071 219 4589, constituency office: Barnstaple 0271 45617)

SPELLER, Bruce C N; s of Maj-Gen Norman Henry Speller, CB, of Church Gate, London SW6, and Barbara Eleanor, *née* Earle, JP; *b* 30 Jan 1953; *Educ* Tonbridge, Christ Church Oxford (MA); *m* 3 Sept 1988, Sarah Mary, *née* Edney; 1 da (Georgina Elizabeth b 1989); *Career* called to the Bar Inner Temple 1976; *Recreations* gardening; *Style—* Bruce Speller, Esq; 7 Bellevue Rd, Barnes, London SW13 (☎ 081 876 2828); Friars Halt, Winchelsea, E Sussex (☎ 0797 226325); 1 Harcourt Bldgs, Temple, London EC4 (☎ 071 353 0375)

SPELMAN, Kenneth John; s of Patrick Joseph Spelman, of Lantern Court, Christchurch Rd, Winchester, and Madge, *née* Simmons; *b* 25 April 1934; *Educ* Brighton Tech Coll (Dip Eng Civil and Structural), Birmingham Coll of Art and Design (Dip TP); *Career* planning offr/borough devpt offr Epsom & Ewell BC 1971-75; city planning offr and engr Gloucester CC 1975-78; principal: KJ Spelman & Assoc, Town Planning & Property Devpt Consultants 1979-; dir Pauntley Properties Ltd 1985-, ptnr The Naturmed Ptnrship 1985-; chm Natural Health Network 1986-; memb: Business Network, Financial Initiative, Br Soc of Dowsers, Anthroposophical Soc, Theosophical Soc, IOD, Medicina Alternativa, Royal Archaeological Inst, Radionic Assoc; FRTPI, FICE, FBIM, FIAS; MIHT; *Recreations* archaeology, walking, reading; *Style—* Kenneth Spelman, Esq; Silver Birches, Private Rd, Rodborough Common, Stroud, Gloucestershire GL5 5BT (☎ 0453 873446/873668, fax 0453 878588, telex 045 383 437105)

SPENCE, Prof Alastair Andrew; s of James Glendinning Spence (d 1964), of Doonfoot, Ayr, and Margaret, *née* Macdonald (d 1986); *b* 18 Sept 1936; *Educ* Ayr Acad, Univ of Glasgow (MB ChB, MD); *m* Maureen Isobel, da of David Aitchison (d 1948), of Prestwick, Ayrshire; 2 s (Andrew b 15 May 1965, Stuart b 17 Sept 1966); *Career* prof and head Univ Dept of Anaesthesia Western Infirmary Glasgow 1969-84, prof of anaesthetics Univ of Edinburgh 1984-; vice pres Coll of Anaesthetists; chm: Bd Br Jl of Anaesthesia, UK Anaesthetic Res Soc; fell Coll of Anaesthetists 1963; *Books* Respiratory Monitoring in Intensive Care (1982), Norris and Campbell's Anaesthesia, Resuscitation and Intensive Care (7 edn, 1989); *Recreations* golf, gardening; *Clubs* Caledonian, London; *Style—* Prof Alastair Spence; Harewood, Kilmacolm PA13 4HX; 3-9 Dun-Ard Gdns, Edinburgh EH9 2HZ (☎ 031 667 0231); Dept of Anaesthetics, Royal Infirmary, Edinburgh EH3 9YW (☎ 031 229 2727, fax 031 229 0437)

SPENCE, Christopher John; s of Brig Ian Fleming Morris Spence, OBE, MC, TD, ADC (d 1966), of London, and Ruth, *née* Peacock (d 1961); *b* 4 June 1937; *Educ* Marlborough; *m* 1, 1960 (m dis 1968), Merle Aurelia, er da of Sir Leonard Ropner, 1 Bt, MC, TD (d 1977); 1 s (Jeremy b 1964 (d 1982)), 1 da (Miranda (Mrs Patrick Barran) b 1963); m 2, 1970, Susan, da of Brig Michael Morley, MBE (d 1990), of Wiltshire; 1 s (Jonathan b 1975), 1 da (Lara b 1972); *Career* 2 Lt 10 Royal Hussars (PWO) 1955-57, Royal Wilts Yeo 1957-66; memb of London Stock Exchange 1959-78, PK English Tst Co Ltd (md 1978-86, dep chm and chief exec 1986-, merchant banker); chm: Tyndall Hldgs plc, Wills Gp plc; *Recreations* racing, shooting, golf; *Clubs* Jockey, Cavalry and Guards', City of London, Swinley Forest Golf; *Style—* Christopher Spence, Esq; Chieveley Manor, Newbury, Berks (☎ 0635 248208); 18A Maunsel Street, London SW1 (☎ 071 828 1484); 12 Carthusian Street, London EC1 (☎ 071 796 1200)

SPENCE, Prof David Allan; s of Allan Lemuel Spence (d 1942), of Auckland, NZ, and Dorothy Louisa, *née* Matthews (d 1982); *b* 3 Jan 1926; *Educ* King's Coll Auckland NZ, Clare Coll Cambridge (MA, PhD), Univ of Oxford (DSc); *m* 19 March 1955, Isobel Begg, da of Robert Maxton Ramsay (d 1957), of Glasgow; 2 s (Paul b 1961, James b 1968), 2 da (Anne (Mrs Young) b 1956, Barbara b 1960); *Career* Nat Serv flying offr RNZAF (Def Sci Branch) 1949-50; sr princ scientific offr Royal Aircraft Estab Farnborough Hants 1963-64 (joined 1952); Univ of Oxford: Dept of Engrg Sci 1964-81, reader in theoretical mechanics 1977-81, fell Lincoln Coll 1964-81 and 1989-; prof of mathematics Imperial Coll London 1981-, ed IMA jl of Applied Mathematics; FRAes, FIMA; *Books* Journal of Fluid Mechanics (contrib); *Recreations* gardening, golf, hill walking; *Clubs* Climbers; *Style—* Prof David Spence; 16 Dunstan Rd, Old Headington, Oxford OX3 9BY (☎ 0865 65663); Deptartment of Mathematics, Imperial College, London SW7 2BZ (☎ 071 589 5111, fax 071 584 7596, telex 261503)

SPENCE, David Lane; s of Dr AS Spence, and Edith F, *née* Lane; *b* 5 Oct 1943; *Educ* Fettes; *m* 1966, Beverley Esther, da of Gp Capt Jasper Cardale (d 1981); 1 s (William b 1978), 2 da (Sally b 1976, Sarah b 1980); *Career* CA; C F Middleton & Co

1962-67; Grant Thornton (formerly Thornton Baker): joined 1967, ptnr 1970, ptnr Euro practice 1974-79, chm Investigations Panel 1975-84 and 1990-, exec ptnr 1984-89; Liveryman Worshipful Co of Glaziers; memb ICAEW, MICAS (Business Legislation Unit); *Recreations* golf, skiing, opera; *Clubs* Caledonian, Royal Mid Surrey Golf, Sunningdale Golf; *Style*— David Spence, Esq; Grant Thornton House, Melton St, Euston Square, London NW1 2EP (☎ 071 383 5100, fax 071 383 4077)

SPENCE, James William (Bill); DL (1988); s of James William Spence, of Stromness, Orkney, and Margaret Duncan, *née* Peace; *b* 19 Jan 1945; *Educ* Firth Jr Secdy Sch Orkney, Leith Nautical Coll Edinburgh, Robert Gordon's Inst Technol Aberdeen (Master Mariner), UWIST Cardiff (BSc); *m* 31 July 1971, Margaret Paplay, da of Henry Stevenson (d 1983), of Stromness, Orkney; 3 s (James b 1976, Steven b 1978, Thomas b 1980); *Career* Merchant Navy 1961-74; apprentice deck offr Watts Watts & Co Ltd 1961-65, certified deck offr P & O Steam Navigation Co Ltd 1965-74; Micoperi SPA 1974-75, temp asst site co-ordinator Scapa Flow Project; John Jolly: mangr 1975, jr ptnr 1976-77, sr ptnr 1977-78, md and proprietor 1978-; vice consul The Netherlands 1978, station hon sec RNLI Kirkwall Lifeboat 1987 (dep Launching Authy 1976-87); memb: Kirkwall Community Cncl 1978-82, Orkney Pilotage Ctee 1979-88; chm: Kirkwall Port Employers' Assoc 1979-87, Bd Tstees Pier Arts Centre Tst Orkney 1989 (tstee 1980), Br House Soc Orkney Riding Club 1985 (memb 1985); MNI 1972, AICS 1979, MRIN 1971; KFO (Cdr Royal Norwegian Order of Merit) 1987; *Recreations* oenophilist, equestrian matters, Orcadian history; *Clubs* Caledonian; *Style*— Bill Spence, Esq, DL; Alton House, Kirkwall, Orkney KW15 1NA; John Jolly, PO Box 2, 21 Bridge St, Kirkwall, Orkney KW15 1HR (☎ 0856 2268, fax 0856 5002, car 0860 761455, telex 75253)

SPENCE, Prof John Edward (Jack); s of John Herbert Spence (d 1946), of Krugersdorp, SA, and Violet, *née* Brown (d 1976); *b* 11 June 1931; *Educ* Boys HS Pretoria SA, Univ of Witwatersrand Johannesburg (BA), LSE (BSc); *m* 27 June 1959, Susanne Hilary; 1 da (Rachel b 1967); *Career* lectr Dept of History and Politics Univ of Natal Pietermaritzburg SA 1958-60, Rockefeller Jr Res Fell LSE 1960-62, reader Dept of Governmental Political Theory Univ Coll Swansea 1972-73 (asst lectr 1962-63, lectr 1963-68, sr lectr 1968-72), prof Dept of Politics Univ of Leicester 1986- (head of Dept of Politics 1974-81, pro vice chllr 1981-85); pres African Studies Assoc UK 1977-78, chm Br Int Studies Assoc 1986-88, memb Hong Kong Cncl for Academic awards 1986-90; memb: Royal Inst of Int Affrs 1961, Int Inst of Strategic Studies 1967; *Books* Republic Under Pressure (1965), Lesotho-Politics of Dependence (1968), Political and Military Framework of Investment in South Africa (1976), British Politics in Perspective (ed with R Borthwick, 1985); *Recreations* collecting Faber poetry volumes, walking dogs, swimming; *Clubs* Travellers; *Style*— Prof J E Spence; Castle View Farm, Bringhurst, nr Market Harborough, Leicestershire; Department of Politics, University of Leicester, University Rd, Leicester LE1 7RH (☎ 0533 522702)

SPENCE, John Francis Gordon; s of Patrick Walter Gordon Spence (d 1974), and Helen Winifred, *née* Fincham (d 1989); *b* 4 April 1934; *Educ* Douai Sch, RMA Sandhurst; *m* 1962, Sheila Veronica, da of Charles Henry Thomas, of Essex; 1 s (Nicholas b 1963), 2 da (Clare b 1965, Cathryn b 1971); *Career* RTR Germany 1955-59; personnel dir Williams Lea Gp Ltd 1970-74; dir personnel servs Hill Samuel Investment Services Group Ltd; dir: Hill Samuel Life Assurance Co Ltd 1981-, Hill Samuel Life Facilities Ltd, Gisborne Life Assurance Co Ltd, NLA Tower Management Ltd; FPIM; *Recreations* painting, walking, theatre; *Style*— John Spence, Esq; 45 Epsom Road, Guildford, Surrey GU1 3LA; Hill Samuel Investment Services Group, NLA Tower, 12-16 Addiscombe Road, Croydon CR9 2DR (☎ 081 686 4355, telex 946929)

SPENCE, Malcolm Hugh; QC (1979); s of Dr Allan William Spence (d 1990), and Martha Lena, *née* Hutchison (d 1981), clan MacDuff; *b* 23 March 1934; *Educ* Stowe, Gonville and Caius Coll Cambridge (MA, LLM); *m* 18 March 1967, (Jennifer) Jane, da of Lt-Gen Sir George Sinclair Cole, KCB, CBE (d 1973); 1 s (Robert William b 1971), 1 da (Annabelle Irene b 1969); *Career* Nat Serv 1 Lt Worcestershire Regt 1952-54; barr Gray's Inn 1958 (James Mould scholar, sr Holker exhibitioner, Lee prizeman), entered Chambers of John Widgery, QC, pupil to Nigel Bridge (now Lord Bridge of Harwich) 1958; chm of Panel Examination in Public of Hartlepool and Cleveland Structure Plans 1979; asst rec 1982, rec 1985, bencher Gray's Inn 1988; landowner (1100 acres); *Books* Rating Law and Valuation (jtly, 1961); *Recreations* trout fishing, golf; *Clubs* Hawks (Cambridge); *Style*— Malcolm Spence, Esq, QC; 23 Ennerdale Rd, Kew, Richmond, Surrey (☎ 081 940 9884); Scamadale, Arisaig, Inverness-shire (☎ 06875 698); 8 New Square, Lincoln's Inn, London WC2 (☎ 071 242 4986, fax 071 405 1166, telex 21785 ADVICE G)

SPENCE, Margaret; *née* Ferguson; da of Robert Ferguson (d 1937), of Longlands, Comber, Co Down, NI, and Sarah Ann, *née* Phillips (d 1981); *b* 17 Sept 1937; *Educ* Bangor Collegiate Sch; *m* 22 Sept 1956, William Herbert (d 1969), s of Herbert Spence (d 1959), of 5 Glenbroom Park, Jordanstown, Co Antrim, NI; *Career* dir: Nat West Ulster Bank Ltd 1985, Laganside Corp (to re-develop Belfast Dockland); chm and md M Ferguson Newtownards (main Ford dealer), female memb Ford Motor Co UK (strategy team-planning); awarded Business Woman of the Year 1984; memb: Local Enterprise Unit LEDU 1980-82, NI Econ Cncl 1981-85; dep chm Newtownards Devpt Cncl 1987, chm Ards Small Business Centre 1988; FIMI 1984, memb IOD 1977; *Recreations* squash; *Clubs* Kiltonga Squash; *Style*— Mrs Margaret Spence; M Ferguson - Newtownards, Regent House, Regent St, Newtownards, Co Down, N Ireland (☎ 0247 812626, fax 0247 818845, car 0836 509573, telex 747923)

SPENCE, Prof Robert; s of Robert Whitehair Spence (d 1988), and Minnie Grace, *née* Wood (d 1984); *b* 11 July 1933; *Educ* Hymers Coll Hull, Hull Coll of Technol (BSc), Imperial Coll London (DIC, PhD, DSc); *m* 18 April 1960, Kathleen, da of George Potts, of 1 Regents Close, Whyteleafe, Surrey; 1 s (Robert b 1963), 1 da (Merin b 1966); *Career* Imperial Coll London: lectr 1962, reader 1968, prof of info engrg 1984-; founding dir and chm Interactive Solutions Ltd 1985; author of numerous papers; FIEE, FIEEE, FCGI, FRSA; FEng; Chevalier De L'ordre Du Palme Academique France 1985; *Books* Linear Active Networks (1970), Tellegen's Theorem and Electrical Networks (1970), Resistive Circuit Theory (1974), Modern Network Theory - An Introduction (1968), Sensitivity and Optimisation (1980), Circuit Analysis by Computer (1986), Tolerance Design of Electronic Circuits (1988); *Recreations* photography, walking; *Style*— Prof Robert Spence; Department of Electrical Engineering, Imperial College of Science Technology and Medicine, Exhibition Rd, London SW7 2BT (☎ 071 225 8505, fax 071 823 8125, telex 929484)

SPENCE, Roy Archibald Joseph; s of Robert Spence (d 1988), of Belfast, and Margaret, *née* Gilmore; *b* 15 July 1952; *Educ* Queen's Univ Belfast (MB BCh, MD); *m* 26 Sept 1979, Diana Mary, da of Dr C Burns, OBE (d 1989), of Ballymoney; 2 s (Robert b 20 July 1982, Andrew b 14 Sept 1984), 1 da (Katharine b 11 Feb 1987); *Career* conslt surgn Belfast City Hosp 1986-; 100 jl papers, 10 chapters in books; memb: Assoc of Surgns, Br Soc of Gastroenterology, BMA; FRCS: (Edinburgh) 1984, (Ireland) 1984; memb World Assoc of Hepato-Biliary Surgns; *Books* Pathology for Surgeons (1986); *Recreations* fishing; *Style*— Roy Spence, Esq; 7 Downshire Crescent, Hillsborough, Co Down, Northern Ireland BT26 6DD (☎ 682362); Level 2, Belfast City Hosp, Lisburn Rd, Belfast BT9 7AB (☎ 0232 329241)

SPENCE, Saxon May; *née* Fairbairn; da of George Frederick Fairbairn (d 1981), and Ann May, *née* Northcott; *b* 25 Feb 1929; *Educ* Ealing Girls GS, UCL (BA), Sch of Educn; *m* 12 May 1952, John George Spence, s of Jack Spence (d 1953); 1 s (Ian b 1961), 1 da (Catherine b 1956); *Career* city cncllr Exeter 1972-74, co cncllr Devon 1973-77 and 1981-, ldr Devon Lab Gp 1985- (former dep ldr 1973-77 and 1981-85); memb: Nat Jt Ctee Working Women's Orgns 1973-85, Nat Lab Women's Ctee 1973-85 (chm 1979-80), Bd SWEB 1978-81, Devon Regnl Ctee Co-op Retail Servs 1978-, Women's Nat Cmmn 1982-85, Devon and Cornwall Area Manpower Bd 1983-88, ACC 1985-89, ACC Educn Ctee 1985-; vice chm: Western Regnl Tport Users' Consultative Ctee 1985-88 (memb 1975-88), ACC Policy Ctee 1989, Exeter and Devon Arts Centre Bd 1989- (memb 1987-), Exeter Cncl of Social Services 1989- (memb 1963-); govr Exeter Coll 1972- (chm of Govrs 1985-89), vice chm of Govrs Rolle Coll 1981-88, govr Further Educn Staff Coll 1986; *Recreations* reading, travelling, theatre, music; *Clubs* Pinhoe and Whipton Labour; *Style*— Mrs Saxon Spence; 5 Regent's Park, Exeter, Devon EX1 2NT (☎ 0392 71 785); Devon CC, County Hall, Exeter, Devon (☎ 0392 382 501, fax 0392 51 096)

SPENCER, Alan Douglas; s of Thomas Spencer, of Dumbleton, Gloucs, and Laura Spencer (d 1977); *b* 22 Aug 1920; *Educ* Prince Henry's GS Evesham; *m* 18 March 1944, Dorothy Joan; 2 da (Sally b 1946, Jocelyn b 1956); *Career* cmmnd Gloster Regt 1940, Green Howards 1940-45, Sch of Inf 1945-47; chm Boots The Chemist 1977-80, vice chm The Boots Co 1978-80, dir Johnson Wax Ltd 1980-90; CBIM 1975; *Recreations* shooting; *Style*— Alan Spencer, Esq; Oakwood, Grange Rd, Edwalton, Notts NG12 4BT (☎ 0602 231722)

SPENCER, Prof Anthony James Merrill; s of James Lawrence Spencer (d 1961), of Streetly, Staffs, and Gladys, *née* Merrill; *b* 23 Aug 1929; *Educ* Queen Mary's GS Walsall, Queens Coll Cambridge (BA, MA, ScD), Univ of Birmingham (PhD); *m* 1 Jan 1955, Margaret, da of Ernest Albert Bosker (d 1949), of Walmley, Sutton Coldfield; 3 s (John b 1957, Timothy b 1960, Richard b 1963); *Career* Private 1 Bn West Yorks Regt 1948-49, res assoc Brown Univ USA 1955-57, sr scientific offr UKAEA 1957-60, prof and head of Dept of Theoretical Mechanics Univ of Nottingham 1965- (lectr 1960-63, reader 1963-65); visiting prof: Brown Univ 1966 and 1971, Lehigh Univ 1978, Univ of Queensland Aust 1982; memb: Mathematics Ctee SRC 1978-81, Mathematical Scis Sub Ctee UGC 1983-87; FRS 1987; *Books* Deformations of Fibre-Reinforced Materials (1972), Engineering Mathematics (2 vols, 1977), Continuum Mechanics (1980); *Style*— Prof Anthony Spencer, FRS; 43 Stanton Lane, Stanton-on-the-Wolds, Keyworth, Nottingham NG12 5BE, (☎ 06077 3134); Dept of Theoretical Mechanics, University of Nottingham, University Park, Nottingham NG7 2RD (☎ 0602 484848, fax 0602 420825, telex 373 UNINOT G)

SPENCER, Aubrey Raymond; s of Isaac Spencer (d 1977), and Leah, *née* Cohen (d 1959); *b* 31 Aug 1924; *Educ* Christ's Coll Finchley, Maidenhead County Boys Sch, Reading Univ (BSc); *m* 13 Sept 1948, Ruth, da of Jack Broder, of 39 Berwyn Rd, Richmond, Surrey; 3 s (Steven Mark Broder b 14 Oct 1949, Daniel Leigh b 19 Oct 1965, Andrew James b 15 July 1967), 1 da (Janine Anne b 12 Feb 1953); *Career* dir: Richmond Metal Co Ltd 1950 (md 1970), Broder Bros Metals Holding Co Ltd 1952; chm and chief exec Richmond Metal Gp 1988; memb Cncl: Br Secdy Metals Assoc 1959-(pres 1980-81), CBI (Smaller Firms); pres Richmond & Barnes Cons Assoc; memb Lloyd's; Freeman City of London 1980, memb Worshipful Co of Fletchers 1980; *Recreations* gardening, tennis, swimming, theatre, opera, reading, music; *Clubs* City Livery, MCC; *Style*— Aubrey Spencer, Esq; Richmond Metal Group, Feltham, Middx TW13 0SQ (☎ 081 890 0981, fax 081 751 6452, telex 934 857)

SPENCER, Barrymore James; CBE; s of James Robert Spencer (decd), and Charlotte Spencer (decd); *b* 14 March 1927; *Educ* Wintringham GS Grimsby, Bradford Tech Coll; *m* 3 Sept 1955, Viola Maria, da of Col Charles Barnet Grandfield; 2 s (Timothy James, Jonathan Maqnus); *Career* non-exec dir British Textile Technology Group, non-exec chm Parkland Textile Holdings plc, ptnr Spencer Farm Produce; chm Parkland Pension Trust, former pres Br Textile Confedn; *Recreations* bridge; *Clubs* Farmers; *Style*— Barrymore James Spencer, Esq, CBE; Parkland Textile Holdings plc, Albion Mills, Green Gates, Bradford, W Yorks BD10 9TQ (☎ 0274 611161, fax 0274 616541, telex 51570)

SPENCER, Hon Mrs (Catherine Anne); *née* Blades; da of 2 Baron Ebbisham, of St Ann's Mere, Warminster, Wilts, and Flavia Mary, *née* Meade; *b* 3 Dec 1955; *Educ* St Mary's Sch Calne, Charterhouse, Wye Coll London (BSc); *m* 1981, Charles James, s of Kenneth Clarke Spencer of St Martin's Farm, Zeals, Warminster, Wilts; 2 s (Thomas James b 1985, Henry Charles Blades b 1990), 1 da (Flora Antonia Blades b 1987); *Career* agric tech advsr; farmer's wife; *Recreations* farming; *Style*— The Hon Mrs Spencer; Search Farm, Stourton, Warminster, Wilts

SPENCER, Christopher Paul; s of Anthony John Spencer, of Cornerstones, Beechwood Ave, Weybridge, Surrey, and Elizabeth, *née* Carruthers; *b* 7 July 1950; *Educ* St Georges Coll Weybridge; *m* 28 June 1975, Margaret Elizabeth, da of Lt-Col Cyril Meredith Battye Howard, OBE, of Rowan Cottage, Rydens Ave, Walton-on-Thames, Surrey; 2 da (Katherine b 13 Aug 1978, Anna Lisa b 24 July 1981); *Career* CA; ptnr: Midgley Snelling Spencer & Co 1978-83, Pannell Kerr Forster (CI) 1984-; hon sec Guernsey Branch IOD; memb: Guernsey C of C, Guernsey Soc of Chartered and Certified Accountants; FCA; *Recreations* sailing, skiing, tennis; *Clubs* United, Guernsey Yacht, Ski Club of GB; *Style*— Christopher Spencer, Esq; La Chimere, George Rd, St Peter Port, Guernsey (☎ 0481 711 040); Pannell Kerr Forster, Suites 13/15, Sarnia House, Le Truchot, St Peter Port, Guernsey (☎ 0481 7279127, fax 0481 710 511, telex 4191177 Panker G)

SPENCER, Derek Harold; QC (1980); s of Thomas Harold Spencer, of Waddington, Lancs, and Gladys, *née* Heslop (d 1989); *b* 31 March 1936; *Educ* Clitheroe Royal GS, Keble Coll Oxford (MA, BCL); *m* 1, 30 July 1960 (m dis), Joan, da of late James Nutter, of Clitheroe, Lancs; 2 s (David b 1966, Andrew b 1970), 1 da (Caroline b 1964); m 2, 26 Nov 1988, Caroline Alexandra, da of Dr Franziskus Pärn, of Hamburg; 1 s (Frederick Thomas Francis b 27 Oct 1990); *Career* 2 Lt KORR 1954-56, served Nigeria; called to the Bar Gray's Inn 1961, rec of Crown Ct 1979-; vice chm St Pancras N Cons Assoc 1977-78; cnclr London Borough of Camden 1978-83, dep ldr Cons Pty 1980-81; MP (C) Leicester South 1983-87, jt sec Cons Back Bench Legal Ctee 1985-86; PPS to Mr David Mellor Min of State Home Off 1986, to Sir Michael Havers Attorney Gen 1986-87; bencher Gray's Inn 1991; *Recreations* reading, swimming, travelling; *Style*— Derek Spencer, Esq, QC; 179 Ashley Gardens, Emery Hill Street, London SW1 (☎ 071 828 2517); 5 King's Bench Walk, Temple, London EC4 (☎ 071 353 4713, fax 071 353 5459)

SPENCER, Geoffrey Thomas; s of James William Spencer, and Doris Winifred, *née* Gillingham; *b* 16 May 1946; *Educ* Cheshunt GS, City of London Coll; *m* 1, 24 June 1974 (m dis 1989), Barbara; 1 s (Alexander James b Oct 1983), 1 da (Hilary Jane, b Sept 1978); m 2, 9 March 1989, Diane, da of Sidney Collins; *Career* Coutts & Co: asst mangr Business Devpt Div 1972-74, account mangr Cavendish Sq branch 1974-78, mangr Kensington branch 1978-82, mangr Mktg and Planning Dept Branch Banking Div 1982-83, head Int Banking Div 1986-88, (sr mangr 1983-84, dep head 1984-86), assoc dir 1986, head Commercial Banking Gp 1988, memb Bd of Coutts Fin Co 1988-90, memb Main Bd 1989-90; dir Coutts & Co (Nassau) Ltd 1985-90, md Coutts Fin

Co 1988-90; London gen mangr CBI-TDG Union Bancaire Privée 1990; ACIB 1970, FCIB 1988; *Recreations* badminton, gardening, travel, music; *Clubs* Overseas Bankers'; *Style—* Geoffrey Spencer, Esq; CBI-TDG Union Bancaire Privée, 39 Upper Brook St, London W1Y 1PE (☎ 071 495 1662, fax 071 499 3059, telex 21169)

SPENCER, (Richard) Harry Ramsay; s of Col Richard Augustus Spencer, DSO, OBE (d 1956), and Maud Evelyn, *née* Ramsay (d 1989); hp (to Barony only), of 3 Viscount Churchill; *b* 11 Oct 1926; *Educ* Wellington, Architectural Assoc (AADip); *m* 1958, Antoinette Rose-Marie, da of Godefroy de Charrière, of Préverenges, Lausanne, Switzerland; 2 s (Michael b 1960, David b 1970); *Career* former Lt Coldstream Gds; ret architect; painter of house portraits; ARIBA; *Recreations* the arts; *Style—* Harry Spencer, Esq; The Old Vicarage, Vernham Dean, Hants (☎ 026 487 386)

SPENCER, Herbert; s of Harold Spencer, and Sarah Ellen, *née* Tagg; *b* 22 June 1924; *m* 23 Sept 1954, Marianne Mols, *née* Dordrecht; 1 da (Mafalda Saskia b 1958); *Career* RAF 1942-45; dir Lund Humphries Publishers 1970-88, prof of graphic arts Royal Coll of Art 1978-85; memb Stamp Advsy Ctee PO 1968-, int pres Alliance Graphique Int 1971-73, Master Royal Designers for Indust and vice pres Royal Soc of Arts 1979-81; conslt: W H Smith Ltd 1973-, Tate Gallery 1981-89; one man exhibitions of paintings: Bleddfa Tst 1986, Gallery 202 London 1988-89 and 1990; one man exhibition of photographs Zelda Cheatle Gallery London 1991; photographs in permanent collection of V & A Museum; ed: Typographica 1949-67, Penrose Annual 1964-73; RDI 1965, FRSA 1965, DrRCA 1970, hon fell RCA 1985; *Books* Traces of Man (photographs, 1967), The Visible Word (1968), London's Canal (2 edn, 1976), Pioneers of Modern Typography (3 edn, 1990), The Liberated Page (2 edn, 1990); *Clubs* Chelsea Arts; *Style—* Herbert Spencer, Esq; 75 Deodar Rd, Putney, London SW15 2NU (☎ 081 874 6352); Runnis Chapel, Dutlas, Knighton, Powys (☎ 054 77 648)

SPENCER, Ivor; DL (London 1985); *b* 20 Nov 1924; *m* 1948, 1 s (Nigel), 1 da (Philippa); *Career* professional toastmaster; life pres Guild of Professional Toastmasters 1956-, princ Ivor Spencer Int Sch for Butler Administrators and Personal Assistants 1981-, princ Ivor Spencer Int Finishing Sch (Hong Kong, London, Paris), chm and md Ivor Spencer Enterprises Ltd; *Recreations* after dinner speaking; *Clubs* IOD; *Style—* Ivor Spencer, Esq; 12 & 14 Little Bornes, Alleyn Park, Dulwich, London SE21 8SE (☎ 081 670 5585, 081 670 8424, fax 081 670 0055, car 0860 313835)

SPENCER, Dr John David; s of Ivor Norman Spencer, of Abingdon House, Mardy Abergavenny, Gwent, and Edna Caroline, *née* Lewis; *b* 9 Nov 1944; *Educ* Tiffin Boy's Sch Kingston, Abingdon Sch, Univ of Birmingham, Univ of London (MB ChB, MSc); *m* 1, 12 April 1969 (m dis 1981), Li Lian; m 2, 1982, Catherine Anne; *Career* sr registrar in radiology Birmingham 1971-75, clinical res fell Inst of Cancer Res 1975-76, conslt radiologist: Northwick Park Hosp 1977-82, Luton and Dunstable Hosp 1982-; chm London Gliding Club; memb: Exec Ctee Br Gliding Assoc, Br Inst of Radiology; FRCR; *Recreations* gliding, shooting; *Clubs* London Gliding, St Hubert of GB; *Style—* Dr John Spencer; Baroona, Swannells Wood, Studham, Bedfordshire LU6 2QB (☎ 0582 872246); Radiology Dept, Luton and Dunstable Hospital, Dunstable Rd, Luton, Beds LU4 0DZ (☎ 0582 491122, fax 0582 598990, car 0836 341928)

SPENCER, John Hall; *b* 17 April 1928; *Educ* Bedford Sch, RNC Greenwich, Harvard Univ; *m* 1 Dec 1953 (m dis 1967), Edite, da of late Gen Jacques Pommes-Barrere; 2 s (William b 1955, Patrick Henri b 1958), 1 da (Catherine M L b 1961); *Career* offr RM 1945-51; William Mallinson & Sons (Australasia) Pty 1952-54, Management Research Groups London 1954-57, Beaverbrook Newspapers 1957-59, Cons Central Office 1959-61, J Walter Thompson 1961-82, md John Spencer Assoc 1982-; chm Activities Ctee London Fedn of Boys Clubs 1982- (memb Exec 1972-), MIPA 1960, MIPR 1961; *Books* The Business of Management (with Sir Roger Falk, 1959), Battle for Crete (1962), The Wall is Strong (1966), The Surgenor Campaign (1972); *Recreations* hunting, golf, travel, the theatre; *Clubs* Carlton, Army & Navy; *Style—* John Spencer, Esq; 24 John Islip St, London SW1P 4LG (☎ 071 828 4886, fax 071 834 6405)

SPENCER, John Loraine; TD (1960); s of Arthur Loraine Spencer, OBE (d 1958), of Woodford Green, Essex, and Emily Maude Spencer, OBE (d 1985); *b* 19 Jan 1923; *Educ* Bancrofts Sch, Gonville and Caius Coll Cambridge (MA); *m* 3 April 1954, Brenda Elizabeth, da of Percy Frederick Loft (d 1949), of Woodford Green, Essex; 2 s (Christopher Loraine b 1955, Nicholas John b 1960), 1 da (Elizabeth Mary b 1957); *Career* Essex Regt 1942-45: serv Normandy landings 1944, Capt (despatches); Offr Haileybury CCF (TA) 1948-61 (Maj); asst master (later housemaster and head of classics) Haileybury 1947-61; headmaster: Royal GS Lancaster 1961-72, Berkhamsted Sch 1972-83; asst dir GAP Activity Projects 1985-; pres Soc of Schoolmasters, memb Bd of Visitors HM YCC Aylesbury; *Clubs* Royal Cwlth; *Style—* John Spencer, Esq, TD; Crofts Close, 7 Aston Rd, Haddenham, Bucks HP17 8AF (☎ 0844 291235)

SPENCER, John Southern; s of Robert Southern Spencer, of Benson Cottage, Hetton, Skipton, N Yorks, and Marjorie Turner, *née* Frankland; *b* 10 Aug 1947; *Educ* Sedbergh, Queens' Coll Cambridge (MA); *m* 8 Dec 1984, Alison, da of Anthony Heap, of Pk Grange Cottage, Threshfield, Skipton, N Yorks; 1 s (David b 1981), 3 da (Suzanne b 1982, Hazel b 1985, Emily b 1988); *Career* slr, ptnr Sugden & Spencer 1975; Rugby Union; formerly: Capt Yorkshire, Capt Univ of Cambridge (3 Blues), Capt Barbarians, Capt England (16 Caps), British Lions Tour 1971; pres Wharfedale RUFC, sec Grassington Angling Club, tstee Upper Wharfedale Immediate Care Scheme, govr Netherside Special School, vice chm Govrs Ermysted's GS Skipton; memb Law Soc; *Recreations* rugby, squash, cricket; *Clubs* The Sportsmans, Wig & Pen, The Rugby; *Style—* John Spencer, Esq; High Pasture, Moor Lane, Threshfield, Skipton, N Yorks BD23 5NS (☎ 0756 752456); 6A Station Rd, Grassington, Skipton, N Yorks BD23 5NQ (☎ 0756 753015)

SPENCER, 8 Earl (GB 1765); (Edward) John Spencer; LVO (1954), DL (Northants 1961); also Viscount Spencer, Baron Spencer (both GB 1761), and Viscount Althorp (GB 1765 & UK 1905); s of 7 Earl Spencer, TD (d 1975) and Lady Cynthia, *née* Hamilton, DCVO, OBE, da of 3 Duke of Abercorn; *b* 24 Jan 1924; *Educ* Eton, RAC Cirencester; *m* 1, 1954 (m dis 1969), Hon Frances Ruth Roche (now Hon Mrs Shand Kydd, *qv*), da of 4 Baron Fermoy, and Ruth, Lady Fermoy, DCVO, OBE, JP, *qv*); 1 s (and 1 s decd), 3 da (Lady Sarah McCorquodale, Lady Jane Fellowes, HRH The Princess of Wales); m 2, 1976, Raine (memb British Tourist Authority 1982-, chm BTA's Spas Ctee 1982-), da of Alexander McCorquodale and his 1 w, Barbara Cartland, *qv*; *Heir* s, Viscount Althorp b 1964; *Career* late Capt Royal Scots Greys; Co Cllr Northants (High Sheriff 1959); patron of 12 livings; temp Equerry to HM King George VI 1950-52 and to HM The Queen 1952-54; ADC to Govr S Australia 1947-50; Dep Hon Col Royal Anglian Regt (TA) 1972-; chm Nene Fndn; memb UK Cncl European Architectural Heritage Year 1975; *Books* Spencers on Spas (1984), Japan and the East (1986); *Recreations* farming, tourism, cricket, music, art, family life; *Clubs* Turf, Brooks's (tstee), MCC, Royal Over-Seas League, Pratt's; *Style—* The Rt Hon the Earl Spencer, LVO, DL; Althorp, Northampton NN7 4HG (☎ 060 4770 760)

SPENCER, John William James; s of Capt John Lawrence Spencer, DSO, MC (d 1967), and Jane Lilian Spencer, *née* Duff; *b* 26 Dec 1957; *Educ* Sedbergh, Magdalene Coll Cambridge (MA); *m* 2 Oct 1987, Jane Elizabeth, da of Andrew Young (d 1974); 1 s (Charles b 1990); *Career* dir: Dewey Warren & Co Ltd 1986-88, PWS North America 1988-89, Ballantyne McKean & Sullivan (Lloyd's Brokers) 1989-; *Style—* J W J Spencer, Esq; Ghyllas, Sedbergh, Cumbria; 9 Defoe Ave, Kew, Surrey (☎ 081 876 0255)

SPENCER, Sir Kelvin Tallent; CBE (1950), MC (1918); s of Charles Tallent Spencer (d 1948), of The Hall, Harmondsworth, Middx, and Edith Elfrida, *née* Swithinbank (d 1946); *b* 7 July 1898; *Educ* UCS, Univ of London (BSc); *m* June 1927, Phoebe Mary (d 1989), da of Henry Wills; 1 s (Geoffrey Tallent b 1929); *Career* 2 Lt RE 1918-19; scientist Royal Aeronautical Estab Farnborough 1923-35; joined Civil Serv 1923; seconded to help start Airworthiness Div of Provisional Int Civil Aviation Orgn (now ICAO) Canada 1946-47, seconded to start Air Registration Bd's tech responsibilities London 1945-46; fndr memb Sci and Med Network; lay memb of Cncl Univ of Exeter 1961-75; Hon LLD Exeter 1975; FCGI 1959, FICE, FRAeS; *Recreations* keeping abreast of progress in relationship between subatomic physics and metaphysics; *Style—* Sir Kelvin Spencer, CBE, MC; Wootans, Branscombe, Devon EX12 3DN; Honeyditches House, Seaton Down Road, Seaton, Devon EX12 2JD

SPENCER, Kirsten Newman; da of Michael John Spencer, of 40 Rownham Mead, Hotwells, Bristol, and Trudy Ann, *née* Jarman; *b* 17 June 1969; *Educ* Bristol GS, Crewe & Alsager Coll of Higher Educn (BEd); *Career* hockey player; Clifton Ladies Hockey Club 1989-, Avon under 16 and under 18, Cheshire under 21 and sr, West under 18, North under 21 and sr; England: under 18 Home Countries tournament Scotland 1987 and Euro Sr Nations tournament Scotland 1987, under 21 BMW tournament Amsterdam 1989 and Home Countries tournament Eire 1990, full team San Sebastian tournament 1990, Euro Squad 1991; Hockey Assoc coaching qualification; *Recreations* windsurfing, canoeing, climbing, potholing; *Style—* Miss Kirsten Spencer; 40 Rownham Mead, Hotwells, Bristol BS8 4YB

SPENCER, Malcolm George; s of Stanley Spencer, of Mansfield, Notts, and Marjorie, *née* Everall; *b* 28 April 1954; *Educ* Queen Elizabeth Boys GS Mansfield, Kingston Poly (Dip mgmnt studies); *m* 6 Sept 1975, Gillian, da of Roy Beeton; 1 s (Christopher Malcolm b 6 Jan 1987), 1 da (Clare Louise b 5 July 1989); *Career* travel clerk 1972-74, clerical offr Mapperley Hosp Notts 1974-75, higher clerical offr King's Mill Hosp Mansfield 1975, gen admin asst Victoria Hosp Mansfield 1975-78, dep admin Parkside Hosp Macclesfield 1978-80; dep sector admin: Gen Hosp Newcastle upon Tyne 1980-83, Gen Hosp Sunderland 1983-85; unit gen mangr: Cherry Knowle Hosp Sunderland 1985-90, Barton Meml Unit Sunderland 1990-91; memb Mgmnt Ctee Sunderland Centre for Counselling Services; NHS Jl Study award 1989, special advsr Nuffield Inst Univ of Leeds; AHSM 1980; *Recreations* squash, swimming, walking; *Style—* Malcolm Spencer, Esq; Focus Management Services, Provincial House, Solly St, Sheffield S1 4BA (☎ 0742 757122, fax 0742 729567)

SPENCER, Paul Samuel John; s of Albert Owen Spencer (d 1986), of Leicester, and Constance Christina, *née* Brass; *b* 24 Oct 1934; *Educ* Wyggeston Sch Leicester, Leicester Colls of Art and Technol, Univ of London; *m* 17 Aug 1957, Avril Dorothy, da of Thomas Spriggs (d 1972), of Leicester; 1 s (Jonathan b 1963), 2 da (Isobel b 1961, Rosemary b 1965); *Career* pre registration pharmacist Middx Hosp London 1957-58, asst lectr Sch of Pharmacy Univ of London 1959-62, princ pharmacologist Allen & Hanburys (now Glaxo Research) Ware Herts 1962-65, sr lectr then reader in pharmacology Sch of Pharmacy Univ of Aston 1965-70, head of sch Welsh Sch of Pharmacy UWIST Cardiff 1978- (prof of pharmacology 1971-), first dean Faculty of Health and Life Sciences Univ of Wales Coll Cardiff 1988-, author of 100 res and professional articles and reviews specialising in pharmacology of psychotropic drugs and pharmaceutical educn; memb: Educn Ctee and various working parties on professional educn and pharmacology RPharmS, various CNAA Ctees; former memb: CRM Psychotropics Sub Ctee, Standing Pharmaceutical Ctee for England and Wales; currently chm Welsh Standing Pharmaceutical Ctee in Welsh Office; FIBiol 1972, FRPharmS 1978, MCPP 1981, CBiol 1984; *Recreations* music, photography, sport; *Style—* Prof Paul Spencer; 4 Long House Close, Lisvane, Cardiff CF4 5XR (☎ 0222 750150); Welsh School of Pharmacy, University of Wales College of Cardiff (UWCC), PO Box 13, Cardiff CF1 3XF (☎ 0222 874781, fax 0222 874149, telex 498635)

SPENCER, Peter John; s of James Leslie Spencer, of Bury St Edmunds, and Kathleen Mary, *née* Kilbride; *b* 22 April 1945; *Educ* Perse Sch for Boys Cambridge, Sidney Sussex Coll Cambridge, St Thomas's Hosp London; *m* 12 April 1969, Susan Mary, da of Leslie George Wellstead, of Cambridge; 1 s (David Charles Peter b 1975), 1 da (Fiona Carolyn Mary b 1979); *Career* conslt obstetrician and gynaecologist W Suffolk Hosp Bury St Edmunds Suffolk 1983-; memb E Anglian Regnl Hosp and Specialists Ctee; FRCS, FRCSEd, FRCOG; *Style—* Peter Spencer, Esq; West Suffolk Hospital, Hardwick Lane, Bury St Edmunds, Suffolk (☎ 0284 763131)

SPENCER, Countess; Raine; da of Alexander McCorquodale (1 cous of 1 Baron McCorquodale of Newton, PC) by his 1 w Barbara Cartland, *qv*; *b* 9 Sept 1929; *m* 1, 1948 (m dis 1976), as his 1 w, 9 Earl of Dartmouth; 3 s (Viscount Lewisham, Hon Rupert Legge, Hon Henry Legge), 1 da (Lady Charlotte Legge); m 2, 1976, as his 2 w, 8 Earl Spencer, LVO, *qv*; *Career* formerly a LCC Voluntary Care Ctee worker in Wandsworth and Vauxhall, and actively involved in the welfare of the elderly in other areas; memb Lewisham W LCC 1958-65; memb: GLC (Richmond) 1967-73, GLC Gen Purposes Ctee 1971-73; former memb BBC Nat Agric Advsy Ctee, chm Govt Working Pty on the Human Habitat for UN Conference on the Environment (which produced The Dartmouth Report, How Do You Want To Live?), and a UK delegate at the Conf in Stockholm 1972; chm: GLC Historic Bldgs Bd 1968-71, Covent Gdn Devpt Ctee 1971-75, UK Exec Ctee of European Architectural Heritage Year 1975; memb: English Tourist Bd 1971-75, BTA Infrastructure Ctee 1972-, Advsy Cncl V & A 1980-, BTA 1982-; chm: BTA Spas Ctee 1981-83, BTA Hotels and Restaurants Ctee 1983-87, BTA Accommodation Ctee 1987-, BTA Commendation Schemes Panel 1982-89, BTA Devpt Ctee 1987-, BTA Come to Britain Awards 1990-, BTA Britain Welcomes Japan Ctee of Honour and Exec Ctee 1989, Ctee for Business Sponsorship of the Arts; awarded a Gold medal for public speaking, and a former guest speaker at Oxford Univ and Cambridge Univ debates; lectr at: Holloway, Maidstone and Wandsworth Prisons; *Books* The Spencers on Spas (with photographs by Earl Spencer); *Style—* The Rt Hon the Countess Spencer; Althorp, Northampton NN7 4HG

SPENCER, Ritchie Lloyd; s of Capt P Lloyd Spencer; *b* 27 Sept 1942; *Educ* St Bees Sch, Univ of Manchester (BA), LSE; *m* 1965, Catherine Dilys, da of Dr John Naish; 3 s (Hal b 1968, Patrick b 1969, James b 1972); *Career* dir Sunderland Shipbuilders Ltd 1972-76, md Reliant Motor plc Tamworth Staffs 1977-87, dir Nash Industries plc 1980-87, chief exec GKN Powder Metallurgy Div 1987-90; chm: Bound Brook Lichfield Ltd 1987-90, Firth Cleveland Sintered Products Ltd 1987-90, Sheepbridge Sintered Products Ltd 1987-90; pres: Bound Brook Italia SpA Brunico 1987-90, Saini SpA Milan 1987-90; dir: Mahindra Sintered Products Pune Ltd India 1987-90, Sintered SA de CV Mexico 1987-90; md: European Industrial Services Ltd 1990-, Nettlefolds Ltd 1990-, Unifix Ltd 1990-, Unifix (Belguim) NV/SA 1990-, Unifix (Netherlands) BV 1990, EIS Depots Ltd 1990-, EIS France SA 1990-; Cncl memb Soc Motor Manufacturers & Traders 1978-87, chm Motor Indust Res Assoc 1984-; MIPM; *Recreations* theatre, gardening, squash, tennis, skiing; *Style—* Ritchie Spencer, Esq; 16 London Rd, Lichfield, Staffs (☎ 0543 262507); Dorlinn View, Argyll Terrace, Tobermory, Isle of Mull (☎ 0688 2324)

SPENCER, Robin Godfrey; s of Eric Spencer, of Chester, and Audrey Elaine, *née* Brown; *b* 8 July 1955; *Educ* King's Sch Chester, Emmanuel Coll Cambridge (MA); *m* 5 Aug 1978, Julia Margaret Eileen, da of Eric John Bennet Burley, of Chester; 3 da (Jennifer b 1983, Susanna b 1984, Laura b 1987); *Career* called to the Bar Grays Inn 1978, practising Wales and Chester Circuit; *Recreations* cricket, music; *Style*— Robin Spencer, Esq, Sedan House, Stanley Place, Chester CH1 2LU (☎ 0244 348282 fax 0244 342336)

SPENCER, Rosemary Jane; CMG (1991); da of Air Vice-Marshal Geoffrey Roger Cole Spencer, CB, CBE (d 1969), and Juliet Mary, *née* Warwick; *b* 1 April 1941; *Educ* Upper Chine Sch, Shanklin IOW, St Hilda's Coll Oxford (BA); *Career* FO 1962-65, Br High Cmmn Nairobi 1965-67, FCO 1967-70, second sec and private sec to Hon Sir Con O'Neill EC negotiating team Brussels 1970-71, first sec UK rep to EC Brussels 1972-73, Br High Cmmn Lagos 1974-77, asst head Rhodesia Dept FCO 1977-79, RCDS 1980, cnsllr Br Embassy Paris 1980-84, external relations UK rep to EC Brussels 1984-87, head of Euro Community Dept External FCO 1987, asst under sec of state Pub Depts FCO 1989-, chm of Governing Bd Upper Chine Sch IOW 1989- (govr 1984); *Recreations* country walking, domestic arts, reading; *Clubs* Oxford & Cambridge, Royal Commonwealth Society; *Style*— Miss Rosemary Spencer, CMG; Foreign and Commonwealth Office, King Charles St, London SW1

SPENCER, Ms Sarah Ann; da of Dr Ian Osborne Bradford Spencer (d 1978), Consultant Physician, and Dr Elspeth Wilkinson, Consultant Psychiatrist; *b* 11 Dec 1952; *Educ* Mount Sch York, King's Sch Tynemouth, Nottingham Univ (BA Hons), Univ Coll London (MPhil); *m* 1978, Brian Anthony, s of Alan Keith Hackland; 1 s (James b 1986); *Career* gen sec Nat Cncl for Civil Liberties 1985; formerly dir The Cobden Tst; *Books* Called to Account: Police Accountability in England and Wales (1985), The New Prevention of Terrorism Act: The Case for Repeal (co-author 1985); *Style*— Ms Sarah Spencer; 21 Tabard St, London SE1

SPENCER, Shaun Michael; QC (1988); s of Edward Michael Spencer, of 37 High Ash Ave, Leeds, and Barbara Joan Patricia Spencer; *b* 4 Feb 1944; *Educ* Cockburn HS, Univ of Durham (LLB); *m* 9 June 1971, Nicola, da of Frederick George Greenwood, of Prince Rupert Drive, Tockwith, N Yorks; 2 s (Robert Phillip b 1972, Samuel James Edward b 1982), 2 da (Eleanor Jane b 1979, Elizabeth Anne b 1980); *Career* lectr in law Univ of Sheffield 1966-68 (asst lectr in law 1965-66), called to the Bar Lincoln's Inn 1968 (Hardwicke & Mansfield scholar), barr N Eastern Circuit 1969-, rec Crown Ct 1985; MFH Claro Beagles 1982-88; *Recreations* beagling, cookery, books, singing; *Style*— Shaun Spencer, Esq, QC; 34A Rutland Drive, Harrogate, N Yorks HG1 2NX (☎ 0423 523162); 6 Park Square, Leeds LS1 2LW (☎ 0532 459763, fax 0532 424395)

SPENCER, Thomas Newnham Bayley; MEP (EDG) Derbyshire 1979-; s of Thomas Henry Newnham Spencer (d 1979); *b* 10 April 1948; *Educ* Nautical Coll Pangbourne, Southampton Univ; *m* 1979, Elizabeth Nan, *née* Bath; 1 da (step); *Recreations* fencing, opera; *Clubs* Carlton; *Style*— Thomas Spencer Esq, MEP; 13 Goulton Rd, London E5 (☎ 081 985 5839); 1 Sant Lane, Doveridge, Derbys

SPENCER, Timothy John; s of John Spencer, of Gt Carleton, Blackpool, Lancs, and Muriel (Miffy), *née* Rowe; *b* 6 Nov 1958; *Educ* Baines GS Poulton Le Fylde Lancs, Downing Coll Cambridge (MA); *m* 3 Sept 1983, (Ann) Fiona, da of James Malcolm Rigg, of Rochdale, Lancs; 1 s (James Charles John b 2 March 1990); *Career* 2 Lt 1 Royal Tank Regt 1978; called to the Bar Middle Temple 1982; *Recreations* following Preston North End and Lancashire CCC, gardening; *Style*— Timothy Spencer, Esq; 2 Crown Office Row, Temple, London EC4Y 7HJ (☎ 071 353 1365, fax 071 353 4591)

SPENCER-CHURCHILL, Lord Charles George William Colin; s of 10 Duke of Marlborough (d 1972); *b* 1940; *Educ* Eton; *m* 1, 1965 (m dis 1968), Gillian, da of Andrew Fuller; m 2, 1970, Elizabeth Jane, da of Capt the Hon Mark Hugh Wyndham, MC; 2 s; *Style*— The Lord Charles Spencer-Churchill

SPENCER-CHURCHILL, Lady Ivor; Elizabeth; *née* Cunningham; er da of late James Cyril Cunningham, of 27 Culross St, London W1; *m* 15 Nov 1947, Lord Ivor Charles Spencer-Churchill (d 1956), yr s of 9 Duke of Marlborough, KG, PC, and his 1 w, Consuelo, *née* Vanderbilt; 1 s (Robert b 1954); *Style*— The Lady Ivor Spencer-Churchill; Fyning House, Rogate, Petersfield, Hants

SPENCER-CHURCHILL, John George Spencer; s of John Strange Spencer Churchill, DSO, TD (yr bro of Sir Winston and 2 s of Lord Randolph Churchill) and Lady Gwendeline Bertie (da of 7 Earl of Abingdon); 2 cous of 10 Duke of Marlborough; bro of Countess of Avon, *qv*; *b* 31 May 1909; *Educ* Harrow, RCA, Central Sch Art, Pembroke Coll Oxford, Ruskin Sch of Art; *m* 1, 1934 (m dis 1938), Angela (*see* Rauf, Bayan), da of Capt George Culme-Seymour (3 s of Sir Michael Culme-Seymour, 3 Bt, GCB, GCVO, and Mary, gda of 2 Baron Sondes); 1 da (Sarah m Colin, bro of Quentin Crewe, *qv*); m 2, 1941 (m dis 1953), Mary, da of Kenneth Cookson (now Mrs Jacob Huizinga); m 3, 1953, Mrs Kathlyn Tandy (d 1957), da of Maj-Gen Walter Beddall, CB, OBE; m 4, 1958, Anna, da of John Janson, of Kristianstad, Sweden, and widow of Granger Boston; *Career* serv WWII Maj RE, GSO2; artist, sculptor, lectr, author; *Recreations* music, travel; *Style*— John Spencer-Churchill Esq; Place du Cros, Grimaud 83360, France (☎ 94 43 21); 15 Cheyne Walk, London SW3 5RB (☎ 071 352 2352)

SPENCER-GREGSON, Dr Richard Nicholas (Nick); s of Capt Cyril Spencer-Gregson (decd), and Mary, *née* Taylor (decd); *b* 8 Dec 1931; *Educ* Haileybury, Kings Coll Newcastle upon Tyne, Univ of Durham (MB BS), Univ of Bradford (MSc), DObstRCOG, FRCOG; *m* Maureen, da of A Millward; 3 da (Fiona, Heather, Rosemary); *Career* Nat Serv Suez Crisis Libya 1956-58, lately Capt RAMC, RMO 5 Royal Tank Regt, 6 Royal Tank Regt, 1 Bn KRRC; asst surgn P&O Steam Navigation Co; res jr doctor appts Royal Victoria Infirmary Newcastle upon Tyne and Princess Mary's Maternity Hosp Newcastle, sr registar St Lukes Bradford and Leeds Royal Infirmary, conslt obstetrician and gynaecologist Grantham and Kesteven Dist Gen Hosp; hon clinical tutor: Univ of Leeds, Bradford Dept of Pharmacology; author of various papers on gynaecological related topics; memb MCC 1956-, chm St Wulframs Ward Cons Assoc; *Recreations* cricket, croquet; *Clubs* Marylebone Cricket, Granthan Cons; *Style*— Dr Nick Spencer-Gregson; Pinfold House, Long Bennington, Newark, Nottinghamshire NG23 5EH (☎ 0400 81356); Grantham and Kesteven District General Hospital, Grantham, Lincs (☎ 0476 65232 ext 4363); Fitzwilliam Private Hospital, Milton Way, Bretton, Peterborough, Cambs PE3 8YQ

SPENCER-JONES, John Franklin; s of Sir Harold Spencer-Jones, KBE (d 1962), and Mary, *née* Owers (d 1970); *b* 17 Jan 1934; *Educ* Gresham Sch Holt Norfolk, Jesus Coll Cambridge (BA, MA); *m* 27 Sept 1956, Ruth Muriel, da of John Edward Arnott Betts, JP, of The Manor House, Hampstead, Norreys, Berks; 3 s (Robert b 17 Feb 1957, Charles b 20 Sept 1959, James b 24 Aug 1968), 1 da (Jane b 12 Nov 1965); *Career* Nat Serv RAF, cmmnd Gen Duties Branch, substantive Pilot Offr 1953-55, RAFVR pilot with CU Air Sqdn (substantive Flying Offr); Aspro Nicholas Ltd 1958-70: export mangr Advance Industrys Ltd 1961, gen mangr ME 1963, md Pakistan Group 1965-70; self employed mgmnt conslt 1970-88 (int assignments in engrg, aviation, energy, pharmaceuticals and hotels industs, especially in ME), dir and co-sec The Heritage Group 1988-; Freeman City of London, Liveryman Worshipful Co of Clockmakers 1962; memb Inst of Export MIEX 1985, ARAeS 1986; *Recreations* collecting, antiques, aviation, history, DIY, travel and exploration; *Style*— John Spencer-Jones, Esq; Merriedene, Dean Lane, Cookham Dean, Maidenhead, Berks SL6 9BG (☎ 062 84 2082); The Heritage Group, 3 Homer St, London W1N 1HN (☎ 071 706 1051/2, fax 071 724 5856)

SPENCER-NAIRN, Angus; s of Michael Alastair Spencer-Nairn, of Baltilly House, Ceres, Fife, and Ursula Helen, *née* Devitt; *b* 23 Jan 1947; *Educ* Eton, RAC (MRAC); *m* 6 July 1968, Christina Janet, da of Col Hugh Gillies, of Kindar House, New Abbey, Dumfriesshire; 1 s (Michael b 1975), 1 da (Fiona b 1974); *Career* CA; sr ptnr Rawlinson & Hunter, in practice St Helier Jersey; *Recreations* motor racing, tennis, deer stalking, golf; *Clubs* Royal and Ancient Golf (St Andrew's), New (Edinburgh); *Style*— Angus Spencer-Nairn, Esq; La Fontaine, Rue Du Pont, St John, Jersey, CI (☎ 0534 61716); Ordnance House, Box 83, 31 Pier Rd, St Helier, Jersey, CI (☎ 0534 75141, fax 0534 32876, telex 4192075)

SPENCER-NAIRN, Sir Robert Arnold; 3 Bt (UK 1933) of Monimail, Co Fife; s of Lt-Col Sir Douglas Leslie Spencer Spencer-Nairn, TD, 2 Bt (d 1970); *b* 11 Oct 1933; *Educ* Eton, Trinity Hall Cambridge; *m* 1963, Joanna Elizabeth, da of late Lt Cdr George Stevenson Salt, RN, s of 2 Bt (cr 1899); 2 s, 1 da; *Heir* s, James Robert Spencer-Nairn b 7 Dec 1966; *Career* late Lt Scots Gds; *Style*— Sir Robert Spencer-Nairn, Bt; Barham, Cupar, Fife

SPENCER ROBERTS, Arthur; s of Arthur Meyrick Roberts (d 1967), and Catherine, *née* Spencer (d 1961); *b* 8 Jan 1920; *Educ* Hastings GS, Hastings Sch of Art, RCA (scholar, Hons Degree in Fine Art); *m* 18 Sept 1946, Mavis Ethel Wynne, da of Capt Cyril Hubert Board (d 1978); *Career* served fighter pilot & artillery 1939-46 Far East, Actg/Capt Mountbattens Staff; Olympic trialist, 100 metres freestyle swimming 1938-39, selected for Olympic team to swim at Helsinki (war interfered); wildlife artist; solo exhibitions incl: Museum Konig and Hammer Gallery NY 1978-79, Tokyo 1982, Bonn 1982, Dallas, London, Bristol; other exhibitions incl: Guildhall London, Las Vegas Houston; mural for Port Lympne Kent 1985-87 (for John Aspinall); paintings in collections of: HRH Duke of Edinburgh, Museum Konig, Bonn, John Aspinall; *Recreations* fishing, swimming, wild life conservation; *Clubs* Game Conservation Int (USA), 20's; *Style*— Arthur Spencer Roberts, Esq; The Boat House, Pett Level, nr Hastings, E Sussex (☎ 0424 813209)

SPENCER-SMITH, Sir John Hamilton; 7 Bt (UK 1804) of Tring Park, Herts; s of Capt Sir Thomas Cospatric Spencer-Smith, 6 Bt (d 1959), and Lucy Ashton, *née* Ingram; *b* 18 March 1947; *Educ* Milton Abbey, Lackham Coll of Agric; *m* 1980, Mrs Christine Sandra Parris, da of late John T C Osborne, of Durrington, Worthing, Sussex ; 1 da (Jessica b 1985); *Heir* kinsman, Peter Spencer-Smith; *Career* owner Hazel House Quarantine Kennels Midhurst; *Recreations* watching polo; *Clubs* Cowdray Park Polo; *Style*— Sir John H Spencer-Smith, Bt; Hazel House Quarantine Kennels, Elsted Marsh, Midhurst, W Sussex

SPENCER-SMITH, Lucy, Lady; Lucy Ashton; da of late Thomas Ashton Ingram; *m* 1944, Sir Thomas Cospatric Hamilton Spencer-Smith, 6 Bt (d 1959); 1 s (7 Bt); *Style*— Lucy, Lady Spencer-Smith; 2 Heathfield Gate, Bepton Rd, Midhurst, Sussex

SPENCER-SMITH, Peter Compton; s of late Lt-Col Michael Seymour Hamilton-Spencer-Smith, DSO, MC (gs of bro of 2 Bt and who did not use surname Hamilton); hp of kinsman, Sir John Spencer-Smith, 7 Bt; *b* 12 Nov 1912; *Educ* Eton, New Coll Oxford; *m* 1950, Philippa Mary, da of late Capt Richard Ford, Rifle Bde; 2 s; *Career* formerly Maj 79 Herts Yeo (Heavy Anti-Aircraft Regt), RA (TA); chm Charles Barker Group plc 1961-72; High Sheriff Hertfordshire 1976; *Style*— Peter Spencer-Smith, Esq; High Down House, Hitchin, Herts

SPENCER WATSON, Mary; da of George Spencer Watson, RA (d 1934), of London, and Hilda Mary Gardiner (d 1953); *b* 7 May 1913; *Educ* Schs of Sculpture: Bournemouth, Slade, Royal Acad (prize winner), Central; Ossip Zadkine Paris; *Career* sculptor; solo exhibitions: Heals Mansard Gallery 1937, Foyles Art Gallery London 1945, Shire Hall Dorchester 1945, Dorset County Museum Dorchester 1976, 1982 and 1991, Civic Centre Southampton 1982, Stour Gallery Blandford 1983, New Art Centre London 1985 and 1990, Pelter Sands Art Gallery Bristol 1988; gp exhibitions incl: Royal Acad London, Fine Art Soc, Woman's Int Soc, Nat Soc, Crafts Centre London, Basle Art Fair, Portland Tout Quarry Dorset, Olympia Art Fair, Hannah Peshar Sculpture Garden Surrey, Roche Ct Sculpture Garden Wilts, Rutherford Art Centre; architectural work for: Guildford Cathedral (two wooden angels in the children's chapel), Harlow New Town, Austin Car Works Longbridge Birmingham, Stevenage New town, Cambridge (two collages), Queen's Hospital Belfast, St Bartholomews Hostel London, Wyke Regis Dorset, St Etheldreda Chesfield Park Herts; teacher 1943-76 at various schs incl Poole Art Coll and Clayesmore Sch; memb: Woman's Int Soc, Nat Soc London; *Recreations* riding; *Style*— Mary Spencer Watson; Dunshay, Langton, Matrayers, Swanage, Dorset BH19 3EB

SPENDER, Prof Sir Stephen Harold; CBE (1962); s of Edward Harold Spender, and Violet Hilda, *née* Schuster; *b* 28 Feb 1909; *Educ* Univ Coll Sch, Univ of Oxford; *m* 1, 1936, Agnes Marie, da of late W H Pearn; m 2, 1941, Natasha Litvin; 1 s, 1 da; *Career* poet and critic; prof of English UCL 1970-77, now emeritus; FRSL; kt 1983; *Publications* The Still Centre (1939), Ruins and Visions (1941), World Within World (autobiography, 1951), Collected Poems (1954), Selected Poems (1965), The Generous Days (1971), Love-Hate Relations (1974), T S Eliot (1975), The Thirties and After (with David Hockney, 1978), Chinese Journal (1980), The Temple (1988), Poems for Spain (1939); editor: D H Lawrence: novelist, poet, prophet (1973), W H Auden: a tribute (1975); *Style*— Prof Sir Stephen Spender, CBE; 15 Loudoun Rd, London NW8 (☎ 071 624 7194)

SPENS, David Patrick; s of Lt-Col Hugh Stuart Spens, MB, MBE, TD (d 1988), and Mary Jean Drake, *née* Reinhold; *b* 2 May 1950; *Educ* Rugby, Univ of Kent (BA); *m* 7 April 1979, Daniele, da of Robert William Irving, MBE; 2 da (Dominique b 1982, Sophie b 1986); *Career* called to the Bar Inner Temple 1973; jr counsel to the Crown at the Central Criminal Ct 1988; *Recreations* tennis, travel, photography; *Style*— David Spens, Esq; 6 Kings Bench Walk, Temple, London EC4Y 7DR (☎ 071 583 0410)

SPENS, Hon (William) David Ralph; s of 2 Baron Spens (d 1984), and Joan Elizabeth, da of late Reginald Goodall; *b* 23 Nov 1943; *Educ* Rugby, Corpus Christi Coll Cambridge; *m* 1967, Gillian, da of Albert Jowett, OBE, MD, FRCS; 1 s (James), 1 da (Tamsin); *Career* barr 1972; *Style*— The Hon David Spens; Marsh Mills Cottage, Over Stowey, Somerset

SPENS, John Alexander; RD (1970), WS; s of T P Spens; *b* 1933; *Educ* BA, LLB; *m* Finella Jane Gilroy; 2 s, 1 da; *Career* Carrick Pursuivant of Arms 1974-85, Albany Herald of Arms 1985-; ptnr Maclay Murray & Spens (Slrs) 1960-90 (conslt 1990-); dir Scottish Amicable; *Style*— John Spens, Esq, RD, WS, Albany Herald of Arms; c/o Lyon Ct, HM New Register House, Edinburgh

SPENS, Dowager Baroness; Kathleen Annie Fedden; da of Roger Dodds, of Bath and Northumberland; *m* 1963, as his 2 w, 1 Baron Spens, KBE, PC (d 1973); *Style*— The Rt Hon the Dowager Lady Spens; Gould, Frittenden, Kent

SPENS, Hon Mallowry Ann; da of 2 Baron Spens; *b* 30 Sept 1949; *Career* int show jumper 1968-72, runs equestrian livery and trg yard; *Recreations* hunting; *Style*— The Hon Mallowry Spens; Missingham Farm, East Brabourne, Ashford, Kent (☎ 023 375 444)

SPENS, 3 Baron (UK 1959); Patrick Michael Rex; s of 2 Baron Spens (d 1984), and Joan Elizabeth, da of late Reginald Goodall; *b* 22 July 1942; *Educ* Rugby, CCC Cambridge (MA); *m* 1966, Barbara, da of Rear-Adm Ralph Fisher, CB, DSO, OBE, DSC; 1 s, 1 da (Hon Sarah b 1970); *Heir* s, Hon Patrick Nathaniel George Spens b 1968; *Career* md Henry Ansbacher & Co 1982-; FCA; *Style—* The Rt Hon Patrick Spens; Gould, Frittenden, Kent

SPENS, Hon (Emily) Susan; MBE (1970); da of William Patrick, 1 Baron Spens, KBE, PC (d 1973), and Hilda Mary, *née* Bowyer (d 1962); William Patrick Spens, KBE, PC, created Baron Spens 1957; *b* 25 April 1924; *Educ* Heathfield Sch Ascot, Birkbeck Coll London (MA); *Career* Serv WWII WRNS 1941-46; secretarial career in BA (formerly BOAC) 1948-53; FCO 1954-72; Int Atomic Energy Agency (IAEA) Vienna Austria 1972-80; *Recreations* classical music, the countryside; *Style—* The Hon E Susan Spens, MBE; Flat 6, 47 The Drive, Hove, E Sussex, BN3 3JE

SPENSLEY, Dr Philip Calvert; s of (John Hackett) Kent Spensley (d 1963), of Ealing, London, and Mary, *née* Schofield (d 1951); *b* 7 May 1920; *Educ* St Paul's, Keble Coll Oxford (MA, BSc, DPhil); *m* 24 Aug 1957, Sheila Ross, da of Alexander Lillingston Fraser (d 1977), of Forres, Morayshire, Scotland; 1 s (Colin b 1958), 3 da (Fiona b 1959, Charis b 1962, Tanya b 1966); *Career* tech offr Royal Ordnance Factories Miny of Supply 1940-45, res chemist Nat Inst for Med Res (MRC) 1950-54, scientific sec Colonial Prods Cncl Colonial Office 1954-58; Tropical Prods Inst DSIR: asst dir 1958-61, dep dir 1961-66, dir overseas devpt admin 1966-81; ed Tropical Science 1984-; memb: Protein Advsy Gp FAO/WHO/Unicef 1968-71, Ctee on Needs of Developing Countries Int Union of Food Sci of Technol 1970-78, CENTO Cncl for Scientific Educn and Res 1970-78, Int Ctee Royal Soc of Chemistry 1982-86, Panel of Chm of Scientific Selection Bds Civil Serv Cmmn 1982-86, Cncl Royal Inst 1985-88, Br Nat Ctee for Chemistry Royal Soc 1986-89; hon treas Keble Assoc Oxford 1987-; Freeman City of London 1951; CChem, FRSC; *Recreations* house and garden development, travel; *Clubs* Athenaeum, RAC, Island Cruising (Salcombe); *Style—* Dr Philip Spensley; 96 Laurel Way, Totteridge, London N20 8HU (☎ 081 445 7895); Pool House, Frogmore, Kingsbridge, S Devon TQ7 2NU; Whurr Publishers, 19B Compton Terrace, London N1 2UN (☎ 071 359 5979, fax 071 226 3652)

SPERRING, Donald James; s of John Roland Sperring, of Sussex, and Edna Joan, *née* Ashton; *b* 5 March 1951; *Educ* Ravensbourne Kent; *m* 18 April 1981, Laura Jane, da of Desmond Champ; 3 s (Ben b 1983, Sam b 1985, Thomas b 1987); 1 da (Alice b 1990); *Career* dir Grandfield Rork Collins (advertising agency) 1981-86, md Young & Rubicam (advertising agency) 1986-; *Recreations* golf, squash; *Clubs* RAC; *Style—* Donald Sperring, Esq; 3 Maywood Close, Beckenham Place Park, Beckenham, Kent (☎ 081 650 9807); Les Fraisiers Sauvages, Avenue D'Auteuil, Le Touquet, France; Young & Rubicam, Greater London House, Hampstead Rd, London NW1

SPERRYN, Simon George; s of George Roland Neville Sperryn of Hampton Lucy, Warwickshire, and Wendy, *née* King; *b* 7 April 1946; *Educ* Rydal Sch Clwydd, Pembroke Coll Cambridge (MA), Cranfield Sch of Mgmnt (MBA); *Career* Chamber of Industry and Commerce: Birmingham 1967-77, chief exec Northants 1979-85, chief exec Manchester 1986-, regnl sec NW 1986-; Joseph Gillott & Sons Ltd 1977-78, dir Manchester Phoenix Initiative Ltd 1989-, chm Manchester Camerata Ltd 1989-; dir Assoc of Br Chambers of Commerce 1990-; FBIM; *Recreations* singing, drawing; *Clubs* St James's (Manchester); *Style—* Simon Sperryn, Esq; Lilac Cottage, Wincle, Macclesfield, Cheshire SK11 0QE (☎ 0260 227 620); Manchester Chamber of Commerce and Industry, 56 Oxford St, Manchester M60 7HJ (☎ 061 236 3210, fax 061 236 4160, telex 667822 CHACON G)

SPICELEY, Peter Joseph; MBE; s of Robert Joseph Spiceley (d 1974), and Lucy Violet, *née* Gore; *b* 5 March 1942; *Educ* Trinity Sch of John Whitgift Croydon; *m* 6 Nov 1965, Cecilia, da of Dr Jorge Emilio Orozco (d 1989); 2 da (Anamaria b 1967, Jaccqueline Suzanne b 1970); *Career* diplomat; FO London 1961, Br Embassy Bogota Colombia 1964-66, Br Embassy Lima Peru 1969-72, Br Embassy Yaoundé Cameroon 1972-74, Br Consulate Douala Cameroon 1976, Br Embassy Quito Ecuador 1976-81, FCO London 1982-86 (1967-69), Br Consulate Miami USA 1986-90; *Style—* Peter Spiceley, Esq, MBE; c/o Foreign & Commonwealth Office, King Charles St, London SW1A 2AH

SPICER, Cdr Bruce Evan; s of Dr Gerald Evan Spicer, MC (d 1976), of Appin, Argyll, and Mary Cecilia, *née* Bethune (d 1983); gs of Sir Evan Spicer and Lt Gen Sir Edward Bethune 'father' of the Territorial Army; *b* 24 March 1927; *Educ* Ludgrove, Britannia RNC Dartmouth; *m* 5 Aug 1954, Susan, da of Maj James Dance, MP, TD (d 1971), of Moreton Morrell, Warwick; *Career* Royal Naval Offr 1940-82; md GB Marine Ltd 1984-; memb of Ctee Royal Humane Soc 1977-; memb Cncls: Hawkley Parish, Hawkley Parochial Church; Freeman City of London, Liveryman Worshipful Co of Fishmongers; memb of Lloyds; OStJ; *Recreations* cricket, golf, shooting, photography, gardening; *Clubs* Royal Scottish Automobile, MCC, Liphook Golf, Free Foresters CC; *Style—* Cdr Bruce E Spicer, RN; Champlers Cottage, Hawkley, Liss, Hampshire GU33 6NG (☎ 073 084 391, fax (M) 073 084 391)

SPICER, Christopher James Evan; s of Adrian Evan Spicer (d 1975); *b* 26 April 1940; *Educ* Eton; *m* 1975, Joanna Grizelda, da of Ven E J G Ward, LVO, Chaplain to HM The Queen; 2 da (Rachel b 1977, Annabel b 1980); *Career* res estate mangr Euston Estate (Duke of Grafton, KG); *Style—* Christopher J E Spicer, Esq; Blackbourne House, Euston, Thetford (☎ 0842 763504); Estate Office, Euston, Thetford, Norfolk (☎ 0842 766366)

SPICER, Sir James Wilton; MP (C) Dorset West Feb 1974-; s of James Spicer and Florence Clara Spicer; *b* 4 Oct 1925; *Educ* Latymer Sch; *m* 1954, Winifred Douglas Shanks; 2 da; *Career* Regular Army 1943-57; contested (C) Southampton Itchen by-election 1971, UK memb Euro Parl 1975-78, MEP (EDG) Wessex 1979-84; chm: Cons Political Centre 1969-72, Cons Gp for Europe 1975-78; chief whip of Cons Gp in Euro Parl 1976-80, memb Select Ctee Agric 1984-85, appointed vice chm Cons Party and chm Int Office 1984-; chm: British-Turkish Parly Gp, British Maltese Parly Gp, dep chm South Africa Club; chm Fitness for Indust, dir Thames and Kennet Marina Ltd; kt 1988; *Style—* Sir James Spicer, MP; Whatley, Beaminster, Dorset (☎ 0308 862337); House of Commons, London SW1A 0AA

SPICER, John Vincent; s of Herbert Gordon Spicer, of Billericay, Essex, and Doreen Mary, *née* Collings; *b* 2 March 1951; *Educ* Billericay Comp Sch, Univ of Sheffield (BA); *m* 23 June 1973, Patricia Ann, da of Raymond Sidney Bracher (d 1986), of Harlow, Essex; *Career* business planner Kodak 1975-77, strategic planner Whitbread & Co plc 1978-82, brewery analyst Grenfell & Colegrave 1982-84, dir Kleinwort Benson Securities Ltd 1986-; memb Stock Exchange; *Recreations* golf, squash, hill walking; *Style—* John Spicer, Esq; Flat 9, 56 Holland Park, London W11 3RS (☎ 071 229 0316); Kleinwort Benson Securities Ltd, 20 Fenchurch St, London (☎ 071 623 8000, telex 922 241)

SPICER, (William) Michael Hardy; MP (C) Worcestershire S 1974-; s of Brig Leslie Hardy Spicer (d 1981), of Whitley Bay, Northumberland, and Muriel Winifred Alice Spicer; *b* 22 Jan 1943; *Educ* Wellington, Emmanuel Coll Cambridge (MA); *m* 1967, Patricia Ann, da of Patrick Sinclair Hunter (d 1981); 1 s, 2 da; *Career* former asst to ed of The Statist, dir Cons Systems Res Centre 1968-70, md Economic Models Ltd 1970-80, PPS to Trade Mins 1979-81, vice chm Cons Pty 1981-83, dep chm Cons Pty 1983-84, Parly under sec of state Dept of Transport 1985-86, Min for Aviation 1986-87, Parly under sec of State Dept of Energy 1987-90, Min for Housing and Planning 1990; *Books* Final Act (1983), Prime Minister, Spy (1986), Cotswold Manners (1989), Cotswold Murders (1991); *Recreations* painting, writing, tennis, squash; *Style—* Michael Spicer, Esq, MP; House of Commons, London SW1 (☎ 071 219 3000)

SPICER, Dr Nicholas Adrian Albert; s and h of (Sir) Peter Spicer, 4 Bt, *qv*; *b* 28 Oct 1953; *Educ* Eton; *Career* medical practitioner; *Style—* Dr Nicholas Spicer; 6 Linton Lane, Bromyard, Herefordshire HR7 4DQ

SPICER, Paul Cridland; s of John Harold Vincent Spicer, of 24 Newcastle Rd, Chester-Le-Street, Co Durham, and Joan Sallie, *née* Hickling; *b* 6 June 1952; *Educ* New Coll Sch Oxford, Oakham Sch Rutland, Univ of London (BMus), Univ of Durham (PGCE), RCM (ARCO, ARCM); *Career* asst dir of music Uppingham Sch 1974-78, dir of music Ellesmere Coll 1978-84, prodr BBC Radio Three 1984-86, sr prodr Radio Three Midlands 1986-90, artistic dir Lichfield Festival 1990-; organ recitalist on Radio Three 1980-; dir: Chester Bach Singers 1982-84, Leicester Bach Choir 1984-, Finzi Singers as composer princ works incl: On The Power of Sound, The Darling of The World; church music incl: Come Out Lazar, Magnificat and Nunc and Dimittis; composer of organ, instrumental and chamber music; cncl memb Assoc of Br Choral Dirs, tstee Finzi Tst, chm Finzi Tst Festivals, dir Abbotsholme Arts Soc; memb RCO; *Recreations* architecture, prints (old and contemporary), promoting British music; *Style—* Paul Spicer, Esq; 1 The Close, Lichfield, Staffs WS13 7LD (☎ 0543 250627); 7 The Close, Lichfield, Staffs WS13 7LD (☎ 0543 257298)

SPICER, Paul George Bullen; s of Col Roy Godfrey Bullen Spicer, CMG, MC (d 1946), and Margaret Ina Frances, *née* Money; *b* 6 Feb 1928; *Educ* Eton; *m* 10 Sept 1954, June Elizabeth Cadogan, da of Antony Fenwick (d 1954), of Kiambu, Kenya, and Brinkburn Priory, Northumberland; 1 s (Rupert b 1955), 1 da (Venetia b 1959); *Career* Lt Coldstream Gds 1945-49; md Overseas with Shell International Petroleum, (served 1949-70), joined Lonrho 1970; (dir Main Bd 1978); *Recreations* books, music, horses; *Clubs* Brooks's; *Style—* Paul Spicer, Esq; Cheapside House, 138 Cheapside, London EC2V 6BL

SPICER, (Sir) Peter James; 4 Bt (UK 1906), of Lancaster Gate, Borough of Paddington, but does not use title; s of Sir Stewart Dykes Spicer, 3 Bt (d 1968); *b* 20 May 1921; *Educ* Winchester, Trinity Coll Cambridge, ChCh Oxford; *m* 1949, Margaret, da of late Sir (James) Steuart Wilson; 1 s, 3 da (and 1 da decd); *Heir* s, Dr Nicholas Spicer; *Career* serv WWII Lt RNVR (despatches); on publishing staff Oxford University Press 1947-81, chm Educational Publishers Cncl 1974-76; appeal dir Mansfield Coll Oxford 1981-85; *Recreations* sailing, walking, gardening, reading, music; *Style—* P J Spicer, Esq; Salt Mill House, Mill Lane, Chichester, W Sussex PO19 3JN (☎ 0243 782825)

SPICER, Hon Mrs (Sarah Margaret); *née* Watkinson; da of 1 Viscount Watkinson, CH, PC; *b* 17 April 1944; *m* 1965, David Bethune Spicer; 4 da; *Style—* The Hon Mrs Spicer; Vingers, West Harting, nr Petersfield, Hants GU31 5NX

SPICKERNELL, Rear Admiral Derek Garland; CB (1974); s of Cdr Sydney Garland Spickernell, RN (ka 1940), and Florence Elizabeth Curtis, *née* March (d 1980); *b* 1 June 1921; *Educ* RNEC Keyham; *m* 1946, Ursula Rosemary Sheila, da of Frederick Cowslade Money (d 1953), of Newbury; 2 s (Richard, John (decd)), 1 da (Susan); *Career* Rear Adm MOD Whitehall 1971-75, dir gen Br Standards Instn 1981-86, vice pres Int Standards Orgn Geneva 1985-; *Recreations* Golf; *Clubs* IOD; *Style—* Rear Admiral Spickernell, CB; Ridgefield, Shawford, Hants (☎ 0962 712157)

ŠPIČKOVÁ, Hon Mrs (Victoria Wentworth); *née* Reilly; o da of Baron Reilly (Life Peer, d 1990), and his 1 w, Pamela Wentworth Martin, *née* Foster; *b* 30 July 1941; *Educ* Francis Holland London, Trinity Coll Toronto Univ (BA); *m* 1973, Daniel Špička, s of Dr Hilar Špička, of Prague; 2 da (Katherine b 1974, Lucie b 1977); *Career* former journalist: Illustrated London News, The Sunday Telegraph; *Recreations* music, travel, reading; *Style—* The Hon Mrs Špičková; U Mrázovky 7, Prague 5, Czechoslovakia 150 00

SPIEGELBERG, Richard George; s of Francis Edward Frederick Spiegelberg (d 1979), and Margaret Neville, *née* Clegg; *b* 21 Jan 1944; *Educ* Marlborough, Hotchkiss Sch USA, New Coll Oxford (MA); *m* 1, 1970 (m dis 1979), Coralie Eve, *née* Dreyfus; 2 s (Rupert b 1971, Maximilian b 1974); m 2, 1980, Suzanne Louise *née* Dodd; 1 s (Assheton b 1981), 1 da (Henrietta b 1984); *Career* Economist Intelligence Unit 1965-67, business journalist and mgmnt ed The Times 1967-74, princ Dept of Indust 1974-75, NEDO 1975-76; assoc dir: J Walter Thompson & Co 1976-80, Coopers & Lybrand 1980-84; dir and jt md Streets Fin 1984-87, exec dir corp communications Merrill Lynch Europe Ltd 1987-; *Books* The City (1973); *Recreations* walking, golf, opera; *Clubs* Brooks's; *Style—* Richard Spiegelberg, Esq

SPIERS, (John) Anthony; *b* 19 Sept 1944; *Educ* Bishop Vesey's GS Sutton Coldfield Warwickshire; *m* 1971, Catherine Anne; 3 s (Jonathan (by first w), Benjamin b 1972, Gerald b 1973), 2 da (Catherine b 1975, Hannah-May b 1981); *Career* slr; ptnr Peter Peter & Wright 1970; clerk to Blanchminster Charity 1976-84; memb Cornwall CC 1981-88, dir Solicitors' Benevolent Assoc; FRSA; *Recreations* fishing, reading, walking; *Style—* Anthony Spiers, Esq; 8 Fore St, Holsworthy, Devon (☎ 0409 253262, fax 0409 254 091)

SPIERS, Donald Maurice; CB (1987), TD (1966); s of Harold Herbert Spiers (d 1968), and Emma, *née* Foster (d 1978); *b* 27 Jan 1934; *Educ* Trinity Coll Cambridge (MA); *m* 13 Dec 1958, Sylvia Mary, da of Sammuel Lowman (d 1963); 2 s (Simon b 1965, Philip b 1969); *Career* 2 Lt RE 1952-54, devpt engr de Havilland 1957-60, operational res Air Miny 1961-66, scientific advsr Far East AF 1967-70, asst chief acientist RAF 1971-78, MOD PE 1978-84, dep controller Aircraft 1984-86, Controller Estabs Res & Nucl 1987-89, Controller Aircraft 1989-; *Style—* Donald Spiers, Esq, CB, TD; MOD, Whitehall, London SW1 (☎ 071 218 7813)

SPIERS, Ven Graeme Hendry Gordon; s of Charles Gordon Spiers (d 1974), of London, and Mary McArthur, *née* Hendry (d 1980); *b* 15 Jan 1925; *Educ* Mercers Sch, Univ of London (ALCD); *m* 17 May 1958, (Patricia) Ann May, da of late Harold Chadwick, of Bournemouth; 2 s (Andrew b 1959, Peter b 1961); *Career* RNVR Sub-Lt 1944, demobbed 1946; ordained: deacon 1952, priest 1953 (Canterbury Cathedral); curate Addiscombe Parish Church Croydon 1952-56, succentor Bradford Cathedral 1956-58; vicar: Speke Liverpool 1958-66, Aigburth Liverpool 1966-80; rural dean Childwall 1976-79, hon canon Liverpool Cathedral 1977-, archdeacon of Liverpool 1979-; chm: Tstees William Edmonds Fund, Josephine Butler Tst; govr St Margaret's C of E Sch Liverpool; *Recreations* reading, gardening, wine making; *Clubs* Liverpool Athenaeum; *Style—* The Ven the Archdeacon of Liverpool; 40 Sinclair Drive, Liverpool L18 3H10 (☎ 051 722 6675); Church House, 1 Hanover St, Liverpool L1 3DW (☎ 051 709 9722)

SPIERS, John Raymond; JP (E Sussex); s of H H Spiers (d 1956), and Kate, *née* Root (d 1973); *b* 30 Sept 1941; *Educ* Red Hill Sch E Sutton, Catford Coll of Commerce, Univ of Sussex (BA); *m* 24 June 1967 (m dis 1983), Prof Margaret Ann Spiers, da of Leonard Forbes Boden, OBE (d 1987); 1 s (Ruskin b 19 June 1968), 1 da (Jehane b 21 Jan 1971); *Career* journalist 1960-64; fndr, chm and md: The Harvester Press Ltd, Harvester Microform Publications Ltd 1973-87; Wheatsheaf Books Ltd 1980-88, fndr and chm John Spiers Publishing Ltd 1988-; memb Advsy Bd Centre for Study of Social History Univ of Warwick 1979-82; chm: Univ of Sussex Alumni Soc

1983-, Brighton Theatre Ltd 1984, Brighton Business Group; tstee: Brighton Festival 1989-, Choice in Educn, Prospect Tst; founding dir Southern Sound Radio 1980-87; dir: Radical Soc 1990-, Center for Intelligence Studies Washington DC 1990-; conslt dir Cons Central Office 1990-, pres elect Brighton Kemp Town Cons Assoc 1990-, memb Advsy Cncl Inst of Econ Affrs Health Unit 1989-; Queen's award for Export Achievement 1986; *Books* The Rediscovery of George Gissing (1971); *Recreations* collecting books, reading them, walking, natural history; *Clubs* Travellers', Athenaeum; *Style—* John Spiers, Esq, JP; John Spiers Publishing Ltd, 30 New Rd, Brighton, Sussex (☎ 0273 26611, fax 0273 23983, telex 87830 HILTON G)

SPIERS, Judith Marilyn (Judi); da of Leonard David Spiers (d 1989), and Fay, *née* Sugarman; *b* 15 March 1950; *Educ* Notre Dame Coll Plymouth, Rose Bruford Coll of Speech and Drama Sidcup Kent; *Career* actress Belgrade Theatre in Education Co Coventry 1973-75, relief announcer then prog presenter Westward TV 1975-85 (franchise taken over by TSW 1982); presenter Bazaar 1985-87, Daytime Live 1987-, Daytime UK 1990; various Guildhall medals for drama; Lombard RAC Rally medal 1989; *Recreations* swimming, reading, cooking, karate, skiing and scubadiving, mimicry and accent learning, travelling, collecting perfume bottles and wooden toys; *Style—* Ms Judi Spiers; Daytime UK, BBC Pebble Mill, Birmingham B5 7QQ (☎ 021 414 8888)

SPIERS, Michael David; s of Montague Spiers, of Middx, and Doris, *née* Pruim; *b* 20 Dec 1949; *Educ* John Lyon Sch Harrow-on-the-Hill; *m* 6 June 1971 (m dis), Carole, da of David Fortuyn (d 1956); 1 s (Daniel b 1979), 2 da (Lisa b 1973, Tanya b 1975); m 2, 9 Oct 1990, Susan, da of Harold Jacobs; *Career* CA 1973, licensed insolvency practitioner 1986; dir: Teampace Hldgs Ltd, Engineering Group; *Recreations* squash, bridge, horse-riding; *Style—* Michael D Spiers, Esq; Highgate Hill, London N19 5NL (☎ 071 281 4474, fax 071 281 3691)

SPIERS, Air Cdre Reginald James; OBE (1972); s of Alfred James Oscar Spiers (d 1963), and Rose Emma Alice, *née* Watson (d 1975); *b* 8 Nov 1928; *Educ* Haberdashers' Askes', RAF Coll Cranwell; *m* 1 Dec 1956, Cynthia Jeanette, da of Arnold S Williams; 2 da ((Sally) Linda b 11 April 1958, Carolyn Deirdre b 30 Sept 1959); *Career* RAF: cmmnd 1949, Pilot 247 (Fighter) Sqdn 1950-52, Day Fighter Ldrs Course 1952, Flt Cdr 64 (Fighter) Sqdn 1952-54 (RAF Aerobatics Team 1953-54), Empire Test Pilots Course RAE Farnborough 1955, Fighter Test Sqdn A & AEE 1955-59, OC 4 (Fighter) Sqdn 1959-61, PSO to C in C RAF Germany 1961-63, RAF Staff Coll 1964, FCO 1965-67, OC RAF Masirah 1967-68, Chief Test Flying Instr ETPS 1968-71, Air Warfare Course 1972, Air Secs Dept MOD 1972-73, MA to Govr Gibraltar 1973-75, CO Experimental Flying Dept RAE Farnborough 1975-78, Staff MOD 1978-79, Cmdt A & AEE Boscombe Down 1979-83; mktg exec GEC Avionics 1984-90; FRAeS 1975; *Recreations* aviation, shooting; *Clubs* RAF; *Style—* Air Cdre Reginald Spiers, OBE; Barnside, Penton Mewsey, nr Andover, Hampshire SP11 0RQ (☎ 026 477 2376)

SPILG, Dr Walter Gerson Spence; s of George Spilg, JP (d 1966), and Fanny, *née* Cohen (d 1978); *b* 27 Oct 1937; *Educ* Hutchesons' GS Glasgow, Univ of Glasgow (MB ChB); *m* 1 Sept 1965, Vivien Anne, da of Edwards Burns (d 1963), of Glasgow; 1 s (Edward George b 1968), 2 da (Sandra Jane b 1966, Jillian Deborah b 1971); *Career* house offr Stobhill Hosp Glasgow 1964-65, registrar in pathology Glasgow Royal Infirmary 1966-68 (Coats Perman Scholar Univ Dept of Pathology 1965-66), lectr in pathology Univ of Glasgow 1969-72, conslt pathologist Victoria Infirmary Glasgow 1972- (sr registrar 1968-69); hon clinical sr lectr Univ of Glasgow; chm Laboratory Med Ctee of W Scot Ctee for Postgraduate Medicinal Educn, memb Greater Glasgow Area Health Bd, memb Area Medical Sub-Ctee in Laboratory Medicine, memb Nat Panel of Specialists; memb: BMA, ACP, Int Acad of Pathology; FRCPath 1982, FRCPG 1988; *Recreations* bridge, reading; *Style—* Dr Walter Spilg; 98 Ayr Road, Newton Mearns, Glasgow G77 6EJ (☎ 041 639 3130); Pathology Dept, Victoria Infirmary, Glasgow G42 9TY (☎ 041 649 4545)

SPILLANE, Mary C; *b* 7 May 1950; *Educ* Harvard Univ (MPA), Simmons Coll (MLIS), Merrimack Coll (BA); *m* 15 Sept 1979, Roger C H Luscombe; 2 da (Anna b 1983, Lucinda b 1985); *Career* started Color Me Beautiful (image consltg firm 1983), formerly in journalism and public affrs, crisis mangr in Carter Admin; active in human and refugee rights, political lobbyist in America & Geneva; *Recreations* running, music, 19 century novels; *Clubs* Network, Metropolitan, IOD; *Style—* Ms Mary Spillane; 45 Abbey Business Centre, Ingate Place, London SW8 3NS

SPILLER, Prof Eric; s of Leonard Spiller, of Wombourne, Staffs, and Helen, *née* Holder; *b* 19 Aug 1946; *m* Carolyn; 2 s (Charles b 12 Sept 1974, Rufus b 8 Nov 1977), 1 da (Nancy b 11 July 1980); *Career* jewellery designer and lectr: pt/t lectr Fashion Dept Harrow Sch of Art 1971-73, lectr in silversmithing and jewellery 1973-75, Dept of Three-Dimensional Studies NI Poly, lectr i/c of jewellery 1975-81 (Dept of Design Grays Sch of Art, Robert Gordons Inst of Technol Aberdeen), prog ldr BA (Combined Studies) Crafts Crewe and Alsager Coll of Higher Educn 1981-83, princ lectr/dep head of dept 1983-85 (Dept of Silversmithing Jewellery and Allied Crafts, Sir John Cass Faculty of Art City of London Poly); head of sch: Sch of Design Portsmouth Coll of Art Design and Further Educn 1985-87, Grays Sch of Art Robert Gordons Inst of Technol Aberdeen 1987-; visiting lectr: Univ of Ulster, West Surrey Coll of Art, Loughborough Coll of Art, S Glamorgan Inst of Higher Educn, Brighton Poly, San Diego State Univ; public collections incl: Goldsmiths Hall, Crafts Cncl, W Midlands Arts, NW Arts, Aberdeen Art Gallery, Scot Crafts Collection; private collections worldwide; numerous exhibitions incl: Craftmans Art (V & A) 1973, Aberdeen Art Gallery 1977, New Jewellery (Royal Exchange Theatre Manchester) 1984, New York 1983, Kyoto 1984, Tokyo 1984-85, Munich 1989; FRSA; *Style—* Prof Eric Spiller; Grays School of Art, Robert Gordon Institute of Technology, Aberdeen (☎ 0224 313247, fax 0224 312723)

SPILLER, Richard John; s of Capt Michael Macnaughton Spiller, of Belfast, and Agnes Gall, *née* Algie; *b* 31 Dec 1953; *Educ* Royal Belfast Academical Inst, Univ of Exeter (LLB), City of London Poly (MA); *m* 17 Sept 1982, Hilary Phyllis, da of William Wright, of Kingston-on-Thames, Surrey; 1 s (James b 1984), 1 da (Emily b 1987); *Career* admitted slr 1980; asst slr: Hedleys 1978-81, Norton Rose 1981-83; ptnr D J Freeman and Co 1983-85; Freeman: City of London 1986, Worshipful Co of Slrs 1986 (dep chm Commercial Law Sub Ctee); memb Law Soc; *Recreations* squash, dining out; *Style—* Richard Spiller, Esq; D J Freeman and Co, 43 Fetter Lane, London EC4A 1NA (☎ 071 583 4055, fax 071 353 7377, telex 894579)

SPILMAN, John Ellerker; JP (1984), DL (Humberside, 1990); s of Maj Harry Spilman, MC, JP, DL (d 1980), and Phyllis Emily, *née* Hind; *b* 9 March 1940; *Educ* Sedbergh, RAC Cirencester; *m* 25 Oct 1975, Patricia Mary, da of Gilbert Sutcliffe (d 1988), of Cleethorpes; 1 s (David b 1984), 1 da (Joanna b 1980); *Career* md farming co, dir Aylesby Manor Farms Ltd; High Sheriff Humberside 1989-90; church warden, tstee Stanford Charity; *Recreations* fishing, shooting, tennis, music; *Clubs* Farmers'; *Style—* John E Spilman, Esq, JP, DL; Aylesby Manor, Grimsby, S Humberside (☎ 0472 71800); Manor Farm, Aylesby, Grimsby (☎ 0472 72550)

SPINK, Ian Alexander; s of John Arthur Spink, of Melbourne, Australia, and Lorna Kathleen, *née* Hart; *b* 8 Oct 1947; *Educ* Highett HS, Aust Ballet Sch; *m* 1, 1972 (m dis 1975), Gail Mae Ferguson; m 2, 1986, Michele Ashmore Smith; *Career* dancer Australian Ballet Co 1968-74, dancer and choreographer Dance Co of NSW 1975-77, dancer Richard Alston & Dancers Co 1978-79, fndr, dancer, dir and choreographer Ian Spink Dance Group 1978-82, co-fndr Second Stride (dance theatre) 1982 (became sole dir 1988), currently freelance choreographer and dir; choreography incl: theatre choreography for RSC, Ro Theatre (Holland) and The Crucible (Sheffield), opera choreography for Opera North, WNO, Royal Opera House, Scot Opera, Opera de Nice, ENO; directed Fugue by Caryl Churchill (channel 4) 1988 and Judith Weir's The Vanishing Bridgegroom (Scot Opera) 1990, directed and choreographed seven maj works for Second Stride incl Heaven Ablaze in his Breast (BBC) 1989 and Lives of the Great Poisoners 1991; *Recreations* music, computers, experimental theatre, housework; *Style—* Ian Spink, Esq; Harriet Cruickshank, 97 Old South Lambeth Rd, London SW8 1XU (☎ 071 735 2933)

SPINKS, *née* White; **Mrs Mary**; da of William White (d 1952), and Mary White (d 1987); *b* 21 Feb 1947; *m* 1968, Henry Spinks; 1 s (Michael b 1975), 1 da (Susanna 1972); *Career* memb: Gen Cncl Nat Asthma Campaign, Asthma Res Cncl; sponsor King's Med Res Tst, fndr and hon organiser of The Starlight Ball 1985-91 (in aid of the Asthma Res Cncl and Nat Asthmas Campaign); voluntary fund raising for Asthma Res Centre at UMDS of Guy's and St Thomas' Hosps London; *Recreations* family life, voluntary fund raising, armchair politics, interest in the younger generation; *Style—* Mrs Henry Spinks; Tantons, Leesons Hill, Chislehurst, Kent BR7 6QH (☎ 0689 838388)

SPIRA, Peter John Ralph; s of Dr Jean-Jacques Spira (d 1970); *b* 2 March 1930; *Educ* Eton, King's Coll Cambridge; *m* 1, 1957, Meriel, *née* Gold; m 2, 1969, Anne Marie Marguerite Renée, *née* Landon; 6 c; *Career* SG Warburg & Co Ltd 1957-74 (vice chm 1971-74, non-exec dir until 1982), fin dir Sotheby Parke Bernet Group plc 1974-82, vice chm Goldman Sachs Int Corpn London 1982-87, dir Société Générale de Surveillance Holding SA Geneva 1987, dep chm County National Westminster Ltd 1988-; memb Nat Film Fin Corpn 1981-86, FCA; *Recreations* music, reading, photography; *Clubs* Buck's; *Style—* Peter Spira, Esq; 63 Bedford Gardens, London W8 7EF (☎ 071 727 5295)

SPITTLE, Leslie; s of Samuel Spittle (d 1942), and Irene, *née* Smith; *b* 14 Nov 1940; *Educ* Acklam Hall GTS, Constantine Coll of Technol, Univ of Hull (LLB); *m* 7 Sept 1963, Brenda, da of Charles Alexander Clayton (d 1961); 3 s (Nicholas b 21 June 1968, Jonathan b 23 Sept 1971, Matthew b 14 Dec 1981); *Career* Univ of Hull Air Sqdn RAFVR; mgmnt trainee 1956-62, lectr and sr lectr Teeside Poly 1965-70; barr Gray's Inn 1970, rec 1990; former: chm Round Table, chm Yarm Sch Assoc, vice-chm govrs Kirklevington Sch, Master Lodge of Freedom; ACIS 1960; *Recreations* amateur dramatics, golf, various charitable bodies; *Clubs* Eaglescliffe GC, Lodge of Freedom, Lodge of Jurists, Rotary (Teeside West); *Style—* Leslie Spittle, Esq; 83 Forest Lane, Kirklevington, Cleveland TS15 9NG (☎ 0642 780195); 4 Paper Bldg, Temple, London; Park Ct Chambers, 40 Park Cross St, Leeds, W Yorks (☎ 0532 433277)

SPITTLE, Dr Margaret Flora; da of Edwin William Spittle (d 1977), of Tunbridge Wells, and Ada Florence, *née* Axam; *b* 11 Nov 1939; *Educ* Kings Coll London, Westminster Hosp Med Sch; *m* 2 Jan 1965 (m dis 1977), Clive Lucas Harmer, s of Cecil Norman Harmer (d 1986), of Westcliff on Sea; 2 da (Kasha Jane Lucas b 1968, Victoria Margaret Lucas b 1971); m 2, 31 May 1986, David John Hare, s of John Robinson Hare (d 1982), of Southrepps; *Career* conslt radiotherapist and oncologist St John's Hosp for Diseases of the Skin and The Cromwell Hosp 1971, dir Meyerstein Inst of Radiotherapy and Oncology The Middlesex Hosp 1987-; memb Cncl of RCR 1987, treas RSM 1988; pres: radiology section RSM 1989, Oncology Section RSM 1987, Head and Neck Oncologists of GB; memb: Govt Ctee on Breast Screening, Royal Colls Gp on HIV Infection, RSM, BMA, RCR; Freeman City of London, Liveryman Worshipful Soc of Apothecaries (memb Ctee); *Recreations* family, golf, music, wind surfing; *Style—* Dr Margaret Spittle; The Manor House, Beaconsfield, Claygate, Surrey KT10 0PW (☎ 03724 65540, fax 03724 70470); Meyerstein Institute of Radiotherapy and Oncology, The Middlesex Hosp, Mortimer St, London W1N 8AA (☎ 071 380 9090, fax 071 636 9044)

SPITTLE, Robert; s of William Charles Spittle, of 24 Shires House, Eden Grove Road, Byfleet, Surrey, and Ellen, *née* Angel; *b* 14 March 1955; *Educ* Highlands CS Sch, Guildford Co Tech Coll, Poly of the South Bank (BSc); *m* 21 May 1977, Lydia Shirley, da of Leonard Taylor; 1 da (Cally b 16 Dec 1980); *Career* design engr in building servs mech engrg Kennedy and Donkin International Consulting Engineers 1971-78, project engr The Raven Group (design and building contractors) 1978-82, project mangr then UK internal mech engrg conslt The Central Consulting Services Group IBM (UK) Ltd, property mgmnt 1982-87, engrg ptnr Building Design Partnership (building design conslts) 1989- (mech engrg assoc 1987-89); memb: Chartered Inst of Building Services Engrs 1982, American Soc of Heating Refrigeration and Air Conditioning Engrs 1986; CEng 1986; *Recreations* swimming, running, squash; *Style—* Robert Spittle, Esq; Building Design Partnership, 16 Greese St, London W1A 4WD (☎ 071 631 4733, fax 071 631 0393, car 0831 475 879)

SPITTLE, (Anthony) Trevor; s of Stanley Spittle (d 1958); *b* 25 Dec 1929; *Educ* Lindisfarne Coll, Univ of Southampton (BCom); *m* 1955, Jennifer Mae, *née* Emery; 2 s (Graham b 1957, Robert b 1962), 2 da (Frances b 1958, Laura b 1964); *Career* ptnr Deloitte Haskins & Sells 1963-76, dep chm Great Universal Stores plc 1976-; FCA; *Recreations* gardening, sport as a spectator (particularly rugby union); *Style—* Trevor Spittle, Esq; Croft House, Cole Hill, S Hanningfield Rd, Rettendon Common, Chelmsford, Essex

SPOKES, Christopher Daniel; s of John Dacre Spokes (d 1976), and Joyce Margaret, *née* Sheppard; *b* 29 July 1947; *Educ* Wellingborough Sch, Northampton Coll of Technol, Northampton Coll of Agric (NCA), Shuttleworth Coll (NDA), UCW Aberystwyth (BSc Econ); *m* May 1983, Gillian Stewart, da of Alec Neil Donaldson; 1 s (Alexander James b Oct 1987), 1 da (Charlotte Kate b April 1985); *Career* articled clerk Cooper Bros (later Coopers & Lybrand) 1973-76; Bidwells chartered surveyors: joined 1977, ptnr 1986, currently head Client Accounting gp; pres Cambridge Soc of Chartered Acocuntants; FCA 1981 (ACA 1976); *Recreations* tennis, billiards, cinema, walking; *Clubs* Farmers'; *Style—* Christopher Spokes, Esq; Brooklands House, 167 Caxton End, Bourn, Cambridge CB3 7ST (☎ 0954 719288); Bidwells, Trumpington Rd, Cambridge CB2 2LD (☎ 0223 841841)

SPOKES, John Arthur Clayton; QC (1973); s of Peter Spencer Spokes (d 1976), of Oxford, and Lilla Jane, *née* Clayton (d 1979); *b* 6 Feb 1931; *Educ* Westminster, Brasenose Coll Oxford (MA); *m* 30 Dec 1961, Jean, da of Dr Robert McLean (d 1972) of Carluke; 1 s (Andrew), 1 da (Gillian); *Career* called to the Bar Gray's Inn 1955, bencher 1985, rec of Crown Ct 1972-; chllr Diocese of Winchester 1985-; chm Data Protection Tbnl 1985-; *Clubs* United Oxford and Cambridge; *Style—* J A C Spokes, Esq, QC; 3 Pump Court, Temple, London EC4Y 7AJ (☎ 071 353 0711, fax 071 353 3319)

SPOKES SYMONDS, Ann; da of Peter Spencer Spokes (d 1976), and Lilla Jane, *née* Clayton (d 1979); *b* 10 Nov 1925; *Educ* The Masters Sch Dobbs Ferry NY, St Anne's Coll Oxford (MA); *m* 1980, (John) Richard Symonds, s of Sir Charles Symonds, KBE, CB (d 1978); twin step s (Jeremy, Peter); *Career* memb Oxford City Cncl 1957-, Parly candidate gen elections of 1959, 1966 and 1970, lord mayor of Oxford 1976-77, chm Oxfordshire CC 1981-83; memb W Regnl Bd Central Independent TV (formerly ATV)

1978- (dir 1978-81), admin Social Servs to 1980, chm ACC Social Servs Ctee 1978-82; memb: Prince of Wales Advsy Gp on Disability 1983-90, Hearing Aid Cncl 1987-89, Bd of Anchor Housing Assn 1976-83 and 1985-; organising sec Age Concern Oxford 1968-80, chm Age Concern England 1983-86 (vice pres 1987-); *Books* Celebrating Age An Authology (1987); *Recreations* photography, travel, lawn tennis, swimming; *Clubs* Royal Overseas League; *Style—* Mrs Ann Spokes Symonds; 43 Davenant Rd, Oxford OX2 8BU

SPON; *see*: de Spon

SPON-SMITH, Robin Witterick; s of Alan Witterick Spon-Smith, and Joyce Margaret, *née* Bache (d 1988); *b* 11 Oct 1942; *Educ* Eltham Coll London; *m* 11 June 1966, Jennifer Dorothy, da of William Frederic Delabere Walker; 2 s (Jolyon b 1973, Phillip b 1975); *Career* 1 Bn London Scottish (TA) 1960-65; slr Supreme Court 1965; called to the Bar Inner Temple 1976; rec 1987; cncllr London Borough Bromley 1968-71, govr Eltham Coll 1974-; Freeman City of London 1980; *Style—* Robin Spon-Smith, Esq; 1 Mitre Court Buildings, Temple, London EC4Y 7BS (☎ 071 353 0434, fax 071 353 3988)

SPOONER, David; s of Samuel Arthur Spooner, MM, of 17 Auckland Rd, Scunthorpe, and Florence, *née* Wilkinson; *b* 30 April 1942; *Educ* Doncaster Rd Secdy Sch; *Career* currently co cncllr Humberside, chm Joint Airports Ctee, Nat UK Ctee rep All Regnl Airports, chm Bd of Dirs Humberside International Airport; pres MENCAP; *Style—* David Spooner, Esq; 78 Lloyds Ave, Scunthorpe, Humberside (☎ 0724 852808) County Hall, Beverley, Humberside (☎ 0482 867131)

SPOONER, Dr David; s of Rev Reginald H Spooner (d 1982), and Lucy Ellen, *née* Read; *b* 12 Jan 1949; *Educ* Magdalen Coll Sch Brackley, Univ of Birmingham (MB, BSc); *m* Diana Lilian, da of Frederick John Mason, of Banbury; 2 s (John, Andrew), 1 da (Rebecca); *Career* res fell Cancer Res Inst Sutton Surrey 1979-81, sr registrar in radiotherapy Royal Marsden Hosp London 1981-82 (registrar 1976-79); conslt in radiotherapy and oncology: Queen Elizabeth Hosp, Birmingham Children's Hosp, Royal Orthopaedic Hosp Birmingham; memb Cncl: Cancerlink, Royal Coll of Radiologists; MRCP, FRCR; *Style—* Dr David Spooner; Dept of Radiotherapy and Oncology, Queen Elizabeth Hospital, Edgbaston B15 2TH (☎ 021 472 1311 ext 3134, fax 021 414 3700)

SPOONER, Dr Derek John; s of Harry Spooner (d 1968), and Vera Lois, *née* Manning; *b* 14 Oct 1943; *Educ* Taunton's Sch Southampton, St Catharine's Coll Cambridge (MA, PhD); *m* 26 July 1969, Christine Elizabeth, da of Arthur Nuttal Simpson, of Looe, Cornwall; 2 da (Catherine b 1974, Helen b 1978); *Career* sr lectr Dept of Geography Univ of Hull 1985- (lectr 1968-85, head dept 1986-89); visiting prof: Univ of Maryland 1976, Univ of W Virginia 1985; ed: Regnl Studies Assoc newsletter 1986-89, Geography (jl of the Geographical Assoc) 1989-; Regional Studies Assoc; Inst of British Geographers; *Books* Mining and Regional Development (1981); *Recreations* cricket, bridwatching, travel; *Clubs* Hull Cricket (capt 1975, 1977, 1990); *Style—* Dr Derek Spooner; School of Geography and Earth Resources, The University, Hull, N Humberside HU6 7RX (☎ 0482 465554, fax 0482 466340)

SPOONER, Doreen Beryl; da of Horace Leonard Spooner (d 1985), of Beckenham, Kent, and Ada Emily, *née* Tribe (d 1983); *b* 30 Jan 1928; *Educ* Hornsey Co Sch London, LCC Sch of Photography (Cert City & Guilds); *m* 1952, Pierre Vandeputte-Manevy (d 1980), s of Raymond Manevy; 1 s (Antony b 2 Oct 1953), 2 da (Jeanne b 5 March 1955, Catherine b 9 Sept 1959); *Career* photographer; asst to Karl Gullers 1947, jr photographer Keystone Press Agency 1948, Mirror Features 1949-50, staff photographer Daily Mirror 1950, travelled USA with Keystone Press 1951, Magnum Paris 1951-52, Daily Mirror 1962-88, freelance photographer 1988-; memb Photographic Bd the Nat Cncl of Training Journalists 1979; FBIPP 1976, FRPS 1979; *Style—* Ms Doreen Spooner; 6 Valley Road, Shortlands, Bromley, Kent BR2 0HD (☎ 081 460 5075)

SPOONER, Prof Frank Clyffurde; s of Harry Gordon Morrison Spooner (d 1967), and Ethel Beatrice, *née* Walden (d 1985); *b* 5 March 1924; *Educ* Christ's Coll Cambridge (BA, MA, PhD, LittD); *Career* WWII RNVR 1942-46, Sub Lt (S); served: HMS Shippigan, HMS Swiftsure, HMS Newfoundland, HMS Rame Head; Chargé de Recherches Centre Nat de la Recherche Scientifique Paris 1949-50, Allen scholar Univ of Cambridge 1951, fell Christ's Coll 1951-57; Cwlth Fund fell: Univ of Chicago 1955-56, Univs of NY, Columbia and Harvard 1956-57, Ecole Pratique des Hautes Etudes Paris 1957-63; lectr: Ctee for Advanced Studies Univ of Oxford 1958-59, in econs Harvard Univ 1961-62; Irving Fisher res prof of econs Yale Univ 1962-63; Univ of Durham: lectr 1963, reader 1964, prof 1966, emeritus prof of econ history 1985, Leverhulme fell 1977-79 and 1985-86; Prix Limantour, Lauréat de l'Académie des Sciences Morales et Politiques (1957); FRHistS 1970, FSA 1983; *Books* L'économie mondiale et les frappes monétaires en France, 1493-1680 (1956), The International Economy and Monetary Movements in France, 1493-1725 (1972), Risks at sea: Amsterdam insurance and maritime Europe, 1766-1780 (1983); *Recreations* music, walking, photography; *Clubs* United Oxford and Cambridge Univ; *Style—* Prof Frank Spooner; 31 Chatsworth Ave, Bromley, Kent BR1 5DP (☎ 081 857 7040); Dept of Economics, 23 Old Elvet, Durham DH1 3HY (☎ 091 374 2272)

SPOONER, Graham Michael; s of Ronald Sidney Spooner (d 1968), of Westcliff-on-Sea, Essex, and Kitty Margaret, *née* Cole (d 1985); *b* 23 Aug 1953; *Educ* Westcliff HS, St John's Coll Cambridge (MA); *Career* joined ICFC (now part of 3i Group plc) 1974: area mangr Nottingham 1983, local dir in London 1986, dir 3i plc 1987-; *Recreations* sports (playing and watching), reading, theatre, travel; *Clubs* United Oxford and Cambridge Univ; *Style—* Graham Spooner, Esq; 4 Hope Close, Canonbury, London N1 (☎ 071 226 6780); 20 Cavendish Rd East, The Park, Nottingham (☎ 0602 472 118); 3i plc, 40 Queen Square, Bristol BS1 4LE (☎ 0272 277412, fax 0272 279433, telex 917844)

SPOONER, Sir James Douglas; o s of Vice Adm Ernest John Spooner, DSO (d 1942), and Megan, *née* Foster (d 1987); *b* 11 July 1932; *Educ* Eton, ChCh Oxford; *m* 1958, Jane Alison, da of Sir Gerald Glover (d 1986); 2 s, 1 da; *Career* former ptnr Dixon Wilson & Co CAs; chm: Coats Viyella 1969-89, Navy Army and Air Force Inst 1973-86, Morgan Crucible 1983-; dir: John Swire & Sons 1970-, J Sainsbury 1981-, Barclays Bank 1983-; pres KIDS (handicapped children's charity); fell and chm Cncl King's Coll London 1986-, dir Royal Opera House Covent Garden 1987-; fell Eton Coll 1990-; FCA; kt 1981; *Recreations* history, music, shooting; *Clubs* White's, Beefsteak; *Style—* Sir James Spooner; Swire House, 59 Buckingham Gate, London SW1E 6AJ

SPOONER, Raymond Philip; s of Henry James Spooner (d 1989), and Ethel, *née* Phillips (d 1986); *b* 31 Aug 1934; *Educ* Addey and Stanhope Sch London, City Univ London (MSc); *m* 23 Oct 1954, Beryl Jean, da of Percy Charles Bratton (d 1973); 1 s (Kevin Paul b 2 Oct 1956, d 1985), 1 da (Yvette Kay Dawn b 14 Oct 1958); *Career* Sgt Intelligence Corps 1952-54, TA 1954-62; sr lectr accountancy and audit Southbank Poly 1982-90 (co sec 1963-67, lectr 1967-82), dir and chief exec Arranbee Consultancy Servs Ltd (conslts in internal auditing and mgmnt control); author of Spooner report (brought about the creation of UK professional qualification for internal auditors); past govr: Inst of Internal Auditors UK 1976-78, SW London Coll 1970-81; past pres Soc Co and Commercial Accountants 1987-88; Freeman: City of London 1978, Worshipful Co of Secs and Admins 1978; MBIM 1967, FSCA 1968, ACIS 1971, FIIA 1986; *Recreations* bridge, DIY; *Style—* Raymond Spooner, Esq; Conifers, Orestan Lane, Effingham, Surrey KT24 5SN (☎ 0372 457248); Arranbee Consultancy Services Ltd, Tredan House, Church Rd, Bookham, Surrey KT23 3JG (☎ 0372 458995)

SPOONER, Richard Hamilton; s of Derek Richard Spooner (d 1978), and Patricia Sackville, *née* Hamilton; *b* 17 Feb 1952; *Educ* Kings Sch Ely, Lanchester Sch of Business Studies (BA); *m* 8 April 1978, Susan Elizabeth Ann, da of Anthony John Rowntree; 3 da (Victoria, Catherine, Elizabeth); *Career* audit mangr Howard Tilly 1976-79, chief accountant Yeoman Aggregates Ltd 1979-83; dir: Yeoman Heavy Haulage Ltd 1980-83, Buckingham Computers Ltd 1981-84, HTA 1983-88; md: Howard Tilly Associates Ltd 1984-88, H T A Property Systems Ltd 1987-, Baker Tilly Management Consultants 1988-; ptnr: Howard Tilly & Co 1986-, Baker Tilly & co 1988-; ACA; memb ICAEW, MInstD, MBIM; *Recreations* tennis, bridge, good food; *Style—* Richard Spooner, Esq; 3 Green Hill, High Wycombe, Bucks (☎ 0494 446 083); Baker Tilly, 2 Bloomsbury St, London WC1B 3ST (☎ 071 413 5100, fax 071 413 5101, car 0831 173 907)

SPOOR, Roger Charlton; OBE (1988), RD, DL (1988); s of Kenneth Spoor (d 1983), of Newcastle and Dorothy, *née* Dickinson; *b* 21 April 1932; *Educ* Sedbergh; *m* 6 Oct 1956, Susan Elizabeth, da of Jack Edmund Daniels; 2 c (Nicola Jane b 9 Jan 1959, Mark b 7 April 1960); *Career* Nat Serv 1955-57; Tyne Div RNR 1950, ret Lieut Cdr 1971; articled clerk Percy F Ward & Co 1950-55; ptnr: J C Graham & Spoor 1958-70, Ernst & Young (formerly Arthur Young) 1970-; memb Exec Ctee Arthur Young 1975-84; dir: Northern Football Ground Co Ltd, Tyneside Economic Development Co Ltd, Tyne & Wear Enterprise Trust, Calvert Trust, Northumbria Calvert Trust Limited, Business in the Community (Tyne, Wear & Northumberland), Tyne and Wear Foundation Limited, Northern RHA; memb Ctee N Soc of Chartered Accountants 1973-80 (pres 1979-80), chm N Soc Courses Ctee 1974-79; memb: N E Electricity Bd 1981-89, Tyne & Wear Residuary Body 1985-88, Northumberland Nat Parks Ctee 1985-90, Ctee IOD (hon sec N Counties Branch 1971-78) 1978-; hon treas Univ of Newcastle 1978- (chm Fin Ctee 1978-), memb TAVR Assoc Employers Liaison Ctee 1987-, chm N Fin Forum 1989-, dir BEAM Ltd (Pinetree Centre) 1990-, Northern Football Club: hon treas 1958-75, memb Mgmnt Ctee 1958-79, pres 1978-79; chm Murray House Community Centre & Youth Club 1972-76 (hon treas 1959-72); Calvert Trust: tstee 1974-, chm Mgmnt Ctee Kielder Adventure Centre 1981-86 (chm Working Party 1979-81), tstee Northumbria Calvert Trust; pres Jubilee Sailing Tst 1989-; Newcastle Upon Tyne Cncl for the Disabled (The Dene Centre): vice chm 1972-86, chm Information & Advsy Ctee 1982-86, chm 1986-; hon sec Ret Offrs Assoc 1981-; Freeman City of Newcastle upon Tyne 1983; FCA 1968 (ACA 1955); *Recreations* fishing, shooting, water colour painting, debating; *Clubs* Army & Navy, Northern Counties, Northumberland Golf; *Style—* Roger Spoor, Esq; 5 Graham Park Road, Newcastle upon Tyne NE3 4BH (☎ 091 285 1238)

SPORBORG, Christopher Henry; s of Henry Nathan Sporborg, CMG (d 1985), of Upwick Hall, Upwick, Albury, Ware, Herts, and Mary, *née* Rowlands; *b* 17 April 1939; *Educ* Rugby, Emmanuel Coll Cambridge; *m* 1961, Lucinda Jane, da of Brig Richard Nigel Hanbury (d 1971), of Hay Lodge, Braughing, Herts; 2 s (William b 1965, Simon b 1972), 2 da (Sarah b 1964, Eliza b 1967); *Career* Nat Serv Lt Coldstream Gds; dep chm Hambros Bank Ltd 1962- (dir 1970, exec dir 1975, currently dep chm); dep chm: Hambros plc (bd memb 1983), Hambro Pacific; chm: Hambro Countrywide plc 1986-, Hambro Australia Ltd 1978-, Hambro America Inc 1985-, Atlas Copco Gp in GB 1984-, BFSS Investmts Ltd 1980-; hon treas BFSS; jt master Puckeridge and Thurlow Foxhounds; landowner; *Recreations* racing, hunting, master of foxhounds; *Clubs* Boodles, Jockey; *Style—* Christopher Sporborg, Esq; Booms Farm , Upwick Green, Ware, Herts (☎ 027 974 444); Hambros Bank Ltd, 41 Towerhill, London EC3N 4HA (☎ 071 480 5000, telex 883851)

SPOTSWOOD, Marshal of the Royal Air Force Sir Denis Frank; GCB (1970, KCB 1966, CB 1961), CBE (1946), DSO (1943), DFC (1942); s of Frank Henry Spotswood (d 1957), of Elstead, Surrey, and Caroline Spotswood (d 1984); *b* 26 Sept 1916; *m* 1942, Ann, da of Solomon Child (d 1968); 1 s; *Career* joined RAF 1936, served WWII in Europe, N Africa and SE Asia (despatches twice), Gp Capt 1954, ADC to HM The Queen 1957-61, Actg Air Cdre 1958, Cdr RAF Coll Cranwell 1958-61, Air Cdre 1960, AVM 1961, Asst COS Air Def Div SHAPE 1961-63, AOC 3 Gp Bomber Cmd 1964-65, C-in-C RAF Germany 1965-68, Cdr 2 Allied TAF 1966-68, Air Marshal 1965, Air Chief Marshal 1968, AOC-in-C RAF Strike Cmd 1968-71, Air ADC to HM The Queen 1970-74, Chief of Air Staff 1971-74, Marshal of the RAF 1974; vice chm Rolls Royce 1974-80, chm Smith's Industs Aerospace Cos 1980-83 (dir 1983-), dir Dowty Gp 1980-87, chm Royal Star and Garter Home 1980-86 (govr 1975-); FRAeS; Offr Legion of Merit (USA); *Recreations* golf, bridge, rugby (spectator), rowing (spectator); *Clubs* RAF, Royal Aeronautical Soc, Phyllis Court, Huntercombe Golf; *Style—* Marshal of the Royal Air Force, Sir Denis Spotswood, GCB, CBE, DSO, DFC; Coombe Cottage, Hambleden, Henley-on-Thames, Oxon

SPOTTISWOOD, Air Vice-Marshal James Donald (Don); CB (1988), CVO (1977), AFC (1971); s of James Thomas Spottiswood (d 1981), of Hartlepool, and Caroline Margaret, *née* Taylor (d 1989); *b* 27 May 1934; *Educ* West Hartlepool GS, Univ of Boston (MA); *m* 3 April 1957, Margaret Maxwell, da of John James Harrison (d 1939), of Wingate; 2 s (Ian b 1960, David b 1963), 1 da (Lynne b 1958); *Career* joined RAF: 1951, 139 Sqdn 1954, CFS 1956 Flt Cdr RAF Halton 1959, Flt Cdr 617 Sqdn 1963, RNSC 1965, Personal SO C-in-C Middle East 1966, Sqdn-Cdr 53 Sqdn 1968, JSSC 1970, Station Cdr RAF Thorney Is 1971, Station Cdr and Dep Capt Queens F1 1974, gp dir RAF Staff Coll Bracknell 1977, RCDS 1978, Int Mil Staff NATO HQ 1979, Dir Gen of Trg 1983, ADC Trg Units 1985, ret 1989; md Airwork Ltd; chm: RAF Gliding and Soaring Assoc 1983-89, Br Gliding Assoc; FBIM; *Recreations* gliding, sailing, golf; *Clubs* RAF; *Style—* Air Vice-Marshal Don Spottiswood, CB, CVO, AFC; c/o Royal Bank of Scotland, Oxford; Airwork Ltd, Bournemouth International Airport, Christchurch, Dorset BH23 6EB (☎ 0202 572271)

SPRAGUE, Christopher William; s of Coulam Alfred Joseph Sprague, of New Malden, Surrey, and Joan Gertrude, *née* Jackson (d 1986); *b* 19 Aug 1943; *Educ* St Edwards Sch Oxford, Christ Church Oxford (MA); *m* 24 April 1971, Clare, da of Dr John Russell Bradshaw (d 1968), of Topsham, Devon; 4 da (Katharine b 1972, Alison b 1974, Hannah b 1979, Alexandra b 1981); *Career* articled Simmons & Simmons, admitted slr 1970; ptnr Ince & Co 1975-, specialist in insur and maritime law, lectr on maritime law and assoc subjects; subscribing memb Assoc of Average Adjusters, supporting memb London Maritime Arbitrators Assoc, memb Law Soc; treas Thames regnl Rowing Cncl, memb Thames Regnl Umpires Cmmn; Liveryman Worshipful Co of Barbers; *Recreations* reading, history, rowing, bellringing; *Clubs* United Oxford and Cambridge, London Rowing, Leander; *Style—* C W Sprague, Esq; Pasturewood, Woodhill Lane, Shamley Green, Guildford, Surrey GU5 0SP

SPRATT, Sir Greville Douglas; GBE (1987), TD (1962, and bar 1968), JP (City Bench 1978), DL (Gtr London 1986); er s of Hugh Douglas Spratt, of Henley-on-Thames, and Sheelah Ivy, *née* Stace; *b* 1 May 1927; *Educ* Leighton Park Sch, Charterhouse; *m* 1954, Sheila Farrow, yst da of late Joseph Wade, of the Old Mill, Langstone, Hants; 3 da; *Career* Coldstream Gds 1945-46, cmmnd 1946, seconded to Arab Legion, served Palestine, Jordan and Egypt 1946-48, GSO III (Ops and Intelligence) 1948; joined HAC as Private 1950, re-cmmnd 1950, Capt 1952, Maj 1954,

CO (Lt-Col) 1962-65, Regtl Col 1966-70, memb Ct of Assts HAC 1960-70 and 1978-; underwriting memb of Lloyd's 1951-; joined J & N Wade Gp of Cos 1961: dir 1969-76, md 1972-76 (when gp sold); regnl dir (City and West End) NatWest Bank, dir Williams Lea Gp; memb City TA&VRA 1960- (vice chm 1973-77, chm 1977-82), vice chm TA&VRA for Gtr London 1980- (memb Exec and Fin Ctee 1977-); Hon Col: City and NE sector London ACF 1983-, 8 Bn The Queen's Fusiliers Cncl 1982-; cncl memb Reserve Forces Assoc 1981-84, pres London Fedn of Old Comrades Assocs 1983-, dep pres London Br Red Cross 1983-; memb: Blackdown Ctee Nat Tst 1977-87, Ctee Guildhall Sch of Music and Drama 1978-80 and 1990- (hon memb GSMD 1988), court City Univ 1981-, Governing Bodies of Girls Schs Assoc 1982-; govr: St Ives Sch 1976- (vice chm 1977-86, chm 1986-), King Edward's Sch Witley 1978- (vice pres 1989), Christ's Hosp 1978-, Bridewell Royal Hosp 1978-, City of London Sch for Girls 1981-82, Malvern Girls' Coll 1982-, St Paul's Cathedral Choir Sch 1985-, Charterhouse 1985- (chm 1989-); life govr Corp of the Sons of the Clergy, patron Int Centre for Child Studies 1985-; vice pres Lest We Forget Assoc 1989-, vice chm Haslemere Royal Br Legion 1989-, chm Action Res for the Crippled Child 1989- (memb Cncl 1982-, memb Haslemere Ctee 1971-82); ADC to HM The Queen 1973-78, Alderman City of London (Castle Baynard Ward) 1978-, Sheriff City of London 1984-85, Lord Mayor of London 1987-88; tstee: Chichester Theatre, Endowment of St Paul's Cathedral, Childrens' Res Int Carthusian Tst, Castle Baynard Educnl Tst; Freeman City of London 1977, Liveryman Worshipful Co of Ironmongers 1977; Hon DLitt 1988; FRSA, KStJ 1987 (OStJ 1985); Chevalier de la Légion d'Honneur 1961, Commandeur de l'Ordre Nationale du Mérite 1984, Cdr Order of the Lion (Malawi) 1985, memb Nat Order of Aztec Eagle (Mexico) 1985; Order of St Olav Norway 1988, Order of Merit Senegal 1988; *Recreations* tennis, music, military history, forestry, stamp, coin and bank note collecting; *Clubs* Cowdray Park Golf and Polo, United Wards, City Livery, Guildhall, City Pickwick; *Style—* Sir Greville Spratt, GBE, TD, JP, DL; Grayswood Place, Haslemere, Surrey GU27 2ET (☎ 0428 4367)

SPRATT, Terence Edward; CBE; s of William Spratt (d 1988), and Nora Spratt (d 1983); *b* 8 Oct 1927; *Educ* St Joseph's Coll London; *m* 1949, Frances; 2 da (Janis b 1956, Lisa b 1958); *Career* retail ops mangr John Gardner Supermarkets 1960-63, chm and md Safeway Food Stores 1975-88 (retail ops dir 1969-75), vice chm Safeway plc 1988-89; currently non-exec dir: Post Office Counters Ltd, Johnson Wax, Argyll Group plc; currently chm Terence Spratt (mgmnt consltss) Ltd; former: chm Food Policy Ctee Retail Consortium, chm and pres Nat Grocers Benevolent Fund, dir Int Assoc Chainstores; FOD, FIGD; *Recreations* golf, gardening, leisure club; *Clubs* Addington Golf; *Style—* Terence Spratt, Esq, CBE; Argyll Group plc, 6 Millington Rd, Hayes, Middx UB3 4AY (☎ 081 848 8744, fax 081 573 1865, telex 934888

SPRECKLEY, HE Sir (John) Nicholas Teague; KCVO (1989), CMG (1983); s of Air Marshal Sir Herbert Spreckley, KBE, CB (d 1963), and Winifred Emery, *née* Teague; *b* 6 Dec 1934; *Educ* Winchester, Magdalene Coll Cambridge (BA); *m* 1958, Margaret Paula Jane, da of late Prof William McCausland Stewart; 1 s (Robin), 1 da (Bridget); *Career* FO: head of Euro community dept (Internal) FCO 1979-83, ambass to Rep of Korea 1983-86, High Cmmr to Malaysia 1986-; *Clubs* Army and Navy; *Style—* HE Sir Nicholas Spreckley, KCVO, CMG; British High Commission, 185 Jalan Ampang, Kuala Lumpur 50450; c/o Foreign and Commonwealth Office, King Charles St, London SW1

SPRIGGE, Prof Timothy Lauro Squire; s of Cecil Jackson Squire Sprigge (d 1959), of Rome and London, and Katriona, *née* Gordon Brown (d 1965); *b* 14 Jan 1932; *Educ* Gonville and Caius Coll Cambridge (MA, PhD); *m* 4 April 1959, Giglia, da of Gavin Gordon (d 1965); 1 s (Samuel Felix b 1961), 2 da (Georgina Nessie b 1960, Lucy Cecilia b 1960); *Career* lectr in philosophy UCL 1961-63, reader in philosophy Univ of Sussex 1963-69 (lectr 1963-70), prof of logic and metaphysics Univ of Edinburgh 1979-89; prof emeritus and endowment fell Univ of Edinburgh 1989-; memb Ctee Scottish Soc for the Prevention of Vivisection; memb: Aristotelian Soc, Mind Assoc, Scots Philosophical Club; *Books* The Correspondence of Jeremy Bentham Vols 1 and 2 (ed, 1968), Facts, Words and Beliefs (1970), Santayana: An Examination of his Philosophy (1974), The Vindication of Absolute Idealism (1983), Theories of Existence (1984), The Rational Foundations of Ethics (1987); *Recreations* backgammon; *Style—* Prof Timothy Sprigge; 31A Raeburn Place, Edinburgh EH4 1HU (☎ 031 315 2443); David Hume Tower, Univ of Edinburgh, George Square, Edinburgh (☎ 031 667 1011 ext 6212)

SPRIGGS, Douglas; s of Harry Spriggs (d 1945), and Maud, *née* Smallwood (d 1947); *b* 12 April 1919; *Educ* Birmingham Sch of Printing; *m* 20 Feb 1949, Gladys Maud, da of Joseph Holliday (d 1972); *Career* RASC 1939-40, 2 Lt RIASC 1940, Capt 1941, Maj 1941-46 (despatches 1942 and 43); md and fndr Kings Norton Press 1946-80, chm Oldfield Press Ltd Wembley 1974-, chm and md KNP Gp Ltd 1980-; pres Midlands Branch Br Fedn of Master Printers 1970; *Recreations* golf; *Clubs* Gay Hill Golf, Ladbrook Park Golf; *Style—* Douglas Spriggs, Esq; KNP Group Ltd, Oxleasow Rd, Redditch D98 0RE (☎ 0527 510000, fax 0527 501735)

SPRING, Hon Mrs (Jane Elizabeth); *née* Henniker-Major; da of 8 Baron Henniker, KCMG, CVO, MC, of Red House, Thornham, Suffolk, and Margaret Osla, *née* Benning (d 1974); *b* 6 July 1954; *Educ* Benenden, Durham Univ, UCL (BA); *m* 1979, Richard John Grenville, s of Herbert John Arthur Spring, of Cape Town; 1 s (Frederick b 1987), 1 da (b 1983); *Career* Magistrate Inner London 1984-87; sec gen Int Federation of Settlements; tstee: Housing the Homeless Central Fund, OSLA Henniker Charitable Tst; *Recreations* opera, riding, tennis; *Clubs* Boodle's (lady memb); *Style—* The Hon Mrs Spring; 124 Cambridge St, London SW1V 4QF (☎ 071 834 1820); Valley Farm, Yaxley, Eye, Suffolk (☎ 037 983 288)

SPRING RICE, Hon Charles James; s and h of 6 Baron Monteagle of Brandon; *b* 24 Feb 1953; *Educ* Harrow; *m* 1987, Mary Teresa Glover; 2 da (Helena Maire b 1987, Charlotte Etain b 1988); *Style—* Charles Spring Rice, Esq; 26 Malvern Rd, London E8 3LP

SPRING RICE, Hon Michael; s of 5 Baron Monteagle of Brandon (d 1946); *b* 1935; *Educ* Harrow; *m* 1959, Fiona, da of James Edward Kenneth Sprot; 1 s, 1 da; *Career* late Lt Irish Gds; Bowmaker Ltd (now Lloyds Bowmaker Fin Gp) 1956-86, Compagnie Bancaire Group 1986-; *Recreations* golf, shooting; *Clubs* Boodle's, Pratt's, Royal Ashdown Forest Golf, Swinley Forest Golf, Royal and Ancient Golf of St Andrews; *Style—* The Hon Michael Spring Rice; Fosseway House, Nettleton Shrub, Chippenham, Wilts SN14 7NL (☎ 0249 782875)

SPRINGBETT, David John; *b* 2 May 1938; *Educ* Dulwich Coll London; *m* ; 3 s (Bruce b 1965, Duncan b 1967, d 1977, Jack b 1985), 4 da (Sally b 1963, Lucy b 1964, Zoe b 1980, Josie b 1981); *Career* reinsurance broker; chm PWS Gp London (fndr memb 1964); underwriting memb Lloyd's; Britain's Salesman of the Year (1981); 3 records in Guinness Book of Records; *Style—* David Springbett, Esq; 52 Minories, London EC3N 1JJ

SPRINGER, Sir Hugh Worrell; GCMG (1984, KCMG 1971), GCVO (1985), KA (1984), CBE (1961, OBE 1954); s of Charles Wilkinson Springer (d 1914), and Florence Nightingale, *née* Barrow (d 1977); *b* 22 June 1913; *Educ* Harrison Coll Barbados, Hertford Coll Oxford; *m* 1942, Dorothy Drinan, 3 da of late Lionel Gittenns; 3 s, 1 da; *Career* called to the Bar Inner Temple 1938; Barbados 1938-47, former memb Colonial Parl and MEC Barbados 1944-47, gen sec Barbados Lab Pty 1940-47, organiser and gen sec Barbados Workers Union 1940-47, registrar Univ of WI 1947-63, dir Univ of WI Inst of Educn 1963-66, acting govr Barbados 1964, Cwlth asst sec gen 1966-70, govr gen Barbados 1984-90; chm Cwlth Caribbean Med Res Cncl 1965-84, sec gen Assoc of Cwlth Universities 1970-80; memb Ct of Govrs: LSE 1970-80, Univ of Exeter 1970-80, Univ of Hull 1970-80, London Sch of Hygiene and Tropical Med 1974-77, Inst of Cwlth Studies 1974-80; vice pres Br Caribbean Assoc 1974-80; memb: Advsy Ctee Science Policy Fndn 1977-, bd dirs United World Colls 1978-90; hon pres Cwlth Human Ecology Cncl 1984- (chm 1971-84); hon fell: Hertford Coll Oxford 1974-, All Souls Coll Oxford 1988- (sr visiting fell 1962-63); Hon DSC Soc Laval; Hon LLD: Victoria (BC), Univ of WI, City Univ, Univ of Manchester, Univ of York, Univ of Ontario, Univ of Zimbabwe, Univ of Bristol 1982, Univ of Birmingham 1983; Hon DLitt: Univ of Warwick, Univ of Ulster, Heriot-Watt Univ, Hong Kong Univ, Univ of St Andrews; Hon DCL: New Brunswick, Univ of Oxford, Univ of E Anglia; Knight of St Andrew (Order of Barbados); *Clubs* Athenaeum, Royal Cwlth Soc; *Style—* Sir Hugh Springer, GCMG, GCVO, KA, CBE; Barclays Bank International, Oceanic House, 1 Cockspur St, London SW1; Gibbes, St Peter, Barbados (☎ 0101 809 4222591)

SPRINGMAN, Nicholas Michael Eyre; s of Paul Michael Eyre Springman, of Bembridge, IOW, and Dame Ann Marcella, *née* Mulloy, DBE (d 1987); *b* 6 Dec 1960; *Educ* Eton, Kingston Poly, Inchbald Sch of Design and Decoration; *Career* Sarah Thomson Designs Ltd 1986-88; dir: Michael Springman Assocs 1987-, Prince Interiors 1989-; Freeman City of London 1983, Liveryman Worshipful Co of Upholders 1983; *Recreations* literature, tennis, music, travel, charity fund raising; *Style—* Nicholas Springman, Esq; 51 Powerscroft Rd, London E5 0PU (☎ 081 985 0539)

SPROAT, Iain MacDonald; s of William and Lydia Sproat; *b* 8 Nov 1938; *Educ* Melrose, Winchester, Magdalen Coll Oxford; *m* 1979, Judith Kernot, *née* King; 1 step s (Charles); *Career* MP (C) Aberdeen S 1970-83, pps to sec of State for Scotland 1973-74; chm Soviet & East Euro Gp of Cons Foreign Affairs ctee 1975-81; leader, Cons Gp on Scottish Select ctee 1979-81; leader Br Parly Delgn to Austria 1980; parly under-sec Trade 1981-83; conslt N M Rothschild & Sons Merchant Bankers Ltd 1983-; chm: Milner and Co Ltd, Cricketers' Who's Who Ltd; dir Ltd; Min: Aviation and Shipping, Tourism; Min responsible for Govt Statistics; distributive retail trader for cinema, film, video; and Board of African Medical and Research Fndn 1987-; special advisr to PM Gen Election 1987; *Books* Wodehouse at War (1981), Cricketers' Who's Who (ed, 1980); *Clubs* Oxford and Cambridge; *Style—* Iain Sproat, Esq; Hedenham Hall, Hedenham, Norfolk NR35 2LE

SPROT OF HAYSTOUN, Lt-Col Aidan Mark; MC (1944), JP (Peeblesshire 1966); yr s of Maj Mark Sprot of Riddell, JP, DL (d 1946), of Riddell, Roxburghshire, and Meliora (d 1979), er da of Sir John Adam Hay, 9 Bt, of Haystoun and Smithfield; *b* 17 June 1919; *Educ* Stowe; *Career* landowner, farmer; Lord-Lt of Tweeddale (formerly Peeblesshire, DL 1966-80) 1980-; Lt-Col served Royal Scots Greys 1940-62; pres Lowlands of Scotland TA & VRA 1986-89; memb: Royal Co of Archers (Queen's Body Guard for Scotland), Peeblesshire CC 1963-75; hon sec Royal Caledonian Hunt 1964-74; dir Peeblesshire Branch Red Cross 1966-74 (now patron); county Cmmr, Peeblesshire Scout Assoc 1968-73 (now pres); pres Lothian Fedn of Boys' Clubs 1988-; *Recreations* country pursuits, motor-cycle touring; *Clubs* New (Edinburgh); *Style—* Lt-Col Aidan Sprot of Haystoun, MC, JP; Crookston, by Peebles EH45 9JQ (☎ 07214 209)

SPROXTON, Rev (Charles) Vernon; s of Alan Sproxton (d 1977), of Hull, and Eleanor, *née* Swales (d 1970); *b* 8 May 1920; *Educ* Riley HS Hull, Univ of Edinburgh, The United Ind (Theol) Coll Bradford; *m* 27 July 1944, Margaret Joan, da of William Ireland (d 1957), of Edinburgh; 2 s (Andrew b 1948 d 1977, David b 1954), 1 da (Ruth b 1951); *Career* sec of Student Christian Movement Univs of Leeds and Sheffield 1944-47, Christian Educn Movement 1947-53; min Waterloo-with-Seaforth Congregational Church 1953-57; radio and TV prodr BBC 1957-77, freelance writer and broadcaster 1977-; writer and prodr of TV biographies on: Pope Paul VI, Saint Augustine, Luther, Erasmus, Jan Hus, Pascal, Kierkegaard, Simone Weil, Dietrich Bonhoeffer; filmed inverviews with great theologians: Karl Barth, Martin Buber, Emil Brunner, Rudolph Bultman, Paul Tillich, Yves Congar; writer of radio features on: C S Lewis, Dorothy Sayers, Reinhold Niebuhr, William Temple, J H Oldham, R H Tawney, Florence Allshorn, H J S Guntrip; occasional contrib to: The Times, The Listener, The Guardian, The New Statesman; film critic: The New Christian; chm Impressions Gallery of Photography York; *Books* Love and Marriage (1970), Teilhard de Chardin (1971), Revelation (1976); *Recreations* photography, metal and woodwork; *Style—* The Rev Vernon Sproxton; The Old Smithy, Tunstall, Richmond, North Yorkshire (☎ 0748 818436)

SPRY, Sir John Farley; s of Joseph Farley Spry (d 1923); *b* 11 March 1910; *Educ* Perse Sch, Peterhouse Cambridge; *m* 1 (m dis 1940); 1 s, 1 da; m 2, 1953, Stella Marie, da of Sydney Carlisle Fichat; *Career* slr; asst registrar of titles and conveyancer Uganda 1936-44, asst dir Land Registration Palestine 1944-48, puisne judge Tanganyika 1961-64, vice pres Court of Appeal East Africa 1970-75 (justice of appeal 1964-70), chm Pensions Appeal Tribunal 1975-76; Gibraltar: chief justice 1976-80, cmmr for revision of laws 1981-85, pres Court of Appeal 1983-; chief justice British Indian Ocean Territory 1981-88, chief justice St Helena 1983-; kt 1975; *Books* Sea Shells of Dar es Salaam (Parts: 1 1961, 2 1964, 3 1968), Civil Procedure in East Africa (1969), Civil Law of Defamation in East Africa (1976); *Recreations* conchology; *Style—* Sir John Spry; 15 de Vere Gardens, London W8

SPURGEON, Maj-Gen Peter Lester; CB (1980); s of Harold Sidney Spurgeon (d 1959), of Suffolk, and Mrs Emily Anne Spurgeon, *née* Bolton; *b* 27 Aug 1927; *Educ* Merchant Taylors Sch Northwood; *m* 1959, da of Cyril Bland Aylward, of Bournemouth (d 1972); 1 s (Simon), 1 da (Nicola); *Career* RM 1946-80; Col Commandant Royal Marines 1987-90; Maj-Gen cmdg Trg and Res Forces RM 1977-80, chief exec Royal Agric Benevolent Inst 1982-91; pres RM Assocn 1986-90; *Recreations* gardening, golf; *Clubs* Army & Navy; *Style—* Maj-Gen P L Spurgeon, CB; c/o Lloyd's Bank, 1 High St, Oxford OX1 4AA

SPURLING, (Susan) Hilary; da of Judge Gilbert Alexander Forrest (d 1977), and Emily Maureen, *née* Armstrong; *b* 25 Dec 1940; *Educ* Clifton HS Bristol, Somerville Coll Oxford; *m* 4 April 1961, John Spurling; 2 s (Nathaniel Stobast b 1974, Gilbert Alexander Fettiplace b 1977), 1 da (Amy Maria b 1972); *Career* Spectator: arts ed 1964-69, lit ed 1966-69; book reviewer: The Observer 1970-87, Daily Telegraph 1987-; *Books* Ivy When Young - The Early Life of I Compton-Burnett 1884-1919 (1974), Handbook to Anthony Powell's Music of Time (1977), Secrets of a Women's Heart - The Later Life of I Compton-Burnett 1919-69 (1984), Elinor Fettiplace's Receipt Book (1986), Paul Scott A Life (1990); *Style—* Ms Hilary Spurling; David Higham Assoc, 5-8 Lower John St, Golden Sq, London W1R 4HA

SPURLING, John Antony; s of Antony Cuthbert Spurling (d 1984), and Elizabeth Frances, *née* Stobart (d 1990); *b* 17 July 1936; *Educ* Dragon Sch, Marlborough, St John's Coll Oxford (BA); *m* 4 April 1961, Susan Hilary, da of Gilbert Alexander Forrest; 2 s (Nathaniel Stobart b 31 May 1974, Gilbert Alexander Fettiplace b 2 Dec 1977), 1 da (Amy Maria b 6 May 1972); *Career* Nat Serv 2 Lt RA 1955-57; plebiscite offr Southern Cameroons 1960-61, BBC Radio announcer 1963-66, freelance writer and broadcaster 1966-, Henfield writing fell Univ of E Anglia 1973, art critic The New Statesman 1976-88; playwright *Plays* for stage: Macrune's Guevara (Nat Theatre) 1969, In the Heart of the British Museum (Traverse Theatre Edinburgh) 1971, The British Empire Part One (Birmingham Repertory Theatre) 1980, Coming Ashore in Guadeloupe (Cherub Co Harrogate, Edinburgh and London) 1982-83; for BBC Radio 3: Dominion Over Palm and Pine 1982, The Christian Hero 1982, The Day of Reckoning 1985, Discobolus 1989 *Books* The Ragged End (novel, 1989); *Style—* John Spurling, Esq; c/o Patricia MacNaughton, MLR, 200 Fulham Rd, London SW10 9PN (☎ 071 351 5442, 071 376 5575, fax 071 351 4560)

SPURR, Margaret Anne (Mrs John Spurr); *née* Spurr; da of John William Spurr, and Anne Spurr; *b* 7 Oct 1933; *Educ* Abbeydale Girls' GS Sheffield, Univ of Keele (BA, PGCE); *m* 7 Nov 1953, John Spurr; 1 s (David b 2 Nov 1959), 1 da (Jane b 26 Aug 1961); *Career* tutor English literature: Univ of Glasgow 1971, Univ of Keele 1972-73, headmistress Bolton Sch Girls Div 1979-; sr examiner Univ of London 1971-80; memb: advsy ctee American studies res centre PCL 1977-89, scholarship selection ctee English Speaking Union 1983-, CBI Schs' Panel 1985-88, nat ctee Women in Indust Year 1986-; chm: PR Ctee Girls' Schs Assoc 1986-88 (pres 1985-86), Nat Isis Ctee 1987-90; fell Midland Div of Woodard Corp 1990; Govr Denstone Coll, Huyton Coll, St Dominics Sch Stone; *Recreations* gardening, theatre, poetry; *Clubs* Univ Womens, Royal Overseas; *Style—* Mrs John Spurr; The Old Vicarage, Croxden, Uttoxeter ST14 5JQ (☎ 088 926 214); Bolton School Girls' Division, Chorley New Rd, Bolton, Lancs BL1 4PB (☎ 0204 40201)

SPURRELL, Dr Roworth Adrian John; s of Ivor Pritchard Spurrell (d 1968), and Marjorie, *née* Cheney; *b* 27 May 1942; *Educ* Oundle, Univ of London (MD, BSc, MB BS); *m* 28 April 1973, Susan Jane, da of George Kemp (d 1984); 2 da (Emma Louise, Clare Alexandra); *Career* registrar in cardiology: St George's Hosp London 1969-70, Nat Heart Hosp 1970-71; sr registrar in Cardiology Guy's Hosp 1971-74, conslt in charge of Cardiology Bart's Hosp 1976- (conslt 1974-); MRCP, FRCP, FACC; *Recreations* sailing, flying; *Clubs* Royal Yacht Squadron, RAC; *Style—* Dr Roworth Spurrell; 10 Upper Wimpole St, London W1M 7TD (☎ 071 935 3922)

SPURRIER, Hon Mrs (Elizabeth Jane); *née* Maude; da of Baron Maude of Stratford-upon-Avon (Life Peer); *b* 1946; *Educ* St Mary's Wantage; *m* 1973, Peter Brotherton Spurrier, *qv*; 2 s (Benedict b 1979, Thomas b 1982); *Career* researcher BBC Radio 4, freelance broadcaster and writer, Southside Magazine 1988; *Style—* The Hon Mrs Spurrier; 15 Morella Rd, Wandsworth Common, London SW12 (☎ 081 675 1431)

SPURRIER, Peter Brotherton; s of Eric Jack Spurrier, MBE, of Storrington Sussex, and Frances Mary, *née* Brotherton; *b* 9 Aug 1942; *Educ* Gayhurst Prep Sch Gerrards Cross, Chetham's Hosp Sch, Manchester Coll of Art and Design (NDD) 1964; *m* 1973, Hon Elizabeth Jane, *qv*, da of Baron Maude of Stratford-upon-Avon; 2 s (Benedict, Thomas), 1 da (Lucinda b 1985); *Career* Portcullis Pursuivant of Arms 1981-; cncl memb The Heraldry Soc; FRSA; Freeman City of London; Freeman and Liveryman Worshipful Co of Painter-Stainers 1985; memb Chartered Soc of Designers; OStJ 1990; Esquire in the Venerable Order of St John; *Recreations* beagling, fishing, painting; *Clubs* City Livery; *Style—* Peter Spurrier, Esq; 15 Morella Rd, Wandsworth Common, London SW12 (☎ 081 675 1431); College of Arms, Queen Victoria St, London EC4 (☎ 071 248 5214)

SPURRIER, Roger Hawley; s of Rev Henry Cecil Marriott Spurrier (d 1954), of Roughton, Lincs, and Olive Victoria, *née* Hawley (d 1981); *b* 15 Feb 1928; *Educ* Marlborough; *m* 1955, Margaret Judith Briony (d 1987), da of John Otto Richards, of NZ; 2 s (Timothy John b 1957, Roger Dermot b 1958); *Career* land agent; sr ptnr Jas Martin & Co; FRICS; *Style—* Roger Spurrier, Esq; The Old Rectory, Blankney, Lincoln (☎ 0526 20483); Jas Martin & Co, 8 Bank St, Lincoln (☎ 0522 510234)

SPURRIER-KIMBELL, David Henry; s of Norman Kenneth Bernard Kimbell, FRCOG (d 1982), of Warmington, N'hants, and Mary Pamela, da of Sir Henry Spurrier; *b* 24 Sept 1944; *Educ* Oundle, Heidelberg Univ; *m* 25 July 1970, Maureen Patricia, da of Dr Eric Charles Elliot Golden; 1 s (Henry b 1986), 2 da (Antonia b 1977, Deborah b 1979); *Career* Br Leyland Motor Corp 1966-78, overseas dir Leyland Vehicles Ltd 1978, joined Spencer Stuart & Assocs Ltd London 1979 (1983 int ptnr, 1985 md UK, 1987 int chm); *Recreations* golf, tennis; *Clubs* Oriental; *Style—* David Spurrier-Kimbell, Esq; Chalkpit House, Ecchinswell, Hants (☎ 0635 298269); 113 Park Lane Lane, London W1 (☎ 071 493 1238)

SPURWAY, (Marcus) John; s of Marcus Humphrey Spurway, of Goudhurst, Kent, and Eva, *née* Mann (d 1980); *b* 28 Oct 1938; *Educ* Archbishop Tenison's Sch Croydon; *m* 23 Oct 1963, Christine Kate, da of Robert Charles Townshend (d 1981), of Canterbury; 2 s (Marcus b 1967, Edward b 1969); *Career* Nat Serv 4 Regt RHA; insur broker; dir Insur Brokers Div Morgan Reid & Sharman Ltd (Lloyd's Brokers, formerly B & C Aviation Insurance Brokers); specialist in aviation insur; *Style—* John Spurway, Esq; Lomeer, Common Rd, Sissinghurst, Kent TN17 2JR; 6 Alie St, London E1 8DD (☎ 071 488 9000, fax 071 480 6914, telex 8811401 and 8954576 COMORE G)

SPYER, David Oswald; s of Samuel Michael Spyer (d 1969); *b* 1 Aug 1927; *Educ* Westham Secdy Sch, Bournemouth Sch, Woodhouse Sch; *m* 1957, Janice Ruth; 1 s, 1 da; *Career* Corp RAF 1945-48; dir: Hill Samuel Securities 1972-80, Lynn Regis Fin 1973-80; chm PHH Leasing Ltd 1977-79 (dir 1975-79), md C E Coates & Co 1980-82, mangr Bank Hapoalim B M 1982-; pres designate The London Soc of Rugby Football Union Referees, vice pres Middx County Rugby Football Union, chm Lensbury RFC; *Recreations* dramatics, philately, rugby football, cricket, squash, table tennis, quizzes; *Clubs* MCC, Lensbury; *Style—* David Spyer, Esq; 36 The Avenue, Hatch End, Middx HA5 4EY

SQUIBB, George Drewry; LVO (1982), QC (1956); s of Reginald Augustus Hodder Squibb (d 1946); *b* 1 Dec 1906; *Educ* King's Sch Chester, Queen's Coll Oxford (BCL, MA); *m* 1, 1936, Bessie, *née* Whittaker (d 1954); 1 da; m 2, 1955, Evelyn May, *née* Higgins; *Career* called to the Bar Inner Temple 1930, bencher 1951, treas 1976, chm Dorset QS 1953-71; jr counsel to Crown in Peerage and Baronetcy Cases 1954-56, hon historical advsr in peerage cases to the Attorney-Gen 1965-, pres Tport Tbnl 1962-81, chief Commons cmmr 1971-85; Norfolk Herald Extraordinary 1959-, Earl Marshal's Lieut, assessor and surrogate in the Court of Chivalry 1976-; Master Worshipful Co Scriveners 1980-81; *Recreations* heraldic and genealogical research; *Clubs* Athenaeum, United Oxford and Cambridge; *Style—* George Squibb, Esq, LVO, QC; The Old House, Cerne Abbas, Dorset DT2 7JQ (☎ 0300 341272)

SQUIRE, David Michael; s of Denis Arthur Squire, of Esher, Surrey, and (Patricia) Mary Joyce, *née* Davis; *b* 26 Feb 1949; *Educ* St Edward's Sch Oxford, Univ Coll Oxford (MA); *m* 1 June 1974, Karen StClair, da of Peter Edward Hook (d 1982); 3 da (Isabelle b 1976, Eleanor b 1980, Madeline b 1982); *Career* CA 1973; joined Price Waterhouse London Office 1970 (ptnr 1981-); FCA 1979; *Recreations* sailing, local history, nautical archaeology; *Style—* David Squire, Esq; 2 St Stephens Ave, London W13 8ES (☎ 071 977 5906); Southwark Towers, 32 London Bridge St, London SE1 9SY (☎ 071 939 3000, 071 939 2255, fax 071 378 0647, telex 884657, 884658)

SQUIRE, Robin Clifford; MP (C) Hornchurch 1979-; *b* 12 July 1944; *Educ* Tiffin Sch Kingston-upon-Thames; *m* Susan Fey, *née* Branch; 1 step s, 1 step da; *Career* cncllr London Borough of Sutton 1968-82 (ldr 1976-79), asst chief accountant Lombard North Central Ltd 1972-79, chm Gtr London Young Cons 1973, vice chm Nat Young Cons 1974-75; contested (C) Havering Hornchurch 1974, sec Cons Parly Euro Affrs Ctee 1979-80; memb: Select Ctee on Environment 1979-83 and 1987- (Tory ldr 1982-83), Select Ctee on Euro Legislation 1985-88; PPS to min of state Dept of Tport 1983-85; vice chm: Cons Parly Trade Ctee 1981-83, Cons Parly Environment Ctee 1985-90 (chm 1990-), chm Cons Action on Electoral Reform 1983-86, memb Bd of Mgmnt Shelter 1982-; successful sponsor of Local Govt (Access to Information) Act 1985; Freedom of Information Award as individual who had most advanced freedom of information in 1985; FCA (ACA 1966); *Books* Set the Party Free (jtly, 1969); *Recreations* bridge, modern music, films; *Style—* Robin Squire, Esq, MP; House of Commons, London SW1A 0AA (☎ 071 219 4526)

SQUIRE, Warwick Nevison; CBE (1982); s of Alfred Squire (d 1956), of Cheltenham, and Elizabeth Ann, *née* Timms (d 1971); *b* 19 July 1921; *Educ* Cheltenham Higher Tech Sch; *m* 8 June 1947, Heidi Elli, da of Wilhelm Behrendt (d 1952) of Essen W Germany; 1 da (Shirley Ann (Mrs Wilton) b 1948); *Career* RA 1942-45, seconded German Control Cmmn 1946; cost accountant Dowty Equipment Ltd 1946-59; Dowty Rotol Ltd: chief accountant 1959-65, fin dir and controller 1965-69, gen mangr 1969-71, md 1971-73, chm 1973-75; gp dir and md Aerospace and Defence Div Dowty Gp Plc 1975-84; former chm Fin Ctee Nat Victims Assoc; Freeman City of Yakima, Washington, USA; FRAeS (1980), FInstD (1980), FRSA (1982); *Recreations* golf, gardening; *Style—* Warwick Squire, Esq, CBE; Highlands, Daisy Bank Rd, Leckhampton Hill, Cheltenham, Glos GL53 9QQ (☎ 0242 521038); Ellwood Exhibitions International, Charlton Kings Industrial Estate, Cirencester Rd, Cheltenham, Glos GL53 8DZ (☎ 0242 524256, fax 0242 222691, telex 43432 DSAG)

SQUIRE, (Clifford) William; CMG (1978), LVO (1972); s of Clifford John Squire (d 1938), of Gt Yarmouth; *b* 7 Oct 1928; *Educ* Royal Masonic Sch, St John's Coll Oxford (MA), Univ of London (PhD), Coll of Europe Bruges; *m* 1, 6 July 1959, Marie José (d 1973), da of René Paul Carlier (d 1978), of Paris; 2 s (Stephen b 1961, Christophe b 1963, decd), 2 da (Catherine b 1960, Anne Louise b 1965); m 2, 22 May 1976, Sara Laetitia, da of Michael Duncan Hutchison, of Richmond, Surrey; 1 s (James b 1977), 1 da (Emma b 1979); *Career* Br Army 2 Lt, Palestine and Greece 1947-49; HM overseas civil serv asst dist offr Nigeria 1953-59; HM Diplomatic Serv Foreign Office, Bucharest, United Nations NY, Bangkok, Washington 1959-79; ambass to Senegal 1979-82, FCO 1982-84, ambass to Israel 1984-88; devpt dir Univ of Cambridge 1988-; *Clubs* Travellers (London); *Style—* William Squire, Esq, CMG, LVO; Royal Bank of Scotland, Holts, Whitehall, London SW1A 2EB; 10 Trumpington St, Cambridge

SQUIRES, Leslie Mervyn; s of Capt Leslie Squires (d 1971), of Folkestone, Kent, and Antoinette, *née* Georgiou; *b* 8 July 1947; *Educ* Gordon Sch; *m* 5 May 1971, Jane Barkby, da of Victor Harold Pochin, of Dartford, Kent; 1 s (Jonathan b 25 May 1975), 1 da (Joanna b 1 Sept 1978); *Career* civil servant in Civil Serv 1964-67, administrative offr Lloyds Register of Shipping 1967-69, New business exec Lloyds & Scottish Ltd 1969-72, regnl Mangr Western Tst & Savings 1972-74, dir Jonathon Wren & Co Ltd 1975-79, md Jonathon Wren City 1977-79, gen mangr fin Recruitment 1979-81, dir and fndr Anderson Squires 1981-; FInstSMM 1980, FInstD 1986, MBIM 1986; *Recreations* travel, current affairs, sport, music; *Clubs* Rugby Football, Bishopsgate Ward; *Style—* Leslie Squires, Esq

SQUIRES, Richard John; s of Richard George Squires (d 1982), of Dulwich, and Lilian Florence, *née* Fuller (d 1987); *b* 9 Dec 1937; *Educ* Alleyns Sch Dulwich; *m* 19 August 1961, Valerie Jean, da of Richard Wotton Wood, of Southfields, Wimbledon; 1 s (Paul Julian b 1970), 1 da (Fiona Jane b 1967); *Career* asst actuary: Imperial Life Assur of Canada 1963-65, Canada Life Co 1965-68; dir Save & Prosper Gp Ltd 1981- (gp actuary 1969-89), ptnr R Watson & Sons 1990-; Freeman City of London, Liveryman Worshipful Co of Actuaries; FIA 1962, ASA 1963; *Recreations* golf, gardening, painting; *Clubs* Tyrrells Wood Golf, City Livery; *Style—* Richard Squires, Esq; 6 The Highway, Sutton, Surrey SM2 5QT (☎ 081 642 7532); R Watson & Sons, Watson House, London Rd, Reigate, Surrey RG2 9PQ (☎ 0737 241144, fax 0737 241496, telex 946070)

SRISKANDAN, Kanagaretnam; s of Kamagaretnam Kathiravelu (d 1980), of Sri Lanka, and Kanmanyammal, *née* Kumaraswamy; *b* 12 Aug 1930; *Educ* Central Coll Jaffna Ceylon, Royal Coll Colombo Ceylon, Univ of Ceylon (BSc, tennis colours); *m* 23 June 1956, Dorothy, da of Louis Harley (d 1964), of Kandy, Sri Lanka; 2 s (Kumar b 1957, Ranjan b 1959), 1 da (Shiranee b 1964); *Career* asst engr: PWD Ceylon 1953-56, Sir William Halcrow & Ptnrs London 1956-58; section engr Tarmac Civil Engineering 1958-59; West Riding of Yorkshire CC: asst engr 1959-61, sr engr 1961-64, princ engr 1964-68; Dept of Transport: Superintending engr Midland Rd Construciton Unit 1968-71, asst chief engr and Head of BES Div 1971-74 (head of BET Div 1974-76), dep chief highway engr 1976-80, chief highway engr 1980-87; divnl dir Mott MacDonald 1988-; CEng 1958, FIHT 1974, FICE 1978, FIStructE 1985; *Publications* numerous papers on Engineering and Management topics; *Recreations* squash, golf; *Style—* Kanagaretnam Sriskandan, Esq; Mott MacDonald Ltd, St Anne House, 20-26 Wellesley Rd, Croydon CR9 2UL (☎ 081 686 5041, fax 081 681 5706, telex 917241 MOTTAY G)

SRIVASTAVA, Awdhesh Chandra; s of Iqbal Bahadur Srivastava of Kanpur, India, and Leela Devi, *née* Srivastava (d 1950); *b* 12 April 1934; *Educ* DPH Higher Secdy Sch Kanpur India, Univ of Lucknow India (MB BS, MD), Univ of Wales (PhD); *m* 10 April 1976, Sandra, da of Donald Bayliss, of South Hiendley, Yorks; 2 s (Avadh b 1976, Atul b 1979), 2 da (Kiron b 1983, Nisha b 1985); *Career* MO Provincial Medical Services India (incl 1 year in Army); registrar in genito-urinary medicine UK 1972-74 (sr registrar 1974-80, conslt 1980-); ed in chief Medical Times; fndr chm AIDS Research Fund Ltd, chm AIDS Care Ethnic Minority UK; fndr pres Overseas Doctors Fedn Ltd; patron Blackliners AIDS Helpline (UK); pres Indian Med Assoc (SW); memb: GMC, BMA, Med Practitioners Union Nat Cncl (chm SW Div), Hosp Conslt and Specialists Assoc; *Recreations* travel, cooking; *Style—* Dr Awdhesh Srivastava; 12 Chainwalk Drive, Truro, Cornwall TR1 3ST (☎ 0872 71696); Dept of Genito-Urinary Medicine, Royal Cornwall Hospital (City), Truro, Cornwall (☎ 0872 41036)

STABB, His Hon Sir William Walter; QC (1968); 2 s of Sir Newton John Stabb, OBE (d 1931), and Ethel Mary, *née* Townsend, DBE (d 1961); *b* 6 Oct 1913; *Educ* Rugby, Univ Coll Oxford; *m* 1940, Dorothy Margaret, *née* Leckie; 4 da; *Career* RAF 1940-46; called to the Bar 1936; bencher Inner Temple 1964- (treas 1985), official referee of the Supreme Court 1969-, circuit judge, sr official referee 1978-85, ret; kt 1981; *Style—* His Hon Sir William Stabb, QC; The Pale Farm, Chipperfield, Kings Langley, Herts (☎ 0923 263124)

STABLE, His Hon Judge (Rondle) Owen Charles; QC (1963); s of Rt Hon Sir Wintringham Stable, MC (d 1977), of Plas Llwyn Owen, Llanbrynmair, Powis, and Lucie Haden, *née* Freeman; *b* 28 Jan 1923; *Educ* Winchester; *m* 6 April 1949, Yvonne Brook, da of Lionel Brook Holliday, OBE (d 1965), of Copgrove Hall, Boroughbridge, Yorkshire; 2 da (Emma (Mrs Hay), Victoria); *Career* WWII Capt RB 1940-46; barr Middle Temple 1948; bencher 1969, dep chm Herts Quarter Sessions 1963-71, recorder of Crown Cts 1972-79, circuit judge 1979; res judge: Wood Green Crown Ct

1980-81, Snaresbrook Crown Ct 1982-; sr circuit judge 1982-; bd of trade inspector: Cadco Gp of Cos 1963-64, HS Whiteside and Co Ltd 1965-67, Int Learning Systems Corpn Ltd 1969-71, Pergamon Press 1969-73; memb: Gen Cncl of the Bar 1962-64, Senate of 4 Inns of Ct 1971-74, Senate of Inns of Ct and the Bar 1974-75; chllr Dio of Bangor 1959-88, memb Governing Body of Church in Wales 1960-88, layreader Dio of St Albans 1961-; chm Horserace Betting Levy Appeal Tbnl 1969-74; *Books* A Review of Coursing (with R M Stuttard, 1971); *Recreations* shooting, listening to music; *Clubs* Boodles; *Style—* His Hon Judge Owen Stable, QC; The Crown Court at Snaresbrook, Holly Bush Hill, London E11 1QW

STABLEFORD, Brian Michael; s of William Ernest Stableford, of Ashton-upon-Lyne, Lancashire, and Joyce Wilkinson; *b* 25 July 1948; *Educ* Manchester GS, Univ of York (BA, DPhil); *m* 1, 1973 (m dis 1983), Vivien Wynne, da of Caradog Owen; 1 s (Leo Michael b 5 April 1975), 1 da (Katharine Margaret b 21 Oct 1978); m 2, 1985, Roberta Jane, da of Charles Cragg; *Career* lectr Sociology Dept Univ of Reading 1976-88; freelance writer (latterly full time); *Books* fiction and science fiction incl: Hooded Swan (series, 1972-78), Realms of Tartarus (1977), Man In a Cage (1976), The Mind Readers (1976), Daedalus (series, 1976-79), The Last Days of the Edge of the World (1978), The Walking Shadow (1979), Asgard (trilogy, 1982-90), The Gates of Eden (1983), The Empire of Fear (1988), The Werewolves of London (1990), Sexual Chemistry: Sardonic Tales of the Genetic Revolution (1991); non-fiction incl: The Science in Science Fiction (1982), The Third Millennium (1985), Scientific Romance in Britain (1985), The Way to Write Science Fiction (1989); contrib to reference books incl; The Encyclopedia of Science Fiction, The Survey of Science Fiction Literature, Anatomy of Wonder, Science Fiction Writers, The Survey of Modern Fantasy Literature, Supernatural Fiction Writers, The Cambridge Guide to Literature In English, Fantasy Literature, Horror Literature; awards incl: European Sci-Fi award 1984, Distinguished Scholarship award, Int Assoc for the Fantastic in the Arts 1987, J Lloyd Eaton award 1987; *Style—* Brian Stableford, Esq; 113 St Peter's Rd, Reading RG6 1PG (☎ 0734 665894)

STABLEFORTH, Dr David Edward; s of Edward Victor Stableforth (d 1975), of Weymouth, Dorset, and Una Alice Stableforth; *b* 23 Feb 1942; *Educ* Truro Sch Cornwall, St Catharine's Coll Cambridge, St Mary's Hosp Paddington; *m* 11 May 1967, Penelope Jane, da of David Ivor Phillips, MC (d 1976), of Finchley, London; 1 s (William b 1973), 2 da (Abigail b 1972, Emily b 1979); *Career* sr med registrar Brompton Hosp and St James Hosp Balham 1973-75, conslt physician E Birmingham Hosp and hon sr lectr Univ of Birmingham 1977-; memb Midland Thoracic Soc; memb: Br Thoracic Soc, BMA, FRCP 1985; *Recreations* walking, cycling, sailing and canoeing, theatre and concert-going; *Style—* Dr David Stableforth; East Birmingham Hospital, Bordesley Green East, Birmingham B9 5ST (☎ 021 766 6611)

STABLER, Arthur Fletcher; s of Edward Stabler (d 1934), of 29 Richard St, Elswick, Newcastle upon Tyne, and Maggie, *née* Churnside (d 1965); *b* 7 Nov 1919; *Educ* Cruddas Park Sch; *m* 30 Oct 1948, Margaret (d 1990), da of John McIntosh (d 1936), of Newcastle upon Tyne; 2 s (Roy b 13 May 1949, David b 5 March 1960); *Career* Nat Serv WWII Royal Northumberland Fus 1939-46; engr Vickers Armstrong Engineering Works 1933-82; memb Supplementary Benefits Cmmn 1976-79, involved in many residents' assocs; hon memb Polish Parachute Regt, pres Polish Solidarity Ctee Tyne and Wear, vice chm Tyne and Wear Fire and Civil Def Authy, vice chm Cityworks Newcastle upon Tyne; city cncllr Newcastle upon Tyne 1963- (dep Lord Mayor 1982-83, Lord Mayor 1983-84); *Books* Gannin Along the Scotswood Road (1976); *Recreations* social work, local history; *Clubs* Polish White Eagle, Pineapple, Maddison's; *Style—* Councillor A F Stabler; 10 Whitebeam Place, Elswick, Newcastle upon Tyne NE4 7EJ (☎ 091 2732362); Civic Centre, Newcastle upon Tyne (☎ 091 2328520)

STACEY, Hon Mrs (Anne Caroline Mary); *née* Bridgeman; e da of 2 Viscount Bridgeman; *b* 30 July 1932; *Educ* Univ of Reading (BSc); *m* 1955, Rev Nicolas David Stacey, er s of David Stacey, of Knaphill Manor, nr Woking (whose mother was Beatrice, sis of 1 Baron Brassey of Apethorpe); 1 s (David Robert b 1958), 2 da (Caroline Jill b 1956, Mary Elizabeth b 1961); *Career* ptnr Eng Homes and Country Tours; memb Nat Tst Regnl Ctee Kent and E Sussex 1984-90; *Style—* The Hon Mrs Stacey; The Old Vicarage, Selling, Faversham, Kent (☎ 022 785 833)

STACEY, Air Vice-Marshal John Nichol; CBE (1972), DSO (1945), DFC (1943); s of Capt Herbert Chambers Stacey (d 1966), of Rhydyfantwn, Moylegrove, nr Cardigan, S Wales, and Brittannia May, *née* Davies (d 1972); *b* 14 Sept 1920; *Educ* Whitgift Middle Sch; *m* 29 April 1950, Veronica, da of Air Vice-Marshal Harry Vivian Satterly, CB, CBE, DFC (d 1982); 2 da (Amanda (Mrs Reuter) b 1953, Caroline (Mrs Russell) b 1956); *Career* served WWII 4 operational tours incl co 160 Liberator Sqdn Ceylon as Wing Cdr 1944-45 (despatches 3 times), asst air attaché Washington DC 1947-48, RAF Staff Coll Bracknell 1949, instructional staff Bracknell 1958-60, CO Royal Malayan AF 1960-63, CO RAF Station Laarbruch Germany 1963-66, Air Offr Cmdg the ATC and Air Cadets 1968-71, AOA Air Support Cmd 1974-75, ret RAF 1975; dir Stanham Housing Assoc 1976-82; memb: Tunbridge Wells Health Authy 1981-85, RAF Housing Assoc 1982-86, Tunbridge Wells and Dist Housing Assoc 1989-; tstee: Housing Assoc Charitable Tst 1978-86, Bedgebury Sch Governing Cncl 1983-, Tunbridge Wells Cancer Help Centre 1983-; MBIM 1966-82; Johan Mangku Negara Malaya 1963; *Recreations* golf, DIY; *Clubs* RAF; Dale Hill Golf, Lamberhurst Golf; *Style—* Air Vice-Marshal John Stacey, CBE, DSO, DFC; Riseden Cottage, Riseden, Goudhurst, Kent TN17 1HJ (☎ 0580 211 239)

STACEY, Prof Margaret Meg; da of Conrad Eugene Petrie (d 1953), and Grace Priscilla, *née* Boyce (d 1949); *b* 27 March 1922; *Educ* City of London Sch for Girls, LSE (BSc); *m* 1945, Frank Arthur Stacey (d 1977); 3 s (Richard John b 1951, Peter Frank b 1955, Michael Read b 1958), 2 da (Patricia Ann b 1948, Catherine Margaret (Kate) b 1954); *Career* lab offr Royal Ordance Factory 1943-44, tutor Oxford 1944-51; Univ Coll Swansea: res offr and fell Lower Swansea Valley Project 1961-63, sr lectr in Sociology 1970-74 (lectr 1963-70), dir Medical Sociology Res Centre 1972-74; Univ of Warwick: prof of sociology 1974-89, chm Dept of Sociology 1974-79, chm Graduate Sch of Interdisciplinary Women's Studies 1985-89, chm Mgmnt Ctee Nursing Policy Studies Centre 1985-89, emeritus prof of sociology 1989-; memb SSRC: Sociology Ctee 1969-71, Panel on Health and Health Policy 1976-77 ; Br Sociological Assoc: memb Exec Ctee 1965-70 and 1975-79, hon gen sec 1968-70, chm 1977-79, pres 1981-83, memb Woman's Caucus 1974-; pres: Soc for the Social History of Medicine 1987-88, Section N (Sociology) BAAS 1990-; memb Cncl: Sci and Soc Working Party on Expensive Med Techniques 1979-82, Nat Acad Awards Health and Med Servs Bd 1980-83, Sci and Soc 1982-91; scientific advsr: Euro Regn Dir WHO 1985-88, Chief Scientist Children's Res Liason Gp and Nat Perinatal Epidemiology Unit DHSS 1980-85, Thomas Coram Unit 1984-, pregnancy studies Thomas Coram Unit Univ of London 1985-89, S Warks RHA Survey of Training Needs of the Mentally Handicapped 1986-88, Res Ctee West Midlands RHA 1987-90, Univ Coll of N Wales Longitudinal Study of Ageing 1987-; memb Editorial Bd: Jl of Med Ethics 1977-82, Sociology 1978-82; ed advsr: Social Sci and Medicine, Jl of the Sociology of Health and Illness, Sociological Review, Jl of Medical Ethics; memb: Welsh Hosp Bd 1970-74 (memb Working Party on Children in Hosp in Wales 1970-72), Michael Davies Ctee Hosp Complaints Procedure 1971-73, GMC 1976-84; pres Assoc for the Welfare of Children in Hosp, govr Coventry Poly 1988-; hon fell Univ Coll Swansea 1987-, Lucile Petry Leone prof Univ of Calif San Francisco 1988; *Books* Tradition and Change: a study of Banbury (1960), Methods of Social Research (1969), Power Persistence and Change: a second study of Banbury (with E Batstone, C Bull and A Murcott, 1975), Health Care and Health Knowledge (co-ed M Reid, C Heath, R Dingwall, 1977), Women, Power and Politics (with Marion Price 1981, Fawcet prize 1982), Concepts of Health, Illness and Disease: a comparative perspective (with Caroline Currer, 1986), The Sociology of Health and Healing (1988), Beyond Separation: further studies of children in hospital (with D Hall, 1979), Overviews of Research on the Care of Children in Hospital (with S Roche, 1984-91); *Recreations* gardening, walking; *Style—* Prof Meg Stacey; 8 Lansdowne Circus, Leamington Spa, Warwickshire CV32 4SW (☎ 0926 312094); Dept of Sociology, University of Warwick, (☎ 0203 523072, fax 0203 461606)

STACEY, Prof Maurice; CBE (1968); s of John Henry Stacey (d 1938), of Bromstead, nr Newport, Shropshire, and Ellen, *née* Titley (d 1955); *b* 8 April 1907; *Educ* Moreton C of E Sch, Adams GS Newport Shropshire, Univ of Birmingham (BSc, PhD, DSc); *m* 29 Jan 1937, Constance Mary (d 1985), da of William Ernest Pugh (d 1961), of Selly Oak, Birmingham; 2 s (Michael John b 21 April 1942, David William b 20 Jan 1951, d 18 Dec 1980) 2 da (Marion Joan b 18 June 1938, Diana Mary b 30 Oct 1946); *Career* Univ OTC 1926-29, Capt Warwicks Regt HG 1942-44; demonstrator Univ of Birmingham 1929-33, Beit Meml fell London Univ 1933-36, lectr in chem Univ of Birmingham 1936-44, res fell Columbia Univ NY 1937; Univ of Birmingham: reader in chem 1944-46, prof of chem 1946-56, Mason prof and head of dept 1956-74, hon sr res fell 1974-76, emeritus prof 1975-; industl conslt 1976-82; memb Weoley Hill Village Cncl and Gardeners Clubs, chief scientific advsr Civil Def (Midlands) 1957-78, originator and organiser Sch Sci Fairs 1959-64, hon memb Assoc for Sci Educn 1972-, chm Jt Recruiting Bd (Midlands) 1954-62, memb: Home Office Sci Cncl 1967-75, Sci Res Cncls; vice pres Edgbaston HS 1984-; former memb ct of govrs Univs: Warwick, Loughborough, Keele; memb missions for Royal Soc Br Lit Cncl: Egypt, Rhodesia, S America; Hon DSc Keele 1977, Grand Award USA Nat Acad Sci 1950, hon fell Mark Twain Soc, emeritus memb American Chem Soc, Bronze Medal Univ of Helsinki 1966, Virtanen Medal Biochem Soc Finland 1964, John Scott Medal City of Philadelphia USA 1969, Medaille d'Honneur Biol Soc France 1974, Catedratico Honor and Medal St Marcus Univ Lima Peru 1962; former vice-pres Royal Soc Chem & Meldola, Tilden & Haworth, lectr and medals Royals Soc Chem; FRS 1950, C Chem, FRSC; *Books* Polysaccharides of Microorganisams (with SA Barker 1961), Carbohydrates of Living Tissues (with Barker 1962); *Recreations* athletics (life memb AAA), antique collecting, horticulture, foreign travel; *Clubs* Athenaeum; *Style—* Prof Maurice Stacey, CBE; 12 Bryony Rd, Weoley Hill, Birmingham B29 4BU (☎ 021 475 2065)

STACEY, Rear Adm Michael Lawrence; CB (1979); s of Maurice Stacey (d 1971), and Dorice Evelyn, *née* Bulling (d 1967); *b* 6 July 1924; *Educ* Epsom Coll; *m* 1955, Penelope Leana, da of Alister Riddoch (d 1968); 2 s (Hugo, Mark); *Career* various sea appts and cmds 1942-70; dep dir Naval Warfare 1970-72, i/c HMS Tiger 1973-75; ADC 1975; asst Chief of Naval Staff (Policy) 1975-76, Flag Offr Gibraltar 1976-79; dir Marine Pollution Control Unit Dept of Tport 1979-88, UK vice pres Advsy Ctee on Protection of the Sea; Younger Brother of Trinity House; memb Ctee of Mgmnt RNLI; *Recreations* fly-fishing, sailing; *Clubs* Army and Navy; *Style—* Rear Adm Michael Stacey, CB; Little Hintock, 40 Lynch Rd, Farnham, Surrey (☎ 0252 713032)

STACEY, Nicholas Anthony Howard; s of Maurus Stacey (d 1945), and Lily, *née* Balkanyi; *Educ* Pietist Gymnasium, Commercial Acad, Univ of Birmingham, Univ of London; *m* 1 (m dis 1986), Gloria Rose Cooklin; m 2, 10 March 1987, Marianne Luise Ehrhardt, *qv*; *Career* editorial staff Financial Times 1945-46, asst sec Assoc of Certified and Corporate Accountants 1947-51, asst ed The Director (jl of IOD) 1953-54, econ and mktg advsr GEC plc 1955-62; chm: Nicholas Stacey Assocs 1960-, Chesham Amalgamations & Investments Ltd 1963-83, Cel-Sci Corp Washington DC 1983-90, Integrated Asset Management 1984; dir Asset Management Fin & Settlement Ltd (NY) 1987-; chm tstees Soc for the Promotion of New Music 1969-86; memb: Consultative Ctee for Indust Bd of Trade 1958-62, US-UK Educnl (Fulbright) Cmmn 1983-90, Governing Ctee Br Fulbright Scholars Assoc 1982-89; fell Chartered Inst of Secretaries and Administrators; *Books* English Accountancy, A Study in Social and Economic History (1954), Changing Pattern of Distribution (1988), Industrial Market Research (1963), Mergers In Modern Business (1976), Living in an Alibi Society (1988); *Recreations* skiing, walking, music, swimming; *Clubs* Reform; *Style—* Nicholas Stacey, Esq; c/o Reform Club, Pall Mall, London SW1Y 5EW

STACEY, Rev Nicolas David; s of David Henry Stacey (d 1986), and Isobel Ewem, *née* Part; *b* 27 Nov 1927; *Educ* RNC Dartmouth, St Edmund Hall Oxford (MA), Cuddesdon Theol Coll Oxford; *m* 19 July 1955, Anne Caroline Mary, eld da of 2 Viscount Bridgeman, KBE, CB, DSO, MC, JP (d 1982); 1 s (David Robert b 10 May 1958), 2 da (Caroline Jill b 28 Aug 1956, Mary Elizabeth b 15 May 1961); *Career* Midshipman RN 1945-46, Sub-Lt 1946-48; asst curate St Marks Portsmouth 1953-58, domestic chaplain to Bishop of Birmingham 1958-60, rector of Woolwich 1960-68, dean London Borough of Greenwich 1965-68, dep dir Oxfam 1968-70; dir social services: London Borough of Ealing 1971-74, Kent CC 1974-85; social services conslt 1985-88, dir Aids Policy Unit 1988-89, ptnr English Homes and Country Tours, govr Reeds Sch Cobham, dir Faversham Oyster Co; patron Terence Higgins Tst, hon sr memb Darwin Coll Univ of Kent, chm Youth Call 1981, dep chm Television South Charitable Tst 1988, six preacher Canterbury Cathedral 1984-90; int sprinter 1948-52, Br Empire Games 1949, Olympic Games 1952, pres Oxford Univ Athletic Club 1951, capt Combined Oxford and Cambridge Athletics Team 1951; *Books* Who Cares (autobiography, 1971); *Recreations* skiing, golf; *Clubs* Beefsteak, Vincents (Oxford), Royal St Georges Golf (Sandwich); *Style—* The Rev Nicolas Stacey; The Old Vicarage, Selling, Faversham, Kent (☎ 0227 752 833)

STACEY, Maj Nigel William; s of William Percival Stacey (d 1972), and Pamela Iris Gledhill, *née* Prudent; *b* 22 Dec 1946; *Educ* Truro Cathedral Sch, Mons Offr Cadet Sch, RMA Sandhurst; *m* 16 March 1973, Pauline Joyce, da of Charles Hallet Taylor (d 1970); 2 s (Simon Nigel James b 1975, Richard Charles George b 1979); *Career* Army Offr Regular Army cmmnd The Light Infantry 1972; Industl Banking 1964-69, stockbroking 1969-71; *Recreations* golf, squash, photography; *Clubs* The Landsdowne, The Light Infantry; *Style—* Maj Nigel Stacey; Coutts & Co, 1 Old Park Lane, London W1Y 4BS

STACEY, Thomas Charles Gerard (Tom); s of David Henry Stacey (d 1986), and Gwen Isobel, *née* Part; *b* 11 Jan 1930; *Educ* Eton, Worcester Coll Oxford; *m* 5 Jan 1952, Caroline Susan, da of Charles Nightingale Clay (d 1961); 1 s (Sam b 1966), 4 da (Emma b 1952, Mathilda b 1954, Isabella b 1957, Tomasina b 1967); *Career* formerly chief roving corr The Sunday Times and others; author and screenwriter; works incl: The Hostile Sun (1953), The Brothers M (1960), Summons to Ruwenzori (1963), To-day's World (1970), The Living and The Dying (1976), The Pandemonium (1980), The Worm in the Rose (1985), Deadline (novel and screenplay, 1988), Bodies and Souls (1989), Decline (1991); chm: Stacey International 1974, Kensington Film Co; fndr and dir Offender's Tag Assoc; awarded John Llewellyn Rhys Meml prize 1953, Granada award (as foreign corr) 1961; FRSL 1977 (memb Cncl 1987); *Recreations* trees, music;

Clubs White's, Beefsteak, Pratt's; *Style*— Tom Stacey, Esq; 128 Kensington Church St, London W8 4BH (☎ 071 221 7166, fax 071 792 9288)

STACK, (Maurice) Neville; s of Maurice Stack (d 1970); *b* 2 Sept 1928; *Educ* Arnold Sch; *m* 1953, Molly, *née* Rowe; 1 s, 1 da; *Career* journalist; Express and Star 1950, Sheffield Telegraph and Kemsley Nat Newspapers 1955, northern news ed IPC Nat Newspapers 1971, sub ed Daily Express 1973, ed Stockport Advertiser 1974, ed-in-chief Leicester Mercury 1974-87, dir F Hewitt & Co Ltd Leicester 1985-88, editorial conslt Straits Times Singapore 1988-89; writer, press conslt, lectr; Hon MA Univ of Leicester 1988; press fell Wolfson Coll Cambridge 1987-88; *Books* The Empty Palace (1977), Editing for the Nineties (1988); *Recreations* writing, travelling, enjoying music and art; *Clubs* Leicestershire; *Style*— Neville Stack, Esq; 34 Main St, Belton-in-Rutland, Leics LE15 9LB (☎ 057 286 645)

STACK, Air Chief Marshal Sir (Thomas) Neville; KCB (1972, CB 1969), CVO (1963), CBE (1965), AFC (1957); s of Thomas Neville Stack, AFC, pioneer airman (d 1949); *b* 19 Oct 1919; *Educ* St Edmund's Coll, RAF Coll Cranwell; *m* 1955, Diana Virginia, da of late Oliver Stuart Todd, MBE; 1 s, 1 da; *Career* cmmnd RAF 1939, served WWII, flying boats 1939-44 (despatches), Coastal Cmd 1945-52, Tport Support Far East (Malaya Ops) and UK 1954-59, Dep Capt The Queen's Flight 1960-62, Tport Support Far East (Borneo Ops) 1962-64, Cmdt RAF Coll Cranwell 1967-70, UK perm mil dep CENTO Ankara 1970-72, AOC-in-C RAF Trg Cmd 1973-75, Air Sec MOD (Air) 1976-78, Air ADC to HM The Queen 1976-78; Gentleman Usher to HM The Queen 1978-89, Extra Gentleman Usher to HM The Queen 1989-; dir gen Asbestos Int Assoc 1978-89; memb Cncl Cancer Res Campaign (CRC) 1979- (memb Exec Ctee 1979-87); govr Wellington Coll 1980-90; pres Old Cranwellian Assoc 1985-; Freeman City of London, Liveryman Guild of Air Pilots and Air Navigators; FRMetS 1945-90, FBIM 1970-88; *Recreations* under-gardening, various outdoor sports; *Clubs* RAF, Boodle's, Hurlingham; *Style*— Air Chief Marshal Sir Neville Stack, KCB, CVO, CBE, AFC; 4 Perrymead St, London SW6 3SP (☎ 071 736 4410)

STACK, (Ann) Prunella (Mrs Brian St Quentin Power); OBE (1980); da of Capt Edward Hugh Bagot Stack, 8 Gurkha Rifles (d 1914), and Mary Meta Bagot Stack (d 1935), fndr Women's League of Health and Beauty 1930; *b* 28 July 1914; *Educ* The Abbey Malvern Wells; *m* 1, 15 Oct 1938, Lord David Douglas-Hamilton (ka 1944), yst s of 13 Duke of Hamilton and 10 Duke of Brandon (d 1940); 2 s (Diarmaid Hugh b 17 June 1940, Iain b 16 Aug 1942); m 2, 22 July 1950, Alfred Gustave Albers (d 1951), o s of late N W Albers, of Newlands, Cape, S Africa; m 3, 15 May 1964, Brian St Quentin Power, 2 s of late Stephen Power, of Querrin, Co Clare; *Career* ldr The Women's League of Health and Beauty 1935 (pres 1982), memb Nat Fitness Cncl 1937-39, vice pres Outward Bound Tst 1980-; *Books* The Way to Health and Beauty (1938), Movement is Life (1973), Island Quest (1979), Zest for Life (1988), Style for Life (1990); *Recreations* poetry, music, travel; *Style*— Miss Prunella Stack, OBE; 14 Gertrude St, London SW10 (☎ 071 351 3393)

STACY, Graham Henry; s of Norman Winny Stacy (d 1980), and Winifred Frances, *née* Wood (d 1985); *b* 23 May 1933; *Educ* Stationers' Company's Sch; *m* 19 July 1958, Mary, da of Cyril Arthur Fereday; 4 c (Richard Graham b 13 June 1963, Julia Caroline b 30 July 1964, Helen Clare (twin) b 30 July 1964, Caroline Jane b 18 Sept 1967); *Career* Nat Serv 1955-57 Sub-Lieut RN; articled clerk Walter Smee Will & Co 1950-55, qualified CA 1955; Price Waterhouse: joined 1957, Brazil and Argentina 1962, ptnr 1968-, nat tech ptnr 1976-88; fndr memb: UK Auditing Practices Ctee 1976-84, UK Accounting Standards Bd 1990-; memb UK Accounting Standards Ctee 1986-90; FCA (ACA 1955); *Recreations* bridge, tennis, DIY; *Style*— Graham Stacy; Price Waterhouse, Southwark Towers, 32 London Bridge St, London SE1 9SY (☎ 071 939 3000)

STACY, Neil Edwin; s of Edwin Frank Dixon Stacy, of Hinton, Gloucestershire, and Gladys Emily, *née* Wallis (d 1980); *b* 15 May 1941; *Educ* Hampton GS, Magdalen Coll Oxford (MA, DPhil); *Career* theatre performances incl: The Soldier's Fortune, A Room with a View, The Importance of Being Earnest, Richard II (Prospect Prodns 1964-68), Enemy (Saville Theatre 1969), The Recruiting Offr (Bristol and Edinburgh Fest 1979), A Patriot for Me (Chichester Festival 1983), Canaries Sometimes Sing (Albery Theatre 1987), Captain Carvallo (Greenwich 1988), Blythe Spirit (Lyric Hammersmith 1989), Single Spies (NT tour 1990); TV performances incl: War and Peace, Barlow at large, Colditz, The Pallisers, To Serve Them all my Days, Shackleton, The Fourth Arm, Duty Free, Three up, Two Down; *Recreations* medieval history; *Style*— Neil Stacy, Esq; c/o Michael Whitehall Ltd, 125 Gloucester Road, London SW7 4TE (☎ 071 244 8466, fax 071 244 9060)

STAËL VON HOLSTEIN, Baron (Sweden 1675); Robert Alexander Karl Constantin; s of Baron Constantin Staël von Holstein (d 1964 in Dawlish) by his w Countess Sylvia von der Recke von Volmerstein, da of (Karl) 4 Count von der Recke von Volmerstein (of a Prussian cr of 1817 by King Frederick William III, though the family originally hailed from Westphalia); the Baron is *chef de famille* and a direct descendant of Madame de Staël, the French authoress; *b* 20 Feb 1928; *Educ* Prebendal Sch Chichester; *m* 15 Sept 1978, (as her 2 husb) Carol, da of Hon Douglas Westwood (2 s of 1 Baron Westwood) and formerly w of Maj John Ralli (whose f John was 3 cous of Sir Godfrey Ralli, 3 Bt); 1 s (Jeremy John Alexander b 1957), 1 da (Victoria Anne b 1962) and 1 step s (Charles Douglas Stephen Ralli b 1968); *Career* exec in construction indust in Africa, S America, M East; consultant in W African economic affairs and planning advsr; *Recreations* tennis, golf; *Clubs* Travellers', Lansdowne; *Style*— Baron Staël von Holstein; 77 Ashworth Mansions, Maida Vale, London W9 1LN (☎ 071 286 7495, telex 296927)

STAFFORD, David Valentine; s of Augustus Everard Stafford (d 1980), and Emily Blanche, *née* Hiscutt (d 1970); *b* 14 Feb 1930; *Educ* Rutlish Sch Merton; *m* 18 April 1953, (Aileen) Patricia, da of Robert Henry Wood, MVO (d 1979); 1 s (Nicholas David b 1954), 1 da (Julia Ann b 1957); *Career* DES 1951-88; sec Open Univ Planning Ctee 1967-69, asst sec DES Higher and Further Educn 1979-88, sec ESRC 1988-90 (sec and acting chm ERSC Feb-Oct 1988), ret; *Recreations* reading, gardening, education research; *Style*— David Stafford, Esq; 3 Bloomfield Park, Bath, Avon BA2 2BY (☎ 0225 312563)

STAFFORD, Hon Mrs (Elizabeth Anne); *née* Richardson; da of Baron Richardson, MVO; *b* 24 July 1937; *m* 1, 1960 (m dis 1970), Angus Jack, s of Brig-Gen James Jack, DSO, DL, by his w, Jeanette, da of Thomas Watson (3 s of Sir John Watson, 1 Bt, JP, DL); 1 s; m 2, 1971, Gregory Stafford; 1 s; *Style*— The Hon Mrs Stafford; 49 Deodar Rd, London SW15

STAFFORD, 15 Baron (E 1640) Francis Melfort William Fitzherbert; s of 14 Baron (d 1986), and Morag Nada, da of late Lt-Col Alastair Campbell, of Altries, Milltimber, Aberdeenshire; *b* 13 March 1954; *Educ* Ampleforth, Reading Univ, RAC Cirencester; *m* 1980, Katharine Mary, 3 da of John Codrington, of Barnes, London SW14; 2 s (Hon Benjamin John Basil b 1983, Hon Toby Francis b 1985), 2 da (Hon Teresa Emily b 1987, Hon Camilla Rose Jane b 1989); *Heir* s, Hon Benjamin Fitzherbert b 8 Nov 1983; *Career* non-exec dir Tarmac Ind Products Div; patron and pres of various orgns in N Staffordshire, non-exec dir Mental Health Fndn Mid Staffs, govr Harper Adams Agric Coll; *Recreations* cricket, shooting, golf; *Clubs* Farmers, Lord's Taverners; *Style*— The Rt Hon Lord Stafford; Swynnerton Park, Stone, Staffordshire SM5 0QE

STAFFORD, Bishop of 1987-; Rt Rev Michael Charles Scott-Joynt; Rt Rev; s of Rev Albert George Scott-Joynt (d 1979), and Bettine, *née* Young; *b* 15 March 1943; *Educ* Bradfield Coll Berks, Kings Coll Cambridge (hon scholar, BA); *m* 24 July 1965, (Mary) Louise, da of Colin White (d 1965); 2 s (Jeremy Charles b 1970, Matthew James b 1970), 1 da (Hannah Margaret b 1968); *Career* curate Cuddesdon Oxon 1967-70, tutor Cuddesdon Coll 1967-72, team vicar Newbury Berks 1972-75, rector Bicester and Islip team miny Oxon 1975-81, dir of ordinands and in-service trg and canon residentiary St Albans Cathedral 1982-87, bishop of Stafford 1987-; memb: Exec Ctee Stoke-on-Trent CAB, Exec Ctee Rural Community, Exec Cncl of Staffordshire; *Recreations* walking, opera; *Style*— The Rt Rev the Bishop of Stafford; Ash Garth, Broughton Crescent, Barlaston, Stoke-on-Trent ST12 9DD (☎ 078 139 3308)

STAFFORD, (Thomas Henry) Michael; s of John Richard Stafford (d 1985), of Atherstone, Warwicks, and Henrietta, *née* Allen (d 1990); *b* 15 July 1926; *Educ* Oakham Sch, Univ of Oxford (MA); *m* 15 July 1950, Lorna Beatrice, da of Douglas James Vero (d 1937), of Atherstone; 2 s (Andrew b 1955, Rupert b 1971), 3 da (Judith b 1951, Alison b 1953, Charlotte b 1959); *Career* aircrew cadet ACI RAF 1945-47; hat mfr; chm Wilson & Stafford Ltd 1985 (dir 1952-); pres Br Felt Hat Manufacturers' Fedn 1959; freemason; *Recreations* gardening, motoring, fishing, singing light opera, reading; *Style*— Michael Stafford, Esq; Limes, 67 South St, Atherstone (☎ 0827 713370); Wilson and Stafford Ltd, Station St, Atherstone, Warwicks (☎ 0827 717941)

STAFFORD, Baroness; Morag Nada; *née* Campbell; yr da of late Lt-Col Alastair Campbell, of Aberdeenshire; *m* 1952, 14 Baron Stafford (d 1986); 3 s (15 Baron, Hon Thomas, Hon Philip), 3 da (Hon Aileen, Hon Caroline, Hon Wendy); *Style*— The Rt Hon Morag, Lady Stafford; Beech Farm House, Beech, Stoke-on-Trent, Staffordshire ST4 8SJ

STAFFORD, Peter Moore; s of Harry Shaw Stafford (d 1981), of Wilmslow, Cheshire, and May Alexandra, *née* Moore; *b* 24 April 1942; *Educ* Charterhouse; *m* 29 Sept 1973, Elspeth Anne, da of James Steel Harvey; 2 c (Gayle b 3 Sept 1975, Christopher b 9 March 1977); *Career* Garnett Crewdson & Co Manchester: articled clerk 1960-64, CA 1964-66; Arthur Andersen 1966-68; ptnr: Garnett Crewdson & Co 1968-71, Spicer & Oppenheim 1971-90 (national managing ptnr 1990), Touche Ross & Co 1990- (all following mergers); memb Partnership Bd 1990-; govr Terra Nova Sch Tst Ltd; FCA (ACA 1965); *Recreations* travel, gardening, restoring antique launches; *Style*— Peter Stafford, Esq; Touche Ross & Co, Abbey House, 74 Mosley St, Manchester M60 2AT (☎ 061 228 3456, fax 061 228 2021, car 0860 629777)

STAHL, Andrew; s of Adam Jack Stahl, of London, and Sheena Penelope, *née* Simms; *b* 4 July 1954; *Educ* Slade Sch of Fine Art; *m* 1988, Jean Oh Mei Yen, da of Henry Oh Sui Hong; *Career* artist; solo exhibitions: Air Gallery London 1981 and 1983, Paton Gallery London 1984 and 1988; gp exhibitions incl: British Drawing (Hayward Gallery) 1982, Pagan Echoes (Riverside Studios) 1983, selections from 10 years at Air (Air Gallery) 1985, 17 International Festival of Painting Cagnes France 1985, Living Art (Ideal Home Exhibition) 1986, Walking & Falling (Interim Art & Kettles Yard Cambridge) 1986, British Painting (touring Malaysia, Singapore, Hong Kong, Thailand) 1987, Artists Choice (V & A Museum) 1987, London Group (RCA) 1988, Figuring out the 80's (Laing Art Gallery Newcastle), Whitechapel Open 1989, Print Show (Flowers East) 1989, Rome Scholars 1980-90, (RCA) 1990, Small is Beautiful (Flowers East) 1990, 19 International Biennale Ljubliana 1991; works in the public collections of: Metropolitan Museum of Art New York, Arts Cncl of GB, Br Cncl, Contemporary Arts Soc, City Museum Peterborough, Leicestershire Educ Authy *Awards* Abbey Major Rome Scholarship 1979-81, Fellowship in Printmaking RCA 1989, Rome award in Painting Br Sch at Rome 1989; *Style*— Andrew Stahl, Esq; 38 Powis Square, London W11 2AY; Acme Studio 69A,105 Carpenters Rd, London E15

STAIB, Hon Mrs (Mary Clare); *née* Kinnaird; da of 13 Lord Kinnaird; *m* 29 May 1988, John Staib, o s of Edward Staib, of Las Palmas, and the Dowager Countess of Dundonald, *qv*; 1 s (James Alexander Christian b 14 Feb 1990); *Style*— The Hon Mrs Staib

STAINER, Michael; s of Peter Stainer (agent to the Duke of Bedford's Estates 1951-67), of The Grand, Folkestone, and Gretl Ilse Emmi Ruth, *née* Gosewisch; *b* 20 Dec 1947; *Educ* Bedford Sch; *Career* CA; Touche Ross & Co 1966-73; own practice 1973-; chm and md The Grand Hotel Ltd 1976-; Freeman City of London 1983, Worshipful Co of CAs; *Style*— Michael Stainer, Esq; The Grand, Folkestone, Kent CT20 2LR (☎ 0303 56789)

STAINTON, Sir (John) Ross; CBE (1971); s of George Stainton, and Helen, *née* Ross; *b* 27 May 1914; *Educ* Malvern; *m* 1939, Doreen Werner; 3 da; *Career* served WWII, RAF; Imperial Airways 1933-40, chm BA 1979-80 (dep chm and chief exec 1977-79, dir 1971-, chm and chief exec BOAC 1972 prior to merger into BA 1974, dir 1968-74, md 1971-72, dep md 1968-71, commercial dir 1964-68, joined 1942); vice pres Private Patients Plan plc; dir Direct Mail Servs Standards Bd; FBIM, FCIT (pres 1970-71); kt 1981; *Style*— Sir Ross Stainton, CBE; c/o Private Patients Plan plc, Tavistock House South, Tavistock Sq, WC1 (☎ 071 388 2468)

STAIR, 13 Earl of (S 1703); Sir John Aymer Dalrymple; 14 Bt of Stair (S 1664) and 10 of Killock (S 1698), KCVO (1978, CVO 1964), MBE (1941); also Viscount Stair, and Lord Glenluce and Stranraer (S 1690); Viscount Dalrymple and Lord Newliston (S 1703), Baron Oxenfoord (UK 1841); s of 12 Earl of Stair (d 1961); *b* 9 Oct 1906; *Educ* Eton; *m* 1960, Davina Katharine, da of late Hon Sir David Bowes-Lyon, KCVO, s of 14 Earl of Strathmore and Kinghorne; 3 s; *Heir* s, Viscount Dalrymple; *Career* Col late Scots Gds, Capt Gen Queen's Bodyguard for Scotland (Royal Co of Archers), Gold Stick for Scotland, Lord-Lt for Wigtownshire 1961-81; *Style*— The Rt Hon the Earl of Stair, KCVO, MBE; Lochinch Castle, Stranraer, Wigtownshire

STAITE, Neil Anthony; s of John Leslie Staite, of Evesham, Worcs, and Patricia Jane Allard, *née* Evesham; *b* 20 Jan 1963; *Educ* Prince Henrys HS, Evesham Coll of Further Educn; *m* 30 Sept 1989, Laura Elizabeth, da of Roger Whittingham; 1 s (Oliver Michael b 9 Feb 1991); *Career* oarsman; Evesham Rowing Club 1977-85, Nottinghamshire Co Rowing Assoc 1985-; rowed in Jr World Championships Bulgaria 1981; achievements incl: Gold medal lightweight four Cwlth Games Edinburgh 1986, Silver medal lightweight four World Rowing Championships Nottingham 1986 and Copenhagen 1987 (Bronze lightweight eight Tasmania 1990), Gold medal lightweight eight Lucerne Int 1984 (Gold lightweight four 1987); Henley Royal Regatta: winner Wyfold Challenge Cup 1987, winner Ladies Plate 1989, winner Thames Challenge Cup 1990; records: Cwlth Games lightweight four 1986, world lightweight eight 1990; asst L Staite & Sons Ltd (horticultural nursery) 1984-; *Recreations* genealogy; *Style*— Neil Staite, Esq; Brookland House, Clayfield Lane, South Littleton, Evesham, Worcestershire WR11 5TG (☎ 0386 830148)

STAKIS, Andros Reo; s of Sir Reo Stakis, of Glasgow, and Annitsa Stakis; *b* 16 April 1956; *Educ* Glasgow Acad, Univ of Edinburgh, Cornell Univ, Sorbonne; *m* Barbara; *Career* trainee Hilton International 1981-82, md Stakis Land & Estates 1983-88, gp md Stakis plc 1988-; *Recreations* shooting, squash, tennis; *Style*— Andros Stakis, Esq; Stakis plc, 58 West Regent St, Glasgow G2 2QZ (☎ 041 332 7773, fax 041 331 1406, telex 779220, car 0836 511470)

STALKER, John Lawson; s of Percy Stalker (d 1958), late of Windermere, Cumbria, and Dorothy, *née* Pickles; *b* 7 Oct 1951; *Educ* Royal Masonic Inst for Boys, Univ of Newcastle (BSc); *m* 20 July 1973, Marie, da of Charles Richard Matterson (d 1980), of Sunderland; 2 da (Rachel Rose b 1983, Naomi Dorothy Ruth b 1987); *Career* ptnr Clark Whitehill CAs; chm Thames Valley Branch Inst of Taxation, lay memb Bucks Family Practitioner Ctee; *Recreations* fishing; *Style*— John Stalker, Esq; 143 Beech Lane, Earley, Reading, Berks (☎ 0734 862352); Clark Whitehill, 4 Priory Rd, High Wycombe, Bucks HP11 1NJ (☎ (0494) 444088)

STALLARD, Baron (Life Peer UK 1983), of St Pancras in the London Borough of Camden; Albert William Stallard; s of Frederick Stallard, of Tottenham; *b* 5 Nov 1921; *Educ* Low Waters Public Sch, Hamilton Acad Scotland; *m* 1944, Julie, da of William Cornelius Murphy, of Co Kerry; 1 s (Hon Richard b 1945), 1 da (Hon Brenda (Hon Mrs Hills) b 1949); *Career* engr 1937-65, tech trg offr 1965-70; memb St Pancras Borough Cncl 1953-59 (alderman 1962-65); chm: Pub Health Ctee 1956-59 and 1962-65, Housing and Planning Dept 1956-59; memb Camden Borough Cncl 1965-70 (alderman 1971-); MP (Lab): St Pancras North 1970-74, Camden Div of St Pancras North 1974-83; PPS: Min of Agric 1973-74, min of Housing and Construction 1974-76; govt whip 1978-79 (asst 1976-78), Lords Cmmr Treasy; memb and chm Camden Town Disablement Advsy Ctee 1951-83, vice pres Camden Assoc of Mental Health; memb AEU Order of Merit (1968), former memb Inst of Trg & Devpt; *Style*— The Rt Hon the Lord Stallard; 2 Belmont St, Chalk Farm, London NW1

STALLARD, Sir Peter Hyla Gawne; KCMG (1961, CMG 1960), CVO (1956), MBE (1945); s of Rev Leonard B Stallard (d 1945), of Ottery St Mary, Devon; *b* 6 March 1915; *Educ* Bromsgrove Sch, CCC Oxford (MA); *m* 1941, Mary Elizabeth, da of Rev H A Kirke of Burnham-on-Sea, Somerset; 1 s, 1 da; *Career* entered Colonial Serv Nigeria 1937, RWAFF (Artillery) W Africa and Burma 1939-45, Lt-Col 1945; sec to PM of Fedn of Nigeria 1957-61, govr and C-in-C Br Honduras 1961-66, Lt-Govr IOM 1966-73, pres Devon and Cornwall Rent Assessment Panel 1976-85; KStJ 1961, Chapter-Gen Order of St John 1976-; *Style*— Sir Peter Stallard, KCMG, CVO, MBE; 18 Henley Rd, Taunton, Somerset (☎ 0823 331505)

STALLARD, Hon Richard; o s of Baron Stallard (Life Peer); *b* 1945; *Educ* Richard Acland Sch London; *m* 1969, Carol, da of William Packman, of Swanley, Kent; 1 s, 1 da; *Style*— The Hon Richard Stallard

STALLWORTHY, Sir John Arthur; s of Arthur John Stallworthy, of NZ; *b* 26 July 1906; *Educ* Auckland GS, Auckland and Otago Univs (NZ); *m* 1934, Margaret Wright, da of John Howie, of Scotland; 1 s, 2 da; *Career* pres: Cancer Information Assoc; Royal Soc of Medicine, Medical Protection Soc, BMA 1975; emeritus prof obstetrics and gynaecology Oxford (prof 1967-73), hon fell Oriel Oxford; MRCOG, FRCS, ERCOG; kt 1972; *Style*— Sir John Stallworthy; 8a College Green, Gloucester GL1 2LX (☎ (0452) 421243)

STALLWORTHY, Jon Howie; s of Sir John Arthur Stallworthy, of College Green, Glos, and Lady Margaret Wright, *née* Howie (d 1980); *b* 18 Jan 1935; *Educ* Rugby, Univ of Oxford (BA, MA, BLitt); *m* 25 June 1960, Gillian (Jill), da of Sir Claude Humphrey Meredith Waldock, CMG, OBE, QC (d 1981); 2 s (Jonathan b 1965, Nicolas b 1970), 1 da (Pippa b 1967); *Career* Nat Serv 1954-55, 2 Lt Oxon and Bucks LI, seconded Royal W African Frontier Force; visiting fell All Souls Coll Oxford 1971-72, dep academic publisher OUP 1972-77, Anderson prof Eng lit Cornell Univ 1977-86, professorial fell Wolfson Coll and reader Eng lit Univ of Oxford; FRSL, FBA 1990; Hon DUniv Surrey; *Books* incl: Between the Lines, WB Yeats's Poetry in the Making (1963), Vision and Revision in Yeats's Last Poems (1969), Alexander Blok, The Twelve and Other Poems (with Peter France, 1970), Wilfred Owen (winner Duff Cooper Meml prize, W H Smith & Son Literary award, E M Forster award, 1974), The Penguin Book of Love Poetry (ed, 1973), Boris Pasternak, Selected Poems (with Peter France, 1984), The Oxford Book of War Poetry (ed, 1984), The Anzac Sonata: New and Selected Poems (1986), First Lines: Poems Written in Youth from Herbert to Heaney (1987); *Style*— Jon Stallworthy, Esq; Long Farm, Elsfield Rd, Old Marston, Oxford OX3 OPR; Wolfson Coll, Oxford OX2 6UD

STALLYBRASS, Hon Mrs (Agnes Mary); *née* Clifford; o da of 11 Baron Clifford of Chudleigh (d 1962), and his 1 w Dorothy, *née* Hornyold (d 1918); *b* 26 Nov 1918; *m* 1944, Robert Weatherhead Stallybrass, 2 s of late Greville Stallybrass; 1 s, 2 da; *Style*— The Hon Mrs Stallybrass; The Old Laundry, Oakhill, nr Bath

STAMER, Sir (Lovelace) Anthony; 5 Bt (UK 1809) of Beauchamp, Dublin; s of Sir Lovelace Stamer, 4 Bt (d 1941), and Mary, *née* Otter (d 1974; her mother Marianne was seventh in descent from 4 Baron North); *b* 28 Feb 1917; *Educ* Harrow, Trinity Coll Cambridge (MA); *m* 1, 1948 (m dis 1953), Stella Huguette, da of Paul Burnell Binnie; 1 s, 1 da; m 2, 1955 (m dis 1959), Margaret Lucy, da of late Maj Belben; m 3, 1960 (m dis 1968), Marjorie June, da of late T C Noakes; m 4, 1983, Elizabeth Graham Smith, da of late C J R Magrath and wid of G P H Smith; *Heir* s, Sqdn Ldr Peter Tomlinson Stamer, RAF (ret); *Career* PO RAF 1939-41, 1 Offr Air Tport Aux 1941-45; exec dir: Bentley Drivers Club Ltd 1969-73, Bugatti and Ferrari Owners Clubs 1973-74; hon tres Ferrari Owners Club 1976-81; *Style*— Sir Anthony Stamer, Bt; White Farm Cottage, White Farm Lane, West Hill, Ottery St Mary, Devon EX11 1XF (☎ 040 481 2706)

STAMER, Peter Tomlinson; s and h of Sir Anthony Stamer, 5 Bt; *b* 19 Nov 1951; *Educ* Malvern, Univ of Southampton; *m* 1979, (m dis 1989) Dinah Louise, da of T S Berry; 1 s (William b 1983), 1 da (Antonia b 1981); *Career* Br Aircraft Corp 1970-71; RAF 1972-89, Sqdn Ldr 1988; Furniture maker/restorer 1990-; *Style*— Peter Stamer, Esq; c/o Lloyds Bank, 31 Sloane Square, London SW1W 8AG

STAMERS-SMITH, Eileen; da of Charles Fairey, and May, *née* Walls; *b* 17 April 1929; *Educ* Castleford GS, Lady Margaret Hall Oxford (MA, DipEd); *m* 19 Dec 1970, Henry Arthur Stamers-Smith, CBE (d 1982), s of Allan Frith Smith, of Bermuda; *Career* Eng teacher: Abbeydale Girls GS Sheffield 1952-57, Cheltenham Ladies' Coll 1957-67; headmistress: Bermuda Girls' HS 1967-71, Malvern Girls' Coll 1984-85; tutor and lectr in garden history and Eng literature and art history: Dept of Continuing Educn Univ of Oxford, WEA Denman Coll, NT, NACF, NADFAS; ed Garden History Soc Newletter 1987-; *Books* R Verey's Countrywoman's Notes (ed); pubns in: Garden History Society Journal and Newsletter, Northern Gardener, HORTUS; *Recreations* Venice, photography, calligraphy, poetry, fell-walking; *Style*— Mrs Eileen Stamers-Smith; 8 Mavor Close, Old Woodstock, Oxon OX7 1YL (☎ 811383)

STAMLER, Samuel Aaron; QC (1971); s of Herman Stamler (d 1962), and Bronia, *née* Rosshandler (d 1973); *b* 3 Dec 1925; *Educ* Berkhamsted, King's Coll Cambridge (MA, LLB); *m* 3 Aug 1953, (Vivienne) Honor, da of Adolph Brotman (d 1970); 2 s (Martin Stephen b 1958, Robin Jacob b 1961), 1 da (Anne Elizabeth b 1957); *Career* called to the Bar Middle Temple 1949, rec Crown Ct 1974, master of the bench Middle Temple 1979; *Recreations* grandchildren, walking; *Clubs* Athenaeum; *Style*— Samuel Stamler, Esq, QC; 47 Forty Avenue, Wembley, Middlesex (☎ 081 904 1714); 1 Essex Court, Temple, London (☎ 071 563 2000)

STAMMERS, Lionel John; s of Frederick Arthur Stammers, and Dorothy Irene, *née* Heales (d 1987); *b* 11 May 1933; *Educ* Harlow Coll London (BSc Econ); *m* 5 Aug 1957, Sybil Ann, da of William James Wescott; 2 da (Jane Emma b 1963, Susan Fiona b 1965); *Career* non exec dir: BTR plc, BBA Group plc, Hays plc, McKechnie plc, Bullough plc, Quadrant Group plc; *Style*— Lionel Stammers, Esq; BTR plc, Silvertown House, Vincent Square, London SW1P 2PL (☎ 071 834 3848, fax 071 834 1841)

STAMP, Hon (Jos) Colin; s of 1 Baron Stamp, GCB, GBE (d 1941, as a result of enemy action); *b* 22 Dec 1917; *Educ* Leys Sch, Queens' Coll Cambridge; *m* 1, 26 June 1940 (m dis 1956), Althea da of late Mrs William Dawes, of Evanston, Illinois, USA; 4 da; m 2, 27 Dec 1958, Gillian Penelope, da of late Guy St John Tatham, of Johannesburg, SA; 2 s; *Career* late Lt RNVR; former dir of mktg servs for Europe of American Express Int; ptnr Martlet Assocs (audiovisual conslts) and Gillian Stamp Assocs (mgmnt conslts); *Productions include* Best Course to Windward (1982; BISFA Silver award), A Gift from Doctor Schweitzer (1983); fndr chm Barnes Community Assoc; *Recreations* sailing, music, photography, lecturing; *Style*— The Hon Colin Stamp; 12 Ullswater Rd, London SW13 (☎ 081 748 2782)

STAMP, David Paul; s of Thomas George Stamp, of Tiptree, Essex, and Betty Caroline, *née* Parnum; *b* 23 June 1955; *Educ* Royal Liberty Sch; *m* 21 July 1979, Helen Mary, da of Harold William Balls (d 1966), of Maldon, Essex; 3 s (James b 1975, Benjamin b 1980, Alastair b 1981); *Career* financier; Euro leasing mangr The Greyhound Gp 1980-85; md Finlease Hldgs Ltd (hldg co of The Finlease Gp) 1985: (UK) Ltd, EFL Ltd, Finance Ltd, Insurance Servs Ltd, Specialised Insurance Servs Ltd; md 1989: United Financial Servs Ltd, Leasepack Ltd, Finlease Travel Ltd, Maple Devpt Ltd; *Recreations* golf, ten-pin bowling; *Style*— David P Stamp; 1 Campbell Drive, Gunthorpe, Peterborough, PE 2RJ (☎ 0733 555855, fax 0733 310227, car 0860 743666)

STAMP, Hon (Nancy) Elizabeth; da of 2 Baron Stamp (d 1941, as a result of enemy action); *b* 1931; *Educ* Univ of St Andrews (MA); *Career* economist Intelligence Unit 1954-59; Maxwell Stamp Associates 1959-62; information offr Oxfam 1963-89; communications advsr Oxfam 1989-, chm The Life Style Movement; *Recreations* skiing, boating; *Style*— The Hon Elizabeth Stamp; 11 Harpes Rd, Oxford OX2 7QJ

STAMP, Ewen George Morrell; TD (1979); s of Col (John George) Morrell Stamp, TD, of Cambridge, and Marian Lomax, *née* Robinson (d 1987); *b* 16 Aug 1939; *Educ* Gordonstoun; *m* 19 Sept 1970, Mary Frances, da of Philip Erskine Hodge, of Lewes, Sussex; 3 da (Jane b 23 Jan 1973, Amy b 8 May 1975, Helen b 7 Dec 1979); *Career* HAC: gunner 1964, 2 Lieut 1968, Capt 1973, ret 1979, memb Ct of Assts 1979-89; CA; articled to Winter Robinson Sisson & Benson 1958-63, with Deloitte Plender Griffiths 1964-68, co sec Blagden & Noakes (Hldgs) Ltd (now Blagden Industries plc), gp fin dir Hemming group Ltd (incl Municipal Journal Ltd, Brintex Ltd, Newman Books Ltd); Freeman City of London 1976; FCA 1977; *Recreations* sailing; *Clubs* HAC, Royal Harwich Yacht; *Style*— Ewen Stamp, Esq, TD; Hemming Group Limited, 32 Vauxhall Bridge Rd, London SW1V 2SS

STAMP, Gavin Mark; s of Barry Hartnell Stamp, of Hereford, and Norah Clare, *née* Rich; *b* 15 March 1948; *Educ* Dulwich, Gonville and Caius Coll Cambridge (MA, PhD); *m* 12 Feb 1982, Alexandra Frances, da of Frank Artley, of Redcar; 2 da (Agnes Mary b 1984, Cecilia Jane b 1986); *Career* architectural historian; lectr Mackintosh Sch of Architecture Glasgow; author; contrib: The Spectator, Daily Telegraph, Independent, Architects Jl, Private Eye; chm Thirties Soc; *Books* The Architects Calendar (1974), The Victorian Buildings of London (with C Amery, 1980), Temples of Power (text only, 1979), Robert Weir Schultz and His Work for The Marquesses of Bute (1981), The Great Perspectivists (1982), The Changing Metropolis (1984), The English House 1860-1914 (1986), Telephone Boxes (1989); *Style*— Gavin Stamp, Esq; 1 Moray Place, Strathbungo, Glasgow G41 2AQ (☎ 041 423 3747)

STAMP, Hon Mrs Maxwell; (Alice) Mary; er da of Walter Richards, of Hereford; *m* 28 Jan 1944, as his 2 w, Hon (Arthur) Maxwell Stamp (d 1984), 3 s of 1 Baron Stamp, GCB, GBE (d 1941); 1 s, 2 da; *Style*— The Hon Mrs Maxwell Stamp; 1 Hollyoaks, Wormingford, Essex CO6 3BD (☎ 0787 228067)

STAMP, Hon (Josiah) Richard; s of 3 Baron Stamp (d 1987); *b* 15 Dec 1943; *Educ* Winchester, Queens' Coll Cambridge; *Style*— The Hon Richard Stamp; Flat B, 11 Lymington Road, London NW6 1HX

STAMP, Terence Henry; s of Thomas Stamp (d 1983), and Ethel Esther *née* Perrot (d 1985); *b* 22 July 1938; *Educ* Plaistow Co GS, Douglas ADA; *Career* actor; films: Billy Budd (1960), The Collector (1964), Far from the Madding Crowd (1966), Tales of Mystery (1967), Theorom (1968), Meeting with Remarkable Men, Superman I and II (1977), The Hit (1984); *Books* Stamp Album (1987), Coming Attractions (1988), Double Feature (1989); *Recreations* film; *Clubs* New York Athletic; *Style*— Terence Stamp, Esq; Julian House, 4 Windmill Street, London W1 (☎ 071 636 4412)

STAMP, 4 Baron (UK 1938) Trevor Charles Bosworth Stamp; s of 3 Baron Stamp (d 1987); *Educ* Leys Sch, Gonville and Caius Cambridge (BA), St Mary's Hosp Med Sch (MB BCh); *m* 1, 1963 (m dis 1971), Anne Carolynn, da of John Kenneth Churchill, of Tunbridge Wells; 2 da; m 2, 1975, Carol Anne, da of Robert Keith Russell, of Farnham, Surrey; 1 s, 1 da; *Heir* s, Hon Nicholas Charles Trevor Stamp b 1978; *Career* consultant physician 1974-; FRCP, MD; *Style*— The Rt Hon the Lord Stamp; Pennyroyal, Village Lane, Hedgerley, Bucks, SL2 3UY; Royal National Orthopaedic Hospital, Stanmore, Middx

STAMPS, Neil; s of Jeffrey Clifford Stamps, of Solihull, W Midlands, and Gillian Rosa, *née* Peat; *b* 21 Aug 1968; *Educ* Tudor Grange Sec Sch, Solihull Sixth Form Coll, Kingston Poly; *Career* wildwater canoeist; Br champion 1989 (under 16 champion 1984, under 18 1984-86); Euro Junior Wildwater Racing Championships: under 16 Gold 1984, under 18 Gold 1984, under 18 team Gold 1986; Silver medallist: World Junior Wildwater Racing Championships Spittal Austria, World Whitewater Championships Maryland USA; *Clubs* Royal Canoe; *Style*— Neil Stamps, Esq; 122 Ulverley Green Road, Solihull, West Midlands B92 8AA (☎ 021 706 0579)

STANBRIDGE, Andrew Morrisroe; s of Arthur George Stanbridge, and Monica Patricia, *née* Morrisroe; *b* 24 May 1951; *Educ* St Michaels Coll Herts; *m* 1982, Helen Maya, da of Vivian Graham Beardsell (d 1982), of Sussex; 1 da (Alexandra b 1986), 1 step da (Christina b 1978); *Career* advertiser; dir Saatchi & Saatchi Compton Ltd; *Style*— Andrew Stanbridge, Esq; 46 Murray Rd, Wimbledon, London SW19 (☎ 081 946 0352)

STANBRIDGE, Air Vice-Marshal Sir Brian Gerald Tivy; KCVO (1979, MVO 1958), CBE (1974), AFC (1952); s of Gerald Edward Stanbridge (d 1966); *b* 6 July 1924; *Educ* Thurlestone Coll Dartmouth; *m* 1, 1949 (m dis 1984), (Kathleen) Diana, *née* Hayes; 2 da; m 2 , 1984, Jennifer Anne; *Career* Air Vice-Marshal, Burma Campaign 1944-45, personal pilot and flying instr to HRH the Duke of Edinburgh 1954-58, sec to COS Ctee 1971-73, defence serv sec to the Queen 1975-79 (ret); dir gen Air Transport Users Ctee 1979-85; *Recreations* bridge, computers, DIY; *Clubs* RAF; *Style*— Air Vice-Marshal Sir Brian Stanbridge KCVO, CBE, AFC; 20 Durrant Way, Sway, Lymington, Hants S041 6PQ (☎ 0590 683030)

STANBRIDGE, Ven Leslie Cyril; *b* 19 May 1920; *Educ* Bromley GS Kent, St John's Coll Durham, Univ of Durham (BA, Dip Theol, MA); *Career* local govt offr 1936-46; served RAPC 1940-45; curate of Erith Kent 1949-51, tutor and chaplain St John's Coll Durham 1951-55, vicar of St Martin Hull 1955-64, rector of Cottingham 1964-72, archdeacon of York 1972-88, canon of York 1968-, succentor canonicorum 1988-; *Recreations* fell walking, cycling; *Style*— The Ven Leslie C Stanbridge; 1 Deangate, York YO1 2JB (☎ 0904 621174)

STANBRIDGE, Dr Raymond John; s of Sidney John Stanbridge, of Herts, and late Dora Margaret Stanbridge; *b* 19 Feb 1947; *Educ* Hemel Hempstead GS, Univ of Leeds (BCom), Univ of Nottingham (MSc), Victoria Univ of Wellington New Zealand (PhD); *m* 1970, Rosemary, da of William Norris, OBE (d 1987); 1 s (Timothy Jonathan b 1974), 2 da (Nicola Josephine b 1976, Felicity Juliet b 1980); *Career* mgmnt conslt Peat Marwick Mitchell & Co 1972-75, head of business planning Nickerson Group 1975-80; md: Stanbridge Mumby and Moore Ltd 1981-, Exchequergate Holdings plc 1987-; *Recreations* cricket, travel; *Style—* Dr Raymond Stanbridge; The Old Vicarage, Nettleham, Lincoln LN2 2RH (☎ 0522 752467); 2A Exchequergate, Lincoln LN2 1PZ (☎ 0522 538081, fax 0522 540940, telex 37688)

STANBROOK, Clive St George Clement; OBE (1988), QC (1989); s of Ivor Robert Stanbrook, MP, and Joan, *née* Clement; *b* 10 April 1948; *Educ* Dragon Sch Oxford, Westminster, UCL (LLB); *m* 3 April 1971, Julia Suzanne, da of Victor Hillary; 1 s (Ivor Victor Hillary), 3 da (Fleur Elizabeth, Sophie Noelette, Isabella Grace); *Career* called to the Bar Inner Temple 1972; bd memb World Trade Center Assoc (London) 1977-83, fndr and sr ptnr Stanbrook & Hooper (int lawyers) Brussels 1977, pres Br C of C for Belgium and Luxembourg 1985-87; *Books* Extradition the Law and Practice (jtly, 1980), Dumping Manual on the EEC Anti Dumping Law (1980), International Trade Law and Practice (co ed, 1984); *Recreations* tennis, sailing; *Style—* Clive Stanbrook, Esq, OBE, QC; Stanbrook & Hooper, 42 Rue du Taciturne, Brussels 1040, Belgium (☎ 230 5059, fax 230 5713, telex 61975 STALAW)

STANBROOK, Ivor Robert; MP (Cons) Orpington 1970-; yr s of Arthur William, and Lilian Stanbrook; *b* 13 Jan 1924; *Educ* Univ of London, Univ of Oxford; *m* 1946, Joan Clement; 2 s; *Career* RAF 1943-46, colonial dist offr Nigeria 1950-60, asst sec Cncl of Ministers Lagos 1954; called to the Bar Inner Temple 1960; contested (C) East Ham S 1966, chm Cons Backbench Constitutional Ctee, chm Cons NI Ctee; chm: Br-Nigerian All Pty Gp, Br-Zambian All Pty Gp, Br-Southern Africa All Pty Gp; memb: Ct of Referees; *Books* Extradition, the Law and Practice (1980), British Nationality, the New Law (1982), A Year in Politics (1987); *Style—* Ivor Stanbrook, Esq, MP; 6 Sevenoaks Rd, Orpington, Kent (☎ 0689 820347)

STANCLIFFE, Very Rev David Staffurth; s of Very Rev Michael S Stancliffe (d 1987 formerly Dean of Winchester), and Barbara Elizabeth, da of Rev Canon Tissington Tatlow; *b* 1 Oct 1942; *Educ* Westminster, Trinity Coll Oxford, Cuddesdon Theological Coll (MA); *m* 17 July 1965, Sarah Loveday, da of Philip Sascha Smith, of Mead House, Great Ayton; 1 s (Benjamin b 1972), 2 da (Rachel b 1968, Hannah b 1969); *Career* asst curate of St Bartholomew's Armley 1967-70, chaplain to Clifton Coll Bristol 1970-77, residentiary canon of Portsmouth Cathedral 1977-82, diocesan dir of ordinands and lay ministry advsr Portsmouth 1977-82, provost of Portsmouth 1982-; memb: Cncl of Chichester Theological Coll 1977-, governing body of the Southern Dioceses Ministerial Training Sch 1977-84; chm: Southern Regional Inst 1979-81 and 1984-89, Diocesan Advsy Ctee 1982-; memb: C of E Liturgical Cmmn 1985-, Gen Synod 1985-, vice pres Assoc European Cathedrals 1986-, Cncl for the Care of Churches; *Recreations* old music, Italy; *Style—* The Very Rev the Provost of Portsmouth; Provost's House, Pembroke Rd, Portsmouth PO1 2NS (☎ 0705 824 400); Portsmouth Cathedral, St Thomas' St, Portsmouth PO1 2HH (☎ 0705 823300)

STANDEN, John Francis; s of Dr Edward Peter Standen (d 1976), and Margaret, *née* O'Shea; *b* 14 Oct 1948; *Educ* St James' Sch Burnt Oak, Univ of Durham (BA); *m* 9 Aug 1975, Kathleen Mary, da of Joseph Quilty, of Co Galway, Ireland; 2 s (Luke b 1981, Owen b 1984), 1 da (Aine b 1979); *Career* dir Barclays Merchant Bank Ltd 1986-, md Corp Fin Barclays de Zoete Wedd Ltd 1990 (dir 1986, dir Property Equity Fund Mgmnt Ltd 1987, head Fin Advsy Unit 1988); ACIB 1974; *Recreations* relaxing, walking, family fun, theatre opera; *Style—* John Standen, Esq; The Blue House, Thorley St, nr Bishops Stortford, Herts CM23 4AL (☎ 0279 508 413); Barclays de Zoete Wedd, Ebbgate House, 2 Swan Lane, London EC4 (☎ 071 623 2323, fax 071 895 1523, telex 923141)

STANDING; *see*: Leon, Sir John, Bt

STANDING, Norman Roy; s of Capt Norman Ebenezer Standing (ka 1943), and Joan Mabel, *née* Cambridge (d 1969); *b* 27 Oct 1938; *Educ* The George Spicer Sch Enfield; *m* 1, 29 Oct 1960 (m dis), Brenda Constance, da of Charles Pickering, of Essex; 1 s (David b 1964), 1 da (Deborah b 1961); m 2, 16 June 1981, Gillian Mary, da of Leonard Richard Wallace, of Cambs; *Career* mktg servs conslt; *Recreations* collecting, travel, walking; *Style—* Norman R Standing, Esq; 8 Burlington Way, Hemingford Grey, Huntingdon, Cambs PE18 9BS (☎ 0480 62654, fax 0480 67563, car phone 0836 204960)

STANDISH, John Victor; s of Albert Victor Standish (d 1981), of Littlehampton, Sussex, and Ethel Alice, *née* Salmon (d 1985); *b* 14 Jan 1930; *Educ* Ilfracombe GS, City of London Coll (DipCAM); *m* 15 Sept 1955, Vivienne Judith, da of Kenneth Lloyd Martin (d 1983), of Wimbledon; 1 s (Miles b 1965), 3 da (Martine b 1956, Amanda b 1957, Jennifer b 1960); *Career* industl res and media conslt 1988-; dir: Ad Group Services Ltd 1978-82, Parker Research Ltd 1978-86, Roles & Parker Ltd 1982-84, Ayer Barker Ltd 1984-86, Interact Communications Ltd 1986-87; urban dist and town cncllr Chesham Bucks 1971-79; memb: ABC Cncl, IPA media panel, Industl Market Res Assoc; MIPA; *Recreations* archaeology, conservation, war gaming; *Clubs* RAC, Wig and Pen, '41'; *Style—* John V Standish, Esq; The Boat House, Lyminster Rd, Littlehampton, W Sussex (☎ 0903 883587); 90 Trinity Court, Gray's Inn Rd, London WC1 (☎ 071 837 9804)

STANDISH, Tony; s of Elias Stern (d 1961), and Gertrud Agnes Alwine Hullebrandt (d 1971); *b* 11 April 1922; *Educ* RG II Gymnasium, Vienna; *m* 12 Jan 1958, Verna Ella, da of Malcolm John Tomlinson, Chief Inspector, Shanghai Police; 3 s (Troy b 1970, Tristan b 1965, Tracy b 1959), 2 da (Tiffany b 1963, Talita b 1970); *Career* Army service 1939-42 Royal Navy German Branch Intelligence; Raymond Gp: 28 dirships 1957-86, incl: Goldmount Houses 1985-87, Goldmount Construction 1982-87, Goldmount Properties 1980-87, M & S T's Supper Room 1972-87, T S Properties 1965-87; chm The Wessex Gp plc 1987; *Recreations* skiing; *Style—* Tony Standish, Esq; Newguards, 30 Western Ave, Branksome Park, Poole, Dorset BH13 7AV; Wessex Bowl, Poole Rd, Bury (☎ 02020 762253)

STANESBY, Rev Canon Derek Malcolm; s of Laurence John Charles Stanesby, of Congleton, Cheshire, and Elsie Lilian, *née* Stean (d 1959); *b* 28 March 1931; *Educ* Orange Hill Sch Edgware, Northampton Poly London, Leeds Univ (BA), Coll of the Resurrection Mirfield, Manchester Univ (MEd, PhD); *m* 29 July 1958, Christine Adela, da of David Payne (d 1985), of Tamworth, Staffs; 3 s (Michael b 1961, Mark b 1963, Peter b 1966), 1 da (Helen b 1959); *Career* RAF 1951-53, PO, Navigator; ordained Norwich Cathedral 1958; curate: Norwich 1958-61, Southwark 1961-63; vicar St Mark Bury 1963-67, rector St Chad Ladybarn 1967-85, canon of Windsor 1985-; memb Archbishops Cmmn on Christian Doctrine; author of various articles; *Books* Science, Reason and Religion (1985); *Recreations* hill walking, sailing, woodwork, idling; *Style—* The Rev Canon Derek Stanesby; 4 The Cloisters, Windsor Castle, Berks SL4 1NJ (☎ 0753 864142)

STANFIELD, Brian John; *b* 12 July 1934; *Educ* LLB (London); *m* 1956, Janet Margery Mary; 1 s, 1 da; *Career* slr 1959; legal dir UK Grand Met plc 1986-; Business in the Community, dep dir LEDU 1990-; pres City of Westminster Law Soc 1979; *Recreations* theatre, music; *Clubs* Savile and Landsdowne; *Style—* Brian Stanfield, Esq; Cheriton, 35 Worple Rd, Epsom, Surrey (☎ 0372 720715); Grand Metropolitan plc; 11/12 Hanover Square, London W1 (☎ 071 629 7488)

STANFIELD, Prof Peter Robert; s of Robert Ainslie Stanfield, of Woodstock, Oxford, and Irene Louisa, *née* Walker; *b* 13 July 1944; *Educ* Portsmouth GS, Univ of Cambridge (MA, PhD, ScD); *m* 21 Sept 1987, Philippa Stanfield, da of Eric Moss of Anderby Creek, Lincolnshire; 2 step s (Edward MacMillan Barrie b 1968, William MacMillan Barrie b 1970); *Career* SRC res fell MBA laboratory Plymouth 1968-69, fell of Clare Coll Cambridge, univ demonstrator in physiology Univ of Cambridge 1969-74; Univ of Leicester: lectr in physiology 1974-81, reader 1981-87, prof 1987-, head of Dept of Physiology 1989-; ed Journal of Physiology 1980-88 (author of scientific papers on physiology of cell membranes Nature and elsewhere); memb Ctee of Physiology Soc 1985-89; memb Physiological Soc 1973-; *Recreations* walking, gardening, music; *Style—* Prof Peter Stanfield; Department of Physiology, University of Leicester, PO Box 138, Leicester LE1 9HN (☎ 0533 523300, fax 0533 523013)

STANFORD, Adrian Timothy James; s of Ven Leonard John Stanford (d 1967), formerly Archdeacon of Coventry, and Dora Kathleen, *née* Timms (d 1939); *b* 19 July 1935; *Educ* Rugby, Merton Coll Oxford (MA); *Career* Nat Serv 2 Lt The Sherwood Foresters 1954-55; merchant banker; dir Samuel Montagu & Co Ltd 1972- (joined 1958); tstee Old Broad St Charity Tst; *Recreations* gardening, architecture; *Clubs* Boodle's, Brooks's; *Style—* Adrian Stanford, Esq; The Old Rectory, Preston Capes, nr Daventry, Northamptonshire NN11 6TE; 47 Ennismore Gardens, London SW7 1AH; Samuel Montagu & Co Ltd, 10 Lower Thames Street, London EC3R 6AE (☎ 071 260 9000)

STANFORD, Julian George; s of Ven Leonard John Stanford (d 1967, formerly Archdeacon of Coventry), and Dora Kathleen, *née* Timms (d 1939); *b* 15 Jan 1933; *Educ* Rugby, Worcester Coll Oxford (MA); *m* 20 April 1963, Elizabeth Constance Julia, da of Francis Basil Aglionby (d 1962), of Tonbridge; 2 s (Henry b 1965, Geoffrey b 1971), 1 da (Lucy b 1967); *Career* Nat Serv trained RB, cmmnd Sherwood Foresters 1951-53; merchant banker; dir Morgan Grenfell & Co Ltd and of other gp cos 1977-86; *Clubs* Brooks's; *Style—* Julian G Stanford, Esq; The Old Rectory, Tendring, Essex (☎ 0255 830287)

STANFORD, Peter James; s of Reginald James Hughes Stanford, of Longridge, Plymyard Ave, Bromborough, Wirral, Merseyside, and Mary Catherine, *née* Fleming; *b* 23 Nov 1961; *Educ* St Anselm's Coll Birkenhead, Merton Coll Oxford (BA); *Career* reporter The Tablet 1983-84, ed The Catholic Herald 1988- (news ed 1984-88), restaurant critic Girl About Town magazine 1986-88, freelance journalist and broadcaster 1984- (incl BBC, The Guardian, The Sunday Times, The Independent, The Independent on Sunday, New Statesman, The Irish Independent); memb Ctee ASPIRE (Assoc for Spinal Res, Rehabilitation and Reintegration); *Books* Hidden Hands: Child Workers Around the World (1988), Believing Bishops (with Simon Lee, 1990), The Seven Deadly Sins (ed, 1990); *Recreations* soap operas, vases, photography, old cars, Cilla Black; *Style—* Peter Stanford, Esq; Fife Cottage, Wellington Way, Bow, London E3 4NE (☎ 081 980 5980); Catholic Herald, Herald House, Lambs Passage, Bunhill Row, London EC1Y 7TQ (☎ 071 588 3101, fax 071 256 9728)

STANFORD, Adm Sir Peter Maxwell; GCB (1986, KCB 1983), LVO (1970); s of Brig Henry Morrant Stanford, CBE, MC (d 1957), of The Stone House, Aldringham, Leiston, Suffolk, and Edith Hamilton, *née* Warren (d 1980); *b* 11 July 1929; *Educ* RNC Britannia; *m* 1957, (Helen) Ann, da of Henry Lingard (d 1935), of Chiengmai, Thailand; 1 s, 2 da; *Career* RN: Flag Offr Second Flotilla 1978-80, Asst Chief of Naval Staff 1980-82, Vice Chief 1982-84, C-in-C Naval Home Cmd 1985-87; *Recreations* field sports, ornithology; *Clubs* Fly-fishers', Naval; *Style—* Adm Sir Peter Stanford, GCB, LVO; c/o Lloyd's Bank Ltd, Cox's and King's Branch, 7 Pall Mall, London SW1Y 5NA

STANFORD-TUCK, Michael David; s of Wing Cdr Roland Robert Stanford-Tuck, DSC, DFC (d 1987), of Sandwich Bay, Kent, and Joyce, *née* Carter (d 1985); *b* 3 Nov 1946; *Educ* Radley, Univ of Southampton (LLB); *m* 30 June 1973, Susan Penelope, da of Raymond John Lilwall, of St Peters, Broadstairs, Kent; 1 s (Alexander b 1976), 2 da (Olivia b 1978, Camilla b 1984); *Career* admitted slr 1972; barr and attorney Supreme Ct of Bermuda 1978; ptnr Appleby Spuling & Kempe Bermuda 1978-83, Taylor Joynson Garrett London 1985-; memb Ctee The Bermuda Soc; Liveryman City of London Slrs Co 1989 (Freeman 1973), Freeman City of London 1989; memb Law Soc; *Recreations* golf, gardening, shooting, skiing; *Clubs* Royal St Georges Golf; *Style—* Michael Stanford-Tuck, Esq; 10 Maltravers St, London WC2 (☎ 071 8368456, fax 071 3797196, telex 268014)

STANFORTH, Prof Anthony William; s of William Reginald Stanforth (d 1979), and Kathleen Helen, *née* Oldham (d 1985); *b* 27 July 1938; *Educ* Ipswich Sch, Univ of Durham (BA, MA), Heidelberg Univ, Marburg Univ (DPhil); *m* 2 Jan 1971, Susan Margaret, da of William James Vale, of Oulton Broad; 2 s (Robert b 16 Feb 1976, Andrew 7 Jan 1979); *Career* asst lectr Univ of Manchester 1964-65, lectr and sr lectr Univ of Newcastle 1965-81 (Earl Grey fell 1961-64), visiting asst prof Univ of Wisconsin 1970-71, prof of languages Heriot-Watt Univ 1981-; FRSA 1983; *Books* Die Bezeichungen für 'gross', 'klein','viel' und 'wenig' im Bereich der Germania (1967); *Recreations* opera; *Style—* Prof Anthony Stanforth; Dept of Languages, Heriot-Watt University, Riccarton, Edinburgh EH14 4AS (☎ 031 4495111)

STANGER, David Harry; OBE (1987); s of Charles Harry Stanger, CBE (d 1987), of Mill Cottage, Knole, Long Sutton, Somerset, and Florence Bessie Hepworth, *née* Bowden; *b* 14 Feb 1939; *Educ* Oundle, Millfield; *m* 20 July 1963, Jill Patricia, da of Reginald Arthur Barnes, of Chessbord, Troutstream Way, Loudwater, Chorley Wood, Herts; 1 s (Edward b 1972); 2 da (Vanessa b 1966, Miranda b 1967); *Career* served RE 1960-66, seconded Malaysian Engrs 1963-66, operational serv Kenya, Nothern Malaysia and Sarawak, Capt RE; joined R H Harry Stanger 1966, ptnr Al Hoty Stanger Ltd 1975; chm: Harry Stanger Ltd 1972-90, Stanger Consultants Ltd 1990-; memb: Steering Ctee NATLAS 1981-85, Advsy Cncl for Calibration and Measurement 1982-87; chm: Assoc of Consulting Scientists 1981-83, NAMAS Advsy Ctee 1985-87, Standards Quality Measurement Advsy Ctee 1987-; sec gen Union Int des Laboratoires 1984-, vice pres IQA 1986 (chm Cncl 1990-), memb Guild of Water Conservators 1989-; chm Br Measurement and Testing Assoc 1990-; UK rep on Cncl Euro Orgn for Testing and Certification 1990; *Recreations* collecting vintage wines; *Clubs* Carlton; *Style—* D H Stanger, Esq, OBE; Summerfield House, Barnet Lane, Elstree, Herts WD6 3HQ (☎ 081 953 0022); Stanger Consultants Ltd, Fortune Lane, Elstree, Herts WD6 3HQ (☎ 081 207 3191, fax 081 207 4706, telex 922262 TESLAB G)

STANGER, Keith Burroughs; s of Eric Alfred (d 1971), of Gildersome, Yorks, and Mary, *née* Burroughs; *b* 17 Sept 1939; *Educ* Leeds GS, Univ of St Andrews (MA), Harvard Business Sch (PHD); *m* 29 April 1967, Susan Margaret, da of Reginald Arthur Banham d (1969), of Buenos Aires; 2 s (Julian Patrick b 1971, Edward Alexander b 1974); *Career* Bank of London and South America (Argentina, Paraguay, Colombia) 1964-72, chief accountant Bank of London and Montreal 1972-76; Lloyds Bank: (Int) USA 1976-80, Uruguay and Brazil 1980-86; Lloyds Bank plc: gen mangr strategic planning 1985-88, gen mangr corp banking and treasy 1988-89, gen mangr fin 1990;

memb Putney Soc, Basset Hound Club, Albany Bassets Club; FRGS; *Recreations* tennis, climbing, walking, antique maps; *Clubs* Montevideo Cricket; *Style*— Keith Stanger, Esq; 9 Spencer Walk, London SW15 (☎ 081 789 1866); 71 Lombard St, London EC3P 3BS (☎ 071 626 1500)

STANGROOM SPRINTHALL, Sonya Mary; da of Samuel Frederick Coates-Sprinthall (d 1973) and Dorothy Mary, *née* Philipson-Atkinson; *b* 19 Aug 1940; *Educ* Lancaster Coll of Art (NDD); *m* 3 Aug 1963 (m dis 1984), James Edward Stangroom, s of Alfred William Stangroom (d 1986); *Career* one woman exhibitions: Holland Park Galleries 1964, Sheffield Indust Exhibition Centre (1965, 1967, 1968), Univ of Sheffield 1965, Philip Frances Gallery Sheffield (1972, 1974), Univ of Sheffield Library Gallery 1980, Saint Edmund's Church Castleton 1980, Edward Mayor Gallery Sheffield (1980, 1982) Abbot Hall Art Gallery Kendal 1987; gp exhibitions incl: Young Contemporaries London 1961, Mansard Gallery London 1969-1975, Richard Bradley Gallery Billingford, Graves Open Exhibition Sheffield, Philip Frances Gallery (8 Sheffield artists), Univ of Sheffield Fine Arts Soc, Mappin Art Gallery (artists Christmas cards), Tate Gallery London (artists Christmas cards); mural cmmns: Sheffield Corpn Dept Education, two murals for Richmond Coll of Educn; portrait cmmns incl: Prof W R Robinson, Prof Sir William Empson, Mrs Hildegard Hertzog; former pres Sheffield Soc for the Encouragement of Art; memb: Br Inst of Persian Studies, Soc for the Promotion of Byzantine Studies, Hawk Tst; *Recreations* archaeology (draughtsman Siraf Persian Gulf 1968), travel, music, Islamic architecture and art, the study of Russian ikons; *Style*— Sonya Stangroom Sprinthall

STANHOPE, Hon Steven Francis Lincoln; s of 11 Earl of Harrington, of Co Limerick, and his 2 w, Anne Theodora, *née* Chute (d 1970); *b* 12 Dec 1951; *Educ* Eton; *m* 1978, Maureen Elizabeth Irvine, da of Maj Harold William Cole, of Poundbury, Dorset; 1 s (Ben b 1978), 1 da (Tara b 1979); *Career* stud farmer, antique dealer, landowner (150 acres); *Recreations* hunting, fishing; *Style*— The Hon Steven Stanhope; Dooneen Stud, Patrickswell, Co Limerick, Ireland (☎ 61 355106)

STANHOPE, Hon William Henry Leicester; s and h of Viscount Petersham; *b* 14 Oct 1967; *Educ* Aysgarth Sch, Aiglon Coll; *Recreations* skiing, fishing, shooting; *Style*— The Hon William Stanhope; Baynton House, Coulston, Westbury, Wiltshire

STANIER, Brig Sir Alexander Beville Gibbons; 2 Bt (UK 1917), of Peplow Hall, Hodnet, Shropshire; DSO (1940 and Bar 1945), MC (1918), JP (Shropshire 1949), DL (1951); patron of two livings; s of Sir Beville Stanier, 1 Bt, JP, DL (d 1921), sometime MP Newport (Shropshire) then Ludlow, and Sarah Constance (d 1948), da of Rev Benjamin Gibbons, of Waresley House, Worcester; *b* 31 Jan 1899; *Educ* Eton, RMC Sandhurst; *m* 1927, Dorothy Gladys (d 1973), da of late Brig-Gen Alfred Douglas Miller, CBE, DSO; 1 s, 1 da; *Heir* s, Beville Douglas Stanier; *Career* served WWI (France 1918); served WWII in France (despatches, American Silver star, Cdr Order of Leopold of Belgium with palms, Belgian Croix de Guerre with palms); Brig (ret) late Welsh Gds (cmding 1945-48); High Sheriff of Shropshire 1951; memb Shropshire CC 1950-58, Cdr Order Legion of Honour (France); CStJ; *Style*— Brig Sir Alexander Stanier, Bt, DSO, MC, JP, DL; Park Cottage, Ludford, Ludlow, Shropshire SY8 1PP (☎ 0584 2675); Hill House, Shotover Park, Wheatley, Oxford 0X9 1QN (☎ 086 77 2996)

STANIER, Capt Beville Douglas; s and h of Brig Sir Alexander Beville Gibbons Stanier, 2 Bt, DSO, MC, JP, DL, and Dorothy Gladys, *née* Miller (d 1973); *b* 20 April 1934; *Educ* Eton; *m* 23 Feb 1963, (Violet) Shelagh, da of Maj James Stockley Sinnott (ka 1942), of Tetbury, Glos; 1 s (Alexander b 1970), 2 da (Henrietta b 1965, Lucinda b 1967); *Career* serv Welsh Gds 1952-60 (2 Lt 1953, Lt 1955, Capt 1958), UK, Egypt, Aust; ADC to Govr-Gen of Aust (Field Marshal Viscount Slim) 1959-60; stockbroker, ptnr Kitcat & Aitken 1960-76; farmer 1974-; conslt Hales Snails Ltd 1976-88; chm Whaddon Parish Cncl; *Recreations* shooting, cricket; *Clubs* MCC; *Style*— Capt Beville Stanier; Kings Close House, Whaddon, Bucks MK17 0NG (☎ 0908 501738); Home Farm, Shotover Park, Wheatley, Oxford OX9 1QP (☎ 08677 2996)

STANIER, Field Marshal Sir John Wilfred; GCB (1982, KCB 1978), MBE (1961), DL (Hampshire 1986); s of Harold Allan Stanier (d 1932), and Penelope Rose, *née* Price (d 1974); *b* 6 Oct 1925; *Educ* Marlborough, Merton Coll Oxford; *m* 1955, Cicely Constance, da of Cmdr Denis Malet Lambert, DSC; 4 da (Emma, Harriet, Miranda, Candia); *Career* cmmnd QOH 1946, served in N Italy, Germany, Hong Kong; cmd: Royal Scots Greys 1966-68, 20 Armoured Bde 1969-71; GOC1 Div 1973-75, Cmdt Staff Coll Camberley 1975-78, Vice CGS 1978-80, Col Royal Scots Dragoon Guards 1979-84, ADC Gen to HM The Queen 1981-85, Col Cmdt RAC 1982-85, C-in-C UKLF 1981-82, CGS 1981-85, Constable HM Tower of London 1990; *Recreations* hunting, fishing; *Clubs* Cavalry and Guards; *Style*— Field Marshal Sir John Stanier, GCB, MBE, DL; c/o Messrs Coutts & Co, 440 Strand, London WC2R 0QS

STANIFORTH, Adrian Martyn Christopher (Kim); s of Adrian Wheatley Staniforth (d 1971), of Todwick, Sheffield, and Doris Annie, *née* Wiles (d 1984); *b* 27 Feb 1936; *Educ* Ackworth Sch, Univ of Manchester (BA); *m* 29 Aug 1964, Margaret, da of James Hardman, of Sheffield (d 1980); 2 s (Dominic b 1965, Rupert b 1969), 2 da (Amanda b 1967, Arabella b 1970); *Career* CA 1960; Spicer and Oppenheim London 1961-62, ptnr Barber Harrison and Platt 1963-; ICAEW: memb Cncl 1973-80, chm Examinations Ctee 1978-80, memb Educn and Trg Directorate 1978-82, memb Ethics Ctee 1985-; chm Cncl St Luke's Hospice 1970-, pres Sheffield Jr C of C 1970-71, chm Yorkshire Regnl Gp of Jr Chambers 1973, memb Rotary Club Sheffield, tstee Sheffield Town Tst; Freeman: City of London 1979, Worshipful Co of CAs 1979; FCA 1960; *Recreations* walking, swimming, skiing, sailing, wine, appreciating the arts; *Clubs* Rotary (Sheffield); *Style*— Kim Staniforth, Esq; 2 Rutland Park, Sheffield S10 2PD (☎ 0724 667171, fax 0742 669846)

STANISZEWSKI, His Excellency Monsieur Stefan; *b* 11 Feb 1931; *Career* Polish ambass to UK 1981- (joined Polish Dip Serv 1960), formerly ambass to Sweden, has also served in Paris; previously chief ed Iskry (Polish publishers); *Style*— HE Monsieur Stefan Staniszewski; Embassy of the Polish People's Republic, 47 Portland Place, W1N 3AG (☎ 071 580 4324/9)

STANLEY, Brian Robert; s of William Augustus Stanley (d 1964), and Elsa Maria Stanley (d 1987); *b* 26 Dec 1935; *Educ* Christ's Hosp; *m* 1 April 1961, Marion, da of Joseph Thacker (d 1961); 1 da (Clair b 1967), 1 s (Sean b 1968); *Career* CA; dir: Harrison-Sons Ltd printers 1965-76, Papla Ltd 1976-; authority on silicone coating; Liveryman Worshipful Co of Stationers; *Recreations* music, sports; *Style*— Brian Stanley, Esq; Zlatorog, Bryants Bottom, Great Missenden, Bucks HP16 0JU; Papla Ltd, York House, Oxford Rd, Beaconsfield, Bucks HP9 1XA (telex 837978)

STANLEY, Hon Charles Ernest; 2 s of 8 Baron Stanley of Alderley; *b* 30 June 1960; *Educ* St Edwards Sch Oxford, Nottingham Univ (BA); *Career* area sales mangr Plessey; *Recreations* sailing, skiing; *Style*— The Hon Charles Stanley; Plessey, 9 Dallington Street, London EC1 (☎ 071 251 6251)

STANLEY, David John; s of Vincent Arthur Stanley (d 1978), of Ruislip, Middlesex, and Joy Harriet Kendall; *b* 15 June 1947; *Educ* Merchant Taylors', Pembroke Coll Cambridge (BA, MA, PhD); *m* 29 July 1972, Meryl Ruth, da of Derwent Mark Atkinson Mercer, of Chandler's Ford, Hampshire; 1 s (Joel b 1985), 3 da (Lydia b 1976, Miriam b 1978, Bethany b 1983); *Career* dir Logica UK Ltd 1982-84; tech dir Logica Space & Def Systems Ltd 1984-86; md Logica Cambridge Ltd; tech dir Logica plc 1985-86; innovation dir Organisation & System Innovations Ltd 1986-; *Recreations* Christian activities, music, gardening; *Style*— Dr David Stanley; 25 Sedley Taylor Rd, Cambridge CB2 2PN (☎ 0223 210468); Oasis, Tectonic Place, Holyport Rd, Maidenhead (☎ 0628 770600, car ☎ 0836 200264)

STANLEY, Edward Richard William; s of Hon Hugh Henry Montagu Stanley (d 1971, gs of 17 Earl of Derby), and Mary Rose (who m 2, A William A Spiegelberg) da of late Charles Francis Birch, of Rhodesia; hp of kinsman, 18 Earl of Derby; *b* 10 Oct 1962; *Educ* Eton, RAC Cirencester; *Career* cmmnd Grenadier Gds 1982-85; Fleming Private Asset Management Ltd; *Clubs* Cavalry and Guards, Turf; *Style*— Edward Stanley, Esq; 90 Old Church Street, Chelsea, London SW3

STANLEY, Hon Mrs (Frances Caroline Burke); *née* Roche; da of 5 Baron Fermoy (d 1984); sis of 6 Baron Fermoy, *qv*; *b* 31 March 1965; *m* 11 Dec 1990, Peter Hugh Charles Stanley, s of Hon Hugh Henry Montagu Stanley (d 1971); *Style*— The Hon Mrs Stanley; New England Stud, Bottisham, Newmarket, Suffolk

STANLEY, Rt Hon Sir John Paul; PC (1984), MP (C) Tonbridge and Malling 1974-; s of Harry Stanley (d 1956), and Maud Stanley; *b* 19 Jan 1942; *Educ* Repton, Lincoln Coll Oxford; *m* 1968, Susan Elizabeth Giles; 2 s, 1 da; *Career* Cons Res Dept (Housing) 1967-68, res assoc IISS 1968-69, fin exec RTZ Corporation 1969-74, memb Parly Select Ctee on Nationalised Industs 1974-76, PPS to Rt Hon Margaret Thatcher 1976-79, min for housing and construction with rank of min of state (DOE) 1979-83, min of state for armed forces MOD 1983-87, min of state for NI 1987-88; kt 1988; *Recreations* music, arts, sailing; *Style*— The Rt Hon Sir John Stanley, MP; House of Commons, London SW1

STANLEY, Louis Thomas; s of Louis Stanley, of Stanley House, Stanley Rd, Hoylake, and Mary Ann, *née* Appelby; *b* 6 Jan 1912; *Educ* Emmanuel Coll Cambridge (MA); *m* 25 May 1955, (Helen) Jean Beech, da of Sir Alfred Owen, of New Hall, Sutton Coldfield; 2 s (Thomas b 1957, Edward b 1961), 2 da (Caroline Jane b 1959, Roberta Marigold b 1963); *Career* economist; dir gen Int Grand Prix Med Servs, chm and jt md BRM; chm Siffert Cncl, hon sec and tres Grand Prix Drivers Assoc, tstee Jim Clark Fndn, memb Royal Inst of Int Affrs; *Books* author of over 70 titles incl: In Search of Genius, Cambridge City of Dreams, Germany After The War, People Places and Pleasures, St Andrews, Public Masks and Private Faces, Newmarket; *Recreations* golf; *Style*— Louis Stanley, Esq; Old Mill House, Trumpington, Cambridge (☎ 0223 840107, 841337)

STANLEY, Oliver Duncan; s of late Bernard Stanley, and Mabel *née* Best; *b* 5 June 1925; *Educ* Rhyl GS, Ch Ch Oxford (MA), Harvard Univ; *m* 7 Sept 1954, Ruth Leah; 1 s (Julian b 1958); 3 da (Nicola b 1955, Katherine b 1960, Sarah b 1963); *Career* served 8 Hussars 1943-47; called to the Bar Middle Temple 1963; HM inspr of Taxes 1952-65, dir Gray Dawes Bank 1966-72; chm Rathbone Bros plc 1987- (dir 1972-87); *Books* Guide to Taxation (1967), Taxology (1971), Creation and Protection of Capital (1974), Taxation Farmers and Landowners (3 edn, 1987); *Recreations* music, tennis, French; *Clubs* Travellers'; *Style*— Oliver Stanley, Esq; University House, London SW1 W0EX

STANLEY, Peter; s of Albert Edward Stanley (d 1964), of Ilkeston, Derbyshire, and Rhoda, *née* Clifford; *b* 20 March 1930; *Educ* Ilkeston GS, Selwyn Coll Cambridge (MA), Univ of Nottingham (PhD); *m* 31 July 1952, Rennie Elizabeth (d 1 June 1954), da of Joseph Wilkinson of Ilkeston, Derbyshire, (d 1933), 1 da (Elizabeth b 4 March 1954); m 2, 5 July 1980, Kathleen Mary (Kate), da of Samuel Evans (d 1981), of Stapleford, Notts; 1 s (Jonathan b 1 July 1982); *Career* Nat Serv 2 Lt RCS 1949-51; tech asst Rolls-Royce Ltd Derby 1954-57; Dept of Mechanical Engrg Univ of Nottingham: sr res asst 1957-61, lectr 1961-71, sr lectr 1971-75, reader 1975-78; prof mechanical engrg Univ of Manchester 1979-, memb Qualifications Bd Award Ctee IMechE; memb: Engrg and Computing Res Degrees Sub Ctee CNAA, ed Bd Jl Strain Analysis, Jt Br Ctee Stress Analysis; MSc Univ of Manchester 1983; FIMechE 1979, MIMechE 1966, CEng, FInstP 1970, AInstP 1959, CPhys; *Books* Computing Developments in Experimental and Numerical Stress Analysis (ed, 1976), Fracture Mechanics in Engineering Practice (ed, 1977), Non-Linear Problems in Stress Analysis (ed, 1978), Stability Problems in Engineering Components and Structures (jt ed, 1979); numerous papers in tech jls; *Recreations* walking, swimming, English Heritaging, Jonathan; *Style*— Peter Stanley, Esq; 7 Croft Road, Wilmslow, Cheshire SK9 6JJ (☎ 0625 527702); Dept of Engineering, University of Manchester, Simon Building, Oxford Rd, Manchester, M13 9PL (☎ 061 275 4303)

STANLEY, Peter Henry Arthur; s of Col F A Stanley, OBE (d 1979), of Bramshott Lodge, Liphook, Hants, and Ann Jane, *née* Collins; *b* 17 March 1933; *Educ* Eton; *m* 1, 7 May 1965 (m dis), Gunilla Margaretha Antonia Sophie, da of Count Wilhelm Douglas (d 1987), of Schloss Langenstein,Baden Wurttemberg; 1 s (Robin b 1968), 1 da (Louisa b 1966); m 2, 21 May 1990, Lucy *née* Barnet Campbell; *Career* Grenadier Gds 1951-53; CA; trainee Dixon Wilson 1953-58, Peat Marwick (NY and Toronto) 1959-60, ptnr Hill Chaplin & Co (stockbrokers) 1961-68, chm and chief exec offr Williams De Broe Hill Chaplin & Co 1984- (dir 1968-); memb Cncl Stock Exchange 1979-86, dir Securities Assoc 1986- (chm Capital Ctee); FCA 1958; *Recreations* tennis, golf, shooting; *Clubs* White's, Swinley Forest Golf; *Style*— Peter Stanley, Esq; Cundall Hall, Helperby, Yorks (☎ 0423 360252); Williams De Broe Ltd, 6 Broadgate, London EC2M 2RP (☎ 071 588 7511, fax 071 588 1702, telex 893277G

STANLEY, Hon Richard Morgan Oliver; s of Lt-Col the Hon Oliver Stanley, DSO (d 1952), and Lady Kathleen Thynne (d 1977), da of 5 Marquess of Bath; raised to rank of a Baron's s 1973 and yr bro of 8 Baron Stanley of Alderley; *b* 30 April 1931; *Educ* Winchester, New Coll Oxford (MA); *m* 27 July 1956, Phyllida Mary Katharine, 3 da of Lt-Col Clive Grantham Austin, JP, DL (d 1974), of Micheldever, and Lady Lilian Lumley, sis of 11 Earl of Scarbrough; 2 s (Martin Thomas Oliver b 1957, Oliver Hugh b 1959), 2 da (Serena Emma Rose b 1961, Laura Sylvia Kathleen b 1968); *Career* Lt Coldstream Gds 1950-51; dir: Metal Box Co Ltd 1979-85, UKPI (dep chm) 1985-86, Friends' Provident Instn 1986-, Gt Venture Investmnt plc 1987-, GA Properties Ltd 1988-, Drawlane Transport Gp plc 1989-; chm: Midland Fox Ltd 1989-, Beeline Buzz Co 1989-; memb Lloyd's; Warden Bradfield Coll; chm Carr Gomm Soc; tstee Disabled Living Fndn; govr Thomas Coram Fndn; Freeman of City of London, Liveryman Worshipful Co of Tinplate Workers; *Recreations* shooting, gardening; *Clubs* Boodle's; *Style*— The Hon Richard Stanley; Wood End House, Ridgeway Lane, Lymington, Hants (☎ 0590 74019); 38 Felden Street, London SW6 5AF (☎ 071 736 5427); Drawlane Transport Group plc, 54 Endless Street, Salisbury (☎ 0722 332153)

STANLEY, Hon Richard Oliver; s and h of 8 Baron Stanley of Alderley; *b* 24 April 1956; *Educ* St Edward's Sch Oxford, Univ Coll London (BSc); *m* 1983, Carla, er da of Dr K T C McKenzie, of Solihull, 1 s (Oliver Richard Hugh b 1986 d 1989), 2 da (Maria Elizabeth Jane b 1988, Imogen Alexandra Ruth b 1990); *Style*— The Hon Richard Stanley

STANLEY, Hon Mrs (Susan Elizabeth Josephine Gabrielle Haden); da of 3 Baron Haden-Guest, and his 1 w, Hilda, *née* Russell-Cruise (d 1980); *b* 12 April 1930; *Educ* St Mary's Convent Ascot; *m* 1953, John Orr Stanley; 4 s (Charles Orr Nicholas b 1954, Martin David Anthony b 1956, Shaun Richard b 1958, Philip Thomas b 1962); *Style*— The Hon Mrs Stanley; Granary House, Holly Hill, London NW3

STANLEY OF ALDERLEY, Kathleen, Baroness; Kathleen Margaret; da of late

Cecil Murray Wright, of Malden, Surrey, and wid of Sir Edmund Frank Crane; *m* 1961, as his 4 w, 6 Baron (d 1971); *Style*— The Rt Hon Kathleen, Lady Stanley of Alderley; 1 Links Court, Grouville, Jersey

STANLEY OF ALDERLEY, 8 Baron (UK 1839); Sir Thomas Henry Oliver Stanley; DL (Gwynedd) 14 Bt (E 1660); also Baron Sheffield (I 1783) and Baron Eddisbury of Winnington (UK 1848); s of Lt-Col the Hon Oliver Hugh Stanley, DSO, JP, DL (d 1952, s of 4 Baron; descended from Sir John Stanley of Weever, yr bro of 1 Earl of Derby), and Lady Kathleen, *née* Thynne (d 1977), da of 5 Marquess of Bath; suc cous, 7 Baron (who preferred to be known as Lord Sheffield) 1971; *b* 28 Sept 1927; *Educ* Wellington Coll; *m* 30 April 1955, Jane Barrett, da of late Ernest George Hartley; 3 s (Richard, Charles, Harry), 1 da (Lucinda); *Heir* s, Hon Richard Stanley; *Career* Capt (ret) Coldstream Gds and Gds Ind Parachute Co; farmer in Anglesey and Oxfordshire; chm Thames Valley Cereals Ltd 1979-81; govr St Edwards Sch Oxford 1979-, RNLI Ctee of Mgmnt 1981- (chm Fund Raising Ctee 1986-); sits as Cons in House of Lords; *Recreations* sailing, fishing, skiing; *Clubs* Farmers'; *Style*— The Rt Hon the Lord Stanley of Alderley; Trysglwyn Fawr, Rhosybol, Amlwch, Anglesey (☎ 0407 830 364); Rectory Farm, Stanton St John, Oxford (☎ 086 735 214)

STANLEY PRICE, His Hon Peter; QC (1956); s of Herbert Stanley Price (d 1957); *b* 27 Nov 1911; *Educ* Cheltenham, Exeter Coll Oxford; *m* 1, 1946, Harriett Ella Theresa, *née* Pownall (d 1948); 2 s (twins); m 2, 1950, Margaret Jane, wid of William Hebditch (d 1941); 1 da; *Career* barr Inner Temple 1936; recorder: Pontefract 1954, York 1955, Kingston-upon-Hull 1958; chm N Riding of Yorks QS 1958-70, bencher Inner Temple 1963, judge of appeal Jersey and Guernsey 1964-69, recorder Sheffield 1965-69, judge of the Chancery Ct of York 1967-, circuit judge (formerly judge of Central Criminal Ct) 1969-84; pres Nat Reference Tbnl: Conciliation Scheme for Deputies employed in Coal-Mining Industry 1967-79, Conciliation Scheme for Coal-Mining Industry 1979-83; *Recreations* birds and trees, gardening, shooting; *Clubs* Brooks's, Yorkshire; *Style*— His Honour Peter Stanley Price, QC; Church Hill, Great Ouseburn, York (☎ 0423 330252)

STANNARD, Timothy John (Tim); s of Henry John Edward Stannard (d 1974), and Betty Pauline Stannard; *b* 29 Oct 1942; *Educ* Cheltenham; *m* 29 Sept 1973, Doreen Ann, da of James Mathias Goff; 2 da (Nicola Zoe, Olivia Ann); *Career* slr; entered in Guinness Book of Records 1991 as having the largest collection of British beermats (over 50,750) as of July 1990; *Recreations* beermat collecting, science fiction, hi-fi, golf; *Clubs* British Beermat Collectors' Soc, Birmingham Science Fiction Gp, Moseley GC; *Style*— Tim Stannard, Esq; Lombard House, 145 Gt Charles St, Birmingham B3 3LP (☎ 021 236 1174)

STANSALL, Paul James; s of James Douglas Stansall (d 1984), of Newark, Notts, and Vera Jean, *née* Hall; *b* 21 Sept 1946; *Educ* Winifred Portland Secdy Techn Sch Worksop Notts, RCA (MA), Leicester Poly (DipArch); *m* 1 Jan 1970, Angela Mary, da of Alexander Burgon (d 1954), of Beeston, Notts; 1 da (Alexandra b 1984); *Career* res asst Univ Coll London (memb Space Syntax Res Team) 1975-80, assoc DEGW Architects Planners and Designers (memb ORBIT 2 Team) 1980-89, visiting prof Cornel Univ 1987-88, founding ptnr Allinson Stansall Partnership conslt artchitects 1989-90, fndr and md Tectus Building and Organisational Analysis 1991-; published numerous res papers and articles 1974-; memb Labour Pty, MRIBA 1987, ARCUK 1981; *Recreations* history of sciences, walking, cooking; *Style*— Paul Stansall, Esq; 25 Harcourt Road, London N22 4XW (☎ 081 8880196), Tectus Building and Organizational Analysis, 12-14 Whitfield St, London W1P 5RD (☎ 071 436 4050, fax 071 436 8451)

STANSBIE, (John) Michael; s of John Albert Stansbie, MBE, of 5 Hays Close, Willersey, Nr Broadway, Worcs, and Norah Lydia, *née* Hopkins; *b* 2 Oct 1941; *Educ* Bolton Sch, Christ Church Oxford (MA), Middlesex Hosp Med Sch (BM BCh); *m* 12 April 1969, Patricia, da of Joseph Arthur Dunn of 12 Fordwich Close, St Arvans, Chepstow, Gwent; 2 s (Nicholas b 1973, Nigel b 1975); *Career* House surgn Middlesex Hosp London 1967, house physican Hillingdon Hosp Middlesex 1967-68, casualty offr Kettering Gen Hosp 1969, ENT registrar and sr ENT house offr Queen Elizabeth Hosp Birmingham 1970-71, sr ENT registrar West Midlands Trg Scheme 1972-76, conslt ENT surgn Coventry and North Warwickshire Health Authorities 1977-; West Midlands regnl advsr in otolaryngology RCS 1988-, chm Coventry and Dist Branch Br Cactus and Succulent Soc 1987-, sec Midland Inst of Otology 1981-90; FRCS 1972, FRSM 1977; *Recreations* natural history, cactus collecting & judging; *Style*— Michael Stansbie, Esq; 76 Bransford Ave, Cannon Park, Coventry CV4 7EB (☎ 0203 416755); ENT Department, Walsgrave Hospital, Clifford Bridge Rd, Coventry (☎ 0203 602020)

STANSBY, John; s of Dumon Stansby (d 1980), and Vera Margaret, *née* Main (d 1972); *b* 2 July 1930; *Educ* Oundle, Jesus Coll Cambridge (MA); *m* 22 July 1966, Anna-Maria, da of Dr Harald Kruschewsky; 1 da (Daniela b 1967), 1 step s (Oliver b 1957), 1 step da (Veronica b 1960); *Career* Nat Serv cmmnd Queens Royal Regt with Somaliland Scouts Br Somaliland 1949-50, Essex Regt TA 1950-55; domestic fuels mktg mangr Shell Mex & BP Ltd 1955-62, sr mktg conslt AIC Ltd 1962-66, dir Rank Leisure Services Ltd 1966-70, dir Energy Div POSN Co 1970-74; chm: Dumon Stansby & Co Ltd 1974-, UIE (UK) Ltd 1974-, SAUR (UK) Ltd 1986-89, Bouygues (UK) Ltd 1986-91, Cementation-SAUR Water Services PLC 1986-88, SAUR Water Services plc 1988-89; dep chm London Tport Exec 1978-80, chm SAUR UK Development plc 1989-91; dir: Stalwart Environmental Services plc 1989-91, Cambrian Environmental Services plc 1990-91; dep chm Energy Resources Ltd 1990-; FInstPet, FCIT, FRSA, MInstM; *Books* Water Privatisation and Management - the UK experience, Privatisation of UK Water and Electricity - the Business Prospect; *Recreations* music, theatre, swimming; *Clubs* Travellers; *Style*— John Stansby, Esq; 19 Brook Green, London W6 7BL (☎ 071 603 0886)

STANSFELD, John Raoul Wilmot; JP (Angus), DL (Angus); s of Capt John de Bourbel Stansfeld, MC, JP, DL (d 1975), of Dunninald, Montrose (*see* Burke's Landed Gentry, 18 edn, vol 3), and Mary Marow, *née* Eardley-Wilmot; *b* 15 Jan 1935; *Educ* Eton, Ch Ch Oxford (MA); *m* 20 Jan 1965, Rosalinde Rachel, da of Desmond Gurney Buxton, DL (d 1987), of Norfolk; 3 s (Edward John Buxton b 1966, Robert George Wilmot b 1967, Nicholas Desmond Morse b 1972); *Career* Lt Gordon Highlanders 1954-58; Salmon Fisheries mangr; chm: North Esk District Salmon Fishery Bd 1967-80, Esk Fishery Bd Ctee 1980-85; vice-chm Assoc of Scottish District Salmon Fishery Bds 1970-85; memb Inst of Fisheries Mgmnt; dir: Joseph Johnston & Sons Ltd 1962-, Atlantic Salmon Tst 1967-77, Dunninald Investmts Ltd 1975-; dir and chm Montrose Chamber of Commerce 1984-; ed Salmon Net Magazine 1978-85; chm Scottish Fish Farmers Assoc 1970-73; sec Diocese of Brechin 1968-76; *Recreations* reading, jigsaw puzzles, working in the woods; *Style*— John R W Stansfeld, Esq, JP, DL; Dunninald, Montrose, Angus DD10 (☎ 0674 74842); 3 America St, Montrose, Angus DD10 (☎ 0674 72666, telex 76332)

STANSFIELD, George Norman; CBE (1985, OBE 1980); s of George Stansfield (d 1975), of Cheadle Hulme, and Martha Alice, *née* Leadbetter; *b* 28 Feb 1926; *Educ* Liscard HS; *m* 1947, Elizabeth Margaret, da of Hugh Williams, of Colwyn Bay, Clwyd; *Career* RAF 1944-47;Miny of Food and Supply 1948-58; personal asst to: Dir-Gen of Armaments Prodn War Office 1958-61, Cwlth Rels Office 1961-62; HM Dip Serv 1965: second sec Calcutta 1962-66 and Port of Spain 1966-68, first sec FCO 1968-71 and (Commercial) Singapore 1971-74; special aide to Earl Mountbatten of Burma on visits to Singapore in 1972 and 1974; HM consul: Durban 1974-78, FCO 1978; cnsllr 1980, head Overseas Estate Dept FCO 1980-82, Br high cmmr Solomon Islands 1982-86, pt/t instr Training Dept FCO 1986-; memb Cncl Pacific Islands Soc; *Recreations* sailing (yacht Tikopia), cine photography, wild life; *Clubs* Royal Cwlth Soc, Royal Southampton Yacht, Civil Serv; *Style*— George Stansfield, Esq, CBE; Deryns Wood, Westfield Rd, Woking, Surrey (☎ 0483 728678)

STANSFIELD SMITH, Colin; CBE (1988); s of Mr Stansfield Smith, and Mary, *née* Simpson; *b* 1 Oct 1932; *Educ* William Hulmes GS, Univ of Cambridge (MA, Dip Arch); *m* 17 Feb 1961, Angela Jean Earnshaw, da of Eric Maw (d 1970), of Rustington, Sussex; 1 s (Oliver b 1970), 1 da (Sophie b 1967); *Career* Nat Serv Intelligence Corps 1951-53; ptnr Emberton Tardrew & Partners 1965-, dep co architect Cheshire CC 1971, co architect Hants 1973, prof of architectural design Sch of Architecture Portsmouth Poly 1990; vice pres RIBA 1983-86; chm Estates Sub Ctee MCC; Royal Gold medal for Architecture; ARIBA; *Recreations* painting, golf; *Clubs* MCC, Hockley GC; *Style*— Colin Stansfield Smith, Esq, CBE; Three Minsters House, High St, Winchester, Hants (☎ 0962 851970)

STANSGATE, Viscountcy of, *see* Benn, Rt Hon Tony (Neil) Wedgwood, MP

STANSGATE, Viscountess; Margaret Eadie; da of Daniel Turner Holmes, late MP for Govan; *m* 1920, 1 Viscount Stansgate (d 1960); 2 s (*see* Rt Hon Tony Benn, MP) and 1 s (decd); *Career* first pres Congregational Fedn of England 1972-73, (now pres emeritus); vice pres Cncl of Christians and Jews; hon fell Hebrew Univ of Jerusalem 1982; *Style*— The Rt Hon Viscountess Stansgate; Stansgate Abbey House, nr Southminster, Essex; 10 North Court, Great Peter St, London SW1P 3LL (☎ 071 222 1988)

STANTON, Alan William; *b* 19 April 1944; *Educ* Architectural Assoc Sch (Dip Arch), Univ of California (MArch); *m* 8 July 1985, Wendy Robin; *Career* architect; medallist, Societé des Architectes, Diplome Par Le Gouvernment Paris; projects: Centre Pompidou Paris 1971-77 (team architect), La Villette Sci Museum Paris 1984-86, as Stanton, Williams, Age of Chivalry Exhibition RA, Issey Miyake Shop; currently: New Gallery Bldg for RIBA London, Winchester Cathedral Museum, Design Museum, London, Birmingham City Museum; *Style*— Alan Stanton, Esq; Studio 9A, 17 Heneage St, London E1 (☎ 071 247 3171/2)

STANTON, Arthur Holbrow; MBE (1944), TD (1945); s of Arthur William Stanton, JP, High Sheriff Gloucestershire 1937 (d 1944), of Field Place, Stroud, Gloucs, and Violet Fairfax, *née* Taylor (d 1957); *b* 20 Jan 1910; *Educ* Marlborough, Staff Coll Haifa; *m* 30 April 1938, Joan Constance, da of Col Edwin Henry Ethelbert Collen, CMG, DSO, RA (d 1943), of Brakeys, Hatfield Peverel, Essex; 3 da (Anne Catharine b 1941, Juliet Mary b 1945, Elizabeth Holbrow b 1948); *Career* cmmnd 2 Lt Royal Gloucs Hussars 1939, WWII, Staff Capt 1 Armd Div 1940-42, serv France 1940, Maj DAQMG 7 Armd Div 1942-43, Lt-Col AA and QMG 50 Northumbrian Div 1944, Maj DAA and QMG 4 Ind Armd Bde 1944-45, serv Western Desert Tripolitania, Tunisia, Italy, France, Belgium, Holland, Germany (despatches twice 1944); md of Nation Discount Co 1962-70, chm Discount Mkt Assoc 1967-69; church warden St Andrew's Hatfield Peverel Essex 1948-80, chm Hatfield Peverel Soc 1970-80; Freeman City of London 1932, Liveryman Worshipful Co of Vintners (Master 1970 and 1974, elected Father of the Court 1989); *Recreations* shooting, painting, travelling, things historical; *Clubs* Naval and Military, 7 Armd Div, Dining, Blackwater SC; *Style*— Arthur Stanton, Esq, MBE, TD; Brakeys, Hatfield Peverel, Chelmsford, Essex CM3 2NY

STANTON, Graeme Clifford; s of Cliff Stanton (d 1981), and Edith, *née* White; *b* 7 June 1939; *Educ* Newcastle Royal GS, Queen Elizabeth's GS, Blackburn; *m* 5 Oct 1966, (Sandra) Heather; 2 s (William b 1970, James b 1972); *Career* journalist; Lancashire Evening Telegraph Blackburn 1957-64, Daily Express and Daily Mail 1964-65, dep ed Evening Echo Watford 1969-70, managing ed Bangkok Post and Bangkok World Thailand 1971-77; ed: The Journal Newcastle 1977-79 (night ed, 1965-69), Evening Chronicle Newcastle 1979-; govr Newcastle Poly, last chm Northern Area Guild of Br Newspaper Eds; *Recreations* golf; *Clubs* Tyneside Golf; *Style*— Graeme Stanton, Esq; 35 Woodlands, Gosforth, Newcastle upon Tyne (☎ 091 284 3451) Evening Chronicle, Thomson House, Groat Market, Newcastle upon Tyne NE1 1ED (☎ 091 232 7500, fax 091 232 2256)

STANTON, Martin; s of Charles Stanton, of Croydon, Surrey, and Herta, *née* Pollack; *b* 11 Jan 1952; *Educ* Whitgift Sch Croydon; *m* 4 May 1985, Jane Mary, da of Douglas Alfred Chandler; 1 da (Jennifer Sarah b 4 Aug 1987); *Career* scientific offr Nat Physical Laboratory 1971-72; sr programmer: Hoskyns Systems Ltd 1973-75, ICL 1975-76, princ tech advsr and sr account mangr Honeywell 1976-82, strategic mktg conslt Pactel 1982-84, sales and mktg dir Feedback Data 1989- (Euro mktg mangr 1984-88); winner Br and German design awards (for Fox Office Terminal); MInstD 1989; *Recreations* horse riding, skiing, music, windsurfing; *Style*— Martin Stanton, Esq; Feedback Data Ltd, Bell Lane, Uckfield, East Sussex TN22 1PT (☎ 0825 761411, fax 0825 768238)

STANTON, Stuart Lawrence; s of Michael Arthur Stanton (d 1968), and Sarah, *née* Joseph; *b* 24 Oct 1938; *Educ* City of London Sch, London Hosp Med Sch (MB BS); *m* 25 Feb 1965; 3 da (Claire b 1967, Talia b 1970, Joanna b 1972); *Career* conslt gynaecologist St George's Hosp 1984-, hon sr lectr St George's Hosp Med Sch 1984-; assoc Br Assoc of Urological Surgns; memb: Blair Bell Res Soc, Int Continence Soc; LRCP 1961, FRCS 1966, (MRCS 1961), FRCOG 1987; *Books* Clinical Gynaecologic Urology (1984), Surgery of Female Incontinence (co ed with Emil Tanagho, 1986), Principles of Gynaecological Surgery (1987), Gynaecology in the Elderly (1988); *Recreations* photography, travel, opera, theatre; *Style*— Stuart Stanton, Esq; Flat 10, 43 Wimpole St, London W1M 7AF (☎ 071 486 0677)

STAPLE, Rev David; s of William Hill Staple (d 1983), and Elsie, *née* King (d 1984); *b* 30 March 1930; *Educ* Watford Boys' GS, Christ's Coll Cambridge (Bishop Gell's Hebrew Prize 1953, MA), Regent's Park and Wadham Coll Oxford (MA), Univ of London (BD external); *m* 23 July 1955, Margaret Lilian, da of Wilfred Ernest Berrington (d 1975); 1 s (Martin Hugh b 1958), 3 da (Rosemary Jane (now Mrs Sherwood) b 1961, Eleanor Ruth (now Mrs Wharton) b 1962, Hilary Margaret (now Mrs Hines) b 1964); *Career* Baptist Minister: West Ham Central Mission 1955-58, Llanishen Cardiff 1958-74, College Road Harrow 1974-86; gen sec Free Church Fed Cncl 1986-; Baptist Missionary Soc Gen Ctee: memb 1965-83, chm 1981-2, hon life memb 1983-; memb Baptist Union Cncl 1970-; memb: Cncl Regent's Park Coll Oxford 1964-, Exec Ctee Regent's Park Coll Oxford 1967-; *Recreations* fellwalking, music; *Style*— The Rev David Staple; The Free Church Federal Council, 27 Tavistock Square, London WC1H 9HH (☎ 071 387 8413, fax 071 383 0150)

STAPLE, George Warren; s of Kenneth Harry Staple, OBE (d 1978), of Paramour Grange, Ash, Kent, and Betty Mary, *née* Lemon; *b* 13 Sept 1940; *Educ* Haileybury; *m* Jan 1968, Olivia Deirdre, da of William James Lowry (d 1952), of Mtoko, Southern Rhodesia; 2 s (Harry b 1976, Edward b 1978), 2 da (Alice b 1969, Polly b 1970); *Career* admitted slr 1964; ptnr Clifford Chance (formerly Clifford-Turner) 1967; inspr DTI: Consolidated Gold Fields plc 1986, Aldermanbury Trust plc 1988; chm of tbnls Securities Assoc; memb: Commercial Ct Ctee 1978-, Ct of Govrs City of London Poly

1982-, Cncl Law Soc 1986- (treas 1989); FCIArb 1985; *Recreations* cricket, hill walking; *Clubs* Brooks's, City of London, MCC; *Style*— George Staple, Esq; Clifford Chance, 19 New Bridge St, London EC4 (☎ 071 353 0211, fax 071 489 0046, telex 887847 LEGIS G)

STAPLE, William Philip; s of Kenneth Harry Staple, OBE (d 1978), and Betty Mary, *née* Lemon; *b* 28 Sept 1947; *Educ* Haileybury, Law Soc Coll of Law; *m* 14 May 1977 (m dis 1986), Jennifer Frances, da of Brig James Douglas Walker, OBE, of Farnham; 1 s (Oliver b 1980), 1 da (Sophia b 1982); *Career* called to the bar 1970-72, exec Cazenove & Co 1972-81, dir N M Rothschild and Sons Ltd 1986- (asst dir 1982-86), non-exec dir Grampian Holdings plc 1984-; *Recreations* fishing, theatre; *Clubs* Whites; *Style*— William Staple, Esq; NM Rothschild & Sons Ltd, New Court, St Swithin's Lane, London EC4P 4DU (☎ 071 280 5000)

STAPLES, (Hubert Anthony) Justin; CMG (1981); s of Francis Hammond (d 1970), of Sussex, and Catherine Margaret Mary, *née* Pownall (d 1981); *b* 14 Nov 1929; *Educ* Downside, Oriel Coll Oxford (BA); *m* 1962, Susan Angela, da of William Langston Collingwood Carter (d 1976), of Oxford; 1 s (Roderick), 1 da (Antonia); *Career* Dip Serv (formerly Foreign Serv) 1954- served in: Bangkok, Berlin, Vientiane, Brussels (UK Delgn NATO), Dublin; HM ambass: Bangkok 1981-86, Helsinki 1986-89; *Recreations* skiing, riding, golf; *Clubs* Travellers'; *Style*— Justin Staples, Esq, CMG

STAPLES, Kenneth Derek; s of Stanley Holt Staples (d 1967), of Rayleigh, Essex, and Catherinee Emma Annie (Nan), *née* Walding (d 1982); *b* 10 Oct 1930; *Educ* Northampton GS, Battersea Poly; *m* 2 April 1955, Jean Mary, da of Walter Henry Creek (d 1981), of Tenterden, Kent; 1 s (Martin William b 2 Oct 1957), 2 da (Jennifer Anne b 8 Aug 1959, Katherine Mary b 10 Jan 1962); *Career* sr civil engr Corpn of London 1957-60, princ civil engr Kershaw & Kaufman 1960-63, sewerage planning engr pub works dept Govt of Singapore 1963-69, engr i/c NE JD & JM Watson 1969-72; ptnr: JD & JM Watson 1972-78, Watson Hawksley Consulting Engrs 1978-; memb ctee on underground construction for Construction Ind Res Info Assoc; FICE 1973 (assoc memb 1956), FIWEM (memb Inst WPC 1970), MConsE; *Recreations* reading photography, gardening; *Style*— Kenneth Staples, Esq; 15 Middle Rd, Aylesbury, Bucks HP21 7AD (☎ 0296 86 488), Watson Hawksley, Terriers House, Amersham Rd, High Wycombe Bucks (☎ 0494 26 240, fax 0494 22 074, telex 83 439 Watson G)

STAPLETON, Sir (Henry) Alfred; 10 Bt (E 1679) of The Leeward Islands; s of Brig Francis Harry Stapleton, CMG (d 1956), and Maud Ellen (d 1960), da of Maj Alfred Wrottesley, gs of 1 Baron Wrottesley; Sir Alfred succeeded his f's 1 cous Sir Miles Talbot Stapleton, 9 Bt, in 1977. Sir Alfred's ggf, Rev Hon Sir Francis Stapleton, 7 Bt, was 4 (but only surviving) s of Sir Thomas Stapleton, 6 Bt, in whose favour the abeyance of the Barony of Le Despencer was terminated 1788. The latter dignity descended to Sir Thomas's eldest son's da Mary, and through her marriage with 6 Viscount Falmouth to the present Viscount; *b* 2 May 1913; *Educ* Marlborough, ChCh Oxford; *m* 1961, Rosslyne Murray, da of Capt Harold Stanley Warren, RN (d 1960), of Parkstone, Dorset; *Heir* none; *Career* served 1939-45 War as Lt Oxfordshire and Bucks LI; *Recreations* cricket umpiring, gardening; *Clubs* Garrick, MCC; *Style*— Sir Alfred Stapleton, Bt; 7 Ridgeway, Horsecastles Lane, Sherborne, Dorset DT9 6BZ (☎ 093 581 2295)

STAPLETON, Anthony Elliott Hopewell; s of Lt-Col B A Stapleton, CBE, MC, TD, of Birralee, Manor Lane, Gerrard Cross, Bucks, and Ann Elliott, *née* Batt (d 1973); *b* 11 Aug 1940; *Educ* Wrekin Coll Wellington Shropshire; *m* 29 Aug 1964, Deana Mary, da of James McCauley; 1 s (Andrew Elliot b 7 April 1969); *Career* trainee Selfridges London 1958-61, asst mangr Lewis's Leicester 1961-62, asst buyer Lewis's London 1962, asst to gen mangr (on acquisition of Ilford Store) 1962-63, sales mangr Lewis's Bristol 1963-67, special accounts controller S Reece & Son Liverpool 1967-68; floor controller: Lewis's Liverpool 1969-70 (asst to promotions dir 1968-69), Lewis's Birmingham 1970-73; asst gen mangr: Lewis's Leicester 1973-74, Lewis's Birmingham 1974-76; gen mángr Selfridges Oxford 1976-79, merchandise dir Selfridges London 1979-85, gen mangr John Radcliffe Hosp Oxford 1985-; chm Oxford Crime Prevention Ctee 1977-79, memb St Traders Assoc 1979-85, memb Steering Ctee Better Made in Britain 1983, exec Textile Benevolent Assoc 1980-85, memb Clothing Panel NEDO 1980-85; *Recreations* family, home brewing, squash, gardening, photography, travel; *Clubs* Oxford Management; *Style*— Anthony Stapleton, Esq; Cedars, Slade End, Brightwell cum Sotwell, nr Wallingford, Oxford OX10 0RQ (☎ 0491 38886); John Radcliffe Hosp, Headington, Oxford OX3 9DU (☎ 0865 741166, fax 0865 741408, car 0860 343381)

STAPLETON, David Eric Cramer; s of Edward Eric Stapleton (d 1957); *b* 7 Nov 1933; *Educ* Ampleforth, RAC Cirencester, Harvard Business Sch; *m* 1960, Annabel Alison, da of Sir Gerald Gordon Ley, 3 Bt, TD, of Lazonby Hall; 4 da; *Career* former ptnr W I Carr and memb Stock Exchange, ret; dir: Pinneys of Scotland (formerly Pinneys Smokehouses Ltd), The Design Solution, Gressingham Ducks plc, Border Financial Servs; farmer; *Recreations* shooting, fishing; *Clubs* The Flyfishers, Buck's; *Style*— David Stapleton, Esq; Armathwaite Place, Armathwaite, Carlisle, Cumbria (☎ 069 92 225); 26 Holland Park Mews, London W11 (☎ 071 243 0052); Border Financial Services, 1 Rosehill Business Park, Carlisle (☎ 0228 514144)

STAPLETON, Air Vice-Marshal Deryck Cameron; CB (1960), CBE (1948), DFC (1941), AFC (1939); s of John Rouse Stapleton, OBE (d 1985), of Sarnia, Natal; *Educ* King Edward VI Sch Totnes; *m* 1942, Ethleen Joan Clifford, da of Sir Cuthbert William Whiteside (d 1969); 3 s; *Career* joined RAF 1936, served Transjordan and Palestine 1937-39, WWII 1939-45 ME, N Africa, UK and Italy, OC 14Sqdn RAF 1940-41, OC 254 Wg RAF 1944-45, asst sec (Air) War Cabinet Offs 1945-46, sec COS Ctee MOD 1947-49; OC: RAF Odiham 1949-51, RAF Oldenburg 1955-57; dir Jt Plans Air Miny 1961-62, chm Jt Def Plans MOD 1963-64, Air Vice-Marshal 1963, AOC No 1 Gp Bomber Cmd 1964-66, Cmdt RAF Staff Coll Bracknell 1966-68, ret 1968; BAC area mangr Libya 1969-70, BAC rep Iran 1970-79, md Irano- Br Electronics 1978-79, BAe rep China and chm British Commercial Cos Assoc Peking 1979-83; *Clubs* White's; *Style*— Air Vice-Marshal Deryck Stapleton, CB, CBE, DFC, AFC; c/o National Westminster Bank, Haymarket, London SW1

STAPLETON, Guy; s of William Algernon Swann Stapleton (d 1981), of Moreton in Marsh, and Joan Denise, *née* Wilson; *b* 10 Nov 1935; *Educ* Malvern; *Career* Govt Serv: with Miny of Tport and Civil Aviation 1954-59, Office of Dir Gen of Navigational Servs 1956-58, Miny of Aviation 1959-65, civil aviation asst Br Embassy Rome 1960-63, private sec to Controller of NATCS 1963-65, MAFF 1965-74 (private sec to jt parly sec 1967-68), Dept of Prices and Consumer Protection 1974-76, MAFF 1976-82, Cabinet Office 1982-85, dir of estabs MAFF 1985-86, chief exec Intervention Bd 1986-; *Books* A Walk of Verse (1961), Poets England (ed), Gloucestershire (1977), Avon and Somerset (1981), Devon (1986), Hertfordshire (with Margaret Tims 1988), Vale of Moreton Churches (1989), Memories of Moreton (ed, 1989); *Recreations* local history, genealogy, topographical verse; *Clubs* Civil Service, Cwlth Tst; *Style*— Guy Stapleton, Esq; Fountain House, 2 Queen's Walk, Reading RG1 7QW (☎ 0734 583626, fax 0734 583626 ext 2370, telex 848302)

STAPLETON, Rev Henry Edward Champneys; s of Edward Parker Stapleton, OBE (d 1979), of The Cottage, Hutton buscel, Scarborough, N Yorks, and Frances Mary, *née* Champneys (d 1981); *b* 17 June 1932; *Educ* Lancing, Pembroke Coll Cambridge (MA), Ely Theol Coll; *m* 14 Nov 1964, Mary Deborah, da of Canon Baldwin Sp Arrow Sapwell (d 1981), of The Rectory, Rockland All Saints, Attleborough' Norfolk; 2 da (Helen Mary Champneys b 1969, Catherine Jane Champneys b 1971); *Career* ordained: decon 1956, priest 1957; curate St Olve's York 1956-59, Pocklington 1959-61; vicar Seaton Ross with Everingham and Brelby and Harswell 1961-67, rural dean Weighton 1966-67, rector Skelton 1967-75, vicar Wroxham & Hoveton St John 1075-81; priest i/c Belaugh 1976-81, Hoveton St John 1979-81; canon residentiary and procentor Rochester Cathedral 1981-88, dean of Carlisle 1988-; tstee: Historic Churches Preservation Tst, Incorporated Church Bldg Soc, Cncl for the Car of Churches; FSA 1976; *Books* Skelton Village - The Coninuity Community (1971), A Skilful Master Builder (1975), Heirs without title (1974), The Model Working Parson (1976), Churchyard Handbook (3 edn, 1988); author of many articles & parish histories; *Recreations* archaeology, genealogy; *Style*— The Very Rev the Dean of Carlisle, FSA; The Deanery, Carlisle, Cumbria CA3 8TZ (☎ 0228 23335)

STAPLETON, Wing Cdr (Erik) Julian; MBE (1981); s of Air Vice-Marshall Frederick Snowden Stapleton, CB, DSO, DFC (d 1974), and Anne Sofie, *née* Schibsted; *b* 5 Jan 1945; *Educ* Farmlingham Coll, RAF Coll Cranwell; *m* 17 Nov 1973, Anne-Sofie da of Bjorn Steenstrup, of Oslo, Norway; 1 s (Stephen b 1976), 1 da (Sonia b 1974); *Career* cmmnd RAF 1967; served UK, Peru, Hong Kong, Malta, Maldive Is, Europe, ADC to AO in C Strike Cmd 1974-76, MOD Harrogate 1976-78, Unit Cdr RAF Church Fenton 1979, HQ RAF Support Cmd 1980-81, RAF Staff Coll 1982, MOD London 1983-84, Dir Staff RAF Staff Coll 1985-86, RAF Staff Coll Chilmark 1987-88, ret RAF 1988; joined Marshall of Cambridge (Engrg) Ltd, head of supply and maintenance 1990-; MInsPet 1988, MInstPS 1988, MBIM 1988; *Recreations* shooting, skiing, tennis, wind-surfing, philately; *Clubs* RAF, Den Norske; *Style*— Wing Cdr Julian Stapleton, MBE; Denham Hall, Denham, Bury St Edmunds, Suffolk IP29 5EL (☎ 0284 811181), Marshall of Cambridge (Engineering) Ltd, Airport Works, Cambridge CB5 8RX (☎ 0223 61133, telex 81208, fax 0223 321032)

STAPLETON, Lt Cdr Nicholas Bryan John; RD (1943); s of Capt Nicholas Stapleton (d 1918), and Mary Jane, *née* Abraham (d 1939); *b* 4 Jan 1909; *Educ* Christ's Hosp, HMS Conway; *m* 3 June 1940, Laetitia Frances Mary, da of Lt-Col Charles à Court Repington, CMG; *Career* serv Midshipman RNR 1926, Navigating Offr (formerly cadet) Canadian Pacific Steamships Ltd 1926-37, marine airport offr Imperial Airways Ltd Southampton 1938; WWII cmd: HMS Brimness, HMS Southern Pride, HMS Amaranthus, HMS Betony, HMS Derg; serv Royal Fleet Aux Serv 1947-69: Master 1957, sr Master Royal Fleet Aux Serv 1968, ret 1969; publicity offr RNLI Brighton & Hove 1973-85; Freeman City of London 1961, Liveryman Hon Co of Master Mariners 1961; *Books* Steam Picket Boats of the Royal Navy (1980); *Recreations* bird watching, watching county cricket; *Style*— Lt Cdr Nicholas Stapleton, RD, RNR; 38 Wilbury Crescent, Hove, E Sussex BN3 6FJ (☎ 0273 733627)

STAPLETON, Nigel John; s of Capt Frederick Ernest John Stapleton, of Winchmore Hill, London, and Katie Margaret, *née* Tyson; *b* 1 Nov 1946; *Educ* City of London Sch, Fitzwilliam Coll Cambridge (BA, MA); *m* 20 Dec 1982, Johanna Augusta, da of Johan Molhoek, of Vienna, Austria; 1 s (Henry James, b 1988) 1 da (Elizabeth Jane Cornelia b 1990); *Career* Unilever plc: various commerical appts 1968-75, devpt dir BOCM Silcock Ltd 1977-80 (corp planning mangr 1975-77), commercial advsr to regnl dir for N America Unilever plc 1980-83, vice pres fin Unilever (US) Inc 1983-86; fin dir Reed International plc 1986-; memb Fin Reporting Review Panel, chm Tech Ctee Hundred Gp of Fin Directors ACMA 1972, FCMA 1987; *Recreations* classical music, travel, tennis, opera; *Clubs* Oxford & Cambridge, Naval & Military; *Style*— Nigel Stapleton, Esq; Reed International plc, 6 Chesterfield Gardens, London W1A 1EJ (☎ 071 491 8269, fax 071 491 8273, car 0860 260 677)

STAPLETON, William Sidney; s of William Henry Stapleton, and Winifred Grace, *née* Lee; *b* 5 July 1923; *Educ* Christ Church Sch London; *m* 5 July 1947, Doris Lilian (Dot), da of Frederick Granger; 1 da (Kay (Mrs Alcina) b 13 Aug 1950); *Career* WWII RN (visual signals) 1942-46; legal exec: Shaen Roscoe & Co 1938-42 and 1946-53, W H Thompson 1953-65; slr 1965, ptnr and sr ptnr Lawford & Co 1965-88 (conslt ptnr 1988-); memb: Lloyds Holborn Law Soc, Legal Aid Area Ctee, Soc of Labour Lawyers; life memb Apex Union; rep player: Surrey Cricket Assoc, Amateur Football Alliance (memb cncl); chm and rep player South Amateur Football League; vice-pres: Southbank Poly Football Club, Southbank Poly Cricket Club; memb Law Soc 1965, FInstLEx; *Recreations* work, cricket, golf, chess, watching and administrating soccer; *Clubs* MCC, Southbank Poly Football, Southbank Poly Cricket, West Kent GC; *Style*— William Stapleton, Esq; 33 Valleyfield Rd, Streatham, London SW16 2HS (☎ 081 769 0899); 15 Devereux Court, Strand, London WC2R 3JJ (☎ 071 353 5099, fax 071 353 5355, telex 892303 FORLAW G)

STAPLETON-COTTON, Hon David Peter Dudley; s of late 4 Viscount Combermere; *b* 6 March 1932; *Educ* Eton; *m* 1955, Susan Nomakepu, da of Sir George Werner Albu, 2 Bt; 2 s (Simon b 1959, Toby James b 1966), 2 da (Nicola Caroline Louisa b 1957, Polly b 1961); *Career* Lt LG (Res); *Clubs* Royal Cape Yacht; *Style*— The Hon David Stapleton-Cotton; Sherwood House, 19 Sherwood Ave, Kenilworth, Cape Town 7700, S Africa

STARK, Sir Andrew Alexander Steel; KCMG (1975, CMG 1964), CVO (1965), DL (Essex 1982); s of Thomas Bow Stark (d 1917), and Barbara Black, *née* Steel (d 1954); *b* 30 Dec 1916; *Educ* Bathgate Acad, Univ of Edinburgh (MA); *m* 24 Sept 1944, (Helen) Rosemary Oxley, da of Lt-Col John Oxley Parker, TD (d 1981), of Faulkbourne, Essex; 3 s (Antony, Michael, Donald b 1953 d 1970); *Career* served WWII Green Howards and staff appts, Maj 1945; entered FO 1948; served Vienna, Belgrade, Rome, Bonn; ambass attached to UK mission UN 1968, under-sec gen UN 1968, ambass Denmark 1971-76, dep under sec FCO 1976-78; dir The Maersk Co 1978-90 (chm 1978-87), Scandinavian Bank 1978-88, Carlsberg Brewery 1980-87; advsr on euro affrs to Soc Motor Mfrs and Traders 1977-; chm: Anglo-Danish Soc 1983-, Anglo-Danish Trade Advsy Bd 1983-, Rural Community Cncl of Essex 1990-; pro-chllr Univ of Essex 1983- (chm cncl 1983-89), pres Br Assoc of Former UN Civil Servants 1989-; DUniv Essex 1990; Grosses Verdienstkreuz German Fed Republic 1965, Grand Cross Order of the Dannebrog (Denmark) 1974; *Recreations* shooting, skiing, tennis; *Clubs* Travellers', MCC; *Style*— Sir Andrew Stark, KCMG, CVO, DL; Fambridge Hall, White Notley, Witham, Essex CM8 1RN (☎ 0376 83117)

STARK, Dame Freya Madeline; DBE (1972, CBE 1953); da of Robert Stark; *Educ* privately, Bedford Coll London, Sch Oriental Studies; *m* 1947, Stewart Perowne, OBE (d 1989); *Career* traveller and writer; CStJ 1981 (OStJ 1949); Hon LLD Glasgow, Hon DLitt Durham; *Style*— Dame Freya Stark, DBE; c/o John Murray, 50 Albemarle St, London W1X 4BD

STARK, Ian David; MBE (1989); s of late Alexander Ross Stark, and Margaret Barrie, *née* Grubb; *b* 22 Feb 1954; *Educ* Galashiels Acad; *m* 30 Nov 1979, Janet Dixon, da of Dr George Ballantyne McAulay; 1 s (Timothy b 8 Aug 1981), 1 da (Stephanie b 3 June 1980); *Career* equestrian; team Silver medallist LA Olympics 1984, team Gold and individual Bronze medallist Euro Championships 1985, team Gold medallist World Championships 1986, champion Badminton Horse Trials 1986, team Gold and individual Silver medallist Euro Championships 1987, first and second place Badminton 1988, team Silver and Individual Silver medallist Seoul Olympics 1988, team

Gold medallist Euro Championships 1989, team Silver and individual Silver medallist Stockholm World Championships 1990; *Books* Flying Scott (with Janet Stark 1988); *Clubs* British Horse Soc; *Style—* Ian Stark, Esq, MBE; Haughhead, Ashkirk, Selkirk, Borders TD7 4NT (☎ 0750 32238)

STARKE, Hon Mr Justice; Sir John Erskine; s of late Hon Sir Hayden Starke, KCMG; *b* 1 Dec 1913; *Educ* Melbourne C of E GS, Melbourne Univ; *m* Elizabeth, da of late Colin Campbell; *Career* Artillery 2 AIF, Mid East and New Guinea WW II; barr Vic 1939, QC 1955, judge of the Supreme Court of Vic 1964-; kt 1976; *Style—* Hon Mr Justice Starke; Supreme Court, Melbourne, Vic 3000, Australia

STARKEY, Hon Mrs (Alleyne Evelyn Maureen Louisa); da of 5 Viscount Templetown (d 1981, when the title became ext); *b* 1921; *m* 1, 1947, Maj John Hackett, late RAOC; 1 s; m 2, 1961, Michael Starkey; *Career* late ATS; *Style—* The Hon Mrs Starkey; Backstreet, Dalry, Castle Douglas

STARKEY, Greville Michael Wilson; s of Arthur Wilson Starkey (d 1986), of Newmarket, and Eileen, *née* Lunn; *b* 21 Dec 1939; *Educ* Lichfield Sch; *m* 20 Jan 1976, (Sonia) Christine, da of Joshua James Simpson (d 1949), of Harrogate, Yorks; 2 da (Helen Noele b 18 July 1975, Anna Christine b 14 Feb 1977); *Career* jockey, ret 1989; owner of Stud Farm; winner: The Arc de Triomphe 1975, The Derby and Oaks England and Ireland 1978; *Recreations* shooting; *Style—* Greville Starkey, Esq; White House Stand, Warren Rd, Kennett, Newmarket, Suffolk CB8 7QP (☎ 0638 750847)

STARKEY, Sir John Philip; 3 Bt (UK 1935) of Norwood Park, Parish of Southwell and Co of Nottingham, DL (Notts 1981); s of Lt-Col Sir William Randle Starkey, 2 Bt (d 1977); *b* 8 May 1938; *Educ* Eton, Ch Ch Oxford (MA), Sloane fell London Business Sch; *m* 1966, Victoria Henrietta Fleetwood, da of late Lt-Col Christopher Herbert Fleetwood Fuller, TD; 1 s, 3 da; *Heir* s, Henry John Starkey b 13 Oct 1973; *Career* cmmnd Rifle Bde 1956-58; merchant banker and agriculturalist; with Antony Gibbs & Son Ltd 1961-71; chm and chief exec Sir William Starkey & Co Ltd 1972-; memb Lloyd's 1961-; chm J L Maltby Ltd; JP Notts 1982-88; Church Cmmr 1985; High Sheriff of Notts 1987-88; memb Exec Ctee and chm E Midlands Region Nat Tst 1986-; chm Notts Branch Country Land Owners Assoc 1977-80 (memb Exec Ctee 1980-85 and 1989-, memb Agric and Land Use Ctee 1986-89); vice-pres (UK) Confederation of European Agric 1988; pres Newark Chamber of Commerce 1980-82; memb Ct Cncl Univ of Nottingham 1980-; memb Archbishop of Canterbury's Cmmn on Rural Affairs (ACORA); *Recreations* cricket; *Style—* Sir John Starkey, Bt, DL; Norwood Park, Southwell, Notts NG25 OPF

STARKIE, Dr Carol Margaret; da of Dr Colin Starkie, and Margaret Joyce, *née* Wrigley, JP; *b* 3 Feb 1939; *Educ* Kidderminster High Sch, Univ of Birmingham (BSc, MB ChB); *m* 18 Aug 1962, Leslie Keith Harding, s of Leslie Charles Harding (d 1964); 1 s (Nicholas b 1969), 1 da (Victoria b 1972); *Career* conslt histopathologist Selly Oak Hosp 1981-; memb Bone Tumour Panel, MRC Soft Tissue Sarcoma Trial; MRCPath 1979, DCH, MRCS, LRCP; *Recreations* museum and art gallery guide; *Style—* Dr C M Starkie; 27 Manor Road North, Edgbaston, Birmingham B16 DJS (☎ 021 4542497), Dept of Histopathology, Selly Oak Hosp, Raddlebarn Rd, Selly Oak, Birmingham B29 6JD (☎ 021 4725313)

STARKIE, James Hugh Nicholas Le Gendre; s of Piers Cecil Le Gendre Starkie (d 1947), and Cicely, *née* de Hoghton (d 1972); *b* 13 Aug 1921; *Educ* Eton, RAC Cirencester; *m* 26 Oct 1963, (Margaret) Jean, da of Francis Graham Grant-Mackintosh; *Career* Lt RNVR 1940-46; farmer; *Recreations* sailing, shooting; *Style—* James Starkie, Esq; Gaulden Manor, Tolland, nr Taunton, Somerset (☎ 09847 213)

STARKIE, (Thomas) Oliver Matthew; s of Dr Ernest Thomas Winstanley Starkie, and Nancey Elizabeth, *née* Colvin; *b* 1 May 1943; *m* 5 Oct 1968, Joan, da of James Ian Ogilvie Brewster, of Short Hill, Livesey Rd, Ludlow, Shrops, 1 s (Christopher James Winstanley b 10 Sept 1971), 1 da (Claire Anne b 24 March 1977); *Career* CA; sr ptnr Starkie & Ptnrs; FCA 1968, ATII 1968; *Recreations* lawn tennis; *Style—* Oliver Starkie, Esq; 7A Harlestone Rd, Northants NN5 7AE (☎ 0604 750080, fax 0604 759927)

STARKIN, Ivan; s of Julian Starkin (d 1972), and Anne Mary, *née* Lewis (d 1978); *b* 3 Dec 1935; *Educ* Northern Poly Sch of Architecture (Dip Arch); *m* 1, 27 March 1960, Lucille Maureen; 2 s (Stewart b 17 July 1961, Jeremy b 11 April 1964), 2 da (Emma b 31 March 1966, Caroline b 22 Oct 1970); m 2, 1 Sept 1976, Jacqueline Susan, *née* Wills; 1 s (Ben b 23 July 1982), 1 da (Samantha b 5 July 1980); *Career* architect, md ICSA Ltd 1982 (specialist in office devpts and private hosps); ARIBA; *Recreations* painting and sketching, theatre; *Style—* Ivan Starkin, Esq; ISCA Ltd, 36 King St, Covent Garden, London WC2E 8JS (☎ 071 836 5153, fax 071 379 0852, telex 22726, car 0831 402493)

STARLING, John Orkney; ISO (1986); s of John Orkney Starling (d 1951), and Janet Mann, *née* Innes (d 1960); *b* 18 Feb 1927; *m* m Sept 1951, Stella Lillian Florence, da of Frederick Ormrod, ISM (d 1976); *Career* asst res engr BP Ltd 1948-52, memb Examining Staff of the Patent Office DTI 1952-87, memb Hampshire CC 1985-; hon life pres Hampshire Fedn of Residents' Assocs, memb Southern Customer Servs Ctee Office of Water Servs 1990-; CEng, MImechE, MSAE (USA), FRSA; *Recreations* golf, swimming, foreign travel; *Style—* John Starling, Esq; Genève, 1 Compton Close, Havant, Hampshire PO9 2DA (☎ 0705 484159); Hampshire County Council, The Castle, Winchester, Hampshire SO23 8UJ (☎ 0962 841 841)

START, Philip Grant; s of Eric Start, of Norfolk, and Beatrice May; *b* 12 June 1946; *Educ* William Grimshaw Sch London; *m* 9 Nov 1974, Jackie, da of William Albery (d 1982); 2 s (Matthew Dunstone b 1970, Rocky William b 1982); *Career* dir Village Gate 1967-74, chm md Woodhouse 1975-; *Recreations* reading, sports, family; *Style—* Philip Start, Esq; 103A Oxford Street, London W11 (☎ 071 439 6785)

STARY, Erica Frances Margaret; da of Eric Halstead Smith (d 1987), and Barbara Maud, *née* Creeke (d 1947); *b* 20 Jan 1943; *Educ* Hunmanby Hall, LSE; *m* 1, 1966; m 2, 1971, Michael McKirdy Anthony Stary, s of John Henry Stary (presumed dead 1939); 1 da (Philippa b 1977); *Career* admitted slr 1965; lectr (later sr lectr) Coll of Law 1966-73, Inland Revenue 1974-75, asst ed (later ed) Br Tax Review 1976-; tech offr Inst of Taxation 1981-86; ptnr: Speechly Bircham 1988-90, Harbottle and Lewis 1990-; chm London Young Slrs Gp 1972; memb Nat Ctee of Young Slrs 1969-77, dir Slrs Benevolent Assoc 1973-77, dir and tstee London Suzuki Gp and Tst 1984-89, asst clerk Second East Brixton Gen Cmmrs of Income Tax 1987-, tstee Nat Children's Orch 1989-, memb Cncl Inst of Taxation 1989-, frequent lectr and author on taxation matters; FTII 1984; *Recreations* sailing, music, theatre; *Style—* Mrs Michael Stary; c/o Barclays Bank, Church St, Weybridge KT13 8DD

STASSINOPOULOS, Mary; da of John Stassinopoulos (d 1975), of Athens, and Pauline, *née* Kalliodis; *b* 9 Jan 1943; *Educ* Greece, Geneva Univ; *m* 1, 1963 (m dis 1977), Michael E Xilas; 1 s (Elias b 1965), 1 da (Irene b 1967); m 2, 1985, John G Carras; *Career* fell Imp Soc of Teachers of Dancing; dir Vacani Sch of Dancing (sch under patronage of HM Queen Elizabeth the Queen Mother), memb Ctee Cecchetti (classical ballet) Soc; *Recreations* theatre, classical music, reading; *Clubs* Harry's Bar; *Style—* Miss Mary Stassinopoulos; 20 Norfolk Rd, London NW8 6HG (☎ 071 586 3691); Vacani Sch of Dancing, 38-42 Harrington Rd, London SW7 (☎ 071 589 6100)

STATHAM, Sir Norman; KCMG (1977, CMG 1967), CVO (1968); s of Frederick Statham, and Maud, *née* Lynes; *b* 15 Aug 1922; *Educ* Seymour Park Cncl Sch, Manchester GS, Gonville and Caius Coll Cambridge; *m* 1948, Hedwig Gerlich; 1 s (and 1 s decd), 1 da; *Career* served WWII and Intelligence Corps until 1947; Manchester Oil Refinery Ltd and Petrochemicals Ltd 1948-50; FO (later FCO) 1951-79: head Euro Economic Integration Dept (rank of cnsllr) 1965-68 and 1970-71, consul-gen São Paulo 1968-70, min (econ) Bonn 1971-75, dep under-sec 1975-77, ambass Brazil 1977-79; vice pres British C of C in Germany 1981-85, pres COBCOE 1982-84, FCO special rep for Br-German Cooperation 1984-86; *Recreations* gardening, reading, birdwatching; *Style—* Sir Norman Statham, KCMG, CVO; 11 Underhill Park Rd, Reigate, Surrey RH2 9LU

STATON, Roger Anthony; s of Harry James Staton (d 1977), of Coventry, and Janet, *née* Palmer; *b* 25 Nov 1945; *Educ* Bablake Sch Coventry, Univ of Manchester (BSc); *m* 23 May 1970, Angela, da of Joesph Armstrong; 2 s (David b 14 Sept 1971, Adam b 5 Aug 1973); *Career* trg offr GEC Telecommunications Ltd Coventry 1968-69 (apprentice 1963-68), prodn ed The Rugby Review 1969-71, dep ed Radio Communication magazine; account exec: Scott Mactaggart Associates 1973-74, Gollen Slater Public Relations 1974-75; fndr Roger Staton Associates 1976-; MIPR; *Recreations* reading, skiing, walking; *Clubs* Wig and Pen; *Style—* Roger Staton, Esq; Roger Staton Associates Ltd, Wellington House, Wellington Rd, Wokingham, Berkshire RG11 2AG (☎ 0734 774858, fax 0734 774854)

STAUGHTON, Rt Hon Lord Justice; Rt Hon Sir Christopher Stephen Thomas Jonathan Thayer Staughton; PC (1988); yr s of Simon Thomas Samuel Staughton, and Edith Madeline, *née* Jones; *b* 24 May 1933; *Educ* Eton, Magdalene Coll Cambridge; *m* 1960, Joanna Susan Elizabeth, er da of George Frederick Arthur Burgess; 2 da; *Career* served 2 Lt 11 Hussars; called to the Bar Inner Temple 1957, QC 1970, rec Crown Ct 1972-81, High Ct judge (Queen's Bench) 1981-87, Lord Justice of Appeal 1987-; kt 1981; *Style—* The Rt Hon Lord Justice Staughton, PC; Royal Courts of Justice, Strand, London WC2A 2LL (☎ 071 936 6000)

STAUGHTON, (Simon) David Howard Ladd; s of Simon Staughton (d 1967), and Madeline Somers-Cox, *née* Jones (d 1974); *b* 24 Jan 1931; *Educ* Eton; *m* 12 Oct 1957, Olivia Katharine , da of Egbert Cecil Barnes (d 1987); 1 s (James b 1959), 2 da (Julia b 1960, Fiona b 1963); *Career* 2 Lt 10 Royal Hussars (PWO); sr ptnr Lee & Pembertons solicitors, chm St Austell Brewery Co Ltd; *Clubs* Cavalry and Guards; *Style—* David Staughton, Esq; The Old Rectory, Latimer, Bucks HP5 1UA (☎ 0494 764567); 45 Pont St, London SW1X 0BX (☎ 071 589 1114)

STAUNTON, Edmund George; s of Maj Reginald Evelyn Boothby (d 1976), of Burwell Hall, Louth, Lincs, and Frances Katherine, *née* Staunton; assumed the name of Staunton by deed poll 1956; *b* 25 April 1943; *Educ* Eton, Royal Agric Coll; *m* 7 March 1970, Elizabeth Anne, da of John Peter Foster, of Harcourt, Hemingford Grey, Hintingdon; 2 s (William B 1972, Robert b 1974); *Career* farming and estate mgmnt; Nottinghamshire: chm Farming and Wildlife Advsy Gp 1981-82, chm Country Landowners Assoc 1984-86, pres Ramblers Assoc 1987-90, pres Fedn of Young Farmers Clubs 1990-91, chm Ctee Celebration of British Food and Farming 1989; ARICS (1970); *Style—* Edmund Staunton, Esq; Staunton Hall, Near Orston, Nottingham

STAUNTON, Marie; da of Austin Staunton, of Grange-over-Sands, Cumbria, and Ann, *née* McAuley; *b* 28 May 1952; *Educ* Larkhill House Sch Preston Lancs, Univ of Lancaster (BA), Coll of Law; *m* 15 March 1986, James Albert Provan, s of William Provan, of Wallaceton, Bridge of Earn, Perthshire; 1 da (Lucy Maryanne b 1987); *Career* slr; dir Br Section Amnesty Int; ed Solicitors Journal; *Recreations* walking, gardening, children, dancing; *Style—* Ms Marie Staunton; 18 Grove Lane, London SE5 (☎ 071 701 9191); Longmans Law Tax and Finance, 21-27 Lamb's Conduit, London WC1N 3NJ (☎ 071 242 2548, fax 071 831 8119)

STAVELEY, Norman Stuart; s of Fred Staveley (d 1959), of Hull, and Mabel Jones (d 1968); *b* 3 Dec 1928; *Educ* Riley HS Hull, Percy Jackson GS Adwick-le-Street; *m* 26 Dec 1959, Gwendoline *née* Leaper; 1 s (Matthew b 9 April 1964); *Career* RAF 1947-48; articled to Lawrence Fawley Judge Hull 1945, CA 1953, in sole practice 1954-67, merged with A J Downs & Co 1967 (became Kidsons 1974 and Kidsons Impey 1990), sometime dep chm Kidsons; served Hull E Yorks and N Lincs Soc of CAs 1953- (pres 1976-77), memb Cncl Humberside Soc on Cncl ICAEW 1974-83, temp cmmr for taxes The Gambia 1971; past treas several musical socs; present treas: Hull Chamber Music Club, Friends of the Brynmonr Jones Library (Univ of Hull), Charles Jacobs Homes (also chm); writer of articles on taxation of authors; memb ACA 1953 (FCA); *Recreations* music, writing; *Clubs* Hull Literary; *Style—* Norman Staveley, Esq; Kidsons Impey, Chartered Accountants, Dunedin House, 45 Percy Street, Hull HU2 8HL (☎ 0482 27406, fax 0482 26957)

STAVELEY, Maj-Gen Robert; s of Brig Robin Staveley, DSO (d 1968), of Fleet, Hants, and Ilys Evelyn, *née* Sutherland (d 1977); *b* 3 June 1928; *Educ* Wellington, RMA Sandhurst, Staff Coll Camberley, RCDS; *m* 15 March 1958, Airlie Jane Rachel, da of Maj-Gen William H Lambert, CB, CBE (d 1978), of Dartmouth, Devon; 1 s (Robin b 3 Feb 1961), 1 da (Anabel Jane (Mrs Merriman) b 9 March 1963); *Career* cmmnd RA 1948, BAOR 1948-51, ADC to GOC Malta 1951-53, pilot Malayan Emergency 1954-57 (despatches), ADC to GOC in C Northern Cmd 1957-58, Indian Staff Coll 1959, SO and missile battery cdr BAOR 1960-65, instr Staff Coll 1966-68, cmd 47 Lt Regt RA UK and Hong Kong 1969-71, CRA 2 Div BAOR 1973-74, RCDS 1975, COS Army Logistic Exec 1979-82, Col Cmdt RA 1982-87, admin controller Norton Rose slrs 1983-; tstee and memb Cncl Douglas Haig Meml Homes 1982-; memb Guild of Air Pilots and Air Navigators 1983, FBIM 1983; *Recreations* offshore sailing, skiing, good food, music; *Clubs* Army and Navy, Royal Ocean Racing, Royal Artillery Yacht (Cdre 1980-83, Adm 1991-); *Style—* Maj-Gen Robert Staveley; Cox & Kings, 7 Pall Mall, PO Box 1190, London SW1Y 5NA

STAVELEY, Adm of the Fleet Sir William Doveton Minet; GCB (1984, KCB 1981); s of Adm Cecil Minet Staveley, CB, CMG (d 1934), and Margaret Adela, *née* Sturdee (d 1960); gs of Gen Sir Charles Staveley and of Adm of the Fleet Sir Doveton Sturdee Bt; *b* 10 Nov 1928; *Educ* West Downs, Winchester, RNC Dartmouth, RNC Greenwich; *m* 1954, Bettina Kirstine, da of L R A Shuter (d 1960); 1 s (Richard), 1 da (Juliet); *Career* joined RN 1942, served HM Yacht Britannia 1957, subsequently in Far East ME and Mediterranean, Dir Naval Plans Naval Staff 1974-76, Flag Offr 2 Flotilla 1976-77, Flag Offr Carriers and Amphibious Ships and NATO Cdr Carrier Striking Gp 2 1977-78, COS to C-in-C Fleet 1978-80, Vice Chief of Naval Staff 1980-82, Allied C-in-C Channel, C-in-C Eastern Atlantic Area and C-in-C Fleet 1982-85, Chief Naval Staff and First Sea Lord 1985-89, First and Princ Naval ADC to HM The Queen 1985-89; chm Royal London Hosp and Assoc Community Servs NHS Tst; dir Br Sch of Osteopathy; tstee and dir: Chatham Historic Dockyard Tst, Florence Nightingale Museum; memb: Ct Univ of Kent, London Advsy Ctee English Heritage; govr Sutton Valence Sch; Freeman City of London, Liveryman Worshipful Co of Shipwrights, yr bro Trinity House; CBIM; *Recreations* gardening, shooting, riding, restoring antique furniture, fishing; *Clubs* Boodle's, RNSA; *Style—* Adm of the Fleet Sir William Staveley, GCB; c/o Lloyds Bank, 83 High St, Sevenoaks, Kent TN13 1LG

STAVERT OF HOSCOTE, Lt-Col Adam William; o s of Ralph Alan Stavert of Hoscote (d 1978), and (Edna) Pearl, *née* Gallagher (d 1985); the Stavert family acquired Hoscote through the marriage (1744) of Thomas Stavert to Elizabeth Pott, whose family had purchased it ca 1728 from the Scotts of Harden, who in their turn had purchased it from 4 Lord Home 1535 (*see* Burke's Landed Gentry, 18 edn, vol III, 1972); *b* 12 Oct 1939; *Educ* Stowe, RMA Sandhurst; *m* 12 Dec 1964, Shuna Nancy, da of Andrew Denis McNab (d 1981), of Tor Bracken, Howwood, Renfrewshire; 2 da (Sarah Vanessa b 30 March 1967, Victoria Gillian b 8 May 1970); *Career* cmmnd 2 Lt KOSB 1959, Platoon Cdr 1960-61, Berlin, Edinburgh, ADC to Govr of Aden 1961-62, CO 2 i/c 1965-68, Malaysia, Borneo, UK, W Germany, Adjt Scottish Inf Depot 1969-70, Army Staff Coll 1971, DAAG MI (A) MOD (Army) 1972-73, Co Cdr 1973-75, Berlin, Belfast, GSO2 HQ 52 Lowland Bde 1976-78 (despatches 1976), Lt-Col and Cdr 2 Bn 52 Lowland Vols 1982-85, ret; regnl appeals dir for Barnardo's (Scotland) 1978-; vice chm Lowland TAVRA (convener Borders Ctee); pres SSAFA Roxburgh Branch 1988-; MBIM, MICFM; *Recreations* tree planting, sailing, shooting; *Clubs* New (Edinburgh), Lansdowne; *Style—* Lt-Col Adam Stavert of Hoscote; Hoscote, Hawick, Roxburghshire TD9 7PN (☎ 045088 217); Barnardo's, 235 Corstorphine Rd, Edinburgh EH12 7AR (☎ 031 334 8765)

STEAD, David; s of Albert Edward Stead (d 1982), and Barbara Valerie Vyall (d 1972); *b* 15 June 1946; *Educ* St Bartholomew's GS Berks, Paston Sch Norfolk, NE London Poly Sch of Architecture (Dip Arch); *m* 1, 27 Dec 1969, Gillian; 1 s (Thomas b 1978), 2 da (Ruth b 1973, Esther b 1975); *m* 2, 14 June 1986, Lynnette Elizabeth; 1 s (Daniel b 1987); *Career* architect; sole princ in own practice; RIBA; FSAI; *Recreations* golf, swimming, work; *Style—* David Stead, Esq; The Dutch House, 18 Austins Grove, Sheringham, Norfolk; Malvern House, 26 Church St, Sheringham, Norfolk

STEADMAN, Anne Mary; da of Victor William Arthur Sheppard, of Bognor Regis, Sussex, and Joyce Helen, *née* Carter; *b* 20 May 1947; *Educ* Colston's Girls' Sch Bristol; *m* 1 Oct 1966 (m dis 1967), Christopher St Jermain Steadman, s of Brian St Jermain Steadman, TD (d 1961); 1 s (James b 1970), 1 da (Millie b 1972); *Career* sr ed Financial Mail Johannesburg SA 1975-79, property corr Financial Weekly 1980-82; dir: Brian Mitchell Assocs Ltd 1982-85, City & Commercial Communications plc 1985-90; ARICS 1970 (hon sec) 1971-73; *Recreations* most sports as a spectator, particularly football; *Style—* Mrs Anne Steadman; 95 High St, Thames Ditton, Surrey (☎ 081 398 0871)

STEADMAN, (Roger) Evan; s of Edward John Steadman (d 1982), and Nellie Maud, *née* Evans (d 1985); *b* 17 Aug 1938; *Educ* Ilford County HS; *m* 22 Dec 1963, Patricia, da of late Peter Reginald Hignett; 1 s (Ben Charles b 1965), 2 da (Rebecca Louise b 1967, Victoria Suki b 1976); *Career* currently chm: MBC Exhibitions Ltd (parent co), Evan Steadman Communications Gp, Bush Steadman & Partners Ltd (PR consits); dir Maxwell Business Communications Ltd, fndr The Evan Steadman Communications Group (sold to Maxwell Communications 1988); former chm The Assoc of Exhibition Organisers; *Books* Earthquake (1968); *Recreations* producing musicals, sponsoring artists, doing nothing in the sunshine; *Style—* Evan Steadman, Esq; 4 Long Rd, Cambridge CB2 2PS (☎ 0223 247692); 37 Chelsea Crescent, London SW10 0XF (☎ 071 352 1001); 15 Passage de la Trinite, Port la Galere, 06590 Theoule, France (☎ 93 75 0221); The Evan Steadman Communications Group, The Hub, Emson Close, Saffron Walden, Essex CB10 1HL (☎ 0799 26699, fax 0799 26088, car 0831 484278)

STEADMAN, Howard Ian; s of Maurice Steadman, and Gertrude Steadman; *b* 17 Dec 1939; *Educ* Kilburn GS, Jesus Coll Oxford (MA); *m* 30 March 1969, Joy Elaine, da of Harry Fisher; 1 s (Richard b 1970), 2 da (Elizabeth b 1973, Victoria b 1980); *Career* McAnally Montogomery and Co stockbrokers 1966-74 (ptnr 1971-74), The British Petroleum Pension Trust Ltd 1974- (portfolio mangr 1982-); memb Stock Exchange 1971-74, AMSIA 1966; *Recreations* bridge, badminton, tennis; *Style—* Howard Steadman, Esq; British Petroleum Pension Services Ltd, Britannic House, Moor Lane, London EC2Y 9BU (☎ 071 920 4280, fax 071 920 3736, telex 888811)

STEAFEL, Sheila; da of Harold Steafel, of S Africa, and Eda, *née* Cohen; *b* 26 May 1935; *Educ* Barnato Park Johannesburg Girls' HS, Univ of the Witwatersrand (BA), Webber Douglas Sch of Drama; *m* 1958 (m dis 1964), Harry H Corbett; *Career* actress; stage roles incl: Billy Liar (1960), How the Other Half Loves (1972), as Harpo in A Day in Hollywood; A Night in the Ukraine (1979), with Players Theatre Old Time Music Hall (1979), revival of Salad Days (1976), Twelfth Night (1983), The Duenna (1983), as the witch in Humperdinck's Hansel and Gretel (1983), with Royal Shakespeare Co as Mistress Quickly in Merry Wives of Windsor (1985), Barbican season (1986), Ivanov (1989), Much Ado About Nothing (1989), Façade with Mozart Players (1988-89); films incl: Baby Love (1969), Some Will Some Won't (1969), Tropic of Cancer (1970), Percy (1971), SWALK (1971), The Waiting Room (1976), Bloodbath in the House of Death (1983); has also appeared in TV series, one woman shows and on radio; *Style—* Ms Sheila Steafel; 6 James Ave, London, NW2 4AJ; Agent: Ken McReddie, 91 Regent St, London W1 (☎ 071 439 1456)

STEANE, Dr Patricia Ann; da of George Glenwright (d 1989), and Louie Margery, *née* Hail (d 1963); *b* 3 April 1938; *Educ* Trowbridge Girls HS, Hitchin Girls GS, Royal Free Hosp Univ of London (MB BS); *m* 15 Oct 1960, Henry Alfred Steane, s of Alfred Steane (d 1986); 1 s (Robert b 2 June 1968), 1 da (Katherine b 23 Oct 1965); *Career* house surgn Royal Free Hosp 1962 (sr house offr anaesthetics 1963-64), house physician Bedford Gen Hosp 1963, registrar anaesthetics W Herts Hosp 1964-65, sr registrar anaesthetics Swansea Hosps 1971-77 (clinical asst 1966-70), conslt anaesthetist Singleton and Morriston Hosps Swansea 1977-; memb: Cncl Med Women's Fedn, Assoc Anaesthetists, BMA, Welsh Med Ctee 1984-86, W Glamorgan Health Authy 1988-90; FFARCS 1971; *Recreations* tennis, music, swimming, skiing; *Clubs* Royal Over-Seas League; *Style—* Dr Patricia Steane; Anaesthetic Dept, Singleton Hospital, Sketty, Swansea SA2 8QA (☎ 0792 205666)

STEARNS, Michael Patrick; s of Cdr Eric Gascoyne Stearns, OBE, and Evelyn, *née* Sherry; *b* 19 Jan 1947; *Educ* Guy's Hosp Univ of London (BDS, MB BS); *m* Elizabeth Jane Elford; *Career* registrar (later sr registrar) Guy's Hosp 1977-84; conslt head and neck surgn and otolaryngologist: Royal Free Hosp 1984-, Barnet Gen Hosp 1984-; sec Euro Acad of Facial Surgery 1989-; fell: Univ of Washington 1982, Univ of Oregon 1983; FRCS 1978, FRSM 1982; *Recreations* flying; *Style—* Michael Stearns, Esq; 97 Harley St, London W1N 1DF (☎ 071 487 4695)

STEARS, Michael John; s of Frank Albert Stears (d 1984), of Hastings, E Sussex, and Elsie Ellis, *née* Munns (d 1985); *b* 25 Aug 1934; *Educ* Harrow Art Coll, Southall Tech Coll; *m* 15 Sept 1960, Brenda Doreen, da of William Albert George Livy, of Stoke Poges, Bucks; 2 da (Jacqueline Anne b 2 March 1961, Janet Madeline b 6 July 1962); *Career* Nat Serv, served RMP (Signals) 1952-54; designer and creator of special effects for films; md Special Effects (World Wide Ltd) 1970-; films incl: Reach for the Sky (1956), Carve Her Name with Pride (1958), Operation Amsterdam (1960), The Guns of Navarone (1961), Dr No (1962), Call Me Bwana (1963), From Russia With Love (1963), Goldfinger (1964), Thunderball (Oscar, 1965), You Only Live Twice (1967), Chitty Chitty Bang Bang (1968), OHMS (1969), Fiddler on the Roof (1971), The Pied Piper (1972), Theatre of Blood (1973), The Black Windmill (1974), That Lucky Touch (1975), One of Our Dinosaurs is Missing (1976), Star Wars (Oscar, 1977) The Martian Chronicles (1979), Outland (1980), Megaforce (1982), Sahara (1984), Haunted Honeymoon (1985), Murder by Illusion (1987), Navy (1988); ACTT 1954, BKSTS 1979; *Recreations* breeding, showing & luring Russian wolf hounds, model aircraft; *Clubs* The Borzoi, The Northern Borzoi Assoc, Soc of Model Aeronautical Engrs; *Style—* Michael Stears, Esq; Welders House, Welders Lane (Jordans), Chalfont St Peter, Bucks (☎ 024 075 505)

STEBLES, Andrew Gordon; s of Capt George Douglas Stebles (d 1983), and Stella Swan (d 1987); *b* 12 March 1950; *Educ* Queen Elizabeth GS Wakefield, Downing Coll Cambridge (BA, MA); *m* 20 Sept 1975, Diane Vivien, da of Gordon William Samuel Johnson of Bromely, Kent; 3 s (Paul Michael Alexander b 15 Aug 1979, Mark Christopher James b 9 July 1981, Jonathan Simon Philip b 17 March 1986); *Career* Blue Circle Industries plc: joined 1972, chief programmer 1978-80, systems assur and standards mangr 1980-83; data admin mangr 1983-85; database admin mangr Corp of Lloyds 1985-86, sr devpt mangr Lloyds Bank plc 1986; *Recreations* cycling, swimming, gardening; *Style—* Andrew Stebles, Esq

STEDALL, Robert Henry; s of Lt-Col M B P Stedall, OBE, TD (d 1982), of Hurstgate, Milford, Godalming, Surrey, and Audrey Wishart, *née* Cottam; *b* 6 Aug 1942; *Educ* Marlborough, McGill Univ Montreal (BCom); *m* 24 June 1972, Elizabeth Jane (Liz), da of C J J Clay (d 1988), of Lamberts, Hascombe, Godalming, Surrey; 2 s (Oliver Marcus b 1976, James Robert b and d 1978), 1 da (Victoria Patricia b 1979); *Career* CA 1967 (articled McClelland Moores & Co 1964-68); Bowater Corporation Ltd 1968-82: cash controller 1968-72, fin dir Far E 1972-75, fin dir Ralli Bros Ltd 1975-82; md Engelhard Metals 1982-84, dir of fin designate Greenwell Montagu 1984-85, fin dir Gartmore Investment Management 1985-88, dir of admin Nat Employers Life Assurance Co Ltd 1989-; memb Dunsfold Parish Cncl; Liveryman Worshipful Co of Ironmongers (Master 1989); FCA; *Recreations* gardening, tennis, golf, bridge; *Clubs* Boodle's; *Style—* Robert Stedall, Esq; Knightons, Dunsfold, Godalming, Surrey GU8 4NU (☎ 048 649 245); National Employers Life Assurance Co Ltd, Milton Court, Dorking, Surrey RH4 3LZ (☎ 0306 887766, fax 0306 881394)

STEDMAN, Patricia Rosamund Kathleen; da of Capt Leonard Gordon Stedman, MC (d 1961), of SA, and Diana Josephine Steere (Mrs Maurice Brown, d 1980); *b* 17 Feb 1938; *Educ* St Mary's Gerrards Cross Bucks, Catherine Judson's Secretarial Coll London; *Career* secretarial then stockbroking asst J A Brewin (later Brewin Dolphin) Stockbrokers London 1957-66, managing exec Brewin Dolphin Jersey 1976-86 (fndr 1973), md Jersey Overseas Invest Mgmnt Ltd (formerly Strabo Investmt Mgmnt Ltd) 1989 (fndr and md 1986), fndr Patricia Stedman Invest Mgmnt 1989; *Recreations* riding, sailing, travelling; *Clubs* Royal Channel Is Yacht; *Style—* Miss Patricia Stedman; The Stable Flat, Northdale, St Ouen, Jersey, Channel Islands JE3 2DU (☎ 0534 83122, fax 0534 85224)

STEDMAN, (Gordon John) Peter; s of Lt Wilson James Stedman (d 1956), of The Butts, Boscastle, Cornwall, and Francis Lilian, *née* Pettengell (d 1979); *b* 3 Jan 1924; *Educ* Sir James Smith's GS Camelford; *Career* Lt RNVR 1941-46, navigating offr MTB in English Channel, gunnery offr SE Asia, proprietor The Wellington Hotel 1982-86 (md 1974-82), conslt Stedman and Co Chartered Accountants 1980-89 (princ 1957-73, sr ptnr 1974-79); memb: RYA, RNSA, BWA, RSPB, Cornwall Beekeepers, RNLI; FCA 1957; *Recreations* yachting, beekeeping, breeding ornamental waterfowl and peacocks, birdwatching; *Style—* Peter Stedman, Esq; The Butts, Boscastle, Cornwall PL35 0AX (☎ 08405 240)

STEDMAN, Baroness (Life Peeress UK 1974), of Longthorpe, in the City of Peterborough; Phyllis Stedman; OBE (1965); da of Percy Adams; *b* 14 July 1916; *Educ* County GS Peterborough; *m* 1941, Henry William Stedman, OBE (d 1988); *Career* branch librarian Peterborough 1932-41, gp offr NFS 1941-44, memb Bd Peterborough Devpt Corpn 1972-75, vice-chm Cambs CC 1973-75 (cncllr 1946-75); Baroness-in-Waiting to HM The Queen (govt whip) 1975-79; govt spokesman in House of Lords on Tport Environment and Trade 1975-79, Parly under-sec Dept of Environment 1979; joined SDP: 1981, whip House of Lords 1981-88, Leader in House of Lords 1988-, spokesman House of Lords on local govt, new towns, Tport, facilities for disabled, environmental protection; memb Cncl of Fire Servs Nat Benevolent Fund 1976-; vice-pres: Nat PHAB 1979-, Assoc of Dist Cncls 1980-, Nat Assoc of Local Cncls 1983-, Assoc of County Cncls 1986-; *Recreations* reading, countryside; *Style—* The Rt Hon the Lady Stedman, OBE; 1 Grovelands, Thorpe Road, Peterborough, Northants PE3 6AQ (☎ 0733 61109); House of Lords, London SW1 (☎ 071 219 3229)

STEED, Mark Wickham; s of Richard David Wickham Steed, and Jennifer Mary, *née* Hugh-Jones; gs of Henry Wickham Steed, editor of the Times; *b* 31 Oct 1952; *Educ* Downside; *m* 3 June 1989, Carola Dawn, da of Dorian Joseph Williams, of Foscote Manor, Buckingham; *Career* CA; dir: Oxford Investments Ltd 1981-86, Beckdest Ltd 1981-88, Colt Securities Ltd 1983-; *Recreations* shooting; *Clubs* Naval and Military; *Style—* Mark Steed, Esq; Grenville Cottage, Gawcott, Buckingham (☎ 0280 813152); 605 Nelson House, Dolphin Square, London SW1 (☎ 071 821 8172)

STEED, Nigel Harry Campbell; s of Cyril Frederick Steed (d 1978), of Great Bealings Suffolk, and Mary Gertrude Millicent, *née* Pausch (d 1989); *b* 11 Oct 1945; *Educ* Felsted; *m* 10 May 1975, Priscilla, da of Eric Geoffrey Pawsey (d 1978), of Braintree, Essex; 1 s (Ian b 1978), 2 da (Susannah b 1976, Nicola b 1980); *Career* admitted slr 1971; lord of the manor of Lavenham, Suffolk; *Recreations* hockey, golf, gardening; *Clubs* Ipswich and Suffolk; *Style—* Nigel Steed, Esq; Drumbeg, 4 Constitution Hill, Ipswich, Suffolk (☎ 0473 254479); Neale House, Neale St, Ipswich, Suffolk (☎ 0473 255556)

STEEDMAN, Air Chief Marshal Sir Alasdair; GCB (1980, KCB 1976, CB 1973), CBE (1965), DFC (1944); s of James Steedman (d 1953); *b* 29 Jan 1922; *Educ* Hampton GS; *m* 1945, Dorothy Isobel (d 1983), da of Col Walter Frederick Todd, late Cameronians; 1 s (Roderick b 1951), 2 da (Lesley b 1947, Jane b 1953); *Career* served WWII 241 242 Sqdns Hurricanes and Spitfires RAF, Station Cdr RAF Lyneham 1962-65, CAS Royal Malatsian Air Force 1965-67, ACAS (Policy) RAF 1969-71, sr Air Staff Offr RAF Strike Cmd 1971-72, Cmdt RAF Staff Coll 1972-75, air memb of Air Force Bd for Supply and Orgn 1976-77, UK mil rep NATO 1977-80, controller RAF Benevolent Fund 1981-88, memb Security Cmmn 1982-; govr Hampton Sch 1976- (chm 1988-), memb Fndn Ctee and govr Gordons Sch 1981-; pres Br Pistol Club 1985-, patron Central Flying Sch RAF 1984-, vice pres Nat Back Pain Assoc 1986-; Liveryman Guild of Air Pilots and Navigators (chm Benevolent Fund 1990-); FRAeS, CBIM; *Recreations* sport, reading, DIY, motoring; *Clubs* RAF; *Style—* Air Chief Marshal Sir Alasdair Steedman, GCB, CBE, DFC; Rutherford, St Chloe, Amberley, near Stroud, Glos GL5 5AS (☎ 0453 872769)

STEEDMAN, Dr Carolyn Kay; da of Ellis Kay Pilling (d 1977), of Streatham Hill and Gypsy Hill, and Edna Dawson (d 1983); *b* 20 March 1947; *Educ* Rosa Bassett GS for Girls London, Sch of Eng and American Studies Univ of Sussex (BA), Newnham Coll Cambridge (MLitt, PhD); *m* 1971 (m dis 1986), Mark Jerome Steedman, s of George Steedman, of Newton under Rawcliffe, Yorks; *Career* class teacher in primary schs in E Sussex and Warwicks 1974-81, project asst Schs Cncl Language in the Multicultural Primary Classroom Project Dept of Eng Univ of London Inst of Educn 1982-83, fell Sociological Res Unit Univ of London Inst of Educn 1983-84, sr lectr Dept of Arts Educn Univ of Warwick 1988- (lectr 1984-88); author of numerous pubns incl: The Tidy House: Little Girls Writing (1982, awarded Fawcett Soc Book prize 1983), Policing the Victorian Community: the Formation of English Provincial Police Forces 1856-1880 (1984), Language Gender and Childhood (jt ed, 1985), Landscape for a

Good Woman (1986), The Radical Soldier's Tale (1988), Childhood Culture and Class In Britain: Margaret McMillan 1860-1931 (1990), ed History Workshop Journal 1983-; memb Panel for Validation and Review Cncl for Nat Academic Awards, external examiner Portsmouth Poly 1990-; *Awards* elected Helen Gamble res student Newnham Coll Cambridge 1970-71, Nuffield Fndn Small Grant in social scis for work on Margaret McMillan (1860-1931) and the idea of childhood 1983, History Twenty Seven Fndn grant Inst of Hist Res 1983, elected Sr Simon res fell Dept of Sociology Univ of Manchester 1990; *Style*— Dr Carolyn Steedman; University of Warwick, Coventry CV4 7Al (☎ 0203 523523 ext 4137)

STEEDMAN, Robert Russell; s of Robert Smith Steedman (d 1950), of Sevenoaks, Kent, and Helen Hope, *née* Brazier; *b* 3 Jan 1929; *Educ* Loretto, School of Architecture Edinburgh Coll of Art (DA), Univ of Pennsylvania (MLA); *m* 1, July 1956 (m dis 1974), Susan Elizabeth, da of Sir Robert Scott, GCMG, CBE (d 1982), of Peebles, Scotland; 1 s (Robert Scott b 1958), 2 da (Helena Elizabeth b 1960, Sarah Aeliz b 1962); m 2, 23 July 1977, Martha, da of Rev John Edmund Hamilton; *Career* Nat Serv Lt RWAFF 1947-48; ptnr Morris and Steedman Edinburgh 1959-; memb: Countryside Cmmn for Scotland 1980-88, Royal Fine Art Cmmn for Scotland 1984-; sec Royal Scottish Acad 1983- (memb Cncl 1981-, dep pres 1982-83), govr Edinburgh Coll of Art 1974-88, memb Edinburgh Festival Soc 1978-; former cncl memb: Royal Incorporation of Architects in Scotland, Soc of Scottish Artists, Scottish Museums 1984-; chm Central Scotland Woodlands Tst 1984-87; awards: Civic Tst ten times 1963-88, Br Steel 1971, Saltire 1971, RIBA (Scotland) 1974, Euro Architectural Heritage Medal 1975, Assoc for the Preservation of Rural Scotland 1983 (1977); elected RSA 1979, RIBA, FRIAS, ALI; *Clubs* New (Edinburgh), Royal and Ancient (St Andrews); *Style*— Robert Steedman, Esq; Muir of Blebo, Bledocraigs, Cupar, Fife (☎ 0334 85 781), 11B Belford Mews, Edinburgh, Lothian; Morris & Steedman, 38 Young St Lane North, Edinburgh (☎ 031 226 6563, fax 031 220 0224)

STEEDS, Prof John Wickham; s of John Henry William Steeds (d 1987), of London, and Ethel Amelia, *née* Tyler; *b* 9 Feb 1940; *Educ* Haberdashers' Aske's, UCL (BSc), Univ of Cambridge (PhD); *m* 7 Dec 1969, Diana Mary, da of Harry Kettlewell (d 1984), of Harlaxton; 2 da (Charlotte b 7 Dec 1971, Lucy b 12 Dec 1973); *Career* res fell Selwyn Coll Cambridge 1964-67; Dept of Physics Univ of Bristol: lectr 1967-77, reader 1977-85, prof 1985-, dir Interface Analysis Centre 1990-; memb Sci and Engrg Cncl Ctees 1982-88, chm Sci Res Fndn Emerson Green 1988-, memb Cmmn on Election Diffraction Int Union of Crystallography; FRS 1988; *Books* Introduction to Anisotropic Elasticity Theory of Dislocations (1973), Election Diffraction of Phases in Alloys (1984); *Recreations* tennis, cycling, travel; *Style*— Prof John Steeds, FRS; 21 Cayngе Square, Clifton, Bristol BS8 3LA (☎ 0272 732183), Physics Dept, Univ of Bristol, Bristol BS8 1TL (☎ 0272 303597, fax 2072 255624, telex 445938 BSUNIV G)

STEEL, Charlotte Elizabeth; da of Lt Cdr David Alan Robert Malcolm Ramsay, OBE, DSC, DSO, RN (d 1981), and Christine Elizabeth Warwick; *b* 29 June 1948; *Educ* St Mary's Sch Wantage; *m* 12 Sept 1970, David William Steel, s of Sir Lincoln Steel (d 1985); 2 s (Jonathan b 1971, Timothy b 1974); *Career* horse trainer and event rider representing England as individual European Championships 1977; dressage judge; previously voluntary worker, ctee memb Stoke Mandeville Hosp, fund raiser Br Paraplegic Sports Soc, SOS Poland helper; *Recreations* theatre, reading, music; *Style*— Mrs David Steel; Chinnor Manor, Chinnor, Oxon OX9 4BG (☎ 0844 51469)

STEEL, (Antony) David; s of Sir James Steel, CBE, JP; *b* 1 May 1938; *Educ* Rugby, Queen's Coll Oxford (MA); *m* 1968, Jane Harriet, da of N C Macpherson, CBE, WS; 1 s, 1 da; *Career* md Coles Cranes Ltd, dir Grove Coles Ltd, Grove Coles France sa, JCB Sales Ltd; FRSA; *Recreations* field sports; *Style*— A D Steel, Esq; The Old Vicarage, Hillesden, Bucks (☎ 0296 730350)

STEEL, Sir David Edward Charles; DSO (1940), MC (1945), TD; s of Gerald Arthur Steel, CB; *b* 29 Nov 1916; *Educ* Rugby, Oxford Univ (BA); *m* 3 Nov 1956, Ann Wynne, da of Maj-Gen Charles Basil Price, CB, DSO, DCM, VD, CD (d 1975); 1 s (Richard), 2 da (Nicola, Caroline); *Career* WWII 9 Queen's Royal Lancers Serv: France, M East, N Africa, Italy; slr Linklaters & Paines 1948, legal asst BP 1950, pres BP N America 1959-61; md: Kuwait Oil 1962-65, BP 1965-75 (dep chm 1972-75, chm 1975-81); dir Bank of England 1978-85; tstee The Economist 1979-, chm Wellcome Trust 1982-89 (tstee 1981-89), pres London Chamber of Commerce and Indust 1982-85; chm govrs Rugby Sch 1984-88; hon fell Univ Coll Oxford, Hon DCL City Univ; kt 1977; *Recreations* golf, gardening; *Clubs* Cavalry and Guards', Royal and Ancient St Andrews; *Style*— Sir David Steel, DSO, MC, TD

STEEL, Rt Hon Sir David Martin Scott; KBE (1990), PC (1977), DL (Ettrick and Lauderdale and Roxburghshire 1990-), MP (Lib Dem) Tweeddale, Ettrick and Lauderdale 1983- (Rosburgh, Selkirk and Peebles 1965-83, Lib 1965-88, Lib Dem 1988-); s of Very Rev Dr David Steel; *b* 31 March 1938; *Educ* Prince of Wales Sch Nairobi, George Watson's Coll Edinburgh, Univ of Edinburgh (MA, LLB); *m* 1962, Judith Mary, da of W D MacGregor, CBE; 2 s (and 1 s adopted), 1 da; *Career* sometime journalist, asst sec Scottish Lib Pty 1962-64, BBC TV interviewer in Scotland 1964-65 and later presenter of religious programmes for STV, Granada and BBC; pres Anti-Apartheid Movement of GB 1966-69, memb Parly Delgn to UN 1967, sponsored Abortion Act 1967, tstee of Shelter 1970- (former chm Shelter Scotland), memb Br Cncl of Churches 1971-74, Lib chief whip 1970-75, spokesman on foreign affrs 1975-76, ldr of Lib Pty 1976-88, memb Select Ctee on Privileges 1979-86; rector Edinburgh Univ 1982-85; Freedom of Tweeddale 1988, Freedom of Ettrick and Lauderdale 1990; Chubb fell Yale Univ 1987, Hon Doctorate Univ of Stirling 1991; *Books* Boost for the Borders (1964), Out of Control (1968), No Entry (1969), The Liberal Way Forward (1975), A New Political Agenda (1976), Militant for the Reasonable Man (1977), A House Divided (1980), Partners in One Nation (1985), Border Country (with Judy Steel, 1985), The Time Has Come (1987), Mary Stuart's Scotland (with Judy Steel, 1987), Against Goliath (1989); *Recreations* vintage cars, fishing; *Style*— The Rt Hon Sir David Steel, KBE, PC, DL, MP; House of Commons, London SW1A 0AA

STEEL, David William; QC (1981); s of Sir Lincoln Steel (d 1985), and Barbara, *née* Goldschmidt; *b* 7 May 1943; *Educ* Eton, Keble Coll Oxford (MA); *m* 1970, Charlotte Elizabeth, da of Lt Cdr David A R M Ramsay, DSM (d 1981); 2 s (Jonathan b 1971, Timothy b 1974); *Career* called to the Bar Inner Temple 1966; jr counsel to Treasury (Admiralty and Common Law) 1978-81; memb: Panel Wreck Cmmrs 1982-, Panel Lloyd's Salvage Arbitrators 1981-; ed: Temperley, Merchant Shipping Acts (1975), Kennedy on Salvage (1985); *Recreations* shooting, fishing; *Clubs* Turf, Beefsteak; *Style*— David Steel, Esq, QC; 2 Essex Court, Temple, London EC4Y 9AP (☎ 071 583 8381, telex 881 2528)

STEEL, Elizabeth Anne; da of William Frederick Steel (d 1961), and Amy Winifred Steel (d 1975); *b* 3 July 1936; *Educ* St Bernard's Convent Sch Slough, Univ of Reading (BSc, MSc); *Career* behavioural endocrinologist; asst in res Sub-Dept of Animal Behaviour Madingley Cambridge 1960, visiting res worker Inst of Animal Behavior Rutgers Univ New Jersey USA 1964, pharmaceutical res Aspro-Nicholas Research Inst Wexham Bucks 1965; Univ of Cambridge: univ asst in res Sub-Dept of Animal Behaviour 1966, chief res officer MRC Unit on Devpt and Integration of Behaviour Madingley 1985-89 (univ sr asst in res 1969), sr res assoc Dept of Psychiatry 1990; *Recreations* riding, walking, taking the lid off things; *Style*— Miss Elizabeth Steel; Department of Zoology, Downing St, Cambridge (☎ 0223 336600)

STEEL, Elizabeth Mary; da of His Hon Judge Edward Steel (d 1976), of Warrington, and Mary Evelyn Griffith, *née* Roberts (d 1987); *b* 28 Nov 1936; *Educ* Howells Sch Denbigh, Univ of Liverpool (LLB); *m* 8 April 1972, Stuart Christie, s of Samuel Albert Christie; 1 da (Elspeth Victoria b 19 Nov 1976), 1 s (Iain Duncan b 17 Feb 1978); *Career* asst slr Percy Hughes & Roberts 1960-67 (articled clerk 1955-60); ptnr: John A Behn Twyford & Co 1968-80 (asst slr 1967-68), Cuff Roberts North Kirk 1980-; recorder 1989; nat vice chm Young Cons 1965-67; memb: Cripps Ctee 1967-69, Race Relations Bd 1970-78, Gen Advsy Cncl BBC 1979-82; chm: N W Advsy Cncl BBC 1979-82, Steering Ctee Hillsborough Slrs Gp 1989-; dep and vice chm Bd of Dirs Liverpool Playhouse 1980-88 (memb 1968); Liverpool Law Soc: vice pres 1988-89, pres 1989-90, memb Ctee, former chm Legal Educn Sub Ctee; non-exec dir Bd Royal Liverpool Univ Hosp Tst; memb: Law Soc 1960, Liverpool Law Soc 1960; *Recreations* theatre (watching professional and performing/directing amateur), music, needlework, cooking, reading, entertaining, being entertained; *Clubs* University Womens Assoc, Athenaeum (Liverpool); *Style*— Miss Elizabeth Steel; Glenisla, 70 Knowsley Road, Cressington Park, Liverpool L19 0PG (☎ 051 427 3760); Cuff Roberts North Kirk, 25 Castle St, Liverpool L2 4TD (☎ 051 227 4181, fax 051 227 2584, car 0860 810265)

STEEL, Her Hon Judge (Anne) Heather; da of His Hon Edward Steel (d 1976), of Cheshire, and Mary Evelyn Griffith, *née* Roberts (d 1987); *b* 3 July 1940; *Educ* Howell's Sch Denbigh North Wales, Univ of Liverpool (LLB); *m* 1967, David Kerr-Muir Beattie, s of Harold Beattie (d 1957), of Manchester; 1 s (Andrew b 1972), 1 da (Elinor b 1970); *Career* called to the Bar Gray's Inn 1963, practised Northern Circuit, prosecuting counsel for DHSS 1984-86, rec Crown Court 1984-86, circuit judge 1986; *Recreations* theatre, art, antiques, gardening; *Style*— Her Hon Judge Heather Steel; The Sessions House, Lancaster Rd, Preston

STEEL, Sir James; CBE (1964), JP (1964), DL (Durham Co 1969); s of Alfred Steel (d 1920), of Thornhill Park, Sunderland, and Katharine, *née* Meikle (d 1943); *b* 19 May 1909; *Educ* Trent Coll; *m* 1935, Margaret Jean, da of Robert Sangster MacLauchlan; 2 s, 2 da; *Career* chm: Steel & Co Ltd 1956-66, CBI Northern Regional Council 1963-66, Washington Development Corporation 1964-77, British Productivity Council 1966-67, Textile Council of GB 1968-72, Natural History Soc of Northumbria 1970-85, Furness Withy & Co Ltd 1975-79, North of England Building Society 1977-85; vice chm: Rea Bros plc 1973-84, Cncl Univ of Durham 1978-1983; dir Newcastle Bd Barclays Bank 1975-82; memb: National Research Development Corporation 1963-73, Northern Econ Planning Cncl 1965-68, Royal Cmmn on the Constitution 1969-73; jt pres Cncl of Order of St John 1974-84; pres: Northumbria Assoc of Youth Clubs 1976-84, TA & VRA for N of Eng 1979-84; vice pres: Durham Co Scout Assoc 1975-, Wildfowl and Wetlands Tst 1982-, Nat Cncl YMCA's NE Div 1968-84; govr: St Aidan's Coll Durham 1967-90, Chad's Coll Durham 1977-83, Trent Coll 1979-83; High Sheriff Co Durham 1972-73, HM Lord-Lieut in the Met Co of Tyne and Wear 1974-84; Queens Silver Jubilee Medal 1977; Freeman Worshipful Co of Founders; Hon DCL Univ of Durham 1978; KJStJ 1981; CBIM; kt 1967; *Books* Bird Quest (1989); *Recreations* ornithology; *Style*— Sir James Steel, CBE, JP, DL; Fawnlees Hall, Wolsingham, Co Durham DL13 3LW (☎ 0388 527307)

STEEL, John Brychan; s of Lt-Col John Exton Steel, of Swindon Hall, nr Cheltenham, Gloucs, and Marianne Valentine, *née* Brychan Rees; *b* 4 June 1954; *Educ* Harrow, Univ of Durham (BSc); *m* 6 June 1981, Susan Rebecca, da of Dr Robert Fraser (d 1979), of Yarm, County Durham; 2 s (Charles John Robert b 1984, Henry James Edward b 1989), 1 da (Sophie Rosanagh b 1986); *Career* Lt Inns of Ct and City yeomanry TA 1977-81; called to the Bar Gray's Inn 1978, appointed to AG list of Bar Supp Panel (common law) 1989; dep chm SCGB, dir Busoga Tst; *Recreations* skiing, walking; *Clubs* RAC, Kandahar, SCGB; *Style*— John Steel, Esq; 61 Abingdon Villas, Kensington, London W8 6XA; Manor Farm Cottage, Ledwell, Oxon OX5 4AN; 4-5 Gray's Inn Sq, Gray's Inn, London WC1R 5AY (☎ 071 404 5252, fax 071 242 7803)

STEEL, (Rupert) Oliver; s of Joseph Steel (d 1959), of Kirkwood, Lockerbie, and Beatrice Elizabeth, *née* Courage (d 1965); *b* 30 April 1922; *Educ* Eton; *m* 1, 1944, Marigold Katharine, da of Percy Roycroft Lowe (d 1952); 2 s (Rupert Michael b 1947, Jonathan Robin b 1949); m 2, 1967, Lucinda Evelyn, da of Arthur Walter James (d 1982); 1 s (James Oliver b 1971), 1 da (Emily Jane b 1970); *Career* Pilot Fleet Air Arm RNVR Lt, Atlantic, Pacific 1941-46 (despatches); Courage & Co Ltd 1946-78, Imperial Group 1975-78, Everards Brewery 1978-84, South Uist Estates Ltd 1980-, Umeco plc 1979-, Lloyds Bank & Subsidiaries 1977-89; *Clubs* Brooks's; *Style*— Oliver Steel, Esq; Winterbourne Holt, Newbury RG16 8AP

STEEL, Patricia Ann; OBE (1990); da of Thomas Norman Steel (d 1970), of Huddersfield, Yorks, and Winifred, *née* Pearson (d 1974); *b* 30 Oct 1941; *Educ* Hunmanby Hall nr Filey, Univ of Exeter (BA); *Career* Parly liaison Chamber of Shipping of UK and Br Shipping Fedn 1968-71; sec: Highway and Traffic Technicians Assoc 1972-73, Inst of Highways and Tportation 1973-90; memb Occupational Pensions Bd 1979-83, non-exec dir London Regnl Tport 1984-; dir: Docklands Light Railway Ltd 1984- (chm 1988-89), Victoria Coach Station Ltd 1988-; memb Street Works Advsy Ctee 1987-; *Recreations* politics, music, travel; *Style*— Miss Patricia Steel, OBE; 7 The Strathmore, 27 Petersham Rd, Richmond, Surrey

STEEL, Richard Hugh Jordan; er s of Sir Christopher Eden Steel, GCMG, MVO (d 1973), of Southrop Lodge, Lechlade, and Catherine (d 1986), er da of Lt-Gen Sir Sidney Clive, GCVO, KCB, CMG, DSO (d 1959); *b* 5 Dec 1932; *Educ* Eton; *m* 1959, Lady Rosemary, *née* Villiers, *qv*, sis of 7 Earl of Clarendon; 2 s (James Thomas Jordan b 1960 (m, 1989, Lindsay J Farrell), Oliver George Nigel b 1962), 1 da (Arabella Rosemary Louise b 1966); *Career* late 2 Lt RHG The Blues; Lazard Bros 1953-73, asst sec HM Treasy 1969-70, Barclays Bank 1973-; *Recreations* gardening, shooting, fishing; *Clubs* Boodle's; *Style*— Richard Steel, Esq; The Glebe House, Notgrove, Cheltenham, Glos (☎ 045 1850 347); Flat 15, Rupert House, Nevern Sq, London SW5 (☎ 071 373 5366)

STEEL, Robert King; s of Charles Leighton Steel III, and Elizabeth Deaton Steel; *b* 3 Aug 1951; *Educ* Duke Univ Durham N Carolina USA (BA), Univ of Chicago (MBA); *m* 30 Aug 1980, Gillian, da of Alexander Hehmeyer; *Career* md Goldman Sachs Int 1988- (vice pres 1976-88); *Style*— Robert Steel, Esq

STEEL, Prof Robert Walter; CBE (1983); s of Frederick Grabham Steel (d 1948), and Winifred Barry, *née* Harrison (d 1974); *b* 31 July 1915; *Educ* Great Yarmouth GS, Cambridge and Co HS, Jesus Coll Oxford (BA, BSc, MA); *m* 9 Jan 1940, Eileen Margaret, da of Arthur Ernest Page (d 1941), of Bournemouth; 1 s (David Robert b 1948), 2 da (Alison Margaret b 1942, Elizabeth Mary b 1945); *Career* Nat Serv WWII Naval Intelligence 1940-45; geographer Ashanti Social Survey Gold Coast 1945-46, lectr (later sr lectr) in cwlth geography Univ of Oxford 1947-56 (fell Jesus Coll 1954-56, hon fell 1982); Univ of Liverpool: John Rankin prof of geography 1957-74, dean Faculty of Arts 1965-68, pro vice-chllr 1971-73; princ Univ Coll Swansea 1974-82, vice chllr Univ of Wales 1979-81; hon dir Cwlth Geographical Bureau 1972-81; chm: Univs' Cncl for Adult and Continuing Educn 1976-80, Lower Swansea Valley Devpt Gp 1979-88, govrs Westhill Coll Birmingham 1981- (vice chm Cncl of Church and Assoc Colls 1988-90, pres 1990-), Wales Advsy Body for Local Authy Higher Educn 1982-86,

Cwlth Human Ecology Cncl 1988-90; Swansea Festival of Music and the Arts 1982-, Swansea Civic Soc 1988-; Hon DSc Univ of Salford 1977, Hon LLD Wales 1983, Hon LLD Univ of Liverpool 1985, Hon DUniv Open Univ 1987, fell Univ Coll of Swansea 1991-; FRGS 1939; memb: Inst of Br Geographers 1939- (pres 1969, ed 1950-61), Geographical Assoc 1946- (pres 1973), African Studies Assoc UK 1963- (pres 1973), Royal African Soc 1939- (vice pres 1977-); *Recreations* walking, gardening, reading, music; *Clubs* Royal Cwlth Soc; *Style—* Prof Robert Steel; 12 Cambridge Rd, Langland, Swansea SA3 4PE (☎ 0792 369 087)

STEEL, Roger Cameron; s of David Ian Steel, of Scarborough, N Yorks, and Sylvia Margaret, *née* Youngman (d 1966); *b* 18 Feb 1952; *Educ* Scarborough HS for Boys, UCL (LLB); *m* 14 June 1975, Harriet Dorothy (Prue), da of George Michael Gee, of Coombe Bissett, Wilts; 2 da (Louise b 1982, Eleanor b 1985); *Career* admitted slr 1976; head of litigation Frere Cholmeley 1988- (articled clerk 1974-76, asst slr 1976, ptnr 1982-); memb: Int Bar Assoc, Holborn Law Soc; memb Law Soc; *Recreations* swimming, photography, travel; *Style—* Roger Steel, Esq; Squirrels Wood, Park Lane, Ashstead, Surrey KT21 1EY (☎ 0372 272083); Frere Cholmeley, 28 Lincoln's Inn Fields, London WC2A 3HH 071 405 7878, fax 071 405 9056)

STEEL, Lady Rosemary Verena Edith; *née* Villiers; posthumous da of late George Herbert Arthur Edward, Lord Hyde (s of 6 Earl of Clarendon, KG, GCMG, GCVO, PC), and Hon Marion Feodorovna Louise Glyn, DCVO (d 1970), er da of 4 Baron Wolverton; raised to the rank of an Earl's da 1956; *b* 29 June 1935,(posthumous); *m* 1959, Richard Hugh Jordan Steel, *qv*, s of Sir Christopher Steel, GCMG, MVO; 2 s (James b 1960, Oliver b 1962), 1 da (Arabella b 1966); *Style—* The Lady Rosemary Steel; The Glebe House, Notgrove, Cheltenham, Glos (☎ 045 15 347)

STEEL, Hon Mrs (Sophia Rose Eileen); *née* Maude; only da of 8 Viscount Hawarden; *b* 20 Jan 1959; *m* 26 June 1982, Timothy Michael Steel, only s of Anthony Steel, of Rock House Farm, Lower Froyle, Alton, Hants; 1 s (Anthony b 1988), 1 da (Isabella b 1984); *Recreations* riding, reading, singing, tennis; *Clubs* Millbrook Golf and Tennis (NY); *Style—* The Hon Mrs Steel; 83 Eaton Terrace, London SW1

STEEL, Vic J; *b* 19 Nov 1938; *Educ* Univ of Liverpool (BA); *Career* salesman rising to dist mangr Crosse & Blackwell Ltd 1960-62, responsible for Vaseline Prods Cheeseborough Ponds Ltd 1962-64, Lyons Bakery 1965-71 (prod mangr, prods gp mangr, mktg gp mangr, mktg dir), Beecham Products 1971-85 (mktg dir Toiletries Div, md Proprietaries Div UK, dir and gen mangr Latin America, vice pres Western Hemisphere, md rising to chm Int Div), md Guiness Beverage Gp Guinness plc 1985-87, currently dir and chm high st subsids Kingfisher plc, currently dir Mansfield Brewery plc; FCIM; *Style—* Vic Steel, Esq; Kingfisher plc, North West House, 119 Marylebone Rd, London NW1 5PX (☎ 071 724 7749, fax 071 724 1160)

STEEL, William Matthew; s of Dr William Steel (d 1964), of Ayr, and Elizabeth Dutch, *née* White (d 1984); *b* 8 June 1933; *Educ* Giggleswick Sch, Univ of Edinburgh (MB ChB); *m* 27 July 1957, Alison Anne, da of William Ramsay Thomson (d 1961), of Dalbeattie; 1 s (Richard b 1961), 1 da (Jane b 1958); *Career* lectr in orthopaedic surgery Univ of Oxford 1967-70, conslt orthopaedic surgn N Staffs Hosps 1970-, reader Sch of Postgrad Med Univ of Keele 1980-; treas Br Orthopaedic Assoc 1985-88, chm Specialist Advsy Ctee of Orthopaedic Surgery 1988-91, memb Jt Ctee of Higher Surgical Trg 1988-91, pres Br Soc for Surgery of Hand 1990; FRCSEd; *Books* Management of Musculoskeletal Problems in the Haemophilias (1972); *Recreations* golf, music, photography; *Clubs* Trentham Golf; *Style—* William Steel, Esq; 11 King St, Newcastle, Staffs ST5 1EH (☎ 0782 618970); Hartshill Orthopaedic Hospital, Stoke on Trent

STEEL, Maj Sir (Fiennes) William Strang; 2 Bt (UK 1938) of Philiphaugh, Co Selkirk, JP (Selkirkshire 1965), DL (1955); eld s of Maj Sir Samuel Strang Steel, 1st Bt (d 1961), by his w Hon Vere Mabel (d 1964), da of 1st Baron Cornwallis; *b* 24 July 1912; *Educ* Eton, RMC Sandhurst; *m* 1941, Joan (d 1982), o da of late Brig-Gen Sir Brodie Haldane Henderson, KCMG, CB; 2 s (1 da decd); *Heir* s, (Fiennes) Michael Strang Steel b 22 Feb 1943; *Career* Maj (ret) 17/21 Lancers (serv 1933-47); convenor Selkirk CC 1967-75; forestry cmmn 1958-73; *Style—* Maj Sir William Strang Steel, Bt, JP, DL; Philiphaugh, Selkirk (☎ 0750 21216)

STEELE, Arthur David McGowan; s of David McGowan Steele (d 1981), of Melbourne, and Agnes Claire, *née* Turner; *b* 16 Dec 1935; *Educ* Geelong Coll, Univ of Melbourne (MB BS); *Career* Active Citizen Military Forces Aust 1954-61, cmmnd Lt 1957; conslt ophthalmic surgn Moorfields Eye Hosp 1976-, author papers on corneal and cataract surgery; treas Ophthalmological Soc of UK 1979-88 (sec 1977-79), hon treas Coll of Ophthalmologists 1988-; Yeoman Worshipful Soc of Apothecaries 1985; FRCS 1971, FRACO 1976, FCOpth 1988; *Books* Cataract Surgery (ed, 1984); *Recreations* music, literature, theatre; *Style—* Arthur Steele, Esq; 62 Wimpole St, London W1M 7DE (☎ 071 637 7400); Moorfields Eye Hospital, City Rd, London EC1V 2PD

STEELE, Hon Mrs (Caroline Mary); *see*: Sargent, Hon Dr

STEELE, John Roderic; CB (1978); s of Harold G Steele (d 1968), of Wakefield, and Doris, *née* Hall (d 1986); *b* 22 Feb 1929; *Educ* Queen Elizabeth GS Wakefield, Queen's Coll Oxford (MA); *m* 22 Sept 1956, (Margaret) Marie, da of Joseph Stevens (d 1963), of Ingleton, Yorks; 2 s (Richard b 1957, David b 1963), 2 da (Alison b 1959, Elisabeth b 1965); *Career* civil serv; asst princ Miny of Civil Aviation 1951-54, private sec to Parly sec 1954-57; princ: Road Tport Div 1957-60, Sea Tport Div 1960-62, shipping policy 1962-64; asst sec shipping policy Bd of Trade 1964-67, cnsllr (shipping) Br Embassy Washington 1967-71, asst sec (Civil Aviation Div) DTI 1971-73; under sec: (Space Div) 1973-74, shipping policy 1974-75; Gen Div Bd of Trade 1975-76, dep sec Bd of Trade 1976-80, dep sec Dept Indust 1980-81, DG (tport) Cmmn of Euro Communities 1981-86; dir P&O Container Line, chm P&O European Transport Service 1989-, memb Dover Harbour Bd 1990-; tport conslt 1986-; FCIT; *Recreations* cricket, tennis, opera; *Clubs* United Oxford and Cambridge, Philippics; *Style—* John Steele, Esq, CB; 7 Kemerton Rd, Beckenham, Kent; Sq Ambiorix 30, BTE 30, 1040 Bruxelles, Belgium; c/o Prisma Transport Consultants, 4 Rue Charles Bonnet Case 269, 1211 Geneve 12, Switzerland

STEELE, Mavis Mary; MBE (1983); da of Alexander McLeod Steele (d 1966), of 45 Kenton Park Ave, Kenton, Harrow, Middx, and Evelyn Violet, *née* Crane (d 1960); *b* 9 Sept 1928; *Educ* Claremont Ave Comp Sch; *Career* int bowler: England Outdoor: singles winner 1961 62 69, pairs winner 1964, 71, triples winner 1968, fours winner 1963-69; Middx: singles winner 1955, 58-59, 1961-62, 1965-70, 1976, 1986; two wood winner 1970-72, 80 pairs winner, 1964, 1967, 1971-72, 1982, 1985; tripples winner 1953, 1968, 1968, 1971, 1973; fours winner 1958, 1963, 1966, 1969, 1976, 1985; Outdoor int 1959-90, Indoor int 1979, 1980, 1981, 1985-91; World Championships NZ singles and pairs Silver medal winner 1973, World Championships Canada fours Gold medal winner and triples Silver medal winner 1973, World Championships Canada fours Gold medal winner and triples Silver medal winner 1981, Cwlth Games Aust triples Bronze medal winner 1982; England indoor: singles winner 1989, two wood triples winner 1989; hon asst sec English Women's Bowling Assoc, hon treas Middx County Women's Bowling Assoc, pres English Women's Indoor Bowling Assoc; *Recreations* bowls; *Clubs* Sunbury Sports Bowls Egham Indoor Bowls; *Style—* Miss Mavis Steele; 45c Woodthorpe Rd, Ashford, Middx TW15 2RP (☎ 0784 259568)

STEELE, Maj-Gen Michael Chandos Merrett; MBE (1972); s of William Chandos Steele (d 1969), of Kingswood, Surrey, and Daisy Rhoda, *née* Merrett (d 1956); *b* 1 Dec 1931; *Educ* Westminster, RMA Sandhurst; *m* 1961, Judith Ann, da of Edward James Huxford, of Grimsby; 2 s (Timothy, Jeremy), 1 da (Elizabeth); *Career* BMRA Welsh Div 1965-67, BM 8 Inf Bde Londonderry 1970-72, CO 22 AD Regt RA 1972-74, GI HQDRA 1974-76, Cmd Artillery Bde 1976-78, BGS Def Sales Organization MOD London 1979-82; Chief Jt Services Liaison Orgn Bonn 1983-86, Col Commandant RA 1988-, Regtl Comptroller RA 1989-; *Recreations* tennis, gardening, walking; *Style—* Maj-Gen Michael Steele, MBE; Elders, Masons Bridge Rd, Redhill, Surrey RH1 5LE (☎ 0737 763982)

STEELE, Prof Raymond; s of William Henry Steele (d 1971), of Southend on Sea, and Madeline Mable, *née* Wilkinson (d 1965); *b* 9 July 1934; *Educ* Univ of Durham (BSc), Loughborough Univ of Technol (PhD, DSc); *m* ; 2 da (Lorna, Susan); *Career* res engr EK Cole 1959-61 (indentured apprentice 1950-55), devpt engr Cossor Radar and Electronics 1961-62, R&D engr Marconi 1962-65; sr lectr: RNC Greenwich 1965-68, Loughborough Univ of Technol 1968-79; scientist Bell Laboratories USA 1979-83, dir Plessey Res Roke Manor 1983-86, prof of communications Univ of Southampton 1983-, md Multiple Access Communications Ltd 1986-; memb DTI Radio Engrg Bd, Euro ed USA IEEE communications magazine; MIEE, SMIEEE, CEng; *Books* Delta Modulation (1975), Digital Communication (contrib, 1986), ed Pentech Press Digital Cellular Radio Series; *Recreations* painting (art), ballroom dancing, music; *Style—* Prof Raymond Steele; Electronic and Computer Science Dept, University of Southampton, Southampton SO9 5NH (☎ 0703 592865, fax 0703 760602); Multiple Access Communications Ltd, Epsilon House, Enterprise Rd, Chilworth Research Centre, Southampton SO1 7NS (☎ 0703 767808, fax 0703 760602)

STEELE, Richard Charles; s of Maj Richard Orson Steele, MBE (d 1984), of Gloucester, and Helen Curtis, *née* Robertson; *b* 26 May 1928; *Educ* Ashburton Coll Devon, Univ Coll of N Wales (BSc), Univ of Oxford; *m* 12 Dec 1956, Anne Freda, da of Hugh White Nelson (d 1978), of New Milton, Hants; 2 s (Richard Hugh b 21 June 1958, John David b 9 Aug 1964), 1 da ((Anne) Mary b 18 Jan 1960); *Career* Gunner 66 Airborne Anti-Tank Regt 1946-48; asst conservator of forests Tanganyika 1951-63, head of Woodland Mgmnt Section Nature Conservancy 1963-72, head of terrestrial and freshwater life sciences NERC 1972-78, head of Div of Scientific Servs Inst of Terrestrial Ecology 1978-80, dir gen Nature Conservancy Cncl 1980-88, conslt in nature conservation and forestry 1988-; memb Cncl: Fauna and Flora Preservation Soc, Nat Tst, Inst of Biology; former pres Inst of Chartered Foresters, memb Southern Advsy Ctee Nat Tst; FICFor 1968, FIBiol 1974, FBIM 1980; *Books* Monks Wood: A Nature Reserve Record (ed 1972); *Recreations* gardening, walking; *Style—* Richard Steele, Esq; Treetops, 20 Deepdene Wood, Dorking, Surrey RH5 4BQ (☎ 0306 883 106)

STEELE, Lt-Col Robert; MBE (1955); s of Robert Steele (d 1969), and Norah Esmé Steele (d 1967); *b* 31 July 1920; *Educ* Marlborough, Freiburg Univ, Sandhurst; *m* 1946, Gyllian Diane, da of Lt-Col Kenneth Greville Williams, OBE (d 1974); 2 s, 1 da; *Career* Grenadier Gds 1939-60, dir Staff Coll Camberley 1956-57, cmd 1 Bn 1957-60, Gentleman-at-Arms HM Body Guard 1969-90 (appointed Harbinger 1987); chm: Boat Showrooms of London 1961-64, Boat Showrooms of Birmingham 1962-66, Speedy Transport (Belgravia) Ltd 1973-82; memb Cncl The Children's Soc 1966-87 (chm 1982-83, vice-chm 1983-84, life vice pres 1987); JP (Hants) 1971-79; *Recreations* shooting, kite flying, collecting Treen; *Clubs* White's, Cavalry and Guards', Pratts; *Style—* Lt-Col Robert Steele, MBE; Church Bottom, Broad Chalke, Salisbury, Wilts SP5 5DS (☎ 0722 780364)

STEELE, Stuart James; s of James Richard Steele (d 1973), of Ealing, London, and Margaret Glass, *née* Leonard (d 1984); *b* 13 Jan 1930; *Educ* Westminster, Trinity Coll Cambridge (MA, MB BChir), Middx Hosp Med Sch; *m* 23 Oct 1965, Jill Westgate, da of Jack Westgate Smith (d 1991), of Watford, Herts; 2 s (Andrew James b July 1968, Alasdair Malcolm b Aug 1970); *Career* Nat Serv Gunner and 2 Lt RA; sr lectr in obstetrics and gynaecology Middx Hosp Med Sch 1969-73; hon conslt: Middx Hosp and the Hosp for Women 1969-, The Margaret Pyke Centre for the Study of Family Planning 1970-; reader in obstetrics and gynaecology: Middx Hosp Med Sch 1973-87, UCL 1987-; dir Dept of Obstetrics and Gynaecology Middx Hosp Med Sch 1973-86, hon conslt UCH 1986-, assoc dir Dept of Obstetrics and Gynaecology UCL 1987-; memb Ctee of Mgmnt Royal Scot Corp, elder Church of Scot; FRCS (1962), FRCOG (1964); *Books* Gynaecology, Obstetrics and the Neonate (1985); *Recreations* gardening, theatre, opera, ballet; *Clubs* RSM; *Style—* Stuart Steele, Esq; Department of Obstetrics and Gynaecology, University College and Middlesex School of Medicine, 86-96 Chenies Mews, London WC1E 6HX (☎ 071 380 9300); The Middlesex Hospital, Mortimer St, London W1N 8AA (☎ 071 387 9433)

STEELE, Tommy; OBE (1979); s of Thomas Walter Hicks (d 1980), and Elizabeth Ellen Bennett (d 1982); *b* 17 Dec 1936; *Educ* Bacon's Sch for Boys Bermondsey; *m* 1960, Ann, *née* Donoughue; 1 da (Emma b 1969); *Career* actor, stage debut Sunderland 1956, London stage debut 1957, New York stage debut 1965; Arthur Kipps in Half a Sixpence (London 1963, New York 1965, film 1967), Hans Andersen in Hans Andersen (London 1974), Don Lockwood in Singin' in the Rain (London 1983 and 1989); *Books* Quincy (1981), The Final Run (1983); *Recreations* squash, painting; *Style—* Tommy Steele, Esq, OBE; c/o ICM Ltd, 388-396 Oxford St, London W1N 9HE (☎ 071 629 8080, fax 071 493 6279)

STEELE-BODGER, Prof Alasdair; CBE (1980); s of Henry William Steele-Bodger, (d 1952), of Lichfield St, Tamworth, Staffs, and Katherine, *née* Macdonald (1983); *b* 1 Jan 1924; *Educ* Shrewsbury, Gonville and Caius Coll Cambridge (BA, MA), Royal Dick Veterinary Coll, Univ of Edinburgh (BSc); *m* 4 Sept 1948, Anne Chisholm, da of Capt Alfred William John Finlayson, RN (d 1957), of Berry Knoll, Burley, Ringwood, Hants; 3 da (Catherine b 1954, Fiona b 1956, Gillie b 1957); *Career* veterinary surgn, gen practice 1948-77, conslt practice 1977-79, prof of veterinary clinical studies Univ of Cambridge 1979-90; dir Bantin & Kingman Ltd 1980; pres Br Veterinary Assoc 1966, pres RCVS 1972, EEC official veterinary expert 1974-; cncl memb Royal Agricultural Soc of Eng 1967-, memb bd of advsrs Univ of London 1984-, memb Home Office Panel of Assessors under Animal (Scientific Procedures) Act 1986-; Cambridge triple blue; MRCVS, FRCVS; *Recreations* walking, fishing, travel; *Clubs* Farmers, Hawks (Cambridge); *Style—* Prof Alasdair Steele-Bodger, CBE; The Bandlands, Clifton Campville, nr Tamworth, Staffs B79 0BE (☎ 082 786 245)

STEELE-PERKINS, Surgn Vice Adm Sir Derek Duncombe; KCB (1966), KCVO (1964); s of Dr Duncombe Steele-Perkins (d 1958), of Honiton, Devon, and Sybil Mary Hill-Jones (d 1953); *b* 19 June 1908; *Educ* Allhallows Sch Rousdon, Royal Coll of Surgns Edinburgh; *m* 1937, Joan (d 1985), da of John Boddan (d 1935), of Heaton Mersey, Lancs; 3 da (Deryn b 1938, Margaret b 1942, Gale b 1944); *Career* joined RN 1932, MO RN 1932-66; sr surgical specialist RN Hosp: Haslar 1939-40, Chatham 1940-44, Sydney 1944-46, Malta 1946-50; MO Royal Cwlth Tours 1951-66, Cmd MO on Staff of C-in-C Portsmouth and med offr in chief RN Hosp Haslar 1961-63, QHS 1961-66, medical dir-gen of the Navy 1963-66, ret as Surgn Vice Adm; FRCS, FRACS, LRCP; *Recreations* sailing, fishing, rugby football; *Clubs* Royal Lymington Yacht (Cdre 1968-71); *Style—* Surgn Vice Adm Sir Derek Steele-Perkins, KCB,

KCVO; 8 The Court, Court Close, Lymington, Hants SO41 8NR (☎ 0590 672 455)

STEELE-WILLIAMS, Kevin; s of Robertus Williams, of Dukinfield, Cheshire (d 1948), and Irene Steele, *née* Budds (d 1983); *b* 18 July 1938; *Educ* St John's C of E Sch Dukinfield, William Hulme's Manchester, Fitzwilliam House Cambridge (BA, MA); *m* 29 Aug 1964, Cicely, da of Edward Twentyman (d 1945); 1 s (Simon Timothy b 1966), 2 da (Nichola Charlotte b 1967, Sophie Louise b 1973); *Career* admitted slr 1966, cmmr for oaths 1972, clerk cmmrs Inland Revenue Altrincham Cheshire and Wythenshawe Manchester 1978-, former ptnr March Pearson & Skelton, currently sr ptnr Sedgley Caldecutt & Co Knutsford; Cambridge Lacrosse blue 1959-61 (toured USA combined Oxford/Cambridge team 1961); tstee (former chm) Ollerton Village Hall Ctee, govr Knutsford County HS; *Recreations* philately, cricket, golf, travel, wine and English cookery; *Clubs* Cambridge Soc; *Style*— Kevin Steele-Williams, Esq; 98 King St, Knutsford, Cheshire (☎ 0565 4234, fax 0565 52711)

STEEN, Anthony David; MP (C) South Hams 1983-; s of Stephen N Steen, of London; *b* 22 July 1939; *Educ* Westminster, Univ of London; *m* Carolyn Padfield; 1 s, 1 da; *Career* social worker, youth ldr; called to the Bar Gray's Inn 1962; fndr dir: Task Force 1964-68, YVF 1968-74; MP Liverpool Wavertree 1974-83; memb Select Ctee Race Relations 1975-79, chm Cons Urban Affrs Ctee 1979-83; vice chm: Social Services Ctee 1979-81, Environment Ctee 1983-86, West Country Members 1987-, Parly Caribbean Gp, Task Force Tst; treas Parly Papua New Guinea Gp; chm: Backbench Sane Planning Ctee, Backbench Urban and Inner City Ctee, Outlandos Tst; memb Parly Population and Devpt Gp; vice pres: Int Centre for Child Studies, Ecology Building Soc, South Hams Young Farmers; memb Cncl: Anglo-Jewish Assoc, Reference Int Cncl for Christian Relief; *Books* New Life for Old Cities (1981), Tested Ideas for Political Success (1983-87), PLUMS (1988); *Clubs* Lords & Commons Cycle; *Style*— Anthony Steen Esq, MP; House of Commons, London SW1A 0AA

STEEN, Martin Gamper; s of Dr Terence Ross Steen (d 1987), and Ingeborg, *née* Gamper; *b* 4 Sept 1954; *Educ* Clifton, Univ of London (LLB); *m* 10 Jan 1977, Charlotte Elizabeth, da of Dr Michael John Goring, of Stanford; 1 s (Michael Terence b 1988), 2 da (Anna Charlotte b 1983, Laura Ingeborg b 1985); *Career* called to the Bar Inner Temple 1976, practising Albion Chambers Bristol 1977-; *Style*— Martin Steen, Esq; Albion Chambers, Broad St, Bristol BS1 1DR (☎ 0272 272144)

STEEN, (David) Michael Cochrane Elsworth; s of Prof Robert Elsworth Steen, MD (d 1981), and Elizabeth Margaret, *née* Cochrane; *b* 5 March 1945; *Educ* Eton, Oriel Coll Oxford (MA); *m* 18 Dec 1971, Rosemary Florence, da of Maj William Bellingham Denis Dobbs; 1 s (Peter b 1977), 3 da (Jane b 1973, Lucy b 1975, Rosalie b 1977); *Career* KPMG Peat Marwick McLintock (formerly Peat Marwick Mitchell & Co) 1968-81 (ptnr 1982-, head of audit servs 1987-90); FCA, ARCM; *Books* Guide to Directors Transactions (1983), Audits & Auditors - What the Public Thinks (1989); *Recreations* music (organ playing), riding, reading; *Clubs* Kildare Street, Carlton, Leander; *Style*— Michael Steen, Esq; Nevilles, Mattingley, Hants RG27 8JU (☎ 025 676 2144); 5 Vicarage Gate, London W8 (☎ 071 937 6558); 1 Puddle Dock, London EC4V 3PD (☎ 071 236 8000, fax 071 248 6552, telex 8811541 PMM LON G)

STEEN, Prof William Maxwell; s of late Stourton William Steen, and Marjorie Gordon, *née* Maxwell; *b* 30 Sept 1933; *Educ* Kingswood Sch Bath, Univ of Cambridge (MA), ICL (PhD); *m* April 1960, Margaret, da of John Thomas Porkess Frankish, of Scunthorpe; 1 s (Philip b 6 Oct 1963), 1 da (Melanie b 6 May 1965); *Career* Nat Serv pilot RAF 1952-54; process engr APV Co Ltd 1958-62, Methodist missionary Soc Bankura Christian Coll India 1962-65, sr lectr ICL 1985 (lectr 1965), James Bibby prof of engrg manufacture Univ of Liverpool 1987-; Freeman City of London 1983, Liveryman Worshipful Co of Goldsmiths; FIM, MIChemE; *Recreations* gardening, swimming, real tennis; *Style*— Prof William Steen; PO Box 147, Liverpool L69 3BX (☎ 051 794 4839/40, fax 051 794 4848, telex 627095)

STEENGRACHT VAN MOYLAND, Mevrouw Jan; Hon Cecily; *née* Somerset; da of 4 Baron Raglan, JP; *b* 10 Aug 1938; *m* 1961, Jonkheer Jan Tewdyr Patrick Steengracht van Moyland, Capt Irish Gds (ret); b 12 March 1933, educ Bradfield; portraitist; memb Cavalry and Guards' Club), yr s of Baron Steengracht van Moyland, of Pant-y-Goitre, Abergavenny; 1 s (Jonkheer Henry Jan Berrington S v M, b 18 Dec 1963), 1 da (Jonkvrouwe Suzanna Cecily S v M, b 3 Nov 1968); *Style*— Mevrouw Jan Steengracht van Moyland; Lanwecha, Llandenny, Usk, Gwent; 14 Addison Ave, London W11 (☎ 071 603 3522)

STEER, Dr Christopher Richard; s of Eric Arthur Steer (d 1975), of Chistlehurst Kent, and Joan, *née* Bowden; *b* 30 May 1947; *Educ* St Olaves GS London, Univ of Edinburgh (BSc, MB ChB, DCH), FRCPEd; *m* 20 Dec 1979 (m dis 1986), Patricia Ann, da of James Gallacher (d 1985); 1 s (Paul Christopher) 1 da (Jane Elizabeth); m 2, 1986, Patricia Mary Lennox; 1 da (Rosemary Gillian); *Career* conslt paediatrician Fife 1983; memb: BMA 1978, Scott Paediatric Soc 1978, Paediatric Res Soc 1978, BPA 1980; FRCPE; *Recreations* gardening; *Style*— Dr Christopher Steer; 14 Bellhouse Rd, Aberdour, Fife KY3 0TL (☎ 0383 860738); Paediatric Department, Victoria Hospital, Hayfield Rd, Kirkcaldy, Fife KY2 5AH (☎ 0592 261155)

STEER, Clive Allen; s of Allan Edwin Steer (d 1986), of Guildford, Surrey, and Majorie, *née* Allen (d 1976); *b* 11 May 1938; *Educ* Northmead Sch Guildford, Royal Aircraft Estab Coll Farnborough, Central Sch of Art & Design London; *m* 24 Feb 1962, Janet, da of Arthur F E Evans, OBE; 1 s (Jonathan b 21 Sept 1967), 3 da (Rebecca b 8 Feb 1966, Georgina b 27 Oct 1970, Jacqueline b 23 Sept 1972); *Career* industl designer; designer GAP Limited (Consultants) London 1960-64, chief industl designer Rediffusion Vision Limited London 1964-69, head of industl design Philips Electrical (UK) Ltd 1969-79, secondment from UK to estab Industrial Design Division Philips Singapore 1979-82, princ Steer Associates (design conslts) 1982-85, sr assoc Business Design Group 1985-89; dir: On the Line Design (conslts) 1989-90, Cumberland Baker Ltd 1990-; speaker on design and mktg at Design Cncl courses; major projects: sr assoc responsible for interior design of Security Pacific Office 1986 and Bank of Boston Office 1987, account dir Ferguson Corporate identity 1990; awards: Design Cncl award for Philips Design Team Product (consumer & contract goods) 1975, 1984 Oscar for Invention and Gold Medal International Exposition of Invention Geneva; former: memb Judging Panel Design Cncl Consumer & Contract Goods Awards, memb Jury Bursary Awards RSA, chm Product Gp (A1) CSD, govr St Martin's Sch of Art; current positions CSD: vice pres, chm Membership Bd, memb Fellowship Bd, memb Cncl; FRSA 1978, FCSD 1979; *Style*— Clive Steer, Esq; Westview, Shere Rd, West Horsley, Leatherhead, Surrey KT24 6EW (☎ 04865 4686); Cumberland Baker Ltd, 5-6 Portman Mews South, London W1H 7AU (☎ 071 493, 1625, fax 071 499 0907)

STEER, Lt-Col Peter Frank; s of Alfred Albert (Peter) Steer, of Bovey Tracey, Devon, and late Gertrude Elizabeth, *née* Murrin (d 1981); *b* 1 May 1933; *Educ* Newton Abbot GS; *m* 21 Aug 1956, Rosina, da of late George William Ethelston, of Oswestry, Salop; 1 s (Martin b 1957), 1 da (Susan b 1960); *Career* cmmnd RA (short serv cmmn) Mons OCS 1952, reg cmmn 1956; Troop Offr 31 Trg Regt RA, 61 Light Regt RA Korea 1953-54, Adventure Trg Instr 64 Trg Regt RA 1954-57, 12 LAA Regt (Adj) BAOR, Regtl Serv 33 Para Light Regt RA and 7 Para Regt RHA Cyprus, Libya, Bahrein and Gulf 1959-83, Canadian Army Staff Coll 1963-65, GS02 (Intelligence) HQ 1Div BAOR 1965-68, cmd 39 (Roberts) Batty of Jr Ldrs Regt RA 1968-69, 7 Para Regt RHA cmd I (Bull's Troop) Batty Malaya and N Ireland 1969-71, Instr Jr Div Staff Coll Warminster 1971-73, Lt-Col and Chief Special Projects HQ Afnorth Oslo 1973, GSOI Review Study Ammunition Rates and Scales MOD 1976, head African Section DI4 Def Int Staff MOD 1976, ret Nov 1979, recalled to serv Dec 1979 as int coordinator mil advsrs staff to Govt of Rhodesia/ Zimbabwe during cease fire and election supervision, ret 1980; conslt reccruitment, gen mangr Securiguard; exec dir Br Schs Exploring Soc 1981- (expdns incl: Greenland 1982-83, Arctic, Norway 1984, Alaska 1985, Papua New Guinea 1987); chm govrs Greenfields Primary Sch Hartley Wintney 1976-90; *Recreations* riding, hill walking, cross country skiing, expeditioning; *Clubs* Special Forces; *Style*— Lt-Col Peter Steer; Nightingales, West Green Rd, Hartley, Wintney, Hants RG27 8RE (☎ 025 126 3688); British Schools Exploring Society, RGS, 1 Kensington Gore SW7 2AR (☎ 071 584 0710)

STEERS, Ian Sydney; s of Sydney Charles Steers (d 1956), and Rosalie Lilian Emily Steers; *b* 11 Sept 1928; *m* 1955, Barbara Joan; 3 s (Austen b 1957, Nigel b 1961, Jeremy b 1964), 1 da (Nicola b 1958); *Career* dir: Tribune Securities, Euro-Clear Clearance Systems plc, United Corporations Ltd, Heronsgate Investmts Ltd, ret; vice-chm Wood Gundy Inc, memb bd of dir of Exec Ctee of Int Primary Mktg Assoc; *Recreations* golf, reading, swimming; *Clubs* National Liberal, City of London, Denham Golf; *Style*— Ian Steers, Esq; Ladywalk, Long Lane, Heronsgate, Rickmansworth, Herts; Wood Gundy Inc, 30 Finsbury Square, London EC2A 1SB (☎ 071 628 4030, telex 886752)

STEFANOU, Stelio H; s of George Stefanou (d 1979), of Surbiton, Surrey, and Katina, *née* Heracleiou; *b* 6 Nov 1952; *Educ* Tiffin GS Kingston upon Thames Surrey, Imp Coll Univ of London (BSc); *m* 3 Sept 1977, Rosemarie Ann, da of Sydney Gordon, of London SE18; *Career* res scientist Johnson Matthey 1974-77, mktg exec Esso UK plc 1977-80, dir John Doyle Construction Ltd 1980-, gp md and chief exec John Doyle Group plc and chm each gp subsid 1987-; memb and gp rep: Confed of Br Industry, Bldg Employers Confed; memb Lighthouse Club; ARCS 1974, FInstD; *Recreations* travel, food, theatre, concerts, opera; *Clubs* IOD; *Style*— Stelio Stefanou, Esq; Potters Bar, Hertfordshire; John Doyle House, Little Burrow, Welwyn Garden City, Herts AL7 2SP (☎ 0707 329 481, fax 0707 328 213)

STEFFENS, Guenter Zeno; OBE; s of Dr jur Guenter Steffens (d 1937), of Berlin, and Ursula Margarete, *née* Lilge (d 1963); *b* 26 Oct 1937; *Educ* Gymnasium Essen Germany, Hermann Lietz Sch Isle of Spiekeroog W Germany; *m* 1 (m dis 1977); 1 s (Christian b 16 July 1965), 1 da (Ursula b 11 May 1964); m 2, 4 Nov 1977, Dorothee Fey Louisa, da of Baron Herbert von Stackelberg (d 1975), of Bonn; *Career* Lt Res W German Luftwaffe 1958-59; Canadian Imperial Bank of Commerce Montreal 1961-62, Swiss Bank Corpn Zurich 1963-64, Credit Commercial de France Paris 1964, Dresdner Bank AG Cologne W Germany 1965-68, gen mangr Dresdner Bank AG London Branch 1968-; chm: German Chamber Indust and Commerce UK 1974-, Foreign Banks Assoc 1978-79, Lombard Assoc 1982-83; Officer's Cross of the Order of Merit of the Federal Repub of Germany 1984; *Clubs* Brooks's, Mid-Atlantic; *Style*— Guenter Z Steffens, Esq, OBE; 30 Thurloe Square, London SW7 2SD (☎ 071 589 5996); Dresdner Bank AG, Dresdner Bank House, 125 Wood St, London EC2 7AQ (☎ 071 606 7030)

STEIN, Christopher Richard (Rick); s of Eric Stein (d 1965), of Cornwall, and Dorothy Gertrude, *née* Jackson; *b* 4 Jan 1947; *Educ* Uppingham, New Coll Oxford (BA); *m* 21 Sept 1975, Jill, da of Jack Newstead; 3 s (Edward b 16 Jan 1979, Jack b 31 Oct 1980, Charles b 14 Sept 1985); *Career* chef and restauranteur; estab (with Jill Stein) The Seafood Restaurant Cornwall 1975-; ratings: 1 Star Egon Ronay Guide, 4/5 Good Food Guide, 1 Rosette AA Guide, Red M Michelin Guide, Black Four Leaf Clover Ackerman Guide; winner Badoit/Decanter Restaurant of the Year award 1989; *Books* English Seafood Cookery (1988, Glenfiddich Food Book of the Year award 1989); *Recreations* surfing; *Style*— Rick Stein, Esq; Trevone House, Trevone, Padstow, Cornwall PL28 8QJ (0841 520504); Seafood Restaurant, Riverside, Padstow PL28 8BY (0841 532485, fax 0841 533344)

STEIN, Cyril; s of late Jack Stein, and late Rebecca, *née* Selner; *b* 20 Feb 1928; *m* 1949, Betty, *née* Young; 2 s, 1 da; *Career* chm and chief exec Ladbroke Group plc; FIOD; *Style*— Cyril Stein, Esq; c/o The Ladbroke Group plc, 10 Cavendish Place, London W1M 9DJ (☎ 071 323 5000, fax 071 436 1300, telex 291268)

STEIN, George Stanley; s of Stephen Stein, and Susan Stein; *b* 23 March 1944; *Educ* Hendon Co GS, UCL (BSc), UCH (MB BS), Kingston Coll, Maudsley Hosp; *m* 27 July 1969, Suzanna Eugenie Siegliende Isabella, da of William Miller (d 1979); 2 s (Benjamin b 5 June 1979, Joseph b 3 Sept 1983); *Career* RCPsych Bronze medal 1980, sr lectr in psychiatry KCH 1981; conslt psychiatrist: Bromley AHA 1981, res centres and post natal depression; author pubns on triptophan metabolism in the maternity blues, asst ed Br Jl of Psychiatry; MRCP, MRCPsych; *Recreations* music; *Style*— George Stein, Esq

STEIN, Keith Peter Sydney; s of Victor Stein (d 1984), and Pearl Stein; *b* 27 July 1945; *Educ* Preston Manor GS, Univ of Leeds (BA), LSE (MSc); *m* 13 Dec 1970, Linda, da of Michael Collins (d 1976); 1 s (Jonathan), 1 da (Nicole); *Career* sr operational res Int Wool Secretariat 1968-70; Unigate Mgmnt Servs Div and Foods Div 1971-76: sr conslt, ops mangr, div planning mangr, special projects dir, commercial accountant, ptnr and nat dir; mgmnt consultancy 1977-86, strategic mgmnt Arthur Young 1986-89, sr ptnr Ernst & Young mgmnt conslts 1989-; FCMA 1976, MIMC 1981; *Recreations* cricket (county, schools and univ), soccer, table tennis, golf, skiing, bridge; *Style*— Keith Stein, Esq; Valley View, Rasehill Close, Rickmansworth, Herts WD3 4EW (☎ 0923 779134); Becket House, 1 Lambeth Palace Road, London SE1 7EU (☎ 071 931 3972, fax 071 928 1345, telex 885234 ERNSLOG)

STEIN, Prof Peter Gonville; JP (1970); s of Walter Oscar Stein (d 1967), of London and Montreux, and Effie Drummond, *née* Walker (d 1969); *b* 29 May 1926; *Educ* Liverpool Coll, Gonville and Caius Coll Cambridge (MA, LLB), Collegio Borromeo Pavia, Univ of Aberdeen (PhD); *m* 1, 22 July 1953 (m dis 1978), Janet Mary, da of Clifford Chamberlain (d 1969), of Manor House, Desborough, Northants; 3 da (Barbara b 1956, Penelope b 1959, Dorothy b 1960); m2, 16 Aug 1978, Anne Mary Howard, da of Harrison Sayer (d 1980), of Seven Dials, Saffron Walden, Essex; *Career* joined RN 1944, Japanese translator 1945, Sub-Lt (sp) RNVR 1945-47; slr of the Supreme Ct 1951; dean Faculty of Law Univ of Aberdeen 1961-64 (prof of jurisprudence 1956-68); Univ of Cambridge: regius prof of civil law and fell of Queens' Coll 1968- (vice pres 1974-81), chm Faculty Bd of Law 1973-76, fell Winchester Coll 1976-; memb: Bd of Mgmnt Royal Cornhill and Assoc (Mental) Hosps 1963-68 (chm 1967-68), Sec of State for Scotland's Working Pty on Hosp Endowments 1966-69, Univ Grants Ctee 1971-75; pres Soc of Pub Teachers of Law 1980-81, memb US-UK Educnl Cmmn (Fulbright) 1985-91; Hon Dr Juris Göttingen 1980; Hon Dott Giur Ferrara 1991; FBA 1974; foreign fell: Accademia di Scienze Morali e Politiche (Naples) 1982, Accademia Nazionale dei Lincei (Rome) 1987; corresponding fell Accademia degli Intronati (Siena) 1988; *Books* Fault in the Formation of Contract in Roman Law and Scots Law (1958), Regulae Iuris: From Juristic Rules to Legal Maxims (1966), Legal Values in Western Society (with J Shand, 1974), Adam Smith's Lectures on Jurisprudence (jt ed, 1978), Legal Evolution (1980), Legal Institutions, the Development of Dispute Settlement (1984), The Character & Influence of the Roman Civil Law: Historical Essays (1988), The Teaching of Roman Law in 12th Century England (with late F de Zulueta, 1991),

Notaries Public in England since the Reformation (ed and contrib, 1991); *Style*— Prof Peter Stein, JP; Wimpole Cottage, Wimpole Rd, Great Eversden, Cambridge CB3 7HR (☎ 0223 262349); Queens' College, Cambridge CB3 9ET (☎ 0223 335569)

STEIN, Richard Jonathan Beaver; s of Leonard Jaques Stein, OBE (d 1973), of 1 Temple Gardens, Middle Temple Lane, London, and Sarah Kitay Stein; *b* 9 Dec 1934; *Educ* Rugby, Pembroke Coll Cambridge (MA); *m* 12 May 1987, Alison Margaret, da of George William Yule (d 1969), of Sevenoaks, Kent; *Career* Nat Serv 1956-58 (jr under offr at Officer Cadet Sch, 2 Lt RE, asst adj of Regt); trainee engr Baker Perkins Ltd 1958-59, articled clerk rising to qualified CA Howard Howes & Co Chartered Accountants 1959-63, mangr Corp Fin Dept Samuel Montagu & Co Ltd 1964-68, jt chief fin offr and dir Fin Ops Reckitt & Colman Ltd 1973-74 (PA to chm 1968-70, asst dir Corp Planning 1970-73, treas 1973), chief fin offr The BOC Group 1975-80, fin dir BOC Limited 1980-86; non-exec dir: Richard Clay plc 1985-86, UDT Holdings Ltd and United Dominions Trust Ltd 1986, Datastream plc 1984, gp fin dir Standard Chartered plc 1986-; currently dir: Standard Chartered Bank, Standard Chartered plc; external memb Fin and Gen Purposes Ctee London Sch of Hygiene and Tropical Medicine 1982-86, memb Ctee of Mgmnt The Robert Fleming Property Unit Tst 1983-; FCA 1974, FCT 1981; *Style*— Richard Stein, Esq; 1 Aldermanbury Square, London EC2V 7SB (☎ 071 280 7017, fax 071 588 5685)

STEIN, Ronald Max; s of Harry Stein (d 1962), of London, and Frances Stein; *b* 24 Nov 1927; *Educ* City of London, Marlborough Coll, Magdalen Coll, Brackley, Christ's Coll Finchley, St Martin's Sch of Art; *m* 21 Sept 1958, Rosalie, da of Cesar Landau (d 1968), of London; 2 da (Val b 26 Feb 1961, Viv b 16 Dec 1964); *Career* RAF 1946-48, Missing Res and Enquiry Serv Italy and Austria, RAF Exhibitons and Displays Park Lane; Leon Goodman Displays London 1944, asst to Art Dir Royds Advertising Agency 1945-55, studio mangr Stowe & Bowden Advertising Agency 1955-59, illustrator The Diabetic Cook Book 1956, designer Eve Club Souvenir Brochure 1959, princ Ronald Stein Advertising Consultancy 1959-, publicity conslt Guild of Glass Engravers 1979-90; Guild of Glass Engravers catalogue St Lawrence Jewry Exhibition 1986; memb: Periodical Proprietors Assoc, Audit Bureau of Circulations, Creative Circle, Publicity Club of London; assoc MInstD; *Recreations* opera, classical music, photography, sketching, international and current affairs; *Clubs* Publicity of London; *Style*— Ronald Stein, Esq; 11 Cleve Rd, W Hampstead, London NW6 3RH (☎ 071 624 8781)

STEINBERG, Prof Hannah; da of late Dr Michael Steinberg, and Marie, *née* Wein; *Educ* Putney HS, Queen Anne's Sch Caversham, Univ of Reading, Denton Secretarial Coll, UCL (BA, PhD); *Career* sec to md Omes Ltd; UCL 1954-: lectr in pharmacology (formerly asst lectr), reader in psychopharmacology, prof in psychopharmacology (first in Western Europe) and head of psychopharmacology gp 1970-; hon consltg clinical psychologist Dept of Psychological Med Royal Free Hosp 1970, visiting prof in psychiatry McMaster Univ Ontario 1971; vice pres: Collegium Internationale Neuro-Psychopharmacologicum 1968-74, Br Assoc for Psychopharmacology 1974-76 (hon memb 1988); convener Academic Women's Achievement Gp 1979-, special tstee Middx Hosp 1988-; memb Editorial Bd: British Journal of Pharmacology 1965-72, Psychopharmacologia 1965-80 Pharmacopsychoecologia 1987-; memb: MRC Working Parties, Experimental Psychological Soc, Br Pharmacological Soc, Assoc for Study of Animal Behaviour, Soc for Study of Addiction, Euro Behavioural Pharmacology Soc (fndr memb 1986), Euro Coll of Neuro-Psychopharmacology (fndr memb 1987); chartered psychologist, fell Br Psychol Soc, distinguished affiliate American Psychol Assoc Div of Psychopharmacology 1978; *Books* Animals and Men (trans and jt ed, 1951), Animal Behaviour and Drug Action (jt ed, 1963), Scientific Basis of Drug Dependence (1968), Psychopharmacology: Sexual Disorders and Drug Abuse (jt ed, 1972); author of numerous scientific and semi-popular articles on pharmacology, physical exercise and mental Health; *Style*— Prof Hannah Steinberg; University College London, Gower Street, London WC1E 6BT (☎ 071 387 7050, 071 380 7232)

STEINBERG, Jack; s of Alexander Steinberg (d 1957), and Sophie Steinberg; *b* 23 May 1913; *Educ* privately, London; *m* 1938, Hannah Anne, da of Solomon Wolfson, JP (d 1941); 2 da; *Career* underwriting memb of Lloyds, pres Steinberg Group (now Alexon Group) 1982-85 (chm 1966-81); memb Nat Econ Devpt Ctee 1966-78, vice pres Br Knitting and Clothing Export Cncl 1984- (chm 1970-78), chm King's Med Res Tst; Freeman City of London, memb Worshipful Co of Plumbers; *Clubs* Brooks's, Portland, Carlton; *Style*— Jack Steinberg, Esq; 74 Portland Place, London W1 (☎ 071 580 5908)

STEINBERG, Dr (Victor) Leonard; s of Nathan Steinberg (d 1947), of London, and Sarah, *née* Bardiger; *b* 26 Aug 1926; *Educ* Shoreham GS, Regent Street Poly, St Bart's Hosp (MB BS, DPhysMed); *m* 25 Jan 1953, Leni, da of Max Ackerman (d 1964), of London; 3 s (Nathan Anthony b 28 Nov 1953, Michael John b 8 Feb 1955, Stephen David b 30 Jan 1960); *Career* conslt rheumatologist: Enfield Gp of Hosps 1959-67, Central Middx Hosp 1960-, Wembley Hosp 1967-; former pres section of rheumatology RSM, pres London Jewish Med Soc; memb: Br Soc of Rheumatology, Harveian Soc of London, Br Med Acupuncture Soc; Freeman City of London, Liveryman Worshipful Soc of Apothecaries of London, BMA, FRCP (London), FRCP (Edinburgh); *Recreations* swimming, walking, opera, theatre; *Clubs* RAC; *Style*— Dr Leonard Steinberg; 22 Holne Chase, London N2 (☎ 081 458 27264); 39 Devonshire Place, London W1 (☎ 071 935 9365)

STEINCKE, Steen; s of Mogens Steincke, of London, and Birte, *née* Bruun (d 1982); *b* 17 Nov 1948; *Educ* Univ of Copenhagen (LLB), Business Sch of Copenhagen (BCom), INSEAD (CEDEP); *m* 7 August 1971, Ebba; 2 da (Anita b 15 Aug 1973, Julie b 30 Sept 1976); *Career* Den Danske Bank Copenhagen 1974-80, gen mangr Danish Banking Dir Scandinavian Bank Ltd 1980-82, sr vice pres i/c funding Nordic Investment Bank Helsinki 1982-83, pres Den Danske Bank London 1983-86, md i/c banking & asset mgmnt Hafnia Trust & Investment Bank Copenhagen 1986-90, jt chief exec Hafnia Holdings (UK) Ltd and md Prolific Financial Management plc 1990-; *Recreations* swimming, tennis; *Clubs* The Danish Club; *Style*— Steen Steincke, Esq; Flat 4, Crown Lodge, 12 Elystan St, London SW3 (☎ 071 823 7226); 18 Nobisvej, 3460 Birkerod, Denmark (☎ 45 821 380); Prolific Financial Management plc, Walbrook House, 23 Walbrook, London EC4N 8LD (☎ 071 280 3700, fax 071 283 8877)

STEINER, Prof George; s of F G Steiner (d 1968), and E Steiner (d 1981); *b* 23 April 1929; *Educ* Paris (BésL), Univ of Chicago (BA), Univ of Harvard (MA), Univ of Oxford (DPhil), Univ of Cambridge (PhD); *m* 7 July 1955, Zara; 1 s (David b 1958), 1 da (Deborah b 1960); *Career* memb staff the Economist London 1952-56, Inst for Advanced Study Princeton 1956-58, Gauss lectr Princeton 1959-60, fell Churchill Coll Cambridge 1961; lectures: Massey 1974, Leslie Stephen Cambridge 1986, W P Ker Univ of Glasgow 1986, Page Barbour Univ of Virginia 1987; Fulbright professorship 1958-69, O Henry short story award 1958, Guggenheim fellowship 1971-72, prof of English and comparative literature Univ of Geneva 1974-; Zabel award of Nat Inst of Arts and Letters of the US 1970, Faulkner Stipend for Fiction PEN 1983, Gifford Lectr 1990, corresponding memb Germany Academy, hon memb American Acad of Arts and Sciences, Legion d'Honneur, doctorate hc Univ of Louvain 1980; Hon DLitt Univs of: East Anglia 1976, Bristol 1989, Glasgow 1990, Liège 1990; FRSL 1964; *Books* Tolstoy or Dostoevsky (1958), The Death of Tragedy (1960), Anno Domini (1964), Language and Silence (1967), Extraterritorial (1971), In Bluebirds Castle (1971), The Sporting Scene: White Knights in Reykavik (1973), After Babel (1975), Heidegger (1978), On Difficulty and other Essays (1978), The Portage to San Cristabal of AH (1981) Antigones (1984), George Steiner, a reader (1984), Real Presences (1989); *Recreations* chess, music, hill walking, old english sheepdog; *Clubs* Athenaeum, Savile, Harvard Club of NYC; *Style*— Prof George Steiner

STEINER, Jeffrey Josef; s of Beno Steiner, and Paula Borstein; *b* 3 April 1937; *Educ* Bradford Inst of Technol Bradford, Yorkshire, London Univ City and Guild; *m* 1, 1957 (m dis 1970), Claude; 1 s (Eric 25 Oct 1961), 2 da (Natalia b 14 Sept 1965, Thierry Tama Tama (foster) b 31 Dec 1970); m 2, 6 March 1976 (m dis 1983), Linda, *née* Schaller; 1 s (Benjamin b 3 April 1978), 1 da (Alexandra b 1980); m 3, 19 March 1987, Irja, *née* Eckerbrant Bonnier; *Career* mangr Metals and Controls Div Texas Instruments 1959-60 (mgmnt trainee 1958-59), pres Texas Instruments 1960-66 (Argentina, Brazil, Mexico, Switzerland, France), pres Burlington Tapis 1967-72, chm and pres Cedec SA Engrg Co 1973-84, chm, pres and chief exec offr Banner Industs Inc (now known as The Fairchild Corporation) 1985- (a NY Stock Exchange Co); hon consul gen of Costa Rica; chm Bd of Govrs Univ of Haifa; memb: Anti-Defamation League, Boys Town of Italy, Montefiore Med Centre; *Recreations* tennis, sailing, art collecting; *Clubs* Annabel's, Polo of Paris, Racing de France, Harry's Bar, St James's, Mark's; *Style*— Jeffrey Steiner, Esq; 6 Cheyne Walk, London SW3; The Fairchild Corporation, 110 East 59th St, NY 10022 USA (☎ 212 3086 and 703 4785805, fax 212 888 5674, telex 971 391 BNR)

STEINER, Prof Robert Emil; CBE (1979); s of Rudolf Steiner (d 1958), of Vienna, and Clary, *née* Nördlinger (d 1921); *b* 1 Feb 1918; *Educ* Theresiamische Academie and Franz Josephs Realgymnasium Vienna, Univ of Vienna, Univ Coll Dublin (MB, ChB, MD); *m* 17 March 1945, Gertrude Margaret, da of Fritz Konirsch (d 1943), of Castlebar, Co Mayo, Ireland; 2 da (Hilary Clare b 1950, Ann Elizabeth b 1953); *Career* WWII; MO Emergency Med Serv: Guys Hosp 1941, Macclesfield Infirmary 1941-42, Winwick Emergency Hosp 1942-44; trainee diagnostic radiologist Sheffield Royal Infirmary 1944, dir Dept of Diagnostic Radiology Hammersmith Hosp 1957-60 (dep dir 1950-57); prof of diagnostic radiology: Dept of Diagnostic Radiology Hammersmith Hosp, Univ of London, Royal Postgrad Med Sch 1960-83 (emeritus prof 1984-); pres: Br Inst of Radiology 1972-73, Royal Coll of Radiologists 1977-79; formerly: dep chm Nat Radiological Protection Bd, civilian conslt radiology to med dir gen (Naval), conslt advsr in radiology to Dept of Health; Hon: FACR 1965, FCRA 1971, FFR, RCSI 1972; DMR 1945, FRCR 1948, FRCP 1965, FRCS 1982; author of over 250 scientific pubns and 5 books; *Recreations* gardening, swimming, walking, music; *Clubs* Hurlingham; *Style*— Prof Robert Steiner, CBE; 12 Stonehill Rd, East Sheen, London SW14 8RW (☎ 081 876 4038); NMR Unit, University of London, Hammersmith Hospital, Du Cane Rd, London W12 OHS (☎ 081 740 3298, 081 743 2030)

STEINER, Rear Adm (Ottakar Harold Mojmir) St John; CB (1967); s of Ferdinand Steiner (d 1961), and Alice Mary Dorothea, *née* Whittington (d 1964); *b* 8 July 1916; *Educ* St Pauls; *m* 1, 1940 (m dis 1974), Evelyn Mary, da of Henry Thomas Young; 1 s (Anthony St John b 1942), 1 da (Angela St John b 1948); m 2, Edith Eleanor Powell, wid of Sqdn Ldr J A F Powell; 1 step s (Jonathan Powell b 1955); *Career* joined RN 1934; served 1935-44: HMS Frobisher, HMS Orion, HMS Southampton, HMS Electra, HMS Courageous, HMS Ilex, HMS Havelock; sqdn torpedo offr HMS Superb 1945-47, staff of C-in-C Far East 1948-50, naval staff Admty 1950-52, exec offr HMS Ceylon 1953-54, exec offr HMS Daedalus 1955-56, naval staff Admty 1956-57, Capt 3 Destroyer Sqdn and CO HMS Saintes 1958-59, NA to UK High Cmmr Canada 1960-62, Capt HMS Centaur 1963-65, asst chief Def Staff 1966-68; ADC to HM The Queen 1965; chm: Whitbread Round the World Races 1972-78, Transglobe Expedition 1979-80, Shipwrecked Fisherman and Mariners Royal Benevolent Soc; cdre RNSA 1974-76 (life vice-cdre 1978); Freeman City of London 1966, memb Worshipful Co of Coachmakers and Coach Harness Makers 1966; *Recreations* sailing, golf, bowls, garden; *Style*— Rear Adm O St John Steiner, CB

STEINFELD, Alan Geoffrey; QC (1986); s of Henry C Steinfeld (d 1967), of London, and Deborah, *née* Brickman; *b* 13 July 1946; *Educ* City of London Sch, Downing Coll Cambridge (BA, LLB); *m* 19 Feb 1976, Josephine Nicole, da of Eugene Gros, of London; 2 s (Martin b 28 Jan 1980, Sebastian b 1 Nov 1981); *Career* barr Lincoln's Inn 1968; *Recreations* lawn tennis, skiing, opera, cinema, lying in Turkish baths; *Clubs* RAC, Cumberland Lawn Tennis; *Style*— Alan Steinfeld, Esq, QC; 29 Boundary Road, St John's Wood, London NW8 OJE (☎ 071 624 8995); Jardin des Hesperides, Antibes, France; 24 Old Buildings, Lincoln's Inn, London WC2 (☎ 071 404 0946, fax 071 405 1360)

STEINFELD, Michael Robert; *b* 3 Dec 1943; *Educ* William Ellis Sch London, Pembroke Coll Oxford (BA); *m* 28 May 1980, Elizabeth Ann, *née* Watson; 2 da (Rebecca Hannah b 25 Feb 1981, Jemimah Francine b 15 Oct 1983); *Career* Titmuss Sainer & Webb: articled clerk 1968-70, asst slr 1970-72, ptnr 1972-; memb Law Soc; *Recreations* sport, food, cinema, newspapers, music, France; *Style*— Michael Steinfeld, Esq; Titmuss Sainer & Webb, 2 Serjeants' Inn, London EC4Y 1LT (☎ 071 583 5353, fax 071 353 3683)

STELL, Christopher Fyson; OBE (1989); s of Herbert Stell (d 1967), of Liverpool, and Caroline Irene, *née* Fyson (d 1982); *b* 26 Jan 1929; *Educ* Liverpool Coll, Univ of Liverpool (BArch, MA); *m* 17 Aug 1957, Dorothy Jean, da of Wilfred Hugh MacKay (d 1986), Havant, Hants; 2 s (John b 1958, Edward b 1962); *Career* conslt Royal Commission on Historical Monuments Eng 1989- (architectural investigator 1955-89); numerous contribs to learned jls; hon vice pres Royal Archaeological Inst; hon sec: Ancient Monuments Soc, The Chapels Soc; memb: Churches Ctee Eng Heritage, Pubns Ctee Soc of Antiquaries, Timberwork Sub-Ctee Cncl for the Care of Churches; ARIBA 1956, FSA 1964; *Books* An Inventory of Nonconformist Chapels and Meeting-Houses in Central England (1986); *Recreations* book binding, photography; *Clubs* Athenaeum; *Style*— Christopher Stell, Esq, OBE; Frognal, 25 Berks Hill, Chorleywood, Herts WD3 5AG (☎ 0923 28 2044); Hob Lane House, Brearley, Luddendenfoot, Halifax, Yorks HX2 6JF; Royal Commission on Historical Monuments (England), Newlands House, 37-40 Berners St, London W1P 4BP (☎ 071 631 5021)

STELLA-SAWICKI, Dr Marek Andrzej; s of Jan Stella-Sawicki (d 1984), of Poland, and Stanislawa, *née* Lissowska; *b* 21 Feb 1948; *Educ* Henry Jordan Sch, Tech Univ Cracow (MSc), King's Coll London (PhD); *m* 27 July 1974, Teresa, da of Capt Antoni Witczak (d 1973), of London; 2 da (Dominika Helena b 1976, Joanna Jadwiga b 1978); *Career* sr systems engr United Biscuits (McVities) Ltd 1975-78, sr projects engr Metal Box PLC 1978-82, projects engrg mangr Computer Field Maintenance Ltd 1982-85, gen mangr DPCE Computer Servs PLC 1985-86, dir engrg ops MBS PLC 1986-88, chief exec and md Computacenter Maintenance Ltd 1988-; conslt Cover Pubns 1976-79, ed Video World 1979-81, publishing dir and ed dir Video Press 1981-85; sponsorship: W Middx Lawn Tennis Club, Video Press Falklands Appeal; FIEE; memb Cncl: Engrg Inst, AFSM USA; *Books* Investigation into Computer Modelling Simulation and Control of the Stirling Engine (1978), Video A-Z (10 vols, 1981-83), A-Z of Personal Computers (10 vols, 1983-86), Which Appliance (2 edns, 1984-86); *Recreations* skiing, shooting, tennis, target shooting (Bisley); *Clubs* Hurlingham, Leander, West Middx Lawn Tennis, 1 Ealing Rifle and Pistol, Nat Rifle Assoc; *Style*—

Dr Marek Stella-Sawicki; Widecombe Lodge, 2 Brentham Way, Ealing, London W5 1BJ (☎ 081 997 4848); Computacenter Maintenance Limited, 8 Woodshots Meadow, The Croxley Centre, Watford, Herts WD1 8YU (☎ 0923 55255, fax 0923 247637, car 0836 681567)

STEMBRIDGE, David Harry; QC (1990); s of Percy Gladstone Stembridge (d 1959), of Droitwich, and Emily Winifred, *née* Wright; *b* 23 Dec 1932; *Educ* Bromsgrove, Univ of Birmingham (LLB); 2 April 1956, Theresa Cecilia, da of Max Furer, of Mulhouse, France; 3 s (Michael b 1957, Peter b 1960, Philip b 1968), 1 da (Helen b 1963); *Career* called to the Bar Gray's Inn 1955, in practice Midland and Oxford Circuit, rec Crown Ct 1977-; *Recreations* organ, sailing; *Clubs* Bar Yacht; *Style—* David Stembridge, Esq, QC; 5 Fountain Ct, Steelhouse Lane, Birmingham B4 6DR (☎ 021 236 5771, fax 021 236 2358)

STEMMER, Philip; s of Emanuel Stemmer, of 21 Parkway, London, and Regina Stemmer; *b* 12 Dec 1949; *Educ* Manchester Jewish GS, Turner Dental Sch Manchester (BDS, represented Univ of Manchester soccer team); *m* 22 Dec 1976, Elissa, da of Myer Freedman; 3 da (Shiri Debra b 12 Aug 1979, Daniella Civia b 15 Dec 1981, Natalie Ruth b 30 Nov 1985); *Career* dental surgn; gen practice (with Phillip Wander) Manchester 1974-76, opened new practice Manchester 1976-84, opened branch practice Droylsden 1982-84, practised in Israel 1984-86 (affiliated to Periodontal Dept Tel Aviv Dental Sch), in private practice Harley St 1986-, owned practice North Finchley 1987-89; distinctions in: pharmacology, orthodontics, oral med, prosthetics; memb: BDA, Alpha Omega, Dental Post Grad Soc of Manchester, Insight Gp; rep Lancs Chess Team 1964 (at board 4 out of 7); *Recreations* swimming, music (opera, cantorial, good modern), chess; *Style—* Philip Stemmer, Esq; 96 Harley St, London W1N 1AF (☎ 071 935 7511/0407, mobile 0831 115406)

STENHAM, Anthony William Paul (Cob); s of Bernard Basil Stenham (d 1972); *b* 28 Jan 1932; *Educ* Eton, Trinity Coll Cambridge (MA); *m* 1, 1966 (m dis), Hon Sheila Marion, *qv*, da of 1 Baron Poole, CBE, TD, PC; m 2, 1983, Anne Martha Mary O'Rawe; 2 da (Polly Elizabeth Josephine b 1986, Daisy Constance b 1990); *Career* chartered accountant and called to the Bar Inner Temple 1954; chm Wiggins Teape Appleton plc 1991-; Bankers Trust Co: md NY, chm Europe Middle East and Africa 1986-90; dep chm VSEL Consortium plc 1986, fin dir Unilever plc and Unilever NV 1970-86, chm ICA 1977-88; dir: Equity Capital for Industry 1976-81, William Baird & Co 1964-69, Capital Radio 1982-, Virgin Group plc 1986-89, The Rank Organisation plc 1987-, Colonial Mutual Life Assurance Group 1987-, Unigate plc 1989, STC plc 1990-; Philip Hill Higginson Erlanger 1962-64, Price Waterhouse 1955-61; govr Architectural Assoc 1982-87, chm Cncl and pro-provost Royal Coll of Art 1979-81 (memb Court 1978-, hon fell 1980); memb: Bd of Govrs Museum of London 1986-, govr Theatres Tst; FCA 1958, FRCA 1980, FRSA 1982; *Recreations* cinema, contemporary art; *Clubs* Turf, Whites; *Style—* Cob Stenham, Esq; 4 The Grove, Highgate, N6 (☎ 081 340 2266, office 071 839 7505)

STENHOUSE, Sir Nicol; s of late John Stenhouse; *b* 14 Feb 1911; *Educ* Repton; *m* 1951, Barbara Heath Wilson (d 1991); 2 s, 1 da; *Career* chm and md Andrew Yule & Co Ltd Calcutta 1959-62; pres Bengal C of C and Indust (Calcutta) and assoc C of C of India 1961-62; kt 1962; *Style—* Sir Nicol Stenhouse; 3 St Mary's Court, Sixpenny Handley, nr Salisbury, Wilts SP5 5PH

STENLAKE, Prof John Bedford; CBE (1985); s of Frank Stenlake (d 1940), of Ealing, London, and Blanche, *née* Bedford (d 1969); *b* 21 Oct 1919; *Educ* Ealing GS, Birkbeck Coll Univ of London (BSc), Sch of Pharmacy Univ of London (PhD, DSc); *m* 14 July 1945, Anne Beatrice, da of Frank Douglas Holder, OBE, MC, JP (d 1978), of Chelmsford; 5 s (Timothy b 1946, Robert b 1948, Christopher b 1951, William b 1953, Richard b 1957), 1 da (Marion b 1961); *Career* WWII RAF Flt Lt 1942-45; Boots The Chemist 1935-39; demonstrator, asst lectr; lectr in pharmaceutical chemistry Sch of Pharmacy Univ of London 1945-52, sr lectr in pharmaceutical chemistry Royal Coll of Sci and Technol Glasgow 1952-61, prof of pharmacy Univ of Strathclyde 1961-82 (hon prof 1982-); inventor of atricurium besylate (Tracium) muscle relaxant used in surgical anaethesia (Queens award for Technol Innovation); memb: Ctee on Safety Meds 1970-79, Lanarkshire Health Bd 1977-83; leader UK delgn to the Euro Pharmacopoeia Cmmn 1980-88, chm Br Pharmacopoeia Cmmn 1980-88 (memb 1963-, vice chm 1978-80), memb Meds Cmmn 1984-; Hon DSc Univ of Strathclyde 1988; CChem, FRSC, FRSE, FRPharmS; *Books* author of several reviews, papers and articles concerned with original res in medicinal and pharmaceutical chemistry; Practical Pharmaceutical Chemistry (with A H Beckett, 1962), Foundations of Molecular Pharmacology (1979), Burger's Medicinal Chemistry (4 edn, 1980), Handbook of Experimental Pharmacology (vol 49, 1986), Medicinal Chemistry, The Role of Organic Chemistry in Drug Research (1986); Foundations of Molecular Pharmacology (1979); *Recreations* reading, gardening; *Clubs* Royal Commonwealth Society; *Style—* Prof John Stenlake, CBE; Mark Corner, Twynholm, Kirkcudbright DG6 4PR (☎ 05576 242); University of Strathclyde, George St, Glasgow G1 1X9 (☎ 041 552 4400)

STENNING, Christopher John William (Kit); s of Col Philip Dives Stenning, of Sunnyside, Elie, Fife, and Cynthia Margaret, *née* Rycroft; *b* 16 Oct 1950; *Educ* Marlborough; *m* 19 Sept 1981, Ruth Marian, da of George Thomas Chenery Draper; 1 s (Jonathan b 1985), 1 da (Rachel b 1983); *Career* slr 1970-82, slr to Prudential Corp 1982-88, dir corp fin David Garrick 1988-90, proprietor Kit Stenning Assocs 1990-; Freeman: City of London 1971, Worshipful Co of Haberdashers 1971; *Books* The Takeover Guide (1988); *Recreations* sport; *Clubs* Hurlingham; *Style—* Kit Stenning, Esq

STENSON, Roger; s of Frederick Stenson (d 1982), of Nottingham, and Mary Agnes, *née* Bagshaw (d 1987); *b* 6 Feb 1936; *Educ* Mundella GS Nottingham, Keble Coll Oxford (MA); *m* 22 July 1960, Janet Elisabeth, da of John Collins McCall (d 1962), of Bookham, Surrey; 2 s (Benjamin James b 22 Oct 1963, Jules Angus b 22 April 1966), 1 da (Kate b 15 Aug 1962); *Career* Nat Serv sr aircraftman RAF 1955-57; md BSG Computer Servs 1977-83, dir mgmnt serv Boots Co plc 1983-87, AGM servs Norwich Union 1987-; FBCS; *Recreations* orienteering, bridge; *Style—* Roger Stenson, Esq; Norwich Union Insurance Gp, 8 Surrey St, Norwich NR1 3NG (☎ 0603 682886)

STEPHEN, Alexander Moncrieff Mitchell; s of Sir Alexander Murray Stephen (d 1974), whose family were shipbuilders 1750-1968, and Katherene Paton, *née* Mitchell (d 1978); *b* 5 March 1927; *Educ* Rugby, Univ of Cambridge (BA); *m* 24 Sept 1954, Susan Mary, *née* Orr, da of James George Orr Thomson (d 1950); 1 s (Graham b 1956); 3 da (Alice d 1959, Susannah b 1960, Alexandra d 1985); *Career* served RN petty offr 1945-48; shipbuilder mainly with Alexander Stephen & Sons Ltd 1951-68 (md 1968), chm Polymer Scotland 1973-; dir: Murray Income Trust plc, Murray Ventures plc, Murray Management Ltd, Murray Johnstone Holdings Ltd, Murray Johnstone Ltd, Murray Smaller Market Trust plc, MJ Finance Ltd, Murray International Trust plc, Scottish Widows' Fund and Life Assurance Society; *Recreations* sailing, shooting, skiing; *Clubs* Western, Royal Northern and Clyde Yacht, Mudhook Yacht (Adm 1984-90), Kandahar Ski; *Style—* Alexander Stephen, Esq; Ballindalloch, Balfron, Stirlingshire (☎ 0360 40202)

STEPHEN, (John) David; s of John Stephen (d 1968), and Anne Eileen Stephen; *b* 3 April 1942; *Educ* Luton GS, King's Coll Cambridge (BA, MA), Univ of Essex (MA); *m* 28 Dec 1968, Susan Dorothy, da of W C G Harris, of Barnstaple, Devon; 3 s (John b 1972, Edward b 1977, Alexander b 1982), 1 da (Sophy b 1974); *Career* Runnymede Tst 1970-75 (dir 1973-75), Latin American regnl rep Int Univ Exchange Fund 1975-77, special advsr to Sec of State for Foreign and Cwlth Affrs 1977-79, freelance writer and conslt 1979-84, memb Gen Mgmnt Bd and dir of corporate rels Cwlth Devpt Corpn 1984-; Parly candidate (Alliance) N Luton 1983 and 1987; *Style—* David Stephen, Esq; 123 Sundon Rd, Harlington, Beds LU5 6LW (☎ 05255 4799); CDC 1 Bessborough Gardens, London SW1 (☎ 071 828 4488, fax 071 828 6505)

STEPHEN, Col George McLaughlin; OBE (1979); s of Dr George Mackie Stephen (d 1951), and Charlotte Baron, *née* McLaughlin (d 1963); *b* 12 May 1938; *Educ* Epsom Coll Epsom Surrey; *m* 1, 26 July 1963 (m dis 1988), Caroline Barbara, *née* Grotrian; 1 s (Aidan Diarmid Grotrian b 3 Sept 1970); m 2, 25 May 1988, Rozanne Shirley, da of Col M P Robinson OBE, TD, DL, of Carleton Lodge, Carleton, W Yorks; *Career* Nat Serv Seaforth Highlanders and Cameronians (Scottish Rifles) 1957-68, Scots Greys 1968-71 (psc RMCS 1972), Scots Dragoon Guards 1971-78 (NDC 1978), Col and CO 13/18 Royal Hussars RAC 1978-81, exchange offr Cmd and Staff Coll Aust 1981-84, Col MOD 1984-88; memb and chief exec Int League for Protection of Horses; memb: cncl Nat Equine Welfare, BHS, BFSS; Queens Body Gd Scot 1987; Hante Dignitaire D'Honneur Grande Chancellerie Int de l'ordre Equestre de Saint Georges de France; *Recreations* riding, shooting, reading, art, music; *Clubs* Cavalry and Guards; *Style—* Col George Stephen, OBE; Overa Farm, Larling, Norfolk (☎ 0953 717 309, fax 0953 717 411)

STEPHEN, Dr (George) Martin; s of Sir Andrew Stephen, KB (d 1980), of Sheffield, and Frances, *née* Barker; *b* 18 July 1949; *Educ* Uppingham, Univ of Leeds (BA), Univ of Sheffield (DipEd, DPhil); *m* 21 Aug 1971, Jennifer Elaine, da of George Fisher, of Polloch Lodge, Polloch, Invernesshire; 3 s (Neill b 26 July 1976, Simon b 31 Aug 1978, Henry b 20 March 1981); *Career* various posts in remand homes 1966-71, teacher of English Uppingham Sch 1971-72, housemaster and teacher of Eng Haileybury Sch and ISC 1972-83, second master Sedbergh Sch 1983-87, headmaster The Perse Sch 1987-; assoc memb of the room Gonville & Coll 1988-; memb HMC 1987-; *Books* An Introductory Guide to English Literature (1982), Studying Shakespeare (1982), British Warship Designs Since 1906 (1984), English Literature (1986), Sea Battles in Close Up (1987), Never Such Innocence (1988), The Fighting Admirals (1990); *Recreations* sailing, fishing, rough shooting, writing, theatre; *Clubs* East India Devonshire Sports & Public School (hon memb); *Style—* Dr Martin Stephen; 80 Glebe Rd, Cambridge CB1 4SZ (☎ 0223 247 964); The Perse Sch, Hils Rd, Cambridge CB2 2QF (☎ 0223 248 127)

STEPHENS, Air Cmdt Dame Anne; DBE (1961, MBE 1946); da of late Gen Sir Reginald Byng Stephens, KCB, CMG; *b* 4 Nov 1912; *Educ* privately; *Career* joined WAAF 1939; WRAF: inspr 1952-54, dep dir 1954-57, dir 1960-63; Hon ADC to HM The Queen 1960-63; *Style—* Air Cmdt Dame Anne Stephens, DBE; The Forge, Sibford Ferris, Banbury, Oxfordshire (☎ 029 578 452)

STEPHENS, Aylwin Kersey (Kerry); s of Sidney Stephens (d 1969), of Dorking, Surrey, and Joan, *née* Kelsey; *b* 16 Jan 1947; *Educ* Truro Sch Cornwall; *m* 1, 28 Nov 1978, Lorraine Naomi Tomlinson (d 1986); m 2, 14 July 1990, Emma Frances Catherine Griffiths, da of Colin Brook; *Career* articled clerk J Hulbert Grove & Co 1964-69; Deloitte Plender & Griffiths (later Deloitte & Co, then Deloitte Haskins & Sells) 1969-85: corporate and int tax specialist, ptnr London Tax Dept 1978, resigned partnership 1985; in private practice specialising in corporate and int tax 1985-87; readmitted ptnr Reading Office Deloitte Haskins & Sells (now Coopers & Lybrand Deloitte) 1987-; FCA 1969; *Recreations* work, walking, good hotels, 50's rock 'n' roll, 16th century; *Style—* Kerry Stephens, Esq; Coopers & Lybrand Deloitte, 9 Greyfriars Rd, Reading, Berkshire RG1 1JG (☎ 0734 607724, fax 0734 607701)

STEPHENS, Brian John; s of George Henry Stephens, of Southampton, and Marie Stephens; *b* 14 Dec 1946; *Educ* King Edward VI GS Southampton; *m* 5 April 1968, Rosemary Ann; 1 s (Marc b 1969), 1 da (Paula b 1970); *Career* BBC: engr 1965, studio mangr 1967, radio prodr 1977, ed of progs Radio 2 1991- (sr prodr 1986); tstee Mother Christmas Charity; *Recreations* cycling, reading, cooking, music on CD; *Style—* Brian Stephens, Esq; Broadcasting House, London W1A 1AA (☎ 071 927 5872)

STEPHENS, Cedric John; s of Col James Edward Stephens (d 1974), of Truro, Cornwall, and Hilda Emily Stephens (d 1972); *b* 13 Feb 1921; *Educ* Univ of London (BSc); *Career* transmission devpt engr STC 1945-51, def research RARDE Fort Halstead and RAE Farnborough 1951-60, dir (Space) Miny of Aviation 1961-64, memb Cncl (chm Tech Ctee) Euro Launcher Devpt Orgn 1962-64, chm Tech Ctee Euro Orgn on Satellite Communications 1964, IDC 1965, dir Signals Res and Devpt Estab MOD 1966-67, chief scientist and dir gen Res Home Office 1969-73 (chief scientific advsr 1967-69), memb Def Scientific Advsy Cncl, chm Civil Serv Engrg Graduate Selection Bds 1973-75, memb Electronics Divnl Bd IEE 1973, dir Exford (Highcliffe) Ltd 1987-; called to the Bar Gray's Inn 1971; memb: Forensic Sci Soc, Hon Soc Grays Inn; CEng, FIEE, FRAeS; *Recreations* playing viola; *Style—* Cedric Stephens; 6 Newlyn Rd, Welling, Kent DA16 3LH; 7 Exeter Court, Wharncliffe Rd, Christchurch, Dorset BH23 5DF; The Athenaeum, Pall Mall, London SW1 (☎ 081 856 1750)

STEPHENS, Lt-Col Charles Frederick Byng; s of Brig Frederick Stephens, CBE, DSO (d 1967), of Ivy Farm, Farringdon, Hants, and Esme Mackenzie, *née* Churchill (d 1987); *b* 12 Nov 1940; *Educ* Haileybury, RMA Sandhurst; *m* 3 Aug 1971, Helen Anne, da of Lt Cdr Sir Godfrey Style, CBE, DSC, RN; 2 da (Alexandra b 1973, Georgina b 1976); *Career* cmmnd Welsh Gds 1961; served: Germany, Aden, Hong Kong; Lt-Col 1983; *Recreations* fishing, hunting, music; *Clubs* Cavalry and Guards'; *Style—* Lt-Col Charles Stephens; Brook House, Amport Andover, Hants (☎ 026477 2635); Headquarters Welsh Guards, Wellington Barracks, London (☎ 071 930 4466 3288)

STEPHENS, Dr John David; s of Sydney Brooke Stephens (d 1982), and Thora Gladys Stephens; *b* 9 April 1944; *Educ* Highfields GS Wolverhampton, Guy's Hosp Med Sch (MB BS, MD); *m* 19 July 1967 (m dis 1976) Amanda; 1 s (Damian b 1 Nov 1969); *Career* house physician and surgn Royal Surrey Co Hosp Guildford 1967-68, house surgn Guy's Hosp 1968-69, house physician Churchill Hosp Oxford 1969-70, registrar in med UCH 1970-72, registrar in cardiology Brompton Hosp 1972-73 (house physician 1970), res fell in cardiology Harvard Univ Med Sch Boston USA 1973-74, sr registrar in cardiology St Bartholomew's Hosp 1974-81, conslt cardiologist Old Church Hosp Romford and London Hosp 1981-; author of pubns in various int med jls on original res in coronary blood flow and congestive heart failure; memb Br Cardiac Soc; MRCP 1970; *Books* Cardiovascular Responses to Vasodilators in Man (1979); *Recreations* squash, opera; *Style—* Dr John Stephens; 29 Devonshire Place, London W1 (☎ 071 637 5881)

STEPHENS, John Lindsay; s of Rev Grosvenor Stephens, of 9 Leasingham Gardens, Bexhill on Sea, E Sussex, and Olive, *née* Voysey-Martin (d 1987); *b* 23 July 1951; *Educ* Christ's Hosp, Lanchester Poly (BA); *m* 30 Aug 1975, Nicola Elizabeth (Nikki), da of Neville Brouard, of Les Eturs, Catel, Guernsey, CI; 1 s (David b 1982), 1 da (Joanna b 1980); *Career* admitted slr 1977; ptnr Simmons and Simmons; memb: Nat Tst, Residents Action Gp WABF, Weald of Kent Preservation Soc, Law Soc; *Recreations* family, music, food and wine, photography, tennis, fitness training; *Clubs* Frittenden Tennis; *Style—* John Stephens, Esq; 14 Dominion St, London EC2M 2RJ (☎ 071 628 2020, fax 071 588 4129, telex 888562 SIMMON G)

STEPHENS, Prof Kenneth Gilbert; s of George Harry Stephens (d 1972), and Christiana, *née* Jackson (d 1986); *b* 3 May 1931; *Educ* Bablake Sch Coventry, Univ of Birmingham (BSc, PhD); *m* 7 Dec 1957 (m dis 1980), Miriam Anne, da of Tom Sim, of Newbury, Berks; 1 s (Ian b 1963), 1 da (Jane b 1961); m 2, Elizabeth Carolynn, da of Howard Jones, of Oxted, Surrey; *Career* res physicist AEI Aldermaston 1955-62, chief physicist Pye Laboratories Cambridge 1963-66; Univ of Surrey: lectr 1966-67, reader 1967-78, prof 1978-, head of dept of electronic and electrical engrg 1983-; govr Royal GS 1977-, chm Blackheath CC; author various articles on ion implantation of materials in scientific jls; FInstP 1972, FIEE 1979; *Recreations* cricket, gardening, music, reading; *Clubs* MCC; *Style—* Prof Kenneth Stephens; 10 Brockway Close, Merrow, Guildford, Surrey GU1 2LW (☎ 0483 575 087); Dept of Electronic and Electrical Eng, Univ of Surrey, Guildford GU2 5XH (☎ 0483 509 135, fax 0483 34 139, telex 859331)

STEPHENS, Malcolm George; CB (1991); s of Frank Ernest, and Annie Mary Janet, *née* Macqueen; *b* 14 July 1937; *Educ* St Michael and All Angels and Shooters Hill GS, St John's Coll Oxford (Gasberd scholar, BA); *m* 5 Dec 1975, Lynette Marie, da of John Patrick Caffery (d 1972); *Career* Dip Serv: joined 1953, Ghana 1959-62, Kenya 1963-65, Exports Credits Guarantee Dept 1965-82, princ 1970, seconded to Civil Service Staff Coll as dir of economics and social admin courses 1971-72, asst sec 1974, estab offr 1977, under sec 1978, head project gp 1978-79, princ fin offr 1979-82; int fin dir Barclays Bank International 1982, export fin dir and dir Barclays Export Servs with Barclays Bank 1983-87, Inst of Credit Mgmnt; pres Int Union of Credit and Investmt Insurers (Berne Union); memb: Overseas Projects Bd 1985-87, British Overseas Trade Bd 1987; chief exec Export Credits Guarantee Dept Ctee Barclays Bank 1987-; FIB, Fell Inst of Export; *Recreations* gardening, reading; *Clubs* Overseas Bankers, Travellers'; *Style—* Malcolm Stephens, Esq, CB; 111 Woolwich Road, Bexleyheath, Kent DA7 4LP (☎ 081 303 6782); ECGD, PO Box 272, Export House, 50 Ludgate Hill, London EC4M 7AY (☎ 071 382 7004)

STEPHENS, His Honour Judge (Stephen) Martin; QC (1982); s of Abraham Stephens (d 1977), of Swansea, and Freda, *née* Ruck; *b* 26 June 1939; *Educ* Swansea GS, Wadham Coll Oxford (MA); *m* 1965, Patricia Alison, da of Joseph Morris (d 1981), of Nottingham; 1 s (Richard b 1966) and 1 s decd, 1 da (Marianne b 1971); *Career* barr 1963-86, circuit judge 1986-; *Recreations* theatre, cricket; *Style—* His Honour Judge Stephens, QC; c/o The Law Courts, Cathays Park, Cardiff

STEPHENS, Meic; s of Herbert Arthur Lloyd Stephens (d 1984), of Pontypridd, and Alma, *née* Symes; *b* 23 July 1938; *Educ* Pontypridd Boys' GS, UCW Aberystwyth (BA), Univ of Rennes (DipFrench), Univ Coll of N Wales Bangor (DipEd); *m* 14 Aug 1965, Ruth Wynn, da of Rev John Ellis Meredith (d 1981), of Aberystwyth; 1 s (Huw b 1981), 3 da (Lowri b 1966, Heledd b 1968, Brengain b 1969); *Career* teacher of French Ebbw Vale GS 1962-66, journalist Western Mail Cardiff 1966-67, lit dir Welsh Arts Cncl 1967-90; ed journalist literary conslt 1990-; hon fell St David's Univ Coll Lampeter 1986; ed Poetry Wales 1965-73; memb: The Kilvert Soc, The Radnorshire Soc, The Hon Soc of Cymmrodorin London; chm Rhys Davis Tst; memb Lit Panel The Br Cncl London; hon memb White Robe Gorsedd of Bards 1976; *Books* Triad (1963), Writers of Wales (75 vols, 1970-), Artists in Wales (3 vols, 1971/73/77), The Welsh Language Today (1973), Exiles All (1973), Linguistic Minorities in Western Europe (1976), Green Horse (ed, 1978), The Curate of Clyro (ed, 1983), The Oxford Companion to the Literature of Wales (1986), A Book of Wales (1988), A Dictionary of Literary Quotations (1989), The Bright Field (ed, 1991); *Style—* Meic Stephens, Esq; 10 Heol Don, Whitchurch, Cardiff (☎ 0222 623359)

STEPHENS, Prof Michael Dawson; s of Walter Nicholas Stephens (d 1973), of Treleigh, and Margaret Edith Ailene Knight (d 1978); *b* 24 Sept 1936; *Educ* Truro Sch, The Johns Hopkins Univ (MA), Univ of Leicester (MEd), Univ of Ediburgh (PhD); *m* 2 Sept 1961, Margaret, da of John Heap, of Euxton; 1 s (David Trethowan b 1965), 2 da (Caroline b 1963, Fiona b 1967); *Career* Nat Serv Ll 1955-57; res fell The John Hopkins Univ 1960-62, demonstrator Univ of Edinburgh 1962-64, head of Adult Educn Division Univ of Liverpool 1966-74 (lectr 1964-66), Robert Peers prof of adult educn Univ of Nottingham 1974-89, over 70 articles in jls; pres Educational Centres Assoc, chm various nat adult educn orgns; FRGS 1961, FRSA 1984; *Books* incl: Teaching Techniques in Adult Education (jt ed, 1971 and 1974), Scientific and Technical Education in Nineteenth Century England (with G W Roderick, 1972), Education and Industry in the Nineteenth Century (with G W Roderick, 1978), Higher Education for All? (co ed, 1980), Post School Education (with G W Roderick, 1984), Culture, Education and the State (ed, 1988), The Education of Armies (ed, 1989), Adult Education (1990), Japan and Education (1991), Education and the Future of Japan (1991); *Recreations* walking the dog, collecting, reflecting; *Clubs* Light Infantry; *Style—* Prof Michael Stephens; 32 Thackeray's Lane, Woodthorpe, Nottingham NG5 4HQ (☎ 0602 262656); University of Nottingham, University Park, Nottingham NG7 2RD (☎ 0602 484848, fax 0602 420825, telex 37346 UNINOTG)

STEPHENS, Rev Prof (William) Peter; s of Alfred Cyril William Joseph Stephens (d 1942), of Prenton, Penare Rd, Penzance, and Jennie Eudora, *née* Trewavas (d 1983); *b* 16 May 1934; *Educ* Truro Sch, Univ of Cambridge (MA, BD), Univ of Strasbourg (Docteur es Sciences Religieuses), Univ of Lund, Univ of Münster; *Career* asst tutor in Greek and New Testament Hartley Victoria Coll Manchester 1958-61, methodist minister Nottingham and univ chaplain 1961-65, minister Shirley Church Croydon 1967-71, Ranmoor chair in church history Hartley Victoria Coll Manchester 1971-73 (Fernley Hartley lectr 1972), Randles chair in historical and systematic theol Wesley Coll Bristol 1973-80, James A Gray lectr Duke Univ N Carolina 1976, res fell Queen's Coll Birmingham 1980-81 (lectr in church history 1981-86, Hartley lectr 1982), prof of history Univ of Aberdeen 1986- (dean Faculty of Divinity 1987-89); memb Bristol City Cncl 1976-83; *Books* The Holy Spirit in the Theology of Martin Buber (1970), Faith and Love (1971), Methodism in Europe (1981), The Theology of Huldrych Zwingli (1986); *Recreations* tennis, squash, skiing, hill-walking, theatre, opera; *Style—* The Rev Prof Peter Stephens; Department of Church History, University of Aberdeen, King's College, Old Aberdeen AB9 2UB (☎ 0224 272383)

STEPHENS, Philip Francis Christopher; s of Haydn Stephens, of London, and Teresa, *née* Martin; *b* 2 June 1953; *Educ* Wimbledon Coll, Worcester Coll Oxford (BA); *Partner* Patricia Jean Hemingway; 1 da (Jessica Rose b 24 Nov 1989); *Career* asst ed Europa Publications 1974-76, ed Commerce International 1976-79, corr Reuters London and Brussels 1979-83, political ed Financial Times 1988- (econs corr 1983-88); Fulbright fell; *Style—* Philip Stephens, Esq; Financial Times, 1 Southwark Bridge, London SE1 (☎ 071 873 3000, House of Commons Press Gallery 071 219 4380)

STEPHENSON, (Robert) Ashley Shute; MVO (1979), LVO (1989); s of James Stephenson (d 1960), and Agnes Maud, *née* Shute (d 1983); *b* 1 Sept 1927; *Educ* Heddon-on-the-Wall Sch, Walbottle Secdy Sch; *m* 21 May 1955, Isabel, da of Edward Dunn (d 1960); 1 s (Ian Ashley b 1964), 1 da (Carol b 1959); *Career* bailiff The Royal Parks 1980-89; freelance gardening corr; some radio and TV appearances; memb Ctee: The London Children's Flower Soc, The Royal Gardeners Benevolent Fund, Rotten Row 300'; memb RHS Floral A Ctee; pres Br Pelargonium and Geranium Soc, chm S East in Bloom Ctee, judge Britain in Bloom, landscape conslt Trusthouse Forte 1989-; MIHort; *Books* The Garden Planner (1981); *Recreations* golf, walking, reading, gardening; *Clubs* Arts; *Style—* Ashley Stephenson, Esq, MVO; 17 Sandore Rd, Seaford, East Sussex BN25 3PZ (☎ 0323 891050)

STEPHENSON, Maj Charles Lyon; TD; s of Col Charles E K Stephenson (d 1971), and Nancy Barbara, *née* Lyon; *b* 15 Aug 1935; *Educ* Eton; *m* 1, 1 March 1960, Margot Jane, da of J Tinker (d 1941); 2 s (George b 1962, Rupert b 1964); 1 da (Belinda b 1963); m 2, 17 Sept 1974, Sarah Merryweather, da of Lt-Gen The Lord Norrie (d 1977), of Berks; *Career* 9 Queens Lancers 1954-55, TA The Yorks Yeo (Maj 1956-68), Maj The Royal Yeo 1969-72 (Sherwood Ranger Sqdn); co dir MD Stephenson Blake (Hldgs) Ltd, non-exec dir Carlton Main Brickworks Ltd; High Sheriff Derbyshire 1984-85; pres Bakewell Agric Show 1980; *Recreations* shooting, fishing, gardening; *Clubs* Cavalry and Guards, MCC, The Sheffield; *Style—* Maj Charles Stephenson, TD; The Cottage, Great Longstone, Derbyshire DE4 1UA (☎ 062987 213); Broombank Road, Chesterfield SA1 9Q5 (☎ 0246 451592)

STEPHENSON, (Robert Noel) David; OBE; s of Capt Arthur Charles Robert Stephenson, MC (d 1965), and Margaret, *née* Smyth (d 1975); *b* 10 June 1932; *Educ* Loretto Sch; *m* 19 Nov 1966, Heather June, da of George Weatherston, of Gosforth, Newcastle upon Tyne; 2 s (Mark b 8 June 1968, John b 3 Oct 1972), 1 da (Julia b 27 July 1969); *Career* CA 1955, Peat Marwick Mitchell Canada 1956-60, Scottish & Newcastle Breweries Ltd 1960-91; bd memb: Tyne & Wear Enterprise Tst 1983-91, Theatre Royal Tst, Tyneside Trg and Enterprise Cncl 1989-91; chm Area Manpower Bd N Tyne 1984-88, Tyneside Stables Project Ltd 1985-91; govr: Loretto Sch, Newcastle-upon-Tyne Poly 1988-91; memb Cncl Univ of Newcastle-upon-Tyne 1984-88; FCA 1960; *Recreations* golf, fishing, gardening; *Clubs* Hon Co of Edinburgh Golfers; *Style—* David Stephenson, Esq, OBE; Newton Low Hall, Felton, Northumberland NE65 9LD (☎ 066 575 617)

STEPHENSON, Franklyn Dacosta; s of Leonard Bruce Young Stephenson, of Barbados, and Violet Stephenson; *b* 8 April 1959; *Educ* St John Baptist Mixed Sch, Samuel Jackman Prescod Poly; *m* 2 April 1981, Julia, da of Clement Ebenezer Josiah Benjamin; 3 da (Ophelia Amanda b 20 Oct 1981, Kathlyn Orissa b 6 Sept 1983, Katrina Alicia Tamara b 1 Nov 1990); *Career* professional cricketer; debut Barbados under 19 level St Vincent 1977 (winner's youth title 1978), W Indies youth tour England 1979 (highest wicket-taker), first class debut Tasmania v Melbourne (took 10 wickets and voted man of the match), Royton 1980 (winner's Central Lancs League), Rawtenstall 1981-82 (winner's Lancs League both seasons), English first class debut Gloucestershire CCC 1982 (7 appearances), full debut Barbados 1982 (scored 165 in first innings), Oldham 1983-84 (record 146 wickets 1983), Fleetwood 1985-86 (winners: Northern league 1985, Lancs knock-out 1986), Greemount 1987 (runners-up Bolton league); Nottingham CCC 1988-: awarded county cap 1988, completed double of 1018 runs and 125 wickets 1988, player of the year 1988; Britannic Assurance player of the year 1988, Notts sportsman of the year 1988, Wetherell award for all-rounder of the year Cricket Soc 1988, Walter Lawrence Swanton trophy for first bowler to take 100 wickets 1980; represented Barbados in Regnl Golf Championships 1986 and 1987, professional golf tournaments 1988-; *Style—* Franklyn Stephenson, Esq; Nottinghamshire CCC, Trent Bridge, Nottingham NG2 6AG (☎ 0602 821525)

STEPHENSON, Geoffrey Charles; s of Edmund Charles Stephenson, and Hilda Rose, *née* Bates; *b* 19 Aug 1943; *Educ* Bromley GS; *m* 3 Sept 1966, Margaret, da of Frank Wirth (d 1989); 1 s (Alistair James b 2 May 1974), 2 da (Louise Elizabeth b 26 March 1970, Rebecca Dorothy b 8 Feb 1972); *Career* Legal and General Assurance Society Ltd 1964-72; called to the Bar Grays Inn 1971, ad eundem Lincoln's Inn; chm Sundridge Park Lawn Tennis and Squash Rackets Club; FCII; *Recreations* sport; *Clubs* Sundridge Park Lawn Tennis and Squash Rackets, British Sub-Aqua; *Style—* Geoffrey Stephenson, Esq; 8 New Square, Lincolns Inn, London WC2 (☎ 071 242 4986, fax 071 406 1166, car 0836 775 208)

STEPHENSON, Prof Geoffrey Michael; s of Maurice Stephenson (d 1958), of Kenton Harrow Middx, and Laura, *née* Sharp (d 1975); *b* 16 April 1939; *Educ* Harrow County GS, Univ of Nottingham (BA, PhD); *m* 1, 14 April 1962 (m dis 1981), Marguerite Ida, da of James Lindsay (d 1986), of Kettering; 1 s (Lawrence James b 1963), 1 da (Katherine b 1965); m 2, 9 July 1982 (m dis 1987) Gillian Sarah, da of Geoffrey Wade, of Cheadle Hulme; m 3, 10 Jan 1989, Jennifer Ann, da of Frederick Williams, of St Mellon, Cardiff; 1 s (David Field William b 1989); *Career* res psychologist Balderton Hosp 1960-61, lectr in psychology Univ of Keele 1962-66, reader in psychology Univ of Nottingham 1976-78 (lectr 1966-74, sr lectr 1974-76), prof and dir of Social and Applied Psychology Res Unit Univ of Kent Canterbury 1978- (dir Inst of Social Psychology 1986-); ed: Br Jl of Social Psychology 1978-84, Social Behaviour Int Jl 1986-; memb: Br Psychological Soc 1960- (chm Social Psychology Section 1977-80), Euro Assoc of Experimental Social Psychology 1972-(pres 1984-87); chm: IBA Advertising Advsy Ctee 1988-, Ind Television Cmmn Advertising Advsy Ctee 1991-; FBPsS 1980-; *Books* The Development of Conscience (1966), The Social Psychology of Bargaining (with Ian Morley, 1976), Industrial Relations: A Social Psychological Approach (with CJ Brotherton, 1978), Progress in Applied Social Psychology Vols 1 and 2 (jtly, 1981 and 1983), Environmental Social Psychology (jt ed, 1988), Introduction to Social Psychology: A European Perspective (jt ed, 1989); *Recreations* sailing, music (violin playing), cooking; *Clubs* LSO, Kent CCC; *Style—* Prof Geoffrey Stephenson; Institute of Social and Applied Psychology, The University, Canterbury, Kent (☎ 0227 764000, telex 965449, fax 0227 763674)

STEPHENSON, Sir Henry Upton; 3 Bt (UK 1936), of Hassop Hall, Co Derby, TD; s of Lt-Col Sir (Henry) Francis Blake Stephenson, 2 Bt, OBE, TD, JP, DL; *b* 26 Nov 1926; *Educ* Eton; *m* 1962, Susan, da of Maj J E Clowes; 4 da; *Heir* 1 cous, Timothy Stephenson; *Career* High Sheriff of Derbyshire 1975; late Capt Yorkshire Yeo; dir Stephenson Blake (Holdings) Ltd and Thos Turton & Sons Ltd; *Style—* Sir Henry Stephenson, Bt, TD; Tissington Cottage, Rowland, Bakewell, Derbyshire

STEPHENSON, Prof (James) Ian Love; s of James Stephenson (d 1979), of Hunwick, Bishop Auckland, and May, *née* Emery (d 1966); *b* 11 Jan 1934; *Educ* Blyth GS, Univ of Durham (BA); *m* 3 Jan 1959, Kate, da of James Robert Brown (d 1987), of Ponteland; 1 s (Stephen b 1964), 1 da (Stella b 1970); *Career* studio demonstrator King's Coll Newcastle upon Tyne (pioneered first modern art fndn course in UK) 1957-58, Boise Sch Italy 1959, visiting lectr Poly Sch of Art London 1959-62, visiting painter Chelsea Sch of Art 1959-66, dir fndn studies Dept of Fine Art Univ of Newcastle (first perceptual and conceptual syllabus) 1966-70, dir postgrad painting Chelsea Sch of Art 1970-, int course ldr Voss Summer Sch 1979, vice pres Sunderland Arts Centre 1982-, first specialist advsr CNAA 1980-83, fine art advsr Canterbury Art Coll 1974-79, RA steward Artists Gen Benevolent Inst 1979-80; memb: Visual Arts Panel Northern Arts Assoc Newcastle 1967-70, Fine Art Panel NCDAD 1972-74, Perm Ctee New Contemporaries Assoc (revived annual nat student exhibitions) 1973-75, Fine Art Bd CNAA 1974-75, sr postgrad examiner Univ of London 1975-83, Advsy Ctee Nat Exhibition of Childrens' Art Manchester 1975-, Working Pty RA Jubilee Exhibition 1976-77, Selection Ctee Arts Cncl Awards 1977-78, Painting Faculty Rome and Abbey Major Scholarships 1978-82, Recommending Ctee Chantrey Bequest 1979-80, Boise Scholarship Ctee UCL 1983; chm Ctee David Murray Studentship Fund 1990, former examiner at various polytechnics; exhibitions incl: Br Painting in the

Sixties London 1963, Mostra di Pittura Contemporanea Amsterdam and Europe (Int Marzotto European prizewinner) 1964-65, 9o Biennio Lugano 1966, 5e Biennale and 18e Salon Paris 1967, recent Br painting London and world tour 1967-75, Junge Generation Grossbritannien Berlin 1968, Retrospective Newcastle 1970, La Peinture Anglaise Aujourd'hui Paris 1973, Elf Englische Zeichner Baden Baden and Bremen 1973, Recente Britse Tekenkunst Antwerp 1973, 13a Bienal Sao Paulo and Latin America 1975, Arte Inglese Oggi Milan 1976, Retrospective London and Bristol 1977, Englische Künst der Gegenwart Bregenz 1977, Br Painting 1952-77 London 1977, Color en la Pintura Britanica Rio de Janeiro and Latin America 1977-79, Abstract Paintings from UK Washington 1978, Retrospective Birmingham and Cardiff 1978, Royal Acad of Arts Edinburgh 1979-80, Art Anglais d'Aujourd'hui Geneva 1980, Br Art 1940-80 London 1980, Colour in Br Painting Hong Kong and Far East 1980-81, Contemporary Br Drawing Tel Aviv and Near East 1980-82, The Deck of Cards Athens and Arabia 1980-82, A Taste of Br Art Today Brussels 1982, Arteder Muestra Internacional Bilbao 1982, La Couleur en la Peinture Britannique Luxembourg and Bucharest 1982-83, Int Print Biennales Bradford 1982 (also 1984 and 1986), 15a Bienale Ljubljana 1983; illustrations: Cubism and After (BBC film) 1962, Contemporary Br Art 1965, Private View 1965, Blow Up (MGM film) 1966, Art of Our Time 1967, Recent Br Painting 1968, Adventure in Art 1969, In Vogue 1975, Painting in Britain (1525-1975) 1976, Br Painting 1976, Contemporary Artists 1977 (also 1983 and 1989), Contemporary Br Artists 1979, Tendenze e Testimonianze 1983; work in collections incl: Birmingham Bristol and Leeds City Art Galleries, Tate Gallery, Gulbenkian Foundation, Madison Art Center, V & A and Welsh Nat Museums; ARA 1975-86, RA 1986; hon memb: Mark Twain Soc 1978-, Accademia Italia 1980-, CAS 1980-81; *Style*— Prof Ian Stephenson; Chelsea School of Art, Manresa Rd, London SW3 6LS (☎ 071 351 3844)

STEPHENSON, His Hon Judge Jim; s of Alexander Stephenson (d 1958), of Heworth, Co Durham, and Norah Stephenson (d 1988); *b* 17 July 1932; *Educ* Royal GS Newcastle upon Tyne, Exeter Coll Oxford (BA); *m* 1964, Jill Christine, da of Dr Edward William Lindeck, of Yew Tree Cottage, Fairwarp, Sussex; 3 s; *Career* barr; rec Crown Ct 1974, circuit judge North-Eastern circuit 1983-; *Recreations* history, walking, music; *Clubs* Durham Co; *Style*— His Hon Judge Stephenson; Newcastle upon Tyne Crown Court, Quayside, Newcastle upon Tyne NE1 3LA (☎ 091 201 2000)

STEPHENSON, Joan, Lady; Joan; eld da of Maj John Herbert Upton, JP, Lord of the Manor of Flamborough, by his 1 w Hilda (3 da of Horace Trelawny, of Shotwick Park, Chester); *b* 20 April 1901; *m* 1925, Lt-Col Sir Francis Stephenson, 2 Bt, OBE, TD, JP, DL (d 1982); 1 s (Sir Henry Stephenson, 3 Bt, *qv*); *Style*— Joan, Lady Stephenson; Hassop Green, Bakewell, Derbyshire

STEPHENSON, Maj-Gen John Aubrey; CB (1982), OBE (1971); s of Reginald Jack Stephenson (d 1976), of 3 Russell Ave, Weymouth, Dorset, and Florence, *née* Pick (d 1947); *b* 15 May 1929; *Educ* Dorchester GS, RMA Sandhurst, RMCS Shrivenham, Staff Coll Camberley, RCDS; *m* 29 July 1953, Sheila, da of Henry Douglas Colbeck (d 1978), of 5 Northumberland Ave, Newcastle upon Tyne; 2 s (Guy b 1957, Peter b 1963), 1 da (Susan b 1955); *Career* joined Royal Artillery (despatches) 1951, pilot 652 Air Op Sqdn RAF 1954-56, Capt 1 Regt RHA 1956-58, Capt 39 Missile Regt 1960-61, Maj Combat Devpt MOD London 1963-64, Batty Cdr (Maj) 25 Field Regt RA 1965-67, CO 16 Light Air Def Regt RA 1969-71, Col project mangr 155 MM Systems 1971-73, Brig Cdr 1 Artillery Bde 1975-77, Brig SMO RARDE 1977-78, Maj Gen DGW/A MOD London 1978-80, VMGO MOD London 1980-81; def conslt 1990-; md Weapon Systems Ltd 1982-90, dir ATX Ltd 1984-86; pres Royal Br Legion Houghton 1987, govr Hardye's Sch Dorchester 1984-, Churchwarden St Peters Stockbridge; FBIM 1977; *Recreations* fishing, sailing, walking, reading, history, travel; *Clubs* IOD, Royal Cwlth Soc; *Style*— Maj Gen John Stephenson, CB, OBE; Collingwood, 27 Trafalgar Way, Stockbridge, Hants SO20 6ET (☎ 0264 810 458, telex 477379 WINSER G)

STEPHENSON, Rt Hon Sir John Frederick Eustace Stephenson; PC (1971); 2 s of Sir Guy Stephenson, CB (er s of Sir Augustus Keppel Stephenson, KCB, KC), by his w Gwendolen, da of Rt Hon John Gilbert Talbot, PC, JP, DL, MP, sometime Parly sec BOT and s in his turn of Hon John Chetwynd Talbot (4 s of 2 Earl Talbot); *b* 28 March 1910; *Educ* Winchester, New Coll Oxford (MA, hon fell); *m* 1951, Hon (Frances) Rose, yr da of Baron Asquith of Bishopstone, PC (*see* Stephenson, Hon Lady); 2 s (David b 1954, Daniel b 1960), 2 da (Mary b 1952, Laura b 1958); *Career* WWII RE and Intelligence Corps served Middle East and NW Europe, Lt-Col 1946; called to the Bar Inner Temple 1934, QC 1960; rec: Bridgwater 1954-59, Winchester 1959-62; chllr Diocese: Peterborough 1956-62, Winchester 1958-62; High Court judge (Queen's Bench) 1962-71, dep chm Dorset QS 1962-71, Lord Justice of Appeal 1971-85; kt 1962; *Books* A Royal Correspondence (1938); *Recreations* reading, music, golf; *Clubs* MCC, Hurlingham, Royal Wimbledon Golf; *Style*— The Rt Hon Sir John Stephenson; 26 Doneraile Street, London SW6 (☎ 071 736 6782)

STEPHENSON, John Patrick; s of Patrick Tinsley Stephenson, of Windmill Orchard, Stebbing, nr Dunmow, Essex, and Evelyn Dorothea Margaret, *née* Orriss; *b* 14 March 1965; *Educ* Felsted, Univ of Durham (BA, Cricket palatinate); *Career* professional cricketer; capt Durham Univ 1986 and Combined Univs 1987; Essex CCC 1984-, debut 1985, awarded county cap 1989, 100 appearances; overseas teams: Fitzroy/Doncaster CC Melbourne 1987-88, Boland CC SA 1988-89, Gold Coast Dolphins and Bond Univ Queensland 1990-91; England: schs tour Zimbabwe 1982-83, 1 Test match v Aust Oval 1989, A tour Zimbabwe 1990, capt under 25 v India 1990; most sixes by an Englishman 1989, shared double hundred opening partnership with Graham Gooch both innings v Northants 1990; honours with Essex CCC: County Championship 1986 (runners up 1989 and 1990), Refuge Cup 1989, runners up Benson & Hedges Cup 1989, runners up John Player League 1986; *Recreations* alternative modern music, modern literature; *Style*— John Stephenson, Esq; c/o Essex CCC, New Writtle St, Chelmsford, Essex (☎ 0245 252420, fax 0245 491607)

STEPHENSON, Lt-Col John Robin; OBE (1976); s of John Stewart Stephenson (d 1975), and Edith Gerda Greenwell Stephenson (d 1975); *b* 25 Feb 1931; *Educ* Christ's Hosp, RMA Sandhurst; *m* 27 Jan 1962, Karen Margrethe, da of August Hansen Koppang (d 1973); 1 s (Robin b 1967), 2 da (Celia b 1963, Kristina b 1964); *Career* cmmnd Royal Sussex Regt 1951, Platoon Cdr Egypt 1951-53, Lt 1953, instr Regtl Depot 1953-54, ADC and Company 2 i/c Korea 1955-56, Company 2 i/c Gibraltar 1956-57, Capt 1957, instr Mons Offr Cadet Sch 1958-60, Company Cdr NI 1960-61, Company Cdr Regtl Depot 1962-64, Maj 1963, GSO3 Libya 1964-65, Company Cdr Germany 1966-67, Infantry rep Sch of Signals 1968-70, Bn 2 i/c NI 1970-72, Lt-Col 1972, Sr Offrs' War Course 1972-73, CO 5 Bn Queen's Regt 1973-76, dep pres Regular Cmmns Bd 1976, SO UK C in C's Ctee 1977-79, ret 1979; sec: MCC 1987- (asst sec 1979-86), Int Cricket Cncl (formerly Conf) 1987-; Order of Orange-Nassau 1972; *Recreations* cricket, rugby, squash, golf, boating and gardening; *Clubs* MCC, IZ, Free Foresters; *Style*— Lt-Col John Stephenson, OBE; Marylebone Cricket Club, Lord's Ground, London NW8 8QN (☎ 071 289 1611-5, fax 071 289 9100, telex 297329 MCCG G)

STEPHENSON, John William; JP (1980); s of Kenneth George Stephenson (d 1979), and Madeline Alice, *née* Ounsworth (d 1974); *b* 23 June 1938; *Educ* Harrow Co Sch; *m* 7 Sept 1963, Lesley Helen, da of Flt Lt Harold Douglas Hopper (d 1980), 2 da (Joanna Margaret b 1968, Sarah Elizabeth b 1970); *Career* surveyor; Fuller Peiser: joined 1959, ptnr 1970, opened Sheffield office 1972, currently sr ptnr Sheffield Office; tstee Sheffield Town 1986, dir and vice chm Sheffield Chamber Music Festival Ltd 1988; FRICS 1970; *Recreations* music, literature, walking; *Clubs* Sheffield; *Style*— John Stephenson, Esq, JP; Borgen, Grindleford, Sheffield S30 1HT (☎ 0433 30288); Fuller Peiser, Chartered Surveyors, Old Bank House, 3 Hartshead, Sheffield S1 2EL (☎ 0742 750161, fax 0742 738226, car 0836 242685)

STEPHENSON, (George) Nigel Primmer; s of Cdr John Keith Burdett Stephenson, OBE (d 1981), and Jane Henrietta, *née* Primmer; *b* 4 Dec 1938; *Educ* St Edward's Sch; *Career* chm London UFO Res Orgn 1960-64 (fndr dir of res 1959), fndr sec Br UFO Assoc 1962-64 (fndr chm 1964-65); *Recreations* ornithology, swimming; *Style*— Nigel Stephenson, Esq; 60 Charles Crescent, Lenzie, Kirkintilloch, Glasgow G66 5HG (☎ 041 776 7279)

STEPHENSON, Paul; s of Paul Stephenson, and Olive Stephenson; *b* 6 May 1937; *Educ* West Hill Coll Birmingham; *m* 21 Nov 1965, Joycelyn, da of Zephaniah Annikie; 1 s (Paul b 26 April 1975), 1 da (Funmicay Joy b 6 July 1977); *Career* sr exec offr and cmmr for racial equality 1972-; vice chm bd of govrs Tulse Hill Sch Lambeth 1974-79; memb: Sports Cncl 1975-81, Press Cncl 1981-; pres: Muhammad Ali Sports Devpt Assoc, Bristol W Indian Parents and Friends Assoc; MIPR 1977-81; *Recreations* overseas travel, cinema, reading, hiking; *Style*— Paul Stephenson, Esq; 12 Downs Park East, Westbury Park, Bristol (☎ 0272 623638); 10-12 Allington St, Elliot House, London SW1 (☎ 071 828 7022)

STEPHENSON, Hon Lady ((Frances) Rose); *née* Asquith; yr da of Baron Asquith of Bishopstone (4 s of 1 Earl of Oxford and Asquith, otherwise H H Asquith, the Liberal PM), and Anne Stephanie, *née* Pollock (d 1964); *b* 4 Oct 1925; *Educ* private; *m* 1951, Rt Hon Sir John Stephenson, *qv*; 2 s, 2 da; *Career* sec War Graves Cmmn; FO 1943-51; chm London Cncl for Welfare of Women & Girls 1959-71; *Style*— The Hon Lady Stephenson

STEPHENSON, Hon Mrs (Sarah Merryweather); *née* Norrie; da of 1 Baron Norrie, GCMG, GCVO, CB, DSO, MC (d 1977); *b* 1943; *Educ* The Guildhall School of Music; *m* 1974, Charles Lyon Stephenson, TD; *Career* Music teacher; *Style*— The Hon Mrs Stephenson; The Cottage, Great Longstone, Bakewell, Derbys DE4 1UA

STEPHENSON, Timothy Congreve; s of Augustus William Stephenson, of Saxbys Mead, Cowden, nr Eden Bridge, Kent, and Mary Gloria (only and posthumous child of Maj William La T Congreve VC, DSO, MC); *b* 7 March 1940; *Educ* Harrow, London Business Sch; *m* 1, 14 April 1966 (m dis 1980), Nerena Anne, d of Maj the Hon William Nicholas Somers Laurence Hyde Villiers; 2 s (Guy b 1969, Frederick b 1978), 2 da (Lucinda b 1967, Henrietta b 1975); m 2, 16 June 1980, Diana-Margaret, da of HE Dr Otto Soltmann, of Coblenz, W Germany; 3 s (Christopher b 1983, William b 1985, James b 1989); *Career* Welsh Gds 1959-65; Gallaher Ltd 1965-79, md Grafton Ltd and chm Grafton Office Products Inc 1980-86, dir IED Assocs Ltd 1985-, md Stephenson Cobbold Ltd 1987-; former memb Industl Tbnls and fndr memb Bd of Lab Rels (ACAS) NI; memb IOD; *Recreations* bridge, shooting, gardening; *Clubs* Brooks's, Beefsteak, Pratt's, City of London; *Style*— T C Stephenson, Esq; c/o Stephenson Cobbold Limited, 84 Palace Court, London W2 4JE (☎ 071 727 5335, 071 243 1383, fax 071 221 2628)

STEPHENSON, Timothy Hugh; TD, JP (Sheffield); only s of William Raymond Shirecliffe Stephenson, himself 2 s of Sir Henry Stephenson, 1 Bt; hp to 1 cous, Sir Henry Stephenson, 3 Bt, TD; *b* 5 Jan 1930; *Educ* Eton, Magdalene Coll Cambridge; *m* 1959, Susan Lesley, yr da of George Harris, of Sheffield; 2 s (Matthew b 1960, Oliver b 1962); *Clubs* Cavalry and Guards', The Sheffield; *Style*— Timothy Stephenson, Esq, TD, JP; Lomberdale Hall, Bakewell, Derbyshire

STEPHENSON, (Augustus) William; s of Sir Guy Stephenson, CB (d 1930), and Gwendolen, *née* Talbot (d 1960); *b* 1 March 1909; *Educ* Harrow; *m* 1, 18 April 1939 (m dis 1952), (Mary) Gloria, da of Maj William La Touche Congreve, VC, DSO, MC (ka 1917); 3 s (Tim b 1940, Martin b 1942, Ben b 1948); m 2, 21 Sept 1962, Elizabeth, da of Arthur James Whittall (d 1971); *Career* RE (TA) 1938, WWII Capt Welsh Gds in N Africa and Italy 1943-45; joined Whitbread & Co 1930 (mangr for Belgium 1935-38), ptnr James Capel & Co 1946-74; memb London Stock Exchange; church warden St Mary Magdalene Cowden 1953-80, pres Cowden and Dist Branch Royal Br Legion, vice pres Falconhurst CC; *Clubs* Army and Navy, MCC, Holtye Golf; *Style*— William Stephenson, Esq; Saxbys Mead, Cowden, Edenbridge, Kent (☎ 0342 850520)

STEPNEY, Bishop of 1978-; Rt Rev James Lawton Thompson; s of Bernard Isaac Thompson, and Marjorie Mary Thompson; *b* 11 Aug 1936; *Educ* Dean Close Sch Cheltenham, Emmanuel Coll Cambridge (MA), Cuddesdon Theol Coll (Gray Theology Essay prize); *m* 1965, Sally Patricia; 1 s (Ben), 1 da (Anna); *Career* Nat Serv 2 Lt 3 RTR 1959-61; curate East Ham 1966-68, chaplain Cuddesdon Theol Coll 1968-71, rector Thamesmead 1971-78, examining chaplain to the Bishop of Southwark 1978-; co-chm Inner Faith Network 1987-; chm: Br Cncl of Churches Ctee for Rels with People of Other Faiths 1983-90, London Diocesan Bd for Social Responsibility 1979-87, Tower Hamlets Assoc for Racial Justice 1979-85, The Urban Learning Fndn 1983-, Social Policy Ctee for the Gen Synod Bd for Social Responsibility 1990-; memb Gen Synod of the C of E, commissary to the Bishop of Namibia, reg broadcaster on radio and TV; jt winner (with Rabbi Gryn) Sir Sigmund Sternberg award 1987; Companion Honour of Orthodox Hospitallers 1987; hon fell Queen Mary Coll London 1986, Hon DLitt E London Poly 1989, FCA; *Books* Origins of Love and Hate (1983), Half Way: Reflections in Midlife (1986), First Aid in Pastoral Care (1987), Trevor Huddleston's Essays on His Life and Work (contrib, 1988), The Lord's Song (1990), Stepney Calling (1991); *Recreations* painting, horses, sport; *Style*— The Rt Rev the Bishop of Stepney; 63 Coborn Road, London E3 2DB (☎ 081 981 2323)

STEPTOE, Roger Guy; s of Charles Steptoe, of Winchester, and Norah Constance, *née* Shaw; *b* 25 Jan 1953; *Educ* Univ of Reading (BA), Royal Acad of Music (LRAM); *Career* composer-in-residence Charterhouse 1976-79, prof of composition RAM 1980-; compositions incl: King of Macedon (opera), symphony, concertos for oboe tuba and clarinet, 2 string quartets, various song cycles for voice and piano, instrumental works for different combinations, oboe quartet, 2 piano sonatas, 2 violin sonatas, In Winters Cold Embraces Dye (for choir and chamber orchestra); works regularly as a soloist, chamber pianist and accompanist, performs compostitions internationally; recordings incl: the songs of Ralph Vaughan Williams with Peter Savidge, the piano quartets of Walton and Frank Bridge; has performed in: UK, IOM, Russia, Sweden, Portugal, Spain, Scotland, W Germany; memb: Inc Soc of Musicians, Royal Philharmonic Soc, Composers' Guild of GB, Royal Soc of Musicians; ARAM 1986; *Recreations* music, gardening, food and drink and seeing friends; *Style*— Roger Steptoe, Esq; c/o Stainer and Bell Ltd, 82 High Rd, London N2 9PW (☎ 081 444 9135)

STERLING, John Adrian Lawrence; s of Francis Thomas Sterling (d 1942), of Melbourne, Aust, and Millicent Lloyd, *née* Pitt (d 1989); *b* 17 April 1927; *Educ* Scotch Coll Melbourne, CEPS Mosman NSW, Barker Coll NSW, Univ of Sydney (LLB); *m* 6 Nov 1976, Caroline Snow, da of Octavius Samuel Wallace (d 1984), of Strabane, Co Tyrone; *Career* admitted to the Bar NSW Aust 1949, called to the Bar Middle Temple 1953, dep DG Int Fedn of Phonographic Indust 1961-73; *Books* various pubns incl: The

Data Protection Act (1984), Copyright Law in the UK and the Rights of Performers Authors and Composers in Europe (1986), Encyclopedia of Data Protection (co-ed, 1991); *Recreations* reading, music; *Style—* J A L Sterling, Esq; Lamb Building, Temple, London EC4Y 7AS (☎ 071 353 6701, fax 071 353 4686, telex 261 511 Jurist G)

STERLING, Prof Michael John Howard; s of Richard Howard Sterling, of 6 Nightingale Rd, Hampton, Middx, and Joan Valeria, *née* Skinner; *b* 9 Feb 1946; *Educ* Hampton GS, Univ of Sheffield (BEng, PhD, DEng); *m* 19 July 1969, Wendy Karla, da of Charles Murray Anstead (d 1978), of Cobbetts Way, Milton Libourne, Wilts; 2 s (Christopher b 1972, Robert b 1975); *Career* res engr GEC Elliot Process Automation 1968-71, sr lectr in control engrg Univ of Sheffield 1978-80 (lectr 1971-78), prof of engrg Univ of Durham 1980-90; vice chllr and princ Brunel Univ 1990-; pres Inst of Measurement and Control 1988; memb: Electricity Supply Res Ctee, SERC Engrg Bd, CEng 1975, FInstMC 1983, FRSA 1984, FIEE 1985; *Books* Power System Control (1978); *Recreations* gardening, DIY, model engineering; *Style—* Prof Michael Sterling; Vice-Chancellor & Principal, Brunel University, Uxbridge, Middlesex UB8 3PH (☎ 0895 74000, fax 0895 32806, telex 261173 G)

STERLING OF PLAISTOW, Baron (Life Peer UK 1991), of Pall Mall in the City of Westminster; Sir Jeffrey Maurice Sterling; CBE (1977); s of Harry and Alice Sterling; *b* 27 Dec 1934; *Educ* Reigate GS, Preston Manor Co Sch, Guildhall Sch of Music; *m* 1985, Dorothy Ann, *née* Smith; 1 da; *Career* advsr: Paul Schweder & Co (Stock Exchange) 1955-57, Geberstadt & Co 1957-62; fin dir Gen Guarantee Corpn 1962-64, md Gula Investmts Ltd 1964-69, chm Sterling Guarantee Tst 1969- (merging with P & O 1985), memb British Airways Bd 1979-82; special advsr to: Sec of State for Indust 1982-83, Sec of State for Trade and Indust 1983-; chm P & O Steam Navigation Co 1983-; chm: Orgn Ctee, World ORT Union (memb Exec 1966-), ORT Tech Servs 1974-; vice pres Br ORT 1978-; dep chm and hon treas London Celebrations Ctee Queen's Silver Jubilee 1975-83; chm Young Vic Co 1975-83, chm govrs Royal Ballet Sch 1983-, govr Royal Ballet 1986-; vice chm and chm of Exec Motability 1977-; vice pres Gen Cncl of Br Shipping 1989-90 (pres 1990); kt 1985; *Recreations* music, swimming, tennis; *Clubs* Garrick, Carlton, Hurlingham; *Style—* The Rt Hon Lord Sterling of Plaistow, CBE; The Peninsular and Oriental Steam Navigation Company, Peninsular House, 79 Pall Mall, London SW1Y 5EJ (☎ 071 930 4343, telex 885551)

STERN, Charles Roger; *b* 16 April 1950; *Educ* Marlborough, Univ of Cambridge (MA), London Business Sch (MSc); *m* 24 July 1973, Nicola Kay; 3 s (Oliver James b 29 May 1978, William Mark b 13 April 1980, Thomas Joseph b 11 May 1984); *Career* planning asst Delta Group Overseas Ltd 1973-76; fin dir: Delta RA Ltd 1976-79, Delta Group Industrial Services Division 1979-84; md Delta Group Australia 1984-86, gp fin dir Aegis Group plc 1986-; ACMA; *Style—* Charles Stern, Esq; Aegis Group plc, 6 Eaton Gate, London SW1 9BL (☎ 071 730 1001, fax 071 823 6852, car 0831 354488)

STERN, (John) Chester; s of Julius Charles Stern (d 1983), of Littlehampton, Sussex, and Bertha Margaret, *née* Baker; *b* 6 Sept 1944; *Educ* Parktown Boys HS Johannesburg SA, Broad Green Coll, Croydon, Surrey; *m* 25 March 1967, Rosemary Ann, da of Wilfred Harold Symons; 2 da (Carolyn Joy b 28 Sept 1969, Paula Jane b 26 Feb 1972); *Career* asst librarian Wills Library Guy's Hospital Medical Sch 1964-65, ed asst Food Processing & Marketing 1965-66, freelance broadcaster BBC Radio London 1970-74, freelance sportswriter The Sunday Telegraph 1973-76, Metropolitan Police New Scotland Yard: publicity asst 1966-68, head of News Gp 1968-71, PRO Traffic Warden Service 1971-74, press and publicity offr London Airport Heathrow 1974-75, press and publicity offr S London 1975-77, head Press Bureau 1977-82; crime corr The Mail on Sunday 1982-; Winston Churchill fell 1975, FRGS 1964, MIPR 1971; *Recreations* badminton, tennis, squash, golf; *Clubs* Scribes, Mensa; *Style—* Chester Stern, Esq; The Mail on Sunday, Associated Newspapers Ltd, Northcliffe House, 2 Derry St, Kensington, London W8 5TS (☎ 071 938 7031)

STERN, Dr Gerald Malcolm; s of Aaron Nathan Stern (d 1975), of London, and Rebecca, *née* Marks (d 1981); *b* 9 Oct 1930; *Educ* Thomas Parmiters Sch, London Hosp Med Coll (MB BS, MD); *m* 28 Sep 1962, Jennifer Rosemary, da of Maj Alfred Charles Pritchard (d 1974); 2 s (Robert Max James b 24 April 1965, Edward Gerald Matthew b 7 April 1972), 1 da (Melanie Rosemary b 6 July 1963); *Career* temp cmmn Surgn Lt RNVR 1956-58; sr conslt neurologist: UCH, Middlesex Hosp; hon conslt neurologist: Nat Hosp Nervous Diseases, St Luke's Hosp for the Clergy; memb: Assoc Br Neurologists 1964-, Assoc Physicians GB and Ireland, bd govrs Nat Hosp Nervous Diseases 1982-, exec bd Parkinson's Disease Soc; FRCP 1970 (memb cncl 1982); Ehrenmitgleid Osterreichishe Parkinson Gesellschaft (1986); *Books* Parkinson's Disease (1989); *Recreations* music, squash; *Clubs* Athenaeum; *Style—* Dr Gerald Stern; 17 Park Village West, Regent's Park, London NW1 (☎ 071 387 7514); 48 Wimpole St, London W1 (☎ 071 388 0640)

STERN, Prof Harold; s of Benjamin Stern (d 1949), and Ann Glushove (d 1959); *b* 15 Oct 1924; *Educ* Queen's Park Secdy Sch Glasgow, Univ of Glasgow (MB ChB, PhD); *m* 2 Jan 1955, Carrol Phyllis, da of Morris Izen, of London; 1 s (David b 1958), 1 da (Beth b 1955); *Career* Capt RAMC 1947-49; hon conslt in virolgy St George's Hosp 1962, ref expert on cytomegalo-viruses Public Health Lab Serv 1967-80, sr ed Journal of Medical Microbiology 1973, chm Bd of Studies in pathology Univ of London 1982-84 (prof of virology 1972), chm Dept of Med Microbiology St George's Hosp Med Sch 1984-; Freeman City of London 1963; FRCPath 1971; *Recreations* ancient history, gardening, walking; *Style—* Prof Harold Stern; Department of Medical Microbiology, St George's Hospital Medical School, Cranmer Terrace, London SW17 0RE (☎ 081 672 9944 ext 55730/1)

STERN, Michael Charles; MP (C) Bristol NW 1983-; s of Maurice Leonard Stern (d 1967), of Finchley, and Rose, *née* Dzialosinski; *b* 3 Aug 1942; *Educ* Christ's Coll GS Finchley; *m* 1976, Jillian Denise, da of Raymond Denis Aldridge, of York; 1 da (Katharine b 1980); *Career* ptnr: Halpern & Woolf 1980-, Percy Phillips & Co 1964-80; chm Bow Group 1977-78; co-opted memb London Borough of Ealing Educn Ctee 1980-83; ACA, FCA; *Recreations* fell-walking, bridge, chess; *Clubs* United & Cecil, Millbank, London Mountaineering; *Style—* Michael Stern Esq, MP; House of Commons, London SW1

STERN, Prof Nicholas Herbert; s of Adalbert Stern, and Marion Fatima, *née* Swann; *b* 22 April 1946; *Educ* Latymer Upper Sch, Cambridge Univ (BA), Oxford Univ (DPhil); *m* 7 Sept 1968, Susan Ruth, da of Albert Edward Chesterton (d 1978), of Pinner, Middx; 2 s (Daniel b 1979, Michael b 1980), 1 da (Helen b 1976); *Career* fell and tutor in econs St Catherine's Coll Oxford, lectr in industl maths Oxford Univ 1970-77; prof of econs: Warwick Univ 1978-85, LSE 1986- (Sir John Hicks prof of econs 1990-); memb: Ctee Oxfam Africa 1974-79, Asia Ctee 1986-89; ed Jl of Public Economics 1981; fell of Econometric Soc 1978; *Books* Crime, the Police and Criminal Statistics (with R Carr-Hill, 1979), Palanpur The Economy of an Indian Village (with C Bliss, 1982), The Theory of Taxation for Developing Countries (with D Newbery, 1987), The Theory and Practice of Taxation for Developing Countries (with E Ahmad, 1991); *Recreations* walking, reading, watching football; *Style—* Prof Nicholas Stern; LSE, Houghton St, London WC2A 2AE (☎ 071 405 7686 ext 3016, fax 071 242 2357, telex 24655 BLPES G)

STERNBERG, Lady Hazel; JP; da of Albert Edward Everett Jones (d 1978), of London, and Kathleen, *née* Oakley; *b* 13 Dec 1927; *Educ* North London Collegiate Sch, St Georgies Harpenden Herts, LSE (BA); *m* 1, 1954, Victor Sternberg (d 1963), s of Benno Sternberg (d 1955), of Israel; 1 s (David b 1961), 1 da (Ruth Anna b 1959); m 2, 4 Feb 1970, Sir Sigmund Sternberg, s of Abraham Sternberg (d 1935), of Hungary; *Career* chm Archway Cruse; involved with: Cruse-Bereavement Care, Relate; *Recreations* gardening, walking; *Style—* Lady Hazel Sternberg, JP; Sternberg Centre for Judaism, The Manor House, 80 East End Rd, London N3

STERNBERG, Michael Vivian; s of Sir Sigmund Sternberg, JP, *qv*, and Beartrice Ruth, *née* Schiff; *b* 12 Sept 1951; *Educ* Carmel Coll Wallingford, Queens' Coll Cambridge (MA, LLM); *m* 20 July 1975, Janine Lois, da of Harold Levinson; 1 s (Daniel Isaiah b 24 Sept 1982), 2 da (Rachel Serena b 2 Feb 1980, Sarah Jessica b 4 Jan 1988); *Career* called to the Bar Gray's Inn 1975; asst sec Family Law Bar Assoc 1986-88; tstee: London Jewish East End Museum, Sternberg Charitable Settlement; memb Cncl of Christians and Jews 1988, Lloyd's underwriter 1978-; Freeman City of London, Liveryman Worshipful Co of Horners 1987; Medaglia D'Argento di Benemenvenza of the Sacred Military Constantinian Order of St George 1990; *Recreations* walking, reading, wine, theatre, amusing children; *Clubs* Reform, City Livery; *Style—* Michael Sternberg, Esq; 3 Dr Johnsons Bldgs, Temple, London EC4Y 7BA (☎ 071 353 4854, fax 071 583 8784)

STERNBERG, Sir Sigmund; JP (Middx 1965); s of Abraham Sternberg (d 1935), of Hungary; *b* 2 June 1921; *m* 1970, Hazel, da of Albert Everett-Jones; 1 s, 1 da, 1 step s, 1 step da; *Career* served WWII; chm: Martin Slowe Estates Ltd 1971-, ISYS plc 1973-; Lloyd's underwriter 1969-; chm Exec Ctee Int Cncl of Christians and Jews, memb Bd Deps of Br Jews, govr Hebrew Univ of Jerusalem, jt hon treas Cncl of Christians and Jews, co-chm Friends of Keston Coll; chm: Function Ctee Inst of Jewish Affairs, Friends of Oxford Centre of Post-Grad Hewbrew Studies; Judge Templeton Prize Fndn, speaker chm Rotary Club of London 1980-83; Hon FRSM 1981, Brotherhood award Nat Conf of Christians and Jews Inc 1980, Silver Pontifical medal 1986; Freeman City of London; Hon FRSM 1981; KCSG 1985, OStJ 1989; OH 1986; kt 1976; *Recreations* golf, swimming; *Clubs* Reform, Rotary, Livery; *Style—* Sir Sigmund Sternberg; The Sternberg Centre for Judaism, 80 East End Rd, London N3 2SY (☎ 071 485 2538, fax , 071 485 4512)

STEUART FOTHRINGHAM, Robert; DL (Angus 1985); eld s of Maj Thomas Scrymsoure Steuart Fothringham (d 1979, 2 s of Lt-Col Walter Thomas James Scrymsoure Steuart Fothringham, of Pourie-Fothringham and Tealing, Angus, and of Grantully and Murthly, Perthshire, who took the name Steuart on succeeding Sir Archibald Douglas Stewart, 8 and last Bt, in the lands of Grantully and Murthly in 1890); *b* 5 Aug 1937; *Educ* Fort Augustus Abbey, Trinity Coll Cambridge, RAC Cirencester; *m* 16 Feb 1962, Elizabeth Mary Charlotte (d 1990), da of Thomas Hope Brendan Lawther, of Earl's Court, London SW5; 2 s (Thomas b 1971, Lionel b 1973), 2 da (Mariana (Mrs Pease) b 1966, Ilona b 1969); *Career* CA; memb Royal Co Archers; *Recreations* shooting, fishing, archery, music; *Clubs* Puffin's, Turf, New (Edinburgh); *Style—* Robert Steuart Fothringham, Esq, DL; Fothringham, Forfar, Angus DD8 2JP (☎ 0307 82 231); Murthly Castle, Murthly, Perth PH1 4HP (☎ 0738 71 397)

STEVEN, Alasdair Robert Malcolm; s of James White Robertson Steven (d 1970), and Helen Mary, *née* Urquhart (d 1989); *b* 1 May 1942; *Educ* Trinity Coll Glenalmond, Univ de Grenoble; *Career* various fin insts 1964-76, ind theatrical prodr 1976-79, freelance journalist 1979-; reviewer opera and ballet Birmingham Post, contrib numerous pubs on the arts; *Recreations* tasting all the cheeses of France ...and trying to remember their names; *Style—* Alasdair Steven, Esq; Poirier, 8a St Dunstan's Rd, London W6 8GB (☎ 081 748 6897); Tomkins, Rue d'Elimeux, Incourt, Picardy, France

STEVEN, Stewart Gustav; s of Rudolph Steven and Trude Steven; *b* 30 Sept 1938; *Educ* Mayfield Coll Sussex; *m* 1965, Inka; 1 s (Jack); *Career* political reporter, central press features 1961-63, political corr Western Daily Press 1963-64; Daily Express: political reporter 1964-65, dip corr 1965-67, foreign ed 1967-72; Daily Mail: asst ed 1972-74, associate ed 1974-82; ed Mail on Sunday 1982; *Books* Operation Splinter Factor (1974), The Spymasters of Israel (1976), The Poles (1982); *Recreations* travel, skiing, writing; *Style—* Stewart Steven Esq; Northcliffe House, 2 Derry St, Kensington, London W8 5TS (☎ 071 938 6000)

STEVEN, Trevor McGregor; s of Donald Richardson Carr Steven, of Berwick-upon-Tweed, Northumberland, and Margaret Rose St Clair, *née* McGregor; *b* 21 Sept 1963; *Educ* Berwick HS; *m* 9 June 1984, Karen, da of John Terence Hindle, of Burnley, Lancs; 2 da (Holly Alexandra b 23 Sept 1986, Christie Raine b 19 March 1990); *Career* footballer; Burnley FC (3 Div champions 1981-82), Everton FC (FA Cup Winners 1983-84, FA Cup runners-up 1984-85, 1988-86, 1 Div league champions 1984-87, Euro Cup Winners Cup 1984-85), Glasgow Rangers FC (Scottish Premier league champions 1989-90, Skol cup runners up 1989-90, Skol cup winners 1990-91); 30 England Caps (memb England Squad Italy World Cup 1990); *Books* Even Stevens (with Gary Stevens, 1988); *Style—* Trevor Steven, Esq; Glasgow Rangers FC, Ibrox Stadium, Edmiston Drive, Glasgow G51 (☎ 041 4275232)

STEVENS, Alan Michael; s of Raymond Alfred George Stevens, of Bournemouth, and Joan Patricia, *née* Drury; *b* 8 April 1955; *Educ* Malvern, Selwyn Coll Cambridge (MA); *m* 2 May 1987, Lynn Sarah, da of Henry B Hopfinger, of Coventry; 1 s (Thomas b 1990), 1 da (Eloise b 1988); *Career* admitted slr 1980; ptnr Linklaters & Paines 1987 (joined 1978); memb Law Soc, Freeman Worshipful Co of Slrs; *Recreations* tennis, skiing, water sports; *Clubs* David Lloyd Slazenger Racquet; *Style—* Alan Stevens, Esq; Putney, London; Linklaters and Paines, Barrington House, 59-67 Gresham St, London EC2V 7JA (☎ 071 606 7080, fax 071 606 5113, telex 884349/888167)

STEVENS, Anne Eileen; da of Wilfred Willett (d 1961), and Eileen Estelle Josephine, *née* Stenhouse (d 1961); *b* 6 May 1923; *Educ* St Clair Tunbridge Wells; *m* 1, Jan 1943, Roger Finney; 1 da (Elizabeth Anne); m 2, Sept 1947, James Palmer; m 3, Jan 1978, Ronald Stevens; *Career* fndr and md Consultus Servs Agency 1962-; *Recreations* gardening; *Style—* Mrs Anne Stevens; The Oast Cottage, Uckfield, E Sussex; Consultus Services Agency, 17 London Rd, Tonbridge, Kent (☎ 0732 355231)

STEVENS, Lady; (Frances) Anne; only child of Capt Christopher Hely-Hutchinson, MC (d 1958; himself 2 s of Rt Hon Sir Walter Hely-Hutchinson, GCMG, 2 s of 4 Earl of Donoughmore), and Gladys Beachy-Head (d 1974); *b* 20 May 1917; *Educ* Southover Manor, Lausanne; *m* 1940, Sir John Stevens, KCMG, DSO, OBE (d 1973), sometime exec dir Bank of England and md Morgan Grenfell; 1 s (John), 2 da (Jane, Mary Anne); *Career* Russian Section Miny of Info 1942-45; Devon rep Nat Art Collection Fund 1977-88, memb Devon Ctee; *Recreations* music, gardening, poetry; *Clubs* Special Forces, Devon and Exeter Inst; *Style—* Lady Stevens; East Worlington House, Crediton, Devon (☎ 0884 860332)

STEVENS, Anthony John (Tony); s of John Walker Stevens (d 1930), and Hilda, *née* Stevens (d 1990); *b* 29 July 1926; *Educ* Long Eaton Co GS, Univ of Liverpool (BSc), Univ of Manchester (Dip Bacteriology); *m* Patricia Frances, da of Robert Gill (d 1974); 1 s (Timothy Mark), 2 da (Carol Anne, Heather Frances); *Career* MAFF: res offr 1952-53, vet investigation offr 1953-65, superintending investigation offr 1965-68, dir vet investigation serv 1968-71, dir vet field servs 1971-78, dir Vet Laboratories 1978-86, conslt and specialist advsr Food and Agricultural Orgn UNO (various periods 1960-90); post grad vet dean London and SE RCVS 1986-, vice pres Zoological Soc of London, pres Surrey Small Shepherds Club, former memb Cncl RCVS; Hon MA Univ of Cambridge 1962; MRCVS; *Books* Handbook of Veterinary Laboratory Diagnosis FAO 1963; *Recreations* farming, archaeology, canals, riding; *Style—* Tony Stevens, Esq; Marigold Cottage, Great Halfpenny Farm, Guildford, Surrey GU4 8PY (☎ 0483 65375)

STEVENS, Brian Turnbull Julius; s of Maj John Osmond Julius Stevens, MBE, and Kathleen, *née* Forman; *b* 3 Nov 1938; *Educ* Eton; *m* 5 Dec 1970, The Hon Henrietta Maria, da of Lt Col 1 Baron St Helens, MC (d 1980); 3 da (Flora Matilda Julius b 25 Feb 1973, Harriet Maria Julius b 11 Jan 1975, Louisa Elizabeth Julius b 15 Oct 1976); *Career* admitted slr 1962; currently ptnr Withers; memb Law Soc; *Recreations* field sports and gardening; *Clubs* Boodle's, Pratts; *Style—* Brian Stevens, Esq; 20 Essex St, London WC2 (☎ 071 836 8400, fax 071 240 2278, telex 24212 WITHER G)

STEVENS, Dr David Laurence; s of Laurence Sydney Stevens (d 1987), of Ampney Crucis, Cirencester, Gloucestershire, and Ida May, *née* Roberts (d 1989); *b* 15 Sept 1938; *Educ* High Pavement Sch, Nottingham and Guys Hosp, Med Sch Univ of London (MB BS, MD); *m* 20 Feb 1965, (Karin) Ute, da of Friedrich Heinrich Rudolf Holtzheimer (d 1966), of Berlin; 2 s (Michael b 1967, Andrew b 1970); *Career* registrar in neurology Derbyshire Royal Infirmary 1966-67, sr registrar in neurology Leeds Gen Infirmary 1967-73, res fell dept of genetics Univ of Leeds 1969-70; conslt neurologist 1973-: Gloucestershire Royal Hosp, Cheltenham Gen Hosp, Frenchay Hosp Bristol; memb ed bd Br Jl of Hosp Med 1985-, assoc ed Journal of Neurological Sciences 1990-; author of articles on neurology in med jls, contribs to various books; World Fedn of Neurology: sec gen res gp on Huntington's chorea 1983-, memb res ctee 1973-; past pres SW England Neurosciences Assoc 1984-85; memb Assoc of Br Neurologists, FRCP 1980 (MRCP 1966); *Books* Handbook of Clinical Neurology (contrib); *Recreations* travel, photography, skiing, talking (a lot); *Style—* Dr David Stevens; Department of Neurology, Gloucestershire Royal Hospital, Gloucester (☎ 0452 394634)

STEVENS, Derek George; s of George William Stevens (d 1967), of London, and Georgina, *née* Crisp (d 1987); *b* 28 Jan 1928; *Educ* Southall Co Sch, Coll of Estate Mgmnt; *m* 5 July 1952, Sheelah Kathleen, da of Frederick Roy Llewelyn Bishop (d 1988); 1 s (Neil Andrew b 1959), 1 da (Susan Elizabeth b 1955); *Career* Corpl RCS 1946-48; surveyor; pupil Knight Frank & Rutley 1944-46 (various appts until 1969), sr ptnr Stickley & Kent 1969-87; London Borough of Harrow: cllr 1967-72 and 1978-86, alderman 1976-78, former chm Housing Ctee; memb NW Valuation Panel, chm and govr of three schs; FRICS; *Recreations* golf, swimming, reading, music; *Style—* Derek Stevens, Esq; 41 Bellfield Ave, Harrow, London (☎ 081 428 4048, car 0831 446 234); Casa Caracus, Campo Mijas 10A Fuengirola, Malaga, Spain (☎ 010 3452 464515)

STEVENS, Handley Michael Gambrell; s of Dr Ernest Norman Stevens, of Highcliffe, Dorset, and Dr Kathleen Emily Gambrell (d 1986); *b* 29 June 1941; *Educ* The Leys Sch, Phillips Acad Andover Mass, King's Coll Cambridge (MA); *m* 5 March 1966, Anne Frances, da of Robert Ross, of Evesbatch, Hereford, Worcester; 3 da (Hilary b 1970, Lucy b 1971, Mary b 1980); *Career* Dip Serv 1964-70 (Kuala Lumpur 1966-69); asst private sec Lord Privy Seal 1970-71, Civil Serv Dept 1970-73, DTI 1973-83, under-sec of int aviation Dept of Tport 1983-87, Fin Dept 1988-; *Recreations* music, walking; *Style—* Handley M G Stevens, Esq; Dept of Transport, 2 Marsham St, London SW1 (☎ 071 276 5259)

STEVENS, Hon Mrs (Henrietta Maria); *née* Hughes-Young; da of 1 Baron St Helens, MC (d 1980); *b* 1940; *m* 1970, Brian Turnbull Julius Stevens; *Style—* The Hon Mrs Stevens

STEVENS, Jocelyn Edward Greville; s of Maj (Charles) Greville Bartlett Stewart-Stevens, formerly Stevens, JP (d 1972, having m subsequently (1936) Muriel Athelstan Hood, *née* Stewart, 10 Lady of Balnakeilly, Perthshire, and adopted (1937) the name Stewart-Stevens), and late Mrs Greville Stevens, da of Sir Edward Hulton (who owned the Evening Standard until 1923, when he sold it to 1 Baron Beaverbrook); *b* 14 Feb 1932; *Educ* Eton, Trinity Cambridge; *m* 1956 (m dis 1979), Jane Armyne, da of John Vincent Sheffield; 2 s (1 decd), 2 da (*see* Delevingne, Charles); *Career* Nat Serv The Rifle Bde 1950-52; journalist; Hulton Press Ltd, chm and md Stevens Press Ltd and ed of Queen Magazine 1957-68, dir Beaverbrook Newspapers 1971-77 (md 1974-77), md Evening Standard Co Ltd 1969-72, md Daily Express 1972-74, dep chm and md Express Newspapers 1975-81, dir Centaur Communications Ltd 1982-85, publisher and ed The Magazine 1982-84, dep chm Independent Television Commission 1991-; govr: ICSTM 1985-, Winchester Sch of Art 1986-89; rector and vice-provost RCA 1984-; Hon DLitt Loughborough; sr fell RCA, hon fell CSD; FRSA; *Recreations* skiing; *Clubs* White's, Buck's, Beefsteak; *Style—* Jocelyn Stevens, Esq; Testbourne, Longparish, nr Andover, Hants SP11 6QT (☎ 026 472 232); 14 Cheyne Walk, London SW3 5RA (☎ work 071 584 5020)

STEVENS, John Christopher Courtney; MEP (C) Thames Valley 1989-; *b* 23 May 1955; *Educ* Winchester, Magdalen Coll Oxford (BA); *Career* foreign exchange dealer Bayerische Hypotheken Wechselbank Munich 1976-77; fin corr: Rome 1978, Paris 1979; foreign exchange dealer Morgan Grenfell & Co Ltd London 1980-84, dir Morgan Grenfell International (and head of Euro Govt Bond Trading) 1985-89; *Books* A Conservative European Monetary Union (1990); *Style—* John Stevens, Esq, MEP; 15 St James's Place, London SW1A 1NW (☎ 071 493 8111, fax 071 493 0673)

STEVENS, Lewis David; MBE (1982), MP (C) Nuneaton 1983-; *b* 13 April 1936; *Educ* Oldbury GS Worcestershire, Univ of Liverpool, Lanchester Coll Coventry; *m* ; 2 s, 1 da; *Career* mgmnt conslt; memb Nuneaton Borough Cncl 1966-72, Parly candidate (C) Nuneaton 1979; *Style—* Lewis Stevens, Esq, MBE, MP; 151 Sherbourne Ave, Nuneaton CV10 9JN (☎ 0203 396105)

STEVENS, Dr (Katharine) Lindsey Haughton; da of Richard Haughton Stevens (d 1977), of Sheringham, Norfolk, and Rachel Vera Joyce, *née* Huxstep; *b* 17 July 1954; *Educ* Harrogate Ladies Coll, Runton Hill and Greshams Schs, Churchill Coll Cambridge (MA), Middx Hosp Med Sch (MB, BCh); *m* 1989, David Barrett McCausland, s of John McCausland, of Pett, Hastings; 1 s (Duncan James Stevens b 1989); *Career* conslt Accident and Emergency Dept St George's Hosp 1985-, hon sr lectr Univ of London 1985-, instr advanced trauma life support RCS 1989, fndr St George's Start-a-Heart campaign and fund 1986; res into: psychological effects of trauma, water safety, resuscitation, cardiac illness, physiotherapy; chm S W Thames Accident and Emergency Conslts Ctee; memb Nat Exec Br Assoc of Accident and Emergency Med (joined 1985), area surgn St John's Ambulance Bde; regnl speciality advsr RCS 1990; MRCP 1983, memb RSM 1989; *Style—* Dr Lindsey Stevens; Accident and Emergency Dept, St Georges Hospital, Blackshaw Rd, London SW17 (☎ 081 672 1255)

STEVENS, Dr Martin John; s of John Frederick Stevens (d 1972), of The Pharmacy, Aldeburgh, Suffolk, and Lucy Thelma, *née* Clark; *b* 5 June 1942; *Educ* The GS Leiston Suffolk, St Thomas's Hosp Med Sch; *m* 1, 13 Sept 1969 (m dis 1977), Virginia Jane, da of Harold Wooley, of Ufton Nervet, Berks; m 2, 14 Oct 1978, (Gwyneth) Sandra George, da of Alec Thomas, of Rotherham, S Yorks; 2 s (John Joseph Benjamin b 23 Aug 1979, James Frederick Martin Zacharia b 18 June 1981); *Career* conslt in the psychiatry of old age E Suffolk Health Authy 1977-; memb exec ctee section for psychiatry of old age of RCPsych, examiner for dip in geriatric med RCP; MRCP 1972, FRCPsych 1986; *Recreations* chorister (bass) St Mary le Tower Church Ipswich; *Style—* Dr Martin Stevens; 55 Henley Road, Ipswich, Suffolk (☎ 0473 251265); Dept of Geriatric Psychiatry, Minsmere House, The Ipswich Hospital, Heath Rd, Ipswich, Suffolk (☎ 0473 712233)

STEVENS, Patrick Tom; s of Tom Stevens, of Norfolk, and Gwendoline, *née* Nurse; *b* 21 Aug 1949; *Educ* Paston GS Norfolk; *m* 24 Aug 1973, Agnes; *Career* tax specialist Coopers & Lybrand 1975-79 (audit specialist 1972-75), sr tax ptnr Finnie & Co 1986- (tax ptnr 1979-86); sec Kytes Theatre Gp; FCA 1972, ATII 1975; *Recreations* theatre; *Style—* Patrick Stevens, Esq; 19 Risebridge Road, Gidea Park, Essex; Finnie & Co, Kreston House, 8 Gate St, London WC2A 3HJ (☎ 071 831 9100, fax 071 831 2666)

STEVENS, Peter Rupert; s of Surgn Capt R W Stevens, RN; *b* 14 May 1938; *Educ* Winchester, Taft Sch (USA); *m* 1963, Sarah Venetia Mary, da of Air Vice-Marshal H A V Hogan, CB, DSO, DFC; 3 children; *Career* 2 Lt KRRC; stockbroker; sr ptnr Laurie Milbank 1981-86 (ptnr 1969-81), head Sterling Fixed Interest and Int Chase Manhattan Gilts Ltd; chief exec GT Mgmnt plc 1989-; memb: Stock Exchange Cncl 1974-87 and 1988- (dep chm 1988-90), Bd of The Securities Assoc 1987-; *Recreations* cricket, tennis, gardening, country pursuits; *Style—* Peter Stevens, Esq; Highmead House, Alton, Hants GU34 4BN (☎ 0420 83945)

STEVENS, Richard; s of C E Stevens (d 1976), of Magdalen Coll Oxford, and Leila, *née* Porter; *b* 9 Dec 1943; *Educ* Winchester, Univ of Cambridge (MA); *Career* investmt mangr; exec dir: Certa Portfolio Management Ltd 1989-, Multitrust plc 1986-90; ACIB; *Recreations* supporting Sunderland FC, railways, music, Georgian architecture; *Clubs* Carlton, Special Forces, IOD; *Style—* Richard Stevens, Esq; The Sheepcote, Bartestree, Hereford HR1 4DE (☎ 0432 850236); 6 Playhouse Yard, London EC4V 5EX (☎ 071 248 9039, fax 071 236 9287)

STEVENS, Prof Stanley James; s of Harold Stevens (d 1987), of 84 Sandalwood Rd, Loughborough, and Gladys Mary, *née* Swain (d 1981); *b* 11 April 1933; *Educ* Bablake Sch Coventry, Univ of Nottingham (MSc), Cranfield Inst of Technol (MSc), Univ of Loughborough (PhD); *m* 1 Sept 1956, Rita Lillian Stevens, da of Charles Lloyd (d 1986), of 5 Meredith Rd, Coventry; 2 da (Carol Anne b 3 June 1961, Kathryn Diane b 3 Nov 1965); *Career* engrg apprenticeship Armstrong-Siddely Motors Ltd 1950-55, project engr Siddeley Engines Ltd Bristol 1955-61; Loughborough Univ of Technol: lectr in aeronautics 1961-70, sr lectr 1970-76, reader 1976-81, prof of aircraft propulsion 1987-; memb: exec ctee Leicestershire Lawn Tennis Assoc, ctee of Royal Aeronautical soc (Loughborough); Freeman City of Coventry 1956: MIMechE, MRAeS, CEng; *Recreations* tennis, walking, water colour painting; *Style—* Prof Stanley Stevens; 101 Valley Road, Loughborough, Leicestershire LE11 3PY (☎ 0509 215139); Head of Dept of Transport Tech, Loughborough University of Tech, Loughborough, Leicestershire (☎ 0509 223404, telex 34319, fax 0509 267613)

STEVENS, Stuart Standish; s of Maj Edward Aloysious Stevens (d 1948), and Virginia Mary, *née* D'Vaz; *b* 30 April 1947; *Educ* St Josephs Euro HS Bangalor S India, Acton County GS, Royal Holloway Coll Univ of London; *m* (m dis); 2 s (Uther Edwards b 1984, Stuart William b 1989), 1 da (Isabella Eda b 1986); *Career* called to the Bar Grays Inn 1970; currently head of Chambers; *Style—* Stuart Stevens, Esq; 3 Kings Bench Walk, Temple, London EC4 (☎ 071 353 2416, fax 071 353 2941)

STEVENS, William David; s of Walter G Stevens, of Corpus Christi, Texas, USA; *b* 18 Sept 1934; *Educ* Texas A & I Univ; *m* 1954, Barbara Ann, *née* Duncan; 4 children; *Career* mgmnt Exxon Co USA 1958-73, asst to pres Exxon 1974-75, dep mangr Producing 1976-78, vice-pres: Esso Gas 1978, Europe 1982; md Esso Petroleum Co Ltd 1978-82; *Recreations* golf, shooting, hiking; *Style—* William Stevens Esq; 24 Harley House, Marylebone Rd, London NW1 (☎ 071 935 6003)

STEVENSON, (William) Bristow; DL (1977); s of James Stevenson, JP, DL (d 1956), of Knockan, Feeny, Co Londonderry, and Kathleen Mary, *née* Young (d 1945); *b* 1 Nov 1924; *Educ* St Edward's Sch Oxford, Trinity Coll Oxford (MA); *m* 1, 25 Nov 1949 (m dis 1958), Barbara Stephanie Boyd, da of Sir William Angus Boyd Iliff, CMG, MBE (d 1974); 2 s (Adrian b 1950, Peter b 1952); m 2, 15 Nov 1958, Julia Heather Margaret , da of Lt-Col Gualter Hugh Rodger Bellingham Somerville, MC; 2 s (James b 1963, Henry b 1970), 1 da (Diana b 1961); *Career* WWII Lt RNVR: Atlantic and Russian Convoys, D Day; admitted slr 1950; farmer; chllr Diocese of Derry and Raphoe 1975-, lay hon sec gen Synod of Church of Ireland 1984-89; pres: Ulster Ram Breeders Assoc, City of Londonderry Slrs Assoc; chm Londonderry Feis 1985-90; High Sheriff Co Londonderry 1971; pres Mental Health Review Tbnl (NI); formerly NI rep on Hill Farming Advsy Ctee; assessor Gen Synod of the Church of Ireland 1988; underwriting memb of Lloyds 1980; formerly vice chm of govrs Foyle & Londonderry Coll; *Recreations* golf, shooting; *Clubs* Northern Counties Londonderry, Naval; *Style—* Bristow Stevenson, Esq, DL; Knockan, Feeny, Co Londonderry (☎ 0504 781265); Court Chambers, 25D Bishop St, Londonderry (☎ 0504 363131/362858)

STEVENSON, Dr David John Douglas; s of Dr Douglas Stuart Stevenson, MBE (d 1951), of Glasgow, and Mary Edith, *née* Lang (d 1981); *b* 6 Jan 1933; *Educ* Ardvreck Sch Perthshire, Oundle, Univ of Cambridge (MA), Univ of Glasgow (MB ChB, MD, DPH), Univ of Liverpool (DTM and H); *m* 29 July 1967, Anna Marie (Rie), da of Povl Sigismund Skadegård (d 1977), of Rungsted Kyst, Denmark; 2 s (Bjorn b 1968, Alan b 1974), 1 da (Ellen b 1969); *Career* house surgn Western Infirmary Glasgow 1957, house physician Stobhill Hosp Glasgow 1957-58, diocesan medical offr Dio of Nyasaland (Univs Mission to Central Africa) 1958-63, govt med offr Malawi 1965-66, lectr in tropical diseases Univ of Edinburgh 1966-72; Sch of Tropical Med Univ of Liverpool: sr lectr in int community health 1972-90 (on loan to Tribhuwan Univ Nepal 1974-75), hon lectr 1990-; Parly candidate (SNP): Glasgow Woodside 1964, Edinburgh South 1970, Euro Parl elections Lothian 1979 and 1984; memb: Inc of Hammermen (Glasgow) 1933, Inc of Bakers (Glasgow) 1942; Freeman City of Glasgow 1933; MFCM 1974; *Books* Davey and Lightbody's The Control of Disease in the Tropics (ed 1987); *Recreations* bagpipe and shawm music, parapsychology; *Clubs* Edinburgh University Staff; *Style—* Dr David Stevenson; 22 Blacket Place, Edinburgh, Scotland EH9 1RL (☎ 031 667 3748); Department of International Community Health, Liverpool School of Tropical Medicine, Pembroke Place, Liverpool L3 5QA (☎ 051 708 9393, fax 051 708 8733)

STEVENSON, (Henry) Dennistoun (Dennis); CBE (1981); s of Alexander James Stevenson, of Scotland, and Sylvia Florence, *née* Inglby; *b* 19 July 1945; *Educ* Edinburgh Acad, Glenalmond, Kings Coll Cambridge; *m* 15 Feb 1972, Charlotte Susan, da of Air Cdre Hon Sir Peter Beckford Rutgers Vanneck, GBE, CB, AFC; 4 s (Alexander, Heneage, Charles, William); *Career* chm: SRU Gp (founded 1972), Aycliffe & Peterlee Corpn 1972-81, Nat Assoc of Youth Clubs 1972-80; dir: Br Technol Gp 1979-, London Docklands Devpt Corpn 1981-88, Tyne Tees TV 1982-87, Pearson plc 1988-, Manpower plc 1988-; chm Intermediate Technol Devpt Gp 1984-90; chm: Docklands Sinfonietta 1989-, Tstees of Tate Gallery 1989-; *Recreations* tennis, violin, reading; *Clubs* MCC, Brooks's; *Style—* Dennis Stevenson, Esq, CBE; SRU Ltd, 78/80 St John St, London EC1M 4HR (☎ 071 250 1131, fax 071 608 0089)

STEVENSON, Dr Derek Paul; CBE (1972); s of Frederick Paul Stevenson (d 1949), and Blanch Maud, *née* Coucher (d 1948); *b* 11 July 1911; *Educ* Epsom Coll, Univ of

London and Guys Hosp; *m* 10 May 1941, Pamela Mary, da of Lt-Col Charles Jervelund, OBE (d 1962); 2 s (John b 1944, Timothy b 1948), 1 da (Wendy b 1942); *Career* regular offr RAMC, MO Sandhurst, overseas serv Malaya, Singpore, China, Capt 1937, WWII served BEF 1939-40, Adj RAMC depot 1940-42, WO 1942-46, Maj 1942, Lt-Col 1943, asst dir gen Army Med Servs WO 1943; sec BMA 1958-76, chm cncl World Med Assoc 1969-71, vice pres Private Patients Plan, conslt Med Insur Agency; cncllr West Sussex CC 1980-85, Chichester Local Health Authy 1983-85, memb Med Servs Bd 1977-79; Hon LLD Univ of Manchester 1964; MRCS, LRCP, BMA; *Recreations* golf, gardening; *Clubs* Athenaeum; *Style*— Dr Derek Stevenson, CBE; 19 Marchwood Gate, Chichester, West Sussex PO19 4HA (☎ 0243 774237)

STEVENSON, George William; s of Harold Stevenson, of Maltby, Yorkshire, and Elsie, *née* Bryan; *b* 30 Aug 1938; *Educ* secdy modern sch; *m* 14 June 1958, Doreen June (d 1989), da of Joseph Parkes; 2 s (Leslie Alan b 8 Jan 1961, Andrew Mark b 19 Feb 1966), 1 da (Jacqueline b 15 Nov 1959); *Career* elected MEP 1984, re-elected 1989; *Recreations* reading, crown green bowling; *Style*— George Stevenson, MEP; 291 Weston Road, Meir, Stoke-on-Trent, Staffordshire ST3 6HA (☎ 0782 326898); Pioneer House, 76-80 Lonsdale St, Stoke-on-Trent, Staffordshire ST4 4DP (☎ 0782 414232, fax 0782 744785)

STEVENSON, Dr Jim; s of George Stevenson (d 1982), and Frances Mildred Groat (d 1974); *b* 9 May 1937; *Educ* Kirkham GS, Univ of Liverpool (BSc, PhD); *m* 5 Jan 1963, Brenda, da of Thomas Edward Cooley (d 1967); 1 s (Michael b 17 Nov 1963), 1 da (Rachel b 21 Nov 1968); *Career* NATO res fell Univ of Trondheim Norway 1963-65, lectr in biochemistry Univ of Warwick 1965-69; BBC Open Univ: prodr 1969-76, ed sci progs 1976-79, head of progs 1979-82; dep sec BBC 1982-83, head of educnl bdcasting services and educn sec BBC 1983-89; chief exec Educnl Bdcasting Services Tst 1988-; memb: Int Inst of Communications, Soc of Satellite Professionals, RTS; *Recreations* television, picture-framing, drawing; *Clubs* Savile; *Style*— Dr Jim Stevenson; 34 Vallance Rd, London N22 4UB (☎ 081 889 6261); The Educational Broadcasting Services Trust, 1-2 Marylebone High St, London W1A 1AR (☎ 071 927 5023, fax 071 224 2426)

STEVENSON, John; CBE (1987); *b* 15 June 1927; *Educ* Henry Smith Sch Hartlepool, Univ of Durham (LLB), Univ of Oxford (MA); *m* 29 March 1956, Kathleen, *née* Petch; 1 s (Mark Petch b 1962), 1 da (Jane Clare b 1960); *Career* admitted slr 1952; clerk of the peace and co slr Gloucestershire CC 1969-74, chief exec Buckinghamshire CC 1974-80, sec Assoc of CCs in Eng and Wales 1980-87; Dep Licensing Authy: Metropolitan and S Eastern Traffic Areas 1988-, Eastern Traffic Area 1990-; vice pres Inst of Trading Standards Admin, visiting fell Nuffield Coll Oxford 1982-90, hon fell Univ of Birmingham 1981-; memb Law Soc; *Style*— John Stevenson, Esq, CBE; 2 Water's Edge, Port La Salle, Yarmouth, Isle of Wight PO41 0XB (☎ 0983 761254); 405 Keyes House, Dolphin Square, London SW1V 3NA (☎ 071 834 2149)

STEVENSON, Juliet Anne Virginia; da of Brig Michael Guy Stevens, MBE, and Virginia Ruth, *née* Marshall; *b* 30 Oct 1956; *Educ* Hurst Lodge Sch Berks, St Catherine's Sch Surrey, RADA; *Career* with RSC 1978-86 (currently assoc artist); roles incl: Titania and Hippolyta in A Midsummer Nights Dream, Isabella in Measure for Measure, Rosalind in As You Like It, Cresida in Troilus and Cressida, Madame de Tourvel in Les Liaisons Dangereuses; other performances incl: Other Worlds (Royal Court Theatre) 1982, Yerma (NT) 1987, Hedda Gabler (NT) 1989; TV appearances incl: Antigone in Antigone, Oedipus at Colonus, The Mallens, Maybury, Freud, Life Story, Out of Love, The March, Aimée, Border Country; films incl: Drowning by Numbers, Ladder of Swords, Truly Madly Deeply; *Books* Clamorous Voices (co-author, 1988); *Recreations* talking, walking, reading, piano, travelling, cinema, theatre, music; *Style*— Ms Juliet Stevenson

STEVENSON, (Donald) Maylin; s of Donald Robert Louis Stevenson (d 1962), of Doncaster, S Yorks, and Idonea Maylin, *née* Vipan (d 1982); *b* 19 Nov 1932; *Educ* Oundle, St Johns Coll Cambridge (MA); *m* 6 June 1981, Veronica Jane, da of Reginald Stephen Loaring (d 1983), of St Peter Port, Guernsey; *Career* Nat Serv 2 Lt E Yorks Regt, Capt W Yorks Regt TA; slr 1959, ptnr Williams Thompson & Co Slrs Christchurch 1975-87, sr ptnr 1984 (conslt 1987-90); *Recreations* sailing, history; *Clubs* Christchurch Sailing; *Style*— Maylin Stevenson, Esq; Laurel Bank, Croft Rd, Bransgore, Christchurch, Dorset (☎ 0425 725 46); 45 Las Araucarias, El Pinaret, Puerto Pollensa, Mallorca

STEVENSON, Maj-Gen Paul Timothy; OBE (1985, MBE 1975); s of Ernest Stevenson, of Wortley, Wotton under Edge, Glos, and Dorothy Trehearn (d 1985); *b* 3 March 1940; *Educ* Bloxham Sch; *m* 26 June 1965, Ann Douglas, da of Col Douglas Burns Drysdale DSO, OBE (d 1990); 1 s (Jonathan b 1970), 1 da (Iona b 1968); *Career* joined RM 1958, 41 Commando 1960-62, 45 Commando (Aden) 1962-63, HMS Mohawk 1965-68, 45 Commando 1973-75, HMS Bulwark 1975-76, Falklands campaign SO1 plans 1982, Co 42 Commando 1983-84, dir personnel 1987-88, Cmd Br Forces Falkland Islands 1989-90; modern pentathlon, Br team 1962-69, biathlon Br team 1965; FBIM; *Recreations* field sports, golf, gardening, skiing; *Clubs* Army and Navy; *Style*— Maj Gen Paul Stevenson, OBE; c/o Lloyds Bank, Wotton under Edge, Glos GL12 7DA

STEVENSON, Robert Wilfrid (Wilf); s of James Alexander Stevenson, and Elizabeth Anne, *née* Macrae; *b* 19 April 1947; *Educ* Edinburgh Acad, Univ Coll Oxford (BA), Napier Poly pt/t (ACCA); *m* 15 April 1972 (m dis 1979), Jennifer Grace, da of David Grace Antonio (d 1986), of Edinburgh; *Career* res offr Univ of Edinburgh Students Assoc 1970-74, sec Napier Poly Edinburgh 1974-87, dir Br Film Inst 1988- (dep dir 1987-88); *Recreations* cinema, hill walking, bridge; *Style*— Wilf Stevenson, Esq; 21 Stephen St, London W1P 1PL (☎ 071 255 1444, fax 071 436 7950, telex 27624 BFILDNG)

STEVENSON, Samuel; s of Samuel Stevenson (d 1989), and Gladys, *née* Daniel (d 1989); *b* 14 March 1933; *Educ* Charterhouse; *m* 18 Dec 1986, Christine Rosemary Nessa, da of Sidney Galkin, of Ruislip, Middx; *Career* Nat Serv Sub Lt RN; ptnr Arthur Young 1962-69; md: Gartmore Investmt Ltd 1969-83, C S Investmt 1983; Freeman City of Glasgow 1935, memb Inc Wrights and Grand Antiquities Soc; MICAS; *Recreations* golf; *Clubs* Brooks's, City of London, MCC; *Style*— Samuel Stevenson, Esq; 149 Pavilion Rd, London SW1X 0BJ (☎ 071 235 6238); CS Investments, 125 High Holborn, London WC1V 6PY (☎ 071 242 1148, fax 071 831 7187, telex 291986)

STEVENSON, Sir Simpson; s of Thomas Henry Stevenson, of Greenock; *b* 18 Aug 1921; *Educ* Greenock HS; *m* 1945, Jean Holmes, da of George Henry; *Career* chm Bd Western Regnl Hosp 1967-73, memb Inverclyde DC 1974-; chm: Scottish Health Servs Common Agency 1973-77, Gt Glasgow Health Bd 1973-83, Consortium of Local Authorities Special Programme 1974-83; memb Royal Cmmn on NHS 1976-79; Hon LLD Univ of Glasgow 1982; kt 1976; *Style*— Sir Simpson Stevenson; The Gables, 64a Reservoir Road, Gourock, Renfrewshire (☎ 0475 31774)

STEVENSON, Hon Mrs (Susan Mary); *née* Blades; da of 2 Baron Ebbisham, TD; *b* 1951; *m* 1980, Peter D Stevenson, 1 s (George b 1987), 1 da (Mary b 1984); *Style*— The Hon Mrs Stevenson; The White House, Whitehouse Loan, Edinburgh EH9 2EY

STEWARD, Rear Adm Cedric John; CB (1984); s of Ethelbert Harold Steward (d 1977), and Anne Isabelle, *née* West (d 1986); *b* 31 Jan 1931; *Educ* Northcote Coll Auckland, Britannia RNC Dartmouth, Greenwich Naval Coll (jssc), RCDS; *m* 1952, Marie Antoinette, da of Arthur Gordon Gurr (d 1951), of Sydney, NSW; 3 s (Mark, Bretton, John); *Career* served Korea 1951 and 1954; Staff Royal Aust Naval Coll Jervis Bay 1959-62, dep head NZ Def Liaison Staff Canberra 1969-73, Capt 11 Frigate Sqdn 1974-75, Dep Chief of Naval Staff 1979-81, Cdre Auckland 1981-83, Chief of Naval Staff 1983-86; proprietor: Fontainebleau Int 1986-, Antric Park Horse Stud 1986-; *Recreations* philately, boating, golf, tennis, equestrian, fishing; *Clubs* Helensville Golf, Auckland RC (Ellerslie); *Style*— Rear Adm Cedric Steward

STEWARD, Maj Charles Anthony; s of Capt Charles Knowles Steward, DSO, MC (d 1929), and Cunitia Charlotte Atwood, *née* Morris, JP (d 1957); *b* 22 June 1919; *Educ* Rugby, RMC Sandhurst; *m* 16 Aug 1941, Feridah Lucretia Mary, da of Lt-Col Edward Francis Jenico Joseph Farrell, JP, DL (d 1951), of Walterstown, Moynalty Kells, Co Meath, Ireland; 1 s (Charles b 26 May 1951), 1 da (Valerie b 8 May 1942 now the Viscountess of Oxfuird); *Career* cmmnd 9 Queens Royal Lancers 1939; WWII served: France 1940, Western Desert 1941, Persia and Iraq 1942-43, India and Burma 1944-45; Staff Coll Camberley 1949, Bde Maj 7 Armd Bde 1950-51, Regtl serv 1952-53, MOD 1954-55, US Cmd and Gen Staff Coll 1956-57, HQ BAOR 1957-59, MOD 1959-60, HQ 1 (Br) Corps 1961-63, ret 1963; cncllr Hartley Wintney RDC 1969-73; Hart DC 1969-80: chm planning 1973-75, vice chm DC 1976-77 (chm 1978-79); fndr and chm Crondall Soc, memb local ctee Cncl for the Protection of Rural Eng, community advsr Crondall Parish; *Recreations* shooting, game fishing; *Style*— Maj C A Steward; The Platt, Crondall, Farnham, Surrey GU10 5NY (☎ 0252 850288)

STEWART; *see*: Shaw-Stewart

STEWART, Sir Alan D'Arcy; 13 Bt (I 1623), of Ramelton, Co Donegal; s (by 1 m) of Sir Jocelyn Harry Stewart, 12 Bt (d 1982); *b* 29 Nov 1932; *Educ* All Saints, Bathurst NSW; *m* 1952, Patricia, da of Lawrence Turner; 2 s, 2 da; *Heir* s, Nicholas Courtney D'Arcy Stewart b 1953; *Career* yacht builder, marine engr; *Style*— Sir Alan Stewart, Bt; One Acre House, Church st, Ramelton, Co Donegal

STEWART, Alastair James; s of Gp Capt James Frederick Stewart, of 34 Beamish Way, Winslow, Bucks and Joan Mary, *née* Lord; *b* 22 June 1952; *Educ* St Augustines Abbey Sch, Univ of Bristol; *m* 8 April 1978, Sally Ann, da of Frederick Harold Rudolph Jung (d 1968); 1 s (Alexander b 1982), 1 da (Clemmie b 1985); *Career* dep pres NUS 1974- 76; Southern ITV: ed trainee 1976, industl reporter and prog presenter incl Energy - What Crisis? 1976-80; ITN: industl corr 1980-82, newscaster incl News at Ten 1982-89 and 1990-; presenter: The Budget 1982-89, General Election 1987, State Opening of Parliament 1988-89, weddings of Prince of Wales and Duke of York; Washington corr 1990; memb NUJ; *Recreations* reading, music, antique maps; *Style*— Alastair Stewart, Esq; ITN, 200 Gray's Inn Road, London W1 (☎ 071 833 3000, fax 071 430 4016)

STEWART, Sheriff Alastair Lindsay; s of Alexander Lindsay Stewart (d 1977); *b* 28 Nov 1938; *Educ* Edinburgh Acad, St Edmund Hall Oxford, Univ of Edinburgh; *m* 1968, Annabel Claire, da of Prof William McCausland Stewart; 2 s; *Career* tutor faculty law Univ of Edinburgh 1963-73, standing jr cncl Registrar of Restrictive Trading Agreements 1968-70, advocate depute 1970-73; Sheriff: South Strathclyde, Dumfries and Galloway at Airdrie 1973-79, Grampian, Highland and Islands at Aberdeen 1979-90, Tayside, Central and Fife at Dundee 1990-; govr Robert Gordon's Inst of Technol 1982-; chm: Grampian Family Conciliation Serv 1984-87, Scottish Assoc of Family Conciliation Servs 1986-89; *Recreations* reading, music; *Style*— Sheriff Alastair Stewart; Sheriff's Chambers, Sheriff Court House, Dundee DD1 9AD

STEWART, Alec James; s of Mickey J Stewart (the England cricket official); *b* 8 April 1963; *Educ* Tiffin Sch; *Career* professional cricketer; Surrey CCC 1981-, awarded county cap 1985; England debut on tour W Indies 1989-90, memb England tour Aust and NZ 1990-91; jt world record 11 catches in a match Surrey v Leics 1989; *Style*— Alec Stewart, Esq; c/o Surrey County Cricket Club, Kennington Oval, London SE11 5SS (☎ 071 582 6660)

STEWART, Alexander Christie; s of Lt-Col Robert Christie Stewart, CBE, of Arndean, Dollar, Clackmannanshire, Scotland, and Ann Grizel, *née* Cochrane; *b* 21 June 1955; *Educ* Gordonstoun; *m* 24 April 1986, Katherine Lake, da of Denys Barry Herbert Domvile; 1 s (Archie b 10 June 1989), 1 da (Georgina b 11 Oct 1987); *Career* racehorse trainer 1983-; trained winners incl: Mtoto, Opale, Waajib, Dubian, Ghariba, Life at the Top, Daarkom, Braashee, Al Maheb; *Recreations* shooting; *Style*— Alexander Stewart, Esq; Clarehaven Stables, Newmarket, Suffolk CB8 7BY (☎ 0638 667323, fax 0638 666389)

STEWART, Alexander Joseph; s of Alexander Stewart (d 1978), of Windsor, Canada, and Mary, *née* Bulloch; *b* 4 Jan 1948; *Educ* McGill Univ Canada (BA), Univ of Oxford (BA, BCL); *m* 25 July 1987, Rosamund Chad, da of Brian James Wilson, of The Spinney, Haughton, nr Tarporley, Cheshire; 1 s (Alexander Robert James); *Career* asst prof of law Univ of Windsor Canada, called to the Bar Gray's Inn 1975, called to the Bar of Upper Canada 1979, joined Lincoln's Inn 1988 ad eundem; *Books* A Casebook on Trusts (1973); *Recreations* tennis, reading; *Clubs* Boulevard; *Style*— Alexander Stewart, Esq; 5 Park Ave, London SW14 8AT (☎ 071 878 7114); 5 New Square, Lincolns Inn, London WC2A 3RJ (☎ 071 404 0404, fax 071 831 6016)

STEWART, Lady Alison Jeannette; da of 6 Earl of Ducie; *b* 9 March 1954; *Educ* Westwings Sch Glos; *m* 1986, Mark Allan Stewart, of Toronto, Canada; 1 s; *Style*— The Lady Alison Stewart

STEWART, (John) Allan; MP (C) Eastwood 1983-; s of Edward MacPherson Stewart by his w Eadie Barrie; *b* 1 June 1942; *Educ* Bell Baxter HS (Cupar), St Andrews Univ, Harvard; *m* 1973, Marjorie Sally (Susie), *née* Gourlay; 1 s, 1 da; *Career* lectr political economy St Andrews Univ 1965-70; CBI 1971-78: head Regnl Devpt Dept 1971-73, dep dir econs 1974, Scottish sec 1974, Scottish dir 1978; cncllr Bromley 1975-76; Parly candidate (C) Dundee East 1970, MP (C) Renfrewshire E 1979-1983; parly under-sec Scottish Office 1981-86 (responsibility for home affrs and environment in Scottish Office April 1982), Scottish min Industry and Educn 1983-86, Scottish min Industry and Local Govt 1990-; *Recreations* golf, bridge; *Style*— Allan Stewart, Esq, MP; Crofthead House, by Neilston, Renfrewshire G78 3NB (☎ 041 881 2892)

STEWART, Andrew Struthers; MP (C) Sherwood 1983-; *b* 1937; *Educ* Strathaven Acad Lanark, West of Scotland Agric Coll; *Career* memb Notts CC 1974-; PPS to John McGregor, Lord Pres and Leader of the House of Commons (also when Sec of State for Educn and Sci, and Min of Agric); memb: Parly Select Ctee for Agric 1985-, All Pty Ctee on Textiles; memb Cons Pty Ctees on Energy and Agric; *Style*— Andrew Stewart, Esq, MP; House of Commons, London SW1

STEWART, Angus; QC; s of Archibald Ian Balfour Stewart, CBE, and Ailsa Rosamund Mary Massey; *b* 14 Dec 1946; *Educ* Edinburgh Acad, Balliol Coll Oxford (BA), Univ of Edinburgh (LLB); *m* 14 June 1975, Jennifer Margaret, da of John Faulds Stewart (d 1980), of Edinburgh; 1 da (Flora b 13 Sept 1981); *Career* barr 1975-; *Style*— Angus Stewart, Esq, QC; 8 Ann Street, Edinburgh EH4 1PJ (☎ 031 332 4083)

STEWART, Barbara Mary; da of Henry Rollinson Bailey (d 1978), of Eccles, Manchester, and Maud Elizabeth, *née* Gurney (d 1984); *b* 9 Aug 1925; *Educ* Pendleton HS for Girls, Manchester Regn Coll of Art Sch of Architecture (DA); *m* 12 July 1952, Dr Geoffrey Stewart, s of Clifford Stewart (d 1965), of Swinton, Lancs; 1 s (Matthew Clifford b 23 Dec 1964); *Career* WRNS 1944-46; architect to Building Design

Partnership 1954-61, lectr Schs of Architecture and Planning Birmingham 1961-64, lectr Extra Mural Dept Univ of Birmingham 1961-70, town cncllr Royal Borough of Bewdley 1965-70, sr architect: Greenwood and Abercrombie 1970-73, Basil Spence and ptnrs 1973-74; Civil Serv: princ architect UGC/Dept of Health 1974-90; Christian Aid organiser Eccles Manchester; World Refugee Year 1959; fndr memb: Avoncraft Museum of Bldgs 1963, Worcs Soc of Architects 1966; vice chm Assoc of Civil Serv Arts Club 1989- (sec dept of Health Art Club 1988-90); voluntary worker Cncl for the Care of Churches 1991-; Bronze medal and commendation of merit for design of Victoria Park Secdy Sch Manchester Soc of Architects 1962; memb RIBA 1949; *Books* Buildings of Bewdley - Historical Research Papers (1967-68); *Recreations* painting and sculpture, photography, gardening; *Clubs* Civil Serv; *Style*— Mrs Barbara M Stewart; 131 London Rd, Ewell, Epsom, Surrey KT17 2BS (☎ 081 393 6554); Dept of Health, Euston Tower, 286 Euston Rd, London NW1

STEWART, Dr (George) Barry; s of Robert Temple Stewart, of 319 Ryhope Rd, Sunderland, Tyne and Wear, and Sarah Alice, *née* Robson; *b* 3 Sept 1943; *Educ* Robert Richardson GS, Univ of Nottingham (LLB), Fitzwilliam Coll and Inst of Criminology Univ of Cambridge (Dip Crim, JD); *Career* called to the Bar Grays Inn 1968, attorney and cnsllr at Law Federal Cts USA, memb Bar of NY 1987, head of chambers, sr memb Cleveland Bar; Methodist preacher, Danby circuit N Yorks accredited 1964; *Recreations* reading, foreign travel; *Style*— Dr G Barry Stewart; Ridge Hall, Ridge Lane, Staithes, Saltburn-by-the-Sea, Cleveland TS13 5DX (☎ 0947 840511); 71A Borough Rd, Middlesbrough, Cleveland TS1 3AA (☎ 0642 226036)

STEWART, Brian Alexander; s of Alexander Bellamy Stewart (d 1977), of West Ridge, Walpole Ave, Chipstead, Coulsdon, Surrey, and Jessie, *née* Hopkins; *b* 7 May 1926; *Educ* Stowe, Trinity Coll Cambridge; *Career* Nat Serv REME 1947-50 (cmmnd Capt, WRS i/c basic section electronics wing REME Trg Centre); memb Lloyds 1949, dir Stewart & Hughman Ltd 1955-87 (joined 1950); dir until 1987: Stewart Grays Inn, Rockall Underwriting Agency, Peninsula Underwriting Agency, Walrond Scarman, Trojan Underwriting Agency; chm River Clyde Holdings plc until 1988; dir: Shopset Ltd (trading as Carsounds) 1987-90, Carsounds (Radio and Stereo Specialists) Ltd 1988-; cdre: Lloyds Yacht Club (adm 1989-), Ocean Cruising Club 1968-75; dep chm In Sail Trg Assoc 1974- (chm schooner ctee 1966-85); *Recreations* sailing; *Clubs* Lloyds Yacht, Royal Thames Yacht, Royal Ocean Racing; *Style*— Brian Stewart, Esq; (☎ 0836 251706, fax 0737 557759)

STEWART, Brian Thomas Webster; CMG (1969); s of Redvers Buller Stewart (d 1976), and Mabel, *née* Sparks (d 1977); *b* 27 April 1922; *Educ* Trinity Coll Glenalmond, Worcester Coll Oxford (MA); *m* Sally Elizabeth, *née* Acland; 1 s (Rory), 3 da (Heather, Anne, Fiona); *Career* Capt Black Watch RHR 1941-46; Colonial Civil Serv (MCS) 1946-57, Dip Serv Asia 1957-79; dir Rubber Growers' Assoc Malaysia 1979-82, dir ops China Racal Electronics 1982-; *Books* All Mens Wisdom (1958); *Clubs* Atheaeum, Special Forces, Hongkong; *Style*— Brian Stewart, Esq, CMG; Broich House, Crieff, Perthshire; 43 High West, 142 Polfulam Rd, Hong Kong; Racal Electronics, 6B Sun House, 90 Connaught Rd (C), Hong Kong

STEWART, Callum John Tyndale; s of Air Vice-Marshal William K Stewart CB, CBE, AFC, QHP (d 1967), of Farnborough, Hants, and Audrey Wentworth, *née* Tyndale (who m 2 1970, Sir Bryan Harold Cabot Matthews, CBE (d 1986); *b* 2 Feb 1945; *Educ* Wellington Coll; *m* 18 July 1975 (m dis 1982), Elaine Alison, da of Francies Bairstow (d 1979); *Career* exec dir Bland Welch & Co Ltd 1963-72; dir: CE Heath (International) Ltd 1972-75, Fielding & Ptnrs 1975-86 (dep chm 1984-86), CE Heath plc 1986-; *Recreations* tennis, jogging, antiques; *Style*— Callum Stewart, Esq; Flat 5, 8 Chelsea Embankment, London SW3 (☎ 071 488 1488); La Petite Tourraque, Bastide Blanche, Ramatuelle, France; c/o CE Heath plc, Cuthbert Heath House, 150 Minories, London EC3M 1NR

STEWART, Colin MacDonald; CB (1983); s of John Stewart, of Glasgow, and Lillias Cecilia MacDonald, *née* Fraser; *b* 26 Dec 1922; *Educ* Queens Park Secdy Sch; *m* 1948, Gladys Edith, da of Ernest Alfred Thwaites, of Barnet, Herts; 3 da; *Career* WWII clerical offr Admty Rosyth Dockyard 1939-42, Fleet Air Arm 1942-46, med serv with 809 Sqdn followed by staff posts in Scotland, Lt (A) RNVR; directing actuary Govt Actuary's Dept 1974-84 (joined 1946), assoc dir (actuarial res) Godwins Ltd 1985-88; FIA 1953; *Books* The Students' Society Log 1960-85; *Recreations* genealogical research; *Style*— Colin Stewart, Esq, CB; 8 The Chase, Coulsdon, Surrey CR5 2EG (☎ 081 660 3966)

STEWART, Lady (Christine) Daphne; *née* Hay; da of 11 Marquess of Tweeddale (d 1967), and Marguerite Christine (d 1946), da of Alexander Ralli, and step da of Lewis Einstein; *b* 29 March 1919; *Educ* at home; *m* 1, 1939 (m dis 1947), Lt-Col David Morley-Fletcher, OBE, TD, yr s of Bernard Morley Morley-Fletcher; 1 s, 1 da; m 2, 1957, Lt-Col Francis Robert Cameron Stewart, late Indian Army, s of late Sir Francis Hugh Stewart, CIE; *Recreations* breeding ponies; *Style*— Lady Daphne Stewart; Middle Blainslie, by Galashiels, Selkirkshire (☎ 089 686 217)

STEWART, Sir David Brodribb; 2 Bt (UK 1960), of Strathgarry, Co Perth, TD (1948); s of Sir Kenneth Dugald Stewart, 1 Bt, GBE (d 1972), and Noel, *née* Brodribb (d 1946); *b* 20 Dec 1913; *Educ* Marlborough, Manchester Coll of Technol (BSc); *m* 14 Sept 1963, Barbara Dykes, da of late Harry Dykes Lloyd, and wid of Donald Ian Stewart; *Heir* bro, Robin Alastair Stewart, *qv*; *Career* cmmd into TA 1934, served WWII France and Belgium 1940 and Italy, cmd Duke of Lancaster's Own Yeo 1952-56, ret as Bt-Col 1956; former md Francis Price (Fabrics) Ltd, ret 1981; *Recreations* gardening; *Style*— Sir David Stewart, Bt, TD; Delamere, Heyes Lane, Alderley Edge, Cheshire SK9 7JY (☎ 0625 582312)

STEWART, David Charles; s of Andrew Graham Stewart (d 1964), of Corsliehill, Houston, Renfrewshire, and Barabel Ethel, *née* Greig (d 1985); *b* 23 June 1936; *Educ* Winchester, Trinity Coll Cambridge (BA); *m* 16 Nov 1978, Wendy Ann, da of John McMillan (d 1951), of Kingswood, Surrey; 1 s (Jonathan b 1979), 3 da (Tara b 1981, Serena b 1983, Fleur (twin) b 1983); *Career* Nat Serv 2 Lt Royal Scots Greys 1956-57; dir: The Victaulic Co Ltd 1965, Stewarts and Lloyds Plastics Ltd 1965; md Victaulic plc 1983-; *Style*— David Stewart, Esq; The Brewery House, Old, Northamptonshire (☎ 0604 781 577); Victaulic plc, 382 Silbury Boulevard, Milton Keynes, Bucks (☎ 0908 691 000)

STEWART, David Howat; s of William Gray Stewart (d 1980), and Helen Dorothy, *née* Howat (d 1986); *b* 27 Oct 1945; *Educ* Grangefield GS Stockton-on-Tees; *m* 1, 14 Sept 1968 (m dis 1985), Gillian; 2 da (Caroline b 1977, Sarah b 1982); m 2, 19 Aug 1985, Susan Andrea, da of Brig George Laing, CBE (ADC to HM The Queen 1962, d 1986); 2 s (Harry b 1985, Frederick George b 1991); *Career* Nat Westminister Bank Group 1963-70, exec dir County Natwest Ltd 1970-87, gen mangr and chief exec Creditanstalt-Bankverein 1987-; ACIB 1967; *Recreations* music; *Style*— David Stewart, Esq; 29 Gresham St, London EC2V 7AH (☎ 071 822 2600, fax 071 822 2663, telex 894 612)

STEWART, Capt David John Christopher; s (by 1 m) and h of Sir Hugh Charlie Godfray Stewart, 6 Bt of Athenree; *b* 19 June 1935; *Educ* Bradfield, RMA Sandhurst; *m* 7 Nov 1959, Bridget Anne, er da of late Patrick Wood Sim; 3 da; *Career* Capt (ret) Royal Inniskilling Fus (seconded Trucial Oman Scouts); sometime dir Maurice James (Hldgs) Ltd; proprietor David Stewart Picture Framing; memb Fine Art Trade Guild; *Clubs* MCC; *Style*— Capt David Stewart; Tower View, 8 Silver St, Wilveliscombe, Somerset

STEWART, David Purcell; s of Maurice Edward Stewart (d 1967), of Epsom, Surrey, and Joyce Ethel Stewart, of Worthing, Sussex; *b* 8 Sept 1941; *Educ* Rutlish Sch Merton Park; *m* 14 Sept 1968, Judith Esther, da of Charles Owen (d 1983), of Bexleyheath; 1 da (Susannah Celia b 23 April 1977); *Career* Coopers & Lybrand Deloitte (formerly Deloitte Haskins & Sells): joined 1958, ptnr 1967, ptnr for nat tax 1982-90, exec ptnr i/c central London office 1990-; Freeman City of London 1982; FCA 1963, FCCA 1981, FIOD 1982; *Recreations* numismatics, theatre, opera; *Clubs* RAC, MCC; *Style*— David Stewart, Esq; The Oast House, Best Beech, Wadhurst, Sussex TN5 6JH; Coopers & Lybrand Deloitte, 128 Queen Victoria St, London EC4 (☎ 071 583 5000)

STEWART, Rt Hon Donald James; PC (1977), MP (SNP) Western Isles 1970-87; *b* 17 Oct 1920; *Educ* Nicolson Inst Stornoway; *m* 1955, Christina Macaulay; *Career* provost of Stornoway 1958-64 and 1968-70; Hon Sheriff 1960; memb Cncl Get Britain Out (EEC), ldr Parly SNP 1974-87; *Style*— The Rt Hon Donald Stewart; Hillcrest, 41 Goathill Rd, Stornoway, Isle of Lewis (☎ 0851 2672)

STEWART, Ewen; s of late Duncan Stewart, of Kinlocheil, and Kate, *née* Blunt; *b* 22 April 1926; *Educ* Univ of Edinburgh (BSc, MA, LLB); *m* 1959, Norma Porteous, da of late William Charteris Hollands, of Earlston; 1 da; *Career* agric economist E of Scotland Coll of Agric 1946-49; practised at Scottish Bar 1952-62, lectr in agric law Univ of Edinburgh 1957-62, former standing jr counsel Miny of Fuel and Power; Parly candidate (Lab) Bannfshire 1962; Sheriff: Wick Caithness 1962-, Dornoch 1977-, Sutherland, Tain Ross and Cromarty 1977-, Stornoway Western Isles 1990; *Style*— Ewen Stewart, Esq; 16 Bignold Court, Wick, Caithness, Highlands KW1 4DL

STEWART, Hon Mrs (Frances Julia); da of Baron Kaldor (Life Peer); *b* 1940; *m* 1962, Michael John Stewart; *Style*— The Hon Mrs Stewart; 39 Upper Park Rd, NW3

STEWART, Prof Sir Frederick Henry; s of Frederick Stewart and Hester, *née* Alexander; *b* 16 Jan 1916; *Educ* Fettes, Univ of Aberdeen (BSc), Emmanuel Coll Cambridge (PhD); *m* 1945, Mary Rainbow (the writer Mary Stewart); *Career* former chm: NERC, Advsy Bd for the Res Cncls; mineralogist ICI Ltd (Billingham Div) 1941-43, lectr in geology Univ of Durham 1943-56, regius prof of geology Univ of Edinburgh 1956-82; tstee Br Museum (Natural History) 1983-87; Hon DSc: Aberdeen, Leicester, Heriot Watt, Durham, Glasgow; FRS, FRSE, FGS; kt 1974; *Style*— Prof Sir Frederick Stewart, FRS, FRSE; 79 Morningside Park, Edinburgh (☎ 031 447 2620); House of Letterawe, Lochawe, Argyll (☎ 083 82 329)

STEWART, George Girdwood; CB (1979), MC (1945), TD (1954); s of Herbert Alexander Stewart (d 1966), and Janetta Dunlop, *née* Girdwood (d 1988); *b* 12 Dec 1919; *Educ* Kelvinside Acad Glasgow, Univ of Glasgow, Univ of Edinburgh (BSc); *m* 1950, Shelagh Jean Morven, da of Dr R R Murray; 1 s (Alan b 1955), 1 da (Sara b 1953); *Career* Cmd Offr 278 (L) Field Regt RA (TA) 1957-60; forestry cmmr 1969-79; pres Scot Ski Club 1971-75, vice-pres Nat Ski Fedn of GB 1975-78; rep Nat Tst for Scotland Perth 1980-88; memb: Environment Panel BR Bd 1980-90, memb Countryside Cmmn for Scot 1981-87; chm Scot Wildlife Tst 1981-87, memb Cairngorm Recreation Tst 1986-; advsr Highlands and Islands Devpt Bd Cairngorm estate 1987-; assoc dir Oakwood Environmental 1991-; FRSA; FICFor, Hon FLI; *Recreations* skiing, tennis, studying Scottish painting; *Clubs* Ski of GB; *Style*— George Stewart, Esq, CB, MC, TD; Stormont House, Mansfield Rd, Scone PH2 6SA (☎ 0738 51815)

STEWART, Gillian; da of Gordon Anderson Stewart (d 1988), and Iris, *née* Ross; *b* 21 Oct 1958; *Educ* Inverness Royal Acad, Univ of Edinburgh (BSc); *Career* golfer; amateur record: Scot under-19 stroke play champion 1975, Scot girl int 1975-77, Br girls champion 1976, Scot women's champion 1979 (1983 and 1984), runner-up Br Championship 1982, runner-up Spanish Championship 1984, IBM Euro Open champion 1984, Helen Holm Trophy winner 1981-84; int appearances: Scot Ladies Home Int 1979-84, Scot Ladies Euro team Championship 1979 (1981, 1983), BG Cwlth team 1979-83, GB Vagliano Trophy Team 1979 (1981, 1983), GB Curtis Cup team 1980-82, GB World Cup team 1982-84, Avia Watches Golfer of the Year 1984; professional golfer 1985-: won Ford Classic at Woburn 1985 (and 1987), fourth in WPGA Order of Merit 1986, seventh in WPGET Order of Merit 1990; memb: Women Professional Golfers Euro Tour, PGA; *Recreations* all aspects of golf, swimming, cookery, keep fit; *Style*— Miss Gillian Stewart; 14 Annfield Road, Inverness, Scotland IV2 3HX (☎ 0463 231477)

STEWART, Gordon; s of Archibald Leitch Stewart, of Luton, Beds, and Christina Macpherson, *née* Taylor (d 1976); *b* 18 April 1953; *Educ* Luton GS, Univ of Durham (BA); *m* 2 Oct 1982, Teresa Violet, da of Sir James Holmes Henry, 2 Bt, CMG, MC, TD, QC, of Hampton, Middx; 2 s (Edmund James b 24 May 1985, Roland Valentine b 16 Jan 1988); *Career* asst slr Slaughter & May 1978-83 (articled clerk 1976-78); ptnr Simmons & Simmons 1985- (asst slr 1983-85); memb Law Soc; *Recreations* food and wine; *Style*— Gordon Stewart, Esq; Simmons & Simmons, 14 Dominion St, London EC2M 2RJ (☎ 071 628 2020, fax 071 588 4129, telex 888562 SIMMON G)

STEWART, (George Robert) Gordon; OBE (1983), WS (1949); s of Capt David Gordon Stewart, MC (d 1967), of Edinburgh, and Mary Grant, *née* Thompson (d 1954); *b* 13 Oct 1924; *Educ* George Watson's Coll Edinburgh, Univ of Edinburgh (MA, LLB); *m* 11 Oct 1952, Rachel Jean, da of Maj John Baxter Morrison (d 1960), of Edinburgh; 2 s (Robert Ian David b 1956, John Douglas b 1961), 1 da (Gillian Mary Jean b 1954); *Career* volunteered Royal Scots 1942, transferred RCS 1944, WWII served Burma, India, Sumatra, SEAC, Capt 1946; admitted slr 1951, ptnr Melville & Lindesay WS Edinburgh 1951-56 (legal asst 1949-50), Notary Public 1952; sec and personnel dir Ideal Standard Ltd Yorks 1975-76 (asst sec 1956-75), legal advsr Inst of CA of Scotland 1985-89 (sec 1976-85); *Recreations* pot gardening, music, walking; *Clubs* Edinburgh Univ Staff; *Style*— Gordon Stewart, Esq, OBE, WS; 15 Hillpark Loan, Edinburgh EH4 7BH (☎ 031 312 7079)

STEWART, Prof Harold Charles; CBE (1975), DL (Gtr London 1967); s of Dr Bernard Halley Stewart (d 1958), and Mabel Florence, *née* Wyatt (d 1968); *b* 23 Nov 1906; *Educ* Mill Hill, Cambridge, UCH; *m* 1, 1929, Dorothy Irene, *née* Löwen (d 1969); 1 s (The Rt Hon Ian Halley Stewart, MP, *qv*), 1 da; m 2, 1970, Audrey Patricia Nicolle, da of Edward le Vavasour dit Durell Nicolle (d 1981), of Jersey; *Career* conslt MOD 1961-74, Gresham prof in physic City of London 1968-70, emeritus prof of pharmacology St Mary's Hosp Med Sch 1974- (head Dept of Pharmacology 1950-74); DG St John Ambulance 1976-78; chm: Sir Halley Stewart Tst for Res 1987- (pres 1978-87), Buttle Tst for Children 1979-; former vice chm Med Cncl Alcoholism (patron 1988-) and vice pres St Christopher's Hosp for Terminal Cases; Guthrie Meml medal for distinguished servs to MOD (Army) 1974; KstJ 1969; *Recreations* genealogy, heraldry, voluntary work; *Clubs* Athenaeum, St John House; *Style*— Prof Harold Stewart, CBE, DL; 41 The Glen, Green Lane, Northwood, Middx HA6 2UR (☎ 09274 248 93)

STEWART, Sir Hugh Charlie Godfray; 6 Bt (UK 1803), of Athenree, Tyrone; DL (Tyrone 1971); s of Sir George Powell Stewart, 5 Bt (d 1945), and Florence Georgina, *née* Godfray (d 1957); *b* 13 April 1897; *Educ* Bradfield, RMC Sandhurst; *m* 1, 1929 (m dis 1942), Rosemary Elinor Dorothy, da of late Maj George Peacocke; 1 s, 1 da; m 2, 1948, Diana Margaret, da of late Capt J E Hibbert, MC, DFC; 1 s (Hugh b 1955), 1 da

(Jane b 1949); *Heir* s by 1 m, Capt David Stewart; *Career* 1914-18 war in France (wounded, first battle Arras 1917), 1939-45 war in France, and as Asst Cmdt Imperial Forces Transhipment Camp, Durban and in Syria; Maj Royal Inniskilling Fusiliers, ret 1945; High Sheriff Tyrone 1955; *Style—* Sir Hugh Stewart, Bt, DL; Cottesbrook, Sandy Pluck Lane, Bentham, Cheltenham

STEWART, Rt Hon (Bernard Harold) Ian Halley; RD (1972), PC (1989), MP (C) N Herts 1983-; s of Prof Harold Stewart, CBE, DL, *qv*, and his 1 w Dorothy Irene, *née* Löwen (d 1969); *b* 10 Aug 1935; *Educ* Haileybury, Jesus Coll Cambridge (MA); *m* 8 Oct 1966, Deborah Charlotte, JP, da of Hon William Buchan (2 s of 1 Baron Tweedsmuir, otherwise known as John Buchan, the author); 1 s (Henry b 1972), 2 da (Lydia b 1969, Louisa b 1970); *Career* served RNVR 1954-56, Lt-Cdr RNR; with Seccombe Marshall & Campion (bill brokers) 1959-60; dir: Brown Shipley & Co (merchant bankers) 1971-83 (joined 1960, asst mangr 1963, mangr 1966), Brown Shipley Holdings 1981-83, Victory Insurance 1976-83; MP (C) Hitchin Feb 1974-83; oppn spokesman Banking Bill 1978-79, PPS to Geoffrey Howe (as Chllr Exchequer) 1979-83, under sec MOD (Def Procurement) Jan-Oct 1983, econ sec Treasy with special responsibility for monetary policy and fin insts 1983-87, min of State for the Armed Forces 1987-88, min of State NI 1988-89, chm The Throgmorton Trust plc 1990-; former jt sec Cons Parly Fin Ctee and memb Pub Expenditure Ctee; memb Br Acad Ctee Sylloge Coins of Br Isles 1967-, vice chm Westminster Ctee Protection Children 1975-, vice pres Herts Soc 1974-; memb Cncl Haileybury 1980- (life govr 1977); tstee Sir Halley Stewart Tst 1978-; LittD Cantab 1978; FBA 1981, FRSE 1986, FSA, FSA Scotland, CStJ 1986 (vice pres St John Ambulance Herts 1978-); *Books* The Scottish Coinage (1955, 1967), Coinage in Tenth-century England (with C E Blunt and C S S Lyon, 1989); *Recreations* history, real tennis; *Clubs* MCC, Hawks; *Style—* The Rt Hon Ian Stewart, RD, MP; House of Commons, London SW1

STEWART, Ian William; s of late Rev William Stewart; *b* 24 March 1923; *Educ* Merchiston Castle; *m* 1953, Jane Alison, *née* Cunningham; 2 c; *Career* Flt Offr Italy; dir William Low & Co Ltd 1952-88, dep chm William Low & Co plc 1982-88, pres Dundee & Tayside C of C 1983-84; *Recreations* shooting, golf, music; *Clubs* New (Edinburgh), Panmure Golf; *Style—* Ian Stewart, Esq; Greenbank, Barry, Carnoustie, Angus (☎ 0241 53043)

STEWART, James Cecil Campbell; CBE (1960); s of late James Stewart, and Mary Stewart; *b* 25 July 1916; *Educ* Armstrong Coll, King's Coll Durham Univ; *m* 1946, Pamela Rouselle, da of William King-Smith; 1 da; *Career* Telecommunication Res Estab 1939-45, AERE Harwell 1946-49, Industl Gp Risley 1949-63, memb Bd of UKAEA and CEGB 1963-69, dir of Nat Nuclear Corpn Ltd 1969-82 (currently conslt); chm: Br Nuclear Forum 1974-, NNC Pension Tstee Ltd 1979-; *Recreations* tending a garden; *Clubs* East India, Les Ambassadeurs; *Style—* James Stewart, Esq, CBE; Whitethorns, Higher Whitley, Warrington, Cheshire WA4 4QJ (☎ 0925 73377)

STEWART, James Harvey; s of Harvey Stewart, of Fochabers, Moray, and Annie, *née* Gray; *b* 15 Aug 1939; *Educ* Peterhead Acad, Univ of Aberdeen (MA), Univ of Manchester (Dip Soc Admin); *m* 24 April 1965, Fiona Maria Maclay, da of John Reid (d 1973), of Peterhead; 3 s (Iain b 1969, Alasdair b 1972, Gordon b 1974), 1 da (Marie b 1966); *Career* hosp sec Princess' Margaret Rose Orthopaedic Hosp Edinburgh 1965-67, dep gp sec York A Hosp Mgmnt Ctee 1968-73 (princ admin asst 1967-68), area admin Northumberland AHA 1973-83, dist admin Northumberland Health Authy 1982-83, regnl admin E Anglian RHA 1983-85, dist gen mangr Barking Havering and Brentwood Health Authy 1985-; AHSM; *Recreations* music, reading, squash, rugby, food, wine; *Clubs* Rotary, Cambridge RUFC, Univ of Cambridge RUFC; *Style—* James Stewart, Esq; The Grange, Harold Wood Hosp, Gubbins Lane, Romford RM3 0BE (☎ 04023 495 11, fax 04023 813 68)

STEWART, James Michael; s of Surgn Lt-Col John M Stewart, and Dr Margaret J W, *née* Robertson; *b* 5 Sept 1960; *Educ* Sedburgh, Univ of Exeter (BA); *Career* KMG Thompson McIntock 1982-86; Peter Leonard Assocs 1986-: fin dir 1987-, md 1989-; FCA; *Recreations* squash, swimming, running, gym; *Style—* James Stewart, Esq; Peter Leonard Assoc Ltd, 535 Kings Rd, London SW10 0SZ (☎ 071 352 1717, fax 071 351 4307)

STEWART, James Simeon Hamilton; QC (1982); s of Henry Hamilton Stewart (d 1970), and Edna Mary, *née* Pulman; *b* 2 May 1943; *Educ* Cheltenham, Univ of Leeds (LLB); *m* 19 April 1972, Helen Margaret, da of (Thomas) Kenneth Whiteley; 2 da (Alexandra b 18 Jan 1974, Georgina b 27 Nov 1975); *Career* called to the Bar Inner Temple 1966, practising N Eastern Circuit and London, rec of Crown Ct 1982-; *Recreations* cricket, gardening, tennis; *Clubs* Bradford, Leeds Taverners; *Style—* James Stewart, Esq, QC; Park Court Chambers, 40 Park Cross St, Leeds S1 2QH (☎ 0532 433277, fax 0532 421285, telex 666135)

STEWART, John Anthony Benedict; CMG (1979), OBE (1973); s of Edward Vincent da Silva Stewart (d 1974), and Emily Veronica, *née* Jones (d 1989); *b* 24 May 1927; *Educ* St Illtyd's Coll Cardiff, Univ of Wales (BSc), Imperial Coll of Sci (DIC); *m* 16 May 1960, Geraldine Margaret, da of Capt Gerald Clifton (d 1975); 2 s (Anthony Vincent Gerald b 20 Dec 1961, Christopher John b and d 1965), 1 da (Drusilla Georgina Jane b 6 June 1967); *Career* midshipman RN 1944-47; Colonial Geological Survey Serv Somaliland Protectorate 1951-55; Colonial Admin Serv: dist offr Somaliland 1955-60, sr dist cmmr N Rhodesia 1960-67; HM Dip Serv: joined 1967, HM Ambass Vietnam 1974-76, HM Ambass Laos 1978, HM Ambass Mozambique 1980-84, high cmmr Sri Lanka 1984-87; chm Civil Serv Selection Bd 1987-; hon treas Tibet Relief Fund of the UK; *Books* The geology of the Mait Area of British Somaliland (1956); *Recreations* fishing, shooting, reading; *Clubs* Flyfishers, Royal Cwlth, Guildford County; *Style—* John A B Stewart, Esq, CMG, OBE

STEWART, Prof John David; s of David Stewart (d 1970), and Phyllis, *née* Crossley (d 1986); *b* 19 March 1929; *Educ* Stockport GS, Balliol Coll Oxford; *m* 27 July 1953, Theresa, da of John Raisman (d 1980); 2 s (David b 7 Oct 1955, Henry b 27 June 1959), 2 da (Lindsey b 16 Feb 1957, Selina b 12 March 1962); *Career* Industl Rels Dept NCB; Inst of Local Govt Studies Univ of Birmingham: sr lectr 1966-67, assoc dir 1970-76, prof 1971-, dir 1976-83; head of Sch of Public Policy Univ of Birmingham 1990-; memb Layfield Ctee on Local Govt Fin, vice pres RIPA; *Books* British Pressure Groups (1958), Management in Local Government (1971), Corporate Planning in Local Government (with R Greenwood, 1974), The Retrospective Local Authority (1974), Approaches in Public Policy (jt ed with S Leach, 1982), The Case for Local Government (with G Jones, 1983), Local Government: Conditions of Local Choice (1983), The New Management of Local Government (1986), Understanding the Management of Local Government (1988), The Future of Local Government (jt ed with G Stoker, 1989); *Style—* Prof John Stewart; 15 Selly Wick Rd, Birmingham B29 7JJ (☎ 021 472 1512)

STEWART, Sheriff John Hall; s of Cecil Francis Wilson Stewart (d 1964), and Mary Fyffe, *née* Wall; *b* 15 March 1944; *Educ* Airdrie Acad, Univ of St Andrews (LLB); *m* 29 Nov 1968, Marion, da of Donald MacCalman (d 1978); 2 s (Alan Brecil b 1973, Rohan Mhairi b 1975), 1 da (Katryn MacCalman b 1978); *Career* enrolled slr 1971-77, appointed Sheriff S Strathclyde Dumfries and Galloway at Airdrie 1985; memb Faculty of Advocates 1978; *Recreations* golf, spectator rugby football and soccor; *Clubs* Uddinton Rugby Football; *Style—* Sheriff John Stewart; 3 Fife Crescent, Bothwell, Glasgow G71 8DG (☎ 0698 853854); Sheriff's Chambers, Sheriff Court House, Graham St, Airdrie ML6 6EE (☎ 0236 51121)

STEWART, Capt John Stephen; OBE; s of William Stewart, JP (d 1987), of Weston Underwood, Bucks, and Theresa, *née* Daniels (d 1948); *b* 14 July 1922; *Educ* Clifton Coll Bristol, Univ of London Med Sch; *m* 15 July 1954, Eileen Mary, da of John Ryan Lahiff (d 1966), of Preston, Lancs; 3 s (Hugh b 1955, Mark b 1956, Kevin b 1959), 1 da (Isabel b 1958); *Career* RM: 2 Lt 1941, Commando Serv Europe 1942-48 (twice wounded), Adj RMB Chatham and Eastney 1948-51, SRMO HMS Implacable Home Fleet Trg Sqdn 1951-53, 45 RM Commando serv Malta and Cyprus (invalided blast injuries), ret 1956; farmer Weston Underwood Bucks 1956-80, dir Nuffield Farming Scholarships Tst 1969-89; chm: Milton Keynes Gen Cmmn of Tax, Arthritis & Rheumatisim Cncl Olney and Dist; life memb Int Wine and Food Soc (past chm and sec Northampton, chm Strasbourg Conf); Nuffield Scholars Beef Prodn Europe 1964, Winston Churchill fell Livestock Husbandry NZ 1974; Freeman City of London, Liveryman Worshipful Co of Farmers 1974; FRAgS 1986; *Recreations* travel by car and caravan, wine and food, reading, watching sport; *Clubs* Farmers'; *Style—* Capt John Stewart, OBE; The Mill House, Olney, Bucks MK46 4AD (☎ 0234 711 381, fax 0234 712 095)

STEWART, John Young (Jackie); OBE (1972); s of Robert Paul Stewart (d 1972), and Jean Clark Young; *b* 11 June 1939; *Educ* Dumbarton Acad; *m* 1962, Helen McGregor; 2 s (Paul b 1965, Mark b 1968); *Career* former racing driver; memb Scottish and Br Team for clay pigeon shooting; former Scottish, English, Irish, Welsh and Br Champion, won Coupe des Nations 1959 and 1960; first raced 1961, competed in 4 meetings driving for Barry Filer Glasgow 1961-62, drove for Ecurie Ecosse and Barry Filer winning 14 out of 23 starts 1963, 28 wins out of 53 starts 1964, drove Formula 1 for Br Racing Motors (BRM) 1965-67 then for Ken Tyrrell 1968-73, has won Australian, NZ, Swedish, Mediterranean, Japanese and many other non-championship maj int motor races, set new world record by winning 26 World Championship Grand Prix (Zandvoort) 1973, 27 (Nürburgring) 1973, third in World Championship 1965, second in 1968 and 1972, World Champion 1969, 1971, 1973; Br Automobile Racing Club Gold Medal 1971 and 1973, Daily Express Sportsman of the Year 1971 and 1973; BBC Sports Personality of the Year 1973, Segrave Trophy 1973, Scottish Sportsman of the Year 1968 and 1973, USA Sportsman of the Year 1973; film: Weekend of a Champion 1972; *Books* World Champion (with Eric Dymock, 1970), Faster! (with Peter Manso, 1972), On the Road (1983), Jackie Stewart's Principles of Performance Driving (with Alan Henry, 1986); *Recreations* tennis, shooting, golf; *Clubs* RAC, RSAC, Br Racing Drivers', Royal and Ancient Golf (St Andrews), Scottish Motor Racing; *Style—* Jackie Stewart, Esq; 24 Rte de Divonne, 1260 Nyon, Switzerland (☎ 010 41 22 610 152, fax 010 41 22 621 096)

STEWART, Keith; s of Alexander James Burness Stewart, of Cathcart, South Africa, and Enid, *née* Soames (d 1973); *b* 6 July 1935; *Educ* Prince of wales Sch Nairobi Kenya, Millfield, Seale Hayne Agric Coll; *m* 16 Sept 1961, Dianna Serena, da of Albert Bidden Allison (d 1989); 4 da (Elaine (Mrs Horne), Karen, Angela, Sylvia); *Career* farmer in Kenya and SA 1956-67, introduced coin-operated washing dry-cleaning and car washing machines in Johannesburg and Pretoria 1967-70, gave exhibitions of kite flying throughout UK 1975-77, has given lectures appeared on TV and written in nat and overseas press 1975-, made first solo crossing of English Channel in a kite powered catameran 1977, invented processes and products (particularly inflatable) used in aeronautical marine and land disciplines 1978-; *Recreations* sailing and skiing with a kite, mallard duck breeding, gardening and study of wines; *Clubs* Sloane; *Style—* Keith Stewart, Esq; Manor Farmhouse, Melbury Osmond, Dorchester, Dorset DT2 0LS (☎ 0935 83592); Manor Farmhouse, Melbury Osmond, Dorchester, Dorset DT2 0LS (☎ 0935 83592, fax 0935 83757)

STEWART, Lady; Mary Florence Elinor; da of Frederick Albert Rainbow (d 1967), and Mary Edith, *née* Matthews (d 1963); *b* 17 Sept 1916; *Educ* Eden Hall Sch Penrith Cumberland, Skellfield Sch Topcliffe Yorks, Univ of Durham (BA, MA); *m* 24 Sept 1945, Sir Frederick Henry Stewart, *qv*, s of Frederick Robert Stewart (d 1974); *Career* pt/t ROC 1941-45; lectr in English Univ of Durham 1941-45 (pt/t lectr 1945-56), novelist 1954-, hon fell Newnham Coll Cambridge 1986; *Books* Madam Will You Talk? (1954), Wildfire at Midnight (1956), Thunder on the Right (1957), Nine Coaches Waiting (1958), My Brother Michael (1959), The Ivy Tree (1961), The Moonspinners (1962), This Rough Magic (1964), Airs Above the Ground (1965), The Gabriel Hounds (1967), The Wind off the Small Isles (1968), The Crystal Cave (1970, Frederick Niven Award), The Little Broomstick (1971), The Hollow Hills (1973), Ludo and the Star Horse (1974, Scottish Arts Cncl Award), Touch Not the Cat (1976), The Last Enchantment (1979), A Walk in Wolf Wood (1980), The Wicked Day (1983), Thornyhold (1988), Frost on the Window and Other Poems (1990), Stormy Petrel (1991); *Recreations* gardening, painting, music; *Clubs* New (Edinburgh); *Style—* Lady Stewart; c/o Hodder and Stoughton Ltd, 47 Bedford Sq, London WC1B 3DD

STEWART, Michael James; s of John Innes MacIntosh Stewart, of Huddersfield, Yorks, and Margaret, *née* Hardwick (d 1979); *b* 6 Feb 1933; *Educ* St Edward's Sch Oxford, Magdalen Coll Oxford (BA, MA); *m* 23 June 1962, Hon Frances Julia, da of Baron Kaldor, FBA (Life Peer d 1986); 1 s (David b 1974), 3 da (Lucy b 1964, Anna b 1966, d 1978, Kitty b 1970); *Career* econ advsr HM Treasy 1961-62 (econ asst 1957-60), sr econ advsr Cabinet Office 1967 (econ advsr 1964-67), econ advsr Kenya Treasy 1967-69, reader in political economics UCL 1969-, special advsr to Foreign Sec 1977-78; *Books* Keynes and After (1967), The Jekyll and Hyde Years (1977), Controlling the Economic Future (1983), Apocalypse 2000 (with Peter Jay, 1987); *Recreations* looking at paintings, eating in restaurants; *Clubs* United Oxford and Cambridge Univ; *Style—* Michael Stewart, Esq; 79 South Hill Park, London NW3 2SS (☎ 071 435 3686); University Coll London, Gower St, London WC1E 6BT (☎ 071 387 7050 ext 2297)

STEWART, Sir Michael Norman Francis; KCMG (1966, CMG 1957), OBE (1948); s of Sir Francis Hugh Stewart, CIE (d 1921); *b* 18 Jan 1911; *Educ* Shrewsbury, Trinity Coll Cambridge; *m* 1951, Katharine Damaris, da of late Capt C H du Boulay, RN; 1 s, 2 da; *Career* asst keeper V & A 1935-39, seconded Miny of Info 1939-41, transferred FO 1941, cnsllr Ankara 1954-59, chargé d'affaires Peking 1959-62, chief civilian instr IDC 1962-64, min Br Embassy Washington 1964-67, ambass Greece 1967-71, dir Ditchley Fndn 1971-76, dir Sotheby's 1977-; *Style—* Sir Michael Stewart, KCMG, OBE; Combe, Nr Newbury, Berks

STEWART, Col (Robert) Michael; OBE (1973), TD (1964), DL (Cleveland, 1975); s of Col Evan George Stewart, DSO, OBE (d 1958), of St Pauls Coll Hong Kong, and Dorothy Sarah, *née* Lander (d 1990); *b* 17 May 1931; *Educ* Monkton Combe Sch, UCL (BSc), Univ of London (Postgrad Dip); *m* 20 Oct 1962, (Vera) Patricia, da of Andrew Catley Hills (1983), of Sevenoaks, Kent; 2 da (Frances b 1963, Isobel b 1965); *Career* Army: cmmnd Royal Signals 1950, served in Austria and Germany 1950-51, CO 34 Signal Regt TA 1970-73 (Col 1973); Dep Cmd: NE Dist TA 1973-76, 12 Signal Bde 1976-79; County Cadet Cmdt 1979-84, Hon Col 34 Regt 1981-88, Col Cmdt Royal Signals 1987-; ICI: plant mangr 1956-59, design engr 1959-66, sec mangr 1966-74, mangr supply dept 1974-77, works engr 1977-78, works mangr 1978-81; gen mangr Phillips-Imperial Petroleum Ltd 1981-, dir Tees and Hartlepool Port Authy 1985-; chm:

Royal Jubilee Tst Ctee for Cleveland 1981-85, Indust Year 1986 Steering Ctee for Cleveland; TAVRAs: chm (N Eng) 1984-90, Cncl chm Jt Civilian Staff Ctee 1987-90, memb Advsy Ctee 1987-90; High Sheriff of Cleveland 1990-91; civil rep Cncl of RFEA 1986-, pres Cleveland SATRO 1990-; memb: MIEE 1960, MInstMC 1962, FRSA 1986; ADC to HM the Queen 1975-80; DL 1975; *Recreations* skiing, sailing, climbing; *Clubs* Army and Navy; *Style*— Col Michael Stewart, OBE, TD, DL; Hutton House, Guisborough, Cleveland TS14 8EQ (☎ 0287 632420); Phillips-Imperial Petroleum Ltd, ICI Headquarters Building, PO Box 90, Wilton, Middlesbrough, Cleveland TS6 8JE (☎ 0642 432033, fax 0642 432666, telex 587461 ICI WILTON)

STEWART, Lady Miranda Katherine; *née* Beatty; da of 2 Earl Beatty, DSC (d 1972), and his 4 w, Diane, *née* Blundell (now Mrs J G Nutting); *b* 18 Feb 1963; *m* 1989, Iain Alan Stewart, yst s of late Sir Dugald L L Stewart of Appin, KCVO, CMG; *Style*— The Lady Miranda Stewart

STEWART, Dame Muriel Acadia; DBE (1968); da of late James Edmund Stewart; *b* 22 Oct 1905; *Educ* Gateshead GS, Univ of Durham (BA); *Career* teacher: Newcastle upon Tyne 1927-29, Northumberland 1929-70; nat pres Nat Union of Teachers 1964-65, headmistress Shiremoor Middle Sch 1969-70; chm Schools Cncl 1969-72, vice chm Bullock Ctee 1972-74, memb Northumberland Educn Ctee 1981-89, pres Lib Democrat Educn Assoc; Hon MEd Univ of Newcastle; *Style*— Dame Muriel Stewart, DBE; 44 Caldwell Rd, Gosforth, Newcastle upon Tyne, NE3 2AX

STEWART, Norman Macleod; s of George Stewart (d 1965), and Elspeth, *née* Stewart (d 1982); *b* 2 Dec 1934; *Educ* Elgin Acad, Univ of Edinburgh (BL); *m* 17 July 1959, Mary Slater, da of William Campbell (d 1977); 4 da (Gillian b 1961, Alison b 1964, Carol b 1967, Morag b 1969); *Career* asst slr Alex Morison and Co WS Edinburgh 1957-58; Allan Black and McCaskie Elgin: asst slr 1959-61, ptnr 1961-84, sr ptnr 1984-; former pres: Edinburgh Univ Club of Moray, Elgin Rotary Club; former chm Moray Crime Prevention Panel, former sec Lossimouth and Hersbruck (Bavaria) Twin Town Assoc, former treas Moray GC; The Law Soc of Scot: cncl memb 1976-89, convenor public rels cmmn 1979-81, convenor professional practice cmmn 1981-84, vice pres 1984-85, pres 1985-86; hon memb American Bar Assoc 1985; memb: Law Soc of Scot, Int Bar Assoc, Cwlth Lawyers Assoc, cncl Soc of Slrs in the Supreme Ct (Scot); *Recreations* travel, music, golf, Spain and its culture; *Clubs* New (Edinburgh); *Style*— Norman Stewart, Esq; Argyll Lodge, Lossiemouth, Moray IV31 6QT (☎ 034381 3150); 151 High St, Elgin, Moray IV30 1DX (☎ 0343 543355, fax 0343 549667)

STEWART, Col Robert Christie; CBE (1983), TD (1962); s of Maj Alexander C Stewart, MC (d 1927), of Arndean, by Dollar, Scotland, and Florence Hamilton, *née* Lighton (d 1982); *b* 3 Aug 1926; *Educ* Eton, Univ of Oxford (BA, MA); *m* 21 May 1953, Ann Grizel, da of Air Chief Marshal Hon Sir Ralph Alexander Cochrane, GBE, KCB, AFC (d 1977); 3 s (Alexander, John, David), 2 da (Catriona (Mrs Marsham), Sara); *Career* Lt Scots Gds 1944-49, 7 Bn Argyll and Sutherland Highlanders TA 1951-65, Lt-Col 1963-66, Hon Col 1/51 Highland Volunteers 1972-75; landowner; Lord Lt Kinross-shire 1966-74; Perth and Kinross CC 1963-73 (memb 1953-75), chm and pres Bd of Govrs East of Scotland Coll of Agric 1970-83; *Recreations* shooting, golf, the country; *Clubs* Royal Perth Golfing Soc; *Style*— Col Robert C Stewart, CBE, TD; Arndean, Dollar, Scotland (☎ 0259 42527)

STEWART, Robin Milton; QC (1978); s of Brig Guy Milton Stewart (d 1943), and Dr Elaine Oenone, *née* Earengey; *b* 5 Aug 1938; *Educ* Winchester, New Coll Oxford (MA); *m* 8 Sept 1962, Lynda Grace, da of Arthur Thomas Albert Medhurst (d 1976); 3 s (Andrew Douglas Lorn b 1964, James Milton b 1966, Sholto Robert Douglas b 1969); *Career* called to the Bar Middle Temple 1963, Kings Inns Dublin 1975; prosecuting counsel to Inland Revenue (NE Circuit) 1976-78, rec Crown Court 1978-, bencher Middle Temple 1988; former memb Hexham UDC and Tynedale DC; Parly candidate (C) Newcastle upon Tyne W 1974; Freeman City of London, Liveryman Worshipful Co of Glaziers 1966; *Recreations* gardens, silver, pictures, opera, Scottish family history; *Clubs* Oriental; *Style*— R M Stewart, Esq, QC; Little Chart, 46 Oak Hill Rd, Sevenoaks, Kent TN13 1NS (☎ 0732 453475); 2 Harcourt Buildings, Temple, London EC4Y 9DB (☎ 071 353 1394, fax 071 353 4134)

STEWART, Sir Ronald Compton; 2 Bt (UK 1937) of Stewartby, Co Bedford; DL (1974); s of Sir (Percy) Malcolm Stewart, 1 Bt, OBE (d 1951); *b* 14 Aug 1903; *Educ* Rugby, Jesus Coll Cambridge; *m* 1936, Cynthia Alexandra, OBE, JP (d 1987), da of Harold Farmiloe (d 1987); *Career* High Sheriff Bedfordshire 1954, DL 1974-88; *Style*— Sir Ronald Stewart, Bt, DL; Maulden Grange, Maulden, Bedfordshire

STEWART, Roy Irvine; CBE (1985), JP (N Tyneside 1978); s of James Irvine Stewart (d 1976), of 31 Percy Gardens, Tynemouth and Ida Vera, *née* Pacey (d 1990); *Educ* South Shields Central HS; *Career* co sec to Bellway plc 1966-85; dir: Mawson & Wareham (Music) Ltd 1972-, Webster & Bell Travel Ltd 1979-; chm Northumbria Ambulance Serv Tst, Diocese of Newcastle Parsonages Bd 1985-, chm Northumbria Cons Euro Constituency 1987-, co cmmr Scout Assoc Co Durham 1972-91, chm Tstees of Newcastle Cathedral 1982-90; Tynemouth and Whitley Bay Cons Assoc: hon treas 1980-83, pres 1983-85, chm 1985-88; High Sheriff Tyne & Wear 1988-89; memb Exec Ctee: Newcastle Cncl for the Disabled, Northumberland Assoc of Boys Clubs; Freeman City of London 1989, memb Worshipful Co of Chartered Accountants, memb ICAEW; *Recreations* music, bridge, motor cycling; *Clubs* Northern Counties; *Style*— Roy I Stewart, Esq, CBE, JP; Brockenhurst, 2 The Broadway, Tynemouth NE30 2LD (☎ 091 2579791); 31 Percy Gdns, Tynemouth NE30 4HQ (☎ 091 2574562)

STEWART, Sir (John) Simon Watson; 6 Bt (UK 1920), of Balgownie; er s of Sir (John) Keith Watson Stewart, 5 Bt (d 1990), and Mary Elizabeth, *née* Moxon; *b* 5 July 1955; *Educ* Uppingham, Charing Cross Hosp Med Sch (MRCP, FRCR, MD); *m* 3 June 1978, Catherine Stewart, da of (Henry) Gordon Bond, of Heyeswood House, Shiplake, Oxon; 1 s ((John) Hamish Watson b 12 Dec 1983), 1 da (Anna Rebecca Watson b 1 May 1987); *Heir* s, (John) Hamish Watson Stewart b 12 Dec 1983; *Career* conslt in clinical oncology St Mary's Hosp Paddington; sr lectr Royal Postgraduate Med Sch Hammersmith Hosp; Freeman City of London 1980, Liveryman Worshipful Co of Merchant Taylors 1980; *Recreations* skiing; *Clubs* Oriental; *Style*— Sir Simon Stewart, Bt; 52 Grosvenor Rd, Chiswick, London W4 4EG (☎ 081 995 2213); Dept of Oncology, St Mary's Hospital, Praed Street, London W2 (☎ 071 725 1132)

STEWART, Sinclair Shepherd; s of Harold Sinclair Stewart (d 1960), of Dolphin Rd, Glasgow, and Frances Marjorie Stewart, of Shields Road, Glasgow; *b* 10 March 1938; *Educ* Glasgow HS; *m* 1961, Avril Marjorie, da of John William Gillott; 2 s, 1 da; *Career* 2 Lt RA; dep md Foote Cone & Belding Ltd 1977-82, md Richard Heath Ltd 1971-74, chm Underline Ltd 1977-82, dep chm Bounty Services Ltd 1982-84, dir Waveney Inns Ltd 1982-, chm Bounty Gift Pax Ltd 1984-; *Recreations* trout fishing, shooting, gardening; *Clubs* Flyfishers'; *Style*— Sinclair Stewart, Esq; 2 Mornington, New Rd, Digswell, Welwyn (☎ 043 871 6509); Bounty Gift Pax Ltd, 3 Theobald Court, Theobald St, Borehamwood, Herts

STEWART, William Gladstone; *b* 15 July 1935; *Educ* Shooters Hill GS London, Woolwich Poly London; *m* 1960 (m dis 1976), Audrey Ann, da of Charles Harrison; 1 s (Nicholas b 1961); 2 other c (Barnaby 1976, Hayley b 1980); *partner*, Laura Calland; 1 da (Isobel b 1989); *Career* RAEC 1952-55, KAR 1958; red coat Butlins 1958, BBC TV 1958-67 (directors course 1965), freelance prodr, broadcaster and writer 1967 (prodns incl: The Frost Programme, David Frost, Live from London, Father Dear Father, Bless This House, The Price is Right, The Thoughts of Chairman Alf, Tickets for the Titanic, The Lady is a Tramp, the Nineteeth Hole, Fifteen-to-One), co-fndr (with Colin Frewin) Sunset and Vine 1976, fndr md Regent Productions 1982-; *Recreations* the English language, music, tennis, riding; *Style*— William G Stewart, Esq; Regent Productions Ltd, 6 Putney Common, London SW15 1HI (☎ 081 789 5350, fax 081 789 5332)

STEWART, Prof William James; s of James W Stewart, of Hindhead, Surrey, and Margaret M Stewart; *b* 13 July 1947; *Educ* Blundell's, Imperial Coll London (BSc, MSc); *m* 1976, Dr Jill A Stewart, da of F E Chapman; 2 c (Alexander b 6 June 1983, Antonia b 1 May 1986); *Career* res exec and special responsibility for all optical work Plessey Research Caswell Limited (joined 1971); visiting prof: UCL, Optical Sciences Centre Univ of Arizona in Tuscon; contrib to numerous books and jls; granted numerous patents for inventions assoc with his field; memb: Ed Bd Journal of Optical Communications, Solid State Devices Sub Ctee SERC, Ctee Photonic Switching Meeting, Euro Optical Switching Programme COST 216; Worshipful Co of Scientific Instrument Makers award for achievement; memb: Optical Soc of America, MIEE, FEng 1989; *Recreations* woodwork; *Style*— Prof William Stewart; Marconi, Caswell, Towcester, Northants NN12 8EQ (☎ 0327 54715, fax 0327 54775)

STEWART, Hon Mrs (Zoë Leighton); *née* Seager; da of 1 Baron Leighton of St Mellons, CBE (d 1963); *b* 28 April 1928; *m* 1, 1955, Malcolm James Peniston (d 1981); 1 s (Douglas), 2 da (Angela, Rosemary); m 2, 1984, Alan Carnegie Stewart; *Style*— The Hon Mrs Stewart; Westwood, Hardgate, Castle Douglas, Kirkcudbrightshire DG7 3LD (☎ 055 666 215)

STEWART-CLARK, Alexander Dudley; s and h of Sir John Stewart-Clark, 3 Bt, MEP, *qv*; *b* 21 Nov 1960; *Educ* Worth Abbey; *Career* md Challenge F Timber Ltd (formerly Douglas Timber Ltd) 1988-; *Books* Hydroscopics of Oak (1987); *Recreations* rugby, tennis; *Style*— Alexander Stewart-Clark, Esq; Puckstye House, nr Cowden, Kent TN8 7ED; 28 Fairfield St, London SW18 1DW

STEWART-CLARK, Jane, Lady; Jane Pamela; da of Maj Arundell Clarke, of Fremington House, N Devon; *m* 1927, Sir Stewart Stewart-Clark, 2 Bt (d 1971); 1 s (Sir John, 3 Bt), 1 da (Mrs Patrick Bowlby); *Style*— Jane, Lady Stewart-Clark; Dundas Castle, S Queensferry, W Lothian

STEWART-CLARK, Sir John (Jack); 3 Bt (UK 1918), of Dundas, W Lothian; MEP (EDG) E Sussex 1979-; s of Sir Stewart Stewart-Clark, 2 Bt (d 1971); *b* 17 Sept 1929; *Educ* Eton, Balliol Coll Oxford, Harvard Business Sch; *m* 1958, Jonkvrouwe Lydia Fredericke, da of Jonkheer James William Loudon, of The Netherlands; 1 s, 4 da; *Heir* s, Alexander Stewart-Clark; *Career* late Coldstream Gds; Parly candidate (C & U) Aberdeen N 1959; treas EDG 1979-; spokesman on: youth, culture, educn, the media and sport; chm EP Delgn to Canada 1979-82, vice-chm EP Delgn to Japan 1986-89, memb EP Delgn to Countries of S America, spokesman Int Affairs 1983-85; dir: Oppenheimer International Ltd until 1984, Low & Bonar 1982-, Cope Allman International Ltd until 1983; AT Kearney Management Consultants 1985-; memb Bd Tstee Savings Bank Scotland 1986-89; md: J & P Coats (Pakistan) Ltd 1961-67, J A Carp's Garenfabrieken (Helmond) Holland 1967-70, Philips Electrical Ltd London 1971-75, Pye of Cambridge Ltd 1975-79; former memb Cncl Royal Utd Servs Inst, chm Supervisory Bd Euro Inst for Security 1984-86, tstee dir Euro Centre for Work and Soc 1983-, vice-chm EPIC (Euro Parliamentarians & Industrialists Cncl) 1984-; pres CRONWE (Conference Regnl Organisations of NW Europe) 1987-; memb Royal Co of Archers (Queen's Bodyguard for Scot); *Recreations* golf, tennis, skiing, music, travel, vintage cars; *Clubs* White's, Royal Ashdown Forest Golf; *Style*— Sir Jack Stewart-Clark, Bt, MEP; Puckstye House, Holtye Common, nr Cowden, Kent (☎ 034 286 541)

STEWART-FITZROY, Capt (William) Wentworth; s of Capt Frederick Henry FitzRoy (d 1937), and Eleanor Lawson Allan (d 1969); *b* 28 Sept 1907; *Educ* NC HMS Worcester, RNC Greenwich; *m* 1, 26 April 1934, Margaret Patricia, da of Douglas Stewart Grant (d 1921), of USA; 3 s (Allan b 1935, James b 1943, Roderick b 1947), 1 da (Anne b 1936); m 2, 23 Jan 1988, Evelyn, da of late James Wallace Nichol, of Washington DC, and wid of Col John Fogg Twombly III, US Army; *Career* serv WWII HMS Warspite 1939-41 (Arctic Patrol 1940, Narvik 1940, Med 1941, Matapan and Crete 1941); cmd destroyers: HMS Buxton (N Atlantic 1941), HMS Valorous (North Sea 1942-43), HMS Arrow (Force Z Med 1943 & Sicily landings), HMS King Alfred (1944, trg), HMS Comet (BR Pacific Fleet 1945-47); naval attaché HM Embassy Belgrade 1947-49, served Korea as Cdr (exec offr) Fleet Flagship HMS Belfast 1950-51, Cdr RN Air Station HMS Seahawk 1951-52; Capt in Policy Plans & Operations Div SHAPE 1952-54; asst dir of Naval Equipment Admty 1954-56, Capt of Dockyard and Queen's harbourmaster Rosyth 1957-58, Cdre HM Dockyard Singapore 1959-61, naval ADC to HM The Queen 1961-62, naval regnl offr MOD for Scotland & NI 1962-72; Hon Sheriff for Sutherland 1974-87; pres Stewart Soc of Clan Stewart 1971-74 (hon vice-pres 1974-); *Recreations* sailing, fishing, golf, amateur petrologist; *Style*— Capt Wentworth Stewart-FitzRoy, RN; 1137 Westmoreland Rd, Alexandria, Virginia 22308, USA

STEWART-LIBERTY, Oliver James; s of Arthur Ivor Stewart-Liberty, MC, TD (d 1990), of Pipers, The Lee, Great Missenden, Bucks, and his 1 w, Rosabel Fremantle, *née* Fynn; *b* 9 Oct 1947; *Educ* Bryanston Sch; *m* 16 Sept 1972, Anne Catherine, da of Frank Arthur Bicknell, of London; 1 s (Charles b 1978), 1 da (Alexandra b 1980); *Career* dir Liberty plc 1977-; *Recreations* shooting, cricket, tennis, boules; *Clubs* Hurlingham; *Style*— Oliver Stewart-Liberty, Esq; 212 Regent Street, London W1R 6AH (☎ 071 734 1234, telex 295850, fax 071 734 8323)

STEWART LOCKHART, Christopher Hallimond; s of Cdr Charles Stewart Lockhart, DSC, RN (d 1963), and Eileen Norton Hallimond (d 1976); *b* 14 July 1922; *Educ* Marlborough; *m* 1951, Kermode, da of Rev Sir William Kermode Derwent, KCMG; 1 s, 1 da; *Career* chm Br-American Tobacco Co Ltd until 1983; dir: BAT Industries plc until 1983, Mardons Packaging Int Ltd, G Percy Trentham Ltd 1983-; *Clubs* MCC; *Style*— Christopher Stewart Lockhart Esq; 108 Oakwood Ct, London W14 8JZ (☎ 071 602 2279); Hop Garden Cottage, Church Rd, Didcot, Oxon (☎ 0235 850513); G Percy Trentham Ltd, Pangbourne, Reading, Berks (☎ 073 57 3333)

STEWART OF ARDVORLICH, Alexander Donald; DL (Perthshire 1988); s of John Alexander McLaren Stewart of Ardvorlich, TD, JP, DL (d 1985), and Violet Hermione, *née* Cameron (d 1979); *b* 18 June 1933; *Educ* Wellington, Univ of Oxford (BA), Univ of Edinburgh (LLB); *m* 4 Dec 1970, Virginia Mary, da of Capt Peter Washington (d 1983), of Pine Farm, Wokingham, Berks; 1 s (James b 1980), 5 da (Sophie b 1972, Emily b 1974, Theresa b 1976, Catrina b 1978, Petra b 1982); *Career* admitted slr (WS) 1961, ptnr McGrigor Donald Glasgow 1965-; dir: Clyde Cablevision Ltd 1984-, Scottish Amicable Life Assurance Soc 1986-; hon consul for Thailand 1983-; *Recreations* field sports, winter sports, music; *Clubs* Puffin's; *Style*— Alexander Stewart of Ardvorlich, DL; Ardvorlich, Lochearnhead, Perthshire (☎ 05673 218); c/o McGrigor Donald, Pacific House, 70 Wellington St, Glasgow G2 6SB (☎ 041 248 6677, fax 041 221 1390)

STEWART OF DALBUIE, George Prince McKean; s of George Stewart (d 1942), of Bothwell, Lanarkshire, and Eileen Eva, *née* Atkinson (d 1942); *b* 2 Nov 1925; *Educ*

Glenalmond, Glasgow Univ (MA); *m* 17 July 1952, Jean Thomson, da of John McNaught (d 1971); 2 s (George b 1953, Roderick b 1961), Ann (b 1956); *Career* served in RNAS 1943-47; dir Alexander Dunn Ltd 1958-70, md Airdun Ltd 1970-87; gen mangr Creda Ltd (Glasgow) 1987-90, dir Midscot Training Services Ltd 1987-; *Recreations* gardening, watercolours, antiquities; *Clubs* Western; *Style—* George Stewart of Dalbuie; Dalbuie, Southend, Argyll

STEWART-PATTERSON, Rev Lady Alison Margaret Katherine Antoinette; *née* Bruce; da of late 10 Earl of Elgin and (14 of) Kincardine, KT, CMG, TD, CD, and Hon Dame Katherine Cochrane, DBE, da of late 1 Baron Cochrane of Cults and Lady Gertrude Boyle, OBE, da of 6 Earl of Glasgow; *b* 1931; *Educ* McGill Univ (BTh, STM), Presbyterian Coll Montreal (Dip); *m* 1957, Cleveland Stewart-Patterson; 2 s, 1 da; *Career* LRAM; ordained min Presbyterian Church in Canada 1977, asst min Church of St Andrew and St Paul Montreal 1977-79, pasteur Eglise Presbytérienne St-Luc Montréal 1980-; *Style—* The Rev Lady Alison Stewart-Patterson; Drishane Farm, 251 Senneville Rd, Senneville, Québec H9X 3L2, Canada

STEWART-RICHARDSON, Alastair Lucas Graham; s of Lt-Col Neil Graham Stewart-Richardson, DSO (d 1934), and Alexandra, *née* Ralli (d 1972); *b* 29 Nov 1927; *Educ* Eton, Magdalene Coll Cambridge (MA); *m* 29 May 1969, (Diana) Claire, da of Brig George Streynsham Rawstorne, CBE, MC (d 1962); 2 s (James George b 1971, Hugh Neil b 1977), 1 da (Sarah Alexandra b 1974); *Career* called to the Bar Inner Temple 1952, bencher 1978; memb: Panel of Arbitrators Lloyd's Form of Salvage Agreement 1983, panel of persons to hear representations for purposes of section 8 and schedule 3 of Food and Environment Act 1985-1988; cmmr of Income Tax for Inner Temple 1982; *Style—* Alastair Stewart-Richardson, Esq; 7 King's Bench Walk, Temple, London EC4Y 7DS (☎ 071 583 0404, fax 071 583 0950, telex 887491 KBLAW)

STEWART-RICHARDSON, Ninian Rorie; s of Sir Ian Stewart Richardson (d 1969), and Audrey Meryl Odlum (who m 2, 1975, Patrick Allan Pearson Robertson, CMG); hp of bro Sir Simon Stewart-Richardson, 17 Bt; *b* 20 Jan 1949; *Educ* Rannoch Sch Perthshire, Commercial Pilot Trg; *m* 21 Oct 1983, Joan Kristina, da of Howard Smee, of Rio de Janeiro; 2 s (Edward Rorie b 22 July 1988, William Howard b 15 Aug 1990), 1 da (Olivia Joan b 16 March 1987); *Career* late commercial air pilot; industrialist Brazil Ultra Violet Application to Indust; *Recreations* sailing, skiing; *Style—* Ninian Stewart-Richardson, Esq; c/o Mrs P A P Robertson, Lynedale, Long Cross, Chertsey, Surrey KT16 0DP; Germetec, Rua Matinore 227 Jacare, Rio de Janeiro (☎ 261 9244)

STEWART-RICHARDSON, Sir Simon Alaisdair (Ian Neile); 17 Bt (NS 1630), of Pencaitland, Haddingtonshire; s of Sir Ian Rorie Hay Stewart-Richardson, 16 Bt (d 1969), by his 2 w, Audrey Meryl Odlum (who m 2, 1975, Patrick Allan Pearson Robertson, CMG); *b* 9 June 1947; *Educ* Trinity Coll Glenalmond; *Heir* bro, Ninian Rorie Stewart-Richardson, *qv*; *Recreations* music, theatre, sailing; *Style—* Sir Simon Stewart-Richardson, Bt; Lynedale, Longcross, nr Chertsey, Surrey KT16 0DP (☎ 093287 2329)

STEWART-SMITH, Christopher Dudley; s of Ean Kendal Stewart-Smith (d 1964), and Edmee, *née* von Wallerstain und Marnegg; *b* 21 Jan 1941; *Educ* Winchester, King's Coll Cambridge, MIT; *m* 1964, Olivia, da of Col John Barstow, DSO; 1 s, 2 da; *Career* Courtaulds Ltd 1962-65, McKinsey & Co Inc 1966-71, Sterling Guarantee Tst 1971-73; chm: Butlers Warehousing and Distribution Ltd 1971-85, Earls Court & Olympia Ltd 1974-85, Sterling Guards Ltd 1974-85, Sutcliffe Catering Gp Ltd 1975-85, P & O Cruises Ltd 1985-86, Swan Hellenic Cruises 1985-86, Conder Gp plc 1987-; dir: Williamson Tea Hldgs plc 1986, George Williamson & Co Ltd 1986-, Reyloc/Reytrace Ltd 1987-; chm: Royal Tournament Ctee 1976-85, Br Exhibitions Promotion Cncl 1984-85, appeal ctee Acad of St Martins in the Fields 1988-89, London C of C and Indust 1988-; vice pres Olympia Int Showjumping 1977-85; friend: RSA 1984-, V & A 1988-; memb: Royal Smithfield Club 1985-, Centre for World Devpt Educn 1988-, Southern Advsy Bd of NatWest Bank plc 1988-; tstee: Conder Conservation Tst 1987-, Res Cncl for Complementary Med 1987-; Liveryman Worshipful Co of Grocers 1972; *Clubs* Travellers', Bucks; *Style—* Christopher Stewart-Smith, Esq; 25/28 Old Burlington Street, London W1X 1LB (☎ 071 734 7701)

STEWART-SMITH, John Ronald; s of Maj James Geoffrey Stewart-Smith (d 1938), of Falcon Hill Kinver, nr Stourbridge, Worcs, and Bertha Mabel Milner, *née* Roberts; *b* 23 Feb 1932; *Educ* Marlborough, Waitaki (NZ); *m* 22 Oct 1955, Catherine May, da of Walter Douglas Montgomery Clarke, JP (d 1948), of Bombay, India; 1 s (Geoffrey b 1958), 2 da (Joanna b 1960, Nicola b 1962); *Career* gp mktg dir Glover Gp Ltd 1976-79, projects dir and co sec Dashwood Finance Co Ltd 1983-, dir Kowloon Shipyard Co Ltd 1983-; CEng, MIMechE 1967, MIMarE 1969, MInst Export 1974, FIMarE 1989; *Recreations* bridge, tennis, skiing; *Style—* John Stewart-Smith, Esq; Dashwood Finance Co Ltd, Georgian House, 63 Coleman St, London EC2R 5BB (☎ 071 588 3215, fax 071 588 4818, telex 885624)

STEWART-WALLACE, (Helen) Mary; da of Edward Schooling (d 1928), of Christchurch Park, Sutton, Surrey (*see* Burke's Landed Gentry, 18 edn, vol II, 1969), and Nellie Vera, *née* Price (d 1959); the firm of Schooling, Lawrence and Schooling were goldsmiths and merchant bankers in the 18th century; *b* 7 March 1914; *Educ* Sutton HS, GPDST, Central Sch of Speech Trg and Dramatic Art, Univ of London (Dip); *m* 4 Nov 1939, Dr Arthur Maurice Stewart-Wallace (conslt neurologist), s of Sir John Stewart-Wallace, CB (d 1963), of The Paddock House, Gerrards Cross, Bucks (*see* Burke's Landed Gentry, 18 edn, vol II, 1969); 1 s (John b 1943), 2 da (Jane b 1940, Elizabeth b 1950); *Career* official speaker for Britain in Europe Referendum Campaign 1975, speaker Cons Nat Womens' Conf; memb: Cons Women's Consultative Ctee, SE Panel of Cons Speakers, House of Lords meeting on educn issues; assoc memb Bruges Gp 1989, former assoc memb Educn Cmmn of Euro Union of Women; writer of genealogical articles and occasional reviews; author of: res paper into secdy educn in comparable western democracies 1978, Research into Secondary Education in Comparable Western Democracies (1978); Freeman City of London, memb Worshipful Co of Goldsmiths; *Recreations* genealogy and family research, educational research, foreign travel; *Clubs* Soc of Genealogists; *Style—* Mrs A M Stewart-Wallace; The Moot House, Ditchling, Sussex

STEWART-WILSON, Lt-Col Blair Aubyn; CVO (1989, LVO 1983); s of Aubyn Harold Raymond Wilson (d 1934), and Muriel Athelstan Hood Stewart-Stevens, *née* Stewart (d 1982); *b* 17 July 1929; *Educ* Eton, RMA Sandhurst; *m* 1962, Helen Mary, da of Maj Wilfred Michael Fox (d 1974), of Taunton; 3 da (Alice b 1963, Sophia b 1966, Belinda b 1970); *Career* dep master of HM Household and Equerry to HM The Queen 1976-; cmmnd Scots Gds 1949; served: UK, Germany, Far East and NZ, Lt-Col 1969; def mil and air attaché Vienna 1975-76; Capt Atholl Highlanders; *Recreations* shooting, fishing; *Clubs* Pratt's and White's; *Style—* Lt-Col Blair Stewart-Wilson, CVO; Buckingham Palace, London SW1 (☎ 071 930 4832)

STEWART-WILSON, Col Ralph Stewart; MC (1944); s of Aubyn Harold Raymond Wilson (d 1934), of Aust, and Muriel Athelstane Hood Stewart-Stevens, *née* Stewart (d 1982); 11 Laird of Balnakeilly; ggs of Charles Wilson, pioneer grazier in NSW and Victoria; *b* 26 Jan 1923; *Educ* Eton; *m* 4 Oct 1949, Rosalind, da of Lt-Col H S O P Stedall, OBE, TD (d 1989), of Oxon; 1 s (Aubyn b 1963), 2 da (Maria b 1952, Lorna b 1954); *Career* soldier and farmer; served Rifle Bde, 60 Rifles, Staffordshire Regt 1941-68; theatres of ops incl: Tunisia 1942-43, Italy and Austria 1944-45, Kenya 1956, Malaya 1956-57; appts incl: BM7 Armd Bde 1954-56, Jt Planning and Def Policy Staffs, 2 i/c 60 Rifles 1963-64, CO 1 Bn The Staffordshire Regt 1964-66; memb Queen's Body Guard for Scotland (Royal Co of Archers), Capt in Atholl Highlanders; former pres Atholl NFU for Scotland, pres The Stewart Soc, memb Br Onithologists Union; *Recreations* ornithology, shooting; *Clubs* Royal and Ancient Golf (St Andrews); *Style—* Col Ralph S Stewart-Wilson of Balnakeilly, MC; Pitlochry, Perthshire PH16 5JJ (☎ 0796 2059)

STEYN, David Andrew; s of John Hofmeyer Steyn, of 3 Louisville Ave, Aberdeen, Scotland, and Daphne Mary, *née* Nelson; *b* 13 Sept 1959; *Educ* Robert Gordon's Coll Aberdeen, Univ of Aberdeen (LLB); *m* 9 June 1990, Tanya Susan, da of Lyon Roussel; *Career* md Quaestor Investment Management Ltd 1989-; *Recreations* theatre, politics; *Style—* David Steyn, Esq; 24 Edge St, Kensington, London W8; Quaestor Investment Management Ltd, River Plate House, Finsbury Circus EC2M 7DH

STEYN, The Hon Mr Justice; Sir Johan; *b* 15 Aug 1932; *Educ* Jan van Riebeeck Sch Cape Town S Africa, Univ of Stellenbosch S Africa (BA, LLB), Univ Coll Oxford (Cape Provine Rhodes scholar, MA); *m* 1; 2 da; m 2, Susan Leonore; 2 s; *Career* barr S Africa 1958-73 (sr counsel), barr England 1973-, QC 1979, bencher Lincoln's Inn 1985, High Court Judge Commercial Court 1985, Supreme Ct Rule Cmmn 1985-89, chm Race Rels Ctee of Bar 1987, presiding judge Northern Circuit 1989-, chm Departmental Advsy Ctee on Arbitration Law 1990- , kt 1985; *Style—* The Hon Mr Justice Steyn; Royal Courts of Justice, Strand, London WC2A 2LL

STEYN, John Hofmeyr; s of Johannes Stephanus Steyn (d 1937), and Blanka (d 1990), *née* Hablutze; *b* 3 Oct 1929; *Educ* Univ of Cape Town (MB ChB), Univ of Aberdeen (PhD); *m* 6 April 1952, Daphne Mary, *née* Nelson; 5 s (John Peter b 1955, David Andrew b 1959, Michael Paul b 1960, Richard Stephen b 1961, Gordon Philip b 1963), 2 da (Anne Scott b 1954, Catherine b 1958); *Career* conslt urologist Aberdeen Royal Infirmary 1967, sr lectr Univ of Aberdeen 1967; FRCS 1957, FRCSEd 1973; OStJ; *Clubs* Carlton; *Style—* John Steyn, Esq; Royal Infirmary, Aberdeen (☎ 0224 681818)

STIBBON, Gen Sir John James; KCB (1988), OBE (1977); s of Jack Stibbon (d 1939), and Elizabeth Matilda, *née* Dixon (d 1968); *b* 5 Jan 1935; *Educ* Portsmouth Southern GS, RMA, RMCS (BSc Eng); *m* 10 Aug 1957, Jean Fergusson, da of John Robert Skeggs, of Newquay, Cornwall; 2 da (Jane b 1958, Emma b 1962); *Career* cmmnd RE 1954, Staff Capt War Office 1962-64, Adj 32 Armd Engr Regt 1964-66, instr RAC Centre 1967-68, OC 2 Armd Engr Sqdn 1968-70, DAA md QMG 12 Mech Bde 1971-72, GSO1 (DS) Staff Coll 1973-75, CO 28 Amphibious Engr Regt 1975-77, Asst Mil Sec MOD 1977-79, Cmd 20 Armd Bde 1979-81, Royal Coll of Def Studies 1982, Cmdt RMCS 1983-85, Asst Chief of Def Staff (operational requirements) MOD 1985-87, Master Gen of the Ordnance 1987-; Col Cmdt: RAPC 1985, RPC 1986, RE 1988; Hon DSc CIT 1989; CEng, FICE 1989; hon vice pres FA; *Recreations* watercolour painting, association football, paleantology; *Clubs* Lansdowne; *Style—* Gen Sir John Stibbon, KCB, OBE; MOD, Whitehall, London (☎ 071 218 6908)

STIBBS, Prof (Douglas) Walter Noble; s of Edward John Stibbs (d 1922), of Sydney, Australia, and Jane, *née* Monro (d 1963); *b* 17 Feb 1919; *Educ* Sydney Boys' HS, Univ of Sydney (BSc, MSc), New Coll Oxford (D Phil); *m* 8 Jan 1949, Margaret Lilian Calvert, da of Rev John Calvert (d 1949), of Sydney, Australia; 2 da (Helen b 1956, Elizabeth b 1959); *Career* lectr Dept of Mathematics and Physics New England Univ Coll Armidale NSW 1942-45, sr sci offr Cwlth Solar Observatory Canberra 1945-51 (res asst 1940-42), Radcliffe travelling fell Radcliffe Observatory Pretoria SA and Univ Observatory Oxford 1951-54, princ sci offr UKAEA Aldermaston 1955-59; Univ of St Andrews: Napier prof of astronomy and dir of Univ Observatory 1959-89, sr prof Senatus Academicus 1987-89, emeritus prof 1990-; visiting prof of astrophysics Yale Univ observatory 1966-67, Br Cncl visiting prof Univ of Utrecht 1968-69, prof Collège de France Paris 1975-76 (Médaille du Collège 1976), visiting fell Australian National Univ Canberra 1990-; memb: Int Astronomical Union 1951- (pres Fin Ctee 1964-67, 1973-76 and 1976-79), Nat Ctee for Astronomy 1964-76, Advsy Ctee for Meteorology in Scotland 1960-69 (also 1972-75 and 1978-80), Science Research Cncl 1972-76, Royal Greenwich Observatory Ctee 1966-70 (memb Bd of Visitors 1963-65), Royal Observatory Edinburgh Ctee 1966-76 (chm 1970-76), Astronomy Space and Radio Bd 1970-76, SA Astronomical Advsy Ctee 1972-76; chm: Astronomy Policy and Grants Ctee 1972-74, N Hemisphere Observatory Planning Ctee 1970-76; FRAS 1942 (memb Cncl 1964-67 and 1970-73, vice pres 1972-73), FRSE 1960 (memb Cncl 1970-72); *Books* The Outer Layers of a Star (with Sir Richard Woolley, 1953); *Recreations* music (organ), ornithology, photography, golf, long distance running (medals for 17 marathons during 1983-87 incl: Athens, Berlin, Boston, Edinburgh 3h 59m 23s, Honolulu, London, Paris); *Clubs* Royal and Ancient Golf (St Andrews); *Style—* Prof D W N Stibbs, FRSE; 75 Gouger St, Torrens, ACT 2607, Australia; Mount Stromlo Observatory, Canberra ACT 2606, Australia

STIBY, Robert Andrew; JP (1980); s of Maj Arthur Robert Charles Stiby, TD, JP (d 1987), of Reigate, and Peggy, *née* Hartley (d 1973); *b* 25 May 1937; *Educ* Marlborough, London Coll of Printing (Dip in Printing Mgmnt); *m* 1, 1962 (m dis 1976); 1 s (Jonathan b 10 May 1963), 1 da (Emma b 17 Sept 1965); m 2, 1980 (m dis 1984), Heather; m 3, 30 May 1986, Julia, da of Sidney Fuller, of Canterbury; (1 da Renata b 5 Nov 1971); *Career* Nat Serv 1955-57; md and chm Croydon Advertiser Gp of Newspapers 1969-83; chm Radio Investments Ltd 1988-; dir: Capital Radio 1972-, Chiltern Radio plc 1980-89, Radio Mercury plc 1983-, United Cable TV Ltd 1984-, Portsmouth & Sunderland Newspapers 1983-87; dep chm Invicta Radio plc 1990-, md Cable Guide Ltd 1987-90; chm of govrs London Coll of Printing 1979; pres Newspaper Soc 1983-84; chm Local News of London Ltd 1972-88; pres Croydon Boys' Club 1988-; *Recreations* sailing, hill walking, painting in oils; *Clubs* MCC, Reigate Heath Golf; *Style—* Robert Stiby, Esq, JP; The White House, Reigate Heath, Surrey RH2 8QR (☎ 0737 242781); Croudace House, 97 Godstone Rd, Caterham, Surrey CR3 6XQ (☎ 0883 341517, fax 0883 341729)

STICKNEY, (Robert) Paul; s of Charles Stickney (d 1966), and Kathleen Mary, *née* Ford (d 1987); *b* 6 Sept 1944; *Educ* Yeovil Sch, Portsmouth Poly Sch of Architecture (Dip Arch); *m* 13 Sept 1969, Dorothy Dawn, da of Alfred Edward Shaw (d 1971); 1 s (Richard b 1972), 1 da (Jenny b 1976); *Career* architect; Portsmouth City Architects Dept 1968-71, sr architect Bailey Piper Stevens Partnership 1971-73; jt managing ptnr Leslie Jones Architects (joined 1973, assoc 1974, ptnr 1977); memb Bd Br Cncl of Shopping Centres; memb RIBA 1970; *Recreations* literature and visual arts; *Style—* Paul Stickney, Esq; Leslie Jones, Leslie House, 3-4 Bentink St, London W1M 5RN (☎ 071 935 5481, fax 071 487 3820, car 0836 274355); Little Court, 25 Ashley Drive, Walton on Thames, Surrey KT12 1JL

STIDDARD, Timothy John Wentworth; s of Capt Jack William Stiddard, MC (d 1986), of Lodewell Farm, Hutton, nr Weston-Super-Mare, Avon, and Joline Olive Wentworth Stiddard, *née* Alexander; *b* 7 April 1957; *Educ* Cheltenham, Lanchester Poly (LLB); *m* 3 April 1982, Joanne Jeanette, da of John Edward White, of 7 Dickenson Rd, Weston-super-Mare, Avon; 1 da (Heather Shona); *Career* slr: Supreme Ct of England and Wales 1981, Weston-Super-Mare Hoteliers Assoc 1981-, Int Audiology Soc 1985-; vice pres Weston-Super-Mare Operative Soc 1983-; treas Weston-Super-Mare Sea Cadet Corps 1979- (civilian instr 1989-); memb: The Law

Soc, Bristol Law Soc; *Recreations* golf, rugby, fishing, philately, freemasonry; *Clubs* Weston Golf, Weston Rugby; *Style*— Timothy Stiddard, Esq; The Lilacs, Burton-Row, Brent Knoll, Somerset (☎ 0278 760771); 19 Boulevard, Weston-super-Mare, Avon (☎ 0934 619000)

STIGWOOD, Robert Colin; s of late Gordon Stigwood, of Beaumont, Adelaide, and Gwendolyn Burrows; *b* 1932; *Educ* Sacred Heart Coll; *Career* theatre, movie, TV and record prodr; came to England 1956, held a variety of jobs incl mangr halfway house for delinquents in Cambridge; opened talent agency in London 1962, first ind record prodr in Eng with release of single Johnny Remember Me (liquidated firm 1965); business mangr Graham Bond Orgn, co-md NEMS Enterprises 1967, fndr Robert Stigwood Orgn 1967, formed RSO Records 1973, dir Polygram 1976; prodr films incl: Jesus Christ Superstar, Bugsy Malone, Tommy, Saturday Night Fever, Grease, Sgt Pepper's Lonely Hearts Club Band, Moment by Moment, The Fan, Times Square, Grease 2, Staying Alive, Gallipoli; prodr stage musicals in England and US incl: Oh! Calcutta, The Dirtiest Show in Town, Pippin, Jesus Christ Superstar, Evita, Sweeney Todd; TV prodr in England and US incl: The Entertainer, The Prime of Miss Jean Brodie (series); Int Prodr of Year ABC Interstate Theatres Inc 1976; *Recreations* sailing, tennis; *Style*— Robert Stigwood, Esq; Robert Stigwood Organisation, 118-120 Wardour St, London W1V 4BT (☎ 071 437 2512, fax 071 437 3674, telex 264267)

STILL, Brig Nigel Maxwell; CBE (1983); s of Brig George Bingham Still, OBE (d 1965), of London, and Violet Winifred, *née* Maxwell (d 1980); *b* 27 March 1936; *Educ* Marlborough, Clare Coll Cambridge (BA); *m* 3 April 1965, Mary Richenda, da of Maj P J D Macfarlane, of 79 Bramley Grange, Guildford, Surrey; 1 s (George b 1973), 1 da (Caroline b 1967); *Career* cmmnd 17/21 Lancers 1958 (Adj 1960), instr RMA Sandhurst 1962, Sqdn Ldr 17/21 Lancers 1965, Army Staff Course 1966, GSO 2 (Armd) HQ Army Strategic Cmd 1968, DAMS Mil Sec's Dept MOD 1972, CO 17/21 Lancers 1975, GSO 1 (Directing Staff) Aust Army Staff Coll 1977, Col GS (OR) 17 MOD 1979, Coll Cdr RMA Sandhurst 1982, Cdr 43 Inf Bde 1984, ret 1987; dir of admin Lyddon (Stockbrokers) Cardiff 1987-88; *Recreations* golf, cricket, rugby football, music; *Clubs* I Zingari (cricket); *Style*— Brig Nigel M Still, CBE; c/o Midland Bank plc, Wellington Square, Minehead, Somerset

STILL, Robert Flisher; s of Robert Herbert Still (d 1955), and Mabel Caroline, *née* Brown (d 1970); *b* 5 March 1923; *Educ* Hove Co GS Sussex; *m* 22 Aug 1944, Gwendoline Jessie, da of Douglas Gordon Everard Barrie (d 1967); 1 s (Christopher Michael b 23 July 1946), 1 da (Lindsay Ann (Mrs Cook) b 10 Oct 1951); *Career* WWII RN Ordinary Seaman HMS Howe 1941, Midshipman 1942, underwater def HMS Osprey and HMS Curlew 1942, Sub Lt 1943, cable laying ops HMS Curlew 1943-46 (N Africa, Sicily, Italy, Belguim, Holland, Germany), Lt 1944, demobbed 1946; clerk Westminster Bank 1940-41; Metway Electrical Industries Ltd Brighton: sales clerk 1946, dir 1947, jt md 1961, md 1967, chm 1987-; life vice pres Sussex Radio and Electrical Industs Golfing Soc, memb Hove Branch Lions Int 1962-, memb Electrical Commercial Travellers Assoc; memb: IOD, Assoc of Supervisory and Exec Engrs; *Recreations* gardening, swimming, walking, theatre; *Style*— Robert Still, Esq; 16 Woodruff Ave, Hove, E Sussex BN3 6PG (☎ 0273 556678); Metway Electrical Industries Ltd, 55 Canning St, Brighton, BN2 2ES (☎ 0273 606433, fax 0273 6677473, telex 877166)

STILL, Dr Ronald McKinnon; s of Ronald Still (d 1980), of Helensburgh, and Nan, *née* McKinnon; *b* 20 March 1932; *Educ* Hermitage Sch Helensburgh, Univ of Glasgow (MB ChB) 1956; *m* 23 Nov 1963 (m dis 1987), Patricia Ann, da of Maj K J Jones (d 1989); 1 s (Jamie b 3 May 1972), 2 da (Sarah b 30 Nov 1966, Shona b 12 June 1969); *Career* short serv commn RAMC, seconded as Capt Malaya Mil Forces 1957-60; house offr: Glasgow Royal Infirmary 1956-57, Oakbank Hosp Glasgow 1961, Queen Mother's Hosp 1962, Western Infirmary 1963; registrar Stobhill and Queen Mother's Hosps 1963-66, sr registrar Glasgow Teaching Hosp 1966-67, conslt obstetrician and gynaecologist Stobhill Hosp Glasgow 1967- (house offr 1961), hon clinical sr lectr Univ of Glasgow; memb Osprey Gynaecological Soc; MRCOG 1963, FRCOG 1973; *Recreations* golf, music; *Clubs* Royal and Ancient (St Andrews), Glasgow Golf, Milngavie Golf; *Style*— Dr Ronald Still; 9/5 Whistlefield Court, 2 Canniesburn Road, Bearsden, Glasgow G61 1PX (☎ 041 942 3097); Stobill General Hospital, Glasgow (☎ 041 588 0111)

STILLWELL, Michael Ian; s of Alan Bertram Stillwell (d 1985), of London, and Dorothy Elizabeth, *née* Peel; *b* 22 Nov 1938; *Educ* Rutlish Sch Merton, Insead Fontainebleau; *m* 1962, Susan, da of William Brown; 2 s (Andrew Michael b 1967 d 1989, Nicholas John b 1968); *Career* CA; articled Clerk Myrus Smith & Walker London 1957-62; Cooper Brothers & Co: Singapore 1963-65, res mangr Ipoh Malaysia 1965-67, ptnr Kuala Lumpur Malaysia 1968-69, ptnr London 1972, seconded to Italian firm Milan 1972-74, ptnr UK 1974-, staff ptnr London 1982-84, dir Human Resources 1985-87, dir Int Affairs 1988-; FCA 1972; *Books* European Financial Reporting - Italy (1976); *Recreations* mountain walking, music, jogging; *Clubs* Barbican Health & Fitness; *Style*— Michael Stillwell, Esq; Snarlton Farm, Wingfield, Wilts BA14 9LH; 11 Belitha Villas, London N1 1PE (☎ 071 609 1982); Coopers & Lybrand Deloitte, Plumtree Court, London EC4A 4HT (☎ 071 822 4589, fax 071 822 4652)

STIMPSON, Peter; s of Victor George Stimpson (d 1958), of Ashington, and Eva, *née* Warne (d 1985); *b* 19 Oct 1935; *Educ* Denstone Coll, Durham Univ (LLB); *m* 14 Oct 1960, Susan Winifred, da of Dr Thomas Young Muir (d 1977), of Gosforth; 2 s (Philip b 1961, Andrew b 1964), 2 da (Jane b 1962, Elizabeth b 1978); *Career* slr; *Recreations* sailing, skiing; *Style*— Peter Stimpson, Esq; Heugh Mill, Stamfordham, Northumberland (☎ 378); 5 Marden Road, Whitley Bay, Tyne and Wear (☎ 091 2530424)

STIMSON, Mark William; s of John William Richard Stimson, of 18 Wychwood Grange, Braidly Rd, Bournmouth, Dorset, and Elizabeth Maureen, *née* Leach; *Educ* Bournmouth Sch, St Edmund Hall Oxford (MA); *m* 1 Sept 1984, Alison, da of Trevor John Masson-Richardson, of 68 Normanhurst Ave, Bournemouth, Dorset; *Career* admitted slr 1983; ptnr Messrs Payne Hicks Beach 1987-; memb Holborn Law Soc, London Young Slrs; memb Law Soc; *Recreations* golf, squash; *Clubs* Fulwell Golf, Colets; *Style*— Mark Stimson, Esq; 62 Milton Road, Hampton, Middx TW12 2LT (☎ 081 783 1834); Messrs Payne Hicks Beach, 10 New Square, Lincoln's Inn, London WC2A 3QG (☎ 071 243 6041, telex 893525 MORLAW G, fax 071 405 0434)

STIMSON, Robert Frederick; s of Frederick Henry Stimson (d 1988), and Gladys Alma, *née* Joel; *b* 16 May 1939; *Educ* Rendcomb Coll, QMC London (BSc, MSc); *m* 12 Aug 1961, Margaret Faith, da of Sydney Francis Kerry; 2 s (James b 1967, Charles b 1969), 1 da (Kerry b 1971); *Career* joined HM Dip Serv 1966; Saigon 1968, Singapore 1970, Cabinet Office 1971-73, Mexico 1974-75, E Germany 1980-81, FO 1982-83 (1967, 1976-79), Dublin 1984-87, govr and cdr in chief St Helena 1988; contrib jl Physics and Chemistry Solids; Order of Aztec Eagle Mexico 1974; *Style*— Robert Stimson, Esq; c/o Foreign & Commonwealth Office, London SW1A 2AH

STINSON, His Hon David John; s of Henry John Edwin Stinson, MC (d 1969), of Beckenham, Kent, and Margaret, *née* Little (d 1969); *b* 22 Feb 1921; *Educ* Eastbourne Coll, Emmanuel Coll Cambridge (MA); *m* 11 Aug 1950, (Eleanor) Judith, da of Kenneth Miles Chance, DSO, DL (d 1980), of Wreay, Carlisle, Cumbria; 3 s (Adam b 13 Dec 1953, Rupert b 21 March 1955 d 25 March 1955, Daniel b 14 Feb 1959), 2 da (Sarah (Mrs Nevill) b 6 March 1952, Emma (Mrs Nash) b 8 July 1956); *Career* 2 Lt 147 Essex Yeo Field Regt RHA 1941, Lt 191 Herts & Essex Yeo Field Regt RA 1942, Actg Capt (despatches) 1944, Actg Capt Air Op Pilot RA 1945-46; called to the Bar Middle Temple 1947; dep chm Herts QS 1965, County Ct judge 1969, circuit judge 1972-86 (appt to Co Cts of Suffolk 1973-86); chllr Diocese of Carlisle 1971-90, chm Ipswich and Dist Family Conciliation Serv 1982-89, pres Parents Conciliation Tst (PACT) in Suffolk 1988-; *Recreations* gardening, sailing, birdwatching; *Clubs* Army and Navy, Waldringfield Sailing; *Style*— His Hon David Stinson; Barrack Row, Waldringfield, Woodbridge, Suffolk IP12 4QX (☎ 0473 36 280)

STINTON, Darrol; MBE (1964); s of Ernest Thomas Stinton (d 1980), and Vera, *née* Hall; *b* 9 Dec 1927; *Educ* Beverley GS; *m* 1, March 1952, Barbara, *née* Chapman; 1 s (Julian b 1957), 1 da (Caroline b 1959); m 2, June 1971, Christine Diane, da of Frederick Miller Roehampton; 1 s (Matthew b 1973); m 3, July 1976, Ann Jacqueline Frances, da of Robert Spence Adair (d 1978), 1 step s (Terence Gent Eggett b 1971), 1 da (Penelope b 1977); *Career* Blackburn and De Havilland aircraft cos; cmmnd RAF 1953-69, Empire Test Pilot Sch 1959, qualified test pilot Air Registration Bd 1969-, Air Worthiness Div of CAA, vice pres Royal Aeronautical Soc 1989-; md Darrol Stinton Ltd Int Aero-Marine Conslts 1982-; CEng, FRAeS, MRINA, MIMechE; *Books* textbooks and papers on aircraft design, flight testing and sailing craft design; *Recreations* subaqua, sailing, writing; *Clubs* RAF, The Tiger; *Style*— Darrol Stinton, Esq, MBE; 40 Castle St, Farnham, Surrey GU9 7JB (☎ 0252 713120)

STIRCH, Eric James; s of Thomas James Stirch, and Margery Ellen, *née* Matthews (d 1968); *b* 13 Jan 1946; *Educ* Ward End Hall Sch; *m* 1, 9 Sept 1967 (m dis), Jean Ann, 2 s (Richard b 1969, Paul b 1972); m 2, Lucy (d 1981), da of James Reginald Wilson (d 1966); *Career* 2 years TA, 5 Battalion Royal Regt of Fusilliers 1975-77; DO mgr GKN Birwelco Ltd 1973-74; dir: Parkside Design Serv Ltd 1974-76, Tamworth Football Club 1978-81; DO Mgr Deritend Eng Co Ltd 1986-88, currently dir Northern Premier Football League; Fell Inst Mgmnt Specialists, MIMechIE; *Recreations* designer and inventor, walking; *Style*— Eric Stirch, Esq; 54 Claremont Road, Tamworth B79 8EW (☎ 0827 63369), Tuke & Bell Ltd, Beacon St, Lichfield WS13 7BB (☎ 0543 41134)

STIRK, James Richard; s of Edward Thomas Stirk, TD, of Clochfaen, Llangurig, Powys and Peggy Isobel Phyllis, *née* Soper; *b* 29 Oct 1959; *Educ* Shrewsbury, Trinity Coll Cambridge (MA); *Career* slr, co sec and co dir; tstee The Curig Charity 1986-, cncl memb The Powysland Club 1987-; *Publications* Works in the Montgomeryshire Collections and the Radnorshire Transactions; *Recreations* writing on historical and legal subjects; *Clubs* Powysland, Radnorshire Soc; *Style*— James Stirk, Esq; Mount Severn, 17 Hunter St, Shrewsbury SY3 8QN (☎ 0743 247 734); Clochfaen, Llangurig, Powys SY18 6RP (☎ 05515 687); Tarmac Quarry Products Ltd, Ettingshall, Wolverhampton WV4 6JP (☎ 0902 353522, fax 0902 402032, telex 338544)

STIRLING, Angus Duncan Aeneas; s of Duncan Alexander Stirling (d 1990), and Lady Marjorie Stirling, *qv*; *b* 1933; *Educ* Eton, Trinity Coll Cambridge; *m* 1959, Armyne Morar Helen Schofield, er da of Mr and Hon Mrs William Schofield of Masham Yorks; 1 s, 2 da; *Career* former dep sec Gen Arts Cncl of GB, dep gen Nat Tst 1983- (dep dir 1979-83), dir Royal Opera House Covent Garden, chm Friends of Covent Garden 1981-; memb: Exec Ctee LSO 1979-89, The Crafts Cncl 1980-85, The Theatres' Tst 1983-, The Byam Shaw Sch of Art Govrs 1965-90, The Samuel Courtauld Tst 1990-; dep chm Royal Ballet Bd 1989- (memb); *Clubs* Garrick, Brooks; *Style*— Angus Stirling, Esq; 25 Ladbroke Grove, London W11

STIRLING, Dr (Thomas) Boyd; s of John Stirling, JP (d 1967), of Aldridge, W Midlands, and Christina Buntin, *née* McNaught (d 1981); *b* 28 Nov 1923; *Educ* Queen Mary's GS, Walsall, Birmingham Univ Med Sch (MB ChB); *m* 11 Nov 1950, Marjory Sarah Glen, da of Alexander Glen McDougall (d 1959), of Bonhill, Dunbartonshire; 2 s (Alistair b 1953, Iain b 1956), 1 da (Fionna b 1959); *Career* Maj RAMC 1947-49; GP 1950-, industl med offr GEC 1959-79, anaesthetist 1951-80, police surgn 1952-83; memb: Walsall Hosp GP Ward 1970-83 (fndr chm), Soc of Occupational Health; BMA; *Recreations* family, walking, reading, golf; *Clubs* Royal Scottish Automobile; *Style*— Dr Boyd Stirling; 15 Northgate, Aldridge, Walsall, W Midlands WS9 8QD (☎ 0922 52201)

STIRLING, Prof Charles James Matthew; s of Brig Alexander Dickson Stirling, DSO (d 1961), and Isobel Millicent, *née* Matthew (d 1984); *b* 8 Dec 1930; *Educ* Edinburgh Acad, Univ of St Andrews (BSc), Kings Coll London (PhD, DSc); *m* 1 Sept 1956, Eileen Gibson, da of William Leslie Powell (d 1974), of Bournemouth; 3 da (Catherine (decd), Julia, Alexandra); *Career* res fell: Civil Serv Porton 1955-57, ICI Edinburgh 1957-59; lectr in chemistry Queens Univ Belfast 1959-65, reader in organic chemistry Kings Coll London 1965-69, head of dept UCNW 1981-90 (prof of organic chemistry 1969-90), prof of organic chemistry Univ of Sheffield 1990-; pres: Perkin Div Royal Soc of Chemistry 1989-91, Section B (Chemistry) Br Assoc for the Advancement of Sci 1990; chm: Menai Bridge Cncl of Churches 1982-83, Bangor Monteverdi Singers 1974-89; FRS 1986, FRSC 1967; *Books* Radicals in Organic Chemistry (1965), Organosulphur Chemistry (ed 1975), Chemistry of the Sulphonium Group (ed, 1982), Chemistry of Sulphones and Sulphoxides (ed with S Patai and Z Rappopost, 1988); *Recreations* choral music, travel, furniture restoration; *Style*— Prof Charles Stirling, FRS; Department of Chemistry, University of Sheffield, Sheffield S3 7HF

STIRLING, (Nicholas) Charles; s of late Hugh Patrick, of Witney House, Leafield, and Anne Marietta Patience; gf Sir Charles Mander Bt, chm Manders' Hldgs plc; *b* 3 Oct 1947; *Educ* Eton; *m* 29 April 1975, Elizabeth Emma, da of Brig V W Barlow DSO, OBE; 1 s (William b 1978), 3 da (Frances b 1980, Patience b 1983, Alexandra b 1988); *Career* sr ptnr N C Stirling & Co; jt master North Pennine Hunt; previously master: Cattistock Hunt (Northumberland), Braes of Derwent Hunt (Nottinghamshire), Haydon Hunt (Dorset), South Notts Hunt; *Recreations* foxhunting, sailing; *Clubs* Northern Counties, Farmers, White Hall; *Style*— Charles Stirling, Esq; Dipton Cottage, Corbridge, Northumberland; Milburn House, Dean St, Newcastle upon Tyne

STIRLING, Derek William; s of William James Stirling (d 1966), of Salisbury, Wilts, and Mary Violet, *née* Phillips (d 1974); *b* 15 Dec 1931; *Educ* Beckenham GS, Poly of Central London, Open Univ (BA); *m* 1958, Margaret Ann, da of Frederick Thomas Davis; 2 s (Christopher Derek b 1960, Julien James b 1962), 1 da (Katrina Jane b 1959); *Career* RAF signals Hong Kong 1950-52, applied photographer MoD 1956-58, head Dept of Photography film and Television Salisbury Coll of Art and Design 1958-; BIPP: chm Educn and Trg Ctee 1984 (memb 1982), memb Cncl 1985, vice pres 1989, pres 1990-91; memb: Cncl Br Photographic Assoc 1989, Vocational Standards Cncl 1987, Br Sound and Television Soc, Royal Photographic Soc; FBIPP 1989 (ABIPP 1962); *Recreations* tennis, badminton; *Style*— Derek Stirling, Esq; Salisbury College of Art and Design, Southampton Rd, Salisbury, Wiltshire SP1 2PP (☎ 0722 26122, fax 0722 331972)

STIRLING, Hugh Gerald; s of Surgn Lt Cdr Hugh Stirling, of Chipping Campden, Glos, and Hilda Irene, *née* Harris; *b* 16 April 1947; *Educ* Glenalmond, Silsoe Coll, West of Scotland Agric Coll (NDAgrE); *m* 24 February 1973, Sheila Janet, da of Lt-Col Patrick Alpin, OBE (d 1974), of Jersey, CI; 1 da (Charlotte b 25 Nov 1973); *Career* RN Aux Serv 1979-, served inshore minesweeper/fast patrol boat; agric engr Coffee Bd of Kenya 1971-75, tech mktg mangr Gunsons Sortex 1975-79, PR exec British

Technology Group (promoting agric innovation) 1979-; FIAgrE 1987, RAS; *Recreations* sailing, shooting, fishing; *Clubs* Farmer's, Muthaiga, Kenya Fly Fishers, RNSA; *Style—* Hugh Stirling, Esq; 67D Shooters Hill Rd, Blackheath, London SE3 (☎ 081 853 2292); British Technology Group, 101 Newington Causeway, London SE1 6BU (☎ 071 403 6666, fax 071 403 7586)

STIRLING, James; s of Joseph Stirling, and Louisa, *née* Frazer; *Educ* Quarry Bank HS, Liverpool Sch of Arts, Univ of Liverpool, Liverpool Sch of Architecture (Dip Arch), Sch of Town Planning and Regnl Res London; *m* 1966, Mary, da of Morton Shand; 1 s, 2 da; *Career* served WWII: Lieut Black Watch and Paratroops (D Day Landing); architect; private practice 1956- (ptnrs: James Gowan 1956-63, Michael Wilford 1971-); visiting teacher: Architectural Assoc London 1957, Regent St Poly London 1958-60, Univ of Cambridge Sch of Architecture 1961; Charles Davenport visiting prof Yale Univ Sch of Architecture USA 1967-84 (visiting critic 1960, 1962); RIBA external examiner for architectural educn: Regent St Poly 1965-68, Barlett Univ of London 1968-71; Bannister Fletcher prof Univ of London 1977, Architectural Assoc external examiner London 1979-81, prof Dusseldorf Kustakademie 1977-; exhibitions incl: Three Building Exhibition (Museum of Modern Art NY) 1969, Drawings Exhibition (RIBA Drawings Collection Gallery London) 1974, Via Arte Della Lana (Orsanmichele Florence) 1977, Manhatten Townhouses Exhibition (NY) 1980, 10 New Buildings Exhibition and Model Futures Exhibitions (ICA London) 1933, Wissenschafts Zentrum (Berlin) 1955, Royal Acad (London) 1986, Tate Gallery 1987, 12 Museums and Galleries (jtly with Wilford, Bologna Museum of Art) 1990; awards: Brunner award Nat Inst of Arts and Letters USA 1976, Alvar Aalto award 1977, RIBA Gold medal for architecture 1980, Pritzker prize 1981, Chicago architecture award 1985, Thomas Jefferson medal (USA) 1986, Hugo Haring prize 1988, Praemium Imperiale award 1990; hon memb: Akademie der Kunste Berlin 1969, Florence Acad of Arts 1979, Accademia Nazionale San Luca Italy 1979, Bund Deutscher Architekten 1983, American Acad and Inst of Arts and Letters 1990; hon fell AIA; hon doctorate: RCA 1979, Univ of Glasgow 1990; architect in residence American Acad in Rome 1982, FRSA 1979, ARA 1985; *Style—* James Stirling, Esq; 8 Fitzroy Square, London W1

STIRLING, Malcolm Douglas; s of Douglas Windebank Stirling (d 1984), of Solihull, W Midlands, and Katharine Anne, *née* Folland; *b* 29 May 1933; *Educ* King Edward's Sch Birmingham; *m* 4 July 1959, Shirley, da of William Clayton Pilkington (d 1980), of Liverpool; 1 s (Alistair b 1960), 2 da (Sian b 1961, Elizabeth b 1966); *Career* Nat Serv cmmnd RA 1957-59; qualified CA 1957, Coopers & Lybrand 1959-61, ptnr Spicer & Oppenheim Birmingham (now Touche Ross & Co) 1961- (managing ptnr Birmingham 1981-90, sr ptnr Birmingham 1986-); hon sec Birmingham CAs Students Soc 1955-56; memb: Midlands Advsy Bd of Legal and Gen Assur Soc 1970-86, Ctee of Birmingham & W Midlands Soc of CAs 1967-78 (pres 1977-78), Midlands Advsy Bd Williams & Glyn Bank 1972-78; dir numerous cos incl Dowding & Mills plc 1974-; govr Schs of King Edward VI Birmingham 1991-; memb Worshipful Co of CAs; *Recreations* squash, dinghy sailing; *Clubs* Birmingham, The Royal Overseas League; *Style—* Malcolm Stirling, Esq; Exhall Court, Exhall, nr Alcester, Warwicks; Touche Ross & Co, Newater House, 11 Newhall St, Birmingham B3 3NY (☎ 021 200 2211, fax 021 236 1515, 021 233 4503)

STIRLING, Lady Marjorie Hilda; *née* Murray; da of late 8 Earl of Dunmore, VC, DSO, MVO; *b* 1904; *m* 1926, Duncan Alexander Stirling (d 1990), former chm Westminster, later Nat Westminster Bank; 2 s (*see* Stirling, Angus); *Career* Order of Mercy; *Style—* The Lady Marjorie Stirling; 20 Kingston House South, Ennismore Gardens, London SW7

STIRLING-AIRD, Lady Margaret Dorothea; *née* Boyle; yst da of Patrick James Boyle, 8 Earl of Glasgow, DSO, DL (d 1963), Capt RN, and Hyacinthe Mary, Countess of Glasgow (d 1977); *b* 20 Nov 1920; *m* 1, 1944 (m dis 1962), Capt Oliver Payan Dawnay, CVO, Coldstream Gds; 2 s, 1 da; m 2, 1973, Peter Douglas Miller Stirling-Aird of Kippendavie, TD; *Style—* The Lady Margaret Stirling-Aird; 9 Lansdowne Road, London W11 3AG

STIRLING-HAMILTON, Sir Malcolm William Bruce; 14 Bt (NS 1673), of Preston, Haddingtonshire; o s of Sir Bruce Stirling-Hamilton, 13 Bt (d 1989), and Stephanie (who m 2, 1990, Anthony Cole Tinsley), eldest da of Dr William Campbell, of Alloway, Ayrshire; *b* 6 Aug 1979; *Heir* kinsman, Robert William Hamilton b 1905; *Style—* Sir Malcolm Stirling-Hamilton, Bt; Afton Lodge, Mossblown, By Ayr, Ayrshire KA6 5AS

STIRLING OF FAIRBURN, Capt Roderick William Kenneth; TD (1965), JP (Ross and Cromarty 1975; s of Maj Sir John Stirling, of Fairburn, KT, MBE (d 1975), of Fairburn, Muir of Ord, Ross-shire, and Marjorie Kythé, *née* Mackenzie of Gairloch; *b* 17 June 1932; *Educ* Harrow, Univ of Aberdeen Sch of Agric; *m* 26 Oct 1963, Penelope Jane, da of Lt-Col Charles Henry Wright, TD, DL (d 1978), of The Cottage, Shadforth, Co Durham, formerly of Tuthill, Haswell, Co Durham; 4 da (Charlotte b 1965, Katharine b 1967, Jane b 1968, Fiona b 1971); *Career* Nat Serv Scots Gds 1950-52, cmmnd 1951, Seaforth Highlanders and Queen's Own Highlanders TA 1953-69, ret Capt; dir: Scottish Salmon and White Fish Co Ltd 1972- (chm 1980-), Moray Firth Salmon Fishing Co Ltd 1973-; vice chm Red Deer Cmmn 1975- (memb 1964-), ret 1989; chm: Highland Ctee Scottish Landowners Fedn 1974-79, Scatwell and Strathconon Community Cncl 1975-88; gen cmmr for income tax 1975-; memb Ross and Cromarty Dist Cncl 1984-; Lord Lieut Ross and Cromarty and Skye and Lochalsh 1988 (DL Ross and Cromarty 1971); *Recreations* field sports, gardening, curling; *Clubs* New (Edinburgh); *Style—* Capt Roderick Stirling of Fairburn, TD, JP; Arcan, Muir of Ord, Ross and Cromarty IV6 7UL (☎ 099 73 207); Fairburn Estate Office, Urray, Muir of Ord, Ross and Cromarty IV6 7UT (☎ 099 73 273)

STIRLING OF GARDEN, Col James; CBE, TD; s of Col Archibald Stirling of Garden, OBE, DL, JP (d 1947); *b* 8 Sept 1930; *Educ* Rugby, Trinity Coll Cambridge; *m* 1958, Fiona Janetta Sophia, da of Lt-Col D A C Wood Parker, OBE, TD, DL (d 1967), of Keithick, Coupar, Angus; 2 s, 2 da; *Career* cmmnd 1 Bn Argyll and Sutherland Highlanders 1950, served Korea (wounded), transferred 7 Bn (TA) 1951, Lt-Col cmdg 1966, CO 3 Bn 1968; hon Col 3/51 Highland Vols TA; Scottish dir Woolwich Building Soc, ptnr Kenneth Ryden and Ptnrs (chartered surveyors), dir Scottish Widows Soc 1976, chm Highland TAVRA 1982-87; DL Stirlingshire 1969, HM Lord-Lt of Central Region (dists of Stirling and Falkirk) 1983-; FRICS; kStJ; *Clubs* New (Edinburgh); *Style—* Col James Stirling of Garden, CBE, TD; Garden, Buchlyvie, Stirling (☎ 036 085 212)

STIRRAT, Prof Gordon Macmillan; s of Alexander Stirrat (d 1989), and Mary Caroline, *née* Hutchinson (d 1987); *b* 12 March 1940; *Educ* Hutchesons GS Glasgow, Univ of Glasgow (MB ChB), Univ of Oxford (MA), Univ of London (MD); *m* 2 April 1965, Janeen Mary, da of Hugh Brown (d 1983); 3 da (Lorna Margaret b 1966, Carolyn Jane b 1967, Lindsay Ann b 1970); *Career* lectr Univ of London 1970-75, clinical reader Univ of Oxford 1975-82, dean Faculty of Med Univ of Bristol 1990- (prof of obstetrics and gynaecology 1982-); memb: South West RHA 1984-90, Bristol & Western Health Authy 1990-, Christian Med Fellowship; FRCOG 1981; *Books* Obstetrics Pocket Consultant - Aids to Obstetrics & Gynaecology; *Recreations* fly fishing, walking, writing; *Clubs* United Oxford & Cambridge University; *Style—* Prof Gordon Stirrat; Department of Obstetrics, University of Bristol, Bristol BS2 8EG (☎ 0272 285622, fax 0272 272792)

STIRRUPS, David Robert; s of Robert James Stirrups (d 1987), and Eunice Nora, *née* Palmer; *b* 23 June 1948; *Educ* Gillingham GS, Univ of Sheffield (BDS), Open Univ (BA), Sheffield Poly (MSc); *m* 22 July 1971, Anne Elizabeth; 1 s (Robert b 1980), 2 da (Kathleen b 1975, Rosemary b 1978, d 1978); *Career* conslt orthodontist Gtr Glasgow Health Bd 1980-; chm Scot Ctee for Hosp Dental Servs 1988; memb: Central Ctee for Hosp Dental Servs 1988, Dental Cncl RCPS Glas 1988; FDS, RCS 1974, RCPS Glas; *Recreations* orienteering; *Clubs* Clydeside; *Style—* David Stirrups, Esq; Glasgow Dental Hospital, 378 Sauchiehall St, Glasgow G2 3JZ (☎ 041 332 7020)

STISTED, Brig (Joseph) Nigel; OBE (1978); o s of Joseph Laurence Heathcote Stisted (d 1975), of Fordlands, Catsfield, Sussex, and Katherine Dorothea, *née* Sayer (d 1977); *b* 23 July 1931; *Educ* Winchester, RMA Sandhurst; *m* 11 Aug 1962, Judith Ann, o da of Col Duncan Arthur Davidson Eykyn, DSO, DL (d 1986), of Howgatemouth, Howgate, Penicuik, Midlothian, Scotland; 2 s (Charles b 21 July 1963, William b 12 April 1965); *Career* joined Army 1950, cmmnd Royal Scots 1952; served 1 Bn: Berlin, Korea, Egypt, Cyprus, Scotland, Suez Ops; Adj Depot Royal Scots 1957-58; ADC to Cdr Br Sector Berlin 1959-60, Instr RMA Sandhurst 1960-61, Staff Coll Camberley 1962, BM 155 (Lowland) Bde 1963-65, cmd 1 Bn Royal Scots 1965-67, Jt Servs Staff Coll 1967, asst mil advsr Br High Cmmn Ottawa 1968-70, 2 IC 1 Bn The Royal Scots 1970-71, CO 1 Bn 1971-73 (despatches 1972), AAG Scot Div Edinburgh 1974-76, cmd New Coll (SMC) RMA Sandhurst 1976-79, Brig Inf HQ UKLF 1980, cmd 52 Lowland Bde 1980-83, ret on med grounds 1983; elected memb Queen's Body Gd for Scotland (Royal Co of Archers) 1966; *Recreations* shooting, stamp collecting; *Clubs* New (Edinburgh), Royal Scots (Edinburgh); *Style—* Brig Nigel Stisted, OBE; c/o The Bank of Scotland, New Town Branch, 103 George Street, Edinburgh EH2 3HR

STITCHER, Gerald Maurice; CBE (1979); s of David Stitcher, OStJ (d 1947), and Eva, *née* Ruda; *b* 25 June 1915; *Educ* St George Monoux GS; *m* 22 Dec 1940, Marie; 1 s (Malcolm David b 1949), 1 da (Carole Linda b 1944); *Career* WWII served RAMC, RAOC and REME 1940-46; dir: Gerimar Ltd, Central Meat Supply Ltd, George Waller Meat Products; former chm Fin Corp of London, chm Lidstone Ltd; chm jt conciliation bd Smithfield Market; cncllr Corp of London 1967- (chief commoner 1979-80); Deputy to the Alderman Farringdon Ward Without; Freeman City of London, memb Worshipful Co of Butchers; Deputy OStJ 1989; *Recreations* debating; *Clubs* City Livery, Guildhall; *Style—* Gerald Stitcher, Esq, CBE; 7 South Lodge, Grove End Road, St John's Wood, London NW8 9ER (☎ 071 286 2462)

STITT, Iain Paul Anderson; s of John Anderson Stitt, of Harrogate, and Elise Marie, *née* Dias; *b* 21 Dec 1939; *Educ* Ampleforth, RNC Dartmouth; *m* 1 July 1961, Barbara Mary, da of Richard Bertram George, of Carlisle (d 1986); 2 s (Jonathan b 1964, Paul b 1965), 3 da (Philippa b 1962, Kristina b 1966, Francesca b 1968); *Career* divnl midshipman RNC Dartmouth 1960, HMS Wotton (Fishery Protection Sqdn) 1960-61, HMS Alert (Far East Despatch Vessel) 1961-63, HMS Yarmouth (Londonderry Sqdn) 1963-64, 1 Lt HMS Fiskerton (Singapore Minesweeping Sqdn) 1964-66; Arthur Andersen & Co 1966-: tax ptnr 1974, office managing ptnr Leeds Office 1975-81, UK dir of tax competence 1981-88, Euro dir of tax competence 1988-89, office managing ptnr EC office in Brussels 1988-; cncl memb Inst of Taxation 1969-89 (pres 1982-84); memb tax ctee: CBI 1980-86, Inst of CA in Eng and Wales 1984-; memb diocesan fin bd Leeds RC Diocese 1987-; memb Hon Co of CAs in Eng and Wales; ATII 1964, FTII 1969, ACA 1970, FCA 1975; *Books* Deferred Tax Accounting (1986), Chapters Contributed to Development Land Tax (1976), Tolley's Tax Planning (1980-88); *Recreations* skiing, classical music; *Clubs* Royal Automobile, Royal Oversea League; *Style—* Iain Stitt, Esq; 2 Hereford Rd, Harrogate HG1 2NP, North Yorkshire (☎ 0423 563 846); Avenue Moliere 204, 1060 Bruxelles, Belgium (☎ 32 2 344 96 26); Arthur Andersen & Co, EC Off, Avenue Des Arts 56, 1040 Bruxelles, Belgium (☎ 32 2 510 42 73, fax 32 2 510 43 08, telex 21678)

STOBART, (George) Alastair; s of Lt Col George Kinnear Stobart, OBE, DL (d 1985), and Ailsa, *née* Craig Cowan (d 1981); *b* 29 Oct 1935; *Educ* Winchester Coll, Trinity Coll Cambridge (BA); *m* 21 Sept 1963, Elizabeth Jean, da of Dr J A G Gulliford, of Cardiff; 2 s (Andrew b 1964, Alexander b 1964), 1 da (Lucy b 1968); *Career* Nat Serv cmmnd DLI 1954-56, Capt TA, ret; Wiggins Teape 1959-72, dir Portals Ltd 1973-; *Recreations* tennis, squash, golf, field sports; *Clubs* Fly Fishers, Lansdowne; *Style—* Alastair Stobart, Esq; Polhampton House, Overton, Basingstoke (☎ 256 770 239, fax 256 771 754); Portals Ltd, Overton, Basingstoke (☎ 256 770, fax 256 771 404, telex 858217 PORTAL G)

STOBO, James; OBE (1983), DL (1987); s of Alexander Hamilton Stobo (d 1968), of Fishwick, and Mary Gilchrist Young (d 1983); *b* 9 Dec 1934; *Educ* Edinburgh Acad; *m* 28 Oct 1963, Pamela Elizabeth Mary, da of James Herriot (d 1941), of Duns; 1 s (Herriot b 1974), 2 da (Laurna b 1966, Carolyn b 1969); *Career* farmer at Fishwick, dir John Hogarth Ltd Kelso, chm Moredun Animal Health Ltd Edinburgh; memb Home Grown Cereals Authy 1971-76; pres: NFU Scot 1973-74, Animal Disease Res Assoc 1980-; past chm and pres Scot Assoc of Young Farmers Clubs; vice pres: Royal Smithfield Club, Scot Nat Fatstock Club; chm: Scot Seed Potato Devpt Cncl, Longridge Towers Sch Govrs; FRAgS 1987; *Recreations* game shooting, photography; *Clubs* Caledonian, Farmers'; *Style—* James Stobo, Esq, OBE, DL; Fishwick, Berwick on Tweed TD15 1XQ (☎ 0289 86224, fax 0289 86384, car 0836 609266)

STOCK, Andrew Nicholas; s of Col Peter William Stock, MBE, of South Godstone, Surrey, and Freda Doreen, *née* Dobson (d 1983); *b* 25 March 1960; *Educ* Sherborne; *m* 15 June 1985, Melanie Louise, da of Michael Vass, of Wargave, Berks; 1 da (Phoebe Helena b 20 June 1990); *Career* artist; one man exhibitions incl: Malcolm Innes Gallery (1981/83/85/87), Alpine Club Gallery, Tryon Gallery; winner: Richard Richardson award 1980, Natural World Fine Art awards 1989 and 1990; PJC award for individual merit 1990; elected youngest memb SWLA 1983, fndr memb SWAN, memb RSPB; *Recreations* fly fishing, walking, tennis, roller-skating; *Style—* Andrew Stock, Esq; Chantry Farm House, Beaminster, Dorset DT8 3SB (☎ 0308 862955); La Gaillardenque, Floressas, Puy L'Eveque, Lot, France

STOCK, Dr Anthony Frederick (Tony); s of Raymond Gilbert Stock (d 1982), of Plymouth, and Lilian; *b* 2 Jan 1947; *Educ* Sutton HS for Boys Plymouth, Univ of Nottingham (PhD), Univ of Surrey (BSc, MPhil); *m* 1, 11 April 1968, Jennifer Mary, da of James Thomas Parcell, of Weston Super Mare; 1 s (Jonathan b 1971), 2 da (Maria b 1970, Rebecca b 1973); m 2, Anne Caroline, da of James Thomas Tynan, of Hartlepool; 2 s (Nathaniel James b 1985, Declan Charles b 1989); *Career* civil engr; res assoc Br Petroleum Co plc BP Res Centre, lectr Civil Engrg Univ of Dundee, sr res asst Univ of Nottingham, published tech papers with the princ topics of pavement design and recycling bituminous materials, major contrib to the tech of recycling bituminous materials within the UK; visiting researcher at Texas Tport Inst 1984-85; *Books* Concrete Pavements (1988); *Recreations* sailing, hill walking, squash; *Clubs* Royal Ocean Racing; *Style—* Dr Tony Stock; Bleak House, 1 Belmont Crescent, Maidenhead, Berks SL6 6LS BP Research Centre, Chertsey Rd, Sunbury-on-Thames, Middlesex TW16 7LN

STOCK, Christopher John Robert; s of Dr John Peter Penderell Stock (d 1973), of Newcastle under Lyme, Staffs, and Sybil, *née* Bashford; *b* 1 May 1938; *Educ* Yarlet Hall, Clifton, Univ of St Andrews (BDS), Univ of London (MSc); *m* 12 Oct 1963,

Diana Mary, da of Reginald Adolph Lovatt Wenger; 2 da (Corinne Alison b 16 July 1968, Sally Penderell b 18 Nov 1971); *Career* Royal Army Dental Corps 1962-78 (ret Lt-Col as clinical advsr in advanced conservation), pt/t in endodontic practice and sr clinical lectr Eastman Dental Hosp London 1978-; memb: Br Endodontic Soc (sec and pres 1982), fedn Dentaire Internationale; fell of Int Coll of Dentists; *Books* Endodontics in Practice (1985, 2 edn 1990), A Colour Atlas of Endodontics (1988); *Recreations* golf, photography, collecting prints; *Clubs* North Hants Golf, St Enodoc Golf; *Style—* Christopher Stock, Esq; Heather House, Pines Rd, Fleet, Hampshire GU13 8NL (☎ 0252 616220); The Endodontic Practice, Lister House, 11/12 Wimpole St, London W1M 7AB (☎ 071 636 7900)

STOCK, Michael (Mike); s of William Ralph Stock (d 1978), and Joan, *née* Stringer; *b* 3 Dec 1951; *Educ* Swanley Comp Swanley Kent, Univ of Hull; *m* 1975, Frances Roberta, da of Kevin Wilcox; 2 s (Matthew b 29 Aug 1982, James b 22 April 1988); *Career* song writer, record producer and musician (signed 1st publishing deal (1970); memb bands: The Pact (sch band), Mirage 1976-84, Nightwork 1981-84; fndr ptnr Stock Aitken Waterman (with Pete Waterman and Matt Aitken) 1984; has won numerous Silver, Gold and Platinum Discs since 1985 for writing and/or producing artists incl: Princess, Hazell Dean, Dead or Alive, Bananarama, Mel and Kim, Sinitta, Rick Astley, Kylie Minogue, Brother Beyond, Jason Donovan, Donna Summer, Sonia, Big Fun, Cliff Richard; *Awards* BPI Best British Producers 1988; Music Week top Producers for: Singles (1st) and Albums (3rd) 1987, Singles (1st) and Albums (1st) 1988 and 1989; Ivor Novello Awards (UK): Songwriters of the Year 1987, 1988 and 1989, Writers of Most Performed Works 1987, 1988 and 1989; BMI Awards (USA) Writers of Most Performed Works 1987, 1988 and 1989; Jasrac Awards (Japan) and Cash Awards (Hong Kong) Writers of the Most Performed Foreign Works 1989; involved with charity work incl SAW Goes to the Albert (Royal Marsden Hosp) and records: Let it Be (Ferry Aid), The Harder I Try (Young Variety Club of GB), Help (Comic Relief), Let's All Chant, I Haven't Stopped Dancing Yet and Use It Up and Wear It Out (Help a London Child), Ferry 'Cross the Mersey (Mersey Aid), Do They Know It's Christmas? (Ethiopia Famine Appeal), You've Got a Friend (Childline); *Recreations* sport; *Style—* Mike Stock, Esq; c/o PWL, 4-7 The Vineyard, Sanctuary St, London SE1 1QL (☎ 071 403 0007, fax 071 403 8202)

STOCKDALE, Dr Elizabeth Joan Nöel; *Educ* Univ of Aberdeen Faculty of Medicine (MB ChB), Dip Med Radiodiagnosis (London 1977); *m* 26 May 1979, Christopher Leo Stockdale; 2 s (David b 1983, Alexander b 1984), 1 da (Jane b 1981); *Career* house surgn Aberdeen Royal Infirmary and house physician Woodend Gen Hosp Aberdeen 1972-73, sr house surgn professorial surgical unit Great Ormond St 1974, registrar and sr registrar dept of diagnostic radiology St Georges Hosp London 1975-79 with appts to The Royal Nat Orthopaedic Hosp, Atkinson Morleys Hosp, The Royal Marsden Hosp and St James Hosp; conslt radiologist to the Grampian Health Bd 1980-, hon clinical sr lectr Univ of Aberdeen 1980-; former pres Aberdeen and NE Branch Med Womens Fedn; memb: S Radiological Soc 1980, Euro Soc of Paediatric Radiologists 1980, Br Paediatric Assoc 1986, S Surgical Paediatric Soc 1980, Br Inst Radiology 1990, Br Med Ultrasound Soc 1990; FRCR 1979; *Recreations* theatre, travel, classical music; *Style—* Dr Elizabeth Stockdale; 1 Grant Road, Banchory, Kincardineshire AB3 3UW (☎ 03302 3096); Department of Diagnostic Radiology, Aberdeen Royal Infirmary, Fosterhill, Aberdeen AB9 2ZG; Department of Diagnostic Radiology, Royal Aberdeen Childrens Hospital, Cornhill Rd, Aberdeen AB9 2ZG (☎ 0224 681818 ext 52697)

STOCKDALE, Hon Lady (Louise); *née* Fermor-Hesketh; da of 1 Baron Hesketh, JP (d 1944); *b* 15 Dec 1911; *m* 1937, Sir Edmund Villiers Minshull Stockdale, 1 Bt, JP (d 1989); 2 s, 1 da (d 1970); *Style—* The Hon Lady Stockdale; Hoddington House, Upton Grey, Basingstoke, Hants (☎ Basingstoke 862 437)

STOCKDALE, (Arthur) Noel; DFM; *Career* former chm Assoc Dairies Ltd; former dir: Adel Investmt Tst, Anzo Hldgs, A R McIndoe Ltd, Austragrades Chemists, Bramhams Foods, Burnley Dairies, Calder Vale Creamery, Club Life Ltd, Craven Dairies Ltd, Farm Stores Ltd, G E M Super Centres Ltd, Gazeley Properties, Grimshawe Hldgs, Halifax Bldg Soc, J Bradbury & Sons, Northern Provincial Dairies, Parkside General Estate, Robert Hardman Ltd, Sandmartin Foods, Steeton Investmts Ltd, Valu Petroleum, Wades Departmental Stores, Wharfedale Creamery Co; former regnl dir Nat West Bank (Eastern bd); kt 1986; *Style—* Sir Noel Stockdale, DFM; c/o Associated Dairies Ltd, Craven House, Kirkstall Rd, Leeds 3, W Yorks (☎ 0532 440141)

STOCKDALE, Sir Thomas Minshull; 2 Bt (UK), of Hoddington, Co Southampton; er s of Sir Edmund Villiers Minshull Stockdale, 1 Bt, JP (d 1989); *b* 7 Jan 1940; *Educ* Eton, Worcester Coll Oxford; *m* 1965, Jacqueline, da of Ha-Van-Vuong, of Saigon; 1 s, 1 da; *Heir* s, John Minshull Stockdale b 13 Dec 1967; *Career* barr 1966; *Recreations* shooting, travel; *Clubs* Turf, MCC; *Style—* Sir Thomas Stockdale, Bt; Conington Hall, Conington, Cambridge CB3 8LT (☎ 095 47 252)

STOCKDILL, Roy; s of Leonard Stockdill (d 1961), of Halifax, Yorks, and Molly, *née* Midgley (d 1983); *b* 4 July 1940; *Educ* Elland GS Yorks; *m* 5 Oct 1963, Stephanie Juliet Ann, da of Horace William Hall, of Coventry; 2 s (Richard Timothy b 15 Aug 1965, Jeremy Robin b 2 Oct 1968); *Career* jr reporter Halifax Courier 1956-60, feature writer Illustrated Chronicle Leicester 1960-61, reporter Coventry Evening Telegraph 1961-64, chief reporter Watford and West Herts Post 1964-65, reporter Sunday Citizen 1965-67; News of the World: reporter 1967-78, asst features ed then dep features ed 1978-85, series/literary ed i/c book serialisations 1985-; memb NUJ (various posts incl chm Watford Branch); *Recreations* genealogy, collecting antique maps, cycling, music/hi-fi; *Clubs* Duffers, Presscala; *Style—* Roy Stockdill, Esq; News of the World, News Group Newspapers Ltd, 1 Virginia St, London E1 (☎ 071 782 4375, fax 071 583 9504)

STOCKEN, (George Hubert) Anthony; s of George Walter Stocken (d 1974), of Wilts, and Olga Germaine, *née* Helson; *b* 30 June 1929; *Educ* Kings Coll Taunton, Royal West of England Acad, Univ of Bristol; *m* 7 Sept 1956, Pauline Denise Cruse, da of Arthur Ford (d 1987), of Hampshire; 1 s (Michael George Anthony b 1956), 1 da (Sarah Ann b 1958); *Career* chartered architect; princ in private arch practice, Architectural Heritage Year Award 1975, Times RICS Conservation Award 1976, Civic Tst Commendation Award 1986; Liveryman and memb of the Ct of Assts of Coach Makers and Coach Harness Makers of London (chm Livery Ctee 1983-85); cncllr Salisbury 1968-74 (dist cncllr 1973-83, chm Dist Cncl 1976-77), mayor of City of Salisbury 1975-76; chm Salisbury Round Table 1966-67, vice chm Nat Assoc of Chartered Tstees; chm: Sarum 76 Salisbury Recreation Centre, Salisbury Branch Nat Fed of Old Age Pensioners Assoc 1975-82 (pres 1982), Salisbury Dist Queen's Silver Jubilee Appeal Fund, Prince's Tst for Wiltshire; tstee Salisbury Almshouse and Welfare Charities, fndr memb Sarum Housing Assoc, fndr chm Rehabilitation Engrg Movement Advsy Panel in Salisbury Dist, chm Workface Community Serv Scheme; memb: Salisbury DHA 1981-83, Salisbury Dist Health Cncl 1983-87; chm of govrs Salisbury Coll of Technol 1979-81, vice chm of govrs Bishop Wordsworth GS 1980-83; govr: Exeter House Sch for Disabled Children, St Martin's CE Junior Aided Sch; fndr chm Cncl for Sport and Recreation in Salisbury Dist, chm Westwood Sports Centre 1970-89, memb Cncl Salisbury Festival; patron: Salisbury Playhouse, St Edmunds Art Centre; chm Wilts Assoc of Boys Clubs and Youth Clubs 1977-89, fndr chm Salisbury Boys Club 1974-76 (pres 1977), memb Nat Cncl of Boys Club 1974-76, chm Nat Devpt of Boys Club 1983-86; ARIBA, FFAS, FRSA, FFB; *Recreations* horse riding, hunting, swimming, walking; *Clubs* Naval, Royal Soc of Arts, RIBA; *Style—* Anthony Stocken, Esq; St Andrew's House, West Street, Wilton, Salisbury, Wilts (☎ 0722 744222); Wilts and Bodrigy, The Lizard, Helston, Cornwall

STOCKEN, Oliver Henry James; s of Henry Edmund West Stocken (d 1980); *b* 22 Dec 1941; *Educ* Felsted, Univ Coll Oxford; *m* 1967, Sally Forbes, da of John Dishon of Aust; 2 s, 1 da; *Career* md Barclays Aust 1982-84; dir: N M Rothschild & Sons 1972-77, Esperanza Ltd 1977-79, Barclays Merchant Bank Ltd 1979-1986, Barclays de Zoete Wedd 1986-; ACA 1967; *Style—* Oliver Stocken Esq; Barclays de Zoete Wedd Ltd, Ebbgate House, 2 Swan Lane, London EC4

STOCKER, Rt Hon Lord Justice; Sir John Dexter; MC (1943), TD; s of late John Augustus Stocker, of Carshalton, Surrey; *b* 7 Oct 1918; *Educ* Westminster, Univ of London (LLB); *m* 1956, Margaret Mary, da of Alexander Patrick Hegarty, of Wimbledon; *Career* 2 Lt Queen's Own Royal West Kent Regt (TA) 1939, served in France 1940, ME 1942-43, Italy 1943-46, DAAG mil mission to Italian Army 1946; called to the Bar Middle Temple 1948, QC 1965, master of the Bench 1971, rec of Crown Ct 1972-73, a judge of High Ct of Justice (Queen's Bench Div) 1973-86, presiding judge SE Circuit 1976-79; Lord Justice of Appeal 1986-; kt 1973; *Clubs* MCC, Naval and Military; *Style—* Sir John Dexter Stocker, MC, TD; Royal Courts of Justice, Strand, London WC2

STOCKER, Col Simon Robin Alonzo; OBE (1982); s of Lt-Col A J Stocker, DSO (d 1950), of Northlands, Chichester, Sussex, and Margaret Aileen, *née* Slane (d 1978); *b* 17 May 1939; *Educ* Wellington, RMA Sandhurst; *m* 25 Sept 1965, Rosemary Victoria, da of Maj Gen George Robert Turner-Cain, CB, CBE, DSO, of Norfolk; 2 s (James b 1967, William b 1969), 1 da (Victoria b 1974); *Career* Col; served in UK, BAOR, Hong Kong, Borneo, Aden, NI; instr RMA Sandhurst 1975-77, CO 1RRW 1980-82, chief G3 Trg HQ NI 1982-84, chief G1 HQ Northern Army Gp 1984-87, NATO Def Coll 1988, currently SBIO and Intelligence Branch Chief SHAPE; chm: Army Hockey 1982-83, BAOR cricket 1985-86; rep army at: cricket 1969 and 1971, hockey 1964 and 1969-70; *Recreations* cricket, hockey, tennis, shooting, singing; *Clubs* MCC; *Style—* Col Simon Stocker, OBE; ANZ and Grindlays Bank plc, 13 St James's Square, London SW1Y 4LF

STOCKS, Alan George Hubert; TD (1971 and clasps 1977 and 1989); s of Hubert Sydney Stocks, and Phyllis Margaret Mary, *née* Knight (d 1972); *b* 22 Sept 1940; *Educ* St John's Leatherhead; *m* 23 March 1974, Marie Georgina, da of George Leander Lowe (d 1956); *Career* Maj: King's Regt (TA) 1959-64, Royal Sussex Regt (TA) 1964-67, Queen's Regt (TA) 1967-; dir: GA Turner & Co 1967-87, Sussex Prints 1987-; memb SE TA&VRA; tstee Marshall's Charity; Freeman City of London 1980; *Recreations* theatre, shooting; *Style—* Alan Stocks, Esq, TD; Old Meadows, Randalls Rd, Leatherhead, Surrey

STOCKS, Hon Helen Jane; JP (Inner London); da of Baroness Stocks (Life Peeress, d 1975), and Prof John Leofric Stocks, DSO (d 1937); *b* 1920; *Style—* The Hon Helen Stocks, JP; 44 Regents Park Rd, London NW1 7SX (☎ 071 586 2431)

STOCKS, Dr Philippa Jane; da of Peter Haldane Robbs, of Kettering, Northants, and Kathleen Elinor, *née* Richardson; *b* 31 March 1951; *Educ* Northampton HS, St Bartholemew's Hosp Med Coll (MB BS); *m* 1, (m dis 1988), Maj Robert Charles Webb; 1 s (Daniel b 6 Jan 1978), 1 da (Nicola b 5 Oct 1980); m 2, 12 Aug 1989, Dr Richard John Stocks, s of James Alfred Stocks of Lincs; *Career* sr registrar in histopathology Leicester Royal Infirmary 1981-87, conslt histopathologist Mansfield 1987-; MRCS, LRCP, MRCPath 1985; *Style—* Dr Philippa Stocks; Dept of Histopathology, Kings Mill Hosp, Mansfield Rd, Sutton in Ashfield, Notts NG17 4RL (☎ 0623 22515)

STOCKTON, 2 Earl of (UK 1984); Alexander Daniel Alan Macmillan; also Viscount Macmillan of Ovenden; s of Rt Hon Maurice Victor Macmillan, PC, MP (Viscount Macmillan of Ovenden, d 1984), and Katharine, Viscountess Macmillan of Ovenden, DBE, *qv*; gs of 1 Earl of Stockton (d 1986); *b* 10 Oct 1943; *Educ* Eton, Ecole Politique Université de Paris, Univ of Strathclyde; *m* 1970, Hélène Birgitte (Bitta), da of late Alan Douglas Christie Hamilton, of Stable Green, Mitford, Northumberland; 1 s (Daniel Maurice Alan b 1974), 2 da (Rebecca b 1980, Louisa b 1982); *Heir* s, Viscount Macmillan of Ovenden; *Career* book and magazine publisher; journalist Glasgow Herald 1965-66, reporter Daily Telegraph 1967, foreign corr Daily Telegraph 1968-69, chief Euro corr Sunday Telegraph 1969-70; dep chm Macmillan Ltd 1972-80, chm Macmillan Publishers 1980-90, pres Macmillan Ltd 1990-; govr English Speaking Union 1978-84 and 1986-; memb Ct of Assts Worshipful Co of Merchant Taylors 1987 (Liveryman 1972), Liveryman Worshipful Co of Stationers 1973-; FBIM, FRSA; *Recreations* shooting, fishing, photography, conversation; *Clubs* Beefsteak, Buck's, Carlton, Garrick, Pratts, White's; *Style—* The Rt Hon the Earl of Stockton; Macmillan Publishers Ltd, 4 Little Essex St, London WC2R 3LF (☎ 071 836 6633)

STOCKTON, Fay (Mrs Millett); da of Capt Albert Reginald Stockton, TD, of Sale, Cheshire, and Maureen, *née* May; *b* 12 Nov 1953; *Educ* Withington Girls Sch, Univ of Manchester (LLB); *m* 25 April 1983, Lawrence Randolph Elijah Millett, s of Elijah Millett (d 1984), of Manchester; 1 s (Mitchell b 25 Jan 1984); *Career* called to the Bar Lincoln's Inn 1976, in practice London and N circuit; *Style—* Miss Fay Stockton; 1 Essex Court, Temple, London EC4Y 9AR (☎ 071 583 2000, fax 071 583 0118, mobile tel 0860 812098, home tel 061 434 7737, fax 061 434 5094)

STODART OF LEASTON, Baron (Life Peer UK 1981), of Humbie, in the District of E Lothian; (James) Anthony Stodart; PC (1974); s of Col Thomas Stodart, CIE, IMS (d 1934), and Mary Alice, *née* Coullie; *b* 6 June 1916; *Educ* Wellington; *m* 1940, Hazel Jean, da of Lt Ronald James Usher, DSC, RN (d 1948); *Career* sits as Cons peer in House of Lords; farmer; MP (C) Edinburgh W 1959-74 (stood as Lib Berwick & E Lothian 1950, C Midlothian and Peebles 1951, Midlothian 1955), under sec of state for Scotland 1963-64, min of state Agric and Fish 1972-74 (Parly sec 1970-72); chm: Agric Credit Corpn 1975-87, Ctee Inquiry Local Govt Scotland 1980, Manpower Review of Vet Profession in UK 1984-85; dir FMC 1980-82; *Recreations* playing golf and preserving a sense of humour; *Clubs* New (Edinburgh), Hon Co of Edinburgh Golfers, Caledonian; *Style—* The Rt Hon the Lord Stodart of Leaston, PC; Lorimers, N Berwick, E Lothian (☎ 0620 2457); Leaston, Humbie, E Lothian (☎ 087 533 213)

STODDARD, Antony Leslie; s of Thomas Leslie Stoddard, of Tavistock, Devon, and Marion, *née* Jones (d 1971); *b* 2 June 1942; *Educ* Kelly Coll Tavistock, St John's Coll Cambridge; *m* Suna; 1 s (David b 1973), 1 da (Anna b 1974); *Career* fndr MA; ptnr Asshetons (solicitors) 1970-86; Shandwick plc: non-exec dir 1985-86, exec dir 1986-90, gp md Jan - Sept 1990, dep chm 1990-; *Style—* Antony Stoddard, Esq; Shandwick plc, 61 Grosvenor St, London W1X 9DA (☎ 071 408 2232, fax 071 493 8365)

STODDARD, Christopher James; s of Frederick Stoddard, of 27 Fenton Close, Congleton, Cheshire, and Millicent, *née* Barnett; *b* 2 June 1947; *Educ* Newcastle HS, Univ of Sheffield (MB ChB, MD); *m* 26 June 1971, Margaret Elizabeth, da of Reginald Bailey (d 1977); 1 s (James Edward b 12 Oct 1977), 1 da (Emma Louise b 3 Oct 1975); *Career* surgical registrar Royal Infirmary Sheffield 1974-76, clinical fell in surgery McMaster Med Centre Hamilton Ontario 1978-79, sr lectr in surgery Liverpool 1981-86, conslt surgn Royal Hallamshire Hosp Sheffield 1986- (lectr in surgery 1977-78); memb: Surgical Res Soc, Br Soc of Gastroenterology; FRCS 1976; *Books* Complications of Minor Surgery (1986), Complications of Upper Gastrointestinal Surgery (1987); *Recreations* golf, gardening; *Style*— Christopher Stoddard, Esq; Braenwern, 12 Slayleigh Lane, Fulwood, Sheffield, S Yorks (☎ 0742 309284); 27 Wilkinson St, Sheffield, S Yorks (☎ 0742 723711)

STODDART, Anne Elizabeth; *b* 29 March 1937; *Career* FO 1960-63 and 1967-70, third then second sec Br Military Govt Berlin 1963-67, first sec econ Br Embassy Ankara 1970-73, head of Chancery Br High Cmmn Colombo 1974-76; asst head: West Indian and Atlantic Dept FCO 1977-78, Maritime Aviation and Environment Dept FCO 1979-81; dep UK Perm Rep to the Cncl of Europe Strasbourg 1981-87, head Import Policy Branch External Euro Policy Div DTI 1987-91, dep perm rep Econ Affairs UK Mission to the UN Geneva 1991-; *Style*— Miss Anne Stoddart; United Kingdom Mission to The United Nations, 37-39 Rue de Vermont, 1211 Geneva 20, Switzerland (☎ 010 4122 734 3800)

STODDART, David Russell; s of Laurence Bowring Stoddart (d 1972), of Cheddington Manor, Leighton Buzzard, Beds, and Gwendoline May Russell; *b* 25 Oct 1937; *Educ* Eton; *m* 27 Nov 1968, Eleanor Mary, da of Samuel Soames; 2 s (Edward Laurence, Jonathan William); *Career* Lt 14/20 Kings Hussars, cmmnd 1956, served BAOR Germany 1956-59; joined Wedd Jefferson 1959 (ptnr 1961-80), joined Tattersalls Ltd 1980 (dir 1983-86); memb Stock Exchange 1961-80; *Recreations* horse racing and breeding, cricket; *Style*— David Stoddart, Esq

STODDART, Prof John Little; s of late John Little Stoddart, and late Margaret Pickering, *née* Dye; *b* 1 Oct 1933; *Educ* South Shields HS for Boys, Univ Coll Durham (BSc), Univ of Wales (PhD), Univ of Durham (DSc); *m* 1957, Wendy Dalton, *née* Leardie; 1 s (decd), 1 da (Janet); *Career* Nat Serv Sgt RA 1954-56 (served UK, Hong kong, Malaya); visiting prof of Reading 1984, dir Welsh Plant Breeding Station Aberystwyth 1987-88 (res scientist 1965-87), res dir AFRC Inst Grassland and Environmental Res 1988-; memb: AFRC Mgmnt Bd, Animals Res Ctee, Plants & Environmental Res Ctee, AFRC/NERC Jt Agriculture & Environment Prog Mgmnt Ctee, Forestry Res Co-ordination Ctee, Biotechnology Jt Advsy Bd, RASE Symposia 1992 Strategy Gp, Sec of State for Wales' Advsy Ctee on Agriculture 1988-; mins memb Cncl of Nat Inst for Agricultural Botany 1978-; Hon Prof Univ Coll of Wales; FIBiol 1984, ARPS 1985; *Publications* contrib author to numerous refereed papers and reviews; *Recreations* photography, golf, model making, swimming; *Style*— Prof John Stoddart; Institute for Grassland and Environmental Research, Plas Gogerddan, Aberystwyth, Dyfed SY23 3EB (☎ 0970 828255, fax 0970 820212)

STODDART, John Maurice; s of Gordon Stoddart (d 1983), of Wallasey, and May, *née* Ledder (d 1969); *b* 18 Sept 1938; *Educ* Wallasey GS, Univ of Reading (BA); *Career* head Dept of Econ and Business Studies Sheffield Poly 1970-72, asst dir NE London Poly 1972-76, dir Humberside Coll 1976-83, princ Sheffield City Poly 1983-; dir Sheffield Sci Park 1988-; memb: Cncl for Educn and Trg in Social Work 1989-, Cncl for Indust and Higher Educn 1990-; CNAA 1980-86, Nat Forum Mgmnt Educn and Devpt 1987-, Ct Univ of Sheffield 1983-; chm Ctee of Dirs of Polys 1990- (vice chm 1988-90); memb Bd Mgmnt Crucible Theatre; hon fell Humberside Coll 1983, companion Br Business Graduates Soc 1984; FBIM 1978, FRSA 1980; author of various articles on education, business education and management; *Recreations* biography, hill walking, squash; *Clubs* Reform; *Style*— John Stoddart, Esq; 58 Riverdale Rd, Sheffield S10 3FB (☎ 0742 683636); Sheffield City Polytechnic, Pond St, Sheffield (☎ 0742 720911)

STODDART, Sir Kenneth Maxwell; KCVO (1989), AE (1942), JP (Liverpool 1952); s of Wilfrid Bowring Stoddart (d 1935), of Liverpool, and Mary Hyslop, *née* Maxwell; *b* 26 May 1914; *Educ* Sedbergh, Clare Coll Cambridge; *m* 5 Sept 1940, Jean Roberta Benson, da of late Dr John Benson Young; 2 da (Jennifer Jean Maxwell (Mrs Jackson) b 1941, Charlotte Maxwell b 1949); *Career* served RAuxAF 1936-45, vice chm (Air) W Lancs T&AFA 1954-64; Lord Lt Merseyside 1979-89 (DL 1974-79, Lancs 1958), High Sheriff Merseyside 1974; chm: Cearns & Brown 1973-84, United Mersey Supply Co 1978-81; chm Liverpool Child Welfare Assoc 1965-81; Hon LLD Liverpool, hon fell Liverpool Poly 1989; KStJ 1979; *Clubs* Liverpool Racquet, Athenaeum; *Style*— Sir Kenneth Stoddart, KCVO, AE, JP; The Spinney, Overdale Rd, Willaston, S Wirral L64 1SY (☎ 051 327 5183)

STODDART, Michael Craig; s of Frank Ogle Boyd Stoddart, of Westbourne, Hants, and Barbara Vincent, *née* Craig; *b* 27 March 1932; *Educ* Marlborough; *m* 15 April 1961, (Susan) Brigid, da of late Capt Denis North-East O'Halloran, RA, of IOW; 2 s (James b 1965, Edward b 1973), 2 da (Phillippa b 1963, Lucinda b 1970); *Career* jt chief exec Singer & Friedlander Ltd 1955-73; chm Electra Investment Trust plc 1986 (dep chm and chief exec 1974-86); chm Electra Kingsway Group 1989, non-exec chm and dir numerous private and public cos; memb: Cncl of Aims of Industry, London Cncl Ironbridge Gorge Museum Tst; tstee All Hallows Church; memb Worshipful Co of Chartered Accountants in England and Wales; FCA 1955; *Recreations* country pursuits, shooting, golf, tennis, theatre, travel; *Clubs* Boodle's; *Style*— Michael Stoddart Esq; Compton House, Kinver, Worcs DY7 5LY; Warwick Lodge, 42 St George's Drive, London SW1V 4BT; Electra Investment Trust plc, 65 Kingsway, London WC2B 6QT (☎ 071 831 6464, telex 265525 ELECG, fax 071 404 5388)

STODDART, Patrick Thomas; s of Thomas Stoddart (d 1987), of Leith, Scotland, and Anne Theresa Power (d 1979); *b* 23 Nov 1944; *Educ* Watford Boys GS; *m* Nicolette, da of Gp Capt A D Murray (RAF ret); *Career* jr reporter Watford Observer 1962, Evening Echo Herts 1967-72, TV Columnist London Evening News 1975-80 (joined as reporter 1972); freelance 1980-85 (various TV series as writer/presenter at TVS and Anglia), TV critic Channel 4 Daily 1989-, currently broadcasting ed and TV critic Sunday Times (joined as broadcasting feature writer 1985); *Recreations* rugby, cricket; *Clubs* Fullerians RFC, Fleet Street Strollers Cricket (chm); *Style*— Patrick Stoddart, Esq; The Sunday Times, 1 Pennington St, London E1 (☎ 071 782 5780, fax 0860 672 885)

STODDART, Peter Laurence Bowring; s of Laurence Bowring Stoddart, JP (d 1973), of Cheddington Manor, Leighton Buzzard Beds, and Gwendolen Mary, *née* Russell; *b* 24 June 1934; *Educ* Sandroyd Sch, Eton, Trinity Coll Oxford; *m* 29 May 1957, Joanna, da of Thomas Adams; 1 s (Clive Laurence Bowring), 2 da (Fiona Gwendolen Jane, Belinda May); *Career* Nat Serv 2 Lt 14/20 Kings Hussars 1952-54; with C T Bowring Group 1955-80; dir: C T Bowring & Co Ltd 1967-80, Singer & Friedlander, Crusader Insurance Co Ltd 1967-80, English & American Insurance Co Ltd 1967-80, Fleming Mercantile Investment Trust plc 1976-90; chm: Greenfriar Investment Co Ltd 1977-90, Robert Fleming Insurance Brokers 1980-90, Capt Bucks CCC 1957-66; Master: Whaddon Chase Hunt 1969-83 Heythrop Hunt 1988-; former Master Worshipful Co of Salters 1986-87; memb Lloyds; *Recreations* field sports & countryside, travel; *Clubs* White's, Cavalry and Guards, MCC; *Style*— Peter Stoddart, Esq; North Rye House, Moreton-in-Marsh, Glos GL56 0XU (☎ 0451 30 636); Robert Fleming Insurance Brokers Ltd, Staple Hall, Stone House Ct, London EC3A 7AX (☎ 071 621 1263, fax 071 623 6175, telex 883 735/6)

STODDART OF SWINDON, Baron (Life Peer UK 1983), of Reading in the Royal Co of Berkshire; David Leonard Stoddart; s of late Arthur Leonard Stoddart, and Queenie Victoria, *née* Price; *b* 4 May 1926; *Educ* St Clement Danes GS, Henley GS; *m* 1, 1946 (m dis 1960), Doreen M Maynard; 1 da (Hon Janet Victoria (Hon Mrs Pudney) b 1947); m 2, 1961, Jennifer, adopted da of late Mrs Lois Percival-Alwyn, of Battle, Sussex; 2 s (Hon Howard David b 1966, Hon Mathwyn Hugh b 1969); *Career* former clerical worker: PO telephones, railways, power station and hosp; former ldr Lab Gp Reading Cncl (memb Reading County Borough Cncl 1954-72); Parly candidate (Lab): Newbury 1959 and 1964, Swindon by-election 1969; MP (Lab) Swindon 1970-83; PPS to Min of Housing and Construction 1974-75, asst govt whip 1975, lord cmmr Treasury 1976-77, oppn spokesman Industry 1982-83, oppn spokesman Energy (Lords) 1983-88, oppn whip (Lords) 1983-88; trade unions: EETPU 1953-, NALGO 1951-70; memb Nat Jt Cncl Electricity Supply Independent 1967-70; *Style*— The Rt Hon the Lord Stoddart of Swindon; Sintra, 37a Bath Rd, Reading, Berks (☎ 0734 576726); House of Lords, London SW1

STOFFBERG, Leon Dutoit; s of William Dutoit Stoffberg, and Yvonne Mei, *née* Robinson; *b* 11 Feb 1951; *Educ* Rondesbosch Boys Sch, Cape Town Univ (CTA); *m* 17 July 1979, Pauline Jean; 1 da (Lisa); *Career* fin dir: Fin Div Great Universal Stores Group 1983-85, Gibbs Insurance Holdings Ltd 1985-; memb Inst of South African CAs; *Style*— Leon Stoffberg, Esq; Bishops Court, Artillery Lane, London E1 7LP (☎ 071 415 0198)

STOGDON, (Edgar) David; MBE (1978); s of Edgar Stogdon (d 1951), of Harrow, and Louise Dalrymple, *née* Dundas (d 1940); *b* 1 Jan 1919; *Educ* Harrow; *m* 1 May 1948, Dorothea Margaret, da of Maj Leonard Haviland (d 1971), of Inveresk Midlothian; 3 s (Matthew b 1949, Henry b 1958, Oliver b 1959), 2 da (Sarah b 1951, Lucy b 1954); *Career* Nat Serv 19 Destroyer Flotilla HMS Brazen 1939, 1 and 15 Destroyer Flotilla HMS Tynedale 1940 (despatches 1940, 1942), 4 Destroyer Flotilla HMS Quality 1943, Br Pacific Fleet 1944, Battle Class Destroyers 1945, demobbed 1946; RNLI 1952-81: div inspr lifeboats, staff inspr, supt of depots; pioneer of inshore lifeboat devpt and rigid-hulled inflatable boats; seconded to Red Cross in cyclone relief work Ganges Delta E Pakistan, awarded Red Cross badge of honour; retained conslt and designer to Royal Dutch Lifeboat Servs; memb RNLI nat ctee on lifeboat preservation; companion Royal Inst of Naval Architects 1982-; *Recreations* sailing, shooting, tennis, church bell ringing, dry stone walling; *Style*— David Stogdon, Esq, MBE; Little Mead, Witchampton, Wimborne, Dorset BH21 5AY (☎ 0258 840 374)

STOKELY, Guy Robert; *b* 30 Oct 1943; *Educ* Forest Sch, Oxford Univ (MA); *m* 4 Oct 1968, Wendy Anne; 3 s (Robert b 1970, Tom b 1979, Tim b 1983), 1 da (Sarah b 1973); *Career* fin vice-pres Manufacturers Life Insur Co 1966-78, gen mangr Saudi Int Bank 1978-; *Recreations* golf, water sports, gardening; *Clubs* RAC; *Style*— Guy Stokely, Esq; The Parsonage, Great Dunmow, Essex CM6 2AT (☎ 0371 2430); 99 Bishopsgate, London EC2M 3TB (☎ 071 638 2323, fax 071 628 8633, telex 8812261/2)

STOKER, Dr Dennis James; s of Dr George Morris Stoker (d 1949), of Mitcham, Surrey, and Elsie Margaret, *née* Macqueen (d 1986); *b* 22 March 1928; *Educ* Oundle, Guy's Hosp Med Sch Univ of London (MB BS); *m* 22 Sept 1951, Anne Sylvia Nelson, da of Norman Forster (d 1962), of Haywards Heath, Sussex; 2 s (Philip b 1954, Neil b 1956), 2 da (Claire b 1952, Catherine b 1958); *Career* cmmnd med branch RAF 1952: RAF Brampton 1952-53, RAF Bridgnorth 1953-55, RAF Hosp W Kirby 1955-56, Med Div RAF Hosp Wroughton 1956-58, i/c Med Div RAF Hosp Akrotiri Cyprus 1958-61, physician i/c Chest Unit RAF Hosp Wroughton 1961-64, Metabolic Unit St Mary's Hosp London 1964-65 (sabbatical), i/c Med Div RAF Hosp Steamer Point Aden 1965-67, i/c Med Div RAF Hosp Cosford Staffs 1967-68, ret Wing Cdr 1968; conslt radiologist: St George's Hosp 1972-87, Royal Nat Orthopaedic Hosp 1972-; dean Inst of Orthopaedics 1987- (dir radiological studies 1975-); ed Skeletal Radiology 1984-, dean Faculty of Clinical Radiology, vice pres Royal Coll of Radiologists 1990-91 (memb of Faculty Bd 1983-85, memb Cncl 1985-88); DMRD, FRCP 1976, FRCR 1975, FRSM 1958; *Books* Knee Arthrography (1980), Orthopaedics: self assessment in radiology (jtly, 1988), Radiology of Skeletal Disorders (jtly, 3 edn 1990); *Recreations* med history, patio gardening, dinghy sailing in warm climates; *Clubs* RAF; *Style*— Dr Dennis Stoker; 4 Waterloo Terrace, Islington, London N1 1TQ (☎ 071 359 0617); 25 Wimpole St, London W1M 7AD (☎ 071 935 4747); Dept of Radiology, Royal Nat Orthopaedic Hosp, 45-51 Bolsover St, London W1P 8AQ (☎ 071 387 5070, ext 269)

STOKER, Linda Beryl; da of Bernard Alistar Dow, and Beryl Georgina Edith, *née* Taylor; *b* 10 July 1954; *Educ* Goffs GS, NE London Poly, memb of Inst of Personnel Mgmnt; *Career* publicity offr The Rank Orgn; trg offr Guy's Health Dist 1975, trg mangr EMI Leisure 1977, trg advsr Hotel and Catering Indust Trg Bd 1979, field organiser Manpower Servs Cmmn 1981, md Dow-Stoker Ltd 1983-, fndr Women Returners Ltd 1990; *Books* A Woman of the Year (1990), Having it All (1991), Women Returners Year Book (1991); *Recreations* sailing, netball; *Style*— Mrs Linda Stoker; Dow-Stoker, The Mill, Stortford Rd, Hatfield Heath, nr Bishop's Stortford, Herts (☎ 0279 730056)

STOKER, Sir Michael George Parke; CBE (1974); *b* 1918 July; *Career* former lectr in pathology Cambridge Univ, fell and dir med studies Clare Coll Cambridge and prof of virology Glasgow Univ, dir Imperial Cancer Research Fund Laboratories 1968-79; former foreign sec and vice-pres Royal Soc 1976-81, former pres Clare Hall Cambridge 1980-87; FRSE, FRS, FRCP; kt 1980; *Style*— Sir Michael Stoker, CBE; Clare Hall, Cambridge

STOKER, Richard; s of Capt Bower Morrell Stoker (d 1983), of Wasdale Manor, Weydale Ave, Scarborough, Yorks, and Winifred *née* Harling; *b* 8 Nov 1938; *Educ* Bredalbane House Sch Castleford, Huddersfield Sch of Music & Sch of Art, RAM, Nadia Boulanger Paris; *m* 1, (m dis 1985), Jacqueline Margaret Trelfer; m 2, 10 July 1986, Gillian Patricia, da of Kenneth Walter Watson, of Stenson Rd, Littleover, Derby; *Career* tutor RAM 1970-80 (prof 1963-85); compositions incl: Johnson Preserv'd (Opera), Three String Quartets, Three Piano Trios, Parfita, Music that Brings Sweet Sleep, Aspects of Flight, Make me a Willow Cabin, Little Organ Book, Three Improvisations, Organ Symphony Three Pieces, Piano Concerto, Piano Variations, Piano Sonata, Two Overtures, Benedictus, Three Violin Sonatas, (Guitar) Sonatina, Improvisation, Diversions, Pastorae, Sonata Concerto; film and stage credits incl: Troilus and Cressida (Old Vic), Portrait of a Town (Standard), End of the Line (Nat Film Sch), Garden Party (Coliseum), My Friend-My Enemy (The Place); ed Composer Magazine 1969-80, memb and treas Steering Ctee Lewisham Arts Festival 1990, memb Composers' Guild 1962- (memb Exec Ctee 1969-80); Mendelssohn scholar 1962, PRS 1962, MCPS 1970, APC 1977, BASCA 1980, memb RSM 1984, memb Blackheath Art Soc 1988, ARAM, ARCM, fell RAM (memb Fellow Assoc 1988); *Books* Portrait of a Town (1974), Words Without Music (1974), Strolling Players (1978), Open Window-Open Door (1985); *Recreations* squash, skiing, tennis, swimming; *Clubs* RAM Guild; *Style*— Richard Stoker, Esq; c/o Ricordi & Co (London) Ltd, The Bury, Church Street, Chesham, Bucks (☎ 0494 78 3311)

STOKES, Dr Adrian Victor; OBE (1983); s of Alfred Samuel Stokes, of 23 Hale Grove Gardens, Mill Hill, London, and Edna, *née* Kerrison; *b* 25 June 1945; *Educ* Orange Hill GS, UCL (BSc, PhD); *m* 3 Oct 1970 (m dis 1978), Caroline Therese, da of Arthur Campbell Miles, of London; *Career* res programmer GEC Computers Ltd

1969-71, res asst/res fell Inst Computer Sci/Dept Stats and Computer Sci UCL 1971-77, sr res fell and sr lectr Sch of Info Sci The Hatfield Poly 1977-81, dir computing St Thomas' Hosp 1981-88 (King's Fund fell 1981-84), hon res fell Dept Computer Sci UCL 1988-, princ consIt NHS Info Mgmnt Centre 1989-; chm Disabled Drivers' Motor Club 1972-82, vice pres Disabled Drivers' Motor Club 1982-, chm Exec Ctee Royal Assoc for Disability and Rehabilitation 1985-, govr and memb Cncl of Mgmnt Motability 1977-, memb Fin and Gen Purposes Ctee Assoc for Spina Bifida and Hydrocephalus 1983-, tstee and memb Cncl of Mgmnt PHAB 1982-90; memb: DHSS Working Party on Mobility Allowance 1975, DHSS Working Party on the Invalid Tricycle Repair Serv 1976-80, DHSS Silver Jubilee Ctee On Improving Access for Disabled People 1977-78, DHSS Ctee on Restrictions Against Disabled People 1979-81, Social Security Advsy Ctee 1980-, Dept of Tport Panel of Advsrs on Disability 1983-85, Disabled Persons' Advsy Ctee 1986-89; pres Hendon North Lib Assoc, 1981-83, candidate for London Borough of Barnet Cncl Mill Hill Ward 1968, 1971, 1974 and 1978; Freeman: City of London 1988, Co of Info Technologists 1988; FBCS 1979, FInstD 1986, CChem 1976, CEng 1990, MRSC 1976, MBIM 1986; *Books* An Introduction to Data Processing Networks (1978), Viewdata: A Public Information Utility (2 edn 1980), The Concise Encyclopaedia of Computer Terminology (1981), Networks (1981), What to Read in Microcomputing (with C Saiady, 1982), A Concise Encyclopaedia of Information Technology (3 edn 1986), Integrated Office Systems (1982), Computer Networks: Fundamentals and Practice (with M D and J M Bacon, 1984), Overview of Data Communications (1985), Communications Standards (1986), The A-Z of Business Computing (1986), OSI Standards and Acronyms (2 edn 1988); *Recreations* philately, science fiction, computer programming; *Style*— Dr Adrian V Stokes, OBE; 97 Millway, Mill Hill, London NW7 3JL (☎ 081 959 6665, car 0860 549 584, fax 081 906 4137); NHS Information Management Centre, 19 Calthorpe Rd, Birmingham B15 1RP (☎ 021 454 1112, fax 021 455 9340)

STOKES, Dr Alistair; *b* 22 July 1948; *Educ* Univ of Wales (BSc, PhD), Univ of Oxford (SRC res fellowship); *m* 22 Aug 1970, Stephanie Mary, da of B H Garland, of Fordingbridge, Hants; 2 da (Charlotte, Samantha); *Career* commercial dir Monsato Co St Louis Missouri USA 1980-82 (joined 1976); Glaxo Pharmaceuticals Ltd: int product mangr 1982-83, mktg and sales dir Duncan Flockhart Ltd 1983-85; gen mangr Yorks Regnl Authy 1985-87; Glaxo Pharaceuticals Ltd: dir business devpt 1987-88, md Glaxo Labs Ltd 1988-89, regnl dir Glaxo Hldgs plc 1989-; memb E Berks Health Authy; *Books* Plasma Proteins (1977); *Recreations* reading, walking, music; *Style*— Dr Alistair Stokes; Glaxo Hldgs plc, Clarges St, London, W17 8DH (☎ 071 493 4060, fax 071 493 4809, car 0836 347477, telex 25456 GLXEPT G)

STOKES, David Mayhew Allen; QC 1989; s of Henry Pauntley Allen Stokes (d 1965), and Marjorie Joan, *née* Mollison; *b* 12 Feb 1944; *Educ* Radley, Inst de Touraine (Tours), Churchill Coll Cambridge (MA); *m* 1970, Ruth Elizabeth, da of Charles Tunstall Evans, CMG, of Sussex; 1 s (Harry b 1974), 1 da (Jennifer b 1978); *Career* called to the Bar Gray's Inn 1968, rec of the Crown Ct 1985-, memb Gen Cncl of the Bar 1989-; guest instr/team ldr Nat Inst of Trial Advocacy York Univ Toronto Canada 1986-; tstee London Suzuki Gp 1988-; *Recreations* amateur dramatics, madrigals; *Clubs* Norfolk (Norwich); *Style*— David M A Stokes, Esq, QC; 5 Paper Buildings Temple EC4Y 7HB (☎ 071 583 6117)

STOKES, Baron (Life Peer UK 1969), of Leyland, Co Palatine of Lancaster; Sir Donald Gresham Stokes; TD (1945), DL (Lancs 1968); s of Harry Potts Stokes (d 1954), of Looe, Cornwall, and Mary Elizabeth Gresham, *née* Yates (d 1969); *b* 22 March 1914; *Educ* Blundell's, Harris Inst of Technol Preston; *m* 25 May 1939, Laura Elizabeth Courteney, da of late Frederick C Lamb; 1 s (Hon Michael Donald Gresham b 13 June 1947); *Career* cmmnd Royal N Lancs Regt 1938, transferred to REME and served WWII with 8 Army in Middle East and Italy with rank of Lt-Col; student apprentice Leyland Motors Ltd 1930 (export mangr 1946, gen sales and service mangr 1950, dir 1954), md and dep chm Leyland Motor Corp 1963, chm and md British Leyland Motor Corp 1967, chm and chief exec British Leyland Ltd 1973, pres 1975, consIt to Leyland Vehicles 1980, chm and dir The Dutton-Forshaw Motor Group Ltd 1980-90, pres Jack Barclay Ltd 1989-90; dir: Suits 1980-, The Dovercourt Motor Co 1982-90, KBH Communications 1985-; pres: CBI 1962, Univ of Manchester Inst of Science and Technol 1972-75, EEF 1967-75; dir: District Bank 1964-69, National Westminster Bank 1969-81, IRC (dep chm 1969-71), EDC for Electronics Industry 1966-68, London Weekend TV 1967-71; chm: Two Counties Radio 1979-84 (pres 1984-90, chm 1990-), GWR Group 1990-; Commodore Royal Motor Yacht Club 1979-81; Freeman of City of London, Liveryman Worshipful Co of Carmen 1964; hon fell of Keble Coll Oxford 1968; Hon LLD Lancaster 1967, Hon DTech Loughborough 1968, Hon DSc Southampton 1969, Hon DSc Salford 1971; FIMI (pres 1962), FIRTE (pres 1982-84), MIRA (pres 1966), FIMechE (pres 1972), SAE (USA), FEng 1976 (CEng 1933), FICE 1984; officier de l'ordre de la Couronne (Belgium) 1964, commandeur de l'ordre de Leopold II (Belgium) 1972; kt 1965; *Recreations* yachting; *Clubs* Royal Motor Yacht, Beefsteak, Army and Navy; *Style*— The Rt Hon the Lord Stokes, TD, DL; Branksome Cliff, Westminster Rd, Poole, Dorset BH13 6JW (☎ 0202 763088); Jack Barclay Ltd, 18 Berkeley Sq, London W1X 6AE (☎ 071 629 7444, fax 071 629 8258, car 0860 415770)

STOKES, Dr John Fisher; s of Dr Kenneth Henry Stokes (d 1962), of Bexhill-on-Sea, and Mary Fisher (d 1973); *b* 19 Sept 1912; *Educ* Haileybury, Gonville and Caius Coll Cambridge (MB BCh, MA, MD), Univ Coll Hosp Med Sch; *m* 21 Sept 1940, (Elizabeth) Joan, da of Thomas Rooke (d 1956); 1 s (Adrian b 1947), 1 da (Jennifer (Mrs Harrison) b 1942); *Career* WWII RAMC 1942-46, 14 Army in Far E, attached to Gen Orde Wingate's 2 Chindit Operation (despatches), demobbed Lt-Col; consIt physician UCH 1947-77; visiting physician: Mass Gen Hosp Boston 1958, Royal Victoria Hosp Montreal 1966; consIt in postgrad med educn in India and Sri Lanka WHO 1967 and 1979, chm Common Examining Bd RCP (UK) 1968-77, sr censor and vice pres RCP London 1969, pres Section of Med RSM London 1972, annual med educn visits to Thailand MOD/FCO Colombo Plan 1969-75; squash racquets runner up: Br Isles Amateur Championship 1937, Br Int 1938; chm Jesters Club 1953-59; Harveian orator RCP London 1981; hon med advsr Leeds Castle Fndn 1977 (tstee 1984); FRCP 1947, FRCPE 1976; *Books* Examinations in Medicine (jtly, 1976 and 1977), MCQ on Lecture Notes on General Surgery (jtly, 1977, 1980 and 1987), MCQ on Clinical Pharmacology (jtly, 1983 and 1988); *Recreations* piano playing, chamber music, cooking, painting; *Clubs* Athenaeum, Savile; *Style*— Dr John Stokes; Ossicles, Newnham Hill, nr Henley-on-Thames, Oxon RG9 5TL (☎ 0491 641526)

STOKES, Sir John Heydon Romaine; MP (C) Halesowen and Stourbridge 1974-; s of late Victor Romaine Stokes, of Hitchin, Herts; *b* 23 July 1917; *Educ* Haileybury Coll, Queen's Coll Oxford; *m* 1, 1939, Barbara Esmé (d 1988), da of late R E Yorke, of Wellingborough, Northants; 1 s, 2 da; m 2, 21 Jan 1989, Mrs E F Plowman (d 1990), wid of John Plowman; m 3, 26 Jan 1991, Ruth Bligh, wid of Sr Timothy Bligh, KBE, DSO, DSC; *Career* army 1939-46: Dakar expedition 1940, wounded N Africa 1943, mil asst to HM Min Beirut and Damascus 1944-46, Maj; personnel offr ICI 1946-51, personnel mangr Br Celanese 1951-59, dep personnel mangr Courtaulds 1957-59, ptnr Clive and Stokes Personnel ConsIts 1959-80; Parly candidate (C): Gloucester 1964, Hitchin 1966; MP (C) Oldbury and Halesowen 1970-74, delegate to Cncl of Europe and WEU 1983-; elected to House of Laity Gen Synod of C of E 1985-90, chm Gen Purposes Ctee Primrose League 1971-85, vice-pres Royal Stuart Soc; kt 1988; *Clubs* Carlton, Buck's; *Style*— Sir John Stokes, MP; Down House, Steeple Claydon, nr Buckingham MK18 2PR

STOKES, Leslie James; s of William James Stokes, and Peggy Florence, *née* Blunsom; *b* 22 May 1951; *Educ* Abbs Cross Tech HS, Sir John Cass Coll, Newcastle upon Tyne Poly (DipAD, RSA travelling bursary prize), RCA (MDes, Braun prize); *m* 1973, Janet Barbara, da of Alfred Johns Victor Hayes; 1 s (William James b 1987), 1 da (Kathryn Louise b 1982); *Career* lectr in 3D design Herts Coll of Art and Design 1976-79, industl design consIt London and Upjohn 1976-81, ptnr London Associates (Industl Design and Product Devpt) 1981; *Awards* Br Design award 1990; memb various jury panels for Design Cncl Design awards; FCSD 1989 (MCSD 1981), memb Design Business Assoc 1986; *Style*— Leslie Stokes, Esq; London Associates, 103 High St, Berkhamsted, Hertfordshire HD4 2DG (☎ 0442 862631, fax 0442 874354)

STOKES, Hon Michael Donald Gresham; s of Baron Stokes, TD (Life Peer); *b* 1947; *Educ* Southampton Univ (BSc); *m* 1970 (m dis 1982), Inger Anita, da of Douglas Percy; 1 s, 1 da; *Style*— The Hon Michael Stokes; 6 Boulters Crt, Maidenhead, Berks

STOKES, Michael George Thomas; s of Michael Philip Stokes (d 1988); *b* 30 May 1948; *Educ* Preston Catholic Coll, Univ of Leeds (LLB); *Career* called to the Bar Gray's Inn 1971; asst lectr Univ of Nottingham 1970-72, in practice Midlands and Oxford circuit 1973-, rec of the Crown Ct 1990 (asst rec 1986); *Recreations* skiing, theatre, riding, breeding thorough bred horses, racing; *Clubs* Northampton and County (Northampton); *Style*— Michael Stokes, Esq; Alpha House, The Marsh, Crick, Northants NN6 7TN (☎ 0788 823484); 1 King's Bench Walk, Temple, London EC4 7DB (☎ 071 353 8436, fax 071 353 2647)

STOKES, Robert Lionel; s of Robert Keith Stokes, of Brecon, Powys, and Eleanor Jean, *née* Edwards; *b* 2 Oct 1954; *Educ* Devonport HS Plymouth, Univ, of Aberdeen (BSc); *Career* radio journalist; Northsound Radio Aberdeen 1982-86, Radio Forth Group Edinburgh 1986-89, Scotland on Sunday 1989-; Silver medallist Int Radio Festival of NY for Radio Forth business prog Money Talks 1989; *Recreations* playing the cello, hillwalking, tennis, cricket; *Style*— Robert Stokes, Esq; Scotland on Sunday, 20 North Bridge, Edinburgh EH1 1YT (☎ 031 243 3607, fax 031 220 2443)

STOLLAR, Derek Arthur; s of Harry Stollar (d 1960), and Grace Elizabeth, *née* Rhodes (d 1975); *b* 18 April 1930; *Educ* City of London Sch, Brixton Sch of Bldg, Architectural Assoc Sch (AA Dip); *m* 1, 1962 (m dis 1971), Carol, da of Flt Lt Hugh Grehan; 1 s (Mark b 9 March 1964), 1 da (Abigail b 31 March 1971); m 2, 18 July 1970, Dawn Virginia, da of Capt Anthony Paul Reiss; 2 step da (Tabitha b 19 Feb 1961, Rachel b 16 May 1963); *Career* Nat Serv writer RN 1948-50; architect 1957-; assoc: Stilman & Eastwick - Field 1960-62, Jan Farber & Bartholomew 1968-72; ptnr David Brian & Stollar 1972-74, princ Derek Stollar 1974-75, ptnr Hugh Roberts Graham & Stollar (later Graham & Stollar) 1975-80, sr dir Graham & Stollar Associates Ltd 1980-89, dir and chm Stollar WRM Associates Ltd 1989-90; memb: Georgian Gp, Soc for Protection of Ancient Bldgs, Bath Preservation Tst, Assoc for Studies in the Conservation of Historic Buildings, Bath Soc; fndr memb Social and Lib Democrats; Freeman City of London 1971; memb AA 1956, FRIBA 1969 (ARIBA 1958); *Recreations* travel, talk, early music (recorder), water colour painting, reading (particularly history); *Style*— Derek Stollar, Esq; 3 Beaufort Place, Bath BA1 6RP (☎ 0225 312801); Rue Mandriére, Alet Les Bains, 11580, Aude, France

STOLLER, Norman Kelvin; MBE (1976); s of Ivor Stoller, of Springhill, Florida, USA, and Sally, *née* Fox (d 1940); *b* 6 Sept 1934; *Educ* Eccles HS; *m* 6 June 1960, Diane, da of Leo Morris (d 1977); 1 s (Martin Jeremy b 1964), 1 da (Linzi Sara b 1962); *Career* RAF 1952-55; dir Seton Prods Ltd 1959, exec chm md Seton Prods Gp 1962, bd chm Sepro Healthcare Inc 1982, exec chm Seton Healthcare Gp 1984; dir Assoc of Br Healthcare Industs Ltd, memb N American Advsy Gp DTI; FInstSMM 1977; Officer of the Most Venerable Order of the Hospital of St John of Jerusalem 1987; *Recreations* sailing; *Clubs* St James's; *Style*— Norman K Stoller, Esq, MBE; Seton Healthcare Gp plc, Tubiton House, Oldham, Gt Manchester OL1 3HS (☎ 061 652 2222, telex 669956 (SETONG), fax 061 626 9090, car 0831 171396)

STOLLERY, Prof John; s of George Stollery, and Emma Stollery; *b* 21 April 1930; *Educ* E Barnet GS, Imp Coll of Sci and Technol London (BScEng, MScEng, DScEng, DIC, CEng); *m* 1956, Jane Elizabeth, da of Walter Reynolds; 4 s; *Career* Aerodynamics Dept De Havilland Aircraft Co 1952-56, reader Aeronautics Dept Imp Coll London 1962 (lectr 1956); Cranfield Inst of Technol: prof of aerodynamics 1973-, head Coll of Aeronautics 1976-86, pro vice-chllr Faculty of Engrg 1982-85 (dean 1976-79); chm: Aerospace Technol Bd MOD 1986-89, Aviation Ctee DTI 1986-; pres RAeS 1987-88; memb Airworthiness Requirements Bd 1990-; visiting prof: Cornell Aeronautical Labs Buffalo USA 1964, Aeronautical Res Lab Wright Patterson Air Force Base 1971, Nat Aeronautical Lab Bangalore India 1977, Peking Inst of Aeronautics and Astronautics 1979, Univ of Queensland 1983; FRAeS 1975, FCGI 1984, FAIAA 1988; *Books* Shock Tube Research (chief ed, 1971); papers in Journal of Fluid Mechanics and Aeronautics; *Recreations* playing tennis, watching football, travelling; *Style*— Prof John Stollery, 28 The Embankment, Bedford (☎ 0234 355087)

STONBOROUGH, John T C; s of John J Stonborough, Villa Toscana, Gmunden, Austria, and Veronica, *née* Morrison-Bell; *b* 20 May 1948; *Educ* Gordonstoun; *m* 29 May 1987, Jane, da of Dr Louis Berger, of USA, wid of Charles Tallents; 1 da (Eloise b 11 March 1988), 1 step s (Hugh Tallents b 27 Nov 1980); *Career* Metropolitan Police 1971-73, journalist and broadcaster 1973-88, md Walborough Consultants Ltd 1988; *awards*: Consumer Journalist of the Year 1982, Radio Reporter of the Year 1984; *Recreations* private pilot, mountaineering, family, entertaining; *Clubs* Annabels, Hurlingham, Compton Abbas Flying; *Style*— John Stonborough, Esq; 14 Bradbourne St, London SW6 3TE (☎ 071 736 7036, car 0860 261352, mobile 0860 579988)

STONE, Dr Alexander; OBE (1988); s of Morris Stone (d 1945), and Rebecca Levi (d 1954); *b* 21 April 1907; *Educ* Hutcheson Boys GS Glasgow, Univ of Glasgow; *m* 26 May 1988, (Phyllis) Bette; *Career* lawyer and banker; chm Combined Capital Ltd; memb: investmt advsy ctee Univ of Glasgow, Scottish Business Gp; vice-pres Scottish Cncl for Spastics; settlor The Alexander Stone Fndn; Hon LLD Univ of Glasgow 1986, Hon DLitt Univ of Strathclyde 1989; Hon memb Royal Glasgow Inst of the Fine Arts; elected AIB (Scot) 1991; *Style*— Dr Alexander Stone, OBE; 62 Sherbrooke Ave, Pollokshields, Glasgow G2 4RY (☎ 041 427 1567); 36 Renfield St, Glasgow G2 1LU (☎ 041 226 4431, fax 041 332 5482, telex 7790570)

STONE, Maj-Gen Anthony Charles Peter; s of Maj (ret) Charles Cecil Stone, of The Coach House, Castle Rd, Salisbury, Wilts, and Kathleen Mons, *née* Grogan; *b* 25 March 1939; *Educ* St Joseph's Coll, RMA Sandhurst, Staff Coll Camberley; *m* 29 July 1967, (Elizabeth) Mary Eirlys, da of Rev Canon Gideon Davies (d 1987), of Little Comberton, Worcs; 2 s (Guy b 1972, Mark b 1979); *Career* RA: cmmnd 1960, serv in Far and M East, BAOR and UK (light, field, medium, heavy, locating and air def artillery), Battery Cdr Q (Sanna's Post) Battery and 2 i/c 5 Regt RA 1974-75, GSO 2 DASD MOD 1976, DS RMCS 1977, CO 5 Regt RA 1980; founded Special Op Troop 1982, Col GS Def Progs Staff MOD 1983, Mil Dir of Studies RMCS 1985, Dir of Operational Requirements (Land) MOD 1986, Dir Light Weapons Projects MOD 1989; DG Policy and Special Projects 1990; *Recreations* shooting, country pursuits, family;

Clubs Army & Navy; *Style*— Maj-Gen Anthony Stone

STONE, Barry Leonard; *b* 19 Feb 1948; *Educ* Univ of London (BSc), Med Coll Bart's (MB BS, LRCP, MRCS); 1 s; *Career* house surgn Frimley Park Hosp 1978 (house physician 1977-78), sr house offr Bethlem Royal Hosp 1978-79, registrar Maudsley Hosp 1979-81, lectr in psychiatry Faculty of Med Univ of Southampton 1981-83, med advsr Upjohn Ltd Michigan USA 1983; locum conslt psychiatrist: Warlingham Park Hosp 1983, Luton and Dunstable Hosp 1983-84, Professorial Unit St Mary's Hosp and Drug Dependancy Unit London 1984, advsr and cnsllr in alcohol and drug abuse Youth Servs Hampshire CC 1985-86, physician BUPA Med Centres (Portsmouth and Croydon) 1986-87, visiting physician BUPA Med Centre London 1989-, conslt psychiatrist Lynbrook Clinic and Windsor Clinic 1990-; in private practice Harley Street London; memb: Br Assoc of Psychopharmacology 1983, Assoc of Pharmaceutical Physicians 1983, Soc for the Study of Addiction 1986-; *Style*— Dr Barry Stone; Acorns, Forest Dean, Fleet, Hampshire GU13 8TT (☎ 0232 620667)

STONE, Brian Lance Dawson; s of Lance Browning Stone (d 1966), of The Old Kennels, Easton, Suffolk, and Susan Caroline, *née* Dawson (d 1962); *b* 9 Sept 1936; *Educ* Charterhouse, ChCh Coll Oxford; *Career* Nat Serv 7 QOH Subalt 1956-57; Mktg Div Sunday Times 1963-66, film indust 1966-67, dir Hamish Hamilton Ltd 1971-76; Hughes Massie Ltd: dir 1977-84, co-owner 1984-86; dir and co-owner Aitken and Stone Ltd 1986-; *Recreations* theatre-going, opera, current affairs; *Clubs* Garrick; *Style*— Brian Stone, Esq; Aitken & Stone Ltd, 29 Fernshaw Rd, London SW10 0TG (☎ 071 351 7561, fax 071 376 3594)

STONE, Carole; da of Harry A Stone (d 1976), and Kathleen Jacques (re-m 1979), *née* Conroy; *b* 30 May 1942; *Educ* Ashford County GS for Girls, Southampton Tech Coll; *Career* joined BBC in 1963 as copytypist in Newsroom BBC South, asst prodr BBC Radio Brighton 1947-70, gen talks prodr BBC Radio 4 1970, prodr BBC Radio 4's Any Questions? programme 1977-89, freelance TV broadcaster 1990-; *Clubs* Reform; *Style*— Miss Carole Stone; Flat 4, The Coach House, 17a Floral St, London WC2E 9DS (☎ 071 379 8664)

STONE, Clive Graham; s of Charles Thomas Stone and Frances Lilian Stone; *b* 7 July 1936; *Educ* Northampton Coll of Advanced Technol, City Univ London; *m* 1957, Pamela Mary; 3 s; *Career* chm Dollond & Aitchison Group plc 1980- (gen mgmnt 1968, md 1973, dep chm 1978); dir: Gallaher Ltd 1981-, Gallaher Pensions Ltd 1984-, Keeler Ltd; chm Theodore Hamblin Ltd; dir Br Retailers Assoc Ltd 1985-; dir Business Action Team (Birmingham) Ltd; govr Royal Nat Coll for the Blind, tstee Fight for Sight; Freeman City of London, memb Ct Worshipful Co of Spectacle Makers; fell Br Coll of Optometrists; *Recreations* sailing, real tennis; *Clubs* Leamington Spa Tennis Court; *Style*— C G Stone, Esq; c/o Dollond & Aitchison Group plc, 1323 Coventry Rd, Yardley, Birmingham B25 8LP (☎ 021 706 2838, fax 021 7062741, telex 339435); Abbey Meads, Forrest Rd, Kenilworth, Warwicks CV8 1LT (☎ 0926 54553)

STONE, David; s of Joseph Stone (d 1972), and Zena, *née* Mindel (d 1987); *b* 27 May 1953; *Educ* Hasmonean GS; *Career* CA in private practice (sole practitioner); personal asst to Norman Tebbit gen elections of 1974 and 1979, cncllr London Borough of Camden 1982-86 (opposition spokesman on leisure servs 1983-86), Parly candidate (Cons) Stoke-on-Trent Central 1987; memb Cons Pty Nat Union Exec Ctee, nat chm Cons Political Centre 1987-90 (vice chm 1984-87); *Recreations* cricket; *Clubs* MCC; *Style*— David Stone, Esq; 16 Goldhurst Terrace, London NW6 (☎ 071 328 4578, car 0836 213413)

STONE, Dorothy Rae Lever; da of Bernard Lever; *b* 9 Oct 1908; *Educ* Manchester HS, Univ of Manchester (LLB); *m* Hyman Stone (decd), 1 Sept 1931; *Career* called to the Bar Middle Temple 1929; memb: Managing Ctee St Bernards Southall 1952-62, Bd of Trade Inter Dept Ctee for Consumer Protection 1959-62, Bd of Govrs Nat Hosp for Nervous Diseases 1962-81, Home Office Ctee (concerning the age of consent) 1979-82; legal advsr Nat Cncl of Women 1962-70; JP North Westminster Div 1966-80; hon treas Jewish Historical Soc of Eng 1961-81 (first woman pres 1982-84); *Recreations* social work, art, music, history, travel; *Style*— Mrs Dorothy Stone; 41 Orchard Court, Portman Square, London W1H 9PA

STONE, Evan David Robert; s of Laurence George Stone (d 1952), and Lillian Stone (d 1955); *b* 26 Aug 1928; *Educ* Berkhamsted Sch, Worcester Coll Oxford (MA); *m* 19 Aug 1959, Gisela Bridget; 1 s (Michael David George b 1960); *Career* Nat Serv cmmnd Army, serv UK and ME 1947-49; called to the Bar Inner Temple 1954, rec of Crown Cts 1979, bencher Inner Temple 1985-, memb Senate of Inns Of Court and the bar 1985-86; former HM dep coroner Inner W London W Middx and City of London; cncllr later alderman London Borough of Islington (dep ldr later ldr of oppn) 1969-74; govr: Moorfields Eye Hosp 1970-79, Highbury Grove Sch 1971-82 (chm govrs 1978-82); chm City and Hackney Health Authority 1984-; memb Criminal Injuries Compensation Bd 1989-; Freeman City of London 1990; *Books* Forensic Medicine (jtly with late Prof Hugh Johnson, 1987); *Recreations* reading, writing, listening to music, sport and games; *Clubs* Garrick, MCC; *Style*— Evan Stone, Esq, QC; 5 Raymond Buildings, Gray's Inn, London, WC1R 5BP (☎ 071 831 0720, fax 071 831 0626)

STONE, Prof Francis Gordon Albert; s of late Sidney Charles Stone and late Florence, *née* Coles; *b* 19 May 1925; *Educ* Exeter Sch, Christ's Coll Cambridge (BA, MA, PhD, ScD), Univ of Southern California (Fulbright scholar, postdoctoral fell); *m* 28 June 1956, Judith Maureen, da of late James Hislop, of Sydney, Australia; 3 s (James Francis b 1957, Peter Gordon b 1961, Derek Charles b 1963); *Career* instr then prof Havard Univ 1954-62, reader in inorganic chemistry Queen Mary Coll London 1962-63, prof of inorganic chemistry and head of dept Univ of Bristol 1963-90, Robert A Welch distinguished prof of chemistry Baylor Univ Texas 1990-; visiting prof: Monash Univ Aust 1966, Univ of Pennsylvania 1968, Carnegie Mellon Univ 1972, Univ of Princeton 1967, Univ of Arizona 1970, Rhodes Univ 1976; lectures: Boomer Univ of Alberta 1965, Firestone Univ of Wisconsin 1970, Tilden Chemical Soc 1971, Ludwig Mond RSC 1982, Reilly Univ of Notre Dame 1983, Waddington Univ of Durham 1984, Sir Edward Frankland prize RSC 1987, G W Watt Univ of Texas (Austria) 1988; Royal Soc of Chemistry: memb Primary Journals Ctee 1964-69, memb Publications Bd 1967, memb Cncl 1967-70 and 1981-83, memb News Publications Ctee 1972-76, pres Dalton Div 1981-83 (vice pres 1983-85); SERC: memb Chemistry Ctee 1972-74 and 1982-85, chm Inorganic Chemistry Panel 1982-85, Royal Soc assessor on Science Bd 1986-88; chm: 4th Int Conf on Organometallic Chemistry Bristol 1969, Royal Soc of Chemistry Conf on the Chemistry of Platinum Metals Bristol 1981, UGC Review of Chemistry in UK univs 1988; memb Advsy Cncl Ramsay Meml Fellowship Tst 1981-90, int assoc Inorganic Syntheses Inc (USA); *awards*: Organometallic Chemistry medal 1972, Transition Metal Chemistry medal RSC 1979, Chugaev medal Inst of Inorganic Chemistry USSR Acad of Scis 1978, American Chemistry Soc award in Inorganic Chemistry 1985, Davy medal Royal Soc 1989, Longstaff medal RSC 1990; FRS 1976, FRSC; *publications* Inorganic Polymers (ed 1962), Hydrogen Compounds of the Group IV Elements (1962), Advances in Organometallic Chemistry (co-ed 1964-89, now in 32 volumes), Comprehensive Organometallic Chemistry (ed 1984); *Recreations* travel; *Style*— Prof Francis Stone, CBE, FRS; 60 Coombe Lane, Bristol BS9 2AY; 1605 South 4th St, Aft 106, Waco Texas 76706 USA (☎ 817 752 7208); Department of Chemistry, Baylor University, Box 7348, Waco Texas 76798-7348 (☎ 817 755 3311, fax 817 755 2403)

STONE, Geoffrey Charles; s of Robert Stone, of London, and Olive Stone; *b* 27 March 1939; *Educ* Leyton Co HS, St David's Coll Lampeter (BA), St Catherines Coll Oxford (MA), Univ of Bristol (PACE), Liverpool Univ (DASE); *m* 30 July 1965, Valerie Anne, da of William Jones (d 1985), of Liverpool; 1 s (Matthew b 1972), 1 da (Rachel b 1975); *Career* asst teacher Ruffwood Sch Kirkby Liverpool 1963-70, dep head teacher Grange Sch Halewood Liverpool 1970-72, warden and head teacher Arthur Mellows Village Coll Glinton Peterborough; headteacher: Parrs Wood HS Didsbury Manchester 1978-90, Bridgewater Co HS Appleton Warrington Cheshire 1990-; memb: Ct Univ of Manchester, Jt Assoc of Classics Teachers, SHA; *Recreations* horticulture, ancient history; *Style*— Geoffrey Stone, Esq; 15 Fog Lane, Didsbury, Manchester; Parrs Wood High Sch, Wilmstow Rd, Didsbury, Manchester M20 1UU (☎ 061 445 8786)

STONE, Georgina Mary (Gina); da of George Leslie de Lacherois, DL, JP (d 1948), and (Catherine Charlotte) Sheila, *née* Blizard (d 1922); *b* 13 Feb 1921; *Educ* Hayes Ct Kent; *m* 19 July 1945, Johan Stone (d 1974); *Career* WWII 1940-45, 3 Offr WRNS 1943-45; farmer and estate owner; fndr and present co chm Abbeyfield Donaghadee Soc, memb Donaghadee UDC 1955-73 (chm 1963-65), chm N Down Area Plan Steering Ctee 1967-73; *Recreations* gardening, swimming; *Style*— Mrs Gina Stone; The Manor House, Donaghadee, Co Down BT21 OHA

STONE, Howard Victor; s of Harold Montague Stone, of 83 Avenue Rd, London, and Niki, *née* Winsor; *b* 9 May 1945; *Educ* Highgate Sch; *m* 17 March 1968, Hilary Louise, da of Alfred Burnett Shindler, of 16 West Heath Ave, London; 1 da (Victoria b 10 Sept 1971); *Career* trainee slr 1964-65 and 1975-78, retail motor indust 1965-75, admitted slr 1978, ptnr Shindler & Co 1981- (asst 1978-81); freelance TV and radio bdcaster on legal matters incl: Moneyspinner, You and Yours, TV am, Breakfast Time, BBC TV News, LBC, Captial Radio; master Billingsgate Ward Club 1988-89 (appointed pres), PR and Parly Liaison offr City of London Law Soc 1989; Freeman City of London; Liveryman Worshipful Cos of: Glovers, Arbitrators, Slrs; ACIArb 1979, memb IBA 1985; *Recreations* reading, travel, theatre; *Clubs* Gresham, City Livery; *Style*— Howard Stone, Esq; Shindler & Co, 37/39 Eastcheap, London EC3M 1AY (☎ 071 283 6376, fax 071 626 5735, car 0836 213 117, telex 924404)

STONE, John Michael; MBE (1991); s of Robert Alfred Stone (d 1983), and Josephine Margery, *née* Sheen; *b* 26 April 1941; *Educ* Framlingham Coll; *m* 2 May 1964, Maxine Campbell, da of John Campbell-Lemon, of The Grange, Aylesbury Rd, Wendover, Bucks; 1 s (Timothy b 1974), 3 da (Karen b 1965, Paula b 1966, Nicola b 1970); *Career* dir E Russell Ltd 1962 (chm 1983), md E Russell (W Country) Ltd 1971; chm: Russell Meats Ltd 1984, Donald Russell Ltd 1984; chm Sims Food Gp plc 1990- (jt chm 1989, chief exec 1988); Freeman: City of London 1964, Worshipful Co of Butchers 1965; memb Inst of Meat; *Books* Meat Buyers Guide for Caterers (1983); *Recreations* shooting, golf, cricket; *Clubs* MCC; *Style*— John Stone, Esq, MBE; Bramleys, Little Kingshill, Great Missenden, Bucks HP16 0EB (☎ 0240 66220, fax 0494 890268); Sims Food Group plc, Douglas House, 32-34 Simpson Rd, Fenny Stratford, Milton Keynes MK1 1BA (☎ 0908 270 061, fax 0908 270 260, car 0860 638 540, telex 27568 DONRUS)

STONE, Sheriff Marcus; s of Morris Stone (d 1945), of Glasgow, and Reva Stone (d 1954); *b* 22 March 1921; *Educ* HS of Glasgow, Univ of Glasgow (MA, LLB); *m* 1956, Jacqueline, da of Paul Barnoin (d 1967), of France; 3 s (Patrick, William, Donald), 2 da (Cynthia, Martine); *Career* WWII served 1939-45, RASC W Africa; advocate 1965; Sheriff: Dumbarton 1971-76, Glasgow 1976-84, Lothian and Borders at Linlithgow 1984-; *Books* Proof of Fact in Criminal Trials (1984), Cross-examination in Criminal Trials (1988), Fact-finding for Magistrates (1990); *Recreations* music, swimming; *Style*— Sheriff Marcus Stone; Sheriffs' Chambers, Sheriff Court House, Court Square, Linlithgow EH49 7EQ (☎ 050 684 2922)

STONE, Martin; s of Abraham Stone (d 1971), of Cardiff, S Wales, and Eva Priscilla, *née* Anstee (d 1988); *b* 28 Feb 1945; *Educ* The Cathedral Sch Llandaff Cardiff, Canton HS Cardiff, Univ of Liverpool (MB ChB, MD); *m* 4 July 1970, Jane, da of Tudor Lloyd-Williams (d 1978), of Mold, N Wales; 2 s (Andrew Martin b 1971, Robert Charles b 1975), 1 da (Louise Jane b 1980); *Career* jr doctor Liverpool Hosps 1968-72, sr house offr Torbay Hosp 1972-73, registrar Charing Cross Hosp 1973-75, res registrar MRC 1975-76; sr registrar: St George's Hosp 1976-77, Southampton Hosp 1977-80; conslt gynaecologist Gwent AHA 1980-; memb: London Obstetric and Gynaecological Soc (chm 1990), Med Advsy Ctee BUPA Hosp Cardiff (Chm 1989); treas Welsh Obstetric and Gynaecological Soc, sr vice pres Caerleon Rotary Club; memb BMA, MRCOG 1973, FRCOG 1986; *Recreations* skiing, red wine, theatre, golf; *Style*— Martin Stone, Esq; Ye Olde Forge, Llanmartin, Newport, Gwent NP6 2EB (☎ 0633 413073); St Joseph's Private Hospital, Harding Ave, Malpas, Newport, Gwent NPT 6QS (☎ 0633 858203); BUPA Hospital, Croescadarn Rd. Pentwyn, Cardiff, S Glamorgan CF2 7XL (☎ 0222 735515)

STONE, Martin Howard; s of Dr Jacob Stone (d 1972), of London, and Gloria Lucille, *née* Supper; *b* 26 May 1949; *Educ* Wanstead Sch; *m* 27 July 1975, Melanie Yvette, da of Joseph Owide, of London; 2 s (Jeremy b 22 Oct 1976, Michael b 23 Nov 1978), 1 da (Emily b 14 Oct 1981); *Career* ptnr Freeda Milston Cedar Baker; currently dir: Wonderworld plc, Bricolpar Ltd, Owide Properties Ltd, Upshire Investmts Ltd, International Resort Holdings plc, FMCB Management Consultants Ltd, The Colquhoun Gp of Co's; hon treas Ravenswood (in aid of mentally handicapped children); FCA 1976; *Recreations* tennis, hockey, reading; *Clubs* Connaught Tennis, Las Brisas, White Elephant; *Style*— Martin Stone, Esq; 42 Upper Grosvenor St, London W1X ODP (☎ 071 491 4864, fax 071 409 3505, car 0860 397 352, telex 21179)

STONE, Michael John Christopher; s of Henry Frederick Stone (d 1979), and Joan Barbara, *née* Da Silva; *b* 10 May 1936; *Educ* Bradfield, Hamburg (Language Course); *m* 8 Jan 1966, Louisa, da of Robert Dyson, of Hawaii; 2 s (Charles b 9 Oct 1966, Andrew b 21 Nov 1970), 1 da (Nicola b 11 Jan 1968); *Career* cmmnd RHA 1955-57, served Germany, cmmnd HAC 1957-63; commodity broker E D & F Man 1957 (gp chm 1983-), chm London Sugar Futures Mkt 1981-84; dir: Farr Man Inc (New York), London Fox (formerly London Commodity Exchange); chm E D & F Man (Sugar) Ltd; *Recreations* shooting, fishing, skiing, farming, gardening; *Clubs* Brooks's, HAC; *Style*— Michael Stone, Esq; Little Mynthurst Farm, Norwood Hill, Nr Horley, Surrey (☎ 0293 862314); E D & F Man Ltd, Sugar Quay, Lower Thames St, London EC3R 6DU (☎ 071 626 8788)

STONE, Prof Norman; s of Flt Lt Norman Stone, RAF (ka 1942), and Mary Robertson, *née* Pettigrew; *b* 8 March 1941; *Educ* Glasgow Acad, Gonville and Caius Coll Cambridge (BA, MA); *m* 1, 2 July 1966 (m dis 1977), Marie Nicole Aubry; 2 s (Nicholas b 1966, Sebastian b 1972); m 2, 11 Aug 1982, Christine Margaret Booker, *née* Verity; 1 s (Rupert b 1983); *Career* Univ of Cambridge: fell Gonville and Caius Coll 1965-71, lectr in Russian history 1968-84, fell Jesus Coll 1971-79, fell Trinity Coll 1979-84; Univ of Oxford: prof of modern history 1984-, fell Worcester Coll 1984-; *Books* The Eastern Front 1914-1917 (1975, Wolfson Prize 1976), Hitler (1980), Europe Transformed 1878-1919 (1983), The Other Russia (with Michael Glenny, 1990); *Recreations* journalism, Eastern Europe, music; *Clubs* Garrick, Beefsteak;

Style— Prof Norman Stone; 18 Thorncliffe Rd, Oxford OX2 7BB

STONE, Maj-Gen Patrick Philip Dennant; CBE (1984, OBE 1981, MBE 1976); s of Dr Philip Hartley Stone (d 1947), and Elsie Maude, *née* Dennant; *b* 2 July 1939; *Educ* Christs Hosp; *m* 5 June 1967, Christine Iredale, da of Gp Capt Leonard Henry Trent, VC (d 1986); 2 s (Edward Patrick Dennant b 1969, Robert Michael b 1972), 1 da (Celia Elizabeth b 1974); *Career* cmmnd East Anglian Regt 1959, Kings African Rifles (Tanzania) 1959-61, Regimental Serv Guyana and S Arabia 1962-64, ADG Governor W Aust 1965-67, Regt Serv UK W Germany and NI 1967-72, RAF Staff Coll 1972, CO 2 Bn Royal Anglian Regt 1977-80, Chief of Staff 1 Armd Div 1981-84, Cdr Berlin Brigade 1985-87, dir Gen Personnel (Army) 1988; *Recreations* country pursuits; *Clubs* Army & Navy; *Style*— Maj-Gen Patrick Stone, CBE; Ministry of Defence, Whitehall, London

STONE, Peter Charles Gray; s of Charles Edwin Stone, and Blodwyn, *née* Griffiths (d 1985); *b* 28 April 1943; *Educ* Trevelyan Secdy Sch Windsor Berks; *m* Janet; 1 s (Lee Martin Gray b 21 April 1968), 1 da (Alexandra Bonnie b 9 March 1973); *Career* photographer; indentured photographer Maidenhead Advertiser 1958, Birmingham Planet Newspaper 1964, Daily Mirror 1964-88; numerous assignments incl: Trans-African Hovercraft Expedition (through West and Central Africa) 1969, overland expedition NY to Argentine World Cup Finals 1978, extensive war coverage, comprehensive coverage of showbiz personalities, photographs of Bob Geldof and the Boomtown Rats in USA, Japan and UK 1978-80, various features; freelance photographer for numerous magazines and newspapers 1988-; awarded Ilford Photographer of the Year for coverage of the Vietnam War 1973; memb NUS 1962; *Books* Having Their Picture Taken-The Boomtown Rats (1980); *Recreations* golf, wining and dining, watching sport in general; *Style*— Peter Stone, Esq; Peter Stone Photography, 82 Ouseley Rd, Wraysbury, Staines, Middx TW19 5JH (☎ 0784 482 914, car 0860 627 849)

STONE, Peter John; s of late Dr Thomas Scott Stone; *b* 24 June 1946; *Educ* King's Sch Canterbury, Christ's Coll Cambridge; *m* 1972, Alison, da of Robert Smith Moffett; 2 s, 2 da; *Career* slr, ptnr Clintons 1972-75; banker Close Brothers Ltd 1975-; dir: Close Brothers Group plc, Close Brothers Holdings Ltd, Close Brothers Ltd, Century Factors Ltd, Close Brothers Trust Ltd, Close Brothers Securities Ltd, Close Brothers Merchant Securities Ltd, Close Nominees Ltd, Clearbook Tst Ltd, Close Investmt Mgmnt Ltd, Air & General Finance Ltd, Safeguard Investmts Ltd, Close Asset Finance Ltd, Shield London Ltd, Prompt Fin Inc (US Co), Jackson - Stops & Staff Ltd; *Recreations* hot-air ballooning, cricket, tennis, real tennis, choral singing, travel, golf, gardening; *Style*— Peter Stone, Esq; c/o Close Brothers Ltd, 36 Great St Helen's, London EC3A 6AP

STONE, Philippa Jane; da of Vivian Harry George Stubbs, of Duston, Northampton, and Merle Josephine Mure McKerrell, *née* Carver; *b* 6 March 1946; *Educ* Notre Dame HS Northampton, Univ of St Andrews, Univ of Oxford (BSc); *m* 1978, (as his 2 w), David Robert Stone, s of Robert Charles Stone; 1 da; *Career* business conslt; memb City Child 1983- (chm 1985-86), Redbridge DHA 1989-90, Mensa Fndn for Gifted Children 1990-; dir: Sharepoint Ltd 1984-88, P J Stone Ltd 1984-; FMS; *Recreations* arts, tennis, sailing, skiing; *Style*— Philippa Stone

STONE, Rex; s of Hiram Stone, of Belper, Derbyshire, and Elsie Lorraine, *née* Taylor; *b* 13 Aug 1938; *Educ* Herbert Strutt GS; *m* 16 Oct 1965, Anita Kay, da of Albert Arthur Hammond (d 1974), of London; 1 s (Alistair b 7 May 1971), 1 da (Rachel b 23 March 1969); *Career* CA; audit mangr Peat Marwick Mitchell & Co 1961-65, co sec RB MacMillan Ltd 1965-69; chm: Alida Holdings plc 1974- (fin dir 1969-72, jt md 1972-74), Chevin Holdings Ltd; dep chm British Polythene Industries plc, dir Fine Colour Packaging Ltd, non-exec dir Derbyshire Building Society 1985-; FCA 1961; *Recreations* travel, game shooting, golf; *Style*— Rex Stone, Esq; Alida Holdings plc, Heanor, Derby DE7 7RG (☎ 0773 530530, fax 0773 530429, telex 377163)

STONE, Richard Frederick; QC (1968); s of Sir Leonard Stone, OBE, QC (d 1978), and Madeleine Marie, *née* Scheffer; *b* 11 March 1928; *Educ* Lakefield Coll Ontario Canada, Rugby, Univ of Cambridge (MA); *m* 1, 1957, late Georgina Maxwell, *née* Morris; 2 da (Victoria b 1958, Diana b 1960); m 2, 1964, Susan, *née* Van Heel; 2 da (Georgina b 1965, Amelia b 1967); *Career* Lt Worcester Regt 1946-48; called to the Bar Gray's Inn 1952; memb: Panel of Lloyds Arbitrators in Salvage 1968, Panel of Wreck Cmmn 1968; bencher Gray's Inn 1974- (vice pres 1991); *Recreations* sailing, windsurfing, diving; *Clubs* Hayling Island Sailing; *Style*— Richard Stone, Esq, QC; 5 Raymond Buildings, Gray's Inn, London WC1R 5BP (☎ 071 242 2697); Queen Elizabeth Building, Temple, London EC4Y 9BS (☎ 071 353 9153, fax 071 583 0126, 262762 (MEMG); 18 Wittering Rd, Hayling Island, Hants PO11 9SP (☎ 0705 463645)

STONE, Hon Richard Malcolm Ellis; s of Baron Stone (Life Peer) (d 1986), and Beryl Florence, *née* Bernstein (d 1989); *b* 1937; *Educ* Univ of Oxford (MA); *m* 1970, Ruth Perry, 1 s (Toby), 2 da (Rebecca, Hannah); *Career* BM, BCh, MRCGP; *Style*— The Hon Richard Stone; 15 Blenheim Rd, London NW8

STONE, Sir (John) Richard Nicholas; CBE (1946); *b* 1913,Aug; *Career* fell King's Coll Cambridge 1945-, P D Leake prof of fin and accounting Cambridge Univ 1955-80; FBA; Nobel prize for Economics 1984; kt 1980; *Style*— Sir Richard Stone, CBE; 13 Millington Road, Cambridge

STONE, Terence Reginald Stewart; s of Harry Victor Stone, of Grey Stones, Dawlish, Devon, and Hilda Mary, *née* Western; *b* 18 Aug 1928; *Educ* Willesden Tech Coll, Coll of Architecture, Regent St Poly; *m* 1952, Beryl Joan, da of Douglas Bramwell Stewart; 4 s, 2 da; *Career* sr architect RAF Air Works Sqdn Air Miny 1947-49; chief architect Costain (W Africa) Ltd 1956-60, chm Terence Stone Gp of Companies 1970-; md: Terence Stone (Devpt) Ltd 1962-, Terence Stone (Construction) Ltd 1975-; FIAS, FRSH, FFB, FBIM; *Recreations* swimming, tennis, badminton, running, motor rallying, skiing, sponsorship and promotion of sport, travel, arts; *Clubs* Rolls Royce Enthusiasts, RAC; *Style*— Terence Stone, Esq; Treston House, Earlstone Place, Dawlish, Devon (☎ 0626 863160); Treston Court, Dawlish, Devon (☎ 0626 862732); Terence Stone Group, Company House, Dawlish, Devon (☎ 0626 863543)

STONEFROST, Maurice Frank; CBE (1983), DL (1986); s of Arthur Stonefrost (d 1980), of Bristol, and Anne, *née* Williams; *b* 1 Sept 1927; *Educ* Merrywood GS Bristol; *m* June 1953, Audrey Jean, da of Charles Fishlock (d 1986); 1 s (Mark), 1 da (Hilary); *Career* Nat Serv RAF 1948-51; local govt: Bristol 1951-54, Slough 1954-56, Coventry 1956-61, W Sussex 1961-64; sec Chartered Inst of Public Fin and Accountancy 1964-73, controller of fin GLC 1973-84, dir gen and clerk GLC and ILEA 1984-85, dir and chief exec BR Pension Fund 1986-90, chm Municipal Insurance Group 1990-; centenary pres Chartered Inst of Public Fin 1984-85, pres Soc of Co Treasurers 1982-83, memb Layfield Ctee on Local Govt Fin 1974-76, memb Ctee on the Future of the Legal Profession 1987-88, chm Public Sector Liaison Ctee of the Accountancy Profession 1987-, managing tstee Municipal Mutual Insur Co 1987-, chm Speakers Cmmn of Citizenship 1988-; Hon DSc City Univ 1987; DPA 1953, CIPIA 1955; *Books* Capital Accounting (1958); *Recreations* walking, gardening; *Style*— Maurice Stonefrost, Esq, CBE, DL; British Rail Pension Fund Company, Broad St House, 55 Old Broad St, London EC3M 1RX (☎ 071 374 0242, fax 071 588 0217)

STONEHAM, Dr (Arthur) Marshall; s of Garth Rivers Stoneham (d 1985), and Nancy Wooler, *née* Leslie; *b* 18 May 1940; *Educ* Barrow-in-Furness GS for Boys, Univ of Bristol (Merchant Venturers' scholar, BSc, PhD); *m* 25 Aug 1962, Doreen, da of John Montgomery (d 1974), of Barrow-in-Furness; 2 da ((Vanessa) Elise b 2 Sept 1963, (Karen) Nicola b 27 Jan 1966); *Career* Harwell Laboratory UKAEA: res fell Theoretical Physics Div 1964-66, sr scientific offr 1966-70, princ scientific offr 1970-74, gp leader Solid State Materials Gp (later Solid State and Quantum Physics Gp) 1974-89, individual merit promotion to Sr Staff Level 1979 (Band Level 1974), head Tech Area Gen Nuclear Safety Res Prog (Core and Fuel Studies) 1988-89, div head Materials Physics and Metallurgy Div 1989-90, dir Res AEA Industrial Technol 1990-; visiting prof Univ of Illinois 1969, Wolfson Industrial Fellow Wolfson Coll Oxford 1985-89 (fell Governing Body 1989-), visiting prof of chemistry Univ of Keele 1988-; Inst of Physics: ed Jl of Physics C - Solid State Physics 1984-88 (dep ed 1982-84), memb Exec Editorial Bd Jl of Physics - Condensed Matter 1989-, memb Editorial Bd Semiconductor Sci and Technol 1986-87, chm Books Editorial Advsy Ctee 1988-, dir Publishing 1988-; memb Polar Solids Gp Ctee RSC; FRS 1989, FInstP 1980; *Books* Theory of Defects in Solids (1975, Russian edn 1978, reprinted 1985); Defects and Defect Processes in Non-Metallic Solids (with W Hayes, 1985), Reliability of Non-Destructive Inspection (with M G Silk and J A G Temple, 1987), Current Issues in Solid State Science (various), Ionic Solids at High Temperatures (1989); *Recreations* music scholarship, orchestral horn playing, reading; *Style*— Dr Marshall Stoneham, FRS; Riding Mill, Bridge End, Dorchester-on-Thames, Wallingford, Oxford OX10 7JP (☎ 0865 340066); AEA Industrial Technology, Harwell Laboratory, Didcot, Oxford OX11 0RA (☎ 0235 432288, telex 83135 ATOMRA G)

STONEHAM, Roger Antony; s of Derrick William Stoneham, and Clara Marjorie, *née* Ryan; *b* 24 May 1944; *Educ* Luton GS, Bedford Modern Sch, Univ of Hull (BSc); *m* 26 Sept 1970, Carole Christine, da of Frank Fosbrook; 1 s (Stephen b 1966), 3 da (Sharon b 1972, Sonja b 1975, Sara b 1981); *Career* CA; Whitbread & Co plc 1975-90; hon treas Mid Anglia Centre of Caravan Club; IPFA, FCCA; *Recreations* caravanning, traction engines, philately, photography, tiddley winks; *Style*— Roger Stoneham, Esq; The Poplars, 8 Spinney Field, Ellington, Huntingdon, Cambs

STONELEY, Dr Robert; s of Dr Robert Stoneley (d 1976), of Cambridge, and Dorothy, *née* Minn (d 1988); *b* 22 July 1929; *Educ* The Leys Sch Cambridge, Pembroke Coll Cambridge (BA, MA, PhD); *m* 22 Oct 1953, Hilda Mary Margaret, da of Dr L R Cox (d 1965); 1 s (Robert Leslie Gayford b 1966), 1 da (Elizabeth Mary Margaret b 1964); *Career* geologist: Falkland Islands Dependencies Survey 1951-53, BP The Br Petroleum Co Ltd 1953-78; prof Imperial Coll of Science & Technol Petroleum Geology Dept Univ of London 1978-; Polar medal; *Recreations* walking, gardening; *Style*— Dr Robert Stoneley; Harestone, Red Cross Lane, Cambridge CB2 2QU; Dept of Geology, Imperial Coll of Science & Technology, Prince Consort Rd, London SW7 2BP

STONER, Roy Frederick; s of Albert Edward Stoner, and Lily, *née* Dowson; *b* 29 Jan 1930; *Educ* Cheltenham GS, Univ of Durham (BSc,); *m* 29 Oct 1952, Alice, da of Mr Dyson; 2 s (Timothy b 1958, Jeremy b 1962), 1 da (Christine b 1954); *Career* RAF Airfield Construction Branch, Flying Offr Detachment Cdr RAF Fassberg Germany 1954-56; chartered civil engr; Sir M Macdonald & Ptnrs: joined 1956, assoc 1969-76, ptnr 1976-87, sr ptnr 1987, gp chm 1987-; chm Groundwater Devpt Consultants Ltd 1984-; FICE 1969 (memb 1956); *Recreations* boating, gardening; *Style*— Roy Stoner, Esq; 10 West St, Comberton, Cambs (☎ 0223 262 455); Demeter House, Station Rd, Cambridge CB1 2RS (☎ 0223 460 660, fax 0223 461 007, telex 817260)

STONHOUSE, Rev Michael Philip; s and h of Sir Philip Allan Stonhouse, 18 Bt; *b* 4 Sept 1948; *Educ* Medicine Hat Coll, Univ of Alberta (BA) [Edmonton], Wycliffe Coll (LTh) [Toronto]; *m* 1977, Colleen Eleanor, da of James Albert Coucill (d 1968), of Toronto, Canada; 2 s (Allan b 1981, David b 1983); *Career* ordained deacon 1977; ordained priest 1978 (both Diocese of Calgary, Canada); asst curate St Peter's, Calgary 1977-80; rector and incumbent Parkland Parish 1980-; *Style*— Rev Michael Stonhouse; Box 539, Elnora, Alberta TOM OYO, Canada (☎ (403) 773 3594)

STONHOUSE, Sir Philip Allan; 18 & 15 Bt (E 1628 & 1670), of Radley, Berkshire; s of Sir Arthur Stonhouse, 17 & 14 Bt (d 1967); *b* 24 Oct 1916; *Educ* W Canada Coll, Queen's Univ, Alberta Univ; *m* 1946, Winnifred, da of John Shield; 2 s; *Heir* s, Michael Stonhouse; *Career* admin mangr; *Recreations* golf, skiing, travel, shooting; *Clubs* Medicine Hat Ski, Connaught Golf; *Style*— Sir Phillip Stonhouse, Bt; 521, 12 St SW, Medicine Hat, Alberta, Canada (☎ 403 526 5832)

STONIER, George; *b* 12 Oct 1946; *m* 14 Feb 1976, Christine Mary; 1 s (Adam b 1982), 1 da (Anna May b 1978); *Career* Wedgwood Ltd 1969-: fin accountant then co sec and industl rels dir; human resources dir Waterford Wedgwood UK plc 1988- (co sec 1986-); vice chm Staffs LEN, memb Mgmnt Bd Staffs Enterprise Agency; ACIS, ACMA; *Recreations* fishing; *Style*— George Stonier, Esq; Waterford Wedgwood UK plc, Barlaston, Stoke-on-Trent, Staffs (☎ 0782 204141, fax 0782 204433, telex 36170, car 0860 620864)

STONOR, Hon Georgina Mary Hope; da of late 6 Baron Camoys; *b* 8 Nov 1941; *Educ* St Mary's Convent Ascot, privately, Reading Coll of Technology and Science; *Career* conslt archivist to nat and private collections, librarian, heritage art researcher and advsr; pres Catholic Family History Soc; OStJ (memb Cncl Oxfordshire); *Style*— The Hon Georgina Stonor; 112 West St, Henley-on-Thames, Oxon RG9 2EA

STONOR, Hon Julia Maria Cristina Mildred; *née* Stonor; eldest da of 6 Baron Camoys (d 1976); eldest gda of Mildred Constance Sherman, Lady Camoys, of Newport, Rhode Island, USA, and ggda of Sophia Augusta Brown, of Providence, Rhode Island; direct descendant of Sir Robert and Lady (Julia) Peel and, in female line, of 1 Baron Camoys, Standard Bearer at Agincourt; god-da of HRH Infanta Maria Cristina of Spain, Countess Marone-Cinzano; resumed her maiden name of Stonor by Deed Poll 1978; *b* 19 April 1939; *Educ* St Mary's Convent Ascot, Reading Tech Coll; *m* 4 May 1963 (m dis 1977 and annulled by Sacred Rota, Rome 1978), Donald Robin Slomnicki Saunders; 1 s (Alexander William Joseph Stonor Saunders b 1964), 1 da (Frances Hélène Jeanne Stonor Saunders b 1966); *Career* traveller and courier, article and short story writer, garden patio designer, landlady, ladies' maid, butcher's asst, public relations and social worker; involved: prison after care, race relations, SOS (charity for the homeless), Age Concern, 2 years in Citizens' Advice Bureau; FRGS; memb: Accademia Italiana, Italian Inst, Fawcett Soc, Irish Peers' Assoc; *Recreations* travel, recusant history, classical music, literature, theatre, fine arts, gardening, continental cookery and catering internationally; *Style*— The Hon Julia Stonor; 90 Burnthwaite Rd, Fulham, London SW6 5BG (☎ 071 385 8528)

STONOR, Air Marshal Sir Thomas Henry; KCB (1989); s of Alphonsus Stonor (d 1959), and Ann Stonor; *b* 5 March 1936; *Educ* St Cuthberts HS Newcastle-upon-Tyne, Kings Coll Univ of Durham (BSc); *m* 31 March 1964, Robin Antoinette, da of Wilfrid Budd (d 1980); 2 s (Jeremy Thomas b 1966, Giles Wilfrid b 1969), 1 da (Alexandra Clare b 1965); *Career* cmmnd RAF 1959, No 3 Sqdn Zataf 1961-64, CFS, No 6 FTS, RAF Coll Cranwell 1964-67, No 231 OCU 1967-69, RAF Staff Coll 1970, HQ RAF Germany 1971-73, OC 31 Sqdn 1974-76, MA to VCDS 1976-78, OC RAF Coltishall 1978-80, RCDS 1981, Inspr Flight Safety 1982-84, Dir of Control (Airspace Policy) 1985-86, Dep Controller Nat Air Traffic Servs 1987-88, Gp Dir CAA and Controller

Nat Air Traffic Servs 1988-91; FCIT; *Recreations* music, gardening; *Clubs* RAF; *Style*— Sir Thomas Stonor, KCB; Barclays Bank PLC, 141 Northumberland St, Haymarket Branch, Newcastle-upon-Tyne NE1 7BH

STOPFORD, Capt Hon Jeremy Neville; LVO (1984); yr s of 8 Earl of Courtown, OBE, TD (d 1975); *b* 22 June 1958; *Educ* Eton, RMA Sandhurst; *m* 1984, Bronwen MacDonald, da of Lt-Col David MacDonald Milner, of Hollycroft, Ashford Hill, Newbury, Berks; 2 da (Clementine Lucy Patricia b 1986, Matilda Rose Philippa b 1988); *Career* Capt Irish Gds; Equerry (temp) to HM Queen Elizabeth The Queen Mother 1982-84; stockbroker 1984-; *Recreations* shooting, photography, squash; *Clubs* Buck's, Annabels; *Style*— Captain The Hon Jeremy Stopford, LVO

STOPFORD, Maj-Gen Stephen Robert Anthony; CB (1989), MBE (1971); s of Cdr Robert Maurice Stopford, DSC, RN (d 1977), and Elsie, *née* Lawson (d 1967); *b* 1 April 1934; *Educ* Downside, Millfield, RMA Sandhurst; *m* 8 Feb 1963, Vanessa, da of Theodore Baron (d 1982); *Career* cmmnd Scots Greys 1954 (Regtl Serv 1954-70), OC D Sqdn Scots DG 1970-72, MOD Central Staff 1972-74, CO Scots DG 1974-77, project mangr MBT 80 1977-79, Col OR 1/10 1979-83, mil attaché Washington 1983-85, dir gen Fighting Vehicles and Engr Equipment (DGFVE) 1985-89; dir David Brown Vehicle Transmissions 1990; AMIEE; *Recreations* shooting, electronics, sailing, diving; *Clubs* Cavalry and Guards'; *Style*— Maj-Gen Stephen Stopford, CB, MBE

STOPFORD, Capt the Hon Terence Victor; s of 7 Earl of Courtown (d 1957), and Cicely Mary Birch (d 1973); *b* 3 Oct 1918; *Educ* Eton; *m* 1951, Sheila Adèle, da of Philip Henry Walter Page (d 1959); 3 s (Henry b 1953, Robert b 1958, James b 1961), 1 da (Catherine b 1965); *Career* RN 1936, HMS Dorsetshire China Sationa 1937-39; WWII HMS Valiant, HMS Scylla, 1945-51 HMS Grenville, HMS Saumarez, HMS Devonshire; Cdr Admty Underwater Weapons and Ops Div 1952, HMS Forth (CO at Suez Ops 1956), naval advsr to UK High Cmmr Ottawa 1959-60, Capt 1960, asst dir Underwater Weapons Admty 1961-63, CO HMS Manxman and Capt Inshore Flotilla Far East Fleet 1963-64, cos to C-in-C Naval Home Cmmd 1965-67, cos offr to Flag Offr Gibraltar 1967-69, Naval ADC to HM 1969, ret; *Recreations* cricket; *Style*— Capt the Hon Terence Stopford, RN; Lake End House, Dorney, Windsor, Berks

STOPFORD, Hon Thomas; s of Baron Stopford of Fallowfield (Life Peer, d 1961); *b* 28 June 1921; *Educ* Manchester GS, Univ of Manchester; *m* 6 July 1943, Mary Howard, da of late Alfred James Small, of Manchester; 1 s; *Career* Capt RA WWII; *Style*— The Hon Thomas Stopford; Mylor, 12 Bazley Rd, Ansdell, Lytham St Annes, Lancs FY8 1AJ (☎ 0253 736844)

STOPFORD SACKVILLE, Lionel Geoffrey; only s of Lt-Col Nigel Stopford Sackville, CBE, TD, JP, DL, by his 1 w, Beatrix (d 1990), da of Col Hercules Pakenham, CMG (gn of 2 Earl of Longford); Col Stopford Sackville was gs of William Bruce Stopford (whose f Richard was 4 s of 2 Earl of Courtown), by William's wife Caroline, da of Hon George Germain and niece and heir of 5 and last Duke of Dorset; *b* 4 Nov 1932; *Educ* Eton; *m* 1, 1960, Susan, da of Jenkin Coles, of the Abbey, Knaresborough; 2 s (Charles b 1961, Thomas b 1968), 1 da (Lucinda b 1963); m 2, 1980, Hon Teresa, *née* Pearson, *qv*; 1 da (Camilla b 1981); *Career* late Lt Northants Yeo, former Lt 14/20 Hussars served Libya; chm: Lowick Manor Farms Ltd, Union Jack Oil plc, Goedhuis & Co Ltd; dir: Dartmoor Investment Trust plc, GT Venture Investmt Co plc, Japan Ventures Ltd, Hughes Lang Corporation; former dir Charter Consolidated; High Sheriff Northants 1976-77; FCA; *Clubs* White's, Pratt's, MCC; *Style*— Lionel Stopford Sackville, Esq; Drayton House, Lowick, Kettering, Northants NN14 3BB; Ranger House, 71 Great Peter St, London SW1P 2BN (☎ 071 222 4363, fax 071 222 5480)

STOPFORD SACKVILLE, Hon Mrs ((Mary) Teresa); *née* Pearson; er da of 3 Viscount Cowdray, TD, by his 1 w, Lady Anne Pamela, *née* Bridgeman; *b* 3 June 1940, HRH The Princess Royal (Princess Mary) stood sponsor; *m* 1980, Lionel Geoffrey Stopford Sackville, *qv*; 1 da (Camilla Anne b 1981); *Recreations* racing, hunting, skiing; *Style*— The Hon Mrs Stopford Sackville; Drayton House, Lowick, Kettering, Northants NN14 3BB; 21 Greville House, Kinnerton St, London SW1X 8EY

STOPPARD, Dr Miriam; da of Sydney Stern, and Jenny Stern; *b* 12 May 1937; *Educ* Newcastle upon Tyne Central HS, Royal Free Hosp Sch of Med London (prize for experimental physiology), King's Coll Med Sch Univ of Durham (MB BS), Univ of Newcastle (MD, MRCP); *m* 1972, Tom Stoppard, *qv*, s of late Eugene Straussler; 2 s, 2 step s; *Career* Royal Victorian Infirmary Kings Coll Hosp Newcastle upon Tyne: house surgn 1961, house physician 1962, sr house offr in med 1962-63; Univ of Bristol: res fell Dept of Chemical Pathology 1963-65 (MRC scholar in chemical pathology 1963-65), registrar in dermatology 1965-66 (MRC scholar in dermatology), sr registrar in dermatology 1966-68; Syntex Pharmaceuticals Ltd: assoc med dir 1968-71, dep med dir 1971-74, med dir 1974-76, dep md 1976, md 1977-81; TV series: Where There's Life (5 series) 1981-, Baby and Co (2 series) 1984-, Woman to Woman 1985, Mirian Stoppard's Health and Beauty Show 1988, Dear Miriam 1989; memb: Heberden Soc, Br Assoc of Rheumatology and Rehabilitation; memb RSM; *Books* Miriam Stoppard's Book of Baby Care (1977), My Medical School (contrib, 1978), Miriam Stoppard's Book of Health Care (1979), The Face and Body Book (1980), Everywoman's Lifeguide (1982), Your Baby (1982), Fifty Plus Lifeguide (1982), Your Growing Child (1983), Baby Care Book (1983), Pregnancy and Birth Book (1984), Baby and Child Medical Handbook (1986), Eveygirl's Lifeguide (1987), Feeding Your Family (1987), Miriam Stoppard's Health and Beauty Book (1988), Every Woman's Medical Handbook (1988), 7 lbs in 7 days (1991), over 40 pubns in med jls; *Recreations* family, skiing, gardening; *Style*— Dr Miriam Stoppard; Iver Grove, Iver, Bucks

STOPS, Leigh Warwick; s of Dr Denis Warwick Stops, of Kingston, Surrey, and Patricia, *née* Hill; *b* 29 May 1946; *Educ* Latymer Upper Sch, Univ of Sussex (BSc), Univ of Lancaster (MA); *m* 3 Dec 1976, Patricia Jane, da of F J Terry; 2 s (Caspar b 1986, Galen b 1988); *Career* advertiser; dir: Colman RSCG & Ptnrs 1984-85, res and planning Allen Brady & Marsh Ltd 1985-90, planning Yellowhammer Advertising Ltd 1991-; *Recreations* sailing, theatre, media, advertisements; *Style*— Leigh W Stops, Esq; 5 Foster Rd, Chiswick, London W4 4NY (☎ 071 436 5000, fax 071 436 4630); Yellowhammer Advertising Ltd, 76 Oxford St, London W1A 1DT

STORER, Prof Roy; s of Harry Storer (d 1980), of Wallasey, and Jessie, *née* Topham (d 1978); *b* 21 Feb 1928; *Educ* Wallasey GS, Univ of Liverpool (LDS, MSc, FDS, DRD); *m* 16 May 1953, Kathleen Mary Frances Pitman, da of Francis Charles Green; 1 s (Michael b 10 March 1961), 2 da (Sheila b 26 Feb 1956, Carolyn b 6 May 1958); *Career* Capt RADC 1951-52 (Lt 1950-51); sr lectr in dental prosthetics Univ of Liverpool 1962-67 (lectr 1954-61), visiting assoc prof Northwestern Univ Chicago 1961-62, hon conslt dental surgn Utd Liverpool Hosps 1962-67; Univ of Newcastle upon Tyne: prof of prosthodontics 1968-, clinical sub-dean Dental Sch 1970-77, dean of dentistry 1977-; sec and cncl memb of Br Soc for the Study of Prosthetic Dentistry 1960-69; memb: Gen Dental Cncl 1977- (chm educn ctee 1986-), Dental Educn Advsy Cncl (UK) 1978-, Bd of Faculty of Dental Surgery RCS 1982-90, dental sub-ctee of Univ Grants Ctee 1982-89, med sub-ctee of Univ Funding Cncl 1989-, EEC Dental Ctee Trg of Dental Practioners 1986-; Univ of Newcastle upon Tyne: memb of Senate, Cncl and Court, chm physical recreation ctee; memb Northern Sports Cncl; memb Br Dental Assoc 1950-; *Recreations* rugby football, cricket, gardening; *Clubs* East India, Athenaeum, MCC; *Style*— Prof Roy Storer; 164 Eastern Way, Darras Hall, Ponteland, Newcastle Upon Tyne NE20 9RH; The Dental Sch, Univ of Newcastle Upon Tyne, Framlington Place, Newcastle Upon Tyne NE2 4BW (☎ 091 2226000)

STOREY, Brian; s of Frederick Stalker (Eric) Storey, of Low Dubwath Farm, Kirklinton, and Lily, *née* Armstrong; *Educ* Irthins Valley Comp Sch Brampton Cumbria; *m* 16 July 1986, Diane Margaret, da of Frances Digby Coulthard; 2 s (Stuart b 11 Nov 1987, Andrew b 14 June 1989); *Career* national hunt jockey; former showjumper: began aged 11, northern jr champion 4 times, qualified for Jr Championships Hickstead and Wembley on Mystic Star 1978; professional nat hunt jockey 1983- (amateur 1981-83), first jockey to win Scot Champion Hurdle (Pat's Jester) and Scot National (Mighty Mark) in same season 1988-89; runs family farm with father; *Recreations* racing; *Style*— Brian Storey, Esq; Woodland View, Kirklinton, Carlisle, Cumbria CA6 6EF (☎ 0228 376); Low Dubwath Farm, Kirklinton (☎ 0228 331)

STOREY, Graham; s of Stanley Runton Storey (d 1971), of Meldreth, Cambs, and Winifred Graham (d 1975); *b* 8 Nov 1920; *Educ* St Edwards Oxford, Trinity Hall Cambridge (MA); *Career* WWII 1941-45 served UK France and Germany, Lt 1942 (despatches); called to the Bar Middle Temple 1950; Trinity Hall Cambridge: fell 1949-88, sr tutor 1958-68, vice master 1970-74, emeritus fell 1988-, reader in English 1981-88 (lectr 1965-81, chm Faculty Bd 1972-74); visiting fell All Souls Coll Oxford 1968; lectr for Br Cncl overseas, Warton lectr Br Acad 1984, Leverhulme Emeritus fellowship, syndic CUP 1983, gen ed Cambridge English Prose Texts 1980-; vice pres G M Hopkins Soc 1971, pres Dickens Soc of America 1983-84; govr: St Edwards Oxford 1959-69, Eastbourne Coll 1965-69; *Books* Reuters' Century(1951), Journals and Papers of G M Hopkins (jt ed 1959), Angel with Horns (ed 1961), Selected Verse and Prose of G M Hopkins (ed 1966), Letters of Dickens (jt ed 1965-), A Preface to Hopkins (1981), Revolutionary Prose of the English Civil War (jt ed 1983), Bleak House A Critical Study (1987); *Recreations* tennis, gardening, theatre, travel; *Style*— Graham Storey, Esq; Crown House, Caxton, Cambs (☎ 0954 719 316); Trinity Hall, Cambridge (☎ 0223 332500)

STOREY, Helen (Mrs Ron Brinkers); da of David Storey, and Barbara, *née* Hamilton; *b* 16 Aug 1959; *Educ* Kingston Poly; *m* 27 Sept 1985, Ron Brinkers, s of Jan Brinkers; 1 s (Luke Dylan Storey-Brinkers); *Career* fashion designer; involved in design studio and publicity coordination and Licensing: Valentino Rome 1981-82, Lancetti Rome 1982-83; own label launched (under umbrella of Amalgamated Talent, Six collections shown) 1984, shop opened (with Karen Boyd and Caroline Coates) Boyd & Storey London 1987, spring/summer collection shown in Designer Forum Umbrella as part of Fashion Week 1988; seasonal exhibitions incl: BDS (London), La Mode aux Tulleries (Paris), Coterie (NY), first catalogue produced 1989, estab Coates & Storey Ltd 1990 (shop re opened as Helen Storey), collection shown as part of London Designer Collections 1990, designer for Jigsaw 1990, first catwalk show for London Fashion Week 1990; clientele incl: Madonna, CAT, Yazz, Bananarama, Cher, Greta Scaachi, Paula Yates; stores sold to incl: Midas, Harrods, Harvey Nichols, Jones, Joseph, Seibu (Japan) Joyce Boutique (Hong Kong), Untitled (NY) and over 80 stores worldwide; nominee Young Designer of the Year award and Best Eveningwear Designer award BFC 1989, winner: (with Karen Boyd) British Apparel Export award 1989, Most Innovative Designer award 1990; memb BICCES; *Style*— Ms Helen Storey; 12 Newburgh St, West Soho (☎ 071 494 3188, fax 071 494 3777)

STOREY, Jeremy Brian; s of Capt James Mackie Storey (d 1976), of Harrogate, N Yorks, and Veronica, *née* Walmsley (d 1978); *b* 21 Oct 1952; *Educ* Uppingham, Downing Coll Cambridge (MA); *m* 19 September 1981, Carolyn, da of Eric Raymond Ansell, of Edenbridge, Kent; *Career* called to the Bar Inner Temple 1974; asst rec (Western Circuit) 1990; *Recreations* travel, theatre, cricket; *Clubs* MCC; *Style*— Jeremy Storey, Esq; 56 Westbere Rd, London NW2 3RU (☎ and fax 071 435 4227); 4 Pump Court, Temple, London EC4Y 7AN (☎ 071 353 2656, fax 071 583 2036)

STOREY, Kenelm; s and h of Sir Richard Storey, 2 Bt, and Virginia Anne, *née* Cayley; *b* 4 Jan 1963; *Educ* Winchester, George Washington Univ USA; *Career* gen mangr The Guardian International Newspaper; *Recreations* football, cricket, tennis, golf, squash; *Clubs* IZ, MCC, Yorkshire Gents Cricket, Butterflies Cricket, Old Wykehamists Cricket; *Style*— Kenelm Storey, Esq; The Grange Farm, Settrington, Malton, Yorkshire; 7 Douro Place, London W8 5PH (☎ 071 937 8823); 300 E 75th St, Apt 33L, NY, NY 10021, USA

STOREY, Leonard Charles; s of Herbert James Storey (d 1944); *b* 12 Aug 1910; *Educ* LCC Cent Sch; *m* 1952, Emily, *née* Hodgson; *Career* RAF 1940-46; CA; dir: Collateral Securities Ltd, Dwelling Devpt Ltd, Linit Flyte Ltd, Silvermoor Property Ltd; dir Kensington Perm Bldg Soc 1954-69; chm St Stephen's Bldg Soc; MRSH, MPCS, FInstD; *Recreations* reading, swimming; *Style*— Leonard Storey Esq; Kensington, 82 Malvern Ave, South Harrow, Middlesex (☎ 422 6008)

STOREY, Maude; CBE (1987); da of Henry Storey (d 1971), and Sarah Farrimond, *née* Davies (d 1981); *b* 30 March 1930; *Educ* Wigan and Dist Mining and Tech Coll, St Mary's Hosp Manchester, Lancaster Royal Infirmary, Paddington Gen Hosp, Royal Coll of Nursing Edinburgh (SRN, SCM, RCI), Queen Elizabeth Coll Univ of London (STD); *Career* domicillary midwife Wigan Co Borough 1953-56, midwifery sister St Mary's Hosp Manchester 1956-59, head nurse Intensive Therapy Unit Mayo Clinic USA 1957-59, théatre sister, clinical instr and nurse tutor Royal Albert Edward Infirmary Wigan 1959-68, lectr in community nursing Univ of Manchester 1968-71, asst and subsequently princ regnl nursing offr Liverpool Regnl Hosp Bd 1971-73, regnl nursing offr Mersey RHA 1973-77, registrar Gen Nursing Cncl for England and Wales 1977-81, chief exec UK Central Cncl for Nursing Midwifery and Health Visiting (UKCC) 1981-87; non-exec dir W Berks Health Authy, memb Cncl Univ of Reading 1989-; pres Royal Coll of Nursing of the UK 1986-90; CStJ 1988; *Recreations* theatre, travel; *Style*— Miss Maude Storey, CBE; 14 Conifer Drive, Tilehurst, Reading, Berks RG3 6YU (☎ 0734 412082)

STOREY, Michael John William; s of Jack Storey, and Pamela Jessamine, *née* Helmore; *b* 30 Dec 1947; *Educ* Wells Cathedral Sch, Central Sch of Speech and Drama; *m* 3 Sept 1976, Virginia, da of Havelock Clive-Smith (d 1964); 2 s (Daniel b 1 Feb 1978, d 1985, Alec b 26 April 1983), 1 da (Florence b 8 March 1987); *Career* composer of music for numerous films incl: Gertler, Another Country, Every Picture tells a Story, The Dress, Coming Up Roses, Hidden City, A Perfect Spy; active memb Greenpeace; *Recreations* tennis, squash, snooker; *Style*— Michael Storey, Esq; Walnut Tree Farm, Bylford, Halesworth, Suffolk IP19 9JX (☎ 050 270 660)

STOREY, Hon Sir Richard; 2 Bt (UK 1960) of Settrington, Co York; s of Baron Buckton (Life Peer, d 1978), and Elisabeth (d 1951), da of late Brig-Gen W J Woodcock, DSO; *b* 23 Jan 1937; *Educ* Winchester, Trinity Coll Cambridge (BA, LLB); *m* 1961, Virginia Anne, da of late Sir Kenelm Henry Ernest Cayley, 10 Bt; 1 s, 2 da; *Heir* s, Kenelm Storey, *qv*; *Career* Nat Serv RNVR 1956; called to Bar Inner Temple 1962, practised until 1969; contested (C) Don Valley 1966 and Huddersfield West 1970; dir: Portsmouth News Shops Limited 1971-, Reuters Holdings Plc 1986-, The Fleming Enterprise Investment Trust Plc 1989-; farms and administers land and woodland; exec chm Portsmouth and Sunderland Newspapers plc 1973- (joined bd

1962, chief exec 1973-86); memb: Newspaper Soc Cncl 1980- (pres 1990-), Press Cncl 1980-86, Regnl Cncl Yorkshire and Humberside CBI 1974-79, Nat Cncl and Exec Ctee CLA 1980-84, Cncl INCA-FIEJ Res Assoc 1983-88, CBI Employment Policy Ctee 1984-88; chm: Yorkshire Executive 1974-76, Regnl Daily Advertising Cncl 1988-89 (fndr chm, dir 1988), Sir Harold Hillier Gardens and Arboretum Mgmnt Ctee 1989-; tstee The Royal Botanic Gardens Kew Fndn 1990-; rep Newspaper Soc Communaute des Associations d'Editeurs de Journaux de le Cee (CAEJ) 1990-; Liveryman Worshipful Co of Stationer's and Newspapermaker's; *Recreations* sport, silviculture; *Style—* The Hon Sir Richard Storey, Bt; 7 Douro Place, London W8 5PH (☎ 071 937 8823); Settrington House, Malton, N Yorks (☎ 09446 400); Portsmouth & Sunderland Newspapers plc, Buckton House, 39 Abingdon Rd, London W8 6AH (☎ 071 938 1066, fax 071 937 1479)

STOREY, Richard Alec; s of Edwin Alexander Storey, of Mundesley-on-Sea, and Minnie Florence, *née* Trundle (d 1988); *b* 2 June 1937; *Educ* Hertford GS, Downing Coll Cambridge; *m* 14 Jan 1961, Jennifer, da of James Clare (d 1990), of Ware; 2 s (Daniel b 1966, Lawrence b 1968), 1 da (Emma b 1969); *Career* local govt admin 1961-3, archivist Historical Manuscripts Cmmn 1963-73, sr archivist Modern Records Centre Univ of Warwick Library 1973-; ed Business Archives 1969-73 and 1975-78; former chm Kenilworth History and Archeology Soc, co-proprietor Odibourne Press; *Books* Primary Sources for Victorian Studies (1977, updated 1987), Ambit (contrib, poetry); *Recreations* literature, cinema, local and transport history; *Style—* Richard Storey, Esq; 32 High St, Kenilworth, Warwicks CV8 1LZ (☎ 0926 57409)

STORIE-PUGH, Col Peter David; CBE (1981, MBE 1945), MC, (1940), TD (1945), DL (1963); s of late Prof Leslie Pugh, CBE, and Paula Storie; *b* 1 Nov 1919; *Educ* Malvern Coll, Queens' Coll Cambridge (MA, PhD), Royal Veterinary Coll Univ of London FRCVS; *m* 1, 1946 (m dis 1971), Alison, da of late Sir Oliver Lyle, OBE; 1 s, 2 da; m 2, 1971, Leslie Helen, da of Earl Striegel; 3 s, 1 da; *Career* served WWII, Queen's Own Royal W Kent Regt (escaped from Spangenberg and Colditz), cmd 1 Bn Cambs Regt, Suffolk and Cambs Regt, Col Dep Cdr 161 Inf Bde, ACF Co Cmdt; lectr Univ of Cambridge 1953-82, UK del EEC Vet Liaison Ctee 1962-75 (pres 1973-75), UK rep Fedn of Veterinarians of EEC 1975-83 (pres 1975-79); chm: Nat Sheepbreeders Assoc 1964-68, Eurovet 1971-73; pres: Cambridge Soc for Study of Comparative Med 1966-67, Int Pig Vet Soc 1967-69 (life pres 1969), Br Vet Assoc 1968-69 and 1970-71, 1 Euro Vet Congress Wiesbaden 1972, RCVS 1977-78; memb: Econ and Social Consultative Assembly of the Euro Communities 1982-89, Parly and Sci Ctee 1962-67, Home Sec's Advsy Ctee 1963-80, Nat Agric Centre Advsy Bd 1966-69, Miny of Agric Farm Animal Advsy Ctee 1970-73; fell Wolfson Coll Cambridge; CChem, FRSC; *Books* Eurovet: an Anatomy of Veterinary Europe (1972), Eurovet 2 (1975); *Clubs* United Oxford and Cambridge University; *Style—* Col Peter Storie-Pugh, CBE, MC, TD, DL; Duxford Grange, Duxford, Cambridge CB2 4QF (☎ 076 382 403)

STORMONT, Viscount; Alexander David Mungo; s and h of 8 Earl of Mansfield and Mansfield; *b* 17 Oct 1956; *Educ* Eton; *m* 1985, Sophia Mary Veronica, only da of Philip Biden Derwent Ashbrooke, of La Grande Maison, St John, Jersey, CI; 1 s (Hon William Philip David Mungo, Master of Stormont b 1 Nov 1988), 1 da (Hon Isabella Mary Alexandra Murray b 1987); *Clubs* White's, Turf, Pratt's; *Style—* Viscount Stormont; Scone Palace, Perthshire

STORMONTH DARLING, Sir James Carlisle (Jamie); CBE (1972), MC (1945), TD, WS (1949); s of Robert Stormonth Darling, WS (d 1956) and Beryl Madeleine, *née* Sayer (d 1955); *b* 18 July 1918; *Educ* Winchester, ChCh Oxford (MA), Univ of Edinburgh (LLB); *m* 1948, Mary Finella, BEM (1945), DL (E Lothian), da of Lt-Gen Sir James Gammell, KCB, DSO, MC (d 1975); 1 s (Angus), 2 da (Caroline, Priscilla); *Career* served WWII KOSB and 52 (Lowland) Div Reconnaissance Regt RAC, Lt-Col 1945; memb Royal Co of Archers (Queen's Bodyguard for Scot) 1958-; dir: Scottish Widows' Fund and Life Assur Soc 1981-89, Nat Tst for Scot (chief exec and dir 1949-83, vice pres emeritus 1985); Scot's Gardens Schemes: exec ctee 1951-, vice pres 1983-; memb Ancient Monuments Bd for Scot 1983-; a vice pres Scot Conservation Projects Tst (former pres); Edinburgh Old Town Charitable Tst: chm 1987-90, tstee 1987-; tstee Scot Churches Architectural Heritage Tst, Hon DUniv Stirling 1983, Hon LLD Univ of Aberdeen 1984; Hon FRIAS 1982; kt 1982; *Recreations* hill walking, gardening, countryside pursuits; *Clubs* New (Edinburgh), Hon Co of Edinburgh Golfers; *Style—* Sir Jamie Stormonth Darling, CBE, MC, TD, WS; Chapelhill House, Dirleton, N Berwick, East Lothian EH39 5HG (☎ 062 085 296)

STORMONTH DARLING, Peter; s of Patrick Stormonth Darling (d 1961), and Edith, *née* Lamb (d 1980); *b* 29 Sept 1932; *Educ* Winchester, New Coll Oxford (MA); *m* 1, 1958 (m dis), Candis Hitzig; 3 da (Candis Christa b 1959, Elizabeth Iona b 1960, Arabella b 1962); m 2, 1970, Maureen O'Leary; *Career* 2 Lt Black Watch 1950-53, served Korean War, Flying Offr RAFVR 1953-56; chm Mercury Asset Management Group plc; dir: S G Warburg Group plc, Orion Insurance plc; *Style—* Peter Stormonth Darling, Esq; 33 King William St, London EC4

STORMONTH-DARLING, Robin Andrew; s of Patrick Stormonth-Darling (d 1960); *b* 1 Oct 1926; *Educ* Abberley Hall, Winchester; *m* 1, 1956 (m dis 1974), Susan, *née* Clifford-Turner; 3 s, 1 da; m 2, 1974 (m dis 1979), Harriet, da of Lt-Gen Sir Archibald Nye, GCSI, GCIE, GCMG, KCB, KBE, MC (d 1967); m 3, 1981, Carola Marion, da of Sir Robert Erskine-Hill, 2 Bt (d 1989), and formerly w of (Richard) David Brooke, *qv*; *Career* Capt 9 Queen's Royal Lancers 1947-54; stockbroker; sr ptnr Laing and Cruickshank 1980-87 (joined 1954, ptnr 1956); memb London Stock Exchange 1955-87, chm Disciplinary Appeals Ctee 1983-90, memb Cncl of Stock Exchange 1978-87, chm Quotations Ctee 1981-85, dep chm Panel on Takeovers of Mergers 1985-87; dir: British Motor Corporation 1960-68, BL Motor Corporation 1968-75, Mercantile House Holdings plc 1984-87 (dep chm 1987), London Scottish Bank plc 1984-, Securities of Investments Bd 1985-87, GPI, Leisure Corp 1986-; chm Tranwood plc 1987-; *Recreations* shooting, skiing, flying, swimming; *Clubs* White's, Perth Hunt, MCC, Hurlingham; *Style—* Robin Stormonth-Darling, Esq; Balvarran, Enochdhu, Blairgowrie, Perthshire, Scotland (☎ 025 081 248); 21 Paradise Walk, London SW3 (☎ 071 352 4161)

STORR, Dr (Charles) Anthony; s of The Rev Vernon Faithfull Storr (d 1940), of Westminster, and Katherine Cecilia Storr (d 1954); gggf Paul Storr (1771-1844) was the Regency Silversmith and also gggf to Laurence and Rex Whistler; *b* 18 May 1920; *Educ* Winchester, Christ's Coll Cambridge (MB BChir, MA); *m* 1, 1942, Catherine, da of late Arthur Cole, of Lincoln's Inn; 3 da (Sophia, Polly, Emma); m 2, 1970, Catherine, da of late A D Peters; *Career* hon conslt psychiatrist Oxford Health Authy, formerly clinical lectr in psychiatry Univ of Oxford, fell Green Coll Oxford 1979 (emeritus fell 1984); FRCPsych, FRCP, FRSL; *Books* The Integrity of the Personality (1960), Sexual Deviation (1964), Human Aggression (1968), Human Destructiveness (1972), The Dynamics of Creation (1972), Jung (1973), The Art of Psychotherapy (1979), Jung: Selected Writings (ed, 1983), Solitude: A Return to the Self (1988), Churchill's Black Dog and Other Phenomena of the Human Mind (1989), Freud (1989); *Recreations* music, journalism, broadcasting; *Clubs* Savile; *Style—* Dr Anthony Storr; 45 Chalfont Rd, Oxford OX2 6TJ (☎ 0865 53348)

STORRS, Dr John Alastair; s of Francis Cecil Storrs, of Hill House, Broadway, Badwell Ash, Suffolk, and Constance Mary, *née* Budd (d 1990); *b* 27 May 1940; *Educ* St Benedict's Abbey Sch Ealing London, Univ of London (MRCS, LRCP, MB BS, DA), Univ of Newcastle upon Tyne; *m* 30 May 1964 (m dis 1989), Maureen Anne, da of late Harry M Hewett; 1 s (Jonathan Amery b 5 March 1965), 1 da (Jacqueline Louise b 8 June 1967); *Career* registrar and sr registrar anaesthetist UCH 1967-70, conslt anaesthetist Royal Victoria Infirmary and assoc hosps Newcastle 1971-, lectr in anaesthesia Univ of Newcastle upon Tyne, invitation lectr Univ of Amsterdam 1974; overseas sec Obstetric Anaesthetists Assoc, chm Div of Anaesthesia Newcastle DHA, warden Eustace Perce Hall Univ of Newcastle; FFA RCS 1969; *Books* Epidural Analgesia in Obstetrics (1974), Current Research on Enflurane: Obstetric Anaesthesia (1981), Controversies in Obstetric Anaesthesia (contrib, 1990); *Recreations* rowing and sailing, music, photography, travel; *Style—* Dr John Storrs; The Royal Victoria Infirmary, Queen Victoria Rd, Newcastle NE1 4LP (☎ 091 232 5131)

STORRY, Kenneth Charles; *b* 11 July 1923; *Educ* Hull GS; *m* 1959, Patricia Irene Frances, *née* McLaughlin; 1 s; *Career* Sub Lt RNVR; dir and md Barclays Unicorn Group Ltd 1977-82, gen mangr Barclays Unicorn Ltd 1974-, district mangr Barclays Bank London (SW dist) 1970-; *Recreations* golf, reading, travel, sailing; *Clubs* Royal Western Yacht, Royal Plymouth, Corinthian Yacht, Yelverton Golf, St Mellion Country; *Style—* Kenneth Storry Esq; 1 Haddington Rd, Stoke, Plymouth, Devon (☎ 0752 569528)

STOTE, Alan Edward Charles; s of Horace Albert Stote, and Frances May, *née* Webb; *b* 16 Sept 1948; *Educ* Lordswood Tech Birmingham; *m* 24 July 1976, Susan Annette Sheila, da of Michael Joseph Carding, of Wolverhampton; 1 s (Richard b 1977), 1 da (Hannah b 1985); *Career* formerly chm and chief exec BTS Group plc; chm CBI Smaller Firms Cncl 1984-86; memb: NEDC 1985-87, Midland CBI Regnl Cncl 1987-; ret; *Recreations* rowing, vintage cars; *Clubs* Bewdley Rowing; *Style—* Alan E C Stote, Esq; Yarhampton House, Yarhampton, Stourport-on-Severn, Worcestershire DY13 0XA (☎ 0299 21 401)

STOTHART, William; s of William Henry Stothart, and Mabel, *née* Owens; *b* 29 Sept 1926; *Educ* Quarry Bank HS Liverpool, Downing Coll Cambridge; *m* 1958, Margaret Elizabeth, *née* Bowden; 1 s (David b 1960), 1 da (Jane b 1963); *Career* co sec and dir Owen Owen plc, ret; treas Univ of Liverpool; *Recreations* golf, fell walking, photography; *Style—* William Stothart, Esq; 6 Croome Drive, West Kirby, Wirral, Merseyside

STOTHER, Ian George; s of John Stother, of Lytham, Lancs, and Joan Lilian, *née* Jones; *b* 12 Feb 1945; *Educ* King Edward VII Sch Lytham, King's Coll Cambridge (MA, MB BChir); *m* 7 April 1969, Jacqueline, da of Alan B Mott, of Heslington, York; 2 da (Lindsay Anne b 21 April 1972, Clare Jennifer (twin) b 21 April 1972); *Career* conslt orthopaedic surgn Gtr Glasgow Health Bd 1978, hon clinical lectr in orthopaedics Univ of Glasgow, hon lectr Biological Engrg Unit Univ of Strathclyde, orthopaedic advsr Scot Ballet Dance Sch for Scotland; memb: Br Orthopaedic Assoc, Br Assoc for Surgery of the Knee, Int Arthroscopy Assoc, Assoc of Surgns of E Africa; FRCSEd 1974 (Glasgow 1981); *Recreations* classic cars, ballet; *Style—* Ian Stother, Esq; Glasgow Nuffield Hospital, 25 Beaconsfield Rd, Glasgow G12 0PJ (☎ 041 334 9441, fax 041 337 1088); Glasgow Royal Infirmary, Glasgow G4 0SF

STOTHERS, Thomas; s of Robert James Stothers (d 1966), and Elizabeth Charlotte Gibson; *b* 24 July 1926; *Educ* Belfast Tech Coll; *m* 1952, Florence Elizabeth, da of Capt William S Simms (d 1960); 2 s (James b 1954, John b 1957); *Career* md H & J Martin Ltd (bldg and civil engrg contracting firm); dir: R J Stothers & Sons Ltd 1947, Teear Ltd, Stothers Holdings Ltd 1976; FCIOB, FASI, FInstD; *Recreations* golf, boating, rugby; *Clubs* Royal Belfast Golf, Malone Rugby, Kirkstown Golf; *Style—* Thomas Stothers, Esq; Cloverlinks, 22 Quarter Road, Cloughy, Co Down; R J Stothers & Sons Ltd, 68 Orby Road, Belfast (☎ 0232 702626)

STOTT, Sir Adrian George Ellingham; 4 Bt (UK 1920), of Stanton, Co Gloucester; s of Sir Philip Sidney Stott, 3 Bt (d 1979), and Lady Stott, *qv*; *b* 7 Oct 1948; *Educ* Univ of British Columbia (BSc, MSc), Univ of Waterloo Ontario (MMaths); *Heir* bro, Vyvyan Philip Stott; *Career* dir of planning (county) 1974-77, town planning conslt 1977-80, real estate portfolio mangr 1980-85, mangr of conservation agency 1985, md of marketing co 1986-88; mgmnt conslt 1989; *Recreations* music, inland waterways, politics; *Clubs* MENSA, Inland Waterways Assoc; *Style—* Sir Adrian Stott, Bt; 1566 Admiral Tyron Boulevard, Parksville, British Columbia V9P 1Y3 (☎ 604 7525774)

STOTT, Lady; Cicely Florence; da of Bertram Ellingham, of Ely House, Hertford; *m* 1947, Sir Philip Sidney Stott, 3 Bt, ARIBA (d 1979); 2 s; *Style—* Lady Stott; 1104 Esquimalt Towers, 1552 Esquimalt Ave, West Vancouver, BC, Canada

STOTT, (Robert Thomas) Dursley; JP (1977); s of Robert Leonard Stott (d 1991), of Onchan, IOM, and Winifrede Anna, *née* Halsall (d 1989); *b* 13 Feb 1935; *Educ* King William's Coll IOM, Magdalene Coll Cambridge (MA); *m* 15 June 1959, Margot, da of George Donald Winston Ashton; 1 s (Paul b 1962), 1 da (Mandy b 1960); *Career* Nat Serv cmmnd 2 Lt 1 Bn The Royal Regt 1955; memb Int Stock Exchange 1962-; chm Dolphin Media; *Style—* Dursley Stott, Esq, JP; Ivydene, Little Switzerland, Douglas, Isle of Man (☎ 0624 21711); 22 Finch Rd, Douglas, Isle of Man (☎ 0624 676969, fax 0624 675655)

STOTT, Rt Hon Lord; George Gordon Stott; PC (1964); s of late Rev Dr G Gordon Stott, and late Flora Corsar Stott; *b* 22 Dec 1909; *Educ* Cramond Sch, Edinburgh Acad, Univ of Edinburgh (MA, LLB, DipEd); *m* 1947, Nancy Deverell, da of late A D Braggins; 1 s, 1 da; *Career* Scottish advocate 1936, advocate-depute 1947-51, KC 1950, sheriff of Roxburgh, Berwick and Selkirk 1961-64, lord advocate 1964-67; a Lord of Session 1967-84; *Style—* The Rt Hon Lord Stott; 12 Midmar Gdns, Edinburgh (☎ 031 447 4251)

STOTT, James Howard; s of Selwyn Stott (d 1962), and Helena, *née* Heap (d 1966); *b* 26 June 1920; *Educ* Barkisland Sch, Sowerby Bridge Secdy Sch, Univ of Manchester (LLB); *m* 23 April 1943, Margery, da of John William Collis (d 1950); 2 s (Richard b 1950, Peter b 1954); *Career* Nat Serv RN 1941, Lt RNVR 1942-46, CO 1943-46; textile dir 1976-84, slr 1949-; *Recreations* singing, gardening; *Style—* James Stott, Esq; 10A Trenance Gdns, Greetland, Halifax (☎ 0422 372166); 13 Harrison Rd, Halifax (☎ 0422 362011)

STOTT, Prof Nigel Clement Halley; s of Maj Halley Harwin Stott, of Natal, and Joyce, *née* Greathead; *b* 27 Nov 1939; *Educ* Univ of Edinburgh (BSc, MB ChB, MRCP); *m* 7 April 1965, (Eleanor) Mary, da of (Townroe) Stephen Collingwood, of Shaftesbury; 2 s (Philip b 19 April 1969, Howard b 25 Nov 1971), 1 da (Paula b 4 June 1967); *Career* registrar Epidemiology Res Unit MRC 1969-70, med offr St Lucy's Hosp Transkei 1970-71, sr lectr Welsh Nat Sch of Med 1972-79, prof of primary med care Southampton 1979-80, prof of gen practice Univ of Wales Coll of Med 1986-; author of numerous chapters and papers; memb: Welsh Postgrad Med and Dental Cncl, Welsh Health Planning Forum, Cncl Univ of Wales Coll of Med; FRCPE 1980, FRCGP 1985 (MRCGP 1979); *Books* Primary Health Care: Bridging the Gap between Theory and Practice (1983), Care of the Dying (1984), Health Checks in General Practice (1988); *Recreations* sailing, gardening; *Clubs* Professional & Academic; *Style—* Prof Nigel Stott; Department of General Practice, University of Wales College of Medicine, Heath Park, Cardiff CF4 4XN (☎ 0222 731671)

STOTT, Prof Peter Frank; CBE; s of Clarence Stott, MC, OBE (d 1981), of London, and Mabel, *née* Sutcliffe; *b* 8 Aug 1927; *Educ* Bradford GS, Clare Coll Cambridge (MA); *m* 5 Sept 1953, Vera, da of Henry Watkins (d 1982), of Norwich; 2 s (Andrew b 1955, Richard b 1958); *Career* ptnr G Maunsell & Partners 1957-63, chief engr London CC 1963-65, dir of highways and transportation and controller of planning and transportation GLC 1965-73, dir gen Nat Water Cncl 1973-83, chm Quality Scheme for Ready Mixed Concrete 1984-; Nash prof of civil engrg 1987-89; pres ICE 1989-90; FEng, FICE, FCIT, FIHT; *Recreations* pottery; *Clubs* Athenaeum; *Style—* Prof Peter Stott, CBE; 7 Frank Dixon Way, Dulwich, London SE21 7BB (☎ 081 693 5121)

STOTT, Richard Keith; s of Fred Brookes Stott (d 1964), and Bertha, *née* Pickford, of Oxford; *b* 17 Aug 1943; *Educ* Clifton; *m* 1970, Penelope Anne, yr da of Air Vice-Marshal Sir Colin Scragg, KBE, CB, AFC and bar (d 1989); 1 s (Christopher b 1978), 2 da (Emily b 1972, Hannah b 1975); *Career* jr reporter Bucks Herald Aylesbury 1963-65, Ferrari News Agency Dartford 1965-68, reporter Daily Mirror 1968-79 (features ed 1979-81, asst ed 1981-84); ed: Sunday People 1984-85, Daily Mirror 1985-89, The People 1990-; md People Publishing Company 1990-; Br Press Award for Reporter of the Year 1977; *Recreations* theatre, reading; *Style—* Richard Stott; c/o The People, 33 Holborn, London EC1P 1DQ

STOTT, Roger; CBE (1979), MP (Lab) Wigan 1983-; s of Richard Stott; *b* 7 Aug 1943; *Educ* Rochdale Tech Coll, Ruskin Coll; *m* 1969 (m dis 1982), Irene Mills; 2 s; *Career* former merchant seaman and PO telephone engr; Rochdale cncllr 1970-74 (chm housing ctee), contested (Lab) Cheadle 1970, MP (Lab) Westhoughton May 1973-1983, sponsored by POEU; PPS to: Indust Sec 1975-76, Rt Hon James Callaghan as PM 1976-79 and as ldr of oppn 1979-1980; vice-chm NW area PLP, memb select ctee Agric 1980-; oppn front bench spokesman: Tport 1981-1983, Trade and Indust 1983-; *Style—* Roger Stott, Esq, CBE, MP; 24 Highgate Crescent, Appley Bridge, Wigan

STOTT, Vyvyan Philip; s of Sir Philip Sidney Stott, 3 Bt (d 1979), and Lady Stott, *qv*; hp of bro, Sir Adrian Stott, 4 Bt; *b* 5 Aug 1952; *Style—* Vyvyan Stott, Esq; 7 Dumbarton Drive, Kenmore, Queensland 4069, Australia

STOUGHTON-HARRIS, Anthony Geoffrey (Tony); CBE (1989); s of Geoffrey Stoughton-Harris (d 1966), and Kathleen Mary, *née* Baker Brown; *b* 5 June 1932; *Educ* Sherborne; *m* 1959, Elizabeth Thackery, da of Joseph Brian White, of Ramsgate; 1 s (Peter), 2 da (Sarah, Helen); *Career* RTR 1956-58; CA 1956; pt/t treas W Herts Main Drainage Authy 1964-70, exec vice chm Nationwide Anglia Bldg Soc 1987-90; dir: Maidenhead and Berkshire Bldg Soc 1967 (md 1975, renamed South of England Bldg Soc 1980, Anglia Bldg Soc in 1983 and Nationwide Anglia Bldg Soc 1987 (dep chm 1990-)), Guardian Royal Exchange 1990-, Southern Electric plc 1990-; chm: Met Assoc of Bldg Socs 1979-80, Northamptonshire Trg and Enterprise Cncl 1990-; gen cmmr Inland Revenue 1982-; memb Cncl Bldg Socs Assoc 1979-90 (chm 1987-89), pt/t memb Southern Electricity Bd 1981-90; dir and chm Electronic Funds Transfer Ltd 1984-89; FCA; *Recreations* sport, gardening, DIY; *Style—* Tony Stoughton-Harris, Esq, CBE; Old Farm House, Blackmile Lane, Grendon, Northants NN7 1JR (☎ 0933 664235); Nationwide Anglia Building Society, New Oxford House, High Holborn, London WC1V 6PW (☎ 071 242 8822 telex 264549)

STOURTON, Hon Charlotte Mary; da of 24 Baron Mowbray, (25) Segrave and (21) Stourton (d 1936); *b* 20 Jan 1904; *Recreations* motoring, walking, dancing; *Clubs* Anglo-Blegium; *Style—* The Hon Charlotte Stourton; 2 Arthington Ave, Harrogate, North Yorkshire

STOURTON, Edward John Ivo; s of Nigel John Ivo Stourton, OBE, of N Yorks, and Rosemary Jennifer Rushworth Abbott, JP; *b* 24 Nov 1957; *Educ* Ampleforth, Trinity Coll Cambridge (MA, pres Cambridge Union); *m* 5 July 1980, Margaret, da of late Sir James Napier Finney McEwen Bt; 2 s (Ivo b 11 June 1982, Thomas b 28 Sept 1987), 1 da (Eleanor b 1 June 1984); *Career* TV journalist 1979-; Washington corr Channel Four News 1986 (fndr memb 1982), Paris corr BBC TV 1988, dip ed ITN 1990; Kt of Honour and Devotion, SMOM; *Recreations* reading; *Clubs* Travellers', Hurlingham, Kenwood (Maryland, USA); *Style—* Edward Stourton, Esq; 73 Hendham Road, London SW17 (☎ 081 767 8584); ITN House, 200 Gray's Inn Road, London WC1 (☎ 071 833 3000)

STOURTON, Hon Edward William Stephen; s and h of 26 Baron Mowbray, 27 Segrave and 23 Stourton; *b* 17 April 1953; *Educ* Ampleforth; *m* 1980, Penelope (Nell) Lucy, da of Dr Peter Brunet, of 4 Rawlinson Rd, Oxford; 3 da (Sarah Louise b 1982, Isabel b 1983, Camilla b 1987); *Style—* The Hon Edward Stourton; 23 Warwick Sq, SW1

STOURTON, Hon James Alastair; s of 26 Baron Mowbray, 27 Segrave and 23 Stourton, CBE, and Jane Faith, *née* de Yarburgh-Bateson, da of Stephen 5 Baron Deramore; *b* 3 July 1956; *Educ* Ampleforth, Magdalene Coll Cambridge (MA); *Career* Sotheby's Picture Dept 1979-, dir Sotheby's London 1987, dir European Valuations Dept 1990; proprietor The Stourton Press; Knight of Honour and Devotion SMO Malta; *Clubs* Pratt's, Beefsteak; *Style—* The Hon James Stourton; 21 Moreton Place, London SW1V 2NL (☎ 071 821 1101); Sotheby's, 34-35 New Bond St, London W1 (☎ 071 493 8080)

STOURTON, Lady Joanna; *née* Lambart; da of Field Marshal 10 Earl of Cavan (d 1946), by his 2 w Hester Joan, Countess of Cavan (d 1976); *b* 8 Dec 1929; *m* 1955, Maj Michael Godwin Plantagenet, s of Hon John Joseph Stourton, s of 24 Baron Mowbray; 2 s (Thomas b 1965, Henry b 1971), 2 da (Julia b 1958, Clare b 1962); *Style—* The Lady Joanna Stourton; The Old Rectory, Great Rollright, Chipping Norton, Oxon (☎ 0608 737385)

STOUT, (John) Bernard; s of John Mitchell Stout (d 1955), of Inkerman Terr, Whitehaven, Cumbria, and Kate Stout (d 1974); *b* 11 Jan 1929; *Educ* Worksop Coll, Pembroke Coll Cambridge (MA); *m* 31 Jan 1959, Elizabeth Clayton, da of David Thomson (d 1954), of Alstonby Hall, Westlinton, Carlisle; 1 s (David Edward b 1960), 2 da (Susan Claire (Mrs Tolson) b 1962, Jennifer Elizabeth b 1969); *Career* Nat Serv RN; admitted slr 1955; ptnr: Blackburn & Main Carlisle 1956-71, Cartmell Mawson & Main Carlisle 1971-88 (latterly sr ptnr); ret 1988; pres Carlisle and Dist Law Soc 1982; chm Carlisle and N Cumbria NSPCC 1986- (pres 1981-85, chm Appeal Ctee 1984); pres Boys Bde Carlisle Dist 1971-76; memb Law Soc; *Recreations* golf, fishing, shooting, fell-walking; *Clubs* Border and County (Carlisle); *Style—* Bernard Stout, Esq; Croft Head, Scotby, Carlisle CA4 8BX (☎ 0228 513 325); Viaduct House, The Viaduct, Carlisle CA3 8EZ (☎ 0228 31561, fax 0228 401 490, telex 64106)

STOUT, Prof David Ker; 31 July 1956, Margaret, da of William Sugden (d 1951); 2 s (Nigel b 1957, Rowland b 1959), 2 da (Lucy b 1961, Eleanor b 1963); *b* 27 Jan 1932; *Educ* Sydney HS Sydney NSW, Univ of Sydney (BA), Magdalen Coll Oxford (BA, Rhodes Scholar); *m* 31 July 1956, Margaret, da of William Sugden (d 1951); 2 s (Nigel b 1957, Rowland b 1959), 2 da (Lucy b 1961, Eleanor b 1963); *Career* Mynors fell and lectr in econs Univ Coll Oxford 1959-76, econ advsr to various govts 1965-76 (Syria, New Hebrides, Aust, Canada), econ dir NEDO 1970-72 and 1976-80, visiting prof of econs Univ of Leicester 1982-(Tyler prof of econs 1980-82), head of Econ Dept Unilever 1982; author of various papers in books and jls on taxation, growth, inflation, balance of payments and other topics; memb: ESRC (chm Indust, Econs and Environment Gp), Bd of Tstees Centre for Economic Policy Res Inst of Fiscal Studies, Exec Ctee (and govr) Nat Inst of Economic and Social Res 1972; *Style—* Prof David Stout; Unilever plc, Blackfriars, PO Box 68, London EC4 (☎ 071 822 6557)

STOUT, Prof Kenneth John; s of John Ernest William Stout (d 1954), of Potters Bar, Hertfordshire, and Florence Stout (d 1987); *b* 3 Aug 1941; *Educ* Mount Grace Comp Sch Potters Bar, Cranfield (MSc), CNAA (PhD, DSc); *m* 30 Nov 1963, Doreen Margaret, da of Francis Hunter (d 1948), of Hull; 2 s (John Hunter b 1965, Steven Charles Hunter b 1969); *Career* reader in precision engrg Leicester Poly 1987-81, head Dept Mfrg Systems Coventry Poly 1981-87, head Sch Mfrg and Mech Engrg Univ of Birmingham 1989- (Lucas prof 1988-); former memb: SERC Ctees Applied Mechanics jt Rolls Royce/SERC and ACME, DTI Advanced Mfrg Techno Ctee; chm Consortium Heads of Prodn Engrg 1988-, memb of Continuing Educn CEI Steering Ctee; FIProdE; *Books* Quality Control in Automation (1985), An Atlas of Surface Topography (1990), Precision Machine Design (contrib, 1990); *Clubs* Nuneaton Golf; *Style—* Prof Kenneth Stout; 24 Golf Drive, Whitestone, Nuneaton, Warwickshire CV11 6LY (☎ 0203 384479); School of Manufacturing and Mechanical Engineering, University of Birmingham, PO Box 363, Birmingham B15 2TT (☎ 021 414 6882, telex 333762 UOBHAM G, fax 021 414 3958)

STOUT, Prof Robert William; s of William Ferguson Stout, CB, of Belfast, and Muriel Stout, *née* Kilner; *b* 6 March 1942; *Educ* Campbell Coll Belfast, Queen's Univ Belfast (MD DSc); *m* 31 Dec 1969, Helena Patricia, da of Frederick William Willis (d 1959), of Comber, Co Down; 2 s (Brian b 1971, Alan b 1972), 1 da (Caroline b 1974); *Career* Eli Lilly Foreign Educn fell Univ of Washington Seattle USA 1971-73, Queen's Univ Belfast; prof of geriatric med Dept of Geriatric Med 1976-; Br Heart Fndn: sr res fell 1974-75, sr lectr 1975-76, dep dean Faculty of Med 1990-91; govr Res Into Ageing, vice pres Age Concern NI, memb Bd of Govrs Methodist Coll Belfast; FRCP 1979, FRCPEd 1988, FRCPI 1989; *Books* Hormones and Atherosclerosis (1982), Arterial Disease in the Elderly (ed, 1984); *Recreations* golf, gardening, reading; *Clubs* Royal Belfast Golf; *Style—* Prof Robert Stout; 3 Larch Hill Drive, Craigavad, Co Down BT18 0JS (☎ 023 172253); Queen's University, Department of Geriatric Medicine, Whitla Medical Building, 97 Lisburn Road, Belfast BT9 7BL (☎ 0232 245133, ext 2152)

STOUTE, Michael Ronald; s of Maj Ronald Audley Stoute, OBE, of Barbados, and Mildred Dorothy, *née* Bowen; *b* 22 Oct 1945; *Educ* Harrison Coll Barbados; *m* 14 June 1969, Joan Patricia, *née* Baker; 1 s (James Robert Michael b 6 June 1974), 1 da (Caroline Elizabeth b 23 Jan 1972); *Career* race horse trainer 1972-, leading flat racing trainer 1981, 1986 and 1989; trained Derby winners: Shergar 1981, Shahrastani 1986; Irish Derby winners: Shergar 1981, Shareef Dancer 1983, Shahrastani 1986; *Recreations* cricket, hunting, skiing; *Style—* Michael Stoute, Esq; Freemason Lodge, Bury Road, Newmarket, Suffolk (☎ 0638 663 801, fax 0638 667 276, telex 817 811)

STOUTZKER, Ian; s of Aron Stoutzker (d 1968), and Dora Stoutzker (d 1968); *b* 21 Jan 1929; *Educ* Berkhamstead Sch, RCM (ARCM), LSE (BSc); *m* 3 Sept 1958, Mercedes; 1 s (Robert b 1962), 1 da (Riquita (Mrs Wade Newmark) b 1960); *Career* Samuel Montagu 1952-56, A Keyser and Co (tutor Keyser Ullmann Ltd) 1956-75, chm London Interstate Bank 1971-75, chm Dawnay Day International 1985-; pres Philharmonia Orch 1976-79 (chm 1972-76); memb: Exec Ctee RCM 1968-, Musicians Benevolent Fund 1980-; chm Live Music Now 1980-; FRCM; *Recreations* music, cross country walking; *Clubs* Carlton; *Style—* Ian Stoutzker, Esq; 33 Wilton Crescent, London SW1X 8RX; 15 Grosvenor Gardens, London SW1W OBD (☎ 071 834 8060, fax 071 828 1984, telex 8955547)

STOVIN-BRADFORD, Frank Randolph; s of William Stovin-Bradford (d 1940), of Golders Green, and Rose Amelia, *née* Phillips (d 1960); *b* 31 Dec 1923; *Educ* Univ Coll Sch London; *m* 20 July 1944, Jacqueline, da of Frank Brown (d 1940), of Temple Fortune; 2 s (Nigel b 1946, Richard Noel b 1957); *Career* Sub Lt (A) RNVR (despatches) Pilot 857 Sqdn RN (Grumman Avengers), HMS Indomitable, East Indian Ocean Fleet and Br Pacific Fleet 1941-45; fell Royal Inst of British Architects; chartered architect in private practice 1957; in 1970 was first architect to bring a successful action in the High Court for breach of copyright since 1934 and the Law affecting copyright was decisively amended as a direct result of this action defining clearly the protection of an architect's drawings; FRIBA; *Recreations* travelling, painting; *Clubs* City Livery, Fleet Air Arm Officers' Assoc; *Style—* Frank R Stovin-Bradford, Esq; 20 Crail View, Northleach, Cheltenham, Gloucestershire GL54 3QH (☎ 0451 60153)

STOVOLD, Andrew (Andy); s of Lancelot Walter Willis-Stovold, of Olveston, Avon, and Doris Patricia, *née* Taylor; *b* 19 March 1953; *Educ* Filton HS, Loughborough Coll of Educn; *m* 30 Sept 1978, Kay Elizabeth; 2 s (Nicholas Craig b 18 June 1981, Neil Andrew b 24 Feb 1983); *Career* professional cricketer; Gloucestershire CCC: debut v Worcs 1973, awarded county cap 1976, benefit 1987, asst coach and second XI capt 1991-; England: schs under 15 and under 19 (tour India 1970-71), Young Cricketers tour W Indies 1972; man of the match awards: Benson & Hedges Cup 9 times incl final 1977, NatWest Trophy 4 times; former schoolboy footballer Bristol Rovers; teacher Tockington Manor Sch 1979-87, fndr Cricket International Ltd 1989-; *Recreations* horse racing, football, winter sports, walking; *Style—* Andy Stovold, Esq; Gloucestershire CCC, Phoenix County Ground, Nevil Rd, Bristol BS7 9EJ (☎ 0272 245216)

STOW, Sir John Montague; GCMG (1966, KCMG 1959, CMG 1950), KCVO (1966); s of Sir Alexander Stow, KCIE, OBE (d 1936), of Netherwood, Newbury, Berks; *b* 1911; *Educ* Harrow, Pembroke Coll Cambridge; *m* 1939, Beatrice, da of late Capt Tryhorne; *Career* entered Colonial Serv (Nigeria) 1934, asst colonial sec Gambia 1938, chief sec Windward Is 1944, admin St Lucia 1947, dir of estab Kenya 1952-55, colonial sec Jamaica 1955-59, govr and C-in-C Barbados 1959-66, govr-gen Barbados 1966-67, ret; KStJ 1959; *Clubs* Caledonian, MCC; *Style—* Sir John Stow, GCMG, KCVO; 26a Tregunter Rd, London SW10 9LH

STOW, Timothy Montague Fenwick; QC (1989); s of Geoffrey Montague Fenwick Stow, LVO (d 1990), of Axenha, Lugar Do Foro, Pineiro De Loures, Portugal, and Joan Fortescue, *née* Flannery (d 1984); *b* 31 Jan 1943; *Educ* Eton; *m* 29 May 1965, Alisoun Mary Francis, da of Paul Walter Homberger, OBE (d 1978); 1 s (Richard Montague Fenwick b 15 Dec 1968), 1 da (Emma Mary b 15 Dec 1972); *Career* called to the Bar 1965, recorder 1989; memb Bar Cncl 1982-85; *Recreations* looking after our country property, tennis, foreign travel, skiing; *Clubs* Travellers'; *Style—* Timothy Stow, Esq QC; 12 Kings Bench Walk, Temple, London EC4Y 7EL (☎ 071 583 0811, fax 071 583 7228)

STOW HILL, Susan, Baroness; Susan Isabella Cloudesley; da of William Auchterlony Hunter, of Spean Bridge, Inverness-shire; *m* 1940, Baron Stow Hill (Life Peer, d 1979); 2 s; *Style—* The Rt Hon Susan, Lady Stow Hill; 19 Church Row, Hampstead, NW3

STOWASSER, Hon Dr (Helen Margaret); *née* Platt; yr da of Baron Platt (Life Peer and 1 Bt, d 1978), and Margaret Irene, *née* Cannon; *b* 16 March 1933; *Educ* Manchester HS for Girls, Newnham Coll Cambridge, Univ of Qld (PhD); *m* 10 July 1954, Cecil Henry Stowasser, s of late Marian Stowasser, of Karlsbad, Czechoslovakia; 3 s; *Career* sr lectr Qld Conservatorium of Music 1987, assoc prof of music educn Univ of Western Australia 1989; *Books* Discover Music 1-3 (1978 and 1983), Discover Music-making (1989); published compositions incl: String Quartet in D, Valse Volante (1987); *Recreations* bushwalking; *Style—* The Hon Dr Stowasser; 1-9

Park Rd, Nedlands, Western Australia 6009, Australia

STOWE, Grahame Conway; s of Harry Stowe (d 1968), and Evelyn, *née* Pester (d 1990); *b* 22 May 1949; *Educ* Allerton Grange Sch Leeds, Univ of Leeds (LLB); *m* 27 Dec 1981, Marilyn Joyce, da of Arnold Morris; 1 s (Benjamin Harry George b 21 May 1988); *Career* admitted slr 1974, commenced own practice 1981, sr ptnr Grahame Stowe Bateson & Co; chm Benefit Appeal Tbnl 1985, pres Mental Health Tbnl 1987, regnl chm Mental Health Tbnl 1991; memb Law Soc, FCIArb 1979; *Recreations* squash; *Style—* Grahame Stowe, Esq; Woodley Chase, Wigton Lane, Leeds 17; Two Willows, 4 Sandmoor Drive, Leeds LS17 7DG; 7 Portland Street, Leeds LS1 3DR (☎ 0532 468163, fax 0532 426632)

STOWE, Sir Kenneth Ronald; GCB (1986, KCB 1980, CB 1977), CVO (1979); s of Arthur Stowe (d 1965), and Emily Stowe; *b* 17 July 1927; *Educ* Dagenham County HS, Exeter Coll Oxford; *m* 1949, Joan Cullen; 2 s (Timothy, Richard), 1 da (Janet); *Career* formerly: DHSS, UNO, Cabinet Office; princ private sec to PM 1975-79, PUS NI Off 1979-81, perm sec DHSS 1981-87, perm sec Cabinet Office 1987; chm Inst of Cancer Res 1987, memb Pres Mugabe's Cmmn to Review Zimbabwe Pub Serv, dep chm English Estates Corporation, life tstee Carnegie UK Tst; *Clubs* Athenaeum; *Style—* Sir Kenneth Stowe, GCB, CVO; c/o Athenaeum Club, Pall Mall, London SW1

STOWELL, Dr Michael James; s of Albert James Stowell (d 1986), of Cardiff, and Kathleen Maud, *née* Poole; *b* 10 July 1935; *Educ* St Julian's HS Newport Gwent, Univ of Bristol (BSc, PhD); *m* 3 March 1962 (m dis 1990), Rosemay, da of Albert William Allen (d 1962); 1 s (George b 1964), 1 da (Heather b 1966); *Career* res mangr TI Res 1978 (res scientist 1960, gp ldr 1968), princ conslt scientist Alcan International Ltd 1989 (res dir 1990); FInstP 1970, FIM, CEng 1981, FRS 1984; *Recreations* music, amateur operatics; *Style—* Dr Michael Stowell, FRS; Alcan International Limited, Banbury Laboratory, Southam Rd, Banbury Oxon OX16 7SP (☎ 0295 272626, telex 837601, fax 0295 274216)

STRABOLGI, 11 Baron (E 1318); David Montague de Burgh Kenworthy; s of 10 Baron (d 1953), by his 1 w, Doris Whitley (d 1988), da of Sir Frederick Whitley-Thomson, JP, MP; co-heir to Baronies of Cobham and Burgh; *b* 1 Nov 1914; *Educ* Gresham's, Chelsea Sch of Art; 3 previous m; m 4, 1961, Doreen Margaret, er da of late Alexander Morgan, of Ashton-under-Lyme, Lancs; *Heir* bro, Rev the Hon Jonathan Malcolm Kenworthy; *Career* Maj and Actg Lt-Col RAOC WWII, Capt Queen's Bodyguard of Yeomen of the Guard; dep chief Govt whip 1974-79, PPS to Ldr of House of Lords and Lord Privy Seal 1969-70, asst oppn whip House of Lords 1970-74; oppn spokesman on: Energy 1979-83, Arts and Libraries 1979-86; dep speaker House of Lords 1986-; memb Br Section Franco-British Cncl 1981; chm Bolton Building Society 1986-87 (dep chm 1983-86, chm 1986-87); Offr de la Légion d'Honneur 1981; *Style—* The Rt Hon the Lord Strabolgi; House of Lords, London SW1A 0PW

STRACEY, Sir John Simon; 9 Bt (UK 1818), of Rackheath, Norfolk; s of Capt Algernon Augustus Henry Stracey (d 1940), and Olive Beryl Stracey (d 1972); Sir John Stracey, 1 Bt, was a recorder of City of London; suc cous, Sir Michael George Motely Stracey, 8 Bt, 1971; *b* 30 Nov 1938; *Educ* Wellington, McGill Univ Montreal; *m* 1968, Martha Maria, da of Johann Egger (d 1936), of Innsbruck, Austria; 2 da; *Heir* cous, Henry Mounteney Stracey; *Career* conslt and designer; specialised in wine trade; own co Vinexperts-Rackheath Inc; *Recreations* yachting (yacht Miss Muffet); *Clubs* Royal St Lawrence Yacht; *Style—* Sir John Stracey, Bt; 652 Belmont Ave, Montréal, PQ H3Y 2W2, Canada (☎ 514 482 9668)

STRACHAN, Alexander George (Alex); s of George Falconer Strachan, and Christina Murray, *née* Dunn; *b* 18 Aug 1945; *Educ* Broughton Sr HS Edinburgh; *m* 1 April 1967, Mary (May) Ewing Strachan, da of James McKinlay; 1 da (Fiona Mary b 28 Jan 1968); *Career* pres Cwlth Gymnastics Fedn 1982-86; pres: Scottish Amateur Gymnastics Assoc 1982-88 (hon life memb), East of Scotland Gymnastics Assoc 1978-82 and 1988-90 (hon life memb): head of delegation GB team 1985 Mens European Championships; GB Olympic gymnastics team mangr Seoul 1988; memb exec ctee Br Amateur Gymnastics Assoc 1988 (memb board of control 1981); gymnastics Personality of the Year (Scotland) 1988; *Recreations* driving, travel, golf; *Style—* Alex Strachan, Esq; 19 Rankeillor St, Edinburgh EH8 9JA (☎ 031 667 9921); City of Edinburgh District Council, City Chambers, High St, Edinburgh EH8 9JA (☎ 031 551 3664)

STRACHAN, Maj Benjamin Leckie (Ben); CMG (1978); s of Charles Gordon Strachan, MC (d 1957), of Crieff, Perthshire, and Annie Primrose, *née* Leckie (d 1972); *b* 4 Jan 1924; *Educ* Rossall Sch Fleetwood Lancs; *m* 1, 5 Dec 1946 (m dis 1957), Ellen, *née* Braasch; 1 s (Christian b 1949); m 2, 29 Nov 1958, Lize, da of Tage Lund (d 1985), of Copenhagen; 2 s (Robert b 1960, James b 1963); *Career* enlisted 1942, Univ of Durham 1942-43, OCTU Sandhurst 1943-44, 2 Lt Royal Dragoons 1944, Lt serv France and Germany (despatches, wounded, POW) 1944-45, Capt instr OCTU 1946-48, Lt 4 QOH serv Malaya (wounded) 1948-51, Capt MECAS 1951-53, Maj GSO2 (int) HQ BT Egypt 1954-55, Capt Sqdn 2 i/c 4 QOH Germany 1955-56 RMSC Shrivenham 1956-58, Maj Sqdn Ldr 10 Royal Hussars 1958-60, GSO2 (int) WO 1960-61, ret to join HM foreign Serv; FO: first sec Info Res Dept 1961-62, info advsr to Govt of Aden 1962-63, asst head of dept Scientific Relations Dept 1964-66, commercial sec Kuwait 1966-69, cnsllr and charge d'affaires of Amman (Jordan) 1969-71, trade cmmr Toronto 1971-74, consul gen Vancouver 1974-76; HM ambass: Sana'a and Djibouti 1977-78, Beirut 1978-81, Algiers 1981-84; special advsr FCO 1990-; vice chm Banchory Branch LSD; Citoyen D'Honneur Grimaud France 1987; *Recreations* sailing, crofting, writing; *Clubs* Lansdowne; *Style—* Maj Ben Strachan, CMG; Mill of Strachan, Strachan, Banchory, Kincardineshire AB3 3NS (☎ 033 045 663)

STRACHAN, Graham Robert; CBE (1977), DL (Co Dunbartonshire 1979); s of George Strachan (d 1985), of Kenmore, Castlegate, W Chiltington, nr Pulborough, Sussex, and Lily Elizabeth, *née* Ayres; third generation of Clydeside engineers since 1872; *b* 1 Nov 1931; *Educ* Trinity Coll Glenalmond, Trinity Coll Cambridge (MA); *m* 1960, Catherine Nicol Liston, da of John Vivian (d 1978); 2 s; *Career* Nat Serv 1955-57, actg Sub-Lt RNVR Far East and Suez 1963-66; engrg dir John Brown and Company (Clydebank) Ltd 1966-68, dir and gen mangr John Brown Engineering Ltd 1968-84 (md 1968, chm 1983), dir Scott Lithgow Ltd; FEng, FIMechE, FIMarE; *Recreations* skiing, golf; *Clubs* Caledonian, Royal Over-Seas League, Buchanan Castle Golf; *Style—* Graham Strachan, CBE, DL; The Mill House, Milndavie Rd, Strathblane, Stirlinghshire G63 9EP (☎ 0360 70220); Scott Lithgow Ltd, Kingston Yard, Port Glasgow, Renfrewshire PA14 5DR (☎ 0475 42101, telex 77195)

STRACHAN, Ian Charles; s of Dr Charles Strachan, of Wilmslow, Cheshire, and Margaret, *née* Craig; *b* 7 April 1943; *Educ* Fettes, Christ's Coll Cambridge (BA, MA), Princeton Univ (MPA), Harvard Univ; *m* 1, 29 July 1967 (m dis 1987), Diane Shafer, da of Raymond P Shafer, of Washington DC, USA; 1 da (Shona Elizabeth b 15 Feb 1970); m 2, 28 Nov 1987, Margaret, da of Dr Hugh Auchincloss, of New Jersey, USA; *Career* VSO Grand Cayman Island BWI 1961-62, assoc Ford Fndn Malaysia 1967-69, various positions Exxon Corporation 1970-86, fin dir Gen Sekiyu Tokyo Japan 1979-82, chm and chief exec Esso Hong Kong and Esso China 1982-83, corp strategy mangr Exxon Corpn NY 1984-86 , chief fin offr and sr vice pres Johnson and Higgins NY 1986-87, fin dir RTZ Corporation plc London 1987-; *Recreations* tennis, reading, oriental antiques; *Clubs* Harvard (NY), Hong Kong; *Style—* Ian Strachan; RTZ Corporation plc, 6 St James's Square, London SW1Y 4LD (☎ 071 930 2399, fax 071 839 6747, telex 24639)

STRACHAN, James Murray; s of Eric Alexander Howieson Strachan, and Jacqueline Georgina; *b* 10 Nov 1953; *Educ* King's Sch Canterbury, Christ Coll Cambridge (BA); *Career* Chase Manhattan Bank 1976-77, md Merrill Lynch Capital Markets 1986-89 (joined 1977); professional photographer 1989-; *Recreations* squash, opera; *Clubs* United Oxford and Cambridge Univ, Groucho; *Style—* James Strachan, Esq; 10B Wedderburn Rd, Hampstead, London NW3 5QG (☎ 071 794 9687, fax 071 794 4593)

STRACHAN, John; JP (1975); s of John Strachan (d 1950), of Craigewan, Fraserburgh, and Annie Isabella, *née* Sutherland (d 1983); *b* 9 Aug 1929; *Educ* Fraserburgh Acad, Univ of Aberdeen (MA, LLB); *m* 21 March 1957, Margaret Campbell (d 1986), da of William Cheyne (d 1976); 1 s (Neil b 5 Feb 1962), 2 da (Pamela Jane b 16 Feb 1965, Caroline Anne b 11 July 1966); 21 March 1957, Margaret (d 1986), da of William Cheyne (d 1963), of Sheildarroch, Cults, Aberdeen; 1s (Neil b 1962), 2 da (Pamela b 1965, Caroline b 1966); *Career* Sub Lt RNVR 1954-56; advocate in Aberdeen; notary public 1960; sr ptnr: Davidson & Garden 1972-89 (ptnr 1958), Peterkins 1990-; dir: William Wilson Hldgs Ltd 1972-, William McKinnon & Co Ltd 1979-, Hunter Construction (Aberdeen) Ltd 1974- (chm 1987-), Osprey Communications plc 1982-; Hon Col Commonwealth of Kentucky 1971, Hon Citizen Louisvile Kentucky 1972; memb: Law Soc of Scotland 1956, Soc of Advocates in Aberdeen 1956; past pres St Andrew's Soc of Aberdeen; FInstD 1969; *Recreations* shooting, salmon fishing; *Clubs* East India, Royal Northern (Aberdeen); *Style—* John Strachan, Esq, JP; 2 Queen's Rd, Aberdeen Scotland (☎ 0224 644276, tel 313906)

STRACHAN, John Charles Haggart; s of late Charles George Strachan, and Elsie Strachan; *b* 2 Oct 1936; *Educ* Univ of London, St Mary's Hosp (MB BS); *m* Caroline Mary, da of John William Parks, MBE, of London; 1 s (James b 1971), 3 da (Alexandra b 1969, Elisabeth b 1972, Cressida b 1983); *Career* conslt orthopaedic surgn New Charing Cross Hosp 1971; surgn to Royal Ballet 1971; FBOA, FRSM, FRCS (Eng). FRCS (Ed); *Recreations* fishing, sailing, stalking; *Clubs* Royal Thames YC, Royal Southern YC, Flyfishers'; *Style—* John Strachan, Esq; 28 Chalcot Square, London NW1 (☎ 071 586 1278); 126 Harley Street, London W1N 1AH (☎ 071 935 0142)

STRACHAN, (Douglas) Mark Arthur; QC (1987); s of Flt-Lt William Arthur Watkin Strachan, of 51 Blockley Rd, Wembley, Middx, and Joyce, *née* Smith; *b* 25 Sept 1946; *Educ* Orange Hill GS Edgware, St Catherine's Coll Oxford (BCL, MA), Nancy Univ France; *Career* called to the Bar Inner Temple 1969; asst rec 1987; contrib to legal jls: Modern Law Review, New Law Journal, Solicitors Journal; *Recreations* France, food, antiques; *Style—* Mark Strachan, Esq, QC; 38 Bedford Gardens, Kensington, London W8 (☎ 071 727 4729); 1 Crown Office Row, Temple, London EC4 (☎ 071 583 9292)

STRACHAN, Michael Francis; CBE (1980, MBE Mil 1945); s of Francis William Strachan (d 1958), and Violet Maude Blackwell, *née* Palmer (d 1927); *b* 23 Oct 1919; *Educ* Rugby, CCC Cambridge (MA); *m* 9 June 1948, Iris, *née* Hemingway; 2 s (Hew b 1949, Gavin b 1952), 2 da (Harriet b 1955, Lucy b 1958); *Career* Army 1939-46, Lt Col 1945; chm and chief exec: Ben Line Steamers Ltd 1970-82 (ptnr WM Thomson & Co mangrs Ben Line Steamers Ltd 1950-60, jt md dir 1964-70), chm Ben Line Containers Ltd 1970-82; chm Assoc Container Transportation Ltd 1971-75; dir: Bank of Scotland 1973-90, EG Thomson Shipping Ltd 1982-; tstee Nat Galleries of Scotland 1972-74, tstee Nat Library of Scotland 1974-90, tstee and memb Exec Ctee Carnegie Tst for Univs of Scotland; memb Queens Bodyguard for Scotland 1966-; FRSE 1979; *Books* The Life and Adventures of Thomas Coryate (1962), Sir Thomas Roe 1581-1644 A Life (1989); *Recreations* country pursuits, silviculture; *Clubs* New (Edinburgh), Naval & Military; *Style—* Michael Strachan, Esq, CBE

STRACHAN, Walter John; s of Bertram Lionel Strachan, and Edith Annie, *née* Gale; *b* 25 Jan 1903; *Educ* Hymers Coll Hull, St Catharine's Coll Cambridge (MA); *m* 7 Aug 1929, Margaret Jason, da of Dr Thomas Jason Wood; 1 s (Geoffrey b 1935), 1 da (Jean b 1932); *Career* poet, author and translator; head Dept of Modern Languages Bishop's Stortford Coll 1928-68 (2 master 1958-68); lectr: Cambridge Coll of Art & Technol 1974-84, Nat Assoc of Fine & Decorative Arts 1975-; fndr Walter Strachan Art Gallery Bishop's Stortford Coll 1990; Chevalier des Arts et des Lettres 1968, Commandeur des Palmes Académiques 1970; *Books* Moments of Time (poetry, 1947), The Artist and the Book in France (1969), Open Air Sculpture in Britain (1984), Towards the Lost Domain, Henry Moore: Animals (1984), A Relationship with Henry Moore 1942-86 (1988); translations incl works of Herman Hesse (Demian, The Prodigy, Peter Camenzind) and Alan Fournier's Letters (1986); *Recreations* drawings in pen and wash of medieval bridges; *Style—* Walter Strachan, Esq; 10 Pleasant Rd, Bishop's Stortford, Herts (☎ 0279 54493)

STRACHEY, (Sir) Charles; 6 Bt (UK 1801), of Sutton Court, Somerset, but does not use title; s of Rt Hon Evelyn John St Loe Strachey (d 1963), and cous of 2 Baron Strachie (d 1973); *b* 20 June 1934; *Educ* Westminster, Magdalen Coll Oxford; *m* 1973, Janet Megan, da of Alexander Miller; 1 da; *Heir* kinsman, Richard Philip Farquhar Strachey, b 10 Aug 1902; *Career* district dealer, rep mangr Ford Motor Co Ltd 1972-75, local govt offr; *Style—* Charles Strachey, Esq; 31 Northchurch Terrace, London N1 4EB

STRACHEY, Hon Mrs Jane Towneley; *née* Strachey; da of late Hon (Thomas) Anthony Edward Towneley Strachey, by his w Mary Sophia, *see* Lady Mary Gore; sis of 4 Baron O'Hagan; *b* 1953; *m* 1972 (m dis 1977), William Stone; reverted to her maiden name; *Style—* The Hon Jane Strachey; 24 Kylestrome House, Cundy Street, London SW1

STRADBROKE, 6 Earl of (UK 1821); Sir (Robert) Keith Rous; 11 Bt (E 1660); also Viscount Dunwich (UK 1821) and Baron Rous (GB 1796); s of 5 Earl of Stradbroke (d 1983, shortly after his brother, 4 Earl) and (1 w) Pamela Catherine Mabell (who d 1972, having obtained a divorce 1941), da of late Capt the Hon Edward James Kay-Shuttleworth (s of 1 Baron Shuttleworth); *b* 25 March 1937; *Educ* Harrow; *m* 1, 1960 (m dis 1976), Dawn Antoinette, da of Thomas Edward Beverley, of Brisbane; 2 s (Viscount Dunwich b 1961, Hon Wesley Alexander b 1972), 5 da (Lady Ingrid Arnel b 1963, Lady Sophia Rayner b 1964, Lady Heidi Simone b 1966, Lady Pamela Keri b 1968, Lady Brigitte Aylena b 1970); m 2, 1977, Roseanna Mary Blanche, da of Francis Reitman, MD (d 1955), and Susan, née Vernon; 5 s (Hon Hektor Fraser b 1978, Hon Maximilian Otho b 1981, Hon Henham Mowbray b 1983, Hon Winston Walberswick b 1986, Hon Yoxford Ulysses Uluru b 1989), 2 da (Lady Zea Katherina b 1979, Lady Minsmere Mathilda b 1988); *Heir* s, Viscount Dunwich, *qv*; *Career* grazier; dir: Rewitu Pty Ltd, Sutuse Pty Ltd; landowner (10,000 acres); *Recreations* making babies; *Style—* The Rt Hon the Earl of Stradbroke; Mount Fyans, RSD Darlington, Victoria 3271, Australia (☎ 055 901 298, and 055 901 294)

STRADLING, Bernard; MBE (1987); s of William James Stradling (d 1962), of Irlam, Manchester, and Hilda, *née* Williams (d 1986); *b* 18 Feb 1930; *Educ* Urmston GS, Manchester Sch of Librarianship; *m* 1, 30 Sept 1957 (m dis 1979), Jean, da of Charles Hedley Hewinson (d 1977), of Ilfracombe; 1 s (Mark b 1964), 1 da (Susan b 1962); m 2, 18 Dec 1981, Christine Young, da of Rev Thomas William Hopwood (d 1964), of Sunderland; 3 step da (Sarah b 1965, Catherine b 1967, Rachel b 1969); *Career* Nat Serv RAF 1948-50; borough librarian Cheltenham 1968-72, co librarian Gloucestershire

1972-90 (rede signated co library arts and museums offr 1987); vice pres Cheltenham Branch WEA, pres Young Arts Centre Cheltenham; FLA 1966, FRSA 1990; *Recreations* photography, wine tasting; *Style—* Bernard Stradling, Esq, MBE; Beechcroft, Kenelm Drive, Cheltenham, Glos GL53 0JR (☎ 0242 516167)

STRADLING, Donald George; s of George Frederick Stradling, of Somerset, and Olive Emily, *née* Simper; *b* 7 Sept 1929; *Educ* Clifton, Magdalen Coll Oxford (MA); *m* 1955, Mary Anne, da of Oscar Cecil Hartridge (d 1983); 2 da(Annette, Marguerite); *Career* master St Albans Sch 1954-55, gp trg and educn offr John Laing & Son Ltd 1955 (gp personnel dir 1969), cmmr Manpower Servs Cmmn 1980-82, dir Bldg and Civil Engrg Holidays Scheme Mgmnt 1984, vice pres Inst of Personnel Mgmnt 1974-76, visiting prof Univ of Salford 1989, vice chm of govrs St Albans HS 1977; memb Cncl: Inst of Manpower Studies 1975-81, CBI 1982, Tyndale House 1977, Fedn of Civil Engrg Contractors 1956; memb: Fedn of Civil Engrg Contractors Wages and Industl Ctee 1978, Nat Steering Gp New Technical & Vocational Educn Initiative 1983, NHS Trg Authy 1986, CBI Employment Ctee 1987; Liveryman Worshipful Co of Glaziers' and Painters of Glass 1983; Hon DPhil; *Publications* contribs on music and musical instruments to New Bible Dictionary 1962; *Recreations* singing (choral music), listening to music (opera), walking; *Clubs* IOD; *Style—* Donald Stradling, Esq; Courts Edge, 12 The Warren, Harpenden, Herts AL5 2NH (☎ 05827 2744); Page Street, Mill Hill, London NW7 2ER (☎ 081 959 3636, telex 263271)

STRADLING, Prof Richard Anthony; s of Harry Wood Stradling (d 1970), of Soilhull, and Jessie Holroyde (d 1978); *b* 19 April 1937; *Educ* Solihull Sch, BNC Oxford (MA, DPhil); *m* 10 Jan 1975, Pamela Mary; 1 s (James b 1976); *Career* offical student tutor and lectr ChCh Oxford 1968-78, prof natural philosophy and chm physics dept Univ of St Andrews 1978-84, prof of physics Imperial Coll London 1984-, dep dir London Univ Interdisciplinary Res Centre 1989-; FRSE 1981; *Style—* Prof Richard Stradling; Two Trees, Hernes Road, Oxford OX2 7PT (☎ 0865 515601), Blackett Laboratory, Prince Consort Rd, Imperial Coll, London SW7 2BZ (☎ 071 589 5111)

STRADLING THOMAS, Sir John; MP (C) Monmouth 1970-; s of Thomas Roger Thomas, of Carmarthen; *b* 10 June 1925; *Educ* Rugby, Univ of London; *m* 1957 (m dis), Freda Rhys, da of Simon Rhys Evans, of Carmarthen; 1 s, 2 da; *Career* farmer; memb HQ Cncl NFU 1963-70; memb Carmarthen Cncl 1961-64; fought (C) Aberavon 1964 and Cardigan 1966; asst govt whip 1971-73, lord cmmr Treasury (govt whip) 1973-74, oppn whip 1974-79, treas of HM Household and dep chief whip 1979-83, min of State Welsh Office 1983-1985; kt 1985; *Style—* Sir John Stradling Thomas, MP; House of Commons, London SW1

STRAFFORD, 8 Earl of (UK 1847); Thomas Edmund Byng; also Baron Strafford (UK 1835), Viscount Enfield (UK 1847); s of 7 Earl of Strafford (d 1984) and his 1 w, Maria Magdalena Elizabeth, da of late Henry Cloete, CMG, of Alpha, S Africa; *b* 26 Sept 1936; *Educ* Eton, Clare Coll Cambridge; *m* 1, 1963 (m dis), Jennifer Mary Denise (she m, 1982, Christopher Bland), da of late Rt Hon William Morrison May, MP; 2 s (Viscount Enfield, Hon James b 1969), 2 da (Lady Georgia b 1965, Lady Harriet b 1967); m 2, 1981, Mrs Judy (Julia Mary) Howard, yr da of Sir Dennis Pilcher, CBE, *qv*; *Heir* s, Viscount Enfield; *Style—* The Rt Hon the Earl of Strafford; 11 St James Terrace, Winchester, Hants (☎ 0962 53905)

STRAIGHT, Lady Daphne Margarita; *née* Finch Hatton; da of 14 (& 9) Earl of Winchilsea and Nottingham by Margaretta, only surviving da of Anthony Joseph Drexel, s of the Anthony Drexel who founded the banks of Drexel, Morgan & Co, New York, and Drexel, Harjes & Co, Paris, also the Drexel Inst of Art, Science & Industry in Philadelphia with an endowment of two million dollars in 1891; *b* 1913; *m* 1935, Air Cdre Whitney Straight (d 1979, a memb of the celebrated American family of Whitney); 2 da; *Style—* Lady Daphne Straight; 3 Aubrey Rd, W8 7JJ (071 727 7822)

STRAKER, Hon Mrs (Ann Geraldine); *née* Milne; da of 2 Baron Milne; *b* 1946; *Educ* Queens Gate Sch London; *m* 1969, Ian Frederick Lawrence Straker; 1 s (Ross b 1977), 1 da (Frances b 1980); *Career* home and publishing; dir Bishopsgate Press London; Liveryman Worshipful Co of Grocers; *Recreations* tennis, skiing, gardening, art, Birman cats; *Style—* The Hon Mrs Straker; Hever Warren, Hever, Kent

STRAKER, Maj Ivan; s of Maj Arthur Coppin Straker (d 1961), of Pawston, Mindrum, Northumberland, and Cicely Longueville, *née* Hayward-Jones (d 1981); *b* 17 June 1928; *Educ* Harrow; *m* 1954, Gillian Elizabeth, da of Lewis Russell Harley Grant (d 1947); 2 s (Hugo b 1955, Simon b 1957), 1 da (Clare b 1960); m 2, Sally Jane, da of Maj William Hastings of Tod-le-Moor, Whittingham, Northumberland; 1 s (Tom b 1977); *Career* RMA Sandhurst, cmmnd 11 Hussars (PAO) 1948, served Germany, NI, M East and Mil Intelligence Staff WO, ret as Maj 1962; chm and chief exec Seagram Distillers plc 1983-, chm: The Glenlivet Distillers Ltd, Hill Thomson and Co Ltd; dir Lothians Racing Syndicate Ltd 1986-, The Western Meetings Club 1989-; *Recreations* horse racing, shooting, fishing, golf; *Clubs* Cavalry and Guards, Boodle's; *Style—* Maj Ivan Straker; 33 Cluny Drive, Edinburgh EH10 6DT (☎ 031 447 6621)

STRAKER, Karen Elizabeth; da of Hugh Charles Straker, of Gaucin, Spain, and Elaine Felicia, *née* Peat; *b* 17 Sept 1964; *Educ* St Anne's HS Wolsingham, St Godric's Coll Hampstead; *Career* int 3-day-event rider; jr Euro Champion 1982, Most Outstanding Young Rider of the Year 1982, Young Riders Euro Silver medalist 1983, int competition Badminton and Burghley 1984-90, Heineken int champion Punchestown 1988; memb Br Equestrian 3 Day Event team: Seoul Olympics (Silver medallist) 1988, World Championships Stockholm (Silver medallist); 4 Euro Championships Burghley 1989; helper Riding for the Disabled, public speaker, instr and demonstrator; memb Br Horse Soc; *Recreations* swimming, tennis, skiing; *Style—* Miss Karen Straker; Wycliffe Grange, Barnard Castle, Co Durham DU2 9TS (☎ 0833 27500)

STRAKER, Sir Michael Ian Bowstead; CBE (1973), JP (Northumberland 1962); yr and only surv s of Edward Charles Straker (d 1943), of High Warden, Hexham, Northumberland, and Margaret Alice Bridget Straker; *b* 10 March 1928; *Educ* Eton; *Career* Coldstream Gds 1946-49; farmer; former chm Newcastle and Gateshead Water Co; chm: (teaching) Newcastle upon Tyne AHA 1973-81, Aycliffe and Peterlee Devpt Corp 1980-, Northumbrian Water Authy 1980-; High Sheriff of Northumberland 1977; chm: Northern Area Cons Assoc 1969-72, Bd of Port of Tyne Authy; Hon DCL Univ of Newcastle upon Tyne 1987; kt 1984; *Style—* Sir Michael Straker, CBE, JP; High Warden, Hexham, Northumberland

STRAKER, Hon Mrs (Sophie Henrietta); *née* Kimball; da of Baron Kimball (Life Peer); *b* 30 Nov 1960; *m* 1982, Reuben Thomas Coppin Straker, 4 and yst son of Hugh Charles Straker, of Spain; 2 da (Camilla Sophie b 1985, Lucy Charlotte b 1988); *Style—* Hon Mrs Straker; Stonecroft, Fourstones, Hexham, Northumberland

STRAKER, Timothy Derrick; s of Derrick Straker (d 1976), of Bickley, Kent, and Dorothy Elizabeth, *née* Rogers; *b* 25 May 1955; *Educ* Malvern, Downing Coll Cambridge (MA); *m* 17 April 1982, Ann, da of Michael Horton Baylis, of Highgate, London; 2 (Rosemary Elizabeth b 1985, Penelope Anne b 1987); *Career* called to the Bar Gray's Inn 1977, Lincoln's Inn ad eundem 1979, memb Local Govt and Planning Bar Assoc, Admin Law Bar Assoc; *Recreations* cricket, reading; *Style—* Timothy Straker, Esq; 11 Southwood Lawn Rd, Highgate, London N6 5SD (☎ 081 3410413, fax 081 3414158), 8 New Sq, Lincoln's Inn, London WC2A 3GP (☎ 071 242 4986, telex 21785 ADVICE G, fax 071 405 1166)

STRANG, Christopher Forrest; s of John Strang (d 1971); *b* 31 May 1926; *Educ* Glasgow Acad, Univ of Glasgow; *m* 1956, Kathleen Mayfield, *née* Fetherston; 1 s, 2 da; *Career* CA; chm Sequa plc; *Recreations* social charity works, golf; *Style—* Christopher Strang Esq; Lyncourt, 4 Clifton Rd, SW19 (☎ 081 946 5765)

STRANG, 2 Baron (UK 1954); Colin Strang; s of 1 Baron Strang, GCB, GCMG, MBE (d 1978), and Elsie Wynne Jones (d 1974); mother's ancestor, Col John Jones, signed Charles I's death warrant; *b* 12 June 1922; *Educ* Merchant Taylors', St John's Coll Oxford (MA, BPhil); *m* 1, 1948, Patricia Marie, da of Meiert C Avis, of Johannesburg, S Africa; m 2, 1955, Barbara Mary Hope (d 1982), da of Frederick Albert Carr, of Wimbledon; 1 da (Caroline b 1957); m 3, 1984, Mary Shewell, da of Richard Miles, of Thornaby-on-Tees; *Heir* none; *Career* prof of philosophy Univ of Newcastle, ret 1982; *Style—* The Rt Hon the Lord Strang; The Manse, Heptonstall Slack, Hebden Bridge, W Yorks HX7 7EZ

STRANG, Gavin Steel; MP (Lab) Edinburgh E 1970-; s of James Steel Strang, of Perthshire; *b* 10 July 1943; *Educ* Morrison's Acad Crieff, Univ of Edinburgh (PhD), Univ of Cambridge (Dip Agric Sci); married, 1 s; *Career* Parly under sec of state Energy March-Oct 1974, Parly sec Agriculture 1974-79; oppn Front Bench spokesman on: Agriculture 1981-82, Employment 1987-89; former scientist with ARC and memb Tayside Econ Planning Consultative Gp; *Style—* Gavin Strang, Esq, MP; House of Commons, London SW1A 0AA (☎ 071 219 5155)

STRANG, Dr John Stanley; s of William John Strang, CBE, of Castle Coombe, Wilts and Margaret Nicholas Strang; *b* 12 May 1950; *Educ* Bryanston, Guy's Hosp Med Sch Univ of London (MBBS); *m* 21 April 1984, Jennifer, da of Edwin Austin Campbell Abbey (d 1975); 2 s (Samuel John b 1985, Robert Luke b 1988); *Career* regnl conslt in drug dependence Manchester 1982-86, conslt psychiatrist in drug dependence Maudsley, Bethlem Royal Hosp 1986-, conslt advsr on drug dependence to Dept of Health 1986-; former conslt WHO, involvement in various nat and local drug orgns; MRCPsych 1977; *Books* AIDS and Drug Misuse: the challenge for policy and practice in the 1990s (ed with G Stimson, 1990); *Recreations* windsurfing; *Style—* Dr John Strang; Drug Dependence Clinical Research and Treatment Unit, The Maudsley Hosp, Denmark Hill, London SE5 8AZ (☎ 071 777 6611 ext 4118, fax 081 777 1668)

STRANG, Richard William; s of Gordon William Strang, of Lymedale, Milford-on-Sea, Hants, and Elizabeth Piercy, *née* Bernard (d 1981); *b* 19 June 1950; *Educ* Radley, CCC Oxford (MA); *Career* CA with Peat Marwick Mitchell London 1971-78, dir Morgan Grenfell & Co Ltd 1986- (joined 1978), non exec dir Morgan Grenfell Aust (Hldgs) Ltd 1987-; FCA 1974; *Recreations* opera, skiing, sailing, tennis, bridge; *Style—* Richard Strang, Esq; 19 Rosary Gardens, London SW7 (☎ 071 373 445); Morgan Grenfell & Co Limited, 23 Great Winchester Street, London EC2P 2AX (☎ 071 826 6827)

STRANG STEEL, Colin Brodie; yr s of Maj Sir William Strang Steel, 2 Bt, of Philiphaugh, Selkirk, *qv*, and Joan Ella Brodie, *née* Henderson (d 1982); *b* 2 June 1945; *Educ* Eton, RAC Cirencester; *m* 24 Oct 1970, April Eileen, da of Aubrey Fairfax Studd, of Cahoo House, Ramsey, IoM; 3 s (James b 1973, Alistair b 1975, Peter b 1977); *Career* chartered surveyor; ptnr Knight Frank & Rutley 1974-; dir Field & Lawn (Marquees) Ltd 1986-; FRICS; *Recreations* cricket, football, squash, tennis, wildlife; *Clubs* MCC, Scottish Cricket Union, New (Edinburgh); *Style—* Colin Strang Steel, Esq; Newlandburn House, Newlandrig, Gorebridge, Midlothian (☎ 0875 20939); 2 North Charlotte St, Edinburgh EH2 4HR (☎ 031 225 7105, fax 031 220 1403)

STRANG STEEL, Jock Wykeham; s of Sir Samuel Strang Steel, 1 Bt (d 1961), of Selkirk, and Hon Vere Mabel (d 1964), da of 1 Baron Cornwallis; *b* 23 April 1914; *Educ* Eton; *m* 14 Nov 1945, Lesley, da of Lt-Col Sir John Reginald Noble Graham, 3 Bt, VC, OBE (d 1980); 1 s (Malcolm Graham b 1946), 2 da (Celia Jane b 1948, Susan Rachel b 1952); *Career* farmer; *Recreations* cricket, shooting; *Style—* Jock W Strang Steel, Esq; Logie, Kirriemuir, Angus (☎ 0575 72249)

STRANG STEEL, Malcolm Graham; WS (1973); s of Jock Wykeham Strang Steel, of Logie, Kirriemuir, Angus, and Lesley, *née* Graham; *b* 24 Nov 1946; *Educ* Eton, Trinity Coll Cambridge (BA), Univ of Edinburgh (LLB); *m* 21 Oct 1972, Margaret Philippa, da of William Patrick Scott, OBE, TD, DL (d 1989), of Kierfiold, Stromness, Orkney; 1 s (Patrick Reginald b 1975), 1 da (Laura b 1977); *Career* slr 1973-; ptnr W & J Burness WS; sec Standing Cncl of Scot Chiefs 1973-83, memb Cncl Law Soc of Scotland 1984-90, tstee Scot Dyslexia Tst; *Recreations* shooting, fishing, skiing, tennis, reading; *Clubs* New (Edinburgh), MCC; *Style—* Malcolm G Strang Steel, Esq, WS; Barrowmore, Mawcarse, Kinross KY13 7SL (☎ 0577 63225); 16 Hope St, Edinburgh EH2 4DD (☎ 031 226 2561, telex 72405, fax 031 225 3964)

STRANG STEEL, Maj (Fiennes) Michael; DL; s and h of Sir William Strang Steel, 2 Bt, JP, DL; *b* 22 Feb 1943; *m* 1977, Sarah Jane, da of late J A S Russell; 2 s, 1 da; *Career* Maj 17/21 Lancers, ret; *Style—* Maj Michael Strang Steel, DL; Ravensheugh, Selkirk

STRANGE, Lady (16 Holder of Title, E 1628) (Jean) Cherry Drummond of Megginch; sr heir-general of 17 Earl of Oxford, Hereditary Great Chamberlain of England, through his da Lady Elizabeth de Vere, mother of 1 Baron Strange; eldest da of 15 Baron Strange (d 1982), and Violet Margaret Florence (d 1975), o da of Sir Robert William Buchanan-Jardine, 2 Bt; suc as 16 holder of the peerage when the abeyance between her and her two sisters was terminated after petition to HM The Queen 1986; *b* 17 Dec 1928; *Educ* Univ of St Andrews (MA), Univ of Cambridge; *m* 2 June 1952, Capt Humphrey ap Evans, MC, who assumed the name of Drummond of Megginch by decree of Lord Lyon 1966, s of Maj James John Pugh Evans, MBE, MC, JP, DL, of Lovegrove, Aberystwyth; 3 s (Maj Hon Adam Humphrey, Hon Dr Humphrey John Jardine b 11 March 1961, Hon John Humphrey Hugo b 26 June 1966), 3 da (Hon Charlotte Cherry b 14 May 1955, Hon Amélie Margaret Mary b 2 July 1963, Hon Catherine Star Violetta b 15 Dec 1967); *Heir* s, Hon Maj Adam Humphrey Drummond of Megginch b 20 April 1953; *Career* pres War Widows of GB Assoc; *Style—* The Rt Hon Lady Strange; Megginch Castle, Errol, Perthshire; 160 Kennington Rd, London SE11

STRANGE, Eric Dawson; s of Stanley Arthur Strange, (d 1959), and Doris Phoebe, *née* Hewett; *b* 3 June 1943; *Educ* Maldon GS, Regent St Poly Sch of Photography (Coll Dip); *m* 25 Sept 1965, Gillian Georgina, yst da of George Edward Read (d 1971), of Burnham on Crouch, Essex; 2 s (David Stanley b 15 May 1966, Jason Leigh b 4 April 1970); *Career* photographic technician Dynacolour Pty Melbourne Aust 1963, Ilford Ltd Ilford Essex 1964, industl photographer Calor Gas Ltd Slough Berks 1964-68, self employed proprietor Dawson Strange Photography Ltd Cobham Surrey 1968-, fndr md Parasol Portrait Photography Ltd Cobham 1977-; dep chm Photography and Photographic Processing Indust Trg Orgn, govr Felton Fleet Sch Cobham; FBIPP 1965; *Clubs* Stoics Cricket, WestEnd Esher Cricket, Cobham FC (chm); *Style—* Eric Strange; Tilt House Cottage, 28 Stoke Road, Cobham, Surrey KT11 3BD (☎ 0932 863316); Parasol Portrait Photography Ltd, Sperry House, 78 Portsmouth Rd, Cobham, Surrey KT11 1JZ (☎ 0932 866722, fax 0932 868591, car 0831 117755)

STRANGE, Raymond Charles; s of Harry Charles Strange (1974); *b* 4 March 1922; *Educ* Raine's Sch; *m* 1950, Margaret Helen, *née* Gummer; 1 da; *Career* Lt RE; chm: A R Stenhouse and Ptnrs Ltd, Stenhouse Reed Shaw Ltd; dir: Stenhouse Holdings Ltd, Reed Stenhouse Co Ltd (Canada); vice pres Societe Generale de Courtage d'Assurances Paris; *Recreations* golf, fishing; *Clubs* Army and Navy; *Style—* Raymond C Strange, Esq; Shepherds Close, Westingto, Chipping Campden, Glos GL55 6EG (☎

0386 841482)

STRANGE, (Frederick Griffiths) St Clair; s of Dr Charles Frederick Strange (d 1927), of 5 Rosslyn Hill, Hampstead, and Olive Cecilia Harrison (d 1970); *b* 22 July 1911; *Educ* Rugby, Royal London Hosp Med Coll, Univ of London; *m* 17 June 1939, Joyce Elsie, da of A Percy Kimber (d 1944), of South Croxted Rd, Dulwich; 1 s (Richard b 1942), 2 da (Diana b 1941, Angela b 1944); *Career* consltg orthopaedic surgn: Kent & Canterbury and Ramsgate Hosps 1947-48, Canterbury and Thanet HMC (later Dist) Areas 1948-75 (hon 1975-); pres Orthopaedic Section RSM 1965-66 (hon memb 1975-); vice pres: RSM 1965-66, Br Orthopaedic Assoc 1971-72; Hunterian prof RCS 1947, Nuffield travelling fell 1948; hon civilian conslt in orthopaedics to the Army at The Royal Herbert Hosp 1967-76; former pres Combined Servs Orthopaedic Soc; Robert Jones Gold medallist Br Orthopaedic Assoc 1943; FRCS (MRCS), LRCP; *Publications* The Hip (1965), The History of the Royal Sea Bathing Hospital (1991), many contribs to orthopaedic lit; *Recreations* photography, philately, travel; *Style*— F G St Clair Strange, Esq

STRANGE, Prof Susan (Mrs Clifford Selly); da of Lt Col Louis Arbon Strange, DSO, OBE, MC, DFC (d 1966), and Marjorie, *née* Beath (d 1968); *b* 9 June 1923; *Educ* Royal Sch Bath, LSE (BSc); *m* 1 Sept 1945 (m dis 1955), Denis McVicar Merritt, s of Sidney Merritt (d 1967); 1 s (Giles b 20 Nov 1943), 1 da (Jane (Mrs Streatfield) b 5 March 1948); m 2, 14 Dec 1955, Clifford Selly; 3 s (Mark b 28 July 1957, Roger b 21 April 1960, Adam b 22 Oct 1963), 1 da (Kate b 24 Oct 1961); *Career* The Economist 1944-46, Washington and UN corr The Observer 1946-48 (econ corr 1951-57), lectr in int relations UCL 1949-64, res fell RIIA 1965-76, German Marshall Fund fell 1976-78, visiting prof Univ of S California 1978, Montague Burton prof of int relations LSE 1978-88, prof of int relations Euro Univ Inst Florence 1989-; *Books* Sterling and British Policy (1971), International Monetary Relations (1976), The International Politics of Surplus Capacity (co ed with R Tooze, 1981), Paths to International Political Economy (ed, 1984), Casino Capitalism (1986), States and Markets (1988); *Recreations* cooking, gardening, tennis, canoeing; *Style*— Prof Susan Strange; Weedon Hill House, Aylesbury, Bucks HP22 YDP (☎ 0296 27772); European University Institute 50016, S Domenico Di Fiesole (FI), Italy (☎ 010 3955 50921)

STRANGER-JONES, Anthony John; s of Leonard Ivan Stranger-Jones (d 1983), and Iris Christine, *née* Truscott (d 1991); *b* 30 Dec 1944; *Educ* Westminster, Christ Church Oxford (MA); *m* 19 June 1976, Kazumi, da of Kazuo Matsuo, of 4500-97 Fukuma-Machi, Munakata-Gun, Fukuoka Pref 811-32, Japan; 1 s (David b 1983), 2 da (Amiko b 1977, Yukiko b 1980); *Career* md Amex Finance (Hong Kong) Ltd 1974-76; dir: Amex Bank Ltd 1976-79, Korea Merchant Banking Corporation 1979-82, Barclays Merchant Bank Ltd 1979-86, Barclays de Zoete Wedd Ltd 1986-; ACIB 1971; *Clubs* MCC; *Style*— Anthony Stranger-Jones, Esq; 33 Randolph Crescent, London W9 1DP (☎ 071 286 7342); Barclays de Zoete Wedd Ltd, Ebbgate House, 2 Swan Lane, London EC4R 3TS (☎ 071 623 2323, fax 071 623 6075, telex 8950851)

STRANRAER-MULL, Rev Gerald Hugh; s of Capt Gerald Stranraer-Mull (d 1955), and Dolena Mackenzie, *née* Workman (d 1986); *b* 24 Nov 1942; *Educ* Woodhouse Grove Sch, King's Coll London (AKC); *m* 30 Dec 1967, Glynis Mary, da of Capt David Kempe, of Iden Green, Kent; 2 s (Michael Paul b and d 1974, Jamie b 1977), 1 da (Clare b 1970); *Career* journalist 1960-66; curate Hexham Abby 1970-72, Corbridge 1972; rector Ellon and Cruden Bay 1972-, canon Aberdeen Cathedral 1981-, dean of Aberdeen and Orkney 1988-; chm: Ellon Schs Cncl 1982-86, Gordon Health Cncl 1982-86; *Books* A Turbulent House - The Augustinians at Hexham (1970), View of the Diocese of Aberdeen and Orkney (1977); *Style*— The Very Rev the Dean of Aberdeen and Orkney; The Rectory, Ellon, Aberdeenshire AB4 9NP (☎ 0358 20366)

STRATFORD, Dr Martin Gould; VRD (1943); s of late Dr Howard Martin Blenheim Stratford, and late Sybil Kathleen Lucy, *née* Gould; *b* 20 Feb 1908; *Educ* Westminster, UCH (MB BS); *m* 15 Sept 1934, da of late Herbert Muir Beddall; 2 s (Muir b 1936, Neil b 1938); *Career* Surgn Lt Cmdr RNVR, served HMS Hermes and RN Hosp Chatham; former physician Charterhouse Rheumatism Clinic, physician St Luke's Hosp for Clergy; *Recreations* cricket, football, golf; *Clubs* MCC, RSM; *Style*— Dr Martin Stratford; 27 Bryanston Square, London W1H 7LS; 42 Harley Street, London W1M 1AB

STRATFORD, (Howard) Muir; JP (1978); s of Dr Martin Gould Stratford, of London, and Dr Mavis Winifred Muir Stratford; *b* 6 June 1936; *Educ* Marlborough; *m* 8 July 1961, Margaret Reid, da of Robert Linton Roderick Ballantine (d 1957); 1 s (Duncan b 1971), 2 da (Gail b 1964, Fiona b 1967); *Career* insur broker; dir Bowring London Ltd 1980-85 and 1986-, chief exec Bowring M K Ltd 1985-86; dir Watford FC 1971-; *Recreations* golf, watching football and cricket; *Clubs* MCC, Moor Park Golf, City Livery; *Style*— Muir Stratford, Esq, JP; Nobles, Church Lane, Sarratt, Herts (☎ 0923 260475); Bowring London Ltd, The Bowring Building, Tower Place, London EC3 (☎ 071 357 1000, fax 071 929 2705, telex 882191, car ☎ 0836 219412)

STRATFORD, Neil Martin; s of Dr Martin Gould Stratford, of London, and Dr Mavis Winifred Muir Stratford, *née* Beddall; *b* 26 April 1938; *Educ* Marlborough, Magdalene Coll Cambridge (BA, MA), Cortauld Inst (BA); *m* 28 April 1966, Anita Jennifer (Jenny), da of Peter Edwin Lewis (d 1980); 2 da (Jemima b 1968, Rebecca b 1971); *Career* Coldstream Gds 1956-58: 2 Lt 1957-58, Lt 1958; trainee Kleinwort Benson Lonsdale 1961-63, lectr Westfield Coll Univ of London 1969-75, keeper of medieval and later antiquities Br Museum 1975-; Liveryman Worshipful Co of Haberdashers 1959-; Académie de Dijon (hon memb) 1975, Soc Nat des Antiquaires, foreign de France (memb) 1985; FSA 1976; *Books* La Sculpture Dubliée De Vezelay (1984); *Recreations* cricket and football, food and wine, music, particularly opera; *Clubs* Garrick, Beefsteak, MCC, IZ, Cambridge Univ, Pitt Hawks; *Style*— Neil Stratford, Esq; 17 Church Row, London NW3 6UP (☎ 071 794 5688); Keeper of Medieval and Later Antiquities, The British Museum, London WC1B 3DG (☎ 071 323 8217)

STRATHALLAN, Viscount; John Eric Drummond; s and h of 17 Earl of Perth, PC; *b* 7 July 1935; *m* 1, 1963 (m dis 1972), Margaret Ann, da of Robert Gordon; 2 s (Hon James, Hon Robert b 7 May 1967); m 2, 6 Oct 1988, Mrs Marion Elliot; *Heir* s, Hon James Drummond; *Style*— Viscount Strathallan; Stobhall, by Perth

STRATHALMOND, Letitia, Baroness; Letitia; da of late Walter Martin Krementz, of Morristown, New Jersey, USA; *m* 1945, 2 Baron, CMG, OBE, TD (d 1976); 1 s, 2 da; *Style*— The Rt Hon Letitia, Lady Strathalmond; 155 Fawn Lane, Portola Valley, California 94028, USA

STRATHALMOND, 3 Baron (UK 1955); William Roberton Fraser; o s of 2 Baron Strathalmond, CMG, OBE, TD (d 1976), and Letitia, *née* Krementz; *b* 22 July 1947; *Educ* Loretto; *m* 1973, Amanda Rose, da of Rev Gordon Clifford Taylor, of St Giles-in-the-Fields Rectory, Gower St, London; 2 s (Hon William, Hon George b 1979), 1 da (Hon Virginia b 22 Dec 1982); *Heir* s, Hon William Gordon Fraser b 24 Sept 1976; *Career* md London Wall Members Agency Ltd 1986- (formerly Bain Dawes Underwriting Agency), dir London Wall Hldgs plc 1986; MICAS 1972; *Style*— The Rt Hon The Lord Strathalmond; Holt House, Elstead, Godalming, Surrey GU8 6LF

STRATHCARRON, 2 Baron (UK 1936); Sir David William Anthony Blyth Macpherson; 2 Bt (UK 1933); s of 1 Baron, KC, PC (d 1937), and Jill, da of Sir George Wood Rhodes, 1 Bt, JP; *b* 23 Jan 1924; *Educ* Eton, Jesus Coll Cambridge; *m* 1, 1947 (m dis 1947), Valerie Cole; m 2, 1948, Diana Hawtry (d 1973), da of late Cdr R H Deane and formerly w of J N O Curle; 2 s; m 3, 1974, Mary Eve, da of late John Comyn Higgins, CIE, and formerly w of Hon Anthony Gerald Samuel, *qv*; *Heir* s, Hon Ian Macpherson; *Career* formerly Flt Lt RAFVR, motoring correspondent of The Field, ptnr Strathcarron & Co; dir: Kirchoffs (London) Ltd, Seabourne Express Co Ltd, Kent Int Airport Ltd; pres: WELPAC plc Driving Instrs Assoc, Nat Breakdown Recovery Club, Guild of Motor Writers, Vehicle Builders and Repairers Assoc Inst of Road Tport Engineers; chm: The Order of the Road; *Books* Motoring for Pleasure; *Style*— The Rt Hon Lord Strathcarron; 22 Rutland Gate, London SW7 1BB (☎ 071 584 1240); Otterwood, Beaulieu, Hants (☎ 0590 612334)

STRATHCLYDE, 2 Baron (UK 1955); Thomas Galloway Dunlop du Roy de Blicquy Galbraith; er s of Hon Sir Thomas Galbraith, KBE, MP (C & Unionist) Glasgow Hillhead 1948-82 (d 1982), by his w, Simone Clothilde Fernande Marie Ghislaine (eldest da of late Jean du Roy de Blicquy, of Bois d'Hautmont, Brabant), whose marriage with Sir Thomas was dissolved 1974; suc gf, 1 Baron Strathclyde, PC, JP (d 1985); *b* 22 Feb 1960; *Educ* Sussex House London, Wellington Coll, Univ of East Anglia (BA), Univ of Aix-en-Provence; *Career* insurance broker Bain Clarkson Ltd (formerly Bain Dawes) 1982-88; Lord in Waiting (Govt Whip House of Lords) 1988-89; spokesman for DTI: parly under sec of state Dept of Employment and min for Tourism 1989-90, parly under sec of state Dept of the Environment July-Sept 1990, parly under sec of state Scottish Office (min for agric, fish, Highlands and Islands); Cons candidate Euro election Merseyside East 1984; *Style*— The Rt Hon Lord Strathclyde; Old Barskimming, Mauchline, Ayrshire KA5 5HB; 2 Cowley St, London SW1 (☎ 071 219 5353)

STRATHCONA AND MOUNT ROYAL, 4 Baron (UK 1900); Donald Euan Palmer Howard; s of 3 Baron Strathcona and Mount Royal (d 1959), and Hon Diana, *née* Loder (d 1985), da of 1 Baron Wakehurst; *b* 26 Nov 1923; *Educ* Eton, Trinity Coll Cambridge, McGill Univ Montreal; *m* 1, 1954 (m dis 1977), Lady Jane Mary, da of 12 Earl Waldegrave, KG, GCVO, TD (*see* Howard, Lady Jane); 2 s, 4 da; m 2, 1978, Patricia, da of late Harvey Evelyn Thomas and wid of John Middleton; *Heir* s, Hon Donald Howard; *Career* sits as Cons in Lords; late Lt RNVR, vice chm Maritime Tst, pres UK Pilots Assoc and Steamboat Assoc of GB, a Lord in Waiting to HM (Govt Whip) 1973-74, parly under sec of state for RAF 1974, jt dep leader of oppn House of Lords 1976-79, min of state MOD 1979-81; dir: Computing Devices Co Ltd, UK Falklands Island Tst, Warrior Preservation Tst; *Recreations* gardening, sailing; *Clubs* Brooks's, Pratt's, RYS, Air Squadron; *Style*— The Rt Hon The Lord Strathcona and Mount Royal; 16 Henning Street, Battersea, London SW11 (☎ 071 223 4318); House of Lords, London SW1; Kiloran, Isle of Colonsay, Scotland (☎ 095 12 301)

STRATHEDEN AND CAMPBELL, 6 Baron (UK 1836 and 1841 respectively); Donald Campbell; o s of 5 Baron Stratheden and Campbell (d 1987), and Evelyn Mary Austen, *née* Smith (d 1989); *b* 4 April 1934; *Educ* Eton; *m* 8 Nov 1957, Hilary Ann Holland, da of Lt-Col William Derington Turner, of Simonstown, S Africa; 1 s (Hon David Anthony), 3 da (Hon Tania Ann b 19 Sept 1960, Hon Wendy Meriel b 27 Jan 1969, Hon Joyce Margaret b 1971); *Heir* s, Hon David Anthony Campbell, *qv*; *Style*— The Rt Hon the Lord Stratheden and Campbell; Ridgewood, MS 1064, Cooroy, Queensland 4563, Australia

STRATHEDEN AND CAMPBELL, Noël, Baroness; Noël Christabel; da of late Capt Conrad Viner; *m* 1, George Vincent; m 2, 21 Dec 1964, as his 2 w, 4 Baron Stratheden and Campbell, CBE (d 1981); *Style*— The Rt Hon Noël, Lady Stratheden and Campbell; 4 Bannisters Field, Church Road, Newick, East Sussex BN8 4JS

STRATHERN, Prof Andrew Jamieson; s of Robert Stratheren (d 1972), and Mary, *née* Sharp; *b* 19 Jan 1939; *Educ* Colchester Royal GS, Trinity Coll Cambridge (Major Entrance Scholar, BA, MA, PhD); *m* 1, 20 July 1973 (m dis 1986), Ann Marilyn Evans; 2 s (Alan Leiper b 1975, Hugh Thomas b 1975), 1 da (Barbara Helen Mary b 1969); m 2, 12 July 1990, Gabriele, da of Dr Peter Sturzenhofecker of Bad Neustadt an der Saale, Germany; *Career* res fell Trinity Coll Cambrige 1965-68, fell Res Sch of Paufic Studies ANU 1970-72 (res fell 1969-70), prof of social anthropology Univ of Papua New Guinea 1973-76, prof and head of Dept of Anthropology UCL 1976-83, dir Inst of PNG Studies Port Moresby PNG 1981-86, emeritus prof Univ of London 1987-, Andrew W Mellon Distinguished prof of anthropology Univ of Pittsburgh 1987-, memb Cncl RAI 1977-80, vice chm Social Anthropology Ctee SSRC 1979-81 (memb 1977-81); FRAI; memb: Assoc of Social Anthropologists of GB and the Cwlth 1967, Assoc for Social Anthropology in Oceania 1987; PNG 10 Anniversary of Ind Medal 1987; *Books* The Rope of Moka (1971), One Father, One Blood (1972), Self - Decoration in Mt Hagen (jtly 1971), Ongka (1979), Inequality in Highlands New Guinea Societies (ed, 1982), A Line of Power (1984), The Mi-Culture of the Mt Hogen People (co-ed, 1990); *Recreations* travel, poetry; *Style*— Prof Andrew Strathern; 1103 Winterton St, Pittsburgh, PA 15206, USA (☎ 412 441 5778); Department of Anthropology, University of Pittsburgh, Pittsburgh PA 15260, USA (☎ 412 648 7519, fax 412 648 5911)

STRATHMORE AND KINGHORNE, 18 Earl of (S 1606 and 1677) Michael Fergus Bowes Lyon; also Lord Glamis (S 1445), Earl of Kinghorne (S 1606), Lord Glamis, Tannadyce, Sidlaw and Strathdichtie, Viscount Lyon and Earl of Strathmore and Kinghorne by special charter (S 1677), Baron Bowes (UK 1887), Earl of Strathmore and Kinghorne (UK 1937); s of 17 Earl of Strathmore and Kinghorne (d 1987), and Mary Pamela, *née* McCorquodale; *b* 7 June 1957; *Educ* Univ of Aberdeen (B Land Econ); *m* 14 Nov 1984, Isobel Charlotte, da of Capt Anthony Weatherall, of Cowhill, Dumfries; 2 s (Simon Patrick (Lord Glamis) b 1986, Hon John Fergus b 1988); *Heir* s, Lord Glamis; *Career* a Page of Honour to HM Queen Elizabeth the Queen Mother (his great aunt) 1971-73; Capt Scots Gds; a Lord in Waiting 1989-; *Clubs* Turf, Pratt's, Perth; *Style*— The Rt Hon the Earl of Strathmore and Kinghorne; Glamis Castle, Forfar, Angus (☎ 030 784 244)

STRATHNAVER, Lord; Alistair Charles St Clair Sutherland; also Master of Sutherland; s (twin) and h of Countess of Sutherland, *qv*; *b* 7 Jan 1947; *Educ* Eton, Christ Church Oxford (BA); *m* 1, 1968, Eileen Elizabeth, o da of Richard Wheeler Baker, of Princeton, USA; 2 da (Hon Rachel b 1970, Hon Rosemary b 1972); m 2, 1980, Gillian Margaret St Clair, da of Robert Murray, of Gourock, Renfrewshire; 1 s, 1 da (Hon Elizabeth b 1984); *Heir* s, Hon Alexander Charles Robert Sutherland b 1 Oct 1981; *Career* constable Met Police 1969-74, IBM UK Ltd 1975-78, Sutherland Estates 1979-; *Style*— Lord Strathnaver; Sutherland Estates Office, Golspie, Sutherland (☎ 040 83 3268)

STRATHSPEY, 5 Baron (UK 1884); Sir Donald Patrick Trevor Grant of Grant; 17 Bt (NS 1625); 32 Chief of the Clan Grant, recognised in the surname of Grant of Grant by decree of Lord Lyon 1950; s of 4 Baron Strathspey (d 1948); *b* 18 March 1912; *Educ* Stowe, SE Agric Coll; *m* 1, 24 Sept 1938 (m dis 1951), Alice, o da of late Francis Bowe, of NZ; 1 s, 2 da; m 2, 1 Sept 1951, Olive, o da of late Wallace Henry Grant, of Norwich; 1 s, 1 da; *Heir* s, Hon James Grant of Grant; *Career* late Lt-Col Gen List; asst chief land agent Def Land Servs, ret; memb: Standing Cncl Scottish Chiefs, Highland Soc London, Clan Grant Socs in USA, Canada, NZ, Australia; pres Civil Serv Motoring Assoc; FRICS; *Books* A History of Clan Grant (1983); *Recreations* sailing, gardening; *Style*— The Rt Hon The Lord Strathspey; Elms Ride, W Wittering, Sussex

STRATTON, David; s of Lawrence James William Stratton (d 1989), and Muriel Elizabeth, *née* Hunt; *b* 16 May 1947; *Educ* Altrincham GS for Boys, Colwyn Bay GS, Univ of Leeds (LLB); *m* 29 May 1971, Ruth Hazel, da of John Eric Delhanty; 3 s (James Anthony b 1 March 1976, Charles Edward b 21 April 1978, Oliver John b 26 Nov 1979), 3 da (Rachael Joanna b 6 May 1981, Rebecca Alice b 30 March 1987, Jessica Rose b 17 June 1990); *Career* admitted slr 1971; articled clerk to Town Clerk Warrington 1969-71, asst rising to princ asst slr Warrington Borough Cncl 1971-72, gp slr Christian Salvesen Properties Limited 1975-79 (asst gp slr 1972-75), currently head Commercial Property Dept and dep sr ptnr Halliwell Landau Solicitors Manchester (ptnr 1979); *Clubs* St James's, IOD; *Style*— David Stratton, Esq; Halliwell Landau, St James's Court, Brown St, Manchester M2 2JF (☎ 061 835 3003, fax 061 835 2994)

STRATTON, (John) Mark; s of Capt Charles Michael Stratton (d 1991), of Brackley, Northants, and Anne Windsor-Lewis, *née* Drummond (d 1985); *b* 27 April 1931; *Educ* Eton, Univ of Lausanne; *m* 1 June 1961, Diana Miranda, da of Eric Martin Smith, MP (d 1951), of Codicote Lodge, Hitchin, Herts; 2 s (James b 1963, Andrew b 1968), 1 da (Kate b 1965); *Career* Army 1949-51 Capt; md: H E Taylor & Co Ltd 1967, Triconfort Ltd 1970-; *Recreations* shooting, fishing, gardening; *Clubs* Boodles; *Style*— Mark Stratton, Esq; Witton Old Rectory, Norwich, Norfolk NR13 5DS (☎ 0603 712425)

STRATTON, Vernon Gordon-Lennox; s of Undecimus Stratton (d 1929), and Muriel Dorothy Phipps, of Boldre, Hants; *b* 26 Oct 1927; *Educ* Eton; *m* 1952, Penelope Anne, da of Sir Geoffrey Lowles; 3 s (James, Charles, Richard), 1 da (Sarah); *Career* 2 Lt 11 Hussars; advertisement mangr Sunday Times Advertisement 1954-56, retail dir Jaeger 1956-64, chm and md Vernon Stratton Ltd 1964-, chm Wilkins Campbell Ltd 1979-86; chm and mangr RYA Olympic Ctee 1977-80, mangr Olympic Sailing 1968, 1972, 1980, Olympic Team (Finn Class) 1960; *Recreations* sailing, skiing, photography; *Clubs* Royal Thames Yacht, Bembridge Sailing; *Style*— Vernon Stratton, Esq; St Helens Station, IOW PO33 1YF (☎ 0983 872865); 15 Donne Place, London SW3 (☎ 071 584 5284); business: 21 Ives St, London SW3 (☎ 071 584 4211)

STRAUGHAN, Dr John (Kenmore); s of Albert Straughan (d 1975), of Goody Hills, Cumbria, and Mary, *née* Martin (d 1987); *b* 31 Oct 1934; *Educ* Keswick Sch, Univ of Durham (MB BS); *m* 1, 5 Jan 1963 (m dis 1972), (Corol) Felicity, da of Geoffrey Hoyles (d 1965), of Jesmond, Newcastle-upon-Tyne; 1 s (Anthony John b 26 March 1965), 1 da (Justina Jane b 31 Oct 1963); m 2, 27 Aug 1975, Patricia Cunningham, da of Maj (Arthur) Colin Bell (d 1942), of Gosforth, Northumbria; *Career* chief MO: Ever Ready Battery Co 1978-82, Occidental Oil 1982-86; med dir Br Rubber Mfrg Assoc 1986-; memb: Nat Rubber Indust Advsy Ctee, Soc Occupational Medicine 1972, MFOM 1982; *Recreations* fly fishing; *Clubs* Northern Counties; *Style*— Dr John K Straughan; Cleobury Ct, Cleobury North, nr Bridgenorth, Shrops WV16 6QQ (☎ 074 633 420); British Rubber Manufacturers' Assoc Ltd, Health Res Unit, Scala House, Holloway Circus, Birmingham B1 1EQ (☎ 021 643 9269, fax 021 631 3297)

STRAUGHAN, Jonathan Nicholson; s of William Christopher Straughan, and Caroline, *née* Nicholson; *b* 29 Dec 1923; *m* 6 Aug 1955, Elizabeth Ruby, da of William Charlton Mason; 1 s (Brian Jonathan), 1 da (Judith Elizabeth); *Career* served Army WWII; fndr ptnr JN Straughan & Co CAS 1953- (conslt 1988-), ptnr Rainbow Straughan & Elliot CAs Sunderland, ptnr John Alderdice & Son CAs; vice chm NE Bd Bradford & Bingley Bldg Soc, former vice chm Stanley Bldg Soc, chm ERESKO Ltd (fin advsy co), fndr Provincial Ind CA Gp; lay preacher Methodist Church, past pres Rotary Club Chester-le-Street, fndr sec Chester-le-Street CAB, past pres Northern Soc of CAS; memb Worshipful Co of Chartered Accountants; FCA, memb Inst of Taxation; *Recreations* golf, tennis, cricket, badminton; *Clubs* Lansdowne; *Style*— Jonathan Straughan, Esq; J N Straughan & Co, Hadrian House, Front St, Chester-le-Street, Co Durham (☎ 091 388 3186)

STRAUSS, Lt Cdr Derek Ronald; s of Ronald Strauss (d 1990), and Theodora, *née* Instone; *b* 16 May 1939; *Educ* Eton; *m* 26 April 1967, Nicola Mary, da of Gp Capt William Blackwood, OBE, DFC; 2 s (James Digby Ronald b 2 July 1969, Toby Anthony Lavery b 21 Sept 1970); *Career* Lt Cdr RNR; with Brown Bros Harriman New York 1961-62; Strauss Turnbull (now SGST Securities Ltd) 1962-; *Recreations* fishing, shooting, skiing; *Clubs* White's, City of London, Pratt's; *Style*— Lt Cdr Derek Strauss, RNR; Societe Generale Strauss Turnbull Securities, Exchange House, Primrose St, Broadgate, London EC2A 2DD (☎ 071 638 5966, fax 071 588 1437, telex 883201)

STRAUSS, Baron (Life Peer UK 1979), of Vauxhall, in the London Borough of Lambeth; George Russell Strauss; PC (1947); s of Arthur Strauss, MP (d 1920), and Minna, *née* Cohen; *b* 18 July 1901; *Educ* Rugby; *m* 1, 1932, Patricia Frances (d 1987), da of F O'Flynn; 2 s (Hon Roger Anthony b 1934, Hon Brian Timothy b 1935), 1 da (Hon Hilary Jane b 1937); m 2, 11 Aug 1987, Mrs Benita Eleonora Armstrong; *Career* MP (L) Vauxhall Div of Lambeth 1929-31, 1934-50 and 1950-79, pps to Min of Tport 1929-31, parly sec Min of Tport 1945-47, and Min of Supply 1947-51; *Style*— The Rt Hon the Lord Strauss, PC; 1 Palace Green, W8 (☎ 071 937 1630)

STRAW, John Whitaker (Jack); MP (Lab) Blackburn 1979-; s of Walter Straw, and Joan Straw; *b* 3 Aug 1946; *Educ* Brentwood Sch Essex, Univ of Leeds; *m* 1, 1968 (m dis 1978), Anthea Weston; 1 da (decd); m 2, 1978, Alice Elizabeth Perkins; 1 s, 1 da; *Career* called to the Bar Inner Temple 1972; pres NUS 1969-71, memb Islington Cncl 1971-78, dep ldr ILEA 1973-74, memb Lab Nat Exec Sub-Ctee Educn and Science 1970, contested (Lab) Tonbridge and Malling 1974; political advsr: Social Servs sec 1974-76, Environment sec 1976-77, Granada TV (World in Action) 1977-79; oppn front bench spokesman: Treasy and Econ Affrs 1981-83, Environment 1983-87; elected to Shadow Cabinet 1987, shadow educn sec 1987-; visiting fell Nuffield Coll Oxford 1990-; *Style*— Jack Straw, Esq, MP; House of Commons, London SW1A 0AA

STRAWSON, Maj-Gen John Michael; CB (1975), OBE (1964); s of Cyril Walter Strawson (d 1937), of London, and Nellie Dora, *née* Jewell (d 1975); *b* 1 Jan 1921; *Educ* Christs Coll Finchley; *m* 29 Dec 1960, Baroness Wilfried Marie, da of Baron Harold von Schellersheim (d 1986), of Rittergut Eisbergen, Germany; 2 da (Viola b 1961, Carolin b 1963); *Career* cmmnd 1941, 4 Queens Own Hussars 1942; served: Middle East, Italy, Germany, Malaya; Staff Coll Camberley 1950, Bde Maj 1951-52, directing staff Camberley 1958-60 (master of Staff Coll Drag Hounds), GSO1 and Col GS WO (later MOD) 1961-62 and 1965-66, cmd The Queens Royal Irish Hussars 1963-65, cmd 39 Inf Bde 1967-68, Imperial Def Coll 1969; chief of staff: SHAPE 1970-72, HQ UKLF 1972-76; ret 1976; Col The Queens Royal Irish Hussars 1975-85; mil advsr Westland plc 1976-85; chm The Friends of Boyton Church, vice pres The Royal Br Legion (Codford); US Bronze Star 1945; *Books* The Battle for North Africa (1969), Hitler as Military Commander (1971), The Battle for the Ardennes (1972), The Battle for Berlin (1974), El Alamein (1981), A History of the SAS Regiment (1984), The Italian Campaign (1987), The Third World War (jtly, 2 vols 1978 and 1982), Gentlemen in Khaki (1989), Beggars in Red (1991); *Recreations* equitation, shooting, tennis, reading; *Clubs* Cavalry and Guards (chm 1984-87); *Style*— Maj-Gen John Strawson, CB, OBE; The Old Rectory, Boyton, Warminster, Wilts BA12 0SS (☎ 0985 50218)

STRAWSON, Sir Peter Frederick; s of late Cyril Walter and Nellie Dora Strawson; *Educ* Christ's Coll Finchley, St John's Coll Oxford; *m* 1945, Grace Hall Martin; 2 s, 2 da; *Career* Waynflete Prof of metaphysical philosophy Univ of Oxford 1968-87, fell Magdalen Coll; FBA; kt 1977; *Style*— Sir Peter Strawson; 25 Farndon Rd, Oxford

STREATFEILD, Lady Moyra Charlotte; *née* Stopford; BEM (1984); da of 7 Earl of Courtown (d 1957); *b* 7 Sept 1917; *m* 1943, Lt Cdr David Henry Champion Streatfeild, RN, s of Rev Claude Arthur Cecil Streatfeild (d 1951); 3 s (Anthony b 1945, Timothy b 1947, Peter b 1954), 1 da (Mary b 1950); *Style*— The Lady Moyra Streatfeild, BEM; Redberry House, Bierton, Aylesbury, Bucks (☎ 0296 82126)

STREATFEILD-JAMES, Capt RN John Jocelyn; s of Cdr Rev E C Streatfeild-James, OBE, and Elizabeth Ann, *née* Kirby (d 1936); *b* 14 April 1929; *Educ* RNC Dartmouth; *m* 11 Aug 1962, Sally Madeline, da of R D Stewart (d 1970); 3 s (David b 22 Oct 1963, Douglas b 13 June 1967, Dominic b 21 April 1969); *Career* naval cadet 1943-47, midshipman 1947-49, Sub Lt Minesweeping and Diving Anti-Bandit Ops Far East 1949-51, Lt rating trg, qualified in undersea warfare, ship and staff duties Far East Exchange Serv RAN 1952-59, Lt Cdr offr trg, nat and NATO undersea warfare ship and staff appts 1960-67, Cdr Staff Coll (JSSC) NATO and nat appts 1968-73, Capt computer project mgmnt, War Coll 1974-77, Cdre and head Br Def Liaison Staff Canada in cmd HMS Howard 1978-80, Capt HMS Excellent 1981-82; clerk to Bd of Govrs RNS Haslemere; vice chm local political pty; FBIM, MNI; *Recreations* painting, carpentry; *Style*— Capt John Streatfeild-James, RN; South Lodge, Tower Rd, Hindhead, Surrey GU26 6SP (☎ 0428 606064); Royal Naval Sch, Haslemere, Surrey GU27 1HQ (☎ 0428 606636)

STREATHER, Bruce Godfrey; s of William Godfrey Streather, of Lakeside, Little Aston Hall, Staffs, and Pamela Mary, *née* Revell; *b* 3 June 1946; *Educ* Malvern, Univ of Oxford (MA); *m* 15 Dec 1973, Geraldine Susan, da of Colin Herbert Clout, of San Franciso, California, USA; 3 da (Charlotte, Annabel, Miranda); *Career* sr ptnr Streathers; memb Law Soc; *Recreations* family, golf; *Clubs* R & A, Moor Hall Golf, Sunningdale Golf, Vincent's, Little Aston Golf, Littlestone Golf; *Style*— Bruce Streather, Esq; 16 Clifford St, London W1 2AY (☎ 071 734 4363, fax 071 734 7539)

STREATOR, Edward; s of Edward Streator (d 1955), of NY, and Ella, *née* Stout (d 1980); *b* 12 Dec 1930; *m* 16 Feb 1957, Priscilla, da of W John Kenney, of Washington; 1 s (Edward b 1958), 2 da (Elinor b 1960, Abigail b 1965); *Career* Lt (jg) USNR 1952-56; joined Foreign Service 1956, third sec US Embassy Addis Ababa 1958-60, second sec US Embassy Lome 1960-62, Office of Intelligence & Res Dept of State 1962-64, staff asst to Sec of State 1984-66, first sec US Mission to NATO (Paris, Brussels) 1966-69, dep dir rising to dir Office of Nato Affairs Dept of State 1969-75, dep US permanent rep to Nato (Brussels) 1975-77, min US Embassy (London) 1977-84, ambass and US rep OECD (Paris) 1984-87, UK rep The Carlyle Group (Washington DC), chm Int Advsy Bd Ruder-Finn (NY); dir: Del Norte Technology (UK) 1988-, Playhouse Theatre Co (London) 1988-, The South Bank (London) 1988-; govr: Ditchley Fndn (UK) 1980-, RUSI 1988-; British-American Arts Assoc 1989-, ESU 1988-; pres American C of C; memb: Exec Ctee Int Inst Strategic Studies (London) 1988-, Exec Ctee The Pilgrims (London) 1988-, Eisenhower Centenial Ctee (UK) 1989-; *Recreations* swimming; *Clubs* Metropolitan (Washington), Brookes's, Buck's, Beefsteak, Garrick, Mill Reef (Antigua); *Style*— Edward Streator, Esq

STREET, Alan Thomas; s of late Thomas Albert Street; *b* 22 Jan 1928; *Educ* Uddingston and Stockport GS; *m* 1953, Betty Diamond, *née* Shaw; 3 da; *Career* dir: J D Williams Gp 1970, Oxendale & Co Ltd 1968, Heather Valley (Woollens) Ltd 1972, Hilton Mailing Services Ltd 1980; MInstM, MCAM; *Recreations* sailing (yacht Milady of Ollerton), skiing; *Clubs* Royal Welsh Yacht, Manchester Cruising Assoc; *Style*— Alan Street, Esq; Ollerton Hall, Knutsford, Cheshire (☎ 0565 650222); J D Williams Group Ltd, 53 Dale St, Manchester M60 6EU (☎ 061 236 3764, telex 667610 BYPOST)

STREET, Brian Frederick; s of Frederick Street, and Ellen, *née* Hollis; *b* 2 June 1927; *Educ* St Philip's GS Edgbaston, Univ of Birmingham (BSc), Harvard Business Sch (AMP); *m* 1951, Margaret Patricia, da of Alderman John William Carleton, JP (d 1951); 1 s (decd), 5 da (Teresa b 1952, Veronica b 1954, Amanda b 1957, Rebecca b 1959, Francesca b 1965); *Career* chartered engr; chief technologist Shell Chemicals UK Ltd 1964-68, dir BCL Group 1972-75, md Air Prods Ltd 1975-80 (chm 1981-), dir Stearns Catalytic Int 1983-86, chm NMC Mgmnt Conslts 1989-, dir Barnus Ltd 1990-; visiting prof: Dept of Chemical and Process Engrg Univ of Surrey 1985-, Univ of Bath 1988-; pres Instn of Chem Engrs 1983-84; memb: CBI Cncl 1983-, Univ of Surrey Cncl 1985- (vice chm 1988-), Engrg Bd SERC 1985-87; hon sec Process Engrg Gp Fellowship of Engrg; chm CBI SE Regnl Cncl 1987-89; chm NEDC Specialised Organics Sector Gp 1990-; Hon DUniv of Surrey 1988; FEng, FIChemE, CBIM, FRSA; *Recreations* sailing, golf, oil painting; *Style*— Brian Street, Esq; Jubilee House, Square Drive, Kingsley Green, Haslemere, Surrey GU27 3LW (☎ 0428 51726); Air Products plc, Hersham Place, Molesey Rd, Walton on Thames, Surrey KT12 4RZ (☎ 0932 249771)

STREET, David Leonard; s of Frederick Sydney Street, of Crawley, and Mary Winifred, *née* Fox; *b* 30 Nov 1955; *Educ* Thomas Bennett Sch, Clare Coll Cambridge (MA); *Career* slr; branch ptnr Donne Mileham & Haddock 1988- (joined 1982, ptnr 1987); memb: No 2 Regnl Duty Slr Ctee 1986-, Liaison Ctee Croydon Crown Ct 1988, Law Soc 1977; *Recreations* photography, music; *Style*— David Street, Esq; 47 Albany Road, West Green, Crawley, West Sussex (☎ 0293 32759), 38/42 High St, Crawley, West Sussex (☎ 0293 552062, fax 0293 543760, telex 87107)

STREETER, David Thomas; s of Reginald David Streeter (d 1976), of East Grinstead, Sussex, and Dorothy Alice, *née* Fairhurst; *b* 20 May 1937; *Educ* Cranbrook Sch, Queen Mary Coll London (BSc); *m* 1, 9 Sept 1967 (m dis 1979), Althea Elizabeth, da of Andrew Haig, of Waldringfield, Suffolk; 1 s (James b 1970); m 2, 5 Jan 1980, Penelope Sheila Dale, da of Gordon Kippax, of Netherfield, Sussex; 2 da (Katharine b 1981, Olivia b 1987); *Career* Univ of Sussex: lectr in ecology 1965-76, reader in ecology 1976-84, dean Sch of Biological Scis 1984-88, pro vice chllr (sci) 1989-; lectr and broadcaster; memb: Gen Advsy Cncl BBC 1975-80, Cncl Royal Soc for Nature Conservation 1963-83, Advsy Ctee for England Nature Conservancy Cncl 1973-83, Countryside Cmmn 1978-84, SE Regnl Ctee Nat Tst 1989-, dep pres Sussex Wildlife Tst 1981-; FIBiol 1986; *Books* Discovering Hedgerows (with R Richardson, 1982), The Wild Flowers of The British Isles (with I Garrard, 1983); *Recreations* natural history, visiting other people's gardens; *Style*— David Streeter, Esq; The Holt, Sheepsetting Lane, Heathfield, East Sussex TN21 0UY (☎ 04352 2849), The Univ of Sussex, Sussex House, Falmer, Brighton BN1 9RH (☎ 0273 678212, fax 0273 678335, telex UNISEX 887159)

STREETER, His Hon John Stuart; DL (Kent 1986); s of Wilfrid Alberto Streeter (d 1962), of Park St, London, and Margaret Law, *née* Stuart (d 1982); *b* 20 May 1920; *Educ* Sherborne; *m* 4 Feb 1956, (Margaret) Nancy, da of Arthur Maurice Richardson (d 1980), of Nutfield, Surrey; 1 s (Graham), 2 da (Coralie, Jacqueline); *Career* WWII Capt RSF (despatches), Hon Maj ACF 1939-53; called to the Bar Gray's Inn 1947, counsel to PO SE Circuit 1959, treas counsel London Sessions 1961; Kent QS: dep chm 1963, perm 1967, chm 1971; circuit judge 1972-86 (res judge Kent 1972-85), dep circuit judge 1986; chm and tstee Sherborne House Day Centre Bermondsey, pres Old Shirburnian Soc 1990; *Style*— His Hon John Streeter, DL; Playstole, Sissinghurst, Cranbrook, Kent TN17 2JN (☎ 0580 712847); Law Courts, Barker Rd, Maidstone, Kent ME16 8EQ (☎ 0622 54966)

STREETER, Patrick Thomas; s of Thomas Thornton Streeter (d 1960), and Nesta, *née* Mavrojani; *b* 1 Aug 1946; *Educ* Harrow; *m* 28 June 1979, Judith Mary, da of Roland Percy Turk; 2 s (George Roland b 1982, Frederick Leopold b 1987), 1 da (Tania Sarah b 1980); *Career* CA; ptnr Streeter Gomme & Co 1970-89; Parly candidate (Lib) Croydon NW 1974-79; cncllr London Borough of Tower Hamlets 1982-90 (ldr opposition 1984-85); chm Bethnal Green Ctee 1986-88; underwriting memb Lloyd's; antiquarian bookseller 1990-; *Recreations* tennis, skiing, reading; *Clubs* RAC; *Style—* Patrick Streeter, Esq; 1 Waterman's End, Matching, Harlow, Essex CM17 0RQ (☎ 0279 730076)

STREETON, Sir Terence George; KBE (1989, MBE 1969), CMG (1981); s of Alfred Victor Streeton, of Northampton, and Edith, *née* Deiton; *b* 12 Jan 1930; *Educ* Wellingborough GS; *m* 1962, Molly, da of Oliver Garley (d 1967), of Leicester; 2 s (Matthew, Simon), 2 da (Sarah, Catherine); *Career* HM Diplomatic Serv, first sec Bonn 1966, FCO 1970, first sec and head of chancery Bombay 1972, cncllr Brussels 1975, FCO 1979, asst under sec of state 1982, Br High Cmmr to Bangladesh 1983-89, ret; chm Int Soc Serv of GB, advsr APS Ltd Singapore; *Recreations* walking, golf; *Clubs* Oriental; *Style—* Sir Terence Streeton, KBE, CMG; The Langtons, Olney, Bucks MK46 5AE (☎ 0234 711761)

STRETCH, James Lionel; s of Edwin Frederick Stretch; *b* 16 Feb 1935; *Educ* Tottenham GS; *m* 1961, Pamela Helen, *née* Minos; 1 s, 1 da; *Career* md Century Power & Light Ltd 1980-87, dir of oil ops Imperial Continental Gas Assoc 1980-87, asst md Agip (UK) Ltd 1987; FCA; *Recreations* squash, walking; *Clubs* City of London; *Style—* James Stretch, Esq; Clibbons, Bulls Green, Datchworth, Herts; Agip (UK) Ltd, 105 Victoria St, London SW1E 6QU (☎ 071 630 1400, telex 8813547)

STRETT, Martin Gerard; s of (Thomas) Brian Strett, and Frances Coleman; *b* 4 April 1968; *Educ* West Park HS, St Helens, Liverpool Poly; *Career* Rugby Union player Orrell RUFC; clubs: West Park RFC 1986-88, Orrell RUFC 1988-; rep: Lancs U16 (capt) 1983, Lancs U18 Schs 1984-85, North of Eng U18 1984-85 (tour Aust 1985-86), Eng Colts 1986-87, Eng Students 1987-, Lancs 1989-90 (County Champions 1990, tour Zimbabwe 1990), North of Eng 1990-91, Eng B 1990; student Liverpool Poly; *Recreations* golf and sport generally; *Style—* Martin Strett, Esq; Orrell RUFC, Edgehall Rd, Orrell, Wigan WN5 8TL

STRETTON, James; *b* 16 Dec 1943; *Educ* Laxton GS, Dundee, Worcester Coll Oxford (BA); *m* 20 July 1968, Isobel Christine; *née* Robertson; 2 da (Lynne b 1970, Gillian b 1973); *Career* dep md Standard Life Assur Co 1988-; FFA 1970; *Style—* James Stretton, Esq; Standard Life Assurance Company, 3 George St, Edinburgh EH2 2XZ (☎ 031 225 2552, fax 031 220 1534, telex 72539)

STREVENS, Frederick Albert John; s of Frank Strevens (d 1968), of Sussex, and Ruby Louise Eliza, *née* Pointing; *b* 24 Oct 1935; *Educ* Steyning GS, Brighton Tech Coll, Harlow Tech Coll; *m* 3 April 1961, Margaret, da of Sidney Walter Westoby (d 1972), of Hertfordshire; 3 s (Andrew b 1963 (decd), David b 1964, Richard b 1968), 1 da (Elizabeth b 1970 (decd)); *Career* mgmnt servs offr; electrical and industl engr NW Thames RHA and Barnet Health Authy 1983-; dir F A Strevens (Industrial Engineering) Ltd 1972-83; memb Inst of Mgmnt Services; Queen's Scout 1953, memb Scout Movement (Gp Scout Ldr, dist advsr Duke of Edinburgh Award); Benemerenti medal 1986, Medal of Merit for Services to Scouting 1988; Kt of St Columba (Past Grand Kt of Cncl 565 Bishop's Stortford); *Recreations* scouting, sailing, mountaineering, drama, reading, DIY; *Style—* Frederick A J Strevens, Esq; 21 Maze Green Road, Bishop's Stortford, Hertfordshire CM23 2PG (☎ 0279 652999); Barnet Health Authy, Management Services Dept, Napsbury Hospital, London Colney, nr St Albans, Herts AL2 1AA (☎ 0727 23333 ext 2909)

STREVENS, Peter; s of Stanley Dawson Strevens (d 1966), and Dorothy Victoria, *née* Compson (d 1987); *b* 18 April 1938; *Educ* Eltham Coll Mottingham London; *m* April 1969, Janet Hyde, da of Lees Hyde Marland (d 1974); 2 s (Nigel Jeremy b 1971, Timothy Maxwell b 1974); *Career* franchise mangr Hertz Int Ltd NY 1963-67; md: United Serv Tport Co Ltd (Hertz Truck Rental) 1969-72 (operations mangr 1967-69), Chatfields-Martin Walter Ltd 1972-; MInstM, MIMI; *Recreations* tennis, golf, gardening; *Clubs* RAC; *Style—* Peter Strevens, Esq; Chatfields-Martin Walter Ltd, Clough St, Hanley, Stoke-on-Trent ST1 4AR (☎ 0782 202591, fax 0782 202171, telex 36253)

STREVENS, Peter Jeffrey; s of Alfred John Strevens (d 1980), of London, and Lilian Ellen, *née* Wiggins (d 1970); *b* 3 Dec 1945; *Educ* Barnsbury Sch; *m* 27 April 1968, Janet Linda, da of George Daniels (d 1982), of Hereford; 1 s (Richard b 1971), 1 da (Emma b 1970); *Career* CA 1968; ptnr: Sydenham & Co 1974, Hodgson Harris 1980, Hodgson Impey 1985, Kidsons Impey 1990; reader Hereford Diocese; memb: Centre for Mgmnt in Agric, Ramblers Assoc; FCA 1968, ACIArb 1989; *Recreations* hill walking, music, wildlife & conservation; *Style—* Peter Strevens, Esq; 7 Admirals Close, Hereford HR1 1BU (☎ 0432 268 585); Kidsons Impey, Elgar House, Holmer Rd, Hereford HR4 9SF (☎ 0432 352 222, fax 0432 269 367, telex 35850)

STRICK, Robert Charles Gordon; s of Charles Gordon Strick (d 1981), of Guildford, and Doris Gwendoline, *née* Bench (d 1981); *b* 23 March 1931; *Educ* Royal GS Guildford, Sidney Sussex Coll Cambridge (MA); *m* 30 May 1960, Jennifer Mary, da of Alec James Hathway, of Dorchester on Thames; 1 s (Charles), 1 da (Catherine); *Career* 2 Lt RA 1950, Lt RA (TA) 1951-55; admin offr HMOCS 1955, sec Cmmn Natural Resources & Population Trends Fiji 1959-60, sec to Govt Kingdom of Tonga 1961-63, devpt offr and divnl cmmr Fiji 1963-67 (sec for Natural Resources 1967-71), under sec Inst of CAs 1971-72, asst sec gen Royal Inst of Chartered Surveyors 1972-80; govr Queen Mary Coll London 1980- (chm Estates Ctee 1984-); Freeman City of London 1977, former clerk to Worshipful Co of Chartered Surveyors 1977-80, clerk Worshipful Co of Drapers (Freeman 1986, Liveryman 1987); *Recreations* walking, cycling, gardening, DIY; *Style—* Robert Strick, Esq; Drapers Hall, Throgmorton St, London EC2N 2DQ (☎ 071 588 5001)

STRICKLAND, Benjamin Vincent Michael; s of Maj-Gen Eugene Vincent Michael Strickland, CMG, DSO, OBE, MM (d 1982), and Barbara Mary Farquharson Meares, da of Maj Benjamin Lamb and gda of Sir John Lamb; *b* 20 Sept 1939; *Educ* Mayfield Coll, Univ Coll Oxford (MA), Harvard Business Sch (Dip AMP); *m* 1965, Tessa Mary Edwina Grant, da of Rear-Adm John Grant, CB, DSO, of Rivermead Court; 1 s (Benjamin Michael John b 1968), 1 da (Columbine Mary Grizel b 1971); *Career* Lt 17/21 Lancers BAOR 1959-60; jr mangr Price Waterhouse & Co 1963-68, dir corp fin J Henry Schroder Wagg & Co 1974-, chm and chief exec Schroders Australia 1978-82, gp md Schroders plc 1983-; FCA, FRSA; *Recreations* travel, military and general history, shooting, theatre; *Clubs* Boodle's, Hurlingham; *Style—* Benjamin Strickland, Esq; 6 Queen's Elm Square, Chelsea, London SW3 6ED (☎ 071 351 0372); 120 Cheapside, London EC2V 6DS (☎ 071 382 6000)

STRICKLAND, Frank; OBE (1986); s of Robert Strickland (d 1972), of Chorley, Lancashire, and Esther, *née* Jackson (d 1974); *b* 4 Feb 1928; *Educ* Harris Inst Preston; *m* 24 Jan 1953, Marian, da of Horace Holt (d 1953), of Chorley, Lancs; 1 da (Barbara b 1954); *Career* Nat Serv RE 1946-48; asst sec Chorley and Dist Bldg Soc, branch mangr Hastings and Thanet Bldg Soc; sec: Corpn Bldg Soc 1962-69, Sunderland and Shields Bldg Soc 1969-75; dir and chief exec North of Eng Bldg Soc 1975-; pres Sunderland & Dist Centre Chartered Bldg Socs Inst, chm Sunderland & Co Durham Royal Inst for Blind, tstee Hudson Charity; chm Bldg Socs Assoc 1989- (cncl memb 1971-), pres Euro Fedn of Bldg Socs; FCBSI 1973; *Clubs* Royal Over-Seas League, MCC, Sunderland; *Style—* Frank Strickland, Esq, OBE; 383 Sunderland Rd, South Shields, Tyne & Wear NE34 8DG (☎ 091 456 1216); North of England Building Society, Fawcett St, Sunderland SR1 1SA, (☎ 091 514 1431)

STRICKLAND, John; s of Thomas Gill Strickland (d 1951), of Westcott, Lodge Lane, Brompton, Northallerton, and Ellen May, *née* Hodgson (d 1958); *b* 2 July 1927; *Educ* Northallerton GS; *m* 2 April 1955, Alice, da of Robert Vincent Hogg (d 1964), of 59 Ainderby Rd, Romanby, Northallerton; 2 s (Thomas Graham b 1959, Paul Julian b 1961); *Career* chartered surveyor; asst surveyor District Bank Ltd 1955-69, property investmt mangr National Westminster Bank Gp 1969-85; Freeman City of London, Liveryman Worshipful Co of Chartered Surveyors; FRICS, FCIArb, FRVA; *Recreations* beekeeping, gardening; *Style—* John Strickland, Esq; Tamarind, Church Lane, Fylingthorpe, Whitby, Yorks YO22 4PN (☎ 0947 880188)

STRICKLAND, (Peel Richard) Jon; s of Douglas Alfred Peel, of Cheltenham, Glos, and Marjory Olive, *née* Hill; *b* 3 Dec 1952; *Educ* Cheltenham GS; *Career* actor; theatre: Steerpike in Gormenghast (world premiere, nat tour), Jesus in The Passion (Theatre Clwyd), Yossarian in Catch 22 (Euro premiere, nat tour), Norman in The Dresser (Duke's Theatre Lancaster), Beralde in The Hypochondriac (Leicester Haymarket), Ned Weeks in The Normal Heart (Nottingham) 1988, Atticus in To Kill A Mocking Bird (Euro premiere, Contact Theatre Manchester) 1987, Douglas Beechey in Man of the Moment (world premiere, Scarborough) 1988, Panaurov in The Parasol (world premiere, Scarborough) 1988, Benny in June Moon (Br premiere, Scarborough) 1989, Bourdon in Wolf At The Door (Br premiere, Scarborough) 1989, Henry Bell in The Revengers' Comedies (world premiere, Scarborough) 1989, Scrooge in A Christmas Carol (Young Vic) 1989, Fagin in Oliver Twist (world premiere, Bristol Old Vic) 1990, Mr Kipps in The Woman In Black (world premiere, Fortune Theatre) 1990-91; TV: Jarvis in Coronation Street (Granada) 1987, Watson in Diary of Rita Patel (BBC) 1988, Taylor in She's Been Away (BBC) 1988, Desmond in London's Burning (LWT) 1989, Stephenson in This Is David Harper (C4) 1990, Sex Politics and Alan Ayckbourn (Landseer/Omnibus) 1990, Popeye in Gone To The Dogs (Central Films) 1991; BBC Radio: Giles Winterbourne in The Woodlanders, Derek Meadle in Quartermaine's Terms, Mr Venus in Our Mutual Friend, Guthrie in Night and Day, Tom in The Norman Conquests, Elj Nielsen in IL Trovarsi, Ulfheim in When We Dead Awaken; BBC Radio Drama Co 1985-86; *Recreations* writing, tennis; *Style—* Jon Strickland, Esq; c/o Sally Long-Innes, ICM/Duncan Heath Associates, 162 Wardour St, London W1V 3AT (☎ 071 439 1471/2111, fax 071 439 7274)

STRICKLAND-CONSTABLE, Edina, Lady; Countess (Ernestine) Edina; da of late (4) Count von Rex (cr of HRE by Francis I 1764, recognised by Elector Frederick Augustus III of Saxony 1765; the family was from Upper Silesia), former Saxon Min in Vienna; *b* 27 Sept 1905,, Vienna; *m* 1929, Sir Henry Marmaduke Strickland-Constable, 10 Bt (d 1975); *Style—* Edina, Lady Strickland-Constable; Wassand Hall, nr Hull, Yorks

STRICKLAND-CONSTABLE, Frederic; s (by 2 m) and h of Sir Robert Strickland-Constable, 11 Bt; *b* 21 Oct 1943; *Educ* Westminster, CCC Cambridge (BA); *Style—* Frederic Strickland-Constable, Esq; Elm Tree Cottage, Rowdow Lane, Otford Hills, Sevenoaks TN16 6XN

STRICKLAND-CONSTABLE, Sir Robert Frederick; 11 Bt (E 1641), of Boynton, Yorkshire; s of Lt-Col Frederick Charles Strickland-Constable (d 1916) (ggs of 7 Bt), and Margaret (d 1959), da of late Rear-Adm Hon Thomas Pakenham, s of 2 Earl of Longford, KP, and bro of 3 and 4 Earls; suc bro, Sir Henry Marmaduke Strickland-Constable, 10 Bt, 1975; *b* 22 Oct 1903; *Educ* Eton, Magdalen Coll Oxford (MA, DPhil); *m* 1, 1929 (m annulled 1931), Rosalind Mary, da of Arthur Webster; m 2, 1936, Lettice, da of late Maj Frederic Strickland (d 1934), (2 s of 8 Bt), and Mary, da of late Sir John Isaac Thornycroft; 2 s (Frederick b 1944, J R F b 1949), 2 da (Miranda b 1938, Elizabeth b 1940); memb Royal Soc of Chem; *Heir* s, Frederick Strickland-Constable; *Career* Lt Cdr RNVR 1940-44; Imperial Coll London Chem Engrg Dept 1948-71 (reader 1963-71); memb Royal Soc of Chemistry; *Books* Kinetics of Crystallisation (1968), contributed to numerous scientific journals; *Recreations* mountaineering, music; *Style—* Dr Robert Strickland-Constable, Bt; c/o Barclays Bank, The Green, Westerham, Kent

STRICKLAND-EALES, David Ian; s of Harry Eales, of 84 Brockley Crescent, Bleadon Hill, Weston-Super-Mare, Avon, and Edith Emily, *née* Smith; *b* 16 Dec 1948; *Educ* Stratton Sch Beds; *m* 1, 22 May 1971 (m dis 1981); 1 s (Oliver b 1976); m 2, 29 July 1983, Gillian Lesley, da of Ernest Washbourne, of Drummonie, Bowring Rd, Ramsey, IOM; 1 da (Chloe b 1984); *Career* Borg Warner Ltd 1965-70, ICL plc 1970-72, IMC Consultancy Group 1972-74, Ladbroke Gp plc 1974-80, chm Chapter One Group Ltd 1980-; chm Nat Fund raising Convention 1990 1991; memb: Age Concern Jubilee Appeal Mktg Ctee 1991, Cheltenham Everyman Theatre Devpt Bd; ICFM; *Recreations* tennis, shooting, carriage driving, gardening; *Clubs* Naval & Military; *Style—* David Strickland-Eales, Esq; Hillfield House, Eldersfield, Gloucester (☎ 045 284 250); Chapter One Group plc, Green Lane, Tewkesbury, Glos GL20 8EZ (☎ 0684 850 040, fax 0684 850 113)

STRIDE, James Tarver; s of George Tarver Stride, and Ivy May Finch; *b* 18 March 1955; *Educ* Dulwich, LSE (B Econ); *m* 1 June 1985, Alexandra Evelyn, da of Luc Louis Clement Smets; 1 s (Sebastian b 1986); *Career* investment mangr; dep chm Selsdon Gp; dir: Trumab Ltd, Jamavik International Ltd; cncllr Buckinghamshire CC 1985-; govr of five schs; author political pamphlets; *Recreations* bridge, gardening; *Clubs* Old Alleynian, Peel; *Style—* James T Stride, Esq; 98 High Street South, Stewkley, nr Leighton Buzzard, Bedfordshire LU7 0HR; 107 Cheapside, London EC2V 6DU (☎ 071 606 7788)

STRIDE, Hon Mrs (Mary Pleasant Lowry); *née* Lamb; 2 da of 1 Baron Rochester, CMG, JP (d 1955), and Rosa Dorothea (d 1979), yr da of late William John Hurst, JP, CC, of Drumaness, Co Down; *b* 13 Oct 1919; *m* 4 Sept 1941, Rev Desmond William Adair Stride (chaplain Heathfield Sch 1967-80, ret), er s of late Cdr Desmond Adair Stride, RN; *Career* LRAM 1939; *Style—* The Hon Mrs Stride; 5 Oakmede Way, Ringmer, Lewes, East Sussex BN8 5JL (☎ 0273 813561)

STRIDE, Hon Mrs (Susan); *née* Macdonald; da of 2 Baron Macdonald of Gwaenysgor; *b* 1947; *m* 1968 (sep 1983), David Hensley Adair Stride; 1 s, 1 da (decd); *Career* fndr and dir Charlwood House Public Relations; *Style—* The Hon Mrs Stride; 73 Swinburne Rd, London SW15

STRIGNER, Andrew Ernest; s of Andrew Strigner (d 1952), and Olimpia Tasselli (d 1964); *b* 5 June 1921; *Educ* St Aloysius Coll Highgate, Guy's Hosp (MB BS), Royal London Homoeopathic Hosp (MFHom); *m* 15 April 1950, Constance, da of George Hackett, submariner (ka 1940); 2 s (Andrew b 1951, Peter b 1952), 1 da (Miriam b 1953); *Career* Army Serv Capt and Flt Cdr Air Ops, RA Europe and India 1941-46; Royal London Homoeopathic Hosp: lectr materia medica, asst physician Paediatric and Cardiological Depts, now physician specialist in hypnosis, nutrition and homoeopathy; cncl memb Inst for the Study and Treatment of Delinquency, chm (now vice pres) The McCarrison Soc for the study of the relationship between nutrition and health; *Clubs* RSM; *Style—* Andrew Strigner, Esq; 17 Harley St, London W1N 1DA (☎ 071 935 4543)

STRINGER, Donald Arthur; OBE (1975); s of Harry William George (d 1963), and Ellen Emily Isted (d 1983); *b* 15 June 1922; *Educ* Bordon GS Sittingbourne Kent; *m* 1945, Hazel, da of William Handley (d 1964); 1 s (David), 1 da (Christine); *Career* Col Engr and Tport Corps RE (TA) 1974; memb Nat Dock Labour Bd 1972-85, chm Nat Assoc of Port Employers 1981-85, dep chm and jt md Assoc British Ports 1985; *Clubs* Army & Navy, Royal Southampton Yacht; *Style*— Donald Stringer, Esq, OBE; Hillcrest, Pinehurst Rd, Bassett, Southampton (☎ 0703 768887)

STRINGER, Frederick Charles; s of late John Stringer; *b* 24 June 1904; *Educ* Taunton Sch; *m* 1, 1931, Elsie, *née* Warrington; 1 s; m 2, 1973, Joan, *née* Trigg; *Career* chm Wadham Stringer Ltd 1969-; fell Inst of Motor Indust 1928-; *Recreations* fishing, swimming, bridge; *Clubs* Royal Naval (Portsmouth); *Style*— Frederick Stringer, Esq; Meonpool, Tanfield Park, Wickham, Hants (☎ 0329 833115)

STRIPLING, William Henry; s of Anthony Edwin (d 1975), of Green Tye, Herts, and Maud Jane, *née* Walsby (d 1974); *b* 31 Aug 1930; *Educ* Penzance Co Sch, Chingford Co HS; *m* 15 June 1957, Doreen, da of William Raymond Duce (d 1982); 3 da (Beverley Ann (Mrs Binney) b 1958, Jacqueline Mary (Mrs Smith) b 1960, Stephanie Jane b 1964); *Career* RAF 1950-52; elected memb: East Herts Dist Cncl (chm 1975-78), Sawbridgeworth Town Cncl (Mayor 1979 and 1990); *Recreations* golf, travel; *Style*— William Stripling, Esq; 19 Hoestock Rd, Sawbridgeworth, Herts CM21 ODZ (☎ 0279 722395); Marshgate Drive, Hertford SG13 7JY (☎ 0992 589491)

STROBEL, Dr Stephan; s of Dr Theodor Martin Maria (d 1983), and Dr Margund Johanna Katharina Strobel, *née* Schroeder (d 1985); *b* 9 Oct 1947; *Educ* Univ of Frankfurt (MD), Univ of Edinburgh (PhD); *m* 29 May 1971, Margarite Magdalena, da of Lotar Neumann, of Chateu de Gingins, Switzerland; 2 s (Patrick b 11 Apr 1975, Chrstian b 16 Sept 1976); *Career* Inst of Child Health London: lectr in paediatrics 1985, sr lectr 1987, hon conslt 1987; assoc prof in peadiatrics Frankfurt 1988- (sr lectr 1984-); author of numerous pubns on related topics; Adalbert von Czerny German Paediatric Assoc 1984; *Recreations* foreign travel, bluewater sailing and racing; *Style*— Dr Stephan Strobel; Dept of Immunology, Institute of Child Health, 30 Guildford St, London WC1N 1EH (☎ 071 2429789)

STROLOGO, Eric Reginald Charles Alexander; s of Lt-Col Reginald Charles Strologo, OBE (d 1958), and Xenia (d 1936), da of Gen Alexander Spiridovitch, Chief of Russian Imperial Gd and sometime Govr of the Crimea; *b* 4 Aug 1920; *Educ* Wellington, RMA Woolwich; *m* 22 July 1946, Marianne Elizabeth, da of Dr Jan Savicki (d 1940), of Czechoslovakia; 1 s (Mark b 1951), 1 da (Jacqueline b 1947); *Career* regular offr RA 1939-58; served: Middle East, 8 Army, RHA, Staff Coll, Europe, Gen Montgomery's HQ 21 Army Gp, ret as Maj; dir Royal Automobile Club 1958-82, special conslt Fédération Internationale de L'automobile Paris 1982-; inventor and patentee of the Carbridge temporary flyover; creator and chm Worldwide Information Service (WISE) Data-Base (the world's first int tourism data-base); hon citizen of New Orleans USA 1972, hon memb Le Jurat de St Emilion France 1973; *Recreations* golf, antiques, travel, architectural and artistic heritage, private pilot's licence; *Clubs* RAC; *Style*— Eric Strologo, Esq; Ravenswood, Mayes Green, Ockley, Surrey RH5 5PN (☎ 0306 70227); Riocaud, Ste Foy-la-Grande, Gironde 33220, France (☎ 57412305); Electronic Mailbox, Microlink, MAG 10066

STRONACH, Prof David Brian; OBE (1975); s of Ian David Stronach (d 1955), of Newstead Abbey Notts, and Marjorie Jessie Duncan, *née* Minto; *b* 10 June 1931; *Educ* Gordonstoun, St John's Coll Cambridge (MA); *m* 30 June 1966, Ruth Vaadia; 2 da (Keren b 1967, Tami b 1972); *Career* Nat Serv Lieut 1 Bn Duke of Wellington's Regt 1950-51; Br Acad archaeological attach'e Iran 1960-61, dir Br Inst of Persian Studies 1961-80, prof of Near Eastern archaeology Univ of Calif Berkeley 1981-, curator Near Eastern archaeology Lowie Museum of Anthropology Univ of Calif Berkeley 1983-; fell: Br Sch of Archaeology in Iraq 1957-59, Br Inst of Archaeology 1958-59; lectureships incl: Hagop Kevorkian visiting lectr in Iranian art and archaeology Univ of Pennsylvania 1967, Rhind lectr Univ of Edinburgh 1973, Charles Eliot Norton lectr American Inst of Archaeology 1980, visiting prof of archaeology and Iranian studies Univ of Arizona 1980-81, Columbia lectr in Iranian studies Columbia Univ 1986, Charles K Wilkinson lectr Metropolitan Museum of Art NY 1990, Victor M Leventritt lectr in art history Harvard Univ 1991; dir of excavations at: Ras al 'Amiya Iraq 1960, Yarim Tepe Iran 1960-62, Pasargadae Iran 1961-63, Tepe Nush-i Jan Iran 1967-78, Shahr-i Quimis/Hecatompylos Iran 1967-78, Nineveh Iraq 1987-90; advsy ed: Iran 1975-, The Jl of Mithraic Studies 1976-79, Iranica Antiqua 1985-, Bulletin of the Asia Institute 1987-, American Journal of Archaeology 1989-; *awards* Ghirshman prize of Acad des Inscriptions et Belles Lettres Paris 1979, Sir Percy Sykes medal Royal Soc for Asian Affrs 1980; corr memb German Archaeological Inst 1966-73; fell: German Archaeological Inst 1973-, Explorers Club NY 1980-, first hon vice pres Br Inst of Persian Studies 1981-, assoc memb Royal Belgian Acad 1988-; FSA 1963; *Books* Pasargadae A Report On The Excavations Conducted By The British institute of Persian Studies from 1961 to 1963 (1978); *Recreations* tribal carpets; *Clubs* Hawks (Cambridge), Explorers (NY); *Style*— Prof David Stronach, OBE, FSA; Department of Near Eastern Studies, University of California, Berkeley, Calif 94720, USA (☎ 415 642 3757)

STRONG, Air Cdre David Malcolm; CB (1964), AFC (1941); s of Theophilus Edgar Strong (d 1952), of Llanishen, Glam, and Margaret, *née* McGregor (d 1955); *b* 30 Sept 1913; *Educ* Cardiff HS; *m* 29 March 1941, Daphne Irene, da of Frederick Arthur Brown (d 1922), of Dover Ct; 2 s (Simon David McGregor b 3 March 1946, Christopher Richard b 14 Aug 1947), 1 da (Carolyn Irene Jane b 7 July 1949); *Career* under trg as pilot 1936, No 166 (B) Sqdn 1936-39, No 10 Operation Trg Unit Abingdon 1940-41, No 104 (B) Sqdn 1941 (POW Germany 1941-45), Co No 5 Air Nav Sch Jurby 1945-46, Co No 10 Air Nav Sch Driffield 1946-47, Air Miny P Staff 1947-48, RAF Staff Coll Bracknell (psa) 1948-49, Air HQ Rhodesian Air Trg Gp 1949-51, directing staff RAF Staff Coll 1952-55, Flying Coll Manby 1956, Co RAF Coningsby 1957-58, Air Miny D of P (A) 1959-61, SASO RAF Germany 1961-63, Cmdt RAF Halton 1963-66; chm RAF RFU 1954-55, chm RAF Golf Soc 1962-63; *Recreations* golf, walking; *Clubs* RAF, Ashridge GC; *Style*— Air Cdre David Strong, CB, AFC; Old Coach House, Wendover, Bucks HP22 6EB (☎ 0296 624 724)

STRONG, John Clifford; CBE (1980); s of Clifford Maurice Strong (d 1967); *b* 14 Jan 1922; *Educ* Beckenham GS, Univ of London; *m* 1942, Janet Doris, *née* Browning; 3 da; *Career* Lt RNVR; HMOCS Tanzania 1946-63, Cwlth Rels Off 1963, first sec Nairobi 1964-68, FCO 1968-73, cnsllr and head Chancery Dar-es-Salaam 1973-78, govr Turks and Caicos Islands 1978-82; *Clubs* Royal Overseas League; *Style*— John Strong, Esq, CBE

STRONG, Michael John; s of Frank James Strong (d 1987), and Ivy Rose, *née* Fruin (d 1964); *b* 27 Dec 1947; *Educ* Rutlish Sch Merton, Coll of Estate Mgmnt; *m* 25 April 1970, Anne Mary, da of Rev William Hurst Nightingale, of Wimbledon, London; 1 s (Jonathan Alexander b 1977); *Career* chartered surveyor, ptnr Richard Ellis; Freeman: City of London 1981, Worshipful Co of Plumbers 1982; FRICS; memb: Royal Acad, Royal Hort Soc; *Recreations* golf, tennis, music, travel, gardens; *Style*— Michael Strong, Esq; The Coolins, Manor House Lane, Little Bookham, Surrey (☎ 0372 52 196); La Borna, Satuna, Begur, Spain; Richard Ellis, Berkeley Square House, Berkeley Square, London W1 (☎ 071 629 6290, fax 071 493 3734)

STRONG, Richard James; s of John Paterson Strong, OBE, of Tilford, Tilbrook, Huntingdon, and Margaret St Claire, *née* Ford (d 1981); *b* 5 July 1936; *Educ* Sherborne, Nat Leather Sellers Coll; *m* 1 May 1963, Camilla Lucretia, da of Maj William Walter Dowding (d 1981); 1 s (James b 30 May 1977), 3 da (Melissa b 30 Dec 1965, Amanda b 13 Nov 1968, Samantha b 28 March 1972); *Career* Nat Serv cmmnd 10 Royal Hussars (PWO); Tanner Strong & Fisher Ltd 1960, md Strong & Fisher (Holdings) plc 1972; govr Bilton Grange Sch Tst, memb E Midlands Industl Cncl; hon treas Oakley Hunt, memb Bletsoe Church PCC; Liveryman Worshipful Co of Grocers; *Recreations* fox hunting, farming, sailing, tennis; *Clubs* Cavalry, Royal Thames Yacht; *Style*— Richard Strong, Esq; Bletsoe Castle, Bletsoe, Beds MK44 1QE; Strong & Fisher (Holdings) plc, 100 Irchester Rd, Rushden, Northants NN10 9XQ (☎ 0933 410 300, fax 0933 410800, telex 31522 AQATAN)

STRONG, Richard Martin; s of Theodore Martin William Strong (d 1978), and Alice Louisa Jean, *née* Spearman, of 8 Woodside Rd, Burton Joyce, Nottingham; the Strongs were originally Sjogrens from Sweden; name changed by Deed Poll on naturalisation in New Zealand 1900; *b* 3 Oct 1929; *Educ* Bedford Sch, Trinity Coll Cambridge (MA); *m* 1, 1956, Ann Georgina; 1 s (Simon Alexander b 1959); m 2, 1971, Venetia Mary, da of Ian Thomson Henderson, CBE (d 1987), of Pond House, Crawley, nr Winchester, Hants; 2 step da; *Career* Nat Serv 2 Lt, Capt TA; CA 1955; dir: Rees Group Ltd 1961-, SEMA Group plc 1977-, RH Group Ltd 1977-, March Med plc 1989-, Resort Hotels plc 1984-, ROCC Corporation Ltd (and subsids) 1984-, Crawford Services Ltd 1985-, County Resort Hotel plc 1987, County Resort Hotels plc 1988; *Recreations* golf, photography, bird watching, walking; *Clubs* Royal Wimbledon Golf; *Style*— Richard Strong, Esq; 25 Newstead Way, Somerset Rd, London SW19 5HR (☎ 081 946 0285)

STRONG, Sir Roy Colin; s of G E C Strong; *b* 23 Aug 1935; *Educ* Edmonton Co GS, Queen Mary Coll London (fell 1975), Warburg Inst (PhD); *m* 1971, Julia Trevelyan Oman, *qv*; *Career* writer and historian, critic (radio, TV and lectures Eng and America); asst keeper Nat Portrait Gallery 1959 (dir, keeper and sec 1967-73); dir (and sec) V & A 1974-87, Ferens prof of fine art Univ of Hull 1972, Walls lectures Pierpont Morgan Library 1974, Shakespeare Prize FVS Fndn Hamburg 1980, vice chm South Bank Bd 1986-90; memb: Arts Cncl of GB 1983-87 (chm Arts Panel), former memb Br Cncl Fine Arts Advsy Ctee, Craft Advsy Cncl, RCA Cncl, Br Film Inst Archive Advsy Ctee, Westminster Abbey Architectural Panel, Historic Bldgs Cncl Historic Houses Ctee; former tstee: Arundel Castle, Chevening; Hon DLitt: Leeds 1983, Keele 1984; sr fell RCA 1983; FSA; kt 1981; *Publications* Portraits of Queen Elizabeth I (1963), Leicester's Triumph (with J A van Dorsten, 1964), Holbein and Henry VIII (1967), Tudor and Jacobean Portraits (1969), The English Icon: Elizabethan and Jacobean Portraiture (1969), Elizabeth R (with Julia Trevelyan Oman, 1971), Van Dyck - Charles I on Horseback (1972), Mary Queen of Scots (with Julia Trevelyan Oman, 1972), Inigo Jones - The Theatre of the Stuart Court (with Stephen Orgel, 1973), Splendour at Court - Renaissance Spectacle and Illusion (1973), An Early Victorian Album; The Hill/Adamson Collection (with Colin Ford 1974), Nicholas Hilliard (1975), The Cult of Elizabeth: Elizabethan Portraiture and Pageantry (1977), And When Did You Last See Your Father? The Victorian Painter and the British Past (1978), The Renaissance Garden in England (1979), Britannia Triumphans: Inigo Jones, Rubens and Whitehall Palace (1980), The English Year (with Julia Trevelyan Oman, 1982), The English Renaissance Miniature (1983); *contrib* Designing for the Dancer (1981), The English Miniature (1981), The New Pelican Guide to English Literature (1982), Artists of the Tudor Court (catalogue 1983), Art and Power (1984), Glyndebourne - A Celebration (1984), Strong Points (1985), Henry Prince of Wales (1986), For Veronica Wedgewood These (1986), Creating Small Gardens (1986), Gloriana (1987), A Small Garden Designer's Handbook (1987), Cecil Beaton The Royal Portraits (1988), Creating Small Formal Gardens, British Theatre Arts Design (1989) Lost Treasures of Briatain (1990), England and the Contiential Renaissance (1990), Sir Philip Sidney's Achievement (1990); *Recreations* gardening, weight training; *Clubs* Garrick, Beefsteak, Arts; *Style*— Sir Roy Strong, FSA; 3cc Morpeth Terrace, London SW1P 1EW

STRONGE, Christopher James; s of late Reginald Herbert James Stronge, and late Doreen Marjorie Stronge; *b* 16 Aug 1933; *Educ* Chigwell Sch, Magdalene Coll Cambridge (MA); *m* 1964, Gabrielle; 1 s (Andrew b 3 Feb 1967), 1 da (Philippa b 9 June 1965); *Career* Deloitte Haskins & Sells: joined 1957, ptnr 1967, dep sr ptnr 1985-90; ptnr (after merger) Coopers and Lybrand Deloitte 1990-; memb: Accounting Standards Ctee 1980-83, Bd Int Accounting Standards Ctee 1986-90; hon treas RIIA 1981-; ACA 1960; *Recreations* sailing, opera, music generally; *Style*— Christopher Stronge, Esq; Coopers & Lybrand Deloitte, 128 Queen Victoria St, London EC4P 4JX (☎ 071 454 8049, 071 583 5000, fax 071 248 3623)

STRONGE, Sir James Anselan Maxwell; 10 Bt (UK 1803), of Tynan, Co Armagh; s of late Maxwell Du Pre James Stronge, and 2 cousin of Capt Sir James Matthew Stronge, 9 Bt (assas 1981); *b* 17 July 1946; *Educ* privately; *Style*— Sir James Stronge, Bt; c/o Helen Allen-Morgan, Manor South, Bishopstone, Sussex BN25 2UD

STROUD, Ven Ernest Charles Frederick; s of Charles Henry Stroud (d 1975), of Bristol, and Irene Doris, *née* Venn (d 1975); *b* 20 May 1931; *Educ* Merrywood GS Bristol, Merchant Venturers Tech Coll, Univ of Durham (BA, Dip Theol), Luton Industl Coll (Dip); *m* 15 Aug 1959, Jeanne Marquerite, da of Alfred Henry Evans (d 1966), of Bristol; 2 da (Teresa b 1961, Bridget b 1963); *Career* ordained: deacon 1960, priest 1961; curate All Saints S Kirkby Pontefract 1960-63, priest i/c St Ninian Whitby 1963-66; incumbent of: All Saints Chelmsford 1966-75, St Margaret Leigh on Sea 1975-83; rural dean Hadleigh 1979-83, hon canon Chelmsford 1982-83, archdeacon of Colchester 1983-; proctor Gen Synod 1980-; chm: Additional Curates Soc, Church Union; memb: C of E Pensions Bd, Essex CC Libraries and Museums Ctee; *Recreations* travel, theatre, gardening; *Style*— The Ven the Archdeacon of Colchester; Archdeacon's House, 63 Powers Hall End, Witham, Essex CM8 1NH (☎ 0376 513 130)

STROUD, Roy Vivian; OBE (1982), JP (Bradford 1972), DL (W Yorks 1983); *Career* chm Stroud Riley Drummond Group Ltd, and various related cos; dir Commerical Union (Bradford Bd); *Style*— Roy V Stroud, Esq, OBE, JP, DL; Ryden House, Esholt Avenue, Guiseley, W Yorks LS20 8AX (☎ 0943 73020)

STROVER, Richard Guy (Dick); *b* 3 July 1941; *Educ* Dragon Sch Oxford, Marlborough; *m* Collette Mary; 1 da (Sara Louise); *Career* articled clerk RF Fraser & Co 1960-65; Harmood Banner & Co 1965-74, Deloitte Haskins & Sells (following merger) 1974-, Coopers & Lybrand Deloitte (following merger); pres Croydon Dist Soc of Chartered Accountants 1990-91; FCA (ACA 1965), MBCS; *Recreations* squash, tennis, sailing, golf, bridge; *Clubs* RAC; *Style*— Dick Strover, Esq; Coopers & Lybrand Deloitte, Melrose House, 42 Dingwall Rd, Croydon CR0 2NE (☎ 081 681 5252, fax 081 760 0897)

STROWGER, Clive; s of Gaston Jack Strowger, OBE, and Kathleen, *née* Gilbert; *b* 4 July 1941; *Educ* Uiv Coll Sch Hampstead London NW3; *m* 23 Jan 1965, Deirdre Majorie, da of Col Bertram Stuart Trevelyan Archer, GC, OBE; 3 s (Timothy b 26 Aug 1968, Andrew b 18 Dec 1969, Stephen b 29 Sept 1980), 1 da (Louise b 2 June 1975); *Career* various managerial positions Ford Motor Coi 1966-71, sr fin mgmnt positions then fin dir BL Int Bl 1971-77; Grand Metropolitan 1977-; md brewing, chief exec consumer sens, chm and chief exec foods, gp fin dir and chief exec retail and property; exec memb Food and Drink Fedn Cncl, companion Br Inst, of Mgmnt; Freeman Worshipful Co of Brewers; FCA 1965, ATII 1965, CBIM 1990; *Recreations* choral singing, family, tennis, skiing; *Style—* Clive Strowger, Esq; Highveld, The Ridge, Woldingham, Surrey CR3 7AX (☎ 088365 2400); c/o Mountleigh Group plc, 49 Grosvenor St, London W1X 9FH (☎ 071 493 5555, fax 071 409 1706)

STROYAN, His Hon Judge (Ronald) Angus Ropner; QC (1972); s of Ronald Strathearn Stroyan (d 1957), of Boreland, and Mary Enid, *née* Ropner (d 1985); *b* 27 Nov 1924; *Educ* Harrow, Trinity Coll Cambridge (BA); *m* 1, 2 June 1952(m dis 1965), Elisabeth Anna, da of Col J P Grant, MC (d 1964), of Rothiemurchus; 2 da (Victoria b 1953, Julia b 1958), 1 s (John b 1955); m 2, 22 Sept 1967, Jill Annette Johnston, da of Sir Douglas Marshall, of Hatt House, Saltash; 1 s (Mark b 1969), 2 step s (Robert b 1952, William b 1963), 2 step da (Lucy b 1954, Henrietta b 1959); *Career* Nat Serv Black Watch (RHR) NW Europe 1943-45, attached Argyll and Sutherland Highlanders Palestine 1945-47, Capt (despatches), serv TA; called to the Bar Inner Temple 1950; dep chm N Riding of Yorks QS 1962-70, chm 1970-71, rec Crown Ct 1972-75; memb Gen Cncl of Bar 1963-67, 1969-73 and 1975; circuit judge 1975-; *Recreations* shooting, fishing, stalking; *Clubs* Caledonian, Yorkshire (York); *Style—* His Hon Judge Stroyan, QC; Boreland, Killin, Perthshire (☎ 05672 252); Chapel Cottage, Whashton, Richmond, North Yorks

STRUTT, Clifford Robert; s of Robert Henry Joslin Strutt (d 1975), of London, and Millicent May, *née* Reynolds (d 1942); *b* 29 Dec 1911; *Educ* Colfe's GS London, Univ of London, Leathersellers Coll London, City and Guilds of London Inst; *m* 13 July 1937, (Mary) Josephine, da of Alexander Heskin, of Lismore, Co Waterford, Ireland; 1 da (Ann Josephine b 1 July 1938); *Career* Dickens Leather Co Ltd: mangr 1936-42, dir 1942-46, jt md 1946-48; chm Carr Tanning Co Ltd 1960- (md 1948-60); assoc Leathersellers Coll 1931; memb: Cncl Br Leather Fedn 1970, Pelman Inst 1942; underwriting memb Lloyd's 1976; FInstD 1963, FBIM 1968, FFA 1988, life memb Soc of Leather Technologists and Chemists 1980; *Style—* Clifford Strutt, Esq; Carr Tanning Co Ltd, Woodchester, Stroud, Glos (☎ 045387 2252, fax 045387 2799, car 0836 597830, telex 43230)

STRUTT, Hon Guy Robert; s of 4 Baron Rayleigh, FRS, JP, DL, by his 2 w, Kathleen, OBE; *b* 16 April 1921; *Educ* Eton, Trinity Coll Cambridge; *Style—* The Hon Guy Strutt; The Old Rectory, Terling, Chelmsford, Essex

STRUTT, Hon Hedley Vicars; s of 4 Baron Rayleigh, by his 1 w, Lady Hilda Mary Clements, da of 4 Earl of Leitrim; *b* 19 Feb 1915; *Educ* Eton, Trinity Coll Cambridge; *Career* Capt Scots Gds (ret), served WWII; *Clubs* Brooks's; *Style—* The Hon Hedley Strutt; Mulroy, Co Donegal, Ireland

STRUTT, Hon Mrs Charles; Hon Jean Elizabeth; *née* Davidson; yr da of 1 Viscount Davidson, GCVO, CH, CB, PC; *b* 19 June 1924; *m* 17 Dec 1952, Hon Charles Richard Strutt (d 1981), s of late 4 Baron Rayleigh; 1 s (6 Baron Rayleigh, *qv*), 2 da (Anne Caroline (Hon Mrs Bernard Jenkin) b 1955, Mary Jean (Mrs Rory Fraser) b 1957); *Career* late Capt WRAC (TA); *Style—* The Hon Mrs Charles Strutt; Berwick Place, Hatfield Peverel, Chelmsford, Essex CM3 2EY (☎ 0245 380321)

STRUTT, Sir Nigel Edward; TD, DL (Essex 1954); s of Edward Jolliffe Strutt (d 1964); *b* 18 Jan 1916; *Educ* Winchester, Wye Agric Coll; *Career* Essex Yeo (Maj) 1937-56, served WWII Capt 104 Essex Yeo RHA (TA) ME 1939-45; former chm and md Strutt & Parker (Farms) Ltd, md Lord Rayleigh's Farms Inc, memb Eastern Electricity Bd 1964-76, chm Advsy Cncl for Agric and Hort 1973-80; pres CLA 1967-69; fell Wye Agric Coll 1970; High Sheriff of Essex 1966; fell Wye Agric Coll 1970; Hon FRASE 1971 (pres 1983); Master Worshipful Co of Farmers 1976; Johann Heinrich von Thunen Gold medal (Univ of Kiel) 1974, Massey-Ferguson Nat award for Servs to UK Agric 1976; Hon DSc Cranfield 1979, Hon DUniv Essex 1981; kt 1972; *Recreations* shooting, skiing; *Clubs* Brooks's, Farmers'; *Style—* Sir Nigel Strutt, TD, DL; Sparrows, Terling, Chelmsford, Essex (☎ 024 533 213); office: Whitelands, Hatfield Peverel, Chelmsford, Essex (☎ 0245 380372)

STRUTT, Hon Peter Algernon; MC, DL; s of late 3 Baron Belper by his 2 w; *b* 1924; *Educ* Eton; *m* 1953, Gay Margaret, da of late Sir (Frank Guy) Clavering Fison, of Crepping Hall, Sutton, Suffolk; 2 s, 2 da; *Career* serv WWII Lt Coldstream Gds; chm Tollemache & Cobbold Brewery Ltd; dir Britannia Building Soc; *Style—* The Hon Peter Strutt, MC, DL; Tollemache & Cobbold Breweries, PO Box 5, Cliff Brewery, Ipswich, Suffolk IP3 0AZ (☎ 0473 56751, telex 987994 Barjon G); The Garden House, Sutton, Ipswich

STRUTT, Hon Richard Henry; s and h of 4 Baron Belper, *qv*; *b* 24 Oct 1941; *Educ* Harrow; *m* 1, 1966 (m dis), Jennifer Vivian, *née* Winser; 1 s, 1 da; m 2, 1980, Mrs Judith Mary de Jonge, da of James Twynam; *Style—* The Hon Richard Strutt; Slaughter Farm, Bourton-on-the-Water, Glos

STRUTT, Hon (Desmond) Rupert; s of late 3 Baron Belper by his 2 w; *b* 1926; *Educ* Eton; *m* 1, 1951 (m dis 1961), Jean Felicity (d 1984), da of Hon Francis Walter Erskine; 2 s; m 2, 1964, Lucy Gwendolen, da of Maj James William Stirling Home Drummond Moray, Scots Gds, of Abercairny, Crieff, Perthshire; 2 s; *Style—* The Hon Rupert Strutt; Rockleys, Goldhanger, Maldon, Essex

STUART; *see*: Burnett-Stuart

STUART, Hon Mrs (Alicia St George); *née* Caulfeild; da of late 12 Visc Charlemont; *b* 1918; *Educ* St George's Sch Montreux Switzerland; *m* 1939, Gp Capt Gordon Hackworth Stuart, MD, RAF; 1 s (Colin Gordon Cameron b 1940); *Recreations* books, theatre, travel; *Style—* The Hon Mrs Stuart; 3 Lovel Hill, Windsor Forest, Berks

STUART, Andrew Christopher; CMG (1979), CPM (1961); s of Rt Rev Cyril Stuart, Bishop of Uganda, (d 1981); and Mary, *née* Summerhayes, OBE; *b* 30 Nov 1928; *Educ* Bryanston, Clare Coll Cambridge (MA); *m* 18 July 1959, Patricia Moira, da of Robert Douglas Kelly (d 1953), of Uganda; 2 s (James b 11 March 1962, Charles b 17 May 1967), 1 da (Fiona Mary (Mrs Farrelly) b 12 Nov 1960); *Career* called to the Bar Middle Temple; HMOCS Uganda 1952-64 (ret judicial advsr); FCO: head of Chancery Helsinki 1968-71, asst S Asian Dept 1971-72, cncllr and head of Dept Hong Kong and India Ocean Dept 1972-75, head of Chancery Jakarta 1975-78, Br resident cmmr New Hebrides 1978-80, HM ambass Finland 1980-83; princ Utd World Coll of the Atlantic 1983-90, conslt VSO 1990-; pres Anglo-Finnish Soc; Order of the Lion of Finland; *Recreations* sailing, gliding, moutaineering; *Clubs* Utd Oxford and Cambridge Univ, Alpine, Jesters; *Style—* Andrew Stuart, Esq, CMG, CPM; 34 Queensgate Terrace, London SW7 5PH (☎ 071 589 7769)

STUART, Viscount; Andrew Richard Charles Stuart; s and h of 8 Earl Castle Stewart; *b* 7 Oct 1953; *Educ* Millfield, Bicton Agric Coll; *m* 1973, Annie Yvette, da of Robert le Poulain, of Paris; 1 da (Hon Celia b 1976); *Career* farmer; *Recreations* flying; *Style—* Viscount Stuart; Combehayes Farm, Buckerell, Honiton, Devon (☎ 0404 850345)

STUART, Lady Arabella; *née* Stuart; da of 18 Earl of Moray (d 1943); *b* 11 July 1934; *m* 1956 (m dis), (Charles) Mark Edward Boxer (Marc the cartoonist, d 1988); 1 s, 1 da; *Career* author, professional name Arabella Boxer; fndr memb Guild of Food Writers; Glenfiddich Food Writer of the Year 1975 and 1977; *Books* First Slice Your Cookbook, Arabella Boxer's Garden Cookbook, Mediterranean Cookbook, The Sunday Times Complete Cookbook; *Style—* The Lady Arabella Stuart; 44 Elm Park Rd, London SW3 6AX

STUART, Hon Charles Rodney Stanford; s of 19 Earl of Moray (d 1974); *b* 1933; *Educ* Stowe, McGill Univ Montreal; *m* 1, 1961 (m dis 1987), Sasha A, da of Lt-Col R G Lewis, of Stow on the Wold; 3 s; m 2, 1987, Frauke Norman, da of Hans Stender, of Marne, Schleswig Holstein; *Career* late 2 Lt The Queen's Bays; *Style—* The Hon Charles Stuart

STUART, Charles Rowell; s of Charles Rowell Stuart, MBE (d 1957); *b* 20 May 1928; *Educ* St Olave's and St Saviours GS, LSE (BScEcon); *m* 1951, Anne Grace, da of Rayond Plimsoll Mingo, of Sidbury, Devon (d 1971); 1 s (Duncan), 2 da (Sheridan, Lindsey b 1962); *Career* serv as Lt in HM Armed Forces in Europe; head of commercial devpt Br Airways; dir; Cyprus Airways Ltd, Br Airtours Ltd, BA Assoc Co Ltd, BA Helicopters Ltd, IAL Ltd; FRAeS, FCIT; *Recreations* marathon running; *Clubs* Oriental, RAC, Rd Runner Clubs of UK and New York, Ranelagh; *Style—* Charles Stuart Esq; Hawthorn Hill Cottage, Warfield, Bracknell, Berks (☎ 03447 2362)

STUART, Cristina Mary; da of Javier Jesus (d 1985), and Eileen Gertrude, *née* Dunn; *b* 11 Aug 1941; *Educ* St Francis Coll Letchworth, Sorbonne, Univ of Barcelona; *m* 1 May 1965, John Arthur Stuart, s of Oscar John Stuart (d 1966); 1 s (John Frederick Douglas b 1966); *Career* md and fndr Speakeasy Trg Ltd; memb: Network, Int Trg in Communications, Inst of Trg and Devpt, Assoc of Mgmnt and Educn Devpt; *Books* Effective Speaking (1988), Video The Complete Presenter (1990); *Recreations* avoiding chocolate; *Style—* Mrs Cristina Stuart; Speakeasy Training Ltd, 17 Clifton Rd, London N3 2AS

STUART, Hon (James) Dominic; s (by 1 m) and h of 2 Viscount Stuart of Findhorn; *b* 25 March 1948; *Educ* Eton, Thames Poly (Dip in Estate Mgmnt); *m* 1979, Yvonne Lucienne, da of Edgar Després, of Ottawa; *Career* business conslt and cnsllr; ARICS; *Recreations* metaphysics, psychology, walking; *Style—* The Hon Dominic Stuart; 15 Stowe Rd, London W12

STUART, Duncan; CMG (1989); s of Ian Cameron Stuart (d 1987), of Burton in Kendal, Lancs, and Patricia Forbes, *née* Hardy (d 1988); *b* 1 July 1934; *Educ* Rugby, BNC Oxford (classical scholar, MA); *m* 29 July 1961, Leonore Luise, da of Dr Carl Liederwald (d 1976), of Berlin; 1 s (James Alexander Cameron b 1965), 1 da (Arabella Mary b 1963); *Career* Nat Serv 2 Lt 1 Bn Oxfordshire and Buckinghamshire LI, served BAOR and Cyprus; joined HM Foreign later Dip Serv 1959, Office of Political Advsr Berlin 1960-61; FO 1961-64, second sec Helsinki 1964-66, head Chancery Dar-es-Salaam 1966-69, FCO 1969-70, first sec Helsinki 1970-74, FCO 1974-80, cnsllr Bonn 1980-83, FCO 1983-86, cnsllr Washington 1986-88, FCO 1989-; *Clubs* Boodle's, United Oxford and Cambridge Univ, MCC; *Style—* Duncan Stuart, Esq, CMG; c/o Foreign & Commonwealth Office, King Charles St, London SW1A 2AH

STUART, Hon James Wallace Wilson; twin s of 19 Earl of Moray (d 1974), of Darnaway Castle, Forres, Moray, and Mable Nelson Maude (d 1969); *b* 30 May 1933; *Educ* Stowe, McGill Univ Montreal; *m* 1958, Jane-Scott, da of Gp Capt Henry Gordon Richards, of Louisville, Kentucky, USA; 1 da (Elizabeth, b 1967); *Career* late 2 Lt, 13/18 Hussars; co dir; *Clubs* Atlantic Cavalry (Montreal), Highland Inverness; *Style—* The Hon James Stuart; Dunphail, Moray IV36 0QG (☎ 030 96 237)

STUART, Hon John Douglas; s of 1 Viscount Stuart of Findhorn, CH, MVO, MC (d 1970) and Lady Rachel, *née* Cavendish (d 1977), da of 9 Duke of Devonshire; *b* 11 June 1925; *Educ* RNC Dartmouth; *m* 1, 1957 (m dis 1958), Mrs Cecile Margaret Tonge, da of G H Barr; m 2, 1969 (m dis 1972), Lady Caroline, *née* Child-Villiers, da of 9 Earl of Jersey and formerly w of Gilbert Edward George Lariston, Viscount Melgund, MBE, now 6 Earl of Minto, *qv*; *Career* Lt RN (ret); *Recreations* golf; *Clubs* White's; *Style—* The Hon John Stuart; 57 Shawfield St, SW3 (☎ 071 351 3000)

STUART, Sir (James) Keith; s of James and Marjorie Stuart; *b* 4 March 1940; *Educ* King George V Sch Southport, Gonville and Caius Coll Cambridge (MA); *m* 1966, Kathleen Anne Pinder, *née* Woodman; 3 s, 1 da; *Career* dist mangr S Western Electricity Bd 1970-72; sec British Transport Docks Bd 1972-75, gen mangr 1976-77, md 1977-82, dep chm 1980-82, chm 1982-83; chm Associated British Ports Holdings plc 1983-; dir Int Assoc of Ports and Harbours 1983, vice pres 1985-87; chm Ctee on Int Port Devpt 1979-85; pres Inst of Freight Forwarders 1983-84; dir: Royal Ordnance Factories 1983-85, BAA plc 1986-; memb Cncl Chartered Inst of Transport 1979-88 (vice pres 1982-83, pres 1985-86); Liveryman Worshipful Co of Clockmakers 1987; FCIT, CBIM, FRSA; kt 1986; *Recreations* music; *Clubs* Brooks's, United Oxford and Cambridge Univ; *Style—* Sir Keith Stuart; Associated British Ports Holdings plc, 150 Holborn, London EC1N 2LR

STUART, Prof Sir Kenneth Lamonte; *b* 16 June 1920; *Educ* Harrison Coll Barbados, McGill Univ Montreal (BA), Queen's Univ Belfast (MB, BCh, BAO); *m* 1958, Barbara Cecille; 1 s, 2 da; *Career* Univ of the WI: dean of Med Faculty 1969-71, head Dept of Med 1972-76; med advsr Cwlth Secretariat 1976-85; chm Ct of Govrs LSHTM 1983; conslt advsr The Wellcome Tst 1984-; memb Bd of Govrs Int Devpt Res Centre of Canada 1985; Hon DSc and Gresham prof of physics Gresham Coll London (MD) 1988-; FRCP, FRCPE, FACP, DTM&H; kt 1977; *Recreations* tennis; *Clubs* St Georges Hill Tennis, Royal Cwlth Soc, RSM; *Style—* Prof Sir Kenneth Stuart; 3 The Garth, Cobham, Surrey (☎ 0932 863826)

STUART, (Charles) Murray; s of Charles Maitland Stuart (d 1984), and Grace Forrester, *née* Kerr (d 1990); *Educ* Glasgow Acad, Univ of Glasgow (MA, LLB); *m* 10 April 1963, Netta Caroline, da of Robert Thomson (d 1981); 1 s (David Charles Thomson b 19 Oct 1970), 1 da (Caroline Alison b 29 Dec 1972); *Career* CA 1961, internal auditor and analyst Ford Motor Company 1962-65, fin dir and sec Sheffield Twist Drill & Steel 1965-69, fin dir and asst md Unicorn Industries Ltd 1969-73, fin dir Hepworth Limited 1973-74, dep md ICL plc 1977-81 (fin dir 1974-77); MB Group plc (formerly Metal Box plc): fin dir 1981-83, dir fin planning and admin 1983-86, gp md 1986-87, gp chief exec 1988-89, chm 1989-90; dir and chief fin offr Berisford International plc 1990-; non-exec dir Scottish Power plc; dep chm Audit Cmmn; memb W Surrey and N E Hants Health Authy; memb Law Soc Scotland 1957; FCT 1984, CBIM 1986, FRSA 1988; *Recreations* sailing, tennis, theatre, ballet; *Style—* Murray Stuart, Esq; Longacre, Guildford Road, Chobham, Woking, Surrey GU24 8EA; Berisford International plc, Berisford Wing, 1 Prescot St, London E1 8AY (☎ 071 481 9144, fax 071 481 8357)

STUART, Nicholas Willoughby; CB (1990); s of Douglas Willoughby Stuart, of Gt Henny, nr Sudbury, Suffolk, and Margaret Eileen, *née* Holms; *b* 2 Oct 1942; *Educ* Harrow, Christ Church Oxford (MA); *m* 1, July 1963 (m dis 1974), Sarah, *née* Mustard; 1 s (Sebastian b 26 Dec 1963, d 8 Dec 1976), 1 da (Henrietta b 21 March 1965); m 2, 29 Dec 1975, Susan Jane, *née* Fletcher; 1 s (Alexander b 1 Feb 1989), 1 da (Emily b 12 Sept 1983); *Career* asst princ DES 1964-68, private sec to Min of Arts 1968-69, princ DES 1969-73; private sec to: Head Civil Serv 1973, PM 1973-76; asst sec DES 1976-79, memb Cabinet of Pres of Euro Cmmn 1979-81, under sec DES 1981-87 (dep sec 1987-); *Style—* Nicholas Stuart, Esq, CB; Dept of Education and Science, Elizabeth House, York Rd, London SE1 (☎ 071 934 9955)

STUART, Sir Phillip Luttrell Stuart; 9 Bt (E 1660), of Hartley Mauduit, Hants; s of late Luttrell Hamilton Stuart and nephew of 8 Bt (d 1959); *b* 7 Sept 1937; *m* 1, 1962

(m dis 1968), Marlene Rose, da of Otto Muth; 2 da; m 2, 1969, Beverley Claire Pieri; 1 s, 1 da; *Heir* s, Geoffrey Phillip Stuart, b 5 July 1973; *Career* Flying Offr RCAF 1957-62; pres Agassiz Industs Ltd; *Style—* Sir Phillip Stuart, Bt; 101-575 East Fifth Street, Vancuver, BC, Canada, V5T1H8

STUART, Lady Sarah Gray; 2 da of 18 Earl of Moray, MC (d 1943); *b* 23 Sept 1928; *m* 9 Aug 1947 (m dis 1977), 4 Baron Hillingdon (d 1978); 1 s (decd 1977), 3 da; *Style—* The Lady Sarah Stuart

STUART, Hon Simon Walter Erskine; s of late 7 Earl Castle Stewart; *b* 22 Aug 1930; *Educ* Eton, Trinity Coll Cambridge; *m* 1973, Deborah Jane, *née* Mounsey; 3 s (Thomas b 1974, Corin b 1975, Tristram b 1977); *Career* former 2 Lt Scots Gds, serv Malaya 1949-50; asst english master Haberdashers' Aske's Sch 1961-78 (formerly King's Canterbury and Stowe); writer 1978-, lectr; *Clubs* Beafsteak; *Style—* The Hon Simon Stuart; 16 Neville Drive, London N2 (☎ 081 458 4149); Windyridge, Wych Cross, Forest Row, Sussex (☎ 034 282 2333)

STUART-FORBES, Sir Charles Edward; 12 Bt (NS 1626), of Pitsligo and Monymusk; s of late Sir Charles Hay Hepburn Stuart-Forbes, 10 Bt; suc bro, Sir Hugh Stuart-Forbes, 11 Bt (d 1937); *b* 6 Aug 1903; *Educ* Ocean Bay Coll; *m* 1966, Ijah Leah MacCabe (d 1974), of Wellington, NZ; *Heir* kinsman, William Daniel Stuart-Forbes; *Career* former co mangr building indust; *Style—* Sir Charles Stuart-Forbes, Bt; 33 Dillons Point Rd, Blenheim, S Island, NZ

STUART-FORBES, William Daniel; s of late William Kenneth Stuart-Forbes, 3 s of 10 Bt; hp of kinsman, Sir Charles Stuart-Forbes, 12 Bt; *b* 21 Aug 1935; *m* 1956, Jannette, da of Hori Toki George MacDonald; 3 s (Kenneth Charles b 26 Dec 1956, Daniel Dawson b 1 April 1962, Reginald MacDonald b 3 Oct 1964), 2 da (Catherine Florence b 1958, Eileen Jane b 1960); *Style—* William Stuart-Forbes, Esq; Omaka Valley, Marlborough, NZ

STUART-HARRIS, Sir Charles Herbert; CBE (1961); s of late Dr Charles Herbert Harris; *b* 12 July 1909; *Educ* King Edward's HS Birmingham, Bart's (MD); *m* 1937, Marjorie Robinson; 2 s (Graham b 1952, Robin b 1951), 1 da (Susan b 1946); *Career* physician Utd Sheffield Hosps 1946-72; Univ of Sheffield: prof of med 1946-72, emeritus prof 1972-, postgraduate dean of med 1972-77; Fogarty scholar-in-res Nat Inst of Health Bethesda Maryland USA 1979 and 1980; FRCP; kt 1970; *Style—* Sir Charles Stuart-Harris, CBE; 28 Whitworth Rd, Sheffield S10 3HD (☎ 0742 301200)

STUART-MENTETH, Charles Grieves; s and h of Sir James Wallace Stuart-Menteth, 6 Bt, by his w, Dorothy Patricia, *née* Warburton; *b* 25 Nov 1950; *m* 1976, Nicola Mary Jane, da of Vincent Charles Raleigh St Lawrence; 3 da; *Style—* Charles Stuart-Menteth Esq; Hillend House, Dalry, Ayrshire (☎ 029 483 3871); work: 75 Durham St, Glasgow (☎ 041 427 6991)

STUART-MENTETH, Sir James Wallace; 6 Bt (UK 1838), of Closeburn, Dumfrieshire, and Mansfield, Ayrshire; s of Sir William Frederick Stuart-Menteth, 5 Bt (d 1952); *b* 13 Nov 1922; *Educ* Fettes, St Andrews Univ, Trinity Coll Oxford (MA); *m* 23 April 1949, (Dorothy) Patricia, da of late Frank Greaves Warburton, of Thorrington, Stirling; 2 s; *Heir* s, Charles Stuart-Menteth; *Career* serv WWII Lt Scots Gds; md alkali and paints div ICI Ltd; *Style—* Sir James Stuart-Menteth, Bt; Nutwood, Auchencairn, Castle Douglas, Kirkcudbrightshire DG7 1QZ

STUART-MOORE, Michael; QC (1990); s of Kenneth Basil Moore (d 1987), and Marjorie Elizabeth, *née* Hodges; *b* 7 July 1944; *Educ* Cranleigh Sch; *m* 8 Dec 1973, Katherine Ann, da of Kenneth William Scott; 1 s (James b 1976),1 da (Zoe-Olivia b 1978)); *Career* called to the Bar Middle Temple 1966; rec of the Crown Ct 1985-; *Recreations* cine-photography, flute, tennis, travel off the beaten track; *Style—* Michael Stuart-Moore, Esq, QC; 1 Hare Ct, Temple, London EC4Y 7BE (☎ 071 353 5324, fax 071 353 0667)

STUART OF FINDHORN, 2 Viscount (UK 1959); David Randolph Moray Stuart; s of 1 Viscount, CH, MVO, MC, PC (d 1971), and Lady Rachel, *née* Cavendish, OBE, da of 9 Duke of Devonshire; through his mother Lord S of F is 1 cous of Rt Hon Maurice Macmillan, PC, MP; *b* 20 June 1924; *Educ* Eton; *m* 1, 1945, Grizel Mary Wilfreda (d 1948), da of late Theodore Fyfe and widow of Michael Gillilan; 1 s; m 2, 1951 (m dis 1979), Marian, da of late Gerald Wilson; 1 s, 3 da; m 3, 1979, Margaret Anne, da of Cdr Peter Du Cane, CBE, RN, and Victoria, sis of Sir John Gawen Carew Pole, 12 Bt, DSO, TD; *Heir* s, Hon (James) Dominic Stuart; *Career* late Lt KRRC, Maj 6/7 Royal Welch Fus (TA), FRICS, Page of Honour to HM 1938-40, DL of Caerns 1963-68, land agent; *Style—* The Rt Hon the Viscount Stuart of Findhorn; 38 Findhorn, nr Forres, Morayshire

STUART OF FINDHORN, Viscountess; Margaret Anne; da of Cdr Peter Du Cane, CBE, RN and Victoria, sis of Sir John Gawen Carew Pole, 12 Bt, DSO, TD; *b* 1932; *m* 1979, 2 Viscount Stuart of Findhorn; *Career* interior designer; *Style—* The Rt Hon the Viscountess Stuart of Findhorn; 6 Winchenden Rd, London SW6

STUART-PAUL, Air Marshal Ronald Ian; KBE (1990, MBE 1967); s of James Grey Stuart-Paul (d 1984), and Isobel Mary McDonald (d 1939); *b* 7 Nov 1934; *Educ* Dollar Acad; *m* 9 Nov 1963, Priscilla Frances, da of George Kay (d 1975); 1 s (Craig b 14 April 1965), 1 da (Rowena b 20 Nov 1969); *Career* RAF Coll Cranwell 1953-56, served various fighter squdns 1957, DA Saudi 1974-75, Cmd RAF Lossiemouth 1976-78, RCDS 1979, NATO 1980-82, MOD 1982-83, AOT 1984-85, DG Al Yamamah 1985; *Clubs* RAF; *Style—* Air Marshall Sir Ronald Stuart-Paul, KBE; 27 Church Way, Little Stukeley, Huntingdon, Cambridgeshire PE17 5BQ (☎ 0480 457660), Castlewood House, 77-91 New Oxford St, London WC1A 1DS (☎ 071 8298505, fax 071 8298536, car 0831 294131)

STUART-SMITH, Hon Mrs (Arabella Clare); *née* Montgomery; only da of 2 Viscount Montgomery of Alamein, CBE; *m* 1982, Jeremy Hugh Stuart-Smith, eldest s of Rt Hon Lord Justice (Rt Hon Sir Murray) Stuart-Smith; 2 s (Edward Murray b 1988, Sam Nicholas b 1990), 2 da (Emma b 1984, Laura b 1986 d 1987); *Style—* The Hon Mrs Stuart-Smith

STUART-SMITH, Dr Deryk Aubrey; s of Lionel Oscar Stuart-Smith (d 1966), and May Marjorie, *née* Fox; *b* 12 April 1927; *Educ* Bishop Cotton Sch, Univ of Glasgow (BSc, MB ChB, MD); *m* 25 Dec 1957, Anne Bennoch, da of Andrew Bennoch Thaw (d 1965); 1 s (Jonathan b 1968), 3 da (Karen b 1961, Tracey b 1964, Susan b 1966); *Career* sr lectr Dept of Med Univ of Glasgow 1970- (MRC res fell Dept of Med 1961-65, lectr 1965-70), dir Bone Metabolism Res Unit Western Infirmary Glasgow 1971 (conslt physician 1970-); pubns on diagnostic procedures in disorders of calcium metabolism; FRCPE 1973, FRCP Glasgow 1977; *Recreations* gardening, theatre, science fiction, science fact; *Style—* Dr Deryk Stuart-Smith; 30 Dolphin Road, Maxwell Park, Glasgow, Scotland G41 4DZ (☎ 041 4232430); Bone Metabolism Research Unit, Dept of Medicine and Therapeutics, Western Infirmary, Glasgow G11 6NT Scotland (041 3398822)

STUART-SMITH, Elizabeth; da of Sir Murray Stuart-Smith, and Joan, *née* Motion; *b* 3 Oct 1961; *Educ* Watford GS for Girls, Queens Coll Harley St, Cordwainers Coll London (travelling scholar); *m* 27 Jan 1990, Adam Beck; *Career* shoe designer; produced private collection in London, has worked with John Galliano and Liza Bruce; currently: manufacturing collection in Italy, design conslt to Diego Dalla Valle Milan; winner Design Cncl awards 1989; *Recreations* travel, food, walking; *Style—* Ms Elizabeth Stuart-Smith; Elizabeth Stuart Smith, 97 North Church Rd, London N1 3ND (☎ 071 704 8019, fax 071 704 8019)

STUART-SMITH, James; CB (1986), QC (1988); s of James Stuart-Smith (d 1937), of Brighton, Sussex, and Florence Emma, *née* Armfield (d 1952); *b* 13 Sept 1919; *Educ* Brighton Coll, London Hosp Med Sch; *m* 28 Dec 1957, Jean Marie Therese, da of Hubert Young Groundsell, of Newport, IOW; 1 s (James b 24 Nov 1959), 1 da (Mary b 11 Nov 1958); *Career* WWII 1939-47, cmmnd 2 Lt KRRC 1940, serv Middle E and Italy 1940-45, staff appts UK 1945-47, demobbed as Actg Lt-Col 1947; called to the Bar Middle Temple 1948, in practice London 1948-55, legal asst to office of Judge Adv-Gen 1955, dep judge advocate 1957, asst judge adv-gen 1968, vice judge adv-gen 1979, judge adv-gen 1984-91; serv: Germany 1959-62, 1971-74 and 1976-79 (as dep judge adv-gen), ME Cmd Aden 1964-65 (as dep judge advocate); rec Crown Ct 1985-; pres Int Soc for Mil Law and the Law of War 1985-91 (vice-pres 1979-85); *Recreations* lawn tennis, writing letters, mowing lawns; *Clubs* RAF; *Style—* James Stuart-Smith, Esq, CB, QC; The Firs, Copthorne, Sussex, RH10 4HH

STUART-SMITH, Lady; Joan Elizabeth Mary; *née* Motion; JP, DL (Herts 1987); da of Maj T A Motion, and Lady Elizabeth Grimston; *b* 14 Feb 1929; *Educ* Univ of Oxford (BA); *m* Rt Hon Lord Justice Stuart-Smith, *qv*; 3 s, 3 da; *Career* High Sheriff (and first woman sheriff) Herts 1983; *Recreations* book-binding, music, propagating plants, building; *Style—* Lady Stuart-Smith, JP, DL

STUART-SMITH, Rt Hon Lord Justice; Rt Hon Sir Murray Stuart-Smith; PC (1988), QC (1970); s of Edward Stuart-Smith, and Doris, *née* Laughland; *b* 18 Nov 1927; *Educ* Radley, CCC Cambridge; *m* 1953, Joan Stuart-Smith, *qv*; 3 s, 3 da; *Career* called to the Bar Gray's Inn 1952, rec Crown Court 1972-81, master of Bench Gray's Inn 1978, High Court Judge Queen's Bench 1981-87, presiding judge Western Circuit 1982-86, Lord Justice of Appeal 1987; memb: Criminal Injuries Compensation Bd 1979-81, Cmmn for Security Servs 1989; kt 1981; *Recreations* playing cello, shooting, building, playing bridge; *Style—* The Rt Hon Lord Justice Stuart-Smith; Royal Courts of Justice, Strand, London

STUART-SMITH, Stephen James Adrian; s of D M Stuart-Smith, of Leics; *b* 18 Aug 1954; *Educ* Denstone Coll, King's Coll London (BA), Univ of London Inst of Educn (PGCE), Univ of Reading (MA); *Career* bookseller 1977-78, asst master secdy schs in London and Hampshire 1978-85; head History Dept: Lord Wandsworth Coll Long Sutton 1985-88, Ditcham Park Sch Petersfield 1988-89; md Enitharmon Press 1987-, freelance ed Macmillan Publishers Ltd and the Royal Acad; fndr and organiser Poetry Festival for schs in Hants, Surrey and Berks 1978-88; memb: Ctee Edward Thomas Fellowship 1986-, Ctee Winchester Literature Network 1989-; FRSA 1990; *Books* Poems from Three Counties (1982, 2 vol 1985), An Enitharmon Anthology (1990); *Recreations* music, choral and solo singing, opera and the theatre, book collecting, walking and travel; *Style—* Stephen Stuart-Smith, Esq; 40 Rushes Rd, Petersfield, Hants GU32 3BW (☎ 0730 62753)

STUART TAYLOR, Hope, Lady; (Ada) Hope; da of Forrest Bertram Leeder, MRCS, FRCP, BC, and widow of Norman Alfred Yarrow; *m* 1959, as his 3 w, Sir Eric Stuart Taylor, 2 Bt, OBE, MD, MRCP (d 1977); *Style—* Hope, Lady Stuart Taylor

STUART TAYLOR, Lady; Iris Mary; da of Rev Edwin John Gargery and Marjorie Grace, *née* Clapp; *b* 8 Oct 1923; *Educ* Micklefield Sch Seaford, Barnett House Oxford (Dip Social Sci), LSE (Dip Mental Health); *m* 1950, Sir Richard Laurence Stuart Taylor, 3 Bt (d 1978); 1 s (Sir Nicholas Richard Stuart Taylor, 4 Bt, *qv*), 1 da (Anne Caroline b 1955); *Career* subaltern ATS; psychiatric social worker 1949-52; *Clubs* Ski Club of Great Britain; *Style—* Iris, Lady Stuart Taylor; White Lodge, Hambrook, Chichester, Sussex PO18 8RG

STUART TAYLOR, Sir Nicholas Richard; 4 Bt (UK 1917), of Kennington, Co London; s of Sir Richard Laurence Stuart Taylor, 3 Bt (d 1978), and Iris Mary Stuart Taylor; Sir Frederick Taylor, 1 Bt was pres of RCP; *b* 14 Jan 1952; *Educ* Bradfield; *m* 1984, Malvena Elizabeth, da of Daniel David Charles Sullivan; 1 da (Virginia Caterina b 1989); *Heir* none; *Career* slr 1977; ptnr Christopher Green & Ptnrs; *Recreations* skiing and other sports; *Style—* Sir Nicholas Stuart Taylor, Bt; 3 Horseshoe Drive, Romsey, Hants; Christopher Green & Ptnrs, 35 Carlton Crescent, Southampton, Hants

STUBBINGS, Betty (Mrs Frederick Ronald); *b* 16 Feb 1929; *m* 19 June 1950, Frederick James Ronald; 3 da (Julia, Linda, Gillian); *Career* lawn bowls player; started playing Pickering Bowls Club 1971, memb Yorkshire Team 1972-90; winner: Nat Singles Championship 1977, Nat Indoor fours 1989; runner-up British Isles Championship 1978; competitor int championships 1978-90; Gold and Silver medallist World Bowls Championships Toronto 1981; Bronze medallist: Commonwealth Games Brizbane 1982, World Bowls Championships Melbourne 1985, Commonwealth Games Edinburgh 1986; *Recreations* reading, walking, dress making; *Style—* Ms Betty Stubbings; 81 Welham Road, Norton Malton, North Yorkshire (☎ 0653 69 3716)

STUBBLEFIELD, Sir (Cyril) James; s of James Stubblefield (d 1926), of Cambridge, and Jane Stubblefield; *b* 6 Sept 1901; *Educ* Perse Sch Cambridge, Chelsea Poly, RCS Univ of London (DSc); *m* 1932, Emily Muriel Elizabeth, da of late L R Yakchee, of Calcutta and Jersey, CI; 2 s; *Career* geology demonstrator Imperial Coll London 1923-28, memb Geological Survey of GB 1928, chief palaeontologist 1947-53, asst dir 1953-60, dir 1960-66; dir: Geological Survey of NI 1960-66, Museum of Practical Geology 1960-66; pres Geological Soc London 1958-60, Palaeontographical Soc 1966-71, 8 Int Congress Carboniferous Stratigraphy and Geology 1968 and ed 4 vol CR; fell Chelsea Coll, Imperial Coll, Kings Coll London; FRS, FGS, FZS, ARCS; kt 1965; *Style—* Sir James Stubblefield, FRS; 35 Kent Ave, Ealing, London W13 8BE (☎ 081 997 5051)

STUBBS, Imogen Mary; da of Robin Desmond Scrivener Stubbs (d 1974), and Heather Mary, *née* McCracken (d 1986); *b* 20 Feb 1961; *Educ* St Paul's Girls', Westminster, Exeter Coll Oxford (scholar, BA), RADA (Silver medallist, John Barton award in Stagefighting); *Career* actress; theatre roles incl: Sally Bowles in Cabaret (Ipswich) 1985, Polly Brown in The Boyfriend (Ipswich) 1985, The Gaoler's Daughter in Two Noble Kinsmen (RSC) 1986-87, Helena in The Rover (RSC) 1986-87, Queen Isabel in Richard II (RSC) 1986-87, Desdemona in Othello (RSC 1989, BBC 1990); tv roles incl: Romy in Deadline (BBC) 1987, Ursula Brangwen in The Rainbow (BBC) 1988, Ginnie in Relatively Speaking (BBC) 1989; films roles incl: Nanou in Nanou (Umbrella Films) 1985, Megan in A Summer Story (ITC Films) 1987, Aud in Erik The Viking (Viking Films) 1988, Sarah in Fellow Traveller (BBC/HBO) 1989, Diana in True Colors (Paramount) 1990; *awards* Critics award for Most Promising Newcomer (for RSC) 1986-87, nominee Laurence Olivier award for Best Newcomer (for RSC) 1987, nominee Best Actress Evening Standard Film Awards (for A Summer Story) 1988, nominee Best Actress Royal Variety Television Awards (for The Rainbow) 1989, Gold medal Best Actress in a Series Chicago Film Festival (for The Rainbow); *Style—* Miss Imogen Stubbs; Michael Foster, c/o Duncan Heath Associates Ltd, 162-170 Wardour St, London W1V 3AT (☎ 071 439 1471)

STUBBS, Sir James Wilfrid; KCVO (1979), TD (1946); eld s of Rev Wilfrid Thomas Stubbs (d 1968), and Muriel Elizabeth, *née* Pope (d 1966); *b* 13 Aug 1910; *Educ* Charterhouse, Brasenose Coll Oxford (MA); *m* 1938, Richenda Katherine Theodora, da of Rt Rev William Champion Streatfeild, Bishop of Lewes (d 1929); 1 s, 1 da (decd); *Career* serv WWII Royal Signals, Lt-Col 1946; asst master St Paul's Sch 1934-46; United Grand Lodge of England: asst grand sec 1948-54, dep grand sec 1954-58, grand sec 1958-80; *Books* The Four Corners (1983), Freemasons' Hall, The

Home and Heritage of The Craft (jtly, 1984), Freemasonry in my Life (1985); *Recreations* travel, family history; *Clubs* Athenaeum; *Style*— Sir James Stubbs, KCVO, TD; 5 Pensioners Court, The Charterhouse, London EC1M 6AU (☎ 071 253 1982)

STUBBS, John Bruford; s of Archibald Edwin Stubbs (d 1965), of Shoreham-by-Sea, and Edith Maud, *née* Jeffery (d 1982); *b* 10 Feb 1932; *Educ* Brighton Coll, Brighton Coll of Art; *m* 30 Sept 1961, Linda, da of George Stanley Hopkinson, of Mill Hill, London; 2 s (Jonathan b 1965, Gerard b 1966), 1 da (Julia b 1963); *Career* Nat Serv Sub/Lt RNVR Submarine Serv 1956-57; deep diving submarine res GPO Res Laboratories with Nat Inst of Oceanography 1959-64; in architectural practice Perth Aust 1965-74, project mangr involved in construction industry and security BSI 1977-; ordinary memb Challenger Soc 1959; ARIBA 1957, Companion RINA 1960, former Fell RAIA 1974; *Books* Construction Industry Guide Specification (WA Chapter with RAIA, 1974); *Recreations* sketching; *Clubs* Naval; *Style*— John Stubbs, Esq; 534 Ben Jonson House, Barbican, London EC2Y 8DL

STUBBS, Dr Michael Wesley; s of Leonard Garforth Stubbs (d 1987), and Isabella Wardrop, *née* McGavin; *b* 23 Dec 1947; *Educ* Glasgow HS for Boys, Kings Coll Cambridge (MA), Univ of Edinburgh (PhD); *Career* lectr in linguistics Univ of Nottingham 1974-85, prof of English in educn Inst of Educn Univ of London 1985-90, prof of English linguistics Univ of Trier Germany 1990-; chm BAAL 1988; *Books* language, schools and classrooms (1976), language and literacy (1980), discourse analysis (1983), educational linguistics (1986); *Recreations* walking; *Style*— Prof Dr Michael Stubbs; FB2 Anglistik, Univ of Trier, 5500 Trier, Germany (☎ 0651 201 2278, fax 0651 251 35)

STUBBS, Una; da of Clarence Stubbs, of Albert Bridge Rd, London SW11, and Kathleen Angela Stubbs; *b* 1 May 1937; *Educ* Baylis Ct Secdy Modern Slough, La Roche Dancing Sch Slough; *m* 1, March 1960 (m dis), Peter Gilmor; 1 s (Jason), m 2, Oct 1969 (m dis), Nicky Henson; 2 s (Christian, Joe); *Career* actress; theatre work incl: (at Theatre Royal Windsor) A Midsummer Night's Dream 1952, Quadrille 1953, The Sun and I (1953), Goody Two Shoes 1953; London Palladium Revue 1954, London Royal Variety Show 1954, London Royal Variety Show 1954, 1972 and 1982, Folies Bergères (Prince of Wales Theatre) 1955, Star Maker (Manchester Hippodrome) 1956, Grab Me A Gondola (Lyric Theatre) 1957, On The Brighter Side (Phoenix Theatre) 1960, Alladin (London Palledium) 1964, Taste of Honey and The Diary of Anne Frank (Westcliffe Theatre) 1966, A Soldiers Tale (Edinburgh Festival and The Young Vic) 1967, The Knack (Golders Green Hippodrome) 1967, Jane Eyre (Adelee Genee Theatre) 1968, Little Malcolm and His Struggle Against The Eunuchs (Young Vic) 1968, Cowardy Custard (Mermaid Theatre) 1972, Cole (Mermaid Theatre) 1974, Irma La Douce (Watford) 1975, Alladin (Richmond Theatre) 1976, Cinderella (Bromley Theatre) 1978, Oh Mr Porter (Mermaid Theatre) 1979, Dick Whittington (Richmond Theatre) 1979, Baggage (Adelphi Theatre) 1980, Worzel Gummidge (Birmingham Rep) 1981 (and Cambridge Theatre London) 1982, The Secret Life of Cartoons (Aldwick Theatre) 1986, Bless The Bride (Sadlers Wells) 1987, It Runs in The Family (Yvonne Arnaud Theatre Guildford) 1988, Run for Your Wife (Criterian) 1988, She Stoops to Conquer (Royal Exchange) 1989, Rumours (Chichester) 1990; TV work incl: Compact (BBC), Wayne and Shuster (BBC), Boy Meets Girl (BBC), Cliff in Scandinavia (BBC), Cole (BBC2), Roy Castle Show (BBC), The Rivals of Sherlock Holmes (BBC), Morecombe and Wise (BBC), Harry Secombe Show (BBC), Happy Families (BBC), Fawlty Towers (BBC), Cool for Cats (Rediffusion), The Dick Emery Show (BBC), It's Cliff Richard (BBC), Worzel Gummidge (Southern ITV), Worzel Cummidge Down Under (Channel 4), Give Us A Clue (Thames ITV), Till Death Do Us Part (BBC), In Sickness And In Health (BBC), Morris Minar's Marvellous Motors (BBC) Tricky Business (BBC); films incl: Summer Holidays, 3 Hats for Lisa, Wonderful Life, Till Death Do Us Part; *books* In Stitches, A Stitch In Time, Una's Fairy Stories; *Recreations* embroidery, dressmaking, cycling; *Style*— Ms Una Stubbs; 17 Whitehall, London SW1 (☎ 071 839 6421)

STUBBS, William Hamilton; s of Joseph Stubbs, and Mary, *née* McNicol; *b* 5 Nov 1937; *Educ* Workington GS Cumberland, St Aloysius Coll Glasgow, Univ of Glasgow (BSc, PhD), Univ of Arizona; *m* 19 Sept 1963, Marie Margaret, da of Joseph Pierce; 3 da (Nadine Ann b 1964, Hilary Jo b 1966, Fiona Mairi b 1967); *Career* Shell Oil Co California 1964-67, teacher in Glasgow 1967-72, asst dir of educn Carlisle 1972-73 and Cumbria 1973-76, dep dir of educn 1976-77, dep educn offr ILEA 1977-82, educn offr and chief exec ILEA 1982-88, chief exec Poly and Colls Funding Cncl; *Style*— William Stubbs, Esq; 122 Cromwell Tower, Barbican, London EC2Y 8DD

STUCKEN, Norah Kathleen Sara; da of Maj Edward Herbert Alexander (d 1958), and Sara Jane, *née* Moore (d 1942); *b* 10 Nov 1912; *Educ* private in Harrogate, Germany and France; *m* 1, 1943, Lionel Sidney Francis Condon (d 1955); 2 s (David b 1949, Jonathan (twin, d 1984)), 1 da (Avril b 1947); m 2, 1957, George Stucken (d 1985); *Career* as Norah Alexander asst literary ed Everybody's Weekly 1934-35, opened Time's first London Office 1935, on Life (Paris and NY) 1935-39, reporter and columnist Sunday Pictorial 1939-45, columnist Daily Mail 1945-48; life pres Grower Publications Ltd 1988- (chm 1955-87); *Recreations* reading, languages, travel; *Style*— Mrs Norah Stucken; 3 South Grove House, London N6 6LP (☎ 081 340 1472)

STUCLEY, Sir Hugh George Coplestone Bampfylde; 6 Bt (UK 1859), of Affeton Castle, Devon; s of Sir Dennis Frederic Bankes Stucley, 5 Bt (d 1983), and Hon Lady Stucley, *qv*; *b* 8 Jan 1945; *Educ* RAC Cirencester; *m* 1969, Angela Caroline, er da of Richard Toller, of Theale, Berks; 2 s, 2 da; *Heir* s, George Dennis Bampfylde Stucley b 26 Dec 1970; *Career* Lt RHG; *Clubs* Cavalry and Guards, Sloane; *Style*— Sir Hugh Stucley, Bt; Affeton Castle, Worlington, Crediton, Devon

STUCLEY, Hon Lady (Sheila Margaret Warwick); *née* Bampfylde; patron of two livings, landowner; da of 4 Baron Poltimore (d 1965), and Cynthia Rachel (d 1961), o da of Hon Gerald Lascelles, CB; *b* 26 Oct 1912; *Educ* privately; *m* 5 Jan 1932, Maj Sir Dennis Frederic Bankes Stucley, 5 Bt, JP, DL (d 1983), s of Sir Hugh Nicholas Granville Stucley 4 Bt (d 1956); 2 s (John b and d 30 July 1933, (Sir) Hugh George Coplestone Bampfylde (6 Bt), *qv*), 4 da (Margaret Cynthia b 3 Sept 1934, Rosemary Anne b 8 Jan 1936, Christine Elizabeth b 25 April 1940, Sarah Susan b 6 Aug 1942); *Career* landowner; Mayoress of Bideford 1954-55; memb: Hartland Church Cncl, Hartland Paris Cncl; pres Garden Show; govr Bideford GS and Bideford Comprehensive Sch (pre-amalgamation); *Recreations* music, gardening; *Style*— The Hon Lady Stucley; Hartland Abbey, Bideford, N Devon EX39 6DT (☎ 02374 41234)

STUDD, Anastasia, Lady; Anastasia; da of Lt-Col Harold Leveson-Gower (d 1972), (6 in descent from 1 Earl Gower and 5 cous of 5 Duke of Sutherland) and Kathleen Leveson-Gower, JP, OBE (d 1984), (da of Sir Murrough Wilson, KBE, JP, DL, by his 1 w, Sybil, 2 da of Sir Powlett Milbank, 2 Bt); *b* 26 Nov 1931; *m* 1958, Capt Sir Kynaston Studd, 3 Bt (d 1977), s of Sir Eric Studd 2 Bt (d 1975); 3 da (Sara Alexandra, Jane Anastasia (Mrs Christopher Hall), Anne Elizabeth); *Style*— Anastasia, Lady Studd; Manor Farm, Rockbourne, Fordingbridge, Hants (☎ 072 53 214)

STUDD, Sir Edward Fairfax; 4 Bt (UK 1929), of Netheravon, Wilts; s of Sir Eric Studd, 2 Bt, OBE, and Kathleen Stephana, da of Lydstone Joseph Langmead; suc bro, Sir (Robert) Kynaston Studd, 3 Bt, 1977; *b* 3 May 1929; *Educ* Winchester; *m* 1960, Prudence Janet, da of Alastair Douglas Fyfe, OBE, of Grey Court, Riding Mill, Northumberland; 2 s, 1 da; *Heir* s, Philip Alastair Fairfax (b 1961); *Career* Subaltern Coldstream Gds, serv Malaya 1948-49; chm Gray Dawes Travel Ltd; memb Ct of Assts Worshipful Co of Merchant Taylors; *Recreations* rural activities; *Clubs* Boodle's, Pratt's; *Style*— Sir Edward Studd, Bt; Kingsbury House, Kingsbury Episcopi, Martock, Yeovil, Somerset TA12 6AU

STUDD, Dr John William Winston; s of Eric Dacombe Studd (d 1941), and Elsie Elizabeth, *née* Kirby; *b* 4 March 1940; *Educ* Royal Hosp Sch Ipswich, Univ of Birmingham (MB BS, MD); *m* 7 May 1980, Dr Margaret Ann Johnson, da of Dr Frederick Johnson, of Hinton Priory, Hinton Charter House, Bath, Avon; 1 s (Thomas b 16 Oct 1981), 1 da (Sarah b 7 Dec 1985); *Career* res fell Univ of Birmingham, lectr in obstetrics and gynaecology Univ Coll of Rhodesia 1972, conslt and sr lectr Univ of Nottingham 1974-75, currently conslt obstetrician and gynaecologist Kings Coll Hosp and Dulwich Hosp London; author papers on: labour, menopause, osteoporosis, premenstrual syndrome; ed British Journal of Obstetrics and Gynaecology, memb Cncl ROCG, vice chm Nat Osteoporosis Soc, vice pres Section of Obstetrics and Gynaecology RSM, pres Int Soc of Reproductive Med; memb; Hosp Consult and Specialists Assoc 1978, BMA 1962; FRCOG 1982 (MRCOG 1967); *Books* Management of Labour (ed, 1985), Management of the Menopause (ed 1988), Progress in Obstetrics and Gynaecology (volumes 1-8), Self asessment in Obstetrics and Gynaecology; *Recreations* tennis, theatre, music, opera; *Style*— Dr John Studd; 27 Blomfield Rd, London W9 1AA (☎ 071 2895817); 120 Harley St, London W1 (☎ 071 4860497, fax 071 2244190, car 0836 526422); Fertility & Endocrinology Centre, Lister Hospital, Chelsea Bridge Rd, London SW1W 8RH (☎ 071 7305433, fax 071 8236108, telex 21283 LISTER G)

STUDD, Paul; s of Michael Keith Studd, and Judith Studd; *b* 9 Oct 1964; *Educ* Read Sch, Wakefield Coll; *Career* water ski champion; memb World team competing USA 1989, silver medal World Games Germany 1989, overall winner Euro Masters UK 1989, Nat jump title held three times incl 1990, overal title 1990; memb Br Water Ski Fedn; *Recreations* tae kwon do, golf, raquet sports, self improvement books; *Style*— Paul Studd, Esq; Honeycutt, A1 Slip Road, Darrington, Pontefract, W Yorks (☎ 0977 708398), 500 A2 Crosswinds Drive, W Palm Beach, Florida, 33413, USA (☎ 010 1 407 642 5243)

STUDD, Sir Peter Malden; GBE (1971), KCVO (1979), DL (Wilts 1983); s of late Brig Malden Studd, DSO, MC, and late Netta, *née* Cramsie; *b* 15 Sept 1916,Dublin; *Educ* Harrow, Clare Coll Cambridge (MA); *m* 1943, Angela, *née* Garnier; 2 s; *Career* RA 1939-45, serv Middle E and Euro Campaigns; De La Rue Co plc 1939-74, dir Lloyds of Scottish plc 1973-84; UK pres Chiropractic Advancement Assoc 1987-90; tstee: Royal Jubilee Tsts 1980-, Arts Educnl Schs 1984-; Capt of cricket Harrow and Cambridge Univ; Lord Mayor London 1970-71 (Alderman 1959, Sheriff 1967); KStJ; past master Worshipful Co of Merchant Taylors, hon Liveryman Worshipful Co of Fruiterers and Plaisterers; Hon DSc City Univ; kt 1969; *Recreations* fishing, shooting, gardening, saving St Pauls, lighting up the Thames; *Clubs* I Zingari, MCC, Houghton; *Style*— Sir Peter Studd, GBE, KCVO, DL; c/o Hoare & Co, 37 Fleet St, London EC4

STUDER, Keith Ronald; s of Ronald Walter Studer, of River Lodge, Goole, Humberside; *b* 15 Sept 1945; *Educ* Ampleforth, Queen's Coll Oxford, Univ of Br Columbia; *m* 1971, Jane Margaret; 1 s, 1 da; *Career* int freight forwarder; chief exec Gellatly Shipping Ltd 1991-; *Style*— Keith Studer, Esq; Dorne House, Chichester Rd, Dorking, Surrey RH4 1LR (☎ 0306 884305); Gellatly Shipping, Sir John Lyon House, Upper Thames St, London EC4

STUDHOLME, Sir Henry William; 3 Bt (UK 1956), of Perridge, Co Devon; er s of Sir Paul Henry William Studholme, 2 Bt, DL (d 1990), and Virginia Katherine, *née* Palmer (d 1990); *b* 31 Jan 1958; *Educ* Eton, Trinity Hall Cambridge (MA); *m* 1 Oct 1988, S Lucy R Deans-Chrystall, o da of Richard S Deans, of Christchurch, NZ, and late Jane R M Deans, of West Wellow, Hants; 1 da (Lorna Jane b 1 June 1990); *Heir* bro, James Paul Gilfred Studholme b 1960; *Career* ACA, ATII; *Style*— Sir Henry Studholme, Bt; Perry's Cottage, Ribston Hall, nr Wetherby, N Yorks LS22 4EZ

STUDHOLME, Joseph Gilfred; s of Sir Henry Gray Studholme, 1 Bt, CVO (d 1987), of Wembury House, Wembury, Plymouth, Devon, and Judith, *née* Whitbread; *b* 14 Jan 1936; *Educ* Eton, Magdalen Coll Oxford (BA, MA); *m* 5 Sept 1959, Rachel, da of Sir William Albemarle Fellowes, KCVO (d 1986), of Flitcham House, Kings Lynn, Norfolk; 3 s (Andrew b 1962, Alexander b 1967, Hugo b 1968); *Career* Nat Serv cmmnd 2 Lt 60 Rifles (KRRC) 1954-56; md King & Shaxson Ltd 1961-63, chm and md Editions Alecto Ltd and subsid cos; chm Cncl of Mgmnt Byam Shaw Sch of Art 1988- (memb 1963-); FRSA; *Clubs* Garrick, MCC; *Style*— Joseph Studholme, Esq; Foudry House, Stratfield Mortimer, Reading, Berks RG7 3NR (☎ 0734 333 000); 46 Kelso Place, London W8 5QG (☎ 071 937 6611, fax 071 937 5795, telex 94012669)

STUDHOLME, Judith, Lady; Judith Joan Mary; *née* Whitbread; o da of Henry William Whitbread (d 1947), of Warminster, Wilts, and Mary, *née* Raymond (d 1926); *b* 15 Nov 1898; *m* 10 April 1929, Sir Henry Gray Studholme, 1 Bt, CVO (d 1987); 2 s, 1 da; *Style*— Judith, Lady Studholme; 30 Abbey Mews, Amesbury Abbey, Amesbury, Wilts SPA 7EX (☎ 0980 624812)

STULTIENS, (Alan) Jeffrey; s of Thomas Stultiens (d 1980), of Syresham, Northants, and Kate, *née* Whittaker; *b* 12 Sept 1944; *Educ* Hutton GS, Tiffin Boys Sch, Kingston Sch of Art, Camberwell Sch of Art and Crafts (DipAD); *partner*, Catherine Knowelden; *Career* fine artist; lectr City of London Poly Sir John Cass Sch of Art 1967-73, sr lectr and leader Fndn Course Hertfordshire Coll of Art & Design 1983-87 (sr lectr 1974-83); exhibitions: John Player Portrait Award (Nat Portrait Gallery) 1984 and 1985, British Portraiture 1980-85 (Fermoy Centre) 1985-86, Portraits for the '80s (Quay Arts Centre) 1986, Royal Portrait Soc 1990; cmmns and collections: Nat Portrait Gallery, Merton Coll Univ of Oxford, Nat Heart and Lung Inst, Servite Houses, private cmmns; awards: Commendation Drawings for All Gainsborough House Soc 1984, first prize John Player Portrait Award Nat Portrait Gallery 1985, Alexon portrait finalist; *Style*— Jeffrey Stultiens, Esq; 26 St George's Close, Toddington, Bedfordshire LU5 6AT (☎ 0525 54120)

STUNELL, (Robert) Andrew; s of Robert George Stunell, of Powick, nr Worcester, and Trixie Stunell; *b* 24 Nov 1942; *Educ* Surbiton GS, Univ of Manchester, Liverpool Poly; *m* 29 July 1967, Gillian Mary Stunell; 3 s (Peter b 1973, Mark b 1974, Daniel b 1979), 2 da (Judith b 1969, Kari b 1970); *Career* architectural asst: various posts 1965-81, freelance 1981-85; cncllrs offr Assoc of Liberal Cncllrs 1985-88, devpt offr Assoc of SLD Cncllrs 1988-90, political sec 1989-; Chester City Cncl 1979, Cheshire CC 1981, Assoc of CC's 1985, ldr SLD GP 1985, vice-chm ACC, Parly candidate Chester (1979, 1983 and 1987); *Books* Guide to Local Government Finance (1985), Success on Balanced Councils (1985), Parish Finance (1986), Success on the Council (1988); *Style*— Andrew Stunell, Esq; 18 Halkyn Rd, Chester CH2 3QE; Assoc of Social & Liberal Democrat Cncllrs, Birchcliffe Centre, Hebden Bridge, W Yorks HX7 8DG (☎ 0422 843 785, fax 0422 843 036)

STUNT, Stewart Robert; s of David James Stunt, of Chichester, Sussex, and Irene Rosina Stunt; *b* 13 Feb 1949; *Educ* Reigate GS, Kingston Poly; *m* 21 April 1971, Celia Mary, da of Dr Andrew Skarbek; 1 da (Sophie Victoria b 1981); *Career* Ogilvy & Mather 1971-72, fndr ptnr The Stewart Stunt Partnership 1979; MInstM; *Recreations* golf, squash, sub-aqua; *Clubs* Long Ashton Golf; *Style*— Stewart Stunt, Esq; The Stewart Stunt Partnership, 10 Saville Place, Bristol BS8 4EJ (☎ 0272 237 877, fax

0272 237 839)

STURDEE, Dr David William; s of Cdr Peter Doveton Sturdee, OBE, of Moray House, Priestlands, Sherborne, Dorset, and Daphne, *née* Langdon; *b* 13 May 1945; *Educ* Sherborne, St Thomas' Hosp Med Sch Univ of London (MB BS, DA, MD); *m* 4 Sept 1971, Elizabeth Morton, da of Dr John Morton Muir (d 1973); 1 s (Simon William b 1973), 1 da (Claire b 1975); *Career* sr registrar W Midlands Rotation 1978-81, conslt obstetrician and gynaecologist Solihull and E Birmingham Hosps 1981-, hon clinical lectr Univ of Birmingham 1981- (res fell Dept of Obstetrics and Gynaecology 1967-77); author of many papers in jls and chapters in books on hormone replacement therapy for menopausal symptoms; memb Cncl: Birmingham and Midlands Obstetric and Gynaecological Soc, Solihull Div BMA; fndr memb: Int Menopause Soc, Br Menopause Soc; memb: higher trg and subspeciality bd ctees RCOG, Int Med Ed Bd Menopause Digest; FRCOG 1988; *Recreations* singing, golf; *Clubs* Copt Heath Golf; *Style*— Dr David Sturdee; 44 Mirfield Rd, Solihull, West Midlands B91 1JD (☎ 021 7051759); Dept of Obstetrics & Gynaecology, Solihull Hosp, Lode Lane, Solihull B91 2JL (☎ 021 7114455)

STURGE, Maj-Gen (Henry Arthur) John; CB (1978); s of Henry George Arthur Sturge (d 1955), and Lilian Beatrice, *née* Goodale) (d 1978); *b* 27 April 1925; *Educ* Wilsons GS Camberwell, QMC London; *m* 18 July 1953, Jean Ailsa, da of John Alfred Mountain (d 1969); 2 s (Simon John b 1959, James Henry b 1962), 1 da (Susan Jean b 1954); *Career* RCS 1945-80; serv in UK, Egypt, Malaya, Hong Kong, BAOR; Army Staff Coll 1955, Jt Servs Staff Coll 1962, regt cmd BAOR 1967-69, Brig cmd UK 1971-73, Chief Signal Offr BAOR 1975-77, ACDS (signals) MOD 1977-80; gen mangr Marconi Space and Def Systems 1981-84 (asst dir 1980), md Marconi Secure Radio Systems 1984-86; princ conslt Logica Space and Def systems 1986-; *Clubs* Army and Navy; *Style*— Maj-Gen John Sturge, CB; Logica Aerospace and Defence Systems Ltd, Cobham Park, Downside Rd, Cobham, Surrey KT11 3LX (☎ 071 637 9111)

STURGEON, Dr David Alexander; s of Flt Lt Alexander Rodger Sturgeon, of Worcs, and Jean, *née* Stansfield; *b* 3 July 1947; *Educ* Hipperholme GS, Univ of Oxford, UCH (BA, MA, BM BCh); *m* 6 Dec 1975, Elizabeth, da of Eric Kurt Lederman, of London; 2 da (Kate b 28 April 1977, Natasha b 29 Aug 1979); *Career* UCH London: Leverhulme jr res fell med sch 1974-75, sr clinical lectr Dept of Mental Health 1977-86, acting head Dept of Mental Health 1981-84, tutor Faculty of Clinical Sciences 1985-87, conslt psychiatrist 1986; author of various papers on family treatment of schizophrenia, psychophysiology of schizophrenia and psychotherapy; psychiatric adviser to: Br Assoc of Cancer United Patients, Breast Care and Mastectomy Assoc; FRCPsych 1986 (memb 1976); *Books* UCH Textbook of Psychiatry (co-ed, 1990); *Recreations* writing; *Style*— Dr David Sturgeon; Department of Psychological Medicine, University College Hospital, Gower Street, London WC1 (☎ 387 9300 ext 8585)

STURGES, James Aldersey Dicken; s of Gp Capt J A D Sturges, RAF (d 1974), and Dorothy Joan Norman; *b* 17 Aug 1945; *Educ* Sherborne, Univ of Durham (BA); *Career* md Past and Present Antiques Totnes Devon, chm Narrows Traders Assoc, memb Disabled Ski Club; *Style*— James Sturges, Esq; Bow Cottage, Tuckenhay, Totnes, Devon

STURGESS, Colin Andrew; s of Alan Paul Sturgess, and Margaret Ann, *née* Crawley; *b* 15 Dec 1968; *Educ* Marian Coll Johannesburg SA; *Career* cyclist; nat champion: 1985 (5 jr titles), 1986 (3 jr titles), 1987 (4000m indiv pursuit), 1988 (3 titles), 1989 (5000m indiv pursuit), 1990 (5000m indiv pursuit and 125 miles road race); world champion 1989 (5000m indiv pursuit); Cwlth Games 1986, Olympic Games 1988; memb Professional Cycling Assoc; *Recreations* music, fashion, reading; *Clubs* Tulip Computers Racing Team, Team Haverhill; *Style*— Colin Sturgess, Esq; c/o 63 Percy Road, Aylestone, Leicester LE2 8FQ

STURGESS-SMITH, Ian Charles; s of Charles Alfred Smith (d 1981), and Doris Ivy, *née* Sturgess; *b* 3 Sept 1937; *Educ* City of Leicester Boy; GS, Univ Coll Hosp Dental Sch (BDS, LDS, RCS); *m* 16 Nov 1989, Christine Ann, da of John Alexander Candlish; *Career* dental surgn in gen practice; memb: BDA, Gen Dental Practioners Assoc; *Recreations* gardening; *Style*— Ian Sturgess-Smith, Esq; 19 Markfield Rd, Groby, Leicester LE6 2FL (☎ 0533 876724); 34 Leicester Rd, Oadby, Leicester LE2 5BA (☎ 0533 714792)

STURGIS, Ann Elisabeth; da of Maj Peter Sturgis, of Dauntsey Park, Chippenham, Wilts (d 1986), and Rachel Sybil, *née* Borthwick; *b* 23 Oct 1945; *Educ* N Forcland Lodge; *Career* estate agent; chm and md Malvern Estate Agents; FCEA 1988; *Recreations* gardening, riding; *Style*— Miss Ann Sturgis; 6 Hyde Park Gdns, London W2 (☎ 071 262 9552); Garden Cottage, Dauntsey Park, Chippenham, Wilts; Malverns, Malvern Court, Onslow Square, London SW7 3HU (☎ 071 589 8122, fax 071 589 4403)

STURRIDGE, Marvin Francis; s of Frank Alexander Leslie Sturridge (d 1978), of Hampstead, London, and Helen Marie, *née* Tucker (d 1980); *b* 12 Sept 1926; *Educ* Ladycross, Univ Coll Sch, Middx Hosp Med Sch Univ of London (MB BS, MS); *m* 8 Feb 1958, June Pamela Linda, da of John Frederick Desmond Rowley (d 1970); 2 s (Paul b 1960, Jonathan b 1966), 2 da (Jacquelin b 1958, Nicola b 1963); *Career* cardiothoracic surgn The Middx Hosp 1967, surgn London Chest Hosp 1967-, hon cardiothoracic surgn Nat Hosp for Nervous Diseases 1970-; memb: Soc of Thoracic and Cardiovascular Surgns of GB and Ireland, Br Cardiac Soc; FRCS 1958; *Recreations* restoration; *Style*— Marvin Sturridge, Esq; 41 Arden Rd, London N3 3AD (☎ 081 346 6394)

STURROCK, Philip James; s of James Cars Sturrock, of 6 Long Fallas Crescent, Brighouse, W Yorks, and Joyce, *née* Knowles; *b* 5 Oct 1947; *Educ* Queen Mary's GS Walsall, Trinity Coll Oxford (MA), Manchester Business Sch (MBA); *m* 5 Aug 1972, Susan, da of (William) Horace Haycock, of 33 Broadstone Ave, Walsall, West Midlands; 1 s (Hugh b 5 May 1981), 2 da (Anna b 23 June 1977, Jane b 3 Jan 1983); *Career* md: IBIS Information Services 1972-80, Pitman Books 1980-83; gp md Routledge and Kegan Paul plc 1983-85, chm and md Cassell plc 1986-; govr Pusey House Oxford, chm Hatfield Philharmonic Orch; Liveryman Worshipful Co of Glaziers; *Recreations* walking, reading, travel; *Clubs* United Oxford and Cambridge; *Style*— Philip Sturrock, Esq; 52 Hill Street, St Albans, Hertfordshire AL3 4QT (☎ 0727 58849), Cassell plc, Villers House, 41-47 Strand, London WC2N 5JE (☎ 071 8394900, fax 071 8391704)

STURROCK, Susan Jean; da of William Horace Haycock, of W Midlands, and Vera, *née* Garbett; *b* 10 April 1950; *Educ* Queen Mary's HS Walsall, Royal Coll of Music (ARCM), Univ of London (BMus, MTC); *m* 5 Aug 1972, Philip James Sturrock, s of James Cars Sturrock, of Yorkshire; 1 s (Hugh b 1981), 2 da (Anna b 1977, Jane b 1983); *Career* music journalist; regular columnist for Review Newspaper Gp, contrib BBC Radio Bedfordshire's Arts Magazine programme, artistic dir Int Organ Festival; co-author and ed of several books; *Books* Musical Instruments of the World (1976), The Book of Music (1978); *Recreations* music, cookery, reading, theatre; *Style*— Mrs Susan Sturrock; 52 Hill St, St Albans, Herts AL3 4QT; Home office (☎ 0727 58849)

STURT, Hon Mrs (Penelope Ann); *née* Mills; da of 3 Baron Hillingdon (d 1952); *b* 1917; *m* 1940, Evelyn Lennox Napier Sturt (d 1945); 1 s, 2 da; *Style*— The Hon Mrs Sturt; Thorn Croft, Chawleigh, Chumleigh, Devon

STURT, Richard Harry Brooke; s of Horace Holford Sturt (d 1962), of Wimborne, Dorset, and Eveline Frances, *née* Brooke; *b* 14 Nov 1939; *Educ* Marlborough, Peterhouse Cambridge (BA, MA); *m* 3 March 1962, Ann Lesley, da of Brig Charles Leslie Morgan, OBE (d 1982), of Walmer, Kent; 4 s ((Richard) Michael Villiers b 1964, Charles (Patrick) Holford b 1966, (Alexander) Fitzgerald Brooke b 1969, Nicholas (Julian) Holford b 1972); *Career* admitted slr 1966, sr ptnr Mowll & Mowll 1984- (ptnr 1967-84); slr: Dover Harbour Bd 1979-, Ind Schs Action Ctee 1980-82; slr and clerk to govrs King's Sch Canterbury 1979-; dep coroner E Kent 1972-79, HM Coroner For Kent (Canterbury and Dover Dist) 1979-, conducted inquest into Herald of Free Enterprise disaster 1987; lectr Police Staff Coll 1990-; memb CAA 1990-; dir: Dover & Folkestone Building Soc 1978-84, Waldershare Park Farms Ltd 1989-; chm: Gateway Broadcasting Ltd 1982-84, Invicta Radio (Invicta Sound plc) 1984-, Mellow 1557 Ltd 1990-; fndr and chm E Kent Holiday Music Tst 1979-; govr: Betteshanger Sch 1978-80, Northbourne Park Sch 1980-85; tstee: Keepershield Charitable Tst, All Saints Waldershare Tst, David Barlow Tst, Cicely Stockmann Memorial Fund, The Invicta Radio Charity; memb: SE England Coroners' Soc (pres 1981-82), Coroners' Soc England and Wales 1972-; FRSA 1990; *Books* Fishery Protection and Foreign Sea Fishing Boats (1973), Halsbury's Laws of England (contrib Fisheries, Ports and Harbours, European Communities, 4 edn), Vaughan on The Law of the European Communities (contrib Fisheries, 1986), The Collision Regulations (2 edn, 1984), The Role of the Coroner in Major Disasters (1988); *Recreations* cricket, singing, bridge, genealogy, fly-fishing; *Clubs* Athenaeum, Flyfishers; *Style*— Richard Sturt, Esq; Kent Cottage, 7 Granville Rd, Walmer, Deal, Kent CT14 7LU (☎ 0304 240250)

STURZAKER, Hugh Gerard; s of George Gerard Sturzaker (d 1971), of Chandlers Ford, Hants, and Gladys Maude, *née* French; *b* 24 June 1940; *Educ* W Buckland Sch Barnstaple Devon, Hertford Coll Oxford (MA), Guy's Med Sch (BM BCh); *m* 30 March 1968, Ann Elizabeth, da of Ernest Philip Featherstone, of South Croydon, Surrey; 3 s (Robert b 1970, John b 1971, James b 1980), 1 da (Nicola b 1973); *Career* house physician and surgn Guy's 1966-67, jr lectr in anatomy Guy's Med Sch 1987-68, surgical registrar Guildford and Guy's Hosps 1968-73, res fell St Mark's Hosp London 1973-74, sr surgical registrar Guy's and Gt Ormond St Hosp for Children, conslt gen surgn Gt Yarmouth and Waverley Health Authy 1979-, clinical teacher Univ of Cambridge; regnl advsr RCS Edinburgh; pres: Oxford Univ Med Soc, Br Med Students Assoc, E Anglian Surgical Club, Gt Yarmouth and Waverley Div BMA; memb: BMA 1966, RSM 1967; FRCSEd 1971, FRCS 1972; *Recreations* windsurfing, gardening, wine and beer making; *Style*— Hugh Sturzaker, Esq; Hobland House, Hobland, Great Yarmouth, Norfolk NR31 9AR (☎ 0493 665287), James Paget Hosptal, Gorleston, Great Yarmouth, Norfolk NR31 6LA (☎ 0493 600611)

STUTTAFORD, Dr (Irving) Thomas; s of Dr William Joseph Edward Stuttaford, MC, (d 1956), of Horning, Norfolk, and Mary Marjorie Dean, *née* Royden (d 1976); *b* 4 May 1931; *Educ* Greshams Sch, BNC Oxford, W London Hosp (MRCS, LRCP, DObstRCOG); *m* 1 June 1957, Pamela Christine, da of Lt-Col Richard Ropner, TD (d 1975), of Aldie, Tain, Rossshire; 3 s (Andrew b 1958, Thomas b 1961, Hugo b 1964); *Career* 2 Lt 10 Royal Hussars (PWO) 1953-55, Lt Scottish Horse TA 1955-59;jr hosp appts 1959-60, gen practice 1960-70, visiting physician BUPA 1970- (asst clincial dir 1979-81); clinical asst venereology: The London Hosp 1974-, Queen Mary's Hosp for the East End 1974-79, Moorfields Eye Hosp 1975-79; sr med advsr The Rank Orgn 1980-85; med columnist The Times 1990- (med corr 1982-90), med columnist Options (magazine), private practice occupational health 1986-; memb: Blofield and Flegg RDC 1964-66, Norwich City Cncl 1969-71; MP (C) Norwich S 1970-74, Parly candidate (C) Isle of Ely 1974 and 1979, sec Cons Health and Social Servs Ctee; memb: Cncl Res Def Soc 1970-79, Built Control Campaign 1970-79, Select Ctee on Sci and Technol; *Books* A Birth Control Plan for Britain (with Mr Alistair Service and Dr John Dunwoody, 1972); author of chapters in: Drinking to Your Health (1989), Which Wine Guide (1991); *Recreations* living in the country, conservation of old buildings; *Clubs* Beefsteak, Athenaeum, Reform, Cavalry and Guard's, Norfolk (Norwich); *Style*— Dr Thomas Stuttaford; The Grange, Bressingham, Diss, Norfolk IP22 2AT (☎ 037 988 245); 8 Devonshire Place, London W1

STUTTAFORD, William Royden; CBE (1989, OBE 1983); s of Dr William Joseph Edward Stuttaford (d 1956), of Horning, Norfolk, and Mary Marjorie Dean, *née* Royden (d 1975); *b* 21 Nov 1928; *Educ* Gresham's, Trinity Coll Oxford (MA); *m* 1, 1958 (m dis), Sarah Jane, da of Philip Legge; 2 s (William Julian b 1962, Dominic Charles b 1964), 2 da (Clare Lucinda b 1960, Melanie Mary b 1964); m 2, 1974 Susan d'Esterre, da of Capt Sir Gerald Curteis, KCVO, RN (d 1972), Broomwood, Sevenoaks, Kent; *Career* Nat Serv 2 Lt 10 Royal Hussars (PWO); memb Stock Exchange 1959-, chm Framlington Gp plc 1983-89, sr ptnr Laurence Prust & Co (stockbrokers) 1983-86; chm: Cons Political Centre 1978-81, East of England Cons Pty 1986-89, Unit Tst Assoc 1987-89; *Clubs* Cavalry and Guard's; *Style*— William Stuttaford, Esq, CBE; Moulshams Manor, Great Wigborough, Colchester, Essex CO5 7RL (☎ 020 635 330)

STUTTARD, Arthur Rupert Davies; s of Harold Stuttard, and Annie Constance, *née* Davies (d 1966); *b* 16 July 1943; *Educ* Accrington GS, ChCh Oxford (MA); *m* 10 Aug 1972, Margaret Evelyn, da of Reginald Wall Sykes; *Career* called to the Bar Middle Temple 1967; practises Northern Circuit, dep stipendiary magistrate Liverpool; *Books* English Law Notebook (1969), author of various articles on Lancs Witchcraft trials; *Recreations* local history, Egyptian and Minoan archaeology; *Style*— Arthur Stuttard, Esq; Acre House, Fence, Near Burnley, Lancs; St James's Chambers, 68 Quay St, Manchester 3 (☎ 061 834 7000)

STUTTARD, John Boothman; s of Thomas Boothman Stuttard (d 1969), and Helena, *née* Teasdale (d 1969); *b* 6 Feb 1945; *Educ* Shrewsbury, Churchill Coll Cambridge (MA); *m* 26 Sept 1970, Lesley Sylvia, da of Thomas Geoffrey Daish, of Kenilworth; 2 s (Thomas Henry Boothman (Tom) b 20 Jan 1975, James Midgley (Jamie) b 21 Aug 1976); *Career* VSO teacher SOAS Brunei 1966-67; Coopers & Lybrand Deloitte (formerly Cooper Brothers & Co): trainee accountant 1967-70, CA 1970, ptnr 1975-, currently dir of corp planning and mktg and chm of Scandinavian mkt gp; accounting advsr to CPRS Cabinet Office Whitehall 1982-83; memb Cambridge Univ Appts Bd 1977-81, treas Totteridge Manor Assoc; FCA; *Recreations* family, travel, squash, Rolls-Royce vintage cars, tennis, theatre; *Clubs* Naval & Military; *Style*— John B Stuttard, Esq; West End House, 56 Totteridge Common, London N20 8LZ (☎ 081 959 1692); Coopers & Lybrand Deloitte, Plumtree Court, London EC4A 4HT (☎ 071 583 5000, fax 071 822 8362)

STYLE, Christopher John David; s of Maj David Carlyle Willoughby Style, MC, TD (d 1978), of Loweswater, Cumbria, and Dr Anne Marion, *née* Phillips; *b* 13 April 1955; *Educ* St Bees Sch Cumbria, Trinity Hall Cambridge (MA), City of London Poly; *m* 7 April 1990, Victoria Jane, *née* Miles; *Career* Linklaters & Paines 1977-: articled clerk 1977-79, slr 1979, asst slr 1979-85, ptnr 1985-; seconded to Sullivan & Cromwell NY 1983; memb London Slrs Litigation Assoc; Freeman City of London 1985, memb City of London Slrs Co; *Books* Documentary Evidence (co-author, 3 edn 1991); *Recreations* fell walking, rock climbing; *Style*— Christopher Style, Esq; 45 Rudall Crescent, London NW3 1RR (☎ 071 435 5711); Linklaters & Paines, Barrington House, 59-67 Gresham St, London EC2V 7JA (☎ 071 606 7080, fax 071 606 5113, telex 884349)

STYLE, Frederick Montague; s of Sir William Style, 12 Bt (d 1981), and La Verne,

Lady Style, *qv*; *b* 5 Nov 1947; *Educ* De Sales Seminary, Marquette Univ; *m* 1971 (m dis 1986), Sharon, da of William H Kurz, of Menomonee Falls, Wisconsin, USA; 2 da (Jennifer b 1977, Christina b 1979); *Style*— Frederick Style, Esq; N 5866 Rockland Beach, Hilbert, WI 54129, USA (☎ 0101 414 439 1643)

STYLE, Lt Cdr Sir Godfrey William; CBE (1961), DSC (1942); er s of Brig-Gen Rodney Style (d 1957; 4 s of Sir William Style, 9 Bt), of Wierton Grange, Boughton-Monchelsea, Kent, and Hélène (d 1975), 2 da of Herman Kleinwort; *b* 3 April 1915; *Educ* Eton; *m* 1, 1942 (m dis 1951), Jill Elizabeth, da of George Bellis Caruth, of Ballymena; 1 s (Montague), 2 da (Helen, Marieka); m 2, 1951, Sigrid Elisabeth Julin (d 1985), da of Per Stellan Carlberg, of Jönköping, Sweden; 1 s (Charles); m 3, 1986, Valerie Beauclerk, da of Cdr Cecil Henry Hulton-Sams, RN, and widow of William Duncan McClure; *Career* joined RN 1933, serv HM Yacht Victoria and Albert 1938, Flag Lt to C-in-C Home Fleet 1939-41, Med 1941-42 (Malta convoys), (wounded 1942, despatches 1940 and 1943), thereafter HQ 4 Gp Bomber Cmd and Admty, invalided from RN 1946; Lloyd's underwriter 1944-; chm Nat Advsy Cncl Employment Disabled People 1963-74, govr Queen Elizabeth's Fndn, memb Cncl Sir Oswald Stoll Fndn 1975-84; dir Star Centre for Youth Cheltenham; kt 1973; *Recreations* field sports, horticulture, lapidary work; *Clubs* Naval and Military; *Style*— Lt Cdr Sir Godfrey Style, CBE, DSC, RN; 30 Carlyle Court, Chelsea Harbour, London SW10 0UQ (☎ 071 352 6512)

STYLE, La Verne, Lady; La Verne; da of Theron Comstock, (d 1985), of Palm Springs, California, and La Verne Comstock (*née* Nehrbas) (d 1983); *b* 17 Feb 1917; *Educ* Marquette Univ; *m* 1941, Sir William Montague Style, 12 Bt (d 1981), s of 11 Bt (d 1942); 2 s (William, Frederick, *qqv*); *Style*— La Verne, Lady Style; 619 Elm St, Hartford, WI 53027, USA (☎ 0101 414 673-5611)

STYLE, Col Rodney Gerald; s of Brig-Gen Rodney Charles Style (d 1957), and Helene Pauline, *née* Kleinwort (d 1974); see Debretts Peerage and Baronetage 1 Bt cr 1627; *b* 28 Oct 1920; *Educ* Eton, Staff Coll Camberley (psc); *m* 18 Oct 1952, Barbara, da of John Austin Hill (d 1950), of Natick, Mass; 3 s (William b 1954, Rodney b 1956, John b 1957), 1 da (Caroline b 1964); *Career* RA, Capt Coldstream Gds 5 Bn and Gds Armd Div, NW Europe 1940-46, Royal Northumberland Fus (Mau Mau Campaign Kenya) 1953-55, Bde Maj 29 Inf Bde (Suez Expdn) 1956; CO 1 Bn Royal Northumberland Fus 1962-65; Col Cmdt Royal Mil Sch of Music Kneller Hall 1973-75; ret 1975; professional photographer 1975-; memb Nat Cncl BIPP (second vice pres 1984-86); Licentiate Br Inst of Professional Photography 1978; *Clubs* Lansdowne; *Style*— Col R Gerald Style; 19 Crooksbury Rd, Farnham, Surrey GU10 1QD (☎ 025 18 2558)

STYLE, Rodney Hill; s of Col (Rodney) Gerald Style, of Runfold, Farnham, Surrey, and Barbara Hill Style; *b* 25 March 1956; *Educ* Eton; *m* 24 April 1982, Georgina Eve, da of John Kinloch Kerr of Abbottrule, of Frocester, Glos; 2 s (George b 1985, Hugo b 1985), 1 da (Elizabeth b 1989); *Career* CA; Spicer and Pegler 1976-85, ptnr Haines Watts 1985-, md Haines Watts Fin Servs Ltd 1987-; Freeman: City of London 1981, Worshipful Co of Grocers 1981, ACA 1981, ATII 1983; *Recreations* skiing; *Style*— Rodney Style, Esq; Greenacre, Steeple Aston, Oxfordshire; Sterling House, 19/23 High St, Kidlington, Oxon OX5 2DH (☎ 08675 78282, fax 08675 77518)

STYLE, Sir William Frederick; 13 Bt (E 1627), of Wateringbury, Kent; s of Sir William Montague Style, 12 Bt (d 1981), and La Verne, Lady Style, *qv*; *b* 13 May 1945; *Educ* (BSc, MEd); *m* 1, 1968, Wendy Gay, da of Gene and Marjory Wittenberger, of Hartford, Wisconsin, USA; 2 da (Shannon b 1969, Erin b 1973); m 2, 1986, Linnea L, da of Donn and Elizabeth Erickson, of Sussex, Wisconsin, USA; 1 da (McKenna b 1987); *Heir* bro, Frederick Montague Style; *Career* public sch teacher; *Recreations* yacht (Summer Style); *Clubs* Fond du Lac Yacht; *Style*— Sir William Style, Bt; 2430 N 3rd Lane, Oconomowoc, WI 53066, USA

STYLER, Granville Charles; s of Samuel Charles Styler, of Shipston-on-Stour, Warwicks, and Frances Joan, *née* Clifford; *b* 9 Jan 1947; *Educ* King Edward VI Sch Stratford-upon-Avon; *m* 11 Sept 1971, Penelope, da of William Arnold Darbyshire, of Lytham St Annes' Lancs; 3 da (Katie b 1974, Sophie b 1977, Emily b 1979); *Career* called to the Bar Gray's Inn 1970, rec 1988; govr St Dominic's Priory Sch Stone; *Recreations* tennis, hockey, jogging, point to point racing; *Style*— Granville Styler, Esq; 5 Fountain Ct, Steelhouse Lane, Birmingham 4 (☎ 021 2365771)

STYLES, Dr John Trevor; s of Capt Sydney Hubert Styles (d 1989), of Rugby, Warks, and Kathleen Joyce, *née* Hutchen; *b* 18 Nov 1939; *Educ* The GS Enfield, UCL (BSc), UCH Med Sch (MB BS); *m* 5 Feb 1966, Hilary Frances, da of Lawrence Rider Simmons (d 1988), of Ringwood, Hants; 1 s (Neville John b 1970), 3 da (Aileen Clare b 1967, Diane Caroline b 1968, Suzanne Catherine b 1971); *Career* registrar anaesthetist: UCH 1967-68, Hosp for Sick Children Gt Ormond St 1968; sr registrar anaesthetist Birmingham Teaching Hosps and Univ of Birmingham 1969-70, hon lectr Dept of Anaesthetics Univ of Birmingham 1970, conslt anaestheist Wolverhampton Hosp 1970-; memb Wolverhampton Health Authy 1982-85; memb Assoc of Anaesthetist of GB and Ireland, fell Coll Anaesthetists; *Recreations* woodworking and renovation of listed building; *Style*— Dr John Styles; Lower Mitton Farm, Penkridge, Stafford ST19 5QW (☎ 0785 780507)

STYLES, Dr William McNeil; s of Sydney James Styles (d 1978), of Bath, and Mary McCallum, *née* McNeil; *b* 22 March 1941; *Educ* City of Bath Boys' Sch, St Catharine's Coll Cambridge (MA, MB BCh), St Mary's Hosp Med Sch; *m* 21 Oct 1967, Jill, da of David Frederick Charles Manderson (d 1988), of Sarisbury Green, Hampshire; 1 s (Robert James b 1970), 3 da (Anna Louise b 1972, Sarah Catharine b 1974, Jane Emma b 1977); *Career* princ in gen med practice 1969-, advsr in gen practice NW Thames RHA 1983-; memb Cncl: Royal Postgrad Med Sch 1976-90, Hammersmith and Queen Charlotte's SHA 1983-90; RCGP (hon sec 1983-89, chm Educn Div 1989-); jt hon sec Jt Ctee Postgrad Trg for Gen Practice 1984-, memb Cncl Med Protection Soc 1990- (chm GP Advsy Bd 1990-); FRCGP; *Recreations* photography, horse riding, reading; *Style*— Dr William Styles; 86 Park Road, Chiswick, London W4 3HL (☎ 081 995 2952), The Grove Health Centre, Goldhawk Rd, London W12 8EJ (☎ 081 743 7153)

SUBAK-SHARPE, Prof John Herbert; s of Robert Subak (killed in the Holocaust 1942), of Vienna, and Nelly, *née* Bruell (killed in the Holocaust 1942); *b* 14 Feb 1924; *Educ* Humanistisches Gymnasium Vienna, Univ of Birmingham (BSc, PhD); *m* 22 Aug 1953, Barbara Naomi, da of late Ernest Harold Morris; 2 s (Robert John b 1956, Ian David b 1970), 1 da (Ann Barbara (Mrs Morton) b 1959); *Career* HM Forces Parachute Regt 1944-47; memb ARC scientific staff Animal Virus Res Inst Pirbright 1956-61, visiting fell California Inst of Technol USA 1961, memb scientific staff MRC Experimental Virus Unit Glasgow 1961-68, visiting prof NIH Bethesda USA 1967-68, prof of virology Univ of Glasgow 1968- (asst lectr 1954-56), hon dir MRC Virology Univ Glasgow 1968-; visiting prof: USUHS Bethesda USA 1985, Clare Hall Cambridge 1986; articles in scientific jls on genetic and molecular studies with viruses and cells; tstee Genetical Soc 1971- (sec 1966-72, vice pres 1972-75); memb: governing body W Scotland Oncology Orgn 1974-, Genetic Manipulation Advsy Gp 1976-80, BRC SHHD Chief Scientist's Orgn 1979-84, governing body AVRI Pribright 1986-88; chm MRC Tap 1986-89; memb: Scientific Advsy Gp Equine Virology Res Fndn 1987-, MRC cell biology and disorders bd 1988-; memb EMBO 1969-, FIBiol 1969, FRSE 1970; *Recreations* travel, bridge; *Clubs* Athenaeum; *Style*— Prof John Subak-Sharpe, FRSE; 17 Kingsborough Gardens, Hyndland, Glasgow G12 9NH (☎ 041 334 1863); Institute of Virology, University of Glasgow, Church St, Glasgow G12 8QQ (☎ 041 334 9555, fax 041 330 4808, telex 777070 UNIGLA)

SUBBA ROW, Raman; CBE (1991); s of Panguluri Venkata Subba Row (d 1954), of Croydon, and Doris Mildred, *née* Pinner (d 1972); *b* 29 Jan 1932; *Educ* Whitgift Sch, Trinity Hall Cambridge (MA, Cricket blue); *m* 1960, Anne Dorothy, da of Ronald Harrison; 2 s (Christopher Gordon b 7 March 1961, Alistair Patrick b 9 May 1965), 1 da (Michele Anne (Mrs Wilson) b 10 Dec 1962); *Career* Nat Serv Pilot Offr RAF 1956-57; cricket administrator; player: Surrey CCC 1953-54, Northants CCC 1955-61 (capt 1958-61), RAF 1956-57 (with tour India 1953-54), represented England 1958-61 (tour Aust 1958 and W Indies 1959); chm Ctee Surrey CCC 1974-79 (memb 1966-); TCCB: chm Mktg Ctee 1968-73, chm Cricket Cncl 1985-90; md Management Public Relations Ltd 1969-; *Recreations* golf, rugby football, management structures; *Style*— Raman Subba Row, Esq, CBE; Surrey CCC, Kennington Oval, London SE11 5SS (☎ 071 582 6660, fax 071 735 7769)

SUBHEDAR, Vasant Yadav; s of Yadav Mahadeo Subhedar, of 4 Sangam Soc, Athwa Lines, Surat, Gurjerat State, India, and Vatsala, *née* Nulkar; *b* 10 June 1936; *Educ* Univ of Bombay (BM BS, MS); *m* 27 Nov 1960, Dr Manisha, da of Vishnu Jaganat Sabnis (d 1975), of Bombay; 1 s (Dr Nimish b 23 Jan 1965), 1 da (Sangeeta (Mrs Ganvir) b 18 April 1962); *Career* conslt surgn Accident and Emergency Dept Dudley Rd Hosp 1978-; memb Exec Ctee Casulty Surgeons Assoc London 1985-88; chm: Accident and Emergency Serv Ctee W Midlands RHA 1985-88, W Midlands Regnl Casulty Surgeons Assoc 1985-88, former vice pres Birmingham Indian Med Assoc, current memb Birmingham Branch Exec Ctee for Overseas Doctors; memb: BMA, Overseas Doctors Assoc, Br Indian Med Assoc, Birmingham Medico legal Soc; *Recreations* photography, music, walking; *Style*— Vasant Subhedar, Esq; Sankey House, 60 Oakham Road, Dudley DY2 7TF (☎ 0384 54849), Dudley Rd Hosp, Dudley Rd, Birmingham B18 7QH (☎ 021 5543801)

SUBRAMANIAN, Dr Bala; s of Venkateswara Iyer (d 1987) of Madurai, India, and Laksmmi, *née* Nageswaran (d 1953); *b* 5 Oct 1940; *Educ* St Mary's HS Dindigul India, All India Inst of Med Sciences New Delhi India (MB BS), Univ of Poona India (MD); *m* 15 July 1965, Shyamala, da of Dr Raja Gopalan; 1 s (Rajiv b 15 Jan 1968), 1 da (Radha b 20 April 1966); *Career* dr of gen med Poona India 1967-1969, lectr in med AFMC Poona India 1969-71, Army Hosp Delhi India 1971-77 (dir gen AFMS Research Pool offr, chief Cardiac Laboratory, Leader High Altitude Research), Northwick Park Hosp and Clinical Res Centre Harrow Middlesex 1977-84 (sr res fell in bio engrg, sr registrar cardiology Br Heart Fndn sr res fell, sr lectr in cardiology, Conslt cardiologist), dir Cardiovascular Res Brunel Univ Uxbridge Middx 1984-89, md Complete Cardiac Care Centre 1989 ICMR award 1973, Maj Gen Amirchand prize (India) 1973, Chief of Army Staff Commendation (India) 1975; FACC 1977, fell American Heart Assoc 1985; memb: Medical Res Soc of UK 1979, British Cardiac Soc 1980, BMA 1981; *Books* Calcium Antagonists in Chronic Stable Angina (1983), author of over 200 orginal research papers; *Recreations* tennis, badminton, photography; *Style*— Dr Bala Subramanian; 34 Devonshire Place, London W1N 1PE (☎ 071 224 0637); Complete Cardiac Care Centre, 34 Devonshire Place, London W1N 1PE (☎ 071 224 0637, fax 071 224 0643)

SUCHAR, Victor Vivian; s of Nicholas Suchar, and Cecile, *née* Filess; *b* 4 June 1938; *Educ* Ecole de Travauz Publics Paris, Columbia Univ Graduate Sch of Business (MBA); *m* 29 June 1967, Elizabeth, da of John Bruce White; *Career* architectural and structural engr NY 1962-69, vice pres and head of corp fin Irving Trust Co NY & London 1970-80; dir: First Chicago Ltd London 1980-85, Lloyds Merchant Bank 1985-86; owner Camden Books Architectural Booksellers 1984; *Books* Essentials of Treasury Management (1980); *Recreations* walking, swimming, reading; *Style*— Victor Suchar, Esq; 14 Prospect Place, Camden Road, Bath BA1 15BL (☎ 0225 337026), Camden Books Architectural Booksellers, 146 Walcot St, Bath BA1 5BL (☎ 0225 461606)

SUCHET, David; s of Jack Suchet, and Joan Suchet; *b* 2 May 1946; *Educ* Wellington, LAMDA; *m* 1976, Sheila Anne, da of William Ferris (d 1986), of Stratford-upon-Avon; 1 s (Robert b 10 May 1981), 1 da (Katherine b 21 July 1983); *Career* actor; began professional career Gateway Theatre Chester 1969; repertory theatres incl: Exeter, Worthing, Birmingham; RSC 1973-; theatre incl: Estragon in Waiting for Godot, John Aubrey in Brief Lives, Timon of Athens (Young Vic), This Story of Yours (Hampstead), Separation (Hampstead then Comedy Theatre); RSC incl: Shylock in Merchant of Venice, Achilles in Troilus and Cressida, Bolingbroke in Richard II, Iago in Othello, Mercutio in Romeo & Juliet, Fool in King Lear, Caliban in The Tempest, Lucio in Measure for Measure, Mole in Toad of Toad Hall; films incl: Trouillfou in Hunchback of Notre Dame, Okana in Falcon and The Snowman, Beria in Red Monarch (for Channel 4), Dyer in Song for Europe, Inspector Japp in Thirteen to Dinner, Lafleur in Harry & The Hendersons, Wil in Why the Whales Came, Muller in A World Apart; tv incl: Edward Teller in Oppenheimer (NNC), Freud in The Life of Freud (BBC), Blott in Blott on the Landscape (BBC), Judge O'Connor in Cause Celebre (Anglia TV), Glougauer in Once in a Lifetime (BBC), Carver in Nobody Here But Us Chickens (Channel 4), Hercule Poirot in Agatha Christie's Poirot (LWT); BBC Radio incl: Ironhand, The Kreuzer Sonata, First Night Impressions, The Shout, Rosenburg in The Trenches, Debusssy, Anton Chekov; awards incl: Best Radio Actor 1979 (for Kreuzer Sonata), Best Actor Marseilles Film Festival 1983 (for Red Monarch), Best Actor Br Indust and Scientific Film Assoc Craft Awards 1986 (for Stress), Best Actor RTS Performance Awards 1986 (for Song for Europe, Freud, Blott on the Landscape, Best Actor nomination in a Supporting Role BAFTA 1989 for A World Apart); dir Canvasback Ltd, assoc artiste RSC, memb Cncl LAMDA, visiting prof of theatre Univ of Nebraska 1975; author of essays in Players of Shakespeare (on Caliban, Shylock, Iago); *Recreations* photography, clarinet, ornithology; *Style*— David Suchet, Esq; c/o The Brunskill Management Ltd, Suite 8, 169 Queens Gate, London SW7 5EH (☎ 071 581 3388, fax 071 589 9460)

SUCKLING, Dr Charles Walter; CBE (1989); s of Ernest Edward Suckling (d 1968), and Barbara, *née* Thompson (d 1986); *b* 24 July 1920; *Educ* Oldershaw GS Wallasey, Univ of Liverpool (BSc, PhD); *m* 25 May 1946, Eleanor Margaret, da of George Finlay Watterson (d 1953); 2 s (Colin b 24 March 1947, Keith b 25 March 1947), 1 da (Karen b 10 March 1952); *Career* ICI PLC 1942-82: res dir Mond Div 1966-69, dep chm Mond Div 1969-72, chm Paints Div 1972-77, gen manager of res tech ICI Group 1977-82; chm Bradbury Suckling and Partners Ltd 1982- (dir 1969-); memb Royal Commission on Environmental Pollution, visiting prof Univ Stirling; DSc Liverpool 1980, D Univ of Stirling 1985; sr FRCA 1986, FRSC, FRS 1978; *Books* Research in the Chemical Industry (jtly, 1969), Chemistry Through Models (jtly, 1978); *Recreations* gardening, music, writing, languages; *Style*— Dr Charles Suckling, CBE, FRS; Willowhay, Shoppenhangers Road, Maidenhead, Berkshire SL6 2QA (☎ 0628 27502)

SUDBURY, John Charles; *b* 7 March 1944; *Educ* E Ham GS, NE London Poly; *m* 1965, Carol Ann, *née* Auker; 1 s, 2 da; *Career* chartered engr, dir Lex Motor Co Ltd; *Recreations* golf, travel, work; *Style*— John Sudbury, Esq; Sycamore, Fishery Rd, Bray, Berks

SUDDABY, Dr Arthur; CBE (1980); s of George Suddaby, of Kingston upon Hull (d 1950), and Alice May, *née* Holmes (d 1970); *b* 26 Feb 1919; *Educ* Riley HS Hull, Hull Tech Coll (BSc), Chelsea Coll (BSc, MSc), QMC London (PhD); *m* 23 Dec 1944, Elizabeth Bullin (d 1965), da of the late Charles Vyse, of Cheyne Row, Chelsea; 2 s (John b 1946, Anthony b 1947); *Career* chem engr 1937-47, sr lectr in chem engrg West Ham Coll of Technol 1947-50; Sir John Cass Coll: sr lectr in physics 1950-61, head of dept 1961-66, princ 1966-70; provost City of London Poly 1970-81; scientific conslt on the carriage of goods by sea until 1990; on various CNAA ctees 1969-81; memb: London and Home Cos Regnl Advsy Ctee on Higher Educn 1971-81, Ct of City Univ 1967-81; chm: Ctee of Dirs of Polys 1976-78, Assoc of Navigation Schs 1972; MIChemE 1944, FRSC 1980; *Recreations* fishing, hunting; *Clubs* Athenaeum; *Style*— Dr Arthur Suddaby, CBE; Castle Hill House, Godshill Wood, Fordingbridge, Hants SP6 2LU (☎ 0425 652234); Flat 3, 16 Elm Park Gardens, Chelsea, London SW10 9NY (☎ 071 352 9164)

SUDDABY, Dominic; s of William Donald Suddaby; *b* 27 Oct 1939; *Educ* St Edwards Sch Oxford; *m* 1964, Sheelagh Maureen, nee Minns; 5 children; *Career* md: Autolease Ltd 1972-74, PHH Servs Ltd and PHH Leasing Ltd 1974-86; dir The Export Fin Co Ltd 1986-; FInstD; *Recreations* shooting, military history, cricket; *Style*— Dominic Suddaby Esq; Troopshill Cottage, Fidges Lane, Eastcombe, nr Stroud, Glos GL6 7DW (☎ 0452 770302)

SUDDARDS, Roger Whitley; CBE (1987), DL (West Yorks 1990); s of John Whitley Suddards, OBE (d 1978), and Jean, *née* Rollitt; *b* 5 June 1930; *Educ* Bradford GS; *m* 1 Aug 1963, Elizabeth Anne, da of Donald Stuart Rayner; 2 da (Jane Elisabeth b 21 June 1965, Helen Victoria b 1 Aug 1967); *Career* RASC 1952-54; slr and sr ptnr Last Suddards 1952-88, conslt Hammond Suddards 1988-; chm: Yorks Bldg Soc, Hammond Suddards Res Ltd 1989-; visiting lectr Leeds Sch of Town Planning 1964-74, memb Planning Law Ctee Law Soc 1964-81, planning law conslt to UN 1974-77, memb Bye-Laws Revision Ctee Law Soc 1984-87, legal memb Royal Town Planning Inst; chm: Advsy Ctee for Land Cmmn for Yorkshire & Humberside, Working Party on Future of Bradford Churches 1978-79, Bradford Disaster Appeal Tst 1985-89, Yorkshire Television Trust Ltd 1990; memb: Ctee Nat Museum of Photography Film and TV 1984-, W Yorks Residuary Body 1986-, Nat Property Advsy Gp NHS 1988-, Eng Heritage Areas Advsy Ctee; tstee: Friends of Bradford Art Galleries 1962-87, Bradford Playhouse of Film Theatre 1962-87, Civic Tst 1988-, Nat Historical Bldg Crafts Inst 1989-; dir: Bradford Breakthrough Ltd, The Independent Broadcasting Television Trust Ltd 1990; pres Bradford Law Soc 1969, pro chllr and chm Cncl Univ of Bradford 1987-, former chm Examinations Bd ISVA; contrib articles: Jl of Planning and Environmental Law (memb Editorial Bd), Law Soc Gazette; hon fell Soc of Valuers of Auctioneers; Liveryman City of London Slrs Co 1968-; *Books* Town Planning Law of West Indies (1974), History of Bradford Law Society (1975), A Lawyer's Peregrination (1984, 2 edn 1987), Bradford Disaster Appeal (1986), Listed Buildings: the Law and Practice (2 edn 1988); *Recreations* theatre, music, reading, travel; *Clubs* Arts, Bradford Club (Bradford); *Style*— Roger W Suddards, Esq, CBE, DL; Low House, High Eldwick, Bingley, W Yorks BD16 3AZ (☎ 0274 564 832); Salts min Saltaire Bradford BD18 3LD (☎ 0274 532 233/588 028, fax 0274 588 848)

SUDELEY, 7 Baron (UK 1838); Merlin Charles Sainthill Hanbury-Tracy; s of Capt David Hanbury-Tracy (gs of 4 Baron) and Colline, da of Lt-Col Collis St Hill; the 1 Baron was chm of the Cmmn for the Rebuilding of the new Houses of Parliament 1835; suc kinsman (6 Baron) 1941; *b* 17 June 1939; *Educ* Eton, Worcester Coll Oxford; *m* 1980 (m dis 1988), Hon Mrs Elizabeth Villiers, da of late Viscount Bury (s of 9 Earl of Albemarle) and formerly w of Alastair John Hanbury-Tracy, *qv*; *Heir* kinsman, (Desmond) Andrew John Hanbury-Tracy, *qv*; *Career* former chm Human Rights Soc (founded by Lord St John of Fawsley to oppose legalisation of euthanasia); introduced debates in the House of Lords on the export of manuscripts 1973, the English Tourist Bd's report "Cathedral & Tourism" 1980, and the teaching & use of the Prayer Bk in Theological colls 1987; patron: Assoc of Bankrupts, Anglican Assoc, St Peter's (Petersham); patron Prayer Book Soc (introduced Prayer Book (Protection) Bill 1981), memb Ctee Manorial Soc; past pres The Montgomeryshire Soc; has contributed to Contemporary Review, London Magazine, Quarterly Review, Vogue, The Universe, Pick of Today's Short Stories, Montgomeryshire Collections, Salisbury Review, Transactions of the Bristol and Gloucs Archaeological Soc, Die Waage (Zeifschrift der Chemie Grünenal), author (with others) The Sudeleys - Lords of Toddlington (1987); vice chllr The Monarchist League; FSA 1989; *Recreations* conversation; *Clubs* Brooks's; *Style*— The Rt Hon the Lord Sudeley, FSA; 25 Melcombe Court, Dorset Square, NW1 (☎ 071 723 7502); c/o Williams & Glyn's Bank, 21 Grosvenor Gardens, SW1

SUENSON-TAYLOR, Hon Christopher John; s and h of 2 Baron Grantchester, QC; *b* 8 April 1951; *Educ* Winchester, LSE (BSc); *m* 1973, Jacqueline, da of Dr Leo Jaffé; 2 s, 2 da; *Career* dairy farmer and cattle breeder; former memb Cncl Holstein Soc Exec, memb Cncl Cheshire Agric Soc; RASE: champion Holstein Cow 1983, Supreme Dairy Female 1990; Master Breeder 1990; 4 All- Britain and 4 Reserve Awards; *Recreations* soccer; *Style*— The Hon Christopher Suenson-Taylor; Lower House Farm, Back Coole Lane, Audlem, Crewe, Cheshire (☎ 0270 811363)

SUENSON-TAYLOR, Hon James Gunnar; 3 and yst s of 2 Baron Grantchester, QC; *b* 30 Sept 1955; *Educ* Eton, Kingston Poly; *m* 1981, Gillian Susan, yr da of Peter Ayling, of Worcester Park, Surrey; 1 s (Andrew James b 1985), 1 da (Katherine Joyce b 1988); *Career* co dir; *Recreations* rowing, shooting, fishing; *Style*— The Hon James Suenson-Taylor; Mole House, 63 Pelhams Walk, Esher, Surrey (☎ 0372 65207)

SUENSON-TAYLOR, Hon Jeremy Kenneth; 2 (twin) s of 2 Baron Grantchester, CBE, QC; *b* 8 April 1951; *Educ* Winchester; *m* Lindsay Anne Kirby, of Leicester; 2 s (Rowan b 1974, Daniel b 1983), 2 da (Laurel b 1979, Zoë b 1982); *Style*— The Hon Jeremy Suenson-Taylor; Hillside Farm, Clutton, nr Bristol, Avon

SUENSON-TAYLOR, Hon Kirsten Victoria Mary; 3 da of 2 Baron Grantchester, QC; *b* 25 Sept 1961; *Style*— The Hon Kirsten Suenson-Taylor; The Gate House, Coombe Wood Rd, Kingston Hill, Surrey

SUESS, Nigel Marcus; *b* 13 Dec 1945; *Educ* Chigwell Sch, Univ of Cambridge; *m* 1978, Maureen, nee Ferguson; 1 da; *Career* banker; dir The British Linen Bank Ltd; *Recreations* mountaineering, chess, ornithology; *Style*— Nigel Suess, Esq; Drumornie, 35 Woodhall Rd, Edinburgh

SUFFIELD, 11 Baron (GB 1786); Sir Anthony Philip Harbord-Hamond; 12 Bt (GB 1745), MC (1950); s of 10 Baron (d 1951), and Nina Annette Mary Crawfuird (d 1955), da of John William Hutchison, of Lauriston Hall, and Edlingham, Kirkcudbrightshire; *b* 19 June 1922; *Educ* Eton; *m* 1952, Elizabeth Eve, da of late Judge (Samuel Richard) Edgedale, QC, of Field Lodge, Crowthorne, Berks; 3 s, 1 da; *Heir* s, Hon Charles Harbord-Hamond; *Career* Maj Coldstream Gds (ret); served: WWII N Africa and Italy, Malaya 1948-50; appointed one of HM Bodyguard of Hon Corps of Gentlemen-at-Arms 1973; *Clubs* Army and Navy, Pratt's; *Style*— The Rt Hon the Lord Suffield, MC; Wood Norton Grange, Dereham, Norfolk (☎ 036 284 235)

SUFFIELD, Sir Henry John Lester; *b* 28 April 1911; *Educ* Camberwell Central Sch; *m* 1940, Elizabeth Mary White; 1 s, 1 da; *Career* serv WWII Maj RASC, with LNER 1926-35, Morris Motor Corpn Canada and USA 1952-64, dep manager and dir Br Motor Corpn Birmingham 1964-68, sales dir BL Motor Corpn 1968-69, head of def sales MOD 1969-76; kt 1973; *Clubs* RAC; *Style*— Sir Henry Suffield; 16 Glebe Court, Fleet, Hants

SUFFOLK, Archdeacon of; *see*: Robinson, Ven Neil

SUFFOLK AND BERKSHIRE, Earl of, 21 of Suffolk (E 1603), 14 of Berkshire (E 1626); Michael John James George Robert Howard; also Viscount Andover and Baron Howard of Charlton (E 1622); s of 20 Earl (k on active serv 1941); the 1 Earl was 2 s of 4 Duke of Norfolk; the 9 Earl's w was mistress of George II, who built Marble Hill House, on the Thames between Twickenham and Richmond, for her (the style is Palladian, designed by Lord Pembroke); *b* 27 March 1935; *Educ* Winchester; *m* 1, 1960 (m dis 1967), Mme Simone Paulmier, da of Georges Litman, of Paris; m 2, 1973 (m dis 1980), Anita Robsham, da of Robin Fuglesang, of Cuckfield, Sussex; 1 s, 1 da (Lady Katharine b 9 April 1976); m 3, 1983, Linda Jacqueline, da of Col Vincent Paravicini and former w of 4 Viscount Bridport; 2 da (Lady Philippa b 1985, Lady Natasha b 1987); *Heir* s, Viscount Andover; *Style*— The Rt Hon the Earl of Suffolk and Berks; Charlton Park, Malmesbury, Wilts (☎ 0666 822206/823200)

SUGDEN, Sir Arthur; s of Arthur Sugden (d 1940), of Manchester, and Elizabeth Ann Sugden (d 1952); *b* 12 Sept 1918; *Educ* Thomas St Sch W Gorton, HS of Commerce Manchester; *m* 1946, Agnes, da of Francis Grayston (d 1930); 2 s; *Career* serv WWII Maj RA, UK and India; certified accountant and chartered sec; chief exec Coop Wholesale Soc Ltd 1973-80, chm Coop Bank 1973-80; FIB; kt 1978; *Recreations* reading, walking, travel; *Style*— Sir Arthur Sugden; 56 Old Wool Lane, Cheadle Hulme, Cheadle, Cheshire SK8 5JA

SUGDEN, Prof David Edward; s of John Cyril Gouldie Sugden (d 1963), and Patricia, *née* Backhouse; *b* 5 March 1941; *Educ* Warwick Sch, Univ of Oxford (BA, DPhil); *m* 9 Aug 1966, Britta Valborg, da of Harald Stridsberg, of Sweden; 2 s (John Peter, Michael Edward), 1 da (Pauline Charlotta); *Career* scientific offr Br Antarctic Survey 1965-66, lectr then reader Univ of Aberdeen 1966-87, prof and head of Geography Dept Univ of Edinburgh 1987-; visiting prof Arctic and Alpine Inst USA; memb: Inst of Br Geographers, Royal Scot Geographical Soc, Royal Geographical Soc, Royal Soc (Edinburgh); *Books* Glaciers and Landscape (with B S John, 1976), Arctic and Antarctic (1982), Geomorphology (with S Schumm and R J Chorley, 1986); *Recreations* hillwalking, gardening, squash; *Style*— Prof David Sugden; Dept of Geography, University of Edinburgh, Drummond St EH8 9XP (☎ 031 650 2521, fax 031 5560544, telex 727442 UNIVEDG)

SUGDEN, Elwyn James; s of Philip Sugden (d 1990), of Swansea, and Vira Jane, *née* Samuel; *b* 21 May 1940; *Educ* Gowerton Boys GS; *m* 31 July 1965, Jean Gaynor, da of Brynmor Thomas; 2 c (Sian Frances b 1 Oct 1969, Rhian Fraser b 9 Feb 1971); *Career* articled clerk Ross Jones & Co Cardiff & Swansea, qualified CA 1969, ptnr NG Thomas & Co Swansea 1969-; chm West Glamorgan and Dyfed Soc of Chartered Accountants; FCA (ACA 1969); *Recreations* music (both classical and jazz), motor sport, badminton, travel, food and the arts in general; *Style*— Elwyn Sugden, Esq; N G Thomas & Co, Chartered Accountants, 7 Wind St, Swansea SA1 1DF (☎ 0792 643591, fax 0792 459047)

SUGDEN, John Christopher; TD (1966); s of Howard Davy Sugden (d 1965), of 3 Prince Arthur Rd, Hampstead, London NW3, and Olive Mary, *née* Brayfield (d 1973); *b* 10 Jan 1933; *Educ* Aldenham; *m* 23 May 1959, Jennifer Jean, da of Ronald George Hilder, of 5 St Christophers Green, Haslemere, Surrey; 1 s (Oliver Davy b 1962), 1 da (Philippa Anne (Mrs Harris-Burland) b 1960); *Career* Nat Serv: Army 1951, cmmnd RASC 1952, served Germany, Capt 1953, 56 London Armd Div TA 1954-67, Duke of Yorks HQ Chelsea BRASCO 1954; export mangr Sharp Perrin & Co 1958-60, self employed retailer 1960-; md Three Counties Toys Ltd 1983-, chm Concorde Toys Ltd 1990- (md 1984-89), vice chm Allied Toy Groups Ltd 1990-; memb: Haslemere Town Cncl 1976-84, Waverley Dist Cncl 1978-82; chm: Dolmetsch Fndn of Early Music, Govrs Shootermill Middle Sch 1979-81, Tstees of Haslemere Hall 1983-; govr Woolmer Hill Sch 1980-; Mayor of Haslemere 1979-80; *Recreations* music, languages; *Style*— John Sugden, Esq, TD; Little Orchard, Kingsley Green, Haslemere, Surrey (☎ 0428 642162) Clotamar, L'Escala, Girona, Spain; 2-4 Petworth Rd, Haslemere, Surrey (☎ 0428 634165, fax 0428 658420)

SUGDEN, Prof Robert; s of Frank Gerald Sugden (d 1987), and Kathleen, *née* Buckley; *b* 26 Aug 1949; *Educ* Eston GS, Univ of York (BA, DLitt), Univ Coll Cardiff (MSc); *m* 26 March 1982, Christine Margaret, da of Leslie Kenneth Upton, of Woking, Surrey; 1 s (Joe b 1984), 1 da (Jane b 1986); *Career* lectr in economics Univ of York 1971-78, reader in economics Univ of Newcastle upon Tyne 1978-85, prof of economics UEA 1985; *Books* The Principles of Practical Cost-Benefit Analysis (with A Williams, 1978), The Political Economy of Public Choice (1981), The Economics of Rights, Cooperation and Welfare (1986); *Recreations* walking, gardening; *Style*— Prof Robert Sugden; School of Economic and Social Studies, Univ of E Anglia, Norwich NR4 7TJ (☎ 0603 592078, fax 0603 58553, telex 975197)

SUGGETT, Gavin Robert; s of Kenneth Frederick Suggett (d 1984), of Weybridge, Surrey, and Nancy, *née* Voss-Bark; *b* 11 May 1944; *Educ* Felsted Sch, Christ's Coll Cambridge (MA), London Business Sch (MSc); *m* 11 Sept 1971, Louise, da of Hon Lord Migdale (d 1983), of Edinburgh and Sutherland; 1 s (Gordon b 1977), 2 da (Clare b 1975, Katie b 1980); *Career* CA; articled clerk Deloittes 1962-66, fin mangr Weir Gp Ltd 1971-73, dir Alliance Tst plc 1987- (co sec 1973-89); pt/t lectr Law Faculty and MBA Course Univ of Dundee; FCA 1971; *Recreations* skiing, gardening, hill walking; *Clubs* New (Edinburgh), Royal Perth Golf; *Style*— Gavin Suggett, Esq; The Alliance Tst, 64 Reform St, Dundee DD1 1TJ (☎ 0382 201700, fax 0382 25133, telex 76195)

SUIRDALE, Viscount; John Michael James Hely-Hutchinson; er s and h of 8 Earl of Donoughmore; *b* 7 Aug 1952; *Educ* Harrow; *m* 1977, Marie-Claire, da of Gerard van den Driessche (d 1985); 1 s (Hon Richard Gregory b 1980), 2 da (Hon Marie-Pierre Joanna b 1978, Hon Tatiana Louise b 1985); *Heir* s, Hon Richard Gregory Hely-Hutchinson b 1980; *Career* dir; *Recreations* shooting, fishing, skiing; *Style*— Viscount Suirdale; 34 Perryn Rd, Acton, London W3 7NA

SULLIVAN, David Dimitri; s of late Walter Terence Sullivan, of Southend-on-Sea, Essex and Xenia Anastasia Sullivan; *b* 19 March 1943; *Educ* Mayfield Coll; *m* 17 June 1967, Lesley June, da of Robert George Berks (d 1968); 1 s (Martyn David b 17 June 1970), 1 da (Karen Susan b 14 Aug 1968); *Career* Herbert Hill & Co (now Stoy Hayward) 1959-65, Clark Battams & Co (now Clark Whitehill) 1965-67, dir N M Rothschild & Sons Ltd 1982- (joined 1967); FCA 1965, ATII 1965; *Recreations* golf, skiing; *Style*— David Sullivan, Esq; New Court, St Swithin's Lane, London EC4P 4DU (☎ 071 280 5000, fax 071 929 1643)

SULLIVAN, Edmund Wendell; s of Thomas James Llewellyn Sullivan (d 1965), of Portadown, and Letitia, *née* Holmes (d 1968); *b* 21 March 1925; *Educ* Portadown Coll, Queen's Univ Belfast, Royal Dick Vet Coll; *m* 1957, Elinor, da of John Wilson Melville (d 1975), of Fife; 2 s (Kenneth, Colin), 1 da (Morna); *Career* vet surgn, gen vet practice 1947-, joined State Vet Serv in NI 1948, MRCVS; *Recreations* hill walking, woodcraft, following rugby & cricket; *Style*— Edmund W Sullivan, Esq; 26 Dillon's Ave, Newtownabbey, Co Antrim (☎ 0232 862323); Dept of Agric for NI, Dundonald House, Upper Newtownards Rd, Belfast (☎ 0232 650111, telex 74578 DEPAGR G)

SULLIVAN, Jeremy Mirth; QC (1982); s of Arthur Brian Sullivan and Pamela Jean, *née* Kendall; *b* 17 Sept 1945; *Educ* Framlingham Coll, King's Coll London (LLB, LLM); *m* 1970, Ursula Klara Marie, da of late Benno August Friederich Hildenbrock; 2 s (Richard b 1974, Geoffrey b 1976); *Career* 2 Lt Suffolk & Cambs Regt (TA) 1963-65; called to the Bar Inner Temple 1968, lectr in law City of London Poly 1968-71; in practice Planning & Local Govt Bar 1971-, memb Parly Bar 1990-, LAMRTPI 1970, LMRTPI 1976, memb Cncl RTPI 1983-87, memb Exec Ctee Georgian Gp 1985-89, recorder 1989-; govr Highgate Sch; *Recreations* walking, railways, canals, reading history; *Style—* Jeremy Sullivan, Esq, QC; 4-5 Grays Inn Square, London WC1R 5JA (☎ 071 404 5252, telex 895 3743 GRAYLAW)

SULLIVAN, Michael Francis; s of Sir Richard Benjamin Magniac Sullivan, 8 Bt (d 1977), and Muriel Mary Paget Pineo (d 1988); *b* 4 April 1936; *Educ* St Andrew Coll SA, Clare Coll Cambridge (MA, MB BChir), St Mary's Hosp Univ of London; *m* 1, 22 Aug 1957 (m dis 1978), Inger, da of Arne Mathieson (d 1984); 1 s (Richard b 9 Jan 1961), 1 da (Nicola b 20 Aug 1965); m 2, 22 Dec 1978, Caroline Mary, da of Maj Christopher Griffin, of Oxborough, Norfolk; 1 da (Lucy b 22 Nov 1980); *Career* spinal surgn Royal Nat Orthopaedic Hosp London 1971-; sec Int Lumbar Spine Surgns 1975-78; pres European Spinal Surgns 1990-91; visiting lectr in spinal surgery: Australia 1985, S Africa 1981, USA 1980, Canada 1982, Japan 1989; author of numerous articles on spinal surgery; FRCS; *Recreations* cricket, sailing, shooting; *Clubs* MCC, Royal Harwich Yacht; *Style—* Michael Sullivan, Esq; 12 Gloucester Crescent, London NW1 7DS (☎ 071 485 4473); High Lodge Farm, Mildenhall, Suffolk (☎ 0638 716664); 95 Harley St, London W1N 1DF (☎ 071 486 4970)

SULLIVAN, (Sir) Richard Arthur; 9 Bt (UK 1804); does not use title; s of Sir Richard Benjamin Magniac Sullivan, 8 Bt (d 1977), and Muriel Mary Paget; *b* 9 Aug 1931; *Educ* Univ of Cape Town (BSc), MIT (MS); *m* 1962, Elenor Mary, da of Kenneth Merson Thorpe, of Somerset W, S Africa; 1 s, 3 da; *Heir* s, Charles Merson Sullivan, b 15 Dec 1962; *Career* civil engr; mangr Woodward Clyde Oceaneering; *Recreations* tennis; *Clubs* Houston Racquet; *Style—* Richard Sullivan, Esq; 1060 Royal York Rd, Toronto, Ontario M8X 2G7, Canada (☎ 0101 416 232 9750); Geocon Inc, 3210 American Drive, Mississanga, Ontario L4V 1B3, Canada (☎ 0101 416 673 1664)

SULLIVAN, Terence Alistair (Terry); s of Cecil Christopher Sullivan (d 1980), of Swansea, and Violet Ann, *née* Green (d 1987); *b* 6 Nov 1935; *m* 29 June 1957, Valerie May, da of Thomas Lewis Williams (d 1988), of Swansea; 1 s (Martin b 10 Oct 1970), 2 da (Linda b 6 March 1964, Carole (twin) b 6 March 1964); *Career* bowls player; champion; Welsh singles (indoor) 1983 and 1986, UK singles (indoor) 1984, World singles (indoor) 1985, Welsh triples (indoor) 1985, Welsh champion of champions (outdoor) 1985 and 1986, Welsh and Br Isles fours (indoor) 1987, Aust Mazda Int Singles (outdoor) 1988; represented Wales in 23 indoor and six outdoor events, Welsh team captain for Br indoor championships 1990, Welsh pairs champion (outdoor) 1990; *Recreations* gardening, walking, reading; *Clubs* Swansea Leisure Centre, Manselton Park (bowling); *Style—* Terry Sullivan, Esq; 6 Ocean View Close, Derwen Fawr, Swansea, West Glamorgan (☎ 0792 204797)

SULTOON, Jeffrey Alan; s of Maurice Sultoon, of London, and Babette, *née* Braun; *b* 8 Oct 1953; *Educ* Haberdashers' Aske's, St Edmund Hall Oxford; *m* 11 May 1985, Vivien Caryl, da of Peter Woodbridge, of Guildford, Surrey; *Career* admitted slr 1978; slr Freshfields 1978-81, ptnr Ashurst Morris Crisp 1986- (slr 1981-86); *Books* Tolley's Company Law (contrib 1990); *Style—* Jeffrey Sultoon, Esq; Ashurst, Morris, Crisp, Broaswalk House, 5 Appold St, London EC2A 2HA (☎ 071 638 1111, fax 071 972 7990, telex 387067)

SULYÁK, Hon Mrs (Rosamund Sybil); *née* Allen; o da of Baron Croham, GBE (Life Peer), *qv*; *b* 1942; *m* 1974, Stephan Sulyák; 1 da (Veronica); *Career* reader (as R S Allen) QMW London; *Books* editions and translations of Medieval texts; *Recreations* riding; *Style—* The Hon Mrs Sulyák; 8A Harewood Road, S Croydon, Surrey CR2 7AL

SUMBERG, David Anthony Gerald; MP (C) Bury S 1983-; s of late Joshua Sumberg and Lorna Sumberg; *b* 2 June 1941; *Educ* Tettenhall Coll Wolverhampton; Coll of Law London; *m* 1972, Carolyn Franks; 1 s, 1 da; *Career* former slr; PPS to Attorney-Gen Sir Patrick Mayhew, QC, MP; memb Manchester CC; contested (C) Wythenshawe Manchester 1979; *Recreations* family and friends; *Style—* David Sumberg, Esq, MP; House of Commons, London SW1A 0AA (☎ 071 219 4459)

SUMMERFIELD, Sir John Crampton Summerfield; CBE (1966, OBE 1961), QC (Bermuda 1963); s of Arthur Frederick Summerfield (d 1941), and Lilian Winifred, *née* Staas (d 1958); *b* 20 Sept 1920; *Educ* Lucton Sch Herefordshire; *m* 11 Aug 1945, Patricia Sandra, da of John Geoffrey Musgrave (d 1926), of Salisbury, Rhodesia; 2 s (John b 1946, Michael b 1948), 2 da (Rosemary b 1955, Margaret (Mrs Goodwin) b 1960); *Career* served WWII, E Africa NFD, Ethiopia and Madagascar, Capt Royal Signals; called to the Bar Gray's Inn 1949; Tanganyika crown counsel/legal draftsman 1949-58, dep legal sec E Africa High Cmmn 1958-62; AG Bermuda 1962-72; chief justice: Bermuda 1972-77, Cayman Islands 1977-87; justice of appeal Court of Appeal Bermuda 1980-88, pres Court of Appeal Belize 1981-82; memb Exec Cncl and MLC Bermuda until 1966; kt 1973; *Recreations* photography, chess; *Clubs* Royal Cwlth Soc; *Style—* Sir John Summerfield, CBE, QC; 3 The Corniche, Sandgate, Folkestone, Kent CT20 3TA (☎ 0303 49479)

SUMMERFIELD, Linda Victoria (Lin); da of Henry Conrad Fullbrook (d 1952), and Rose Iris, *née* Hollings; *b* 24 Feb 1952; *Educ* Sudbury HS for Girls; *Career* author; works published incl: Count the Days (1989, shortlisted for John Creasey prize), Never Walk Behind Me (1990), various short stories; *Recreations* reading, walking, sketching, opera, worrying; *Style—* Ms Lin Summerfield; 52 Butt Rd, Great Cornard, nr Sudbury, Suffolk CO10 0DP; c/o Heather Jeeves, 15 Campden Hill Square, London W8 J7Y (☎ 071 727 1699, fax 071 376 2778)

SUMMERFIELD, Peter William; s of Frank Summerfield (d 1984), and Margot; *b* 3 June 1933; *Educ* William Ellis Sch, Pembroke Coll Oxford (MA); *m* 1, 15 July 1962, Susan Evelyn (d 1990) da of late Willy Wharton, of Ealing, London; 2 s (Mark Steven b 1965, David Michael b 1968), 1 da (Amanda Deborah b 1965); m 2, 5 July 1973, Marianne Dorothee, da of Hans Granby, of Hendon, London; *Career* Nat Serv, Egypt and Malta 1952-54; admitted slr 1960; ptnr: Oppenheimer Nathan and Vandyk 1965-88 (articled clerk 1957-60, asst slr 1960 -65), Nabarro Nathanson 1988-; chm Int Bd of Advrs Univ of the Pacific McGeorge Sch of Law (visiting prof 1987); memb: Law Soc of Eng and Wales, Euro Gp of Law Soc, Int Bar Assoc, American Bar Assoc, Br-German Jurists' Assoc, IOD, Bd of Visitors McGeorge Sch of Law Univ of the Pacific USA, Soc of Eng and American Lawyers, American C of C UK, Anglo-Austrian Soc, Anglo-German, Anglo-Swiss Soc, Br-Swiss C of C, Br C of C in Germany, German Chamber of Indust and Commerce UK, Franco-Br Chamber of Indust and Commerce, Br C of C in Spain, Japan Assoc, Finnish-Br Trade Guild, Norwegian C of C, Swedish C of C; *Books* Dispute Resolution for the International Commercial Lawyer (co-ed, 1988); *Recreations* tennis; *Style—* Peter Summerfield, Esq; Nabarro Nathanson, 50 Stratton St, London W1X 5FL (☎ 071 4939933, fax 071 6297900, telex 8813144 NABARO G)

SUMMERHAYES, Gerald Victor; CMG (1979), OBE (1969); s of Victor Samuel Summerhayes, OBE (d 1977), and Florence Ann Victoria Summerhayes (d 1978); *b* 28 Jan 1928; *Educ* Kings' Sch Ely, BNC Oxford; *Career* admin offr Col Serv 1952-60, Overseas Civil Serv 1960-83, permenant sec Sokoto State Nigeria 1970-81, various ministries including Cabinet Office, Health and Local Govt, ret 1983; *Style—* Gerald Summerhayes, Esq, CMG, OBE; Bridge Cottage, Bridge St, Sidbury, Devon EX10 0RU (☎ 039 57 311); Box 172, Sokoto, Nigeria

SUMMERS, David Lewis; s of Maj Lewis Summers (d 1948), and Beatrice, *née* Greenaway; *b* 25 Nov 1941; *Educ* Mundella Sch Nottingham, St Edmund Hall Oxford (MA); *m* 24 Dec 1966, Veronica Yvonne Elizabeth, da of Cyril Clarence King (d 1970); 2 s (Jonathan b 1971, Benjamin b 1973); *Career* RN Lt 1963-66; Longmans 1966-69, Butterworth & Co Publishers Ltd 1969-, md Butterworth Scientific 1981-86, chief exec UK Legal Publishing 1986-, dir Reed International Books 1990; contrib various chapters to professional pubns; memb: Harvard Business Club, Soc of Bookmen, Anglo-Finnish Soc; Freeman City of London 1988, Liveryman Worshipful Co of Stationers 1989; *Recreations* tennis, squash, cross-country skiing, theatre, music; *Clubs* Garrick; *Style—* David Summers, Esq; Fir Tree Farm, Golford Rd, Cranbrook, Kent TN17 3NW (☎ 0580 713377); 88 Kingsway, London WC2B 6AB (☎ 071 405 6900, fax 071 831 8110)

SUMMERS, Eric William; *b* 10 Dec 1914; *Educ* Dartford Tech Coll; *m* 1939, Janet; 2 children; *Career* CIBS; chm Courtney, Pope (Hldgs) Ltd; fell Inst of Plant Engrg, companion CIBS; FRSA; *Clubs* RAC, Livery; *Style—* Eric Summers, Esq; Muskoday, 29 The Meadow, Chislehurst, Kent BR7 6AA (☎ 081 467 8047); Courtney, Pope (Holdings) Ltd, Amhurst Park Works, South Tottenham, London N15 6RB (☎ 081 800 1270)

SUMMERS, Felix Roland Brattan; 2 Bt (UK 1952), of Shotton, Co Flint; s of Sir Geoffrey Summers, 1 Bt, CBE, JP, DL (d 1972); *b* 1 Oct 1918; *Educ* Shrewsbury; *m* 1945, Anna Marie Louise, da of late Gustave Demaegd of Brussels; 1 da; *Heir* none; *Career* serv 8 Army (Middle E, N Africa, France and Belgium) 1937-45; *Style—* Felix Summers, Esq; Warren House, 16 Warren Lane, Friston, Eastbourne, Sussex

SUMMERS, Jonathan; *b* 2 Oct 1946; *Educ* Macleod HS Melbourne Aust, Prahan Tech Coll Melbourne; *m* 29 March 1969, Lesley; 3 c; *Career* baritone; professional debut title role Rigoletto (Kent Opera) 1975; major debuts: The Royal Opera House Covent Garden (Der Freischütz) 1977, The Aust Opera Sydney (La Traviata) 1981, Paris Opera (Lohengrin) 1982, Hamburg State Opera (Don Carlos) 1986, Teatro Communale Florence (La Boheme) 1987, Nat Theatre Munich (Figaro) 1988, Metropolitan Opera NY (La Boheme) 1988, Tokyo La Scala Milan on tour (La Boheme) 1988, Glyndebourne (Falstaff) 1990, Lyric Opera Chicago (Lucia di Lammermoor) 1990; recent performances incl: title role Onegin (ENO) 1989, A Masked Ball (ENO) 1989, title role Macbeth (ENO) 1990, La Boheme Royal Opera House Covent Garden 1990; concert repertoire incl: Elijah (Mendelssohn), Requiem (Faure and Brahms), The Kingdom, The Apostles, The Dream of Gerontius (Elgar), Carmina Burana (Orff), Sea Symphony (Vaughan Williams), Das Knaben Wunderhorn (Mahler), A Mass of Life (Delius); has performed with: Orchestre de Paris, Berlin Philharmonic, Orchestre Symphonie de Montreal and most Br orchs; recordings incl: Peter Grimes (Grammy 1979), Samson et Delila, La Boheme (Leoncavallo), The Bohemian Girl, Carmina Burana, A Sea Symphony; videos incl: Samson et Delila, Der Rosenkavalier, Il Travatore; Green Room Theatre award for leading male artist (Melbourne Aust) 1988; *Style—* Jonathan Summers, Esq; c/o Patricia Greenan, 19b Belsize Park, London NW3 4DU (☎ 071 794 5954, fax 071 431 3503)

SUMMERS, (Robert) Michael; s of Leslie Summers, and Sophie, *née* Joel; *b* 4 May 1940; *Educ* Haberdashers' Aske's Hampstead Sch; *m* Cilla; 1 s (Raphael b 1979), 3 da (Gaye b 1966, Dawn b 1969, Coral b 1984); *Career* fin dir London City & Westcliff Properties Ltd 1966-77; md: Sterling Publishing Gp plc 1978-, Debrett's Peerage Ltd 1988-; FCA; *Recreations* family, music, literature, scrabble; *Clubs* Old Haberdashers' Assoc; *Style—* Michael Summers, Esq; 6 Woodtree Close, Hendon, London NW4 1HQ (☎ 081 203 3351); Sterling Publishing Gp plc, Garfield House, 86/88 Edgware Road, London W2 2YW (☎ 071 258 0066, fax 071 723 5766)

SUMMERS, Nicholas; s of Henry Forbes Summers, CB, of Tunbridge Wells, and Rosemary, *née* Roberts; *b* 11 July 1939; *Educ* Tonbridge, CCC Oxford (BA, MA); *m* 3 April 1965, Marian Elizabeth (Mandy), da of Stanley George Ottley, of Fairlight; 4 s (Timothy b 1966, William b 1968, Michael b 1973, Stephen b 1977); *Career* Civil Serv; Dept of Educn and Sci (formerly Miny of Educn): asst princ 1961-66, princ 1966-74, asst sec 1976-81, under sec 1981-; asst sec Cabinet Office 1975-76 (princ 1974-75); *Recreations* music; *Style—* Nicholas Summers, Esq; Dept of Education and Science, Elizabeth House, York Rd, London SE1 7PH (☎ 071 934 9928)

SUMMERS, Sue; da of DAvid Summers, of Monte Carlo, and Honey Beatrice, *née* Phillips; *Educ* Queen's Coll London, Univ of Bristol (BA); *m* 1, 1979 (m dis 1989), Rod Allen; m 2, Philip Norman; 1 da (Jessica Rose b 22 Nov 1990); *Career* journalist; trainee Thomson Regional Newspapers, trainee reporter Reading Evening Post, tv and film corr Screen International, tv ed London Evening Standard, ed screen pages Sunday Times, arts ed London Daily News, ed 7 Days Sunday Telegraph; memb: Broadcasting Press Guild, Thames TV Theatre Writers' Award Scheme, Ctee Edinburgh TV Festival 1990; judge Sony Radio Awards 1991; *Recreations* opera, telephoning; *Style—* Ms Sue Summers; Telegraph Newspapers, South Quay, 181 Marsh Wall, London E14 (☎ 071 538 5000)

SUMMERS, William Hamilton; LVO (1990, MVO 1974); s of Dr Maxwell Hamilton Summers, DSO, OBE (d 1989), and Evelyne Elizabeth, *née* Baird; *b* 4 Oct 1930; *Educ* King's Sch Bruton Somerset; *m* 1959, Rosemarie Jean, da of Thomas Norman Hutchison (d 1982), of Chile; 1 s (John b 1964), 2 da (Alison Jane b 1961, Catherine b 1969); *Career* jeweller; dir Garrard & Co 1972; fell Gemologists Assoc; FGA; *Recreations* walking, reading; *Style—* William Summers, Esq, LVO; National Westminster Bank, 1 New Bond St, London W1Y 0HU; Garrard & Co Ltd, 112 Regent St, London W1 2JJ (☎ 071 734 7020, fax 071 439 9197, telex 8952365 REGENT G)

SUMMERSCALE, David Michael; s of Noel Tynwald Summerscale (d 1960), and Beatrice, *née* Wilson; *b* 22 April 1937; *Educ* Sherborne, Trinity Hall Cambridge; *m* 19 July 1975, Pauline Gabrielle Marie-Thérèse, da of Prof Michel Fleury; 1 s (Tristan Edward Fleury b 1985), 1 da (Emily Noelle Fleury b 1982); *Career* lectr in English Literature and tutor St Stephen's Coll Univ of Delhi 1959-63, head of English and housemaster Charterhouse 1963-75, master Haileybury 1976-86, head master Westminster Sch 1986-; memb: Managing Ctee Cambridge Mission to Delhi 1965, CF Andrews Centenary Appeal Ctee 1970, Headmasters Conf Academic Policy Sub-Ctee 1982-86, Cncl Charing Cross & Westminster Med Sch 1986-; vice chm English Speaking Union Scholarship Ctee 1982-; govr: The Hall Sch Hampstead 1986-, Arnold House Sch St John's Wood 1988-; nominated memb Sch Ctee Merchant Taylor's Co 1988-, staff advsr Governing Body Westminster Abbey Choir Sch 1989-, conslt and govr Assam Valley Sch India 1990-, awarder and reviser in English Oxford & Cambridge Schs Examination Bd; FRSA 1984; *Publications* articles on English and Indian literature; dramatisations of novels and verse; *Recreations* music, play production, reading, mountaineering, squash, golf, cricket, tennis, rackets; *Clubs* Athenaeum, I Zingari, Free Foresters, Jesters, Alpin Suisse; *Style—* David Summerscale, Esq; 17 Dean's Yard, Westminster, London SW1P 3PB (☎ 071 222 6904, fax 071 222 9019)

SUMMERSCALE, (Jack) John Nelson; s of Sir John Percival Sumerscale, KBE (d

1980), and Nelle Blossom, *née* Stogsdall (d 1977); *b* 27 July 1944; *Educ* Bryanston Sch, Pembroke Coll Cambridge (BA); *m* 1, 15 March 1969, Cordelia Isobel, da of Sir Alexander Lees Mayall, KCVO, GCMG, of Sturford Mead, Walminster, Wilts; 2 s (Aaron b 26 Aug 1969, Gideon b 24 Dec 1970); m 2, 25 July 1981, Lynda Susan, da of Eric Stewart, of 36 Allbrook House, Roehampton, London; *Career* AC, Coopers & Lybrand 1965-69, Market Investigations Ltd 1969-70, de Zoete & Bevan 1970-86, dir Barclays de Zoete Wedd Securities 1986-; head UK res Barclays de Zoete Wedd 1989-; treas Fulham Parents and Children; FCA 1968; *Style—* Jack Summerscale, Esq; 23 Chelverton Rd, London SW15; Barclays De Zoete Wedd, Ebbgate House, 2 Swan Lane, London EC4 (☎ 071 623 2323, fax 071 626 1753)

SUMMERSCALE, Peter Wayne; *b* 23 April 1935; *Educ* Rugby, New Coll Oxford (Exhibitioner, MA), Russian Res Centre Harvard Univ, Centre for British Russian Studies Univ of Cambridge; *m* 3 c; *Career* HM Dip Serv 1960-: served Tokyo, Belgrade and Bahrain, dep head of mission Santiago Chile, Cabinet Office Assessments Staff, dep head of Mission British Embassy Brussels 1978-81, ambass Costa Rica and Nicaragua 1983-86, head of Dept for East-West Security Negotiations FCO and dep leader UK Delegation to Euro Security and Cooperation Conf 1986-90; fin advsr Hill Samuel Investment Services; *Recreations* art, architectrue, travel, sailing, skiing, tennis, squash, bridge; *Style—* Peter Summerscale, Esq; 5 Grove Terrace, London NW5 1PH (☎ 071 267 8406, office 071 210 6058)

SUMMERSKILL, Hon Michael Brynmor; s of Baroness Summerskill, of Kenwood, CH, PC, MRCS, LRCP (Life Peeress, d 1980), and Dr Edward Jeffrey Samuel, MB BS (d 1983); *b* 28 Nov 1927; *Educ* St Paul's, Merton Coll Oxford (BCL, MA); *m* June 1951, Florence Marion Johnston, da of Sydney Robert Elliott, of Glasgow; 1 s (Ben b 1961), 2 da (Anna b 1959, Clare (twin) b 1961); m 2, 1972, Audrey Alexandra Brontë Blemings; m 3, 1983, Maryly Blew LaFollette, da of Earle Blew; *Career* called to the Bar Middle Temple 1952; former dir Thomas Miller & Co and ptnr Thos R Miller & Son, former pres London Maritime Arbitrators' Assoc 1983-85; FCIArb, ACII; *Books* Penguin Dictionary of Politics (with Florence Elliott), Laytime, Oil Rigs, China on the Western Front; *Clubs* Chelsea Arts, Colony Room, Reform; *Style—* The Hon Michael Summerskill; 4 Millfield Lane, London N6 (☎ 081 341 7531)

SUMMERSKILL, Dr the Hon Shirley Catherine Wynne; da of Baroness Summerskill, CH, PC (Life Peeress, d 1980), and Dr Edward Jeffrey Samuel, MB, BS (d 1983); *b* 9 Sept 1931; *Educ* St Paul's Girls' Sch, Somerville Coll Oxford, St Thomas' Hosp; *m* 1957 (m dis 1971), John Ryman, barr; *Career* MP (L) Halifax 1964-83, parly under-sec of state Home Office 1974-79; oppn spokesman on: Home Affairs 1979-83, Health 1970-74; UK del UN Status of Women Cmmn 1968 & 1969, memb Br Delgn Cncl Europe & WEU 1968 & 1969; chm PLP Health Gp 1969-70 (vice-chm 1964-69), memb Lab Nat Exec Ctee 1982-83; in practice as Physician 1960- (MA, BM BCh, resident house surgn, subsequently house physician St Helier Hosp Carshalton 1959); fought Blackpool N (by-election) 1962; med offr Nat Blood Transfusion Serv; *Style—* Dr the Hon Shirley Summerskill

SUMMERSON, Sir John Newenham; CH (1987), CBE (1952); s of Samuel James Summerson (d 1907), of Darlington; *b* 25 Nov 1904; *Educ* Harrow, UCL; *m* 1938, Elizabeth Alison, da of late Herbert Raikes Hepworth, CBE, of Leeds; 3 s; *Career* dep dir National Buildings Record 1941-45, curator Sir John Soane's Museum 1945-84; Slade prof of fine art: Oxford 1958-59, Cambridge 1966-67; lectr in history of architecture Birkbeck Coll and AA London 1950-67, chm Nat Cncl for Diplomas in Art and Design 1961-70, tstee Nat Portrait Gallery 1966-73; Royal Gold Medal for Architecture 1976; FBA, FSA, ARIBA; kt 1958; *Clubs* Athenaeum; *Style—* Sir John Summerson, CH, CBE; 1 Eton Villas, London NW3 (☎ 071 722 6247)

SUMNER, Bernard; *b* 4 Jan 1956; *Educ* Salford GS; *Career* fndr memb and guitarist Joy Division 1978-79 (albums Unknown Pleasures (1978), Closer (1979)); New Order: formed (after death of Joy Division singer Ian Curtis) 1980, debut performance The Beach Club Manchester 1980, major tours of the USA 1986, 1987 and 1989; started solo project alongside Johnny Marr and the Pet Shop Boys 1988, debut performance Electronic 1990; gold albums: Power Corruption and Lies (UK), Low-life (UK), Brotherhood (UK), Technique (UK, USA); platinum album Substance (UK, USA); Blue Monday best selling 12 inch single of all time; co owner: Hacienda nightclub Manchester (winner Courvoisier best venue award), Dry Bar Manchester; played at Gala performance for TRH The Duke and Duchess of York at UK Festival LA; *Recreations* skiing, yachting, clubs; *Style—* Bernard Sumner, Esq; 11 Hastings Ave, Chorlton, Manchester (☎ 061 861 8403, fax 061 881 4152)

SUMNER, His Hon Judge Christopher John; s of His Hon (William) Donald Massey Sumner, OBE, QC (d 1990), of High Halden, Kent, and Muriel Kathleen, *née* Wilson; *b* 28 Aug 1939; *Educ* Charterhouse, Sidney Sussex Coll Cambridge (MA); *m* 24 Sept 1970, Carole Ashley, da of John Ashley Mann (d 1985), and Alison Mann; 1 s (William Mark b 30 Nov 1978), 2 da (Claire Louise b 6 Sept 1972, Emma Jane b 29 Oct 1974); *Career* called to the Bar Inner Temple 1961, asst rec 1983, rec 1986, circuit judge 1987; *Recreations* reading, theatre, sport; *Clubs* Hurlingham; *Style—* His Hon Judge Christopher Sumner

SUMNER, Christopher Kent; s of George Tomlinson Sumner (d 1979), and Alice Mary Bettley, *née* Brown (d 1989); *b* 28 Sept 1943; *Educ* The King's Sch Chester, Univ of Durham (BA, MA); *m* 3 Aug 1967, Marjorie, da of George Prince, of 12b Derwent Court, Troutbeck Rd, Liverpool 18; 2 s (Stuart b 1970, Edward b 1974); *Career* slr; chm Social Security Appeal Tbnls 1984-; Parly candidate (Lib) Runcorn 1970; *Recreations* squash, scouting; *Style—* Christopher K Sumner, Esq; 4 Mossgiel Ave, Ainsdale, Southport (☎ 0704 73153); Adler Sumner Moore, 23 Hoghton St, Southport (☎ 0704 547247, 0704 530990)

SUMNER, David Moorcroft; s of Allan Summer (d 1967), and Clara, *née* Sanderson; *b* 28 July 1936; *Educ* Blackpool GS, Rossallo Sch; *m* 1, 1963 (m dis 1980); 1 s (David St John Moorcroft b 1968), 2 da (Elizabeth Victoria Moorcroft b 1965, Virginia Helen Moorcroft b 1966); m 2, 19 Feb 1982, Susan Margaret, da of May Horgan, of Altringham, Cheshire; 1 s (Harry Jocelyn Moorcroft b 1981), 1 da (Bethany Lloyd b 1986), 2 step da (Ana-Paula Ramos-Pereira Lloyd b 1974, Elisa Mary Ramos-Pereira Lloyd b 1976); *Career* served King's Regt 1955-57; called to the Bar Lincoln's Inn 1963, dep circuit judge 1978-82, rec Crown Ct 1982; *Recreations* fly-fishing; *Style—* David Sumner, Esq; David Sumner's Chambers, Rational House, 64 Bridge St, Manchester 3 (☎ 061 8325701)

SUMNER, Francis Ian; s of Guy Chadwick Sumner (d 1986), and Margaret Hilliard, *née* Wilson; *b* 25 Oct 1942; *Educ* Tonbridge; *m* 29 Dec 1978, Diana Harriman, da of John Ernest Newman; 2 s (Edward John b 18 Nov 1979, Richard William b 12 May 1981), 1 da (Nicola Margaret b 6 Dec 1983); *Career* asst slr Slaughter & May 1966-72 (articled clerk 1961-66), ptnr Norton Rose 1973- (asst slr 1972-73); Freeman City of London Solicitors Co; memb Law Soc; *Recreations* golf, gardening, fishing, shooting; *Style—* Francis Sumner, Esq; Norton Rose, Kempson House, Camomile St, London EC3A 7AN (☎ 071 283 2434, fax 071 588 1181)

SUMNER, Hazel Mary; da of Charles Fox Cullwick, of Sheriffhales, Shropshire, and Enid May, *née* Rogers, of Gresford, Clwyd; *b* 17 April 1930; *Educ* Priory GS Shrewsbury, Leicester Coll of Domestic Sci, Univ of Birmingham, LSE (BScEcon, MSc); *m* 14 Aug 1954, Herbert Sumner; 1 da (Katherine b 25 March 1960); *Career* teacher 1951-61, lectr in educn 1961-71, sr res offr Univ of Liverpool 1971-74, teacher educn co-ordinator and chief asst to controller BBC educn 1975-90; educn conslt 1990-; memb of various curriculum devpt gps linking with educn and indust; author of various papers on educn; *Recreations* conversation, entertaining, reading biographies, music, walking; *Clubs* Univ Women's; *Style—* Ms Hazel Sumner; The Ark, St Weonards, Hereford; BBC Education, Villiers House, Ealing Broadway, London W5 2PA (☎ 081 991 8084, fax 081 840 6720)

SUMNER-FERGUSSON, (William) Howard David; s of William Graham Sumner-Fergusson (d 1945), and Catharine Mary, *née* Sumner (d 1984); *b* 11 March 1946; *Educ* Elston Hall Newark, The Oratory; *m* 1, 1975, Felicia Clare Hedley (d 1975), da of late Andro C Roberts, of Leicestershire; m 2, 1979, Lucienne Gay Elizabeth, da of William Hilder (d 1986), of Valentines, Hurstbourne, Tarrant, and of Chiswick; 1 s (William Rupert Giles b 1982), 1 da (Rebecca Sophie b 1980); *Career* dir: Anglesey Rd Development Ltd 1974-85, Salmon Charles (London and Home Counties) Ltd 1986-87, Quality Fare 1987, Everards Brewery Ltd, John Sarson Ltd, John Sarson Wines Ltd 1974-85, Clensouth Ltd 1989-; md Gibbs Mew plc 1989; *Recreations* gardening, shooting, bridge; *Clubs* Naval; *Style—* Howard Sumner-Fergusson, Esq; Cleeve House, Broad Chalke, Salisbury, Wilts SP5 5DN (☎ 0772 780135)

SUMNERS, Dr David George; s of George William Sumners, of 113 Walmington Fold, London, and Irene Florence, *née* Kelly; *b* 23 Sept 1952; *Educ* William Ellis Sch, UCL (BSc, MB BS); *m* 12 June 1976, Susan Mary, da of Thomas Arthur Bourn, of 111 Grangewood Rd, Nottingham; 1 s (William David b 28 Feb 1985), 1 da (Emily Mary b 23 March 1982); *Career* conslt psychiatrist: Edgware Gen Hosp and Napsbury Hosp 1988-, Grovelands Priory Hosp 1988-; dir NW Thames RHA Brain Injury Rehabilitation Unit 1988-; dir Tranx (UK) Ltd; MRCPsych 1983; *Recreations* opera; *Style—* Dr David Sumners; Grovelands Priory Hosp, The Bourne, London N14 6RA (☎ 081 8828191)

SUMPTION, Jonathan Philip Chadwick; QC (1986); s of Anthony James Sumption, DSC, and Hedy, *née* Hedigan; *b* 9 Dec 1948; *Educ* Eton, Magdalen Coll Oxford (MA); *m* 26 June 1971, Teresa Mary, da of Jerome Bernard Whelan; 1 s (Bernard b 1981), 2 da (Frederique b 1979, Madeleine b 1983); *Career* fell Magdalen Coll Oxford 1971-75, called to the Bar Middle Temple 1975, bencher 1990; *Books* Pilgrimage An Image of Medieval Religion (1975), The Albigensian Crusade (1978), The Hundred Years War (1990); *Recreations* music, history; *Style—* Jonathan Sumption, Esq, QC; 34 Crooms Hill, London SE10 (☎ 081 858 4444); 1 Brick Court, Temple, London EC4 (☎ 071 583 0777, fax 071 583 9401 (Group 3), telex 892687 IBRICK G)

SUMSION, John Walbridge; OBE (1991); s of Dr Herbert Whitton Sumsion, CBE, sometime organist of Gloucester Cathedral, composer and Prof Royal Coll of Music, and Alice Hartley, *née* Garlichs; *b* 16 Aug 1928; *Educ* Rendcomb Coll, Clare Coll Cambridge (MA), Yale Univ (MA), Cornell Univ; *m* 1, 1961 (m dis 1979), Annette Dorothea, *née* Wilson; 2 s (Christopher b 1965, Michael b 1968), 2 da (Bridget b 1963, Kate b 1970); m 2, 1979, Hazel Mary, *née* English; *Career* dir K Shoemakers Ltd 1962-81, registrar of Public Lending Right 1981-91, dir Library & Info Statistics Unit Univ of Loughborough 1991-; hon fell Library Assoc 1990; author of various jl articles; *Books* PLR In Practise (1988); *Recreations* music (singing, flute), walking, tennis; *Clubs* United Oxford and Cambridge Univ; *Style—* John Sumsion, Esq, OBE; Appleton Wiske, Northallerton, N Yorks (☎ 060 981 408); office: Bayheath House, Prince Regent St, Stockton-on-Tees, Cleveland

SUNDERLAND, Alistair John; s of Dr Robert Slater Sunderland, and Marion, *née* Wilson; *b* 24 March 1949; *Educ* Lewis' Sch for Boys, Liverpool Poly; *m* Glenys, da of Gwylim Thomas; 2 s (Adam Thomas, Geraint John), 2 da (Sian Marion, Rhian Alice); *Career* ptnr Austin-Smith Lord 1974-; memb RIBA 1978, ARCUK; *Recreations* jogging, sailing; *Clubs* Liverpool Architectural Soc; *Style—* Alistair Sunderland, Esq; Austin-Smith: Lord, 5-6 Bowood Court, Calver Rd, Warrington, Cheshire WA2 8QZ

SUNDERLAND, Prof Eric; s of Leonard Sunderland (d 1990), of Ammanford, Dyfed, and Mary Agnes, *née* Davies; *b* 18 March 1930; *Educ* Amman Valley GS, Univ Coll Wales Aberystwyth (BA, MA), UCL (PhD); *m* 19 Oct 1957, (Jean) Patricia, da of George Albert Watson (d 1972), of Cardiff; 2 da (Rowena, Frances); *Career* res asst NCB 1957-58; Univ of Durham: lectr in anthropology 1958-66, sr lectr 1966-71, prof 1971-84, pro vice-chllr 1979-84; princ Univ Coll of N Wales Bangor 1984-; patron Schizophrenia Assoc GB 1985-, hon memb Gorsedd of Bards Royal Nat Eisteddfod of Wales, dir Gregynog Press 1986, chm Welsh Language Educn Devpt Ctee 1987, memb Welsh Language Bd 1988, vice-pres Gwynedd branch Gt Ormond St Hosp Appeal 1988; FIBiol 1975; memb: RAI (hon treas 1985-89, pres 1989-91), SSHB, Biosocial Soc; Int Union of Anthropological and Ethnological Scis 1978-; Hrdlička medal for Anthropological Res 1976, hon fell Croatian Anthropological Soc Gorjanovic-Krambergeri medal; *Books* Genetic Variation in Britain (1973), The Operation of Intelligence: Biological Preconditions for Operation of Intelligence (1980), Genetic and Population Studies in Wales (1986); *Recreations* book collecting, watercolours, gardening, music, travelling; *Clubs* Athenaeum; *Style—* Prof Eric Sunderland; Bryn, Ffriddoedd Rd, Bangor, Gwynedd LL57 2EH; Principal's Office, University College of North Wales, Bangor, Gwynedd LL57 2DG (☎ 0248 351 151 ext 2000, fax 0248 370451, telex 61100 UCNWSL G)

SUNDERLAND, Eric Edgar; JP (1978); s of Edgar Sunderland (d 1928), and Ida Evelyn (d 1985); *b* 16 Nov 1927; *Educ* Queen Elizabeth GS Horncastle, Bradford Inst Technol; *m* 1958, Irene Mary, *née* Beecroft; *Career* gp md Homfray & Co Textile Div 1972-76, md Henry Mason Ltd 1976-80, chm and chief exec Contessa Cars & Electro-Acoustic Devpts Ltd 1976-, gp md E & T Wall Ltd 1980-, dir Nottingham Wine Buying Gp 1983-, vice chm Bradford Hosp Fund (now Sovereign Health Care) 1974-, vice pres Bradford S Constituency Cons Assoc 1989, fell Inst of Plant Engrs; *Recreations* music, cars, chess, railway preservation; *Clubs* Cons (Bradford); *Style—* Eric Sunderland, Esq, JP; Sundial House, 5 Manscombe Rd, Allerton, Bradford, West Yorks BD15 7AQ (☎ 0274 546 568, office 0535 602738)

SUNDERLAND, (Arthur) John; s of His Honour Judge George Frederick Irvon Sunderland (d 1984), and Mary Katherine, *née* Bowen (d 1983); *b* 24 Feb 1932; *Educ* Marlborough, London Coll of Printing; *m* 6 Sept 1958, Audrey Ann, da of George Henry Thompson (d 1980); 3 s (Andrew John, Timothy James, Richard Mark); *Career* Nat Serv 2 Lt RE 1953-55; dir: James Upton Ltd 1963-69, Surrey Fine Art Press Ltd 1963-69, Sunderland Print Ltd 1969-84, Alday Green & Welburn Ltd 1978-84, Randall Bross Ltd 1970-84, Foxplan Ltd 1984-87, Rapidflow Ltd 1985-89; chm Ladypool Rd Neighbourhood Centre Birmingham 1970-76, govr W House Sch Birmingham 1973-; St John Ambulance Bde W Midlands: dep co cmmr 1976-78, co cmmr/cdr 1978-86, cmmr-in-chief 1986-90; KStJ (1986, OStJ 1978, CStJ 1982); memb Field Survey Assoc 1955-; *Recreations* walking, sport; *Style—* John Sunderland, Esq; Cherry Hill House, Cherry Hill Rd, Barnt Gn, Birmingham B45 8LJ (☎ 021 445 1232)

SUNDERLAND, John Michael; s of Harry Sunderland, and Joyce Eileen, *née* Farnish; *b* 24 Aug 1945; *Educ* King Edward VII Lytham, Univ of St Andrews (MA); *m* Sept 1965, Jean Margaret, da of Col Alexander Grieve (d 1975); 3 s (Jonothan b 1969, Robin b 1972, Ben Alexander b 1978), 1 da (Corianne b 1966); *Career* md Trebor Bassett Ltd; *Style—* John Sunderland, Esq; Woodlands, Penn St, Bucks (☎ 0494 713235); 1-4 Connaught Place, London W1 (☎ 071 262 1212)

SUNNUCKS, James Horrace George; DL (Essex 1990); s of Stanley Lloyd Sunnucks (d 1953), and Edith Vera Constance, *née* Sendell (d 1979); *b* 20 Sept 1925; *Educ* Wellington, Trinity Hall Cambridge (MA); *m* 1 Oct 1955, Rosemary Ann (Tessa), da of Col J W Borradaile (d 1946); 4 s (William b 2 Aug 1956, John b 4 March 1959, David b 4 April 1961, Andrew b 3 May 1965); *Career* RNVR 1943-46; called to the Bar Lincoln's Inn 1950, bencher 1980, memb Senate Inns of Ct and Bar; pres Inst of Conveyancers 1988-89 (memb 1974-); licensed reader diocese of Chelmsford 1954, memb Parole Review Ctee Chelmsford Prison (later chm) 1970-82; asst Parly boundary cmmnr (Wandsworth, Camden, Wilts) 1975-85; Freeman: City of London 1986, Worshipful Co of Gardeners 1986; pres County of Essex (Eastern Area) Order of St John 1990; *Books* Williams and Mortimer on Executors (ed), Halsbury's Laws of England (ed); *Recreations* gardening, local history, sailing; *Clubs* United Oxford and Cambridge Univ, Garrick, Norfolk; *Style*— James Sunnucks, Esq, DL; East Mersea Hall, Colchester, Essex CO5 8TJ (☎ 0206 383 215); 5 Hale Court, Lincoln's Inn, London WC2 (☎ 071 242 4764); 5 New Square, Lincoln's Inn, London WC2A 3RJ (☎ 071 404 0404, fax 071 831 6016); Octagon House, Colegate, Norwich

SUPER, Dr Maurice; s of Eric Simon Super, MM (d 1979), of Johannesburg, and Aida, *née* Marsden (d 1980); *b* 17 Oct 1936; *Educ* King Edward VII Sch Johannesburg, Univ of the Witwatersrand (MB BCh), Univ of Cape Town (MD), Univ of Edinburgh (MSc, DCH); *m* 16 Dec 1958, Anne Monica, da of Jan Gliksman; 2 s (Michael b 18 March 1960, Jonathan b 21 Oct 1966), 1 da (Beth b 4 April 1969); *Career* paediatric trg Baragwanath Hosp Johannesburgh 1959-67, conslt paediatrician to SW African Admin and SW African Railways and Harbours 1967-78, conslt paediatric geneticist Royal Manchester Children's Hosp 1979-; numerous articles on cystic fibrosis; English rep EEC Initiative on Cystic Fibrosis Genetics, fndr SA Cystic Fibrosis Assoc; FRCPE 1977; *Books* Cystic Fibrosis: The Facts (1987, 2 edn, 1991); *Recreations* tennis, bridge; *Clubs* Northern Lawn Tennis, Manchester Bridge; *Style*— Dr Maurice Super; Dept of Clinical Genetics, Royal Manchester Children's Hospital, Manchester M27 1HA (☎ 061 7944696, fax 061 7945929)

SUPPLE, Robert John (Robbie); s of William Joseph Supple, and Mary Phyllimena, *née* Dore; *b* 2 Feb 1967; *Educ* Ballyduff Boys Nat Sch, Ballybunion Secdy Sch; *Partner* Shona Mitchell; *Career* National hunt jockey; apprentice to J S Bolger Co Carlow Ireland, rode first winner on flat 1984 (Special Display), total 4 winners on flat, first winner over hurdles Punches Town 1987 (on Frank O'Brien's Catsrock); based England 1987-, rode 5 winners for G A Hubbard 1987-88, moved to J J O'Neill's yard 1989, rode 34 winners 1989-90 (runner up conditional jockeys' table); currently retained by John Upson; *Recreations* hunting, wildlife; *Style*— Robbie Supple, Esq; c/o Roy Briggs, Esq (☎ 0609 748241, car 0836 229366)

SUPRAMANIAM, Ganesan; s of Snell Aseervatham Supramaniam (d 1952), and Ranganayki, *née* Ramasamy-Pillai (d 1985); *b* 31 Oct 1943; *Educ* Royal Coll Colombo Ceylon, Univ of Ceylon (MB BS), Univ of London (MSc); *Career* paediatric registrar St Georges Hosp 1979-80, sr registrar St Marys Hosp 1981-84, currently conslt peadiatrician Watford Gen Hosp; various pubns in jls; ctee memb Cystic Fibrosis Holiday Fund, memb Br Diabetic Assoc, regnl med advsr Cystic Fibrosis Res Tst; memb: BPA, BMA; DCH 1975, MRCP 1977; *Recreations* squash, cricket, badminton; *Style*— Ganesan Supramaniam, Esq; 86 Carlton Avenue West, Wembley, Middlesex HAO 3QU (☎ 081 9046671); Watford General Hospital, Vicarage Rd, Watford, Herts WD1 8HB (☎ 0923 217695, fax 0923 55080)

SURATGAR, David; s of Prof Lotfali Suratgar (d 1969), of Tehran, and Prof Edith Olive, *née* Hepburn (d 1985); *b* 23 Oct 1938; *Educ* Silcoates Sch Yorks, New Coll Oxford (BA, MA), Columbia Univ NY (MIA); *m* 6 Aug 1962, Barbara Lita (d 1990), da of Donald Telfer Low, of Wytham Abbey, Wytham, Oxford; 1 s (Karim Donald Hepburn b 4 Aug 1966), 1 da (Roxanne Christina Noelle b 25 Dec 1964); *Career* Legal Dept UN Secretariat 1961-62, Sullivan & Cromwell (lawyers) NYC 1963-64, legal counsel World Bank 1964-73, adjunct prof of law Univ of Georgetown 1966-73, dir Morgan Grenfell & Co Ltd 1973-88 (gp dir 1988-), legal counsel Bank of England and Nat Water Cncl 1976, conslt Jones Day Reavis & Pogue (lawyers) 1988-; dir: Societe Internationale Financiere Pour Investissements et le Developpement en Afrique 1981-, Oxford Playhouse Tst 1989, Northern Ballet Theatre 1981-83, Garsington Opera Co 1991-, Oxford International Institute 1990-; chm West India Ctee (Royal Charter) 1987-89 (vice pres 1989-); memb: Bd Major Projects Assoc Templeton Coll Oxford, Bodleian Library Appeal 1987-; sr res fell Int Law Inst Washington DC; memb: Gray's Inn, Int Bar Assoc, Br Inst of Int and Comparative Law; *Books* Default and Rescheduling - Sovereign and Corporate Borrowers in Difficulty (1984), International Financial Law (jlty, 1980); *Recreations* shooting, book collecting, theatre, travelling; *Clubs* Travellers, Chelsea Arts; *Style*— David Suratgar, Esq; 265 Woodstock Road, Oxford OX2 7AE; Morgan Grenfell & Co Ltd, 23 Gt Winchester St, London EC2P 2AX (☎ 071 588 4545, fax 071 826 6155, telex 893511)

SURMAN, Martyn; s of Leslie Charles Surman (d 1970), of Brighton, and Irene Grace, *née* Rogers; *b* 21 Nov 1944; *Educ* Varndean GS for Boys, Brighton Coll of Technol, Coll of Estate Mgmnt; *m* 1, 1 Oct 1966 (m dis); 1 s (David Keith b 20 Jan 1968), 1 da (Tracey Deborah (twin)); m 2, 13 March 1976 (m dis); m 3, 14 Sept 1990, Irene Florence, da of Sidney William Hart (d 1986); *Career* trainee building surveyor Watney Mann Brewers 1963-69, sr architectural asst and dep to Borough Architect Hove Borough Cncl Architect's Dept 1973-78 (joined 1969); PSA Services: troubleshooter Building Advsy Branch Croydon 1978, area design mangr Portsmouth 1984, planning mangr (head Gp Planning Team) Portsmouth 1986, gp building surveyor 1989, dep head of profession building surveyors PSA Servs HQ Croydon Jan 1990, superintending building surveyor July 1990, head of profession building surveyors Oct 1990; pres Building Surveyors Div RICS 1990-91; FRICS 1986 (ARICS 1975); *Recreations* photography, sport, travelling, theatre; *Style*— Martyn Surman, Esq; PSA Services, Room 1515, Apollo House, 36 Wellesley Rd, Croydon, Surrey CR9 3RR (☎ 081 760 8758, fax 081 760 8157); Bramblehurst, Limes Lane, Potters Green, Buxted, E Sussex TN22 4PB (☎ 0825 813111)

SURRELL, Hon Mrs (Maureen Dawn); *née* Vernon; da of 5 Baron Lyveden (d 1973); *b* 1926; *m* 1946, Noel Surrell; 1 s; *Style*— The Hon Mrs Surrell; 539 Pukehina Parade, RD9, Te Puke, New Zealand

SURREY, Christopher Durden (Kit); s of Stephen James Surrey, of Southampton, Hampshire, and Frances Vera, *née* Durden, of Sturminster Newton, Dorset; *b* 23 June 1946; *Educ* Tauntons GS Southampton, Southampton Art Coll, Wimbledon Sch of Art (DipAD); *m* 19 July 1969, Margaret Jullian, da of Leslie Arnold Grealey; 1 s (Thomas Hamo b 7 May 1973), 1 da (Charlotte Sarah b 18 Sept 1975); *Career* theatre designer, film and TV art dir; asst designer Citizens Theatre Glasgow 1968, London 1969, Fringe 1970; designer: York Theatre Royal 1971-72, Northcott Theatre Exeter 1972-74; freelance since 1974; prodns incl: The Master Builder, Jumpers, Death of a Salesman, Toad of Toad Hall (all for Theatre Clwyd), One Flew over the Cuckoo's Nest, Taking Steps, Shades of Brown, The Wizard of Oz, Bunter, Alice in Wonderland (all Northcott Exeter), Rosmersholm (Royal Exchange Manchester), Turkey Time and John Bull (Bristol Old Vic), Peter Grimes and The Queen of Spades (New Sussex Opera); prodns for RSC incl: Dingo (1976), Captain Swing, Sore Throats, A Doll's House, The Accrington Pals, Men's Beano, The Suicide, Lear, Golden Girls, The Comedy of Errors, The Merchant of Venice, Twelfth Night, Cymbeline, The Churchill Play, Playing with Trains, Much Ado about Nothing; exhibited at Soc of Br Theatre Designers: Central Sch of Art 1976, The Roundhouse 1979, Riverside Studios 1983 and 1987; GB rep Int Orgn of Scenographers and Theatre Technicians E Berlin 1981 and Moscow 1982; memb Soc of Br Theatre Designers; *Books* Artswest (contrib 1988), British Theatre Design - The Modern Age (contrib 1989); *Recreations* walking and climbing; *Style*— Kit Surrey, Esq; 77 Queens Road, St Thomas, Exeter, Devon EX2 9EW (☎ 0392 70240)

SURTEES, Anthony Conyers; s of Conyers A Surtees, of Clare Park, Cromdall, Hants, and Betty W, *née* Strange; *b* 2 Sept 1935; *Educ* Rugby, Balliol Coll Oxford (BA); *m* 1967, Anne, da of Capt E G S Smallwood; 1 s (Benedick b 1972), 2 da (Virginia b 1969, Charlotte b 1970); *Career* articled clerk Norton Rose Greenwell and Co 1957-60, ptnr Norton Rose 1965- (asst slr 1960-); dir Solicitors' Benevolent Assoc (chm 1987), lectr and writer on legal aspects of equipment leasing and of golf course projects; memb: City of London Solicitors Co, Law Soc 1960-; *Recreations* playing golf tennis and bridge, collecting antiquarian books; *Style*— Anthony Surtees, Esq; Potters Hatch House, Crondall, Hants GU10 5PW; Norton Rose, Kempson House, Camomile St, London EC3A 7AN (☎ 071 283 2434, fax 071 588 1181)

SURTEES, John; MBE (1959); *b* 11 Feb 1934; *m* Jane; 2 da (Edwina b 1987, Leonora b 1989); *Career* motorcycle and racing car driver; apprentice Vincent HRD Co Stevenage; won first race Vincent Grey Flash (built by himself) 1951, competed in first int world championship 1952, raced on maj Br Circuits 1952-54, Br champion 1954-55, commenced riding in world championships 1956; driving racing cars 1960-68, Formula 1 world champion 1964; winner: Canadian American Championship Sports Car Series 1966, Japanese Grand Prix 1972, Imola Shell Formula 2 championship 1972; became a car constructor 1968 (Formula 2 Euro champion car constructor 1972); currently motor sport and engrg conslt and property developer; Freeman: City of London 1990, Worshipful Co of Carmen 1990; *Style*— John Surtees, Esq, MBE; Enterprise Way, Station Rd, Edenbridge, Kent TN8 6EW (☎ 0732 865496, fax 0732 866945)

SURTEES, Maj John Freville Henry; OBE (1975), MC (1940); s of Maj Robert Lambton Surtees,OBE, JP (d 1968), of Littlestone-on-Sea, Kent, and Anne Olive Marguerite, *née* Beck (d 1944); *b* 26 Jan 1919; *Educ* Eton, RMC Sandhurst; *m* 1, 1946 (m dis 1967), Audrey, da of Maj Basil Baillie Falkner (d 1964); 2 da (Anna, Christian); m 2, 1969 (m dis 1985), Anne, da of Sir Edward Denham, GCVO, KBE (d 1938); *Career* 2 Lt 1 Bn The Rifle Bde 1939 (POW wounded), Calais 1940-45, 2 Bn Rifle Bde 1945-46, GSO 2 Allied Liaison Branch BAOR 1946-47, ret 1948; md: Percy Fox & Co (Wine Importers) 1962 (chm 1970-73), Garvey (London) Ltd 1973-84; govr Oundle Sch; memb Inst of Masters of Wine 1956; Master Worshipful Co of Grocers 1966-67; *Recreations* fishing, racing, music; *Clubs* Boodle's, Green Jackets, White's; *Style*— Maj John Surtees, OBE, MC; Down House, Wylye, Warminster, Wiltshire BA12 0QN

SURTEES, Richard Vere Norman; s of Maj Vere Nathaniel Faber Surtees (*see* Surtees of Dinsdale on Tees, Burke's Landed Gentry, 18 edn, vol 2), of The Old Farm House, Hopesay, Craven Arms, Shropshire, and Mary Petronilla, er da of Sir Ninian Comper, architect (d 1957); *b* 9 April 1924; *Educ* Shrewsbury, Pembroke Coll Cambridge (BA); *m* 8 Dec 1951, Elizabeth Vivienne, da of Capt F C Ainley, MBE (ka 1938, The Green Howards); 2 s (Nicholas Vere b 28 June 1953, Jonathan Michael b 9 Feb 1957), 1 da (Frances Mary b 28 Feb 1956, d 19 March 1956); *Career* served WWII Lt Grenadier Gds, cmmnd 1943 (wounded 1945), served NW Germany 1 Bn (Gds Armd Div); asst sec Burt Boulton & Haywood Ltd 1952-61, staff and office mangr Antony Gibbs & Sons Ltd (merchant bankers) 1961-69, Nat Farmers Union (Agric House, Knightsbridge) 1969-84, exec Fedn of Agric Co Ops (UK) Ltd (UK Euro rep body); sec: Br Agric Cncl, Nat Fedn of Pest Control Socs Ltd, Fedn of Syndicate Credit Cos, ret 1984; tstee Plunkett Fndn for Co-op Studies in Oxford 1984-; Ctee memb: Land Tsts Assoc, The RS Surtees Soc; Hon BA Cambridge; *Recreations* gardening, art, music, travel; *Clubs* Brooks's, Farmer's; *Style*— Richard Surtees, Esq; Grove End, Byfleet Rd, Cobham, Surrey KT11 1DS (☎ 0932 62575)

SUSCHITZKY, (John) Peter; s of Wolfgang Suschitzky, and Ilona, *née* Donath; *b* 6 April 1940; *Educ* Mountgrace Sch, Inst des Hautes Etudes Cinématographiques Paris; *m* June 1964 (m dis 1982), Johanna Roeber; 1 s (Adam b 1972), 2 da (Anya b 1969, Rebecca b 1974); *Career* dir of photography films incl: Charlie Bubbles 1966, Leo The Last 1967, The Rocky Horror Picture Show 1974, The Empire Strikes Back 1978, Falling in Love 1984, Dead Ringers 1988; memb: Br Soc of Cinematographers, Dirs Guild of America; *Recreations* music, playing the transverse flute, history, cooking; *Style*— Peter Suschitzky, Esq; 13 Priory Rd, London NW6 4NN (☎ 071 624 3734)

SUSMAN, Peter Joseph; s of Albert Leonard Susman, of London, and Sybil Rebecca, *née* Joseph; *b* 20 Feb 1943; *Educ* Dulwich, Lincoln Coll Oxford (MA), Law Sch Univ of Chicago (JD); *m* 5 June 1966, Peggy Judith, da of Harvey Stone, of New Jersey, USA; 1 s (Daniel b 13 Feb 1979), 1 da (Deborah b 16 Nov 1976); *Career* barr 1967-70 and 1972-; assoc New York City Law Firm 1970-72; *Style*— Peter Susman, Esq; New Court, Temple, London EC4Y 9BE (☎ 071 583 6166, fax 071 583 2827)

SUSSMAN, Prof Max; s of Hans Sussman (d 1948), of London, and Erna, *née* Hirsch; *b* 12 Oct 1932; *Educ* Highbury Co Sch, Univ of Leeds (BSc, PhD); *m* 12 June 1960, Jean Margaret, da of late Dr Rudolf Heinrich Golde, of London; 1 s (Jonathan), 1 da (Judith); *Career* asst bacteriologist Western Infirmary Glasgow 1958-60, memb sci staff MRC 1960-64, sr lectr Welsh Nat Sch of Med Cardiff 1970-75 (lectr 1964-70), prof of bacteriology Med Sch Newcastle upon Tyne 1975-89, ret 1989; vice pres Inst of Biology 1984-86 (memb Cncl 1975-79, hon treas 1979-84), chief ed Bd Soc for Applied Bacteriology 1985- (sr ed 1982-84); CBiol, FIBiol 1975, FRCPath 1989, FRSA 1989; *Books* The Virulence of Escherichia COli (1985), The Release of Genetically-Engineered Microorganisms (1988); *Recreations* music, walking, talking; *Clubs* East India; *Style*— Prof Max Sussman; Dept of Microbiology, Medical School, Newcastle upon Tyne NE2 4HH (☎ 091 2227596, fax 091 2227736)

SUSSMAN, Norman Frederick; CBE (1988, OBE 1981); s of Samuel Sussman (d 1941), of London, and Miriam, *née* Eisen; *b* 19 Jan 1925; *Educ* Univ Coll Sch Hampstead; *m* 8 Feb 1953, Iris, da of Maurice Williams; 1 da (Valerie b 21 March 1958); *Career* WWII Capt RA 1943-47; joined family co L S & J Sussman Limited 1941 (currently chm); memb Clothing Econ Devpt Cncl 1968-88, chm Shirt, Collar & Tie Manufacturers' Fedn 1968 and 1972 (memb Exec Ctee 1962), pres Appeal Textile Benevolent Assoc 1974-75, chm Br Clothing Industry's Jr Cncl 1977-80, fndr chm Br memb Clothing Indust Assoc 1980-87 (pres 1987), BCIA rep CBI Cncl 1987-; memb: Devon and Cornwall Trg and Enterprise Cncl 1989 (chm Northern Area Bd), Bd Clothing and Allied Products Indust Trg Bd Tst 1990, Cncl Apparel, Knitting and Textile Alliance, memb Clothing Manufacturers Wages Cncl 1990, Cncl Br Knitting and Clothing Confederation 1991; chm: Bill Cole Meml Tst, Br Clothing Indust Assoc Pension Fund Mgmnt Ctee; former positions incl: pres Clothing and Footwear Inst 1980-81, memb Cncl WIRA, chm Shirley Inst Clothing Ctee, memb Bd Clothing Industry's Productivity Resources Agency, memb Bd Br Clothing Centre, memb Shirt Making Wages Cncl; Univ of Bradford: hon visiting fell, chm Steering Ctee for Clothing Degree Course, memb Advsy Ctee Dept of Industl Technol 1991-; memb Cons Pty (ward chm Hendon South Constituency); *Style*— Norman Sussman, Esq, CBE; Montana, Winnington Rd, Finchley, London N2 0TX (☎ 081 455 9394); L S & J

Sussman Limited, Albany House, 12 Albany Rd, London E10 7EN (☎ 081 539 8373, fax 081 556 9653)

SUTCH, Andrew Lang; s of Rev Canon Christopher Lang Sutch, of 18 Linden Rd, Bristol, and Gladys Ethelwyn, *née* Larrington; *b* 10 July 1952; *Educ* Haileybury Coll, Oriel Coll Oxford (MA); *m* 22 May 1982, Shirley Anne, da of Gordon Alger Teichmann, of 47 Lexden Rd, Colchester; 2 s (James b 12 Dec 1983, Francis b 24 Aug 1986); *Career* Lt Intelligence Corps TA 1976-86; admitted slr 1979, ptnr Stephenson Harwood 1984- (employed 1977-); memb Law Soc 1979; *Recreations* theatre, running; *Style—* Andrew Sutch, Esq; Stephenson Harwood, One St Paul's Churchyard, London EC4M 8SH (☎ 071 329 4422, fax 071 606 0822)

SUTCLIFF, Cdr (Archibald) Edward; OBE (1958), DSC (1944); s of Capt Archibald Alfred Sutcliff, RAMC (d 1915), and Mary Natalie Vaughan (d 1967); *b* 12 June 1911; *Educ* RNC Dartmouth; *m* 11 Aug 1944, Dinah Sarah Joanna, da of Lawrence Metelerkamp (d 1961), of Johannesburg; 1 s (Edward b 1946), 1 da (Sarah b 1949); *Career* regular RN offr 1928-58, navigation specialist; serv WWII continuously at sea: Atlantic, Arctic, Antarctic, Indian & Pacific Oceans; ret cmdr RN 1958; mangr then gen mangr ME Navigation Aids Serv; *Recreations* fly-fishing, birdwatching, hill walking, listening to music; *Clubs* Naval & Military; *Style—* Cdr Edward Sutcliff, OBE, DSC; Creach, Aros, Isle of Mull, Argyll PA72 6JZ (☎ 068 85 242)

SUTCLIFF, Rosemary; OBE (1975); da of Capt George Ernest Sutcliff, RN (d 1966), and Nessie Elizabeth, *née* Lawton (d 1955); *b* 14 Dec 1920; *Educ* Bideford Sch of Art; *Career* historical and childrens' novelist; FRSL 1982; *Books* incl: The Eagle of the Ninth (1954), Sword at Sunset (1962), The Lantern Bearers (1958), Song for a Dark Queen (1976), The Shining Company (1990); *Recreations* none except dogs and staring into the middle distance; *Style—* Miss Rosemary Sutcliff, OBE; Swallowshaw, Walberton, Arundel, Sussex BN18 0PQ (☎ 0243 5513616)

SUTCLIFFE, Allan; *b* 30 Jan 1936; *Educ* Neath GS, UCL (LLB); *m* 17 June 1983, Pauline; *Career* various fin positions Br 1960-70 (graduate trainee 1957-60), dir fin Wales Gas Bd 1972-80 (chief accountant 1970-72); dep chm Br Gas: W Midlands 1980-83, N Thames 1983-86; md fin Br Gas plc 1987- (designate 1986-87); Freeman City of London 1986; FCMA, CBIM, CIGasE; *Recreations* reading, music, old buildings; *Clubs* RAC; *Style—* Allan Sutcliffe, Esq; British Gas Plc, Rivermill Hse, 152 Grosvenor Rd, London SW1V 3JL (☎ 071 821 1444)

SUTCLIFFE, Prof Charles Martin Sydenham; s of Gordon Edward Sutcliffe, and Florence Lillian, *née* Cole; *b* 5 Jan 1948; *Educ* KCS Wimbledon, Univ of Reading (BA); *Career* International Computers Ltd 1965-68, Unilever 1971-73, lectr Univ of Reading 1973-86, Northern Soc prof of accounting and fin 1986-90, prof of accountancy Univ of Southampton 1990-; memb Berkshire CC 1981-85; ACMA 1985, AT11 1968, MInstAM 1968; *Books* The Dangers of Low Level Radiation (1987); *Recreations* cycling; *Style—* Prof Charles Sutcliffe; Department of Accounting and Management Science, The University, Southampton SO9 5NH (☎ 0703 595000)

SUTCLIFFE, (Charles Wilfred) David; s of Max Sutcliffe (d 1976), of Shipley, W Yorks, and Mary Doreen Sutcliffe (d 1977); *b* 21 June 1936; *Educ* Uppingham, Univ of Leeds (BA); *m* 6 May 1960, Hanne, da of Carl Olaf Carlsen (d 1967), of Copenhagen, Denmark; 2 s (Charles Peter David b 1961, John Mark Benson b 1963); *Career* Lt 4 Royal Tank Regt; chm and jt md Benson Turner Ltd 1978- (jt md from 1968), chm Benson Turner (Dyers) Ltd 1976-78; dir: Bradford Microfirms Ltd 1981-88, Enterflow Ltd 1983-, Bradford Breakthrough Ltd 1990-, Bradford Training & Enterprise Cncl 1991-; pres Bradford C of C 1983-85, memb High Steward's Cncl York Minster 1980- (tstee York Minster Fund 1987-), fndr and chm Bradford Enterprise Agency 1983-89, pres Bradford Textile Soc 1987-88; memb Co Merchants of the Staple of England 1979, Freeman City of London, Liveryman Guild of Framework Knitters 1983; hon fell Bradford & Ilkley Community Coll 1985; C Text, FTI; *Recreations* golf, shooting, sailing; *Clubs* Brooks's; *Style—* David Sutcliffe, Esq; Ivy House Farm, Kettlesing, nr Harrogate, N Yorks HG3 2LR (☎ 0423 770561); 133 New Kings Rd, London SW6 4SL (☎ 071 731 8417); Benson Turner Ltd, Station Mills, Wyke, Bradford, West Yorks BD12 8LA (☎ 0274 601122, fax 0274 691170, telex 517683 BENTUR G)

SUTCLIFFE, Hon Mrs (Helen); *née* Rhodes; da of Baron Rhodes, KG, DFC, PC, DL; *b* 15 Aug 1929; *m* 1954, John Sutcliffe, JP, DL, s of Herbert Sutcliffe, of Colwyn Bay; 2 s, 1 da; *Style—* The Hon Mrs Sutcliffe; Lower Carr, Diggle, Dobcross, Oldham, Lancs

SUTCLIFFE, Ian Sharp; s of Harold Nelson Sutcliffe (d 1962), of Houghton Hall, Houghton, Carlisle, and Isabella Fox, *née* Jerdan; *b* 30 Jan 1931; *Educ* Marlborough, Emmanuel Coll Cambridge (MA, LLM, Hockey blue); *m* 10 June 1960, Anne Lyon, da of Robert Lyon Wyllie, CBE, JP, DL, of Cockermouth, Cumbria; 3 s (Andrew Robert Nelson b 6 May 1962, (Ian) Jonathan Wyllie b 11 Feb 1967, Nicholas Richard b 27 Nov 1968); *Career* 2 Lt RASC (Water Tport Div) 1950-51, RARO 1952-60; admitted slr 1958; NP 1958, conslt Mounseys (formerly Mounsey Bowman & Sutcliffe) 1960, sr ptnr 1964-90; Metrorural Properties Ltd 1987-; registrar and legal sec to Bishopric of Carlisle 1963-, clerk to Dean and Chapter of Carlisle Cathedral 1963-; played: squash for Cumbria 1955-60, hockey for Northumberland 1955-64; memb: Law Soc, Soc of Notaries Pub; *Recreations* golf, tennis; *Clubs* R and A Golf (St Andrew's), County and Border (Carlisle); *Style—* Ian S Sutcliffe, Esq; Mulcaster House, Stanwix, Carlisle, Cumbria (☎ 0228 26314); 19 Castle St, Carlisle, Cumbria (☎ 0228 25195)

SUTCLIFFE, James Stocks; s of Peter S Stucliffe, and Hon Mrs (Dora) Valerie Patricia, *née* Canning, *qv*; *b* 9 March 1953; *Educ* Stowe, Grimsby Tech Coll (HND); *m* 18 June 1988, Susan Diana, da of John Beaumont, of Legbourne, Louth, Lincs; 1 s (William Goerge b Oct 1989), 1 da (by previous m) (Hannah Elizabeth b 20 April 1983); *Career* chm and dir: John Sutcliffe & Son (Holdings) Ltd, John Sutcliffe & Son (Grimsby) Ltd, Sutcliffe International Ltd, John Sutcliffe (Heavy) Ltd, John Sutcliffe (International Transport) Ltd, Sutcliffe Travel Ltd, Confill (UK) Ltd, Docks Motor Engineering Co Ltd, Furncliffe Freight Forwarders Ltd, Sutcliffe Solloway & Co Ltd, Sutcliffe Solloway (Life & Pensions) Ltd, Solloway Group Pensions Schemes Ltd; MInstD; *Recreations* motor sport; *Style—* James Sutcliffe, Esq; John Sutcliffe & Son (Holdings) Ltd, Sutcliffe House, Market St, Grimsby, S Humberside DN31 1QT (☎ 0472 359101, telex 52502 SUTGBY G, fax 0472 241935)

SUTCLIFFE, Martin Rhodes; s of John Sutcliffe, JP, DL, of Oldham, Lancashire, and the Hon Helen, *née* Rhodes; gs of late Lord Rhodes of Saddleworth, KG, DFC, PC, DL; *b* 21 Sept 1955; *Educ* Hulme GS (house capt, represented sch in swimming & athletics), Univ of Sheffield (BA, DipArch); *m* 26 July 1980, Gillian Margaret, da of Arthur Price, of Rochdale, Lancashire; 1 s (Henry Ellis b 16 April 1987), 1 da (Hannah Sarah Rhodes b 19 April 1982); *Career* architect; Skidmore Owings and Merrill Chicago 1977-78, Montague Assocs Derby 1980-81, Derek Latham and Assocs Derby 1981-85 (assoc 1983-); projects incl: St Michaels Derby, Veterinary Hospital Derby, Heights of Abraham Cable Car Project and Wirksworth Heritage Centre (Civic Tst award commendations); Building Design Partnership (BDP): joined 1985, assoc 1988, ptnr 1990; projects incl: Pescod Square Boston, Reedswood Centre Walsall, Cheshire Oaks Regnl Shopping Centre, Carbrook Hall Office Park Sheffield, Ryton Centre Worksop; registered architect and MRIBA 1981-; *Recreations* family and home, visual and performing arts, places of architectural and historic interest, the countryside, Derbyshire well dressing; *Style—* Martin Sutcliffe, Esq; Building Design Partnership, Fountain Precinct, Balm Green, Sheffield S1 2JA (☎ 0742 731641, fax 0742 701878, car 0831 476116)

SUTCLIFFE, Col Patrick Malcolm Brogden; CBE (1983, MBE 1966), TD, DL (Hants 1973); s of William Francis Sutcliffe (d 1959), and Edna Mary, *née* Brogden (d 1978); *b* 21 Oct 1922; *Educ* Marlborough Coll, Pembroke Coll Cambridge (MA); *m* 1950, Dorothy Anne Daly, da of Arnold Daly Briscoe, TD, of Woodbridge, Suffolk; 2 s, 1 da; *Career* Berks Yeo 1942-60, Berks & Westminster Dragoons 1961-67, Lt-Col Royal Berks Territorials 1967-69, Col TA & VR E and S E District 1969-74, vice-chm (Hants) Eastern Wessex TA & VRA 1974 (chm 1975-84 and vice-chm Cncl 1981-84); ADC to HM The Queen 1970; FRICS; *Clubs* Army and Navy; *Style—* Col Patrick Sutcliffe, CBE, TD, DL; Burntwood Farm, Winchester, Hants (☎ 0962 882384)

SUTCLIFFE, Serena; *m* David Peppercorn; *Career* translator UNESCO; author, conslt and expert on wine; pubns: Wines of The World, Great Vineyards and Winemakers, The Wine Drinker's Handbook, The Pocket Guide to the Wines of Burgundy, A Celebration of Champagne (Decanter book of the year award, 1988); dir Peppercorn and Sutcliffe 1988-91 (non-exec dir 1991-), conslt to multinational cos, wine estates, ind investmt cos and other instns; dir Wine Dept Sotheby's 1991-; Chevalier dans L'Ordre des Arts et des Lettres; memb Inst Masters of Wine; *Style—* Ms Serena Sutcliffe; Director Wine Department, Sotheby's, 34 & 35 New Bond Street, London W1A 2AA

SUTCLIFFE, Hon Mrs ((Dora) Valerie Patricia); *née* Canning; elder da of 4 Baron Garvagh (d 1956); *b* 31 Oct 1919; *m* 1, 13 Jan 1942, Philip Anthony Wellesley Colley, Lt RA (ka 1944); 2 da; m 2, 28 Aug 1950, Peter Stocks Sutcliffe, o s of Ernest Sutcliffe, of Stewton House, Louth, Lincs; 1 s; *Style—* The Hon Mrs Sutcliffe; La Serena, Quartiers Les Clots, Clavier, Le Var, France

SUTHERLAND, David George Carr; CBE (1974), MC (1942, and bar 1943), TD, DL (Tweeddale 1974); s of Lt-Col Arthur Henry Carr Sutherland, OBE, MC (d 1962), of Cringletie, Peebles, Scotland, and Ruby, *née* Miller (d 1982); *b* 28 Oct 1920; *Educ* Eton, Sandhurst RMA; *m* 1, Sept 1945, Jean Beatrice (d 1963), da of Evelyn Henderson, of Sedgwick Park, Nr Horsham, Sussex; 1 s (Michael b 1946), 2 da (Sarah (twin) b 1946, Fiona b 1953); m 2, May 1964, Christine Alexandra Hotchkiss, author, of New York; *Career* served WWII Black Watch and SAS: Dunkirk, Western Desert, Aegean, Adriatic (wounded, despatches); various cmd and staff appts 1945-55 incl: Br Mil Mission to Greece, instr Sandhurst, Gold Staff Offr at HM The Queen's Coronation; ret 1955, Cmdr 21 SAS Regt (Artists Rifles) TA 1956-60; MOD 1955-80, landowner and farmer 1962-, non-exec dir Asset Protection International Ltd 1981-85, conslt Control Risks Group Ltd 1985-; memb Queen's Bodyguard for Scotland (Royal Co of Archers) 1949-; FRGS; Greek War Cross 1944 and 1945; *Recreations* fishing, shooting, walking; *Clubs* Brooks's, Special Forces; *Style—* David Sutherland, Esq, CBE, MC, TD, DL; 51 Victoria Rd, London W8; Ferniehaugh, Dolphinton, Tweeddale

SUTHERLAND, (Ian) Douglas; s of Col Francis Ian Sinclair Sutherland, OBE, MC, ED (d 1962), of Moffat and Ceylon, and Helen Myrtle Sutherland (d 1988); *b* 23 Oct 1945; *Educ* St Bees Sch Cumberland; *m* 11 Oct 1975, Kathyrn, da of John Henry Wallace (d 1989), of Haltwhistle, Northumberland; 1 s (Jonathan b 6 Nov 1976), 1 da (Iseabail b 13 July 1972); *Career* D M Hall & Son 1965-: trainee surveyor, ptnr 1975; memb Co of Merchants of the City of Edinburgh; FRICS 1980; *Clubs* New Edinburgh, Royal Scots Edinburgh; *Style—* Douglas Sutherland, Esq; 2 Ormidale Terr, Edinburgh EH12 6EQ (☎ 031 337 5584); D M Hall & Son, Chartered Surveyors, 13-15 Morningside Drive, Edinburgh EH10 5LZ (☎ 031 452 8811, fax 031 452 8619, car 0836 705 000)

SUTHERLAND, Countess of (24 in line, S circa 1235); Elizabeth Millicent Sutherland Janson; also Lady Strathnaver (strictly speaking a territorial style, but treated as a Lordship for purposes of use as courtesy title for heir to Earldom since the end of the sixteenth century); adopted surname of Sutherland under Scots law 1963; Chief of the Clan Sutherland; o da of Lord Alistair St Clair Sutherland-Leveson-Gower, MC (d 1921, s of 4 Duke of Sutherland, KG, and Lady Millicent St Clair-Erskine, da of 4 Earl of Rosslyn), and Elizabeth Hélène, *née* Demarest (d 1931); suc to Earldom of Sutherland held by unc, 5 Duke of Sutherland, KT, PC, 1963 (thus came about precisely the contingency that might have caused objection to be made when the Dukedom was so named on its creation 130 years earlier in 1833, *viz* that because the latter was heritable in tail male while the Earldom not only could be held by a female but actually was (by the 1 Duke's wife) at the time of the cr, the two might become separated; the then Countess of Sutherland in her own right (gggg mother of present Countess) was known as the 'Duchess-Countess' in a style analogous to that of the Spanish Count-Duke Olivares of the seventeenth century; *b* 30 March 1921; *Educ* Queen's Coll Harley St, abroad; *m* 5 Jan 1946, Charles Noel Janson, DL, eldest s of late Charles Wilfrid Janson, of 16 Wilton Crescent, London SW1; 2 s (Alistair, Martin (twins)), 1 s (Matthew decd), 1 da (Annabel); *Heir* s, Lord Strathnaver; *Career* serv Land Army 1939-41; hosp lab technician: Raigmore Hosp Inverness, St Thomas's Hosp London; chm: Northern Times 1963-88 (dir 1988-), Dunrobin Sch Ltd 1965-72, Dunrobin Castle Ltd 1972-; *Recreations* reading, swimming; *Style—* The Rt Hon the Countess of Sutherland; 39 Edwardes Sq, London W8 (☎ 071 603 0659); Dunrobin Castle, Golspie, Sutherland; House of Tongue, by Lairg, Sutherland

SUTHERLAND, Dr George Roberton (Roy); s of George Roberton Sutherland, of 33 Elm Court, Glasgow Rd, Milgavie, Glasgow, and Barbara Barnett, *née* Smith; *b* 15 Dec 1931; *Educ* George Heriot's Sch Edinburgh, Univ of Edinburgh (MB ChB); *m* 22 March 1963, Lorna Hunter, da of Dr Thomas Rodger Murray (d 1989), of Glasgow; 2 da (Fiona b 1965, Karen b 1968); *Career* Flt Lt RAF 1957-58 (Flying Offr 1956-57); Univ of Edinburgh: lectr Dept of Med 1959-64, hon clinical lectr Dept of Radiology 1966-68; conslt radiologist: S Gen Hosp Glasgow 1968-77, (i/c) Stobhill Gen Hosp Glasgow 1977-87, (i/c) Royal Infirmary and Stobhill Gen Hosp Glasgow 1987-; hon clinical lectr Dept of Radiology Univ of Glasgow 1972-; former pres Scottish Radiological Soc, chm Standing Scot Ctee RCR (memb Faculty Bd, chm Computer Ctee); memb: Governing Body The Queen's Coll Glasgow, BMA, RSGB; elder St George's-Tron Church Glasgow; FRCR 1968, FRCPE 1973, FRCPG 1986; *Books* Textbook of Radiology by Sutton (contrib chapter on Eye and Orbit); *Recreations* golf, classic cars, electronics, boating; *Clubs* Royal Air Force; *Style—* Dr Roy Sutherland; 22 Montrose Drive, Bearsden, Glasgow G61 3LG (☎ 041 9427802), Tigh Na Lachan, Stuckrioch, by Strachur Strathlachlan, Argyllshire; Radiology Dept, Royal Infirmary, Glasgow (☎ 041 5523535); Glasgow, Nuffield Hospital, Beaconsfield Rd, Glasgow (☎ 041 334 9441, car 0860 454518)

SUTHERLAND, Prof Ian Oxley; s of Maxwell Charles Sutherland (d 1983), and Margaret, *née* Seabrook (d 1943); *b* 11 Dec 1931; *Educ* Ilford Co HS, Pembroke Coll Cambridge (BA, MA, PhD); *m* 31 March 1956, Sheila Margaret, da of Dr Morris Lord Yates, of Caldy, Wirral; 2 s (John b 1962, Andrew b 1968) 1 da (Elizabeth b 1959); *Career* lectr Univ of Bristol 1961-63, reader Univ of Sheffield 1969-77 (lectr 1963-69); Univ of Liverpool: prof of organic chemistry 1977-86, Heath-Harrison prof of organic chemistry 1986-, dean of science 1986-88; FRSC, CChem, memb American Chemical Soc; *Recreations* gardening, photography; *Style—* Prof Ian Sutherland; Dept of Chemistry, University of Liverpool, PO Box 147, Liverpool L69 3BX (☎ 051

7943501, telex 627095 UNILPL G, fax 051 7086502)

SUTHERLAND, James; CBE (1974); s of James Sutherland, JP (d 1951), and Agnes, *née* Walker; *b* 15 Feb 1920; *Educ* Queen's Park Secdy Sch Glasgow, Glasgow Univ (MA, LLB, LLD); *m* 1, 6 Sept 1948, Elizabeth Kelly Barr; 2 s (David b 1949, Malcolm b 1952, d 1975); m 2, 27 Sept 1984, Grace Williamson Dawson; *Career* Royal Signals 1940-46; ptnr McClure Naismith Anderson & Gardiner (solicitors) Glasgow and Edinburgh 1951-87, conslt 1987-90; examiner in Scots Law Glasgow Univ 1951-55, mercantile and industrial law 1968-69; chm Glasgow South Nat Insurance Tribunal 1964-66; memb Law Soc of Scotland Cncl 1959-77 (vice-pres 1969-70, pres 1972-74); memb Int Bar Assoc Cncl 1972- (chm Gen Practices Section 1978-80, sec gen 1980-84, pres 1984-86); dean of Royal Faculty of Procurators in Glasgow 1977-80; chm Glasgow Maternity and Women's Hosps 1966-74; vice-chm Glasgow Eastern Health Cncl 1975-77; memb: Gen Dental Cncl 1975-89, Ct of Strathclyde Univ 1977-; Deacon Incorporation of Barbers Glasgow 1962-63; Hon LLD Glasgow 1985; *Recreations* golf; *Clubs* Royal and Ancient, Western (Glasgow); *Style*— Dr James Sutherland, CBE; Greenacres, 20/21 Easter Belmont Road, Edinburgh EH12 6EX (☎ 031 337 1888, fax 031 346 0067); Johnston Court, St Andrews, Fife

SUTHERLAND, (Robert) James Mackay; s of James Fleming Sutherland (d 1932), of Knockbrex, Kirkcudbright, Scot, and Edith Mary, *née* Meredith (d 1964); *b* 3 Nov 1922; *Educ* Stowe, Trinity Coll Cambridge (BA); *m* 7 June 1947, Anthea, da of John Christopher Hyland (d 1961), of Donegal, Ireland; 2 da (Chloe Helena Meredith b 15 Sept 1952, Sabina Rachel b 20 Nov 1954); *Career* RNVR 1943-46, Lt, demobbed 1946; asst civil engr: Sir William Halcrow & Partners 1946-56, A J Harris 1956-58; Harris & Sutherland: ptnr 1958-87, active conslt 1987-; author of various chapters and papers on engineering and engineering history; memb Royal Fine Art Cmmn, former pres Newcomen Soc for the Study of Hist of Sci and Technol 1987-89; memb various ctees incl: Br Standards Inst, English Heritage; FEng, FICE, FIStructE (vice pres 1980-82); *Recreations* engineering history, architectural travel and photography; *Clubs* Travellers'; *Style*— James Sutherland, Esq; 4 Pitt St, London W8 4NX (☎ 071 937 7961); Harris & Sutherland, 82-83 Blackfriars Rd, London SE1 8HA (☎ 071 928 0282, fax 071 927 0785)

SUTHERLAND, Lady (Jeanne Edith); *née* Nutt; da of Thomas Dixon Nutt, of Linden Barn, Gazeley, nr Newmarket, Suffolk; *b* 9 Dec 1927; *Educ* Univ of London (MA); *m* 1955, Sir Iain Johnstone Macbeth Sutherland, KCMG (d 1986); 1 s, 2 da; *Career* former attaché Br Embassy Moscow, lectr Poly N London, chm Greek Animal Welfare Fund (GAWF-UK), ctee memb and treas UK Study Gp on Soviet Educn; memb Bd of Visitors Pentonville Prison; *Recreations* travel, theatre, literature, tennis; *Style*— Lady Sutherland; 24 Cholmeley Park, Highgate, London N6 5EU

SUTHERLAND, Dame Joan; AC (1975), DBE (1979, CBE 1961); da of William Sutherland, of Sydney; *b* 7 Nov 1926; *Educ* St Catherine's Waverley; *m* 1954, Richard Bonynge; 1 s; *Career* opera singer; debut Sydney 1947, Royal Opera House Covent Garden 1952; performed in operas at: Glyndebourne, La Scala Milan, Vienna State Opera, Metropolitan Opera NY; has made numerous recordings; *Style*— Dame Joan Sutherland, AC, DBE; c/o Ingpen & Williams, 14 Kensington Court, London, W8 5DN

SUTHERLAND, 6 Duke of (UK 1833); Sir John Sutherland Egerton; 13 Bt (E 1620), TD, DL (Berwicks); also 5 Earl of Ellesmere (UK 1846), which known as 1944-63 (when he inherited the Dukedom); also Baron Gower (GB 1703), Earl Gower and Viscount Trentham (GB 1746), Marquess of Stafford (GB 1786), Viscount Brackley (UK 1846); s of 4 Earl of Ellesmere (d 1944), and Lady Violet Lambton, da of 4 Earl of Durham; *b* 10 May 1915; *Educ* Eton, Trinity Coll Cambridge; *m* 1, 1939, Lady Diana Percy (d 1978), da of 8 Duke of Northumberland; m 2, 1979, Evelyn, da of late Maj Robert Moubray (whose w Claire was gda of Sir Charles Morrison-Bell, 1 Bt); *Heir* Cyril Egerton, *qv*; *Career* late Capt RAC (TA), serv WWII (POW); *Style*— His Grace The Duke of Sutherland, TD DL; Mertoun, St Boswell's, Melrose, Roxburghshire; Lingay Cottage, Hall Farm, Newmarket, Suffolk

SUTHERLAND, Dr Mackenzie Stewart; s of Sinclair Millar Sutherland (d 1969), of Carluke, Scot, and Elsie, *née* Shand; *b* 31 March 1933; *Educ* Univ of Aberdeen (MB ChB, DPM, Dip Psycotherapy); *m* 20 June 1962, Una Marguerite, da of John George Weir (d 1982) of Aberdeen; 1 s (Grant b 1969), 1 da (Shona b 1963); *Career* RAC 5th Royal Tank Regt Korea 1952-54; jr med posts 1962-72; N Tees Gen Hosp: conslt psychiatrist 1972-, sr conslt 1987-, chm div of psychiatry 1988-90; MRCPsych 1972; *Recreations* squash, golf, philately; *Style*— Dr Mackenzie Sutherland; 70 Chestnut Drive, Marton, Cleveland (☎ 0642 315712), Department of Psychiatry, North Tees General Hosp, Stockton, Cleveland (☎ 0642 672122)

SUTHERLAND, Margaret, Lady; Margaret; JP; da of Albert Owen (d 1965), of Chalfont St Giles Bucks, and Elsie Owen, *née* Wright (d 1964); *b* 3 June 1916; *Educ* Ilford GS Essex; *m* 1944, as his 2 w, Sir Ivan Sutherland, 2 Bt (d 1980), of Thurso House, Newcastle upon Tyne; 3 s (William, Owen, Ben); *Career* magistrate 1966, Northumberland CC 1961-74, cncllr Embleton Parish 1964-74; Alnwick dist cncllr 1960-74; pres: Northumberland Assoc of Local Cncls, Seahouses Lifeboat Guild, Seahouses Harbour cmmr; vice pres Community Cncl of Northumberland; *Recreations* handbell ringing, embroidery, yoga; *Style*— Margaret, Lady Sutherland, JP; The Smithy, Embleton, Alnwick, Northumberland (☎ 066 576 467)

SUTHERLAND, Sir Maurice; s of Thomas Daniel Sutherland (d 1953); *b* 12 July 1915; *Educ* Stockton Secdy Sch; *m* 1, 1941, Beatrice Skinner; 1 s; m 2, 1960, Jane Ellen; 1 step da; m 3, 1984, Ellen Margaret; 1 step s; *Career* slr; ldr Teesside County Boro Cncl 1968-74, (mayor 1972-73) ldr Cleveland CC 1974-77 (ldr of oppn 1977-81, ldr 1981); kt 1976; *Style*— Sir Maurice Sutherland; 8 Manor Close, Low Worsall, Yarm, Cleveland; work: PO Box 100A, Municipal Buildings, Middlesbrough, Cleveland TS1 2QH (☎ 0642 248155)

SUTHERLAND, (David) Michael; s of Sir Benjamin Ivan Sutherland, Bt (d 1980), of Embleton, Alnwick, and Marjorie Constance Daniel Bousfield, *née* Brewer (d 1980); *b* 14 June 1940; *Educ* Sedbergh Sch, St Catharine's Coll Cambridge (MA); *m* 11 Aug 1966, Caroline Mary, da of Robert S Hogan (d 1944); 3 da (Julia Ruth b 1967, Serena Louise b 1971, Polly Anne b 1975); *Career* farmer; *Recreations* tennis, curling; *Style*— Michael Sutherland, Esq

SUTHERLAND, (John Alexander) Muir; s of John Alexander Sutherland (d 1988), and Eleanor, *née* Muir (d 1936); *b* 5 April 1933; *Educ* Trinity Coll Glenalmond, Hertford Coll Oxford (MA); *m* 26 March 1970, Mercedes Gonzalez; 2 s (Alejandro b 1 July 1971, Stuart b 2 May 1974); *Career* Nat Serv 2 Lt Highland Light Infantry 1951-53; head of presentation and planning Border Television 1963-66, prog coordinator ABC Television 1966-68; Thames Television: prog coordinator 1968-72, controller int sales 1973-74, md Thames TV International 1975-82, dir of progs 1982-86; dir Celtic Films Ltd 1986-; *Recreations* golf; *Clubs* Club De Campo (Madrid); *Style*— Muir Sutherland, Esq; Celtic Films Ltd, 1/2 Bromley Place, London W1P 5HB (☎ 071 637 7651, fax 071 436 5387, telex 264639)

SUTHERLAND, Peter Berkeley Douglas; s of late Douglas Sutherland, and late Ethel, *née* Page; *b* 13 Feb 1925; *Educ* Shrewsbury, St Catharine's Coll Cambridge (MA), UCL (DipArch), Royal Acad; *m* 16 March 1962, Diane Marie, da of Charles Joseph Wyatt (d 1986), of Somers Rd, Reigate; 1 s (Justin Charles Berkeley b 1966), 1 da (Belinda Marie b 1968); *Career* Royal Devon Yeo RA 1943-47, Capt India and Malaya; architect; chm Henley Cons Assoc 1967 (pres 1971), Henley Cmmrs of Taxes 1974- (chm 1983), coach Univ of Oxford Olympic VIII 1960; Desborough medal; RIBA 1954; *Recreations* rowing, punting; *Clubs* Leander (past capt and life memb), MCC, Upper Thames Rowing (pres and fndr), Phyllis Court; *Style*— Peter Sutherland, Esq; Bird Place, Henley-on-Thames (☎ 0491 572033); Saragossa House, New Street, Henley-on-Thames (☎ 0491 573003)

SUTHERLAND, Peter Denis William; s of William George Sutherland, of Dublin, and Barbara, *née* Nealon; *b* 25 April 1946; *Educ* Gonzaga Coll, Univ Coll Dublin (BCL), Hon Soc of the Kings Inns; *m* 18 Sept 1971, Maruja Cabria Valcarcel, da of Paulino Cabria Garcia, of Reinosa, Santander, Spain; 2 s (Shane b 1972, Ian b 1974), 1 da (Natalia b 1979); *Career* barr: Kings Inns 1968, Middle Temple 1976, attorney of New York Bar, admitted to practice before the Supreme Ct of the US, practising memb of Irish Bar 1968-81 (Sen Cncl 1980); tutor in law Univ Coll Dublin 1969-71, memb Cncl of State of Ireland and attorney-gen of Ireland 1981-Aug 1982 and Dec 1982-1984; Cmmr of EC for Competition and Relations with Euro Parl 1985-89; visiting fell Kennedy Sch of Govt Univ of Harvard 1989; chm Allied Irish Banks 1989-; chm Shannon Aerospace plc; memb bds of: GPA plc, James Crean plc, CRH plc, BP; Bencher of Hon Soc of King's Inns Dublin; memb bd of govrs Euro Inst of Public Admin Maastricht; Hon LLD St Louis Univ 1985; Gd Cross Order of Leopold II (Belgium), Gd Cross of Civil Merit (Spain); *Books* 1er Janvier 1993 - ce qui va changer en Europe (1988); *Recreations* tennis, reading; *Clubs* FitzWilliam Lawn Tennis (Dublin), Lansdowne Rugby Football, Royal Irish Yacht; *Style*— Peter Sutherland, Esq; Allied Irish Banks plc, Bankcentre, Ballsbridge, Dublin 4, Republic of Ireland (☎ 0001 600 311, fax 0001 603 063)

SUTHERLAND, Dr Sheena; da of John William Robertson (d 1975), and Christian, *née* McLeman; *b* 4 Dec 1938; *Educ* Fraserburgh Acad, Univ of Aberdeen (MB ChB); *m* 1 Aug 1964, Prof Stewart Ross Sutherland, *qv*, 1 s (Duncan Stewart b 1970), 2 da (Fiona Mair b 1966, Kirsten Ann b 1968); *Career* registrar Inst of Virology Glasgow 1975-77, lectr Middx Hosp Med Sch 1978-84, conslt virologist Public Health Laboratory Dulwich 1985-, hon sr lectr King's Coll Sch of Med and Dentistry 1985-, hon conslt Camberwell Health Authy 1985-; MRCPath 1982; *Recreations* weaving, gardening, crafts, theatre; *Clubs* Royal Soc of Med; *Style*— Dr Sheena Sutherland; Virology Laboratory, Dulwich Hospital, East Dulwich Grove, London SE22 (☎ 693 3377 ext 3202, fax 299 0233)

SUTHERLAND, Prof Stewart Ross; s of George Arthur Caswell Sutherland (d 1974), of Aberdeen, and Ethel, *née* Masson; *b* 25 Feb 1941; *Educ* Robert Gordons Coll Aberdeen, Univ of Aberdeen (MA), Corpus Christi Coll Cambridge (MA); *m* 1 Aug 1964, Sheena, da of John Robertson (d 1975), of Fraserburgh; 1 s (Duncan Stewart b 9 March 1970), 2 da (Fiona Mair b 11 Dec 1966, Kirsten Ann b 20 Aug 1968); *Career* asst lectr UCNW 1965-68; Univ of Stirling: lectr 1968, sr lectr 1972, reader 1976-77; Kings Coll London: prof of history and philosophy of religion 1977-85, vice-princ 1981-85, princ 1985-90; vice chancellor Univ of London 1990-; C of E Bd of Educn 1980-84; chm: Br Academy Postgrad Studentships Ctee 1987-, cncl of Royal Inst of Philosophy 1988-; vice chm Ctee of Vice Chancellors and Principals 1989-91; memb Worshipful Co Goldsmiths 1986; Hon LHD: Wooster Ohio USA, CCC, Univ of Bangor, Univ of Aberdeen; *Books* Atheism and Rejection of God (1977), God, Jesus and Belief (1984), Faith and Ambiguity (1984), The World's Religions (ed, 1988); *Recreations* tassie medallions, jazz, theatre; *Clubs* Athenaeum; *Style*— Prof Stewart Sutherland; University of London, Senate House, Malet St, London WCIE 7HU (☎ 071 636 8000)

SUTHERLAND, Prof (Norman) Stuart; s of Norman McCleod Sutherland (d 1979), and Celia Dickson, *née* Jackson; *b* 26 March 1927; *Educ* King Edward's HS Brimingham, Univ of Oxford (BA, BA); *m* 3 July 1954, Jose Louise, da of Michael Fogden; 2 da (Gay b 3 March 1959, Julia Claire b 7 Aug 1961); *Career* Sergeant RAF 1949-1951; Univ of Oxford: fell Magdalen Coll 1954-58, res dir in experimental psychology 1959-64, fell Merton Coll 1959-64; prof Mass Inst Technol USA 1960-61 and 1962-63, dir Centre for Res in Perception and Cognition Univ of Sussex 1969- (prof of experimental psychology 1964-); memb: Soc of Experimental Psychology, Int Brain Soc; *Books* Quartly Jl Experimental Psychology Monograph (contrib, 1961), Animal Discrimination Learning (ed with R M Gilbert, 1969), Mechanisms of Animal Discrimination Learning (with N J Mackintosh, 1971), Brain and Behaviour (with O Wolthuis, 1972), National Attitudes held by European Executives (with V Selwyn, 1974), Tutorial Essays in Psychology (ed, 1975), Breakdown: A Personal Crisis and a Medical Dilemma (1976, revised 1987), Prestel and the User (1980), Discovering the Human Mind (1982), Men Change Too (1987), Macmillan Dictionary of Psychology (1989); *Recreations* buildings; *Style*— Prof Stuart Sutherland; Experimental Psychology, Sussex University, Brighton (☎ 0273 678304)

SUTHERLAND, Veronica Evelyn; CMG (1988); da of Lt-Col M G Beckett KOYLI (d 1949), and Constance Mary, *née* Cavanagh-Mainwaring; *b* 25 April 1939; *Educ* Royal Sch Bath, Univ of London (BA), Univ of Southampton (MA); *m* 29 Dec 1981, Alex James, s of James Sutherland (d 1969); *Career* third later second sec FCO 1965, second sec Copenhagen 1967, first sec FCO 1970, first sec Devpt New Delhi 1975, FCO 1978; cnsllr and perm UK del UNESCO Pans 1981, cnsllr FCO 1984, HM Ambassador Abidjan 1987; asst under sec of State (Dep Ch Clerk) FCO 1990-; *Recreations* painting; *Style*— Mrs Veronica E Sutherland, CMG; c/o FCO, London SW1

SUTHERLAND, Sir William George MacKenzie; QPM; *b* 12 Nov 1933; *Educ* Inverness Technical HS; *m* Jennie; 2 da; *Career* Cheshire Police 1954-73, Surrey Police 1973-75, Hertfordshire Police 1975-79; chief constable: Bedfordshire Police 1979-83, Lothian and Borders Police 1983; kt 1988; *Recreations* squash, hill-walking; *Style*— Sir William Sutherland, QPM; Chief Constable, Lothian and Borders Police, Police Headquarters, Fettes Avenue, Edinburgh EH4 1RB (☎ 031 311 3131)

SUTHERLAND JANSON, Hon Martin Dearman; s (yr twin) of Countess of Sutherland; *Educ* Eton; *m* 1974, Hon Mary Ann, *qv*; 5 s; *Style*— The Hon Martin Sutherland Janson; Meadow Cottage, Christmas Common, Watlington, Oxon OX9 5HR

SUTHERLAND JANSON, Hon Mrs (Mary Ann); *née* Balfour; da of 1 Baron Balfour of Inchrye, MC, PC (d 1988), and Mary, Baroness Balfour of Inchrye, *qv*; *m* 1974, Hon Martin Sutherland Janson, *qv*; 5 s; *Style*— The Hon Mrs Sutherland Janson; Meadow Cottage, Christmas Common, Watlington, Oxon OX9 5HR

SUTRO, Joan Maud; da of Arthur Bertram Colyer (d 1976), and Florence Maud, *née* Maycroft (d 1982); *Educ* Farnborough Hill Convent, Bedford HS, Coll De Jeunes Filles, Dreux; *m* 29 March 1941, Edward Leopold, MC, s of Leopold Sutro (d 1943); 1 s (decd), 2 da (Caroline Alexandra b 1943, Rosemary Jane b 1945); *Career* WWII served Balkans 1939-41; memb: Godstone Rural Dist Cncl 1948-52, Surrey Div Exec for Educn; chm: Int Spring Fair 1974-79, Women's Cncl 1981-87 (chm of Delegation to China 1982); translated play Auguste by Raymond Castans produced by BBC Radio and for the Stage in S Africa; memb Royal Inst Affrs 1944-; govr: Oxted Co Sch 1950-71, Central Sch of Speech & Drama 1956-; vice pres Anglo-Turkish Soc 1983-; *Recreations* travel to remote places, theatre; *Style*— Mrs Edward Sutro; 12 South Eaton Place, London SW1W 9JA

SUTTIE, Amanda Margaret; da of Alexander Gordon Wanniarachy, of Boxford, Suffolk, and Cynthia Elizabeth, *née* Cogswell; *b* 2 May 1958; *Educ* Fyfield Sch Ongar Essex, Norland Nursery Trg Coll Denford Park Hungerford Berks (NNEB, RSH,

Norland Dip); *m* 23 May 1987, Dr Donald George Suttie, s of George Fraser Suttie, of Christchurch, NZ; 1 da (Alice Jemima b 29 Sept 1989); *Career* proprietor Canonbury Nannies Agency 1983-87 and 1990-, dir and princ Canonbury Nannies Ltd 1987-89, writer nanny helpline column Nursery World Magazine 1987-89, organiser first UK Nanny Fair 1988 (radio, TV nat and int press coverage, second fair 1989); memb Highgate Soc 1981-83, exec memb Bethnal Green and Stepney Cons Assoc 1984-86 (candidate local cncl elections 1986), sch govr Columbia Rd Nursery Sch London 1985-87; memb: Georgian Gp 1985-88, Nat Art Collection Fund 1987-88; currently: memb S Suffolk Cons Assoc, involved in fund raising activities for Nedging and Boxford Churches Suffolk; memb Fedn of Recruitment and Employment Servs; *Recreations* theatre, ballet, film, literature, art, antiques, ancient historic bldgs, interior design, wine tasting, cookery; *Style—* Mrs Amanda Suttie; 6 Northampton Grove, Islington, London N1; Apple Tree Cottage, Nedging, Suffolk; (☎ 071 704 0639/071 226 3194)

SUTTIE, Ian Alexander; s of John Alexander Suttie, of Aberdeen, and Christina Mary, *née* Mackie; *b* 8 June 1945; *Educ* Robert Gordons Coll Aberdeen, Univ of Aberdeen (CA); *m* 1 Dec 1971, Dorothy Elizabeth, da of Charles John George Small; 1 s (Martin b 1978), 2 da (Julia b 1974, Fiona b 1976); *Career* chm and md Wellserv plc, md Offshore Rentals Ltd, md Offshore Rentals Norge AS, dir Elbora Ltd, dir Handling Equipment Services Ltd, dir IDJ Properties Ltd; *Recreations* golf, curling, swimming; *Clubs* Aberdeen Petroleum; *Style—* Ian A Suttie, Esq; Parklea, North Deeside Rd, Pitfodels, Aberdeen AB1 9PB (☎ 0224 861389); Souterhead Rd, Altens, Aberdeen

SUTTILL, Bernard Roy (Rab); *b* 17 June 1919; *Educ* Univ Coll Sch, Royal Coll of Science (DIC, BSc, ARCS); *m* 1947, Ruth, 2 s, 3 da; *Career* served WW II RAF 1941-46 Fl Lt; oil exec Shell 1947-74, md Shell Co of Quatar, ret; Thompson North Sea Ltd 1974-; *Clubs* RAF; *Style—* Rab Suttill Esq; c/o Thomson North Sea Ltd, 75 Davies Street, London W1Y 1FA (☎ 071 493 7541); Stoke Park Farm, Abbotswood, Guildford GU1 1UT

SUTTON; *see*: Foster-Sutton

SUTTON, Alan John; s of William Clifford Sutton (d 1964), of Abertillery, and Emily, *née* Batten; *b* 16 March 1936; *Educ* Hafod-Y-Ddôl GS, Bristol Univ (BSc); *m* 7 Sept 1957, Glenis, da of George Henry (d 1986), of Ebbw Vale; 1 s (Andrew Jonathan b 1964), 1 da (Lisa Jayne b 1963); *Career* chief engr Eng Electric 1957-62, sales mangr Solartron 1962-69, md AB Connectors 1969-76, industl dir Welsh Off 1976-79, exec dir Welsh Devpt Agency 1979-88, chm and chief exec Anglolink Ltd 1988-; MIEE 1962; *Recreations* golf, walking; *Style—* Alan Sutton, Esq; Brockton House Heol-y-Delyn, Lisvane, Cardiff CF4 5SR (☎ 0222 753 194, fax 0222 747 037)

SUTTON, Andrew; s of William Stanley Sutton, of Birkenhead, Merseyside, and Evelyn Margaret, *née* Kitchin; *b* 27 Aug 1947; *Educ* Jesus Coll Cambridge (MA); *Career* ptnr Price Waterhouse London 1978-; vice pres Opportunities for the Disabled, cncl chm Bede House Assoc; Freeman City of London 1988; ACA 1971, FCA 1979; *Recreations* walking, opera, music, reading; *Clubs* Oxford and Cambridge; *Style—* Andrew Sutton, Esq; 53 Fitzjames Ave, London W14 0RR (☎ 071 603 5881); Southwark Towers, 32 London Bridge St, London SE1 9SY (☎ 071 407 8989, fax 071 378 0647, telex 884657)

SUTTON, Andrew Waugh; s of Edward James Sutton, of Leamington Spa, and Joyce Christine, *née* Plant; *b* 6 July 1945; *Educ* Leamington Coll for Boys, RCA (MDes, Leverhulme scholarship); *Career* freelance design conslt; ctee memb: Design and Industs Assoc, Industl Bldgs Preservation Tst, CSD; *Style—* Andrew Sutton, Esq; 136 Coldharbour Lane, Camberwell, London SE5 9PZ (☎ 071 274 6345); Sutton 231 Camberwell New Rd, London SE5 0TH (☎ 071 701 6002)

SUTTON, Andrew William; *b* 4 Oct 1939; *Educ* Brentwood Sch, Univ of Birmingham, Univ of Aston; *m* 13 July 1964, Kay, da of Lionel Edge, of Birmingham; 1 s (Benjamin b 21 Feb 1969), 1 da (Rebecca b 6 April 1967); *Career* psychologist: Newport (Mon) 1965-67, Birmingham 1968-84; Univ of Birmingham: hon lectr in educnl psychology 1970-84, assoc Centre for Russian & E Euro Studies 1980-, hon res fell Dept of Psychology 1984-; dir: Fndn for Conductive Educn 1986-, Questions Publishing Co; hon conductor Peto Inst Budapest 1990-; tstee Kids Charity; *Books* Home, School and Leisure in the Soviet Union (1980), Reconstructing Psychological Practice (1981), Conductive Education (1985); *Recreations* gardening, garden-railways; *Style—* Andrew Sutton, Esq; 78 Clarendon St, Leamington Spa, Warks CV32 4PE (☎ 0926 311966); The Foundation For Conductive Education, The University, Birmingham B15 2TT (☎ 021 414 4947, fax 021 414 3971, telex 333 762)

SUTTON, Barry Bridge; JP (Taunton); s of Albert Sutton (d 1976), of Taunton, and Ethel Ada, *née* Bridge; *b* 21 Jan 1937; *Educ* Eltham Coll, Peterhouse Coll Cambridge (MA), Univ of Bristol (DipEd); *m* 12 Aug 1961, Margaret Helen, da of (Edward) Thomas Palmer (d 1986); 1 s (Mark b 1964), 2 da (Clare b 1965, Jane b 1968); *Career* housemaster and sr history master Wycliffe Coll Stonehouse Glos 1961-75; headmaster: Hereford Cathedral Sch 1975-87, Taunton Sch 1987-; memb Ctee of the Cncl of Scout Assoc, a treas Somerset Scout Cncl; former JP Hereford; memb: HMC, Historical Assoc; *Recreations* mountain walking; *Clubs* E India, Devonshire, Sports, Pub Sch; *Style—* Barry Sutton, Esq; Headmaster's House, Private Rd, Staplegrove, Taunton TA2 6AJ (☎ 0823 272 588); Taunton Sch, Taunton TA2 6AD (☎ 0823 284 596)

SUTTON, Colin Bertie John; QPM (1985); s of Bertie Sydney Russel Sutton (d 1978), and Phyllis May, *née* Edkins, of Warwickshire; *b* 6 Dec 1938; *Educ* King Edward VI GS, UCL (LLB); *m* 1960, Anne Margaret, da of Henry Edward Davis, of Warwickshire; *Career* asst chief constable Leics Constabulary 1977-81, asst cmmr Metropolitan Police 1984-87 (dep asst cmmr 1981-84); Freeman City of London 1989, Liveryman Worshipful Co of Fletchers; FBIM; Serving Bro OStJ 1989; *Recreations* golf, fishing, music, reading, conservation, fellow of RSPB; *Clubs* RAC; *Style—* Colin Sutton, Esq, QPM; Police Requirements for Sci & Technol, Home Office, Horseferry House, Dean Ryle St, London SW1P 2AW

SUTTON, Dr George Christopher; *b* 4 Feb 1934; *Educ* Rugby, Corpus Christi Coll Cambridge (MD, MA), UCH Med Sch London; *m* 7 Feb 1959, Angela Elizabeth, *née* Dornan-Fox; 3 da (Sarah-Jane b 1962, Caroline b 1965, Rachel b 1967); *Career* med registrar St George's Hosp London 1963-67 (Addenbrooke's Hosp Cambridge 1962-63), fell in cardiology Univ of N Carolina Chapel Hill Med Sch 1965-66, sr registrar in cardiology Brompton Hosp London 1987-71, conslt cardiologist Hillingdon Hosp Middx 1972-, hon conslt Harefield Hosp Middx 1972-, sr lectr in cardiology Nat Heart and Lung Inst London 1972-, hon conslt Brompton Royal and Nat Heart and Lung Hosp London 1972-; author of various scientific papers in cardiology; memb: Br Cardiac Soc (cncl 1982-86), Euro Soc of Cardiology; FRCP 1977, FACC 1977; *Books* Physiological and Clinical aspects of Cardiac Auscultation, An audio-visual programme (1967), Slide Atlas of Cardiology (1978), An Introduction to Echocardiography (1978), Clinical and Investigatory Features of Cardiac Pathology (1988); *Recreations* watching cricket, golf, music, photography; *Clubs* MCC; *Style—* Dr George Sutton; Cardiology Dept, Hillingdon Hosp, Pield Heath Rd, Uxbridge, Middx UB8 3NN (☎ 0895 56509, fax 0895 56509)

SUTTON, Graham Charles; s of Charles James Sutton (d 1975), and Ruby Ethel, *née* Moorecroft (d 1984); *b* 29 Aug 1942; *Educ* Brentwood Sch, Coll of Estate Mgmnt; *m* 12 March 1966, Elizabeth Anne, da of Robert Woodman, of 21 Reed Pond Walk, Gidea Pk, Essex; 2 s (Matthew b 1968, Christopher b 1971); *Career* articled pupil asst Stanley Hicks & Son 1959-66, asst surveyor Debenham Tewson & Chinnocks 1966-68, sr ptnr Freeth Melhuish 1982- (asst surveyor 1969-72, ptnr 1972-82); Freeman City of London 1982, Liveryman Worshipful Co of Coopers; FRICS 1965, FRVA 1971; *Recreations* shooting, golf, skiing, windsurfing; *Clubs* City Livery, Harpenden Common Golf, Surveyors 1894, Soc of Old Brentwoods; *Style—* Graham Sutton, Esq; 32 Milton Rd, Harpenden, Herts AL5 5LS (☎ 05827 3489); 24 Holywell Hill, St Albans, Herts AL1 1BZ (☎ 0727 48680, fax 0727 51745)

SUTTON, James; s of Thomas Alfred Victor Sutton (d 1982), of Poynton, Cheshire, and Emily, *née* Firth (d 1967); *b* 12 Jan 1923; *Educ* Kingswood Sch Bath; *m* 21 June 1950, Joan, da of Ezra Wainwright (d 1956); 1 s (Michael b 5 July 1955), 1 da (Angela (Mrs Fendall) b 5 May 1959); *Career* WW II RAF meteorologist 1942-47; meteorologist Air Miny 1941-42, asst gen mangr Vernon Building Soc 1948; qualified CA 1953, ptnr TAV Sutton & Co 1953-, dir and chief exec Vernon Building Soc 1971 (gen mangr 1970), dir Deanwater Hotel (Cheshire) Ltd; chm NW Building Socs Assoc 1986; chm Poyntonf Sports Club 1962-83 (memb 1948-83); FCA 1953; *Recreations* travel, gardening; *Style—* James Sutton, Esq; 26 St Petersgate, Stockport, Cheshire SK1 1HD (☎ 061 477 9797, fax 061 480 3414)

SUTTON, Prof John; s of Gerald John Sutton (d 1958), and Kathleen Alice, *née* Richard, MBE; *b* 8 July 1919; *Educ* King's Sch Worcester, Imperial Coll London (BSc, PhD, DSc); *m* 1, 13 June 1949, Janet Vida, (d 1985), da of Prof David Meredith Seares Watson; m 2, 21 Aug 1985, Betty Middleton-Sandford, da of James Middleton Honeychurch; *Career* cmmnd 2 Lt RAOC 1941, transferred to REME 1942, Capt 1944, served AA cmd UK 1941-46; Imperial Coll: lectr in geology 1948-58, prof of geology 1958-64, head of geology dept 1964-74; dean Royal Sch of Mines 1965-68 and 1974-77, Centre for Enviromental Technol 1976-83, pro-rector 1980-83; fell Imperial Coll; FRS 1966; *Recreations* gardening; *Style—* Prof John Sutton, FRS; The Manor House, Martinstown, Dorchester, Dorset DT2 9JN

SUTTON, Air Marshal Sir John Matthias Dobson; KCB (1986, CB 1980); s of Harry Rowston Sutton (d 1990), of Alford, Lincs, and Gertrude, *née* Dobson (d 1979); *b* 9 July 1932; *Educ* Queen Elizabeth GS Alford Lincs; *m* 1, 25 Sept 1954 (m dis 1968), Delia Eleanor, *née* Woodward; 1 s (Shaun b 13 Feb 1961), 1 da (Shenagh b 22 Jan 1957); m 2, 23 May 1969, Angela Faith, da of Wing Cdr G J Gray, DFC, of Fowey, Cornwall; 2 s (Mark b 13 April 1971, Stephen b 8 Oct 1972); *Career* joined RAF 1950, pilot trg (cmmnd) 1951, fighter sqdns UK and Germany 1952-61, staff coll 1963, CO 249 sqdn 1964-66, asst sec Chief of Staff's Ctee 1966-69, OC 14 sqdn 1970-71, asst chief of staff (plans and policy) HQ 2ATAF 1971-73, staff chief of def staff 1973-74, RCDS 1975, cmdt Central Flying Sch 1976-77, asst chief of air staff (policy) 1977-79, dep Cdr RAF Germany 1980-82, asst chief of def staff (commitments) 1982-84, asst chief of def staff (overseas) 1985, AOC-in-C RAF Support Command 1986-89; Lt-Govr of Jersey designate (to take up appointment May 1990), tstee Oakham Sch; *Recreations* golf, skiing; *Clubs* RAF, Luffenham Heath Golf; *Style—* Air Marshal Sir John Sutton, KCB; c/o Holts Bank, Kirkland House, Whitehall, London SW1A 2EB

SUTTON, Linda; *b* 14 Dec 1947; *Educ* Southend Coll of Technol, Winchester Sch of Art, RCA (MA); *Career* artist; solo exhibitions: Galerij de Zwarte Panter Antwerp 1971, Bedford House Gallery London 1974, L'Agrifoglio Milan 1975, World's End Gallery London 1978, Ikon Gallery Birmingham 1979, Chenil Gallery London 1980, Royal Festival Hall London 1984, Stephen Bartley Gallery London 1986, Beecroft Gallery Westcliff-on-Sea (with Carel Weight, CBE, RA) 1987, Jersey Arts Centre St Helier Channel Islands 1988, Christopher Hull Gallery London London 1988, Beaux Arts Bath 1988, Austin/Desmond Fine Art Bloomsbury; gp exhibitions incl: Royal Acad Summer Exhibitions 1972-90, British Painting 1952-57 (Royal Acad) 1977, Contemporary Arts Soc Market 1984, Contemporary Arts Fair (Barbican) 1984, Bath Festival 1985 and 1988, Jonleigh Gallery Guildford 1987, The Lefevre Gallery London 1988, Art 90 (Business Art Centre Islington) 1990 (and Art 91 1991), Int Art Fair Olympia 1990 and 1991, Directors Choice (New Academy Gallery) 1990, Academia Italia 1990; awards: prizewinner GLC Spirit of London (Royal Festival Hall) 1979, 1980 and 1981, first prize Contemporary Arts Soc 1981, third prize Nat Portrait Gallery 1982, prizewinner Royal Acad Summer Exhibition 1987; *Clubs* Chelsea Arts, Colony Room; *Style—* Miss Linda Sutton; 192 Batttersea Bridge Rd, London SW11 3AE

SUTTON, Michael Antony (Tony); MC (1944); s of Brig William Moxhay Sutton, DSO, MC (d 1949), of Bath, and Barbara Marie, *née* Corballis; *b* 29 March 1921; *Educ* Ampleforth, Worcester Coll Oxford (MA, Rugby blue, Cricket blue); *m* 12 April 1958, Bridget Gillian Mary, da of Brig Walter Lindley Fawcett, MC (missing presumed ka 1942), of Yorks and India; 2 s (Philip b 8 Dec 1966, Michael b 9 Feb 1968), 3 da (Veronica Ford b 3 March 1959, Bridget Swithinbank b 3 Sept 1960, Teresa Pim b 24 Jan 1962); *Career* Capt Westminster Dragoons 1941-45, Normandy to Germany via Belgium and Holland 1944-45; Capt North Somerset Yeo 1948-53; admitted slr 1951, ptnr and conslt Tozers 1952-; rep Barbarians RFC 1946, rugby referee Devon Soc; tstee and govr of ind schs; memb Law Soc 1951; KCSG Papal 1969; *Recreations* member Magic Circle, keeping fit, Times crossword; *Clubs* Vincent's (Oxford), MCC; *Style—* M A Sutton, Esq, MC; Duncombe, Landscore Rd, Teignmouth, Devon TQ14 9JS (☎ 0626 774453); 2 Orchard Gdns, Teignmouth, Devon TQ14 8DR (☎ 0626 772376)

SUTTON, Michael Phillip; s of Charles Phillip Sutton, of Worksop, Notts, and Maisie, *née* Kelsey; *b* 25 Feb 1946; *Educ* Haileybury and ISC; *m* 24 July 1971, Susan Margaret, da of John Turner, JP, DL, of Lound, Notts; *Career* CA 1970, Old Broad St Securities Ltd 1970-71, md Singer and Fridlander Ltd 1983 (joined 1971); Freeman: City of London 1978, Worshipful Co of Pipe Tobacco Makers and Blenders (memb Ct of Assts 1982) FCA 1976; *Recreations* shooting, fishing, horse racing, gardening; *Clubs* Turf; *Style—* Michael Sutton, Esq; West Bank, Gamston, Retford, Notts (☎ 077 783 387); 55 Cathorpe Rd, Birmingham B15 ITL (☎ 021 456 3311, car 0860 207 998/0860 334 293)

SUTTON, Capt Oliver Peter; CBE (1978); s of Albert Bernard Sutton (d 1961), of Chile, and Joan Firth, *née* Brewster (d 1981); *b* 17 Jan 1926; *Educ* RNC Dartmouth; *m* 16 Dec 1962, Gay, da of Charles Owen (d 1949); 2 s (Matthew b 5 Feb 1964, Simon b 31 Oct 1968); *Career* RN: Cadet 1939, Cdre 1978, specialist in navigation, ret as COS to Flag Offr Plymouth; dir Br Radio and Electronic Equipment Mfrs Assoc 1978-, sec Euro Assoc of Consumer Electronics Mfrs 1987-90, chm JRS Associates EMC Consultancy 1991-; FBIM; *Recreations* fishing, tennis, gardening; *Style—* Capt Oliver Sutton, CBE; British Radio and Electronic Equipment Manufacturers' Association (BREMA) Landseer House, 19 Charing Cross Rd, London WC2H 0ES (☎ 071 932 3206, fax 071 839 4613, telex 296215 BREMA G)

SUTTON, Peter John; s of Charles James Sutton (d 1975), and Ruby Ethel, *née* Moorecroft (d 1984); *b* 29 Aug 1942; *Educ* Brentwood Sch, Clare Coll Cambridge; *m* 12 April 1969, Marjorie, da of Robert Howe; 1 s (David Robert b 22 May 1973), 1 da (Catherine Fiona b 19 Oct 1970); *Career* sr accountant and mangr Deloitte Plender Griffiths & Co 1967-73 (articled clerk 1964-67), mangr Black Geoghegan & Till 1973-74; Spicer and Pegler (name changed to Spicer & Oppenheim 1988, merged to become part of Touche Ross & Co 1990): mangr 1974-76, ptnr 1976-; hon treas Cambridgeshire Lawn Tennis Assoc; FCA 1968; *Style—* Peter Sutton, Esq; 2 West Hill Rd, Foxton, Cambridge CB2 6SZ (☎ 0223 870721); Touche Ross & Co, Leda House, Station Rd, Cambridge CB1 2RN (☎ 0223 460222, fax 0223 350839)

SUTTON, Philip John; s of Louis Sutton (d 1976), and Ann, *née* Lazarus (d 1980); *b* 20 Oct 1928; *Educ* Slade Sch of Fine Art UCL (Dip Fine Art); *m* 11 July 1953, Heather Minifie Ellis, da of Arthur Owen Ellis Cooke; 1 s (Jacob b 11 May 1954), 3 da (Imogen b 21 Feb 1956, Saskia b 19 Jan 1958, Rebekah b 30 Sept 1960); *Career* aircraftsman RAF 1947-49; artist, designer and painter; designed poster and flag for RA summer show 1979, exhibition of painted ceramics at Odette Gilbert Gallery 1987, painting of William Shakespeare for Int Shakespeare Globe Centre 1988, exhibition of paintings at RA summer show 1988; ARA 1977; RA 1988; *Recreations* running, swimming; *Style—* Philip Sutton, Esq; 10 Soudan Rd, London SW11 4HH (☎ 071 622 2647); 4 Morfa Terr Manorbier, Tenby, Dyfed

SUTTON, Dr Richard; s of Dick Brasnett Sutton (d 1981), of Newport, Gwent, and Greta Mary, *née* Leadbeter; *b* 1 Sept 1940; *Educ* Gresham's, King's Coll London, King's Coll Hosp London (MB BS); *m* 28 Nov 1969, (Anna) Gunilla, da of Carl-Axel Cassö (d 1976), of Stockholm, Sweden; 1 s (Edmund b 24 April 1967); *Career* house offr: Plymouth Gen Hosp 1964-65, Kings Coll Hosp 1965, St Stephen's Hosp 1966, London Chest Hosp 1966-67; registrar St George's Hosp 1967-68, fell in cardiology Univ N Carolina USA 1968-69, registrar (later sr registrar and temporary conslt) Nat Heart Hosp 1970-76, conslt cardiologist Westminster and St Stephen's Hosps 1976-; ed European Journal of Cardiac Pacing and Electrophysiology; hon conslt cardiologist: Italian Hosp 1977-89, SW Thames RHA 1979-, St Luke's Hosp for the Clergy 1980-; Govr's award American Coll of Cardiology 1979 and 1982; pres, co fndr and former sec Br Pacing and Electrophysiology Gp; Hon DSc Univ of London 1988; FRCP 1982 (MRCP 1967); memb: BMA, RSM, Br Cardiac Soc, American Coll of Cardiology, American Heart Assoc, Euro Soc of Cardiology; *Books* Pacemakers (chapter in Oxford Textbook of Medicine, 1987), Foundations of Cardiac Pacing (ed, 1991); *Recreations* opera, tennis, cross-country skiing; *Style—* Dr Richard Sutton; 149 Harley St, London W1N 1HG (☎ 071 935 4444, fax 071 486 3782, telex 263250)

SUTTON, Sir Richard Lexington; 9 Bt (GB 1772), of Norwood Park, Nottinghamshire; s of Sir Robert Lexington Sutton, 8 Bt (d 1981); *b* 27 April 1937; *Educ* Stowe; *m* 1959, Fiamma, da of G M Ferrari, of Rome; 1 s, 1 da; *Heir* s, David Robert Sutton, b 26 Feb 1960; *Style—* Sir Richard Sutton, Bt; Moor Hill, Langham, Gillingham, Dorset

SUTTON, Richard Manners; s of John Charles Ludlow Manners Sutton, of Willerby Lodge, Staxton, Scarborough, North Yorks, and Daphne Agnes, *née* Wormald (d 1961); *b* 5 May 1947; *Educ* Charterhouse; *m* 1, 1972 (m dis 1979), Mary, *née* Diebold; m 2, 1979, Penelope Jane, *née* Quinlan; 2 s (William b 1980, Thomas b 1982); *Career* slr i/c intellectual property Dibb Lupton Broomhead; *Style—* Richard Sutton, Esq; Dibb Lupton Broomhead, 117 The Headrow, Leeds LS1 5JX

SUTTON, Robert Hiles; s of John Ormerod Sutton, of The Old School House, Tichborne, Hants, and Margaret Patricia, *née* Buckland; *b* 19 Jan 1954; *Educ* Winchester, Magdalen Coll Oxford (BA); *m* 8 Aug 1981, Carola Jane (Tiggy), da of Sir Anthony Dewey, 3 Bt, of The Rag, Galhampton, Yeovil, Somerset; 2 s (Patrick William b 1984, Jonathan David Ormerod b 1990), 1 da (Joanna Kate b 1987); *Career* Macfarlanes Slrs 1976- (ptnr 1983-); memb Law Soc and IBA; *Recreations* rackets, poker; *Clubs* City; *Style—* Robert Sutton, Esq; Macfarlanes, 10 Norwich St, London EC4 A1BD (☎ 071 831 9222, fax 071 831 9607)

SUTTON, Stephen John; s of Stephen John Sutton (d 1990), of Mill Lane, Hartington, and Ursula Jean, *née* Howson; *b* 16 April 1961; *Educ* Queen Elizabeth GS Ashbourne; *m* 7 July 1990, Helen Jean, da of David Thomas Sanders; 1 step da (Amy Crystal Lucic b 6 April 1983); *Career* professional footballer; Nottingham Forest 1977-: turned professional 1979, debut v Norwich City 1980, over 265 appearances; on loan: Mansfield Town 1980 (9 appearances), Derby County 1982 (14 appearances); represented Derbyshire Schs at football and rugby; winner's medals: Littlewoods Cup 1989 and 1990, Simod Cup 1989, Mercantile Credit, Soccer Six; *Style—* Stephen Sutton, Esq; City Ground, Pavillion Rd, Nottingham (☎ 0602 822202)

SUTTON, Thomas Francis (Tom); *b* 9 Feb 1923; *Educ* King's Sch Worcester, St Peter's Coll Oxford (MA 1953); *m* 1, 23 June 1950 (m dis 1974), Anne, *née* Fleming; 1 s (Jonathan b 1951), 2 da (Nicola b 1954, Alison b 1959); m 2, 1 Sept 1982, Maki, *née* Watanabe; *Career* res offr BR Mkt Res Bureau Ltd 1949-51, advtg mangr Pasolds Ltd 1951-52, md J Walter Thompson GmbH Frankfurt 1952-59; dir: J Walter Thompson Co Ltd 1960-73 (md 1960-66), J Walter Thompson Co (New York) 1965-83 (exec vice-pres Int Operations 1966-72), md J Walter Thompson Co (Japan) 1972-80; pres J Walter Thompson (Asia/Pacific) 1980-81, chm E A Int NY 1981-, chm Lansdown Euro Advertising Ltd 1983; pt/t lectr in advtg and mktg: Rutger's Univ New Jersey 1968-71, Columbia Univ NY 1971-73, Sophia Univ Tokyo 1974-81; winner Int Advertising Man of the Year award 1970; *Recreations* chess, riding, reading; *Clubs* Princeton (New York), Walton Hall (Warks), Pudding (Mickleton); *Style—* Tom Sutton, Esq; Rushway House, Willington, Shipston-on-Stour, Warwickshire

SUZMAN, Janet; da of Saul Peter Suzman, of Johannesburg, SA, and Betty *née* Sonnenberg; *b* 9 Feb 1939; *Educ* Kingsmead Coll Johannesburg, Univ of the Witwatersrand (BA); *m* 1969 (m dis 1986), Trevor Robert Nunn; 1 s (Joshua b 1980); *Career* actress; performances incl: The Wars of the Roses 1964, The Relapse 1967, The Taming of the Shrew 1967, A Day in the Death of Joe Egg 1970, Nicholas and Alexandra (Acad Award nomination) 1971, Antony and Cleopatra 1972, Hello and Goodbye (Evening Standard Award) 1973, Three Sisters (Standard Award 1976), Hedda Gabler 1978, The Greeks 1980, The Draughtsman's Contract 1981, Vassa 1985, Mountbatten Viceroy of India 1986, The Singing Detective 1987, Andromache 1988, A Dry White Season 1989; directed Othello (Market Theatre Johannesburg 1987, TV 1988), Another Time 1989-90; hon MA Open Univ 1986, hon DLitt Univ of Warwick 1990; *Recreations* yacht 'Chicken Sloop'; *Style—* Miss Janet Suzman; William Morris, 31/32 Soho Square, London W1 (☎ 071 434 2191)

SVENNINGSON, Hon Mrs (Daphne Rose); *née* Canning; da of 4 Baron Garvagh (d 1956); *b* 1922; *m* 1950, Bancroft Svenningson; 1 s, 2 da; *Style—* The Hon Mrs Svenningson; 53 Ferdon Ave, Westmount, Montreal, Canada

SWAAB, Roger Henry; s of Cyril Henry Swaab, of Shrewsbury, and Betty Joan Swaab, *née* Moore; *b* 6 June 1944; *Educ* Brewood GS, Birmingham Sch of Arch (Dip Arch); *m* 12 July 1968, Elizabeth Kay, da of William Edward Smith Penlon, of Staffs; 1 s (Christian b 1973), 1 da (Beth b 1973); *Career* architect; snr ptnr Hickton Madeley & Ptnrs; dir: Hickton Madeley Interiors Ltd 1986, Hickton Madeley Landscape Ltd 1989-, Hickton Madeley Project Management Ltd 1988-; ACIArb; *Recreations* golf; *Clubs* Shrewsbury Golf, Nefyn & Dist Golf; *Style—* Roger H Swaab, Esq; 24 Hatherton Rd, Walsall WS1 1XP (☎ 0922 645400, fax 0922 647359 HMP)

SWAEBE, Barry James; s of Albert Victor Swaebe (d 1967), and Sophy Estlin Hancock, *née* Grundy (d 1982); *b* 12 May 1923; *m* 28 May 1966, Miriam Isobel, da of Robert Owen Morgans; 2 da (Sophy Anna b 1 Jan 1967, Clare Isobel b 9 Jan 1968); *Career* WWII RAF; social and portrait photographer AV Swaebe Ltd 1946-; photographs in numerous pubns incl: Tatler, Harpers and Queen; exhibition photographs of Barbados Harrods 1965; *Style—* Barry Swaebe, Esq; 16 Southwood Lane, Highgate Village, London N6 5EE (☎ 081 348 6010)

SWAFFIELD, David Richard; s of Sir James Cheseborough Swaffield, CBE, DL, RD, *qv*; *b* 11 Nov 1951; *Educ* Dulwich, Downing Coll Cambridge (MA); *m* 20 Oct 1979, (Barbara) Dianne, da of Albert Ernest Pilkington (d 1988), JP, of Wilmslow, Cheshire; 2 s (James b 1983, Robin b 1988); *Career* investment analysis Rowe & Pitman 1973-75, admitted slr 1979, ptnr Hill Dickinson & Co 1982-89 (slr 1979-82), dir Grayhill Ltd 1984-85, ptnr Hill Dickinson Davis Campbell 1989; *Style—* David Swaffield, Esq; Brentwood, 12 Meols Drive, Hoylake, Wirral L47 4AQ (☎ 051 6321389); Hill Dickinson Davis Campbell, Equity & Law House, 47 Castle St, Liverpool L2 9UB (051 2723151, telex 051 2271352)

SWAFFIELD, Sir James Chesebrough; CBE (1971), RD (1967), DL (Greater London 1978); s of Frederick Swaffield (d 1970); *b* 1924; *Educ* Cheltenham GS, Haberdashers' Aske's Sch, London Univ (MA, LLB); *m* 1950, Elizabeth Margaret Ellen, da of Albert Victor Maunder (d 1965); 2 s, 2 da; *Career* WWII Lt-Cdr RNVR Atlantic and NW Europe; asst slr: Norwich Corpn 1949-52, Cheltenham Corpn 1952-53, Southend on Sea Corpn 1953-56; dep town clerk Blackpool 1956-61 (town clerk 1961-62); sec Assoc of Municipal Corpns 1962-72, dir-gen and clerk GLC 1973-84, clerk to ILEA 1973-84, clerk of Lieutenancy for Gtr London 1973-84; chm: BR Property Bd 1984-, Outward Bound Tst; Distinguished Service Award (Int City Mgmnt Assoc) 1984; hon fell Inst Local Govt Studies Birmingham Univ; OStJ; FRSA; kt 1976; *Clubs* Reform, Naval; *Style—* Sir James Swaffield, CBE, RD, DL; 10 Kelsey Way, Beckenham, Kent

SWAIN, Marilyn Janice; da of Percival Harold Swain, of Grantham, and Alice Maud, *née* George (d 1969); *b* 3 May 1931; *Educ* Berkhamsted Sch for Girls, Bartlett Sch of Architecture, Univ Coll London; *Career* Phillip's auctioneers London 1960-70, Bonhams 1970-73, freelance valuer and lectr 1973-78, Neales of Nottingham 1978-82 (head of dept), md Fine Art Div William H Brown 1982-; memb BBC Antiques Roadshow team 1991; memb RICS furniture and Works of Art Ctee 1984-, fndr memb and hon sec Derby Porcelain Int Sec, hon sec Soc of Fine Art Auctioneers 1985-, fell Gemmological Assoc of GB 1967, FRSA 1972, FRICS 1981; *Recreations* fair weather sailing and walking, embroidery, giving and receiving dinner parties; *Style—* Miss Marilyn Swain; Westgate Hall, Westgate, Grantham, Lincolnshire NG31 6LT (☎ 0476 68861, fax 0476 590317)

SWAINE, Anthony Wells; s of Albert Victor Alexander Swaine (d 1972), of Cornwall, and Hilda May Allen (d 1983); *b* 25 Aug 1913; *Educ* Chatham House, Ramsgate; *Career* architect; in private practice specialising in historic bldgs; architectural advsr to: Faversham old town (author Faversham conserved), Historic Churches Preservation Tst (memb panel hon conslt architects); architectural advsr historic bldgs responsible for old Margate, pt/t teacher of architecture Canterbury Coll of Art (responsible for cathedral and precincts); memb of cncl and tech panel Ancient Monuments Soc (reps the Soc on Int Cncl), patron Venice in Peril, author report on conservation Il Problema di Venezia to UNESCO, served on Int Confe for Stone Conservation Athens; memb SPAB, FRIBA, FSA; *Recreations* travelling, languages, lecturing (as memb of panel of speakers of Civic Tst), history as applied to architecture, drawing, painting, photography; *Style—* Anthony Swaine, Esq; 19 Farrier St, Deal, Kent (☎ 0304 366369); Latchmere House, Watling St, Canterbury, Kent (☎ 0277 462680)

SWAINE, Richard Carter; s of Charles Frederick Swaine (d 1980), of Cottingham, Hull, and Kathleen Mary Swaine, *née* Battye (d 1987); *b* 2 July 1933; *Educ* Oakham Sch Rutland, Hull Sch of Architect, RIBA; *Career* RAF (Nat Sev) navigator; architect, own business 1969-; awards: Save Commendation, Civic Tst Commendation 1978, Euro Heritage Team Commendation 1974, E Yorkshire Planning Award 1982; *Recreations* sculpture, photography, all sport, town planning; *Clubs* Brough Golf, Welton Hockey and Cricket; *Style—* Richard Swaine, Esq; 1 Creyle Lane, Welton, Brough, N Humberside HU15 1NQ

SWAINSON, Capt (John) Anthony Rowland; OBE (1971); s of Charles John Graind'orge Swainson (d 1968), and Marion Alice Vining, *née* Rudrum (d 1966); *b* 29 Oct 1921; *Educ* St Paul's, RAF Staff Coll Bracknell; *m* 1 (m dis 1961), Crystal Alison Frances; 1 s (Adam b 16 May 1952), 1 da (Nicola b 29 Dec 1950); m 2, 26 Oct 1964 (Marie-Thérèse) Délia, da of Antoine Pintur, of Chatou, Paris, France; 1 da (Caroline b 3 Oct 1965); *Career* Nat Serv RN 1941, cmmnd Sub Lt RNVR 1943 (despatches 1944), Lt (reg cmmn) 1948, served in frigates, destroyers, cruisers, aircraft carriers, action in atlantic convoys, D Day and Suez; appointed dir The Lord's Taverners 1972; non exec dir: Good Books Ltd, Dowson & Salisbury Management Consultants; memb Cricket Cncl Fund, exec memb Nat Cricket Assoc; *Books* Please Give Generously (1987); *Recreations* golf, tennis, gardening, music; *Clubs* MCC, RAF, Garrick; *Style—* Capt Anthony Swainson, OBE, RN; 48 Springhead, Tunbridge Wells, Kent TN2 3NZ (☎ 0892 30786); Lord's Taverners, 1 Chester St, London SW1X 7HP (☎ 071 245 6466, fax 071 8231479)

SWAINSON, Charles Patrick; s of John Edward Swainson, of Winchcombe, Glos, and Diana Patricia, *née* O'Rorke; *b* 18 May 1948; *Educ* White Friars Sch Cheltenham, Univ of Edinburgh (MB ChB); *m* 4 July 1981, Marie Adele, da of Charleton Irwin; 1 s (Andrew b 1983); *Career* sr lectr Univ of Otago NZ 1981-86, conslt physician Royal Infirmary 1986-, pt/t sr lectr dept of med Univ of Edinburgh 1986-; FRCP 1984; *Recreations* wine, singing, skiing, mountaineering; *Style—* Charles Swainson, Esq; Renal Unit, Royal Infirmary, Edinburgh EH3 9YW (☎ 031 2292477)

SWAINSON, Eric; CBE (1981); *b* 5 Dec 1926; *Educ* Univ of Sheffield (BMet); *m* 1953, Betty Irene; 2 da; *Career* md IMI plc (metals fabricating and gen engrg) 1974-86, dir Birmingham Broadcasting Ltd 1973-, dir Midlands Radio Hldgs plc 1988-, memb review bd for govt contracts 1978-, chm Lloyds Bank (Birmingham & W Mids Regnl Bd) 1985- (memb 1979-); dir: Lloyds Bank plc 1986-, Fairey Gp 1987-, Amec plc 1987-; chm W Mids Indust Devpt Bd; pro-chllr Aston Univ 1981-86; Hon DSc (Aston) 1986; *Style—* Eric Swainson Esq, CBE; Paddox Hollow, Norton Lindsey, Warwick CV35 8JA (☎ 092 684 3190)

SWAINSON, Richard Gallienne; TD (1946); s of John Gallienne Swainson (d 1958), of Marshrange, Lancaster, and Edith, *née* Barrett (d 1954); *b* 16 Oct 1911; *Educ* Lancaster Royal GS, Corpus Christi Coll Cambridge (MA); *m* Aug 1950, Stella Margaret, da of Edwin Charles Colborn, of Spalding, Lincs; 1 s (William), 3 da (Margaret, Caroline, Sarah), 1 step da (Diana); *Career* 88 FD Regt RA (TA) 1939-46, Capt France 1939-40 (POW Malaya 1942-45); slr 1936-88; NP 1946-89; govr LRGS; *Recreations* golf; *Style—* Richard G Swainson, Esq, TD; Marshrange, Lancaster LA1 1YQ (☎ 0524 65347)

SWALES, Prof John Douglas; s of Frank Swales (d 1969), of Leicester, and Doris Agnes, *née* Flude (d 1959); *b* 19 Oct 1935; *Educ* Wyggeston GS Leicester, Univ of Cambridge (MA, MD); *m* 7 Oct 1967, Kathleen Patricia, da of Cdr Edward Townsend (d 1986), of Dublin; 1 s (Philip Patrick Richard b 1972), 1 da (Charlotte Rachel b 1975); *Career* sr lectr med Univ of Manchester 1970-74, prof med Univ of Leicester 1974; ed: Clinical Sci 1980-82, Jl of Hypertension 1982-87; pres Br Hypertension Soc 1984-86, censor RCP 1985-87; chm: Assoc Clinical Profs of Med 1987-, Fedn of Assoc Clinical Profs 1987-; FRCP; *Books* Sodium Metabolism in Disease (1975), Clinical Hypertension (1979), Platt versus Pickering: and Episode in Medical History (1985);

Recreations bibliophile; *Clubs* Athenaeum; *Style*— Prof John Swales; 21 Morland Avenue, Leicester, Leicestershire LE2 2PF (☎ 0533 707161), Dept of Medicine, Clinical Sciences Building, Royal Infirmary, PO Box 65, Leicester LE2 7LX (☎ 0533 523182, fax 0533 523107)

SWALES, Prof Martin William; s of Peter John Swales (d 1978), and Doris, *née* Davies (d 1989); *b* 3 Nov 1940; *Educ* King Edward's Sch Birmingham, Christ's Coll Cambridge, Univ of Birmingham; *m* 23 Sept 1966, Erika Marta, da of Ernst Meier (d 1988), of Basel, Switzerland; 1 s (Christopher b 1970), 1 da (Catherine b 1973); *Career* lectr in German Univ of Birmingham 1964-70, reader in German King's Coll London 1972-75, prof of German Univ of Toronto 1975-76 (assoc prof 1970-72), dean of arts UCL 1982-85 (prof of German 1976-), hon dir Inst of Germanic Studies Univ of London 1989-; *Books* Arthur Schnitzler (1971), The German Novelle (1977), The German Bildungsroman (1978), Thomas Mann (1980), Adalbert Stifter (with E M Swales, 1984), Goethe - The Sorrows of Young Werther (1987); *Recreations* music, theatre, film, amateur dramatics; *Style*— Prof Martin Swales; 11 De Freville Avenue, Cambridge CB4 1HW (☎ 0223 352510), Dept of German, Univ College, Gower St, London WC1E 6BT (☎ 071 387 7050)

SWALES, Peter Brian; s of Ernest Wilfed Swales (d 1956), of Leamington Spa, and Gladys Mildred, *née* Wright (d 1962); *b* 25 July 1929; *Educ* Warwick Sch, St Catharine's Coll Cambridge (MA); *m* 9 April 1960, Jean Brenda, da of Rowell Vines (d 1962), of Leamington Spa; 2 s (David b 1963, Peter b 1969), 3 da (Catharine b 1961, Alison b 1965, Nicola b 1967); *Career* Nat Serv RAF 1948-49; dir: Irvin GB 1970-73, Chiswell Wire Co Ltd 1977-; md Swales Mgmnt Consultancy 1973-77; memb Letchworth Cons Pty; MICE 1956, MIMechE 1960, CEng 1960; *Recreations* golf, fishing, hill walking; *Style*— Peter Swales, Esq; 302 Norton Way South, Letchworth, Herts (☎ 0462 685 971); Garthlwyd, Landderfel, Bala, Gwynedd; Chiswell Wire Co Ltd, Sandown Rd, Watford, Herts (☎ 0923 35412, fax 0923 54754, telex 924588)

SWALLOW, Charles John; s of John Cuthbert Swallow (d 1968), and Irene Dupont, *née* Rée; *b* 29 July 1938; *Educ* Charterhouse, Lincoln Coll Oxford (MA), Wolfson Coll Oxford (MSc); *m* 28 July 1961, Susanna Janet, da of Maj Kenneth Arnold Gibbs Crawley (d 1988); 1 s (Mark b 18 Sept 1963), 1 da (Amanda b 28 Feb 1967); *Career* Ensign Scots Guards 1956-58; asst master Harrow Sch 1961-73, history teacher Bicester Sch 1973-76, headmaster Mount Grace School 1976-84; dir Vanderbilt Racquet Club 1974-; Open Racquets Champion of British Isles 1970, Open Real Tennis Doubles Champion of British Isles 1971, 1972 and 1973; High Sheriff Oxfordshire 1986-87; memb: Gen Advsy Cncl IBA 1977-83, Educn for Capability Ctee; RSA, FRSA; *Books* The Sick Man of Europe, The Decline of The Ottoman Empire 1789-1923 (1972); *Recreations* music, theatre, travel, ball games; *Clubs* All England LTC, MCC, Izingari, Whites, Pratts; *Style*— Charles Swallow, Esq; Manor Barn House, Wendlebury, Bicester, Oxon OX6 8PP (☎ 0869 253179); Vanderbilt Racquet Club, 31 Sterne St, London W12 8AB (☎ 081 743 9822)

SWALLOW, Dr Michael William; s of William Percy Swallow (d 1940), of Worthing, and Evelyn Farmer (d 1963); *b* 11 Dec 1928; *Educ* Westminster Abbey Choir Sch, Magdalen Coll Sch Oxford, Univ of London (MB BS); *m* 2 June 1956, Barbara Mary, da of James Drummond-Smith (d 1945), of Daventry; 2 da (Nicola b 1958, Gemma b 1961); *Career* Nat Serv; Capt RAMC 1954-56, Maj RAMC (TA) 1956-69; med registrar Westminster Hosp 1959-60, sr registrar in neurology (former registrar) Nat Hosp London 1960-63, sr registrar UCH 1963-64, conslt neurologist Royal Victoria Hosp Belfast 1964-89; pres 1 Neurological Assoc 1987 (memb 1965-), vice pres Br Soc for Music Therapy, memb Assoc Br Neurologists 1965, sec NI Music Therapy Tst; FRCP; *Books* Collected Papers of Louis J Hurwitz (ed, 1972); *Recreations* music, european travel, music with disabled people; *Style*— Dr Michael Swallow; 15 Deramore Drive, Belfast BT9 5JQ (☎ 0232 669042)

SWALLOW, (Jake Brangwyn) Sheridan; s of Hereward Stanley Swallow, OBE, TD (d 1986), and Barbara Brangwyn, *née* Corfield (d 1984); *b* 4 Sept 1949; *Educ* Radley, Magdalene Coll Cambridge (MA); *m* 30 Aug 1975, Sarah-Jane Emma, da of Arthur Henry Miskin, of Ifield Court, Cobham, Kent; 1 s (Hereward John b 1980), 1 da (Louisa Meregan Sarah b 1984); *Career* Turquand Youngs and successor firms 1971-77; Imperial Gp plc 1977-84; dir and gen mangr Saccone & Speed Int Ltd, dir Imp Hotels & Catering Ltd; Cullens Hldgs plc 1984-86, Bellhouse & Joseph Investmts Ltd 1987-; Freeman City of London, Liveryman Worshipful Co of Haberdashers; FCA; *Recreations* country life; *Clubs* Oriental; *Style*— Sheridan Swallow, Esq

SWALLOW, Sir William; s of late W T Swallow; *b* 2 Jan 1905; *m* 1929, Kathleen Lucy, *née* Smith; *Career* chm and md: General Motors Ltd 1953-61, Vauxhall Motors Ltd 1961-66; kt 1967; *Recreations* golf; *Style*— Sir William Swallow; Alderton Lodge, Ashridge Park, Berkhamsted, Herts (☎ 044 284 2284)

SWALWELL, (John) Anthony; s of Anthony Swalwell, MM (d 1967), and Ann Winifred, *née* Unsworth (d 1985); *b* 5 Dec 1931; *Educ* Wigan GS, Victoria Univ of Manchester (LLB); *m* 2 April 1956, Sylvia Mary, da of Albert George Mount; 1 s (William b 1957), 1 da (Alison b 1960); *Career* asst slr Manchester Corp 1956-69, ptnr Rhodes & Swalwell 1969-, dep coroner Greater Manchester (W Dist) 1974-, acting stipendiary magistrate Liverpool 1986-; pres Wigan Law Soc 1982-83; hon slr: Royal Br Legion (Wigan Town Branch), Bellingham (Wigan) Bowling Green Ltd; memb Law Soc; *Recreations* cricket, crown green bowling; *Clubs* Bellingham Bowling (Wigan), Lancs CCC; *Style*— Anthony Swalwell, Esq; 1 Kingsmede, Wigan Lane, Wigan, Lancashire (☎ 0942 42118); Rhodes & Swalwell, 30 Market Place, Wigan WN1 1PJ (☎ 0942 491227, fax 0942 820083)

SWAN, Conrad Marshall John Fisher; CVO (1986); s of Dr Henry Swan (*née* Swenciski or Swiecicki), of Vancouver (whose f, Paul, emigrated from Poland, where the family had long been landed proprietors and from time to time represented in the Senate of pre-Partition Poland); *b* 13 May 1924; *Educ* St George's Coll Weybridge, SOAS Univ of London, Univ of Western Ontario, Peterhouse Cambridge; *m* 1957, Lady Hilda Susan Mary, *qv*, da of 3 Earl of Iddesleigh; 1 s, 4 da; *Career* Rouge Dragon Pursuivant 1962-68, York Herald of Arms 1968-, sr herald and registrar Coll of Arms 1982-; genealogist of Order of Bath 1972-; KStJ (genealogist of Grand Priory, Order of St John 1976-), hon genealogist Order of St Michael & St George 1989-; Kt of Honour & Devotion SMO Malta 1979; FSA; lectr; *Books* Canada: Symbols of Sovereignty (1977), The Chapel of the Order of the Bath (1978); *Style*— Conrad Swan, Esq, CVO, York Herald of Arms; Boxford House, Boxford, Colchester, Essex (☎ 0787 210208)

SWAN, Lady Hilda Susan Mary; *née* Northcote; da of 3 Earl of Iddesleigh (d 1970), and Elizabeth, Dowager Countess of Iddesleigh, *qv*; *b* 1937; *m* 1957, Conrad Swan, CVO, *qv*, York Herald; 1 s (Andrew), 4 da (Elizabeth Magdalen b 1959, (Hilda) Juliana b 1961, Catherine b 1962, Anastasia b 1966); *Career* East Suffolk County Chm RDA; County Pres Suffolk St John Ambulance; Dame of Honour and Devotion Sov Mil Order of Malta 1979; *Style*— The Lady Hilda Swan; Boxford House, Boxford, Colchester (☎ 0787 210208)

SWAN, Richard Roland Seymour; s of Capt Seymour Lankester Swan, RM (d 1988), and Ethel Hayward, *née* Drew; *b* 21 April 1937; *Educ* Cranleigh, Sidney Sussex Coll Cambridge (MA); *m* 1, 16 Sept 1961 (m dis 1967), Penelope Ann, da of Anthony Urling Clark, of Gwelhale, Rock, nr Wadebridge, Cornwall; 2 s (Mark b 1963, Rupert b 1965); m 2, 14 Oct 1967, Hedwig Erna Lydia, da of Dr Franz Pesendorfer (d 1944), of Vienna, Austria; 1 s (Michael b 1969), 2 da (Caroline b 1968, Olivia b 1970); *Career* Nat Serv Royal Sussex Regt, 2 Lt 1956, Lt 1959 East Surrey Regt; admitted slr 1963; sr ptnr Heald Nickinson Milton Keynes 1979-; non- exec dir Scantronic Hldgs plc; memb Youth and Community Sub Ctee Bucks CC, dir Milton Keynes and Dist C of C and Indust 1981- (pres 1986-88, chm 1984-88), memb Norman Hawes Educnl Tst; NP; chm: Buckinghamshire Assoc Boys Clubs 1986-, City Gallery Arts Tst 1982- (chm 1987-90); memb Cncl Nat Assoc Boys Clubs; memb Law Soc 1963; *Recreations* book collecting, reading, walking; *Clubs* Naval and Military, Woburn Golf and Country; *Style*— Richard Swan, Esq; Five Pines, Wood Lane, Aspley Guise, Milton Keynes MK17 8EL (☎ 0908 583 495); Chancery House, 199 Silbury Boulevard, Grafton Gate East, Central Milton Keynes MK9 1LN (☎ 0908 662 277, fax 0908 675 667, car 0836 742 932, telex 826480); 48 Bedford Sq, London WC1B 3DS

SWANN, Maj Derek Lord; s of Capt Thomas Lord Swann (d 1965), of Bramhall, Cheshire, and Maimie Mellis Birch, *née* Wald (d 1966); *b* 26 Nov 1930; *Educ* William Hulme's GS, Manchester Coll of Art; *m* 3 May 1958, Joan Mary, da of Capt Ronald Gardner (d 1959), of Bridge of Weir; 1 s (David James Lord b 16 July 1959); *Career* TA (attached 8 MANC) 1949-55, Nat Serv 2 Lt RE 1955, 2 Lt RE (TA) 1957, Maj RE (T) 1965, ret 1968; princ ptnr Norman Jones Sons & Rigby 1989- (ptnr 1968-89); chm local ctee ABF; memb: RYA, RNLI, Wildfowl Tst; MRIBA; *Recreations* watching rugby, sailing, birdwatching and sketching; *Clubs* Army and Navy, Union (Southport); *Style*— Maj Derek Swann; Norman Jones Sons & Rigby, 57 Houghton St, Southport, Lancs PR9 9PG (☎ 0704 31252, fax 0704 32833)

SWANN, Donald Ibrahim; s of late Dr Herbert William Swann, of Richmond, Surrey, and Naguimè, *née* Sultan; *b* 30 Sept 1923; *Educ* Westminster, Christ Church Oxford (MA); *m* 1955 (m dis 1983), Janet Mary, *née* Oxborrow; 2 da; *Career* conscientious objector WWII, served Quaker Friends Ambulance Unit; pianist, composer and entertainer; contrib of music to revues and musical plays incl: Airs on a Shoestring 1953-54, Wild Thyme (with Michael Flanders accompanist of own compositions) 1955, At the Drop of a Hat (London, Edinburgh Festival, Broadway, and tours of US, Canada, GB and Ireland) 1957-63, At the Drop of Another Hat (Haymarket, Globe, and tours of Aust, NZ and US) 1963-67; concerts of Solo work and work with other artists: Set by Swann, An Evening in Crete, Soundings by Swann, Between the Bars, A Crack in Time (in search of peace); fndr Albert House Press 1974; *Compositions* incl: Lucy and the Hunter, London Sketches 1958, Festival Matins 1962, Perelandra 1961-62, Settings of John Betjeman Poems 1964, Requiem for the Living 1969, The Rope of Love (around the earth in song) 1973, The Five Scrolls 1975, Round the Piano with Donald Swann 1979, The Yeast Factory 1979, South African Song Cycle 1982; Songs and Operas incl: The Song of Caedmon (with Arthur Scholey) 1971, Singalive 1978, Wacky and his Fuddlejig 1978, Candle Tree 1980, Baboushka 1980, The Visitors 1984, Brendan A-hoy 1985; Mamahuhu 1986, Envy 1986, Victorian Song Cycle 1987, William Blake and John Clare Song Cycle 1989; various activities incl musical events and compositions in aid of peace UK and abroad; *Books* Sing Round The Year (Book of New Carols for Children, 1965), The Space Between the Bars (reflections, 1967), The Road Goes Ever On (with J R R Tolkien, 1968, revised edn 1978), Swann's Way Out: a posthumous adventure (1974), Omnibus Flanders and Swann Songbook (1977), Alphabetaphon-Essays (1987), Soliloquy...as told to Lyn Smith (autobiography, 1991); *Recreations* Greek travel; *Style*— Donald Swann, Esq; 13 Albert Bridge Rd, London SW11 4PX

SWANN, Dr Ian Lonsdale; s of Dr Geoffrey Swann, and Ida, *née* Lonsdale; *b* 13 March 1947; *Educ* Liverpool Coll, Univ of St Andrews (MB ChB, DCH); *m* 4 Aug 1973, Alison Gleave, da of Charles Edward Brownlow, of Burnley, Lancs; 1 s (Alexander David b 1977), 1 da (Gayle Penelope b 1980); *Career* sr house offr paediatrics to prof R G Mitchell Dundee 1973; registrar: Chalmers Unit Edinburgh Royal Infirmary 1973-74, Royal Hosp for Sick Children Edinburgh 1975-77; sr registrar and clinical tutor Univ Hosp of Wales 1978-80, conslt paediatrician NW RHA 1980-; MRCP 1974, FRCPE 1985, memb Br Paediatric Assoc; *Books* The Asthmatic Child in Play and Sport (contrib); *Recreations* walking, skiing, music, oil painting; *Style*— Dr Ian Swann; Burnley General Hospital, Casterton Ave, Burnley, Lancs (☎ 0282 25071)

SWANN, Dr James Cyprian; s of Ven Cecil Gordon Aldersey Swann (d 1969), and Hilda, *née* McMahon (d 1978); *b* 10 July 1931; *Educ* Gosfield Sch, The London Hosp Med Coll (MB BS, DMRD); *m* 28 Jan 1961, Josephine Margaret, da of Joseph Winston Ellis (d 1975); 3 da (Rachel b 1963, Laura b 1965, Clare b 1972); *Career* 2 Lt RA; conslt radiologist: The London Hosp 1968-76, The Royal Masonic Hosp 1970-84, Bromley Health Authy 1976-; chm Bromley Health Dist CAT Scanner Appeal; FFR, memb Br Inst Radiology 1965, FRCR 1975; *Recreations* painting in oils, photography, gardening; *Clubs* BMA; *Style*— Dr James Swann; 104 Hayes Way, Beckenham, Kent BR3 2RT (☎ 081 650 3673); Department of Radiology, Farnborough Hospital, Farnborough Common, Orpington, Kent BR6 8ND (☎ 0689 53333)

SWANN, Hon Mrs (Lydia Mary); *née* Hewitt; eldest da of 8 Viscount Lifford; *b* 10 May 1938; *m* 24 April 1965, Michael Christopher Swann, o s of Sir Anthony Charles Christopher Swann, 3 Bt, CMG, OBE; 2 s, 1 da; *Style*— The Hon Mrs Swann

SWANN, Sir Michael Christopher; 4 Bt (UK 1906), of Prince's Gardens, Royal Borough of Kensington, TD; s of Sir Anthony Charles Christopher Swann, 3 Bt, CMG, OBE (d 1991), and Jean Margaret, *née* Niblock-Stuart; *b* 23 Sept 1941; *Educ* Eton; *m* 1, 1965 (m dis 1985), Hon Lydia Mary Hewitt, da of 8 Viscount Lifford; 2 s (Jonathan Christopher b 1966, Toby Charles b 1971), 1 da (Tessa Margaret b 1969); m 2, 1988, Marilyn Ann, *née* Morse; *Heir* s, Jonathan Christopher Swann b 1966; *Career* late 60 Rifles; insurance broker; *Style*— Sir Michael Swann, Bt, TD; 100 Hurlingham Rd, London SW6 3NR

SWANN, Dr the Hon (Gavin Michael) Peter; s of Baron Swann (Life Peer, d 1990), and Teresa Ann, *née* Gleadowe; *b* 25 April 1955; *Educ* Edinburgh Academy, St Andrews Univ (MA), Bristol Univ, LSE; *m* 1 April 1989, Jenny, da of Prof Walter Elkan; 1 da (Caroline Susan Teresa b 22 Feb 1991); *Career* lectr Brunel Univ; *Recreations* sailing; *Style*— Dr the Hon Peter Swann; 28 Winscombe Crescent, London W5

SWANN, Hon Richard Meredith; er s of Baron Swann (Life Peer, d 1990), and Teresa Ann, *née* Gleadowe; *b* 31 Aug 1944; *Educ* Edin Acad, Trin Coll Cambridge, UCL; *m* 1969, Julia, da of Ronald Coke-Steel; 1 s (Robert); *Career* architect; *Recreations* sailing; *Style*— The Hon Richard Swann; 1 Carmel Court, Holland St, London W8

SWANNELL, John; *b* 27 Dec 1946; *Career* professional photographer; began career as photographic asst Vogue Studios former asst to David Bailey, fashion photographer (Vogue, Harpers & Queen, Tatler, Ritz newspaper); exhibition: several at the Nat Portrait Gallery London (which holds 40 Swannell Photographs in their Permanent Collection), fashion photography 1974- (Royal Photographic Soc Bath) July-Sept 1990; personalities photographed incl: HRH Princess Royal, Joan Collins, George Michael, Grace Jones, Jane Seymour, Shikira Caine, Yasmin Le Bon, Brian Ferry, Patsy Kensit and Pete Townsend; dir over 50 commercials since 1984 specialising in high fashion and beauty; awards: Gold award incl: Best Commercial of the Year 1984 (for Boots No 7), Silver award at Cannes for Best 40 Second Commercial (Rimmel Cosmetics) No 1 Commercial NY 1990 (for Johnsons); *Books* Fine Line (1982), Naked Landscape

(1982); *Style—* John Swannell, Esq; John Swannell Studios, 5 Charlotte Mews, London W1P 1LP (☎ 071 436 2797, fax 071 436 2679); Chalk Farm Studios, 10 A Belmont St, London NW1 (☎ 071 482 1003)

SWANNELL, Robert William Ashburnham; s of Maj David William Ashburnham Swannell, MBE, and Pamela Mary, *née* Woods; *b* 18 Nov 1950; *Educ* Rugby; *m* Jan 1982, Patricia Ann, da of John Ward; 1 s (William), 1 da (Alicia); *Career* CA 1973; Peat Marwick Mitchell & Co 1969-73, Inns of Ct Sch of Law 1973-76, called to the Bar Lincoln's Inn 1976, dir J Henry Schroder Wagg & Co 1985-; *Style—* Robert Swannell, Esq; 120 Cheapside, London EC2 (☎ 071 382 6000, fax 071 382 6459)

SWANSEA, 4 Baron (UK 1893); Sir John Hussey Hamilton; 4 Bt (UK 1882), DL (Powys 1962); s of 3 Baron Swansea, DSO, MVO, TD (d 1934), and Hon Winifred Hamilton, da of 1 Baron HolmPatrick; *b* 1 Jan 1925; *Educ* Eton, Trinity Coll Cambridge; *m* 1, 1956 (m dis 1973), Miriam (d 1975), da of Anthony Caccia-Birch, MC; 1 s, 2 da; m 2, 1982, Mrs Lucy Temple-Richards, da of Rt Rev Hugh Gough and Hon Mrs (M E) Gough, *qqv*; *Heir* s, Hon Richard Anthony Hussey Vivian b 24 Jan 1957; *Career* vice-pres and vice-chm of cncl of Nat Rifle Assoc; pres: Shooting Sports Tst, Welsh Rifle Assoc; chm Br Shooting Sports cncl; *Recreations* shooting, fishing, rifle shooting; *Style—* The Rt Hon the Lord Swansea, DL; Chapel House Cottage, Alltmawr, Builth Wells, Powys (☎ 098 23 662)

SWANSTON, Andrew Roger; s of James Alexander Swanston (d 1988), and Olive Dora, *née* May, of Great Yarmouth, Norfolk; *b* 15 Nov 1948; *Educ* Great Yarmouth GS, Brunel Univ (BTech), St Batholemew's Hosp Med Coll Univ of London (MB BS, LRCP); *m* 11 March 1978, Dorothy Jean, da of John Gibson Robson; 1 s (James Andrew b 4 July 1979), 1 da (Kathryn Elizabeth b 18 Jan 1982); *Career* primary FRCS (England) 1980, FRCS in Otolaryngology (England) 1983, sr registrar in ENT Surgery Royal Nat Throat Nose and Ear Hosp (also Great Ormond Street Hosp for Sick Children, Royal Berkshire Hosp Reading) 1984-87, Janet Nash res fellowship Univ of Zurich 1987, conslt ENT surgn St Bartholemew's Hosp 1987-; hon conslt ENT surgn Newham Gen Hosp London 1987-; VSO Cameroon West Africa 1967-68, memb cncl Br Assoc of Otolaryngologists 1990; MRCS 1978, memb BMA 1980, FRSM 1980, FRCS 1983; *Books* Otolaryngology volume 4 Rhinology (contrib, 5 edn 1987); *Recreations* trout fishing, classic car restoration; *Style—* Andrew Swanston, Esq; Oak House, Coopers Green Lane, St Albans, Herts (☎ 0727 830655); 59 Harley Street, London W1 (☎ 071 580 9746, 071 580 5200)

SWANSTON, Roy; s of Robert Trotter Swanston, of Lincoln, and Margaret Anne, *née* Paxton; *b* 31 Oct 1940; *Educ* Berwick upon Tweed GS, Coll of Estate Mgmnt; *m* Doreen, da of late John William Edmundson; 1 s (Philip b 17 Oct 1968), 1 da (Heather b 1 Dec 1966); *Career* various quantity surveying posts Sunderland CBC 1958-67, sr quantity surveyor CLASP Development Group Nottingham 1967-71, asst chief quantity surveyor Nottinghamshire CC 1971-74, directing surveyor Durham CC 1974-75, dir Dept of Architecture Cheshire CC 1982-87 (dir of Building Economics 1975-82), mgmnt conslt Peat Marwick McLintock 1987-88; dir: Bucknall Austin plc 1988-90, Properties in Care English Heritage 1990-; RICS: pres Quantity Surveyors Div 1982-83, hon treas 1986-90, vice pres 1990-, chm Educn and Membership Ctee 1990-; FRICS; *Recreations* fell walking, watching soccer (supporter of Sunderland AFC), lay preacher with Methodist Church; *Clubs* Royal Over-Seas League; *Style—* Roy Swanston, Esq; English Heritage, Keysign House, 429 Oxford St, London W1R 2HD (☎ 071 973 3000, fax 071 973 3430)

SWANTON, Ernest William (Jim); OBE (1965); s of William Swanton (d 1966), of Malvern, Worcs, and Lillian Emily, *née* Walters (d 1953); *b* 11 Feb 1907; *Educ* Cranleigh Sch; *m* 11 Feb 1958, Ann Marion Carbutt, da of R H de Montmorency (d 1938), of Wentworth, Surrey; *Career* served WWII 1939-45, Actg Maj 148 FD Regt Bedfords Yeo RA (captured Singapore POW 1942-45); journalist author and bdcaster 1924-; journalist Evening Standard 1927-39, rugby corr Daily Telegraph 1984-64 (cricket corr 1946-75); played cricket for Middx 1937-38; managed own X1: W Indies 1956 and 1961, Malaya and Far East 1964; ctee memb MCC 1975-85, Kent CCC 1971-89; pres: Cricket Soc 1976-83, Sandwich Town CC 1977-, Forty Club 1983-86, The Cricketer 1988-; *Books* A History of Cricket (with HS Altham, 1938), Denis Compton a Cricket Sketch (1948), Elusive Victory (1951), Cricket and the Clock (1952), Best Cricket Stories (1953), West Indian Adventure (1954), Victory in Australia 1954/55 (1955), Reports from South Africa (1957), West Indies Revisited (1960), The Ashes in Suspense (1963), World of Cricket (ed, 1966, 1980, 1986), Cricket from All Angles (1968), Sort of a Cricket Person (1972), Swanton in Australia (1975), Follow On (1985), As I Said at the Time (anthology, 1984), Kent Cricket a Photographic History 1744-1984 (with CH Taylor, 1985), Back Page Cricket (1987), The Essential E W Swanton (anthology, 1990); *Recreations* golf, watching cricket; *Clubs* MCC, Vincent's (Oxford), Naval and Military, 1 Zingari; *Style—* Jim Swanton, Esq, OBE; Delf House, Sandwich, Kent CT13 9HB

SWANTON, Dr (Robert) Howard; s of Robert Neil Swanton (d 1976), and Susanne, *née* Baldwin; *b* 30 Sept 1944; *Educ* Monkton Combe Sch, Queen's Coll Cambridge (fndn scholar, MA, MB BChir, MD), St Thomas's Hosp Med Sch (exhibitioner, Mead medal in med, Bristowe medal pathology); *m* Lindsay Ann, da of Arnold Jepson, of Blackburn, Lancashire; 1 s (Robert Charles b 24 Feb 1972), 1 da (Josephine Kate b 23 Jan 1975); *Career* house physician St Thomas's Hosp 1969, house surgn St Peter's Hosp Chertsey 1970; sr house offr: Hammersmith Hosp 1970-71, Nat Heart Hosp 1971; med registrar Poole Hosp 1971-72, sr med registrar St Thomas's Hosp London 1975-77 (cardiac registrar 1972-74), sr registrar in cardiology Nat Heart Hosp 1977-79; conslt cardiologist Middlesex Hosp 1979-, King Edward VII Hosp for Offrs 1984-; Br Cardiac Soc: memb 1979-, asst sec 1986-88, sec 1988-; FRCP 1984 (MRCP 1971); *Books* Pocket Consultant in Cardiology (1 edn 1984, 2 edn 1989); *Recreations* music, photography; *Clubs* St Albans Medical; *Style—* Dr Howard Swanton; Kent Lodge, 10 Dover Park Drive, Roehampton, London SW15 5BG (☎ 081 788 6920); Dept of Cardiology, Middlesex Hospital, Mortimer St, London W1N 8AA (☎ 071 380 9055); 25 Upper Wimpole St, London W1M 7TA (☎ 071 486 7416)

SWANWICK, Sir Graham Russell; MBE (1944); s of Eric Drayton Swanwick (d 1955), of Whittington House, Chesterfield, and Margery Eleanor, *née* Norton (d 1959); *b* 24 Aug 1906; *Educ* Winchester, Univ Coll Oxford; *m* 1, 1933 (m dis 1945), Helen Barbara Reid (d 1970); 2 s (Richard, Anthony); m 2, 1952, Mrs Audrey Celia Parkinson (d 1987), da of H C Hextall of Ford, Ashurst, Steyning, Sussex (d 1987); 1 step s (Richard) (and 1 step s (Dale) decd); *Career* WWII Wing Cdr RAFVR 1940-45 (despatches); called to the Bar Inner Temple 1930, QC 1956, bencher 1962; rec of: Lincoln 1957-59, Leicester 1959-66; dep chm Lincs QS (parts of Kesteven) 1960-63, chm Derbyshire QS 1963-66 (dep chm 1966-71), judge Jersey and Guernsey Cts of Appeal 1964-66, judge of High Ct of Justice (Queen's Bench Div) 1966-80, presiding judge Midland and Oxford circuit 1975-78; kt 1966; *Recreations* shooting; *Clubs* RAF; *Style—* Sir Graham Swanwick, MBE; Burnett's Ashurst, Steyning, W Sussex BN44 3AY (☎ 0403 710241)

SWAPP, Dr Garden Hepburn; s of Garden Hepburn Swapp, DSC (d 1967), of Stonehaven, Scotland, and Frances Elizabeth, *née* McRobie (d 1977); *b* 21 Nov 1929; *Educ* Mackie Acad Stonehaven, Fordyce Acad Banffshire, Univ of Aberdeen (DCH); *m* 3 July 1954, Anne Margaret, da of Robert Begg Gillespie, of Stonehaven; 3 s (Garden b and d 1960, George b 1966, David b 1968), 1 da (Helen b 1964); *Career* Sqdn Ldr RAF Medical Branch 1954-67; obstetrician and gynaecologist; registrar Aberdeen Gen Hosps 1961-64, clinical sr lectr Univ of Aberdeen 1970- (lectr 1964-66, sr lectr 1966-70), conslt Grampian Health Bd 1970-; former memb Scot and BMA; Burgess City of Aberdeen; BMA 1954, FRCOG 1976; *Recreations* walking; *Clubs* Royal Northern Univ, Aberdeen Rotary; *Style—* Dr Garden Swapp; 38 Gray St, Aberdeen AB1 6SE (☎ 0224 318302); Royal Infirmary, Aberdeen AB9 2ZB (☎ 0224 681818)

SWARBRICK, Dr Edwin Thornton; s of Richard Thornton Swarbrick, and Mary Elizabeth, *née* Cooper; *b* 29 April 1945; *Educ* Pocklington Sch Yorks, Wilbraham Acad Mass USA, St George's Med Sch London (MM BS, MD, FRCP); *m* 3 March 1984, (Angela) Corinne, da of Kenneth Hamer; 2 s (Benjamin Thornton b 8 Jan 1985, Matthew Thornton b 9 Feb 1987); *Career* house physician and surgn St Georges Hosp London 1968-69, sr house offr Brompton Hosp 1970-71; registrar The London Hosp 1971-72, and St Mark's Hosp 1972-74; res fell Inst of Child Health London 1974-76, lectr in gastroenterology St Bart's Hosp 1976-80, conslt physician Wolverhampton 1980; memb Br Soc Gastroenterology; memb BMA, FRSM, FRCP; *Recreations* equestrian sports, skiing, music, the arts; *Style—* Dr Edwin Swarbrick; Coppice Green, Shifnal, Shropshire (☎ 0952 462226); Nuffield Hospital, Wood Rd, Tettenhall, Wolverhampton (☎ 0902 754177)

SWARBRICK, Prof James; s of George Winston Swarbrick, and Edith, *née* Cooper; *b* 8 May 1934; *Educ* Sloane GS, Chelsea Coll London (BPharm, PhD, DSc); *m* 1960, Pamela Margaret Oliver; *Career* lectr Chelsea Coll 1964 (asst lectr 1962), visiting asst prof Purdue Univ 1964; Univ of Conn: assoc prof 1966, prof and chm Dept of Pharmaceutics 1969, asst dean 1970; dir product devpt Sterling-Winthrop Res Inst NY 1972, First prof of Pharmaceutics Univ of Sydney 1975-76, Dean Sch of Pharmacy Univ of London 1976-78, prof of pharmacy Univ of South Calif LA 1978-81, chm Div Pharmaceutics and prof of pharmaceutics Univ of North Carolina 1981-; visiting scientist Astra Laboratories Sweden 1971, indust conslt 1965-72 and 1975-, conslt Aust Dept of Health 1975-76, memb Ctee on Specifications Nat Formulary 1970-75, chm Jt US Pharmacopoeia Nat Formulary Panel on Disintegration 1971-75; memb: Ctee on Graduate Programs American Assoc Colls of Pharmacy 1969-71, Practice Trg Ctee Pharmaceutical Soc of NSW 1975-76, Acad Bd Univ of Sidney 1975-76, Collegiate Cncl 1976-78, Educn Ctee Royal Pharmaceutical Soc GB 1976-18, Working Pty on Pre-Registration Training 1977-78; Pharmaceutical Mfrs Assoc Fndn: memb Basic Pharmacology Advsy Ctee 1982-, chm Pharmaceutics Advsy Ctee 1986-, memb Sci Advsy Ctee 1986-; memb Editorial Bd: Jl of Biopharmaceutics and Pharmacokinetics 1973-79, Drug Devpt Communications 1974-82, Pharmaceutical Technol 1978-, Biopharmaceutics and Drug Disposition 1979; series ed: Current Concepts in the Pharmaceutical Sciences, Drugs and the Pharmaceutical Sciences; CChem, FRSC, FAAS 1966, FRIC 1970; fell: Acad of Pharmaceutical Sciences, Royal Pharmaceutical Society of GB 1978 (memb 1961), American Assoc of Pharmaceutical Scientists 1987; *Publications* Physical Pharmacy (with A N Martin and A Cammarata, 2 edn, 1969, 3 edn, 1983), Encyclopedia of Pharmaceutical Technology (jt ed), contrib to various pharmaceutical books and jls; *Recreations* woodwork, listening to music, golf; *Style—* Prof James Swarbrick; School of Pharmacy, University of North Carolina, Beard Hall B 7360, Chapel Hill NC 27599 7360, USA (☎ 919 962 0092)

SWASH, Dr Michael; s of Edwin Frank Swash, of Milford on Sea, Hants, and Kathleen, *née* Burton; *b* 29 Jan 1939; *Educ* Forest Sch, Snaresbrook London, London Hosp Med Coll Univ of London (MD), Univ of Virginia Med Sch Charlottesville, VA USA; *m* 22 Jan 1966, Caroline Mary, da of Edward Payne, of Box, Nistroud, Glos; 3 s (Jesse Edward, Thomas Henry, (Edmond) Joseph); *Career* current positions held: med dir The Royal London Hosp and Assoc Community Servs NHS Tst, conslt neurologist The London Hosp and Newham Gen Hosp 1972-, hon conslt neurologist St Mark's Hosp London and St Luke's Hosp for the Clergy London, neurologist-adjunct Cleveland Clinic Fndn Ohio USA 1980-, sr lectr in neuropathology The London Hosp Med Coll 1981-; hon sec Section of Neurology RSM 1974-77, hon sec NETRHA Advsy Ctee for Neurology and Neurosurgery 1975-78, hon sec Assoc Br Neurologists 1979-84, chm Southwark and Camberwell Multiple Sclerosis Soc 1985-, memb Neuroscience Bd MRC 1986-91; memb: NY Acad of Scis, Br Neuropathological Soc, RSM, Br Soc Clinical Neurophysiology, Assoc of Br Neurologists, American Acad of Neurology, American Neurological Assoc, Austral Neurological Assoc, Pathological Soc GB, Br Soc Gastroenterology; membre d'honneur de la Société Nationale Française de Colo Proctologie; Liveryman Worshipful Co of Apothecaries 1989; MRCPath, FRCP 1977 (memb 1972); *Books* incl: Clinical Neuropathology (jtly, 1982), Muscle Biopsy Pathology (jtly, 1984, 2 edn, 1984), Scientific Basis of Clinical Neurology (jtly, 1985), Neuromuscular Diseases (jtly, 2 edn, 1988), Hierarchies in Neurology (jtly, 1989), Neurology: a concise clinic text (jtly, 1989), Clinical Neurology (2 vols, jtly 1991); *Recreations* walking, music, rowing, theatre, opera; *Clubs* London Rowing, Athenaeum; *Style—* Dr Michael Swash; Dept of Neurology, The Royal London Hospital, London E1 1BB (☎ 071 377 7472, fax 071 377 7008, 071 377 7949, car 0836 258751)

SWATMAN, Philip Hilary; s of Philip Stenning Swatman Parkstone Dorset and Patricia Meeson; *b* 1 Dec 1949; *Educ* St Edwards Sch Oxford, ChCh Oxford (BA); *m* Rosemary Anne; 1 s (Richard Oliver b 14 Oct 1981,), 2 da (Elizabeth Harriet b 16 Aug 1978, Rowena Jane b 16 April 1984); *Career* KPMG Peat Marwick Mclintock 1971-77, National Enterprise Board 1977-79; dir: NM Rothschild & Sons 1986-87 (joined 1979), of corp fin Chase Property Holdings plc 1987-88, NM Rothschild & Sons Ltd 1988-; FCA; *Recreations* sailing, squash, shooting, opera, theatre; *Style—* Philip Swatman, Esq; Hamblings, Church Rd, Ham Common, Surrey TW10 5HG; NM Rothschild & Sons Ltd, New Court, St Swithins Lane, London EC4P 4DU (☎ 071 210 5332, fax 071 283 4275)

SWAYNE, Sir Ronald Oliver Carless; MC (1945); s of Col Oswald Rocke Swayne, DSO (d 1948) of Tillington Court, nr Hereford, by his w, Brenda (d 1956), yr da of Arthur Butler, of Brooklyn, Chislehurst; *b* 11 May 1918; *Educ* Bromsgrove Sch Worcester, Oxford Univ; *m* 1941, Charmian (d 1984), da of Maj W E P Cairnes (d 1953), of Eardsley, Herefords; 1 s (Giles b 1946);1 da (Amanda b 1951); *Career* served WWII Herefords Regt and 1 Commando; chm Overseas Containers 1973-82 (md 1978-82); dir Ocean Tport & Trading, Nat Freight Co 1973-85; pres: Inst of Freight Forwarders 1980, Gen Cncl Br Shipping 1978-79; vice-chm Br Shipping Fedn 1976; former pres Ctee des Assocs d'Armateurs EEC; kt 1979; *Clubs* Flyfishers (London), Houghton (Stockbridge); *Style—* Sir Ronald Swayne, MC; Puddle House, Chicksgrove, Tisbury, Salisbury, Wilts SP3 6NA (☎ 072 276 454)

SWAYTHLING, 4 Baron (UK 1907) David Charles Samuel Montagu; 4 Bt (UK 1894); s of 3 Baron Swaythling, OBE (d 1990), and his 1 w, Mary Violet, *née* Levy; *b* 6 Aug 1928; *Educ* Eton, Trinity Coll Cambridge (BA); *m* 14 Dec 1951, Christiane Françoise (Ninette), yr da of Edgar Dreyfus (d 1976), of Paris; 1 s (Hon Charles Edgar Samuel b 1954), 2 da (Fiona Yvonne b 1952 (d 1982), Hon Nicole Mary (Hon Mrs Campbell) b 1956); *Heir* s, Hon Charles Edgar Samuel Montagu b 20 Feb 1954; *Career* chm Samuel Montagu & Co Ltd 1970-73, chm and chief exec Orion Bank Ltd 1974-79; chm: Ailsa Investment Trust plc 1981-87, Rothmans International plc 1988-; dir: Daily Telegraph plc, Horserace Totalisator Bd; pres Assoc for Jewish Youth;

Recreations shooting, racing, theatre; *Clubs* White's, Pratt's, Portland, Knickerbocker (New York), Union (Sydney); *Style*— The Rt Hon the Lord Swaythling; 14 Craven Hill Mews, Devonshire Terrace, London W2 3DY (☎ 071 724 7860); Rothmans Int plc, 15 Hill St, London W1X 7FB (☎ 071 491 4366, telex 24764)

SWAYTHLING, Dowager Lady; Jean Marcia; *née* Leith-Marshall; CBE (1943); da of late G G Leith-Marshall; *b* 14 Aug 1908; *m* 1 (m dis), Sqdn Ldr G R M Knox, RAF; 1 da; m 2, 13 Aug 1945, as his 2 w, 3 Baron Swaythling, OBE (d 1990); *Career* Chief Controller and Dir ATS 1941-43; *Style*— The Rt Hon the Dowager Lady Swaythling, CBE; Terwick Hill House, Rogate, Petersfield, Hampshire

SWEENEY, Michael Anthony (Mike); s of Michael Dominick Sweeney (d 1969), of Nottingham, and Madaleine, *née* Beatty; *b* 14 Oct 1944; *Educ* Becket Sch, St John's Coll Cambridge (rowing blue); *m* 3 August 1968, Tina, *née* Marson; 1 s (Paul Michael b 29 Nov 1971), 1 da (Claire Helena 15 April 1970); *Career* Boat Race: stroke 1965, stroke and pres 1966, umpire 1984, 1986, 1988 and 1990; GB eights Euro championships 1967, GB coxless pairs World championships 1970, chm GB Selection Bd 1972-76, team mangr: GB rowing teams 1973-79, Olympic rowing teams 1980 and 1984; elected Henley steward 1974, int (FISA) umpire 1982-, chm of Regattas Cmmn World Rowing (FISA) Cncl 1990; civil engr construction indust 1967-70, district mangr Severn Trent Water Ltd 1987- (river engr 1970-86); Henley medals: Ladies' plate 1966, Visitors' 1966, Wyfold 1967, Stewards' 1968; *Recreations* squash, tennis, skiing, golf; *Style*— Mike Sweeney, Esq; 36 The Ropewalk, Nottingham NG1 5DW (☎ 0602 474690); Severn Trent Water Ltd, Sherwood District, Great Central Rd, Mansfield NGI 82RG (☎ 0623 421321, fax 0623 27971)

SWEENEY, Patrick John (Pat); s of Patrick John Sweeney, Sr, of London and Alice Betty, *née* Scopes; *b* 12 Aug 1952; *m* 21 April 1990, Martha Elizabeth, da of James Plessas; *Career* rowing coach and competitor; began rowing 1964, winner over fifty int titles; major UK titles: nat champion 10 times, head of the river 7 times, Prince Philip Henley Royal Regatta 1971, Grand Henley Royal Regatta 1975; honours with Br nat team: Silver medal coxed fours World Youth Championships 1968, Silver medal eights World Championships 1974, Silver medal eights Olympic Games 1976, Gold medal lightweight eights World Championships 1986, Gold medal coxed pairs World Championships 1986 (Silver 1987), Bronze medal coxed pairs Olympic Games 1988; head coach: Burnaby Lake Aquatic Club Canada 1978-79, Univ of Calif at Berkeley 1979-86, Oxford Univ 1989-90; coach to Br men's pair Roberts/Clark 1977 and Redgrave/Pinsent 1990; asst coach: M Spracklen 1987-89, Br nat squad 1987-88 (incl men's pair Redgrave/Holmes), Br men's pair Redgrave/Pinsent 1990; memb coaching staff US Olympic and nat devpt teams 1979-86; achievements as coach incl: Boat Race winners Oxford Univ 1989 and 1990, various Canadian and US Collegiate titles, various men's pair Olympic and World Championships medals; *Style*— Pat Sweeney, Esq; 9 Southmead Road, Wimbledon Park, London SW19 6SS (☎ 081 788 4559)

SWEENEY, Dr Thomas Kevin; s of John Francis Sweeney (d 1975), of Clontarf, Dublin, and Mildred, *née* Forbes (d 1987); *b* 10 Aug 1923; *Educ* O'Connell Sch Dublin, Nat Univ Coll Dublin (MB Bchir, BAO, FFCM, DTM&H, TDD); *m* 25 Jan 1950, Eveleen Moira, da of Driryan (d 1959), of 27 Fitzwilliam Sq, Dublin; 2 s (Niall b 1950, Paul b 1962), 2 da (Geainne (Mrs Hedges) b 1956, Maedb (Mrs Newman) b 1958); *Career* princ med offr Colonial Med Serv 1950-65, asst sr med offr Welsh Hosp Bd 1965-68; Dept of Health: med offr 1968-88, sr princ med offr 1979-83, sr med offr 1983-88; QHP 1984-87; memb BR Med Assoc; *Recreations* golf, cathedrals, gardening, reading; *Style*— Dr Thomas Sweeney; The White House, Sheerwater Ave, Woodham, Weybridge, Surrey KT15 3DD (☎ 093 234 3559)

SWEETBAUM, Henry Alan; s of Irving Sweetbaum (d 1985), and Bertha Sweetbaum (d 1952); *b* 22 Nov 1937; *Educ* Wharton Sch Univ of Pennsylvania (BSc); *m* 1, 29 May 1960, late Suzanne, *née* Milburn; m 2, 8 Nov 1971, Anne Betty Leonie, *née* de Vigier; 4 s (Jeffrey Alan b 15 Aug 1961, Barry Jay b 31 March 1964, Peter Mark b 13 Dec 1967, James William Mark b 21 Nov 1974); *Career* mangr cost accounting Mohican Corporation 1959-60, sales rep Underwood Corp 1960-62, exec vice pres and dir Leasco Corporation (Reliance Group) 1962-69, exec dir Plessey Company Ltd 1970-71, fndr chm Huntington Securities Limited 1971-, pt/t chm Data Recording Instrument Company Ltd 1976-82 (non-exec dir 1973-76), non-exec dir: Decision Data Corporation 1980-83, Ashton-Tate Corporation 1986, Silicon Systems Inc 1988-89; chm Wickes International Corporation 1982-87, chm and chief exec Wickes plc 1986-; dir: Centre for Strategic Mgmnt Studies Wharton Sch Univ of Pennsylvania, Undergraduate Advsy Bd Wharton Sch Univ of Pennsylvania; *Books* Restructing: The Management Challenge (contrib, 1990); *Recreations* shooting, swimming; *Clubs* Reform; *Style*— Henry Sweetbaum, Esq; Wickes plc, 19-21 Mortimer St, London W1N 7RJ (☎ 071 631 1018, fax 071 637 1784)

SWEETEN, Anthony Ricardo; s of Benjamin Arthur Sweeten (d 1975); *b* 24 Oct 1941; *Educ* Clare Hall Coll Halifax, Tech Coll Halifax, Bradford Univ; *m* 1966, Marion Brenda Mary, *née* Hayter; 2 s, 1 da; *Career* dir TS Harrison & Sons Ltd 1975-; *Recreations* golf, shooting, fishing; *Clubs* Lightcliffe Golf, Leeds Serv Rifle; *Style*— Anthony Sweeten, Esq; Green Acre, Bramley Lane, Lightcliffe, Halifax, W Yorkshire (☎ 0422 201467)

SWEETMAN, Mrs Ronald; Jennifer Joan; *see*: Jennifer Dickson

SWEETMAN, John Francis; CB (1990), TD (1964); s of Thomas Nelson Sweetman (d 1982), and Mary Monica, *née* D'Arcy-Reddy; *b* 31 Oct 1930; *Educ* Cardinal Vaughan Sch, St Catharines Coll Cambridge (MA); *m* 1, 31 March 1959 (m dis 1981), Susan Manley, *qv*, da of Lt Col Manley (d 1986); 1 s (Edward John D'Arcy b 4 March 1969), 1 da (Jane Frances b 17 Jan 1960; m 2, Celia Elizabeth, da of Sir William Nield, *qv*; 2 s (Thomas William b 27 Aug 1984, James Benedict b 24 Sept 1987); *Career* 2 Lt RA serv in Gibraltar 1949-51, TA (City of London RA) and AER 1951-65; House of Commons: clerk 1954-, clerk of Select Ctees on Nationalised Industs and on Sci and Technol 1962-65 and 1970-73, second clerk Select Ctees 1979-83, clerk of Overseas Office 1983-87, clerk asst 1987-90, clerk of Ctees 1990-; memb Oxford and Cambridge Catholic Educn Bd 1964-84; *Books* contrib to: Erskine Mays' Parliamentary Practice, Halsbury's Laws of England (4 edn); ed Cncl of Europe Procedure and Practice of the Parliamentary Assembly (9 edn, 1990); *Clubs* MCC; *Style*— John Sweetman, Esq, CB, TD; 41 Creffield Road, London W5 3RR (☎ 081 992 2456); House of Commons, London SW1A OAA (☎ 071 219 3313)

SWEETNAM, (David) Rodney; CBE (1990); s of Dr William Sweetnam (d 1970), of Broadlands Ave, Shepperton, Middx, and Irene, *née* Black (d 1967); *b* 5 Feb 1927; *Educ* Clayesmore, Univ of Cambridge, Middlesex Hosp Med Sch (MA, MB BChir); *m* 23 May 1959, Patricia Ann Staveley, da of A Staveley Gough, OBE; 1 s (David Ian Staveley b 9 May 1963), 1 da (Sarah Ann Staveley b 20 March 1961); *Career* Surgn Lt RNVR 1950-52; conslt orthopaedic surgn: Middx Hosp 1960-, King Edward VII Hosp for Offrs 1964-, (hon) Royal Hosp Chelsea 1974-, (hon) Royal Nat Orthopaedic Hosp 1983-; hon civil conslt in orthopaedic surgery to the Army 1974-, conslt advsr in orthopaedic surgery to DHSS 1981-90, chm MRC Working Pty on Bone Sarcoma 1980-85, dir Medical Sickness Annuity and Life Assurance Society 1982-, orthopaedic surgn to HM the Queen 1982-, dir and dep chm Permanent Assurance Co 1988-; fell Br Orthopaedic Assoc 1960- (pres 1985-86), div sec and treas Br Ed Soc of Bone and Joint Surgery 1975-, memb and former pres Combined Servs Orthopaedic Soc 1983-; memb: Cncl RCS 1985-, Exec Ctee Arthritis and Rheumatism Cncl 1985-; FRCS; *Books and Publications* The Basis and Practice of Orthopaedic Surgery (jt ed), Essentials of Orthopaedics (1970), Osteosarcoma (British Medical Journal, 1979), papers on bone tumours and gen orthopaedic surgery and fractures; *Publications* The Basis and Practise of Orthopaedics (jtly 1980), 'Osteosarcoma' Br Medical Journal (1979), papers on bone tumours and gen orthopaedic surgery and fractures; *Recreations* garden labouring; *Style*— Rodney Sweetnam, Esq, CBE; 23 Wimpole St, London W1M 7AD

SWEETNAM, (Robert) William; s of George William Sweetnam, of Chardstock, Devon, and Elisabeth Ann, *née* Randolph; *b* 25 Nov 1954; *Educ* Clifton Coll Bristol (LLB); *m* 26 April 1980, Philippa Mary, da of John Eastell, of Ingatestone, Essex; 1 s (James William b 1982), 1 da (Jeniffer Susan b 1985); *Career* slr 1978-; dir Dryfield Finance Ltd 1983; ptnr Battern & Co Slrs 1983-; *Recreations* skiing, sailing, classic cars, carpentry; *Style*— William Sweetnam, Esq; 33 Glenavon Park, Sneyd Park, Bristol; 2 St Pauls Road, Clifton, Bristol (☎ 0272 737848, fax 272 237040)

SWETENHAM, John Foster; s of Brig John Edmund Swetenham, DSO (d 1982), and Alison Ann, yst da of Col the Hon Guy Greville Wilson, CMG, DSO; descended from Elias de Swetenham living in the reigns of Richard I, John and Henry III. Family received land at the Somerford Booths 1298, land sold 1930's; *b* 16 Jan 1939; *Educ* Eton, Sandhurst; *m* 1964, Marion Sylvia, yr da of George Alfred Parker (d 1982); 1 s, 1 da; *Career* Mil Serv 1956-70, adjutant Royal Scots Greys 1965-67, Capt, ret 1970 memb Stock Exchange 1973-; *Recreations* sailing, country pursuits, skiing; *Clubs* Royal Yacht Sqadron, Royal Ocean Racing, Cavalry and Guards', Pratt's; *Style*— Foster Swetenham, Esq; Pound Farmhouse, Rayne, Braintree, Essex CM7 5DJ (☎ 0376 26738); 84 Campden St, London W8 (☎ 071 727 5176); office: William de Broe plc, 6 Broadgate, London EC2 (☎ 071 588 7511)

SWIFT, Brian Paul; s of Ronald C Swift, of Eastbourne, and Constance M Swift; *b* 19 Feb 1947; *Educ* William Hulme's Sch Manchester, Bablake Sch Coventry, Univ of Manchester (BSc); *m* 30 Dec 1970, Wenche, da of Boerge Flate Skogly, of Hamar, Norway; 1 s (Nicholas b 30 Nov 1971), 2 da (Charlotte b 25 Sept 1974, Camilla b 13 June 1988); *Career* acting pilot offr RAFVR 1967; currently Sr Capt BA; memb BALPA, vice chm Gt Park Cons Assoc; *Style*— Brian Swift, Esq; PO Box 10, Heathrow, London TW6 2JA

SWIFT, Prof Cameron Graham; s of Rev Graham Swift (d 1973), and Victoria, *née* Williamson; *b* 5 April 1946; *Educ* Lawrence Sheriff Sch Rugby, Univ of London (MB BS), Univ of Dundee (PhD); *m* Margaret Rosemary, da of Henry K Vernon; *Career* MRC Res Fell in clinical pharmacology Univ of Dundee 1977-80, conslt physician Dept of Med for the elderly N Humberside 1980-84, dir of postgraduate med educn N Humberside 1982-84, conslt physician and sr lectr Dept of Geriatric Med Univ of Wales Coll of Med 1984-86, prof of health care of the elderly Univ of London 1986-; conslt physician; Kings Coll Hosp, Dulwich Hosp 1986-; hon prof of health care Univ of Kent 1986-; chm trg ctee and pharmacology and therapeutic section of Br Geriatric Soc; bd memb: Age Concern, King's Coll Inst of Gerontology; memb: Sub Ctee on efficacy and adverse reactions, Ctee on Safety of Meds, Br Pharmacological Soc, Br Geriatrics Sco; FRCP 1988; *Books* Clinical Pharmacology in the Elderly (Ed, 1987); *Recreations* music, ornithology, hill walking; *Style*— Prof Cameron Swift; Kings College School of Medicine and Dentistry, Kings College Hospital, Denmark Hill, London SE5 9RS (☎ 081 693 3377 ext 3312)

SWIFT, Graham Colin; s of Lionel Allan Stanley Swift, and Sheila Irene, *née* Bourne; *b* 4 May 1949; *Educ* Dulwich, Queens' Coll Cambridge, Univ of York; *Career* author; Geoffrey Faber Meml Prize, Guardian Fiction prize, RSL Winifred Holtby award 1983, Booker McConnell prize nominee 1983, Premio Grinzane Cavour Italy 1987; FRSL 1984; *Books* novels: The Sweet Shop Owner 1980, Shuttlecock 1981, Waterland 1983, Out of this World 1988; short stories: Learning to Swim 1982, The Magic Wheel (anthology, ed with David Profumo, 1986); *Recreations* fishing; *Style*— Graham Swift, Esq

SWIFT, Lionel; QC (1975); s of Harris Swift (d 1971), and Bassie Swift; *b* 3 Oct 1931; *Educ* UC London (LLB), Brasenose Coll Oxford (BCL), Univ of Chicago Law Sch (JD); *m* 1966, Elizabeth, da of Max Herzig, of Montreal; 1 da (Allison b 1968); *Career* jr counsel to Treasy in Probate 1974; barr, rec 1979; bencher Inner Temple 1984; chm Institute of Laryngology and Otology 1985; *Style*— Lionel Swift, QC; 4 Paper Buildings, Temple, London EC4Y 7EX (☎ 071 353 3420)

SWIFT, Malcolm Robin; QC (1988); s of Willie Swift, Huddersfield, W Yorks, and Heather May Farquhar Swift, OBE, *née* Nield; *b* 19 Jan 1948; *Educ* Colne Valley HS W Yorks, King's Coll London (LLB); *m* 20 Sept 1969, (Anne) Rachael, da of Ernest Rothery Ayre, of Bolton-by-Bowland, Lancs; 1 s (Daniel b 1977), 2 da (Joanna b 1972, Catherine b 1975); *Career* called to the Bar Gray's Inn 1970, practice NE Circuit, recorder Crown Ct 1987, co-opted memb Remuneration Ctee of Bar Cncl 1978-89, vice chm Brighouse Civic Tst; *Recreations* squash, cycling, music, theatre; *Style*— Malcolm Swift, Esq, QC; Park Court Chambers, 40 Park Cross St, Leeds LS1 2QH (☎ 0532 433277, fax 0532 421285, telex 666135 DX Leeds 26401)

SWIFT, Dr Peter George Furmston; s of Herbert Swift (d 1988), and Catherine Nell, *née* Edwards (d 1977); *b* 22 Jan 1943; *Educ* Wyggeston GS for Boys, Downing Coll Cambridge (MA), Guy's Hosp London (DCH); *m* 19 Sept 1970, Heather, da of Douglas Hillhouse (d 1970); 3 da (Kate b 1973, Lucy Jane b 1974, Elizabeth Anne b 1976); *Career* sr house offr neonatal paediatrics UCH 1971, registrar paediatrics Sheffield Children's Hosp 1972-74; sr registrar: Royal Hosp for Sick Children Bristol 1974-77, Exeter Hosps 1977-78; conslt paediatrician with special interest in endocrinology and diabetes Leicester Gen Hosp 1979-; chm: Children and Young Person's Advsy Ctee Br Diabetic Assoc 1983-86, working pty on servs for diabetic children Br Paediatric Assoc 1987-89; FRCP; memb: Br Paediatric Assoc, BDA, GMC; *Recreations* sports; *Clubs* Leicester Squash, Leicester Univ Sports; *Style*— Dr Peter Swift; 21 Westminster Rd, Leicester LE2 2EH (☎ 0533 705360); Leicester General Hospital, Gwendolen Rd, Leicester LE5 4PW (☎ 0533 490490)

SWIFT, Robert; s of Max Swift (d 1960), and Leah, *née* Seigle (d 1978); *b* 13 Aug 1941; *Educ* John Marshall HS, Los Angeles, Univ of London (LLB); *m* 23 Sept 1963, Hilary, da of Simon Bernard Casson (d 1971); 2 s (Mark b 1969, Simon b 1972); 1 da (Miranda b 1976); *Career* slr; Patent & Trademark Dept EMI Ltd 1967-71, Linklaters & Paines 1971-75, legal asst White and Case NY 1975, ptnr Linklaters & Paines 1976-; vice chm City of London Law Soc Intellectual Property Sub Ctee; memb: Jt Bar-Law Soc Working Pty on Intellectual Property Law, Patent Slrs Assoc, Computor Law Gp; memb: Worshipful Co of Slrs 1976, Law Soc 1967; *Recreations* music, books, walking; *Clubs* Riverside; *Style*— Robert Swift, Esq; Linklaters & Paines, Barrington House, 59-67 Gresham St, London EC2V 7JA

SWIFT, Ronald Cephas; s of James Swift (d 1981), and Maud Mary, *née* Coleman (d 1981); *b* 4 Aug 1920; *Educ* Haberdasher's Aske's, Hatchman London; *m* 16 Oct 1943, Constance Maude (Connie), da of Frederick William Edwards (d 1970); 2 s (Peter Michael b 12 Dec 1944, Brian Paul b 19 Feb 1947); *Career* RNVR 1938-39, RN 1939-46; mktg mangr Foil-James Booth Aluminium Ltd 1963-65 (sales promotion mangr 1962-63), gen mangr Foil Div Foil-Alcan Booth Industs Ltd 1965-77, dir Alcan Foils Ltd 1971-77, commercial dir and gen mangr Foil-Alcan Booth Sheet Ltd 1977-82 (company name changed to Alcan Plate Ltd 1978), chm Promotion Ctee Euro Aluminium Foil Assoc 1978-82; memb and former pres Past Rotarians Club Eastbourne and dist; fndr chm and past pres Bablake Sch Parents Assoc; memb: Probus Club Eastbourne, PO and Telephone Advsy Ctees Eastbourne, Glyndebourne Festival Soc, Exec Bd British Airways, Friends of Eastbourne Hosps; Freeman City of London, Liveryman Worshipful Co of Marketors; FCIM; *Clubs* Wig and Pen, City Livery, Surrey CCC; *Style—* Ronald Swift Esq; 15 Tavistock, Devonshire Place, Eastbourne, E Sussex BN21 4AG (☎ 0323 35282)

SWIFT, Timothy John; s of Kenneth Alan Swift, of Great Glen, Leicestershire, and Olive Mary, *née* Brown; *b* 1 July 1957; *Educ* Beauchamp Coll Oadby, Univ of Leicester (BSc); *m* 10 Feb 1979, Diane Elizabeth, da of David Bryant, of Stafford; 1 s (Owen b 1987); *Career* sr analyst GEC Gas Turbines 1978-85, res technologist GEC ERC Whetstone 1985-90; ccncllr Leics 1981- (gp ldr 1981-88), Oadby and Wigston Borough cnclIr 1983-, Parly candidate Harborough 1983 and 1987, memb ACC 1985-, chm social servs ctee ACC 1988-89, organising sec Assoc of SLD Cncllrs 1990-; *Recreations* squash, badminton, country walking; *Style—* Timothy Swift, Esq; 31 Cheshire Drive, South Wigston, Leicester LE8 2WA (☎ 0533 786844)

SWINBURN, Brig David Henry Amyatt; CBE (1989); s of Maj-Gen Henry Robinson Swinburn, CB, OBE, MC (d 1981), and Naomi Barbara, *née* Hull, of Amesbury Abbey, Amesbury, Wilts; bro, Lt-Gen Sir Richard Swinburn, KCB, *qv*; *b* 15 July 1934; *Educ* Wellington. Univ of Cambridge (MA); *m* 1, 7 Jan 1961, Belinda Marion, *née* Stainton (d 13 June 1961); m 2, 17 Sept 1966, Gillian Adair, MVO, da of Col Adair Murray, of Winchester; 2 s (Jonathan b 1969, Christopher b 1970), 1 da (Joanna b 1970); *Career* cmmnd RE 1954, Lt-Col and CO 26 Engr Regt 1974, Brig and Cmmnd RE of Corps 1979, RCDS course 1981; MOD: dir NATO 1982, dir Engr Servs 1984, dir Exams and Courses 1986, ADC to HM The Queen 1986-89, ret 1989; gp trg mangr Mott MacDonald Consltg Engrs 1989-; FBIM, Companion of Inst of Civil Engrs; *Recreations* squash, skiing, fishing, gardening; *Style—* Brig David Swinburn, CBE; Mott MacDonald Consultants Ltd, St Anne House, 20-26 Wellesley Rd, Croydon CR9 2UL (☎ 081 686 5041, fax 081 686 5706, telex 917241 MOTTAY G)

SWINBURN, Lt-Gen Sir Richard Hull; KCB (1991); s of Maj-Gen Henry Robinson Swinburn, CB, OBE, MC (d 1981), and N R (Barbara); bro, Brig D H A Swinburn, CBE, *qv*; *b* 30 Oct 1937; *Educ* Wellington, RMA Sandhurst; *m* 29 Aug 1964, Jane Elise, da of A B Brodie (ka 1942); *Career* cmmnd 1957, cmmnd 17/21 Lancers 1979-82, cmmnd 7 Armoured Bde 1983-85, GOC 1 Armoured Div 1987-89, Asst Chief of Gen Staff MOD 1989-; huntsman RMA Sandhurst Beagles 1956-57, master and huntsman Dheklia Draghounds 1971, memb Hampshire Hunt 1974-, master and huntsman Staff Coll Draghounds 1985-86, chm Army Beagling Assoc 1988-; *Recreations* hunting, lurchers; *Clubs* Cavalry and Guards; *Style—* Lt-Gen Sir Richard Swinburn, KCB; Ministry of Defence, Main Building, London SW1 (☎ 071 230 7191)

SWINBURNE, Prof Richard Granville; s of William Henry Swinburne, of Colchester, and Gladys Edith Swinburne (d 1988); *b* 26 Dec 1934; *Educ* Exeter Coll Oxford (BA, MA, BPhil); *m* 1960, Monica; 2 da (Caroline b 1961, Nicola b 1962); *Career* Fereday fell St Johns Coll Oxford 1958-61, Leverhulme res fell Leeds Univ 1961-63, lectr Hull Univ 1963-69 (sr lectr 1969-72), visiting assoc prof of philosophy Maryland Univ 1969-70, prof of philosophy Keele Univ 1972-84, Nolloth prof of philosophy of the Christian religion Oxford Univ 1985-; visiting lectureships: Wilde lectr Oxford Univ 1975-78, Marrett Meml lectr Exeter Coll Oxford 1980, Gifford lectr Aberdeen Univ 1982-83 and 1983-84, Edward Cadbury lectr Birmingham Univ 1987; distinguished visiting scholar Univ of Adelaide 1982, visiting prof of philosophy Syracuse Univ 1987; *Books* Space and Time (1968), The Concept of Miracle (1971), An Introduction to Confirmation Theory (1973), The Coherence of Theism (1977), The Existence of God (1979), Faith and Reason (1981), Personal Identity (with Sydney Shoemaker 1984), The Evolution of the Soul (1986), Responsibility and Atonement (1989); ed: The Justification of Induction (1974), Space, Time and Causality (1983), Miracles (1988); *Style—* Prof Richard Swinburne; Oriel College, Oxford OX1 4EW (☎ 0865 276 589)

SWINBURNE, Prof Terence Reginald; s of Reginald Swinburne, of Gravesend, Kent, and Gladys Hannah, *née* Shrusbsall; *b* 17 July 1936; *Educ* Kent Co GS for Boys Gravesend, Imp Coll of Sci and Technol Univ of London (BSc, PhD, DSc); *m* 23 Aug 1958, Valerie Mary, da of Daniel Parkes; 2 s (Julian Edward b 25 Sept 1965, Nigel David b 17 Jan 1968); *Career* reader Faculty of Agric Queens Univ of Belfast 1977 (joined 1960), sr princ sci offr Plant Pathology Res Div Dept of Agric NI 1979-80, head of Crop Protection Div E Malling Reo Station 1980-85, dir AFRC Inst of Hort Res 1985-; memb Br Mycological Soc, Assoc of Applied Biologists, Inst of Biol; FIHort; *Books* Iron, Siderophores and Plant Diseases; *Recreations* sailing; *Clubs* Farmers; *Style—* Prof Terence Swinburne; Tan House, Frog lane, West Malling, Kent (☎ 0732 846 090); AFRC Institute of Horticultural Research, Bradbourne House, East Malling, Kent (☎ 0732 843 833)

SWINDELLS, Maj-Gen (George) Michael Geoffrey; CB (1985); s of George Martyn Swindells (d 1960), and Marjorie, *née* Leigh (d 1991); *b* 15 Jan 1930; *Educ* Rugby; *m* 8 July 1955, Prudence Bridget Barbara, da of William Scarth Carlisle Tully, CBE (d 1987); 1 s (Adam b 1975), 2 da (Diana Harris b 1956, Georgina b 1961); *Career* cmmnd 5 Royal Inniskilling Dragoon Gds 1949, cmd 9/12 Royal Lancers 1968-71, Cdr 11 Armd Bde 1975-76, RCDS 1977, chief Jt Servs Liason Orgn Bonn 1980-83, dir Mgmnt and Support of Intelligence 1983-85, Col 9/12 Royal Lancers 1990-; controller Army Benevolent Fund 1987-; chm governing body Royal Sch Hampstead 1985-89, liaison Variety Club of GB; *Recreations* country life; *Clubs* Cavalry and Guards, Army & Navy; *Style—* Maj-Gen Michael Swindells, CB; Wilcot Lodge, Pewsey, Wilts; 41 Queen's Gate, London SW7 5HR (☎ 071 584 5232)

SWINDELLS, Robert; JP (Ashton-upon-Lyne 1977); s of William Swindells (d 1962), and Mary Alice Swindells; *b* 27 May 1928; *Educ* Glossop GS Derbys, John Dalton Coll of Technol Manchester; *m* 2 July 1965, Annette, da of Harold Greenwood, of Audenshaw, Manchester; 3 s (Jonathan b 13 March 1966, David b 12 June 1968, Christopher b 2 May 1970); *Career* fndr dir Berwin Rubber Co Ltd 1953, chm and md Berwin Polymer Processing Gp Ltd 1958-83; HM gen cmmr for income tax Oldham dist 1981; memb: Longdendale Footpath Preservation Soc, Masonic Club Ashton-upon-Lyne; FPRI 1979; *Recreations* music, wildlife, charities, travelling; *Clubs* Lancs Cricket, Country Gentlemans Assoc Travel; *Style—* Robert Swindells, Esq, JP; Minorca House, Hollingworth, via Hyde, Cheshire SK14 8HY (☎ 0457 62396)

SWINDEN, (Thomas) Alan; CBE (1971); s of Dr Thomas Swinden (d 1944), of Sheffield, and Ethel Taylor, *née* Thompson (d 1978); *b* 27 Aug 1915; *Educ* Rydal Sch, Univ of Sheffield (BEng); *m* 21 June 1941, Brenda Elise, da of Frederick John Roe (d 1961), of Epsom; 1 da (Gail b 1950); *Career* Rolls Royce Ltd 1937-55 (seconded armd fighting vehicle div Miny of Supply 1941-45); dir: Engrg Employers Fedn 1964-65 (joined 1955), Engrg Indust Trg Bd 1965-70, dep dir-gen CBI 1970-78, chm Inst Manpower Studies 1977-86, dir Kingston Regnl Mgmnt Centre 1980-84; memb: Cncl ACAS 1974-84, Consultative Gp on Industl and Business Affrs BBC 1977-83; chm Derby No 1 Hosp Mgmnt Ctee 1953-55, chm govrs N E Surrey Coll Technol 1986- (govr 1973-); *Recreations* gardening, golf, reading; *Clubs* RAC; *Style—* Alan Swinden, Esq, CBE; 85 College Rd, Epsom, Surrey KT17 4HH (☎ 03727 720848)

SWINDLEHURST, Alison Jean; da of Michael James Swindlehurst, of 71 Harewood Ave, Boscombe, Bournemouth, and Jean, *née* Pierce; *b* 10 Aug 1970; *Educ* Avonbourne Sch for Girls Bournemouth; *Career* hockey player; Bournemouth and Parkstone Club 1985-90, Clifton Club 1990-, Dorset sr 1989-90 (under 16 and under 18 1985-88), West sr 1989-90 (under 21 1988-89), 2 GB caps Wellington NZ 1990; England: under 21 1988-90 (played at first Jr World Cup Ottowa 1989), sr B 1989-90, 3 full caps Aberdeen 1990; gym instructor Burlington Sports & Health Club 1986-88, cashier Tesco 1990-; runner-up Dorset sports personality of the year 1990; *Recreations* keeping fit, listening to music, all sports; *Style—* Miss Alison Swindlehurst; Apartment A, Preston Court, 44 Windsor Rd, Penarth, South Glamorgan CF6 1JJ; c/o Mrs Sue Slocombe, 2 Coombeside, Folleigh Lane, Long Ashton, Bristol (☎ 0222 220221)

SWINDLEHURST, Rt Rev Owen Francis; s of late Francis Swindlehurst, and late Ellen, *née* Woods; *b* 10 May 1928; *Educ* Ushaw Coll Durham, Gregorian Univ Rome (PhL, STL, DCL); *Career* ordained priest 1954; curate: St Matthew's Ponteland 1959-69, St Bede's Newcastle 1969-73; parish priest Holy Name Newcastle 1973-78, appointed auxiliary bishop of Hexham and Newcastle Diocese and ordained bishop 1977; *Recreations* reading, geriatric squash, walking; *Style—* The Rt Rev Owen Swindlehurst; Oaklea, Tunstall Rd, Sunderland SR2 7JR (☎ 091 514 1158)

SWINDON, Archdeacon of; *see*: Clark, Ven Kenneth James

SWINEY, Col David Alexander; s of Maj Gen Sir Neville Swiney KBE, CB, MC, ADC (d 1970), of Bourton-on-the-Water, Glos, and Ena Margery Le Poer, *née* Power (d 1975); *b* 22 Jan 1924; *Educ* Cheltenham Coll, ASC Camberley, Joint Services Staff Coll Latimer; *m* 9 Sept 1950, Hazel Anne Elisabeth, da of Col Arthur Joynes, MC (d 1978), of Frinton-on-Sea; 1 s (Michael b 1951), 2 da (Amanda b 1954, Tessa b 1958); *Career* WWII cmmnd RA, Lt 75 Anti-Tank Regt NW Europe 1944-45, 8 Field Regt India 1945-46 (despatches 1945), pilot trg UK 1946-47, Capt 651 AOP Sqdn RAF (Palestine, Jordan, Tripoli, Egypt) 1947-50, Instr Mons OCS 1951-54, Adj 37 Regt Malta 1956-58, Maj staff of Dir Ops Cyprus 1958-60, 2 i/c 36 Guided Weapons Regt 1960-62 Germany, planning staff HQ BAOR Germany 1963-65, Lt-Col CO Lovat Scouts Scotland 1965-67, staff naval C in C Plymouth 1967-69, Col Ops Plans and Logistics HQ FARELF Singapore 1969-71, trng staff UKLF 1972-74, MOD 1975-78; admin Glos Red Cross, co-ordinator Glos Co Jt Emergency Exec Ctee, chm Bourton Hosp Friends; pres Bourton Vale CC; MBIM; *Recreations* shooting, fishing, history, Cotswold churches; *Clubs* MCC, Lansdowne; *Style—* Col David Swiney; Nethercote House, Bourton-on-the-Water, Glos GL54 2DT (☎ 0451 20354)

SWINFEN, Averil, Baroness Swinfen; Averil Kathleen Suzanne; da of late Maj William Marshall Hickman Humphreys and formerly w of Lt-Col Andrew Knowles, TD; *m* 1950, as his 2 w, 2 Baron (d 1977); *Style—* The Rt Hon Averil, Lady Swinfen; Keentlea, Clifden, Corofin, Co Clare, Ireland

SWINFEN, 3 Baron (UK 1919); Roger Mynors Swinfen Eady; s of 2 Baron (d 1977), and Mary Aline, da of late Col Harold Mynors Farmar, CMG, DSO; *b* 14 Dec 1938; *Educ* Westminster, RMA Sandhurst; *m* 24 Oct 1962, Patricia Anne, o da of Frank D Blackmore (d 1968), of Dublin; 1 s, 3 da (Hon Georgina b 1964, Hon Katherine b 1966, Hon Arabella b 1969); *Heir* s, Hon Charles Roger Peregrine Swinfen Eady b 8 March 1971; *Career* Lt Royal Scots; memb Direct Mail Services Standard Bd 1983-; ARICS 1970-; chm Parly Gp Video Enquiry Working Party 1983-85; JP (Kent) 1983-86; Fell Indust and Parly Tst 1983; pres SE Region - Br Sports Assoc for the Disabled 1986-; *Style—* The Rt Hon the Lord Swinfen; House of Lords, London SW1

SWINGLAND, Owen Merlin Webb; QC (1974); s of Charles Swingland (d 1941), of Kent, and Maggie Eveline , *née* Webb (d 1961); family moved from Worcestershire ca 1680 to parish of St Margaret Pattens, Eastcheap, London, lived in Kent about 200 years; *b* 26 Sept 1919; *Educ* Haberdashers' Aske's, King's Coll London; *m* 1941, Kathleen Joan Eason, da of late Frederick William Parry; 1 s (Charles), 2 da (Diana, Carole); *Career* barr; bencher of Gray's Inn, gen cmmr of income tax; a church cmmr for England 1982-90; Master Worshipful Co of Haberdashers' 1987; memb Lincoln's Inn 1978; *Recreations* reading, music, theatre, gardening; *Style—* Owen Swingland, Esq, QC; Redwings House, Bayleys Hill, Weald, Sevenoaks, Kent (☎ 0732 451 667)

SWINGLEHURST, John James Hutton; s of Hutton Swinglehurst (d 1986), of Broadwell House, Market Lavington, Wilts, and Margaret Lascelles, *née* Reynolds (d 1989); *b* 27 Dec 1931; *Educ* St Bees Sch; *m* 1 (m dis), Hazel Anne, *née* Godfrey-Faussett; 2 s (Anthony b 25 Nov 1958, Richard b 21 Aug 1960); m 2, 4 Dec 1964, Patricia Maureen, da of Daniel John Bowen, of Bolnore, Cuckfield, Sussex; 1 s (Hutton b 28 July 1970); *Career* insur broker; dir: Sedgwick Overseas Investmts 1975-, Sedgwick Gp plc 1979-, Sedgwick Gp Africa Property Ltd 1982-, Sedgwick Ltd 1986-, Sedgwick Hldgs RV 1987-; chm Sedgwick Group Pension Scheme Trustees Limited 1990-; *Recreations* skiing, tennis, swimming, music; *Style—* John Swinglehurst, Esq; 26 Holland St, London W8 (☎ 071 937 1995); Sedgwick Gp plc, Sedgwick House, The Sedgwick Centre, London E1 8DX (☎ 071 377 3138, fax 071 377 3292, car 0836 224 043, telex 882131)

SWINGLER, Raymond John Peter; s of Raymond Joseph Swingler (d 1942), of Christchurch, NZ, and Mary Elizabeth, *née* Alexander (d 1975); *b* 8 Oct 1933; *Educ* St Thomas's Acad Oamaru NZ, St Bede's Coll Christchurch NZ, Univ of Canterbury NZ; *m* 11 July 1960, Shirley (d 1980), da of Frederick Wilkinson (d 1962), of Plymouth; 2 da (Elisabeth-Jane b 1 July 1961, Claire-Louise b 6 Oct 1963); *Career* journalist: The Press (NZ) 1956-57, Marlborough Express 1957-59, Nelson Mail 1959-61, freelance Middle East 1961-62, Cambridge Evening News 1962-79; memb: Press Cncl 1975-78, Press Cncl Complaints Ctee 1976-78, Nat Exec Cncl NUJ 1973-75 and 1978-79, Prov Newspapers Indust Cncl 1976-79; chm Gen Purposes Ctee 1974-75, sec Press Cncl 1980-89 (asst dir 1989-90), asst dir The Press Complaints Cmmn 1991-; *Recreations* travel; *Style—* Raymond Swingler, Esq; The Press Complaints Commission, No 1 Salisbury Square, London EC4Y 8AE (☎ 071 353 1248, fax 071 353 8355)

SWINLEY, Margaret Albinia Joanna; OBE (1980); da of Capt Casper Silas Balfour Swinley, DSO, DSC, RN (d 1983), and Sylvia Jocosa, *née* Carnegie; *b* 30 Sept 1935; *Educ* Southover Manor Sch Lewes Sussex, Univ of Edinburgh (MA); *Career* English teacher/sec United Paper Mills Ltd Jämsänkoski Finland 1958-60; joined Br Cncl 1960: Birmingham Area Office 1960-63, Tel Aviv 1963, Lagos 1963-66; seconded to London HQ of VSO 1966-67, New Delhi 1967-70, dep rep Lagos 1970-73, dir Tech Cooperation Trg Dept 1973-76, rep Israel 1976-80, asst (later dep) controller Educn Med & Sci Div 1980-82; controller: Africa and Middle East Divn 1982-86, Home Div 1986-89; memb Soroptimist Int of Greater London (pres 1988-89), tstee Lloyd Fndn, advsr overseas projects and memb Overseas Ctee Help The Aged; govr: Westbury-on-Severn C of E Primary Sch (chm 1990-), Int Students House London, Hosting for Overseas Students; *Recreations* theatre going, country life, keeping dogs and shire horses; *Clubs* Cwlth Tst, Soroptimist Int of Greater London; *Style—* Miss M A J Swinley, OBE

SWINNERTON, Col Iain Spencer; TD, JP, DL (W Midlands 1976); s of James Percy Swinnerton (d 1977), and Lilian, *née* Spencer (d 1935); *b* 23 April 1932; *Educ* King Edward VI Sch Stourbridge, RMA Sandhurst; *m* 1958, Angela, da of Maurice Bent Sellers; 1 s, 2 da; *Career* proprietor The Swinford Press; magistrate Worcs 1972-; sr vice pres and chm of cncl Birmingham & Midland Inst 1987-; govr: King Edwards Sch

1976-88, The Royal Sch Wolverhampton 1987-; div pres St John Ambulance 1977-85; pres Birmingham & Midland Soc for genealogy and Heraldry 1972-, chm Br Fedn of Family History Socs 1974-77 (pres 1978-), tstee Inst of Heraldic and Geneological Studies 1977-88 (Gold Medal 1977), fell Soc of Genealogists 1975; *Publications* A History of the Worcestershire Artillery, Heraldry can be Fun, also many papers on genealogy and heraldry; *Recreations* genealogy, heraldry, travel; *Clubs* Army and Navy, Old Edwardian; *Style*— Col Iain Swinnerton, TD, JP, DL; Owls Barn, Bridgnorth Rd, Stourton, nr Stourbridge, W Midlands DY7 6RS (☎ 0384 872717)

SWINNERTON-DYER; *see*: Dyer

SWINSON, Christopher; s of Arthur Montagu Swinson, of 52 Green Moor Link, Winchmore Hill, London, and Jean, *née* Dudley; *b* 27 Jan 1948; *Educ* Wadham Coll Oxford (BA, MA); *m* 9 Sept 1972, Christine Margaret, da of Walter Yeats Hallam (d 1973); 1 s (Timothy b 1987); *Career* mangr Price Waterhouse 1970-78, nat manging ptnr Binder Hamlyn 1989- (sr mangr 1978-81, ptnr 1981-); memb Cncl and chm Fin Reporting and Auditing Gp ICEAW, hon treas Naval Records Soc; Freeman City of London 1985, memb Worshipful Co of CAs; FCA 1974; *Clubs* Athenaeum; *Style*— Christopher Swinson, Esq; 2 Seymour Close, Hatch End, Pinner, Middx; BDO Binder Hamlyn, 20 Old Bailey, London EC4M 7BH (☎ 071 489 6261, fax 071 489 6281)

SWINSON, Sir John Henry Alan; OBE (1973); s of Edward Alexander Swinson (d 1944), of Knock, Belfast, and Mary Margaret, *née* McLeod (d 1966); *b* 12 July 1922; *Educ* Royal Belfast Acad Inst; *m* 1944, da of John Gallagher (d 1958), of Castlereagh, Belfast; 2 s (Alan, Peter); *Career* commercial dir Ireland Trusthouse Forte plc 1962-; dir various subsid cos; chm: NI Tourist Bd 1980-88 (memb 1970-80), Livestock Mktg Cmmn 1970-85, Catering Indust Trg Bd (NI) 1966-75, NI Trg Exec 1975-83; kt 1984; *Recreations* sailing; *Clubs* Royal NI Yacht; *Style*— Sir John H A Swinson, OBE; 10 Circular Road East, Cultra, Co Down BT18 0HA, N Ireland (☎ 02317 2494); c/o Trusthouse Forte plc, Conway Hotel, Dunmurry, Belfast BT17 9ES (☎ 0232 612101)

SWINSON, Margaret Anne; da of John Godfrey Ball, of Bewdley, Worcs, and Pamela Margaret, *née* Moody; *b* 16 Dec 1957; *Educ* Alice Ottley Sch Worcester, Univ of Liverpool (BA); *m* 5 Sept 1981, Michael Albert Swinson, s of Albert Henry Swinson, of Macclesfield, Cheshire; 1 s (Thomas), 1 da (Rebecca); *Career* self employed account and tax practitioner and music teacher; memb Gen Synod of C of E, tstee Church Urban Fund; treas Liverpool Family Serv Unit and Crossfire Festivals; ACA 1981, ATII 1983; *Recreations* music; *Style*— Mrs Margaret Swinson

SWINTON, 2 Earl of (UK 1955); David Yarburgh Cunliffe-Lister; JP (N Yorks 1971), DL (1978); also Viscount Swinton (UK 1935), Baron Masham (UK 1955); s of late Maj the Hon John Yarburgh Cunliffe-Lister, eldest s of 1 Earl, GBE, CH, MC, MP; suc gf 1972; *b* 21 March 1937; *Educ* Winchester, RAC Cirencester; *m* 1959, Susan Lilian Primrose (Baroness Masham of Ilton, *qv*), da of late Sir Ronald Norman John Charles Udny Sinclair, 8 Bt (cr 1704); 1 s, 1 da (both adopted); *Heir* bro, Hon Nicholas Cunliffe-Lister; *Career* sits as Cons in House of Lords, Capt HM's Body Guard of Yeomen of the Guard (dep govt chief whip in Lords) 1982-86; ccnllr: N Riding Yorks 1961-74, N Yorks 1973-77; countryside cmmr 1987-; *Clubs* White's, Leyburn Market; *Style*— The Rt Hon the Earl of Swinton, JP DL; Dykes Hill House, Masham, N Yorks (☎ 0765 689241); 46 Westminster Gdns, Marsham St, London SW1 (☎ 071 834 0700)

SWINTON, Maj-Gen Sir John; KCVO (1979), OBE (1969), JP (Berwicks 1989); the family of Swinton of that Ilk, now represented by the Kimmerghame branch, has owned land in the Swinton area of Berwickshire since the eleventh century; s of Brig A H C Swinton, MC (d 1972), of Kimmerghame, Duns, Berwicks, and Mrs I D Erskine, of Swinton, Berwickshire; *b* 21 April 1925; *Educ* Harrow; *m* 1954, Judith Balfour, da of Harold Killen, of Merribee, NSW; 3 s, 1 da; *Career* served Scots Gds 1943-71, Lt-Col 1970-71, cmd 4 Gds Armd Bde 1972-73, Brig Lowlands 1975-76, GOC London Dist and Maj-Gen i/c The Household Div 1976-79, ret 1979; Brig Royal Co of Archers Queen's Body Guard for Scotland, Hon Col 2 Bn 52 Lowland Volunteers 1983-90; nat chm Royal Br Legion Scotland 1986-89 (vice chm 1984-86); chm: Berwickshire Civic Soc 1982-, Scottish Ex-Serv Charitable Orgns SESCO 1988-89; tstee: Scottish Nat War Meml 1984- (vice-chm 1988-), Army Museums Ogilby Tst 1978-90, Royal Br Legion Scotland Housing Assoc; memb Centl Advsy Ctee on War Pensions 1986-89, chm Thirlestane Castle Tst 1984-90; Lord Lt Berwicks 1989- (DL 1980-89); *Clubs* New (Edinburgh), Pratt's; *Style*— Maj-Gen Sir John Swinton, KCVO, OBE, JP; Kimmerghame, Duns, Berwicks TD11 3LU (☎ 0361 83277)

SWINTON OF THAT ILK, John Walter (Jack); s of Liulf Swinton of that Ilk (d 1977), of Henderson, Nevada, USA, and Alice Gertrude Kidney (d 1977); suc f as Chief of the Name of Swinton 1977; *b* 6 Oct 1934; *Educ* Montana State Univ (BArch); *m* 1956, Marlene Louise, da of Charles Herbert Wakelen (d 1976), of Lethbridge, Alberta; 1 s (Rolfe b 1971); *Heir* s, Rolfe William Swinton, b 1970; *Career* princ and pres Swinton Architects Ltd; *Recreations* skiing, fishing, tennis; *Clubs* Rotary West Calgary, Calgary Burns; *Style*— John Swinton of that Ilk; 123 Superior Ave SW, Calgary, Alberta T3C 2H8, Canada (☎ 403 245 3631); 5917 - 1A Street SW, Calgary, Alberta, Canada T2H 0G4 (☎ AC 403 255 1125)

SWIRE, Sir Adrian Christopher; yr s of John Kidston Swire, DL (d 1983), of Hubbards Hall, Old Harlow, Essex, by his w Juliet Richenda (d 1981), da of Charles Barclay, bro of Sir John A Swire, CBE, *qv*; *b* 15 Feb 1932; *Educ* Eton, Univ Coll Oxford (MA); *m* 1970, Lady Judith, *qv*; 2 s, 1 da; *Career* Nat Service Coldstream Gds 1950-52, RAFVR and Royal Hong Kong AAF 1953-61; joined Butterfield & Swire Far East 1956; John Swire & Son Ltd: dir 1961, dep chm 1966, chm 1987; dir: Swire Pacific, Cathay Pacific Airways, Brooke Bond Gp 1972-82; NAAFI 1972-86; pres Gen Cncl of Br Shipping 1980-81, chm Int Chamber of Shipping 1982-87; memb: Gen Ctee Lloyd's Register, London Advsy Ctee Hong Kong and Shanghai Banking Corp 1990-; visiting fell Nuffield Coll Oxford 1981-89; Hon Air Cdre RAuxAF, trustee RAF Museum 1983-; DL (Oxon) 1989; Elder Brother Trinity House 1990; *Clubs* White's, Brooks's, Pratt's; *Style*— Sir Adrian Swire; John Swire & Sons Ltd, Swire House, 59 Buckingham Gate, London SW1E 6AJ (☎ 071 834 7717)

SWIRE, Hugo George William; s of Humphrey Roger Swire, and Philippa Sophia, *née* Montgomerie; *b* 30 Nov 1959; *Educ* St Aubyn's Rottingdean, Eton, Univ of St Andrews, RMA Sandhurst; *Career* Lt 1 Bn Grenadier Guards 1980-83; head Nat Gallery Tst 1988-; *Clubs* Pratt's; *Style*— Hugo Swire, Esq; 4 Beechmore Rd, London SW11 (☎ 071 627 3237); The National Gallery, Trafalgar Square, London WC2N 5DN (☎ 071 839 3321)

SWIRE, Sir John Anthony; CBE (1977); s of John Kidston Swire (d 1983); bro of Sir Adrian Swire, *qv*; *b* 1927; *Educ* Eton, Univ Coll Oxford; *m* 1961, Moira Ducharne; 2 s, 1 da; *Career* served Irish Gds (UK and Palestine) 1945-48; joined Butterfield & Swire Hong Kong 1950; John Swire & Sons Ltd: joined 1955, chm 1966-87, hon pres and exec dir 1987-; former dir: Royal Insurance Co, British Bank of the Middle East, Ocean Transport & Trading Ltd; dir James Finlay & Co plc 1976-; memb: London Advsy Ctee Hongkong and Shanghai Banking Corpn 1969-89, Euro-Asia Centre Advsy Bd 1980-, Advsy Cncl Sch of Business Stanford Univ 1981-90; memb Cncl Univ of Kent 1989; hon fell St Antony's & Univs Colls Oxford; Hon DL Hong Kong 1989; kt 1990; *Style*— Sir John Swire, CBE; Luton House, Selling, nr Faversham, Kent; John Swire & Sons Ltd, Swire House, 59 Buckingham Gate, London SW1E 6AJ (☎ 071 834 7717)

SWIRE, Lady Judith; *née* Compton; er da of 6 Marquess of Northampton, DSO (d 1978), and his 2 w, Virginia, da of Col David Heaton, DSO; *b* 26 Sept 1943; *Educ* RCM, London Univ; *m* 1970, Sir Adrian Swire, *qv*; 2 s, 1 da; *Style*— The Lady Judith Swire; 59 Buckingham Gate, London SW1E 6AJ

SWIRE, Rhoderick Martin; s of Patrick Douglas Swire, (d 1960), of Shropshire, and Joan Mary, *née* Allison (d 1970); *b* 27 March 1951; *Educ* Eton, Univ of Birmingham (BSc); *m* 11 June 1977, Georgina Mary, da of Christopher Ronald Thompson, qv, of Shropshire; 1 s (Hugh b 1979), 2 da (Henrietta b 1981, Camilla b 1985); *Career* Peat Marwick Mitchell 1972-76; John Swire & Sons Ltd 1976-81: gp accountant Hong Kong 1976-79, asst to chm Aust 1979-81, London 1981; GT Mgmnt plc: mangr unquoted investmt 1981-88, dir main bd 1987; md GT Venture Mgmnt Hldgs; FCA 1980 (ACA 1975); *Recreations* shooting, tennis, gardening; *Clubs* Boodles; *Style*— Rhoderick Swire, Esq; Aldenham Park, Bridgnorth, Shropshire; 43/44 Albemarle St, London W1X 3FF (☎ 071 493 5685, fax 071 629 0844)

SWISS, Sir Rodney Geoffrey; OBE (1964), JP (Middlesex 1949); s of Henry Herbert Swiss (d 1958), of Devonport, Devon; *b* 4 Aug 1904; *Educ* Plymouth Coll, Dean Close Sch Cheltenham, Guy's Hosp; *m* 1928, Muriel Alberta Gledhill (d 1985); *Career* dental surgn, pres Br Dental Assoc 1971-, pres Gen Dental Cncl 1974-79; FDSRCS; kt 1975; *Style*— Sir Rodney Swiss, OBE, JP; Shrublands, 23 West Way, Pinner, Middx (01 866 0621)

SWITHENBANK, Prof Joshua (Jim); s of Joshua Swithenbank (d 1971), and Ethel Eva, *née* Foster; *b* 19 Oct 1931; *Educ* Friend's Sch Wigton Cumberland, Univ of Birmingham (BSc), Univ of Sheffield (PhD); *m* 29 March 1958, Margaret Elizabeth Anderson, da of Rev James Herbert Manson; 1 s (Joshua Ross b 11 July 1962), 3 da (Elizabeth b 7 May 1960, Christine b 28 March 1965, Shirley Joyce b 20 May 1966); *Career* engr Res and Devpt Dept Rolls Royce Ltd 1953-58, engr Design Dept Canadair 1958, assoc prof Mechanical Engrg 1958-61, prof Dept of Mechanical and Process Engrg Univ of Sheffield 1961-; author of over 100 articles in scientific jls and books; fndr memb Watt Ctee on Energy Ltd 1975-, memb ACORD 1988-90, gen superintendent res Int Flame Res Fndn 1989-91; memb: American Inst of Chemical Engrg, American Inst of Astronautics and Areonautics; FEng 1978, FInstE (pres 1987-88), FIChemE; *Recreations* scuba diving, photography, travel; *Clubs* British Sub Aqua, Athenaeum; *Style*— Prof Jim Swithenbank; Department of Mechanical and Process Engineering, Sheffield University, Western Bank, Sheffield S10 2TN (☎ 0742 768555 ext 5342)

SWORD, Robert Arthur Hallifax; s of James Michael Sword, JP, and Diana Dominica *née* Hallifax; *b* 16 May 1952; *Educ* Southern Highlands Sch Tanzania, St Edmunds Sch Hindhead Surrey, Bradfield Coll Reading Berks, RAC Cirencester Glos; *m* 22 July 1978, Rosemary, da of Richard Arthur Bedford-Payne, of Grassington, N Yorks; 2 s (Edmund James Bedford b 1984, Sam Richard b 1986); *Career* chartered surveyor and land agent; ptnr Humberts (Yorks) 1983-; memb Co of the Merchants of the Staple of Eng, fell Agric Assoc of Valuers; FRICS; *Recreations* shooting, gardening; *Clubs* York's, Farmers'; *Style*— Robert Sword, Esq; Wood Cottage, Scackleton, Hovingham, York YO6 4NB (☎ 0653 628 304); Humberts, 37 Mickelgate, York YO1 1JH (☎ 0904 611828)

SWORN, Dr Michael John; s of Ernest James Sworn (d 1942), and Clarice, *née* Heath; *b* 12 April 1942; *Educ* All Saint's Sch Bloxham, London Hosp Med Coll, Univ of London (MB BS, LLB); *m* 9 Sept 1967, Bridget Mary, da of John Shanahan, of Somerville, New Jersey, USA; 1 da (Sarah Louise b 1973); *Career* jr lectr in morbid anatomy Inst of Pathology The London Hosp 1967-69, sr registrar in morbid anatomy United Sheffield Hosps 1969-70, lectr in pathology Univ of Sheffield 1970-73, conslt pathologist The Royal Hampshire Co Hosp 1974-, examiner for the primary fellowship RCS 1983-89, examiner in pathology The Examining Bd England 1983-89; memb: Pathological Soc 1972, Assoc Clinical Pathologists 1973, Br Soc Clinical Cytology 1975; asst sec then sec Winchester Div BMA 1976-82, liaison offr Assoc of Clinical Pathologists for Winchester 1983-; MRCS, LRCP, FRCPath; *Recreations* golf; *Style*— Dr Michael Sworn; Barncliffe, 28 Chilbolton Ave, Winchester, Hants SO22 5HD (☎ 0962 853558); Royal Hampshire County Hospital, Romsey Rd, Winchester, Hants SO22 5DG (☎ 0962 63535)

SWYNNERTON, Sir Roger John Massy; CMG (1959), OBE (1951), MC (1941); s of Charles Francis Massy Swynnerton, CMG (d 1938), and Norah Aimee Geraldine Smyth (d 1963); *b* 16 Jan 1911; *Educ* Lancing, Gonville and Caius Cambridge (BA, Dip Agric), Imperial Coll of Tropical Agric Trinidad (AICTA); *m* 1943, Grizel Beryl, da of Ralph William Richardson Miller, CMG (d 1958), of Lushoto, Tanganyika; 2 s (John, Charles); *Career* 2 Lt OC CUOTC Artillery Batty 1932-33, TARO 1933-60, served with 1/6 KAR (Kenya, Italian Somaliland, Abyssinia) 1939-42, temp Capt Colonial Agric Serv Tanganyika 1934-51, seconded to agric duties Malta 1942-43, Kenya 1951-63 (asst dir of agric 1951, dep 1954, dir 1956-60, perm sec Miny of Agric 1960-62, temp min 1961, MLC 1956-61, ret 1963); memb Advsy Ctee on Devpt of Economic Resources of Southern Rhodesia 1961-62, agric advsr and memb Exec Mgmnt Bd Cwlth Devpt Corpn 1962-76, self-employed conslt in tropical agric and devpt 1976-85; dir Booker Agriculture International Ltd 1976-88; Univ of Southampton: visiting lectr 1977-88, memb Advsy Bd on Irrigation Studies 1980-88; pres Swynnerton Family Soc 1982-, Tropical Agric Assoc 1983-89; kt 1976; *Publications* All About KNCU Coffee (1948), A Plan to Intensify the Development of African Agriculture in Kenya (1954); *Clubs* Royal Overseas League, Royal Cwlth Soc; *Style*— Sir Roger Swynnerton, CMG, OBE, MC; Cherry House, 2 Vincent Rd, Stoke D'Abernon, Cobham, Surrey KT11 3JB

SYBORN, Victor Jack; s of Arthur Robert Syborn (d 1974), and Alice, *née* Coles (d 1979); *b* 18 July 1920; *Educ* Ealing Coll; *m* 1 April 1950, Patricia Eveleen, da of Harold Blomeley (d 1972); 1 s (Philip Charles b 7 Aug 1954), 1 da (Veronica Frances b 22 Aug 1956); *Career* Army 1941-47: cmmnd 5 Regt 1943, seconded RM 1944 (Normandy Landing), serv 5 Regt RHA and 7 Armd Div 1944-46, Air Liaison Offr 2 Gp RAF 1946-47; TA 1947-54; princ Syborn & Atkinson Chartered Architects 1951-88; Freeman City of London 1975, Liveryman Worshipful Co of Gardeners 1975; ARIBA 1951, FRIBA 1964; *Recreations* travel, sailing; *Clubs* RAC, Royal Lymington Yacht; *Style*— Victor Syborn, Esq; The Shepherd's House, The Sands, Farnham, Surrey GU10 1JN (☎ 02518 2080); Syborn & Atkinson, 4 Pratt Walk, London SE11 6AR (☎ 071 735 2071, fax 071 735 9799)

SYCAMORE, Phillip; s of Frank Sycamore, of Lancaster, Lancs, and Evelyn Martin, *née* Burley; *b* 9 March 1951; *Educ* Lancaster Royal GS, Univ of London (LLB); *m* 22 June 1974, Sandra, da of Peter Frederick Cooper (d 1986), of Morecambe, Lancs; 2 s (Thomas b 1980, Jonathan b 1983), 1 da (Hannah b 1978); *Career* admitted slr 1975; ptnr with Lonsdale slrs Blackpool Lancs; memb The Law Soc Remuneration and Practice Devpt Ctee; *Clubs* Royal Lytham and St Annes Golf; *Style*— Phillip Sycamore, Esq; 213 Clifton Drive South, Lytham St Annes (☎ 0253 728532); 342 Lytham Road, South Shore, Blackpool, Lancs (☎ 0253 45258, fax 0253 48943)

SYDENHAM, Colin Peter; s of Herbert Willmott Sydenham (d 1975), of Croydon, Surrey, and Veronica Margery, *née* Denny (d 1988); *b* 13 Dec 1937; *Educ* Eton, King's Coll Cambridge (BA); *m* 15 Sept 1964, (Priscilla) Angela, da of Anthony

Tannett, of Aldeburgh, Suffolk; 2 s (Simon b 1 Jan 1967, Rupert b 16 July 1968), 1 da (Katharine b 9 July 1969); *Career* Nat Serv RA 1956-58 (2 Lt 1958); called to the Bar 1963, pt/t chm of industl tbnls 1975-81; memb: Br Chess Problem Soc (memb Ctee 1976, vice-pres 1986, pres 1989-90), Horatian Soc (hon sec 1980-); *Recreations* chess problems, mediaeval sculpture, dinghy sailing; *Clubs* MCC; *Style*— Colin Sydenham, Esq; 4 Stone Buildings, Lincolns Inn, London WC2A 3XT (☎ 071 242 5524, fax 071 831 7907, telex 892300)

SYKES, Allen; s of Jack Sykes, of Slaithewaite, Yorks, and Dorothy, *née* Main (d 1956); *b* 26 Dec 1931; *Educ* Texas Country Day Sch Dallas, Selhurst GS, LSE (BSc); *m* 17 Jan 1959, Dorothy June, da of Wilfred Hugh Moore (d 1982), of Sutton, Surrey; 1 s (Jeremy Jonathan Nicholas b 1961), 1 da (Caroline Emma Jane b 1964); *Career* cmmnd Sub Lt Exec Branch Nat Serv 1953-55, Lt RNVR 1951-65; economist and mgmnt trainee Econs Dept Unilever 1955-60, head project evaluation RTZ 1960-70, md RTZ Devpt Enterprises (in charge of Channel Tunnel Project for RTZ and Br Channel Tunnel Co) 1970-72; dir Willis Faber plc 1972-86: advsr to govts, banks, utilities, mining and oil cos on major int projects, non exec positions 1986-; md Consolidated Gold Fields plc 1986-89 (responsible for devpt Br and part of N America, advsr then non-exec dir 1972-86), promoter of several maj int technol projects 1989-; dir Willis Carroon plc, Lawson Mardon Group Ltd; fndr and memb Cncl Br Major Projects Assoc 1981- (fndr Canadian Assoc 1984); *Publications* Finance & Analysis of Capital Projects (with A J Merrett, 1963 and 1972), Housing Finance 1965 (with A J Merrett), Successful Accomplishment of Giant Projects (1979), Privatise Coal (with Colin Robinson, 1987), Current Choices - Ways to Privatise Electricity (with Colin Robinson, 1987), Corporate Takeovers - The Need for Fundamental Rethinking (1990); *Recreations* tennis, chess, opera; *Clubs* ESU, Gresham, RAC; *Style*— Allen Sykes, Esq; Mallington, 29 The Mount, Leatherhead, Surrey KT22 9EB (☎ 0372 375851, fax 0372 362693)

SYKES, Audrey, Lady; Audrey Winifred; da of Frederick Thompson, of Cricklewood; *m* 1935, Sir Hugh Sykes, 2 Bt (d 1974); *Style*— Audrey, Lady Sykes; 19 Bouverie Gdns, Harrow, Middx

SYKES, Bonar Hugh Charles; s of Maj-Gen Rt Hon Sir Frederick Sykes, GCSI, GCIE, GBE, KCB, CMG (d 1954), and Isabel Harrington, *née* Law (d 1969), da of Rt Hon Andrew Bonar Law; *b* 20 Dec 1922; *Educ* Eton, Queen's Coll Oxford (MA); *m* 28 Sept 1949, Mary, da of Rt Hon Sir Eric Phipps, GCB, GCMG, GCVO (d 1945); 4 s (Hugh b 1950, David b 1953, James b 1956, Alan b 1960); *Career* Lt RNVR 1942-46; trainee Tractor Div Ford Motor Co 1948-49; Dip Serv 1949-69: second sec Prague 1951, second sec (later first sec) Bonn 1953-57, first sec (later cnsllr) Tehran 1961-65, cnsllr Ottawa 1966-68; farming in Wilts 1969-; tstee Wilts Archaeological & Nat History Soc (pres 1975-85); cncl memb: Area Museums Cncl for SW 1975-86, Museums Assoc 1981-84; memb bd of visitors Erlestoke Prison 1977-87 (chm 1983-85); High Sheriff Wiltshire 1988-89; FSA 1985; *Style*— Bonar Sykes, Esq, FSA; Conock Manor, Devizes, Wiltshire (☎ 0380 84 227)

SYKES, David Michael; s of Michael le Gallais Sykes (d 1981; yr s of Capt Stanley Edgar Sykes, who was yr s of Sir Charles Sykes, 1 Bt, KBE), and his 1 w, Joan, *née* Groome; hp of unc, Sir John Charles Anthony le Gallais Sykes, 3 Bt; *b* 10 June 1954; *m* 1974 (m dis 1987), Susan Elizabeth, 3 da of G W Hall; 1 s (Stephen David b 1978); m 2, 1987, Margaret Lynne, da of J T McGreavy; 1 da (Joanna Lauren b 1986); *Style*— David Sykes Esq; The Chestnuts, Middle Lane, Nether Broughton, Leics LE14 3HD

SYKES, Dr Elizabeth Ann Bowen; da of Sir Francis Godfrey Sykes, Bt (d 1990), and Eira Betty, *née* Badcock (d 1970); *b* 17 Sept 1936; *Educ* Howell's Sch Denbigh, Bedford Coll London (BSc, MSc), Univ of Edinburgh (PhD); *Career* res staff Nat Inst of Industl Psychology 1959-62, res assoc Dept of Psychological Med Univ of Edinburgh 1962-65, lectr Dept of Psychology Univ Coll of N Wales 1965-74; Middx Poly: sr lectr in psychology 1974-86, princ lectr 1986-90, reader 1990-, acting head School of Psychology 1991-92; Univ Coll London: hon res fell Dept of Pharmacology 1977-79, hon res fell Dept of Psychology Psychopharmacology Gp 1979-; articles on psychopharmacology, physical exercise and mental health in learned jls; memb Assoc for Study of Animal Behaviour 1963, sci fell Zoological Soc of London 1975, memb Br Assoc for Psychopharmacology 1978, fndr memb European Behavioural Pharmacology Soc 1986, assoc fell Br Psychological Soc 1988, C Psychol 1990; *Style*— Dr Elizabeth Sykes; 19 Torriano Cottages, off Leighton Rd, London NW5 2TA; School of Psychology, Middx Polytechnic, Queensway, Enfield, Middx EN3 4SF (☎ 081 368 1299, fax 081 805 0702)

SYKES, Eric; OBE; s of Vernon Sykes, and Harriet Sykes; *b* 4 May 1923; *m* 14 Feb 1952, Edith Eleanore, da of Bruno Milbradt; 1 s (David Kurt b 2 June 1959), 3 da (Katherine Lee b 6 Sept 1952, Susan Jane b 20 Sep 1953, Julie Louise b 2 July 1958); *Career* wireless operator mobile signals unit RAF 1941-47; comic actor, writer and dir; varied TV and film career (20 feature films); numerous TV appearances incl writing and lead role Sykes Show for 20 years; silent film writer and dir: The Plank (V), Rhubarb, Mr H is Late; Freeman City of London; *Recreations* golf; *Clubs* Royal and Ancient Golf; *Style*— Eric Sykes, Esq, OBE; 9 Orme Court, Bayswater, London W2 (☎ 071 727 1544)

SYKES, Gerard William; s of William Joshua Sykes (d 1987), and Dorothy Lily, *née* Freeman; *b* 3 Dec 1944; *Educ* Sir Roger Manwoods Sandwich Kent; *m* 1974, Rosalind Mary Louise, da of S Peter Meneaugh; *Career* articled clerk Percy Gore & Co Margate, qualified chartered accountant 1966 mangr Hurdman and Cranstoun 1968-71 ptnr Thornton Baker (now Grant Thornton) 1973- (int mangr 1971-73); Freeman City of London 1977; ACA 1966; *Recreations* vintage cars, skiing; *Clubs* RAC; *Style*— Gerard Sykes, Esq; Grant Thornton, Grant Thornton House, Melton St, Euston Square, London NW1 2EP (☎ 071 383 5100)

SYKES, Sir (Francis) John Badcock; 10 Bt (GB 1781), of Basildon, Berks; o s of Sir Francis Godfrey Sykes, 9 Bt (d 1990), and his 1 w, Eira Betty, *née* Badcock (d 1970); *b* 7 June 1942; *Educ* Shrewsbury, Worcester Coll Oxford (MA); *m* 1966, Susan Alexandra, da of Adm of the Fleet Sir Edward Ashmore, GCB, DSC, by his w Elizabeth, da of Sir Lionel Sturdee, 2 and last Bt, CBE; 3 s (Francis Charles b 1968, Edward William b 1970, Alexander Henry Ashmore b 1974); *Heir* s, Francis Charles Sykes b 1968; *Career* slr 1968, ptnr in legal firm of Townsends, Swindon and Newbury; *Style*— Sir John Sykes, Bt; Kingsbury Croft, Kingsbury St, Marlborough, Wilts SN8 1HU (☎ 0672 512115)

SYKES, Dr John Bradbury; s of Stanley William Sykes (d 1961), of Margate, and Eleanor, *née* Bradbury (d 1967); *b* 26 Jan 1929; *Educ* Wallasey GS, Rochdale HS, St Lawrence Coll, Univ of Oxford (MA, DPhil); *m* 1955 (m dis 1988); 1 s (Steven); *Career* lexicographer, translator; head of translations office AERE Harwell 1958-71; ed Concise and Pocket Oxford Dictionaries 1971-81, head German Dictionaries OUP 1981-89, gen ed Shorter Oxford English Dictionary 1989-; memb Translators' Guild, 1960-88 (chm 1984-88); fell: Inst of Linguists 1960-86, Inst of Translation and Interpreting (chm 1986-); Hon DLitt City Univ 1984; *Recreations* crosswords (Times national champion 1972-75, 1977, 1980, 1983, 1985, 1989, 1990); *Clubs* Pen; *Style*— Dr John Sykes; 68 Woodstock Close, Oxford OX2 8DD (☎ 0865 57532); Oxford University Press, Walton Street, Oxford OX2 6DP (☎ 0865 56767)

SYKES, Sir John Charles Anthony le Gallais; 3 Bt (UK 1921), of Kingsknowes, Galashiels, Co Selkirk; s of Capt Stanley Sykes (yr s of Sir Charles Sykes, 1 Bt, KBE, JP, MP Huddersfield) and Florence Anaïse, da of François le Gallais, of Jersey; suc unc, Sir Hugh Sykes, 2 Bt, 1974; *b* 19 April 1928; *Educ* Churchers' Coll; *m* 1954 (m dis 1969), Aitha Isobel, da of Lionel Dean, of Huddersfield; *Heir* nephew, David Sykes; *Career* gen export merchant; *Recreations* wine, food, travel, bridge; *Style*— Sir John Sykes, Bt; 58 Alders View Drive, E Grinstead, W Sussex RH19 2DN (☎ 0342 322027); Sir John Sykes and Co, PO Box 200, East Grinstead, W Sussex RH19 2YN

SYKES, (John) Keith; *b* 5 Feb 1933; *Educ* Wrekin Coll, Univ of Leeds, Grays Inn; *m* 1958, Undine, *née* Hodgetts; 1 s, 4 da; *Career* chm Keith Ceramic Materials Ltd; dir: Television South West plc, CPA Holdings Ltd, Ferro (GB) Ltd, British Ceramic Research Ltd; *Recreations* fishing; *Style*— J Keith Sykes, Esq; Keith Ceramic Materials Ltd, Fishers Way, Crabtree Manor Way, Belvedere, Kent

SYKES, Prof (Malcolm) Keith; s of Prof Joseph Sykes, OBE, (d 1967), and Phyllis Mary Sykes (d 1972); *b* 13 Sept 1925; *Educ* Magdalene Coll Cambridge (MA, MB BChir), Univ Coll Hosp London (DA); *m* 14 Jan 1956, Michelle June, da of William Ewart Ratcliffe (d 1951); 1 s (Jonathan b 1964), 3 da (Karen b 1957, Virginia b 1958, Susan b 1967); *Career* cmmnd RAMC 1950-52, Capt, served BAOR; prof of clinical anaesthesia Royal Post Graduate Med Sch London 1970-80 (lectr, sr lectr then reader 1958-70); Nuffield prof of anaesthetics and fell Pembroke Coll Oxford 1980-; Rickman Godlee travelling scholar and fell in anaesthetics Massachusetts Gen Hosp Boston USA 1954-55; pres Section of Anaesthetics Royal Soc of Med 1989-90; vice pres Assoc of Anaesthetists 1990-92, former vice pres and senator Euro Acad of Anaesthesiology; FFARCS (Hon FFARACS 1978), Hon FFA (SA) 1989; memb: BMA, RSM; *Books* Respiratory Failure (1965, 1976), Principles of Measurement for Anaesthetists (1970), Principles of Clinical Measurement (1981), Principles of Clinical Measurement and Monitoring (1991); *Recreations* walking, sailing, birdwatching, gardening; *Style*— Prof Keith Sykes; 10 Fitzherbert Close, Iffley, Oxford OX4 4EN (☎ 0865 771152); Radcliffe Infirmary, Woodstock Rd, Oxford OX2 6HE 0865 311188)

SYKES, Hon Mrs (Laura Catherine); *née* James; er da of Baron Saint Brides, GCMG, CVO, MBE, PC (Life Peer, d 1989), and his 1 w, Elizabeth Margaret Roper, *née* Piesse (d 1966); *b* 1948; *Educ* Univ of Sussex (BA); *m* 1981, Robert Lacy Tatton Sykes, s of Geoffrey Sykes, of Kirribilli, NSW, Australia; *Style*— The Hon Mrs Sykes; 6 Hans Cres, London SW1X OLJ (☎ 071 589 6463)

SYKES, Lady; Norah; da of J E Staton, of Clowne; *m* 1930, Sir Charles Sykes, CBE, FRS, FInstP, DSc, PhD, DMe, sometime chm Firth Brown Ltd and pro-chllr Sheffield Univ (d 1982); 1 s (Howard), 1 da (Patricia); *Style*— Lady Sykes; Upholme, Blackamoor Crescent, Dore, Sheffield

SYKES, Lady Pauline Anne; *née* Ogilvie-Grant; da of Countess of Seafield (12 in line), and Derek Studley-Herbert (who assumed by deed poll additional surnames of Ogilvie-Grant); *b* 1944; *m* 1, 1964 (m dis 1970), James Henry Harcourt Illingworth (whose sis m 1, Earl of Seafield, *qv*); m 2, 1972 (m dis 1976), Sir William Gordon Cumming, 6 Bt; m 3, 1976, Hugh Richard Sykes; 1 s; *Style*— Lady Pauline Sykes; Revack Lodge, Grantown-on-Spey, Morayshire

SYKES, Phillip Rodney; s of Sir Richard Adam Sykes, KCMG, MC (d 1979), and Lady Ann Georgina, *née* Fisher; *b* 17 March 1955; *Educ* Winchester, Ch Ch Oxford (MA); *m* 26 June 1982, Caroline Frances Gordon Sykes, da of Michael Dawson Miller, of 52 Scarsdale Villas, London W8; 2 s (Richard b 1985, Christopher b 1988); *Career* ptnr BDO Binder Hamlyn 1986- (joined 1976), seconded fin services section Nat West Bank plc 1985-86; ACA 1986; *Recreations* field sports, tennis, reading, theatre; *Style*— Phillip Sykes, Esq; BDO Binder Hamlyn, 20 Old Bailey, London EC4M 7BH (☎ 071 489 9000, telex 24276)

SYKES, Dr Richard Brook; *b* 7 Aug 1942; *Educ* Royds Hall GS Huddersfield, Paddington Tech Coll, Chelsea Coll, Queen Elizabeth Coll Univ of London, Bristol Univ; *Career* head Antibiotic Res Unit Glaxo Research UK 1972-77; The Squibb Inst for Med Res: asst dir Dept of Microbiology 1977-79, dir Dept of Microbiology 1979-83, assoc dir 1981-86, vice pres Infectious Diseases and Metabolic Diseases 1983-86; chm and chief exec Glaxo Group Research Ltd 1987- (dep chief exec 1986), res and devpt dir Glaxo Holdings plc 1987-; chm Dev of Antimicrobial Chemotherapy American Soc of Microbiology 1985-86; memb Ed Bds of various jls; visiting prof King's Coll London; author of numerous scientific articles and lecture papers; *Style*— Dr Richard Sykes; Glaxo Holdings plc, Lansdowne House, Berkeley Square, London W1X 6BP (☎ 081 422 3434, fax 081 966 4277)

SYKES, Richard Hugh; s of John George Sykes (d 1971), of York, and Dorothy Eleanor Chamberlin, *née* Chilman; *b* 11 April 1943; *Educ* Winchester, Trinity Coll Oxford (scholar, MA); *m* 26 April 1969, Linda, da of Richard Saxby-Soffe; 2 s (Thomas Richard b 1 April 1971, John Nicholas b 1 Jan 1975), 1 da (Eleanor Mary b 30 Sept 1977); *Career* teacher St Joseph's Coll Chidya in Masasi Diocese Tanzania 1964-65; Allen & Overy: articled clerk, asst slr 1969-74, ptnr 1974-; memb Co of Merchant Adventurers of City of York; memb: Law Soc, City of London Solicitors Co; *Recreations* reading, walking; *Clubs* Brooks's; *Style*— Richard Sykes, Esq; Allen & Overy, 9 Cheapside, London EC2V 6AD (☎ 071 248 9898, fax 071 236 2192)

SYKES, (James) Richard; QC (1981); s of Philip James Sykes (d 1985), and Lucy Barbara, *née* Cowper (d 1981); *b* 28 May 1934; *Educ* Charterhouse, Pembroke Coll Cambridge (MA); *m* 27 Aug 1959, Susan Ethne Patricia, da of Lt Col Joan Manchester Allen (ka 1941); 1 s (Christopher James b 1965), 3 da (Annabel Mary b 1961, Camilla Jane b 1963, Rosemary Anne b 1969); *Career* RASC 1952-54, 2 Lt 1953; called to the Bar Lincoln's Inn 1958, bencher Lincoln's Inn 1989; memb: Law Soc Standing Ctee on Co Law 1973-, City Co Law Ctee 1974-79, City Capital Markets Ctee 1980-, Mgmnt Ctee International Exhibition Cooperative Society Ltd 1986-, Exec Ctee VSO 1987-; chm Judging Panel: Accountants and Stock Exchange Annual Awards 1982-89, Int Stock Exchange and Inst of Chartered Accountants Annual Awards for Published Accounts 1990-; *Books* Gore-Browne on Companies (conslt ed, 42 edn 1972, 43 edn 1977, 44 edn 1986), The Conduct of Meetings (jt ed, 20 edn 1966, 21 edn 1975); *Style*— Richard Sykes, Esq, QC; Erskine Chambers, 30 Lincoln's Inn Fields, London WCA 3PF (☎ 071 242 5532, fax 071 831 0125)

SYKES, Roger Ian; s of Arthur Sykes, and Ada, *née* Thompson (d 1937); *b* 9 Jan 1935; *Educ* King James' Almondbury, Huddersfield, City & Guilds Coll, Imperial Coll of Sci and Technol London (BSc); *m* 12 Oct 1957, Sheenagh Anne, da of Charles Harold Barry, CBE, of Alderley Edge, Cheshire; 1 s (Christopher Shaun Franklin b 1958), 2 da (Jennifer Anne b 1959, Fiona Carole b 1962); *Career* Nat Serv Pilot Univ of London Air Sqdn 1954-56; Bristol Aeroplane Co: tech engr of aerodynamics 1957-59, section ldr flight trails performance 1959-64, mangr flight trials assessment 1964-66, hd of systems analysis 1966-71; hd of mgmnt servs Br Air Corpn (GW) Bristol 1971-86, divnl computor systems mangr (naval and electronic systems div) 1986-87, hd of mgmnt servs Br Aerospace (dynamics) Ltd Bristol; chm W England Br Interplanetary Soc; CEng, ACGI, FBIS, FRAeS; *Recreations* miniature steam locomotives, music (guitar and keyboards), art; *Clubs* BSMEE; *Style*— Roger Sykes, Esq; Cloisters, Manor Way, Failand, Bristol BS8 3UY (☎ 0272 393800); British Aerospace (Dynamics) Ltd, PO Box 5, Filton, Bristol BS12 7QF (☎ 0272 693831, fax 0272 692055, telex 449452)

SYKES, Maj Roy Forester; TD (1950 and clasp), DL (Northants 1983); s of Lt-Col Vincent Harold Sykes (d 1976), and Olive Annie Louise, *née* Webb (d 1966); *b* 29 July 1916; *Educ* The Leys Sch, Emmanuel Coll Cambridge (MA, LLM); *m* 1947, Pamela Anne Mary, da of Wing-Cdr Arthur Leslie Horrell (d 1981); 3 da (Carolyn, Diana, Judith); *Career* cmmnd 5 Bn Northamptonshire Regt TA 1934, served WW II Maj UK & NI, TARO 1948-66; admitted slr 1946-; clerk to the Justices of Oundle-Thrapston Courts 1957-74; diocesan reader C of E 1949-, Archbishop's diploma 1958; Northants co pres Royal Br Legion 1976-; E Midlands area pres Royal Br Legion 1982-83 and 1987-88; *Recreations* game shooting, history, gardening; *Style—* Maj Roy Sykes, TD, DL; Tavern Cottage, Aldwincle, Kettering, Northants

SYKES, Sir Tatton Christopher Mark; 8 Bt (GB 1783), of Sledmere, Yorkshire; s of Lt-Col Sir (Mark Tatton) Richard Tatton-Sykes, 7 Bt (d 1978; assumed additional surname of Tatton by deed poll 1977, discontinued at his demise); *b* 24 Dec 1943; *Educ* Eton, Université d'Aix Marseilles, RAC Cirencester; *Heir* bro, Jeremy John Sykes; *Clubs* Brooks's; *Style—* Sir Tatton Sykes, Bt; Sledmere, Driffield, Yorkshire

SYLVESTER, Timothy Oliver; s of Oliver Andrew Sylvester (d 1980), of Cedar Lodge, Lambridge, Bath, and Grace Dorothy (Jane), *née* Biggs; *b* 11 Sept 1946; *Educ* King Edwards GS Bath, Univ of Sheffield (BA); *Career* currently sr ptnr Sylvester Groves & Co (having formed practice 1975), dir and chm Queen Sq Admin Ltd 1983, dir and exec vice pres Renewable Resources Inc USA 1983, chm and dir Sylvester Groves Properties 1984; dir: QSA (Malaysia) Ltd 1988, Dawes Coatings Ltd 1988; sec The Palladium Tst 1980, treas Assoc of Old Edwardians Bath; IOD 1980, FCA 1981 (ACA 1975), memb FIMBRA; *Recreations* clay pigeon shooting, squash, travelling; *Style—* Timothy Sylvester, Esq; 15 Queen Sq, Bath BA1 1EG (☎ 0225 464551, fax 0225 444687)

SYLVESTER BRADLEY, Hon Mrs (Elizabeth Mary Jean); *née* Annesley; eldest da of 14 Viscount Valentia, MC; *b* 6 May 1926; *m* 1948, Maj James Terence Ralphe Sylvester Bradley (d 1987), s of late Lt-Col Charles Reginald Sylvester Bradley, of the Manor House, Langton Herring, Dorset; 1 s (Charles b 1959), 3 da (Fiona b 1949, Heather b 1951, Catherine b 1957); *Style—* The Hon Mrs Sylvester Bradley; Knighton Manor, Durweston, Blandford, Dorset

SYME, Dr James; s of James Wilson Syme (d 1988), of Edinburgh, and Christina Kay, *née* Marshall; *b* 25 Aug 1930; *Educ* Beath HS, Univ of Edinburgh (MB ChB); *m* 15 Dec 1956, Mary Pamela, da of Peter McCormick (d 1957), of Bolton, Lancs; 1 s (Peter James b 1959), 1 da (Victoria Claire b 1961); *Career* Capt RAMC in W Africa 1955-57; conslt paediatrician Edinburgh 1965- hon sr lectr Univ of Edinburgh 1965-, author of articles in med pres and textbooks; vice pres RCPE(d) 1985-89 (cncl memb 1976-81), chm and memb of several ctees and working parties of med profession; FRCPE 1968 (memb 1958), FRCPG 1978; *Books* approx 30 articles in medical press, including three contributions to textbooks; *Recreations* walking, church history and architecture; *Clubs* New (Edinburgh); *Style—* Dr James Syme; 13 Succoth Park, Edinburgh EH12 6BX (☎ 031 337 6069); 17 Riverside Walk, Airton by Skipton, N Yorks BD23 4AF (☎ 07293 568); Medical Paediatric Unit, Western General Hospital, Edinburgh (☎ 031 332 2525)

SYMES, Dr David Millman; s of Henry Millman Symes (d 1978), and Harvey Gwendoline, *née* Davies (d 1975); *b* 20 June 1936; *Educ* Hove Co GS, St Mary's Hosp London, Univ of London (MB BS, MRCS, LRCP); *m* (m dis) Jose Ann Symes; 2 da (Kathryn Ann b 6 June 1960, Tiffany Jane b 19 Sept 1964); *Career* princ and sr ptnr gen practice 1960-, visiting MO Morgan Crucible Co 1961-62, MO Columbia Pictures 1964, ship surgn Blue Star Line 1965, euro med conslt Whittaker Int 1976-84; med advsr: John Brown Engrg 1978-83, Tate & Lyle Group 1982-90; examining med practitioner DHSS 1978-; yacht master (ocean) 1982; Chevalier De L'Ordre de Coteaux de Champagne 1988, Freeman City of London 1971, Liveryman Worshipful Soc of Apothecaries 1972; memb: Soc Occupational Med 1983, BMA 1990, Br Medical Acupuncture Soc 1990; *Recreations* tennis, sailing; *Clubs* Cruising Assoc, Wimbledon Westside Tennis, Royal Yachting Assoc, Emsworth Slipper Sailing, City Livery Yacht; *Style—* Dr David Symes; 3 Ditton Reach, Thames Ditton, Surrey KT7 OXB (☎ 081 398 0958); 138 Harley St, London W1; Tate & Lyle plc, Lower Thames St, London EC3 (☎ 071 935 0054)

SYMES, Prof Martin Spencer; s of Oliver Edward Symes, of Juniper Cottage, Burcombe, Sailsbury, Wilts, and Beatrice Mary, *née* Spencer; *b* 19 Aug 1941; *Educ* Dauntsey's Sch, Cambridge Univ (BA, MA, DipArch), Architectural Assoc (PlanDip), Univ of London (PhD); *m* 23 June 1964, Valerie Joy, da of Harold James Willcox (d 1979); 1 s (Benedick b 1967), 1 da (Francesca b 1971); *Career* architectural asst: London CC 1963, Eero Saarinen Assocs 1964, Yorke Rosenberg Mardall 1965-67; architect Arup Assocs 1968-73, conslt Duffy Eley Giffone Worthington 1975-82, visiting fell Princeton Univ 1980, sr lectr UCL 1983-89 (lectr 1973-83), res fell of Melbourne 1985, prof Univ of Manchester 1989 visiting prof Tokyo Univ 1990; sec IAPS Int Assoc for the Study of People and their Physical Suroundings 1984-88, chm RIBA Professional Literature Ctee 1988-; memb RIBA 1967; *Books* Architects Journal Handbook on the Reuse of Redundant Industrial Buildings (jt ed, 1978), Journal of Architectural and Planning Research (jt ed, 1984); *Style—* Prof Martin Symes; 27 Corner Green, Blackheath, London SE3 9JJ (☎ 071 852 6834); British Gas Chair of Urban Renewal, School of Architecture, The University, Manchester M13 9PL (☎ 061 275 6912)

SYMINGTON, Prof Sir Thomas; s of James Symington (d 1919), of Muirkirk, Ayrshire, and Margaret Steven Symington (d 1967); *b* 1 April 1915; *Educ* Cumnock Acad, Glasgow Univ (BSc, MB ChB, MD); *m* 1943, Esther Margaret, da of John Forsyth, of Viewfield Farm, Bellshill (d 1951); 1 s (and 1 s decd), 1 da; *Career* Maj RAMC, served Malaya 1947-49; prof of Pathology Univ of Glasgow 1954-70, prof of Pathology Univ of London 1971-77, dir Inst of Cancer Res Royal Cancer Hosp London 1970-77; visiting prof of Pathology Stanford Univ 1965-67; Hon Dr of Med Szeged Univ Hungary (1971), Hon DSc McGill Univ Canada 1983; kt 1978; *Recreations* golf, gardening; *Clubs* Roy Troon Golf; *Style—* Prof Sir Thomas Symington; Greenbriar, 2 Lady Margaret Drive, Troon KA10 7AL (☎ 315 707)

SYMON, Prof Lindsay; TD (1967); s of William Lindsay Symon (d 1972), of Innellan, Argyllshire, and Isabel, *née* Shaw (d 1967); *b* 4 Nov 1929; *Educ* Aberdeen GS, Univ of Aberdeen (MB ChB); *m* 14 Aug 1953, Pauline Barbara, da of William Rowland (d 1970), of Liverpool; 1 s (Lindsay b 17 March 1955), 2 da (Barbara Rosemary b 6 July 1956, Fiona Margaret b 12 May 1959); *Career* Capt RAMC 1953-55, Maj RAMC TA 1955-69; prof of neurological surgery, sr neurological surgn Nat Hosp for Nervous Diseases Queen Square and Maida Vale; hon conslt neurological surgn: St Thomas' Hosp, Hammersmith Hosp, Royal Nat Nose Throat and Ear Hosp; civilian advsr in neurological surgery to the RN 1979-, chief ed Advances and Technical Standards in Neurosurgery; pres World Fedn of Neurosurgical Socs 1989; Freeman City of London 1982; FRCSEd 1957, FRCS 1959; *Books* Operative Surgery (Neurosurgery) (1989); *Recreations* golf; *Clubs* Caledonian, Royal and Ancient, Rye, South Herts, Tidworth; *Style—* Prof Lindsay Symon, TD; The National Hospital, Queen Square, London WC1N 3BG (☎ 071 278 1091, fax 071 278 5069)

SYMONDS, Kenneth Thomas; s of Percival Harold Symonds (d 1980), and Gladys Symonds (d 1942); *b* 11 March 1928; *Educ* Queen Elizabeth's GS Barnet; *m* 11 March 1958, Gunvor, da of Rudolf Orre (d 1976); *Career* chm Gradus Ltd 1986- (md 1966-86); *Recreations* travel, cinema, theatre; *Style—* Kenneth Symonds, Esq; 27 Chapel Side, Moscow Rd, London W2 4LE (☎ 071 727 9296); Gradus Ltd, 298 Westbourne Grove, London W11 2PS (☎ 071 229 4352, fax 071 221 4466)

SYMONDS, Prof (Edwin) Malcolm; s of Edwin Joseph Truman Symonds, MBE (d 1985), of Adelaide, S Aust, and Eugene Mary Symonds; *b* 6 Nov 1934; *Educ* St Peter's Coll Adelaide, Univ of Adelaid (MB BS, MD); *m* 26 April 1958, (Beverley) Sue, da of Rex Bertram Martin, of Adelaide, S Aust; 4 s (Ian Martin b 1959, David Malcolm b 1963, Thomas Rex b 1967, Matthew Richard Edwin b 1973); *Career* sr registrar and clinical lectr Liverpool 1963-66, sr lectr and reader Univ of Adelaide 1967-71, fndn prof of obstetrics and gynaecology Univ of Nottingham 1972-; cmmr Cwlth Scholarships Cmmn, cncl memb RCOG; hon fell: American Gynaecological and Obstetrical Soc, Polish Gynaecological Soc, Hungarian Gynaecological Soc, Italian Perinatal Soc; former memb: Nottingham Dist Health Authy, Trent RHA; FRCOG; *Books* Hypertension in Pregancy (1985), Essential Obstetrics and Gynaecology (1986), In Vitro Fertilization Past, Present Future (1986), Chorion Villus Sampling (1987); *Recreations* cricket, golf, classical music and travel; *Style—* Prof Malcolm Symonds; Department of Obstetrics and Gynaecology, D Floor, East Block, University Hospital, Queen's Medical Centre, Nottingham NG7 2UH (☎ 0602 709240 fax 0602 709234)

SYMONDS, Dr Michael Anthony Edward; s of Edward Samuel Symonds (d 1983), of Chingford, London E4, and Marjorie Symonds (d 1960); *b* 1 April 1929; *Educ* Trent Coll Derbyshire, St Thomas's Hosp Med Sch; *m* 6 Nov 1957, Rowena, da of Fred Thornley (d 1980), of Walton-on-the-Naze, Essex; 2 s (William b 1958, James b 1961), 1 da (Joanna b 1964); *Career* house appts 1958-60, conslt physician in genito-urinary med City and Hackney Health Authy 1969-, conslt physician in genito-urinary med Herts and Essex Gen Hosp Bishops Stortford (also physician i/c) 1974-, hon conslt physician in genito-urinary med St Thomas's Hosp London 1976-, conslt advsr in genito-urinary med BUPA Med Centre London 1981-, physician i/c genito-urinary med Barts 1982-; convener to examiners in genito-urinary med Soc of Apothecaries of London 1987- (examiner 1980-); govr St Aubyn's Sch Woodford Green Essex 1982-; MRCP 1968, FRCP 1981; *Recreations* people, jogging, wine; *Clubs* RSM; *Style—* Dr Michael Symonds; 9 Beulah Rd, Epping, Essex CM16 6RH (☎ 0378 72614); 138 Harley St, London W1N 1AH (☎ 071 486 3979)

SYMONDS, Dr (Raymond) Paul; TD (1982); s of Raymond Symonds, of 1 Montgomery Rd, Barnard Castle, Co Durham, and Muriel May, *née* Smith; *b* 27 Dec 1948; *Educ* Univ of Newcastle (MB BS, MD); *m* 2 Aug 1975, Jennifer, da of Norman Willis, of 17 Newbridge Ave, Sunderland, Tyne and Wear; 1 s (Peter b 9 Aug 1977), 2 da (Catherine Sarah b 26 March 1980, Victoria Jane b 15 May 1985); *Career* Maj TA RAMC (vol) 1970-87; conslt in radiotherapy and oncology Beatson Oncology Centre Glasgow, visiting prof Hahnemann Med Coll Philadelphia Pa USA 1981; author of papers on head and neck and on gynaecological cancer; MRCP 1975, FRCR 1981, FRCP Glasg 1989; *Books* The Management of Bladder Cancer (contrib, 1988), Management of Cancer in the Elderly (contrib, 1990); *Recreations* walking, cycling, shortwave radio; *Style—* Dr Paul Symonds, TD; 1 Douglas Gardens, Bearsden, Glasgow G61 2SJ (☎ 041 942 4627); Beatson Oncology Centre, Western Infirmary, Glasgow G11 6NT (☎ 041 339 8822)

SYMONDS, (John) Richard (Charters); s of Air Vice-Marshal Sir Charles Symonds (d 1978), and Janet, *née* Poulton (d 1919); *b* 2 Oct 1918; *Educ* Rugby, Corpus Christi Coll Oxford (MA); *m* Ann Spokes; *Career* UN 1946-63, 1968-79; sr res offr Oxford Univ Inst of Cwltt Studies 1963-65, professorial fell Inst of Devpt Studies Univ of Sussex 1966-69, sr assoc memb St Anthony's Coll Oxford 1979-, hon dir UN Career Records Project 1989-; *Books* The Making of Pakistan (1950), The British and Their Successors (1966), International Targets of Development (with M Carder 1970), The United Nations and the Population Question (1973), Oxford and Empire (1986), Alternative Saints (1988); *Recreations* walking, travel; *Clubs* Royal Commonwealth Society; *Style—* Richard Symonds, Esq; 43 Davenham Rd, Oxford OX2 8BU (☎ 0865 515661)

SYMONS, Christopher John Maurice; QC (1989); s of Clifford Louis Symons, and Pamela Constance, *née* Vos; *b* 5 Feb 1949; *Educ* Clifton Coll, Univ of Kent (BA); *m* 13 July 1974, Susan Mary, da of Gordon Teichmann; 1 s (Nicholas b 1978), 1 da (Samantha b 1980); *Career* called to the Bar Middle Temple 1972; memb supplemental panel of Jr Counsel to The Crown (common law) 1982-85, called to the Gibraltar Bar 1985, Jr Counsel to The Crown Common Law 1985-89, called to the Irish Bar 1988, called to the Northern Ireland Bar 1990, asst rec 1990; *Recreations* hitting balls; *Clubs* Hurlingham, Roehampton, Sotogrande; *Style—* Christopher Symons, Esq, QC; 3 Gray's Inn Place, Gray's Inn, London WC1R 5EA (☎ 071 831 8441, fax 071 831 8479, telex 295119 LEXCOL G)

SYMONS, Dr John Charles; s of Dr Percy Symons (d 1969), of Reading, Berks, and Constance Mary, *née* Dyer (d 1982); *b* 13 May 1938; *Educ* Oratory Sch, Trinity Coll Cambridge (BA, MA), St Thomas' Med Sch (MB BChir); *m* 3 Aug 1968, Louisa Beverley McKenzie, da of Dr S G M Francis, of Sudbury, Suffolk; 1 s (James b 1977), 2 da (Emma b 1970, Rebecca b 1973); *Career* house offr: surgery (later med) Burton on Trent 1962-63, obstetrics St Thomas' Hosp 1963-64; sr house offr (later registrar) paediatrics Royal Berks Hosp 1964-67, paediatric specialist Corner Brook Newfoundland 1967-68, princ gen practice Wonersh Guildford 1968-69, med registrar Prospect Park Hosp Reading 1969-71; sr registrar: Jenny Lind Hosp Norwich 1971-73, Brompton Hosp 1973-75; conslt paediatrician Colchester 1975-, hon clinical tutor Guys Hosp Med Sch 1985-, dir Child Health Servs NE Essex District Health Authy 1990-; memb Colchester Med Soc 1975; chm: Colchester Action for Epilepsy, Colchester branch Liver Fndn; med advsr local branches Asthma Soc & Diabetic Assoc, aeromedical advsr St Johns, church warden Colchester, parish Cncllr Colchester; RCOG 1964, DCH 1967; memb: BMA 1962, Br Paediatric Assoc 1968; FRCP 1987 (MRCP 1971); *Recreations* game fishing, cricket; *Style—* Dr John Symons; Moors Farm, Assington, Suffolk CO6 5NE (☎ 0787 227 379); Colchester Gen Hosp, Turner Rd, Colchester, Essex (☎ 0206 853 853 535); Rooms: 29 Oaks Drive, Colchester

SYMONS, Julian Gustave; s of Morris Albert Symons (d 1929), and of Minnie Louise, *née* Bull (d 1963); *b* 30 May 1912; *m* 25 Oct 1941, Kathleen, da of Sydney Hatch Clark (d 1967); 1 s (Marcus Richard Julian b 1951), 1 da (Sarah Louise b 1948 d 1976); *Career* RAC 1942-44; freelance author; chm Crime Writers Assoc 1958-59, pres The Detection Club 1976-85, pres Conan Doyle Society 1989-; grand master: Mystery Writers of America 1982, Swedish Acad 1978; Crime Writers Assoc: Golden Dagger award 1957, Silver Dagger award 1960; Mystery Writers of America Edgar award 1960 and 1963, Cartier Diamond Dagger award 1990; FRSL 1976; *Books* incl: The Colour of Murder (1957), The Progress of a Crime (1960), Bloody Murder (1972); *Recreations* walking in cities; *Clubs* Detection; *Style—* Julian Symons, Esq; Groton House, 330 Dover Rd, Walmer, Deal, Kent CT14 7NX (☎ 0304 365209)

SYMONS, Prof Leslie John; *b* 8 Nov 1926; *Educ* London Sch of Economics and Political Sci (BSc), Queens Univ of Belfast (PhD); *m* 24 March 1954, Gloria Lola Colville; 2 da (Alison b 28 Feb 1956, Jennifer b 16 Oct 1962); *Career* asst and lectr Queens Univ of Belfast 1953-62; Univ of Canterbury New Zealand: visiting lectr 1960, sr lectr 1962-70; Simon sr res fell Univ of Manchester 1967-68; Univ Coll of Swansea:

sr lectr, reader, prof of geography 1970-; *Books* Land Use in Northern Ireland (ed, 1963), Agricultural Geography (1967), Northern Ireland, A Geographical Introduction (with L Hanna, 1967 and 1978), Russian Agriculture, A Geographical Survey (1972), Russian Transport, An Historical and Geographical Survey (ed with C White, 1975), The Soviet Union, A Systematic Geography (ed, 1982 and 1990), Soviet and East European Transport Problems (ed with J Ambler and D Shaw, 1985), Transport and Economic Development, Soviet Union and Eastern Europe (ed with J Ambler and J Tismer, 1987); *Recreations* mountain walking, flying, landscape painting; *Style—* Prof Leslie Symons; Squirrels' Jump, 17 Wychwood Close, Langland, Swansea SA3 4PH (☎ 0792 369675); Ard Tigh An T'Sruthain, Laggan Bridge, Newtonmore, Invernessshire; Dept of Geography, University Coll of Swansea, Swansea SA2 8PP (☎ 0792 295231, fax 0792 205556, telex 48358)

SYMONS, Prof Martyn Christian Raymond; s of Stephen White Symons (d 1972), and Marjorie, *née* Le Brassuer (d 1958); *b* 12 Nov 1925; *Educ* John Fisher Sch Purley Surrey, Battersea Poly London (BSc, PhD, DSc); *m* 1, Joy Lendon (d 1963); 1 s (Richard b 1957), 1 da (Susan b 1954); m 2, 12 Jan 1972, Janice (Jan) Olive, da of George O'Connor; *Career* Army 1946-49, Actg Capt 1948; lectr in chemistry Battersea Poly 1949-53, lectr in organic chemistry Univ of Southampton 1953-60, prof of physical chemistry Univ of Leicester 1960-89, res prof of chemistry and dir Career Res Campaign Electric Spin Resonance Gp Univ of Leicester; author of 2 books and over 900 original sci papers; FRSC 1949, FRSA 1965, FRS 1985; *Recreations* water colour painting, piano playing; *Style—* Prof Martyn Symons, FRS; 144 Victoria Park Rd, Leicester LE2 1XD (☎ 0533 700 314); Dept of Chemistry, The University, Leicester (☎ 0533 522 141, fax 0533 522 200, telex LIECWL 341198)

SYMONS, Michael John; s of Kenneth Francis Symons, and Aileen Joyce, *née* Winship (d 1972); *b* 23 Nov 1947; *Educ* Sir William Borlase's Sch Marlow Bucks, Trinity Coll Cambridge (MA); *m* 10 Dec 1974, Gwendoline Winifred Symons; *Career* gp fin dir Ridgeon Gp; FCA, MCT; *Recreations* athletics, making money; *Style—* Michael Symons, Esq; Cyril Ridgeon & Son Ltd, Tenison Rd, Cambridge CB1 2DS (☎ 0223 467467)

SYMONS, Patrick Stewart; s of Norman Holding Symons (d 1977), of East Dean, Sussex, and Nora, *née* Westlake (d 1934); *b* 24 Oct 1925; *Educ* Bryanston, Camberwell Sch of Arts and Crafts; *Career* artist; visiting teacher Chelsea Sch of Art 1977-85 (i/c fndn course 1960-77), teacher Camberwell and St Albans Schs of Art 1953-59; exhibitions: New Art Centre 1960, William Darby Gallery 1975-76, Browse and Darby 1982 and 1989; Major Works: Wimbledon Oaks (Doncaster Museum), Oak Arch Grey Wimbledon Common (Tate), Mary Iliffs Viola played by Electric Light and Drawn by Gas Light (David Workman, Connecticut), Beech Elder and Nettles (Browse and Darby); winner: jt first prize Tolly Cobbold 1981, prize for drawing New English Art Club 1987, RA Summer Show Wollaston award 1990; ARA 1983; *Recreations* botany, mathematics; *Style—* Patrick Symons, Esq; 20 Grove Hill Rd, Camberwell, London SE5 8DG (☎ 071 274 2373); Browse and Darby, 19 Cork St, London W1X 2LP (☎ 071 734 7984)

SYNGE, Sir Robert Carson; 8 Bt (UK 1801), of Kiltrough; s of late Neale Hutchinson Synge and n of 7 Bt (d 1942); *b* 4 May 1922; *m* 1944, Dorothy Jean, da of Theodore Johnson, of Cloverdale, BC, Canada; 2 da; *Heir* cousin, Neale Francis Synge, b 28 Feb 1917; *Style—* Sir Robert Synge, Bt; 19364 Fraser Valley Highway, RR4 Langley, BC, Canada

SYPNIEWSKI, Ferdinand-Josef Volpier; s of Joseph-Ferdinand Sypniewski, of Theodor Kocher Strasse 11, CH 2502 Bienne, and Lieselotte Elsa Maria, *née* Gaebisch; *b* 15 Jan 1956; *Educ* Int Sch Walterswil Baar, Coll Saint Michel Fribourg Switzerland, Universite de Fribourg (DipTheol), Dartmouth Coll Hanover NH USA; *Career* pp cnllr US Army Munich 1977-81; co fndr: Hanover Music Festival, Rollins Chapel Organ Recitals Hanover New Hampshire USA 1984-85; dir Volpier Designs 1985-89, procurement and contract admin Goldman Sachs Int Ltd 1989-; Hospitaller OStJ; *Books* Whistling to the Tune (1983); *Recreations* hiking, writing, collecting oddities; *Clubs* London House; *Style—* Chevalier Ferdinand Sypniewski

SYRUS, David; s of William Henry Syrus (d 1978), and Amie Sills (d 1987); *b* 13 Oct 1946; *Educ* Hastings GS, Queen's Coll Oxford (MA); *m* 27 July 1972, Lorna, da of Stanley Miller, of Kinross, Scotland; 2 s (Daniel b 15 Jan 1976, Oliver b 25 May 1977), 1 da (Emma b 30 July 1979); *Career* music staff Royal Opera House 1971-81 (head 1981), asst conducter Bayreuth Festival 1977-84, accompanist Carnegie Hall 1985 (also London, Montreal, Paris, Vienna), continuo player (Monte Carlo, Munich, London, Paris, Cologne, Frankfurt); conducter 'Ariadne auf Naxos' Royal Opera House 1985, world premieres of 'Tailor of Gloucester' and 'Pig Organ', British premieres of 'The Boy Who Grew Too Fast' (Menotti) and 'Pollicino' (Henze); recordings for EMI Phonogram and TV; *Recreations* swimming, walking, reading; *Style—* David Syrus, Esq; 95 Alric Avenue, New Malden, Surrey KT3 4JP (☎ 081 949 2432); Royal Opera House, London WC2 (☎ 071 240 1200)

SYSON, William Watson Cockburn (Bill); s of William Cockburn Syson (d 1939), of Edinburgh, and Mary Jane, *née* Watson (d 1983); *b* 12 Sept 1930; *Educ* Broughton; *Career* Nat Serv Army 1949-51, TA 1951-58; joined Bank of Scotland 1947, sr managerial positions Edinburgh 1969-81, chief mangr head off 1981-90, asst gen mangr 1987-90; chm Bank of Scotland Edinburgh & District Mangrs and Officials Circle 1978; dir: Great Western Resources Inc 1990-, The British Real Estate Group plc 1990-, First International Leasing Corporation Ltd 1990-, Resent Investment Trust Ltd 1991-; chm City Site Estates plc 1991-; former lectr Heriot Watt Coll and Univ, former examiner and moderator Inst of Bankers Scotland; world sen jr Chamber Int 1970, sr vice-pres Edinburgh and Midlothian Bn Boys' Bde 1970-90 (actg pres 1987-88), chm City Centre Christian Outreach 1981-82; hon treas: East of Scotland branch Br Red Cross 1974-82 (memb Scottish Fin Ctee 1976-81), Scottish branch Soldiers Sailors and Airmen's Families Assoc 1974-82, Victoria League Scotland 1969-75, Scottish Churches Architectural Heritage Tst 1980-84; treas and memb Cncl The Prince Tst East of Scotland and Borders Area 1978-84; FIB Scot 1979 (memb 1954); *Books* Interpretation of Balance Sheets (1957), Sources of Finance (1973), Forestry (1985); *Recreations* art, music, reading, hill walking, sport; *Clubs* New (Edinburgh), Cronies, Edinburgh Academicals Sports; *Style—* Bill Syson, Esq; 27 Succoth Park, Edinburgh EH12 6BX (☎ 031 337 1321)

SYSONBY, 3 Baron (UK 1935); John Frederick Ponsonby; s of 2 Baron, DSO (d 1956); *b* 5 Aug 1945; *Heir* none; *Style—* The Rt Hon the Lord Sysonby; c/o Friars, Whitefriars, Chester

SZPIRO, Richard David; s of George Szpiro of Belgrave Place, London, and Halina Szpiro; *b* 11 Aug 1944; *Educ* St Paul's Sch, Churchill Coll Cambridge (MA); *m* annulled; 2 s (Toby b 1971, Jamie b 1973); *Career* merchant banker; md: Wintrust plc 1969-, Wintrust Securities plc; *Recreations* golf, tennis; *Clubs* Mark's, Hurlingham; *Style—* Richard Szpiro, Esq; 15 Holland Park Ave, London W11 (☎ 071 236 2360)

T

TABERNER, Michael John; s of Ernest Taberner, and Una, *née* Dean; *b* 5 June 1950; *Educ* King Henry VIII Sch Coventry, Oxford Univ (MA); *m* 9 Oct 1976, Siobain Mary, da of Donald Gillespie Macnab; 1 s (Richard James Philip b 1983), 1 da (Sarah Alexandra b 1987); *Career* slr; admitted to Law Soc 1974, ptnr Angel & Co Coventry 1980; govr St Thomas More's Sch Coventry, tstee Coventry and Warwicks Cancer Treatment Fund; *Recreations* rugby football, theatre, hill-walking; *Clubs* Old Coventrians Assoc, Old Coventrians RFC; *Style*— Michael Taberner, Esq; Leamount, 74 St Martins Rd, Finham, Coventry (☎ 0203 419171); Angel & Co, 117 New Union St, Coventry (☎ 0203 252211)

TABOR, Charles James; er s of Robert Charles Tabor (d 1985), of Great Codham Hall, Shalford, nr Braintree, Essex, and Beryl Nora, *née* Lewis; *b* 15 March 1946; *Educ* Summer Fields Oxford, Cokethorpe Sch Witney Oxon, RAC Cirencester (NCA); *m* 23 Oct 1968, Gillian, da of John Buckley (d 1966), of Hartsmead, Ashton Keynes, Wilts; 2 s (Christopher Charles Robert b 26 Sept 1970, Oliver Charles John b 7 Oct 1978), 1 da ((Sarah) Claire Buckley b 26 Jan 1973); *Career* dir Tabor Farms Ltd; memb: Essex Farming and Wildlife Advsy Gp, Essex Farmers' Union, Essex Co Landowners' Assoc; dir Rolls Royce Enthusiasts' Club, tstee The Sir Henry Royce Meml Fndn; *Clubs* Farmers', Essex; *Style*— Charles Tabor, Esq; Sutton Hall, Rochford, Essex SS4 1LQ (☎ 0702 545730)

TABOR, Maj-Gen David St John Maur; CB (1977), MC (1944); yst s of Harry Ernest Tabor; *b* 5 Oct 1922; *Educ* Eton, RMA Sandhurst; *m* 1, 27 July 1955, Hon Pamela Roxane Nivison (d 1987), 2 da of 2 Baron Glendyne (d 1967); 2 s; m 2, 4 Oct 1989, Marguerite, widow of Col Peter Arkwright; *Career* 2 Lt RHG 1942, served NW Europe WWII (wounded), Lt-Col cmdg Household Cavalry and Silver Stick in Waiting 1964, Brig 1966, Cdr Berlin Inf Bde 1966, Cdr Br Army Staff and mil attaché Washington 1968, RCDS 1971, Maj-Gen 1972, defence attaché Paris 1972-74, GOC Eastern Dist 1975-77; vice chm ACFA 1979; *Recreations* shooting, fishing, gardening; *Clubs* MCC, Turf, RAC; *Style*— Maj-Gen David Tabor, CB, MC; Lower Farm, Compton Abdale, Glos GL54 4DS

TABOR, John Edward; OBE (1944), DL (Essex 1972); s of Edward Henry Tabor; *b* 31 March 1911; *Educ* Westminster, Felsted, Emmanuel Coll Cambridge (MA); *m* 1, 1945, Marjorie Lorenzen (d 1953); 1 s, 3 da; m 2, 1960, Margaret Anne Turner, *née* Benson; *Career* Civil Service 1932-45, farmer, landowner, pro chancellor (and chm to 1983) Cncl Univ of Essex, memb Essex CC 1952-77, High Sheriff Essex 1980; Hon DUniv Essex 1984; *Recreations* hunting, travel; *Clubs* Farmers'; *Style*— John Tabor Esq, OBE, DL; Bovingdon Hall, Braintree, Essex (☎ 0371 850205)

TACKABERRY, John Antony; QC (1982); s of Thomas Raphael Tackaberry (d 1971), and Mary Catherine, *née* Geoghegan (d 1985); *b* 13 Nov 1939; *Educ* Downside, Trinity Coll Dublin, Downing Coll Cambridge (MA, LLM); *m* Penelope, da of Seth Holt (d 1971); 2 s (Christopher b 1966, Antony b 1968); *Career* lectr: Chinese Min of Further Educn 1963-64, Poly of Central London 1965-67; called to the Bar 1967 (Republic of Ireland Bar 1987, Californian Bar 1988); rec 1988; pres: Soc of Construction Law 1987-85, Euro Soc of Construction Law 1985-87; memb arbitral panels of Los Angeles Center for Commercial Arbitration 1987; vice pres Chartered Inst of Arbitrators 1988; author of numerous articles; FCIArb, FFB; *Recreations* good food, good wine, good company, windsurfing, photography; *Clubs* Athenaeum; *Style*— John Tackaberry, Esq, QC; 22 Willes Road, London NW5 (☎ 071 267 2137, fax 071 482 1018); Atkin Building, Grays Inn, London WC1R 3J (☎ 071 404 0102, fax 071 405 7456, telex 298623 HUDSON)

TADDEI, Hon Mrs (Charlotte Mary); da of 2 Baron Piercy (d 1981), and Oonagh Lavinia Baylay; *b* 24 May 1947; *Educ* Badminton Sch, Univ of Florence; *m* 1966, Paolo Emilio Taddei, s of Enrico Taddei; 1 s, 1 da; *Career* teacher; *Style*— The Hon Mrs Taddei; Via Lorenzo il Magnifico 70, Florence, Italy

TADIÉ, Prof Jean-Yves; s of Henri Tadié (d 1980), of Paris, and Marie, *née* Férester (d 1988); *b* 7 Oct 1936; *Educ* Coll St Louis de Gonzague (Jesuits) Paris, Lic à lettres Sorbonne D'Etudes Agrégation de Lettres Ecole Normale Supérieure Docteur ès Lettres Sorbonne; *m* 13 June 1962, Arlette-Gabrielle, da of H Khoury (d 1964), of Cairo; 3 s (Alexis b 27 March 1963, Benoit b 13 Feb 1968, Jerome b 28 April 1972); *Career* French Mil Serv 1963-64; lectr Univ of Alexandria 1962, asst prof Faculte Lettres de Paris 1967-68, prof Université de Caen 1968, (and de Tours 1969), prof of French Lit Université de la Sorbonne Nouvelle (Paris III) 1970- (and Univ of Cairo 1972-76), dir French Inst London 1976-81, Marshal Foch prof of French lit and fell All Souls Coll Oxford 1988; Ordre National du Mérite (Chevalier), Palais Académiques 1975, Grand Prix de l'Académie Francaise 1988, offr Ordre de la Couronne de Belgique 1979; *Books* Proust et le Roman (1971), Introduction la Vie Litt XIX siècle (1970), Le Recit Poètique (1978), Le Roman d'Aventures (1982), Proust (1983), La Critique Littéraire au XX siècle (1987), Le Roman du XX Siècle (1990), Portrait de l'Artiste (1990), ed Proust: A La Recherche du Temps Perdu, Bibl de la Pléiade (4 vol, 1987-89); *Recreations* tennis, golf, cinema, opera, music; *Clubs* Reform; *Style*— Prof Jean-Yves Tadié; All Souls College, Oxford OX1 4AL (☎ 0865 279 289); 4 rue Dupont des Loges, 75007 Paris; La Croix d'Ouault, 37310 Tauxigny, France

TADMAN, Colonel John; s of George Ronald Tadman, of Hampton-on-Thames, and Phyllis Selena, *née* Laker; *b* 1 April 1933; *Educ* Hampton Sch, RMA Sandhurst, Staff Coll, Nat Def Coll; *m* 8 April 1961, Corinna Mary, da of Cdr Charles William Medlicott Vereker, RN (ret), of Wylye, Wiltshire; 1 s (Miles William Vereker b 1966), 2 da (Carey Joanna b 1962, Fenella Jane b 1964); *Career* professional soldier 1951-84, Cdr 5 Bn Royal Anglian Regt, head of Secretariat to UK C in C's Ctee; md Dyas (Marquees) Ltd 1984; dir Julianas Leisure div 1987-; *Recreations* sailing, shooting; *Clubs* Hampshire CCC; *Style*— Col John Tadman; West End Mill, Donhead St Andrew, Shaftesbury, Dorset SP7 9YY (☎ 074 788 346); Dyas (Marquees) Ltd, Unit 3, Nursling Ind Estate, Southampton

TAGENT, Michael Edward; s of Edward Rene Tagent (d 1975), of Amersham, Bucks, and Joan Gladys Tagent; *b* 2 June 1943; *Educ* Merchant Taylors'; *m* 19 Sept 1970, Jacqueline Mary (Jackie), da of Lancelot Lea Schofield (d 1988), of Amersham, Bucks; 1 s (John b 6 Feb 1978), 2 da (Catherine b 17 Sept 1971, Elizabeth b 3 July 1973); *Career* articled to Whinney Smith & Whinney CA's 1961-66, asst mangr Whinney Murray & Sons Pans 1966-69, audit mangr Neville Russell & Co 1969-73, co sec and accountant Dugdale Underwriting Ltd 1973-75, fin mangr The HP Motor Policies at Lloyds 1975-83; chief exec: mgmnt servs John Poland Group 1983-87, HGP Motor Policies at Lloyds 1987-88; md HGP Managing Agency Ltd 1989, gp fin controller Delta Doric Group 1990; Anglican reader 1968-, formerley chm Amersham Deanery Synod, currently churchwarden parish of Chesham Bois; FCA 1966, MBIM 1975, FCII 1983 (ATII 1966); *Recreations* walking, photography; *Style*— Michael Tagent, Esq; 46 Long Park, Chesham Bois, Amersham, Bucks HP6 5LA (☎ 0494 727675)

TAGER, Romie; s of Osias Tager, of London, and Minnie Tager (d 1974); *b* 19 July 1947; *Educ* Hasmonean GS Hendon London, UCL (LLB); *m* 29 Aug 1971, Esther Marianne, da of Rev Leo Sichel, of London; 2 s (Joseph b 23 Oct 1980, Simon (twin) b 23 Oct 1980); *Career* called to the Bar Middle Temple 1970; head of own chambers in Serjeant's Inn 1987- (formerly in Inner Temple), memb Hon Socs of Middle and Inner Temples and Int Bar Assoc; *Recreations* opera, theatre, travel; *Clubs* Peak; *Style*— Romie Tager, Esq; 33 Ingram Avenue, London NW11 6TG (☎ 081 455 2827, fax 081 455 5905); Fifth Floor, 1 Serjeants Inn, Fleet St, London EC4 (☎ 071 353 7571, fax 071 353 5966)

TAGG, Alan; s of Thomas Bertram Tagg, and Annie, *née* Hufton; *b* 13 April 1928; *Educ* Mansfield Coll of Art Old Vic Theatre Sch; *Career* freelance theatre designer; asst to Cecil Beaton, Oliver Messel, first play Charles Morgan's The River Line 1952, worked for HM Tennent Ltd, fndr memb English Stage Co 1956; designed: first prodn Look Back in Anger 1956, The Entertainer (with Lawrence Oliver) 1957, fifteen other prodns at Royal Court Theatre, four prodns for RSC incl Graham Green's The Return of AJ Raffles 1975, twelve prodns at Chichester Festival Theatre incl Dear Antoine (with Edith Evans) 1971 and Waters of the Moon (with Ingrid Bergman) 1977, prodns of nine plays by Alan Ayckbourn, ten prodns for NT, 93 West End prodns (incl Billy Liar 1959, How the Other Half Loves 1970, The Constant Wife 1973, Alphabetical Order 1975, Donkeys Years 1976, The Kingfisher 1977, Candida 1977, The Millionairess 1978, Peter Shaffer's Lettice and Lovage (with Maggie Smith) 1987), eleven prodns on Broadway (incl Peter Shaffer's Black Comedy 1967 and Lettice and Lovage (with Maggie Smith) 1990), prodn of Look Back in Anger Moscow Arts Theatre; worked with dirs incl: Lindsay Anderson, Michael Blakemore, John Dexter, John Gielgud, Tony Richardson and Michael Rudman; exhibitions designed incl: Shakespeare Stratford-upon-Avon 1964, Hector Berlioz 1969, 25 Years of Covent Garden, V & A Museum 1971, Byron 1974; *Recreations* living in France; *Clubs* Groucho; *Style*— Alan Tagg, Esq; 19 Parsons Green, London SW6 4UL (☎ 071 731 2787)

TAGGART, Dr Hugh McAllister; s of Dr James Taggart, of 27 Kensington Rd, Belfast, and Margaret Helen, *née* Thompson; *b* 29 Nov 1949; *Educ* Campbell Coll Belfast, Queen's Univ of Belfast (MB, MD); *m* 5 July 1974, Grace Ann Margretta, da of James Campbell (d 1982); 1 s (Christopher b 24 Oct 1978), 1 da (Kathryn b 19 July 1981); *Career* sr post doctoral res fell Univ of Washington Seattle USA 1979-80, sr lectr geriatric med Queen's Univ of Belfast 1980-, conslt physician Belfast City Hosp 1980-(sr registrar geriatric med 1977-79); memb: Med Advsy Bd Nat Osteoporosis Soc, Sci Ctee Br Geriatics Soc; memb BMA, fell Ulster Med Soc; *Recreations* golf, skiing, swimming, tennis; *Clubs* Royal Belfast Golf; *Style*— Dr Hugh Taggart; 1 Crawfordsburn Wood, Crawfordsburn, Bangor, Co Down BT19 1XB; Department of Geriatric Medicine, Whita Medical Building, 97 Lisburn Rd, Belfast BT9 7BL NI (☎ 0232 245133 ext 2158)

TAGHIZADEH, Abdosamad; s of Reza Taghizadeh (d 1980), of Iran, and Kafayat Taghizadeh (d 1985); *Educ* Univ of Tehran Med Sch (MD), Univ of London (PhD); *m* 20 Nov 1964, Forough, da of Mohsen Kiasati, of Tehran; 3 children (Arash b 20 Dec 1967, Hadi b 10 Oct 1969, Sattar b 4 Jan 1975); *Career* pres Nat Univ of Iran 1979-81 (prof of pathology 1979-82), lectr and hon sr lectr UCH 1966-81; contrib to numerous learned jls; FRSM 1962; memb: Pathological Soc of GB and Ireland 1962, Paediatric Pathological Soc 1970, BMA 1985; *Style*— Dr Abdosamad Taghizadeh; Dept of Pathology, Oldchurch Hospital, Romford, Essex RM7 OBE (☎ 0708 46090 ext 3287)

TAGOE, Emmanuel Ayitey; s of Emmanuel Okai Tagoe Gbese, Accra, Ghana, W Africa, and Agnes Kuokor Ashie (d 1968); *b* 20 Jan 1949; *Educ* Odorgonno Secdy Sch Accra, Inst of African Studies Legon Accra; *m* 23 Dec 1989 Janice, da of Horace Hayde; 2 s (Samuel Nii Okai b 14 May 1973, Emmanuel Nii Okai b 26 Feb 1974), 2 da (Agnes Dedeikuokor b 27 Nov 1968, Elizabeth Dedei b 30 Dec 1974); *Career* master drummer and musical dir; apprentice drummer Ashiedu Keteke Cultural Troupe 1965-68, troupes played with incl: Voice of Germany Cultural Troupe, master drummer and asst tutor Unity Cultural Troupe, Arts Cncl of Ghana Dance Troupe, Arts Cncl Folkloric Co 1972, master and asst ldr Dabuo Dance Co (toured GB and Germany 1977), joined Steel and Skins 1977 (toured Ireland, Britain, Denmark, Germany, France, Holland, Sweden), fndr and asst tutor Yaa Asentewa (winners Andy Anderon Award of Endeavour Committment and Achievement 1982 and 1983), currently musical dir and co fndr Adzido; awarded best musician in black music and dance Black People Devpt Tst 1989; *Recreations* music, dance, travel, football; *Style*— Emmanuel Tagoe, Esq; 161 Wigan House, Warwick Grove, Upper Clapton, London E5 9JD (☎ 081 806 8962); Adzido Pan African Dance Ensemble, The Trade Centre, Unit IOB, 202-208 New North Rd, Islington, London N1 7BL (☎ 071 359 7453, fax 071 704 0300)

TAHANY, Lady Caroline Ann; da (by 1 m) of 7 Earl Cadogan; *b* 1946; *m* 1965 (m dis 1975), Euan Woodruffe Foster; 2 s; assumed name Tahany in lieu of Foster 1981; *Style*— The Lady Caroline Tahany; 78 New Walk, Leicester

TAIT, Andrew Wilson; OBE (1967); s of Dr Adam Tait (d 1934), of Fife, and Jenny Tait (d 1925); *b* 25 Sept 1922; *Educ* George Watson's Coll Edinburgh, Univ of Edinburgh; *m* 1954, Betty Isobel, da of Finlay Maclennan (d 1960); 2 da (Jane, Susan); *Career* ldr writer The Scotsman 1947-48, Scottish Office 1948-64; chm Nat Housebuilding Cncl and Housing Res Fndn 1964-87 (D G 1985-87); advsr on housing in USA, Canada and Aust 1973-81, chm World Housing and Home Warranty Conf 1987-; chm: New Homes Environmental Group, Johnson Fry Property; dir Barratt plc; *Recreations* golf, tennis; *Clubs* Caledonian; *Style*— Andrew Tait, Esq, OBE; Orchard Croft, Grimmshill, Great Missenden, Bucks

TAIT, Brian Sharland; s of Ernest Waldegrave Tait (d 1953), of Vaila, Killara, NSW,

Aust, and Florence Eva, *née* Sharland (d 1975); *b* 13 Jan 1918; *Educ* Sydney C of E GS, Sydney Tech Coll Univ of NSW (Assoc in Arch); *m* 16 March 1944, Marjorie Joan, da of Tom Lewis Lawrence (d 1970), of Court House, Kenilworth Ave, Gloucester; 1 s (James b 1948), 2 da (Amanda (Mrs Chamberlayne) b 1947, Joanna (Mrs Russell) b 1952); *Career* Mil Serv 1940 with Aust Light Horse Regt awaiting call up to RAAF; 1940-45 RAAF, Sqdn Ldr, two operational tours as pilot and Flt Cdr 202 Sqdn, RAF Coastal Cmd (flying boats) Gibraltar, W Africa, Shetlands and N Ireland; architect: ptnr Moore & Ward, Sydney Aust 1946-48, asst County Arch Glos 1948-49, own practice 1950-65, ptnr ASTAM Design Partnership 1965-72, own practice 1972-, conslt to Dyer Assocs 1982-; memb cncl RIBA 1962-68; pres Glos Arch Assoc; 1962-64: fndr chm Gloucester Civic Design Gp 1957, chm Gloucester Civic Tst 1978-81; dir Gloucester Historic Bldgs Ltd 1979-90, Gloucestershire Historic Churches Preservation Tst 1981-90, tstee Gloucestershire Heritage Tst 1985-90; clerk to Tirley Parish Cncl 1985-90; FRIBA; *Recreations* painting (watercolours), golf; *Clubs* Rotary (Gloucester), Conservative (Gloucester), Tewkesbury Park and Country; *Style—* Brian Tait, Esq; Prince's Plume Cottage, Tirley, Gloucester GL19 4ET (☎ 045 278 335); Old Pitch, Tirley, Gloucester GL19 4ET

TAIT, Eric; MBE (Mil 1980); s of William Johnston Tait (d 1959), and Sarah, *née* Jones; *b* 10 Jan 1945; *Educ* George Heriots Sch, RMA Sandhurst, Univ of London (BSc), Univ of Cambridge (MPhil); *m* 29 March 1967, Agnes Jane Boag, da of Capt Henry George Anderson (d 1958); 1 s (Michael b 1969), 1 da (Eva b 1973); *Career* Lt Col RE, served BAOR, Middle East, Caribbean, N Ireland (despatches 1976); dir Euro ops Pannell Kerr Forster 1989-; ed in chief The Accountants Magazine; sec Inst of CA's of Scotland 1984-89; memb of exec Scottish Cncl Devpt and Indust 1984-89; *Recreations* hillwalking, swimming, reading, writing; *Style—* Eric Tait, Esq, MBE; Pannell Ker Forster Worldwide, 78 Hatton Garden, London EC1N 8JA (☎ 071 831 7393, fax 071 405 6736, telex 295998)

TAIT, Ivan Ballantyne; TD (1967), KStJ (1982); s of Ivan Tait (d 1976), and Elise Alexander, *née* Forsyth (d 1972); *b* 14 Sept 1928; *Educ* Glasgow Acad, Daniel Stewart's Coll, Univ of Edinburgh (MB ChB); *m* 3 July 1965, Jocelyn Mary Connel, da of Lt-Col William Michael Leggatt, DSO (d 1946); 1 s ((Ivan) Alexander Legatt b 12 June 1974), 1 da (Arabella Elizabeth b 24 Oct 1968); *Career* Nat Serv PMO Gurkha Rifles, RAMC 1952-54 (despatches 1953), Col L RAMC (Vol) TA 1955-, hon surgn (TA) to HM The Queen; Edinburgh Royal Infirmary and St Mary's Hosp London 1951-64, Univ of Kentucky 1965-67, conslt surgn Tayside Health Bd 1967-72, conslt dept of genitourinary med Edinburgh 1973-82, conslt in admin charge of genitourinary med services West of Scot 1982-; memb: business ctee of Gen Cncl Univ of Edinburgh, Scot Primory Chapter OStJ; Liveryman Worshipful Soc of Apothecaries 1959, Hammerman Glasgow 1986; FRCS Glasgow, Edinburgh and London; KLJ 1980, UN Cyprus Medal 1984; KStJ 1982; *Recreations* TA, charitable Socs; *Clubs* New, (Edinburgh); *Style—* Ivan B Tait, Esq, TD; 6 Lennox Row, Edinburgh EH5 3HN; Department of Genitourinary Medicine, Glasgow Royal Infirmary, Alexandra Parade, Glasgow (☎ 041 552 3535 ext 5572)

TAIT, James Francis; s of Herbert Tait (d 1935), and Constance Hevinia, *née* Brotherton (d 1974); *b* 1 Dec 1925; *Educ* Darlington GS, Univ of Leeds (BSc, PhD); *m* 1 Sept 1956, Sylvia Agnes Sophia, da of James W Wardropper (d 1947); *Career* Dept of Physics Middx Hosp Med Sch: lectr 1948-55, external sci staff MRC 1955-58, Joel prof and head of Dept 1970-82, jt head of Biophysical Endocrinology Unit 1970-86; sr scientist Worcester Fndn for Experimental Biology Mass USA 1958-70 (chm Sci Cncl 1968-70), emeritus prof Univ of London 1982-; sec Laurentian Hormone Ctee; memb: Gen Med Bd US PHS Study Section USA 1967-70, Ed Bd Clincical Endocrinology USA, Cncl Soc for Endocrinology 1971-74, Grant in Aid Ctee Royal Soc 1979-82, Steroid Reference Ctee MRC 1972-79; hon memb Faculty of Radiology UK; awards: Soc of Endocrinology medal 1969, Tadeus Reichstein award of Int Endocrine Soc 1976, Gregory Pincus Meml medal 1977, CIBA award Cncl for High Blood Pressure 1977, Dale medal Soc for Endocrinology 1979, Res Career award United Public Health Serv 1962-70; gave Douglas Wright Lecture Melbourne Aust 1989; elected to: American Acad of Arts and Scis 1958-70; Hon DSc Univ of Hull; FRS 1959, FRSM 1971-; *Pubns* many chapters in books, 200 scientific papers; *Recreations* photography, gardening, walking dog, bowling; *Clubs* Royal Society, RSM; *Style—* Prof James Tait, FRS; Moorlands, Main Road, East Boldre, Nr Brockenhurst, Hants SO42 7WT (☎ 059 065 312)

TAIT, Sir James Sharp; s of William Blyth Tait; *b* 13 June 1912; *Educ* Royal Tech Coll Glasgow, Univ of Glasgow (BSc, PhD); *m* 1939, Mary Cassidy, da of Archibald Linton, of Kilmaurs, Ayrshire; 2 s, 1 da; *Career* princ: Woolwich Poly 1951-56, Northampton Coll of Advanced Technol London 1956-66; vice chllr and princ The City Univ 1966-74; Hon LLD Univ of Strathclyde, Hon DSc City Univ; kt 1969; *Style—* Sir James Tait; 23 Trowlock Avenue, Teddington, Middx

TAIT, Lady Katharine Jane; *née* Russell; da of 3 Earl Russell (Bertrand Russell) by his 2 w, Dora; *b* 29 Dec 1923; *m* 1948, Rev Charles Tait; 4 s, 1 da; *Style—* The Lady Katharine Tait; Falls Village, Conn 06031, USA

TAIT, Marion Hooper (Mrs Marion Morse); da of Charles Arnold Browell Tait, OBE (d 1962), of London, and Betty Maude, *née* Hooper; *b* 7 Oct 1950; *Educ* Royal Acad of Dancing, Royal Ballet Sch; *m* 9 Oct 1971, David Thomas Morse, s of Thomas Walter Morse (d 1984); *Career* former princ dancer with Sadler's Wells Royal Ballet, princ dancer The Birmingham Royal Ballet; worked with leading choreographers and had roles created by: Sir Kenneth MacMillan, Sir Frederick Ashton, David Bintley, Christopher Bruce, Joe Layton; danced all maj classical roles; guest dancer: The Houston Ballet, Munich Ballet, Japan, Poland (Polich Ballet's Bicentenial medal of Honour); *Recreations* singing, tap dancing, needlework; *Style—* Ms Marion Tait; c/o Birmingham Royal Ballet, Hippodrome Theatre, Thorp Street, Birmingham B5 4AU

TAIT, Simon John Anderson; s of William Anderson Tait (d 1973), and Alice Mary, *née* Crowther; *b* 30 Jan 1948; *Educ* Hawes Down Secdy Modern Sch; *m* 1979, Ann Sandra, da of George William Hugh Williams (d 1990); 1 s (Adam Anderson b 1988); *Career* journalist; Croydon Advertiser 1966-70, Brighton Evening Argus 1970, Newham Recorder 1971, Manchester Evening News 1972, writer Government Info Serv 1975, head of PR servs V & A 1980, Telegraph Sunday Magazine 1984, freelance writer 1985, The Times 1988; author of many newspaper and magazine articles on the arts and museums; *Books* Palaces of Discovery (Story of British Museums) (1989), Times Guide to Museums and Galleries 1989-90 and 1990-91; *Recreations* telling fantasy as it really is; *Clubs* Reform; *Style—* Simon Tait, Esq; The Times, 1 Pennington St, London E1 9XN (☎ 071 782 5950)

TALBOT, Clifford Heyworth; s of Frank Heyworth Talbot, QC, of 9 Westfield, Little Abington, Cambridge, and Mabel, *née* Williams (d 1956); *b* 22 April 1925; *Educ* Leighton Park Sch, Univ of Cambridge (MA), Guys Hosp (MChir, FRCS); *m* 17 June 1950, Margaret Hilda, da of Wallace Samuel Hooper (d 1972); 1 s (David b 1952), 2 da (Mary b 1953, Jennifer b 1959); *Career* Nat Serv Capt RAMC 1949-51; sr surgical registrar Bristol 1957-61, conslt surgn Sheffield 1961-90, regnl advsr in surgery Trent region 1985-89; former memb Bd of Govrs United Sheffield Hosp, memb Sheffield Health Authy 1981-84; town tstee Sheffield 1978-; fell Assoc of Surgns of GB and Ireland; *Recreations* sailing, fishing; *Style—* Clifford Talbot, Esq; Morlands Farm, Moorlands Lane, Froggatt, Calver, nr Sheffield S30 1ZF (☎ 0433 31876)

TALBOT, Hon Mrs (Cynthia Edith); *née* Guest; da of 1 Viscount Wimborne, JP, and Hon Alice Grosvenor, da of 2 Baron Ebury; *b* 24 Oct 1908; *m* 1933, Capt Thomas Talbot, CB, QC, *qv*; 1 s, 3 da; *Style—* The Hon Mrs Talbot; Falconhurst, Edenbridge, Kent (☎ 0342 850 641, fax 0342 850 940)

TALBOT, Vice Adm Sir (Arthur Allison) FitzRoy; KBE (1964), CB (1961), DSO (1940 and bar 1942), DL (Somerset 1973); s of Capt Henry FitzRoy George Talbot, DSO, RN (gs of Rev Henry Talbot by his w Mary, da of Maj-Gen Hon Sir William Ponsonby, KCB (ka Waterloo 1815, 2 s of 1 Baron Ponsonby of Imokilly, cr 1806 & extinct 1866) by his w Georgiana, da of 1 Baron Southampton. The Rev Henry Talbot was eldest s of Very Rev Charles Talbot, Dean of Salisbury, by his w Lady Elizabeth Somerset, da of 5 Duke of Beaufort. The Dean was 2 s of Rev and Hon George Talbot, 3 s of 1 Baron Talbot (cr 1833) and unc of 1 Earl Talbot (of the 1784 cr); *b* 22 Oct 1909; *Educ* RNC Dartmouth; *m* 1, 1940, Joyce Gertrude, er da of late Frank Edwin Linley, of Fowey; 2 da (Anthea Jane b 1944, m 1969 James Charrington; Elizabeth Ann b 1945, m 1969 Michel Shuttleworth); m 2, 1983, Elizabeth Mary, da of Rupert Charles Ensor, of Co Armagh, and formerly w of (1) Capt Richard Steele, RN (m dis 1951), (2) Sir Esmond Otho Durlacher (d 1982), stockbroker; *Career* served RN 1922-67: Channel, East Coast UK, Mediterranean, Western Isles during WWII, Staff Offr Ops to C-in-C Br Pacific Fleet & Far East Station 1947-48, Capt 1950, Naval Attaché Moscow & Helsinki 1951-53, IDC 1954, Cdre RN Barracks Portsmouth 1957-59, Rear Adm 1960, Flag Offr Arabian Seas & Persian Gulf 1960-61, ME 1961-62, Vice Adm 1962, C-in-C S Atlantic & S America 1963-65, C-in-C Plymouth 1965-67; *Style—* Vice Adm Sir FitzRoy Talbot, KBE, CB, DSO, DL

TALBOT, Sir Hilary Gwynne; s of Rev Prebendary A Talbot, RD; *b* 22 Jan 1912; *Educ* Haileybury, Worcester Coll Oxford; *m* 1963, Jean Whitworth, JP, da of Kenneth Fisher; *Career* served WWII RA; barr 1935, dep chm Northants Quarter Sessions 1948-62, chm Derbyshire Quarter Sessions 1958-63, judge of County Cts 1962-68, dep chm Hants Quarter Sessions 1964-71, High Court judge Queen's Bench 1968-83, judge Employment Appeals Tbnl 1978-81, memb Parole Bd 1980-83, dep chm Boundary Cmmn Wales 1980-83; memb Rule Ctee Supreme Ct until Nov 1981; kt 1968; *Style—* Sir Hilary Talbot; Old Chapel House, Little Ashley, Bradford on Avon, Wilts BA15 2PN (☎ 022 16 2182)

TALBOT, John Michael Arthur; s of John Edward Lightfoot Talbot (Capt WWI and WWII, d 1974), of 22 Chepstow Place, London, and Muriel Emily Mary, *née* Horsley; *b* 29 Dec 1934; *Educ* Sherborne, Trinity Hall Cambridge (MA); *m* 9 Sept 1961, Adrienne Mary, da of Capt R F T Stannard, CBE, DSC, RN (d 1969), of Little Barley Mow, Headley, Hants; 1 s (Michael b 1962), 1 da (Claire b 1964); *Career* Nat Serv 2 Lt Middx Regt; sr ptnr Bower Cotton & Bower 1982- (ptnr 1964-); clerk to govrs Highgate Sch; vice pres Blackheath FC; memb Law Soc; *Recreations* swimming, walking, wine, history; *Clubs* Blackheath FC, Teddington CC; *Style—* John Talbot, Esq; 51 Culmington Rd, Ealing, London W13 9NJ (☎ 081 567 4905); 36 Whitefriars St, London EC4Y 8BH (☎ 071 353 3040)

TALBOT, Patrick John; QC (1990); s of John Bentley Talbot, MC, of Farnham, Surrey, and Marguerite Maxwell, *née* Townley; *b* 28 July 1946; *Educ* Charterhouse, Univ Coll Oxford (MA); *m* 8 May 1976, Judith Anne, da of David Percival Urwin; 1 s (William Patrick Charles b 2 June 1983), 2 da (Sophie Camilla b 28 Nov 1977, Alexandra Claire Maxwell b 8 Nov 1979); *Career* called to the Bar Lincoln's Inn 1969, in practice Chancery Bar 1970-; memb: Senate of Inns of Court and the Bar 1974-77, Cncl of Legal Educn 1977-; *Recreations* cricket, skiing, collecting old toys; *Clubs* MCC, Wimbledon Wanderers Cricket; *Style—* Patrick Talbot, Esq, QC; 22 West Park Rd, Kew, Richmond TW9 4DA (☎ 081 878 3516); 31 Farm Lane, Great Bedwyn, Marlborough, Wilts SN8 3LU (☎ 0672 870974); 13 Old Square, Lincoln's Inn, London WC2A 3UA (☎ 071 242 6105, fax 071 405 4004)

TALBOT, Hon Rose Maud; da of late Col the Hon Milo George Talbot, CB (4 s of late 4 Baron Talbot de Malahide), and sis of 7 Baron Talbot de Malahide (d 1973, when the UK Barony became ext); *b* 1915; *Style—* The Hon Rose Talbot; Malahide, Fingal, Tasmania, Australia 7214

TALBOT, Thomas George; CB (1960), QC (1954); s of Rt Hon Sir George Talbot, PC (ggs of Hon John Talbot, QC, 4 s of 2 Earl Talbot, which title is now merged with Earldom of Shrewsbury), and Gertrude, *née* Cator; *b* 21 Dec 1904; *Educ* Winchester, New Coll Oxford; *m* 1933, Hon Cynthia Guest (*see* Hon Mrs Talbot); 1 s, 3 da; *Career* served WWII RE (TA) and Scots Gds; called to the Bar Inner Temple 1929, bencher 1960, asst subsequently dep parly counsel to Treasy 1944-53, counsel chm Ctees House of Lords 1953-77 (asst counsel chm 1977-82); *Clubs* Brooks's; *Style—* Thomas Talbot, Esq, CB, QC; Falconhurst, Edenbridge, Kent (☎ 0342 850 641)

TALBOT OF MALAHIDE, 10 Baron (I 1831); Reginald John Richard Arundell; DL (Wilts); also Hereditary Lord Adm of Malahide and the Adjacent Seas (a distinction dating by charter from 5 March in the 15 year of the reign of Edward IV). The mother of the 2 and 3 Barons, who was the first holder of the title, was, to use the full designation, cr Baroness Talbot of Malahide and Lady Malahide of Malahide; s of Reginald John Arthur Arundell (changed his surname to Arundell 1945, s of Reginald Aloysius Talbot, ggs of Baroness Talbot of Malahide), and Mabile Arundell, gda of 9 Baron Arundell of Wardour; suc kinsman 9 Baron Talbot of Malahide (d 1987); *b* 9 Jan 1931; *Educ* Stonyhurst, RMA Sandhurst; *m* 1955, Laura Duff (d 1989), yr da of Gp Capt Edward Tennant, DSO, MC, JP (n of 1 Baron Glenconner), and his 2 w, Victoria Duff, MBE, o da of Sir Robert Duff, 2 Bt; 1 s (Richard), 4 da (Juliet, Catherine, Rose, Lucy); *Heir* s, Hon Richard John Tennant Arundell b 1957; *Career* chm St John Cncl for Wilts; KStJ 1988 (CStJ 1983, OStJ 1978); Kt of Honour and Devotion SMOM 1977; hon citizen of State of Maryland; *Style—* The Rt Hon Lord Talbot of Malahide, DL; Hook Manor, Donhead St Andrew, Shaftesbury, Dorset (☎ 0747 828270)

TALBOT-PONSONBY, Michael Clement; s of Col J A Talbot-Ponsonby, of Todenham Manor, Moreton-in-Marsh (d 1969), and Elizabeth Frances, *née* Fraser (d 1980); *b* 3 Jan 1932; *Educ* Eton; *m* 28 Jan 1956, Judith Katherine (d 1985), da of Bishop T S Gibson, of, Kimberley, SA (d 1953); 4 da (Caroline Frances (Mrs Patrick Dilkington) b 1958, Charlotte Jane b 1963, Lucy Elizabeth b 1965, Katherine Louisa b 1967); *Career* dir Ogilvy & Mather 1968-78; chm: Mather's Advertising Foster Turner & Benson 1978-83, Alexander Fraser Parva Properties; non-exec dir Phoenix Advertising 1984-86; memb various charitable ctees; *Recreations* riding, hunting, racing, gardening; *Clubs* Turf; *Style—* Michael Talbot-Ponsonby, Esq; 10 Westmoreland Place, London SW1V 4AD (☎ 071 834 5218); Hinton Manor, Hinton Parva, nr Swindon (☎ 0793 790507)

TALBOT-PONSONBY, Nigel Edward Charles; s of Edward Fitzroy Talbot-Ponsonby (ggs of Adm Sir Charles Talbot, KCB, who was s of Very Rev Charles Talbot, Dean of Salisbury, by Lady Elizabeth Somerset, da of 5 Duke of Beaufort; the Dean was n of 3 Baron and 1 Earl Talbot, which two dignities are now held by the Earl of Shrewsbury); *b* 24 Sept 1946; *Educ* Harrow; *m* 1977, Robina, da of Lt Cdr Henry Bruce, JP, DL, RN ret (gs of 9 Earl of Elgin & 13 ofX Kincardine), of Barley Down House, Alresford; 3 s (Henry b 1981, James b 1986, Alexander b 1987); *Career* chartered surveyor; ptnr Humberts (chartered surveyors) and managing ptnr Humberts Int Leisure Div (the firm which handled the sale of Highgrove to HRH The

Prince of Wales (Duchy of Cornwall) 1981 and the purchase of Lands End for Peter de Savary 1987); dir Singleton Open Air Museum Sussex; former memb Recreation and Leisure Mgmnt Ctee Royal Inst of Chartered Surveyors; memb Land Decade Cncl; FRICS; *Recreations* sailing, field sports; *Clubs* Royal Thames Yacht, Lloyds; *Style*— Nigel Talbot-Ponsonby, Esq; Langrish Lodge, Langrish, Petersfield, Hants GU32 1RB ((☎ 0730 63374); 25 Grosvenor Street, London W1X 9FE (☎ 071 629 6700, telex 27444)

TALBOT-RICE, Nigel; s of Mervyn Gurney Talbot-Rice (d 1979), and Eleanor Butler Adair, *née* Williamson (d 1965); *b* 14 May 1938; *Educ* Charterhouse, ChCh Oxford (MA, DipEd); *m* 20 July 1968, (Rosfrith) Joanna Sarah, da of Air-Cdr F J Manning, CB, CBE, RAF (d 1988); 1 s (Samuel b 17 March 1982), 4 da (Sarah b 24 Oct 1969, Caroline b 26 Sept 1971, Rebecca b 2 Sept 1973, Helena b 28 Jan 1977); *Career* Nat Serv Coldstream Gds 1957-58; asst master Papplewick Sch Ascot 1961-64, headmaster Summer Fields Sch Oxford 1975- (asst master 1965-71, asst headmaster 1971-75); memb IAPS 1971; *Books* Survey of Religion in Preparatory Schools (1965); *Recreations* golf, gardening; *Style*— Nigel Talbot-Rice, Esq; Beech House, Mayfield Rd, Oxford; Cool Bawn, Thurlestone, Devon; Summer Fields, Oxford OX2 7EN (☎ 0865 54433)

TALBOT WILLCOX, Peter Desmond Ropner; s of George Talbot Willcox, MC (d 1968), and Constance Winsome, *née* Ropner (d 1988); *b* 17 March 1927; *Educ* Eton; *m* 31 March 1950, Jennifer April, da of Lt-Col E Holt, OBE, MC (d 1969), of Little Tew, Oxon; 1 s (Paul b 1952), 3 da (Jane b 1955, Lucy b 1957, Henrietta b 1964); *Career* Lt Irish Gds 1946-48; chm: Wilks Shipping Co Ltd 1966-, Eggar Forrester Group 1966-90 (dir Eggar Forrester and Verner Ltd 1955-66); dir Gallic Management Co Ltd 1979-, chm Douglas and Gordon Ltd 1979-90; pres Inst of Chartered Shipbrokers 1986-88, chm of Centre for Spiritual and Psychological Studies 1987-89; *Recreations* meditation, painting, walking, gardening, reading, practising Tai Chi, listening to music; *Clubs* City of London; *Style*— Peter Talbot Willcox, Esq; Thanescroft, Shamley Green, Guildford, Surrey GU5 0TJ; Eggar Forrester Holdings Ltd, Rodwell House, Middlesex St, London E17 7HJ (☎ 071 377 9366, telex 8811671)

TALINTYRE, Douglas George; s of Henry Matthew Talintyre (d 1962), and Gladys, *née* Gould; *b* 26 July 1932; *Educ* Harrow Co GS for Boys, LSE (BSc, MSc); *m* 29 Dec 1956, Maureen Diana, da of Edward Lyons (d 1978); 1 s (John b 1963), 1 da (April b 1965); *Career* NCB 1956-66, princ Navy Dept MOD 1966-69; Cmmn on Industl Rels: sr industl rels offr (princ) 1969-71, dir of industl rels (asst sec) 1971-74; asst sec Trg Servs Agency 1974-75, cnsllr (Lab) HM Embassy Washington DC 1975-77, head of policy and planning MSC 1977-80; Dept of Employment: asst sec 1980-86, dir of fin and res mgmnt and princ fin offr (undersec) 1986-89; dir Office of Manpower Economics 1989-; Freeman Co of Cordwainers Newcastle upon Tyne, 1952; *Clubs* Reform; *Style*— D G Talintyre, Esq; Office of Manpower Economics, 22 Kingsway, London WC2B 6JY (☎ 071 405 5944)

TALLBOYS, Richard Gilbert; CMG, OBE; s of Harry Tallboys (d 1963), and Doris Gilbert (d 1967); *b* 25 April 1931; *Educ* Palmers Sch, Univ of London (LLB), Univ of Tasmania (BCom); *m* 1954, Margaret Evelyn, da of Brig Horace William Strutt DSO, ED (d 1985), of Tasmania; 2 s (Roger, Peter), 2 da (Prudence, Sarah); *Career* Lt Cdr RANR; Merchant Navy 1947-55, accountant in Aust 1955-62, with Aust Govt Trade Cmmn 1962-68 (served in: Johannesburg, Singapore, Jakarta), with HM Dip Serv 1968-88 (serv in Brasilia and Phnom Penh), commercial cnsllr Seoul 1976-80, HM consul-gen Houston 1980-85, HM ambass Hanoi 1985-87; chief exec World Coal Inst 1988-; Freeman City of London 1985; FCA, FCIS, FACPA; *Books* Doing Business with Indonesia (1968); *Recreations* skiing; *Clubs* Travellers, Naval, Tasmanian; *Style*— Richard G Tallboys, Esq, CMG, OBE

TALLON, David Seymour; s of Claude Reginald Tallon, of London, and Blanche Mary, *née* Mahony (d 1984); *b* 7 Oct 1940; *Educ* Rugby; *m* Jillian Valerie, da of Jack Perry; 2 s (Alastair James b 14 May 1965, Timothy Paul b 6 July 1967), 2 da (Victoria Kate Rebecca b 1 March 1969, Elizabeth Jane Biddy b 16 May 1970); *Career* CA 1964; articled clerk Deloitte Plender Griffiths 1958-64, then Dearden Harper Miller 1969 (tax mangr 1967-69), sr ptnr Dearden Farrow 1986-87 (ptnr 1977, nat tax ptnr 1982-86), managing ptnr Bristol office BDO Binder Hamlyn 1990- (dep sr ptnr 1987-89); Freeman City of London 1976, Liveryman Worshipful Co of Needlemakers; memb IOD, FCA; *Books* Capital Transfer Tax Planning (2 edn 1976, 3 edn 1978), Inland Revenue Practices & Concessions (1980); *Recreations* golf; *Clubs* Gresham, Bristol Commercial Rooms, Hampstead Cricket, Butterflies Cricket, Frogs Cricket, Hendon Golf; *Style*— David Tallon, Esq; BDO Binder Hamlyn, Narrow Quay House, Prince Street, Bristol BS1 4PQ (☎ 0272 279936)

TAMBLIN, Air Cdre Pamela Joy; CB (1980); *b* 1926; *Career* RAF 1951; dir Women's RAF 1976-80; *Style*— Air Cdre Pamela Tamblin, CB; 2 Carlton Court, Eastbury Rd, Watford, Herts

TAMLIN, Keith Maxwell; s of Sydney Thomas Tamlin (d 1946), and Madeline Isabel, *née* Prowse; *b* 19 July 1928; *Educ* Ruthin Sch, Univ of Wales (LLB); *m* 21 June 1954, Marian, da of Thomas Roberts; 2 da (Helen Susan b 25 May 1955, Karen Michele b 26 April 1958); *Career* Nat Serv King's (Liverpool) Regt RASC 1947-49 (cmmnd 1948, served ME); slr Supreme Ct of Judicature 1954, ptnr North Kirk & Co Slrs Liverpool 1959 (joined 1954), currently sr ptnr Cuff Roberts North Kirk Slrs Liverpool; dir: Everton Football Club Co Ltd 1974-, H Samuel plc 1979- (and other cos within H Samuel Group), Watches of Switzerland plc, several cos within Distributive Sector, various cos dealing with racehorse breeding; pres: Liverpool Jr C of C 1960, Liverpool Round Table 1965; chm Jt Ctees organising Charity Gala Performances at Liverpool Playhouse 1964-65 (to raise funds for Liverpool Central Boys' Club, Liverpool Maternity Hosp and the Br Red Cross and Women's Hosp), memb and slr Ctee Liverpool and Dist Family Servs Unit 1963-82, sec The Mail Order Traders' Assoc of GB 1967- (dir 1974); memb: PO Users' Nat Cncl 1970-, Trg Ctee Distributive Indust Bd 1971-, Cncl Retail Consortium 1973-, Cncl Advtg Assoc 1982-, Cncl CBI 1988-; nominated by HM Govt as a Gp 1 Employers' Rep to Econ and Social Ctee Brussels 1983; memb: Liverpool Law Soc, The Law Soc (pres 1984); *Recreations* walking, swimming, golf, watching football and professional golf; *Clubs* Athenaeum (Liverpool), East India; *Style*— Keith Tamlin, Esq; Cuff Roberts North Kirk, 25 Castle St, Liverpool L2 4TD (☎ 051 227 4181, fax 051 051 227 2584)

TAMM, Mary; da of Endel Tamm, of Surrey, and Raissa, *née* Kisseliev (d 1989); *b* 22 March 1950; *Educ* Bradford, RADA; *m* 14 Jan 1978, Marcus Jonathan Hardman Ringrose, s of Wing Cdr Richard Ringrose, DFC (d 1973), of London; 1 da (Lauren Zoe b 18 Nov 1979); *Career* actress; journalist: freelance writer for Moncy Mail, stories for magazines; theatre appearances incl: Mother Earth, The Bitter Tears of Petra Von Kant, Cards on the Table, Good Morning Bill, Swimming Pools at War, Present Laughter; films incl: Witness Madness, Odessa File, The Likely Lads, The Doubt, Rampage, Three Kinds of Heat; TV appearances incl: Donati Conspiracy, Warship, Girls of Slender Means, Not the Nine O'Clock News, The Assassination Run, The Treachery Game, Hunter's Walk, Jane Eyre, Bergerac, The Hello Goodbye Man, Coronation Street, A Raging Calm, Public Eye, Whodunnit, The Inheritors, Only When I Laugh, Quest for Love, Return of the Saint, World's Beyond, Hercule Poirot, Casualty, The Bill, Perfect Scoundrels; assoc of RADA memb Assoc's Ctee; *Recreations* riding, piano, reading, theatre, opera, art; *Style*— Ms Mary Tamm; Barry Langford Associates, Garden Studios, 11-15 Batterton St, London WC2H 9PB

TAMPIN, James Sidney; s of Horace Tampin (d 1966), and Jessie Harris, *née* Chamberlain; *b* 24 Aug 1940; *Educ* St Peters Devizes; *m* 28 March 1964, Stella Mary, da of Thomas Alfred Smith; 2 s (Stuart Peter b 13 Feb 1968; Christopher James b 15 July 1976); *Career* Sgt and PR photographer RAOC 1959-65; photographer; apprentice Wiltshire Gazette 1955-59; chief photographer: Herts & Essex Observer 1965-72, Rhodesia Herald 1972-76; freelance photographer 1977-79, chief photographer Doncaster Evening Post 1979-84, staff photographer Western Gazette 1984-89, chief photographer Dorset Evening Echo 1989-; BIPP: memb Cncl 1985-, nat pres 1988-89, chm Sector 4 Admin and Qualifications Bd, led negotiations with BT for sponsorship of Br Press Photographer of the Year Awards; former award winner World Press Photo Competition; FBIPP 1976 (memb 1966); *Style*— James Tampin, Esq; 28 Corfe Rd, Redlands, Weymouth, Dorset DT3 5RH (☎ 0305 812742); Dorset Evening Echo, St Thomas St, Weymouth, Dorset DT4 8EU (☎ 0305 784804, fax 0305 782593)

TAMS, Gerald Raymond; s of Peter Tams (d 1977), and Olive Margaret, *née* Simmons; *b* 11 Sept 1939; *Educ* Ratcliffe Coll Leicester, N Staffs Coll of Technol; *m* Angela Margaret, da of Alan Gibbons Weston, RE; 2 s (Robert William b June 1967 d 1968, Stephen Charles b 4 Dec 1969), 1 da (Catherine Monica b 11 Aug 1971); *Career* currently md: John Tams Ltd (joined 1960), A T Finney & Sons Ltd; currently chm and md John Tams Group plc; former pres Br Ceramic Mfrs Fedn, memb Nat Jt Cncl Br Ceramic Indust; *Recreations* golf, garden, Jaguars; *Clubs* Jaguar Drivers, Alvis Owners, Trentham Golf; *Style*— Gerald Tams, Esq; Fradswell Hall, Stafford ST18 0EX; John Tams Group plc, Longton, Stoke-on-Trent (☎ 0782 599226, fax 0782 599149, telex 367162 TAMS G)

TAMWORTH, Viscount; Robert William Saswalo Shirley; s and h of 13 Earl Ferrers; *b* 29 Dec 1952; *Educ* Ampleforth; *m* 21 June 1980, Susannah Mary, da of Charles Edward William Sheepshanks, of Arthington Hall, Otley, W Yorks; 2 s (Hon William Robert Charles b 10 Dec 1984, another b 2 June 1990), 1 da (Hon Hermione Mary Annabel b 11 Dec 1982); *Heir* s, Hon William Shirley; *Career* teaching in Kenya under CMS Youth Service Abroad Scheme 1971-72; articled to Whinney Murray & Co (chartered accountants) 1972-76; asst mangr Ernst & Whinney (now Ernst & Young) 1976-82; gp auditor and sr treasy analyst with BICC plc 1982-86, gp fin controller Viking Property Gp Ltd 1986, dir Viking Property Gp Ltd 1987-88, dir Norseman Holdings Ltd (formerly Ashby Securities Ltd) 1987- and assoc cos 1988-; FCA; *Recreations* the countryside and related activities, gardening; *Clubs* Boodle's; *Style*— Viscount Tamworth; The Old Vicarage, Shirley, Derby DE6 3AZ (☎ 0335 60815)

TAN, Melvyn; s of Tan Keng Hian, of Singapore, and Wong Sou Yuen; *b* 13 Oct 1956; *Educ* Yehudi Menuhin Sch Surrey, Royal Coll of Music; *Career* classical musician, fortepiano/harpsichord; interpreter of Baroque, classical and early Romantic works; repertoire incl: Weber, Mendelssohn, Chopin; debut Wigmore Hall 1977; played in all major UK venues with the Acad of Ancient Music, Eng Chamber Orch, RPO, London Classical Players; US tour playing Beethoven 1985, concert series with Roger Norrington and London Classical Players 1987 1988; festivals in 1989 incl: The Beethoven Experience (Purchase NY, with Roger Norrington and London Classical Players), Midsummer Mozart Festival in San Francisco (also Aldeburgh, Bath, Holland, Helsinki, and Kuhmo Finland); performed in 1990: San Francisco, toured France and Japan, Queen Elizabeth Hall; recordings for EMI incl: Beethoven's Waldstein, Appassionata and Les Adieux sonatas Schubert Impromptus, Beethoven Piano Concertos (with Roger Norrington and the London Classical Players), Salonkonzert (with Eric Hoeprich, Michel Garcin-Marrou and Konrad Hünteler; *Style*— Melvyn Tan, Esq; c/o Valerie Barber, Fifth Floor, 24 Chancery Lane, London WC2A 1LS (☎ 071 404 2266/2277, fax 071 831 2724)

TANCRED, Dr William Raymond (Bill); s of Adrian Nicholas Tancred, of 433 Nacton Rd, Ipswich, Suffolk, and Elsie Catherine Jane, *née* Donovan; *b* 6 Aug 1942; *Educ* Army Sch of Physical Training, Loughborough Coll of Education (CertEd), Loughborough Univ (MSc), West Virginia Univ (NATO scholar, PhD); *m* 12 Sept 1970, Angela Joyce, da of John Lloyd Moore; 3 da (Nicola Anne b 27 March 1972, Andrea Sacha b 4 Nov 1973, Joanna Louise b 20 July 1975); *Career* represented GB: Euro Championships (discus) 1966, 1969 and 1974, Cwlth Games (discus) 1966 and 1970 (Bronze medal) and 1974 (Silver medal), discus event 1968/72 Olympic Games; AAA Champion discus 1966, 1967, 1968, 1969, 1970, 1972 and 1973, AAA Champion shot (indoors) 1969 and 1973, current UK discus record holder 64.32m (1974), represented GB in 54 full Internationals; physical trg and recreation instr attached to I E Anglian Regt 1961-63, physical trg instructor Br Mil Garrison in Aden 1964-65, physical trg and recreation staff instr RMA Sandhurst 1965-68, head Physical Educn Dept Tower Ramparts Sch Ipswich 1970-71, lectr and head Dept of Physical Educn and Recreation W Bridgeford Coll of Further Educn 1973-75, sr lectr Nottingham Coll of Educn/Trent Poly 1975-78, dir of physical educn and recreation The Univ of Sheffield 1980-; Winston Churchill fell 1989, fell Br Assoc of Physical Trg 1986, memb Inst of Leisure and Amenity Mgmnt 1988, sr memb Br Inst of Sports Coaches; *Books* Weight Training For Sport (1984), Olympic Games (1984), Health Related Fitness (1987); Leisure Management (1991); *Recreations* walking in the Peak District, watching all sports, keeping fit; *Clubs* The International Athletes (chm); *Style*— Dr Bill Tancred; The University of Sheffield, Department of Physical Education and Recreation, Goodwin Athletics Centre, Northumberland Rd, Sheffield S10 2TZ (☎ 0742 768555, ext 6257/8)

TANDY, David John; s of Ernest Tandy, of Bexhill, and Ivy Eleonor Tandy (d 1969); *b* 25 June 1944; *Educ* Bexley GS, Univ of London (LLB); *m* Catherine Mary; 2 da (Philippa Siobhan b 31 July 1970, Elizabeth Virginia b 31 July 1972); *Career* Capital Taxes Ofice 1967-73, ptnr Titmuss Sainer and Webb 1976- (joined 1973); memb City of London Solicitors Co; memb Law Soc 1975; *Recreations* shooting; *Style*— David Tandy, Esq; Titmuss Sainer & Webb, 2 Serjeants' Inn, London EC4Y 1LT (☎ 071 583 5353)

TANG, Charles Michael Whitton; s of Peter Whitton Tang (d 1977), and Ruby Winifred, *née* Woon-Sam; *b* 17 April 1940; *Educ* Queen's Coll Guyana, UCL (LLB), The Queens Coll Oxford (BCL); *m* 13 Sept 1975, Denise Margaret, da of John Hall (d 1970); 3 s (Peter Whitton b 4 Nov 1980, Edward James Whitton b 4 Sept 1985, Charles Michael Whitton b 4 May 1988), 1 da (Bethany Louise b 6 Sept 1978); *Career* slr 1970, sr ptnr Michael Tang and Co Slrs; Oxford blue at tennis 1964 and 1965, played int lawn tennis tournament circuit 1965-66, played Davis Cup 1965; memb Law Soc; *Books* Matrimonial Law - The Financial Aspects (1989); *Recreations* golf, tennis; *Clubs* RAC, Hurlingham, Vincents, Gerrards Cross Golf; *Style*— Michael Tang, Esq; Purbeck, Martinsend Lane, Great Missenden, Bucks; Michael Tang & Co, 66-70 Shaftesbury Ave, London W1V 7DG (☎ 071 437 6154)

TANGLEY, Hon Peter Meldrum; s of Baron Tangley (Life Peer, d 1973); *b* 1936; *m* 1961, Annabel Binnie; *Style*— The Hon Peter Tangley; Byways, Little London, Witley, Surrey

TANGYE, Lady; Clarisse Renée Elisabeth; da of Baron Victor Schosberger de Tornya, of Tura, Hungary; *m* 1924, Sir Basil Tangye, 2 & last Bt (d 1969); 1 da; *Style*— Lady Tangye; Flat 15, High Point, Richmon Hill Rd, Edgbaston, Birmingham

15

TANGYE, Derek Alan Trevithick; s of Lt-Col Richard Trevithick Gilbertson Tangye (d 1944), and Sophie Elizabeth Frieda, *née* Kidman (d 1954); *b* 29 Feb 1912; *Educ* Harrow; *m* 20 Feb 1943, Jean Everald (d 1986), da of Frank Nicol (d 1952); *Career* enlisted Duke of Cornwall's Light Inf 1939, transferred MI (Capt) 1940-50; *Books* Time Was Mine (1941), Went The Day Well (ed, 1942), One King (survey of the Br Cwlth, 1944), The Minack Chronicles incl: A Gull on the Roof (1961), The Way to Minack (1968), Jeannie (1988), The Evening Gull (1990); *Recreations* contemplation; *Style—* Derek Tangye, Esq; Dorminack, nr Lamorna, Penzance, Cornwall

TANGYE, Lady Marguerite Rose; *née* Bligh; da of 9 Earl of Darnley (d 1955), and Daphne Rachel (d 1948), da of Hon Alfred John Mulholland (yst s of 1 Baron Dunleath); *b* 24 April 1913; *m* 1, 3 Aug 1934 (m dis 1941), Claud Dobré Strickland (ka 1941); m 2, 30 April 1942 (m dis 1951), Wing-Cdr Gordon Stanley Keith Haywood, RAF; 1 s, 1 da (twins); m 3, 5 May 1951 (m dis 1963), as his 2 w, Nigel Trevithick Tangye (d 1988); *Style—* The Lady Marguerite Tangye; 52 Redcliffe Gardens, London SW10 (☎ 071 351 4875)

TANKARD, Geoffrey; s of Arnold Tankard (d 1952), of Westfield, Halifax, and Ada Tankard (d 1937); *b* 25 Jan 1929; *Educ* Batley GS, Univ of Leeds (LLB); *m* 3 Aug 1956; 1 s (Julian b 13 March 1961), 1 da (Penelope b 3 Oct 1958); *Career* Nat Serv 1952-54; admitted slr 1952; currently ptnr Harrison Tankard & Mossmans Bradford (princ of form 1955-88, currently conslt); former master Ben Rhyudding Masonic Lodge; memb Law Soc 1951; *Recreations* golf; *Clubs* Shipley Golf; *Style—* Geoffrey Tankard, Esq; Wheatleys, 74 Wheatley Lane, Ben Rhydding, Ilkley, W Yorks LS29 8SF (☎ 0943 600466); Apartment 2D Olimpo 2, Paeso Maritimo, Caravajal, Torre Blanca; 8 Duke St, Piccadilly, Bradford, W Yorks (☎ 0274 722285, fax 0274 731905)

TANKEL, Henry Isidore; s of Hyman William Tankel (d 1946), of Glasgow, and Bertha, *née* Sacks (d 1968); *b* 14 Jan 1926; *Educ* Glasgow HS, Univ of Glasgow (MB ChB, MD); *m* 2 Oct 1956, Judith Benita, da of Edward Woolfson (d 1982), of Glasgow; 2 s (Jeremy b 1957, Alan b 1961), 2 da (Belinda b 1964, Laura b 1968); *Career* Capt: RAMC 1950-51 (Lt 1949-50), TA 1951-54; Fulbright scholar Mount Sinai Hosp NY 1954-55, conslt surgn Southern Gen Hosp Glasgow 1962-91; memb: Cncl RCPSGlas 1977-82, Nat Panel Specialists 1978-82 and 1987-90; treas Scot Ctee Hosp Med Servs 1978-, invited to address Gen Assembly Church of Scotland 1984; chm: Surgery Ctee W of Scotland Ctee Postgrad Med Educn 1985-89, Scot Jt Conslts Ctee 1989-; former pres Glasgow Jewish Rep Cncl, jt chm Christian Jewish Consultation gp Church of Scotland, memb Scot Health Serv Advsy Cncl; FRCSE 1954, FRCSGlas 1962; *Recreations* walking, making model boats; *Style—* Henry Tankel, Esq; 26 Dalziel Drive, Glasgow G41 4PU (☎ 041 423 5830)

TANKERVILLE, Countess of; Georgiana Lilian Maude; *née* Wilson; da of late Gilbert Wilson, DD, PhD of Vancouver, BC; *Educ* Univ of Br Columbia (BA), BLS Univ of Toronto; *m* 1954, as his 2 w, 9 Earl of Tankerville (d 1980); *Career* WRCNS, 1944-46; Librarian: BC Provincial Library, Victoria Public Library, The Hamlin School San Francisco, UNICEF, San Francisco; *Style—* The Rt Hon the Countess of Tankerville; 139 Olympia Way, San Francisco, Calif, USA, 94131

TANKERVILLE, 10 Earl of (GB 1714); Peter Grey Bennet; also Baron Ossulston (E 1682); s of 9 Earl of Tankerville (d 1980), and Georgiana Lilian Maude, *née* Wilson; *b* 18 Oct 1956; *Educ* Grace Cathedral Sch San Francisco (chorister), Oberlin Conservatory Ohio (BMus), San Francisco State Univ (MA); *Heir* uncle, Rev the Hon George Arthur Grey Bennet; *Career* musician San Francisco; *Style—* The Rt Hon the Earl of Tankerville; 139 Olympia Way, San Francisco, Calif 94131, USA (☎ 415 826 6639)

TANKERVILLE, Dowager Countess of; Violet; da of Erik Pallin, of Stockholm; *m* 1930, as his 2 w, 8 Earl of Tankerville (d 1971); 1 s, 1 da; *Career* Order of Vasa of Sweden; JP (Northumberland) 1942-, pres Chillingham Wild Cattle Assoc Ltd 1972-; *Style—* The Rt Hon the Dowager Countess of Tankerville; Estate House, Chillingham, Alnwick, Northumberland NE66 5NW

TANLAW, Baron (Life Peer UK 1971), of Tanlawhill, Co Dumfries; Hon Simon Brooke Mackay; yst s of 2 Earl of Inchcape (d 1939), and Leonora Margaret Brooke, da of HH the 3 Rajah of Sarawak (Sir Charles Vyner Brooke (d 1963)); *b* 30 March 1934; *Educ* Eton, Trinity Coll Cambridge (MA); *m* 1, 1959, Joanna Susan, o da of Maj John Henry Hirsch (d 1983), of Sungrove Lodge, Newbury, Berks; 1 s (Hon James Brooke b 1961) (and 1 s decd), 2 da (Hon Iona Héloïse (Hon Mrs Hudson) b 1960, Hon Rebecca Alexandra b 1967); m 2, 1976, Rina Siew Yong, yst da of late Tiong Cha Tan, of Kuala Lumpur, Malaysia; 1 s (Hon Brooke Brooke b 1982), 1 da (Hon Asia Brooke b 1980); *Career* sits as Ind (formerly Lib) in House of Lords; 2 Lt 12 Royal Lancers 1952-54; chm and md Fandstan Gp of private cos, dir Inchcape plc, pres Sarawak Assoc 1972-75; memb of govrs LSE 1980-, hon fell Univ of Buckingham 1981; Hon DUniv Buckingham 1983; nat appeal chm of the Elizabeth FitzRoy Homes for the Mentally Handicapped 1985-; *Clubs* White's, Oriental, Buck's, Puffin's; *Style—* The Rt Hon the Lord Tanlaw; Tanlawhill, Eskadalemuir, By Langholm, Dumfriesshire; 31 Brompton Square, London SW3; work: 36 Ennismore Gardens, London SW7

TANNER, Adrian Christopher; s of Alfred Charles Tanner, and Betty Margaret Tanner; *b* 13 Oct 1946; *Educ* Skinners Sch Tunbridge Wells; *m* 1969, Anna Margaret, *née* Shepherd; 2 da; *Career* marine insur broker; dir Alexander Howden Insurance Brokers Ltd 1978-81, Robert Fleming Marine Ltd 1982-; memb Lloyd's; *Style—* Adrian Tanner Esq; Wallington House, Smarden, Kent

TANNER, Amoret Frances Venables; da of Col Thomas Venables Scudamore (d 1951), and Joyce Carr, *née* Shields (d 1977); Rev James Venables, Vicar of Buckland Newton, Dorset, received Horticultural Soc's Silver medal for first treatise on making compost 1816; *b* 27 March 1930; *Educ* Uplands Sch Dorset; *m* 1, 4 April 1953, Christopher Scott; m 2, 13 Aug 1985, Ralph Esmond Selby Tanner; *Career* fndr memb The Ephemera Soc, tstee Fndn for Ephemera Studies; *Books* Hedgerow Harvest (1979), Murmur of Bees (1980); with Christopher Scott: Dummy Board Figures (1966), Antiques as an Investment (1967), Treasures in Your Attic (1971), Discovering Stately Homes (1973, 1975, 1981, 1988); *Recreations* collecting printed ephemera pre-1920, garden history, plant collecting; *Clubs* Royal Cwlth Soc; *Style—* Mrs Amoret Tanner; The Footprint, Padworth Common, Reading RG7 4QG (☎ 0734 701190)

TANNER, Bruce Winton; s of Lt Denis Frank Winton Tanner, MC, and Gladys, *née* Colegrove; *b* 21 Feb 1931; *Educ* King Edward's Sch Birmingham, St Catherine's Coll Oxford (BA); *m* 4 April 1960, Alma, da of Harold Athur Stoddard; 3 da (Jane b 1963, Ruth b 1965, Judith b 1968); *Career* 2 Lt RASC 1950; md Horizon Midlands Ltd 1965-74, chm and chief exec Horizon Travel Ltd 1974-85, chm Horizon Travel plc 1985-87, chm Chimes Restaurants (UK) plc 1987-, dir Birmingham Cable Corp 1988-; pres Int Fedn of Tour Operators 1980-83, dep chm Birmingham Hippodrome Theatre Devpt Tst 1990- (chm 1982-90), memb Cncl Birmingham Chamber of Indust and Commerce 1984-, dep chm Birmingham Cons Assoc 1987-89; *Recreations* theatre, tennis; *Style—* Bruce Tanner, Esq; 37 St Agnes Rd, Moseley, Birmingham B13 9PJ (☎ 021 449 3953); Flat 10, 4 Hans Place, London SW1X 0EY

TANNER, Dr John Ian; CBE (1979); s of R A Tanner, and I D M Tanner; *b* 2 Jan 1927; *Educ* Switzerland, City of London Library Sch, Univ of London (BA), Univ of Nottingham (MA, PhD), Univ of Oxford (MA); *m* 1953, April, *née* Rothery; *Career* archivist and librarian Kensington Library 1950-51, curator Leighton House Art Gallery and Museum 1951-53, curator librarian and tutor RAF Coll 1953-63, extra-mural lectr in history of art Univ of Nottingham 1959-63; founding dir: RAF Museum 1963-87, Battle of Britain Museum 1978-87, Cosford Aero-Space Museum 1978-87, Bomber Cmd Museum 1982-87; sr res fell Pembroke Coll Oxford 1982- (hon archivist 1980-); Walmsley lectr City Univ 1980, visiting fell Wolfson Coll Cambridge 1983-; prof Univ of Poland 1988-; chm Int Air Museum Ctee; pres: Anglo-American Ecumenical Assoc, Bd of Advsrs Battle Harbour Fndn's Anglican Serv, Trg and Religious Orgn, USAF Euro Meml Fndn; founding tstee Manchester Air and Space Museum, memb Founding Ctee All England Lawn Tennis Museum, memb Advsy Cncl Inst of Heraldic and Genealogical Studies, hon sec Old Cranwellian Assoc 1956-64; Hon DLitt City Univ, Hon LLD Univ of Poland, Freeman City of London 1966; Liveryman: Worshipful Co of Gold and Silver Wyre Drawers 1966, Worshipful Co of Scriveners 1978; Freeman Guild of Air Pilots and Air Navigators 1979; FLA, FMA, FRHistS, FRAeS, FSA; hon memb Collegio Araldico of Rome 1963, Tissandier Award Fedn Aeronautique Int 1977; OStJ 1964, KStJ 1978, St John Serv Medal 1985, KCSG 1977 (star 1985), Cross of Merit Order of Malta 1978, Nile Gold Medal Egypt 1987, Grand Cdr OM Holy Sepulchre Vatican, Constantinian Order 1988; *Books* List of Cranwell Graduates (ed second edn 1963), Encyclopaedic Dictionary of Heraldry (jtly, 1968), How to Trace Your Ancestors (1971), Man in Flight (1973), The Royal Air Force Museum: one hundred years of aviation history (1973), Badges and Insignia of the British Armed Forces (with W E May and W Y Carmen, 1974), Charles I (1974), Who's Famous in Your Family (second edn 1979), Wings of the Eagle (exhibition catalogue, 1976), The Fell in the Battle (1980), Sir William Rothenstein (exhibition catalogue, 1985), RAF Museum - a combined guide (1987); gen ed: Museums and Librarians, Studies in Air History; *Recreations* cricket, opera, reading; *Clubs* Athenaeum, Beefsteak, Reform, MCC, RAF; *Style—* Dr John Tanner, CBE; Flat One, 57 Drayton Gardens, London SW10 9RU

TANNER, Prof Paul Anthony (Tony); *b* 18 March 1935; *Educ* Raynes Park County GR, Jesus Coll Cambridge (BA), Univ of Calif Berkeley; *Career* Intelligence Corps 1953-55; dir English Studies King's Coll Cambridge 1961- (fell 1960-), ACLS fell Univ of Calif Berkeley 1962-63, lectr Univ of Cambridge 1966- (asst lectr 1964-66), visiting Concora lectr Northwestern Univ 1967, visiting prof Univ of Venice 1969; lectr: Kyoto Seminar Japan 1972, Salzburg Seminar Austria 1973; visiting fell Center for Twentieth Century Studies Univ of Wisconsin 1974, fell Center for Advanced Study in the Behavioral Sciences Stanford Calif 1974-75, univ lectr Univ of Cambridge 1975-76, prof John Hopkins Univ, univ lectr with responsibility for American lit Univ of Cambridge 1977-80, reader Univ of Cambridge 1980-; *Publications* Lord Jim (1963), Saul Bellow (1965), City of Words: American Fiction 1950-70 (1970), Adultery in the Novel (1979), Thomas Pynchon (1982), Jane Austen (1986), Henry James, Subjective Adventurer (Essays and Studies 1963), Robert Musil (London Magazine 1965), Malamud's New Life (critical Quarterly 1968), My Life in American Literature (Tri Quarterly 1974), The Ever-Dying, Ever-Living Novel (Lugano Review 1981), Conrad and the Last Gentleman (Critical Quarterly 1986); *Style—* Prof Tony Tanner; King's College, Cambridge (☎ 0223 350411)

TANQUERAY, David Andrew; s of David Yeo Bartholemew Tanqueray (d 1944), and Majorie Edith, *née* Macdonald; *b* 23 May 1939; *Educ* Rugby, Clare Coll Cambridge (MA), Univ of California Berkeley; *m* 20 Aug 1966, Tamsin Mary, da of Air Cdre Cyril Montague Heard; 1 s (David b 1981), 2 da (Venetia b 1974, Tabitha b 1977); *Career* conslt Control Data Ltd 1969-84, Floating Point Systems UK Ltd 1985-; awarded Harkness Fellowship 1966; *Recreations* music; *Style—* David Tanqueray, Esq; 27 Cheriton Ave, Twyford, Berks RG10 9DB (☎ 0734 341544); Floating Point Systems UK Ltd, Apex House, London Rd, Bracknell, Berks RG12 2TE (☎ 0344 56921)

TANSLEY, Sir Eric Crawford; CMG (1946); s of William Tansley; *b* 1901; *Educ* Mercer's Sch; *m* 1931, Iris, da of Thomas Richards, of Eltham; 1 s, 1 da; *Career* entered Civil Serv 1939, mktg dir W African Produce Control Bd Colonial Office 1940-47, ret 1947; dir Cwlth (formerly Colonial) Development Corporation 1948-51 and 1961-68, md Ghana Cocoa Marketing Co 1961, advsr Nigerian Produce Marketing Co to 1961; dir: Standard Bank, Bank of W Africa, Standard and Chartered Banking Group 1972, chm Plantation and Colonial Products until 1972, ret; kt 1953; *Style—* Sir Eric Tansley, CMG; 11 Cadogan Sq, London SW1 (☎ 071 235 2752)

TANT, Russell Byron; s of Melvyn John Tant (d 1970), and Sadie Jacobs (d 1989); *b* 20 March 1949; *Educ* Orange Hill Co GS, UCH London (BDS, capt UCH CC); *m* 1981 (m dis 1990), Elizabeth Mary Lorimer; 2 s (Radleigh Lewis Byron b 6 Oct 1983, Sebastian Charles Russell b 5 July 1985); *Career* gen dental practice Knightsbridge 1972-76, commenced practice Harpenden Herts 1978, fully private practice Wimpole Street 1985; pres London Dental Study Club 1983; *Recreations* cricket, golf, skiing, squash, music; *Clubs* Marylebone Cricket, Royal Cinque Ports Golf, Harpenden Golf; *Style—* Russell Tant, Esq; 39 Silsoe House, Park Village East, London NW1 (☎ 071 387 8445); 17 Upper Wimpole St, London W1M 7TB (☎ 071 935 0087)

TANTAM, Prof Digby John Howard; s of Donald Harry Tantam, of Cheam, Surrey, and Daphne, *née* Winterbone; *b* 15 March 1948; *Educ* St Paul's, Univ of Oxford (MA, BM BCh), Univ of Harvard (MPhil), Univ of London (PhD); *m* 6 July 1974, Sheila Jean, da of Richard Geoffrey Hunt Salkeld; 1 s (Robert John Geoffrey b 1978), 1 da (Grace Ruth b 1980); *Career* St George's Hosp 1974-75, Harvard Med Sch 1976-77, Maudsley Hosp 1977-83, Dept of Psychiatry Univ of Manchester 1983-90, prof psychotherapy Univ of Warwick 1990-; MRCPsych; *Books* Making Sense of Psychiatric Cases (with M Greenberg and G Szmukler, 1986), Public Health Impact of Mental Illness (with D Goldberg, 1990); *Recreations* cycling, reading, cooking, gardening, philosophy; *Style—* Prof Digby Tantam; Department of Psychology, University of Warwick, Coventry CV4 7AL)

TAPLEY, (David) Mark; s of John Randolph Tapley (d 1972), of Stafford, and Nancy Doris Rathbone (d 1986); *b* 24 March 1946; *Educ* King Edward VI Sch Stafford, Oriel Coll Oxford (BA), London Business Sch (MBA); *m* April 1970, Judith Ann, da of Basil Wilford, of Stafford; 1 s (Richard Paul b March 1979), 1 da (Charlotte Emily b June 1977); *Career* systems engr ICL 1969-72, investmt analyst and portfolio mangr JP Morgan 1974-84 (vice pres 1982), dir of equities American Express Asset Management (later Shearson Lehman Global Asset Management and Posthorn Global Asset Management) 1984-90, md London and Bishopsgate International plc 1990-; reg speaker at conferences seminars and trg courses on devpts in investmt mgmnt indust; memb NY Soc of Investmt Analysts 1974, ASIA 1976; *Books* International Portfolio Management (ed and contrib 1986); *Recreations* running, theatre, music; *Style—* Mark Tapley, Esq; London & Bishopsgate Investment plc, 12th Floor, 76 Shoe Lane, London EC2R 3JB (☎ 071 583 1978, fax 071 353 0040, portable 0831 411654)

TAPLEY, William Donald Thomas; s of Albert Edward Tapley (d 1972), and Florence Louisa, *née* Lavers (d 1957); *b* 19 Jan 1924; *Educ* St Boniface Sch; *m* 4 June 1949, Betty Mary, *née* Way; 2 s (Andrew Donald b 31 July 1950, Richard Charles b 10 Sept 1953); *Career* Nevill Hovey Smith & Co (CA's) Plymouth 1940-50, asst accountant J Sainsbury Ltd (now plc) 1950-53, Avon Rubber Co Ltd (now plc) 1953-65: asst accountant, chief accountant, production mangr, works mangr, works dir, dir and gen mangr Tyre Div; BTR plc 1966-89: gen mangr of productivity servs 1966, dir and gen mangr of hose and belting 1966, dir and gen mangr Leyland Gp 1969, gp chief exec for many subsids 1972, dep md 1975, chm European Reg 1984, non-exec dir 1989; dep chm Automotive Products plc 1984-, non-exec dir Epwin Gp plc 1984-, appointed to regnl bd (now western advsy bd) Natwest Bank plc 1984-, non-exec dir BBA Gp plc 1986-89; pres: Br Rubber Manufacturers Assoc 1981-83, Plastics and Rubber Inst 1988-90; treas Rubber and Plastics Res Assoc 1988-; *Recreations* golf; *Clubs* Royal Over-Seas League; *Style*— William Tapley, Esq; 26 Sloane Gardens, London SW1W 8DJ; Hombeams, Higher Park Rd, Braunton, Barnstaple, Devon EX33 2LF

TAPNER, John Walter; s of Walter Frederick Searle Tapner (d 1977), and Margot Elizabeth, *née* Pellant (d 1979); *b* 12 June 1929; *Educ* King's Coll Taunton, Univ of London (LLB); *m* 26 Jan 1957, Cherry, da of Capt Ralph Joseph Moreton (d 1957); 2 s (Rory b 1959, Paul b 1963), 1 da (Michelle b 1961); *Career* slr; dep sr ptnr Slaughter and May 1986-90 (ptnr 1964-90); *Recreations* music, various spectator sports; *Style*— John W Tapner, Esq; The Coach House, Branches Park, Cowlinge, nr Newmarket, Suffolk CB8 9HN

TAPP, David Redvers; s of Horace Redvers Tapp (d 1965), of Chelmsford, Essex, and Jessie Margaret, *née* Davis (d 1978); *b* 26 Feb 1930; *Educ* King Edward VI GS Chelmsford Essex, Chelmsford Sch of Architecture; *m* 10 July 1954, Irene Theodosia, da of Charles Smith (d 1982), of Essex; 1 s (Christopher b 1961), 1 da (Alison b 1958); *Career* RE Cyprus 1956-57; chartered architect; princ in own architect's practice 1969-, bdcaster on timber frame housing BBC; ARIBA; *Recreations* tennis, cricket, gardening, wine; *Clubs* Phyllis Court (Henley), Rotary, Jaguar Drivers; *Style*— David R Tapp, Esq; Shandi, Hop Gardens, Henley on Thames, Oxon (☎ 0491 575730); 13 Fair Mile, Henley on Thames (☎ 0491 576336)

TAPPER, Colin Frederick Herbert; s of Herbert Frederick Tapper (d 1977), and Florence, *née* Lambard (d 1976); *b* 13 Oct 1934; *Educ* Bishopshalt GS, Magdalen Coll Oxford (Vinerian scholar); *m* 1 April 1961, Margaret, da of Harold White (d 1978); 1 da (Lucy b 22 Jan 1973); *Career* called to the Bar Gray's Inn 1961; lectr LSE 1959-65, reader in law All Souls Oxford 1979-, vice pres Magdalen Coll Oxford 1991- (fell 1965-); visiting prof: Univ of Alabama and Univ of NY 1970, Stanford Univ 1976, Monash Univ 1984, Univ of Northern Kentucky 1986, Univ of Sydney 1989, Univ of Western Aust 1991; dir: Butterworth 1979-85, Butterworth Telepublishing 1979-90; conslt: Butterworths 1968-90, Masons (Solicitors) 1990-; *Books* Computer Law (1978, 4 edn 1990), Computers and The Law (1983), Cross on Evidence (7 edn 1990); *Recreations* reading, writing, computing; *Style*— Colin Tapper, Esq; Corner Cottage, Stonesfield, Oxford OX7 2QA (☎ 0993 891284); Magdalen College, Oxford OX1 4AU (☎ 0865 276055, fax 0865 276103)

TAPPIN, Andrew Brice; s of Walter Philip Tappin, of Bridport, Dorset, and Daphne Mary, *née* Brice; *b* 27 Jan 1945; *Educ* Willington Sch, Stamford Sch, Tiffin Sch; *m* 4 Sept 1971, Barbara Jane, da of late Clive Edward Midwinter; 1 s (Rupert Clive b 22 Feb 1972), 1 da (Laura Rachel b 22 Oct 1974); *Career* qualified sr Annan Dexter & Co 1967-71 (articled clerk 1963-67); ptnr: Dearden Lord Annan Morrish 1972, Dearden Farrow (after merger) 1977-, BDO Binder Hamlyn (after merger) 1987-; govr E Sheen Primary Sch; FCA 1977 (ACA 1967); *Books* Capital Transfer Tax Planning (jtly, 1975), Financial Planning for Clients (jtly, 1979); *Recreations* squash, running, education, music; *Style*— Andrew Tappin, Esq; BDO Binder Hamlyn, 7-17 Lansdowne Rd, Croydon CR9 2PL (☎ 081 688 4422, fax 081 760 0315)

TAPPS-GERVIS-MEYRICK, Ann, Lady; Ann; *née* Miller; yr da of Edward Clive Miller (d 1956), of Melbourne, Aust; *m* 20 March 1940, Sir George David Eliott Tapps-Gervis-Meyrick, 6 Bt, MC (d 1988); 1 s (Sir George, 7 Bt, *qv*), 1 da (Caroline Susan Joan (Mrs Hulse) b 30 April 1942); *Style*— Ann, Lady Tapps-Gervis-Meyrick; Waterditch House, Bransgore, Christchurch, Dorset

TAPPS-GERVIS-MEYRICK, Sir George Christopher Cadafael; 7 Bt (GB 1791), of Hinton Admiral, Hampshire; o s of Sir George David Eliott Tapps-Gervis-Meyrick, 6 Bt, MC (d 1988); *b* 10 March 1941; *Educ* Eton, Trinity Coll Cambridge; *m* 14 March 1968, Jean Louise, yst da of Lord William Walter Montagu Douglas Scott, MC (d 1958), 2 s of 7 Duke of Buccleuch; 2 s, 1 da; *Heir* s, George William Owen Tapps-Gervis-Meyrick b 1970; *Style*— Sir George Meyrick, Bt; Hinton Admiral, Christchurch, Dorset

TAPSCOTT, Paul Mais; s of Henry John Tapscott (d 1960), and Marjorie Phyllis, *née* Brooks; *b* 23 May 1919; *Educ* Uppingham, Trinity Coll Cambridge (BA); *m* 1946, Babette Alison, da of Joseph Blackham, of Birmingham (d 1941); 1 da; *Career* economist and memb Stock Exchange 1956-85; chm: Laurence Scott Ltd 1961-80, Lesney Products & Co Ltd 1960-80, Associated Fisheries Ltd 1969-78; dir Friends Provident Life Office 1964-90, chm and dep chm Francis Industries Ltd 1964-84; *Recreations* swimming, gardening, DIY; *Clubs* Phyllis Court; *Style*— Paul Tapscott, Esq; Brampton, Green Dene, E Horsley, Leatherhead, Surrey KT24 5RF (☎ 048 65 2058); 256 Southbank House, Black Prince Rd, London SE1 7SJ (☎ 071 587 1571)

TAPSELL, Sir Peter Hannay Bailey; MP (C) East Lindsey 1983-; s of late Eustace Tapsell, and Jessie Maxwell Hannay, *qv*; *b* 1 Feb 1930; *Educ* Tonbridge, Merton Coll Oxford, hon postmaster, MA, hon fell 1989; *m* 1, 1963 (m dis 1971), Hon Cecilia, 3 da of 9 Baron Hawke; 1 s (decd); m 2, 1974, Gabrielle, da of late Jean Mahieu, of Normandy, France; *Career* 2 Lt Royal Sussex Regt Middle East 1948-50, hon life memb 6 Sqdn RAF 1971; librarian Oxford Union 1953 (rep on debating tour of USA 1954); PA to PM (Sir Anthony Eden) election campaign 1955, Cons Res Dept 1954-57, memb London Stock Exchange 1957-, advsr to commercial and central banks in Third World and Japan; contested (C) Wednesbury By Election 1957; MP (C): Nottingham W 1959-64, Horncastle Lincs 1966-83; oppn front bench spokesman on: foreign and cwlth affrs 1976-77, treasy and econ affrs 1977-78; chm: Coningsby Club 1957-58, Br Caribbean Assoc 1963-64; hon treas Anglo-Chinese Parly Gp 1970-74; memb: Cncl Inst for Fiscal Studies, Trilateral Cmmn, Organising Ctee Zaire River Expedition 1974-75, Ct Hull Univ; hon memb Investmt Advsy Bd Brunei Govt 1976-85, Brunei Dato (Datuk) 1971, vice pres Tennyson Soc 1966-, hon vice chm Mitsubishi Tst Oxford Fndn 1988-; kt 1985; *Clubs* Athenaeum, Carlton, Hurlingham; *Style*— Sir Peter Tapsell, MP; c/o House of Commons, London SW1 (☎ 071 219 3000)

TARASSENKO, Lady Ann Mary Elizabeth; da (by 2 m) of late 6 Earl of Craven; *b* 9 April 1959; *m* 1978, Dr Lionel Tarassenko; 1 s (Luke Ivan Thomas b 1988), 1 da (Naomi Rachel Elizabeth b 1989); *Style*— The Lady Ann Tarassenko; 12 Squitchey Lane, Oxford

TARDIF, Graham Mackenzie de Putron; s of Frederick Graham Charles Tardif (d 1972), and Mabel Marion, *née* Mackenzie (d 1987); *b* 27 June 1935; *Educ* Tonbridge; *m* 1, 9 April 1960 (m dis 1971), Judith Livock; 1 s (Simon b 1963, d 1987), 1 da (Michele b 1962); m 2, 8 Jan 1972, Lucinda, da of John Hoskyns-Abrahall; 1 s (Ben b 1972), 2 da (Kate b 1975, Lucy b 1981); *Career* Nat Serv RAF 1953-55; dir: J H Minet UK 1968, Frank B Hall UK 1970, Wigham Poland UK 1973, Frizzell Group 1976; pres and chief exec Canadian International Insurance Management Ltd Bermuda USA 1981, chm Soberbiew Ltd and Graham Tardif Assoc Ltd, Leslie & Godwin UK Ltd 1990; Freeman City of London 1989; *Recreations* golf, rugby football, dog-walking, cooking; *Clubs* Royal St Georges Golf, Richmond FC (pres 1989), London Rowing; *Style*— Graham Tardif, Esq; The Gate House, Dell Quay, Chichester, W Sussex PO20 7EE (☎ 0243 784197)

TARLING, Nikolas Daniel; s of Keith Ellis Tarling, of Yarlet, Stafford, and Ethel Marjorie Joy, *née* Harris (d 1967); *b* 1 May 1941; *Educ* Repton, Univ of Oxford (MA); *m* 14 Feb 1969, Elizabeth Helen Margaret, da of Maj Alexander David Duncan Lawson, MBE, of Blinkbonny, Newburgh, Fife; 3 da (Rebecca, Camilla, Serena); *Career* admitted slr 1966; Freshfields: ptnr 1974-, resident ptnr Paris 1974-75, Euro ptnr London 1988-; *Recreations* fishing, skiing, music, old master drawings; *Clubs* City of London, Hurlingham; *Style*— Nikolas Tarling, Esq; 13 Markham Sq, London SW3 4UY; Fontaine St Donat, 06140 Vence; Whitefriars, London EC4Y 1HT

TARLOW, Dr Michael Jacob; s of Dr Samuel Tarlow, of London, and Fanny, *née* Yankelevitch (d 1987); *b* 27 Dec 1939; *Educ* Haberdashers' Aske's, London Guy's Hosp Med Sch (MB BS), Univ Coll London (MSc); *m* Olwynne, da of Harry Frank (d 1963), of Darlington; 3 c (Sarah b 1967, Joanna b 1969, Ben b 1973); *Career* various jr hosp appts 1962-68, house physician and registrar Hosp for Sick Children Gt Ormond St 1968-70, fell Mayo Clinic Rochester USA 1970-72, sr registrar Royal Aberdeen Hosp for Sick Children 1972-74, sr lectr paediatrics and hon conslt paediatrician Univ of Birmingham Med Sch 1974-; memb Ed Bd: Archives of Disease in Childhood 1984-90, British Journal of Hospital Medicine 1984-; FRCP 1982; *Books* Paediatric Revision (with Dr K C Chin, 1989); *Recreations* chess, squash, hillwalking; *Style*— Dr Michael Tarlow; 43 Silhill Hall Rd, Solihull, W Midlands B91 1JX (☎ 021 705 4197); Dept of Paediatrics, East Birmingham Hospital, Bordesley Green East, Birmingham B9 5ST (☎ 021 766 6611)

TARN, Prof John Nelson; s of Percival Nelson Tarn (d 1976), and Mary Isabell, *née* Purvis (d 1972); *b* 23 Nov 1934; *Educ* Royal GS Newcastle Upon Tyne, Kings Coll Newcastle (BArch), Gonville and Caius Coll Cambridge (PhD); *Career* architectural asst W B Edwards and Ptnrs Newcastle 1960-63, sr lectr in architecture Univ of Sheffield 1970 (lectr 1963-70), prof of architecture and head of Dept Univ of Nottingham 1970-73, Roscoe prof of architecture since 1974 and head of Liverpool Sch of Architecture 1974-86, head of Liverpool Sch of Architecture and Building Engrg 1986-90, pro-vice-chllr Liverpool Univ 1988; memb Peak Park Planning Bd 1973-86: chm Planning Control Ctee 1979-, vice chm of Bd 1981-86, co-opted memb Planning Control Ctee 1986-; RIBA: chm Examinations Sub Ctee 1975-, memb Professional Literature Ctee 1968-77, memb Educn and Professional Devpt Ctee 1978-; memb: Countryside Cmmn Review Ctee on Nat Parks 1989-90, Technol Ctee UGC 1974-84, Architecture Ctee CNAA 1981-86, Built Environment Ctee 1986-89; ARCUK: chm Bd of Educn 1983-86, vice chm Cncl 1985-86, chm 1987-90; FRIBA, FRHistS, FSA, FRSA; *Books* Working Class Housing in Nineteenth Century Britain (1971), Five Per Cent Philanthropy (1973), The Peak District, Its Architecture (1973); *Clubs* Athenaeum; *Style*— Prof John Tarn; 2 Ashmore Close, Barton Hey Drive, Caldy, Wirral, Merseyside L48 2JX; Piping Stones, Stanton in Peak, Matlock, Derbyshire DE4 2LR; Liverpool School of Arch and Building Engrg, Liverpool University, PO Box 147, Liverpool L69 3BX (☎ 051 794 2602, fax 051 708 6502, telex 627095 UNILPL G)

TARNOPOLSKY, Alex; s of Samuel Tarnopolsky, of Buenos Aires, and Raquel, *née* Jacuboff (d 1972); *b* 17 Oct 1939; *Educ* Univ of Buenos Aires (MD); *m* 17 Nov 1968, Alma, da of Victor Petchersky (d 1967); 2 s (Matias b 1970, Damian b 1976); *Career* res psychiatrist Policlinico Lanus Buenos Aires Argentina 1967-71, sr lectr Inst Psychiatry London 1977-81, conslt psychotherapist Maudsley Hosp 1981-, visiting prof of psychiatry Univ of Toronto 1988-89, prof of psychiatry McMaster Univ Canada 1991; conslt: WHO 1972-73 and 1977, Swedish Med Res Cncl 1979, dept of psychiatry Univ of Mass Pittsfield 1984 and 1987; FRCPsych, memb Br Psychoanalytical Soc 1984; author of over 60 scientific papers on psychiatric epidemiology and personality disorders; *Recreations* painting, photography; *Style*— Dr Alex Tarnopolsky; 3 Hemstal Rd, London NW6 2AB (☎ 071 624 9143); The Maudsley Hosp, Psychotherapy Unit, Denmark Hill, London SE5 8AZ (☎ 071 703 6333, fax 071 703 0179)

TARRANT, Christopher John (Chris); s of Maj B A Tarrant, MC, and Joan Ellen, *née* Cox; *b* 10 Oct 1946; *Educ* Kings Sch Worcester, Birmingham Univ (BA); *m* 1, Aug 1977 (m dis 1982), Sheila Margaret, da of Maj Ralph Roberton (d 1982); m 2, Ingrid; 3 da (Helen Victoria, Jennifer Mary, Samantha Charlotte); *Career* prodr/presenter of TV progs incl: ATV Today (1972), Tiswas (1974), OTT (1982), Everybody's Equal (1989), PSI (1989); presenter of Capital Radio's Breakfast Show 1987-; patron: Duke's Trust, Phoenix Centre for Physically Handicapped; *Books* Ken's Furry Friends (1986), Fishfriars Hall Revisited (1987); *Recreations* fishing, cricket; *Clubs* White Swan Piscatorials, Lords Taverners; PVA Ltd, Alpha Tower, Birmingham B1 1TT (☎ 021 643 4011)

TARRANT, Lucius Frederick Charles; s of Hugh Sherrard Tarrant (d 1963), of Cork, Ireland, and Doreen Kathleen Beatrice, *née* Harvey (d 1981); *b* 17 Aug 1928; *Educ* Cork GS, Portora Royal Sch, Univ of Dublin (BA, BAI); *m* 16 March 1956, Yvonne Anne, da of George Stephen Sheffield (d 1956); 2 da (Sally-Ann b 1957, Julie b 1959); *Career* Public Works Dept Nigeria 1950-52, md Costain Group plc 1952-89; FICE; *Recreations* sailing, gardening; *Clubs* Bosham Sailing; *Style*— Lucius Tarrant, Esq; Ilex Cottage, The Street, West Clandon, Surrey GU4 7TJ

TARRANT, Peter Elliot; s of Cuthbert Easton Tarrant (d 1985), of Auckland, NZ, and Maud, *née* Dotchin (d 1989); *b* 19 May 1925; *Educ* Takapuna GS, Auckland Univ Coll, Univ of NZ (Dip Journ); *m* July 1951, Noeline Margaret Anne, *née* Harris; 1 s (Richard Peter b 1955), 1 da (Robyn Penelope Anne (Mrs Bailey) b 1953); *Career* ed various NZ Magazines 1948-50, dir Cuthbert E Tarrant Ltd NZ 1952-58, press offr Colonial Office London 1959-61 (info offr 1951-52), press and info offr The De La Rue Group 1961-63, PR mangr International Computers Ltd 1963-69; md: Tarrant Wilkinson and Partners Ltd 1970-71, Peter Tarrant & Associates Ltd UK 1972-88; dir A Plus Group Ltd UK 1988-; awarded: Dip CAM, Inst PR President's prize 1977, IPR Sword of Excellence award 1988; memb Chartered Inst of Journalists 1950, MIPR 1963, memb CAM Graduates Assoc 1977; *Books* British Dependencies in the Caribbean and the North Atlantic (co-author, 1952), Handbook of Consumer Sales Promotion (exec ed, 1974), Clean Up-It's Good Business (1986); *Recreations* golf, reading; *Clubs* United Oxford and Cambridge Univ, Burhill Golf; *Style*— Peter Tarrant, Esq; A Plus Group Ltd, Tithe Barn, Tithe Court, Langley, Berks SL3 8AS (☎ 0753 586655, fax 0753 586223)

TARRING, Trevor John; s of Leslie Herbert Tarring (d 1964), of Cobham Surrey, and Ethel Anne, (d 1976), *née* Rosser; *b* 5 July 1932; *Educ* Brentwood Sch, Brasenose Coll Oxford (MA); *m* 21 March 1959, Marjorie Jane, da of John Henry Colbert (d 1966), of Malvern, Worcs; 1 da (Emma Jane b 1964); *Career* dir Metal Bureau Ltd 1964, chief exec Metal Bulletin 1987- (jt ed 1968, md 1978); Freeman Stationers Co; MinstMet 1963; *Books* Trading in Metals (1953), Nonferrous Metal Works of the World (ed 1974); *Recreations* vintage car competitions; *Clubs* Vintage Sports Car; *Style*— Trevor Tarring, Esq; Metal Bulletin plc, PO Box 28E, Worcester Park, London KT4 7HY (☎ 081 330 4311, fax 081 337 8943, telex 21 383)

TARUSCHIO, Franco Vittorio; s of Giuseppe Taruschio (d 1974), of Italy, and Apina Cecati (d 1988); *b* 29 March 1938; *Educ* GS Osimo, Hotel Sch, Bellagio Como Italy; *m* 9 Nov 1963, Emily Ann Dunant, da Dr Gerald Owen Forester, 1 da (Sasha Dunant b and d 1976), 1 adopted da (Pavinee Mia b 27 Feb 1977); *Career* restaurateur; formerly at: Hotel Splendide Lugano, Restaurant La Belle Meunière Clermont-Ferrand, Three Horse Shoes Hotel Rugby; Walnut Tree Inn Gwent 1963-; Gold medal for services to tourism in Wales 1985, Egon Ronay Restaurant of the Year award 1987; *Recreations* swimming and walking; *Style—* Franco Taruschio, Esq; Walnut Tree Inn, Llandewi Skirrid, Abergavenny, Gwent, Wales NP7 8AW (☎ 0873 2797)

TASKER, John Mellis (Jack); MBE (1954); s of Sir Theodore James Tasker, CIE, OBE, ICS (d 1981), of Southover Swanage, Dorset, and Lady Jessie Helen Tasker (d 1974); *b* 18 Jan 1919; *Educ* Westminster, Trinity Coll Cambridge (BA); *m* 8 Oct 1949 (m dis 1988), (Cecile) Juliet, da of George Walter Frederick McGwire (d 1959), of Hayes, Durlston, Swanage, Dorset; 3 s (Nigel b 1950, Richard b 1959, Patrick b 1961), 2 da (Madeline b 1952, Elizabeth b 1956); *Career* cmmnd 2 Lt RA 1939, Lt 1941, Capt 1942, demobbed 1946; HMOCS 1947-69: asst sec Gibraltar 1947-51, admin offr The Gambia 1951-56, under sec Kenya 1956-69; sec to the bd Milton Keynes Devpt Corp 1969-81, ret 1981; *Style—* Jack Tasker, Esq, MBE; Brook Farm House, Milton Keynes Village, Milton Keynes (☎ 0908 665 360)

TASKER, Sidney H; *Educ* Univ of Manchester; *Career* Nat Serv RE; architect; trainee architect 1947, architect Grenfell-Baines 1955- (became Building Design Partnership 1961), ptnr Building Design Partnership 1964-; projects incl: Shell Admin HQ at Stanlow Oil Refinery Cheshire 1955-60, works restaurant for Mobil Oil Birkenhead 1957-60, telephone exchange, offices and workshop Preston 1958-62, devpt plan Univ of Bradford 1964-65 and all academic residential and other bldgs on the campus up to 1991; conslt to City of Chester 1962-75; project ptnr: ICI Petrochemicals Div Admin and Res HQ Teeside 1969-75, Northgate Area Leisure Centre Chester 1972-77; project ptnr and project mangr for proposed Leyland Cars Res Design and Devpt Centre 1976-78; architect ptnr various projects Sellafield for British Nuclear Fuels plc 1970s-80s, conslt architect Yorkshire Sculpture Park Bretton Hall nr Wakefield 1984-, jt job ptnr Building Design Partnership Team designing major building installations for Br Army Mount Pleasant Air Base Falkland Is 1983-85; project ptnr: (and architect) New Crown Cts Kingston upon Hull 1985-, The Pyramids Birkenhead 1989; architect Kirklees Priory 1988, project ptnr and architect Lawrence Batley Centre Nat Art Educn Archive Bretton Hall Coll 1988-, project ptnr devpt plan Lancashire Poly 1990 and Sports Complex Ingol Preston 1990; conslt to Local Govt Bd IOM during pub inquiry into Summerland fire disaster 1973, ldr consortium of conslts on cmmn from DOE to recast Building Regulations for Eng and Wales 1981 (work was fndn of Building Regulations 1985), lectr on various aspects of architecture and architectural practice, contrib to tech press and author of a guide to building regulations; *Awards* Office of the Year award 1973, RIBA Regnl award 1976; Hon Doctorate Univ of Bradford 1989, MRIBA; *Style—* Sidney H Tasker, Esq; Building Design Partnership, Vernon St, Moor Lane, Preston PR1 3PQ

TATCH, Brian; s of David Tatch, of London and formerly of Glasgow (d 1958), and Gertrude Tatch (now Gertrude Alper); *b* 24 April 1943; *Educ* Central Fndn Grammar, UCL (BSc); *m* 1965, Denise Ann, da of William Eugene Puckett (d 1979), of London and formerly of Louisville, Kentucky; 2 s, 1 da; *Career* consulting actuary; ptnr Clay & Partners 1975-; fndr memb Assoc of Pensioner Tstees (chm 1981-85); chm: Clay Clark Whitehill Ltd 1987- (jt chm 1985-87), The Bridford Group Ltd 1987; FIA, FPMI; *Style—* Brian Tatch, Esq; c/o Clay & Partners, 61 Brook St, London W1Y 2HN (☎ 071 408 1600, telex 27167); 4 Eversley Crescent, London N21 1EJ (☎ 081 360 6243)

TATE, Alan George; s of George Tate (d 1967), of Beckenham, Kent, and Margaret Grace, *née* Holmes (d 1988); *b* 19 Nov 1927; *Educ* Colfe's GS Lewisham, Univ of London (BSc); *m* 14 June 1952, Barbara Victoria, da of Donald Mason (d 1973), of Nottingham; 1 s (Neil), 2 da (Jill, Karen); *Career* dir G Tate and Son Ltd civil engrg contractors 1949-63, fndr ptnr A G Tate & Ptnrs conslt civil and structural engrs 1963-; Master Worshipful Co Paviors 1990-91; FICE 1964, FIStructE 1961, MConsE 1967; *Recreations* photography, foreign travel; *Clubs* City Livery; *Style—* Alan Tate, Esq; 17 Orchard Rd, Bromley, Kent BR1 2PR (☎ 081 464 2830); 39-41 High St, Bromley, Kent BR1 1LE (☎ 081 464 7438)

TATE, David Alfred; s of Alfred James Tate (d 1982), of Hastings, Sussex, and Marie, *née* Coe (d 1985); *b* 23 Oct 1934; *Educ* Latymer Upper Sch Hammersmith; *m* 21 June 1958, Doreen Hilda, da of Wilfrid George Wilson (d 1985), of Wembley, Middx; 2 s (Nigel David b 1963, Peter Robert b 1966), 1 da (Jennifer Mary b 1968); *Career* CA; clerk to the Worshipful Co of Joiners and Ceilers 1978; FCA; *Style—* David Tate, Esq; Parkville House, Bridge St, Pinner, Middx, HA5 3JD, (☎ 081 429 0605, fax 081 866 8856, car 0836 261282)

TATE, David Henry; s of Charles Bertram Tate (d 1941), of Whitley Bay, and Edith Atkinson (d 1980); *b* 18 May 1929; *Educ* St Peters Sch York, Kings Coll Univ of Durham (LLB); *m* 27 May 1955, Norah Joyce, da of Mitchell Millar Graham (d 1953), of Edinburgh; 3 da (Caroline, Stephanie, Nicola); *Career* slr; ptnr: Clifford-Turner 1962-87, Clifford Chance 1987-; tstee Royal Philharmonic Orch Tst; memb: Law Soc, Int Bar Assoc; *Recreations* the arts, bridge, gardening, fishing; *Style—* David Tate, Esq; Royex House, Aldermanbury Square, London EC2V 6BY (☎ 071 600 0808, fax 071 489 0046, telex 8959991)

TATE, David Read; s of Maurice Tate, of Penarth, S Glam, and Florence, *née* Read; *b* 10 Feb 1955; *Educ* Penarth GS, Jesus Coll Oxford (BA), UCL (MSc); *Career* Deloitte Haskins & Sells CAs 1977-80 (Mgmnt Consultancy Div 1980-83), dir Corporate Fin Div Chartered WestLB Ltd; ACA 1980; *Recreations* golf, hillwalking, opera, theatre; *Clubs* Royal Porthcawl Golf, United Oxford and Cambridge; *Style—* David Tate, Esq; Chartered WestLB Ltd, 33-36 Gracechurch St, London EC3V 0AX (☎ 071 623 8711, fax 071 626 5262, telex 884689)

TATE, Sir Henry; 4 Bt (UK 1898), TD, DL (Rutland 1964); s of Sir Ernest William Tate, 3 Bt, JP, DL (d 1939); *b* 29 June 1902; *Educ* Uppingham, RMC; *m* 1, 1927, Lilian Nairne (d 1984), da of late Col Saxon Gregson-Ellis, JP; 2 s; m 2, 6 Aug 1988, Edna, *née* Stokes; *Heir* s, (Henry) Saxon Tate; *Career* formerly Lt Grenadier Gds, Hon Lt-Col RWF; cncllr Rutland CC 1958-69, 1970-74; High Sheriff of Rutland 1949-50, jt master Cottesmore Foxhounds 1946-58, pres Cottesmore Hunt 1974-, dep pres Burghley Horse Trials 1960-82, chm Rutland Agric Soc 1946-66; *Recreations* hunting, fishing, gardening, shooting; *Clubs* Buck's; *Style—* Sir Henry Tate, Bt, TD, DL; Preston Lodge, Withcote, Oakham, Rutland, Leics LE15 8DP; The Cottage, Galltfaenan, Trefnant, Clwyd

TATE, (William) Nicolas; yr s of Lt-Col Sir Henry Tate, 4 Bt, TD, DL, *qv*; *b* 19 Nov 1934; *Educ* Eton, Ch Ch Oxford (MA); *m* 7 Dec 1960, Sarah, er da of Lt-Col Angus John Campbell Rose (d 1980), of Dunira Garden House, Comrie, Perthshire; 2 s (Rupert Sebastian b 13 Nov 1962, Adrian b 27 July 1966, d 1966), 2 da (Melissa Nairne b 4 July 1964, d 1969, Georgina Nairne b 8 March 1969); *Career* cmmnd Grenadier Gds 1956, Lt 1958; dir CBI 1972-81; dir gen Salisbury Cathedral Spire Tst 1985-89, chief exec Anastasia Tst for the Deaf 1989-; *Style—* Nicolas Tate, Esq; Sauvey Castle Farm, Withcote, Oakham, Rutland LE15 8DT

TATE, (Henry) Saxon; CBE (1991); s and h of Lt-Col Sir Henry Tate, 4 Bt, TD, DL; *b* 28 Nov 1931; *Educ* Eton, Ch Ch Oxford; *m* 1, 3 Oct 1953 (m dis 1975), Sheila Ann, da of Duncan Robertson; 4 s (Edward Nicholas b 1966, Duncan Saxon b 1968, John William b 1969, Paul Henry (twin) b 1969); m 2, 31 Jan 1975, Virginia Joan Sturm; *Career* 2 Lt Life Guards 1949-51 (Lt Special Reserve 1951-); prodn trainee Tate & Lyle Liverpool 1952, various appts to refiner dir 1958-65, chief exec offr Redpath Industs 1965-73, md and chm Exec Ctee Tate & Lyle plc 1973-80 (vice chm 1980-92), chief exec Industl Devpt Bd for NI 1982-85, chm and chief exec London Future and Options Exchange (trading as London Fox) 1985-; *Clubs* Buck's; *Style—* Saxon Tate, Esq, CBE; 26 Cleaver Square, London SE11 4BA (☎ 071 582 6507); 1 Commodity Quay, St Katherines Dock, London E1 9AX (☎ 071 481 2080, fax 071 702 9923, telex 884370)

TATHAM, Amanda Jane (Mrs Miles Hockley); da of Christopher Trevor Caton Tatham, of Winchester, and Regine Marien, *née* Legge; *b* 13 March 1953; *Educ* St Paul's Girls, London Coll of Printing (BA); *m* 1988, Julian Miles Hockley, s of Alan John Hockley; *Career* graphic design asst Pentagram Design 1975-79, designer SMS Design 1979-80, fndr and proprietor Amanda Tatham Design Ltd 1980-84, fndr ptnr Lambton Place Design 1984-87, co fndr and ptnr Tatham Pearce Ltd 1987-; corporate brochure, print and annual report accounts worked on incl: Cambridge Electronic Industries 1980-, George Wimpey 1981-, Woolworths 1983, Reckitt & Colman 1983 and 1984, Lloyds Bank 1985-, Dalgety 1986 and 1987, Hepworth/Next 1984-88, WCRS 1987, Asda 1989, The Broadgate Club 1989-, Eurotherm 1989-, Ratners Group 1990-, Seagram Europe 1990-, Mitsubishi Finance International 1990-; corporate indentity accounts worked on incl: Framlington 1982-87, Lloyds Bank 1985-, Healey & Baker 1989-, The Broadgate Club 1989-, LWT and TVS (sales merger) 1990-; awarded: Communication Arts Award for Design Excellence 1979, Spicer & Oppenheim Effective Finance Communications Award 1988; memb: Design Business Assoc (Cncl of Mgmnt 1988-90), D&AD 1978; FCSD 1986 (memb Cncl 1990-); *Recreations* food, wine, classical and contemporary music, the visual arts; *Clubs* 2 Brydges Place; *Style—* Ms Amanda Tatham; Tatham Pearce Ltd, 9 Hatton St, London NW8 8PL (☎ 071 706 4303, fax 071 262 0486)

TATHAM, Maj (Clifford Jackson) John; MBE (1946); s of Maj Clifford Tatham (d 1960), of Charnwood, Cotes Rd, Barrow-upon-Soar, nr Loughborough, Leics, and Gertrude Elizabeth, *née* White (d 1962); *b* 27 Aug 1916; *Educ* Rawlins Sch Quorn, Loughborough Sch; *m* 27 June 1942, (Mary) Noëlle, da of William Edward Carr Lazenby, CBE (d 1968), of 38 Cotes Rd, Barrow-upon-Soar, nr Loughborough, Leics; 2 da (Angela (Mrs Murphy) b 28 Sept 1949, Jemma (Mrs Peters) b 24 May 1954); *Career* WWII: TA 1939, 2 Lt 11 AA Div 1941, Capt 27 S/L Regt RASC Platoon 1942, A/Lt-Col 79 Armd Div 1945 (Maj 1944), demob, transferred to RASC Res of Offrs 1945; John Ellis & Sons Ltd: laboratory technician 1931, i/c Laboratory New Pipe Works Potters Marston 1934-36, departmental mangr 1946, commercial mangr 1950, gen mangr 1951; dir Redland Holdings (take over co) 1960-70, chm Emalux of Leicester Ltd 1970-76; chief recruitment offr Bldg Employers Confedn 1976-, chm Barrow-upon-Soar RDC 1968-72, 1 Mayor Charnwood Borough Cncl; chm 1971-: Br Butterfly Conservation Soc, Leics Rail Servs Action Gp, Nat Paving and Kerb Assoc Midlands area; fell Royal Entomological Soc London; *Recreations* philately, motor racing, natural history, butterflies; *Clubs* RCT, Lighthouse, Loughborough Naturalists, BBCS; *Style—* Maj John Tatham, MBE; Tudor House, 102 Chaveney Rd, Quorn, nr Loughborough, Leics LE12 8AD (☎ 0509 412870); Building Employers' Confederation, 82 New Cavendish St, London W1M 8AD (☎ 071 580 5588, fax 071 631 3872, telex 265763)

TATHAM, Nigel John; s of Col Eric Tillyer Tatham (d 1982), and Hon Lettice Theresa (d 1967), eldest da of 10 Baron Digby; *b* 10 Oct 1927; *Educ* Pinewood, Rothesay Collegiate Sch; *m* 7 July 1951, Elizabeth Anne, da of Sir (William) Errington Keville, CBE; 4 da (Joanna b 1956, Caroline b 1958, Edwina b 1962, Charlotte b 1966); *Career* shipping co dir; dir: Subsidiaries of Furness Withy & Co Ltd 1959-72, Furness Withy & Co Ltd 1970-72; vice pres Sea Containers Ltd 1973-90; *Recreations* skiing, sailing, golf, tennis, gardening, music; *Style—* Nigel Tatham, Esq; 5 Avenue Ct, Draycott Ave, London SW3 (☎ 071 589 3379); Sea Containers House, 20 Upper Ground, London SE1 (☎ 071 928 6969)

TATHAM, Capt Richard Heathcote; s of Lt-Col William Heathcote Tatham, OBE, TD (d 1955), of Marylea, Heathside Rd, Woking, Surrey, and Mary, *née* Leigh-Wood (d 1975); *b* 19 Aug 1932; *Educ* Eton; *m* 6 Aug 1962, Ilona Eva, da of Janos Zelei (d 1988), of 61 Hungaria Krt, Budapest, Hungary; 1 s (William b 1964), 1 step da (Melinda (Mrs Lowe) b 1953); *Career* cmmnd Coldstream Gds 1951, Captain 1955, ADC to Govr of Tasmania 1957-58, ADC to Govr of S Aust 1958-60, ret 1962; dir Omnia Hldgs Gp 1962-68, chm Overland Gp 1968-76, mangr Pub Affrs George Wimpey plc 1990- (Corp Rels Dept 1976-); memb Cncl People's Dispensary for Sick Animals; Freeman City of London, Liveryman Worshipful Co of Merchant Taylors 1970; *Recreations* collecting militaria, gardening; *Clubs* Cavalry and Guards, 1900 Club, Household Div Yacht; *Style—* Capt Richard Tatham; 47 Strawberry Vale, Twickenham, Middx TW1 4RX (☎ 081 892 6775); Corporate Relations Dept George Wimpey PLC, 26 Hammersmith Grove, London W6 7EN (☎ 081 748 2000, fax 081 741 4596)

TATTERSALL, David Nowell; s of David Lawrence Tattersall (d 1979), and Mary Ellen, *née* Gott (d 1979); *b* 12 April 1930; *Educ* The Leys School Cambridge; *m* 29 Aug 1959, Susan Elisabeth, da of John Heap (d 1961); 2 s (John b 1972, Michael b 1973); *Career* Nat Serv RAPC 1953-55; articled clerk Waterworth Rudd & Hare Blackburn 1947-53, dir James Tattersall & Sons Ltd Nelson 1955-57, accountant English Sewing Cotton Co Ltd 1957-70, fin dir Overseas Div English Calico Ltd 1970-73, gp accountant Tootal Ltd 1973-79, dir Tootal Group plc 1979-83, ptnr Dastat CAs 1983-; hon treas Family Welfare Assoc of Manchester Ltd; FCA 1956; *Recreations* motoring, gardening, photography; *Style—* David Tattersall, Esq; Greycot, Castle Hill, Prestbury, Macclesfield, Cheshire, SK10 4AS (☎ 0625 829664)

TATTERSALL, John Hartley; s of Robert Herman Tattersall (d 1958), of Roewen, Conwy, Gwynedd, and Jean, *née* Stevens; *b* 5 April 1952; *Educ* Shrewsbury, Christ's Coll Cambridge (MA); *m* 8 Sept 1984, Madeleine Virginia, da of Robert Edward Hugh Coles, of Caversham, Berks; 2 s (Robert b 1985, Luke 1987), 1 da (Clare b 1990); *Career* ptnr Coopers & Lybrand Deloitte (formerly Coopers & Lybrand, joined 1975) 1985-; memb Banking Sub Ctee ICAEW 1989-; churchwarden St Jude's Church London 1984-, dir London City Ballet Tst Ltd 1987-; Freeman Worshipful Co of Horners 1980; ACA 1978, FCA 1989; The Investment Business: Compliance with the Rules (1990); *Recreations* walking, opera, ballet; *Style—* John Tattersall, Esq; 3 St Ann's Villas, Holland Park, London, W11 4RU (☎ 071 603 1053); Coopers & Lybrand Deloitte, Plumtree Ct, London, EC4A 4HT (☎ 071 583 5000, fax 071 822 4652, telex 887470 COLYLN G)

TATTERSALL-WALKER, George; s of George Tattersall-Walker (d 1947); *b* 2 Sept 1920; *Educ* The Leys Sch; *m* 1947, Edith; 2 s; *Career* CA 1949; exec brewery and hotels 1950-; planning dir John Smith's Tadcaster Brewery Ltd 1969-83, dir James Hole & Co Ltd 1975-90; chm: Anchor Hotels & Taverns Ltd 1977-82, Cantrell & Cochrane Pension Tst 1977-89, John Smith's Brewery SA Belgium 1970-82, Immo Smiths SA Brussels 1972-82, Vivaldi SA Brussels 1972-82, H&G Simmonds Pension Tst Ltd 1972-87, BIM Regnl Bd 1980-90, CAs Tstees Ltd 1986-; pres: West Yorkshire Soc CAs 1980-81, York Soc CAs 1988-89; lectr accountancy 1950-; lay preacher 1944-; memb Cncl Inst of CAs 1966-85; co archivist 1984-; memb Br Cncl of Archives 1988-; FBIM 1990; *Recreations* gardening, donkeys, public speaking; *Clubs* Anglo-Belgian, Over-Seas; *Style—* George Tattersall-Walker, Esq; Woodside, Oaks

Lane, Boston Spa, W Yorks LS23 6DS (☎ 0937 842250)

TATTERSFIELD, Prof Brian; s of Norman Tattersfield (d 1959), and Marian, *née* Rogers; *b* 12 April 1936; *Educ* Heckmondwike GS, Batley Sch of Art (NDD), RCA (ARCA); *m* 20 April 1963, (Elizabeth) Mary Tindall, da of Richard Newton Wakelin (d 1964), of Richmond, Surrey; 2 da (Jane Charlotte Wakelin b 1964, Emma Louisa Wakelin b 1972); *Career* art dir Young and Rubicam Ltd 1962-63, designer Fletcher Forbes Gill 1963, co-fndr Minale Tattersfield 1964 (ptnr and creative head 1964-), visiting lectr RCA 1978, visiting prof in design Brighton Poly 1988-, govr Norwich Sch of Art; design awards incl: Typomundus Canada 1964, creativity on paper NY 1966, Silver award D&ADA 1968 (1970 and 1974-84), Gold award Art Dir Club NY 1975, Poster award Warsaw Biennale 1969, Br Poster Design award 1970, Liderman Gold award for graphic design Madrid 1983, Civic Tst award 1985, D&ADA president's award for outstanding contrib to Br design 1987; exhibitions: Museum of Modern Art NY 1978, London Design Centre 1981, Glasgow Design Centre 1981, Museum of Modern Art Milan 1983, Cultural Centre of Madrid 1985, Axis Gallery Tokyo 1988; various articles in Br and int jls; memb: D&ADA, Art and Design Panel CNAA, Design Panel BR; hon fell RCA, FCSD, FRSA; *Style*— Prof Brian Tattersfield; Sarisberie Cottage, The Street, W Clandon, Surrey GU4 7ST (☎ 0483 222908); 178 High St, Aldeburgh, Suffolk; Minale, Tattersfield & Ptnrs Ltd, The Courtyard, 37 Sheen Rd, Richmond, Surrey TW9 1AJ (☎ 081 948 7999, fax 081 948 2435, telex 22397 MINTAT G)

TATTON-BROWN, Lady Kenya Eleanor; *née* Kitchener; da of Viscount Broome (d 1928), by his w Adela Mary Evelyn; sis of 3 Earl Kitchener of Khartoum; *b* 12 July 1923; *Educ* Open Univ (BA); *m* 1947, as his 2 wife, John Stewart Tatton-Brown (d 1971), s of Eden Tatton-Brown, CB, of Westergate Wood, Chichester; 3 da; *Career* War Serv 3 Offr WRNS; MCSP, state registered physiotherapist, chartered physiotherapist in private practice 1946-; govr Whitelands Coll, Putney; *Recreations* tennis; *Style*— The Lady Kenya Tatton-Brown; Westergate Wood, Level Mare Lane, Chichester, W Sussex PO20 6SB (☎ 024 354 3061)

TATUM, Kelvin Martin; s of Martin Tatum, of Pheasants, Thakeham Rd, Coolham, W Sussex, and Janet, *née* Reeve; *b* 8 Feb 1964; *Educ* Brighton Coll; *m* 12 March 1988, Deborah Ann, da of David Edward Rule, of 63 Berrywood Gardens, Hedge End, Hants; *Career* 3 times Br schoolboy scramble champion; showjumper; debut Wimbledon British League 1983, Young Rider of the Year 1983 and 1985, third place Individual World Final Poland Katowice 1986, Br and Cwlth champion 1987 and 1988, Eng Capt 1989 (winners of World Team Cup Final 1989), Inter-Continental champion 1989, Br and Cwlth champion 1990; *Recreations* golf; *Style*— Kelvin Tatum, Esq; Coventry Speedway, Brandon Rd, Brandon, nr Coventry (☎ 0203 542395)

TATUM, Hon Mrs (Marguerite Betty); *née* Cadman; 1 da of 1 Baron Cadman, GCMG, FRS; *b* 1913; *m* 1940, Rev John Tatum (d 1966); 2 s, 1 da; *Style*— The Hon Mrs Tatum; Gorsedown, Birling Gap, Eastbourne, Sussex

TAUBER, Peter; s of Nandor Tauber, and Ilona, *née* Tubor (d 1990); *b* 13 Jan 1927; *Educ* Univ of Budapest, Univ of Zürich, St Andrews Univ; *m* 18 Oct 1952, Martha, da of Emeric Balazs; 1 s (Robert John Michael b 9 Nov 1956); *Career* fndr and proprietor Peter Tauber Press Agency 1950- (major literary and syndication agency placing books about and by the famous worldwide); *Recreations* reading, travel, art, antiques, music; *Style*— Peter Tauber, Esq; Peter Tauber Press Agency, 94 East End Rd, London N3 2SX

TAUNTON, Bishop of; Rt Rev Nigel Simeon McCulloch; s of Pilot Offr Kenneth McCulloch, RAFVR (ka 1943), and Audrey Muriel, *née* Ball; *b* 17 Jan 1942; *Educ* Liverpool Coll, Selwyn Coll Cambridge (BA, MA), Cuddesdon Theol Coll Oxford; *m* 15 April 1974, Celia Hume, da of Rev Canon Horace Lyle Hume Townshend, of Norwich, Norfolk (*see* Burke's Irish Family Records, 1976); 2 da (Kathleen b 1975, Elizabeth b 1977); *Career* ordained 1966, curate of Ellesmere Port Merseyside 1966-70, chaplain Christ's Coll Cambridge 1970-73, dir theol studies Christ's Coll Cambridge 1970-75 (permission to officiate Dio of Liverpool 1970-73); diocesan missioner Norwich Diocese 1973-78, chaplain Young Friends of Norwich Cathedral 1974-78, rector St Thomas's and St Edmund's Salisbury 1978-86, archdeacon of Sarum 1979-86, hon canon Salisbury Cathedral and prebendary of Ogbourne 1979-86, prebendary of Wanstrow in Wells Cathedral 1986-; chm Cambridge War on Want 1971-73, chm C of E Decade of Evangelism Steering Gp 1989-; memb: Br Cncl of Churches USA Exchange (Church Growth) 1972-75, Archbishops Cncl for Evangelism, res and trg Gp 1974-79; govr: Westwood St Thomas, St Edmund & St Mark's Salisbury 1979-86, Salisbury-Wells Theol Coll 1981-82, Royal Sch of Church Music 1984-, Marlborough Coll 1985-, Kings Bruton 1987-, Somerset Coll of Art and Technol 1987-; pres Somerset Rural Music Sch 1986-; memb: Gen Synod Working Gp Organists & Choirmasters 1984-85, Bath and Wells Zambia Link Programme 1987-; chm Fin Ctee ACCM 1987-; memb: C of E Gen Synod 1990-, House of Bishops 1990-; *Recreations* music, walking in the Lake District, broadcasting, gardening; *Clubs* Royal Cwlth Soc; *Style*— The Rt Rev the Bishop of Taunton; Sherford Farm House, Taunton TA1 3RF (☎ 0823 288759)

TAUNTON, Terence Grosvenor; s of Hugh Grosvenor Taunton (d 1986), of Whitstable, Kent, and Dorothy Edna, *née* Fulcher; *b* 16 Aug 1938; *Educ* Faversham GS; *m* Kay, da of late James Herbert Rochester; 2 s (Kevin James b 21 April 1967, Toby Edwin b 20 July 1969); *Career* Nat Serv RN 1956-58; insur broker Bland Payne (later Sedgewicks) 1958-82 (dir Bland Payne International 1978-), Fenchurch Insurance Brokers Ltd 1982- (md 1984-), dir Fenchurch Construction Brokers 1982-; ACII 1968; *Recreations* sailing, golfing, gardening, walking; *Clubs* Hampton Pier Yacht, Herne Bay Golf; *Style*— Terence Taunton, Esq; 15 Spenser Rd, Herne Bay, Kent CT6 5QL (☎ 02273 61823); Fenchurch Insurance Brokers Ltd, 89 High Rd, South Woodford, London E18 2RH (☎ 081 505 3333, fax 081 505 5014)

TAUSIG, Peter; s of Dr Walter Charles Tausig (d 1969), and Judith, *née* Morris; *b* 15 Aug 1943; *Educ* Battersea GS, UCL (BSc); *m* 28 June 1987, Geraldine Angharad Alice, da of Leslie Stanley, of Chelsea, London; 2 da (Eva Lily Ibolya b 3 April 1988, Katja Francesca b 30 Dec 1990); *Career* economist: Aust Bureau of Census and Statistics 1965-69, CBI 1969, Bank of London and S America 1970-74, International Marine Banking Co 1974-76, S G Warburg/Warburg Securities 1976-88 (dir 1983); exec dir UBS Phillips & Drew 1989-; *Recreations* theatre, literature, music, walking, skiing, travel; *Clubs* Groucho; *Style*— Peter Tausig, Esq; Elm Lodge, 2 Elm Row, Hampstead, London NW3 1AA (☎ 071 435 7099); UBS Phillips & Drew, 100 Liverpool St, London EC2M 2RH (☎ 071 901 3333)

TAUSKY, Vilem; CBE (1981); s of Dr Emil Tausky (d 1945), of Czechoslovakia, and Josephine, *née* Ascher (d 1935); *b* 20 July 1910; *Educ* Janacek Conservatoire Brno Czechoslovakia, Meisterschule Prague Czechoslovakia; *m* 1 Jan 1948, Margaret Helen, *née* Powell (d 1982); *Career* Czechoslovak Army; served: France 1939-40, England 1940-45; conductor Brno Opera House 1929-39, musical dir Carl Rosa Opera 1945-49; guest conductor: Royal Opera House 1951-, Sadlers Wells 1953-; dir of opera Guildhall Sch of Music 1977-87; Freeman: City of London, Worshipful Co of Musicians; FGSM 1979; Czechoslovakia Military Cross 1944, Czechoslovkia Order of Merit 1945; *Books* Vilem Tausky Tells His Story (1979), Leos Janacek - Leaves from his Life (1982), Concerto (1957), Concertino for Harmonica and Orchestra (1963), Soho Scherzo for Orchestra (1966), Divertimento for Strings (1966); *Style*— Vilem Tausky, Esq, CBE; 44 Haven Green Court, Ealing, London W5 2UY (☎ 081 997 6512)

TAVARÉ, Christopher James; s of Andrew K Tavaré, and June, *née* Attwood; *b* 27 Oct 1954; *Educ* Sevenoaks Sch, St Johns Coll Oxford; *m* 22 March 1980, Vanessa, da of Edward L Leary; *Career* cricketer; Kent CCC: debut 1974, capt 1983-84; Somerset CCC: debut 1989, capt 1990-; memb: England Schools Cricket Assoc 1973, England Young Cricketers 1974; England career: 31 Test Matches 1980-89, 29 One Day International 1980-84; overseas tour: India and Sri Lanka 1981-82, Australia and NZ 1982-83, Fiji NZ and Pakistan 1983-84; Save & Prosper Group 1979-81, N M Schroder Financial Management Ltd 1986-88, ADAS Ministry of Agriculture Fisheries and Food 1989-; *Recreations* golf, American football, zoology, films, woodwork; *Style*— Christopher Tavaré, Esq; Somerset County Cricket Club, The County Ground, Taunton, Somerset TA1 1JT (☎ 0823 272946)

TAVARÉ, Sir John; CBE (1983); s of Leon Alfred Tavaré (d 1976), and Grace Tavaré (d 1976); *b* 12 July 1920; *Educ* Chatham House Ramsgate, King's Coll London Univ (BSc); *m* 1949, Margaret Daphne Wray; 3 s; *Career* PA mgmnt conslt 1948-58, Unilever plc 1958-70, chm and md Whitecroft plc 1970-85; kt 1989; *Recreations* golf; *Clubs* Prestbury Golf; *Style*— Sir John Tavaré, CBE; The Gables, Macclesfield Rd, Prestbury, Cheshire (☎ 0625 829778)

TAVENER, Prof John Kenneth; s of Charles Kenneth Tavener, and Muriel Evelyn, *née* Brown (d 1985); *b* 28 Jan 1944; *Educ* Highgate Sch, RAM; *m* 17 Nov 1974 (m dis 1980), Victoria (d 1990), da of Dr Costas Marangopoulos, of Athens; *Career* composer; organist St John's Church London 1960-75, prof of composition Trinity Coll of Music 1968-; compositions incl: Cain and Abel (First prize Prince Rainier of Monaco 1965) 1965, The Whale (London) 1968, Celtic Requiem, Ultimos Ritos (Holland Festival) 1974, Akhmatova Requiem 1980 (Edinburgh Festival), Antigone, Thérèse (Covent Garden) 1979, Palintropos (Moscow) 1989, Sappho Fragments, Towards the Son, Mandelion, A Gentle Spirit, Ikon of Light (Tallis Scholars) 1984, Liturgy of St John Chrysosstom, Risen!, In Memory of Cats, Let Not the Prince be Silent, Requiem for Father Malachy, Two Hymns to the Mother of God, Kyklike Kinesis, Collegium Regale (King's Coll Cambridge) 1987, Hymn to the Holy Spirit, Acclamation for His All Holiness the Ecumenical Patriarch Demetrios I (Canterbury Cathedral) 1988, Akathist of Thanksgiving (Westminster Abbey) 1988, Ikon of St Seraphim (Truro Cathedral) 1988, The Protecting Veil (Royal Albert Hall) 1989, Resurrection (Glasgow Cathedral) 1990, European City of Culture 1990; memb Russian Orthodox Church; Hon: FRAM, FTCL; Hon Doctorale New Delhi Univ India for services to the Sacred in Art; *Recreations* travelling in Greece, collecting ikons; *Style*— Prof John Tavener

TAVENER, Philip Brandon; s of George Frederick Tavener (d 1985), of Kingsbridge, Devon, and Muriel Edith Kathleen, *née* Jensen; *b* 17 May 1943; *Educ* Haberdashers' Aske's, Hertfordshire Coll of Agric; *m* 1, 26 July 1969, Pamela Denise, da of Arthur Sutherland; 1 da (Sarah b 1974); m 2, 6 May 1978, Sally, da of John McNeil (d 1956); 1 s (Andrew b 1982); *Career* agrochemical conslt; chm and md Chiltern Farm Chemicals 1980-; *Recreations* gardening, conservation, bird watching, renovating old property; *Style*— Philip Tavener, Esq; Chiltern Farm Chemicals, 11 High St, Thornborough, Buckingham MU18 2DF (☎ 0280 822400, fax 0280 822082)

TAVENER, Robin Frederick; s of Harold William Tavener (d 1969); *b* 20 Nov 1929; *Educ* Leighton Park Sch Reading; *m* 1955, Pamela Beatrice, *née* Austin; 2 s, 1 da; *Career* fin dir ITT 1965-69; Stone-Platt Industs: fin dir and chm Electrical Div 1969-74, md and chief exec 1980-81; ldr of Mgmnt Team organised by Candover Investmts to purchase the electrical div of Stone-Platt Indust, chief exec Stone Int plc 1982-87, non-exec dep chm Claudius Peters AG Hamburg 1987-; exec chm: INS Ltd, Toat Hill Garage Ltd; FCCA, CBIM, FRSA; *Recreations* theatre, music, travelling, sailing, skiing; *Clubs* RAC; *Style*— Robin F Tavener, Esq; The Mill House, Wonersh, Guildford, Surrey (☎ and fax 0483 894120)

TAVERNE, Dick; QC (1965); s of Dr Nicolaas Jacobus Marie Taverne (d 1966), and Louise Victoria, *née* Koch; *b* 18 Oct 1928; *Educ* Charterhouse, Balliol Coll Oxford; *m* 6 Aug 1955, Janice, da of late Dr Robert Stuart Fleming Hennessey; 2 da (Suzanna b 1960, Caroline b 1963); *Career* called to the Bar 1954; MP (Lab) Lincoln 1962-72: Parly sec Home Office 1966-68, min of state Treasy 1968-69, fin sec 1969-70, resigned Labour Party 1972; re-elected Independent Social Democrat MP Lincoln 1973-74; first dir Inst for Fiscal Studies 1971 (chm 1979-83), chm Public Policy Centre 1984-87, Br memb Spierenburg Ctee to examine working of Euro Cmmn 1979; dir: Equity & Law 1972-, BOC Group 1975-, PRIMA Europe 1987-; chm OLIM Convertible Tst 1989-; *Books* The Future of the Left (1974); *Recreations* sailing, marathon running; *Style*— Dick Taverne, Esq, QC; 60 Cambridge Street, London SW1V 4QQ (☎ 071 828 0166); PRIMA Europe Ltd, 14 Soho Square, London W1V 5FB (☎ 071 287 6676)

TAVISTOCK, Marquess of; Henry Robin Ian Russell; DL (Beds 1985); s and h of 13 Duke of Bedford; *b* 21 Jan 1940; *Educ* Le Rosey Switzerland, Harvard; *m* 20 June 1961, Henrietta Joan, da of Henry Frederic Tiarks; 3 s; *Heir* s, Lord Howland; *Career* chm: Berkeley Devpt Capital Ltd 1985-, chm Bd Tstees Kennedy Meml Fund 1985-90; dir: Trafalgar House plc 1977-90, TR Property Investment Tst plc 1982-, United Racecourses 1977-, Berkeley Govett plc 1985-; pres Woburn Golf and Country Club; *Clubs* White's, Jockey Club Rooms, The Brook (NY); *Style*— Marquess of Tavistock, DL; Woburn Abbey, Woburn, Bedfordshire MK43 0TP (☎ 0525 290 666)

TAYAR, Graham Joseph; s of Robert Alfred Victor Tayar (d 1958), of Birmingham, and Muriel Sara, *née* Aaron (d 1977); *b* 5 March 1933; *Educ* King Edwards Sch Birmingham, Jesus Coll Cambridge (BA, MA); *m* 1, 7 July 1956 (m dis 1966), (Alice) Meriel, da of Clarendon Monsell (d 1936); 2 da (Penelope (Mrs Simon Vevers) b 1957, Imogen (Dr Bloor) b 1958); m 2, July 1969 (m dis 1983), Lynn Hilary, da of J Kramer; 1 step s (Daryl Leon b 1966); m 3, Dec 1983, Christina Elizabeth, da of Darsie Rawlins, and Hon Mrs Rachel, *née* Irby, *qv*; *Career* schoolmaster Birmingham 1956-59, schoolmaster (later dep head and sec Nat Curriculum Ctee) Addis Ababa Ethiopia 1959-64; extra mural univ lectr: Haile Selassie Univ Addis Ababa 1960-63, London Univ 1968-71; freelance journalist and broadcaster 1962-65: BBC, Observer, Daily Telegraph, AFP NBC (NY); BBC radio prodr: Birmingham 1965-66, Bush House (African and World Serv) 1966-69; sr radio prodr 1969-80, exec prodr Broadcasting House 1980-89, broadcasting conslt and head of radio/audio SAGE 1989-; fndr ldr and pianist Crouch End Allstars New Orleans Jazz Band 1971-, prodr various records incl Sunday Best, (Jazzology US) 1985, organizer of jazz festivals and jazz band balls, literary ed New Middle East 1970-73; poetry published: Tribune, Extra Verse, Envoi, Poetry and Audience; memb: Kentish Town Police and Community Crime Panel (ed Neighbourhood Watch Magazine), Advsy Ctee W Sussex Inst Maths Centre 1986-89, Media Studies Ctees BTEC and C & G, FRSA 1989; *Books* Personality And Power (ed, 1971), Education at Home and Abroad (with Prof J Lauwerys, 1972), Living Decisions (1973); *Recreations* playing jazz, writing occasional verses; *Clubs* BBC, The Academy, Cambridge Union; *Style*— Graham Tayar, Esq; 25 Fortess Rd, Kentish Town, London NW5 1AD (☎ 071 485 0578); 17 Middle St, Port Isaac, Cornwall; The SAGE Consortium, 10 Woodlawn Rd, Fulham, London SW6 6NQ (☎ 071 385 5069)

TAYAR, Dr René Benedict; s of Oscar Tayar, of Artmaur, 32 Hughes Hallett St, Sliema, Malta, and Violet, *née* Riccardi; *b* 3 Oct 1945; *Educ* St Aloysius' Coll Malta, Royal Univ of Malta (MD), Royal Coll of Radiologists London; *m* 25 Jan 1971,

Margaret Rose, da of Louis Francis Tortell, of 2 Ghar il-Lembi St, Sliema, Malta; 1 s (Benjamin b 8 Sept 1978); *Career* sr registrar in radiology Bristol Royal Infirmary 1977-81 (registrar in radiology 1974-77), conslt radiologist Merton and Sutton Health Authy 1981, hon sr lectr St Georges' Hosp Med Sch 1988; conslt radiologist Parkside Hosp Wimbledon; fndr memb Sir Harry Secombe Scanner Appeal, sec Med Staff Ctee St Helier Hosp Carshalton Surrey, memb Guildford Bone Tumour Registry; FRCR 1980; *Recreations* tennis, music, literature; *Style—* Dr Rene Tayar; 45 Epsom Lane South, Tadworth, Surrey KT20 5TA (☎ 0737 813582); Dept of Radiodiagnosis, St Helier Hospital, Wrthye Lane, Carshalton, Surrey SM5 1AA (☎ 081 644 4343)

TAYLOR, Alan Broughton; s of Valentine James Broughton Taylor, of 34 Norman Ave, Birmingham, and Gladys Maud, *née* Williams (d 1988); *b* 23 Jan 1939; *Educ* Malvern, Univ of Geneva, Univ of Birmingham (LLB), BNC Oxford (MLitt); *m* 15 Aug 1964, Diana, da of Dr James Robson Hindmarsh (d 1970), of Peach Cottage, Lytchett Matravers, Dorset; 2 s (Stephen James b 30 Nov 1965, Robert David b 21 Feb 1968); *Career* called to the Bar Gray's Inn 1961, in practice 1962-, rec 1979-; govr St Matthew's Sch Smethwick W Mids 1988-; *Books* A Practical Guide to the Care of the Injured by P S London (contrib, 1964); *Recreations* philately, fell walking; *Style—* Alan Taylor, Esq; 94 Augustus Rd, Edgbaston, Birmingham B15 3LT (☎ 021 454 8600); 2 Fountain Court, Birmingham B4 6DR (☎ 021 236 3882, fax 021 233 3205)

TAYLOR, Andrew John Robert; s of The Rev Arthur John Taylor, of Monmouth, and Hilda Mary, *née* Haines; *b* 14 Oct 1951; *Educ* The King's Sch Ely, Woodbridge Sch Suffolk, Emmanuel Coll Cambridge (BA), UCL (MA); *m* 8 Sept 1979, Caroline Jane, da of Ian George Silverwood; 1 s (William John Alexander b 6 March 1989), 1 da (Sarah Jessica b 9 June 1986); *Career* writer; various jobs ranging from boatbuilding to teaching 1973-76, freelance sub ed for London publishers 1975-84, library asst then asst librarian London Borough of Brent 1976-81, self-employed writer 1981-; author of books for children (under name of John Robert Taylor) incl: Hairline Cracks (1988), Private Nose (1989), Snapshot (1989), Double Exposure (1990); books for adults (under name of Andrew Taylor) incl: Caroline Minuscule (1982), Waiting for the End of the World (1984), Our Fathers' Lies (1985), An Old School Tie (1986), Freelance Death (1987), The Second Midnight (1988), Blacklist (1988), Blood Relation (1990), Toyshop (1990); *Awards* (for Caroline Minuscule) John Creasey meml award of Crime Writers' Assoc 1982 and Edgar nomination from Mystery Writers of America, Our Fathers' Lies shortlisted for Gold Dagger of Crime Writers Assoc 1985, Snapshot shortlisted for NatWest Children's Book of the Year award 1989; memb: The Soc of Authors, The Crime Writers' Assoc; *Style—* Andrew Taylor, Esq; The Carriage House, 13 Lords Hill, Coleford, Gloucestershire GL16 8BG (☎ 0594 33923); Richard Scott Simon Ltd, 43 Doughty St, London WC1N 2LF

TAYLOR, Andrew Robert; s of Benjamin Clive Taylor, of 13 Inkerman Terrace, Tredegar, Gwent, and Enid, *née* Jones; *b* 14 Feb 1961; *Educ* Tredegar Comp Sch, Univ Coll Cardiff (BSc), Inns of Court Sch of Law; *Career* called to the Bar Gray's Inn 1985; chm Abergavenny Lawn Tennis Club 1987-89, sec Tredegar RFC 1987-88; parly candidate (Cons) Blenenau Gwent 1987, currently prospective candidate S Wales Euro Constituency; *Recreations* rugby, tennis, theatre; *Style—* Andrew Taylor, Esq; 13 Inkerman Terrace, Tredegar, Gwent NP2 3NP (☎ 0495 253630); 49 Westgate Chambers, Commercial St, Newport NPT 1JP (☎ 0633 67403, 0633 55855, car 0836 724 938)

TAYLOR, (Winifred) Ann; MP (L) Dewsbury 1987-; *b* 2 July 1947; *Educ* Bolton Sch, Bradford Univ, Sheffield Univ; married; 1 s (b 1982), 1 da (b 1983); *Career* oppn front bench spokesman 1981- (educn 1979-81), asst govt whip 1977-79; PPS to: Def Sec 1976-77, Sec State DES 1975-76; MP (L) Bolton W 1974-87; former teacher, pt/t tutor Open Univ; *Books* Political Action (with Jim Flin, 1978); *Style—* Mrs Ann Taylor, MP; Glyn Garth, Stoney Bank Rd, Thongsbridge, Huddersfield, Yorks

TAYLOR, Annita; da of Romola Piapan (d 1967), of Switzerland, and Rosalia Smak Piapan (d 1984); *b* 21 Sept 1925; *Educ* Avviamento Professionale Tecnico di Monfalcone Italy; *m* 10 Nov 1946, Alfred Oakley Taylor, s of George Oakley Taylor; 1 da (Ligmoi Hannah b 18 Oct 1947); *Career* md ABBA DG Co Ltd 1983-90 (dir 1978-90); dir: Liglets Co Ltd 1982-, Rosalia Mgmnt Servs Co Ltd 1989-90; involved with: Riding for the Disabled, Red Cross; *Recreations* racing, polo, shooting; *Clubs* Guards Polo, Jockey, Racehorse Owners Assoc; *Style—* Mrs Annita Taylor; Wadley Manor, Faringdon, Oxon; 19 Millers Court, Chiswick Mall, London W4 (☎ 0367 20556, 081 748 2997)

TAYLOR, Dr Arnold Joseph; CBE (1971); s of Dr John George Taylor (d 1942), of Battersea, and Mary Matilda, *née* Riley (d 1965); *b* 24 July 1911; *Educ* Sir Walter St John's Sch Battersea, Merchant Taylors', St John's Coll Oxford (MA); *m* 19 April 1940, Patricia Katharine, da of Samuel Arthur Guilbride (d 1950), of Victoria, BC; 1 s (John Guilbride b 1947), 1 da (Katharine Mary b 1953); *Career* RAF Intelligence served in UK, N Africa, Italy 1942-46; asst master Chard Sch Somerset 1934-35, HM Office of Works Inspectorate of Ancient Monuments 1935, chief inspr of ancient monuments and historic bldgs Miny of Public Bldgs 1961, ret 1972; pres Soc of Antiquaries 1975-78 (gold medal 1988); memb: Ancient Monuments Bds for Eng Wales & Scotland 1973-81, Cathedrals Advsy Ctee 1964-80, Advsy Bd for Redundant Churches 1973-81 (chm 1975-77), Westminster Abbey Architectural Advsy Panel 1979-; cmmr Royal Cmmns on Historic Monuments Wales 1956-83 (Eng 1963-78); Freeman: City of London, Worshipful Co of Merchant Taylors; Hon DLitt Wales 1969, Hon DUniv Caen 1980; FBA 1972, FSA; *Recreations* observing the built environment, music; *Style—* Dr Arnold Taylor, CBE, FSA; Rose Cottage, Chiddingfold, Surrey (☎ 042 879 2069)

TAYLOR, Basil Horace; s of Horace Webb Taylor (d 1964), and Lilian Matilda, *née* Johnson (d 1960); *b* 11 July 1924; *Educ* Whitgift Sch Croydon, Sch of Building; *m* 16 July 1955, Cynthia Joan, da of William Marsh Gill (d 1986); 1 s (Julian Matthew Corfield b 1962); *Career* served RN 1943-46; CA; sr ptnr Paton Pitt Taylor & Assocs London 1978-; worked in: Aust 1963, Oman and Malaysia 1975-86; currently in UK; ARIBA; *Clubs* Directors; *Style—* Basil H Taylor, Esq; Paton Pitt Taylor & Assocs, 26 Wilfred Street, London SW1E 6PL (☎ 01 834 8707)

TAYLOR, Baz; s of Alfred William Taylor, of 51 Newton Rd, Tankerton, Whitstable, Kent, and Marjorie, *née* Steventon; *b* 30 Aug 1944; *Educ* Simon Langton GS Canterbury, Queen's Coll Oxford (MA); *m* 16 May 1970, (Marianne) Valerie, da of Eiddfryn James (d 1957), of Caemorgan, Cardigan, Dyfed, Wales; 2 da (Alice Jane b 28 May 1971, Katharine Elizabeth b 4 Nov 1972); *Career* prodr World in Action Granada TV 1968, dir The Christians 1975 (NY Film and TV Festival Award); dir, prodr and exec prodr of numerous notable prodns incl: Talent with Julie Walters (NY Film and TV Award), Auf Wiedersehn Pet (1983 Br Press and Broadcasting Award and 1989 Drama of the Decade Award), Shine on Harvey Moon, Young Charlie Chaplin Thames TV (1989 Emmy nomination USA), Near Mrs (feature film) 1991; memb: Friends of the Earth, Nat Tst, BAFTA 1975; elected memb Cncl Dir's Guild of GB 1990; *Books* Cash and Carrie (1986), Love Me, Love My Dog (1987); *Recreations* sailing, walking, skiing; *Clubs* BAFTA; *Style—* Baz Taylor, Esq; 17 Alexander St, London W2 5NT (☎ 071 727 1191, fax 071 229 1256, tlx 263361)

TAYLOR, Hon Bernard Alfred; o s of Baron Taylor of Mansfield (Life Peer); *b* 7 Feb 1922; *m* 1952; *Style—* The Hon Bernard Taylor; 126 Mansfield St, Sherwood, Nottingham

TAYLOR, Bernard David; s of Thomas Taylor, of Coventry, and Winifred, *née* Smith; *b* 17 Oct 1935; *Educ* John Gulson GS Coventry, Univ of Wales Bangor (BSc), London Business Sch; *m* 5 Sept 1959, Nadine Barbara, da of Ben Maile, of Devoran, Cornwall; 2 s (Johnathan b 5 Oct 1964, Michael b 5 Nov 1966), 2 da (Sian b 30 Sept 1960, Sarah b 10 Oct 1962); *Career* md Glaxo Aust 1972-83, md Glaxo Pharmaceuticals UK 1984-86, chief exec Glaxo Hldgs plc 1985-89; cncllr Victorian Coll of Pharmacy 1976-82; memb: CBI Europe Ctee 1987-, Br Overseas Trade Bd 1987-; fell London Business Sch 1988; *Style—* Bernard Taylor, Esq

TAYLOR, Bernard John; s of John Taylor (d 1962), and Evelyn Frances Taylor; *b* 2 Nov 1956; *Educ* Cheltenham, St John's Coll Oxford (MA); *m* 16 June 1984, Sarah Jane, da of John Paskin Taylor, of Paris; *Career* dir Med Div Smiths Industries plc 1983-85 (business planning and acquisitions 1979-82), exec dir Baring Bros & Co Ltd 1985 (mangr and asst dir Corp Fin Dept); non-exec dir New Focus Healthcare 1986; memb: RPS 1971, RSC 1972; *Books* Photosensitive Film Formation on Copper (I) (1974), Photosensitive Film Formation on Copper (II) (1976), Oxidation of Alcohols to Carbonyl Compounds, Synthesis (1979); *Recreations* photography, gardening, wine; *Clubs* United Oxford and Cambridge Univ; *Style—* Bernard Taylor, Esq; 8 Bishopsgate, London EC2N 4AE (☎ 071 283 8833)

TAYLOR, Prof Brent William; s of Robert Ernest Taylor (d 1971), of Christchurch, NZ, and Norma Gertrude, *née* Collett; *b* 21 Nov 1941; *Educ* Christchurch Boys HS, Otago Univ (MB ChB, MRCP), Univ of Bristol (PhD); *m* 17 Jan 1970, Moira Elizabeth, da of Thomas Richard Hall (d 1983), of Palmerston North, NZ; 1 s (Samuel b 1973), 1 da (Katherine b 1975); *Career* jr med posts Christchurch NZ 1967-71, res and trg posts Great Ormond Street and Inst of Child Health London 1971-74, sr lectr in paediatrics Christchurch NZ 1975-81, conslt sr lectr in social paediatrics and epidemiology Univ of Bristol and visiting paediatrician and epidemiologist Riyadh Mil Hosp 1981-84, conslt sr lectr in child health St Mary's Hosp Med Sch London 1985-88, prof of community child health Royal Free Hosp Sch of Med Univ of London 1988-; FRCP 1985, FRACP 1981 (MRACP 1970); *Recreations* opera, personal computing; *Style—* Prof Brent Taylor; 6 Bradley Gardens, London W13 8HF (☎ 081 991 1371); Department of Child Health, Royal Free Hospital/School of Medicine, London NW3 2QG (☎ 071 794 0500)

TAYLOR, Hon Mrs ((Lavender Lilias) Carole); *née* Alport; yr da of Baron Alport, TD, PC, DL (Life Peer), and Rachel Cecilia, *née* Bingham (d 1983); *b* 13 Dec 1950; *m* 1974, Ian Colin Taylor, MBE, MP, *qv*; 2 s (Arthur Lawrence Alport b 1977, Ralph George Alport b 1980); *Style—* The Hon Mrs Taylor; Lane End Cottage, Cranmore Lane, West Horsley, Surrey KT24 6BW (☎ 04865 5449)

TAYLOR, Cavan; s of Albert William Taylor, and Muriel, *née* Horncastle (d 1985); *b* 23 Feb 1935; *Educ* King's Coll Sch Wimbledon, Emmanuel Cambridge (MA, LLM); *m* 1962, Helen, da of late Everard Tinling; 1 s (Sean b 1965), 2 da (Karen b 1963, Camilla b 1970); *Career* Nat Serv 2 Lt RASC 1953-55; admitted slr 1961, ptnr Lovell White Durrant (dep sr ptnr 1990-), dir Tissunique Ltd; former chm Cooper Estates Ltd, former dir Hampton Gold Mining Areas plc; memb: Governing Body of King's Coll Sch Wimbledon 1970- (chm 1973-90), Law Soc, Int Bar Assoc; *Recreations* reading, sailing, gardening; *Clubs* Travellers'; *Style—* Cavan Taylor, Esq; Lovell White Durrant, 65 Holborn Viaduct, London EC1A 2DY (☎ 071 236 0066, fax 071 248 4212); Covenham House, Broad Highway, Cobham, Surrey KT11 2RP (☎ 64258)

TAYLOR, Charles Edward; s of William Charles Taylor (d 1953), of Walsall, and Alice Maud Mary, *née* Gay (d 1987); *b* 16 May 1920; *Educ* Queen Mary's GS Walsall, Univ of London; *Career* serv WWII RA 1939-45; athletics coach 1960-; has produced 28 int athletes (incl seven membs GB Olympic team) who have competed for GB and won medals at every level; qualified FA coach, BAAB Master Coach; *Recreations* books, theatre, music, wine; *Style—* Charles Taylor, Esq; 7 Somers Road, Walsall, West Midlands WS2 9AU (☎ 0922 26453); BAAB Edgbaston House, 3 Duchess Place, Hagley Rd, Birmingham B16 8NM (☎ 021 456 4050, fax 021 456 4069)

TAYLOR, Hon Charles Richard Herbert; yr s of Baron Taylor (Life Peer); *b* 27 Jan 1950; *Educ* Highgate, King's Coll Cambridge, Queen's and St Antony's Colls Oxford, Wharton Sch Pennsylvania; *m* 1977, Mary-Ellen, da of late John Feeney, of Pa, USA; *Career* devpt economist World Bank to 1981, private economic conslt 1981-; *Clubs* Washington Squash and Racquets; *Style—* The Hon Charles Taylor; 3911 Argyle Terrace, Washington DC 20011, USA

TAYLOR, Charles Spencer; s of Leonard Taylor, and Phyllis Rose, *née* Emerson (d 1982); *b* 18 Jan 1952; *Educ* William Fletcher Sch Bognor Regis, Univ of Hull (LLB); *m* 7 Sept 1973, Elizabeth Mary (Liz), da of Ernest Richard Stephens; 2 s (Leo John Julius b 5 June 1987, Jack Michael Marius b 10 Feb 1990); *Career* called to the Bar Middle Temple 1974, in practice SE Circuit; memb Hon Soc of the Middle Temple 1969; *Recreations* gardening; *Style—* Charles Taylor, Esq; 3 East Pallant, Chichester, Sussex PO19 1TR (☎ 0243 784538, fax 780861)

TAYLOR, Dr Christopher Michael; s of Harry Taylor (d 1983), and Margaret Elizabeth, *née* Leigh; *b* 27 July 1952; *Educ* Hutton GS, Christ Coll Cambridge (MA), Kings Coll Hosp Med Sch Univ of London (MB BChir); *m* 4 Nov 1978, Soopamah, da of Arnasalon Munisami, of Mauritius; 2 s (Michael Khrisnen b 1983, Andrew James Silven b 1987), 1 da (Rachel Kevina b 1980); *Career* conslt psychiatrist Leeds Eastern Health Authy 1986-; MRCPsych; *Style—* Dr Christopher Taylor; St James's University Hospital, Beckett St, Leeds, W Yorks LS9 7TF (☎ 0532 433 144)

TAYLOR, Clifford; s of Fred Taylor (d 1985), of Wombwell, Yorkshire, and Annie Elizabeth, *née* Hudson (d 1986); *b* 6 March 1941; *Educ* Barnsley Coll of Mining & Technol; *m* 21 Nov 1962, Catherine Helen, da of Charles Thomas Green (d 1968), of Hoyland, Yorkshire; 2 da (Amanda b 8 Sept 1965, Susan b 11 June 1967); *Career* CA NCB 1957-65, Midlands Counties Dairy 1965-68, BBC 1968-; dep dir fin 1984-86, dir Resources TV 1986-; assoc memb Chartered Inst of Management Accountants; *Recreations* squash, walking, horse racing, sport, theatre; *Clubs* Rugby, MCC (assoc memb); *Style—* Clifford Taylor, Esq; BBC TV Centre, Wood Lane, London W12 (☎ 081 576 7788)

TAYLOR, Sir Cyril Julian Hebden; s of Rev Cyril Eustace Taylor (d 1935), of Switzerland, and Marjory Victoria, *née* Hebden; *b* 14 May 1935; *Educ* St Marylebone GS London, Roundhay Sch Leeds, Trinity Hall Cambridge (MA), Harvard Business Sch (MBA); *m* 5 June 1965, June Judith (Judy), da of Earl Denman (d 1970); 1 da (Kirsten Livia Hebden b 1970); *Career* Nat Serv 1954-56 (cmmn with E Surrey Regt seconded to 3 Bn King's African Rifles in Kenya during Mau Mau emergency); brand mangr Procter & Gamble Cincinnati Ohio 1961-64, fndr chm AIFS Inc 1964- (cos incl: American Inst for Foreign Study, Camp America, Au Pair in America, Richmond Coll, English Language Services), chm City Technology Colleges Trust 1987-, advsr to Sec of State for Educn and Sci 1987-; Parly Candidate (C) Huddersfield E Feb 1974 and Keighley Oct; Gtr London Cncl for Ruislip Northwood: memb 1977-86, chm Profession and Gen Servs Ctee 1978-81, opposition spokesman for tport, policy and resources 1981-86, dep ldr of the opposition 1983-86; memb Bd of Dirs Centre for Policy Studies 1984-; pres: Ruislip Northwood Cons Assoc 1986-, Harvard Business Sch Club of London 1990-; chm Lexham Gdns Residents Assoc; FRSA; kt 1989; *Books and Pamphlets* The Guide to Study Abroad (with prof John Garraty and Lily von

Klemperer), Peace has its Price (1972), No More Tick (1974), The Elected Member's Guide to Reducing Public Expenditure (1980), A Realistic Plan for London Transport (1982), Reforming London's Government (1984), Quangoes Just Grow (1985), London Preserv'd (1985), Bringing Accountabiltiy Back to Local Government (1985), Employment Examined: The Right Approach to More Jobs (1986) Raising Educational Standards (1990); and author of numerous pamphlets; *Recreations* keen tennis player, swimmer, gardener and theatre goer; *Clubs* Carlton, Chelsea Arts, Hurlingham, Harvard (New York), Racquet and Tennis (New York); *Style—* Sir Cyril Taylor; 1 Lexham Walk, London W8 5JD (☎ 071 370 2081); American Institute for Foreign Study, 37 Queen's Gate, London SW7 5HR (☎ 071 581 2733, fax 071 589 6721)

TAYLOR, David George Pendleton; s of George James Pendleton Taylor (d 1972), and Dorothy May Taylor, *née* Williams (d 1978); *b* 5 July 1933; *Educ* Clifton, Clare Coll Cambridge (MA); *Career* Sub Lt (Special) RNVR 1952-54; dist offr and subsequently sr local govt offr Tanganyika (now Tanzania) 1958-63; with Booker plc 1964-89 (sr mgmnt post and dir, chm and chief exec Booker (Malawi) 1976-77); seconded as chief exec Falkland Islands Govt 1983-87 and 1988-89 (on an interim basis), govr Montserrat 1990-; memb: Royal Cwlth Soc, Royal Inst of Affairs, RGS, Royal African Soc; *Recreations* painting, reading; *Clubs* Br Sportsman's, MCC, United Oxford and Cambridge; *Style—* David Taylor, Esq; 53 Lillian Road, London SW13 9JF

TAYLOR, David John; s of Charles Stanley Taylor (d 1980), of Bath, and Eileen Florence Taylor (d 1980); *b* 7 July 1943; *Educ* The King's Sch Ottery St Mary, Kingswood GS Bristol; *Career* CA 1967; articled clerk Ricketts Cooper & Co 1961-67; Cooper Bros & Co (now Coopers & Lybrand Deloitte): audit sr Bristol office 1967, audit sr Accra Ghana office 1967, audit mangr office 1969, secondments to Monrovia Liberia, memb of World Bank funded mgmnt consultancy (working on project for Electricity Corp of Ghana); founding ptnr Robson Taylor 1969-90, fndr mgmnt consultancy 1990-; holds several non-exec directorships; chm Fin Ctee and memb of Cncl of Mgmnt of Bath Festival Soc Ltd 1984-90, pres W of Eng Soc of CAs 1990-91; FCA 1974; *Recreations* skiing, horse riding, wine, travel, theatre; *Clubs* MCC, St James', Bath RFU, Landsdown CC, Forty Club; *Style—* David Taylor, Esq; 31 Sion Hill, Bath, Avon BA1 2UW (☎ 0225 424509); David Taylor, Chartered Accountant, 1 North Parade Passage, Bath, Avon BA1 1NX (☎ 0225 420808, car 0836 642808, fax 0225 482825)

TAYLOR, David Mills; s of Donald Charles Taylor (d 1940), and Elsa Marjorie Taylor (d 1967); *b* 22 Dec 1935; *Educ* Royal Commercial Travellers Schs; *m* 1960, Gillian Irene, da of George Edward Washford; 4 da; *Career* gp fin dir: Brooke Bond Oxo Ltd 1968-71, The Guthrie Corporation Ltd 1971-79, Trafalgar House plc 1979-87; fin dir The Fitzroy Robinson Partnership 1987-90; FCA, FCT; *Recreations* golf, oriental cooking, music; *Style—* David M Taylor, Esq; Fairwood House, Fairmile Park Rd, Cobham, Surrey KT11 2PG (☎ 0932 863520)

TAYLOR, David Samuel Irving; s of Samuel Donald Taylor (d 1970), of Pulborough, Sussex, and Winifred Alice May, *née* Marker; *b* 6 June 1942; *Educ* Dauntsey's Sch, Univ of Liverpool (MB ChB); *m* 5 July 1969, Anna, da of Air Cdr John Rhys-Jones (d 1972), of Nutbourne Manor, Pulborough, Sussex; 2 s (Matthew Samuel b 1970, Nicholas James b 1972); *Career* res surgn Moorfields Eye Hosp 1971-74, fell in neurophthalmology Univ of California San Francisco 1976-77, conslt ophthalmologist Nat Hosp for Nervous Diseases London 1976-89, conslt paediatric ophthalmologist Hosp for Sick Children Gt Ormond St London 1976-, hon sr lectr Inst Child Health London 1976-; memb Cncl Royal London Soc for the Blind, fndr and organiser Help a Child to See; memb: BMA 1970, RSM 1974, American Acad Ophthalmology 1976; FRCS 1973, FRCP 1984, FCOphth 1988; *Books* Paediatric Ophthalmology (jtly, 2 edn 1990); *Recreations* sailing, tennis, skiing, forestry; *Clubs* Athenaeum; *Style—* David Taylor, Esq; 23 Church Rd, Barnes, London SW13 9HE (☎ 081 878 0305); 1 Harmont Hse, 20 Harley St, London W1N 1AL (☎ 081 935 7916)

TAYLOR, Denise Marilyn; *Educ* Belvedere Sch Liverpool, Liverpool Sch of Dental Surgery Univ of Liverpool (BDS), DipOrth RCS, Cert of Specialist Training in Orthodontics for EC purposes, Cert of Accreditation of Br Soc of Med and Dental Hypnosis; *Career* house offr Liverpool Dental Hosp and Liverpool Royal Infirmary; sr house offr: in oral and maxillofacial surgery Walton Hosp and Liverpool Dental Hosp, in children's dentistry and orthodontics St Georges Hosp and Royal Dental Hosp; registrar in orthodontics Southampton Gen Hosp, clinical orthodontist Middx Hosp London, currently clinical orthodontist at Whipps Cross Hosp Leytonstone and Wexham Park Hosp Slough, in private practice Wimpole St London; dental sec Section of Hypnosis and Psychosomatic Medicine RSM; memb: Br Assoc of Orthodontists, BDA, RSM, Br Soc of Med and Dental Hypnosis; *Recreations* ice skating, skiing, tennis, riding, photography, art; *Style—* Ms Denise Taylor; 20 Wimpole Street, London W1 (☎ 071 636 4132)

TAYLOR, Dennis James; s of Thomas Taylor, of 24 Mourne Cres, Coalisland, Co Tyrone, NI, and Annie, *née* Donnelly (d 1984); *b* 19 Jan 1949; *Educ* Prima Dixon Sch; *m* 30 March 1970, Patricia Ann, da of Robert Burrows; 2 s (Damian Thomas b 26 June 1973, Brendon Martin b 21 Oct 1976), 1 da (Denise Ann b 27 April 1971); *Career* snooker player; turned professional 1971; winner: Rothmans Grand Prix 1984, Embassy World Championship 1985, BCE Canadian Masters 1985, Kit Kat Break for World Champions 1985, Carlsberg Challenge 1986, Benson & Hedges Masters 1987, Carting Champions 1987, Labatts Canadian Masters 1987, Matchroom Championship 1987; Irish Professional Champion 1982, 1985, 1986 and 1987; involved with the Snooker Golf Soc; *Style—* Dennis Taylor, Esq; c/o Barry Hurn, Ground Floor, 1 Arcade Place, South Street, Romford, Essex (☎ 0708 730 480)

TAYLOR, Derek Edmund; s of Jack Evans Taylor, and Mary Jane, *née* Quigley; *b* 30 Nov 1925; *Educ* Farnworth GS, Royal Tech Coll (now Univ of Salford) (ARTCS), Univ of London (BSc); *m* 28 Sept 1965, Pamela Margaret, da of John Seymour (d 1974), of Australia; 2 da (Margaret Jane b 1966, Kathleen Anne b 1968); *Career* physicist ICI 1951-56, sr scientist NCB 1956-58, sr conslt HB Maynard Inc Pittsburgh 1958-61, md English Velvets Ltd 1961-64, sr supervisory conslt Coopers & Lybrand Assoc Ltd 1965-73, md Scandinavian Inst for Admin Res Planning Ltd 1973-75; dir mgmnt and bus devpt Kingston Regnl Mgmnt Centre 1975-90; non-exec dir: Roehampton Club Ltd, Glaxo Insurance (Bermuda) Ltd, Market Garages (Spitalfields) Ltd, Stategic Planning Soc; md Derek Taylor Assoc Ltd 1991-; Freeman: City of London, Worshipful Co of Bakers; CPhys 1985, MInstP 1978, FIMC 1986, FBIM 1978, FInstD 1965; *Books* New Organisations From Old; *Recreations* golf, skiing, bridge, opera music; *Clubs* Roehampton, Royal Wimbledon Golf, City Livery; *Style—* Derek Taylor, Esq; 6 Ridgway Gardens, Wimbledon, London SW19 4SZ (☎ 081 946 0585)

TAYLOR, Edward (Teddy) Macmillan; MP (C) Southend E 1980-; s of Edward Taylor (d 1962), and Minnie Hamilton Taylor; *b* 18 April 1937; *Educ* Glasgow HS, Univ of Glasgow (MA); *m* 1970, Sheila, da of Alex Duncan, of 80 Wimborne Rd, Southend-on-Sea; 2 s, 1 da; *Career* journalist with Glasgow Herald 1958-59, industl rels offr with Clyde Shipbuilders' Assoc 1959-64, MP (C) Glasgow Cathcart 1964-79, parly under-sec Scottish Office 1970-71 and 1974; opposition spokesman for: Trade 1977, Scottish Affrs 1977-79; *Recreations* golf, chess; *Style—* Teddy Taylor, Esq, MP; 12 Lynton Rd, Thorpe Bay, Southend, Essex (☎ 0586 586282); House of Commons, London SW1 (☎ 071 219 3476)

TAYLOR, Eric; s of Sydney Taylor (d 1979), of Wigan, Lancs, and Sarah Helen, *née* Lea (d 1982); *b* 22 Jan 1931; *Educ* Wigan GS, Univ of Manchester (LLB, LLM); *m* 7 April 1958 (Margaret) Jessie, da of Thomas Brown Gowland (d 1951); *Career* admitted slr 1955, ptnr Temperley Taylor 1957-, rec Crown Ct 1978-; pt/t lectr law Univ of Manchester 1958-80 (hon special lectr in law 1981-), examiner Law Soc Final Exam 1968-81 (chief examiner 1978-83); chm: Manchester Young Slrs Gp 1963, Manchester Nat Insur Appeal Tbnl 1967-73; pres Oldham Law Assoc 1970-72; Law Soc: memb Cncl 1972-91, chm Educn and Trg Ctee 1980-83, chm Criminal Law Ctee 1984-87; govr Coll of Law 1984-; memb: CNAA Legal Studies Bd 1975-84, Lord Chancellor's Advsy Ctee on Trg of Magistrates 1974-79; memb Law Soc 1955; *Books* Modern Conveyancy Precedents (2 edn, 1989), Modern Wills Precedents (1969, 2 edn 1987); *Recreations* horse riding, dressage; *Clubs* Farmers; *Style—* Eric Taylor, Esq; 10 Mercers Rd, Heywood, Lancs L10 2NP (☎ 0706 66630); Suffield House, Middleton, Manchester M24 4EL (☎ 061 643 2411, fax 061 655 3015)

TAYLOR, Dr Eric Andrew; s of Dr Jack Andrew Taylor, of Bruton, Somerset, and Grace, *née* Longley; *b* 22 Dec 1944; *Educ* Clifton, Univ of Cambridge (MA, MB BChir), Harvard Univ, Middx Hosp Med Sch; *m* Dr Anne Patricia Roberts, da of Edgar Roberts, of 73 Pondfield Crescent, St Albans; 2 s (Thomas b 1976, Paul b 1980); *Career* reader in developmental neuropsychiatry Univ of London 1987-, ed Journal of Child Psychology and Psychiatry 1983-, memb scientific staff MRC 1990-; hon conslt child and adolescent psychiatry 1978-: Bethlem Royal Hosp, Maudsley Hosp, KCH; memb exec Assoc Child Psychology and Psychiatry; FRCP 1986, FRCPsych 1988; *Books* The Overactive Child: Clinics in Developmental Medicine No 97 (1986), The Hyperactive Child: A Parent's Guide (1986); *Style—* Dr Eric Taylor; Institute of Psychiatry, De Crespigny Park, London SE5 (☎ 071 703 5411)

TAYLOR, Hon Mrs (Frances Rochelle); *née* Bellow; er da of Baron Bellwin (Life Peer); *b* 1951; *m* 1971, Stephen Taylor; 3 s (Daniel Mark b 1973, Benjamin Paul b 1974, Edward David b 1976); *Career* co dir; *Style—* The Hon Mrs Taylor

TAYLOR, Chief Constable Francis William (Frank); QPM (1989), DL (Durham 1990); *b* 27 March 1933; *m* 17 Dec 1955, Sylvia; 2 s (Andrew b 17 Nov 1959, John b 6 June 1965), 1 da (Julie b 18 Feb 1957); *Career* chief superintendent Gtr Manchester Police 1958-82 (prev constable Manchester City Police), asst chief constable Lincolnshire Police 1982-85; Durham Constabulary: dep chief constable 1985-88, chief constable 1988-; memb and vice pres Upper Teesdale and Weardale Fell Rescue Assoc; memb Help the Aged and Rotary Club; FBIM 1981; *Recreations* reading, music, swimming, walking; *Style—* Frank Taylor, Esq, QPM, DL; Durham Constabulary, Chief Constable's Office, Aykley Heads, Durham DH1 5TT (☎ 091 386 4929, telex Durpol 53530, fax 091 386 3913, car 0836 329691)

TAYLOR, Frank Henry; s of George Henry Taylor (d 1935), of Garden Ave, Mitcham, Surrey, and Emma Rebecca, *née* Hodder (d 1965); *b* 10 Oct 1907; *Educ* Rutlish Sch Merton London; *m* 1, 1936, Dora Mackay (d 1944); 1 da (Margaret MacKay b 10 July 1938); m 2, 1948, Mabel Hills (d 1974); 2 s (Martin Henry b 11 Feb 1951, Frank Nicholas b 14 June 1953); m 3, 28 Jan 1978, Glenys Mary Edwards, MBE, da of William Edwards (d 1924), of Bethesda, N Wales; *Career* Lt-Col 1 Caernarvonshire Bn HG 1943; CA 1930, fin dir of tea coffee cocoa and yeast Miny of Food 1942, fin rep Miny of War Tport Overseas 1944, visited over 40 countries on fin and political missions, princ Frank H Taylor & Co London CA, chm Wimbledon South West Finance plc 1959-; parly candidate (C): contested Newcastle under Lyme 1955, Chorley 1959; MP (C) Manchester Moss Side 1961-74; govr Rutlish Sch 1951-90; played rugby for Surrey Co, golf capt RAC 1962, sculling Thames Champion 1931, punting several Thames championships; Freeman Guild Co of Air Pilots, Liveryman and former Master Worshipful Co of Bakers; FCIS 1929, FCA 1930; *Recreations* rugby sculling, punting, shooting, golf; *Clubs* RAC, City Livery, British Sportsmans; *Style—* Frank Taylor, Esq; 4 Barrie House, Lancaster Gate, London W2 (☎ 071 262 5684); 114 Hewgate St, London EC1A 7AE (☎ 071 606 9485)

TAYLOR, Frank William; s of Frank Taylor (d 1963), and Mary Gibson, *née* Steward; *b* 7 Oct 1937; *Educ* Birkenhead Inst; *m* 3 Aug 1963, Ann Taylor; 1 s (Michael b 13 Oct 1965), 1 da (Steffanie b 28 April 1968); *Career* ptnr Ernst & Young CA's, pres Insolvency Practioners Assoc 1973; FCA; *Recreations* golf; *Clubs* Heswall; *Style—* Frank Taylor, Esq; Stableford, Brook Lane, Parkgate, Wirral, Cheshire; Ernst & Young, Silkhouse Court, Tithebarn St, Liverpool L2 2LE

TAYLOR, Geoffrey Newton (Geoff); s of William Henry Taylor, of Bovingdon Green, Bucks, and Elsie May Taylor; *b* 25 April 1938; *Educ* Royal GS High Wycombe, Oxford Univ (MA); *m* 1, 1963, Julia Nora Barnes; 2 s (Scott Geoffrey b 1967, Jon Michael b 1970); m 2, 1976, Janice Darleen Swett; *Career* dir: Investors In Indust plc 1985-90, Rodime plc 1981-89, LSI Logic (Europe) 1985-; chm 3i Corp 1990; *Recreations* music, tennis, pilot; *Clubs* IOD; *Style—* Geoff Taylor, Esq; The Hill, Penn Rd, Beaconsfield, Bucks HP9 2TS; Investors in Industry plc, 91 Waterloo Rd, London SE1 8XP (telex 917844, fax 071 928 3131)

TAYLOR, Geoffrey William; s of Joseph William (d 1980), of Heckmondwike, Yorks, and Doris, *née* Parr (d 1984); *b* 4 Feb 1927; *Educ* Heckmondwike GS, Univ of London (BCom); *m* 21 July 1951, Joyce, da of George Clifford Walker, (d 1952), of Liversedge, Yorks; 3 s (Nigel b 1954, Christopher b 1957, Julian b 1959), 1 da (Ruth b 1966); *Career* RN 1945-47; Midland Bank 1943-86: md Midland Bank Fin Corp 1967-72, gp treas 1972-73, asst chief gen mangr 1974-80, dep gp chief exec 1980-81, gp chief exec 1982-86; chm Daiwa Europe Bank plc 1987-, memb Banking Servs Law Review Ctee 1987-88, dir Y J Lovell Hldgs plc; memb Fin Devpt Bd NSPCC; Freeman City of London 1984; FCIOB 1975, FBIM 1979; *Recreations* golf, reading, music; *Style—* Geoffrey Taylor, Esq; The Mount, Parkfields, Stokesheath Road, Oxshott, Surrey KT22 OPW (☎ 037 842991); Daiwa Europe Bank plc, Level 19, City Tower, 40 Basinghall St, London EC2V 5DE (☎ 071 315 3900, fax 071 782 0875, telex 9419121 DIAFIN G)

TAYLOR, Sir George; s of George William Taylor, of Edinburgh; *b* 15 Feb 1904; *Educ* George Heriot's Sch Edinburgh, Univ of Edinburgh (DSc); *m* 1, 1929 (m dis 1965), Alice Helen (d 1977), da of Thomas William Pendrich, of Edinburgh; 2 s; m 2, 1965, Norah (d 1967), da of William Christopher English, of Carrycoats Hall, Northumberland; m 3, 1969, Beryl, Lady Colwyn (d 1987); m 4, 1989, June Maitland; *Career* keeper of botany Br Museum 1950-56, botanical sec Linnean Soc 1950-56 (vice pres 1956), dir Royal Botanic Gardens Kew 1956-71, visiting prof Univ of Reading 1969-, dir Stanley Smith Hort Tst 1970-89, conslt Stanley Smith Hort Tst 1989-; vice pres and prof of botany Royal Hort Soc 1974-, pres Botanical Soc of Br Is; FRS, FRSE, FLS; kt 1962; *Recreations* angling, gardening; *Clubs* New (Edinburgh); *Style—* Sir George Taylor; Belhaven House, Dunbar, East Lothian (☎ 0368 62392/63546)

TAYLOR, Sir (Arthur) Godfrey; DL (Gtr London, 1988); *b* 1925,Aug; *Career* formerly: borough cncllr, alderman, chm London Borough Assoc; chm Assoc of Met Authy 1978-80, managing tstee Municipal Mutual Insurance Ltd 1979-86; chm: Southern Water Authy 1981-85, London Residuary Body 1985-; kt 1980; *Style—* Sir Godfrey Taylor, DL; 23 Somerhill Lodge, Somerhill Rd, Hove, E Sussex

TAYLOR, Gordon; s of Alec Taylor (d 1980), of Ashton under Lyne, Lancs, and Mary, *née* Walsh; *b* 28 Dec 1944; *Educ* Ashton under Lyne GS, Univ of London (BSc); *m* 27 July 1968, Catharine Margaret, da of Frederick Johnston, of Bury, Lancs; 2 s (Simon

Mark b 1970, Jonathan Peter b 1973); *Career* professional footballer: Bolton Wanderers 1960-70, Birmingham City 1970-76, Blackburn Rovers 1976-78, Vancouver Whitecaps (N American Soccer League) 1977, Bury 1978-80; sec and chief exec Professional Footballers Assoc 1981- (chm 1978-80); Hon MA Loughborough Univ; *Recreations* theatre, music, reading, watching sport, squash; *Style—* Gordon Taylor, Esq; Professional Footballers Association, 2 Oxford Court, Bishopsgate, Manchester M2 3WQ (☎ 061 236 0575, fax 061 228 7229)

TAYLOR, Gordon William; s of William Herbert Taylor (d 1973), and Elizabeth Ann, *née* Tucker (d 1946); *b* 26 June 1928; *Educ* Army Technical Sch Arborfield, Univ of London (BSc Eng, PhD); *m* 3 April 1954, Audrey Catherine, da of Arthur Bull (d 1976), of Blackheath, London; 3 s (Mark b 1961, Zachary b 1962, Matthew b 1965), 2 da (Gemma b 1964, Katie b 1966); *Career* Kellogg Int Corp 1954-59, WR Grace 1960-62; gen mangr: Nalco Ltd 1962-66, BTR Industs 1966-68; md: Kestrel Chemicals 1968-69, Astral Mktg 1969-70; Robson Refractories 1971-87; md Firemarket Ltd 1987-; Alderman GLC 1972-77, memb Croydon Central 1977-80; chm: Public Servs Ctee 1977-78, London Tport Ctee 1978-79; MICE, MIMechE, AMIEE; *Recreations* reading, theatre, opera, tennis; *Clubs* Holland Park Lawn Tennis; *Style—* Gordon Taylor, Esq; 33 Royal Ave, Chelsea, London SW3 4QE (☎ 071 730 3045)

TAYLOR, Rev Canon Humphrey Vincent; s of Maurice Humphrey Taylor, MBE (d 1987), and Mary Patricia Stuart, *née* Wood; *b* 5 March 1938; *Educ* Harrow, Pembroke Coll Cambridge (BA, MA), Univ of London (MA); *m* 24 April 1965, Anne Katharine, da of Thomas Henry Dart, of Woking, Surrey; 2 da (Katharine b 1966, Elizabeth b 1968); *Career* Nat Serv PO Tech Branch 1956-58; curate: Hammersmith 1963-64, N Kensington 1964-66; rector Lilongwe Malawi 1966-71, chaplain and lectr Bishop Grosseteste Coll Lincoln 1972-74, sec for chaplaincies in higher educn Gen Synod Bd of Educn 1974-80, sec USPG 1984- (mission progs sec 1980-84); hon canon: Bristol Cathedral 1986-, Province of Southern Africa 1989-; *Style—* The Rev Canon Humphrey Taylor; Partnership House, 157 Waterloo Road, London SE1 8XA (☎ 071 928 8681, fax 071 928 2371, telex 8590 907 Ang Com G)

TAYLOR, Iain Scott; TD; s of John Ross Taylor (d 1963), of Kerryston House, Kellas, by Dundee, Angus, and Annie, *née* Scott Paterson (d 1982); *b* 1 June 1931; *Educ* Dundee HS, Merchiston Castle Sch; *m* 8 Aug 1956, Nancy Christine, da of Dr William Allison (d 1979), of Elmbank, 154 City Rd, Dundee; 2 s (Alastair b 1958, Andrew b 1964), 2 da (Shirley b 1960, Sandra b 1962); *Career* Nat Serv RAF Regt 1950-52 (Pilot Offr 1951, Sqdn Adj 23 LAA Sqdn 1951-52, Flt Cdr 1952); TA 1953-75; FFYEO: Troop Ldr 1953-56, Troop Ldr (FFY Scottish Horse) 1956-66, Maj Sqdn Cdr 1966-71, 2 i/c 1971; Highland Yeo Offr commanding at disbandment 1975; ACF 1976-: Lt-Col Cmdt Angus-Dundee Bn 1976-79, Col 1979-89, cadet Force Medal 1988, Brig 1989, Cmdt Scotland 1989-; WS Taylor & Co Ltd 1952-56, sole ptnr A Watson & Co 1956-63, jt ptnr Taylor Stewart Ltd 1961-66, fin dir John Cooper & Sons Ltd; non-exec dir: Century Aluminium Co Ltd 1969-77, Kinnes Oilfield Services Ltd 1974-80, schs liaison offr Tayside Region Dundee Chamber of Commerce 1983; chm Lord Armistead Tst, tstee and memb exec and Scottish Veterans; Residencies, chm Rosendael House Ctee, hon treas (formerly founding chm) Murroes & Wellbank Community Cncl, elder Murroes Parish Church; curling, memb: RCCC Cncl 1981-84, memb Scottish Team in Switzerland 1980; *Recreations* shooting, curling, swimming, sailing, philately, militaria; *Style—* Iain Taylor, Esq, TD; Tigh-Na-Torr, Kellas, Dundee DD5 3PD (☎ 082 625 327)

TAYLOR, Ian Charles Boucher; s of Leslie Charles Taylor, of Kidderminster, Worcs, and Freda May, *née* Bell; *b* 24 Sept 1954; *Educ* Queen Elizabeth GS Hartlebury Worcs, Borough Road Coll, West London Inst of Higher Educn Univ of London (BEd, Cert Ed); *m* 25 Oct 1980, Julie Ann, da of James William Whitehead, of Whitestone, Nuneaton, Warwicks; 2 s (Simon Christopher b 16 Nov 1984, Oliver Sebastian b 9 Nov 1986); *Career* England hockey career: World Cup Buenos Aires 1978, Euro Cup Hanover 1979 (Bronze), World Cup Bombay 1982-83, Euro Cup Amsterdam 1983, World Cup London 1986 (Silver); Euro Cup Moscow 1987 (Silver); GB career Champion's Trophy: Lahore 1978, Karachi 1981, 1982, 1984 (Bronze), Perth 1985 (Silver), Lahore 1986, Amsterdam 1987, Lahore 1988; Los Angeles Olympics 1984 (Bronze), Seoul Olympics 1988 (Gold), voted best goalkeeper for 11 consecutive years, captained World XI 12 times; 'ministers' nominee on Regnl Sports Cncl, memb Hockey Assoc Tech Ctee; *Books* Taylor On Hockey (1988), Behind The Mask (1989); *Recreations* golf, antiques; *Style—* Ian Taylor, Esq; c/o British Olympic Assoc, 1 Wandsworth Plain, London SW18 1EH

TAYLOR, Ian Colin; MBE (1974), MP (C) Esher 1987; s of Horace Stanley Taylor, and Beryl, *née* Harper; *b* 18 April 1945; *Educ* Whitley Abbey Sch Coventry, Univ of Keele (BA), LSE; *m* 17 June 1974, Hon Carole Alport, da of Baron Alport (Life Peer), *qv*, of The Cross House, Layer de la Haye, Colchester, Essex; 2 s (Arthur b 1977, Ralph b 1980); *Career* co dir incl: Mathercourt Securities Ltd 1980-91, Mathercourt Group plc 1990-; conslt Commercial Union plc 1988-, PPS to Rt Hon William Waldegrave MP 1990-; memb Cons Nat Union Exec Ctee 1967-75 and 1990-, nat chm Fedn of Cons Students 1968-69, chm Euro Union of Christian Democratic and Cons Students 1969-70, hon sec Br Cons Assoc in France 1976-78; Foreign Affrs Select Ctee 1987-90; chm: Cons Gp for Europe 1985-88, Cwlth Youth Exchange Cncl 1980-84 (vice-pres 1984-), Cons Back Bench Euro Affrs Ctee 1988-89 and Foreign and Cwlth Cncl 1990-; assoc Soc of Investmt Analysts 1972; *Pamphlets* Under Some Delusion (1972), Fair Shares for all the Workers (1988), Releasing the Community Spirit (1990); *Recreations* playing cricket, opera, shooting; *Clubs* Carlton; *Style—* Ian Taylor, Esq, MBE, MP; House of Commons, London SW1A 0AA (☎ 071 219 5221)

TAYLOR, Ian Compton; s of Colin Vaughan Taylor, (d 1940), and Marjorie Lydia (d 1968); *b* 4 July 1937; *Educ* Wellington, The Sorbonne, Christ's Coll Cambridge (MA); *m* 27 Nov 1965, Marylou Anne Jane, da of Cdr A J Watson, OBE, RN; 2 s (Leo P C Compton b 20 Sept 1966, Ian D C Compton b 30 Aug 1967), 2 da (Samantha J C Compton b 10 March 1970, Jennifer J C Compton b 27 Aug 1971); *Career* Lt Intelligence Corps 1955-57, Army Emergency Reserve 1957-88; export dir British SIDAC Ltd 1961-72; md Corruplast Ltd 1972-74, Charter Cars Ltd 1977-80; dep md Midland Montagu Ventures Ltd 1980-; *Recreations* tennis, foreign travel, family; *Clubs* Hurlingham; *Style—* Ian Taylor, Esq; 1 Weltje Road, London W6 (☎ 081 748 9646); c/o Midland Montagu Ventures Ltd, 10 Lower Thames St, London EC3R 6AE (☎ 071 260 9836, fax 071 270 7265, car 0860 378004, telex 887213)

TAYLOR, Prof Irving; s of Samual Taylor, and Fay, *née* Valcovitch; *b* 7 Jan 1945; *Educ* Roundhay Sch Leeds, Univ of Sheffield Med Sch (MB ChB, MD, ChM); *m* 31 Aug 1969, Berenice Penelope, da of Dr Henry Brunner, of Slough; 3 da (Justine Samantha, Tamara Zoe, Gabrielle Rivka); *Career* sr registrar surgery Sheffield 1973-77 (registrar surgery 1971-73, res registrar 1973), sr lectr in surgery Liverpool 1977-81, prof of surgery and head of Dept Surgery Univ of Southampton 1981-89, Hunterian prof RCS 1981; sec: Surgical Res Soc 1985-87, Assoc of Profs of Surgery 1988; ed sec Assoc of Surgns 1987; FRCS 1972, memb RSM 1982; *Books* Complications of Surgery of Lower Gastrointestinal Tract (1985), Progress in Surgery 1 (1985), Progress in Surgery 2 (1987), Progress in Surgery 3 (1989), Benign Breast Disease (1989); *Recreations* tennis, swimming, gardening, squash; *Style—* Prof Irving Taylor; University Surgical Unit, Centre Block F Level, Southampton Gen Hosp, Tremona Rd, Southampton SO9 4XY (☎ 0703 777222 ext 4305)

TAYLOR, Hon Judge Ivor Ralph; QC (1973); s of Abraham Taylor, and Ruth Taylor; *b* 26 Oct 1927; *Educ* Stand GS Whitefield, Univ of Manchester; *m* 1, 1954 (m dis 1974), Ruth Cassel; 1 s, 1 da; m 2 (m dis); m 3, 1984, (Audrey) Joyce Goldman, *née* Wayne; *Career* RAF 1945; called to the Bar Grays Inn 1951; standing counsel to Inland Revenue N Circuit 1969-73, rec 1972-76; chm of Enquiry into Death of Baby Brown at Rochdale Infirmary; *Recreations* golf, walking; *Style—* His Hon Judge Ivor Taylor, QC; 5 Eagle Lodge, 19 Harrop Rd, Hale, Altrincham, Cheshire WA15 9DA (☎ 061 941 5591)

TAYLOR, Sir James; MBE (1945); s of James Taylor, of Sunderland; *b* 16 Aug 1902; *Educ* Bede Coll Sunderland, Rutherford Coll Newcastle upon Tyne, Univ of Durham, Sorbonne, Univ of Utrecht, Univ of Cambridge; *m* 1929, Margaret Lennox, da of Robert Stewart, of Newcastle upon Tyne; 2 s, 1 da; *Career* dir ICI 1952-64; chm: Imperial Aluminium Co Ltd 1959-64, Imperial Metals Ltd 1962-64 (chm Yorkshire 1958-64); dep chm: Royal Ordnance Factories Bd 1959-72, Pyrotenax Ltd 1965-67; dir: BDH Gp Ltd 1965-67, Oldham Int 1965-72, Fulmer Res Inst (chm 1976-78); chm Chloride Silent Power Ltd 1975-81; pres Inst of Physics and Physical Soc 1966-68; memb: steering ctee Nat Physical Laboratory 1966, advsy cncl on Calibration and Measurement 1966, ct Brunel Univ 1967-82; chm cncl RSA 1969-71 (vice-pres 1969-87, vice-pres emeritus 1987-); FRSC; kt 1966; *Style—* Sir James Taylor, MBE; Culvers, Seale, Nr Farnham, Surrey (☎ 025 182210)

TAYLOR, Prof James Allan (Jim); s of John William Taylor (d 1949), of 125 Moss Bank Rd, St Helens, Merseyside, and Ethel, *née* Middlehurst (d 1972); *b* 20 June 1925; *Educ* Prescot GS, Univ of Liverpool (BA, MA, DipEd); *m* 31 March 1962, Sylvia Brenda, da of William Reginald Parr (d 1963), of Gaydene, The Park, Chistleton, Chester; 1 s (Marcus b 31 Aug 1966), 1 da (Amanda b 29 March 1964); *Career* geography master: Pudsey GS Yorks 1946-47, Farnworth GS Bolton Lancs 1947-49; UCW Aberystwyth Dept of Geography 1950-: lectr, sr lectr, reader, prof; moderator for geography A'level with ULESB 1978-, environmental conslt 1980-88 (1968-79), dir and sec Environmental Conslts Ltd (incl six assoc conslts) 1989-; chm Int Bracken Gp 1986-, chm Prescot GS Old Boys Annual Reunions; memb: Geographical Assoc 1948, Inst Br Geographers 1950, Assoc of Br Climatologists 1970, Biogeography Study Gp 1976; *Books* incl: British Weather in Maps (with R A Yates, 1958), Weather and Agriculture (ed, 1967), Weather Economics (ed, 1970), Climatic Resources and Economic Activity (ed, 1974), Culture and Environment in Prehistoric Wales (ed, 1980), Themes in Biogeography (ed, 1984); *Recreations* contributions to radio and television on environmental issues, golf, jazz piano, walking; *Style—* Prof James Taylor; Glyn Ceiro, Dole, Bow St, Aberystwyth, Dyfed, Wales SY24 5AE (☎ 0970 828436/0970 622599)

TAYLOR, Dr James Francis Nuttall; s of Evan Nuttall Taylor, of 34 Andorra Court, Bromley, Kent, and Margaret Susie, *née* Howes (d 1979); *b* 19 Oct 1938; *Educ* Sherborne, Queens' Coll Cambridge (MA BChir, MD), St Thomas' Hosp Med Sch; *m* 18 Sept 1965, Ann, da of Ernest Ensor (d 1985); 4 s (Jonathan James b 30 May 1969, Andrew David b 10 Aug 1970, Richard Paul b 31 Jan 1973, Michael Christopher b 14 June 1974); *Career* res fell: Yale Univ Sch Med New Haven Conn 1971-72, Br Heart Assoc 1972-75; conslt paediatric cardiologist Hosp for Sick Children 1975-, sr lectr Inst Child Health 1975-, hon conslt paediatric cardiologist E Anglian RHA 1978-; memb Bd Govrs Hosps for Sick Children 1982-84 and 1985-90; memb: Br Paediatric Assoc 1970, Br Cardiac Soc 1971, Assoc Euro Paediatrics Cardiologists 1975; FRCP 1978, FACC 1979, FRSM 1985; Knight Order of Falcons Iceland 1981; *Recreations* music, photography, walking; *Style—* Dr James Taylor; 1 Bolton Gardens, Bromley, Kent BR1 4ES (☎ 081 464 8027); Hospital for Sick Children, Cardiac Wing, Great Ormond St, London WC1N 3JH (☎ 071 405 9200 ext 5294)

TAYLOR, Hon Mrs ((Mary) Jane); da of Baron McAlpine of West Green (Life Peer), *qv*, by his 1 w, Sarah Alexandra, da of late Paul Hillman Baron; *b* 1965; *m* 9 Dec 1987, Simon J E du B Taylor, eldest s of Timothy Taylor, of Meadle, Bucks; *Style—* The Hon Mrs Taylor; Callow Street, London SW3 6BJ

TAYLOR, Dame Jean Elizabeth; DCVO (1978); da of late Capt William Taylor (ka 1917); *b* 7 Nov 1916; *Career* joined Office of Private Sec to HM The Queen 1958, chief clerk 1961-78; *Recreations* music, walking, looking at old buildings; *Style—* Dame Jean Taylor, DCVO; Church Cottage, Frittenden, Cranbrook, Kent

TAYLOR, Hon Jeremy Stephen; s of Baron Taylor (Life Peer); *b* 1940; *Educ* Highgate; *m* 1964, Christina, da of late John Bruce Holmes; children; *Career* television executive; *Style—* The Hon Jeremy Taylor; 19 Ayresome Av, Leeds LS8 1BB

TAYLOR, (Margaret) Jessie; OBE (1989); da of Thomas Brown Gowland (d 1951), of Middleton, Manchester, and Ann Goldie, *née* Brighouse (d 1962); *b* 30 Nov 1924; *Educ* Queen Elizabeth GS Middleton, Univ of Manchester (BA, DipEd); *m* 7 April 1958, Eric Taylor, s of Sydney Taylor (d 1979), of Wigan; *Career* jr classics teacher Cheadle Hulme Sch 1946-49; N Manchester GS for Girls: sr classics teacher 1950, sr mistress 1963, actg headmistress 1967; dep headteacher Wright Robinson HS 1967-75, headmistress Whalley Range HS for Girls 1976-88, chm Manchester HS Heads 1982-88; dir Piccadilly Radio 1980-; memb Cncl Examining Ctee Assoc Lancs Schs Examining Bd 1976-89, conslt course tutor NW Educn Mgmnt Centre 1980-82; memb: Nurse Educn Ctee S Manchester Area 1976-88, Williams Ctee (Home Office Ctee on Obscenity and Censorship) 1977-79, Ct of Univ of Salford 1982-88, Northern Examining Assoc (NEA) Examinations Ctee 1988-, UNICEF 1988, Northern Dressage Gp, Middleton Musical Soc NE, Cheshire Drag Hunt, Middleton Parish Church; FRSA 1979; *Recreations* music, riding; *Clubs* Leigh Riding, Rochdale Riding; *Style—* Mrs Jessie Taylor, OBE; 10 Mercers Rd, Hopwood, Heywood, Lancs OL10 2NP (☎ 0706 66630)

TAYLOR, Hon Joan Evelyn; *née* Underhill; da of Lord Underhill, Baron of Leyton, CBE (Life Peer), and Flora Janet, *née* Philbrick; *b* 11 April 1944; *Educ* Warren Farm Secdy Sch Birmingham, Brooklyn Tech Coll Birmingham, Open Univ; *m* 1, 9 Oct 1965 (m dis 1973), Edwin Fennell; m 2, 28 July 1973 (m dis 1989), Ian Robert Taylor; 3 s (Adrian b 5 July 1969, Patrick b 11 May 1975, David b 1 Nov 1979); *Career* private sec Labour Party HQ 1960-64; memb: Nottingham City Cncl 1972-74, Nottinghamshire CC 1973-77 and 1983-, Assoc of CCs 1987- (sec of Lab Gp, dep lab spokesman on social services); memb Selston PC 1983-87 (chm 1986-87); active memb and office holder GMB/APEX (TU); memb: GMB's Parly Panel, Regnl Exec Ctee Labour Party, private sec Labour Pty HQ 1960-64; memb: Nottingham City Cncl 1972-74, Nottinghamshire CC 1973-77 and 1983-, Assoc of CCs 1987- (sec of Lab Gp, dep Lab Spokesman on Social Servs), Selston PC 1983-87 (chm 1986-87), GMB Parly Panel, Regnl Exec Ctee Lab Pty; chm Social Servs Ctee 1983-, active memb and office holder GMB/APEX (TU); Lab Pty candidate at Gen Election 1991/92; *Recreations* politics, bobbin lace making, jogging, reading; *Style—* The Hon Joan Taylor; 22 Royal Oak Drive, Selston, Notts NG16 6QF (☎ 0773 812655); County Hall, West Bridgford, Nottingham NG2 7QD (☎ 0602 823823, telex 37485)

TAYLOR, Sir Jock (John) Lang; KCMG (1979, CMG 1974); s of Sir John William Taylor, KBE, CMG; *b* 3 Aug 1924; *Educ* Prague, Vienna, ISC Windsor; *m* 1952, Molly, only da of James Rushworth; 5 s; *Career* Foreign Serv 1949-84; ambass: to Bonn 1981-84, The Hague 1979-81, Venezuela 1975-79; under-sec Dept Energy

1974-75, asst under-sec FCO 1973-74; has also served Saigon, Hanoi, Beirut, Prague, Montevideo, Bonn, Buenos Aires; *Style*— Sir Jock Taylor, KCMG; The Old Flint, Boxgrove, nr Chichester, West Sussex

TAYLOR, John; MBE (1981); s of Percival Henry Taylor (d 1969), and Florence, *née* Jeffries (d 1981); *b* 4 March 1928; *Educ* Peter Symonds, Winchester; *m* 1, 1949, Joyce, da of Harold Hodson (d 1970); 3 s (Patrick b 1950, Ian b 1953, Andrew b 1964), 2 da (Janet b 1956, Jillian b 1960); m 2, 1980, Christiane, da of Capt Edouard Jean Talou (d 1947); *Career* cmmnd RE 1947; chartered architect and designer; fndr: Taylor & Crowther (princ) 1952, John Taylor Architects (sole princ) 1963, Marshman Warren Taylor (jt princ) 1968, MWT Architects (chm) 1972, MWT Planning 1975, MWT Landscapes 1982, MWT Design 1986; fndr and chm The Co of Designers plc 1986-90, fndr and sole princ Precept Project Assessment 1991-; 7 times Gold medallist DOE Housing Award, 5 times Civic Tst Award; FRIBA, FCSD; *Recreations* sailing, travel; *Style*— John Taylor, Esq, MBE; Milbury Barton, Exminster, Exeter (☎ 0392 832151); Precept Project Assessment, Priests Court, Exminster, Exeter (☎ 0392 823718)

TAYLOR, Brig John; s of John Taylor (d 1957), and Isabella Christie Dunlop, *née* Allan; *b* 26 July 1937; *Educ* Greenock Acad, Univ of Glasgow; *m* 28 July 1961, Elaine, da of Alec Baden Warren (d 1988); 2 s (Angus John b 1964, Alasdair Niall b 1965), 1 da (Louise Alix b 1968); *Career* Capt 1962, Maj 1964, Lt-Col 1975, Col 1983, Brig 1989-; memb Law Soc of Scotland; *Recreations* sailing, bird watching, walking; *Style*— Brig John Taylor; Army Legal Group UK, HQ UKLF

TAYLOR, John Arthur Frederick; TD (1966); s of Col F E A Taylor, TD, and Minnie, *née* Eckford (d 1973); *b* 12 Aug 1933; *Educ* Dulwich; *m* 26 Oct 1963, Sally May, *née* Reogh; 2 s (Toby b 1968, Timothy (twin)); *Career* Nat Serv cmmnd RA 1952-54, TA HAC 1954-56, ret as Maj; tea taster and buyer 1954-61, produce broker London Corn Exchange and Baltic Exchange 1961-66, chm and md Hang-it Framing Systems 1966; govr Meridian Sch Greenwich; memb Cncl: City of London Branch Royal Soc of St George, Nat Art Collections Fund; Freeman City of London 1957, Master Worshipful Co of Wheelwrights 1987 (Freeman 1957), Liveryman Worshipful Co of Painters-Stainers, Sheriff City of London 1990-91; *Recreations* family, theatre, opera, skiing, foreign travel, gardening (badly); *Style*— John Taylor, Esq, TD; 225 Greenwich High Rd, Greenwich, London SE10 8NB (☎ 081 858 2312, fax 081 853 2133)

TAYLOR, Rt Rev John Bernard; *see*: St Albans, Bishop of

TAYLOR, Prof John Bryan; s of Frank Herbert Taylor (d 1978), and Ada, *née* Stinton (d 1973); *b* 26 Dec 1928; *Educ* Oldbury GS, Univ of Birmingham (BSc, PhD); *m* 18 Aug 1951, Joan Margaret, da of Ivor William Hargest (d 1957); 1 s (Paul Robert John b 1961), 1 da (Helen Margaret b 1957); *Career* Flying Officer RAF 1950-52; head of Theoretical Physics Div and chief physicist UK AEA Culham Laboratory 1962-89, chm Plasma Physics Div Inst of Physics 1972-73, Fondren fndn prof of plasma theory Univ of Texas at Austin 1989-; numerous contribs to jls; FInstP 1969, FRS 1970, fell American Physical Soc 1984; *Recreations* model engineering, gliding; *Style*— Prof John Taylor, FRS; Institute of Fusion Studies, University of Texas at Austin, Robert Lee Moore Hall, Austin, Texas 78712 (☎ 512 471 6127/1322, fax 512 471 6715)

TAYLOR, John Charles; QC (1984); s of Sidney Herbert Taylor (d 1977), of St Ives, Cambridgeshire, and Gertrude Florence, *née* Law; *b* 22 April 1931; *Educ* Palmers Sch Essex, Queens' Coll Cambridge (MA, LIB), Harvard Univ USA (LIM); *m* 1964, Jean Aimée, da of William Rankin Monteith (d 1976), late of Purston Manor, Brackley, Northants; 1 da (Victoria b 1967); *Career* memb Stevens Ctee on Minerals Planning Control 1972-74; chm EIP Panel for Leics and Rutland Structure Plan 1985; *Recreations* country pursuits, boardsailing, skiing, sailing; *Clubs* Athenaeum, Travellers'; *Style*— John Taylor, Esq, QC; Clifton Grange, Clifton, Shefford, Beds; 2 Mitre Court Buildings, Temple, London EC4

TAYLOR, Rt Hon John David; PC (NI 1970), MP (UU) Strangford 1983-; s of George David Taylor, of Armagh (d 1979), and Georgina, *née* Baird (d 1986); *b* 24 Dec 1937; *Educ* Royal Sch Armagh, Queen's Univ Belfast (BSc); *m* 1970, Mary Frances, da of Ernest Leslie Todd (d 1985); 1 s (Jonathan), 5 da (Jane, Rachel, Rowena, Alex, Hannah); *Career* MP (UU) S Tyrone NI Parl 1965-73, min of state Miny of Home Affrs 1970-72; memb (UU): Fermanagh and S Tyrone, NI Assembly 1973-75; memb: (UU) N Down NI Constitutional Convention 1975-76, (UU) N Down NI Assembly 1982-86; MEP NI 1979-89; chartered engr; dir: West Ulster Estates Ltd 1968-, Bramley Apple Restaurant Ltd 1974-, Ulster Gazette (Armagh) Ltd 1983-, Gosford Housing Assoc (Armagh) Ltd 1978-, Cerdac Print (Belfast) Ltd, Tyrone Printing Ltd, Tyrone Courier Ltd, Sovereign Properties (NI) Ltd, Tontine Rooms Holding Co Ltd; *Clubs* Armagh County, Armagh City, Farmers' (Whitehall London); *Style*— The Rt Hon John D Taylor, MP; Mullinure, Portadown Road, Armagh, N Ireland (☎ 0861 522409)

TAYLOR, John Edward; s of Jesse Taylor (d 1977), of Hadleigh, Suffolk, and Clarice Bowron, *née* Watling; *b* 11 Nov 1931; *Educ* Cockburn Sch Leeds, Leeds Coll of Technol, RAF Tech Coll Henlow; *m* 25 Aug 1956, Marion Eveline, da of Francis Charles Jordon (d 1932); 3 da (Valerie b 1957, Patricia b 1959, Carol (twin) b 1959); *Career* RAF 1952-55: tech offr RAF Butzweilerhof 1953-54, M & E offr Airfield Construction Branch RAF Wildenrath 1954-55; contracts engr AEI Ltd 1956-66, sales mangr Distribution Transformers 1965-66, commercial mangr Eastern Electricity Bd 1976-80, central dir mktg Electricity Cncl 1980-90; dir: Br Electrical Approvals Bd 1984-, Chloride-RWE 1990; chm Airfield Construction Offrs Assoc 1982; CEng 1966, MIEE 1963, FBIM 1989; *Recreations* motor cruising, photography; *Clubs* RAF; *Style*— J E Taylor, Esq; Hill House, 59 Henley Rd, Ipswich IP1 3SN (☎ 0473 252094); Chloride-RWE, Clifton Juncton, Swinton, Manchester M27 2LR (☎ 061 794 4611, fax 061 793 6606)

TAYLOR, Prof John Gerald; s of Dr William Taylor (d 1984), and Elsie, *née* Boyd (d 1986); *b* 18 Aug 1931; *Educ* Lancaster GS, Blackburn GS, Chelmsford GS, Mid Essex Tech Coll (BSc), Christs Coll Cambridge (BSc, BA, MA, PhD); *m* 1 (m dis), Patricia Kenney; m 2, Pamela Nancy, da of late Matthew Cutmore; 2 s (Geoffrey, Robin), 3 da (Frances, Susan, Elizabeth); *Career* Cwlth fell Inst for Advanced Study Princeton NJ USA 1956-58, res fell Christ's Coll Cambridge 1958-60 (asst lectr Faculty of Mathematics 1959-60); memb: Inst Hautes Études Scientifiques Paris 1960-61, Inst for Advanced Study Princeton 1961-63; sr res fell Churchill Coll Cambridge 1963-64, prof of physics Rutger Univ NJ USA 1964-66, lectr in Mathematics Inst and fell Hertford Coll Oxford 1966-67, lectr and reader QMC London 1967-69, prof of physics Univ of Southampton 1969-71, prof of mathematics King's Coll London 1971-, euro ed in chief Neural Networks 1990-; chm: Mathematics and Physics Gp Inst of Physics 1981-86 (vice chm 1988-), Jt Euro Neural Networks Initiative Cncl 1990-; convenor Br Neural Network Soc 1988-; fell Cambridge Philosophy Soc, FInstP, FRAS; *Books* Quantum Mechanics (1969), The Shape of Minds to Come (1971), The New Physics (1972), Black Holes: The End of the Universe? (1973), Superminds (1975), Special Relativity (1975), Science and the Supernatural (1980), The Horizons of Knowledge (1982), and over 200 sci papers and numerous radio and TV programmes on popular science; *Recreations* travelling, listening to music, theatre, reading, swimming; *Style*— Prof John Taylor; 33 Meredyth Rd, Barnes, London SW13 0DS (☎ 081 876 3361); Dept of Mathematics, Kings Coll, Strand, London WC2R 2LS (☎ 071 836 5454, fax 071 836 1799)

TAYLOR, John Mark; MP (C) Solihull 1983-; s of Wilfred Taylor and Eileen Taylor; *b* 19 Aug 1941; *Educ* Bromsgrove, Coll of Law; *m* 1979, Catherine Ann Hall; *Career* admitted slr 1966; memb: Solihull Cncl 1971-74, W Mid CC 1973-86 (ldr 1977-79); contested (C) Dudley E Feb and Oct 1974; govr Univ of Birmingham 1977-81, MEP (EDG) Mids E 1979-84, dep chm Cons Gp Euro Parl 1981-82; memb House of Commons Environment Select Ctee 1983-87, PPS to Chllr of the Duchy of Lancaster 1987-88, asst govt whip 1988-89, Lord Cmmr of the Treasy (whip) 1989-90, Vice-Chamberlain HM's Household 1990-; *Recreations* cricket, golf and reading; *Clubs* Carlton, MCC; *Style*— John Taylor, Esq, MP; 211 Bernards Rd, Solihull, W Mids (☎ 021 707 1076)

TAYLOR, Dr John Michael; s of Eric John Taylor (d 1979), and Dorothy Irene, *née* Spring; *b* 15 Feb 1943; *Educ* King Edward's Sch Birmingham, Emmanuel Coll Cambridge (MA, PhD); *m* 14 Aug 1965, Judith, da of Maurice Moyle; 2 s (Michael James b 21 April 1967, David Charles b 21 April 1971), 2 da (Miranda Elizabeth b 14 Feb 1969, Lydia Jane b 7 March 1976); *Career* student apprentice GEC Telecommunications Coventry 1961-62, res engr GEC Hirst Res Centre 1965-66; UK Govt 1969-84: sr scientific offr Signals R & D Estab (SRDE) Christchurch 1969-70, sr scientific offr SRDE Communications Res Div 1970-73, princ scientific offr SRDE 1973-77, sr princ scientific offr and supt of Fixed Networks and Data Systems Div SRDE 1977-79 (SRDE merged with RRE Malvern 1978), supt Computer Applications Div RSRE Malvern 1979-81, dep chief scientific offr and head of Command Control and Communications Dept Admiralty Surface Weapons Estab (became Admiralty Res Estab 1983) 1982-84 (head Command Systems Div 1981-82); Hewlett-Packard Laboratories dir Info Systems Laboratory 1984-86, dir Bristol Res Centre 1986-90, dir Hewlett-Packard Laboratories Europe 1990-; visiting industl prof Univ of Bristol 1985-; memb: Advsy Bd A1 Applications Inst Univ of Edinburgh 1985-89, Res and Technol Ctee CBI 1988-; chm: Systems Architecture Ctee Info Technol Advsy Bd UK DTI and SERC 1988-, Computing and Control Divnl Bd UK IEE 1989-90; visiting prof Imp Coll of Sci Technol and Med Univ of London 1990-; FEng 1986, FIEE, FRSA, CEng, MBCS; *Recreations* family, music, theatre, photography, sailing; *Style*— Dr John Taylor; dir Hewlett-Packard Laboratories, Filton Rd, Stoke Gifford, Bristol BS12 6QZ (☎ 0272 799910, fax 0272 236975)

TAYLOR, John Richard Creighton; s of Richard Henry Chase Taylor (d 1987), and Rachel Loveday, *née* Creighton; *b* 17 Dec 1942; *Educ* Malvern Coll, Ecole des Hautes Etudes Commerciales Paris; *m* 7 Feb 1970, Sarah Barbour, da of Peter Thomas Simon Brown; 2 s (Oliver b 1973, Humphrey b 1981), 2 da (Eliza b 1972, Sophie b 1976); *Career* dir: Vine Products and Whiteways 1981-84, Grants of St James 1984-, London Wine Bars 1984-, Trouncer Wine and Spirit Merchants 1985-; chm and md Hatch Mansfield and Co 1984-; memb: Distillers Co 1980, Inst of Masters of Wine 1972; *Recreations* opera, theatre, walking, foreign interests, all sports; *Clubs* RAC; *Style*— John Taylor, Esq; Grants of St James's, St James's House, Guildford, Business Park, Guildford, Surrey GU2 5AD (☎ 0483 64861, fax 0483 506691, telex 859328)

TAYLOR, John Russell; s of Arthur Russell Taylor (d 1966), of Dover, Kent, and Kathleen Mary, *née* Picker; *b* 19 June 1935; *Educ* Dover GS, Jesus Coll Cambridge (BA 1956, MA 1959), Courtauld Inst of Art London; *Career* The Times: sub-ed Educnl Supplement 1959-60, ed asst Literary Supplement 1960-62, film critic 1962-73, art critic 1978-; prof of cinema div Univ of Southern California 1972-78, ed Films and Filming 1983-90; memb: Critics Circle 1962, Private Libraries Assoc 1967 (pres 1986-88), Assoc Art Historians 1985; AICA 1978; *Books Incl:* Anger and After (1962), Cinema Eye Cinema Ear (1964), The Art Nouveau in Britain (1966), The Rise and Fall of the Well-Made Play (1967), The Art Dealers (1969), The Hollywood Musical (1971), The Second Wave (1971), Graham Greene on Film (ed 1972), Directors and Directions (1975), Hitch (1978), Impressionism (1981), Strangers in Paradise (1983), Alec Guinness (1984), Edward Wolfe (1986), Orson Welles (1986), Bernard Meninsky (1990), Impressionist Dreams (1990); *Recreations* buying books, talking to strange dogs; *Style*— John Russell Taylor, Esq; The Times, 1 Pennington St, London E1 9XN (☎ 071 782 5000, fax 071 488 3242)

TAYLOR, John Stephen; s of Maj Gerald Howard Taylor (d 1963), and Helen Mary Rivett, *née* Harrington; *b* 26 Dec 1928; *Educ* Stowe, Trinity Coll Cambridge (MA), Architectural Assoc London (Dip Arch); *m* 1, 1956 (m dis 1963), Tye Pagan, da of Tully Grigg, of Biot, France; 1 s (Fred b 1963), 1 da (Nona b 1960); m 2, 1965 Susan Marriott Sweet; *Career* joined Irish Gds 1947, serv GHQ FARELF Singapore RE, Capt Cheshire Yeo 1949-58; sr ptnr Chapman Taylor Ptnrs whose London bldgs incl: Caxton House DOE, One Drummond Gate (Met Police), Lansdowne House Berkeley Sq; planning conslts and princ architects to Crown Cmmrs Millbank Estate; govr Stowe Sch 1962-90 (chm 1975-81), chm Allied Schs Cncl 1982-88; Freeman Worshipful Co of Chartered Architects; *Recreations* gardens, boats; *Clubs* Royal Thames Yacht; *Style*— J S Taylor, Esq; 35 Kinnerton St, London SW1X 8ED; Castell Gyrn, Llanbedr, Ruthin, Clwyd, N Wales; 11 Capri Close, Avalon, NSW 2107, Australia; Isle of Scalpay, Harris, Western Isles, Scotland PA84 3YB; Chapman Taylor Partners, 96 Kensington High St, London W8 4SG (☎ 071 938 3333, fax 071 937 1391)

TAYLOR, John William Ransom; OBE (1991); s of Victor Charles Taylor (d 1976), of Ely, Cambs, and Florence Hilda, *née* Ransom (d 1969); *b* 8 June 1922; *Educ* Ely Cathedral Choir Sch, Soham GS Cambs; *m* 7 Sept 1946, Doris Alice, da of George Arthur Haddrick (d 1933), of London; 1 s (Michael John Haddrick b 1949), 1 da (Susan Hilda Haddrick b 1947); *Career* design offr Hawker Aircraft Ltd 1941-47, air corr Meccano Magazine 1943-71, publicity offr Fairey Aviation Gp 1947-55, ed Air BP Magazine Br Petroleum 1956-72; ed, ed-in-chief and ed emeritus Jane's All the World's Aircraft 1959-, contrib ed Air Force Magazine (US) 1971-, jt ed Guinness Book of Air Facts and Feats 1974-83; dist cmmr Surbiton Scout Assoc 1965-69, dep warden and warden Christ Church Surbiton Hill 1971-80, pres Chiltern Aviation Soc Ruislip; vice pres: Horse Rangers Assoc, Guild Aviation Artists, Croydon Airport Soc, Surbiton Scout Assoc; memb Central Flying Sch Assoc; awards: Paul Tissandier Diploma Fédération Aéronautique Internationale 1990, Lauren D Lyman Award Aviation/Space Writers Assoc 1990; Freeman City of London 1987, Liveryman Guild Air Pilots and Air Navigators 1987 (Freeman 1983); memb Académie Nationale de l'Air et l'Espace (France) 1985-; FRAeS, FRHistS; *Books* 231 incl: Spitfire (1946), Aircraft Annual (1949-75), Civil Aircraft Markings (1950-78), Picture History of Flight (1955), CFS Birthplace of Air Power (1958, revised 1987), Combat Aircraft of the World (1969), Westland 50 (1965), Encyclopaedia of World Aircraft (with M J H Taylor 1966), Pictorial History of the Royal Air Force (3 vols 1968-71, revised 1980), Aircraft Aircraft (1967), The Lore of Flight (1971), Spies in the Sky (with D Mondey 1972), History of Aviation (with K Munson 1973), Soviet Wings (1991); *Recreations* historical studies, travel, philately; *Clubs* City Livery, RAF, Royal Aero; *Style*— John W R Taylor, Esq, OBE; 36 Alexandra Drive, Surbiton, Surrey KT5 9AF (☎ 081 399 5435)

TAYLOR, Jonathan Francis; s of Sir Reginald William Taylor (d 1971), of Great Haseley, Oxford, and Lady (Sarah) Ruth, *née* Tyson; *b* 12 Aug 1935; *Educ* Winchester, CCC Oxford (BA, MA); *m* 8 April 1965, (Anthea) Gail, da of Robert Vergette Proctor (d 1985), of Sheffield; 3 s (Luke b 1968, Matthew b 1970, James b

1972); *Career* Nat Serv 2 Lt KAR 1954-56; Booker plc: joined 1959, chm Agric Div 1976-80, dir 1980, chief exec 1984; pres IBEC Inc (USA) 1980-84, dir Tate & Lyle plc 1988, chm Arbor Acres Farm Inc USA 1991; memb Advsy Cncl UNIDO 1986, govr SOAS 1988, curator Bodleian Library 1989; CBIM 1984, FRSA 1990; *Recreations* travel, skiing, collecting watercolours; *Clubs* Travellers', Knickerbocker (NY); *Style—* Jonathan Taylor, Esq; Booker plc, Portland House, Stag Place, London SW1E 5AY (☎ 071 828 9850, fax 071 630 8029, telex 888169)

TAYLOR, Jonathan Jeremy Kirwan; s of Sir Charles Stuart Taylor, TD, DL *qv*; *b* 12 Oct 1943; *Educ* Eton, St Edmund Hall Oxford (MA); *m* 1966, Victoria Mary Caroline, da of Hon John Francis McLaren (d 1953); 4 da (Arabella b 1969, Lucinda b 1972, Caroline b 1976, Katherine b 1979); *Career* called to the Bar Middle Temple 1968; dir Baring Asset 1989- (formerly Baring Int Investmt Mgmnt Ltd) and other Baring Investmt Gp Cos, md Onyx Country Estates Ltd; *Recreations* skiing (Br Olympic Team 1964), tennis, boating; *Clubs* Turf, Royal Thames Yacht, Hong Kong; *Style—* Jonathan Taylor, Esq; Baring Asset Management Ltd, 155 Bishopsgate, London EC2M 3XY (☎ 071 628 6000, fax 071 638 7928, telex 885888 BAMUK G)

TAYLOR, Hon Joyce; has retained maiden name for business purposes; da of Baron Taylor of Gryfe (Life Peer); *b* 14 March 1948; *Educ* Hutcheson's Girls' GS Glasgow, Strathclyde Univ; *m* 1, 1969, Alan Begbie; 1 s (Alasdair b 1970), 1 da (Caroline b 1972); m 2, 1982, John Huw Lloyd Richards; *Style—* The Hon Joyce Taylor; 19 Kessington Drive, Bearsden, Glasgow (☎ 041 942 1454); 1 Woodland Rise, Muswell Hill, London N10 3UP (☎ 081 444 1291)

TAYLOR, Judy Julia Marie (Mrs Richard Hough); MBE (1971); adopted da of Gladys Spicer Taylor; *b* 12 Aug 1932; *Educ* St Paul's Girls Sch; *m* 1980, Richard Hough; *Career* writer and publisher; The Bodley Head: joined (specialising in children's books) 1951, dep md 1971-80, dir 1967-84; Chatto, Bodley Head & Jonathan Cape Ltd 1973-80, Chatto, Bodley Head & Jonathan Cape Australia Pty Ltd 1977-80; Publishers Assoc: chm Children's Book Gp 1969-72, memb Cncl 1972-78; memb: Book Devpt Cncl 1973-76, Unicef Int Art Ctee 1968-70, 1976 and 1982-83, Unicef Greeting Card Ctee 1982-85; conslt to Penguin (formerly to Frederick Warne) on Beatrix Potter 1981-87 and 1989-; assoc dir Western Woods Inst USA 1984-, consulting ed Reinhardt Books 1988-; *Books* Sophie and Jack (1982), Sophie and Jack Help Out (1983), My First Year: a Beatrix Potter Baby Book (1983), Sophie and Jack in the Snow (1984), Beatrix Potter: Artist, Storyteller and Countrywoman (1986), Dudley and the Monster (1986), Dudley Goes Flying (1986), Dudley in a Jam (1986), Dudley and the Strawberry Shake (1986), That Naughty Rabbit: Beatrix Potter and Peter Rabbit (1987), My Dog (1987), My Cat (1987), Dudley Bakes a Cake (1988), Beatrix Potter and Hawkshead (1988), Sophie and Jack in the Rain (1989), Beatrix Potter and Hill Top (1989), Beatrix Potter's Letters: a Selection (1989), The Adventures of Dudley Dormouse (1990); author of numerous articles; *Recreations* collecting early children's books, gardening; *Style—* Ms Judy Taylor, MBE; 31 Meadowbank, Primrose Hill, London NW3 1AY (☎ 071 722 5663, fax 071 722 7750)

TAYLOR, Dr Keith Henry; s of George Henry Philip Taylor (d 1980), and Vera May, *née* Jones; *b* 25 Nov 1938; *Educ* King Edward VI Sch Stratford-upon-Avon, Univ of Birmingham (BSc, PhD); *m* 28 Sept 1964, Adelaide; 1 s (Mark b 1969), 1 da (Karen b 1966); *Career* various positions Esso Petroleum Co Ltd 1964-80, div ops mangr Exxon Co New Orleans USA, exec asst to chm Exxon Corporation NY 1984-85; md: Esso Exploration & Prodn UK Ltd 1985- (prodn mangr 1982-84), Esso UK plc; dir: Esso Petroleum Company Limited, Quadrant Gas Ltd; pres UK Offshore Operators Assoc 1988 and 1989, memb Offshore Indust Advsy Bd 1989-; CBIM 1985, MInstD 1986, memb Soc Petroleum Engrs 1987, FRSA; *Recreations* walking, hunting, fishing, watching rugby and golf; *Style—* Dr Keith Taylor; Esso Exploration & Prodn UK Ltd, Esso Hse, 94 Victoria St, London SW1E 5JW (☎ 071 245 3280 fax 071 245 3154 telex 24942)

TAYLOR, Ken; s of Edgar Mason Taylor (d 1931), of Bolton and Helen Agnes, *née* Higgin (d 1978); *b* 10 Nov 1922; *Educ* Gresham's; *m* 1, 1946 (m dis 1951), Elizabeth Jane, *née* Tillotson; 1 da (Pamela b 1948); m 2, 28 March 1953, Gillian Dorothea, da of Harry Erskine Black (d 1971), of Sidmouth; 2 s (Matthew (qv) b 1963, Simon b 1964), 1 da (Victoria b 1956); *Career* TV dramatist; TV plays incl: China Doll, Into the Dark, The Long Distance Blue, The Slaughtermen, The Devil and John Brown, The Seekers, Shoulder to Shoulder, The Poisoning of Charles Bravo; TV adaptions incl: The Melancholy Hussar, The Girls of Slender Means, The Birds Fall Down, Mansfield Park, The Jewel in the Crown; BAFTA Writer of the Year Award 1964, Writers' Guild Best Original Teleplay Award 1964, Royal TV Soc Writer's Award 1984 for The Jewel in the Crown; memb Writers' Guild of GB; *Recreations* walking, music; *Style—* Ken Taylor, Esq; 17 Creighton Ave, London N10 1NX (☎ 081 883 9058); Quilkin Cottage, Gwithian, Hayle, Cornwall TR27 5BX (☎ 0736 752287)

TAYLOR, Kenneth; JP (1983); s of Kenneth Warburton Taylor (d 1989) and Kathleen, *née* Dilworth; *b* 26 Jan 1941; *Educ* Accrington Tech Sch, Burnley Coll (HNC), Openshaw Coll (IHVE); *m* 10 June 1960, Jean, da of Dr Staff (d 1956); 1 s (John b 1961), 1 da (Jeanette b 1962); *Career* design engr Burnley Co Borough 1963-71, princ Taylor Marren and Haslam (consltg engrs) 1971-85, chief building serv engr Oldham Met Borough 1985-88, chm Taylor Assoc Ltd (consltg engrs) 1988-; expert witness and arbitrator; several pubns in professional jls on legal matters; memb: Magistrates Assoc, Ctee of CIBSE, Manchester Coll Advsy Panel; CEng, FCIBSE, FIPlantE, FIHospE, FSE, FIOP, FBIM, ACIArb, MConsE; memb: Soc of Construction Law, American Soc of Heating Refrigerating and Air Conditioning Engrs; *Books* Plant Engineers Reference Book (jt author); *Recreations* church activities, lectures on legal matters; *Clubs* Foreign Travel; *Style—* Kenneth Taylor, Esq, JP; 40 Wilkie Ave, Glen View, Burnley, Lancs BB11 3QE (☎ 0282 33872); 1 Manchester Rd, Burnley, Lancs BB11 1HQ (☎ 0282 52111, DX 23880 BURNLEY, fax 0282 24217, car 0860 289156)

TAYLOR, Dr Kenneth George; s of George Edward Taylor (d 1990), of Grange Hill House, Halesowen, and Kathleen Anne, *née* Weaver (d 1989); *b* 9 Dec 1944; *Educ* Laytmer Upper Sch Hammersmith, St Bartholomew's Hosp Med Coll (MB BS, MD); *m* 5 July 1969, Gwendoline, da of Thomas Edward Wilson (d 1979), of Mitton, nr Clitheroe, Lancashire; *Career* res fell and hon sr registrar Bart's London 1975-78, sr registrar in med The Gen Hosp Birmingham 1978-81, hon sr clinical lectr Univ of Birmingham 1981-, conslt physician Dudley Rd Hosp Birmingham 1981-; sec Birmingham Div BMA, chm Birmingham Conslts for the Rescue of the NHS 1988-90; memb Cruising Assoc, FRCP 1988; *Books* Diabetic Eye Disease (jtly, 1984), Diabetes and the Heart (ed, 1987); *Recreations* coastal cruising, classical music; *Clubs* Walton and Frinton Yacht; *Style—* Dr Kenneth Taylor; Dudley Road Hosp, Birmingham B18 7QH (☎ 021 554 3801)

TAYLOR, Prof Kenneth MacDonald (Ken); s of Hugh Baird Taylor, of Garwyn, Marketgate, Crail, Fife, Scotland, and Mary, *née* MacDonald (d 1978); *b* 20 Oct 1947; *Educ* Jordanhill Coll Sch Glasgow, Univ of Glasgow (MB ChB, MD); *m* 14 May 1971, Christine Elizabeth, da of John Buchanan (d 1986), of Ullapool, Ross-shire, Scotland; 1 s (Iain b 1972), 1 da (Kirstin b 1975); *Career* Hall Fell in surgery Western Infirmary Glasgow 1971-72, sr lectr cardiac surgery Royal Infirmary Glasgow 1980-83 (lectr 1974-79), prof of cardiac surgery Royal Post Grad Med Sch Hammersmith Hosp 1983-; memb: Assoc of Profs of Surgery, Specialist Advsy Ctee in Cardiothoracic Surgery; dir Sch of Perfusion Sciences, govr Drayton Manor HS London; memb: Surgical Res Soc 1977, Soc of Cardiothoracic Surgns of GB and Ireland 1979, British Cardiac Soc 1983, Soc of Thoracic Surgns of America 1986, Euro Assoc for Cardiothoracic Surgery 1988, American Assoc for Thoracic Surgery 1989; pres Soc of Prefusionists GB and Ireland 1989-; FRCS (Eng), FRCS (Glasgow); *Books* Pulsatile Perfusion (1982), Handbook of Intensive Care (1984), Cardiopulmonary Bypass - Principles and Management (1986), Principles of Surgical Research (1989), Perfusion (ed, 1984-); *Recreations* family, church, music; *Style—* Prof Ken Taylor; 129 Argyle Rd, Ealing, London W13 0DB; Cardiac Surgery Unit, Royal Postgrad Med Sch, Hammersmith Hosp, Ducane Rd, London W12 0HS (☎ 081 740 3214, fax 081 740 3167)

TAYLOR, Prof Laurence John (Laurie); s of Stanley Douglas Taylor, and Winifred Agnes, *née* Cooper; *Educ* St Mary's Coll Liverpool, Rose Bruford Coll, Birkbeck Univ of London (BA), Univ of Leicester (MA); *m* 1; 1 s (Matthew b 5 Dec 1960); m 2, 16 Dec 1988, Catherine, da of Harold Francis Mahoney; *Career* librarian Liverpool City Cncl 1952-54, salesman Br Enka Ltd 1954-57, teacher Forest Hill Comp 1961-64, actor Theatre Workshop Stratford 1960-61; Univ of York: lectr 1965-70, sr lectr 1970-73, reader 1973-75, prof 1975-; *Books* Psychological Survival (1972), Escape Attempts (1976), In The Underworld (1984), Professor Lapping Sends His Apologies (1986); *Recreations* football, jazz; *Clubs* The Groucho, The Rathbone; *Style—* Prof Laurie Taylor; c/o Department of Sociology, University of York, Heslington, York YO1 5DD (☎ 0904 430000)

TAYLOR, Hon Mrs (Marilyn Ruth); da of Baron Fisher of Camden (Life Peer, d 1979); *b* 1940; *Educ* BA; *m* 1960, Mervyn Taylor, slr; *Style—* The Hon Mrs Taylor; 4 Springfield Rd, Templeogue, Dublin

TAYLOR, Martin Francis (Frank); s of Dr Albert William Taylor (d 1982), of Lamberhurst, Kent, and Margaret Oyston (d 1989); *b* 19 Jan 1944; *Educ* Sidcot Sch, Queen Mary Coll Univ of London; *m* 8 Aug 1970, Margaret Anne, da of Frederick William Harris (d 1975), of Beckenham, Kent; 1 s (Jeremy b 1975), 1 da (Claire b 1972); *Career* town planner, ptnr T P Bennett Partnership 1979- (joined 1966, assoc 1970-79); MRTPI; *Recreations* travel, gardening, choral singing, family life; *Style—* Frank Taylor, Esq; T P Bennett Partnership, 262 High Holborn, London WC1V 7DU (☎ 071 405 9277, fax 071 405 3568, telex 21671)

TAYLOR, Martin Gibbeson; s of Roy Gibbeson Taylor (d 1955), of Worthing, Sussex, and Vera Constance, *née* Farmer; *b* 30 Jan 1935; *Educ* Haileybury, St Catharine's Coll Cambridge (MA); *m* 18 June 1960, Gunilla Chatarina, da of Nils Bryner (d 1962), of Stockholm, Sweden; 2 s (Thomas b 1963, Seth b 1967); *Career* 2 Lt RA 1953-55; with Mann Judd & Co (CA) 1958-62, co sec Dow Chemical UK 1963-69, Hanson plc 1969-: dir 1976-, vice chm 1988-; non-exec dir: Vickers plc, National Westminster Bank PLC; memb: Panel on Take-overs and Mergers, Cncl CBI; govr The Mall Sch; FCA 1961; *Recreations* pictures, books, theatre, sport; *Clubs* MCC; *Style—* Martin G Taylor, Esq; Hanson plc, 1 Grosvenor Place, London SW1X 7JH (☎ 071 245 1245, fax 071 245 9795, telex 917698)

TAYLOR, Prof Martin John; s of John Maurice Taylor, of Leicester, and Sheila Mary Barbara, *née* Comacho; *b* 18 Feb 1952; *Educ* Wyggeston GS, Pembroke Coll Oxford (MA), King's Coll London (PhD); *m* 1 Dec 1973, Sharon Lynn, da of Harold Marlow; 2 s (Andrew b 19 March 1981, James b 3 July 1983), 2 da (Rebecca b 28 July 1977, Deborah b 9 May 1979); *Career* res asst Kings Coll London 1976-77, jr lectr Oxford 1977-78, lectr QMC 1978-81, professeur associé Besançon 1979-80, fell Trinity Coll Cambridge 1981-85, chair in pure mathematics UMIST 1985-; chm Bramhall Cncl of Churches; memb Cncl London Mathematics Soc: jr Whitehead prize 1982, Adams prize 1983; *Books* Classgroups of Group Rings (1983), Elliptic Functions and Rings of Integers (with P H Cassoll-Nogués); *Style—* Prof Martin Taylor; Dept of Mathematics, UMIST, PO Box 88, Manchester M60 1QD (☎ 061 200 3640)

TAYLOR, Martyn Graeme; s of John William Havelock Taylor (d 1977), of Calne, Wilts, and Betty Evelyn, *née* Clarke; *b* 8 June 1938; *Educ* Marlborough, Pembroke Coll Oxford (MA); *m* 23 May 1964, Jean, da of Thomas Topping (d 1983), of Churchill, Somerset; 2 s (Jeremy b 1966, Bruce b 1968), 1 da (Kirsty b 1972); *Career* CA; ptnr Coopers & Lybrand Deloitte 1972- (memb staff 1959-72); reader C of E, memb Winchester Diocesan Bd of Fin 1984-; FCA; *Books* Financial Times World Survey of Bank Annual Reports (jtly, 1982), Banks: An Accounting and Auditing Guide (jtly, 1983); *Recreations* fell walking, history and statistics of cricket; *Style—* Martyn Taylor, Esq; Coopers & Lybrand Deloitte, PO Box 207, 128 Queen Victoria St, London, EC4P 4JX (☎ 071 583 5000, fax 071 248 3623, telex 894941)

TAYLOR, Matthew Owen John; MP (Liberal Democrats) Truro 1987; s of Kenneth Heywood Taylor, and Gillian Dorothea, *née* Black; *b* 3 Jan 1963; *Educ* St Pauls Sch, Tremorvah Sch, Treliske Sch, Univ Coll Sch, Lady Margaret Hall Oxford (BA); *Career* pres Univ of Oxford Student Union 1985-86; econ res asst Parly Lib Pty 1986-87 (attached to late David Penhaligon MP); Parly spokesman for: Energy 1987-88, Local Govt, Housing and Tport 1988-89, Trade and Indust 1989-90, Educn 1990-; *Style—* Matthew Taylor, Esq, MP; 11a New Bridge St, Truro, Cornwall (☎ 0872 73478); House of Commons London, SW1 (☎ 071 219 3483)

TAYLOR, Hon Mrs (Melinda Charlotte); da of 2 Viscount Brookeborough, PC, DL; *b* 13 April 1958; *m* 1982, Nicholas Taylor, eldest s of Ronald Taylor, of Bighton Wood, Alresford, Hants; 1 s (Christopher Martin b 1990), 1 da (Alice b 1988); *Style—* The Hon Mrs Taylor; Holly Lodge, 79 Larkhall Rise, London SW4 6H5

TAYLOR, Rev Michael Hugh; s of Albert Taylor and Gwendoline Taylor; *b* 8 Sept 1936; *Educ* Northampton GS, Univ of Manchester (MA), Union Theological Seminary NY (BD, STM); *m* 1960, Adele May, *née* Dixon; 2 s, 1 da; *Career* baptist min 1960-69 (North Shields Northumberland, Hall Green Birmingham), princ Northern Baptist Coll Manchester 1970-85, lectr in theology and ethics Univ of Manchester 1970-85, examing chaplin to Bishop of Manchester 1975-85; chm Audenshaw Fndn Tstees 1979-, dir Christian Aid 1985-; memb cmmn on Theological Educn, vice-moderator World Cncl of Churches 1985 (memb 1972); Fulbright Travel award 1969; *Books* Variation on a Theme (1971), Learning to Care (1983), Good for the Poor (1990); *Recreations* walking, theatre, cooking; *Style—* The Rev Michael Taylor; 58 Woodland Rise, London N10 3UN (☎ 081 883 7217)

TAYLOR, Michael Paul Gordon; s of Gordon Taylor, and Stella, *née* Marsh; *b* 2 March 1949; *Educ* Altrincham GS, St Johns Coll Cambridge (LLB); *m* 11 June 1977, Angela Evelyn Llewellyn, *née* Morris; 2 da (Catherine Elizabeth b 2 May 1981, Eleanor Frances b 7 Aug 1983); *Career* ptnr Norton Rose 1979-; Freeman City of London Slrs Co; memb: Int Bar Assoc, Law Soc; *Recreations* sport, theatre, reading; *Clubs* RAC; *Style—* Michael Taylor, Esq; Kempson House, Camomile St, London EC3A 7AN (☎ 071 283 2434)

TAYLOR, Neil Royston; s of Leonard Bertram Taylor, and Audrey Margaret, *née* Wilson; *b* 21 July 1959; *Educ* Cray Valley Tech HS; *m* 25 Sept 1982, Jane Claire, da of Frank Cecil Fitzearle; 2 da (Amy Louise b 7 Nov 1985, Lauren Francesca b 21 July 1988); *Career* cricketer; played: Kent Schs Under 15's, 16's and 19's, England Schs Under 19's Tour to India 1977-78, Young England v Young W Indies 1978; Kent CCC XI: debut 1979, played over 200 matches, highest partnership (with Simon Hinks) 366 Kent v Middlesex 1990; played England v Pakistan 1982; winner: seven Benson &

Hedges Man of the Match awards, Kent Player of the Season 1989 and 1990; winner of seven Benson & Hedges Man of the Match Awards; *Recreations* golf, rugby union, reading, music, working for Radio Kent; *Style*— Neil Taylor, Esq; Kent County Cricket Club, St Lawrence Ground, Old Dover Rd, Canterbury, Kent (☎ 0227 456886)

TAYLOR, Neville; CB (1989); s of late Frederick Herbert Taylor, and late Lottie, *née* London; *b* 17 Nov 1930; *Educ* Sir Joseph Williamson's Mathematical Sch Rochester, Coll of Commerce Gillingham; *m* 4 Sept 1954, Margaret Ann, da of late Thomas Bainbridge Vickers; 2 s (Andrew b 1956, Martin b 1958); *Career* RCS 1948-50; journalist 1950-58; press offr Admty 1958-63, fleet info offr Far E Fleet Singapore Malaysia 1963-65, chief press offr MOD 1966-68, info advsr NEDO/NEDC London 1968-70, dep dir PR RN 1970, head of info MAFF 1971-72, dir info DOE 1974-79 (dep dir 1972), DHSS 1979-82, chief of PR MOD 1982-85, dir gen COI and head of Govt Info Serv 1985-88, princ assoc Defence Public Affairs Consultants Ltd 1989-; freelance journalist 1989-; *Recreations* fishing, bird watching; *Clubs* Castle, Rochester; *Style*— Neville Taylor, Esq, CB; Crow Lane House, Crow Lane, Rochester, Kent (☎ 0634 842 990)

TAYLOR, Nicholas Roy; s of Stanley Arthur Taylor (d 1988), and Jessie Rose, *née* Pickett (d 1969); *b* 2 Sept 1948; *Educ* Hampton GS; *m* 1972 (m dis 1985), Valerie, *née* Parr; 1 s (Peter Nicholas b 20 March 1981), 2 da (Deborah Joanne b 8 Oct 1978, Beth Eloise Kim b 10 Oct 1984); *Career* articled clerk Bolton Colby & Co Staines 1965-70, CA Fuller Jenks Beecroft & Co 1970-73, mangr Arthur Young & Co HK 1973-75, ptnr Haines Watts 1978- (joined 1976), lectr on Taxation and Fin matters; FCA (ACA 1970); *Recreations* flying, skiing; *Style*— Nicholas Taylor, Esq; Haines Watts, Sterling House, 165-175 Farnham Road, Slough, Berkshire SL1 4UZ (☎ 0753 30333, fax 0753 76606)

TAYLOR, (Lilian) Patricia; MBE (1981); da of Clarence Harold Lawson Gibbon (d 1962), of Southampton, and Aileen Colthurst, *née* Persson (d 1961); *b* 4 Nov 1921; *Educ* Southampton GS for Girls, Bishop Otter Trg Coll Chichester; *m* 30 July 1947, George Edward (Roger) Taylor, s of John Edward Taylor (d 1972), of Eastbourne; 2 s (David Roger b 21 March 1963, John Patrick b 24 Oct 1964); *Career* mangr England Netball Team: Trinidad 1978, Aust 1981 and 1985; rep to GAISF 1983-89, memb Cncl IFNA 1975, 1979 and 1983, first vice pres Int Fedn Netball 1983-, pres AENA 1986- (vice chm 1967-72, chm 1972-86); Oscar State award World Games 1985; teacher of mathematics 1940-82; Silver Jubilee Medal 1977; *Recreations* golf, crosswords, reading; *Clubs* Christchurch and Roos; *Style*— Mrs Patricia Taylor, MBE; 15 Surrey Rd, Felixstowe, Suffolk IP11 7SB (☎ 0394 282609); All England Netball Association Ltd, Francis House, Francis St, London SW1P 1DE (☎ 071 828 2176)

TAYLOR, (John) Patrick Enfield; s of Arthur Hugh Enfield Taylor, RNVR (d 1983), of Midhurst, W Sussex, and Monica Soames, *née* Cooke; *b* 3 April 1948; *Educ* Eton; *m* 1972, Heather Diana, da of Col Roger Barratt, of Cowmire Hall, Crosthwaite, nr Kendal, Cumbria; 1 s (Rupert b 1979), 3 da (Melissa b 1976, Pippa b 1980, Hermione b 1983); *Career* ptnr Coopers & Lybrand 1980-86 (qualified 1972), fin dir Langdale Group plc 1986-88, gp fin dir Capital Radio plc 1988-; chm Bd of Govrs Inhurst House Sch; FCA; *Recreations* tennis, swimming, sailing, skiing; *Style*— Patrick Taylor, Esq; Capital Radio plc, Euston Tower, London NW1 3DR (☎ 071 380 6166, fax 071 380 6184, car 0831 409006)

TAYLOR, Paul Duncan; JP (1969); s of Edward Duncan Taylor; *b* 25 April 1936; *Educ* Mill Hill Sch; *m* 1964, Lindsay Veronica Moncrieff, *née* Smith; 2 s; *Career* CA; ptnr Touche Ross, chm Wagon Industry Holdings plc; dir: John Foster Son plc, Leeds and Holbeck Building Society; *Clubs* The Leeds; *Style*— Paul Taylor, Esq, JP; Oakwood House, Upper Batley, Batley, W Yorks

TAYLOR, Hon Paul Nurton; s of Baron Taylor of Blackburn (Life Peer); *b* 1953; *m* 1978, Diane Brindle; *Style*— The Hon Paul Taylor; 601 Preston Old Rd, Blackburn, Lancs

TAYLOR, Peter; *b* 1942; *Educ* Scarborough HS, Pembroke Coll Cambridge (BA); *m* Susan McConachy; 2 s (Ben, Sam); *Career* TV presenter; reporter: This Week (Thames TV) 1967-80, Panorama (BBC TV) 1980-86; presenter: Brass Tacks (BBC 2) 1986, Newsnight (BBC 2) 1987, Public Eye (BBC 2) 1989-91; writer and presenter Families at War and The Maze-Enemies Within (BBC 1) 1989-90; *awards* RTS: Best Home Documentary (for Stalker-Conspiracy or Coincidence) 1987, Best Home Documentary (for Families at War) 1990, Best Home Documentary (for Inside Story - The Maze) 1991; Broadcasting Press Guild Best Single Documentary (for Inside Story - The Maze) 1990; *Books* Beating The Terrorists (1981, Cobden Trust award), Smoke Ring - The Politics of Tobacco (1988, World Health Orgn Gold Medallion); *Style*— Peter Taylor, Esq; British Broadcasting Corporation, Lime Grove Studios, Lime Grove, Shepherds Bush, London W12 7RJ (☎ 081 743 8000, fax 081 746 0789)

TAYLOR, Peter Cranbourne; s of Maurice Ewan Taylor, OBE, of St Andrews, and Mary Ann, *née* Gorst; *b* 11 Aug 1938; *Educ* Univ of Edinburgh (MA); *m* 27 June 1970, Lois Mary, da of Anthony Godard Templeton, TD (d 1986), of St Andrews; 1 s (Christopher b 13 Nov 1975), 1 da (Kerrie b 18 Dec 1972); *Career* CA 1962; ptnr: Romanes & Munro Edinburgh 1964-74, Deloitte Haskins & Sells 1974- (now Coopers & Lybrand Deloitte); convenor ICAS, Memb Servs Ctee 1984-90, sec and treas Scottish Nat Blood Transfusion Assoc 1981-, memb Scot Dental Practice Bd 1991-; *Recreations* shooting, country pursuits; *Clubs* New (Edinburgh), Lansdowne; *Style*— Peter Taylor, Esq; Erskine House, 68 Queen Street, Edinburgh

TAYLOR, Peter Duncan; s of Capt Arthur Gilbert Taylor (d 1968), of Manchester, and Amy Margaret, *née* Duncan (d 1958); *b* 4 May 1925; *Educ* Oakham Sch, Univ of St Andrews; *m* 20 June 1956, Barbara, da of Daniel Greenaway (d 1968); 1 s (John); *Career* pilot RAF; Simon Engrg plc, dir Simon-Carves Ltd and Lodge-Cottell Ltd 1951-72, dir and sec Turriff Corpn plc 1972-; FCA 1951; *Recreations* golf, antiques, bridge; *Style*— Peter Taylor, Esq; Tanglewood, 6 Woodside Way, Solihull, W Mids B91 1HB; Turriff Corpn plc, Budbrooke Rd, Warwick CV34 5XJ (☎ 0926 410 400, fax 0926 497 315, car 0836 525 799)

TAYLOR, Rt Hon Lord Justice; Rt Hon Sir Peter Murray Taylor; PC (1988), QC (1967); s of Herman Louis Taylor (d 1966), of Newcastle upon Tyne; *b* 1 May 1930; *Educ* Newcastle Royal GS, Pembroke Coll Cambridge; *m* 1956, Irene Shirley, da of Lionel Harris, of Newcastle; 1 s, 3 da; *Career* called to the Bar Inner Temple 1954; QC 1967, rec of Huddersfield 1969, dep chm Northumberland QS 1970; recorder of: Teesside 1970-71, Crown Ct 1972-80; bencher 1975, High Ct Judge Queen's Bench Div 1980-87; presiding judge North Eastern Circuit 1984-87 (ldr 1975-80), Lord Justice of the Ct of Appeal 1987-, pres Inns of Ct Cncl 1991-; chm Hillsborough Disaster Inquiry 1989; controller Royal Opera House Devpt Land Tst 1990-; Hon LLD Univ of Newcastle; kt 1980; *Style*— The Rt Hon Lord Justice Taylor; Royal Courts of Justice, The Strand, London WC2

TAYLOR, Philippe Arthur; s of Arthur Peach Taylor, (d 1974), of St Andrews, Fife, and Simone, *née* Vacquin; *b* 9 Feb 1937; *Educ* Trinity Coll Glenalmond, St Andrews Univ; *m* 10 Feb 1973, Margaret Nancy, s of Arnold Frederick Wilkins, OBE (d 1985), of Framlingham, Suffolk; 2 s (Rupert Arthur James b 1975, Charles Philip b 1976); *Career* Proctor and Gamble 1961-66, Masius Int 1966-70, Br Tourist Authy 1970-75; chief exec: Scottish Tourist Bd 1975-81, Birmingham Convention Bureau 1982-; chm Br Assoc of Conference Towns 1988-, vice chm Ikon Gallery 1988-, Chevalier de L'Ordre des Couteaux de Champagne 1985; FTS 1975; *Books* Captain Crossjack and the Lost Penguin (1969); *Recreations* sailing, painting, tourism, making things; *Clubs* Royal Northumberland YC, Orford Sailing; *Style*— Philippe Taylor, Esq; Cadogan House, Beauchamp Ave, Leamington Spa, 2 Perth St, Edinburgh (☎ 0926 831 925); 9 The Wharf, Birmingham, W Mids (☎ 021 631 2401, fax 021 643 5001)

TAYLOR, Phillip; s of Harry Sidney Taylor, of Newcastle, and Elisabeth, *née* Telford; *b* 27 Sept 1948; *Educ* Anfield Palin Boys Sch, Newcastle Coll; *m* 30 Sept 1972, Iris, da of John Harland (d 1979); 2 s (Christopher b 29 June 1977, Michael James b 16 Aug 1978), 1 da (Leigh b 21 Oct 1974); *Career* Minories Garages Ltd: gen mangr 1974-78, dir 1978, chm 1990-; gp dir Appleyard Group plc 1990-; *Recreations* golf, sailing, skiing; *Clubs* Slaley Golf, Whickham Golf, Fontburn Ski, Beadnell Yacht; *Style*— Phillip Taylor, Esq; 63 Cornmoor Road, Whickham, Newcastle upon Tyne NE16 4PU (☎ 091 488 4192); Minories Garages Limited, Retail World, Team Valley Trading Estate, Gateshead, Tyne & Wear NE8 1BS (☎ 091 491 0343, fax 091 491 0744)

TAYLOR, Phyllis Mary Constance; da of Cecil Tedder (d 1974), and Constance, *née* Price (d 1984); *b* 29 Sept 1926; *Educ* Sudbury HS, Girton Coll Cambridge (BA,MA); *m* 31 Dec 1949, Peter Royston Taylor, s of John William Edward Taylor (d 1972); 1 s (Julian Peter Gerald Royston b 10 Nov 1954); *Career* head of history Loughton HS 1951-58 (asst mistress 1948-51), mistress Lancaster Royal Grammar Sch for Boys 1959; head of history: Casterton Sch Kirby Lonsdale 1960, Lancaster Girls GS 1961 (mistress 1960-61); dep head Carlyle Sch Chelsea 1962-64; headmistress: Walthamstow HS 1964-68, Walthamstow Sr HS 1968-76, Wanstead HS 1976-82; candidate (Lib): Essex CC 1982, Dunmow DGI 1987; chm Dunmow Lib Pty 1986-88; memb UGC 1978-83; *Books* under pen name Julianne Royston: The Penhale Heiress (1988), The Penhale Fortune (1989); *Recreations* horses, gardening, theatre, ecology; *Style*— Mrs Phyllis Taylor; White Horses, High Roding, Gt Dunmow, Essex CM6 1NS (☎ 0371 3161)

TAYLOR, Richard; s of Horace Christopher Taylor (d 1933) of Hampstead Gardens Suburb, and Dulcie Muriel, *née* Marriott; *b* 16 June 1929; *Educ* UCS London, Univ Coll Oxford (exhibitioner, BA); *Career* Larkins Studio: animation trainee 1953, dir i/c prodn 1957, md 1959-66; fndr Richard Taylor Cartoon Films Ltd 1966; animation course dir RCA 1989 (head of Animation Dept 1986); producer designer and/or dir: Mr Finley's Feelings (Metropolitan Life, US) 1956, commercials for Barclay's Bank (winner Grand Prix SAWA and Coppa di Venezia) 1956-66, industl films 1966-76, educnl material BBC TV 1976-85, Muzzy in Gondoland (BBC) 1985, Muzzy Comes Back (BBC) 1988; pres ASIFA UK 1986-; memb: GBA, BAFTA; *Style*— Richard Taylor, Esq; Royal College of Art, Kensington Gore, London SW7 2EU (☎ 071 584 5020)

TAYLOR, Richard; *b* 6 Feb 1945; *Educ* Corpus Christi Coll Oxford (MA); *Career* admitted slr 1969; McKenna & Co: articled clerk 1967-69, asst slr 1969-74, on secondment to lawyers' cos in Germany France Holland Jan 1973 - June 1973, ptnr 1974-, memb Bd of Ptnrs 1984-, fndr Brussels office 1988 (shares responsibility with res ptnr David Marks); specialist in competition law and EEC law, has pleaded before Euro Ct of Justice Luxembourg; author of various articles on competition and EEC law, ed McKenna & Co monthly bulletin on EEC law; memb Ctee Solicitors Euro Gp; *Style*— Richard Taylor, Esq

TAYLOR, Lt-Col Richard Ian Griffith; DSO, MC, DL; s of Lt-Col Thomas George Taylor, DSO (d 1946); *b* 5 June 1911; *Educ* Harrow, Oxford Univ; *m* 1934 (m dis 1951), Hon Sylvia Alice, da of late 2 Baron Joicey; 2 s (Simon, James), 1 da (Valerie); m 2, 1952, Hon Cecily Eveline (d 1975), widow of Patrick Magor Leatham, MC, and da of 1 and last Baron Buckland; 2 da; *Career* Lt-Col; serv Greece, Western desert, France, Germany; farmer, landowner; *Recreations* shooting, fishing, hunting; *Style*— Lt-Col Richard Taylor, DSO, MC, DL; Chipchase Castle, Wark on Tyne, Northumberland

TAYLOR, His Hon Judge Robert Carruthers; s of John Houston Taylor, CBE (d 1983), and Barbara Mary, *née* Carruthers; *b* 6 Jan 1939; *Educ* Wycliffe Coll, St John's Coll Oxford (MA); *m* 16 April 1968, Jacqueline Marjorie, da of Nigel Geoffrey Randall Chambers, of West Yorks; 1 s (John b 1972), 1 da (Susannah b 1969); *Career* called to the Bar Middle Temple 1961, practised NE Circuit 1962-84, rec 1976-84, chm Agric Land Tbnl (Lancs/Yorks/Humberside) 1979-; *Recreations* reading, music, gardening, exercising whippets; *Clubs* Yorks CCC; *Style*— His Hon Judge Robert Taylor; The Courthouse, 1 Oxford Row, Leeds LS1 3BE

TAYLOR, Robert Julian Faussitt; s of Col GF Taylor, MBE; *b* 21 June 1929; *Educ* Dragon Sch, Trinity Coll Cambridge; *m* 1967, Jacqueline, *née* Castaing; 2 s; *Career* md Manchester Ship Canal Co 1980-, dir Ocean Tport & Trading 1964-79, Br Antartic Survey 1953-57, the Wildfowl Survey 1973-81, RSPB Cncl 1978-81; *Recreations* the countryside, birds, deer, gardening, climbing, reading; *Clubs* Travellers'; *Style*— Robert Taylor, Esq; Bridgewater House, Runcorn, Ches; Home Lodge, Cholderton, Wilts

TAYLOR, Sheriff-Principal Robert Richardson; QC; s of James Stevens Taylor (d 1949), of Lanarkshire, and Agnes Richardson (d 1942); *b* 16 Sept 1919; *Educ* Glasgow HS, Univ of Glasgow (MA, LLB, PhD); *m* 1949, Birgitta, da of Ivan Bjorkling (d 1954); 2 s (Richard, Hamish), 1 da (Kristina); *Career* called to the Bar: Scotland 1944, Middle Temple 1948; lectr in int private law Univ of Edinburgh 1947-69; Sheriff-Princ: Stirling Dumbarton & Clackmannan 1971-75, Tayside Central & Fife 1975-90; contested (U & NL): Dundee E 1955, Dundee W 1950 & 1963; chm: Central and Southern Region Scottish Cons Assoc 1969-71, Sheriff Cts Rules Cncl 1982-89, Northern Lighthouse Bd 1985-86; *Recreations* fishing, lapidary and mineral collecting; *Style*— Sheriff-Principal Robert Taylor, QC; 51 Northumberland St, Edinburgh, (☎ 031 556 1722)

TAYLOR, Dr Robert Thomas; s of George Taylor (d 1973), of Derwent Rd, Warrington, Lancs, and Marie Louise, *née* Fidler (d 1986); *b* 21 March 1933; *Educ* Boteler GS, Univ of Oxford (BA, MA, DPhil); *m* 1, 20 Aug 1954 (m dis 1965), Ina, *née* Wilson; 1 s (Timothy b 1959); m 2, 25 Sept 1965, Rosemary Janet, da of Charles Leonard Boileau, of 36 Ryders Bolt, Bexhill on Sea, Sussex; 2 s (Aubrey b 1967, Christopher 1968), 1 da (Alison b 1973); *Career* res assoc in Randall laboratory physics Univ of Michigan USA 1957-58, lectr in physics Univ of Liverpool 1959-61 (ICI res fell 1958-59); The Br Cncl: asst regnl rep Madras 1961-64, sci offr Spain 1964-69, dir staff recruitment 1969-73, regnl rep Bombay 1973-77, rep Mexico 1977-81, personnel controller London 1981-86, rep Greece 1986-90, ADG 1990-; examiner in physics: Oxford Local Bd 1956-61, Oxford and Cambridge Bd 1957; chief examiner physics NUJMB 1961 (examiner 1960); *Books* contrib Chambers Encyclopaedia (1967); *Recreations* war games, computers, theatre; *Style*— Dr Robert T Taylor; Mark Haven, High St, Cranbrook, Kent TN17 3EW (☎ 0580 714212); The British Council, 10 Spring Gardens, London SW1A 2BN (☎ 071 389 4875, fax 071 389 4971, telex 8952201 BRICON G)

TAYLOR, (Robert Hunter) Robin; s of Robert Louis Taylor (d 1970), of Milngavie, Dunbartonshire, Scotland, and Jean Allan (d 1954); *b* 5 Nov 1932; *Educ* Aberdeen GS, Kelvinside Acad; *m* 11 Sept 1964, Kathleen Mabel, da of Capt Harold Percival Gibbs (d 1950), of Dundee, Scotland; 2 s (Philip b 1966, Colin b 1968); *Career* builders merchant; chm md Scott RAE Stevenson Ltd, nat pres The Builders Merchants Fedn 1988-89; Freeman: City of London, City of Glasgow; Liveryman Worshipful Co of Builders Merchants; FInstD, FInstBM (fndr memb); *Recreations* golf, gardening, photography, walking, reading, philately; *Clubs* Buchanan Castle Golf, Rotary (Strathendrick), BA Exec; *Style—* Robin Taylor, Esq; The Rowans, Killearn, Stirlingshire G63 9LG (☎ 0360 50388); Scott Rae Stevenson Ltd, 265 Pollokshaws Rd, Glasgow G41 1PT (☎ 041 423 5461)

TAYLOR, Roger Heath; s of Frederick George Taylor (d 1969), of Kingston-Upon-Thames, and Gladys Florence, *née* Heath; *b* 29 Nov 1944; *Educ* Surbiton GS, Brunel Univ (BSc); *m* 5 Oct 1968, Ann Joan, da of Leslie Ernest Leonard, of Bramford, Suffolk; 2 s (James Hrothgar Heath b 4 May 1976, Samuel St John Cedric Edmond Heath), 1 da (Donna Katrina Heath); *Career* res chemist Metal Box Co 1965-66, prodn supervisor Harrington Bros 1966-69, sales mangr Reeve Angel Scientific 1969-74, dir and jt owner Int Chemicals Trading Co Interchem UK Ltd 1974-; vice chm Parish Cncl; chm: Playing Field Charity Tst, Community Covers, Govrs Co Sch & Educnl Ctee; involved in local politics; *Recreations* squash, Motorsport; *Style—* Roger Taylor, Esq; Tintern, The Street Copdock, Suffolk (☎ 0473 86 439); B 10/11 Farthing Rd, Indust Estate, Ipswich, Suffolk (☎ 0473 463 701, fax 0473 43 521, car 0860 366 567)

TAYLOR, Ronald George; CBE (1988); s of Ernest Noel Taylor (d 1978), of Bristol, and May Elizabeth, *née* Besant (d 1955); *b* 12 Dec 1935; *Educ* Cotham GS Bristol, Jesus Coll Oxford (BA); *m* 14 June 1960, Patricia, da of Septon Stoker, of Hemingbrough; 1 s (David Robert b 1963), 2 da (Gillian Mary b 1961, Alison Catherine b 1965); *Career* Nat Serv 2 Lt Royal Signals 1957-59; dir Leeds C of C and Indust 1974 (joined 1959), dir-gen Assoc of Br C of C 1984; FSAE 1988, FRSA 1988; *Recreations* bridge, rugby union football; *Style—* Ronald Taylor, Esq, CBE; 2 Holly Bush Lane, Harpenden, Herts (☎ 0582 712139); Assoc of British Chambers of Commerce, Sovereign House, 212 Shaftesbury Ave, London (☎ 071 240 5831, fax 071 379 6331, telex 265871)

TAYLOR, (Robert Murray) Ross; s of Dr George Ross Taylor (d 1940), and Helen Bailey, *née* Murray (d 1989); *b* 10 Dec 1932; *Educ* Coatbridge Secondary Sch, Univ of Glasgow (MB ChB, ChM); *m* 7 Jan 1959, Margaret Rose, da of Capt Albert Henry Cutland (d 1975); 1 s (Bill b 1965), 3 da (Linda b 1960, Jill b 1962, Anne b 1964); *Career* Capt RAMC 23 Para Field Ambulance and 2 Bn Parachute Regt 1957-59; registrar bishop Auckland Gen Hosp 1959-62, res fell Univ of Newcastle upon Tyne 1964-65, conslt surgn Royal Victor Infirmary Newcastle 1970- (registrar in surgery 1962-64, sr registrar 1965-70); tstee Gt North Run 1984-; chm and tstee: Transplant Patients Assoc of GB, Transplant Olympic Assoc of GB 1984-; fndr memb: Euro Soc for Organ Transplantation, Int Transplantation Soc, Br Transplantation Soc (pres 1986-89); Pres N of England Surgical Soc 1990-91; *Recreations* golf, jogging, charity fundraising; *Clubs* Northumberland Golf; *Style—* Robert Taylor, Esq; Ward One Office, Royal Victoria Infirmary, Queen Victoria Rd, Newcastle upon Tyne NE1 4LP (☎ 091 2325131 ext 24662, fax 091 2210081)

TAYLOR, Russell Colin; s of Cyril Wilfred Taylor (d 1971), and Ruby Phillis Taylor (d 1977); *b* 27 Sept 1945; *Educ* City of Oxford GS, Birmingham Coll of Commerce; *m* 29 July 1967, Sheila Mary; 2 s (Adrian Keith b 25 July 1975, Philip Russell b 17 June 1978); *Career* asst prod mangr Cadbury Schweppes (formerly Cadbury Brothers Ltd) 1968-70 (mgmnt trainee 1964-68), brand mangr CWS Ltd Manchester 1970-72; Anglia Canners: mktg mangr 1972-73, sales and mktg mangr 1973-75, mktg dir 1975-77, sales and mktg dir 1977-79, dep md 1979-81, md 1981-87; chief exec Armitage Brothers plc 1987-; memb ICSA; *Recreations* sport, music, current affrs, card games, quizzes; *Style—* Russell Taylor, Esq; 8 The Banks, Bingham, Nottingham NG13 8BL (☎ 0949 837577); Armitage Brothers plc, Armitage House, Colwick, Nottingham NG4 2BA (☎ 0602 614984, fax 0602 617496, telex 377921 ARMBRO G)

TAYLOR, Prof Samuel Sorby Brittain; s of late Samuel Stephen Taylor, and Elsie Irene, *née* Chappell; *b* 20 Sept 1930; *Educ* High Storrs GS Sheffield, Univ of Birmingham (MA, PhD); *m* 15 Aug 1956, (Agnes) Nan McCreadie, da of late Peter Ewan, of Dundee; 2 da (Moira Elizabeth b 13 Aug 1959, Dorothy Frances b 1 Feb 1962); *Career* Nat Serv 1956-58, Sub Lt RNVR 1957-; personnel res offr Dunlop Rubber Co 1958-60, res fell (for Voltaire's correspondence vols 66-98, under Theodore Besterman) Institut et Musée Voltaire Geneva 1960-63; Univ of St Andrews: asst 1963, lectr 1964, reader 1972, personal chair 1977; author of studies of Voltaire, memb Ed Ctee Voltaire's Complete Works; sec gen Soc for Eighteenth Century Studies 1967-68; chm: Nat Cncl for Modern Languages 1981-85 (memb 1979-), Scottish Nat Working Pty on Standard Grade; memb: Examinations Bd Inst of Linguists 1986, Scottish Univs French Language Res Assoc; Officier dans L'Ordre des Palmes Académiques 1986; contrib to: Voltaire's Correspondence (1953-63), Rousseau's Contemporary Reptutation in France (1963), New Cambridge Bibliography of English Literature Vol 2 (1971), The Definitive Text of Voltaire's Works: The Leningrad Encadrée (1974), Voltaire's Humour (1979), Re-appraisals of Rousseau: Studies in Honour of RA Leigh (1980), Modern Swiss Literature: Unity and Diversity (1985); Le français en faculté (jtly, 1980), En Fin de Compte (jtly, 1988); *Recreations* grade 1 SAAA timekeeper for athletics, photography; *Clubs* Fife Athletic, Paris University, Hallamshire Harriers; *Style—* Prof Samuel Taylor; 11 Irvine Crescent, St Andrews, Fife KY16 8LG (☎ 0334 72588); Department of French, University of St Andrews, St Andrews KY16 9PH (☎ 0334 76161, fax 0334 74674, telex 9312110846 SA G)

TAYLOR, Hon Mrs (Sarah Lovell); *née* Rippon; 2 da of Baron Rippon of Hexham, PC, QC (Life Peer); *b* 10 March 1950; *Educ* Sherborne Sch of Girls Dorset, St Paul's Girls' Sch London, St Anne's Coll Oxford (MA); *m* 1978, Michael Taylor; 2 s (James Geoffrey Bethune b 1979, Alexander Edward Yorke b 1982); *Career* admitted slr 1978; called to the NY Bar 1980; Messrs Theodore Goddard Solicitors 1974-77, Nixon Hargraves Devans & Doyle NY (Lawyers) 1980-84; dir: Robert Fraser Group Ltd 1986-, Robert Fraser & Partners Ltd and subsid 1986-; *Style—* The Hon Mrs Taylor; 22 Elmstone Rd, London SW6 5TN (☎ 071 736 1759); Robert Fraser Group Ltd, 29 Albermarle St, London W1X 3FA (☎ 071 493 3211)

TAYLOR, Selwyn Francis; s of Alfred Petre Taylor (d 1958), of Brook Cottage, Combe, Malborough, S Devon, and Emily, *née* Edwards (d 1965); *b* 16 Sept 1913; *Educ* Keble Coll Oxford (MA), Kings Coll Hosp London, Stockholm, Harvard; *m* 14 Oct 1939, Ruth Margaret, da of Sir Alfred Bakewell Howitt, CVO, MP (d 1950), of Wolfhall Manor, Burbage, Wilts; 1 s (Simon b 8 Sept 1945), 1 da (Jane b 18 Nov 1950); *Career* serv RNVR 1940-45, Surgn Lt Cdr 1944; surgical specialist: Kintyre, E Africa, Mobile Surgical Unit Malaya, Sydney; univ lectr and consIt surgn: Royal Postgrad Med Sch Hammersmith Hosp 1947-78, KCH 1951-65; dean Royal Postgrad Med Sch 1965-75; Rockefeller travelling fell Harvard 1948-49; visiting prof: Duke Univ, UCLA, Cincinnati, Chapel Hill, Hong Kong, S Africa; memb: Gen Med Cncl, senate Univ of London, Euro Thyroid Assoc (fndr memb), Cncl RCS 1965 (vice pres 1976-78); pres: Harveian Soc, Med Educn Sec, RSM; first pres Int Assoc Endocrine Surgns 1978-81; chm London Thyroid Club, corresponding fell American Thyroid Assoc; Gold Staff Offr Coronation 1953; Freeman City of London, Liveryman Worshipful Soc of Apothecaries; Hon FRCSEd, Hon FCM S Africa; DM MCh, FRCS; *Books* Recent Advances in Surgery (edns 5-10, 1959-80), Short Text Book of Surgery (edns 1-7,1960-80), Surgical Management (1984); *Recreations* sailing, tennis, gardening, wine; *Clubs* Garrick, Hurlingham, RN Sailing Assoc, Bosham Sailing (tstee), Saintsbury; *Style—* Selwyn Taylor, Esq; Trippets, Bosham, Chichester PO18 8JE (☎ 0243 573387)

TAYLOR, Simon John; s of John Kenneth Taylor, of Chesterfield, and Ruth Marjorie, *née* Standeven; *b* 28 Dec 1950; *Educ* Ripton, St Peter's Coll Oxford (BA); *m* 9 May 1981, Elizabeth Frances, da of Stanley Jefferson (d 1989), of Cranleigh; *Career* articled clerk Gordon Dadds & Co 1975-77, admitted slr 1977, ptnr Sinclair Roche & Temperley 1983- (asst slr 1977-83); memb Law Soc; *Recreations* fishing, riding, theatre; *Style—* Simon Taylor, Esq; Sinclair Roche & Temperley, Stone House, 128-140 Bishopsgate, London EC2M 4JP (☎ 071 3747 9044, fax 071 377 1528, telex 889281)

TAYLOR, Stanley Thomas; Charles Taylor (d 1948), and Eleanor Miriam, *née* North (d 1969); *b* 26 Sept 1923; *Educ* Archbishop Tenisons's GS; *m* 12 Feb 1955, Valerie Mary, da of Ernest Whitmarsh-Everiss (d 1972), of Bristol; 1 s (Stephen Charles b 1960), 1 da (Helen Frances b 1956); *Career* war serv cmmnd RAFVR; admin of Hertfordshire Health Authy until 1979, chief exec and sec Children's Film & Television Fndn 1980-; Freeman City of London, fndr memb Worshipful Co Chartered Secretaries and Administrators; FHSM 1968, FCIS 1970; *Recreations* golf, reading (biographies), walking; *Clubs* RAF; *Style—* Stanley T Taylor, Esq; 22 Stakers Ct, Milton Rd, Harpenden, Herts AL5 5PA (☎ 058 27 5287); Children's Film & Television Foundation Ltd, Elstree Studios, Borehamwood, Herts WD6 1JG (☎ 081 953 0844)

TAYLOR, Hon Mrs (Sylvia Alice); da of 2 Baron Joicey (d 1940); *b* 1908; *m* 1934 (m dis 1951), Lt-Col Richard Ian Griffith Taylor, DSO, MC (d 1984); 2 s, 1 da; *Style—* The Hon Mrs Sylvia Taylor

TAYLOR, Hon Mrs Sylvia Alice; 2 da of 2 Baron Joicey (d 1940) and Georgina Wharton (d 1952), da of Maj Augustus Edward Burdon; *b* 5 Aug 1908; *m* 28 April 1934 (m dis 1951), Lt-Col Richard Ian Griffith Taylor, DSO, MC, eld s of late Lt-Col Thomas George Taylor, DSO, of Chipchase Castle, Wark-on-Tyne; 2 s, 1 da; *Style—* The Hon Mrs Taylor

TAYLOR, Thomas Francis Frederick (Tom); s of Dennis Bentley Taylor (d 1963), of London, and Joan, *née* Nixon; *b* 9 Aug 1937; *Educ* The Dragon Sch, Rugby, Univ Coll Oxford (MA); *m* 18 Sept 1965, Gillian, da of Rev Alan Joslin; 4 s (Richard Stephens b 17 Feb 1967, Thomas Benedict (Ben) b 19 May 1968, (Christopher) Luke b 26 March 1971, Barnaby Mark b 1 July 1974); *Career* Midshipman RN 1955-57; articled clerk Field Roscoe & Co 1960-63, asst slr Bentley Taylor & Goodwin 1963-64, Denton Hall Burgin & Warrens 1964-; memb Worshipful Co of Grocers; memb Law Soc; *Recreations* choral singing, gardening, fishing; *Style—* Thomas Taylor, Esq; Five Chancery Lane, Clifford's Inn, London EC4A 1BU (☎ 071 242 1212, fax 071 404 0087)

TAYLOR, Lady Ursula Daphne; *née* Brudenell-Bruce; da of 6 Marquess of Ailesbury, DSO, TD (d 1961), and Caroline Sydney Anne, *née* Madden (d 1941); *b* 21 Oct 1905; *Educ* at home; *m* 1944, Alec Taylor; 2 s (and 1 s decd); *Career* chiropodist 1944-; *Recreations* motoring; *Style—* The Lady Ursula Taylor; 18 Cresswell Rd, Newbury, Berks (☎ Newbury 35957)

TAYLOR, Wendy Ann (Mrs Bruce Robertson); CBE (1988); da of Edward Philip Taylor, and Lilian Maude, *née* Wright; *b* 29 Jan 1945; *Educ* St Martin's Sch of Art (LDAD); *m* 1982, Bruce Robertson, s of Maurice Robertson; 1 s (Matthew Thomas b 1984); *Career* sculptor; one man exhibitions: Axiom Gallery London 1970, Angela Flowers Gallery London 1972, 24 King's Lynn Festival Norfolk and World Trade Centre London 1974, Annely Juda Fine Art London 1975, Oxford Gallery Oxford 1976, Oliver Dowling Gallery Dublin 1976 and 1979, Building Art The Process (Building Centre Gallery 1986; shown in over 100 gp exhibitions 1964-82; represented in collections in: GB, USA, Rep of Ireland, NZ, Germany, Sweden, Qatar, Switzerland, Seychelles; maj cmmns: The Travellers London 1969, Gazebo (edn of 4 London, NY, Oxford, Suffolk) 1970-72, Triad Oxford 1971, Timepiece London 1973, Calthae Leics 1977, Octo Milton Keynes 1979, Counterpoise Birmingham 1980, Compass Bowl Basildon 1980, Sentinel Reigate 1982, Bronze Relief Canterbury 1981, Equatorial Sundial Bletchley 1982, Essence Milton Keynes 1982, Opus Morley Coll 1983, Gazebo Golder's Hill Park London 1983, Network London 1984, Geo I and Geo II Stratford-upon-Avon 1985, Landscape and Tree of the Wood Fenhurst Surrey 1986, Pharos Peel Park E Kilbride 1986, Ceres Fenhurst Surrey 1986, Nexus Corby Northants 1986, Globe Sundial Swansea Maritime Quarter 1987, Spirit of Enterprise Isle of Dogs London 1987, Silver Fountain Guildford Surrey 1988, The Whirlies E Kilbride 1988, Pilot Kites Norwich Airport 1988, Fire Flow Hamilton Scotland 1988, Armillary Sundial Basildon Essex 1989, Pharos II E Kilbride 1989, Phoenix E Kilbride 1990, Globe Sundial London Zoological Gardens Continuum Guildford; awards: Walter Neurath 1964, Pratt 1965, Sainsbury 1966, Arts Cncl 1977, Duais Na Riochta (Kingdom prize), Gold medal Rep of Ireland 1977, winner silk screen Barcham Green Print Competition 1978; examiner Univ of London 1982-83, memb Ct RCA 1982-, memb Cncl Morley Coll 1985-88, conslt New Town Cmmn Basildon (formerly Basildon Devpt Corpn) 1985-, specialist advsr Fine Art Bd CNAA 1985- (memb 1980-85, memb Ctee for Art Design), memb Royal Fine Art Cmmn 1981-, design conslt London Borough of Barking and Dagenham 1989-; memb London Docklands Design Advsy Bd 1989-; memb PCFC 1989-; FZS 1989; *Recreations* gardening; *Style—* Ms Wendy Taylor, CBE; 73 Bow Rd, Bow, London EC3 2AN (☎ 081 981 2037)

TAYLOR, William; s of Abraham Taylor (d 1962), of Newcastle upon Tyne, and Isabella Oliver, *née* Franks (d 1983); *b* 31 Dec 1921; *Educ* Rutherford Coll Newcastle upon Tyne, AA Sch of Architecture (AADipl, SADG); *m* 16 April 1949, Stella (d 1984), da of Edwin George Wilkins (d 1954), of Marnhull, Dorset; 1 s (Randolph b 1960); *Career* lectr in architecture Univ of Durham 1945-47, private practise 1947-52, RIBA bursar Br Sch of Archaeology Athens 1957, visiting prof Sch of Architecture Univ of Virginia USA 1959-60, princ lectr Sch of Architecture Oxford 1964- (sr lectr 1952-), sr tutor Dept of Architecture Oxford Poly 1970-81, assoc architect Br Sch of Archaeology at Knossos Crete 1977; examiner in history of architecture: RIBA, Univ of Oxford Delegacy of Local Examinations; ARIBA 1945, FRIBA 1970; *Books* A Bibliography on Romanesque Architecture (1960), Greek Architecture (1971), History of Architecture (contrib 18 edn, 1975), The Worlds Great Architecture (contrib, 1980), The Bronze Age Palace at Knossos (jtly, 1981); *Recreations* music, ancient history, archaeology; *Style—* William Taylor, Esq; 23 Gallerton Court, Ponteland, Northumberland NE20 9EN (☎ 0661 72588)

TAYLOR, Prof Sir William; CBE (1982); s of Herbert Taylor (d 1969), and Maud Ethel, *née* Peyto (d 1972); *b* 31 May 1930; *Educ* Erith GS, LSE (BSc), Westminster Coll London (PGCE), Univ of London Inst of Educn (DipEd, PhD); *m* 30 Dec 1954, Rita, da of Ronald Hague (d 1957); 1 s (Richard William James b 27 July 1964), 2 da (Anne Catherine (Mrs Mitchell) b 12 April 1958, Rosemary Caroline (Mrs Williams) b 11 March 1960); *Career* Nat Serv Royal West Kent Regt 1948-49, Intelligence Corps 1950-53, 135 Field Security Section TA; teacher in Kent 1953-59, dep head Slade Green Secdy Sch 1956-59, sr lectr St Luke's Coll Exeter 1959-61, princ lectr and head of Educn Dept Hilde and Bede Coll Durham 1961-64, tutor and lectr in educn Univ of Oxford 1964-66, prof of educn Univ of Bristol 1966-73, dir Univ of London Inst of

Educn 1973-83, princ Univ of London 1983-85, vice-chllr Univ of Hull 1985-91; chm: Educnl Advsy Cncl of the IBA 1977-83, Univs Cncl for the Educn of Teachers 1976-79, Ctee for Educnl Res Cncl of Europe 1968-71, Nat Fndn for Educnl Res 1984-88, Cncl for the Accreditation of Teacher Educn (CATE) 1984-, Univs Cncl for Adult and Continuing Educn 1986-90, NFER/Nelson Publishing Co 1988-; dir Fenner plc 1988-; pres Assoc of Colls of Further and Higher Educn 1985-88; Freeman City of London 1986, Liveryman Worshipful Soc of Apothecaries 1986; Hon DSc Aston Univ 1977, Hon LittD Univ of Leeds 1979, Hon DCL Univ of Kent 1981, Hon DUniv Open Univ 1983, Hon DLit Univ of Loughborough 1984; FCP 1977, FCCEA 1978, FWACEA 1979; kt 1990; *Books* The Secondary Modern School (1963), Educational Administration and the Social Sciences (ed jtly 1969, Japanese edn 1970), Society and the Education of Teachers (1969), Towards a Policy for the Education of Teachers (ed 1969), Policy and Planning in Post Secondary Education (1971), Theory into Practice (1972), Heading for Change (1973), Research Perspectives in Education (ed 1973), Education 1973: Perspectives and Plans for Graduate Studies (with Downey, Daniels and Baker 1973), Educational Administration in Australia and Abroad (jt ed with Thomas and Farquhar, 1975), Research and Reform in Teacher Education (1978), Education for the Eighties - the Central Issues (ed with Simon, 1981), New Zealand - Reviews of National Policies for Education (with assistance from P H Karmel and Ingrid Eide, 1983), Metaphors of Education (ed, 1984), Universities under Scrutiny (1987); *Recreations* books, music; *Style*— Prof Sir William Taylor, CBE; Council for the Accreditation of Teacher Education, Elizabeth House, York Road, London SW1 7PH (☎ 071 934 0746, fax 071 934 0736)

TAYLOR, (Brian) William (Bill); s of Alan Stuart Taylor (d 1975), of Chatham, Kent, and Dora Frances Mary, *née* Betts (d 1968); *b* 29 April 1933; *Educ* Emanuel Sch Wandsworth; *m* 15 Aug 1959, Mary Evelyn, da of William Henry Buckley (d 1976), of Great Bookham, Surrey; 2 s (Jeffrey William b 16 Feb 1967, Michael John b 20 Jan 1972), 2 da (Helen Mary (Mrs Compston) b 28 Jan 1963, Gillian Elizabeth (Mrs Cooksley) b 30 Oct 1964); *Career* Miny of Nat Insur: exec offr 1952, higher exec offr 1963, princ 1968, asst sec 1976, under sec 1982; on secondment from Dept of Social Security; Civil Service Comm 1990-; *Recreations* music, theatre, literature, tennis; *Clubs* Royal Cwlth Soc; *Style*— Bill Taylor, Esq; Civil Service Commission, 24 Whitehall, London SW1A 2ED (☎ 071 210 6674, fax 071 210 6793)

TAYLOR, William Bernard; s of Francis Augustus Taylor (d 1956), of Swansea, and Mary Elizabeth, *née* George; *b* 13 Dec 1930; *Educ* Dynevor Sch Swansea, Univ of Kent (MA); *m* 26 April 1956, Rachel May, da of Daniel Brynmor Davies (d 1959), of Godre Rhiw, Morriston, Swansea; 1 s (Simon b 1965), 2 da (Kim b 1959, Deborah b 1961); *Career* Nat Serv 1949-51, cmmnd RNVR 1950, Sub Lt RNVR 1951-53; Dist Audit Serv 1951-61, treas Llwchwr UDC 1967-68 (dep treas 1961-67), asst educn offr Fin and Mgmnt Manchester Corp 1969-72, co treas Kent 1980-87 (asst co treas 1972-73, dep co treas 1973-80), specialist local authy advsr Arthur Young Management Consultants 1987-89, MIM Ltd, Lombard N Central plc, Sedgwick James (Nat) Ltd 1987-, dir Interlake DRC Ltd 1989-, non-exec memb Medway Health Authy 1990- (chm Fin and Review Ctee 1990-); author of numerous articles for learned magazines; memb Exec Ctee Soc of Co Treas 1983-86, fin advsr to Social Servs Ctee of Assoc of CCs 1983-86, Lloyds Underwriter 1988-; memb: Maidstone Rotary Club, Union St Methodist Church; life memb W Kent speakers Club, hon treas SE Eng Tst Bd 1980-87, govr Kent Inst of Art and Design (chm Fin Ctee 1989-); FRSA, memb IPFA; *Books* Terotechnology & The Pursuit of Life Cycle Costs (1980); *Recreations* public speaking, tennis, cricket, watching rugby; *Style*— William Taylor, Esq; Selby Shaw, Heath Rd, Boughton Monchelsea, Maidstone, Kent ME17 4JE (☎ 0622 7450 22)

TAYLOR, (Peter) William Edward; QC (1981); s of Peter Taylor (d 1963), of Winchester, and Julia Anne, *née* North (d 1989); *b* 27 July 1917; *Educ* Peter Symonds' Sch Winchester, Christ's Coll Cambridge (MA); *m* 2 Jan 1948, Julia Mary, da of Air Cdre Sir Vernon Brown, CB (d 1986), of Chelsea, London SW3; 2 s (Malcolm b 1950, Nigel b 1952); *Career* cmmd TA 1937; served RA 1939-46: France and Belgium 1939-40, N Africa 1942-43, N W Europe 1944-45 (despatches), acting Lt-Col 1945; Hon Maj TARO 1946; called to the Bar Inner Temple 1946, Lincoln's Inn 1953, in practice 1947-, lectr in construction of documents Cncl of Legal Educn 1952-70, Conveyancing Counsel of the Ct 1974-81, bencher Lincoln's Inn 1976-; memb: Gen Cncl of the Bar 1971-74, Senate of the Inns of Ct and the Bar 1974-75, Inter-professional Ctee on Retirement Provision 1974-, Land Registration Rule Ctee 1976-81, Standing Ctee on Conveyancing 1985-87, Inc Cncl of Law Reporting 1977-87 (vice chm 1988-); *Recreations* sailing, music; *Style*— William Taylor, Esq, QC; 46 Onslow Sq, London SW7 3NX (☎ 071 589 1301); Carey Sconce, Yarmouth, Isle of Wight, PO41 OSB

TAYLOR, Dr William Halstead; s of late Thomas Halstead Taylor, of Wardle, Lancashire, and late Alice May, *née* Hallett; *b* 26 April 1924; *Educ* Manchester GS, Ch Ch Oxford (MA), Radcliffe Infirmary Univ of Oxford (BCh, DM); *m* 7 Sept 1950, June Helen, da of late Tom Edward Thorniley, of Wilmslow, Cheshire; 1 s (John b 1954), 3 da (Susan b 1951, Philippa b 1955, Rowena b 1958); *Career* chemical pathologist and physician (formerly lectr and sr lectr in clinical biochemistry) Univ of Oxford 1949-59, fell and tutor in natural sci St Peter's Coll Univ of Oxford 1957-59, head of dept of Chemical Pathology United Liverpool Hosps and Liverpool Health Authy 1959-89, dir of studies in chemical pathology Univ of Liverpool 1962-74, dir of Mersey Regnl Metabolic Unit 1965-89, pt/t asst physician Halton Gen Hosp Runcorn 1989-; memb: Med Res Soc, Assoc of Clinical Biochemists, Assoc of Clinical Pathologists; former memb Ed Bd Clinical Science; 41 Club of Liverpool, Liverpool Rotary; FRCP 1971; *Books* Fluid Therapy and Disorders of Electrolyte Balance (1965); *Recreations* music, fly-fishing, walking, philately; *Style*— Dr William H Taylor; 16 Salisbury Rd, Cressington Park, Liverpool L19 0PJ (☎ 051 427 1042); Department of Medical Microbiology, Royal Liverpool Hospital, Liverpool L7 8XW

TAYLOR, William Horace; GC (1941), MBE (1973); s of William Arthur Taylor (d 1945), and Hilda Jane, *née* Nicholson; *b* 23 Oct 1908; *Educ* Manchester GS; *m* 19 Sept 1946, Joan Isabel, da of John Skaife D'Ingerthorpe; 1 s (William Norman b 1949), 3 da (Susan Rosemary b 1948, Jane Elizabeth b 1951, Belinda Mary b 1954); *Career* Dept of Torpedoes and Mines Admty (despatches and comendation for brave conduct 1941), fndr memb Naval Clearance Divers, HMS Vernon 1944; travelling cmmr Sea Scouts UK 1946, field cmmr SW Eng Scout Assoc 1952-74, estate mangr 1975-84; *Recreations* scouting, boating, music; *Style*— William Horace Taylor, Esq, GC, MBE; The Bungalow, Carbeth, Blanefield, Glasgow G63 9AT (☎ 0360 70847)

TAYLOR, William James; QC (1986); s of Cecil Taylor, of 15 Drumblair Crescent, Inverness, and Ellen, *née* Daubney; *b* 13 Sept 1944; *Educ* Robert Gordon's Coll, Univ of Aberdeen (MA, LLB); *Career* admitted Faculty of Advocates 1971, standing jr DHSS 1978-79, standing jr counsel FCO 1979-86, called to the Bar Inner Temple 1990; *Recreations* sailing, skiing, hillwalking, theatre, opera, music; *Style*— William Taylor, Esq, QC; Hill House, 69 Dirleton Avenue, North Berwick, East Lothian EH39 4QL (☎ 0620 5111); Parliament House, Parliament Square, Edinburgh, EH1 1RF (☎ 031 226 2881); 11 South Square, Gray's Inn, London WC1R 5EU (☎ 071 831 2311, fax 071 404 4939)

TAYLOR, William McCaughey; s of William Taylor (d 1959), of Ballyhalbert, Co Down, and Georgina Lindsay, *née* McCaughey (d 1983); *b* 10 May 1926; *Educ* Campbell Coll Belfast, Trinity Coll Oxford (MA); *m* 1955, June Louise, da of William Ewart Macartney (d 1971), of Ballymena, Co Antrim; 2 s (Dwayne b 1963, Heath b 1966), 2 da (Karin b 1956, Nicola b 1958); *Career* served WWII Lt Royal Inniskilling Fus 1944-47; chief exec N Ireland Police Authy (detached under sec NI Office) 1979-86; chm NI Coal Importers Assoc 1986-; *Recreations* golf, bridge, gardening, piano; *Clubs* Royal Belfast Golf; *Style*— William McCaughey Taylor, Esq; 1 Knocktern Gardens, Belfast BT4 3LZ (☎ 0232 653400); Northern Ireland Coal Importers Association, 51 Upper Arthur St, Belfast BT1 4GT (☎ 0232 241153)

TAYLOR-DOWNES, Michael; s of Lt-Col Francis Algernon Taylor-Downes (d 1951), of Colwyn Bay, N Wales, and Lillias Elsie, *née* Banks (d 1966); *b* 30 Dec 1930; *Educ* The Downs Sch Colwall, Westminster; *m* 1, 2 Dec 1950, Pamela Jane Firkins (d 1972); 2 da (Elizabeth Jane (Hon Mrs Ian Wills) b 1952, Amanda Charlotte b 1955); m 2, 5 Oct 1963, Audrey Elizabeth Jackson (d 1984); m 3, 29 Nov 1983, Remony Charmian, da of late Sir Charles Gerald Stewkley Shuckburgh 12 Bt, TD, DL; *Career* The Life Gds 1949-52, Inns of Ct Regt (TA) 1952-59; underwriting memb of Lloyds 1956; vice chm Cotswold District Cncl 1975-80; master: The Garth Fox Hounds 1955-60, Cotswold Vale Fox Hounds 1962-63, Hawkstone Otter Hounds 1965-72, Wye Valley Otter Hounds 1969-72; *Recreations* hunting, shooting, fishing, coursing, racing; *Style*— Michael Taylor-Downes, Esq; The Cottage, Sherbourne, Warwick, CV35 8AA (☎ 0926 624 073)

TAYLOR-JONES, Dr Thomas Henry Edward; DL (Kent 1981); s of Henry Taylor-Jones (d 1939); *b* 6 Feb 1906; *Educ* Dulwich, Univ of London (DCH); *m* 1931, Dorothy Amy (d 1990), da of John Corbett (d 1922); 1 s (decd), 1 da; *Career* late orthopaedic house surgn Belgrave Hosp for Children, MO West View Hosp Tenterden; MRCS, LRCP; *Recreations* gardening; *Clubs* Band of Brothers; *Style*— Dr Thomas Taylor-Jones, DL; The Garden, St Michaels, Tenterden, Kent (☎ 05806 3193)

TAYLOR OF BLACKBURN, Baron (Life Peer UK 1978), of Blackburn, Co Lancaster; Thomas Taylor; CBE (1974, OBE 1969), JP (Blackburn 1960); s of James Taylor; *b* 10 June 1929; *Educ* Blakey Moor Higher Grade Sch; *m* 1950, Kathleen, da of John Edward Nurton; 1 s (Hon Paul Nurton b 1953); *Career* memb Blackburn Town Cncl 1954-76 (ldr, and chm Policy and Resources Ctee 1972-76), dep pro chllr Lancaster Univ 1974-, chm Govt Ctee of Enquiry into Mgmnt and Govt of Schs, past chm Juvenile Bench, pres Free Church Cncl 1962-68, memb Norweb Bd and Select Ctee on Sci and Technol; dir and dep chm Themes International plc; dir and conslt to several other cos; *Style*— The Rt Hon the Lord Taylor of Blackburn, CBE, JP; 34 Tower Rd, Feniscliffe, Blackburn, Lancs

TAYLOR OF GRYFE, Baron (Life Peer UK 1968), of Bridge of Weir, Renfrewshire; Thomas Johnston Taylor; DL (Renfrewshire 1970); s of John Sharp Taylor, of Glasgow; *b* 27 April 1912; *Educ* Bellahouston Acad Glasgow; *m* 1943, Isobel, da of William Wands; 2 da (Hon Jill (Hon Mrs Wäber) b 1945, Hon Joyce (Hon Mrs Richards) b 1948); *Career* sits as Lab Peer in House of Lords; chm: The Forestry Cmmn 1970-76, Econ Forestry Gp 1976-82, Morgan Grenfell (Scotland) Ltd 1973-86, Scottish Railways Bd 1971-80, Scottish Peers Assoc 1987-; memb: BR Bd 1968-80, Bd Scottish Television Ltd 1968-82; dir: Scottish Civic Tst, Whiteaway Laidlaw & Co Ltd (Bankers) 1971-90, Friends' Provident Life Office 1972-82, Scottish Metropolitan Property Co Ltd 1972-90, BR Property Bd 1972-82; Hon LLD Strathclyde 1974; chm Isaac and Edith Wolfson Tst, tstee The Dulverson Tst 1980-, vice chm Scot Cncl Devpt and Indust; FRSE; *Clubs* Caledonian, Royal and Ancient (St Andrews); *Style*— The Rt Hon the Lord Taylor of Gryfe, DL, FRSE; 33 Seagate, Kingsbarns, Fife KY16 8SC

TAYLOR OF HADFIELD, Baron (Life Peer UK 1982), of Hadfield in the Co of Derby; Frank (Francis) Taylor; s of Francis Taylor and Sarah Ann Earnshaw; *b* 7 Jan 1905; *m* 1, 1929 (m dis); 2 da (Hon Audrey Evelyn (Hon Mrs Trafford) b 1932, Hon Gillian Doreen (Hon Mrs Marlar) b 1934); m 2, 1956, Christine Enid, da of Charles Hughes; 1 da (Hon Sarah (Hon Mrs Melville) b 1961); *Career* fndr, life pres: Taylor Woodrow Gp (md 1921-79, chm 1937-74), Taylor Woodrow Hldgs USA Ltd, pres Aims 1978-; former dir BOAC; FCIOB (hon fell 1979); Hon DSc Salford; hon: FICE, FFB; kt 1974; *Style*— The Rt Hon the Lord Taylor of Hadfield; 86 Gloucester Mews West, London W2 6DY (☎ 071 262 0581, fax 071 723 7290)

TAYLOR OF MANSFIELD, Baron (Life Peer UK 1966), of Mansfield, Co Nottingham; Harry Bernard Taylor; CBE (1966); s of late Henry Taylor, of Mansfield Woodhouse, Notts; *b* 18 Sept 1895; *Educ* Oxclose Lane Sch Mansfield Woodhouse; *m* 1921, Clara Annie (d 1983), da of John Ashley, of Mansfield Woodhouse; 1 s (Hon Bernard Alfred b 1922); *Career* MP (L) Mansfield Div of Nottinghamshire 1941-66, PPS to Min of Nat Insur 1945, parly sec Miny of Nat Insur 1950-51; *Books* Uphill all the Way (autobiog, 1973); *Style*— The Rt Hon the Lord Taylor of Mansfield, CBE; 47 Shakespeare Ave, Mansfield Woodhouse, Nottinghamshire (☎ 0623 2392)

TAYLOR-SCHOFIELD, Annette Ainscough; da of Brian Wormald, and Maureen Daphne, *née* Goodman; *b* 26 July 1953; *Educ* Mill Mount GS for Girls York; *m* 1, 2 Jan 1971, (m dis 1977), Nigel Griffiths Ainsclough, s of Thomas Griffiths Ainsclough, of Bracknell Berks; 1 s (Matthew Sean b 1971), 1 da (Kathryn b 1973); m 2, 3 Aug 1978, (m dis 1983), Timothy (Julian) Taylor-Schofield; *Career* sales mangr Impact Insulation Ltd 1975-76 (mktg mangr 1974-75), sales dir Solarwall Ltd 1976-78, property renovator 1978-80, Insulation Agency 1980-83; co-owner Ziggy's Nightclub & Staircase Restaurant York 1983- (winner Disco Mirror awards 1986-88, runner up Disco & Club Int award 1987, Yorks Disco of the Year 1988, runner up Club Mirror award), chm and md Taylor-Schofield Leisure Ltd 1987-, dir and co sec Bellerby's Ltd York 1989-; memb mgmnt ctee One Parent Families Assoc; film Women Mean Business by York Film Workshop; Network (1987), The Int Alliance (1989); *Recreations* snow skiing, canoeing, mountain walking, fitness training, tennis, music; *Clubs* Viking Leisure Club; *Style*— Ms A A Taylor-Schofield; Taylor Schoffield Leisure Ltd, 31-33, North Moor Rd, Huntingdon, York YO3 9QN (☎ 0904 764 399 & 763 131/2); Ziggy's Nightclub, Micklegate, York - evenings (☎ 0904 620 602)

TAYLOR-SMITH, John Roderick; s of Harold Wilfred Taylor-Smith (d 1990), and Kathleen, *née* MacDonald; *b* 14 July 1959; *Educ* Rongotai Coll Wellington NZ, Univ of Otago (BDS), Univ of Sheffield (surgery and prosthetics course); *m* 16 Jan 1988, Janice Wendy, da of Stuart Withell; *Career* house surgeon Wellington Public Hosp NZ 1983-84, sr house surgeon Plastics and Maxillo-Facial Unit Lower Hutt Hosp NZ 1984-85, proprietor dental practice Wimpole St 1990- (dental surgeon London 1985-); memb: BDA, Br Soc Occlusal Studies 1988; *Recreations* cricket, rugby, golf, squash, tennis, skiing, scuba diving, riding; *Clubs* Roehampton, London New Zealand Cricket, Old Riegations Rugby; *Style*— John Taylor-Smith, Esq; John Taylor-Smith, Dental Surgeon, 30A Wimpole St, London W1 M7AE (☎ 071 224 4432)

TAYLOR THOMPSON, (John) Derek; CB (1985); s of John Taylor Thompson (d 1964), of Herts, and Marjorie Bligh, *née* Westcott; *b* 6 Aug 1927; *Educ* St Peter's Sch York, Balliol Coll Oxford (MA); *m* 2 Oct 1954, Helen Margaret, da of George Laurie Walker (d 1934), of Wimbledon; 2 da (Catherine b 1957, Bopha b 1960); *Career* memb Bd Inland Revenue 1973-87; chm: Fiscal Affs Ctee, Orgn for Econ Co-op and Devpt 1984-89; sec Churches Main Ctee 1990-; *Recreations* rural pursuits, reading, writing;

Clubs United Oxford and Cambridge Univ; *Style*— Derek Taylor Thompson, Esq, CB; Jessops, Nutley, E Sussex TN22 3PD

TAYLORSON, John Brown; s of John Brown Taylorson (d 1945), and Edith Maria Taylorson (d 1981); *b* 5 March 1931; *Educ* Forest Sch Snares Brook Essex; *m* 1, 1960 (m dis), Barbara June Hagg; 2 s (Jonathan, James), 1 da (Sally); m 2, 1985, Helen Anne; *Career* Flying Offr RAF 1959-61; md: Int Div Gardner Merchant Food Services 1974-77, Fedics Food Services Pty 1977-80; chief exec Civil Serv Catering Orgn 1980-81, head of catering BA plc 1981-89; md: John Taylorson Association 1990-, Inflight Marketing Services 1990-; pres Int Flight Catering Assoc 1983-86, chm Int Serv Indust Search 1990-; *Recreations* golf, walking, theatre, crosswords; *Clubs* Escorts, Jesters, Burhill Golf, Wanderers; *Style*— John Taylorson, Esq; Deer Pond Cottage, Highfields, East Horsley, Surrey KT24 5AA; John Taylorson Group of Companies, One Heathrow Boulevard, 286 Bath Rd, West Drayton, Middlesex UB7 0DQ

TE ATAIRANGIKAAHU, Te Arikinui Dame Arikinui; DBE (1970); da of Koroki Te Rata Mahuta V; *b* 23 July 1931; *Educ* Waikato Diocesan Secdy Sch for Girls Hamilton; *m* 1952, Whatumoana Paki, QSO; 2 s, 5 da; *Career* Hon Doctorate (Waikato); The Maori Queen 1966-; Te Atairangikaahu (the soaring bird of the dawn); ONZ (1988), OStJ (1986); *Style*— Te Arikinui Dame Te Atairangikaahu, DBE; Turangawaewae Marae, Turongo House, Ngaruawahia, NZ

TE KANAWA, Dame Kiri Janette; DBE (1982, OBE 1973); da of Thomas Te Kanawa, of Auckland, NZ, and late Elanor Te Kanawa; *b* 6 March 1944, Gisborne, NZ; *Educ* St Mary's Coll Auckland, London Opera Centre; *m* 1967, Desmond Stephen Park, s of Joseph Frank Park, of Brisbane, Aust; 1 s, 1 da; *Career* opera singer; studied singing under Dame Sister Mary Leo, *qv* 1959-65; has sung major roles at: Royal Opera House (Covent Garden), Metropolitan Opera (New York), Paris Opera, San Francisco Opera, Sydney Opera, Cologne Opera, La Scala (Milan); sang at Royal Wedding of HRH Prince of Wales to Lady Diana Spencer 1981; Hon LLD Dundee; Hon DMus: Durham 1982, Oxford 1983; *Style*— Dame Kiri Te Kanawa, DBE; c/o Basil Horsfield, L'Estoril (B), Avenue Princess Grace 31, Monte Carlo, Monaco

TEAGUE, (Edward) Thomas Henry; s of Harry John Teague, of Kelsall, Cheshire, and Anne Elizabeth, *née* Hunt; *b* 21 May 1954; *Educ* St Francis Xavier's Coll Liverpool, Christ's Coll Cambridge (MA); *m* 8 Aug 1980, Helen Mary Bernadette, da of Daniel Matthew Howard (d 1974); 2 s (Michael b 1983, Dominic b 1985); *Career* called to the Bar Inner Temple 1977; in practice on Wales and Chester circuit 1978-; memb Soc of Dorset Men, co fndr and memb Soc of St Edmund Campion; *Recreations* playing the cello, fly-fishing, stargazing; *Style*— Thomas Teague, Esq; Campion House, Becketts Lane, Chester CH3 5RW (☎ 0244 311520); 40 King St, Chester CH1 2AH (☎ 0244 323 886/329 273, fax 47732)

TEALL OF TEALLACH, Dr Dennistoun Gordon; s of Bernard John Teall (d 1966), of Radford Semele, and Agnes Mary, *née* Cottrell (d 1977); *b* 8 Aug 1924; *Educ* Warwick Sch, Cooper's Hill Coll (Ed Cert), Univ of Leicester (MEd, PhD), Coll of Preceptors (LCP); *m* 4 Oct 1946, Eleanor Joan, da of John Thomas Ackland (d 1967), of Quadring; 2 s (David b 1947, Richard b 1962), 2 da (Maryon b 1950, Christine b 1956); *Career* serv WWII despatch rider Civil Def 1940-43, radio offr Merchant Navy 1945-46 (cadet 1943-44); works chemist Colas Products Ltd 1946-47; headmaster: Yarwell Sch 1952-60, Priory Prep Sch 1960-62, princ Priory Coll 1962-84; chm: Midlands area Independent Schs Assoc 1982-85, NE England and Scotland Independent Schs Assoc 1982-85; hon exec pres Scottish Tartans Soc 1983- (patron 1978-, chm 1979-83); memb: Manorial Soc of GB, Noble Leet of Feudal Lords, Royal Scottish Country Dance Assoc, Calesonian Soc Edinburgh, Scottish Railways Preservation Soc; chm bd of tstees Scottish Tartans Museum N Caroline USA 1988-; memb Lloyd's of London; cncllr: Oundle and Thrapston RDC 1961-67, Barnack RDC 1965-68, Nassington Parish Cncl 1958-66, St Martins Without Parish Cncl 1965-68; hon memb Clan Grant, memb House of Gordon; Lord of the Manor of Croyland; feudal superior Gordon Schs Huntly Aberdeenshire; Royal Humane Soc's Award for Gallantry in Saving Life, certificate of honour California State Senate 1990; MIOD, FCS 1945, FSA Scot 1978, FSTS 1981; Hon Lt-Col Militia of the State of Georgia 1987; *Books* May Festivals (1963), The Tradesmen and Corporation of Stamford 1485-1750 (1975), The Manx Tartans (1981), The District Tartans of Scotland (jtly, 1988), A Brief History of The Scottish Tartans Society (1988); *Recreations* sailing in strong winds, windsurfing in light airs, horse riding, scottish dancing, mountain walking, swimming in warm waters; *Clubs* Univ Centre (Cambridge), Manx Sc; *Style*— Dr Gordon Teall of Teallach; Cornaa House, Maughold, IOM (☎ 0624 813580); Scottish Tartans Museum, Comrie, Perthshire PH6 2DW (☎ 0724 70779, car 0860 640 234)

TEAR, Robert; CBE (1984); s of Thomas Arthur Tear, of Barry, S Glam, and Edith Marion Tear; *b* 8 March 1939; *Educ* Barry GS, King's Coll Cambridge (MA); *m* 10 Jan 1961, Hilary, da of William Thomas, of Cwmbran, Gwent; 2 da (Rebecca b 22 Nov 1961, Elizabeth b 11 Feb 1966); *Career* opera/concert singer and conductor; regular appearances: throughout America, Covent Garden, Munich, Park, Salzburg, Brussels and Geneva; holder of Chair of Int Vocal Studies at RAM; hon fell King's Coll Cambridge 1988, RAM, RCM; *Recreations* anything interesting; *Clubs* Garrick, Beefsteak; *Style*— Robert Tear, Esq, CBE; Harold Holt Ltd, 31 Sinclair Rd, London W14 0NS (☎ 071 603 4600)

TEARE, Nigel John Martin; s of Eric John Teare (d 1980), and Mary Rackham, *née* Faragher (d 1985); *b* 8 Jan 1952; *Educ* King William's Coll Castletown IOM, St Peter's Coll Oxford (BA, MA); *m* 16 Aug 1975, (Elizabeth) Jane, da of Alan James Pentecost, of Beaulieu, Derby Rd, Nottingham; 2 s (Roland b 1981, David b 1984), 1 da (Charlotte b 1982); *Career* called to the Bar Lincoln's Inn 1974, junior counsel to treasy in Admty matters 1989-; *Recreations* collecting Manx paintings, golf, squash, tennis; *Clubs* RAC; *Style*— Nigel Teare, Esq; The Towers, Hawkshill Place, Portsmouth Rd, Esher, Surrey KT10 9HY (☎ 0372 464552); 2 Essex Ct, Temple, London (☎ 071 583 8381, fax 071 353 0998, telex 8812528 ADROIT)

TEASDALE, Anthony Laurence; s of John S Teasdale, of Beverley, N Humberside, and Pauline, *née* Tomlinson (d 1983); *b* 4 June 1957; *Educ* Slough GS, Balliol Coll Oxford (MA), Nuffield Coll Oxford (MPhil); *Career* res asst to Rt Hon Nigel Lawson MP 1978-79; lectr in politics: Corpus Christi Coll Oxford 1980-81, Magdalen Coll Oxford 1982; policy advsr Euro Democratic Gp (of Cons MEPs) Brussels and London 1982-86, asst to Dir Gen for Econ and Fin Affrs EC Cncl of Mins Brussels 1986-88; political advsr to Rt Hon Sir Geoffrey Howe QC MP 1988-90; *Books* Righting The Balance: A New Agenda for Euro-Japanese Trade (with James Moorhouse MEP, 1987); *Recreations* music, reading, travel; *Clubs* Carlton, St Stephen's, IOD; *Style*— Anthony Teasdale, Esq; 34 Buckingham Palace Road, London SW1W 0QP (☎ 071 828 3153)

TEASDALE, Lt Cdr (Raymond) Geoffrey; s of Canham Teasdale (d 1977), of Aldbrough, Yorks, and Alma Arabella, *née* Hobbs; *b* 5 Sept 1931; *Educ* Hymers Coll Hull, RNC Dartmouth; *m* 22 Aug 1980, Michele Evadne, da of Capt Godfrey Charles Gale; *Career* RN 1949-81; chief counter-pollution advsr MOD 1981; chm Nautical Inst (Avon) 1986; FInstPet; MNI; *Recreations* fishing, golf, shooting; *Clubs* RN Sailing Assoc; *Style*— Lt Cdr Geoffrey Teasdale; 11 St Martins Park, Marshfield, Avon (☎ 0225 891764; MOD (Navy), Ensleigh, Bath (☎ 0225 467694)

TEBB, Robert Maxwell; s of Capt Harry Raymond Tebb (d 1978), of Scarborough, and Kathleen, *née* Cheveley (d 1979); *b* 9 Feb 1927; *Educ* Leeds GS; *Career* food distributor; md Leigh Lineham & Sharphouse Ltd 1967-, chm Leigh Lineham 1983-; chm City of Leeds Coll of Music 1990, dir Eng Summer Sch of Light Opera, dep admin Harveys Leeds Inst Pianoforte Competition; *Recreations* theatre, music; *Style*— Robert Tebb, Esq; Grove Court, Holt Ave, Church Lane, Adel, Leeds 16, W Yorks (☎ 0532 679666); Leigh Lineham Ltd, 7 Cottage Rd, Headingley, Leeds LS6 4DD (☎ 0532 782319)

TEBBIT, Sir Donald Claude; GCMG (1980, KCMG 1975, CMG 1965); s of Richard Claude Tebbit (d 1967), of The Old Farm, Toft, Cambridge; *b* 4 May 1920; *Educ* Perse Sch Cambridge, Trinity Hall Cambridge (MA); *m* 1947, Barbara, da of Rev Norman Matheson (d 1952), of Beauly, Inverness-shire; 1 s, 3 da; *Career* Nat Serv WWII RNVR; entered FO 1946, min Br Embassy Washington 1970-72, chief clerk FCO 1972-76, high cmmr Aust 1976-80, ret; chm Dip Appeals Bd 1980-87, dir gen British Property Federation 1980-85, dir Rio Tinto Zinc Corporation 1980-90; pres: (UK) Australian-British C of C 1980-85, Old Persean Soc 1981-82; govr Nuffield Hosps 1980-90 (dep chm); chm Marshall Aid Commemoration Cmmn 1985-, memb Appeals Bd Cncl of Europe 1981-; chm: ESU of the Cwlth 1983-87, Jt Cwlth Socs Cncl 1987-; *Clubs* Travellers', Gog Magog Golf; *Style*— Sir Donald Tebbit, GCMG; Priory Cottage, Toft, Cambridge CB3 7RH

TEBBIT, Rt Hon Norman Beresford; CH (1987), PC 1981, MP (C) Chingford 1974-; 2 s of Leonard Albert and Edith Tebbit, of Enfield; *b* 29 March 1931; *Educ* Edmonton Co GS; *m* 1956, Margaret Elizabeth, da of Stanley Daines, of Chatteris; 2 s, 1 da; *Career* RAF 1949-51, RAuxAF 1952-55; journalist 1947-49, publishing and advertising 1951-53, airline pilot 1953-70 (memb BALPA and former official); MP (C): Epping 1970-74, Waltham Forest, Chingford 1974-1983; former: memb Select Ctee Science and Technol, chm Cons Aviation Ctee, vice chm and sec Cons Housing and Construction Ctee, sec New Town MPs; PPS to Min of State for Employment 1972-73, Parly under sec state for Trade 1979-81, min of state for Indust 1981, sec of state for Employment 1981-Oct 1983, sec of state for Trade and Indust Oct 1983-85; dir: BET plc, BT plc, Sears plc, JCB Excavators Ltd, Onix Group Ltd; cnllr of Duchy of Lancaster 1985-87, chm Cons Pty 1985-87; *Books* Upwardly Mobile, an autobiography (1988); *Style*— The Rt Hon Norman Tebbit, CH, MP; House of Commons, SW1

TEBBUTT, Michael Laurence; s of Laurence Tebbutt (d 1983), and Joan, *née* Payne (d 1989); *b* 23 July 1931; *Educ* Stamford Sch Lincs; *m* 23 May 1959, Hazel, da of Andrew Taylor, of Braidhaugh, Roxburghshire; 4 da (Fiona Joan (Mrs Woodcock) b 1960, Nicola Jane Dorothy (Mrs Cork) b 1962, Davina Dawn b 1963, Rowena Morag b 1965); *Career* RN; serv HMS: Vanguard 1950, Finisterre 1951, Vanguard 1953; FOSM Staff 1954, 3 Submarine Sqdn 1955, HMS Dolphin 1957; with Outward Bound Tst 1957-61, trg offr Jt Iron Cncl 1961-63, gen mangr Bowes Lyon House 1963-67, gen sec NFYFC's 1967-69, comptroller Knebworth House 1969-72; admin: Weston Park 1972-82, Culzean (NTS) 1982-; vice pres Wrekin Decorative and Fine Arts Soc; chm: Ayrshire Decorative and Fine Arts Soc (exec memb), Ayrshire and Burns Country Tourist Bd, Culzean Arts Guild; MBIM 1985; *Recreations* mountaineering, sailing, music; *Clubs* Glasgow Art; *Style*— Michael Tebbutt, Esq; Culzean Castle, Maybole, Ayrshire KA19 8LE (☎ 06556 274, fax 06556 615)

TEDDER, John Anthony; s of Ronald Sidney Tedder, RAF (ka 1943), and Florence Eva, *née* Buist; *b* 15 Sept 1943; *Educ* St Dunstan's Coll London, Ravensbourne Coll of Art, Birmingham Coll of Art and Design (BA); *m* 22 Dec 1970, Vera Jean, da of Douglas Osmonde; 2 da (Germaine b 23 March 1974, Lauren b 28 Dec 1977); *Career* asst design mangr John Harper & Co Ltd 1968-70, designer Taylor Law & Co Stourbridge 1970-71, ideas progressor Frido Div Friedland Doggart Ltd Stockport; sr indust designer: Corning (UK) Ltd Sunderland 1973-78, Rank Radio Int Plymouth 1978-81; product design assoc TACP Architects Liverpool 1981-84, owner Tedder Associates (industrial designers) 1984-, assoc lectr in product design N Staffs Poly 1987-; licenciate memb SIAD 1967 (past chm various regions, former hon sec), FCSD 1976 (currently vice chm); *Recreations* photography, videography, getting away from England; *Style*— John Tedder, Esq; Tedder Associates, 37 Westbourne Rd, West Kirby, Wirral L48 4DQ (☎ 051 625 1498, fax 051 625 2548)

TEDDER, 2 Baron (UK 1946); John Michael Tedder; s of Marshal of the RAF 1 Baron Tedder, GCB, AOC-in-C M East 1941-42 & Med 1943, Dep Supreme Cmdr Allied Expeditionary Force 1943-45, Chief Air Staff 1946-49 and Chllr Cambridge Univ 1950-67 (d 1967); *b* 4 July 1926; *Educ* Dauntsey's Sch, Magdalene Coll Cambridge (ScD), Univ of Birmingham (PhD, DSc); *m* 1952, Peggy Eileen, da of Samuel George Growcott, of Birmingham; 2 s, 1 da; *Heir* s, Hon Robin John Tedder; *Career* Purdie prof of chemistry St Salvator's Coll St Andrews Univ 1969-89; memb RSC 1980-89; FRSE, FRSC; *Style*— The Rt Hon the Lord Tedder, FRSE; Little Rathmore, Kennedy Gdns, St Andrews, Fife, Scotland (☎ 0334 73546)

TEDDER, Hon Mina Una Margaret; da of 1 Baron Tedder, GCB (d 1967); *b* 1920; *Career* Womens Auxiliary Air Force 1939-47; asst librarian British Embassy Washington USA 1950-54, BBC TV 1954-57, Scottish TV Glasgow 1957-65, dist cmmr Nat Savings Alnwick Northumberland 1970-74, asst house mistress St Leonards Sch 1979-81; *Style*— The Hon Mina Tedder

TEDDER, Philip Anthony; s of Arthur Henry Tedder (d 1988), and Winifred May, *née* Marshall; *b* 3 Sept 1945; *Educ* Sutton Co GS, Univ Coll of Wales; *m* 6 July 1968, Pauline, da of William Richarson, of Manchester; 1 s (Richard b 1977); *Career* Coopers & Lybrand Deloitte (formerly Deloitte Haskins & Sells): joined 1968, Panel on take-overs and mergers 1979-81, ptnr CA's 1981-; FCA; *Recreations* tennis, swimming, walking, photography; *Clubs* MCC, RAC; *Style*— Philip Tedder, Esq; Coopers & Lybrand Deloitte, PO Box 207, 128 Queen Victoria St, London EC4P 4JX (☎ 071 583 5000, fax 071 248 3623, telex 894941)

TEDDER, Hon Robin John; s and h of 2 Baron Tedder; *b* 6 April 1955; *m* 1, 1977, Jennifer Peggy (d 1978), da of John Mangan, of Christchurch; m 2, 1980, (Rita) Aristea, da of John Frangidis, of Sydney, NSW, Australia; 2 s (Benjamin John, b 1985, Christopher Arthur b 1986), 1 da (Jacqueline Christina b 1988); *Career* stockbroker/merchant banker; md: Australian Gilt Securities, Australian Gilt Equities, Australian Gilt Futures Ltd, Dublin Financial Services Ltd; *Recreations* sailing, golf; *Clubs* Royal Sydney Yacht Squadron, Royal & Ancient Golf (St Andrews), Cromer Golf, The Australian Golf; *Style*— The Hon Robin Tedder

TEDDY, Peter Julian; s of Francis Gerald Teddy, of Rhyl, N Wales, and Beryl Dorothy Fogg; *b* 2 Nov 1944; *Educ* Rhyl GS, Univ of Wales (BSc), Univ of Oxford (MA, DPhil, BM BCh); *m* 1 June 1974 (dis 1988), Fiona Margaret, da of Richard Edward Millard, CBE, JP; 2 s (Alexander Francis b 1982, William Peter b 1986), m 2, 1989, Rosalee Margaret Elliott, 1 s (Timothy James Elliott b 1990); *Career* conslt neurological surgn: Radcliffe Infirmary Oxford, Nat Spinal Injuries Centre Stoke Mandeville Hosp 1981-; sr res fell St Peter's Coll Oxford 1971-, clinical lectr, dir of clinical studies Univ of Oxford Med Sch; *Recreations* tennis, dinghy sailing, squash; *Style*— Peter Teddy, Esq; Dept of Neurological Surgery, Radcliffe Infirmary, Oxford OX2 6HE (☎ 0865 311188)

TEE, (Brian) Nicholas; s of James Haselden Tee, of Churchdown, Glos, and May, *née* Kent; *b* 19 Oct 1950; *Educ* The Kings Sch Glos, Univ of Manchester,

Loughborough Univ; *m* 1 s (Charles Nicholas b 1984); *Career* princ Nicholas Tee CAs; FICA; *Recreations* property maintenance, redevelopment, swimming; *Style*— Nicholas Tee, Esq; Little Orchard, Lansdown Parade, Cheltenham, Glos GL50 2LH; The Old School House, Leckhampton Road, Cheltenham, Glos GL53 0AX (☎ 0242 513232, car 0836 608183)

TEED, Roy Norman; s of Thomas Westcott Teed (d 1983), and Jeannette Sutton (d 1956); *b* 18 May 1928; *Educ* Kings Coll Sch Wimbledon, RAM; *m* 30 Dec 1981, Jennifer, Ann, da of Frederick Perry, of 56 Mersea Rd, Colchester, Essex; 1 s (Paul Lennox Perry b 26 Oct 1982), 2 da (Lucy Charlotte Emily b 16 Sept 1985, Trudy Sarah Jane b 4 March 1988); *Career* Nat Serv RAF 1946-49; composer; compositions incl: Fanfares and March, Piano Trio, Serenade for 10 winds, Concertino for treble recorder and strings, Piece for a Special Occasion, A Celebration Overture, Scena for clarinet and piano, Toccata for organ, Elegy and Tarantella for violin and piano, Sextet Variations, Overture for organ, Overture, The Overcoat: an opera in 2 acts, Music Fills The Air, Music of the Seasons, Te Deum, Music for a Ballet, A Trip to the Zoo, Elegy Scherzo and Trio, The Pardoner's Tale, Five Funny Songs, Five Epitaphs; prof RAM 1966- (former freelance musician); author articles in RAM magazine 1983 and 1985; FRAM 1977; *Recreations* walking, reading, theatre, swimming, playing with my children, gardening; *Clubs* RAM; *Style*— Roy Teed, Esq; 63 Egret Crescent, Longridge Park, Colchester, Essex CO4 3FP (☎ 0206 870839); Royal Academy of Music, Marylebone Rd, London NW1 (☎ 071 935 5461, fax 071 487 3342)

TEELING SMITH, Prof George; OBE (1986); s of Herbert Teeling Smith, of Edinburgh, and Jessie Sybil, *née* Dickson (d 1983); *b* 20 March 1928; *Educ* Bryanston, Clare Coll Cambridge (BA), Heriot Watt Coll; *m* 6 Sept 1967, Diana, *née* St John Stevas; *Career* Nat Serv 1946-48; various pharmaceutical indust appts then dep md Winthrop Laboratories 1960-62, dir Office of Health Econ 1962-, assoc prof of health econ res gp Brunel Univ 1980-; memb NEDO Pharmaceutical WP 1975-77, chm Int Sci Policy Fndn 1988-; M Pharm Univ of Bradford 1977; FRPharmS 1978; *Books* How to use the NHS (1970), Health Economics, Prospects for the Future (1987), Measuring Health: A Practical Approach (1989); MRPharmS; *Recreations* gardening, collecting prints; *Style*— Prof George Teeling Smith, OBE; 65 Castelnau, London SW13 9RT (☎ 081 748 4254); Office of Health Economics, 12 Whitehall, London SW1A 2DY (☎ 071 930 9203)

TEELOCK, HE Dr Boodhun; s of Ramessur Teelock (d 1945), and Sadny Jugdharree (d 1926); *b* 20 July 1922; *Educ* Edinburgh Univ (MB ChB), Liverpool Univ (DTM & H), DPH (England); *m* 9 Jan 1956, Riziya, da of Anand Mohan Sahay, of India; 3 da (Vijayalakshmi b 29 Oct 1956, Neena b 24 March 1959, Sajni b 31 Aug 1960); *Career* sch med offr Mauritius 1952-59; princ med offr Mauritius 1960- 68; regnl advsr Public Health WHO and regnl offr for Africa at Brazzaville 1968-71; rep WHO: Tanzania 1971-74, Kenya and Seychelles 1974-79; immunisation med offr Air Mauritius 1980-89; High Cmmr for Mauritius in UK 1989-; memb BMA and Mauritius Med Assoc; *Style*— HE Dr Boodhun Teelock; Mauritius High Commission, 32-33 Elvaston Place, London SW7 5NW (☎ 071 581 0294)

TEELOCK, Lady; Vinaya Kumari; *née* Prasad; *Educ* BA; *m* Sir Leckraz Teelock, CBE (d 1982), High Cmmr for Mauritius in UK 1968-82 and Doyen of Dip Corps at his death; 1 s, 1 da; *Career* barr Middle Temple; *Style*— Lady Teelock; Flat 1, Chelsea House, Lowndes St, SW1

TEGNER, Ian Nicol; s of Sven Stuart Tegner, OBE (d 1971); *b* 11 July 1933; *Educ* Rugby; *m* 1961, Meriel Helen, da of Maurice Stanley Lush, CB, CBE, MC; 1 s, 1 da; *Career* CA (Scotland) 1957; Clarkson Gordon & Co Toronto Canada 1958-59, Barton Mayhew & Co 1959-71 (ptnr 1965), fin dir Bowater Industries plc 1971-86, dir gp fin Midland Bank plc 1987-90, chm The 100 Gp of Fin Dirs 1988-90; dir: Control Risks Group Ltd 1990-, Wiggins Teape Appleton plc 1990-; pres elect Inst of CA's of Scotland 1991-92; *Recreations* book collecting, walking, choral singing, family life, travel; *Style*— Ian Tegner, Esq; 44 Norland Square, London W11 4PZ (☎ 071 229 8604); Keepers Cottage, Kilninver, Argyll

TEIGNMOUTH, Baroness; Pamela; s of Harry Edmonds-Heath; *m* 1, George Meyer; m 2, 1979, as his 2 w, 7 & last Baron Teignmouth, DSC & bar (d 1981); *Style*— The Rt Hon the Lady Teignmouth

TEJAN-SIE, Sir Banja; GCMG (1970, CMG 1967); s of Alpha Ahmed Tejan-Sie (d 1957), and Ayesatu Tejan Sie (d 1958); *b* 7 Aug 1917; *Educ* Bo Sch, Prince of Wales Sch Sierra Leone, LSE; *m* 1945, Admire Stapleton; 5 s (1 s decd), 3 da; *Career* called to the Bar Lincoln's Inn 1951, vice pres Sierra Leone People's Pty 1953-56; speaker Sierra Leone House of Reps 1962-67, chief justice 1967-70; actg govr gen and govr gen Sierra Leone 1967-70; hon treas Int African Inst London; GCON (Nigeria) 1970, Grand Band Star of Africa (Liberia) 1969, Order of Cedar (Lebanon) 1966, Special Grand Cordon (Taiwan) 1967; *Clubs* Commonwealth; *Style*— Sir Banja Tejan-Sie, GCMG; 3 Tracey Ave, London NW2 4AT (☎ 081 452 2324)

TELFER, Capt Bryan Geoffrey (Bryn); s of Alfred Telfer, of Portland Court, Hythe, Kent, and Ivy Georgina, *née* Nanson (d 1974); *b* 10 June 1938; *Educ* John Ruskin GS Croydon; *m* 2 Jan 1960, Hazel Olive, da of Herbert Arthur Pellatt, of Willow Cres, Preston, Weymouth, Dorset; 2 s (Simon David b 9 July 1964, James Andrew b 19 Aug 1967), 1 da (Sally Jane b 18 June 1961); *Career* joined RN as meterologist in Fleet Air Arm 1956, NATO staff Malta 1960-62, serv aircraft carriers Bulwark and Centaur 1962-66, cmmnd Sub Lt 1966, flt deck offr Eagle 1966, transferred gen serv 1970, qualified princ warfare offr 1972, ops offr and above water warfare offr Glamorgan and Blake 1972-76, cdr Greenwich Staff Course 1976, cmd mgmnt servs offr to C in C Nav Home 1977, Cdr (X) Intrepid Operation Corporate 1980-82, dep intelligence staff MOD London 1982-84, Capt 1984, ACOS to Cdr Allied Naval Forces S Reg Naples 1984-87, dep dir Naval Ops and dir Shipping Trade MOD 1987-, appt to NATO Int Mil Staff Brusels HQ 1990; FBIM 1977; *Recreations* yachting, drama, golf; *Clubs* Royal Dorset Yacht; *Style*— Capt Bryn Telfer, RN; Deputy Director Naval Operations & Trade, Room 5357, Ministry of Defence, Main Building, Whitehall, London (☎ 071 218 3510)

TELFER, (Frederick) Charles Edmund; s of Edmund Telfer (d 1953); *b* 10 Nov 1931; *Educ* Millfield, Pembroke Coll Oxford; *m* 1965, Patricia Mary, da of John George Abraham, TD (d 1973); 3 s, 1 da; *Career* stockbroker 1957; ptnr: Joseph Sebag & Co 1965-, Carr Sebag & Co 1979-, ptnr Laurie Millbank & Co 1983-; memb Cncl Stock Exchange 1975-81, Chase Manhattan Securities 1986; *Recreations* sailing, shooting, skiing; *Clubs* City of London, Royal Thames Yacht, Royal London Yacht, Royal Southern Yacht; *Style*— Charles Telfer, Esq; West End House, Frensham, Surrey (025125 3549)

TELFER, Dr the Hon Mrs (Laetitia Mary); *née* Bruce; JP (Newcastle upon Tyne); da of 7 Lord Balfour of Burleigh (d 1967), and Violet Dorothy Evelyn, MBE (d 1976), yr da of late Richard Henry Done, of Salterswell, Tarporley, Cheshire; *b* 29 Dec 1920; *Educ* St Andrews Univ (MB ChB); *m* 8 July 1955, Dr Ian Metcalfe Telfer (d 1988), er s of John Telfer, FSAA, of Kingarth, Moorside, Fenham, Newcastle upon Tyne; 2 s (John Bruce b 15 June 1956, George Metcalfe b 9 Oct 1961), 1 da (Mary Daubeny b 30 March 1958); *Career* pres W Northumberland Branch NSPCC 1988; vice-pres NE Cncl on Addictions 1989; *Style*— Dr the Hon Mrs Telfer, JP; Wallbottle Hall, Newcastle upon Tyne NE15 8JD

TELFER, Dr Robert Gilmour Jamieson (Rab); CBE (1985); s of James Telfer (d 1987), of Edinburgh, and Helen Lambie, *née* Jamieson (d 1977); *b* 22 April 1928; *Educ* Bathgate Acad, Univ of Edinburgh (BSc, PhD); *m* 8 July 1953, Joan Audrey, da of George William Gunning (d 1964), of Swansea; 3 s (James Gilmour b 26 June 1957, Robin Gunning b 26 Jan 1959, John Telfer b 26 July 1961); *Career* shift chemist AEA 1953-54; ICI 1954-81 (R and D dir Petrochemical Div, dep chm 1975-76, chm 1976-81); dir: Phillips Imp Petroleum Ltd 1976-81, Manchester Business Sch 1984-88, Renold plc 1984-, Volex Group plc 1985-; chm and md Mather and Platt Ltd 1981-84, chm Euro Industrial Services Ltd 1988-89, exec chm BSI Standards 1989-; chm Advsy Cncl on Energy Conservation 1982-84, personal advsr to SOS for Energy 1984-87; memb: Advsy Cncl on R and D for Fuel and Power 1981-87, Civil Serv Coll Advsy Cncl 1985-90; sr visiting fellowship Manchester Business Sch Univ of Manchester; hon MBA Univ of Manchester; CBIM; *Recreations* poetry, gardening, walking, swimming, supporting Middlesborough FC; *Clubs* Caledonian; *Style*— Dr Rab Telfer, CBE; Downings, Upleatham, Redcar, Cleveland TS11 8AG; B51, 2 Park St, London W1A 2BS (☎ 071 629 9000, telex 266933 BSILON G)

TELFER BRUNTON, Dr (William) Andrew; JP; s of Robert Brunton (d 1973), and Sarah Hamilton, *née* Telfer (d 1961); *b* 23 Feb 1948; *Educ* Edinburgh Acad, Strathallan Sch, Univ of Edinburgh (BSc, MB ChB); *m* 8 Dec 1977, Patricia, da of Leslie Noble, of Broadstairs; 3 da (Lisa b 1981, Anne b 1984, Fiona b 1985); *Career* lectr in bacteriology Univ of Edinburgh, conslt med microbiologist, dir Truro Public Health Laboratory; memb: Assoc of Medical Microbiologists, The Br Soc for the Study of Infection, The Pathological Soc; memb Cncl Assoc of Clinical Pathologists, dep Wines and Spirits Educn Tst, memb The Grand Antiquity Soc Glasgow; Freeman Burgess of Incorporation of Gardeners Glasgow; *Recreations* gardening, wine; *Style*— Dr Andrew Telfer Brunton, JP; Public Health Laboratory, Royal Cornwall Hospital (City), Infirmary Hill, Truro, Cornwall TR1 2HZ (☎ 0872 79361)

TELFER SMOLLETT OF BONHILL, Georgina Myra Albinia; da of Sir Gifford Wheaton Grey Fox, 2 Bt (d 1959), and his 1 w, Hon Myra Newton, da of 1 Baron Eltisley, KBE; *b* 1930; *m* 1951, Patrick Telfer Smollett of Bonhill, MC, DL, *qv*; 1 s (David), 1 da (Gabrielle); *Style*— Mrs Patrick Telfer Smollett of Bonhill; Cameron, Alexandria, Dunbartonshire (☎ 0389 56226); 9 Cleveland Row, London SW1 (☎ 071 930 6319)

TELFER SMOLLETT OF BONHILL, Patrick Tobias Telfer; MC (1940), DL (Dunbartonshire 1957); s of Maj-Gen Alexander Patrick Drummond Telfer Smollett of Bonhill, CB, CBE, DSO, MC (d 1954) and late Marian Lucy, da of George Herbert Strutt, of Bridgehill, and of Kingairloch, Argyll; descendant of John Smollett, of Dunbartonshire, shipowner, who was instrumental in the destruction of the Florida, one of the ships of the Armada, off the Island of Mull 1588; also descendant of Tobias Smollett, historian and novelist, and of Sir James Smollett, signatory to the Act of Union; *b* 26 Dec 1914; *m* 1951, Georgina Myra Albina, *qv*, da of Sir Gifford Fox, 2 and last Bt, MP; 1 s, 1 da; *Heir* s, David Telfer Smollett yr of Bonhill b 1953; *Career* 2 Lt HLI 1936, served India 1936, Palestine 1938; serv: Eritrea, Egypt and Italy WWII, Mil Mission to Egypt 1942, Allied Kommandatura Berlin 1948-51, Cyprus 1955-56, Egypt 1956, Maj 1945, ret 1959; memb Royal Co of Archers (Queen's Bodyguard for Scotland) 1956; vice-cdre Loch Lomond Rowing Club, vice-pres Loch Lomond Motor Cycle Club; KJStJ; *Recreations* skiing, animal husbandry, conservation of rare animals; *Style*— Patrick Telfer Smollett of Bonhill, Esq, MC, DL; Cameron, Alexandria, Dunbartonshire (☎ 0389 56226); 9 Cleveland Row, SW1 (☎ 071 930 6319)

TELFORD, Sir Robert; CBE (1967), DL (Essex 1981); s of Robert Telford; *b* 1 Oct 1915; *Educ* Quarry Bank HS Liverpool, Queen Elizabeth GS Tamworth, Christ's Coll Cambridge (MA); *m* 1, 1941 (m dis 1950); 1 s; m 2, 1958, Elizabeth Mary, da of F W Shelley; 3 da; *Career* md: Marconi Co 1965-81 (previously md and mangr various Marconi subsids), GEC-Marconi Electronics Ltd 1968-84; dir: GEC plc 1973-84, Ericsson Radio Systems (Sweden), Canadian Marconi Co (Canada); chm: The Marconi Co Ltd 1981-84 (hon life pres 1984-), Marconi Avionics Ltd 1981-85, Prelude Technol Investmts Ltd 1984-, CTP Investmts Ltd 1987-; pres Marconi Italiana (Italy) 1983-85; advsr to Comett Prog of Euro Community 1989-; memb: Engrg Indust Trg Bd 1968-82, Electronics Econ Devpt Ctee 1980-85, cncl Univ of Essex 1980-88, cncl Industl Soc 1982-86, cncl Fellowship of Engrg 1983-86, Business and Technician Educn Cncl 1984-86, Engrg Bd SERC 1985-88, Info Technol Advsy Gp DTI 1985-88, Engrg Cncl 1986-89, Industl Res and Devpt Advsy Ctee to Euro Community 1987-; chm: Electronics Avionics Requirements Bd of DOI 1981-85, Alvey Steering Gp 1983-88, Teaching Co Mgmnt Cmmn 1984-88, Cwlth Engrs Cncl 1989-; pres: Electronic Engrg Assoc 1963-64, Instn of Prodn Engrs 1982-83; visitor to Hatfield Poly 1987-; Freeman City of London 1984; Hon DSc: Salford 1981, Cranfield Inst of Technol 1982, Bath 1984, Aston 1985; Hon DEng: Bradford 1986, Birmingham 1986; Hon DTech Anglia Inst 1989; hon: FIMech 1983, FIEE 1986; CBIM, FEng, FIProdE, FRSA; kt 1978; *Style*— Sir Robert Telford, CBE, DL; Marconi House, Chelmsford, Essex CM1 1PL (☎ 0245 275780); Rettendon House, Rettendon, Chelmsford, Essex CM3 8DW (☎ 0268 733131)

TELLING, Arthur Edward; s of Arthur Henry Telling, OBE (d 1972), and Eleanor Mary, *née* Soles (d 1955); *b* 22 April 1920; *Educ* William Ellis Sch London, Jesus Coll Oxford (MA); *m* 21 March 1959, Diana, da of William John Almond (d 1967), of Hessle, E Yorks; *Career* res asst (later asst sec) Bldg Indust Nat Cncl 1941-48; called to the Bar Inner Temple 1949, asst sec and legal advsr Nat Fedn of Property Owners 1949-52, in private practice 1953-; lectr Trent Poly 1964-82; memb: Utd Reformed Church, Rotary Club (Nottingham, Rotary fndn offr Dist 122 1974-76, chm N dist London Congregational Union 1958-60); *Books* Planning Applications Appeals and Inquiries (jtly, 1953), Planning Law and Procedure (8 edns 1963-90), Water Authorities (1974); contrib Halsbury's Laws of England (3 and 4 edns); *Recreations* reading, watching TV; *Style*— Arthur Telling, Esq; 43 Harrow Rd, W Bridgford, Nottingham NG2 7DW (☎ 0602 231889); 24 The Ropewalk, Nottingham NG1 5EF (☎ 0602 472581, fax 0602 476532)

TELLING, David Malcolm; s of Alfred Caleb Victor Telling, CBE, of Barley Farm, Branches Cross, Wrington, Avon, and Dorothy Lillie, *née* Miller (d 1974); *b* 12 Aug 1938; *Educ* Cheltenham; *m* 26 Sept 1964, (Margaret Elizabeth) Jane, da of Maj-Gen Francis James Claude Piggott, CB, CBE, DSO, *qv*; 2 da ((Jane Emma) Louise b 12 Aug 1965, (Lucy Jane) Susy b 12 Aug 1969); *Career* serv RM May-Dec 1957, cmmnd 1 Bn KOSB Dec 1957, served in Malaya and Berlin until May 1959; HAT Gp plc:1 dir 1969-86, jt md 1973-76, chief exec 1976-86, chm 1983-86; chm and md Mitie Group plc 1988-; chm: S Western Industl Cncl 1983-87, Avon Branch Game Conservancy 1987; memb Soc of Merchant Adventurers Bristol 1966; Freeman City of London 1959, Liveryman of Worshipful Co of Plaisterers; FCIOB; *Recreations* stalking, shooting, skiing, water skiing; *Style*— David Telling, Esq; 9/25 Lowndes Square, London SW1; Meeting House Farm, Long Lane, Wrington, Bristol, Avon BS18 7SP; The Estate Office, The Stable Block, Barley Wood, Wrington, Avon BS18 7SA (☎ 0934 862006, fax 0934 862239)

TELLWRIGHT, Hon Mrs (Caroline Fiona); *née* Fitzherbert; 2 da of 14 Baron Stafford (d 1986); *b* 13 Oct 1956; *Educ* Sacred Heart Convent, Woldingham; *m* 1981, Kirkland Tellwright, er s of William Tellwright (d 1986), of Market Drayton,

Shropshire; 2 da (Turia Mary b 1984, Laura Caroline b 1987); *Career* housewife; *Recreations* hunting, point-to-point, racing; *Style—* The Hon Mrs Tellwright; The Sydnall Farm, Woodseaves, Market Drayton, Shropshire

TELTSCHER, Bernard Louis; s of Felix Teltscher (d 1978), of Kingston Upon Thames, and Lillie, *née* Knoepfmacher (d 1961); *b* 18 Feb 1923; *Educ* Czech GS Breclav, UC London (BSc), Trinity Coll Cambridge (MA); *m* 1, 11 Sept 1963 (m dis), Irene Gladys Valerie, da of George Nathaniel Hotten, of Carshalton, Surrey; 1 da (Lisa decd); m 2, 10 Nov 1978 (m dis), Jill Patricia, da of Ivor Cooper, of Cornwall Gdns, London SW7; 1 s (Mark b 1980), 1 da (Natalie b 1981); *Career* wine importer; dir: Teltscher Bros Ltd 1958-, (chm 1978-), Ducal Vinery Ltd 1947-, Latymer Wine Shippers Ltd 1974-, Lutomer Bonded Warehouse Co Ltd 1981-, Lutomer Wine Co Ltd 1958-, St James's Bridge Club Ltd 1982-, Wine & Spirit Assoc of GB & NI 1985-86, Wine Devpt Bd 1983-86; Yugoslav Flag with Gold Star; *Recreations* bridge; *Clubs* St James's Bridge, Hurlingham; *Style—* Bernard Teltscher, Esq; 17 Carlyle Square, London SW3 6EX (☎ 071 351 5091); Lutomer House, West India Dock, Prestons Road, London E14 9SB (fax 071 515 3957, telex 887896 TELBROG)

TEMKIN, Prof Jennifer (Mrs Graham Zellick); da of Michael Temkin, of London, and Minnie, *née* Levy; *b* 6 June 1948; *Educ* South Hampstead HS for Girls, LSE, Univ of London (LLB, LLM); *m* 18 Sept 1975, Prof Graham John Zellick, s of Reginald H Zellick, of Windsor, Berks; 1 s (Adam b 1977), 1 da (Lara b 1980); *Career* called to the Bar Middle Temple 1971, lectr in law LSE 1971-89, visiting prof of law Univ of Toronto 1978-79, dean Sch of Law Univ of Buckingham 1989- (prof of law 1989-); memb: Ed Advsy Gp Howard Jl of Criminal Justice 1984-, Scrutiny Ctee on Draft Criminal Code Old Bailey 1985-86, editorial bd Jl of Criminal Law 1986-, Home Sec's Advsy Gp on Use of Video Recordings in Criminal Proceedings 1988-89, Ctee of Heads Univ Law Schs 1989-; FRSA 1989; *Books* Rape and the Legal Process (1987); *Style—* Prof Jennifer Temkin; Sch of Law, Univ of Buckingham, Buckingham MK18 1EG (☎ 0280 814080)

TEMPERLEY, Prof Howard Reed; s of Fred Temperley (d 1972), of Sunderland, and Eva May Temperley (d 1965); *b* 16 Nov 1932; *Educ* Newcastle Royal GS, Magdalen Coll Oxford, Yale; m, 1966, Rachel Stephanie (d 1990), da of Rowley S Hooper (d 1951), of Toronto; 1 s (Nicholas b 1971), 2 da (Alison b 1962, Rebecca b 1969); *Career* Nat Serv 2 Lt Armoured Corps 1951-53; asst lectr Univ Coll of Wales Aberystwyth 1960-61, lectr Univ of Manchester 1961-67, prof Univ of East Anglia 1981-; chm Br Assoc for American Studies 1986-89; *Books* British Antislavery 1833-1870 (1972), Lieut Colonel Joseph Gubbins's New Brunswick Journals of 1811 and 1813 (ed), Introduction to American Studies (ed jtly, 2 edn 1989); *Recreations* jogging; *Clubs* Norfolk; *Style—* Prof Howard Temperley; Arlington House, Arlington Lane, Norwich NR2 2DB (☎ 0603 628497); School of English and American Studies, University of East Anglia, Norwich NR4 7TJ (☎ 0603 56161, fax 0603 58553, telex 976197)

TEMPERLEY, Tom Groome; OBE (1970); s of Thomas Temperley (d 1960), of Bolton, and Mabel Alberta (d 1971); *b* 22 Nov 1930; *Educ* Bolton Co GS, Bolton Coll of Technol, Etude Universitaires Luxemburg; *m* 11 Jan 1961, Edith, da of Edmund Kay, of Bolton; 1 s (Tom Gaskell b 10 Dec 1961), 1 da (Elizabeth Katherine b 1 June 1967); *Career* chem Br Electricity Authy 1948-54, chief chem and tech advsr Kuwait Miny of Electricity and Water 1954-70, princ Temperley & Assoc 1957-, pres Conam Servs Inc 1970-79, advsr to and authority on ME; past pres Euro Desalination Assoc, fndr bd memb Int Desalination Assoc, patron fndr memb and former chm Continental Sch Jeddah, fndr Temperley Awards (encouraging handicapped to improve themselves physically); life memb: Nat Amateur Body-Builders Assoc, Assoc of Strength Athletes; fndr memb Br Business Gp Jeddah Saudi Arabia, elected Desalination Engr of Year by Int Desalination & Environmental Assoc in Tokyo 1978; life patron Continental Sch Jeddah; life memb: AWWA, ACE, AACE; CEng, Eur Ing, FIE, FINucE, FI Corr S&T, FID, MAChem E, FRSH, FIPet; *Recreations* weight trg, swimming; *Clubs* RAC; *Style—* Dr Tom Temperley, OBE; Loveley Hall, Salesbury, Blackburn, Lancashire BB1 9EQ (☎ 0254 48630); 213 Darwen Rd, Bromley Cross, Bolton, Lancashire; PO Box 5114, Ruwis Muscat, Sultanate of Oman; PO Box 3240, Jeddah, Saudi Arabia

TEMPEST, Henry Roger; DL (N Yorks 1981); Lord of the Manors of Broughton, Burnsall and Thorpe; yr but only surviving s of Brig-Gen Roger Tempest, CMG, DSO, JP, DL; inherited Broughton Hall Estate on death of elder bro in 1970; *b* 2 April 1924; *Educ* Oratory Sch, Ch Ch Oxford; *m* 1957, Janet Evelyn Mary, da of Harold Longton, of Johannesburg; 2 s (Roger Henry b 1963, Piers b 1973), 3 da (Bridget b 1957, Anne b 1959, Mary b 1961); *Career* Scots Gds 1943-47, serv NW Europe (wounded 1945), apptd to Q Staff HQ Gds Div 1945, Staff Capt 1946; Britannia Rubber Co Ltd 1947-51; emigrated to Lusaka (then in Northern Rhodesia) 1952, incorporated cost accountant (AACWA) S Africa 1959; returned to UK 1961, fin offr Univ of Oxford Dept of Nuclear Physics 1962-72; memb: N Yorks Co Cncl 1973-85, Skipton Rural Dist Cncl 1973-74, Br Computer Soc 1973, Exec Ctee CLA Yorks 1973-87, Cncl Order of St John N Yorks 1977-87, pres Skipton Branch Royal Br Legion 1974; govr: Craven Coll of Further Educn 1974-85, Skipton Girls' HS 1976-85; ACIS 1958, FCIS 1971; Knight of Malta; *Clubs* Lansdowne, Pratt's; *Style—* Henry Tempest Esq, DL; Broughton Hall, Skipton, N Yorks BD23 3AE (☎ 0756 792267, fax : 0756 792362)

TEMPEST, (Albert) John; s of Allan Tempest (d 1969), and Ruth, *née* Kettlewell (d 1974); *b* 7 Oct 1938; *Educ* Giggleswick Sch, Leeds Coll of Art (DipArch, DipTP); *m* 29 Aug 1969, Susan Dorothea, da of Arthur Rooke (d 1983); 1 s (Matthew b 20 Jan 1973), 1 da (Caroline b 31 Aug 1975); *Career* chartered architect and town planner; formerly with BR property bd and GLC; joined John Brunton & ptnrs 1971, dir John Brunton plc 1976-; pres Br Architectural Students Assoc 1961-62, cncl memb TCPA 1973-76, vice pres RIBA 1985-87 (cncl memb 1982-85), chm architectural competitions RIBA 1989-; memb RIBA, MRTPI; *Recreations* arts, literature, architectural history, design, photography; *Style—* John Tempest, Esq; John Brunton plc, Arndale House, Headingley, Leeds, West Yorkshire LS6 2UU (☎ 0532 787201, fax 0532 751925)

TEMPEST-MOGG, Dr Brenden Dayne; JP (New S Wales 1967); s of Alan Reginald Mogg, JP (NSW), Capt RAAF, and Ethyl Mavis Tempest-Hay; *b* 10 April 1945; *Educ* The Scots Coll Sydney, Univ of NSW (BA), Essex Univ (MA), Hertford Coll Oxford (MLitt), George Washington Univ Washington DC (EdD); *m* 27 May 1984 (m dis 1990), Galina, da of Ivan Mikhailovich Kobzev, of Frunze, USSR; 1 da (Gloria Dela Hay b 27 Feb 1987); *Career* pres Warnborough Coll (The American Coll in Oxford) 1973-; visiting lectr in Aust, India and USA 1976-; guest ed Sociological Perspectives 1982-; conslt on higher educn admin 1988-; *Recreations* sailing, polo, travel, tennis; *Clubs* The Victoria League for Cwlth Friendship, United Oxford and Cambridge, Cowdray Park Polo, Cirencester Park Polo; *Style—* Dr Brenden Tempest-Mogg, JP; Warnborough College (The American College in Oxford), Boar's Hill, Oxford OX1 5ED (☎ 0865 730901, fax 0865 327796, telex 837574)

TEMPLE, Anthony Dominic Afamado; QC; s of Sir Rawden John Afamado Temple, CBE, QC, *qv*, and Margaret, *née* Gunson (d 1980); *b* 21 Sept 1945; *Educ* Haileybury and ISC, Worcester Coll Oxford (MA); *m* 28 May 1983, Susan Elizabeth, s of Ernst Bodansky (d 1990), of Millmead, Broadbridge Heath, Sussex; 2 da (Jessica Elizabeth b 11 Dec 1985, Alexandra Louise b 21 Aug 1988); *Career* called to the Bar Inner Temple 1968; Crown Law Off W Aust 1968-69; UK practice 1970; asst recorder 1982, rec 1989; *Recreations* modern pentathlon, travel; *Style—* Anthony Temple, Esq, QC; 4 Pump Court, London EC4 (☎ 071 353 2656, fax 071 583 2036)

TEMPLE, Lt-Col Guy; MC (1953); s of Maj-Gen B Temple, CB, CMG, MC (d 1973), and Dulcibella, *née* Radcliffe (d 1982); *b* 16 Sept 1928; *Educ* Radley, RMA Sandhurst; *m* 7 Jan 1956, Caroline, da of Capt H F Bone, DSO, DSC, RN (d 1982); 1 s (Piers b 1963), 3 da (Deborah (Mrs Rudd) b 1956, Bridget (Mrs Ter Haar) b 1958, Miranda (Mrs Leenen) b 1961); *Career* cmmnd Gloucestershire Regt 1948, served Jamaica 1949 and Korea (Battle of Imjin) 1950-53, dist mil intelligence offr Kenya 1955-57, Cyprus 1958-60, HQ Libya 1963-66, HQ Army Strategic Cmd 1968-70, Univ of Glasgow 1970-72, Dubai Def Force 1972-79, dir of logistics HQ Central Cmd Dubai 1979-; fndr Dubai Offshore SC; Dubai Medal 1976, UAE Medal 1980; *Recreations* sailing, tennis, skiing; *Style—* Lt-Col Guy Temple, MC; HQ Central Mil Command, PO Box 854, Dubai, United Arab Emirates, Arabian Gulf (☎ 010 971 494763, fax 010 971 440237)

TEMPLE, John Graham; s of Joseph Henry Temple, and Norah, *née* Selby (d 1987); *b* 14 March 1942; *Educ* William Hulme's GS Manchester, Univ of Liverpool (MB ChB, ChM); *m* 11 April 1966, (Margaret) Jillian Leighton, da of Robert Leighton Hartley (d 1966), of Wigan; 2 s (Robert b 27 Oct 1967, Christopher b 5 July 1972), 1 da (Caroline b 29 Dec 1969); *Career* conslt surgn Queen Elizabeth Hosp Birmingham 1979-; dep postgrad dean Univ of Birmingham 1987- (hon sr clinical lectr 1979-); regnl advsr in surgery RCS 1990-; memb: BMA 1965, Assoc Surgns GB 1974; FRCS Ed, FRCS; *Recreations* skiing, sailing; *Style—* John Temple, Esq; Wharncliffe, 24 Westfield Rd, Edgbaston, Birmingham B15 3QG (☎ 021 454 2445); Queen Elizabeth Hospital, Edgbaston, Birmingham B15 2TH (☎ 021 472 1311)

TEMPLE, Sir John Meredith; JP (Cheshire 1949), DL (1975); s of Tom Temple (d 1955); *b* 9 June 1910; *Educ* Charterhouse, Clare Coll Cambridge; *m* 1942, Nancy Violet, da of Brig-Gen Robert Hare, CMG, DSO, DL; 1 s, 1 da; *Career* farmer, landowner; memb Lloyd's 1938; MP (C) Chester 1956-74, special rep from House of Commons at UN XXVI Gen Assembly 1971; High Sheriff Cheshire 1980-81; kt 1982; *Recreations* travel; *Clubs* Carlton, Army and Navy, Racquet (Liverpool); *Style—* Sir John Temple, JP, DL; Picton Gorse, Chester (☎ 0244 300239)

TEMPLE, Prof John Tempest; s of Oscar Vincent Athelstan Temple (d 1960), of Wealdstone, and Mary Ethel Tempest, *née* Butler (d 1948); *b* 29 July 1927; *Educ* Harrow County Sch, St Catharine's Coll Cambridge (MA,PhD, ScD); *m* 15 July 1964, Dorothy Mary, da of Harold Thompson (d 1956) of Didsbury; 1 s (Richard John b 21 Sept 1965), 1 da (Jane Sarah (twin b 21 Sept 1965)); *Career* asst lectr UCL 1950-54, asst lectr Bedford Coll London 1956, prof of geology Birkbeck Coll London 1984- (lectr 1956-71, reader in palaeontology 1971-84); fell Geological Soc London 1951; memb: Palaeontological Assoc, Palaeontological Soc; *Books* Early Llandovery Brachiopods of Wales (1987); *Recreations* reading, walking; *Style—* Prof John Temple; 105 Chapel St, Billericay, Essex CM12 9LR (☎ 0277 656565); Birkbeck College, Department of Geology, Malet St, London WC1E 7HX (☎ 071 580 6622)

TEMPLE, Kenneth James Noel; s of Richard James Temple; *b* 10 Dec 1919; *Educ* Godalming Surrey; *m* 1943, Kathleen Mary; 1 child; *Career* RAF 1940-45, Flt Engr; sales rep 1951-76, dir Drake & Son Ltd 1976-, md 1980- (Weymouth, Torquay, Exeter, Yeovil); *Books* Travel; *Style—* Kenneth Temple, Esq; 42 Brunel Rd, Elberry Cove, Paignton, Devon TQ4 6HW

TEMPLE, Marie, Lady; Marie Wanda; da of late F C Henderson, of Bombay, India; *m* 1939, as his 2 w, Sir Richard Durand Temple, 3 Bt, DSO (d 1962); *Style—* Marie, Lady Temple

TEMPLE, Nina Claire; da of Landon Royce Temple, and Barbara Joan Temple; *b* 21 April 1956; *Educ* Imperial Coll London (BSc); *m* Partner John Davies, s of Stanley Davies; 1 s (Oliver b 1988), 1 da (Rebecca 1986); *Career* full time worker Communist Party, nat sec Communist Party GB 1990-; ARSM; *Recreations* rambling, swimming, gardening, movies; *Style—* Ms Nina Temple; 16 St John St, London EC1 (☎ 071 251 4406, fax 071 250 3654)

TEMPLE, Ralph; s of Harry Temple (ka 1941), and Julia, *née* Glassman; *b* 15 Nov 1933; *Educ* Hackney Downs GS; *m* 22 May 1955, Patricia Yvonne, da of Samuel Gould (d 1975), of London; 2 s (Graham Robin b 23 April 1958, Howard Jeremy b 28 March 1960); *Career* managing clerk Wilson Wright and Co CA's 1955-61; Tesco plc: sr exec 1961-73, gp fin dir 1973-83, jt gp md 1983-85; md Temple Conslts (fin conslts) 1986-; Freeman City Of London; FCA 1956; *Recreations* travel, bridge, keep fit; *Style—* Ralph Temple, Esq; 2 Culverlands Close, Stanmore, Middx, HA7 3AG

TEMPLE, Sir Rawden John Afamado; CBE (1964), QC (1951); *b* 1908; *Educ* King Edward's Sch Birmingham, Queen's Coll Oxford (MA, BCL); *m* 1936, Margaret (d 1980), da of Sir James Gunson, CMG, CBE; 2 s; *Career* barr 1931, master of Bench Inner Temple 1960 (treas 1983); chief social security cmmr 1975-81, child benefit referee 1976-; vice chm Gen Cncl of the Bar 1960-64, memb Industl Injuries Advsy Cncl; kt 1980; *Recreations* fishing; *Style—* Sir Rawden Temple, CBE, QC; 3 North King's Bench Walk, Temple, EC4 (☎ 071 353 6420)

TEMPLE, Richard; s and h of Sir Richard Antony Purbeck Temple, 4 Bt, MC; *b* 17 Aug 1937; *m* 1964, Emma Rose, da of late Maj-Gen Sir Robert Edward Laycock, KCMG, CB, DSO; 3 da; *Style—* Richard Temple, Esq; The Temple Gallery, 6 Clarendon Cross, London W11 4AP

TEMPLE, Sir Richard Anthony Purbeck; 4 Bt (UK 1876), MC (1941); s of Sir Richard Durand Temple, 3 Bt, DSO (d 1962); *b* 19 Jan 1913; *Educ* Stowe, Trinity Hall Cambridge; *m* 1, 1936 (m dis 1946), Lucy Geils, da of late Alain Joly de Lotbiniere, of Montreal; 2 s; m 2, 1950, Jean, da of late James T Finnie, and widow of Oliver P Croom-Johnson; 1 da; *Heir* s, Richard Temple; *Career* serv WWII (wounded), former Maj KRRC; *Clubs* Army and Navy; *Style—* Sir Richard Temple, Bt, MC; c/o The National Westminster Bank Ltd, 94 Kensington High St, London W8

TEMPLE, His Hon Judge Sir (Ernest) Sanderson; MBE (1946), QC (1969); s of Ernest Temple (d 1957); *b* 23 May 1921; *Educ* Kendal Sch, Queen's Coll Oxford; *m* 1946, June Debonnaire, *née* Saunders; 1 s, 2 da; *Career* served Army, India and Burma Temp Lt-Col (despatches); called to the Bar Gray's Inn 1943; chm Westmorland QS 1968-71 (dep chm 1967-68), former asst rec Salford and Blackburn, rec Crown Court 1971-77, hon rec of Kendal 1972, circuit judge and rec of Liverpool 1977-, hon rec Lancaster 1987; former memb Bar Cncl, dep chm Agric Land Tbnl, jt master Vale of Lune Harriers 1963-85, vice chm Br Harriers Racing Club; pres: Royal Lancs Agric Soc 1991, NW Dining Club; hon fell Clerks of Works Soc; *Recreations* farming and horses; *Clubs* Racquet Liverpool, kt 1988; *Style—* His Hon Judge Sir Sanderson Temple, MBE, QC; Yealand Hall, Yealand Redmayne, nr Carnforth LA5 9TD (☎ 0524 781200)

TEMPLE-MORRIS, Peter; MP (C) Leominster 1974-; s of His Honour Sir Owen Temple-Morris (d 1985), and Vera, *née* Thompson (d 1986); *b* 12 Feb 1938; *Educ* Malvern, St Catharine's Coll Cambridge; *m* 1964, Taheré, er da of H E Senator Khozeimé Alam, of Teheran; 2 s, 2 da; *Career* called to the Bar Inner Temple 1962, Hampstead Cons Political Centre 1971-73, second prosecuting counsel Inland Revenue SE Circuit 1971-74, PPS to Sec of State for Tport 1979; chm: Br Iranian Parly Gp, Br Lebanese and Br Netherlands Parly Gps, Br Gp Inter-Parly Union 1982-85 (exec 1976-); vice chm: Cons Parly Foreign Affrs Ctee, Cons Parly N Ireland Ctee, UK-

USSR and UK-Argentine Parly Gps, All Pty Southern Africa Gp; nat treas UN Assoc Cncl, memb Cncl GB-USSR Assoc, memb Commons Select Ctee on Foreign Affrs 1987-90, first Br co-chm Br-Irish Inter-Parly Body; *Recreations* shooting, wine, food, family; *Style*— Peter Temple-Morris, Esq, MP; House of Commons, London SW1A 0AA (☎ 071 219 4181)

TEMPLE OF STOWE, 8 Earl (UK 1822); (Walter) Grenville Algernon Temple-Gore-Langton; o s of Cdr Hon Evelyn Arthur Grenville Temple-Gore-Langton, DSO, RN (d 1972; yst s of 4 Earl), and Irene, *née* Gartside-Spaight (d 1967); suc his cousin 7 Earl Temple of Stowe 1988; *b* 2 Oct 1924; *Educ* Nautical Coll Pangbourne; *m* 1, 24 July 1954, Zillah Ray (d 1966), da of James Boxall, of Fir Grove, Tillington, Petworth, Sussex; 2 s (James Grenville, Lord Langton b 1955, Hon Robert Chandos b 1957), 1 da (Lady Anna Clare b 1960); m 2, 1 June 1968, (Margaret) Elizabeth Graham, o da of Col Henry William Scarth of Breckness, of Skaill House, Orkney; *Heir* s, Lord Langton, *qv*; *Style*— The Rt Hon the Earl Temple of Stowe; Garth, Outertown, Stromness, Orkney; The Cottage, Easton, Winchester, Hants

TEMPLE-RICHARDS, Susan Mary; da of Capt Neville Roland Joseph Bradshaw (d 1975), of Withypool, Lewes, Sussex, and Dorothy Mary Arnold, *née* Saunders; *b* 8 June 1932; *Educ* Cheltenham Ladies Coll, Badminton Sch Bristol, Westfield Coll London (BA); *m* 6 June 1964, Peter Henry John Temple-Richards (d 1975), s of Brig Harold Beecham Temple-Richards (d 1969), of Hindringham Hall, Fakenham, Norfolk; *Career* MOD 1956-58 and 1974-86, PA to Lord Hunt (formerly Sir John Hunt) 1960-62, self employed charitable organiser 1966-74; fundraiser Duke of Edinburgh's Tstee Office 1962-66, tst memb Arts Educnl Schs 1976, chm Newbury Duke of Edinburgh's Award Ctee 1977-80, memb Cncl Br Epilepsy Assoc 1982-89; sec Br Soviet Pamirs Expdn 1962; Freeman City of London 1976, memb Ct of Assets Cripplegate Ward 1989; FRGS 1963; *Recreations* gardening, travelling, opera; *Clubs* Lansdowne; *Style*— Mrs Susan Temple-Richards; 13 Culmstock Rd, London SW11 6LZ (☎ 071 228 9815)

TEMPLE-GORE-LANGTON, Hon Robert Chandos; yr s of 8 Earl Temple of Stowe, *qv*; *b* 22 Nov 1957; *Educ* Eton; *m* 1985, Susan Penelope, er da of David Cavender, of The Manor House, Dowlish Wake, Ilminster, Somerset; 1 s (Louis Grenville b 19 Dec 1990), 1 da (Georgia Ray b 15 April 1989); *Career* journalist; *Style*— The Hon Robert Temple-Gore-Langton; 52 Archbishop's Place, London SW2

TEMPLEMAN, Hon Michael Richard; yr s of Baron Templeman, MBE, PC (Life Peer); *b* 1951; *m* 1974, Lesley Frances, da of Henry Davis; issue; *Style*— The Hon Michael Templeman

TEMPLEMAN, The Rev the Hon Peter Morton; er s of Baron Templeman, MBE, PC (Life Peer); *b* 1949; *Educ* Ch Ch Oxford (BA 1971, MA 1975, BTh 1975), Wycliffe Hall Oxford; *m* 1973, Ann Joyce, da of Peter Williams; 3 children; *Career* deacon 1976, priest 1977; Chaplain St John's Coll Cambridge 1979-84; priest-in-charge: St Paul Finchley 1984-85, St Luke Finchley 1984- 85; Incumbent St Paul and St Luke Finchley 1985-; *Style*— The Rev the Hon Peter Templeman; St Paul's Vicarage, 50 Long Lane, London N3 2PU (☎ 081 346 8729)

TEMPLEMAN, Baron (Life Peer 1982), of White Lackington, Co Somerset; Sydney William Templeman; MBE (1946), PC (1978); s of Herbert William Templeman; *b* 3 March 1920; *Educ* Southall GS, St John's Coll Cambridge; *m* 1946, Margaret Joan (d 1988), da of Morton Rowles; 2 s (Rev Hon Peter Morton b 1949, Hon Michael Richard b 1951); *Career* called to the Bar 1947, QC 1964, memb Middle Temple & Lincoln's Inn, former memb Bar Cncl, bencher Middle Temple; tres 1987; Lord Justice of Appeal 1978-82, Lord of Appeal in Ordinary 1982-, High Ct judge (Chancery) 1972-78, attorney-gen Duchy Lancaster 1970-72, pres Bar Assoc for Commerce Fin & Indust 1982-86; hon fell St John's Coll Cambridge 1982; Hon DLitt Reading 1980, Hon LLD Birmingham 1986, Hon LLD CNAA Huddersfield Poly 1990, visitor Univ of Exeter 1990-; hon memb Canadian & American Bar Assocs; former pres Senate of Inns of Ct & Bar; kt 1972; *Style*— The Rt Hon Lord Templeman, MBE, PC; Manor Heath, Knowl Hill, Woking, Surrey (☎ 0483 761930)

TEMPLER, Maj-Gen James Robert; CB (1989), OBE (1978, MBE 1973); s of Brig Cecil Robert Templer, DSO (d 1986), and Angela Mary, *née* Henderson; *b* 8 Jan 1936; *Educ* Charterhouse, RMA Sandhurst; *m* 1, 1963 (m dis 1979); 2 s (William b 1964, Tristram b 1969), 1 da (Sophie b 1966); m 2, 18 July 1981, Sarah Ann (Sally), da of Capt W K Rogers, DSC, RM, of Nether Wallop; *Career* 2 Lt 41 and 4 Regt BAOR 1956-59, Lt Kings Troop RHA 1960-63, Capt 6 Regt Borneo 1964-66, Staff Coll 1967, Maj GSO2 3 Div UK 1968-69, BC 5 and 3 Regt NI 1970-72, GSO2 Sch of Artillery 1973, Lt-Col instr Staff Coll 1974-75, CO 42 Regt 1976, CO 5 Regt 1977, GSO1 MOD 1978, Col (later Brig) CRA 2 Armd Div 1979-81, Study Artillery in 90's 1982, RCDS 1983, ACOS Trg HQ UKLF 1984-86, Maj-Gen ACDS MOD 1986-89, ret 1990; Br Nat Cross Country Ski Champion 1958; riding, winner of: Euro Individual Championship 3 day event 1962, RA Gold Cup Sandown 1962 and 1963, Burghley 1962, Munich 1963, Badminton 1964; memb Br Olympic 3 day event team Tokyo; FBIM 1988; *Recreations* riding, sailing, skiing, gardening, shooting, fishing; *Style*— Maj-Gen James Templer, CB, OBE; c/o Lloyds Bank Ltd, Crediton, Devon

TEMPLETON, Prof (Alexander) Allan; s of Richard Templeton (d 1968), of Aberdeen, and Minnie, *née* Whitfield; *b* 28 June 1946; *Educ* Aberdeen GS, Univ of Aberdeen (MB ChB, MD); *m* 17 Dec 1980, Gillian Constance, da of Geoffrey William John Penney, of Eastbourne; 3 s (Richard b 1981, Robert b 1983, Peter b 1987), 1 da (Katherine b 1985); *Career* lectr and sr lectr Univ of Edinburgh 1976-85; regius prof of obstetrics and gynaecology Aberdeen Univ 1985-; author of various pubns on Human Infertility and Gynacological Endocrinology; MRCOG 1974, FRCOG 1987; *Books* The Early Days of Pregnancy (1987), Reproduction and the Law (1990); *Recreations* mountaineering; *Clubs* Royal Northern and Univ; *Style*— Prof Allan Templeton; Knapperna House, Udney, Aberdeenshire (☎ 06513 2481); Dept of Obstetrics and Gynaecology, Univ of Aberdeen, Foresterhill, Aberdeen (☎ 0224 681818)

TEMPLETON, (William) Berry; s of Douglas Joseph Templeton (d 1948), and Elizabeth Jane, *née* Caton (d 1964); *b* 13 Sept 1925; *Educ* Birkenhead Sch, Univ of Liverpool; *m* 1, 5 Oct 1946 (m dis 1961), Sheila Joan, da of the Arthur Leuty; m 2, 3 April 1962, Adele Monica, da of late Louis Arthur Westley; *Career* chm W Berry Templeton Ltd 1963-, vice chm Gateway Building Soc 1985-88; dir: Woolwich Equitable Building Soc 1988-, Woolwich Homes 1988-, Woolwich Assured Homes (1987) Ltd 1989-; KStJ; Freeman City of London, memb Guild of Freemen; memb AMInstBE, MCIOB, FFB; *Recreations* horse racing, polo, music, ballet; *Clubs* Oriental, Guards' Polo; *Style*— Berry Templeton, Esq; 39 York Terrace East, Regent's Park, London NW1 4PT (☎ 071 486 2209)

TEMPLETON, Sir John; s of late Harvey Maxwell Templeton, and late Vella, *née* Handly; *b* 29 Nov 1912; *Educ* Yale (BA), Balliol Coll Oxford (Rhodes scholar, MA); *m* 1, 17 April 1937, Judith Dudley Folk (d 1951); 2 s (John Marks b 1939, Christopher Winston b 1947), 1 da (Anne Dudley (Mrs Zimmerman) b 1941); m 2, 31 Dec 1958, Irene Reynolds; *Career* vice pres National Geographical Co 1937-40; pres: Templeton Dobbrow and Vance Inc 1940-60, Templeton Growth Fund Ltd 1954-85, Templeton Investment Counsel Ltd Edinburgh 1976-, Templeton World Fund Inc 1978-87; chartered fin analyst 1965-, chm Templeton Galbraith and Hansberger Ltd 1986-; sec Templeton Fndn 1960-; fndr: Templeton Prizes for Progress in Religion 1972, Templeton UK Project Tst 1984; pres Bd of Tstees Princeton Theol Seminary 1967-73 and 1976-85, memb Cncl Templeton Coll (formerly Oxford Centre for Mgmnt Studies) 1983-; Hon LLD: Beaver Coll 1968, Marquette Univ 1980, Jamestown Coll 1983, Maryville Coll 1984; Hon DLitt Wilson Coll 1974, Hon DD Buena Vista Coll 1979, Hon DCL Univ of the South 1984, Hon DLitt Manhattan Coll 1990; memb Soc of Security Analysts; kt 1987; *Books* The Humble Approach (1981), The Templeton Touch (jtly, 1985), The Templeton Plan (1987), Global Investing (1988), The God Who Would be Known (1989), Riches for the Mind and Spirit (1990); *Clubs* Athenaeum, Lansdowne, Royal Over-seas League, United Oxford and Cambridge Univ, England; *Style*— Sir John Templeton; Templeton Galbraith & Hansberger Ltd, Lyford Cay, PO Box N-7776, Nassau, Bahamas (☎ 809 362 4600, fax 809 362 4880)

TEMPLETON, Richard; s of Capt John Templeton (d 1953), of Maelsllech Farm, Radyr, Cardiff, and Janet, *née* Morgan; *b* 11 April 1945; *Educ* Clifton, Univ of Reading (BA), Univ of Bradford (MSc); *m* Belinda Susan, da of Tim Timlin, of Harewood House, Scotland End, Hook Norton, Oxon; *Career* trainee analyst Philips & Drew stockbrokers 1969-71, dir Robert Fleming Ltd 1980- (joined 1971); Freeman Town of Llantrisant; ASIA 1972; *Recreations* beagling, reading; *Clubs* Turf, MCC; *Style*— Richard Templeton, Esq; 25 Copthall Ave, London, EC2R 7DR (☎ 071 638 5858, 071 638 9100)

TENBY, 3 Viscount (UK 1957) William Lloyd-George; JP (Hants); s of 1 Viscount Tenby, TD, PC (d 1967), s of 1 Earl Lloyd George; suc bro, 2 Viscount 1983; *b* 7 Nov 1927; *Educ* Eastbourne Coll, St Catharine's Coll Cambridge (BA); *m* 1955, Ursula, da of late Lt-Col Henry Edward Medlicott, DSO; 1 s (Timothy b 1962), 2 da (Hon Sara Gwenfron b 1957, Clare Mair b 1961); *Heir* s, Timothy Henry Gwilym *qv*; *Career* Capt RWF (TA); chm St James Public Relations, dir Williams Lea & Co; *Style*— The Rt Hon the Viscount Tenby, JP; Triggs, Crondall, nr Farnham, Surrey GU10 5RU (☎ 0252 850592)

TENCH, David Edward; OBE (1987); s of Henry George Tench (d 1971), and Emma Rose, *née* Orsborn (d 1980); *b* 14 June 1929; *Educ* Merchant Taylors'; *m* 1, 17 Aug 1957, Judith April Seaton Gurney (d 1986); 2 s (Matthew David Gurney b 1960, Daniel John Gurney b 1966), 1 da (Emma Rose Caroline (Mrs Reid) b 1962); m 2, 2 April 1988, Elizabeth Ann Irvine Macdonald; *Career* slr 1952; in private practice 1954-58, slr Inland Revenue 1958-69, head Legal Dept Consumers' Assoc (publishers of Which?) 1988- (legal advsr 1969-); broadcaster on consumer affairs 1964-; chm Domestic Coal Consumers' Cncl, energy cmmr 1977-79; *Books* The Law for Consumers (1962), The Legal Side of Buying a House (1965), Wills and Probate (1968), Towards a Middle System of Law (1981); *Recreations* gardening, music; *Style*— David Tench, Esq, OBE; 2 Marylebone Rd, London NW1 4DS (☎ 071 486 5544)

TENCH, William Henry; CBE (1980); s of Henry George Tench (d 1970), and Emma Rose, *née* Orsborn (d 1980); *b* 2 Aug 1921; *Educ* Portsmouth GS; *m* 4 Nov 1944, Margaret, da of Harry Edwin Ireland (d 1966); 1 da (Ann Margaret (Mrs Kingston) b 1950); *Career* RN 1939-46, pilot 1940-, released Lt (A) RNVR 1946; airline pilot 1947-55, inspr of accidents Miny of Tport 1955-73, chief inspr of accidents Dept of Trade 1974-81, ret 1981; conslt on aircraft accident investigation MOD 1986, advsr on air safety to Cmmr for Tport EEC; FRAeS; *Books* Safety is no Accident (1985); *Recreations* sailing, music; *Style*— William Tench, Esq, CBE; Seaways, Restronguet Point, Feock, Cornwall TR3 6RB (☎ 0872 865 434)

TENISON; *see*: King-Tenison

TENNANT, Anthony John; s of Maj John Tennant, TD (d 1967), and Hon Antonia Mary Roby Benson (later Viscountess Radcliffe, d 1982), da of 1 Baron Charnwood; *b* 5 Nov 1930; *Educ* Eton, Trinity Coll Cambridge (BA); *m* 1954, Rosemary Violet, da of Col Henry Charles Minshull, of Stockdale (d 1982); 2 s (Christopher, Patrick); *Career* cmmnd Scots Guards, served in Malaya; account exec Ogilvy & Mather 1953; dir: Mather & Crowther 1960-66, Tennant & Sturge 1966-70, Watney Mann & Truman 1970-76; dep md International Distillers & Vintners 1976; md: International Distillers & Vintners Ltd 1977-83, Bd of Grand Metropolitan plc 1977-87; gp md Grand Metropolitan plc 1983-87, chm International Distillers & Vintners Ltd 1983-87; dir: Guardian Royal Exchange plc 1989-, Guardian Royal Exchange Assurance plc 1989-, BNP UK Holdings Ltd 1991-; chm Guiness plc 1990- (gp chief exec 1987); memb Cncl Food From Britain 1983-86; *Clubs* Boodle's; *Style*— Anthony Tennant Esq; Guinness plc, 39 Portman Square, London W1H 9HB (☎ 071 486 0288, telex 23368)

TENNANT, Hon Charles Edward Pevensey; s and h of 3 Baron Glenconner; *b* 15 Feb 1957; *Style*— The Hon Charles Tennant; 50 Victoria Rd, London W8

TENNANT, Lady Emma; *née* Cavendish; da of 11 Duke of Devonshire, MC, PC; *b* 1943; *m* 1963, Hon Tobias William Tennant (s by 2 m of late 2 Baron Glenconner); 1 s, 2 da; *Style*— The Lady Emma Tennant; Shaws, Newcastleton, Roxburghshire

TENNANT, Hon Mrs Emma Christina; *née* Tennant; da of late 2 Baron Glenconner by his 2 w; *b* 20 Oct 1937; *Educ* St Paul's Girls Sch; *m* 1, 1957 (m dis 1962), Sebastian, s of Henry Yorke and Hon Mrs (Adelaide) Yorke, *qv*, da of 2 Baron Biddulph; m 2, 1963 (m dis), Christopher Booker, journalist and author, *qv*; m 3, 1968 (m dis 1973), Alexander, s of Claud Cockburn, the journalist, *qv*, and Patricia, da of John Arbuthnot, MVO, ggs of Sir William Arbuthnot, 1 Bt; *Career* novelist (as Emma Tennant); author of 8 novels, incl The Bad Sister, Wild Nights; latest work: The House of Hospitalities (1983), Sisters' Strangers (1989), Frankenstein's Baby; founder ed literary newspaper Bananas; FRSL; *Recreations* exploring, walking in Dorset; *Style*— The Hon Mrs Emma Tennant; c/o A D Peters Ltd

TENNANT, Lady Harriot; *née* Pleydell-Bouverie; da of 7 Earl of Radnor, KG, KCVO, JP, DL (d 1968), by his 1 w; *b* 18 Dec 1935; *m* 11 Dec 1965, Mark Iain Tennant of Balfluig, *qv*; 1 s (Lysander Philip Roby b 1968), 1 da (Sophia Roby b 1967); *Style*— Lady Harriot Tennant; Balfluig Castle, Alford, Aberdeenshire AB3 8EJ

TENNANT, Sir Iain Mark; KT (1986), JP (Morayshire 1961); s of Lt-Col John Edward Tennant, DSO, MC (ka 1942; gs of Sir Charles Tennant, 1 Bt, and n of 1 Baron Glenconner), of Innes House, Elgin, and his 1 w, Georgina Helen, da of Sir George Kirkpatrick, KCB, KCSI; *b* 11 March 1919; *Educ* Eton, Magdalene Coll Cambridge; *m* 11 July 1946, Lady Margaret Helen Isla Marion, *née* Ogilvy (*see* Lady Margaret Tennant); 2 s (Mark b 1947, Christopher b 1950), 1 da (Emma (Mrs Cheape) b 1954); *Career* Capt Scots Gds 1941, served N Africa 1940-42; memb Royal Co of Archers (Queen's Body Guard for Scotland) and Ensign 1981, Lt 1988; HM Lord-Lt for Morayshire 1963- (DL 1954); chm: Bd of Govrs of Gordonstoun Sch 1957-72, Glenlivet Distillers 1964-84, Scottish Northern Investmt Tst 1964-84, Grampian TV 1967-89, Seagram Distillers 1979-84; Crown Estate Cmmr 1970-90; Lord High Cmmr to Gen Assembly of the Church of Scotland 1988 and 1989; dir: Clydesdale Bank 1968-89, Abbey National Building Society 1981-89 (chm Scottish Advsy Bd 1981-89, memb 1968-89); former dir Times Publishing Co Ltd, memb Newspaper Panel Monopolies and Mergers Cmmn; Hon LLD Univ of Aberdeen 1990; FRSA 1971, CBIM 1983; *Recreations* country pursuits; *Style*— Sir Iain Tennant, KT, JP; Lochnabo House, Lhanbryde, Morayshire (☎ 0343 84 2228); Innes House, Elgin, Morayshire (☎ 0343 84 2410)

TENNANT, Hon Mrs (Irene Adelaide); *née* Gage; da of 5 Viscount Gage and Leila, *née* Peel (great niece of Sir Robert Peel, the PM); *b* 9 Feb 1898; *m* 1, 1923 (m annulled 1928), Capt Murray Shuldham-Legh; m 2, 1928, Maj Frederick Bull (m dis 1950); 1 s (decd), 1 da; m 3, 1950, Ernest Tennant, OBE (d 1962, kinsman of the

Barons Glenconner); *Style—* The Hon Mrs Tennant; Grove House, Great Bardfield, Essex (☎ 0371 810398)

TENNANT, Hon James Grey Herbert; 2 s of late 2 Baron Glenconner by his 1 w; *b* 5 March 1929; *Educ* Eton, Trinity Coll Cambridge; *m* 1962, Elizabeth, da of W J Daloøes, of Toronto; *Career* 2 Lt RHG, Asst Adj 1949; Gold Staff Offr at Coronation of HM The Queen 1953; chm Tennant Guaranty Ltd; has Coronation Medal 1953; FRGS; *Recreations* shooting, riding, painting; *Clubs* White's, RAC; *Style—* The Hon James Tennant; 25 St Leonard's Terrace, London SW3 4QG

TENNANT, Julian William Fiaschi; s of Ernest William Dalrymple Tennant (s of William Tennant, who was 4 cous of 1 Baron Glenconner, Margot Asquith, Baroness Elliot of Harwood, late Lady Ribblesdale and late Lady Crathorne); *b* 1 Aug 1924; *Educ* Eton; *m* 1954, Miranda, da of Capt Sidney Fairbairn, of Steventon Rectory (a previous occupant of which was Jane Austen), Steventon, nr Basingstoke; 1 s (Mungo), 2 da (Nell, Angela); *Career* served Capt Coldstream Gds (Gds Armd Div); chm: C Tennant & Sons 1973-80, Ingersoll Locks 1956-80, Daphne's Restaurant 1970-, Jermyn Street Travel 1981-; *Recreations* gardening, good food; *Clubs* Saints & Sinners, White's; *Style—* Julian Tennant, Esq; 112 Draycott Ave, London SW3 (☎ 071 589 9898); Plush Manor, Plush, Dorchester, Dorset (☎ 030 04 516)

TENNANT, Lady Margaret Isla Marion; *née* Ogilvy; 2 da of 12 Earl of Airlie, KT, GCVO, MC (d 1968), and Lady Alexandra Coke (d 1984), da of 3 Earl of Leicester; *b* 23 July 1920; *m* 11 July 1946, Sir Iain Mark Tennant, KT, JP, *qv*; 2 s, 1 da; *Career* formerley with WRNS; vice chm Cancer Relief 1981 (chm Scotland 1981-); *Style—* The Lady Margaret Tennant; Lochnabo House, Elgin, Morayshire (☎ 034 384 2228)

TENNANT, Sir Peter Frank Dalrymple; CMG (1958), OBE (1944); s of late G F D Tennant, of St Margaret's, Herts; *b* 29 Nov 1910; *Educ* Marlborough, Trinity Coll Cambridge (MA); *m* 1, 1934 (m dis 1952), da of Prof Fellenius, of Stockholm; 1 s, 2 da; m 2, 1953, Galina Bosley, da of K Grunberg, of Helsinki; 1 step s; *Career* fell and univ lectr Queens' Coll Cambridge 1934-39, press attaché Br Legation Stockholm 1939-45, info cnsllr Br Embassy Paris 1945-50, dep cmdt Br Sector Berlin 1950-52, overseas dir FBI 1952-63, dep DG FBI 1963-64; formerly memb Cncl of Industl Design, DG Br Nat Export Cncl 1965-71; dir: Barclays Bank SA Paris, Prudential Assurance Co 1973-81, Prudential Corporation 1979-86, C Tennant Sons & Co Ltd, Anglo-Rumanian Bank, Northern Engineering Industries (International) Ltd, International Energy Bank; industl advsr Barclays Bank International 1972-81; chm Gabbitas Thring Educn Tst, pres and chm London C of C, memb Bd Centre for International Briefing, actg chm Wilton Park Academic Cncl to 1983, former chm UK Ctee Euro Culture Fndn, tstee and former chm Heinz Koeppler Tst for Wilton Park, memb Cncl Impact Fndn, fell The Linnean Soc of London; kt 1972; *Books* Ibsen's Dramatic Technique, The Scandinavian Book, Vid Sidan Av Kriget (Swedish translations of Touchlines Of War, 1989); *Recreations* painting, writing, talking; *Clubs* Travellers'; *Style—* Sir Peter Tennant, CMG, OBE; Blue Anchor House, Linchmere Rd, Haslemere, Surrey GU27 3QF (☎ 0428 3124)

TENNANT, Hon Tobias William; s of late 2 Baron Glenconner by his 2 w; *b* 1 June 1941; *Educ* Eton, New Coll Oxford; *m* 1963, Lady Emma Cavendish, er da of 11 Duke of Devonshire, MC, DL; 1 s, 2 da; *Career* sometime pres OUBC; *Style—* The Hon Tobias Tennant; Shaws, Newcastleton, Roxburghshire (☎ 038 73 241)

TENNANT OF BALFLUIG, Mark Iain; Baron of Balfluig; s of Maj John Tennant, TD (d 1967), of Budds Farm, Wittersham, Kent, and Hon Antonia Mary Roby Benson (later Viscountess Radcliffe; d 1982), da of 1 Baron Charnwood; *b* 4 Dec 1932; *Educ* Eton, New Coll Oxford (MA); *m* 11 Dec 1965, Lady Harriot Pleydell-Bouverie, da of 7 Earl of Radnor, KG, KCVO, JP, DL (d 1968); 1 s (Lysander Philip Roby b 1968), 1 da (Sophia Roby b 1967); *Career* Lt The Rifle Bde (SRO); called to the Bar Inner Temple 1958, master of the Bench 1984, rec Crown Ct 1987, master of the Supreme Ct, Queen's Bench Div 1988; chm Royal Orchestral Soc for Amateur Musicians 1989; *Clubs* Brooks's; *Style—* M I Tennant, Esq; Balfluig Castle, Aberdeenshire AB3 8EJ; Royal Courts of Justice, Strand, London WC2A 2LL

TENNENT, (John) Michael; s of Capt John Harvey Tennent, MC (d 1978), and Mary Lilian, *née* Stevenson (d 1958); *b* 5 Feb 1929; *Educ* Charterhouse; *m* 8 Sept 1956, Rosalind Jane Mallord, da of Charles Wilfrid Mallord Turner (d 1979); 2 s (Richard Michael b and d 1960, John Charles Roger b 1964), 1 da (Julie Rosalind Mary b 1962); *Career* cmmnd Lt 1947-49; qualified CA 1954; md Corporate Advisers Ltd, chm various cos; memb Ctee: NASDIM, FIMBRA; Liveryman Worshipful Co of Coach Makers 1956; memb ICEAW 1954; *Books* Practical Liquidity Management (1974), The Hesitant Heart (1988); *Recreations* yachting, tennis; *Clubs* Cumberland Tennis, IOD; *Style—* Michael Tennent, Esq; 4 Brendon Close, Esher, Surrey (☎ 0372 464283)

TENNYSON, 4 Baron (UK 1884); Harold Christopher Tennyson; s of 3 Baron Tennyson (d 1951; a notable cricketer who captained Hants and (in four Test Matches v Australia in 1921) England; he was in turn gs of the Victorian Poet Laureate and 1 Baron), and of the Hon Clarissa, *née* Tennant (d 1960), da of 1 Baron Glenconner; *b* 25 March 1919; *Educ* Eton, Trinity Coll Cambridge (BA); *Heir* bro, Hon Mark Aubrey Tennyson, DSC, RN (ret); *Career* employed WO 1939-46; co-fndr (with Sir Charles Tennyson, CMG) of Tennyson Res Centre Lincoln; Hon Freeman City of Lincoln 1964; *Clubs* White's, Special Forces (life memb), RAC, Travellers' (hon memb); *Style—* The Rt Hon the Lord Tennyson; 314 Grosvenor Square, Duke St, Rondebosch 7700, Cape Town, South Africa

TENNYSON, Cdr the Hon Mark Aubrey; DSC (1943); s of 3 Baron Tennyson (d 1951), and hp of bro, 4 Baron; *b* 28 March 1920; *Educ* RNC Dartmouth; *m* 1964, Deline Celeste Budler; *Career* 1939-45 War (despatches), Cdr RN 1954; *Clubs* White's, Royal Yacht Squadron; *Style—* Cdr The Hon Mark Tennyson, DSC; Mellaston, 13 Cumnor Avenue, Kenilworth 7700, Cape Town, SA

TENNYSON-D'EYNCOURT, Lady; Juanita; *née* Borromeo; eldest da of late Fortunato Borromeo and Lydia, *née* Montero; *b* 5 March 1944; *Educ* Univ de Santo Tomás Philippines (BS); *m* 1966, Sir Giles Gervais Tennyson-d'Eyncourt, 4 Bt (d 1989); 1 s (Sir Mark Gervais, 5 Bt); *Style—* Lady Tennyson-d'Eyncourt; c/o Hyde Mahon Bridges, 52 Bedford Row, London WC1R 4UH

TENNYSON-d'EYNCOURT, Sir Mark Gervais; 5 Bt (UK 1930), of Carter's Corner Farm, Parish of Herstmonceux, Co Sussex; o s of Sir Giles Gervais Tennyson-d'Eyncourt, 4 Bt (d 1989); *b* 12 March 1967; *Educ* Charterhouse, Kingston Poly (BA); *Heir* none; *Career* fashion designer; Freeman City of London 1989; *Style—* Sir Mark Tennyson-d'Eyncourt, Bt; 775 Wandsworth Rd, London SW8 3JG

TENNYSON-D'EYNCOURT, Norah, Lady; Norah; *née* Gill; da of late Thomas Gill, of Sheffield; *m* 1977, as his 3 w, Sir (John) Jeremy Eustace Tennyson-d'Eyncourt, 3 Bt (d 1988); *Style—* Norah, Lady Tennyson-d'Eyncourt; Bayons House, Hinton St George, Somerset

TENNYSON-D'EYNCOURT, Vinnie, Lady; Vinnie Lorraine; da of late Andrew Pearson, of Minneapolis, USA; *m* 1, Robert J O'Donnell (decd); m 2, 1964, as his 2 w, Sir (Eustace) Gervais Tennyson-d'Eyncourt, 2 Bt (d 1971); *Style—* Vinnie, Lady Tennyson-d'Eyncourt; Catalino Pueblo, 2556 Avenida Maria, Tucson, Arizona 85718, USA

TEO, Sir (Fiatau) Penitala; GCMG (1979), GCVO (1982), ISO (1970), MBE (1956); *b* 21 July 1911; married with children; *Career* govr gen Tuvalu 1978-86; *Style—* Sir Penitala Teõ, GCMG, GCVO, ISO, MBE; Alapi, Funafuti, Tuvalu

TER HAAR, Roger Eduard Lound; s of Dr Dirk Ter Haar, and Christine Janet Ter Haar; *b* 14 June 1952; *Educ* Felsted, Magdalen Coll Oxford (BA); *m* 10 Sept 1977, Sarah Anne, da of Peter Leysham Martyn; 2 s (James b 1978, Harry b 1983), 1 da (Amilla b 1980); *Career* called to the Bar Inner Temple 1974; memb Hascombe PCC; *Recreations* gardening, golf; *Clubs* Dunsfold Tennis, Brooks's; *Style—* Roger Ter Haar, Esq; 2 Crown Office Row, Temple, London EC4Y 7HS (☎ 071 353 9337, fax 071 583 0589, telex 8954005)

TERENGHI, Mario; s of Emilio Giuseppe Terenghi, and Luigia, *née* Ripamonti; *b* 28 May 1927; *Educ* HS of Commerce Monza, Universita Cattolica Milan; *m* 8 Dec 1983, Airdrie Melba Joyce, da of Robert Lloyd George Armstrong (d 1959); *Career* exec dir Orion Banking Gp 1975-80; dir: Orion Multinat Servs Ltd 1975-80 (chm), Orion Pacific Ltd Hong Kong 1975-80, Orion Leasing Hldgs Ltd 1975-80, Libra Banks Ltd 1975-84; sr mangr Credito Italiano SpA 1981-84 (1946-75), md Credito Italiano Int Ltd 1984-; FInstD; Knight of the Italian Republic; *Style—* Mario Terenghi, Esq; Lombard Assoc, Foreign Banks Assoc, 21 Redcliffe Rd, London SW10 9NP; Credito Italiano Int Ltd, 95 Gresham St, London EC2V 7NB (☎ 071 600 3616, fax 071 826 8927, telex 8814392)

TERRAS, Antony Michael; s of Fredrick Richard Terras (d 1974), and Katherine Joan, *née* Anning; *b* 18 Aug 1934; *Educ* Uppingham, Univ of Manchester (BA); *m* 9 April 1960, Ann, da of George William Cartwright; 1 da (Jenny Katherine b 9 Jan 1966); *Career* Nat Serv 1958-60; qualified chartered accountant 1958, ptnr Deloitte (formerly Deloitte Plender Griffiths & Co) 1973 (joined 1965), ptnr Coopers & Lybrand Deloitte 1990- (following merger); hon treas Manchester C of C and Indust 1989-; FCA (ACA 1958); *Recreations* drawing, painting, golf, walking; *Clubs* St James's (Manchester); *Style—* Antony Terras, Esq; Coopers & Lybrand Deloitte, Abacus Court, 6 Minshull St, Manchester M1 3ED (☎ 061 236 9191, fax 061 247 4000)

TERRAS, (Christopher) Richard; s of Frederick Richard Terras (d 1976), and Katherine Joan, *née* Anning; *b* 17 Oct 1937; *Educ* Uppingham, Univ Coll Oxford (MA); *m* 27 Oct 1962, Janet Esther May, da of Leslie Harold Sydney Baxter (d 1980); 1 s (Nicholas b 1965), 3 da (Clare b 1964, Penelope b 1968, Joanna b 1971); *Career* CA; ptnr: Swanwick Terras & Co 1963-65, Abbott & Son 1963-65, Arthur Andersen & Co 1971-; *Recreations* cricket (played for Cheshire); *Clubs* Free Foresters, Cheshire Gentlemen, Leicestershire Gentlemen, Vincent's, Forty, St James's (Manchester); *Style—* Richard Terras, Esq; Frog Castle, Macclesfield Rd, Alderley Edge, Cheshire (☎ 0625 583118); Arthur Andersen & Co, Bank House, 9 Charlotte St, Manchester MI 4EU (☎ 0836 609 615)

TERRINGTON, Derek Humphrey; s of Douglas Jack, of Bury St Edmunds, and Jean Mary, *née* Humphrey; *b* 25 Jan 1949; *Educ* Sea Point Boys HS, Univ of Cape Town (MA); *m* 15 July 1978, Jennifer Mary, da of late Leslie Vernon Jones; 1 da (Sarah b 29 Sept 1984); *Career* assoc ptnr Grievson Grant 1984 (dir 1991), dir Phillips & Drew 1988 (asst dir 1987); memb: Soc of Investmt Analysts, Int Stock Exchange; *Style—* Derek Terrington, Esq; 16 St Winifred's Road, Teddington, Middlesex TW11 9JR; Phillips & Drew Ltd, 100 Liverpool St, London EC2M 2RM (☎ 071 901 3333)

TERRINGTON, 4 Baron (UK 1918); James Allen David Woodhouse; s of 3 Baron Terrington, KBE (d 1961); *b* 30 Dec 1915; *Educ* Winchester, RMC Sandhurst; *m* 1942, Suzanne, da of Col T S Irwin, JP, DL, late Royal Dragoons, of Justicetown, Carlisle, and Mill House, Holton, Suffolk; 3 da (Hon Mrs Bolton, Hon Georgina W, Countess Alexander of Tunis); *Heir* bro, Hon Christopher Montague Woodhouse, DSO, OBE; *Career* Staff Coll Haifa 1944, psc 1944, served WWII in India, N Africa and Middle East (wounded); sits as Independent Peer in House of Lords; Maj (ret) Royal Norfolk Regt and Queen's Westminster Rifles (King's Royal Rifle Corps) TA, an ADC to GOC Madras 1940; former memb Stock Exchange, partner in Sheppards and Chase 1952-80, dep chm of Ctees House of Lords 1961-63; exec memb Nat Listening Library (talking books for the disabled); vice pres Small Farmers Assoc memb: Ecclesiastical Ctee since 1979, Int Advsy Bd of the American Univ Washington DC USA; exec memb Wider Share Ownership Cncl (formerly dep chm); *Recreations* fishing, gardening; *Clubs* Boodle's; *Style—* The Rt Hon the Lord Terrington; The Mill House, Breamore, Fordingbridge, Hampshire

TERRIS, John Marlin; s of Dr John Marlin Terris, of Bearsden, Scotland, and Edith Helen Douglas, *née* Robertson; *b* 21 Nov 1948; *Educ* Glasgow Acad, Hamilton Acad, Univ of St Andrews (Rugby colours and cap); *m* 7 Dec 1974, Amanda, da of late Leonard Eason; 2 s (James b 19 Sept 1977, Andrew b 8 Nov 1979); *Career* advertising exec; media asst Wasey Campbell-Ewald 1972-73; media mangr: Wasey Financial 1973-74, Foster Turner & Benson 1974-75; media dir: Universal McCann 1975-80, Dorland Advertising 1980-82, MWK & P 1982-84; vice chm CIA Group plc 1986- (business devpt dir CIA Group 1984-86); *Recreations* walking, snooker, board games, movies; *Style—* John Terris, Esq; Chemin Blanc, La Rocque-Baignard, Cambremer, France (☎ 010 33 3163 1441); 14 Pinewood Close, Shirley, Croydon, Surrey CR0 5EX (☎ 081 654 6607); CIA Group plc, 1 Paris Garden, London SE1 8NU

TERRY; *see*: Imbert-Terry

TERRY, Prof Arthur Hubert; s of Arthur Terry (d 1962), of York, and Beatrice, *née* Hardisty (d 1983); *b* 17 Feb 1927; *Educ* St Peter's Sch York, Trinity Hall Cambridge (BA, MA); *m* 25 June 1955, Mary (Molly) Gordon, da of Dr John Sellar (d 1963), of Markinch, Fife; 2 s (Richard, Philip), 1 da (Sally); *Career* Nat Serv 1947-49, Sgt-instr RAEC; prof of Spanish Queen's Univ of Belfast 1962-72 (asst lectr 1950-54, lectr 1954-60, sr lectr 1960-62), prof of lit Univ of Essex 1973-, special prof Univ of Nottingham 1990-, sr res fell Inst of Romance Studies 1990-; pres: Int Catalan Studies Assoc 1982-88, Br Comparative Lit Assoc 1986-; Cross of St George 1982 (awarded by Catalan Govt for work as critic and historian of Catalan lit and services to Catalan culture); *Books* La Poesia de Joan Maragall (1963), An Anthology of Spanish Poetry 1500-1700 (2 vols, 1965 and 1968), Catalan Literature (1972), Antonio Machado: Campos de Castilla (1973), Selected Poems of Ausiàs March (1976), Joan Maragall, Antologia Poètica (1981), Sobre poesia catalana contemporània: Riba, Foix, Espriu (1985); *Recreations* music; *Style—* Prof Arthur Terry; 11 Braiswick, Colchester CO4 5AU (☎ 0206 851807); Department of Literature, The University of Essex, Wivenhoe Park, Colchester CO4 3SQ (☎ 0206 873333, fax 0206 873598, telex 98440 UNILIB G)

TERRY, David Robins; s of Joseph Robins Terry (d 1977), of Little Hall, Heslington, York, and Mary Patricia Colston, *née* Douty; *b* 11 Nov 1942; *Educ* Rishworth Sch Halifax; *m* 19 Nov 1986, Katharine Ruth, da of Amos Eastham, of Selby; 2 s (Nigel Joseph Douty b 15 June 1970, Oliver Stuart Robins b 6 May 1972); *Career* Army Serv 4 and 7 Royal Dragoon Gds 1961; CA 1968; articled clerk John Gordon Walton & Co Leeds 1962-67; Price Waterhouse: joined Leeds Office 1969, ptnr 1980, transferred to Birmingham 1980, specialist in business servs 1986-, gp ldr 1986-; pres Cncl of Dudley and Dist C of C 1989-90 (memb 1985-), chm Mgmnt Ctee Dudley Nat Pianoforte Competition 1987-, govr St Richards Hospice Worcester 1991; Merchant Adventurer of Co of Merchant Adventurers of City of York; ATII 1971, FCA 1978; *Recreations* poor golf, music, family, assitant church organist; *Clubs* Landsdowne; *Style—* David Terry, Esq; Tapenhall House, Porters Mill, Droitwich, Worcester WR9 OAN

TERRY, Sir George Walter Roberts; CBE (1976), QPM (1967), DL (E Sussex 1983); s of Walter George Tygh Terry; *b* 29 May 1921; *Educ* Peterborough; *m* 1942,

Charlotte Elisabeth, da of Stanley Kresina; 1 s; *Career* Nat Serv Capt Italy Northants Regt; chief constable: Pembrokeshire 1958-65, E Sussex 1965-67, Lincs 1970-73, Sussex 1973-83 (dep chief constable 1968-69); pres Assoc of Chief Police Offrs 1980-81 (chm Traffic Ctee 1976-79), memb Cncl Inst Advanced Motorists 1974; tstee: Disabled Housing Tst 1986, Coll of Driver Educn 1989; CStJ 1982; kt 1981; *Style—* Sir George Terry, CBE, QPM, DL; c/o National Westminster Bank plc, 173 High St, Lewes, E Sussex BN7 1YF (☎ 0273 471211)

TERRY, (Robert) Jeffrey; s of Robert James Terry, of Stockport, and Emily, *née* Davison (d 1975); *b* 10 Sept 1952; *Educ* William Hulme's Sch Manchester, King's Coll London (LLB), City of London Poly (MA); *m* 15 July 1978, Susan Terry, da of Reginald Trevor Kingston Gregory, of Bath; 2 da (Sarah Louise b 7 Aug 1983, Anna May Emily b 7 May 1987); *Career* called to the Bar 1976, community lawyer Southend CAB 1976-78, in private practice London 1978- and Manchester 1989-; memb: Hon Soc Lincoln's Inn 1975, Northern Chancery Bar Assoc; *Recreations* walking, photography, reading lit, classics, history; *Style—* Jeffrey Terry, Esq; Hall Stones Green Farm, Cross Stone, Todmorden, W Yorks (fax 0706 815745); Cairnside, 43 Canonbie Road, London SE23; 8 King St, Manchester (☎ 061 834 9560, fax 061 834 2733); Lamb Building, Temple, London EC4 (☎ 071 353 6701, fax 071 353 4686)

TERRY, Sir John Elliott; s of late Ernest Fairchild Terry, OBE, of Pulborough, Sussex; *b* 11 June 1913; *Educ* Mill Hill Sch, Univ of London; *m* 1940, Joan Christine, da of late Frank Alfred Ernest Howard, of Stoke D'Abernon, Surrey; 1 s, 1 da; *Career* business mangr Film Prodrs Guild 1946-47; slr: Legal Dept Rank Organisation 1947-49, Nat Film Fin Corpn 1949-57 (sec 1956-57, md 1958-78); conslt Denton Hall & Burgin 1979-89; govr: Nat Film Sch 1970-81, Royal Nat Coll for the Blind 1980-, London Int Film Sch 1982-89; pres Copinger Soc 1981-83; kt 1976; *Style—* Sir John Terry; Still Point, Branscombe, Devon

TERRY, John Victor; s of Norman Victor Terry (d 1981), and Mary Josephine Terry; *b* 6 Sept 1942; *Educ* Leys Sch Cambridge, Jesus Coll Cambridge (MA), Harvard Business Sch (MBA); *m* 3 April 1965, Jane Gillian, da of Donald Pearson, of Cambridge; 2 s (Nicholas b 11 Jan 1969, Simon b 6 May 1971); *Career* gen mangr Herbert Terry and Sons Ltd 1971-75; purchased and formed independent co of Anglepoise Lighting 1975: md 1975-88, chm 1988-; pres: Harvard Business Sch Assoc of Midlands 1983-85, Lighting Indust Fedn 1988-89; Freeman Worshipful Co of Lightmongers 1985; sec Frazer Nash Section Vintage Sports Car Club; *Recreations* windsurfing, cars, sailing, real tennis; *Clubs* Royal London Yacht, Barnt Green SC, Leamington TC, British Racing Drivers; *Style—* John Terry, Esq; Wasperton House, Warwick CV35 8EB (☎ 0926 624264); Anglepoise Lighting, Redditch B97 8DR (☎ 0527 63771, fax 0527 61232, telex 336918, car 0836 757523)

TERRY, Nicholas John; s of John Edmund Terry (d 1978), of Nottingham, and Winifred Nina, *née* White (d 1970); *b* 12 Nov 1947; *Educ* Peveril Sch Nottingham, Bilborough GS Nottingham, Bath Univ Sch of Architecture (BSc, BArch); *m* 27 June 1970, Dorothy, da of Leslie Atkins; 1 da (Alexandra Louise Terry b 31 Dec 1977); *Career* architect; Terry Associates Bath 1970; Building Design Partnership Manchester: architect (work incl Manchester Museum, Durham Millburngate and Albert Dock Liverpool) 1972-75, conslt design architect 1978, architect ptnr 1990; Arthur Erickson Architects Canada (Provincial Law Courts Vancouver BC) 1975-77, John S Bonnington Partnership St Albans (Cyprus Govt Centre and Kuwait Stock Exchange) 1978-81, dir of architecture and md Heery Architects and Engineers London 1983-89 (architect for Citibank HQs London and Frankfurt 1981-83); design awards for Durham Millburngate (Building Design Partnership): RIBA award 1977, Civic Trust award 1978, Europa Nostra award 1978; Honour award for Robson Square Law Courts (Arthur Erickson Architects) 1980; *Exhibitions* Durham Millburngate: Royal Acad Summer Exhibition 1974, Museum of Modern Art NY 1979; Albert Dock Royal Acad Summer Exhibition 1975, Kuwait Stock Exchange RIBA 1982; MRIBA 1973; memb: RAIC 1976, Architectural Inst of BC 1976, Soc of American Mil Engrs 1976; MInstD 1988; *Recreations* swimming, walking, gardening, architecture, reading; *Style—* Nicholas Terry, Esq; Building Design Partnership, PO Box 4WD, 16 Gresse St, London W1A 4WD (☎ 071 631 4733, fax 071 631 0393)

TERRY, (Vivian) Paul; s of Charles Michael Terry, of Titchfield, Hampshire, and Patricia Mary, *née* Newell; *b* 14 Jan 1959; *Educ* Millfield; *m* 4 June 1986, Bernadette Mary, da of Liam Sutcliffe; 1 da (Siobhan Catherine b 13 Sept 1987); *Career* professional cricketer; Hampshire CCC 1978-; captain Eng Sch Cricket Assoc tour to India 1977-78; played for Young England v WI and Aust; played twice v England v WI 1984; *Recreations* soccer, golf, squash, most sports, music; *Style—* Paul Terry, Esq; Hampshire Cricket Club, Northlands Road, Southampton SO9 2TY (☎ 0703 333788, fax 0703 330121)

TERRY, Air Chief Marshal Sir Peter David George; GCB (1983, KCB 1978, CB 1975), AFC (1968); s of (James) George Terry (d 1968), and Laura Chilton, *née* Powell (d 1980); *b* 18 Oct 1926; *Educ* Chatham House Sch Ramsgate; *m* 1946, Betty Martha Louisa, da of Arthur Thompson; 2 s (Stephen, David (decd)), 1 da (Elizabeth); *Career* RAF 1945-84, cmmnd 1946, dir Air Staff Briefing MOD 1970-71, dir Forward Policy RAF 1971-75, asst COS Policy and Plans 1975-77, vice chief Air Staff 1977-79, C-in-C RAF Germany and Cdr 2 Allied Tactical AF 1979-81, dep C-in-C AFCENT 1981, Dep Supreme Allied Cdr Europe 1981-84, Govr and C-in-C Gibraltar 1985-89; Queen's Commendation for Valuable Service in Air 1959 and 1962; *Recreations* golf; *Clubs* RAF; *Style—* Air Chief Marshal Sir Peter Terry, GCB, AFC

TERRY, (John) Quinlan; s of Philip John Terry, of Suffolk, and Phyllis May Whiteman; *b* 24 July 1937; *Educ* Bryanston, Arch Assoc; *m* 9 Sept 1961, Christina Marie-Therese, da of Joachin Tadeusz de Ruttié (d 1968); 1 s (Francis Nathaniel b 1969), 4 da (Elizabeth b 1964, Anna b 1965, Martha b 1979, Sophia b 1982); *Career* architect in private practice; works incl: country houses in the classical style, Richmond Riverside Devpt, New Howard Bldg Downing Coll Cambridge; *Recreations* sketching; *Style—* Quinlan Terry, Esq; Old Exchange, High St, Dedham, Colchester

TESLER, Brian; CBE; s of David Tesler (d 1972), and Esther Tesler; *b* 19 Feb 1929; *Educ* Chiswick Co Sch for Boys, Exeter Coll Oxford (MA); *m* 1959, Audrey Mary; 1 s; *Career* former TV prodr/dir; dir of progs: ABC 1963-68, Thames TV 1968-74; LWT: dep chief exec 1974, md 1976, chm and md 1984; dir: ITN 1979-90, Channel 4 1980-84, Oracle Teletext Ltd 1980-, Services Sound and Vision corp 1980-; chm: LWT Ltd 1984- ITV Super Channel Ltd 1986-88, LWT International Ltd 1990-, LWT Production Facilities 1990-; dep chm LWT (Holdings) plc 1990-; govr: Nat Film and TV Sch 1977-, BFI 1986; memb Br Screen Advsy Cncl 1977; chm: ITCA Cncl 1980-82, ITV Film Purchase Ctee 1988-90; *Recreations* books, theatre, cinema, music; *Style—* Brian Tesler, Esq, CBE; LWT Ltd, South Bank Television Centre, Upper Ground, London SE1 9LT (☎ 071 261 3000, fax 071 261 1290)

TESTA, Dr Humberto Juan; s of Orestes Miguel Angel Testa (d 1956), of Buenos Aires, Argentina, and Victoria Juana, *née* Vidal; *b* 11 Dec 1936; *Educ* Sch of Med Buenos Aires Univ (MD, PhD); *m* 18 Dec 1964, Nydia Esther, da of Victor Anibal D Garcia (d 1982), of Neuguen, Argentina; 1 s (Fernando Julio b 31 Dec 1965), 2 da (Cecilia b 27 Nov 1973, Paula b 2 May 1982); *Career* Manchester Royal Infirmary: res offr 1967-68, res registrar 1968-70, fell nuclear med 1970-73, conslt nuclear med 1974-; pt/t lectr diagnostic radiology and nuclear med Univ of Manchester 1977-; fell: Manchester Med Soc, Br Nuclear Med Soc, Euro Nuclear Med Soc, Br Inst of Radiology; FRCP 1968, FRCR 1989; *Books* Nuclear Medicine in Urology and Nephrology (ed with O'Reilly and Shields, 1986); *Recreations* squash, music and reading; *Style—* Dr Humberto Testa; 27 Barcheston Rd, Cheadle, Cheshire SK8 1LJ (☎ 061 428 6873); Dept of Nuclear Med, Royal Infirmary, Oxford Rd, Manchester M13 9WL (☎ 061 276 4820)

TESTA, Dr Nydia Esther Garcia; da of Victor Anibal Garcia (d 1981), and Manuela, *née* Barreiros; *b* 15 Feb 1938; *Educ* Univ of Buenos Aires, Univ of Manchester (PhD); *m* 18 Dec 1964, Humberto Juan Testa, s of Orestes Testa (d 1955); 1 s (Fernando b 1965), 2 da (Cecilia b 1973, Paula b 1981); *Career* res fell Cncl of Scientific and Tech Investigations Buenos Aires 1963-67, visiting res fell Paterson Laboratories 1967-74, scientist and sr scientist Paterson Inst for Cancer Res 1974-; author numerous scientific pubns in jls and books; *Style—* Dr Nydia Testa; Paterson Institute for Cancer Research, Christie Hospital (☎ 061 445 2596, fax 061 434 7728, telex 93499 TXLINKG, car MBX 614458123)

TETLEY, Brian; s of Herbert Tetley (d 1957), of Little Gomersal, and Gladys, *née* Holliday (d 1985); *b* 5 Sept 1937; *Educ* Heckmondwike GS; *m* 29 Aug 1959, Winifred Mary, da of William Sylvester O'Neill (d 1981), of Birkenshaw, Bradford; 2 s (Mark Richard b 1963, Neil Jon b 1966); *Career* CA; fin dir and co sec The Bradford Property Tst plc; dir: Margrave Estates Ltd, Faside Estates Ltd, Bradwa Ltd, Ashday Property Co Ltd, Sydenham Estates Ltd, and dir of various other cos; FCA; *Recreations* Rotary, golf; *Clubs* The Bradford; *Style—* Brian Tetley, Esq; Reighton, 123 Huddersfield Rd, Liversedge, W Yorks WF15 7DA; 69 Market St, Bradford BD1 1NE (☎ 0274 723 181)

TETLEY, Glen; s of Glenford Andrew Tetley (d 1985), and Mary Eleanor Byrne; *b* 3 Feb 1926; *Educ* Franklin and Marshall Coll, NY Univ (BSc); *Career* choreographer of ballets incl: Pierrot Lunaire 1962, The Anatomy Lesson 1964, Mythical Hunters 1965, Ricercare 1966, Ziggurat 1967, Circles 1968, Embrace Tiger and Return to Mountain 1968, Arena 1968, Field Figures 1971, Laborintus 1972, Gemini 1973, Voluntaries 1973, Sacre du Printemps 1974, Greening 1975, Sphinx 1978, The Tempest 1979, Firebird 1981, Revelation and Fall 1984, Alice 1986; artistic associate National Ballet of Canada 1987-; Queen Elizabeth II Coronation Award 1981, Prix Italia 1982, Tennant Caledonian Award Edinburgh Fest 1983, Ohloana Career Medal 1986-; dir Glen Tetley Dance Co 1962-69, co dir Nederlands Dans Theater 1969-71; dir Stuttgart Ballet 1972-74; choreographer: Royal Ballet Covent Garden, Ballet Rambert, Festival Ballet, American Ballet Theatre, Nat Ballet of Canada, Royal Danish Ballet, Royal Swedish Ballet, Nat Ballet of Norway, Australian Ballet, Stuttgart Ballet, Paris Opera, La Scala, Ater Balletto; *Style—* Glen Tetley, Esq; Highbank, Green Lane, Old Bosham, Chichester, W Sussex PO18 8NT; Susan Bloch and Co, 25 Charles St, New York, NY 10014 USA (☎ 212 807 6480, telex 65204)

TETLEY, Sir Herbert; KBE (1965), CB (1958); s of Albert Tetley (d 1926), of Leeds, and Mary Tetley (d 1947); *b* 23 April 1908; *Educ* Leeds GS, Queen's Coll Oxford (MA); *m* 1941, (Nancy) Agnes MacLean MacFarlane, da of John Macphee of Glasgow; 1 s; *Career* jt actuary Nat Provident Inst 1946-53, govt actuary 1958-73 (dep govt actuary 1953-58); chm: Civil Serv Insur Soc and assoc socs 1961-73, Ctee on Econs Road Res Bd 1962-65; pres Inst of Actuaries 1964-66, memb Res Ctee on Road Traffic 1966-72; *Style—* Sir Herbert Tetley, KBE, CB; 37 Upper Brighton Rd, Surbiton, Surrey KT6 6QX (☎ 081 399 3001)

TETLEY, Lady Patricia Maud; *née* Bowes-Lyon; raised to the rank of an Earl's da 1974; da (twin) of late Hon Michael Claude Hamilton Bowes-Lyon, 5 s of 14 Earl of Strathmore and Kinghorne; sis of 17 Earl; *b* 1932; *m* 1964 (m dis 1970), Oliver Robin Tetley; 1 s (Alexander b 1965); *Style—* The Lady Patricia Tetley; Abbey Lodge, Chruch St, Wymondham, Norfolk (☎ 0953 602355)

TETLEY, Richard James; s of Brig James Noel Tetley, DSO, TD, ADC, DL, LLD (d 1970), of Moor House, Moortown, Leeds, and Joyce Carine, *née* Grierson; *b* 15 April 1930; *Educ* Bradfield, Queen's Coll Oxford (MA); *m* 24 Aug 1963, Margaret Claire, da of Prof Allwyn Charles Keys (d 1985), of Auckland, NZ; 4 s (Douglas b 1964, Andrew b 1966, Stuart b 1968, Iain b 1970); *Career* dir Allied Breweries 1969-79, with ICL plc 1983-; memb Cncl Univ of Leeds 1965-88; *Style—* Richard J Tetley, Esq; Beacon Croft, Shaw Lane, Lichfield, Staffs WS13 7AG (☎ 0543 263 304)

TETT, Sir Hugh Charles; s of James Charles Tett (d 1955); *b* 28 Oct 1906; *Educ* Hele's Sch Exeter, Univ Coll Exeter, Royal Coll of Sci (BSc, DIC, ARCS); *m* 1, 1931, Katie Sargent (d 1948); 1 da; m 2, 1949, Joyce Lilian, *née* Mansell (d 1979); 1 da; m 3, 1980, Barbara Mary, *née* Mackenzie; *Career* Esso Petroleum Co 1928-: dir 1951, chm 1959-67; chm Cncl Inst of Petroleum 1947-48; memb: CSIR 1961-64, Advsy Cncl Miny of Technol 1964-67; chm Econ Devpt Ctee for Motor Mfrg Indust 1967-69; pro-chllr Univ of Southampton 1967-79; fell Imp Coll of Sci and Technol 1964; Hon DSc Univs of: Southampton 1965, Exeter 1970; kt 1966; *Clubs* Athenaeum; *Style—* Sir Hugh Tett; Primrose Cottage, Bosham, Chichester, W Sussex PO18 8HZ (☎ 0243 572705)

TETT, Peter Alfred; s of Norman Noel Tett, CBE (d 1979), and Irene Constance, *née* Edwards; *b* 5 Nov 1939; *Educ* Oundle, Clare Coll Cambridge (MA), Carnegie Melloń Univ Pittsburgh USA (MSc); *m* 15 Aug 1964, Romaine Joy Carley, da of Dr John Carley Read (d 1969); 1 s (Richard b 1969), 1 da (Gillian b 1967); *Career* dir: Halma plc 1984, London & European Group plc 1978-82; *Recreations* golf, skiing, theatre; *Clubs* Moor Park Golf, E Devon Golf; *Style—* Peter A Tett, Esq; 5 Bedford Rd, Moor Park, Northwood, Middx HA6 2BA (☎ 092 74 22622); Misbourne Court, Rectory Way, Amersham, Bucks HP7 0DE (☎ 0494 721111)

TETTENBORN, Richard Garstin; s of Philip Arthur De Gleichen Tettenborn (d 1990), of Belper, Derbyshire, and Helena Louise, *née* Sharpe (d 1971); *b* 23 Sept 1940; *Educ* Herbert Strutt Sch Belper, Brasenose Coll Oxford (MA); *m* 15 Jan 1983, Susan Margaret, da of John Crew (1983), of Keynsham; 1 s (Mark b 1986); *Career* trainee accountant Derbyshire CC 1963-67, gp accountant London Borough of Sutton 1967-70, asst county treas W Sussex CC 1970-76, dep country treas Mid-Glamorgan CC 1976-79, county treas S Glamorgan CC 1980-; tres S Wales Police Authority 1991-, vice pres Soc of County Treasurers, memb Cncl CIPFA; memb: CIPFA 1967, Soc of County Treasurers 1980; chm Venture Link Investors M H Syndicate Review Ctee; *Recreations* golf, theatre, family; *Clubs* United Oxford and Cambridge University; *Style—* Richard Tettenborn, Esq; County Hall, Atlantic Wharf, Cardiff CF1 5UW (☎ 0222 872200, fax 0222 872333)

TEVERSON, Hon Mrs (Joanna Rosamond Georgina); da of Baron Gore-Booth GCMG, KCVO (Life Baron) (d 1984), and his w, Patricia Mary, da of late Montague Ellerton, of Yokohama, Japan; *b* 1954; *Educ* Sherborne Sch, New Hall Cambridge (BA); *m* 1978, Paul Richard Teverson; 1 s (Richard Hugh b 1984), 1 da (Cathryn b 1986); *Style—* The Hon Mrs Teverson; 25 Silverton Road, Hammersmith, London W6 9NY

TEVIOT, 2 Baron (UK 1940); Charles John Kerr; s of 1 Baron Teviot, DSO, MC (d 1968, himself ggs of 6 Marquess of Lothian), by his 2 w Angela (d 1979), da of Lt-Col Charles Villiers, CBE, DSO (ggn of 4 Earl of Clarendon) by his w Lady Kathleen Cole (2 da of 4 Earl of Enniskillen); *b* 16 Dec 1934; *Educ* Eton; *m* 1965, Patricia Mary, da of late Alexander Harris; 1 s, 1 da (Hon Catherine b 1976); *Heir* s, Hon

Charles Robert Kerr b 19 Sept 1971; *Career* memb Advsy Cncl on Public Records 1974-82, dir Debrett's Peerage Ltd 1977-83; fell Soc of Genealogists 1975; *Recreations* genealogy, walking; *Style*— The Rt Hon the Lord Teviot; 12 Grand Ave, Hassocks, W Sussex (☎ 079 18 4471)

TEWKESBURY, Bishop of 1986-; Rt Rev (Geoffrey David) Jeremy Walsh; s of Howard Wilton Walsh, OBE (d 1969), and Helen Maud Walsh, *née* Lovell (d 1985); *b* 7 Dec 1929; *Educ* Felsted, Pembroke Coll Cambridge (MA), Lincoln Theol Coll; *m* 1961, Cynthia Helen, da of Francis Philip Knight (d 1985); 2 s (David b 1962, Andrew b 1967), 1 da (Helen b 1964); *Career* vicar St Matthew's Bristol 1961-66; rector: Marlborough 1966-76, Elmsett with Aldham Suffolk 1976-80; archdeacon of Ipswich 1976-86; *Recreations* golf, gardening, bird-watching; *Style*— The Rt Rev the Bishop of Tewkesbury; Green Acre, 166 Hempsted Lane, Gloucester GL2 6LG (☎ 0452 521824)

TEYNHAM, 20 Baron (E 1616); John Christopher Ingham Roper-Curzon; s of 19 Baron Teynham, DSO, DSC (d 1972), by his 1 w Elspeth (m dis 1956, she d 1976, having m 2, 1958, 6 Marquess of Northampton, DSO); *b* 25 Dec 1928; *Educ* Eton; *m* 1964, Elizabeth, da of Lt-Col the Hon David Scrymgeour-Wedderburn, DSO (ka 1944) 2 s of 10 Earl of Dundee; 5 s of 6 Duke of Buccleuch; 5 s (Hon David, Hon Jonathan b (twin) 27 April 1973, Hon Peter b 20 Nov 1977, Hon William b 27 July 1980, Hon Benjamin b 15 Sept 1982), 5 da (Hon Emma b 19 Sept 1966, Hon Sophie b 30 Nov 1967, Hon Lucy b 23 July 1969, Hon Hermione b (twin) 27 April 1973, Hon Alice b 18 Dec 1983); *Heir* s, Hon David John Henry Ingham Roper-Curzon, b 5 Oct 1965; *Career* late Capt The Buffs (TA) and 2 Lt Coldstream Gds, active serv Palestine 1948, ADC to Govr of Bermuda 1953 and 1955, ADC to Gov of Leeward Islands 1955 (also private sec 1956), ADC to govr of Jamaica 1962; pres Inst of Commerce 1972-, vice-pres Inst of Export, memb Cncl Sail Training Assoc 1964; memb Cncl of l'Orchestra du Monde 1987-; land agent; OStJ; *Clubs* Turf, House of Lords Yacht, Ocean Cruising, Beaulieu River Sailing, Puffin's (Edinburgh); *Style*— The Rt Hon the Lord Teynham; Pylewell Park, Lymington, Hants

THACKARA, John Alexander; s of Alexander Daniel Thackara, of Bath, and Eleanor Hazel, *née* Miller; *b* 6 Aug 1951; *Educ* Marlborough, Univ of Kent (BA), Univ of Wales (Dip Journ); *m* 20 April 1989, Hilary Mary, da of late Bowyer Arnold, DFC; 1 da (Kate Eleanor b 1989); *Career* commissioning ed Granada Publishing 1975-79, manging ed NSW Univ Press 1979-80, ed Design Magazine 1981-85, freelance design critic 1985-87, fndr and dir Design Analysis Int 1987, dir of res RCA 1989; FRSA 1987; *Books* New British Design (1987), Design after Modernism (1988); *Recreations* the baby, travel; *Clubs* Groucho; *Style*— John Thackara, Esq; 88 Kensington Park Rd, London W11 2PL (☎ 071 734 0314); 15 Greek St, London W1V 5LF; Royal College of Art, Kensington Gore, London SW7 (☎ 071 734 0314, fax 071 437 2700)

THACKER, Arthur Doe; s of Gilbert Doe Dwyer Way Thacker (d 1986), and Judith Mary St Leger, *née* Fagan (d 1980); *b* 19 June 1931; *Educ* Haileybury, ISC, Christ's Coll Cambridge (BA, MA); *m* 18 June 1960, Maude April Beatrice Evelyn, da of Frederick Croysdale Waud (d 1949); 2 s (Thomas b 1962, Geoffrey b 1970), 2 da (Bridget b 1963, Judith b 1966); *Career* RCS 1949-56, actg Capt and adjt; Wiggins Teape GP 1954-88; territorial dir Far East; dir: Wiggins Teape Overseas Ltd 1977, Overseas Hldgs Ltd 1978, and Wiggings Teape Hong Kong 1978, Malaysia 1978, NZ 1978, Japan 1978, Singapore 1978, Far East Hldgs 1980, Australia 1983, Computer Forms Toppan Moore Pty Ltd, Singapore 1985; proprietor ADT Business Consultancy 1988-90; memb Inst Admin Mgmnt 1974-, borough cncllr St Mary Bourne Ward of Basingstoke and Deane Borough Cncl 1979, 1983 and 1987, chm Housing Ctee 1988-; *Recreations* golf, contract bridge, tennis, gardening, philately; *Clubs* The Hong Kong, Royal Hong Kong Golf, Royal Hong Kong Yacht, Royal Selangor Golf, The Lake (Kuala Lumpur), Tidworth Garrison Golf, Valderrama Golf (Sotogrande, Spain); *Style*— Arthur D Thacker, Esq; Bourne House, St Mary Bourne, Andover, Hants SP11 6AP (☎ 0264 738 464)

THAIN, Gregory Neil David; *b* 12 Feb 1957; *Career* chief exec International Communication and Data Ltd; *Recreations* gliding, cricket; *Clubs* El Cid, Stocks, IOD; *Style*— Gregory Thain, Esq; International Communications & Data, 29 Corsham Street, London N1 6DR (☎ 071 251 2883)

THAIN, Leslie Alister; s of Alexander Simpson Thain (d 1966); *b* 22 Aug 1939; *Educ* Fettes, Univ of Edinburgh (MA, LLB); *m* 1968, Katherine Mary, *née* Hudson; 1 s, 1 da; *Career* slr, co dir; WS; *Recreations* golf, tennis, freemasonry, gardening; *Style*— Leslie Thain, Esq, WS; The Dean, Longniddry, E Lothian (☎ 0875 53272, office 031 226 6703)

THATCHER, Anthony Neville; s of Edwin Neville Thatcher (d 1978), and Elsie May, *née* Webster; *b* 10 Sept 1939; *Educ* Sir John Lawes Sch Harpenden, Luton Tech Coll, Univ of Manchester (MSc); *m* 20 Oct 1968, Sally Margaret, da of Henry Joseph Clark, of Norfolk; *Career* student apprentice Haywards Tyler & Co Luton 1956-64, project engr Smiths Indust London 1964-65, Ultra Electronics 1967-77, md Dowty Electronics Controls Ltd 1978-82, gp chief exec Dowty Group plc 1986- (md Electronics Div 1982-86, memb Bd 1983); memb: Cncl Electronics Engrg Assoc 1983- (pres 1986), Cncl Soc of Br Aerospace Cos 1986-, Bd SW Electricity Bd 1989-, Engrg Cncl 1989-, RARDE Mgmnt Bd (industl) 1986-, Mgmnt Bd Engrg Employers Fedn 1988- (vice pres 1990), Electronics and Avionics Requirements Bd of DTI 1981-85, Innovation Advsy Bd DTI 1988-, Engrg Mkts Advsy Ctee DTI 1988-90; memb Cncl The Cheltenham Ladies Coll; Liveryman Worshipful Co of Glass Sellers; CEng, FIMechE; *Recreations* art, jazz piano, opera, fishing, gardening, bird watching; *Style*— Anthony Thatcher, Esq; Dowty Group plc, Arle Ct, Cheltenham, Glos GL51 0TP (☎ 0242 533614, fax 0242 533277, telex 43176)

THATCHER, Sir Denis; 1 Bt (UK 1991), of Scotney, Co Kent, MBE, TD; *b* 10 May 1915; *Educ* Mill Hill; *m* 1, 1942 (m dis 1946), Margaret Doris (who m 2, 1948, Sir (Alfred) Howard Whitby Hickman, 3 Bt, who d 1979), o da of Leonard Kempson, of Potters Bar, Middx; m 2, 1951, Rt Hon Margaret Hilda, OM, FRS, MP, *qv*, yr da of late Alfred Roberts, of Grantham, Lincs; 1 s (Mark), 1 da (Carol b (twin) 15 Aug 1953); *Heir* s, Mark Thatcher b 15 Aug 1953; *Career* served WWII as Maj RA; vice-chm Attwoods plc 1983-, dir Quinton Hazell plc; formerly dir Burmah Castrol; *Style*— Sir Denis Thatcher, Bt, MBE, TD; c/o Attwoods plc, The Pickeridge, Stoke Common Road, Fulmer, Bucks SL3 6HA

THATCHER, Grant Ashley; s of Stephen Thatcher, of Llandudno, North Wales, and Doreen, *née* Lambton; *b* 24 Nov 1962; *Educ* Rodway Comp, Filton Tech Coll, RADA; *Career* actor, theatre work incl: Jacques and Phoebe in As You Like It (Cherub Co), Valentine in Twelfth Night (Sheffield Crucible), Marchbanks in Candida (Arts Theatre West End), Rt Hon Alan Howard in French Without Tears (Leicester Haymarket); RSC 1990-91: Anfriso in The Last Days of Don Juan, Diomedes in Troilus and Cressida, Gaveston in Edward II; TV work incl: Peter Wessel in The Diary of Anne Frank (BBC TV), Bonds in Aliens in the Family (BBC TV), Hannay (Thames TV), documentary on Mike Leigh (Omnibus BBC TV); film work incl Strapless; *Recreations* gardening; *Style*— Grant Thatcher, Esq; c/o John Wood at Hope & Lyne, 108 Leonard Street, London EC2 (☎ 071 739 6200)

THATCHER, Rt Hon Margaret Hilda; OM (1990), PC (1970), MP (C) Finchley 1987-; yr da of late Alfred Roberts, grocer, of Grantham, Lincs, sometime borough cncllr, alderman and mayor of Grantham, and Beatrice, *née* Stephenson; prefers to be known as Mrs Thatcher rather than Lady Thatcher; *b* 13 Oct 1925; *Educ* Huntingtower Primary Sch Grantham, Kesteven and Grantham Girls' Sch, Somerville Coll Oxford (MA, BSc, hon fellow 1970); *m* 1951, as his 2 w, Sir Denis Thatcher, 1 Bt; 1 s (Mark b 15 Aug 1953), 1 da (Carol (twin) b 15 Aug 1953, radio journalist, presenter (freelance) with LBC); *Career* former research chemist; called to the Bar Lincoln's Inn 1954 (hon bencher 1975), contested (C) Dartford 1950 and 1951; MP (C): Finchley 1959-74, Barnet, Finchley 1974-1983 and 1983-87; jt parly sec Miny of Pensions and National Insurance 1961-64, memb Shadow Cabinet 1967-70 (spokesman on: Tport, Power, Treasury matters, Housing and Pensions), chief oppn spokesman educn 1969-70, sec of state Educn and Science (and co-chm Women's National Cmmn) 1970-74, chief oppn spokesman environment 1974-75, leader of the Opposition Feb 1975-79, prime minister and first lord of Treasury (first woman to hold this office) 4 May 1979-28 Nov 1990; minister for the Civil Service Jan 1981-Nov 1990; Freedom of Borough of Barnet 1980; hon Freeman of Worshipful Co of Grocers 1980; Freedom of Falkland Islands 1983; Donovan Award USA 1981, US Medal of Freedom 1991; FRS 1983; *Style*— The Rt Hon Margaret Thatcher, OM, FRS, MP; House of Commons, London SW1

THAYER, Pamela Patricia; ISO; da of Albert Harold Thayer (d 1969), of Gt Wood Cottage, Ibstone Common, Bucks, and Kathleen, *née* Holloway (d 1984); *b* 9 Sept 1925; *Educ* Notting Hill and Ealing High Sch, GPDST, Girton Coll Cambridge (MA), Bedford Coll London (Social Science Cert), LSE (Child Care Cert); *Career* Children's Dept Inspectorate Home Office 1954-70, asst chief inspector Social Servs Inspectorate DHSS 1970-85, child care consIt 1985-; govt advsr Gibraltar 1970 and 1978 (Thayer Report 1970), dir Comparative Study of Child Care Cncl of Europe 1986-87, vice pres Pre-Sch Playgroups Assoc, hon memb NSPCC Cncl, chm Advsy Gp Barnardo's High/ Scope, memb Ctee ISS; *Books* Forms of Child Care (1988); *Recreations* politics, writing, theatre, music; *Clubs* Oriental; *Style*— Miss Pamela Thayer, ISO; Great Wood Cottage, Ibstone Common, Buckinghamshire HP14 3XU; 60 Lord's View, London NW8 7HQ

THELLUSSON, Hon Peter Robert; s of Lt-Col Hon Hugh Thellusson, DSO, by his w Gwynnydd, da of Brig-Gen Sir Robert Colleton, 9 and last Bt, CB; bro of 8 Baron Rendlesham and was raised to rank of a Baron's s 1945; *b* 25 Jan 1920; *Educ* Eton; *m* 1, 1947 (m dis 1950), Pamela (d 1968), da of Oliver Parker (2 s of Hon Francis Parker, 4 s of 6 Earl of Macclesfield by Lady Mary Grosvenor, da of 2 Marquess of Westminster, KG) and former w of Maj Timothy Tufnell, MC; m 2, 1952, Celia, da of James Walsh; 2 s; *Career* served WWII, Capt KRRC; *Style*— The Hon Peter Thellusson; 29 Bramham Gdns, SW5

THELWELL, Norman; s of Christopher Thelwell (d 1974), and Emily, *née* Vick (d 1964); *b* 3 May 1923; *Educ* Rock Ferry HS, Liverpool Coll of Art (ATD); *m* 1948, Rhona Evelyn, da of Harold Clyde Ladbury (d 1961); 1 s (David), 1 da (Penelope); *Career* artist & cartoonist; lectr Wolverhampton Coll of Art 1950-56; regular contributor to Punch 1952-77, cartoonist to News Chronicle, Sunday Express, Sunday Dispatch, and many other publications; *Books* Angels on Horseback (1957), Thelwell Country (1959), Thelwell in Orbit (1961), A Place of Your Own, A Leg at Each Corner, Thelwells Riding Academy, Top Dog, Up the Garden Path, The Compleat Tangler (1967), Thelwell's Book of Leisure (1968), This Desirable Plot (1970), The Effluent Society (1971), Penelope (1972), Three Sheets in the Wind, Belt Up (1974), Thelwell Goes West (1975), Thelwell's Brat Race (1977), Thelwell's Gymkhana, A Plank Bridge by a Pool (1978), A Millstone Round My Neck (1981), Pony Cavalcade, Some Damn Fool's Signed the Rubens Again (1982), Thelwell's Magnificat (1983), Thelwells Sporting Prints (1984), Wrestling with a Pencil (autobiography, 1986), Play It As It Lies (1987); *Recreations* trout fishing; *Style*— Norman Thelwell, Esq; Herons Mead, Timsbury, Romsey, Hants SO51 0NE (☎ 0794 68238)

THEMEN, Arthur Edward George; s of Dr Lambert Christian Joseph Themen (d 1945), of 13 Glodwick Rd, Oldham, Lancs, and Ethel Elizabeth, *née* Nadin; *b* 26 Nov 1939; *Educ* Manchester GS, St Catharine's Coll Cambridge (MA), St Mary's Hosp Med Sch Univ of London; *m* 8 Jan 1968 (m dis 1979), Judith Frances Anquetil, da of Frank Alexander Arrowsmith, OBE, of Oxford; 2 s (Daniel b 1971, Benjamin b 1972), 1 da (Justine b 1969); *Career* former house surgn St Mary's Hosp, RPMS; surgical registrar Royal Northern Hosp 1969, sr registrar St Mary's and Royal Nat Orthopaedic Hosps 1971-74, currently conslt orthopaedic surgn Royal Berks Hosp and assoc surgn Nuffield Orthopaedic Centre Oxford; special interest incl spinal and jt replacement surgery; various articles on joint replacement in professional jls; musical career as jazz musician; memb prize winning Cambridge Univ Jazz Gp 1958 (best soloist 1959), involved with early Br Blues movement; worked with: Mick Jagger, Rod Stewart, Georgie Fame; UK rep in Int Jazz Orch Festival Zurich 1965; began long assoc with Stan Tracey 1974; toured and recorded with: Charlie Parker alumni, Al Haig, Red Rodney; most recent tours incl Chicago and NY Jazz Festivals; records incl: Captain Adventure 1975, Under Milk Wood 1976, Expressly Ellington 1978 (with Al Haig), Spectrum 1982, Playing in the Yard 1986, Genesis 1987 (with Stan Tracey); memb Contemporary Music Ctee Arts Cncl; Fell Br Orthopaedic Assoc 1974, FRSM; *Recreations* skiing, sailing; *Clubs* Ronnie Scott's; *Style*— Arthur Themen, Esq; 6 The Blades, Lower Mall, Hammersmith, London W6 (☎ 081 741 7066); 21 Eldon Square, Reading, Berks (☎ 0734 573555); Orthopaedic Dept, Royal Berkshire Hospital, London Rd, Reading, Berks (☎ 0734 584711)

THEOBALD, Prof Michael Francis; s of George Charles Theobald, of Sanderstead, Surrey, and Elsie Dorothy, *née* Baker; *b* 1 Sept 1946; *Educ* King's Coll London, Univ of Manchester (BSc, MA, PhD); *m* 26 Oct 1972, Pauline Florence, da of Capt Christopher Herbert Harman (d 1989), of St Leonards, nr Ringwood; 1 s (Jonathan Harman b 3 Sept 1978), 1 da (Sarah Pauline b 5 June 1981); *Career* CA; Price Waterhouse & Co London 1968-72, (Buenos Aires 1972-74), Univ of Manchester 1974-85, Peat Marwick prof and head Dept of Accounting and Finance Univ of Birmingham 1985-; articles published in: Journal of Finance, Journal of Financial and Quantitave Analysis, Journal of Banking and Finance, Journal of Portfolio Management; memb: Res Bd of the Inst of Chartered Accountants, Training and Qualifications Cmmn of the Euro Fedn of Financial Analysts Socs; conslt to the ESRC; FCA 1972; *Recreations* sport, maintaining equilibrium; *Style*— Prof Michael Theobald; Deparment of Accounting and Finance, University of Birmingham, PO Box 363, Birmingham B15 2TT (☎ 021 414 6540)

THEOBALD, (George) Peter; JP (1974); s of George Oswald Theobald (d 1952), of Surrey, and Helen, *née* Moore (d 1972); *b* 5 Aug 1931; *Educ* Betteshanger Sch, Harrow; *m* 1955, Josephine Mary, da of Wilfrid Andrew Carmichael Boodle (d 1961); 2 s (Carmichael, Christopher), 3 da (Caroline, Jane, Kate); *Career* cmmnd 5 Regt RHA 1950-52, Lt 290 City of London Regt RA (TA) 1953-59; gp chief exec Robert Warner plc 1953-74; dir: Moran Holdings plc 1977-, Moran Tea Co (India) plc 1981-; memb: Tport Users Consultative Ctee for London 1969-84 (dep chm 1978-79), London Regnl Passengers Ctee 1984-90; church cmmnr for England 1978-79, licensed asst diocese of Guildford 1970-; Alderman City of London 1974-79; govr: Bridewell Royal Hosp 1974-, Christs Hosp 1976-, King Edwards Sch Witley 1974- (tstee Educn Tst 1977-), St Leonards Mayfield Sch 1982-88; memb: Harrow Club 1978-, Nat Flood and Tempest

Distress Fund 1977-; memb Ct of Assts Worshipful Co of Merchant Taylors 1983- (Master 1989-90); *Recreations* gardening, transport, walking; *Clubs* Oriental, MCC; *Style—* Peter Theobald, Esq, JP; Towerhill Manor, Gomshall, Guildford, Surrey GU5 9LP (☎ 048 641 2381)

THEODOROU, Skevos Gregory; s of Gregory Alfred Theodorou (d 1970), and Irene, *née* Alakouzos (both of shipping families); *b* 12 Oct 1939; *Educ* Le Rosey Switzerland, Neuchâtel Univ (Dip Business Admin); *m* 1, 1968 (m dis), Gillian Geraldine Anne, da of Maj-Gen Sir (Harold) John Crossley Hildreth, KBE, and sis of Jan Hildreth (sometime dir gen of IOD); 1 s (Alexander John (Skevos) Hildreth b 11 May 1976), 1 da (Charlotte Amanda Joanna Hildreth b 26 Oct 1978); m 2, Antonia Henriette de Galard Brassac de Béarn, eldest da of Count Jean de Béarn; 1 s (Gregory b 23 Oct 1986), 1 da (Clementine Eléonore b 6 Sept 1990); *Career* shipping, memb Baltic Exchange 1964-, md Transmarine SA Paris 1967-79, dir Clarkson & Co Ltd 1975-; *Recreations* shooting, sailing; *Clubs* Royal Thames Yacht, Royal Hellenic Yacht (Athens); *Style—* Skevos Theodorou, Esq; 58d Blomfield Rd, London W9 2PA

THESIGER, Hon Frederic Corin Piers; s and h of 3 Viscount Chelmsford; *b* 6 March 1962; *Style—* The Hon Frederic Thesiger; 26 Ormonde Gate, London SW3 4EX

THESIGER, Wilfred Patrick; CBE (1968), DSO (1941); eld s of Capt the Hon Wilfred Gilbert Thesiger, DSO (d 1920), and Kathleen Mary, *née* Vigors, CBE (d 1973); *b* 3 June 1910; *Educ* Eton, Magdalen Coll Oxford (MA); *Career* hon attaché Duke of Gloucester's Mission to Haile Selassie's Coronation 1930; explored Danakil Country and Aussa Sultanate of Abyssinia 1933-34; Sudan Political Serv Darfur 1935-37, and Upper Nile 1938-40, Sudan Def Force Abyssinian Campaign 1940-41, Maj SOE Syria 1941-42, SAS Regt W Desert 1942-43, advsr to the Crown Prince in Ethiopia 1944; explored in Southern Arabia 1945-50 (twice crossed the Empty Quarter by camel), lived with the Madan in the marshes of Southern Iraq 1950-58; awarded Back Grant RGS 1935, Founder's Medal RGS 1948, Lawrence of Arabia Medal RCAS 1955, Livingstone Medal RSGS 1962, W H Heinemann Award RSL 1964, Burton Meml Medal Royal Asiatic Soc 1966; hon fell: Magdalen Coll Oxford 1982, Br Acad 1982; Hon DLitt Univ of Leicester; FRSL 1966; Star of Ethiopia third class 1930; *Books* Arabian Sands (1959), The Marsh Arabs (1964), Desert, Marsh and Mountain (1979), The Life of My Choice (1987), Visions of a Nomad (1987); *Recreations* travel in remote areas, photography; *Clubs* Travellers', Beefsteak; *Style—* Wilfred Thesiger, Esq, CBE, DSO; 15 Shelley Court, Tite St, London SW3 4JB (☎ 071 352 7213)

THETFORD, Bishop Suffragan of 1981-; Rt Rev Timothy Dudley-Smith; s of Arthur and Phyllis Dudley Smith, of Buxton, Derbys; *b* 26 Dec 1926; *Educ* Tonbridge, Pembroke Coll Cambridge (BA), Ridley Hall Cambridge (MA), Lambeth (MLitt); *m* 1959, (June) Arlette MacDonald; 1 s, 2 da; *Career* ordained 1950, archdeacon of Norwich 1973-81; *Publications* Christian Literature and the Church Bookstall (1963), What Makes a Man a Christian? (1966), A Man Named Jesus (1971), Someone who Beckons (1978), Lift Every Heart (1984), A Flame of Love (1987), Songs of Deliverance (1988), Praying with The English Hymn Writers (1989); contributor to various hymn books; *Recreations* reading, verse, woodwork, family and friends; *Clubs* Norfolk (Norwich); *Style—* The Rt Rev the Bishop of Thetford; Rectory Meadow, Bramerton, Norwich NR14 7DW (☎ 050 88 251)

THEVA, Dr Rajaluxmi; da of Thuraiappa Santhirasegaram (d 1964), of Sri Lanka, and Nallamah, *née* Sinnaiah; *Educ* Chundikuli Girls' Sch Jaffna Ceylon, Med Sch Univ of Ceylon (DPM, MB BS); *m* 1968, Murugesam Pillai Theva, s of Sinnaiah Murugesam Pillai (d 1984), of Sri Lanka; 1 s (Skantha Ruben b 1973), 1 da (Geetha b 1971); *Career* conslt psychiatrist St Lawrence's Hosp Caterham Surrey 1985- (clinical asst 1974-85); advsr on mental handicap to MIND; memb: MIND, MENCAP, Med Protection Soc 1974; MRCPsych 1985; *Recreations* golf, badminton; *Style—* Dr Rajaluxmi Theva; Croydon Mental Handicap Unit, Croydon, Surrey

THIMBLEBY, Prof Harold William; s of Peter Thimbleby, of Rugby, Warwicks, and Angela Marion, *née* Hodson; *b* 19 July 1955; *Educ* Rugby, Univ of London (BSc, MSc, PhD); *m* 16 Feb 1980, Prudence Mary (Prue), da of Capt Arundel Charles Barker, of Matlock, Derbyshire; 3 s (William, Samuel, Isaac), 1 da (Emma b 1987); *Career* lectr in computer sci Univ of York 1982-88, prof of info technol Univ of Stirlingshire 1988-; co-inventor of Liveware (technique for exploiting computer viruses) 1989; Br Computer Soc Wilkes medal 1987; memb St John's Church Alloa; *Books* Formal Methods In Human-Computer Interaction (ed with M D Harrison, 1989), User Interface Design (1990); *Recreations* hill walking, woodwork; *Style—* Prof Harold Thimbleby; Dept of Computing Science, Stirling University, Stirling FK9 4LA (☎ 0786 73171 ext 7421, fax 0786 63000, telex 777557 STUNIV G)

THIMBLEBY, Peter; s of Arthur Wilfrid Thimbleby, and Gertrude Mary, *née* Fovargue; *b* 12 Sept 1927; *Educ* Rugby, Leicester Sch of Architecture; *m* 16 Sept 1950, Angela Marion (d 1990), da of Walter Harold Hodson (d 1982); 1 s (Harold William b 1955), 1 da (Elizabeth Angela b 1953); *Career* Grenfell Bains Gp 1951-57, princ in private practice 1957-; FRIBA, FIAAS; *Recreations* caravanning; *Style—* Peter Thimbleby, Esq; Ryedale, 9 Overslade Lane, Rugby CV22 6DU (☎ 0788 815019); 62 Regent St, Rugby CV21 2PS (☎ 0788 544513)

THIN, Dr (Robert) Nicol Traquair; s of Robert Traquair Thin (d 1990), of Bromley, Kent, and Annie Dempster, *née* Snowball; *b* 21 Sept 1935; *Educ* Loretto, Univ of Edinburgh Med Sch (MB ChB, MD); *m* 1962, (Agnes) Ann, da of Alexander William Graham, OBE (d 1964), of Inverness; 2 s (Sandy b 1964, Iain b 1968); *Career* cmmnd into RAMC 1964, Malaya, Singapore and UK, ret Maj; Maj TA 1974-76; venereologist BMH Singapore 1969-71, conslt venereologist Edinburgh Royal Infirmary 1971-73, conslt in genitourinary med St Bartholomew's Hosp London 1973-81, conslt venereologist St Peter's Hosps London 1975-, civilian conslt in genitourinary Med to the Army 1981-, hon sr lectr Inst of Urology and conslt in genitourinary med St Thomas' Hosp London 1982-, personal conslt advsr in genitourinary med to The CMO at The Dept of Health; ed British Journal of Venereal Diseases 1975-80, contrib specialist and general textbooks incl Lecture Notes on Sexually Transmitted Diseases; pres Med Soc of Venereal Diseases 1987-89 (memb 1968-), chm Specialist Advsy Ctee on Genitourinary Medicine of the Jt Ctee on Higher Med Training 1982-83 (memb 1976-81, sec 1981-82), examiner for Dip in Genitourinary Med for The Soc of Apothecaries of London 1981-, pres Soc of Health Advsrs in Sexually Transmitted Diseases 1983-86, memb Expert Advsy Gp on AIDS 1985-87, external examiner of Dip in Venereology for Univ of Liverpool 1987-89, memb Genitourinary Med Sub Ctee of RCP 1987-; memb Nat Tst; former: postgrad dean St Bartholomew's Hosp Med Coll, pres Edinburgh Univ Boat Club; vice pres St Thomas' Hosp Boat Club; memb: BMA 1960-, Med Soc of Venereal Diseases 1968-; FRSM 1988-, FRCP, FRCPE; *Recreations* music, reading, overseas travel; *Clubs* City Volunteer Officers; *Style—* Dr Nicol Thin; Teratak, 13 Park Ave, Bromley, Kent BR1 4EF (☎ 081 464 9278); Dept of Genitourinary Medicine, St Thomas' Hospital, London SE1 7EH (☎ 081 928 9292 ext 2429, fax 081 922 8079, telex 27913 STHLDN G)

THIRLWALL, Prof Anthony Philip; s of Isaac Thirlwall (d 1960), and Ivy, *née* Ticehurst (d 1988); *b* 21 April 1941; *Educ* Clark Univ USA (MA), Univ of Leeds (BA, PhD); *m* 26 March 1966, Gianna, da of Bruno Paoletti (d 1985), of Trieste; 2 s (Lawrence b 1967, Adrian b and d 1975), 1 da (Alexandra 1974); *Career* asst lectr in economics Univ of Leeds 1964, lectr in economics Univ of Kent 1966, prof of applied economics 1976-; econ advsr Dept of Employment 1968-70; memb: Action Aid, Royal Econ Soc 1964; *Books* Growth and Development: With Special Reference to Developing Economies (1972, 4 edn 1989), Inflation, Saving and Growth in Developing Economies (1974), Regional Growth and Unemployment in the United Kingdom (with R Dixon, 1975), Financing Economic Development (1976), Keynes and International Monetary Relations (ed, 1976), Keynes and Laissez Faire (ed, 1978), Keynes and the Bloomsbury Group (ed with D Crabtree, 1980), Balance of Payments Theory and the United Kingdom Experience (1980, 3 ed 1986), Keynes and Economic Development (ed, 1987), Nicholas Kaldor (1987), Collected Essays of Nicholas Kaldor Volume 9 (ed with F Targetti, 1989), The Essential Kaldor (ed with F Targetti, 1989), European Factor Mobility: Trends and Consequences (ed with I Gordon, 1989), Deindustrialisation (with S Bazen, 1989); *Recreations* athletics; *Style—* Prof Anthony Thirlwall; 14 Moorfield, Canterbury, Kent (☎ 0227 769904); Keynes College, University of Kent, Canterbury, Kent (☎ 0227 764000, fax 0227 459025, telex 965449)

THISELTON, Rev Dr Anthony Charles; s of Eric Charles Thiselton (d 1979), of Woking, Surrey, and Hilda Winifred, *née* Kevan (d 1969); *b* 13 July 1937; *Educ* City of London, King's Coll London (BD, MTh), Univ of Sheffield (PhD); *m* 21 Sept 1963, Rosemary Stella, da of Ernest Walter Harman (d 1979), of Eastbourne, Sussex; 2 s (Stephen b 1964, Martin b 1969), 1 da (Linda b 1966); *Career* curate Holy Trinity Sydenham 1960-63, chaplain Tyndale Hall Bristol 1963-67, recognised teacher in theology Univ of Bristol 1965-70, sr tutor Tyndale Hall 1967-70, lectr in biblical studies Univ of Sheffield 1970-79 (sr lectr 1979-85), visiting prof and fell Calvin Coll Grand Rapids 1982-83; princ: St John's Coll Nottingham 1985-88, St John's Coll Univ of Durham 1988-; memb: C of E Doctrine Cmmn 1976, C of E Faith and Order Advsy Gp 1971-81 and 1986-, CNAA Ctee for Arts and Humanities 1983-87, CNAA Ctee for Humanities 1987-90, Revised Catechism Working Pty 1988-89, Studiorum Novi Testamenti Societas, Soc for the Study of Theology, American Acad of Religion; examining chaplain to: Bishop of Sheffield 1976-80, Bishop of Leicester 1979-86; *Books* Language, Liturgy and Meaning (1975), The Two Horizons: New Testament Hermeneutics and Philosophical Description (1980), The Responsibility of Hermeneutics (jtly 1985), New Horizons in Hermeneutics (1991); contrib: Believing in the Church, We Believe in God, Their Lord and Ours; *Recreations* organ, choral music, the sea; *Clubs* National Liberal; *Style—* The Rev Dr Anthony Thiselton; 20a South St, Durham DH1 4QP; St John's College, Durham DH1 3RJ (☎ 091 374 3579/ 3561, fax 091 374 3740)

THISTLETHWAITE, Prof Frank; CBE (1979); s of Lee Thistlethwaite (d 1973), of Bibury, Glos, and Florence Nightingale, *née* Thornber (d 1982); *b* 24 July 1915; *Educ* Bootham Sch York, St John's Coll Cambridge (MA), Univ of Minnesota USA; *m* 11 Aug 1940, Jane, da of Harry Lindley Hosford (d 1946), of Lyme, Connecticut, USA; 2 s (Stephen Lee b 1944 d 1951, Miles b 1949), 3 da (Jill (Mrs Pellew) b 1942, Harriet b 1953, Sarah Lee (Mrs More) b 1956); *Career* RAF 1941-45, seconded to Offices of War Cabinet 1942-45; Br Press Serv NY 1940-41; fell St John's Coll Cambridge 1945-61, lectr Faculty of Econs and Politics Univ of Cambridge 1949-61, Inst for Advanced Study Princeton Univ 1954; founding chm Br Assoc for American Studies 1955-59, founding vice chllr UEA 1961-80; visiting fell Henry E Huntingdon Library California 1973, chm Ctee of Mgmnt Inst of US Studies Univ of London, Hill visiting prof Univ of Minnesota 1986; memb: Inter-Univ Cncl for Higher Educn Overseas 1962-81 (chm 1977-81), Marshall Aid Commoration Cmmn 1964-80, Bd (formerly Exec Ctee) Br Cncl 1971-82; pres Friends of Cambridge Univ Library 1983-; Hon LHD Univ of Colorado 1972, hon fell St John's Coll Cambridge 1974, Hon DCL UEA 1980, hon prof of history Univ of Mauritius; Hon FRIBA 1985, FRHistS 1963; *Books* The Great Experiment an Introduction to the History of the American People (1955), The Anglo-American Connection in the Early Nineteenth Century (1958), Dorset Pilgrims: The Story of West Country Puritans who went to New England in the 17th Century (1989); *Recreations* playing the piano, historical writing; *Clubs* Athenaeum; *Style—* Prof Frank Thistlethwaite, CBE; 15 Park Parade, Cambridge CB5 8AL (☎ 0223 352680); Island Cottage, Winson, Glos

THISTLETHWAITE, John; s of late Robert Thistlethwaite, of Salterforth, and Edith Mary, *née* Pickles; *b* 5 March 1943; *Educ* Ashville Coll Harrogate; *m* 18 June 1966 (m dis 1976); 1 s (Simon b 1968); *Career* CA; co sec: Dale Electric International 1967-70, Suter Electrical Ltd 1970-, Pennine Motor Group 1970-73, Evans of Leeds plc 1984-87; sr ptnr John Thistlethwaite and Co CAs 1975-; dir: R Thistlethwaite Ltd 1959-60, Simon James Motors Ltd 1972-78, Skipton Finance Ltd 1973-, F R Evans (Admin) Ltd 1985-87, Erskine Systems Ltd 1968-70, Dale Electrical Installations Ltd 1968-70, Dale Plant Hire Ltd 1968-70, Skipton Sports Cars Ltd 1978-85; FCA 1966, FSCA 1968, MICM 1975; *Recreations* cricket, music, snooker, motoring; *Clubs* Crosshill Cons, Craven Gentlemens, Skipton; *Style—* John Thistlethwaite, Esq; Hunters Moon, Embsay, Skipton, N Yorkshire (☎ 0756 795052)

THISTLETHWAYTE, John Robin; JP; s of Lt Cdr Thomas Thistlethwayte, RNVR (d 1956), of Bursledon Lodge, Old Bursledon, Hants, and Hon Eileen Gwladys (d 1955), *née* Berry; eld da of 1 and last Baron Buckland; *b* 8 Dec 1935; *Educ* Bradfield, RAC Cirencester; *m* 22 Jan 1964, Mary Katharine Grasett, da of Lt-Gen Sir (Arthur) Edward Grasett KBE, CB, DSO, MC, of Adderbury, Oxfordshire; 2 s (Mark b 1964, Hugo b 1967), 1 da (Sophy b 1973); *Career* chartered surveyor; ptnr Savills 1961-86, conslt to Savills Ltd 1986-; Mayor of Chipping 1964 and 1965; chm: Chipping Norton Petty Sessional Div 1984 and 1985, N Oxfordshire and Chipping Norton PSD 1989-; FRICS; *Recreations* shooting, travel; *Clubs* Boodles, St James; *Style—* J Robin Thistlethwayte, Esq, JP; Sorbrook Manor, Adderbury, Oxfordshire OX17 3EG; The Estate Office, Southwick, Fareham, Hants PO17 6EA; Savills Ltd, 21 Horse Fair, Banbury, Oxfordshire (☎ 0295 3535, telex 837291 SAVBAN, fax 0295 50784)

THISTLETHWAYTE, Maj (Thomas) Noel; s of Lt Cdr Thomas Arthur Donald Claude Thistlethwayte, RNVR (d 1956), and Ethel Mary, *née* Hickie (d 1934); *b* 18 Oct 1925; *Educ* Eton; *m* 10 Oct 1953, Ann Patience Wallop, da of Capt Newton William-Powlett, DSC, RN, of Cadhay, Ottery-St-Mary, Devon; 1 s (Rupert b 19 Jan 1955), 1 da (Jane b 2 June 1957); *Career* cmmd 60 Rifles KRRC 1944, seconded Para Regt 1947-50, serv Palestine, N Africa, Egypt, Borneo, BAOR, Lt-Col dir staff Army Staff Coll 1961-64, ret 1965; dir: Rupert Chetwynd & Partners Advertising 1968-77, Chetwynd Streets Financial Advertising and Chetwynd Streets (Holdings) Ltd 1973-77; govr Royal West of Eng Residential Sch for the Deaf, local chm Devon Historic Churches Tst; MIPA 1968-77; *Recreations* sailing, shooting; *Clubs* Naval & Military; *Style—* Maj Noel Thistlethwayte; Summerhayes, Throwleigh, Okehampton, Devon (☎ 064 723 425)

THOM, Timothy Ritchie; JP (1982); s of David Ritchie Thom (d 1957), and Edna Beryl, *née* May (d 1986); *b* 20 May 1940; *Educ* Bedford Sch; *m* 8 Feb 1964, Diana Monica Mae, da of Edward James Morrow Tait (d 1973); 2 da (Fiona b 1965, Belinda b 1967); *Career* CA; ptnr Price Waterhouse Bristol; memb: Cncl of the Univ of Bristol, bd Bristol Devpt Bd; FCA (1964); *Recreations* golf, fishing, gardening; *Clubs* Clifton, Burnham and Berrow Golf; *Style—* Timothy Thom, Esq, JP; The Forge, Lower Langford, Bristol BS18 7HU (☎ 0934 862356); c/o Clifton Heights, Triangle

West, Bristol BS8 1EB (☎ 0272 293701)

THOMANECK, Dr Jürgen Karl Albert; JP; *b* 12 June 1941; *Educ* Altes Gymnasium Flenburg, Univ of Kiel, Univ of Tübingen, Univ of Aberdeen (MEd, DPhil); *m* 3 Aug 1964, Guinevere, *née* Ronald; 2 da (Yasmin Helene b 6 Dec 1964, Naomi Morwenna b 20 May 1977); *Career* head of German Dept Univ of Aberdeen 1984-88 and 1989- (lectr 1969-87, sr lectr 1987-); pres Aberdeen Trades Cncl, Grampian regnl cncllr (leader Lab Gp); *Books* Deutsches Abiturienten Lexikon (4 edn jtly, 1974), Fremdsprachenunterricht und Soziolinguistik (1981), Police and Public Order in Europe (1984), Ulrich Plenzdorf's Die neuen Leiden des Jungen W (1988), The German Democratic Republic: Politics, Government and Society: Basic Documents (1989); *Recreations* reading, soccer; *Clubs* Aberdeen Trades Council; *Style—* Dr Jurgen Thomaneck, JP; 17 Elm Place, Aberdeen AB2 3SN (☎ 0224 637744); Univ of Aberdeen, Dept of German, Taylor Buildings, King's College, Old Aberdeen AB9 2UB (☎ 0224 272487)

THOMAS, Dr Adrian Mark Kynaston; s of Prof Peter Kynaston Thomas, of Highgate, London, and Mary Truscott Cox (d 1977); *b* 1 April 1954; *Educ* Christ Coll Finchley, UCL (MB BS, BSc, MRCP); *m* 8 July 1978, Susan Margaret, da of Arthur Oliver Viney, of Amersham, Bucks; 2 s (Gareth Kynaston b 1985, Owen Matthew Truscott b 7 July 1990), 1 da (Charlotte Mary Truscott b 1988); *Career* sr registrar Hammersmith Hosp 1981-87; conslt radiologist 1987-: Bromley Hosp, Beckenham Hosp, Farnborough Hosp, Sloane Hosp; memb: Radiology History Ctee, Bromley MENCAP, Bromley Learning Disabilities Forum, Milton Soc of America, Cncl Charles Williams Soc; memb: BMA 1976, RSM 1981, Br Inst of Radiology 1981, RCR 1982, Christian Med Fellowship 1989; FRCR; *Books* Self Assessment in Radiology and Imaging: Nuclear Medicine (jt ed, 1989); *Recreations* music, bonsai, life and works of John Milton and Charles Williams; *Style—* Dr Adrian Thomas

THOMAS, Prof Adrian Tregerthen; s of Rev Owen George Thomas, and Jean Tregerthen, *née* Short; *b* 11 June 1947; *Educ* Kingswood Sch Bath, Univ of Nottingham (BMus), Univ Coll Cardiff (MA), Kraków Acad of Music; *Career* Hamilton Harty prof of music Queen's Univ Belfast 1985 (lectr 1973, sr lectr 1982); compositions: Intrada (orchestra, 1981), Elegy (violin and piano, 1983), Rau (string octet, 1985), Black Rainbow (acappella choir, BBC Cmmn, 1989); conductor Br première Lutoslawski's Trois Poèmes d'Henri Michaux 1969, head of music BBC Radio 3 1990-; memb Bd Arts Cncl NI 1980-89; chm: Music and Opera Ctee ACNI 1986-89, Central Music Advsy Ctee BBC 1987-89; memb Gen Advsy Ctee BBC 1988-90; FRSA 1988; medal Polish Composers' Union for Outstanding Servs to Contemporary Polish Music 1989; *Books* Grażyna Bacewicz: Chamber and Orchestral Music (1985); *Recreations* mountain walking, entomology; *Style—* Prof Adrian Thomas

THOMAS, (John) Alan; s of Idris Thomas, of Langland, Swansea, and Ellen Constance Thomas; *b* 4 Jan 1943; *Educ* Dynevor Sch Swansea, Univ of Nottingham (BSc); *m* 1966, Angela, da of Fersil Owain Taylor (d 1969); 2 s (Andrew James b 1971, Alexander Michael b 1974); *Career* md Data Logic Ltd 1973-85, pres and chief exec offr Raytheon Europe 1985-89, vice pres Raytheon Co (US); seconded to MOD as head of Def Export Servs Orgn 1989-, dir various Raytheon subsid cos 1978-89; pres Computing Servs Assoc 1980-81; visiting prof Poly of Central London 1982- (govr 1989-); Freeman City of London 1988; CEng, MIProdE, FCMA (prizewinner); *Recreations* music, sport; *Clubs* Annabel's, Ambassadeurs, Athenaeum; *Style—* Alan Thomas, Esq; Head of Defence Export Services, Ministry of Defence, Main Building, Whitehall, London SW1A 2HB (☎ 071 218 3042, telex 22241)

THOMAS, Alston Havard Rees; s of Ebenezer Gwyn (d 1971), of Longworth, Oxford, and Mary Ann, *née* Morris (d 1974); *b* 8 July 1925; *Career* reporter: West Wales Guardian 1939-44, Wiltshire Times 1944-46; Bristol Evening Post: local govt specialist writer (also sport and ecclesiastical affrs) 1946-70, Diary ed 1970-84, fin and property writer 1984-88; pres Inst of Journalists 1985-86 (memb 1974, chm 1981-84); memb: Press Cncl 1979-90, Cncl of Newspaper Press Fund 1987-; pres Bristol and West of England Press Fund; memb: Wales and West of England Newspaper Trg Cncl, Avon Cncl of St John Ambulance; *Books* Muddling Through (jtly, 1988); *Recreations* rugby football; *Clubs* Savages (Bristol); *Style—* Alston Thomas, Esq; Havene, Maysmead Lane, Langford, Bristol BS18 7HX (☎ 0934 862515)

THOMAS, Angus Arnold; s of late David Arnold Thomas, of Cardiff, and late Dorothy Mabel, *née* Angus; *b* 7 Sept 1927; *Educ* Bryanston, Clare Coll Cambridge (MA); *m* 11 April 1953, Margaret Ruth, da of late Frank Bird, of Cardiff; 1 s, 2 da; *Career* joined Davy and United Engrg Co (presently Davy Corp) 1951 (director of sales 1961, gen mangr 1970), dir Davy Ashmore Benson Pease and Co, dep chm Davy Ashmore Int, dir Loewy Robertson Engrg Co, joined Head Wrightson and Co Ltd, md BS Massey Ltd 1972, chm Head Wrightson Machine Co Ltd 1974, dir Head Wrightson Process Engrg 1976, dir of marketing Davy McKee Sheffield (following Head Wrightson merger with Davy) 1978, chief exec Process Engrg and Non Ferrous Div Davy McKee Stockton 1982, dir Davy McKee in HK 1986-87, dir Davy McKee Int 1990; chm Br Metalworking Plantmakers Assoc 1976-77; memb: Capital Goods Ctee 1979-85, Br and South Asian Trade Assoc BOTB; Freeman: Worshipful Co of Cutlers in Hallamshire, City of London, Worshipful Co of Tin Plate Workers alias WireWorkers; FIMechE, CEng; *Recreations* field sports, photography, music; *Clubs* United Oxford and Cambridge Univ; *Style—* Angus Arnold Thomas, Esq; Oswaldkirk, York

THOMAS, Capt (John Anthony) Bruce; RN; s of John Haydn Thomas (d 1987), of Crowborough, and Hove, and Barbara Ann, *née* Jones (d 1974); *b* 15 Nov 1929; *Educ* Warden House, RNC Dartmouth, RNC Greenwich; *m* 30 Nov 1957, Genevieve Margaret, da of Walter Frederick Whiting (d 1985), of Felixstowe; 1 da (Rachel b 1965); *Career* Sub Lt 1949, Lt 1952, Lt Cdr 1960, Cdr 1964, in cmd HMS Houghton and Sr Offr 6 M Sqdn 1964-66, JSSC 1966/67, MOD (N) 1967-68, Exec Offr HMS Albion 1968-71, Dir Serv Intelligence FE Cmd 1971-72, Capt 1972, i/c HMS Phoebe 1973-74, ACOS (ops) NAVSOUTH 1974-76, i/c HMS Hermione and Capt 5 Frigate Sqdn 1977-78, Cdre 1978, Cdre Naval Ship Acceptance and dir of Naval Equipment 1978-82, naval advsr BAE Mil Aircraft Bristol; ADC to HM The Queen 1981-82; memb Bd Br Marine Equipment Cncl 1987- (vice pres 1990-); *Recreations* golf, shooting, sailing; *Clubs* Army & Navy, Lansdown Golf, Royal Naval; *Style—* Capt Bruce Thomas, RN; Church End, Hawkesbury Upton, Badminton GL9 1AU (☎ 045423 707)

THOMAS, Dr Cedric Marshall; CBE (1991, OBE 1983); s of David John Thomas (d 1958), of Birmingham, and Evis Margaret, *née* Field (d 1946); *b* 26 May 1930; *Educ* King Edward's Sch Birmingham, Univ of Birmingham (BSc, PhD); *m* 1, 12 June 1954, (Dora) Ann (d 1975), da of Walter Pritchard (d 1975), of N Wales; 1 s (Nicholas b 1955), 1 da (Sarah b 1957); m 2, 19 Sept 1976, Margaret Elizabeth, *née* Shirley; 1 step s (Michael b 1954), 3 step da (Carolyn b 1952, Beth b 1959, Helen b 1961); *Career* NCB 1954-59, Morgan Crucible Co Ltd 1960-61, chief exec Johnson Progress Group 1970-77 (joined 1961), business conslt 1977-80, chief exec Benjamin Priest Group 1983-84 (joined 1980), dir and chief exec Engineering Employers W Midlands Assoc 1984-; memb Mgmnt Bd EEF 1972-80, govr N Staffs Poly 1973-80, pres Engineering Employers W Midlands Assoc 1976-78, chm Special Programmes Area Bd 1978-83, memb: Health and Safety Cmmn 1980-90, CBI Health and Safety Policy Cmmn 1983-; chm: Area Manpower Bd 1986-88; fell Minerals Engrg Soc, FIMinE, CEng; *Recreations* tennis, walking; *Style—* Dr Cedric Thomas, CBE; Parkfields House, Tittensor, Staffs ST12 9HQ (☎ 078139 3677); St James's House, Frederick Rd, Edgbaston, Birmingham B15 1JJ (☎ 021 456 2222, fax 021 454 6745, telex 334037)

THOMAS, (Antony) Charles; CBE (1991), DL (Cornwall 1988); s of Donald Woodroffe Thomas (d 1959), of Lowenac, Camborne, Cornwall, and Viva Warrington, *née* Holman (d 1980); *b* 26 April 1928; *Educ* Winchester, CCC Oxford (MA, DLitt), Inst of Archaeology (Dip Prehistoric Archaeology); *m* 1 July 1959, Jessica Dorothea Esther, da of Prof Frederick Alexander Mann, of 56 Manchester St, London; 2 s (Charles Richard Vivian b 1961, Martin Nicholas Caleb b 1963), 2 da (Susanna Charlotte Elizabeth b 1966, Lavinia Caroline Alice b 1971); *Career* Army Serv 1946-48; lectr in archaeology Univ of Edinburgh 1957-67, prof of archaeology Univ of Leicester 1967-71, prof of Cornish studies Univ of Exeter 1972-; pres: CBA 1970-73, Royal Inst of Cornwall 1970-72, Soc for Medieval Archaeology 1986-89, Cornwall Archaeological Soc 1984-88; chm: Cornwall Ctee for Rescue Archaeology 1974-88, BBC's SW Regnl Advsy Cncl 1975-80, DOE Area Archaeology Ctee Devon and Cornwall 1975-79; acting chm Royal Cmmn on the Hist Monuments of Eng 1988- (memb 1983-); hon memb Royal Irish Acad 1973; FSA: Scotland 1957, London 1960; Frend medal London Soc 1982; hon fell Royal Soc of Antiquaries of Ireland 1975; FRHistS 1982; *Books* Christian Antiquities of Camborne (1967), The Early Christian Archaeology of North Britain (1971), Britain and Ireland in Early Christian Times (with A Small and D M Wilson, 1971) St Ninian's Isle and its Treasure (with D Ivall, 1973), Military Insignia of Cornwall (1974), Christianity in Roman Britain to AD 500 (1981), Exploration of a Drowned Landscape (1985), Celtic Britain (1986), Views and Likenesses: photographers in Cornwall and Scilly 1939-70 (1988); *Recreations* military history, bibliophily, archaeological fieldwork; *Style—* Prof Charles Thomas

THOMAS, Christopher (Chris); s of Neofitos Theophilou, of London, and Mary, *née* Mouzouris; *b* 1 Sept 1963; *Educ* Highgate Wood Sch London; *Career* Bd dir MJP/Carat International 1989- (joined as trainee media exec 1980); dir Int Advertising Assoc (UK Chapter) 1990 (joined 1981); *Style—* Chris Thomas, Esq; MJP/Carat International, 2-6 Fulham Broadway, London SW6 7AA (☎ 071 381 8010, fax 071 385 3233)

THOMAS, Christopher Peter (Chris); s of Cecil Stevens Thomas, of Highcliff, Dorset, and Ruth Ela, *née* Roberts; *b* 13 Jan 1947; *Educ* Upper Latimer, RAM (jr exhibitioner); *m* (m dis); 1 s (Jan Stevens b 29 Sept 1970), 1 da (Carla b 22 Nov 1971); partner, Tine Steincke; 1 s (Michael James b 15 May 1988), 1 da (Mia b 1 Feb 1991); *Career* pop music prodr; credits incl: Climax Blues Band (Climax Chicago Blues Band, The Climax Blues Band Plays On, A Lot of Bottle, Tightly Knit), Nirvana (Dedicated to Markos III), Procol Harum (Home, Broken Barricades, Live with The Edmonton Symphony Orchestra, Grand Hotel, Exotic Birds and Fruit), Mick Abrahams Band (Mick Abrahams Band, At Last), Christopher Milk (Some People Will Drink Anything), John Cale (Paris 1919), Roxy Music (For Your Pleasure, Stranded, Siren, Viva Roxy Music), Badfinger (Ass, Badfinger, Wish You Were Here), Sadistic Mika Band (Black Ship, Hot! Menu), Kokomo (Kokomo), Bryan Ferry (Let's Stick Together), Krazy Kat (China Seas), Eno (Here Comes The Warm Jets), The Sex Pistols (Never Mind the Bollocks), Frankie Miller (Full House), Chris Spedding (Hurt), Tom Robinson Band (Power in the Darkness), Wings (Back to The Egg), The Pretenders (Pretenders, Pretenders II, Learning to Crawl), Pete Townshend (Empty Glass, All The Best Cowboys Have Chinese Eyes, White City), Elton John (The Fox, Jump Up, Too Low For Zero, Breaking Hearts, Reg Strikes Back, Sleeping With the Past), INXS (Listen Like Thieves, Kick, X), Dave Stewart & The Spiritual Cowboys); mixing credits incl: Pink Floyd (Dark Side of the Moon), Roxy Music (Country Life), Ronnie Lane (One for the Road); 24 albums produced went silver, gold, platinum; winner: Rolling Stone Critics award 1980, Best Single Prodr Billboards 1988, Best Prodr Brit Awards 1990; *Recreations* travelling, meeting people; *Style—* Chris Thomas, Esq; c/o Steve O'Rourke, 43 Portland Road, London W11 4LJ (☎ 071 221 2046, fax 071 229 5445)

THOMAS, Christopher Sydney; QC (1989); s of John Raymond Thomas (d 1982), and Daphne May, *née* Thomas; *b* 17 March 1950; *Educ* King's Sch Worcester, Univ of Kent at Canterbury (BA); *m* 28 May 1979, Patricia Jane, da of Leslie Heath, of Gillingham, Kent; 1 s (Alexander), 1 da (Felicity); *Career* called to the Bar Lincoln's Inn 1973, appointed QC 1989, arbitrator for building and civil engrg disputes and arbitration; *Recreations* farming; *Style—* Christopher Thomas, Esq, QC; 10 Essex St, Outer Temple, London WC2R 3AA (☎ 071 240 6981, fax 071 240 7722, telex 8955650 IIKBWG)

THOMAS, Christopher Wilson; CBE; *b* 29 April 1927; *Educ* Sherborne, Pembroke Coll Cambridge; *Career* currently: non-exec dep chm Bristol Waterworks Company, non-exec dir Bristol & West Building Society, chm Bristol Development Corporation; *Style—* Christopher Thomas, Esq, CBE; Bristol Development Corporation, Techno House, Redcliffe Way, Bristol BS1 6NX (☎ 0272 255222, fax 0272 252666)

THOMAS, D M; s of Harold Redvers Thomas, and Amy, *née* Moyle; *b* 27 Jan 1935; *Educ* New Coll Oxford (BA, MA); 2 s (Sean, Ross), 1 da (Caitlin); *Career* novelist; head of English Dept Hereford Coll of Educn 1973-75; *Books* The Flute-Player (1978), Birthstone (1979), The White Hotel (1981), Ararat (1983), Swallow (1984), Sphinx (1986), Summit (1987); Lying Together (1990); Memories and Hallucinations (autobiography, 1988); poetry: Dreaming in Bronze (1979), Selected Poems (1982); *Style—* D M Thomas, Esq; Coach House, Rashleigh Vale, Truro, Cornwall TR1 1TJ (☎ 0872 78885)

THOMAS, Dr Dafydd Elis; MP (Plaid Cymru) Meirionnydd Nant Conwy 1983-; *b* 18 Oct 1946; *Educ* Univ Coll of North Wales; *Career* former adult educn tutor, writer and broadcaster; memb TGWU; Parly candidate (Plaid Cymru) Conway 1970; Pty spokesman: Social, Educn and Social Policy 1975, Agric and Rural Devpt 1974; Plaid Cymru vice pres 1979-81; hon sec: All Pty Mental Health Gp, Mind, Inst for Workers Control and Shelter; memb Select Ctee Educn, Science and Arts; *Style—* Dr Dafydd Thomas, MP; Bryn Meurig, Y Lawnt, Dolgellau, Gwynedd LL40 1DS

THOMAS, Prof David; s of William Thomas, and Florence Grace Thomas; *b* 16 Feb 1931; *Educ* Bridgend GS, UCW Aberystwyth (BA, MA), Univ of London (PhD); *m* 1955, Daphne Elizabeth Berry; 1 s, 1 da; *Career* Nat Serv RAF 1949-51; UCL 1957-70: asst lectr, lectr, reader, sec AUT 1963-65, convenor non-professorial staff 1968-70, chm Arts and Laws Library Ctee 1969-70; Saint David's Univ Coll 1970-78: prof and head of Dept, dean Faculty of Arts 1971-73, chm Computer Users' Ctee 1971-75, memb Cncl Univ of Wales 1971-74, chm Student Health and Welfare Ctee 1977-78 (also Safety Ctee), dep princ 1977-78; Univ of Birmingham 1978-: prof and head of Dept 1978-86, prof of geography 1987-, chm Field Course & Vacation Grants Ctee 1983-86, pro vice chllr 1984-89, univ rep on Jt Matriculation Bd 1989-, chm Jt Safety Advsy Ctee 1990-; visiting prof: Federal Sch in Euro Geography Minnesota 1968, Univ of Minnestota 1975; memb: Field Studies Cncl 1972-74 and 1978-, Br Nat Ctee for Geography of the Royal Soc 1972-74 and 1976-78, W Midlands Cncl for Further Educn 1984-86; memb Cncl: RGS 1987-91, Inst of Br Geographers 1972-74 (hon sec 1976-78, jr vice pres 1986, sr vice pres 1987, pres 1988); sec and convenor Conf of Geography Heads of Depts 1972-74, chm 18+ Ctee for Geography of Secondary Examinations Cncl 1983-89, vice chm Nat Curriculum Geography Working Gp 1989-90; *Books* Agriculture in Wales during the Napolonic Wars (1963), London's Green Belt

(1970), Man and His World: an Introduction to Human Geography (with J A Dawson, 1975), Wales, The Shaping of a Nation (with P Morgan, 1984); *Recreations* music, wine; *Style—* Prof David Thomas; 6 Plymouth Drive, Barnt Green, Birmingham B45 8JB (☎ 021 445 3295); School of Geography, University of Birmingham, Edgbaston, Birmingham B15 2TT (☎ 021 414 5540)

THOMAS, Rev David; s of Rt Rev John James Absalom Thomas, DD, of Woodbine Cottage, St Mary Street, Tenby, and Elizabeth Louise, *née* James; *b* 22 July 1942; *Educ* Christ Coll Brecon, Keble Coll Oxford, St Stephen's House Oxford (BA, MA); *m* 1 April 1967, Rosemary Christine, da of Arthur Louis Calton, of 6 Eastern Rd, West End, Southampton; 1 s (John Dyfrig b 1971), 1 da (Felicity Jane b 1968); *Career* curate Hawarden 1967-69, chaplain St Michael's Coll Llandaff 1970-75 (tutor 1969), vice princ St Stephen's House Oxford 1975-79 and 1982-87, vicar of Chepstow 1979-82, vicar of Newton 1987-; memb: Church in Wales Liturgical Cmmn 1969 (sec 1970-75), Church in Wales Doctrinal Cmmn 1975-, Church in Wales Standing Liturgical Advsy Ctee 1987-, Working Gp on Authy 1987-88, Working Gp on Healing 1987-88; managing tstee St Michael's Coll Llandaff 1988-, Governing Body of the Church in Wales 1972-75, 1980-82 and 1989-; *Books* The Ministry of the Word (contrib, 1979); *Recreations* music, history, travel in Europe, walking, anything to do with the sea; *Style—* The Rev David Thomas; The Vicarage, Mary Twill Lane, Newton, Swansea SA3 4RB (☎ 0792 368348)

THOMAS, David Arthur; s of David Martell Thomas (d 1960), of Hampton, Middx, and Sybil Elizabeth, *née* Perry; *b* 7 April 1938; *Educ* RCA (DES RCA); *m* 1, 8 Aug 1976 (m dis 1986), Georgina Anne Caroline, da of Dr Joseph Linhart, of London; 1 s (Edward b 14 Feb 1977); m 2, 12 Sept 1987, Gillian Mary, da of Norman Duncan Mussett (d 1983); 1 da (Jessica b 5 Jan 1988); *Career* md David Thomas Design Ltd 1965- (designing and producing fine jewellery and silver); one man exhibitions: St Louis and NY USA, Sydney Aust, Tokyo Japan, Goldsmiths' Hall London, Florence Italy; princ cmmns: Masters' badge Grocers' Co, Ladies badge of Goldsmiths' Co, Sheriffs' badges for City of London, trophy for King George VI and Queen Elizabeth II stakes; jewellery in perm collections: Worshipful Co of Goldsmiths, De Beers Diamonds, V & A; chm Goldsmiths' Craft Cncl 1986-88; Freeman City of London 1964, Liveryman Worshipful Co of Goldsmiths 1985; FRSA 1964; *Style—* David Thomas, Esq; 65 Pimlico Rd, London SW1 (☎ 071 730 2389); Steep Cottage, Marle Hill, Chalford, Glos (☎ 0453 88 4058)

THOMAS, David Emrys; s of Emrys Thomas (d 1979), of Guildford, and Elsie Florence, *née* Brown; *b* 9 July 1935; *Educ* Tiffin GS Kingston upon Thames; *m* 1 June 1957, Rosemary, da of Alexander De'Ath, of Hampton, Middlesex; 2 s (Guy b 1963, Mark b 1964), 1 da (Caroline b 1967); *Career* local govt admin 1951-63, Admin Office Local Govt Trg Bd 1968-69, co personnel offr Surrey CC 1970-77 (dep estab offr 1969-70), under sec for manpower Assoc of Met Authys 1977-81, sec LACSAB 1987-91 (indust rels offr 1963-68, dep sec 1981-87), employers' sec Nat Jt Negotiating Cncls in Local Govt 1987-91, management and personnel conslt 1991-; Dip in Municipal Admin, FIPM; fndr pres Soc of Chief Personnel Offrs in Local Govt; *Recreations* unskilled gardening, the musical theatre; *Style—* David Thomas, Esq; The White House, Three Pears Rd, Merrow, Guildford, Surrey GU1 2XU (☎ 0483 69588)

THOMAS, David Gavin; s of Cecil Goring Thomas (d 1974), of Penarth, and Vera Winifred, *née* Wilson; *b* 30 Jan 1943; *Educ* Wycliffe; *m* 14 Aug 1971, Jane Annette, da of John Edward Verdon (d 1984); 1 s (William David b 24 Dec 1976), 2 da (Joanna Louise b 10 April 1975, Laura Anne b 6 July 1979); *Career* qualified clerk Peat Marwick Mitchell 1966-68 (articled clerk 1960-66), fin accountant GKN (S Wales) Ltd 1972-73 (mgmnt accountant 1968-72), chief accountant Nova Jersey Knit Ltd 1973-74; Golley Slater & Partners Ltd: co sec 1974-75, fin dir 1976-87, gp fin dir 1987; ACA 1966; *Recreations* golf, sailing, bridge; *Clubs* Cardiff and County, Glamorganshire Golf, Penarth Yacht; *Style—* David G Thomas, Esq; 20 Clinton Road, Penarth, South Glamorgan CF6 2JD (☎ 0222 705677); Golley Slater Group, 9/11 The Hayes, Cardiff, South Glamorgan CF1 1NU (☎ 0222 388621, fax 0222 238729)

THOMAS, David Glyndor Treharne; s of Dr John Glyndor Treharne Thomas, MC (Capt RAMC, d 1955), of Fairways, Hills Rd, Cambridge, and Ellen, *née* Geldart (d 1970); *b* 14 May 1941; *Educ* Perse Sch Cambridge, Gonville and Caius Coll Cambridge (BA, MA, MB BChir); *m* 29 Dec 1970, Hazel Agnes Christina, da of William John Cockburn (d 1977), of 15 Tylney Rd, Paisley, Renfrewshire; 1 s (William b 1972); *Career* St Mary's Hosp London: house surgn 1966, asst lectr in anatomy 1967-68, sr house offr in neurology 1969, casualty offr 1969; Royal Post Grad Med Sch Hammersmith Hosp London: sr house offr in surgery 1970, registrar in cardio-thoracic surgery 1970-71; Inst of Neurological Scis Southern Gen Hosp Glasgow: registrar, sr registrar and lectr in neuro surgery 1972-76; sr lectr Inst of Neurology and conslt neurosurgn Nat Hosps for Nervous Diseases and Northwick Park Hosp Harrow 1976-; memb: Med Acad Staff Ctee BMA 1981-82, Jt Hosp Med Servs Ctee 1981-82; chm EORTC Experimental Neuro-Oncology Gp 1986-88; Freeman City of London 1969, Liveryman Worshipful Soc of Apothecaries 1971; MRCS 1966, MRCP 1970, FRCSEd 1972, FRCPG 1985; *Books* Brain Tumours: Scientific Basis, Clinical Investigation and Current Therapy (ed with DI Grahamm, 1980), Biology of Brain Tumour (ed with MD Walker, 1986), Neurooncology: Primary Brain Tumours (ed, 1989); *Recreations* military and naval history; *Clubs* Athenaeum, RSM; *Style—* David Thomas, Esq; 34 Oppidans Rd, Primrose Hill, London NW3 3AG (☎ 071 586 2262); The National Hospital, Queen Square, London WC1 3BG (☎ 071 837 3611 ext 3154/071 829 8765, fax 071 278 7894)

THOMAS, David Graeme; s of Edgar Henry Edwin Thomas (d 1974), and late Freda Dorothy Thomas; *b* 22 Oct 1925; *Educ* St Paul's; *m* 23 Aug 1961, Annie Muriel (d 1988); *Career* Scots Gds 1943-47, cmmnd 1944; Whinney Murray CAs 1951-56, sec Hill Samuel & Co 1956-63, dir Robert Fleming & Co 1963-86, chm Aberdare Holdings 1971-74; dep chm: HAT Holdings 1974-86, Robert Fleming Holdings 1981-86, chm Fleming Enterprise Investment Tst plc 1986-; *Recreations* golf; *Clubs* Pratt's, Naval and Military; *Style—* David Thomas, Esq; Bubblewell House, Minchinhampton, Gloucestershire GL6 9AT (☎ 0453 882531); 25 Copthall Ave, London EC2R 7DR (☎ 071 638 5858, telex 297451, fax 071 588 7219)

THOMAS, David John Godfrey; s and h of Sir Godfrey Michael David Thomas, 11 Bt; *b* 11 June 1961; *Educ* Harrow; *Career* dir; *Recreations* squash (Eng Int), tennis; *Clubs* Hurlingham, MCC, Jesters, Escorts; *Style—* David Thomas, Esq; 30 Orbain Rd, London SW6 7JY

THOMAS, Hon David Nigel Mitchell; er s of Baron Thomas of Gwydir, PC, QC (Life Peer), *qv*; *Style—* The Hon David Thomas; 72 Jerningham Road, London SE14

THOMAS, David Richard; DL (Derbyshire 1987); s of Richard Ernest Thomas (d 1975), of Watford, and Beryl Edna, *née* Elliott; *b* 11 June 1937; *Educ* Watford GS, St George's Hosp Med Sch (MB BS); *m* 18 Sept 1965 (m dis 1990), Josephine Anne, *née* Newton; 3 da (Charlotte b 12 June 1966, Emily b 28 March 1968, Amanda (twin) b 28 March 1968); *Career* house surgn St George's Hosp 1961-62, registrar St Thomas' Hosp 1965-66, sr registrar Sheffield Hosp 1969-72, surgn Derby Hosps and clinical tutor surgery Univ of Nottingham 1973-; chm: Derby Scanner Appeal, Derby HS; memb BMA, Assoc Surgns GB and Ireland, FRCS; author of Transplantation of Islets of Langerhans (article in Nature Magazine, 1973); *Recreations* computing; *Style—* David Thomas, Esq, DL; 145 Duffield Rd, Derby DE3 1AF (☎ 0332 363000); East Midlands Nuffield Hosp, Littleover, Derby (☎ 0332 517891)

THOMAS, David William Penrose; s of David Churchill Thomas, CMG, and Susan Petronella Thomas, OBE, *née* Arrow; *b* 17 Jan 1959; *Educ* Eton, King's Coll Cambridge (BA); *m* 28 June 1986, Clare Elizabeth, da of John Jeremy, MBE; 2 da (Holly b 1988, Lucy b 1989); *Career* Young Journalist of the Year Br Press Awards 1983-84; ed: The Magazine 1984-85, Sunday Today Magazine 1986; chief feature writer You Magazine 1986-88 (formerly asst ed), ed Punch 1989-; Columnist of the Year Magazine Publishing Awards 1989; features incl: Sunday Times, Observer, Daily Mail, Tatler, The Face, Rolling Stone, GQ (US); *Books* Bilko, the Fort Baxter Story (1984), Fame & Fortune (1988), Sex and Shopping (1988), Great Sporting Moments (1989); *Clubs* Groucho, Hogarth; *Style—* David Thomas, Esq; Punch, Ludgate House, 245 Blackfriars Rd, London 8E1 (☎ 071 921 5905, fax 071 928 2874)

THOMAS, Rev (Edward Walter) Dennis; s of Edward John Thomas (d 1970), of Pontardawe, nr Swansea, and Roseline Jane, *née* Matthias (d 1970); *b* 16 June 1932; *Educ* Bible Coll of Wales, Neath Tech Coll, St Michael's Theol Coll Cardiff; *m* 25 June 1955, Phyllis Evelyn, da of John George Alexander Japp (d 1959), of Trebanos, nr Swansea; 3 s (Christopher b 1957, Andrew b 1960, Simon b 1962), 1 da (Siân b 1971); *Career* RAF (air-wireless) 1951-54; with International Nickel Co (Mond) Ltd 1954-61; curate of Loughor 1963-69; vicar: Ystradfellte 1969-74, St Mark & St Luke Dunkinfield 1974-; chaplain to: Mayor of Tameside 1977-79 and 1990-, High Sheriff of Gtr Manchester 1987-88; divnl police chaplain 1977-, chaplain to Special Constabulary of Gtr Manchester 1986-, officiating chaplain HM Forces 1988-; county cnclr Breconshire 1970-74; chm: Ystradfellte Parish Cncl 1972, Ystradfellte Community Cncl 1973; co-fndr Tameside Play Cncl; memb: Community Prog, YTS, Age Concern, Crime Prevention 1978-, Community Health Cncl 1985-91; govr High Sch 1975-; *Recreations* helping unemployed, raising money for charity, police, health, sport, education; *Style—* The Rev Dennis Thomas; The Vicarage, Church St, Dukinfield Cheshire SK16 4PR (☎ 061 330 2783)

THOMAS, Sir Derek Morison David; KCMG (1987, CMG 1977); s of Kenneth Peter David Thomas (1982), of Hill House, Hempstead, Saffron Walden, Essex, and Mali McLeod, *née* Morison (d 1972); *b* 31 Oct 1929; *Educ* Radley, Trinity Hall Cambridge (MA); *m* 1956, Lineke, da of Thijs Van der Mast (d 1988), of Eindhoven, Netherlands; 1 s (Matthew b 1967), 1 da (Caroline b 1963); *Career* Sub Lt RNVR 1955 (Midshipman 1953-55); articled apprentice Dolphin Industry Developments Ltd 1947; entered Dip Serv 1953; served in: Moscow, Manila, Brussels, Sofia, Ottawa, Paris, Washington; dep under sec of state for Europe and political dir FCO 1984-87, Br ambass to Italy 1987-89; Euro advsr N M Rothschild & Sons 1990; dir: Rothschild Italia 1990, Christow Consultants 1990; assoc CDP Nexus 1990; *Style—* Sir Derek Thomas, KCMG; 12 Lower Sloane Street, London SW1W 8BJ

THOMAS, Derek Walter; s of Walter John Thomas (d 1974); *b* 18 Oct 1936; *Educ* Portsmouth Southern GS; *m* 1960, Maureen Janet, *née* Smith; 1 s, 1 da; *Career* md: D W Thomas (Pensions) Ltd, D W Thomas (Investmts) Ltd; memb Assoc Pensioner Tstees, FIMBRA, FIA; *Recreations* squash, cricket, singing, music; *Style—* Derek Thomas, Esq; Allingtons, 43 Beech Rd, Reigate, Surrey

THOMAS, Douglas Ronald; s of Harry Leonard Thomas; *b* 15 Feb 1925; *m* Shirley Edith Frances, da of Archibald Dixon; 1 s (David), 2 da (Susan (Mrs Taylor), Sally (Mrs Demaine)); *Career* served Sgt RAF; ret; FCIS, FBIM; *Clubs* Arts; *Style—* Douglas Thomas, Esq

THOMAS, Prof (James) Edward; s of James Edward Thomas (ka 1941), of Portfield, Haverfordwest, Pembrokeshire, and Margaret Elizabeth, *née* Absalom (d 1981); *b* 20 Dec 1933; *Educ* Haverfordwest GS, Univ of Oxford, Univ of London, Univ of York; *m* 24 Aug 1957, Olwen, da of John Yolland (d 1980), of Colby, Wiston, Pembrokeshire; 2 s (Simon b 24 Oct 1958, Philip b 6 June 1961); *Career* Nat Serv RA 1952-54; admin offr Govt of N Rhodesia 1957-60, govr HM Prison Serv 1960-67, lectr and sr lectr Univ of Hull 1967-78; Univ of Nottingham 1978-: reader, prof, dean of educn, pro vice chllr; bursar Imp Rels Tst 1970, fell Japan Soc for Promotion of Sci, former chm Standing Conf on Univ Teaching and Res in Educn of Adults, vice chm Univ Cncl on Adult and Continuing Educn; FRSA; *Books* The English Prison Officer since 1950: a study in conflict (1972), Imprisonment in Western Australia: Evolution Theory and Practice (with A Stewart, 1978), The Exploding Prison: Prison Riots and the case of Hull (with R Pooley, 1980), Radical Adult Education: Theory and Practice (1982), International Biography of Adult Education (with B Elsey, 1985), Learning Democracy in Japan: The Social Education of Japanese Adults (1986), House of Care: Prisons and Prisoners in England 1500-1800 (1988), A Select Biography of Adult Continuing Education (with J H Davis, 5 edn 1988); *Recreations* music, walking, cinema; *Style—* Prof Edward Thomas; University of Nottingham, University Park, Nottingham NG7 2RD (☎ 0602 484848, fax 0602 420825, telex 37346 UNINOT 2)

THOMAS, Prof Edward John; s of John Henry Thomas (d 1958), of Plymouth, Devon, and Lily Elizabeth Jane Thomas; *b* 25 Nov 1937; *Educ* Devonport HS, Keble Coll Oxford (MA), Univ of London (MSc), Univ of Manchester (PhD); *m* 12 Sep 1964, Erica Jean, da of Eric Distin (d 1977), of Salcombe, Devon; 1 s (Gerard William b 1969), 1 da (Katherine Grace b 1965); *Career* res scientist GEC plc 1962-64, lectr Univ of Manchester 1964-68, currently dir of continuing educn Univ of Bristol (staff tutor 1969-80, sr lectr 1980-81, prof of adult educn 1981-); treas Univs Cncl for Adult and Continuing Educn; MInstP 1972, FRSA 1983; *Books* Type II Superconductivity (1969), From Quarks to Quasars (1977); *Recreations* reading, writing, eating, drinking, talking; *Style—* Prof Edward Thomas; Dept for Continuing Education, The University, Bristol BS8 1HR (☎ 0272 303627, fax 0272 254975, telex 445938)

THOMAS, (John) Frank Phillips; s of John Phillips Thomas (d 1948), and Catherine Myfanwy, *née* Williams (d 1979); *b* 11 April 1920; *Educ* Christ's Coll Finchley, Univ of London (BSc); *m* 12 Dec 1942, Edith Victory, da of Alexander Caskie Milne (d 1958); 1 s (Paul Alexander b 1945), 1 da (Jane Margaret b 1947); *Career* BT: dir network planning 1972-78, dir overseas liaison 1978-81; dir Frank Thomas Conslts 1981-; vice pres Rickmansworth LT Club; MIEE; *Recreations* fly fishing; *Style—* Frank Thomas, Esq; 24 Moneyhill Road, Richmansworth, Herts WD3 2EQ (☎ 0923 772992)

THOMAS, Dr Gareth; s of Rev Evan George Thomas, and Nina Mary, *née* Clargo; step s of Olwen Elizabeth, *née* Jones; *b* 3 Nov 1945; *Educ* Merchant Taylors', St Mary's Hosp Med Sch (MB BS), Univ of London (MD); *m* 20 Sept 1969, Alison Muir, da of late David Muir Kelly, of Haile, Cumbria; 3 s (Mark b 1971, Robert b 1973, James b 1976), 2 da (Anna b 1980, Abigail b 1982); *Career* obstetrician and gynaecologist; house physician St Mary's Hosp London 1969; resident med offr: Queen Charlotte's Hosp London 1970-71, Samaritan Hosp London 1971-72; lectr and hon registrar UCL 1972-75, hon lectr Univ of Oxford 1975-77, sr registrar Oxfordshire RHA 1975-79, conslt Ipswich and East Suffolk 1979-, clinical dir Dept of Gynaecological and Maternity Servs 1991-; memb Bd Christchurch Park Hosp Ipswich, examiner Univ of London 1988-; MRCS 1969, MRCOG 1974 FRCOG 1987; *Recreations* sailing; *Clubs* Royal Harwich Yacht, The Ipswich Rotary, Association Broadcasting Doctors; *Style—* Dr Gareth Thomas; 49 Graham Rd, Ipswich, Suffolk IP1 3QF (☎ 0473 232718)

THOMAS, Air Vice-Marshal Geoffrey Percy Sansom; CB (1970), OBE (1945); s of

Reginald Ernest Sansom Thomas (d 1949); *b* 24 April 1915; *Educ* King's Coll Sch Wimbledon; *m* 1940, Sally, *née* Biddle; 1 s (Garth Michael Geoffrey b 1941), 1 da (Deborah Diana b 1946); *Career* cmmnd RAF 1939, served with Turkish Air Force 1950-52, served with RAAF 1960-62, Air Cdre 1965, dir of Movements 1965, Air Vice-Marshal 1969, SASO Maintenance Cmd 1969-71, ret 1971; *Style—* Air Vice-Marshal Geoffrey Thomas, CB, OBE; Elms Wood House, Elms Vale, Dover, Kent (☎ 0304 206375)

THOMAS, (Lionel) George; s of Joseph Thomas, of Northland, New Zealand, and Akinihi, *née* Wanoa; *b* 26 May 1950; *Educ* Kaitaia Coll Northland NZ, Univ of Auckland NZ (BCom); *m* 12 Aug 1983, Sandra Patricia, da of Maurice Wylie Hunt; 2 da (Catherine Koa b 9 May 1984, Sarah Jean b 24 April 1986); *Career* asst cost accountant Downer Construction NZ 1970, accountant Golden Chemical Products Ltd 1971, co sec City & West End News Ltd 1972, fin and cost accountant Dulux (NZ) Ltd 1973-76, self employed conslt in UK 1976-84, fin ptnr Fitzroy Robinson Partnership 1985-; ACA 1976; *Recreations* tennis; *Clubs* Riverside Raquet, London Rugby; *Style—* George Thomas, Esq; 77 Portland Place, London W1N 4EP (☎ 071 636 8033, fax 071 580 3996)

THOMAS, Gerald Cyril; s of Samuel Thomas (d 1966), of Montpelier Court, London W5, and Freda Ann, *née* Cohen (d 1983); *b* 10 Dec 1920; *Educ* St Brendan's Coll Clifton, Middlesex Univ Coll, Arlington Park Coll; *m* 15 Aug 1957, Barbara Evelyn, da of Frederick Tarry; 3 da (Sarah Evelyn b 28 April 1962, Deborah Jane b 3 Oct 1965, Samantha Anne b 5 Jan 1967); *Career* served WWII KRRC and Royal Sussex Regt in France Belgium Holland Germany and ME; film director; asst ed then ed Denham studios; worked on: Hamlet, The October Man, The Flying Dutchman, Madness of The Heart, Tony Draws A Horse, Doctor In The House, Appointment with Venus, Venetian Bird, A Day To Remember, The Sword And The Rose; second unit dir: Mad About Men, Above Us The Waves; assoc prodr: After The Ball, Passionate Stranger; dir: Circus Friends, Time Lock, The Vicious Circle, Chain of Events, Solitary Child, The Duke Wore Jeans, Please Turn Over, Watch Your Stern, No Kidding, Raising The Wind, Twice Around The Daffodils, The Iron Maiden, Nurse On Wheels, The Big Job, Bless This House, Second Victory and 30 Carry On films; tv work: Carry On Laughing (for ATV), Carry On Christmas (Thames TV), Odd Man Out (Thames TV), Just for Laughs (Thames TV), What A Carry On (BBC); *awards* British Comedy Awards Lifetime Achievement award for Br Comedy 1990; govr High March Sch Beaconsfield; memb: Dirs' Guild of GB, BAFTA, BFI; *Recreations* motor sport, travel, food and wine; *Clubs* Leander, RAC, Lord's Taverners, Variety, Annabel's, Harry's Bar, The Queen's Regt Officers'; *Style—* Gerald Thomas, Esq; GT Productions Limited, Pinewood Studios, Iver Heath, Buckinghamshire SL0 0NH (☎ 0753 654341, fax 0753 656844, car 0860 206880)

THOMAS, Gervase Alan; s of Alan Ernest Wentworth Thomas, DSO, MC (d 1969); *b* 19 April 1930; *Educ* Eton, Clare Coll Cambridge; *m* 1961 (m dis 1984), Jane Elizabeth, *née* Ross-Lowe; 2 s, 2 da; m 2, 1988, Carey Yulan Adria Corner, *née* Ross; *Career* 2 Lt Grenadier Gds; *Recreations* fox hunting, shooting, boating, golf; *Clubs* Boodle's, MCC; *Style—* Gervase Thomas, Esq; 42 Eaton Square SW1W 9BD (☎ 071 235 7276)

THOMAS, Glyn Collen; s of Graham Lewis Thomas, of Budleigh Salterton, Devon, and Pegi Joan, *née* Bingham; *b* 30 July 1951; *Educ* BEC GS London, Cardiff HS Glamorgan, Univ of Wales Cardiff (BSc); *m* 9 Sept 1983, Heather Audrey, da of Thomas Alexander Kerslick, of Fulham, London; 1 s (Gregory Lewis b 30 March 1984), 1 da (Chloe Elizabeth b 3 June 1988); *Career* Peat Marwick Mitchell 1972-76, Rothmans International London and Zug 1976-86, Kingfisher plc 1986-; memb Chalfonts and Gerrards Cross Gp SDP, memb Assoc Corporate Treasy 1982; FCA 1975 (ACA); *Recreations* skiing, squash; *Style—* Glyn Thomas, Esq; 6 Old Mead, Chalfont St Peter, Bucks SL9 0SE (☎ 02407 3691); Kingfisher plc, 119 Marylebone Rd, London NW1 5PX (☎ 071 724 7749, fax 071 724 1160)

THOMAS, Godfrey Slee; s of Harold Charles Thomas, of Walberton, Arundel, West Sussex, and Freda Elisabeth, *née* Slee; *b* 14 Feb 1946; *Educ* Brighton Coll, New Coll Oxford (BA, MA); *m* 5 Nov 1977, Caroline Anne, da of Leslie Gordon Glynn Warne (d 1962); 2 da (Charlotte b 21 Nov 1978, Verity b 9 March 1981); *Career* dir: Cap Scientific Ltd 1980-82, Cap Industry Ltd 1982-88, Dowty-Sema Ltd 1988-, Aerosystems International Ltd 1988-, md Sema Group Systems Ltd 1988-; *Recreations* squash, singing, riding; *Style—* Godfrey Thomas, Esq; Sema Scientific, Scientific House, 40-44 Coombe Rd, New Malden KT3 4QF (☎ 071 942 9661, fax 071 949 8067, telex 28863)

THOMAS, Graham Stuart; OBE (1975); s of William Richard Thomas (d 1947), of 169 Hills Rd, Cambridge, and Lilian, *née* Hays (d 1951); *b* 3 April 1909; *Educ* Botanic Garden Univ of Cambridge; *Career* foreman later mangr T Hilling & Co 1931, assoc dir Sunningdale Nurseries Windlesham Surrey 1968-71 (mangr 1956), gardens conslt Nat Tst 1974- (advsr 1954-74); vice pres: Garden History Soc, Br Hosta and Hemerocallis Soc; vice patron Royal Nat Rose Soc; RHS: Veitch Meml Medal 1966, Victoria Medal of Hon 1968; Dean Hole Medal Royal Nat Rose Soc 1976, hon memb Irish Garden Plant Soc 1983; *Books* The Old Shrub Roses (1955), Colour in the Winter Garden (1957), Shrub Roses of Today (1962), Climbing Roses Old and New (1965), Plants for Ground Cover (1970), Perennial Garden Plants (1976), Gardens of the National Trust (1979), Three Gardens (1983), Trees in the Landscape (1983), Recreating the Period Garden (ed, 1984), A Garden of Roses (1987), The Complete Paintings and Drawings of Graham Stuart Thomas (1987), The Rock Garden and its Plants (1989); *Recreations* music, painting flowers, reading; *Style—* Graham Thomas, Esq, OBE; Briar Cottage, 21 Kettlewell Close, Horsell, Woking, Surrey (☎ 048 6271 4042)

THOMAS, (John) Harvey Noake; CBE (1990); s of Col John Humphrey Kenneth Thomas (d 1984), of Leamington Spa, and Olga Rosina, *née* Noake; *b* 10 April 1939; *Educ* Westminster, Univ of Minnesota, Univ of Hawaii, North Western Bible Coll Minnesota; *m* 22 Dec 1978, Marlies, da of Erich Kram, of Wölmersen, Germany; 2 da (Leah Elisabeth b 1984, Lani Christine b 1986); *Career* Billy Graham Evangelistic Assoc 1960-75, int PR conslt 1976-, dir presentation and promotion Cons Party 1985-, field dir PM's Election Tour 1987, dir The London Cremation Co 1984-; memb: Oakwood Baptist Church N London, Salvation Army Advsy Bd London; fell: Inst of PR, Inst of Journalists; memb Assoc of Conf Execs; *Books* In The Face Of Fear (1985), Making an Impact (1989); *Recreations* family, travel; *Clubs* IOD; *Style—* Harvey Thomas, Esq, CBE; 105A High Rd, Wood Green, London N22 6BB (☎ 081 889 6466)

THOMAS, Hilary Joan; *née* Thompson; da of John MacMillan Thompson, of Shaftesbury, Dorset, and Vivienne Josephine, *née* Thomson; *b* 27 May 1935; *Educ* St Cyprian's Sch Cape Town; *m* 15 June 1963, Rowland Humphrey Thomas, s of Leonard Tennant Thomas (d 1968); 1 s (David James Hamilton b 1970), 1 da (Caroline Josephine b 1966); *Career* SRN St Thomas' Hosp 1958; journalist; historical researcher and genealogist 1970-; *publications*: travel books, nursing articles, research on biographies, genealogies; *Recreations* travel, theatre, music, books, country walking; *Clubs* Soc of Genealogists; *Style—* Mrs Hilary Thomas; 27 Grasvenor Ave, Barnet, Herts EN5 2BY (☎ 081 440 5662)

THOMAS, Prof Howard Christopher; s of Harold Thomas (d 1986), and Hilda, *née* Pickering (d 1980); *b* 31 July 1945; *Educ* Thornbury GS, Univ of Newcastle upon Tyne (BSc, MB BS, Phillipson prize in med), Univ of Glasgow (PhD); *m* 31 May 1975, Dilys, da of John Andrew Ferguson (d 1979); 1 s (Robin James b 4 Oct 1978), 1 da (Lucy b 18 Feb 1980); *Career* lectr in immunology at univ 1971-74; Royal Free Hosp Med Sch London: lectr in med 1974-78, sr Wellcome fell in clinical sci 1978-83, reader in med 1983-84, prof of med 1984-87; prof and chm of med: St Mary's Hosp Med Sch, Imp Coll London; conslt physician and hepatologist St Mary's Hosp 1987-; Humphry Davy Rolleston lectr RCP 1986; Br Soc of Gastroenterology Res medal 1984, Hans Popper Int prize for Distinction in Hepatology; FRCP, FRCPS, MRCPath; *Books* Clinical Gastrointestinal Immunology (1979), Recent Advances in Hepatology (jt ed Vol 1 1983, Vol 2 1986), author of various publications on Hepatology; *Recreations* tennis and golf; *Style—* Prof Howard Thomas; Department of Medicine, St Mary's Hospital, Praed Street, London W2 1PG (☎ 071 725 1606)

THOMAS, (David) Hugh; s of David Rogers Thomas (d 1980), of Ammanford, Dyfed, and Mary, *née* Jones; *b* 1 April 1937; *Educ* Amman Valley GS, Univ Coll of Wales; *m* 22 Aug 1963, Beryl Dorothy, da of David Garth Williams (d 1951), of Penrhyndeudraeth, Gwynedd; 1 da (Nia b 29 May 1971); *Career* slr; asst slr: Carmarthenshire CC 1961-64, Llanelli RDC 1964-65; dep town clerk Port Talbot 1965-74, dep county clerk W Glamorgan CC 1974-80; hon sec Court of the Royal Nat Elsteddfod 1975-, chm St Johns Cncl M Glamorgan 1984-, hon sec Welsh Counties Ctee 1985-90, memb Welsh Arts Cncl 1986- (chm of Arts Ctee); OStJ; Cross of the Order of Merit Federal Republic of Germany 1990; *Recreations* rugby, bowls, music, art; *Style—* Hugh Thomas, Esq; Llys Gwyn, 70 Brynteg Ave, Bridgend, Mid Glamorgan CF31 3EL (☎ 0656 657204); Mid Glamorgan County Hall, Cathays Park, Cardiff, S Glamorgan (☎ 0222 780001)

THOMAS, (Edward) Hugh Gwynne; s of Edward Gwynne Thomas, OBE, VRD (d 1976), and Lisbeth Helen Mair, *née* Thomas (d 1950); *b* 12 Dec 1938; *Educ* Canford; *m* 1 Dec 1973, Annemary Perry, da of Lawrence Walter Dixon, of Poole, Dorset; 3 da (Juliet b 16 Oct 1974, Annabel b 15 May 1977, Louisa b 30 July 1979); *Career* slr 1963, ptnr Keene Marsland 1966-; Freeman: City of London 1966, Worshipful Co of Slrs 1966; memb Law Soc 1963; *Recreations* golf, sailing; *Clubs* Beaconsfield Golf; *Style—* Hugh Thomas, Esq; Orchard Corner, Curzon Ave, Beaconsfield, Bucks HP9 2NN (☎ 0494 671056); Dragoon House, 37 Artillery Lane, Bishopsgate, London E1 7TL (☎ 071 375 1581, fax 071 375 0318)

THOMAS, Hugh Miles; s of Dr Gwilym Dorrien Thomas, of 47 Ty Rhŷs, The Parade, nr Camarthen, and late Dorothy Gertrude, *née* Jones; *b* 14 Oct 1944; *Educ* Clifton, Univ of Southampton (BSc); *m* 10 Sept 1966, Alison Mary, da of Lt-Col Richard Ryder Davies (d 1968); 2 s (Simon b 1 July 1970, Ryder b 24 May 1973); *Career* CA 1969; Price Waterhouse: articled clerk 1966, ptnr 1978-, ptnr in charge Wales 1983-; pres S Wales Inst of CAs 1987-88; memb: Cncl UWIST 1983-88, Cncl Univ of Wales Coll of Cardiff 1988 and 1991-, Mgmnt Ctee Cardiff Business Sch, Sports Cncl for Wales, Prince of Wales' Ctee (chm Fin and Gen Purposes Ctee); vice pres: Cardiff Business Club, The Welsh Inst of Int Affrs; FCA 1979; *Recreations* sailing, farming; *Clubs* Cardiff Co; *Style—* Hugh Thomas, Esq; Penprysg, Llangenny, Crickhowell, Powys (☎ 0873 811387, fax 0873 811405); Price Waterhouse, Haywood House, Dumfries Place, Cardiff CF1 4BA (☎ 0222 376255, fax 0222 374124)

THOMAS, Hon Huw Maynard Mitchell; yr s of Baron Thomas of Gwydir, PC, QC (Life Peer), *qv*; *m* Jane, *née* Perman; 2 da; *Style—* The Hon Huw Thomas; 2 Porden Rd, London SW2

THOMAS, Huw Owen; s of Goronwy Evan Thomas (d 1984), and Morfydd Owen, *née* Jones; *b* 11 May 1941; *Educ* Liverpool Coll, Welsh Nat Sch of Med (MB BCh), Univ of Liverpool (MChOrth); *m* 25 Oct 1975, Judith Audrey; 2 s (Tom Owen Thomas b 11 March 1977, Tristan Goronwy b 26 Jan 1979); *Career* Capt TA RAMC 1970-73; house surgn Cardiff Royal Infirmary 1966, sr house offr Liverpool 1967-69, prosecutor RCS 1967, sr registrar Liverpool & Wrightington Hosp for Hip Surgery 1974-78, conslt orthopaedic surgn Wirral AHA 1978-; memb Medical Appeals Tbnl; FRCS Ed 1971, FRCS 1972, FRSM; author of articles on: Metallic Implants from Crematoria, Isolated Dislocation of Scaphoid, Recurrent Dislocation of Patella; *Recreations* fishing, shooting, music; *Style—* Huw Thomas, Esq; Pinwydden, 18 Pine Walks, Prenton, Wirral L42 8NE (☎ 051 608 3909); Arrowe Park Hosp, Wirral; Clatterbridge Hosp, Wirral; Bupa Murrayfield Hosp, Wirral (☎ 051 678 5111)

THOMAS, Ian David; s of Evan Morgan Thomas (d 1984), of Cardiff, and Nancy, *née* Watkin (d 1970); *b* 16 March 1932; *Educ* Haverfordwest GS, Trinity Coll Univ of Dublin (MA); *Career* Sub Lt Instructor Branch RN 1957, Lt 1958; legal asst S Wales Electricity Bd 1961-63, princ asst The Electricity Cncl 1963-66, sr offr The Gas Cncl 1966-68, dir gen Int Fedn of the Phonographic Indust 1982- (legal advsr 1968-74, dep dir gen 1974-82); memb: Middle Temple London, King's Inns Dublin, Bar Assoc for Commerce, Indust and Fin; *Clubs* Oriental London, Kildare St and Univ Dublin; *Style—* Ian Thomas, Esq; IFPI Secretariat, 54 Regent St, London W1R 5PJ (☎ 071 434 3521, fax 071 439 9166, telex 919044 IFPI G)

THOMAS, Ian Mitchell; s of John Bythell Thomas (d 1977), of Sutton Coldfield, and Gladys Ethel, *née* Miller; *b* 17 May 1933; *Educ* Liverpool Coll, Selwyn Coll Cambridge (MA); *m* 1, 20 Aug 1960 (m dis 1976), Jenifer Diana, da of Dr George Thomas Lance Fletcher Morris, of Coggeshall, Essex; 2 s (James b 1961, Mark b 1965), 2 da (Emma b 1963, Victoria b 1969); m 2, 24 Oct 1977, Diana Lesley Kathryn, wid of Nicholas Thorne (d 1976), and da of Donald William Leslie (d 1984), of Wimbledon; 1 step s (Alexander b 1972), 1 step da (Camilla b 1976); *Career* Nat Serv 4 KORR 1952-54 (2 Lt 1953), PA to COS Br Cwlth Forces Korea 1953, Capt The Liverpool Scottish Queen's Own Cameron Highlanders TA; asst md Hobson Bates and Ptnrs 1965 (dir 1963), jt md Cavenham Foods Ltd 1965-67, md Fabbri and Ptnrs Ltd 1968-70, chm Culpeper Ltd 1972- (md 1972-); cncllr (C) Islington Cncl 1968-70, vice pres Herb Soc 1986-87 (memb Cncl 1978-87); *Books* Culpeper's Book of Birth (1985), How to Grow Herbs (1988), Culpeper Herbal Notebook (1991); *Recreations* running, tennis, skiing, gardening; *Style—* Ian Thomas, Esq; Floriston Hall, Wixoe, Halstead, Essex CO9 4AR (☎ 044 085 229); Culpeper Ltd, Hadstock Rd, Linton, Cambridge CB1 6NJ (☎ 0223 891196, fax 0223 893104, telex 81698)

THOMAS, Irene; da of Edmund Roberts Ready (d 1956), and Ethel, *née* Crapnell (d 1970); *b* 28 June 1920; *Educ* The County Sch Ashford Middx; *m* 1, 1940 (m dis 1949), Wesley J C Baldry; m 2, 23 Jan 1950, Edward Kenfig Thomas, s of Walter Thomas of Porth, Rhondda; *Career* NFS 1940-45, Covent Garden Opera 1946-49, freelance singer 1950-68; broadcaster of progs incl: Brain of Britain 1961, Brain of Brains 1962, Round Britain Quiz 1967 and 1973-, Round Europe Quiz, Transatlantic Quiz, The Gardening Quiz 1988-; tv progs incl: The 60-70-80 show (with Roy Hudd) 1974-80, About Face 1986; regular contrib Woman & Home Magazine; Hon MUniv Open Univ 1987; *Books* The Bandsman's Daughter (1979), The Almost Impossible Quiz Book (1982); *Recreations* watching cats, thinking; *Style—* Mrs Irene Thomas; c/o BBC, Broadcasting House, London W1A 1AA

THOMAS, Hon (Henry) Isambard Tobias; 2 s of Baron Thomas of Swynnerton; *b* 28 Jan 1964; *Educ* Latymer Upper Sch, London Coll of Printing, St Martin's Sch of Art; *Career* design executive Thames & Hudson Publishers Ltd 1988-; *Style—* The Hon Isambard Thomas; 29 Ladbroke Grove, London W11 3BB (☎ 071 727 2288); c/o Thames & Hudson, Publishers, 30-34 Bloomsbury Street, London WC1B 3QP (☎ 071

636 5488, fax 071 636 4799)

THOMAS, Hon Mrs (Jacqueline); yst da of Baron Cooper of Stockton Heath (Life Peer, d 1988); *b* 1946; *m* 1972, J Bradford Thomas; 3 s (Samuel Spencer b 1975, Alexander Benjamin b 1976, Jeremy Edward b 1980); *Style—* The Hon Mrs Thomas; 54 Stanley Road, East Sheen, London SW14 7DZ

THOMAS, James Alfred; s of Robert Thomas (d 1962), of Shrewsbury, Shrops; and Margarett, *née* Griffiths (d 1989); *b* 31 March 1927; *Educ* Univ of Sussex (MPhil), Brighton Sch of Architecture (Dip Arch); *m* 21 March 1951, Cynthia, da of John Rance Goddard (d 1984), of Brighton, Sussex; 1 s (James); *Career* Royal Signals 1 Air Support Central Mediterranean 1945-48, RAF(VR) 1948-52; electricity supply indust 1950-63, Electricity Council scholar 1960-63, univ architect and engr Univ of Sussex 1964-81 (responsible for tech planning and devpt of univ bldgs, conslt architect to the univ 1981-), currently sr lectr Brighton Sch of Architecture and in private practice with James Thomas Architects & Environmental Consultants); memb Energy Ctee RIBA; ARIBA 1964, CEng 1972, fell Inst of Energy 1972, fell CIBSE 1974; *Recreations* swimming, looking at mostly old buildings; *Style—* James Thomas, Esq; 3 Lewes Crescent, Brighton, Sussex (☎ 0273 607100)

THOMAS, Jeffrey; QC (1974); s of John Thomas and Phyllis, *née* Hile; *b* 12 Nov 1933; *Educ* Abertillery GS, King's Coll London; *m* 1, 1960 (m dis 1981), Margaret Jenkins; m 2, 1987, Valerie Ellerington; *Career* barr (Gray's Inn) 1957, Crown Court recorder 1975-, served RCT from 1959 and as Maj Dep Assist Directorate Army Legal Servs BAOR HQ 1961; fought Barry (Lab) 1966; MP (Lab to Dec 1981, thereafter SDP) Abertillery 1970-83; pps to Sec of State Wales 1977-79, memb Labour Party 1986, vice chm Br Gp IPU, oppn spokesman on legal affrs 1979-81; chm Br-Caribbean Assoc 1979-83 (now vice pres), memb Court Univ of London until 1986; *Style—* Jeffrey Thomas Esq, QC; 3 Temple Gdns, Temple, London EC4 (☎ 071 583 0010); 26 Ellington St, London N7

THOMAS, Jeremy Jack; s of Maj Phillip Thomas, MC, and Joy Eveleyn, *née* Spanjer; *b* 26 July 1949; *Educ* Millfield; *m* 1, (m dis 1977), Claudia Frolich; m 2, 1982, Vivien Patricia, da of Adolph Coughman; 2 s (Jack Felix, Joshua Kit), 1 da (Jessica Emily); *Career* film prodr; films incl: Mad Dog Morgan (1976), The Shout (1977), The Great Rock 'n Roll Swindle (1979), Bad Timing (1979), Eureka (1982), Merry Christmas Mr Lawrence (1982), The Hit (1983), Insignificance (1984), The Last Emperor (1988, winner of nine Academy awards incl one for Best Picture), Everybody Wins (1989), The Sheltering Sky (1990); *Style—* Jeremy Thomas, Esq; The Recorded Picture Co, 8-12 Broadwick Street, London W1V 1FH (☎ 071 439 0607, fax 071 434 1192, telex 941 9035 RECORD G)

THOMAS, Dr John Anthony Griffiths; s of William Thomas, of 37 Lynton Walk, Rhyl, Clwyd, and Bernice Margaret, *née* Griffiths (d 1989); *b* 28 Aug 1943; *Educ* Alun GS Clwyd, Univ of Leeds (BSc), Univ of Keele (PhD); *m* 16 Aug 1965, Sylvia Jean, da of Robert Norman (d 1983); 2 da (Rachel b 1971, Emily b 1974); *Career* dir (former ed and publisher) Reed Business Publishing Ltd 1970-86 (dep md IPC Sci and Technol Press Ltd 1977-78, publishing dir IPC Business Press Ltd 1978-84, md Update Gp Ltd 1984-85, md Update-Siebert Ltd 1985-86), dir BBC Enterprises Ltd 1986-; chm: Redwood Publishing Ltd 1986-, Hartog Hutton Publishing Ltd 1986-, World Publications Ltd, BBC Frontline Ltd; dir Periodical Publishers Assoc Ltd; *Books* Energy Today (1977), The Quest for Fuel (1978), Energy Analysis (ed, 1978); *Recreations* jogging, swimming, reading; *Style—* Dr John Thomas; BBC Enterprises Ltd, 35 Marylebone High St, London W1A 4MM (☎ 071 927 4675)

THOMAS, (Roger) John Laugharne; QC (1984); s of Roger Edward Laugharne Thomas (d 1970), of Ystradgynlais, and Dinah Agnes, *née* Jones; *b* 22 Oct 1947; *Educ* Rugby, Trinity Hall Cambridge (BA), Univ of Chicago Law Sch (JD); *m* 6 Jan 1973, Elizabeth Ann, da of Stephen James Buchanan (d 1984), of Ohio; 1 s (David b 1978), 1 da (Alison b 1980); *Career* teaching asst Mayo Coll India 1965-66; called to the Bar Gray's Inn 1969, QC Eastern Carribean Supreme Ct 1986, recorder 1987; faculty fell Univ of Southampton 1990-; *Recreations* gardens, travel, walking, opera; *Style—* John L Thomas, Esq, QC; 4 Essex Court, Temple, London, EC4Y 9AJ (☎ 071 583 9191, fax 071 353 2422, telex 888465 COMCAS)

THOMAS, John Richard; s of David Edgar Thomas (d 1954), of Talog, Manor Way, Petts Wood, Kent, and Daisy Thomas (d 1949); *b* 11 Sept 1927; *Educ* Dulwich; *m* 4 July 1953, Pamela Mary, da of Owen Henry White (d 1959), of Three Chimneys, Fittleworth, West Sussex; 2 s (Mark David b 2 May 1955, Richard Jeremy b 19 Sept 1958); *Career* Royal W Kent Regt: Private 1946, cmmnd 2 Lt 1947, demobilised 1948; chm and sr ptnr Baxter Payne & Lepper Chartered Surveyors 1973-87 (ptnr 1959, conslt 1987-90); dir: South of England Building Society 1967-82, Nationwide Anglia Society 1987-, Surveyors Holdings (RICS) Ltd 1986-; dep chm Anglia Building Society 1985-87 (vice chm 1982-85); chm: Nationwide Anglia Estate Agents 1987-, Peter Ling plc (bldg contractors); chm Gtr London (SE) Scout Cncl 1973-, hon sec Bromley Literary and Music Soc 1970-85; pres Gen Practice RICS 1977-78 (memb Gen Cncl 1974-88), magistrate SE Cmmn 1975-; fndr memb Worshipful Co of Chartered Surveyors 1977-; FRICS 1954, FRSA 1973; *Books* Valuations for Loan Purposes (1981), Estate Agents Act 1979 (1982); *Recreations* golf, music, gardening; *Clubs* St Stephen's, Ham Manor Golf, Sundridge Park Golf; *Style—* John Thomas, Esq; 6 Glenbyrne Lodge, Albemarle Rd, Beckenham, Kent (☎ 081 464 1181); Nationwide Anglia Building Society, Chesterfield House, Bloomsbury Way, London (☎ 071 242 8822/071 379 0101)

THOMAS, Prof (William) John; s of Trevor Roylance Thomas (d 1975), of Dinas Powys, S Glam, Swansea and Carmarthen, and Gwendoline Novello, *née* Williams (d 1984); *b* 13 July 1929; *Educ* Dynevor GS Swansea, Univ Coll Swansea, Univ of Wales (BSc, DSc), Imperial Coll London (PhD); *m* 11 June 1955, Pamela Heather, da of Clifford Rees; 1 s (Mark b 1959), 1 da (Clare b 1963); *Career* scientific offr Int Nickel Co 1954-55, lectr Univ Coll Swansea 1955-58 and 1960-68, sr scientific offr Atomic Energy Authy Harwell 1958-60, prof of chem engrg Univ of Bath 1968-, pro vice chllr Univ of Bath 1988; vice pres Inst of Chem Engrg 1988-90; FIChemE contrib scientific books; vice pres Inst of Chem Engrg 1988-90; FIChemE; *Books* Introduction to the Principles of Heterogeneous Catalysis (1969), contrib to scientific books; *Recreations* former Welsh Rugby Union (WRU) referee, assistant organist at Bathampton Parish church; *Style—* Prof John Thomas; School of Chemical Engineering, University of Bath, Claverton Down, Bath BA2 7AY (☎ 0225 826575, fax 0225 462508, telex 449097)

THOMAS, Keith Henry Westcott; CB (1982), OBE (1962); s of Henry Westcott Thomas (d 1957), and Norah Dorothy, *née* Stone (d 1985); *b* 20 May 1923; *Educ* Southern Secdy Sch for Boys Portsmouth, Royal Dockyard Sch Portsmouth, RN Engrg Coll Manadon, RNC Greenwich; *m* 31 Aug 1946, Brenda Jeanette, da of William Royston Crofton (d 1964); 2 s (Michael b 1948, David b 1951); *Career* RCNC 1946-: asst constructor Admty Experiment Works Haslar 1946-49, professional sec to Dir of Naval Construction Admty 1949-52, constructor Admty (HM Yacht Britannia) 1952-53, constructor on staff of tactical dir and Staff Requirements Div Admty 1953-56, constructor large carrier design Admty Bath 1956-60, constructor HM Dockyard Portsmouth 1960-63, chief constructor 1963-66, dep planning mangr HM Dockyard Devonport 1966-68 (project mangr 1968-70), dir gen Naval Design Canberra Aust 1970-73, planning mangr HM Dockyard Rosyth 1973-75 (gen mangr 1975-77), gen mangr HM Dockyard Devonport 1977-79, chief exec Royal Dockyards (head RCNC) 1979-83, ret 1983; pres Portsmouth Royal Dockyard Historical Soc, chm Hayling Island Gp Civil Serv Retirement Fellowship; FEng 1981, FRINA 1970, FIIM 1981; *Recreations* painting, music, lapidary; *Style—* Keith Thomas, Esq, CB, OBE, FEng; 6 Wyborn Close, Hayling Island, Hants PO11 9HY (☎ 0705 463 435)

THOMAS, Keith Sinclair; s of John Harold Thomas, of Sefton Court, St Annes-on-Sea, Lancs, and Elsie Maud, *née* Lewis; *b* 29 May 1946; *Educ* King Edward VII Sch Lytham, Merton Coll Oxford (BA); *m* 9 Aug 1973, Ann, da of late Eric John Parry, of Stanley Ave, Farington, Leyland, Preston; 1 s (Gareth Richard b 13 May 1979), 1 da (Clare Rachel b 27 May 1976); *Career* called to the Bar Gray's Inn 1969; head of Chambers Winckley Squaree Preston; memb: Lancs RUFC, Vale of Lune Harriers; hon sec Vale of Lune Point-to-Point; *Recreations* sport (racing, rugby, football); *Style—* Keith Thomas, Esq; Kay's Barn, Ribchestere, Preston PR3 3XE (☎ 0254 878 049); 14 Winckley Square, Preston PR1 3JJ (☎ 0772 52828); 5 Essex Court, London

THOMAS, Sir Keith Vivian; s of Vivian Jones Thomas (d 1987), and Hilda Janet Eirene, *née* Davies (d 1979); *b* 2 Jan 1933; *Educ* Barry Co GS, Balliol Coll Oxford (MA); *m* 16 Aug 1961, Valerie June, da of Eric Charles Little, of Beaconsfield, Bucks; 1 s (Edmund b 1965), 1 da (Emily b 1963); *Career* fell: All Souls Coll Oxford 1955-57, St John's Coll Oxford 1957-86; prof of modern history Univ of Oxford 1986 (reader 1978-85), pres CCC Oxford 1986-, pro vice chllr Univ of Oxford 1988-; del OUP 1980-, vice pres Royal Hist Soc 1980-84 (jt literary dir 1970-74, memb Cncl 1975-78); memb: Br Acad (memb Cncl 1985-88), ESRC 1985-90, Reviewing Ctee on Exports of Works of Art 1990-; Hon DLitt: Univ of Kent 1983, Univ of Wales 1987; Hon LLD Williams Coll Mass 1988; FRHist 1970, FBA 1979; kt 1988; *Books* Religion and the Decline of Magic (1971), Man and the Natural World (1983); *Recreations* visiting secondhand bookshops; *Clubs* Utd Oxford and Cambridge; *Style—* Sir Keith Thomas; The President's Lodgings, Corpus Christi College, Oxford OX1 4JE (☎ 0865 250738); Corpus Christi College, Oxford OX1 4JF (☎ 0865 276739, fax 0865 793121)

THOMAS, Kelvin Einstein; s of George Harold Thomas (d 1975), and Nora, *née* Gourdin (d 1976); *b* 11 Nov 1926; *Educ* Woodstock Sch Mussoorie UP India, John Hopkins Univ Baltimore Maryland USA (BA), Guy's Hosp Univ of London (MB BS, DLO); *m* 4 Aug 1956, Diana Mary, da of Rev Ernest Allen; 1 s (Stephen b 23 April 1961), 1 da (Anna b 3 March 1967); *Career* clinical teacher Faculty of Med Univ of Nottingham and conslt ear, nose and throat surgn Univ Hosp Nottingham 1966-; memb: BMA 1955, Med Art Soc; FRSM 1966, FRCS, FRSA 1990; *Recreations* sculpture; *Style—* Kelvin Thomas, Esq; University Hospital, Queen's Medical Centre, Nottingham (☎ 0602 421421)

THOMAS, Leslie; s of David James Thomas, MN (ka 1943), and Dorothy Hilda Court (d 1943); *b* 22 March 1931; *Educ* Dr Barnardo's Kingston-on-Thames, Kingston Tech Sch; *m* 1, 1956 (m dis 1971), Maureen, da of Charles Crane; 2 s (Mark, Gareth), 1 da (Lois); m 2, Nov 1971, Diana Miles; 1 s (Matthew); *Career* Nat Serv Singapore, Malaya 1949-51; journalist 1951-63: Exchange Telegraph 1955-57, London Evening News 1957-63; many radio and tv appearances; *Books* This Time Next Week (1964), The Virgin Soldiers (1966), Some Lovely Islands (1968), Tropic of Ruislip (1974), The Magic Army (1981), The Hidden Places of Britain (1981), A World of Islands (1983), In My Wildest Dreams (1983), The Dearest and The Best (1984), The Adventures of Goodnight and Loving (1986), The Loves and Journeys of Revolving Jones (1991); *Recreations* cricket, music, antiques, stamp collecting; *Clubs* Lord's Taverners, Wig and Pen; *Style—* Leslie Thomas, Esq

THOMAS, Sir (John) Maldwyn; s of Daniel Thomas (d 1930), and Gladys Thomas Davies (d 1954); *b* 17 June 1918; *Educ* Porth Glamorgan GS; *m* 1975, Maureen Elizabeth; *Career* called to the Bar Gray's Inn 1954 (re-admitted 1986), admitted slr 1965; chm Rank Xerox Ltd 1972-79 (co sec 1964, md 1970), dir Xerox Corporation 1974-79, non exec dir Int Military Servs 1978-84; non exec dep chm John Brown plc 1984-86, non exec dir Westland plc 1985-, memb Cncl The Richmond Fellowship 1984-; vice pres: London Welsh Rugby FC, London Welsh Tst 1988-; tstee London Welsh Sch 1989-; kt 1984; *Clubs* Reform; *Style—* Sir Maldwyn Thomas; 9 Chester Terrace, Regent's Park, London NW1 4ND (☎ 071 486 4368)

THOMAS, Margaret; da of Francis Stewart Thomas (d 1971), of London, and Grace Darling, *née* Whetherly (d 1978); *b* 26 Sept 1916; *Educ* Slade, Royal Acad Schs; *Career* artist and painter; solo shows: Leicester Galleries London (1949 and 1951), five shows at Aitken Dotts and Scot Gallery Edinburgh (1952-82), Howard Roberts Cardiff, Canaletto Gallery London, Minories Colchester, Mall Galleries London, Octagon Gallery Belfast, Sally Hunter Fine Arts 1988, Maltings Concert Hall Gallery Snape; work in numerous public collections incl: Chantrey Bequest, Miny of Educn, Robert Fleming Holdings Ltd, Lloyd's of London, Exeter Coll Oxford, Univ of Bath, Scot Nat Orchestra, Edinburgh City Corp, Mitsukshi Ltd Tokyo; reg exhibitor at Royal Acad and Royal Scot Acad (painting purchased by HRH Prince Philip), winner Hunting Gp award Oil Painting of the Year 1981; memb: Royal W of Eng Acad, RBA, NEAC; *Recreations* gardening, dogs, vintage cars; *Style—* Miss Margaret Thomas; 8 North Bank St, Edinburgh (☎ 031 225 3343); Ellingham Mill, Bungay, Suffolk (☎ 050 845 656)

THOMAS, Mark David Clement; s of Clem Thomas, of Swansea, and Anne, *née* Barter; *b* 23 June 1964; *Educ* Gowerton Comprehensive Sch, Univ of Loughborough (BA), Magdalene Coll Cambridge (BA, 2 Rugby blues); *Career* Rugby Union winger Rosslyn Park FC; County Schs Champion (W Glamorgan) 100m 200m 4x100m javelin; clubs: Swansea RFC 1983-88, Loughborough Univ RFC 1982-85, Vail RFC Colorado USA 1985-87, Cambridge Univ RFC 1985-88, Durban HSOB SA 1988, Harlequins FC 1988-89, London Welsh RFC 1989-90, Rosslyn Park 1990-91; rep: Welsh Students 1985, Welsh Exiles 1991, Swiss Barbarians 1990, Crawshays Welsh 1983-90, Middx 1990, Public Sch Wanderers 1989; surveyor Richard Ellis; *Recreations* water skiing, skiing, golf, travel, good food and wine; *Style—* Mark Thomas, Esq; Rosslyn Park FC, Priory Lane, Roehampton, Barnes, London SW15 (☎ home 081 675 3981)

THOMAS, Meyric Leslie; OBE (1987); s of Lt-Col Charles Leslie Thomas (d 1979), of Horton, Gower, Glamorgan, and Edith Annie Thomas (d 1983); *b* 17 Nov 1928; *Educ* Clifton, Jesus Coll Oxford (MA); *m* 2 March 1956, Jillian Hamilton, da of Lt-Col Robert William Armstrong (d 1975), of Oxford; 2 s (Peter Leslie b 1956, Charles Leslie b 1958), 1 da (Clare Leslie b 1960); *Career* Nat Serv 2 Lt Glos Regt 1947-49; admitted slr 1953, ptnr LC Thomas & Son 1953-91 (conslt 1991-); Neath Harbour Cmmrs' Clerk Neath Div Income Tax Cmmrs; Oxford Rowing blue 1952 and 1953, pres OUBC 1953, former pres and chm Neath RFC; pres: Neath Br Legion, Neath Cons Assoc; *Clubs* Vincent's, Neath Constitutional; *Style—* Meyric Thomas, Esq, OBE; 13 Westernmoor Rd, Neath, W Glamorgan (☎ 0639 643322); LC Thomas & Son, 19 London Rd, Neath, W Glamorgan (☎ 0639 645061, fax 0639 646792)

THOMAS, Michael David; CMG (1985), QC (1973); s of D Cardigan Thomas and Kathleen Thomas; *b* 8 Sept 1933; *Educ* Chigwell Sch Essex, LSE; *m* 1, 1958 (m dis 1978), Jane Lena Mary, eldest da of late Francis Neate; 2 s, 2 da; m 2, 1981 (m dis 1986), Mrs Gabrielle Blakemore; m 3, 1988, Lydia Dunn; *Career* barr Middle Temple 1955 (bencher 1982), jr counsel to Treasury in admiralty matters 1966-73, wreck cmmr and salvage arbitrator Lloyd's 1974-83, attorney-gen Hong Kong 1983-88; memb of Exec and Legislative Cncls Hong Kong 1983-88; *Style—* Michael Thomas, Esq, CMG, QC; 2 Essex Court, Temple, London EC4Y 9AP; Temple Chambers, One Pacific Place, 88 Queensway, Hong Kong

THOMAS, Sir (Godfrey) Michael David; 11 Bt (E 1694), of Wenvoe, Glamorganshire; s of Rt Hon Sir Godfrey John Vignoles, 10 Bt, PC, GCVO, KCB, CSI (d 1968); *b* 10 Oct 1925; *Educ* Harrow; *m* 1956, Margaret Greta, da of John Cleland, of Stormont Court, Godden Green, Sevenoaks; 1 s, 2 da (of whom 1 s and 1 da are twins); *Heir* s, David John Godfrey Thomas; *Career* Capt The Rifle Bde 1944-56; memb Stock Exchange 1959-88; *Clubs* MCC, Hurlingham; *Style—* Sir Michael Thomas, Bt; 2 Napier Avenue, London SW6 3PS (☎ 071 736 6896)

THOMAS, Prof Michael Frederic; s of Hugh Frederic Thomas (d 1987), and Kathleen Helena Doris, *née* Phelps (d 1981); *b* 15 Sept 1933; *Educ* Royal GS Guildford, Univ of Reading (BA, MA), Univ of London (PhD); *m* 29 Dec 1956, (Elizabeth) Anne, da of Harry Guest Dadley (d 1955); 1 s (Graham Hugh b 13 Oct 1959), 1 da (Gillian Anne, b 31 March 1965); *Career* asst lectr Magee Univ Coll Londonderry NI 1957-60, lectr Univ of Ibadan 1960-64, sr lectr in geography Univ of St Andrews 1974-79 (lectr 1964-74), fndn prof of environmental sci Univ of Stirling 1980-; memb Cncl Royal Scot Geographical Soc, memb Management Ctee Scot Environmental Educn Cncl; FGS 1985, FRSE 1988; *Books* Environment & Land Use in Africa (jtly and jt ed, 1969), Tropical Geomorphology (1974), Land Assessment in Scotland (jt ed, 1980), Evaluation of Land Resources in Scotland (jtly and jt ed, 1990); *Recreations* listening to classical music, jazz, hill walking, travel; *Style—* Prof Michael Thomas, FRSE; Dept of Environmental Science, Univ of Stirling, Stirling FK9 4LA (☎ 0786 73171, fax 0786 63000, telex 777557 STUNIV G)

THOMAS, Michael Gavin Lynam; s of (Theodore) Lynam Thomas (d 1976), and Margaret Evelyn, *née* Astbury; *b* 14 Aug 1936; *Educ* Dragon Sch Oxford, Rugby, Trinity Coll Oxford (MA); *m* 11 April 1964, Jane Angela Elizabeth, da of Capt Richard Stafford Allen (d 1943); 1 s (Archie b 1969, d 1985), 1 da (Emily b 1966); *Career* army 1955-57, cmmnd S Staffordshire Regt 1956, served Cyprus; Bank of England 1961-68, dir Avoncroft Museum of Bldgs 1968-; regnl chm Cncl and Exec Ctee Nat Tst, tstee Landmark Tst; memb: Cncl Assoc of Ind Museums, Cncl W Midlands Area Museums Assoc, Diocesan Advsy Ctee; *Recreations* tennis, concerts, historic buildings, museums; *Clubs* Vincent's; *Style—* Michael Thomas, Esq; 2 Stephenson Terrace, Worcester WR1 3EA (☎ 0905 20518); Avoncroft Museum of Buildings, Stoke Heath, Bromsgrove, Worcs B60 4JR (☎ 0527 31886)

THOMAS, Prof Michael James; *b* 15 July 1933; *Educ* King Edward's Sch Birmingham, UCL (BSc), Graduate Sch of Business Indiana Univ (MBA); *m* Nancy, *née* Yeoman; 1 s (Huw), 1 da (Helen); *Career* cmmnd Br Army 1952, served Royal Warwickshire Regt, seconded W African Frontier Force Nigeria Regt 1952-53, army res offr 1953-56; market res mangr The Metal Box Co Ltd London 1957-60, Faculty Sch of Mgmnt Syracuse Univ 1960-71 (assoc prof), assoc dir Syracuse Univ Exec Devpt Prog, Sch of Mgmnt Univ of Lancaster 1971-86 (head Dept of Mktg 1972-77), chm Sch Governing Body 1975-79, memb Univ Cncl 1979-85; senate rep: Sch of Mgmnt 1985, Academic Promotions Ctee 1985-86; dep chm Sch of Mgmnt 1986-87, dir MCom degree (Marketing for Industrialising Countries) 1987-88, head Dept of Mktg Univ of Strathclyde 1988- (prof 1987-); visiting prof: Syracuse Univ 1977, Univ of Nigeria 1979, Temple Univ Philadelphia 1980, Univ of Gdansk 1977, 1978, 1980, 1983 and 1988: adjunct prof Syracuse Univ 1980-, various pubns in jls, md Silverdale Ltd Editorial Prints; sr conslt: Silverdale Mktg Consits, Mktg Consultancy Res Servs; memb Nat Cncl Chartered Inst of Mktg 1974 (memb Nat Exec Ctee 1990-), dep chm Gas Consumers' Cncl for the Northwest 1977-86: chm mktg: Educn Bd Inst of Mktg 1979-86, Mktg Educn Gp of GB and Ireland 1986-90; ed Mktg Intelligence and Planning Jl; memb Editorial Bd: Jl of Marketing Mgmnt, Jl of MRS, Quarterly Review of Marketing, Nigerian Jl of Marketing; chm Jt Parish Ctee Arnside-Silverdale Area of Outstanding Nat Beauty 1975-85; FRSA, FCIM; *Books* International Marketing Management (1969), International Marketing (1971), Modern Marketing Management (1970-73), Management Sales and Marketing Training (contrib, 1984), The Pocket Guide to Marketing (1986), The Marketing Book (1987), The Marketing Digest (1988), The Marketing Handbook (1989); *Recreations* book collecting, bird watching, the study of Polish politics; *Clubs* Scottish Ornithologists; *Style—* Prof Michael Thomas; Department of Marketing, University of Strathclyde, Stenhouse Building, 173 Cathedral St, Glasgow G4 0RQ (☎ 041 552 4400, fax 041 552 2802, telex 77472 UNSLIB G)

THOMAS, Col Michael John Glyn; s of Glyn Pritchard Thomas (d 1985), and Mary, *née* Moseley (d 1987); *b* 14 Feb 1938; *Educ* Haileybury and ISC, Univ of Cambridge (MA, MB BChir), St Bart's; *m* 23 May 1969, (Sheelagh) Jane, da of Harold Thorpe (d 1979); 1 da (Fleur b 1970); *Career* RMO 2 Bn Para Regt 1964-67, trainee in pathology BMH Singapore 1967-71; specialist in pathology: Colchester MH 1971-74, Singapore 1974-76; sr specialist in pathology and 2 i/c Army Blood Supply Depot (ABSD) 1977-82, exchange fell Walter Reed Army Medical Centre Washington DC 1982-83, offr i/c Leishman Lab 1984-87, CO ABSD 1987-; BMA memb: Cncl 1973-74 and 1977-82, Armed Forces Ctee 1971-82 and 1988-, Jr Membs Forum 1971-78 (chm 1974), Bd of Sci and Educn 1987-, Rep Body 1972-82 and 1987-, Expert Ctee on AIDS 1986-, EEC Ctee 1989-; memb Ctee on Transfusion Equipment Br Standard Inst, expert witness on gene mapping ESC; memb: Assoc of Clinical Pathologists 1971, Br Blood Transfusion Soc 1987, Inst of Medical Ethics 1987; LMSSA, DTM & H; *Books* co-author: Control of Infection (1989), Nuclear Attack, Ethics and Casualty Selection (1988), Handbook of Medical Ethics (1979 and subsequent edns), A Code of Practice for the Safe Use and Disposal of Sharps; Dictionary of Medical Ethics (contrib), AIDS and Human Rights a UK Perspective (contrib); *Recreations* DIY, photography, philately; *Clubs* Tanglin (Singapore); *Style—* Col Michael J G Thomas, L/RAMC; Army Blood Supply Depot, Ordnance Rd, Aldershot, Hants GU11 2AF (☎ 0252 347140/1, fax 0252 347147)

THOMAS, Sir (William) Michael Marsh; 3 Bt (UK 1918), of Garreglwyd, Anglesey; s of Major Sir William Eustace Rhyddlad Thomas, 2 Bt, MBE (d 1958), and Enid Helena Marsh (d 1982); *b* 4 Dec 1930; *Educ* Oundle; *m* 1957, Geraldine, da of Robert Drysdale, of Trearddur Bay, Anglesey; 3 da; *Heir* none; *Career* formerly md Gors Nurseries Ltd; *Style—* Sir Michael Thomas, Bt; Belan, Fawr, Rhosneigr, Anglesey (☎ 0407 810541)

THOMAS, Michael Stuart (Mike); s of Arthur Edward Thomas, and Mona, *née* Parker; *b* 24 May 1944; *Educ* Latymer Upper Sch, King's Sch Macclesfield, Univ of Liverpool (BA); *m* 31 July 1975, Maureen Theresa, da of Denis Kelly; 1 s by 1 m (Paul b 1973); *Career* pres Liverpool Univ Guild of Undergrads 1965, memb Nat Exec NUS, head Res Dept Co-Op Pty 1966-68, sr res assoc Policy Studies Inst 1968-73, dir The Volunteer Centre 1973-74; MP (Lab and Co-op 1974-81, SDP 1981-83) Newcastle upon Tyne East 1974-1983; PPS to Rt Hon Roy Hattersley MP 1974-76, memb Commons Select Ctee Nationalised Industs 1975-79, chm PLP Trade Gp 1979-81, SDP spokesman on Health and Social Security 1981-83, SDP candidate Exeter 1987; memb: SDP Policy Ctee 1981-83 and 1984-90, SDP Nat Ctee 1981-90; chm SDP Orgn Ctee 1981-88 (Fin Ctee 1988-89), communications consit 1978-, dir Dewe Rogerson Ltd 1984-88, md Corporate Communications Strategy Ltd 1988-, dir BR Western Region 1985-; fndr Parliament's weekly jl The House Magazine 1976, ed The BBC Guide to Parliament 1979 and 1983, author various articles, reviews and pamphlets; memb US DAW; *Recreations* collecting election pottery and medals, walking, countryside; *Clubs* Devon and Exeter Inst; *Style—* Mike Thomas, Esq; 9 King St, London WC2E 8HN (☎ 071 836 1111)

THOMAS, Neil Philip; s of Simon David Thomas, of 149 Stanmore Hill, Stanmore, Middx, and Jessie, *née* Blagborough; *b* 29 April 1950; *Educ* Stowe, Univ of London (BSc); *m* 1, 25 Jan 1974, Mary Josephine Christian (d 1977), da of A V M Patrick Joseph O'Connor, CB, OBE; 1 da (Joanna b 19 June 1977); m 2, 29 April 1979, Julia Vera, da of J J Ashken; 1 s (James b 17 March 1981), 1 da (Gemma b 15 Oct 1982); *Career* late sr registrar in orthopaedics: Royal Nat Orthopaedic Hosp, UCH and the Westminster Hosp; consit orthopaedic surgn N Hants Health Authy; memb: Int Knee Soc, Euro Soc of Knee and Arthroscopic Surgery, Br Assoc of Surgery of the Knee; RCS rep Engrg in Med Gp Ctee; Sir Herbert Seddon Prize and Medal 1986, President's Medal Br Assoc of Surgery of the Knee 1985-86; FRCS 1978, FRSM, fell Br Orthopaedic Assoc; *Recreations* golf, horticulture, wine, fishing; *Style—* Neil Thomas, Esq; Little Bullington House, Bullington, Sutton Scotney, Winchester, Hampshire SO21 3QQ (☎ 0962 760233); The Hampshire Clinic, Basing Rd, Basingstoke, Hampshire (☎ 0256 819222)

THOMAS, Lt Cdr Neil Ronald Lindley; RD (1969, and Clasp 1980); s of Henry Ronald Thomas (d 1989), and Edith Lindley, JP, of 4 Links Close, Wallasey; *b* 31 Jan 1934; *Educ* Wallasey GS, Jesus Coll Cambridge; *Career* Nat Serv RN 1953-55, Sub Lt RNR 1955, Lt RNR 1958, Lt Cdr RNR 1966, ret 1985; mgmnt trainee N Greening and Sons Warrington (wire weavers and metal perforators) 1957, various mgmnt posts in sales 1959-76, fund raiser Voluntary and Christian Serv (Help the Aged) 1977-78, dir Serve Wirral (youth trg) 1979, sec and chief exec Serve Wirral Tst Co Ltd (charitable co providing vocational trg to young and unemployed) 1985; Lib Cncllr: Wallasey Borough Cncl 1971-74, Wirral Met Cncl (dep gp leader) 1973-79; Lib Parly candidate: Ellesmere Port and Bebington 1974, Wallasey 1979; dist commissioner for scouts Wallasey Dist 1973-79; capt: Wallasey GS Boat Club 1952-53, Liverpool Victoria Rowing Club (14 times) 1959-85; chm: Merseyside Regatta Ctee 1959-85, NW Rowing Cncl 1967-85 (former sec); memb Exec Amateur Rowing Assoc Cncl 1969-85 (divnl rep 1968-85), int rowing umpire 1972-, chm Nat Umpires' Commission 1976, pres Amateur Rowing Assoc 1985-, chm Nat Assoc of Trg Agencies 1987-90, chm Nat Trg Fedn 1990-; *Recreations* rowing, music, politics; *Clubs* Leander, Liverpool Victoria Rowing, Hollingworth Lake Rowing; *Style—* Lt Cdr Neil Thomas, RD; 7 Marine Terrace, Wallasey, Merseyside L45 7RE (☎ 051 630 2533); Serve Wirral Trust Co Ltd, Liscard Hall, Central Park, Wallasey, Merseyside L44 0BT (☎ 051 691 2070, fax 051 691 1073)

THOMAS, (Robert) Neville; QC (1975); s of Robert Derfel Thomas (d 1983), of Clwyd, and Enid Anne, *née* Edwards (d 1990); *b* 31 March 1936; *Educ* Ruthin Sch, Univ of Oxford (MA, BCL); *m* 28 March 1970, Jennifer Anne, da of Philip Henry Akerman Brownrigg, CMG, DSO, OBE, TD, *qv*; 1 s (Gerran b 19 March 1973), 1 da (Meriel b 21 Aug 1975); *Career* Lt Intelligence Corps 1955-57; called to the Bar Inner Temple 1962, rec Crown Ct 1975-82, master of the Bench Inner Temple 1985; *Recreations* fishing, walking, gardening; *Clubs* Garrick; *Style—* Neville Thomas, Esq, QC; Glansevern, Berriew, Welshpool, Powys; 38 Courtfield Gardens, London SW5; 3 Gray's Inn Place, London WC1R 5EA (☎ 071 831 8441, 071 831 8479, fax 071 831 8479, telex 295119 LEXCOL G)

THOMAS, Nicholas Andrew; s of Stanley Thomas (d 1971), of Plymouth, Devon, and Phyllis Doreen, *née* Larman (d 1990); *b* 14 April 1953; *Educ* Kelly Coll Tavistock Devon, Exeter Coll Oxford (BA); *Career* admitted slr 1977; Macfarlanes: articled clerk 1975-77, asst slr 1977-82, ptnr 1982-; memb: City of London Slrs Co, Law Soc; *Recreations* golf, walking, classical music, opera; *Style—* Nicholas Thomas, Esq; 8 Oxford Rd North, Chiswick, London W4 4DN (☎ 081 995 6921); Macfarlanes, 10 Norwich St, London EC4A 1BD (☎ 071 831 9222, fax 071 831 9607, telex 296381 MACFAR G)

THOMAS, (James) Nigel; s of Charles Walter Thomas (d 1956), of Bradford, Yorks, and Kathleen, *née* Lister; *b* 11 May 1944; *Educ* Bradford GS, St Edmund Hall Oxford (MA), Univ of Oxford Med Sch (BM, BCh); *m* 1 April 1968, Gerda, da of Gustav Oelgeklaus (d 1967) of Lengerich, Westphalia, Germany; 1 s ((Charles Walter) Christian b 31 May 1978), 2 da ((Julia Elizabeth) Kirsten b 22 Sept 1970, (Heide Alicia) Katrin b 28 Aug 1972); *Career* consit ENT specialist Groote Schuur Hosp Capetown SA 1974-76, first asst Radcliffe Infirmary Oxford 1976-79, consit ENT surgn Kings Coll 1979-; George Herbert Hunt fellowship Univ of Oxford 1978; memb Camberwell Health Authy, pres Osler House Club 1967-68; FRCS 1972; *Books* Mawson's Diseases of the Ear (contrib, 1988); *Recreations* rugby, squash, music; *Style—* Nigel Thomas, Esq; Kings College Hospital, Denmark Hill, Camberwell, London SE5 9RS (☎ 071 326 3194)

THOMAS, Prof Noel L'Estrange; s of Richard Gratton Thomas (d 1971), of Sale, Manchester, and Gladys L'Estrange (d 1978); *b* 5 Dec 1929; *Educ* Sale Co GS for Boys, Univ of Manchester (BA), Univ of Liverpool (MA), Univ of Salford (PhD); *m* 20 Feb 1954, Norma, da of Robert Brown (d 1950), of Manchester; 2 da (Katharine b 1962, Ruth b 1965); *Career* master Das erste Bundesrealgymnasium Graz 1951-52, asst master German Canon Slade GS Bolton 1959-64 (Holt HS for Boys Liverpool 1953-59); Univ of Salford Dept of Modern Languages: lectr in German 1964-73, sr lectr 1973-83, prof 1983-, chm 1984-89; dir Language-Export Ltd; memb conf of Univ Teachers of German, memb Assoc for Study of German Politics, memb AUT; *Books* Modern Prose Passages for Translation into German (with G Weischedel, 1968), Modern German Prose Passages (with G Weischedel, 1972), The Narrative Works of Günter Grass - a critical interpretation (1983), Interpreting as a Language Teaching Technique (ed with Richard Towell, 1985), Grass: Die Blechtrommel (1985); *Recreations* fell walking, choral singing; *Style—* Prof Noel Thomas; 5 Whiting Grove, Deane, Bolton BL3 4PU (☎ 0204 652424); Department of Modern Languages, University of Salford, Salford M5 4WT (☎ 061 745 5614, fax 061 745 59999, telex 668680)

THOMAS, Norman; CBE; s of Bowen Thomas (d 1961), of Edmonton, London N18, and Ada, *née* Redding (d 1987); *b* 1 June 1921; *Educ* Latymer's Sch Edmonton, Camden Trg Coll Camden London; *m* 24 Dec 1942, Rose Matilda, da of Jack Henshaw (d 1954), of Islington, London; 1 s (Paul b 1955), 1 da (Jill (Mrs Singer) b 1947); *Career* commerce and indust 1936-47, primary sch teacher London and Herts 1948-56, primary sch head teacher Stevenage Herts 1956-61, HM inspr of schs Lincs and SE 1962-69, HM staff inspr primary educn 1969-73, HM chief inspector primary educn 1973-81, chm ILEA enquiry into primary educn in central London with report published 1985, advsr House of Commons Select Ctee 1984-86, memb Task Gp on Assessment and Testing in the Nat Curriculum 1987-88, contrib books on primary educn; *Books* Handbook of Primary Education in Europe (contrib 1989), Primary Education from Plowden to the 1990's (1990); *Recreations* photography, reading; *Style—* Norman Thomas, Esq, CBE; 19 Langley Way, Watford, Herts WD1 3EJ (☎ 0923 223766)

THOMAS, Pamela; OBE (1983); da of Rev Llewlyn Thomas (d 1959), of All Saints'

Vicarage, Glasbury, Powys, and Betty, *née* Williams (d 1971); *b* 15 May 1929; *Educ* Roedean, King's Coll London; *Career* barr, broadcaster, co dir, lectr; called to the Bar Lincoln's Inn 1955, head of chambers 1983; visiting lectr in law Poly of Central London 1959-75; memb Performing Rights Tbnl 1987, sec Soc of Cons Lawyers 1963-82, chm political devpt ctee SOCL 1982-85, fndr memb Bow Gp; Parly candidate: St Pancras N for LCC 1958, (C) Swansea East 1963, (C) Willesden West 1966; former govr: Chelsea Sch for Boys, Chelsea-Hurlingham Comprehensive Sch; former vice chm PCC St Augustine's Queen's Gate, vice pres Old Roedeanians Assoc 1982-88, govr Roedean Sch 1983, memb Copywright Tbnl 1989, govr designate Fulham Adult Educn Coll; *Style*— Miss Pamela Thomas, OBE; 2 Clareville Court, Clareville Grove, London SW7 (☎ 071 373 6947); Broomfield, Glasbury-on-Wye, via Hereford (☎ 049 74 338); 3 New Square, Lincoln's Inn, London WC2 (☎ 071 242 3436)

THOMAS, Patricia, Lady; Patricia; *née* Larkins; *m* 1957, as his 3 w, Major Sir William Eustace Rhyddlad Thomas, 2 Bt, MBE (d 1958); *Style*— Patricia, Lady Thomas

THOMAS, Patricia Anne; da of Frederick Sidney Lofts (d 1978), of Mitcham, Surrey, and Ann Elizabeth, *née* Brown (d 1982); *b* 3 April 1940; *Educ* Mitcham Co GS for Girls, King's Coll London (LLB, LLM), Univ of Illinois; *m* 20 July 1968, (Joseph) Glyn Thomas, s of Joseph Ernest Thomas of Holmesfield, Derbyshire (d 1975); 1 s (Paul b 1972), 2 da (Jacqueline b 1969, Ruth b 1970); *Career* lectr Univ of Leeds 1962-63 and 1964-68, sr lectr (later princ lectr) Preston Poly 1973-78, head Sch of Law Lancs Poly 1978-85; Gtr Manchester and Lancs Rent Assessment Panel: memb 1975-85, vice pres 1984-85, pres 1985; cmmr Local Admin 1985-, chm Blackpool Supplementary Benefit Appeal Tbnl 1980-85; *Books* Law of Evidence (1972); *Recreations* walking, cooking, reading, travel; *Style*— Mrs Patricia Thomas; Greenbank Farm, Over Kellet, Carnforth, Lancashire LA6 1BS (☎ 0524 733296); Commission for Local Administration in England, Beverley House, 17 Shipton Rd, York YO3 6FZ (☎ 0904 630151)

THOMAS, Patricia Eileen; da of Ieuan Gwynn Thomas (d 1989), and Lovice Eileen, *née* Phillips; *b* 3 June 1949; *Educ* St Joseph's Convent Reading, St Hugh's Coll Oxford (MA); *Career* slr; ptnr: Denton Hall Burgin & Warrens (formerly Denton Hall & Burgin) 1982-88, S J Berwin & Co 1988-; chm: Environmental Law Ctee, Int Bar Assoc; memb: Planning Law Ctee, Law Soc, Environmental Law Sub Ctee Law Soc; memb Worshipful Co of Slrs; *Books* Surveyors Factbook (contrib 1990), Planning Factbook (ed and contrib 1991); *Recreations* architecture, fly-fishing, flying; *Style*— Miss Patricia Thomas; S J Berwin & Co, 236 Grays Inn Rd, London WC1X 8HB (☎ 071 278 0444, fax 071 833 2860)

THOMAS, Patrick James; s of Frederick George Thomas (d 1978), of Swindon, Wilts, and Ruby Ethel, *née* Bright; *b* 31 Aug 1941; *Educ* Commonwealth GS Swindon, Univ of Kent at Canterbury (MA); *m* 22 Aug 1964, Patricia Mary, da of John Edward Hughes (d 1985), of Swindon; 2 da (Sara Jane b 1965, Nicola Anne b 1967); *Career* exec engr PO Telephones 1959-61, process technician Plessey Semiconductors Ltd 1961-62, trainee accountant Swindon Corporation 1962-65, accountant Reading Corporation 1965-69; Kent CC: asst computer mangr 1969-73, data processing mangr 1973-86, asst head of computing and mgmnt servs 1986-87, head of technol servs 1987-; memb: Exec Ctee Telecommunications Users Assoc, Nat Computing Centre, Inst of Quality Assurance, Inst of Advanced Motorists 1987; memb: CIPFA 1966, BIM 1983; *Recreations* philately, clay pigeon shooting, gliding, squash, golf, driving; *Style*— Patrick Thomas, Esq

THOMAS, Pauline Ann; da of Rupert Augustus Thomas, of Georgia, USA, and Beryl Leone Thomas; *b* 6 Feb 1956; *Educ* Saker Baptist Coll and CCAST W Cameroon, LSE (LLB); *m* 19 April 1986, Stephen Neil Mobbs, s of Noel Edward Henry Mobbs, of Norwich, Norfolk; *Career* mgmnt conslt Intermatrix Ltd 1984-86, practice devpt mangr Lovell White & King 1986-88, mktg mangr Grant Thornton 1989-; *Recreations* travel, theatre, reading, classical music; *Style*— Ms Pauline Thomas; Grant Thornton, Melton St, Euston Square, London NW1 2EP (☎ 071 383 5100, fax 071 383 4715, telex 289848)

THOMAS, Prof Peter David Garner; s of David Thomas (d 1967), and Doris, *née* Davies (d 1962); *b* 1 May 1930; *Educ* St Bees Sch Cumberland, Univ Coll of N Wales (BA, MA), UCL (PhD); *m* 21 March 1963, Sheila; 2 s (Alan b 1963, Michael b 1965, d 1983), 1 da (Sally b 1970); *Career* lectr Univ of Glasgow 1959-65 (asst lectr 1956-59); Univ Coll Wales: lectr 1965-68, sr lectr 1968-71, reader 1971-75, prof 1976-; chm: Dyfed LTA 1981-, Aberystwyth Lib Democrats 1988-; FRHistS 1971; *Books* The House of Commons in the Eighteenth Century (1971), British Politics and the Stamp Act Crisis (1975), Lord North (1976), The American Revolution (1986), The Townshend Duties Crisis (1987); *Recreations* lawn tennis; *Style*— Prof Peter Thomas; 16 Pen-Y-Craig, Aberystwyth, Dyfed SY23 2JA (☎ 0970 612053); History Department, University College of Wales, Aberystwyth, Dyfed SY23 3DY (☎ 0970 622663)

THOMAS, Peter Roy; *b* 29 March 1946; *Career* Garland Compton Advertising 1968-70, Lyons Marketing 1970-72; chief exec: Purchasepoint 1972-90, Lopex 1990-; *Style*— Peter Thomas, Esq; Lopex plc, Alliance House, 63 St Martin's Lane, London WC2N 4BH (☎ 071 836 0281)

THOMAS, Dr Philip Frederic; *b* 1 April 1949; *Educ* Univ of Manchester (MB ChB), Univ of Edinburgh (MPhil); *Career* conslt psychiatrist, hon assoc lectr psychiatry at Manchester Royal Infirmary, clinical interests incl community psychiatry, substance misuse problems and ethnic minority groups; res interests incl pubns in psycholinguistics, human communications and methods of serv delivery; MRCPsych 1980; *Style*— Dr Philip Thomas; Manchester Royal Infirmary, Department of Psychiatry, Rawnsley Building, Oxford Rd, Manchester M13 9WL (☎ 061 276 5335)

THOMAS, Ralph Philip; MC (1942); *Educ* Telisford Sch Clifton; *m* 1944, Joy, *née* Spanjer; 1 s, 2 da; *Career* film director; WWII 1939-44 Maj 9 Lancers, Instr RMC 1944-46; film industry 1932-39 (all prodn depts incl editing), Rank Organisation Trailer Dept 1946-48, Gainsborough Pictures 1948-; dir: Once Upon a Dream, Travellers Joy; dir at Pinewood Studios: The Clouded Yellow, Appointment with Venus, The Venetian Bird, A Day To Remember, Doctor In The House, Mad About Men, Above Us The Waves, Doctor At Sea, The Iron Petticoat, Checkpoint, Doctor at Large, Campbell's Kingdom, A Tale of Two Cities, The Wind Cannot Read, The 39 Steps, Upstairs and Downstairs, Conspiracy of Hearts, Doctor In Love, No My Darling Daughter, No Love for Johnnie, The Wild and the Willing, Doctor in Distress, Hot Enough for June, The High Bright Sun, Doctor in Clover, Deadlier Than The Male, Nobody Runs Forever, Some Girls Do, Doctor In Trouble, Quest, Percy, It's a 2 foot 6 inch Above The Ground World, Percy's Progress, A Nightingale Sang in Berkeley Square, Doctor's Daughters, Pop Pirates; *Clubs* Garrick; *Style*— Ralph Thomas, Esq, MC

THOMAS, Dr Reginald; s of Dr Leopold Thomas (d 1956), and Irma Thomas, *née* von Smekal; *b* 28 Feb 1928; *Educ* Vienna Univ (DL); *m* 26 Nov 1960, Ingrid Renate, da of Dr Franz Helmut Leitner (d 1976), late ambass; 3 s (Alexander b 1963, George b 1966, Michael b 1970), 1 da (Elisabeth b 1962); *Career* entered Austrian foreign service 1951, Austrian Legation Berne 1952-56, legal advsr Miny Foreign Affairs Vienna 1956-59, Austrian Embassy Tokyo 1959-62, head of office of sec gen for Foreign Affairs Vienna 1962-68, ambassador Pakistan and concurrently accredited to the Union of Burma 1968-71, ambass to Japan 1971-75, Miny of Foreign Affairs Vienna: head of Personnel Dept 1975-76, head of Dept of Admin 1976-82; Austrian Ambass to the Court of St James' 1982-87; Grand Cross Order of the Rising Sun (Japan), Order of Diplomatic Service (Korea), Independence Order (Jordan), Order of F de Miranda (Venezuela), Hilal-o-Quaid-i-Azam (Pakistan); *Clubs* Queen's, Hurlingham, Austrian Assoc for Foreign Policy and Internat Relations; *Style*— Dr Reginald Thomas; A-1010 Wien, Schwarzenbergstrasse 8; Federal Ministry of Foreign Affairs, Ballhausplatz 2, A-1014 Wien, Austria

THOMAS, Richard; CMG (1990); s of Anthony Hugh Thomas, JP, of The Old School, Stone-In-Oxney, Tenterden, Kent and Molly, *née* Bourne, MBE; *b* 18 Feb 1938; *Educ* Leighton Park, Merton Coll Oxford (MA); *m* 12 Feb 1966, Catherine Jane, da of Daniel Hayes, (d 1969), of Richmond, NSW; 1 s (Alexander James b 1969), 2 da (Phoebe Elizabeth b 1967, Corinna Jane b 1971); *Career* Nat Serv 2 Lt RASC 1959-61; HM Diplomatic Serv: asst pte FCO 1961, private sec to Parly Under Sec 1962-63; second sec: Accra 1963-65, Lomé 1965-66; second later first sec: UK Delgn NATO Paris and Brussels 1966-69, FCO 1969-72, New Dehli 1972-75, FCO (asst head of Dept) 1976-78; FCO visiting res fell RIIA 1978-79, cnsllr Prague 1979-83, ambass Iceland 1983-86, overseas inspr 1986-89, ambass Bulgaria 1989-; *Books* India's Emergence as an Industrial Power: Middle Eastern Contracts (1982); *Recreations* foreign parts, gossip, skiing; *Style*— Richard Thomas, Esq, CMG; Foreign and Commonwealth Office, King Charles St, London SW1

THOMAS, Richard James; s of Daniel Lewis Thomas, JP, of Southend on Sea, Essex, and Norah Mary, *née* James; *b* 18 June 1949; *Educ* Bishop's Stortford Coll, Univ of Southampton (LLB); *m* 18 May 1974, Julia Delicia Thomas, da of Dr Edward Granville Woodchurch Clarke, MC, of Shurlock Row, Berks; 2 s (Andrew b 1977, Christopher b 1983), 1 da (Gemma b 1979); *Career* articled clerk and asst slr Freshfields 1971-74, slr CAB Legal Serv 1974-79, legal offr and head of resources gp Nat Consumer Cncl 1979-86, dir Consumer Affrs Off Fair Trading 1986-; author of reports, articles and broadcasts on a range of legal and consumer issues; tstee W London Fair Housing Gp 1976-79; memb: Mgmnt Ctee Gtr London CAB Serv 1977-79, Lord Chllr's Advsy Ctee on Civil Justice Review 1985-88; memb Law Soc; *Recreations* family, maintenance of home and garden, travel; *Style*— Richard Thomas, Esq; Office of Fair Trading, Field House, Breams Buildings, London EC1A 1PR (☎ 071 242 2858)

THOMAS, Adm Sir (William) Richard Scott; KCB (1987), OBE (1974); s of Cdr William Scott Thomas, DSC, RN (d 1983), and Mary Hilda Bertha, *née* Hemelryk (d 1990); *b* 22 March 1932; *Educ* Downside; *m* 1959, Patricia Margaret, da of Dr John Henry Cullinan (d 1957), of Fressingfield, Suffolk; 4 s (Dominic b 1972, Gareth b 1967, George b 1973, Gavin (decd)), 4 da (Victoria b 1970, Emma b 1974, Harriet b 1968, Jemima b 1970); *Career* Naval Off; CO HM Ships: Buttress 1958, Wolverton 1960-61, Greetham 1962, Torquay 1965, Troubridge 1966-68, Fearless 1977-78; Naval Sec 1983-85, Flag Offr Second Flotilla 1985-87, Dep SACLANT 1987-89, Adm 1989, UK mil rep of NATO 1989-; student of Naval Staff Coll, Jt Servs Staff Coll and RCDS; *Recreations* family and gardening; *Style*— Adm Sir Richard Thomas, KCB, OBE

THOMAS, Richard Stephen; s of Richard Thomas (d 1979), and Leah Mary, *née* Bowen (d 1988); *b* 13 June 1943; *Educ* Pentre GS, UWIST; *m* 23 Sept 1967, Sandra, da of Norman Bishop (d 1990); 1 s (Christopher Richard b 11 Sept 1969), 1 da (Sarah Elizabeth b 7 Sept 1973); *Career* clerical offr Welsh Hosp Bd 1961-63, admin asst Cardiff N Hosp Mgmnt Ctee 1963-65, admin offr Cardiff Royal Infirmary 1965-69, commissioning asst Univ Hosp of Wales 1969-71, commissioning offr Merthyr and Cynon Valley Hosp Mgmnt Ctee 1971-73, project mangr Welsh Health Tech Servs Orgn Cardiff 1974-75, personnel offr West Glamorgan Health Authy 1975-78, area personnel offr Dyfed Health Authy 1978-85, unit gen mangr E Dyfed Health Authy 1987- (planning offr 1985-86, asst gen mangr 1986-87); AHSM 1966, MIPM 1971, hon sec Welsh Assoc of Health Authorities 1986-88; (chm SW Wales Branch IHSM); *Recreations* golf, walking, music, sport spectating; *Clubs* Carmarthen Round Table, Carmarthen Ex Round Tablers, Towy Carmarthen, Rotary Club; *Style*— Richard Thomas, Esq; 7 Llygad-Yr-Haul, Llangunnor, Carmarthen, Dyfed SA31 2LB (☎ 0267 231635); East Dyfed Health Authority, West Wales General Hospital, Glanwili, Carmarthen, Dyfed (☎ 0267 235151)

THOMAS, Robert Ernest (Bob); s of William Edward Thomas (d 1965), and Laura Jane, *née* Willoughby; *b* 15 Sept 1932; *Educ* Bedford Modern Sch, King's Coll London, Univ of Lancaster (MA); *m* 1 (m dis 1972), Barbara, *née* Levelle; 1 s (Adam Teirnan b 1963), 1 da (Sarah Jane b 1959); m 2, Aug 1972, Jacqueline Phyllis (d 1990), da of Prof Guy Marrian, CBE (d 1981); m 3, Dec 1990, Shaké, da of Reupen Metrabian (d 1977); *Career* Nat Serv 2 Lt Royal Signals 1950-52; head of mktg Univ of Lancaster 1969-71, client and programme dir Ashridge Mgmnt Coll 1974-, chm t2 Solutions Ltd 1982-87, dir Deeko plc 1983-86; chm: BCCH Ltd 1984-, Rockliffe Leisure Ltd 1984-, Team One Ltd 1987-, Edgemount Ltd 1989-; dir Sherwood Computer Group plc 1988-; founding govr communications Advertising and Mktg Educn Fndn, served on two Indust Trg Bds; MCAM 1980; *Recreations* photography, music; *Clubs* IOD; *Style*— Bob Thomas, Esq; Cadman Square, Shenley Lodge, Milton Keynes MK5 7DN (☎ 0908 678 456); Ashridge Management College, Berkhamsted, Herts HP4 1NS (☎ 044 284 3491, fax 044 284 2382, telex 826434 ASHCOL G)

THOMAS, Sir Robert Evan; JP (Manchester 1948), DL (County Palatine of Greater Manchester 1974); s of Jesse Thomas, of Leigh, Lancs; *b* 8 Oct 1901; *Educ* St Peter's Leigh, Univ of Manchester (MA) 1974; *m* 1924, Edna, da of William Isherwood, of Leigh; 1 s, 1 da; *Career* former bus driver and trade union official; Lord Mayor of Manchester 1962-63, DL County Palatine of Lancaster 1967-73, dep chm Manchester Ship Canal until 1974, ldr Greater Manchester Met CC 1973-77, chm Assoc of Met Authorities 1974-77; kt 1967; *Books* Sir Bob; *Recreations* Golf; *Clubs* Heaton Moor Golf; *Style*— Sir Robert Thomas, JP, DL; 29 Milwain Road, Manchester M19 2PX

THOMAS, Robin Edwin; s of Arthur Edwin Thomas (ka 1942), and Joan Cicely, *née* Parsons; *b* 17 Oct 1940; *Educ* Stowe, Lincoln Coll Oxford (BA, MA), Harvard Business Sch (MBA); *m* 2 Sept 1972, Janine Penelope Russell, da of James Robert Maitland Boothby (d 1974); 1 da (Aurelia b 1975); *Career* md Thomas & Edge Ltd 1962-71, mangr Continental Illinois Ltd 1973-77, vice pres Continental Illinois Nat Bank 1977-; *Recreations* opera, bridge, skiing, tennis; *Style*— Robin Thomas, Esq; Worsley House, 4 West Side, London SW19 4TN (☎ 081 946 7187), Continental Bank, 162 Queen Victoria St, London, EC4V 4BS (☎ 01 860 5444, fax 01 860 5484, telex 887019)

THOMAS, Roger Geraint; s of Geraint Phillips Thomas (d 1989), and Doreen Augusta, *née* Cooke (d 1975); *b* 22 July 1945; *Educ* Penarth Co Sch, Leighton Park Sch Reading, Univ of Birmingham (LLB); *m* 23 Oct 1971, Rhian Elisabeth Kenyon, da of Erith Kenyon Thomas (d 1975), of Cardigan; *Career* ptnr Phillips & Buck slrs 1969-; memb: ct Nat Museum of Wales 1983- (cncl memb 1985-), Welsh Cncl CBI 1987-; vice chm Techniquest Cardiff, chm Cardiff branch BIM 1988-90; memb Law Soc 1969, FBIM 1984; *Recreations* sailboarding, hill walking; *Clubs* Cardiff and County, Penarth Yacht; *Style*— Roger G Thomas, Esq; Phillips & Buck, Fitzalan House, Fitzalan Rd, Cardiff CF2 1XZ; 1 Gunpowder Square, Printer St, London EC4A 3DE (☎ 0222 471147, fax 0222 464347, telex 497625)

THOMAS, Roger Lloyd; s of Trevor John Thomas (d 1972), of Barry, S Glam, and Eleanor Maud, *née* Jones (d 1973); *b* 7 Feb 1919; *Educ* Barry County Sch, Magdalen

Coll Oxford (MA); *m* 27 Oct 1945, Stella Mary, da of Reginald Ernest Willmett (d 1957), of Newport; 3 s (Julian b 1947, Andrew b 1948, Rupert b 1951), 1 da (Ursula b 1950); *Career* WWII enlisted RA 1939, cmmnd RA 1940; seconded to 2 Indian Field Regt 1940; served 1941-43: India, Iraq, Syria, Egypt, Libya; Capt 1942; staff offr intelligence: GHQ Paiforce, GHQ ME, AFHQ Algiers 1943-44, HQ Allied Armies in Italy 1944-45 (Maj 1944), SHAEF Frankfurt 1945-46; civil servant: Miny of Fuel and Power 1948-50, Home Office 1950-60 (private sec, permanent under sec of state 1950-51, Parly under sec of state 1951-53); sec: Interdepartmental Ctee on Powers of Subpoena 1960, Treasy 1960-62, Home Office 1962-64, Welsh Office 1964-67, Aberfan Inquiry Tbnl 1966-67, Miny of Housing 1967-70; chm Working Party on Building by Direct Labour Orgns 1968-69, gen mangr Housing Corp 1970-73, asst sec DOE 1974-79, advsr Central Policy Review Staff Cabinet Office 1979, sr clerk Ctee Office House of Commons 1979-84, clerk to Select Ctee on Welsh Affairs 1982-84, ret 1984; *Style*— R Lloyd Thomas, Esq; 5 Park Ave, Caterham, Surrey CR3 6AH (☎ 0883 342080)

THOMAS, Rosalind Mary; da of John Wyndham Pain (d 1963), of Howey Hall, Llandrindod Wells, Powys, and Nina Owena, *née* Lankester (d 1980); *b* 28 May 1921; *Educ* RCM; *m* 1, 16 Dec 1941, Lt John Stewart Hallam, KRRC (ka 1943): 1 da (Nina b 7 March 1943); *m* 2, 21 March 1952, Edward Llewelyn Thomas (d 1963), s of Capt Edward Aubrey Thomas (d 1952), of Cefndyrys, Builth Wells, Powys; 1 s (Evan David b 19 Jan 1953), 1 da (Celia b 22 April 1954); *Career* Powys CC: memb Cncl 1973-, chm 1987-88; co cncllr Radnor 1964-73; memb: Radnor LEA 1964-73, Powys LEA 1973-; memb Brecon & Radnor HMC 1956, memb Powys Health Authy 1973-, chm Adoption Panel Powys Social Servs 1974-87, chm Govrs Llandrindod Wells HS 1980-, former pres Radnor Fedn of YFCs, former pres Brecon & Radnor CLA (memb Exec Ctee and Cncl 1987), chm SE Wales Arts Cncl, High Sheriff of Powys 1987-88, memb Gen Advsy Cncl BBC 1988; *Style*— Mrs Edward L Thomas; Pengraig, Cefndyrys, Builth Wells, Powys LD2 3TF (☎ 0982 552726)

THOMAS, Roydon Urquhart; QC (1985); s of Rowland Donald Thomas (d 1957), and Jean Milne, *née* Leslie; *b* 17 May 1936; *Educ* Fettes, Sidney Sussex Coll Cambridge (BA); *m* ; 2 s (Peter Urquhart Milne b and d 1960, Guy Roydon Patrick b 1984), 1 da (Rosemary Urquhart b 1964); *Career* called to Bar Middle Temple, practising barr, SE Circuit, rec 1986-; *Recreations* golf, fishing, skiing; *Clubs* Hurlingham; *Style*— Roydon Thomas, Esq, QC; 1 Essex Court, Temple, London EC4Y 9AR (☎ 071 583 2000, fax 071 583 0118/353 8958)

THOMAS, Dr Sarah Elizabeth; da of Dr Alfred Evan Thomas, and Lucy Shaw, *née* Bradbury; *b* 29 June 1951; *Educ* Nottingham Bluecoat Sch, Univ of Sheffield Med Sch (MB ChB); *m* 1 Oct 1977, Dr Nigel Hugh Pereira, s of Sir Charles Pereira, CB, FRS; 3 da (Rebecca Lucy b 27 Nov 1980, Bridget Jane b 20 July 1983, Frances Elizabeth (twin) b 20 July 1983); *Career* lectr in med Univ of Nairobi Kenya 1980-81, conslt dermatologist Barnsley Hosp and Trent Regnl Health Authy 1986-; memb: BMA, MDU, Br Dermatological Soc 1986-; MRCP; *Recreations* music (piano and cello); *Style*— Dr Sarah Thomas; Dermatology Dept, Barnsley General Hospital, Gawber Rd, Barnsley

THOMAS, Simon; *b* 3 Feb 1960; *Educ* Plymouth Coll of Art & Design (fndn course), Ravensbourne Coll of Art & Design (BA), RCA (MA); *Career* sculptor; asst to: John Maine for Arena on S Bank London 1983-84, Philip King on Docklands Sculpture Project Canary Wharf 1984; stone carving asst to Hamish Horsley for Lewisham Borough Cncl cmmn 1985, Kemijarvi Int Wood Carving Symposium Kemijarvi Finnish Lapland 1987, Peterborough festival of carving 1988, lecture tour Finnish Lapland centering on Art and Soc Symposium Sarestoniemi Art Museum (for Lappish Summer Univ) 1989; solo exhibition Albermarle Gallery London 1989; gp exhibitions: Toute Quarry Portland Sculpture Park Dorset 1983, Quarries (Camden Arts Centre London) 1983, Landscape Work in Snowdonia National Park, Llandudno Art Gallery 1984, RCA Sculpture and Drawing Show (Central Sch of Art & Design) 1986, RCA Final Year Show 1988, Sculptors of Fame and Promise (Chichester Cathedral) 1988, New Milestones (Dorchester Co Musem) 1988, Concept 88 - Reality 89 (Univ of Essex) 1989, Dartmoor (Plymouth City Art Gallery) 1989, Trees Woods and the Green Man (Craft Cncl Gallery and tour) 1989, Art at Your Fingertips (St Mary Tradescant Museum of Garden History Lambeth) 1990; cmmns: New Milestones (Common Ground on Coastal Walk Durdle Moor Dorset) 1985, Three Large Wood Carvings (London Wildlife Tst) 1986, Burning Bush (Louisville Kentucky USA) 1990; Madame Tussauds award 1988; *Style*— Simon Thomas, Esq; Albemarle Gallery, 18 Albemarle St, London W1X 3HA (☎ 071 355 1880, fax 071 493 9272)

THOMAS, Stephen Richard; s of Maj Norman Arthur Thomas (d 1974), of E Horsley, and Norah Margaret, *née* Cooke; *b* 9 June 1947; *Educ* Elizabeth Coll Guernsey; *m* 17 July 1971, Felicity Ruth, da of Harold Arthur George Quaintance (Flt Sgt RAF Bomber Cmd), of Rowlstone; 2 s (Daniel b 1973, Peter b 1979), 2 da (Hannah b 1975, Elizabeth b and d 1977); *Career* Coopers Deloitte: joined 1965, ptnr 1981-, chm Coopers Deloitte Building Socs Indust Gp, Japanese liaison ptnr, fin servs sector ptnr, sr accounting advsr seconded to HM Treasy 1981-83; memb Alton Evangelical Free Church and Odiham Soc; FCA 1969; *Recreations* cricket, riding and tennis with family; *Style*— Stephen Thomas, Esq; Coopers & Lybrand Deloitte, 128 Queen Victoria St, London EC4P 4JX (☎ 071 583 5000, fax 071 248 3623, telex 894941)

THOMAS, Sir Swinton Barclay; s of Brig William Bain Thomas, CBE, DSO (d 1967), and Mary Georgina Thomas (d 1986); *b* 12 Jan 1931; *Educ* Ampleforth, Lincoln Coll Oxford (MA); *m* 1967, Angela Rose Elizabeth, wid of Sir Anthony Cope, 15 Bt, da of James Alfred Snarey Wright (d 1975); 1 s (Dominic), 1 da (Melissa); *Career* Lt Cameronians (Scottish Rifles); barr Inner Temple 1955, AC 1975, bencher Inner Temple 1983; judge of the High Ct 1985, presiding judge Western Circuit 1987-91; kt 1985; *Recreations* reading, travel; *Clubs* Garrick; *Style*— The Hon Sir Swinton Thomas; Royal Courts of Justice, Strand, London WC2 (☎ 071 936 6884)

THOMAS, Dr Trevor Anthony; s of Arthur William Thomas (d 1981), and Gladys MAry Gwendoline, *née* Hulin (d 1986); *b* 16 March 1939; *Educ* Bristol GS, Univ of St Andrews (MB ChB); *m* 10 July 1965, Yvonne Mary Louise, da of Percival Charles Branch (d 1946); 1 s (Jeremy Simon b 1969); *Career* sr conslt anaesthetist Bristol Maternity Hosp 1975-, chm Anaesthesia Div United Bristol Hosp 1977-80 (conslt anaesthetist 1972), South Western regnl assessor in anaesthesia for confidential enquires into maternal deaths 1978-, hon clinical lectr Univ of Bristol 1980-, examiner for Part 1 Fellowship of the Coll of Anaesthetists 1985-, chm Hosp Med Ctee Bristol and Western Health Dist 1988-, memb SW Regnl Hosp Med Advsy Ctee 1989-; ed Anaesthesia Points West 1976-80; hon sec: Obstetric Anaesthetists Assoc 1981-84, Soc of Anaesthetists of the South Western Regn 1985-88; memb: Cncl of Anaesthesia Sect RSM 1989-, Obstetric Sub-Ctee World Fedn of Socs of Anaesthesiology 1988-; FFARCS 1969, fell Coll of Anaesthetists 1989; *Books* Prescribing in Pregnancy (ed by Gordon M Stirrat and Linda Beeley in: CLinics of Obstetrics and Gynaecology 1986), Problems in Obstetrics Anaesthesia (ed by B M Morgan 1987), Cardiopulmonary Resuscitation (ed by P J F Baskett 1989); *Recreations* swimming, archery, music, theatre; *Style*— Dr Trevor Thomas; 14 Cleeve Lawns, Downend, Bristol BS16 6HJ (☎ 0272 567620); Sir Humphrey Davy Dept of Anaesthesia, Bristol Royal Infirmary, Mauldin St, Bristol BS2 8HW (☎ 0272 230000)

THOMAS, Dr Tudor Ewart; s of William Ewart Thomas (d 1980), and Phyllis, *née* Bevan (d 1986); *b* 27 Nov 1944; *Educ* Amman Valley GS, UCW Aberystwyth (BSc), Univ of Salford (PhD); *m* 27 July 1968, Brenda, da of Emlyn Davies; 1 s (Huw Glyn b 14 April 1972), 1 da (Carys Wyn b 3 Oct 1973); *Career* Unilever: mgmnt trainee 1968-70, area prodn mangr Unichema Chemicals Ltd 1970-74 (co prodn mangr 1974-78), divnl head Unichema International West Germany 1978-82, tech dir Vinyl Products Ltd 1982-85; unit gen mangr Mid Surrey Health Authy 1986-90, chief exec Epsom Health Care NHS Tst 1991-; magistrate Epsom 1988, elder United Reform Church 1986; FRSC 1982, CChem 1982; *Recreations* gardening, rugby; *Style*— Dr Tudor Thomas; Epsom Health Care NHS Trust, Epsom General Hospital, Dorking Road, Epsom, Surrey KT18 7EG (☎ 0372 726100)

THOMAS, Hon Mrs (Ursula Nancy); *née* Eden; da of 7 Baron Henley (d 1977); *b* 1950; *m* 1978, William Thomas; *Style*— The Hon Mrs Thomas

THOMAS, William Ernest Ghinn; s of Kenneth Dawson Thomas, of Sheffield, and Monica Isobel, *née* Markham; *b* 13 Feb 1948; *Educ* Dulwich, King's Coll London (BSc), St George's Hosp Med Sch (MB BS); *m* 30 June 1973, Grace Violet, da of Alfred Henry Samways (d 1979), of London; 2 s (Christopher b 1977, Benjamin b 1985), 3 da (Nicola b 1974, Jacqueline b 1979, Hannah b 1983); *Career* Hunterian prof RCS 1987 (Arris and Gale lectr 1982, Bernard Sunley fell 1977), Moynihan fell Assoc of Surgns 1982, conslt surgn Royal Hallamshire Hosp Sheffield 1986; exec ed Current Practice in Surgery 1988; memb: BMA 1974, BSG 1980; nat pres Gideons Int 1987-90; Royal Humane Soc award for Bravery 1974, Dr of the Year award 1985, European Soc prize for Surgical Res 1981; FRCS 1976, SRS 1981; *Books* Preparation and Revision for the FRCS (1986), Self-assessment Exercises in Surgery (1986), Nuclear Medicine: Applications to Surgery (1988); *Recreations* skiing, photography, oil painting; *Style*— William Thomas, Esq; Ash Lodge, 65 Whirlow Park Rd, Whirlow, Sheffield, S Yorks S11 9NN (☎ 0742 620 852); Royal Hallamshire Hospital, Glossop Rd, Sheffield, S Yorks S10 2JF (☎ 0742 766 222)

THOMAS, Sir William James Cooper; 2 Bt (UK 1919), of Ynyshir, Co Glamorgan, TD, JP (Monmouthshire 1958), DL (1973); s of Sir (William) James Thomas, 1 Bt (d 1945); *b* 7 May 1919; *Educ* Harrow, Downing Coll Cambridge; *m* 1947, Freida Dunbar (d 1990), da of late F A Whyte, of Montcoffer, Banff; 2 s, 1 da; *Heir* s, William Michael Thomas; *Career* served RA WW II; called to the Bar Inner Temple 1948; High Sheriff Co Monmouthshire 1973-74; *Clubs* Army and Navy; *Style*— Sir William Thomas, Bt, TD, JP, DL; Tump House, Llanrothal, Monmouth, Gwent (☎ 0600 2757)

THOMAS, Ven William Jordison; s of Henry William Thomas (d 1978), of Middlesbrough and Italy, and Dorothy Newton (d 1968); *b* 16 Dec 1927; *Educ* Homewood Prep Sch, Acklam Hall, Giggleswick Sch, King's Coll Cambridge (MA); *m* 23 Nov 1953, Kathleen Jeffrey, da of late William Robson, of Northumberland; *Career* Nat Serv RN 1946-48; ordained: deacon 1953, priest 1954; asst curate: St Anthony Newcastle 1953-56, Berwick-upon-Tweed 1956-59; vicar: Alwinton with Holystone and Alnham and Lordship of Kidland 1959-70, Alston with Garrigill, Nenthead and Kirkhaugh 1970-80; priest i/c Knaresdale 1973-80, team rector Glendale 1980-82, archdeacon of Northumberland and canon residentiary 1982-; harbour cmmr N Sunderland 1990; *Recreations* making pictures and magic, sailing; *Clubs* Victory Ex-Services; *Style*— The Ven the Archdeacon of Northumberland; 80 Moorside North, Fenham, Newcastle-upon-Tyne NE4 9DU (☎ 091 273 8245); Wark Cottage, Whittingham, Alnwick (☎ 066 574 300)

THOMAS, Wyndham; CBE (1982); s of Robert John Thomas (d 1959), and Hannah Mary, *née* Davies (d 1931); *b* 1 Feb 1924; *Educ* Maesteg GS, Cardiff Training Coll, Carnegie Coll, LSE; *m* 17 May 1947, Elizabeth Terry (Betty), *née* Hopkin; 1 s (Gareth b 1962), 3 da (Sally b 1956, Jenny b 1958, Tessa b 1960); *Career* RA and RCS 1943-45, cmmnd RWF 1945, demob Lt 1947; chm Inner City Enterprises plc 1983-; dir Town and Country Planning Assoc 1955-67, chm Housebuilders' Fedn's Independent Cmmn on Private Housebuilding and the Inner Cities; memb: Cmmn for the Towns 1964-68, DOE Property Advsy Gp 1974-90, London Docklands Devpt Corp 1981-88, Urban Investment Review Group DOE 1985-87, RIBA Inner Cities Working Pty 1987-88, Cncl RTPI 1989-; gen mangr Peterborough Devpt Corp 1968-83, conslt Letchworth Garden City Corp 1985-; mayor and bailiff Borough of Hemel Hempstead 1959-60, pres Thorpewood Golf Club 1975-, hon memb Royal Town Planning Inst 1980; Offr of the Order of Orange Nassau 1982; *Recreations* golf, running, restoring old furniture; *Clubs* Royal Over Seas League; *Style*— Wyndham Thomas, Esq, CBE; 8 Westwood Park Rd, Peterborough, Cambridgeshire (☎ 0733 64399); Inner City Enterprises plc, 52 Poland St, London W1V 3DF (☎ 071 287 5858)

THOMAS-EMBERSON, Steve; s of Colin Thomas-Emberson, of Carisbrooke, Stoneygate, Leics, and Jean, *née* Vezey-Walker (d 1986); *b* 4 June 1956; *Educ* The Bosworth Sch; *Career* mergers and acquisitions conslt; dir: Carter Hargrave Ltd 1987-, Pioneer Holdings Ltd 1988-, Grey Cat Communications Ltd 1988-, Goodyear Music Co Ltd 1989-, Goodyear Publishing Ltd 1989-, Glenway Investmts plc 1990-, Glenway Corp Ltd 1990-; fndr memb Boswell St James Dining Soc, tstee Young Dancers Fund; *Recreations* living well, conversation with intelligent ladies; *Clubs* Great Windsor and Ascot Yacht (hon Cdre); *Style*— Steve Thomas-Emberson, Esq; Alconleigh Cottage, Weir Rd, Kibworth Beauchamp, Leics (☎ 0533 793679); 14 Devonshire Sq, London EC2 (☎ 071 377 2800)

THOMAS-EVERARD, Christopher Philip; s of Maj Charles Richard Thomas, MA (ka 1944), and Prunella Peel Lewin-Harris, *née* Bentley-Taylor (d 1979); *see* Burke's Landed Gentry, 18 edn, vol 1, 1965; *b* 19 March 1941; *Educ* Stowe, RAC; *m* 1966, Rohaise Harriet Julia, da of Maj Eudo Tonson Rye; 1 s (Guy Richard), 2 da; *Career* farmer, landowner, chartered surveyor, owner of Miltons Estate and Broford Farm 1966-, chm: W Som NFU 1978-80, Som NFU Hill Farming Ctee 1981-82, Devon and Som Exmoor Hill Farming Ctee 1985-88; SW rep on MAFF Hill Farming Advsy Ctee 1979-; memb of MAFF SW Regnl Panel 1977-83; underwriting memb of Lloyd's 1973-; *Recreations* sailing, hunting; *Style*— Christopher Thomas-Everard, Esq; Broford Farm, Dulverton, Somerset (☎ 0398 23569)

THOMAS OF GWYDIR, Baron (Life Peer UK 1987), of Llanrwst, Co Gwynedd; Peter John Mitchell Thomas; PC (1964), QC (1965); o s of late David Thomas, of Llanrwst, Denbighshire, and Anne Gwendoline, *née* Mitchell; *b* 31 July 1920; *Educ* Epworth Coll Rhyl, Jesus Coll Oxford (MA); *m* 1947, Frances Elizabeth Tessa (d 1985), o da of late Basil Dean, CBE, the theatrical producer, by his 2 w, Lady Mercy Greville, 2 da of 5 Earl of Warwick; 2 s (Hon David Nigel Mitchell b 1950, Hon Huw Basil Maynard Mitchell b 1953), 2 da (Hon Frances Jane Mitchell b 1954, Hon Catherine Clare Mitchell b 1958); *Career* served WW II with RAF (prisoner); barr Middle Temple 1947; memb Wales and Chester Circuit, dep chm Cheshire Quarter Sessions 1966-70, Denbighshire Quarter Sessions 1968-70, bencher Middle Temple 1971, rec Crown Court 1974-88, arbitrator of ICC Court of Arbitration Paris 1974-88; MP (C): Conway 1951-66, Hendon S 1970-87; PPS to Solicitor Gen 1954-59, parly sec Min of Labour 1959-61, parly under-sec of state for Foreign Affairs 1961-63, min of state for Foreign Affairs 1963-64, opposition front bench spokesman on Foreign Affairs and Law 1964-66; chm Conservative Party Organisation 1970-72, sec of state for Wales 1970-74; pres Nat Union of Cons and Unionist Assocs 1974-76; *Clubs* Carlton; *Style*— The Rt Hon Lord Thomas of Gwydir, PC, QC; Millicent Cottage, Elstead, Surrey; 37 Chester Way, London SE11 (☎ 071 735 6047)

THOMAS OF SWYNNERTON, Baron (Life Peer UK 1981), of Notting Hill in Greater London; Hugh Swynnerton Thomas; s of Hugh Whitelegge Thomas, CMG (d 1960; s of Rev T W Thomas and sometime of the Colonial Serv, sec for Native Affairs in the Gold Gold Coast; chief commissioner Ashanti 1932 and UK rep to League of Nations *re* Togoland Mandate Report 1931 & 1934), and Margery Angelo Augusta, *née* Swynnerton; *b* 21 Oct 1931; *Educ* Sherborne, Queens' Coll Cambridge (MA); *m* 1962, Hon Vanessa Mary Jebb, *qv*, da of 1 Baron Gladwyn; 2 s (Hon Charles Inigo Gladwyn b 1962, Hon Henry Isambard Tobias b 1964), 1 da (Hon Isabella Pandora b 1966); *Career* sits as Conservative in House of Lords; historian; with Foreign Office 1954-57, lecturer Sandhurst 1957, prof history Reading Univ 1966-76; chm Centre for Policy Studies 1979-; memb Amnesty International; *Books Incl:* The Spanish Civil War (1961, revised 1977), Cuba (1971), An Unfinished History of the World (1979, revised 1982); *Clubs* Beefsteak, Garrick, Travellers' (Paris); *Style—* The Rt Hon Lord Thomas of Swynnerton; 29 Ladbroke Grove, London W11 3BB (☎ 01 727 2288)

THOMAS OF SWYNNERTON, Baroness; Hon Vanessa Mary; *née* Jebb; er da of 1 Baron Gladwyn, GCMG, GCVO, CB, and Cynthia, da of Sir Saxton William Armstrong Noble, 3 Bt; *b* 1931; *m* 1962, Baron Thomas of Swynnerton (Life Peer), *qv*; 2 s, 1 da; *Style—* The Rt Hon the Lady Thomas of Swynnerton; 29 Ladbroke Grove, London W11 3BB

THOMASON, Prof George Frederick; CBE (1982); s of George Frederick Thomason (d 1967), of Hawkshead, Lancs, and Eva Elizabeth, *née* Walker (d 1977); *b* 27 Nov 1927; *Educ* Kelsick GS Ambleside, Univ of Sheffield (BA), Univ of Toronto (MA), Univ of Wales (PhD); *m* 5 Sept 1953, Jean Elizabeth, da of Henry Horsley (d 1982), of Montreal, Canada; 1 s (Geraint b 25 Nov 1960), 1 da (Sian b 1 March 1957); *Career* RASC 1946-48; Univ Coll Cardiff: res asst 1953-54, asst lectr 1954-56, res assoc 1956-59, lectr 1959-60, sr lectr 1963-69, head of dept 1966-84, reader 1969, prof 1969-84, prof emeritus 1984-; asst to md Flex Fasteners Ltd 1960-62; dir: Enterprise & Training Development Ltd 1989-; dep chm Wales Cncl for Voluntary Action; memb: Opportunities for Volunteering (Wales) Ctee, Mgmnt Ctee Family Care Housing Assoc, Ct and Cncl Univ of Wales Coll of Cardiff, ACAS Panel of Industl Rels Arbitrators, two pay review bodies Drs, Dentists, Nurses, Midwives & Health Visitors; CIPM 1975, FBIM 1975; *Books* Textbook of Human Resource Management (1988), Textbook of Industrial Relations Management (1984), Professional Approach to Community Work (1969); *Recreations* gardening; *Clubs* Athenaeum, Cardiff and County; *Style—* Prof George Thomason, CBE; 149 Lake Rd, West, Cardiff CF2 5PJ (☎ 0222 754236)

THOMASON, Prof Harry; s of (Joseph) Alfred Thomason (d 1982), of Croston, and Edna, *née* Penwarden; *b* 29 Feb 1940; *Educ* Hutton GS, Chester Coll, Loughborough Univ of Technol (DLC, PHD), Univ of Salford (MSc); *m* 5 Aug 1966, Marie, da of Herbert Flintoff (d 1975), of Newburgh; 1 s (Timothy Simon b 26 Jan 1968); *Career* lectr Royal Coll of Advanced Technol Salford 1963-66, sr lectr Univ of Salford 1974-77 (lectr 1966-74); Loughborough Univ of Technol: founding prof and head Dept of Physical Educn and Sports Sci 1977-87, pro vice chllr 1987-90, pro vice chllr External Rels 1990-; Br Assoc of Sport and Med: memb Cncl and treas, memb Exec Ctee 1964-80 and 1987-; memb Med Sub-Ctee of BOA, assessor Assoc of Cwlth Univs Scholarship Scheme 1984-, dir Loughborough Consultants Ltd 1989-, advsr to Miny of Educn Singapore 1983-87 and 1990-, Miny of Sports rep E Midlands Region 1983-89; FRSM 1970, FRSA 1990; *Books* Sports Medicine (contrib, 1976), Basic Book of Sports Medicine (contrib, 1978), Science and Sporting Performance (contrib, 1982); *Recreations* skiing, hill walking, learning to sail; *Clubs* Athenaeum, Royal Windemere Yacht Club; *Style—* Prof Harry Thomason; Loughborough University of Technology (☎ 0509 223440, 09662 3557)

THOMASON, (Kenneth) Roy; OBE (1986); s of Thomas Roger Thomason (d 1989) of Ringwood, Hants, and Constance Dora, *née* Wilcox; *b* 14 Dec 1944; *Educ* Cheney Sch Oxford, Univ of London (LLB); *m* 6 Sept 1969, Christine Ann, da of William Richard Parsons (d 1985), of Queen's Park, Bournemouth; 2 s (Richard b 1972, Edward b 1974); 2 da (Julia b 1978, Emily b 1981); *Career* sr ptnr Horden & George Bournemouth 1979-; dir various cos; ldr Bournemouth Borough Cncl 1974-82 (memb 1970); Cons Pty: constituency chm Bournemouth West 1981-82, chm Wessex Area Local Govt Advsy Ctee 1981-83, memb Nat Local Govt Advsy Ctee 1981- (vice-chm 1989-), memb Nat Union Exec 1989-; Assoc of Dist Cncls: memb Cncl 1979, Cons gp ldr 1981-87, chm Housing and Environmental Health Ctee 1983-87, chm 1987-; *Recreations* sailing, architectural history; *Style—* Roy Thomason, Esq, OBE; Culross House, 18 Wellington Rd, Bournemouth (☎ 0202 292113); 23 Chapter St, London SW1 (☎ 071 233 6868)

THOMPSON, Prof Alan Eric; s of Eric Joseph Thompson (d 1956), and Florence, *née* Holmes (d 1974); *b* 16 Sept 1924; *Educ* Univ of Edinburgh (MA, PhD); *m* 3 Dec 1960, da of Frank Long (d 1963); 3 s (Matthew b 1962, Andrew b 1967, Hamish b 1971); *Career* WWII (served with Infantry and Br Forces Network in Centl Med Forces, Italy and Austria); lectr in economics Univ of Edinburgh 1953-59 and 1964-71, AJ Balfour prof of economics Heriot Watt Univ 1972-87, visiting prof Stanford Univ USA 1966 and 1968; Parly advsr: Scottish TV 1966-67, Pharmaceutical Gen Cncl Scotland 1985-; pres Edinburgh Amenity and Port Assoc 1970-75, hon vice-pres Assoc of Nazi War Camp Survivors 1960-; chm: Northern Offshore (Maritime) Resources Study 1974-84, Newbattle Abbey Coll, Edinburgh Ctee Peace Through NATO 1984-; govr Leith Nautical Coll 1981-84; memb: Royal Fine Art Cmmn for Scotland 1975-80, Local Govt Boundaries Cmmn (Scotland) 1975-82, Jt Military Educn Ctee Edinburgh and Heriot-Watt Univs 1975-, Scottish Cncl for Adult Educn in HM Forces 1973-; MP (Lab) Dunfermline 1959-64, Parly candidate (Lab) Galloway 1950 and 1951; FRSA 1972; *Books* Development of Economic Doctrine (jtly, 1980); *Recreations* bridge, croquet, writing children's stories, plays; *Clubs* New (Edinburgh), Edinburgh University Staff, Loch Earn Sailing; *Style—* Prof Alan Thompson; 11 Upper Gray Street, Edinburgh EH9 1SN; Ardtrostan Cottage, St Fillan's, Perthshire (☎ 031 667 2140, 076 485 275); School of Business and Financial Studies, Heriot-Watt Univ, 31-35 Grassmarket, Edinburgh EH1 2HJ

THOMPSON, Alec Geoffrey; OBE (1984); s of Alexander William Thompson (d 1968), and Edna May Thompson (d 1980); *b* 25 April 1926; *Educ* Preston GS, Manchester GS, Univ of Manchester (BSc); *m* 1949, Irene Lilian, da of James Eatock; 2 s (John, Peter); *Career* dir: J Bibby & Sons Ltd 1977-87, Majorfinch Ltd 1985-; md J Bibby & Sons plc 1979-82; vice-chm: J Bibby & Sons plc 1982-87, Petranol plc 1984-86, Fothergill-Harvey plc 1985-86; chm: Westmorland Smoked Foods Ltd 1985-, Gilbert Gilks & Gordon Ltd 1989-; hon treas and memb Cncl Univ of Lancaster 1983-; chm: Francis Scott Charitable Tst 1985-, Lancaster & Dist Health Authy 1985-; CBIM, FRSA; *Recreations* fishing, shooting, travel; *Clubs* Carlton; *Style—* Alec Thompson, Esq, OBE; Barcaldene, Leighton Drive, Beetham, Milnthorpe, Cumbria (☎ 044 82 2276)

THOMPSON, Ann Frances (Fran); da of Kenneth Charles Thompson, of Binsted, Hampshire, and Mary Philomena, *née* Rex; *b* 3 Feb 1955; *Educ* Farnborough Hill Convent Sch, UCW (BA); partner, Patrick Nils Connellan, s of Michael Anthony Connellan; 1 s (Ruari Svend b 20 Jan 1991); *Career* theatrical designer; assoc designer: Wolsey Theatre Ipswich 1980-81 (Saved, Pear Gynt), Nuffield Theatre Southampton 1981-83 (A Midsummer Night's Dream, Summer and Smoke, Dead Men, Adventures of Alice, Working Class Hero, Just a Kick in the Grass, The Dealer); The Importance of Being Earnest (opening of Wilde Theatre Bracknell) 1984; head of design Palace Theatre Watford: Trumpets and Rasberries (1984), Chance Visitor (premiere, 1984), Lulu (1984); freelance: Comedians (Everyman Theatre Liverpool) 1987, All's Well That Ends Well (Playhouse Theatre Leeds) 1987, Young Vic Theatre London (Julius Caesar 1987, Romeo and Juliet 1987, Enemy of the People 1988, Measure for Measure 1989), Passion Play (Playhouse Theatre Liverpool) 1988, Picture Palace (premiere, Women's Theatre Group) 1988, Twelfth Night (Theatre Royal Stratford East) 1988, A Winters Tale (Open Air Theatre Regent's Park) 1988, La Traviata (WNO) 1989, The Price (Young Vic Theatre) 1990, Pericles (RSC, Swan Theatre, Pit Theatre Barbican) 1989-90, Safe In Our Hands (W Yorkshire Playhouse Leeds) 1990, All My Sons (Birmingham Repertory Theatre) 1990; *Style—* Ms Fran Thompson; 97 Leahurst Rd, Lewisham, London SE13 5HY (☎ 081 463 9188); agent, Peter Murphy, Curtis Brown and John Farguharson, 161-168 Regent St, London W1R 5TB (☎ 071 872 0331)

THOMPSON, Anthony Arthur Richard; QC (1980); s of William Frank McGregor Thompson (d 1934), and Doris Louise, *née* Hill (d 1988); *b* 4 July 1932; *Educ* Latymer Sch, Univ Coll Oxford (MA), Sorbonne; *m* 1958, Francoise Alix Marie, da of Joseph Justin Reynier (d 1981); 2 s (Richard, Mark), 1 s decd, 1 da (Melissa); *Career* called to the Bar Inner Temple 1957; chm Bar Euro Gp 1984-86, recorder of the Crown Ct 1985, bencher Inner Temple 1986; avocat of the Paris Bar 1988; *Recreations* food & wine, theatre, cinema, lawn tennis; *Clubs* Roehampton; *Style—* Anthony Thompson Esq, QC; Coln Manor, Coln St Aldwyns, Gloucestershire GL7 5AD; 1 Essex Court, Temple, London EC4Y 9AR (☎ 071 583 2000, telex 889109 ESSEX G, fax 071 583 0118)

THOMPSON, Dr Catriona; da of John MacIntosh (d 1938), and Kate Ann, *née* Mackinnon (d 1975); *b* 29 May 1937; *Educ* Portree HS Isle of Skye, Univ of Edinburgh (MB ChB); *m* 16 July 1964, Douglas Theophilus Thompson, s of George Batchin Thompson, MBE (d 1958); 2 s (Hal b 1 Sept 1968, Andrew b 20 Jan 1975); *Career* hon lectr Dept Anaesthetics Univ of Zimbabwe 1972-76; conslt anaesthetist: Harare Central Hosp Zimbabwe 1967-77, Parirenyatwa Gp of Hosps Harare Zimbabwe 1970-82, Ayrshire and Arran Health Bd Crosshouse Hosp 1988-; first nat pres Zimbabwe Assoc of Univ Women 1980-82, memb Br Fedn of Univ Women 1986-, convener Membership Ctee Int Fedn of Univ Women 1989-; memb NW Regnl Pain Soc 1986-; FFARCS 1970; *Recreations* golf, badminton, walking, bridge; *Clubs* Crosby Hall; *Style—* Dr Catriona Thompson; Crosshouse Hospital, Crosshouse, Kilmarnock, Ayrshire KA2 0BE (☎ 0563 21133)

THOMPSON, Sir Christopher Peile; 6 Bt (UK 1890), of Park Gate, Guiseley, Yorks; s of Lt-Col Sir Peile Thompson, OBE, 5 Bt (d 1985), and his wife, Barbara Johnson, da of late Horace Johnson Rampling; *b* 21 Dec 1944; *Educ* Marlborough, RMA Sandhurst, Staff Coll; *m* 22 Nov 1969, Anna Elizabeth, da of late Maj Arthur George Callander, of Silbury House, Avebury, Wilts; 1 s (Peile Richard b 1975), 1 da (Alexandra Lucy b 1973); *Heir* s, Peile Richard Thompson b 3 March 1975; *Career* 11 Hussars (PAO), then Royal Hussars (PWO), cmmnd 1965, CO Royal Hussars 1985-87, ret 1990; private sec to HRH Prince Michael of Kent 1990- (equerry 1989); *Recreations* fishing, shooting, sailing, windsurfing, skiing, reading, gardening, cresta; *Clubs* Cavalry and Guards', RAC, St Moritz Toboganning; *Style—* Sir Christopher Thompson, Bt; Old Farm, Augres, Trinity, Jersey, CI

THOMPSON, Christopher Ronald; s of Col S J Thompson, DSO, DL (d 1956); *b* 14 Dec 1927; *Educ* Shrewsbury, Trinity Coll Cambridge; *m* 1949, Rachael Mary, *née* Meynell; 2 s (1 s decd), 1 da; *Career* sr ptnr Aldenham Business Services, chm Fillermist International Ltd; dir: Isotron plc, Barclay's Bank Ltd, Saraswati Syndicate India, G T Japan Investment Trust plc, Mappa Mundi plc; chm: Anglo Venezuelan Soc 1982-85, Sino-British Trade Cncl 1981-85, John Sutcliffe (Shipping) Ltd 1985-88; memb Cncl Shropshire Regnl Ctee CLA; High Sheriff Shropshire 1984-85; *Recreations* fly-fishing, shooting, gardening; *Clubs* Boodle's; *Style—* Christopher Thompson, Esq; Aldenham Park, Bridgnorth, Shrops (☎ 074 631 218); Estate Off Aldenham Park (☎ 074 631 351)

THOMPSON, Clive Malcolm; *b* 4 April 1943; *Educ* Clifton Coll, Univ of Birmingham (BSc); *Career* gp chief exec Rentokil Group plc; non-exec dir: MB-Caradon plc, Farepak plc; dep chm SE Regnl Cncl CBI; *Style—* Clive Thompson, Esq; Rentokil Group plc, Felcourt, East Grinstead, West Sussex

THOMPSON, David; s of Bernard Thompson, of Castleford, and Violet, *née* Laidler; *b* 28 Oct 1944; *Educ* King's Sch Pontefract; *m* 24 Oct 1970, Glenys, da of Harry Colley, of Badsworth, nr Pontefract; 2 s (Anthony David b 24 Aug 1972, Richard Martin b 17 Feb 1976); *Career* John Gordon Walton CAs until 1967, sr ptnr Buckle Barton 1981- (ptnr 1978-81); fin dir and sec: Safe Hands Creche Ltd 1985-, Securicloak Ltd 1986-; fin dir Bradford City AFC 1986- (vice chm 1990-); chm: Omnis Associates Ltd 1986-, DT Financial Consultants Ltd 1986-; fin dir and sec: Grandma Batty Holdings Ltd (formerly Wondercourt Ltd) 1987-; dir and sec: Grandma Batty's Emporiums Ltd 1988-, Grandma Batty's Restaurants Ltd 1990-, Creches for Business Ltd 1990-, Portercase Ltd 1990-, Tropical Sno Ltd 1990-, Safe Hands (Franchised Creches) Ltd 1990-, Novelgrove Ltd 1990-; dep songster ldr Castleford Corps Salvation Army; ACA 1969, FCA 1979; *Recreations* football, most sports; *Clubs* Regency (Leeds), Napoleon's (Bradford); *Style—* David Thompson, Esq; Stone Lea, Badsworth Court, Badsworth, Pontefract, W Yorks WF9 1NW (☎ 0977 645467); Sanderson House, Station Rd, Horsforth, Leeds LS18 5NT (☎ 0532 588 216/ 581 640, fax 0532 390 270, car tel 0836 265 365)

THOMPSON, David William Moffat; s of Rev William Meredith Drew Thompson, of Oxnam Manse, Jedburgh, Roxburghshire, and Vida Faerrie, *née* Sloan; *b* 14 Feb 1950; *Educ* Shrewsbury, Kent Sch Conn USA, ChCh Oxford (MA); *Career* ptnr KPMG Peat Marwick McLintock 1987; memb Exec Ctee People and Churches Together; FCA 1975, Certified Public Accountant Calif 1981; *Clubs* New (Edinburgh); *Style—* David Thompson, Esq; Pear Tree Cottage, Rodmell, Lewes, East Sussex (☎ 0273 472113); KPMG Peat Marwick McLintock, Queen Square House, Queen Square, Brighton, E Sussex (☎ 0273 820042, fax 0273 23723)

THOMPSON, Derek Paul; s of Stanley Moorhouse Thompson (d 1985), and Lilian, *née* Forster; *b* 31 July 1950; *Educ* Fyling Hall, Guisborough GS; *m* 19 Oct 1979, Janie, da of Bill McLaren, MBE, of Hawick, Scotland; 2 s (Alexander McLaren b 5 June 1982, James Gordon b 5 Nov 1984); *Career* sports commentator and presenter; BBC Radio Sport 1972-81, ITV Sport 1981-85, Channel 4 Racing 1985-; *Recreations* tennis, golf, jogging; *Clubs* Moor Park Golf; *Style—* Derek Thompson, Esq; Chalfont St Giles, Bucks (☎ 02407 2163, car 0860 711526, 0831 422021)

THOMPSON, Donald; MP (C) Calder Valley 1983-; s of Geoffrey Thompson; *b* 13 Nov 1931; *Educ* Hipperholme GS; *m* 1957, Patricia Hopkins; 2 s; *Career* farmer, md Armadillo Plastics; memb: West Riding and West Yorkshire CC, Calderdale DC 1967-79; chm Cons Candidates' Assoc 1972-74; contested (C): Batley and Morley 1970, Sowerby Feb and Oct 1974, MP (C) Sowerby 1979-1983, Govt whip and Lord Cmmr of the Treas 1981-86 , parly sec MAFF 1986-89, Govt whip COE and WEU 1990-;

Style— Donald Thompson, Esq, MP; Moravian House, Lightcliffe, nr Halifax, W Yorks (☎ 0422 202920)

THOMPSON, Donald James (Don); MBE (1970); s of Laurie James Thompson (d 1974), of Cranford, nr Hounslow, and Doris Alice, *née* Denny (d 1978); *b* 20 Jan 1933; *Educ* Hounslow Coll, Open Univ (BA); *m* 26 May 1967, Margaret, da of John Bell; 1 s (David James b 11 July 1979), 1 da ((Sarah) Helen b 5 July 1975); *Career* former international athlete; jr cross country and road running athlete Thames Valley Harriers 1948-50, jr and sr race walker Metropolitan Walking Club 1950-68, sr cross country runner Thames Valley Harriers 1966- (also road runner Folkestone Athletics Club 1968-); Gold medal 50km walk Olympic Games Rome 1960 (also competed Melbourne 1956 and Tokyo 1964), Bronze medal 50km walk Euro Games Belgrade 1962 (also competed Stockholm 1958 and Budapest 1966), fourth place 20 mile walk Cwlth Games Kingston 1966, UK 50km walk champion 8 times 1956-62 and 1966, winner London to Brighton walk 9 times 1955-62 and 1967 (broke record 1957); achieved 100,000 miles of recorded racing and training 1951-90; fire insurance clerk: Pearl Assurance 1950-53, Commercial Union 1953-69 (also accounts clerk); teacher training coll 1969-72, primary sch teacher Battersea 1972-75, Secdy sch teacher Kent 1975-83, salesman Kleeneze 1983-84, self-employed gardener 1984-; Fire Branch ACII 1969; *Recreations* athletics first and last, keen unskilled decorator; *Style*— Don Thompson, Esq, MBE

THOMPSON, Dudley Stuart; s of Joel Percy Thompson (d 1964), and Joan Evelyn, *née* Anstey (d 1984); *b* 4 Nov 1942; *Educ* Whitgift Sch; *m* 27 June 1970, Anne Elizabeth, da of John Egerton Coope (d 1964); 1 s (Paul Dudley Fitzgerald b April 1975), 2 da (Karen Juliette b July 1973, Hazel Joan b Sept 1978); *Career* sr mangr Touche Ross & Co 1969-78, gp chief accountant Imperial Continental Gas Assoc 1978-87, gp fin dir Goode Durrant plc 1988-; chm Merstham Village Tst, pres Merstham Village Club; FCA 1965, FCT 1982, MBIM 1985; *Recreations* golf, theatre, sailing, gardening; *Clubs* Walton Heath Golf, Hunstanton Golf; *Style*— Dudley Thompson, Esq; The Georgian House, Rockshaw Rd, Merstham, Surrey RH1 3DB; Goode Durrant plc, 22 Buckingham St, London WCRN 6PU (☎ 071 782 0010)

THOMPSON, Lt-Col Sir Edward Hugh Dudley; MBE (1945), TD, DL (Derby 1978); s of Neale Dudley Thompson; *b* 12 May 1907; *Educ* Uppingham, Lincoln Coll Oxford; *m* 1, 1931, Ruth Monica, *née* Wainwright; 2 s; m 2, 1947, Doreen Maud, *née* Tibbitt; 1 s, 1 da; *Career* Lt-Col 1939-45; slr 1931-36; asst md Ind Coope & Co Ltd 1937-39 (chm 1955-62), chm Allied Breweries Ltd 1961-68; chm Brewers Soc 1959-61; High Sheriff Derby 1964; Dr of Laws Univ of Nottingham 1984; kt 1967; *Recreations* farming; *Clubs* Boodle's; *Style*— Lt-Col Sir Edward Thompson, MBE, TD, DL; Culland Hall, Brailsford, Derby (☎ 0335 60247)

THOMPSON, Eric John; s of Herbert William Thompson (d 1990), of Beverley, N Humberside, and Florence, *née* Brewer (d 1937); *b* 26 Sept 1934; *Educ* Beverley GS, LSE (BSc); *Career* Pilot Offr RAF 1956-58; statistician in computer industry 1958-60, oil indust 1960-65, Gen Register Office 1965-68, GLC 1967-74 (asst dir intelligence 1972-74), chief statistican Central Statistical Office (ed Social Trends) 1975-80; dir of Statistics Dept of Tport 1980-89, dep dir Office of Population Censuses and Surveys 1989-; memb: E Yorks Local History Soc, Housman Soc, Richard III Soc (Exec Ctee 1984-), Friends of Nat Libraries, Selden Soc, Richard III and Yorkist History Tst (tstee); *Recreations* reading, collecting books, British medieval history, English literature; *Style*— Eric J Thompson, Esq; Office of Population Censuses and Surveys, St Catherine's House, London WC2B 6JP (☎ 071 242 0262)

THOMPSON, Ernest Gerald (Tommy); OBE (1973); s of Joseph Thompson (d 1943), of Goodmayes, Essex, and Rhoda Annie, *née* Messenger (d 1970); *b* 22 Nov 1925; *Educ* Brentwood Sch, Trinity Coll Cambridge; *m* 14 Sept 1968, Janet Muriel, da of Philip Andrew Smith (d 1977), of Blackmore House, Blackmore, Essex; 1 s (Richard Michael b 1971); *Career* Flt Lt navigator and bomb aimer RAF 1943-47; Int Secretariat of the Euro Movement Paris 1951-55, joined Baird & Tatlock Ltd 1955 (instrument sales mangr 1962-68), dir Dannatt SA Paris 1963-68, chm and md Chemlab Instruments Ltd 1968-86, chm Chemlab Mfrg Ltd, chm and md Chemlab Scientific Prod Ltd 1986-; memb Hon Lecturing Faculty Inst of Mktg 1966-78, hon sec Britain in Europe 1958-68, vice chm Cons Gp for Europe 1967-75; memb: Gen Cncl of Cons Gp for Europe 1975-, nat exec of the Euro Movement 1969-83, nat cncl of Euro Movement 1983-, Int Fed Ctee of Union Européen des Fédéralistes 1974-; Honorary Senator of the Belgium Movement for the Utd States of Europe; Freeman City of London 1979; LRSC 1968, FInstD; *Recreations* music, swimming, travel, gardening; *Style*— Tommy Thompson, Esq, OBE; Yew Tree House, Morgan Crescent, Theydon Bois, Essex (☎ 0992 812486); Los Ruisenores, Son Pieras, Calviá, Mallorca, Spain; Chemlab Scientific Products Ltd, Construction House, Grenfell Ave, Hornchurch, Essex RM12 4EH (☎ 04024 76162, fax 04024 37231)

THOMPSON, Estelle Margaret; *b* 8 June 1960; *Educ* Sheffield City Poly (BA), Royal Coll of Art (MA); *Career* artist; pt/t lectr: Winchester Sch of Art, Christies Fine Art Course, Ruskin Sch of Art, Royal Coll of Art; solo exhibitions incl: Pomeroy Purdy Gallery 1989 and 1991, Eastbourne Clarke Gallery Florida 1989 and 1990; group exhibitions incl: Three Painters from the RCA (Paton Gallery) 1985, Women and Water (Odette Gilbert Gallery) 1988, Homage to the Square (Flaxman Gallery) 1989 and 1990, The Theory and Practice of the Small Painting (Anderson O'Day Gallery) 1990, Whitechapel Open 1990, Art in Worship (Worcester Cathedral and Tewkesbury Abbey) 1991; work in the collections of: The Arts Cncl, The Br Cncl, Towner Art Gallery Sussex, Arthur Andersen Collection, The Contemporary Art Soc, County Nat West, Reed Int, Unilever, Coopers & Lybrand Deloitte; *Style*— Ms Estelle Thompson; c/o Pomeroy Purdy Gallery, Jacob Street Film Studios, Mill St, London SE1 (☎ 071 237 6062, fax 071 252 0511)

THOMPSON, Frank Robert; s of Corpl Arthur Robert Thompson (d 1964), of Newark, Notts, and Margaret Ellen, *née* Fordham; *b* 1 Jan 1938; *Educ* Magnus GS Newark, Univ of Hull (BA, DipEd); *m* 21 Dec 1963, (Janet) Deirdre, da of Robert Fraser Skinner, of Melton Mowbray, Leicestershire; 1 s (Alastair b 1966), 1 da (Virginia b 1965); *Career* dep head Park Further Educn Centre Swindon 1969-70, head Westbourne Further Educn Centre Swindon 1971-72; Pontypool Coll: head gen studies 1975-82, sr lectr Dept of Arts and Gen Studies 1982-90; Parly candidate (Lab): S Norfolk 1964, Wells 1970, Monmouth 1974; memb Univ of Bristol Ct 1981-86; Glos CC: cncllr for Coleford 1981-, dep ldr 1982-85, gp ldr 1985-, rep on Assoc of CCs 1985, memb Planning and Transportation Ctee (now Environment Ctee) 1985-90, dep spokesman Lab Gp 1990-; Staunton Parish Cncl: memb 1979-87 (chm 1981-87), rep Forest of Dean CAB Mgmnt Ctee 1979-87; chm Govrs: Royal Forest of Dean GS 1982-85, Lakers Sch 1985-; memb NATFHE 1973-; *Recreations* long distance walking, swimming, chess, listening to music; *Style*— Frank Thompson, Esq; Steep Meadow, Staunton, Coleford, Gloucestershire GL16 8PD (☎ 0594 33873); Pontypool Coll, Blaendare Rd, Pontypool, Gwent (☎ 049 55 55141)

THOMPSON, Gabriel Piers; s of James Thompson, of Kings Norton, Birmingham, and Mary Josephine, *née* McAndrew; *b* 8 March 1962; *Educ* The Reading Bluecoat Sch Sonning-on-Thames Berkshire; *m* 20 Aug 1982, Martina Josephine, da of Francis Joseph Devlin; *Career* Reading Evening Post: trainee reporter 1981, sub-ed 1982, passed NCTJ proficiency test 1983, sr reporter 1983; sub-ed: Middlesborough Evening Gazette 1984, Newcastle Journal 1985; The Independent: layout sub-ed 1986, foreign sub-ed 1987, foreign prodn ed 1989; prodn ed The Independent on Sunday 1990- (chief sub-ed 1990); *Recreations* smoking, drinking, eating, falling in love, walking on desks; *Clubs* The Irish National Foresters (County Tyrone); *Style*— Gabriel Thompson, Esq; 27 Greek Street, Soho, London W1V 5LL; Mullaghmore, County Sligo, Republic of Ireland; The Independent on Sunday, 40 City Road, London EC1Y 2DB

THOMPSON, Dr Geoffrey Stuart; s of Frank Vincent Thompson (d 1975), of Oldham, Lancashire, and Maud Partington, *née* Hague (d 1989); *b* 26 June 1926; *Educ* Manchester GS, Trinity Coll Cambridge (MA, MD); *m* 28 April 1962, Angela Mary Stewart, da of Dr David Brown, CBE (d 1973), of Bootle, Lancashire; 1 s (Jonathan Richard b 1967), 1 da (Jane Elizabeth b 1969); *Career* Nat Serv Flt Lt RAF 1952-54; house surgn UCH 1951, house physician then registrar then sr registrar Liverpool Teaching Hosps 1954-65, conslt physician S Manchester DHA 1965-; memb med and scientific section Br Diabetic Assoc, fell Manchester Med Soc; memb BMA; *Recreations* swimming, walking; *Style*— Dr Geoffrey Thompson; 41 The Downs, Altrincham WA14 2QG (☎ 061 928 2471)

THOMPSON, Dr Gilbert Richard; s of Lt-Col Richard Louis Thompson (d 1976), and Violet Mary, *née* Harrison (d 1955); *b* 20 Nov 1932; *Educ* Downside, St Thomas's Hosp Med Sch (MB BS, MRCP), Univ of London (MD); *m* 14 June 1958, Sheila Jacqueline Mary, da of Melchior Deurvorst (d 1977); 2 s (Mark b 1961, Philip b 1971), 2 da (Anna b 1959, Jennifer b 1977); *Career* Lt RAMC Royal Army Med Coll Millbank 1957-58; Capt RAMC mil hosp: Accra Ghana 1959-61, Millbank 1961-63; registrar and sr registrar in med Hammersmith Hosp 1963-66, res fell Harvard Med Sch and Mass Gen Hosp Boston 1966-67, lectr in med Royal Postgrad Med Sch and conslt physician Hammersmith Hosp 1967-72, asst prof Baylor Coll of Med and Methodist Hosp Houston 1972-73, sr lectr in med Royal Postgrad Med Sch 1972-74, conslt MRC Lipid Metabolism Unit Hammersmith Hosp 1975-83, visiting prof Royal Victoria Hosp Montreal 1981-82, currently conslt MRC lipoprotein team Hammersmith Hosp; chm Br Hyperlipidaemia Assoc; FRCP 1973; *Books* A Handbook of Hyperlipidaemia (1989); *Recreations* squash, skiing, fly-fishing; *Style*— Dr Gilbert Thompson; MRC Lipoprotein Team, Hammersmith Hospital, Ducane Rd, London W12 0HS (☎ 081 740 3262, fax 081 746 0586)

THOMPSON, Guy Charles Wallace; s of Cdr John Lionel Wallace Thompson (d 1987), and Patricia June, *née* Etchells; *b* 23 Nov 1952; *Educ* Sutton Valence, Univ of Newcastle upon Tyne (BA, BArch); *m* 2 Aug 1975, Gillian Edna, da of P R Brown; 1 da (Amy Charlotte b 21 Nov 1982); *Career* architectural asst PSA Edinburgh 1974-75, design conslt Planning Dept Tyne and Wear Cncl (Highways and Environmental Works Team Section) 1977; Norman & Dawbarn: architectural asst 1977, assoc 1983, ptnr 1989; projects incl: operating theatre RAF Hosp Ely 1978, mil works force accommodation Chilwell 1984, Southwood Business Park Farnborough, Consulate and Cultural Centre Queensgate, Kensington Laboratories for PSA; *awards* Northern Brick Fedn Design award 1977, competition winner Hawth Centre for the Performing Arts 1986; memb ARCUK 1978, ARIBA 1978; *Recreations* squash, walking, architecture; *Style*— Guy Thompson, Esq; 53 Wodeland Ave, Guildford, Surrey GU1 4JZ (☎ 0483 31097); Norman & Dawbarn, College House, Woodbridge Rd, Guildford, Surrey GU1 4RT (☎ 0483 33551, fax 0483 506459)

THOMPSON, Harry William; s of Gordon William Thompson, of Nant Ddu, Rhandirmwyn, Llandovery, Dyfed, and Brenda, *née* Houghton; *b* 6 Feb 1960; *Educ* Highgate, BNC Oxford (MA); *Career* BBC TV: researcher (Chronicle, Not the 9 O'Clock News) 1981-82, dir (Film 83, Destination D Day, Nationwide) 1982-84; script ed and sr prodr radio comedy (incl The News Quiz, Weekending, The Mary Whitehouse Experience, Lenin of The Rovers, Beachcomber.....by the Way, The Miles & Millner Show) 1985-; writer of TV documentaries incl: Decibels of the Decade, The Man in the Iron Mask; TV prodr Have I got news for you 1990; contrib to: Spitting Image, Not The 9 O'Clock News, Private Eye, The Independent, The Listener; *Books* The Prejudice Library (1986), The Man in the Iron Mask (1987), The News Quiz Book (1987), The Spitting Image Book (contrib, 1988), Tintin - Hergé and his creation (1991); *Recreations* cricket, old bookshops, pig keeping, travel; *Clubs* Captain Scott; *Style*— Harry Thompson, Esq; Alexandra House, St Mary's Terr, London W2 1SF (☎ 071 402 2157); BBC, 16 Langham St, London W1 (☎ 071 927 4867)

THOMPSON, (James) Howard; OBE (1985); s of James Alan Thompson (d 1982), and Edna, *née* Perkins; *b* 26 March 1942; *Educ* Northampton GS, Magdalene Coll Cambridge (BA), Stanford Univ (MA); *m* 11 Sept 1965, Claire Marguerite, da of Thomas Hayes Dockrell, TD (d 1970), of Northampton; 1 s (Hayes Benedict b 1972), 1 da (Catherine Frances b 1967); *Career* English language offr Br Cncl Yugoslavia 1965-69, assoc prof of English Regnl Inst of English Chandigarh India 1970-73, advsr Schs and Further Educn Br Cncl London 1978-80, educn attache Br Embassy Washington 1980-84; Br Cncl: dep controller Sci Technol and Educn Div London 1984-87, controller Educn and Sci Div London, dir Indonesia 1981-91; chm Educn and Trg Export Ctee 1987-89; *Books* Teaching English; *Recreations* travel, photography; *Style*— Howard Thompson, Esq, OBE; British Council, Widjojo Centre, J L Jendral Sudirman 71, Jakarta (☎ 570 6334, fax 582743, 45246 BRICON JKT)

THOMPSON, Dr Ian McKim; s of John William Thompson (d 1976), of Solihull, and Dr Elizabeth Maria, *née* Williams; *b* 19 Aug 1938; *Educ* Epsom Coll, Univ of Birmingham (MB ChB); *m* 8 Sept 1962, Dr (Veronica) Jane, da of John Dent Richards (d 1987), of Fladbury; 2 s (David b 1966, Peter b 1969), 1 da (Suzanne b 1972); *Career* lectr in pathology Univ of Birmingham 1964-67, conslt forensic pathologist to HM Coroner City of Birmingham 1966-, dep sec BMA 1969-, lectr Dept of Adult Educn Keele Univ 1985-; fndr memb AMEC, memb GMC 1979-; hon memb Collegiate Med Coll of Spain 1975; BMA 1961, FRSM 1988; *Books* The Hospital Gazeteer (ed, 1972), BMA Handbook for Trainee Doctors in General Practice (ed 1985), BMA Handbook for Hospital Junior Doctors (ed, 1985); *Recreations* inland waterways, rambling; *Style*— Dr McKim Thompson; Weir Cottage, Fladbury, Pershore, Worcs WR10 2QA (☎ 0386 860 668); BMA House, Tavistock Square, London WC1H 9JP (☎ 071 383 6005)

THOMPSON, James Craig; s of Alfred Thompson, of Newcastle upon Tyne, and Eleanor, *née* Craig; *b* 27 Oct 1933; *Educ* Heaton GS, Rutherford Coll Newcastle; *m* 4 Sept 1957, Catherine, da of James Warburton, of Newcastle upon Tyne; 1 s (Roderic b 1959), 1 da (Fiona b 1963); *Career* pres: The Maidstone Minor League 1976-, The Eastern Professional Floodlight League 1976-; chm: The Southern Football League 1977-79, The Alliance Premier Football League 1979-89; memb Cncl FA 1982-; pres The Kent League 1984-89, pres The Football Conf 1989-; chm and md: Maidstone United Football Club Ltd 1970-, Adverkit International Ltd 1987-90; commercial exec: Belfast Telegraph, Newcastle Chronicle and Journal, Scotsman Publications, Liverpool Post and Echo 1960-76; advertising and mktg mangr Kent Messenger Gp 1976-79 (dir 1972-79), md South Eastern Newspapers 1975-79, chm Harvest Publications Ltd 1983-, dir Weekly Newspaper Advertising Bureau 1977-; life govr Kent County Agric Soc 1976-, hon life memb Kent County CC 1978; memb: MCC, Catenian Assoc (pres Maidstone Circle 1974-75); *Recreations* walking, Northumbrian history; *Clubs* East India, Maidstone; *Style*— James Thompson, Esq; Prescott House, Otham, Kent (☎

0622 861606); Maidstone United FC Ltd, Bowerdene House, Number One Bower Terrace, Maidstone, Kent (☎ 0622 754403, fax 0622 685803)

THOMPSON, Rt Rev James Lawton; *see*: Stepney, Bishop of

THOMPSON, Prof (John) Jeffrey; CBE (1989); s of John Thompson (d 1968), of Southport, Lancs, and Elsie May, *née* Wright; *b* 13 July 1938; *Educ* King George V Sch Southport, St John's Coll Cambridge (MA), Balliol Coll Oxford (MA), Hatfield Poly (PhD); *m* 6 April 1963, Kathleen Audrey, da of Francis Arthur Gough (d 1989), of Southport, Lancs; 3 da (Karen b 1965, Alison b 1966, Lynda 1971); *Career* schoolmaster Blundell's Tiverton 1961-65, head of chemistry Watford GS 1965-69, lectr KCL 1968-69, Shell fell UCL 1969-70, lectr and tutor Dept Educnl Studies Oxford 1970-79, lectr in chemistry Keble Coll Oxford 1970-76, pro-vice chllr Univ of Bath 1986-89 (prof of educn 1979-); dep chm Sch Examinations and Assessment Cncl, vice pres and gen sec Br Assoc for the Advancement of Sci; chm: Assoc for Sci Educn 1981, Examining Bd Int Baccalaureate 1984-89; memb: Cncl Wildfowl and Wetlands Tst, Royal Soc Educn Ctee, Assoc for Sci Educn; FRSC, FRSA (1984); *Books* An Introduction to Chemical Energetics (1967), Study of Chemistry Programmes (1972), Modern Physical Chemistry (1982), A Foundation Course in Chemistry (1982), Dimensions of Science (ed, 1986), The Chemistry Dimension (1987); *Recreations* N country art and music, collecting sugar wrappers; *Style*— Prof Jeffrey Thompson, CBE; School of Education, University of Bath, Claverton Down, Bath BA2 7AY

THOMPSON, Jeremy Sinclair; s of Norman Sinclair Thompson, CBE, of Shadrach House, Burton Bradstock, Dorset, and Peggy, *née* Sivil; *b* 6 April 1954; *Educ* Durham Sch, Keble Coll Oxford (MA); *m* 12 June 1982, Lucy Jane Thompson, da of Peter Joseph Wagner (d 1983); 2 da (Victoria b 1986, Poppy b 1989); *Career* Peat Marwick Mitchell 1976-80, dir accounting servs Air Florida Europe Ltd 1980-82, conslt Coopers & Lybrand Assocs 1982-84; md: Sinclair Thompson Assocs 1985-86, Tranwood Earl & Co Ltd 1986-; dir Tranwood plc 1987-; ACA 1980; *Recreations* rowing, sailing; *Clubs* Leander, Royal Ocean Racing; *Style*— Jeremy Thompson, Esq; Hill Barn Farm, Broomers Hill, Pulborough, W Sussex (☎ 07982 2778); Tranwood Earl & Co Ltd, 123 Sloane St, London SW1 (☎ 071 730 3412, fax 071 730 5770, telex 932016)

THOMPSON, John; MP (Lab) Wansbeck 1983-; s of Nicholas Thompson, of Ashington, Northumberland (d 1966), and Lilian Thompson; *b* 27 Aug 1928; *Educ* Bothal Sch; *m* 1952, Margaret, da of John Robert Clarke (d 1974), of Newbiggin-by-Sea, Northumberland; 1 s, 1 da; *Career* electrical engineer 1966-83; dist cncllr 1970-79, co cncllr 1974-85, ldr and vice chm Northumberland Co Cncl 1974-83, memb Bd Northumbrian Water Authority 1981-83, alternate memb Parly Assembly Cncl of Europe and W Euro Union 1987-; *Recreations* caravanning, listening; *Style*— John Thompson, Esq, MP; House of Commons, London SW1 (☎ 071 219 4048); 20 Falstone Crescent, Ashington, Northumberland (☎ 0670 817830)

THOMPSON, John; s of John Thompson, of Myrtle Bank, Kersal Rd, Prestwich, Lancs (d 1964), and Ellen Anne, *née* Evans (d 1954); *b* 10 May 1932; *m* 2 April 1955, Eileen Joan, da of Ernest Neate, of Amesbury, Wilts; *Career* md Wincanton Motor Gp, operations, dir Arlington Motor Hldgs, exec dir: United Service Garages Ltd, Turnbulls (Plymouth) Ltd; dir: Zenith Motors Ltd, Wincanton Garages Ltd, Vogal Motors Ltd, Hewitts Garages Ltd, Kays Ltd, Charnwood Trucks Ltd, Shepshed Engr Ltd, Wincanton Body Works (Westbury) Ltd; Freemasonry Rank 1987, past provincial sr Grand Deacon (Prov of East Lancashire); acting rank-prov Grand Steward 1985-86; FBIM, FIMI; *Recreations* motor racing, golf, horse riding, all aspects sports; *Clubs* Directors Lodge, RAC, Inst Directors, Mansion House (Poole), Bramshaw Golf, BARC; *Style*— John Thompson, Esq; Whisper Wood, The Warren, Chalfont Heights, Gerrards Cross (☎ 0753 885263); Arlington Motor Hldgs, Ardent House, Gateway, Stevenage SG1 3NF (telex 825548, car ☎ 0860 522 908)

THOMPSON, John; MBE (1975); s of Arthur Thompson, and Josephine, *née* Brooke; *b* 28 May 1945; *Educ* St Nicholas GS, Central London Poly (DMS); *m* 9 July 1966, Barbara, da of Ernest Hopper; 1 da (Ailsa b 1967); *Career* FCO: vice consul Dusseldorf 1966-69, Abu Dhabi 1969-72, Phnom Penh 1972-74; DTI 1975-77; FCO: first sec consul and head of chancery, Luanda 1979-82; consul Sao Paulo 1982-85; asst head: South Pacific Dept, Aid Policy Dept; high cmmr Vanuatu 1988-; *Recreations* philately, reading, walking, bridge; *Clubs* Commonwealth Tst; *Style*— John Thompson, Esq, MBE; c/o Foreign and Cwlth Office, London SW1A 2AH

THOMPSON, Sir John; s of Donald Thompson; *b* 16 Dec 1907; *Educ* Bellahouston Acad, Univ of Glasgow, Oriel Coll Oxford; *m* 1934, Agnes, da of John Drummond, of Glasgow; 2 s; *Career* called to the Bar Middle Temple 1933; QC 1954, vice chm Gen Cncl Bar 1960-61, cmmr assize Birmingham 1961, judge High Court (Queen's Bench) 1961-82; kt 1961; *Recreations* golf; *Clubs* R & A, Sundridge Park Golf; *Style*— Sir John Thompson; 73 Sevenoaks Rd, Orpington, Kent BR6 9JN (☎ 0689 822339)

THOMPSON, John Brian; CBE (1980); s of Jack Thompson (d 1985), of Chilton, Bucks, and Lilian Elizabeth, *née* Sutton (d 1981); *b* 8 June 1928; *Educ* St Paul's Pembroke Coll Oxford (MA), LSE; *m* 12 Dec 1957, Sylvia Gough (Sally), da of Thomas Waterhouse, CBE (d 1961), of Holywell, N Wales; 2 s (Piers b 1959, Barnaby b 1961), 1 da (Eliza b 1963); *Career* ed Observer Colour Mag 1966-70, sr advsr (radio) to Min of Posts and Telecomm 1971, dir of radio IBA 1972-87, vice chm (radio) Euro Bdcasting Union 1986-88, judge Booker Fiction prize 1987, ed The Viewer 1988-, independent dir The Observer 1989-; *Clubs* Garrick, Groucho; *Style*— John Thompson, Esq, CBE; 4 Edith Grove, London SW10 ONW (☎ 071 352 5414)

THOMPSON, John Handby; CB (1988); s of Rev John Thomas Thompson (d 1931), and Clara, *née* Handby (d 1974); *b* 21 Feb 1929; *Educ* Silcoates Sch Wakefield, St John's Coll Oxford (MA), Univ of Sheffield (PhD); *Career* Intelligence Corps 1947-49; Civil Serv: joined 1953, Inland Revenue 1953-64, Dept of Educn and Sci 1964-88 (under sec 1978, dir of establishments 1984), Cabinet Office 1988- (ceremonial offr 1988); conslt Educn Management Information Exchange, govr Poly of North London; *publications* The Free Church Army Chaplain 1830-1930 (thesis); *Recreations* reading, nonconformist history; *Clubs* Reform; *Style*— John Thompson, Esq, CB

THOMPSON, Col John Keith Lumley; CMG (1982), MBE (mil 1965), TD (1961, Bar 1963 and 1971); s of John Vere Valentine Thompson, (d 1968), of Wallsend, Tyne and Wear, and Gertrude, *née* Herrington (d 1977); *b* 31 March 1923; *Educ* Wallsend GS, King's Coll Durham Univ (BSc); *m* 21 Nov 1950, Audrey, da of George Henderson (d 1977), Grantham; 1 s (John Robert b 1951); *Career* served WWII 2 Lt (later Lt then Acting Capt) REME NW Europe; TAVR 1948-78: Maj 44 Para Bde (v) BEME 1948-70, Lt-Col Dep Inspr REME (v) Southern Cmd 1970-72, Col Dep Cdr 44 Para Bde (v) 1972-75, ADC to HM The Queen 1974-78; res scientist: Road Res Lab (DSIR) 1948-55, AWRE (Aldermaston) 1955-64; memb staff Lord Zuckerman chief sci advsr MOD 1964-65, head E Mids Regnl Office Miny of Technol 1965-70, head Int Affrs Atomic Energy Div Dept of Energy 1972-74, regnl dir W Mids and Northern Regnl Offices DTI 1974-78 (formerly 1970-72), cnsllr (sci & technol) Br Embassy Washington USA 1978-83, pres Lumley Assocs Conslt 1983-89; Br Legion: vice pres Baston and Langtoft Branch, pres Bourne and Dist, hon rep Offrs Assoc Bourne and Dist; FBIM 1975, memb American Soc Automotive Engrs 1983; *Recreations* outdoor sports, riding, skiing, windsurfing; *Style*— Col John Thompson, CMG, MBE, TD; Clewer Cottage, 7 School Lane, Baston, Peterborough PE6 9PD (☎ 077 836 374)

THOMPSON, John Michael Anthony; s of George Edward Thompson (d 1982), of Deganwy, Gwynedd, N Wales, and Joan, *née* Smith; *b* 3 Feb 1941; *Educ* William Hulme's GS Manchester, Univ of Manchester (BA, MA); *m* 24 July 1965, Alison Sara, da of Walter Bowers, of Cheadle Hulme, Greater Manchester; 2 da (Hannah Jane b 19 March 1973, Harriet Mary b 13 Feb 1976); *Career* res asst Whitworth Art Gallery 1964-66, keeper Rutherston Collection Manchester City Art Gallery 1966-68; dir: NW Museum and Gallery Serv 1968-70, Arts and Museums Bradford 1970-75, Tyne and Wear Co Museums and Galleries 1975-86, Tyne and Wear Jt Museums Serv 1986-; fndr memb and hon sec Gp of Dirs of Museums in Br Isles, pres Museums North 1990-, advsr Assoc of Met Authorities, jt sponsor Shipbuilding Exhibition Centre South Tyneside, memb Standards Steering Ctee Museums Trg Inst 1990- (chair Curatorship Gp 1990-); FMA 1977, (AMA 1970); *Books* Manual of Curatorship, A Guide to Museum Practice (ed, 2 edn 1986); *Recreations* running, travel, visiting exhibitions; *Clubs* Museum Assoc; *Style*— John Thompson, Esq; 21 Linden Rd, Gosforth, Newcastle upon Tyne; Blandford House, Blandford Sq, Newcastle upon Tyne

THOMPSON, Prof John Quentin Warburton; s of Frederick John Warburton Thompson (d 1951), of Ealing, London, and Ethel Georgina Eleanor, *née* Wade (d 1966); *b* 7 Nov 1924; *Educ* City of London Sch, London Hosp and Univ of London (MB BS, PhD); *m* 3 Oct 1969, Judith Russell, da of Harry Hick, of Wakefield, Yorks; 1 s (Jonathan b 29 March 1972), 1 da (Georgina b 13 Feb 1974); *Career* Nat Serv Flt Lt RAF Med Branch 1949-51; res asst Dept of Applied Pharmacology Med Unit Univ Coll Hosp and Dept of Pharmacology UCL 1952-54, lectr Dept of Pharmacology Inst of Basic Med Sciences RCS 1954-64, sr lectr in pharmacology Med Unit St George's Hosp London 1961-64, prof of pharmacology Dept of Pharmacological Sciences Med Sch Newcastle 1964-90, conslt clinical pharmacologist Royal Victoria Infirmary 1964-90 (conslt in charge pain relief clinic 1979-90); dir of studies St Oswald's Hospice 1989-; memb: Br Pharmacological Soc 1958, Intractable Pain Soc of GB and Ireland 1978, Int Assoc for the Study of Pain 1981, Br Med Acupuncture Soc, Assoc for Palliative Med 1985; pres Tyne and Wear branch Nat Back Pain Assoc; hon master of Chinese Med China Acad Taiwan; memb BMA 1948, FRCP 1981; *Books* Textbook of Dental Pharmacology and Therapeutics (jtly, 1989); *Recreations* music, photography, DIY; *Style*— Prof John Thompson; dir of Studies and Honorary Physician, St Oswald's Hospice, Regent Ave, Newcastle upo Tyne NE3 1EE (☎ 091 2850063)

THOMPSON, (Thomas D'Eyncourt) John; s and h of Sir Lionel Tennyson Thompson, 5 Bt; *b* 22 Dec 1956; *Educ* Eton; *Style*— John Thompson, Esq; c/o Sir Lionel Thompson, Bt, 16 Old Buildings, Lincolns Inn, London WC2

THOMPSON, Rear Adm John Yelverton; CB (1960), DL (Cornwall 1973); s of Sir John Perronet Thompson, KCSI, KCIE, ICS (d 1935), and Ada Lucia, *née* Tyrrell (d 1957); *b* 25 May 1909; *Educ* Mourne Grange, Kilkeel Co Down, RNC Dartmouth (psc 1946); *m* 15 Dec 1934, Barbara Helen Mary Aston, da of Dr Benjamin William Martin Aston Key, OBE (d 1961), of Southsea; 2 s (Richard b 1935, Martin b 1939); *Career* Lt Cdr HMS Anson N Atlantic 1941-43, Cdr Naval Ordnance Dept Admty 1943-45, US 5 Fleet 1946, Liverpool 1947, Newcastle 1948; Capt Ordnance Bd 1948-50, Unicorn (Korean War) 1951-52 (despatches), dir Gunnery Div, Naval Staff 1952-54, IDC 1955; Cdre RN Barracks Portsmouth 1956-57; ADC to HM The Queen 1957-58; Rear Adm Admty Interview Bd 1958, Adm Supt HM Dockyard Chatham 1958-61 (ret); naval advsr Elliott-Automation 1961-66; govr Aldenham Sch 1967-75; chm Herts Scout Cncl 1962-71; DL Hertfordshire 1966-73; American Legion of Merit (1953); *Style*— Rear Adm J Y Thompson, CB, DL; Flushing Meadow, Manaccan, nr Helston, Cornwall (☎ 032 623 354)

THOMPSON, Jonathan Charles Arthur; s of William Arthur Lisle Thompson, of Liverpool and Anglesey, and Margaret Elizabeth; *b* 27 May 1954; *Educ* Liverpool Coll, Blackpool Coll (HND); *m* 4 Oct 1986, Caroline Jane, da of John Albert Howard; 2 da (Elizabeth Jane b 3 March 1989, Emily Louise b 25 Sept 1990); *Career* industl release Gleneagles Hotel 1973 and Abernant Lake Hotel 1974, dep mangr Birmingham Centre Hotel 1976-77 (mgmnt trainee 1975-76), hotel mangr Palm Beach Hotel Aquaba Jordan 1977-78, dep gen mangr The Compleat Angler Hotel Marlow 1978-81, gen mangr Stratton House Hotel Cirencester 1981-83; Historic House Hotels 1983- (gen mangr Bodysgallen Hall 1983-88, dir and gen mangr Hartwell House 1989-); past memb: Overseas Mktg Intelligence Ctee, Welsh Div BMRCA, Llandrillo Tech Coll Consultative Ctee; memb: Thames and Chilterns Div BMRCA (rep for Buckinghamshire), Hotel Catering and Institutional Mgmnt Assoc, Restauranteurs Assoc of GB, Confrerie des Cheus de Tastevin; Master Innholder 1990-; AA Red Stars 1983-, RAC Blue Ribbons 1988, Hotel of the Year Andrew Hayer's Hideaway Report 1985-87, Welsh Tourist Bd award for services to tourism 1986-, Queen's award for export achievement 1987, Good Hotel Guide Cesar award for outstanding restoration and first class hotel mgmnt 1988, Egon Ronay Guide 1989, Good Food Guide Buckinghamshire County Restaurant of the Year 1989; MHCIMA; *Recreations* history and heritage, my family; *Style*— Jonathan Thompson, Esq; Awelfor, FFordd Llechi, Rhosneigr, Isle of Anglesey, Gwynedd LL64 5JY (☎ 0407 810289); Historic House Hotels, Hartwell House, Oxford Rd, Aylesbury, Buckinghamshire HP17 8NL (☎ 0296 747444, fax 0296 747450)

THOMPSON, Joseph Lefroy Courtenay; s of Joseph Matthew Thompson, of Belfast (d 1976); *b* 4 April 1943; *Educ* Rugby, Trinity Coll Dublin; *m* 1967, Joan Lesley, *née* Love; 1 s, 1 da; *Career* md Charleville Hldgs Ltd; dir: William Ewart Investmt Ltd Hicks Bullick Ltd, Sydney Pentland Ltd, Industl Therapy Orgn (Ulster) Ltd; govr Princes Gardens Sch; *Clubs* Lansdowne; *Style*— J L Thompson Esq; Charleville, 39 Manse Rd, Castlereagh, Belfast (☎ 0232 792412)

THOMPSON, (Rupert) Julian de la Mare; s of Rupert Spens Thompson (d 1952), and Florence Elizabeth de la Mare; *b* 23 July 1941; *Educ* Eton, King's Coll Cambridge (MA); *m* 6 March 1965, Jacqueline Mary, da of John William Linnell Ivimy; 3 da (Rebecca b 1966, Sophia b 1968, Cecilia b 1971); *Career* Sothebys: dir 1969-, dep chm Sothebys (UK) 1987- (chm 1982-86); *Style*— Julian Thompson, Esq; 43 Clarendon Rd, London W11 4JD (☎ 071 727 6039); Crossington Farm, Upton Bishop, Ross-on-Wye, Hereford (☎ 098 985 363); Sotheby's 34-45 New Bond St, London W1A 2AA (☎ 071 493 8080)

THOMPSON, Maj-Gen Julian Howard Atherden; CB (1982), OBE (1978); s of Maj A J Thompson, DSO, MC (d 1966), of Cornwall, and Mary Stearns, *née* Krause (d 1978); *b* 7 Oct 1934; *Educ* Sherborne; *m* 1960, Janet Avery, da of Richard Robinson Rodd, of Devon; 1 s (David), 1 da (Henrietta); *Career* CO 40 Commando RM 1975-78; Cdr 3 Commando Bde 1981-83, including Falklands Campaign 1982, Maj-Gen cmd Training and Special Forces Royal Marines; sr research fell Kings Coll London; *Books* No Picnic (1985), Ready for Anything: The Parachute Regiment at War 1940-82 (1989); *Clubs* Army and Navy; *Style*— Maj-Gen Julian Thompson, CB, OBE; Lloyds Bank plc, 8 Royal Parade, Plymouth

THOMPSON, Keith Anthony; s of Charles Basil Thompson, of 21 Glenavon Rd, Kings Heath, Birmingham, and Emalie Viola Thompson; *b* 24 April 1965; *Educ* Brandwood Secondary Sch; *m* 13 Nov 1988, Marian, da of Severino Diaz Carbojosa; *Career* professional footballer; Coventry City 1980-85 and 1988- (debut v Birmingham City 1983), Real Oviedo Spain 1985-88; on loan: 3 appearances Wimbledon, 10 appearances Northampton Town; 2 England youth caps; *Recreations* karate, swimming, cinema; *Style*— Keith Thompson, Esq; Coventry City Football Club, Highfield Rd

Stadium, King Richard St, Coventry CV2 4FW (☎ 0203 57171, 312132)

THOMPSON, Keith Bruce; s of Charles Bruce Thompson (d 1982), and Eva Elizabeth, *née* Vidler (d 1966); *b* 13 Sept 1932; *Educ* Bishopshalt Sch Hillingdon, New Coll Oxford (MA), Oxford Dept of Educn (DipEd), Univ of Bristol (MEd); *m* 17 Aug 1956, Kathleen Anne, da of Sydney Reeves, OBE (d 1982); 1 s (Bruce b 1959), 1 da (Fiona b 1961); *Career* RAOC 1950-52; schoolmaster City of Bath Boys' Sch 1956-62, lectr Newton Park Coll Bath 1962-67, head of dept Philippa Fawcett Coll Streatham 1967-72, princ Madeley Coll Staffs 1972-78, dep dir Staffs Poly (formerly N Staffs Poly) 1986- (dep dir 1978-86); chm: Standing Conf on Studies in Educn 1980-82, Undergraduate Initial Trg Bd (Educn) CNAA 1981-85, Polys' Central Admissions System 1989-; memb Nat Advsy Body for Public Sector of Higher Educn 1983-88 (chm Teacher Educn Gp 1983-85); *Books* Education and Philosophy (1972), Curriculum Development (jtly, 1974), Education for Teaching 1968-74 (ed-journal); *Recreations* sport, music; *Style—* Keith Thompson, Esq; Staffs Poly, Beaconside, Stafford ST18 OAD (☎ 0785 52331, fax 0785 45441)

THOMPSON, Dr (Malcolm) Keith; s of Ralph Whittier Thompson (d 1962), of London, and Ethel Eva, *née* Smith (d 1972); *b* 30 June 1921; *Educ* Trinity Sch of John Whitgift, Univ of St Andrews (MB ChB), Univ of London (DObst); *m* 24 Oct 1953, Jeanne Sophie Auguste, da of Jean Bernard Struys (d 1971), of Brussels; 1 da (Chantal (Mrs Blake-Milton) b 18 July 1957); *Career* Friend's Ambulance Unit 1943-45; house physician to Sir Ian Hill 1952-53, house surgn in obstetrics & gynaecology Wanstead Hosp 1953, princ in GP Woodside Health Centre London SE25 1955-86; examiner for MRCGP examination 1976-86, RCP examiner for diploma in geriatric med 1984-; Nuffield travelling fell 1970, Med Gilliland travelling fell 1984; fndr assoc memb RCGP 1953; med ed: Medical Opinion 1978-79, Geriatric Medicine 1984-86; med corr Yours newspaper 1974-, lectr Coll of GP HK 1987; advsr: WHO Copenhagen 1979, DHSS 1980; distinctions: Butterworth Gold medal 1967, Hunterian Socs Gold medal 1968; med advsr Help the Aged; memb: Governing Body Age Concern, Med Advsy Panel Parkinsons Disease Soc of GB (pres Croydon Branch), BMA, Br Geriatrics Soc 1971; RCOG 1954, MRCGP 1965, FRCGP 1977, FRSM; *Books* Geriatrics and the General Practitioner Team (1969), Geriatrie Voor Die Huisarts (1971), The Care of the Elderly in General Practice (1984), Caring for an Elderly Relative (1986), Commonsense Geriatrics (1990); *Recreations* swimming, golf, music, theatre, walking; *Style—* Dr Keith Thompson; 28 Steep Hill, Stanhope Rd, Croydon CR0 5QS (☎ 081 686 7489)

THOMPSON, Sir (Thomas) Lionel Tennyson; 5 Bt (UK 1806), of Hartsbourne Manor, Hertfordshire; s of Lt-Col Sir Thomas Raikes Lovett Thompson, 4 Bt, MC (d 1964), and of late Millicent Ellen Jean, da of late Edmund Charles Tennyson-d'Eyncourt, of Bayons Manor, Lincs; *b* 19 June 1921; *Educ* Eton; *m* 1955 (m dis 1962), Mrs Margaret van Beers, da of late Walter Herbert Browne; 1 s, 1 da; *Heir* s, Thomas d'Eyncourt John Thompson; *Career* WWII Flying Offr RAFVR (invalided), and subsequently Able Seaman Royal Fleet Auxiliary (1939-45, and Aircrew (Europe) stars, Defence and Victory Medals); barr Lincoln's Inn 1952; *Style—* Sir Lionel Thompson, Bt

THOMPSON, Lucy Ellen; da of William Chidgey (d 1956), and Elizabeth, *née* Lightfoot (d 1972); *b* 25 June 1924; *Educ* Buckingham Gate Secdy Sch; *m* 3 April 1954, Jack Evans Thompson, s of Ralph Dean Henry Thompson (d 1946); *Career* sec Lloyds Bank 1947-54; md: RHD Thompson & Co Ltd 1954-89, Thompson Hydribind Equipment Co Ltd 1963-, Marine and Tidal Power Ltd 1973-; *Recreations* Scottish country dancing; *Clubs* Royal Highland Yacht, British Motor Yacht; *Style—* Mrs Lucy Thompson; 27B Rydens Grove, Whalton On Thames, Surrey (☎ 0932 226351); Maelstroma, Kilmelford By Oban, Argyll; RHD Thompson & Co Ltd, Hersham Trading Estate, Walton on Thames, Surrey (☎ 0932 226 351)

THOMPSON, Michael; s of Eric Thompson, of Brenchley, and Mary, *née* Shuttleworth; *b* 18 June 1954; *Educ* Bradford GS, Trinity Coll Cambridge (MA); *Career* RAF Reservist 1973-76; Freshfields: articled clerk 1977-79, asst slr 1979-85, ptnr Corporate Tax Dept 1985-; memb Law Soc's Revenue Law Sub Ctee on Petroleum Taxation; rep City Deanery Synod, memb PCC St Helen's Church Bishopsgate; Freeman of City of Worshipful Co Slrs 1987; memb Law Soc; *Recreations* sailing, fell walking; *Style—* Michael Thompson, Esq; Whitefriars, 65 Fleet St, London EC4Y 1HT (☎ 071 963 4000, fax 248 3487/8/9, telex 889292)

THOMPSON, Prof (Francis) Michael Longstreth; s of Francis Longstreth-Thompson, OBE (d 1973), of Little Waltham, Essex, and Mildred Grace, *née* Corder (d 1963); *b* 13 Aug 1925; *Educ* Bootham Sch York, Queen's Coll Oxford (MA, DPhil), Merton Coll Oxford; *m* 11 Aug 1951, Anne Longstreth, da of Maj John Lovibond Challoner, TA, of Northumberland (d 1970); 2 s ((Francis) Jonathan Longstreth b 1958, Matthew Longstreth b 1964), 1 da (Suzanna Jane Longstreth b 1959); *Career* WWII 1943-47, Lt 1944, 7 Indian Field Regt RIA India and Sumatra 1945-46, Staff Capt 26 Indian Div E Bengal 1946-47, Capt 1946-47; reader in economic history UCL 1963-68 (lectr in history 1951-63), prof of modern history Bedford Coll London 1968-77, dir Inst of Historical Res and prof of history London Univ 1977-90; emeritus prof of history London Univ 1990; pres: Economic History Soc 1984-87, Royal Historical Soc 1988-, Br Agric History Soc 1989-; sec Br Nat Ctee of Historians 1977-, Br Acad rep humanities Ctee Euro Sci Fndn 1983-, hon treas Int Econ History Assoc 1986-; ed Econ History Review 1968-80; FRHistS 1963, ARICS 1968, FBA 1979; *Books* English Landed Society in the Nineteenth Century (1963), Victorian England: The Horse Drawn Society (1970), Chartered Surveyors: The Growth of a Profession (1968), Hampstead: Building a Borough (1974), The Rise of Suburbia (ed, 1982), Horses in European Economic History (ed, 1983), The Rise of Respectable Society (1988), The Cambridge Social History of Britain 1750-1950 (3 vols, ed, 1990), The University of London and the World of Learning, 1836-1986 (ed, 1990); *Recreations* gardening, walking, carpentry; *Style—* Prof Michael Thompson; Institute of Historical Research, University of London, Senate House, London WC1E 7HU (☎ 071 636 0272)

THOMPSON, Michael Reginald; s of Frederick John Thompson, of Bramcote, Notts, and Dorothy, *née* Greensmith (d 1987); *b* 19 July 1943; *Educ* High Pavement GS, Univ of Sheffield (MB ChB, MD); *m* 3 Jan 1970, Judith Ann, da of John Hatchett Glover (d 1987), of Stratford-upon-Avon; 3 da (Hannah Louise b 28 April 1972, Emma Judith b 14 Nov 1975, Victoria Jillian b 24 March 1977); *Career* lectr in surgery Univ of Manchester Med Sch 1972-75, res fell VA Centre Wadsworth UCLA USA 1974-75 (Dept of Physiology Univ of Michigan 1973-74), sr registrar Bristol Hosps 1975-81, conslt surgn Portsmouth and S E Hants 1981-; memb Wessex Regnl Med Advsy Ctee, memb Br Soc of Gastroenterology; memb: Assoc of Surgns, BMA, RSM; FRCS 1971; *Recreations* sailing, windsurfing, theatre; *Clubs* The 82, Surgical Travelling; *Style—* Michael Thompson, Esq; St Andrews, 9 Eastern Parade, Southsea, Hants PO4 9RA (☎ 0705 756938; 31 Mill Lane, Sheet, Petersfield; St Mary's Hospital, Milton, Portsmouth (☎ 0705 822331); BUPA Hospital, Havant, Portsmouth (☎ 0705 454511)

THOMPSON, (John) Michael Strutt; s of John Thompson (d 1951), of Dale Farm, Weald, Sevenoaks, Kent, and Donnie Agnes Beatrice, *née* Strutt (d 1979); *b* 14 Dec 1931; *Educ* Felsted; *m* 24 Oct 1959, Fiona Mary, da of Wing Cdr Malcolm Glassford Begg, MC (d 1969), of Armsworth Park Farm, Alresford, Hants; 1 s (Marcus Peter Strutt b 1961), 1 da (Julia Mariette (Mrs Gallagher) b 1963); *Career* Nat Serv 2 Lt cmmnd Rifle Bde 1956-58; res sub agent RH & RW Clutton Hursley Estate Hants 1958-65, agent and sec Ernest Cook Tst Fairford Glos 1965-73, chief agent Fitzwilliam Estates Milton Park Peterborough Cambs 1974-; pres local Cons branch 1981-, gen cmmr Income Tax Peterborough 1981, pres Land Agency and Agric Div RICS 1985-86; chm Landowners Gp 1987-, vice chm Cambs CLA 1988-; FRICS 1956, FAAV 1986; *Recreations* fishing, shooting, sailing; *Clubs* Farmers; *Style—* Michael Thompson, Esq; Stibbington House, Wansford, Peterborough, Cambs PE8 6JS (☎ 0780 782043); Estate Office, Milton Pk, Peterborough, Cambs PE6 7AH (☎ 0733 267740, fax 0733 331200)

THOMPSON, Michael Warwick; s of Kelvin Warwick Thompson (d 1985), of Cotherstone, Co Durham, and Madeleine, *née* Walford; *b* 1 June 1931; *Educ* Rydal Sch, Univ of Liverpool (BSc, DSc, Oliver Lodge prizewinner); *m* 1956, Sybil Noreen, da of John Rosser Spooner (d 1959); 2 s (Andrew Warwick b 5 Dec 1957, Paul Warwick b 9 Aug 1959); *Career* res scientist AERE Harwell 1953-65, prof of experimental physics Univ of Sussex 1965-80 (pro vice chllr 1972-78), vice chllr Univ of E Anglia 1980-86, vice chllr and princ Univ of Birmingham 1987-; non-exec dir Alliance & Leicester Building Society 1978-; author of one book and numerous papers in sci jls; Inst of Physics CV Boy's prizewinner 1972; memb: E Sussex Educn Ctee 1973-78, E Sussex Area Health Authy 1973-80, W Midlands Regnl Health Authy 1987, Physics Ctee SRC 1972-79 (memb, chm) FInstP 1964; kt 1991; *Style—* Prof Sir Michael Thompson; Meadowcroft, 43 Edgbaston Park Rd, Birmingham B15 2RS (☎ 021 454 6565); University of Birmingham, Edgbaston, Birmingham B15 2TT (☎ 021 414 4536, fax 021 414 4534)

THOMPSON, Nanne, Lady; Nanne; *née* Broome; JP; da of late Charles Broome, of Walton, Liverpool; *b* 24 July 1912; *m* 1936, Sir Kenneth Pugh Thompson, 1 Bt (d 1984, formerly MP (C) for Walton Liverpool and Asst Postmaster Gen 1957-59); 1 s (Paul, 2 Bt, *qv*), 1 da; *Style—* Nanne, Lady Thompson, JP; Atherton Cottage, via Kirklake Rd, Formby, Merseyside L37 2DD (☎ 070 48 72486)

THOMPSON, Nicholas Annesley Marler; s and h of Sir Richard Hilton Marler Thompson, 1 Bt; *b* 19 March 1947; *m* 1982, Venetia Catherine, yr da of John Horace Broke Heathcote, of Conington House, nr Peterborough; 2 s (Simon b 1985, Charles b 1986); *Career* admitted slr 1973; memb Westminster City Cncl 1978-86; dep Lord Mayor of Westminster 1983-84; Cons candidate for Newham South 1983 general election; *Recreations* foreign travel, skiing, riding, tennis, walking, theatre, reading; *Clubs* Carlton; *Style—* Nicholas Thompson, Esq; Maxgate, George Rd, Kingston-upon-Thames, Surrey KT2 7NR (☎ 081 942 7251); 5 Chancery Lane, Clifford's Inn, London EC4A 1BU (☎ 071 242 1212)

THOMPSON, Nicolas de la Mare; s of Rupert Spens Thompson (d 1951), and Florence Elizabeth, *née* de la Mare; *b* 4 June 1928; *Educ* Eton, Christ Church Oxford (MA); *m* 13 Sept 1956, (Fenella Mary) Erica, da of Powlett Pennell (d 1970); 2 s (Rupert b 1962, Simon b 1964), 1 da (Sarah b 1960); *Career* RAF 1949-51; md George Weidenfeld & Nicolson Ltd 1956-70, publishing dir Pitman plc 1976-84, md Heinemann Gp of Publishers Ltd 1985-87; dir: Octopus Publishing Gp plc 1985-, Reed International Books Ltd 1989-; chm: Heinemann Educational Books Ltd, Octopus Publishing Group Australia Ltd; chm Book Devpt Cncl 1984-86; *Style—* Nicolas Thompson, Esq; Flat A, 8 Ennismore Gardens, London SW7 (☎ 071 584 9769); Michelin House, 81 Fulham Rd, London SW3 (☎ 071 581 9393)

THOMPSON, Dr Noel Brentnall Watson; s of George Watson Thompson (d 1980), and Mary Henrietta, *née* Gibson (d 1944); *b* 11 Dec 1932; *Educ* Manchester GS, Univ of Cambridge (MA), Imperial Coll London (MSc, PhD); *m* Jan 1957, Margaret Angela Elizabeth, da of Ernest William Baston (d 1967), of Bristol; 1 s (Gareth b 1972); *Career* Sub Lt RN 1951-53; sec Nat Libraries Ctee 1967-69, lectr Univ of Birmingham 1961-65, under sec Dept of Educn and Sci 1980-88, Cabinet Office Secretariat 1977-79, chief exec Nat Cncl for Educnl Technol 1988-; *Recreations* railways of all sizes, electronics, mechanics, music, photography, walking; *Style—* Dr Noel B W Thompson; National Council for Educational Technology, 3 Devonshire St, London W1N 2BA (☎ 071 636 4186)

THOMPSON, (Charles) Norman; CBE (1978); s of Robert Norman Thompson (d 1962), of 85 Temple Rd, Prenton, Birkenhead, Cheshire, and Evelyn Tivendale, *née* Woods (d 1956); *b* 23 Oct 1922; *Educ* Birkenhead Inst, Univ of Liverpool (BSc); *m* 8 June 1946, Pamela Margaret, da of Alfred Christopher Francis Wicks, MBE (d 1971), of 94 Aigburth Hall Ave, Liverpool; 1 da (Fiona Jane b 1954); *Career* res chemist Shell UK Ltd 1943, personnel supt Shell Int Petroleum Ltd 1958-61, dir res admin Shell Research Ltd 1961-78, head of res and devpt Shell UK Ltd 1978-82; chm Res Advsy Ctee Inst of Petroleum 1961-78, Tech Educn Cncl 1974-81, Ct Univ of Surrey 1978-; pres RIC 1976-78 (memb Cncl 1972-80); memb Bd Thames Water Authy 1980-87, chm Professional Affrs Bd RSC 1980-84; memb CSTI (chm 1981-83, chm Health Care Sci Advsy Ctee 1986-); CChem, FRSC 1971; *Recreations* golf, travel, theatre-going, bridge, bowls, photography; *Clubs* West Byfleet Golf, Wey Valley Indoor Bowling (Guildford); *Style—* Norman Thompson, Esq, CBE; Delamere, Horsell Park, Woking, Surrey GU21 4LW (☎ 0483 714939)

THOMPSON, Norman Sinclair; CBE (1980); s of, Norman Whitfield Thompson (d 1955), and Jane, *née* Robinson (d 1967); *b* 7 July 1920; *Educ* Middlesbrough HS; *m* 14 July 1945, Peggy, da of Alfred Sivil (d 1946); 2 s (Paul Sinclair b 1947, Jeremy Sinclair b 1954), 1 da (Gillian Margaret b and d 1953); *Career* radio offr Merchant Navy 1940-45, asst sec Patons & Baldwins Ltd 1946-55, commercial mangr Cowans Sheldon & Co Ltd 1955-57, gp sec Richardsons Westcarth & Co Ltd 1957-61, fin dir David Brown & Sons 1961-63; Swan Hunter Group: gen mangr 1963-67, dir 1964-70, overseas dir 1967-69, dep md 1969-70; md The Cunard Steam Ship Co Ltd 1970-74; chm: Mass Transit Railway Corporation Hong Kong 1975-83, C-Fin Group of Companies Hong Kong 1983-, Poole Harbour Commissioners 1984-86; dir: Hong Kong Bank 1978-85, British Shipbuilders 1983-86; dep chm New Hong Kong Tunnel Co 1986-; FCA 1947, ACMA 1949; Order of Rising Sun and Sacred Treasure (Japan) 1983; *Recreations* sailing, music; *Clubs* Oriental, Royal Ocean Racing, Royal Hong Kong Yacht, Hong Kong; *Style—* Norman Thompson, Esq, CBE; Shadrach House, Burton Bradstock, Bridport, Dorset DT6 4QG (☎ 0308 897670); 8 Floor, Baskerville House, 22 Ice House St, Hong Kong (☎ 5239058, fax 8101056)

THOMPSON, (Hugh) Patrick; MP (C) Norwich North 1987-; s of Gerald Leopold Thompson, of 11 Gretton Court, Girton, Cambridge, and Kathleen Mary Landsdown Thompson; *b* 21 Oct 1935; *Educ* Felsted, Emmanuel Coll Cambridge (MA); *m* 1 Sept 1962, Kathleen, da of Thomas Falkingham Howson (d 1963); *Career* Nat Serv 2 Lt KOYLI 1957-59; TA 1959-65; jr engr English Electric Valve Co Chelmsford 1959-60; physics master: The Manchester GS 1960-65, Gresham's Sch Holt 1965-83 (Gresham's CCF, Cadet Force Medal, Major); contested (C): Bradford North Feb and Oct 1974, Barrow-in-Furness 1979; MP (C) Norwich North 1983-, pps to Min of State for Transport 1987-88; pps to Min of State for Social Security and the Disabled 1988-89, fndr memb All Pty Gp for Engrg Devpt 1985-; MInstP; *Recreations* travel, music, gardening; *Clubs* The Norfolk; *Style—* Patrick Thompson, Esq, MP; House of Commons, London SW1A OAA (☎ 071 219 6398)

THOMPSON, Paul; s of Frank Thompson, and Dorothy, *née* Mahoney; *b* 3 Aug 1960; *Educ* Lampton Comp Hounslow Middx; *m* 27 Aug 1983, Julie Margaret, da of Alfred Henry Almond; 1 s (Richard b 9 Feb 1987), 1 da (Kathryn Emma b 2 June 1990);

Career 3 year indentures West London Observer 1980-83, reporter Shepherds Bush Gazette 1983-84, freelance reporter 1984-85, reporter Daily Express 1985-; *Recreations* tennis, cinema, football; *Style—* Paul Thompson, Esq; Branksome, Albert Rd, Hampton Hill, Middlesex (☎ 081 979 1390); Daily Express, Ludgate House, 245 Blackfriars Rd, London SE1 9UX (☎ 071 922 7088, fax 071 620 1654, car 0831 237056)

THOMPSON, Sir Paul Anthony; 2 Bt (UK 1963), of Walton-on-the-Hill, City of Liverpool; s of Sir Kenneth Pugh Thompson, 1 Bt (d 1984; MP (C) for Walton Liverpool 1950-64, Asst PMG 1957-59), and Nanne, Lady Thompson, JP, *qv*; *b* 6 Oct 1939; *m* 1971, Pauline Dorothy, da of Robert Orrell Spencer, of Tippett House, Smithills, Bolton, Lancs; 2 s (Richard, David), 2 da (Karena, Nicola); *Heir* s, Richard Thompson; *Career* co dir; *Style—* Sir Paul Thompson, Bt; 28 Dowhills Rd, Blundellsands, Liverpool L23 8SW

THOMPSON, Prof Paul Richard; *b* 1935; *Educ* Bishop's Stortford Coll, Corpus Christi Coll Oxford, Queen's Coll Oxford (MA, DPhil); *m* 1, Thea, *née* Vigne; 1 s, 1 da; m 2, Natasha Burchardt; 1 da; *Career* jr res fell Queen's Coll Oxford 1961-64; Univ of Essex: lectr sociology 1964-69, sr lectr 1969-71, reader 1971-88, res prof social history 1988-; sr res fell Nuffield Coll Oxford 1968-89, visiting prof art history John Hopkins Univ 1972, Hoffman Wood Prof architecture Univ of Leeds 1977-78, Benjamin Meaker prof Univ of Bristol 1987; dir Nat Life Story Collection 1987-; ed: Victorial Soc Conf Reports 1965-67, Oral History 1970-, Life Stories 1985-89; *Books* History of English Architecture (jtly 2 edn, 1979), The Work of William Morris (new edn, 1977 & 1991), Socialists Liberal and Labour: The Struggle for London 1880-1914 (1967), William Butterfield (1971), The Edwardians: The Remaking of British Society (1975), The Voice of the Past: Oral History (2 edn, 1988), Living the Fishing (1983), I Don't Feel Old (1990), The Myths We Live By (1990); *Recreations* cycling, drawing, music, friendship, travel; *Style—* Prof Paul Thompson; 18 Lonsdale Rd, Oxford OX2 7EW (☎ 0865 510840)

THOMPSON, (Anthony) Peter; s of Thomas George Thompson (d 1974), of Liverpool, and Florence Mary, *née* Bucke (d 1972); *b* 16 May 1928; *Educ* Liverpool Inst, Lancaster Royal GS, Shrewsbury, Downing Coll Cambridge (MA); *m* 1 , 6 Sept 1952, Norma Rachel (d 1973), da of Frederick Sidney Banks; 1 s (Anthony b 1959), 2 da (Rosemary b 1954, Pippa b 1962); m 2, 18 June 1988, Jenifer Mischa (Jenny), da of Col James William Power Saunders; *Career* 2 Lt RASC 1946-48; CA; ptnr: head of res Sheppards & Co 1961-64, de Zoete & Gorton, de Zoete & Bevan 1964-86; dir Barclays de Zoete Wedd 1986-88 (conslt 1988-); FCA; *Recreations* skiing, sailing, music, theatre; *Style—* Peter Thompson, Esq; BZW Ebbgate House, Swan Lane, London EC4

THOMPSON, Sir Peter Anthony; s of late Herbert Thompson and Sarah Jane Thompson; *b* 14 April 1928; *Educ* Bradford GS, Leeds Univ (BA Econ); *m* 1, 1958, Patricia Anne Norcott (d 1983); 1 s, 2 da; m 2, 1986, Lydia Mary Kite, *née* Hodding; 2 da (Emma Elizabeth, Harriet Claire); *Career* formerly with: Unilever, GKN, Rank Organisation, British Steel Corpn, British Road Services; exec vice chm National Freight Corpn (later Company) 1976-77, dep chm and chief exec 1977-82, chm and chief exec National Freight Consortium 1982-90; chm: Community Hospitals plc, FI Group, Child Base Ltd; former pres Inst of Freight Forwarders; exec chm National Freight Consortium plc 1984-, pres Inst of Logistics and Distribution Mgmnt; dir: Pilkington plc, Granville & Co Ltd, Smiths Industries plc, Wembley plc; FCIT, CBIM; kt 1984; *Recreations* golf, walking, music; *Clubs* RAC; *Style—* Sir Peter Thompson; Tickford House, Silver St, Newport Pagnell, Bucks MK16 0EX (☎ 008 216660, fax 0908 211698)

THOMPSON, Prof Peter John; s of George Kenneth Thompson (d 1982), of 2 Sambar Rd, Deer Park, Fazeley, Staffs, and Gladys Pamela, *née* Partington (d 1987); *b* 17 April 1937; *Educ* Chance Tech Coll, Aston Univ (BSc, MSc), CNAA (DTech); *m* 9 Sept 1964, (Dorothy) Ann, da of Frank Smith (d 1969), of 191 Stourbridge Rd, Holly Hall, Dudley; 1 s (Mark b 1965), 1 da (Nicola b 1968); *Career* student apprentice Tube Investments Birmingham 1953-61, lectr and sr lectr Harris Coll Preston 1961-65 and 1968-70, sr sci offr UKAEE Preston 1965-68, princ lectr in prodn engrg Sheffield City Poly 1970-77, dean and head Dept of Engrg Trent Poly Nottingham 1977-83, chief exec Nat Cncl Vocational Qualifications 1986-; memb: Mfrg Mech and Prodn Engrg Bd CNAA 1978-85, Ctee for Engrg in Polys 1981-85, Engrg Scis Divnl Bd IMechE 1982-84, Further Educn Unit 1989-, Cncl Open Coll 1987-89; CEng, MIMechE 1970, FIMechE 1980, MIProdE 1979, FIPlantE 1982, FITD 1987, FRSA 1986; *Recreations* golf, geneology; *Style—* Prof Peter Thompson; 222 Euston Rd, London NW1 2BZ (☎ 071 387 9898, fax 071 687 0978)

THOMPSON, Peter John Stuart (Nimble); s of late Douglas Stuart Thompson, and Irene Agnes, *née* Laird, OBE; *b* 28 Sept 1946; *Educ* Rossall Sch, Univ of Leeds (LLB); *m* 18 July 1970, Morven Mary, da of late Guy Hanscombe; 1 s (Angus Iain Stuart b 1973 d 1988), 1 da (Siona Catherine Stuart b 1975); *Career* articled clerk Rowe and Maw London 1969-71, admitted slr 1971, managing ptnr Hepworth and Chadwick (a memb of Eversheds) 1989- (ptnr 1973-); dir: TEP Stores Ltd, Eversheds; chm NE Branch CIArb 1987-88; memb Law Soc, ACIArb, FID, MBIM; *Recreations* fishing, walking and talking; *Clubs* RAC, Leeds; *Style—* Nimble Thompson, Esq; The Grange, Kirkby Malzeard, Ripon, N Yorks (☎ 076 583 398); Hepworth and Chadwick, Cloth Hall Court, Infirmary St, Leeds LS1 2JB (☎ 0532 430391, fax 0532 456188)

THOMPSON, Peter Kenneth James; s of Rt Rev Kenneth George Thompson (d 1976), first Bishop of Sherwood, and Doreen May Latchford; *b* 30 July 1937; *Educ* Worksop Coll, Christ's Coll Cambridge (MA, LLB); *m* 10 Aug 1970, Sandy Lynne, da of Wallace Harper (d 1970); 2 da (Helena b 1978, Gemma b 1981); *Career* called to the Bar Lincoln's Inn 1961, practised at Common Law Bar 1961-73, lawyer in Government Serv 1973-, slr to Depts of Health and Social Security 1989-; *Recreations* writing; *Style—* Peter K J Thompson, Esq; Richmond House, 79 Whitehall, London SW1A 2NS (☎ 071 210 5244)

THOMPSON, (William) Pratt; s of Philip Amos Thompson, and Regina Beatrice, *née* Kirby; *b* 9 Feb 1933; *Educ* Princeton, Columbia Univ (BA), Univ of Geneva (MBA); *m* 1963, Jenny Frances Styles; 2 da; *Career* vice pres AMF Incorporated 1968-73 (exec assignments in NY, Geneva, Tokyo, Hong Kong and London 1959-68), dep md Bowthorpe Holdings plc 1973-78, md Jaguar Rover Triumph Ltd 1978-79, chm BT International Ltd 1979-81, dir Metalurgica de Santa Ana SA Madrid 1978-81, vice chm Colbert Group Geneva 1981-84, vice chm: AIDCOM International plc 1983-86 (dir 1982-86), AIDCOM Technology Ltd 1982-86, Husky Computers Ltd 1982-86; md Unitech plc 1989- (dir 1987-), non-exec chm Gallex Ltd 1989-; memb: Cncl SMMT 1978-81, Cncl on Foreign Rels USA 1980-89, London Advsy Ctee Barnardos 1989-; advsr Int Centre for Child Studies Univ of Bristol 1982-84; *Clubs* Brooks's, Hurlingham, Knickerbocker (NY); *Style—* Pratt Thompson, Esq; 29 Palace Gardens Terrace, London W8 4SB

THOMPSON, Prof Raymond; CBE (1988); s of William Edward Thompson (d 1946), and Hilda, *née* Rowley (d 1990); *b* 4 April 1925; *Educ* Longton HS, Univ of Nottingham (MSc, PhD), Imperial Coll (DIC); *Career* dir Borax Holdings Ltd 1969-87, md Borax Research Ltd 1980-86 (dep chm 1986-90), dir Boride Ceramics and Composites Ltd 1988-; conslt to: Borax Holdings, Rhone-Poulenc Chemicals, CRA Ltd 1988-; special prof of inorganic chemistry Univ of Nottingham 1975-, hon prof of chemistry Univ of Warwick 1975-; govr Kingston-upon-Thames Poly 1978-88; Freeman City of London; Liveryman: Worshipful Co of Glass Sellers 1983, Worshipful Co of Engineers 1987; FEng 1985, FRSC 1957, FIMM 1972, FRSA 1985; *Books* Mellor's Comprehensive Treatise, Boron Supplement (1979), The Modern Inorganic Chemicals Industry (1977), Speciality Inorganic Chemicals (1980), Energy and Chemistry (1981), Trace Metal Removal from Aqueous Solution (1986), The Chemistry of Wood Preservation (1991); *Recreations* gardening; *Style—* Prof Raymond Thompson, CBE; The Garth, 7 Winchester Close, Esher Place, Esher, Surrey KT10 8QH (☎ 0372 64428); Borax Research Ltd, Cox Lane, Chessington, Surrey KT9 1SJ (☎ 081 397 5141, fax 081 391 5744, telex 929612)

THOMPSON, Richard Henry; s of Lt-Col Richard Louis Thompson (d 1976), and Violet Mary, *née* Harrison (d 1955); *b* 6 Aug 1936; *Educ* Downside, St Catharine's Coll Cambridge (County Major scholarship, MA); *m* 14 July 1962, Cynthia Joan, da of Col Robert Nicholas Hurst, MC; 2 da (Emma Catharine b 16 April 1963, Lucinda Mary b 20 Aug 1966); *Career* Nat Serv cmmnd RE 1954-56; qualified with Sir Alexander Gibb & Partners 1959-63, exec dir P E Consulting Group Limited 1964-75, chief exec New Court & Partners Limited 1976-77, co fndr and chm Thompson Clive & Partners Ltd 1978-; pt/t chm: GT Venture Management Holdings Ltd, Medicom International Ltd, Phonic Ear Holdings Inc; CEng, MICE 1963, FIMC 1975; *Recreations* literature, music, fishing, tennis, golf; *Clubs* Brooks's, RAC, Roehampton, Tidworth Golf; *Style—* Richard Thompson, Esq; Thompson Clive & Partners, 24 Old Bond Street, London W1X 3DA (☎ 071 409 2062)

THOMPSON, Sir Richard Hilton Marler; 1 Bt (UK 1963), of Reculver, Co Kent; s of Richard Smith Thompson (d 1952), and Kathleen Hilda, *née* Marler (d 1916), of London and Calcutta; *b* 5 Oct 1912; *Educ* Malvern; *m* 9 Aug 1939, Anne Christabel de Vere, da of late Philip de Vere Annesley (bro of 13 Viscount Valentia); 1 s; *Heir* s, Nicholas Annesley Marler Thompson, *qv*; *Career* RNVR 1940-46, cmmnd 1941 (despatches 1942), Lt Cdr 1944; publishing business in India 1930-39; MP (C) Croydon West 1950-55, asst-govt whip 1952, Lord Cmmr of the Treasy 1954, MP (C) Croydon South 1955-66 and 1970-74, vice chamberlain of HM Household 1956, Parly sec Miny of Health 1957-59, under-sec of state CRO 1959-60, Parly sec Miny of Works 1960-62; tstee Br Museum 1951-84, memb Cncl Nat Tst 1978-84; dir: Rediffusion TV Ltd and Rediffusion Holdings Ltd 1966-83; fndr memb and first elected pres Br Museum Soc 1970-74, chm Capital Counties Property Co Ltd 1971-77; pres Br Property Fedn 1976-77; *Recreations* gardening, country pursuits, reading; *Clubs* Carlton, Army and Navy; *Style—* Sir Richard Thompson, Bt; Rhodes House, Sellindge, Kent

THOMPSON, Richard Kenneth Spencer; s and h of Sir Paul Thompson, 2 Bt, of Walton-on-the-Hill, City of Liverpool; *b* 27 Jan 1976; *Style—* Richard Thompson, Esq

THOMPSON, Dr Richard Paul Hepworth; s of Stanley Henry Thompson (d 1966), and Winifred Lilian Collier; *b* 14 April 1940; *Educ* Epsom Coll, St Thomas's Hosp Med Sch, Univ of Oxford (MA, DM); *m* 1974, Eleanor Mary, da of Timothy Noel Joseph Hughes (d 1979); *Career* conslt physician St Thomas's Hosp 1972-; examiner in med Soc of Apothecaries 1976-80, examiner Faculty of Dental Surgery RCS 1980-87, memb Mgmnt Ctee Inst of Psychiatry 1985-89, govr Guy's Hosp Med Sch 1980-82, physician to the Royal Household 1982-, King Edward VII Hosp for Offrs 1982-; FRCP; *Recreations* gardening; *Style—* Dr Richard Thompson; 36 Dealtry Rd, London SW15 (☎ 081 789 3839); St Thomas' Hospital, London SE1 (☎ 071 928 9292, ext 2650)

THOMPSON, Sir Robert Grainger Ker; KBE (1965), CMG (1961), DSO (1945), MC (1943); s of Rev Canon William Grainger Thompson (d 1966); *b* 12 April 1916; *Educ* Marlborough, Sidney Sussex Coll Cambridge; *m* 1950, Merryn, da of Sir Alec Newboult, KBE, CMG, MC (d 1964); 1 s, 1 da; *Career* Wing Cdr RAF 1939-45; Malayan Civil Serv 1938-61, sec for Def 1959-61, head Br Advsy Mission Vietnam 1961-65; author and conslt; *Recreations* all country pursuits; *Style—* Sir Robert Thompson, KBE, CMG, DSO, MC; Pitcott House, Winsford, Somerset

THOMPSON, Robert Patrick Werner; s of (Hugh Reginald) Patrick Thompson, of Rugby, Warwickshire, and Eva Maria; *b* 6 Aug 1965; *Educ* Cheltenham, Univ of London (BA), Univ of Buckingham; *Career* hockey player; first cap GB v Malaysia IPOH 1987, first cap Eng v Wales in Dublin 1987, Euro Cup Silver medal Moscow 1987, Olympic reserve Seoul Olympics 1988; *Recreations* cricket, tennis, rugby; *Style—* Robert Thompson, Esq

THOMPSON, (David) Robin Bibby; TD (1987); s of Noel Denis Thompson (d 1967), of Sansaw Hall, Clive, Shrewsbury, and Cynthia Joan, *née* Bibby (d 1971); *b* 23 July 1946; *Educ* Uppingham; *m* 21 July 1971, Caroline Ann, da of Lt-Col O H J Foster, of Ardraccan House, Navan, Co Meath, Ireland; 1 s (James Peter Bibby b 1975), 1 da (Alexandra Jane b 1976); *Career* Mons OCS 1964-65, cmmnd QRIH 1965-71, ADC to HE Govr Victoria 1970-71, cmd Queen's Own Yeo TA 1984-87 (cmmnd 1974), Col TA 1987, ADC to HM The Queen 1988; farmer and landowner 1971-, dir Bibby Line Ltd 1974-87; memb Salop CLA Ctee 1971-, chm NAC Housing Assoc 1983-86; memb: Rural Devpt Cmmn 1986-, Bd Housing Corpn 1989-, Cncl RASE 1985; High Sheriff Shropshire 1989-90; *Recreations* skiing, gardening, conservation, horses; *Clubs* Cavalry and Guard's; *Style—* Robin Thompson, Esq, TD; Sansaw Hall, Clive, Shrewsbury, Salop SY4 3JR; Estate Office, Hadnall, Shrewsbury SY4 3DL, (☎ 09397 226)

THOMPSON, (Peter) Robin; s of Robert Leslie Thompson (d 1967), of Bristol, and Ellen Mabel, *née* Gibbons (d 1966); *b* 30 Sept 1941; *Educ* Farmor's Sch Gloucestershire, Hinckley Sch Leicestershire; *m* 27 March 1965, Pauline Ann, da of Frederick Box; 2 s (Julian Guy b 25 July 1967, Dominic Giles b 23 Jan 1971); *Career* chief reporter Wilts and Gloucestershire Standard 1963 (joined 1958), sr journalist Bristol Evening Post 1967-73 (acted as corr for most nat media, subsequently specialised in Gloucestershire Regt), first PR Offr (incl promotion of the Hexagon) Reading Borough Cncl 1973-78, PR mangr to six cos Vickers Ltd 1978-80, sr practitioner design consultancy 1980-81, founding ptnr Contact Marketing Services (subsequently Earl & Thompson Marketing Ltd) 1981 (now chm and jt md); *awards* commemorative certificate presented by HRH The Prince of Wales (in appreciation of work for the Prince's Tst and Volunteers); MIPR 1979, memb PR Conslts Assoc 1989; *Recreations* Prince's Tst work, travel, reading, football, my business; *Clubs* Rotary (Cirencester), Cirencester Town FC; *Style—* Robin Thompson, Esq; Green Gables, 11 Chesterton Lane, Cirencester, Gloucestershire GL7 1XU (☎ 0285 654106); Earl & Thompson Marketing Limited, The Creative Centre, 1 Hucclecote Rd, Barnwood, Gloucester GL3 3TH (☎ 0452 372000, fax 0452 371344, studio 0452 371422, car 0860 726399)

THOMPSON, Dr Ronald Augustine; MBE (1962), TD (1982); s of Lionel Wellesley Thompson, MBE (d 1989), of Surrey, and Eileen Charlotte, *née* Byrne (d 1978); *b* 28 Aug 1933; *Educ* Karachi GS, Univ Coll Hosp London (BSc, MBBS); *m* 8 Sept 1962, Anthea Georgina Erica, da of Eric George Midwinter (d 1981), of Whitton; 1 s (Richard b 1968), 2 da (Juliet b 1963, Suzanne b 1965); *Career* Nat Serv RAMC, seconded to Ghana AMC 1960-62, TA RAMC (vol) 1967-88, Col RAMC, CO 202 Midland Gen Hosp RAMC (vol) 1985-88; med registrar Univ Coll Hosp London 1963-65, sr registrar Univ of Birmingham Med Sch 1965-68, lectr in immunology Univ of

Birmingham 1968-69, conslt immunologist and dir Regnl Immunology Laboratory E Birmingham Hosp 1969-; memb: E Birmingham DHA 1978-82, Cncl RCPath 1977-80; treas Br Soc for Immunology 1979-85; FRCP 1979, FRCPath 1981; *Books* Practice of Clinical Immunology (1974), Techniques in Clinical Immunology (1977), Clinical and Experimental Immunology (ed, 1989); *Recreations* squash, tennis, music; *Clubs* Edgbaston Priory; *Style—* Dr Ronald Thompson, MBE, TD; Regional Immunology Department, East Birmingham Hospital, Birmingham B9 5ST (☎ 021 766 6611, fax 021 766 6879)

THOMPSON, Stuart Gordon; s of George Douglas Thompson, of Studley Green, High Wycombe, Bucks, and Irene, *née* Taws; *b* 28 Nov 1953; *Educ* John Hampden GS High Wycombe Bucks; *m* 19 June 1976, Angela Elizabeth, da of Norman Albert Leslie Keeping, of Wymondham, nr Norwich, Norfolk; *Career* marine broker Golding Adam Ltd (insur brokers) 1972-73, underwriting asst HL Price (marine syndicate 920) 1973-80, asst underwriter (marine) London and Hull Maritime Insur Co 1980-82, dir Octavian Syndicate Management; RAF Macmillan & Co Ltd: dep marine underwriter (for syndicates 80, 83, 843, 180) 1982, dir and underwriter (of 843) 1986, underwriter (80 and 843) 1989-91; *Recreations* clay pigeon shooting, walking, Britain's Inland Waterways; *Style—* Stuart Thompson, Esq; Field End, 2 Manor Farm Cottages, Marsworth, nr Tring, Herts (☎ 0296 661698); Octavian Underwriting Ltd, 1 Aldgate, London EC3 N 1RE

THOMPSON, Terence James; s of James Andrew Thompson (d 1984), of Burton upon Trent, and Irene, *née* Smith (d 1974); *b* 19 Jan 1928; *Educ* Birmingham Sch of Music; *m* 18 Aug 1951 (m dis 1957); *Career* Band of 1 Bn S Staffs Regt 1946-48; music master W Bromwich Tech HS 1950-59, clarinet teacher Sch of St Mary and St Anne Abbots Bromley 1957-, head of music March End Sch Wednesfield 1960-66, lectr W Midlands Coll of Higher Educn 1965-89, sr teacher Wolverhampton Music Sch 1968-; professional clarinettist and saxophonist, numerous published works; memb: Composers Guild of GB, Schs Music Assoc, Clarinet and Saxophone Soc, Assoc of Woodwind Teachers, Black Country Soc, Performing Rights Soc, Mechanical Copyright Protection Soc; *Recreations* motoring, philately, the canal scene; *Style—* Terence Thompson, Esq; 58 Willeshall Rd, Bilston, W Midlands WV14 6NW (☎ 0902 495646)

THOMPSON, Prof William; s of William Thompson (d 1969), and Amelia Thompson; *b* 2 Feb 1937; *Educ* Wallace HS Lisburn Co Antrim NI, Queen's Univ Belfast (BSc, MB, BCh, BAO, MD); *m* 8 July 1961, Anne Elizabeth, da of Professor James Morrison, OBE (D 1987); 1 s (Andrew James b 1964), 3 da (Christine Louise (Mrs Gordon) b 1963, Gillian Claire b 1968); *Career* lectr in obstetrics and gynaecology Univ of Singapore 1968-69, sr lectr and conslt obstetrician and gynaecologist Royal Maternity Hosp Belfast 1970-80, prof and head Dept of Obstetrics and Gynaecology Queen's Univ of Belfast 1980-, conslt obstetrician and gynaecologist Royal Maternity and Royal Victoria Hosps Belfast 1980-; dep sec gen Int Fedn of Fertility Socs, memb Area Health Bd, chm Med Staff Ctee Royal Maternity Hosp Belfast; memb: Br Med Soc, Gynaecological Visiting Soc; FRCOG; *Books* Fertility and Sterility (1986), Perinatal Medicine (1988); *Recreations* gardening, travelling, photography; *Style—* Prof William Thompson; Institute of Clinical Science, Dept of Obstetrics and Gynaecology, Grosvenor Rd, Belfast, Northern Ireland BT12 6BJ (☎ 0232 240 503 ext 2506, fax 0232 247 895, telex 74487)

THOMPSON HANCOCK, Dr Percy Ellis; s of Dr Frank Ryder Thompson Hancock (d 1957), and Ethel Cullen, *née* Ellis (d 1972); *b* 4 Feb 1904; *Educ* Wellington, Gonville and Caius Coll Cambridge, Bart's (MB, BChir); *m* 1, 4 June 1932, Dorothy Doris (d 1953), da of William Henry Barnes (d 1931); 2 da (Judith b 1933, Caroline b 1939); m 2, 3 March 1955, Laurie Newton Sharp, da of William Henry Charles Newton (d 1936); *Career* hon conslt physician: Nat Temperence Hosp London 1936, Potters Bar and Dist Hosp 1937, Royal Marsden Hosp London 1937, Royal Free Hosp and Sch of Medicine 1938; dir Dept of Clinical Res Royal Marsden Hosp and Inst of Cancer Res 1963-72, external examiner in med Univ of London 1963-72; memb Grand Cncl Cancer Res Campaign 1948, rep RCP on Imp Cancer Res Fund, memb Exec Ctee Action on Smoking and Health (ASH) 1973, hosp visitor King Edward's Hosp Fund for London; hon fell RSM 1945 (pres oncology section 1974-75), MRCS, LRCP, FRCP, MRCP; hon memb: American Gastroscopic Soc 1958, Societa Italiana Cancerologia 1967, Sociedad Chileana di Cancerologia 1969, Sociedad Chileana di Haematlogia 1969, Sociedad Medica di Valparaiso; *Recreations* dining and wining; *Style—* Dr Percy Ellis Thompson Hancock; 23 Wigmore Place, London WIH 9DD (☎ 071 631 4679)

THOMSEN, Leif; s of Orla Thomsen and Kirsten, *née* Caver; *b* 15 March 1936; *Educ* Gentofte Statsskole Denmark, Denmark Tech; *m* 1962, Anne Elisabeth, *née* Naested; *Career* civil engr Denmark and Peru 1960-63, mgmnt and commercial engrg positions F L Smidth & Co (Denmark) 1963-79; md: F L Smidth & Co Ltd (UK) 1979-84, F L Smidth & Co (SA)(Pty) Ltd 1988-; gen mangr Tanga Cement Co Tanzania 1987-88; *Recreations* archaeology; *Style—* Leif Thomsen, Esq; 19 St Bernards, Chichester Rd, Croydon, Surrey

THOMSON; *see*: Hyde-Thomson, White-Thomson

THOMSON, Sir Adam; CBE (1976); s of Frank Thomson and Jemima Roger; *b* 7 July 1926; *Educ* Rutherglen Academy, Coatbridge Coll, Royal Tech Coll (Univ of Strathclyde) Glasgow; *m* 1948, Dawn Elizabeth Burt; 2 s (Scott, Anthony); *Career* chm Gold Stag Ltd, chm and chief exec Caledonian Aviation Gp 1961-, Br Caledonian Airways until 1988; dep chm Martin Currie Pacific Tst 1985; non-exec dir: Royal Bank of Scotland Gp 1982-89, Metropolitan Estates Property Co 1982 until 1989; dir: Br Caldeonian Hotel Mgmnt Ltd until 1988, Br Caldeonian Helicopters Ltd until 1988, Bachelors Abroad Ltd, The Royal Bank of Scotland Gp plc; sr dir Stanford Res Int until 1989, chm Assoc of Euro Airlines 1977-78, won Scottish Free Enterprise Award Aims for Freedom and Enterprise 1976, Businessman of the Yr 1971; Hon LLD: Univ of Glasgow 1979, Univ of Sussex 1984, Univ of Strathclyde 1986; FRAeS; kt 1983; *Recreations* golf, sailing; *Clubs* Caledonian, Walton Heath Golf, Royal and Ancient Golf St Andrews; *Style—* Sir Adam Thomson, CBE; 154 Buckswood Drive, Crawley, W Sussex; Caledonian House, Crawley, West Sussex (☎ 0293 27890)

THOMSON, Alexander McEwan; s of James Aitchison Thomson (d 1956), and Agnes McEwan, *née* Walls (d 1975); *b* 13 Nov 1917; *Educ* Daniel Stewart's Coll, George Heriot's Sch, Univ of Edinburgh; *m* 10 May 1942, Marjorie May, da of John William Wood, MBE (d 1974); 2 s (Keith Robert b 1947, Neil Gordon b 1952), 1 da (Maureen Barbara b 1950); *Career* RASC 1939, N Ireland 1940-42, Sch of Artillery India 1942, cmmnd 1942 Madras 1942-44; ptnr: Fairbairn & Thomson 1956-60, Drummond & Reid 1960-69, Drummond & Co WS 1969-83 (sr ptnr 1970-83); slr: Gen Teaching Cncl for Scotland 1966-83, Edinburgh Assessor 1969-83; pres SSC Soc 1979-82; *Recreations* reading, tv; *Style—* Alexander Thomson, Esq

THOMSON, Dr Allan David; s of Reginald William Thomson (d 1953), of Ascot, and Florence, *née* Pestell (d 1984), of London; *b* 22 Dec 1936; *Educ* Univ of Edinburgh Med Sch (BSc, MB ChB, PhD); *m* 1, 28 Dec 1963 (m dis 1987), Jocelyn, da of F Price, of Sedgley, Dudley; 2 s (Simon Bruce b 28 Feb 1964, Jeremy Alexander b 14 June 1976); m 2, 12 May 1988, Wendy Phyllis Nesbit Howard, *née* Evans; *Career* asst prof of med Coll of Med & Dentistry New Jersey USA 1970, conslt physician and gastroenterologist Greenwich Dist Hosp London 1974-, hon sec lectr KCH London 1975-, recognised teacher Univ of London 1983-; ed in chief of res jl of Med Cncl on Alcoholism - Alcohol and Alcoholism; pres Greenwich & Bexley BMA 1974, memb Nat Ctee of RCS 1984-86; Freeman City of London; Liveryman: Worshipful Co of Basketmakers, Worshipful Soc of Apothecaries; FRCP 1984 (MRCP 1973); memb: American Assoc for Study of Liver Disease, Med Cncl on Alcoholism, RCPE, Euro Assoc for Study of the Liver; *Books* over 120 res articles and books relating to gen gastroenterology and alcoholic brain damage; *Recreations* music, reading, walking, photography; *Clubs* Brooks's, Med Soc of London; *Style—* Dr Allan Thomson; AMI Blackheath Hospital, 40-42 Lee Terrace, London SE3 9UD (☎ 081 318 4900)

THOMSON, Andrew Edward; s of Andrew Thomson, of 42 Glenlyon Rd, Leven Fife, Scotland, and Margaret Gordon Cairns, *née* Trainer; *b* 26 Nov 1955; *Educ* Kirkland HS; *m* 18 Sept 1982, Linda June, da of Tony Gerlad Leeves; 2 s (Edward Thomas b 24 Aug 1986, David Andrew b 27 Sept 1990); *Career* bowls player; memb Cyphers Indoor Bowling Club, first tournament win Buckhaven Bowls Club Championship 1972; titles: Thames Cockney Classic 1986, Ely Masters Singles 1988, Tennants Welsh Classic 1989; represented Scotland 1979; represented England 1981-: sixth place singles Cwlth Games Edinburgh 1986, fifth place pairs Cwlth Games Auckland 1990; records: nat singles indoor 1989 and 1990 (outdoor 1981), pairs indoor 1986, triples indoor 1981, fours indoor 1983, 1984, 1988, 1989, 1990; *Recreations* football, cricket; *Style—* Andrew Thomson, Esq; 71 Gerda Road, New Eltham, London SE9 3SJ (☎ 081 850 4798); Cyphers Indoor Bowling Club, Kingshall Rd, Beckenham, Kent BR3 1LP (☎ 081 778 3889)

THOMSON, Andrew Gordon; s of James Thomson (d 1981), of 12 Duke St, Cromarty, Scotland, and Anne, *née* Skinner (d 1981); *b* 20 July 1928; *Educ* Nigg Sch, Tain Royal Acad Scotland; *m* 27 March 1954, Jean Ann, da of Leonard Walter Collison, MBE, (d 1974), of 19 Elmgate Gardens, Edgware, Middx; 1 s (Stuart), 1 da (Susan); *Career* Nat Serv 1946-48; Waterman Partnership Ltd (formerly HL Waterman and Partners): engr, sr engr 1959, assoc 1961, ptnr 1962, sr ptnr 1983, chm 1988; memb Worshipful Co of Fletchers, Freeman City of London 1982; MSocIS France (Memb of Societe des Ingenieurs et Scientifiques de France); *Recreations* golf; *Clubs* St Stephens, City Livery, St George's Hill Golf; *Style—* Andrew Thomson, Esq; 46-47 Blackfriars Rd, London SE1 8PN (☎ 071 928 7888, fax 071 928 3033, telex 24157)

THOMSON, Babs; da of Robert G Lunine (d 1973), and Margaret Mary, *née* McCue (d 1991); *b* 24 June 1945; *Educ* S Miami HS Miami USA, Univ of Bryn Mawr Pennsylvania, Univ of Miami (BA); *m* 1, John Altoon (d 1969); m 2, Paul Douglas Thomson (d 1987); *Career* dir Multiples Gallery LA USA 1970-72, head of Painting Dept Sotheby's LA USA 1973-77; dir: Thomson & Samuel Continental Watercolours London 1978-80, Christies London 1985-90; winner Woman of the Year award for contrib to art 1975; *Style—* Mrs Babs Thomson

THOMSON, Caroline Agnes Morgan; da of Lord Thomson of Monifieth, KT, and Grace, *née* Jenkins; *b* 15 May 1954; *Educ* Mary Datchelor GS London, Univ of York (BA); *m* 1, 12 Nov 1977 (m dis 1981), Ian Campbell Bradley; m 2, 30 July 1983, Roger John Liddle; 1 s (Andrew b 29 Oct 1988); *Career* prodr BBC Radio and TV progs incl Analysis and Panorama 1975-82, political asst to Rt Hon Roy Jenkins, MP 1982-83, head of corp affrs Channel 4 TV 1990- (commissioning ed 1984-90); memb RTS 1985, BAFTA 1988; *Recreations* music and cooking; *Style—* Ms Caroline Thomson; Channel 4 Television, 60 Charlotte St, London W1 (☎ 071 631 4444)

THOMSON, Charles Grant; s of William Eddie Spalding Thomson, of 23 Thorn Drive, Bearsden, Glasgow, and Helen Donaldson, *née* Campbell; *b* 23 Sept 1948; *Educ* Jordanhill Coll Sch, Univ of Glasgow (BSc); *m* 11 July 1970, Pamela Anne, da of Frederick Simpson Mackay (d 1987), of 38 Ballater Drive, Bearsden, Glasgow; 1 s (Richard b 1979), 1 da (Susan b 1975); *Career* Scot Mutual Assur Soc: joined 1969-, various official and exec appts 1974-, gen mangr (fin) and appointed actuary Scot Mutual Gp 1990-; Faculty of Actuaries: memb of Cncl 1983-86 and 1989-, chm Faculty Examinations Bd 1989- (memb 1982-, sec 1985-89); FFA 1973; *Recreations* golf, swimming; *Clubs* Glasgow Golf, Windyhill Golf; *Style—* Charles Thomson, Esq; St Fillans, Ralston Rd, Bearsden, Glasgow; 109 St Vincent St, Glasgow G2 5HN (☎ 041 248 6321, fax 041 221 1230, telex 777145)

THOMSON, Christopher James; s of Ronald Stuart Thomson (d 1948), and Heather Mary Shrimpton; *b* 30 Jan 1933; *Educ* Wellington, Merton Coll Oxford (MA); *m* 1976, Daphne Moyna, da of Edward Maguire; 2 step da; *Career* 2 Lt Coldstream Guards (Egypt); md Bowater UK Paper Co Newsprint Div; dir Lamco Paper Sales 1983-; *Clubs* White's; *Style—* Christopher Thomson, Esq; 65 Arlington Ave, Westmount, Quebec H3Y 2W5 (☎ 514 935 2255)

THOMSON, Clive Benjamin; JP (Gloucester, 1986); s of Benjamin Alfred Thomson, of Brighton, and Ivy Grace, *née* Smith; *b* 29 May 1935; *Educ* Westminster; *m* 11 Jan 1959, Mary Lilian (Molly), da of Eric Clements (d 1985); 1 s (Michael Clive b and d 1963), 2 da (Deborah Jane b 1962, Victoria Louise b 1965); *Career* Nat Serv 2 Lt Royal Berks Regt 1953-55, Capt Royal Berks Regt (TA) 1955-65, Capt HAC 1980-91; dir and gen mangr Ecclesiastical Insur Office plc; JP Richmond 1975-85; former chm: Wesbury Cons Assoc, Twickenham Cons Assoc, London SW Euro Cons Assoc; former dep chm Gtr London Cons Assoc, former pres Surbiton Griffins FC; memb Nat Exec Nat Assoc Voluntary Hostels, chm East Gloucestershire NHS Tst; Freeman City of London 1980; Liveryman Worshipful Co of: Insurers 1980, Marketors 1991; FInstM 1988; *Recreations* walking, politics, racing; *Clubs* United, Cecil; *Style—* Clive Thomson, Esq, JP; Chota Koti, Oakley Rd, Cheltenham, Glos GL52 6PA (☎ 0242 582 936); Ecclesiastical Insurance Group, Beaufort House, Brunswick Rd, Glos (☎ 0452 419 221)

THOMSON, David; s of George Thomson (d 1972), and Frances Mary, *née* Eade (d 1983); *b* 20 Sept 1932; *Educ* Royal HS Edinburgh; *m* 10 Sept 1957, Dorothy Patricia, da of Edward Waterhouse (d 1978); 2 s (Michael b 1964, Ian b 1969), 1 da (Anne b 1959); *Career* Nat serv 2 Lt RASC; CA; dir NRDC 1976-81, md Systems Programmes Holdings 1981-83; dir Syntech Information Technology Fndn; *Recreations* walking, music, antiques, books; *Style—* David Thomson, Esq; Swanston, Burtons Way, Chalfont St Giles, Bucks; 120 Wigmore St, London (☎ 071 487 3870, fax 071 487 3860, car 0836 526702)

THOMSON, Sir (Frederick Douglas) David; 3 Bt (UK 1929), of Glendarroch, Co Midlothian; s of Sir (James) Douglas Wishart, 2 Bt (d 1972), and Bettina, er da of late Lt Cdr David William Shafto Douglas, RN; *b* 14 Feb 1940; *Educ* Eton, Univ Coll Oxford (BA); *m* 1967, Caroline Anne, da of Maj Timothy Stuart Lewis, Royal Scots Greys; 2 s, 1 da; *Heir* s, Simon Douglas Charles Thomson b 16 June 1969; *Career* dir Ben Line Steamers Ltd 1964-89; chm: Jove Investment Trust plc 1983-, Britannia Steamship Insurance Assoc Ltd (dir 1965-), Through Transport Mutual Insurance Assoc Ltd (dir 1973-), Abtrust News European Investment Trust plc 1990-, The Castle Cairn Investment Trust Co plc 1990-; dir: Life Assoc of Scotland Ltd 1970-, Martin Currie Pacific Tst plc 1985-, Danae Investment Trust plc 1979-, Cairn Energy plc 1971-, G & G Kynoch plc 1990-; memb Royal Co of Archers (Queen's Body Guard for Scotland); *Style—* Sir David Thomson, Bt; Glenbrook House, Balerno, Midlothian EH14 7BQ (☎ 031 449 4116); Newhaven House, 39 Western Harbour, Leith, Edinburgh EH6 6NX (☎ 031 553 4044, fax 031 554 3051, telex 72519)

THOMSON, David John; s of David Barron Thomson, of Monifieth, Dundee (d 1979), and Margaret Seath Baxter (d 1955); gf David Thomson, of Anstruther, Capt of last windjammer to sail under British flag Garthpool; *b* 21 Feb 1941; *Educ* Forest Sch London, Glasgow Univ (MA); *m* 1966, Marjorie Rose, da of William Clifford Utting; 2 s (Andrew b 1967, Mark b 1970), 1 da (Kathryn b 1970); *Career* marketing dir: European Div Rowntree plc Ltd 1980-, Grocery Div 1975-80; dep chm Rowntree Europe 1985; md Rowntree Snack Foods 1986-; *Recreations* golf, gardening, sea fishing, walking, reading, light opera; *Clubs* Yorkshire, York Golf; *Style*— David Thomson, Esq; Ashurst, Usher Park Rd, Haxby, York (☎ 0904 769537); Rowntree plc, York YO1 1XY (☎ 0904 53071); Rowntree Snackfoods, Cottage Beck Rd, Scunthorpe, S Humberside DN16 1TT (☎ 0724 281222)

THOMSON, Hon David Kenneth Roy; s and h of 2 Baron Thomson of Fleet; *b* 12 June 1957; *Style*— The Hon David Thomson

THOMSON, David Kinnear; CBE 1972 (MBE 1945), TD (1945), JP (1955), DL (Perth and Kinross 1966-77 and 1980); s of Peter Thomson, and Jessie, *née* Kinnear; *b* 26 March 1910; *Educ* Perth Acad, Strathallan Sch; *Career* former pres Peter Thomson (Perth) Ltd whisky blenders and exporters; memb Perth Local Authy 1949-72, Lord Provost of Perth 1966-72, hon Sheriff of Perth 1966-; memb: ITA Scottish Branch 1968-73, Scottish Econ Cncl; chm Bd of Mgmnt Perth Tech Coll 1972-75, dir Scottish Transport Gp 1972-76, memb Scottish Opera 1973-81, chm Tayside Health Bd 1973-77, memb Ct Univ of Dundee 1975-79, chm Scottish Licensed Trade 1981-82, pres Perth Festival of the Arts 1985-90 (chm 1973-85); Freeman of Perth and Kinross 1982; CStJ 1984; *Recreations* golf, walking, listening to music; *Clubs* Royal Perth Golfing Soc; *Style*— David Thomson, Esq, CBE, TD, JP, DL; Fairhill, Oakbank Rd, Perth (☎ 0738 26593)

THOMSON, David Paget; s of late Sir George Thomson, FRS, Nobel Laureate; *b* 19 March 1931; *Educ* Rugby, Trinity Coll Cambridge; *m* 1959, Patience Mary, da of late Sir Lawrence Bragg, CH, MC, FRS, Nobel Laureate; 2 s, 2 da; *Career* Lt Cdr RNR, joined Lazard Bros & Co Ltd 1956, md 1966, seconded HM Foreign Service 1971-73, economic counsellor Bonn, Lazards 1973-86; chm: Jutcrest Ltd 1985-88, F & C Germany Investment Tst PLC 1990-; cncl chm The Royal Instn 1985-87, memb MMC 1985-, tstee Portsmouth Naval Base Property Tst 1986-, dir and gen Br Invisible Exports Cncl 1987-, tstee Lucy Cavendish Coll Cambridge 1987, chm Fitzwilliam Museum Tst Cambridge 1988-, dir Med Sickness Soc 1990; *Clubs* Athenaeum; *Style*— David Thomson, Esq; Little Stoke House, North Stoke, Oxon (☎ 0491 37161)

THOMSON, Prof Derick S; s of James Thomson (d 1971), and Christina, *née* Smith (d 1968); *b* 5 Aug 1921; *Educ* Nicolson Inst Stornoway, Univ of Aberdeen (MA), Emmanuel Coll Cambridge (BA), UCNW Bangor; *m* 31 March 1952, Carol MacMichael, da of Daniel Galbraith (d 1943); 5 s (Dòmhnall Ruaraidh b 1954, Daniel (James) b 1956, Ranald b 1963, Roderick b 1969, Calum b 1974), 1 da (Tia b 1960); *Career* WWII serv RAF 1942-45; asst in Celtic Univ of Edinburgh 1948-49, lectr in Welsh Univ of Glasgow 1949-56, reader in Celtic Univ of Aberdeen 1956-63, prof of Celtic Univ of Glasgow 1963-; former memb Scottish Arts Cncl; chm: Gaelic Books Cncl 1968-, Catherine McCaig Tst; pres Scottish Gaelic Texts Soc; Ossian Prize FVS Fndn Hamburg 1974; Hon DLitt Univ of Wales 1987; FRSE 1977; *Books* Gairm (ed, 1952-), An Introduction to Gaelic Poetry (1989), The Companion to Gaelic Scotland (1983), Creachadh na Clàrsaich/Plundering the Harp (collected poems) (1982); *Recreations* publishing, travel; *Clubs* Glasgow Arts; *Style*— Prof Derick Thomson, FRSE; 19 Bemersyde Ave, Mansewood, Glasgow G43 1DA (☎ 041 632 7880); Dept of Celtic, Univ of Glasgow, Glasgow G12 1DA (☎ 041 339 8855 ext 4222)

THOMSON, Dr Duncan; s of Duncan Murdoch Thomson (d 1958), and Jane McFarlane, *née* Wilson (d 1982); *b* 2 Oct 1934; *Educ* Airdrie Acad, Univ of Edinburgh (MA, PhD), Edinburgh Coll of Art; *m* 15 July 1964, Julia Jane, da of Donald Campbell MacPhail (d 1962); 1 da (Rebecca b 1974); *Career* art teacher 1959-67, keeper Scottish Nat Portrait Gallery 1982- (asst keeper 1967-82); *Recreations* literature; *Style*— Dr Duncan Thomson; 3 Eglinton Crescent, Edinburgh EH12 5DH (☎ 031 225 6430); Scottish National Portrait Gallery, 1 Queen St, Edinburgh EH2 1JD

THOMSON, Edward Arthur; s of Arthur Percival Thomson (d 1976), of Bognor Regis, and Lilian Emily, *née* Lawther (d 1976); *b* 2 March 1915; *Educ* Stationers' Co Sch London; *m* 1, 29 April 1939, (Madge) Beryl (d 1983), da of late George William Manly, of Hornsey; 2 s (Ian b 1947, Peter b 1950); m 2, 1983, Ramchuan, *née* Pungsomboon; *Career* TA 61 AA Bde 1937, cmmnd RA 1942; md later chm EA Thomson (Gems) Ltd 1958, chm Morris Goldmam Gems Ltd 1971-, Precious Stone Trade Section London C & C 1982-83; pres Precious Stone Cmmn Int Confed of Jewellers Precious Stone Dealers Retailers and Wholesalers 1979-84, chm of govrs Southwark Coll of FE 1968-71, vice chm Finchley Boxing Club 1987-91; Freeman City of London 1975, Liveryman Worshipful Co of Wheelwrights 1975, Freeman Worshipful Co of Stationers and Newspaper Makers 1987; Hon FGA 1985; *Recreations* gardening, travel; *Clubs* Directors, Oriental, City Livery; *Style*— Edward Thomson, Esq; EA Thomson (Gems) Ltd, Chapel House, Hatton Place, Hatton Garden, London EC1N 8RX, (☎ 071 242 3181, fax 071 831 1776, telex 27726 THOMCO G)

THOMSON, (Hon) Mrs (Elizabeth Frances); *née* Williams; da of Baron Francis-Williams (Life Peer, d 1970); does not use courtesy prefix of Hon; *m* 1963, George Alexander Thomson; children; *Style*— Mrs Thomson; 27 Haverfield Gdns, Kew, Richmond, Surrey

THOMSON, Bettina, Lady; Evelyn Margaret Isobel; *née* Douglas; eld da of late Lt-Cdr David William Sholto Douglas, RN; *b* 1 Jan 1915; *Educ* private; *m* 25 Sept 1935, Sir (James) Douglas Wishart Thomson, 2 Bt (d 1972); 2 s, 3 da; *Style*— Bettina, Lady Thomson; Old Caberston, Walkerburn, Peeblesshire

THOMSON, Grant Hugh; s of Albert Edward Thomson (d 1976), of Toronto, Canada, and Muriel Frances, *née* Craggs (d 1986); *b* 11 Nov 1935; *m* 1, 1959 (m dis), Vera Anne, da of H Cibula; 1 da; m 2, 1985, Mary Rayleigh, da of Harold Stanfield Strutt; *Career* served HM Forces RAF photographer II 1954-60, photographer Guided Weapons and Aircraft Divs BAC 1960-64, photographic mangr BKS Surveys Ltd 1964-67, tech servs product specialist (aerial) Ilford Ltd 1967-72, lectr Int Inst for Aerospace Survey and Earth Scis (ITC) Enschede The Netherlands 1972-74; photographic engr: Hunting Technical Services Ltd, Hunting Surveys and Consultants Ltd 1974-; author of numerous pubns relating to aerial photography in various photographic jls; FRPS 1985, FBIPP 1987; *Style*— Grant H Thomson, Esq; Hunting Technical Services Ltd, Thamesfield House, Boundary Way, Hemel Hempstead, Herts HP2 7SR (☎ 0442 231800, fax 0442 219886)

THOMSON, (Henry) Harron; s of late Robert Molland Thomson, and late Annabella MClean, *née* Harron; *b* 3 March 1927; *Educ* Leyton County HS, King's Coll London, St George's Hosp Med Sch (MB BS), FRCS, FRCOG; *m* 26 Jan 1957, Sybil Jean; 2 s (Timothy b 1959, Toby b 1964), 1 da (Stephanie b 1962); *Career* conslt gynaecologist: Clementine Churchill Hosp Harrow Middx, Bishops Wood Private Hosp Northwood Middx; memb: Thoroughbred Breeders Assoc, Racehorse Owners Assoc, Chelsea Clinical Soc, Hunterian Soc; *Recreations* breeding and racing thoroughbred horses; *Style*— Harron Thomson, Esq; 9 Deerings Drive, Eastcote, Pinner, Middx HA5 2NZ (☎ 081 429 1482); Consulting Rooms: Clementine Churchill Hospital, Harrow, Middx (☎ 081 422 3464), Bishops Wood Private Hospital, Rickmansworth Rd, Northwood, Middx HA6 2JW (☎ 0923 835 814, fax 0923 835181)

THOMSON, Ian Gray; s of Norman Gray Thomson, JP (d 1965), and Doris Inez, *née* Perring; *b* 7 June 1927; *Educ* Sherborne; *m* 24 June 1966, Bridget Anne, da of Harold Keith, of Bournemouth; 1 s (Andrew James Gray b 1967), 1 da (Alexandra Bridget b 1969); *Career* RA (AA) 1945-48, cmnd 105 HAA Regt 1947; md John Perring Ltd 1964-88 (joined 1948, dir 1957-88); dir: Perring Furnishing Ltd 1967-88, Avenue Trading Ltd 1986-, Perring Fin Ltd 1986-; govr Adams GS Newport Shropshire; Liveryman: Worshipful Co of Haberdashers 1948, Worshipful Co of Furniture Makers 1961; *Recreations* gardening, travel, game fishing; *Clubs* RAC, City Livery; *Style*— Ian Thomson, Esq; Seafield Hse, Wood Gason Lane, Hayling Is, Hants PO11 0RL; 6 Willow Lodge, River Gardens, Stevenage Rd, Fulham, London SW6 6NW; Woodcock House, 36 High St, Wimbledon Village SW19 (☎ 081 944 1777, fax 081 944 1717)

THOMSON, Sir Ian Sutherland; KBE (1985, MBE mil 1945), CMG (1968); s of William Sutherland Thomson (d 1966), of Glasgow, and Jessie McCaig, *née* Malloch (d 1982); *b* 8 Jan 1920; *Educ* Glasgow HS, Univ of Glasgow (MA); *m* 1 Sept 1945, Nancy Marguerite (d 1988), da of William Kearsley (d 1956), of Suva, Fiji; 7 s (Andrew b 1947, Peter b 1948, John b 1950, David b 1953, Richard b 1954, Mark b 1956, Douglas b 1960), 1 da (Sally b 1958); m 2, 1989, Nancy Caldwell, da of Robert Smyth McColl, of Glasgow; *Career* The Royal Highland Regt The Black Watch 1940, Fiji Mil Forces, ret Capt 1945; HM Colonial Admin Serv Fiji 1946-54, seconded to W Africa Dept and Civil Aviation Dept Colonial Office 1954-56, chm Native Lands and Fisheries Cmmn Fiji 1957-63 (cmmr for native reserves), cmmr Western Div Fiji 1963-66, actg chief sec and ldr of govt business Fiji Legislative Cncl 1966, admin Br Virgin Is 1966-70, independent chm Fiji Sugar Indust 1971-84; chm: Fiji Econ Devpt Bd 1981-86, Air Pacific Ltd 1984-87, Sedgwick (Fiji) Ltd 1984-87, Thomson Pacific Resources Ltd 1988-; Freeman City of Glasgow 1946; fell Inst Mgmnt 1984-87; kt 1985; *Recreations* golf, gardening; *Style*— Sir Ian Thomson, KBE, CMG; Sonas, Ardentallen, by Oban, Strathclyde PA34 4SF (☎ 0631 628 46)

THOMSON, Lady Jacqueline Rosemary Margot; *née* Rufus Isaacs; da of 3 Marquess of Reading, MBE, MC (d 1980); *b* 10 Nov 1946; *Educ* Southover Manor Lewes, Int Sch Geneva, Madrid Univ; *m* 1976, Sir Mark Wilfrid Home Thomson, 3 Bt, *qv*; 3 s, 1 da; *Style*— The Lady Jacqueline Thomson; 42 Glebe Place, London SW3 5JE (☎ 071 352 5015)

THOMSON, Lt-Col James Currie; MBE (Mil 1945), TD (1946), JP (Hertfordshire 1956), DL (1975); s of James Thomson (d 1961), of Leith, Edinburgh, and Nell Gertrude, *née* Hutt (d 1943); *b* 4 Feb 1911; *Educ* Marlborough, Pembroke Coll Cambridge (MA); *m* 12 May 1945, Letitia Blanche, wid of Capt M V Fleming (POW d of wounds 1940), and da of Hon Malcolm Algernon Borthwick (d 1941), of Woodcote House, Oxon; 1 s (James Borthwick b 9 Feb 1946), 1 da (Clare Nell (Hon Mrs R C Denison-Pender) b 9 Feb 1946 (twin)), 3 step s (Valentine Patrick b 1 Aug 1935, Christopher Michael b 8 May 1937, David Algernon b 24 Nov 1938 d 1975), 1 step da (Gillian (Mrs N C Newbury) b 28 Jan 1940); *Career* London Scottish Regt: joined 1936, cmmnd 2 Lt 1938, Adj 1 Bn 1940 serv UK and PAIFORCE 1939-42, on staff N Africa and Italy 1943-44 (despatches), 2 i/c then CO 2 Bn Queens Own Cameron Highlanders (wounded) serv Italy Greece Austria 1944-45, hon rank Lt-Col; Charles Mackinlay & Co Ltd: apprentice 1932, dir then chm 1970-76; cnclr Hertford RDC 1948-66, chm Stevenage Bench 1980; High Sheriff 1971-72; chm Herts Soc 1974-80; Master Worshipful Co of Founders 1964-65; *Clubs* Boodle's; *Style*— Lt-Col James Thomson, MBE, TD, JP, DL; Stable Court, Walkern, nr Stevenage, Herts SG2 7JA

THOMSON, Sir John; KBE (1972), TD (1944); s of late Guy Thomson, JP; *b* 3 April 1908; *Educ* Winchester, Magdalen Coll Oxford; *m* 1, 1935, Elizabeth, *née* Brotherhood, JP (d 1977); m 2, 1979, Eva Elizabeth Dreaper, *née* Russell; *Career* Bt-Col Cmd Oxfordshire Yeo Regt RA 1942-44 and 1947-50; dir Union Discount Co of London Ltd 1960-74; chm: Barclays Bank Ltd 1962-73 (dir 1947-78), Morland and Co Ltd 1979-83; pres Br Bankers Assoc 1964-66; memb: Royal Cmmn on Trade Unions and Employees Assocs 1965-68, BR Nat Export Cncl 1968; steward Jockey Club 1974-71, dep steward Univ of Oxford, curator Univ of Oxford Chest 1949-74, chm Nuffield Med Tstees 1951-82; High Sheriff Oxon 1957, DL Oxon 1947-57, vice Lord-Lt Oxon 1957-63, Lord-Lt Oxon 1963-79; Freeman City of Oxford; Hon DCL Oxford 1957, hon fell St Catherine's Coll Oxford; FIB; KStJ (1973); *Recreations* steeplechase horse owner and breeder; *Clubs* Cavalry and Guard's, Jockey, Overseas Bankers' (pres 1968-69, currently vice pres); *Style*— Sir John Thomson, KBE, TD; Manor Farm House, Spelsbury, Oxford (☎ 0608 810266)

THOMSON, Sir John Adam; GCMG (1985, KCMG 1978, CMG 1972); s of Sir George Paget Thomson, FRS (d 1975), sometime Master CCC Cambridge, and Kathleen Buchanan, *née* Smith (d 1941); *b* 27 April 1927; *Educ* Phillip's Exeter Acad USA, Univ of Aberdeen, Trinity Coll Cambridge; *m* 1953, Elizabeth Anne McClure (d 1988); 3 s, 1 da; *Career* joined FO 1950, head of Planning Staff FO 1967, on secondment to Cabinet Office as chief of Assessments Staff 1968-71, min and dep perm rep N Atlantic Cncl 1972-73, head UK Delgn MBFR Exploratory Talks in Vienna 1973, asst under sec FCO 1973-76, high cmmr India 1977-82, UK perm rep UNO NY and UK rep Security Cncl (with personal rank of ambass) 1982-87; dir Grindlays Bank 1987-; princ 21 Century Trust London 1987-90, memb Cncl Int Inst of Strategic Studies 1987-; memb Governing Body: Inst of Devpt Studies, Overseas Devpt Inst, 21 Century Tst; assoc memb Nuffield Coll Oxford; *Books* Crusader Castles (co-author with R Fedden, 1956); *Recreations* hill walking; *Clubs* Athenaeum, Century (New York); *Style*— Sir John Thomson, GCMG; c/o Heads of Mission Section, Foreign and Commonwealth Office, King Charles St, London SW1

THOMSON, John M; s of John Wilson Thomson, and Catherine, *née* Murray Phillips; *b* 30 Jan 1928; *Educ* Falkirk HS, Univ of Edinburgh (MA); *m* Ingrid, Erich Haugas; 1 s (Ian b 24 June 1961), 1 da (Clare b 1 Sept 1964); *Career* Lazard Bros & Co Ltd 1950-59, Manufacturers Hanover Trust Company 1959-66, dep chief exec Brook Bond Group plc 1966-84; currently non-exec dir: Thames Water plc, Scottish & Newcastle Breweries plc, C Czarnikow Holdings Ltd; also currently: non-exec chm London & Manchester Group plc, non-exec vice chm J Bibby & Sons plc; *Recreations* reading, walking, theatre, foreign travel; *Style*— John M Thomson, Esq; London and Manchester Group plc, Eldon House, Eldon St, London EC2M 7LB (☎ 071 247 2000, fax 071 247 2859, telex 4726 ASSUR)

THOMSON, Prof Joseph McGeachy; s of James Thomson, of Davaar Ave, Campbeltown, and Catherine Morrans, *née* McGeachy; *b* 6 May 1948; *Educ* Keil Sch Dumbarton, Univ of Edinburgh (LLB); *Career* lectr: Univ of Birmingham 1970-74, Kings Coll London 1974-84; prof of law Univ of Strathclyde 1984-90, Regius prof of Law Univ of Glasgow 1991, dep gen ed Stair Meml Encyclopaedia of the Laws of Scotland 1985-; *Books* Family Law in Scotland (1987); *Recreations* opera, ballet, food and wine; *Style*— Prof Joseph Thomson; 140 Hyndland Rd, Glasgow G12 9PN (☎ 041 334 6682); The Law School, Stair Building, Univ of Glasgow (☎ 041 339 8855)

THOMSON, Malcolm George; QC (1987); s of George Robert Thomson, OBE (d 1987), and Daphne Ethel, *née* Daniels; *b* 6 April 1950; *Educ* The Edinburgh Acad, Univ of Edinburgh (LLB); *m* 18 March 1978, Susan Gordon, da of Gordon Aitken, of 18 Northanger Court, Grove St, Bath; 2 da (Victoria b 1982, Jacqueline b 1989); *Career* advocate at the Scottish Bar 1974; standing jr counsel 1982-87: Dept of Agriculture and Fisheries for Scotland, The Forestry Cmmn Scotland; case ed Scottish

Current Law 1977-, ed Scots Law Times Reports 1989-; *Recreations* sailing, skiing; *Clubs* New (Edinburgh); *Style—* Malcolm Thomson, Esq, QC; 10 Avon Grove, Edinburgh EH4 6RF (☎ 031 336 5261); Advocates Library, Parliament House, Edinburgh EH1 1RF (☎ 031 226 5071)

THOMSON, Sir Mark Wilfrid Home; 3 Bt (UK 1925), of Old Nunthorpe, Co York; s of Sir Ivo Wilfrid Home Thomson, 2 Bt (d 1991), and his 1 w, Sybil Marguerite, *née* Thompson; *b* 29 Dec 1939; *m* 1976, Lady Jacqueline Rosemary Margot Rufus Isaacs, o da of 3 Marquess of Reading; 3 s (Albert Mark Hume b 1979, Jake Michael Alfred b 1983, Luke Ivo Charles b (twin) 1983), 1 da (Daisy Jacqueline Carol b 1977); *Heir* s, Albert Mark Home Thomson b 3 Aug 1979; *Style—* Sir Mark Thomson, Bt; 42 Glebe Place, London SW3 5JE (☎ 071 352 5015; office: 071 408 1592)

THOMSON, Brig Michael; MBE (1974); s of George MacDonald Thomson, of Glen Eden, Auchendoon Rd, Newton Stewart, Wigtownshire, and Winifred Carol, *née* Delmhorst (d 1971); *b* 13 Feb 1936; *Educ* Gordonstoun; *m* 30 Oct 1965, Maryelle Therese Madeleine, da of Col Baron Leonce de Curieres de Castelmau, of Chateau d'Aguesseau, Trouville sur Mer, France; 3 s (Patrick b 1967, Roderick b 1970, Nicholas b 1974); *Career* cmmnd King's Own Scot Borderers 1959, CO 1976-78, instr Staff Coll 1979-81, cmdt Zimbabwe Staff Coll 1981-83, cdr 52 Lowland Bde 1986-89; *Recreations* shooting, skiing; *Clubs* Army and Navy; *Style—* Brig Michael Thomson, MBE; Clos de Callenville, Chemin de Callenville, 14360 Trouville, France (☎ 010 33 31 88 18 77); Flat 1, 80 Claverton St, London SW1

THOMSON, (George) Michael Mackinnon; s of Wing Cdr George Reid Thomson (d 1986), of Kinellar House, and Phyllis Sarah, *née* Mackinnon (d 1985); *b* 29 March 1940; *Educ* Rugby, Heriot-Watt Univ (Dip Town Planning); *m* 3 June 1967, Caroline Mary, da of Lt-Col George Harold Hay (d 1967), of Berwickshire; 1 s (Jolyon b 1970), 1 da (Mary b 1970); *Career* principal of Mackinnon Thomson Planning; MRTPI, FFAS, ARIBA, ARIAS; *Recreations* films, filming, skiing; *Clubs* Royal Northern; *Style—* Michael Thomson, Esq; Mackinnon Thomson Planning, Moray House, 145 Crown Street, Aberdeen

THOMSON, Dr Neil Campbell; s of Prof Adam Simpson Turnbull Thomson, of Ayr, and Margaret Campbell, *née* Templeton; *b* 3 April 1948; *Educ* Spiers Sch Beith, Univ of Glasgow (MB ChB, MD); *m* 15 Aug 1973, Lorna Jean, da of William Sim Walker Fraser, of Perth; 2 s (David Fraser b 10 July 1976, Andrew Campbell b 8 May 1978), 1 da (Jennifer Lorna b 22 May 1985); *Career* jr hosp doctor Glasgow Teaching Hosps 1972-80, res fell McMaster Univ Hamilton Ontario Canada 1980-81, conslt physician Western Infirmary Glasgow 1982-; memb Res Ctees: The Chest Heart and Stroke Assoc, The Nat Asthma Campaign; FRCP; memb: Br Thoracic Soc (hon sec), American Thoracic Soc, Scot Soc of Physicians, Br Soc for Allergy and Clinical Immunology; *Books* Asthma: Basic Mechanisms and Clinical Management (1988), Handbook of Clinical Allergy (1990); *Recreations* fishing, gardening, hill walking; *Style—* Dr Neil C Thomson; Dept of Respiratory Medicine, Western Infirmary, Glasgow G11 6NT

THOMSON, Sheriff Nigel Ernest Drummond; s of Rev James Kyd Thomson (d 1939), of Edinburgh, and Joan Drummond (d 1929); *b* 19 June 1926; *Educ* George Watson's Boys' Coll Edinburgh, Univ of St Andrews (MA), Univ of Edinburgh (LLB); *m* 1964, Snjólaug, da of Consul Gen Sigursteinn Magnússon (d 1982), of Edinburgh; 1 s (Diggi b 1969), 1 da (Ingalo b 1967); *Career* Lt Indian Grenadiers; advocate; Sheriff at: Hamilton 1966-1976, Edinburgh 1976-; chm Music Ctee Scottish Arts Cncl 1979-1984; chm Edinburgh Youth Orchestra 1986-; hon pres: Scottish Assoc for Counselling 1984-88, Strathaven Arts Guild 1976-, Tenovus-Edinburgh 1985-; *Recreations* music, woodwork, golf; *Clubs* New (Edinburgh), Bruntsfield Golf, Strathaven Arts; *Style—* Sheriff Nigel Thomson; 50 Grange Rd, Edinburgh (☎ 031 667 2166); Sheriff Court, Lawnmarket, Edinburgh (☎ 031 226 7181)

THOMSON, Oliver Campbell Watt; s of (James) Oliver Thomson OBE (d 1972), of Milngavie, and Linda Marie, *née* Kelly; *b* 28 Feb 1936; *Educ* King Edward VI Sch Birmingham, Trinity Coll Cambridge (MA); *m* 10 Sept 1960, Jean Patricia Dawson, da of James Sellar Christie, CBE (d 1986), of Glasgow; 2 s (Calum b 1961, Iain b 1964), 1 da (Margaret b 1967); *Career* RN 1954-56, Lt RNR 1964-70; dir McCallum Advertising 1972-75, md Charles Barker Scotland 1975-85, mktg dir Holmes McDougall 1985-87, md Levy McCallum Ltd 1987-; chm Four Acres Charitable Tst; dir Westbourne Sch; MCAM, FBIM, FIPA; *Books* The Romans in Scotland (1965), Persuasion in History (1970); *Recreations* sailing, hillwalking; *Clubs* RSAC; *Style—* Oliver Thomson, Esq; 3 Kirklee Terr, Glasgow G12 (☎ 041 339 7453); Levy McCallum Advertising Agency, 203 St Vincent St, Glasgow, Strathclyde G2 5QF (☎ 041 248 7977, fax 041 221 5803)

THOMSON, Peter Alexander Bremner; CVO (1986); s of Alexander Bremner Thomson (d 1976), and Dorothy Davison, *née* Scurr; *b* 16 Jan 1938; *Educ* Canford, RNC Dartmouth, SOAS (BA, MPhil); *m* 31 July 1965, Lucinda Coleman, da of Colin Sellar (d 1965), of Morayshire; 3 s (Philip b 1970, Nicholas b 1972, Christopher b 1978); *Career* RN 1954-75; Sub Lt and Lt in HM Ships: Albion, Plover, Tiger, Ark Royal, Eagle; Lt Cdr ashore Hong Kong and Taiwan; Dip Serv 1975-; first sec: London, Lagos, Hong Kong; cnsllr Peking; *Recreations* sailing, walking; *Clubs* Travellers, Hong Kong; *Style—* Peter Thomson, Esq, CVO; The Red House, Charlton, Horethorne, Sherborne, Dorset (☎ 096 322 301); c/o FCO, King Charles Street, SW1

THOMSON, Robert Walter; s of Robert Clow Thomson, of Kirkabister, Shore Rd, Whiting Bay, Arran, and Anne, *née* Watson; *b* 3 Feb 1936; *Educ* Rutherglen Acad, Glasgow Sch of Art, Glasgow Coll of Tech (B Arch, Dip TP); *m* 1 Sept 1960, Janet Wilson, da of Thomas Ross Menzies, JP (d 1976); 1 s (Eric Douglas b 1964), 1 da (Kay Anne b 1966); *Career* chartered architect and planning conslt in private practice 1964-; FRIAS, RIBA, MRTPI, ACIArb, FFB; *Recreations* hill climbing; *Style—* Robert Thomson, Esq; 11 Calderwood Rd, Newlands, Glasgow G43 2RP (☎ 041 637 5345)

THOMSON, Stanley; CBE (1989); s of William Ingram Thomson (d 1971), and Annie Blanche Thomson (d 1975); *b* 23 June 1926; *Educ* Robert Gordon's Coll Aberdeen; *m* 8 June 1956, Elizabeth Wright, da of Erick Knox Wilson, of Scotland; 1 s (David Bruce b 1960); *Career* certified accountant; exec dir Ford Motor Co Ltd 1980-90 (dir of fin 1967-90); pres Chartered Assoc of CAs 1987-88 (fell 1952, memb Cncl 1974); memb: Industl Devpt Advsy Bd 1978-86, Cncl Univ of Essex 1988-, Bd Int Accounting Standards Ctee 1990-, Fin Reporting Cncl 1990-; vice chm Accounting Standards Ctee (memb 1982-85); FCCA, CBIM; *Recreations* gardening, reading; *Style—* Stanley Thomson, Esq, CBE; 6 Belvedere Rd, Brentwood, Essex (☎ 0277 226111)

THOMSON, Sue; da of Basil Raymond Hamilton (d 1942); *b* 6 Aug 1938; *Educ* Christ's Hosp; *m* 1978, André Davis; 1 da (Susannah b 1978); *Career* exec dir Octopus Publishing Gp Ltd 1971-, md Octopus Books Ltd 1971-77; dir Mandarin Publishers Ltd Hong Kong 1971-; *Recreations* family life, early domestic architecture; *Clubs* University Women's; *Style—* Miss Sue Thomson; 59 Grosvenor St, London W1 (☎ 071 493 5841)

THOMSON, Dr Thomas James; CBE (1983, OBE 1978); s of Thomas Thomson (d 1949), of Stoer Park, Airdrie, Scotland, and Annie Jane, *née* Grant (d 1968); *b* 8 April 1923; *Educ* Airdrie Acad, Univ of Glasgow (MB ChB); *m* 10 Jan 1948, Jessie Smith, da of George Edward Shotbolt (d 1955), of Balmaha, Seafield Drive, Ardrossan, Scotland; 2 s (Ian b 1954, Alan b 1960), 1 da (Shona b 1955); *Career* Flt-Lt RAF 1946-48; conslt physician and gastroenterologist Stobhill Gen Hosp Glasgow 1961-87; Dept of Materia Medica Univ of Glasgow: lectr 1953-61, hon lectr 1961-87; postgrad advsr to Glasgow Northern Hosps 1961-80, sec Specialist Advsy Ctee for Gen Internal Med UK 1970-74; chm: Medica - Pharmaceutical Forum 1978-80 (chm Educn Advsy Bd 1979-84); Conf of Royal Colls and Faculties in Scotland 1982-84, Nat Med Consultative Ctee for Scotland 1982-87; pres RCPSGlas 1982-84 (hon sec 1965-73), active in postgrad med educn ctees locally nationally and in EEC; chm Gtr Glasgow Health Bd 1987- (memb 1985-); Hon Fell American Coll of Physicians 1983, Hon LLD Univ of Glasgow 1988; FRCP (Glasgow) 1964, FRCP (London) 1969, FRCP (Edin) 1982, FRCP (Ireland) 1983; *Books* Dilling's Pharmacology (jt ed 1969), Gastroenterology - an integrated course (1972, 3 edn 1983); *Recreations* swimming, golfing; *Clubs* RAF London, RSAC (Glasgow); *Style—* Dr Thomas Thomson, CBE; 1 Varna Rd, Glasgow G14 9NE (☎ 041 959 5930); Gtr Glasgow Health Bd, 112 Ingram St, Glasgow G1 1ET (☎ 041 552 6222)

THOMSON, William Chalmers; s of William Thomson (d 1968), of Glasgow, and Catherine, *née* Chalmers (d 1943); *b* 22 Feb 1929; *Educ* Royal Coll of Science and Technol Strathclyde (Dip Arch, Dip Town Planning); *m* 2 April 1955, Elizabeth Penman, da of John Sinclair (d 1972), of Glasgow; 1 s (Alan Sinclair b 1963), 1 da (Karen Jane b 1966); *Career* architect/planner East Kilbride Devpt Corp 1954-56; Cumbernauld Devpt Corp 1957-61, acting chief architect and planning offr Basingstoke Devpt Corp 1962-64; dir Colin Buchanan and Ptnrs 1964-89, dir Development Management Group Paris 1989-90, design conslt 1991-; RIBA, FRTIP; *Recreations* riding, target shooting, cycling; *Style—* William C Thomson, Esq; 19 rue des Reservoirs, 78000 Versailles, France (☎ 1 3953 4972)

THOMSON, Dr William Oliver; s of Capt William Crosbie Thomson (d 1955), of Glasgow, and Mary Jolie, *née* Johnstone (d 1953); *b* 23 March 1925; *Educ* Allan Glen's Sch Glasgow, Univ of Glasgow (MB ChB, MD, DPH, DPA); *m* 5 April 1956, Isobel Lauder Glendinning, da of Capt John Glendinning Brady (d 1942), of Montreal and Glasgow; 2 s (John b 2 Sept 1957, David b 18 Jan 1960); *Career* Capt RAMC 1948-50; public health 1953-60, appts in admin med 1960-73, chief admin med offr Lanarkshire Health Bd 1973-88; involved in: recording for blind, cancer res; Dip Worshipful Soc of Apothecaries, hon Dip Scottish Cncl for Health Educn Edinburgh 1979; FRCP, FFPH; *Recreations* keeping busy; *Style—* Dr William O Thomson; 7 Silverwells Court, Bothwell G71 8LT

THOMSON GLOVER, Lady Sarah Jane; *née* Craven; da of 6 Earl of Craven (d 1965), and his 1 w, Irene Meyrick (who m 2, 1961, late Sir Andrew MacTaggart); *b* 9 Jan 1940; *m* 1961, David John Traill Thomson Glover; 2 da; *Style—* The Lady Sarah Thomson Glover; La Gratitude, 6 de Villiers Street, Somerset West, 7130, Cape Province, South Africa

THOMSON OF FLEET, 2 Baron (UK 1964), of Northbridge in the City of Edinburgh; Kenneth Roy Thomson; s of 1 Baron Thomson of Fleet, GBE (d 1976), fndr of the Thomson newspapers; *b* 1 Sept 1923; *Educ* Upper Canada Coll Toronto, Cambridge Univ (MA); *m* 1956, Nora Marilyn, da of Albert Vernard Lavis, of Toronto; 2 s, 1 da; *Heir* s, Hon David Kenneth Roy Thomson; *Career* serv WWII RCAF; began in editorial dept Timmins Daily Press 1947, newspaper proprietor, chm: Int Thomson Orgn Ltd 1978-, Thomson Orgn 1976-78, co-pres Times Newspapers Ltd 1971-81, chm and dir Thomson Newspapers Ltd (owners of 38 daily newspapers in Canada), chm Thomson Newspapers Inc (owners of 82 newspapers in the US), dir Toronto Dominion Bank, Scottish and York Ltd, Abitibi Price Inc, Hudson's Bay Co, Simpsons Ltd; vice pres and dir: Cablevue (Quinte) Ltd, Veribest Products Ltd; pres and dir of many other newspapers and communications companies; *Recreations* collecting paintings and works of art, walking; *Clubs* York (Toronto), National Hunt, Granite (Toronto), York Downs; *Style—* The Rt Hon the Lord Thomson of Fleet; 8 Kensington Palace Gdns, London W8; 8 Castle Frank Rd, Toronto, Ontario M4W 2Z4, Canada; offices: Thomson Newspapers Ltd, 65 Queen Street West, Toronto Ontario M5H 2M8, Canada; Thomson Corp plc, 1st Floor, The Quadrangle, PO Box 4YG, 180 Wardour St, London W1A 4YG

THOMSON OF MONIFIETH, Baron (Life Peer UK 1977), of Monifieth in the District of the City of Dundee; George Morgan Thomson; KT (1981), PC (1966); s of late James Thomson, of Monifieth, Angus; *b* 16 Jan 1921; *Educ* Grove Acad Dundee; *m* 1948, Grace, da of Cunningham Jenkins, of Glasgow; 2 da (Hon Caroline Agnes Morgan (Hon Mrs Liddle) b 1954, Hon Ailsa Ballantine (Hon Mrs Newby) b 1956); *Career* on staff of Dandy rising to chief sub-ed 1930s; asst ed then ed Forward 1946-53; MP (L) Dundee East 1952-72, min of State FO 1964-66, chllr of Duchy of Lancaster 1966-67 and 1969-70, joint min of State FO 1967, sec of State for Cwlth Affrs 1967-68, min without portfolio 1968-69, shadow def min 1970-72; EEC cmmnr 1973-77; chm: Euro Movement in Br 1977-80, Advertising Standards Authy 1977-80; dir: Royal Bank of Scotland Group 1982-90, ICI plc 1977-90, Woolwich Equitable Building Soc 1979-91; First Crown Estate cmmnr 1978-80, chm IBA 1981-88, vice-pres Royal TV Soc 1982-, chllr Heriot Watt Univ 1977-; Hon LLD Dundee 1967, Hon DLitt Heriot-Watt 1973, Hon DSc Aston 1976, Hon DLitt New Univ of Ulster 1984; tstee: Pilgrim Trust, Thomson Fndn, Leeds Castle Fndn; *Clubs* Brooks's; *Style—* The Rt Hon the Lord Thomson of Monifieth, KT, PC; 9 Cavendish Place, London W1M 9DL (☎ 071 636 6667)

THORBEK, Erik; s of Kai Birch (d 1988), and Dr Agro Grete Thorbek; *b* 10 Jan 1941; *Educ* Billum Coll Denmark; *m* 6 April 1963, Susan Margaret, da of Sidney Gair (d 1977); 2 s (Alexander b 1964, Nikolas b 1973), 2 da (Francesca b 1966, Natasha b 1975); *Career* chm and chief exec 1977- H & T Walker Group of Companies (dir 1964-72, md 1972-77); *Recreations* golf, skiing, horse racing, shooting, sailing, travel; *Clubs* Turf, Helford River Sailing, Nevill Golf; *Style—* Erik Thorbek, Esq; Maynards, Matfield, Kent TN12 7DU (☎ 0892 72 3966); Walker House, London Rd, Riverhead, Sevenoaks, Kent TN13 2DN (☎ 0732 450712, fax 0732 459288)

THORBURN, Andrew; s of James Beresford Thorburn (d 1972), and Marjorie Clara Thorburn (d 1987); *b* 20 March 1934; *Educ* Univ of Southampton (BSc); *m* 1957, Margaret Anne, da of Reginald Crack (d 1964); 1 s (Edward), 2 da (Jenny, Anna); *Career* county planning offr of E Sussex 1973-83, chief exec English Tourist Bd 1983-85, chm Grant Thornton 1990- (head of tourism and leisure 1986-90); dir Sussex Heritage Tst, pres Royal Town Planning Inst 1982; *Books* Planning Villages (1971); *Recreations* sailing; *Style—* Andrew Thorburn, Esq; Hyde Manor, Kingston, Lewes, E Sussex BN7 3PB (☎ 0273 476019)

THORBURN, Eric Walter Andrew; s of Walter Thorburn (d 1987), of Giffnock, Glasgow, and Catherine Graham, *née* Wales (d 1988); *b* 7 Feb 1940; *Educ* Leeds GS, Allan Glens Sch Glasgow, Royal Coll of Sci and Technol Glasgow (DA); *m* 2 March 1966, Elizabeth Anne, da of Robert Paton Brown (d 1975), of Mansewood, Glasgow; 1 s (Alan Graham Robert b 1969), 1 da (Rhona Elizabeth b 1967); *Career* chartered architect; Eric Thorburn Assoc 1986-; sr ptnr Thorburn Twigg Brown & Ptnrs 1980-86; assoc Ian Burke Assoc 1979; princ bldgs: Mitchel House Glasgow, Extension to King's Theatre Glasgow, Shopping Centre Polmont; RIBA 1967; ARIAS, FFB; *Recreations* swimming, curling; *Style—* Eric Thorburn, Esq; 5 Wellesley Crescent, Hairmyres, E Kilbride G75 8TS (☎ 03552 32833); 5 Claremont Terrace, Glasgow G3

7XR (☎ 041 333 9250)

THORBURN, Paul Huw; s of Geoffrey George Thorburn, and Pauline Hughes, *née* Jenkins; *b* 24 Nov 1962; *Educ* Hereford Cathedral Sch, Univ Coll Swansea; *m* 5 Oct 1987, Sharon Elizabeth Ann, da of Thomas Conlin; 1 da (Kelly Elizabeth Ann b 17 March 1990); *Career* Rugby Union full back Neath RFC and Wales (34 caps); clubs: Ebbw Vale RFC, Neath RFC 1984- (186 appearances), Welsh Universities, UAU RFC, capped Wales B 1984; Wales: debut v France 1985, scored record 52 points Five Nations Championship 1986, Triple Crown winners 1988, capt 4 times, third place World Cup 1987, kicked 70 yard penalty v Scotland (longest in int match) 1986; *Recreations* waterskiing, squash, golf; *Style—* Paul Thorburn, Esq; 15 Heol-Y-Waun, Pontlliw, Swansea; Neath RFC, Gnoll Park Road, Neath, West Glamorgan (☎ 0639 636547)

THORBURN, Eur Ing Prof Samuel; OBE (1987); s of Samuel Thorburn, MBE (d 1984), of Strathclyde, and Isabella Thorburn (d 1983); *b* 15 Oct 1930; *Educ* Hamilton Acad, Royal Technical Coll (now Univ of Strathclyde); *m* 1953, Margaret Elizabeth May; 1 s (David John b 1958), 1 da (Lynne Margaret b 1967); *Career* trainee M Mackenzie Limited 1947-51, design and construction engr Colvilles Limited 1951-58, chief engr Whatlings Foundations Ltd 1958-61; engrg dir: Caledonian Foundations Limited 1961-64, GKN Foundations Limited 1964-66; dir: Thorburn Associates 1966-90 (fndr 1966), Thorburn PLC 1990-; visiting prof Univ of Strathclyde; memb: ICE Engrg Ctee, ICE Ground Engrg Bd, Euro Community Advsy Panel, Working Gp on EC Liaison, Tech Ctee on Penetration Testing Int Soc of Soil Mechanics and Fndn Engrg; memb: Assoc of Consltg Engrs, American Concrete Inst, German Soc for Soil Mechanics and Fndn Engrg; conslt Dept of Energy, advsr Br design and construction of bridge fndns; former memb Tech Advsy Ctee: BSI, CIRIA, Science and Res Cncl, DOE, Dept of Energy; former chm of Tech Ctee: IStructE, ICE; Oscar Faber award IStructE 1970, Eur Ing; Freeman of the City of Glasgow; FICE 1967, FIStructE 1970, FASCE 1971, FEng 1985; *Books* Underpinning (1985), author of numerous papers and contribs to publications on engrg; *Recreations* offshore cruising, golf, painting, public speaking; *Clubs* Reform, Royal Scottish Automobile; *Style—* Eur Ing Prof Sam Thorburn, OBE; 32 Lochbroom Drive, Newton Mearns, Eastwood, Strathclyde, Scotland O77 5PF (☎ 041 639 2724); Thorburn Plc, Kinneil House, 243 West George St, Glasgow G2 4QE (☎ 041 226 3611, fax 041 248 3773)

THORLEY, Simon Joe; QC (1989); s of Sir Gerald Thorley, TD (d 1988), and Beryl Preston, *née* Rhodes; *b* 22 May 1950; *Educ* Rugby, Keble Coll Oxford (MA); *m* 7 May 1983, Jane Elizabeth, da of Frank Cockcroft, of Saltburn by Sea, Cleveland; 2 s (Matthew b 1984, Nicholas b 1985), 1 da (Francesca b 1988); *Career* called to the Bar Inner Temple 1972- (specialising in patent matters); church warden of St Margaret's Wicken Bonhunt; *Books* Terrell on Patents (jt ed, 13 edn); *Recreations* family, shooting, walking; *Style—* Simon Thorley, Esq, QC; 6 Pump Ct, Temple, London EC4Y 7AR (☎ 071 353 8588, fax 071 583 1516)

THORN, Jeremy Gordon; s of James Douglas Thorn, of Appleton, nr Warrington, Cheshire, and Daphne Elizabeth, *née* Robinson; *b* 23 March 1948; *Educ* Mill Hill, Univ of Leeds (BSc), European Coll of Marketing (Dip), Cranfield Sch of Mgmnt; *m* 24 July 1971, Eilis Anne, da of Christopher Maurice Coffey, of Street, Somerset; 4 da (Jessica b 1977, Rachel b 1982, Alicen b 1984, Stephanie b 1987); *Career* former fencing team capt: Univ of Leeds, Warwickshire, W Midlands, Yorkshire; former Warwickshire épée and sabre champion and W Midlands and Yorkshire sabre champion; dir sales and mktg: Baugh & Weedon Ltd 1978-81, Bradley & Foster Ltd 1981-83, Spear & Jackson Ltd 1984-86; chm Bristol Wire Rope Ltd 1988-, md Bridon Ropes Ltd 1989- (dir int mktg and distribution 1986-89); dir and dep chm Barnsley/Doncaster Trg and Enterprise Cncl, chm Manpower and Soc Affrs Ctee of Br Ind Steel Prodrs Assoc; former memb W Midlands Sports Cncl, former chm W Midlands region Amateur Fencing Assoc; chm Fedn of Wire Rope Manufacturers of GB, UK spokesman Euro Wire Rope Info Serv; CEng, MIM, FBIM; *Books* How to Negotiate Better Deals (1989), The First Time Sales Manager (1990); *Recreations* music, sport; *Style—* Jeremy Thorn, Esq; Bridon Ropes Ltd, Carr Hill, Doncaster, S Yorks DN9 8DG (☎ 0302 382498, fax 0302 382578, telex 547981)

THORN, John Leonard; s of Stanley Leonard Thorn (d 1951), and Winifred Thorn; *b* 28 April 1925; *Educ* St Paul's, CCC Cambridge; *m* 1955, Veronica Laura, da of Sir Robert Maconochie, OBE, QC (d 1962); 1 s, 1 da; *Career* schoolmaster; asst master Clifton Coll 1949-61; headmaster: Repton Sch 1961-68, Winchester Coll 1968-85; dir Royal Opera House Covent Garden 1972-78, tstee Br Museum 1980-85; dir Winchester Cathedral Tst 1986-88 and 1990-; memb: Bd The Securities Assoc 1987-91, Exec Ctee Cancer Res Campaign 1987-90, Hampshire Bldgs Preservation Tst 1987- (vice-chm 1990-); chm of govrs Abingdon Sch 1991-; *Books* A History of England (jtly, 1961), Road to Winchester (1989), and numerous articles; *Recreations* all the arts; *Clubs* Garrick; *Style—* John Thorn, Esq; 6 Chilbolton Avenue, Winchester SO22 5HD (☎ 0962 855990)

THORN, Roger Eric; QC (1990); s of James Douglas (Pat) Thorn, of Appleton, Cheshire, and Daphne Elizabeth Thorn; *b* 23 March 1948; *Educ* Mill Hill Sch London, Univ of Newcastle upon Tyne (LLB); *Career* called to the Bar Middle Temple 1970 (Harmsworth scholar and Major exhibitioner); memb NE Circuit; memb Bd Faculty of Law Univ of Newcastle upon Tyne; *Books* A Practical Guide to Road Traffic Accident Claims (1987), Road Traffic Accident Claims (1990), Negotiating Better Deals (legal contrib, 1988); *Recreations* theatre, music, walking, bridge, learning patience; *Clubs* Durham County, Old Millhillians; *Style—* Roger Thorn, Esq, QC

THORN, Gp Capt Timothy Gane (Tim); AFC (1983); s of Jack Gane Thorn (d 1985), of Little Blakenham, nr Ipswich, Suffolk, and Ivy May, *née* Chapli (d 1985); *b* 21 Sept 1942; *Educ* Ipswich Sch, RAF Coll Cranwell; *m* 2 Oct 1971, (Elisabeth) Rosemary, da of Donald Garmon Meredith (d 1969); 1 s (Christopher b 18 Oct 1974), 1 da (Jennifer b 2 Oct 1976); *Career* won minor cos cricket championhip with Suffolk 1960, offr trg RAF Coll 1961-64, PO 1964, played rugby for RAF 1964-66, Flying Offr 1965, played for Blackheath RFC 1965, ejected from aircraft after mid-air collision 1966, Flt Lt 1967, bronze medal at Euro bobsleigh championships 1968, GB rep in bobsleigh at Grenoble Winter Olympics 1968, Sqdn Ldr 1972, landed without parachute from 500 feet at night 1973, Indian Def Servs Staff Coll 1975, Flt Cdr number 41 (F) Sqdn 1976-79, Wing Cdr 1979, Queen's Commendation for Valuable Serv In the Air 1979, CO number II (AC) Sqdn 1980-83, operational requirements MOD 1983-86, Gp Capt 1986, CO RAF Cranwell 1986-88, Gp Capt Flying Trg HQ RAF Support Command; qualified parachutist, qualified mil and civil flying instr; MRAeS 1986; *Clubs* Royal Air Force, Adastrian CC; *Style—* Gp Capt Tim Thorn, AFC; Royal College of Defence Studies, Seaford House, 37 Belgrave Square, London SW1X 8NS (☎ 071 235 1091)

THORNALLEY, Helen Theresa; da of Robert Houseman Thornalley (d 1987), of Skegness, Lincolnshire, and Bride Theresa Slater, *née* McDanial; *b* 10 Sept 1968; *Educ* Skegness Secdy Modern, North Lincs Coll, West London Inst of Higher Educn (BA); *Career* hockey player; Skegness Ladies Club 1981-86, Slough Ladies Club 1989-; Lincs: under 18 1983-86, under 21 1984-88, sr 1984-88; East: under 18 1983-86, under 21 1984-88, sr 1987-89; England: 12 under 18 caps 1983-86, 25 under 21 caps 1984-88 (Silver medal Euro Cup Paris 1988), sr World Cup and Euro Cup training squad 1989-91, indoor squad 1991; 1 cap Home Countries Aberdeen 1990, 6 caps Br Colls Squad 1988-91, 5 caps World Student Games Squad 1990-91; winners Nat League Championship Slough 1990; pt/t receptionist Cafe Royal London; *Recreations* art, music; *Style—* Miss Helen Thornalley; c/o Slough Sports Club, Chalvey Rd East, Slough, Berks (☎ 0753 20982)

THORNBER, Iain; JP (1988), DL (Lochaber, Inverness and Badenoch and Strathspey); s of James Thornber (d 1982), of Morvern, Argyll, and Jeannie Easton Campbell, *née* Stenhouse; *b* 3 Feb 1948; *Educ* Glenhurich Public Sch; *Career* company factor Glensanda Estate Morvern (Foster Yeoman Ltd) 1980; life memb W Highland Museum Fort William; memb: Forestry Cmmn local advsy panel, Morvern Red Deer Mgmnt Gp, Inverness Prison Visiting Ctee, Country Life Museums Tst; rep memb Royal Soc for Nature Conservation Rahoy Hills Nature Res; Lochaber dist cncllr for Ardgour Sunart and Morvern; FSA Scot 1973, FRSA 1987; FSA (London) 1990; *Books* The Castles of Morvern Argyll (1975), The Sculptured Stones of Cill Choluimchille Morvern Argyll (1975), The Gaelic Bards of Morvern (1985), Rats (1989), Bronze Age Cairns in the Aline Valley Morvern Argyll (jt author, Proceedings of the Soc of Antiquaries of Scot vol 106, 1974-75), The Gaelic Bards of Morvern (1985), Cairn 3, Acharn, Morvern, Argyll (jt author, Proceedings of the Society of Antiquaries of Scot vol 118, 1988), Moidart, Or Among the Clanranalds (ed 1989 edn); *Recreations* deer stalking, salmon fishing, photography, local history research; *Style—* Iain Thornber, Esq, JP, DL, FSA; Knock House, Morvern, Oban, Argyll PA34 5UU (☎ 096 784 651); Glensanda Estate, Morvern, Argyll (☎ 063 173 415, fax 063 173 460, telex 777792)

THORNE, Angela Margaret Leslie; da of Lt-Col Dr William Herbert Alfred Thorne, OBE (d 1982), and (Leslie) Sylvia (May) Thorne; *b* 25 Jan 1939; *Educ* Farlington House Horsham Sussex; *m* 22 Sept 1967, Peter David Penry-Jones, s of Rev David Penry-Jones; 2 s (Rupert William b 22 Sept 1970, Laurence David b 18 Aug 1977); *Career* actress; roles incl: Gloria Claudon in You Never Can Tell (Theatre Royal) 1966, Julia in The Rivals (Theatre Royal) 1966, Portia in The Merchant of Venice (Theatre Royal) 1967, Io in Prometheus Bound (Mermaid Theatre) 1971, Vanessa in Yahoo (Queens Theatre) 1976, Mrs Thatcher in Anyone for Dennis (Whitehall Theatre) 1981, Lady Gay Spanker in London Assurance (Theatre Royal) 1989; Betty Smith in the film Oh What a Lovely War 1968, tv roles incl Marjorie Frobisher in To the Manor Born and Daphne in Three Up Two Down; memb: The Actor's Charitable Tst, The Theatrical Ladies Guild; *Style—* Miss Angela Thorne; Michael Whitehall Ltd, 125 Gloucester Rd, London SW7 4TE (☎ 071 244 8466)

THORNE, Lady Anne Patricia; *née* Pery; o da of 5 Earl of Limerick, GBE, CH, KCB, DSO, TD (d 1967), and Angela Olivia, Countess of Limerick, GBE, CH, LLD, *née* Trotter (d 1981); *b* 3 Oct 1928; *Educ* North Foreland Lodge, St Hugh's Coll Oxford (MA, DPhil); *m* 16 May 1959, Sir Peter Francis Thorne, KCVO, CBE, ERD *qv*; 1 s, 3 da; *Career* sr lecturer Imperial Coll of Science and Technology; memb various scientific ctees and editorial bds of scientific journals; memb bd European Gp for Atomic Spectroscopy 1979-85 (chm 1982-85); memb governing bodies of various schs, past and present; *Books* Spectrophysics (second edn 1988), author of about 40 papers published in scientific journals; *Style—* The Lady Anne Thorne; Chiddinglye Farmhouse, West Hoathly, East Grinstead, Sussex RH19 4QS (☎ 0342 810338)

THORNE, Clive (Duncan); s of Desmond Clive Thorne, of Eastbourne, and May, *née* Davey; *b* 21 Jan 1952; *Educ* Eastbourne GS, Trinity Hall Cambridge (BA, MA); *m* 1, 11 Oct 1975 (m dis 1982), Catherine Sykes; m 2, 12 July 1986, Alison Mary Healy, da of Cdr Michael Healy, of Beaulieu Sur Mer, France; *Career* articled clerk Clifford Turner 1975-77, slr England 1977-84, slr Hong Kong 1984-87, barr and slr Victoria Aus 1985, currently ptnr and head of Intellectual Property Gp Denton Hall Burgin and Warrens; various articles Euro Intellectual Property Review and other jls; memb: Cons and U party, Law Soc; *Books* Sony Guide to Home Taping (contrib 1983), Intellectual Property - The New Law (1989); *Recreations* English music, reading, walking, flute playing; *Clubs* United Oxford and Cambridge Univ; *Style—* Clive Thorne, Esq; Five Chancery Lane, Cliffords Inn, London EC4A 1BU (☎ 071 242 1212, fax 071 404 0087)

THORNE, Maj-Gen Sir David Calthrop; KBE (1983, CBE 1979, OBE 1975); s of Richard Everard Thorne (d 1957), and Audrey Ursula, *née* Bone; identical twin bro of Brig Michael Thorne, CBE, *qv*; *b* 13 Dec 1933; *Educ* St Edward's Sch Oxford, RMA Sandhurst; *m* 1962, Suzan Anne, da of Edward Eaton Goldsmith; 1 s, 2 da; *Career* cmmnd Royal Norfolk Regt 1952, cmd 1 Bn Royal Anglian Regt 1972-74, Bde Cdr 3 Infantry Bde NI 1977-79, Maj-Gen 1981, Vice QMG 1981-82, Cdr British Forces Falkland Islands 1982-83, cmd 1 Armd Div 1983-85; Dep Col Royal Anglian Regt 1981-87, dir of Infantry 1986-88, Col Cmdt Queen's Div 1986-88; dir gen Cwlth Tst 1989-; *Recreations* cricket, squash, butterfly collecting; *Clubs* Army and Navy, MCC, I-Zingari, Free Foresters, Jesters; *Style—* Maj-Gen Sir David Thorne, KBE; c/o Barclays Bank, 52 Abbeygate St, Bury St Edmunds, Suffolk IP33 1LL

THORNE, Maj George; MC (1945), ERD, DL (Oxfordshire 1961); 2 s of Gen Sir (Augustus Francis) Andrew Nicol Thorne, KCB, CMG, DSO, DL (d 1970), of Knowl Hill House, nr Reading (*see* Burke's Landed Gentry, 18 edn, vol II, 1969), and Hon Margaret Douglas-Pennant (d 1967), 10 da of 2 Baron Penrhyn; *b* 1 July 1912; *Educ* Eton, Trinity Coll Oxford; *m* 18 April 1942, Juliet Agnes, o da of Hon (Arthur) George Villiers Peel, JP, DL (d 1956), 2 s of 1 Viscount Peel, and Lady Agnes Lygon, da of 6 Earl Beauchamp; 2 s (Robert George (Robin) b 7 Feb 1943, Ian David Peel b 14 Oct 1944), 1 da (Viola Georgina Juliet (Mrs Nicholas Halsey) b 20 Sept 1948, *qv*); *Career* Maj late Grenadier Guards (SR), serv WWII, ADC to GOC 1 Div (Maj-Gen Hon Harold Alexander) 1939-40, OC No 3 Co 1 Bn Gren Gds 1941-45, Capt The King's Co 1 Bn Gren Gds 1945 (despatches); memb sales staff McVitie & Price Ltd 1934-39 and 1946-67; farmer 1950-; memb: Royal Br Legion (Peppard), Dunkirk Veterans Assoc (Henley); *Recreations* shooting, sailing, cricket; *Clubs* Farmers'; *Style—* Maj George Thorne, MC, ERD, DL; Blounts Farm, Sonning Common, Reading, Berks (☎ 0734 723191)

THORNE, Ian David Peel; s of Maj George Thorne, MC, ERD, DL, *qv*; *b* 14 Oct 1944; *Educ* Eton, RMA Sandhurst, Trinity Coll Oxford (MA); *Career* served in Grenadier Gds 1965-73 (ret as Capt); country landowner 1974-; chm Promise (Film) Production Co; pres Newark and Notts Agric Soc 1989-90, vice pres Notts Assoc of Boys' and Keystone Clubs, former chm of various ctees; High Sheriff of Notts 1986-87; *Publications* Purple Patches; *Recreations* shooting, travel; *Clubs* Boodle's, I Zingari; *Style—* I D P Thorne, Esq

THORNE, Matthew Wadman John; s of Robin Horton John Thorne, CMG, OBE, of the Old Vicarage, Old Heathfield, E Sussex, and Joan Helen, *née* Wadman; *b* 27 June 1952; *Educ* Dragon Sch, King's Sch Canterbury, Trinity Coll Oxford (MA); *m* 1978, Sheila Leigh, da of Col Hon Robert George Hugh Phillimore, OBE (d 1984), 3 s of 2 Baron Phillimore, MC, DL; 3 s (Robin b 15 Feb 1983, Andrew b 27 Feb 1986, Edward b 16 July 1989), 1 da (Aelene b 17 June 1981); *Career* Price Waterhouse 1975-78, County Natwest 1978-83, Beazer plc 1983-91; FCA 1978; *Style—* Matthew Thorne, Esq; The Mount, Bannerdown Rd, Batheaston, Bath, Avon

THORNE, Dr Napier Arnold; s of Arnold Thorne (d 1959), of Kenilworth, Cape Town, SA, and Wilhelmina Rosa, *née* Ayson (d 1970); *b* 26 Dec 1920; *Educ* Eastbourne Coll, Univ of London, Barts Hosp (MB BS, MD); *m* 16 May 1953, Pamela Joan, da of Robert Thomas Frederick Houchin, of Turves, Ruckinge, Kent; 1 s (Robert Napier b 1959), 3 da (Susan b 1954, Jane b 1957, Katherine b 1959); *Career* conslt dermatologist: Prince of Wales Hosp 1955-85, London Hosp 1968-81; hon conslt dermatologist: Italian Hosp London 1969-89, Hosp of St John and St Elizabeth 1976-; sen Univ of London 1970-80, pres Inst of Trichologists 1972-, tstee and chm Philological Fndn 1982-; Freeman City of London; Liveryman: Worshipful Co of Farriers 1965, Worshipful Co of Apothecaries 1978; MRCS 1945, LRCP 1945, memb BMA 1945, fell Hunterian Soc 1947, MRCP 1949, FRSM 1949, fell Med Soc of London 1961, FRCP 1972, FRSA 1983; *Recreations* gardening, music, sailing, travelling; *Clubs* RSM; *Style—* Dr Napier Thorne; 106 Orchard Rd, Tewin, Herts AL6 0LZ (☎ 043 879 294); 96 Harley St, London W1N 1AF (☎ 071 935 4811, car 0860 335 729)

THORNE, Neil Gordon; OBE (1980), TD (1969), MP (C), Ilford South 1979-; s of Henry Frederick Thorne (d 1964); *b* 8 Aug 1932; *Educ* City of London Sch, Univ of London; *Career* TA 1952-82, Lt-Col RA; chartered surveyor 1961-, sr ptnr Hull & Co 1962-76; Borough of Redbridge: cnclIr 1965-68, alderman 1975-78; memb GLC and chm Central Area Bd 1967-73, Silver Jubilee Medal 1977; CO London Univ OTC 1976-80; chm: Nat Cncl of Civil Def 1982-86, St Edward's Housing Assoc 1985-, Armed Forces Parly Scheme 1987-; memb Ct of Referees 1987-; OStJ (1988); *Recreations* riding, walking, tennis; *Clubs* Carlton; *Style—* Neil Thorne, Esq, OBE, TD, MP; 60 Gyllyngdune Gardens, Seven Kings, Ilford, Essex IG3 9HY (☎ 081 590 3262)

THORNE, Sir Peter Francis; KCVO (1981), CBE (1966), ERD; s of Gen Sir (Augustus Francis) Andrew Nicol Thorne, KCB, CMG, DSO (d 1970); *b* 6 Aug 1914; *Educ* Eton, Trinity Coll Oxford; *m* 16 May 1959, Lady Anne Patricia Pery, *qv*, da of 5 Earl of Limerick, GBE, CH, KCB, DSO; 1 s, 3 da; *Career* Hon Lt-Col Grenadier Guards 1945 (serv WWII France and SE Asia); with ICI Ltd 1946-48; asst serjeant at arms House of Commons 1948-57, dep serjeant at arms 1957-76, serjeant at arms 1976-82; *Publications* The Royal Mace in the House of Commons (1990); *Clubs* Cavalry and Guards', Royal Yacht Sqdn; *Style—* Sir Peter Thorne, KCVO, CBE, ERD; Chiddinglye Farmhouse, West Hoathly, East Grinstead, Sussex RH19 4QS (☎ 0342 810338)

THORNE, Peter Geoffrey; s of Ernest Geoffrey Thorne (d 1976), of Duncliffe, Saunton, N Devon, and Edwina Mary, *née* Wilkinson; *b* 2 June 1948; *Educ* Clifton, (slrs finals, Sir George Fowler prize for Best Qualifier from Devon); *m* Jane Frances, da of John David Henson, MC, OBE; 1 s (Benjamin David Geoffrey b 11 July 1981), 1 da (Lucy Frances Alice b 18 Jan 1984); *Career* articles Messrs Sargent & Probert Slrs of Exeter 1965-70, qualified slr 1971; Norton Rose (then Norton Rose Botterell & Roche) 1971-: specialist in asset (particularly ship and aircraft) fin, ptnr 1977, Hong Kong office 1981-83; memb: City of London Slrs Co, Law Soc, Int Bar Assoc; ARAeS; *Recreations* flying, fishing, philately, skiing; *Style—* Peter Thorne, Esq; Norton Rose, Kempson House, Camomile St, London EC3A 7AN (☎ 071 283 2434, fax 071 588 1181)

THORNE, Robert George; s of Maj George Thorne, MC, DL; *b* 7 Feb 1943; *Educ* Eton, RAC Cirencester; *Career* local dir Barclays Bank Ltd: Bristol 1973-76, Newcastle upon Tyne 1977-80, London Northern 1980-83, Pall Mall 1983-; *Recreations* country pursuits; *Clubs* Brooks's; *Style—* Robert Thorne, Esq; Blounts Farm, Sonning Common, Reading, Berks

THORNE, Robin Horton John; CMG (1966), OBE (1963); s of Sir John Anderson Thorne, KCIE, CSI (d 1964), of Sherrald, Sedlescombe, E Sussex, and Lady Dorothy Thorne, *née* Horton (d 1944); *b* 13 July 1917; *Educ* Dragon Sch Oxford, Rugby, Exeter Coll Oxford (MA); *m* 18 May 1946, Joan Helen, da of Edwin Trangmar Wadman, OBE, JP (d 1972), of Priesthawes, Polegate, E Sussex; 1 s (Matthew b 27 June 1952); *Career* WWII, Devonshire Regt and Kings African Rifles; served: E Africa, Abyssinia, Madagascar, ME, Burma; Capt 1939-46; Colonial Admin Serv and HM Overseas Serv 1946-67: Tanganyika 1946-58, Aden 1958-67, asst chief sec (Colony) MLC and memb Govrs Exec Cncl 1959-63, ministerial sec to Chief Min 1963-65, asst high cmmr 1966-67; tstee Aden Port Tst 1959-66, memb Ctee Vice Chllrs and Princs UK Univs (CVCP) 1967-77 (asst sec 1968-77), pt/t admin vice chllrs office Univ of Sussex 1978-81; chm Staines Tst 1979-86 (tstee 1976-86), memb Mgmnt Ctee Sussex Housing Assoc for Aged 1983-88; *Recreations* travel, ornithology, gardening, books; *Clubs* Royal Cwlth Soc; *Style—* Robin Thorne, Esq, CMG, OBE; The Old Vicarage, Old Heathfield, Heathfield, E Sussex TN21 9AD (☎ 04352 3160)

THORNE, Rosemary Prudence; da of Arnold Rex Bishop, of Clevedon, Avon, and Brenda Prudence, *née* Withers; *b* 12 Feb 1952; *Educ* Univ of Warwick (BSc); *m* 10 Jan 1976 (m dis 1984), Peter Humphrey Thorne; *Career* accountant BOC Limited 1974-77, chief accountant Mothercare plc 1977-82, chief accountant then gp fin controller Habitat Mothercare plc 1982-85, gp fin controller Storehouse plc Jan-Sept 1986, fin and dir co sec House of Fraser plc (Harrods Ltd) 1986-90, gp fin conroller Grand Metropolitan Finance plc 1990-; dir: Watney Mann & Truman Holdings plc 1990-, Grand Metropolitan plc 1990-; memb Cncl CIMA, FCMA 1984, MCT 1986; *Style—* Mrs Rosemary Rhorne; Grand Metropolitan plc, 11-12 Hanover Square, London W1A 1DP (☎ 071 629 7488/2804, fax 071 495 0786, telex 299606, car 0836 376523)

THORNELY, (Gervase) Michael Cobham; s of Maj John Thornely, OBE, and Hon Muriel (granted rank of Baron's da 1917, although her f did not survive to enjoy the Barony of Cobham called out of abeyance in 1916), *née* Alexander, yr sis of 12 and 13 (or 15 and 16 but for attainder) Barons Cobham; in remainder to abeyant Barony through his mother (who became a coheiress after the death of the 13 (or 16) Baron in 1951); *b* 21 Oct 1918; *Educ* Rugby, Trinity Hall Cambridge (MA); *m* 1954, Jennifer, da of Sir (Charles) Hilary Scott (solicitor and former pres Law Soc), of Knowle House, Addington, Surrey; 2 s (Richard b 1957, Charles b 1958), 2 da (Elizabeth b 1960, Jacqueline b 1965); *Career* headmaster Sedbergh Sch 1954-75 (asst master 1940-54); FRSA; *Recreations* music, fishing; *Style—* Michael Thornely, Esq; High Stangerthwaite, Killington, Sedbergh, Cumbria (☎ 05396 20444)

THORNELY TAYLOR, Edward John; s of John Thornely Taylor, JP (d 1960); *b* 27 May 1924; *Educ* Uppingham; *Career* landowner; Lord of The Manor: Scaftworth (Notts), Hoylandswaine, Thurnscoe and Oxspring (Yorks); High Sheriff S Yorks 1975-76; *Recreations* shooting, cricket; *Clubs* MCC, Farmers'; *Style—* Edward Thornely Taylor, Esq; Scaftworth Hall, nr Doncaster DN10 6BL (☎ 0302 710323)

THORNEYCROFT, Hon John Hamo; s of Baron Thorneycroft, CH, PC (Life Peer), and his 1 w Sheila Wells Page; *b* 24 March 1940; *Educ* Eton, Cambridge, Univ of Wales Inst of Science and Technology (DipArch); *m* 1971, Delia, da of Arthur William Lloyd (d 1977), of Penallt, Monmouth; 1 s (Richard b 1977), 1 da (Eleanor b 1974); *Career* principal architect; Dept of Ancient Monuments and Historic Buildings (English Heritage); memb Order of Orange-Nassau 1982; *Style—* The Hon John Thorneycroft; 21 St Peters St, Islington, London N1 8JD (☎ 071 226 0578)

THORNEYCROFT, John Patrick; s of Gerald Hamo Thorneycroft (d 1967), of Park House, Codsall Wood, Staffs, and Kathleen Mary, *née* Wilson (d 1985); *b* 9 Dec 1939; *Educ* Wellington, Pembroke Coll Cambridge (MA); *m* 16 Oct 1965, Rev Philippa Hazel Jeanetta (Pippa), da of Philip Fitzgerald Mander (d 1972), of The Folley Stableford, nr Bridgnorth, Shropshire; 2 s (Hugh b 1967, Martin b 1977), 2 da (Veryan b 1971, Naomi b 1975); *Career* sr ptnr in legal ptnrship, Lichfield diocesan registrar, legal sec to Bishop of Lichfield; *Recreations* tennis, squash, walking; *Style—* John Thorneycroft, Esq; Kemberton Hall, nr Shifnal, Shropshire (☎ 0952 580 588); Manby & Steward, 9th Floor, Mander House, Wolverhampton, West Midlands (☎ 0902 772711, fax 0902 24321, car 0836 69563)

THORNEYCROFT, Dr Malcolm; s of Alec Charles Thorneycroft (d 1974); *b* 7 June 1936; *Educ* Wellingborough GS, Univ of Nottingham; *m* 1960, Margaret Rose, *née* Fisher; 1 s, 2 da; *Career* chartered electrical engr, engrg dir TI Churchill Ltd 1976-85, TI Machine Tools Ltd 1985-87, Matrix Churchill Ltd 1987-; *Recreations* swimming, walking; *Clubs* 41 Club, Coventry; *Style—* Dr Malcolm Thorneycroft; 1 Riverford Croft, Kenilworth Grange, Coventry

THORNEYCROFT, Baron (Life Peer 1967), of Dunston, Co Stafford; (George Edward) Peter Thorneycroft; CH (1979), PC (1951); s of late George Thorneycroft, DSO, of Dunston Hall, Staffs; *b* 26 July 1909; *Educ* Eton, RMA Woolwich; *m* 1, 1938 (m dis 1949), Sheila Wells, da of E W Page, of Tettenhall; 1 s; m 2, 1949, Countess Carla Roberti, da of late Count Malagola Cappi, of Ravenna, Italy; 1 da; *Career* RA 1930, resigned cmmn 1933; barr Inner Temple 1935; MP (C): Stafford 1938-45, Monmouth 1945-66; Parly sec Miny of War Tport 1945, pres BOT 1951-57, chllr of the Exchequer 1957-58, resigned, min of Aviation 1960-62, min of Def 1962-64; chm Cons Pty 1975-81; chm: Pirelli General Cable Works Ltd, Pirelli Ltd 1970-87 (pres 1987-), Pirelli UK plc 1987-89, Trusthouse Forte Ltd 1970-82 (pres 1982-), British Insurance Co Ltd 1980-87, Cinzano (UK) Ltd 1982-85; memb Royal Soc of Br Artists 1978; Order of the Sacred Treasure (1 Class, Japan) 1983; *Recreations* painting; *Clubs* Army and Navy; *Style—* The Rt Hon the Lord Thorneycroft, CH, PC; 42c Eaton Square, London SW1; House of Lords, London SW1 (☎ 081 748 5843)

THORNHILL, Andrew Robert; QC (1985); s of Edward Percy Thornhill, of Bristol, and Amelia Joy Thornhill; *b* 4 Aug 1943; *Educ* Clifton, CCC Oxford; *m* 5 Aug 1971, Helen Mary, da of George William Livingston, of Gainsborough; 2 s (George Percy b 1 Dec 1973, Henry Robert b 26 May 1977), 2 da (Emily Mary b 12 June 1972, Eleanor Clare b 19 June 1980); *Career* called to the Bar Middle Temple 1969, joined chambers of H H Monroe 1969; *Recreations* sailing, walking, education; *Clubs* Oxford and Cambridge, Tamesis, Chew Valley Lake Sailing; *Style—* Andrew Thornhill, Esq, QC; 37 Canynge Rd, Clifton, Bristol; St Agnes, Cranshaws, by Duns, E Lothian; 4 Pump Ct, Temple, London EC4 (☎ 071 583 9770)

THORNHILL, Lt-Col (Edmund) Basil; MC (1918), DL (Cambs and Isle of Ely 1957-); s of Edmund Henry Thornhill (d 1936), of Manor House, Boxworth, Cambs, and Violet Nina, *née* Campbell (d 1922); *b* 27 Feb 1898; *Educ* St Bee's Cumberland, RMA Woolwich; *m* 1934, Diana Pearl Day, *née* Beales (d 1983), da of Hubert Day Beales (d 1950), of St Margaret's Rd, Cambridge; 2 s, 1 da; *Career* Lt RA (France, Belgium) 1917-18, WWII Lt-Col 1939-45 (France, Western Desert, Italy), ret; dep cmdt then cmdt Cambs and Isle of Ely Army Cadet Force 1948-55, chm Cambridge and Isle of Ely Territorial Assoc 1957-62, Vice Lord-Lt Cambs and Isle of Ely 1965-75; *Clubs* Army and Navy; *Style—* Lt-Col Basil Thornhill, MC, DL; Manor House, Boxworth, Cambridge CB3 8NF (☎ 095 47 209)

THORNHILL, (George Edmund) Peter; s of Lt-Col Edmund Basil Thornhill, MC, of Manor House, Boxworth, Cambs, and Diana Pearl Day, *née* Beales (d 1983); descendant in unbroken male line of the family of Thornhill of Thornhill, Yorkshire (landowners); *b* 13 April 1935; *Educ* Eton, Trinity Coll Cambridge (MA); *m* 12 Sept 1959, Margaret Daughne, o da of Cdr William Geoffrey Barnard Hartley (d 1983), of Houghton Hill House, Huntingdon; 1 s (Edmund George William b 1969), 3 da (Vanessa (Mrs John Fairhead) b 1960, Claire (Mrs Christopher Hill) b 1962, Harriet b 1965); *Career* Nat Serv 1953-55, 2 Lt RA; landowner; former ptnr Smith-Woolley and Co chartered surveyors and chartered land agents, resigned 1975, dir Thornhill Yorkshire Estates Co, chm Huntingdon/Peterborough Branch CLA 1983-85 (vice chm Nottinghamshire Branch 1990-); FRICS, formerly FLAS; *Recreations* shooting; *Clubs* Farmers, Cambridge County, Eton Vikings; *Style—* Peter Thornhill, Esq; The Grove, Winthorpe, Newark, Notts NG24 2NR (☎ 0636 703577, fax 0636 640609); Estate Office, The Gardens, Diddington, Huntingdon, Cambs PE18 9XU (☎ 0480 810240)

THORNHILL, Richard John; s of Richard Norwood Thornhill, and Eleanor Louise, *née* Hoey; *b* 13 Nov 1954; *Educ* Malvern, St John's Coll Oxford (MA); *m* 30 Aug 1980, Nicola, da of Peter John Dyke, of Cumbria; 1 s (Hugo b 1989); *Career* Slaughter & May: articled clerk 1977-79, admitted slr 1979, ptnr 1986- (admitted Hong Kong Supreme Court 1982 and practised Hong Kong office 1982-84); memb Law Soc; *Recreations* walking, water skiing, theatre, opera; *Style—* Richard Thornhill, Esq; 36 Chipstead St, London SW6 (☎ 071 736 4091); 35 Basinghall St, London EC2V 5DB (☎ 071 600 1200, fax 071 726 0028)

THORNING-PETERSEN, Rudolph Anton; s of Erik Thorning-Petersen (d 1946), and Helga, *née* Westergaard (d 1978); *b* 17 July 1927; *Educ* Univ of Copenhagen (Masters Degree); *m* 30 June 1949, Britta, da of Pierre Leyssac (d 1946); 1 s (Erik b 1953), 1 da (Eva b 1956); *Career* joined Danish Min of Foreign Affrs 1952; ambass: Beirut, Baghdad, Amman, Damascus, Nicosia 1975-80, Peking 1980-83, Moscow 1983-89, London 1989-; Cdr Order of the Dannebrog Denmark 1981; *Style—* His Excellency the Ambassador of Denmark; Royal Danish Embassy, 55 Sloane St, London SW1X 9SR (☎ 071 333 0200, telex 28103, fax 071 333 0270)

THORNTON, Adrian Heber; s of Nigel Heber Thornton, Croix de Guerre (d 1941), and Margaret Marion Gwendolen, *née* Gault; *b* 17 Sept 1937; *Educ* Eton, Pembroke Coll Camb (MA), INSEAD (MBA); *m* 8 Feb 1972, Margaret Barbara, da of Cyril Arthur Wales (d 1983); 1 s (Jasper b 1975), 2 da (Emily b 1973, Rebecca b 1979); *Career* 2 Lt Green Jackets Cyprus 1956-58; md: Gallic Management Ltd, Gallic Shipping Ltd; *Clubs* City of London; *Style—* Adrian Thornton, Esq; 31 Cheyne Row, London SW3 5HW (☎ 071 352 6290); Gallic Shipping Ltd, Bell Court House, 11 Blomfield St, London EC2M 7AY (☎ 071 628 4851, fax 071 374 0408, telex 913062 GALLIC G)

THORNTON, Allan Charles; s of Robert Charles Thornton, and Jessie, *née* Waldram (d 1966); *b* 17 Nov 1949; *Educ* Banff School of Arts Canada; *Career* co-ordinator creative writing programme Banff Sch of Arts 1975-76, co-fndr Greenpeace UK and Rainbow Warrior 1976-78, exec dir Greenpeace UK 1978-81 and 1986-88, chm Environmental Investigation Agency 1988- (fndr and exec dir 1984-86); dir: Greenpeace Ltd UK, Greenpeace Charitable Fndn Canada; *Books* To Save the Elephants (1990); *Recreations* wildlife safaris in Tanzania and saving wildlife generally; *Style—* Allan Thornton, Esq; Environmental Investigation Agency Ltd, 208-209 Upper St, London N1 1RL (☎ 071 704 9441, fax 071 226 2888)

THORNTON, Anthony Christopher Lawrence; QC (1988); s of Maj Richard Thornton (d 1983), and Margery Alice Clerk, CBE; *b* 18 Aug 1947; *Educ* Eton, Keble Coll Oxford (MA, BCL); *m* 18 Feb 1983, Lyn Christine, da of Lawrence Thurlby, of 39 Halifax Rd, Cambridge; 1 s (Matthew James b 12 June 1983); *Career* called to the Bar Middle Temple 1970; in practice 1970, asst recorder 1988, QC 1988, memb Gen Cncl of the Bar 1988 (treas 1990-91); Freeman: City of London 1976, Worshipful Co of Leathersellers 1976; assoc of Inst of Arbitrators 1987; *Books* Halsbury's Laws - Volume 4: Building Contracts (jt ed and contrib, 1972), Construction Law Review (jt ed), Burns - The Expert Witness (contrib, 1989); *Recreations* family, opera, cricket;

Clubs RAC; *Style—* Anthony Thornton, Esq, QC; 1 Cannons Field, Marston, Oxford OX3 0QR (☎ 0865 725038); 1 Atkin Building, Gray's Inn, London WC1R 5BQ (☎ 071 404 0102, fax 071 405 7456, telex 298623 HUDSON)

THORNTON, Christopher Cholmondeley; s of Reginald Trelawny Thornton, MBE, MC (d 1968), and Elsie Barbara Anson, *née* Tate (d 1979); *b* 28 Sept 1933; *Educ* St Andrews Sch Pangbourne, Marlborough; *m* 17 June 1961, Jennifer, da of Ernest Charles Goldsworthy (d 1986); 1 s (Philip Charles b 1965), 1 da (Julia Lucy b 1967); *Career* Nat Serv Midshipman HMS Perseus and HMS Excellent RN 1952-54; slr's articled clerk Mackrell Maton & Co 1954-60, admitted slr 1960, Stephenson Harwood Linklaters & Paines 1963-65, mangr Hill Samuel & Co Ltd 1965-68; dir: Rediffusion (West Indies) Ltd 1970-, Rediffusion plc 1984-88 (exec 1968-84), Rediffusion (Hong Kong) Ltd 1985-; chm: Telcommunications Network Ltd 1990-; chm WI Trade Advsy Gp to BOTB 1983-85, vice chm W India Ctee 1985-; cnclr Sevenoaks UDC 1967-70, chm Dartford and Gravesham DHA 1990-; Liveryman City of London Slrs Co 1967; memb Law Soc 1960, fell IOD 1987; *Recreations* fly fishing, tennis, choral singing, gardening; *Clubs* East India; *Style—* Christopher Thornton, Esq; Kettleshill House, Under River, Sevenoaks, Kent TN15 0RX

THORNTON, Clive Edward Ian; CBE (1983); s of Albert Thornton (d 1963), of Newcastle upon Tyne, and Margaret, *née* Coil; *b* 12 Dec 1929; *Educ* St Anthony's Newcastle upon Tyne, Coll of Commerce Newcastle upon Tyne, Univ of London (LLB); *m* 17 March 1956, Maureen Carmine, da of Michael Crane (d 1975), of London; 1 s (Richard b 1963), 1 da (Elizabeth b 1957); *Career* admitted slr 1962, slr to First Nat Fin Corp 1964-67, chief slr Abbey Nat Building Soc 1967-78 (dep chief exec 1978, chief exec and dir 1979-83), ptnr Stoneham Langton and Passmore Solicitors 1985-87; dir: Housing Corp 1980-86, Investment Data Services Ltd 1986-90, Melton Mowbray Building Soc 1988-, Mirror Newspapers 1983-84; chm: Financial Weekly 1983-87, Thamesmead Town Ltd 1986-90, Universe Publications 1986-, Ind Radio Thamesmead Ltd 1989-90, chm Armstrong Capital Hldgs Ltd 1988-, Burgin Hall Ltd 1988-, Thorndale Benedict Ltd 1988-; *Recreations* breeding Devon cattle; *Clubs* City Livery; *Style—* Clive Thornton, Esq, CBE; The Old Rectory, Creeton, Grantham, Lincs (☎ 078 081 401); Northington St, Grays Inn, London WC1N 2JG

THORNTON, Hon Mrs (Diana Cara); da of 3 Baron Fairhaven, JP; *b* 1961; *m* 1983, Guy D Thornton, eld s of B M Thornton, of Stansted House, Stansted, Essex; *Style—* The Hon Mrs Thornton; 40/42 Harcourt Terrace, London SW10

THORNTON, Ian Charles; s of Charles William Thornton (d 1977), and Fay, *née* Eastwood; *b* 23 March 1934; *Educ* Manchester GS, Schs of Architecture/Civic Design Univ of Liverpool (BArch, MCD); *m* 1 Oct 1959, Mary Doreen, da of Robert Thomas Evans (d 1956); 2 da (Jacqueline b 1960, Jennifer b 1962); *Career* asst architect Morter & Dobie 1956-59, ptnr Bruxby & Evans 1959-61, assoc and ptnr Ronald Fielding Ptnrship 1961-70, ptnr and dir Alec French Partnership 1970-84; fndr dir Thornton Hartnell 1985-; nat pres: Faculty of Bldg 1982-84, Concrete Soc 1985-86; vice-pres RIBA (practice) 1986-87; cncl memb RIBA 1984-87; vice-pres Bristol FC (Rugby); Freeman: Worshipful Co of Constructors, Worshipful Co of Chartered Architects; FRIBA, FFB; *Recreations* rugby, cricket, golf, snooker, walking; *Clubs* MCC, Royal Western Yacht; *Style—* Ian Thornton, Esq; Old Manor Farm, Ingst, Olveston, Bristol BS12 3AP (☎ 04545 2353); Thornton Hartnell, 7 Park St, Bristol BS1 5NF (☎ 0272 272525, fax 0272 297847)

THORNTON, John Henry; OBE (1987), QPM (1980); s of Sidney Thornton (d 1968), and Ethel, *née* Grinnell (d 1972); *b* 24 Dec 1930; *Educ* Prince Henry's GS Evesham; *m* 1, 13 Dec 1952 (m dis 1972), Norma Lucille, da of Alfred James Scrivenor, of Eltham, London SE9; 2 s (Christopher b 1954, Jonathan b 1963); m 2, 7 Jan 1972, Hazel Ann, da of William Butler, of Blackheath, London SE3; 2 s (James b 1974 d 1976, Joseph b 1976), 1 da (Amy b 1973); *Career* RN 1949-50; Metropolitan Police 1950, supt 1965, vice pres Br Section Int Police Assoc 1969-79, cdr 1976, head of Community Rels 1977-80, Royal Coll of Defence Studies 1981, dep asst cmmnr 1981, dir of Info 1982-83, head of Trg 1983-85, dep asst cmmnr Metropolitan Police North West Area 1985-86; vice pres British Section Int Police Assoc 1969-79; lay canon of St Albans Cathedral 1988-; chm: Breakaway Theatre Co St Albans 1987-, Int Organ Festival 1988; Liveryman Worshipful Co of Glaziers 1983; CStJ 1985; *Recreations* music, gardening, learning; *Style—* John Thornton, Esq, OBE, QPM; Cathedral and Abbey Church of St Albans, Sumpter Yard AL1 1BY

THORNTON, Prof (Robert) Kelsey Rought; s of Harold Thornton (d 1975), and Mildred, *née* Brookes; *b* 12 Aug 1938; *Educ* Burnley GS, Unvi of Manchester (BA, MA, PhD); *m* 1, 3 Aug 1961 (m dis 1976), Sarah Elizabeth Ann, da of Hendri Griffiths; 3 s (Jason b 1965, Ben b 1968, Thomas b 1982), 1 da (Amy b 1979); m 2, 22 Sept 1989, Eileen Valerie, da of Maurice Davison; *Career* prof Univ of Newcastle Upon Tyne 1984-89 (lectr 1965-75, sr lectr 1975-84), prof and head Sch of Eng Univ of Birmingham 1989-; chm John Clare Soc 1987-90; *Books* incl: The Decadent Dilemma (1983), Gerard Manley Hopkins: The Poems (1973), All My Eyes See: The Visual World of Gerard Manley Hopkins (1975), Ivor Gurney Collected Letters (1991); *Recreations* water colour painting, book collecting; *Style—* Prof Kelsey Thornton; School of English, University of Birmingham, Edgbaston, Birmingham B15 2TT (☎ 021 414 5667)

THORNTON, (George) Malcolm; MP (C) Crosby 1983-; s of George Edmund Thornton by his w Ethel; *b* 3 April 1939; *Educ* Wallasey GS, Liverpool Nautical Coll; *m* 1, 1962; 1 s; m 2, 1972, Sue Banton (decd 1989); m 3, 1990, Rosemary, *née* Hewitt; *Career* former River Mersey pilot; memb: Wallasey County Borough Cncl 1965-75, Wirral Metropolitan Cncl 1973-79 (ldr 1974-77); chm Merseyside Dists Liaison Ctee 1975-77; vice-pres: Assoc Met Authys, Burnham Ctee 1978-79; chm: AMA Educn Ctee 1978-79, Cncl Local Educn Authys 1978-79; MP (C) Liverpool Garston 1979-83; sec: C Parly Shipping and Shipbuilding Ctee 1979-81, C Parly Educn Ctee; memb Select Ctee on Environment 1979-81; PPS to: Rt Hon Patrick Jenkin (as Indust Sec) 1981-1983 and (as Environment Sec) 1983-84; chm Select Ctee on Educn, Sci and the Arts; *Style—* Malcolm Thornton, Esq, MP; House of Commons, London SW1 (☎ 071 219 4489)

THORNTON, Margaret; da of Cyril Arthur Wales (d 1983), and Anna Margaret Wales, MBE, *née* Chang; *b* 28 Jan 1940; *Educ* Burgess Hill PNEU Sussex, Mary Wray Secretarial Coll Sussex; *m* 1972, Adrian Heber Thornton, s of Nigel Heber Thornton, Croix de Guerre (d 1941); 1 s (Jasper Hamilton b 1975), 2 da (Emily Harriet b 1973, Rebecca Louise b 1980); *Career* jt md Redfern Gallery; exhibitions selected and organised incl: Paul Wunderlich 1968, British Sculptors 1972, Graham Sutherland - From the Douglas Cooper Collection 1976, 65 Years of British Painting (The Rotunda Exchange Square, Hong Kong) 1988; organised visit of Patrick Procktor to China (first Br artist since Cultural Revolution) 1980; memb The Canadian High Cmmn Advsy Ctee of Visual Arts; *Recreations* visiting galleries, museums and antique markets; *Style—* Mrs Margaret Thornton; The Redfern Gallery, 20 Cork Street, London W1 (☎ 071 734 1732, 071 734 0578, fax 071 494 2908)

THORNTON, Michael Stanley; s of Joseph Stanley Thornton, of The Close Farm, Ashbourne, Derbyshire, and Jeanetta, *née* Jamieson (d 1982); *b* 1 Aug 1936; *Educ* Uppingham; *m* 1, 3 Sept 1960 (m dis 1977), Marie Margaret, *née* Pepper; 2 da (Jill Susan b 18 Aug 1961, Sally-Ann Margaret b 6 March 1964); m 2, 1977, Jane Susan Hinckley, *née* Bourne; 1 s (Matthew Michael b 11 Sept 1978); *Career* Nat Serv, cmmnd RASC 1955, Lt 1956; family business JW Thornton Ltd (Thorntons plc 1988): joined 1957, dir 1963, now dep chm, chief exec and co sec; non-exec dir Derbs Cablevision Ltd; tstee The Bishop of Derby's Urban Fund; vice pres: The Arkwright Soc, NSPCC Ctee (Derby Branch); hon memb NSPCC Cncl; chm: Prince's Tst Ctee (Derbyshire), Amber Valley Groundwork Tst; pres Ashbourne Shire Horse Soc, Chieften Asbourne Highland Gathering, past pres Matlock Rugby Club; FCIS 1977 (Assoc 1963); *Style—* Michael Thornton, Esq; Thorntons plc, Thornton Park, Somercotes, Derbyshire DE55 4XJ (☎ 0773 608822, fax 0773 540842, telex 377835)

THORNTON, Peter Anthony; s of Robert Thornton (d 1990), and Freda, *née* Willey; *b* 8 May 1944; *Educ* Bradford GS, Univ of Manchster (BSc); *m* 1969 (m dis 1987); 1 s (James William b 1976), 2 da (Victoria Jane b 1973, Charlotte Sarah b 1974); *Career* chartered surveyor and engineer; jt md Greycoat plc; FRICS, FICE, FCIOB; *Recreations* squash, tennis, water skiing; *Clubs* RAC, Hurlingham, Riverside, Princes; *Style—* Peter Thornton, Esq; Van Buren Cottage, Queens Ride, Barnes Common, London SW13 0JF (☎ 081 7881969); 27 Old Jewry, London EC2R 8DQ (☎ 071 606 0818, car 0836 508549)

THORNTON, Sir Peter Eustace; KCB (1974); s of D O Thornton; *b* 1917; *Educ* Charterhouse, Gonville and Caius Cambridge; *m* 1946, Rosamond Hobart Myers; 2 s, 1 da; *Career* BOT 1946, asst under-sec of State Dept of Economic Affrs 1964-67, under-sec Cabinet Office 1967-70, dep sec 1970-72, dep sec DTI 1972-74, second perm sec Dept of Trade 1974, perm sec 1974-77; dir: Laird Gp 1978-, Courtaulds, Rolls Royce, Hill Samuel Gp 1977-87; pro-chllr Open Univ 1979-83; *Style—* Sir Peter Thornton, KCB; 22 East St, Alresford, Hants SO24 9EE

THORNTON, Peter Kai; s of Sir Gerard Thornton (d 1977), of Kingsthorpe Hall, Northampton, and Gerda Nörregaard, of Copenhagen; *b* 8 April 1925; *Educ* Bryanston, De Havilland Aeronautical Tech Sch, Trinity Hall Cambridge (BA); *m* 22 Aug 1950, Mary Ann Rosamund, da of Arthur Helps (d 1976), of Cregane, Rosscarbery, Co Cork; 3 da; *Career* served Intelligence Corps Austria 1945-48; asst keeper V & A: Dept of Textiles 1954-62, Dept of Furniture and Woodwork 1962-84 (keeper 1966-84); keeper-in-charge Ham House and Osterley Park, curator Sir John Soane's Museum 1984-; memb: Cncl Nat Tst 1983-84, London Advsy Ctee Eng Heritage 1986-88; chm Furniture History Soc 1974-84; FSA 1976; *Books* Baroque and Rococo Silks (1965), Seventeenth Century Decoration (1978), The Furnishing and Decoration of Ham House (with M Tomlin), Authentic Decor - The Domestic Interior 1620-1920 (1984), Musical Instruments as Works of Art (1968), The Italian Renaissance Interia 1400-1600 (1991); *Style—* Peter Thornton, Esq, FSA; 15 Cheniston Gardens, London W8 (☎ 071 937 8868); Cahergal, Union Hall, Co Cork, Rep of Ireland; Sir John Soane's Museum, 13 Lincoln's Inn Fields, London WC2 (☎ 071 405 2107)

THORNTON, Peter Leonard; s of Walter Lawrence Thornton (d 1958), of Basingstoke, Hants, and Alice, *née* Latham (d 1954); *b* 9 Aug 1945; *Educ* Queen Mary's GS Basingstoke, Regent St Poly, Sch of Modern Languages London; *m* 6 Sept 1976, Gabrielle Mary, da of Theodore Cortazzi, of San Jose, Costa Rica; *Career* journalist: Associated Newspapers 1965-67, Daily Telegraph 1967-73; news ed LBC Radio 1973-77, ed Independent Radio News 1977-83, editorial dir LBC Radio 1983-89, md and chief ed LBC and Independent Radio News 1989-; *Style—* Peter Thornton, Esq; LBC Radio, Crown House, 72 Hammersmith Rd, London W14 8YE (☎ 071 371 1515, fax 071 371 2133)

THORNTON, Peter Norman; s of William Norman Thornton (d 1984), and Muriel Thornton; *b* 5 May 1933; *Educ* Repton; *m* 4 April 1983, Jocelyn Bernice, da of William Henry Poole (d 1969); 1 s (Miles b 1968), 2 da (Sarah b 1962, Samantha b 1965); *Career* Lt Royal Signals Malaya 1951-55, Hallamshire Bn (Maj) 1955-61, GSM; dir (ret as chm) J W Thornton Ltd 1962-87, dir and chm Peter Thornton Assocs (venture capital and mgmnt consultancy); dir Buxton International Festival Soc 1983-; chm: Midland Asthma & Allergy Res Assoc 1976-79, Confectioners Benevolent Fund 1990-; fndr and tstee Sheffield Asthma Soc 1977; fndr memb SDP; FIIM (1976), FIOD (1981); *Recreations* offshore sailing, small boat racing, music; *Clubs* IOD, Ogston Sailing; *Style—* Peter Thornton, Esq; Field Farm, Wensley, Matlock, Derbyshire DE4 2LL (☎ 0629 732598); Peter Thornton Associates, The Archway, Crown Square, Matlock, Derbyshire DE4 3AT (☎ 0629 584422, car 0836 212713)

THORNTON, Richard Chicheley; s of Capt Edward Chicheley Thornton, DSC, RN (d 1959), of Titchfield, Hants, and Margaret Noel, *née* Terry (d 1970); *b* 5 July 1931; *Educ* Stowe, Keble Coll Oxford; *m* 1, 1958 (m dis 1987), Jennifer Mary, da of Col Leo Dominic Gleeson, DSO (d 1976); 1 s (Henry Dominic Chicheley b 1963), 2 da (Mary Virginia Chicheley (Mrs Morton) b 1959, Lucy Margaret Chicheley (Mrs Torrington) b 1960); m 2, 4 March 1989, Susan Joy, *née* Middleton; *Career* Nat Serv cmmnd 2 Lt Royal Signals 1950; Capt Royal Signals TA 1952-58; called to the Bar Gray's Inn 1957; fndr: GT Mgmnt 1969, Thornton & Co 1985; hon fell Keble Coll Oxford 1986; hon treas: Marine Soc, Inst of Child Health; memb Worshipful Co of Watermen and Lightermen 1987, Freeman City of London 1987; *Recreations* sailing; *Clubs* The Garrick, Royal Thames Yacht; *Style—* Richard Thornton, Esq; Thornton Management Ltd, 33 Cavendish Square, London W1M 7HF (☎ 071 493 7262, fax 071 409 0590, telex 923061, car 0860 597360)

THORNTON, Robert Luke Grant (Bob); er s of Rev Canon Cecil Grant Thornton, of Leicester, and Winifred Dorothy, *née* Fawkes; *b* 22 Dec 1923; *Educ* Bromsgrove; *m* 1953, Helen, da of Rev C B Hodson; 3 s (James, John, Peter), 1 da (Catherine); *Career* Capt RIASC 1942-45, India 1942-43, 36 Br Div in N Burma 1944, with 3 Commando Bde Hong Kong 1945; combined dental med course Guy's Hosp 1946, orthodontic house surgn Royal Dental Hosp 1952, gen dental practitioner Salisbury 1952, dental surgn WDHO Wills Bristol 1953-79; gen dental practitioner Almondsbury 1978-; hon treas (and life memb) Assoc of Industl Dental Surgns 1968-78; fndr JOGLE Club raising £102,000 in aid of the Nat Star Centre for Disabled Youth Cheltenham having walked 3 times and cycled once between John O'Groats and Lands End since 1972; *Recreations* amateur potter, foreign travel, gardening, reading about Sir Winston Churchill, raising money for the Star Centre; *Style—* Bob Thornton, Esq; 3 Red House Lane, Almondsbury, Bristol BS12 4BB (☎ 0454 612300)

THORNTON, Dr Robert Ribblesdale; CBE (1973); s of Thomas Thornton (d 1970), of 102 Filey Rd, Scarborough, and Florence, *née* Gatenby (d 1959); *b* 2 April 1913; *Educ* Leeds GS, St John's Coll Cambridge (BA, LLB, LLM, MA); *m* 27 Jan 1940, Ruth Eleonore, da of William Tuckson (d 1938), of Beaconsfield Road, New Southgate, London; 1 s (Peter b 1946), 1 da (Ann Sparling b 1941); *Career* serv WWII 1940-46; Adj 86 Field Regt 1943-45, Bde Maj RA 3 Divn 1945, 53 (Welsh) Divn 1945-46; asst slr: Leeds 1938-40 and 1946-47, Bristol 1947-53; dep town clerk Southampton 1953-54; town clerk: Salford 1954-66, Leicester 1966-73; chief exec Leicestershire CC 1973-76, dep chm Local Govt Boundary Cmmn for England 1982 (memb 1976-82); pres Soc of Town Clerks 1971, treas Univ of Leicester 1980-85; DL (Leics) 1974-85; Hon LLD Univ of Leicester 1987; Solace 1974; *Recreations* sport (watching), music (listening); *Style—* Dr R R Thornton, CBE; 16 St Marys Close, Winterborne Whitechurch, Blandford Forum, Dorset DT11 0DJ (☎ 0258 880 980)

THORNYCROFT, Col Guy Mytton; DL (Shropshire 1967); s of Lt-Col Charles Mytton Thornycroft, CBE, DSO (d 1948); *b* 1 April 1917; *Educ* Shrewsbury, RMA

Sandhurst; *m* 1947, Kathleen, *née* Evans; 2 s; *Career* Col King's Shropshire LI 1937-60, Bde-Col LI 1959-60; High Sheriff Shropshire 1975; *Recreations* shooting, cricket; *Clubs* MCC; *Style—* Col Guy Thornycroft, DL; Bank Cottage, Kenley, Shropshire

THOROGOOD, Alfreda; da of Edward Thorogood (d 1966), and Alfreda, *née* Langham; *b* 17 Aug 1942; *Educ* Lady Eden's Sch, Royal Ballet Sch (Jr and Upper); *m* 1 Aug 1967, David Richard Wall, CBE, s of Charles Wall; 1 s (Daniel b 12 Dec 1974), 1 da (Annaliese b 15 Oct 1971); *Career* princ dancer Royal Ballet Co touring section 1968 (joined 1960, soloist 1966), transferred to resident co 1970, danced all leading roles in major classical ballets; created roles for: Sir Frederick Ashton, Sir Kenneth MacMillan, Anthony Tudor, Geoffrey Cauley; danced roles choreographed by: Dame Ninette de Valois, Glen Tetley, Jerome Robins, Rudolf Nureyev, Leonide Massine, John Cranko, John Neumier, David Bintley, André Howard; left Royal Ballet 1980; dir Bush Davies Sch 1988 (sr teacher 1982-85, dep ballet princ 1985-88), artistic advsr Royal Acad of Dancing 1989-; ARAD, Dip PDTC; *Style—* Miss Alfreda Thorogood

THOROLD, Capt Sir Anthony Henry; 15 Bt (E 1642), OBE (1942), DSC (1942, and bar 1945), JP (Lincs 1961), DL (1959); s of Sir James Ernest Thorold, 14 Bt (d 1965), and Katharine (d 1959), eldest da of Rev William Rolfe Tindal-Atkinson, formerly vicar of St Andrew's, Burgess Hill; *b* 7 Sept 1903; *Educ* RNC: Osborne, Dartmouth; *m* 1939, Jocelyn Elaine Laura, da of Sir Clifford Edward Heathcote-Smith, KBE, CMG (d 1963); 1 s, 2 da; *Heir* s, (Anthony) Oliver Thorold; *Career* RN 1917, served WWII in Home and Med Fleets as SO, ops in Force H and Western Approaches, Capt 1946, Cdre in Charge Hong Kong 1953-55, ADC to The Queen 1955-56, ret 1956; CC Kesteven 1958-74, High Sheriff Lincolns 1968, ldr Lincs CC 1973-81; chm: Grantham Hosp Mgmnt Ctee 1963-74, Lincoln Diocesan Tst and Bd of Fin 1966-71; *Recreations* shooting; *Clubs* Army and Navy; *Style—* Capt Sir Anthony Thorold, Bt, OBE, DSC, JP, DL; Syston Old Hall, Grantham, Lincs NG32 2BX (☎ 0400 50270)

THOROLD, (Anthony) Oliver; s and h of Sir Anthony Thorold, 15 Bt, OBE, DSC; *b* 15 April 1945; *Educ* Winchester, Lincoln Coll Oxford; *m* 1977, Genevra, da of John L Richardson, of Broadshaw, W Calder, W Lothian; 1 s (Henry b 1981), 1 da (Lydia b 1985); *Career* barr Inner Temple 1971; *Style—* Oliver Thorold, Esq; 8 Richmond Cres, London N1 (☎ 071 609 0437); Dr Johnson's Bldgs, Temple, London EC4 (☎ 071 353 9328)

THOROLD, Peter Guy Henry; s of Sir Guy Thorold, KCMG (d 1970); *b* 20 April 1930; *Educ* Eton, New Coll Oxford; *m* 1964, Anne, da of Robert Fender; 4 children; *Career* dir Bain Dawes Ltd 1972-; *Clubs* Buck's; *Style—* Peter Thorold, Esq; 25 Stanley Cres, London W11 2NA

THOROLD, Hon Mrs (Phyllis Margaret); *née* Russell; OBE (1946); da of 2 Baron Ampthill, GCSI, GCIE, and Margaret, *née* Lygon, GBE, GCVO; *b* 3 June 1909; *Educ* RCM (LRAM, ARCM); *m* 1940 (m annulled on her petition 1942), Capt William Thorold (d 1943, gggs of Sir John Thorold, 9 Bt, MP); *Career* serv WWII Dep Cmmr Jt War Orgn Order of St John and Br Cross Soc; served: N Africa (despatches), Russia, Manila, Hong Kong; musician, embroideress; OStJ 1941; *Style—* The Hon Mrs Thorold; 55 Ebury Mews, London SW1W 9NY (☎ 071 730 9097)

THORP, James Noble; s of Arthur Thorp (d 1953), and Annie, *née* Rollinson (d 1975); *b* 27 Oct 1934; *Educ* Rothwell GS, Leeds Coll of Art Sch of Architecture; *m* 18 Jan 1958, Jean, da of Arthur Brown (d 1972); 2 s (Ian James b 1958, Julian Alexander b 1969), 2 da (Sally Ann b 1961, Jayne Stella b 1964); *Career* architect, estab private practice 1961; lectr in design 1964-87: Leeds Coll of Art, Leeds Poly, Sheffield Univ; Civic Tst assessor; awards: Leeds Gold medal 1964, DOE Award for Design 1976, Civic Tst Commendation 1987; ARIBA; *Recreations* skiing, amateur theatre, scenic design, music; *Style—* James Thorp, Esq; 73 Church St, Woodlesford, Leeds 26 (☎ 0532 826303); Design Studio, James Thorp & Partners, 21 Park St, Leeds 1 (☎ 0532 455451)

THORP, Jeremy Walter; s of Walter Thorp (d 1977), of Dublin, and Dorothy Bliss (d 1989); *b* 12 Dec 1941; *Educ* King Edward VII Sch Sheffield, CCC Oxford (MA); *m* 15 Sept 1973, Estela Maria, da of Alberto Lessa (d 1968), of Montevideo, Uruguay; *Career* HM Treasy 1963-78: asst private sec to Sec of State for Econ Affrs 1967-69, financial attaché HM Embassy Washington 1971-73; FCO 1978-: first sec head of Chancery and consul gen HM Embassy Lima Peru 1982-86, dep head of mission HM Embassy Dublin 1988-; *Recreations* music, buying paintings, walking, swimming, travel, reading; *Clubs* Kildare Street and Univ (Dublin); *Style—* Jeremy Thorp, Esq

THORPE; *see*: Gardner-Thorpe

THORPE, Adèle Loraine; da of Lionel Raphael Lewis Thorpe, and Bettie Louise, *née* Frome; *b* 29 Sept 1952; *Educ* Henrietta Barnett; *m* 16 April 1982, Simon Peter Thorpe, s of Stanley Thorpe; 1 da (Katy b 1987); *Career* northern euro accountant Amdahl (UK) Ltd 1978-81; fin dir: Tandem Computer Ltd 1981-87, Sybase Software Ltd 1987-; chm Slough Branch BIM 1985-87; memb: Cncl Inst Chartered Secretaries and Administrators BBO Branch 1984-88, Thames Water Customer Servs Ctee; Liveryman Worshipful Co of Chartered Secretaries and Administrators; memb IOD, FCIS, FBIM; *Style—* Mrs Adèle Thorpe; Harmony House, St Hubert's Close, Gerrards Cross, Bucks

THORPE, Adrian Charles; s of Prof Lewis Guy Melville Thorpe (d 1977), and (Eva Mary) Barbara, da of Alfred Reynolds; *b* 29 July 1942; *Educ* The Leys Sch, Christ's Coll Cambridge (BA, MA); *m* 26 Oct 1968, Miyoko, da of Taketaro Kosugi (d 1950), of Japan; *Career* entered HM Dip Serv 1965; Tokyo 1965-70, FCO 1970-73, Beirut 1973-76 (head of Chancery 1975-76), FCO 1976, Tokyo 1976-81, FCO 1981-85 (cnsllr and head of Info Technol Dept 1982-85); econ cnsllr Bonn 1985-89; dep high cmmr Kuala Lumpur 1989-; FRSA; *Recreations* opera, travel, bookshops, comfort; *Clubs* Tokyo (Japan), Royal Selangor Golf; *Style—* Adrian Thorpe, Esq; c/o FCO, King Charles St, London SW1A 2AH (☎ 071 270 3000); British High Commission, 185 Jalan Ampang, 50450 Kuala Lumpur, Malaysia (☎ 03 248 2122, fax 03 248 0880, telex MA 35225)

THORPE, (James) Andrew Charles; s of R L Thorpe, of Fairways, Silverstone Drive, Manchester, and Gertrude, *née* Sutton; *Educ* Giggleswick Sch Settle Yorkshire, Univ of Leeds (MB ChB); *Career* currently conslt cardiothoracic surgn Northern Gen Hosp Sheffield; author of articles on cardiothoracic surgery; FRCS 1977, FRCSEd 1977; *Style—* Andrew Thorpe, Esq; 8 St Alban's Drive, Fulwood, Sheffield S10 4DL (☎ 0742 434343); Cardio Thoracic Unit, Northern General Hospital, Sheffield S5 7AV (☎ 0742 434343)

THORPE, Clifford Malcolm (Mick); s of Clifford Padgett Thorpe (d 1977), of Hull, and Phyllis Ivy, *née* Atkins (d 1980); *b* 2 April 1931; *Educ* Marist Coll Hull, Univ of Manchester (LLB); *m* 4 April 1961, Sheila Muir, da of Arthur Thomson Macfarlane; 5 s (Martin Peter b 1962, Christopher Paul b 1963, Richard Michael b 1963, Malcolm James b 1965, Gregory Neil b 1969), 1 da (Fiona Mary b 1966); *Career* admitted slr 1954; fndr Thorpe and Co slrs 1955-; pres Scarborough Law Soc 1965, clerk to Gen Tax Cmmrs 1974-, memb Law Soc 1954-; dir Hull City AFC plc 1984-; chm: Scarborough Round Table 1966, Area 15 Round Table 1969; pres: Nat Assoc of Round Tables 1971, Scarborough Catenian Assoc 1962, Yorks Coast Pastoral Cncl 1985-88; fndr pres Rotary Club of Scarborough Cavaliers 1978, vice chm St Catherines Hospice Tst 1986-; *Recreations* walking, music, skiing, travel; *Style—* Mick Thorpe, Esq; 46 Stone Quarry Rd, Burniston, Scarborough YO13 ODF (☎ 0723 871155); Thorpe and Co Slrs, 17 Valley Bridge Parade, Scarborough YO11 2JX (☎ 0723 364321, fax 0723 500459)

THORPE, Edward; s of Ronald Thorpe, of Hythe, Southampton (d 1986), and Helen Mary Thorpe (d 1987); *b* 14 June 1936; *Educ* Kemp-Welch Sch Parkstone Poole Dorset, RADA (special dip); *m* Sept 1955, Gillian (qv), da of Dr Jack Freeman; 2 da (Harriet Amelia b June 1957, Matilda Helen Rachel b May 1960); *Career* child actor Italia Conti prodn Where The Rainbow Ends; actor: Old Vic Company, various repertory theatres; freelance writer (specialising in dance); *Books* The Other Hollywood (1970), The Night I Caught The Santa Fé Chief (1971), Kenneth MacMillan (biography, 1987), Black Dance (1989); *Recreations* watching motor racing; *Style—* Edward Thorpe, Esq

THORPE, Geoffrey Digby; s of late Gordon Digby Thorpe, of Scotland, and Agnes Joyce Saville, *née* Haines; *b* 24 Sept 1949; *Educ* Windsor GS for Boys, Architectural Assoc Sch of Architecture (AA Dip); *m* 29 Sept 1973, Jane Florence, da of James Hay McElwee, of Havant, Hampshire; 1 da (Holly b 1980); *Career* indust gp architect; Milton Keynes Devpt Corp 1974-78, asst co architect East Sussex 1978-80, chm Thorpe Architecture Ltd 1980-; dir: Prospace Ltd; memb: RIBA 1975, ARCUK 1975, AA; *Recreations* fly and game fishing; *Style—* Geoffrey Thorpe, Esq; Lower Farm, Madehurst, Arundel, West Sussex BN18 0NU (☎ 0243 65 531); Bonefish Yacht Club, 95 Coco Plum Drive, Marathon, Florida Keys FL 33050 USA; Tarrant St, Arundel, West Sussex BN18 9SB (☎ 0903 883 500, fax 0903 882 188, car 0836 646 570)

THORPE, Rt Hon (John) Jeremy; PC (1967); s of Capt John Henry Thorpe, OBE, KC, JP (d 1944), sometime MP (C) for Rusholme and dep chm Middx QS (eldest s of Ven John Thorpe, Archdeacon of Macclesfield), and Ursula, JP, er da of Sir John Norton-Griffiths, 1 Bt, KCB, DSO, sometime MP for Wednesbury and Wandsworth Central; *b* 29 April 1929; *Educ* Eton, Trinity Coll Oxford (pres Oxford Union 1951); *m* 1, 1968, Caroline (d 1970), da of Warwick Allpass, of Kingswood, Surrey; 1 s; m 2, 1973, Marion, Countess of Harewood (*see* Harewood, Earl of), da of Erwin Stein (d 1958); *Career* called to the Bar Inner Temple 1954; MP (Lib) N Devon 1959-79, ldr Lib Pty 1967-76 (hon treas 1965-67); chm Jeremy Thorpe Assoc Ltd (Devpt Conslts), conslt Stramit Ltd; vice pres Anti-Apartheid Movement 1969-76, exec chm UN Assoc 1976-80; memb Devon Sessions; hon fell Trinity Coll Oxford, Hon LLD Univ of Exeter; FRSA; *Clubs* Nat Lib; *Style—* The Rt Hon Jeremy Thorpe, PC; 2 Orme Square, London W2 4RS

THORPE, John Grafton; s of Grafton Gould Thorpe (d 1963), of West Hill, Epsom, Surrey, and Ivy Dorothy, *née* Locks; *b* 29 Oct 1932; *Educ* St John's Sch Leatherhead, City of Freeman Sch; *m* 30 March 1957, Pamela, da of Thomas Francis Faithfull, of Leatherhead, Surrey; 1 s (Martin John Richard b 9 Sept 1958), 1 da (Caroline Jane b 31 May 1960); *Career* underwriter: Lloyd's 1963, St Quintin Syndicate 1979-85; dir Alexander Howden Underwriting 1979-84, underwriter Coster Syndicate 1986-90; vice pres Leatherhead CC; Freeman City of London 1955; Liveryman: Worshipful Co of Glass Sellers 1955 (apprentice 1950-55 memb Ct 1989, Master 1990), Worshipful Co of Makers of Playing Cards 1979 (Steward 1984-86, elected to Ct 1986, Junior Warden 1988, Sr Warden 1989); *Books* The Playing Cards of the Worshipful Company of Makers of Playing Cards (1980); *Recreations* playing cards, watching cricket; *Clubs* MCC; *Style—* John Thorpe, Esq; Epsom Rd, Leatherhead, Surrey; Lloyd's, London EC3 (☎ 071 623 7100)

THORPE, Hon Mr Justice; Sir Mathew Alexander; yr s of late Michael Alexander Thorpe, of Restory Gate House, Petworth, Sussex, and Dorothea Margaret, *née* Lambert; *b* 30 July 1938; *Educ* Stowe, Balliol Coll Oxford; *m* 1, 30 Dec 1966, Lavinia Hermione, da of Maj Robert James Buxton (d 1968); 3 s (Gervase b 1967, Alexander b 1969, Marcus b 1971); m 2, 3 Aug 1989, Mrs Carola Millar; *Career* called to the Bar Inner Temple 1961, QC 1980, rec 1982, High Ct judge 1988; memb Matrimonial Causes Rule Ctee 1978-83; bencher Inner Temple 1985; *Style—* The Hon Mr Justice Thorpe; Royal Courts of Justice, Strand, London WC2

THORPE, Richard Malin; s of Capt Bernard Thorpe (d 1987), and Hilda Mary Thorpe (d 1971); *b* 15 Oct 1926; *Educ* Cranleigh Sch, Trinity Coll Cambridge (MA); *m* 31 Dec 1948, Alice Daisy, da of Henry Samuel Adlam; 1 s (Malin b 1950); *Career* cmmnd Irish Gds 1944, demob 1947; joined family firm Bernard Thorpe & Ptnrs land agents and surveyers 1951, managing ptnr and chm Main Equity Partnership 1973, chm and sr ptnr Nat Partnership 1983, churchwarden Parish church of St Lawrence Bidborough, former co and dist cncllr Kent, vice chm Citicare St Clememts; pres: Cons Assoc Constituency (Tunbridge Wells), local cons Assoc (Southborough), West Kent Hunt Supporters Club (former master Kent Hunt); former memb Westminster Cncl Fin & Gen Purposes ctee; Master of Worshipful Co of Gold and Silver Wyre Drawers 1987 (Freeman and memb ct), Freeman and Liveryman Worshipful Co of Farmers 1967; FRICS 1954; *Recreations* gardening; *Clubs* Oriental; *Style—* Richard Thorpe, Esq; Home Farm, London Rd, Southborough, Tunbridge Wells, Kent TN4 0UH (☎ 0732 354744)

THORPE-TRACEY, Maj Stephen Frederick; s of Rev Julian Stephen Victor Thorpe-Tracey (d 1949), of the Rectory, Monkokehampton, Devon, and Faith Catherine Gwendoline, *née* Powell; *b* 27 Dec 1929; *Educ* Plymouth Coll; *m* 1 Jan 1955, Shirley, da of Lt-Col George Frederick Byles (d 1951), of The Old Forge, Stoodleigh, Tiverton, Devon; 1 s (Jeremy), 2 da (Catherine, Barbara); *Career* emergency cmmn 1948, short serv cmmn 1950, regular cmmn DLI 1952, Staff Coll Camberley 1960 (psc), GSO2 Def Operational Res Estab 1961-63, Trg Maj 8 DLI TA 1964-65, Maj 1 DLI 1965-66, GSO2 MOD 1966-70; direct entry Civil Serv: princ 1970-77, asst sec 1977-86, under sec and controller Newcastle Central Office DHSS 1986-89; memb Prescription Pricing Authy 1990-, hon sec Civil Serv Chess Assoc 1974-77, cdre Goring Thames SC 1981-82, chm Northern Gp Royal Inst of Public Admin 1988-89; *Recreations* chess, golf, sailing, fell walking; *Clubs* Naval and Military; *Style—* Maj Stephen Thorpe-Tracey; 12 Woodbine Avenue, Gosforth, Newcastle upon Tyne NE3 4EU (☎ 091 284 5491)

THORSTVEDT, Erik; s of Harald Thorstvedt, of Stavanger, Norway, and Liv Ingrid, *née* Jörpeland; *b* 28 Oct 1962; *m* Tove Helen; 1 da (Charlotte b 31 Oct 1986); *Career* professional footballer; Eik IF Norway 1982-84, Viking Norway 1984-86, Borussia Möenchengladbach Germany 1986-88, IFK Gothenburg Sweden 1988-89, Tottenham Hotspur 1989-; Norwegian caps: 4 youth, 5 under 21, 64 full; *Recreations* film, music; *Style—* Erik Thorstvedt, Esq; Tottenham Hotspur FC, 748 High Road, Tottenham, London N17 OAP (☎ 081 808 8080)

THOULD, Dr Anthony Keith; s of Harry Bevis Thould (d 1974), of Idless Mill, Truro, Cornwall, and Daisy, *née* Behenna; *b* 4 Oct 1930; *Educ* Stowe, St Bartholomew's Hosp (MB BS, MD); *m* 24 Aug 1957, Bernine Tivey, da of Harold Hughes Furner (d 1984), of Cooma, New South Wales, Aust; 3 s (Anthony Julian b 1958, Geoffrey Robert b 1959, Jeremy Bevis b 1962); *Career* house physican Norfolk and Norwich Hosp 1955, clinical offr RAMC in Med 33 Gen Hosp HK 1955-57, later Surgn Lt Cdr RNR, med registrar UCH 1960-62, sr med registrar Bart's 1962-65 (house surgn 1954, jr med registrar 1958, res fell 1959), conslt physician and rheumatologist Royal Cornwall Hosp Truro 1965-; Med-Gilliland fell Stanford Univ USA 1983; memb: Cncl Br Soc for Rheumatology 1985-, Herberden Soc 1967-85, Paleopathology Soc 1982-; FRCP; *Books* Copeman's Textbook of Rheumatology (contrib, 1986), Annals of Rheumatic Diseases (ed, 1988); numerous pubns in scientific literature; *Recreations* N American history, architecture, travel, reading, gardening, walking; *Style—* Dr Anthony Thould; Idless Mill, Truro, Cornwall TR4 9QS (☎ 0872 72593); Duke of Cornwall Dept of Rheumatology, Royal Cornwall Hospital (City), Truro, Cornwall (☎ 0872 74242, fax 0872 222857)

THOURON, Sir John Rupert Hunt; KBE (1976, CBE 1967); s of John Longstreth Thouron, and Amelia Thouron; *b* 10 May 1908; *Educ* Sherborne; *m* 1 (m dis); 1 s; m 2, 1953, Esther duPont, da of Lammot duPont; *Career* Br Army Offr, serv WWII Major Black Watch; with Lady Thouron, fndr of Thouron Univ of Pennsylvania Fund for British-American Student Exchange 1960; *Recreations* gardening, horticulture, racing, hunting, fishing, golf; *Clubs* Vicmead, Seminole, Jupiter Island, The Brook (all US), White's, Sunningdale, Royal St George's; *Style—* Sir John Thouron, KBE; Summer: DOE RUN, Unionville, Chester County, Pa 19375, USA (☎ 215 384 5542); Winter: 416 South Beach Rd, Hobe Sound, Florida 33455, USA (☎ 407 546 3577); office: 3801 Kennett Pike, Greenville, Delaware 19807, USA (☎ 302 652 6350)

THREADGOLD, Andrew Richard; s of Stanley Dennis Threadgold, of Brentwood, Essex, and the late Phyllis Ethel, *née* Marsh; *b* 8 Feb 1944; *Educ* Brentwood Sch, Nottingham Univ (BA), Melbourne Univ (PhD); *m* 21 May 1966 (sep), Rosalind Threadgold; 2 s (Richard b 1967, Matthew b 1971); *Career* mangr econ info Int Wool Secretariat 1971-74, advsr Econ Div Bank of England 1974-84, on secondment chief economist Postel Investmt Mgmnt Ltd 1984-86, head fin supervision Gen Div Bank of England 1986-87; chief exec and dir securities investmnt Postel Investmt Mgmnt 1987-; *Style—* Andrew Threadgold, Esq; 5 Barnsbury St, London N1 1PW (☎ 071 354 0583); Postel Investment Management Ltd, Standon House, 21 Mansell St, London E1 8AA (☎ 071 702 0888, fax 071 702 9452, telex 8956577, 888947)

THRELFALL, (Richard) Ian; QC (1965); s of William Bernhard Threlfall (d 1965), and Evelyn Alice, *née* Maconochie (d 1987); *b* 14 Jan 1920; *Educ* Oundle, Gonville and Caius Coll Cambridge (BA); *m* 9 Sept 1948, Annette, da of George Cowper Hugh Matthey (d 1972); 3 s (George, Aidan (decd), Hugh), 3 da (Emma (Mrs Antonatos), Alexandra (Mrs Holloway), Victoria (Mrs Bathurst)); *Career* serv WWII Indian Armd Corps Probyn's Horse, staff appts GS02 HQ 14 Army 1945 (despatches twice); called to the Bar Lincoln's Inn 1947, bencher 1973; memb: E Surrey Health Authy 1982-90, Surrey Family Practioner Ctee 1982-90; Liveryman Worshipful Co of Goldsmiths 1964 (memb Ct of Assts 1969, Prime Warden, 1978-79); FSA 1949; *Style—* Ian Threlfall, Esq, QC, FSA; Pebble Hill House, Limpsfield, Oxted, Surrey (☎ 0883 712452)

THRELFALL, (John) Peter; s of William Emmett Threlfall (d 1976), of Yorks, and Edith, *née* Jackson; *b* 11 Oct 1936; *Educ* Ilkley GS; *m* 16 Sept 1967, Karin Hedda, da of Gerhard Johannes Rothkamn, of Halle; 2 s (Jörn Peter b 11 Sept 1968, Axel Christopher (twin) b 11 Sept 1968); *Career* Nat Serv 2 Lt RAPC 1960-62, trainee accountant 1954-59, CA Cooper Brothers & Co London 1962-71, ptnr Coopers & Lybrand Deloitte 1971-; FCA 1969 (ACA 1959); *Recreations* travel, theatre, music; *Style—* Peter Threlfall, Esq; Coopers & Lybrand Deloitte, Hillgate House, 26 Old Bailey, London EC4M 7PL (☎ 071 583 5000, fax 071 236 2367)

THRESHER, Stuart Edward; s of Ronald Stanley Thresher, of Kent, and Patricia Leslie, *née* Fulton; *b* 8 Feb 1963; *Educ* Sevenoaks Sch; *Career* Rugby Union full-back Harlequins FC; clubs: Nat West Bank RFC 1981-83, United London Banks RFC 1981-85, Harlequins FC 1983- (150 appearances, winner John Player Cup 1988, winner Middx Sevens 1989 and 1990, vice capt 1990), Barbarians RFC; rep: London Division (Divnl winners 1988, beat Aust 1988), Eng B (debut v Aust 1988, 2 caps); National Westminster Bank 1982-85; moneybroker: Godesll Ashley Pearce 1985-86, Butler Harlow Weda 1986-; *Recreations* cricket, golf, Chelsea FC; *Style—* Stuart Thresher, Esq; Harlequins FC, Stoop Memorial Ground, Craneford Way, Twickenham, Middlesex (☎ 081 892 0822)

THRING, Jeremy John; DL (Avon); o s of late Christopher William Thring, MBE, TD, of King Meadow, Upton Lovell, Warminster, Wilts, and Joan Evelyn, *née* Graham; *b* 11 May 1936; *Educ* Winchester; *m* 30 June 1962, Cynthia Kay, da of late Gilbert Kikpatrick Smith, of Bath; 2 da (Lucinda Katharine b 8 Aug 1963, Candida Sara b 11 May 1965); *Career* Nat Serv cmmnd 3 Kings Own Hussars 1955; admitted slr 1962; local dir Coutts Bank 1989; NP 1962, govr Bath HS; chm: Royal Nat Hosp for Rheumatic Diseases, NHS Trust; tstee: Bath Inst for Res into Care of the Elderly, Nat Eye Res Centre, Avon and Bristol Red Cross Tst Fund; memb: Law Soc, Soc of Prov Notaries; *Recreations* stalking, shooting, fishing; *Clubs* Bath and Co; *Style—* Jeremy Thring, Esq, DL; Belcombe House, Bradford-on-Avon, Wilts (☎ 02216 2295); Thrings & Long, 4-5 North Parade, Midland Bridge, Bath BA1 2HQ (☎ 0225 448494, fax 0225 319735/319660, telex 444712)

THRING, John Gale Wake; s of Walter Leonard Howard Thring, of New Place Stables, Lingfield, Surrey, *see* Burke's Landed Gentry, 18 Edn vol 3), and Elizabeth Mary Ann, *née* Vandenbergh; *b* 2 May 1943; *Educ* Wellington Coll, The Hill Sch USA; *m* 1 Oct 1966, Dianne Elizabeth, da of William Henry Jones, of Wembury Park, Newchapel, Surrey; 3 da (Victoria Elizabeth Sarah b 1967, Arabella Caroline b 1969, Henrietta Charlotte Anne b 1971); *Career* property developer; govr Fonthill Sch 1983; *Style—* John Thring, Esq; Rosslyn House, Dormansland, Surrey RH7 6QR (☎ 0342 833 587)

THRING, Prof Meredith Wooldridge; s of Capt W H Thring, CBE, RN (d 1949), and Dorothy Wooldridge (d 1922); *b* 17 Dec 1915; *Educ* Malvern, Trinity Coll Cambridge (BA, ScD); *m* 14 Dec 1940, (Alice) Margaret (d 1986), da of Robert Hooley (d 1949), of London; 2 s (John b 1944, Robert b 1949), 1 da (Susan (Mrs Kalaugher) b 1942); *Career* HG 1941-45; scientific offr Br Coal Utilisation Res Assoc 1937-46, head Physics Dept Br Iron & Steel Res Assoc 1944-53 (asst dir 1953), prof fuel technol and chem engrg Univ of Sheffield 1953-64, prof mechanical engrg QMC London 1964-81; lectured in: Aust, Canada, USA, France, Holland, Italy, Russia, Argentina, Mexico, W Germany, Bulgaria, Hungary, Czechoslavakia and Poland; Hadfield medal Iron and Steel Inst 1949; jt fndr Int Flame Res Fndn 1949; memb: Clean Air Cncl 1957-62, Advsy Cncl R & D Miny of Power 1960-66, Fire Res Bd 1961-64, Educn Ctee RAF 1968-76, UNESCO Cmmn to Bangladesh 1979; Hon D Open Univ 1982; FInstP 1944, FIMechE 1968, FIEE 1968, FIChemE 1972, FEng 1976, SFInstFuel 1951 (pres 1962-63); memb: Royal Norwegian Scientific Soc 1974, corr memb Nat Acad of Engrg Mexico 1977; *Books* The Science of Flames and Furnaces (1952, 2 edn 1962), Machines - Masters or Slaves of Man? (1973), Man, Machines and Tomorrow (1973), How to Invent (1975), The Engineer's Conscience (1980), Robots and Telechirs (1983); *Recreations* wood carving, arboriculture; *Clubs* Athenaeum; *Style—* Prof Meredith Thring; Bell Farm, Brundish, Suffolk IP13 8BL (☎ 0379 384296)

THRING, Peter Streatfeild; TD (1970); s of Jack Reddie Thring (d 1975), and Eirene Helen, *née* Streatfeild (d 1983); *b* 31 Dec 1933; *Educ* Winchester, Univ of Oxford (MA); *m* Joanna Elizabeth, da of Charles Gordon Duff, MC (d 1968); 1 s (Christopher b 1964), 1 da (Katharine b 1966); *Career* Nat Serv 2 Lt 157 Div Locating Batty RA 1952-54, 254 City of London Field Regt RA TA 1954-71, Maj 1969; CA; ptnr Ernst & Young; hon treas: The Mothers Union 1972-86, Oxford Soc 1977-; FCA 1970; *Recreations* bee-keeping, sailing, gardening; *Clubs* United Oxford and Cambridge; *Style—* Peter Thring, Esq, TD; Old School House, Cheverells Green, Markyate, St Albans, Herts AL3 8AB (☎ 0582 840501); Rolls House, 7 Rolls Buildings, Fetter Lane, London EC4A INH (☎ 071 931 1225, fax 071 405 2147/4610)

THROCKMORTON, Sir Anthony John Benedict; 12 Bt (E 1642); s of Capt Herbert John Anthony Throckmorton, RN (d 1941, 3 s of 10 Bt), and Ethel Mary, *née* Stapleton-Bretherton (d 1929); suc cousin, Sir Robert George Maxwell Throckmorton, 11 Bt, 1989; *b* 9 Feb 1916; *Educ* Beaumont; *m* 1972, Violet Virginia, da of late Anders William Anderson; *Heir* none; *Style—* Sir Anthony Throckmorton, Bt; 2006 Oakes Avenue, Everett, Washington 98201, USA; University of Washington, Seattle, Washington 98195 (☎ 206 543 8757)

THROCKMORTON, Lady Isabel Violet Kathleen; *née* Manners; da of 9 Duke of Rutland (d 1940), and Kathleen, *née* Tennant (d 1989); *b* 5 Jan 1918; *m* 1, 1936 (m dis 1951), Gp Capt Loel Guinness, OBE (d 1988); 1 s (William Loel Seymour Guinness, *qv*), 1 da (Marchioness of Dufferin and Ava, *qv*); m 2, 1953, Sir Robert Throckmorton, 11 Bt (d 1989); *Style—* The Lady Isabel Throckmorton; Molland, S Molton, N Devon; Coughton Court, Alcester, Warwicks

THROWER, David John; s of Edward Thrower (d 1972), and Gladys Naomi Maude, *née* Talbot; *b* 19 Nov 1932; *Educ* St Joseph's Coll, Cranfield Sch of Mgmnt; *m* 10 Aug 1955, Marie Jeanette, da of Frederick White (d 1975); 1 s (Graham David b 1969), 4 da (Amanda Jane b 1956, Christine Alyson b 1959, Karen Denise b 1961, Michelle Susan b 1967); *Career* RAF aircrew, sr NCO, Gunnery Offr; dir H Bradley Ltd 1957-(md 1967-74), fndr Nailpak Ltd 1972 (md 1974), fndr and chm Thrower Bros Group (Holdings) Ltd 1974- (also chief exec 1991-), dir Thrower Leasing Ltd 1983-86, ptnr Lebrad Properties Syndicate 1967-87; pres Upper Norwood Rotary Club 1977-78, life pres 2nd Croydon Scout Gp, chm CBI S London Region; FCIS, FBIM; *Recreations* golf, reading, touring; *Clubs* Upper Norwood Rotary, IOD, Croydon Dining, Air Gunners Assoc; *Style—* David J Thrower, Esq; Heatherdene, Harewood Rd, S Croydon, Surrey; 32 Church Rd, London SE19

THRUSH, Prof Brian Arthur; s of Arthur Albert Thrush (d 1963), of Hampstead, London, and Dorothy Charlotte, *née* Money (d 1982); *b* 23 July 1928; *Educ* Haberdashers' Aske's, Emmanuel Coll Cambridge (BA, MA, PhD, ScD); *m* 31 May 1958, Rosemary Catherine, da of George Henry Terry (d 1970), of Ottawa, Canada; 1 s (Basil Mark Brian b 1965), 1 da (Felicity Elizabeth b 1967); *Career* conslt to US Nat Bureau of Standards 1957-58; Univ of Cambridge: demonstrator in physical chemistry 1953-58, asst dir of res 1959-64, lectr 1964-69, reader 1969-78, prof of physical chemistry 1978-, head of chemistry dept 1988-, vice-master Emmanuel Coll 1986-90 (fell 1960-); visiting prof Chinese Acad of Sci 1980-; memb: Lawes Agric Tst Ctee 1979-89, Natural Environment Res Cncl 1985-90, Cncl of the Royal Soc 1990-92; Tilden lectr of Chemical Soc 1965, Michael Polanyi medallist Royal Soc of Chemistry 1980; FRS 1976, FRSC 1977, memb Academia Europaea 1990; *Recreations* wine, walking; *Clubs* Athenaeum; *Style—* Prof Brian Thrush, FRS; Brook Cottage, Pemberton Terrace, Cambridge CB2 1JA (☎ 0223 357 637); University of Cambridge, Dept of Chemistry, Lensfield Rd, Cambridge CB2 1EW (☎ 0223 336 458, fax 0223 336 362, telex 81240); Emmanuel College, Cambridge CB2 3AP (☎ 0223 334 268)

THUBRON, Colin Gerald Dryden; s of Brig Gerald Ernest Thubron, DSO, OBE, of Pheasants Hatch, Piltdown, Uckfield, Sussex, and Evelyn Kate Mary, *née* Dryden; *b* 14 June 1939; *Educ* Eton; *Career* editorial staff: Hutchinson & Co 1959-62, Macmillan Co NY 1964-5; freelance filmmaker 1962-64; author; *Books* Mirror to Damascus (1967), The Hills of Adonis (1968), Jerusalam (1969), Journey Into Cyprus (1975), The God in the Mountain (1977), Emperor (1978), Among the Russians (1983), A Cruel Madness (1984, Silver Pen Award), Behind the Wall (1987, Hawthorncle Prize, Thomas Cook Award), Falling (1989); FRSL 1969; *Style—* Colin Thubron, Esq; Garden Cottage, 27 St Ann's Villas, London W11 4RT (☎ 071 602 2522)

THUM, Maximilien John Alexandre (Max); s of Maximilien Francois Thum (d 1972), of Geneva, Switzerland, and Kathleen Isabel, *née* Crouch (d 1972); *b* 15 Feb 1933; *Educ* Ecole Internationale de Genéve, Chigwell Sch Essex, Law Socs Coll of Law; *m* 1, 15 Feb 1958 (m dis 1981), Freda, *née* Wray; 2 s (Nicolas Charles Maximilien b 3 Feb 1959, Jonathan Richard Alexandre b 25 March 1962), 1 da (Annabel Maxine Elizabeth b 26 Nov 1963); m 2, 25 Feb 1982, Valerie, *née* Kay; *Career* RAF 1955-57, cmmnd Pilot Offr 1956; admitted slr of Supreme Court 1955, asst slr Lewis and Lewis and Gisborne 1955, slr Rodyk and Davidson Singapore 1957-60, called to Singapore Bar 1958, Professional Purposes Dept Law Soc 1961, ptnr Sharpe Pritchard and Co London 1962-66, sr litigation ptnr Ashurst Morris Crisp London 1967-; memb: Int Bar Assoc, American Bar Assoc; *Recreations* photography, opera, swimming, tennis, shooting; *Clubs* RAC; *Style—* Max Thum, Esq; Fosters, Mattingley, Hants; 24 Stanhope Gardens, London SW7; Ashurst Morris Crisp, Solicitors, Broadwalk House, 5 Appold St, London EC2A 2HA (☎ 071 638 1111, fax 071 972 7990, telex 887067 ASHLAW)

THURLOW, Dr Alexander Cresswell; s of Maurice Cresswell Thurlow (d 1940), and Despina Alexandra, *née* Evangelinou; *b* 13 April 1940; *Educ* E Sussex GS, St Marys Hosp Med Sch (MB BS); *m* 29 June 1963, Joanna, da of Stefan Woycicki, of Wiltshire; 2 da (Susan Kristina b 1965, Jane b 1966); *Career* sr registrar anaesthesia St Thomas' Hosp and Hosp For Sick Children 1969-72; conslt anaesthetist: St Georges Hosp 1972-, Royal Dental Hosp 1972-82; asst prof of anaesthesia Stanford Univ California USA 1975-76, tutor and lectr anaesthesia Coll of Anaesthetists 1977-; memb Assoc of Anaesthetists, cncl memb Assoc of Dental Anaesthetists; memb BMA, FFARCS 1968; *Books* contrib: Clinics In Anaesthesiology (1983), A Practice of Anaesthesia (1984), Anaesthesia and Sedation in Dentistry (1983); *Recreations* swimming, skiing, opera, theatre; *Style—* Dr Alexander Thurlow; Dept of Anaesthesia, St Georges Hospital, Blackshaw Rd, London SW17 (☎ 081 672 1255)

THURLOW, David George; OBE (1987); s of Frederick Charles Thurlow (d 1986), of Bury St Edmunds, and Audrey Isabel Mary, *née* Farrow; *b* 31 March 1939; *Educ* King Edward VI Sch Bury St Edmunds, Dept of Architecture Cambridge Coll of Art, Sch of Architecture Canterbury Coll of Art, Univ of Cambridge (MA); *m* 19 Dec 1959, Pamela Ann, da of Percy Adolphous Rumbelow; 3 da (Suzanne Elizabeth, Jane Ann, Emma Louise); *Career* fndr ptnr: Cambridge Design Group 1970, Cambridge Design Architects 1975, Design Group Cambridge 1988; Faculty of Architecture Univ of Cambridge 1970-77, exhibitor Royal Acad Summer Exhibition 1983-87; awards incl: RIBA Award 1976, 1984 and 1986, Civic Tst Award 1978 and 1986, DOE Housing Award 1985; fndr memb: Granta Housing Soc, Cambridge Forum for the Construction Indust 1981 (chm 1985-86); assessor: RIBA Awards 1979, 1984, 1986 and 1990, Civic Tst Awards 1979-88; memb PSA Design Panel 1987-; ARIBA 1965; *Recreations* cricket, golf, food; *Clubs* Athenaeum; *Style—* David Thurlow, Esq, OBE; 9 Sylvester Rd, Cambridge (☎ 0223 316 378); Design Group Cambridge, Merlin Place, Milton Rd, Cambridge CB4 4DP (☎ 0223 420 228, fax 0223 420 566)

THURLOW, 8 Baron (GB 1792); Francis Edward Hovell-Thurlow-Cumming-Bruce; KCMG (1961, CMG 1957); 2 s of Rev 6 Baron Thurlow (d 1952), and Grace Catherine, *née* Trotter (d 1959); suc bro, 7 Baron Thurlow, CB, CBE, DSO, 1971; *b* 9 March 1912; *Educ* Shrewsbury, Trinity Coll Cambridge (MA); *m* 13 Aug 1949, Yvonne Diana (d 1990), da of late Aubyn Harold Raymond Wilson, of Westerlee, St Andrews, Fife, and formerly w of Mandell Creighton Dormehl; 2 s, 2 da; *Heir* s, Hon Roualeyn Robert Hovell-Thurlow-Cumming-Bruce; *Career* Dept of Agric for Scotland 1935-37, sec to British High Cmmn in NZ 1939-44 and Canada 1944-45; private sec to

Sec of State for Commonwealth Relations 1947-49, cnsllr British High Cmmn in New Delhi 1949-52, advsr to Govr of Gold Coast 1955; dep high cmmr in Ghana 1957 and Canada 1958; high cmmr for UK in NZ 1959-63 and Nigeria 1963-66; dep under sec FCO 1964, govr and C-in-C of Bahamas 1968-72; chm Inst of Comparative Study of History, Philosophy and the Sciences 1975; chm Khiron Educnl Tst 1988; KStJ; *Recreations* chess; *Clubs* Travellers'; *Style—* The Rt Hon the Lord Thurlow, KCMG; 102 Leith Mansions, Grantully Road, London W9 1LJ (☎ 071 289 9664)

THURNHAM, Peter Giles; MP (C) Bolton North-East 1983; s of Giles Rymer Thurnham (d 1975), and Marjorie May, *née* Preston; *b* 21 Aug 1938; *Educ* Oundle Sch, Peterhouse Cambridge, Harvard Business Sch, Cranfield Inst of Tech; *m* 1963, Sarah Janet, da of Harold Keenlyside Stroude (d 1974); 1 s, 3 da, 1 s adopted; *Career* professional engr running own business 1972-; memb S Lakeland Dist Cncl 1982-84; *Recreations* Lake Dist, family life; *Style—* Peter Thurnham, Esq, MP; Hollin Hall, Crook, Kendal, Cumbria LA8 9HP (☎ 0539 821 382); House of Commons, London SW1

THURSBY-PELHAM, Brig (Mervyn) Christopher; OBE (1986); s of Nevill Cressett Thursby-Pelham (d 1950), of Danyrall, Carmarthenshire, *see* Burke's Landed Gentry, 18 Edn, vol 1, and Yseulte, *née* Peel (d 1982); *b* 23 March 1921; *Educ* Wellington, Merton Coll Oxford; *m* 16 Jan 1943, Rachel Mary Latimer, da of Sir Walter Stuart James Willson (d 1952), of Tonbridge, Kent; 1 s (David Thomas Cressett b 1948), 1 da (Philippa Rachel Mary b 1943); *Career* cmmnd Welsh Gds 1941; serv 3 Bn: N Africa, Italy, Austria 1943-45, 1 Bn serv Palestine and Egypt, graduate Staff Coll Camberley 1950, GSO2 (Ops) 6 Armd Div BAOR 1951-53, Regtl Adj Welsh Gds 1956-57, DS Coll Camberley 1957-60, Cmdt Gds Depot Pirbright 1960-63, GSO1 (Ops) Allied Staff Berlin 1963-64, Regtl Lt-Col cmdg WG 1964-67, COS Br Forces Gulf 1967-69, COS London Dist 1969-72, Dep Fortress Cdr Gibraltar 1972-74, Dep Cdr Midwest Dist UK 1974-76; ADC to The Queen 1972-76; dir gen Br Heart Fndn 1976-86 and 1988-90, co pres Royal Br Legion Berks 1985-91; pres Welsh Gds Assoc Monmouthshire branch 1987, Gds Assoc Reading branch 1991-; *Recreations* fishing, sailing, skiing, travel; *Clubs* Cavalry and Gds, Royal Yacht Sqdn; *Style—* Brig Christopher Thursby-Pelham, OBE; Ridgeland House, Finchampstead, Berks RG11 3TA; King's Quay, Whippingham, IOW PO32 6NU

THURSFIELD, John Richard; s of Maj Rupert MacNaghten Cecil Thursfield (d 1979), and Elizabeth Margaret Mary, *née* Gunning; *b* 2 Oct 1937; *Educ* Rugby Sch; *m* 29 April 1961, Sarah, da of Charles Clinton Dawkins (d 1985); 2 s (Peter John b 1964, Robert Charles b 1967), 2 da (Mary Elizabeth b 1963, Rachel Sarah b 1969); *Career* dir Union Discount Co Ltd; *Recreations* skiing; *Style—* John Thursfield, Esq; Hodges Farm, Lower Froyle, Alton, Hants, GU34 4LL (☎ 0420 23294); 39 Cornhill, London, EC3V 3NU (☎ 071 623 1020)

THURSO, 2 Viscount (UK 1952); Sir Robin Macdonald Sinclair; 5 Bt (GB 1786), JP (Caithness 1959); s of 1 Viscount Thurso, KT, CMG, PC (d 1970, leader, as Sir Archibald Sinclair, of Lib Pty 1935-45), and Marigold (da of Lt-Col James Forbes, gs of Sir Charles Forbes, 3 Bt, by the Col's 1 w Lady Angela St Clair-Erskine, da of 4 Earl of Rosslyn); *b* 24 Dec 1922; *Educ* Eton, New Coll Oxford, Edinburgh Univ; *m* 1952, Margaret Beaumont, da of late Col Josiah James Robertson, DSO, TD, JP, DL, of Norwood, Wick, Caithness, and widow of Lt Guy Warwick Brokensha, DSC, RN; 2 s, 1 da; *Heir* s, Hon John Archibald Sinclair; *Career* sits as Lib peer in House of Lords; Flt Lt RAF 1939-45; farmer; memb Caithness CC 1949-61 and 1965-73, town cncllr Thurso 1957-61 and 1965-73, baillie 1960 and 1969, dean of Guild 1968, police judge 1971; chm: Sinclair Family Tst Ltd, Lochdhu Hotels Ltd, Thurso Fisheries Ltd; dir Stephens (Plastics) Ltd; fndr & 1 chm Caithness Glass Ltd; Lord-Lieut Caithness 1973- (DL 1952, Vice-Lt 1964-73); pres Highland Soc of London 1980-83; Boys Bde 1985-; North Country Cheviot Sheep Soc 1951-54; Assoc of Scottish Dist Fishery Bds 1975-; chm Caithness & Sutherland Youth Employment Ctee 1957-75, memb Red Deer Cmmn 1965-74; *Recreations* shooting, fishing, amateur drama; *Clubs* RAF, New (Edinburgh); *Style—* The Rt Hon the Viscount Thurso, JP; Thurso East Mains, Thurso, Caithness, Scotland (☎ 0847 62600); Dalnawillan, Altnabreac, Caithness

THURSTON, Dr John Gavin Bourdas; s of Gavin Leonard Bourdas Thurston (d 1980), and Ione Witham, *née* Barber (d 1967); *b* 8 April 1937; *Educ* Haileybury Coll, Guy's Hosp (MB BS, MRCS, LRCP, MRCP); *m* 1, Felicity, *née* Neal; 1 s (Gavin b 1962), 1 da (Georgette Margaret (Mrs McCready) b 1959); m 2, Joy Elizabeth, *née* Leech; 3 s (Gareth b 1966, John b 1969, Andrew b 1972); m 3, 25 July 1986, Stephanie Sarah, da of John Henry Mayo; *Career* house physician and surgn: Guy's 1961-62, Lewisham Hosp 1962; house physician Brompton Hosp 1962-63, registrar Westminster Hosp 1964-66, res sr registrar Br Heart Fndn 1967-68, sr cardiology registrar Westminster Hosp 1968-78, conslt Accident and Emergency Dept Queen Mary's Univ Hosp Roehampton 1979-; disaster doctor RFU Twickenham; med offr: Surrey Co RFC, Rosslyn Park RFC; med companion Grand Order of Water Rats, conslt physician PPP Med Centre London; pres A/E Section RSM 1980-90, hon sec Br Assoc of A/E Med 1984-90; Freeman City of London 1965, Liveryman Worshipful Soc of Apothecaries 1963; memb: BMA 1962, Br Assoc of A/E Med 1979; FRSM 1986; *Books* Hyperbaric Medicine (co-author 1977), Scientific Foundations of Anaesthesia (co-author 1976); *Recreations* eating, drinking, rugby, humour, after-dinner speaking, study of good English; *Clubs* Snowball, Rosslyn Park RFC, Grand Order of Water Rats; *Style—* Dr John Thurston; 164 Upper Richmond Rd West, East Sheen, London SW14 8AW (☎ 081 878 9875); Queen Marys University Hospital, Roehampton, London SW15 5PN (☎ 081 789 6611)

THURSTON, Julian Paul; s of Ronald Thurston, of Dunstable, Beds, and Eileen Joyce Thurston, *née* Salmon; *b* 11 May 1955; *Educ* Bedford Sch, Merton Coll Oxford (MA); *m* 11 July 1981, Julia Sarah, da of Thomas George Kerslake (d 1966); 1 s (Thomas b 1989), 1 da (Sarah b 1987); *Career* admitted slr 1979; ptnr McKenna & Co 1986-; *Style—* Julian Thurston, Esq; McKenna & Co, Inveresk House, 1 Aldwych, London WC2R 0HF (☎ 071 836 2442, fax 071 379 3059, telex 27251)

THWAITE, Ann; da of A J Harrop (d 1963), and Hilda Mary, *née* Valentine (d 1990); *b* 4 Oct 1932; *Educ* Marsden Sch Wellington NZ, Queen Elizabeth's GS Barnet, St Hilda's Coll Oxford (MA); *m* 4 Aug 1955, Anthony Thwaite, OBE, *qv*; 4 da (Emily b 1957, Caroline b 1959, Lucy b 1961, Alice b 1965); *Career* writer; reg reviewer of children's books 1963-85 in TLS, currently in The Guardian, TES; children's books incl: The Camelthorn Papers (1969), Tracks (1978), Allsorts 1-7 (ed, 1968-75), Allsorts of Poems (1978); publications: Waiting for the Party: the life of Frances Hodgson Burnett (1974), My Oxford (ed, 1977), Edmund Gosse: a literary landscape (1984), A A Milne: his life (1990), Portraits from Life: essays by Edmund Gosse (ed, 1991); winner: Duff Cooper Memorial award (for Edmund Gosse) 1985, Whitbread Biography prize (for A A Milne) 1990; FRSL; *Recreations* other people's lives, punting on the Tas; *Clubs* PEN, Soc of Authors, Royal Over-Seas League, Children's Books History Soc; *Style—* Ann Thwaite; The Mill House, Low Tharston, Norfolk NR15 2YN (☎ 050 841 569); c/o Curtis Brown, 162 Regent St, London W1R 5TB (☎ 071 872 0332)

THWAITE, Anthony Simon; OBE (1990); s of Hartley Thwaite, JP (d 1978), of Yorks, and Alice Evelyn, *née* Mallinson; *b* 23 June 1930; *Educ* Kingswood Sch Bath, ChCh Oxford (MA); *m* 4 Aug 1955, Ann Barbara, *qv*, da of Angus John Harrop (d 1963), of NZ and London; 4 da (Emily b 1957, Caroline b 1959, Lucy b 1961, Alice b 1965); *Career* Nat Serv Sgt Instr Rifle Bde and RAEC 1949-51; lectr English lit Univ of Tokyo 1955-57, prodr BBC radio 1957-62, literary ed The Listener 1962-65, asst prof English Univ of Libya Benghazi 1965-67, literary ed New Statesman 1968-72, co ed Encounter 1973-85, dir Andre Deutsch Ltd 1986-; Richard Hillary Meml Prize 1968, Cholmondeley Award for Poetry 1983, chm of judges Booker Prize 1986; former memb: Ctee of Mgmnt Soc of Authors, Cncl RSL, Lit Panel Arts Cncl of GB; current memb Lit Advsy Ctee Br Cncl; Hon LittD Univ of Hull 1989; FRSL 1978; *Books* Poems 1953-83 (1984), Six Centuries of Verse (1984), Poetry Today (1985), Letter From Tokyo (1987), Philip Larkin: Collected Poems (ed, 1988), Poems 1953-88 (1989); *Recreations* archaeology, travel; *Style—* Anthony Thwaite, Esq, OBE; The Mill House, Low Tharston, Norfolk (☎ 050 841 569)

THWAITES, Prof Sir Bryan; s of Ernest James Thwaites (d 1978), and Dorothy Marguerite, *née* Dickeson; *b* 6 Dec 1923; *Educ* Dulwich, Winchester, Clare Coll Cambridge (MA, PhD); *m* 11 Sept 1948, Katharine Mary, da of H R Harries (d 1946); 4 s (Barnaby Christopher b 1953, Quentin Mark b 1956, Dominic John b 1958, Jacoby Michael b 1963), 2 da (Eleanor Jane b 1951, Matilda Bridget b 1966); *Career* sci offr Nat Physical Lab 1944-47, lectr Imperial Coll London 1947-51, asst master Winchester Coll 1951-59, prof of mathematics Univ of Southampton 1959-66, princ Westfield Coll of London 1966-83; fndr Sch of Mathematics Project (SMP) 1961 (chm of Tstees 1968-83, life pres 1984); JP 1963-66; chm: Mgmnt Ctee Northwick Park Hosp 1970-74, Brent and Harrow AHA 1973-82, Wessex RHA 1982-88; tstee Forbes Tst 1986-, memb City Technol Colls Tst 1987-, chm Friends of Winchester Coll 1980-, dir Brendoncase Fndn 1990-; hon prof Univ of Southampton 1983-; FIMA (pres 1966); kt 1986; *Books* Incompressible Aerodynamics (1960), On Teaching Mathematics (1961), The SMP: The First Ten Years (1973), Education 2000 (1983); *Recreations* sailing, music; *Clubs* IOD; *Style—* Prof Sir Bryan Thwaites; Milnthorpe, Winchester, Hampshire SO22 4NF (☎ 0962 852394)

THWAITES, Hon Mrs (Flora Margaret); yr da of Baron Jenkin of Roding, PC (Life Peer), *qv*; *b* 1962; *Educ* St John's Coll Durham; *m* 12 May 1990, Jacoby Michael Thwaites, yst s of Prof Sir Bryan Thwaites, of Milnthorpe, Winchester, Hants; *Style—* The Hon Mrs Thwaites; 32 Fairfield Road, London E3 2QB

THWAITES, Jacqueline Ann; JP (South Westminster 1976); da of late Sonia Whitaker, *née* Pentney; *b* 16 Dec 1931; *Educ* Convent of the Sacred Heart Brighton, House of Citizenship London; *m* 1, 1955 (m dis 1963), Michael Inchbald; 1 s (Courtenay Charles b 1958), 1 da (Charlotte Amanda b 1960); m 2, 2 June 1974, Brig Peter Trevenen Thwaites, s of late Lt-Col Norman Graham Thwaites, CBE, MVO, MC; *Career* fndr and princ: Inchbald Sch of Design 1960, Inchbald Sch of Fine Arts 1970, Inchbald Sch of Garden Design 1972; memb: Monopolies Cmmn 1972-75, Whitford Ctee on Copyright and Design 1974-76, London Electricity Conservation Cncl 1973-76, Westminster City Cncl (Warwick Ward) 1974-78, Visiting Ctee RCA 1986-90; tstee St Peter's Res Tst 1987-90, acting pres Int Soc of Interior Designers (London Chapter 1987-90); chm Int Soc of Interior Designers 1990-; *Books* Directory of Interior Designers (1966), Bedrooms (1968), Design & Decoration (1971); *Recreations* fishing, travel; *Style—* Mrs Jacqueline Thwaites, JP; Inchbald School of Design, 32 Eccleston Square, London SW1V 1PB (☎ 071 630 9011, fax 071 976 5979)

THWAITES, Brig Peter Trevenen; s of Lt-Col Norman Graham Thwaites, CBE, MVO, MC (d 1956), of Barley End, Tring, Herts, and Eleanor Lucia, *née* Whitridge; *b* 30 July 1926; *Educ* Rugby; *m* 1, 7 Oct 1950 (m dis), Ellen Theresa (d 1976), da of William J King (d 1970); 2 s (Thomas b 1952 d 1960, Christian b 1958), 2 da (Allegra (Mrs Martin) b 1956, Grania b 1959); m 2, Jacqueline Ann Inchbald, *née* Bromley; *Career* cmmnd Grenadier Gds 1944; served: Germany, Egypt, Br Cameroons, Br Guyana; memb Sir William Penney's scientific pty UK atomic trials S Aust 1956, Staff Coll 1958, Bde Maj 1 (later 2) Fed Inf Bde Malaya 1959-60, Jt Servs Staff Coll 1965, MOD 1965-67, Aden 1967, cmd Muscat Regt Sultan of Muscat's Armed Forces Dhofar Campaign 1967-70, AQMG HQ London Dist 1970-71, Col cmd Br Army Staff Singapore and govr Singapore Int Sch 1970-73, dep dir Def Operational Plans (Army) 1973-74, Brig 1975, head of MOD logistics survey team to Saudi Arabia 1976, ret 1977; chm Jt Staff Sultan of Oman's Armed Forces 1977-81; playwright: Love or Money (with Charles Ross, 1958), Master of None (1960), Roger's Last Stand (1976), Caught in the Act (with Charles Ross, 1981), Relative Strangers (1984); chm Individual Sch Direction Ltd 1981-; chm Hurlingham Polo Assoc 1982-; Sultan of Oman's Bravery Medal, Sultan's Commendation, Sultan of Oman's Distinguished Service Medal for Gallantry; *Recreations* shooting; *Clubs* White's, Beefsteak, Cavalry and Guards'; *Style—* Brig Peter Thwaites; The Manor House, Ayot St Lawrence, Herts; 32 Eccleston Sq, London SW1; 7 Eaton Gate, London SW1W 9BA (☎ 071 730 5508)

THWAITES, Ronald; QC (1987); s of Stanley Thwaites, of Stockton-on-Tees, and Aviva, *née* Cohen; *b* 21 Jan 1946; *Educ* Richard Hind Secdy Tech Sch Stockton, Grangefield GS Stockton, Kingston Coll of Technol (LLB); *m* 7 Aug 1972, Judith Adelaide Foley, da of Barry Baron Myers, of Surbiton; 3 s (George b 1973, David b 1976, Richard b 1981), 1 da (Stephanie b 1980); *Career* called to the Bar Gray's Inn (ad eundem Inner Temple) 1970; *Recreations* swimming, squash, lighting bonfires; *Style—* Ronald Thwaites, Esq, QC; 10 Kings Bench Walk, Temple, London EC4Y 7EB (☎ 071 353 2501, fax 071 353 0658)

THYKIER, Hans; s of Svend Thykier (d 1986), and Emilie Marie Johansen (d 1980); *b* 22 April 1931; *Educ* Ostre Borgerdyd Skole Copenhagen Denmark, Univ of Copenhagen; *m* 1971, Gertrud Ilona Birgitta, da of Baron Oscar Didrik Staël von Holstein (d 1969); 4 children; *Career* A H Riise Copenhagen Denmark 1957-66, Mobil Europe Inc (in Denmark, Austria, Switzerland and the UK) 1966-71, mktg dir in Europe for Occidental International Oil Inc 1971-74, exec dir Int Planned Parenthood Fedn (IPPF) 1974-76, American Express Co 1976-85, vice pres American Express Bank (in Europe, ME and Africa) 1983-85; dir Foreign & Colonial Management (Jersey) Ltd 1985-88, John Govett & Co Management (Jersey) Ltd, John Govett (CI) Ltd 1988-; *Recreations* tennis, yachting; *Clubs* Brooks's, Oriental, Royal Thames Yacht, Royal Danish Yacht, Danish; *Style—* Hans Thykier, Esq; 14 Beaumont St, London W1 (☎ 071 486 3041); Naylands, Slaugham, W Sussex, (☎ 0444 400270); Casa Ararat, Penedo, Sintra, Portugal; 20 Dalen, FANO, Vesterhavsbad, FANO, Denmark

THYNE, Malcolm Tod; s of Andrew Tod Thyne (d 1982), and Margaret Melrose, *née* Davidson (d 1984); *b* 6 Nov 1942; *Educ* Leys Sch Cambridge, Clare Coll Cambridge (MA); *m* 31 July 1969, Eleanor Christine, da of James Fleming Scott, of Edinburgh; 2 s (Douglas b 1973, Iain b 1976); *Career* asst master: Edinburgh Acad 1965-69, Oundle Sch 1969-80 (housemaster 1972-80); headmaster: St Bees Sch Cumbria 1980-88, Fettes Coll 1988-; HMC 1980; *Books* Periodicity, Atomic Structure and Bonding (1976), contribs to Nuffield Chemistry pubns; *Recreations* mountaineering; *Style—* Malcolm Thyne, Esq; The Lodge, Fettes College, Edinburgh EH4 1QX; Fettes College, Edinburgh EH4 1QX (☎ 031 332 2281)

THYNNE, Lord Christopher John; 2 s of 6 Marquess of Bath, ED, by his 1 w, Hon Daphne Vivian, da of 4 Baron Vivian; *b* 9 April 1934; *Educ* Eton; *m* 1968, Antonia, da of Maj Sir Anthony Palmer, 5 Bt; 1 da; *Career* late 2 Lt Life Guards; runs Longleat House; *Recreations* photography, drawing; *Style—* The Lord Christopher Thynne; The

Hermitage, Horningsham, Wilts; Longleat, Warminster, Wilts (☎ 0985 844 551)

THYNNE, Lady; Liese-Maria; da of late Kenneth William Dennis, of Bristol, and Mrs George Jackaman, of Malta; *b* 1 May 1939; *Educ* Abbeydale Sch Sheffield; *m* 1977, as his 3 w, Lord Valentine Thynne (d 1979), s of 6 Marquess of Bath, ED; 1 da (Natasche Charlotte-Lara Luist Wolsley b 1986) da of Thomas Gerrard Wolsley, of New York; *Career* artist; *Recreations* reading, painting, gardening, cooking, listening to baroque music, medieval architecture, keeping house; *Style—* The Lady Valentine Thynne; Bridge House, St John Street, Wells, Somerset

THYSSEN-BORNEMISZA, Baroness Francesca; da of Baron Heinrich von Thyssen, of the German steel family, and Fiona Campbell-Walter, the mannequin; *b* 1958; *Educ* Le Rosey Switzerland, St Martin's Art Sch, ICA; *Career* photographer, singer and mannequin; apprentice to family business; *Style—* Baroness Francesca Thyssen-Bornemisza; 28 Seymour Walk, London SW10 (☎ 071 352 7913)

TIARKS, Anthony John Phipps; er s of Lt Cdr John Desmond Tiarks, RN; *b* 28 July 1952; *Educ* Millfield, City Univ (BSc); *m* 1979, Lesley, da of Dr Ian Verner, of 67 Harley Street, London; 1 da (Venetia b 1985); *Career* jt dep md ACLI Int Commodity Servs (UK subsid of Donaldson Lufkin Jenrette, a Wall Street investment banking firm) 1982-; md Tide (UK) Ltd; landowner; *Recreations* shooting, sailing; *Style—* Anthony Tiarks, Esq; c/o ACLI International Commodity Services Ltd, 52 Mark Lane, London EC3 (☎ 071 623 5811); The Old Manor, Chawton, nr Alton, Hants; 2 South Audley Street, London W1 (☎ 071 409 3500)

TIBBALDS, Francis Eric; s of late William Eric Tibbalds, of Beckenham, Kent, and Elsie Agnes, *née* Wood; *b* 16 Oct 1941; *Educ* Farnham GS, Regent St Poly (Dip Arch), Univ of London (MPhil); *m* 6 Sept 1969, Janet Grace, da of Kenneth Malcolm McDonald, of Hayes, Bromley, Kent; 2 s (Adam Dominic b 1971, Benedict Malcolm b 1973); *Career* sr architect planner Llewelyn-Davies Weeks Forestier-Walker & Bor 1969-70, princ architect planner Westminster City Cncl 1970-72, dep chief planning offr Lambeth Borough 1972-74, jt project dir Gp Five (Nigeria) 1974-75, dir of planning Llewelyn-Davies Weeks 1975-78, fndr ptnr Tibbalds Partnership 1978, Tibbalds Colbourne Karski Williams Ltd Architects and Planners 1990-; visiting prof Bartlett Sch of Architecture and Planning UCL 1989-; pres Univ of London Town Planning Soc 1968, fndr Urban Design Gp (chm 1979-86), hon sec RTPI 1990- (pres 1988); memb: Cncl (and chm Environment Ctee) RSA 1989, London Advsy Ctee and Historic Areas Advsy Ctee English Heritage (The Historic Buildings and Monuments Cmmn) 1990-; sr vice pres Euro Cncl of Town Planners 1990-; Freeman City of London 1988, memb Worshipful Co of CAs; RIBA 1968, FRTPI 1970, FRSA 1980, FFB 1985; *Books* Urban Sketchbook (1988); *Recreations* sketching, choral singing; *Style—* Francis E Tibbalds, Esq; 37 Kelsey Park Ave, Beckenham, Kent BR3 2NL (☎ 081 658 3479); Tibbalds Colbourne Karski Williams Ltd, 39 Charing Cross Rd, London WC2H 0AW (☎ 071 439 9272, fax 071 439 0323)

TIBBELLS, John Terence; s of William Shearer Tibbells (d 1949), of Liverpool, and Martha, *née* Fox (d 1973); *b* 5 May 1931; *Educ* Liverpool Coll; *m* 12 March 1964, Sheila Myfanwy, da of Robert Ivor Roberts (d 1958), of Dyserth Hall, Dyserth, Clwyd; 2 da (Sally b 1967, Nicola b 1970); *Career* Subaltern S Lancs Regt (PWV) 1955-57, 24 Bde Barnard Castle and Berlin Ind Bde; CA Glass and Edwards Liverpool 1949-58, other professional firms 1962-67; sec Liverpool cos in Seagram Gp 1958-61, accountant of wine cos John Holt Gp 1961-62, princ J T Tibbells and Co 1968-; FCA, ATII; *Recreations* country life, travel, rugby; *Clubs* Liverpool St Helens FC (RU), Old Lerpoolian Soc; *Style—* John Tibbells, Esq; Clarence House, Bryniau, Dyserth, Rhyl, Clwyd LL18 6BY; J T Tibbells & Co Chartered Accountants, Clarence House, Bryniau, Dyserth, Rhyl, Clwyd LL18 6BY

TIBBER, His Hon Judge Anthony Harris; s of Maurice Tibber (d 1969), and Priscilla, *née* Deyong (d 1970); *b* 23 June 1926; *Educ* Univ Coll Sch Hampstead, Magdalen Coll Sch Brackley; *m* 1954, Rhona Ann, da of Julius Salter; 3 s (Peter, Clifford, Andrew); *Career* rec Crown Ct 1976, circuit judge 1977; *Style—* His Hon Judge Tibber; c/o Edmonton County Ct, Fore St, London N18 2TN (☎ 081 807 1666)

TIBBITS, Capt Sir David Stanley; DSC (1943); s of Hubert Tibbits (d 1933), of Warwick, and Edith Lucy, *née* Harman (d 1965); *b* 11 April 1911; *Educ* Wells House Sch Malvern Wells, RNC Dartmouth; *m* 1938, Mary Florence, da of Harry St George Butterfield, of Bermuda; 2 da; *Career* joined RN 1925, served WWII, Navigating Offr, started RN Radar Plotting Sch 1943, Cdr 1946, Capt 1953, Dir Radio Equipment Dept Admty 1953-56, i/c HMS Manxman, Dryad and Hermes 1956-61, ret 1961; elder bro of Trinity House 1961 (dep master and chm of Bd 1972-76), fndr chm The Pilots' Nat Pension Fund 1967-76, tstee Nat Maritime Museum 1973-77, govr Pangbourne Coll 1973-78, lay vice pres Missions to Seamen 1973-, hon sec King George's Fund for Sailors 1974-80, memb Bermuda Port Authy & chm Pilotage Ctee, pres Bermuda Soc for the Blind, lay memb BDA Diocesan Synod and Cathedral Vestry 1982-88; Liveryman Worshipful Co of Shipwrights 1973 (memb Ct 1976); FNI 1979 (fndr memb 1972); kt 1976; *Recreations* sailing (yacht Beacon of Bermuda), photography, music; *Clubs* Army and Navy, Royal Yacht Sqdn, Hurlingham, Royal Bermuda Yacht, Royal Hamilton Amateur Dinghy; *Style—* Capt Sir David Tibbits, DSC, RN; Harting Hill, PO Box HM 1419, Hamilton, Bermuda HM FX (☎ 80929 54394)

TIBBS, (Geoffrey) Michael Graydon; OBE (1987); s of Rev Geoffrey Wilberforce Tibbs (d 1957), vicar of Lynchmere, Sussex, and Margaret Florence, *née* Skinner (d 1952); *b* 21 Nov 1921; *Educ* Berkhamsted Sch, St Peter's Coll Oxford (BA, MA); *m* 6 Oct 1951, Anne Rosemary, da of Donald Jocelyn Wortley (d 1981), of Bunchfield, Lynchmere, Sussex; 2 s (Philip b 1955, Christopher b 1957); *Career* serv WWII; ordinary seaman HMS Cottesmore 1940; RNVR: Midshipman 1941, Sub Lt HMS Sheffield 1941, Lt HMS/M Tantulus 1943, HMS/M Varne 1945-46, (despatches); Sudan Political Serv 1949-55 (dist cmmr), seconded ME Centre of Arab Studies 1950; personnel orgn and overseas depts Automobile Assoc 1955-68, memb Lynchmere PCC and Parish Cncl, local pantomime prodr; sec: RCP 1968-86 (hon fell 1986), Faculty of Community Med 1971-72 (hon fell 1987), Faculty of Occupational Med 1978-86 (hon fell 1987); Freeman City of London 1986; FRGS 1948, MIPM 1960, FInstM 1971 (memb 1959); *Books* A Look in Lynchmere; *Recreations* local affairs, producing pantomimes, making bonfires; *Clubs* Naval; *Style—* Michael Tibbs, Esq, OBE; Welkin, Lynchmere Ridge, Haslemere, Surrey GU27 3PP (☎ 0428 643120)

TIBBUTT, Dr David Arthur; s of Sidney Arthur William Tibbutt (d 1955), of Wadhurst, Sussex, and Dorothy Ellen, *née* Lay; *b* 8 March 1941; *Educ* The Skinners' GS Tunbridge Wells, St Peter's Coll Oxford (MA, BM BCh, DM); *m* 26 Nov 1966, Jane, da of Air Vice-Marshal Sir George David Harvey, KBE, CB, DFC (d 1969), of Over Worton, Oxon; 2 s (Mark David b 1968, William George b 1970); *Career* jr hosp doctor United Oxford Hosp 1968-76, conslt physician Worcester Royal Infirmary 1976-, various pubns on thromboembolic disease 1974-, visiting lectr Makerere Univ Med Sch Kampala Uganda 1965-81, post grad clinical tutor (Worcester Dist) 1987-; chm Worcester Dist Clinical Audit Ctee, memb Local Exec Ctee BMA, pres Worcester Dist Br Heart Fndn, tstee Worcestershire Hosp Tst; memb: BMA 1968, W Midlands Physicians Assoc 1976; MRCP 1971, FRCP 1983; *Books* Pulmonary Embolism: Current Therapeutic Concepts (1977); *Recreations* water colour painting, gardening, philately, enjoying Scotland; *Style—* Dr David Tibbutt; Perry Point, 4 Whittington Rd, Worcester WR5 2JU (☎ 0905 355451); Keeper's Cottage, East Kinnauld, Rogart, Sutherland; Worcester Royal Infirmary, Worcester (☎ 0905 763333)

TICKELL, Sir Crispin Charles Cervantes; GCMG (1989), KCVO (1983, MVO 1958); s of Jerrard Tickell, and Renée Oriana, *née* Haynes; *b* 25 Aug 1930; *Educ* Westminster, Christ Church Oxford (MA); *m* 1, 1954 (m dis 1976), Chloë, da of Sir James Gunn, RA; 2 s, 1 da; m 2, 1977, Penelope, da of Dr Vernon Thonre; *Career* serv Lt Coldstream Gds 1952-54; joined Dip Serv 1954-; fell Center for Int Affrs Harvard Univ 1975-76, chef de cabinet to Roy Jenkins as Pres of EEC Cmmn 1977-81, visiting fell All Souls Coll Oxford 1981, ambass Mexico 1981-83, dep under sec FCO 1983-84, perm sec Overseas Devpt Admin 1984-87, perm rep and ambass UN 1987-90; warden Green Coll Oxford 1990-, pres Royal Geographical Soc 1990-; chm: Climate Inst of Washington DC 1990, Int Inst of Environment and Devpt 1990; Offr Order of Orange Nassau Netherlands 1958; *Books* Climatic Change and World Affairs (2 edn, 1986); *Recreations* climatology, paleohistory, art (especially precolumbiana), mountains; *Clubs* Brooks's; *Style—* Sir Crispin Tickell, GCMG, KCVO; Warden's Lodgings, Green College, Oxford OX2 6HG

TICKELL, Maj-Gen Marston Eustace; CBE (1973, MBE 1955), MC (1945); s of Maj-Gen Sir Eustace Francis Tickell, KBE, CB, MC (d 1972), and Mary Violet, *née* Buszard; *b* 18 Nov 1923; *Educ* Wellington, Peterhouse Cambridge; *m* 1961, Pamela Vere, da of Vice Adm Arthur Duncan Read, CB (d 1976); *Career* RE 1944, Engr-in-Chief (Army) 1972-75, Cmdt RMCS 1975-78, ret as Maj-Gen 1978; Col-Cmdt RE (pres Inst 1979-82), Hon Col Engr and Tport Staff Corps 1983-88; *Recreations* sailing; *Clubs* Royal Ocean Racing, Army and Navy; *Style—* Maj-Gen Marston Tickell, CBE, MC; The Old Vicarage, Branscombe, Seaton, Devon

TICKLE, Brian Percival; CB (1985); s of William Tickle, and Lucy, *née* Percival; *b* 31 Oct 1921; *Educ* The Judd Sch Tonbridge; *m* 3 March 1945, Margaret Alice; 1 s (John b 1948), 1 da (Margaret (Mrs Schofield) b 1949); *Career* WWII RCS 1941-46; Civil Serv 1938-70; sr registrar Family Div High Court of Justice 1982-88 (registrar 1970-), ret 1988; co-chm Independent Schools Tribunal 1988-; capt Nevill Golf Club 1975 (tstee 1974-); *Books* Rees Divorce Handbook (ed 1963), Atkins Court Forms and Precedents Probate (2 edn, 1984); *Recreations* golf; *Clubs* Cwlth Tst, Nevill Golf; *Style—* B P Tickle, Esq, CB; 1A Royal Chase, Tunbridge Wells, Kent, TN4 8AX

TICKTIN, Dr Stephen Jan; s of Benjamin Isaac Ticktin, of Toronto, Canada, and Syme Rebecca, *née* Slavner; *b* 30 March 1946; *Educ* Vaughan Rd Collegiate Toronto Canada, Univ of Toronto (MA, MD); *m* 2 Sept 1988, Olga Evaldovna, da of Evalid Moiseyevich Dvorkin, of Leningrad, USSR; *Career* drug dependence unit UCH 1985-89, dept of child psychiatry Central Middx Hosp 1987-; London ed of Asylum magazine for democratic psychiatry; memb London Alliance for Mental Health Action and Survivors Speak Out, assoc memb Philadelphia Assoc; memb: Soc for Existential Analysis, Nat Mind (med dir Brent Mind); MRCPsych; *Recreations* American folk music, badminton; *Style—* Dr Stephen Ticktin; 26 Marlborough Rd, London N19 4NB (☎ 071 272 6059); Dept of Child Psychiatry, Central Middlesex Hospital, Acton Lane, Park Royal, London NW10 7NS (☎ 081 453 2357)

TIDBOROUGH, Hon Mrs (Christine Gray); *née* Addison; yr da of 2 Viscount Addison (d 1976), and Brigit Helen Christine, *née* Williams (d 1980); *b* 3 Sept 1946; *m* 28 Feb 1966, Terry Frederick Tidborough, s of Victor Tidborough, of Cullompton, Devon; *Style—* The Hon Mrs Tidborough; 2 Silver Street, Willand, Cullompton, Devon

TIDBURY, Sir Charles Henderson; DL (Hants 1989); s of late Brig O H Tidbury, MC, and Beryl, *née* Pearce (decd); *b* 26 Jan 1926; *Educ* Eton; *m* 1950, Anne, da of late Brig Hugh Edward Russell, DSO, and Dorothy (d 1989) (who m 2, 1963, Gen Sir Richard Nugent O'Connor, KT, GCB, DSO, MC, d 1981); 2 s, 3 da; *Career* servd KRRC 1943-52, Palestine 1946-48 (despatches), Queen's Westminster TA 1952-60; chm: Whitbread & Co 1978-84, Brickwoods Brewery Ltd 1966-71; dir: Whitbread & Co plc 1959-88, Nabisco Gp Ltd 1985-88, Whitbread Investment Co plc, Barclays Bank plc 1985-91, Barclays plc 1978-91, Mercantile Credit Co Ltd 1985-91, Vaux Gp plc 1985-91, ICL Europe 1985-91, Pearl Group plc 1986-, Mercantile Gp plc 1988-91, George Gale & Co Ltd 1991-; pres: Shire Horse Soc 1986-88, Inst of Brewing 1976-78 (vice pres 1978), Br Inst of Innkeeping 1985-; chm: Brewers Soc 1982-84 (vice pres 1985-), Brewing Res Fndn 1985-, Master Brewers' Co 1988-89, Mary Rose Tst 1980-, William & Mary Tercentenary Tst 1985-; tstee Nat Maritime Museum 1984-; govr: The Nat Heart & Chest Hosps 1988-90, Portsmouth Poly 1988-; memb Centre for Policy Studies; kt 1989; *Recreations* family, sailing, shooting, countryside; *Clubs* Brooks's, Royal Yacht Sqdn, Island Sailing, Bembridge Sailing; *Style—* Sir Charles Tidbury, DL; 22 Ursula St, London SW11 3DW; Crocker Hill Farm, Forest Lane, Wickham, Hants PO17 5DW; 20 Queen Anne's Gate, London SW1H 9AA (☎ 071 222 7060)

TIDMARSH, John Alan; s of Charles Frederick Tidmarsh (d 1962), and Violet Beatrice, *née* Bishopp (d 1984); *b* 13 Aug 1928; *Educ* Cotham; *m* 29 March 1955, Patricia Charlotte, da of Gp Capt Norman Charles Pleasance (d 1943); 1 s (Patrick Charles Holden b 19 April 1962), 1 da (Emma Charlotte b 16 Nov 1960); *Career* Nat Serv RAF 1946-48, sports reporter Western Daily Press 1948-53; BBC: reporter Western Region 1953-55, TV news reporter and reader 1955-66; freelance news reporter 1966-68, presenter BBC World Service Outlook programme 1966-; Geese Theatre Co of GB, Windsor Community Arts Centre; *Recreations* cricket, gardening, cooking, travel; *Clubs* MCC, BBC Bushmen Cricket; *Style—* John Tidmarsh, Esq; 23 Gloucester St, London SW1V 2DB (☎ 071 834 8816)

TIDY, William Edward (Bill); *b* 9 Oct 1933; *m* 1960, Rosa; 2 s (Nick, Robert), 1 da (Sylvia); *Career* cartoonist; Mil Serv RE 1952-56; worked in advtg agency 1956-57, professional cartoonist 1957-; cartoon strips incl: Chelm of Tryg (Punch) 1966-67, The Cloggies (Private Eye) 1967-81, (The Listener) 1985-86, Doctor Whittle (General Practitioner) 1970-, Grimbledon Down (New Scientist) 1970-, The Fosdyke Saga (The Daily Mirror) 1971-85, Kegbuster (What's Brewing) 1976-, The Sporting Spagthorpes (Titbits) 1976-79, Intergalatic Mirror (The Mirror Group) 1979-81, The Last Chip Shop (Private Eye) 1981-85, The Crudgingtons (Today) 1986-87, Billy Bucket (Private Eye) 1988-89, Savage Sports (The Mail On Sunday) 1988-89, God's Own County (Yorkshire Post) 1989-90; tv presenter: Weekend (Granada), Three Days Last Summer (BBC 2), Tidy Up Walsall (BBC 1), Tidy Up Naples (BBC 2), It's My City (BBC 1); numerous tv guest appearances incl This Is Your Life 1975; radio presenter Tidy Answers (BBC Radio 4), several radio guest appearances; playwright: The Great Eric Ackroyd Disaster (Oldham Coliseum), The Cloggies (Theatre Clwyd), The Fosdyke Saga (Bush Theatre and Arts Cncl Tour); writer and illustrator: Laugh with Bill Tidy, Tidy's World, The Fosdyke Saga (15 vols), The World's Worst Golf Club, Robbie And The Blobbies, A Day At Gringemound School, The Incredible Bed, Draw Me 387 Baked Beans; illustrator: The Exploding Present (by John Wells), Napoleon's Retreat From Wigan (by Mike Harding), The Book of Heroic Failures (by Stephen Pile), Everbody's Doing It (by Max Hodes), Fisherman's Friend (by Bill Tidy and Derrick Geer), Rosa Tidy's Pasta Book (by Rosa Tidy), Fine Glances (by Mike Seabrook), Food For All The Family (by Magnus Pike), Service Banking (by Michael Hanson), Justices of the Peace Guide to Procedure, Improving Relationships Between the Public and Civil Servants (COI), EEC Hygiene Rules on the Preparation and Serving of Foodstuffs; after-dinner speaker for numerous orgns incl pub cos and charities; designer of stage sets and costumes; fndr (with Sylvia Tidy) Tidy

Publications Ltd 1988; *awards* Granada TV's What The Papers Say award for Cartoonist of the Year 1974 and The Soc of Strip Illustrators award 1980; *Recreations* supporting Everton FC, cultivating peas and beans, watching ships and aircraft, playing cricket, looking after various dependents and independent furry friends and masses of goldfish; *Clubs* Cartoonist's of GB, Lord's Taverners, Armed Forces Benevolent Fund; *Style—* Bill Tidy, Esq; The Yews, 59 High Street, Kegworth, Derby DE7 2DA (☎ 0509 673939, fax 0509 674763, car 0836 509805)

TIEMAN, Ross; s of John Eric Tieman, of Tonbridge, Kent, and Gladys Hilda, *née* Osbourne; *b* 25 Feb 1957; *Educ* Maidstone GS, UEA (BA); *Career* journalist; trainee reporter Kent Messenger 1980-82, reporter Kent Evening Post 1982-84; dep city ed Birmingham Post 1986-89 (industl reporter 1984-86), business news ed Daily Express 1989-90, industl corr The Times 1990; *Recreations* sailing, skiing, cycling; *Style—* Ross Tieman, Esq; 14 Thorndean St, London SW18 4HE (☎ 081 879 3159); The Times, 1 Pennington St, London E1 9XN (☎ 071 782 5092/5109, fax 071 782 5112)

TIERNEY, Sydney; JP (1965); s of James Tierney (d 1977), and Eleanor, *née* Mould (d 1979); *b* 16 Sept 1923; *Educ* Pearne Secondary Modern Sch, Platter Coll Oxford; *m* 5 Sept 1957, Audrey (d 1981), da of Alfred Duffield; 2 da (Susan b 14 Sept 1958, Patricia b 17 April 1960); m 2, 5 Dec 1985, Margaret Olive, *née* Hannah; *Career* WWII RAF 1942-46 (served SE Asia Command, SA, Pakistan, India, Bangladesh); Trade Union organiser US DAW 1953-74, Labour MP Yardley Birmingham 1974-79, pres USDAW 1977- (nat offr 1979-87); memb Nat Exec Ctee Labour Party 1978-90; *Recreations* fell walking, natural history, sport; *Style—* Sydney Tierney, Esq, JP; 56 Priory Lane, Grange Over Sands, Cumbria LA11 7BJ (☎ 05395 34935); Oakley, 188 Wilsmlow Rd, Manchester M14 6LJ (☎ 061 224£ 2804, fax 061 257 2566)

TIGHE, Anthony Rodger; s of Brian Anthony Michael Tighe, of Bear Park, Foxhouse Lane, Maghull, Lancs, and Paula Angela, *née* Capper; *b* 9 March 1951; *Educ* St Edward's Coll Liverpool, Thames Poly; *Career* salesman Berger Paints 1972-74, in family business 1974-76; Wilsons Brewery Manchester: joined as salesman 1976, area sales mangr 1978-80, sales promotion mangr 1980-82, PR mangr 1982-83; head of PR Grand Metropolitan Brewing North 1983-84, fndr md Greenwood Tighe Public Relations 1984-88, chief exec GTPR (now part of KLP Group plc) 1988-, dir KLP Scotland Ltd 1988-; *awards* first winner Inst of PR Sword of Excellence for product rels 1984, Inst Sales Promotion award 1987, Inst of PR Certificate of Excellence 1989; MIPR 1984, MInstD 1988; *Recreations* golf, Everton FC; *Clubs* Mere Golf and Country; *Style—* Anthony Tighe, Esq; Mendips, 6 Ulviet Gate, The Belfry, High Legh, Knutsford, Cheshire (☎ 0925 75 3336); Greenwood Tighe Public Relations, Osbourne Place, The Downs, Atrincham, Cheshire (☎ 061 928 3535, fax 061 927 7103, car 0836 362 362)

TIKARAM, Hon Justice Sir Moti; KBE (1980); s of Tikaram and Singari; *b* 18 March 1925; *Educ* Marist Bros HS Suva, Victoria Univ Wellington NZ (LLB); *m* 1944, Satyawati (d 1981); 2 s, 1 da; *Career* started law practice 1954, stipendiary magistrate 1960, puinse judge 1968; acted as chief justice 1971 and 1990, ombudsman Fiji 1972-87; Court of Appeal judge 1988-; patron Fiji Lawn Tennis Assoc; *Publications* articles in The Pacific Way and in Recent Law 131; *Recreations* tennis; *Clubs* Fiji, Fiji Golf (Suva); *Style—* The Hon Justice Sir Moti Tikaram, KBE; PO Box 514, 45 Domain Road, Suva, Fiji; office: PO Box 2215, Suva (☎ 211489)

TIKARAM, Tanita; *b* 12 Aug 1960; *Career* singer and songwriter 1987-; first solo performance (Mean Fiddler) 16 Dec 1987, first UK tour Sept-Oct 1988, first Euro tour Jan-March 1989, first USA tour May-June 1989, first World tour Feb-Sept 1990; written over 70 songs; multi platinum disc (worldwide except USA) for Ancient Heart LP 1988 and 1989, gold disc (worldwide except USA) for The Sweet Keeper LP 1990; Twist in my Sobriety single: platinum disc Germany Switzerland Aust, gold disc France Italy Sweden; various other int awards from music indust; *Recreations* books, theatre, go-karting, travelling, snooker, American arts and crafts furniture collecting; *Style—* Miss Tanita Tikaram; c/o Paul Charles, Asgard, 125 Parkway, London NW1 7PS (☎ 071 387 5090, fax 071 387 8740)

TILBERIS, Elizabeth Jane; da of Thomas Stuart-Black Kelly, of Bath, and Janet Storrie, *née* Caldwell; *b* 7 Sept 1947; *Educ* Malvern Girls' Coll, Jacob Kramer Coll Leeds, Leicester Coll of Art (BA); *m* 17 July 1971, Andrew Tilberis, s of Theodore Symeon Tilberis (d 1986); 2 s (Robert b 1981, Christopher b 1985); *Career* Vogue Magazine: fashion asst 1970, fashion ed 1974, exec fashion ed 1981, fashion dir 1987, ed 1987, ed-in-chief 1989-; memb Exec Ctee Br Fashion Cncl (chm Press Ctee 1989); *Recreations* gardening, music; *Style—* Mrs Andrew Tilberis; Vogue Magazine, Vogue House, Hanover Square, London W1 (☎ 071 499 9080)

TILBURY, Alan George; CBE (1966, OBE 1962); s of George Tilbury (d 1945); *b* 9 Dec 1925; *Educ* Sutton Co GS, Natal SA, Univ of London; *m* 1949, Jean-Mary McInnes, *née* Pinkerton; 3 da; *Career* advocate; entered Colonial Legal Serv 1954; attorney-gen Botswana (formerly known as Bechuanaland) 1963 and 1966-69; The Brewers Soc London: head Legal Dept 1970-72, dep sec 1972-82, sec 1982-, dir 1990; chm UK Botswana Soc; *Recreations* sailing (yacht Arabella), music; *Clubs* Tollesbury Cruising, Blackwater Sailing; *Style—* Alan Tilbury, Esq, CBE; Oakwood, Tolleshunt Major, Essex (☎ 0621 860656)

TILEY, Timothy Francis Thornhill; s of Rev George Edward Tiley (d 1985), and Cecilia Frances Mystica Thornhill (d 1982); descended from ancient family of Thornhill, of Thornhill in Yorkshire, which can trace continuous line of descent from saxon theign Eisulf de Thornhill (1080-1165), membs of the family of Jordan de Thornhill (s of Eisulf) are portrayed in a group of the most famous of the 13 century miracle windows in the Trinity chapel of Canterbury Cathedral; *b* 6 June 1949; *Educ* Malvern, St Peter's Coll Oxford (MA); *Career* fndr and md Tim Tiley Ltd (publishers of philosophical and religious prints) 1978-; co-fndr of Brass Rubbing Centres: Oxford 1973, Bristol 1974, Stratford upon Avon 1974, London 1975, Edinburgh 1976, Bath 1976, Glastonbury 1977, Washington DC 1977; *Recreations* piano, reading, cycling, travelling, historical studies; *Clubs* Royal Cwlth Soc; *Style—* Timothy Tiley, Esq; Eblana Lodge, 157 Cheltenham Rd, Bristol, Avon BS6 5RR (☎ 0272 423397)

TILL, Brian Marson; TD (1946); s of Thomas Marson Till, OBE (d 1957), of The Old Rectory, Inkpen, Berks, and Gladys Rhoda Alice, *née* Stedman (d 1963); *b* 17 July 1913; *Educ* Marlborough, Trinity Hall Cambridge (MA); *m* 1, 16 Aug 1950, Amy Anne Elkington (d 1981), da of late Laurence Craigie Maclagan Wedderburn, of N Berwick; 2 s (Thomas Laurence b 29 Aug 1953, William Dominic b 29 Dec 1954); m 2, 27 Nov 1982, Lydia Margaret Gardner, da of late Charles Burnett Morgan, of King Somborne, Hants, wid of Lt Cdr JRN Gardner; *Career* joined TA 52 HAA Regt RA 1938, served WW11, Maj 1943, demob 1945; qualified CA 1939, sr ptnr Black Geoghegan & Till 1957 (ptnr 1939-), ret 1978; memb Worshipful Co of Fishmongers 1935 (Prime Warden 1979-80); *Recreations* fishing, shooting, stalking, skiing; *Clubs* Flyfishers; *Style—* Brian Till, Esq, TD; The Granary, Piddletrenthide, Dorset DT2 7QX

TILL, Ian Jeremy; s of Francis Oughtred Till, of Ilkley, Yorks, and Kathleen Emily, *née* Munt; *b* 6 Sept 1938; *Educ* Ghyll Royd Sch Ilkley, The Leys Sch (JDip MA); *m* 25 July 1964, Caroline Elizabeth Minden, da of Ronald Minden Wilson (d 1987), of Capetown, SA; 2 s (Rodger, Rupert); *Career* CA; formerly with: Robson Rhodes, Deloittes Haskins & Sells, Crompton Parkinson, Courtaulds, Air Products; gp chief accountant Shepherd Building Group Ltd 1975-; dir The Centre for Software Engineering Ltd; cncl memb ICEAW, memb Bldg Employers Confedn Jt Tax Ctee; hon auditor Barbarian FC, govr Univ Coll of Ripon and York St John, treas St Paul's Church Holgate, memb Old Leysian Lodge; FCA; *Recreations* chess, rambling, music, financial markets; *Style—* Ian Till, Esq; 21 Hamilton Way, Acomb, York, N Yorks; Shepherd Building Group Ltd, Blue Bridge Lane, York, N Yorks

TILL, Ven Michael Stanley; s of Maj Stanley Brierley Till (d 1985), of Sunderland, and Charlotte Mary, *née* Pearse; *b* 19 Nov 1935; *Educ* Brighton Hove and Sussex GS, Lincoln Coll Oxford (BA), Westcott House Cambridge; *m* 1965, Theresa Sybil Henriette (Tessa), da of Capt Stephen Wentworth Roskill, CBE, DSC, RN (d 1982), of Cambridge; 1 s (Tobias b 21 April 1969), 1 da (Sophie Elizabeth b 18 May 1971); *Career* Nat Serv 2 Lt RASC HQ NID 1955-57; asst curate St Johns Wood Parish Church 1964-67, dean and fell King's Coll Cambridge 1970-81 (chaplain 1967-70), vicar All Saints Fulham 1981-86, rural dean Hammersmith and Fulham 1982-86, archdeacon of Canterbury 1986-; memb: ACCM (selector) 1975-, General Synod 1986-; chm Canterbury Arts Cncl, prior of St Nicholas Hosp Harbledown; govr: The King's Sch, St Edmund's Sch Benenden; *Recreations* painting, walking, art and music appreciation, building; *Style—* The Ven the Archdeacon of Canterbury; Chillenden Chambers, 29 The Precincts, Canterbury, Kent CT1 2EP (☎ 0227 463036)

TILLARD, Andrew John; s of Maj Gen Philip Blencowe Tillard, CBE, and Patricia Susan Tillard (d 1988); *b* 19 Oct 1956; *Educ* Bradfield Coll; *m* 7 June 1987, Sara-Jane Clare, da of Christopher Wysock-Wright; 2 da (Katie b 22 Feb 1988, Natasha b 21 Feb 1989); *Career* Sandhurst 1976, 1318 Royal Hussars 1976-80; sales and mktg exec Procter and Gamble 1980-82, sr exec Int Mktg and Promotions 1982-83, md Decisions Gp 1983-, dir Ind Software Marketplace 1985-91; memb BDMA; *Recreations* tennis, shooting; *Clubs* Raffles, Mark Cox; *Style—* Andrew Tillard, Esq; 54 Elmfield Rd, Balham, London SW17 (☎ 081 673 7849, fax 071 731 7768); Release Pen, Chailey, Sussex; 19 Worple Rd, London SW19 4JS (☎ 081 879 7766, fax 081 879 7700)

TILLARD, Maj-Gen Philip Blencowe; CBE (1973, OBE 1967); s of Brig John Arthur Stuart Tillard, OBE, MC (d 1975), and Margaret Penelope, *née* Blencowe (d 1966); *b* 2 Jan 1923; *Educ* Winchester, Staff Coll Camberley, Jt Servs Staff Coll; *m* 21 March 1953, Patricia Susan (d 1988), da of Leslie Wiliam Rose Robertson (d 1957), of Snitterfield, Warwicks; 3 s (James b 1954, Andrew b 1956, Richard b 1961), 1 da (Melinda b 1963); *Career* WWII cmmnd KRRC 1942, served 11 Bn (Syria, Italy, Greece) 1943-45, ADC to GOC 2 Div and Army Cdr Malaya 1946, ADC to GOC N Mid Dist 1947, transferred to 13/18 Royal Hussars 1947, served Libya, Malaya 1950 (despatches) and 1960, Adj Warwicks Yeo 1951-53, BAOR 1954-55 and 1961-62, cmd 13/18 Hussars 1964-66, DAQMG (ops) 2 Div 1957-59, GSO2 Int WO 1963, GSO1 Princ Admin Offrs Secretariat MOD 1966-67, Brig Cdr RAC 3 Div Tidworth 1967-69, dep dir Army Trg WO 1970-73, Maj-Gen COS HQ BAOR 1973-76; asst/actg dir resort servs Brighton Borough Cncl 1977-84 (asst to chief exec 1985-87); pres Chailey Sports Assoc 1975-, chm East Sussex Br Field Sports Soc 1988-; ADC to HM The Queen 1970-73; *Publications* Tillard Report on RMA Sandhurst (1972), Suffield report on setting up Army tank training area in Canada; *Recreations* family, shooting and country pursuits, estate; *Clubs* Farmers, Sussex; *Style—* Maj-Gen P B Tillard, CBE; Church House, North Chailey, nr Lewes, E Sussex BN8 4DA (☎ 082572 2759)

TILLER, Rev John; s of Harry Maurice Tiller, and Lucille Tiller; *b* 22 June 1938; *Educ* St Albans Sch, Ch Ch Oxford (MA), Univ of Bristol (MLitt); *m* 5 Aug 1961, Ruth Alison, da of Charles Arthur Watson (d 1966); 2 s (Andrew b 1964, Jonathan b 1967), 1 da (Rachel b 1965); *Career* lectr Trinity Coll Bristol 1967-73, priest in charge Christ Church Bedford 1973-78, chief sec Advsy Cncl for the Church's Miny 1978-84, chllr and canon residentiary of Hereford Cathedral 1984; *Books* A Strategy for the Church's Ministry (1983), The Gospel Community (1987); *Style—* The Rev Canon John Tiller; Canon's House, 3 St John St, Hereford HR1 2NB (☎ 0432 265 659)

TILLEY, Clifford James; CBE (1981); s of Henry James Tilley (d 1952), of Burnham on Sea, Somerset, and Zenobia Ruth Tilley (d 1959); *b* 23 Oct 1911; *Educ* Wycliffe Coll, St John's Coll Oxford (BA); *m* 1936, Ingeborg Hildegard Erna, da of Dr Heinrich Hoepker (d 1958), of Berlin; 2 s (Christopher, Stephen); *Career* WWII Maj RA AA Cmd 1939-44, Staff Coll Camberley 1944, HQ Allied Land Forces Norway 1945; chm Willett & Son (Corn Merchants) Ltd Bristol 1962-88; pres: Grain & Feed Trade Assoc London 1976-77 and 1988-89, Bourse de Commerce Européenne Strasbourg 1976-78, Comité du Commerce des Céréales et des Aliments du Bétail de la Communauté Européenne Brussels 1978-79 and 1981-83 (hon pres 1983); *Recreations* travel; *Style—* Clifford Tilley, Esq, CBE; 17 Dennyview Rd, Abbots Leigh, Bristol BS8 3RD (☎ 027 537 2307)

TILLEY, John Vincent; MP (Lab) Lambeth Central April 1978-; *b* 1941,June; *Career* memb Lambeth Police Monitoring Gp 1981-82; oppn front bench spokesman Home Affrs 1981-82 (sacked for opposing official Lab policy on Falklands crisis); fought Kensington Oct and Nov 1974; former memb Wandsworth Borough Cncl; memb: NUJ, Co-Op Pty, Fabian Soc; *Style—* John Tilley, Esq, MP; House of Commons, London SW1A 0AA

TILLEY, Martin; s of Raymond Tilley, of Lutterworth, Leics, and Georgina, *née* Cottrell; *b* 14 March 1960; *Educ* Lutterworth GS, Southfields Coll, Preston Poly (BA); *Career* graphic designer: Wolff Olins 1983-84, Michael Peters & Ptnrs 1985-86, Trickett & Webb 1986-87, Pentagram 1987-89, McIlroy Coates 1990-; D&AD awards 1982, 1987 and 1988, RSA bursary first 1984, D&AD student award 1986; memb RSA 1985; *Recreations* cycling; *Clubs* Edinburgh Road; *Style—* Martin Tilley, Esq; McIlroy Coates, 10 Bernard St, Leith, Edinburgh EH6 6PP (☎ 031 555 1342, fax 031 555 1343)

TILLOTSON, Maj-Gen Henry Michael; CB (1983), CBE (1976, OBE 1970, MBE 1956); s of Henry Tillotson (d 1967), of Keighley, W Yorks, and May Elizabeth Tillotson (d 1977); *b* 12 May 1928; *Educ* Chesterfield Sch, RMA Sandhurst; *m* 1956, Angela Jane, da of Capt Bertram Wadsworth Shaw, TD (d 1978), of Swanland, E Yorks; 2 s, 1 da; *Career* cmmnd E Yorks Regt 1948; served: Austria 1948-50, Germany 1951-52, Indo-China 1953, Malaya 1953-56, Germany 1956-57 and 1961-63, Malaysia 1964-65, S Arabia 1965-67, Cyprus 1970-71, Hong Kong 1974-75; COS UN Force Cyprus 1976-78, Maj-Gen 1980, COS to C-in-C UK Land Forces 1980-83, Col Prince of Wales's Own Regt of Yorks 1979-86; regnl dir SE Asia Int Mil Servs Ltd 1983-86; res ed Army Quarterly & Def Journal 1987, chm SKY-NET PR 1990; *Recreations* travel, birds, listening to music; *Clubs* Army & Navy; *Style—* Maj-Gen H M Tillotson, CB, CBE; c/o Lloyds Bank, 16 St James's St, London SW1A 1EY

TILLY, John; s of Charles Selby Tilly, of Park House, Greatham, Hartlepool, and Allison, *née* MacFarlane; *b* 22 April 1940; *Educ* Repton Sch, Coll of Law Guildford; *m* 27 Feb 1965, Veronica Evelyn, da of Harold Pallister (d 1965), of Cambridge Rd, Middlesbrough; 1 s (Nicholas Charles b 1966), 1 da (Kate Fiona b 1969); *Career* slr 1972, dir The Hartlepools Water Co 1975, Notary Public 1970; pres Hartlepool Law Soc 1982 (memb 1972), memb Soc of Prov Notaries 1970; *Recreations* farming; *Style—* John Tilly, Esq; York Chambers, York Rd, Hartlepool (☎ 0429 264 101, fax 0429 274 796, telex 58349)

TILLY, Brig (Alfred) John; CBE (1953), DL (Cornwall 1961); s of Alfred Tilly (d 1937), of Henleaze Gardens, Westbury, Bristol, and Elizabeth, *née* Trounson (d 1952); *b* 27 Aug 1909; *Educ* Clifton, Sandhurst; *m* 22 Aug 1936, Joy Viola (d 1986), da of

William Arthur Jeboult (d 1947); 2 da (Vanessa, Rosemary); *Career* cmmnd 2 DCLI 1930, Staff Coll Camberley 1940, Bde Maj 136 Inf Bde 1940, DAAG 1 Corps 1940, instr Staff Coll 1940, 2 i/c 5 DCLI 1942, GSO1 combined ops 1943, 2 i/c 8 Para 1944, CO 12 Air Landing Bn Devons 1944, CO 6 Royal Welsh Para 1945 (despatches NW Europe 1945), Jt Servs Staff Coll 1947, AAG WO 1948, instr Jt Servs Staff Coll, GSO1 Br Troops Egypt 1950, Cdr Quetta Staff Coll (Pakistan) 1951, Cdr 31 lorried Inf Bde 1954, Brig AQ 1 Corps 1956; TA sec Cornwall 1958, dep sec Western WX TAVR Assoc 1965-74; *Recreations* music, painting, horology, swimming, tennis; *Style*— Brig John Tilly, CBE, DL; Moonsgreen, Elysian Fields, Sidmouth, Devon EX10 8UH

TILLYER, Graham Ernest; s of Ernest Horace Tillyer (d 1983), of Exeter, and Betty Alice, *née* Toms; *b* 23 Sept 1939; *Educ* Exeter Sch, Univ of Manchester (BSc); *m* 27 Feb 1965, Margaret Hazel, da of John Farbon Moultrie, CBE, JP, of Hornchurch, Essex; 3 da (Elizabeth Margaret b 1965, Anne Charlotte b 1967, Sarah Louise b 1971); *Career* M1 motorway work with Sir Owen Williams & Partners: bridge design 1961-64, supervision of construction 1965-68, design of cement works tunnels and railway; office devpts with Oscar Faber Partnership 1969-70 and 1974-77; supervision of construction of int telephone exchange with Mondial House City of London Property Servs Agency 1971-74; chief civil engr BPA Ltd; design of works for aviation fuel distribution on behalf of MOD and BP; Liveryman Worshipful Co of Bakers 1972; MICE 1967, memb Inst of Highways and Transportation 1969; *Recreations* sailing, horticulture, foreign travel; *Clubs* Old Exonian; *Style*— Graham Tillyer, Esq; 5 Ben Austins, West Common, Redbourn, Herts AL3 7DR (☎ 058285 4639); Lord Alexander House, Hemel Hempstead, Herts HP1 1EJ (☎ 0442 218862)

TILLYER, William; *b* 25 Sept 1938; *Educ* Middlesbrough Coll of Art, Slade Sch of Fine Art, Atelier 17 Paris; *Career* artist; lectr; Central Sch of Art 1964-70, Bath Acad of Art 1964-72, Watford Sch of Art 1970-73, Goldsmiths Coll 1975-76, Loughborough Sch of Art 1975-76; visiting prof Rhode Island Sch of Brown Univ 1975-76; visiting lectr: Reading Coll of Art 1975-76, St Martins Sch of Art 1980; artist in residence Univ of Melbourne Aust 1981-82; *solo exhibitions incl:* Arnolfine Gallery Bristol 1970-73, Serpentine Gallery 1971, Galerie Theodor Hoss Stuttgart 1974, Museum of Contemporary Art Utrecht 1975, ICA 1975, Sunderland Arts Centre 1975-79, Melbourne Univ Gallery Aust 1982, Jan Turner Gallery LA 1987, Smith Anderson Gallery Calif 1989, Bernard Jacobson Gallery 1989 and 1991; selected group exhibitions incl: Young Contemporaries (ICA) 1959 and 1961, Forty Christmas Trees (Arnolfini Gallery) 1972, Recent Aquisitions (V & A) 1973, Le Jeune Gravure Contemporaine (Musee d'Art Madame Paris) 1974, British Painting 1952-77 (RA, New Dehli, touring) 1977, British Art since 1960 (Kunsthalle, Lund Univ Sweden) 1979, Eight British Artists (Bernard Jacobson Gallery NY) 1980, Four British Artists (Jan Turner Gallery LA) 1988; work in the collections of: V&A, Arts Cncl of GB, The Br Cncl, Tate, Manchester City Art Gallery, Reading of Univ, MOMA NY, Brooklyn Art Museum NY, Boston Museum of Art, Fort Worth Art Museum Texas, Northern Arts Assoc, Museum of Contemporary Art Friedrickstad Norway, Museum of Art Lodz Poland, Museum of Contemporary Art Ultrecht Holland, Westminster Bank London, Bank of America, Univ of Melbourne, Federal Savings Bank LA, The Art Gallery of Western Aust; *Style*— William Tillyer, Esq; Bernard Jacobson Gallery, 14A Clifford Street, London W1X 1RF (☎ 071 495 8575)

TILNEY, Dame Guinevere (Lady Tilney); DBE (1984); yst da of Sir Alfred Hamilton Grant, 12 Bt, KCSI, KCIE (d 1937); *b* 8 Sept 1916; *Educ* Westonbirt Girls Sch; *m* 1, 19 Feb 1944, Capt K Lionel Hunter, Royal Canadian Dragoons (d 1947); 1 s; *m* 2, 3 June 1954, Sir John Tilney, *qv*; *Career* former 2 Offr WRNS; former DL Lancs (later Merseyside); memb BBC Gen Advsy Cncl 1967-75, pres Nat Cncl of Women of GB 1968-70, chm Women's Nat Cmmn 1969-71, Br rep of UN Status of Women Cmmn 1970-73, co-chm Women Caring Tst 1972-75; served in private and political office of Rt Hon Margaret Thatcher 1975-83; *Recreations* writing, reading, making soup; *Style*— Dame Guinevere Tilney, DBE; 3 Victoria Sq, London SW1W 0QY (☎ 071 828 8674)

TILNEY, Sir John Dudley Robert Tarleton; TD, JP (Liverpool 1946); yr s of Col R H Tilney, DSO, of Tattenhall, Cheshire; *b* 1907; *Educ* Eton, Magdalen Coll Oxford; *m* 3 June 1954, Dame Guinevere, DBE, *qv*, wid of Lionel Hunter, and da of Sir Alfred Hamilton Grant, 12 Bt, KCSI, KCIE (d 1937); 1 step s; *Career* WWII served 59 (4 W Lancs) Medium Regt RA and 11 Medium Regt (despatches, Croix de Guerre with Gilt Star 1945), Lt-Col 1947, Col 1961, Cdr 359 (4 W Lancs) Medium Regt RA (TA) 1947-49, formerly Hon Col 470 (3 W Lancs) LAA Regt RA (TA); former memb Utd Stock Exchange; MP (C) Liverpool Wavertree 1950-74; PPS to: sec state for War 1951-55, PMG 1957-59, min Tport 1959; chm Inter-Parly Union 1959-62, parly under sec State Cwlth Relations Office 1962-63 and for Cwlth Relations and Colonies 1963-64, memb Exec Ctee Nat Union of Cons and Unionist Assocs 1965-74, treas Cwlth Parly Assoc UK 1968-70, memb Select Ctee on Foreign Affrs and Def Sub Ctees 1971-74; chm Airey Neave Meml Tst until 1983; memb Cncl Imperial Soc Kts Bachelor 1978-89, Legion of Honour 1960; pres Assoc of Lancastrians in London 1980-81; kt 1973; *Clubs* Pratt's, Liverpool Racquet; *Style*— Sir John Tilney, TD, JP; 3 Victoria Square, London SW1 WOQZ (☎ 071 828 8674)

TILSON, Jake; s of Joe Tilson, of Wiltshire, and Jos, *née* Morton; *b* 14 Feb 1958; *Educ* Holland Park Sch, Chippenham GS, Chelsea Sch of Art (BA), Royal Coll of Art (MA); *m* Jennifer Elizabeth, da of Ernest McLean Bovelle Lee; *Career* artist; lectr: Illustration Dept RCA, Painting Dept Ruskin Sch of Art Oxford; co-ed Laza 7 magazine 1978; ed and publisher: Cipher magazine 1979-81, Atlas magazine 1985-; solo exhibitions: Xerographies 1977-83 (Galerie Jet J Donguy Paris) 1983, Excavator-Barcelona-Excavador (Nigel Greenwood Gallery) 1986, One World (Warehouse London & Liverpool) 1987, Collages 1986-89 (Stylt Goteborg Sweden) 1989, How Far is an Hour (Nigel Greenwood Gallery) 1989, East Village Vendors (Ruskin Sch of Drawing Oxford) 1990, How Far is an Hour (Galleria Cavalino Venice Italy) 1990, The Terminator Line (Nigel Greenwood Gallery) 1990; group exhibitions: Northern Young Contemporaries (Whitworth Gallery Manchester) 1977, Ecritures (Fndn Nat des Arts Graphiques et Plastiques Paris) 1980, Groupe TZ 85 (Inst Audio Visual Paris) 1980, Arst Machina (La Maison de la Culture de Rennes) 1982, Xerographers Gallery London 1982, Paris Bienale 1982, Br Artists Books (Atlantis Gallery), New Media 2 (Malmo Konsthall Sweden) 1984, Copyart Biennale Barcelona 1985, Br Art & Design (Vienna) 1986, Artist as Publisher (Crafts Cncl) 1986, Int Contemporary Art Fair (London) 1986 and 1989 (LA) 1987, Artist's Books (Univ of Nevada touring) 1986, Rencontres Autour de la Revue Luna-Park (Centre Georges Pompidou) 1987, Br Artists Books (Centre for the Book Arts NY) 1987, Bath Contemporary Art Fair (Bath) 1987, London Print Fair (Royal Acad) 1987, Art in Prodn (Manchester City Art Gallery) 1988 and 1989, Exhibition Road-150 Years (RCA) 1988, Bound Image (Milton Keynes and touring) 1988, 20 Years of Br Art from the Sackner Archive (BASS Museum Miami Florida) 1988, Atlas 3 (Nigel Greenwood Gallery) 1988, Echtzeit (Kasseler Kunstverein) 1988, Paper (Amics Tokyo) 1988, London Original Print Fair (Royal Acad) 1988, 2 Bineal Int de Electrografia Y Copy Art Valencia 1988, Editioned Clocks (Libertys) 1989, Scottish Connections Sculpture (Colchester & Edinburgh) 1989, Original Copies (MOMA Kyoto Tokyo, RCA) 1990; Artists' books incl: Light and Dark (1979), Exposure (1980), 8 Views of Paris (1980), The V Agents (1980), World Atlas (1984), Excavator-Barcelona-Excavador (1986), Breakfast Special (1989); London Arts Assoc Literature grant 1980, Art Cncl Arts Publishing subsidy 1981, Hugh Dunn award 1983, Unilever prize 1983, Major Travelling scholarship RCA 1983, first prize Royal Over-Seas League Exhibition 1988; *Style*— Jake Tilson, Esq; Nigel Greenwood Gallery, 4 New Burlington St, London W1 (☎ 071 434 3795)

TILSON, Joseph Charles (Joe); s of Frederick Arthur Edward Tilson (d 1973), and Ethel Stapeley Louise, *née* Saunders (d 1982); *b* 24 Aug 1928; *Educ* St Martins Sch of Art, RCA, Br Sch at Rome; *m* 2 Aug 1956, Joslyn, da of Alistair Morton (d 1963); 1 s (Jake b 1958), 2 da (Anna Jesse b 1959, Sophy Jane b 1965); *Career* RAF 1946-49; painter, sculptor, printmaker; worked in Italy and Spain 1955-57; visiting lectr 1962-63: Slade Sch of Art, Kings Coll London, Univ of Durham; teacher Sch of Visual Arts NY 1966, visiting lectr Staatliche Hochschule für Bildende Kunste Hamburg 1971-72; memb Arts Panel and Cncl 1966-71; exhibitions incl Venice Biennale 1964; work at: Marlborough Gallery 1966, Waddington Galleries; retrospective exhibitions: Boymans Van Beuningen Museum Rotterdam 1973, Vancouver Art Gallery 1979, Volterra 1983; Biennale prizes Krakow 1974 and Ljubljana 1985, subject of TV films 1963 (and 1968 and 1974); ARCA 1955, ARA 1985; *Recreations* planting trees; *Style*— Joe Tilson, Esq; c/o Waddington Galleries, 11 Cork St, London W1X 1PD (☎ 071 437 8611, fax 071 734 4146, telex 266772)

TIMBERS, Brig Kenneth Alan; s of Capt Arthur Robert Timbers (d 1942), of Woodchurch, Suffolk, and Nancy Gwendoline, *née* Smith (d 1985); *b* 11 July 1935; *Educ* Harvey GS Folkestone, RMA Sandhurst; *m* 21 Sept 1957, (Ursula) Bridget, da of Canon Eric Arthur Newman (d 1970); 2 s (Stephen b 1961, Michael b 1962), 1 da (Tricia b 1959); *Career* cmmnd RA 1956, gunnery staff course 1963-64, army staff course 1966-68, promoted Maj 1967, Lt-Col 1974, cmd 47 Field Regt RA 1976-78, GSOI (W) HQDRA 1978-81, promoted Col 1981, project mangr 155 mm Systems 1981-85, promoted Brig 1985; dir Quality Assurance 1985-88, ret 1988; hist sec of the RA Inst; dir: RA Museum, Museum of Artillery in The Rotunda, RA Medal Collection, RA Library 1988; FBIM 1985; *Recreations* fine arts; *Style*— Brig K A Timbers; Royal Artillery Institution, Old Royal Military Academy, Woolwich, London SE18 4DN (☎ 081 854 2242 ext 5623)

TIMBRELL, Christopher John; s of Sidney Benjamin Timbrell (d 1973), of Kings Heath, Birmingham, and Marion Leah, *née* Bailey (d 1976); *b* 17 July 1941; *Educ* Kings Coll Taunton; *m* 12 Sept 1967, Margaret Joy, da of Phillips William Doleman Winkley; 1 s (Philip Benjamin Christopher b 2 June 1973), 1 da (Kerstin Margaret Leah b 9 Feb 1970); *Career* articled clerk Charlton & Co (chartered accountants) Birmingham 1960, mangr Newmam Biggs Charlton & Co Birmingham 1972, currently ptnr i/c trust & executorship BDO Binder Hamlyn Birmingham (formerly Josolyne Layton-Bennett & Co Birmingham) (ptnr 1976-); dep church warden St Philips Cathedral Birmingham 1986-, govr St John's Sch Sparkhill Birmingham 1987-, trustee various local Birmingham charities; FCA 1978 (ACA 1969); *Recreations* listening to music, genealogy, amateur radio licencee; *Clubs* Old Aluredian; *Style*— Christopher Timbrell, Esq; 92 Honeyborne Rd, Sutton Coldfield, West Midlands B75 6BN (☎ 021 378 0731); BDO Binder Hamlyn, The Rotunda, 150 New St, Birmingham B4 2PD (☎ 021 643 5544, fax 021 643 4665)

TIMBURY, Dr Morag Crichton; da of William McCulloch (d 1975), of Glasgow, Scotland, and Dr Esther Sinclair, *née* Hood (d 1981); *b* 29 Sept 1930; *Educ* St Bride's Sch Helensburgh, Univ of Glasgow (MB, MD, PhD); *m* 5 Oct 1954, Dr Gerald Charles Timbury (d 1985), s of Montague Timbury (d 1980), of Glasgow; 1 da (Judith Susan (Mrs Sawyer) b 16 Nov 1959); *Career* sr lectr and reader in virology Inst of Virology Glasgow, prof of bacteriology Univ of Glasgow Royal Infirmary 1978-88, head Regnl Virus Laboratory Ruchill Hosp Glasgow 1983-88, dir Central Public Health Laboratory Colindale London 1988-; FRSE, FRCPath, FRCP (Glasgow); memb: BMA, Soc for Gen Microbiology; *Books* Notes on Medical Virology (9 edn, 1991), Notes on Medical Bacteriology (3 edn, 1990); *Recreations* reading, fortified houses & castles, military history; *Clubs* RSM; *Style*— Dr Morag Timbury, FRSE; 9-2 Antrim Grove, Belsize Park, London NW3 4XR; St Rules, South St, Elie, Fife; Central Public Health Laboratory, 61 Colindale Ave, London NW9 5HT (☎ 081 200 4400, fax 081 200 7874, telex 8953942 DEFEND G)

TIMMINS, Derek John; s of Ronald Timmins (d 1979), and Ann, *née* Mulville; *b* 7 Oct 1953; *Educ* UP Holland GS, Univ of Liverpool (BM, MB BS, ChB); *Career* appointed conslt physician Liverpool Health Authy 1988; MRCP, MRCGP, DRCOG; *Recreations* music, gardening, sports, walking, photography; *Style*— Derek Timmins, Esq; Felicitas, 8 Douglas Rd, West Kirby, Wirral, Merseyside L48 6EB; The Royal Liverpool Hospital, Prescot St, Liverpool L7 8XP (☎ 051 709 0141 ext 2088)

TIMMINS, Col John Bradford; OBE (1973), TD (1968 and bar 1974), JP 1987; Lord Lt of Gtr Manchester 1987-; s of Capt John James Timmins (d 1972); *b* 23 June 1932; *Educ* Dudley GS Worcs, Aston Univ Birmingham (MSc); *m* 1956, Jean, *née* Edwards; 5 s, 1 da; *Career* Col TA; ADC to HM The Queen 1975-80, Hon Col 75 Engr Regt 1980-; civil engr and chartered builder, chm Warburton Properties Ltd 1973-; chm Greater Manchester Co Ctee TAVRA 1980-88, vice-pres TA & VRA for NW England and IOM 1987-; KStJ 1988, Co pres Order of St John 1988-, High Sheriff Co of Gtr Manchester 1986-87, former cdre Manchester Cruising Assoc; Hon DSc Salford 1990; *Recreations* gardening, sailing (yacht Blue Octopus); *Clubs* Army and Navy, Manchester Literary and Philosophical, REYC; *Style*— Col John Timmins, OBE, TD, JP; The Old Rectory, Warburton, Lymm, Cheshire

TIMMS, Ven George Boorne; s of George Timms (d 1936), and Annie Elizabeth, *née* Boorne (d 1939); *b* 4 Oct 1910; *Educ* Derby Sch, St Edmund Hall Oxford (MA), Coll of the Resurrection Mirfield; *Career* clerk in Holy Orders; deacon 1935, priest 1936; curacies: St Mary Magdalen Coventry 1935-38, St Bartholomew Reading 1938-49; Oxford diocesan inspr of schs 1944-49, sacrist Southwark Cathedral 1949-52, vicar St Mary the Virgin Primrose Hill 1952-65, rural dean Hampstead 1959-65, prebendary St Paul's Cathedral 1964-71, proctor in convocation 1955-59, 1965-70 and 1974-80, dir ordination trg and examining chaplain to Bishop of London 1965-81, archdeacon Hackney 1971-81 (emeritus 1981-); chm and dir The English Hymnal Co Ltd 1968-; chm Alcuin Club 1968-87, pres Sion Coll 1980-81; *Books* Dixit Cranmer (1946), The Liturgical Seasons (1965), The Cloud of Witnesses (1982), The New English Hymnal (ed, 1986); *Style*— The Ven George B Timms; Cleve Lodge, Minster-in-Thanet, Ramsgate, Kent CT12 4BA (☎ 0843 821777)

TIMMS, Neil Richard Frederick Charles; s of Maj John Charles Timms, OBE, of The Old Rectory, Sutton Benger, Wilts, and Margaret Hazel, *née* Roberts; *b* 23 April 1949; *Educ* Forest Sch, Stockport GS, St Catharine's Coll Cambridge (MA); *m* 23 Dec 1983 (m dis 1987), Yolande Pelly Victoria, *née* Sziedlar; 2 da (Georgina b 1984, Victoria b 1986); *Career* called to the Bar Inner Temple 1974, practises SE circuit, memb MO circuit; *Style*— Neil Timms, Esq; 6 Kings Bench Walk, Temple, London EC4 (☎ 071 353 9901, fax 071 583 2033 Groups 2 & 3)

TIMNEY, Janet Susan Patricia (Sue); s of Maj A L Carruthers, of Dumfries, Scotland, and Jetta Hutton; *b* 9 July 1950; *Educ* Jarrow GS, Univ of Newcastle (BA), Heriot Watt Univ, RCA (MA); *m* 1, 1968 (m dis), John, s of Jack Timney, of Workington, Cumberland; 1 da (Alix b 1974); m 2, 1981, Grahame Fowler; 3 s (Louis b 1980, Max b 1984, Todd b 1986); *Career* photography and graphics asst 1967-71, estab Timney-Fowler partnership with Grahame Fowler 1979- (developing range of prods, retail outlets and contracts especially in Japan and USA); perm collections: V & A, Cooper-Hewitt Museum NY, Art Inst of Chicago; visiting lectr RCA 1979-; memb: Textile Ctee Design Cncl, Ctee for Young Designers into Indust RSA, Scot Devpt Cncl; Roscoe award (USA) Surface Decoration Category 1988 and 1989; memb Interior Designers and Decorators Assoc 1986, FCSD 1989; *Recreations* my family; *Clubs* Chelsea Arts; *Style—* Ms Sue Timney; Timney Fowler Ltd, 388 Kings Road, London SW3 5UZ (☎ 071 352 2263, fax 071 352 0351)

TIMPERLEY, Dr Walter Richard; s of Capt Walter Alonzo Timperley, RAMC (d 1965), and Rosalie Mary, *née* Randles (d 1967); *b* 16 June 1936; *Educ* Oundle, Univ of Oxford (MA, BM BCh, DM); *m* 1 April 1961, Rosalind Marjorie, da of late Frederick Norman Baron; 2 da (Jane Clare b 8 Feb 1964, Anne Louise b 29 June 1965); *Career* lectr in neuropathology Univ of Manchester 1967-71, conslt neuropathologist Sheffield Health Authy 1971-, hon clinical lectr Univ of Sheffield 1971-; hon sec Assoc of Clinical Pathologists 1985 (cncl memb 1984), cncl memb RCPath 1987-; memb: BMA, Br Neuropathological Assoc, Pathological Soc, Int Neuropathological Soc, World Assoc & Socs of Pathology, Assoc of Br Neurologists; *Books* Neurological Complications in Clinical Haematology (1980); *Recreations* walking, photography, reading, ornithology; *Style—* Dr Walter Timperley; Dept of Neuropathology, Royal Hallamshire Hospital, Glossop Rd, Sheffield S10 2JF (☎ 0742 766222 ext 2038)

TIMPSON, (John) Alastair Livingston; MC (1942); s of Capt Lawrence Timpson (d 1937), of Maizeland, Barrytown on Hudson NY and Appleton Manor, Abingdon, and Katharine, *née* Livingston (d 1933), of Clermont, Tivoli on Hudson, NY; *b* 23 May 1915; *Educ* Eton, Trinity Coll Cambridge (BA); *m* 1, 25 May 1940 (m dis 1956), (Elizabeth) Phoebe, da of Sir George Houstoun-Boswall (ka 1915), of Blackadder House, Berwickshire; 3 s (Nicholas b 1941, Rupert b 1945, Gerard b 1946), 1 da (Veronica b 1950); m 2, 3 April 1965, Aline Rosemary, da of Lt-Col David Hunter Blair (d 1959); *Career* cmmnd Scots Gds 1940, served London Egypt Libya Tunisia and Italy in 2 Bn, 17 months in Guards Patrol LRDG (despatches 1942 and 1943), invalided out 1946; sec Bongold Mines Bulawayo 1939, ptnr Earnshaw Haes & Co 1946, Cazenove & Co 1948-55, dir merchant fin co Robinson Frere & Co London and Beirut 1955-58, ptnr Orme and Eykyn (later merged to form Stock Beech & Co) 1959-83; Cons chm Co Dist Chelmsford Constituency 1951-55; memb: Soc of Investment Analysts, Stock Exchange 1946; *Recreations* shooting, fishing, gardening; *Clubs* Boodle's, Pratt's; *Style—* Alastair Timpson, Esq, MC; Preedy's Cottage, Castle Combe, Wiltshire SN14 7HX (☎ 0249 782730); Lewis Briggs International, 19 Cavendish Square, London W1M 9AD (☎ 071 491 3057)

TIMPSON, John Harry Robert; OBE (1987); s of John Hubert Victor Timpson (d 1955), and Caroline Willson (d 1970); *b* 2 July 1928; *Educ* Merchant Taylors'; *m* 1951, Muriel Patricia, da of Albert Edward Whale (d 1962); 2 s (Jeremy, Nicholas); *Career* reporter Eastern Daily Press 1951-59, radio and TV reporter BBC News 1959-70, co-presenter Today programme Radio 4 1970-86, chm Any Questions? Radio 4 1984-87; *Books* Today and Yesterday (1976), The Lighter Side of Today (1983), The John Timpson Early Morning Book (1986), Timpson's England - A Look Beyond The Obvious (1987), Norwich - A Fine City (1988), Paper Trail (1989), Requiem For a Red Box (1989), Timpson's Towns of England and Wales (1989), Timpson's Travels in East Anglia (1990); *Recreations* enjoying Norfolk; *Clubs* Durrants (Old Merchant Taylors' Soc); *Style—* John Timpson, Esq, OBE; The Ark Cottage, Wellingham, King's Lynn, Norfolk

TIMPSON, Lady Selina Catherine; *née* Meade; eldest da of 6 Earl of Clanwilliam (d 1989); *b* 1950; *m* 1972, Nicholas George Lawrence Timpson, gs of Sir George Reginald Houstoun-Boswall, 4 Bt (d 1914); 1 s (Lawrence b 1974), 1 da (Catherine b 1979); *Style—* The Lady Selina Timpson; Ardington Croft, Wantage, Oxon

TIMSON, Mrs Rodney; Penelope Anne Constance; *see*: Keith, P A C

TIMSON, (Christopher) Rodney Grosvenor; s of Albert Ernest Timson, and Mary Clare Timson, *née* Elliott; *b* 6 July 1942; *Educ* Dean Close Sch Cheltenham; *m* Angela Susan Kift; *Career* md Abbey Dropforgings Ltd 1974-82, non-exec dir T L Elliott & Co Ltd 1979, chm and md Tom Smith Gp 1989-, chm Afterfield Ltd 1989-; ind memb Parole Review Ctee Stafford Prison 1978-82, memb Br Pyrotechnists Assoc 1987-, Royal Warrant Holder 1989-; *Recreations* fishing, shooting, restoration of steam traction engines; *Style—* Rodney Timson, Esq; Rose Cottage, Wramplingham, Norfolk NR18 0RZ (☎ 0603 812385); Tom Smith Group, Salhouse Rd, Norwich (☎ 0603 404904, fax 0603 401750, telex 975378)

TINDALE, Gordon Anthony; OBE (1983); s of George Augustus Tindale (decd), and Olive Sarah, *née* Lansdowne (decd); *b* 17 March 1938; *Educ* Highgate Sch, Trinity Coll Oxford (BA), Birkbeck Coll London (MA); *m* June 1960, Sonia Mary, da of Arthur Bertram Spencer Soper (decd); 1 s (Stephen Christopher b March 1963), 1 da (Helen Frances b Nov 1960); *Career* Nat Serv 1956-58, 2 Lt RCS, Lt reserve serv 23 SAS; language training MECAS Amman Baghdad London 1961-71, Br Cncl rep Lesotho Botswana Swaziland 1975-78, dir Middle East Dept 1978, Br Cncl rep Lusaka Zambia 1979-83, head Mgmnt Div 1983-87, Br Cncl rep Cairo Egypt 1987-89 (asst cultural attaché 1971-74), cultural cnsllr Washington DC USA 1989-; *Recreations* golf, music, theatre; *Clubs* Hendon Golf, West Heath Tennis; *Style—* Gordon Tindale, Esq, OBE; 23 Heath Hurst Rd, London NW3 2RU; 2921 Garfield Terrace NW, Washington DC 20008, USA (☎ 010 1 202 328 1714); British Embassy, 3100 Massachusetts Ave, Washington DC, 20008 USA (☎ 010 1 202 898 4330, fax 010 1 202 898 4255)

TINDALE, Lawrence Victor Dolman; CBE (1971); s of John Stephen Tindale, and Alice Lilian Tindale; *b* 24 April 1921; *Educ* Latymer Upper Sch; *m* 1946, Beatrice Mabel; 1 s, 1 da; *Career* CA; chm: C & J Clark Ltd, Edbro plc; dep chm 3i Gp plc; dir BTG; *Recreations* opera lover; *Clubs* Reform, St James's (Manchester); *Style—* Lawrence Tindale, Esq, CBE; 3 Amyand Park Gardens, Twickenham, Middx TW1 3HS (☎ 081 892 9457); office: 91 Waterloo Road, London SE1 8XP (☎ 081 928 3131, telex 917844)

TINDALE, Patricia Randall; da of Thomas John Tindale (d 1986), and Princess May, *née* Uttin (d 1986); *b* 11 March 1926; *Educ* Blatchington Ct Sch, Architectural Assoc Sch of Architecture (AA Dip); *Career* architect; Miny of Educn: Welsh Dept 1949-50, Devpt Gp 1951-61; Miny of Housing and Local Govt R & D Gp 1961-72; DOE: head of Bldg Regulations Professional Div 1972-74, head Housing Devpt Directorate, dir Central Unit of the Built Environment 1980-81, chief architect 1982-86; architectural conslt 1986-, chair Housing Design Awards 1986-; ARIBA 1950; *Books* Housebuilding in the USA (1965); *Recreations* weaving, sailing; *Clubs* Reform; *Style—* Miss Patricia Tindale; 34 Crescent Grove, London SW4 7AH (☎ 071 622 1926)

TINDALL, Gillian Elizabeth; da of D H Tindall; *b* 4 May 1938; *Educ* Univ of Oxford (BA, MA); *m* 1963, Richard G Lansdown; 1 s; *Career* novelist/biographer/historian; freelance journalist; occasional articles and reviews for: The Observer, Guardian, New Statesman, London Evening Standard, The Times, Encounter, Sunday Times, The Independent, New Society; occasional broadcaster BBC; FRSL, FRSA; *Books* novels: No Name in the Street (1959), The Water and the Sound (1961), The Edge of the Paper (1963), The Youngest (1967), Someone Else (1969, 2 edn 1975), Fly Away Home (1971, Somerset Maugham award 1972), The Traveller and His Child (1975), The Intruder (1979), Looking Forward (1983), To the City (1987), Give Them All My Love (1989); short stories: Dances of Death (1973), The China Egg and Other Stories (1981); biography: The Born Exile (George Gissing, 1974); other non fiction: A Handbook on Witchcraft (1965), The Fields Beneath (1977), City of Gold: the biography of Bombay (1981), Rosamond Lehmann: an Appreciation (1985), Architecture of the British Empire (contrib, 1986), Countries of the Mind: the meaning of place to writers (1991); *Recreations* keeping house, foreign travel; *Style—* Ms Gillian Tindall; c/o Curtis Brown Ltd, 162-168 Regent Street, London, W1

TINDLE, David; s of Ernest Edwin Cook (d 1975), and Dorothy, *née* Smith (who m 2, 1946, William Tindle, and d 1974); assumed surname of Tindle 1946; *b* 29 April 1932; *Educ* Coventry Secdy Mod Sch, Coventry Sch of Art; *m* 3 Jan 1969, Janet Freda, da of Felix Trollope (d 1988); 1 s (Nathan b 1975), 2 da (Saskia b 1970, Charlotte b 1972); *Career* artist: visiting tutor many art schs 1956-, tutor RCA 1972-83; Ruskin Master of Drawing and Fine Art Oxford 1985-87 (MA 1985); many one man exhibitions incl: Piccadilly Gallery 1954-83, Coventry City Art Gallery 1957, Galerie du Tours San Francisco 1964, Northern Art Gallery 1972, Fischer Fine Art 1985 and 1989 (also important one man show at Gallery XX Hamburg: 1974, 1977, 1980 and 1985); represented in exhibitions: Royal Acad 1954, 1968, 1970-83 (Winne Johnson Wax Award 1983), Salon de la Jeune Peinture (Paris) 1967, Internationale Biennale of Realist Art (Bologna) 1967; work represented at: The Tate Gallery, The Arts Cncl, Chantrey Bequest DOE, London Museum, De Beers Collection, Royal Acad, Nat Portrait Gallery; designed stage set for Tchaikovsky's Iolanta (Aldeburgh Festival) 1988; hon fell St Edmund Hall Oxford 1988; ARA 1973, RA 1979, FRCA 1981, hon FRCA 1983; *Style—* David Tindle, Esq; 56A Leam Terrace, Leamington Spa CV31 1DE; Studio Flat 1, 61 Holly Walk, Leamington Spa, Warwickshire CV32 4JG; c/o Fischer Fine Art Ltd, 30 King St, St James's, London SW1 (☎ 071 839 3942)

TINDLE, Ray Stanley; CBE (1987, OBE 1974), DL (Surrey); s of John Robert Tindle (d 1975), and Maud, *née* Bilney (d 1952); *b* 8 Oct 1926; *Educ* Torquay GS, Strand Sch; *m* 8 Oct 1949, Beryl Julia, da of David Charles Ellis (d 1968); 1 s (Owen Charles b 1956); *Career* Capt Devonshire Regt 1944-47, served Far East; chm: Tindle Newspapers Ltd, Surrey Advertiser Newspaper Holdings Ltd; dir Guardian & Manchester Evening News Ltd and 36 other newspaper cos; fndr Tindle Enterprise Centres for the Unemployed 1984, treas Newspaper Soc (pres 1971-72); memb: MMC Newspaper Panel, Cncl Cwlth Press Union; vice pres Newspaper Press Fund; Master Worshipful Co of Stationers and Newspaper Makers 1985-86; FCIS, FCIArb; *Style—* Ray Tindle, Esq, CBE, DL; Devonshire House, 92 West St, Farnham, Surrey GU9 7EN; Tindle Newspapers Ltd, Newspaper House, 114/115 West St, Farnham, Surrey GU9 7HL (☎ 0252 725224, fax 0252 724951)

TINHAM, Alan Clement John; s of Victor Robert Sydney Tinham (d 1964), of Broadstairs, Kent, and Ethel Mabel, *née* Clements (d 1985); *b* 25 Jan 1948; *Educ* Chatham House GS Ramsgate; *m* 27 Sept 1969, Margaret Catherine, da of John Handford, of Broadstairs, Kent; 1 s (Richard b 1975), 3 da (Rebecca b 1973, Victoria b 1979, Ruth b 1987); *Career* managing ptnr Margate branch of Reeves & Neylan CAs; FCA, ATII; *Recreations* windsurfing, sea angling; *Style—* Alan Tinham, Esq; Spindrift, Marine Drive, Kingsgate, Broadstairs, Kent CT10 3LU (☎ 0843 63450); Reeves and Neylan, Cecil Sq House, Cecil Sq, Margate, Kent (☎ 0843 227937)

TINKER, Dr (Philip) Bernard Hague; s of Philip Tinker (d 1978), and Gertrude, *née* Hague (d 1977); *b* 1 Feb 1930; *Educ* Rochdale HS, Univ of Sheffield (BSc, PhD), Univ of Oxford (Bsc, PhD); *m* 27 Aug 1955, Maureen, da of Francis Ellis (d 1952); 1 s (John Philip b 1956), 1 da (Amanda Jane b 1960); *Career* overseas res serv 1955-62, Rothamsted Experimental Station 1962-65, lectr in soil sci Univ of Oxford 1965-71, prof of agric botany Univ of Leeds 1971-77, head of Soils Div and dep dir 1977-85, Rothamsted Experimental Station, dir of sci NERC 1985-; FIBiol 1976, FRSC 1985, memb Norwegian Acad of Sci 1987; *Books* Solute Movement in the Soil-Root System (1977), Endomycorrhizas (1977), Advances in Plant Nutrition (vol I 1984, vol II 1985, vol III 1988); *Recreations* gardening, map collecting; *Clubs* Farmers'; *Style—* Dr Bernard Tinker; The Glebe House, Broadwell, nr Lechlade, Glos GL7 3QS (☎ 036 786 436); Natural Environment Res Cncl, Polaris House, North Star Ave, Swindon, Wilts SN2 1EU (☎ 0793 411523, fax 0793 411502, telex 444293 ENVRE G)

TINKER, Rev Prebendary Eric Franklin; OBE (1989); s of Frank Stanley Tinker (d 1923), and Margaret Louise, *née* Wiseman (d 1981); *b* 29 June 1920; *Educ* Lambrook, Radley, Exeter Coll Oxford (BA, MA), Lincoln Theol Coll; *m* 29 Dec 1956, Anthea Margaret, da of Lt Cdr James Collins, RN, of Melton Mowbray; 2 s (Jonathan b 1959, Andrew b 1960), 1 da (Rachel b 1964); *Career* curate: Great Berkhamsted 1944, Rugby Parish Church 1946; chaplain to the Forces 1948, London sec Student Christian Movement 1949, chaplain Univ of London 1951; vicar: St James Handsworth 1955, Enfield Parish Church 1965; sr chaplain Univs and Polys in London 1969-90, dir of educn Dioceses of London and Southwark 1972-80, prebendary St Paul's Cathedral London 1969-90 (emeritus 1990); vice chm All Saints Educnl Tst; Hon DD City Univ 1987, Hon DD Univ of London 1989; Freeman City of London 1980; *Style—* The Rev Prebendary Eric Tinker, OBE; 35 Theberton Street, London N1 0QY (☎ 071 359 4750)

TINKER, Prof Hugh Russell; s of Sgt Clement Hugh Tinker (d 1973), of Marlow, Bucks, and Gertrude Marian Tinker (d 1983); *b* 20 July 1921; *Educ* Taunton Sch, Sidney Sussex Coll Cambridge (MA); *m* 23 Aug 1948, Elisabeth McKenzie, da of Charles Frederick Willis; 3 s (Jonathan b 1950, Mark b 1952, David b 1957, ka 1982); *Career* WWII RAC 1939, IA 1941-46; SOAS Univ of London 1948-69 (lectr, reader, prof), dir Inst of Race Rels 1969-72, prof of politics Univ of Lancaster 1977, now emeritus prof; Parly candidate (Lib) 1964, 1966, 1979, vice pres of the ExServ Campaign for Nuclear Disarmament; *Books* The Union of Burma; A Study of the First Years of Independence (1957), South Asia: A Short History (1966), Race, Conflict and the International Order (1977), Burma: The Struggle for Independence (vol I 1983, vol II 1984), Men Who Overturned Empires; Fighters, Dreamers and Schemers (1988); *Recreations* walking, writing; *Style—* Prof Hugh Tinker; Montbegon, Hornby, Lancaster LA2 8JZ (☎ 0468 21130)

TINKER, Jack Samuel; s of Edward Smith Tinker (d 1977), and Lily, *née* Pierce; *b* 15 Feb 1938; *Educ* Hulme GS for Boys Oldham; *m* 14 Feb 1961, (m dis 1969), Mavis Ann, *née* Page; 3 da (Victoria-Jane b 31 Oct 1961, Camilla Caroline Page b 24 April 1963, Charlotte Verity Ingham b 12 March 1966, d 1990); *Career* trainee journalist The Surrey Advertiser 1957-60; Evening Argus (Sussex) 1960-70: drama critic, leader writer, film critic, feature writer; ed Diary Column Daily Sketch 1970-71, drama critic and feature writer Daily Mail 1971-; British Press Awards: highly commended 1980, Critic of the Year 1982 and 1989; memb Critics' Circle 1972 (chm Drama Panel 1986-87); *Books* The Television Barons (1980), Coronation Street - 25 Years (1985); *Recreations* petit point, attending theatres; *Clubs* Wig and Pen, Scribes West; *Style—* Jack Tinker, Esq; Daily Mail, Northcliffe House, 2 Derry St, London WC2 (☎ 071 938 6364)

TINLEY, Gervase Edmund Newport; s of Robert Gervase William Newport Tinley; *b* 16 June 1930; *Educ* HMS Worcester; *m* 1965, Jean Lengden, *née* Allen; 2 s, 2 da; *Career* served MN 1946-51 and 1956-58; schoolmaster 1959-60; dir: Stewart Wrightson Assur Conslts 1973-, Army Dependants Assur Tst 1973-, Naval Dependents Income & Assur Tst 1976-; chm Electoral Reform Soc 1979- (dep chm

1977); dep chm: Centurion Housing Assoc 1980-, Cromwell Assoc; master mariner; fell Pensions Mgmnt Inst, FBIM; *Clubs* Reform, Mensa; *Style—* Gervase Tinley, Esq; Kingston Bridge House, Church Grove, Kingston upon Thames, Surrey; office: Kingston Bridge House, Church Grove, Kingston upon Thames, Surrey KT1 4AG (☎ 081 977 8888)

TINTON, Stephen Christopher Ben; s of Ben Howard Tinton, and Joan Wanda Tinton; *b* 19 July 1948; *Educ* Royal GS High Wycombe, St Catharine's Coll Cambridge (BA); *m* 9 Dec 1972, Dr Marilyn Margaret, da of Reginald St George Stead, FRCS, of Highcliffe, Dorset; 1 s (Paul b 27 May 1980), 1 da (Sarah b 24 June 1978); *Career* teacher Dehra Dun India 1967; audit and business advsy ptnr Price Waterhouse 1982- (audit mangr 1976-82); *Recreations* sport, music, theatre; *Clubs* RAC; *Style—* Steve Tinton, Esq; Price Waterhouse, Southwark Towers, 32 London Bridge St, London SE1 (☎ 071 939 3000, fax 071 378 0647)

TIPPET, Vice Adm Sir Anthony Sanders; KCB (1984); s of W Tippet and H W Kitley, *née* Sanders; *b* 2 Oct 1928; *Educ* W Buckland Sch Devon; *m* 1950, Lola, *née* Bassett; 2 s (1 s decd), 1 da; *Career* RN 1946, Rear Adm 1979, Asst Chief of Fleet Support MOD 1979-81, Chief Naval Supply and Secretariat Offr 1981-83, Flag Offr and Port Adm Portsmouth 1981-83, Vice Adm 1983, Chief of Fleet Support 1983-87; called to the Bar Grays Inn 1958; gen mangr Hosps for Sick Children London 1987, memb Bd of Govrs W Buckland Sch; memb: RN Sailing Assoc 1986, RN Lay Readers Soc; CBIM; *Style—* Vice Adm Sir Anthony Tippet, KCB; c/o Barclays Bank, 46 North St, Taunton TA1 1LZ

TIPPETT, Sir Michael Kemp; KBE (1966, CBE 1959), OM (1983), CH (1979); s of late Henry William Tippett; *b* 2 Jan 1905; *Educ* Stamford Sch, RCM; *Career* composer; RCM 1923-28, private lessons with RO Morris 1930, dir of music Morley Coll London 1940-51, artistic dir Bath Festival 1969-74, pres London Coll of Music 1983-; imprisoned for 3 months as conscientious objector Wormwood Scrubs 1943, pres Peace Union, hon pres Bath CND; works incl: String Quartets 1-4, Piano Sonatas 1-4, Symphonies 1-4; operas: The Midsummer Marriage 1947-52, King Priam 1958-61, The Knot Garden 1966-70, The Ice Break 1973-76, New Year 1985-88; choral works incl: A Child of Our Time 1939-41, The Vision of St Augustine 1965, The Mask of Time 1980-82; chamber works: Sonata for Four Horns 1955, The Blue Guitar 1982; brass: Festal Brass with Blues 1983; Hon DMus: Univ of Cambridge 1964, Trinity Coll Dublin 1964, Univ of Leeds 1965, Univ of Oxford 1967, Univ of Leicester 1968, Univ of Wales 1968, Univ of Bristol 1970, Univ of London 1975, Univ of Sheffield 1976, Univ of Birmingham 1976, Univ of Lancaster 1977, Univ of Liverpool 1981, RCM 1982, Melbourne Univ 1984, Univ of Keele 1986, Univ of Aberdeen 1987; FRCM 1961; memb: Akademie der Künste Berlin 1976, American Acad of Arts and Letters 1976; Gold Medal Royal Philharmonic Soc 1976, Prix de Composition (Monaco) 1984; Cdr de l'Ordre des Arts et des Lettres (France) 1988; *Books* Moving into Aquarius (1974), Music of the Angels (1980); *Style—* Sir Michael Tippett, KBE, OM, CH; c/o Schott & Co, 48 Great Marlborough St, London W1

TIPPING, Hon Mrs (Catherine Joy); *née* Davies; da of 2 Baron Darwen, of White Lodge, Sandelswood End, Beaconsfield, Bucks, by his w Kathleen Dora; *b* 10 July 1948; *Educ* High Wycombe HS, Univ of Cardiff (BA), PGCE; *m* 1, 1970 (m dis 1976), Robert Nienhuis; m 2, 1976, Richard George Tipping; 2 s (Damian Richard George b 1977, Gregory Luke Darius b 1980); *Career* pt/t lectr in English literature and English language; chm Droitwich Poetry Gp 1988-91; *Recreations* ballet, writing poetry, theatre-going; *Style—* The Hon Mrs Tipping; Coombe Cottage, 44 Worcester Rd, Droitwich, Worcs WR9 8AJ (☎ 0905 775051)

TIPPING, Robert Marsh; s of Harry Neville Derek Tipping, of the Chase, Chigwell Row, Essex, and Anne Marsh, *née* Fletcher; *b* 22 July 1944; *Educ* privately, Chard Sch Chard Somerset; *Career* stockbroker; ptnr Smith Keen Cutler 1973, Membs and Clerks Panel 1977, advsr to Govt and Central Bank Barbados 1979-81, asst lectr Jesus Coll Cambridge 1981, dir of various private cos; memb London Stock Exchange 1971-79; Freeman: City of London 1977, Worshipful Co of Pattenmakers 1978; FBISL 1981; *Recreations* fishing, sailing; *Clubs* City Livery, City Yacht; *Style—* Robert Tipping, Esq; Millers Farm, Grove Lane, Chigwell Row, Essex (☎ 081 500 6596)

TIPTAFT, David Howard Palmer; JP (1972-); s of C Paxman Tiptaft, MC, JP (d 1984), of Wentworth, S Yorks, and Irene, *née* Palmer (d 1968); *b* 6 Jan 1938; *Educ* Goldsborough Hall N Yorks, Shrewsbury; *m* 1 June 1963, Jennifer Cherry, da of Gerald Richard Millward (d 1967), of Khartoum; 2 s (Justyn b 30 Sept 1965, Quintin b 19 June 1970), 2 da (Elgiva b 10 March 1964, Genovefa b 20 Dec 1966); *Career* qualified CA 1962, Arthur Young 1961-64, princ Tiptaft Smith & Co 1966-; chm Don Valley Cons Assoc 1964-75, treas Rother Valley Cons Assoc 1976-83, chm Wentworth Cons Assoc 1983-, Yorks area treas Cons Central Office 1988-; govr Denaby Main Jr Sch, memb Redundant Churches Uses Ctee Sheffield Diocese; FCA 1973; *Recreations* flying, tennis, opera, Wagner, horticulture; *Style—* David Tiptaft, Esq, JP; Ashcroft House, Wentworth, nr Rotherham, S Yorks (☎ 0226 742 972); Tiptaft Smith and Co, Waveney House, Adwick Rd, Mexborough, S Yorks (☎ 0709 582991)

TIRARD, Lady Nesta; *née* FitzGerald; da of 8 Duke of Leinster; *b* 1942; *m* 1977, Philip Tirard; 2 da; *Style—* The Lady Nesta Tirard; Coolnabrune, Borris, Co Carlow, Ireland

TITCHENER, John Lanham Bradbury; CMG (1955), OBE (1947); s of Alfred Titchener (d 1956); *b* 28 Nov 1912; *Educ* City of London Sch, RCM; *m* 1958, Britta Frederikke Marian, da of Carl Bendixsen (hon consul); 2 step s; *Career* BBC TV prodr 1938-39, talks prodr 1939-43; seconded to HM Armed Forces 1943-46; HM Diplomatic Serv 1947-57, cncllr 1954-57 (resigned); dir: Int Insur Service (Iran) 1974-79, Hamworthy Engrg (Iran) 1974-79, Hagen Int A/S; *Recreations* music, gardening, fishing; *Clubs* Travellers'; *Style—* Lanham Titchener, Esq, CMG, OBE; 3 Impasse Du Chateau, 06190 Roquebrune Village, CM France (☎ France 93 35 07 85); Weysesgade 13, 2100 Copenhagen (☎ 01 200 871)

TITCHENER-BARRETT, Lt-Col Sir Dennis Charles; TD (1953 and 2 Bars); s of Charles William George Barrett (d 1974), and Edith Lambert Titchener (d 1964); *m* 1940, Joan Florence, da of Albert Robert Wilson, of Coleherne Court, Old Brompton Rd, London; 1 s (Robert), 3 da (Georgina, Caroline, Jacqueline); *Career* WWII RA 1939-46, cmd 415 Coast Regt RA (TA) 1950-56, memb Kent T & AFA 1950-56; ILEA sch govr 1956-73; memb: RUSI 1947-, Gtr London Central Valuation Panel 1964-75, Cons Bd of Finance 1968-75, Gen Purposes and Nat Exec Ctees 1968-75, Cons Central Cncl 1968-78, Cons Policy Gp for Gtr London 1975-78, Kensington Cons Assoc 1975-; chm: S Kensington Cons Assoc 1955-58, tstee and chm Woodstock (London) Ltd 1962-89; treas Gtr London Area Cons and Unionist Assoc 1968-75, chm Gtr London area Cons and Unionists Assoc 1975-78, vice pres Nat Soc Cons Agents Gtr London Area 1975- (vice pres Gtr London Area 1978-); underwriting memb Lloyds 1977-; High Sheriff Gtr London 1977-78; kt 1981; *Clubs* Carlton; *Style—* Lt-Col Sir Dennis Titchener-Barrett, TD; 8 Launceston Place, London W8 5RL (☎ 071 937 0613)

TITCHMARSH, Alan Fred; s of Alan Titchmarsh (d 1986), of Ilkley, Yorkshire, and Bessie, *née* Hardisty; *b* 2 May 1949; *Educ* Shipley Art and Tech Inst, Hertfordshire Coll of Agriculture and Horticulture (Nat Cert Horticulture), Royal Botanic Gardens Kew (Dip in Horticulture, Sir Joseph Hooker prize, Keith Jones Cup for public speaking); *m* 1975, Alison Margaret, da of Geoffrey Herbert Needs; 2 da (Polly Alexandra b 1980, Camilla Rose b 1982); *Career* apprentice gardener Parks Dept Ilkley Urban District Cncl 1964-68, staff training supervisor Royal Botanic Gardens Kew 1972-74, asst ed Gardening Books Hamlyn Publishing Group 1974-76, dep ed Amateur Gardening magazine 1978-79 (asst ed 1976-78); freelance writer, presenter, interviewer and broadcaster 1979-; BBC Radio progs: You and Yours 1975-82, Down to Earth 1982-89, A House In A Garden 1987-, Alan Titchmarsh Show 1989-; BBC TV progs: Nationwide (gardening expert) 1980-83, Breakfast Time (gardening expert) 1983-86, Open Air 1986-87, Daytime Live 1987-90, Scene Today 1990-, Chelsea Flower Show 1983-, Grow Biz Quiz 1989, More Than Meets The Eye 1990, Songs of Praise 1989-; gardening corr: Woman's Own 1987-85, Daily Mail 1985-; gardening ed Homes and Gardens 1985-89; winner of: Gardening Writer of the Year 1980 and 1983, Royal Horticultural Soc's Gold medal Chelsea Flower Show 1985; Freeman City of London 1989, Liveryman Worshipful Co of Gardeners 1989; memb Inst Horticulture; author of various books incl: Gardening Under cover (1979), Climbers and Wall Plants (1980), Garden Techniques (1981), The Allotment Gardener's Handbook (1982), The Rock Gardener's Handbook (1983), Supergardener (1983), Alan Titchmarsh's Avant-Gardening (1984), Daytime Live Gardening Book (1990); *Recreations* theatre, reading, gardening, riding; *Clubs* Lord's Taverners; *Style—* Alan Titchmarsh, Esq; c/o Arlington Enterprises, 1-3 Charlotte St, London W1P 1HD (☎ 071 580 0702)

TITCOMB, (Simon) James; s of Geoffrey Cowley Baden Titcomb (d 1960), of Brighton, and Molly Gwendolyn Titcomb (d 1985); *b* 10 July 1931; *Educ* Brighton Coll; *m* 1957, Ann Constance, da of Gerald Bernard Vokins; 2 s, 1 da; *Career* Lt Nat Serv 1955-57; memb Stock Exchange 1962, ptnr de Zoete & Bevan (Stockbrokers) 1962-76 (sr ptnr 1976-86); dir of public and private companies; FCA, CBIM; *Recreations* golf, tennis, bridge, travel, wild life; *Clubs* Brooks's, City of London; *Style—* James Titcomb, Esq; Plummerden House, Lindfield, Sussex RH16 2QS (☎ 044 47 2117); Barclays de Zoete Wedd, Ebbgate House, 25 Swan Lane, London EC4R 3TS (☎ 071 623 2323)

TITE, Prof Michael Stanley; s of Arthur Robert Tite (d 1985), and Evelyn Francis Violet, *née* Endersby (d 1971); *b* 9 Nov 1938; *Educ* Trinity Sch of John Whitgift Croydon, ChCh Oxford (Exhibitioner, MA, DPhil); *m* 10 June 1967, Virgina Byng, da of Rear Adm Gambier John Byng Noel, CB, of Woodpeckers, Church Lane, Haslemere, Surrey; 2 da (Sarah Beatrice b 1970, Alice Evelyn Byng b 1972); *Career* ICI res fell Univ of Leeds 1964-67, lectr Univ of Essex 1967-75, keeper Res Laboratory British Museum 1975-89, prof of archaeological sci Univ of Oxford 1989-; memb: Panel on Sci and Conservation Eng Heritage, Sci-based Archaeology Ctee SERC; FSA 1977; *Books* Methods of Physical Examination in Archaeology (1972); *Recreations* walking, gardening, travel; *Style—* Prof Michael Tite, FSA; Research Laboratory for Archaeology and the History of Art, 6 Keble Rd, Oxford OX1 3QJ (☎ 0865 515211)

TITE, Nicholas William Spencer; s of William Timpson Tite (d 1970), and Stephanie Frances, *née* Spencer; *b* 29 July 1950; *Educ* Wellingborough Sch, Northampton Sch of Art (travelling scholar), Winchester Sch of Art (Dip AD, first year painting prize); *Career* Studio Prints Queen's Crescent London 1974-76, etching technician Central Sch of Art 1976-78, Editiono Alecto (working on Tom Phillip's Dante's Inferno) 1978, creation of Talfourd Press (prodn controller Tom Phillip's Dante's Inferno) 1980-83, ed RA Magazine 1983-; responsible for exhibitions in Friends' Room at Royal Acad incl: Ghika, Bryan Kneale, Carelweight, S W Hayler, Lenord McComb, RAs Through the Lens, Etchings by Academicians 1988-; *Recreations* cricket; *Style—* Nicholas Tite, Esq; RA Magazine, Royal Academy of Arts, Burlington House, London W1V 0DS (☎ 071 287 2906, fax 071 287 9023)

TITLEY, Gary; s of Wilfred James Titley, and Joyce Lillian Titley; *b* 19 Jan 1950; *Educ* Univ of York (BA, PGCE); *m* 1975, Maria (Charo) Rosario; 1 s (Adam), 1 da (Samantha); *Career* various positions until 1973 incl: bus conductor, delivery driver, postman, security guard, labourer and barman; TEFL Bilbao 1973-75, history teacher Earls High Sch Halesowen 1976-84; campaign mangr to Terry Pitt MEP (and later John Bird MEP) 1983-89; Parly candidate (Lab): Bromsgrove 1983, Dudley West 1987; memb Bolton West CLP; West Midlands CC 1981-: vice chm Econ Devpt Ctee 1981-84, vice chm Consumer Servs Ctee 1984-86; Euro Parliament activities: chief whip Euro Parly Lab Party, memb External Rels Ctee, memb Economic and Monetary Ctee, memb Budget Control Ctee, memb S American Delgn, & Socialist Group spokesman on EFTA rels; dir W Midlands Enterprise Bd 1982-89; chm: W Midlands Co-op Finance Co 1982-89, Black Country Co-op Development Agency 1982-88; *Recreations* family, reading, sport; *Clubs* Halesowen Lab (W Midlands), Springvale Sports and Social (Bilston), Little Lever (Bolton); *Style—* Gary Titley, Esq, MEP; 16 Spring Lane, Radcliffe, Manchester M26 9TQ (☎ 061 724 4008)

TITMAN, John Edward Powis; CVO, JP (Surrey 1971); s of late Sir George Titman, CBE, MVO; *b* 23 May 1926; *Educ* City of London Sch; *m* 1953, Annabel Clare, da of late C F Naylor; 2 s; *Career* sec The Lord Chamberlain's Office 1978-, Serjeant at Arms to HM The Queen 1982-; Freeman Worshipful Co of Wax Chandlers (Master 1984); *Clubs* RAC, MCC; *Style—* John Titman, Esq, CVO, JP; Friars Garth, The Parade, Epsom, Surrey (☎ 037 272 2302)

TITTERINGTON, David Michael; s of Geoffrey Bridge Titterington, of Beverley, East Yorks, and Claire Elizabeth, *née* Parsons; *b* 10 Jan 1958; *Educ* Hindley & Abram GS, Northern Sch of Music, Pembroke Coll Oxford (BA, organ scholar), Conservatoire: Rueil-Malmaison Paris; *Career* organist; debut Royal Festival Hall 1986; concert and concerto performances at maj festivals & venues worldwide incl: Bicentennial festival of Sydney 1988, Hong Kong, Istanbul, Schleswig-Holstein, Cheltenham; Proms debut 1990; orchestras played with incl: BBC Scottish Symphony Orchestra, Bournemouth Sinfonietta, English Sinfonia, Berlin Symphony Orchestra; giver of master classes internationally; numerous recordings made incl complete works of César Franck (for BBC), also recorded for Hyperion Records and Multi Sonic Label; world premiere performances incl: Petr Eben's Job 1986, Naji Hakim's Rubaiyat 1990, Diana Burrell's Arched Forms with Bells (Proms cmmn) 1990; Ian Fleming Award 1983; French Government Scholarship 1983-4; Arts Council Bursary 1984, Premier Prix 1984; Prix d'Excellence 1985 (Rueil-Malmaison Conservatoire, Paris), professor of organ Royal Academy of Music 1990- general editor 'organ repertoire series': united music publishers, London 1987-; *Style—* David Titterington, Esq; Clarion/Seven Muses, 64 Whitehall Park, London N19 3TN (☎ 071 272 4413, fax 071 281 9687)

TIVERTON, Viscount; *see*: Giffard, Adam Edward

TIZARD, Prof Barbara Patricia; *née* Parker; da of Herbert Parker, and Elsie, *née* Kirk, sis to His Honour Judge Michael Clynes Parker, *qv*; *b* 16 April 1926; *Educ* St Paul's, Somerville Coll Oxford (BA), Inst of Psychiatry London (PhD); *m* 15 Dec 1947, Prof Jack Tizard (d 1979), s of John Marsh Tizard, of Stratford, NZ; 3 s (William b 3 Jan 1951, John b 10 Dec 1952, d 1983, Martin b 17 Nov 1966, d 1975), 2 da (Jenny b 17 Dec 1955, Lucy b 26 Jan 1968); *Career* co ed Br Jl of Psychology 1975-, memb ed bd Jl Child Psychology and Psychiatry, reader in educn Inst of Educn 1978-80, dir Thomas Coram Res Unit 1980-, emeritus prof of educn Univ of London 1982-; former chm Assoc Child Psychology and Psychiatry; fell Br Psychological Soc; *Publications*: Early Childhood Education (1975), Adoption a Second Chance (1977), Involving

Parents in Nursery and Infant Schools (1981), Young Children Learning (with M Hughes, 1984), Young Children at School in the Inner City (with P Blatchford, J Burke, C Farquhar, I Plewis 1988); *Style—* Prof Barbara Tizard; Institute of Education, 27 Wobourn Square, London WC1H OAA (☎ 071 636 1500, fax 071 436 2186)

TIZARD, HE Dame Catherine Anne; da of Neil McLean, and Helen McLean; *b* 4 April 1931; *Educ* Matamata Coll, Univ of Auckland (BA); *m* 1951 (m dis 1983), Rt Hon Robert James Tizard; 1 s (Nigel Robert), 3 da (Anne Frances, Linda Catherine, Judith Ngaire); *Career* sr tutor in zoology Univ of Auckland 1963-83; JP 1980, elected memb Auckland City Cncl 1971, Mayor of Auckland City Cncl 1971, Mayor of Auckland 1983-90, Govr Gen NZ 1990-; occasional radio, tv and newspaper commentator; Winston Churchill fell 1981; fndn chairperson S Auckland Marriage Guidance Cncl, patron and memb of numerous community and arts orgns; former memb: Cncl of Auckland War Meml Museum and Inst, Auckland City Art Gallery, Auckland City Library, Auckland Theatre Tst, ASB Community Tsts, Auckland Maritime Museum Tst, Eastern Scdy Schs Bd of Govrs, Auckland Teachers Coll Cncl, Univ of Auckland Cncl; prior OStJ (NZ) 1990, NZ 1990 medal; *Style—* Her Excellency Dame Catherine Tizard, GCMG, DBE; Government House, Private Bag, Wellington, New Zealand (☎ 010 64 04 898 055, fax 010 64 04 895 536)

TIZARD, Prof Sir (John) Peter Mills; eld s of Sir Henry Tizard, GCB, AFC, FRS (d 1959), sometime pres Magdalen Oxford and memb Cncl of Min of Aircraft Production during WWII, Lady (Kathleen Eleanor) Tizard, *née* Wilson (d 1968); *b* 1 April 1916; *Educ* Rugby, Oriel Coll Oxford and Middx Hosp (BM BCh, MRCP, DCH); *m* 1945, Elisabeth Joy, da of Clifford Taylor; 2 s, 1 da; *Career* serv WWII RAMC (Temp Maj); prof paediatrics Univ of Oxford and fell Jesus Coll Oxford 1972-83 (hon fell 1983-), hon conslt children's physician Oxford AHA 1972-83, prof of paediatrics Inst Child Health Royal Postgrad Medical Sch London Univ 1964-72, hon conslt children's physician Hammersmith Hosp 1954-72, chm Hammersmith Hosp Medical Ctee 1970-71; pres Br Paediatric Assoc 1982-85, memb Neonatal Soc 1959- (pres 1975-78), pres Harveian Soc 1977 (memb 1974-), memb Br Paediatric Neurological Assoc; Worshipful Soc of Apothecaries: memb Ct of Assts 1971, Master 1983-84; FRCP, FRSocMed; kt 1982; *Style—* Prof Sir Peter Tizard; Jesus College, Oxford OX1 3DW; Holly Cottage, Court Drive, Hillingdon, Middx UB10 0BN (☎ 0895 811055)

TOALSTER, John Raymond; s of Chief Petty Offr John Edward Toalster, RNVR (ka 1944), and Adeline Enid, *née* Smith; *b* 12 March 1941; *Educ* Kingston HS Hull N Humberside, LSE (BSc); *m* 21 Sept 1963, Christine Anne, da of Edward Percy Paget (d 1970); 1 s (Quentin Simon Edward b 1966), 2 da (Rachel Jane b 1969, Bethan Claire b 1981); *Career* lectr in economics Univ of Sierra Leone 1964-67, corp planner Mobil Oil 1967-69, sr analyst (oils) stockbroking 1970-77, corporate fin mangr Kuwait International Investment Co 1977-81, energy specialist stockbroking 1982-90; dir: Hoare Govett 1982-90, Security Pacific, Société General Strauss Turnbull 1990-; FInstPet 1988; private circulation to clients; *Recreations* swimming, sailing, badminton; *Style—* John Toalster, Esq; Fig St Farm, Sevenoaks, Kent (☎ 0732 453357); Société General Strauss Turnbull, Exchange House, Primrose St, London EC2A (☎ 071 638 5699, fax 071 588 1437)

TOBE, Prof Martin Leslie; s of Charles Tobe (d 1989), and Anne, *née* Felpert (d 1952); *b* 22 May 1930; *Educ* Kilburn GS, UCL (BSc, PhD, DSc); *m* 18 Dec 1952, Rosalie Maureen, da of Moss Dancyger, CBE (d 1964); 1 s (Alan b 1955, d 1987), 2 da (Andrea b 1958, Michelle (Mrs Thomas) b 1964); *Career* res asst Univ of Durham 1954-56, lectr UCL 1956-65, Rose Morgan prof Univ of Kansas 1965-66; UCL: reader 1966-71, prof 1971-; FRSC 1953; *Books* Inorganic Reaction Mechanisms (1972); *Style—* Prof Martin Tobe; Chemistry Department, University College London, 20 Gordon Street, London WC1H 0AJ (☎ 071 387 7050)

TOBIAS, Dr Jeffrey Stewart; s of Gerald Joseph Tobias, of Bournemouth, and Sylvia, *née* Pearlberg; *b* 4 Dec 1946; *Educ* Hendon GS, Gonville and Caius Coll Cambridge (MA, MD); *m* 16 Nov 1973, Dr Gabriela Jill Tobias, da of Hans Jaecker, of Otford, Kent; 2 s (Benjamin Alexander b 1980, Max William Solomon b 1983), 1 da (Katherine Deborah b 1978); *Career* fell in med Harvard Med Sch 1974-75, sr registrar Royal Marsden Hosp and Inst of Cancer Res 1976-80, conslt clinical oncology UCH and Middlesex Hosps London 1981-; hon sec Br Oncological Assoc, chm UK Co-ordinating Ctee for Cancer Res Head and Neck Working Pty; memb: Medical Res Cncl Working Pty in Gynaecological and Brain Tumors, Cancer Res Campaign Working Pty in Breast Cancer; fell American Soc for Therapeutic Radiology; FRCP, FRCR; *Books* Primary Management of Breast Cancer (1985), Cancer and its Management (with R L Souhami, 1986), Cancer - A Colour Atlas (1990); *Recreations* music, theatre, walking; *Clubs* Albatross Wind and Water; *Style—* Dr Jeffrey Tobias; 48 Northchurch Rd, London N1 (☎ 071 249 2326); The Green, 34 The Kymin, Monmouth, Gwent; Dept of Radiotherapy and Oncology, University College Hospital, London WC1 (☎ 071 387 9300)

TOBIN, Julian Jacob; s of John Tobin (d 1966), and Georgina Tobin (d 1972); *b* 13 Aug 1927; *Educ* Great Yarmouth GS, Cambridge and Co HS, Magdalene Coll Cambridge (MA, LLM); *m* 6 Dec 1959, Jocelyne, da of Bernard Prevezer (d 1958), of 30 Green St, London W1; 1 s (Rupert b 1963), 2 da (Sasha b 1965, Annabel b 1968); *Career* admitted slr 1953; sr ptnr Pritchard Englefield & Tobin 1973-, admitted slr Hong Kong, ptnr Robert W H Wang & Co and Pritchard Englefield & Wang 1983-; memb: Hampstead Borough Cncl 1956-65, Camden Borough Cncl 1964- (dep ldr of Cons gp: 1968-73, 1974-79, 1985-; ldr of Cons gp 1979-81); tstee: Athlone Tst 1979-Lib Jewish Synagogue 1989- (treas 1984-89); special tstee: London Hosps 1981-88, Univ Coll Hosps 1986-; govr Univ Coll Sch 1981-87, dir Andre Deutsch Ltd 1983-, former chm Hampstead Cons Assoc (now sr tstee), former memb Home Office Ctee on Juveniles and Ctee on Rent Rebates and Rent Allowances DOE; memb Nat Advsy Property Ctee Cons Party; *Recreations* reading, watching cricket, opera, music generally; *Clubs* Carlton, Garrick, Savile; *Style—* Julian Tobin, Esq; 18 Eton Villas, Hampstead, London NW3 (☎ 071 722 8000); Orchard Cottage, Thicket Rd, Houghton, Huntingdon; 23 Great Castle St, London W1 (☎ 071 629 8883, fax 071 493 1891)

TOBIN, Capt Nicholas John; DSC (1982); s of Lt-Col PA Tobin, MBE, of Haslemere, Surrey, and Rosemary Nicoll, *née* Armitage; *b* 1 Jan 1945; *Educ* Duke of York Sch Nairobi Kenya, Britannia RNC Dartmouth; *m* 7 Aug 1976, Josephine Anne, da of Lt-Col JG Fisher, OBE (d 1976); 1 da (Naomi b 1983); *Career* naval offr; HM ships 1963-74: Glasserton, Victorious, Aisne, London, Dryad; CO HMS Beachampton and HMS Wolverton 1974, HMS Ark Royal 1976, dir staff RN Staff Coll 1979, CO HMS Antelope 1981, naval and def staff MOD 1982, def and naval attache Tokyo 1987, with the Admiralty 1990; *Recreations* sailing, golf, walking; *Clubs* Royal Navy; *Style—* Capt Nicholas Tobin, DSC, RN, MOD (Navy); Old Admiralty Building, Spring Gardens, London SW1A 2BE (☎ 071 218 3635)

TODD, Hon Alexander Henry; o s of Baron Todd, OM (Life Peer); *b* 11 Nov 1939; *Educ* The Leys Sch Cambridge, Oriel Coll Oxford (DPhil); *m* 1, 12 May 1967 (m dis), Joan Margaret, da of Frederick Wilbur Koester, of Campbell, California, USA; m 2, 3 Oct 1981, Patricia Mary, da of late Brig A Harvey Jones, of Somerford Booths, Cheshire; *Style—* The Hon Alexander Todd; The Chestnuts, Crown Lane, Lower Peover, Knutsford, Cheshire WA16 9QB (☎ 0565 722297)

TODD, Baron (Life Peer UK 1962), of Trumpington, Cambs; Alexander Robertus Todd; OM (1977); el s of Alexander Todd, JP (d 1952), of Glasgow; *b* 2 Oct 1907; *Educ* Allan Glen's Sch Glasgow, Univ of Glasgow (DSc), Frankfurt-on-Main Univ (PhD), Univ of Oxford (DPhil); *m* 1937, Alison Sarah (d 1987), da of Sir Henry Hallett Dale, OM, GBE, (d 1968); 1 s (Hon Alexander Henry b 1939), 2 da (Hon Helen Jean (Hon Mrs Brown) b 1941, Hon Hilary Alison b 1946); *Career* prof of chemistry: Univ of Manchester 1938-44, Univ of Cambridge 1944-71; master of Christ's Coll Cambridge 1963-78, managing tstee Nuffield Fndn 1950-79 (chm 1973-79), chllr Strathclyde Univ 1964-91, chm Croucher Fndn (Hong Kong) 1980-88 (pres 1988-); FRS 1942 (pres 1975-80); Hon LLD: Glasgow, Melbourne, Edinburgh, Manchester and California; Hon DSc Durham; Hon DLitt Sydney; Nobel prize for Chemistry 1957; kt 1954; *Recreations* golf; *Style—* The Rt Hon the Lord Todd, OM, FRS; 9 Parker St, Cambridge CB1 1JL (☎ 0223 356688)

TODD, Dr (William Taylor) Andrew; s of James McArthur Todd, of 28 Forrester Road, Edinburgh, and Jean Morley, *née* Smith; *b* 14 July 1953; *Educ* George Heriot's Sch, Univ of Edinburgh (BSc, MB ChB); *m* 1 July 1978, Morag Jennifer, da of Trevor John Ransley, of Edinburgh; 3 da (Jennifer b 1980, Rachel b 1983, Anna b 1987); *Career* Royal Infirmary Edinburgh: res house offr 1972, SHO in med 1978, registrar 1981-82, sr registrar 1985; City Hosp Edinburgh: registrar 1979-81, sr registrar 1984; visiting lectr Univ of Zimbabwe 1983, conslt physician 1985-; elder Church of Scotland; memb Br Soc for Study of Infection 1981; FRCPE; *Recreations* curling, hill walking; *Style—* Dr Andrew Todd; 57 Blairbeth Rd, Burnside, Glasgow G73 4JD (☎ 041 634 4328); Infections Diseases Unit, Monklands District General Hospital, Airdrie, Lanarkshire, Scotland ML6 0JS (☎ 0236 69344)

TODD, Anthony Clive; s of George William Todd (d 1967), and Clarissa, *née* Looker (d 1984); *b* 18 Oct 1928; *Educ* Palmers Grays Essex, UCL (Dip Arch, Dip TP); *m* 13 Aug 1966, Theresa, da of Hugh Kelly, of Co Sligo; 2 s (Andrew b 1967, Richard b 1970); *Career* mil serv: architectural instructor No 3 Army Coll Welbeck Abbey; chartered architect and town planning conslt; ptnr: Anthony Todd & Associates (architects); Freeman of the City of London, memb Worshipful Co of Constructors; RIBA; FRTPI; FFB; *Recreations* music, motor sports; *Style—* Anthony C Todd; 1 Macaulay Court, Caterham, Surrey CR3 5HS (☎ 0883 342781)

TODD, Daphne Jane; da of Frank Todd (d 1976), of Whitstable, and Annie Mary, *née* Lord; *b* 27 March 1947; *Educ* Simon Langton GS for Girls Canterbury, Slade Sch of Fine Art (DFA, Higher Dip in Fine Art); *m* 31 Aug 1984, Lt-Col (Patrick Robert) Terence Driscoll, s of Patrick Driscoll (d 1979); 1 da (Mary Jane b 12 Nov 1977); *Career* artist; dir of studies Heatherley Sch of Art 1980-86; work in the collections of: Regtl HQ Irish Guards, Univ of Cambridge, Univ of London, Univ of Oxford, Royal Holloway Museum and Art Gallery, Bishop's Palace Hereford, Royal Acad, Nat Portrait Gallery, Science Museum; second prize John Player Portrait Award Nat Portrait Gallery 1983, first prize Oil Painting of the Year Hunting Gp Nat Art Prize Competition 1984; retrospective exhibition Morley Gallery 1989; memb NEAC 1984, RP 1985, hon sec 1990; *Clubs* Chelsea Arts; *Style—* Miss Daphne Todd; Salters Green Farm, Mayfield, East Sussex TN20 6NP (☎ 089 285 2472)

TODD, Sir Ian Pelham; KBE (1989); s of late Alan Herapath Todd, and late Constance Edwards; *b* 23 March 1921; *Educ* Sherborne, Bart's Med Coll, Toronto Univ (MRCS, LRCP, FRCS, MD, MS, DCH); *m* 25 July 1946, Jean Audrey Ann, da of late James Morton Noble; 2 s (Neil b 1947, Stuart b 1957), 3 da (Jocelyn b 1948, Jane b 1952, Caroline b 1955); *Career* Maj RAMC; consltg surgn King Edward VII Hosp for Offrs, hon consltg surgn Barts and St Marks Hosps; former pres RCS, vice pres Imperial Cancer Res Fund, pres Med Soc of London; hon memb: Academie de Chirurgie de Paris, Assoc of Surgns of India, Hellenic Surgical Assoc, American Soc Coloproctology, RACS (sec Coloproctology), Acad of Med Malaysia; Hon: FCS SA 1986, FACS 1988, FRACS 1988, FRCS Can 1989, FRCPS Glasgow 1989; Star of Jordan 1973; FRGS; *Recreations* music, travel, philately, skiing; *Clubs* RSM; *Style—* Sir Ian P Todd, KBE; 34 Chester Close North, London NW1 4JE (☎ 071 486 7776)

TODD, James; s of Robert Nicol Todd (d 1959), and Catherina Buchanan, *née* Semple (d 1990); *b* 3 July 1894; *Educ* John Street Sr Secdy Sch Glasgow, Harvard Business Sch; *m* 2 Oct 1953, Isabella Smith Jack, da of John Green (d 1985); 1 s (Jeffrey b 1958), 3 da (Gail b 1960, Julie b 1963, Lindsay b 1966); *Career* RCS 1950-52; dir Lazard Brothers & Co Ltd 1977, exec vice pres Korea Merchant Banking Corporation Seoul 1982-86; dir: Lazard Brothers & Co Ltd Jersey 1987 (Guernsey 1987), Marehome 1988; ACIB 1963; *Clubs* RAC; *Style—* James Todd, Esq; Old Letton Court, Letton, nr Hereford; 10 Morgans Walk, Battersea Bridge Rd, London SW11 (☎ 071 228 7556) Lazard Brothers & Co Ltd, 21 Moorfields, London EC2 (☎ 071 588 2721)

TODD, John Gordon; s of George Todd, and Janet Brown, *née* Glass; *b* 7 June 1958; *Educ* Stewarts Melville Coll Edinburgh; *Career* Habitat Designs Ltd 1978-79, Wine Importers (Edinburgh) Ltd 1979-80, Scottish Industrial & Trade Exhibitions Ltd (currently chief exec and dir) 1980-, Industrial & Trade Exhibitions (NI) Ltd 1987-; dir: Art in Partnership (Scot) Ltd 1986-90, Edinburgh's Capital Ltd 1989-, IFEX Ltd (Dublin) 1989-, Edinburgh C of C & Manufactures 1989-; *Recreations* music, art, friends; *Style—* John Todd, Esq; 46A Blacket Place, Edinburgh, EH9 1RJ (☎ 031 667 2998); Scottish Industrial & Trade Exhibitions Ltd (SITE), 10 Blenheim Place, Edinburgh EH7 5JH (☎ 031 556 5152, fax 031 556 8896, telex 728117 SELEH G)

TODD, (Thomas) Keith; s of Thomas William Todd, and Cecile Olive Francis, *née* Hefti; *b* 22 June 1953; *m* 19 May 1979, Anne Elizabeth, da of Hilson Adam Henfrie, of Edinburgh; 2 s ((Thomas) Christopher b 1984, Andrew Adam Paul b 1986), 2 da (Fiona Elizabeth b 1980, Nicola Anne b 1982); *Career* chief fin offr Cincinnati Electronics 1981-86; fin dir: The Marconi Co 1986-87, ICL 1987-; FCMA; *Recreations* golf, swimming; *Style—* Keith Todd, Esq; ICL, 1 High St, Putney, London SW15 1SW (☎ 081 788 7272)

TODD, Prof Malcolm; s of Wilfrid Todd (d 1980), of Durham, and Rose Evelyn, *née* Johnson; *b* 27 Nov 1939; *Educ* Henry Smith Sch, Univ of Wales (BA, DLitt), BNC Oxford (Dip); *m* 2 Sept 1964, Molly, da of Alexander John Tanner (d 1987), of London; 1 s (Malcolm Richard b 1966), 1 da (Katharine Grace b 1965); *Career* res asst Rheinisches Landesmuseum Bonn 1963-65, reader Univ of Nottingham 1977-79 (lectr 1965-74, sr lectr 1974-77), prof of archaeology Univ of Exeter 1979-; visiting fell: All Souls Coll Oxford 1984, BNC Oxford 1990-91; vice pres Roman Soc 1984-; memb: Royal Cmmn on Historical Monuments 1986-, Cncl Nat Tst 1986-, German Archaeological Inst 1977; sr res fell Br Acad 1990-91; FSA 1970; *Books* The Northern Barbarians (1975, 3 edn 1987), Roman Britain (1981 and 1985), The South-West To AD 1000 (1987), Britannia (ed, 1984-89), Research on Roman Britain: 1960-89 (ed 1989), Les Germains Aux frontiers de l'empire romain (1990); *Recreations* reading, writing; *Style—* Prof Malcolm Todd, FSA; The University, Exeter, Devon EX4 4QH (☎ 0392 264 351)

TODD, Mark James; MBE (1984); s of Norman Edward Todd, of Cambridge, NZ, and Lenore Adele Todd, *née* Nickle; *b* 1 March 1956; *Educ* Cambridge HS, Waikato Tech Inst (DipAg); *m* 29 Nov 1986, Carolyn Faye; 1 da (Lauren b 1988); *Career* Equestrian: winner Badminton Horse Trials 1980, Gold medal winner LA Olympics 1984, Br Open

Champion 1985, 1988, 1989, winner of the German Championship at Luhmuhlen 1986; Burghley Horse Trials: winner and runner-up 1987, winner 1990; Gold medal winner and team Bronze medal winner Seoul Olympics 1988, winner of Int Three Day Events Stockholm Achelswang and Boekelo 1989, Scot Champion 1989, team Gold medalist World Three Day Event Championships 1990; number one in the world 1984, 1988, 1989; *Books* Charisma (1989); *Recreations* swimming, skiing, tennis, squash; *Style*— Mark Todd, Esq, MBE; Cholderton Equestrian Centre, Cholderton, Salisbury, Wiltshire SP4 0DW (☎ 0980 64 615)

TODD, Paul Rodney; s of Thomas Robert Todd (d 1977), of Spalding, and Gladys, *née* Blyth; *b* 17 Nov 1952; *Educ* Spalding GS, Univ of Leeds (BEd, DipEd); *Career* composer and music dir: Leeds Playhouse 1974-75 and 1978, Newcastle Univ Theatre 1976, Backworth Drama Centre 1977, Stephen Joseph Theatre Scarborough 1978-88, Royal NT 1985-88; scriptwriter and lyricist; memb: Musicians' Union, Equity, Performing Right Soc, Br Acad of Songwriters, Composers and Authors; *Books* Suburban Strains (with Alan Ayckbourn, 1982); *Recreations* cricket, crosswords; *Style*— Paul Todd, Esq; 10 Garibaldi St, Scarborough, N Yorks YO11 1RW (☎ 0723 352073)

TODD, Richard Andrew Palethorpe; s of Maj Andrew William Palethorpe Todd, MC (d 1941), of Clevedon Lodge, Wimborne, Dorset, and Marvilla Rose, *née* Agar-Daly; *b* 11 June 1919; *Educ* Norwood Sch Exeter, Shrewsbury, Queen Elizabeth's Wimborne, and privately; *m* 1, 13 Aug 1949 (m dis 1970), Catherine Stewart Crawford, da of William Grant-Bogle (d 1967); 1 s (Peter Grant Palethorpe b 1952), 1 da (Fiona Margaret Palethorpe b 1956); m 2, 1970, Virginia Anne Rollo, da of Colin Cotterill Rollo Mailer; 2 s (Andrew Richard Palethorpe b 1973, Seumas Alexander Palethorpe b 1977); *Career* WWII Serv: RMC Sandhurst 1940, cmmnd KOYLI 1941, seconded Parachute Regt 1943, D Day with 7 (LI) Para Bn Normandy, GSO3 (ops) 6 Airborne Div 1944, served Battle of the Bulge and Holland Rhine crossing, 2 i/c 3 Para Bde Def Co Palestine 1945-46; actor, prodr and dir 1937-; entered film indust 1948 making many Br and American films incl: The Hasty Heart (with Ronald Reagan), Disney's Robin Hood, Rob Roy, The Dam Busters, The Virgin Queen, A Man Called Peter, Yantze Incident, Chase a Crooked Shadow, D Day the 6th of June, The Longest Day; awarded Br Nat Film award, Oscar nomination and Hollywood Golden Globe for The Hasty Heart 1950; returned to theatre 1965 in An Ideal Husband, fndr dir Truimph Theatre Prodns 1970, led RSC N American tour of The Hollow Crown 1975, subsequent theatre appearances incl The Business of Murder London 1981-88; former Worshipful Master Lodge of Emulation no 21 (former Grand Steward); pres: Henley and Dist Agric Assoc 1963, Thames Valley Branch Save The Children Fund 1958-64, Grantham Branch Inst of Advanced Motorists; life pres Friends of Smith Hosp Henley, pres Birmingham Age Concern 1989-; *Books* Caught In The Act (1986), In Camera (1989); *Recreations* shooting, fishing, working; *Clubs* Army & Navy; *Style*— Richard Todd, Esq; Chinham Farm, Faringdon, Oxfordshire SN7 8EZ

TODD, Ronald (Ron); s of George Thomas Todd, and Emily Todd; *b* 11 March 1927; *Educ* St Patrick's Sch Walthamstow; *m* 1945, Josephine Tarrant; 1 s, 2 da; *Career* WWII RM Commandos (incl time in Hong Kong); dep convenor Ford Motor Company 1954-62; memb Exec Bd Unity Trust Bank plc; TGWU: joined 1946, full time offr Metal Engineering & Chemical Section 1962, regnl offr 1969, regnl sec London and SE 1976 (appointed 1975), nat organiser 1978, gen sec 1985- (elected 1984); memb: TUC Gen Cncl, TUC Econ Ctee, Fin and Gen Purposes Ctee, TUC Health Servs Ctee, Ctee on Euro Strategy, Employment Policy Organisation Ctee, TUC Energy Ctee, TUC/LP Liaison Ctee, TUC Environment Action Gp, TUC Gen Cncl NEDC, The Cncl for Charitable Support, President's Ctee Business in the Community; chm of TUC Int Ctee; hon vice pres CND, trade union rep Anti Apartheid Ctees, memb and tstee of TUFL; tstee: Tribune, CTUC Tst, Arts for Labour; vice pres Inst of Employment Rights, patron Bernt Carlsson Tst; *Recreations* collecting Victorian music covers, archaeology; *Style*— Ron Todd, Esq; Transport & General Workers' Union, Transport House, Smith Square, London SW1P 3JB (☎ 071 828 7788)

TODD, Ronald Stanley; s of William Stanley Todd (d 1977), and Dorothy Margaret, *née* Cooke; *b* 16 Feb 1930; *Educ* Merchant Taylor's, Univ of Liverpool (MB ChB, DObst, RCOG); *m* 7 Jan 1966, Gillian Margaret, da of William George Drinkwater (d 1966); 2 s (James b 1967, Richard b 1968), 1 da (Susan b 1966); *Career* Nat Serv 1948; fell Hanneman Hosp Philadelphia 1960, lectr in surgery Univ of Liverpool 1962 (demonstrator in anatomy 1956), conslt surgn Wrexham N Wales 1965 (ret); memb: Ct of Examiners RCS 1972, med appeal tbnls 1988; memb Cncl Assoc of Surgns of GB and I, pres N Wales Ileostomy Assoc 1975; FRCSEd 1960, FRCS 1961; *Style*— Ronald Todd, Esq; Rosebank, 18 Sandy Lane, Chester CH3 5UL (☎ 0244 351561)

TODD, Rev Dr (Andrew) Stewart; s of William Stewart Todd (d 1977), of Alloa, Clackmannanshire, and Robina Victoria, *née* Fraser (d 1988); *b* 26 May 1926; *Educ* Stirling HS, Univ of Edinburgh (MA, BD), Univ of Basel; *m* 17 Sept 1953, Janet Agnes Brown, da of John Smith, JP, DL, of Woodemailing, Symington, Lanarkshire; 2 s (David b 1956, Philip b 1960), 2 da (Diana b 1955, Jane b 1958); *Career* asst min St Cuthbert's Edinburgh 1951-52; min: Symington Lanarkshire 1952-60, N Leith 1960-67, St Machar's Cathedral Old Aberdeen 1967-; memb Church Hymnary Revision Ctee 1963-73, convenor Gen Assembly's Ctee on Public Worship and Aids to Devotion 1974-78, moderator Aberdeen Presbytery 1980-81, convenor Gen Assembly's Panel on Doctrine 1988-; Hon DD Univ of Aberdeen 1982; hon pres: Church Serv Soc, Scottish Church Soc; memb Societas Liturgica; *Recreations* music, gardening; *Style*— Rev Dr Stewart Todd; 18 The Chanonry, Old Aberdeen (☎ 0224 483688); Culearn, Balquhidder, Perthshire (☎ 08774 662)

TODHUNTER, Michael John Benjamin; s of Brig Edward Joseph Todhunter (d 1976), and Agnes Mary, *née* Swire (d 1975); *b* 25 March 1935; *Educ* Eton, Magdalen Coll Oxford (MA); *m* 1959, Caroline Francesca, da of Maj William Walter Dowding (d 1980); 1 s (Charles), 2 da (Nicola (Mrs James Denoon Duncan), Emily); *Career* 2 Lt 11 Hussars (PAO); banker; London advsr Yasuda Trust and Banking Co Ltd, chm Clyde Shipping Co Ltd; dir: James Finlay plc, SH Lock & Co (Holdings) Ltd, Kleinwort Development Fund plc, Newbury Racecourse plc; special tstee Great Ormond Street Hosp, dir Inst of Child Health; *Recreations* shooting; *Clubs* White's, Pratt's, City of London, Western (Glasgow); *Style*— Michael Todhunter, Esq; The Old Rectory, Farnborough, Wantage, Oxon OX12 8NX (☎ 048 82 298); The Studio, 4 Lowndes St, London SW1 (☎ 071 235 6421); office: 12 Cocklane, London EC1A 9BU

TOFIELD, Terence Greville William; s of Herbert Russell Tofield (d 1981), and Mary Josephine Tofield (d 1971); *b* 5 July 1936; *Educ* Latymer Upper; *Career* PR dir Rumasa and Augustus Barnett & Son Ltd (now Lawlers Ltd); tstee: City of London Univ, Wine and Spirit Educn Tst; Officier Ordre des Coteaux France; Liveryman Worshipful Co of Distillers; *Recreations* tennis, shooting, skiing; *Clubs* Hurlingham, RAC, Mardens; *Style*— Terence Tofield, Esq; 77 Swan Court, Chelsea Manor St, London SW3 5RY (☎ 071 352 3444); Lionsmead House, Shalbourne nr Marlborough, Wilts SN8 8DD; 88/92 South St, Dorking, Surrey (☎ 0306 884412 and 0672 870440)

TOFT, Dr Anthony (Douglas); s of William Vincent Toft (d 1982), of Newport, Salop, and Anne, *née* Laing; *b* 29 Oct 1944; *Educ* Perth Acad, Univ of Edinburgh (BSc, MB ChB, MD); *m* 23 July 1968, Maureen Margaret, da of John Darling (d 1986), of Perth; 1 s (Neil b 1970), 1 da (Gillian b 1972); *Career* conslt physician gen med and endocrinology 1978-, chief MO Scottish Equitable Life Assurance Society 1988-; FRCPE 1980 (memb Cncl 1985-88), memb Assoc of Physicians of GB and I 1984, vice pres RCPE 1990-; *Books* Diagnosis and Management of Endocrine Diseases (1982); *Recreations* golf, gardening, hill walking; *Style*— Dr Anthony Toft; 41 Hermitage Gardens, Edinburgh EH10 6AZ (☎ 031 447 2221); Dept of Medicine, Royal Infirmary, Edinburgh EH3 9YW, (☎ 031 229 2477)

TOFT, Ashton Reginald Marson (Rex); s of Thomas Marson Toft (d 1971), of Kendal, Cumbria, and Mary, *née* Webb; *b* 13 July 1934; *Educ* Lancaster Royal GS, Univ of Manchester; *m* 1, (m dis), Mary Elizabeth; 3 da ((Beverley) Jane b 31 May 1962, (Suzanne) Michelle b 18 April 1965, Lisa Mary Stacey b 14 June 1971); m 2, Joyce Foster, da of Albert Pickthall (d 1970); 2 step s (Alasdair Kilpatrick b 1974, Andrew Kilpatrick b 1978); *Career* slr: ptnr Bleasdale & Co; memb Cumbria CC; chm Friends of Sellafield Soc, Port of Workington Ctee; dir W Cumbria Ground Work Tst; Parly candidate (Cons) 1987; memb Law Soc (former chm W Cumbria Law Soc); *Recreations* politics, sport, reading; *Style*— Rex Toft, Esq; Gopeland House, Gosforth, Cumbria (☎ 094 67 25217); 14 Scotch St, Whitehaven, Cumbria; 2 Denton Hill, Gosforth, Cumbria (☎ 0946 69 2165)

TOGHILL, Dr Peter James; s of John Walter Toghill, of Bushey, Hertfordshire, and Lena Mary, *née* Jow (d 1985); *b* 16 June 1932; *Educ* Watford GS, Univ Coll Hosp Med Sch (MB BS), Univ of London (MD, LRCP); *m* 25 April 1964, Rosemary Anne, da of Alfred Samuel Cash, of Whatton, Nottinghamshire; 3 da (Claire Elizabeth b 1966, Helen Louise b 1969, Joanna Mary b 1972); *Career* Capt RAMC 1956-58; sr med registrar Kings Coll Hosp 1964-68, conslt physician Gen Hosp Nottingham 1968-, clinical dean Univ of Nottingham Med Sch 1977-80, currently sr conslt physician Univ Hosp Nottingham (conslt physician 1968-91); pro-censor RCP London 1991; memb Assoc of Physicians of GB and I, FRCP, FRCPE, MRCS; *Books* Examining Patients (1990); *Recreations* Nottinghamshire cricket, growing roses; *Style*— Dr Peter Toghill; 119 Lambley Lane, Burton Joyce, Nottingham NG14 5BL (☎ 0602 31 2446); 9 Regent St, Nottingham NG1 5BS (☎ 0602 472906)

TOLAN, Peter Graham; s of Daniel Tolan (d 1954), and Marjoie, *née* Goode; *b* 9 Sept 1944; *Educ* Ullathorne GS Coventry, Birmingham Coll of Commerce; *m* 26 Oct 1968, Christine Elizabeth, da of Kenneth Murray; 1 s (Mark Damien b 30 Jan 1971), 1 da (Danielle Elizabeth b 6 Oct 1972); *Career* trainee reporter Warwick and Warwickshire Advertiser 1961-67, sr reporter Nuneaton Evening Tribune 1967-68, freelance jounalist and broadcaster 1968-75, press and PR offr TI Machines (Int) 1975-77, PR conslt Harrison Cowley Public Relations (Brimingham) 1978-85 (dep md 1983), dir of PR Rex Stewart (Bristol) 1985, md Rex Stewart PR Ltd 1988, chief exec Rex Stewart Grayling Ltd Group 1990-, dir Bd Grayling International 1990-; MIPR 1988; *Recreations* rugby union (memb Warwickshire Soc of Referees); *Style*— Peter Tolan, Esq; 7 Gloster Drive, Mount Royal, Kenilworth CV8 2TU (☎ 0926 512349); Rex Stewart Grayling, Centre Court, 1301 Stratford Rd, Hall Green, Birmingham B28 9HH (☎ 021 702 2220, car 0836 722517)

TOLEMAN, Norman Edward (Ted); s of Albert Edward Toleman (d 1966), of Cherry Acre, 2 Courtland Drive, Chigwell, Essex, and Kathleen Eardley, *née* Templeton; *b* 14 March 1938; *Educ* Clarke's Ilford Essex; *m* 8 July 1961, Dianne Joan da of George Walter Prior, of Willow Cottage, Hoe, Dereham, Norfolk; 2 s (Gary b 1961, Michael (twin) b 1961); *Career* powerboat racing: Br Nat Champion 1980-83, Euro Champion 1980; 1981 Australian Champion, fifth in American Championship, set new Class 1 World Speed Record of 97.65 mph; 1982: runner-up World Championship, winner London-Calais-London race, set new Class 1 World Speed Record of 110.41 mph Lake Windermere; 1983: European Championships Sweden and Italy, raised World Speed Record to 120.95 mph Lake Windermere; conceived and skippered the initial Spirit of Britain Transatlantic Challenge (Virgin) 1985; motor sport: formed Toleman Gp Motorsport 1969, 1 and 2 place Tolemen Gp Motorsport Formula Two Championship 1980, entered Formula One motor racing 1981, 2 position Monaco Grand Prix 1984, entered Paris-Dakar rally to promote Br tech leadership; business acquisition of: A & C McLennan 1969, James Car Deliveries 1973, Samual Eden 1977, Cougar Marine (UK largest vehicle tportation Co) 1980; vice pres Stowmarket FC; patron racing for BR; Freeman City of London 1984; memb Worshipful Co of Carmen; CBIM 1990; *Recreations* int driver, rallying, bob sleigh driving, motor and offshore power racing; *Clubs* Royal Southern Yacht, Br Racing Drivers; *Style*— Ted Toleman, Esq, JP; Abilene Lodge, Drinkstone Rd, Gedding, Bury St, Edmunds, Suffolk, IP30 0QD (☎ 044 937 831); Toleman House, St Thomas Rd, Brentwood, Essex CM14 4ES (☎ 0277 226 060, fax 0277 220 343, car 0836 341424, telex 995259)

TOLER, Maj-Gen David Arthur Hodges; OBE (1963), MC (1945), DL (1982); s of Maj Thomas Clayton Toler, JP, DL (d 1940), of Swettenham Hall, Congleton, Cheshire, and Gertrude Marianna, *née* Wilkinson (d 1962); *b* 13 Sept 1920; *Educ* Stowe, Ch Ch Oxford (MA); *m* 11 Sept 1951, Judith Mary, da of late Maj James William Garden, DSO, of Aberdeen; 1 s (Hugh b 1953), 1 da (Jane b 1955); *Career* WWII 2 Lt Coldstream Gds 1940; served in WWII in N Africa and Italy 1942-45; Adj RMA Sandhurst 1958-60, Br liaison offr US Continental Army Cmd (Col) 1960-62, cmd 2 Bn Coldstream Gds 1962-64, cmd Coldstream Gds 1964-65, cmd 4 Gds Bde 1965-68, Brig 1966, dep cmdt Staff Coll Camberley 1968-69, Maj-Gen 1969, GOC E Midland Dist 1970-73; Dep Hon Col Lincs Royal Anglian Regt 1979-84; co emergency planning offr Lincs 1974-77; chm Lincoln Diocesan Advsy Ctee 1981-86; hon clerk to the Lieutenancy (Co of Lincoln) 1983-90; chm Lincs TA & VR Ctee 1984-86; *Recreations* shooting, fishing; *Clubs* Army and Navy; *Style*— Maj-Gen David Toler, OBE, MC, DL; Rutland Farm, Fulbeck, Grantham, Lincs NG32 3LG

TOLKIEN, Emma Katherine de Cusance; da of Anthony de Cusance Cussans, of The Hosp of St Cross, Winchester, and Cecilia Anne, *née* Ratcliffe; *b* 20 July 1953; *Educ* St Mary's Convent Shaftesbury Dorset, Holland Park Comp London, Univ of Manchester (BA); *m* 19 Oct 1985, Michael Geoffrey Stuart Tolkien, s of Stuart Frederick Gerald Tolkien (d 1978), of Staverton, Devon; 2 s (Edmond Michael de Cusance b 6 April 1990, Oliver Bertram de Cusance (twin) b 6 April 1990); *Career* Yachting Monthly Magazine: features ed 1981-85, organiser outside events triangle race 1986 (also 1988 and 90), classic yacht rally 1989; ed: Tall Ships News 1983-, West Country Cruising 1988, East Coast Rivers 1989; memb: Topsham Museum Soc, Topsham Soc, Devon Valuation and Community Charge Tbnl; memb Yachting Journalists Assoc 1982; *Recreations* sailing, dog walking; *Clubs* Royal Western Yacht of England, Royal Torbay Yacht, Topsham Sailing; *Style*— Mrs Michael Tolkien; 2 Swains Court, Topsham, Exeter, Devon EX3 OHH (☎ 039287 7979)

TOLKIEN, Faith Lucy Tilly; da of Frank Thomas Faulconbridge (d 1973), and Gladys Lilian, *née* Tilly (d 1946); *b* 9 June 1928; *Educ* St Felix Sch Southwold, St Anne's Coll Oxford (MA), Oxford City Art Sch; *m* 1, 2 April 1951 (m dis 1967), Christopher Reuel Tolkien, s of John Ronald Reuel Tolkien (d 1973); 1 s (Simon Mario Reuel Tolkien b 12 Jan 1959), m 2, Tracy Steinberg; 1 s (Nicholas Faulconbridge Reuel b 20 Aug 1990)); *Career* sculptor; teacher 1964-79; portrait heads incl: The Rt Hon Lord Jenkins of Hillhead, Sir Richard Doll, C S Lewis, J R R Tolkien, Dame Iris Murdoch, DBE, Sir Michael Oppenheimer, Bt, Lady Oppenheimer; has exhibited in the Royal Acad exhibition; church works incl: Madonna and Child in Univ of Birmingham RC Chapel, Stations of the Cross in Corpus Christi Church Oxford and bronze relief for shrine of

St John Wall in St Mary's Church Harvington Worcs, crucifixion sculpture in the chapel of the Sacred Heart St John's Seminary Wonersh Surrey; *Recreations* novels, poetry, biography, scripture and theology, bird watching, walking, travelling, visiting pubs; *Style—* Mrs Faith Tolkien; 28 Church St, Watlington, Oxford OX9 5QR (☎ 049161 2514); Studio, c/o Alec Ryman, Sculpture Castings, Ellery Rise, Frieth, Nr Henley-on-Thames (☎ 0494 881988)

TOLLEMACHE, Hon Hugh John Hamilton; s of 4 Baron Tollemache (d 1975); *b* 1946; *Educ* Eton; *m* 1986, Rosie, da of Hon Anthony Cayzer; 1 s (b 1 Sept 1989); *Style—* The Hon Hugh Tollemache; 19 Clarendon St, SW1

TOLLEMACHE, Sir Lyonel Humphry John; 7 Bt (GB 1793), JP (Leics), DL (Leics); s of Maj-Gen Sir Humphry Thomas Tollemache 6 Bt, CB, CBE, DL (d 1990), and Nora Priscilla, *née* Taylor (d 1990); *b* 10 July 1931; *Educ* Uppingham, RAC Cirencester; *m* 6 Feb 1960, Mary Joscelyne, da of Col William Henry Whitbread, TD; 2 s (Lyonel Thomas b 1963, Richard John b 1966), 2 da (Katheryne Mary b 1960, Henrietta Joscelyne b 1970); *Heir* s, Lyonel Thomas Tollemache b 23 Jan 1963; *Career* cmmnd Coldstream Gds, Maj; High Sheriff of Leicestershire 1978-79, CO cncllr Leicestershire 1985-; FRICS; *Style—* Sir Lyonel Tollemache, Bt, JP, DL; Buckminster Park, Grantham, Lincs NG33 5RU (☎ 0476 860 349; office 0476 860 471)

TOLLEMACHE, Hon Michael David Douglas; s of 4 Baron Tollemache (d 1975); *b* 23 Aug 1944; *Educ* Eton, Trinity Coll Cambridge (MA); *m* 5 Feb 1969, Thérèsa, da of Peter Bowring; 2 s (twins), 1 da; *Career* dir: Michael Tollemache Ltd 1967-, David Carritt Ltd 1983-, Artemis Fine Arts Ltd 1983-; *Clubs* White's; *Style—* The Hon Michael Tollemache; Framsden Hall, Helmingham, Stowmarket, Suffolk (☎ 071 930 8733)

TOLLEMACHE, Hon (John) Nicholas Lyonel; s of 4 Baron Tollemache (d 1975); *b* 13 June 1941; *Educ* Eton, Trinity Coll Cambridge (MA), Harvard (MBA); *m* 1, 1971 (m dis 1974), Heide Eva Marie, da of Gunther Wiedeck, of Bonn; m 2, 1982, Dietlinde Hannelore, da of Hannelore Riegel of Muncih, W Germany; *Style—* The Hon Nicholas Tollemache; 1114 San Ysidro Drive, Beverly Hills, CA 90210, USA

TOLLEMACHE, 5 Baron (UK 1876); Timothy John Edward Tollemache; DL (Suffolk 1984); s of 4 Baron Tollemache (d 1975); *b* 13 Dec 1939; *Educ* Eton; *m* 1970, Alexandra Dorothy Jean, da of Col Hugo Meynell, MC, JP, DL (d 1960); 2 s (Hon Edward, Hon James b 1980), 1 da (Hon Selina b 1973); *Heir* s, Hon Edward John Hugo Tollemache b 12 May 1976; *Career* cmmnd Coldstream Gds 1959-62; chm NRG Victory Holdings Ltd; dir AMEV Holdings (UK) Ltd 1980, and other companies; farmer; pres: Suffolk Assoc of Local Cncls 1978-, Friends of Ipswich Museums 1980-, Cheshire Cereal Soc 1983-, Suffolk Agric Assoc 1988; chm: HHA (E Anglia) 1979-83, Cncl St John (Suffolk) 1982-89; vice pres Cheshire BRCS 1980-, St Edmundsbury Cathedral Appeal 1986-90; patron Suffolk Accident Rescue Services 1983-; CStJ 1988; *Recreations* shooting, fishing; *Clubs* White's, Pratt's, Special Forces; *Style—* The Rt Hon Lord Tollemache, DL; Helmingham Hall, Stowmarket, Suffolk (☎ 047 339 217)

TOLLER, Mark Geoffrey Charles; s of Capt Charles Bolton Toller, and Eleanor Ann, *née* Pease; *b* 23 Oct 1950; *Educ* Harrow; *m* 22 May 1981, Anna Caroline, da of James Alastair McGregor; 1 s (Edward b 4 June 1983), 2 da (Annabel b 14 Jan 1987, Katharine b 7 Aug 1989); *Career* asst dir Guinness Mahon & Co Ltd 1983-87, dir Br and Cwlth Merchant Bank plc 1987-; memb ICA; *Recreations* horse racing, golf, shooting; *Style—* Mark Toller, Esq; British and Commonwealth Merchant Bank plc, 19 Motcomb St, London SW1 (☎ 071 245 6616, fax 071 235 2048)

TOLLEY, David Anthony; s of Frank Stanley Tolley, of Sale, Cheshire, and Elizabeth, *née* Dean; *b* 29 Nov 1947; *Educ* Manchester GS, Kings Coll Hosp Med Sch (MB BS); *m* 4 July 1970, Judith Anne, da of Wing Cdr Dennis Martin Finn, DFC (d 1983), of Salisbury; 3 s (Nicholas, Christopher, Jeremy), 1 da (Felicity Jane); *Career* conslt urological surgeon: Royal Infirmary Edinburgh 1980-91, Western General Hospital 1991-; die the Scottish Lithotriptor Centre Deaconess Hosp Edinburgh 1991-; memb Urological Cancer Working Pty MRC; FRCS (England and Edinburgh); *Recreations* golf, motor racing, music; *Style—* David Tolley, Esq; 14 Moray Place, Edinburgh EH3 6DT (☎ 031 225 5320)

TOLLEY, Rev Canon George; s of George Enoch Frederick Tolley (d 1971), of Old Hill, Staffs, and Elsie, *née* Billingham (d 1977); *b* 24 May 1925; *Educ* Halesowen GS Worcs, Birmingham Central Tech Coll, Princeton Univ, Lincoln Theol Coll, London Univ (BSc, MSc, PhD); *m* 21 June 1947, Joan Amelia, da of Isaac Grosvenor (d 1984), of Blackheath, Worcs; 2 s (Christopher b 1951, Martin b 1952), 1 da (Jane b 1955); *Career* chief chemist Metallisation Ltd 1947-51, Chemistry Dept Birmingham Coll of Advanced Technol 1951-58 (head of dept 1954-58), head of research Allied Ironfounders Ltd 1958-61, princ Worcester Tech Coll 1961-65, sr dir of studies RAF Coll Cranwell 1965-66, princ Sheffield Poly 1966-82; Manpower Services Cmmn: dir of open technol, head of Quality Branch, chief offr Review of Vocational Qualifications 1987, conslt in educn and training 1988-; ordained priest C of E 1968, hon canon Sheffield 1976; one of twelve Capital Burgesses of the Commonality of Sheffield 1980-; memb Yorks and Humberside Economic Planning Cncl 1974-79, hon sec Assoc of Colls of Higher and Further Educn 1974-83; pres Inst of Home Econs 1987-90; chm: Further Educn Unit 1977-83, Cncl Selly Oak Colls 1983-, Educn-Industry Forum Industry Matters 1984-88; memb: CNAA 1973-82, Cncl RSA 1985-, Cncl S Yorks Fndn 1986-; Hon DSc: Univ of Sheffield 1983, Open Univ 1983, CNAA 1986; hon fell: City and Guilds of London, Sheffield Poly, Coll of Preceptors, Columbia Pacific Univ, Inst of Trg and Devpt; FRSC 1954, fell Plastics and Rubber Inst 1973, CBIM 1978; *Books* Meaning and Purpose in Higher Education (1976); *Recreations* music, hill walking, bird watching; *Clubs* Athenaeum; *Style—* The Rev Canon George Tolley; 74 Furniss Ave, Dore Sheffield S17 3QP (☎ 0742 360 538)

TOLLIT, Mark Frederick; MBE (1985); s of C Clifton Tollit (d 1965), of Middx, and Francis F, *née* Green (d 1977); *b* 7 Sept 1925; *Educ* Eastbourne Coll, London Sch of Printing; *m* 1, 24 April 1948, Mary Jamieson (d 1971), da of J J Reid, OBE (d 1964); 2 s (Mark Nigel b 1950, Ian Clifton b 1952), 1 da (Clare Margaret b 1958); m 2, 24 Aug 1974, Gillian Marigold, da of Bertram Savage (d 1975); *Career* Capt Queens Royal Regt UK and Egypt; chm Tollit & Harvey Ltd (Norfolk), dir W Norfolk Enterprise Trust Ltd (Kings Lynn); Master Worshipful Co of Stationers and Newspaper Makers; FID 1958; *Recreations* sailing, gardening, affinity with four legged creatures; *Clubs* Sloane; *Style—* Mark Tollit, MBE; Tollit & Harvey Ltd, Oldmedow Rd, Kings Lynn, Norfolk PE30 4LW (☎ 0553 760774, fax 0553 767235)

TOLMAN, Jeffery Alexander Spencer; s of Gerald James Spencer, of Cornwall, and Doris Rosaline, *née* Lane (d 1966); *b* 12 July 1950; *Educ* St Clement Danes GS, Univ of Wales Sch of Int Politics; *Career* product mangr Birds Eye Foods (Unilever) 1971-73, account exec Ogilvy & Mather 1973-74; McCann Erickson 1974-79: account supervisor, account dir, assoc dir, dir; fndr ptnr Grandfield Rork Collins 1979-85, chief exec (Strategy) Saatchi & Saatchi Advertising 1990- (gp account dir 1985-86, dep chm 1987-); MIPA; *Recreations* walking, eating, drinking, politics; *Clubs* Reform, RAC, Grouchos; *Style—* Jeffery Tolman, Esq; 12 Stonor Rd, London W14 8RZ (☎ 071 603 6697); Lushers, Whitsbury, Hampshire; Saatchi & Saatchi Advertising, 80 Charlotte St, London W1 (☎ 071 636 5060, fax 071 637 8489, telex 261580, car 0836 677 871)

TOLSTOY, Dimitry (full surname Tolstoy-Miloslavsky); QC (1959); s of Michael Tolstoy-Miloslavsky (d 1947); *b* 8 Nov 1912; *Educ* Wellington, Trinity Coll Cambridge; *m* Frieda Mary, da of late Howard Wicksteed; 1 s (Nikolai T-M, *qv*), 1 da (Natasha or Natalie m 1974 Patrick John Bucknell); m 2, 1943, Natalie, da of Captain Vladimir Deytrikh (d 1951); 1 s (Andrei T-M, *qv*), 1 da (Tania or Tatiana (Mrs Illingworth)); *Career* called to the Bar Gray's Inn 1937, lectr in divorce to Inns of Court 1952-68; author; *Publications* Tolstoy on Divorce (7 edns, 1946-71); *Style—* Dimitry Tolstoy Esq, QC

TOLSTOY-MILOSLAVSKY, Count Andrei; s of (Count) Dimitry Tolstoy-Miloslavsky, QC, and Natalie; half-bro of Count Nikolai Tolstoy-Miloslavsky, *qv*; *b* 12 May 1949; *Educ* French Lycée, Wellington Coll, Univ of Surrey; *m* 1976, Carolinda Beatrice Catherine, da of Maj Ralph Pilcher, Welsh Gds, of Hay Place, Binsted, Hants; 2 s (Igor b 1985, Oleg b 1986), 1 da (Liubov b 1979); *Career* businessman; *Recreations* tennis, sailing, running, reading, guitar; *Clubs* Beefsteak, RAC; *Style—* Count Andrei Tolstoy-Miloslavsky; 8 Orlando Rd, London SW4 0LF (☎ 071 720 6687)

TOLSTOY-MILOSLAVSKY, Count Nikolai Dmitrievich; s of (Count) Dimitry Tolstoy, *qv*; *b* 23 June 1935; *Educ* Wellington, Trinity Coll Dublin (MA); *m* 1971, Georgina Katherine, da of Maj Peter Brown, of Longworth, Berkshire; 1 s (Dmitri b 1978), 3 da (Alexandra b 1973, Anastasia b 1975, Xenia b 1980); *Heir* (Count) Dmitri Nikolaevich Tolstoy-Miloslavsky; *Career* pres Assoc for a Free Russia; chm the Monarchist League; author, historian, biographer; *Books*: The Founding of Evil Hold School (1968), Night of The Long Knives (1972), Victims of Yalta (1978), The Half-Mad Lord (1978), Stalin's Secret War (1981), The Tolstoys (1983); The Quest for Merlin (1985), The Minister and the Massacres (1986), The Coming of the King (1988), also monographs on Celtic studies; FRSL; *Recreations* walking, archery, broadsword-and-buckler play; *Style—* Count Nikolai Tolstoy-Miloslavsky; Court Close, Southmoor, Abingdon, Berks (☎ 0865 820186)

TOM, Peter William Gregory; s of John Gregory Tom, of Bardon House, Bardon Hill, Leicester, and Barbara, *née* Lambden; *b* 26 July 1940; *Educ* Hinckley GS; *m* 28 Jan 1985 (m dis 1990), Patrice Alison, da of Ronald S Chandler, of Markfield, Leics; 1 s (decd), 2 da (Saffron b 1972, Layla b 1975) by previous m; *Career* chm and chief exec Bardon Group PLC; *Recreations* tennis, theatre, golf; *Style—* Peter W G Tom, Esq; Bardon Group PLC, Bardon Hill, Leicester LE6 2TL (☎ 0530 510088, fax 0530 510259)

TOMALIN, Air Cdre Charles Douglas; CBE (1966, OBE 1953), DFC (1943, AFC 1942); s of Frederick Tomalin (d 1933); *b* 20 Aug 1914; *Educ* William Ellis Sch, RAF Staff Coll, US Armed Forces Staff Coll, IDC; *m* 1941, Margaret, da of Rev J J Ellis (d 1962); 2 s; *Career* joined RAF 1936, dir Intelligence (A) 1961-63, head Br Def Liaison Staff and Air Attaché S Africa 1963-66, ret Air Cdre; represented England in diving events in the Br Empire Games: 1930, 1934, 1938 (1 Gold, 3 Silver medals); represented GB in high diving event in the 1936 Olympic Games; *Clubs* RAF; *Style—* Air Cdre Charles Tomalin, CBE, DFC; Rauceby, Nascot Wood Rd, Watford, Herts WD1 3SD (☎ 0923 229539)

TOMALIN, Claire; da of Emile Delavenay, and Muriel Emily, *née* Herbert (d 1984); *b* 20 June 1933; *Educ* Lycée Français de Londres, Girls GS Hitchin, Dartington Hall Sch, Newnham Coll Cambridge (BA, MA); *m* 17 Sept 1955, Nicholas Osborne Tomalin (d 1973), s of Miles Ridley Tomalin (d 1983); 2 s (Daniel b and d 1960, Thomas Nicholas Ronald b 1970), 3 da (Josephine Sarah b 1956, Susanna Lucy b 1958 d 1980, Emily Claire Elizabeth b 1961); *Career* publishers ed, reader, journalist 1953-67; literary ed: New Statesman 1974-78 (dep literary ed 1968-70), Sunday Times 1980-86; FRSL 1974; *Books* Life and Death of Mary Wollstonecraft (1974), Shelley and His World (1980), Katherine Mansfield: A Secret Life (1987), The Invisible Woman: The Story of Nelly Ternan and Charles Dickens (1990); play: The Winter Wife (1991); *Style—* Mrs Claire Tomalin; 57 Gloucester Crescent, London NW1 7EG

TOMBA, Hon Mrs (Henrietta Jane); *née* Piercy; yst da of 2 Baron Piercy (d 1981); *b* 1951; *Educ* Badminton Sch, Univ St Andrews (MA); *m* 1985, Tullio Luigi Giuseppe Tomba, s of Gualfardo Tomba (d 1945), of Udine, Italy; 2 s (Tommaso Piercy b 1987, Francesco Piercy b 1989); *Style—* The Hon Mrs Tomba; Via Corona 40, Campoformido (Udine) Italy (☎ 0432 662260)

TOMBS, Baron (Life Peer UK 1990), of Brailes in the County of Warwickshire; Sir Francis Leonard Tombs; s of Joseph Tombs; *b* 17 May 1924; *Educ* Elmore Green Sch Walsall, Birmingham Coll of Technol, Univ of London (BSc); *m* 1949, Marjorie Evans; 3 da (Hon Catherine Barbara b 22 April 1950, Hon Elisabeth Jane b 18 Dec 1952, Hon Margaret Clare b 25 Nov 1958); *Career* trained with: GEC Ltd Birmingham 1939-45, Birmingham Corp electricity supply dept 1946-47, Br Electricity Authy 1948-57; gen mangr GEC Ltd Kent 1958-67, dir and gen mangr James Howden & Co Glasgow 1967-68; South of Scotland Electricity Bd: dir of engrg 1969-73, dep chm 1973-74, chm 1974-77; chm: Electricity Cncl for England and Wales 1977-80, Weir Group plc 1981-83, Turner & Newall plc 1982-89, Rolls-Royce plc 1985-, The Engineering Cncl 1985-88, The Advsy Cncl on Sci and Technol 1987-90, Molecule Theatre Co 1985-; dir: N M Rothschild & Sons Ltd 1981-, Rolls-Royce Ltd 1982-, Turner & Newall International Ltd 1982-89, Turner & Newall Welfare Trust Ltd 1982-89, Shell-UK Ltd 1983-; pro chllr and chm Cncl Cranfield Inst of Technol 1985-, vice pres Engrs for Disaster Relief 1985-; Liveryman and Assistant Warden Worshipful Co of Goldsmith's, Freeman City of London; Hon LLD Univ of Strathclyde (visiting prof); Hon DSc: Aston Univ, Lodz Univ (Poland), Cranfield Inst of Technol, The City Univ London, Univ of Bradford, Queen's Univ Belfast, Univ of Surrey, Univ of Nottingham, Univ of Cambridge; Hon DTech Loughborough Univ of Techmol, Hon DEd CNAA; FEng (past vice pres), FIEE (past pres), Hon FIMechE, Hon FICE, Hon FIChemE, Hon FIProdE, Hon memb Br Nuclear Energy Soc; kt 1978; *Style—* The Rt Hon the Lord Tombs; Honington Lodge, Honington, Shipston-upon-Stour, Warwickshire CV36 5AA; Rolls-Royce plc, 65 Buckingham Gate, London SW1E 6AT (☎ 071 222 9020, telex 918091)

TOMKINS, Prof Cyril Robert; s of Charles Albert Tomkins (d 1955), of Southampton, and Gladys Rose Sylvester; *b* 27 May 1939; *Educ* Price's Sch, Univ of Bristol (BA), LSE (MSc); *m* 10 Aug 1963, Dorothy, da of Sydney Parker (d 1988), of Portsmouth; 2 s (Neil b 1967, Stephen b 1969); *Career* accountant for four years, lectr Univ of Hull 1969-70, sr res offr and lectr Univ Coll of N Wales 1970-73, sr lectr Univ of Strathclyde 1973-75, prof accounting and finance Univ of Bath 1975-; numerous journal articles, govt reports and other papers: The Devpt of Relevant Accounting Reports (1969), Constructing Social Accounts (1970), Lease Finance In Industrial Markets (1980), The Everyday Accountant and Researching His Reality (1983), Materiality In Local Government Auditing (1985), Changing Attitudes To Innovation In The Civil Service (1989), Making Sense of Cost-Plus Transfer Prices (1990); reviews incl: Frontiers of Investment Analysis (1970), Public And Local Authority Accounts (1974), The Lease-Purchase Decision (1978), Planning And Control Of Municipal Revenues And Expenditures (1984), Management Accounting - The Challenge of Technological Innovation (1990); funded res projects incl: local govt financial control, comparison of investment decision making in UK and German cos, developed fin mgmnt in central govt; memb of Ed Bd: Accounting and Business Research, Auditing and Accountability, Journal of Accounting and Business Finance, Financial Management and Accountability; chm: Br Accounting Assoc 1989; CIPFA 1967, FCCA; *Books* Financial Planning In Divisionalised Companies (1974), An Economic Analysis of The Financial Leasing

Industry (jt 1979), Issues In Public Sector Accounting (jt 1984), Achieving Economy Efficiency And Effectiveness In The Public Sector (1987), Corporate Resources Allocation - strategy and finance (1991); *Recreations* travel, gardening, reading, walking; *Style—* Prof Cyril Tomkins; Univ of Bath, Sch of Management, Bath, Avon BA2 7AY (☎ 0225 826028)

TOMKINS, Sir Edward Emile; GCMG (1975, KCMG 1969, CMG 1960), CVO (1957); s of Lt-Col Ernest Leith Tomkins; *b* 16 Nov 1915; *Educ* Ampleforth, Trinity Coll Cambridge; *m* 15 Nov 1955, Gillian, da of Air Cdre Constantine Evelyn Benson, CBE, DSO (yr bro of late Sir Rex Benson), by his w Lady Morvyth, *née* Ward (2 da of 2 Earl of Dudley and sis of 1 Viscount Ward of Witley); 1 s (Julian b 1956), 2 da (Sarah b 1958, Rosemary b 1961); *Career* served WWII 1940-43 (liaised with French Free Forces); diplomat, joined Foreign Service 1939; served: Moscow 1944-46, FO 1946-51, Washington 1951-54, cnsllr (Information) Paris 1954-59, FO 1959-63, min Bonn 1963-67, min Washington 1967-69; ambass: Netherlands 1970-72, France 1972-75, ret; memb Bucks CC 1977-, chm Friends of Univ Coll of Buckingham 1977; Croix de Guerre, Grand Officer Légion d'Honneur 1984; *Clubs* Turf, Garrick; *Style—* Sir Edward Tomkins, GCMG, CVO; Winslow Hall, Winslow, Bucks (☎ (029 671) 2323)

TOMKINS, Dr Peter Maurice; s of Rowland Maurice Tomkins, of Leeds, Yorks, and Gwendoline Mary, *née* Dunkley; *b* 29 Nov 1941; *Educ* Leeds Modern Sch, Univ of Bradford (BTech), Univ of Leeds (PhD); *m* 14 May 1988, Rosemary Anne, da of John Gale Harrison, of Stockport, Cheshire; 1 da (Amber Lauren b 17 Oct 1990); *Career* R & D scientist Albright & Wilson plc 1963-64, univ demonstrator then fell Univ of Leeds 1964-67, dept mangr (mfrg, R & D devpt, brands) Mars Confectionary Ltd 1967-69, mangr then princ conslt Arthur Young & Co 1969-71, vice pres and gen mangr Encyclopaedia Britannica International Ltd 1971-73, chief exec and dir D M Management Consultants Ltd (strategic direct mktg consultancy) 1973-, non-exec gp dir Charlwell Industrial Holdings Ltd 1973-; vice pres Youth Clubs UK (former dep chm), chm Community Indust Bd (Nat Assoc of Youth Clubs) 1975-78, fndr tstee Charity Effectiveness Review Tst 1984-90, memb SW Thames RHA 1986-90; Lloyds Underwriting Name 1978-; memb RSC 1968, CChem 1970, FBIM 1972, memb Br Direct Mktg Assoc 1979-, FInstD 1980, FIMC 1982; author of mgmnt and mktg articles in various jls; *Recreations* squash, skiing, jogging, yoga, charity work; *Clubs* IOD, Roehampton; *Style—* Dr Peter Tomkins; D M Management Consultants Ltd, 19 Clarges St, London W1Y 7PG (☎ 071 499 8030, fax 071 491 9408, car 0836 244288)

TOMKINSON, John Stanley; CBE (1981); s of Harry Stanley Tomkinson (d 1981), of Stafford, and Katie Mills, *née* Cliff (d 1979); *b* 8 March 1916; *Educ* Rydal Sch, Univ of Birmingham Sch of Med, St Thomas' Hosp (MB ChB); *m* 31 March 1954, Barbara Marie, da of Tom Pilkington (d 1966), of Eastbourne; 2 s (Barnaby John b 1957 d 1986, Matthew James b 1958), 1 da (Claudia (Mrs Finlay) b 1955); *Career* Surgn Lt RNVR 1942-46; conslt surgn (obstetrics and gynaecology): Queen Charlotte's Maternity Hosp, Chelsea Hosp for Women and Guy's Hosp London 1953-79; sec gen Int Fedn of Gynaecology and Obstetrics 1976-85, now hon sec gen, conslt advsr in obstetrics and gynaecology DHSS 1966-81; former memb Cncl RCS England and RCOG, dep chm Central Midwives Bd; visiting prof Spanish Hosp Mexico City 1972; former examiner: Univ of Oxford, Univ of Cambridge, Univ of London, Univ of Birmingham, Univ of Belfast, Univ of Tripoli, Univ of Addis Ababa, Univ of Singapore, E Africa Univs; memb: RCOG Conjoint Bd and Central Midwives Bd; hon fell and memb Continental Gynaecological Club of America (also Canada, Colombia, Nigeria, S Africa, Brazil, Jordan, Korea, Italy, Spain, Poland, Romania); ed Queen Charlotte's Textbook of Obstetrics; Copernicus medal Acad of Med Cracow Poland, medal of Polish Nation for Aid and Cooperation in Med; FRCS, FRCOG; *Recreations* fly fishing, needlework, bird watching; *Clubs* Athenaeum, Flyfishers', MCC; *Style—* John Tomkinson, Esq, CBE; 3 Downside, St John's Ave, London SW15 2AE (☎ 081 789 9422); Rose Cottage, Up Somborne, Stockbridge, Hants SO20 6QY (☎ 0794 388 837); Keats House, Guy's Hospital, London SE1 (☎ 071 407 8579)

TOMKINSON, Robert Charles; s of William Robert Tomkinson (d 1980), and Helen Mary, *née* Blane, MBE; *b* 14 July 1941; *Educ* Marlborough, Univ of Oxford (MA); *m* 15 June 1968, Joanna Sally, da of Maj William Philip Stuart Hastings; 2 s (James Robert b 1970, Simon William b 1972); *Career* mangr Peat Marwick Mitchell & Co 1966-75, dep md Scrimgeour Hardcastle & Co Ltd 1975-79, fin dir Intercontinental Fuels Ltd 1979-81; gp fin dir: Automotive Products plc 1982-86, Electrocomponents plc 1986-; non-exec dir Lloyd Thompson Gp plc 1987-; FCA 1966, FCT 1985; *Recreations* salmon fishing, riding, skiing; *Clubs* Boodle's; *Style—* Robert Tomkinson, Esq; Home Farm, Wappenham, Towcester, Northants NN12 8SJ (☎ 0327 860439); Electrocomponents plc, 21 Knightsbridge, London SW1X 7LY (☎ 071 245 1277, fax 071 235 4487, car 0860 261937)

TOMKYS, Sir (William) Roger; KCMG (1991, CMG 1984); s of William Arthur Tomkys (d 1973), of Harden, Yorks, and Edith Tomkys (d 1984); *b* 15 March 1937; *Educ* Bradford GS, Balliol Coll Oxford (MA); *m* 1963, Margaret Jean, da of Norman Beilby Abbey (d 1964), of Barrow-in-Furness; 1 s, 1 da; *Career* Foreign Serv 1960-; seconded to Cabinet Office 1975, head Near East and N Africa Dept FCO 1977-80, head chancery and cnsllr Rome 1980-81, ambass and consul gen to Bahrain 1981-84, ambass to Syria 1984-86, princ fin offr FCO 1986-89, dep under sec of state 1989-; also served: Athens, Benghazi, Amman; studied MECAS; Commendatore Dell'Ordine Al Merito Italy 1980, Order of Bahrain (first class) 1984; *Clubs* United Oxford and Cambridge Univ, Royal Blackheath Golf; *Style—* Sir Roger Tomkys, KCMG; c/o Foreign & Commonwealth Office, King Charles Street, London SW1

TOMLIN, Ivan; s of Fred Tomlin (d 1961), and Alice, *née* Weston (d 1967); *b* 7 Aug 1924; *Educ* Broom Leys Sch Coalville, Leicester Coll of Art and Technol; *m* 18 March 1950, Patricia Anne, da of Leo Peter McCarthy (d 1974); 1 s (Stephen b 1953), 1 da (Susan b 1954); *Career* Bevan Boy 1944-46; joined Howard Farrow Ltd (bldg and civil engrg contractors) 1948: md 1962, company acquired by ICI and reorganised 1966, md Farrow Group Ltd 1970, dir Farrow Property Devpts Ltd; chm: F Rendell & Sons Ltd, Devizes Farrow Construction Ltd, Heery Farrow Ltd; bldg and devpt conslt (managing devpts in and around City of London) 1978; Inst of Bldg: chartered 1980, chm London region 1970-71, nat pres 1974-75, chm Professional Practice Bd 1975-81, hon tres 1981-86; chm Harrow Round Table 1965, fndr memb Golders Green Rotary Club 1967, dep chm Bd of Govrs Tottenham Tech Coll 1973-77; gen cmmr of income tax 1970, JP Gore Div Middx 1968; Freeman City of London 1968, Liveryman Worshipful Co of Farriers 1968; AIOB 1959, FAIB 1974; *Books* guest ed of the Architect's Journal for a Series on The Cost of Building (1975-77); *Recreations* trout and salmon fishing; *Clubs* City Livery; *Style—* Ivan Tomlin, Esq; 3 Anselm Rd, Hatch End, Pinner, Middx HA5 4LN (☎ 081 428 4025)

TOMLINS, Christopher David Corbett; s of Maj David Corbett Tomlins, of Bosham, West Sussex, and Pamela Gertrude, *née* Steele; *b* 15 Aug 1940; *Educ* Bradfield, Guys Hosp Med and Dental Sch (BDS, MB BS), Univ of London (FDS, LRCP, MRCS); *m* 28 Oct 1972, Gillian Joan, da of Spencer Charles Cawthorn (d 1974); 4 s (David b 1974, Julian b 1976, Roger b 1976 (twin), Michael b 1979); *Career* dental house surgn Edgware Gen Hosp and Guys Hosp 1964, orthopaedic house surgn Guys Hosp 1970, house physician St Luke's Hosp Guildford 1970; registrar: Eastman Dental Hosp 1971-72, Westminster and Queen Mary's Roehampton 1972-73; sr registrar Westminster, Queen Mary's and Univ Coll Hosp 1973-76, visiting registrar Univ of Witswatersrand Johannesburg 1976, conslt oral and maxillofacial surgn Royal Berks Hosp Reading 1976-; hon treas BMA 1988 (chm 1984, vice chm W Berkshire dist 1986), chm Reading section BDA 1986 (chm Hosps Gp Oxford div 1978); memb: Berkshire Dist Dental Advsy Ctee (vice chm 1988), Reading Pathological Soc; fell BAOMS 1976; *Recreations* sailing, skiing, walking, photography; *Style—* Christopher Tomlins, Esq; Silbury, 50 Shinfield Rd, Reading, Berkshire RG2 7BW (☎ 0734 871566); 13 Bath Rd, Reading, Berkshire RG1 6HJ (☎ 0734 584711)

TOMLINSON, Sir Bernard Evans; CBE (1981), DL (1989); s of James Arthur Tomlinson (d 1980), and Doris Mary, *née* Evans (d 1985); *b* 13 July 1920; *Educ* Brunts Sch Mansfield Notts, UCL (MB BS), UCH (MD); *m* 9 Aug 1944, Betty, da of Edgar Oxley (d 1941); 1 s (David Andrew b 1945), 1 da (Elizabeth Oxley (Mrs Peerless) b 1950); *Career* Maj RAMC specialist pathologist 1947-49; trainee pathologist (EMS) 1943-47, conslt neuropathologist Gen Hosp Newcastle upon Tyne 1972-85 (conslt pathologist 1949-55, sr conslt pathologist 1955-82), prof emeritus pathology Univ of Newcastle 1985- (hon prof pathology 1972-85); pres Br Neuropathological Soc, chm Northern RHA 1982-90, memb and vice chm Newcastle Health Authy 1975-80, pres Northern Alzheimer Disease Soc 1986-; author of numerous book chapters and articles on the pathology of the brain in old age and the pathology of dementia; FRCP, FRCPath; kt 1988; *Recreations* golf, gardening, walking, music; *Clubs* Army & Navy, Pall Mall; *Style—* Sir Bernard Tomlinson, CBE, DL; Greyholme, Wynbury Rd, Low Fell, Gateshead, Tyne & Wear NE9 6TS (☎ 091 487 5227)

TOMLINSON, Prof (Alfred) Charles; s of Alfred Tomlinson, DCM (d 1973), of Stoke-on-Trent, and May, *née* Lucas (d 1972); *b* 8 Jan 1927; *Educ* Longton HS, Queens' Coll Cambridge (BA, MA), Univ of London (MA); *m* 23 Oct 1948, Brenda, da of Edwin Albert Raybould (d 1977), of Stoke-on-Trent; 2 da (Justine, Juliet); *Career* visiting prof Univ of New Mexico 1962-63, O'Connor prof Colgate Univ NY 1967-68 and 1989-90, visiting fell of humanities Princeton Univ 1981, prof of Eng lit Univ of Bristol 1982- (lectr 1956-68, reader 1968-82), Lamont prof Union Coll NY 1987; numerous public lectures and poetry readings throughout the world 1960-; graphics exhibited at Grimpel Fils and Leicester Galleries, one man shows at OUP London 1972 and Clare Coll Cambridge 1975, Arts Cncl touring exhibition The Graphics and Poetry of Charles Tomlinson opened at the Hayward Gallery London then toured England, Canada and the USA 1978-; Hon fell Queens' Coll Cambridge 1976; Hon DLitt: Univ of Keele 1981, Colgate Univ NY 1981, Univ of New Mexico 1986; hon prof Univ of Keele 1989-, hon fell Royal Holloway and Bedford New Coll 1991; FRSL 1975; *Books* incl: Collected Poems (1987), The Return (1987), Annunciations (1989), Renga and Airborn (with Octavio Paz), Some Americans (1981), Poetry and Metamorphosis (1983), Selected W C Williams (ed, 1976), Selected Octavio Paz (ed, 1979), Selected George Oppen (ed, 1990), Oxford Book of Verse in English Translation (ed, 1980); graphics incl Eden (1985); *Recreations* music, gardening, walking, travel; *Style—* Prof Charles Tomlinson; English Department, University of Bristol, 3-5 Woodland Rd, Bristol, Avon (☎ 0272 303030)

TOMLINSON, Claire Janet; da of Lascelles Arthur Lucas (d 1988), of Woolmers Park, nr Hertford, Herts, and Ethel Barbara, *née* Daer; *b* 14 Feb 1944; *Educ* Wycombe Abbey, Millfield, Somerville Coll Oxford (MA); *m* 16 March 1968, (George) Simon Tomlinson, s of George Antony Tomlinson (d 1954); 2 s (Luke b 27 Jan 1977, Mark b 25 March 1982), 1 da (Emma b 30 Oct 1974); *Career* polo player; Oxford half blue 1964-66, first women to play against Cambridge, capt Oxford Univ team 1966, pioneered breakthrough for woman to be allowed in high-goal polo 1978, memb winnning team Queen's Cup 1979; highest rated woman polo player in the World, has achieved higher handicap than any other woman (5 goals in 1986, currently 3 goals); fencing: Oxford half blue 1963-66, capt Oxford ladies team 1965-66, memb England under-21 team 1962-63; squash: Oxford half blue 1964-66; *Style—* Mrs Claire Tomlinson; Down Farm, Westonbirt, nr Tetbury, Glos (☎ 066 688 214)

TOMLINSON, David Cecil MacAlister; s of Clarence Samuel Tomlinson (d 1978), of New Bond St, London and Folkestone, and Florence Elizabeth Sinclair Thomson (d 1968); maternal uncle Albert Borlase Armitage (1864-43) was second in cmd on Scott's first Antarctic Expedition 1901-04; uncle Sir Cecil Hamilton Armitage (1867-1933) Govr of Gambia 1924-30; *b* 7 May 1917; *Educ* Tonbridge; *m* 1953, Audrey, da of Walter Redvers Freeman, of S Yorks; 4 s (David, James, William, Henry); *Career* Grenadier Gds 1935-36, WWII Flt Lt RAF (pilot), demob 1946; actor; chief roles incl: Henry in The Little Hut (Lyric 1950-53), Clive in All Mary (Duke of Yorks 1954-55), David in Dear Delinquent (Westminster and Aldwych 1957-58), Tom in The Ring of Truth (Savoy, July 1959), Robert in Boeing-Boeing (Apollo 1962); acted and directed: Mother's Boy (Globe 1964), A Friend Indeed (Cambridge 1966), On the Rocks (Dublin Festival 1969), A Friend Indeed and A Song at Twilight (SA) 1973-74, The Turning Point (Duke of Yorks 1974); first appeared in films 1939, since then appeared in leading roles in over 50 films; *Recreations* putting my feet up; *Clubs* Garrick; *Style—* David Tomlinson Esq; Brook Cottage, Mursley, Bucks MK17 0RS (☎ 029 672 213); 610 Chelsea Cloisters, Sloane Ave, London SW3 (☎ 071 589 7303)

TOMLINSON, David Redvers; s of David Cecil Macalister Tomlinson, and Audrey, *née* Freeman; *b* 6 April 1954; *Educ* Lord Williams' Sch Univ of Leeds (LLB); *m* 8 Nov 1988, Theresa Jane, da of John Packer; *Career* called to the Bar Inner Temple 1977, practising South East Circuit; *Style—* David Tomlinson, Esq; 9 Kings Bench Walk, Temple, London EC4 7DX (☎ 071 353 5638, fax 071 353 6166)

TOMLINSON, Elvira Mary (Molly); da of Domingo Riccardo Busi (d 1962), and Mary Wright, *née* Webster (d 1968); *b* 13 Sept 1922; *Educ* Westonbirt Sch Tetbury Glos; *m* 31 May 1947, (John) Michael Tomlinson, s of Henry Harrison Tomlinson (d 1944); *Career* chm: Busi & Stephenson Ltd 1968-90, dir Busi & Stephenson Ghana Ltd; dir C Zard & Co Ltd Nigeria; vice chm Conservative W Africa Ctee; FInstD; *Recreations* gardening; *Clubs* Royal Ocean Racing, Liverpool Racquet, Irish Cruising; *Style—* Mrs Michael Tomlinson; Apartment 224, The Colonnades, Albert Dock, Liverpool L3 4AA

TOMLINSON, John; s of Frank Tomlinson, of Whitecliff, Longsdon, Stoke-on-Trent, Staffs, and Barbara, *née* Mayer (d 1986); *b* 30 Jan 1941; *Educ* Lawton Hall, Alsager; *m* 31 March 1962, Christine Ann, da of Thomas Evan Jones, of Clifton Drive, Stafford; 2 s (Nicholas John b 1963, David Nigel b 1964), 1 da (Lisa Ann b 1969); *Career* dep chief exec London Scottish Bank plc; dir: London Scottish Bank plc and subsidiaries, Refuge Lending Co (N) Ltd, Reliance Guarantee Co Ltd, Robinson Way & Co Ltd, Dupant Bros Ltd, Glengall Est Ltd; MBIM 1972, FInstAA 1975; *Recreations* shooting, fishing; *Style—* John Tomlinson, Esq; Ford Hall Farm, Ford, nr Leek, Staffs (☎ 05388 304 342); Arndale House, Manchester

TOMLINSON, Prof John Race Godfrey; CBE (1983); s of John Angell Tomlinson (d 1968), and Beatrice Elizabeth Race, *née* Godfrey; *b* 24 April 1932; *Educ* Stretford GS, Univ of Manchester (BA, MA), Univ of London; *m* 27 March 1954, Audrey Mavis, da of John Barrett (d 1935); 2 s (John b 1958, Graham b 1962), 2 da (Susan b 1959, Janet b 1960); *Career* Flt Lt RAF 1955-58; teacher 1958-60; educn offr: Shropshire LEA 1960-63, Lancs LEA 1963-67; dir of educn Cheshire LEA 1972-84 (dep dir 1967-71), dir Inst of Educn Univ of Warwick 1985-; pres Soc Educn Offrs 1982-83; chm: Further Educn Curriculum Devpt Unit 1976- 78, Schs Cncl 1978-82, Tstees Schs Curriculum

Award 1982-, RSA Examinations Bd 1985-89, Cncl RSA 1989-91 (memb Cncl 1980-); fell Coll of Preceptors, memb Royal Northern Coll of Music, FBIM 1977, FRSA 1976; *Books* Additional Grenville Papers (ed 1962), The Changing Government of Education (ed with S Ranson, 1986), Teacher Appraisal: A Nationwide Approach (ed with A Evans 1989); *Recreations* walking, music, gardening; *Clubs* Atheneum, Army and Navy, Royal Over-Seas League; *Style—* Prof John Tomlinson, CBE; Institute of Education, University of Warwick, Westwood, Coventry CV4 7AL (☎ 0203 523821, telex 317472 UN IREG)

TOMLINSON, John Rowland; s of Rowland Tomlinson, of Park Rd, Scotby, Carlisle, and Ellen Tomlinson, *née* Greenwood (d 1969); *b* 22 Sept 1946; *Educ* Accrington GS, Univ of Manchester (BSc), Royal Manchester Coll of Music; *m* 9 Aug 1969, Moya, da of William Joel (d 1978); 1 s (Joseph b 3 March 1976), 2 da (Abigail 27 Aug 1971, Ellen Tamasine 15 Feb 1973); *Career* princ opera singer: Glyndebourne festival 1971-74, English Nat Opera 1974-80; has made several appearances at The Royal Opera House Covent Garden 1976-, sang Wotan and the Ring in Bayreuth in 1988 and 1989; several int concert appearances: Paris, Berlin, Vienna, Amsterdam, Lisbon and San Francisco; *Recreations* tennis; *Style—* John Tomlinson, Esq; Music International, 13 Ardilaun Rd, Highbury, London N5 2QR (☎ 071 359 5183)

TOMLINSON, Maj-Gen Michael John; CB 1981, OBE (1973, MBE 1964); s of Sidney Cyril Tomlinson (d 1983), and Emily Rose, *née* Hodges (d 1986); *b* 20 May 1929; *Educ* The Skinners' Sch Tunbridge Wells, RMA Sandhurst; *m* 24 June 1955, Lily Patricia, da of Lt-Col A Rowland, OBE, MC (d 1971); 1 s (Peter b 1958), 1 da (Jane (Mrs Wallis) b 1962); *Career* cmmnd RA 1949; served 1950-60 (Tripoli, Canal Zone, Jordan, Germany), GS02 ops to dir of ops Brunei 1964-62 (despatches); dep asst mil sec 1966-68, instr Staff Coll Camberley 1968-70, CO 2 Field Regt RA 1970-72, Col GS Staff Coll Camberley 1972-73, CRA 3 Div 1973-75, dep mil sec 1976-78, dir of manning (Army) 1978-79, Vice Adj Gen 1979-81, DRA 1981-84, rct May 1984; Col Cmdt RA 1982-, Hon Col 104 Regt RA (V) 1985-87, Hon Regt Col 2 Field Regt RA 1985-89; vice pres Nat Artillery Assoc 1984-, pres central branch RA Assoc 1988-90; sec The Dulverton Tst 1984-; FBIM 1984, FRSA 1985; *Recreations* gardening, music; *Clubs* Army and Navy; *Style—* Maj-Gen Michael Tomlinson, CB, OBE; The Dulverton Trust, 5 St James's Place, London SW1A 1NP (☎ 071 629 9121, fax 071 495 6201)

TOMLINSON, Prof Richard Allan; s of James Edward Tomlinson (d 1963), and Dorothea Mary, *née* Grellier (d 1983); *b* 25 April 1932; *Educ* King Edward's Sch Birmingham, St John's Coll Cambridge (BA, MA); *m* 14 Dec 1957, Heather Margaret, da of Ernest Fraser Murphy (d 1965); 3 s (Nicholas John b 1959, Peter Brian b 1962, Edward James b 1965), 1 da (Penelope Ann b 1961); *Career* asst Dept of Greek Univ of Edinburgh 1957-58; Univ of Birmingham: asst lectr 1958-61, lectr 1961-69, sr lectr 1969-71, prof of ancient history and archaeology 1971-; memb: Victorian Soc, Managing Ctee Br Sch at Athens (and editor Annual); FSA; *Books* Argos and the Argolid (1972), Greek Sanctuaries (1976), Epidauros (1980), Greek Architecture (1989); *Recreations* walking; *Style—* Prof Richard Tomlinson, FSA; Department of Ancient History and Archaeology, University of Birmingham, Birmingham B15 2TT (☎ 021 414 5497)

TOMLINSON, Prof Sally; da of Clifford Gilmore Entwistle (d 1966), and Alice Nora, *née* Stubbs (d 1974); *b* 22 Aug 1936; *Educ* Macclesfield HS, Univ of Liverpool (BA), Univ of Birmingham (MSoc Sci), Univ of Warwick (PhD); *m* 31 Aug 1957, Sqdn Ldr Brian Joseph Tomlinson (RAF ret); 1 s (Simon b 1962), 2 da (Susan b 1960, Joanna b 1963); *Career* lectr and sr lectr W Midlands Coll of Educn 1969-73, sr res fell Univ of Warwick 1974-77, prof of educn Univ of Lancaster 1984-91 (lectr and sr lectr 1978-84), prof of educn Univ of Wales Swansea 1991-, sr assoc memb St Antony's Coll Oxford 1984-85; memb Univ Cncl for educn of teachers 1984-, res assoc Inst for Public Policy Res 1990-; *Books* Colonial Immigrants in a British City - a class analysis (with John Rex, 1979), Education Subnormality - A Study in Decision Making (1981), Special Education: Policy Practices and Social Issues (jt ed, 1981), A Sociology of Special Education (1982), Ethnic Minorites in British Schools: A Review of the Literature 1960-1982 (1983), Home and School in Multicultural Britain (1984), Special Education and Social Interests (ed with Len Barton, 1984), Affirmative Action and Positive Policies in the Education of Ethnic Minorities (ed with Abraham Yogev, 1989), The School Effect: A Study of Multi-Racial Comprehensives (with David Smith, 1989), Multi-Cultural Education in White Schools (1990); *Recreations* riding; *Style—* Prof Sally Tomlinson; Dept of Education, University College of Swansea, Swansea (☎ 0792 295154)

TOMLINSON, Sir (Frank) Stanley; KCMG (1966, CMG 1954); s of John Tomlinson (d 1955); *b* 21 March 1912; *Educ* High Pavement Sch, Univ of Nottingham; *m* 1959, Nancy, *née* Gleeson-White; *Career* former: cnsllr Br Embassy Washington, head of SE Asia Dept FO, dep to GOC (Br Sector) Berlin; min UK Delgn to NATO 1961-64, consul-gen NY 1964-66, high cmmr Ceylon 1966-69, dep under-sec state FCO 1969-72; Hon LLD Nottingham 1970; *Style—* Sir Stanley Tomlinson, KCMG; 32 Long Street, Devizes, Wilts

TOMLINSON, Prof Stephen; s of Frank Tomlison, of 31 Crompton Ave, Bolton, Lancs, and Elsie, *née* Towler; *b* 20 Dec 1944; *Educ* Hayward GS Bolton, Univ of Sheffield (MB ChB, MD); *m* 14 Oct 1970, Christine Margaret, da of George Hope, of 8 Mather Ave, Sheffield, Yorks; 2 da (Rebecca b 1974, Sarah b 1977); *Career* Wellcome Tst sr lectr in clinical sci 1980-85 (sr res fell 1977-80), reader in med Univ of Sheffield 1982-85, prof of med Univ of Manchester 1985-, chm Sch of Med Servs Univ of Manchester Med Sch; pubns on mechanisms of hormone action, and intacellular signalling and orgn of health care in diabetes; sec Assoc of Physicians of GB and I 1988-, dir Central Manchester Hosps Tst; FRCP; *Style—* Prof Stephen Tomlinson; Mackants Farm, Blackburn Rd, Eagley Bank, Bolton BL1 7LH (☎ 0204 54765); The Manchester Diabetes Centre, 130 Hathersage Rd, Manchester M13 0HZ; The Univ Dept of Med, Manchester Royal Infirmary Oxford Rd, Manchester M13 9WL (☎ 061 276 4182)

TOMLINSON, Stephen Miles; QC (1988); s of Capt Enoch Tomlinson, of Winslow, Bucks, and Mary Marjorie Cecelia, *née* Miles; *b* 29 March 1952; *Educ* King's Sch Worcester, Worcester Coll Oxford (MA); *m* 15 March 1980, Joanna Kathleen, da of Ian Joseph Greig; 1 s, 1 da; *Career* called to the Bar Inner Temple 1974, bencher 1990; *Recreations* cricket, gardening, walking, family; *Clubs* Travellers', MCC; *Style—* Stephen Tomlinson, Esq, QC; 7 King's Bench Walk, Temple, London EC4Y 7DS (☎ 071 583 0404, fax 071 583 0950, telex 887491)

TOMPSON, Hon Mrs (Margaret-Ann Michelle); *née* Donaldson; er da of Baron Donaldson of Lymington, PC (Life Peer), *qv*; *b* 1946; *Educ* St Paul's Girls' Sch, London Sch of Occupational Therapy (Dip OT), Univ of Saskatchewan (MCEd); *m* 1969, Conal Tompson; 1 s (Douglas Conal b 4 Jan 1974), 1 da (Caroline Margaret b 11 Dec 1975); *Style—* The Hon Mrs Tompson; 736 University Drive, Saskatoon, Saskatchewan S7N 0J4, Canada

TOMS, Anthony Roger; s of Albert Raymond Toms (d 1982), of Redruth, Cornwall, and Lilian Mae, *née* Roberts (d 1971); *b* 9 Aug 1940; *Educ* Truro Sch, Okehampton GS; *Career* asst co treas W Midlands MCC 1975, gen mangr I53 SCC 1989, computer serv mangr London Borough of Islington 1969; former pres Unisys User Assoc Euro Africa, former chm Nat Computing Centre Regnl Ctee; FBCS 1971; *Recreations* golf, horse riding; *Style—* Anthony Toms, Esq; I53, Surrey County Council, Kingston upon Thames, Surrey KT1 2DE (☎ 081 541 9700, fax 081 541 9727, telex 263312)

TOMS, Carl; OBE (1969); s of Bernard Toms (d 1947), of Mansfield, Notts, and Edith Toms; *b* 29 May 1927; *Educ* Sch of Art Mansfield, RCA, Old Vic Sch; *Career* conscript WWII; asst to Oliver Messel 1953-59; first design cmmn Suzanna's Secret Glyndebourne 1960; theatre designer 1960- (interior Theatre Royal Bath), design conslt for investiture of Prince of Wales at Caernarvon Castle, Tony award for prodn of Sherlock Holmes for the RSC in 1975, head of design Young Vic Theatre until 1980 (dir), Olivier award for the Provoked Wife for NT 1981, worked on 14 prodns for the NT, 10 prodns for the Burg Theatre and Statsoper Vienna, and also for NY City Opera, Metropolitan Opera, San Francisco Opera, and many West End prodns; active in charitable work; FRSA; *Recreations* work, theatre, art, architecture, gardens; *Clubs* Groucho; *Style—* Carl Toms, Esq, OBE; The White House, Beaumont, nr Wormley, Broxbourne, Herts EN10 7QJ (☎ 0992 463961)

TOMS, Edward Ernest; s of Alfred William Toms (d 1981), and Julia, *née* Harrington (d 1980); *b* 10 Dec 1920; *Educ* St Boniface's Coll; *m* 1946, Veronica Rose, da of Francis Rose (d 1951), and Bridget Rose (d 1972), of Dovercourt, Essex; 3 s (Duncan, David, James), 1 da (Rosemary); *Career* RTR 1940-43, Special Forces 1943-45, Regt Offr Seaforth Highlanders 1943-59, Bde Maj Berlin Inf Bde 1959-61, Col Gen Staff UK C-in-C Ctte 1966-69; asst sec Dept of Employment 1969-77, cnsllr Br Embassy Bonn and Br Embassy Vienna 1977-81, int labour advsr FCO 1981-83, dir Porcelain & Pictures Ltd 1983-; chm Nat Framers and Retailers Ctee, memb of Ct of Fine Art Trade Guild 1987; *Recreations* hill walking, picture framing; *Clubs* Army & Navy, Special Forces; *Style—* Edward Toms, Esq; c/o Clydesdale Bank, Chief Office, 5 Castle St, Aberdeen

TOMS, Dr Rhinedd Margaret; da of David Peregrine Jones (d 1983), of Llanelli, Dyfed, and Margaret Edith, *née* Davies; *b* 18 June 1942; *Educ* Howells Sch Denbigh, Girton Coll Cambridge (MA), Westminster Med Sch (MB BChir); *m* 19 Oct 1968, Brian Frank Toms (d 1985), s of Harold Frank Toms (d 1989), of Rushden, Northamptonshire; 1 s (David b 1971), 1 da (Eleanor b 1969); *Career* clinical med offr London Borough of Southwark 1968-71, sr med offr Lambeth Lewisham and Southwark AHA 1973-75, trg posts in psychiatry 1976-84, conslt psychiatrist NE Essex Health Authy 1984-; hon conslt St Luke's Hosp for the Clergy, clinical tutor in psychiatry Br Postgrad Med Fedn 1988-, hon conslt Colchester Branch of Relate; memb Exec Ctee Phoenix Gp Homes; memb BMA; *Recreations* gardening, music, choral singing; *Style—* Dr Rhinedd Toms; 45 Oaks Drive, Colchester, Essex CO3 3PS (☎ 0206 549547); The Lakes Unit, Colchester General Hospital, Colchester, Essex CO4 5JL (☎ 0206 853535)

TOMSETT, Alan Jeffrey; OBE (1974); s of Maurice Jeffrey Tomsett (d 1987), and Edith Sarah, *née* Mackelworth (d 1953); *b* 3 May 1922; *Educ* Trinity Sch of John Whitgift Croydon, Univ of London (BCom); *m* 1948, Joyce May, da of Walter Albert Hill (d 1959); 1 s (Ian), 1 da (Ann); *Career* served WWII 1941-46 with RAF (Middle East 1942-45); Hodgson Harris & Co Chartered Accountants London 1938, Smallfield Rawlins & Co 1951, Northern Mercantile & Investmt Corpn 1955, William Baird & Co Ltd 1962-63; fin dir Br Tport Docks Bd 1974-83 (chief accountant and fin controller 1964-73), dir Assoc Br Ports Hldgs plc 1983- (fin dir 1983-87); FCA, FCMA, JDipMA, FCIS, FCIT (hon treas 1982-88); *Recreations* gardening; *Style—* Alan Jeffrey Tomsett, Esq, OBE; 102 Ballards Way, Croydon, Surrey CR0 5RG

TONGE, Hon Mrs (Judith Felicity); *née* Allen; da of Baron Allen of Fallowfield, CBE (Life Peer; d 1985); *b* 1946; *m* 1973, Graham Tonge; 1 s (Daniel Allen b 1974), 1 da (Lucy Clare b 1977); *Style—* The Hon Mrs Tonge; Little Hilliers, Innhams Wood, Crowborough, E Sussex TN6 1TE

TONGUE, Carole; MEP (Lab) London East 1984-; da of Walter Archer Tongue, of Lausanne, Switzerland, and Muriel Esther, *née* Lambert; *b* 14 Oct 1955; *Educ* Brentwood Co HS, Loughborough Univ of Technol (BA); *Career* asst ed Laboratory Practice 1977-78, courier for Sunsites Ltd in France 1978-79, Robert Schumann Scholarship for res in social affrs Euro Parl 1979-80, sec and admin asst in Socialist Gp Secretariat of Euro Parl 1980-84, dep ldr Br Labour Gp in Euro Parl; memb: Inst for the Study of Drug Dependence (ISDD), CND, END, One World, Friends of the Earth, Greenpeace, Fabian Soc; vice chm; AMA, SERA; memb: Euro Parl: full memb Econ and Monetary Ctee, subst memb Political Affairs Ctee; memb RIIA; *Recreations* piano, cello, tennis, squash, riding, cinema, theatre, opera; *Style—* Ms Carole Tongue, MEP; London East European Constituency Office, 97a Ilford Lane, Ilford, Essex IG1 2RJ (☎ 081 514 0198, fax 081 553 4764)

TONKIN, Derek; CMG (1982); s of Henry James Tonkin (d 1947), and Norah, *née* Wearing; *b* 30 Dec 1929; *Educ* High Paverent GS Nottingham, St Catherine's Coll Oxford (MA); *m* 1953, Doreen, da of Horace Samuel Rooke (d 1967); 2 s (Christopher (decd), Jeremy), 2 da (Caroline, Susan); *Career* HM Diplomatic Service 1952-89; ambass to Vietnam 1980-82, min to S Africa 1983-85, ambass to Thailand and Laos 1986-89 (ret); chm: Advsy Bd Centre for SE Asian Studies, Gen Ctee Ockenden Venture; dir Thai Holdings Ltd; *Recreations* tennis, music; *Clubs* Royal Bangkok Sports; *Style—* Derek Tonkin, Esq, CMG; Heathfields, Berry Lane, Worplesdon, Guildford, Surrey GU3 3PU (☎ 0483 232955)

TONKING, (Russel) Simon William Ferguson; s of Lt Col John Wilson Tonking, MBE, TD, of Felindre, Llanidloes, Powys, and Mary Oldham, *née* Ferguson (d 1971); *b* 25 March 1952; *Educ* The Kings Sch Canterbury, Emmanuel Coll Cambridge (MA); *m* 10 July 1976, (Sylvia) Mithra, da of Colin Ian McIntyre, of 47 Smith St, Chelsea, London SW3; 1 s (William b 1988), 1 da (Flora b 1984); *Career* called to the Bar Inner Temple 1975; steward Lichfield Cathedral (head steward 1984-86); *Recreations* music, old motor cars, painting; *Clubs* Vintage Sports Car; *Style—* Simon Tonking, Esq; 4 Fountain Court, Steelhouse Lane, Birmingham B4 6DR (☎ 021 236 3476)

TONKS, Dr Clive Malcolm; s of Clarence Tonks (d 1989), of York, and Annie, *née* Holt; *b* 21 March 1932; *Educ* Normanton GS, Univ of Leeds (MB ChB); *m* 25 Oct 1958, Dr Joyce Margaret Handby, da of Clarence Handby (d 1983); 1 s (David b 1964), 2 da (Susan b 1960, Alison b 1962); *Career* conslt psychiatrist St Mary's Hosp and Med Sch 1969-; hon clinical sr lectr Imperial Coll of Sci Technol and Med (previously sr lectr in psychiatry Univ of Leeds); assoc prof of psychiatry Yale; chm Med Staff Paddington & North Kensington Health Authy 1983-87; author of papers and chapters on psychiatric topics; memb various standing ctees Royal Coll of Psychiatry; memb Parole Bd 1989; FRCP, FRCPsych, DPM Univ of London; *Recreations* geology, opera, walking; *Clubs* RSM; *Style—* Dr Clive M Tonks; 10 Anselm Rd, Pinner, Middlesex (☎ 081 428 3894); St Mary's Hospital, Praed St, London W2 (☎ 071 725 6666)

TONKS, John; s of late John Henry Tonks, of Brewood Staffs, and late Gladys Mary, *née* Maddocks; *b* 14 Aug 1927; *Educ* Dudley GS, Birmingham Coll of Art (maj scholar, NDD Sculpture, art teacher's Dip); *m* 14 July 1951, Sylvia Irene, da of Thomas William Taylor; 1 s (Julian Matthew John b 19 April 1953), 1 da (Caroline Louise Sylvia Mary b 12 April 1956); *Career* specialist art teacher in secdy schs 1952-65, lectr rising to sr lectr and princ lectr in sculpture W Midlands Coll of Higher Educn 1965-82, freelance sculptor 1982-; solo exhibitions incl: V B Gallery St Louis USA 1981, Oriel 31

Welshpool 1983, Ombersley Gallery Worcs 1983, Britain Salutes New York (Poole Willis Gallery NY) 1983, Helias Gallery Birmingham 1984, Univ of Birmingham 1984, Liverpool Int Garden Festival 1984; pub cmmns: Statue of Virgin Mary (St Mary's Church, Enville, Staffs), Sculpture of the Risen Christ (Wombourne Parish Church Staffs), The Family (Alexander Hosp, Redditch, Worcs); fell RSBS 1978 (assoc 1967, vice pres 1990); *Recreations* walking and work; *Style*— John Tonks, Esq; Downshill Cottage, Comhampton, Stourport-on-Servern, Worcester DY13 9ST (☎ 0905 620718)

TONKS, Julian Matthew John; s of John Tonks, of Comhampton, Worcs, and Sylvia Irene, *née* Taylor; *b* 19 April 1953; *Educ* Dudley GS, Trinity Coll Oxford (MA, MLitt); *m* 14 Aug 1980, Ann Miles, da of James Miles Henderson, of Granite City, Illinois, USA; *Career* admitted slr 1982; asst slr Freshfields 1982-86, tax ptnr Pinsent & Co 1987- (articled clerk 1980-82); *Recreations* growing apples, collecting photographs, cricket, wine; *Clubs* Worcestershire CC; *Style*— Julian Tonks, Esq; Poyle Court, Hampton Poyle, Oxon OX5 2QF; Pinsent & Co, Solicitors, Post & Mail House, 26 Colmore Circus, Birmingham B4 6BH (☎ 021 200 1050, fax 021 200 1040)

TONYPANDY, 1 Viscount (UK 1983), of Rhondda, Co Mid Glamorgan; Rt Hon (Thomas) George Thomas; PC (1968); s of Zachariah Thomas (d 1932), of Tonypandy, S Wales, and Emma Jane Thomas; *b* 29 Jan 1909, Port Talbot; *Educ* Tonypandy GS, Univ Coll Southampton; *Career* former schoolmaster and vice pres Methodist Conference 1959-60; MP (Lab): Cardiff Central 1945-50, Cardiff W 1950-83; PPS to min of Civil Aviation 1951, chm Welsh Labour Party 1950-51, parly under sec Home Office 1964-66, first chm Welsh Parly Grand Ctee, min of state Welsh Office 1966-67, Cwlth Office 1967-68, sec of state for Wales 1968-70, speaker of House of Commons 1976-83 (dep speaker and chm Ways and Means Ctee 1974-76); hon master bencher of the bench Gray's Inn 1982-; pres: Nat Children's Home 1990- (formerly chm), Br Heart Fndn; Freeman: Rhondda, City of Cardiff, City of London; hon memb: Worshipful Co of Blacksmiths 1977, hon fell St Hugh's Coll Oxford 1983, hon memb Cambridge Students Union 1982, hon fell Hertford Coll Oxford 1983; pres Coll of Preceptors 1983-87; Hon LLD: Asbury Coll Kentucky, Univ of Southampton, Univ of Wales, Birmingham, Oklahoma USA, Liverpool, Leeds; Hon DCL Oxford, Hon DD Shreveport Louisiana; Hon LLD Open Univ; Dato Setia Negara Brunei 1971, Grand Cross of Peruvian Congress 1980, Gold Award for Work of Democracy, State of Carinthia, Austria 1982, hon fell Univ Coll Cardiff 1982; Hon LLD Warwick 1984; Hon LLD Keele 1984; *Books* Christian Heritage in Politics (1960), Memoirs of a Speaker (1985), My Wales (1986); *Recreations* travel; *Clubs* Travellers', Reform, United Oxford and Cambridge Univ, County Club (Cardiff); *Style*— The Rt Hon the Viscount Tonypandy, PC; House of Lords, London SW1

TOOGOOD, James Anthony Gordon; s of Maj Leonard Gordon Toogood (d 1988), of St Albans, Herts, and Muriel Frances Georgina, *née* Robinson (d 1987); *b* 12 July 1932; *Educ* Aldenham, St John's Coll Cambridge (MA); *m* 12 Oct 1963, (Anne) Margaret, da of Charles Wilfred Robbins (d 1977), of St Albans, Herts; 3 s (Michael b 1964, Paul b 1967, Oliver b 1970); *Career* Nat Serv RA 1951-53, Capt Herts Yeo 1953-59; admitted slr 1959; sr ptnr Forrester & Forrester 1977-; Mayor of Malmesbury 1978; chm Bd of Govrs Malmesbury Sch 1970-75 and 1988-; memb Law Soc; *Recreations* music, country pursuits, chairing ctees; *Style*— James Toogood, Esq; Riversdale, Malmesbury, Wiltshire (☎ 0666 822120); 59 High Street, Malmesbury, Wiltshire (☎ 0666 822671)

TOOGOOD, John; QPM (1977); s of James Waller Giddings Toogood (d 1964), of Chippenham, Wilts, and Katherine Mary, *née* Winter (d 1956); *b* 19 Aug 1924; *Educ* Chippenham GS, Kings Coll London (LLB, LLM); *m* 1, 19 Oct 1946 (m dis 1949), June, da of Leslie Llewellyn Rowlands (d 1970), of Plymouth, Devon; m 2, 20 Dec 1951, Josephine, *née* Curran (d 1984); 1 da (Katherine b 3 Sept 1962); m 3, 23 July 1986 (remarried), June Martin (Rowlands); *Career* RM 1942-46; Met Police 1946-83 (ret as Cdr); called to the Bar Gray'F Inn 1957, practice at bar 1983-; memb Medico-Legal Soc 1955; admitted as Serving Brother to the Order of St John 1984; *Recreations* family; *Style*— John Toogood, Esq, QPM; 4 Kings Bench Walk, Temple, London EC4V 7DL (☎ 071 353 0478)

TOOGOOD, John; s of Raymond George Toogood, of 44 Steep Hill, Lincoln, and Joan Charlotte, *née* Wallis; *b* 17 Dec 1944; *Educ* Lincoln Sch, Bristol Old Vic Theatre Sch; *m* 26 Oct 1973, Maris Deborah, da of Maj Joseph Frank Sharp (d 1964), of 153 Warm Lane, London NW2; 1 s (Julian Frank b 13 April 1976), 2 da (Rachel Louise b 29 March 1978, Rebecca Sarah b 25 June 1982); *Career* Lincoln Theatre Royal 1958-63, Bristol Old Vic 1963-66, Liverpool Playhouse 1966-71, Greenwich Theatre 1971-72, co mangr No 1 Tours 1972-74, freelance co mangr West End (1974-78 and 1980-81), prodn mangr The King and I Palladium 1979-80, asst tech dir MMA 1981-86, gen mangr Prince Edward Theatre 1986-; chm Stage Mgmnt Assoc, memb cncl Assoc of Br Theatre Technicians; *Recreations* allotment, cycling; *Style*— John Toogood, Esq; 13 Arran Road, London SE6 2LT (☎ 081 698 5775); Prince Edward Theatre, Old Compton Street, London W1 (☎ 071 437 2024)

TOOK, Barry; s of Charles William Took (d 1961), of Worthing, and Kate Louie Rose, *née* Cox (d 1969); *b* 19 June 1928; *Educ* Stationers Cos' Sch; *m* 1, 10 Aug 1950 (m dis 1965), Dorothy Bird, da of Richard Bird (d 1965), of Lincoln; 2 s (Barry b 1951, David b 1961), 1 da (Susan b 1956); m 2, 29 Oct 1965, Lynden L, da of Mark Leonard (d 1967), of Scunthorpe; 1 da (Elinor b 1968); *Career* Nat Serv RAF 1946-49; broadcaster: Late Extra 1959-60, Bootsie and Snudge 1960-63, Round the Horne 1964-68, Marty 1968-69, Rowan and Martins Laugh In 1969-70, On the Move (adult literacy project) 1975-79, Points of View 1979-86; conslt Comedy Dept Thames TV 1968-69, advsr BBC TV 1969-70, head of light entertainment LWT 1971-72; hon cncllr NSPCC, vice pres NDCS; *Books* Laughter in the Air (1976), Tooks Eye View (1983), Comedy Greats (1989), A Point of View (autobiography, 1990); *Recreations* golf, travel; *Clubs* Garrick, MCC; *Style*— Barry Took, Esq; 17 Hanover House, St Johns Wood, London NW8 7DX (☎ 071 722 8049, fax 071 483 2834)

TOOKE, Brian Cecil; CBE (1983), JP (Suffolk 1965); s of Cecil George Tooke (d 1982), and Violet Mabel, *née* Rolfe (d 1988); *b* 29 Dec 1933; *Educ* St Joseph's Coll Ipswich; *m* 4 July 1959 (m dis 1987), Patricia Ann; 2 s (Robert James b 1964, Julian Charles George b 1968), 2 da (Clarissa Jane b 1961, Melissa Mary b 1972); *Career* chm Sadler Hldgs Ltd, chm Local Bd of Commercial Union Assur plc; chm East of England Area Young Cons 1962-64; memb: Cons Party Nat Union Exec 1962-64 and 1975-84, Nat Union GP Ctee 1980-83, Cons Party Nat Advsy Ctee for Local Govt 1968-77; memb Ipswich CBC 1959-74, pres East of England Area Cons Assoc 1987-90 (chm 1980-83), chm Ipswich and Suffolk Industl Advsy Cncl 1985-88 (fndr memb 1972-), pres, tstee, former chm and fndr Suffolk Cncl Nat Assoc of Boys Clubs 1962-, memb Cncl East Anglian TAVR Assoc 1985- (memb Suffolk Ctee TAVR 1980-); chm: Ipswich and dist Appeal Ctee Suffolk Tst for Nature Conservations 1983-85, chm East Anglian Region C of C 1984-87; govr St Joseph's Gp Coll Ipswich 1963-88; *Recreations* theatre, architecture; *Clubs* Carlton; *Style*— Brian Tooke, Esq, CBE, JP; Chattisham Hall, Suffolk IP8 3PX; Sadler Holdings Ltd, PO Box 21, Richmond House, Sproughton Rd, Ipswich, Suffolk IP1 5AW

TOOKEY, Christopher David; s of Alan Oliver Tookey, of Sunnyside, Lingfield, Surrey, and Winifreda, *née* Marsh; *b* 9 April 1950; *Educ* Tonbridge, Exeter Coll Oxford (MA, ed of Isis, pres Oxford Union); *m* 3 Sept 1989, Frances Anne, da of Henry Robert Heasman; *Career* writer and composer of musicals; prodns incl: Hard Times 1973, Room with A Revue 1974, Retrogrim's Progress 1974, Hanky Park 1975, Dick Whittington 1975 and 1976, An Evening with Noel and Gertie 1975 and 1976, The Resurrection of the British Musical 1977, Him 'n' Her 1979, Ladies and Jurgen 1980; asst theatre dir Belgrade Theatre Co 1973-74, Haymarket and Phoenix Theatre Leicester 1974-75, TV prodr and dir Associated Television 1975-82, weekend ed and assoc features ed TV-am 1982-83, freelance TV dir 1983-; credits incl: After Dark, Network 7, various rock videos; as freelance journalist: Books and Bookmen 1983-86, film critic Sunday Telegraph (freelance feature writer 1986, TV critic 1987-89), TV critic for Daily Telegraph 1989- (feature writer 1986-); freelance broadcaster 1989- (credits incl Book Choice (C4) and First Edition (BSB); *Recreations* writing musicals, composing music, reading; *Style*— Christopher Tookey, Esq; Chris Tookey Productions, 4 Alwyne Villas, London N1 2HQ (☎ 071 226 2726, fax 071 354 2574)

TOOLEY, Alan Hunter; s of Henry Hunter Tooley (d 1972), of Middlesbrough, and Josephine; *b* 13 May 1930; *Educ* Falmouth and East Ham GS, Univ of London (MB BS); *m* 1, 1 March 1958 (m dis 1976), Mary Josephine, *née* Aitken; 1 s (Timothy Hunter b 13 June 1964), 2 da (Elizabeth Mary b 29 Oct 1958, Fiona Margaret (twin)); m 2, 3 June 1977, Barbara Elizabeth, da of William Miller (d 1960), of Coventry; *Career* surgn cdr RN Med Serc 1955-68; conslt surgn South Tees Health Dist 1968-; examiner in anatomy for Primary FRCS 1978-84, regnl advsr in surgery RCS 1983; memb: Darlington Health Authy 1983-, ct of examiners in surgery Final RCS 1985-, pres N of Eng Surgical Soc 1987-88, chm regnl sub ctee in surgery Northern region 1989; memb vasular soc, fell assoc of surgns; LRCP, FRCS, AKC; *Recreations* music, woodturning; *Clubs* Army and Navy; *Style*— Alan Tooley, Esq; 26 The Avenue, Linthorpe, Middlesbrough, Cleveland TS5 (☎ 0642 818750); South Cleveland Hospital, Marton Rd, Middlesbrough, Cleveland (☎ 0642 850850)

TOOLEY, Sir John; yr s of late H R Tooley; *b* 1 June 1924; *Educ* Repton, Magdalene Coll Cambridge; *m* 1, 1951 (m dis 1965), Judith Craig Morris; 3 da; m 2, 1968 (m dis 1990), Patricia Janet Norah, 2 da of late G W Bagshawe; 1 s; *Career* served Rifle Bde 1943-47; sec Guildhall Sch of Music and Drama 1952-55; Royal Opera House: asst to gen administrator 1955-60, asst gen admin 1960-70, gen admin 1970-80, gen dir 1980-88; vice chm ARMA Ltd, chm ARMA Insur Brokers Ltd, arts conslt 1988-; govr Repton Sch; Commendatore Italian Republic 1976; Hon FRAM, Hon GSM, Hon RNCM; kt 1979; *Recreations* walking, theatre; *Clubs* Garrick, Arts; *Style*— Sir John Tooley; 32 First Street, London SW3 2LD

TOOLEY, Dr Peter John Hocart; s of Dr Patrick Hocart Tooley, of Kapri, Houmet Lane, Vale, Guernsey, CI, and Brenda Margaret, *née* Williams (d 1939); *b* 28 Feb 1939; *Educ* Elizabeth Coll Guernsey, St Georges Sch Harpenden, Univ of London, London Hosp Med Coll London Univ (MB BS, DObst RCOG, DMJ); *m* 1, 22 Sept 1966 (m dis 1983), Elizabeth Monica, da of Percy Roche, of 164 London Rd, Twyford, Reading, Berks; 1 s (Patrick b 1969), 2 da (Lucy b 1967, Josephine b 1971); m 2, 1987, Diana Edith, *née* Sturdy; *Career* sr ptnr gen practise Twyford Berks 1974-90 (princ 1966, trainer 1977-81), MO Marks & Spencer plc Reading 1980-90, asst dep coroner Borough of Reading 1984-89, sr med advsr Janssen Pharmaceutical Ltd 1990- (med conslt gen practice affrs 1986-90); MO Oxfordshire RFU 1970-; memb: Berks Local Med Ctee 1978-86, Reading Pathological Soc; chm Reading Med Club 1980-83 and 1987-90 (fndr memb), vice-chm Polehampton Charities 1986-90 (tstee 1975); Freeman City of London, Liveryman Worshipful Soc of Apothecaries 1965; MRCS, LRCP 1963, MRCGP 1971; memb: BMA, Br Acad of Forensic Scis, Br Assoc of Pharmaceutical Physicians, Pharmaceutical Marketing Soc; FRSM; *Recreations* sports, gardening, travel; *Style*— Dr Peter Tooley; Siplak House, Station Rd, Lower Shiplake, Henley on Thames, Oxon RG9 3NY (☎ 0734 403545); Janssen Pharmaceutical Ltd, Grove, Wantage, Oxon OX12 0DQ (☎ 0235 772966, fax 0235 772 121, telex 0235 837301 E-MAIL BT GOLD JPL 004, car 0831 161 178)

TOONE, Dr Brian Kenneth; s of Donald Freer Thomas (d 1979), and Mary Mable Ethel, *née* Downing; *b* 1 July 1937; *Educ* St Laurence Coll Ramsgate, King's Coll and St George's Hosp Med Sch London (MB BS, MPhil); *m* 28 Sept 1965 (m dis 1979), Megan Reece; *Career* conslt Dept of Psychological Med KCH 1980-, hon conslt The Maudsley and Bethlem Royal Hosp 1980-, hon sr lectr Inst of Psychiatry 1986- (sub-dean 1984-87, currently recognised teacher Univ of London); chapters and scientific articles on organic psychiatry and psychiatric aspects of epilepsy; MRCP 1967, MRCPsych 1973, FRCP 1988, FRCPsych 1988; *Recreations* tennis, squash, photography; *Style*— Dr Brian Toone; King's College Hospital, Dept of Psychological Medicine, Denmark Hill, London SE5 9RS (☎ 071 326 3228, 071 326 3226, fax 071 326 2586)

TOOP, Alan James; s of James Cecil Toop (d 1973), of Clephane Rd, London, and Elsie Ada, *née* Lavers; *b* 25 Feb 1934; *Educ* Highbury GS, UCL (BA); *m* 12 Sept 1964, Tessa Peggy Elaine, da of Richard Eric Widdis (d 1966), of Kenton, Middx; 1 s (Adam b 1965), 2 da (Annie b 1968, Rose b 1972); *Career* chm The Sales Machine Ltd 1970-, account dir J Walter Thompson 1967-70, mktg mangr Lever Bros 1961-65, brand mangr Wall's Ice Cream 1958-61; FInstM; *Books* Choosing The Right Sales Promotion (1966), Positioning Brands Profitably (co-author, 1987); *Recreations* exercise; *Clubs* IOD; *Style*— Alan Toop, Esq; 93 Riverview Gardens, London SW13 9RA; The Sales Machine Ltd, 75-79 York Rd, London SE1 7NP (☎ 071 928 3355, fax 071 928 2484)

TOOP, David; s of Leslie John Toop, of Waltham Cross, Herts, and Doris Ada May, *née* Purver; *b* 5 May 1949; *Educ* Broxbourne GS, Hornsey Coll of Art, Watford Coll of Art; *m* 30 May 1987, Kimberley, da of Les Leston; 1 da (Juliette Angelica b 13 Feb 1990); *Career* music journalist and musician; played with Paul Burwell 1970-80, gave three illustrated music talks BBC Radio 3 1971-75, recorded three pieces for The Obscure Label 1975, launched record label Quartz 1978, recorded with Flying Lizards 1979, publisher and co-ed Collusion magazine 1981-83, pop music critic The Sunday Times Newspaper 1986-88; currently: monthly music columnist and feature writer The Face 1984-, music columnist The Tatler, music critic The Times; contrib to Arena, Details, Sunday Times Magazine and various books; *Books* The Rap Attack (1984); *Style*— David Toop, Esq

TOOTAL, Christopher Peter; s of Charles Stanley Albert Tootal, of Plaxtol, Kent, and Patricia Mary, *née* Swanson; *b* 10 March 1936; *Educ* Repton, Queen's Coll Oxford (Robert Styring scholar, BA, BSc); *m* 20 April 1968, Alison Jane, da of late Archibald James Forbes; 1 s (Alastair James David b 22 April 1970), 1 da (Joanna Helen Natacha b 13 March 1974); *Career* tech asst Frank B Dehn & Co 1958-60, chartered patent agent Gill Jennings & Every 1962-64 (tech asst 1960-62); Herbert Smith: articled clerk 1964-67, asst slr 1967-68, ptnr 1968-; Liveryman Worshipful Co of Tallow Chandlers 1965-; chm Patent Solicitors' Assoc, pres Br Gp of Int Assoc for Protection of Industl Property; *Books* The Law of Industrial Design - Registered Designs, Copyright and Design Right (1990); *Recreations* music, sailing, photography; *Clubs* Royal Harwich Yacht; *Style*— Christopher Tootal, Esq; Herbert Smith, Exchange House, Primrose St, London EC2A 2HS (☎ 071 374 8000, fax 071 496 0043)

TOOTH, Simon John Geoffrey; s of Cyril John Tooth (d 1936), and Irene, *née* O'Connor (d 1976); *b* 27 May 1934; *Educ* Downside Coll Bath; *m* 1959, Melissa Mary (d 1981), da of Col Colwell Carney (d 1978), of Palm Beach, Florida; 1 s (John), 3 da

(Tata, Clare, Alexa); *Career* memb London Stock Exchange 1959-84, exec research conslt 1982-84; London mangr Trans City Hldgs, Aust Investmt Bank 1985-; *Recreations* golf, sailing, deep sea fishing; *Clubs* IOD, Hurlingham; *Style*— Simon Tooth, Esq; 52 St Mary Abbots Court, Warwick Gardens, London W14 8RA; 32 Lombard Street, London EC3 (☎ 071 929 2141)

TOPLEY, Donald Thomas; s of Thomas Aland Topley (d 1990), and Rhoda Millicent, *née* Ayres; *b* 25 Feb 1964; *Educ* Royal Hosp Sch Holbrook Ipswich; *Career* cricketer Essex CCC 1985-; clubs: Surrey CCC 1985 (1 appearance), Noodsberg (Natal) 1985-86, Roodepoort City SA 1986-87, Griqueland West 1987-88, Harare Sports Club Zimbabwe 1990-91; Essex: best batting 66 v Yorks 1987, took 7 for 75 v Derbyshire 1988, taken over 300 first class wickets, Nat West winners, John Player League winners and third place, Benson and Hedges runners up, Co Champions, won Refuge A Cup winners; Benson and Hedges Gold award, Nat West Man of the Month; young professional staff HCC Leeds 1981-84, qualified Advanced Coach in Cricket, nat coach Zimbabwe; Eng: twelfth man at Lords many times, held one handed catch v WI (Lords second test) 1984; *Recreations* photography, eating out; *Style*— Donald Topley, Esq

TOPLIS, Philip John; s of Ivor Toplis, of Penarth, Glamorgan, and Theresa Mary, *née* Williams (d 1986); *b* 6 March 1950; *Educ* Christ's Coll Brecon, Univ of Bristol (MB ChB); *m* 12 March 1983, Catherine Diana Suzanne, da of Robert Pierre Marcel Lassalle; 2 s (Gareth b 1983, Alexander b 1989), 1 da (Laura (twin) b 1983); *Career* conslt obstetrician and gynaecologist W Surrey and NE Hants HA 1986-; memb BMA 1973, FRCS 1979, MRCOG 1980, FRSM 1984; *Books* Alcohol and Coffee Consumption in Pregnancy (1982), Colposcopy and the Postmenopausal Woman (1986); *Recreations* golf, skiing, pianoforte; *Clubs* RSM; *Style*— Philip Toplis, Esq; Millstream, Hagley Rd, Fleet, Hants GU13 8LH (☎ 0252 615886); Frimley Park Hospital, Camberley, Surrey (☎ 0276 69277)

TOPOLSKI, Daniel; s of Feliks Topolski (d 1989), of London, and Marion Everall Topolski (d 1985); *b* 4 June 1945; *Educ* French Lycee London, Westminster, New Coll Oxford; *partner*, Susan Gilmore, da of James Gilbert; 2 da (Emma Sheridan b 30 Jan 1987, Tamsin Lucy Gilbert b 17 Nov 1990); *Career* rower and rowing coach; memb: London rowing Club 1964-, Univ of Oxford Isis Boat Club 1965-, Leander Club 1965-, Tideway Scullers 1965-, Upper Thames Rowing Club 1986-; participant Oxford v Cambridge Boat Race 1967 (winner) and 1968; Henley Royal Regatta: competitor 1962-89 (record holder for 74 rows), winner 1969-70 and 1976-77, record holder for Britannia Cup 1976-86; maj championships: 5 place VIIIs N American Championships (St Catherine's, Canada) 1967, 12 place Coxless IVs Euro Championships (Klagenfurt, Austria) 1969, 7 place Lightweight Coxless IVs World Championships (Lucerne, Switzerland) 1974, 2 place Lightweight Coxless IVs World Championships (Nottingham, UK) 1975, winner Coxed IVs Home International (Cork, Eire) 1976, Gold medallist Lightweight VIIIs World Championships (Amsterdam, Holland) 1977, 7 place Lightweight Double Sculls World Championships (Copenhagen, Denmark) 1978; chief coach to Oxford Univ for Boat Race 1973-87 (won 12, longest ever Oxford winning sequence (10), 3 course records 1974 1976 and 1984 (16mins 45secs)), coach to Nat Women's Rowing Squad 1978-80; maj championships as coach: 8 place VIIIs World Championships (Bled, Yugoslavia) 1979, 5 place VIIIs Olympics (Moscow) 1980, 12 place Men's Pairs and 10 place Women's Pairs World Championships (Lucerne) 1982, 12 place Mens Pairs Olympics (Los Angeles) 1984; prodr BBC TV 1969-73, expedition leader Iran and Turkey 1973-74, writer on travel and sport, TV and radio presenter, journalist, photographer; Churchill fell; *Books* Mazungu: One Man's Africa (1976), Travels with My Father (1983), Boat Race (1985), True Blue (1989), Henley the Regatta (1989); *Style*— Daniel Topolski, Esq; 69 Randolph Avenue, London W9 1DW (☎ 071 289 8939)

TOPP, Air Cdre Roger Leslie; AFC (1950, and 2 Bars 1955 and 1957); s of Horace William Topp (d 1972), and Kathleen, *née* Peters; *b* 14 May 1923; *Educ* North Mundham Sch, RAF Cranwell; *m* 21 April 1945, Audrey Jane, da of Arther Stanley Jeffery (d 1969); 1 s (Jeffery b 12 Aug 1950), 1 da (Marilyn b 24 March 1946); *Career* WWII: cmmnd RAF 1944, Glider Pilot Regt E Sqdn Rhine Crossing Operation Varisity 1945; pilot Nos 107 and 98 Mosquito Sqdns BAFO Germany 1947-50, Empire Test Pilots Sch Farnborough 1950; lead test pilot: Armament and structures flights Farnborough, Comet Flight tests after disasters 1951-55; OC No 111 Fighter Sqdn, formed and led Black Arrows aerobatic team 1955-58; ops staff: HQ AAFCE Fontainbleau 1959, HQ Brockzetel Sector Control Germany 1960-61; jssc Latimer 1961; OC: Fighter Test Sqdn Boscombe Down 1952-64, RAF Coltishall 1964-66; Canadian Nat Def Coll Ontario 1966-67; staff Ops Requirements MOD (air) 1966-67, Cmdt Aeroplane & Armament Experimental Estab Boscombe Down 1970-72, dep gen mangr NATO Multi-role Combat Aircraft Mgmnt Agency Munich 1972-78 (head mil factors 1969-70), ret RAF 1978; conslt: Ferranti Defence Systems Edinburgh 1978-88, Br Indust for mil aviation, avionic and gen equipment 1988-; *Recreations* golf, yachting; *Clubs* RAF, Royal Fowey Yacht; *Style*— Air Cdre Roger Topp, AFC; Cedar Lodge, Meadow Drive, Hoveton St John, Norfolk (☎ 0603 783887); Fairview, The Espanade, Fowey, Cornwall

TOPPIN, Leo Christian; s of Aubrey John Toppin, CVO (d 1969, formerly Norroy and Ulster King of Arms), and Agnes Louise (d 1951); *b* 14 June 1916; *Educ* Harrow; *m* 1938, Heather Mary, da of Capt Eric Schooling (d 1914), of Royal Warwickshire Regt; 2 s; *Career* Army Serv 1939-42, Mid East Cmd 1942-46, Maj; former dir: Kelani Valley Rubber Estates Ltd, Hunasgeria Tea Estates Ltd (chm), Tea Corporation Ltd, Deviturai Tea and Rubber Estates Ltd (chm and md), Highfields Ceylon Ltd, Consolidated Commercial Ltd (chm), Liverpool Grain Storage & Transit Ltd, Liverpool & Manchester Investment Tst Ltd, London and Manchester Securities plc, and other cos; underwriting memb Lloyd's 1938-; chm: Leo C Toppin (Investmnts) Ltd, Carlton Real Estates 1982-83 (dir until 1982); *Recreations* swimming; *Clubs* Naval and Military; *Style*— Leo Toppin, Esq; The Gables, 8 Herbrand Walk, Cooden, Bexhill-on-Sea, East Sussex

TOPPING, Rev Francis (Frank); s of Francis Bede Topping (d 1982), of Birkenhead, and Dorothy Veronica, *née* Kelly (d 1985); *b* 30 March 1937; *Educ* St Anselm's Coll Birkenhead, The North West Sch of Speech and Drama Southport, Didsbury Coll Bristol; *m* 15 April 1958, June, da of Alfred Sydney Berry; 2 s (Simon b 1961, Mark b 1963), 1 da (Anne b 1959); *Career* Nat Serv RAF Cyprus 1955-57, temp officiating Chaplain RSME Regt 1983-84; stage mangr, electrician, asst carpenter and actor Leatherhead Repertory Co 1957-58, stage mangr and actor Wolverhampton Grand Theatre 1959-60, played Krishna in Dear Augustine (Royal Court Theatre) 1959, actor and stage mangr Touring Co 1960-; Granada TV: stage hand, TV floormangr 1960, first asst film dir 1962-64; Theological Coll 1964-67, probationer Methodist min Woodingdean Brighton and univ chaplin Univ of Sussex 1967-70, freelance bdcaster BBC Radio Brighton 1967-70, ordained Methodist min 1970, prodr BBC Radio Bristol 1970-72 (and short story ed and presenter), asst religious progs organizer for all religious progs in N Manchester BBC Network Centre 1972-73, nat ed London 1973-80; progs on BBC radio incl: Good Morning Sunday, Thought for the Day, Pause for Thought; presenter: Sunday Best (ITV), Topping on Sunday (ITV) 1982-84, The 5 Minute Show (TVS) 1989; nat chaplain Toch 1984-86 (hon chaplain 1985-), chaplain Kent Coll 1988-; with Donald Swann wrote songs and sketches for Radio and TV and Swann with Topping (Ambassadors Theatre); presented three one-man plays; *Books* Lord of the Morning (1977), Lord of the Evening (1979), Lord of my Days (1980), Working at Prayer (1981), Pause for Thought - with Frank Topping (1981), Lord of Life (1982), The Words of Christ, 40 Meditations (1983), God Bless You Spoonbill (1984), Lord of Time (1985), An Impossible God (1985), Wings of the Morning (1987), Act Your Age (1989); *Recreations* sailing, sketching, watercolours; *Clubs* Naval, Hurst Castle Sailing; *Style*— The Rev Frank Topping; Browning Lodge, Kent College, Pembury, Tumbridge Wells, Kent (☎ 0892 82 3870); 3 Springfield Cottages, Brede, Rye, E Sussex

TOPPING, John; s of John Topping ISO (d 1970), of Edinburgh, and Margaret May, *née* Cunningham; *b* 22 July 1936; *Educ* George Heriot's Edinburgh; *m* 27 March 1967, Anne Fyfe; 2 da (Julia b 1969, Amy b 1974); *Career* fin dir and co sec Early's of Witney plc 1988-; CA, FCT; *Recreations* golf; *Clubs* Ashridge Golf, Copt Heath Golf; *Style*— John Topping, Esq; Windleshaw, Whiteleaf, Princes Risborough, Bucks HP17 0LX (☎ 08444 4097); Early's of Witney plc, Witney Mill, Witney, Oxon OX8 5EB (☎ 0993 703131)

TORA, Brian Roberto; adopted s of Ernest Carlo Tora, and Betty Lilian, *née* Squires (d 1971); *b* 21 Sept 1945; *Educ* Bancroft's Sch Woodford Green Essex; *m* 4 July 1975 (m dis 1988), Jennifer, da of (Julius) Dennis Israel Blanckensee (d 1951); 2 s (Matthew b 26 Dec 1977, Thomas b 5 June 1979); m 2, 20 Oct 1989, Elizabeth Mary, *née* Edgecombe; *Career* Grieveson Grant 1963-74, investmt mangr Singer & Friedlander 1974-79; investmt dir: Van Cutsem & Assocs 1979-82, Touche Remnant Fin Mgmnt 1982-85; head of retail mktg James Capel & Co 1985-; dir: James Capel Unit Trust Management 1985-, James Capel Financial Services 1986-; tstee The Mobility Tst, reg bdcaster; contrib articles on personal fin to several jls; memb Stock Exchange; *Recreations* bridge, reading, food and wine; *Style*— Brian Tora, Esq; Enniskillen Lodge, Little Waldingfield, Suffolk C010 0SU (☎ 0787 247 783); James Capel & Co, James Capel House, 6 Bevis Marks, London EC3A 7JQ (☎ 071 621 0011, fax 071 621 0496)

TORBET, Dr (Thomas) Edgar; JP (E Kilbride); s of Sqdn Ldr Harry Torbet (d 1968), of Tekka, Crieff, and Agnes Edgar, *née* McClemont (d 1974); *b* 15 March 1930; *Educ* Morrison's Acad Crieff, Univ of Glasgow (MB ChB); *m* 12 Aug 1960, Helen Fiona, da of Philip Murdoch Graham (d 1981), of Hardwar Millhouse, Tighnabruaich, Argyll; 1 s (Alastair Edgar Graham b 1962); *Career* Nat Serv RAF Sqdn Ldr Med Branch 1954-56; conslt obstetrician and gynaecologist Southern Gen Hosp Glasgow and hon clinical lectr Univ of Glasgow 1967-; FRCSEd 1966, FRCOG 1973 (MRCOG 1960); *Recreations* sailing, skiing; *Style*— Dr Edgar Torbet, JP; 10 Easter Rd, Busby, Clarkston, Glasgow G76 8HS (☎ 041 644 1099); Department of Obstetrics and Gynaecology, Southern General Hospital, Glasgow G51 4TF (☎ 041 445 2466)

TORDOFF, Baron (Life Peer UK 1981), of Knutsford, Co Cheshire; Geoffrey Johnson Tordoff; s of Stanley Acomb Tordoff, of Marple, Cheshire; *b* 11 Oct 1928; *Educ* Manchester GS, Manchester Univ; *m* 1953, Mary Patricia, da of Thomas Swarbrick, of Leeds; 2 s (Hon Nicholas Gregory b 1958, Hon Mark Edmund b 1962), 3 da (Hon Mary Catherine b 1954, Hon Frances Jane b 1956, Hon Paula Mary b 1960); *Career* contested (Lib) Northwich 1964, Knutsford 1966 and 1970; chm Lib Party 1976-79, pres 1983-84; chm Campaigns and Elections Ctee 1982; Lib Chief Whip 1984-88; Lib Democrat Chief Whip 1988-; *Style*— The Rt Hon the Lord Tordoff; House of Lords, London SW1

TOREN, Amikam; s of Benjamin Toren and Alisa Toren; *b* 18 May 1945; *m* 1972, Christina, da of Ian Camden Pratt; 1 s (Manuel b 5 Nov 1973); *Career* lectr Brighton Poly 1990-, visiting lectr: Byam Shaw Sch of Art, Dep of Fine Art Goldsmiths Coll; artist; individual exhibitions incl: Annely Juda Fine Art London 1973, Serpentine Gallery London 1976, Replacing (ICA London) 1979, If Painting then... (Riverside Studios London) 1981, Actualities (Matt's Gallery London) 1984, unnamed exhibitions Anthony Reynolds GAllery London 1985 and 1991, Pidgin Paintings 1987, Stacks 1989; Ikon Gallery Birmingham 1990, Arnolfini Gallery Bristol 1991, Gabrielle Maubrie Paris 1991, Chisenhale Gallery London 1991; particpated in numerous gp exhibitions 1967-; *Style*— Amikam Toren; Anthony Reynolds Gallery, 37 Cowper St, London EC2 4AP (☎ 071 253 5575, fax 071 253 5621)

TORINO, Peter Antony; s of Nello Torino (d 1955), and Anna, *née* Victoria; *b* 15 Sept 1954; *Educ* Cotton Coll, Univ of Bristol (BSc); *m* 2 Jan 1977, Moira, da of Martin Augustine Ansbro, of Reading; *Career* CA; mangr Peat Marwick McLintock 1981-84, UK accountant Control Data 1984-85, fin dir Grayling Gp 1985-; memb ICEAW; *Recreations* travel, squash, reading; *Style*— Peter Antony Torino, Esq; 29 Hartley Rd, London E11 (☎ 081 989 2413); 4 Bedford Sq, London WC1 (☎ 071 255 1100, fax 071 631 0602)

TORNBOHM, (Peter) Noel; s of Eric Anthony Tornbohm (d 1986), of Darlington, and May, *née* Barrow (d 1969); *b* 11 Jan 1943; *Educ* Queen Elizabeth GS Darlington, UCL (LLB); *m* 1, 29 May 1965 (m dis 1982), Yvonne Hamilton (Mrs Way), da of Wilfred Vincent Miller, of Darlington; 1 s (Paul b 28 March 1971), 1 da (Catherine b 16 June 1969); m 2, 1983, Maureen Roberta (Mo), da of Frank Griffin, of Mickleover, Derby; *Career* admitted slr 1967; ptnr Smith Roddam & Co 1968-71 (joined 1967), sr ptnr Gadsby Coxon & Copestake 1983 (joined 1971); former memb City & Derby 126 Round Table; memb: Derby Beaujolais Fellowship, Derby S and W Derbys Cons Assoc; chm Derby 41 Club 1990-91 (memb); memb Law Soc slrs Benevolent Assoc; *Recreations* playing & listening to music, walking, keeping dogs; *Style*— Noel Tornbohm, Esq; Hillbank House, 2 The Common, Quarndon, Derby DE6 4JY (☎ 0332 553376); Gadsby Coxon & Copestake, Sterne House, Lodge Lane, Derby (☎ 0332 372372, fax 0332 365715)

TORNEY, Thomas William; JP (Derby 1969); *b* 2 July 1915; *Educ* elementary sch; *Career* joined Lab Pty 1930; election agent: Wembley North 1945, Derby West 1964; Derby and Dist area organiser USDAW (sponsored by same) 1946-1970, MP (Lab) Bradford South 1970-87 (ret); memb: Parly Select Ctee Race Relations and Immigration 1970-, Select Ctee on Agric 1979-, Wine and Spirit Liaison Ctee; chm: PLP Agric Fish and Food Gp 1981-; *Style*— Thomas Torney, Esq, JP; 8 Wesley Court, 2 Beckwith Rd, London SE24 (☎ 071 274 6822)

TOROBERT, Sir Henry Thomas; KBE (1981); *Career* mangr Reserve Bank 1972, govt advsr on currency, first govr Bank of Papua New Guinea 1973- (and instrumental in its foundation); *Style*— Sir Henry ToRobert, KBE; PO Box 898, Port Moresby, Papua New Guinea

TORODE, John Arthur; s of Alfred Charles Torode (d 1980), gen sec Sign and Display Trades Union, and Dorothy Amelia Torode (d 1966); *b* 4 Jan 1939; *Educ* Lincoln Coll Oxford (BA), Cornell Univ Ithaca NY; *m* 1974, Naseem Fatima, da of Dr Abdul Wasi Khan (d 1977); 1 s from previous marriage (Jonathan b 1970), 1 s (George b 1976), 1 da (Amelia b 1975); *Career* policy editor The Independent 1986-; political leader writer and columnist The Guardian 1977-86 (labour ed 1967-72, diary ed 1974-77), memb Younger Ctee on Privacy 1969-72, memb editorial bd New Statesman 1969-72, jt presenter Weekend World 1972, conslt India for UN World Food Programme 1982, chm Labour and Industl Corrs Gp 1969-72; Parly candidate: (Lab) Kingston on Thames 1979, (SDP) Saffron Walden 1983; memb Exec Ctee Friends of Cyprus 1982-; hon citizen of Huntsville Alabama; *Recreations* swimming, amateur archaeology; *Clubs* Reform, Zoological Society of London; *Style*— John Torode, Esq; 25 Platt's Lane, Hampstead, London NW3 7NP (☎ 071 435 6105); The Independent, 40 City Rd, London EC1

TORPHICHEN, Master of; Douglas Robert Alexander Sandilands; s of late Hon Walter Alexander Sandilands (s of 12 Lord Torphichen, d 1966), and hp of cous, 15 Lord Torphichen; *b* 31 Aug 1926; *m* 1, 1949, Ethel Louise Burkitt; 1 s; m 2, Suzette Véva, *née* Pernet; 2 s; *Style*— The Master of Torphichen; 109 Royal George Road, Burgess Hill, W Sussex

TORPHICHEN, 15 Lord (S 1564); James Andrew Douglas Sandilands; s of 14 Lord Torphichen (d 1975); *see also* Sir Francis Sandilands; *b* 27 Aug 1946; *Educ* King's Sch Canterbury, Univ of Birmingham; *m* 1976, Margaret Elizabeth, da of William Alfred Beale (d 1967), of Boston, Mass; 4 da (Margaret b 1979, Mary b 1981, Anne b 1985, Alison b 1990); *Heir* Master of Torphichen, *qv* (first cous once removed); *Career* electronics engr; *Style*— The Rt Hon the Lord Torphichen; Calder House, Mid-Calder, West Lothian EH53 0HN

TORPHICHEN, Pamela, Lady; Pamela Mary; da of late John Howard Snow, and widow of Thomas Hodson-Pressinger; *b* 11 July 1926; *Educ* Old Palace Mayfield Sussex; *m* 1973, as his 3 w, 14 Lord Torphichen (d 1975); *Career* LRAM, cncllr Hampstead Borough Cncl 1949-52; pres Ladies of Charity (Westminster) 1975-; *Recreations* writes music, interested in Russian ikons; *Style*— The Rt Hon Pamela, Lady Torphichen; 16 Moore St, London SW3

TORRANCE, (David) Andrew; s of James Torrance, of Blundellsands, Liverpool, and Gladys, *née* Riley; *b* 18 May 1953; *Educ* Merchant Taylors' Sch Crosby, Emmanuel Coll Cambridge (MA), London Business Sch (MSc); *m* 30 Dec 1983, Ann Lesley, da of George Tasker (d 1972), of Bebington, Wirral; 1 s (James b 1987), 1 da (Lucy b 1984); *Career* vice-pres and dir Boston Consulting Gp Ltd (joined 1976, mangr 1981); *Recreations* cars, tennis, food, wine; *Style*— Andrew Torrance, Esq; 117 Lansdowne Rd, London W11 2LF (☎ 071 727 9019); The Boston Consulting Group Ltd, Devonshire House, Mayfair Place, London W1 (☎ 071 753 5353, fax 071 499 3660, telex 28975)

TORRANCE, (Henry) Bruce; s of Maj Thomas Stirling Torrance (d 1976), of Edinburgh, and Isobel Smith Torrance (d 1981); *b* 12 March 1927; *Educ* Edinburgh Acad, Univ of Edinburgh (MB ChB); *m* 15 Sept 1955, Isobel Marjorie, da of Maj Jack Parr (d 1963), of Edinburgh; 2 s (Anthony b 9 July 1959, Fergus b 10 May 1968), 2 da (Caroline b 26 Sept 1956, Juliet b 26 July 1961); *Career* Sqdn Ldr (surgical specialist) RAF 1950-52; conslt surgn (later sr surgn and hon lectr) Manchester Royal Infirmary 1959-89; memb: Pancreatic Soc, North of England Gastroenterology Soc, James IV Assoc of Surgns; vice pres and hon sec Br Digestive Fndn; FRCS Ed 1953, FRCS 1961; *Recreations* sailing, golf; *Clubs* Wilmslow Golf, West Linton Golf; *Style*— Bruce Torrance, Esq; Persilands, Biggar, Lanarkshire MS12 6LX (☎ 0899 20813)

TORRANCE, Prof John Steele (Jack); s of Robert Torrance (d 1941), of Belfast NI, and Charlotte Robinson Torrance (d 1982); *b* 11 Jan 1929; *Educ* Belfast Coll of Technol (MBA); *m* 8 Sept 1948, Rosetta Fitz-Simons, da of Thomas Patterson Shepherd (d 1980), of Donaghadee, NI; 4 da (Sharon Rose b 1952, Cheryl Sara b 1954, Candida Eleanor b 1956, Dara Rosetta b 1960); *Career* seconded DNC Bath 1946; trainee Harland & Wolfe Belfast 1941-50, sr engr GN Haden and SRW Murland 1950-60, sr ptnr Steensen Varming Mulcahy & Partners Edinburgh 1972-85 (associate then ptnr 1960-72); involved in design for major projects incl: hosps, univs, banks, insur cos, commercial offices, swimming and leisure complexes; visiting prof Univ of Strathclyde 1988-, prof Heriot-Watt Univ 1989-; contrib numerous articles in tech jls; FCIBSE (nat pres 1985-86), FCIArb, MBAE, MConsE; *Recreations* music, reading, golf; *Clubs* Sloane; *Style*— Prof Jack Torrance; 1 Southbank Ct, Easter Park Drive, Edinburgh EH4 6JR (☎ 031 312 6923)

TORRANCE, Very Rev Prof Thomas Forsyth; MBE (1944); s of Rev Thomas Torrance (d 1959), of Edinburgh, and Annie Elizabeth, *née* Sharp; *b* 30 Aug 1913; *Educ* Canadian Sch Chengdu, Bellshill Acad Scotland, Univ of Edinburgh (MA, BD, DLitt), Univ of Basel (Dr Theol), Oriel Coll Oxford; *m* 2 Oct 1946, Margaret Edith, da of George Frederick Spear (d 1946), of Combe Down, Bath; 2 s (Thomas Spear b 3 July 1947, Iain Richard b 13 Jan 1949), 1 da (Alison Meta Elizabeth b 15 April 1951); *Career* Chaplain Church of Scotland MEF and CMF 1943-45, Combined Ops and 10 Indian Div, Emergency Serv Palestine Police Force May 1936; prof systematic theol Auburn NY 1938-39, minister Alyth Barony Parish Perthshire 1940-47, minister Beechgrove Parish Church Aberdeen 1947-50, prof church history New Coll Univ of Edinburgh 1950-52, prof christian dogmatics Univ of Edinburgh 1952-79, moderator of the Gen Assembly of the Church of Scotland 1976-77; fndr and co-ed Scottish Journal of Theology 1948-82; memb: Academic Inst de Philosophie des Sciences 1976-, Kuratorium Das Deutsche Inst für Bildung and Wissen Paderborn and Berlin, Europaeische Akademie für Umweltfragen Tübingen, Cmmn of Faith and Order of the World Cncl of Churches 1952-62, Bd Center of Theological Inquiry Princeton 1979-; pres Academie Int des Sciences Religieuses 1972-81; Hon DD Presbyterian Coll Montreal 1950, Hon DTheol Univ of Geneva 1959, DTheol Faculté Libre Paris 1959, Hon DD St Andrews 1960, Hon DTheol Oslo 1961, Hon DSc Heriot-Watt Univ 1983, Hon DTheol Debrecen Reformed Coll Hungary 1988; FRSE Edinburgh 1977, FBA 1982; Cross of St Mark Patriarchate of Alexandria 1973, Proto-Presbyter of the Greek Orthodox Church Patriarchate of Alexandria 1973, Cross of Thyateira 1977; *Books include* The Doctrine in the Apostolic Fathers (1946 and 1948), Kingdom and Church (1956), When Christ Comes and Comes Again (1957), The Mystery of the Lord's Supper (1958), The School of Faith (1959), Conflict and Agreement in the Church, Vol 1 Order and Disorder (1959), The Apocalypse Today (1959), Conflict and Agreement in the Church, Vol II The Ministry and the Sacraments of the Gospel (1960), Theology in Reconstruction (1965), Theological Science (1969), Space Time and Incarnation (1969), God and Rationality (1971), Theology in Reconciliation (1975), Space, Time and Resurrection (1976), The Ground and Grammar of Theology (1980), Christian Theology and Scientific Culture (1980), Divine and Contingent Order (1981), Reality and Evangelical Theology (1982), Judicial Law and Physical Law (1982), The Mediation of Christ (1983), Transformation and Convergence in the Frame of Knowledge (1984), The Christian Frame of Mind (1985, 2 edn 1989), Reality and Scientific Theology (1985), The Trinitarian Faith (1988), The Hermenentics of John Calvin (1988), Karl Barth Biblical and Evangelical Theologian (1990); works edited: Karl Barth Church Dogmatics (with G Bromiley, 1956-77), Calvin's Tracts and Treatises (1959), Calvin's New Testament Commentaries (with D W Torrance, 1959-73), Belief in Science and the Christian Life (1980), Christian Theology and Scientific Culture (1980-83), James Clerk Maxwell, A Dynamical Theory of the Electromagnetic Field (1982), Theology and Science at the Frontiers of Knowledge (1985-90); *Recreations* fishing; *Clubs* Edinburgh Univ Staff, New (Edinburgh); *Style*— The Very Rev Prof Thomas Torrance; 37 Braid Farm Road, Edinburgh EH10 6LE (☎ 031 447 3224)

TORRANCE, Prof Victor Brownlie; s of Thomas Brownlie Torrance (d 1969), and Mary King Torrance, MBE, *née* Miller; *b* 24 Feb 1937; *Educ* Wisham High Sch, Heriot-Watt Univ (BSc, MSc), Univ of Edinburgh (PhD); *m* 1, (m dis 1982) Mary McParland; 1 s (Andrew Brownlie b 19 March 1968), 2 da (Adrienne Joan b 20 Sept 1964, Deirdrie Ann b 15 March 1967), 1 step s (Ross William Hall), 1 step da (Kirsty Ann Hall); m 2, 18 Oct 1982, Inez Marjorie Ann, da of William Jack (d 1971); *Career* sr lectr i/c Bldg Div Sch of Architecture and Bldg Singapore Poly Singapore 1966-68, assoc prof and head of Dept of Bldg and Estate Mgmnt Faculty of Architecture and Bldg Nat Univ of Singapore 1968-72, William Watson prof of bldg Dept of Bldg Engrg and Surveying Heriot-Watt Univ 1972-, ptnr Bldg and Design Conslts 1976-; memb: Bd of Govrs Edinburgh Coll of Art 1973-88, Civil Engrg and Transport Ctee and Bldg Sub-Ctee Science Res Cncl 1975-78, CNAA Technol Res Ctee 1982-85, Scot Bldg Standards Advsy Ctee Res Sub-Ctee 1982-85; chm RIAS Res Steering Ctee 1982-85, memb Panel of Visitors to the Bldg Res Estab 1983-89, conslt of Bldg Investigation Centre 1987-, dir Lloyds Surveyors 1989-; chm Cncl of Props of Bldg 1987-, pres Chartered Inst of Bldg 1988-89; chm: Advsy Bd of Wimlas Testing Servs, Geo Wimpey Laboratories 1988-, chm CIOB Environment Gp 1990-; FCIOB 1972, FBIM 1972, FRSA 1973, Hon ARICS 1986; *Style*— Prof Victor Torrance; Kerry, 3 Craiginnan Gardens, Dollar, Clackmannshire FK14 7JA (☎ 02594 2240); Department of Building Engineering and Surveying, Heriot-Watt University, Riccarton, Edinburgh EH14 4AS (☎ 031 449 5111, fax 031 451 3161)

TORRE DIAZ, 7 Conde (Count; cr of 1846 by Queen Isabel II of Spain); Paul Gerald de Zulueta; only s of Maj Peter Paul John de Zulueta, (Welsh Gds (d 1982; whose mother, Dora, m as her 2 husband, 5 Marquess of Bristol) by his w Tessa, who m as 2 husb, 2 Viscount Montgomery of Alameia, er da of late Lt-Gen Sir Frederick Browning, GCVO, KBE, CB, DSO, and Daphne du Maurier, the novelist; *b* 12 April 1956; *Educ* Ampleforth, RMA Sandhurst; *m* 18 June 1988, Susan, o da of Dr G J Pritchard, of The Old Mill House, Stanwell Moor; 1 s (Guy Peter b 26 Aug 1990); *Career* Maj Welsh Gds 1979, Adj 1983-85; Robert Fleming & Co 1987-89, ptnr The Mast Organisation 1990-; *Recreations* skiing, mountaineering, loafing; *Clubs* Royal Fowey Yacht, Pratts; *Style*— P G de Zulueta; 15 Henniker Mews, London SW3

TORRENS-SPENCE, Capt (Frederick) Michael Alexander; DSO, DSC (1941, AFC 1944), JP; s of Lt-Col Herbert Frederick Torrens-Spence (d 1937), of Rosstulla, Whiteabbey, Co Antrim, and Eileen Torrens (d 1983); *b* 10 March 1914; *Educ* RNC Dartmouth; *m* 1944, Rachel Nora, da of Edward Stanley Clarke, JP, DL (d 1960), of Ballyaughlis Lodge, Lisburn, Co Down; 3 s, 1 da; *Career* cmmnd Sub Lt RN 1934, served Med 1940-42, chief instr Empire Test Pilots Sch 1947-48, dep dir Air Warfare Div Naval Staff 1952-54; cmd: HMS Delight 1955-56, RNAS Lossiemouth 1956-58, HMS Albion 1959-61; County Cmdt Ulster Special Constabulary 1961-70, CO 2 Bn UDR 1970-71; ADC to HM The Queen 1961; High Sheriff Co Armagh 1979, Lord-Lt Co Armagh 1981-89 (formerly DL); landowner 115 acres; DFC Greece 1943; *Clubs* MCC; *Style*— Capt Michael Torrens-Spence, DSO, DSC, AFC, JP, RN; Drumeullen House, Ballydugan, Downpatrick, Do Down, N Ireland

TORRINGTON, 11 Viscount (GB 1721); Sir Timothy Howard St George Byng; 11 Bt (GB 1715); Baron Byng of Southill (GB 1721); s of Hon George Byng, RN (d on active service 1944, himself s of 10 Viscount, whom present Viscount suc 1961), and Anne Yvonne Bostock, *née* Wood; *b* 13 July 1943; *Educ* Harrow, St Edmund Hall Oxford (BA); *m* 1973, Susan Honour, da of Michael George Thomas Webster, of The Vale, Windsor Forest, Berks; 3 da (Hon Henrietta Rose b 1977, Hon Georgina Isobel b 1980, Hon Malaika Anne b 13 April 1982); *Heir* kinsman, John Cranmer-Byng, MC; *Career* chm Moray Firth Exploration plc, Exploration & Production Services (Hldgs) Ltd (Expro); dir Flextech plc; memb House of Lords Select Ctee on Euro Community; *Recreations* travel and field sports; *Clubs* White's, Pratts, Muthaiga (Nairobi); *Style*— The Rt Hon the Viscount Torrington; Great Hunts Place, Owslebury, Winchester, Hants (☎ 096 274 234); London office: (☎ 071 245 6522)

TORY, Sir Geofroy William; KCMG (1958, CMG 1956); s of William Frank Tory, of Sheffield, and Edith Wreghitt; *b* 31 July 1912; *Educ* King Edward VII Sch Sheffield, Queens' Coll Cambridge; *m* 1, 1938, Emilia Strickland; 2 s, 1 da; m 2, 1950, Florence Hazel (d 1985), da of Arthur William Thomas, of Halifax, Nova Scotia; *Career* IDC, WWII serv RA; entered Dominions Office 1935, PPS to Sec State Dominion Affrs 1945-46, sr sec Office of UK High Cmmr Canada 1946-49, cnsllr Br Embassy Dublin 1950-51; dep UK high cmmr: Pakistan (Peshawar) 1953-54, Australia 1954-57; asst under sec state Cwlth Rels Office 1957, UK high cmmr Fedn of Malaya 1957-63, Br ambass Eire 1963-66, UK high cmmr Malta 1967-70, ret 1970; PMN (Malaysia) 1963; *Style*— Sir Geofroy Tory, KCMG; 17 Barrowgate Rd, London W4 4QX

TOSH, Malcolm Charles; s of Charles William Tosh (d 1976), of London, and Marjorie Ann, *née* Grant; *b* 14 May 1934; *Educ* Clifton; *m* 3 Dec 1960, Elizabeth Jane Holmes, da of Raymond Hugh Scott Piercy, of Walton-on-Thames; 2 s (David b 1964, Philip b 1967), 2 da (Lucinda b 1963, Camilla b 1970); *Career* RA 1957-59, Lt 1958; trainee accountant Peat Marwick McLintock 1952-57, CA 1957, ptnr Kidsons Impey 1963- (joined 1959); qualified 1959-63); church warden; Liveryman Worshipful Co of Glaziers 1981 (hon treas 1988-); *Recreations* bridge, opera, tennis, golf, fell walking; *Clubs* City of London, Naval and Military, MCC, London Scottish; *Style*— Malcolm Tosh, Esq; Little Clandon, West Clandon, Surrey GU4 7ST (☎ 0483 222561); 20 Cursitor St, London EC4A 1HY (☎ 071 405 2088, fax 071 831 2206)

TOSSWILL, (Timothy Maurice) Stephen; s of Timothy Dymond Tosswill (d 1991), of Cullompton, Devon, and Sigrid, *née* Bohn (d 1985); *b* 28 April 1949; *Educ* Rugby, St Paul's, Univ of London (LLB, LLM); *Career* criminal lawyer, admitted slr 1976; ptnr Tosswill & Co 1976-, memb Crown Cts Liaison Ctee 1984-, author of articles in Criminal Law Review and New Law Journal; *Recreations* music, photography, skiing, scuba diving, supporting Wimbledon FC; *Style*— Stephen Tosswill, Esq; 260 Brixton Hill, London SW2 1HP (☎ 081 674 9494, fax 081 671 8987)

TOTMAN, Edward Bartram; s of Edward Bartram Totman (d 1989), of 41 Mayfield Rd, Sutton, Surrey, and Joan Cecilia Mary, *née* McCamley; *b* 28 June 1942; *Educ* Wimbledon Coll King's Coll London (LLB); *m* 25 July 1970, Colette Maria, da of Vincent Aloysius Jackson (d 1962), of Wickham Ave, Cheam, Surrey; 1 s (Julian b 1971), 3 da (Marissa b 1973, Siobhan b 1976, Carmel b 1979); *Career* admitted slr 1970; articled clerk then slr GLC 1965-72, Abbey National Building Society 1972-74, Mercantile Credit Co Ltd 1974-79, ptnr D J Freeman & Co 1981- (joined 1979); memb The Catenian Assoc; memb Law Soc 1970; *Recreations* tennis, swimming, photography, reading; *Style*— Edward Totman, Esq; 91 The Green, Ewell, Epsom, Surrey KT17 3JX (☎ 081 393 3530); D J Freeman & Co, 1 and 43 Fetter Lane, London EC4A 1BR (☎ 071 583 5555 fax 071 583 3232, telex 913434)

TOTTENHAM, Rev Lady Ann Elizabeth; da of 8 Marquess of Ely; *b* 21 July 1940; *Educ* Trinity Coll Toronto Univ (BA STB), Union Seminary New York (MTB); *Career* headmistress Bishop Strachan Sch, Toronto; *Style*— The Rev the Lady Ann Tottenham

TOTTENHAM, Lord Richard Ivor; s (by 1 m) of 8 Marquess of Ely; *b* 1954; *Educ* Univ of Western Ontario (BA); *m* 1978, Virginia Murney, da of William Murney Morris (decd), of Toronto, Ontario; 2 da (Elizabeth b 1983, Katherine b 1985); *Style*— The Lord Richard Tottenham; 819 Grace St, Newmarket, Ontario, L3Y 2L6 Canada

TOTTENHAM, Lord Timothy Craig; 2 s of 8 Marquess of Ely; *b* 17 Jan 1948; *Educ* Ottawa Teachers' Coll; *m* 1973, Elizabeth Jane, da of Grant McAllister, of Ottawa, Ontario; 2 s (Scott b 1977, John b 1981); *Career* teaching principal St Michaels Univ Sch Victoria BC Canada; *Recreations* sailing, windsurfing, gardening; *Style*— The Lord Timothy Tottenham

TOUCHE, Sir Rodney Gordon; 2 Bt (UK 1962), of Dorking, Surrey; s of Rt Hon Sir Gordon Cosmo Touche, 1 Bt (d 1972); *b* 5 Dec 1928; *Educ* Marlborough, Univ Coll Oxford; *m* 30 April 1955, Ouida Ann, er da of late Frederick Gerald MacLellan, of Moncton, New Brunswick, Canada; 1 s, 3 da; *Heir* s, Eric MacLellan Touche; *Style—* Sir Rodney Touche, Bt; 1100 8th Ave (Apt 2403), Calgary, Alberta, Canada (☎ 403 233 8800)

TOULMIN, John Kelvin; QC (1980); s of A H Toulmin, and late B Toulmin, *née* Fraser; *b* 14 Feb 1941; *Educ* Winchester, Trinity Hall Cambridge (BA, MA), Univ of Michigan Law Sch (LLM); *m* 13 May 1967, Carolyn Merton, da of Merton Gullick (d 1953); 1 s (Geoffrey b 1969), 2 da (Alison b 1972, Hilary b 1975); *Career* called to the Bar 1965; bencher Middle Temple 1986, memb Bar Cncl/Senate 1971-77, 1978-81 and 1986-, memb Supreme Court Rules Ctee 1976-80, rec Crown Ct 1984, called to the Bar N I 1989; govr The Maudsley and Bethlem Royal Hosps 1979-87, memb Ctee of Mgmnt Inst of Psychiatry 1982-, chm Young Barr Ctee 1973-75, bar rep UK delegation to Cncl of the Bars and Law Socs of Europe (CCBE) 1983-90) (ldr of the UK delegation 1987-90), vice pres CCBE 1991-; chm of Bar Int Practice Ctee 1987; *Books* DHSS report into Unnecessary Dental Treatment in NHS (co author 1986), articles on rights of estab & recognition of diplomas in Europe, Butterworths Banking Encyclopaedia (ed Euro Law Section); *Recreations* cricket, listening to music; *Clubs* MCC; *Style—* John Toulmin, Esq, QC; 3 Grays Inn Place, Grays Inn, London WC1R 5EA (☎ 071 831 8441, fax 071 831 8479)

TOULSON, Roger Grenfell; QC (1986); s of Stanley Kilsha Toulson, of Redhill, Surrey, and Lilian Mary Toulson (d 1985); *b* 23 Sept 1946; *Educ* Mill Hill Sch, Jesus Coll Cambridge (MA, LLB); *m* 28 April 1973, Elizabeth, da of Henry Bertram Chrimes, of Bracken Bank, Dawstone Rd, Heswall, Wirral, Merseyside; 2 s (Henry b 1979, Thomas 1984), 2 da (Susanna b 1975, Rachel b 1977); *Career* called to the Bar Inner Temple 1969, rec 1987; *Recreations* skiing, tennis, gardening; *Style—* Roger Toulson, Esq, QC; Billhurst Farm, Wood St Village, nr Guildford, Surrey GU3 3DZ (☎ 0483 235 246); 2 Crown Office Row, Temple, London EC4Y 7HJ (☎ 071 583 8155, fax 071 583 1205)

TOUZEL, Michael John; s of Harold Winter Touzel (d 1957), and Dorothy Ena, *née* Cabot (d 1965); *b* 26 July 1937; *Educ* Victoria Coll Jersey; *m* 26 July 1962, Odette Kathleen, da of Joseph Maurice (d 1982); 1 s (Ian Michael b 15 Aug 1963); *Career* sales rep Country Gentleman's Assoc (Jersey) Ltd 1955-59, clerical salesman Jago Tweedle & Co Ltd 1959-63, formed own Insurance Brokers now known as MJ Touzel Insurance Brokers Ltd; ctee memb IOD Jersey Branch, FBIIBA 1979, FIOD 1979, MBIM 1988, memb Chartered Insur Inst; *Recreations* bowling, motor yachting; *Clubs* Jersey Bowling, St Helier Yacht; *Style—* Michael Touzel, Esq; M J Touzel (Insurance Brokers) Ltd, West House, Peter St, St Helier, Jersey, Channel Islands 0534 36451, fax 0534 36998)

TOVEY, Sir Brian John Maynard; KCMG (1980); s of Rev Collett John Tovey (d 1967), and Kathleen Edith Maud Maynard (d 1972); *b* 15 April 1926; *Educ* St Edwards Sch Oxford, St Edmund Hall Oxford, Sch of Oriental and African Studies London (BA); *m* 1989, Mary Helen, *née* Lane; *Career* dir Govt Communications HQ 1978-83; Plessey Electronics Systems Ltd: def systems conslt 1983-85, defence and political advsr 1985-88; chm: Creswell Associates Ltd 1988-, Fujitsu Europe Telecom R & D Centre Ltd 1990-; *Recreations* music, walking, 16th Century Italian art; *Clubs* Naval & Military; *Style—* Sir Brian Tovey, KCMG; 8 Creswell Gardens, London SW5 OBJ

TOVEY, Dr Geoffrey Harold; CBE (1974); s of Harold John Tovey (d 1976), of Midsomer Norton, and Gertrude, *née* Taylor (d 1936); *b* 29 May 1916; *Educ* Wycliffe Coll, Univ of Bristol (MB ChB, MD); *m* 6 Sept 1941, Margaret Beryl, da of Frederick Charles Davies (d 1941), of Abertysswg; 2 s (Charles b 1943, d 1973, Stuart b 1946); *Career* RAMC 1941-46, 8 Field Ambulance 1941-42, Army Blood Transfusion Serv 1942-46, OC No 3 Base Transfusion Unit India Cmd 1945-46; dir SW Regnl Blood Transfusion Serv 1946-79, conslt advsr in blood transfusion DHSS 1978-81, hon conslt in blood transfusion MOD 1978-82, fndr and dir UK Transplant Serv 1969-79, conslt physician Southmead Hosp Bristol 1946-79, clinical lectr in haematology Univ of Bristol 1947-79; pres: Int Soc of Blood Transfusion 1973-76, Br Soc for Haematology 1977-78; Hellenic Soc for Transplantation award 1976, Oliver Memorial award 1977, Alwyn Zoutendyk Memorial Award Medal SA Inst for Med Res 1979; memb: Select Ctee of Experts on Histocompatability Cncl of Europe 1970-79, Select Ctee of Experts on Immunohaematology 1978-81; fndr Rehabilitation at Home Serv for Adult Brain Damaged Eastbourne 1989, memb Eastbourne Dist Med Soc; FRCPath 1963, FRCP 1968; *Books* Technique of Fluid Balance (1957); *Recreations* walking, foreign travel; *Style—* Dr Geoffrey Tovey, CBE; Lynton, 1B St John's Rd, Eastbourne, E Sussex

TOVEY, Dr Stuart John; s of Dr G H Tovey, CBE, of Eastbourne, and Margaret Beryl, *née* Davies; *b* 21 May 1946; *Educ* Wycliffe Coll, Univ of Bristol; *Career* Acting PO RAFVR 1965-69; conslt in charge of genito-urinary med Guys Hosp London; MRCP 1981, MRCGP 1982; *Recreations* yachting; *Style—* Dr Stuart Tovey; The Lloyd Clinic, Guy's Hospital, St Thomas St, London SE1 9RT (☎ 071 955 5955)

TOWER, Hon Mrs (Victoria Marion Ann); *née* Lever; 2 da of 3 Viscount Leverhulme, KG, TD; *b* 23 Sept 1945; *m* 1, 1966 (m dis 1973), (John) Richard Walter Reginald Carew Pole, o s of Sir John Gawen Carew Pole, 12 Bt, DSO, TD; m 2, 1975 (m dis 1987), (Robert) Gordon Lennox Apsion; 2 s, 1 da; m 3, 6 Feb 1990, Brig Peter Tower, CBE; *Style—* The Hon Mrs Tower; 8 Mulberry Walk, Chelsea, London SW3

TOWERS, Dr David Anthony; s of George Thomas Towers (d 1970), of Winsford, Cheshire, and Joyce Leigh, *née* Sadler; *b* 27 May 1947; *Educ* Verdin GS Winsford Cheshire, Univ of Newcastle upon Tyne (BSc), Univ of Leeds (PhD); *m* 8 Sept 1973, Lorna Mary, da of Samuel Hoole (d 1954), of Winsford, Cheshire; 2 s (Martin b 1968, Timothy b 1974), 1 da (Ailsa b 1976); *Career* temp lectr Univ of Sheffield 1973-74 (jr res fell 1971-73); Univ of Lancaster: lectr 1974-88, sr lectr 1988-, head of mathematics 1989-; res assoc Univ of California Berkeley 1978-79, various papers on algebra and mathematical educn; ed: Proceedings of Undergraduate Mathematics Teaching Conf Univ of Nottingham, Macmillan Guides Series in Mathematics; memb London Mathematical Soc 1972; *Books* Guide to Linear Algebra (1988); *Recreations* singing, opera, theatre, reading, sport; *Style—* Dr David Towers; Department of Mathematics, Lancaster University, Lancaster LA1 4YF (☎ 0524 65201 ext 3944, fax 0524 841710, telex 65111 LANCUL G)

TOWERS, Jonathan Henry Nicholson; s of John Richard Hugh Towers, of Lund House, Lund House Green, Harrogate, North Yorkshire, and Gwynneth Helen Marshall, *née* Nicholson; *b* 5 April 1939; *Educ* Radley, Clare Coll Cambridge (MA); *m* 29 Sept 1979, Vanessa Catherine, da of John Francis Milward, of Barlow Woodseats Hall, Nr Chesterfield, Derbyshire; 2 s (Edward b 1982, Harry b 1988); *Career* sr ptnr Grays slrs York 1987, under sheriff Yorkshire and Hallamshire 1988; memb Law Soc 1966; *Recreations* golf, shooting, walking, reading, skiing; *Clubs* Yorkshire (York); *Style—* Jonathan Towers, Esq; Grays, Solicitors, Duncombe Place, York YO1 2DY (☎ 0904 634 771, fax 0904 610 711)

TOWERS, (William) Lennox; s of John Maxwell Towers, of Peebles, and Elizabeth Torrance Aitchison, *née* Moodie (d 1977); *b* 24 Sept 1946; *Educ* Hutchesons' Boys' GS Glasgow, Leeds GS, Univ of Exeter (LLB); *m* 23 Sept 1972, Jan Elaine, da of Frank Morrill, of Menston, W Yorks; 2 s (Alexander b 1977, Edmund b 1985), 1 da (Francesca b 1980); *Career* ptnr Booth & Co Slrs Leeds 1974- (managing ptnr 1990), chm H Foster & Co (Stearines) Ltd Group 1978-, dir M 5 Ltd 1988-89; memb Law Soc 1971; *Recreations* family pursuits; *Style—* Lennox Towers, Esq

TOWILL, Prof Denis Royston; *b* 28 April 1933; *Educ* Univ of Bristol (BSc), Univ of Birmingham (MSc, DSc); *m* 27 March 1961, Christine Ann Forrester; 2 s (Jonathan b 2 Dec 1964, Edwin b 17 May 1970), 1 da (Rachel b 22 Dec 1962); *Career* engr; dynamic analyst Br Aerospace Weston/Filton 1957-59, conslt Norris Consultants Bristol 1959-62, sr lectr RMCS Shrivenham, prof and head of dept UWIST Cardiff (reader 1966-69, prof 1970-81), prof and head of Sch of Electrical, Electronic and Systems Engrg Univ of Wales Coll of Cardiff 1988-; served on various SERC and IFAC ctees, memb exec cmmn to oversee formation of Univ of Wales Coll of Cardiff 1987-88, memb IEE Cncl, chm IEE Mgmnt and Design Bd 1990-91; MIProdE 1964, FIEE 1972, FEng 1988; distinguished overseas scientist fell of Eta Kapa Nu 1978; awarded Clerk Maxwell Laughem Thompson and McMichael Premiums by IERE; *Books* Transfer Function Techniques for Control Engineers (1970), Coefficient Plane Models for Control System (1981), Analysis and Design; *Recreations* music, sport; *Clubs* Bristol Rovers Presidents, Radyr CC (vice pres); *Style—* Prof Denis Towill; School of Electrical, Electronic, and Systems Engineering, University of Wales, College of Cardiff (☎ 0222 874422, fax 0222 874192, telex 497368)

TOWLE, Peter Frederic Harold; DSC 1945; s of Frederic Statham Towle, of Sutton Courtenay, Berks (d 1963), and Gwendolen Lucy Hippisley (d 1965); *b* 8 July 1923; *Educ* Shrewsbury, Brasenose Coll Oxford; *m* 31 March 1951, Kathleen Mary, da of William Vickers BSc, of Cranleigh, Surrey; 2 s (Simon b 1952, Nicholas b 1954), 1 da (Helen b 1956); *Career* Lt (A) RNVR, N Atlantic 1944, Indian Ocean and Pacific 1945; chm: Buttons Ltd 1962-64, Brough Nicholson and Hall Ltd 1962-64; md: AFA Minerva EMI Ltd 1968-71, International Time Recording Co Ltd 1972-75; dir: Brocks Group plc 1972-75, Securicor Ltd 1976-88, Securicor Group plc 1978-, Security Services plc 1978-, Telecom Securicor Cellular Radio Ltd 1984-, Datatrak Ltd 1986-, Serco plc 1987-; chm Securicor Ltd 1985-88, gp chief exec Securicor Group plc 1985-88, exec consultant 1988-; *Recreations* sailing, shooting; *Clubs* Royal London Yacht, Royal Solent Yacht; *Style—* Peter Towle, Esq; 80 Eccleston Square, London SW1; Sutton Park House, Sutton, Surrey (☎ 081 770 7000)

TOWLER, Peter Jeremy Hamilton; s of Stuart Hamilton-Towler, MBE, of E Skirdle, Waterrow, nr Taunton, Somerset, and Betty Irene, *née* Hardwidge; *b* 21 March 1952; *Educ* Peter Symonds Winchester, Clare Coll Cambridge (BA, MA); *m* 15 Sept 1979, Dr Martha Crellin, da of Norman Langdon-Down, of River Lodge, Dunally Park, Shepperton-on-Thames, Middx; 1 s, 1 da; *Career* called to the Bar Middle Temple 1974 (Harmsworth scholar); memb: Western Circuit 1976-, (memb Circuit and Wine Ctee 1990-), Admin Law Bar Assoc 1987-, Local Govt and Planning Bar Assoc 1988-; fndr memb and chm Ampfield Cons Tst 1988-; churchwarden 1988-; memb: Romsey Deanery Synod 1985-88; Liveryman Worshipful Co of Weavers 1982, Freeman City of London 1982; ACIArb 1984; *Recreations* cricket, tennis, skiing, conservation; *Clubs* MCC; *Style—* Peter Towler, Esq; 17 Carlton Crescent, Southampton SO9 5AL (☎ 0703 636036, fax 0703 223877)

TOWNELEY, Simon Peter Edmund Cosmo William; JP (Lancs 1956); f assumed surname of Worsthorne by deed poll in 1923, but reverted to Koch de Gooreynd in 1937; Simon (Towneley) discontinued by deed poll the name of Worsthorne, and assumed by Royal Licence of 1955 the arms of Towneley, by reason of descent from the eldest da and sr co-heiress of Col Charles Towneley of Towneley; ancestors of the Towneley family were Lay Deans of Whalley Abbey and were granted lands near Burnley by Roger de Lacy, Earl of Lincoln, c 1200; s of Alexander Koch de Gooreynd, OBE, late Irish Gds (s of Manuela, da of Alexandre de Laski, and Joaquima, Marquessa de Souza Lisboa, herself da of José Marques Lisboa, sometime min Plenipotentiary of Emperor of Brazil to Court of St James), and Priscilla, now Baroness Norman, *qv*; er bro of Peregrine Worsthorne; *b* 14 Dec 1921; *Educ* Stowe, Worcester Coll Oxford (MA, DPhil); *m* 30 June 1955, Mary, 2 da of Cuthbert Fitzherbert (d 1987); 1 s (Peregrine b 1962), 6 da (Alice b 1956, Charlotte b 1957, Katharine b 1958, Victoria b 1964, Cosima b 1967, Frances b 1969); *Career* served KRRC Italy 1941-46; lectr in history of music Worcester Coll Oxford 1949-55; cncllr Lancs 1961-66, High Sheriff Lancs 1971-72, HM Lord-Lt and Custos Rotulorum Lancs 1976-, Hon Col Duke of Lancaster's Own Yeomanry 1979-88; non exec dir Granada TV 1981-, live pres Northern Ballet Theatre; memb Ct and Cncl: Univ of Manchester, Royal Northern Coll of Music; memb Cncl Duchy of Lancaster 1986-, tstee Br Museum 1988-; KStJ 1976, KCSG (Papal decoration); *Books* Venetian Opera in the Seventeenth Century; *Clubs* Beefsteak, Pratt's, Boodle's; *Style—* Simon Towneley, Esq, JP; Dyneley, Burnley, Lancs (☎ 0282 23322)

TOWNELEY STRACHEY, Hon Richard; s of Hon (Thomas) Anthony Edward Towneley Strachey (d 1955), by his w (now Lady Mary Gore, *qv*); hp of bro 4 Baron O'Hagan; *b* 29 Dec 1950; *Educ* Eton; *m* 1983, Sally Anne, yr da of Frederick Cecil Cross, of Upcompton, Compton Bishop, Somerset; *Style—* Hon Richard Towneley Strachey; 23 Thomas St, Bath

TOWNEND, James Barrie Stanley; QC (1978); s of Frederick Stanley Townend (d 1967), of Deal, Kent, and Marjorie Elizabeth, *née* Arnold; *b* 21 Feb 1938; *Educ* Tonbridge, Lincoln Coll Oxford (MA); *m* 20 June 1970, Airelle Claire, da of Hermann Dail Nies, of Wimbledon; 1 step da (Pascale Jéhanne Lucie Sallée-Townend); *Career* Nat Serv in BAOR and UK 1955-57, Lt RA; called to the Bar Middle Temple 1962, rec Crown Court 1979-; memb: Kingston and Esher DHA 1983-86, Senate of the Inns of Court and Bar 1984-86, Gen Cncl of the Bar 1984-88; chm: Family Law Bar Assoc 1986-88, Supreme Ct Procedure Ctee; bencher Middle Temple 1987; fell Int Acad of Matrimonial Lawyers; *Recreations* fishing, sailing, writing verse; *Clubs* Bar Yacht; *Style—* James Barrie Stanley Townend, QC; 1 King's Bench Walk, Temple, London EC4Y 7DB (☎ 071 583 6266)

TOWNEND, John Coupe; s of Harry Norman Townend (d 1988), of Sherborne, Dorset, and Joyce Dentith, *née* Coupe; *b* 24 Aug 1947; *Educ* Liverpool Inst, LSE (BSc Econ, MSc); *m* 15 March 1969, Dorothy, da of David William Allister (d 1971); 3 s (Andrew, Jonathan, Christopher); *Career* Bank of Eng 1968- (head of Wholesale Mkts Supervision Div 1986-90, head Gilt-Edged and Money Mkts Div 1990-); contrib articles to various economic jls; *Recreations* running, fell walking, opera, birds; *Style—* John Townend, Esq; Bank of England, Threadneedle St, London EC2R 8AH

TOWNEND, John Ernest; MP (C) Bridlington 1979-; s of Charles Hope, and Dorothy Townend; *b* 12 June 1934; *Educ* Hymers Coll Hull; *m* 1963, Jennifer Ann; 2 s, 2 da; *Career* CA 1951-56, divnl chm Haltemprice and Beverley Young Conservatives 1952-54; RAF 1957-59, govr Hymers Coll, chm J Townend & Sons (Hull) Ltd 1977- (dir and sec 1959-67, md 1967-77), memb Hull CC 1966-74, chm Humber Bridge Bd 1969-71, Parly candidate (C) Kingston upon Hull North 1970, ldr Humberside CC (memb and Cons ldr of oppn 1973-77) 1977-79, PPS to Hugh Rossi Min of State for the Disabled 1981-1983; dir: Merchant Vintners Ltd, AAH Holdings PLC, Surrey Building Society (vice chm); vice chm Backbench Fin Ctee 1983-, chm Cons Small Business Ctee 1987-; memb Treasy and Civil Service Select Ctee; memb Lloyds; FCA; *Clubs* Carlton; *Style—* John Townend Esq, MP; Sigglesthorne Hall, Sigglesthorne, Hull, N Humberside

TOWNEND, Hon Mrs; (Katharine Patricia); *née* Smith; da of 3 Viscount Hambleden and Lady Patricia Herbert, da of 15 Earl of Pembroke; *b* 1933; *m* 1, 1961, Ivan Moffat; 2 s; m 2, 1973, Peter Robert Gascoigne Townend; *Style*— The Hon Mrs Townend; 122 Hurlingham Rd, London SW6 (☎ 071 736 1530)

TOWNING HILL, Richard; s of Rupert Albert Hill (d 1972), and Henrietta Towning (d 1974); *b* 5 Feb 1922; *Educ* Wells Cathedral Sch, Wells Blue Sch, Univ of Birmingham, Arch Assoc London; *m* 1956 (m dis 1980), Claude Diane, da of Dr Pierre-Alfred Chappuis (d 1960), of Switzerland; 1 s (Alexander b 1960), 1 da (Josephine b 1957); *Career* Capt RE 14 Army England, India, Assam and Burma 1940-45; architect; work incl: devpt of St James Barton Bristol with Sun Life Court, Malborough House, Avon House North, Barton House, York House, redevpt Welbeck House Brunswick Square (in conjunction with Eng Heritage); public and private housing with design winning awards at: Pitch and Pay Park Bristol, Colemans Farm Calne Wilts; works illustrated in: RIBA Jl, Architects Jl, The Times, Daily Telegraph; ARIBA 1949, FRIBA 1957; *Recreations* travel, writing, photography, swimming; *Clubs* MCC; *Style*— Richard Towning Hill, Esq; 7 Clifton Wood Court, Clifton Wood Road, Bristol BS8 4UL

TOWNS, Robin Peter; s of Harold George Towns, and Mildred, *née* Evans; *b* 3 Nov 1943; *Educ* Ilford Co HS, UCL (LLB); *m* 10 Aug 1968, (Isabel) Susan, da of Albert Partington (d 1966), of Bolton, Lancs; 3 da (Emma b 1971, Sarah b 1973, Rebecca b 1976); *Career* admitted slr 1968, memb Legal Section Private Banking and Fin Servs Div Lloyds Bank plc (sr legal advsr 1980-); govr: Harlands Primary Sch Haywards Heath 1988- (chm 1989), Haywards Heath Sixth Form Coll 1988-; chm Friends of Haywards Heath Coll 1988-90; *Recreations* listening to music, collecting Vanity Fair prints; *Style*— Robin P Towns, Esq; Llechwedd, 65 Lincoln Wood, Haywards Heath, W Sussex RH16 1LJ (☎ 0444 412 393); Capital House, 1/5 Perrymount Rd, Haywards Heath, W Sussex RH16 3SP

TOWNSEND, Andy David; s of Donald Edward Townsend, and Thelma, *née* Leaver; *b* 23 July 1963; *Educ* Upton Co Primary Sch, Bexleyheath Secdy Sch; *m* Jacqueline Sheila, da of Norman Evans; 1 s (Daniel Andrew b 19 June 1986), 1 da (Kelly Louise b 10 July 1989); *Career* professional footballer; debut Southampton v Aston Villa 1985, 101 appearances Southampton 1985-88, 85 appearances Norwich City 1988-90, transferred for £1,200,000 to Chelsea 1990-; Republic of Ireland: 22 full caps, 2 goals, played in World Cup Italy 1990 (scored penalty v Romania); transferred from Welling Utd to Weymouth for record non-league fee at time (£13,500); *Recreations* snooker, golf, playing guitar; *Style*— Andy Townsend, Esq; Chelsea FC, Stamford Bridge, London SW6 1HS (☎ 071 385 5545)

TOWNSEND, (John) Anthony Victor; s of John Richard Christopher Townsend, of Eaton Place, London, and Carla Hillerns, *née* Lehmann (d 1990); *b* 24 Jan 1948; *Educ* Harrow, Selwyn Coll Cambridge (MA); *m* 16 April 1971, Carolyn Ann, da of Sir Walter Salomon (d 1987); 1 s (Christopher b 26 Feb 1974), 1 da (Alexandra b 26 Feb 1976); *Career* Brown Shipley & Co Ltd bankers 1969-74; Rea Brothers Ltd bankers 1974-78; John Townsend & Co (Holdings) Ltd 1979-87; Finsbury Asset Management Ltd (investment banking) 1988-; dir: Rea Brothers Group plc (dep chm), Blue Ridge Real Estate Co (USA), Immuno International A G (Switzerland); memb Lloyd's 1972-; govr Cranleigh Sch 1989-; tstee Harrow Club 1989-, memb Ct Worshipful Co of Pattenmakers 1988-; *Recreations* tennis, shooting, skiing; *Clubs* Gresham, RAC, Doubles (New York); *Style*— Anthony Townsend, Esq; The Coach House, Winterfold, Barhatch Lane, Cranleigh, Surrey GU6 7NH (☎ 0483 271366); Finsbury Asset Management Ltd, Neptune House, Triton Court, 14 Finsbury Square, London EC2A 1BR (☎ 071 256 8873, fax 071 638 0541, telex 8958024)

TOWNSEND, Bruce Arnold; s of James Townsend (d 1978), of Rugby, and Hilda Norah, *née* Parker; *b* 25 July 1929; *Educ* Rugby, UCL (BSc); *m* 7 July 1956, Gillian Rosina, da of Norman Powell; 2 s (Matthew Gavin Bruce b 27 Sept 1958, Adam Robert James b 4 July 1962), 1 da (Hannah Gillian Ruth b 23 March, 1966); *Career* Lt Royal Warwicks Regt 1949-54 (seconded to 3 Battalion Nigeria Regt Royal W African Frontier Force 1949-51); Chemical Engrg Dept Courtaulds Coventry 1954-69 (head of dept 1967-69), chm Accrington Brick and Tile 1969-76, md Ashton Brothers Hyde 1969-75, chm Talbot Weaving Chorley 1972-76, md Robert Usher Drogheda 1975-76, chm Processing Div Courtaulds Nuneaton 1976-79, chief exec Courtaulds Research Coventry 1986- (gen mangr 1980-86); dir: Biwater Desalination 1983-87, Usutu Pulp Co Ltd Swaziland 1985-90, SAICCOR Natal SA 1987-89; Queen's award for technol 1989; FIChemE 1968 (memb Cncl 1982-85), FEng 1984 (memb Cncl 1987-90); *Recreations* art, history, wine-making, cycling; *Style*— Bruce Townsend, Esq; Long Lea, Castle Lane, Woolscott, Rugby, Coventry CV23 8DE (☎ 0788 810348); Courtaulds Research, PO Box 111, 101 Lockhurst Lane, Warwicks CV6 5RS (☎ 0203 688771, fax 0203 680623)

TOWNSEND, Bryan Sydney; s of Sydney Townsend, of Derbyshire, and Gladys Clara, *née* Russel; *b* 2 April 1930; *Educ* Wolverton Tech Coll; *m* Betty Eileen; 1 s (Nicholas), 2 da (Lynn Jane (Mrs Punter), Sally (Mrs Carmichael)); *Career* Royal Marines 1950-52; Southern Electricity: dist engr 1964-66, dist mangr 1966-68, area engr 1968-70, asst chief engr plant and design 1970-73; dep chief engr S E Electricity 1973-76, chief engr S Wales Electricity 1976-78, dep chm SW Electricity 1978-1986, chm Midlands Electricity plc 1986-; memb Cncl: West Midlands Region CBI, Birmingham C of C & Indust; FIEE; *Recreations* golf; *Clubs* Labrook Park Golf; *Style*— Bryan Townsend, Esq; Midlands Electricity plc, Mucklow Hill, Halesowen, W Midlands B62 8BP (☎ 021 423 2345, fax 021 422 2777, telex 338092, car 0831 296269)

TOWNSEND, Charles Peter; s of Major Sam Fletcher Townsend, MC, of Lowick Bridge, Cumbria, and Katherine Mary, *née* Reynolds; *b* 19 Nov 1949; *Educ* Ampleforth, Univ of Manchester (BSc); *m* 7 Oct 1972, Barbara Anne, da of Robert William Bowes (d 1983); 1 s (Hugo b 1979), 2 da (Sophy b 1976, Emma b 1982); *Career* BOC Ltd 1971-81, chm and md Townsend Croquet Ltd 1981; The Croquet Assoc: cncl memb 1986, chm publicity ctee 1989-; ed Croquet News 1989-; *Books* Five Simple Business Games (1977), Townsend's Croquet Almanack (with John Walters, 1988-90); *Recreations* croquet, performing magic tricks; *Clubs* Croquet Assoc, Harwich Town Sailing; *Style*— Charles Townsend, Esq; 30 West St, Harwich, Essex CO12 3DD (☎ 0255 553 408); Townsend Croquet Ltd, Claire Rd, Kirby Cross, Frinton-on-Sea, Essex CO13 0LX (☎ 0255 674 404, fax 0255 850977)

TOWNSEND, Cyril David; MP (C) Bexleyheath 1974-; s of Lt-Col Cyril Moseley Townsend, and Lois, *née* Henderson; *b* 21 Dec 1937, Woking; *Educ* Bradfield, RMA Sandhurst; *m* 1976, Anita Sarah Weldon, da of late Lt-Col F G W Walshe, MC; 2 s (Hugh, John); *Career* cmmnd Durham LI 1958; served: Berlin, UK, Cyprus, Borneo; Adj DLI 1966-68, ADC to Govr and C-in-C Hong Kong (Sir David Trench GCMG, MC) 1964-66; PA to Lord Plummer and the Rt Hon Edward Heath 1968-1970, CRD 1970-74; memb Select Ctees on: Violence in the Family 1975, Foreign Affrs 1982-83, Armed Forces Bill (chm) 1981-; PPS to Min of State DHSS (Rt Hon Reg Prentice) 1979, sponsor of Protection of Children Act 1978; vice chm: Cons Parly Def Ctee (jt sec 1982-85), Friends of Cyprus 1980-; chm All Pty Freedom for Rudolf Hess Campaign, jt chm Cncl for Advancement of Arab-Br Understanding 1982-; chm: British-Cyprus CPA Gp 1983-, and co fndr S Atlantic Cncl 1983-, the Bow Gp Standing Ctee on Foreign Affairs 1977-84; vice chm Hansard Soc 1988-, memb SE London Industl Consultative Gp 1975-83, vice chm of Cons ME Cncl 1988-; fell of Ind and Parly Tst, Br Parly Observer at presidential election in Lebanon 1982, ldr Parly delgn to Iran (first since revolution) 1988; *Publications* Helping Others To Help Themselves: Voluntary Action In The Eighties (1981); contribs to Contemporary Review, political jls and a Middle East newspaper; *Style*— Cyril Townsend, Esq, MP; House of Commons, London SW1

TOWNSEND, Brig Ian Glen; s of Kenneth Townsend, of Leamington Spa, Warwickshire, and Irene Dorothy, *née* Singleton; *b* 7 Feb 1941; *Educ* Dulwich, RMA Sandhurst, Staff Coll; *m* 1, 19 Sept 1964 (m dis 1988), Loraine Jean, da of William A H Birnie (d 1978), of USA; 2 da (Lucie b 1966, Helen (twin) b 1966); m 2, 17 Feb 1989, Susan Natalie, da of Cdr Frank AL Heron-Watson, of Dalbeattie, Scotland; 2 step s (Anthony b 1965, Ben b 1969); *Career* regtl and staff appts in UK, Germany, NI, Belgium 1961-81 incl: mil asst to UK, mil rep NATO HQ 1979-81, CO 27 Field Regt RA 1981-83, Col operational requirements MOD 1983-86, Cdr artillery 1 Armoured Div 1986-88, asst chief of staff trg HQ UKLF 1988-; FBIM 1988; *Recreations* skiing, golf, painting, music; *Clubs* Army and Navy; *Style*— Brig Ian Townsend; Headquarters, United Kingdom Land Forces, Wilton, Salisbury, Wilts (☎ 0722 433666)

TOWNSEND, Joan; da of Emlyn Davies (d 1971), of Shotton, North Wales, and Amelia Mary, *née* Tyrer (d 1987); *b* 7 Dec 1936; *Educ* Wigan Girls' HS, Hawarden GS, Somerville Coll Oxford (Beilby scholarship, BA, MA), Univ Coll of Swansea (MSc); *m* 23 April 1960, Prof (William) Godfrey Townsend, s of William Hughes Townsend (d 1976), of Swansea; 2 da (Frances Mary (now Mrs Walker) b 1965, Helen Louise b 1967); *Career* various sch teaching and lecturing appts incl: tutor Open Univ 1971-75, pt/t lectr Oxford Poly 1975-76, head of mathematics Sch of St Helen and St Katharine Abingdon 1976-81, headmistress Oxford HS GPDST 1981-; tstee Westminster Centre Oxford; FRSA; *Publications* paper in Quarterly Journal of Mathematics and Applied Mechanics 1965, various articles on education; *Recreations* music (singing and piano), walking, skiing, dressmaking, reading; *Style*— Mrs Joan Townsend; Silver Howe, 62 Iffley Turn, Oxford OX4 4HN (☎ 0865 715807); Oxford High School GPDST, Belbroughton Rd, Oxford OX2 6XA (☎ 0865 59888, fax 0865 52343)

TOWNSEND, Jonathan Richard Arthur; s of David Charles Humphrey Townsend, and Honor Stobart, *née* Hancock (d 1967); *b* 30 Nov 1942; *Educ* Winchester, Corpus Christi Coll Oxford (BA); *m* Sarah Elizabeth, da of Cdr Gordon Chalmers Fortin, RN, of Lavenham, Suffolk; 2 da (Honor Sarah b 2 Sept 1968, Louise Rosamond b 12 March 1971); *Career* prodn mangr DRG plc 1961-62 and 1965-68, ptnr Laing and Cruickshank 1972-73 (joined 1969), ptnr de Zoete and Bevan 1973-86, md Barclays de Zoete Securities 1986, dir in charge of business devpt Kleinwort Benson 1990-; *Recreations* cricket, tennis, shooting, bridge; *Clubs* Brooks's, MCC, Vincents; *Style*— Jonathan Townsend, Esq; Mount Farm, Thorpe Morieux, Bury St Edmunds, Suffolk; 73 Gloucester St, London SW1 (☎ 071 834 8650); Kleinwort Benson Ltd, 20 Fenchurch St, London EC3P 3DP (☎ 071 623 8000, fax 071 929 2657)

TOWNSEND, Lady Juliet Margaret; *née* Smith; LVO (1981); da of 2 Earl of Birkenhead, TD (d 1975); *b* 9 Sept 1941; *Educ* Westonbirt, Somerville Coll Oxford; *m* 1970, John Richard Townsend, s of Lt-Col Clarence Henry Southgate Townsend, OBE, MC, TD, MRCVS (d 1953); 3 da; *Career* lady-in-waiting to HRH The Princess Margaret, Countess of Snowdon 1965-71, extra lady-in-waiting 1971-; *Style*— The Lady Juliet Townsend, LVO; Newbottle Manor, Banbury, Oxon (☎ 0295 811295)

TOWNSEND, Rear Adm Sir Leslie William; KCVO (1981), CBE (1973); s of William Bligh Townsend and Ellen, *née* Alford; *b* 22 Feb 1924; *Educ* Regent's Park Sch Southampton; *m* 1947, Marjorie Bennett; 1 s, 3 da; *Career* joined RN 1942, cmmnd 1943; sec to: Vice-Chief of Naval Staff 1967-70, First Sea Lord and Chief of Naval Staff 1970-71; mil asst to: Chief Def Staff 1971-73, chm NATO Military Ctee 1974; dir Naval and WRNS Appointments 1976, Rear Adm 1979, sec Defence Services 1979-82, ret 1982; memb of Lord Chllr's Panel of Independent Inspectors 1982-; *Style*— Rear Adm Sir Leslie Townsend, KCVO, CBE; 21 Osborne View Rd, Hill Head, Fareham, Hants PO14 3JW (☎ 0329 663446)

TOWNSEND, Peter; s of Lewis William Townsend, of Canterbury, and Jessie Gertrude, *née* Ramsey; *b* 24 Aug 1919; *Educ* King's Sch Canterbury, Worcester Coll Oxford (exhibitioner); *m* 1949, Rose, *née* Yardumian (d 1990); 2 da (Sarah Moore b 1954, Catherine Ross b 1957); *Career* Friends Ambulance Unit 1940-43; exec sec Int Ctee Chinese Industl Co-ops 1942-51; journalism from Shanghai for BBC, The Spectator, National Guardian US 1949; asst ed Far East Trade (London) 1954-65, ed Studio International 1965-75, fndr and co-ed Art Monthly 1976-, fndr and ed Art Monthly Aust 1987-; fndr memb Air and Space 1967 (former chm Art Servs Grant), former chm Greater London Arts Assoc *Publications* Art Within Reach: a survey of public art (1979); *Style*— Peter Townsend, Esq; Art Monthly, 36 Great Russell St, London WC1 (☎ 071 580 4168, fax 071 240 5958); Art Monthly Australia, Art Centre, Arts Centre, Australian National University, Canberra (☎ 06 248 0321)

TOWNSEND, Prof Peter Brereton; s of Flt Lt Philip Brereton Townsend, of Knaresborough, N Yorks, and Alice Mary, *née* Southcote; *b* 6 April 1928; *Educ* Univ Coll Sch, St John's Coll Cambridge (BA), Free Univ Berlin; *m* 1, 18 June 1949 (m dis 1974), Ruth, *née* Pearce; 4 s (Matthew b 1952, Adam b 1953, Christian b 1957, Benjamin b 1962); m 2, 14 June 1976 (m dis 1980), Joy, *née* Skegg; 1 da (Lucy b 1976); m 3, 4 Jan 1985, Jean Ann Corston, da of Laurie Parkin, of Yeovil; *Career* RASC and RAEC 1946-48; res sec Political and Econ Planning 1952-54, res offr Inst of Community Studies Bethnal Green 1954-57, res fell (later lectr) LSE 1957-63, prof of sociology Univ of Essex 1963-81 (pro vice-chllr 1975-78), prof of social policy Univ of Bristol 1982-, Michael Harrington prof of sociology (International Poverty) City Univ of NY 1991-2; chm Child Poverty Action Gp 1969-89 (pres 1989-), chm Disability Alliance 1974-; former pres Psychiatric Rehabilition Assoc 1967-85, pres Mencap SW region 1990-; pt/t govr advsr and conslt; memb: exec ctee Fabian Soc 1958-89 (chm 1965-66, vice-pres 1989-), chief scientists' ctee DHSS 1976-79, res Working Gp on Inequalities in Health 1977-80, Br Sociological Assoc 1961-90, Social Policy Assoc 1978-90; Hon DUniv Essex 1990; *Books* incl: Cambridge Anthology (ed 1952), The Family Life of Old People (1957), The Last Refuge: A Survey of Residential Institutions and Homes for the Aged in England and Wales (1962), The Poor and Poorest (with Brian Abel-Smith, 1965), The Aged in the Welfare State (with Dorothy Wedderburn, 1965), Old People in Three Industrial Societies (with Ethel Shanas and others, 1968), The Concept of Poverty (ed, 1970), The Social Minority (1973), Disability Rights Handbook (jtly, 1973 and 1976-84), Sociology and Social Policy (1975), Poverty in the United Kingdom (1979), Inequalities in Health (with Sir Douglas Black and others, 1980), Disability in Britain (with Alan Walker, 1982), Responses to Poverty: Lessons from Europe (with Roger Lawson and Robert Walker, 1984), Health and Deprivation: Inequality and the North (with Peter Phillimore and Alastair Beattie 1987), Poverty and Labour in London (with Paul Corrigan and Ute Kowarzik, 1987); *Recreations* athletics, gardening; *Style*— Prof Peter Townsend; Department of Social Policy and Social Planning, University of Bristol, 40 Berkeley Square, Bristol BS8 1HY (☎ 0272 297403)

TOWNSEND, Sue; *Career* author and playwright; joined Writers Group Phoenix Arts Centre 1978 (winner Thames Television Bursary as writer in residence for

Womberang); *Plays* Womberang (Soho Poly) 1979, The Ghost of Daniel Lambert (Phoenix Arts Centre and Leicester Haymarket Theatre) 1981, Dayroom (Croydon Warehouse Theatre) 1981, Captain Christmas and the Evil Adults (Phoenix Arts Centre) 1982, Bazaar and Rummage (Royal Court Theatre Upstairs) 1982, Groping for Words (Croydon Warehouse Theatre) 1983, The Great Celestial Cow (Royal Court Theatre and tour) 1984, Ten Tiny Fingers, Nine Tiny Toes (Library Theatre, Manchester) 1989, Ear Nose and Throat (Arts Theatre Cambridge) 1988, Disneyland it Ain't (Royal Court Theatre Upstairs) 1989; *Books* The Secret Diary of Adrian Mole aged 13 3/4, The Growing Pains of Adrian Mole, The True Confessions of Adrian Albert Mole Margaret Hilda Roberts and Susan Lilian Townsend (1989), Rebuilding Coventry (1988), The Secret Diary of Adrian Mole aged 13 3/4 - The Play, Bazaar and Rummage, Groping for Words, Womberang: Three Plays by Sue Townsend, Great Celestial Cow (1984), Mr Bevan's Dream; tv works incl: contrib Revolting Women (BBC) 1981, Bazaar and Rummage (BBC) 1983, The Secret Diary of Adrian Mole (Thames TV) 1985, The Growing Pains of Adrian Mole (Thames TV) 1987, The Refuge (Channel 4) 1987; Best Selling Author of the Decade; *Style—* Ms Sue Townsend; Anthony Sheil Associates Ltd, 43 Doughty Street, London WC1N 2LF

TOWNSEND-ROSE, Lady Katherine Patricia; 3 da of 6 Earl of Erne; *b* 4 Nov 1962; *m* 16 Sept 1989, Jonathan C Townsend-Rose, s of Colin Townsend-Rose, of Midlem, by Selkirk; *Style—* The Lady Katherine Townsend-Rose

TOWNSHEND, Prof Alan; s of Stanley Charles Townshend, of 77 Pontamman Rd, Ammanford, Dyfed, and Betsy, *née* Roberts; *b* 20 June 1939; *Educ* Pontadawe GS, Univ of Birmingham (BSc, PhD, DSc); *m* 11 Aug 1962, Enid, da of Harold Horton (d 1990), of 1 Prospect Cottages, S Kirkby, Pontefract, W Yorks; 3 s (Robert Michael b 1966, Peter Charles b 1967, Gareth Richard b 1970); *Career* lectr in chemistry Univ of Birmingham 1964-80, dean of Sch of Chemistry Univ of Hull 1989- (sr lectr then reader in analytical chemistry 1980-84, prof 1984); Royal Soc of Chemistry Silver medal 1975 (Gold medal 1991), AnalaR gold medal 1987, Theophilus Redwood lectr 1988; memb Analytical Div Ctee Int Union of Pure and Applied Chemistry; CChem, FRSC 1978; *Books* Inorganic Reaction Chemistry: Systematic Chemical Separation (1980), Inorganic Reaction Chemistry: Reactions of the Elements and their Compounds Part A: Alkali Metals to Nitrogen (1981), Inorganic Reaction Chemistry: Reactions of the Elements and their Compounds Part B: Osmium to Zirconium (1981); *Recreations* walking, food and wine; *Clubs* Savage; *Style—* Prof Alan Townshend; School of Chemistry, Univ of Hull, Hull HU6 7RX North Humberside (☎ 0482 465027, fax 0482 46610)

TOWNSHEND, Lady Carolyn Elizabeth Ann; has resumed surname Townshend; da of 7 Marquess Townshend; *b* 27 Sept 1940; *Educ* Univ of Florence Italy; *m* 13 Oct 1962 (m dis 1971), Antonio Capellini; 1 s (Vincenzo Charles Townshend); *Career* International Promotions & PR; md Carolyn Townshend & Associates; FRSA; *Recreations* classical music, painting, skiing; *Clubs* Arts; *Style—* The Lady Carolyn Townshend

TOWNSHEND, 7 Marquess (GB 1787); Sir George John Patrick Dominic Townshend; 11 Bt (E 1617); also Baron Townshend of Lynn Regis (E 1661) and Viscount Townshend of Raynham (E 1682); s of 6 Marquess (d 1921) whose forebear, 1 Marquess and Field Marshal commanded the field of Quebec after the death of Gen Wolfe; *b* 13 May 1916; *Educ* Harrow; *m* 1, 1939 (m dis 1960; she m 1960, Brig Sir James Gault, KCMG, MVO, OBE), Elizabeth Pamela Audrey, da of Maj Thomas Luby, late judicial cmmr ICS; 1 s, 2 da; m 2, 1960, Ann Frances (d 1988), da of late Arthur Pellew Darlow; 1 s, 1 da; *Heir* s, Viscount Raynham; *Career* Norfolk Yeomanry 1936-40, Scots Gds 1940-45; chm: Anglia TV Ltd 1958-86, Anglia TV Gp plc 1976-86, Survival Anglia Ltd 1971-86, AP Bank Ltd 1975-, Raynham Farm Co Ltd 1957-, Norfolk Agric Station 1973-87; dir: Norwich Union Life Insur Soc Ltd 1950-86 (vice chm 1973-86), Norwich Union Fire Insur Soc Ltd 1950-86 (vice chm 1975-86), Riggs National Corporation 1987-89; DL Norfolk 1951-61; DCL 1989, FRSA 1990; *Clubs* White's, MCC, Norfolk, Pilgrim's; *Style—* The Most Hon the Marquess Townshend; Raynham Hall, Fakenham, Norfolk (☎ 0328 862133)

TOWNSHEND, Lord John Patrick; s of 7 Marquess Townshend; *b* 1962; *Educ* Eton, London Univ; *m* 12 Sept 1987, Rachel Lucy, da of Lt-Gen Sir John Chapple, KBE; *Career* advertising copywriter; *Recreations* advertising, drumming, Norfolk; *Style—* The Lord John Townshend

TOWNSHEND, Timothy John Hume; s of Canon Horace Lyle Hume Townshend, of The Close, Norwich, Norfolk, and Lorna Ethel, *née* Lutton; *b* 20 May 1949; *Educ* Ipswich Sch, Pembroke Coll Cambridge (BA, MA); *Career* called to the Bar Lincoln's Inn 1972, practises SE circuit; memb Ctee Broadland Housing Assoc; *Recreations* sailing, skiing, gardening; *Clubs* Norfolk, (Norwich); *Style—* Timothy Townshend, Esq; 24 Newmarket Rd, Norwich, Norfolk NR2 2LA (☎ 0603 661519); Octagon House, 19 Colegate, Norwich, Norfolk (☎ 0603 623186, fax 0603 760519)

TOWNSIN, Michael Farndon; s of Reginald Townsin, and Mary, *née* Tebbs; *b* 7 April 1940; *Educ* Kings Sch Peterborough; *m* 1, 17 June 1967 (m dis 1977), Denise Margaret, da of George Ellicott (d 1972), of Peterborough; 1 s (Luke William), 3 da (Tara Sophie, Talitha Lucy, Georgina Sarah); m 2, 3 Jan 1981, Christine Noelle, da of Leonard Barker (d 1969), of Perth, W Aust; *Career* exec offr DHSS 1960-64; jt md and dep chm Young & Rubicam 1980-83 (media exec 1964-74, media dir and bd dir 1974-80), chm and chief exec offr Havas Conseil Marsteller 1983-86, advertising and mktg conslt 1986-; FIPA; *Recreations* swimming, reading, films; *Clubs* Annabel's, Mark's, Harry's Bar; *Style—* Michael Townsin, Esq; 21 Denbigh Gardens, Richmond, Surrey TW10 6EN (☎ 081 948 2829, car 0836 216282)

TOWNSLEY, Barry Stephen; s of Dr William Townsley; *b* 14 Oct 1946; *Educ* Hasmonean GS; *m* 3 Nov 1975, Hon Laura Helen, da of Lord Wolfson of Marylebone (Life Peer); 1 s (Charles Philip Wolfson b 2 June 1984), 2 da (Alexandra Jane Wolfson b 3 May 1977, Georgina Kate Wolfson b 26 May 1979); *Career* W Greenwell & Co 1964-69; dir Astaire & Co 1969-76; fndr and sr ptnr Jacobson Townsley & Co 1976-; tstee Serpentine Gallery London; memb Int Stock Exchange; *Recreations* contemporary art; *Clubs* Carlton; *Style—* Barry Townsley, Esq; Jacobson Townsley & Co, 44 Worship St, London EC2A 2JT (☎ 071 377 6161, fax 071 375 1380)

TOY, Rev Canon John; s of Sidney Toy, (d 1967), of London, and Violet Mary, *née* Doudney (d 1952); *b* 25 Nov 1930; *Educ* Epsom Co GS, Hatfield Coll Durham (BA, MA), Univ of Leeds (PhD); *m* 1963, Mollie, da of Eric Tilbury (d 1987), of Ross-on-Wye; 1 s (Paul Bernard James b 1964), 1 da (Katherine Violet b 1966); *Career* priest C of E 1956, curacy in London 1955-58, travelling sec with Student Christian Movement 1958-60, chaplain and lectr Ely Theol Coll 1960-64, chaplain St Andrew's Gothenburg Sweden 1965-69, lectr, sr lectr and princ lectr in theol St John's Coll York 1969-83, canon residentiary and chllr York Min 1983-; *Publications* Cathedral Booklets; Jesus: Man for God (1988); *Recreations* music, architecture, travel; *Clubs* Yorkshire (York); *Style—* The Rev Canon John Toy; 10 Precentor's Court, York YO1 2EJ (☎ 0904 620877)

TOYE, Bryan Edward; JP; s of Herbert Graham Donovan Toye (d 1969), and Marion Alberta, *née* Montignani; *b* 17 March 1938; *Educ* Stowe; *m* 8 Oct 1982, Fiona Ann, da of Gordon Henry James Hogg, of Wellington, NZ; 2 s (Charles Edward Graham b 16 Dec 1983, Frederick b 6 Jan 1988), 1 da (Elisabeth Fiona Ann b 27 July 1985); *Career* Hon Col 55 Ordnance Co RAOC (Volunteers); joined Toye & Co 1956, dir Toye Kenning & Spencer 1962-, dir Toye & Co 1966, chm Toye and Co plc & 23 assoc subsid cos 1969-; govr: Bridewell Royal Hosp, Christs Hosp; estates and sch govr King Edward's Sch Witley; tstee: Queen Elizabeth Scholarship Tst, Britain-Australia Bicentennial Tst; steward Henley Royal Regatta 1980; alderman the Ward of Lime St 1983 (pres Lime St Ward Club), pres City Livery Club 1988-89, Master Worshipful Co of Gold & Silver Wyre Drawers 1984; memb Ct of Assts: Worshipful Co of Broderers, Guild of Freemen of the City of London; Liveryman Worshipful Co of Goldsmiths; hon memb Ct of Assts Hon Artillery Co, memb cncl Royal Warrant Holders Assoc 1982; FInstD 1966, FBIM 1983, FRSA; memb Lloyds; OStJ 1980; *Recreations* swimming, tennis, gardening, music, entertaining; *Clubs* Leander, Wig and Pen, RAC, Middx Co RFC, Wasps FC (tstee and vice pres); *Style—* Bryan Toye, Esq, JP; Toye & Co plc, 19-21 Great Queen St, London WC2B 5BE (☎ 071 242 0471, fax 071 831 8692, telex 261285)

TOYE, Col (Claude) Hugh; OBE (1962, MBE 1947); s of Rev Percy Sheffield Toye (d 1968), and Sarah, *née* Griffiths (d 1966); *b* 28 March 1917; *Educ* Kingswood Sch Bath, Queens' Coll Cambridge (BA, MA); *m* 28 April 1958, Betty, da of Lionel Hayne (d 1932), of Oulton Broad, Suffolk; 1 s, decd; *Career* enlisted Private RAMC (TA) 1938, Field Ambulance France 1940 (despatches), cmmnd RA 1941, Capt, instr Intelligence Sch Karachi 1943-44, Maj CSDIC (India) 1944-46, GSO 11 (Intelligence) HQ ALFSEA 1946-47, staff Coll Camberley 1948, 14 Fd Regt RA Hongkong 1949-51 (Adj), DAA and QMG HQ 56 Armd Div (TA) 1951-53, 115 Locating Battery RA BAOR 1954-56, GSO II Political Office MEF Cyprus 1956-58, Cmd 36 Battery RA Cyprus 1958 (UK 1959), Lt-Col Mil Attaché Vientiane 1960-62, GSO I (SD) SHAPE Paris 1962-64, Gwilym Gibbon res fell Nuffield Coll Oxford (DPhil) 1964-66, Col UK mil advsr's rep HQ SEATO Bangkok 1966-68, def advsr UK Mission to UN NY 1969-70, Dep Cdr Br Army Staff Washington 1970-72, ret 1972; reviewer of books on Indo-China 1965-75 (mostly for TLS); *Books* The Springing Tiger, a study of Subhas Chandra Bose (1959), Laos: Buffer State or Battleground (1968); *Recreations* gardening, music, history of S E Asia; *Clubs* Army and Navy; *Style—* Col Hugh Toye, OBE; 5, Farm Close Lane, Wheatley, Oxford OX9 1UG

TOYE, Prof John Francis Joseph; s of John Redmond Toye, of Sketty, Swansea, S Wales, and Adele, *née* Francis (d 1972); *b* 7 Oct 1942; *Educ* Christ's Coll Finchley, Jesus Coll Cambridge (BA, MA), Harvard, SOAS (MSc, PhD); *m* 18 March 1967, Janet, da of Richard Henry Reason, of Harrow, London; 1 s (Richard b 1973), 1 da (Eleanor b 1970); *Career* asst princ HM Treasy 1965-68, res fell SOAS London 1970-72, fell (later tutor) Wolfson Coll Cambridge 1972-80 (asst dir of devpt studies 1977-80); dir: Commodities Res Unit Ltd 1980-82, Centre for Devpt Studies Univ Coll Swansea 1982-87, Inst of Devpt Studies Univ of Sussex (professorial fell) 1987-; memb: Wandsworth Community Rels Cncl 1968-72, Cambridge Cncl of Community Rels 1972-80, W Glamorgan Equal Opportunities Gp 1983-87; *Books* Taxation and Economic Development (1978), Trade and Poor Countries (1979), Public Expenditure and Indian Development Policy (1981), Dilemmas of Development (1987), Does Aid Work in India? (1990); *Recreations* music, walking, theatre; *Style—* Prof John Toye; Institute of Development Studies, University of Sussex, Falmer, Brighton, Sussex BN1 9RE

TOYE, Wendy; da of Ernest Walter Toye and Jessie Crichton, *née* Ramsay; *b* 1 May 1917; *Educ* privately; *m* Edward Selwyn Sharp (m dis); *Career* choreographer, actress, dir and dancer; studied dancing as a child and first appeared at the Royal Albert Hall in 1921, produced a ballet at the Palladium when only ten years of age, made her first appearance on the stage at the Old Vic as Mustard Seed in a Midsummer Night's Dream 1929, Marigold in Toad of Toad Hall, choreographer Mother Earth (Savoy) 1929, numerous roles with Ninette de Valois Vic-Wells Ballet Co 1930, princ dancer in The Golden Toy, toured with Anton Dolin 1934-35; choreographed for princ dancer: Markora Dolin Co, Rambert Ballet Co; arranged the dances for George Black's prodns 1937-44 (incl Black and Blue, Black Velvet, Strike a New Note and Strike It Again), Gay Rosalinda (Palace) 1945; directed prodns of Big Ben, Bless the Bride and Tough at the Top for Sir Charles Cochran (Adelphi) 1946, played princ girl in the pantomime Simple Simon (Birmingham) 1947, sent her co Ballet-Hoode Wendy Toye to Paris for a season 1948, directed Lady at the Wheel 1958 and many more; recent prodns incl: This Thing Called Love (Ambassadors) 1984, Noel and Gertie (Princess Grace Theatre Monte Carlo) 1984, assoc prodr Barnum (Victoria Palace), tribute to Joyce Grenfell 1985; Shaw Festival Theatre Canada: Celemare, Mad Woman of Chaillot; assoc prodr Torvill & Dean Ice Show World Tour 1985, Singing In The Rain (London Palladium), dir and choreographer Kiss Me Kate (Copenhagen) and Unholy Trinity (Stephenville Festival) 1986, Laburnham Grove (Watford Palace) 1987, Miranda (Chichester Festival Theatre) 1987, Songbook (Watermill Theatre) 1988, Ziegfeld (London Palladium) 1988, Mrs Dot (Watford Palace) 1988, Family and Friends (Sadlers Wells) 1988, When That I Was (Manitoba Theatre Center) 1988, Oh (Coward Playhouse Hong Kong) 1989, Cinderella (Palace Waterford), Till We Meet Again Concert (Festival Hall) 1989, Retrospective Season of Films Directed by Wendy Toye (Festival de Films des Femmes International, Paris) 1990, Penny Black (Wavendon) 1990, Moll Flanders (Watermill Theatre) 1990, Captain Beaky's Heavens Up (Playhouse) 1990, 2 Operas (Aix en Provence Festival) 1991, The Drummer (Watermill Theatre) 1991; ENO prodns incl: Bluebeards Castle, The Telephone, Russalka, La Vie Parisienne, Orpheus In The Underworld, Italian Girl In Algiers, Fledermaus; Seraglio, The Impresario For Yehudi Menuhin's Bath Festival (with Menuhin conducting); directed films: The Stranger Left No Card (first prize Cannes Film Festival), On The Twentieth Day, Raising A Riot, We Joined The Navy, Three Cases of Murder, All For Mary, True As A Turtle, The King's Breakfast; lectured in Australia 1977, memb cncl LAMDA, original memb Accreditation Bd instigated by NCDT for Acting Courses 1981-84, served Equity Cncl as first dirs rep 1974 (dirs sub ctee 1971); memb: Grand Cncl Royal Acad of Dancing, Ctee for Wavenden All Music Scheme, Vivian Ellis Award Scheme, Richard Stillgoe Award Scheme; Queen's Silver Jubilee Medal 1977; *Recreations* embroidery, gardening; *Style—* Wendy Toye; c/o Jay Benning & Coy, Canberra House, 315 Regent St, London W1R 7YB

TOYN, His Hon Judge (Richard) John; s of Richard Thomas Millington Toyn (d 1961), of Leamington Spa, Warwicks, and Ethel, *née* Crimp (d 1981); *b* 24 Jan 1927; *Educ* Solihull Sch, Bristol GS, Univ of Bristol (LLB); *m* 20 Aug 1955, Joyce Evelyn, da of Harold Llewelyn Goodwin (d 1970), of Solihull, W Midlands; 2 s (Andrew b 1956, Richard b 1960), 2 da (Julia b 1958, Louise b 1964); *Career* RASC 1948-50; called to the Bar 1950; circuit judge; memb Parole Bd for England and Wales 1978-80; contributing ed Butterworths County Court Precedents and Pleading; *Style—* His Hon Judge Toyn; c/o Queen Elizabeth II Law Courts, Birmingham

TOYNBEE, Lawrence Leifchild; s of Arnold Joseph Toynbee (d 1975), of London, and Rosalind Mary, *née* Murray (d 1967); *b* 21 Dec 1922; *Educ* Ampleforth, New Coll Oxford, Ruskin Sch of Drawing and Fine Arts (Cert in Fine Art); *m* 20 April 1945, Jean Constance, da of Brig Gen The Hon Arthur Melland Asquith, DSO (d 1939), of Clovelly Court, Bideford, Devon; 6 da (Rosalind (Mrs Pennybacker) b 1946, Celia (Mrs Caulton) b 1948, Clare (Mrs Huxley) b 1949, Rachel (Mrs Fletcher) b 1950,

Sarah (Mrs Towler) b 1953, Frances (Mrs Wilson) b 1957); *Career* Sandhurst, WWII Lt 4 Bn Coldstream Gds 1942-44; art master St Edwards Sch Oxford 1947-62, visiting tutor Ruskin Sch of Drawing Oxford 1947-62, lectr Oxford Sch of Art 1960-63, sr lectr in painting Bradford Sch of Art 1963-67, dir fine art Morley Coll London 1967-72; one man exhibitions: Leicester Galleries 1961, 1963, 1965, 1967 and 1972 (and at Mayor Gallery), Agnews 1980, Fine Art Soc 1985 and 1989; various minor charitable works; *Clubs* MCC, IZ, FF, Vincents; *Style—* Lawrence Toynbee, Esq; Chapel Cottage, Ganthorpe, Terrington, York YO6 4QD (☎ 065 384 383)

TOYNBEE, Michael Robert; JP, DL (E Sussex 1989); s of Ralph Victor Toynbee (d 1970); *b* 26 Nov 1925; *Educ* Winchester; *m* 1953, Yvonne Norah, *née* Cleland; 1 s, 1 da; *Career* Capt Rifle Bde 1945-52, WO 1949-52; chm: Jessel Toynbee & Gillett plc 1977-84 (dir 1953-77), Alexanders Discount 1984-88; chm Sch Cncl Ardingly Coll; High Sheriff East Sussex 1985; treas Univ of Sussex 1987-; *Recreations* shooting, fishing, tennis; *Style—* Michael Toynbee, Esq, JP, DL; Westerleigh, Wadhurst, E Sussex (☎ 089 288 3238)

TOYNBEE, Polly (Mrs Peter Jenkins); da of Philip Toynbee (d 1981), and Anne Barbara Denise, *née* Powell; *b* 27 Dec 1946; *Educ* Badminton Sch, Holland Park Comprehensive, St Anne's Coll Oxford; *m* 28 Dec 1970, Peter George James Jenkins, s of Kenneth Jenkins; 3 children (Millicent b 5 Dec 1971, Flora b 17 Dec 1975, Nathaniel b 10 Jan 1985), 1 step da (Amy b 29 Oct 1964); *Career* reporter The Observer 1968-71, ed The Washington Monthly USA 1971-72, feature writer The Observer 1973-77, columnist The Guardian 1977-88, social affrs ed BBC 1988-; SDP candidate Lewisham East 1983; *Books* Leftovers (1966), A Working Life (1970), Hospital (1977), The Way We Live Now (1982), Lost Children (1985); *Recreations* children; *Style—* Ms Polly Toynbee; BBC Television, Television Centre, Wood Lane, London W12 (☎ 081 576 7487)

TOYNBEE, Simon Victor; s of Ralph Victor Toynbee (d 1970), and Bridget, *née* Monins; *b* 30 Jan 1944; *Educ* Winchester; *m* 12 Aug 1967, Antoinette Mary, da of John Walter Devonshire, of Santa Monica, California, USA; 3 da (Georgina, Elizabeth, Susannah); *Career* 2 Lt The RB 1963-65; Jessel Toynbee and Co Ltd 1966-72, Singer and Friedlander Ltd 1973 82 (dir Investmt Dept 1977-82), Henderson Administration Ltd 1982-90 (dir 1986-90), Mercury Asset Management plc 1990-; dir Mercury Private Investors Ltd, investmt dir Mercury Fund Managers Ltd; hon investmt advsr Royal Greenjackets Funds and Church Army; *Recreations* gardening, deerstalking; *Clubs* Royal Greenjackets, MCC; *Style—* S V Toynbee, Esq; Old Tong Farm, Brenchley, Kent TN12 7HT (☎ 0892 723552); 33 King William St, London EC4R 9AS (☎ 071 280 2254, fax 071 280 2827)

TOYNE, Prof Peter; DL (Merseyside 1990); s of Harold Toyne, and Lavinia Doris, *née* Smith (d 1968); *b* 3 Dec 1939; *Educ* Ripon GS, Univ of Bristol (BA); *m* 2 Aug 1969, Angela, da of Rev John Alroy Wedderburn; 1 s (Simon b 1970); *Career* Univ of Exeter: lectr in geography 1965-75, sr lectr 1975-80, sub dean of social studies 1976-79; dir Dept of Educn and Sci Educnl Credit Transfer Feasibility Study 1977-80, dep dir W Sussex Inst of HE 1980-83, dep rector N E London Poly 1983-86, rector The Liverpool Poly 1986-; vice chm Ctee Dirs of Polys, chm BBC Radio Merseyside; memb: BBC NW Advsy Cncl, Bd The Liverpool Playhouse, Ctee of Business Opportunities on Merseyside (BOOM), Merseyside Enterprise Forum, Educnl Activities Ctee Royal Liverpool Philharmonic Orchestra; chm Access Courses Recognition Gp CVCP/CNAA, memb Ctee for Int cooperation in HE Br Cncl, chm ECCTIS 2000 Advsy Ctee, Theological Coll inspr House of Bishops; *Books* World Problems (1969), Techniques in Human Geography (1971), Recreation and Environment (1974), Organisation, Location and Behaviour (1974), Toyne Report on Credit Transfer (1979), and 35 articles in various professional jls; *Recreations* music (orchestral and churchmusic), railways, gardening, travel; *Clubs* Liverpool Athenaeum; *Style—* Prof Peter Toyne, DL; The Liverpool Poly, 2 Rodney St, 70 Mount Pleasant, Liverpool L3 5UX (☎ 051 709 3676, fax 051 709 0172)

TOYNE SEWELL, Maj Gen Timothy Patrick; s of Brig Edgar Patrick Sewell, CBE (d 1956), and Elizabeth Cecily Mease, *née* Toyne, MBE; *b* 7 July 1941; *Educ* Bedford Sch, RMA Sandhurst; *m* 7 Aug 1965; 1 s (Patrick b 1967), 1 da (Melanie b 1969); *Career* cmmnd King's Own Scottish Borderers 1961; served: Aden, Malaysia, BAOR, NI; Staff Coll 1973, CO IKOSB 1981-83, COS HQ British Forces Falkland Island 1983-84, Cdr 19 Inf Bde 1985-87, RCDS 1988, Cdr BMATT Zimbabwe 1989-91, Cmdt RMA Sandhurst 1991; chm Army Tennis Rackets Assoc 1981-88; *Recreations* rackets, tennis, squash, golf, fishing; *Clubs* Army and Navy; *Style—* Maj Gen Timothy Toyne Sewell

TOYNTON, Peter A; *b* 28 Aug 1943; *m* ;4c; *Career* Binder Hamlyn & Co 1961-72; gp fin dir: Ocan Inchcape Ltd (int offshore oil services gp) 1972-87, CIA Group (advertising media specialists) 1987-90; *Recreations* musician; *Style—* Peter Toynton, Esq; IDK Media Limited, 1 Wardock Street, London W1V 3HE

TRACEY, Eric Frank; s of Allan Lewis Tracey, of Auckland, NZ, and late Marcelle Frances, *née* Petrie; *b* 3 July 1948; *Educ* Mount Albert GS Auckland NZ, Univ of Auckland (BCom, MCom); *m* 16 May 1970, Patricia, da of late G S (Bill) Gamble, of Hatch End, Middx; *Career* Inland Revenue NZ 1965, lectr Univ of Auckland 1970-72, Touche Ross & Co London 1973- (ptnr 1980-); ACA (NZ) 1970, FCA 1975, ACIS 1972; *Recreations* walking, rugby, cricket, cooking, certain roses, NZ plants; *Style—* Eric Tracey, Esq; 6 De Beauvoir Sq, De Beauvoir Town, London N1 4LG (☎ and fax 071 254 6057); Touche Ross & Co, Hill House, 1 Little New St, London EC4A 3TR (☎ 071 936 3000, fax 071 583 8517)

TRACEY, Richard Patrick; JP (1977), MP (C) Surbiton 1983-; s of P H (Dick) Tracey (d 1959), of Stratford upon Avon, and Hilda, *née* Timms; *b* 8 Feb 1943; *Educ* King Edward VI Sch Stratford upon Avon, Univ of Birmingham (LLB); *m* Katharine R, da of John Gardner (d 1969), of Ealing; 1 s, 3 da; *Career* ldr writer Daily Express 1964-66, presenter of current affrs programmes BBC Radio and TV 1966-78, documentaries BBC 1974-76, dep chm Gtr London Cons Pty 1981-83, Parly under sec of state for Environment and min for Sport 1985-87; chm: Select Ctee on Televising the House of Commons 1988-, London Cons MPs 1990-; Cons London Election Coordinator 1989-; vice chm Special Olympics UK 1989-; Freeman City of London 1984; *Books* The World of Motor Sport (with R Hudson-Evans), Hickstead - the first Twelve Years (with M Clayton); *Recreations* boating, riding, wildlife conservation; *Clubs* Wig and Pen; *Style—* Richard Tracey, Esq, JP, MP; House of Commons, London SW1A 0AA (☎ 071 219 5196)

TRACEY, Stanley William; OBE (1986); s of Stanley Clark Tracey (d 1957), and Florence Louise, *née* Guest (d 1984); *b* 30 Dec 1926; *m* 1, 1946 (m dis), Joan Lower; m 2, 1957 Jean Richards (m dis 1960); m 3, 24 Dec 1960, Florence Mary (Jackie), da of Douglas Richard Buckland (d 1970), of London; 1 s (Clark b 1961), 1 da (Sarah b 1962); *Career* served RAF 1946-48; composer of over 300 titles incl: Under Milkwood Suite 1965, Genesis and some 40 albums; resident pianist Ronnie Scotts Club London 1960-66, ptnr (with wife) Steam Record Co 1975-, toured ME 1982, S America 1980 with own quartet, pianist/leader quartet, quintet, sextet (Hexad), octet and 15 piece orchestra; hon RAM; memb RSM & JB; *Style—* Stanley Tracey, Esq, OBE; 12 Cotlandswick, London Colney, Herts, AL2 1EE (☎ 0727 23286)

TRAFFORD, Edward Willoughby; s of Maj S W Trafford (d 1953), of Wroxham Hall, Norwich, Norfolk, and Lady Elizabeth, *née* Bertie, OBE (d 1987); *b* 2 July 1924; *Educ* Harrow, Downside, RAC Cirencester; *m* 3 April 1952, June Imelda, da of Richard Harding, of Echo Valley, Springbrook, Queensland, Aust; 3 s (Michael Francis b 1953, Bernard Edward b 1955, Andrew Martin b 1960), 1 da (Amanda Gabriel Mary b 1959); *Career* served Scots Gds 1942-47; St Faith and Aylshal RDC 1966-74; Norfolk Local Valuation Panel 1967 (chm 1984, dep chm 1979); Broadland DC 1974-88 (chm 1983-86); pres Valuation and Community Charge Tribunal 1989; Knight of Honour and Devotion Sovereign Military Order of Malta; *Recreations* shooting, opera; *Clubs* Brooks's, Royal Automobile; *Style—* Edward Trafford, Esq; Broad House, Wroxham, Norwich NR12 8TS (☎ 0603 782616)

TRAFFORD, Ian Colton; OBE (1967); s of Dr Harold Trafford, of Warlingham, Surrey, and Laura Dorothy, *née* Porteous (d 1965); bro of Baron Trafford (Life Peer; d 1989); *b* 8 July 1928; *Educ* Charterhouse, St John's Coll Oxford (BA); *m* 20 July 1949 (m dis 1964), Nella, da of Petros Georgara (d 1958), of Athens, Greece; m 2, 12 Dec 1972, Jacqueline Carole, *née* Trenque; *Career* Intelligence Corps 1946-48, cmmnd 1947, Actg Capt 1948, GSO3 Br Mil Mission to Greece 1948; feature writer (subsequently features ed and industl corr); The Financial Times 1951-58, UK corr Barrons Weekly NY 1954-60, md Industl and Trade Fairs Hldgs 1966-71 (dir 1958-); dir gen Br Trade Fairs: Peking 1964, Moscow 1966, Bucharest 1968, Sao Paolo 1969, Buenos Aires 1970; md The Economist Newspaper Ltd 1971-81, chm The Economist Intelligence Unit Ltd 1971-79, local dir W London Branch Commercial Union Insur 1974-83; publisher 1981-88: The Times Educnl Supplement, The Times Higher Educnl Supplement, The Times Literary Supplement; ret 1988; *Recreations* gardening; *Style—* Ian Trafford, Esq, OBE; Grafton House, Westhall Rd, Warlingham, Surrey CR3 9HF (☎ 0883 622048)

TRAFFORD, Roger Samuel; s of Jack Trafford, of St Cleer, Liskeard, Cornwall, and Sylvia, *née* Holmwood (d 1979); *b* 12 Feb 1939; *Educ* Forest Sch London (Eng schoolboys in football and hockey), Hertford Coll Oxford (MA, Univ football team); *m* 24 July 1971, Cheryl Anne, da of Gordon Robert Ellis Norbrook, of Barnes, London; 2 s (James Richard Ellis b 11 Nov 1973, George Roger Ellis b 21 April 1976); *Career* Eng teacher The Fessenden Sch Boston Mass 1962-65, housemaster and head of Eng St Paul's Prep Sch London 1965-73; headmaster: King's Coll Prep Sch Taunton Somerset 1973-82, Clifton Coll Prep Sch Bristol 1982-; Walter Hines Page scholarship to USA 1987; vice chm ISIS South and West 1977-82, memb Cncl IAPS 1982-84, 1987-89, 1990-92 (chm 1991-92); govr: Cheam Sch, Park Sch Bath; memb: NAHT, Oxford Soc; *Books* The Heads Guide (1989); *Recreations* rackets, skiing, windsurfing, an avid supporter of rugby and yet dedicated to Manchester Utd since birth; *Style—* Roger Trafford, Esq; Matthew's, 12 The Avenue, Clifton, Bristol BS8 3HE (☎ 0272 733541); Clifton College Preparatory School, The Avenue, Clifton, Bristol (☎ 0272 737264, fax 0272 466826)

TRAHERNE, Sir Cennydd George; KG (1970), TD (1950); s of late Cdr Llewellyn Edmund Traherne, RN, and Dorothy, *née* Sinclair, gda of Sir John George Tollemache Sinclair, 3 Bt of Ulster; *b* 14 Dec 1910; *Educ* Wellington, BNC Oxford; *m* 1934, Olivera Rowena, OBE, JP (d 1986), da of James Binney (d 1935) and The Lady Marjory, *née* Brudenell-Bruce, da of 5 Marquess of Ailesbury; *Career* served WWII Capt RA & CMP Home & NW Europe (despatches); called to the Bar Inner Temple 1938, dir Cardiff Building Society 1953-85, dir Wales Gas Board 1958-71, chm Wales Gas Consultative Cncl 1958-71, pres Welsh Nat Sch & Univ of Wales Coll of Medicine 1970-87 (fell 1989), dir Commercial Bank of Wales 1972-88; HM Lt of Glamorgan 1952-74 and of Mid, S and W Glamorgan 1974-85; pres Cambrian Archaeological Assoc 1983-84; Hon Col Glamorgan Army Cadet Force 1983-85, memb Gorsedd of the Bards of Wales, hon master Bench of Inner Temple 1983; kt 1964; *Recreations* fishing, walking; *Clubs* Athenaeum, Cardiff and County; *Style—* Sir Cennydd Traherne, KG, TD; Coedarhydyglyn, nr Cardiff, CF5 6SF (☎ 0446 760321)

TRAILL, Sir Alan; GBE (1984), QSO (1990); s of George Traill, and Margaret Eleanor, *née* Matthews; *b* 7 May 1935; *Educ* St Andrew's Sch Eastbourne, Charterhouse, Jesus Coll Cambridge (MA); *m* 1964, Sarah Jane, *née* Hutt; 1 s; *Career* dir Morice Tozer & Beck 1960-63; chm: Traill Allenborough Ltd 1978-81 (founding dir 1973-76), Lyon Holdings 1981-86; dir: Lyon Jago Webb 1981-86, Lyon Traill Attenborough (Lloyds Brokers) 1981-86, PWS Holdings 1986-87, Aegis Insurance Brokers 1987-89; md Colburn Traill Ltd 1989-; memb: Lloyd's 1964-, Ct of Common Cncl City of London 1970, London Ct of Int Arbitration 1981-86; memb Cncl Br Insur Brokers Assoc 1978-79 (chm Reinsurance Brokers Ctee 1978); Alderman Langbourn Ward 1975-, Sheriff 1982-83, Lord Mayor of London 1984-85; dir City Arts Tst 1980-, almoner Christ's Hosp Fndn 1980-, govr King Edwards Sch Witley 1980-, tstee RSC 1982-, Chllr City of London Univ 1984-85 (DMus 1984); Master Worshipful Co of Cutlers 1979-80; *Recreations* shooting, skiing, DIY, travel, opera, assisting education; *Clubs* City Livery; *Style—* Sir Alan Traill, GBE, QSO; 19-21 Great Tower St, London EC3R 5AQ

TRAIN, Andrew John; s of David Walter Train, of Glen Villa, Fladbury, Worcs, and Eileen, *née* Dobbing; *b* 21 Sept 1963; *Educ* Pershore HS, Univ of Birmingham (LLB); *m* 30 July 1988, Alison Ann, da of Arthur Patrick Peters, of Walnut Way, Hyde Heath, Amersham, Bucks; 1 da (Hannah Catherine b 10 Oct 1990); *Career* pairs canoeist with brother Stephen Train: GB team Olmpic Games 1984 and 1988, Silver medal World Sprint Championships 1985, Bronze medal World Sprint Championships 1987, Gold medal World Cup Marathon 1989, World Marathon Champion 1988-89; singles canoeist: nat champion 1989; trainee slr New Saunders Smith & Roberts Solicitors (Evesham); memb Nat Olympic Trg Squad; *Recreations* canoe coaching, swimming, family; *Clubs* Fladbury Canoe and Kayak; *Style—* Andrew Train, Esq; 1 Fern Cottages, Butchers Walk, Fladbury, Pershore, Worcs WR10 2PY

TRAIN, Christopher John; CB (1986); s of Keith Sydney Sayer Train (d 1985), and Edna Ashby, *née* Ellis; *b* 12 March 1932; *Educ* Nottingham HS, ChCh Oxford (BA, MA); *m* 24 Aug 1957, Sheila Mary, da of Wilfred Watson (d 1950); 1 s (Nicholas b 1959), 1 da (Helen (Mrs McCartney) b 1961); *Career* Sub Lt RNVR 1955-57; asst master St Paul's Sch 1957-67; Home Office 1968-: sec Royal Cmmn on Criminal Procedure 1978-80, princ fin offr 1981-83, dir gen of Prison Serv of England and Wales 1983-; *Recreations* jogging, cooking, cricket; *Clubs* Vincent's (Oxford), Reform; *Style—* Christopher Train, Esq, CB; Home Office, Queen Anne's Gate, London SW1 (☎ 071 273 3000)

TRAIN, Stephen David; s of David Walter Train, and Eillen, *née* Dobbing; *b* 23 Feb 1962; *Educ* Pershore High Sch; *m* 8 April 1985, Lisa Jean, da of Albert William Beeby (1983); 1 s (James b 5 May 1986); *Career* singles canoeist: 6 place 1000m CI and 9 place 1000m C2 Olympic finals 1984; pairs canoeist with brother Andrew Train: World Silver medal C2 10000m 1985, World Bronze medal C2 10000m 1987, Olympic semifinalist 1988, World Champion Gold medal C2 marathon 1989; *Clubs* Fladbury Canoe and Kayak; *Style—* Stephen Train, Esq; Train for Canoeing Ltd, c/o T L Elliott, Univ 5C, Ashcurch Business Centre, Tewkesbury, Glos (☎ 0684 298418)

TRANCHELL, Christopher Peter John (Chris); s of Allan George Small, of 1 Redhill, Bassett, Southampton, and Irene Rose Kathleen, *née* Trowbridge; *b* 13 April 1941; *Educ* Portswood Rd Secdy Modern, Southampton Tech Coll, Bristol Old Vic Theatre Sch; *m* 1 s (Benedick George b 21 March 1969), 2 da (Sophi b 22 Aug 1964,

Imogen Lucy b 24 Aug 1967); *Career* actor; fndr memb Margate Stage Company 1962; theatre work: Romeo in Romeo and Juliet (Lincoln), Sergius in Arms and the Man (Margate) Biff in Death of a Salesman (Worcester), Frank in Forget-me-not Lane by Peter Nichols (Worcester), Nathan in Guys and Dolls by Frank Loesser (Worcester), Aydak in Caucasian Chalk Circle by Brecht (Orange Tree), Shamrock Wombs in All Walks of Leg by John Lennon, Friar Lawrence in Romeo and Juliet, The Real Inspector Hound by Tom Stoppard (Young Vic), Ken in Whose Life is it Anyway (Salisbury), Houst in Bent (for Theatre Clwyd), Not Just a War (Lyric Studio Hammersmith), Ten Years of Freedom 1989, Merlin in Morte D'Arthur by David Freeman 1990; BBC TV: Dr Who, Play School, The Survivors, The Bill; films: Oh What a Lovely War! The Battle of Britain, The Hiding Place; memb Bd of DITS Lyric Theatre Hammersmith 1983-89 (currently hon patron), fndr memb Arts for Labour 1981; *Recreations* singing, sailing, travel in Europe, the USSR, the USA & South America; *Clubs* West London Trades, Actor Centre; *Style*— Chris Tranchell, Esq; 52 Dewhurst Road, Hammersmith, London W14 OES (☎ 071 603 6493); Clare Fox Associates Limited, 9 Plymouth Rd, London NW6 7EH (☎ 071 372 2301)

TRANGMAR, Donald George; s of George Edward Trangmar (d 1975), of Barrow-in-Furness, and Mabel Winifred, *née* Rose; *b* 16 Nov 1939; *Educ* Barrow-in-Furness GS; *m* 1, 1968 (m dis 1986), Norma, *née* Denison; 1 da (Natalie Jane b 26 Dec 1981); m 2, 14 Oct 1988, Christabelle, *née* Mitchell; *Career* joined Marks and Spencer 1965 (dir 1983-); *Recreations* cricket; *Style*— Donald Trangmar, Esq; Marks and Spencer plc, Michael House, 57 Baker St, London W1A 1DN (☎ 071 935 4422)

TRANMIRE, Baron (Life Peer UK 1974), of Upsall, Co N Yorkshire; Robin (Robert) Hugh Turton; KBE (1971), MC (1942), PC (1955), JP (N Riding Yorks 1936), DL (1962); 2 s of late Maj Robert Bell Turton, JP, DL, of Kildale Hall, Yorks, Lord of the Manor and Patron of the Living of Kildale (himself 2 s of Edmund Turton, JP, DL, by his w Lady Cecilia Leeson, yr da of 4 Earl of Milltown, KP; Following the death without issue of Lady Cecilia's 3 er bros, 5, 6 and 7 Earls (latter d 1891) the dignity has been dormant); Maj Robert Turton m Marion Edith, da of Lt-Col Godfrey Beaumont by Anne Maria (da of Sir Edmund Blackett, 6 Bt); *b* 8 Aug 1903; *Educ* Eton, Balliol Coll Oxford (BA); *m* 1928, Ruby Christian, da of late Robert Thomas Scott, of Beechmont, Sevenoaks, Kent; 3 s (Hon Michael Andrew b 1929, Hon Timothy Robert Scott b 1934 d 1989, Hon Gerald Christopher b 1937), 1 da (Hon Gillian Hermione Christian (Hon Mrs Wells) b 1930); *Career* served WWII Lt-Col Green Howards; called to the Bar Inner Temple 1926; MP (C) Thirsk and Malton 1929-74, Parly sec Miny of Nat Insur 1951-53, Min of Pensions and Nat Insur 1953-54, jt parly under-sec state for Foreign Affrs 1954-55, Min Health 1955-57; *Style*— The Rt Hon the Lord Tranmire, KBE, MC, PC, JP, DL; Upsall Castle, Thirsk, N Yorks YO7 2QJ (☎ 0845 537202); 15 Grey Coat Gardens, London SW1P 2QA (☎ 071 834 1535)

TRANT, Patrick Murray; s of Philip Trant (d 1984), and Jane, *née* Wackley; *b* 31 Jan 1953; *Educ* St Marys Coll Southampton, Prestentation Coll Reading; *Career* co chm Trant Gp of Cos; *Recreations* horse racing, tennis, golf, greyhound breeding; *Clubs* Turf; *Style*— Patrick Trant, Esq; Stoneham Park Hse, Stoneham, Eastleigh, Hants SO5 3HT (☎ 0703 768 955)

TRANT, Gen Sir Richard Brooking; KCB (1982, CB 1979); s of Richard Brooking Trant, and Dora Rodney, *née* Lancaster; *b* 28 March 1928; *m* 1957, Diana, da of Rev Stephen Zachary Edwards; 1 s (Richard b 1967), 2 da (Diana b 1962, Sarah b 1965); *Career* cmmnd RA 1947, Def Servs Staff Coll India 1962-63, Brig Maj Aden Protectorate Levies FRA 1963-65, Cmd 3 RHA 1968-71, sr instr Army Staff Coll 1971-72; cmd 5 Air Portable Bde 1972-74, cmd Landforces NI 1977-79, Dir Army Staff Duties 1979-81, GOC SE dist 1982-83, Land Dep C-in-C Falklands 1982; QMG and Gen 1983-86, Col Cmdt RAEC 1979-86, RA 1982-87, RAOC 1984-88, HAC 1984-, cmmr Duke of Yorks Royal Mil Sch 1987-; sr def advsr Short Bros Belfast, conslt Peat Marwick McKlintock 1986-88, dep chm Wilson's Hogg Robinson 1988-, chm Hunting Engrg Ltd 1988-, chm Def Div Hunting plc 1988-; cmmr Royal Hosp Chelsea 1988-, memb Armed Forces Pay Review Body 1988; vice pres Defence Manufacturers Assoc 1987; Freeman City of London 1984; memb Soc Br Aerospace Cos 1988-; *Recreations* field sports, sailing, golf; *Clubs* Army and Navy, Royal Fowey Yacht; *Style*— Gen Sir Richard Trant, KCB; c/o Lloyds Bank, Newquay, Cornwall

TRANTER, Nigel Godwin; OBE (1983); s of Gilbert Tredgold Tranter (d 1929), of Edinburgh, and Eleanor Annie Cass (d 1933); *b* 23 Nov 1909; *Educ* George Heriot's Sch Edinburgh, Univ of Edinburgh (Hon MA); *m* 1933, May Jean Campbell (d 1979), da of Thomas Douglas Grieve (d 1925), of Edinburgh; 1 s (Philip, d 1966), 1 da (Frances-May); *Career* author and novelist; published over 100 books, fiction and non-fiction; hon pres Scottish Pen Club; former chm: Soc of Authors Scotland, Nat Book League Scotland, St Andrew Soc of E Lothian, Nat Forth Rd Bridge Ctee 1953-57, E Lothian Lib Assoc 1960-70; D Litt Univ of Strathclyde 1990; *Books* Robert the Bruce Trilogy (1965-69), The Fortified House in Scotland (5 vols, 1962-71), Nigel Tranter's Scotland (1981), Columba (1987), The Story of Scotland (1987), Flowers of Chivalry (1988), Mail Royal (1989), Warden of The Queen's March (1989), Kenneth (1990); *Recreations* walking, historical research, knighthood; *Clubs* PEN; *Style*— Nigel Tranter, Esq, OBE; Quarry House, Aberlady, East Lothian, Scotland EH32 0QB (☎ 087 57258)

TRAPNELL, Dr David Hallam; s of Hallam Trapnell (d 1982), of Clifton, Bristol, and Ruth Louisa, *née* Walker; *b* 21 June 1928; *Educ* Clifton, Gonville and Caius Coll Cambridge (MA, MD), Middx Hosp; *m* 14 Nov 1959, Mary Elizabeth, da of John Gray (d 1976), of Whitby, Yorkshire; 2 s (Simon, Philip); *Career* Nat Serv Capt RAMC (formerly Lt) 1954-56; registrar and sr registrar Bart's 1957-61; conslt radiologist: Queen Mary's Hosp Roehampton, Westminster Hosp 1962-84, London Clinic 1978-84; pres: Br Inst of Radiology 1980-81, Int Fleischner Soc 1983-84, Br Postmark Soc 1970-75; George Simon lectr RCR 1983; churchwarden All Souls Church Langham Place London W1 1967-84, fndr chm Soc for Wildlife Art of the Nations 1982-, hon dir Nature in Art Int Centre for Wildlife Art Gloucester 1987-; Winston Churchill travelling fellowship 1985; FRCP 1975, FRCR 1975, FRSA 1990; *Books* Principles of X-Ray Diagnosis (1967), Dental Manifestations of Systemic Disease (jtly 1973), Radiology in Clinical Diagnosis (ed series), Health Disease and Heating in Illustrated Bible Dictionary (1980), Nature in Art A Celebration of 300 Years of Wildlife Art (1991); *Recreations* postal history, natural history; *Style*— Dr David Trapnell; Nature in Art, The International Centre for Wildlife Art, Wallsworth Hall, Sandhurst, Gloucester GL2 9PA (☎ 0452 731 422)

TRAPNELL, Rev Stephen Hallam; s of Hallam Trapnell (d 1982), of Clifton, Bristol, and Ruth, *née* Walker; *b* 10 June 1930; *Educ* Clifton, Gonville and Caius Coll Cambridge (MA), Ridley Hall Cambridge, Virginia Seminary Alexandria Va USA (MDiv); *m* 6 May 1961, Ann Mary Hensleigh, da of Lt-Col Eric H L H Walter, of Chaldon, Surrey; 2 s (Andrew b 1964, Mark b 1967), 2 da (Rachel b 1962, Lydia b 1965); *Career* 2 Lt RASC 1949; ordained priest 1957; curate of: St Matthias Upper Tulse Hill London 1956-59, St Mary's Reigate 1969-61; vicar of: Christ Church Richmond Surrey 1961-72, Holy Trinity Sydenham London 1972-80; rector of Worting Basingstoke Hants 1980-; surrogate for marriages; *Publications* Teaching The Familes (1973), More for all the Family (contrib, 1990); *Recreations* the study of wild flowers (especially orchids); *Clubs* The Co of All Faithful People (life memb); *Style*— The Rev Stephen Trapnell; The Rectory, Glebe Lane, Basingstoke RG23 8QA (☎ 0256 22095)

TRAPP, Prof Joseph Burney; CBE (1990); s of Henry Mansfield Burney Trapp (d 1957), and Frances Melanie, *née* Wolters (d 1950); *b* 16 July 1925; *Educ* Dannevirke HS, Victoria Univ NZ (MA); *m* 9 June 1953, Elayne Margaret, da of Sir Robert Alexander Falla, KCMG, of Days Bay, Wellington, NZ (d 1979); 2 s (Michael b 1957, James b 1959); *Career* asst librarian Alexander Turnbull Library Wellington 1946-50; asst lectr: Victoria Univ Coll 1950-51, Univ of Reading 1951-53; Warburg Inst Univ of London: asst librarian 1953-66, librarian 1966-76, dir 1976-90; FSA 1978, FRSA 1978, FBA 1980; *Books* The Apology of Sir Thomas More (ed 1979); *Style*— Prof J B Trapp, CBE; The Warburg Institute, Woburn Square, London WC1H OAB (☎ 071 580 9663)

TRASENSTER, Maj Michael Augustus Tulk; CVO (1954); s of Major William Augustus Trasenster, MC (d 1950), of Meonstoke, and Brenda de Courcy, *née* Barrett (d 1987); *b* 26 Jan 1923; *Educ* Winchester; *m* 11 Jan 1950, Fay Norrie, da of Thomas Darley (d 1982), of Yorks; 2 da (Anna b 1953, Julia b 1955); *Career* serv 4/7 Royal Dragoon Gds 1942, Normandy and NW Europe 1944-45, Middle East 1946; ADC to Govr S Aust 1947-49, Sch of Tank Technol and Tech Staff 1951; military sec and comptroller to Govr Gen of NZ 1952-55; involved in brewing indust 1955-60; contributed photographs to various pubns; ARPS 1960; Chev Order Leopold II with palm 1944, Croix de Guerre with palm; *Recreations* art, painting, reading; *Style*— Maj Michael Trasenster, CVO; c/o Royal Bank of Scotland, High St, Winchester, Hampshire

TRASLER, Prof Gordon Blair; JP (Hants 1978); s of Frank Ferrier Trasler (d 1978), and Marian, *née* Blair (d 1940); *b* 7 March 1929; *Educ* Bryanston, Univ Coll Exeter (MA); *m* 19 Sept 1953, Kathleen Patricia, da of Gerald Richard Fitzarthur Fegan (d 1955); *Career* Nat Serv Royal Fusiliers and RCS 1947-49; asst in statistics Univ Coll Exeter 1952-53, psychologist HM Prison Winchester 1956-57 (HM Prison Wandsworth 1955-56); Univ of Southampton: lectr 1957-64, prof of psychology 1964-, dean of social sciences 1970-73; ed in chief British Journal of Criminology 1981-86, memb Winchester Health Authy 1982-90, vice pres Inst for the Study and Treatment of Delinquency 1987- (chm 1982-87); Sellin-Glueck award for outstanding contributions to criminology American Society of Criminology 1990; FBPsS 1964, CPsychol 1988; *Books* In Place of Parents (1960), The Explanation of Criminality (1962), The Shaping of Social Behaviour (1967), The Formative Years (jtly, 1968), Behaviour Modification with Offenders (with DP Farrington, 1980); *Recreations* writing, photography, reading, music; *Style*— Prof Gordon Trasler, JP; Fox Croft, Old Kennels Lane, Oliver's Battery, Winchester, Hants SO22 4JT (☎ 0962 852345); Department of Psychology, The University, Southampton SO9 5NH (☎ 0703 592582, fax 0703 593939, telex 47661)

TRAVERS, David; s of George Bowes Travers (d 1966), and Gertrude Colbert, *née* Chrunside; *b* 19 March 1957; *Educ* Spennymoor Secdy Sch, Kings Coll London (LLB, AKC, LLM); *m* 13 Oct 1984, Sheila Mary, da of Martin Killoran, CBE, QFSM; 1 da (Rosamond b 11 Oct 1988); *Career* called to the Bar Middle Temple 1981, Harmsworth scholar Northern Circuit, pt/t lectr Accountancy Tuition Centre Manchester and Liverpool until 1983, memb exec Northern circuit 1985-87, occasional lectr Dept of Mgmnt Scis UMIST 1986-87, occasional libel reader Express newspapers 1987-88, exec ed King's Counsel 1979 (ed 1978), joined chambers Birmingham 1988, Royal Inst Scholar 1975, memb Delegacy Governing Body King's Coll London 1977-78, sabbatical pres King's Coll London Union of Students 1979-80, pres Middle Temple Students Assoc 1980-81; memb: Family Law Bar Assoc, Hon Soc of the Middle Temple 1978-; hon life memb King's Coll London Union of Students 1980; *Recreations* food, wine, words; *Style*— David Travers, Esq; 3 Fountain Ct, Steelhouse Lane, Birmingham B4 6DR (☎ 021 236 5854, 021 236 2286, document exchange: DX 16079, fax 021 236 7008)

TRAVERS, William Inglis Linden (Bill); MBE (1945); s of William Halton Lindon Travers (d 1966), of Newcastle upon Tyne, and Florence, *née* Wheatley; *b* 3 Jan 1922; *Educ* Governess GS Newcastle upon Tyne, Hannah and Gash Private Sch Sunderland; *m* 1, 1950 (m dis 1957), Patricia Raine; 1 da (Anna Louise Linden b 28 Jan 1951); m 2, 19 Sept 1957, Virginia Anne, *qv*, da of Terence Morrell McKenna (d 1948); 3 s (William Morrell Linden b 4 Nov 1958, Justin McKenna Linden b 6 March 1963, Daniel Inglis Linden b 27 Feb 1967), 1 da (Louise Annabella b 6 July 1960); *Career* enlisted Royal Northumberland Fus 1940, cmmnd 9 Gurkha Rifles 1941, Lt Razmak NW Frontier India Pathan tribal warfare 1942, Wingate's second Chindit campaign India 1943 (cdr recce gp, promoted Capt in field), SOE 1944 (Maj i/c re-formed 2/9 Gurkha Bn Force 136, parachuted behind enemy lines into Perak Malaya to organise Malayan Peoples Anti-Japanese Army, remained in Malaya until Allied troops landed), Maj Hiroshima Japan 1946; actor of stage and screen; films incl: Geordie 1954, Bhowani Junction 1955, Born Free 1966, Ring of Bright Water (also wrote screenplay) 1968, The Belstone Fox 1973: tv incl: Lorna Doone BBC TV 1963, The Admirable Crichton (Acad Award nomination for best actor) 1967, Wild Dogs of Africa (documentary) 1973, Bloody Ivory (prodr and writer) 1980; stage appearances incl: A Cook for Mr General (Playhouse Theatre NYC) 1961, (RSC Stratford upon Avon) 1962, Abraham Cochrane (Broadway NYC) 1964, Peter Pan (London) 1970; pres Beauty Without Cruelty UK, patron Captive Animals Protection Soc, fndr Zoo Check Charitable Tst; Freeman City of Houston 1966; *Books* On Playing with Lions (with Virginia McKenna, 1966), Beyond the Bars (jtly 1987); *Recreations* travelling, photography, gardening; *Clubs* Special Forces; *Style*— Bill Travers, Esq, MBE

TRAVERSE-HEALY, Prof Tim; OBE (1989); s of John Healy, MBE, and Gladys, *née* Traverse; *b* 25 March 1923; *Educ* Stonyhurst, St Mary's Hosp London Univ (Dip CAM); *m* 8 March 1946, Joan, da of Sidney Thompson (d 1968), of London and Sussex; 2 s (Sean b 1947, Kevin b 1949), 3 da (Sharon (Mrs Butterfield) b 1951, Corinne (Mrs Russell) b 1953, Jeannine b 1954); *Career* WWII RA Territorial Res, RM Commandos and Special Forces 1941-46; memb Public and Social Policy Ctee Nat Westminster Bank, sr ptnr Traverse-Healy Ltd Corporate Affrs Counsel 1947-, memb bd Centre for Public Affrs Studies 1969-; dir Charles Barker Holdings Ltd 1987-; (UK) PR Educn Tst 1990-; hon prof: Univ of Stirling, Univ of Wales; visiting prof Baylor Univ Texas USA; vice-pres Euro PR Confedn 1965-69, memb Professional Practices Ctee (UK) PR Conslts Assoc 1988-; Int PR Assoc: fndr sec 1950-61, cncl memb 1961-68, pres 1968-73, emeritus memb 1982, Presidential Gold medal 1985, pres World PR congress Tel Aviv 1970 and Geneva 1973; PR congress fndr lectures: Boston 1976, Bombay 1982, Melbourne 1988; pres: Int Fndn for PR Res and Educn 1983-85, Int Fndn for PR Studies 1986-87 (tstee 1987-88); memb (US) Public Affairs Cncl 1975-; PR News award 1983, PR Week award 1987, (US) Page Soc award 1990; Hon FIPR 1988 (Tallents Gold medal 1985); memb: RM Officers Assoc, Commandos Assoc, London Flotilla; tstee London City Ballet Co; MIPR 1948, FIPR 1956 (pres 1967-68), FIPA 1957, FRSA 1953; *Recreations* Irish soc, French politics; *Clubs* Athenaeum, Philippics, Norwegian, RAC; *Style*— Prof Tim Traverse-Healy, OBE; 8 Rockwells Gardens, Dulwich Wood Park, London SE19; Griffoul, 82150 Montaigu de Quercy, Tarn et Garonne, France

TRAVIS, Ernest Raymond Anthony; s of Ernest Raymond Travis, and Constance Mary Travis; *b* 18 May 1943; *Educ* Harrow; *m* 1, 1967 (m dis 1977), Hon Rosemary

Gail, *qv*, da of Baron Pritchard, of Haddon; m 2, 1978, Jean Heather, da of John MacDonald (d 1983); m 3 Peta Jane, da of Sir Peter Foster; *Career* called to the Bar Inner Temple 1965; chm Travis Perkins plc; *Style—* Anthony Travis, Esq; 320 Fulham Rd, London SW10; Pitters Farm, Naish Hill, Chippenham, Wilts; Travis Perkins plc, 149 Harrow Rd, Paddington, London W2 (☎ 071 402 0081)

TRAVIS, John Anthony; s of Leonard Kirkbride Travis, of Brighton, Sussex, and Elsie Travis (d 1961); *b* 18 Aug 1945; *Educ* Brighton Sch of Music & Drama, Doris Iscaccas Sch of Dancing, Royal Ballet Sch, Univ of Manchester (Dip in Theatre Archives); *Career* dancer Covent Garden Opera Ballet; London Festival Ballet: dancer then leading soloist 1966-77, created London Festival Ballet Archive 1979, prog presenter Educn Dept 1980-84; on secondment to study at V & A Museum 1977, studied at Lincoln Centre NY 1978-79; teaching: annually at Nat Festivals of Youth Dance to classes and repertoire at all levels, at community centres and theatres in five Brazilian Cities 1982, at first Summer Sch in Dominica 1990, currently at Northern Sch of Contemporary Dance Leeds; guest classes: West St, Northern Ballet Sch Manchester; lectr on history of dance; artistic co-ordinator Dance Advance 1988 - (touring mangr for China visit 1989), dir of 3 Youth Dance Spectaculars for Greater London Arts at the Place and Opening Gala of Northern Sch of Contemporary Dance; dir Phoenix Dance Co; patron: East London Regnl Dance Cncl, Harehills Dance Umbrella; memb Ctee: Nat Festivals of Youth Dance, Dance and Mime Panel Eastern Arts Assoc; memb: Dirs Advsy Panel Br Ballet Orgn; Bd Northern Ballet Theatre; *Style—* John Travis, Esq

TRAVIS, Norman John; s of Frederick Pickles (d 1949), of Bristol, and Ada Alice, *née* Travis (d 1947); *b* 7 March 1913; *Educ* Clifton, Trinity Coll Oxford (MA, BSc); *m* 25 Feb 1939, Mary Elizabeth, da of Alan Dale-Harris (d 1962), of Iver, Bucks; 4 s (Rupert b 1940, Julian b 1942, Michael b 1947, Mark b 1955); *Career* cmmnd 2 Lt RE 1940, navigator RAF 1942, demob Sqdn ldr 1945; md Borax (Holdings) Ltd 1966-70; dir: First Inter State Bank of California 1967-80, Rio-Tinto-Zinc Corp Ltd 1968-79; chm: US Borax & Chemical Corporation Los Angeles 1966-80, RTZ-Borax Ltd 1970-79; memb: Bd Dirs American Mining Congress, Cncl Chem Indust Assoc, Bibliographical Soc, Assoc Internationalle dc Bibliophile; chm Clifton Coll Cncl 1971-78; *Books* The Tincal Trail (jtly, 1984); *Recreations* collecting antiquarian books, golf, real tennis; *Clubs* RAF, MCC, Los Angeles CC; *Style—* Norman Travis, Esq; Howe Green Hall, Hertford, Herts SG13 8LH (☎ 0707 261243)

TRAVIS, (Henry) Stuart; s of Sidney Travis (d 1956), of Accrington, Lancs, and Mary Travis; *b* 7 Dec 1945; *Educ* Peel Park Sch Accrington, Accrington GS; *m* March 1969, Margaret, da of Frederic Ryden (d 1960), of Oswaldtwistle, Lancs; 3 da (Joanne b 1972, Sally b 1975, Susannah b 1977); *Career* William Deacons Bank Ltd 1963-69, sr mangr Liverpool City Office Williams & Glyns Bank Ltd 1983-85 (joined 1970, mangr Torquay 1978-83); Arbuthnot Latham Bank Ltd: asst dir 1985-86, dir UK Banking 1986-88, dir head of Banking Dept 1988-89; chm Arbuthnot Asset Finance 1987-89, chief exec Arbuthnot Leasing International Ltd 1988, chm Mablewest Ltd; dir: Capital Sourcing Ltd, Lamanstore Ltd; vice pres Torbay Inst of Bankers 1983; memb: Round Table 1968-86, Rotary 1981-87; *Recreations* shooting, sailing, bowling; *Clubs* Royal Torbay Yacht; *Style—* Stuart Travis, Esq; Warberry Court, Torquay, Devon; Maplewest Ltd, Recreation Rd, Plymouth, Devon

TREACHER, Adm Sir John Devereux; KCB (1975); s of late Frank Charles Treacher, of Bentley Grove, Suffolk; *b* 23 Sept 1924,Chile; *Educ* St Paul's; *m* 1, 1953 (m dis 1968), Patcie, da of Dr F McGrath, of Evanston, Illinois; 1 s, 1 da; m 2, 1969, Kirsteen Forbes, da of D F Landale, of Dumfries; 1 s, 1 da; *Career* served RN 1941-77 (qualified pilot 1946, Capt 1962, Rear Adm 1970, Vice Adm 1972, Vice Chief Naval Staff 1973-75, Adm 1975, C-in-C Fleet & Allied C-in-C Channel & E Atlantic 1975-77); non-press memb Press Cncl 1978-81, chief exec Nat Car Parks 1977-81 (dir 1977-85); dir: Westland Group plc 1978-89 (vice chm 1984, dep chm 1986), Meggitt plc 1979-; FRAeS 1973; *Clubs* Boodle's; *Style—* Adm Sir John Treacher, KCB; 22 Newton Rd, London W2 5LT

TREACHER, William Charles (Bill); s of William Charles Treacher (d 1960), and Minnie, *née* Chapal; *b* 4 June 1930; *Educ* The Webber Douglas Drama Acad; *m* 1 Dec 1971, Katherine Glyn, da of Glyn Kessey (d 1986), of Perth, Western Aust; 1 s (Jamie b 6 Nov 1974), 1 da (Sophie b 24 Oct 1978); *Career* LAC RAF 1948-50; MN 1951-55; actor; Brian Rix Theatre of Laughter Garrick Theatre 1966-79, Murder at the Vicarage (Fortune Theatre 1977-79), Arthur Fowler in Eastenders (BBC 1985-); extensive theatre and TV experience; memb The Mental Health Fndn; *Recreations* sailing, reading; *Style—* William Treacher, Esq; BBC TV Centre, Clarendon Road, Borehamwood, Herts WD6 1JF (☎ 081 953 6100, fax 081 207 0657)

TREACY, Colman Maurice; QC (1990); s of Dr Maurice Colman Treacy, and Mary Teresa, *née* Frisby; *b* 28 July 1949; *Educ* Stonyhurst, Jesus Coll Cambridge (open scholar, MA); *m* 28 July 1976, Laura Elizabeth, da of Henry Daniels; 1 s, 1 da; *Career* called to the Bar Middle Temple 1971, in practice Midlands and Oxford Circuit; *Style—* Colman Treacy, Esq, QC; 3 Fountain Court, Steelhouse Lane, Birmingham B4 6DR (☎ 021 236 5854, fax 021 236 7008)

TREADGOLD, Hazel Rhona; da of Edward Ernest Froude-Bailey (d 1979), of Hassocks, Sussex, and Cora May, *née* Baker; *b* 29 May 1936; *Educ* Millers Secdy Coll; *m* 20 June 1959, John David Treadgold, *qv*, dean of Chichester, s of Oscar Threadgold, of Nottingham; 2 s (Marcus Edward Newton b 1961, Simon John Newton b 1964), 1 da (Joanna Clare b 1968); *Career* memb Women's Cncl, central pres Mother's Union 1983-88, co-ordinator for The Archbishop of Canterbury of The Bishops Wives' Conf at Lambeth Conf 1988, govr of Bishop Wilton C of E Comp Sch Chichester 1990, vice pres Chichester Relate Ctee 1990; *Recreations* swimming, tennis, flower arranging, gardening; *Style—* Mrs Hazel Treadgold; The Deanery, Chicester, W Sussex PO19 1PX (☎ 0243 783286), 4 Washington St, Chichester, W Sussex

TREADGOLD, Very Rev John David; LVO (1990); *b* 30 Dec 1931; *Educ* Univ of Nottingham (BA), Wells Theol Coll; *m* Hazel Rhona, *née* Bailey; 2 s, 1 da; *Career* deacon 1959, priest 1960, vicar choral of Southwell Minster 1959-64, CF (TA) 1962-67, rector of Wollaton Nottingham 1964-74, CF (TAVR) 1974-78, vicar of Darlington 1974-81, surrogate 1976-81, canon of Windsor and chaplain of The Royal Chapel Windsor Great Park 1981-89; chaplain to HM The Queen 1983-89; FRSA 1990; *Style—* The Very Rev John Treadgold, LVO; The Deanery, Chichester, W Sussex PO19 1PX (☎ 0243 783286)

TREADWELL, Lt-Col Gerald William; OBE (1964); s of Claude Mallam Treadwell (d 1931), and Emily Dorothy, *née* Mixer (d 1911); *b* 26 Nov 1905; *Educ* Stamford, King's Coll London; *m* 25 Jan 1941 (in Jerusalem Cathedral), Margaret, da of Frederick Rogers (d 1972), of Llanusk, Usk, Mon; 1 s (John b 1950), 1 da (Ann b 1945); *Career* Lt-Col serv Middle E (1 Cav Div), Italy and Austria 1939-48, mil prosecutor, Jerusalem Mil Court 1943-44; slr; pres: City of Westminster Law Soc 1969-70, Blackheath CC 1971-76; chm Bromley Cons Assoc 1958-62; *Books* Military Courts Manual; *Clubs* Cavalry and Guard's, Blackheath Cricket (vice pres), Blackheath Rugby (vice pres); *Style—* Lt-Col Gerald Treadwell, OBE; Ashlawn, Bickley Rd, Bickley, Kent BR1 2ND

TREANOR, Frances Mary Elizabeth; da of George Francis Treanor (d 1978), of London, and Biddy, *née* Maunsell (d 1964); *b* 16 April 1944; *Educ* Convent of the Sacred Heart HS For Girls Hammersmith, Goldsmiths Coll London (NDD), Hornsey Coll of Art (ATC); *m* 1, 9 Oct 1965 (m dis 1969), Francis John Elliott, s of Aubrey Elliott (d 1988), of Wales; 1 da (Lizzie Taylor b 1966); m 2, 30 Oct 1969 (m dis 1982), (Thomas) Anthony Taylor, s of Thomas Taylor (d 1984), of Cornwall; *Career* artist; *Commissions* Volvo purchase 1987, govt purchase Art of Govt Scheme Derry's Gift 1987, govt print purchase Inland Revenue and Custom & Excise 1988, set design OUDS prodn of Shakespeare's As You Like It summer tour Japan, USA and England 1988, 3i Commercial Property 1988, Capital & Counties 1988, Dean Witter International 1989, Woolwich 1989, Japan Development Bank 1990, Bruce McGaw Graphics NY 1990; *Awards* L'Artiste Assoifée 1975, George Rowney Pastel 1982, Frank Herring award for Merit 1984, Willi Hoffman-Guth award 1988; ILEA teacher DES 1966, pt/t teacher of art ILEA 1967-87, sessional lectr in art and design at American Coll in London 1979-87; vice chm Blackheath Art Soc 1974, memb Steering Gp Greenwich Lone Parent Project 1984, area coordinator Neighbourhood Watch Scheme 1988-89; memb Cncl Pastel Soc, FBA 1982 and 1986; *Books and Publications* Pastel Painting Technique (1987), The Medici Society (1987), Choosing & Mixing Colours (1988), Drawing With Colour (J Martin, 1990), Static (card pubns, 1990), Women's Artist Diary (1988), Something Fishy (pastel painting for card pubn, 1990), Flower Show (1990); *Recreations* tv, conversation, antique markets; *Style—* Miss Frances Treanor; 121 Royal Hill, Greenwich, London SE10 8SS (☎ 081 692 3239)

TREANOR, Mark; s of John Treanor, of 34 Beauly Rd, Baillieston, Glasgow, and Elizabeth, *née* Scade; *b* 1 April 1962; *Educ* St Ambrose RC Secdy Sch Coatbridge; *m* 25 June 1983, Mary Helen, da of William John Davie; 3 s (Mark b 16 July 1985, Michael John b 21 Aug 1988, Kieran b 6 Dec 1989); *Career* professional footballer; over 300 appearances Clydebank 1979-89, over 50 appearances St Johnstone 1989-; Scot Div 1 Championships 1990; *Recreations* swimming, boxing, snooker; *Style—* Mark Treanor, Esq; St Johnstone FC, McDiarmid Stadium, Crieff Rd, Perth (☎ 0738 26961)

TREASE, (Robert) Geoffrey; s of George Albert Trease (d 1932), of Nottingham, and Florence Trease; *b* 11 Aug 1909; *Educ* Nottingham HS, Queens Coll Oxford (open classical scholar); *m* 1933, Marian Haselden Granger Boyer (changed name to Boyer by deed poll), da of Henry Haselden Granger; 1 da (Jocelyn Heather (Mrs Norman Payne) b 1936); *Career* served WWII KORR, AEC; freelance writer 1933-, author of 101 books, published in 20 languages, 16 for adults and 85 for older children books incl: Bows Against the Barons (1934), Walking in England (1935), Such Divinity (1939), Cue for Treason (1940), Only Natural (1940), Tales Out of School (1949), Snared Nightingale (1958), The Italian Story (1963), The Condottieri (1970), A Whiff of Burnt Boats (autobiography, 1971), Laughter At The Door (autobiography, 1974), Portrait of a Cavalier: William Cavendish, first Duke of Newcastle (biography, 1979), Tomorrow Is A Stranger (1987), The Arpino Assignment (1988), Shadow Under The Sea (1990), Calabrian Quest (1990), Aunt Augusta's Elephant (1991); Welwyn Drama Festival New Play prize 1938 (for After The Tempest published in Best One Act Plays of 1938), New York Herald Tribune Book award 1966 (for This Is Your Century); chm Soc of Authors 1972-73 (perm memb Cncl 1974-), fndr chm Children's Writers Group; fell PEN, FRSL 1979; *Recreations* walking, theatre; *Clubs* Royal Over-Seas League; *Style—* Geoffrey Trease, Esq; c/o Murray Pollinger, 222 Old Brompton Rd, London SW5 0BZ (☎ 071 373 4711, fax 071 373 3775)

TREASURE, Fred; s of Fred Treasure (d 1959), of Preston, Lancs, and Ann Mary, *née* Sadler (d 1966); *b* 5 May 1919; *Educ* Preston GS; *m* 21 Oct 1940, Doris Dixon, da of Harry Howarth (local artist, d 1964), of Preston, Lancs; 1 s (John Philip b 1947), 1 da (Judith Ann b 1943); *Career* RAF 1939-46, Sgt; qualified accountant 1950, ptnr Ashworth Treasure & Co 1957-70, in private practice 1951-57 and 1970-89 (ret); co sec and dir Sadlers (Lytham) Ltd engrs until 1990 (now ret); pres Lytham St Annes and Flyde YMCA 1978- (chm 1968-78); *Recreations* football and cricket for sch, RAF and local clubs post-war; *Clubs* Rotary of Lytham (pres 1965-66); *Style—* Fred Treasure, Esq; 72 Clifton Drive, Fairhaven, Lytham St Annes, Lancashire (☎ 0253 737828)

TREASURE, Prof John Albert Penberthy; s of Harold Paul Treasure (d 1969), and Constance Frances, *née* Shapland (d 1987); *b* 20 June 1924; *Educ* Cardiff HS, Univ of Wales (BA), Univ of Cambridge (PhD); *m* 30 March 1954, Valerie Ellen, da of Lawrence Bell (d 1981); 2 s (Julian Paul b 1958, Simon John Richard b 1960), 1 step s (Jonathan Edward b 1948); *Career* md British Market Research Bureau Ltd 1957-60; marketing dir J Walter Thompson Co London 1960-66 (chm 1967-77); dean City Univ Business Sch 1978-81; vice chm Saatchi & Saatchi London 1983-89; tstee Charity Aid Foundation 1983-88; chm History of Advertising Tst 1985-90; Freeman City of London 1981, Liveryman Worshipful Co of Marketors 1981; CBIM 1980, FIPA 1967; *Recreations* golf, tennis; *Clubs* Queen's, Hurlingham, Royal Mid-Surrey; *Style—* Prof John Treasure; Saatchi & Saatchi Ltd, 80 Charlotte St, London W1A 1AQ (☎ 071 636 5060, fax 071 637 8489)

TRECHMAN, Gavin; s of Capt John Ronald Gordon Trechman, RN, and Phyllis Morva Trechman; ggs of Lord Charles Greenway; *b* 4 March 1942; *Educ* Charterhouse; *m* 3 Dec 1975, Angela de Carvalho, da of late Arnaldo Luiz; 1 s (Richard b 1977), 1 da (Sara b 1978); *Career* oil exec, dir Alexander Duckham & Co; *Recreations* golf, tennis; *Clubs* Royal Wimbledon Golf, Hurlingham; *Style—* Gavin Trechman, Esq; 8 Paultons St, London SW3 5DP (☎ 071 352 9118); BP (Switzerland), Kalkbreitestrasse 51, 8023 Zurich 3 (☎ 01 468 1201)

TREDINNICK, David; MP (C) Bosworth 1987-; *b* 19 Jan 1950; *Educ* Eton, Mons Offr Cadet Sch, Graduate Business Sch, Cape Town Univ (MBA), St John's Coll Oxford (MLitt); *m* Rebecca; 1 s (Thomas, b 6 July 1989), 1 da (Sophie); *Career* Grenadier Gds 1968-71; chm Anglo-East Euro Trading Co; chm Br Atlantic Gp of Young Politicians 1989-, jt sec Cons Backbench Defence and Foreign Affrs Ctee 1990; *Recreations* skiing, tennis, golf, backgammon, rifle and shotgun shooting, windsurfing, travel; *Style—* David Tredinnick, Esq, MP; House of Commons, London SW1 (☎ 071 219 4514)

TREDINNICK, Noël Harwood; s of Harold James Tredinnick, of Beckenham, Kent, and Nola Frewin, *née* Harwood; *b* 9 March 1949; *Educ* St Olave's GS for Boys, Southwark Cathedral, Guildhall Sch of Music and Drama, Inst of Educn London Univ (Dip Ed); *m* 3 July 1976, Fiona Jean, da of James Malcolm Couper-Johnston, of Beckenham, Kent; 1 da (Isabel Jane b 1983); *Career* school master Langley Park Sch for Boys Beckenham 1971-75, prof and memb Acad Bd Guildhall Sch 1975-, organist and dir of music All Souls Church Langham Place London 1972-, artist dir Langham Arts 1987-; composer, orchestrator and conductor: Beckenham Chorale 1971-72, All Souls Orch 1972-, BBC Concert Orch 1985-, BBC Radio Orch 1988-; musical dir: BBC Radio (Religious Dept), Songs of Praise BBC TV; fndr and conductor Prom Praise; numerous recordings and performances with Cliff Richard, Mary O'Hara and Wendy Craig; memb: Archbishop's Cmmn on Church Music, Cncl Music in Worship Tst; *Recreations* theatre, architecture, country-walking; *Clubs* ACG; *Style—* Noël Tredinnick, Esq; 2 All Souls Place, London WIN 3DB (☎ 071 580 0898, fax 071 436 3019)

TREDRE, Roger Ford; s of Alec Ford Tredre, and Angela Joyce, *née* Morris; *b* 9 March 1962; *Educ* Epsom Coll, Sidney Sussex Coll Cambridge (scholar, MA); *Career*

journalist; staff writer The Bulletin Brussels 1984-86, dep editor Fashion Weekly 1989 (news ed 1987-88), fashion corr The Independent 1989-; freelance work for: Vogue, GQ, Business, radio and TV; *Recreations* travel; *Style—* Roger Tredre, Esq; 64 Huntingdon St, London N1 1BX (☎ 071 607 4616); The Independent, 40 City Rd, London EC1 2DB (☎ 071 253 1222)

TREE, Lady Anne Evelyn Beatrice; *née* Cavendish; da of late 10 Duke of Devonshire, KBE, MBE, TD; *b* 1927; *m* 1949, Michael Lambert Tree, *qv* ; 2 adopted da (Isabella, Esther); *Style—* The Lady Anne Tree; 75 Eaton Square, London SW1 (☎ 071 235 1320); Shute House, Donhead St Mary, nr Salisbury, Wilts (☎ 034 788 253)

TREE, (Arthur) Jeremy; s of Arthur Ronald (d 1976), and bro of Michael, *qv*; *b* 21 Dec 1925; *Educ* Eton; *Career* 2 Lt 1 Household Cavalry 1945-47; owner and former trainer of racehorses; *Clubs* Turf; *Style—* Jeremy Tree, Esq; Beckhampton House, Marlborough, Wilts (☎ 067 23 244 204)

TREFFRY, David Charles; OBE (1966); yr s of Col Roger Carpenter Treffry, MC, TD, RA (d 1945), and Dorothy Emma, *née* Gundry Mills (d 1970); descended from an old Cornish family which acquired the manor of Fowey and the house of Place by marriage with an heiress *ca* 1300 (*see* Burke's Landed Gentry, 18 edn, vol I, 1965); *b* 7 Oct 1926; *Educ* Marlborough, Magdalen Coll Oxford (MA); *Career* Capt Frontier Force Regt IA 1945-48; joined HM Overseas Colonial Serv 1952, political offr S Arabia 1952, asst chief sec Aden 1959, perm sec Miny of Finance S Arabian Fedn 1963, cabinet sec S Arabian Fedn 1966, ret 1968; Int Monetary Fund 1968-87; fin advsr Indonesia 1971-73; memb: Cncl Royal Inst of Cornwall, Regnl Ctee Nat Tst Devon and Cornwall; High Sheriff of Cornwall 1991; *Clubs* Travellers'; *Style—* David Treffry, Esq, OBE; Place, Fowey, Cornwall; 1684 32nd Street NW, Washington, DC 20007, USA

TREFGARNE, 2 Baron (UK 1947); David Garro Trefgarne; PC (1989); s of 1 Baron Trefgarne (d 1960), and Elizabeth (who m 2, 1962 (m dis 1966), Cdr Anthony Tosswill Courtney, OBE (d 1988); and 3, 1971, Hugh Cecil Howat Ker (d 1987)), da of late Charles Edward Churchill, of Ashton Keynes, Wilts; *b* 31 March 1941; *Educ* Haileybury, Princeton Univ USA; *m* 1968, Rosalie, da of Baron Lane of Horsell (Life Peer); 2 s (George, Justin b 1973), 1 da (Rebecca b 1976); *Heir* s, Hon George Garro Trefgarne b 4 Jan 1970; *Career* awarded Royal Aero Club Bronze medal (jtly) for flight UK to Aust and back in light aircraft 1963; oppn whip House of Lords 1977-79, a Lord in Waiting (Government Whip) 1979-8; under-sec state: Dept of Trade 1981, FCO 1981-82, DHSS 1982-83, Def (for Armed Forces) 1983-85, Min of State Def (for Def Support) 1985-86, Min of state (Def Procurement) 1986-89, min for Trade DTI 1989-90; *Recreations* flying, photography; *Style—* The Rt Hon the Lord Trefgarne, PC; House of Lords, London SW1

TREFGARNE, Hon Gwion George Garro; s of 1 Baron Trefgarne (d 1960), and Elizabeth, *née* Churchill; *b* 2 April 1953; *Educ* Milton Abbey Sch, Merrist Wood Agric Coll, Usk Coll of Agric; *m* 6 Sept 1986, Jacqueline Louise, da of Alan Rees, of Woodspring, Brockweir, Chepstow, Gwent; 1 s (Samuel Ivor Garro b 1987), 1 da (Hannah Elizabeth b 1989); *Career* served TAVR; tree surgn; memb Severn Area Rescue Assoc; *Style—* The Hon Gwion Trefgarne; Cherry Croft, Hewelsfield, nr Lydney, Glos

TREFGARNE, Hon Trevor Garro; 2 s of 1 Baron Trefgarne (d 1960), and Elizabeth, *née* Churchill; *b* 18 Jan 1944; *Educ* Cheltenham; *m* 1, 1967 (m dis 1979), Diana Elizabeth, da of late Michael Gibb, of Forge House, Taynton, Oxon, by his w Ursula (whose f, Maj Guy Gibbs, TD, was 1 cous of 1st Baron Wraxall); 2 s (Rupert b 1972, Oliver b 1974), 1 da (Susannah Julia b 1976); m 2, 1979, Caroline France, da of Michael Gosschalk, of Monte Carlo; 1 s (Mark b 1982); *Career* Cranfield Sch of Management 1968-69, chm Nesco Investments plc; *Style—* The Hon Trevor Trefgarne; 17 Avenue de l'Annonciade, Monaco

TREFUSIS, Lt Cdr Nicholas John; JP (Cornwall); s of Henry Trefusis (d 1975), of Trefusis, and Sheila Margaret, *née* Bryan; *b* 21 Oct 1943; *Educ* Sherborne, Lincoln Coll Oxford; *m* 23 Oct 1973, Servane Marie, da of M Louis Melenec, of Brest, France; 1 s (Jan b 27 April 1977), 1 da (Tamara b 19 Dec 1974); *Career* RN 1964-81; specialised as hydrographic surveyor, exchange serv Royal Danish Navy 1977-80, CO HMS Egeria and sr offr Inshore Survey Sqdn 1980-81; farmer and landowner 1982-; pres: Royal Cornwall Poly Soc, Friends of Glasney; *Recreations* music, sailing; *Style—* Lt Cdr Nicholas Trefusis, JP, RN; Trefusis, Flushing, Falmouth, Cornwall TR11 5TD (☎ 0326 75351)

TREGLOWN, Jeremy Dickinson; s of Rev Geoffrey Leonard Treglown, MBE, Hon CF, of 36 Christ Church Rd, Cheltenham, Glos, and Beryl Miriam; *b* 24 May 1946; *Educ* Bristol GS, St Peter's Coll Saltley Birmingham, St Peter's Coll Oxford (MA, BLitt), UCL (PhD); *m* 1970 (m dis 1982), Rona Mary Bower; 1 s, 2 da; m 2, 1984, Holly Mary Belinda Eley, *née* Urquhart; *Career* lectr in English Lincoln Coll Oxford 1973-76; ed Times Literary Supplement 1982-90 (asst ed 1980-82); contrib to: Sunday Times, Observer and many other jls; visiting fell All Souls Coll Oxford, Mellon visiting assoc California Inst of Technol, fell Huntington Library California 1988, fell and memb Cncl RSL 1989-, hon res fell UCL 1991-; *Publications* (ed) The Letters of John Wilmot, Earl of Rochester (1980), Spirit of Wit (1982), The Lantern-Bearers: Essays by Robert Louis Stevenson (1988); general ed Plays in Performance series 1981-85; author of various articles on poetry, drama and literary history; *Style—* Jeremy Treglown, Esq; 102 Savernake Rd, London NW3

TREGONING, Christopher William Courtenay; s of Lt-Col John Langford Tregoning, MBE, TD (d 1976), of Windrush House, Inkpen, Newbury, and Sioned Georgina Courtenay, *née* Strick; *b* 15 June 1948; *Educ* Harrow, Fitzwilliam Coll Cambridge (MA); *m* 15 Sept 1973, Antonia Isabella Mary, da of Maj John Albert Miles Critchley-Salmonson, of The Manor House, Great Barton, Bury St Edmunds; 3 s (Harry John William b 28 Jan 1976, Daniel Christopher Leonard b 30 Dec 1977, Thomas Anthony Cecil b 26 Jan 1982); *Career* Thomson McLintock & Co 1970-74, Barclays Bank Ltd 1974-79, dep md Den Norske Bank plc (formerly Nordic Bank plc) 1986 (1979-91); FCA 1974; *Recreations* field sports, racing; *Style—* Christopher Tregoning, Esq; Den Norse Bank plc, 20 St Dunstan's Hill, London EC3R 8HY (☎ 071 621 1111, fax 071 626 7400)

TREGONING, Julian George; s of John L Tregoning, MBE, TD (d 1976), and Sioned, *née* Strick; *b* 24 Oct 1946; *Educ* Harrow; *m* Tessa Jane, da of Cdr Norman Lanyon, DSC (d 1982); 2 s (Oliver b 1973, Guy b 1975); *Career* RN 1965-68; dir Save & Prosper Group Ltd 1985- (joined 1968); treas Royal UK Beneficent Assoc (RUKBA); memb Ctee City of London Club; Liveryman Worshipful Co of Grocers; *Recreations* tennis, sailing, skiing, water colours; *Clubs* City of London, MCC, St Moritz Tobogganing; *Style—* Julian Tregoning, Esq; Save & Prosper Group Ltd, 1 Finsbury Ave, London EC2M 2QY (☎ 071 588 1717, fax 071 247 5006, telex 883838 SAVPRO G)

TREHANE, Sir (Walter) Richard; s of James Trehane (d 1949), of Hampreston Manor Farm, Wimborne, Dorset, and Muriel Yeoman Cowl; *b* 14 July 1913; *Educ* Monkton Combe Sch (govr 1957-), Univ of Reading; *m* 1948, Elizabeth Mitchell, da of Martin Shaw, MC; 2 s; *Career* mangr Hampreston Manor Farm 1936-; dir: Rivers Estate Co 1964-88, Southern TV 1968-81, Rank Orgn 1971-84; former memb: Dorset War Agric Exec Ctee, Milk Mktg Bd 1947-77 (chm 1958-77), Dorset CC; former chm: English Country Cheese Cncl 1955-77, UK Dairy Assoc; pres Int Dairy Fedn 1968-72; pres Euro Assoc Animal Prodn 1961-67 (hon pres 1967-); chm Alfa-Laval Co 1982-85 (dir 1977-85); Hon DSc Univ of Reading; FRAgS; Cdr Order of Merit France 1964; kt 1967; *Style—* Sir Richard Trehane; Hampreston Manor Farm, Wimborne, Dorset

TREHARNE, Jennet Mary Lloyd (Mrs Stephen Warren); da of William Alan Treharne, of Penarth, S Glamorgan, and Janet Gwendoline, *née* Lloyd; *b* 6 Sept 1953; *Educ* Sir Frederick Osborn Sch Welwyn Garden City, Mid Essex Tech Coll, London Univ (external LLB); *m* 15 March 1980, Dr Stephen Willis Warren, s of Philip Warren; 1 s (Huw b 18 Aug 1982), 1 da (Siân b 9 Jan 1984); *Career* called to the Bar Middle Temple 1975, moved to Abergavenny 1981; memb Newport Chambers and criminal practitioner S Wales 1987-; *Recreations* family, walking in W Wales; *Style—* Miss Jennet Treharne; Glaslyn, Avenue Rd, Abergavenng, Gwent (☎ 0873 5539); 73 Blue Anchor Way, Dale, Dyfed; 12 Clytha Park Rd, Newport, Gwent (☎ 0633 67403)

TREISTER, Suzanne; s of Maksymilian Treister, of London, and June Mary, *née* Scott; *b* 22 Nov 1958; *Educ* Brighton Poly, St Martin's Sch of Art (BA), Chelsea Sch of Art (MA); *Career* solo exhibitions: Edward Totah Gallery London 1985 1988 and 1990, Ikon Gallery Birmingham and tour 1990, Kerlin Gallery Dublin 1990; gp exhibitions incl: Stowells Trophy (Royal Academy London) 1981, Chapter Two Gallery London 1982, Images for Today (touring) 1982-83, Whitechapel Open (Whitechapel Art Gallery) 1984, 10 Painters (St Martin's Sch of Art) 1986, 4 British Artists (Edward Bates Gallery Chicago USA) 1986, Something Solid (Cornerhouse Manchester), New Brits: Contemporary British and Scottish Painting (The Contemporary Arts Centre Cincinnati Ohio USA and touring) 1988, Figuring out the 80's (Laing Art Gallery Newcastle upon Tyne) 1988, Its a still-life (Arts Council Collection London and touring) 1988, John Moores (3rd prize winner) 1989, Decoy (Serpentine Gallery London) 1990, Global Art (Brent Gallery and Galleria, Houston Texas) 1990; pub collections: Leics Co Cncl, Leeds City Cncl, Arts Cncl of GB, Saatchi Collection, Br Cncl, Nordstern Koln; *Style—* Miss Suzanne Treister; c/o Edward Totah, Edward Totah Gallery, 13 Old Burlington St, London W1 (☎ 071 734 0343, fax 071 287 2186)

TREITEL, Prof Guenter Heinz; QC (1983); s of Theodor Treitel (d 1973), and Hanna, *née* Levy (d 1951); *b* 26 Oct 1928; *Educ* Kilburn GS, Magdalen Coll Oxford (BA, MA, BCL, DCL); *m* 1 Jan 1957, Phyllis Margaret, da of Ronald Cook; 2 s (Richard James b 1958, Henry Marcus b 1960); *Career* asst lectr LSE 1951-53, lectr Univ Coll Oxford 1953-54, fell Magdalen Coll Oxford 1954-79, All Souls reader in Eng law 1964-79, Vinerian prof Eng law 1979-, fell All Souls Coll Oxford 1979-; visiting lectr/prof 1964-89 Univs of: Chicago, Houston, Southern Methodist, Virginia, Santa Clara, W Aust; tstee Br Museum 1983-, memb Cncl Nat Tst 1984-; hon bencher Gray's Inn 1982; FBA 1977; *Books* The Law of Contract (1962, 7 edn 1987), An Outline of the Law of Contract (1975, 4 edn 1989), Remedies for Breach of Contract, A Comparative Account (1988); jt ed of: Benjamin's Sale of Goods (1975, 3 edn 1987), Chitty on Contracts (23 edn 1968 - 26 edn 1989), Dicey (& Morris) Conflict of Laws (7 edn 1958, 8 edn 1967); *Recreations* reading, music; *Style—* Prof H Treitel, QC; All Souls College, Oxford OX1 4AL (☎ 0865 279379, fax 0865 279299)

TRELFORD, Donald; s of Thomas Staplin Trelford, of Coventry, and Doris, *née* Gilchrist; *b* 9 Nov 1937; *Educ* Bablake Sch Coventry, Selwyn Coll Cambridge (MA); *m* 1, Janice; 2 s, 1 da; m 2, 1978, Katherine Louise, da of John Mark, of Guernsey; 1 da; *Career* ed Times of Malawi 1963-66; corr in Africa: The Observer, The Times, BBC; ed and dir The Observer 1975- (dep ed 1969-75), regular bdcasts on radio and television; memb Br exec ctee Int Press Inst, vice pres Br Sports Tst; memb: Defence Press and Bdcasting Ctee, Olivier Awards Ctee, MCC ctee 1988-91; Hon DLitt Univ of Sheffield; FRSA ; Freeman City of London; Liveryman Worshipful Co of Stationers; *Publications* County Champions (contrib, 1982), Sunday Best (ed, annual anthology 1981-83), Siege (jt author, 1980), Snookered (1986), Child of Change (with Garry Kasparov, 1987), Saturday's Boys (contrib, 1990), Fine Glances (contrib, 1990); *Recreations* golf, tennis, snooker; *Clubs* Garrick, Beefsteak, RAF, MCC; *Style—* Donald Trelford, Esq; The Observer, Chelsea Bridge House, Queenstown Road, London SW8 4NN (☎ 071 350 3306, fax 071 498 3874)

TREMAIN, Rose; da of Keith Nicholas Thomson, and Viola Mabel, *née* Dudley; *b* 2 Aug 1943; *Educ* Sorbonne, Univ of East Anglia (BA); *m* 1, 7 May 1971 (m dis 1976), Jon Tremain; 1 da (Eleanor Rachel b 16 July 1972); m 2, 2 Aug 1982, Jonathan Dudley; *Career* pt/t lectr in creative writing UEA; author; winner: Dylan Thomas Prize 1984, Giles Cooper Award 1985, Angel Prize 1985 and 1989, Sunday Express Book of the Year Award 1989; memb bd of dirs Book Tst; FRSL 1983; *Books* Sadlers Birthday (1975), Letter to Sister Benedicta (1978), The Cupboard (1980), The Colonel's Daughter (1982), The Swimming Pool Season (1984), The Garden of The Villa Mollini (1986), Restoration (1989); *Recreations* gardening, yoga; *Style—* Ms Rose Tremain; 2 High House, South Ave, Thorpe St Andrew, Norwich NR7 0EZ (☎ 0603 39682)

TREMLETT, Timothy Maurice (Tim); s of Maurice Fletcher Tremlett (d 1984), of Southampton, and Melina Mae, *née* Cousins; *b* 26 July 1956; *Educ* Bellemoor Secdy Modern, Richard Taunton Sixth Form Coll; *m* 28 Sept 1979, Carolyn Patricia, da of Terence Michael Hickley; 3 s (Christopher Timothy b 2 Sept 1981, Alastair Jonathan b 1 Feb 1983, Benjamin Paul b 2 May 1984); *Career* cricket administrator; represented W of England under 15; player Hampshire CCC 1976-: debut v Sussex 1976, awarded county cap 1983, 200 first class appearances; tours: England B to Sri Lanka 1986, English Cos to Zimbabwe 1984-85; former sales asst in furriers, currently cricket and coaching administrator Hampshire CCC; *Recreations* golf, table tennis, most sports; *Style—* Tim Tremlett, Esq; Hampshire CCC, Northlands Rd, Southampton, Hampshire SO9 2TY (☎ 0703 333788, fax 0703 330121)

TRENCH, Sir Peter Edward; CBE (1964, OBE (Mil) 1945), TD (1949); s of James Trench; *b* 16 June 1918; *Educ* privately, Univ of London and Cambridge; *m* 1940, Mary St Clair Morford; 1 s, 1 da; *Career* served WWII Queen's Royal Regt; former md Bovis Ltd, chm Y J Lovell Holdings until 1983; former dir: Capital & Counties plc, LEP Group plc, Nationwide Building Society, Crendon Concrete, The Builder Group plc, Haden plc, Trench & Ptnrs Ltd; former chm Construction & Housing Res Advsy Cncl, Nat House Bldg Cncl 1978-84; vice pres Bldg Centre, hon memb Architectural Assoc; former memb Cncl: CBI, RSA; visiting prof of construction mgmnt Univ of Reading 1981-88, former memb Ct Govrs LSE, former Hon Sec St Mary's Hosp Med Sch; Hon DSc; JP Inner London 1963-71; FCIArb, FRSA, CBIM, Hon FCIOB, Hon FRIBA; kt 1979; *Style—* Sir Peter Trench, CBE, TD; 4 Napier Close, Napier Rd, London W14 8LG (☎ 071 602 3936)

TRENCH, Hon Roderick Nigel Godolphin; o s and h of 7 Baron Ashtown, KCMG; *b* 17 Nov 1944; *Educ* Eton, Stanford Univ USA; *m* 1, 1967, Janet (d 1971), da of Harold Hamilton-Faulkner, of Redwood City, California, USA; 1 s (Timothy Roderick Hamilton b 29 Feb 1968); m 2, 1973, Susan Barbara, da of Lewis Frank Day, FRCS, DLO, of Cooden, Sussex; 1 da (Victoria Susan b 24 Aug 1977); *Style—* The Hon Roderick Trench; Bassetts, Coggins Mill Lane, Mayfield, Sussex

TRENCHARD, 3 Viscount (UK 1936); Sir Hugh Trenchard; 3 Bt (UK 1919); also Baron Trenchard (UK 1930); s of 2 Viscount Trenchard, MC (d 1987), and of Patricia, da of Adm Sir Sidney Bailey, KBE, CB, DSO; *b* 12 March 1951; *Educ* Eton, Trinity Coll Cambridge; *m* 1975, Fiona Elizabeth, da of Hon James Ian Morrison, TD, DL, *qv*, s of 1 Baron Margadale; 2 s (Hon Alexander Thomas b 1978, Hon William James b 1986), 2 da (Hon Katherine Clare b 1980, Hon Laura Mary b 1987); *Heir* s, Hon

Alexander Thomas Trenchard b 1978; *Career* Capt 4 Royal Green Jackets, TA 1973-80; dir Kleinwort Benson Ltd 1986- (joined 1973, chief rep in Japan 1980-85); pres Kleinwort Benson Int Inc 1988- (gen mangr Tokyo 1985-88); dir Dover Japan Inc 1985-87; memb: Gen Affairs Ctee Japan Security Dealers Assoc 1977-88, Japan Assoc of Corp Execs 1987-; *Style*— The Rt Hon the Viscount Trenchard; 85 Thurleigh Rd, London SW12 8TY

TRENCHARD, Hon John; 2 s of 2 Viscount Trenchard, MC (d 1987); *b* 13 March 1953; *Educ* Eton; *m* 9 June 1983, Clare, yst da of E de Burgh Marsh, of The Old Rectory, Salcott, Essex; 1 s (Thomas Edward b 13 May 1988), 1 da (Emma Clare b 31 Jan 1991); *Style*— The Hon John Trenchard

TREND, Hon Michael St John; er s of Baron Trend, GCB, CVO, PC (Life Peer, d 1987); *b* 1952; *m* 28 Feb 1987, Jill E, er da of L A Kershaw; 1 da (Faith Charlotte b 1988); *Style*— The Hon Michael Trend

TREND, Baroness; Patricia Charlotte; da of late Rev Gilbert Shaw; *m* 1949, Baron Trend, GCB, CVO, PC (Life Peer, d 1987); 2 s, 1 da; *Style*— The Rt Hon the Lady Trend

TREND, Hon Patrick St John; yr s of Baron Trend, GCB, CVO, PC (Life Peer, d 1988); *Style*— The Hon Patrick Trend; Michaelmas House, 28 Tangier Rd, Guildford, Surrey GU1 2DF (☎ 0483 576187); Arthur Andersen & Co, 1 Surrey St, London WC2R 2PS (☎ 071 836 1200, fax 071 831 1133)

TRENDELL, Derek; s of Clifford Trendell, of Chew Magna, Somerset, and Joyce Mabel, *née* Hunt; *b* 7 May 1945; *Educ* Keynsham GS; *m* 7 Sept 1968, Diane Pamela, 2 da (Joanna Catherine b 19 Nov 1969, Sarah Louise b 1 March 1973); *Career* trainee Grace Derbyshire & Todd of Bristol 1962-68; Price Waterhouse: Kingston Jamaica 1969-73, London 1973-79, Nottingham 1979-88; ptnr i/c: Leicester 1988-90, East Midlands 1991-; FCA 1967; *Recreations* golf, walking, ornithology, wine; *Clubs* The Leicestershire Golf; *Style*— Derek Trendell, Esq; Price Waterhouse, Southgate House, Millstone Lane, Leicester (☎ 0533 531981, fax 0533 532697)

TRENEMAN, Dr Richard Howard Wotton; s of Harry Ewart Treneman (d 1970), of Ley, Plympton, Plymouth, and Gladys Helena, *née* Treleaven; *b* 21 Oct 1925; *Educ* St Boniface's Coll Plymouth, Univ of Liverpool, Royal Coll of Surgeons Ireland; *m* 13 Oct 1956, Claire, da of Michael John O'Neil Quirk (d 1967), of Cregg Cottage, Carrick-on-Suir, Tipperary; 3 s ((Richard) Christopher Michael b 8 Dec 1960, Oliver b 15 May 1964, Brian b 21 Nov 1966), 3 da (Nichola b 12 April 1958, Jill b 4 May 1959, Judy b 4 Aug 1965); *Career* house offr Shrewsbury and Copthorne Hosps 1955-56, casualty offr Salisbury Gen Infirmary 1956-58; registrar ENT surgery: Salisbury Hosp Gp 1958-60, Brighton and Lewes Hosps 1960-62; civilian med practitioner MOD (Army) Bulford and Tidworth Garrisons 1962-63, cmmnd Maj RAMC 1963, registrar accident and emergency dept Tidworth Mil Hosp 1963-66, postgrad sr med offr course Royal Army Med Coll London 1966-67, sr med offr Med Reception Station Sennelager W Germany 1967-68, 2 i/c 30 Field Ambulance RAMC 1968-69, Lt-Col 1969, sr med offr Br Forces Sharjah 1970, CO 7 Field Ambulance RAMC and sr med offr 12 Mechanised Bde 1970-73, dep asst dir gen Army Med Dept MOD 1973-75; asst dir Med Servs: Rhine Area BAOR 1975-76, HQ UKLF 1976-78, SE Dist 1978; dep dir Med Servs FARELF 1978-80, Col 1979, CO Br Mil Hosp Rinteln BAOR 1980-86, Col Enviromental Med and Res Def Med Servs Directorate 1986-87, med advsr (Army) Chemical Def Estab Porton Down 1987-89, Dept of Gen Practice Royal Army Med Coll 1989-; govr Christ the King Sch Amesbury; OStJ 1986; LRCPI, LRCSI; memb: BMA 1955, Salisbury Med Soc 1986; assoc memb RCGP 1981; *Recreations* music, theatre, reading, gardening, travel; *Style*— Dr Richard Treneman; The Grange, Idmiston, Nr Salisbury, Wilts SP4 0AP (☎ 0980 610374)

TRENERRY, Hon Mrs (Jennifer); *née* Hill; da of Baron Hill of Luton, PC (Life Peer; d Aug 1989), and Marion Spencer, *née* Wallace (d Nov 1989); *b* 1933; *Educ* Sch of St Mary and St Anne Abbots Bromley, and London Univ; *m* 1, 1960 (m dis), Robert Duncan Barnaby Leicester, MB; 2 s (Andrew b 1961, Stephen b 1963), 2 da (Sarah b 1963, Gillian b 1968); m 2, 1974, Thomas Trenerry; *Career* medical practitioner in paediatrics and community health; hon paediatric registrar Westmead Hosp, Sydney; child medical offr Parranatta Child Health Centre, Sydney; *Recreations* tennis, bush-walking, crafts; *Style*— The Hon Mrs Trenerry; 33 Day Rd, Cheltenham, New South Wales, Australia

TRENERRY, Michael John Boulden; s of Leslie Trenerry, and Margaret Trenerry; *b* 27 March 1953; *Educ* Truro Sch, Essex Inst of Higher Educn, Bristol Poly, Poly of South West (LLB, Dip ES, Cert Ed); *m* 19 July 1975, Elizabeth Mary, da of Benny Pearce; 2 da (Samantha b 1980, Rebecca b 1985); *Career* formerly slr in private practice; md Michael Trenerry Ltd; sr lectr in legal and mgmnt studies; memb Int Bar Assoc; *Recreations* numismatics, horses, art; *Style*— Michael Trenerry, Esq; Newhaven, 1 Northfield Drive, Truro, Cornwall TR1 2BS (☎ 0872 77977)

TRENOUTH, Dr Michael John; s of John Trenouth, of Grange-over-Sands, and Marjorie Trenouth; *b* 2 June 1946; *Educ* Friend's Sch Lancaster, Univ of Manchester (BSc, BDS, MDS, PhD, DOrth, DDO, FDS, RCPS); *Career* Manchester Dental Hosp: house offr 1971-72, lectr in oral surgery 1972-75, lectr dental anatomy and hon registrar orthodontics 1975-78, lectr orthodontics and hon sr registrar orthodontics 1978-85; conslt orthodontist Preston Royal Hosp 1985-; treas Manchester and Region Orthodontic Study Gp 1980-85; FDS, RCPS; *Recreations* ice skating; *Style*— Dr Michael Trenouth; Royal Preston Hospital, PO Box 66, Sharoe Green Lane, Preston PR2 4HT (☎ 0772 710597)

TRESS, Dr Ronald Charles; CBE (1968); s of Stephen Charles Tress (d 1953), and Emma Jane, *née* Blewitt (d 1975); *b* 11 Jan 1915; *Educ* Gillingham Co Sch, Univ Coll Southampton, Univ of London (BSc), St Deiniol's Library Hawarden, Univ of Manchester; *m* 25 July 1942, Josephine Kelly, da of Hubert James Medland (d 1968); 1 s (Thomas b 1949), 2 da (Sarah b 1944, Janet b 1946); *Career* asst lectr econs Univ Coll of SW Exeter 1938-41, econ asst War Cabinet Offices 1941-45, econ advsr Cabinet Sec 1945-47, reader in public fin Univ of London 1947-51, prof of political economy Univ of Bristol 1951-68, master Birkbeck Coll London 1968-77; dir The Leverhulme Tst 1977-84, SW Econ Planning Cncl 1965-68, devpt cmmr 1959-81, tstee City Parochial Fndn 1974-77 and 1979-89, govr Christ Church Coll Canterbury 1975-91, memb Cncl Univ of Kent Canterbury 1977-, vice pres Royal Econ Soc 1979- (sec gen 1975-79), chm Lord Chllr's Advsy Ctee on Legal Aid 1979-84; Hon: DSc Bristol 1968, LLD Furman S Carolina 1973, DUniv Open Univ 1974, LLD Exeter 1976, DSc Southampton 1978, DCL Univ of Kent at Canterbury 1984; *Clubs* Athenaeum; *Style*— Dr R C Tress, CBE; 22 The Beach, Walmer, Deal, Kent CT14 7HJ (☎ 0304 373254)

TRETHOWAN, (Henry) Brock; s of Michael Trethowan, OBE (d 1968), of Hampshire, Phyllis Franklin, *née* Miles (d 1981); *b* 22 June 1937; *Educ* Sherborne; *m* 11 April 1970, Virginia, da of Lt-Col Geoffrey Charles Lee, of Farnham, Surrey; 2 da (Rebecca b 1966, Henrietta b 1977); *Career* slr; ptnr Trethowans of Salisbury; rec County and Crown Ct; pres Wilts Valuation and Community Charge Tbnl 1989-, vice pres Euham Village Centre; tstee Salisbury Hospice Care Tst 1981- (vice chm 1988-); *Recreations* family, gardening, food and wine; *Style*— Brock Trethowan, Esq; 10 Hartwood Rd, Salisbury, Wilts; College Chambers, New St, Salisbury, Wilts (☎ 0722 412512, fax 0722 431300)

TRETHOWAN, Prof Sir William Henry; CBE (1975); s of William Henry Trethowan (d 1933), of Hampstead, and Joan Durham, *née* Hickson (d 1949); *b* 3 June 1917; *Educ* Oundle, Clare Coll Cambridge (MB BChir), Guy's Hosp; *m* 1, 1940, Pamela (d 1985), da of Jack Waters (d 1946); 1 s, 2 da; m 2, 1988, Heather Dalton; *Career* serv RAMC 1944-47, BAOR, India, Maj; prof of psychiatry: Sydney Univ Aust 1956-62, Univ of Birmingham 1962-82 (emeritus 1982-); hon conslt psychiatrist: Central Birmingham Health Dist 1962-82, Hollymoor Hosp 1964-82, Midland Centre for Neurosurgery 1975-82; dean of Med Faculty Univ of Birmingham 1968-74; hon fell Royal Aust and NZ Coll of Psychiatry; Hon DSc Chinese Univ of Hong Kong; Hon FRCPsych; FRCP, FRACP; kt 1980; *Books* Textbook of Psychiatry (with A C P Sims), Uncommon Psychiatric Syndromes (with M D Enoch); *Recreations* music; *Clubs* Birmingham Med Inst; *Style*— Prof Sir William Trethowan, CBE; 99 Bristol Rd, Edgbaston, Birmingham B5 7TX (☎ 021 440 7590)

TREUHAFT, Hon Mrs (Jessica); *see*: Mitford, Jessica

TREUHERZ, Julian Benjamin; s of Werner Treuherz and Irmgard, *née* Amberg; *b* 12 March 1947; *Educ* Manchester GS, ChCh Oxford (MA), Univ of East Anglia (MA); *Career* Manchester City Art Gallery: trainee 1971, asst Keeper of Fine Art 1972, Keeper of Fine Art 1974; keeper of Art Galleries (Walker Art Gallery, Liverpool and Lady Lever Art Gallery, Port Sunlight) 1989-; publications: Pre-Raphaelite Paintings from the Manchester City Art Galllery 1981, Hard Times: Social Realism in Victorian Art 1987, Country Houses of Cheshire (jtly with Peter de Figueiredo, 1988); various articles in art-historical jls; memb: Museums Assoc 1971, Victorian Soc 1971 (hon sec Manchester Group 1972-9, chm Manchester Group 1980-83); ctee memb Contemporary Art Soc 1990, ctee memb Liverpool Univ Fine Arts Sub-Gp 1990-; *Recreations* playing the piano, cooking, opera; *Style*— Julian Treuherz, Esq; Walker Art Gallery, William Brown St, Liverpool L3 8EL (☎ 051 207 0001)

TREVELYAN, Dennis John; CB (1981); s of John Henry Trevelyan (d 1982), and Eliza Trevelyan; *b* 21 July 1929; *Educ* Enfield GS, Univ Coll Oxford; *m* 1960, Carol, da of John Coombes (d 1944); 1 s, 1 da; *Career* entered Home Office 1950, princ private sec to Lord Pres and Ldr of House 1964-67, asst under-sec state NI Office 1972-76, asst under sec state Home Office Broadcasting Dept 1976-77, dep under-sec of state Home Office and dir-gen Prison Serv 1978-83, first Civil Serv cmmr 1983-89 (responsible to the Queen and the Privy Cncl for keeping unqualified persons out of the Civil Service); princ Mansfield College Oxford 1989-; memb: City of London Univ Business Sch Cncl 1986, Exec Ctee of Industl Participation Assoc 1987-; govr London Contemporary Dance Tst 1986-; *Recreations* music, sailing; *Clubs* Athenaeum, MCC; *Style*— Dennis Trevelyan, Esq, CB; Mansfield College, Mansfield Road, Oxford OX1 3TF

TREVELYAN, Edward Norman; s and h of Sir Norman Trevelyan, 10 Bt; *b* 14 Aug 1955; *Style*— Edward Trevelyan, Esq

TREVELYAN, Geoffrey Washington; s of late Rt Hon Sir Charles P Trevelyan, 3 Bt; hp of bro, Sir George Trevelyan, 4 Bt; *b* 4 July 1920; *Educ* Oundle, Univ of Cambridge (MA); *m* 1947, Gillian Isabel, da of late Alexander Wood; 1 s, 1 da; *Career* de Havilland AC Co Ltd 1941-61; dir: Chatto & Windus Ltd, Hogarth Press Ltd 1962-78, Chatto, Bodley Head and Jonathan Cape Ltd 1970-78; chm Thames North Regn of Abbeyfield Soc, technical writer, hon treas Family Planning Assoc 1975-90; dir: Family Planning Sales Ltd 1985-90, The Lake Hunts Ltd; *Style*— Geoffrey Trevelyan, Esq; Silkstead, 3b Abbey Mill End, St Albans, Herts (☎ 0727 864866)

TREVELYAN, Sir George Lowthian; 4 Bt (UK 1874), of Wallington, Northumberland; s of Rt Hon Sir Charles Philips Trevelyan, 3 Bt, PC, JP (d 1958), and Mary Katharine, OBE, JP (d 1966), yst da of Sir Hugh Bell, 2 Bt; *b* 5 Nov 1906; *Educ* Sidcot Sch, Trinity Coll Cambridge (MA); *m* 1940, Editha Helen, da of Col John Lindsay-Smith, CBE; 1 da (adopted); *Heir* bro, Geoffrey Washington Trevelyan; *Career* WWII Capt RB, transferred to GHQ Travelling Wings for Home Guard Trg Adj Highland Home Guard; taught at No1 Army College Dalkeith 1945-47; craftsman-designer of furniture Peter Waals workshops 1929-31, trained and qualified to teach F M Alexander Technique for re-education 1931-36, taught at Gordonstoun and Abinger Hill Sch 1936-41, princ Attingham Park, the Shropshire Adult Coll 1947-71; fndr and pres Wrekin Tst (an educnl charity concerned with spiritual nature of man and the universe) with Malcolm Lazarus as co-dir ran weekend courses and conferences countrywide 1971-83; presented with the Right Livelihood Award in Stockholm 1982; lectures widely in Britain and abroad; *Books* Twelve Seats at the Round Table (with Edmund Matchett, 1976), A Vision of the Aquarian Age (1977), The Active Eye in Architecture (1977), Magic Casements (1980), Operation Redemption (1981), Summons to a High Crusade (1986); *Style*— Sir George Trevelyan, Bt; The Barn, Hawkesbury, Badminton, Avon GL9 1BW (☎ 045 423 359)

TREVELYAN, Sir Norman Irving; 10 Bt (E 1662), of Nettlecombe, Somerset; s of Edward Trevelyan (gggs of Sir John Trevelyan, 4 Bt); suc 3 cous, Sir Willoughby Trevelyan, 9 Bt, 1976; *b* 29 Jan 1915; *m* 1951, Jennifer Mary, da of Arthur E Riddett, of Long Orchards, Copt Hill Lane, Burgh Heath, Surrey; 2 s, 1 da; *Heir* s, Edward Norman Trevelyan; *Style*— Sir Norman Trevelyan, Bt; 1041 Adella Av, Coronada, Calif 92118, USA

TREVELYAN, (Walter) Raleigh; s of Col Walter Raleigh Fetherstonhaugh Trevelyan (d 1953), and Olive Beatrice, *née* Frost (d 1976); *b* 6 July 1923; *Educ* Winchester; *Career* Capt Rifle Bde Nat Serv WWII; publisher 1948-88: Collins, Hutchinson, Michael Joseph (as ed dir), Hamish Hamilton, Jonathan Cape, Bloomsbury; translator from Italian (John Florio Prize 1967), reviewer; contrib: Apollo, Connoisseur, John Rylands Bulletin; FRSL (memb Cncl); *Books* The Fortress (1955), A Hermit Disclosed (1960), The Big Tomato (1966), Princes Under The Volcano (1972), The Shadow of Vesuvius (1976), A Pre-Raphaelite Circle (1978), Rome '44 (1982), Shades of the Alhambra (1984), The Golden Oriole (1987); *Recreations* travel, gardening; *Clubs* Brooks's, Groucho; *Style*— Raleigh Trevelyan, Esq; 18 Hertford St, London W1Y 7DB (☎ 071 629 5879); St Cadix, St Veep, Lostwithiel, Cornwall PL22 0PB (☎ 0208 872313)

TREVELYAN, Baroness; Violet Margaret; o da of late Gen Sir William Henry Bartholomew, GCB, CMG, DSO; *m* 10 Nov 1937, Baron Trevelyan, KG, GCMG, CIE, OBE (Life Peer, d 1985); 2 da; *Style*— The Rt Hon the Lady Trevelyan; 24 Duchess of Bedford House, London W8 7QN

TREVERTON-JONES, Ronald; s of Dennis Ford Treverton-Jones (d 1950), of Newport, Gwent, and Alison Joy Bielski, *née* Morris-Prosser; *b* 1 Aug 1949; *Educ* Malvern, Univ of Wales Swansea (BSc); *m* 1, 31 July 1970 (m dis 1985), Margaret Jean, da of Donald John Purser, of Northfield, Brimingham; 2 s (Peter b 1976, Michael b 1978); m 2, 17 Oct 1987, Jacqueline Diane, da of James Leslie Beckingham Welch (d 1974), of Quinton, Birmingham; *Career* graduate trainee National Westminster Bank 1970-72, trainee N Lea Barham & Brooks 1970-74, ptnr Harris Allday Lea & Brooks 1976- (assoc memb 1974-76); vice chm The Bow Group London 1979-80, chm Birmingham Bow Group 1979-90, sec Round Table Nat Conference Birmingham, tstee Avoncroft Museum Devpt Tst 1989; memb Stock Exchange 1975; *Books* Financing our Cities (with Edwina Currie and Peter McGauley, 1976), Right Wheel - A Conservative Policy for the Motor Industry (1977); *Recreations* country pursuits, woodland managment, travel; *Clubs* Birmingham; *Style*— Ronald Treverton-Jones, Esq; Ravenhill Court, Lulsley, Knightwick, Worcs (☎ 0886 21242), La Bartelle Basse, Pont De

Russac, 46170, Castelnau-Montratier, France; Harris Allday Lea & Brooks, 33 Great Charles St, Birmingham B3 3JN (☎ 021 2331222, fax 021 2362587)

TREVES, Vanni Emanuele; s of Giuliano Treves (ka 1944), and Marianna, *née* Baer; *b* 3 Nov 1940; *Educ* St Paul's, Univ of Oxford (MA), Univ of Illinois (LLM); *m* 7 Jan 1971, Angela Veronica, da of Lt-Gen Sir Richard Fyffe, DSO, OBE, MC (d 1971); 2 s (Alexander b 1973, William b 1975), 1 da (Louise b 1983); *Career* slr; ptnr Macfarlanes 1970 (sr ptnr 1987); dir: Oceonics Group plc 1984, Saatchi & Saatchi Co plc 1987-90, BBA Group plc 1987 (chm 1989-), Fiskars Ltd 1989; dep chm McKechnie plc 1990-; tstee: J Paul Getty Jr Charitable Tst, 29th May 1961 Charitable Tst; hon treas London Fedn of Boys' Clubs; *Recreations* walking, eating, watercolours; *Clubs* Boodle's, City of London; *Style—* Vanni Treves, Esq; 10 Norwich St, London EC4A 1BD (☎ 071 831 9222, fax 071 831 9607, telex 296381)

TREVETHIN, Baron; *see*: Oaksey, Baron

TREVETT, Peter George; s of George Albert Trevett, of 56 Berrylands, Surbiton, Surrey, and Janet, *née* Ayling; *b* 25 Nov 1947; *Educ* Kingston GS, Queens' Coll Cambridge (MA, LLM); *m* 12 July 1972, Vera Lucia; 2 s (Thomas b 1973, Philip b 1978), 1 da (Jessica b 1982); *Career* called to the Bar Lincoln's Inn 1971, practising revenue barr 1973-; memb Hon Soc of Lincoln's Inn; author of various articles in professional jls; *Recreations* golf, collecting cactaceae, gardening, book collecting, reading; *Clubs* Woking Golf; *Style—* Peter Trevett, Esq; 11 New Sq, Lincoln's Inn, London WC1A 3QB (☎ 071 242 4017, fax 071 831 2391, telex 894189 TAXLAW G)

TREVILIAN; *see*: Cely-Trevilian

TREVOR, 4 Baron (UK 1880); Charles Edwin Hill-Trevor; JP (Clwyd 1959); s of 3 Baron Trevor (d 1950, himself gs of 3 Marquess of Downshire); *b* 13 Aug 1928; *Educ* Shrewsbury; *m* 1967, Susan Janet Elizabeth, da of Ronald Ivor Bence, DSC, VRD, BEM, of Birmingham; 2 s (Hon Marke Charles b 1970, Hon Iain Robert b 1971); *Heir* s, Hon Marke Charles Hill-Trevor; *Career* chm Berwyn Petty Sessional Division; tstee: Royal Forestry Soc of England, Wales & N Ireland, Inst of Orthopaedics Robert Jones & Agnes Hunt Orthopaedic Hospital; memb: Awe District Salmon Fishery Bd, River Orchy Fishery Assoc, N Wales Police Authy; patron of 2 livings; CStJ; *Recreations* fishing, shooting; *Clubs* East India; *Style—* The Rt Hon the Lord Trevor, JP; Brynkinalt, Chirk, Wrexham, Clwyd (☎ 0691 773425); Auch, Bridge of Orchy, Argyllshire (☎ 083 84 282)

TREVOR, John Clyfford; s of Clyfford Trevor (d 1970), and Louisa Ryder, *née* Airey; *b* 16 Aug 1932; *Educ* USA, Millfield; *m* 14 Sept 1957, Jane Carolyn, da of Capt Charles Houstoun-Boswall (d 1946), Royal Scots Greys (*see* Baronetage); 2 s (Mark b 1961, Richard b 1969), 2 da (Carolyn b 1959, Emma b 1963); *Career* Nat Serv 2 Lt First Bn East Surrey Regt 1952-53, serv Libya and and Egypt; sr ptnr J Trevor and Sons 1972-88 (exec chm 1988-); chm: Central London branch RICS 1978-79, gen practice div of the Central London Branch RICS 1973-74, RICS Working Pty on Conveyancing 1986-, J Trevor Mortleman and Poland Ltd, Lloyds Brokers 1985-88; memb Gen Practice Divisional Gen Cncl 1985-; FRICS, ACIArb; *Recreations* furniture restoration, gardening; *Clubs* Naval and Military, MCC; *Style—* John Trevor, Esq; J Trevors & Sons, 58 Grosvenor St, London W1X 0DD

TREVOR, Phyllis, Baroness; Phyllis; da of J A Sims, of Ings House, Kirton-in-Lindsey, Lincs; *m* 1927, 3 Baron Trevor (d 1950); *Career* OStJ; *Style—* The Rt Hon Phyllis, Lady Trevor; The Holt, Chirk, Wrexham

TREVOR, William; CBE (1977); *b* 24 May 1928; *Educ* St Columba's Coll Dublin, Trinity Coll Dublin; *m* 1952, Jane, da of C N Ryan; 2 s; *Career* writer; books: The Old Boys (1964), The Boarding House (Hawthornden Prize, 1965), The Love Department (1966), The Day We Got Drunk on Cake (1967), Mrs Eckdorf in O'Neill Hotel (1969), Miss Gomez and the Brethren (1971), The Ballroom of Romance (1972), Elizabeth Alone (1973), Angels at the Ritz (Royal Soc of Lit Award, 1975), The Children of Dynmouth (Whitbread Award, 1976), Lovers of Their Time (1978), The Distant Past (1979), Other People's Worlds (1980), Beyond the Pale (1981), Fools of Fortune (Whitbread Award, 1983), A Writer's Ireland (1984), The News from Ireland (1986), The Silence in the Garden (Yorkshire Post Book of the Year Award, 1989), Family Sins (1990); Allied Irish Banks' Prize 1976; Hon D Litt: Univ of Exeter 1984, Trinity Coll Dublin 1986, Queen's Univ Belfast 1989, Nat Univ of Ireland (Cork) 1990; memb Irish Acad of Letters; *Style—* William Trevor, Esq, CBE; c/o A D Peters, 5th Floor, The Chambers, Chelsea Harbour, London SW10

TREVOR-ROPER, Patrick Dacre; s of Dr Bertie William Edward Trevor-Roper (d 1978), of Alnwick, Northumberland, and Kathleen Elizabeth Trevor-Roper (d 1965); *b* 9 June 1916; *Educ* Charterhouse, Clare Coll Cambridge (MA, MD), Westminster Med Sch; *Career* Capt NZ Med Corps, served Italy 1943-46; conslt ophthalmic surgn: Westminster Hosp 1947-82, Moorfields Eye Hosp 1963-81; teacher Univ of London 1949-82; ed Transactions of the Ophthalmic Soc UK 1949-88; pres Ophthalmic Section RSM 1978-80, vice pres Ophthalmic Soc of UK, chm Ophthalmic Qualifications Ctee BMA; Freeman City of London, Liveryman Worshipful Co of Spectacle Makers; FRCS 1947, FRGS, FRZS, FRSA; *Books* The World Through Blunted Sight (1970), The Eye and its Disorders (2 edn, 1984), Lecture notes in Ophthalmology (8 edn, 1991), Recent Advances in Ophthalmology (1975); *Recreations* music, travel; *Clubs* Athenaeum, Beefsteak; *Style—* Patrick Trevor-Roper, Esq; 3 Park Sq West, London NW1 4LS (☎ 071 935 5052)

TREW, Anthony Leslie Gwynn; s of Howel Douglas Gwynn Trew, of Ivy Cottage, Burwash, E Sussex and Madeline Louisa, *née* Daniel (d 1987); *b* 20 March 1942; *Educ* Haileybury and Imperial Service Coll; *m* 24 April 1976, Angela Rosalind Drury, da of late Gerald Drury Culverwell; 1 s (Charles b 1989), 3 da (Cressida b 1981, Annabel b 1985, Felicity b 1987); *Career* admitted slr 1968, ptnr Richards Butler 1974-, res ptnr Abu Dhabi 1978-; govr Al Khubairat Community Sch; Freeman City of London 1977; memb Law Soc; *Recreations* swimming, walking, talking, reading, desert driving; *Clubs* Reform, Abu Dhabi Marina, Law Soc; *Style—* Anthony Trew, Esq; PO Box 46904, Abu Dhabi, UAE (☎ 010 971 2 778600, fax 010 971 2 778630, telex 22261 RBLAW EM); Richards Butler, Beaufort House, 15 St Botolph St, London EC3A 7EE (☎ 071 2476555, fax 071 2475091, telex 949494 RBLAW G); Flitterbrook Barn, Rushlake Green, Heathfield, E Sussex TN21 9PL (☎ 0435 830643)

TREW, Francis Sidney Edward; CMG (1984); s of Major Harry Francis Trew (d 1968), and Alice Mary, *née* Sewell (d 1972); *b* 22 Feb 1931; *Educ* Taunton's Sch Southampton; *m* 1958, Marlene Laurette, da of late George Peter Regnery, of Stratford, Conn, USA; 3 da; *Career* HM Dip Serv; served in: Lebanon 1952, Amman 1953, Bahrain 1953-54, Jedda 1954-56; vice consul Philadelphia 1956-58, second sec Kuwait 1959-62, consul Guatemala City 1965-70, first sec Mexico City 1971-74, consul Algeciras 1977-79, high cmmr Belmopan Belize 1981-84, HM ambass Panama 1984-88; Order of Aztec Eagle (Mexico) 1975; *Recreations* fishing, carpentry; *Style—* Francis Trew, Esq, CMG; Higher Trickeys, Morebath Tiverton, Devon EX16 9AL

TREW, Peter John Edward; s of Antony Francis Trew, DSC, and Nora, *née* Houthakker; *b* 30 April 1932; *Educ* Diocesan Coll Cape, RNC Dartmouth; *m* 1, 1955 (m dis 1985), Angela Margaret, da of Kenneth Patrick Rush, CBE (d 1981); 2 s (Robin b 1957, Martin b 1959), 1 da (Sarah b 1961); m 2, 1985, Joan, da of Allan Howarth; *Career* RN 1950-54; MP (C) for Dartford 1970-74; dir Rush-Tompkins Gp plc 1973-90; *Style—* Peter Trew, Esq; 1 Painshill House, Cobham, Surrey (☎ 0932 863315)

TREWBY, Vice Adm Sir (George Francis) Allan; KCB (1974); s of Vice Adm George Trewby, CMG, DSO (d 1953), of Richmond, Surrey; *b* 8 July 1917; *Educ* RNC Dartmouth, RNEC Keyham, RNC Greenwich; *m* 1942, Sandra Coleridge, da of late G C Stedham, of Kenya; 2 s; *Career* joined RN 1931, Cdr 1950, Capt 1959, Rear Adm 1968, asst controller (Polaris) MOD 1968-71, Vice Adm 1971, Chief of Fleet Support and memb of Admty Bd 1971-74, ret 1974; mangr Messrs Foster Wheeler Ltd 1975-77, conslt 1977-87, ret 1987; *Style—* Vice Adm Sir Allan Trewby, KCB; 2 Radnor Close, Henley-on-Thames, Oxon

TREWBY, Dr Peter Nicholas; s of Vice Adm sir Allan Trewby, KCB and Sandra Coleridge, *née* Stedham; *b* 12 Dec 1946; *Educ* Marlborough, Churchill Coll Cambridge (MA, MB BChir, MD); *m* Catherine Scott, da of Capt A S Falconer, of Sedbergh, Cumbria; 1 s (Thomas Joseph b 1985, Hannah Jane b 1983); *Career* conslt physician and clinical tutor Darlington Meml Hosp; FRCP 1985; *Recreations* carpentry, campanology, gardening, walking; *Style—* Dr Peter Trewby; Darlington Memorial Hosp, Darlington, Co Durham (☎ 0325 380100)

TREWIN, Ion Courtenay Gill; s of John Courtenay Trewin, OBE (d 1990), the theatre critic and author, and Wendy Elizabeth, *née* Monk; *b* 13 July 1943; *Educ* Highgate; *m* 7 Aug 1965, Susan Harriet, da of Walter Harry Merry (d 1953), of 48 Cholmeley Cres, Highgate, London; 1 s (Simon b 1966), 1 da (Maria b 1971); *Career* reporter: The Independent & South Devon Times Plymouth 1960-63, The Sunday Telegraph 1963-67; The Times: ed staff 1967-79, ed The Times Diary 1969-72, literary ed 1972-79; ed Drama Magazine 1979-81, editorial dir Hodder & Stoughton 1985- (sr ed 1979-85); chm: Library Ctee Highgate Literary & Scientific Inst 1974-90, Soc of Bookmen 1986-88; chm of judges Booker Prize for fiction 1974; memb: Arts and Library Ctee MCC 1988-, Lit Panel Arts Cncl of GB 1975-78; Mgmnt Ct Booker prize 1989-; author of introductions to new edns of classic novels (for Leslie Charteris, Sapper and Darnford Yates); *Books* Journalism (1975), Norfolk Cottage (1977); *Recreations* restoring clocks, watching cricket, gossip; *Clubs* Garrick, MCC; *Style—* Ion Trewin, Esq; 48 Cholmeley Cres, Highgate, London N6 5HA (☎ 081 348 2130); Bank Cottage, Surrey St, Wiggenhall St Germans, King's Lynn, Norfolk PE34 3EX; Hodder & Stoughton Ltd, 47 Bedford Sq, London WC1B 3DP (☎ 071 636 9851, 0732 450111, fax 071 631 5248, 0732 460134, telex 885887, 95122)

TRIBBLE, Norman Reginald; s of Frederick John Tribble (d 1972), of Exeter, and Alice Maud, *née* Hooper (d 1980); *b* 17 Feb 1927; *Educ* St Luke's Coll Sch Exeter, Univ of London (BSc); *m* 20 July 1946, Christine Mary, da of Stuart Allen Moore (d 1960), of Folkestone; 1 da (Hilary b 1953); *Career* Lt 1 Bn Devonshire Regt 1945-48, served Singapore 1946 and Hong Kong 1947; accountant Inst Prodn Engrs 1948-53; mgmnt accountant Shell-Mex and BP Ltd 1953-60, dir and proprietor Manchester Exchange and Investment Bank Ltd 1960-89; chm Schlesinger & Co Ltd; dir: London Advsy Bd, Bank Julius Baer & Co Ltd, Reliance Bank Ltd; hon life pres ACT (fndn chm 1979), chm Patrons Club, Cons Assoc Tunbridge Wells; churchwarden, memb The Archbishop's Cncl for the Church Urban Fund; Liveryman Worshipful Co of Musicians; FCCA 1953; *Recreations* music, sport; *Clubs* Naval and Military, Overseas Bankers; *Style—* Norman Tribble, Esq; 237 Forest Rd, Tunbridge Wells, Kent TN2 5H7 (☎ 0892 20149); Manchester Exchange and Investment Bank, International House, 1 St Katherine's Way, London E1 9UN (☎ 071 488 4888, fax 071 488 3480, telex 261238)

TRIBE, John Edward; s of George Edward Tribe, of March, Cambs, and Gwendoline, *née* Morton; *b* 24 March 1946; *Educ* Oundle, Univ of Reading (BSc); *Career* joined family farming businesses 1969-; dir: Marcam & MDS Supplies Ltd 1978-, United Farmers Trading Agency 1989- (chm designate 1990); first chm March and CHATTERIS Trg Gp 1978-80; chm: March branch NFU 1985-86, Agric Trg Bd Cambridgeshire Area Trg Ctee 1987-90, Fenland Crime Prevention Panel 1988-89, Cambridgeshire Co NFU 1990, East of England Agric Soc Safety Ctee 1990- (memb Cncl 1990-); memb Bd ATB West Anglia (LATB9) 1990-, dir Cambs Tec (Central and Southern Cambs Trg and Enterprise Cncl) 1990-; *Style—* John Edward Tribe, Esq; Stapleford Grange, Stapleford, Cambridge CB2 5ED (☎ 0223 843098); 59 Elwyn Rd, March, Cambs PE15 9BY (☎ 0354 53180)

TRICE, John Edward; s of Edward Victor Trice (d 1962), of Pembroke, Dyfed, and Denise Mary, *née* Bray (d 1975); *b* 29 Jan 1941; *Educ* Pembroke GS, Gonville and Caius Coll Cambridge (BA, LLM, MA); *Career* Legal Dept Manchester Corp 1963-66, jt fndr Cambrian Law Review 1970, hon lectr in law UCW Aberystwyth 1989 (lectr 1966-89), emeritus ed Cambrian Law Review 1989; author of numerous articles and reviews in legal periodicals; sec UCW Music Club 1973-88, memb World Congress of Legal Editors 1982, external examiner to Univs of Dundee Birmingham and London; hon memb Soc Public Teachers of Law; *Books* English and Continental Systems of Administrative Law (jtly, 1978); *Recreations* music, cats, walking, travel; *Clubs* UCW Staff House; *Style—* John Trice, Esq; Ty Penfro, Llvest Mews, Llanbadarn Fawr, Aberystwyth SY23 3AU (☎ 0970 623787), Law Faculty, UCW (Univ College of Wales), Aberystwyth (☎ 0970 623111)

TRICKETT, Lynne; da of Dr Jack Fishman, of London, and Eileen, *née* Slonims; *b* 19 May 1945; *Educ* St Martin in the Fields HS for Girls, Chelsea Coll of Art; *m* 8 March 1968, Terence Wilden Trickett;1 s (Alexander Wilden b 9 Aug 1973), 2 da (Polly Kate b 4 Nov 1977, Rosey Anna b 22 Dec 1983); *Career* designer: Planning Unit 1966-67, Wiggins Teape 1967-69, FFS Advertising Agency NY 1969-70; fndr ptnr Trickett & Webb 1971-; work exhibited and published throughout the world, winner of numerous awards in D&AD, Donside and National Calender awards; frequent memb: Jury D&ADA, Bursary Jury RSA; external examiner CNAA (memb Graphic Design Ctee 1986-87), memb Nat Business Calender Award Ctee, chm Nat Graphic Design & Print Awards 1990; FCSD, FRSA; *Recreations* reading, collecting Russian avant garde art, modern British art, ephemera, toys; *Style—* Ms Lynne Trickett; 9 Hamilton Terrace, London NW8 9RE (☎ 071 286 5209); Trickett & Webb Limited, The Factory, 84 Marchmont St, London WC1 (☎ 071 388 5832, fax 071 387 4287)

TRICKETT, Peter; s of late Henry Alexander Trickett, and Irene, *née* Hallam; *b* 25 March 1955; *Educ* Burnage GS, Stockport Coll of Technology, Birmingham Poly (BA); *m* 1980, Sarah Cardine, da of William Leonard Humpage; 1 s (Thomas Peter b 14 March 1986), 2 da (Emma Caroline b 2 June 1988, Lucy Alice b 23 Aug 1990); *Career* with John Hunt Associates 1977, with Conran Associates 1978, founding dir The Design Solution 1984-; memb Design & Art Directors Club of GB 1986; *Recreations* sailing; *Style—* Peter Trickett, Esq; The Design Solution, 20 Kingly Court, London W1R 5LE (☎ 071 434 0887, fax 071 434 0269)

TRICKETT, (Mabel) Rachel; da of James Trickett, and Margaret, *née* Hesketh; *b* 20 Dec 1923; *Educ* Lady Margaret Hall Oxford (BA, MA); *Career* asst to curator Manchester City Art Galleries 1945-46, lectr Univ of Hull 1946-49 and 1950-54, Cwlth Fund fell Yale 1949-50, fell St Hugh's Coll Oxford 1954-73 (princ 1973-91); *Books* The Return Home (1952), The Course of Love (1954), Point of Honour (1958), A Changing Place (1952), The Elders (1966), The Honest Muse (1967), A Visit to Timon (1970); *Style—* Miss Rachel Trickett; St Hugh's Coll, Oxford OX2 6LE (☎ 0865 274900)

TRIDGELL, (Francis) Peter; TD (1954); s of Arthur Ernest Tridgell (d 1980), of Tottenham, and Florence Tridgell (d 1974); *b* 12 Feb 1925; *Educ* Tottenham Co Sch; *m* 17 March 1950, Lois Audrey, da of Leonard Hugh Cooper (d 1970), of Tottenham;

1 s (Mark b 1955, d 1968), 3 da (Helen b 1952, Rhona b 1957, Kathryn b 1962); *Career* RAFVR 1943, Royal Signals 1944, i/c communications United Provinces Indian Signals 1946, Sqdn Cdr Royal Signals TA 1948-62; Nat Westminster Bank: area dir N and E London 1969-75, transmission mangr 1975-78, dep gen mangr Business Devpt and Planning 1978-85; memb Eurocheque Working Gp Brussels 1975-78, vice-pres Euro Fin Mktg Assoc 1983-85, govr and treas Middx Poly, fndr memb Enfield Nat Tst Assoc; Freeman City of London 1976, Liveryman Worshipful Co of Painter Stainers 1976; FCIB 1981, FInstM 1986; *Recreations* dinghy racing, tennis, singing; *Clubs* Livery; *Style—* Peter Tridgell, Esq, TD; 100 Prince George Ave, London N14 4ST (☎ 081 360 7158)

TRIER, Peter Eugene; CBE (1980); s of Ernst Joseph Trier (d 1938), and Nellie Marie, *née* Bender (d 1979); *b* 12 Sept 1919; *Educ* Mill Hill Sch, Trinity Hall Cambridge (Mathematical Wrangler); *m* 1946, Margaret Nora, da of Frederick James Holloway (d 1964), of Shoreham-by-Sea; 3 s; *Career* RN Scientific Serv 1941-50; dir: Mullard Research Labs 1953-69, Philips Electronics 1969-85; chm Def Sci Advsy Cncl 1981-85, pro chllr Brunel Univ 1980- (chm Cncl 1973-79), pres Inst of Mathematics 1982 and 1983; Hon DTech Brunel 1975; Glazebrook medal and prize Inst of Physics 1984; FEng; *Recreations* travel, sailing, railway history, Trier family history; *Clubs* Savile; *Style—* Peter Trier, Esq, CBE; Yew Tree House, Bredon, Tewkesbury, Glos GL20 7HF (☎ 0684 72200)

TRIGER, David Ronald; s of Dr Kurt Triger (d 1968), of Abertillery, Gwent, and Olga, *née* Adler; *b* 19 Sept 1941; *Educ* Cheltenham, St John's Coll Oxford (MA, BM BCh, DPhil); *m* 10 Aug 1972, Jennifer Ann, da of Prof Albert Francis Norman, of Hull; 3 s (Simon b 1977, Richard b 1982, Michael b 1982), 1 da (Sara b 1980); *Career* lectr in med Univ of Southampton Med Sch 1972-77, MRC travelling fell Univ of S California 1975-76, reader in med Univ of Sheffield Med Sch 1984- (sr lectr 1977-84); sec Br Assoc for Study of the Liver 1984-87, memb Cncl Br Soc of Gastroenterology 1985-88; FRCP 1980, memb Assoc of Physicians GB and I 1984; *Books* Practical Management of Liver Disease (1981), Clinical Immunology of the Liver and Gastrointestinal Tract (1986), Liver Disease in Gall Stones: The Facts (1987); *Recreations* gardening, Indian cooking; *Style—* David Triger, Esq; Dept of Medicine, Royal Hallamshire Hospital, Sheffield S10 2JF (☎ 0742 766222, fax 0742 721104)

TRIGG, Prof Roger Hugh; s of The Rev Ivor Trigg, of Taunton, Somerset, and Muriel Grace, *née* Collins; *b* 14 Aug 1941; *Educ* Bristol GS, New Coll Oxford (MA, DPhil); *m* 12 July 1972, Julia da of Wilfred Gibbs, of Taunton, Somerset; 1 s (Nicholas b 10 May 1973 d 1990), 1 da (Alison b 26 Jan 1977); *Career* Univ of Warwick: lectr 1966-74, sr lectr 1974-78, reader 1978-87, chm of Dept of Philosophy, dir of Centre for Res in Philosophy and Literature, prof of philosophy 1987-; *Books* Pain and Emotion (1970), Reason and Commitment (1973), Reality at Risk (1980, revised edn 1989), The Shaping of Man (1982), Understanding Social Science (1985), Ideas of Human Nature (1988); *Clubs* Somerset and Worcestershire CCC; *Style—* Prof Roger Trigg; Department of Philosophy, University of Warwick, Coventry CV4 7AL (☎ 0203 523019)

TRIGGER, Ian James Campbell; s of Lt Walter James Trigger (d 1961), and Mary Elizabeth, *née* Roberts (d 1984); *b* 16 Nov 1943; *Educ* Ruthin Sch Wales, Univ Coll of Wales Aberystwyth (LLB), Downing Coll Cambridge (MA); *m* 28 Aug 1971, Jennifer Ann, da of Harry Colin Downs (d 1986); 2 s (Ieuan Mungo Campbell b 12 Oct 1973, Simon Huw Campbell b 21 April 1977); *Career* law lectr UWIST 1967-70, called to the Bar Inner Temple 1970, Northern circuit 1970-, asst rec 1986-; pt/t chm: Social Security Appeal Tbnl 1983-, Med Appeal Tbnl 1989-; churchwarden St Saviour's Church Oxton 1986-88; *Recreations* preserving the countryside from the ravages of greed and the Church from mediocrity; *Style—* Ian Trigger, Esq; Alyn Bank, Llanarmon-yn-ial, Mold, Clwyd; Oriel Chambers, 5 Covent Garden, Liverpool L2 8UD (☎ 051 236 7191)

TRIGGS, Helen Lois; da of Robert Roy Triggs, of Hull, and Ethel, *née* Pettican (d 1974); *b* 16 Nov 1950; *Educ* Beverley HS Yorkshire, Univ of Leicester (BA), Hull Coll of Commerce (LCC private sec's Dip); *Career* editorial asst Orbis Publishing 1973, account exec Bell Capper Assoc 1975; Leslie Bishop Co: account exec 1978, dir 1981, jt md 1985, md 1988; dep chm Shandwick PR Ltd (acquired Leslie Bishop Co 1990-); FIPR, memb Mktg Soc; *Recreations* dressage, travel; *Clubs* British Horse Soc Dressage Group; *Style—* Ms Helen Triggs; Garden Flat, 40 Elsham Rd, London W14 8BH (☎ 071 603 8573); Shandwick PR Co Ltd, 114 Cromwell Road, London SW7 4ES (☎ 071 835 1001, fax 071 373 4311, car 0860 385860)

TRILLING, Capt Ossia; s of Sam Trilling (d 1950), and Rachel, *née* Kaplan (d 1968); *b* 22 Sept 1913; *Educ* St Paul's, St John's Coll Oxford (BA); *m* 11 July 1951, Marie-Louise, da of Harald Otto William Crichton-Fock (d 1978); *Career* WWII enlisted RA 1940, cmmnd 2 Lt 1942, demob Actg Capt 1946; co fndr and dir Chesham Repertory Theatre 1939-40; ed: Theatre Newsletter 1946-51, Theatre News Agency 1946; regular contrib Theatre World 1954-65, theatre and music corr The Times; obituary contrib: The Times, The Daily Telegraph, The Independent; regular contrib: The Stage, BBC arts programmes, BBC World Serv, various Euro radio stations (ret 1989); corr numerous papers and pubns, translator of foreign language dramas; lectr Br Cncl; vice pres Int Assoc of Theatre Critics 1956-77; memb Bd of Dirs Theatre Royal Stratford East 1975-89; memb Cncl: Critics' Circle (UK), Br Theatre Inst; Offr Royal Order of the North Star Sweden 1980, kt first class Order of the Finnish Lion Finland 1983; *Books* International Theatre (1946); *Recreations* swimming, walking, theatre-going, piano playing; *Style—* Capt Ossia Trilling; Flat 7, 9A Portland Place, London W1N 3AA (☎ 071 580 6440)

TRIMBLE, Prof (Edward) Geoffrey; s of Robert James Trimble (d 1968), of Bristol, and Kathleen Annie, *née* Dicks (1976); *b* 17 Nov 1923; *Educ* Weston-super-Mare GS, Univ of Bristol (BSc); *m* 30 June 1965, Gerda Hee, da of Osvaid Nikolas Rasmussen, of Horsens, Denmark; 1 s (Ian b 23 Feb 1958), 1 da (Christine b 1 June 1961); *Career* RAE 1943-45; appts with civil engrg contractors and conslt 1964-67, conslt PE Management Consultant Ltd 1960-64, dep chief exec Nat Bldg Agency 1964-67, prof of constructive mgmnt Loughborough Univ 1967-89, projects dir Euro Construction Inst 1989, fndr and pres Assoc of Project Mangrs UK, vice pres Internet Int Zurich, chm Construction Mgmnt Steering Gp SERC 1978-86; FICE, MIMechE, MIStructE; *Recreations* skiing, windsurfing; *Style—* Prof Geoffrey Trimble; Forest Lodge, Woodhouse Eaves, Leicestershire LE12 8RE (☎ 0509 890389, fax 0509 890159); Dept of Civil Engineering, Univ of Technology, Loughborough LE11 3TU (☎ 0509 222620, fax 0509 610231, telex 34319 UNITEC G)

TRIMLESTOWN, 20 Baron (I 1461); Anthony Edward Barnewall; s of 19 Baron Trimlestown (d 1990), and his 1 w, Muriel, *née* Schneider (d 1937); *b* 2 Feb 1928; *Educ* Ampleforth; *m* 1, 1963 (m dis 1973), Lorna Margaret Marion (d 1988), da of late Charles Douglas Ramsay; m 2, 1977, Mary Wonderly, er da of late Judge Thomas F McAllister, of Grand Rapids, Michigan, USA; *Heir* bro, Hon Raymond Charles Barnewall b 1930; *Career* late Irish Gds; *Style—* The Rt Hon the Lord Trimlestown; Ada, Michigan 49301, USA

TRINDER, Frederick William; s of Charles Elliott Trinder (d 1970), and Grace Johanna, *née* Hoadly (d 1974); *b* 18 Nov 1930; *Educ* Ruskin Coll Oxford, LSE (BSc); *m* 17 Oct 1974, Christiane Friederike Brigitte, da of Joachim Hase (d 1952); 1 s (Stefan Charles b 1979); *Career* admitted slr 1966, dep charity cmmr 1974-84 (cmmr 1984-85); tstee Charities Official Investmt Fund, John Hunt award Tst; memb: BBC Central Appeals Advsy Ctee, IBA Appeals Advsy Ctee; *Recreations* travel, reading; *Clubs* Royal Overseas League; *Style—* Frederick Trinder, Esq; 37 The Common, W Wratting, Cambridge CB1 5LR (☎ 0223 290469)

TRINGHAM, David Lawrence; s of George William Tringham (d 1986), of Grasse, France, and Madeleine Joyce, *née* De Courcy (d 1987); *b* 13 March 1935; *Educ* Bedford Modern, Preston Manor GS; *m* 24 Oct 1962, Annette Alberte, da of Raymond Andre Schmitt (d 1987), of Paris; 2 da (Andréa Fréderique b 18 March 1966, Gaia Frances b 3 April 1970); *Career* Nat Serv Bombardier 39 Heavy Field Regt 1953-55; entered film indust under Sir Michael Balcon at Ealing Studios 1955, asst dir Lawrence of Arabia 1961-62; first asst dir working with: David Lean, Joseph Losey, Richard Lester, Sidney Lumet, Don Siegel, Peter Hyams amongst others; writer of numerous screenplays, adaptor and dir The Last Chapter; *Recreations* painting and drawing, cycling, reading and writing in the sun; *Style—* David Tringham, Esq; 40 Langthorne St, London SW6 6JY

TRINICK, (George Edward) Michael; OBE (1984), DL (Cornwall 1988-); s of Cdr G W Trinick, OBE, RD, RNR (d 1959), of Mylor, Falmouth, Cornwall, and Rosamond Frances, *née* Lloyd; *b* 10 July 1924; *Educ* Haileybury, Christ's Coll Cambridge, RAC; *m* 30 Sept 1950, (Maud) Elizabeth Lyon, da of Arthur Bickersteth Hutchinson (d 1952), of Godalming, Surrey; 2 s (Marcus b 1952, William b 1965), 2 da (Mary b 1954, Cecily b 1956); *Career* RE 1942-47, Substantive Lt, attached Bombay Sappers and Miners 1946-47; land agent Nat Tst Cornwall 1953, sec Nat Tst Ctee for Devon and Cornwall 1958-84, ret; pres Royal Inst of Cornwall 1971-72; High Sheriff of Cornwall 1989-90; fell Chartered Land Agents Soc 1947, FLAS 1969, FRICS 1970; *Recreations* shooting; *Clubs* Farmer's; *Style—* Michael Trinick, Esq, OBE, DL; Newton House, Lanhydrock, Bodmin, Cornwall PL30 4AH (☎ 0208 72543)

TRIPONEL, Hon Mrs (Angela Caroline); da of Baron Harris of High Cross (Life Peer); *m* 1977, Roland Triponel, of Lyon, France; 4 da; *Style—* The Hon Mrs Triponel; Oakhurst, 21 Warwick Rd, Hale, Cheshire WA15 9NS (☎ 061 928 8409)

TRIPP, Rt Rev Howard George; s of Basil Howard Tripp (d 1981), and Alice Emily, *née* Haslett (d 1985); *b* 3 July 1927; *Educ* The John Fisher Sch Purley, St John's Seminary Wonersh Guildford; *Career* asst priest: St Mary's Blackheath SE3 1953-56; Our Lady Queen of Peace E Sheen 1956-62; asst fin sec RC Diocese of Southwark 1962-68, parish priest Our Lady Queen of Peace E Sheen 1965-71, dir Southwark Catholic Children's Soc 1971-80, auxiliary bishop Southwark and titular bishop of Newport 1980-; *Recreations* vegetable gardening; *Style—* The Rt Rev Howard Tripp; 8 Arterbury Road, London SW20 8AJ (☎ 081 946 4609)

TRIPPIER, David Austin; RD, JP (Rochdale 1975), MP (Cons) Rossendale and Darwen 1983-; s of Austin Trippier MC; *b* 15 May 1946; *Educ* Bury GS; *m* 1975, Ruth Worthington; 3 s; *Career* cmmnd Offr Royal Marine Reserve 1968; sec: Cons Parly Def Ctee, All Pty Parly Footwear Ctee; ldr Cons Gp Rochdale Cncl 1974-76 (memb Cncl 1969-78); memb Stock Exchange 1968-; MP (C) Rossendale 1979-1983, nat vice-chm Assoc Cons Clubs 1980, PPS to Kenneth Clarke as Min State (Health) DHSS 1982-83; parly under-sec state: Trade and Indust 1983-85, Dept of Employment 1985-87, Dept of the Environment 1987-89; Min of State DOE 1989-; dep chm Cons Pty May-Dec 1990; *Style—* David Trippier, Esq, RD, JP, MP; House of Commons, London SW1 (☎ 071 219 4186)

TRISTRAM, Maj Uvedale Francis Barrington; Major; s of Uvedale Barrington Tristram (d 1926), and Edla Mary, *née* Guarracino (d 1960); *b* 20 March 1915; *Educ* St George's Coll Surrey; *m* 8 Sept 1939, Elizabeth Frances, da of Capt Harold-Eden-Pearson (d 1945); 1 da (Carolyn Frances, b 23 Oct 1940); *Career* cmmnd RASC 1941, Capt 1942; mil observer Italian Campaign: 7 Armd Div, 1 Inf, 46 Inf, 6 Armd Div; Maj GSO2 8 Br Armd Corps 1945, DADPR Eastern Cmd 1946, SO2 (PR) War Off 1947-48, RARO (Intelligence Corps) 1948-65; BP: dep mangr PR Tehran 1948-49, mangr PR oilfields Iran 1949-50, staff London 1950-60; managing ed Hulton Publications 1960-61, editorial mangr Longacre Press 1961-62, dir of info Govt of Basutoland (colonial serv) 1962-66, head Info Servs UK Freedom from Hunger Campaign 1967-73, fndr and ed World Hunger; press advsr: Voluntary Ctee on Overseas Aid & Devpt 1973-76, Catholic Fund for Overseas Devpt 1976-77; Master of the Keys (Guild of Catholic Writers) 1988-, memb Inst of Journalists; *Books* Adventure in Oil (with Henry Longhurst, 1959), Saint John Fisher (Mazenod Press Basutoland, 1966); *Clubs* Press, Naval; *Style—* Maj Uvedale Tristram; 19 Mallards Reach, Weybridge, Surrey KT13 9HQ (☎ 0932 248411)

TRITTON, Alan George; s of George Henton Tritton, of Lyons Hall, Essex, and Iris Mary, *née* Baillie; *b* 2 Oct 1931; *Educ* Eton; *m* 1, 1958 (m dis), Elizabeth Clare d'Abreu, QC, *qv*; 2 s; m 2, 1972, Diana Marion Spencer; *Career* memb Br Schs Exploring Soc Expedition N Norway 1949; serv 1 Bn Seaforth Highlanders Malaya 1950-52 (wounded in action Pahang); memb Falkland Islands Dependencies Survey 1952-54; Barclays Bank: joined 1954, local dir 54 Lombard St 1964, dir Barclays Bank UK Management Ltd 1972, dir Barclays Bank Ltd 1974-, dir Barclays Bank plc 1974-; dir Mercantile Credit Co Ltd 1973-, vice pres Equitable Life Assurance Soc 1983- (dir 1976-); Royal Geographic Soc: a vice pres 1983-, memb Cncl 1975-, hon treas 1984-; chm: Westminster Abbey Investmt Ctee 1976-, Calcutta Tercentenary Tst 1989-; cmmr Public Works Loan Bd 1970-74; memb: Ctee Br Trans-Atlantic Expedition 1966-69, Ctee Br Everest SW Face Expedition 1974-75, Ctee of Mgmnt Mount Everest Fndn 1976-, Friends Ctee Scott Polar Res Inst 1976-80, Governing Body Br Nat Ctee Int Chamber of Commerce 1975-90 (hon treas 1985), Cncl Essex Agric Soc 1973-76, Indo-Br Industrialists Forum; *Style—* Alan Tritton, Esq; Barclays plc, 54 Lombard St, London EC3P 3AH

TRITTON, Maj Sir Anthony John Ernest; 4 Bt (UK 1905); s of Maj Sir Geoffrey Ernest Tritton, 3 Bt, CBE (d 1976); *b* 4 March 1927; *Educ* Eton; *m* 1957, Diana, da of Rear Adm St John Aldrich Micklethwait, CB, DSO; 1 s, 1 da (Clarissa); *Heir* s, Jeremy Ernest Tritton; *Career* Maj (ret) The Queen's Own Hussars; farmer; *Recreations* shooting, fishing; *Clubs* Cavalry and Guards'; *Style—* Maj Sir Anthony Tritton, Bt; River House, Heytesbury, Warminster, Wilts BA12 0EE

TRITTON, (Elizabeth) Clare (Mrs McLaren); QC (1988); da of Col A L D'Abreu, CBE (d 1976), of Congleton Warwickshire, and Elizabeth Throckmorton (d 1970); *b* 18 Aug 1935; *Educ* Convent of The Holy Child, Mayfield St Leonards, Univ of Birmingham (BA); *m* 1, Alan George Tritton, *qv* (m dis 1971); 2 s (Guy b 18 Nov 1963, Charles b 12 May 1965), 1 da (Christina Margaret (Mrs Birch) b 24 Sept 1960); m 2, 2 Dec 1973, Andrew McLaren; *Career* called to the Bar 1968; chm The Bar European Group 1982-84, UK rapporteur to FIDE Sept 1988, vice chm Int Practice Ctee Bar Cncl 1988-; fndr Bar European News, author of numerous legal articles; memb: Euro Ctee Br Invisible Exports Cncl, Ind Cncl FIMBRA 1991; *Books* Towards A Community Air Transport Policy (contrib, 1989); *Recreations* travelling, gardening, reading; *Style—* Mrs Clare Tritton, QC; 18 Battersea Square, London SW11 3JF (☎ 071 228 7140), Coughton Court Coughton, Alcester, Warwickshire (☎ 0789 762542), The Manor, Molland, S Molton, N Devon (☎ 07697 325), European Law Chambers, 5 Paper Buildings, Temple, London EC4Y 7HB (☎ 071 583 9275, fax 071 583 1926, car 0860 564320)

TRITTON, Hon Mrs (Georgina Anne); *née* Ward; da of 1 Viscount Ward of Witley, PC by his 1 w Anne Capel; *b* 12 March 1941; *Educ* Lawnside, Sorbonne; *m* 1, 1963 (m dis 1971), Alastair Forbes, the writer and journalist, s of late James Forbes, of Boston; m 2, Patrick Tritton, *qv*; 2 s; *Career* actress; *Recreations* bullfighting, reading; *Style—* The Hon Mrs Tritton; Quintana 23, Gustavo Madero, La Villa, Mexico City, Mexico

TRITTON, Jeremy Ernest; s and h of Sir Anthony Tritton, 4 Bt; *b* 6 Oct 1961; *Style—* Jeremy Tritton, Esq; 2A Beechmore Rd, London SW11 4ET (☎ 071 627 8056)

TRITTON, Patrick Claude Henry; 2 s of Patrick Arthur Tritton (gn of Sir Charles Tritton, 1 Bt) by his 1 w, Judith, *née* Hurt; *b* 18 May 1934; *Educ* Eton, Cambridge Univ; *m* 1, 1962 (m dis), as her 2 husb, Nancy, da of Sir Harry Oakes, 1 Bt (*see* Nancy Oakes); m 2, Hon Georgina Ward, *qv*, da of 1 Viscount Ward of Witley, PC, and former w of Alastair Forbes; *Career* broker; *Recreations* bullfighting, falconry, reading; *Clubs* White's, Pratt's, Boodle's; *Style—* Patrick Tritton, Esq

TRITTON, Peter Robert Jolliffe; s of Lt-Col J H Tritton, MBE (d 1988), and Pamela, *née* Skewes-Cox; *b* 22 May 1951; *Educ* Charterhouse; *m* 9 Sept 1975, Hon Sally Louise, da of 2 Baron Nelson of Stafford; 1 s (Jonathan James Hedley b 1981), 1 da (Emma Pamela Louise b 1986); *Career* memb Lloyds 1981-; dir: Alexander Howden Insurance Brokers 1980-85, P/R Alexander Howden Gp 1985-, P/R Alexander & Alexander Europe plc 1988-; *Recreations* shooting, skiing, organ music, good food; *Style—* Peter Tritton, Esq; Weasel Cottage, Brent Pelham, Herts (☎ 0279 777584); 8 Devonshire Square, London EC2M 4PL (☎ 071 623 5500, fax 071 626 1178, telex 882171 HOWDEN G, car 0831 111619)

TRODDEN, Paul John; s of Lawrence Trodden (d 1962), of Birmingham, and Lilian Jane Trodden; *b* 17 April 1950; *Educ* St Philips GS Birmingham; *m* 22 Dec 1973, Patricia Mary, da of Daniel Francis Duffy (d 1983), of Birmingham; 1 s (Matthew Lawrence b 1979), 2 da (Laura Cathrine b 1981, Kate Elizabeth b 1985); *Career* chartered and certified accountant; ACA; *Style—* Paul J Trodden, Esq; 4 Eachway Lane, Rednal, Birmingham; 30 St Mary's Row, Birmingham B13 8JG (☎ 021 449 8121)

TROKE, Helen Suzanne; MBE (1987); da of Graham Ronald Troke, of 9 Cerdic Mews, Hamble, Southampton SO35 LW, and Diana Rosemary, *née* Hudd; *b* 7 Nov 1964; *Career* int badminton player: 91 Eng caps, 82 titles; Euro championships: gold medals in singles 1984 and 1986, gold and silver medals in team competition, under 18 singles medals 1981 and 1983; cwlth games: 2 singles gold medals, 2 team gold medals; German Open Grand Prix singles champion 1989; mini olympics for mentally and physically handicapped: deaf badminton; *Recreations* golf, swimming, tennis; *Style—* Miss Helen Troke, MBE; 12 Hamble Manor, The Green, Hamble, Southampton (☎ 0703 454359)

TROLLOPE, Sir Anthony Simon; 17 Bt (E 1642), of Casewick, Co Lincoln; o s of Sir Anthony Owen Clavering Trollope, 16 Bt (d 1987), and Joan Mary Alexis, *née* Gibbes; *b* 31 Aug 1945; *Educ* Sydney Univ (BA); *m* 1969, Denise, da of Trevern Thompson, of N Sydney, NSW, Australia; 2 da (Kellie Yvette b 1970, Analese Christine b 1972); *Heir* bro, Hugh Irwin Trollope, b 31 March 1947; *Style—* Sir Anthony Trollope, Bt; Churinga Lodge, 28 Midson Rd, Oakville, NSW 2765, Australia

TROLLOPE, Hugh Irwin; yr s of Sir Anthony Owen Clavering Trollope, 16 Bt (d 1987); bro and hp of Sir Anthony Simon Trollope, 17 Bt, *qv*; *b* 31 March 1947; *m* 1971, Barbara Anne, da of William Ian Jamieson, of Lawley Crescent, Pymble, NSW, Australia: 1 s (Andrew Ian b 1978), 2 da (Edwina Anne b 1976, Jennifer Kate b 1980); *Style—* Hugh Trollope, Esq; 26 Bayswater Road, Lindfield, NSW 2070, Australia

TROLLOPE, Dowager Lady; Joan Mary Alexis; *née* Gibbs; da of Alexis Robert Gibbs, of Manly, NSW, Autralia; *m* 1942, Sir Anthony Owen Clavering Trollope, 16 Bt (d 1987); 2 s; *Style—* The Dowager Lady Trollope; Clavering, 77 Roseville Ave, Roseville, NSE, Australia

TROLLOPE, Joanna (Mrs Curteis); da of Arthur George Cecil Trollope, of Overton, Hampshire, and Rosemary, *née* Hodson; *b* 9 Dec 1943; *Educ* Reigate Co Sch For Girls, St Hugh's Coll Oxford (MA); *m* 1, 14 May 1966 (m dis 1985), David Roger William Potter, s of William Edward Potter, of Durweston, Dorset; 2 da (Louise b 15 Jan 1969, Antonia b 23 Oct 1971); m 2, 12 April 1985, Ian Bayley Curteis, s of John Richard Jones, of Lydd, Romney Marsh; *Career* writer; Info Res Dept FO 1965-67, English teacher in various schs, feature writer Harpers and Queen, freelance work for maj newspapers; memb: Soc of Authors, PEN, Ctee Trollope Soc; *Books* Parson Harding's Daughter (Historical Novel of the Year, 1980), The Taverners' Place (1986), Britannia's Daughters (1983), The Choir (1988), A Village Affair (1989), A Passionate Man (1990), The Rector's Wife (1991); *Style—* Miss Joanna Trollope; The Mill House, Coln St Aldwyns, Cirencester, Gloucestershire

TROMANS, Christopher John; s of Percy Tromans (d 1979), and Phyllis Eileen, *née* Berryman; *b* 25 Nov 1942; *Educ* Truro Sch, St Edmund Hall Oxford (MA); *m* 31 May 1969, Gillian, da of John Delbridge Roberts (d 1966); 1 s (Andrew b 1972), 1 da (Sarah b 1970); *Career* admitted slr 1968; ptnr: Sitwell Money and Murdoch Truro 1971-79, Murdoch Tromans and Hoskin Truro and Redruth 1979-88, Murdoch Tromans Truro 1988-; NP 1970; memb No 4 SW Legal Aid Area Ctee and Appeals Panel, dep high ct and co ct registrar W Circuit 1987-90, dep district judge 1991-; memb Lions Club of Truro, dep chm of govrs Truro Sch, memb Royal Inst of Cornwall; ACIArb 1978, FRSA 1990; *Recreations* boating, practical theatre, travel, military history; *Clubs* Oxford Union, Cornwall Farmers (Truro); *Style—* Christopher Tromans, Esq; 17 Knights Meadow, Carnon Downs, Truro, Cornwall TR3 6HU (0872 863 695); Murdoch Tromans, Richmond Villa, 37 Edward St, Truro, Cornwall TR1 3AJ (☎ 0872 79474, fax 0872 79137)

TROMPETER, Dr Richard Simon; s of Nysen Trompeter, and Betty, *née* Rubin; *b* 27 Jan 1946; *Educ* Orange Hill Co GS for Boys London, Guys Hosp Med Sch (MB BS); *m* 26 March 1978, Barbara Ann, da of Ervin Blum; 2 s (Alexander b 1979, Nicholas b 1981), 1 da (Rebecca b 1986), 1 step da (Sara b 1973); *Career* house surgn Guys Hosp and house physician St Mary Abbots Hosp 1970-71; sr house offr 1971-74: Renal Unit Royal Free Hosp, paediatrics Guys Hosp and The London Hosp, neonatal paediatrics John Radcliffe Hosp, Gt Ormond St Hosp; registrar Hosps for Sick Children Gt Ormond St 1975-77, res fell Dept of Immunology Inst of Child Health 1977-78, hon sr registrar and lectr in paediatrics Guys Hosp Med Sch 1979-84, sr lectr in paediatrics Royal Free Hosp Sch Med 1984-87, conslt paediatric nephrologist The Royal Free Hosp 1986-89 (hon sr lectr Sch of Med), conslt paediatric nephrologist Hosps for Sick Children Gt Ormond St 1986-89 (princ appt 1989-); ed Guys Hosp Gazette 1969-70, memb RCP Standing Ctee of Membs 1976-78, jr staff rep Br Paediatric Assoc Cncl 1982-83, clinical rep Conf of Med Academic Reps 1982-83, govr ILEA Royal Free Hosp Sch 1985-89; memb: Bd of Studies in Med Univ of London 1986-89, Div of Physicians Hosps for Sick Children Gt Ormond St 1987-; chm Div of Child Health Hampstead Authy 1987-89 (memb Div of Physicians 1984-89, memb Exec Ctee 1988-89); memb: Library Ctee Royal Free Sch of Med Univ of London 1988-89 (memb: Academic Staff Assoc 1984-87, Educn Cncl 1984-89, Sch Cncl 1986-87), Exec Ctee and Cncl Renal Assoc 1989; FRCP 1989 (MRCP 1973); *Recreations* literature, theatre; *Style—* Dr Richard Trompeter; 1 Holt Close, London N10 3HW (☎ 081 444 8985); Hospitals for Sick Children, Great Ormond St, London WC1 3JH (☎ 071 405 9200, fax 071 829 8643)

TROOSTWYK, David Koos; s of Joseph Koos Troostwyk (d 1976), and Beatrice Isobel, *née* Thornborough (d 1978); *b* 5 Aug 1929; *Educ* Royal Coll of Art (travelling scholar, ARCA); *Career* artist; solo exhibitions: Univ of Southampton 1966, Gulbenkian Gallery 1969, Kasmin Ltd 1971, ICA 1974, Felicity Samuel Gallery 1977, Inst of Modern Art Brisbane 1979, Matt's Gallery 1979, 1981, 1984, Akumulatory Gallery Poznan 1980; group exhibitions incl: Kursaal Ostende 1968, Galerie 20 Amsterdam 1968, Annely Juda Gallery 1969, Axiom Gallery 1970, Alfred Schmela Dusseldorf 1972, Int Poezie Rotterdam 1974, Int Art Fair Basle 1975, Biannual Sydney 1976, ICA LA 1978, Tate Gallery (books) 1982, Barcelona (books) 1983, Artspace Sydney 1984; collections: Arts Cncl, Tate Gallery; head of painting Winchester Sch of Art 1964-67, head of sculpture Sydney Coll of Arts 1977-79, former visiting lectr Slade and Chelsea Sch of Arts; trading in photographic paper images 1980-; *Style—* David Troostwyk, Esq; Apartment 4, 3 Chester Way, London SE11 4UT (☎ 071 735 9278); Matt's Gallery, 10 Martello St, London Fields, London E8 3PE

TROTMAN, Palma Noreen Sarah; da of Algernon Bernard Harcourt (d 1941), of Jersey, and Irene Priscilla, *née* McFarling (d 1951); *Educ* Jersey Ladies Coll, St Anne's Coll Oxford (MA); *m* 1945, Jack Harry Walter Trotman, s of Harry Walter Trotman (d 1964); *Career* novelist; formerly with British FO, sometime tutor Queen's Univ Kingston Ontario and magazine ed; author of 18 diplomatic thrillers under Palma Harcourt pseudonym, novels published in UK, USA and translated into numerous languages; most recent books: Double Deceit (1990), The Reluctant Defector (1991); memb Crime Writers' Assoc; *Recreations* reading and writing; *Style—* Ms Palma Harcourt; Murray Pollinger Literary Agency, 222 Old Brompton Rd, London SW5 0BZ (☎ 071 373 3711, fax 071 373 3775)

TROTMAN-DICKENSON, Sir Aubrey Fiennes; s of Edward Newton Trotman-Dickenson, MC (d 1977), of Airesford, and Violet Murray, *née* Nicoll; *b* 12 Feb 1926; *Educ* Winchester, Balliol Coll Oxford (MA, BSc), Univ of Manchester (PhD), Univ of Edinburgh (DSc); *m* 11 Aug 1953, Danusia Irena, da of Maj Eugeniusz Karel Hewell (d 1955), of Warsaw; 2 s (Casimir b 1955, Dominic b 1961), 1 da (Beatrice b 1957); *Career* tech offr EI Pont de Nemours USA 1953-54, lectr Univ of Edinburgh 1954-60, prof of chemistry Univ Coll of Wales Aberystwyth 1960-68; princ: UWIST 1968-88, Univ Coll Cardiff 1987-88, Univ of Wales Coll Cardiff 1988-; memb Wales Gas Bd 1966-72, chm Job Creation Scheme 1975-78, govr Christ Coll Brecon 1985-88; kt 1989; *Style—* Sir Aubrey Trotman-Dickenson; Radyr Chain, Llandaff, Cardiff (☎ 0222 563263); PO Box 68 Cardiff CF1 3XA (☎ 0222 874835, fax 0222 874478, telex 498635)

TROTT, John Francis Henry; s of Francis Herbert Trott (d 1969), of 31 The Ridge, Coulsdon, Surrey, and Ellen Jane, *née* Tilbury; *b* 23 Jan 1938; *Educ* Whitgift Sch, Merton Coll Oxford (BA); *m* 24 April 1965, Averil Margaret, da of Harold Charles Milestone, of 13 Loxford Way, Caterham, Surrey; 2 s (Christopher John b 1966, Jeremy Charles b 1973), 1 da (Nicola Margaret b 1968); *Career* merchant banker; dir Kleinwort Benson Ltd 1972-86, dir Standard Life Assurance Co 1974-, chm and chief exec Kleinwort Benson International Investment Ltd 1986, chm Kleinwort Overseas Investmt Tst; dir: Merchants Tst, Brunner Investmt Tst; *Recreations* golf, tennis; *Clubs* Union, New York; *Style—* John Trott, Esq; Odstock, Castle Square, Bletchingley, Surrey RH1 4LB (☎ 0883 743 100); Kleinwort Benson Ltd, 10 Fenchurch St, London EC3

TROTT, Philip David Anthony; s of Sqdn Ldr Sydney Harold Trott (d 1985), of Fareham, and Ruth, *née* Neubauer; *b* 5 June 1952; *Educ* Oxford Poly, UCL (LLB); *Career* admitted slr 1979; Dale Parkinson & Co 1977-78; Lawford & Co: articles 1978-79, asst slr 1979-82, ptnr 1982-89; ptnr Thomson Snell & Passmore 1989-; lectr and speaker at various legal conferences and seminars; memb Industl Law Soc 1978-, hon legal advsr Kings Cross CAB 1979-, advsr to Art Law 1983-84, memb Exec Immigration Law Practitioners Assoc 1984-90 (chm 1986-88); occasional author of legal articles on immigration and employment law; memb Law Soc; *Recreations* sailing, swimming, playing squash, hill walking, flying, travel; *Style—* Philip Trott, Esq; Thomson Snell & Passmore, Tower House, 8-14 Southampton St, London WC2E 7HA (☎ 071 379 0921, fax 071 379 3526)

TROTTER, Alexander Richard; DL (Berwicks 1987); s of Maj H R Trotter (d 1962), of Charterhall, Duns, Berwicks, and Rona M, *née* Murray; *b* 20 Feb 1939; *Educ* Eton, City of London Tech Coll; *m* 1 June 1970, Julia Henrietta, da of Sir Peter McClintock Greenwell, 3 Bt (d 1979); 3 s (Henry b 1972, Edward b 1973, Rupert b 1977); *Career* served Royal Scots Greys 1958-68; mangr Charterhall Estate and Farm 1969, chm Mortonhall Park Ltd 1973-, dir Timber Growers' GB Ltd 1977-82, vice chm Border Grain Ltd 1984-; memb Berwickshire CC 1969-75 (chm Roads Ctee 1974-75), memb Cncl Scot Landowners' Fedn 1975- (chm Land Use Ctee 1975-78, convener 1982-85), memb Dept of Agric Working Party on the Agric Holding (Scotland) Legislation 1981-82, chm Cncl Scottish Ctee of Nature Conservancy 1985-90, memb UK Ctee for Euro Year of the Environment 1986-88; memb Royal Co of Archers (Queen's Body Guard for Scotland); FRSA 1987; *Recreations* skiing, riding, shooting; *Clubs* New (Edinburgh), Pratt's; *Style—* Alexander Trotter, Esq; Charterhall, Duns, Berwickshire TD11 3RE (☎ 089 084 210, office ☎ 089 084 301)

TROTTER, Colin John Richard; s of Maj Frederick Liddel (d 1961), and Evelyn Grace, *née* Oxley; *b* 12 Sept 1932; *Educ* Eton, RAC Cirencester; *m* 10 July 1964, Elizabeth Mary, da of Richard Joseph Stallard, (d 1986), of Monte Carlo; 1 s (Rupert Alexander John b 1965); *Career* Nat Serv 2 Lt KRRC; asst to Messrs Rylands & Co Cirencester 1956-60, res agent Wherwell Estate Andover 1961-64; owner-mangr: Mells Park Estate Frome 1964-79, Attington Stud Oxford 1979-; chm: Bristol Bd Commercial Union Assur Gp 1977-84, EDECO Holdings Ltd 1985-89; High Sheriff of Somerset 1972; memb: Co Agric Ctee Somerset 1968-74, cncl Royal Bath and W Agric Soc 1970-82, panel Agric Lands Tbnl 1970-89; FRICS 1970, FBIM; *Recreations* racing, shooting; *Style—* C J R Trotter, Esq; Attington Stud, Tetsworth, Oxfordshire OX9 7BY (☎ 084428 206)

TROTTER, Geoffrey Wensley; OBE (1988); s of Alfred Wensley Trotter (d 1936), of Calver, Derbys, and Gladys, Styring (d 1980); *b* 31 Dec 1924; *Educ* High Storrs GS Sheffield, HMS St Vincent Gosport Hants; *m* 26 June 1948, Mary Elizabeth, da of Capt Gerald Fountaine Sanger, CBE, JP (d 1981), of Willingham Cottage, Send, Surrey; 2 s (John Geoffrey b 1951, Andrew James b 1954), 1 da (Rosemary Clare (Mrs Heaton) b 1958); *Career* Seaman HMS St Vincent 1943, Sub Lt USN 1944-46, Lt Pilot Fleet Air Arm 1946-48; md London Cab Co Ltd 1958-; London Serv Stations Ltd 1958-: dir Datacab Ltd 1986, badge examiner Boy Scouts Assoc, parish cncllr; chm: London Taxi Bd 1958-, London Motor Cab Proprietors Assoc 1958-; FIMI, CEng; *Recreations* golf, squash, tennis, gardening; *Clubs* RAC; *Style—* Geoffrey Trotter, Esq, OBE; 74 Manor Drive, Surbiton, Surrey (☎ 071 735 7777); 1-3 Brixton Rd, London SW9 (☎ 071 735 2000)

TROTTER, Neville Guthrie; JP (Newcastle upon Tyne 1973), MP (Cons) Tynemouth 1974-; s of Capt Alexander Trotter (d 1940), and Elizabeth, *née* Guthrie; *b* 27 Jan 1932; *Educ* Shrewsbury, Univ of Durham (BCom); *m* 1983, Caroline, da of Capt John Darley Farrow, OBE, RN, and Oona, *née* Hall; 1 da (Sophie b 1985); *Career* RAF

1955-58; CA; ptnr Thornton Baker & Co 1962-74 (now conslt Grant Thornton), chm Cons Parly Shipping and Shipbuilding Ctee 1979-85 (vice chm 1976-79); memb: Select Ctee on Tport, US Naval Inst, RUSI; conslt to: Br Marine Equipment Cncl, Northern Gen Tport; dir: William Baird plc, Darchem Ltd; private bills passed on Consumer Safety, Licensing Law, Glue Sniffing; memb Newcastle City Cncl 1963-74 (Alderman 1970-74); formerly: memb Tyne & Wear Met Cncl, memb CAA Airline Users Ctee, vice chm Northumberland Police Authy, mil sec Cons Parly Aviation Ctee; memb: Northern Econ Planning Cncl, Tyne Improvement Cmmn, Tyneside Passenger Tport Authy; memb Cncl RUSI, FCA; *Recreations* aviation, gardening, fell walking; *Clubs* RAF, Northern Counties, Newcastle upon Tyne, Whitley Bay, Tynemouth Cons; *Style*— Neville Trotter, Esq, JP, MP; Grant Thornton, Higham House, Higham Place, Newcastle upon Tyne NE1 6LB (☎ 091 261 2631)

TROTTER, Thomas Andrew; s of His Hon Richard Stanley Trotter (d 1974), of Heswall, Merseyside, and Ruth Elizabeth, *née* Pierce (d 1982); *b* 4 April 1957; *Educ* Malvern, RCM, Univ of Cambridge (MA); *Career* concert organist; scholar RCM 1974; organ scholar: St George's Chapel Windsor 1975-76, King's Coll Cambridge 1976-79; organist: St Margaret's Church Westminster 1982-, to the City of Birmingham 1983-; debut Royal Festival Hall 1980, Prom Royal Albert Hall 1986, festival performances in UK and Europe; tours to: USA, Aust, and the Far East; recording artist for Decca 1989-; first prize winner: Bach Prize, St Albans Int Organ Competition 1979, Prix de Virtuosité, Conservatoire Rueil-Malmaison Paris 1981; ARCM, FRCO; *Style*— Thomas Trotter, Esq; c/o The Town Hall, Birmingham B3 3DQ (☎ 021 235 3942)

TROTTER, Timothy Hugh Southcombe; s of Antony Stuart Trotter (d 1976), of Brandsby, North Yorkshire, and Marie Louise, *née* Brook; *b* 7 Jan 1959; *Educ* Wellington, Ealing Coll London (BA, capt of Tennis, capt of Rugby); *m* 31 May 1986, Caroline, da of Peter Edney Brewer; 1 s (Alexander Antony Stuart b 16 May 1989); *Career* marketing mangr: Lanier Business Products Inc 1980-83, Fraser Henderson Limited 1983-85; ptnr and dep md Hill Murray Limited 1985-91, fndr and md Ludgate Communications Limited 1991-; MCIM 1984, MIPR 1986; *Recreations* tennis, skiing, shooting, backgammon, equestrianism, theatre; *Clubs* City of London, Queen's, Harlequins RFC, O W Tennis; *Style*— Timothy Trotter, Esq; Ludgate Communications Limited, 111 Charterhouse St, London EC1M 6AA (☎ 071 253 2252, fax 071 253 4717, car 0831 148390)

TROTTER, Maj William Kemp; CBE (1989), DL (Co Durham 1990); s of Lt-Col William Dale Chaytor Trotter (d 1983), of Gorst Hall, Staindrop, Darlington, Durham, and Gladys Mona, *née* Brendon; *b* 4 Sept 1929; *Educ* Canford; *m* 6 Aug 1960, (Mary) Virginia, da of Maj Sir Reginald Culcheth Holcroft, 2 Bt (d 1978); 3 s (James William Dale b 1964, Henry Edward Dale b 1966, Philip George Dale b 1969), 1 da (Victoria Mary (Mrs Nicholas James Thomas) b 1962); *Career* cmmnd 11 Hussars (PAO) 1948, Capt 1956, Maj 1963, serv Malaya, NI, Aden, BAOR; ret 1972; chm: Bishops Auckland Constituency Cons Assoc 1974-79, Northern Area Cons Assoc 1987-; High Sheriff Co Durham 1977; *Recreations* field sports; *Clubs* Army and Navy; *Style*— Maj William Trotter, CBE, DL; The Deanery, Staindrop, Darlington, Co Durham DL2 3LD (☎ 0833 60253)

TROUBRIDGE, Thomas; s of Vice Adm Sir Thomas Hope Troubridge, KCB, DSO, RN (d 1949); uncle of Sir Thomas Troubridge, 7 Bt; *b* 26 Dec 1939; *Educ* Eton; *m* 1, 1971 (m dis 1977), Baroness Marie Christine, da of Baron Günther von Reibnitz, and now Princess Michael of Kent (*see* Royal Family); m 2, 1981, Mrs Petronella Forgan; *Career* Kleinwort Benson Ltd; *Recreations* shooting; *Clubs* White's, The Brook (New York); *Style*— Thomas Troubridge, Esq; 1b Gertrude St, SW10 0JN (☎ 071 352 6049)

TROUBRIDGE, Sir Thomas Richard; 7 Bt (GB 1799); s of Sir Peter Troubridge, 6 Bt (d 1988), and Venetia, the Hon Lady Troubridge, *née* Weeks, da of 1 Baron Weeks; *b* 23 Jan 1955; *Educ* Eton, Univ Coll Durham; *m* 1984, Hon Rosemary Douglas-Pennant, da of 6 Baron Penrhyn, DSO, MBE, *qv*; 1 s (Edward Peter b 1989), 1 da (Emily Rose b 1987); *Heir* s, Edward Peter Troubridge b 10 Aug 1989; *Career* CA, ptnr Price Waterhouse; *Recreations* sailing ("Spreadeagle"), skiing; *Clubs* White's, RAC, Itchenor Sailing; *Style*— Sir Thomas Troubridge, Bt; 28 Lilyville Rd, London SW6 5DW (☎ 071 736 5739); Price Waterhouse, Southwark Towers, 32 London Bridge St, London SE1 9SY

TROUBRIDGE, Hon Lady (Venetia Daphne); *née* Weeks; da of Lt-Gen 1 and last Baron Weeks, KCB, CBE, DSO, MC, TD (d 1960), and Baroness Weeks (d 1985); *b* 29 Aug 1933; *m* 10 April 1954, Sir Peter Troubridge, 6 Bt (d 1988); 1 s, 2 da; *Style*— Venetia, The Hon Lady Troubridge; The Manor House, Elsted, Midhurst, West Sussex

TROUGHTON, Alistair Anthony James Lionel; s of Capt James Cecil Martin Troughton, of High Wych, Sawbridgeworth, Herts, and Georgina Mary, *née* Madell; *b* 8 Jan 1954; *Educ* Wellington; *m* 24 April 1976, (Helen) Mary Claire, da of George Xenophon Constantinidi, of Marsh Mills House, Wargrave Rd, Henley-on-Thames, Oxon; 2 s (James Anthony George Lionel b 16 May 1980, Albert Henry William (Bertie) b 19 Aug 1987), 2 da (Sarah Emily Jane b 22 May 1978, Lucy Mary b 16 July 1982); *Career* Bland Welch and Sedgwick Payne 1973-79, Seascope Insurance Services 1979-82 (dir 1981), Steel Burrill Jones GP plc 1983- (dir 1988); *Recreations* shooting, racing, fishing, cricket; *Clubs* Boodle's, MCC; *Style*— Alistair Troughton, Esq; The Old Rectory, Grafham, nr Huntingdon, Cambs PE18 0BB (☎ 0480 810 261); Steel Burrill Jones, Bankside House, 107-112 Leadenhall St, London EC3 (☎ 071 247 8888, fax 071 621 1848, car 0836 260 741, mobile phone 0836 722 545, telex 887830 SBJ G)

TROUGHTON, Sir Charles Hugh Willis; CBE (1966), MC (1940), TD (1959); s of Charles Vivian Troughton (d 1955), of Woolleys Hambleden, Henley on Thames, and Constance Lilla, *née* Tate (d 1973); *b* 27 Aug 1916; *Educ* Haileybury, Trinity Coll Cambridge; *m* 1947, Constance Gillean, yr da of Col Philip Mitford (7 in descent from Humphrey Mitford, whose yr bro John became a merchant in London and was ancestor of the Barons Redesdale) by his w Constance, da of Sir John Fowler, 2 Bt; 3 s (Peter b 1948, James b 1950, Simon b 1953), 1 da (Katrina b 1956); *Career* joined TA 1938, served WWII Oxon and Bucks LI (POW); barr 1945, chm Br Cncl 1977-84; dir: Electric & General Investment Co 1967-86 (chm 1977-80), William Collins & Sons 1977-88, Whitbread & Co 1978-85, Whitbread Investment Co 1981-; independent nat dir Times Newspaper Holdings 1983-88; former chm W H Smith & Son (Holdings) 1972-77; govr LSE 1975-; kt 1977; *Clubs* Garrick, MCC; *Style*— Sir Charles Troughton, CBE, MC, TD; Little Leckmelm House, Lochbroom, by Garve, Ross-shire

TROUGHTON, Sarah Hope; da of Robert Modan Thorne Campbell-Preston, of Ardchattan Priory, Oban, Argyll, and Angela, *née* Pearson (d 1981); *b* 7 March 1951; *Educ* Hornsey Coll of Art, Chelsea Sch of Art, English Sch of Gardening; *m* 1973, James Michael Troughton, s of Sir Charles Troughton; 1 s (Robert Charles Peter b 2 Dec 1982), 2 da (Jane Hope b 21 Oct 1977, Claire Gillean b 16 April 1980); *Career* practising artist 1976-, garden designer 1990-; solo exhibitions: Southampton Univ 1978, Macrobert Centre Stirling 1980, Corranhalls Oban 1980, Centre 181 Hammersmith 1982, Air Gallery London 1984, Sue Rankin Gallery London 1988; Silver Lion Ski Club GB 1970; memb Br Ski Team 1969-71; patron of New Art Tate 1986-; memb RHS, PHO; *Recreations* skiing, gardening, collecting art; *Clubs* Ski Club of GB; *Style*— Mrs Sarah Troughton; 1A St John's Gardens, London W1 2NP (☎ 071 727 0943)

TROUP, His Hon Judge Alistair Mewburn; s of William Annandale Troup, MC, and Margaret Lois, *née* Mewburn (d 1966); *b* 23 Nov 1927; *Educ* Merchant Taylors', New Coll Oxford; *m* 1969, Marjorie Cynthia, da of Francis Graham Hutchinson (d 1976); by prev marriages, 1 s (Alistair b 1964), 3 da (Victoria b 1953, Rosalind b 1955, Claudia b 1956); *Career* called to the Bar Lincoln's Inn 1952, crown counsel Tanganyika 1955-62, sr counsel 1962-64, dep circuit judge 1975-77, rec Crown Ct 1977-80, circuit judge 1980-; *Recreations* walking, gardening, golf; *Clubs* Sloane, Seaford Golf, Wildernesse (Sevenoaks); *Style*— His Hon Judge Alistair Troup; Lewes Crown Ct, High St, Lewes, E Sussex (☎ 0273 480400)

TROUP, Vice Adm Sir (John) Anthony Rose; KCB (1975), DSC (1943) and bar (1945); s of Capt H R Troup, RN; *b* 18 July 1921; *Educ* RNC Dartmouth; *m* 1, 1943 (m dis 1952), Joy Gordon-Smith; 2 s, 1 da; m 2, 1953, Cordelia Mary, da of W K T Hope, of Newbury, Berks; 2 s, 1 da; *Career* joined RN HMS Worcester and RNC Britannia 1934-38, HMS Cornwall 1939-40, submarine specialist 1941, war period in Submarines Turbulent H32 and Strongbow (despatches 1943), Capt 1959, Rear Adm 1969, Flag Offr Sea Trg 1969-71, Cdr Far E Fleet 1971-72, Flag Offr Submarines and NATO Cdr Submarines E Atlantic Area 1972-74, Flag Offr Scotland and N Ireland and NATO Cdr N Atlantic 1974-77; def advsr Scicon (UK) 1979-88; *Recreations* sailing, shooting, gardening; *Clubs* Army and Navy, Royal Yacht Sqdn; *Style*— Vice Adm Sir Anthony Troup, KCB, DSC; c/o Army and Navy Club, Pall Mall, London

TROUP, Donald Alexander Gordon; OBE (1988); s of Francis Gordon Troup (d 1984), of Haslemere, and Olive Mary Katharine, *née* Mosse (d 1959); *b* 20 Dec 1927; *Educ* Radley, Corpus Christi Coll Cambridge; *m* 1, 22 May 1954, Alison Joyce (d 1985), da of Dr Clement Neve (d 1939), of Croydon; 3 s (Robert James b 1955, Andrew Richard b 1957, Nigel Francis b 1960); m 2, 20 Dec 1986, Anne Hanson Barnes, wid of Brian Dearden Barnes (d 1982), da of Walter Hanson Freeman, MC, TD (d 1949); *Career* ptnr Porter & Cobb 1963-85, dir Cobbs 1985-86, exec conslt G A Property Servs 1986-90, conslt Caxtons 1990-; memb Cncl RURAL 1984-, pres RICS 1986-87; tstee Richard Watts and City of Rochester Almhouse Charities 1969-; Freeman Worshipful Co of Chartered Surveyors 1978; FRICS 1954, FAAV 1970; *Books* Agricultural Holdings Act (1984); *Style*— Donald Troup, Esq, OBE; Lees Lodge, Yalding, Kent (☎ office: 0622 812064, home 0622 814169)

TROUP, (John) Edward Astley; s of Vice Adm Sir Anthony Troup, KCB, DSC, and Lady Cordelia Mary; *b* 26 Jan 1955; *Educ* Oundle, CCC Oxford (MA, MSc); *m* 16 Dec 1978, Siriol Jane, da of Lt Col John Samuel Martin, OBE; 2 s (Lawrence 18 May 1985, Madoc 19 May 1989), 1 da (Mabyn 9 April 1987); *Career* admitted slr 1981; memb Law Soc Revenue Ctee; Freeman Worshipful Co of Grocers, Freeman City of London 1980; ATII; *Recreations* cinema, Wagner, reading Moby Dick, sleep; *Style*— Edward Troup, Esq; Simmons & Simmons, 14 Dominion Street, London EC2M 2RJ (☎ 071 6282020, fax 071 5884129)

TROUP, Prof Malcolm; s of William John Troup (d 1971), of Toronto, and Wendela Mary, *née* Seymour Conway (d 1960); *b* 22 Feb 1930; *Educ* Royal Conservatory of Music Toronto (ARCT), Saarlandisches Konservatorium, Univ of York (DPhil Mus), Guildhall Sch of Music and Drama (FGSM); *m* 24 Feb 1962, Carmen Lamarca-Bello Subercaseaux, da of Arturo Lamarca-Bello (d 1963), of Paris, Santiago and San Francisco; 1 da (Wendela b 1963); *Career* concert pianist 1954-70; toured world wide, int festivals incl: Prague, Berlin, York, Belfast, Montreal Expo, CBC Toronto, Halifax, Cwlth Arts Festival London; played with leading orchestras incl: LSO, Hallé, Berliner-Sinfonie, Hamburg, Bucharest, Warsaw, Oslo Philharmonic, Bergen Harmonien, Toronto, Winnipeg, Sao Paulo, Lima, Santiago; first performances of important modern works, numerous recordings; dir music Guildhall Sch of Music and Drama 1970-75, prof music and head dept City Univ London 1975-; judge of: CBC Nat Talent Competition, Chopin Competition of Aust 1988, Eckhard-Grammaté Piano Competition, Young Musicians of the Year; govr Music Therapy Charity Tst, chm Euro Piano Teachers Assoc, ed Piano Journal 1987-; external examiner: King's Coll London, Univ of York, Univ of Keele; music advsr: Royal Netherlands Govt, Br Cncl, Canada Cncl; Freeman City of London 1971, Liveryman Worshipful Co of Musicians 1973; hon prof Univ of Chile 1966, Hon LLD Meml Univ of Newfoundland Canada 1985; FRSA 1986, memb RSM 1988; *Books* Serial Strawinsky in 20 Century Music; author of various articles in: Composer, Music and Musicians, Music Teacher, Piano Journal, Revista Universitaria de Chile; *Style*— Prof Malcolm Troup; Dept of Music, The City University, Northampton Square, London EC1V 0HB (☎ 071 253 4399 ext 3271/3284, fax 071 250 0837)

TROWBRIDGE, Hon Mrs ((Dorothy) Frances Lucy St George); *née* Caulfeild; er da of 12 Viscount Charlemont (d 1979); *b* 28 Sept 1915; *Educ* Queens Gate London, Brillantmont Lausanne; *m* 1945, Robert Hender Trowbridge, late Flt Lt RAAF; 2 s (Mark Robert b 1947, Richard Keith Giles b 1950); *Clubs* Overseas; *Style*— The Hon Mrs Trowbridge; Drumcairn, Lane End, Elmstead Market, Essex CO7 7BB (☎ 0206 22 2726)

TROWBRIDGE, Martin Edward O'Keeffe; CBE (1987); s of Edward Stanley Trowbridge (d 1962), of London, and Ida, *née* O'Keeffe (d 1981); *b* 9 May 1925; *Educ* Royal Coll of Sci, City and Guilds Coll, Imperial Coll London (BSc), American Mgmnt Assoc Coll NY (Dip Business Studies); *m* 1946, Valerie Ann, da of Royden Glazebrook (d 1948), of Eastbourne, Sussex; 1 s (Sean); *Career* dir (later gp md) Pennwalt International Corporation Philadelphia USA 1953-72, gp md Pegler Hattersley Ltd 1972-73, chm and md Martin Trowbridge Ltd 1972-; dir gen Chem Industs Assoc 1973-87; dir: Nat Radiological Protection Bd 1987-, Investmt Mangrs Regulatory Orgn 1987-; memb: Conseil d'Administration CEFIC Brussels 1973-87 (later chm), Advsy Ctee Euro Business Inst 1985-90; tstee Catalyst Nat Chem Museum 1986-90; Hinchley medal Inst of Chem Engrs, Int medal Soc of Chem Indust; CEng, FIChemE, ACGI, FCGI, MSCI; *Books* Poems (1953), Exhibiting for Profit, Centrifugation, Economics of the Process Plant Industry, The Purification of Marine Oils; *Recreations* shooting, painting and relief printing, mineralogy, studying Italian literature, wooden boxes; *Clubs* Old Siberians, Frensham Gun, Boffles (NYC); *Style*— Martin Trowbridge, Esq, CBE; 51A Moreton Terrace, London SW1V 2NS

TROWBRIDGE, Rear Adm Sir Richard John; KCVO (1975); s of Albert George Trowbridge (d 1970); *b* 21 Jan 1920; *Educ* Andover GS; *m* 1955, Anne Mildred, da of Francis W Perceval; 2 s; *Career* joined RN 1935, serv WWII (despatches), Cdr 1953 (destroyer Carysfort 1956-58); exec offr: HMS Bermuda 1958-59, HMS Excellent 1959-60; Capt 1960, cmd Fishery Protection Sqdn 1962-64, Rear Adm 1970, Flag Offr Royal Yachts 1970-75; extra equerry to HM the Queen 1970-; yr bro Trinity House 1972; govr Western Australia 1980-83; KStJ 1980; *Recreations* sailing, golf, fishing; *Clubs* Army and Navy; *Style*— Rear Adm Sir Richard Trowbridge, KCVO; Old Idsworth Garden, Finchdean, Portsmouth, Hants (☎ 070 541 2714)

TROWELL, Dr Joan Mary; da of Gordon Watson Trowell (d 1984), and Vera, *née* Kilham (d 1969); *b* 2 Jan 1941; *Educ* Walthamstow Hall Sevenoaks, Royal Free Hosp Med Sch London (MB BS), MRCP; *m* 31 Oct 1970, John Percy Perry (d 1985), s of Percy Perry (d 1964); 1 s (Mark b 1972), 1 da (Helen b 1974); *Career* house physician London: Royal Free Hosp 1964, Royal Northern Hosp 1965, Brompton Hosp 1967, Hammersmith Hosp 1967; med registrar: Addenbrookes Hosp Cambridge 1968,

Hammersmith Hosp 1969; lectr in med Nuffield Dept of Clinical Med Oxford 1971, hon conslt physician John Radcliffe Hosp Oxford 1981; exec of Oxon Cncl for Alcohol and Drug Use, memb Alcohol Concern, regnl and univ rep Med Cncl on Alcoholism; Hon MA Oxford 1971; FRCP 1987; *Books* Topics in Gastroenterology (1975), Oxford Textbook of Medicine (contrib, 1986), Oxford Textbook of Pathology (contrib, 1990); *Style—* Dr Joan Trowell; John Radcliffe Hospital, Headington, Oxford OX3 9DU (☎ 0865 741166)

TROWER, Anthony Gosselin; s of Sir William Gosselin Trower (d 1963), of Stanstead Bury, Ware Herts, and Hon Joan Olivia, *née* Tomlin (d 1986, er da of Baron Tomlin of Ash, Lord of Appeal in Ordinary); *b* 12 July 1921; *Educ* Eton; *m* 27 June 1957, Catherine Joan, da of Col John Philip Kellett, DSO, MC; 4 s (Jonathan b 1958, William b 1959, Christopher b 1964, Richard b 1966) 1 da (Charlotte b 1961); *Career* joined TA 1939 and serv WWII gunner Herts Yeomanry (cmmnd RA) Middle E and India (Intelligence Corps), Western Europe (1 SAS Regt) 1939-45; admitted slr 1949; ptnr Trower Still & Keeling subsequently Trowers and Hamlins (now sr ptnr and third generation in firm) 1952-90; *Recreations* field sports, mountain walking, birds, most things to do with preserving the Herts countryside, beautifying my house; *Clubs* Travellers', St James's (Manchester), The Alpine; *Style—* Anthony G Trower, Esq; Stanstead Bury, Ware, Hertfordshire (☎ 027 979 3205); Towers & Hamlins, 6 New Square, Lincoln's Inn, London WC2A (☎ 071 831 6292)

TROWER, John; s of Geoffrey Arthur Owen Trower, of 1 Mongers mead, Barcombe, Lewes, E Sussex, and Lillian Helen, *née* Watts; *b* 6 Feb 1956; *Educ* Chailey Co Secdy Sch, Lewes Priory Comp, Loughborough Univ (BSc); partner, Karen Angela, da of Graham Peter Dawson; 1 s (Thomas George b 19 June 1986), 2 da (Sophie Lily b 24 May 1985, Harriet Daisy b 11 April 1990); *Career* athletics coach; competitive career (javelin): joined Brighton & Hove Athletics Club 1970, participated in English Sch Championships 1970-72 (winner 1972 with schs record), B int England v France 1978, 6 full int appearances for England 1979-83 (debut v USSR), ret from competitive athletics through injury 1983; sr nat javelin coach Amateur Athletic Assoc 1987-; played cricket soccer and rugby at under 19 county level; recreation offr Telford Devpt Corp 1980-85; Wrekin Cncl: dep mangr 1985-87, mangr 1987-89, area mangr 1989-; Post Office Counters coach of the month Oct 1989; *Recreations* my family, athletics; *Style—* John Trower, Esq; 1 Moorland Rd, Newport, Shropshire TF10 7PH (☎ 0952 811802)

TROY-DAVIES, (Christine) Karen; da of Christopher Anthony Troy (d 1986), of Burnham-on-Sea, Somerset, and Christina Sylvia, *née* Richards; *b* 1 Nov 1957; *Educ* Sexeys GS Blackford Somerset, St Catherine's Coll Oxford (BA), Univ of Virginia (LLM); *m* 29 July 1989, Peter Jonathan Troy-Davies, s of Edward Davies, of Blackpool, Lancs; *Career* called to the Bar: Lincoln's Inn 1981, Washington DC 1982; assoc attorney Ely Ritts Pietrowski and Brickfield Washington DC 1982-84, conslt Centre for Oceans Law and Policy Univ of Virginia 1984-86, lectr in energy law Centre for Commercial Law Studies Univ of London 1984-87, in practice 1987-; memb: Popular Flying Assoc, Southern (Autogyro) Strut, Lawyers Flying Assoc; chm: Cierva Club; *Books* Articles Only (asst ed, 1985-86), Commercial Law Bulletin (corr, 1985-86), International Journal of Estuarine and Coastal Law (ed, 1986-87), Oil and Gas Law and Taxation Review (contrib); *Recreations* travel, reading; *Style—* Mrs Karen Troy-Davies; 4 Essex Court, Temple, London EC4Y 9AJ (☎ 071 583 9191, fax 071 583 2422, telex 888465 COMCAS G

TRUBSHAW, Ernest Brian; CBE (1970, OBE 1964), MVO (1948); s of Maj Harold Ernest Trubshaw, JP, DL (d 1952), of Pembrey, Carmarthenshire, and Lumley Victoria, *née* Carter (d 1980); *b* 29 Jan 1924; *Educ* Winchester; *m* 21 April 1973, Yvonne Patricia, wid of R H Edmondson, and da of late John Arthur Clapham, of Harrogate, Yorks; *Career* RAF 1942-50, Bomber Cmd 1944, Tport Cmd 1945, The King's Flt 1946-48, Empire Flying Sch 1949, RAF Flying Coll 1949-50; Vickers-Armstrong: experimental test pilot 1950-53, dep chief test pilot 1953-60, chief test pilot 1960-66; dir flt testing and chief test pilot BAC/BAE 1966-80, gen mangr Br Aerospace 1980-86, pt/t memb CAA Bd 1986-, dir A J Walker (Aviation) Ltd 1986-, aviation conslt 1986-; Freeman City of London, Warden Guild of Air Pilots and Air Navigators 1958-61, memb Worshipful Co of Coachmakers and Coach Harness Makers; Hon DTech Loughborough 1986; Fell: Royal Aeronautical Soc, Soc of Experimental Test Pilots; Derry and Richards Memorial Medal 1961 and 1964, Richard Hansford Burroughs Memorial Trophy (USA) 1964, R P Alston Medal 1964, Seagrave Trophy 1970, Air League founders Medal 1971, Iven C Kincheloe Award (USA) 1971, Harmon Trophy 1971, Bluebird Trophy 1973, French Aeronautical Medal 1976; *Clubs* RAF, MCC; *Style—* Ernest Trubshaw, Esq, CBE, MVO; The Garden House, Dodington, nr Chipping Sodbury, Avon BS17 6SG (☎ 0454 323 951, car 0836 270 432)

TRUDEAU, Rt Hon Pierre Elliott; CH (1984), PC (Canada), QC (Canada); responsible for repatriation of British North American Act 1982; s of Charles-Emile Trudeau and Grace, *née* Elliott; *b* 18 Oct 1919; *Educ* Jean-de-Brébeuf Coll Montreal, Univ of Montreal, Harvard Univ, Ecole des Sciences Politiques Paris, LSE; *m* 1971, Margaret, da of James Sinclair, of Vancouver; 3 s (Justin, Emmanuel 'Sasha', Michel); *Career* barr Quebec 1943; prof of law Univ of Montreal 1961-65; MP (Lib) 1965-84, parly sec to PM of Canada (Rt Hon Lester Pearson) 1966-67, Min Justice and attorney-gen 1967-68, ldr of Lib Pty of Canada 1968-84, PM of Canada 1968-79 and 1980-84; founding memb Montreal Civil Liberties Union; Hon LLD Univ of Alberta; hon fell LSE 1969; Freeman City of London; FRSC; *Books* Deux Innocents en Chine Rouge (1961; Two Innocents in Red China 1969), Le Fédéralisme et la Société Canadienne-Française (1968; Federalism and the French Canadians 1968), Réponses (1968); *Recreations* swimming, skiing, canoeing, scuba diving; *Style—* The Rt Hon Pierre Trudeau, CH, QC; House of Commons, Ottawa, Ontario K1A 0A2, Canada

TRUE, Dr Rodney Charles; s of Charles William True, of Fairland, Green Lane, Rayners Park GS Wimbledon, Univ of Leeds (MB ChB, DPM); *b* 22 June 1942; *m* 8 Aug 1966, Christine Maureen; 1 s (Simon Rodney b 6 Feb 1968), 1 da (Sarah Jane b 4 Dec 1966); *Career* sr registrar W Midlands RHA 1974-77, conslt psychiatrist Mersey RHA 1977-; memb Soc of Clinical Psychiatrists; MRCPsych; *Recreations* organ playing, music, tropical plants; *Style—* Dr Rodney True; Leighton Hosp, Crewe, Cheshire (☎ 0270 255141)

TRUEMAN, Frederick Sewards; OBE; s of Alan Thomas Trueman (d 1970), of Maltby, S Yorks, and Ethel Bennett, *née* Stimpson; *b* 6 Feb 1931; *Educ* Stainton Cncl Sch, Maltby Hall Mod Sch; *m* 1, (m dis 1972), Enid Elizabeth, *née* Chapman; 1 s (Rodney Fredrick Bennett b 1965), 2 da (Karen (Mrs Slight) b 1960, Rebecca Elizabeth Jane b 1965); m 2, 28 Feb 1973, Veronica; *Career* played cricket for Yorkshire 1949 and England 1952, world record holder Christchurch NZ 1963 (243 test wickets), first man to reach 300 test wickets at Oval v Aust 1964, ret 1968; currently worldwide broadcaster, journalist and after dinner speak; memb: Lord Taverners, Variety Club of GB; *Recreations* golf, wildlife (chiefly birds); *Style—* Fredrick Trueman, Esq, OBE; Bay Tree Cottage, Flasby, Gargrave, Skipton, N Yorks BD23 3PU (fax 0756 748235)

TRUESDALE, Geoffrey Ashworth; s of Reginald Truesdale (d 1934), and Ellen, *née* Ashworth (d 1974); *b* 16 March 1927; *Educ* King Edward's HS Birmingham, Bishop Vesey's Sch Sutton Coldfield, Univ of London (BSc); *m* 5 May 1951, Beryl, da of Leslie Charles Hathaway (d 1988); 1 s (David Geoffrey b 1953), 1 da (Carolyn (Mrs Mitchell) b 1957); *Career* tech offr Water Pollution Res Laboratory (now Water Res Centre) 1947-68, chemical inspr DOE 1968-70, conslt Balfours Consulting Engrs 1988- (joined 1970, ptnr 1976-88); chm Conslts in Environmental Sciences Ltd; pres: Euro Water Pollution Control Assoc 1984-87, Inst of Water and Environment Mgmnt (UK) 1988-89 (fell 1987); Freeman City of London 1989; memb Guild of Water Conservators; FIWEM 1987, predecessor bodies FIWPC 1959, FIPHE 1966, FIWES 1979-87; *Recreations* music, gardening; *Style—* Geoffrey Truesdale, Esq; Bracebridge, Oast Rd, Oxted, Surrey RH8 9DX (☎ 0883 717473)

TRUETT, Philip Arthur; s of William Arthur Truett (d 1945), of Croydon Surrey, and Nancy, *née* Reid; *b* 14 Oct 1942; *Educ* Cranleigh Sch, Grenoble Univ; *m* 29 Dec 1973, Juliet Anne, da of Joseph Dennison Macadam, MBE, of Buenos Aires Argentina; 2 da (Emma b 1977, Victoria b 1981); *Career* Lloyd's underwriting agent; Lloyd's 1961, dir Furness-Houlder (Reinsurance) Ltd and dir Furness-Houlder (Overseas Insurance Services) Ltd 1971-80, MWE Underwriting Agencies Ltd 1980-83, dir Fenchurch Underwriting Agencies Ltd 1983-; memb Lloyd's 1973- (memb House Ctee 1989-); hon sec Lloyd's GC 1985, former capt Old Cranleighan Golf Soc, vice pres SE Junior Golf Soc, fndr ctee memb Br Golf Collectors Soc, hon librarian The Truett Golf Library, memb Ctee Annual Nat Serv for Seafarers; *Recreations* golf, golf history, golf book collecting, skiing; *Clubs* Royal and Ancient Golf, Walton Heath Golf, Rye Golf, W Sussex Golf, Royal Cinque Ports Golf, Lloyds Golf, Kandahar Ski; *Style—* Philip Truett, Esq; Woodbine House, 12 Spencer Road, South Croydon, Surrey CR2 7EH (☎ 081 686 1080); Fenchurch Underwriting Agencies Ltd, 136 Minories, London EC3N 1QN (☎ 071 488 2388, fax 071 481 9467, telex 884442)

TRUGLIA, Lucia; da of Franco Truglia, of Rome, and Anna Mancini Truglia (d 1990); *b* 19 Jan 1949; *Educ* Lydia Johnson Ballet Sch, Scuola di Ballo dell Teatro dell' Opera di Roma (dir Attilia Radice); *Career* soloist and princ: Rome Opera 1972-79 (joined Corps de Ballet 1967), New London Ballet 1979; London Festival Ballet (now Eng Nat Ballet): soloist 1979-81, princ 1981, sr princ 1982-90; princ Eng Nat Ballet Sch 1990; *principal roles* Rome Opera: The Seven Deadly Sins, Day Dream, Queen of Spades, Four Temperaments; New London Ballet: Soft Blue Shadows, Faust; London Festival Ballet (Eng Nat Ballet): Giselle, Odette/Odile, Juliet in Romeo and Juliet, Olga in Onegin, Sasha/Sugar Plum fairy and Tanya in Nutcracker, Swanilda in Coppelia (opposite Nureyev), Vivette in L'Arlesienne (opposite Schaufuss), Pimpinella in Pulcinella, Bruce's Land, Apollo, Sanguine Fan, Dvorak Variations; prizes incl: Saracebno d'Oro 1972, Premio Campidoglio 1973, Premio Riccione 1977-78, Premio Internazionale Feyer des Artiste 1978, Premio La Velca d'Oro 1971, 1978, Gonfalone d'Oro 1972; *Style—* Ms Lucia Truglia; English National Ballet, Markova House, 39 Jay Mews, London SW7 2ES (☎ 071 581 1245, 071 225 0425, fax 071 225 0827)

TRUMAN, Prof Aubrey; s of Edwin Truman (d 1966), of 27 The Greenway, Wolstanton, Newcastle-under-Lyme, Staffs, and Nellie, *née* Nixon (d 1972); *b* 9 Dec 1943; *Educ* Wolstan CGS, Univ Coll Oxford (MA, DPhil); *m* 24 July 1965, Jane, da of Harold Pratt; 1 s (Thomas b 29 Aug 1977), 2 da (Rachel b 12 Nov 1968, Emma b 26 July 1970); *Career* sr lectr dept of maths Heriot Watt Univ 1978-82 (lectr 1969-78), chm IT ctee 1984-, organiser IX Int Congress on Mathematical Physics 1988 (memb sci advsy ctee), dean of faculty of sci Univ Coll Swansea 1989- (prof of maths 1982-, head of dept of maths and computer sci 1985-), ed books on stochastic processes and applications and proceedings of IXI Int Congress on Mathematical Physics, physics ed Europhysics letters, ctee memb S Wales Maths Assoc (pres 1985-88); FRSE, FIMA; *Recreations* walking and bridge; *Style—* Prof Aubrey Truman; Dep of Maths and Computer Science, Univ Coll Swansea, Singleton Park, Swansea SA2 8PP (☎ 0792 295458)

TRUMPINGTON, Baroness (Life Peer UK 1980), of Sandwich, Co Kent; Jean Alys Barker; da of late Maj Arthur Edward Campbell-Harris, MC, and Doris Marie, *née* Robson; *b* 23 Oct 1922; *Educ* privately in England and France; *m* 1954, William Alan Barker (d 1988); 1 s (Hon Adam Campbell b 1955); *Career* sits as Cons peer in House of Lords; cons cllr Cambridge City Cncl Trumpington Ward 1963-73, Mayor of Cambridge 1971-72, Dep Mayor 1972-73, cons cllr Camb Trumpington Ward 1973-75, hon cllr City of Cambridge 1975-; JP: Cambridge 1972-75, S Westminster 1976-82; UK delegate to UN Status of Women Cmmn 1979-81, hon fell Lucy Cavendish Coll Cambridge 1980; Baroness-in-Waiting to HM The Queen 1983-85; parly under-sec of State: DHSS 1985-87, MAFF 1987-89; min of State MAFF 1989-; *Recreations* bridge, racing, golf, antique hunting; *Style—* The Rt Hon the Baroness Trumpington; House of Lords, London SW1

TRURO, 13 Bishop of 1990-; Rt Rev Michael Thomas Ball; patron of 2 archdeaconries, 24 canonries, 64 livings, one alternately with the Crown, one other alternately and three jointly; The See of Cornwall existed independently 865-1050, whereafter merged with Diocese of Exeter until 1876, when the See refounded; It comprises the old archdeaconry of Cornwall within the Diocese of Exeter; s of Thomas James Ball (d 1966), of Eastbourne, and Kathleen Obena Bradley, *née* Morris (d 1980); *b* 14 Feb 1932; *Educ* Lancing, Queens' Coll Cambridge (BA, MA); *Career* schoolmaster 1955-75; chaplain for higher educn in Brighton Area 1975-80, curate Whiteshill Stroud 1971-75, parish priest Stanmer and Falmer 1975-80; prior of Stroud Glos 1963-75, co fndr Community of the Glorious Ascension 1960; involved in: governing body various ind schools, drug rehabilitation unit, school for violent or difficult children; pres local hospice; fell Woodward Corpn, provost N Div Woodward Schs 1985-86; bishop of Jarrow 1980-90, bishop of Truro 1990-; *Recreations* sport, music, housework; *Style—* The Rt Rev the Bishop of Truro; Lis Escop, Feock, Truro, Cornwall TR3 6QQ (☎ 0872 862657, fax 0872 862680)

TRUSCOTT, Sir George James Irving; 3 Bt (UK 1909), of Oakleigh, East Grinstead, Sussex; s of Sir Eric Homewood Stanham Truscott, 2 Bt (d 1973); *b* 24 Oct 1929; *Educ* Sherborne; *m* 1, 1954 (m dis 1958), Irene Marion Craig Barr Brown; m 2, 1962, Yvonne Dora, da of late Frank Edward Nicholson; 1 s, 1 da; *Heir* s, Ralph Eric Nicholson Truscott b 21 Feb 1966; *Style—* Sir George Truscott, Bt; BM QUILL, London WC1N 3XX

TRUSLER, Colin Harold; s of Harold Sidney Trusler (d 1973), and Alice Joan, *née* Angell; *b* 11 July 1942; *Educ* Loughborough GS, Wadham Coll Oxford (scholar, MA), Harvard Business Sch; *m* 1, 1965, Jill Vivienne, *née* Bullen; 2 s (Rupert Charles b 1969, Simon Edward b 1973), 1 da (Phillipa Sarah b 1971); m 2, 1982, Fiona Innes, *née* Parsons; 2 s (Felix Colin Innes b 1986, Barnaby Colin Innes b 1991); *Career* graduate trainee Public Relations Partnership 1963-66, conslt Brook Hart Ruder & Finn International 1966-69; Lloyds Bank: PR advsr 1969-72, mktg mangr 1972-78, head of mktg 1978-86; Shandwick Consultants: dir 1986-88, md 1988-90, chm and chief exec 1990-; dir: Shandwick Public Affairs 1987-, Fairfax Design Company 1989-, Shandwick Europe plc 1990-; MCIM 1980; *Recreations* family life; *Style—* Colin Trusler, Esq; Shandwick Consultants Ltd, Dauntsey House, Frederick's Place, Old Jewry, London EC2R 8AB (☎ 071 726 4291, fax 081 696 0882)

TRUSSLER, John; s of Thomas Herbert Trussler (d 1969), of Middx, and Lillian Frances, *née* Bailey (d 1986); *b* 11 July 1937; *Educ* Willesden Coll of Technol, Harvard Graduate Business Sch; *m* 2 June 1962, Anne Patricia, da of Henry Vincent Sheriff (d

1971), of Middx; 2 s (Andrew John b 1966, Jonathan David b 1971); *Career* md: Kyle Stewart Ltd (and chm of numerous subsid cos), Lakers Mechanical Services; chm: Appin House Motors Ltd, Arlingdrive Ltd, Lakers Process Engineering Ltd, London Open Golf Ltd, Robin Alexander Plant Hire Ltd, Wembley Laboratories Ltd; dir: Kyle Stewart Holdings Inc, Andrew Murray Joinery Ltd, Ardshiel Contractors Ltd, Ardshiel Ltd, Rakehit Ltd, Silver One Ltd, Stewart-Usborne Developments Ltd, Chertsey Boulevard Management, Droitwich Leisure Ltd, Lockton Developments plc; govr Willesden Coll of Technol; FCIBS, FRSA; *Recreations* travel, gardening, photography, reading, music; *Clubs* IOD, Harvard Business Sch of London; *Style—* John Trussler, Esq; Cobblestones Wood End Road, Harpenden, Hertfordshire AL5 3ED; Kyle Stewart Ltd, Ardshiel House, Empire Way, Wembley, Middlesex HA9 0NA

TRUST, Peter; s of Ernest Jones Travis (d 1979), and Lillian Varley, *née* Perason; *b* 1 March 1936; *Educ* Salford GS, Salford Royal Tech Coll, art apprenticeship Spain; *m* 7 April 1970, Doreen, MBE, da of Ernest Duckett Runcorn (d 1973); *Career* artist and illustrator; charity fndr and chm; 29 one man shows; Art into Industry; murals; public portraits and commissions; paintings in public and private collections; creator 'Art Constructions' (pre-cursor to concrete poetry); lectr on disfigurement and guidance; memb Soc of Authors; *Recreations* detective novels, walking dog; *Style—* Peter Trust, Esq; Hillview, Wester Kinsleith, Luthrie, Fife KY15 4NR (☎ 03377 281); Disfigurement Guidance Centre, Guild House, 1 George Street, Cellardyke, Fife KY10 3AS (☎ 0333 312350)

TRUSTRAM EVE, Col Hon Peter Nanton; OBE (Mil 1978); yr twin s of 1 Baron Silsoe, GBE, MC, TD, QC (d 1976), by his 1 w Marguerite (da of Sir Augustus Meredith Nanton); *b* 2 May 1930; *Educ* Winchester, ChCh Oxford; *m* 1, 1961, Petronilla Letiere Sheldon, da of Jannion Steele Elliott, of Dowles Manor, Bewdley, Worcs; 2 s (Richard b 1963, Nicholas b 1965); m 2, 1988, Albinia Julia, da of Christopher Diggle, of Old Warden, Beds; *Career* late RWF, RB and RGJ, CO Oxford Univ OTC 1973, def and mil attaché Brussels 1980, gen mangr Churchill Hosp Oxford 1985-88; Offr of the Order of Leopold (Belgium, 1990); *Recreations* skiing, collecting antiques (particularly sixteenth and seventeenth century maps); *Clubs* Ski of GB, Anglo-Belgian; *Style—* Col the Hon Peter Trustram Eve, OBE; Barton End Hall, nr Nailsworth, Glos GL6 0QQ (☎ 045383 3471); 82 Shuttleworth Rd, London SW11 (☎ 071 585 1012)

TRYON, 3 Baron (UK 1940); Anthony George Merrik Tryon; s of 2 Baron Tryon, GCVO, KCB, DSO, PC (d 1976), and Ethelreda (da of Sir Merrik Burrell, 7 Bt, CBE); *b* 26 May 1940; *Educ* Eton; *m* 1973, Dale Elizabeth, da of Barry Harper, of Melbourne, Aust; 2 s (Charles, Edward (twin) b 1979), 2 da (Zöe b 1974, Victoria (twin) b 1979); *Heir* s, Hon Charles George Barrington Tryon, b 15 May 1976; *Career* page of honour to HM The Queen 1954-56; Capt Royal Wilts Yeo; dir Lazard Bros & Co Ltd 1976-83, chm English & Scottish Investors Ltd 1977-87; *Recreations* fishing, shooting; *Clubs* White's, Pratt's; *Style—* The Rt Hon the Lord Tryon; Ogbury House, Great Durnford, Salisbury (☎ 0722 73225)

TRYON, Hon Aylmer Douglas; s of 1 Baron Tryon (d 1940); *b* 16 July 1909; *Educ* Eton, Trinity Coll Cambridge (BA); *Career* formerly Capt Grenadier Gds; fndr Tryon Gallery; *Books* Kingfisher Mill, Wildfowlers Year, The Quiet Waters By; *Recreations* fishing, shooting, natural history; *Clubs* Boodle's, Flyfisher's, Pratt's; *Style—* The Hon Aylmer Tryon; Kingfisher Mill, Great Durnford, Salisbury, Wilts

TRYON, Ethelreda, Baroness; Ethelreda Josephine; da of Sir Merrik Burrell, 7 Bt, CBE, JP, by his 2 w, Coralie (da of John Porter, DL, of Belle Isle, Co Fermanagh and Clonbalt, Co Longford); *b* 20 June 1909; *m* 1939, Brig 2 Baron Tryon, GCVO, KCB, DSO, PC (d 1976); 1 s, 1 da; *Style—* The Rt Hon Ethelreda, Lady Tryon; Church Farm, Great Durnford, Salisbury, Wilts (☎ 072 273 281)

TRYTHALL, Maj-Gen Anthony John (Tony); CB (1983); s of Eric Stewart Trythall (d 1963), and Irene, *née* Hollingham; *b* 30 March 1927; *Educ* Lawrence Sheriff Sch Rugby, St Edmund Hall Oxford (BA, DipEd), Kings Coll London (MA); *m* 2 Aug 1952, Celia, da of Sidney Richard Haddon, of Rugby; 2 s (Timothy b 1960, Peter b 1961), 1 da (Susan b 1967); *Career* Royal Army Educnl Corps Offr 1948-49 and 1953-84, serv Egypt, Transjordan, Malaya, W Germany, UK, Chief Inspr and Col Research 1973-74, Chief Educn Offr UK Land Forces 1976-80, Dir Army Educn 1980-84; md Brassey's Defence Publishers 1984-87, exec dep chm 1988-; memb: Cncl Royal Utd Services Inst 1978-84, Bd of War Studies London Univ 1983-, Gallipoli Meml Lecture Tst 1984- (chm 1986-89); publisher to Int Inst for Strategic Studies 1989-, Centre for Euro Policy Studies 1990-, Centre for Defence Studies 1990-; cncl memb RUSI 1978-84; First Prize Trench Gascoigne Essay 1969; *Books* Boney Fuller: The Intellectual General 1878-1966 (1977), The Downfall of Leslie Hore-Belisha in the Second World War (1982), articles in military and historical journals; *Recreations* garden, family, good food and wine, military thoughts; *Clubs* Naval and Military; *Style—* Maj-Gen Anthony Trythall, CB; c/o Royal Bank of Scotland, Whitehall Branch, Kirkland House, Whitehall, London SW1A 2EB; 50 Fetter Lane, London EC4A 1AA (☎ 071 377 4885, 071 377 4888)

TSUNEMATSU, Samuel Ikuo (Sammy); s of Takashi Tsunematsu (d 1966), of Satsuma, Japan, and Toyono, *née* Nakanoue; *b* 4 Oct 1951; *Educ* Obirin Univ Tokyo Japan (BA); *m* 15 Feb 1985, Yoshiko, da of Dr Kiyoshi Yorifuji, of Hokkaido, Japan; *Career* dir Gendai Travel Ltd 1980, md Soseki Museum London 1984, dir Y & S Co; fndr Anglo Satsuma Soc London; *Books* Soseki in London (1985), Life of Yoshio Markino (1989), The World of Yoshio Markino (1989), Yoshio Markino - A Japanese Artist in London (1990); Japanese translations: Watashimo London Paris Rome Inshoki 1990, Waga Riso no Eikokujosei Tachi 1990, Kirimo London 1991; *Recreations* reading the ancient Chinese Latin and Greek classics in order to forget the modern civilisation; *Clubs* The Nat Lib; *Style—* Sammy Tsunematsu, Esq; 48 Elliott Road, Croydon, Surrey CR4 7QA (☎ 081 6834058), 80 The Chase, London SW4 0NG (☎ 071 7208718, fax 071 6849925); Urbanisation 'La Colina 35', Calle Eucaliptus 15, Buzon 2824, 03734 Moraira (Alicante) (☎ and fax 346 574 4682)

TUBY, John; OBE; s of Joseph Tuby (d 1983), and Georgette, *née* Ismalun (d 1970); *b* 17 June 1923; *Educ* Private; *m* 29 May 1958, (Edith) Joan Redmayne, da of Col William Eric Walker, CBE, TD (d 1949); *Career* WWII Army 1941-47: Western Desert, Eritrea, Palestine, Syria and Three Force; sr exec Feeds Sales Div Quaker Oats Ltd 1953-63, exec dir of subsidiary of Thomas Tilling Gp 1963-83, dir gen Franco-Br C of C and Indust 1988-89 (pres 1982-84), govr Br Sch of Paris 1985-, pres The Br Luncheon Club (1916) 1981; *Style—* John Tuby, Esq, OBE; 60850 Le Coudray Saint Germer (Oise), France (☎ 44 81 62 18)

TUCK, Dr (John) Anthony; s of Prof John Philip Tuck, of Chillingham House, Gt Gransden, Sandy, Beds, and Jane Adelaide, *née* Wall; *b* 14 Nov 1940; *Educ* Royal GS Newcastle upon Tyne, Jesus Coll Cambridge (BA, MA, PhD); *m* 17 July 1976, Amanda Jane, da of Dr Lawrence John Cawley, of the Old Hall, Carlton Husthwaite, Thirsk, Yorks; 2 s (Robert James b 1979, Michael Richard b 1982); *Career* sr lectr in history Univ of Lancaster 1975-87 (lectr 1965), master Collingwood Coll Univ of Durham 1978; reader in medieval history Univ of Bristol 1987-; FRHistS 1987-90, Prof of medieval history Univ of Bristol 1990-; FRHistS 1987; *Books* Richard II and the English Nobility (1973), Crown and Nobility 1272-1461 (1985), Royal Grammar School, Newcastle Upon Tyne (with B Mains and others, 1986); *Style—* Dr Anthony Tuck; 66 A Hill View, Henleaze, Bristol BS9 4PU (☎ 0272 622 953); Department of History, University of Bristol, 13 Woodland Rd, Bristol BS8 1TB (☎ 0272 303 030)

TUCK, Sir Bruce Adolph Reginald; 3 Bt (UK 1910); s of Major Sir (William) Reginald Tuck, 2 Bt (d 1954, s of Sir Adolph Tuck, 1 Bt, who was gs of Raphael Tuck, fine art publisher and chm and md of Raphael Tuck and Sons); *b* 29 June 1926; *Educ* Canford; *m* 1, 1949 (m dis in Jamaica 1964), Luise, da of John C Renfro, of San Angelo, Texas, USA; 2 s; m 2, 1968, Pamela Dorothy, da of Alfred Michael Nicholson, of London; 1 da; *Heir* s, Richard Bruce Tuck; *Career* Lt Scots Gds 1945-47; with Miller-Carnegie; *Clubs* Lansdowne; *Style—* Sir Bruce Tuck, Bt; Montego Bay, PO Box 274, Jamaica

TUCK, Richard Bruce; s and h of Sir Bruce Tuck, 3 Bt; *b* 7 Oct 1952; *Educ* Millfield; *Career* Firearm Sales; *Recreations* shooting, fishing; *Clubs* Ducks Unlimited; *Style—* Richard Tuck, Esq; 9449 Briar Forest, Houston, Texas 77056, USA

TUCKER, Alistair John James; s of James Charles Henry Tucker (d 1982), and Mary Hannah, *née* Featherstonehaugh (d 1975); *b* 17 Feb 1936; *Educ* Southend HS, Keble Coll Oxford (BA, MA); *m* 2 Sept 1967, Deirdre Ann Forster, da of George Moore, of Amersham, Bucks; 1 s (Alistair b 1976), 1 da (Hannah b 1972); *Career* Subaltern The Green Howards 1958-60; exec dir within Transport Holding Co 1967-70, md Alistair Tucker Halcrow and Assoc (conslts in the mgmnt, economics, regulation and strategic planning of the air tport indust) 1970-; visiting prof Univ of Surrey 1987-; MCIT 1972, MRAeS 1980; *Recreations* walking, travel, archaeology; *Clubs* Athenaeum; *Style—* Alistair Tucker, Esq; 50 Primrose Gardens, London NW3 4TP (☎ 071 586 0027); Vineyard House, 44 Brook Green, London W6 7BY (☎ 071 602 7282, fax 071 603 0095, telex 916148)

TUCKER, Christopher Francis John; s of Sidney Francis George Tucker, of Brixham, Devon, and Lilian Joyce, *née* Hitchcock; *b* 1 Oct 1957; *Educ* Exeter Coll Oxford (MA), Univ of London (MSc); *Career* planning engr Dept of Corporate Strategy HQ CEGB 1983-85 (res offr physics 1979-83), asst dir Kleinwort Benson Securities 1989 (Investmt Analyst Electronics and Telephone Networks Sectors 1986-89), dir investmt res electronics and telephone networks Kitcat and Aitken 1989-90, Carr Kitcat & Aitken 1990-; MInstP 1984, MIEE 1986; *Recreations* travel, skiing, opera; *Clubs* United Oxford & Cambridge Univ; *Style—* Christopher Tucker, Esq; Carr Kitcat & Aitken, 1 London Bridge, London SE1 9TJ (☎ 071 378 7050 ext 2127, fax 071 403 0755, telex 8956121)

TUCKER, Christopher Robby; s of Lt Leslie Freeman Tucker, JP, of Kemsing, Kent, and Leila Annie, *née* Ison; *b* 23 March 1941; *Educ* Eversley Sch Southwald Suffolk, Elizabeth Coll Guernsey CI, Guildhall Sch of Music and Drama London; *m* 29 July 1971 (m dis 1977), Marion Edith, da of Philip John Flint, of Wellingborough; *Career* princ special make-up effects on: films: Star Wars 1976, Boys from Brazil 1978, Elephant Man 1979, Quest for Fire 1980, Company of Wolves 1983, High Spirits 1988; TV: I Claudius 1975, Holocaust 1976, Lillie Langtry 1979, Prince Regent 1980, War and Remembrance 1986; theatre: Richard III and Cyrano de Bergerac 1984, Phantom of the Opera 1986; active involvement in local history, archaeology, natural history; Freeman City of London 1962, Freeman Worshipful Co of Haberdashers 1962; BFI 1982, BAFTA 1982, AIP 1984; *Recreations* antiquarian books, opera, antiquities; *Style—* Christopher Tucker, Esq; Bere Ct, Pangbourne, Berks RH8 8HT (☎ 07357 2393); Agent-Eric L'Epine-Smith, 10 Wyndham Place, London W1H 1AS (☎ 071 724 0739/0)

TUCKER, Clifford Lewis; JP (Inner London) 1960-; s of Rev Frederick Charles Tucker (d 1950), of Monmouth, and Phoebe, *née* Thomas (d 1939); *b* 18 Dec 1912; *Educ* Monmouth, St Davids' Univ Coll Lampeter (BA); *Career* industl relations staff ICI plc 1936-46, mangr Industl Relations Dept Head Office BP plc 1951-65 (M E 1946-51), industl relations advsr 1965-71, conslt industl relations 1971-80, memb Arbitration Panel ACAS 1972-82; memb ILO Petroleum Ctee Geneva 1948-51; alderman: Met Borough of Stepney 1952-57, St Pancras 1960-64, Camden 1964-71; tstee: Whitechapel Art Gallery 1953-88, Tonybee Hall 1953-, tstee Wells and Camden Tst 1964-; charter dep Mayor Camden 1964-66, lectr Ford Fndn Int Conference Industl Relations 1965; memb: Appeals Ctee Inner London Quarter Sessions 1968-78, Peter Bedford Tst 1971-, City of London Mitchell Fndn 1974-; chm Thames Div Magistrates 1976-81, dep chm Inner London Magistrates Ctee 1979-81, visiting lectr on industl relations UK and German univs; companion IPM; *Recreations* trying to fight poverty and prejudice; *Clubs* Reform, RAC; *Style—* Clifford Tucker, Esq, JP; 2 Streatley Place, Hampstead, London NW3 1HP (☎ 071 794 4778)

TUCKER, Colin Patrick; s of Douglas Edwin Allen Tucker (d 1981), and Bridget Tucker (d 1969); *Educ* Prior Park Coll Bath, Univ of Cambridge (BA); *m* 18 June 1986, Sarah Madeline, da of Stanley Owen Fisher (d 1986); 3 da (Rebecca Jane b 1969, Abigail b 1971, Hannah Matilda b 1976); *Career* fell Univ of Manchester 1964-65, BBC Radio Drama Dept 1969-74, script ed BBC TV Play for Today 1975-77; prodr BBC TV: Prince Regent 1978, Fair Stood the Wind for France 1979, Shadow of the Noose 1988-89, Portrait of a Marriage 1989-90; prodr LWT Drummonds 1984-85; memb: BAFTA, Assoc of Ind Prodrs; *Style—* Colin Tucker, Esq; 86 Church Rd, Richmond, Surrey TW10 6LW (☎ 081 940 4561)

TUCKER, Herbert Harold; OBE (1965); o s of late Francis Tucker and late Mary Ann Tucker; *b* 4 Dec 1925; *Educ* Queen Elizabeth's Lincs, Rossington Main Yorks; *m* 1948, Mary Stewart, *née* Dunlop; 3 s; *Career* Econ Info Unit Treasy 1948-49, Daily Telegraph 1949-50, FO 1951, cnsllr and dir Br Info Servs Canberra 1974-78, consul-gen Vancouver 1979-83, disarmament info co-ordinator FCO 1983-84, ret; Roberts Centre 1984-; conslt Centre for Security and Conflict Studies 1986-89, Dulverton Tst 1988-; *Style—* Herbert Tucker, Esq, OBE; Pullens Cottage, Leigh Hill Rd, Cobham, Surrey KT11 2HX

TUCKER, (John) Keith; s of Reginald John Tucker (d 1976), and Nancy, *née* Harker; *b* 24 March 1945; *Educ* Haberdashers' Aske's, Charing Cross Hosp Med Sch (MB BS); *m* 4 Oct 1975, Jill Margaret, da of Dr Thomas Oliphant McKane (d 1972), of Gtr Easton Essex; 3 s (Timothy b 1977, Alexander b 1979, Ian b 1981); *Career* house surgn Charing Cross Hosp 1969, registrar Addenbrookes Hosp Cambridge 1971-73, sr registrar St Bartholomews Higher Orthopeadic Training Scheme 1973-77; hon clinical tutor in med Univ of Cambridge; author of various scientific papers, co-designer of The Norwich Hip Replacement System 1982-; examiner for the Intercollegiage Bd in Orthopaedic Surgery 1989; memb: The Br Hip Soc, Br Orthopaedic Assoc; hon MD Univ of Murcia Spain 1985; memb: BMA, RSM; MRCS, FRCS, LRCP; *Recreations* family; *Style—* Keith Tucker, Esq; 77 Newmarket Rd, Norwich (☎ 0603 614016)

TUCKER, Louis Newton; s of Sidney Tucker (d 1968), of Aust, and Elsie Louise Marion, *née* Newton (d 1971); *b* 3 Aug 1925; *Educ* Christs Hosp Horsham; *m* 1, Nov 1949 (m dis 1963), Beryl, da of Reginald White, of Epsom; 1 s (Nicholas b 6 July 1951); m 2, 19 Oct 1966, Vera Catherine Watkins, da of George Frederick Goodwin; 1 s (Marcus Newton b 12 July 1967), 1 da (Sarah b 6 March 1969); *Career* Maj N Staffs Regt 1942-46, serv Middle E; slr 1953, sr ptnr Helder Roberts & Co; dir: New Estates Ltd 1950-, Estates Property Investmt Co plc 1961-88, Property Security Investmt Tst plc 1961-, govr Christs Hosp; Freeman Worshipful Co of Merchant Taylors 1950; memb Law Soc, MIOD; *Recreations* tennis, gardening; *Style—* Louis Newton Tucker, Esq; Helder Roberts & Co, Ormond House, 2 High St, Epsom,

Surrey (☎ 037 27 26567)

TUCKER, His Hon Judge; (Henry John) Martin; QC (1975); s of Percival Albert Tucker (d 1959), of Hereford House, Hinton Rd, Bournemouth, and Dorothy Effie Mary, *née* Hobbs (d 1990); *b* 8 April 1930; *Educ* Downside, Ch Ch Oxford (MA); *m* 17 Aug 1957, Sheila Helen, da of Hugh Thomas Wateridge (d 1988), of 5 Lower Marine Parade, Dovercourt, Essex; 1 s (Adrian Mark b 1958), 4 da (Helen Mary b 1959, Elizabeth Frances b 1963, Catharine Clare b 1964, Philippa Rose b 1968); *Career* called to the Bar Inner Temple 1954, dep chm Somerset QS 1971, rec 1972-81, judge Western Circuit 1981-; *Recreations* walking occasionally, gardening gently, listening to music; *Clubs* Hampshire (Winchester); *Style—* His Hon Judge Tucker, QC; Chingri Khal, Sleepers Hill, Winchester, Hants SO22 4NB (☎ 0962 853927)

TUCKER, Peter Edward; s of Edward Albert George Tucker, of Park Lane, Newmarket, Suffolk, and Hilda Frances, *née* Brown; *b* 29 Oct 1941; *Educ* The Kings Sch Ely Cambs; *m* 26 March 1966, Brigid Elisabeth, da of Col James Michael Lind (d 1986); 1 da (Caroline Clare b 6 Aug 1969); *Career* Bank of America 1969-79, dir Investment and Mortgages Ltd Kenya 1980-, dir and chief exec Mount Banking Corpn Ltd London 1982-, chm Hytex Rubber Co Ltd Rotherham UK 1985-, dir Deacon Hoare Co Ltd Bristol 1988-; AIB 1962; *Recreations* golf, shooting, fishing, reading; *Clubs* Oriental, Hankley Common Golf (Surrey), Muthaiga (Nairobi Kenya); *Style—* Peter Tucker, Esq; Larchfield, Jumps Road, Churt, Surrey GU10 2JZ (☎ 025125 2904), Flat 5A, 5 Mount St, Mayfair, London W1Y 5AA; Mount Banking Corp Ltd, 5 Mount St, Mayfair, London W1Y 5AA (☎ 071 4091613, telex 21662, fax 071 4931604)

TUCKER, Ravenna Michele; da of John William Tucker, MBE, of Malaysia, and Valerie Saw, *née* Hong Bee; *Educ* King George V Sch Hong Kong; *Career* ballet dancer with Birmingham Royal Ballet (formerly Sadlers Wells Royal Ballet); first solo role Pas de Trois in Swan Lake 1980; other roles incl: title role in Requiem, Juliet in Romeo and Juliet, title role in Ondine, Aurora in Sleeping Beauty, Nikiya in La Bayadere, Odette and Odile in Swan Lake, title role in Giselle, Sugar Plum Fairy in Nutcracker, Rhapsody, Afternoon of A Funn; involved with: Action Aid, Royal Ballet educn projects for schs and hosps; *Recreations* painting, swimming, reading, needlepoint; *Style—* Miss Ravenna Tucker; Birmingham Royal Ballet, Birmingham Hippodrome, Thorpe St, Birmingham B5 4AU

TUCKER, Hon Mr Justice; Sir Richard Howard; s of His Hon Judge Howard Archibald Tucker (d 1963), and Margaret Minton, *née* Thacker (d 1976); *b* 9 July 1930; *Educ* Shrewsbury, Queen's Coll Oxford (MA); *m* 1, 1958 (m dis 1974), Paula Mary Bennett Frost; 1 s (Stephen), 2 da (Anneli, Gemma); m 2, 1975, Wendy Kate Standbrook (d 1988); m 3, 16 Sept 1989, Mrs Jacqueline S R Thomson, wid of William Thomson; *Career* barr Lincoln's Inn 1954, bencher 1979, rec 1972-85, judge of the High Ct Queen's Bench Div 1985-, presiding judge Midland and Oxford Circuit 1986-90; *Recreations* shooting, gardening, sailing (yacht Classmate of Beaulieu); *Clubs* Garrick, Leander, Bar Yacht; *Style—* Sir Richard Tucker; Royal Courts of Justice

TUCKER, Dr Sam Michael; s of Harry Tucker (d 1970), and Ray Tucker (d 1982); *b* 15 Oct 1926; *Educ* Benoni HS SA, Witwatersrand Univ (MB BCh); *m* 13 Dec 1953, Barbara Helen, da of M Kaplan; 2 s (Mark b 1957, Trevor b 1962), 1 da (Dana b 1956); *Career* conslt paediatrician Hillingdon Hosp Uxbridge and 152 Harley St London, clinical tutor and examiner RCP; memb Hillingdon Dist Health Authy, pres Section of Paediatrics RSM 1987-88, chm Med Advsy Ctee Portland Hosp 1987-88; assoc prof Brunel Univ Uxbridge 1988-; *Recreations* football, golf; *Clubs* RSM; *Style—* Dr Sam Tucker; 65 Uphill Rd, Mill Hill, London NW7 4PT; 152 Harley St, London W1

TUCKEY, Andrew Marmaduke Lane; s of Henry Lane Tuckey (d 1982), and Aileen Rosemary, *née* Newsom-Davis; *b* 28 Aug 1943; *Educ* Plumtree Sch Zimbabwe; *m* 24 June 1967, Margaret Louise, da of Dr Clive Barnes (d 1979); 1 s (Jonathan b 1970), 2 da (Clara b 1972, Anna b 1982); *Career* chm Baring Bros & Co Ltd, dir various Baring subsids; dir and treas Friends of Covent Garden, tstee Esmee Fairbairn Charitable Tst; *Recreations* music, tennis, windsurfing; *Clubs* Roehampton, City of London; *Style—* Andrew Tuckey, Esq; 36 Lonsdale Rd, Barnes, London SW13 9QR (☎ 081 748 9893); Baring Brothers & Co Ltd, 8 Bishopsgate, London EC2N 4AE (☎ 071 280 1000, fax 071 283 0447)

TUCKEY, Simon Lane; QC (1981); s of Henry Lane Tuckey (d 1982), and Aileen Rosemary *née* Newsom-Davis; *b* 17 Oct 1941; *Educ* Plumtree Sch Zimbabwe; *m* 1964, Jennifer Rosemary, da of Sir Charles Edgar Matthews Hardie, of Henley-on-Thames; 1 s (William b 1966), 2 da (Camilla b 1965, Kate b 1970); *Career* called to the Bar Lincoln's Inn 1964, rec 1984, chm review panel Fin Reporting Cncl 1990; *Recreations* sailing ('Java'), tennis; *Style—* Simon Tuckey, Esq, QC; 6 Regents Park Terrace, London NW1 (☎ 071 485 8952); 4 Pump Court, Temple, London EC4 (☎ 071 353 2656)

TUCKMAN, Frederick Augustus (Fred); OBE; s of Otto Tuchmann (d 1930), of Magdeburg, Germany, and Amy Tina, *née* Adler (d 1966); *b* 9 June 1922; *Educ* LSE (BSc); *m* 22 July 1966, Patricia Caroline, da of Sidney Sim Myers, of 40 High Mount, Hendon, London NW4; 2 s (Michael David b 25 March 1968, Jeremy Francis Henry b 4 Feb 1971), 1 da (Jane Tina b 11 March 1970); *Career* Flt Sgt RAF (Education) 1942-46; departmental mangr Marks & Spencer 1950-54, co sec and personnel mangr British & International Address Ltd 1955-63, asst co sec Temple Press 1963-65, mgmnt conslt Hay Group 1965-85, ptnr Hay Associates 1975-85; MEP (EDG) for Leicester 1979-89; Cons spokesman Social and Employment Ctee 1984-89, led Cons in Latin American Delgn 1982-87; chm Int Gp Small Business 1985, pres Anglo-Jewish Assoc 1989-; awarded Cross of the Order of Merit of the Federal Republic of Germany 1990; FCIS, FIPM, FBIM, MInstM; *Recreations* reading, music, walking, discussion, family; *Clubs* Carlton, Athenaeum; *Style—* Fred Tuckman, Esq, OBE; 6 Cumberland Rd, Barnes, London SW13 9LY (☎ 081 748 2392)

TUCKWELL, Barry Emmanuel; OBE (1963); s of Charles Robert Tuckwell (d 1986), and Elizabeth Jane, *née* Hill; *b* 5 March 1931; *Educ* Sydney Conservatorium; *m* 1, 1958 (m dis 1970), Dr Sally Newton; 2 s (David Michael, Thomas James), 1 da (Jane Madeleine); m 2, 1970 (m dis 1988); *Career* princ horn LSO 1955-68, princ conductor Tasmanian Symphony Orch 1980-83, music dir and conductor Maryland Symphony Orch 1982-; Hon RAM, Hon GSM; FRSA; *Clubs* Athenaeum; *Style—* Barry Tuckwell, Esq, OBE; c/o Harold Holt Ltd, 31 Sinclair Rd, London W14 ONS (☎ 071 603 4600)

TUCKWELL, Dr Gareth David; s of Sir Edward Tuckwell, KCVO (d 1988), and Phyllis Courthope, *née* Regester (d 1970); *b* 3 Dec 1946; *Educ* Charterhouse, Univ of London and St Bartholomew's Hosp Med Coll (MB BS, DObstRCOG, LRCP); *m* 4 Aug 1973, (Susan) Mary, da of Dr Hugh Wilfred Sansom, OBE, of 29 Holmewood Ridge, Langton Green, Kent; 2 s (Jonathan b 1977, Paul b 1984), 1 da (Deborah b 1976), 1 adopted da (Alexandria b 1984); *Career* princ in gen practice 1974-86, clinical tutor in gen practice St Bartholomew's Hosp Med Coll 1976-86; dir Dorothy Kerin Tst 1986-, med dir of Burrswood Tunbridge Wells 1986-, vice pres Phyllis Tuckwell Memorial Hosp Farnham; memb: Working Pty on The Churches Miny of Healing in the Light of Hospice Experience, Caring Professions Concern; tstee The Burrswood Endowment Tst, Coke Hole Tst Drug Rehabilitation Centre; memb and area rep Christian Med Fellowship; editorial advsr Healing and Wholeness magazine; Freeman City of London, Liveryman Worshipful Soc of Apothecaries 1971; MRCS 1971, MRCGP; memb: Assoc of Palliative Medicine, BMA; *Recreations* photography, walking, gardening; *Style—* Dr Gareth Tuckwell; St Luke's House, Burrswood, Groombridge, Tunbridge Wells, Kent TN3 9PY (☎ 0892 864349); Burrswood, Groombridge, Tunbridge Wells, Kent TN3 9PY (☎ 0892 863637)

TUCKWELL, Paul Hamilton; s of Bernard Sydney Tuckwell, of Steyning Sussex, and Betty, *née* Richardson; *b* 3 Sept 1956; *Educ* Eastbourne Coll, Univ of Loughborough (BSc); *m* 5 April 1980, Maria del Rosario (Rosie), da of Agodofredo Casera; 1 da (Micaela Holly Anne b 1987); *Career* Lloyds Bank Int Ltd 1978-84, dir NM Rothschild & Sons Ltd 1989- (joined 1984); *Recreations* music, theatre, walking; *Style—* Paul Tuckwell, Esq; NM Rothschild & Sons Ltd, New Court, St Swithin's Lane, London EC4P 4DU (☎ 071 280 5731, telex 888031)

TUDOR, Anne Jennifer; da of George Tudor, of Newport, Gwent, and Nancy, *née* Leahy; *b* 23 June 1956; *Educ* St Josephs HS Newport Gwent, South Bank Poly (BA); partner, Geoffrey Taylor; *Career* various journalist and advtg positions, assoc dir Yellow Hammer Advertising; dir: Generator Marketing Ltd 1987-89, The Leisure Process Ltd 1989-; *Recreations* tennis, golf; *Clubs* Surrey Tennis and Country; *Style—* Ms Anne Tudor; 29 Bracken Avenue, London SW12 8BJ (☎ 081 673 7677); The Leisure Process, 126 Great Portland St, London W1N 5PH (☎ 071 631 0666, fax 071 631 3753, car 0836 768423)

TUDOR, Rev Dr (Richard) John; s of Rev Charles Leonard Tudor (d 1986), and Ellen, *née* Clay (d 1981); *b* 8 Feb 1930; *Educ* Clee GS Grimsby, Queen Elizabeth's Barnet, Univ of Manchester (BA); *m* 21 July 1956, Cynthia Campbell, da of Richard Anderson (d 1951); 1 s (Peter b 1964), 1 da (Helen b 1967); *Career* RAF 1948-51; jr Methodist minister East Ham London 1954-57, ordained Newark 1957, minister Thornton Cleveleys Blackpool 1957-60; supt minister: Derby Methodist Mission 1960-71, Coventry Methodist Mission 1971-75, Brighton Dome Mission 1975-81, Westminster Central Hall 1981-; free church chaplain Westminster Hosp 1982-, chm Westminster Christian Cncl 1988-90, chaplain to Int Charity Stewards Ancient Order of Foresters Friendly Soc; Hon Texan 1965, Freeman Fort Worth Texas 1970, Freeman Arkansas 1987; Hon DD Texas Wesleyan Univ Fort Worth Texas 1981; *Recreations* motoring, cooking, photography, the delights of family life; *Style—* The Rev Dr R John Tudor; Westminster Methodist Central Hall, Storey's Gate, London SW1H 9NU (☎ 071 222 8010, fax 071 222 6883)

TUDOR, (Alwyn) Kenneth; s of Alwyn Ieuan Tudor, CBE (d 1984), and Edith Eleanor, *née* Taylor (d 1981); *b* 9 April 1921; *Educ* Felsted; *m* 9 July 1949, Hazel Edith; 1 s (David b 1959), 1 da (Wendy b 1961); *Career* served WWII 1941-46, cmmnd RSC 1942, Temp Maj 1946; London Life Assoc Ltd (life assur co) 1939-81: actuary and mangr 1966, dir 1977, ret gen mangr 1981, ret dir 1985; Freeman City of London 1979, Liveryman Worshipful Co of Actuaries 1980 (Hon Clerk 1981-89, Court Asst 1989); FIA 1951, MInstD 1977; *Recreations* bowls, gardening, walking, travelling holidays; *Style—* Kenneth Tudor, Esq

TUDOR-CRAIG, Pamela, Lady; Pamela (Pamela, Lady Wedgwood); *m* 1, James Tudor-Craig, FSA (d 1969), o s of Maj Sir Algernon Tudor Tudor-Craig, KBE, FSA (d 1943); m 2, 1982, as his 2 w, Sir John Hamilton Wedgwood, 2 Bt, TD (d 1989); *Career* art historian; prof of art history: Univ of Evansville at Harlaxton Coll 1979-89 (fndr Annual Int Symposium on Inter-disciplinary Eng Medieval Studies 1984), Lansdowne Coll Palace Gate London 1990-; speaker in confs at Poitiers and Regensburg; lecture tours of America: Kalamazoo, Smithsonian and Nat Gallery Washington, Museum of Fine Arts Harvard Univ, Metropolitan Museum NY (twice), Univ Museum in Philadelphia, Stamford Univ; TV work: Richard III with Barlow and Watt 1976, Light of Experience 1976, Round Table at Winchester (Horizon) 1977, Richard III for Timewatch 1983, Trial of Richard III for ITV (nominated as programme of the year) 1984, The Secret Life of Paintings BBC 2 1986; ctee memb to advise conservation West Front at: Wells Cathedral 1973-85, Exeter Cathedral 1979-86; memb: Cathedrals Advsy Cmmn for Eng, Architectural Advsy Panel Westminster Abbey, Panel Paintings Ctee Cncl for the Care of Churches (chm Wallpaintings Ctee), Cncl Soc of Antiquaries 1989-, Cultural Affrs Ctee ESU 1991-; vice chm Fabric Ctee Southwell Minster, fndr Cambridgeshire Historic Churches Tst; FSA; *Publications incl* The Secret Life of Paintings (with Richard Foster, 1986), New Bell's Cathedral Guide to Westminster Abbey (jtly, 1986), reg contributor to Arts Page of Church Times; *Style—* Pamela, Lady Wedgwood, FSA; Home Farm, Leighton Bromswold, nr Huntingdon, Cambs PE18 OFL (☎ 0480 890340)

TUDOR EVANS, Hon Mr Justice; Sir Haydn; s of John Edgar Evans by his w, Ellen Stringer; *b* 20 June 1920; *Educ* Cardiff HS, W Monmouth Sch, Lincoln Coll Oxford; *m* 1947, Sheilagh Isabella, *née* Pilkington; 1 s; *Career* served WWII RNVR; called to the Bar 1947, QC 1962, bencher Lincoln's Inn 1970, rec Crown Ct 1972-74, High Ct judge Family Div 1974-78, Queen's Bench Div 1978-, judge Employment Appeal Tbnl 1982-; kt 1974; *Clubs* Garrick, MCC, RAC; *Style—* The Hon Mr Justice Tudor Evans; c/o Royal Courts of Justice, Strand, London WC2

TUDOR JOHN, William; s of Mr Tudor John, of Castle House, Llantrisant, Mid Glamorgan, and Gwen, *née* Griffiths (d 1969); *b* 26 April 1944; *Educ* Cowbridge Sch, Downing Coll Cambridge; *m* 25 Feb 1967, Jane, da of Peter Clark, of Cowbridge, Mid Glam; 3 da (Rebecca b 1971, Katherine b 1974, Elizabeth b 1980); *Career* Allen & Overy: articled clerk 1967-69, asst slr 1969-70, ptnr 1972-; banker Orion Bank Ltd 1970-72; non-exec chm: Suttons Seeds Ltd 1978-, Horticultural and Botanical Holdings Ltd 1985-; appeal steward Br Boxing Bd of Control 1980-; assoc fell Downing Coll Cambridge 1986-; Freeman City of London, Liveryman City of London Slrs Co 1972; memb: Law Soc 1969, Int Bar Assoc 1976; *Recreations* shooting, rugby football, reading, music; *Clubs* The Justinians, Cardiff and County; *Style—* William Tudor John, Esq; Willian Bury, Willian, Herts SG6 2AF (☎ 0462 683532); Allen & Overy, 9 Cheapside, London EC2V 6AD (☎ 071 248 9898, fax 071 236 2192, telex 8812801, car 0836 730 128)

TUDOR-POLE, Edward Felix; s of David Wellesly Tudor-Pole, of South of France, and Shirley Cecila, *née* Brown; *b* 6 Dec 1955; *Educ* KESW, RADA; *Career* actor; theatre roles incl: Scullery in Road (Royal Ct) 1986, Churchill in Sink The Belgrano 1987, Rt Hon Ernest Wooley in The Admirable Crichton (Theatre Royal Haymarket) 1988, Riff Raff in Rocky Horror Show (Piccadilly Theatre) 1990; several tv appearances on Top of the Pops (BBC1) with Tenpole Tudor 1981-82, The Money Men (LWT) 1988, radio appearances in Radio I Airplay 1980-90; films incl: The Great Rock and Roll Swindle, Absolute Beginners, Straight to Hell, Walker, White Hunter Black Heart; writer and performer Who Killed Bambi? (with The Sex Pistols), awarded Silver disc for recording of The Swords of 1000 Men; *Recreations* long distance running, playing the guitar; *Style—* Edward Tudor-Pole, Esq; Michael Foster, Duncan Heath Associates, Paramount House, Wardour St, London W1 (☎ 071 439 1471)

TUDOR-WILLIAMS, Robert; s of David Tudor-Williams (d 1990), of Cleddau Lodge, Haverfordwest, and Nanette Llewellin; *b* 4 Nov 1945; *Educ* Haverfordwest GS, Guy's (BDS, LDS, RCS); *m* 1971, Margaret Ann, da of Arthur Hector Morris; 2 s (Laurence b 6 April 1973, Dylan b 8 April 1974), 1 da (Rebecca b 16 Jan 1979); *Career* asst house surgn Guy's 1970, house surgn King's Coll Hosp 1970-71, sr hosp dental offr Eastman Dental Hosp 1972, gen practice in City and West End 1970-72, princ of gp practice Fulham 1972-80, clinical asst in oral Surgery Charing Cross Hosp 1974-87, in private practice Fulham and Esher Surrey 1980-88, in private practice Harley St 1988-;

special interests: cosmetic dentistry, headaches, migraines and disorders of the TMJ 1988-; lectr Hammersmith and W London Coll: to med secs 1978-87, to dental surgery assts 1977-88; lectr and course dir to dental surgery assts BDA 1988-, radio dentist LBC 1989-; memb Panel of Examiners: RCS (Edinburgh) 1988-, Examining Bd for Dental Surgery Assts 1982-; memb: BDA 1970- (chm Kingston and Dist Section 1983-84), Br Soc of Periodontology 1985-, L D Pankey Assoc 1985-, Br Dental Migraine Study Gp 1985-, Br Soc of Gen Dental Surgery 1986-, Health Fndn 1988-, Fedn Dentair Int 1990-; MGDS RCS (Ed) 1986, FRSM 1986; *Recreations* sailing, gardening, theatre, swimming, cycling, shooting, fishing; *Style—* Robert Tudor-Williams, Esq; The Birches, 50 Grove Way, Esher, Surrey KT10 8HL (☎ 081 398 5953); 73 Harley St, London W1N 1DE (☎ 071 224 3848, fax 071 224 1706, mobile 0831 293763)

TUDWAY, Dr David Christie; s of Dr Robert Christie Tudway (d 1991), of Haddenham nr Aylesbury, and Winifred Mary, *née* Littler; *b* 28 April 1947; *Educ* Clifton Coll, Middlesex Hosp Med Sch; *m* 31 May 1980, Kathleen Joyce, da of Leslie Oakes, of Audley nr Stoke-on-Trent; 1 da (Penelope); *Career* jr med posts 1971-78, trainee radiologist 1978-83, conslt radiologist E Birmingham Hosp 1983-, dir of radiology E Birmingham dist 1988-; memb W Midlands Soc of Radiologists; MRCP 1976, FRCR 1982; *Recreations* yachting, walking; *Clubs* Dartmouth Yacht; *Style—* Dr David Tudway; Dept of Radiology, East Birmingham Hospital, Bordesley Green East, Birmingham B9 5ST (☎ 021 766 6611)

TUDWAY QUILTER, David Cuthbert; *see*: Quilter, David Cuthbert

TUFFIN, Alan; *b* 2 Aug 1933; *Career* former postal and telegraph worker; Union of Communication Workers: elected to Exec Cncl 1966, full time offr 1969, dep gen sec 1979, gen sec 1982-; dir: Unity Trust, Trade Union Unit Trust; TUC: memb Gen Cncl, memb Fin and Gen Purposes Ctee, memb Econ and Int Ctee, memb Health and Safety Cmmn, chm Social Insurance and Industl Welfare Ctee; memb Exec Ctee Postal Telegraph and Telephone Inf; memb Exec Ctee Duke of Edinburgh Cmmwlth Study Conf; *Style—* Alan Tuffin, Esq; UCW House, Crescent Lane, London SW4 9RN

TUFNELL, Hon Mrs (Anne Rosemary); *née* Trench; da of late 5 Baron Ashtown, OBE (d 1979), by his 1 w, Ellen Nancy (d 1949), da of late William Garton; *b* 1936; *m* 1, 1958, Capt Timothy Patrick Arnold Gosselin, Scots Gds (d 1961); 1 da (Nicola Jane Gosselin b 1960); m 2, 1962, Col Greville Tufnell, *qv*; 3 da; *Style—* The Hon Mrs Tufnell; Quenington Court, Quenington, Cirencester, Glos GL7 5BN (☎ 0285 750511)

TUFNELL, Hon Mrs (Georgina Mary); *née* Cavendish; yr da of 5 Baron Chesham, PC, TD (d 1989); *b* 8 Sept 1944; *m* 1967, (Michael) Wynne Tufnell; 3 s; *Style—* The Hon Mrs Tufnell; High Dell Farmhouse, Bighton, Alresford, Hants SO24 9RB (☎ 0962 73 3970)

TUFNELL, Col Greville Wyndham; s of Maj K E M Tufnell, MC (d 1976); *b* 7 April 1932; *Educ* Eton, RMA Sandhurst; *m* 1962, Hon Anne, *qv*; 3 da; *Career* 2 Lt Grenadier Gds 1952, Adj 2 Bn 1959-61, GSO 3 WO (MO2) 1962-63, Staff Coll 1964, Maj 1965, DAQMG London Dist 1966-67, GSO 2 HQ Div 1969-71, Lt-Col 1971, cmdg 1 Bn Grenadier Gds 1971-73 (despatches 1972), Bde Maj Household Div 1974-76, Col 1976, cmdg Grenadier Gds 1976-78, Yeoman of the Guard Exon 1979, Ensign 1985, Clerk to the Cheque and Adjutant 1987; devpt offr Nat Star Centre for Disabled Youth 1982-; Liveryman Worshipful Co of Grocers', Freeman City of London; FBIM; *Clubs* Cavalry and Guards, MCC; *Style—* Col G W Tufnell; Quenington Court, Quenington, Cirencester, Glos GL7 5BN (☎ 0285 750511)

TUFNELL, Capt Michael Neville; CVO (1976), DSC (1940); er s of Col Neville Charsley Tufnell (d 1951), of Fairfield, Sunninghill, Ascot, and Sybil Carlos, *née* Clarke (d 1958); *b* 28 Jan 1914; *Educ* RNC Dartmouth, Greenwich; *m* 1941, Patricia Wynne, da of Edward Wynne Chapman (ka 1914), of NZ; 1 s, 2 da; *Career* RN 1927, serv WWII, Cdr 1946, Capt 1953, naval attaché Tokyo 1952-54, CO HMS Decoy 1954-56, naval advsr Australia 1958-60, CO HMS St Vincent Jrs Trg Estab 1960-62, ret; gentleman usher to HM The Queen 1965, extra gentleman usher to HM The Queen 1984-; Freeman City of London, Liveryman Worshipful Co of Grocers; *Recreations* cricket; *Clubs* Royal Yacht Sqdn, Naval and Military, MCC; *Style—* Capt M N Tufnell, CVO, DSC; Curdridge Grange, Curdridge, Southampton, Hants (☎ 048 92 782454)

TUFNELL, Maj Timothy; MC (1945), ERD; s of Col Neville Charsley Tufnell (d 1951), of Fairfield, Sunninghill, Ascot; *b* 1920; *Educ* Eton; *m* 1944 (m dis 1947), Pamela Dione, only da of Oliver Parker (d 1967); *Career* serv WWII 1939-46: Grenadier Gds, Capt 1941, Maj 1944; underwriting memb Lloyd's, conslt Knight Frank & Rutley; chm St John Cncl for Berks, memb Cncl Order of St John; Liveryman Worshipful of Grocers; C St J; *Recreations* backgammon, racing; *Clubs* Bucks, MCC; *Style—* Major Timothy Tufnell, MC, ERD; Hernes Keep, North St, Winkfield, Windsor, Berks SL4 4BY

TUGENDHAT, Sir Christopher Samuel; er s of Dr Georg Tugendhat (d 1973), of London; *b* 23 Feb 1937; *Educ* Ampleforth, Gonville and Caius Coll Cambridge; *m* 1967, Julia Lissant, da of Kenneth D Dobson, of Keston, Kent; 2 s; *Career* ldr and feature writer Financial Times 1960-70; MP (C): Cities of London and Westminster 1970-74, City of London and Westminster South 1974-76; dir Sunningdale Oils 1971-76, conslt Phillips Petroleum International Ltd 1972-1976, former conslt to Wood Mackenzie & Co Stockbrokers; Br EEC cmmr (responsible for budget, fin control, personnel and admin) 1977-81, vice pres Cmmn of Euro Communities (responsible for budget, fin control, fin insts and taxation) 1981-85; author of pamphlets incl: Britain, Europe and the Third World (1976), Conservatives in Europe (1979), Is Reform Possible ? (1981); dir: The BOG Group 1985-, Commercial Union Assurance Co plc 1988-; chm: CAA 1986-, Royal Inst of Int Affrs Chatham House 1986-; dep chm Nat Westminster Bank 1990 (dir 1985-); kt 1990; *Books* Oil: The Biggest Business (1968), The Multinationals (1971), Making Sense of Europe (1986), Options for British Foreign Policy in the 1990's (with William Wallace, 1988); *Recreations* conversation, reading, being with my family; *Clubs* Buck's, Carlton, Anglo-Belgian; *Style—* Sir Christopher Tugendhat; 35 Westbourne Park Rd, London W2 5QD

TUGENDHAT, Michael George; QC (1986); s of Dr Georg Tugendhat (d 1973), and Maire, *née* Littledale; *b* 21 Oct 1944; *Educ* Ampleforth, Gonville & Caius Coll Cambridge (MA), Yale; *m* 6 June 1970, Blandine Marie, da of Comte Pierre-Charles Menche de Loisne, of France, 4 s (Charles b 1972, Thomas b 1973, Gregory b 1977, Henry b 1986); *Career* called to the Bar Inner Temple 1969, MO Circuit, bencher Inner Temple; *Clubs* Brooks's; *Style—* Michael Tugendhat, Esq, QC; 10 South Square, Gray's Inn, London WC1R 5EZ (☎ 071 242 2902)

TUGHAN, Frederick Charles; CBE (1968); s of William Tughan (d 1912); *b* 24 Jan 1909; *Educ* Bangor GS, Queen's Univ Belfast; *m* 1935, Mildred, *née* Patterson; 2 s, 3 da (1 decd); *Career* slr 1930, Mayor of Bangor 1956-60, chm Seed Potato Bd NI 1961-68, dir: Lamont Life Assoc Co, Ulster Scot Friendly Soc, Bangor Provident Tst; *Recreations* golf; *Clubs* Royal Belfast; *Style—* Frederick Tughan, Esq, CBE; 40 Kylestone Rd, Bangor, Co Down (☎ 0232 883993); Ralborough Securities Ltd, 20 Victoria St, Belfast BT1 3PD

TUGWELL, John; s of John James Arthur Tugwell, of Hove, Sussex, and Vera Olive, *née* Mockford (d 1984); *b* 1 Oct 1940; *Educ* Hove Co GS; *m* 12 May 1962, Janice Elizabeth, da of Leslie Walter Santer (d 1979); 1 s (Matthew b 8 Dec 1969), 1 da (Jane b 11 Oct 1965); *Career* dir and chief exec int business National Westminster Bank plc (gen mangr business devpt div 1987-88, regnl gen mangr exec office N America 1984-87); memb: America Europe Community Assoc; ACIB; *Recreations* cricket, gardening, walking; *Style—* John Tugwell, Esq; Roundways, 13 Oak Bank, Lindfield, West Sussex RH16 1RR (☎ 0444 450 019); National Westminster Bank plc, 41 Lothbury, London EC2P 2BP (☎ 071 726 1970)

TUGWELL, Richard Stuart; s of Reginald Wilfred Tugwell, of Cirencester, Glos, and Sarah, *née* Burrow (d 1982); *b* 5 Nov 1947; *Educ* Cirencester GS, Bognor Regis Coll of Educn; *m* 30 May 1970, Elisabeth Mary, da of Maj Garth Douglas Curtis, OBE, of Winchester, Hants; 2 da (Lisa b 15 Nov 1970, Anna b 3 May 1974); *Career* journalist Wilts & Glos Standard 1969-84 (sports ed 1978-84), sports ed Oxford Times 1984, Br Sportswriters Assoc/Sports Cncl Award, Weekly Newspaper Sports Writer of the Year 1987; *Recreations* cricket, golf; *Clubs* Cirencester Cricket (Capt), Cirencester Golf, Glos Gypsies Cricket, S Oxfordshire Amateurs Cricket; *Style—* Richard Tugwell, Esq; Oxford and County Newspapers Ltd, Osney Mead, Oxford OX2 0EJ (☎ 0865 244 988)

TUITE, Sir Christopher Hugh; 14 Bt (I 1622), of Sonnagh, Westmeath; s of Sir Dennis George Harmsworth Tuite, 13 Bt, MBE (d 1981), descended from the Sir Richard de Tuite or Tuitt, who was one of Strongbow's followers in his invasion of Ireland in 1172); *b* 3 Nov 1949; *Educ* Wellington Coll, Leeds Univ (BSc), Bristol Univ (PhD); *m* 1976, Deborah Ann, da of A E Martz, of Pittsburgh, USA; 2 s (Thomas Livingstone b 1977, Jonathan Christopher Hannington b 1981); *Heir* s, Thomas Livingstone Tuite; *Career* res offr The Wildfowl Tst 1978-81; pres Spirutec Inc (Arizona) 1982-; *Style—* Sir Christopher Tuite, Bt; 1521 East June, Mesa, Arizona 85203, USA

TUITE, Margaret, Lady; Margaret Essie; da of Col Walter Leslie Dundas, DSO, of Farnham; *m* 1947, Sir Dennis Tuite, 13 Bt, MBE (d 1981); 3 s; *Style—* Margaret, Lady Tuite; 7 Vicarage Gardens, Grayshott, Hindhead, Surrey GU26 6NH (☎ 0428 605026)

TUITE, Thomas Robert Henry Stratford; OBE (1989, MBE 1974); s of Capt Thomas Mark Hardress Stratford Tuite, MC, JP (d 1976), of Dublin, and Ethel Mary, *née* Wilson (d 1988); *b* 12 July 1923; *Educ* educated privately, Trinity Coll Dublin (BA, MA); *m* 12 Sept 1957, (Maria) Rosario Briales de Leon, da of Col German Briales Lopez (d 1964), of Malaga; 5 s (Thomas b 1958, Jaime b 1960, Gerard b 1961, Mark b 1963, Patrick b 1968); *Career* called to the Bar Kings Inn Dublin 1945, called to the Bar Gray's Inn 1951, admitted barr and slr of Alberta Canada 1954; practised in Ireland 1946-48, legal asst Control Cmmn Germany 1948-49, legal offr FO Admin of African Territories Eritrea 1950-52, memb Attorney Gen's Dept Alberta 1953-54, Br consul Malaga 1969-89 (vice consul 1962-69), chm Thomas Wilson SA Lloyd's Agents Malaga 1982-; *Recreations* swimming, fishing; *Style—* Thomas Tuite, Esq, OBE; Los Pinos, Calle Ricardo Leon 5, 29017 Malaga, Spain (☎ 010 34 52 292137); c/o Thomas Wilson SA, Calle Vendeja 6, 29080 Malaga, Spain (☎ 010 34 52 212195, telex 79090 TWIE, fax 010 34 52 210158)

TUIVAGA, Hon Mr Justice; Hon Sir Timoci Uluiburotu; *b* 1931,Oct; *Career* acting chief justice of Fiji 1974-80, chief justice 1980-; kt 1981; *Style—* Hon Mr Justice Tuivaga; 228 Ratu Sukuna Rd, Suva, Fiji

TUKE, Sir Anthony Favill; s of Anthony Tuke; *b* 22 Aug 1920; *Educ* Winchester, Magdalene Coll Cambridge; *m* 1946, Emilia Mila Antic; 1 s, 1 da; *Career* chm: Savoy Hotel plc 1984- (dir 1982-), RTZ Corpn 1981-85 (dir 1980-91); dir: Barclays Bank 1965-90 (chm 1973-81), Barclays Bank UK 1971-81, Barclays Bank Int 1965-87 (chm 1972-79), Urban Fndn 1980-86, Merchants Tst 1969-, Royal Insur 1978- (dep chm 1985-), Whitbread Investmt Co plc 1984-; memb Trilateral Cmmn 1973-90; govr Motability 1978-84, former vice-pres Inst of Bankers and Br Bankers Assoc; kt 1979; *Clubs* MCC (pres 1982-83, memb ctee, chm fin ctee 1983-90); *Style—* Sir Anthony Tuke; Freelands, Wherwell, Andover, Hants

TUKE, Peter Godfrey; s of Dr Reginald Godfrey Tuke (d 1973), of Bournemouth, and Dorothy Beatrice, *née* Underwood (d 1948); *b* 14 June 1944; *Educ* Radley, Keble Coll Oxford (MA, Rowing blues), Poly of Central London (Dip Arch); *m* 21 June 1975, Susan, da of Edward Albert Hamilton Lawrence (d 1978), of Handcross, Sussex; 2 s (Edward b 1978, William b 1980); *Career* corporate planning BP 1967-71, architect and ptnr Prior Manton Tuke Ptnrship 1981-; MRIBA 1979; *Recreations* theatre, sailing, walking; *Clubs* Vincents, Leander; *Style—* Peter Tuke, Esq; 48 Brodrick Rd, London SW17 (☎ 081 672 8678); 15 Prescott Place, London SW4 (☎ 071 627 8085, fax 071 627 2658)

TULLO, Carol Anne; da of Edward Alan Dodgson, of Woolton, Liverpool, and Patricia, *née* Masterson; *b* 9 Jan 1956; *Educ* Holly Lodge, Univ of Hull (LLB); *m* 5 May 1979, Robin Brownrigg Tullo, s of James Francis Swanzy Tullo, of Highgate, London; 1 da (Alice b 1986); *Career* called to the Bar Inner Temple 1977; dir: Stevens 1985, Sweet & Maxwell Ltd 1988, ESC Publishing Ltd 1990; *Recreations* motherhood; *Style—* Mrs Robin Tullo; 38 Friern Park, London N12 9DA (☎ 081 445 9689); South Quay Plaza, 183 Marsh Wall, London E14 9FT (☎ 071 538 8686, fax 071 538 8625, telex 9290 89)

TULLOCH, Alastair Robert Clifford; s of James Richard Moore Tulloch, and Heather Netta (d 1989); *b* 1 Oct 1955; *Educ* St Andrew's Coll SA, Magdalen Coll Oxford; *m* 15 Aug 1987, Hilary, da of Rev Alisdair MacDonell, of St Mary's Haddington, Scotland; 1 da (Emma Heather b 1988), 2 s (Robin b and d 1989, Hugh Gordon b 1991); *Career* asst slr: Lovell White and King 1980-82 (articled 1978-80), McNeil and Co Dubai 1982-84, Clifford Turner 1984-86; ptnr Frere Cholmeley 1987-; memb Law Society; *Recreations* DIY, skiing, sailing, hill-walking; *Style—* Alastair Tulloch, Esq; 46 Laurier Road, London NW5 1SJ (☎ 071 482 0820), Frere Cholmeley, 28 Lincoln's Inn Fields, London WC2A 3HH (☎ 071 405 7878, fax 071 405 9056)

TULLOCH, Iain William Patrick; s of Maj William Alexander Tulloch, (d 1988), of Southwood House, Monkton, Ayrshire, and Margaret Edith Phyllis, *née* Farquhar (d 1968); *b* 12 Dec 1940; *Educ* Rugby, Brown Univ Providence Rhode Island USA; *m* 5 Oct 1967, Charmian Mary, da of Michael Anthony Callender of Gaston Cottage, Alton, Hants; 1 s (Gillem b 1971), 1 da (Leesa b 1969); *Career* Lt Ayshire Yeomanry 1966; CA 1966; dir Murray Johnstone 1987, non exec dir Leveraged Opportunity Trust 1989, IFG Group 1990; *Recreations* royal tennis, squash, golf, gardening; *Clubs* Prestwick Golf, Western; *Style—* Iain Tulloch, Esq; Swallow Ha', Symington, Ayrshire; Murray Johnstone Ltd, 7 West Nile St, Glasgow (☎ 041 2263131, fax 014 2485636, telex 778667)

TULLOCH, William Paul; s of William Andrew Tulloch, of Sydney, Australia, and Ada Imelda, *née* Ratcliffe; *b* 26 Sept 1956; *Educ* Marcellin Coll Randwick Sydney, Univ of NSW (BSc, BArch); *m* 28 Sept 1985, Melanie Susan, da of James Sutherland Dag McKay; 1 s (William David b 30 Jan 1989); *Career* architect; Mitchell Giurgola & Thorp Canberra (projects incl New Parliament House Canberra) 1982, Maurice Meyersohn & Assocs London (projects incl Kensington Palace Hotel) 1981-82, Alexander Flinder Ashley Partnership (projects incl St James Hotel) 1983-84, Rolfe Judd Group Practice London (projects incl refurbishment of listed building Sackville of London) 1984; ptnr The Fitzroy Robinson Partnership 1989- (sr architect 1985-86, assoc 1986-88, sr assoc 1988-89) projects incl: Robert Fleming & Co headquarters 1985, offices and hotel No 1 Knightsbridge and St Georges 1985, retail devpt Oracle Reading 1986-87, office devpt Bridge St Plaza Reading 1985-87, new industl complex Redland Plasterboard Factory 1987, res and devpt headquarters Computing Devices

Eastbourne 1987-88, office and retail devpt Scottish Widows 1988, office and retail devpt Swire House Hong Kong 1988-89, merchant bank fitting-out Hambros 1988, office and retail devpt New Islington Square 1989, leisure complex The Battersea 1989, Solent Business Park 1989, office devpt Station Rd Croydon 1989-90, office and retail devpt Fleet St Square 1989-91; memb: RIBA, ARCUK; *Recreations* sailing, skiing, rugby; *Style*— William Tulloch, Esq; The Fitzroy Robinson Partnership, 77 Portland Place, London W1 (☎ 071 636 8033)

TULLY, David John; s of William Scarth Carlisle Tully, CBE (d 1987), and Patience Treby, *née* Betts; *b* 13 March 1942; *Educ* Twyford, Sherborne; *m* 7 May 1965, Susan Patricia, da of (James) Geoffrey Arnott; 1 s (James Herbert b 1967), 2 da (Louise Patience b 1969, Clare Jane b 1972); *Career* slr, ptnr Addleshaw & Sons Latham Manchester 1969-; formerly chm: Manchester Young Slrs, Nat Young Slrs, The St James's Club; formerly pres Manchester Law Soc; dir Cobden Gp of Cos 1975; govr Manchester GS; *Recreations* shooting, fishing, golf; *Clubs* St James's (Manchester), Racquets (Manchester); *Style*— David Tully, Esq; 2 Warwick Drive, Hale, Altrincham, Cheshire WA15 9EA (☎ 061 928 3029); Dennis House, Marsden St, Manchester M2 1JD (☎ 061 832 5994, fax 061 832 2250)

TULLY, (William) Mark; OBE (1985); s of late William Scarth Carlisle Tully, CBE, and Patience Treby, *née* Betts; *b* 24 Oct 1935; *Educ* New Sch Darjeeling India, Twyford Sch Winchester Hants, Marlborough, Trinity Hall Cambridge (MA); *m* 13 Aug 1960, (Frances) Margaret, da of late Frank Howard Butler; 2 s (Sam b 1965, Patrick b 1967), 2 da (Sarah b 1961, Emma b 1963); *Career* Nat Serv 2 Lt 1 Royal Dragoons 1954-56; regnl dir Abbey Field Soc for housing old people 1960-64; BBC: Personnel Dept 1964-65, asst then acting rep BBC Delhi 1965-69, Hindi prog organiser External Servs London 1969-70, chief talks writer External Servs 1970-71, chief of Bureau 1972-; winner of: Dimbleby Award BAFTA 1984, Radio and Critics Bdcasting Press Guild Radio Award 1984; *Books* Amritsar Mrs Gandhis Last Battle (with Satish Jacob, 1985), Raj to Rajiv (with Zareer Masani, 1988); *Recreations* reading, fishing, bird watching; *Clubs* Oriental, Press and Gymkhana (Delhi); *Style*— Mark Tully, Esq, OBE; 1 Nizamuddin East, New Delhi 110013 (☎ 616108, 693069, 693066, telex 51 66227, fax 616102)

TUMIM, His Hon Judge Stephen; s of Joseph Tumim, CBE (d 1957), and Renée Tumim (d 1941); *b* 15 Aug 1930; *Educ* St Edwards Sch Oxford, Worcester Coll Oxford; *m* 1 Feb 1962, Winifred Letitia, da of Col Algernon Borthwick (d 1976), of Essex; 3 da (Matilda b 1963, Emma b 1964, Olivia b 1968); *Career* called to the Bar Middle Temple 1955, rec Crown Ct 1977-78, circuit judge 1978-; chm Friends of Tate Gallery 1983-90, pres Royal Literary Fund 1990-; HM chief inspr of prisons for England and Wales 1987-; *Books* Great Legal Disasters (1983), Great Legal Fiascos (1985); *Clubs* Garrick, Beefsteak; *Style*— His Hon Judge Tumim

TUMIM, Winifred Letitia; da of Lt-Col Algernon Malcolm Borthwick MC (d 1975), of Braintree, Essex, and Edith Wilde, *née* Addison (d 1975); *b* 3 June 1936; *Educ* North Foreland Lodge Sch, Lady Margaret Hall Oxford (BA, MA), Univ of London (Dip Linguistics, Dip Soc Studies); *m* Feb 18 1962, Stephen Tumim, s of Joseph Tumim, CBE, of Headington, Oxford; 3 da (Matilda Edith (Mrs Prendergast), Emma Renee (Mrs Iliffe), Olivia Blanche); *Career* author of articles and reviews in pubns incl: TES, Nursing, Where?, Higher Educn; memb: Govt Ctee of Enquiry on educn of handicapped children 1974-78, Ealing Hammersmith and Hounslow AHA 1978-82, Hammersmith and Fulham DHA 1982-85, Dept of Employment Govt advsy ctee on employment of disabled people 1987-, mgmnt ctee Family Housing Assoc; parly candidate (SDP) Wantage 1983 and 1987; govr Mary Hare GS for the Deaf 1974-, tstee Hearing and Speech Tst 1981-, chm RNID 1985, chm of tstees Independent Living Fund 1988-, tstee City Parochial Fndn 1989-; Nat Deaf Children's Soc: first chm W London branch (fndr 1974), chm educn ctee 1974-80, FRSA; *Books* Weekly Boarding, Why & How (1974), Parents as Partners (1980), A Pre-School Service of Deaf Children and their Parents (1981), Bibliography of Literature for and about Young People with Special Needs (1981), National Book League, International Year of the Child–Notebook for School Leavers with Special Needs (1985); *Recreations* walking, talking, gardening, opera, watercolor painting; *Clubs* National Lib Club; *Style*— Mrs Winifred Tumim; River House, 24 Upper Mall, London W6 9TA (☎ 081 748 5238); Royal National Institute for the Deaf, 105 Gower St, London WC1 (☎ 071 387 8033)

TUNBRIDGE, Lady; Dorothy; da of Henry Gregg, of Knottingley; *Educ* Univ of Leeds (MSc, MA, DipEd); *m* 1935, Sir Ronald Ernest Tunbridge, OBE, JP (d 1984, prof of med Leeds Univ 1946-71); 2 s; *Career* vice pres Yorks Ladies Cncl of Educn (hon sec 1960-71), chm Univ of Leeds Convocation 1953-56, memb Leeds (GP B) Hosp Mgmnt Ctee (vice chm 1972-74), first pres Knottingley Civic Soc; *Style*— Lady Tunbridge; 9 Ancaster Rd, Leeds LS16 5HH

TUNBRIDGE, Dr (William) Michael Gregg; s of Sir Ronald Ernest Tunbridge, OBE (d 1984), of Leeds, and Dorothy, *née* Gregg; *b* 13 June 1940; *Educ* Kingswood Sch Bath, Queens' Coll Cambridge (MA, MD), UCH; *m* 28 Aug 1965, Felicity Katherine Edith, da of Arthur Myers Parrish (d 1987), of Bangor; 2 da (Clare b 1968, Anne b 1970); *Career* conslt physician Newcastle Gen Hosp 1977-, sr lectr in med Univ of Newcastle upon Tyne; memb Br Diabetic Assoc; FRCP 1979; *Recreations* hockey; *Style*— Dr Michael Tunbridge; Newcastle General Hosp, Westgate Rd, Newcastle upon Tyne NE4 6BE (091 2738811)

TUNE, Laurence Kenneth; s of Elijah Thomas Tune, and Catherine Tune; *b* 30 Sept 1939; *Educ* Holywell GS, Univ of Wales (BSc); *m* 1964, Ann Bridget, da of Thomas William Jackson (d 1953), of Northwich; 1 s (Christopher b 1971), 1 da (Helen b 1969); *Career* dir: PA Mgmnt Conslts Ltd 1979-83, Coopers & Lybrand Assocs Ltd 1983-, Coopers & Lybrand Deloitte Exec Resourcing; memb Chartered Inst Mktg, FIMC; *Recreations* literature, theatre, cinema; *Clubs* Portico Library, Manchester Literary & Philosophical Soc; *Style*— Laurence Tune, Esq; 8 Dane Bank Rd, Lymm, Ches (☎ 092 575 3154); Coopers & Lybrand Deloitte Ltd, Abacus Ct, 6 Minshull St, Manchester M1 3ED (☎ 061 236 9191, fax 061 247 4000, telex 667257)

TUNNEY, Kieran Patrick; s of Patrick Adam Tunney, and Julia O'Callaghan, *née* Clancy; *b* 14 Oct 1922; *Educ* Rep of Ireland, England and France; *Career* offr cadet Grenadier Gds 1942; theatre corr, playwright author; plays: The Patriot Cork Ireland 1938, Day After Tomorrow Q Theatre and Fortune Theatre 1946, The Marriage Playground Q Theatre 1946, A Priest in the Family (observer Play of the Season) Family Westminster Theatre 1951, The Wedding Ring Manchester Opera House 1952, Royal Exit Cambridge 1953, God and Kate Murphy Broadway 1959 (Best Record of the Theatrical Year), A House of Glass London 1963; screenplays: The Rasputin Yousoupoff Affair, The Red Prophet, Justice Deferred; theatre critic: Daily Sketch, Queen Magazine, News Chronicle, Tatler, Truth Ballet; memb Dramatisis Guild NY; *Books* Tallulah Darling of the Gods, Interupted Autobiography & Aurora (1990); *Recreations* walking, tennis, reading; *Style*— Kieran Tunney, Esq; 510 Beatty House, Dolphin Square, London SW1V 3PL (☎ 071 798 8285)

TUNNICLIFFE, Jonathan Frederick; s of William Frederick Tunnicliffe (d 1979), of Grassington, Skipton, N Yorks, and Doris, *née* Thompson (d 1966); *b* 20 Sept 1929; *Educ* Chesterfield GS, Queen Elizabeth GS Wakefield, Univ of Leeds (BSc, ICI Mining prize); *m* 1 Sept 1951, Enid Barbara, da of Edward Richardson; 2 s (William Richard b 3 Feb 1952, Jonathan Edward b 4 May 1965), 2 da (Susan Carol b 21 April 1953, Anne Elizabeth b 1 May 1957); *Career* mine underofficial NCB 1956-57 (mgmnt trainee 1954-56); colliery mangr: Snydale Colliery 1959-64, Newmarket Silkstone Colliery 1964-68 (colliery undermanager 1957-59); area safety engr N Yorks Area NCB 1973-75; colliery gen mangr: Prince of Wales Colliery 1968-73, Lofthouse Colliery 1975-78, Selby Coalfield 1978-82; Milburn prof of mining engrg and head of Dept of Mining Engrg Univ of Newcastle 1982-90, prof of mining engrg and head of Dept of Mining and Mineral Engrg Univ of Leeds 1990-; pres Midland Inst of Mining Engrs 1978-79 (awarded Thomas Adam medal 1983), nat pres Inst of Mining Engrs 1987-88 (EIMCO-McArthur award 1983, Sir Andrew Bryan award 1989), currently chm Chamber of Engrs of Mining and Minerals; MIME 1952, FEng 1989; *Recreations* walking, reading, Gilbert and Sullivan Soc, sport; *Clubs* St John House; *Style*— Prof Jonathan Tunnicliffe; 10 The Russets, Sandal, Wakefield, West Yorkshire WF2 6JF (☎ 0924 256675); Department of Mining and Mineral Engineering, The University of Leeds, Leeds LS2 9JT (☎ 0532 332789, fax 0532 467310)

TUNSTALL, Anthony Richard; s of Samuel Thomas Tunstall, and Edith Gwendoline Tunstall; *b* 14 Sept 1924; *Educ* Alleyns Sch Dulwich, King's Coll Cambridge; *m* 1, (m dis), (Gwladys Amy) Monica Mary, da of Harold Sinclair; 3 s (Nicholas b 1954, Oliver b 1955, Alexander b 1961), 3 da (Helen b 1952, Angela b 1956, Sarah b 1958); m 2, Helene Bichon; 1 s (Anthony b 1982); *Career* cmmn Coastal Forces RNVR; princ horn palyer Royal Opera House Covent Garden London; *Clubs* The Savage; *Style*— Anthony Tunstall, Esq; 12 Albert Square, London SW8 1BT (☎ 071 735 5807)

TUNSTALL-PEDOE, Prof Hugh David; s of Prof Dan Pedoe, of Minneapolis, USA, and (Bessie Maude) Mary, *née* Tunstall (d 1965); *b* 30 Dec 1939; *Educ* Haberdashers' Aske's, Hampstead Sch, Dulwich, King's Coll Cambridge, Guy's Hosp Med Sch (MB BChir, MA, MD); *m* 24 June 1967, Jacqueline Helen, da of Kenneth B Burbidge, of Felmersham, Bedfordshire; 2 s (William b 1969, Oliver b 1973), 1 da (Susan b 1971); *Career* house physician 1964-66: Guy's, Brompton Hosp, Nat Hosp for Nervous Diseases; jr registrar Guy's 1967, clinical scientific staff Social Med Unit MRC 1969-71, lectr in med London Hosp 1971-74 (registrar in gen med 1968-69); St Mary's Hosp 1974-81: sr lectr in epidemiology, conslt physician, hon community physician; Univ of Dundee Ninewells Med Sch 1981-: dir Cardiovascular Epidemiology Unit, prof of cardiovascular epidemiology, sr lectr in med; conslt cardiologist and specialist in public health med Tayside Health Bd 1981; various pubns in jls; chm Working Gp on Epidemiology and Prevention Euro Soc of Cardiology 1983-85, memb Resuscitation Cncl of UK; FRCP 1981, FFPHM 1981, FRCPE 1987, FESC 1988; *Books* Multiple Choice Questions in Epidemiology and Community Medicine (with W C S Smith, 1987); *Recreations* golf, bee-keeping, jogging; *Clubs* RSM; *Style*— Prof Hugh Tunstall-Pedoe; 4 Hill Street, Broughty Ferry, Dundee DD5 2JL (☎ 0382 77358), Cardiovascular Epidemiology Unit, Ninewells Hosp and Medical Sch, Dundee DD1 9SY (☎ 0382 644255, fax 0382 641095)

TUOHY, Denis John; s of John Vincent Tuohy (d 1976), of Scariff, Co Clare, and Anne Mary, *née* Doody; *b* 2 April 1937; *Educ* Clongowes Wood Coll Ireland, Queen's Univ Belfast (BA, Blayney exhibition prize, Peel prize, debating medal); *m* 1960 (m dis 1988), Eleanor Moya, da of Felix Charles McCann; 2 s (Mark b 12 June 1962, Christopher b 3 April 1964), 2 da (Eleanor b 14 July 1969, Catherine b 21 Oct 1974); *Career* tv reporter, presenter and writer; presenter and reporter: BBC NI 1960-64 (also actor), 24 Hours (BBC 1) 1967-71 (also prodr), Panorama (BBC 1) 1974-75, TV Eye (Thames) 1979-86; presenter: Late Night Line Up (BBC 2) 1964-67, People and Politics (Thames) 1973, Midweek (BBC 1) 1974, Tonight (BBC 1) 1975-79, Reporting London (Thames) 1981-82, The Garden Party (BBC 1) 1990; reporter: Man Alive (BBC 2) 1971-72, This Week (Thames) 1972-74 and 1987-; special documentaries as presenter writer and narrator: Lord of the Rings (BBC 1) 1974, A Life of O'Reilly (BBC 1) 1974, Mr Truman Why Did You Drop the Second Bomb? (BBC 1) 1975, Do You Know Where Jimmy Carter Lives? (BBC 1) 1977, To Us a Child (Thames, UNICEF) 1986, The Blitz (Thames) 1990; Eisenhower travelling fellow (survey of public tv in USA) 1967, special prize for documentary To Us a Child (Third World film/tv festival Algiers) 1987; memb NUJ 1970-; *Recreations* watching rugby and cricket, theatre, cinema, running; *Clubs* Harlequins RFC, London Irish RFC; *Style*— Denis Tuohy, Esq; 3 Elleray Rd, Teddington, Middlesex TW11 0HG (☎ 081 977 3561); c/o Jon Roseman Associates Ltd, 103 Charing Cross Rd, London WC2H 0DT (☎ 071 439 8245)

TUPPER, Capt Anthony Charles; DSC (1945); s of Lt-Col Geoffrey William Henry Tupper, TD (d 1936), of Putney, and Alicia Mary, *née* Livingstone-Learmonth (d 1947); *b* 28 March 1915; *Educ* RNC Dartmouth and Greenwich; *m* 14 Nov 1942, Agnes Anne, da of Lt-Col Sir Edward Hoblyn Warren Bolitho, KBE, CB, DSO (d 1969); *Career* Naval Offr Med Fleet 1932-34, China 1934-35 and 1936-38, Atlantic and Home Fleets 1939-45, Home Fleet 1945-49, Admty MOD 1950-52, Far E and America, WI Station 1954-55, Admty Naval Staff Gunnery Div 1955-57, CSO to Flag Offr Malta 1958-59, Reserve Fleet Plymouth 1959-61, ret 1961; dairy farming (Jersey cattle) 1961-; cmmr of Irish Lights 1971 (chm 1988-89); *Recreations* shooting, fishing; *Clubs* Army and Navy, Kildare St and Univ (Dublin), Pratt's; *Style*— Capt Anthony Tupper, Esq, DSC, RN; Lyrath, Kilkenny, Co Kilkenny, Republic of Ireland (☎ 353 56 21382)

TUPPER, Sir Charles Hibbert; 5 Bt (UK 1888), of Armdale, Halifax, Nova Scotia; s of Sir James Macdonald Tupper, 4 Bt (d 1967), and Mary Agnes Jean, *née* Collins; Sir Charles, 1 Bt (d 1915), was PM of Nova Scotia 1864-67 (encompassing date of Union), PM of Canada 1896, ldr of oppn 1896-1900; *b* 4 July 1930; *m* 1959 (m dis 1975); 1 s; *Heir* s, Charles Hibbert Tupper b 10 July 1964; *Career* asst cmmr (ret); *Style*— Sir Charles Tupper, Bt; Suite 1101, 955 Marine Drive, W Vancouver, BC V7T 1A9, Canada

TUPPER, Simon Richard Farquhar; s of John Otway Richard Tupper, of Blandford Forum, Dorset, and Suzanne Denise Boswell, *née* Tonks; *b* 17 April 1952; *Educ* Canford; *m* 24 Feb 1979, Sally, da of Col Eustace Frank Alfred, OBE, RM (d 1976); 1 s (Tobias b 1984), 1 da (Joanna b 1980); *Career* photographer and journalist specialising in agric and livestock 1981-, official championship photographer for RASE 1987-88; accredited photographer: Rare Breeds Survival Tst, Dairy and Beef Breed Socs, Nat Pig Breeding Assoc; *Recreations* hunting, trout fishing, shooting, photography; *Style*— Simon R F Tupper, Esq; c/o Barclays Bank, High St, Burford, Oxon

TURBERFIELD, Alan Frank; CBE (1990); s of Frank Turberfield, of 59 The Glebe, Cumnor, Oxford, and Agnes, *née* Jackson (d 1970); *b* 24 Sept 1930; *Educ* Ashby de la Zouch Boys' GS, St John's Coll Oxford (Open scholar, MA); *m* 4 Aug 1956, Gillian Doris, da of Leonard William George Markwell (d 1973), of Bexhill; 1 s (Paul b 1961), 1 da (Alison b 1963); *Career* Staff Sgt RAEC 1952-54; asst master: King Edward VII Sch Sheffield 1954-58, Birkenhead Sch 1958-63; head of classics Portsmouth GS 1963-68, HM Inspectorate of Schs 1968-90, staff inspr of classics (Secdy Sch) 1977-90), dir sch and coll awards Royal Anniversary Tst 1990-; memb: 20 Club, DES, Assoc HMI, Jt Assoc of Classical Teachers, Virgil Soc, Br Sch of Athens; *Books* Voyage of Aeneas (with D A S John, 1968); *Recreations* theatre, theology, travel in China and Greece; *Style*— Alan Turberfield, Esq, CBE; 75 Hurst Rise Rd, Cumnor Hill, Oxford OX2 9HF (☎ 0865 864450, fax 0865 864025); Royal Anniversary Trust,

Horsley Towers, East Horsley, Surrey KT24 6DU (☎ 04865 5268, fax 04865 5783)

TURBOTT, Sir Ian Graham; CMG (1962), CVO (1966), JP (1971); s of Thomas Turbott (d 1956), of Auckland, NZ; *b* 9 March 1922; *Educ* Takapuna GS, Auckland Univ, Jesus Coll Cambridge, LSE; *m* 1952, Nancy, da of Lyman Lantz (d 1935), of Sacramento California; 3 da; *Career* Capt 2 NZEF (W Pacific and Italy) WWII, 1939-45 Star, Pacific Star, Italy Star, War Medal, Def Medal, NZ Medal; FRSA; entered Colonial Serv 1947, admin offr Gilbert and Ellice Islands 1947-56, seconded Colonial Office 1956-58; admin and HM The Queen's rep: Antigua 1958-64, Grenada 1964-67; govr Assoc State of Grenada 1967-68; chm: Chloride Batteries Australia Ltd 1974-84, Advsy Bd American Int Underwriters (Aust) Pty Ltd 1976-89, TNT Security Pty Ltd 1976-, The Triple M Broadcasting Group Pty Ltd 1976-, Penrith Lakes Developement Corporation Pty Ltd 1980-, Essington Ltd 1984-89, Spencer Stuart & Assoc Pty Ltd 1970-82, the Sydney Int Piano Competition 1977-86, Duke of Edinburgh's Award Scheme (NSW) 1984-, Trade Mission Japan 1982, Trade Mission Yugoslavia 1986; dep chm: Stereo F/M Ltd (NZ), Hoyts Media Ltd 1987-; dir: Carita Financial Group 1977-89, Standard Chartered Bank Ltd 1980-, Hoyts Entertainment Ltd 1990-; tstee: Australian Cancer Res Fndn for Med Res, World Wildlife Fund Australia; fndn chllr Univ of S Sydney 1989-, govr NSW Conservatory of Music 1976-90, hon memb Japanese Dist 1972; *award* Father of the Year 1986; kt 1968; *see Debrett's Handbook of Australia and New Zealand for further details*; *Recreations* farming, fishing, tennis, cricket; *Clubs* Australia (Sydney), Royal Sydney Yacht Sqdn; *Style—* Sir Ian Turbott, CMG, CVO, JP; 27 Amiens Road, Clontarf, NSW 2093, Australia (☎ 02 949 1566)

TURCAN, Henry Watson; s of Henry Hutchison Turcan, TD (d 1977), of Lindores House, Newburgh, Fife, and Lilias Cheyne (d 1975); *b* 22 Aug 1941; *Educ* Rugby, Trinity Coll Oxford (MA); *m* 18 April 1969, Jane, da of Arthur Woodman Blair, WS, of Dunbar, E Lothian; 1 s (Henry b 1974), 1 da (Chloë b 1972); *Career* called to the Bar Inner Temple 1965; legal assessor Gen Optical Cncl 1982-; rec Crown Ct 1985-; *Recreations* hunting, shooting, fishing, golf; *Clubs* Royal and Ancient Golf (St Andrews), Hon Co of Edinburgh Golfers Muirfield; *Style—* Henry Turcan, Esq; 4 Paper Buildings Temple, London EC4 (☎ 071 353 3420)

TURING, Sir (John) Dermot; 12 Bt (NS 1638), of Foveran, Aberdeenshire; s of John Ferrier Turing (d 1983), and his 2 w, Beryl Mary Ada, *née* Hann; suc kinsman Sir John Leslie Turing, 11 Bt, MC (d 1987); *b* 26 Feb 1961; *Educ* Sherborne, King's Coll Camb (MA), New Coll Oxford (DPhil); *m* 26 July 1986, (Dr) Nicola Jane, da of Malcolm Douglas Simmonds, of Paris; 2 s (John Malcolm Ferrier b 5 Sept 1988, James Robert Edward b 6 Jan 1991); *Heir* s, John Malcolm Ferrier Turing b 5 Sept 1988; *Style—* Sir Dermot Turing, Bt; 35 Tavistock Avenue, London E17 6HP

TURL, Philip Austin; s of Lt-Col Henry William Turl RAOC (d 1988), of North Finchley, London, and Clara, *née* Pinnell (d 1980); *b* 23 May 1932; *Educ* City of London Sch, Jesus Coll Cambridge (MA); *m* 5 April 1969, Wendy Rosemary, da of Rev Frank Jones, of Dereham Norfolk; 2 s (Graham b 1970, Andrew b 1977), 1 da (Catherine b 1973); *Career* Lt RAOC (res); called to the Bar Middle Temple 1959; Freeman: City of London 1952, Worshipful Co of Glass Sellers; memb Methodist Church, Christian Youth Worker; *Books* Praises in Sorrow and Praises in Faith, fifth book of Psalms (1962); *Clubs* Wig and Pen; *Style—* Philip Turl, Esq; 22 Wolstonbury, Woodside Park, London N12 7BA; 1 Harcourt Bldgs, Temple, London EC4Y 9DA (☎ 071 353 9371, fax 071 583 1656)

TURLE, Arish Richard; MC (1974); s of Rear Adm Charles Edward Turle, CBE, DSO (d 1966), and Janes Gillies, *née* Gray; *b* 4 April 1939; *Educ* Wellington; *m* 7 Sept 1969, Susan De Witt, da of Jack Leslie Keith Brown; 1 s (Edward b 1974), 1 da (Serena b 1973); *Career* RMA Sandhurst 1958-59, 2 Lt Rifle Bde 1960, Capt 22 SAS Regt 1964, Base Ecole Des Troupeś Aeroportes (BETAP) France 1970-71, Army Staff Coll Camberley 1971-72, Maj 22 SAS 1973, ret 1977; Control Risks Ltd: joined 1977, md 1979, resigned 1987; md (int) Kroll Assocs Ltd 1988; FBIM; *Recreations* golf; *Clubs* Boodle's, Special Forces; *Style—* Arish Turle, Esq, MC; Kroll Assocs Ltd, Leconfield House, Curzon St, London W1Y 7FB (☎ 071 408 0766, fax 071 493 7954)

TURLIK, Piotr (Peter) Zbigniew Vincent de Paulo; s of Zbigniew Tomasz Turlik (d 1943 in Majdanek Concentration Camp), of Warsaw, Poland, and Teresa Zofia, *née* Majewska; *b* 15 Jan 1943; *Educ* The John Fisher Sch Purley Surrey, Coll of Estate Mgmnt Kensington London; *m* 9 Sept 1967, Marie-Madeleine, da of Theodor Radosky (d 1947), of Beauvoir sur Noirt, France; *Career* asst dir Gtr London Cncl (Docklands Jt Ctee) 1978-80, asst sec seconded to Dept of Environment 1980-81, dir of strategic affairs London Docklands Devpt Corp 1989- (dir of industrial devpt 1981-84, dir of business devpt 1984-89); vice-pres Docklands Business Club 1989 (jt chm 1984-89), govr Hackney Coll 1984-, memb Working Party on Urban Regeneration RICS 1988-; ARICS 1971; *Recreations* travel, reading (biographies, history), small scale gardening; *Clubs* East India, Ognisko (Polish Hearth); *Style—* Peter Turlik, Esq; 12 Wincott St, Kennington, London SE11 4NT (☎ 071 5823045), 4 Chemin du College, Clavette-la Jarrie, France 17220; London Docklands Development Corporation, Thames Quay, 191 Marsh Wall, London E14 9TJ (☎ 071 512 3000, fax 071 512 0777, telex 894041 LDDC G)

TURMEAU, Dr William Arthur; CBE; s of Frank Richard Turmeau (d 1972), of Stromness, Orkney, and Catherine Lyon, *née* Linklater; *b* 19 Sept 1929; *Educ* Stromness Acad, Univ of Edinburgh (BSc), Moray House Coll of Educn, Heriot-Watt Univ (PhD); *m* 4 April 1957, Margaret Moar, da of Arthur Burnett; 1 da (Rachel Margaret b 1967); *Career* Nat Serv RCS 1947-49; res engr Northern Electric Co Ltd Montreal 1952-54, mechanical engr USAF Goose Bay Labrador 1954-56, contracts mangr Godfrey Engineering Co Ltd Montreal 1956-61, lectr Bristo Tech Inst Edinburgh 1962-64; Napier Coll Edinburgh: lectr and sr lectr 1964-68, head of Dept of Mechanical Engrg 1968-75, asst princ and dean of Faculty of Technol 1975-82, princ 1982-; memb Ctee: Scottish Econ Cncl, Br Cncl Inter-Univ Poly Cncl, Br Cncl Ctee for Cooperation in Higher Educn, Euro Engrg Educn, Ctee of Dirs of Polys, IMechE standing Ctee for Degree Accreditation, Scot Examination Bd, Scot Action on Smoking and Health, Manpower Policy Ctee Scot Cncl Devpt and Indust; FIMechE, CEng, FRSE; *Recreations* study of Leonardo da Vinci, modern jazz; *Clubs* Caledonian; *Style—* Dr William Turmeau, CBE, FRSE; 71 Morningside Park, Edinburgh EH10 5EZ (☎ 031 447 4639); Napier Polytechnic of Ediburgh, 219 Colinton Rd, Edinburgh EH14 1DJ (☎ 031 444 2266)

TURNBERG, Prof Leslie Arnold; s of Hyman Turnberg (d 1985), and Dora, *née* Bloomfield; *b* 22 March 1934; *Educ* Stand GS, Univ of Manchester (MB ChB, MD); *m* 30 Jan 1968, Edna, da of Berthold Barme (d 1981); 1 s (Daniel b 1970), 1 da (Helen b 1971); *Career* lectr Royal Free Hosp 1966-67, res fell Univ of Texas Dallas 1967-68, prof of med Univ of Manchester 1973- (sr lectr 1968-73, dean of Faculty of Med 1986-89); memb: GMC, Cncl RCP, Med Advsy Ctee of Vice Chllrs and Princs Ctee, MRC; memb: Br Soc of Gastroenterology, Assoc of Physicians GB; FRCP 1973; *Books* Intestinal Transport (1981), Electrolyte and Water Transport Acros Gastro-Intestinal Epithelia (1982), Clinical Gastroenterology (1989); *Recreations* reading, painting, walking; *Style—* Prof Leslie Turnberg; Department of Medicine, University of Manchester School of Medicine, Hope Hospital, Salford M6 8HD (☎ 061 7897373, fax 061 7877432)

TURNBULL, Andrew; CB (1990); s of Anthony Turnbull (d 1984), and Mary, *née* Williams; *b* 21 Jan 1945; *Educ* Enfield GS, Christ's Coll Cambridge (BA); *m* 8 Sept 1967, Diane Elizabeth, da of Roland Clarke; 2 s (Adam b 1974, Benet b 1977); *Career* economist Govt of Zambia 1968-70; HM Treas: asst princ 1970-72, princ 1972-76, seconded to IMF Washington 1976-78, asst sec 1978-83, under sec 1985-88; princ private sec to the PM (Mrs Thatcher 1988-90, Mr John Major 1990-) (private sec econ affrs 1983-85); *Recreations* watching football, playing cricket, fell walking, running, opera; *Style—* Andrew Turnbull, Esq, CB; 10 Downing St, London SW1 72AA

TURNBULL, (Charles Colin) Andrew; s of Charles Elliot Turnbull, of Ilkley, Yorkshire, and Vera Mavis, *née* Clarke; *b* 10 May 1950; *Educ* Leeds GS, Coll of Estate Management Univ of Reading, Univ of Liverpool (BA Econ), Univ of Birmingham (MSc); *m* 31 July 1976, Una Jane, da of Arnold Raymond Humphrey; 3 da (Hannah Elizabeth 6 24 Sept 1981, Holly Katherine 6 13 March 1984, Lydia Helen 6 13 June 1988); *Career* British Airways 1973-78: joined 1973, cargo marketing offr 1974, passenger traffic forecasts offr 1975, sr forecasts offr 1977; project work in: Ecuador, Venezuela, USA, Ghana, Ivory Coast, Sudan, SA, Saudi Arabia, Abu Dhabi, Dubai; Graham Poulter Partnership 1979-: joined as res mangr 1979, head of res 1981, dir of res and planning 1983-, ptnr 1985-; awarded Communications, Advertising and Marketing Dip 1979, Kelliher Cup (Communications Advertising and Marketing Fndn) for paper on int advtg 1979; memb: Market Res Soc 1980-, Account Planning Group 1989-; *Recreations* sailing, tennis, music, three young daughters; *Style—* Andrew Turnbull, Esq; Low Rigg, 15 Clifton Road, Ben Rhydding, Ilkley, West Yorkshire LS29 8TU (☎ 0943 609367); The Graham Poulter Partnership, Poulter House, 2 Burley Rd, Leeds LS3 1NJ (☎ 0532 469611, fax 0532 448796, car 0860 747126)

TURNBULL, (George) Anthony Twentyman; s of Stuart John Twentyman Turnbull (d 1991), and Hilda Joyce, *née* Taylor (d 1983); *b* 26 June 1938; *Educ* Charterhouse, ChCh Oxford; *m* 14 June 1962, Petronel Jonette Rene Turnbull, JP, da of Maj James Williams Thursby Dunn (d 1969), of St Leonards Lodge, Clewer, Windsor, Berks; 2 s (Robert Edward Twentyman b 1965, Timothy William John b 1970), 1 da (Victoria Jonette b 1963); *Career* called to the Bar 1962; Debenham Tewson & Chinnocks: joined 1962, ptnr 1965, chief exec 1987; Freeman Worshipful Co of Fruiterers; FRICS; *Recreations* theatre, conversation, playing games; *Clubs* Savile, Brook St, London W1; *Style—* Anthony Turnbull, Esq; Park Cottage, Downside Rd, Downside, Cobham, Surrey KT11 3LZ; 67A Aylesford St, London SW1; 44 Brook St, London W1A 4AG (☎ 071 408 1161)

TURNBULL, Christopher James; s of Rev Captin James Turnbull, of Glastonbury, and Rosemary Erskine Turnbull; *b* 15 April 1950; *Educ* Haileybury, Queens Coll Cambridge (MA, MB BChir), Westminster Med Sch; *m* 5 Jan 1974, Susan Mary, da of Roger Avery Lovelock, Horsell, Woking; 2 s (James Edward b 1979, Luke Christopher b 1985), 1 da (Claire Elizabeth b 1982); *Career* GP vocational trainee Sandhurst Berks 1976-79, registrar in med Wellington Hosp NZ 1979-81, sr registrar in geriatric med Liverpool rotations 1981-83, conslt physician geriatric med Wirral 1983-, clinical dir for the elderly 1988-89; author of articles on: glaucoma in the elderly, postural hypotension in the elderly, Parkinsons Disease in the elderly, diabetism in the elderly; chm: Wirral Assoc for Care of the Elderly 1983-, Wirral Planning GP for the Elderly 1988-90; memb: Br Geriatrics Soc, Br Assoc for Serv to the Elderly; MRCP, MRCGP; *Recreations* dinghy sailing, windsurfing, renaissance music; *Style—* Christopher Turnbull, Esq; Arrowe Park Hospital, Arrowe Park Road, Upton, Wirral, Merseyside L49 5PE (☎ 051 0785111 ext 2134)

TURNBULL, Sir George Henry; s of late Bartholomew Turnbull, of 34 Rochester Rd, Earlson, Coventry, and late Pauline Anne, *née* Konrath; *b* 17 Oct 1926; *Educ* King Henry VIII Sch Coventry, Univ of Birmingham (BSc); *m* 14 March 1950, Marion, da of Henry George Wing (d 1969); 1 s (Robert), 2 da (Deborah, Penny); *Career* Standard Motors Ltd: PA to Tech Dir 1950-51, exec i/c Experimental Dept 1954-55, divnl mangr (cars) 1956-59, gen mangr 1959-62; work mangr Petters Ltd 1955-56, dir and gen mangr Standard-Triumph International 1962-; BL Motor Corpn: dir 1967, dep md 1968-73, md 1973; md BL Austin Morris 1968-73, chm BL Truck and Bus Div 1972-73, vice pres and dir Hyundai Motors Seoul S Korea 1974-77, dep md Iran National Motor Co Tehran 1978-79 (conslt advsr to Chm 1977-78), chm Talbot UK 1979-84; Inchape plc: gp md 1984-86, gp chief exec 1985-86, chm and chief exec 1986-; Freeman City of Coventry 1948; memb SMMT, FIMechE, FIProdE; kt 1990; *Books* Report on Future of the Korean Car Industry (1976); *Recreations* skiing, tennis, golf, fishing; *Clubs* Moreton Morrell Tennis Court, Conventry RFC, Finham Park Golf, Royal and Ancient Golf; *Style—* Sir George Turnbull; Morrell House, Moreton Morrell, Warwick CV35 9AL (☎ 0926 651 278); Inchcape plc, St James's House, 23 King St, London SW1Y 6QY (☎ 071 321 0110, fax 071 321 0604, car 0860 365 425, telex 885395)

TURNBULL, Jeffrey Alan; CBE (1991); s of Alan Edward Turnbull (d 1986), of Monkseaton and Carlisle, and Alice May, *née* Slee (d 1940); *b* 14 Aug 1934; *Educ* Newcastle upon Tyne Royal GS, Liverpool Coll of Technology (DipTE); *m* 7 Aug 1957, Beryl, da of Walter Griffith (d 1974), of Crewe; 2 s (Martin John b 1964, Andrew Malcolm b 1972), 1 da (Alison Denise b 1962); *Career* Nat Serv Corpl RE 1956-58; jr engr Cheshire CC 1951-55, engr Herefordshire CC 1955-59, res engr Berks CC 1959-66; Mott Hay & Anderson 1966-89: dep chief designer (roads) 1966-68, chief designer (roads) 1968-78, assoc 1973-78, dir (int) 1975-89, dir 1978-89, dir (hldgs) 1983-89, chief exec (hldgs) 1987-89; chm and dir Mott MacDonald Gp Ltd 1989-; memb Editorial Bd New Civil Engrg 1979-82; CEng 1959, FIHT 1966, FICE 1973, MInstD; *Books* Civil Engineers Reference Book (contrib 4 edn, 1988), numerous papers to PIARC and IRF confs; *Recreations* cruising, visiting France, walking; *Clubs* RAC, IOD; *Style—* Jeffrey Turnbull, Esq, CBE; 63 Higher Drive, Banstead, Surrey SM7 1PW (☎ 081 393 1054); Mott MacDonald Gp Ltd, St Anne House, 20/26 Wellesley Rd, Croydon, Surrey CR9 2UL (☎ 081 686 5041, fax 081 681 5706/081 688 1814, telex 917241 MOTTAY G)

TURNBULL, Lt-Col John Hugh Stephenson; MC (1943,45); s of Lt-Col Sir Hugh Turnbull, KCVO, KBE, of Reidhaven, Grantown-on -Spey, Morayshire, and Jean, *née* Grant; *b* 10 Jan 1916; *Educ* Haileybury; *m* 7 Nov 1964, Sophie Penelope, da of Frederick Bryan Landale, of Coopers Ground, E Knoyle, Wilt; 1 da (Penelope); *Career* London Scottish 1936, 1 Commando 1941-46 (cmmd Far E 1945-46), cmmnd Gordon Highlanders 1945, Staff Coll 1946, 2 Para Bn 1948-51, various staff & regtl appts until ret 1960; memb Royal Co of Archers; *Style—* Lt-Col John Turnbull, MC; Rossdhal, Comrie, Perthshire (☎ 0764 70301); 27 Nelson St, Edinburgh; 24 Onslow Sq, London SW7

TURNBULL, Hon Mrs (Mary Elizabeth); *née* Parnell; eldest da of 6 Baron Congleton (d 1932); *b* 21 Feb 1919; *Educ* private and boarding sch; *m* 20 July 1956, Percy Purvis Turnbull (d 1976) pianist/composer; *Career* Govt salary, modern school teacher 1947-51; ARCM; *Recreations* music; *Clubs* English Speaking Union, Special Forces, New Cavendish, British Music Soc, Turnbull Memorial Trust; *Style—* The Hon Mrs Turnbull; West Wing, Dean House, West Dean, Salisbury, Wilts SP5 1JQ

TURNBULL, Sir Richard Gordon; GCMG (1962, KCMG 1958, CMG 1953); s of Richard Francis Turnbull (d 1963); *b* 1909; *Educ* Univ Coll Sch, UCL, Magdalene Coll Cambridge; *m* 1939, Beatrice, da of John Wilson (d 1986); 2 s, 1 da; *Career* entered Colonial Admin Serv 1931, dist offr Kenya 1931, provincial cmmr 1948, provincial cmmr Northern Frontier Province 1948-53, min for Internal Security and Def 1954, chief sec and govr's dep Kenya 1955-58, govr and c-in-c Tanganyika Territory 1958-61 (govr gen and c-in-c 1961-62), chm Central Land Bd Kenya 1963-64, high cmmr for Aden and Protectorates of South Arabia 1965-67; fell UCL, hon fell Magdalene Coll Cambridge; KStJ 1958; *Style—* Sir Richard Turnbull, GCMG; Friars Neuk, Jedburgh, Roxburghshire TD8 6BN

TURNBULL, Steven Michael; s of Philip Peveril Turnbull (d 1987), of Rock, Cornwall, and Dorothy June Turnbull; *b* 24 Oct 1952; *Educ* Monkton Combe Sch, Univ Coll Oxford (BA); *m* 22 Sept 1985, Mary Ann, da of David M Colyer, of Cheltenham, Glos; 1 s (Matthew b 11 July 1987), 1 da (Clare b 21 Aug 1988); *Career* Linklaters & Paines: joined 1975, slr 1978, joined Corporate Dept, ptnr 1985; memb Law Soc, memb City of London slrs Co; *Recreations* golf, tennis, family; *Clubs* Oxford and Cambridge Golfing Soc, Royal Wimbledon Golf; *Style—* Steven Turnbull, Esq; Linklaters & Paines, Barrington House, 59-67 Gresham St, London EC2V 7JA (☎ 071 606 7080)

TURNBULL, William; *b* 11 Jan 1922; *Educ* Slade Sch of Art; *Career* artist; solo exhibitions: Hanover Gallery 1950, 1952, ICA 1957, Molton Gallery 1960, 1961, Marlborough-Gerson Gallery NY 1963, Art Inst Detroit 1963, Bennington Coll Vermont 1965, Galeric Muller Stuttgart 1965, 1974, Pavilion Gallery Balboa Calif 1966, Waddington Galleries 1967, 1969, 1970, 1976, 1981, 1982, 1985, 1987, IX Bienal Sao Paolo Brazil touring 1967-68, Hayward Gallery 1968, Tate Gallery 1973, Scottish Arts Cncl 1974, Waddington and Tooth Galleries 1978, The Scottish Gallery Edinburgh 1981, Galerie Kutter Luxembourg 1983, Nat Museum Art Gallery Singapore 1984, Terry Dintenfass Inc NY 1988, John Berggruen Gallery San Francisco 1988-89, Arnold Herstand Gallery NY 1989, Sculpture on the Close (Jesus Coll Cambridge) 1990; selected group exhibitions: Venice Biennale (Br Pavilion, Venice) 1952, Pittsburgh Int (Carnegie Inst Pittsburg Pa) 1958, 1961, 1962, Situation (RBA Galleries) 1960, Second Int Exhibition of Sculpture (Musee Rodin Paris) 1961, Hirshhorn Collection (Guggenheim Museum NY) 1962, Seventh Int Art Exhibition Tokyo 1963, Guggenheim Int NY 1964, Br Sculpture in the Sixties (Tate Gallery) 1965, First Int Exhibition of Modern Sculpture (Hakone Open Air Museum Japan) 1969, McAlpine Collection (Tate Gallery) 1971, Art Inglese Oggie (Palazzo Reale Milan), Tate 79 (Tate Gallery) 1979, Br Sculpture in the twentieth century: part 2 symbol and imagination 1951-80 (Whitechapel Art Gallery 1982, Forty Years of Modern Art 1945-85 (Tate Gallery) 1986, Br Art in the Twentieth Century: The Modern Movement (Royal Acad and touring) 1987, Britannica: Trente Ans de Sculpture 1960-88 (Musee de Beaux Arts, Le Havre) 1988, Modern Br Sculpture from the Collection (Tate Liverpool) 1988, Scottish Art Since 1900 (Scottish Nat Gallery of Modern Art Edinburgh and Barbican Art Gallery) 1989, The Independant Group: Postwar Britain and the Aesthetics of Plenty (ICA) 1990-91; works in the collections of: Albright - Knox Art Gallery Buffalo, Arts Cncl of GB, Art Gallery of Ontario, Br Cncl, Contemporary Arts Soc, Dundee Museum and Art Gallery, Franklin P Murphy Sculpture Garden UCLA, Glasgow Museum and Art Gallery, Hirshorn Museum and Sculpture (Smithsonian Inst) Washington DC, Univ of Hull, McCrory Corp NY, Museum of Contemporary Art Tehran, Nat Gallery of Art Washington DC, Scottish Nat Gallery of Modern Art Edinburgh, Stadtisches Museum Leverkusen Germany, Sydney Opera House, Tate Gallery, V&A, Westfalisches Landesmuseum Munster; *Style—* William Turnbull, Esq; c/o Waddington Galleries Ltd, 11 Cork Street, London W1X 1PD (☎ 071 437 8611, fax 071 734 4146)

TURNER, Adrian Geoffrey Leslie; LVO (1986); er s of Leslie Bertram Turner, MBE (d 1979), and Lillian Augusta, *née* Broad; *b* 28 April 1927; *Educ* Highgate, Clayesmore, Univ of London; *Career* Dip Serv 1948-87: Lahore, Pakistan 1955-57 (also broadcaster western music Radio Pakistan and external examiner Univ of the Punjab), Colombo Sri Lanka 1960-63 (also broadcaster Radio Ceylon), Asuncion, Paraguay 1969-71, Holy See 1971-73; memb Br delegation: Int Lab Conf Geneva 1959, UN Gen Assembly New York 1965, UN Conf on the Law of Treaties Vienna 1969, head Hons Section FCO 1979-87; memb: Cncl Heraldry Soc 1947-86 (hon fell 1954), Hon Cncl of Mgmnt The Royal Philharmonic Soc 1981-86 (fell 1951), Cncl St John Historical Soc 1985-90, Conslt False Orders Ctee Orders of St John of Jerusalem 1987; Freeman City of London 1978, Liveryman Worshipful Co of Scriveners; Sovereign Mil Order of Malta 1972, Knight of Obedience 1981, OStJ 1988; FRSA 1987; *Recreations* music, heraldry, genealogy, reading, the study of the Orders of St John and of the legality of Roman Catholic territorial titles; *Clubs* Royal Over-Seas League; *Style—* Adrian Turner, Esq, LVO; Shelsley, 135 Cranley Gdns, Muswell Hill, London N10 3AG

TURNER, Amédée Edward; QC (1976), MEP (EDG) Suffolk and SE Cambs 1984-; s of Frederick William Turner (d 1945), and Ruth Hempson (d 1970); mother's side Huguenot Swiss; *b* 26 March 1929; *Educ* Ch Ch Oxford; *m* 1960, Deborah Dudley, da of Dr Philip Owen: 1s, 1 da; *Career* called to the Bar Inner Temple 1954; practised patent bar 1954-57, assoc Kenyon & Kenyon patent attorneys NY 1957-60, in practice in London 1960-; contested (C) Norwich N gen elections 1964, 1966 and 1970, Euro Parl; vice chm Legal Ctee 1979-84; memb: Econ and Monetary Ctee 1979-84, Tport Ctee 1981-84, Energy Ctee 1983-89, ACP Jt Ctee, 1989 Chief Whip Euro Democratic Gp, MEP (C) Suffolk and Harwich 1979-84; *Books* The Law of Trade Secrets (1962, supplement 1968), The Law of the New European Patent (1979), many Cons Pty study papers on defence, oil and Middle East; *Recreations* garden designs, painting; *Clubs* Carlton, Coningsby, United and Cecil; *Style—* Amédée Turner, Esq, QC, MEP; 3 Montrose Place, London SW1X 7DU; The Barn, Westleton, Saxmundham, Suffolk (☎ 072 873 235)

TURNER, Hon Mrs (Anne Mary Cameron); *née* Corbett; da of 3 Baron Rowallan, and Eleanor Mary, only da of late Capt George Frederic Boyle; *b* 3 Sept 1953; *m* 1972, Rodney John Turner; 2 s, 2 da; *Recreations* hunting; *Style—* The Hon Mrs Turner; Leigh Court, Angersleigh, Somerset (☎ 82342 700)

TURNER, Ven Antony Hubert Michael; s of Frederick George Turner (d 1960), and Winifred Frances Turner (d 1956); *b* 17 June 1930; *Educ* Royal Liberty Sch Romford, Univ of London (Dip Theol); *m* 5 July 1956, Margaret Kathleen, da of Reginald McKenzie Phillips, of 133 Balgores Lane, Gidea Park, Essex; 1 s (Michael b 1961), 2 da (Ruth b 1958, Susan b 1960); *Career* ordained deacon 1956, curate St Ann's Nottingham 1956-59, curate in charge St Cuthbert's Cheadle Diocese of Chester 1959-62, vicar Christ Church Macclesfield 1962-68, home sec Bible Churchmen's Missionary Soc 1968-74, vicar St Jude's Southsea 1974-86, rural dean Portsmouth 1979-84, archdeacon of the IOW 1986-; church cmmr 1983-; vice chm C of E Pensions Bd; ACA 1952, FCA 1962; *Recreations* photography, caravanning; *Style—* Ven the Archdeacon of the IOW; The Archdeaconry, 3 Beech Grove, Ryde, IOW PO33 3AN

TURNER, Prof Barry Arthur; s of Arthur Turner (d 1981), of Birmingham, and Doris, May, *née* Bromfield; *b* 27 June 1937; *Educ* Kings Norton GS, Univ of Leeds, Univ of Birmingham (BSocSc), Univ of Exeter (PhD); *m* 1 April 1961, Janet Howd; 2 da (Victoria b 1963, Louise b 1966); *Career* res fell Indust Sociology Unit Imperial Coll Univ of London 1966-69, sr res fell CUSSR Longhborough Univ of Technol 1969-70, dean of Faculty of Social Studies Univ of Exeter 1981-84 (lectr for the Dept of Sociology 1970-78, reader in the sociology of organization 1978-90, head of dept 1980-89), prof of Euro business Middx Business Sch; author of numerous academic articles; memb Br Sociological Assoc, Fell Br Middle Eastern Studies Soc; *Books* Exploring the Industrial Subculture (1971), Industrialism (1972), Man-Made Disasters (1978), The Way of the Thesis (1989), Organizational Symbolism (1990); *Recreations* tai chi chuan, painting; *Style—* Prof Barry Turner; Middlesex Business School, Middlesex Polytechnic, The Burroughs, London NW4 4BT (☎ 081 368 1299, fax 081 202 1539)

TURNER, (Charles) Brian Godsell; s of Ernest Joseph Turner (d 1964), of Holmwood, Clarendon Rd, Harpenden, and Bertha, *née* Harris (d 1968); *b* 26 Oct 1913; *Educ* Tottenham GS; *m* 1941, Helen, da of Cecil Robert Slowe (d 1968), of Tabley, Wadhurst, Sussex; 2 s, 1 da; *Career* HAC (TA) 1930, cmmnd KOYLI 1939, Capt 1940, transferred to RA 1941; serv WWII: UK, France, Belgium, Holland, Germany; CA London 1950-74, ret; chm: Bournemouth & Dist Water Co 1977, Mid Kent Water Co 1980-87, Eastbourne Waterworks Co 1987; hon tres Nat Assoc of Parish Cncls 1958-73; FRSA; FCA; *Recreations* gardening, philately, travel; *Style—* Brian Turner, Esq; Dellside, Tongswood Drive, Hawkhurst, Kent TN18 5DS (☎ 058 075 3145)

TURNER, Brian James; s of Lawrence Turner, of Morley, Leeds, and late Lily, *née* Riley; *b* 7 May 1946; *Educ* Morley GS, Leeds Coll of Food Technol, Borough Poly, Ealing Hotel Sch; *m* Denise, da of Alan Parker, of 5 Manor Rd, Wood Lane, Rothwell, Leeds, Yorks; 2 s (Simeon James b 18 Nov 1974, Benjamin Jon b 5 July 1977); *Career* chef; Simpsons Strand London 1964-66, Savoy Hotel London 1966-69, Beau-Rivage Palace Lausanne-Ouchy Switzerland 1969-70, Claridges Hotel London 1970-71, Capital Hotel London 1971-86, Turners of Walton Street London 1986-; FHCIMA 1988- (MHCIMA 1980-88); *Style—* Brian Turner, Esq; Venturite Ltd, T/A Turner's, 87-89 Walton Street, London SW3 2HP (☎ 071 584 6711)

TURNER, Prof Cedric Edward; CBE (1987); s of Charles Turner (d 1949), and Mabel Evelyn, *née* Berry (d 1962); *b* 5 Aug 1926; *Educ* Brockenhurst County GS, Univ of Southampton (BSc), Univ of London (PhD, DSc); *m* 29 Aug 1953, Margaret (Peggy) Dorothy, da of Edward Percy Davies (d 1976), of Airlie, 21 Holford Rd, Merrow, Guildford, Surrey; 1 s (Jeffrey b 1961), 2 da (Hazel b 1956, Gillian b 1959); *Career* prof of materials in mechanical engineering Imperial Coll 1975- (lectr 1951-66, reader 1966-75, asst dir 1966-73, seconded to Nat Physical Laboratory 1976-78, seconded to Br Aerospace 1978-79); memb of Industl Advsy Ctee on Fracture Avoidance; silver medal The Plastics Inst 1963, James Clayton Prize Inst of Mech Engrs 1981, hon prof Shenyang Inst of Aeronautical Engineering People's Republic of China 1986, Leverhulme sr res fell 1990-92; FIMechE 1976, FEng 1989; *Books* Introduction to Plate & Shell Theory (1967), Post-Yield Fracture Mechanics (jtly, 2 edn, 1985); *Recreations* walking, gardening, fracture mechanics; *Style—* Prof Cedric Turner, CBE; Mechanical Engineering Dept, Imperial Coll, London SW7 2BX (☎ 071 589 5111 ext 6181, fax 071 584 7596, telex 09294484)

TURNER, Christopher; s of Harry Turner, and Margaret Rowen Muriel, *née* Archer; *b* 28 July 1940; *m* 23 May 1969, Caroline Sue Hodgeson, da of late George Potts, of Pontefract; 2 da (Rachel Louise b 21 June 1975, Lucy Georgina b 30 June 1979); *Career* ptnr Robson Rhodes CA's, Leeds & Bradford 1972- (chm 1984-85); govr Leeds Girls' HS, circuit steward Methodist Church Horsforth and Bramley; FCA; *Recreations* golf; *Clubs* Headingly Golf, Bradford; *Style—* Christopher Turner, Esq; Windy Lea, 36 Lee Lane East, Horsforth, Leeds LS18 5RE (☎ 0532 582520), Robson Rhodes, St George House, 40 Great George St, Leeds (☎ 0532 459631 fax 0532 452823)

TURNER, Christopher Gilbert; s of Theodore Francis Turner, QC (d 1986), and Hon Elizabeth Alice, *née* Schuster (d 1983), da of 1 and last Baron Schuster, GCB (d 1956), permanent sec of the Lord Chancellor and Clerk of the Crown in Chancery 1915-44; *b* 23 Dec 1929; *Educ* Winchester, New Coll Oxford; *m* 3 Aug 1961, Lucia, da of Prof Stephen Ranulph Kingdon Glanville (d 1956, provost of King's Coll Cambridge and Herbert Thompson Prof of Egyptology); 1 s (Matthew b 1964), 2 da (Rosalie b 1962, d 1989, Catherine b 1967); *Career* head of classics: Radley until 1961, Charterhouse 1961-68; headmaster: Dean Close Sch 1968-79, Stowe 1979-89; Dio Lay Reader; chm of Govrs Beachborough Sch, Aldro Sch, Elstree Sch; *Books* History in Comparative Study in Greek and Latin Literature (Chapter 10, 1969); *Recreations* violin playing, music generally, walking, manual labour, repairing books, reading; *Style—* Christopher Turner, Esq; Rosemullion, High St, Great Rollright, Chipping Norton, Oxon OX7 5RQ

TURNER, Colin Francis; s of Francis Sidney Turner (d 1987), of Penge, and Charlotte Clara, *née* Hathaway (d 1968); *b* 11 April 1930; *Educ* Beckenham GS, Kings Coll London (LLB); *m* 14 April 1951, Josephine Alma, da of Charles Henry Jones (d 1924); 2 s (Christopher b 1956, Paul b 1957), 1 da (Elizabeth b 1952); *Career* entered Princ Probate Registry 1949, dist probate registrar York 1965-68, sr dist judge (formerly sr registrar) Family Div of High Ct 1988-91 (registrar 1971-88); ret; memb: Supreme Ct Procedure Ctee, Matrimonial Causes Rule Ctee; *Books* Rayden on Divorce (jt ed of edns 9, 11, 12, 13), Supreme Court Practice (ed), Precedents in Matrimonial Causes and Ancillary Matters; *Recreations* birding, fishing; *Style—* C F Turner, Esq; Lakers, Church Rd, Redhill, Surrey RH1 6QA (☎ 0737 761807); Principal Registry Family Division Somerset House, Strand, London WC2 (☎ 071 936 6934)

TURNER, Colin William Carstairs; CBE (1984), DFC (1944); s of Colin Carstairs William Turner (d 1963), of Enfield, Middx, and Phebe Marianne Miller (d 1945); *b* 14 Jan 1922; *Educ* Highgate Sch; *m* 7 May 1949, Evelyn Mary, da of Claude Horatio Buckard (d 1966), of Enfield; 3 s (Anthony b 18 Feb 1954, Nigel b 7 Jan 1956, Christopher b 1 Aug 1964), 1 da (Susan b 23 Aug 1951); *Career* air observer RAFVR, volunteered 1940, ITW Torquay 1941, 47 Air Sch Queenstown SA 1941, 31 Air Sch E London SA 1941, 70 OTU Nakuru Kenya 1942, 223 Sqdn Baltimores Desert Air Force Egypt 1942 (cmmnd 1943), Tunisia 1943, Malta 1943, Sicily 1943, Italy 1943, returned UK 1944, 527 Sqdn Digby Lincs (crashed 1944), RAF Hosp Northallerton and Rehabilitation Centre Loughborough 1944-45, invalided-out as Flying Offr 1946; Colin Turner Group of Cos (family co): joined 1940, dir 1945, md 1964-84, chm 1985-87, life pres 1988-; Overseas Press and Media Assoc: fndr pres 1965-67, hon treas 1974-82, life pres 1983-; ed Overseas Media Guide 1968-74; Cwlth Press Union: assoc memb 1963-, chm PR Ctee 1970-87, memb Fin Ctee 1972-87, Exec Ctee 1988-; memb Nat Exec Cons Pty 1946-53, 1968-73 and 1976-82; chm Cons Cwlth and Overseas Cncl 1976-82 (vice-pres 1984-), Parly candidate (C) Enfield East 1950 and 1951, MP (C) West Woolwich 1959-64; pres Enfield Branch RAFA 1947-58 and 1966- (memb 1945-), chm 223 Sqdn Assoc 1947-; pres Old Cholmeleian Assoc 1985-86 (Highgate Sch Old Boys), ed The Cholmeleian 1982-; *Recreations* DIY, gardening, sailing, fishing; *Clubs* North Enfield Conservative; *Style—* Colin Turner, Esq, CBE, DFC; 55 Rowantree Rd, Enfield, Middx EN2 8PN (☎ 081 363 2403)

TURNER, David George Patrick; s of George Patrick Turner (d 1988), of Londonderry, and Elsie Bamford, *née* McClure; *b* 11 July 1954; *Educ* Foyle Coll Londonderry, King's Coll London (LLB, AKC), Coll of Law London; *m* 4 March 1978, Jean Patricia, da of Gerald William Hewett, of Carleton, Rode, Norfolk; 2 s (Robert b 7 Oct 1980, Richard b 30 Oct 1982); *Career* called to the Bar Grays Inn 1976, S Eastern Circuit; dir and co sec Whimbrel Pubns Ltd; churchwarden and lay reader All Souls' Langham Place, memb Marylebone Deanery Synod; tstee: Langham Tst, St

Paul's Tst (Portman Square); memb: Family Law Bar Assoc, Criminal Bar Assoc, Ecclesiastical Soc Law; *Recreations* reading, swimming, family; *Style—* David Turner, Esq; 14 Chatterton Road, London N4 2DZ (☎ 071 226 7357); 14 Grays Inn Square, Grays Inn, London WC1R 5JP (☎ 071 242 0858, fax 071 242 5434)

TURNER, David John; s of Frederick Turner, of 66 Osmaston Rd, Prenton, Birkenhead, Merseyside, and Sheila Margaret, *née* Collinson; *b* 7 Feb 1945; *Educ* Birkenhead Sch; 1 s (Jonathon Frederick b 23 March 1978), 2 da (Sarah Frances b 28 Feb 1970, Catherine Margaret b 19 Feb 1974); *Career* CA: Cook & Co Liverpool 1963-68, Touche Ross & Co London 1968-69; mgmnt auditor Mobil Oil Corpn 1969-71, chief accountant Mobil Servs Ltd 1971-73, special projects co-ordinator Mobil Europe Inc 1973-74, fin dir Booker plc (formerly Booker McConnell Ltd) 1975-; FCA; *Recreations* squash, tennis, skiing; *Clubs* Surbiton Lawn Tennis and Squash; *Style—* David Turner, Esq; Portland House, Stag Place, London SW1 5AY (☎ 071 828 9850, fax 071 630 8029, telex 888169)

TURNER, Dr David John; s of Edward John Versey Turner, and Maud Beatrice, *née* Fisher; *b* 13 Feb 1935; *Educ* Felixstowe Country GS, Univ of Edinburgh (MB ChB); *m* 25 July 1959, Jill, da of John Walter Lewis; 2 s (John b 1962, Scott b 1964); *Career* sr housr offr and registrar in anaesthetics 1963-66: Ipswich Hosp, E Suffolk Hosp; registrar and sr registrar in anaesthetics Royal Infirmary Edinburgh 1966-69, conslt anaesthetist to Gt Yarmouth and Waveney Dist at James Paget Hosp 1969-; memb: BMA, E Anglia Assoc of Anaesthetics, Obstetric Anaesthetists assoc, Br Intractable Pain Soc; FFARCS; *Recreations* sailing, birdwatching, squash; *Clubs* Royal Norfolk and Suffolk Yacht, Waveney and Oulton Broad Yacht, Gunton Park Squash; *Style—* Dr David Turner; Gosford House, 3 Noel Rd, Oulton Broad, Lowestoft, Suffolk NR32 3JS (☎ 0502 564263); Dept of Anaesthesia, James Paget Hospital, Lowestoft Rd, Gorleston, Gt Yarmouth, Norfolk (☎ 0493 600611)

TURNER, David Roy; s of Robert Edward Turner, of 17 Derriads Lane, Chippenham, Wiltshire, and Evelyn Peggy, *née* Summers; *b* 5 Feb 1949; *Educ* Chippenham Secondary Modern Sch; *m* 18 Feb 1977, Henriette, da of Hendrik Ockert Burger (d 1960); 1 da Nicola Marianna (b 15 March 1984); *Career* cricketer; Hampshire CCC: debut 1966, 416 First Class matches, 39 Nat West competition matches, 256 Refuge Assurance league matches, 79 Benson & Hedges Cup matches, Benefit Year 1981; Western Province SA 1977-78 (5 matches); winner: Championship medal 1973, Sunday League Winners medal 1975, 1978 and 1986, Currie Cup Winners medal (SA) 1978, Benson & Hedges Cup Winners medal 1988, 4 Benson & Hedges Gold awards for Man of the Match, 1 Gillette Cup Man of the Match Gold award 1976; holder of record for Benson & Hedges Cup Competition for 285 2nd wicket partnership with C G Greenridge (Hants v Minor Counties (South), Amersham) 1973; Westinghouse Brake & Signal Co Ltd (engrg firm) 1966-71, coach to PAARL CC 1973-80, worked in family shoe business 1989-91; *Recreations* chess, watching films (preferably war films), golf, gardening; *Style—* David Turner, Esq; Shoe Box, 72A Sheldon Rd, Chippenham, Wiltshire

TURNER, Prof David Warren; s of Robert Cecil Turner (d 1983), of Leigh on Sea, Essex, and Constance Margaret, *née* Bonner (d 1969); *b* 16 July 1927; *Educ* Westcliff HS, Univ of Exeter (BSc), Imperial Coll Univ of London (PhD, DIC); *m* 11 Sept 1954, Barbara Marion, da of Cyril Fisher (d 1982), of Oxford; 1 s (Paul b 1958), 1 da (Susan b 1963); *Career* reader in organic chemistry Imperial Coll Univ of London 1965 (lectr 1958); Univ of Oxford: fell and tutor Balliol Coll 1967, lectr in physical chemistry 1968, reader in physical chemistry 1978, prof of electron spectroscopy 1984; memb IUPAC cmmn on Molecular Spectroscopy; Hon DTech Royal Tech Inst Stockholm 1971, Hon DPhil Univ of Basel 1980; FRS 1973; *Books* Molecular Photoelectron Spectroscopy (1970); *Recreations* music, gardening, tinkering with gadgets; *Style—* Prof David Turner, FRS; Balliol College, Oxford

TURNER, Dennis; MP (Lab) Wolverhampton SE 1987; s of Thomas Herbert Turner (d 1981), and Mary Elizabeth, *née* Peasley (d 1974); *b* 26 Aug 1942; *Educ* Stonefield Secdy Sch Bilston W Mids, Bilston Coll of Further Educn; *m* 19 June 1976, Patricia Mary, da of Joseph Henry Narroway (d 1984), of Bilston; 1 s (Brendon Robert b 1977), 1 da (Jenny Mary b 1980); *Career* chm: Springvale Co-op Ltd Bilston, Springvale Trg Ltd Bilston; dir: W Mids Co-op Fin Ltd, Black Country Devpt Agency; dep ldr Wolverhampton MDC 1979-86; former chm: Socl Servs Ctee, Housing Ctee, Further Educn Ctee, Econ Devpt Ctee; memb W Mids CC 1975-; pres: Bilston Community Assoc, Bradley Community Assoc, Ettingshall Darts League, Bradley and Wultrun Corps of Drums; sec and tstee Bradley and Dist Sr Citizens Centre; *Recreations* compereing, beer tasting, all card games; *Clubs* New Springvale Sports & Social (Bilston); *Style—* Dennis Turner, Esq, MP; Ambleside, King St, Bradley, Bilston, W Mids (☎ 0902 41822); Springvale House, Millfields Rd, Bilston, W Mids (0902 42364)

TURNER, Brig Dame Evelyn Marguerite; DBE (1965, MBE 1946), RRC (1956); da of late Thomas Turner, and Molly, *née* Bryan; *b* 10 May 1910; *Educ* St Bartholomew's Hosp London; *Career* joined QAIMNS (later QARANC) 1937, served WWII (POW Sumatra 1942-45), matron-in-chief and dir Army Nursing Service 1964-68, ret; Col Cmdt QARANC 1969-74; CStJ 1966; *Style—* Brig Dame Margot Turner, DBE, RRC; 2 Chantry Court, Frimley, Surrey (☎ 0276 22030)

TURNER, Admiral Sir (Arthur) Francis; KCB (1970, CB 1966), DSC (1945); s of Rear Adm A W J Turner (d 1964), and Agnes Maria Lochrane (d 1958); *b* 23 June 1912; *Educ* Stonyhurst; *m* 1963, Elizabeth Clare, da of Capt Hubert E F and Hon Mrs de Trafford, of Villa Bologna, Malta; 2 s (Francis b 1966, Michael b 1969); *Career* joined RN 1931, serv WWII Atlantic and Pacific, Capt 1956, Rear Adm 1964, DG Aircraft (Naval) MOD 1966-67, Chief of Fleet Support MOD 1967-71, Vice Adm 1968, Adm 1970; *Clubs* Army and Navy, Union (Malta); *Style—* Adm Sir Francis Turner, KCB, DSC; Plantation House, Ockham Rd South, East Horsley, Surrey

TURNER, Frank; s of Frank Turner (d 1976), of Earby, Yorkshire, and Marion, *née* Robinson; *b* 7 June 1943; *Educ* Keighley Tech Coll, Univ of Salford (BSc), Columbia Univ Business Sch NY (long distance running trophy); *m* 1967, Byrnece, da of Jack Crawshaw; 1 s (Julian Mark b 4 July 1977), 1 da (Suzanne Nicola b 5 Feb 1972); *Career* Rolls Royce Ltd: apprentice 1959, graduate apprentice 1963-67, machine tool devpt engr 1967-69, tech asst and prog mangr RB211 1969-72, fin controller Rolls Royce 1971 Ltd Barnoldswick 1972-73, prodn products mangr Barnoldswick 1973-75, product centre mangr Derby 1975-78, gen mangr prodn 1978-80, dir mfrg 1980-83, dir mfrg engrg 1983-85, dir industl and marine Ansty 1985-87, chm Cooper Rolls Inc 1985-87, dir Civil Engines Rolls Royce plc 1987-, dir International Aero Engines AG 1987-, appointed to Main Bd Rolls Royce plc 1988, memb Bd Rolls Royce Inc 1987-90; *Awards* Mensforth Gold medal of Inst of Prodn Engrs for contrib to Br mfrg technol 1985, James Clayton award Inst of Mechanicla Engrs for contrib to design, devpt and mfr of aero gas turbines; FEng 1985, fell Inst of Prodn Engrg 1986, FInstMechE 1986, fell Royal Aeronautical Soc 1989; *Recreations* family, sailing, running, windsurfing, keep fit, music, golf; *Style—* Frank Turner, Esq; Rolls Royce plc, PO Box 31, Moor Lane, Derby (☎ 0332 249637, fax 0332 248856)

TURNER, Geoffrey Howard; s of Charles William Turner (d 1990), of Willaston-in-Wirral, and Evelyn Doris, *née* Harris; *b* 23 July 1945; *Educ* The Kings's Sch Chester, St Edmund Hall Oxford (BA, MA); *m* 31 May 1975, Margaret Linda, da of John Aitken Donaldson, of Sedgley, West Midlands; 2 da (Katherine b 1978, Charlotte b 1981); *Career* Stock Exchange: mangr Membership Dept 1975-78 (asst mangr 1973-75), sec Wilson Evidence Ctee 1978, sec Planning Ctee 1977-78, sec Restrictive Practices Case Ctee 1978-83, head of membership 1983-86; int stock dir of membership Int Stock Exchange 1986-90, dir of membership, Securities Assoc Ltd 1986- (sec 1986-88); chm govrs Wood End Jr and Infant Schs Harpenden; Freeman City of London 1980; *Recreations* visiting country churches, collecting books and prints; *Clubs* Vincents (Oxford), Leander; *Style—* Geoffrey Turner, Esq; 44 Roundwood Lane, Harpenden, Herts (☎ 0582 769882); The Securities Association Ltd, Stock Exchange Tower, Old Broad St, London EC2N 1EQ (☎ 071 256 9000, fax 071 334 8943)

TURNER, Air Cdre Graham Charles; s of Harold George Turner, of Southrey, Lincs, and Constance May, *née* Peachey (d 1984); *b* 13 May 1932; *Educ* Chesterfield Sch, Univ of Sheffield Med Sch (MB, ChB); *m* 26 Oct 1957, Anne Shirley, da of Arthur Miller (d 1962), of Sheffield; 1 s (Mark b 1960), 2 da (Karen b 1958, Fiona b 1963); *Career* RAF: cmmnd 1958, conslt physician 1967, CO RAF Ely 1988-; FRCP 1977; *Recreations* skiing, sailing, ornithology, gardening; *Clubs* Royal Air Force; *Style—* Air Cdre Graham Turner; Anadry, Sevenhampton, Swindon SN6 7QA (☎ 0793 762615); Ely House, Royal Air Force, Ely, Cambs CB6 1DN (☎ 0353 665781); The Princess of Wales Hospital, Royal Air Force, Ely Cambs (☎ 0353 665781)

TURNER, Graham John; s of David Turner, and Phylis, *née* Newcombe; *b* 5 Oct 1947; *Educ* Stanney Lane Secdy Modern; *m* Carol Ann, da of Alfred Lawrence Prideaux; 3 s (Christopher Neil b 15 Sept 1970, Graham Mark b 4 Oct 1972, Andrew Jonathan b 16 Nov 1979), 1 da (Samantha Ann b 29 March 1974); *Career* professional football manager; player: 77 appearances Wrexham 1964-68, 215 appearances Chester City 1968-73, 342 appearances Shrewsbury Town 1973-84 (player-mangr 1978-84, 3 Div Championship 1978-79); mangr: Aston Villa 1984-86, Wolverhampton Wanderers 1986-; England youth caps; Div 4 Championship 1987-88, Sherpa Van Trophy winner, Div 3 Championship 1988-89; *Books* The Only Way Is Up (1989); *Recreations* fly fishing, golf, reading; *Style—* Graham Turner, Esq; Wolverhampton Wanderers FC, Molineux, Waterloo Rd, Wolverhampton, W Midlands (☎ 0902 712181)

TURNER, Grant; s of Mark John Victor Turner, of Essex, and Joyce Eileen, *née* Boddens; *b* 30 Oct 1957; *Educ* Brentwood Sch, Florida State Univ Tallahassee (BSc); *m* 14 Nov 1987, Judy Johnson Turner, da of Dr James Henry Johnson; *Career* professional golfer; amateur career: represented England & GB boys and youth teams 1975-77, selected for NCAA All American Coll Team 1979-81, winner Belgian Amateur Championship 1977, winner French Jr Championship; turned professional 1982, player PGA Euro tour 1983-, winner Calberson Classic France 1985, winner Zimbabwe Open 1990; course record Golf du Chantilly France (score 63) 1989, rookie of the Year 1983; *Recreations* tennis, reading; *Style—* Grant Turner, Esq; PGA European Tour, Wentworth Club, Wentworth Drive, Virginia Water, Surrey GU25 4LS (☎ 0245 251160, fax 0245 283725)

TURNER, Prof Grenville; s of Arnold Turner, of Todmorden, and Florence Turner; *b* 1 Nov 1936; *Educ* Todmorden GS, St Johns Coll Cambridge (BA, MA), Balliol Coll Oxford (DPhil); *m* 8 April 1961, Kathleen, da of William Morris (d 1986), of Rochdale; 1 s (Patrick b 1968), 1 da (Charlotte b 1966); *Career* asst prof Univ of California Berkeley 1962-64, res assoc California Inst of Technol 1970-71, prof of physics Univ of Sheffield 1980-88 (lectr 1964-74, sr lectr 1974-79, reader 1979-80), prof of isotope geochemistry Univ of Manchester 1988-; memb Ctees: SERC, Br Nat Space Centre; FRS 1980 (memb Cncl 1990-); *Recreations* photography, walking, theatre; *Style—* Prof Grenville Turner, FRS; The Royd, Todmorden, Lancs OL14 8DW (☎ 0706 818 621); Dept of Geology, The Univ of Manchester M13 9PL (☎ 061 275 3800, fax 061 275 3947, telex 666517 UNIMAN)

TURNER, Harry Edward; s of Harry Turner (d 1967), of London, and Bessie Marguerite Jay (d 1984); *b* 28 Feb 1935; *Educ* Sloane Sch Chelsea; *m* 2 June 1956, Carolyn Louie, da of Frank Bird (d 1958), of Guernsey, CI; 1 s (Gregory Alexander b 1957), 1 da (Jane Louie b 195 9); *Career* RA 1953-55, cmmnd 2 Lt 1 Bn Middx Regt 1934; Westward TV: sales exec 1962, gen sales mangr 1966, head of sales 1970, dir of sales 1972; md TSW 1985 (joined 1981), dir ITN; vice chm The Advertising Assoc; FRSA 1986; *Books* The Man Who Could Hear Fishes Scream (1978), The Gentle Art of Salesmanship (1985), So You Want to be a Sales Manager (1986); *Recreations* skiing, riding, tennis, writing; *Clubs* English Speaking Union, The White Elephant, Tramp, Mannheim (NY); *Style—* Harry Turner, Esq; Four Acres, Lake Road, Deepcut, Surrey GU16 6RB; Villa Cortayne, Benalmadena, Spain (☎ 0252 835527); TSW, Derrys Cross, Plymouth, Devon (☎ 0752 663322)

TURNER, (Robert) Ian; s of Major Lewis John Turner, of Grove House, Singleton, nr Chichester, W Sussex, and Jean Cleghorn, *née* Dashwood; *b* 22 Oct 1940; *Educ* Eton; *m* 4 May 1974, Alexandra Susan, da of Brig Peter Chamber Hinde, DSO (d 1983); 1 s (Peter b 1975), 1 da (Katharine b 1977); *Career* dir Fuller, Smith & Turner plc 1967; *Recreations* shooting, skiing; *Style—* Ian Turner, Esq; Fuller, Smith & Turner plc, Griffin Brewery, Chiswick, London W4 2QB (☎ 081 994 2691, telex 912000)

TURNER, James; s of James Gordon Melville Turner, GC (d 1967), and Peggy Pamela, *née* Masters; *b* 23 Nov 1952; *Educ* Bexhill GS, Univ of Hull (LLB); *m* 7 July 1979, Sheila, da of John Barclay Green, OBE, of Woking, Surrey; 3 s (George b 27 Jan 1981, Roderick b 1 Nov 1986, Felix b 1 Feb 1991), 1 da (Phoebe b 23 Nov 1983); *Career* called to Bar Inner Temple 1976; *Recreations* eating, drinking, reading, law; *Style—* James Turner, Esq; 1 King's Bench Walk, Temple, London EC4Y 7DB (☎ 071 583 6266, fax 071 583 2068)

TURNER, James Francis; s of Rev Percy Reginald Turner, of The Old Rectory, Wem, Salop; *b* 14 March 1915; *Educ* Marlborough, Pembroke Coll Cambridge; *m* 1968, Hon Joanna Elizabeth, *née* Piercy; *Career* served WWII pilot and navigator RN, Ark Royal, including sinking of Bismarck, also in Caribbean, Coastal Command; commanded 828 and 830 Sqdns Malta, on staff Flag Offr Naval Air Stations 1944; mangr Estate Duties Investmt Tst 1958 (dir 1973-80); dir: Henry Boot & Sons 1973-, Bermaline and Bermaline Foods 1972-, Bloxwich Lock & Stamping 1973-; md Cavendish Mercantile Co 1981-; hon treas Friends of the Elderly 1976-82, formed Gourley Charitable Tst 1970, memb Cncl Arts Educnl Schools 1972-; *Recreations* work, charities; *Clubs* Boodle's; *Style—* James F Turner, Esq; The Old Coach House, Burford, Oxon OX8 4HZ (☎ 099 382 2368)

TURNER, Janet Mary (Mrs Griffin); da of Cecil Sidney Turner, and Gwendoline Joyce, *née* Loseby; *b* 16 Nov 1957; *Educ* Wycombe Abbey Sch, Univ of Bristol (LLB); *m* 16 April 1983, Paul Griffin, s of Reginald Stuart Griffin; *Career* called to the Bar Middle Temple 1979; Harmsworth Scholar, practising barr; sec of London Common Law and Commercial Bar Assoc, memb Commercial Bar Assoc; *Recreations* collecting art, books, antique furniture and ephemera, travel, music, wine, gardening, skiing; *Style—* Miss Janet Turner; 3 Gray's Inn Place, Gray's Inn, London WC1 R5EA (☎ 071 831 8441, fax 071 831 8479, telex 295119 LEXCOL G)

TURNER, Hon Mrs ((Dorothy) Joan); *née* Yerburgh; er da (by 1 w) of 1 Baron Alvingham (d 1955); *b* 12 April 1913; *m* 12 March 1934, Lt-Col William Aspinall Turner, late The Queen's Bays; 1 s, 1 da; *Style—* The Hon Mrs Turner; Rectory Cottage, Cheselbourne, Dorchester, Dorset

TURNER, Hon Mrs (Joanna Elizabeth); 2 da of 1 Baron Piercy, CBE (d 1966); *b* 10

Jan 1923; *Educ* St Paul's, Somerville Coll Oxford; *m* 1968, James Francis Turner, *qv*; *Career* classics teacher: Downe House 1944-46, Gordonstoun 1947-48, Badminton Sch Bristol 1948-65; headmistress Badminton Sch 1966-69; JP Inner London Juvenile Courts Panel 1970-75; classics teacher Ellesmere Coll 1975-79; *Style*— The Hon Mrs Turner; The Old Coach House, Burford, Oxon (☎ 099382 2368)

TURNER, Prof John Derfel; s of Joseph Turner (d 1962), of Manchester and Southport, and Dorothy Winifred, *née* Derfel (d 1979); *b* 27 Feb 1928; *Educ* Manchester GS, The Univ of Manchester (BA, MA, DipEd); *m* 6 June 1951, Susan Broady, da of Robert Baldwin Hovey, MC, OBE (d 1974), of Wheelock, Cheshire; 2 s (Stephen b 1953, Leigh b 1959); *Career* Educn Offr RAF 1948-50; teacher Prince Henry's GS Evesham 1951-53, sr lectr in educn Nigerian Coll of Arts Sci and Technol 1956-61 (lectr in English 1953-56), lectr in educn Inst of Educn Univ of Exeter 1961-64, prof of educn and dir Sch of Educn Univ of Botswana Lesotho and Swaziland 1964-70 (pro vice chllr 1966-70, emeritus prof 1970), prof of adult and higher educn Univ of Manchester 1976-85 (prof of educn and dir Sch of Educn 1970-76), rector Univ Coll of Botswana Univ of Botswana and Swaziland 1981-82 (vice chllr 1982-84); Univ of Manchester: dir Sch of Educn, dean Faculty of Educn; memb: UK Nat Cmmn UNESCO 1975-81, IUC Working Parties on E and Central Africa and on Rural Devpt 1975-81, Educn Sub-ctee UGC 1980-81, Working Pty on Academic Devpt of Univ of Juba 1977-78; chm: Cncl Social Studies Advsy Ctee Selly Oak Colls 1975-81, Ed Bd Int Journal of Educn and Devpt 1978-81, Univ's Cncl for Educn of Teachers 1979-81 and 1988 (vice-chm 1976-79), Bd Govrs Abbotsholme Sch 1980-, Cncl of Validating Univs 1990-, Pres Cmmn on HE in Namibia 1991-; methodist local preacher; Hon LLD Ohio Univ 1982; Hon FCP 1985, hon fell Bolton Inst of Technol 1988; *Recreations* reading, music, theatre, walking; *Clubs* Royal Cwlth Soc, Royal Overseas League; *Style*— Prof John Turner; 13 Firswood Mount, Gatley, Cheadle, Cheshire SK8 4JY (☎ 061 428 2734); Sch of Educn, Univ of Manchester, Oxford Rd, Manchester M13 9PL (☎ 061 275 3458, fax 061 275 3519)

TURNER, John Frayn; s of late George Francis Turner, and late Daisy Louise, *née* Frayn; *b* 9 Aug 1923; *Educ* Royal GS Guildford; *m* 9 Aug 1945, Joyce Isabelle, da of late Wilfred Ernest Howson; 1 da (Francesca Lynn b 1947); *Career* served Admty and RN 1941-47; journalist; writer and ed 1948-63, responsible for RAF publicity MOD 1963-73, sr ed pubns COI 1973-83; managing ed 1984-85: Art and Artists, Dance and Dancers, Films and Filming, Music and Musicians, Plays and Players; *Books* Service Most Silent (1955), VCs of the Royal Navy (1956), Prisoner at Large (1957), Hovering Angels (1957), Periscope Patrol (1958), Invasion '44 (1959), VCs of the Air (1960), Battle Stations (1960), Highly Explosive (1961), The Blinding Flash (1962), VCs of the Army (1962), A Girl Called Johnnie (1963), Famous Air Battles (1963), Fight for the Sky (with Douglas Bader, 1973), Destination Berchtesgaden (1975), British Aircraft of World War 2 (1975), Famous Flights (1978), The Bader Wing (1981), The Yanks Are Coming (1983), Frank Sinatra (1983), The Bader Tapes (1986), The Good Spy Guide (1988), Rupert Brooke - The Splendour and the Pain (1990); *Recreations* music, theatre, films, art; *Style*— John Frayn Turner, Esq; Apartment 302, The Metropole, Folkestone, Kent (☎ 0303 50144)

TURNER, John R; s of Walter George Turner (d 1985), and Sarah Leonora, *née* Radley (d 1967); *b* 28 Jan 1939; *Educ* Rugby, Univ of Cambridge (MA, MusB); *Career* asst master Cheltenham Coll 1961-65, organist and dir of music Glasgow Cathedral, lectr Royal Scot Acad of Music and Drama, organist Univ of Strathclyde 1965-; has produced various gramophone records and toured in Italy and USA; Hon MA Univ of Strathclyde 1990; *Recreations* motor-caravaning, gardening; *Style*— John Turner, Esq; 2 Cathkin Cottage, Burnside Rd, Glasgow G73 5RD (☎ 041 634 3083)

TURNER, Prof John Richard George; s of George Hugh Turner (d 1983), of Liverpool, and Elsie Ellen, *née* Booth; *b* 11 Sept 1940; *Educ* Quarry Bank HS Liverpool, Univ of Liverpool (BSc), Univ of Oxford (DPhil, DSc); *m* 3 April 1967, Sandra Fordyce, da of Alexander Thomson Millar, of Dundee; 1 s (Richard b 1970), 1 da (Lois b 1977); *Career* lectr in biology Univ of York 1965-72, assoc prof of biology Stony Brook Campus NY State Univ 1971-77, princ scientific offr Rothamsted Experimental Station Harpenden 1977-78, prof of genetics Univ of Leeds 1987- (lectr 1978-81, reader in evolutionary genetics 1981-87); circa 100 papers in scientific jls; contrib books on: evolution, ecology, genetics, butterflies, history of science; radio and TV appearances; fndr memb Conservation Soc, jt sec Cncl for Academic Autonomy; memb: Yorkshire Wildlife Tst, Yorkshire Naturalists Union; memb American Soc of Naturalists 1971; FRES 1962; *Recreations* opera, swimming, philately, wildlife, drawing, translating poetry,r spoonerising; *Style*— Prof John Turner; Department of Genetics, University of Leeds, Leeds LS2 9JT (☎ 0532 333095, fax 0532 441175, telex 556473 UNILDS G)

TURNER, John Warren; CBE (1988); s of Thomas Henry Huxley Turner, CBE (d 1973), of Cardiff, and Phebe Elvira, *née* Evans; *b* 12 Oct 1935; *Educ* Shrewsbury, St John's Coll Cambridge; *m* 8 Oct 1966, Jillian Fiona Geraldine, da of Thomas Ouchterlony Turton Hart; 1 s (Gavin b 1972); *Career* 2 Lt RE Middle East 1957-59, TA 1959-66, Capt ret; construction conslt; former chm and md E Turner and Sons Ltd (dir 1964-89); chm Bldg Regulations Advsy Ctee BRAC 1985- (memb 1971-), memb Cncl Br Bd of Agrément (BBA) 1980-, chm Cncl for Bldg and Civil Engrg BSI 1985-, dir Principality Bldg Soc 1985-; pres: Bldg Employers Confedn 1985-86, Concrete Soc 1976-77, Wales Div IOD 1981-86; govr Christ Coll Brecon 1981-84, memb Wales Cncl CBI 1980-86; JP 1979-85; CBIM, FCIOB; *Recreations* golf; *Clubs* Cardiff and County, Leander, Royal Porthcawl Golf, Royal and Ancient Golf; *Style*— John Turner, Esq, CBE; 38 Victoria Rd, Penarth, S Glamorgan CF6 2HX (☎ 0222 707924)

TURNER, Jonathan David Chattyn; s of Maxwell Turner, and Naomi, *née* Myers; *b* 13 May 1958; *Educ* Rugby, Corpus Christi Coll Cambridge (BA, MA), Université Libre de Bruxelles (Lic Sp Dr Eur); *m* 23 Nov 1986, Caroline Frances Esther, da of Lawrence Sam Berman, CB, qv; 1 s (Jacob b 1988), 1 da (Camilla b 1990); *Career* called to the Bar Gray's Inn 1982 (currently specialising in intellectual property, competition and computer law); promoter of competition law reform; *Books* Halsbury's Laws of England, EC Competition Law (1986), European Patent Office Reports (1986-1991), Forms and Agreements on Intellectual Property and International Licensing (1979-89), Law of the European Communities Service (1990-1); *Recreations* walking, theatre; *Style*— Jonathan Turner, Esq; 3 Pump Court, Temple, London EC4Y 7AJ

TURNER, Kenneth Edward; s of Frank Turner (d 1967), of 8 Queens Rd, Portsmouth, Hants, and Dorothy Lilian May, *née* Poling (d 1967); *b* 8 Nov 1920; *Educ* Taunton Sch; *m* 6 July 1946, Norah (Mona), da of Patrick Hearns (d 1960), of Mill St, Ballina, Co Mayo, Ireland; 2 s (John b 1947, Michael b 1949), 2 da (Catherine (Mrs Osborne) b 1954, Margaret b 1957); *Career* Rifleman KRRC 1940, 2 Lt Somerset LI 1941, Capt RIASC 1942-46; admitted slr 1947, Turner Garett & Co 1950, currently sr ptnr Mackrell Turner Garett; Lib cncllr Woking 1963-66, former chm Botleys Park Hosp Chertsey, chm Second Achilles Housing Assoc; memb Law Soc 1950; *Recreations* sailing, golf; *Clubs* Royal Cwlth Soc, Woking Golf; *Style*— Kenneth Turner, Esq; The Well House, Firbank Lane, St Johns, Woking, Surrey (☎ 0483 723048, fax 0483 755 818, telex 858 070 MTG LAW G)

TURNER, Prof Kenneth John; s of Graham Leslie Turner (d 1970), of Glasgow, and Christina McInnes, *née* Fraser; *b* 21 Feb 1949; *Educ* Hutchesons Boys GS, Univ of Glasgow (BSc), Univ of Edinburgh (PhD); *m* 15 Sept 1973, Elizabeth Mary Christina, da of Rev William James Hutton, of Glasgow; 2 s (Duncan b 1979, Robin b 1981); *Career* data communications conslt 1980-86, prof of computing sci 1986; memb BSI; *Books* Formal Description Techniques (ed 1988); *Recreations* choral activities, handicrafts; *Style*— Prof Kenneth Turner; Dept of Computing Science, Univ of Stirling, Stirling FK9 4LA (☎ 0786 73171, fax 0786 63000, telex 777557 STUNIV G)

TURNER, Lawrence Frederick; OBE (1982); s of Frederick Thomas Turner (d 1967), of Warwicks, and Edith Elizabeth Turner (d 1975); *b* 28 Jan 1929; *Educ* Moseley GS, Univ of Aston (BSc, CEng); *m* 5 June 1954, Jeanette, da of Wilfred Edwin Clements (d 1967), of Warwicks; 2 s (Adrian Richard Lawrence b 1957, (Anthony) Christopher b 1959), 1 da (Susan Kathryn b 1965); *Career* chartered electrical engr; chm Static Systems Group plc 1964; pres Inst Hosp Engrg 1979-81; Freeman City of London 1986; memb: Worshipful Co of Fanmakers, Worshipful Co of Engineers; FIEE, FCIBSE; *Recreations* sailing, music, opera, rowing; *Clubs* Athenaeum, Royal Dart Yacht; *Style*— Lawrence Turner, Esq, OBE; Harborough Hall, Blakedown, Worcs (☎ 0562 700129); Static Systems Group plc, Heath Mill Rd, Wombourn, Staffs (☎ 0902 895551)

TURNER, Dr Leslie Howard; MBE (Mil); s of Aubrey Howard Turner (d 1958), of Raynes Park, and Elsie Louise, *née* Anderson (d 1962); *b* 30 Nov 1916; *Educ* King's Sch Canterbury, Middx Hosp Univ of London (MB BS, MD); *m* 1 Aug 1940, Kathleen Elizabeth (Nancy), da of Maj Denis Connors (d 1956), of Southsea; 1 s (Michael); *Career* WWII Lt 3 Field Ambulance Federated Malay States Vol Force 1942-45 (POW Singapore and Siam Burma Railway F Force); Colonial Med Serv Malaya 1940-59: MO i/c med and admin in hosps 1946-52, MO Inst for Med Res 1952-59; conslt (yaws) WHO 1959; reference expert leptospirosis Wellcome Laboratories of Tropical Med 1960-64, dir Leptospirosis Reference Laboratory Public Health Laboratories Serv and memb gp WHO 1964-78, sec Taxonomic Sub Ctee on Leptospirosis 1960-78; memb: BMA 1946, RSM 1962; *Recreations* reading (gardening is a chore, not recreational); *Clubs* Royal Overseas League; *Style*— Dr Leslie Turner, MBE

TURNER, Lowri; da of Merfyn Lloyd Turner, of 24 Harberton Rd, London, and Shirley Elizabeth, *née* Davis; *b* 31 Dec 1964; *Educ* Greycoat Hospital Westminster, Camden Sch for Girls, St Martins Sch of Art, Newcastle Poly; *Career* fashion asst Observer 1987-90, fashion ed Evening Standard 1990-; *Recreations* champagne lifestyle; *Style*— Miss Lowri Turner; Fashion Editor, The Evening Standard, Northcliffe House, 2 Derry St, Kensington, London W8 5EE (☎ 071 938 7597/8, fax 071 937 2648)

TURNER, Brig Dame Margot; *see*: Turner, Brig Dame Evelyn Marguerite

TURNER, Mark George; s of Jeffrey Farrar Turner, of Kendal, Cumbria, and Joyce, *née* Barkas; *b* 27 Aug 1959; *Educ* Sedbergh, Queen's Coll Oxford (BA); *m* 23 Jan 1988, Caroline Sophia, da of George Haydn Bullock, of Richmond, Surrey; 1 da (Alice Elizabeth b 29 Oct 1989); *Career* called to the Bar Gray's Inn 1981, tenant Deans Ct Chambers Manchester 1982-, called to the Bar Northern Circuit 1982; memb: Manchester and District Medico-Legal Soc, Hon Soc of Gray's Inn, Union Internationale des Avocats; *Recreations* classical music, history, general knowledge quizzes; *Clubs* Mastermind (semi finalist 1988); *Style*— Mark Turner, Esq; Manor Farm Cottage, 1 Hall Lane, Woodley, nr Stockport SK6 1PP (☎ 061 430 2524); 1 Deans Court, Cumberland House, Crown Square, Manchester M3 3HA (☎ 061 834 4097)

TURNER, Martin Neely; s of Robert Gabriel Barnard Turner (d 1969), of Bourton on the Water, and Dorothy Margaret, *née* Neely; *b* 12 Dec 1954; *Educ* Solihull Sch, Birmingham Poly Coll of Commerce (HND), Manchester Business Sch (MBA); *m* 18 Sept 1982, Stephanie Pamela, da of Albert William Edmonds; 2 da (Claire b 24 April 1985, Penny b 16 June 1988); *Career* CA; mangr Peat Marwick McLintock Birmingham until 1985, co sec and co accountant of insur pensions and personal fin planning Fraser Tudor Ltd 1985-87, gp fin analyst Littlewoods Organisation plc 1987-90, fin dir NW Estates plc 1990, princ M N Turner CAs; memb Solihull Centre Nat Tst; FCA 1980, FInstD 1990, ATT 1990; *Recreations* rambling, squash; *Clubs* The Old Silhillians (Solihull), The Fentham (Hampton-in-Arden); *Style*— Martin Turner, Esq; 54 Grenfell Pk, Parkgate, Neston, South Wirral L64 6TT (☎ 051 336 7079); North West Estates plc, 7-8 Brickfield Business Centre, 60 Manchester Rd, Northwich, Cheshire CW9 7LS (☎ 0606 49800, fax 0606 49324, car 0836 518770)

TURNER, Martin William; s of William Alexander Turner (d 1972), of 24 Marshall Rd, Rainham, Kent, and Enine Felicity, *née* McCabe; *b* 3 Oct 1940; *Educ* Gravesend Tech Sch, Medway Coll of Art (Nat Dip in Design); *Career* artist; mural paintings cmmnd by: MOD 1971, GEC Ltd 1976, Rochester upon Medway Civic Centre 1987; series of paintings and limited edition prints based on the Medway Towns and exhibited regularly at Royal Acad 1960-; chm local youth club 1957-65; memb ROI 1975; *Recreations* photography, walking, model making; *Style*— Martin Turner, Esq; 24 Marshall Rd, Rainham, Kent (☎ 0634 319 94)

TURNER, (Francis) Michael; s of Francis Richard Turner (d 1978), of Leicester, and Rosalie, *née* Gudger; *b* 8 Aug 1934; *Educ* City of Leicester Boys GS, Leicester Colls of Art and Technol; *m* Patricia Irene, da of Sidney James Coley; 1 s (Michael James b 2 July 1958), 2 da (Helen Louise b 23 April 1962, Susan Jane b 25 Feb 1964); *Career* cricket administrator; Leicestershire CCC: player 1951-58, asst sec 1959-60, sec 1960-69, sec and mangr 1969-85, chief exec 1985-; TCCB: memb Exec Ctee 1968-, memb Cricket Cncl 1968-; Hon MA Univ of Leicester 1985; *Style*— Michael Turner, Esq; Leicestershire CCC, County Ground, Grace Road, Leicester LE2 8AD (☎ 0533 832128)

TURNER, Michael James; s of James Henry Turner (d 1966), and Doris May, *née* Daniels (d 1983); *b* 8 July 1939; *Educ* BEC GS London, Imperial Coll London (BSc, ARCS), London Business Sch, Harvard Business Sch; *m* 29 Dec 1962, Elizabeth Joyce, da of George Edward Hanselman (d 1969); 1 s (David b 1964), 1 da (Anne b 1966); *Career* gen mangr Sun Life Assurance Society plc 1989 (joined 1960); dir: Sun Life Financial Associates, Sun Life Financial Services, Sun Life Direct Marketing, Sun Life Broker Services, The Bristol Initiative, Sun Life Pensions Management Ltd, Suntrust, Sun Life Unit Assurance; elder Redland Park Utd Reformed Church; *Recreations* rambling, overseas travel; *Style*— Michael Turner, Esq; Grey Roofs, The Scop, Almondsbury, Bristol; Sun Life Assurance Society plc, Sun Life Court, St James Barton, Bristol BS99 7SL (☎ 0272 426 911, fax 0272 441 453)

TURNER, Michael John; s of Gerald Mortimer Turner, of Wood Cottage, Ashtead Woods, Ashtead, Surrey, and Joyce Isobel Marguerite, *née* Healy; *b* 12 June 1951; *Educ* Eton; *m* 17 July 1982, Diana Mary St Clair, da of David Michael St Clair Weir; 3 s (Freddie b 1985, Max b 1987, Harry b 1989); *Career* dir: Fuller Smith and Turner plc 1985-, Ringwoods Ltd 1985-, Fuller Smith and Turner Estates Ltd 1985; chm Leonard Tong 1986-87 (dir 1982-); FCA; *Recreations* skiing, shooting, golf, tennis, motor racing, travel; *Clubs* Aldeburgh Golf, Eton Vikings, Wine Trade Sports; *Style*— Michael Turner, Esq; 5 Bowerdean St, London SW6 3TN; Fuller Smith & Turner plc, Griffin Brewery, Chiswick, London W4 2QB

TURNER, The Hon Mr Justice Turner; Hon Sir Michael John; QC (1973); s of Theodore Francis Turner, QC (d 1986), and Elizabeth Alice, *née* Schuster (d 1983); *b*

31 May 1931; *Educ* Winchester, Magdalene Coll Cambridge (BA); *m* 26 July 1956 (m dis 1965), Hon Susan Money-Coutts, da of 7 Baron Latymer (d 1987); 1 s (Mark b 1958), 1 da (Louise b 1959); m 2, 1965, Frances Deborah, da of The Rt Hon Sir David Powell Croom-Johnson; 2 s (David b 1966, James b 1967); *Career* called to the Bar Inner Temple 1955, recorder 1970, chm E Midlands Agric Laws Tribunal 1972, High Ct judge 1985-; memb Judicial Studies Bd 1988-, co-chm Civil & Family Ctee Judicial Studies Bd 1988; Kt 1985; *Recreations* listening to music, horses; *Clubs* Army & Navy; *Style*— The Hon Mr Justice Turner; c/o Royal Courts of Justice, Strand, London WC2A 2AA

TURNER, Michael Ralph; *b* 26 Jan 1929; *Educ* BA; *Career* gp md and chief exec Associated Book Publishers plc 1982-87, chm Methuen Inc New York 1981-87, sr vice-pres publishing/information gp Int Thomson Organisation Ltd 1987-; pres Publishers Assoc 1987-; *Books* The Bluffer's Guide to the Theatre (1967); with Antony Miall: Parlour Poetry (1967), The Parlour Song Book (1972), Just a Song at Twilight (1975), The Edwardian Song Book (1982), Gluttony, Pride and Lust and Other Sins for the World of Books (with Michael Geare, 1984); translation of Tintin books (with Leslie Lonsdale-Cooper, 1958-); *Recreations* theatre, writing, maritime art; *Clubs* Garrick; *Style*— Michael Turner, Esq; International Thomson Organisation Ltd, First Floor, The Quadrangle, 180 Wardour Street, London W1A 4YG (☎ 071 437 9787)

TURNER, Dr Michael Skinner; s of Sir Michael William Turner, CBE (d 1980), of Egerton Gardens, London, and Lady (Wendy), *née* Stranack; *b* 12 Aug 1947; *Educ* Dragon Sch, Marlborough, Univ of London and St Thomas's Hosp (MB BS, MRCS, LRCP), Washington (MD); *m* 8 July 1972, Amanda Baldwin, da of John Baldwin Raper, DFC, of Sloane Ave, London; 4 da (Lucinda b 6 Dec 1974, Nara b 9 Oct 1976, Camilla b 3 July 1980, Alexia b 29 Jan 1984); *Career* chief med advsr: Texaco, Vickers Ltd, Citibank, Inchcape, BZW, Henlys Ltd, Robert Fleming, Lloyds Register of Shipping, Hoare Govett/Security Pacific; med advsr: Hong Kong and Shanghai Bank, Sedgwick Group, ANZ/Grindlays Bank; memb med advsy ctee: UKOOA, Inst Petroleum; hon chief med advsr Br Ski Fedn 1974, dep dir of med servs BOA, Alpine team doctor Winter Olympics Calgary 1988; Freeman City of London 1971, Liveryman Worshipful Co of Skinners; BASM 1975, BMA 1976, FZS 1981; memb: RSM, Soc Occupational Med, Assur Med Soc, Med Book Soc; *Recreations* skiing, shooting, fishing, tennis; *Style*— Dr Michael Turner; 4 Tite St, London SW3 4HY; The City Medical Centre, 17 St Helens Place, London EC3A 6DE (☎ 071 588 5477, fax 071 256 5295)

TURNER, Hon (Edward) Neil; s of 1 Baron Netherthorpe (d 1980), and Margaret Lucy, *née* Mattock; *b* 27 Jan 1941; *Educ* Rugby, RAC Cirencester, Univ of London; *m* 12 Oct 1963, Gillian Mary, da of Christopher John King (d 1963); 1 s (Charles b 3 May 1966), 1 da (Sara b 4 Feb 1971); *Career* chm Edward Turner and Son Ltd 1971-; vice-chm Yorks and Humberside Devpt Assoc 1989-; memb: Yorks and Humberside Econ Planning Cncl 1975-79, Residuary Body for S Yorks 1985-89, Cncl BIM 1976-81 and 1982-88, Regnl Cncl CBI 1989-; gen cmmr of Taxes 1973-; High Sheriff S Yorks 1983-84, Freeman Co of Cutlers in Hallamshire; FRICS, QALAS, Dip FBA (Lond), FBIM, FRSA; *Recreations* shooting, golf; *Clubs* Lindrick Golf; *Style*— The Hon Neil Turner; The Limes, Crowgate, South Anston, nr Sheffield, S Yorks S31 7AL; 312 Petre St, Sheffield S4 8LT (☎ 0742 430291)

TURNER, Paul; s of Albert Leslie Turner, of 13 Greenfield Terrace, Newbridge, Gwent, and Elsie May, *née* Evans; *b* 13 Feb 1960; *Educ* Newbridge GS, Greenfield Secdy; *m* 16 July 1985, Janine Christina, da of Melville Greenway (d 1977); 1 s (Thomas Paul b 31 Aug 1986); *Career* Rugby Union fly-half and full-back Newport RFC and Wales (3 caps); clubs: Crumlin RFC 1978-79 (50 appearances, 200 points scored), Newbridge RFC 1979-87 (250 appearances, record 2, 500 points scored), London Welsh RFC 1987- (13 appearnces), Newport RFC 1990- (debut 1985, 110 appearances, record 368 points scored 1986); club records: record number of drop goals (23) in a season in Wales 1982-83, record 105 drop goals in first class career, top points scorer in Britain 1980-90; rep: Wales B (debut 1985), Japanese Presidents XV (v NZ 1987), FNB Int Squad SA 1989; Wales: debut v Ireland 1989; *Recreations* any sport; *Style*— Paul Turner, Esq; Westholm, 32 Edward St, Griffithstown, Pontypool, Gwent (☎ 0495 753626); c/o Newport RFC, Rodney Rd, Newport, Gwent (☎ 0633 258193)

TURNER, Prof Paul; s of Leonard Parcy Turner (d 1980), of Ascot, and Florence Maud, *née* Yates (d 1973); *b* 16 April 1933; *Educ* Roan Sch Greenwich London, Univ of London (MB BS, BSc, MD); *m* 1, 17 July 1954 (m dis 1968), Margaret; 1 da (Karen b 1968); m 2, 21 March 1968, Kathleen, da of Joseph Weaver (d 1988), of Nantwich; 1 da (Emma b 1970); *Career* lectr in pharmacology St Bartholemew's Hosp 1963-64, prof in clincial pharmacology 1972- (lectr 1964-65, sr lectr 1965-57, reader 1967-72); pres Fellowship of Postgrad Med, chm Ctee of Toxicity for Dept of Health, vice chm of Br Pharmacopoeia Cmmn; Freeman Worshipful Soc of Apothecaries; MRCP 1962, FRCP 1973, Hon MRPharmS 1977, memb RSM; *Books* Clinical Aspects of Autonomic Pharmacology (1968), Clinical Pharmacology (1986), Drug Treatment in Psychiatry (1988); *Recreations* piano and organ, travel, food and wine; *Clubs* Athenaeum; *Style*— Prof Paul Turner; 2 Englemere Wood, Kings Ride, Ascot, Berks SL5 8DE; 62 Defoe House, Barbican, London EC2Y 8DN; Dept of Clinical Pharmacology, St Bartholemew's Hospital, London EC1A 7BE (☎ 071 601 7423, fax 071 601 8134)

TURNER, Dr Peter Breen; s of Douglas Patrick Breen Turner, of Uppingham, Leics, and Dorothy Allen, *née* Glenn; *b* 6 Jan 1953; *Educ* Rossall Sch, Univ of London (MB BS); *m* Elizabeth Mary Alice, da of Edward Salmon, of Lapworth, Warwicks; 1 s (Henry), 1 da (Cassandra); *Career* St Georges Hosp Med Sch London 1971-76, various house offr and sr house offr posts 1976-81, registrar in psychiatry Notts AHA 1981-82; Leics AHA: sr registrar in psychiatry 1982-85, conslt gen psychiatrist 1985-; *Recreations* golf, fishing; *Clubs* Leicestershire Golf; *Style*— Dr Peter Turner; Carlton Hayes Hospital, Narborough, Leics (☎ 0533 863481)

TURNER, Peter John; s of John Hope Turner, of Seacrest, St Bees, Cumbria, and Nell, *née* Dansie; *b* 5 Nov 1939; *Educ* St Bees Sch; *m* 28 Sept 1968, Gabrielle Mary Ann (Gay), da of Robert Gash (d 1967); 1 s (James Hope b 1974), 2 da (Anna Louise b 1972, Alice Rebecca b 1983); *Career* articled clerk Peat Marwick Mitchell & Co 1959-64, asst accountant Distington Engineering Co Ltd 1965-67, accountant E H Marley & Partners Ltd 1967-69, chm H Edgard & Sons London Ltd 1969-88; dir: Bothel Limestone & Brick Co Ltd 1984-88, Pitchfine Ltd 1987-; princ Peter J Turner & Co CAs 1989-; FICA 1975; *Recreations* golf, tennis, snooker; *Clubs* Cockermouth Cons, Workington Golf, Old St Beghians; *Style*— Peter Turner, Esq; Lane Head, Cockermouth, Cumbria CA13 0DS (☎ 0900 823476); 21B Station St, Cockermouth, Cumbria CA13 9QW (☎ 0900 827676)

TURNER, Philip; CBE (1975); s of George Francis Turner (d 1957), of Alverstoke, Hants, and Daisy Louise, *née* Frayn; *b* 1 June 1913; *Educ* Peter Symonds Sch Winchester, Univ of London (LLB); *m* 1938, Hazel Edith, da of Douglas Anton Benda (d 1923); 1 da (and 1 da decd); *Career* Lt Cdr RNVR WWII (Atlantic convoys, Scapa Flow, Far East); admitted slr 1935, asst slr GPO Slr's Dept 1953-62, princ asst slr GPO 1962-72, slr to Post Office 1972-75; chm: Civil Service Legal Soc 1957-58, Int Bar Assoc Ctee on Public Utility Law 1972-77; private practice in: Infields, Hampton Wick, Surrey; FRSA; *Recreations* piano, golf; *Clubs* Naval, Royal Automobile, Hants and Surrey CC, Law Soc; *Style*— Philip Turner, Esq, CBE; 8 Walters Mead, Ashtead, Surrey KT21 2BP (☎ 0372 273656)

TURNER, Surgn Rear Adm Philip Stanley; CB (1963); s of Frank Overy Turner, of Tunbridge Wells, and Ellen Mary, *née* Holder; *b* 31 Oct 1905; *Educ* Cranbrook, Guy's Hosp (LDS, RCS); *m* 1934, Marguerite (d 1990), da of John Donnelly, of Glasgow; 1 s (Ian d 1966), 1 da (Sarah); *Career* entered RN as Surgn Lt 1928, Surgn Capt (D) 1955, Surgn Rear Adm (D) 1961, sr specialist in Dental Surgery 1946-60, dir of dental services RN Admiralty and MOD 1961-64, QHDS 1960-64; fndn fell Br Assoc of Oral Surgns 1962, ret 1964; *Style*— Surgn Rear Adm Philip Turner, CB

TURNER, Prof Raymond; s of Mrs Winifred Howe; *b* 28 April 1947; *Career* Univ of Mass USA: Sloan fell in cognitive sci 1982, sr res fell 1986 and 1989, visiting prof Univ of Rochester NY USA 1982, visiting fell Centre for Study of Language and Information Stanford Univ California USA 1984 (conslt in sci 1982), prof of computer sci Univ of Essex 1985- (lectr 1973-85), visiting prof Univ of Texas Austin USA 1987; *Books* Logics for Artificial Intelligence (1984), Truth and Modality for Knowledge Representation (1990); *Style*— Prof Raymond Turner; Dept of Computer Science, University of Essex, Colchester, Essex (☎ 0206 87 2342)

TURNER, Raymond Edward; *b* 3 Aug 1946; *Educ* Fairfax HS Southend, Braintree and Chelmsford Tech Coll (HNC), Leeds Coll of Art (BA); *m* 16 Aug 1969, Sandra Rosemary; 2 da (Alice b 27 Feb 1971, Coral b 6 April 1973); *Career* sr creative designer Gillette Industries 1974-77; Kilkenny Design - Nat Design Authy of Ireland: ind design mangr 1978-80, mangr of design 1980-83, head of design consultancy and asst chief exec 1983-85; design dir London Regnl Transport 1985-88, md Wolff Olins 1988-; external assessor Sheffield Poly; design mgmnt advsr RCA; *Recreations* shooting, music, theatre, outdoor pursuits; *Style*— Raymond Turner, Esq; Wolff Olins, 22 Dukes Rd, London WC1H 9AB (☎ 071 387 0891, fax 071 388 6639/388 0498, telex 261438)

TURNER, Richard Timmis; OBE (1978); s of Dr John Richard Timmis Turner, of Rose Farm, Worleston, Nantwich, Cheshire CW5 6DS, and Alison Elizabeth, *née* Bythell; *b* 17 Aug 1942; *Educ* Shrewsbury, Univ of Manchester (BA); *m* 11 Sept 1982, Margaret Rose Mary, da of Dr Ivor Corbett (d 1982); 2 da (Catherine b 1983, Rebecca b 1985); *Career* joined Rolls-Royce Ltd 1965, commercial mangr Rolls-Royce Inc NY 1971-74, mktg exec civil engines Rolls-Royce Ltd 1977, commercial dir civil engines Rolls Royce plc 1986, dir STC plc 1989- (gp mktg dir 1988-); assoc of Royal Aeronautical Soc, memb IOD; *Recreations* opera, music, rugby, farming; *Style*— Richard Turner, Esq, OBE; STC plc, Corporate Headquarters, 1B Portland Place, London W1N 3AA (☎ 071 323 1000, fax 071 323 1000 ext 245, car 0836 271248, telex 22385 STC HOG)

TURNER, Robert Lockley; s of Capt James Lockley-Turner, OBE (d 1954), of Purley, Berks, and Maud Beatrice, *née* Hillyard; *b* 2 Sept 1935; *Educ* Clifton, St Catharine's Coll Cambridge (MA); *m* 5 Oct 1963, Jennifer Mary, da of Alan Guy Fishwick Leather, TD, of Chester; 1 s (Guy Lockley b 1967), 1 da (Claire Henrietta b 1969); *Career* barr; cmmnd Gloucestershire Regt 1959, Army Legal Serv 1959-66 (Maj 1962); practised Midland and Oxford Circuit 1967-84, rec Crown Ct 1981-84, master Queen's Bench Div of Supreme Ct 1984-; hon Steward Westminster Abbey 1985-; *Publications* The Office and Functions of Queen's Bench Masters (1990), Supreme Court Practice (ed jtly, 1991); *Recreations* sailing, gardening; *Clubs* Royal Fowey Yacht; *Style*— Robert Turner, Esq; Royal Courts of Justice, Strand, London WC2A 2LJ

TURNER, Prof (James Charles) Robin; s of James William Cecil Turner, MC (d 1968), of Cambridge, and Beatrice Maude, *née* Stooke (d 1987); *b* 14 July 1930; *Educ* Greshams, Trinity Coll Cambridge (ScD, MA, PhD); *m* 20 Dec 1958, (Margaret) Anne, da of George Binford Sellwood (d 1937), of Cullompton; 1 s (Michael b 1962), 2 da (Julia b 1960, Caroline b 1962); *Career* Nat Serv RAEC 1948-49; lectr Univ of Cambridge 1955-79, fell Pembroke Coll Cambridge 1962-79, prof of chemical engrg Univ of Exeter 1979-; visiting prof: Austin Texas 1965, Sydney 1970, Seattle 1975, Christchurch NZ 1978, Bahia Blanca 1980; former chm SW Branch Inst Chemical Engrs; memb: Engrg Profs Conf Ctee, Tst Panel of CIBA-GEIGY; chemical engr, FIChemE; *Books* Chemical Reactor Theory (with K G Denbigh, 1971); *Recreations* watching sport, playing golf, choral singing, gardening, philately and antiques; *Style*— Prof Robin Turner; School of Engineering, University of Exeter, Exeter, Devon (☎ 0392 263651, fax 0392 217965, telex 42894 EXUNIV G)

TURNER, Roger Burton; s of Jack Burton Turner, of 18 Compton Fields, Bishops Croft, Ely, Cambridgeshire, and Jean, *née* Trevor; *b* 28 July 1947; *Educ* Hawes Down Co Secdy Sch, King's Coll London (BD, MTH), Univ of London Inst of Educn (PGCE), Univ of Kent (MA); *Career* asst master Ashford GS 1972-77, lectr in new testament studies La Sainte Union Coll of Higher Educn Southampton 1977-80, called to the Bar Gray's Inn 1982, in practice SE Circuit 1983-; memb Ecclesiastical Law Soc; *Recreations* drawing, church history and doctrine, reading; *Clubs* Sion Coll; *Style*— Roger Turner, Esq; 44 Claverton St, London SW1V 3AU (☎ 071 630 6510); 10 Bolt Court, Fleet St, London EC4A 3DB (☎ 071 583 0510, fax 071 583 7770)

TURNER, Lady Rose Mary Sydney; *née* Yorke; da of 9 Earl of Hardwicke; *b* 1951; *Educ* St Mary's Convent Ascot; *m* 1 (m dis), Kenneth Delbray; resumed maiden name of Yorke; m 2, 1981 (m dis 1985), (Herbert) Richard Vaughan (publisher, d 1987); 1 da (Katharine Sarah Tahlita Valour Yorke b 6 June 1985); m 3, 8 Dec 1990, Tony Turner; *Style*— The Lady Rose Turner; Penscoits, Myny Tho, Pwllheli, Gwynedd LL53 7PS (☎ 0758 740384)

TURNER, Wilfred; CMG (1977), CVO (1979); s of Allen Turner (d 1966), and Eliza, *née* Leech (d 1955); *b* 10 Oct 1921; *Educ* Heywood GS, Univ of London (BSc); *m* 26 March 1947, June Gladys, da of Leonard Ham Tite, MBE (d 1983); 2 s (Nicholas Hugh b 1950, Matthew Julian b 1955), 1 da (Harriet Louise Macrae b 1960); *Career* REME: cmmnd 2 Lt 1942, Capt 1945, demobbed 1947; Miny of Lab 1938-60 (asst lab advsr India 1955-59), Miny of Health 1960-66 (sec Ctee of Safety of Drugs 1963-66), HM Dip Serv 1966-81 (Br high cmmr Botswana 1977-81), dir Southern Africa Assoc 1983-88, non exec dir Transmark (BR) 1987-90; memb: Royal Inst of Int Affrs, Royal African Soc, Exec Ctee Zambia Soc, Central Ctee Royal Cwlth Soc; *Recreations* hill walking; *Clubs* Royal Cwlth Soc; *Style*— Wilfred Turner, Esq, CMG, CVO; 44 Tower Rd, Twickenham, Middlesex TW1 4PE (☎ 081 892 1593)

TURNER CAIN, Maj-Gen (George) Robert; CB (1967), CBE (1963), DSO (1944); s of Wing Cdr George Turner Cain (d 1967), and Jesse Mary Smith (d 1927); *b* 16 Feb 1912; *Educ* Norwich Sch, Sandhurst; *m* 1938, Lamorna Maturin, da of Col G B Hingston (ka 1916); 1 s (Michael), 1 da (Rosemary); *Career* gazetted Norfolk Regt 1932, India 1933-38, NW Frontier Waziristan Camp 1937 (despatches), WWII 1 Royal Norfolk and 1 Hereford, BLA 1944-45, BAOR 1945-48, Berlin Airlift 1948, Hong Kong communist China 1953-54, cmd 1 Fed IB Malaya 1957-59, BGS HQ BAOR 1961-64, MGA HQ FARELF 1964-66 (Confrontation of Indonesia), ADC to HM The Queen 1960-64; chm and dir: F & G Smith Ltd Maltsters, Walpole & Wright Ltd, Crisp Maltings Ltd and EDME Ltd, Anglia Maltings Gp (Hldgs) Ltd 1947-82; pres Anglia Maltings (Hldgs) Ltd 1982-; Croix de Guerre avec Palme 1945, Star of Kedah 1959; *Style*— Maj-Gen Robert Turner Cain, CB, CBE, DSO; Holbreck, Hollowlane, Stiffkey, Wells-next-the-Sea, Norfolk NR23 1QG (☎ 0328 830280)

TURNER-OXENHAM, (John) Brent; s of John Eric Turner Oxenham, and Eileen Madge, *née* Maycock; *b* 13 June 1938; *Educ* Kent Coll, Caius Coll Shoreham, Steyning GS; *m* 17 Dec 1971, Sandra Elizabeth, da of Maj Harold Roden, of 5 Promenade Reine Astrid, Menton, France; 2 da (Victoria Elizabeth b 1974, Rebecca Jane b 1976); *Career* independent professional antiques valuer and restorer; *Recreations* travelling, theatre, gardening, Dartmoor, countryside exploration; *Clubs* RAC, CGA; *Style—* John Turner-Oxenham, Esq; Huxbear House, Chudleigh, S Devon TQ13 0NY (☎ 0626 852 948)

TURNER-SAMUELS, David Jessel; QC (1972); s of Moss Turner-Samuels, MP, of London, and Gladys Deborah, *née* Belcher; *b* 5 April 1918; *Educ* Westminster; *m* 5 Nov 1939 (m dis 1976), Norma, da of Philip Verstone, of Worthing (d 1971); 1 s (Michael b 17 Aug 1946), 1 da (Elizabeth b 28 March 1958); m 2, 10 April 1977, Norma Florence, da of George David Shellabear (d 1973), of Devon; *Career* WWII RA 1939-46; barr Middle Temple 1939, bencher Middle Temple, attorney at law Trinidad and Tobago; *Style—* David Turner-Samuels, Esq, QC; Cherry Tree Cottage, Petworth Rd, Haslemere, Surrey GU27 3BG; New Court, Temple, London EL4Y 9BE; Cloister, Temple, London EC4Y 7AA (☎ 071 583 0303, fax 071 583 2254)

TURNER-WARWICK, Prof Dame Margaret Elizabeth Harvey; DBE (1991); da of William Harvey Moore, QC, and Maud Kirkdale, *née* Baden-Powell; *b* 19 Nov 1924; *Educ* City of London, Maynard, St Pauls Sch for Girls, Lady Margaret Hall Oxford (scholar, MA, DM), UCH Univ of London (PhD); *m* 21 Jan 1950, Richard Trevor Turner-Warwick, s of William Turner-Warwick (d 1949); 2 da (Gillian (Mrs Bathe) b 1953, Lynne (Dr Turner-Stokes) b 1955); *Career* conslt physician Elizabeth Garrett Anderson Hosp 1960-67, conslt physician London Chest Hosp and Brompton Hosp 1967, dean of Cardiothoracic Inst 1984-87 (sr lectr 1963-72, prof 1972-87); emeritus prof of med (thoracic) Univ of London; memb Bd of Govrs Nat Heart and Chest Hosps 1971-88, pres Br Thoracic Soc 1982-83, non-exec memb SHA 1990; memb: Systems Bd MRC 1982-85, Senate Univ of London 1983-87, Med Advsy Ctee CORDA 1985-88, Imperial Cancer Res Fund Cncl 1988-, NW Thames RHA 1988-90; chm Asthma Res Cncl 1988-89; memb: Mgmnt Ctee Cardiothoracic Inst, Assoc of Physicians; Hon DSc: Univ of Exeter, Univ of London, NY Univ; RCP: fell 1969, second vice pres 1988 (pres 1989-), FRACP 1983, FRCPEd 1988, FACP 1988, FRCP Canada 1989, FFOM, FFPHM 1990; memb Alpha Omega Alpha (USA) 1988; *Recreations* family and their hobbies, classical music, watercolour painting; *Style—* Prof Dame Margaret Turner-Warwick, DBE; 55 Fitzroy Park, Highgate, London N6; 61 Harley House, Marylebone Road, London NW1 (☎ 071 935 2550)

TURNER-WARWICK, Dr Richard Trevor; s of William Turner-Warwick, FRCS (d 1949), and Dr Joan Margaret Warwick (d 1990); *b* 21 Feb 1925; *Educ* Bedales, Oriel Coll Oxford (pres Boat Club Oxford Crew), Middlesex Hosp (Broderip scholarship); *m* 21 Jan 1950, Prof Dame Margaret Turner Warwick, DBE, PRCP, *qv*, da of W Harvey Moore, QC (d 1965); 2 da (Gillian (Mrs Bathe) b 1953, Lynne (Dr Turner-Stokes) b 1955); *Career* surgn; Hunterian prof RCS 1957 and 1977; conslt surgn Middlesex Hosp 1960, Royal Nat Orthopaedic Hosp 1962, conslt urologist St Peter's Hosp 1964, King Edward VII Hosp for Officers 1964, Royal Prince Alfred Hosp Sydney 1978, Robert Luff Fndn fell in reconstructive urology 1990-, numerous scientific pubns and contrib to urological texts, Freeman City of London, Liveryman Soc of Apothecaries; Hon DSc NY 1985, Hon FRACS 1986; memb: Cncl RCS 1978-92, Cncl RCOG 1990, American Assoc of Genito-Urinary Surgns 1978, FRCS 1957, FACS 1978, fell Aust Urological Soc 1987, FRCP 1987, FRCOG 1990; *Recreations* fishing, gardening, family; *Clubs* Vincent's (Oxford), Leander, The Houghton; *Style—* Dr Richard Turner-Warwick; 61 Harley House, Marylebone Rd, London NW1 (☎ 081 935 2550)

TURNEY, Alan Harry; CB; s of Harry Landrey Turney (d 1951), and Alice Theresa, *née* Bailey; *b* 20 Aug 1932; *Educ* St Albans GS, LSE (BSc Econ); *m* 22 June 1957, Ann Mary, da of George William Dollimore (d 1988); *Career* Home Office 1961-; private sec to Home Sec (Henry Brooke) 1962-64, princ Police, Prison and Gen Depts 1964-76, asst sec Broadcasting Dept 1976-81, Rayner Review of Forensic Sci Service 1981, Criminal and Prison Depts 1981-86, asst under sec of state Fire and Emergency Planning Dept 1986-; sec Hertfordshire RFU 1969-77; *Recreations* rugby union football (now spectating!); *Style—* Alan Turney, Esq, CB; 74 Kimpton Road, Blackmore End, Wheathampstead, Herts AL4 8LX (☎ 0438 832636); Home Office, 50 Queen Anne's Gate, London SW1H 9AT (☎ 071 273 2798)

TURNHAM ELVINS, Rev Mark Anthony Lawrence; s of Rev Stanley William Gordon Elvins (Maj Royal Army Chaplains Dept and former rector of Dover Castle, d 1973), and Eileen Margaret Elvins, *née* Turnham; *b* 26 Nov 1939; *Educ* Dover Coll, Ruskin Sch of Drawing, St Stephen's House Oxford, Beda Coll, Gregorian Univ Rome; *Career* HAC 1962-91, Capt Royal Army Chaplains Dept TA; St James's Gallery Jermyn St 1961, asst ed Debrett's Peerage Ltd 1962-64, reading theology at Oxford and Rome 1965-73, ordained priest Arundel Cathedral 1973 (asst priest and chantry priest to Duke of Norfolk 1973-79); fndr: Assoc for English Worship 1975, St Thomas Fund for the Homeless 1980; opened first hostel for recovering drug misusers Sussex 1986; memb Heraldry Soc; Chaplain of Magistral Obedience SMOM; FAMS; Cdr of Grace the Constantinian Order of St George; *Books* Old Catholic England (1978), Arundel Priory 1390-1980 (1981), The Sussex Martyrs (1983), The Church's Response to the Homeless (1985), Drugs - How the Church Can Help (with Teresa Searle, 1987), Cardinals and Heraldry (1989); *Recreations* historical flights of fancy; *Clubs* Sion College (City Livery); *Style—* The Rev Mark Turnham Elvins; The Priest's House, Tanyard, Henfield, West Sussex BN5 9PE

TURNOR, Maj Anthony Richard; CBE (1973), DL (Wiltshire 1982-); s of Lt-Col Algernon Turnor, MC (d 1930), and Beatrice Mildred Denison (d 1981); *b* 4 Feb 1914; *Educ* Eton, RMC Sandhurst; *m* 6 Oct 1952, Joyce Winifred, da of William James Osborn, of Spinney Green, Little Over, Derby; 1 s (Richard b 1956), 1 da (Carey b 1954); *Career* Kings Royal Rifle Corps 1934, Palestine medal 1936-37, WWII Italy 1943-44, No 2 Army Commando Italy Yugoslavia Albania, wounded 1945, retired 1947; memb Wiltshire CC 1974-81, High Sheriff Wiltshire 1977-78, farmer at Foxley; chm: Malmesbury RDC 1964-69, Chippenham Cons Assoc 1962-65, Wessex Area Cons 1969-72; pres Royal Br Legion Wilts Co 1985-89; *Recreations* shooting, fishing, skiing; *Clubs* Army and Navy; *Style—* Maj Anthony Turnor, CBE, DL; Foxley Manor, Malmesbury, Wiltshire (☎ 0666 824607)

TURNOR, Richard William Corbet; s of Maj Anthony Richard Turnor, CBE, DL, and Joyce Winnifred, *née* Osborn; *b* 15 March 1956; *Educ* Maidwell Hall Sch, Eton, Keble Coll Oxford (BA); *m* 31 Dec 1985, Louisa Mary, da of Andrew Garden Duff Forbes; 1 s (William Michael Francis b 1988), 1 da (Elizabeth Beatrice b 1990); *Career* admitted slr 1980; ptnr Allen & Overy 1985- (joined 1979); memb Law Soc 1981; *Recreations* field sports, skiing, growing trees, conservation; *Clubs* Buck's; *Style—* Richard Turnor, Esq; Messrs Allen & Overy, 9 Cheapside, London EC2V 6AD (☎ 071 248 9898, fax 071 236 2192, telex 8812801)

TURPIN, (James) Alexander; CMG (1966); s of Samuel Alexander Turpin (d 1944), of Dublin, and Marie Louise, *née* Mitchell (d 1921); *b* 7 Jan 1917; *Educ* The King's Hospital Dublin, Trinity Coll Dublin (MA); *m* 1942, Kathleen Iris, da of Thomas Tait Eadie (d 1968), of Co Kerry; 1 da (Alexa); *Career* Royal Irish Fus 1942-46, Capt; HM Foreign (later Dip) Serv 1947; served: Paris, Warsaw, Tokyo, The Hague, New Delhi, Manila; ambass Manila 1972-76; chm Br Philippine Soc 1986-88; *Publications* New Society's Challenge in the Philippines (1980), The Philippines: Problems of the Ageing New Society (1984); *Recreations* music, cookery, wine, tennis, swimming; *Style—* Alexander Turpin, Esq, CMG; 12 Grimwood Rd, Twickenham, Middlesex

TURPIN, Maj-Gen Patrick George; CB (1962), OBE (1943); s of Rev Julian James Turpin, MA, BD (d 1936), Vicar of Misterton Somerset, and Emily Hannah Bryant (d 1960); *b* 27 April 1911; *Educ* Haileybury, Exeter Coll Oxford (BA, MA); *m* 1947, Cherry Leslie Joy, da of Maj Kenneth Sydney Grove (d 1949), of Bleadon, Somerset; 1 s (Richard), 1 da (Annabel); *Career* cmmnd RASC 1933; served WWII: Egypt, Western Desert, Sicily, Italy and Germany; AQMG 30 Corps 1943, AA & QMG 5 Div 1943-44, DA & QMG (Brig) 1 Corps BLA 1945, DAG HQ BAOR 1956-59, Brig 17 Gurkha Div Malaya 1959-60, dir of supplies and tport WO 1960-63, dir of movements MOD 1963-66, psc 1941, jssc 1949, idc 1955, Col Cmdt RCT 1965-71, Col Gurkha Army Serv Corps 1960-65, Col Gurkha Tport Regt 1965-73; sec gen ABTA 1966-69; pres Army Lawn Tennis Assoc 1968-73; govr Royal Sch for Daughters of Officers of the Army Bath 1963-83; FCIT, FRHS; *Recreations* lawn tennis (rep Somerset and Army, Somerset Co Champion 1948), squash rackets (rep Bucks and Army), golf; *Clubs* Oxford Union Soc, All England Lawn Tennis, Int Lawn Tennis, Escorts Squash Rackets; *Style—* Maj-Gen Patrick Turpin, CB, OBE

TURRILL, Hon Mrs (Jean Phyllis); *née* Wise; da of 1 Baron Wise, DL; *b* 11 July 1914; *m* 1939, Lt-Col John Turrill, OBE, TD; 1 s, 2 da; *Style—* The Hon Mrs Turrill; 94 Albert Rd, Caversham, Reading

TURTLE, Dr Mark Jonathan; s of Edgar Ernest Turtle, MBE, of 97 Charlton Lane, Cheltenham, Gloucs, and Kathleen, *née* Furlong; *b* 28 Jan 1952; *Educ* Surbiton Co GS, Univ of London (MB BS, LRCP); *m* 26 May 1979, Lynette Caryn, da of Lewis Malcolm Llewellyn, of Parc Yr Onen, Llwyn Meredydd, Camarthen; *Career* conslt anaesthetist and specialist in chronic pain relief, previously sr registrar Bristol and SW Regn and registrar Salford Manchester; memb: Assoc of Anaesthetists, Pain Soc, Intensive Care Soc, Soc Anaesthetists of Wales; FFARCS 1981, MRCS; *Style—* Dr Mark Turtle; Nant-Y-Grove, Llangynog, Carmarthen, Dyfed SA33 5DE (☎ 0267 211 391); West Wales General Hospital, Camarthen, Dyfed SA31 2AF (☎ 0267 235151)

TURTON, Eugenie Christine (Genie); da of Arthur Turton (d 1973), and Georgina, *née* Fairhurst; *b* 19 Feb 1946; *Educ* Nottingham Girls HS (GPDST), Girton Coll Cambridge (MA); *m* 1, 20 July 1968 (m dis 1972), Richard Lindsay Gordon; m 2, 14 June 1974 (m dis 1978), Gerrard Flanagan; *Career* princ private sec to Sec of State for Tport 1978-80, memb Channel Link Financing Group Midland Bank 1981-82, head of machinery Govt Div Cabinet Office 1982-85, dir heritage and royal estate DOE 1987 (under sec Housing Gp 1986-87), under sec innercities DOE 1990-; non-exec dir Woolwich Building Soc 1987-; FRSA 1986; *Recreations* music, books; *Style—* Miss Genie Turton; DOE, 2 Marsham St, London SW1 (☎ 071 276 3836)

TURTON, Hon Gerald Christopher; s of Baron Tranmire (Life Peer), and Ruby Christian, *née* Scott; *b* 12 May 1937; *Educ* Eton, RAC Cirencester; *m* 1967, Alexandra Susan, da of Lt-Col S Oliver, of Richmond, Yorks; 1 s, 2 da; *Career* farmer; *Style—* The Hon Gerald Turton; Park House, Upsall, Thirsk, N Yorks (☎ 0845 537383)

TURTON, Richard Charles; s of Charles Ernest Turton (d 1978), of Epperstone, Notts, and Aline Audrey Turton (d 1983); *b* 17 Dec 1936; *Educ* Uppingham; *m* 1, 15 Aug 1961 (m dis 1969), Rosemary Margaret, da of Arthur J C Moore, of Uppingham, Rutland; 2 s (Andrew b 20 June 1962, Philip b 6 Feb 1965); m 2, Susan Katharine, da of Capt Edward Norman Allan (d 1944); 1 s (Paul b 29 May 1970); *Career* qualified CA 1961; ptnr: Turton Ross & Co 1961-63, Chamberlain Turton & Dunn 1963-75, Spicer & Oppenheim (formerly Spicer & Pegler) 1975-90, Touche Ross & Co 1990-; chm Insolvency Practitioners Assoc 1975-76, pres Insol International 1985-89; sec Nottingham Glyndebourne Assoc 1967, memb Fin Ctee Glyndebourne 1980-; pres Nottingham Hockey Club 1975-80, memb Cncl ICAEW 1986-90; Freeman City of London, memb Worshipful Co of CAs; FCA 1966, FIPA, MICM; *Books* Meet the Receiver (1985); *Recreations* singing, violin, listening to classical music, gardening, hockey, tennis; *Style—* Richard Turton, Esq; Touche Ross & Co, 1 Woodborough Rd, Nottingham NG1 3FG (☎ 0602 500511, fax 0602 590181, car 0836 610 130, telex 377013 ESANO G)

TURTON-HART, Sir Francis Edmund; KBE (1963, MBE 1942); s of David Edwin Hart (d 1947), of New Hextalls, Bletchingley, Surrey, and Zoe Evelyn Turton (d 1964); *b* 29 May 1908; *Educ* Uppingham; *m* 1947, Margaret Frances Edith, da of Richard Hathorn Greaves (d 1955), of Cairo; 1 da; *Career* Hon Maj E Africa 1924-38, served WWII RE, ME Western Desert, Italy, Nigeria 1947-65; dir: Amalgamated Engrg Co Ltd Nigeria 1949-59, Dorman Long (Nigeria) Ltd 1959-65; memb Nigerian Federal House of Representatives 1956-60, pres Lagos C of C 1960-63; *Recreations* shooting, golf; *Clubs* Thurlestone Golf (pres); *Style—* Sir Francis Turton-Hart, KBE; 28 Vincent Rd, Kingsbridge, Devon TQ7 1RP (☎ 0548 2872)

TURVEY, Garry; s of Henry Oxley Turvey (d 1981), and Annie Maude, *née* Braley; *b* 11 Oct 1934; *Educ* Morecambe GS, Manchester Business Sch; *m* 11 June 1960, Hilary Margaret, da of Walter Saines; 3 s (Ian Michael b 1961, Peter Geoffrey b 1964, David Mark b 1965); *Career* Nat Serv RAF 1954-56; sec Traders Rd Tport Assoc 1966-68 (asst sec 1960-66); Freight Tport Assoc: sec 1969-74, dep dir gen 1974-83, dir gen 1984-; FCIS 1959, FCIT 1983, FILDM 1988; *Recreations* cricket, gardening; *Clubs* RAC; *Style—* Garry Turvey, Esq; 139 Imberhorne Lane, E Grinstead, W Sussex RH19 1RD (☎ 0342 325829); Freight Transport Association Ltd, Hermes House, St Johns Rd, Tunbridge Wells, Kent (☎ 0892 26171, fax 0892 34989, telex 957158, car 0836 591581)

TURVEY, Peter James; s of Douglas Ronald Turvey, of Croydon, and Kathleen Mildred, *née* Smith; *b* 9 May 1943; *Educ* Whitgift Sch, Brasenose Coll Oxford (MA); *m* 23 Oct 1965, (Norah) Louise, da of Dr Peter O'Flynn, of Croydon; 1 s (Andrew b 1968), 3 da (Marie-Louise b 1967, Caroline b 1972, Fiona b 1975); *Career* asst gen mangr Swiss Re (UK) 1972-87, princ Mercer Fraser 1987-; vice pres Inst of Actuaries 1988-91 (hon sec 1984-86), chm Staple Inn Actuarial Soc 1988-90; chm Croydon HS Scholarship Tst; Master Co of Actuaries 1990-91; FIA 1968; *Recreations* jogging, skiing, windsurfing, bridge; *Style—* Peter Turvey, Esq; William M Mercer Fraser Ltd, Telford House, 14 Tothill St, London SW1H 9NB (☎ 071 222 9121, fax 071 799 2449, telex 8813544)

TURVILL, Peter Barry; s of William Herbert Turvill (d 1988), of Worthing, W Sussex, and Evelyn Margaret, *née* Kennard (d 1970); *b* 16 Aug 1945; *Educ* Kingsway Coll London; *m* 8 April 1972, Jane Alexandra, da of Alexander John Langley, of Yapton, Sussex; 2 da (Joanne b 1976, Caroline b 1979); *Career* accountant; fin dir R A Marshall Ltd 1972-; *Recreations* charitable activities, reading, music; *Style—* Peter B Turvill, Esq; 127 Clarence Avenue, Clapham Park, London SW4 8LX (☎ 081 674 1756); Century House, 33 Station Road, London SE25 5AH (☎ 081 771 5119)

TURVILLE CONSTABLE-MAXWELL, Robert John; s of David Turville Constable-Maxwell (d 1985), and Mary Alethea Elizabeth Evelyn; *b* 4 Oct 1933; *Educ* Ampleforth; *m* 23 April 1960, Susan Mary, da of Stephen Francis Gaisford St Lawrence (d 1957), of Howth Castle, Co Dublin; 2 s (Anthony Nicholas b 1961, Stephen Bernard b 1963), 1 da (Alice Marion b 1969); *Career* Lt Grenadier Gds 1952-

54; Allied Lyons 1956-84, underwriting memb Lloyds; vice chm Harborough Cons Assoc, pres Husbands Bosworth Sheepdog Trial Assoc, ctee memb local CLA; High Sheriff Leicestershire 1991-92; Freeman City of London 1975, memb Brewers Court; *Recreations* golf, shooting, tennis; *Clubs* Cavalry & Guards, Pratts; *Style—* Robert Turville Constable-Maxwell, Esq; Bosworth Hall, Husbands Bosworth, Nr Lutterworth, Leics LE15 7LZ (☎ 0858 880 730); Brewing Products, The Malt Extract Factory, Kirkliston, West Lothian EH29 9DN (☎ 031 333 3261)

TUSA, John; s of John Tusa, OBE, of Dorset, and Lydia, *née* Sklenarova; *b* 2 March 1936; *Educ* Gresham's, Trinity Coll Cambridge (BA); *m* 1960, Ann Hilary, da of Stanley Dowson, of Lancs; 2 s (John, James); *Career* presenter: Newsnight BBC 2 1980-86, Timewatch BBC 2 1982-84; md BBC World Service 1986-; Royal Television Soc Journalist of the Year 1984, BAFTA Richard Dimbleby Award 1984; tstee Nat Portrait Gallery; *Books* The Nuremberg Trial (co-author with Ann Tusa, 1984), The Berlin Blockade (co-author with Ann Tusa, 1988), Conversations with the World (1990); *Recreations* squash, tennis, opera, music; *Clubs* United Oxford and Cambridge Univ; *Style—* John Tusa, Esq; 21 Christchurch Hill, London NW3 1JY (☎ 071 435 9495)

TUSHINGHAM, Rita; da of John Tushingham, of Liverpool, and Enid Ellen, *née* Lott; *b* 14 March 1942; *Educ* La Sagesse Convent Liverpool; *m* 1, 1 Dec 1962 (m dis 1976), Terence William Bicknell; 2 da (Dodonna b 1 May 1964, Aisha b 16 June 1971); m 2, 27 Aug 1981, Ousama Rawi, s of Najib El-Rawi, of Geneva, Switzerland; *Career* actress; began career Liverpool Repertory Theatre 1958, first film A Taste of Honey 1961 (Best Actress Cannes Film Festival), New York Film Critics Award, Golden Globe Award); other films incl: Gin with Green Eyes 1965 (Best Actress Variety Club of GB), The Knack 1965 (Best Actress Mexican Film Festival), Doctor Zhivago 1966, The Trap 1967, The Guru 1968, Bedsitting Room 1969, A Judgement in Stone 1986, Resurrected 1988, Hard Days Hard Nights 1989; tv incl: Bread 1988, Dante and Beatrice in Liverpool 1989, Sunday Pursuit 1990; *Recreations* incl care and protection of animals, cooking, painting, gardening; *Style—* Miss Rita Tushingham; c/o Michael Anderson, ICM, 388 Oxford St, London WIN 9HE (☎ 081 885 974)

TUTIN, Dorothy; CBE (1967); da of John Tutin, and Ada Evelyn Friars; *b* 8 April 1930; *Educ* St Catherine's Bramley, RADA (Dip); *m* 1964, Derek Barton-Chapple (stage name Derek Waring), s of Wing Cdr Harry John Barton-Chapple; 1 s (Nicholas b 1966), 1 da (Amanda b 1965); *Career* stage and film actress; began stage career 1959; stage rôles incl: many Shakespearian parts, Sally Bowles in I am a Camera; film rôles incl: Polly Peachum in The Beggar's Opera, Cecily in The Importance of Being Earnest, Lucie Manette in A Tale of Two Cities, Sophie Breslea in Savage Messiah, The Shooting Party; Variety Club of Gt Britain Film Actress Award 1972; *Style—* Miss Dorothy Tutin, CBE; c/o Michael Whitehall, 125 Gloucester Rd, London SW7 4TE

TUTT, Leo Edward; s of Leo Edward Tutt (d 1975), of Sydney, NSW, Australia, and Dorothy, *née* M C Adam (d 1985); *b* 6 April 1938; *Educ* Knox GS NSW Aust; *m* 21 Oct 1961, Heather Elphistone, da of Charles Walter Coombe (d 1965), of Sydney, NSW, Australia; 2 s (Leo, James), 1 da (Katie); *Career* CA in pub practice 1966-73, jt md Tutt Bryant Ltd 1973-74, dir and chief exec Escor Ltd 1974-78; non-exec dir Friends Provident Life Office 1987-, chief exec Bowater plc 1978-, chm and chief Bowater Industries Australia 1974-, non-exec dep chm Bundaberg Sugar Company Limited (Aust Listed Co) 1984-; dir: State Rail Authy NSW 1989-, The Graduate Sch of Mgmnt and Pub Policy Fndn, Univ of Sydney 1989; FCA 1966, FAIM 1966; *Recreations* sailing, golf; *Clubs* American, Avondale Golf, Elanora Country, Royal Prince Alfred Yacht, Royal Sydney Yacht Squadron; *Style—* Leo Tutt, Esq; Sedlescombe, 9a Arterial Rd, St Ives, NSW 2075, Australia; Bay Cottage, 36 Hudson Pde, Clareville Beach, NSW 2071, Australia (☎ 010 61 2 440 8171, 010 61 2 918 8513); Bowater Industries Australia Limited, Level 13, 131 Macquarie St, Sydney, NSW 2000, Australia (☎ 010 61 2 251 6133, fax 010 61 2 251 1065)

TUTT, Dr Leslie William Godfrey; s of Charles Leslie Tutt, of London, and Emily Ditcham, *née* Wiseman; *b* 13 Oct 1921; *Educ* RMC of Sci (pac), Univ of London (MSc, PhD); *Career* RA 1940-46, Maj SO 1944; actuary and mathematical statistician in private practice; lectr; writer; contrib numerous res papers and tech articles to actuarial, statistical and fin jls 1950-; Inst of Statisticians: memb Cncl 1968-74 and 1975-81, vice chm 1981-84, chm 1984-87, vice pres 1987-; memb: Exec Ctee Pensions Res Accountants Gp 1976-85, Cncl Nat Assoc Pension Funds 1979-83, Bd of Examiners Faculty of Actuaries 1980-90 (Cncl 1975-78); examinations assessor CII 1980-; Liveryman: Worshipful Co of Loriners 1975, Worshipful Co of Actuaries 1979; FFA 1949, FSS 1951, FIS 1951, assoc Soc of Actuaries USA 1968, FPMI 1976; *Books* Private Pension Scheme Finance (1970), Pension Schemes, Investment, Communications and Overseas Aspects (1977), Pension Law and Taxation (1985), Financial Aspects of Pension Business (1986), Financial Aspects of Life Business (1987), Financial Services Marketing and Investor Protection (1988), Life Assurance (1988), Pensions (1988), Financial Advisers' Competence Test (jtly, 1989), Taxation and Trusts (1990), Personal Investment Planning (1990), Corporate Investment Planning (1991); *Recreations* running, riding the cresta run, bobsleighing, golf; *Clubs* Athenaeum, City Livery, New (Edinburgh); *Style—* Dr L W G Tutt; 21 Sandilands, Croydon, Surrey CR0 5DF (☎ 081 654 2995)

TUTT, Penny; da of Frank Robert Pennell (d 1945), and Edith May, *née* Bingham; *b* 23 March 1925; *Educ* King Edward VI HS for Girls Birmingham; *m* 24 Aug 1956 (m dis 1986), Norman Leslie Tutt, s of George Tutt (d 1964), of Ealing, London; 1 s (Simon b 19 Feb 1960), 1 da (Sarah b 30 Sept 1962); *Career* Midland Bank 1943-46, Nat Cncl of Soc Servs 1946-49, Sigmund Pumps 1949-50, winner Britain's Perfect Air Girl Award 1950 (travelled Aust, featured on radio and tv), passenger relations offr BOAC 1953-59 (air hostess 1950-53); FI Gp 1969-90: PA to fndr, co sec, mangr, exec dir to subsids, dir Community Relations; fndr chm: tstees Women into Information Technol, National Employers Advsy Cncl Apex Tst; memb: Commerce/Indust Liaison Ctee Royal Jubilee Tst 1987-89, Exec Ctee Industl Soc 1988-89, Business in the Community, Women into Econ Devpt Initiative 1988-90 (conslt 1990-); MBIM 1981, AMJI 1983; *Recreations* family, talking with people; *Style—* Mrs Penny Tutt; Arrow Hills, Bittell Farm, Barnt Green, Worcestershire B45 8BP

TUTT, Sylvia Irene Maud; da of Charles Leslie Tutt, of London, and Emily Ditcham, *née* Wiseman; *Career* chartered sec and admin in private practice; author of numerous technical articles in professional and financial journals 1956-; Inst of Chartered Secs and Admins: memb Benevolent Fund Mgmnt Ctee 1975-, memb Cncl 1975-76 and 1980-82, memb Educn Ctee 1980-82, memb Pubns and PR Ctee 1980-82, rep memb Crossways Tst 1977-, pres Women's Soc 1975-76 (memb Ctee 1968-71 and 1976-87, hon sec 1971-74, vice pres 1973-75), chm London Branch 1984-85 (memb Ctee 1974-82 and 1985-87, vice chm 1982-84); sr examiner CII 1975-, pres Soroptimist Int of Central London 1976-78 (vice pres 1974-76); Liveryman Worshipful Co of Scriveners 1978, Freeman Guild of Freemen City of London 1976; Worshipful Co of Chartered Secs and Admins: Liveryman 1977, memb Ct of Assts 1977-, jr Warden 1981-82, sr Warden 1982-83, Master 1983-84; managing tstee Charitable Tst 1978-; ACIS 1956, FRSA 1983; *Books* Private Pension Scheme Finance (jtly, 1970), Pensions and Employee Benefits (contrib, 1973), Pension Law and Taxation (jtly, 1985), Financial Aspects of Pension Business (jtly, 1986), Financial Aspects of Life Business (jtly, 1987), A Mastership of a Livery Company (1988), Financial Aspects of Long Term Business (1991); *Recreations* horse riding, golf, winter sports; *Clubs* City Livery, Royal Over-Seas League; *Style—* Miss Sylvia I M Tutt; 21 Sandilands, Croydon, Surrey CRO 5DF(☎ 081 654 2995)

TUZO, Gen Sir Harry Craufurd; GCB (1973, KCB 1971), OBE (1961), MC (1945), DL (Norfolk 1983); s of John Tuzo, and Annie, *née* Craufurd; *b* 26 Aug 1917; *Educ* Wellington, Oriel Coll Oxford (MA); *m* 1943, Monica Salter; 1 da; *Career* WWII RA, on staff Far East 1946-49, RHA, Staff Sch Inf, GSO1 WO, Cdr 51 Gurkha Bde, IDC, COS BAOR 1967-69, dir RA 1969-71, GOC and dir of ops NI 1971-73, Gen 1973, cdr N Army Gp and C-in-C BAOR 1973-76, Dep Supreme Allied Cdr Europe 1976-78, ADC Gen to HM The Queen 1974-77; Col Cmdt RA 1971-83, and RHA 1976-83; chm: Royal Utd Servs Inst 1980-83, Marconi Space and Def Systems 1976-83; master gunner St James's Park 1977-83; hon fell Oriel Coll Oxford; memb Cncl of Inst for Study of Conflict; govr Wellington Coll 1977-87; chm: King's Lynn Festival and Fermoy Centre 1982-87, Pensthorpe Wildfowl Tst 1986-; pres Norfolk Soc 1987-; *Clubs* Army and Navy; *Style—* Gen Sir Harry Tuzo, GCB, OBE, MC, DL; c/o Army and Navy Club, Pall Mall, London SW1 1JJ

TWEED, Jill (Mrs Hicks); da of late Maj Jack Robert Lowrie Tweed, and Kathleen Janie, *née* Freeth; *b* 7 Dec 1935; *Educ* Slade Sch of Art (BA); *m* Philip Lionel Sholto Hicks, s of Brig P Hicks; 1 s (David b 1971), 1 da (Nicola b 1960); *Career* sculptor; solo and gp exhibitions incl: New Grafton Gallery 1975, Royal Acad 1979, Embankment Gallery 1979, Poole-Willis Gallery NYC 1984, Barbican Centre 1990, Flowers East Gallery 1991; cmmns incl: HM Queen Elizabeth Queen Mother 1980, HRH Prince Charles and Lady Diana Spencer 1981, HE The Governor of Guernsey; ARBS; *Recreations* horse riding; *Style—* Ms Jill Tweed; 15 Cleveland Rd, Barnes, London SW13 0AA (☎ 081 876 7889)

TWEED, (David) John; s of William Tweed (d 1989), and Margaret, *née* Gittus (d 1984); *b* 14 Dec 1946; *Educ* The King's Sch Chester, Univ of Manchester (BA, BArch); *m* 26 April 1980, Helen Elspeth Hamilton, da of Dr Frank Hamilton-Leckie, MC, TD, of Monklands, Uddingston, Glasgow; 1 da (Hilary b 1986); *Career* founded John Tweed Assocs Architects Chester; memb Cncl: RIBA NW Region 1983-87, Chester Sports and Leisure Assoc 1984-; chm Mgmnt Ctee Claverton Ct Chester 1985-, pres Cheshire Soc of Architects 1985-86; memb Cncl: The Architects Benevolent Soc 1986-, Chester Civic Tst 1986, Info and Interpretation Gp and memb Steering Ctee Presenting Chester; memb: RIBA NW Educn Ctee 1987-, Bd Chester Historic Bldgs Preservation Tst 1987-; RIBA 1974, ACIArb 1983; *Recreations* rowing, sailing, squash, boatbuilding; *Style—* D John Tweed, Esq; Ivy House, Hob Hill, Tilston, nr Malpas, Cheshire SX14 7DU (☎ 0829 250301); Duncraig House, Salen, Argyll; Tweed Nuttal Partnership, Chapel House, City Road, Chester CH1 3AE (☎ 0244 310388, fax 0244 325643)

TWEEDIE, Prof David Philip; s of Aidrian Ian Tweedie, of Doncaster, and Marie Patricia, *née* Phillips; *b* 7 July 1944; *Educ* Grangemouth HS, Univ of Edinburgh (BCom, PhD); *m* 6 June 1970, Janice Christine, da of George Haddow Brown; 2 s (Ross Steven b 10 June 1976, Mark David b 25 May 1977); *Career* apprentice and qualified asst Mann Judd Gordon & Co Chartered Accountants Glasgow 1969-72; Univ of Edinburgh: lectr Dept of Accounting and Business Methods 1973-78, dir of studies 1973-75, assoc dean Faculty of Social Scis 1975-78; tech dir Inst of Chartered Accountants in Scotland 1978-91, nat res ptnr KMG Thomson McLintock 1982-87, nat tech ptnr Peat Marwick McLintock 1987-90; chm Accounting Standards Bd 1990- (ex officio memb Fin Reporting Cncl); Univ of Lancaster: visiting prof of accounting Int Centre for Res in Accounting (ICRA) 1978-88, tstee ICRA 1982-, dep chm Bd of Tstees ICRA 1986-; visiting prof of accounting Dept of Economics Univ of Bristol 1988-; memb Cncl ICAEW 1989 (memb Auditing Res Fndn 1988-90), chm CCAB Auditing Practices Ctee 1989-90 (vice chm 1986-88, memb 1985-90), UK and Irish rep Int Auditing Practices Ctee 1983-88, UK and Irish tech advsr International Accounting Standards Ctee 1979-81; *Books* The Private Shareholder & the Corporate Report ICAEW (with TA Lee, 1977), Financial Reporting Inflation and The Capital Maintenance Concept ICRA (1979), The Institutional Investor & Financial Information ICAEW (with TA Lee, 1981), The Debate on Inflation Accounting (with G Whittington, 1984); *Style—* Prof David Tweedie; Accounting Standards Board, Holborn Hall, 100 Gray's Inn Rd, London WC1X 8AL (☎ 071 404 8818, fax 071 404 4497)

TWEEDIE, James Hamilton; s of George Carrick Tweedie (d 1978), of Anchor Farm, Little Ellingham, Norfolk, and Gladys Mary, *née* Telford; *b* 31 March 1950; *Educ* Loughborough Coll, Bart's (BSc, MB BS, MS); *m* 17 Feb 1973, Julia Evelyn, da of Eric Raymond Workman, of Gloucester; 1 s (George b 1973), 1 da (Juliette b 1975); *Career* conslt surgn Stoke Mandeville Hosp; memb: BMA, RSM; FRCS Ed, FRCS; *Recreations* golf, skiing; *Clubs* Grey Turner Surgical; *Style—* James Tweedie, Esq; Loosley House, Loosley Row, Bucks HP17 0PF (☎ 08444 6819); Stoke Mandeville Hospital, Aylesbury, Bucks (☎ 0296 84111)

TWEEDIE, Hon Mrs (Prudence Mary); *née* Addington; er da of 6 Viscount Sidmouth; *b* 11 June 1916; *m* 1 July 1939, Lt Cdr Hugo Edward Forbes Tweedie, DSC, RN (d 1986), s of late Adm Sir Hugh Tweedie, KCB; 4 s, 3 da; *Style—* The Hon Mrs Tweedie; 14 Fernbank, St Stephen's Rd, Bournemouth BH2 6JP

TWEEDIE-SMITH, John Ian; s of Leslie Tweedie-Smith; *b* 17 Feb 1929; *Educ* Stowe; *m* 1954, Gillian Mary; 4 c; *Career* co dir; memb London CC 1961-65; md Rawlplug Co Ltd 1968-73, chm E H Mundy & Co Ltd 1977- (gp md 1973-75); *Recreations* swimming, golf; *Style—* John Tweedie-Smith, Esq; c/o EH Mundy & Co Ltd, 2 City Business Centre, Basin Rd, Chichester, West Sussex PO19 2DU

TWEEDSMUIR, 2 Baron (UK 1935); John Norman Stuart Buchan; CBE (1964, OBE 1945), CD (1964); s of 1 Baron Tweedsmuir, GCMG, GCVO, CH, sometime Govr-Gen Canada (the writer John Buchan, d 1940) and Susan Charlotte (d 1977), da of Hon Norman Grosvenor (s of 1 Baron Ebury); *b* 25 Nov 1911; *Educ* Eton, BNC Oxford; *m* 1, 1948, Priscilla Jean Fortescue (later Baroness Tweedsmuir of Belhelvie, PC; d 1978); 1 da; m 2, 1980, Jean Margharita, da of late Capt Humphrey Douglas Tollemache, RN (gs of 1 Baron Tollemache), and widow of Capt Sir Francis Cullen Grant, 12 Bt; *Heir* bro, Hon William De L'Aigle Buchan; *Career* late Lt-Col Canadian Infantry Corps; HM Colonial Serv Uganda 1934-36; rector Univ of Aberdeen 1948-51; chm Jt East and Central African Bd 1950-52, UK delegate UN Assembly 1951-52, Council of Europe 1952, pres Cwlth and British Empire Chambers of Commerce 1955-57, warden Neidpath Castle 1958; govr: Cwlth Inst 1958-77 (tstee 1977-), Ditchley Fndn; pres: Inst of Rural Life at Home and Overseas 1951-84, London branch Oxford Soc, Inst of Export 1964-67, British Schs Exploring Soc 1964-85; chm: Advertising Standards Authy 1971-74, Cncl on Tbnls 1973-80, British Rheumatism and Arthritis Assoc 1971-78 (pres 1978-), West End bd Sun Alliance Insurance plc; Hon LLD: Aberdeen, Queen's (Canada); FRSA, FRSE; *Recreations* fishing, forestry; *Clubs* Carlton, Travellers', Flyfishers'; *Style—* The Rt Hon the Lord Tweedsmuir, CBE, CD; Kingston House, Kingston Bagpuize, Oxon (☎ 0865 820259)

TWEEDY, Colin David; s of Clifford Harry Tweedy, of Abbotsbury, Dorset, and Kitty Audrey, *née* Matthews; *b* 26 Oct 1953; *Educ* City of Bath Boys Sch, St Catherine's Coll Oxford (MA); *Career* mangr Thorndike Theatre Leatherhead 1976-78, corp fin offr Guinness Mahon 1978-80, asst dir Streets Financial PR 1980-83, DG Assoc for

Business Sponsorship of the Arts 1983-; memb: UK Nat Ctee Euro Cinema and TV Year 1988-89, Cncl Japan Festival 1991; dir Oxford Stage Co, tstee Crusaid; Freeman City of London 1978; FSA; *Books* A Celebration of Ten Years' Business Sponsorship of the Arts (1987); *Clubs* Utd Oxford and Cambridge Univ; *Style—* Colin Tweedy, Esq, FSA; 60 Gainsford St, Butlers Wharf, London SE1 2NY (☎ 071 378 8143)

TWEEDY, Brig (Oliver) Robert; s of Cdr G J D Tweedy, OBE, RN (d 1969), and V E Maurice (d 1984); *b* 4 Feb 1930; *Educ* Sedbergh, RMA Sandhurst; *m* 11 Aug 1956, April Dawn, da of E T Berrangé; 2 s (Christopher b 1962, Andrew b 1964), 1 da (Sareth b 1959); *Career* cmmnd The Black Watch 1949; CO 1 BW Scotland, N Ireland and Hong Kong 1971-73; cdr British Advsy Team Nigeria 1980-82; cdr 51 Highland Brigade 1982-84; ADC to HM The Queen 1983-85, ret 1985; *Recreations* golf, country pursuits; *Style—* Brig Robert Tweedy; Inverbraan, Little Dunkeld, Perthshire PH8 0AD; Commandant, Queen Victoria Sch, Dunblane, Perthshire FK15 0JY

TWELVETREES, Hon Mrs (Catherine Simonne); *née* du Parcq; da of late Baron du Parcq (Life Peer); *m* 1939, Leslie Twelvetrees; children; *Style—* The Hon Mrs Twelvetrees; 14 Overdale Rd, Leicester

TWEMLOW, William Antony (Tony); s of Richard Lawrence Twemlow, of West Kirby, Wirral, and Sylvia Doreen Twemlow; *b* 2 Dec 1943; *Educ* Calday Grange GS, Downing Coll Cambridge (MA); *m* 12 Oct 1968, Margaret, da of William Thompson Scollay (d 1979); 2 s (Roy William b 15 Dec 1971, James Antony b 28 Sept 1982), 1 da (Laura Jane b 6 July 1973); *Career* Cuff Roberts: articled clerk 1965-68, asst slr 1968-71, ptnr 1971-, managing ptnr 1986-; licensed insolvency practitioner 1987; chm: Liverpool Young Slrs Gp 1969-70, Young Slrs Gp Law Soc 1978-79, Liverpool Bd of Legal Studies 1988-; dir Slrs Benevolent Assoc 1980-, memb Remuneration and Practice Devpt Ctee Law Soc 1980-; memb Royal Liverpool Philharmonic Choir 1965-, dep vice chm Royal Liverpool Philharmonic Soc 1988- (memb Bd 1986-); dir Hoylake Cottage Hosp Tst Ltd 1989-; memb: Law Soc 1968, Liverpool Law Soc 1968, Insolvency Lawyers Assoc 1989, Insolvency Practitioners Assoc 1990; *Recreations* music, tennis; *Clubs* Lyceum (Liverpool); *Style—* Tony Twemlow, Esq; 10 Eddisbury Road, West Kirby, Wirral, Merseyside L48 5DS (☎ 051 632 2545); Cuff Roberts, 100 Old Hall Street, Liverpool L3 9TD (☎ 051 227 4181, fax 051 227 2584)

TWIGG, David Joseph; s of John Twigg (d 1960), of Tothby Manor, Lincs, and Edith Mary, *née* Waterfield (d 1982); *b* 7 March 1934; *Educ* Queen Elizabeth's Sch Lincs; *m* 1, 9 May 1970 (m dis 1987), Hilary Ann, da of Maj Ronald Hedley Vickers (d 1977), of Gloucester; m 2, 15 July 1988, Nina, da of Ivan Prokopenko, of Moscow; *Career* Nat Serv RE 1958-60, serving Mil Engrg Experimental Estab Christchurch and No 1 Bomb Disposal Unit; civil engr Lincs and Bucks CC 1953-62, sr civil engr Huntingdonshire CC 1962-65, sr appts with consulting engrs 1965-70; ptnr: Donovan H Lee and Ptnrs Consulting Engrs 1970-79, The Henderson Busby Partnership Consulting Engrs (dir) 1979-82; fndr and sr ptnr: David Twigg Assocs 1983-, DTA Transportation Consulting Engrs and Planners 1987-; co-fndr Twigg Graham Rail; chm Merton Community Rels Cncl 1983; various offices Kingston Lib Assoc 1976-88, Lib Dem cncllr Kingston upon Thames 1990; Parly candididate Wimbledon: (Lib) 1979, (Alliance) 1983; contested London SW Euro Seat 1984; CEng 1963, FICE 1973, FIHT 1968, MCONSE 1986; *Recreations* tennis, cricket, history; *Clubs* Nat Lib; *Style—* David Twigg, Esq; 87 Blenheim Gardens, Kingston upon Thames, Surrey KT2 7BJ (☎ 081 549 3690); 91 East Hill, Wandsworth, London SW18 2QD (☎ 081 874 0834/3291, fax 081 877 1390)

TWIGG, Dr Graham Ira; s of John Twigg (d 1938), of Moscar, Derbyshire, and Lois, *née* Dearden (d 1975); *b* 15 Nov 1927; *Educ* Lady Manners Sch Bakewell, Univ of Sheffield (BSc, PhD); *m* 29 Sept 1956, Mary Elizabeth, da of John William Hancock (d 1956), of Burrs Mount, Great Hucklow; 1 s (Dr John David Twigg); *Career* RAF 1945-48; colonial rodent liaison offr Colonial Office 1958-59, lectr Univ of London 1959-; former sec and capt Royal Ascot Cricket Club; FZS 1960; *Books* The Brown Rat (1975), The Black Death: A Biological Reappraisal (1984); *Style—* Dr Graham Twigg; 6 Wentworth Way, Ascot, Berks SL5 8HU (☎ 0344 884442); Dept of Biology, Royal Holloway & Bedford New College, Egham, Surrey (☎ 0784 335553)

TWIGG, Patrick Alan; QC (1986); s of Alan Oswald Twigg, of W Linton, Scotland, and Gwendoline Mary, *née* Slocock; *b* 19 May 1943; *Educ* Repton, The Sorbonne, Pernjia Univ Italy, Univ of Bristol (LLB), Univ of Virginia (scholar, LLM); *m* 24 July 1974, Gabrielle Madeline Bay, da of Anthony Green; 1 s (Henry Matthew Edmund b 25 July 1983), 1 da (Venetia Madeline (twin) b 25 July 1983); *Career* called to the Bar Inner Temple (maj scholar) 1967, rec 1987, practice specialising in commercial and construction law UK and abroad 1987-; memb Western Circuit; memb: Old Stagers 1970-, Bd of the Canterbury Festival; vice pres Friends of the Canterbury Festival, pres Bishops Borne CC; *Recreations* family, house, planting trees, music, composition, amateur dramatics, piano, landscape gardening; *Clubs* Delta Theta Phi Fraternity; *Style—* Patrick Twigg, Esq, QC; 1st Floor, 2 Temple Gardens, Temple, London EC4Y 9AY (☎ 071 583 6041, fax 071 583 2094)

TWINCH, Richard William; s of Richard Herbert Twinch, of Burleydam House, Burleydam, Whitchurch, Salop, and Roma Bayliss, *née* Silver; *b* 29 Oct 1950; *Educ* Wellington, Clare Coll Cambridge (MA, Architectural Assoc AADip); *m* Hazel Cecilia, da of James Herbert Merrison (d 1987); 1 s (Oliver b 1975), 2 da (Jemila b 1977, Anna b 1981); *Career* architect and special technol conslt; author of tech software for architects incl: Condensation Control 1981-90, Heat Loss Performance 1983-90; dir: Richard Twinch Design, Chisholme Inst Beshara Sch of Esoteric Educn; commentator to Beshara Magazine, lectr and consit in CAD; MA external examiner Visual and Traditional Arts Unit RCA 1990; computer columnist to Building Design and Atrium magazines, author of numerous articles on CAD in architectural press, papers incl Thermal Insulation and Condensation and Building Materials (1988); RIBA; *Recreations* listening to music, walking, tennis; *Style—* Richard Twinch, Esq; 9 Redan St, Ipswich, Suffolk IP1 3PQ (☎ 0473 254605/210001)

TWINING, Hon John Peter; s of Baron Twining (Life Peer d 1967); *b* 8 June 1929; *Educ* Charterhouse, BNC Oxford; *m* 1954, Mary Avice, da of Brig Joseph Hector Dealy Bennett, CBE (d 1979); 2 s; *Career* Colonial Serv 1953-63; admin offr City & Guilds of London Inst 1963-78, chm Guildford Educnl Servs; ed: EDUCA, Open Learning for Technicians (1982); *Style—* The Hon John Twining; 3 The Ridgeway, Guildford, Surrey

TWINING, Prof William Lawrence; s of Baron Twining (Life Peer d 1967); *b* 1934; *Educ* Charterhouse, BNC Oxford, Chicago Univ (JD, LLD, DCL); *m* 1957, Penelope Elizabeth, da of Richard Wall Morris; 1 s, 1 da; *Career* prof of jurisprudence Queen's Univ Belfast 1965-72, prof of law Univ of Warwick 1972-82, Quain prof of jurisprudence UCL 1983-; pres Soc of Public Teachers of Law 1978-79, chm Cwlth Legal Educn Assoc 1983-; *Books* Karl Llewellyn and the Realist Movement (1973), How to do Things with Rules (2 edn, with David Miers, 1982), Theories of Evidence: Bentham & Wigmore (1985), Rethinking Evidence (1990); *Style—* Prof William Twining; 10 Mill Lane, Iffley, Oxford OX4 4EJ

TWINN, Dr Ian David; MP (C) Edmonton 1983-; s of David Twinn, of Cambridge, and Gwynneth Irene, *née* Ellis; *b* 26 April 1950; *Educ* Netherhall Secdy Mod Sch Cambridge, Cambridge GS, Univ Coll of Wales Aberystwyth, Univ of Reading (BA, PhD); *m* 28 July 1973, Frances Elizabeth, da of Godfrey Nall Holtby (d 1988), of Poltesco, Cornwall; 2 s (David b 1983, John b 1986); *Career* sr lectr in town planning Poly of the South Bank 1975-83; PPS to: Rt Hon Sir Peter Morrison, MP 1985-90, David Trippier, MP 1990-; jt chm Br Parly Lighting Gp, hon sec all-party Parly Greek Ctee; Freeman of City of London 1981; MIBG 1972, FRSA 1989; *Recreations* antique furniture restoration, collecting second-hand books, bookcase building; *Style—* Dr Ian Twinn, MP; House of Commons, London SW1A 0AA (☎ 071 219 3000)

TWISK, Russell Godfrey; s of K Y Twisk, of Twisk, Holland, and Joyce, *née* Brunning; *b* 24 Aug 1941; *Educ* Salesian Coll Farnborough; *m* 1965, Ellen Elizabeth Bambury; 2 da; *Career* Harmsworth Press: dep ed Golf Illustrated 1960, sub ed Sphere; freelance journalist 1962; BBC: joined Editorial Staff Radio Times 1966, dep ed Radio Times 1971, devpt mangr 1975, ed The Listener 1981-87, ed numerous BBC pubns; ed in chief British Reader's Digest 1988-; dir: The Reader's Digest Assoc Ltd 1989-, Berkeley Magazines Ltd 1990-; radio critic The Observer 1989, publisher BBC Adult Literacy Project, deviser Radio Times Drama Awards; govr London Coll of Printing 1967-87 (chm 1974 and 1978); chm: The Reader's Digest Tst 1988, Br Soc of Magazine Eds 1989, Nat Leadership Ctee Charities Aid Fndn 1991; memb Advsy Cncl ASH 1989-, vice pres Media Soc 1991-; *Recreations* running, map reading; *Clubs* Reform, Groucho; *Style—* Russell Twisk, Esq

TWISLETON-WYKEHAM-FIENNES *see also*: Fiennes

TWISLETON-WYKEHAM-FIENNES, Audrey, Lady; Audrey Joan; da of Sir Percy Wilson Newson, 1 and last Bt; sis of Dowager Lady Napier and Ettrick; *b* 21 July 1912; *Educ* Heathfield; *m* 1931, Lt-Col Sir Ranulph Twisleton-Wykeham-Fiennes, 2 Bt, DSO (d of wounds received in action 1943), s of Col Hon Sir Eustace T-W-F 1 Bt (2 s of 17 Baron Saye and Sele); 1 s (present Bt), 3 da (Susan, m 1957 Lt-Col John Scott, Blues and Royals, Celia, m 1963 Dr Robert Brown, Gillian m 1960 Timothy Hoult); *Style—* Audrey, Lady Twisleton-Wykeham-Fiennes; Robins, Lodsworth, W Sussex GU28 9DE

TWISLETON-WYKEHAM-FIENNES, Sir John Saye Wingfield; KCB (1970, CB 1953), QC (1972); 3 s of Gerard Twisleton-Wykeham-Fiennes, CBE (d 1926, s of Rev Hon Wingfield Twisleton-Wykeham-Fiennes, 4 s of 16 Baron Saye and Sele); *b* 14 April 1911; *Educ* Winchester, Balliol Coll Oxford; *m* 1 Sep 1937, Sylvia (d 1979), da of Rev Charles McDowall (d 1956); 2 s, 1 da; *Career* barr; served Parly Counsel Office 1939-76, first Parly counsel 1968-72; *Style—* Sir John Twisleton-Wykeham-Fiennes, KCB, QC; Mill House, Preston St Mary, Sudbury, Suffolk (☎ 0787 247125)

TWISLETON-WYKEHAM-FIENNES, Very Rev the Hon Oliver William; s of 20 Baron Saye and Sele, OBE, MC (d 1968), and Hersey Cecilia Hester (d 1968), da of Capt Sir Thomas Dacres Butler, KCVO; *b* 17 May 1926; *Educ* Eton, New Coll Oxford (MA); *m* 26 June 1956, Juliet, yr da of Dr Trevor Braby Heaton, OBE; 2 s, 2 da; *Career* late Lt Rifle Bde; ordained 1954, rector of Lambeth 1963-68, dean of Lincoln 1968-89, dean emeritus 1989; CStJ; *Style—* The Very Rev the Hon Oliver Twisleton-Wykeham-Fiennes; Home Farm House, Colsterworth, nr Grantham, Lincs NG33 5NE (☎ 0476 860811)

TWISLETON-WYKEHAM-FIENNES, Sir Ranulph; 3 Bt (UK 1916), of Banbury, Co Oxford; s of Lt-Col Sir Ranulph Twisleton-Wykeham-Fiennes, 2 Bt, DSO (d 1943, gs of 17 Baron Saye and Sele), and Audrey, Lady Twisleton-Wykeham-Fiennes, *qv*; *b* 7 March 1944, (posthumously); *Educ* Eton, Mons; *m* 11 Sept 1970, Virginia Frances, da of Thomas Pepper (d 1985); *Career* Capt Royal Scots Greys, Capt 22 SAS Regt 1966; Capt Sultan of Oman's Armed Forces 1968-70; author and explorer; leader of first polar circumnavigation of earth, the Transglobe Expedition that arrived back in UK in Sept 1982 after 3 years non-stop travel; Man of the Year award 1982; exec conslt for Western Europe to Chm Occidental Petroleum Corporation 1984-90; awarded: French Parachute Wings 1968, Gold medal of New York Explorers Club 1984, Livingstone Gold medal by Royal Scottish Geographical Soc 1983, Fndr's medal of RGS 1984, ITV award for event of the decade 1990; Hon DSc Loughborough; Dhofar Campaign medal 1968, Sultan of Oman's Bravery medal 1970; awarded the Polar medal by HM The Queen 1987 (wife was first woman to receive Polar medal); *Books* Talent for Trouble (1968), Icefall in Norway (1971), The Headless Valley (1972), Where Soldiers Fear to Tread (1975), Hell on Ice (1978), To the Ends of the Earth: Transglobe Expedition 1979-82 (1983), Bothie The Polar Dog (1984, co written with wife), Living Dangerously (1987); *Recreations* skiing, photography; *Clubs* Guild of Vintners; *Style—* Sir Ranulph Twisleton-Wykeham-Fiennes, Bt

TWISS, Charles Edward Hartley; s of Edward Whalley Twiss (d 1983), of Grappenhall, Cheshire, and Margaret Gertrude, *née* Hartley; *b* 10 April 1943; *Educ* Boteler GS Warrington Cheshire, Hertford Coll Oxford (MA); *m* 6 Oct 1967, Sylvia, da of Frank Ellis (d 1968), of Elland, W Yorks; 1 s (Simon Charles Ellis b 1971), 1 da (Rebecca Catherine b 1973); *Career* admitted slr 1967; ptnr Streat Daunt & Farmiloe Southampton 1969-76, asst controller (legal) London Borough of Harrow 1976-80, slr to Bd Eastern Electricity 1980-85, dir of legal servs British Gas plc 1985-; *Recreations* tennis, sailing, music; *Clubs* Royal Harwich Yacht; *Style—* Charles Twiss, Esq; Old Barn, Old Barn Rd, Mount Bures, Suffolk CO8 5AH (☎ 0787 228342); British Gas plc, Rivermill House, 152 Grosvenor Rd, London (☎ 071 821 1444, telex 938529)

TWISS, Admiral Sir Frank Roddam; KCB (1965, CB 1962), KCVO (1978), DSC (1945); s of Col E K Twiss, DSO, and Margaret Edmondson Twiss, *née* Tate (d 1950); *b* 7 July 1910; *Educ* RNC Dartmouth; *m* 1, 1936, Prudence (d 1974), da of Rear Adm John de Mestre Hutchison, CMG (d 1932); 2 s, 1 da; m 2, 1978, Rosemary Maitland, *née* Howe, wid of Capt Denis Chilton, RN; *Career* joined RN 1924, Rear Adm 1960, Naval Sec to First Lord of Admty 1960-62, Flag Offr Flotillas Home Fleet 1962-64, Cdr Far E Fleet 1965-67, Adm 1967, Second Sea Lord and Chief of Naval Personnel 1967-70; Gentleman Usher of the Black Rod House of Lords 1970-78 (Serjeant-at-arms House of Lords and Sec to Lord Great Chamberlain 1971-78), memb Cwlth War Graves Cmmn 1970-79; younger bro of Trinity House 1956-; *Clubs* Army and Navy; *Style—* Admiral Sir Frank Twiss, KCB, KCVO, DSC; East Marsh Farm, Bratton, nr Westbury, Wilts

TWISS, (Lionel) Peter; OBE (1956), DSC (1942, and bar 1943); s of Col Dudley Cyril Twiss, South Staffordshire Regt (d 1964), of Lindfield Sussex, and Laura Georgina Smith, *née* Chapman (d 1980); *b* 23 July 1921; *Educ* Sherborne; *m* 1, Oct 1944; m 2, 1949; 2 da (Joanna d 1954, Sarah b 1954); m 3, 1960; 1 da (Miranda b 1961); m 4, 4 Nov 1964, Heather Linda (d 1988), da of Strachan Goldingham (d 1981), of Palmerston North, NI, New Zealand; *Career* fleet air arm 804 sqdn 1939-46, Med Convoys 807 Sqdn, Nightfighters 1 Seafire Sqndn N Africa Op Torch, NFIU, Br Air Cmmn Patuxent River USA, A & AEE Boscombe Down Empire Test Pilots Sch, Naval Test Sqdn A & AEE Lt RNVR; Fairey Aviation test pilot 1946-60 (chief test pilot 1957); Worlds absolute air speed record 1956; Fairey Marine sales mangr; dir: Fairey Marine, Fairey Yacht Harbours; gen mangr and dir Hamble Point Marina; marine conslt; *Recreations* ornithology, yachting, gardening; *Clubs* Royal Southern Yacht, Island Sailing; *Style—* Peter Twiss, Esq, OBE, DSC; Nettleworth, 33 South St, Titchfield, Hampshire PO14 4DL

TWIST, Stephen John; s of James Twist, of Darlington, Co Durham, and Kathleen Marion, *née* Gamble; *b* 26 Sept 1950; *Educ* Queen Elizabeth GS Darlington, Univ of Liverpool (LLB); *m* 4 May 1990, Ann, *née* Stockton; *Career* former police offr Met Police; called to the Bar Middle Temple 1979; memb: Hon Soc of Middle Temple, Hon Soc Gray's Inn; *Style—* Stephen Twist, Esq; York Chambers, 14 Toft Green, York

YO1 1JT; 2 Harcourt Buildings, Temple, London EC4Y 9DB

TWISTON DAVIES, David James; s of Mervyn Peter Twiston Davies, of Somerset, and Isabel Anne, *née* Fox; *b* 23 March 1945; *Educ* Downside; *m* 10 June 1970, Margaret Anne (Rita), da of Francis Gerard Montgomery (d 1978); 3 s (Benedict, James, Huw), 1 da (Bess); *Career* journalist; East Anglian Daily Times 1966-68, Winnipeg Free Press 1968-70; The Daily Telegraph: news sub ed 1970-77, asst literary ed 1977-86, dep obituaries ed 1986-88, ed Peterborough column 1988-89, letters ed 1989-; Freeman City of London; *Recreations* defending reputation of the British Empire; *Clubs* Travellers'; *Style*— David Twiston Davies, Esq; 20 Warwick Park, Tunbridge Wells, Kent (☎ 0892 30341); The Daily Telegraph, 181 Marsh Wall, London E14 (☎ 071 538 6458, fax 071 538 6455)

TWISTON-DAVIES, Audley William; s of William Anthony Twiston-Davies, DL (d 1989), of The Mynde, Much Dewchurch, Herefordshire, and Rosemary, *née* Archdale; *b* 13 Nov 1950; *Educ* Radley; *m* 9 Feb 1985, Hon Caroline Harbord-Hamond, da of Lord Suffield, of Wood Norton, Dereham, Norfolk; 2 da (Antonia Rose b 22 Oct 1987, another b 13 Feb 1990); *Career* dir: For & Colonial Mgmnt Ltd, Brazilian Securties Ltd, Brazilain Investmt Co; Liveryman Haberdashers Co; *Clubs* City; *Style*— Audley Twiston-Davies, Esq; 67 Oakley Gardens, London SW3 (☎ 071 351 4796); 1 Laurence Pountney Hill, London EC4 (☎ 071 929 2701, fax 071 621 9589)

TWITCHETT, John Anthony Murray; s of Joseph Ernest James Twitchett (d 1959), of Westdene, Forest Lane, Chigwell, Essex, and Olive Jessie, *née* Lidford (d 1986); *b* 26 July 1932; *Educ* Chigwell Sch Essex; *m* 1, 30 March 1960, Doricka Edith (d 1963), da of late Henry Edmund Palfreman, of London; m 2, 25 Jan 1964 (m dis 1972), Rosemary, da of Joseph Hallam, of Cowley Moor, Wellswood, Torquay, S Devon; 2 da (Elizabeth Anne b 24 Nov 1964, Caroline Mary b 11 June 1966); *Career* former landowner Woodeaton Oxon, ptnr David John Ceramics 1970-, curator Royal Crown Derby Museum 1972-; int lectr venues incl: V&A, Canadian Nat Gallery Ottawa, Royal Ontario Museum Toronto, Musée des Beaux Arts Montréal; memb Cncl Derby Porcelain Int Soc, memb Ctee Burford and Dist Refugee Aid Soc; memb: Nat Tst, NFU; vice pres Melbourne Male Voice Choir, life tstee The Royal Crown Derby Museum Tst 1988; FRSA 1975; *Books* Royal Crown Derby (1976), Derby Porcelain (1980), Landscapes on Derby and Worcester (with Henry sandon, 1984), Painters and the Derby China Works (with John Murdoch, 1987); *Recreations* golf; *Clubs* Public Schools; *Style*— John Twitchett, Esq; 5 Swan Lane Close, Burford, Oxford OX8 4SP; David John Ceramics, 11 Acre End St, Eynsham, Oxford OX8 1PE (☎ 0865 880786)

TWITE, Robin; OBE; s of Reginald John Twite (d 1973), of Rugby, Warwicks, and May Elizabeth Twite (d 1963); *b* 2 May 1932; *Educ* Lawrence Sheriff Sch Rugby, Balliol Coll Oxford (MA); *m* 1, July 1955 (m dis 1979), Sally Patricia, *née* Randall; 1 s (Daniel b 7 Feb 1963); m 2, 25 March 1980, Sonia, *née* Yaari; *Career* RCS 1950-52; Br Cncl 1955-87: sec overseas students fees awards scheme 1966-68, rep Israel 1968-73, rep Calcutta 1980-84, controller books libraries and info 1984-87, resigned 1987; sec Open Univ of Israel 1973-76; currently advsr to chm Hebrew Univ Res and Devpt Authy Jerusalem; *Recreations* travel, meditation, freelance journalism; *Style*— Robin Twite, Esq, OBE; 45 Christchurch Ave, London NW6; 36 Gimel, Ein Kerem, Jerusalem, Israel; c/o Chairman, Hebrew Univ, Research and Dev Authority, Hebrew Univ, Jerusalem

TWIVY, Paul Christopher Barstow; s of Dr Samuel Barstow Twivy, of Dunstable, and Sheila, *née* Webster; *b* 19 Oct 1958; *Educ* Haberdashers' Aske's Sch, Magdalen Coll Oxford (BA); *m* 31 July 1982 (m dis), Martha Mary Sladden; 2 s (Samuel b 1985, Joshua b 1988); *Career* bd dir Hedger Mitchell Stark 1982-83, md Still Price Court Twivy D'Souza Lintas 1984-; memb: Steering Ctee Comic Relief, Exec Ctee The Healthcare Fndn, Cncl IPA; spokesman for: advtg indust, RCN, Healthcare Fndn; memb Mktg Soc, MIPA; *Recreations* freelance comedy writer, playwright, poetry, reading, swimming, music (guitar and piano); *Clubs* Oxford Union, Groucho's; *Style*— Paul Twivy, Esq; Flat 2, 13 Belsize Park Gardens, London NW3 4JG; Still Price Court Twivy D'Souza: Lintas, 84 Eccleston Square, London SW1V 1PX

TWYFORD, Donald Henry; CB (1990); s of Henry John Twyford (d 1982), of Ferring and Crowborough, Sussex, and Lily Hilda, *née* Ridler (d 1977); *b* 4 Feb 1931; *Educ* Wembley Co Sch; *Career* Nat Serv RAF Educn Branch 1949-51; Civil Serv: joined Export Credits Guarantee Dept 1949, sr principal (chief underwriter) 1968, asst sec 1972, establishment offr 1976, under sec 1979, chm EC Policy Co-ordination Gp 1981; *Recreations* growing citrus fruits in Spain, travel, music; *Style*— Donald Twyford, Esq, CB; c/o PO Box No 272, 50 Ludgate Hill, London EC4M 7AY

TWYFORD, Sidney Hamilton; s of Robert James Twyford (d 1924), and Sarah Hamilton, *née* Taylor (d 1937); *b* 6 Oct 1906; *m* 16 Feb 1943, Williamina, da of Donald Campbell MacDonald (d 1936); 3 s (Robert b 28 March 1945, John b 20 June 1946, d 1946, Kenneth b 2 Oct 1947); *Career* WWII 1939-45: hon artillery boy 1939, cmmnd 2 Lt RA 1940, Acting Maj, War Substantive Capt 1945; md Campbell Hamilton & Co Ltd 1950-86, memb Lloyds 1977; Freeman City of London 1977, Liveryman Worshipful Co of Upholders 1977; MIOD 1958; *Recreations* rugby, hockey, cricket; *Clubs* RAC, Caledonian, The City Livery; *Style*— Sidney Twyford, Esq; Flat 2, Braidley, Cliffe Drive, Canford Cliffs, Dorset; Longwood House, Heather Close, Kingswood (☎ 0737 832 947)

TWYMAN, Paul Hadleigh; s of late Lawrence Alfred Twyman, and Gladys Mary, *née* Williams; *b* 24 July 1943; *Educ* Chatham House Sch Ramsgate, Univ of Sheffield (BA), LSE (MSc); *Career* schoolmaster 1963-64; Civil Serv: asst princ Bd of Trade 1967-71, memb Secretariat Cmmn on the Third London Airport 1969-71, private sec to Sec of State for Trade and Indust 1971-73, princ anti-dumping unit DTI 1976-78, asst sec and head of overseas projects gp DTI 1978-81, civil aviation div 1981-83, Dept of Tport 1983, Cabinet Office 1984, under sec and dir enterprise and deregulation unit Dept of Employment 1985-87; econ advsr to chm of Cons Pty and head of econ section Cons Res Dept 1987, chm Political Strategy Ltd 1988; dir: Anglia Building Society 1983, Nationwide Anglia Bldg Soc 1987-; non-exec dir D'Arcy Masius Benton and Bowles; Euro Parly candidate Greater Manchester West 1989; FBIM; *Recreations* hill walking, gardening, observing gorillas; *Style*— Paul Twyman, Esq; 2 St James's Sq, London SW1Y 4JN (☎ 071 839 3422)

TYACKE, Maj-Gen David Noel Hugh; CB (1970), OBE (1957); s of Capt Charles Noel Walker Tyacke (ka 1918), and Phoebe Coulthard (d 1969); *b* 18 Nov 1915; *Educ* Malvern, RMA Sandhurst; *m* 1940, Diana, da of Aubrey Hare Duke (d 1972); 1 s (Nicholas); *Career* cmmnd DCLI 1935 RA, cmd 1 Bn DCLI 1957-59, cmd 130 Inf Bde (TA) 1961-63, GOC Singapore Dist 1966-70; *Recreations* walking, motoring, bird watching; *Style*— Maj-Gen David Tyacke, CB, OBE; c/o Lloyds Bank, 7 Pall Mall, London SW1Y 5NA

TYACKE, Maj Humphry John; s of Col Ashley John Tyacke (d 1985), of Grayswood, Fareham, Hampshire, and L M A Tyacke (d 1984); direct descendant of Sir Joseph Paxton, creator of the Crystal Palace; *b* 4 Dec 1930; *Educ* Wellington, RMA Sandhurst; *m* 17 Sept 1980, Barbara Mary, da of W E Hunter (surgeon) (d 1980), of Cefn Mawr Hall, nr Mold, Flintshire; 2 step s (Anthony b 1951, Michael b 1954); *Career* Maj 13/18 Royal Hussars (Queen Mary's Own): Malaya, Aden, Malaysia, Falkland Islands; *Recreations* sailing; *Style*— Maj Humphry Tyacke; Crossways, Hoe, Dereham, Norfolk (☎ 860550); Mijas (Spain)

TYDEMAN, John Peter; s of George Alfred Tydeman (d 1960), of Cheshunt, Herts, and Gladys Florence Beatrice, *née* Brown (d 1982); *b* 30 March 1936; *Educ* Hertford GS, Trinity Coll Cambridge (MA); *Career* 2 Lt 1 Singapore Regt RA 1954-56, served Malaya; head of drama radio BBC 1986- (radio drama prodr 1960-79, asst head radio drama 1979-86); awarded: Prix Italia 1970, Prix Futura 1979 and 1983, Bdcasting Press Guild Award for outstanding radio prodn 1983; stage prodns incl: Objection to Sex and Violence (Royal Ct) 1975, The Bells of Hell (Garrick Theatre) 1977, Falstaff (Fortune Theatre) 1984; *Recreations* swimming, foreign places, theatre; *Clubs* Garrick; *Style*— John Tydeman, Esq; 88 Great Titchfield St, London W1P 7AG (☎ 071 636 3886); Broadcasting House, Portland Place, London W1 (☎ 071 927 4605, tlx 265781, fax 071 580 5780)

TYDEMAN, Prof William Marcus; s of Henry Marcus Tydeman, MBE (d 1975), of East Malling, Kent, and Elizabeth Mary, *née* Shepherd (d 1988); *b* 29 Aug 1935; *Educ* Maidstone GS, Univ Coll Oxford (BA, MA, MLitt); *m* 29 July 1961, Jacqueline Barbara Anne, da of Robert Lewis Jennison (d 1957); 2 da (Josephine b 1963, Rosalind b 1966); *Career* RCS 1954-56, cmmnd 2 Lt 1955; head Sch of English and Linguistics UCNW Bangor 1989- (asst lectr in Eng 1961-64, lectr 1964-70, sr lectr 1970-83, reader 1983-86, head of Dept of English 1983-89, prof 1986); *Books* English Poetry 1400-1580 (ed, 1970), The Theatre in the Middle Ages (1978), Four Tudor Comedies (ed, 1984), Dr Faustus: Text and Performance (1984), English Medieval Theatre 1400-1500 (1986), The Welsh Connection (ed, 1986), The State of the Art: Christopher Marlowe (jtly, 1989); *Recreations* theatre, local history; *Style*— Prof William Tydeman; Sch of English & Linguistics, Univ Coll of N Wales, Bangor, Gwynedd LL57 2DG (☎ 0248 351151 ext 2101)

TYE, Alan; *b* 18 Sept 1933; *Educ* Regent St Poly Sch of Architecture (Dip Arch); *m* 1966, Anita Birgitta, Goethe-Tye; 2 s (Nicolas b 1969, Kevin b 1973), 1 da (Madeleine b 1967); *Career* formed Alan Tye Design 1962-; civic tst award assessor 1968 and 1969, visiting tutor RCA 1978-83 (external assessor 1987-), specialist advsr on Ind Design CNAA 1980, London regnl assessor RIBA 1981, RSA bursary judge 1983-; recipient Int Design prize Rome 1962, Cncl of Ind design award 1965 (1966 and 1981), Br Aluminium Design award 1966, memb Selection Ctee Cncl of Industl Design 1967, 1 prize GAI award 1969, Observer (London) design award 1969, Ringling Mus of Art (Fla) award 1969, Gold medal graphic design 1970, 1 Prize GAI award Int Bldg Exhibition 1971, British Aluminium Eros Trophy 1973, 4 awards for design excellence Aust 1973, commendation for arch 1977, IBD Int Award (NY) 1982, Internat Bldg Exhibits top design award 1983 (1985), Royal Designer for Indust 1986; memb RIBA; *Recreations* tai chi, aikido, badminton, fly dressing; *Style*— Alan Tye, Esq; Great West Plantation, Tring, Herts HP23 6DA (☎ 044282 5353, telex 826715 Aero G, fax 044282 7723)

TYE, James; *b* 21 Dec 1921; *Educ* Upper Hornsey LCC Sch, Br Safety Cncl (Dip Safety Mgmnt); *m* 1950, Mrs Rosalie Hooker; 1 s, 1 da; *Career* WWII RAF 1940-46; advtg agent and contractor 1946-50; md 1950-62: Sky Press Ltd, Safety Publications Ltd, Press Transworld Ltd, Industrial Services Ltd; dir gen Br Safety Cncl 1968- (exec dir 1962-68), chm Bd of Govrs Int Inst of Safety Mgmnt 1975-, memb Parly All Party Freedom of Info Campaign; Freeman City of London 1976, Liveryman Worshipful Co of Basketmakers, memb Guild of Freemen City of London; fell Inst of Accident Prevention Zambia, vice pres Jamaica Safety Cncl, assoc Inst of Occupational Safety & Health; memb: American Soc of Safety Engrs, American Safety Mgmnt Soc; FBIM, FRSA, FID; *Books* Communicating the Safety Message (1968), Management Introduction to Total Loss Control (1971), Safety-Uncensored (with K Ullyet; 1971), The Management Guide to Product Liability (with Bowes Egan, 1979); handbooks: Industrial Safety Digest (1953), Advanced Driving (1957), Why Imprison Untrained Drivers? (1980); papers and reports on numerous aspects of safety to Parly gps and British Safety Cncl membs; *Recreations* squash, badminton, skiing, golf, sailing; *Clubs* City Livery, RAC; *Style*— James Tye, Esq; 55 Hartington Road, Chiswick W4 3TS (☎ 081 995 3206); British Safety Council (☎ 081 741 1231)

TYERS, Anthony Gordon; s of Arthur Tyers, of Sunbury on Thames, Surrey, and Marion Joan, *née* Cheal; *b* 14 Sept 1944; *Educ* Hampton Sch, Charing Cross Hosp Univ of London (MB BS); *m* 7 Oct 1983, Renée Constance Barbara, da of Frits De Waard, of Waalre, Netherlands; 2 s (Jonathan Richard Duncan b 30 July 1986, Richard Christopher James b 30 April 1989); *Career* registrar Univ Coll Hosp London 1973-76, sr registrar Moorfields Eye Hosp 1978-81, fell Massachusetts Eye and Ear Infirmary Boston USA 1981-82, sr registrar Moorfields Eye Hosp and Middx Hosp London 1982-86, conslt ophthalmic surgn Salisbury Gen Hosps 1986-; tstee Salisbury Hosps Tst, sec Wessex Regnl Advsy Ctee for Ophthalmology; memb: BMA, RSM, Euro Soc of Ophthalmic Plastic and Reconstructive Surgery, Southern Ophthalmological Soc; FRCS 1974, FRCSEd 1980, FCOphth 1989; *Books* Basic Clinical Ophthalmology (contrib 1984); *Recreations* squash, skiing, clarinet, campanology; *Style*— Anthony Tyers, Esq; Odstock Hospital, Salisbury SP2 8BJ (☎ 0722 336262); New Hall Hospital, Salisbury SP5 4EY (☎ 0722 331021)

TYLDESLEY, Reginald George; s of Bertrand Joseph Jennings Tyldesley (d 1966), of Woking, and Isabel, *née* Hughes (d 1972); *b* 4 Sept 1923; *Educ* Lancing; *Career* RAC; Sandhurst 1943-44, cmmnd 1944, attached Royal Mil Police 1944-47, served in India, Malaya, French Indochina, Java, appt Capt and Dep Asst Provost Marshall 1945, dep asst cmmr of Police Batavia Djakarta 1946; CA 1949, Deloitte Haskins & Sells 1947-84, ret as sr mangr; dir Friends of St Paul's Enterprises Ltd 1987-; memb: Cncl Friends of St Paul's Cathedral (tstee), Royal Horticultural Soc, Horsell Common Preservation Soc, Surrey & Hampshire Canal Soc, Soc of Genealogists; Freeman City of London 1959, Liveryman Worshipful Co of Goldsmiths 1959; FCA 1949; *Recreations* genealogy, gardening, fine arts, conservation, cookery; *Clubs* Royal Over-Seas League; *Style*— Reginald Tyldesley, Esq; Craigmore, Horsell Park, Woking, Surrey GU21 4LW (☎ 0483 772496)

TYLDESLEY, Robert John Ross; s of John Tyldesley; *b* 3 Feb 1935; *Educ* Headlands GS, LSE; *m* Cynthia Ann; 1 s, 1 da; *Career* former md F Hewitt & Son Ltd, dir and gen mangr Wester Morning News Co Ltd Plymouth, md Western Mail & Echo Cardiff, Thomson Regnl Newspapers Ltd Watford; cncl memb: Newspaper Soc, Cwlth Press Union; *Recreations* skiing, shooting; *Clubs* Royal Western Yacht, Cardiff and County; *Style*— Robert Tyldesley, Esq; Glan Avon Lodge, Peterston Super Ely, South Glamorgan

TYLER, Brig Arthur Catchmay (Hugh); CBE (1960), MC (1945), DL (Surrey 1968); s of Hugh Griffin Tyler, JP (d 1953), of Cleddon House, nr Monmouth, and Muriel Barnes (d 1976); *b* 20 Aug 1913; *Educ* Allhallows Sch, RMC Sandhurst; *m* 1938, Sheila Maysie, da of James Kinloch, of Meigle, Perthshire; 3 s, 1 da; *Career* served WWII Africa, Burma (despatches), Bt-Lt-Col 1953, Col 1957, Brig 1960, sec British Jt Servs Mission Washington 1952-54, WO 1957-60, sr UK liaison offr and mil advsr to High Cmmr Canada 1960-63, asst COS Allied Forces Central Europe 1963-65, sec Cncl of TA and VR Assocs 1965-72, Hon Col 7 (V) Bn The Queens Regt 1971-75; govr Allhallows Sch 1967 (chm 1976-79); Mil Knight of Windsor 1978-; *Style*— Brig A C Tyler, CBE, MC, DL; 19 Lower Ward, Windsor Castle, Berks SL4 1NJ (☎ 0753 851471)

TYLER, Maj-Gen Christopher; CB (1989); s of Maj-Gen Sir Leslie Tyler, KBE, CB, *qv*, of Liphook, Hants, and Louie Teresa, *née* Franklin (d 1950); *b* 9 July 1934; *Educ* Beaumont Coll Old Windsor, RMA Sandhurst, Trinity Coll Cambridge (MA); *m* 12 July 1958, Suzanne, da of (Hubert John) Patrick Whitcomb (d 1962); 1 s (William 1959), 3 da (Catherine b 1961, Louisa b 1965, Sophie b 1967); *Career* cmmnd REME 1954, Army Staff Coll 1966-67, Lt-Col CO 1 Parachute Logistic Regt 1974-76, Asst Mil Sec (MS6) 1976-77, Col Asst Adj Gen (AG21) 1977-80, Chief Aircraft Engr Army Air Corps 1980-82, Brig Dir EME Mgmnt Servs 1982-83, cdr Maintenance 1 (BR) Corps 1983-85, Dep Cmdt Royal Mil Coll of Sci 1985-87, Maj-Gen Dep Chief of Staff (Support) HQ AFNORTH 1987-89; resident govr and keeper of the Jewel House HM Tower of London; hon sec RFU Referee Advsy Panel 1979-83; Liveryman Worshipful Co of Turners 1979; CEng 1964, FRAES 1981, FIMechE 1982, FBIM 1982; *Recreations* most sports but especially Rugby Union Football; *Clubs* Lansdowne, Hawks, Br Sportsman's; *Style—* Maj-Gen Christopher Tyler, CB; Queen's House, HM Tower of London EC3N 4AB (☎ 071 480 6593)

TYLER, John William; s of Joseph Thomas Tyler (d 1975), of Newark, Notts, and Clara Gertrude, *née* Martin (d 1979); *b* 21 Nov 1931; *Educ* The Magnus Sch Newark Notts, Univ of Nottingham (BA), Coll of Law; *m* 8 Jan 1955, Patricia, da of John Reginald Neal (d 1966), of Hove, E Sussex; 2 s (Timothy John Neal b 30 Oct 1957 d 1978, Gavin Thomas b 6 Dec 1960), 1 da (Nicola Patricia (Mrs Hulm) b 3 March 1965); *Career* Flt Lt Adjs Branch RAF 1952-58; dir and co sec Atcost Gp of Co's 1958-69; admitted slr 1973; ptnr Cripps Harries Hall 1974- (joined 1970); NP; chm Jones Clifton Gp of Co's 1985 (dir 1975-); chm Local Advsy Ctee Nuffield Hosp Tunbridge Wells, dir Heathlands House Ltd (private charity for severely disabled young people); Freeman City of London, Liveryman Worshipful Co of Carmen 1977; memb Law Soc; *Recreations* golf, skiing, gardening; *Style—* John Tyler, Esq; 14 Blatchington Rd, Tunbridge Wells, Kent TN2 5EG (☎ 0892 27822); Cripps Harries Hall, 84 Calverley Rd, Tunbridge Wells, Kent TN1 2UP (☎ 0892 515121, fax 0892 515444)

TYLER, Maj-Gen Sir Leslie Norman; KBE (1961, OBE 1942), CB (1955); s of Maj Norman Tyler, RA (TA) (d 1931), and Aurora Tyler (d 1930); *b* 26 April 1904; *Educ* Diocesan Coll S Africa, RNC Osborne and Dartmouth, King's Coll London (BSc); *m* 1, 1930, Louie Teresa (d 1950), da of Lt-Col R J Franklin (d 1944); 1 s, 1 da; m 2, 1953, Sheila, wid of Maj-Gen L H Cox, CB, CBE, MC (d 1949); 2 s, 2 step da; *Career* Lt RAOC 1927, transfd REME 1942, Brig WWII, served Malta, NW Europe; DEME War Office 1957-60 (ret); regnl dir Miny of Public Bldg and Works Central Mediterranean 1963-69, chm and vice chm Royal Hosp and Home for Incurables Putney 1970-81; Master Worshipful Co of Turners 1982-83 (Upper Warden 1981-85); FIMechE, FKC; *Recreations* music, watching rugby football, cricket, lawn tennis; *Clubs* Army and Navy; *Style—* Maj-Gen Sir Leslie Tyler, KBE, CB; 51 Chiltley Way, Liphook, Hants GU30 7HE (☎ 0428 722335)

TYLER, Paul Archer; CBE (1985); s of Oliver Walter Tyler (d 1957), of Elm Park, Broadhempston, Totnes, Devon, and (Ursula) Grace Gibbons, *née* May; *b* 29 Oct 1941; *Educ* Mount House Sch Tavistock, Sherborne, Exeter Coll Oxford (MA); *m* 27 June 1970, Nicola Mary (Nicky), da of Michael Warren Ingram, OBE, of the Manor House, S Cerney, Cirencester, Glos; 1 s (Dominick b 1975), 1 da (Sophie b 1972); *Career* dep then dir of public affrs RIBA 1966-73, regnl organiser and bd memb Shelter 1975-76, md Courier Newspaper Group 1976-81, dir then sr conslt Good Relations Ltd 1982-, md Western Approaches PR Ltd 1987-; Devon co cncllr 1964-70, memb Devon and Cornwall Police Authy, vice chm Dartmoor Nat Park; MP (Lib) 1974; Lib Pty: contested Totnes seat 1966, contested Bodmin seat 1970, 1974 and 1979, chm 1983-86; contested Cornwall and Plymouth for Euro Parl as Lib Democrat 1989; PPC N Cornwall 1990; MIPR 1987; *Recreations* sailing, walking, cornish ancestry; *Clubs* Nat Lib; *Style—* Paul Tyler, Esq, CBE; Western Approaches, 14 Addison Rd, North Hill, Plymouth PL4 8LL (☎ 0752 222181, fax 0752 261664)

TYLER, Richard Michael Townsend; s of James Tyler-Stewart-Mackenzie (d 1956), of Brahan, Cononbridge, Ross-shire, and Kathleen Audrey, *née* Townsend (d 1941); *b* 9 Nov 1916; *Educ* Charterhouse, RWA Sch of Arch; *m* 15 July 1944, Anne Henrietta, er da of Cdr Sir Geoffrey Cecil Congreve, 1 Bt, DSO (ka 1942), of Congreve Manor, Staffs; 2 s (Christian b 1945, Felix b 1954), 2 da (Camilla b 1946, Amelia b 1950); *Career* served RE WWII, Capt, wounded 1941 W Desert; architect; ptnr Bird and Tyler Assocs 1954-83, principally engaged on country houses and buildings for the disabled; Civic Tst awards; ARIBA; *Clubs* Boodles; *Style—* Richard Tyler, Esq; Brachamfield House, Burstock, Beaminster, Dorset

TYLOR, John Edward; s of Maj Vyvian Alfred Tylor, MC (d 1968), and M S Tylor; *b* 1 July 1942; *Educ* Eton, Trinity Coll Dublin (MA); *m* 18 Oct 1975, Heather Catherine, da of Richard Alan Budgett, of Kirtlington, Oxon; 2 s (Sam Vyvian b 1980, Hugo Alexander b 1985); *Career* slr Herbert Smith & Co 1967-73, Samuel Montagu & Co 1973-, exec dir Corp Fin Dept 1981-; *Recreations* field sports, polo; *Style—* John Tylor, Esq; Stud Farm, Chesterton, Bicester; 10 Lower Thames St, London EC2 (☎ 071 260 9000)

TYNAN, Kathleen; da of Matthew Henry Halton (d 1956), of Canada, and Jean Joslin Campbell Halton; *b* 25 Jan 1940; *Educ* Queens' Coll Harley St London, Sorbonne, Univ of Oxford, Univ of London (BA); *m* 30 June 1967, Kenneth Tynan, s of Sir Peter Peacock; 1 s (Matthew Blake), 1 da (Roxana Nell); *Career* writer; researcher Newsweek magazine NY 1960, features writer and reporter arts column The Observer London 1962-64, features writer Sunday Times London 1964-67, freelance journlist and TV interviewer 1967-75, author 1975-; runner up NCR Literature award for non-fiction 1988; memb: Writers Guild, PEN; *Books* The Summer Aeroplane (1975), Agatha (screenplay 1978, novel 1979), The Life of Kenneth Tynan: biography (1987), Profiles (ed, 1989); *Recreations* reading, travel; *Style—* Mrs Kathleen Tynan; Peters Fraser & Dunlop, The Chambers, Chelsea Harbour, Lots Rd, London SW10 0XF (☎ 071 376 7676, fax 071 352 7356)

TYNAN, Prof Michael John; s of Sqdn Ldr Jerry Joseph Tynan, MBE (d 1990), and Florence Ann (d 1964); *Educ* Bedford Modern Sch, London Hosp Med Coll (FRCP); *m* Eirlys Pugh, da of Ernest Williams; *Career* sr resident Childrens Hospital Boston Mass, teaching fell Harvard Med Sch 1961, lectr Inst of Child Health London 1968-71; conslt paediatric cardiologist: Newcastle Gen Hosp 1971-77, Guys Hosp 1977-82; prof paediatric cardiology Guys Hosp 1982, hon conslt paediatric cardilogist Cambridge Mil Hosp; memb Physiological Soc; Freeman Worshipful Soc of Apothecaries; *Books* Paediatric Cardiology (jtly 1988); *Clubs* Athenaeum; *Style—* Prof Michael Tynan; 5 Ravensden St, London SE11 4AQ (☎ 071 735 7119); Guy's Hospital, St Thomas St, London SE1 9RT (☎ 071 378 7351)

TYNAN, Prof Oliver; s of John Tynan (d 1949), and Ethelwyn Tynan, MBE (d 1980); *b* 3 April 1928; *Educ* Dragon Sch Oxford, Marlborough, Univ of Oxford (BA), Univ of London; *m* 1 Sept 1959, Carol, da of late Arthur James Penrose Booth, of Craven Arms, Shropshire; 1 s (Christopher b 1957), 1 da (Clare b 1959); *Career* advsr on the human aspects of industry; visiting prof Brunel The Univ of W London; dir Work Res Unit ACAS 1979-86; *Recreations* wine making, gardening, goose breeding; *Clubs* Devonshire House Management; *Style—* Prof Oliver Tynan; Tudor Cottage, Brockley, Bury St Edmunds, Suffolk IP29 4AG (☎ 0284 830321)

TYREE, Daniel C; *b* 4 June 1948; *Educ* St Louis Univ (BA), Rutgers Grad Sch of Business (MBA), Rutgers Law Sch (JD) Degrees; *m* 1975, Teri L, da of Dwight Pattee, of 2079 Lincoln Lane, Salt Lake City, Utah, USA; 1 s (Ian Stuart b 19 Dec 1982), 1 da (Heather Alise b 7 Jan 1980); *Career* practised law on Wall St 1974-75; Salomon Brothers Inc 1975-: head equipment of lease fin gp, head of transportation fin and equipment gps, head of project fin gp, md head of int investmt banking 1984-; memb: NY and New Jersey Bar Assoc, Int Advsy Ctee NY Stock Exchange; *Clubs* Mark's, Annabel's, The Down Town Assoc of NY; *Style—* Daniel C Tyree, Esq; 45 Eaton Place, London SW1X 8DE; Salomon Brothers Int Ltd, Victoria Plaza, 111 Buckingham Palace Rd, London SW1W OSB (☎ 071 721 3777, fax 071 222 7062, telex 886441)

TYREE, Sir (Alfred) William; KCVO, OBE (1971); s of J V Tyree; *b* 4 Nov 1921; *Educ* Auckland GS, Sydney Tech Coll; *m* 1946, Joyce, da of F Lyndon; 2 s, 1 da; *Career* fndr Tyree Industs Ltd 1956; chm and fndr: Westralian Transformers and subsids (ret 1981), Alpha Air (Sydney) P/L, CPR Constructions P/L, CPR Investmts P/L, CPR Properties P/L, Technical Components P/L, Tycan Australia P/L, Tyree Hldgs P/L, Tyronsea Plastics P/L, A W Tyree Transformers P/L, Wirex P/L, A W Tyree Fndn (incl MEDICHECK Referral Centre, Sydney Square Diagnostic Breast Clinic, Tyree Chair of Electrical Engrg Univ of NSW, chair of otolaryngology Univ of Sydney); kt 1975; *Style—* Sir William Tyree, KCVO, OBE; 3 Lindsay Ave, Darling Point, NSW 2027, Australia

TYRELL-KENYON, Hon Lloyd; s and h of 5 Baron Kenyon, CBE; *b* 13 July 1947; *Educ* Eton, Magdalene Coll Cambridge; *m* 1971, Sally Carolyn, da of J F P Matthews, of The Firs, Thurston, Bury St Edmunds; 2 s; *Style—* The Hon Lloyd Tyrell-Kenyon; Gredington, Whitchurch, Shropshire SY13 3DH (☎ 094874 550)

TYRER, His Hon Judge Christopher John Meese; s of Jack Meese Tyrer, of 57 Thornhill Rd, Rhiwbina, Cardiff, South Glamorgan, Wales, and Margaret Joan, *née* Wyatt; *b* 22 May 1944; *Educ* Wellington, Univ of Bristol (LLB); *m* 9 Feb 1974, (Monica) Jane Tyrer, JP, da of Peter Beckett, of Daisy Nook, Carleton, Pontefract, Yorkshire; 1 s (David b 1981), 1 da (Rebecca b 1979); *Career* called to the Bar Inner Temple 1968; dep judiciary 1979 (dep judge 1979-82), asst rec 1982-83, rec 1983-89; vice chm St John's Sch Lancs Green 1989- (govr 1984-), chm Speen Sch 1989- (govr 1984-), memb Bucks Assoc of Govrs of Primary Schs 1989, chm High Wycombe Div 1989-; *Recreations* music, reading, photography, growing things; *Style—* His Hon Judge Christopher Tyrer; Randalls Cottage, Loosley Row, Princes Risborough, Aylesbury, Bucks HP17 0NU (☎ 084 44 4650)

TYRIE, Peter Robert; s of Capt W M B Tyrie (d 1964), and Kitty J Tyrie; *b* 3 April 1946; *Educ* Enfield GS, Westminster Coll Hotel Sch (BSc); *m* 29 Jan 1972, Christine Mary, da of Merton Bacon; 3 s (Simon, Nicholas, Tristan), 1 da (Sophie); *Career* mangr Inverurie Hotel Bermuda 1969-71, res mangr Portman Hotel London 1971-73, project dir Pannell Kerr Forster 1973-77, ops dir Penta Hotels 1977-80; md: Gleneagles Hotel plc 1980-86, Mandarin Oriental Group 1986-89, Balmoral International Ltd 1989-; dir Bell's Whiskey 1983-86, Edinburgh Fund Managers Dragon Trust 1989-; FHCIMA; *Recreations* squash, shooting, fishing, rugby, classic cars; *Style—* Peter Tyrie, Esq; The Balmoral Hotel, Princes St, Edinburgh (☎ 031 557 8688, fax 031 557 6333)

TYRONE, Earl of; Henry Nicholas de la Poer Beresford; s and h of 8 Marquess of Waterford by his w Lady Caroline Wyndham-Quin, da of 6 Earl of Dunraven and Mount-Earl; *b* 23 March 1958; *Educ* Harrow; *m* 1986, Amanda, da of Norman Thompson, of The Castle, Boris in Ossory, Co Laois; 2 s (Baron le Poer, Hon Marcus Patrick b 23 April 1990); *Heir* s, Richard John, Baron le Poer b 19 Aug 1987; *Style—* Earl of Tyrone; Garden House, Curraghmore, Portlaw, Co Waterford, Republic of Ireland (☎ 051 87 186)

TYRREL, John Frederick Eagle; s of Wing Cdr Frederick William Duffet (d 1974), and Doris Ethel, *née* Eagle (1985); *b* 1 Oct 1934; *Educ* Watford GS, Webber-Douglas Sch of Singing and Dramatic Art London; *m* 1, 28 Nov 1958 (m dis 1984), Mirabelle Elaine, da of Richard Leonard Thomas (d 1981); 1 s (Nöel b 1959), 1 da (Rebecca b 1960); m 2, 10 April 1985, Virginia Frances, da of Berkely Alexander Smith, of Forest Lodge, Swanmore, Bishop's Watham, Hants; *Career* Nat Serv RAPC Egypt 1953-55; actor: Hamlet (Laertes) 1957, Inherit this Wind 1960, Pygmalion 1960, The Reluctant Debutante 1961; dir: The Summer People 1962, Present Laughter 1964, Blithe Spirit 1965; author: Cinderella 1964; broadcaster 1977-: World of Sport, ITV Racing, Channel 4 Racing; *Books* Racecourses on the Flat (1989), Chasing Around Britain (1990); *Recreations* gardening; *Clubs* East India; *Style—* John Tyrrel, Esq; 15 Doris Street, Newmarket, Suffolk CB8 0LD (☎ 0638 663274)

TYRREL, Rebecca Amanda; da of John Frederick Tyrrel, and Mirabelle Elaine, *née* Thomas; *b* 8 Nov 1960; *Educ* La Retraite Convent Salisbury Wiltshire; *Career* asst fashion ed The Times 1984-87, dep Fashion ed The Independent 1987-88, fashion corr The Sunday Times 1988-89, fashion and IQ ed The Mail on Sunday 1989-; *Style—* Ms Rebecca Tyrrel; Mail On Sunday, Northcliffe House, 2 Derry St, London W8 5TS (☎ 071 938 6000, fax 071 937 0081)

TYRRELL; *see*: Smyth-Tyrrell

TYRRELL, Alan Rupert; QC (1976), MEP (EDG) London East 1979-84; *b* 1933,June; *Career* barr Gray's Inn 1956, bencher 1986, rec Crown Ct 1972-; MEP (EDG) London East 1979-84, chm Bar European Gp 1986-88; chm Int Practice Ctee Bar Cncl 1988, Lord Chancellor's legal visitor 1990-; memb Cncl Medical Protection Soc 1990-; *Style—* Alan Tyrrell Esq, QC, MED; 15 Willifield Way, Hampstead Garden Suburb, London NW11; 42 Rue du Taciturne, 1040 Bruxelles, Belgium; Francis Taylor Bldg, Temple, London EC4

TYRRELL, Lady Caroline Susan Elizabeth; da of late Lt-Col Lord Edward Douglas John Hay (3 s of 10 Marquess of Tweeddale) and sis of 12 Marquess; raised to the rank of a Marquess's da 1970; *b* 1930; *m* 1, 1953 (m dis 1970), Richard Noel Marshall Armitage; 2 s; m 2, 1970, Reginald Charles Tyrrell; *Style—* The Lady Caroline Tyrrell; Capplegill, Moffat, Dumfriesshire

TYRRELL, Dr David Arthur John; CBE (1980); s of late Lt-Col Sidney Charles Tyrrell, of Stalham, Norfolk, and Agnes Kate, *née* Blewett (d 1990); *b* 19 June 1925; *Educ* Ashford Co Sch Middx, King Edward VII Sch Sheffield, Univ of Sheffield (MB ChB, MD); *m* 15 April 1950, (Betty) Moyra, da of Dr John Wylie, MC, of Woodlands, Doncaster, Yorks; 1 s (Stephen b 1955 d 1979), 2 da (Frances b 1951, Susan b 1953); *Career* res registrar Sheffield Utd Hosps 1950-51, asst physician and res asst Rockefeller Inst Hosp NY 1951-54, memb MRC scientific staff Virus Res Laboratory Univ of Sheffield 1954, Common Cold Unit Salisbury 1957 (head 1962), dir of WHO Virus Reference Laboratory 1962-90, head Div of Communicable Diseases Clinical Res Centre Harrow 1967-84 (dep dir 1970-84); hon conslt physician: West Hendon Hosp 1967-70, Northwick Park Hosp Harrow 1970-85, Wessex RHA 1985-90; dir MRC Common Cold Unit Salisbury 1982-90; chm ACDP; memb: Governing Body Animal Virus Disease Res Inst Pirbright, hon chm Biological Prods Sub Ctee of Ctee on Safety of Med, tstee Nuffield Fndn, memb Steering Ctee MRC AIDS Directed Prog; The Rock Carling Lecture 1982, The Leewenhoek Lecture; author of numerous scientific pubns; Hon DSc Univ of Sheffield 1979; Hon MD Southampton 1990; FRCP 1965, FRS 1970, FRCPath 1971, memb Assoc of Physicians; hon memb: Infectious Disease Soc of America, Australian Soc of Infectious Diseases, American Assoc of

Physicians; *Books* Common Colds and Related Diseases (1965), Interferon and its Clinical Potential (1976), The Abolition of Infection: Hope or Illusion (1982); *Recreations* music, gardening, walking; *Style—* Dr David Tyrrell, CBE, FRS; Ash Lodge, Dean Lane, Whiteparish, Salisbury SP5 2RN (☎ 0749 884 352)

TYRRELL, George Edward; s of William George Tyrrell (d 1937); *b* 21 Sept 1920; *Educ* Whitgift Middle Sch Croydon; *m* 1950, Mildred Hilda; 1 s, 1 da; *Career* consulting engr; former dir of John Miles & Partners (London) Ltd; Freeman City of London; CEng, FIEE; *Recreations* shooting; *Clubs* IOD; *Style—* George E Tyrrell, Esq; 1 Leigham Court, Dawlish, Devon (☎ 0626 867054)

TYRRELL, Jean Margaret; OBE (1982), DL (W Yorks 1983); da of Fredrick Harrap (d 1960), of Woodthorpe House, Wakefield, and Bertha Harrap (d 1977); *b* 1 July 1918; *Educ* St Leonards St Andrews Fife, Univ of Geneva; *m* 15 July 1944, James Hall Tyrrell, s of Robert Tyrrell (d 1942); 3 da (Susan Gaye (Mrs Ainslie), Anne Maureen (Mrs Upsdell), Carolyn Jane); *Career* served WWII with Mechanised Tport Corps; joined Harrap Bros (Sirdar Wools) Ltd 1939, chm and md Sirdar plc 1960 (dir 1953, jt md 1959); The Times Veuve Cliquot Business Woman of the Year 1980; former memb: local MSC, Advsy Ctee on Womens Employment (Dept of Employment); gen cmmr of taxes; hon vice chm Br Hand Knitting Assoc; Doctor of Laws honoris causa Univ of Leeds 1988, Hon LLD Univ of Leeds 1988; MInstD; *Recreations* golf, sailing, bridge; *Clubs* Wakefield Golf; *Style—* Mrs Jean Tyrrell, OBE, DL; Sirdar Group, Bective Mills, Alverthorpe, Wakefield, W Yorks (☎ 0924 371501, fax 0924 290506, telex 557426); Invermor, 23 Woodthorpe Lane, Wakefield, W Yorks WF2 6JC (☎ 0924 255468); Keewaydin, Golf Rd, Abersoch, Gwynedd, N Wales

TYRRELL, Sir Murray Louis; KCVO (1968, CVO 1954), CBE (1959), JP; s of late Thomas Michael Tyrrell, and Florence Evelyn Tyrrell; *b* 1 Dec 1913; *Educ* Orbost HS, Melbourne HS; *m* 1939, Ellen St Clair, da of late E W St Clair Greig; 1 s, 2 da; *Career* private sec to mins of the Crown 1939-47, official sec to govr-gen of Australia 1947-74, comptroller 1947-53; attached Royal Household Buckingham Palace 1962; KStJ; *Style—* Sir Murray Tyrrell, KCVO, CBE

TYRRELL, Prof (Henry John) Valentine; s of John Rice Tyrell (d 1954), of Prittlewell, Essex, and Josephine Magdalene, *née* MacGuinness (d 1960); *b* 14 Feb 1920; *Educ* Newport HS, Jesus Coll Oxford (MA, BSc, DSc); *m* 1, 15 July 1947, Sheila Mabel, da of Philip Henry Straw (d 1985), of London; 3 s (Michael b 1948, Patrick b 1950, Sebastian b 1961), 3 da (Jennifer b 1951, Philippa b 1956, Fiona b 1965); m 2, Sept 1986 Bethan, da of Ben Davies; *Career* WWII RA 1939 (transfd to res) discharged 1942; scientific offr: ICI General Chemicals 1943-45, Br Non-Ferrous Metals Res Assoc 1945-47; memb academic staff Univ of Sheffield 1947-65, prof of physical chemistry Chelsea Coll Univ of London 1965-84 (princ 1984-85), vice princ Kings Coll KQC Univ of London 1985-87; Royal Inst of GB: hon sec 1978-84, memb Cncl 1986-89, chm 1986-89; chm Cncl Greenacre Sch Banstead Surrey 1989; fell Royal Soc of Chemistry 1968; *Books* Diffusion and Heat Flow in Liquids (1961), Thermometric Titimetry (1968), Diffusion in Liquids (1984); *Recreations* music, walking, gardening; *Clubs* Athenaeum (memb Gen Ctee 1986-89); *Style—* Prof Valentine Tyrrell; Fair Oaks, Coombe Hill Rd, Kingston upon Thames, KT2 7DU (☎ 081 949 6623)

TYRWHITT, John Edward Charles; s of Adm Sir St John Reginald Joseph Tyrwhitt, 2 Bt, KCB, DSO, DSC and bar, and bro of Sir Reginald Tyrwhitt, 3 Bt; *b* 27 July 1953; *Educ* Worth Sch, Magdalene Coll Cambridge (MA); *m* 1978, Melinda Ngaire, da of Capt Anthony Philip Towell, MC, of Ridge Rd, Long Island, NY, USA; 3 s (St John b 5 Jan 1980, Oliver b 9 May 1982, Alexander b 15 Feb 1984); *Career* ACA; *Style—* John Tyrwhitt, Esq

TYRWHITT, Brig Dame Mary Joan Caroline; DBE (1949, OBE 1946), TD; er da of Adm of the Fleet Sir Reginald Tyrwhitt, 1 Bt, GCB, DSO; *b* 27 Dec 1903; *Career* sr controller ATS (dir 1946-49), Brig WRAC 1949-50; Hon ADC to George VI 1949-50, asst admin WRVS Southern Region 1953-72; *Style—* Brig Dame Mary Tyrwhitt, DBE, TD

TYRWHITT, Sir Reginald Thomas Newman; 3 Bt (UK 1919), of Terschelling, and of Oxford; s of Adm Sir St John Reginald Joseph Tyrwhitt, 2 Bt, KCB, DSO, DSC (d 1961), and Nancy Veronica, da of Charles Newman Gilbey (gn of Sir Walter Gilbey, 1 Bt); Sir St John's gf's gf, Richard, was 3 s of Capt John Tyrwhitt, RN (d 1812), of Netherclay House, Somerset, by his w Katherine (paternal gda of Lady Susan Clinton, da of 6 Earl of Lincoln (a dignity now subsumed in the Duchy of Newcastle); Richard's er bro was (Sir) Thomas, *née* Tyrwhitt, who assumed (1790) the name of Jones (although subsequent holders of the Btcy appear to have been known as Tyrwhitt) & was cr a Bt 1808; Sir Thomas's ggs, Sir Raymond Tyrwhitt, 4 Bt, inherited his mother's Barony of Berners, *qv*, the Btcy becoming extinct 1950; John Tyrwhitt of Netherclay was seventh in descent from Marmaduke Tyrwhitt, yr s of Sir William Tyrwhitt, of Kettilby; *b* 21 Feb 1947; *Educ* Downside; *m* 1972 (m dis 1980 and annulled 1984), Sheila Gail, da of William Alistair Crawford Nicoll, of Liphook, Hants; m 2, 1984, Charlotte, o da of Capt Angus Jeremy Christopher Hildyard, DL, RA, *qv*; 1 s (Robert St John Hildyard b 1987), 1 da (Letitia Mary Hildyard b 1988); *Heir* s, Robert St John Hildyard b 1987; *Career* 2 Lt RA 1966, Lt 1969, RARO 1969; *Style—* Sir Reginald Tyrwhitt, Bt; c/o Lloyds Bank, 2 Silver St, Kingston-upon-Hull

TYSER, Hon Mrs (Susan Frances); *née* Remnant; da of 2 Baron Remnant, MBE (d 1967); *b* 9 May 1938; *m* 29 March 1967, Alan Tyser, s of Granville Tyser, of Park Lane, London W1; 1 s; *Style—* The Hon Mrs Tyser; West Hanney House, Wantage, Oxon

TYSON, Dr Alan Walker; CBE (1989); s of Lt Henry Alan Maurice Tyson (d 1975), of Edinburgh, and Dorothy Allan, *née* Walker (d 1959); *b* 27 Oct 1926; *Educ* Rugby, Magdalen Coll Oxford (BA, MA), Univ Coll London and Univ Coll Hosp Med Sch (MB BS); *Career* sr res fell All Souls Coll Oxford 1971- (fell 1952-), on editorial staff standard edn of Freud's works 1952-74, visiting lectr in psychiatry Montefiore Hosp NY 1967-68, lectr in psychopathology and developmental psychology Oxford Univ 1968-70, visiting prof of music Columbia Univ NY 1969, James PR Lyell reader in bibliography Oxford Univ 1973-74, Ernest Bloch prof of music Univ of California Berkeley 1977-78, memb Inst for Advanced Studies Princeton 1983-84, visiting prof of music Graduate Center City Univ of NY 1985; assoc memb Br Psychoanalytical Soc 1957-, MRCPsych 1972, FBA 1978; *Books* The Authentic English Editions of Beethoven (1963), English Music Publishers' Plate Numbers (with O W Neighbour, 1965), Selected Letters of Beethoven (ed 1967), Thematic Catalogue of the Works of Muzio Clementi (1967), Beethoven Studies (ed Vol 1 1973, Vol 2 1977, Vol 3 1982), The Beethoven Sketchbooks (with D Johnson and R Winter, 1985), Mozart: Studies of the Autograph Scores (1987); *Style—* Dr Alan Tyson, CBE; 7 Southcote Road, London N19 5BJ (☎ 071 609 2981); All Souls College, Oxford OX1 4AL (☎ 0865 279363)

TYSON, John Vernon; s of Gilbert John Gilbanks Tyson (d 1942), and Caroline, *née* Smith (d 1985); *b* 16 Feb 1937; *Educ* Keswick Sch, Fitzwilliam Coll Cambridge (MA); *m* 30 July 1966, Nigella Jane, da of Frederick John Sewry (d 1978); 1 s (Robin Timothy Gilbanks b 1971), 2 da (Rachel Caroline b 1969, Helen Mary b 1976); *Career* asst master Abingdon Sch 1960-66, head of mathematics and headmaster's admin asst Bradfield Coll 1966-78, headmaster St Edmund's Sch Canterbury 1978-; chm: Canterbury Cathedral Old Choristers' Assoc, Ellis Ctee Mathematics Panel 1980-84; memb Cncl ISCO 1989-; *Books* School Mathematic Project (books 1-5 co-author), Individualised Mathematics (co-author); *Recreations* music, chess, crossword, printing, DIY; *Style—* John V Tyson, Esq; Pontigny, University Rd, Canterbury, Kent CT2 8HU (☎ 0227 454575)

TYZACK, David Ian Heslop; s of Ernest Rudolf Tyzack, MBE (d 1973), and Joan Mary, *née* Palmer; *b* 21 March 1946; *Educ* Allhallows Sch, St Catharine's Coll Cambridge (MA); *m* 27 Jan 1973, Elizabeth Ann, da of Maj Henry Frank Cubitt, TD, Sutherlake Barton, Broadclyst, Exeter, Devon; 1 s (William b 12 June 983), 1 da (Anna b 6 April 1981); *Career* called to the Bar Inner Temple 1970; in practice Western Circuit; memb: The Hon Soc of the Inner Temple 1970; *Recreations* gardening, walking, skiing, church; *Style—* David Tyzack, Esq; 25 Southernhay East, Exeter, Devon (☎ 0392 55777, fax 0392 412001, car 0860 649686)

TYZACK, Margaret; OBE (1970); da of Thomas Edward Tyzack, and Doris, *née* Moseley; *Educ* St Angela's Ursuline Convent, RADA; *m* 26 March 1958, Alan Stephenson, s of Thomas Stephenson; 1 s (Matthew b 10 Aug 1964); *Career* actress; Royal Court Theatre: Progress to the Park, the Ginger Man, Tom and Viv (also Public Theatre New York, nominated for US Drama Desk Award); RSC: Coriolanus, Julius Caesar, Titus Andronicus, Summerfolk (also New York, Stratford, Ontario), Ghosts, Richard III, All's Well that End's Well, Lower Depths (at Art's theatre); other theatre work incl: The Cherry Orchard and Sisters Exeter and UK tour, A Man for All Seasons and Macbeth Nottingham and European tour, Find your Way Home, Open Space, Vivat Vivat Regina Piccadilly Theatre, People are Living There Royal Exchange Manchester, Veronica's Room Palace Watford, Mornings at Seven Westminster Theatre, An Inspector Calls and Night Must Fall Greenwich Theatre; SWET Best Actress Award for Martha in Who's Afraid of Virginia Woolf? National Theatre, Tony Nomination for the countess in All's Well that Ends Well RSC New York, Variety Club Best Actress Award for Lettice and Lovage Globe Theatre; films incl: Prick Up Your Ears, 2001, A Clockwork Orange, A Touch of Love, The Whisperers, Ring of Spies, The Wars, Mr Love; tv incl: The Forsyte Sage, The First Churchills (BAFTA Best Actress Award), Cousin Bette (US Emmy Nomination), A Winter's Tale, I Claudius, The Reason of things, Another Man's Life, Waters of the Moon, The Silver Box, Dear Octopus, Amelia Edwards, The Flowering Cherry, An Inspector Calls; *Style—* Ms Margaret Tyzack, OBE; c/o Joyce Edwards, 275 Kennington Road, London SE11 (☎ 071 735 5736)

U

UCHIDA, Mitsuko; da of Fujio Uchida, of Tokyo, and Yasuko Uchida; *b* 20 Dec 1948; *Educ* Hochschule fur Musik und Daistellende Kunst Wien; *Career* pianist; performed complete Mozart piano sonatas in London, Tokyo, Germany and NY; extensive work with English Chamber Orchestra incl complete Mozart piano concertos, has played with most major int orchs; recordings incl: complete Mozart piano sonatas, numerous Mozart piano concertos, Mozart quintet for piano and winds, Chopin Piano Sonatas 2 and 3, Debussy 12 Études; *awards* first prize Int Beethoven Competition Wien, second prize Int Chopin Competition Warsaw; numerous record prizes incl: The Gramaphone prize, Edison prize (Holland); *Recreations* music; Van Walsum Management, 26 Wadham Road, London SW15 2LR (☎ 081 874 6344, fax 081 877 0077)

UDAL, John Oliver; JP (Inner London 1966); s of Nicholas Robin Udal, CBE (d 1964), of Tunbridge Wells, and Margaret Ruth, *née* Oliver (d 1969); *b* 2 May 1926; *Educ* Winchester, New Coll Oxford (MA); *m* 1, 27 June 1959 (m dis 1979), Ann Leone Murray, *née* Hopkins; 2 s (Nicholas b 1960, Adrian b 1960), 1 da (Joanna b 1964); m 2, 17 May 1979, Ann Marie, da of Albert Edward Bridges Webb (d 1970); *Career* Irish Guards BAOR and Palestine 1944-48 (2 Lt 1945, Lt 1946); Sudan Political Serv 1950-55, asst dist cmmr Khartoum and Upper Nile MECAS 1951, first class magistrate 1953; Cons Res Dept 1955-66 (head cwlth affrs); shipbroker 1966-76, princ Baltic Mercantile and Shipping Exchange 1970-79, dir Eggar Forrester Hldgs Ltd 1970-79 (md Eggar Forrester Ltd, chm Terminal Operators Ltd); shipping conslt 1980-84, vice pres Jebsens UK Ltd 1980-82; liaison dir Central Cncl Econ League 1984-89 (ret 1989); memb LCC (S Kensington) 1961-65, Parly candidate Leeds South by election 1963, alderman GLC 1967-73; memb: City Parochial Fndn 1973- (chm Estates Ctee 1977-87), Tst for London 1988-, Exec Gordon Sch Fndn 1967- (govr 1969-81 and 1989-); Freeman City of London; *Books* Paying for Schooling (with T E Utley 1975); *Recreations* tennis, lower fell walking; *Clubs* Athenaeum; *Style—* John Udal, Esq, JP; 5 Soudan Rd, London SW11 4HH (☎ 071 627 1887)

UDALL, David Victor; s of George Edward Udall, of Woldingham, Surrey; *b* 8 Nov 1937; *Educ* Hampton GS; *m* 1974, Ann, da of John Daniel Ellwood; 2 s, 1 da; *Career* CA (own practice); md: Casetrend Ltd, Casetrend Property Investment Co Ltd; fin dir: Ellwall Properties Ltd, Ellwall Hldgs Ltd, Dereham Produce Co Ltd; *Recreations* tennis, landscape gardening, travelling; *Style—* David Udall, Esq; Dukes Edge, Lunghurst Rd, Woldingham, Surrey (☎ 088 365 2340)

UDALL, (Patricia) Jane; da of Dennis Udall, of Llangwnnadl, Gwynedd, North Wales, and Joan Irene, *née* Bayliss; *b* 24 March 1956; *Educ* Brierley Hill GS, Univ of Wales Aberystwth (BSc); *Career* CA 1981: fin dir Tibbatts & Co Design Gp Ltd 1986- (co sec 1984-86); memb ICAEW, ctee memb Design Business Assoc; *Recreations* sailing, tennis, skiing, netball, tapestry; *Clubs* Local Sports; *Style—* Miss Jane Udall; Apple Dorne, Greensforge Lane, Stourton, Nr Stourbridge, W Midlands DY7 5AB (☎ 0384 873828); 1 St Paul's Sq, Birmingham B3 1QU (☎ 021 233 2871, fax 021 236 8705)

UDOMA, Hon Sir (Egbert) Udo; CFR (1978); s of Chief Udoma Inam of Ibekwe Ntanaran Akama, Ikot Abasi, Akwa Ibom State, Nigeria, and Adiaha Edem; *b* 21 June 1917; *Educ* Methodist Coll Uzuakoli, Trinity Coll Dublin, St Catherine's Coll Oxford (LLB, MA, PhD); *m* 1950, Grace Bassey; 5 s (and 1 s decd), 1 da; *Career* barr Gray's Inn 1945, practised as barr and slr Supreme Ct Nigeria 1946-61, MHR Nigeria 1952-59, High Ct judge Lagos 1961-63, govr gen 1963, chief justice of Uganda 1963-69, justice Supreme Ct of Nigeria 1969-82, ret; nat pres Ibibio State Union 1947-61, memb Nigeria Mktg Co 1952-54, mangr ctee W Africa Inst for Oil Palm Research 1953-63, chm bd of tstees King George V Memorial Fund 1964-69, patron Nigeria Soc of Int Law 1968, chllr Ahmadu Bello Univ 1972-75, chm Constituent Assembly Nigerian Constitution 1977-78, dir and presiding justice Seminar for Judges Nigeria 1980 and 1981, memb Nigerian Inst of Int Affrs 1979-; awarded title of Obong Ikpa Isong Ibibio 1961; Hon LLD: Univ of Ibadan 1967, Ahamadu Bello Univ 1972, Trinity Coll Dublin 1973; kt 1964; *Publications* The Lion and the Oil Palm and other essays (1943), The Human Right to Individual Freedom - a Symposium on World Habeas Corpus (jty 1970), The Story of the Ibibio Union (1987); *Clubs* Metropolitan, Island (both Lagos); *Style—* Hon Sir Udo Udoma, CFR; Mfut Itiat Enin, 8 Dr Udoma St, Ikot Abasi, Akaw Ibom State, Nigeria

UFF, Dr John Francis; QC (1983); s of Frederick Uff (d 1981), and Eva Uff (d 1969); *b* 30 Jan 1942; *Educ* Stratton Sch Biggleswade, King's Coll London (BSc, PhD); *m* 29 July 1967, Diana Murial, da of Prof Ronald Graveson, CBE; 2 s (Alexander John b 1973, Christopher Edward b 1975), 1 da (Leonora Meriel b 1977); *Career* civil engr 1966-70, called to the Bar 1970, appointed arbitrator in many UK and foreign commercial disputes (mostly engrg and construction), visiting prof and dir Centre of Construction Law and Mgmnt King's Coll London 1987; FICE 1982, FCIArb 1982; *Books* Construction Law (4 edn, 1985), ICE Arbitration Practice (1985), Construction Contract Policy (1989), International and ICC Arbitration (1991); *Recreations* violin making, farming; *Style—* Dr John Uff, QC; 6 Southwood Lane, Highgate, London N6 (☎ 081 340 5127); Ashstead Farm, Selside, Cumbria

UFLAND, Richard Mark; s of Bertram Ufland, and Shirley, *née* Gross; *b* 4 May 1957; *Educ* St Paul's Sch, Downing Coll Cambridge (MA); *m* 20 Oct 1985, Jane Camilla, da of Louis Rapaport, 2 s (James b 1987, William b 1990); *Career* ptnr Stephenson Harwood 1986- (articled 1979-81, asst slr 1981-86); Freeman: City of London, Worshipful Co of Solicitors of the City of London; memb Law Soc; *Recreations* classical music, bridge, skiing; *Style—* Richard Ufland, Esq; 10 Folly Close, Radlett, Herts WD7 8DR (☎ 0923 854378); One St Paul's Churchyard, London EC4M 8SH (☎ 071 329 4422, fax 071 606 8822, telex 886789 SHSPC G)

UGLOW, Euan Ernest Richard; s of Ernest Uglow, of London, and Elizabeth Jane, *née* Williams; *b* 10 March 1932; *Educ* Strand GS for Boys, Univ Coll, Slade Sch of Fine Art; *Career* work represented in following public collections: Tate Gallery, Arts Cncl, Ferens Art Gallery, Cardiff Art Gallery, Govt Art Collection; fell Univ Coll London; artist tstee National Gallery London 1990-; *Clubs* Garrick; *Style—* Euan Uglow, Esq; c/o Browse & Darby Ltd, 19 Cork St, London W1X 2LP (☎ 071 734 7984)

UHLMAN, Hon Mrs (Nancy Diana Joyce); da of 1 Baron Croft, CMG, TD, PC (d 1947), and Hon Nancy, da of 1 Baron Borwick; *b* 1912; *m* 1936, Dr Manfred Uhlman (d 1985); 1 s (Francis Raymond Croft b 1943), 1 da (Caroline Ann b 1940); *Style—* The Hon Mrs Uhlman; Croft Castle, nr Leominster, Herefordshire HR6 9PW

ULLATHORNE, Peter Lindley; s of Philip Stanley Ullathorne (d 1990), and Mary Lindley Ullathorne; *b* 6 Aug 1948; *Educ* Chesterfield GS, City of Leicester Poly, AA Sch of Architecture, RIBA (AA Dip); *Career* architect; Richard Rogers Partnership 1971-74, Louis De Soissons Partnership 1974-77, GMW Partnership 1977-80, YRM Architects 1980-83, DEGW Architects 1983-86, md First Architectual Group plc 1986-89, gp dir McColl Gp Limited 1989-, visiting prof Univ of Cincinatti 1985; Freeman City of London 1990, Liveryman Worshipful Co of Chartered Architects; memb AA 1971, MRIBA 1974, FRSA 1989; *Recreations* reading, opera, country life; *Clubs* RAC, London Library; *Style—* Peter Lindley Ullathorne, Esq; 136 Somerset Rd, Wimbledon, London SW19 5HP (☎ 081 879 1208); 1 South Lodge Court, Brampton, Chesterfield, Derbyshire S40 3QG

ULLMAN, Hon Mrs (Julian Mary); *née* Russell; da of Baron Russell of Killowen, PC; *b* 1935; *m* 1, 1955 (m dis 1974), Anthony Allfrey, s of Lady Holman, *qv*, by her 1 husb Capt Basil Allfrey; 1 s, 2 da; m 2, Mr Ullman, of Norfolk, Virginia, USA; *Style—* The Hon Mrs Ullman

ULLMAN, Tracey; da of Anthony John Ullman (d 1966), and Dorin, *née* Cleaver; *b* 30 Dec 1959; *Educ* The Italia Conti Stage Sch Brixton; *m* 27 Dec 1983, Allan John McKeown, s of late Victor McKeown; 1 da (Mabel Ellen b 2 April 1986); *Career* dancer: Gigi (Theatre des Westerns Berlin) 1976, Second Generation (Blackpool and Liverpool) 1977; musicals: Elvis (Astoria) 1978, Oh Boy (Astoria) 1978, Rocky Horror Show (Comedy Theatre) 1979; theatre: Talent (Everyman Liverpool) 1980, Dracula (Young Vic) 1980, Four in a Million (Royal Court) 1981, She Stoops to Conquer (Lyric Hammersmith) 1982, The Taming of the Shrew (NY Shakespeare Festival Broadway) 1990, The Big Love (one woman show) 1991; tv incl: Three of a Kind 1981-83, A Kick up the Eighties 1981 and 1983, The Young Visitors 1984, Girls on Top 1985, The Tracey Ullman Show 1987-90; films: Plenty 1984, I Love You to Death 1989; recordings: various top ten singles 1981-84, You Broke my Heart in Seventeen Places (album, Gold record); Most Promising New Actress London Theatre Critics award 1981, Best Light Entertainment Performance BAFTA 1983, five American comedy awards 1988-90, Best Female Comedy Performance Golden Globe awards USA 1988; Emmy awards (USA): Best Variety Show tv 1989, Best Writing 1990, Best Performance in a Variety or Music Show 1990; *Recreations* hiking, riding, finding unspoilt areas of the earth and being quiet; *Style—* Miss Tracey Ullman; Duncan Heath Associates Ltd, 162-170 Wardour St, London WIV 3AT

ULLMANN, Prof Julian Richard; s of Richard Edwin Ullmann (d 1988), of West Hoathly, Sussex, and Thelma Beatrice, *née* Ford; *b* 21 June 1936; *Educ* Eastbourne Coll, Pembroke Coll Cambridge (MA), Imperial Coll London (PhD); *m* 7 Nov 1964, Margaret Evelyn, da of Dr Gerald Beeston (d 1968); 1 s (David b 1967), 1 da (Karen b 1969); *Career* princ scientific offr Nat Physical Laboratory 1970 (scientific offr 1959), head Dept of Computer Sci Univ of Sheffield 1980 (prof 1975), head and prof of computer sci Royal Holloway and Bedford New Coll Univ of London 1986, head of Dept of Computing and prof of computer sci King's Coll Univ of London 1989-; chm: British Pattern Recognition Assoc 1976-84, Alvey MMI Pattern Analysis Ctee 1983-87; CEng, FBCS; *Books* Pattern Recognition Techniques (1973), Micro Computer Technology (1982), A Pascal Database Book (1986); *Recreations* serious music; *Style—* Prof Julian Ullmann; Dept of Computing, King's College London, Strand, London WC2R 2LS (☎ 071 873 2595)

ULLSTEIN, Augustus Rupert Patrick Anthony; s of Frederick Charles Leopold Ullstein (d 1988), of Chiswick, and Patricia, *née* Guinness; *b* 21 March 1947; *Educ* Bradfield, LSE (LLB); *m* 12 Sept 1970, Pamela Margaret, da of Claude Wells (d 1974), of Woodford, Essex; 2 s (William b 3 July 1980, George b 29 April 1983), 2 da (Elizabeth b 1 June 1977, Caroline b 28 Oct 1978); *Career* called to the Bar Inner Temple 1970, dep registrar Family Div 1987; dir Saxon Radio 1980-87; Freeman City of London 1982, Liveryman Worshipful Co of Bowyers 1982; *Books* The Law of Restrictive Trade Practices and Monopolies (second supplement to second edn, 1973), Matrimonial and Domestic Injunctions (1982); *Recreations* after dinner speaking, television, my children; *Clubs* Farmers; *Style—* Augustus Ullstein, Esq; 74 Duke's Ave, Chiswick, London W4; 5 Paper Buildings, Temple, London EC4 (☎ 071 353 8494, fax 071 583 1926, car 0836 250 954)

ULLSWATER, 2 Viscount (UK 1921); Nicholas James Christopher Lowther; s of Lt John Arthur Lowther, MVO, RNVR (d 1942); suc ggf, 1 Viscount Ullswater, GCB (s of late Hon William Lowther, bro of late 3 Earl of Lonsdale), 1949; *b* 9 Jan 1942; *Educ* Eton, Trinity Coll Cambridge; *m* 1967, Susan, da of James Howard Weatherby, of Salisbury, Wilts, by his w Mary (4 da of Sir Hereward Wake, 13 Bt, CB, CMG, DSO, JP, DL); 2 s (Hon Benjamin b 1975, Hon Edward b 8 Oct 1981), 2 da (Hon Emma b 1968, Hon Clare b 1970); *Heir* s, Hon Benjamin James Lowther b 26 Nov 1975; *Career* Capt Royal Wessex Yeo TAVR 1973-78; a Lord in Waiting 1989-90; Parly under-sec of state Dept of Employment 1990-; farmer; *Style—* The Rt Hon the Viscount Ullswater; Barrow Street House, nr Mere, Warminster, Wilts BA12 6AB (☎ 0747 860621)

ULRICK, Alan Henry; s of Henry Alexander Ulrick, of Hayes, Middlesex, and the late Ivy Beatrice, *née* Wright; *b* 25 June 1928; *Educ* Principal Sch, Chiswick Poly; *m* 10 Sept 1961, (Lily) Bronwen Gwen, da of the late Robert Lee; 2 da (Caroline Louise b 1963, d 1971, Susannah Elizabeth b 1965); *Career* Nat Serv RAF 1946-49; Chase Manhattan Bank NA London: joined 1944, asst gen mangr 1977, sr vice-pres capital mkts and foreign exchange sector 1987-90; *Recreations* bridge, sailing, horse racing (owner), gardening; *Clubs* Overseas Bankers, Int Forex Assoc; *Style—* Alan Ulrick, Esq; Twintops, 38 Oatlands Chase, Weybridge, Surrey (☎ 0932 223 316)

ULYATE, Hon Mrs (Frances Margaret); *née* Douglas; da of Baron Douglas of Barloch, KCMG (d 1980), by 1 w, Minnie, *née* Smith (d 1969); *b* 22 May 1920; *Educ* St Pauls Girls Sch, London Sch of Medicine for Women; *m* 1943, Kenneth Ulyate, PhD, MSc; 2 s, 1 da; *Career* conslt anaesthetist (ret); memb RSM; *Books* contributed to Active Learnings in Hospitals (R W Revans); *Recreations* music, gardening, embroidery; *Style—* The Hon Mrs Ulyate; 8 Cambridge Rd, London SW11 4RS (☎ 071 228 2247); 8 Market Place, Tetbury, Glos GL8 8DA (☎ 0666 54009)

ULYATE, Hon Mrs (Katharine Hilda); *née* Borwick; da of 3 Baron Borwick (d 1961), by 1 w, Irene Phyllis (d 1969), da of Thomas Main Patterson; *b* 1914; *m* 1938, Ashton Jack Ulyate; 2 s (Stanley b 1939, Raymond b 1955), 1 da (Sandra (Mrs Berry) b 1945); *Style*— The Hon Mrs Ulyate; 5 Elgarth, 19 St Patrick Road, Pietermaritzburg 3201, Natal, S Africa

UNDERHILL, Prof Allan Edward; s of Albert Edward Underhill (d 1977), and Winifred, *née* Bailey (d 1982); *b* 13 Dec 1935; *Educ* Derby Sch Derby, Univ of Hull (BSc, PhD), Univ of Wales (DSc); *m* 13 Aug 1960, Audrey Jean, da of Harry Foster (d 1973); 1 s (David b 1964), 1 da (Ann b 1963); *Career* res chemist ICI Ltd 1961-62, lectr Univ of Loughborough 1962-65, prof Univ of Wales Bangor 1983- (lectr 1965-74, sr lectr 1974-83); SERC 1988-: memb Chem Ctee, memb Molecular Electronics Ctee, memb Nat Ctee for Superconductivity, coordinator initiative on materials for the 21 century; FRCS 1972; *Recreations* photography, badminton, theate; *Style*— Prof Allan Underhill; Meifod, 46 Ffiddoedd Rd, Bangor, Gwynedd LL57 2TW (☎ 0248 370929); Department of Chemistry, University of Wales, Bangor, Gwynedd LL57 2UW (☎ 0248 351151, fax 0248 370528)

UNDERHILL, Kenneth; s of Frederick William Underhill (d 1934), and Gladys, *née* Thompson (d 1984); *b* 2 July 1928; *Educ* Rutherford Coll Newcastle, Br Coll of Naturopathy and Osteopathy; *m* 15 Aug 1953, Evelyn Ellen, da of Albert Edward Barnard (d 1986); 4 s (Nicholas Peter, Simon Barry, Christopher Andrew, Carl Philip), 1 da (Melanie Jane); *Career* Nat Serv Corpl PT Instr RAF 1946, memb RAF gymnastic display team; lectr in differential diagnosis Br Coll of Naturopathy and Osteopathy 1955-65, visiting osteopath Windmill Theatre 1955 - closure; int lectr on cranial osteopathy, TV appearances; memb: Cranial Osteopathy Assoc, Acupuncture Assoc; Freeman City of London 1988; Hon Dr in Acupuncture France; MRO; *Recreations* golf, tennis, windsurfing, water-skiing; *Clubs* Muswell Hill Golf; *Style*— Kenneth Underhill, Esq; Glenside Vineyards Rd, Northaw, Herts EN6 4PF (☎ 0707 87 4446); 7 Park Crescent, Regents Park, London W1N 3HE (☎ 071 402 4430)

UNDERHILL, Nicholas Peter; s of Kenneth Underhill, and Evelyn Ellen, *née* Barnard; *b* 15 Jan 1955; *Educ* William Ellis Sch; *m* 28 July 1973, Julie Ann Evelyn, da of Wilfred Augustus Michael Chard, of London; 3 s (Matthew, James, Julian), 1 da (Lyndsey); *Career* property advtg mangr Evening Standard 1974-75, ptnr Druce & Co 1978-81, equity ptnr Hampton & Sons 1986-87, md Hamptons (estate agents) 1988-89; chm Underhill Group of Companies 1989-; memb Hampstead and Highgate Cons Assoc; MLandInst; *Recreations* shooting, rugby, skiing, opera, power boating; *Clubs* Carlton, MCC, Saracens RFC, Lords Taverners; *Style*— Nicholas Underhill, Esq; Wellfield Ave, London N10 (☎ 081 444 2248); Villa Sous Colline, 5 Rue De L'Occident, Port Grimaud, S France; Underhill Group, Kit Cat House, 89 Heath Street, Hampstead, London NW3 6UG (☎ 071 435 4343, fax 071 794 4558, car 0860 560 997)

UNDERHILL, Baron (Life Peer UK 1979), of Leyton, Greater London; (Henry) Reginall Underhill (Reg); CBE (1976); s of Henry James Underhill (d 1943), and Alice Maud Underhill (d 1957), of Walthamstow; *b* 8 May 1914; *Educ* Tom Hood Central Sch Leytonstone; *m* 1937, Flora Janet, da of Leonard George Philbrick; 2 s (Hon Terry Leonard b 1938 m 1959 Dorothy Askew, Hon Robert b 1948 m 1970 Christine Ann Vinson), 1 da (Hon Joan Evelyn (Hon Mrs Taylor) b 1944); *Career* takes Labour whip in House of Lords; memb APEX 1931-; propaganda offr Lab Pty 1947, regional organiser W Midlands 1948, asst nat agent 1960, nat agent of the Lab Pty 1972-79, advsr to Home Sec 1980-84, memb Parly delgn to Zimbabwe 1980, memb IPU delgn to USSR 1986, dep ldr Lab Oppn 1982-89, oppn spokesman (Lords) Electoral Affairs and Transport 1980-; pres Assoc of Metropolitan Authorities; memb: Houghton Ctee on Financial Aid to Political Parties 1975-76, Kilbrandon Ctee on New Ireland Forum 1984; *Recreations* golf, life-long supporter Leyton Orient FC; *Style*— The Rt Hon the Lord Underhill, CBE; 94 Loughton Way, Buckhurst Hill, Essex IG9 6AH (☎ 081 504 1910)

UNDERHILL, Hon Robert; s of Baron Underhill, CBE (Life Peer); *b* 26 Feb 1948; *Educ* Handsworth GS, Chingford County HS, Queen Mary Coll London (BSc); *m* 1970, Christine Ann, da of Ernest Edward Lawrence Vinsen; 1 s (Bruce), 1 da (Helen); *Career* sr mangr Touche Ross & Co; fin dir and co sec: Ritz Design Gp plc 1986-87, Campbell & Armstrong plc; FCA; *Recreations* gardening, sport and other outdoor pursuits; *Style*— The Hon Robert Underhill; Campbell & Armstrong plc, Broom House, Highfield Rd, Levenshulme, Manchester M19 3WD

UNDERHILL, Hon Terry Leonard; s of Baron Underhill, CBE (Life Peer); *b* 1938; *m* 1960, Dorothy, da of late Edwin Askew; 3 s (Philip b 1964, Richard b 1967, Duncan b 1969); *Style*— The Hon Terry Underhill; Fairlight, Mill Cross, Rattery, S Brent, Devon TQ10 9LB (☎ 036 47 2314)

UNDERWOOD, Derek Leslie; MBE (1981); s of Leslie Frank Underwood (d 1978), of Kent, and Evelyn Ann, *née* Wells; *b* 8 June 1945; *Educ* Dulwich Coll Prep Sch, Beckenham and Penge GS; *m* 1973, Dawn, da of Gerald Daniel Sullivan, of Surrey; 2 da (Heather b 1976, Fiona b 1977); *Career* cricketer; joined Kent 1962, County Cap 1964, England debut 1966, left-arm spin bowler, 86 Test matches - 297 test wickets; yst player ever to take 100 wickets in debut season, ret from first class cricket 1987; dir Club Surfaces Ltd (artificial grass surfaces co); pres Met Dist Assoc of Kent CCs; *Style*— Derek Underwood, MBE; Kent County Cricket Club, St Lawrence Ground, Canterbury, Kent (☎ 0227 456886)

UNDERWOOD, Grahame John Taylor; s of Wing Cdr Shirley Taylor Underwood, OBE, of Elstone, nr Newark, and Joyce Mary, *née* Smith; *b* 1 July 1944; *Educ* Ashby De La Zouch GS, Poly of N London (Dip Arch); *m* 4 May 1968, Christine Elva, da of Sqdn Ldr Cecil Reginald Long, MBE, DSM (d 1972); 2 s (Christopher Taylor b 1971, Toby Grahame b 1972), 1 da (Lucy Jane b 1974); *Career* Watkins Gray Int: architect and planner 1969-72, assoc 1972-83, ptnr 1983, dir 1983-; dir: Watkins Gray Peter Jones 1983-, Watkins Gray Int Ltd 1983-, Watkins Gray Ho & Ptnrs 1989-; princ designs incl: Royal Masonic Hosp, Nat Heart and Chest Hosps London and Baghdad, Dammam and Unayzah Hosps Saudi Arabia, Bromley Hosp, Orpington Hosp; fndr memb Care Health Planning; chm Edgbaston Round Table 1984; memb: BSI Tech Ctee, RIBA 1973; *Books* Architects Jl Handbook of Ironmongery (1979), The Security of Buildings (1984), numerous tech articles; *Recreations* gliding (holder int silver cert); *Clubs* Midland Gliding; *Style*— Grahame Underwood, Esq; Watkins Gray Int, Alexander House, Spur Rd, Orpington, Kent BR6 0QR (☎ 0689 870521, fax 0689 835151)

UNDERWOOD, Rory; s of late James Ashley Underwood, and Anne Tan; *b* 19 June 1963; *Educ* Barnard Castle Sch; *m* 19 Sept 1987, Wendy, da of Laurence Sydney Blanshard; 1 da (Rebecca Jennifer Anne b 25 June 1990); *Career* Rugby Union wing threequarter Leicester FC and England (38 caps); clubs: Middlesborough RUFC, Leicester FC, RAF RFC, Barbarians RFC; rep: Eng Colts, Eng U23, Eng B (debut 1982); England: debut v Ireland 1984, memb World Cup squad 1987 (3 appearances), tour Aust 1988 (2 test appearances), tour Romania 1989; Br Lions tour Aust 1989 (3 test appearances); Eng records: most capped back and wing, most tries in internationals (22), most tries in an international (jtly held, 5 v Fiji 1989); cmmnd RAF 1983, awarded wings 1985, 360 Sqdn 1986; *Recreations* crosswords, reading, music; *Style*— Rory Underwood, Esq; Gembira, 6 Primrose Way, Witham Meadows, Grantham, Lincs NG31 7HS (☎ 0476 74681); c/o Rugby Football Union, Twickenham, Middlesex (☎ 081 892 8161)

UNGER, Michael Ronald; s of Ronald Unger, CBE, of Carvoeiro, Algarve, Portugal, and Joan Maureen Unger; *b* 8 Dec 1943; *Educ* Wirral GS; *m* 20 Aug 1966, Eunice; 1 s (Paul b 1973), 1 da (Sarah decd); *Career* ed: Daily Post Liverpool 1977-82, Liverpool Echo 1982-83, Manchester Evening News 1983-; dir: the Guardian & Manchester Evening News plc 1983-; tstee the Scott Tst 1986-; *Books* The Memoirs of Bridget Hitler; *Recreations* reading, walking; *Clubs* Press (Manchester); *Style*— Michael Unger, Esq; 164 Deansgate, Manchester (☎ 061 832 7200)

UNMACK, Timothy Stuart Brooke; s of Randall Carter Unmack (d 1978), and Anne Roberta, *née* Stuart (d 1972); *b* 5 Aug 1937; *Educ* Radley, Christ Church Oxford (MA); *m* 21 May 1966, Eleanor Gillian, da of George Aidan Drury Tait (d 1970); 2 s (Guy Douglas b 13 March 1975, Neil Alexander b 29 July 1977); *Career* Nat Serv RN; admitted slr 1965, sr ptnr Beaumont & Son 1987 (ptnr 1968-); memb ctee on legal aspects of air traffic control of Int Law Soc; former chm Royal Philanthropic Soc Redhill; memb Worshipful Co of Barbers; memb: Law Soc 1965, Royal Aeronautical Soc 1987, Royal Soc for Asian Affairs 1987; *Recreations* squash, sailing, languages; *Clubs* Utd Oxford & Cambridge Univ; *Style*— Timothy Unmack, Esq; Lloyds Chambers, 1 Portsoken St, London E1 8AW (☎ 071 481 3100, fax 071 481 3353, telex 889018 BOSUN G)

UNSWORTH, Sir Edgar Ignatius Godfrey; CMG (1954), QC (N Rhodesia, now Zambia, 1951); s of John Unsworth; *b* 18 April 1906; *Educ* Stonyhurst, Manchester Univ; *m* 1964, Eileen, widow of Raymond Ritzema; *Career* barr Gray's Inn 1930, fought Farnworth (C) 1935 Gen Election; Crown counsel: Nigeria 1937, N Rhodesia 1942 (slr-gen 1946, then slr-gen Malaya Fedn), attorney-gen N Rhodesia 1951-56, attorney-gen Nigeria 1956-60, federal justice Supreme Court of Nigeria 1960-62; CJ: Nyasaland 1962-64, Gibraltar 1965-76; justice appeal Gibraltar 1976-81; kt 1963; *Style*— Sir Edgar Unsworth, CMG, QC; Pedro el Grande 9, Sotogrande, (Cadiz), Spain

UNSWORTH, Michael Anthony; s of Lt Cdr John Geoffrey Unsworth, MBE, of Hayling Island, Hants, and Joan Rhyllis, *née* Clemes; *b* 29 Oct 1949; *Educ* St John's Coll Southsea Hants, Enfield Coll of Tech (BA); *m* 1 Dec 1973, Masa, da of Prof Zitomir Lozica, of Orebic, Yugoslavia; 2 da (Tania Elizabeth b 10 Oct 1978, Tessa Joanna b 27 June 1981); *Career* res analyst Grieveson Grant & Co 1972-79, ptnr Scott Goff Hancock & Co 1981-86 (sr oil analyst 1979-81, Scott Goff Hancock merged with Smith Bros to form Smith New Ct), dir i/c of res Smith New Ct 1989- (dir i/c of energy res 1986-); memb Stock Exchange; assoc: Soc of Investmt Analysts, Inst of Petroleum; memb: London Oil Analysts Gp (former chm), Nat Assoc of Petroleum Investmt Analysts (USA), Edinburgh and Leith Petroleum Club; *Recreations* sailing, opera, theatre; *Clubs* Little Ship, Cruising Assoc; *Style*— Michael Unsworth, Esq; Smith New Court plc, Smith New Court House, 20 Farringdon Road, London EC1M 3NH (☎ 071 772 1000, fax 071 772 2908)

UNSWORTH, Dr Philip Francis; s of Stephen Unsworth (d 1959), of Manchester, and Teresa *née* McElin; *b* 18 Sept 1947; *Educ* St Bede's Coll, Univ of Manchester (BSc, MB ChB); *Career* doctor; house surgn and physician Manchester Royal Inf 1971-72; lectr: Middlesex Hosp 1972-75, St Thomas Hosp 1975-76; microbiologist: Colindale 1977-79, Tameside and Glossop DHA 1979-; *Recreations* sports and walking, music, reading; *Style*— Dr Philip Unsworth; 1 Pine Rd, Didsbury, Manchester M20 0UY (☎ 061 445 6480); Dept Microbiology, Tameside General Hospital, Ashton-U-Lyne, Lancs OL6 9RW (☎ 061 330 8373)

UNSWORTH, Walter (Walt); *b* 16 Dec 1928; *Educ* Wigan Tech Coll, Chester Coll (LCP); *m* 2 June 1952, Dorothy Winstanley; 1 s (Duncan b 1958), 1 da (Gail b 1953); *Career* RA 1947-49; sci teacher 1951-73, editorial dir Cicerone Press 1968, ed Climber and Rambler Magazine 1974-86; hon vice pres Lancashire Mountaineering Club, memb Soc of Authors 1970, pres Outdoor Writers Guild 1979, memb Br Guild of Travel Writers 1988; *Books* The English Outcrops (1944), The Young Mountaineer (1959), Tiger in the Snow (1966), The Book of Rock Climbing (1968), North Face (1969), Portrait of the River Derwent (1971), Encyclopaedia of Mountaineering (1975), Peaks, Passes and Glaciers (1981), Everest (1981), The Pennine Playground (1984), Savage Snows (1986), Classic Walks in the Lake District (1988), Classic Walks in the Yorkshire Dales (1989); *Recreations* travel, mountain walking, photography; *Clubs* Alpine; *Style*— Walt Unsworth, Esq; Harmony Hall, Milnthorpe, Cumbria LAY 7QE (☎ 05395 62112); Cicerone Press, 2 Police Square, Milnthorpe, Cumbria LA7 7PY (☎ 05593 62069, fax 05395 63417)

UNWIN, Sir (James) Brian; KCB; s of Reginald Unwin (d 1975), and Winifred Annie, *née* Walthall (d 1989); *b* 21 Sept 1935; *Educ* Chesterfield Sch, New Coll Oxford (MA), Yale Univ (MA); *m* 5 May 1964, Diana Susan, da of Sir David Aubrey Scott, GCMG, *qv*; 3 s (Michael Alexander, Christopher James, Nicholas Edward); *Career* HM Civil Serv: asst princ CRO 1960, second later first sec Br High Cmmn Salisbury Southern Rhodesia 1961-64, first sec Br High Cmmn Accra 1964-65, FCO 1965-68, HM Treasy 1968-81 (asst sec 1972, under sec 1975), dep sec Cabinet Off 1985-87 (under sec 1981-83), dep sec HM Treasy 1983-85, chm of the bd HM Customs & Excise 1987-; UK dir Euro Investmt Bank 1983-85, hon sec bd of dirs ENO 1987-; chm Civil Serv Sports Cncl 1989-; CBIM 1988; *Recreations* bird watching, opera, Wellington, Trollope; *Clubs* Reform, Vincents, Kingswood Village (Surrey); *Style*— Sir Brian Unwin, KCB; HM Customs & Excise, New King's Beam House, 22 Upper Ground, London SE1 9PJ (☎ 071 382 5001)

UNWIN, David Charles; s of Peter Charles Unwin, and Rosemary Gwendolen Winifred, *née* Locket; *b* 12 May 1947; *Educ* Clifton, Trinity Coll Oxford (BA); *m* 16 Aug 1969, Lorna, da of Richard Frank Bullivant; 1 s (James b 1978), 1 da (Catherine b 1974); *Career* called to the Bar Lincoln's Inn 1971, treasy jr counsel in charity matters 1987-; *Recreations* music, mountaineering, sailing; *Style*— David Unwin, Esq; 7 Stone Bldgs, Lincoln's Inn, London WC2 (☎ 071 405 3886, fax 071 242 8502)

UNWIN, David Storr; s of Sir Stanley Unwin, KCMG (d 1968), and Alice Mary Storr (d 1971); *b* 3 Dec 1918; *Educ* Abbotsholme Sch Derbys; *m* 31 July 1945, Bridget Mary Periwinkle, da of Capt (E) Sydney Jasper Herbert, RN (d 1941); 1 da (Phyllida b 1950), 1 s (Corydon b 1950); *Career* author; *Books Incl:* The Governor's Wife (1954), A View of the Heath (1956), Fifty Years with Father (biography, 1982); books for children: Rickafire! (1942), Dream Gold (1948), Drumbeats (1953), The Future Took Us (1957), Foxy-Boy (1959), The Girl in the Grove (1974), The Wishing Bone (1977); *Recreations* travel; *Clubs* Pen; *Style*— David S Unwin, Esq; Garden Flat, 31 Belsize Park, London NW3 4DX (☎ 071 435 5198)

UNWIN, Ven Kenneth; s of Percy Unwin (d 1971), and Elsie, *née* Holmes (d 1979); *b* 16 Sept 1926; *Educ* Chesterfield Sch, St Edmund Hall Oxford (MA); *m* 1958, Beryl, da of Arthur Riley (d 1990), of Leeds; 1 s (Michael b 1973), 4 da (Katharine b 1959, Helen b 1961, Sarah b 1963, Ruth b 1965); *Career* vicar: St John Baptist Dodworth 1959-69, St John Baptist Royston Barnsley 1969-73, St John Baptist Wakefield 1973-82; archdeacon of Pontefract 1981-; *Style*— Ven The Archdeacon of Pontefract; Pontefract House, 19a Tithe Barn Street, Horbury, Wakefield WF4 6LJ (☎ 0924 263777)

UNWIN, HE Peter William; CMG (1981); s of Arnold Unwin, and Norah Unwin; *b* 20 May 1932; *Educ* Ampleforth, Ch Ch Oxford (MA); *m* 1955, Monica Steven; 2 s, 2 da;

Career army 1954-56; entered Foreign Office 1956, cnsllr (econ) Bonn 1973-75, head Personnel Policy Dept FCO 1976-78, min (econ) Bonn 1980-82, ambass to Hungary 1983-86, ambass to Denmark 1986; *Style*— HE Mr Peter Unwin, CMG; British Embassy, Kastelsvet 40, Copenhagen, Denmark; Foreign and Commonwealth Office, King Charles St, London SW1

UNWIN, Rayner Stephens; CBE; s of Sir Stanley Unwin (d 1968), and Alice Mary Storr (d 1971); *b* 23 Dec 1925; *Educ* Abbotsholme Sch, Trinity Coll Oxford (MA), Harvard (MA); *m* 1952, Carol Margaret, *née* Curwen; 1 s (Merlin b 1954), 3 da (Camilla b 1955, Tamara b 1958, Sharon b 1958); *Career* publisher; *Recreations* skiing downhill, hill walking, birds, gardens; *Clubs* Garrick; *Style*— Rayner Unwin, Esq, CBE; Limes Cottage, Little Missenden, Nr Amersham, Bucks; 19 New Row, London WC2

UNWIN, Vicky; da of Thomas Michael Unwin, of Milverton, Somerset, and Sheila Margaret Findlay Mills; *b* 3 Nov 1957; *Educ* Wycombe Abbey, Oxford HS, Girton Coll Cambridge (BA); *m* 18 June 1983, Ross Brett Cattell, s of Dr William Ross Cattell, of London; 1 s (Thomas William b 21 Jan 1988); *Career* dir Heinemann Educnl Boleswa 1987-, publishing dir Heinemann Educnl Books 1987-90 (graduate traineeship 1979-80), md Heineman International Literature and Textbooks 1990-; sec Int Charity Assoc for Teaching Caribbean and African Lit 1984-87; *Recreations* skiing, walking, riding, gardening, reading; *Style*— Ms Vicky Unwin; 3 Manor Cottages, Westbrook St, Blewbury, Oxon (☎ 0235 851032); Heinemann ILT, Halley Ct, Jordan Hill, Oxford OX2 8EJ (☎ 0865 311366, fax 0865 310043, telex 837292 HEBOXF G)

UPHAM, Charles Hazlitt; VC (1943) and Bar (1943), JP; s of John Hazlitt Upham (barr, d 1951), and Agatha Upham (d 1975); *b* 21 Sept 1908; *Educ* Christ's Coll NZ, Lincoln Agric Coll (Post Grad Land Valuation); *m* 1945, Mary, da of James McTamney (d 1916); 3 da; *Career* Capt WWII (POW Colditz, amongst others camps); sheep farmer 1700 acres, now semi-retired; *Recreations* riding, fishing, reading; *Clubs* Christchurch, Canterbury and Officers (all NZ); hon memb Sydney RSL; *Style*— Charles Upham, Esq, VC, JP; Landsdowne, Parnassus Rd, N Canterbury, New Zealand

UPSHALL, John; s of Reginald Charles Upshall (d 1981), and Lucy May, *née* Spicer; *b* 1 May 1942; *Educ* Latymer Upper Sch Hammersmith London; *m* 8 May 1965, Frances Anne, da of Eric Randell Cooper (d 1986); 2 s (Richard b 1970, Craig b 1973); *Career* co sec Lilly Industries Ltd 1988- (fin controller 1979-88); memb Rotary Club of Basingstoke; FCA 1964; *Recreations* amateur drama, riding; *Style*— John Upshall, Esq; 17 Franklin Ave, Hartley Wintney, Basingstoke, Hampshire RG27 8RV (☎ 0251 264299); Lilly Industries Limited, Kingsclere Rd, Basingstoke, Hampshire RG21 2XA (☎ 0256 473241, fax 0256 485900)

UPSHON, Laurence Marshall; s of Lt-Col Hector Llewellyn Marshall Upshon (d 1957), and Hilda Winifred, *née* Southgate; *b* 21 June 1950; *Educ* St Peter's Sch Yerrow Guildford Surrey; *m* 18 July 1970, Heide Maria, da of Gustav Hawlin, of Salzburg, Austria; 2 s (Rupert b 1977, Robin b 1979), 1 da (Claire b 1976); *Career* asst gp ed Stratford Express Gp 1974-76, Southern TV 1976-87 (features ed 1980), exec prodr news and current affairs TUS 1982-84 (sr prodr 1981), ed Coast and Coast 1984-85, head of news Central TV 1989- (ed central news 1985); memb: RTS, BAFTA, ABE, RTNDA(US); *Recreations* sport (cricket), painting, reading, music; *Style*— Laurence Upshon, Esq; Whitlenge House, Hartlebury, Worcestershire DY10 4HD (☎ 0299 250567); Central Television plc, Broad St, Birmingham B1 2JP (☎ 021 643 9898, fax 021 616 1633, car 0836 532279)

UPTON, Prof Anthony Frederick; s of C A Upton (d 1936), and S G, *née* McCarthy (d 1980); *b* 13 Oct 1929; *Educ* Windsor Co Boy's Sch, Queen's Coll Oxford (MA), Duke's Univ USA (AM); *m* 12 Aug 1951, Sirkka Rauha, da of Onni Pöllänen, of Helsinki, Finland; 3 s (Nicholas b 3 July 1957, Timothy b 19 Dec 1958, Jeremy b 11 Jan 1963); *Career* asst lectr in modern history Univ of Leeds 1953-56; Univ of St Andrews 1956-: lectr in modern history 1956, sr lectr 1966, reader 1974, prof of Nordic history 1983, chm Modern History Dept 1987; memb: Lab Pty, Hist Assoc, Socialist Educn Assoc; fell Porthan Soc Univ of Turku Finland; FRHistS; *Books* Sir Arthur Ingram (1961), Finland in Crisis 1940-41 (1964), The Communist Parties of Scandinavia and Finland (1973), Finland 1939-40 (1974), The Finnish Revolution 1917-18 (1980); *Recreations* promoting the demise of capitalism; *Style*— Prof Anthony Upton; 5 West Acres, St Andrews, Fife (☎ 0334 73358); Dept of Modern History, University of St Andrews, St Andrews, Fife KY16 9AL (☎ 0334 76161 ext 358)

UPTON, Prof Brian Geoffrey Johnson; s of Harry Johnson Upton, and Constance Ethel, *née* Bailey; *b* 2 March 1933; *Educ* Reading Sch, Oxford (BA, MA, DPhil); *m* 13 Sept 1958, Bodil, da of Svend Aalbaek Madsen; 2 s (Peter Lawrence Johnson b 16 Dec 1961, Michael Geoffrey b 12 March 1964), 1 da (Melanie Jane b 15 June 1975); *Career* geological survey of Greenland 1958-60, post-doctoral fell California Inst of Technol 1961-62; Univ of Edinburgh: lectr geology 1962-72, reader geology 1972-82, prof petrology 1982-; memb edirorial bd: Scottish Journal of Geology 1969-73, Transactions RSE Earth Sciences 1983-89, Journal of Petrology (exec ed) 1983-; chm Royal Soc Sub Ctee on Volcanology British Nat Ctee for Geodesy and Geophysics; memb: Geological Soc London 1967, RSF 1980; *Recreations* painting, gardening, wild life conservation; *Style*— Prof Brian Upton; Dept of Geology and Geophysics, West Mains Rd, Edinburgh EH9 3JW (☎ 031 667 1011, fax 3563, telex 727 442)

UPTON, Prof Graham; s of William Upton, of Sydney, Aust, and Edna May, *née* Groves; *b* 30 April 1944; *Educ* Univ of Sydney (MA, Dip Ed), Univ of NSW (MEd), Univ of Wales (PhD); *m* 1 (m dis 1984), Jennifer Ann; 1 s (Stuart Ingham b 10 Jan 1969), 1 da (Sonja Cape b 13 March 1970); ptnr 2 common law w, Elizabeth Mary Hayward, da of Jack Speed; 1 s (James Llewellyn b 20 Dec 1986), 1 da (Hermione Catherine b 19 Jan 1988); *Career* schoolteacher NSW 1966-71, lectr in special educn Leeds Poly 1972-74; Univ Coll Cardiff 1974-88: lectr, sr lectr, reader, head Dept of Educn, dean Faculty of Educn; prof Univ of Birmingham 1988-; memb: Nat Cncl for Special Educn, Assoc for Child Psychology and Psychiatry, Assoc of Workers for Maladjusted Children; AFBPS 1983; *Books* Physical & Creative Activities for the Mentally Handicapped (1979), Educating Children with Behaviour Problems (1983); *Style*— Prof Graham Upton; School of Education, University of Birmingham, Edgbaston, Birmingham B15 2TT (☎ 021 414 4831, fax 021 414 4865

UPTON, John; s of Ernest Upton (d 1940); *b* 3 Dec 1905; *m* 1951, Kathleen Ruth; 2 s, 2 da; *Career* md The Liverpool Warehousing Co Ltd, chm The Br Public Warehousekeepers Ctee 1979-80; dir: Lukwa Storage Ltd, North West Storage Co, Cheshire Storage; *Recreations* golf; *Clubs* Royal Birkdale Golf; *Style*— John Upton Esq; 5 Westbourne Rd, Birkdale, Southport

UPTON, Dr Julian John Mainwaring; s of Cecil Mainwaring Upton (d 1980), of Baronscroft, Milner Rd, W :st Cliff, Bownemouth, and Dodo, *née* Bremridge (d 1954); *b* 14 July 1937; *Educ* Clifton Coll Bristol, Peterhouse Cambridge (BA), Guy's Hosp (MB BChir); *m* 15 Feb 1964, Angela, da of Walter Bernard Hicklin (d 1985), of Pearl Court, Knaphill, Surrey; 3 s (Timothy Julian Mainwaring b 19 April 1966, Mark Richard Mainwaring b 17 Feb 1969, Alexander James Mainwaring b 5 April 1973); *Career* house posts Guildford Hosps 1963-65, final training Leeds Gen Infirmary and St James Univ Hosp 1968-75, conslt otolaryngologist Taunton and Somerset Hosps and Yeovil Hosp 1975-; author various papers published in the Journal of Laryngology; memb: Peterhouse Soc, Old Cliftonian Soc, Camelot Med Soc, Br Med Laser Assoc, Br Assoc Otolaryngology; memb: RSM, BMA; FRCS 1969, FRCSEd 1972; *Recreations* golf, ornithology, gardening, walking, books, botanical and nature studies; *Clubs* Univ, West Somerset Med; *Style*— Dr Julian Upton; c/o ENT Dept Taunton and Somerset Hospital, Musgrove Park, Taunton, Somerset TA1 5DA (☎ 0823 333444 ext 2167); Yeovil District Hosp, Higher Kingston, Yeovil, Somerset; Nuffield Hospital, Staplegrove Elm, Taunton TA2 6AN

UPTON, Peter Thomas; s of Frank Harry Upton (d 1985), of Wilts, and Rachel Amelia, *née* Cain; n of Charles W Cain the artist known as the 'Etcher of the East'; *b* 1 Jan 1937; *Educ* Headlands GS Wilts, Newlands Park Coll (Art Teachers Cert), Reading Univ (Post Grad Res in Psychology); *m* 14 Aug 1963, Janet Harnell, da of Maj Thomas Joyce Parry (d 1958); 1 s (Simon Dominic b 1966), 1 da (Fiona Sorolla b 1964); *Career* artist; equestrian painter and sculptor; exhibition and 1 man shows held in London, America, France, Sweden, Dubai, Saudi Arabia; works in private and Royal collections; head of art and housemaster Pierrepont Sch 1961-89; pres Arab Horse Soc of GB 1986-87, int judge and expert on the Arab Horse, breeder and judge of Dartmoor ponies; *Books* Desert Heritage (1980), The Classic Arab Horse (1987), The Arab Horse A Complete Record of all Horses Imported From the Desert to the UK (1989), author of numerous articles on the Arab horse for nat and int magazines; *Recreations* travelling in the deserts of Arabia, falconry, riding, hunting, an avid bibliophile; *Style*— Peter T Upton, Esq; The Old Vicarage, Clun, Shropshire

UPTON, Robin James; JP (1969); s of Col Philip Valentine Upton, MBE, TD, JP, DL (d 1985), of Park Lodge and Coptfold, Margaretting, Essex, and Veronica Rosemary, da of Lt-Col Leslie Heber Thornton, CMG, DSO, of Lewes, Sussex; *b* 18 March 1931; *Educ* Trinity Coll Glenalmond, Trinity Coll Cambridge (MA); *m* 1961, Priscilla Mary, yr da of Dr William Sydney Charles Copeman, CBE, TD (d 1970), of 12 Hyde Park Place, London W2; 2 s (Hugo, Simon), 1 da (Victoria); *Career* farmer, magistrate; dir: R J Upton Farms Ltd 1969-, Reed & Upton Ltd 1971-, Mereacre Farms Ltd 1983-, Assoc Farmers plc 1983-90; county chm Suffolk Country Landowners Assoc 1981-84, High Sheriff of Suffolk 1988-89; Master Worshipful Co of Farmers 1990; *Recreations* conservation, shooting, fishing; *Style*— R J Upton, Esq, JP; Park Farm, Herringswell, Bury St Edmunds, Suffolk (☎ 0638 750317)

UPTON, Roger Charles; s of Frank Harry Upton (d 1985), of Wilts, and Rachel Amelia, *née* Cain; *b* 1 Jan 1937; *m* 9 Aug 1961, Jean, da of Andrew Robert Turnell (d 1982), of Ogbourne, Marlborough, Wilts; 2 s (Mark Lundy, Guy); *Career* Royal Horse Gds; artist and sculptor; works in: USA, UK, Arabia, Europe; contrib of articles on: falconry, coursing, the Middle East, poetry; memb advsy ctee to HO and DOE on Protection of Birds 1967-80; *Books* A Bird In The Hand, O For A Falconers Voice; *Recreations* falconry, coursing, hunting, punting, driving horses; *Clubs* British Falconers'; *Style*— Roger Upton, Esq; (☎ 067 286 656)

URE, Alan Willis; CBE (1984), RD (1969); s of Colin McGregor Ure (d 1963), and Edith Hannah Eileen Willis Swinburne (d 1945); *b* 30 March 1926; *Educ* Kelvinside Acad, Merchiston Castle Sch, Pembroke Coll Cambridge; *m* 1953, Mary Christine, *née* Henry; 1 s, 2 da; *Career* memb Construction Indust Trg Bd 1982-85, pres Nat Fedn of Bldg Trades Employers 1981-82, memb Royal Cmmn on Civil Liability and Compensation for Personal Injury 1974-78; chm Nat Jt Cncl for the Bldg Industry 1989-, formerly dep md Trollope and Colls Hldgs, md Trollope and Colls Ltd and Trollope and Colls Mgmnt Ltd; vice pres Fedn Internationale Européenne de Constructon 1982-85; *Recreations* vintage motoring, bell ringing, walking, reading, sailing; *Clubs* Naval; *Style*— Alan Ure, Esq, CBE, RD; 28 Hambleside Court, Hamble SO3 5QE; 20 Eastbourne Terrace, London W2 6LE

URE, Sir John Burns; KCMG (1987), LVO (1968); s of Tam Ure, MBE (d 1963), and Mary Jeanie, *née* Bosworth (d 1963); *b* 5 July 1931; *Educ* Uppingham Sch, Magdalene Coll Cambridge (MA), Harvard Business Sch (AMP); *m* 1972, Caroline, da of Charles Allan, of Roxburghshire; 1 s (Alasdair b 1978), 1 da (Arabella b 1981); *Career* 2 Lt Cameronians (Scot Rifles) 1949-51, active serv during Emergency in Malaya; Lt London Scot (Gordon Highlanders) 1951-55 (TA), served at Br Embassies in Moscow, Leopoldville, Santiago and in the Foreign and Cwlth Office in London 1956-71; cncllr and chargé d'affaires at Lisbon 1972-77; head of S America Dept FCO 1977-79, ambass to Cuba 1979-81, asst under-sec of state FCO 1981-84, ambass to Brazil 1984-87, ambass to Sweden 1987-91; commr-gen for Expo '92 1990-; Cdr of Military Order of Christ (Portugal) 1973; *Books* Cucumber Sandwiches in the Andes (1973), The Trail of Tamerlane (1980), The Quest for Captain Morgan (1983), Trespassers on the Amazon (1986), Prince Henry The Navigator (1977), book reviews for TLS; *Recreations* travelling uncomfortably in remote places and writing about it comfortably afterwards; *Clubs* Whites, Beefsteak, Royal Geographical Soc; *Style*— Sir John Ure, KCMG, LVO; Netters Hall, Hawkhurst, Kent TN18 5AT (☎ 0580 752191)

UREN, (John) Michael Leal; s of Arthur Claude Uren (d 1977), of Rickmansworth, Herts, and Doris May, *née* Leal (d 1983); *b* 1 Sept 1923; *Educ* Sherborne, Imperial Coll London (BSc, ACGI); *m* 26 Nov 1955, Serena Anne, da of Edward Raymond Peal, of Salisbury; 2 s (David Richard b 1960, (Robert) Mark b 1962); *Career* RN 1943-46; cmmnd Sub-Lt RNVR, air engr offr Fleet Air Arm; civil engr; Sir Alexander Gibb and Ptnrs Persia (now Iran) 1946-51, The Cementation Company Ltd Scotland 1951-53, Holland & Hannen and Cubitts NZ 1953-55, Industl Complex for Pressed Steel Co Swindon 1955-56, British European Airways Base Heathrow 1956-58, Dowsett Engineering Construction Ltd (dir 1958, md 1961); fndr memb and dir (later chm) Civil and Marine Ltd; currently chm: Civil & Marine Holdings Ltd, Camey SA Dunkirk France, German D'Hoore NV Brugges Belgium, Purfleet Aggregates Ltd Purfleet; dir: Blackwall Aggregates Ltd Greenwich, Evered plc; chm Royal London Soc for the Blind 1981- (cncllr 1974-); Freeman City of London 1958, Master Worshipful Co of Cordwainers 1990-91 (Liveryman 1958, Second Warden 1988, Sr Warden 1989); CEng, MICE, MIStructE, MIWEM, FRICS; *Recreations* 15th and 16th century timber framed buildings, country pursuits, farming (pedigree Romney sheep, cereals and linseed); *Clubs* Naval and Military; *Style*— Michael Uren, Esq; Priory Farm, Appledore Rd, Tenterden, Kent TN30 7DD (☎ 05806 4161); Civil & Marine Ltd, Johnson's Wharf, King Edward Rd, Greenhithe, Kent DA9 9AD (☎ 0322 844646, fax 0322 847211)

URIBE, Anne Finlay; da of John Roff Finlay Best, of Jersey, CI, and Mary Dorothy, *née* Kean; *b* 10 June 1945; *m* Julian Uribe, s of Federico Uribe; 2 s (Frederick John b 24 April 1980, Philip George b 15 April 1983); *Career* Sotheby Parke-Bernet NY 1968-72, dir The Mayor Gallery London 1973-86, art conslt to collectors, artists and institutions 1986-; *Recreations* art, archaeology, long distance running; *Style*— Mrs Anne Uribe

URQUHART, Barry; s of Kenneth Hector Urquhart, of Horsham, Sussex, and Lillian Rosina, *née* Batten (d 1983); *b* 19 Oct 1943; *Educ* St Paul's Sch, Poly of N London (Dip Arch); *m* 23 Nov 1977, Susan Corrie, da of Henry William Albert Griffiths (d 1985), of Spindrift Cottages, Roedean Way, Brighton; 1 s (David Alexander b 29 Nov 1985), 1 da (Rebecca Elizabeth b 8 March 1983); *Career* formed own architecture practice 1977; chm: BUA Surveyors, BUA Design Ltd; nat and int lectr in designing for the mentally ill and mentally handicapped; contrib to learned jls; elder Living Water Fellowship; memb: Weybridge Soc, IOD; RIBA, FASI, FIAA; *Clubs* Old Pauline, St

George's Hill Lawn Tennis; *Style*— Barry Urquhart, Esq; 80 Onslow Rd, Burwood Park, Walton on Thames, Surrey KT12 5AY (☎ 0932 229 463); BUA Barry Urquhart Assocs, 23 Monument Green, Weybridge, Surrey KT13 8QW (☎ 0932 856 551, fax 0932 859 735); 12 Chequers Rd, Basingstoke, Hants; 7 Prior Park Buildings, Widcombe, Bath BA2 4NP

URQUHART, Sir Brian Edward; KCMG (1986), MBE (1945); s of Murray Urquhart (d 1977), and Bertha Rendall Urquhart (d 1984); *b* 28 Feb 1919; *Educ* Westminster, Ch Ch Oxford; *m* 1, 1944 (m dis 1963), Alfreda, da of Constant Huntington (d 1964), of London; 2 s (Thomas b 1944, Robert b 1948), 1 da (Katherine b 1946); m 2, 1963, Sidney, da of Sidney Howard (d 1939), of USA; 1 s (Charles b 1967), 1 da (Rachel b 1963); *Career* Maj Dorset Regt and Airborne Forces Africa and Europe 1939-45; UN Secretariat 1945-86 (under sec gen special political affrs 1972-86), scholar in residence Ford Fndn 1986-; hon DCL Oxford; *Books* Hammarskjold (1972), A Life in Peace and War (1987), Decolonization and World Peace (1989), A World in Need of Leadership: Tomorrow's United Nations (1990); *Recreations* reading, writing; *Clubs* Century (New York); *Style*— Sir Brian Urquhart, KCMG, MBE; 131 East 66th St, New York 10021; Howard Farm, Tyringham, Massachusetts 01264; The Ford Foundation, 320 East 43rd St, New York, New York 10017 (☎ 212 573 4952)

URQUHART, Dennis Alexander; *b* 5 March 1929; *Educ* King Edward VI Sch Southampton, The Queen's Coll Oxford (BA); *m* 24 Aug 1957, Chrystal Walton; 2 s, 2 da; *Career* dir Bass plc; *Recreations* music, opera, English cricket, Welsh rugby; *Style*— Dennis Urquhart, Esq; Bisterne Lodge, Bisterne Close, Burley, Ringwood, Hants BH24 4BA; Bass plc, 66 Chiltern St, London W1M 1PE

URQUHART, James Graham; CVO (1983); s of James Urquhart (d 1982), of Edinburgh, and Mary, *née* Clark (d 1984); *b* 23 April 1925; *Educ* Berwickshire HS; *m* 1 Oct 1949, Margaret, da of Earnest Hutchinson (d 1982), of Rock Ferry; 2 da (Janet b 10 May 1952, Alison b 18 May 1955); *Career* BR 1949-86: mgmnt trainee 1949-52, dist traffic supt Perth 1960-62, divnl mangr Glasgow 1964-67, asst gen mangr York 1967-69, chief operating offr BR HQ 1969-72, personnel dir 1972-74, gen mangr London Midlands Region 1975-77, memb Ops and Productivity Bd 1977-85, memb Exports Bd 1985-86; chm: British Transport Police 1977-86, BR Engineering 1982-86, Transmark 1983-86, Freightliner 1983-86; dir: Park Air Electronics Ltd 1986-89, Waterslides plc 1987-, Systems Connection Group 1988-, OFIOX Ltd 1989-, CUC Ltd 1989-; MIT 1978, MIMH 1979, CBIM 1982, FIPersonnel 1983; *Recreations* golf, reading; *Style*— James Urquhart, Esq, CVO; 10 Wychcotes, Caversham, Reading (☎ 0734 479 071); 22A High St, Hungerford (☎ 0448 84141)

URQUHART, Lawrence McAllister; s of Robert Urquhart, of 3 Chesterton House, Chesterton Way, Cirencester, Glos, and Josephine McEwan, *née* Bissell (d 1988); *b* 24 Sept 1935; *Educ* Strathallan Sch Perthshire, Kings Coll London (LLB); *m* 26 Aug 1961, Elizabeth Catherine, da of William Burns (d 1952); 3 s (Douglas b 1964, Ross b 1965, Guy b 1971), 1 da (Caroline b 1972); *Career* CA; appts: Price Waterhouse 1957-62, Shell International Petroleum 1962-64, PA Mgmnt Conslts 1964-68; sr gp exec Charterhouse Gp Ltd 1968-74; gp fin dir: Tozer Kemsley and Millbourn Hldgs 1974-77, Burmah Oil Co Ltd 1977-82; chief exec Castrol Ltd 1982-85, gp chief exec Burmah Oil plc 1988-90 (gp md 1985-88), chm and chief exec Burmah Castrol plc; Liveryman Worshipful Co of Coachmakers and Coach Harness Makers 1984; CBIM, FInstPet; *Recreations* golf, music; *Clubs* Lilley Brook Golf, Frilford Heath Golf; *Style*— Lawrence Urquhart, Esq; Burmah Castrol plc, Burmah Castrol House, Pipers Way, Swindon, Wiltshire, SN3 1RE (☎ 0793 511 521, car 0836 526878, telex 449221)

URQUHART, Peter William; s of Maj-Gen Ronald Walton Urquhart, CB, DSO, DL (d 1968), of Meredith, Tibberton, Gloucestershire, and Jean Margaret, *née* Moir; *b* 10 July 1944; *Educ* Bedford Sch, Pembroke Coll Cambridge (BA, MA); *m* 1 May 1976, The Hon Anne Serena, da of Lord Griffiths, of Kensington, London; 1 s (James b 1980), 3 da (Katherine b 1978, Flora b 1981, Serena b 1984); *Career* RMA Sandhurst 1963-64, Lt RE 1964-69; stockbroker: James Capel 1969-75, Gilbert Elliot 1975-76, Sheppards & Chase 1976-79, Mercury Asset Management (formerly Warburg Investment Management) 1981- (dir 1984-); *Recreations* field sports, racing, golf, gardening; *Style*— Peter Urquhart, Esq; 33 King William St, London EC4 (☎ 071 280 2187)

URQUHART, Dr Ranald Pirie Macdonald; s of Duncan Hector Urquhart (d 1989), and Sarah Macdonald Urquhart (d 1982); *b* 27 Dec 1929; *Educ* Abbey Sch Fort Augustus, Univ of Edinburgh (MB ChB); *m* Marie, da of James Larney (d 1975), of Winchester; 3 s (James b 1971, Andrew b 1972, Ian b 1976); *Career* Nat Serv, Lt RAMC 1954, Capt RAMC 1955-56, Korea, Japan, Malaya, Suez; house surgn RNI Inverness 1953, house physician Eastern Gen Hosp Edinburgh 1953, sr house offr and registrar Royal Edinburgh Hosp 1956-58; registrar in 1959-64: RHSC Edinburgh, CGTC London, Hertfordshire; sr registrar Earls Ct CGU 1964-67, conslt child psychiatrist Hillingdon Hosp and CG Clinics 1967-; staff: Hampstead Clinic 1970-75, Brent Consultation Centre 1975-; chm NW Thames child psychiatrists 1987-89; Fell RSM 1956, memb foreign psychoanalytical Soc 1981, FRCPsych 1982; *Recreations* fishing, golf; *Style*— Dr Ranald Urquhart; 12 Langbourne Ave, London N6 6AL (☎ 081 348 3693); Hillingdon Hospital, Uxbridge, Middx (☎ 0865 38282)

URQUHART, Hon Ronald Douglas Lauchlan; yr s of Baron Tayside, OBE (Life Peer d 1975), and Hilda Gwendoline, *née* Harris; name of Lauchlan derives from ancestor in 1745 rebellion nicknamed 'the Big Sword' or 'Lauchlan'; *b* 20 Feb 1948; *Educ* Fettes, Edinburgh Univ (LLB); *m* 1975, Dorothy May Jackson; *Career* chartered accountant; fin dir Jardine Insurance Services Ltd; dir of various gp cos 1984-; *Recreations* golf, backgammon; *Clubs* Caledonian, Hong Kong, Gresham; *Style*— The Hon Ronald Urquhart; Ash Park, East Prawle, nr Kingsbridge, Devon TQ7 2BX; 6 Crutched Friars, London EC3

URQUHART, Hon William James Lauchlan; s of Baron Tayside (Life Peer, d 1975); *b* 18 Oct 1944; *Educ* Fettes, Univ of Glasgow (BSc); *m* 1967, Wendy Helen Cook; 3 da (Carolyn, Suzanne, Jacqueline); *Career* CA, company dir; ATTI; *Style*— The Hon William Urquhart; Magicwell House, Balmullo, St Andrews, Fife

URRY, (John) Brian Marshall; s of John Marshall Urry (d 1972); *b* 11 March 1938; *Educ* Solihull Sch, Univ of Aston (BSc); *m* 1968, Carol Elizabeth, *née* Blakely; 2 s; *Career* chm and md: Powell-Piggott Ltd, Hudson Edmunds & Co Ltd, Peerless Stampings Ltd, Outward Tools Ltd; hon sec Warwicks Union of Golf Clubs, jt hon sec Public Schs Old Boys Golf Assoc; *Recreations* golf; *Clubs* St Pauls (Birmingham), Olton Golf, St Enodoc Golf, R&A Golf; *Style*— Brian Urry, Esq; Dormers, Dickens Heath Rd, Shirley, Solihull, W Midlands (☎ 056 482 3114); Newman Tonks Metals Division, Priory Rd, Aston, Birmingham B6 7LF (☎ 021 328 5665, telex 339987)

URSELL, Bruce Anthony; s of Stuart Ursell, of Edgware, London, and Nancy, *née* Fallowes; *b* 28 Aug 1942; *Educ* William Ellis Sch Highgate; *m* 19 Feb 1966, Anne Carole, da of John Pitt (d 1970); 1 s (Piers John b 1971), 2 da (Philippa Anne b 1972, Virginia Anne b 1974); *Career* mangr Standard Chartered Bank 1961-68, gen mangr Western American Bank 1968-74, md Guiness Mahon & Co Ltd 1984-87 (dir 1974-84), chm Lockton Developments Plc 1985, dir Surrey Broadcasting (USA) 1986-, chief exec British & Commonwealth Merchant Bank plc 1987-90, dir British & Commonwealth Holdings plc 1987-90; *Recreations* tennis, theatre, cinema, reading; *Style*— Bruce Ursell, Esq; Roundwood Park, Harpenden, Hertfordshire (☎ 0582 712784); 66 Cannons St, London EC4N 6AE (☎ 071 248 0900, fax 071 248 0917, telex 884 040)

URSELL, Rev Philip Elliott; s of Clifford Edwin Ursell, of Porthcawl, S Wales, and Hilda Jane, *née* Tucker; *b* 3 Dec 1942; *Educ* Cathays HS Cardiff, Univ Coll Cardiff (BA), St Stephen's House Oxford (MA); *Career* ordained Llandaff Cathedral: deacon 1968, priest 1969; asst curate Newton Nottage 1968-71, asst chaplain Univ Coll Cardiff 1971-77, chaplain The Poly of Wales 1974-77, fell chaplain and dir of studies in music Emmanuel Coll Cambridge 1977-82, princ Pusey House Oxford 1982-, fell St Cross Coll Oxford 1982-, warden Soc of the Holy and Undivided Trinity Ascot Priory 1986-, examining chaplain to the Bishop of London 1986-; *Style*— The Rev Philip Ursell; Pusey House, Oxford OX1 3LZ (☎ 0865 278415, fax 0865 270708); Ascot Priory, Berks SL5 8RT (☎ 0344 885157)

URWICK, Sir Alan Bedford; KCVO (1984), CMG (1978); s of Col L F Urwick; *b* 2 May 1930; *Educ* The Dragon Sch, Rugby, New Coll Oxford (MA); *m* 1960, Marta Yolanda, da of Adhemar Montagne (formerly Peruvian ambass in London 1969-78); 3 s (Christopher, Richard, Michael); *Career* FO 1952-89; served: Brussels, Moscow, Baghdad, Amman, Washington, Cairo; memb Central Policy Review Staff Cabinet Office 1973-75, head Near East and N Africa Dept FCO 1975-76, min Madrid 1977-79; ambass: Jordan 1979-84, Egypt 1984-87; high cmmr Canada 1987-89, Sgt at Arms House of Commons 1989-; KStJ 1983; Jordanian Order of Independence 1 Class 1984; *Clubs* Garrick; *Style*— Sir Alan Urwick, KCVO, CMG; Speaker's Court, House of Commons, London SW1

URWIN, (Charles) Harry; s of Thomas Urwin (d 1958), and Lydia Urwin; *b* 24 Feb 1915; *Educ* Elementary CC Sch Durham; *m* 31 May 1941, Hilda; 1 da (Marion b 22 Jan 1942); *Career* dep gen sec TGWU 1969-80 (dist offr Coventry 1947-59, regnl offr Midlands 1960-69), dist sec CSEU Coventry 1955-60; memb: Gen Cncl TUC 1969-80, Industl Devpt Advsy Bd 1972-78, Cncl MSC 1974-78, Cncl Nat Enterprise Bd 1975-78, Standing Cmmn Pay Comparability 1978-81; assoc fell IRRU Univ of Warwick 1980; *Recreations* walking; *Style*— Harry Urwin, Esq, 4 Leacliffe Way, Aldridge, Walsall WS9 0PW (☎ 021 353 3363)

URWIN, Peter Michael; s of Denis John Urwin (ka 1943), of Longthorpe Peterborough, and Vera May, *née* Frost; *b* 22 April 1941; *Educ* Stamford Sch, Kings Peterborough; *m* 27 April 1968 (sep), Jean Maureen, da of J J George W Jepson, of Christchurch, Hants; 2 s (Simon Christopher James b 1977, James Alexander Edward b 1980); *Career* Royal Insurance 1959-65, Shaw & Sons Insurance Brokers 1965-66, United Africa Co (Unilever) Freetown Sierra Leone 1966-71, dir own cos incl Peter Urwin Holdings Ltd 1971-; md Birchgrey Ltd (promoters of Euro Open Golf Championship) 1981-; Sierra Leone Open Golf Champion 1970, capt Freetown GC 1970; ACII 1962; *Recreations* golf, bridge, philately; *Clubs* Roehampton, Kingswood Golf; *Style*— Peter Urwin, Esq; Hallega Folly, Hurst Close, Headley, Epsom, Surrey; Broadway House, The Broadway, Wimbledon, London SW19 1RL (☎ 081 542 9048, fax 081 543 0314)

USBORNE, (Thomas) Peter; s of Thomas George Usborne, and Gerda, *née* Just; *b* 18 Aug 1937; *Educ* Summerfields Sch, Eton, Balliol Coll Oxford, INSEAD (MBA); *m* 30 Oct 1964, Cornelie, da of Alfred Tüecking, of Munich; 1 s (Martin b May 1973), 1 da (Nicola b 12 Dec 1969); *Career* 2 Lt Rifle Brigade, seconded VI KAR 1956-58; co-fndr and md Private Eye Magazine 1962-65, sr scientist Metra Sigma Martech Management Consultancy, publishing dir Macdonald Educational 1968-73, fndr and md Usborne Publishing Ltd; *Recreations* sailing, gliding; *Clubs* Garrick; *Style*— Peter Usborne, Esq; Usborne Publishing Ltd, Usborne House, 83-85 Saffron Hill, London EC1 (☎ 071 430 2800)

USHER, Andrew Michael; s of Francis George Usher; *b* 15 Oct 1938; *Educ* Cheltenham Coll; *m* 1964, Anne, *née* Whittington; 3 s, 1 da; *Career* slr 1964; sec Br Investmt Tst plc 1979-86, dir The Fleming Fledgeling Investmt Tst plc 1978-, ptnr Baillie Gifford & Co 1986-; *Recreations* genealogy, music, golf; *Clubs* New (Edinburgh), memb Hon Co of Edinburgh Golfers Muirfield; *Style*— Andrew Usher, Esq; 12 Blackford Rd, Edinburgh EH9 2DS

USHER, Peter Joseph; CBE (1990, OBE 1980); s of Philip Usher, of Dymchurch, Kent (d 1960), and Gertrude, *née* Capon (d 1964); *b* 28 July 1926; *Educ* Maidstone Tech Sch, Royal Naval Coll Greenwich; *m* 31 March 1951, Pamela; 2 s (Martin b 1952, David b 1954); *Career* constructor cdr RN Staff of Flag Offr (submarines) 1960-64, Naval constructor overseer 1964-66; Vosper Thornycroft (UK) Ltd: tech gen mangr 1966-68, tech dir 1968-74, dep md 1974-81, md 1981-89, dep chm 1989-90, chm 1990-; FEng, FRINA, RCNC; *Recreations* golf, music; *Clubs* Naval and Military; *Style*— Peter Usher, Esq, CBE; Vosper Thornycroft (UK) Ltd, Victoria Rd, Woolston, Southampton SO9 5GR (fax 0703 421539, telex 47682 VT WOOL (G))

USHER, (Thomas) Raymond; s of Thomas Edward Usher (d 1987), of Easington, Co Durham, and Catherine, *née* McGourley; *b* 10 April 1932; *Educ* Ryhope Robert Richardson GS Co Durham, Univ of Sheffield (BA); *m* 11 Feb 1956, Clare (d 1990), da of Antony Wear Elliott, of Durham (d 1976); 1 s (Antony Edward b 1965); *Career* dir: Nat Employers Gen Insurance Co Ltd (S Africa) 1972-86, Nat Employers Life Assoc Co Ltd (UK) 1976-84, Nat Underwriters (Reinsurance) Ltd (Bermuda) 1979-85, Nat Employers' Mutual Gen Insurance Assoc (UK) Ltd 1976-88, The Chancellor Group Ltd (Canada) 1986-90, American Family Ltd 1985-, American Family Health & Sec Co Ltd 1985-, American Family Life Assoc Co Ltd 1985-, East West Insur Co Ltd 1987-; chm: Chancellor Insur Co Ltd (UK) 1985-90, Usher Insurance Services Ltd 1988-; *Recreations* golf, sailing, horse racing; *Clubs* Royal Thames Yacht, City Livery; *Style*— Raymond Usher, Esq; Parsonage Farmhouse, Church Rd, Wanborough, Wiltshire SN4 0BZ (☎ 0793 790 818); 6 Kinnerton Place, North London SW1 (☎ 071 235 4518); CE Heath Plc, 150 Minories, London EC3 (☎ 071 488 2488)

USHER, Sir Robert Edward; 6 Bt (UK 1899), of Norton, Midlothian, and of Wells, Co Roxburgh; s of Sir Robert Stuart Usher, 4 Bt (d 1962); suc bro, Sir Peter Lionel Usher, 5 Bt (d 1990); *b* 18 April 1934; *Heir* kinsman, (William) John Tevenar Usher b 1940; *Style*— Sir Robert Usher, Bt; Hallrule, Hawick, Roxburghshire

USHER, Shaun David; s of John Gray Usher (d 1988), of Clevedon, Avon, and Judith Usher (d 1986); *b* 18 May 1937; *Educ* Clevedon Secdy Modern Sch; *m* Sylvia May, da of Arthur Joseph White; 1 s (Peter b 19 March 1963); *Career* trainee reporter Clevedon Mercury 1953-54 and 1957-59, Western Daily Press 1954-55, Bristol Evening Post/Western Daily Press 1959-61, entertainments ed Daily Sketch 1970-71 (broadcasting corr 1964-70); Daily Mail: entertainments ed 1971-72, TV critic 1972-78, foreign corr and sr feature writer 1978-83, film critic and video columnist 1983-; Best Short Story prize Crime Writers Assoc 1976 and 1977; *Recreations* reading and writing; *Style*— Shaun Usher, Esq; Entertainments Dept, Daily Mail, 2 Derry St, London W8 5TT (☎ 071 938 6365)

USHERWOOD, Nicholas John; s of Stephen Dean Usherwood, of London and Hazel, *née* Weston (d 1968); *b* 4 June 1943; *Educ* Westminster, Courtauld Inst of Art Univ of London (BA); *m* 1, 1979 (m dis 1990), Henrietta Mahaffy; 1 s (Theodore Patrick John b 1981), 1 da (Constance Hazel Kate b 1985); m 2, 1991, Jilly Szaybo; *Career* lectr in art history Portsmouth and Wimbledon Colls of Art 1965-68, res under Sir Nikolaus Pevsner on Pelican History of Art 1966-68, admin Royal Acad of Arts 1969-77 (exhibitions sec 1974-77), dep keeper i/c exhibitions and PR British Museum 1977-78; freelance writer, critic, lectr and exhibition organiser and curator 1978-; curator and catalogue of exhibitions incl: David Inshaw (Brighton Gallery and Museum) 1978, Algernon Newton RA (Sheffield and Royal Acad of Arts) 1980, The Ruralists (Arnolfini Bristol and Camden Arts Centre) 1981, Tristram Hillier (Bradford and Royal Acad of Arts) 1983, Julian Trevelyan (Watermans Art Centre) 1985, Peter Blake - Commercial Art (Watermans Art Centre Brentford) 1986, Mass Observation (Watermans Art Centre Brentford) 1987, Richard Eurich War Paintings (Imp War Museum) 1991; exhibitions organized: Athena Art Awards 1985-88, Images of Paradise 1989, New Generation (Bonhams London) 1990, Painting Today (Bonhams London) 1991; regular contrib to: Daily Telegraph, Arts Review, RA Magazine, Galleries, The Art Newspaper; regular lectr at Sothebys and regnl art schs; admin Turner Bicentennary Exhibition (RA) 1974; Picker Fell and critic in residence Kingston Poly 1990-91, memb: CNAA 1976-78, Int Assoc of Art Critics 1989-; Chevalier Order of Leopold II of Belgium 1972; *Recreations* maps (new), music, poetry, new places (town and country), cricket, talking to painters; *Style—* Nicholas Usherwood, Esq; 17a Abinger Road, Bedford Park, London W4 1EU (☎ 081 994 2604)

USHERWOOD, Stephen Dean; s of John Frederick Usherwood (d 1964), and Grace Ellen, *née* Crush (d 1966); *b* 14 Sept 1907; *Educ* St Dunstan's Coll London, Oriel Coll Oxford (MA); *m* 1, 27 July 1935, Hazel Doreen, *née* Weston (d 1968); 1 s (Nicholas John b 1943), 1 da (Susan Clare b 1939); m 2, 24 Oct 1970, Elizabeth Ada, *née* Beavington; *Career* Flt Lt RAF attached GCHQ 1941-46; sch master 1931-41; Educn and Current Affrs Depts BBC 1946-68; author, coll lectr and broadcaster 1968-; *Books* Reign by Reign (1960), The Bible, Book by Book (1962), Shakespeare, Play by Play (1967), History from Familiar Things (1969-71), Britain, Century by Century (1972), Europe, Century by Century (1972), Food, Drink and History (1972), The Great Enterprise, The Story of the Spanish Armada (1982); with Elizabeth Usherwood: Visit Some London Catholic Churches (1982), The Counter Armada 1596: The Journal of the Mary Rose (1983), We Die For The Old Religion (1987); *Recreations* travel, theatre, music; *Clubs* Soc of Authors; *Style—* Stephen Usherwood, Esq; 24 St Mary's Grove, Canonbury, London N1 2NT (☎ 071 226 9813)

USTINOV, Sir Peter Alexander; CBE (1975); s of late Iona Ustinov, journalist, and late Nadia Benois, painter (niece of Alexandre Benois, the stage designer); *b* 16 April 1921; *Educ* Westminster, London Theatre Sch; *m* 1, 8 Aug 1940 (m dis 1950), Isolde Denham, actress, da of Reginald Denham, actor (and half-sister of Angela Lansbury, *qv*); 1 da (Tamara b 1945); m 2, 15 Feb 1954 (m dis 1971), Suzanne Cloutier; 1 s (Igor b 1956), 2 da (Pavla b 1954, Andrea b 1959); m 3, 21 June 1972, Hélène du Lau d'Allemans; *Career* Nat Serv WWII 1942-46 Royal Sussex Regt, Army Kinematograph Service, Directorate of Army Psychiatry; actor, prodr, dir, author and playwright; plays incl: House of Regrets (1942), Blow Your Own Trumpet (1943), The Banbury Nose (1944), The Indifferent Shepherd (1946), Man in the Raincoat (1949), The Love of Four Colonels (1950), The Moment of Truth (1951), High Balcony (1952), Romanoff and Juliet (1956), Paris Not So Gay (1956), Photo Finish (1962), Half Way Up the Tree (1967), The Unknown Soldier and His Wife (1967), Overheard (1981), Beethoven's Tenth (1983); films written incl: The Way Ahead (1942), School for Secrets (1946), Private Angelo (1949), Billy Budd (1962), The Lady L (1964), Hot Millions (1968), Memed My Hawk (1982); books incl: Add A Dash of Pity (1960), The Loser (1961), Krumnagel (1971), Dear Me (1977), My Russia (1983), Ustinov in Russia (1987), The Disinformer (1989), The Old Man and Mr Smith (1990); TV includes: History of Europe (BBC), Einstein's Universe (1979), The Well Tempered Bach (1985, nominated for an Emmy), 13 At Dinner (1985), Deadman's Folly (1986), Appointment With Death (1987), Peter Ustinov in China (1987), Peter Ustinov's Russia (1987); films incl: Private Angelo (1949), Odette (1950), Quo Vadis (1951), Beau Brummel (1954), We're No Angels (1955), The Spies (1955), The Sundowners (1960), Spartacus (1960), Romanoff and Juliet (1961), Billy Budd (1962), Topkapi (1963), Blackbeard's Ghost (1967), The Comedians (1967), Hot Millions (1968), Hammersmith Is Out (1971), One of Our Dinosaurs Is Missing (1974), Purple Taxi (1977), Death on the Nile (1977), The Thief of Baghdad (1978), Ashanti (1979), Charlie Chan and the Curse of the Dragon Queen (1980), Evil Under the Sun (1981), Memed My Hawk (1982), The French Revolution (1989); phonographic recordings incl: Mock Mozart, Peter and the Wolf, Hary Janos, The Old Man of Lochnagar; also dir several operas incl: The Magic Flute (Hamburg 1968), Les Brigands (Berlin 1978), The Marriage (Piccola Scala 1981), Mavra (1982), Katja Kabanowa (Hamburg 1985); Benjamin Franklin medal RSA 1957, Hon DMus Cleveland Inst of Music 1967, Hon LLD Univ of Dundee 1969 (rector 1968 and 1971-73), Hon LLD La Salle Coll of Philadelphia 1971, Hon DLitt Lancaster Univ 1972, Hon DUniv Lethbridge Canada 1974, Hon DUniv Georgetown Washington 1988, Hon DUniv Toronto 1984, Hon DUniv Carlton Ottawa 1991; UNICEF award for Distinguished Service 1978, Prix de la Butte (French award for 'Dear Me' 1978), Variety Club award of GB for Best Actor 1979, Commandeur de Arts et des Lettres 1985, Elected to Acad of Fine Arts 1988; kt 1990; *Recreations* sailing, music, motor cars; *Clubs* Garrick, Arts Theatre, Queens, Royal Automobile; *Style—* Sir Peter Ustinov, CBE; 11 Rue de Silly, 92100 Boulogne, France (☎ 010 3314 603 8753)

UTIGER, Ronald Ernest; CBE; *b* 1926; *Educ* Shrewsbury, Worcester Coll Oxford (MA); *m* 1953, Barbara von Mohl; 1 s, 1 da; *Career* economist Courtaulds Ltd 1950-61; Br Aluminium Ltd: fin controller 1961-64, comm dir 1965-68, md 1968-79, chm 1979-82; dir: Br Alcan Aluminium plc 1982-, Ultramar plc 1983-, National Grid Co plc 1990-; chm TI Group 1984-89 (md 1982-86, dep chm and md 1982-84); pres NIESR 1986-; memb Br Library Bd 1987-; FRSA, CBIM; *Style—* Ronald Utiger, Esq, CBE; 9 Ailsa Rd, St Margaret's, Twickenham, Middx

UTTING, Prof John Edward; JP; s of Henry Alphege Utting (d 1979), of Liverpool, and Theresa Gladys, *née* Mullins (d 1983); *b* 17 March 1932; *Educ* Liverpool Coll, Peterhouse Cambridge (MA, MB BChir); *m* 27 Oct 1958, Dr Jean Oliver Utting, da of James Gerrard, JP, of St Andrews, Fife; 1 s (James Henry b 14 Aug 1965), 3 da (Clare Helen b 10 Aug 1959, Mary Elizabeth (Mrs White) b 11 Aug 1960, Catherine Emily (Mrs Grace) b 17 Jan 1962); *Career* Univ of Liverpool: sr lectr in anaesthesia 1970-77, prof of anaesthesia 1977-, pro vice chllr 1987-; chm: Govrs Liverpool Coll, Linacre Centre for Study of Med Ethics; memb: Liverpool Med Instn, RSM; *Books* General Anaesthesia (jtly, 5 edn), various papers on anaesthesia; *Style—* Prof John Utting, JP; Sanjo, Green Lane, Liverpool L18 2EP (☎ 051 722 0501); Univ Dept of Anaesthesia, The University, PO Box 147, Liverpool L69 3BX (☎ 051 709 0141, fax 051 708 6502, telex 627095 UNILPL G)

UTTING, Sir William Benjamin; CB (1985); s of John William Utting (d 1968), of Great Yarmouth, and Florence Ada Anne, *née* Thompson (d 1961); *b* 13 May 1931; *Educ* Great Yarmouth GS, New Coll Oxford (BA, MA), Barnett House Oxford (Cert Social Work); *m* 27 Dec 1954, Mildred Sadie, da of David Whiteford Jackson (d 1967), of Grantham; 2 s (Andrew John b 1956, Patrick William b 1964), 1 da (Sarah Anne b 1959); *Career* probation offr: Durham 1956-58, Norfolk 1958-61; sr probation offr Durham 1961-64, princ probation offr Newcastle upon Tyne 1964-68, lectr in social studies Univ of Newcastle upon Tyne 1968-70, dir of social servs Royal Borough of Kensington & Chelsea 1970-76, chief inspector Social Servs Inspectorate DHSS 1985- (chief social work offr 1976-85); tstee: Mental Health Fndn, Joseph Rowntree Fndn; memb: Assoc of Dirs of Social Servs, Br Assoc of Social Workers, Social Care Assoc; Kt 1991; *Recreations* literature, art, music; *Style—* Sir William Utting, CB; Department of Health, Richmond House, 79 Whitehall, London SW1A 2NF (☎ 071 210 5569, fax 071 210 5572)

UTTLEY, Hon Mrs (Katherine Barbara); da (by 1 m) of late 18 Baron St John of Bletso; *b* 1907; *m* 1945, George William Uttley (d 1986), late Flt Lt RAF; 1 da; *Career* S/O WAAF; *Style—* The Hon Mrs Uttley; 44 Heath Crescent, Free School Lane, Halifax HX1 2PW

UTTLEY, Roger Miles; s of James Stuart Uttley, and Peggy, *née* Howarth; *b* 11 Sept 1949; *Educ* Montgomery Secondary Modern, Blackpool GS, Northumberland Coll of Educ (CertEd), North London Poly (MA); *m* 1971, Kristine, da of Arthur Samuel Gibbs; 2 s (Simon b 1976, Benjamin b 1978); *Career* dir of physical education Harrow Sch; England RFU player 1973-80, 23 Caps, Capt season 1976-77, British Lions 1974 tour S Africa, played all four test matches; *Books* Pride in England (autobiography), Captaincy in Rugby Football; *Style—* Roger Uttley, Esq; 1 Deyne Court, Harrow Park, Harrow on Hill, Middlesex (☎ 081 869 1207); Harrow Sch Sports Centre, Football Lane, Harrow on Hill (☎ 081 422 2196, fax 081 423 3112)

UTTON, Prof Michael Arthur; s of Arthur Leslie Utton (d 1987), and Lucy Eileen, *née* Gepp; *b* 19 Sept 1939; *Educ* Westcliff HS, Univ of Nottingham (BA), Univ of Reading (PhD); *m* 11 Oct 1963, Vera, da of Robert Georg Niebler, of Langenfield; 3 s (Ralph b 1966, Oliver b 1968, Tim b 1970); *Career* asst Univ of Glasgow 1961-62, res Economist Intelligence Unit 1962-64; conslt: Nat Inst of Economic and Social Res 1970-84, Euro Cmmn 1985-87; prof dept of econs Univ of Reading 1986- (lectr 1964-79, reader 1979-86), conslt OECD 1987-88; *Books* Industrial Concentration (1970), Diversification and Competition (1979), The Political Economy of Big Business (1982), The Profits and Stability of Monopoly (1986), The Economics of Regulating Industry (1986); *Recreations* opera, theatre, cycling; *Style—* Prof Michael Utton; Department of Economics, University of Reading, Whiteknights, PO Box 218, Reading RG6 2AA (☎ 0734 318231, fax 0734 750236)

UVAROV, Dame Olga; DBE (1983, CBE 1978); da of Nikolas Uvarov, and Elena Uvarov; *Educ* Royal Veterinary Coll; *Career* private veterinary practice 1934-53, clinical res pharmaceutical indust 1953-70, head of veterinary advsy dept Glaxo Laboratories 1967-70, Br Veterinary Assoc Tech Info Serv 1970-76, worked on MAFF ctees (under Medicines Act 1968) 1972-77, advsr on tech info BVA 1976-78, memb Medicines Cmmn 1978-82; pres: Soc of Women Veterinary Surgeons 1947-49, Central Veterinary Soc 1952-53, Assoc of Veterinary Teachers and Res Workers 1967-68, Comparative Medicine Section RSM 1967-68 (sec Int Affairs 1983-86), Royal Coll of Veterinary Surgeons 1976-77 (memb Cncl 1968-88), Laboratory Animal Science Assoc 1984- (vice pres 1983-85); vice pres: Res Def Soc 1982 (hon sec 1978-82), Inst of Animal Technicians 1983, Univ Fedn of Animal Welfare 1986-91 (memb Cncl 1983); Hon DSc Guelph Canada 1976, FRCVS 1973 (memb 1934, memb Cncl 1968-88), fell RVC 1979, hon fell RSM 1982, FIBiol 1983; Victory Gold Medal Central Veterinary Soc 1965; *Books* The Veterinary Annual, Int Encyclopaedia of Veterinary Medicine, many publications in the Veterinary Record and other journals; *Style—* Dame Olga Uvarov, DBE; 76 Elm Park Ct, Elm Park Rd, Pinner, Middx HA5 3LL

UXBRIDGE, Earl of; Charles Alexander Vaughan Paget; s and h of 7 Marquess of Anglesey, DL; *b* 13 Nov 1950; *Educ* Eton, Exeter Coll Oxford; *m* 1986, Georganne Elizabeth Elliott, da of Col John Alfred Downes, MBE, MC, of Tudor Cottage, Whittlesford, Cambs; 1 s (Lord Paget de Beaudesert b 11 April 1986), 1 da (Cara Elizabeth Isis); *Heir* s, Lord Paget de Beaudesert; *Style—* Earl of Uxbridge; Plas Newydd, Llanfair PG, Anglesey, Wales

UZIELL-HAMILTON, Her Hon Judge; Adrianne Pauline; da of late Dr Marcus Grantham, and Ella Grantham; *b* 14 May 1932; *Educ* Maria Gray's Acad for Girls; *m* 1952, Mario Reginald Uziell-Hamilton; 1 s, 1 da; *Career* called to the Bar Middle Temple 1965 (ad eundem Inner Temple 1976-), head of chambers 1976-, rec Crown Ct 1985-, circuit judge S E Circuit 1990-; memb: Legal Aid Panel 1969-, Gen Cncl of the Bar 1970-74 (exec ctee 1973-74); govr Poly of N London 1986-; author of various articles on marriage contracts; FRSA; *Recreations* collecting theatre and ballet costume design, cooking, conversation; *Clubs* Lloyds; *Style—* Her Hon Judge Uziell-Hamilton; 3 Dr Johnson's Bldgs, Temple, London EC4 (☎ 071 353 8778)

UZIELL-HAMILTON, Mario Reginald; s of Don Nino Uziell (d 1951), and Dona Louisa Sevilla de Uziell (d 1976); *b* 4 May 1922; *Educ* Brentwood, Sorbonne, St Catharine's Coll Cambridge; *m* 1952, Adrianne Pauline, da of Prof Marcus Grantham (d 1975); 1 s (Fabian b 1955), 1 da (Amanda b 1956); *Career* Intelligence Corps 1942-46; barr Middle Temple 1951, slr 1959-, sr ptnr Hooper Holt & Co (slrs London, Redhill, Marbella Spain); chm: Fabian Properties Ltd, Commercial & Continental Ltd; dir Mercantile Asset Corpn Ltd; chm: Anglo Ivory Coast Soc 1973-, Anglo Afrique Gp 1983-86; trustee National Benevolent Fund for the Aged 1984-; Cruz Vermeila Portugal 1945, Ordre National Cote d'Ivoire 1983; *Recreations* watching football (particularly Queens Park Rangers); *Style—* Mario Uziell-Hamilton, Esq; 12 Jeymer Ave, London NW2 4PL (☎ 081 450 6462); office: One Beaumont Court, 38-40 Beaumont St, London WIN 1FA (☎ 071 486 1366); Chandos St, Cavendish Square, London W1M 0HP (☎ 071 580 6562)

UZIELLI, (William) John; s of Herbert Rex Uzielli, CIE, JP, ICS (d 1961); *b* 2 March 1937; *Educ* Marlborough, Trinity Coll Oxford (MA); *m* 1968, Angela Mary, *née* Carrick; 1 s, 1 da; *Career* insur broker, memb Lloyd's, dir Hogg Group plc; *Recreations* golf, gardening; *Clubs* Royal and Ancient Golf, Berkshire Golf, Trevose Golf, City of London; *Style—* John Uzielli, Esq; Buckhurst Park Cottage, Cheapside, Ascot, Berks (☎ 0344 22932, office 071 480 4000)

V

VACHER, Peter John; s of Edwin John Vacher, of Westcott, Surrey, and Deira Beatrice, *née* Paxman; *b* 28 June 1942; *Educ* Marlborough, London Sch of Printing (Dip Mgmnt); *m* 11 June 1966, Mary Anne (Polly), da of Gerald King, of Britannia RNC, Dartmouth; 3 s (Julian, Clive, Brian); *Career* md Burgess & Son (Abingdon) Ltd 1972- (joined 1963); held various posts in BPIF and PIRA 1970-; chm Oxford Section Rolls Royce Enthusiasts 1987; *Recreations* restoration of vintage motor cars; *Style—* Peter Vacher, Esq; Gilbournes Farm, Drayton, Abingdon, Oxon OX14 4HA (☎ 0235 531540); Burgess & Son (Abingdon) Ltd, Thames View, Abingdon, Oxon OX14 3LE (☎ 0235 555555, fax 0235 555544, car 0860 836851, telex 837316)

VADASZ, Dr Imre Mihall; s of Imre Vadasz (d 1944), of Budapest, Hungary, and Renee, *née* Rasko; *b* 8 March 1938; *Educ* Guys' Hosp Med Sch, Univ of London (MB BS); *m* 22 April 1989, Bridget Christine, da of Raymond Joseph Mannion (d 1974); *Career* sr registrar Guys Hosp 1967-70, conslt physician and rheumatologist Dartford and Gravesend Hosps 1970-, clinical tutor Univ of London 1973-81; cncl memb Nat Assoc of Clinical Tutors 1977-81; FRCP 1972 (MRCP 1966); *Recreations* sailing, flying; *Clubs* Royal Ocean Racing; *Style—* Dr Imre Vadasz; Legge Lodge, Legge Lane, Briling, nr Maidstone, Kent ME18 5JH (☎ 0634 240213)

VAES, Baron Robert R L; Hon KCMG 1968; *Educ* Brussels Univ (LLD); *m* 22 July 1947, Anne Albers; 1 da (Corinne (Lady John Wellesley)); *Career* joined Belgian Dip Serv 1946; served: Washington, Paris, Hong Kong, London, Rome Madrid; personal priv sec to Min of Foreign Trade 1958-60, dir-gen of political affairs 1964-66, perm under-sec Min of Foreign Affairs (Foreign Trade and Devpt Cooperation 1966-72); ambass: Spain 1972-76, UK 1976- 84; dir Sotheby's 1984-; cr Baron (Kingdom of Belgium) 1985; Grand Offr Order of Leopold Belgium, Grand Offr Legion of Honour France, Grand Cross Order of Isabel the Catholic Spain; *Recreations* bridge; *Clubs* White's, Beefsteak, Pratt's, Anglo-Belgian; *Style—* Baron Vaes, KCMG; The Orangery Cottage, Langley Park, Bucks; Sotheby's, 34/35 New Bond St, London W1A 2AA (☎ 071 4085378)

VAIL, John Richard; s of Lionel Stuart Vail, JP, and Catherine Grace, *née* Ridler; *b* 7 May 1937; *Educ* Clifton Coll; *m* 21 Oct 1961, Anne, da of Cdr Peter Ward, RN, of 2 Herne Court, Petersfield, Hampshire; 2 s (Paul Dominic b 29 Sept 1962, Thomas Edward b 19 Jan 1967), 1 da (Joanna b 5 Nov 1964); *Career* chartered surveyor; ptnr LS Vail & Son Fareham 1961-88 (sr ptnr 1966 -88), sr ptnr Vail Williams Conslt Surveyors and Commercial Property Agents 1988-; farmer; dir Portsmouth Building Soc; govr Farleigh Sch, memb cncl St Dismas Soc; RICS Galsworthy Prize 1961; former player Rugby Union for Hampshire; FRICS 1961; *Recreations* fox hunting, tennis, shooting; *Clubs* Carlton; *Style—* John Vail, Esq; The Old Rectory, Upham, Hants, SO3 1JH; 20 Brunswick Place, Southampton SO1 2AQ (☎ 0703 631973, fax 0703 223884, car 0836 221 485)

VAILE, (Philip) Bryn; MBE (1989); s of Philip Edward Burdock Vaile, of Lymington, Hants, and Florence, *née* Hughes (d 1983); *b* 16 Aug 1956; *Educ* Belfairs HS, Singapore Int Sch, Thames Poly, Portsmouth Poly; *m* 4 Feb 1989, Erika, da of Erik Lessmann, of São Paulo, Brazil; *Career* Mobil Oil Co Ltd: retail mktg 1978-, credit controller 1982-, liquid petroleum gas mktg admin 1986-; sales mangr Mondosport Ltd 1989, mktg exec PNTA 1990; sec Int Star Class Solent Fleet 1990; *Recreations* yacht racing, golf, photography, music, walking; *Clubs* Royal Lymington Yacht; *Style—* Bryn Vaile, Esq, MBE; 22 Terrington Hill, Marlow, Bucks SL7 2RF (☎ 0628 476082); 94a High St, Sevenoaks, Kent TN13 1LP (☎ 0962 741742, fax 0962 741141)

VAISEY, David George; s of William Thomas Vaisey, and Minnie, *née* Payne (d 1987); *b* 15 March 1935; *Educ* Rendcomb Coll Glos, Exeter Coll Oxford (BA, MA); *m* 7 Aug 1965, Maureen Anne, da of August Alfred Mansell (d 1939); 2 da (Katharine b 1968, Elizabeth b 1969); *Career* Nat Serv 1954-56, 2 Lt Glos Regt, seconded KAR 1955-56 serv Kenya; archivist Staffs CC 1960-63, asst (later sr asst) librarian Bodleian Library Oxford 1963-75, dep keeper Univ of Oxford Archives 1966-75, keeper of western manuscripts Bodleian Library Oxford 1975-86 (Bodley's librarian 1986-); professorial fell Exeter Coll Oxford 1975-, visiting prof library studies UCLA 1985, memb Royal Cmmn on Historical Manuscripts 1986-, hon res fell Sch of Library Archive and Info Studies UCL 1987-, chm Nat Cncl on Archives 1988-; Encomienda Order of Isabel la Católica (Spain) 1989; FRHistS 1973, FSA 1974; *Books* Staffordshire and the Great Rebellion (jtly, 1964), Probate Inventories of Lichfield and District 1568-1680 (1969), Victorian and Edwardian Oxford from Old Photographs (jtly, 1971), Oxford Shops and Shopping (1972), Art for Commerce (jtly, 1973), Oxfordshire, A Handbook for Local Historians (jtly, 1973, 2 edn 1974), The Diary of Thomas Turner 1754-65 (1984, revised 1985); *Style—* David Vaisey, Esq, FSA; 12 Hernes Rd, Oxford, OX2 7PU (☎ 0865 59258); Bodleian Library, Oxford OX1 3BG (☎ 0865 277 166, fax 0865 277 182, telex 83656)

VAIZEY, Baroness; Marina Alandra; da of Lyman Stansky, of New York, USA; *b* 16 Jan 1938; *Educ* Brearley Sch New York, Putney Sch Putney Vermont, Radcliffe Coll, Harvard Univ (BA), Girton Coll Cambridge (MA); *m* 1961, Baron Vaizey (Life Peer, d 1984); 2 s, 1 da; *Career* art critic: Financial Times 1970-74, Sunday Times 1974-; dance critic Now! 1979-81; tstee Imperial War Museum 1991-; author, broadcaster, occasional exhibition organiser, lecturer, ctee memb; *Books* 100 Masterpieces of Art (1979), Artist as Photographer (1982), Peter Blake (1985); *Recreations* arts, travel; *Style—* The Rt Hon the Lady Vaizey; 24 Heathfield Terrace, London W4 4JE (☎ 081 994 7994)

VAIZEY, Hon Polly; o da of Baron Vaizey (Life Peer, d 1984); *b* 3 Dec 1962; *Educ* St Paul's Girls' Sch, Lady Margaret Hall; *Career* stockbroker; *Style—* The Hon Polly Vaizey

VAIZEY, Hon Thomas Peter John; er s of Baron Vaizey (Life Peer, d 1984); *b* 1964; *Educ* St Paul's, Worcester Coll Oxford (BA), City Univ (Dip Law); *Career* called to the Bar Inner Temple 1988; *Recreations* travel; *Style—* The Hon Thomas Vaizey

VALDINGER, Jan Robin; s of Maj Stefan Valdinger-Vajda, MC, of Chertsey, Surrey, and Peggy, *née* Chadwick; *b* 28 Sept 1945; *Educ* Univ of Newcastle upon Tyne (LLB); *m* 28 Sept 1974, Rosemary Jane, da of Brendan O'Conor Donelan, of Esher, Surrey; 1 s (Stefan b 1975), 2 da (Anna b 1977, Juliet b 1980); *Career* articled clerk Pinsent & Co 1968-70, slr Clifford Turner & Co 1970-74, corporate fin exec Morgan Grenfell & Co 1974-79; Standard Chartered Merchant Bank Ltd (now known as Chartered West L B Ltd): chief exec Merchant Banking Div India 1979-83, md Hong Kong 1983-87, dir Advsy Servs London 1987-; memb Law Soc; *Clubs* Hong Kong, Royal Hong Kong Jockey; *Style—* Jan Valdinger, Esq; Michael Court, More Lane, Esher, Surrey KT10 8AJ (☎ 03724 68362); Chartered West L B, 33-36 Gracechurch St, London EC3V 0AX (☎ 071 623 8711, fax 071 626 1610, telex 884689)

VALE, Dr (John) Allister; s of John Richard Vale, of Grappenhall, Cheshire, and Ellen, *née* Warburton; *b* 13 June 1944; *Educ* Co GS Altrincham, Guy's Hosp London (MB BS, MD); *m* 4 Sept 1971, Elizabeth Margaret Hastings, da of Brig Leonard Walter Jubb (d 1979), of Chislehurst, Kent; 2 da (Fiona b 1974, Katherine b 1975); *Career* conslt physician and dir: W Midlands Poisons Unit, Dudley Road Hosp Birmingham 1982-; sr clinical lectr Dept of Med Univ of Birmingham 1982-, sec Part 1 MRCP (UK) Examining Bd 1982-; memb: Poison Bd Home Office, W Birmingham Health Authy 1985-90; vice pres Euro Assoc of Poisons Centers and Clinical Toxicologists; FRCP 1984, fell American Acad of Clinical Toxicology 1988, fell RSM; memb: Br Pharmacological Soc, Br Toxicology Soc; *Books* Poisoning - Diagnosis and Treatment (with T J Meredith, 1979), A Concise Guide to the Management of Poisoning (with T J Meredith, 1981); *Recreations* reading, photography; *Clubs* Nat; *Style—* Dr Allister Vale; West Midlands Poison Unit, Dudley Road Hospital, Birmingham B18 7QH (☎ 021 554 3801, fax 021 523 6526); Royal College of Physicians, St Andrews Place, Regents Park, London NW1 4LE (☎ 071 935 1174 ext 326)

VALE, Brian; OBE (1977); s of Leslie Vale, of Headcorn, Kent (d 1986), and May, *née* Knowles (d 1983); *b* 26 May 1938; *Educ* Sir Joseph Williamson's Mathematical Sch Rochester, Univ of Keele (BA, DipEd), King's Coll London (MPhil); *m* 12 Dec 1966, Margaret Mary, da of Thomas Ernest Cookson, of Cockerham, Lancs (d 1983); 2 s (Nicholas b 1970, Jonathan b 1977); *Career* Overseas Civil Serv: Northern Rhodesia 1960-63, asst cmmr N Rhodesia London 1964, educn attaché Zambia High Cmmn London 1964-65; Br Cncl: Rio de Janiero 1965-68, Appts Div London 1968-71, Educn and Sci Div 1972-75, rep Riyadh Saudi Arabia 1975-78, dep controller Educn and Sci Div London 1978-83, dir gen TETOC 1980-81, controller Sci Technol and Educn Div, rep and cultural cnsllr Cairo Embassy 1983-87, asst dir gen Br Cncl London 1987-91, dir Spain and cultural attaché Madrid Embassy 1991-; *Recreations* reading, talking, naval history; *Clubs* Travellers; *Style—* Brian Vale, Esq, OBE; 40 Gloucester Circus, Greenwich, London SE10; 10 Spring Gardens, London SW1A 2BN (☎ 071 930 8466)

VALENTIA, Gladys, Viscountess; Gladys May Kathleen; da of Uriah Fowler (d 1941), and Emily (d 1938); *b* 19 Feb 1903; *Educ* Ridley Hall Cambridge; *m* 1938, 13 Viscount Valentia (d 1951); *Style—* The Rt Hon Gladys, Viscountess Valentia; 34 Uphills, Bruton, Somerset (☎ 074 981 1524)

VALENTIA, 15 Viscount (I 1642, with precedence of 1622); Sir Richard John Dighton Annesley; Bt (I 1620, Premier Baronet of Ireland); also Baron Mountnorris (I 1628); s of 14 Viscount Valentia (d 1983), and Joan, Viscountess Valentia (d 1986); *b* 15 Aug 1929; *Educ* Marlborough, RMA; *m* 10 Aug 1957, Anita Phyllis, o da of William Arthur Joy, of Bristol; 3 s, 1 da; *Heir* s, Hon Francis Annesley, *qv*; *Career* Capt RA (ret); *Style—* The Rt Hon the Viscount Valentia

VALENTIN, Dr Friedrich Heinrich Hermann; s of Kurt Heinrich Valentin (d 1940), and Margarete Hedwig Eva, *née* Beermann (d 1957); *b* 10 Jan 1918; *Educ* Grunewald Gymnasium Berlin, Univ of Edinburgh, Univ of Witwatersrand (BSc, MSc, PhD); *m* 31 Jan 1953, Nancy, da of George Henry Hitchin (d 1962), of Bury, Lancs; 2 s (Peter Henry b 1959, Leo Kurt b 1964), 1 da (Claire Marguerite b 1955); *Career* offr S African MOD 1942-45, lectr Univ of Natal 1946-49, chem engr Petrocarbon Ltd 1949-51, sr chem engr British Oxygen Co Ltd 1951-55, sr lectr Univ of Cape Town 1955-56, prof of chem engrg Univ of Natal 1957-62, dep dir (res) Warren Spring Labs 1970-82 (head chem engrg 1962-69); consltg chem engr 1982-; Eur Ing, C Eng, FIChemE, FIWEM, MConsE, MBAE; memb: Nat Soc Clean Air, Filtration Soc Inst of Environmental Assessment, Int Professional Assoc for Environment Affrs, Environmental Law Assoc; *Books* Absorption in Gas Liquid Dispersions (1965), Odours, Working Party Reports Parts 1 and 2 (ed, 1974-75), Odour Control - A Concise Guide (1980), Silos - Draft Design Code for Silos, Bins, Bunkers and Hoppers (1987); *Recreations* gardening, yoga, jogging, walking, family, writing computer programs, travel; *Style—* Dr Friedrich Valentin; Elm Tree House, Letchworth Lane, Letchworth, Herts SG6 3ND (☎ 0462 684940, fax 0462 671436)

VALENTINE, David Aitken; s of David Aitken Valentine (d 1979), of Balgrummo, Perth, and Isabella, *née* Dow (d 1983); *b* 31 Jan 1939; *Educ* Perth Acad, CPU California (BA, MBA); *m* 15 Nov 1963, Sheena Mairi, da of John McLean (d 1984), of Perth; 1 da (Janine Lynne b 12 July 1966); *Career* corporate planning mangr and lectr in Aust 1972, Airfix Prods Ltd 1973-76, BSG Int (special and subsids) 1976-80, chief exec Bullers plc and subsids 1983-88, dir Valentine Associates 1988-; FRSA; *Books* Insolvency Prevention (1985); *Recreations* shooting, water colour painting; *Clubs* Carlton, RAC, Phyllis Ct; *Style—* David Valentine, Esq; Sussex House, Berkeley Gardens, Claygate, Esher, Surrey (☎ 0372 468430, fax 0372 464956); Res Gordon Bennett, Boulevard Gordon Bennett, Beaulieu-sur- Mer, Cote d'Azur, France (☎ 010 33 93 01 10 87)

VALENTINE, Dr Donald Graham; s of Rev Cyril Henry Valentine (d 1957), and Ada Grace, *née* Herington (d 1982); *b* 5 Nov 1929; *Educ* East Grinstead Co GS, Trinity Coll Cambridge (BA, MA, LLB), Utrecht Univ Netherlands (Dr Jur); *m* 25 March 1961, Vera Ruth, da of Robert Klinger (d 1954); 2 da (Tessa, Jill); *Career* asst lectr LSE 1954, called to the Bar Lincolns Inn 1956, lectr LSE 1957, prof of law Univ of Nigeria 1966-67, reader in law LSE 1967-81; Freeman: Worshipful Co of Arbitrators 1985, City of London 1988; FCIArb; *Books* The Court of Justice of the European Coal and Steel Community (1956), The Court of Justice of the European Communities (2 vols, 1966); *Recreations* greenhouse gardening; *Clubs* Garrick; *Style—* Dr D G Valentine; 3 Park Lane, Appleton, Oxfordshire (☎ 0865 864658); 1 Atkin Building, Gray's Inn, London WC1 (☎ 071 404 0102, fax 071 405 7456, telex 298623 HUDSON)

VALENTINE, Hon Mrs (Janet Sibella); *née* Weir; da of 2 Viscount Weir, CBE; *b* 13 April 1947; *m* 1978, Francis Anthony Brinsley Valentine, 2 s of Dr Francis Valentine and Lady Freda, *née* Butler, half-sis of 9 Earl of Lanesborough, TD, JP, DL; 1 s (b

1983), 1 da (b 1981); *Style*— The Hon Mrs Valentine; The Gate House, Astrop, Banbury, Oxon

VALENTINE, Michael Robert; s of Alfred Buyers Valentine, CB (d 1970), and Violet Elise; *b* 16 Jan 1928; *Educ* Shrewsbury, Corpus Christi Coll Cambridge (MA); *m* 1957, Shirley Josephine, *née* Hall; 1 s (James b 1964), 2 da (Josephine b 1958, Helen b 1960); *Career* Lt RCS; sr mangr Cooper Brothers & Co CAS 1957-60; dir: S G Warburg & Co Ltd 1966-88 (vice-chm 1986-88), Mercury Securities Ltd 1974-86, S G Warburg Gp plc 1986- (non exec 1988-); Croda International plc: non-exec dir 1982-86, vice-chm 1986-89, chm 1989-; non exec dir Reckitt & Colman plc 1986-; FCA; *Recreations* opera, vintage cars, social life, travel; *Style*— Michael Valentine, Esq; 2 Finsbury Ave, London EC2M 2PA (☎ 071 860 1090)

VALÈRE, Hon Mrs (Gloria Theresa); da of Baron Constantine (Life Peer; d 1971); *b* 2 April 1928; *Educ* St Andrew's Univ (MA), Inst of Educn London Univ (DipEd); *m* 1954, André Joseph Valère; 1 s; *Career* public service Medal of Merit of Order of the Trinity 1982 (MOM); *Style*— The Hon Mrs Valère; 202A Terrace Vale, Goodwood Park, Point Cumana, Trinidad and Tobago (☎ 637 4840)

VALIOS, Nicholas Paul; *b* 5 May 1943; *Educ* Stonyhurst; *m* 2 Sept 1967, Cynthia Valerie; 1 s (Mark b 11 Sept 1973), 1 da (Natalie b 6 Aug 1969); *Career* called to the Bar Inner Temple 1964; asst rec 1981, rec of Crown Ct 1986; *Recreations* windsurfing; *Style*— Nicholas Valios, Esq; Francis Taylor Building, Temple, London EC4Y 7BY (☎ 071 353 7768, fax 071 353 0659)

VALLANCE, Prof Elizabeth Mary; da of William Henderson McGonnigill, and Jane Brown, *née* Kirkwood; *b* 8 April 1945; *Educ* Univ of St Andrews (MA), LSE (MSc), Univ of London (PhD); *m* 5 Aug 1967, Iain David Thomas Vallance, *qv*, s of Edmund Thomas Vallance, CBE, ERD; 1 s (Edmund William Thomas b 1975), 1 da (Rachel Emma b 1972); *Career* Sloan fell London Business Sch; univ lectr, visiting prof in politics Queen Mary and Westfield Coll Univ of London (head Dept of Political Studies 1985-88); dir HMV Gp; author; *Books* The State, Society and Self-Destruction (1975), Women in the House (1979), Women of Europe (1985), Member of Parliament (jtly, 1987, 2 edn 1990); *Style*— Prof Elizabeth Vallance; c/o Macmillans Ltd, 4 Little Essex St, London WC2

VALLANCE, Michael Wilson; s of Vivian Victor Wilson Vallance (d 1967), of Wandsworth and Helston, Cornwall, and Kate, *née* Edwards (d 1986); *b* 9 Sept 1933; *Educ* Brighton Coll, St John's Coll Cambridge (MA); *m* 1 April 1970, Mary Winifred Ann, da of John Steele Garnett (d 1969) of Runcorn, Cheshire; 1 s (Vivian b 1974), 2 da (Rachel b 1971, Emma b 1972); *Career* staff memb Utd Steel Cos Ltd 1952-53; asst master: Abingdon Sch 1957-61, Harrow Sch 1961-72; headmaster: Durham Sch 1972-82, Bloxham Sch 1982-; chm: Ctee of Northern ISIS 1976-77, NE Div of Headmasters Conf 1981-82; tstee Bloxham Project 1988-; memb: Steering Ctee Bloxham Project 1986-, Headmasters Conf 1972; *Recreations* books, cricket, the sea; *Clubs* MCC, Jesters; *Style*— Michael Vallance, Esq; Bloxham Sch, nr Banbury, Oxfordshire OX15 4PE (☎ 0295 720 206)

VALLANCE-OWEN, Prof John; s of Edwin Augustine Owen (d 1973), of Bangor, N Wales, and Julia May, *née* Vallance (d 1974); *b* 31 Oct 1920; *Educ* Friars Sch Bangor N Wales, Epsom Coll Surrey, St John's Coll Cambridge, The London Hosp (MA, MD); *m* 24 June 1950, Renee, da of Harold Thornton (d 1952), of Stanmore, Middx; 2 s (Andrew b 1951, Colin b 1963), 2 da (Sarah b 1954, Catherine b 1961); *Career* ROC 1939-43; pathology asst and med first asst to Sir Horace Evans London Hosp 1946-51, Rockefeller travelling fell Univ of Pennsylvania Philadelphia USA 1955-56, sr med registrar to Prof Russell Fraser Royal Postgrad Med Sch London Hammersmith Hosp 1956-58 (liaison physician Obstetric Dept 1951-55); Royal Victoria Infirmary Newcastle upon Tyne: conslt physician and lectr in med Univ of Durham 1958-64, conslt physician and reader in med Univ of Newcastle upon Tyne 1964-66; conslt physician and prof of med Queen's Univ Royal Victoria Hosp Belfast NI 1966-82; Prince of Wales Hosp Shatin NT Hong Kong: fndn prof and chm Dept Med Chinese Univ of Hong Kong 1983-88; assoc dean Faculty Med Chinese Univ of Hong Kong, hon conslt med to Hong Kong Govt 1984-88, hon conslt med Br Army Hong Kong 1985-88, currently visiting prof Royal Postgrad Med Sch Hammersmith Hosp, conslt physician London Ind Hosp 1988-; memb Northern Health and Social Servs Bd DHSS NI 1973-82 (memb Standing Med Advsy Ctee 1969-73); cncllr: RCP London 1976-79 (regnl advsr NI 1970-75), RCP Ireland 1976-82; memb: RSM, RCPath; *Books* Essentials of Cardiology (1961, 2 edn 1968), Diabetes: Its Physiological & Biochemical Basis (1975); *Recreations* tennis, golf, music; *Clubs* E India, Utd Servs Recreation (Hong Kong); *Style*— Prof John Vallance-Owen; 17 St Matthews Lodge, Oakley Sq, London NW1 1MB (☎ 071 388 3644); 10 Spinney Drive, Gt Shelford, Cambridge CB 5ZY (☎ 0223 842767); Cuildochart, Killin, Perthshire (☎ 05672 337); London Ind Hosp, Beaumont Sq, London E1 (☎ 071 790 0990)

VALLAT, Prof Sir Francis Aimé; GBE (1981), KCMG (1962, CMG 1955), QC (1961); s of Col Frederick Vallat, OBE (d 1922); *b* 25 May 1912; *Educ* Univ Coll Toronto, Gonville and Caius Coll Cambridge; *m* 1, 1939 (m dis 1973), Mary Alison, da of F H Cockell, of Barnham, Sussex; 1 s, 1 da; m 2, 1988, Patricia Maria, da of Capt Hamish Morton Anderson, MB ChB, RAMC; *Career* serv WWII as Flt Lt RAFVR; barr Gray's Inn 1935; joined FO 1945, legal advsr Perm UK Delegation to UN 1950-54, dep legal advsr FO 1954-60, legal advsr 1960-68, visiting prof McGill Univ 1965-66; dir Int Law Studies King's Coll London 1968-76, reader Int Law London Univ 1969-70 (prof 1970-76, prof emeritus 1976-); bencher Gray's Inn 1971-; memb: Int Law Cmmn 1973-81 (chm 1977-78), Permanent Ct of Arbitration 1981-, Curatorium Hague Acad of Int Law 1982-, vice pres Inst of Int Law 1989-91; Dr en dr hc Univ of Lausanne 1979; *Clubs* Hurlingham; *Style*— Prof Sir Francis Vallat, GBE, KCMG, QC; 3 Essex Court, Temple, London EC4 (☎ 071 583 9294); 17 Ranelagh Grove, London SW1W 8PA (☎ 071 730 6656)

VALLINGS, Vice Adm Sir George Montague Francis; KCB (1986); s of Robert Archibald Vallings, DSC (d 1970), of Perth, Scotland, and Alice Mary Joan, *née* Bramsden (d 1964); *b* 31 May 1932; *Educ* Belhahen Hill Dunbar, RNC Dartmouth; *m* 12 Sept 1964, Tessa Julia, da of Bernard Delacourt Cousins (d 1963), of Haslemere; 3 s (Sam b 10 Jan 1966, Tom b 1 Oct 1968, Andrew b 28 June 1970); *Career* Cdr 1965, CO HMS Defender 1967-68, Exec Offr HMS Bristol 1970-73, Capt 1974, NA Canberra Aust 1974-76, Capt 2 Frigate Sqdn 1977-78, dir Naval Op and Trade 1978-80, Cdre Clyde 1980-82, Rear Adm 1983, Flag Offr Gibraltar 1983-85, Vice Adm 1985, Flag Offr Scotland and NI 1985-87; sec Chartered Inst Mgmnt Accountants 1987-, chm Race Ctee Sail Trg Assoc; cncl memb: Royal Nat Mission to Deep Sea Fisherman, Bede House Assoc (Bermondsey); MNI 1976; *Recreations* various sports; *Clubs* Woking Golf, Royal Ocean Racing; *Style*— Vice Adm Sir George Vallings, KCB; Meadowcroft, 25 St Marys Rd, Long Ditton, Surrey KT6 5EU (☎ 081 398 6932); 63 Portland Place, London W1 4AB (☎ 071 637 2311)

VALLINGS, Robert Ross; s of Lt Cdr Robert Archibald Vallings, DSC, RNVR (d 1969), of Perth, Scotland, and Alice Mary Joan, *née* Bramsdon (d 1964); *b* 18 Nov 1943; *Educ* Rugby; *m* 12 May 1973, Penelope Claire, da of Dr Thomas Parham Lalonde (d 1982), of Romsey, Hants; 1 s (Timothy b 1974), 1 da (Claire b 1975); *Career* admitted slr 1969; ptnr Rodcliffes & Co 1970-; *Recreations* sport; *Clubs* Naval and Military, Richmond FC, Hurlingham; *Style*— Robert Vallings, Esq; 4 Halsey St, Chelsea, London SW3 2QH (☎ 071 589 7912); Rodcliffes & Co, 5 Great Coll St, Westminster, London SW1P 3SJ (☎ 071 222 7040, fax 071 222 6208, telex 919302)

VALLIS, Rear-Adm Michael Anthony; CB (1986); s of Ronald William Harvey Vallis (d 1980), of Frome, Somerset, and Sarah Josephine (d 1964); *b* 30 June 1929; *Educ* RNC Dartmouth, RNEC Manadon, RNC Greenwich; *m* 1959, Pauline Dorothy, da of George Abbott (d 1967), of Wymondham, Leics; 3 s, 1 da; *Career* dir Naval Recruiting 1979-82, dir-gen Surface Ships MOD 1983-84, dir-gen Marine Engrg MOD 1984-86 and sr naval rep Bath 1983-86, dir Darchem Ltd 1987, pres Inst of Marine Engrs 1991; FEng; *Recreations* fishing, walking, music, theatre; *Clubs* Royal Overseas League; *Style*— Rear-Adm Michael Vallis, CB; 54 Bloomfield Park, Bath BA2 2BX (☎ 0225 314286)

VALLS, HE Don Rafael Francisco Jose; LVO (1986); s of Aurelio Valls, (d 1968), and Maria de los Angeles, *née* Carreras (d 1970); *b* 10 Jan 1912; *Educ* Chamatin De La Rosa Madrid, Stonyhurst, Madrid Univ; *m* 1 March 1947, Diana Seymour, da of John Chadwick Greaves (d 1950); 2 s (Rafael Rhidian b 1948, Juan Aurelio b 1949); *Career* called to the Bar Middle Temple 1933, barr Spanish Bar Madrid 1934, practising barr Spanish and English Law 1934-75, legal advsr to Spanish Embassy London 1939, legal attache to Spanish Embassy London 1975-; Blackstone prizeman 1931, 1932; memb: various Spanish Govt Delegations for negotiating Legal Conventions, Bar Cncl Foreign Relations Ctee 1965-70; rep Spanish Bar Cncl 1950-73; memb: British Maritime Law Assoc, Spanish Maritime Law Assoc; Kt Grand Cross Order of Civil Merit Spain 1986, Kt Car Order of Isabel the Catholic Spain 1970, Car Order Civil Merit 1954 Spain; *Books* many articles on Spanish law, author of 35 summaries of relevant Spanish laws currently available; *Recreations* music, sailing, motoring; *Clubs* Pegasus, Bar Yacht, Royal Southern Yacht; *Style*— HE Don Rafael Valls, LVO; 26 Hans Crescent, London SW1 (☎ 071 235 5555); Casa Bermudas, Altea, Spain; Spanish Embassy, 24 Belgrave Square, London SW1X 89A

VALMAN, Dr (Hyman) Bernard; s of Samuel Valman, and Lillian, *née* Schwoltz; *b* 10 Feb 1934; *Educ* Charterhouse, Univ of Cambridge (MA, MD); *m* 24 May 1964, Thea, da of Maj Weiss (d 1958); 1 s (Martin David 29 Dec 1969), 1 da (Nadia Deborah b 11 Jan 1968); *Career* Nat Serv Capt RAMC 1959-61; sr registrar The Hosp for Sick Children Gt Ormond St 1969-72, conslt paediatrician Northwick Park Hosp and Clinical Res Centre Harrow 1972-; ed Archives of Disease in Childhood 1982-; memb Soc of Authors, sec to paediatric ctee of RCP (chm of examining bd for dip in child health); memb: RSM, BPA; FRCP; *Books* Keeping Babies and Children Healthy (1985), 1-7 (3 edn, 1988), The First Year of Life (3 edn, 1989); *Recreations* gardening, editing, writing; *Style*— Dr Bernard Valman; Northwick Park Hospital, Harrow, Middx HA1 3UJ (☎ 081 864 3232)

VALPY, Peter Francis; s of Kenneth Francis Valpy (d 1986), of Blackheath London, and Freda Frances, *née* Stone; *b* 4 June 1938; *Educ* King's Canterbury, Univ of Swansea; *m* 13 Jan 1962, Virginia Judith, da of Michael Carter Gower Ringer; 1 s (Edward Francis Ringer b 5 Jan 1970), 2 da (Tessa Frances b 23 Oct 1963, Lisa Frances b 1 Jan 1966); *Career* Nat Serv Cyprus 2 Lt Royal W Kent Regt Queen's Own 1958-60; sr buyer C & A Modes 1967-69 (trainee mangr 1960-67), merchandising mangr Freemans (Liverpool) Ltd 1969-71, merchandising controller Peter Robinson Ltd (part of Burton Group) 1971-74, md Country Casuals Ltd (part of Coats Patons) 1977-86 (gen mangr 1974-77), conslt Textile Market Studies 1986-87, dir Br Knitting and Clothing Export Cncl 1991 (exec dir 1987-91); pres Old Kings Scholars Assoc; Freeman City of London, Liveryman Worshipful Co of Woolmen; memb: Twenty Club, IOD, English Vineyards Assoc, NFU, CLA, Game Conservancy; FRSA, FBIM; *Recreations* shooting, wine; *Clubs* Leander, London Rowing, Henley Royal Regatta Stewards; *Style*— Peter Valpy, Esq; British Knitting & Clothing Export Council, British Apparel & Textiles Centre, Oxford Circus, 7 Swallow Place, London W1R 7AA (☎ 071 493 6622, fax 071 493 6276)

VAN 'T HOFF, Dr Walter; s of Robert van 't Hoff (d 1979), and Petronella Charlotte Antoinette Wilhelmina, *née* Hooft (d 1979); *b* 21 May 1924; *Educ* Bryanston, Queens' Coll Cambridge, Guy's Hosp Med Sch (MA, MB BChir); *m* 14 Jan 1956, Rosemary Anne, da of Dr William Francis Cooper (d 1950), of Kingston-upon-Thames; 3 s (William b 1958, Hugh b 1960, Graham b 1961); *Career* RAMC 1947-49, RMO 2 Bn Grenadier Gds 1948-49, memb Rhine Army Ski Team; sr med registrar Westminster Hosp 1955-62, res fell med Peter Bent Brigham Hosp Harvard Univ 1956-57, conslt physician N Staffs Hosp Centre 1962-89, sr lectr endocrinology Univ of Keele 1980-89, chm jt liaison ctee Br Endocrine Socs 1984-86; memb: quality assur ctee King Edwards Hosp Fund London 1986-88, cncl RCP 1979-82; pres: W Midlands Physicians Assoc 1987-88, section of endocrinology RSM 1982-84; memb: Assoc Physicians GB and Ireland, Soc for Endocrinology, Thyroid Club; MRCP 1952, FRCP 1971; *Recreations* sailing, travel, photography; *Clubs* Royal Soc of Med, Ski GB, Hardway Sailing, Cruising Assoc; *Style*— Dr Walter van 't Hoff; Granida, 9 East St, Hambledon, Hants PO7 4RX (☎ 0705 632382)

VAN ALLAN, Richard; s of Joseph Arthur Jones, of Mansfield, Notts, and Irene Hannah, *née* Taylor; *b* 28 May 1935; *Educ* Brunts GS Mansfield, Worcester Coll of Educ (Dip Ed), Birmingham Sch of Mus; *m* 1, 1963 (m dis 1974), Elizabeth Mary, da of Bib Peabody (d 1983), of Leamington Spa; 1 s (Guy Richard b 1967); m 2, 31 Dec 1976 (m dis 1987), Elisabeth Rosemary, da of Richard Pickering, DM, of Cape Town SA; 1 s (Robert Tristan b 1979), 1 da (Emma Mary b 1983); *Career* police constable, Sgt Special Investigation Branch, RMP 1953-56; sch teacher, opera singer (debut 1964); principal bass at: Glyndebourne, WNO, ENO, Scottish Opera, Royal Opera House Covent Garden, Nice, Bordeaux, Paris, Marseille, Bruxelles, San Diego, Miami, Boston, Seattle, Metropolitan NY, Buenos Aires; dir Nat Opera Studio; Hon RAM; *Recordings* Cosi Fan Tutte, Don Alfonso (Grammy award), Don Giovanni, Leporello (Grammy nomination); *Recreations* cricket, golf, shooting; *Style*— Richard Van Allan, Esq; 18 Octavia St, London SW11 3DN (☎ 071 228 8462)

VAN CULIN, Rev Canon Samuel; *Educ* Princeton Univ (AB), Virginia Theol Seminary (BD); *Career* curate St Andrew's Catholic Honolulu 1955-56, canon precenter and rector Hawaiian congregation Honolulu 1956-58, asst rector St John's Washington DC 1958-60, gen sec Lyman Int Washington DC 1960-61, asst sec Overseas Dept Exec Cncl of Episcopal Church USA 1968-76, exec World Mission Episcopal Church USA 1976-83, sec gen Anglican Consultative Cncl 1983-; hon canon: Canterbury 1983, Jerusalem 1983, Ibadan Nigeria 1984, Cape Town SA 1989; Hon DD Virginia Theol Seminary 1977; *Recreations* music, swimming; *Clubs* Athenaeum, Princeton (NY); *Style*— The Rev Canon Samuel Van Culin; Anglican Consultative Council, Partnership House, 157 Waterloo Rd, London SE1 8UT (☎ 071 620 1110, fax 071 620 1070, telex 8950907 ANGCOM G)

VAN CUTSEM, Geoffrey Neil; yr s of Bernard van Cutsem (d 1975), and Mary (d 1989), da of Capt Edward Compton, JP, DL (s of Lord Alwyne Compton, 2 s of 4 Marquess of Northampton, KG), of Newby Hall, Ripon; yr bro of Hugh van Cutsem, *qv*; *b* 23 Nov 1944; *Educ* Ampleforth; *m* 30 Oct 1969, Sarah, only da of Alastair McCorquodale, *qv*; 2 da (Sophie b 5 Aug 1975, Zara b 11 Dec 1978); *Career* served RHG (Blues and Royals) 1963-68, Capt 1967; joined Savills 1969, exec dir 1987-; memb Nat Appeals Ctee Cancer Res Campaign; FRICS 1973; *Clubs* White's, Pratt's; *Style*— Geoffrey van Cutsem, Esq; 9a Elm Park Rd, London SW3 6BP (☎ 071 352

8281); The Old Rectory, Old Somerby, Grantham, Lincs NG33 4AG (☎ 0476 63167); Savills, 20 Grosvenor Hill, London W1X 0HQ (☎ 071 499 8644)

VAN CUTSEM, Hugh Bernard Edward; s of Bernard van Cutsem (d 1975), and Mary, da of Capt Edward Compton, JP, DL (himself s of Lord Alwyne Compton, 2 s of 4 Marquess of Northampton, KG), of Newby Hall, Ripon; er bro of Geoffrey van Cutsem, *qv*; *b* 21 July 1941; *Educ* Ampleforth; *m* 1971, Jonkvrouwe Emilie Elise Christine, da of Jonkheer Pieter Quarles van Ufford (Netherlands cr of Willem I 1814), of Ackworth House, E Bergholt, Suffolk; 4 s; *Career* Lt Life Gds; bloodstock breeder, farmer, co chm; *Clubs* White's, Jockey; *Style*— Hugh van Cutsem, Esq; Northmore, Exning, Newmarket, Suffolk CB8 7JR (☎ 063 877 332)

VAN CUYLENBURG, Peter; s of Flt Lt Brian Van Cuylenburg, of Auckland, NZ, and Margaret, *née* Budd; *b* 5 March 1948; *Educ* Sir William Borlase Marlow Bucks, St John's Singapore, Bristol Poly; *m* 5 Aug 1972, Mary-Rose, da of Harry Sabberton, of Cambridge (d 1984); 1 s (Jeremy b 1981), 1 da (Nicola b 1984); *Career* md Texas Instruments Ltd 1984-87; vice-pres: Data Systems Gp, Texas Instruments 1987-89; chief exec Mercury Communications Ltd 1989; CBIM; *Recreations* sailing; *Style*— Peter van Cuylenburg, Esq; Mercury Communications Ltd, New Mercury House, Red Lion Square, London WC1R 4HQ (☎ 071 528 2300)

VAN DER NOOT, Hon Mrs (Barbara Mary); *née* Cokayne; da of late 1 Baron Cullen of Ashbourne and Grace, da of the late Rev the Hon John Marsham (s of 3 Earl of Romney); *b* 1905; *m* 1929, Maj Gilbert Edgar Francis Van der Noot (d 1981); 1 da; *Style*— The Hon Mrs Van der Noot; Oak Cottage, Hartley Wintney, Hants

VAN DER WATEREN, Jan Floris; s of Jacob van der Wateren (d 1981), of Pretoria, and Wilhelmina, *née* LaBuschagnè; *b* 14 May 1940; *Educ* Univ of Potchefstroon SA (MA), Univ of Sussex, UCL (Dip in Library Studies); *Career* managing librarian RIBA Library 1976-83, dir and Sir Banister Fletcher librarian Br Architectural Library 1984-87, keeper and chief librarian Nat Art Library 1988-; ALA; *Style*— Jan Floris van der Wateren, Esq; 52 Blenheim Crescent, London W11 1NY (☎ 071 221 6221); National Art Library, Victoria & Albert Museum, London SW7 2RL (☎ 071 938 8303, fax 071 938 8461, telex 268831 VICART G)

VAN DER WERFF, His Hon Judge Jonathan Ervine; s of James van der Werff (d 1960), of London, and Clare Poupart, *née* Ervine; *b* 23 June 1935; *Educ* Harrow, RMA Sandhurst; *m* 17 Sept 1968, Katharine Bridget, da of Maj James Colvin, of Newland House, Withypool, Somerset; 2 da (Olivia b 1971, Claudia b 1976); *Career* joined Coldstream Gds 1953, RMA Sandhurst 1954-55, cmmnd 1955, Adj 1 Bn 1962-64, Maj 1967, ret 1968; called to the Bar Inner Temple 1969, rec 1986, circuit judge 1986, res judge Croydon Combined Court Centre 1989; *Clubs* Pratt's, Bembridge Sailing, Something; *Style*— His Hon Judge van der Werff; The Law Courts, Altyre Rd, Croydon CR9 5AB

VAN DER WYCK, Jonkheer Herman Constantyn; s of Jonkheer Hendrik Lodewyk van der Wyck, OBE (d 1986), Col Royal Netherlands Artillery, and Berendina Johanna van Welderen, Baroness Rengers (d 1963); *b* 17 March 1934; *Educ* Inst for Int Studies Univ of Geneva (MA), Rotterdam and Ann Arbour Business Sch (MA); *m* 1, 1959 (m dis 1969), Danielle Mourgue d'Algue; 1 s (Patrick Henri Louis b 5 Dec 1962), 1 da (Edina Nathalie b 8 Aug 1960); m 2, 1977 (m dis 1988), Viviana Olga Paulina van Reigersberg Versluys; 2 s (Edzard Lorillard b 10 Oct 1980, Alexander Lodewyk b 5 Aug 1985); *Career* ret Capt Royal Dutch Cavalry; chm S G Warburg & Co Ltd, vice chm S G Warburg Gp plc; dir: Automobiles Peugeot, Peugeot Talbot UK Ltd, Energy Int NV; *Recreations* skiing, water skiing, swimming, tennis, reading, music; *Style*— Herman C van der Wyck, Esq; 27 South Terrace, London SW7 (☎ 071 584 9931); S G Warburg Group plc, 1 Finsbury Avenue, London EC2 (☎ 071 382 4086)

VAN GEEST, Leonard Waling; s of Leonard van Geest; *b* 1 April 1950; *Educ* Spalding GS; *m* 1978, Gillian Denise, *née* Fox; 1 s; *Career* chm Geest plc; non-exec chm The Littlewoods Organisation; *Recreations* tennis; *Style*— Leonard van Geest Esq; Wool Hall, Cross Gate, Wykeham, Spalding (☎ 0775 766256)

VAN HEE, David William; s of Victor George Van Hee (d 1990), of Coventry, Warwickshire, and Vera, *née* Gibson; *b* 26 Feb 1949; *Educ* King Henry VIII Sch Coventry, Downing Coll Cambridge (MA, LLB); *Career* called to the Bar Middle Temple 1972, barr South Eastern circuit; *Recreations* gliding; *Clubs* Utd Oxford and Cambridge; *Style*— David Van Hee, Esq; 3 Dr Johnson's Buildings, Temple EC4 (☎ 071 353 4854, fax 071 583 8784)

VAN KLAVEREN, Dr George (John); s of Wilhelm Gottfried van Klaveren (d 1963), and Gladys Joan van Klaveren, *née* Bickmore (d 1962); *b* 9 May 1925; *Educ* Marlborough, Univ of Cambridge, St Mary's Hosp (MRCS, LRCP); *m* 10 Aug 1949, Doreen Maud, da of William Benjamin Riceveal Berriman (d 1964); 1 s (Geoffrey b 1960), 1 da (Juliana b 1952); *Career* Flt Lt RAF 1950-52, physician and surgn in gen practice 1952-70; sr med offr to Br Rail Bd 1986-90, chm Br Coll of Acupuncture 1986-; *Recreations* badminton, philately, gardening; *Clubs* AA; *Style*— Dr George van Klaveren; Hunting Delight, 3 Rotherfield Rd, Henley-on-Thames, Oxon RG9 1NR (☎ 0491 575736)

VAN KOETSVELD, Hon Mrs (Margaret Ross); *née* Geddes; o da of 2 Baron Geddes, KBE (d 1975), and Enid, Baroness Geddes, *qv*; *b* 5 May 1934; *Educ* Benenden; *m* 6 May 1961, Ralph Emilius Quintus van Koetsveld, s of Johan Emilius van Koetsveld, of Rotterdam; 3 s (Michael, Guy, Dirk); *Career* memb Assoc of Occupational Therapists; chm Hydon Hill Cheshire Home, Godalming 1984-88; tstee Leonard Cheshire Fndn; *Recreations* needlework, canalling, singing; *Style*— The Hon Mrs van Koetsveld; Northacre, Grenville Rd, Shackleford, Godalming, Surrey GU8 6AX

VAN MARLE, (Johan) Tyo; s of Tyo Henrik van Marle and Catharina Alida van Marle of St Jeaume, Chateauneuf, AM France; *b* 20 Oct 1940; *Educ* Baarns Lyceum, Amsterdam Univ, Harvard Bus Sch USA; *m* 1972, Isabella Christina, da of Rudolph Maximillian Crommelin; 3 s (John b 1977, Francis b 1980, Arthur b 1989); *Career* mangr Pierson Heldring and Pierson (bankers) Amsterdam 1966-72; dir J Henry Schroder Wagg and Co Ltd (merchant bankers) 1972-82, md Schroder & Chartered (merchant bankers) Hong Kong 1982-84, exec dir Credit Suisse First Boston (Investmt Bankers) 1984-89, chief exec offr Credit Suisse First Boston Nederland NV Amsterdam 1987-; *Recreations* opera, golf, skiing; *Clubs* Sunningdale Golf, Annabelle's, Hong Kong, Sheh-OGC; *Style*— Tyo van Marle, Esq; Jagtlust Eemnesserweg 38B, 1261 HJ Blaricum, The Netherlands, (☎ 02153 11706); Herengracht 478, 1017 CB Amsterdam (☎ 020 556 7222, telex 14517 CSFB NL)

VAN PRAAG, Louis; CBE (1986); s of Barend Van Praag (d 1976), of London, and Rosalie Van Praag, *née* Monnickendam (d 1978); *b* 9 Aug 1926; *Educ* Owens Sch, Univ of Paris; *m* 1, 19 Nov 1947 (m dis 1963), Angela, da of Archibald McCorquodale (d 1925), of Kildary, Scotland; 2 s (Lucas b 1950, Nicholas b 1952), 1 da (Josephine b 1953); m 2, 11 Sept 1964, Kathy, da of Leonard Titelman, of Fayence, France; 1 s (Joshua b 1979), 2 da (Katharine b 1969, Lucy b 1974); *Career* dir Sabre Group 1958-87 (chm International Group 1976-87), dir Franklin Stores Inc USA 1976-82, sr ptnr Strategic Design Consultants 1988-; memb: Nat Cncl for Dips Art and Design 1971-74, Cncl CNAA 1974-83; chm Design Res Ctee 1976-79, govr Winchester Coll of Art 1976-79, memb Art and Design Nat Advsy Body 1981-83, chm DTI Working Party on Mgmnt of Design 1982-84; memb: Financial Times Design Mgmnt Ctee 1987-, Ct RCA 1980- (chm RCA Enterprises 1977-83, memb Cncl 1979-83, hon fell 1980); chm Museum of Modern Art Oxford 1984-88; memb: Cncl Ecole Nationale Sup De Creation Industriel (Paris) 1986-, Advsy Bd Ashmolean Museum 1988-; chm: DTI Steering Ctee In-House Trg Managing Design 1988-, Lead Industl Body for Design 1989-; memb: Advsy Cncl Design Museum 1989-, Advsy Ctee London Business Sch 1989-; RSA Bicentenary medal 1989; hon: FRCA 1980, Dr DES (CNAA) 1987; FCSD; *Recreations* walking, skiing, music of many kinds; *Style*— Louis Van Praag, Esq, CBE; Design Resource, 53 St John Street, Oxford OX1 2LQ (☎ 0856 516159)

VAN RAALTE, Hon Mrs (Mary Anne); *née* Berry; eldest da of 2 Viscount Kemsley; *b* 30 April 1934; *m* 26 July 1960, Charles Henry van Raalte, s of late Noel van Raalte; 1 s, 2 da; *Style*— The Hon Mrs van Raalte; 7 Meadowcourt Road, Oadby, Leicester

VAN RIJSBERGEN, Prof Cornelis Joost; s of Jacob Adam van Rijsbergen (d 1987), and Gerritdina, *née* Verheij; *b* 17 Oct 1943; *Educ* Univ of W Aust (BSc), Univ of Cambridge (PhD); *m* 22 May 1965, Juliet Hilary, da of Ernest Arthur Clement Gundry, of Perth, Aust; 1 da (Nicola b 1973); *Career* tutor in mathematics Univ of W Aust 1966-68, lectr Monash Univ 1973-75, Royal Soc res fell Univ of Cambridge 1975-79 (sr res offr King's Coll 1969-72); prof computer sci: Univ Coll Dublin 1980-86, Univ of Glasgow 1986-; MBCS 1971, FIEE 1987; *Books* Information Retrieval (2 edn, 1979); *Recreations* swimming, cinema, travel, fiction; *Clubs* Utd Oxford & Cambridge Univ; *Style*— Prof Cornelis van Rijsbergen; 14 Park Parade, Cambridge CB5 8AL: 18A Westbourne Gardens, Glasgow G12 9XD (☎ 0223 60318, 041 3398331); Dept of Computing Science, University of Glasgow, Glasgow G12 8QQ (☎ 041 3304463, fax 041 3304913, telex 777070 UNIGLA)

VAN STRAUBENZEE, Sir William Radcliffe; MBE (1954); s of late Brig A B van Straubenzee, DSO, MC, and Margaret Joan, da of A N Radcliffe, of Bag Park, Widecombe-in-the-Moor, Newton Abbot, S Devon; *b* 27 Jan 1924; *Educ* Westminster; *Career* serv WWII Maj RA; slr 1952; former memb Gen Synod C of E, chm Dioceses Cmmn 1978-86, church cmmr 1968-87; MP (C) Wokingham 1959-87; PPS to Min Educn 1960-62, jt parly under sec of State Dept of Educn and Sci 1970-72, Min State NI 1972-74, second church estates cmmr 1979-87, chm YCs Nat Advsy Ctee 1951-53; chm: Cons Parly Educn Ctee 1979-83, Select Ctee Assistance to Private Membs 1975-77; memb Exec 1922 Ctee 1979-87; former chm Nat Cncl for Drama Trg; kt 1981; *Clubs* Carlton, Garrick; *Style*— Sir William van Straubenzee, MBE; York House, 199 Westminster Bridge Rd, London SE1 (☎ 071 928 6855)

VAN VEEN, Marcella; da of Marcel Fresco, of Holland, and Barbara, *née* Zoeteman; *b* 28 March 1943; *Educ* Holland; *m* 4 Aug 1963, Peter Vincent, s of Johan van Veen; 1 s (Robert b 1964), 1 da (Julie b 1968); *Career* md: DAC (Dial a Char) Ltd, DAC Prods Ltd; *Recreations* theatre, opera, travel; *Clubs* IOD; *Style*— Mrs Marcella Van Veen; 46 Goffs Park Rd, Crawley, Sussex (☎ 0293 518416); DAC Ltd, 77 London Rd, East Grinstead, Sussex (☎ 0342 315556, car ☎ : 0836 514017)

VAN ZUYDAM, Paul Johannes; *b* 13 March 1938; *m* 4 children; *Career* chm chief exec Prestige Gp plc 1983-; dir Gallaher Ltd 1986-; *Clubs* Hurlingham; *Style*— Paul van Zuydam, Esq; The Prestige Gp plc, Prestige House, 14-18 Holborn, London EC1N 2LQ (☎ 071 405 6711, telex PRESLOW G 24162)

VANCE, Charles Ivan; s of E Goldblatt; *b* 1929; *Educ* Royal Sch Dungannon, Queen's Univ Belfast; *m* 1966, Hon Imogen Moynihan, *qv*; 1 da (Jacqueline); *Career* actor and theatrical dir/prodr/publisher and ed; dep chm Festival of Br Theatre 1974-, chm Standing Advsy Ctee on Local Authy and the Performing Arts 1973-; chm Prestige Plays Ltd, pres Theatrical Mgmnt Assoc 1971-76; vice-chm: Theatres Advy Cncl 1974-; dir: Grand Opera House York 1987-89, Top Hat Catering 1986-90; chm Platform Pubns Ltd 1987-; FRSA, FInstD; *Books* Amateur Stage (ed), Br Theatre Directory (1971-75), Br Theatre Review (1973), Amateur Theatre Yearbook (1990), Stage Adaption: Jane Eyre and Wuthering Heights; *Recreations* travel, cooking, sailing (in 1956 single handed crossing Atlantic), dog breeding; *Clubs* RAC, Kennel, Hurlingham, Green Room, Variety Club of GB, Wig and Pen; *Style*— Charles Vance, Esq; Oak Lodge, Farway, nr Colyton, E Devon EX13 6DH

VANCE, Hon Mrs (Imogen Anne Ierne); *née* Moynihan; da of 2 Baron Moynihan, OBE, TD (d 1965); *b* 1932; *m* 1, 1953 (m dis 1965), Michael Edward Peter Williams; m 2, 1965, Charles Ivan Vance, *qv*; 1 da; *Style*— The Hon Mrs Vance; Oak Lodge, Perry Hill, Farway, nr Colyton, E Devon EX13 6DH

VANDEN-BEMPDE-JOHNSTONE; *see*: Johnstone

VANDER ELST, Philip Denis Andrew; *b* 25 June 1951; *Educ* Bryanston, Exeter Coll Oxford (MA); *m* 17 Sept 1977, Rachel Jane, *née* Tingle; *Career* Centre for Policy Studies 1977-78, Inst of Econ Affrs 1979-80; ed Freedom Today; pubns: Freedom and Free Enterprise (US Industl Cncl, 1977), Br Collectivism: The Bitter Harvest (American Con Union, 1978), Capitalist Tech for Soviet Survival (Inst of Econ Affrs, 1981), The Future of Freedom (Freedom Assoc, 1987), Idealism Without Illusions: A foreign policy for freedom (Freedom Assoc 1989), Resisting Leviathan: The Case Against A European State (1991); *Recreations* walking, swimming, reading; *Style*— Philip Vander Elst, Esq; Freedom Association, 35 Westminster Bridge Rd, London SE1 7JB (☎ 071 9289925, fax 071 9289524)

VANDER-MOLEN, Jack; s of Leon Vandermolen (d 1941), of Berwick St, London W1, and Rosetta, *née* Defries (d 1952); *b* 9 Aug 1923; *Educ* Archibishop Tenisons GS; *m* 23 March 1950, Muriel, da of Louis Walters (d 1981), of Edgware, Middx; 3 s (Jonathan Mark b 1954, Paul Nicholas b 1956 d 1985, Leon Richard b 1960), 1 da (Lesley Rebecca b 1952); *Career* WWII RM 1942-46 (ME combined ops 1943-45); orthotic conslt V-M Orthopaedics Ltd 1948- (chm and md 1963-), pt/t conslt Camp Ltd; chm of tstees Paul Vander-Molen Fndn 1986-, expedition ldr Breakthrough Disability 1986 (expedition to Iceland involving disabled explorers) collaborated with Channel 4 in making film A Different Frontier; hon orthotic conslt to Sandy Gall Afghanistan Appeal; Br Surgical Trade Assoc: chm 1984-87, pres 1987-90, vice pres 1990-; pres IV Hendon Scouts and Guides, hon vice pres Hendon and Edgware Dist Scouts and Guides, awarded Chief Scouts Medal of Merit for outstanding servs to Scouting 1984; Freeman City of London 1973, memb: Worshipful Co of Basketmakers 1973, Guild of World Traders in London 1986, United Wards 1973; FRGS 1986, fell Br Inst Surgical Technologists 1958; *Books* Iceland Breakthrough (jt author, 1985); *Recreations* outdoor adventure activities, music (organ playing), writing, boating; *Style*— Jack Vander-Molen, Esq; The Model Farm House, Church End, London NW4 4JS; 10 Garrick Ait, Hampton on Thames, Middx (☎ 081 203 1214, 081 203 2344)

VANDER SPIEGEL, Joseph Anthony; OBE; s of Joseph Vander Spiegel (d 1977), of Grimsby, and Helen, *née* Kelly (d 1948); *b* 2 July 1923; *Educ* Wintringham GS Grimsby; *m* 15 Oct 1949, Margaret Mary, da of Clarence Twaites (d 1971), of London; 1 s (Mark b 1954), 2 da (Catherine b 1951, Josephine b 1957); *Career* Corpl RASC 1942-47; Charringtons Solid Fuel: dir 1974, md 1976-86; pres Coal Merchants Fedn GB 1985-86; chm Chamber of Coal Traders 1985-; Freeman City of London 1984, memb Worshipful Co of Fuellers 1985; *Recreations* tennis, allotment gardening; *Clubs* Nat Lib, Cricketers; *Style*— Joseph Vander Spiegel, Esq, OBE; 44 Drapers Rd, Enfield, Middx EN2 8LY (☎ 081 367 6248); Victoria House, Southampton Row, London WC1B 4DH (☎ 071 405 8218)

VANDERFELT, Sir Robin Victor; KBE (1973, OBE 1954); s of Sydney Vanderfelt, OBE; *b* 24 July 1921; *Educ* Haileybury, Peterhouse Cambridge; *m* 1962, Jean Becker, da of John Steward; 2 s; *Career* serv WWII Burma and India; asst sec Cwlth Parly Assoc UK branch 1949-59 (sec 1960-61, sec-gen 1961-86); *Recreations* gardening; *Clubs* Cwlth Tst, Royal Overseas League; *Style—* Sir Robin Vanderfelt, KBE; No 6 Saddler's Mead, Wilton, Salisbury, Wilts SP2 0DE

VANDERSTEEN, Martin Hugh; s of William Martin Vandersteen (d 1983), and Dorothy Margaret, *née* Leith; *b* 9 Aug 1935; *Educ* Harrow Co GS; *m* 3 April 1967, Catherine Susan Mary, da of John Cansdale Webb; 2 s (Anthony b 1970, William b 1973); *Career* managing ptnr regnl Andersen Consulting 1989 (joined 1957, ptnr 1968-, UK managing ptnr 1973-86); chm UK Mgmnt Consulting Assoc 1981, FCA; *Recreations* sailing, fishing, golf, swimming; *Clubs* Royal Ocean Racing, Royal Southern Yacht, RAC, Royal Wimbledon Golf, Otter Swimming; *Style—* Martin Vandersteen, Esq; 2 Bristol Gardens, Putney Heath, London SW15 3TG (☎ 081 788 9026); 2 Arundel St, London WC2R 3LT (☎ 071 438 3106)

VANDORE, Peter Kerr; QC (Scotland, 1982); s of James Vandore (d 1977), and Janet Kerr Fife, of Frenchie, Fife; *b* 7 June 1943; *Educ* Berwickshire HS, Univ of Edinburgh (MA, LLB); *m* 5 Sept 1970, Hilary Anne, da of Clement Davies (d 1990), of Huddersfield; 2 da (Emma Mary b 13 March 1975, Sara Elizabeth b 15 Sept 1977); *Career* called to the Scottish Bar 1968, standing counsel to Sec of State for Scotland for private legislation procedure 1975-86; memb: Legal Aid Central Ctee 1972-85, Cncl Cockburn Assoc 1988-; chm Central New Town Assoc (CENTA) 1989-90 (memb 1980-90); *Style—* Peter Vandore, Esq, QC; 17 Kings Stables Lane, Edinburgh, Scotland EH1 2LQ (☎ 031 228 1683); Advocates Library, Parliament House, Parliament Square, High Street, Edinburgh (☎ 031 226 5071)

VANE, Hon Christopher John Fletcher-; yr s of 1 Baron Inglewood, TD (d 1989); *b* 27 March 1953; *Educ* Eton, Trinity Coll Cambridge; *m* 23 June 1990, Margaret M, da of late Dr Paul Eisenklam; *Career* called to the Bar Inner Temple 1976; *Clubs* Travellers', Northern Counties (Newcastle-upon-Tyne); *Style—* The Hon Christopher Vane; Morton House, Morton, Calthwaite, Penrith, Cumbria (☎ 076 885 241); 3c Lambton Rd, Newcastle-upon-Tyne NE2 4RX (☎ 091 2810930)

VANE, Hon Gerald Raby; yr s of 10 Baron Barnard, CMG, OBE, MC, TD (d 1964); *b* 2 Dec 1926; *Educ* Eton, Trinity Coll Cambridge (BA); *Career* Durham LI; chm Watermill Theatre Bagnor Newbury 1975-83; memb: Southern Arts Assoc, Exec Ctee Friends of the Bowes Museum; chm: Western Area Planning Newbury DC 1979-82, Devpt Servs Ctee Newbury DC 1983-86; tstee Richmondshire Preservation Tst 1989-; *Recreations* politics, local govt, architecture, gardens; *Style—* The Hon Gerald Vane; 1 Hartforth, Gilling West, Richmond, N Yorks DL10 5JR (☎ 0748 2716)

VANE, Hon Henry Francis Cecil; s and h of 11 Baron Barnard, TD, JP, and Lady Davina, *née* Cecil, da of 6 Marquess of Exeter; *b* 11 March 1959; *Educ* Edinburgh Univ (BSc); *Style—* The Hon Henry Vane

VANE, Sir John Robert; s of Maurice Vane, and Frances Florence, *née* Fisher; *b* 1927; *Educ* King Edward's HS Birmingham, Univ of Birmingham (BSc), St Catherine's Coll Oxford (BSc, DPhil, DSc); *m* 1948, Elizabeth Daphne Page; 2 da; *Career* RCS: sr lectr in pharmacology Inst of Basic Med Scis 1955-61, reader in pharmacology 1961-65, prof of experimental pharmacology 1966-73; gp res and devpt dir The Wellcome Fndn 1973-85; chm The William Harvey Res Inst 1986-; tstee Migraine Tst 1988- (and memb Scientific Advsy Ctee); recipient of numerous int prizes and awards incl: Nobel Prize for Physiology or Med (jt) 1982, Royal Medal of the RS 1989; FRS; kt 1984; *Recreations* underwater swimming and photography; *Clubs* Athenaeum, Garrick; *Style—* Sir John Vane, FRS; St Bartholomew's Hosp Medical Coll, Charterhouse Sq, London EC1M 6BQ (☎ 071 982 6119, fax 071 251 1685)

VANE PERCY, Christopher David; s of Kenneth Vane Percy, of 6 Days Lane Biddenham, Bedfordshire, and Jean Farquharson, of The Mews House, Island Hall, Godmanchester, Cambs; *b* 15 March 1945; *Educ* Bedford Sch; *m* 17 May 1973, The Hon Linda Denise, da of late Robert Egerton Grosvenor 5 Baron Ebury; 1 s (Maximilian Egerton b 1979), 1 da (Grace Dorothy Denise b 1981); *Career* interior designer; *Books* The Glass of Lalique - A Collector's Guide (1977); *Style—* Christopher Vane Percy, Esq; Island Hall, Godmanchester, Cambs PE18 8BA (☎ 0480 459676); CVP Designs Ltd, 27 Burton Place, London W1X 7AB (☎ 071 4937995, fax 071 3554006)

VANE PERCY, Hon Mrs (Linda Denise); *née* Grosvenor; da of late 5 Baron Ebury, DSO, by 2 w, Hon Denise Yarde-Buller (da of 3 Baron Churston); *b* 1948; *m* 1973, Christopher D Vane Percy; 1 s (Maximillian b 1979), 1 da (Grace Dorothy b 1981); *Style—* The Hon Mrs Vane Percy

VANE-TEMPEST-STEWART, Lord Reginald Alexander; 2 s of 9 Marquess of Londonderry, and his 2 w, Doreen, *née* Wells; *b* 1977; *Style—* The Lord Reginald Vane-Tempest-Stewart

VANN JONES, Dr John; s of John Jones (d 1975), and Elizabeth, *née* Kelly; *b* 8 May 1945; *Educ* Hyndland Sch Glasgow, Univ of Glasgow (MB ChB, PhD); *m* 23 Sept 1970, Anne Margaret, da of Andrew Abercrombie, of Glasgow; 2 s (Richard John, Simon Andrew), 2 da (Kerstin Anne, Caroline Patricia); *Career* lectr in cardiology Univ of Glasgow 1972-77 (res fell 1969-72), MRC travelling fell Univ of Gothenburg 1975-76, reader in cardiovascular med Univ of Oxford 1980-81 (lectr 1977-80), conslt cardiologist Bristol 1981-90; memb: Br Cardiac Soc, Br Hypertension Soc, Med Res Soc, Physiological Soc; FRCP 1987; *Books* Scientific Foundations of Cardiology (1983), Outline of Cardiology (1983); *Recreations* golf, table tennis, swimming; *Clubs* Bristol Clifton Golf; *Style—* Dr John Vann Jones; Hawthorne House, Silver Street, Chew Magna, Avon BS18 8RE (☎ 0272 332164), Cardiology Dept, Royal Infirmary, Bristol (☎ 0272 230000)

VANNECK, Hon Joshua Charles; s and h of 6 Baron Huntingfield; *b* 10 Aug 1954; *Educ* Eton, Magdalene Coll Cambridge (MA); *m* 1982, Arabella Mary, da of Maj Alastair Hugh Joseph Fraser, MC, of Moniack Castle, Kirkhill, Inverness; 4 s (Gerard Charles Alastair b 12 March 1985, John Errington b 1988, Richard Fraser b 1990, David Guise b 1990 (twin)), 1 da (Vanessa Clare b 1983); *Career* accountant; *Clubs* Pratt's; *Style—* The Hon Joshua Vanneck; Flat 1, Clanricarde Mansions, Clanricarde Gdns, London W2

VANNER, Michael John; s of Walter Geoffrey Vanner (d 1933), of Winkfield, Berks, and Doris Ellen, *née* Hall (d 1977); *b* 6 Dec 1932; *Educ* Blundell's, Sidney Sussex Coll Cambridge (BA, MA); *m* 1 July 1961, Myra, da of William John Sharpe (d 1982), of Fetcham, Surrey; 2 s (Luke b 1967, Guy b 1970); *Career* res engr Electrical Res Assoc 1955-64, chief devpt engr BICC Construction Co Ltd 1964-75, engrg conslt Balfour Beatty Power Construction Ltd 1981-86 (engrg mangr 1973-81), princ Construction and Material Servs (int consulting) 1986-; chm IEE PG Power Cables and Overhead Lines 1988- (memb 1985-); CEng, MIEE 1984, CPhys, MInstP 1962, MBGS 1961; *Books* The Structure of Soil and A Critical Review of The Mechanisms of Soil Moisture Retention And Migration (1961); *Recreations* walking in the country, sailing; *Style—* Michael Vanner, Esq; 17 Wolsey Way, Loughborough, Leics LE11 1PR (☎ 0509 236 877); Construction And Material Services, 1 Blanford Rd, Reigate, Surrey RH2 7DP (☎ 0737 222 173)

VANSTONE, Hon Mrs (Mary Rose); *née* Brock; da of Baron Brock (Life Peer, d 1980) and Baroness Brock, *qv*; *b* 1933; *m* 1959, Keith Vanstone; children; *Style—* The Hon Mrs Vanstone; Blakes Farm, Ashurst, Steyning, W Sussex

VARAH, Prebendary Dr (Edward) Chad; OBE (1969); s of Canon William Edward Varah (d 1945), of Barton on Humber, and Mary, *née* Atkinson (d 1965); *b* 12 Nov 1911; *Educ* Worksop Coll Notts, Keble Coll Oxford, Lincoln Theological Coll; *m* 1940, Doris Susan, OBE, da of Harry Whanslaw (d 1961), of Putney; 4 s (Michael, Andrew, David, Charles), 1 da (Felicity); *Career* staff scriptwriter Eagle 1950-62; C of E clerk in holy orders; rector Lord Mayor's Parish Church of St Stephen Walbrook 1953-; fndr: The Samaritans 1953, Befrienders Int 1974; pres Ctee Publishing Russian Church Music 1960-80; chm: The Samaritans Inc 1963-66, Befrienders Int 1974-83 (pres 1983-86); patron: Outsiders Club 1984, Terrence Higgins Tst 1987; preb St Paul's 1975-; Albert Schweitzer Gold medal 1972, Louis Dublin award American Assoc Suicidology 1974, Prix de l'Inst de la Vie 1977, Roumanian Patriarchal Cross 1968; Liveryman Worshipful Co of Carmen; Hon LLD Univ of Leicester, hon fell Keble Coll Oxford; *Recreations* reading, writing autobiography, watching TV nature programmes; *Clubs* Oxford Union, Sion Coll (City); *Style—* Preb Dr Chad Varah, OBE; St Stephen Walbrook, London EC4N 8BN (☎ 071 283 4444, 071 626 8242)

VARCOE, Jeremy Richard Lovering Grosvenor; CMG (1989); s of Ronald Arthur Grosvenor Varcoe, TD, of Florida, USA, and Zöe Elizabeth, *née* Lovering (d 1971); *b* 20 Sept 1937; *Educ* Charterhouse, Lincoln Coll Oxford (MA); *m* 30 Dec 1961, Wendy Anne (d 1991), da of Robert F Moss, MBE (d 1973); 2 da (Francesca b 1964, Lucy b 1966); *Career* Nat Serv 2 Lt 4 RTR 1956-58; dist offr HMOCS Swaziland 1962-65, called to the Bar Gray's Inn 1966, asst legal advsr GKN Ltd 1966-67, lectr in law Univ of Birmingham 1967-70; HM Dip Serv 1970-: first sec FCO 1970-71, dep sec gen Pearce Cmmn on Rhodesian Opinion 1971-72, first sec (Info) Ankara 1972-74, head of Chancery Lusaka 1974-78, first sec FCO 1978-79, cnsllr (Commercial) Kuala Lumpur 1979-82, head Southern Africa Dept FCO 1982-84, cnsllr Ankara 1984-85, Standard Chartered Bank Istanbul (unpaid leave from FCO) 1985-86, HM ambass Somalia 1987-89, min and dep high cmmr Lagos 1989-90, asst under-sec coordinator London Economic Summit 1991; *Books* Legal Aid In Criminal Proceedings - A Regional Survey (with Prof G F Borrie, 1970); *Recreations* sailing, golf, public affairs; *Clubs* Royal Cwlth Tst; *Style—* Jeremy Varcoe, Esq, CMG; Flat 2, Neate House, 52 Lupus St, London SW1V 3EE (☎ 071 821 6731); c/o Foreign & Commonwealth Office, King Charles St, London SW1A 2AH (☎ 071 270 3597, fax 071 270 3622)

VARCOE, (Christopher) Stephen; s of Philip William Varcoe, OBE (d 1980), of Lanescot, Par, Cornwall, and Mary Northwood, *née* Mercier; *b* 19 May 1949; *Educ* King's Sch Canterbury, King's Coll Cambridge (BA, MA), Guildhall Sch of Music; *m* 22 April 1972, Melinda, da of William Arthur Davies, of 11 Sackville Road, Cheam, Surrey; 3 s (Josiah b 6 March 1979, Amyas b 16 Nov 1982, Leander 26 March 1986 d 1986), 2 da (Flora b 22 Nov 1975, Oriana b 9 April 1988); *Career* baritone, freelance concert opera singer 1970-; Calouste Gulbenkian Fndn Fellowship 1977; *Recreations* building, painting, gardening; *Style—* Stephen Varcoe, Esq; Ron Gonsalves, 10 Dagnan Rd, London SW12 9LQ (☎ 081 673 6507, fax 081 675 7276, telex 265871 MONREF G REF MUS033)

VARDE, John; s of Shamrao Varde (d 1949), and Helen, *née* Leontzini; *b* 2 Jan 1935; *Educ* Malvern; *m* 1964, Elizabeth Lilian, da of James Hudson Foskett (d 1985); 1 s (Andrew b 1965), 1 da (Nicola b 1967); *Career* mechanical and mfrg engr; md Westland Helicopters Ltd 1987-; FIMechE 1985, FIProdE 1989 (vice pres 1989); *Recreations* music; *Style—* John Varde Esq; 32 Richmond Road, Sherborne, Dorset; Westland Helicopters Ltd, Yeovil, Somerset BA20 2YB (☎ 0935 702500, telex 46277)

VARDY, Peter Christian; s of Mark Vardy; *b* 29 July 1945; *Educ* Charterhouse, Southampton Univ, King's Coll London; *m* 1974, Anne Maree, da of Patrick Moore; 2 s, 3 da; *Career* management consultant; chm H Young Holdings Gp 1979-; dir of various cos; FCA; *Recreations* philosophy of religion, forestry, walking, travel; *Clubs* East India, Sports & Public Schools; *Style—* Peter Vardy Esq; 14 Croft Gdns, Alton, Hants

VARLEY, Hon Mrs (Elizabeth Susan); *née* Douglas-Scott-Montagu; da of 2 Baron Montagu of Beaulieu, KCIE, CSI (d 1929); *b* 1909; *m* 1962, Col Arthur Noel Claude Varley, CBE (d 1985); *Style—* The Hon Mrs Varley; The Mill Race, Beaulieu, Hants

VARLEY, Baron (Life Peer UK 1990), of Chesterfield in the County of Derbyshire; Eric Graham Varley; PC (1974), DL; s of Frank and Eva Varley; *b* 11 Aug 1932; *Educ* Ruskin Coll Oxford; *m* 1955, Marjorie Turner; 1 s; *Career* worked in engineering and mining industry; branch sec NUM 1955-64 (memb Derbys Area Exec Ctee 1956-64); MP (Lab) Chesterfield 1964-84, asst govt whip 1967-68, PPS to Harold Wilson as PM 1968-69, min of state Technology 1969-70; energy sec 1974-75, industry sec 1975-79; chief oppn spokesman Employment 1979-83, treas Lab Pty 1981-83, oppn front bench spokesman Employment 1981-83; chm and chief exec Coalite Gp 1984- (dep exec chm 1983-84); steward and bailiff of the Manor of Northstead 1984-; *Style—* The Rt Hon Lord Varley, PC, DL

VARLEY, Ian Mansergh; s of William Mansergh Varley (d 1956), of Brighton, and Hephzibah, *née* Walker (d 1957); *b* 25 June 1926; *Educ* Brighton Coll, Brighton Tech Coll, Univ of London (BSc); *m* 1 Sept 1951, Jean Margaret, da of Jack Spencer Searle (d 1956), of Brighton; 1 s (Christopher Mansergh b 1960), 1 da (Alison Elizabeth b 1954); *Career* chartered engr; ptnr: Chester & Varley Singapore 1953-60, Steen Sehested & Partners Singapore 1960-65, TF Burns & Partners London & Hove 1965- (conslt 1986-); dist govr Rotary Int Dist 125, memb Cncl Brighton Poly 1985; CEng, FICE 1963, MConsE 1963, FIE (Malaysia); *Recreations* sailing, golf, gardening, rotary; *Clubs* Dyke Golf (Brighton); *Style—* Ian Varley, Esq; Newtimber, The Common, Henfield, W Sussex BN5 9RL (☎ 0273 492 538); TF Burns & Partners, 41 Portland Road, Hove, E Sussex BN3 5DQ (☎ 0273 720 626, fax 0273 735 292)

VARLEY, Dame Joan Fleetwood; DBE (1985, CBE 1974); da of Fleetwood Ireton Varley (d 1941), of London, and Harriet Elizabeth, *née* Heenan; *b* 22 Feb 1920; *Educ* Cheltenham Ladies, LSE (BSc); *Career* WAAF Corpl Fighter Cmd radio operator, section offr Fighter Cmd Meteorological Offr; Cons; dep agent Warwick & Leamington Constituency 1949-52, agent Shrewsbury Constituency 1952-56, CPC offr W Midlands Area Cons Central Office 1956-57, Dep Central Office agent NW Area 1957-64, dep chief orgn offr Cons Central Office 1965-66, dep dir of orgn Cons Central Office 1966-74, chief asst to dir gen and chief woman exec 1974-75, dir of central admin Cons Central Office 1975-76, dir of local govt orgn 1976-84; churchwarden St Clements & St James Norlands Jt Parish, chm Friends of St James Norlands Assoc, memb Brighter Kensington & Chelsea Scheme Ctee; govr Thames Poly 1980 (vice-chm Ct of Govrs 1986-), pt/t memb VAT Appeals Tbnl 1986-; *Recreations* gardening, walking; *Clubs* St Stephens, United and Cecil; *Style—* Dame Joan Varley, DBE; 9 Queensdale Walk, Holland Park, London W11 4QQ (☎ 071 727 1292)

VARLEY, (John) Philip; TD; s of John Varley (d 1952), of Leamington Spa, and Frances, *née* Gould (d 1976); *b* 14 May 1920; *Educ* Downside, Univ of Birmingham (LLB); *m* 12 July 1952, Jacqueline Mary, da of Lt Col George Taylor, DSO, TD, DL (d 1983), of Kirkheaton, nr Huddersfield; 1 s (John Silvester b 1956), 1 da (Mrs Philippa Jane O'Gorman b 1954); *Career* Maj Royal Warwicks Regt, Europe, POW 1940-45; slr; conslt Varley Hibbs and Co; pres Warwicks Law Soc 1984-85; OStJ; *Recreations* shooting; *Clubs* Army and Navy; *Style—* Philip Varley, Esq; Garden House, Barford Hill, Barford, nr Warwick; 16 Hamilton Terrace, Leamington Spa, Warwickshire (☎ 0926 881251)

VARMA, Dr Alakh Niranjan; s of Phulan Prasad Varma (d 1957), of India, and Karepati Varma (d 1989); *b* 27 Feb 1932; *Educ* Patna Univ of India (BSc, MB BS, DPM), Univ of Edinburgh (DPM); *m* 17 Nov 1959, Dr Sashi Bala Varma, da of Anjani Bir Prasad (d 1960), of Lucknow, India; 2 s (Niraj b 1 Oct 1960, Anu Ranjan b 14 June 1964); *Career* asst MO India 1957-60, sr MO Ghana Africa 1961-68, conslt in child and adolescent psychiatry 1973-, psychiatrist BC Canada 1981-82; MRCPsych, FRSH; *Recreations* travelling, photography; *Style*— Dr Alakh Varma; 149 Grantham Road, Sleaford, Lincolnshire NG34 7NR (☎ 0529 303681), Rauceby Hosp, Sleaford, Lincs NG34 7PP (☎ 05298241)

VARNEY, Lady Mary Bethune; *née* Lindesay-Bethune; yr da of 14 Earl of Lindsay (d 1985); *b* 11 Dec 1935; *m* 14 Dec 1956, Capt Owen Buckingham Varney; 2 s, 1 da; *Style*— The Lady Mary Varney; Hill House, Dedham, nr Colchester, Essex CO7 6EA

VARNEY, Michael Arthur; s of Sydney Albert Varney (d 1986), and Vera Margaret, *née* Fisher (d 1962); *b* 19 Nov 1933; *Educ* Ealing County GS; *m* 4 Sept 1965 (m dis 1988), Carol Elizabeth, da of John Little; 1 s (Andrew Michael), 1 da (Joanne Claire); *Career* Nat Serv SAC 1952-54; asst sec Globe Building Society 1965-70, exec accountant London Investment Building Society 1970-76, asst accountant East Surrey Building Society 1976-80, gen mangr and sec Bexhill-on-Sea Building Soc 1980-; memb Ctee Bexhill Horticultural Soc; FCBSI 1971, FCIS 1975; *Recreations* computers, badminton, photography, bridge; *Style*— Michael Varney, Esq; Badgers, 5 Woodland Way, Crowhurst, Battle, East Sussex TN33 9AP (☎ 0424 83 286); 2 Devonshire Square, Bexhill-on-Sea, East Sussex TN40 1AE (☎ 0424 210 542)

VARTAN, John Brian Robertson; s of Dr Ronald Hepworth Vartan; *b* 13 Sept 1937; *Educ* Uppingham, Gonville and Caius Coll Cambridge; *m* 1963, Frances Margaret, *née* Bowser; 2 children; *Career* stockbroker; memb Cncl The Stock Exchange 1976-83, chm Provincial Unit of Stock Exchange 1980-83; memb Central Exec Ctee NSPCC 1972-81; *Recreations* shooting, fishing, golf, tennis; *Clubs* IOD; *Style*— John B R Vartan Esq; Castor Heights, Castor, Peterborough (☎ 073 121 315)

VARTY, Prof (Ernest) Kenneth Charles; s of Ernest Varty (d 1986), and Doris, *née* Hollingworth (d 1962); *b* 18 Aug 1927; *Educ* Bemrose Sch Derby, Univ of Nottingham (BA, PhD), Univ of Keele (DLitt); *m* 26 Sept 1988, Hedwig Hermine Juliane (Hety), da of Ludwig Beninghoff (d 1966); 2 da (Anne, Catherine); *Career* RAF 1946-48; serv in UK, Egypt, Southern Rhodesia; asst lectr then lectr in French Univ of Keele 1953-56, lectr then sr lectr Univ of Leicester 1961-66, dean of Faculty of Arts Univ of Glasgow 1979-82 (Stevenson professor of French 1968-90); visiting lectr Univ of Warwick 1967, visiting res fell Univ of Oxford 1974, visiting prof Univ of Jerusalem 1977, elected life memb Clare Hall Univ of Cambridge 1986 (visiting res fell 1984); jt ed The Bibliographical Bulletin of Int Arthurian Soc 1969-76; chm Bd of Studies for Modern Languages Univ of Glasgow 1974-77, vice pres Br Branch The Int Arthurian Soc 1976- (formerly sec 1969-76), hon pres Int Reynard Soc (pres 1974-87), hon life memb of Hon Soc Phi Kappa Phi 1989; FSA 1969; Chevalier dans l'Ordre des Palmes Académiques 1988; *Books* Reynard The Fox: A Study of the Fox in Medieval English Art (1967), A la Recherche du Roman de Renart (1987); *Recreations* photography, travel; *Style*— Prof Kenneth Varty, FSA; 4 Dundonald Road, Glasgow G12 9LJ (☎ 041 339 1413), French Dept, Univ of Glasgow, Glasgow G12 8QL

VASARY, Tamas; s of Josef Vasary (d 1975), and Elisabeth, *née* Baltazar (d 1977); *b* 11 Aug 1933; *Educ* Franz Liszt Music Acad Budapest; *m* 30 March 1967, Ildiko, da of Lajos Kovács, of Sao Paulo, Brazil; *Career* pianist and conductor, first concert at age of 8, asst prof Budapest Music Acad at 21; prizes at int competitions: Paris 1955, Warsaw 1955, Brussels 1956, Rio de Janeiro 1957; debut in London 1960 (New York 1961); recording incl: Chopin, Liszt, Brahms, Mozart, Rachmaninoff; conducting debut 1969; conducted many major orchestras incl: Berlin Philharmonic, London Symphony, Royal Philharmonic; music dir Northern Sinfonietta 1979-82, princ conductor Bournemouth Sinfonietta 1989-; Awarded Bach and Poaderewski medals 1961; *Recreations* yoga, writing; *Style*— Tamas Vasary, Esq; 9 Village Road, London N3 1TL (☎ 081 346 2381); Harold Holt Ltd, 31 Sinclair Road, London W14 0NS (☎ 071 603 4600)

VASQUEZ, Sir Alfred Joseph; CBE (1974), QC (1986); s of Alfred J Vasquez (d 1971), of Gibraltar, and Maria Josefa, *née* Rugeroni (d 1942); *b* 2 March 1923; *Educ* Mount St Mary's Sch, Millfield, Fitzwilliam Coll Cambridge (MA); *m* 10 April 1950, Carmen, da of Lt-Col Robert Michael Sheppard-Capurro, OBE, JP, of Cloister Ramp, Gibraltar; 3 s (Alfred b 1951, Robert b 1952, Peter b 1953), 1 da (Mrs Maurice Sewe b 1958); *Career* served Gibraltar Def Force 1943-45, Gibraltar Regt 1957-64, Capt; barr Inner Temple 1950, sr ptnr Vasquez Benady and Co, barristers and solicitors; speaker Gibraltar House of Assembly 1970-, Mayor of Gibraltar 1970-76; chm: Gibraltar Regt Assoc, Gibraltar Bursary and Scholarship Bd, Cwlth Parly Assoc Gibraltar Branch; memb: Gibraltar Public Serv Cmmn, Ctee Gibraltar Lawyers Assoc, Ctee Gibraltar Soc for Cancer Relief; kt 1987; *Recreations* golf, shooting, bridge; *Clubs* Sotogrande Golf (Cadiz), Mediterranean Racing (Gibraltar), Calpe Rowing; *Style*— The Hon Sir Alfred Vasquez, CBE, QC; 2 St Bernards Road, Gibraltar (☎ 010 350 73710); 26A St Georges Drive, London SW1 (☎ 01 821 0987); Cloister House, Fountain Ramp, Gibraltar (☎ 010 350 76108)

VASSAR-SMITH, John Rathborne; s and h of Sir Richard Vassar-Smith, 3 Bt, TD; *b* 23 July 1936; *Educ* Eton; *m* 1971, Roberta Elaine, da of Wing Cdr Norman Williamson; 2 s (Richard b 1975, David b 1978); *Career* runs St Ronans Prep Sch; *Style*— John Vassar-Smith, Esq; St Ronans, Hawkhurst, Kent

VASSAR-SMITH, Sir Richard Rathborne; 3 Bt (UK 1917), of Charlton Park, Charlton Kings, TD (1950); s of late Maj Charles Martin Vassar-Smith (2 s of 1 Bt); suc unc, Sir John George Lawley Vassar-Smith (d 1942); *b* 24 Nov 1909; *Educ* Lancing, Pembroke Coll Cambridge; *m* 1932, Dawn Mary, da of Sir Raymond Wybrow Woods, CBE (d 1943); 1 s, 1 da (and 1 child decd); *Heir* s, John Rathborne Vassar-Smith; *Career* Maj RA 1939-45; St Ronans Prep Sch: ptnr 1946-57, ptnr with son John Vassar-Smith, *qv* 1957-, headmaster 1957-; *Recreations* golf; *Clubs* Hawks (Cambridge), Rye Golf; *Style*— Sir Richard Vassar-Smith, Bt, TD; Orchard House, St Ronans, Hawkhurst, Kent (☎ 058 05 2300)

VASSILTCHIKOV, Prince George; s of Prince Illarion Vassiltchikov (d 1969), and Princess Lydia Viazemsky (d 1948); descended from one Indris, who is said to have arrived in Russia in the 14th c; Boyars of the Great Princes of Muscovy since the late 15th c; Anna Vassiltchikova was the 5th wife of Tsar Ivan IV 'the Terrible'; in senior court, state, and military positions in Russia from the 16th c until 1917; *b* 22 Nov 1919; *Educ* secdy educn in France (Lycée Condorcet) & Lithuania (Russian gymnasium), Univ Education in Italy (Rome), Germany (Berlin), France (Paris Ecole Libre des Sciences Politiques et Sociales); *m* 1964, Barbarina, da of Ambass Guy de Keller, of Rougemont, Switzerland; 1 s (Alexander b 1966), 1 da (Nathalia b 1965); *Career* Agence France-Presse (Paris) 1944-45; Int Military Tribunal (Nüremberg) 1945-46, UN Secretariat 1948-60 and 1966-77, in business 1977-; *Books* author (pseud 'Geoffrey Bailey' The Conspirators (1960/61); ed The Berlin Diaries 1940-45, of Marie ('Missie') Vassiltchikov (1985); *Recreations* reading, writing, music, travel; *Clubs* Beefsteak; *Style*— Prince George Vassiltchikov; 73 Durrels House, Warwick Gardens, London W14; 7 Grande Rue, Rolle, Vaud, Switzerland

VASUDEV, Dr Kadaba Srinath; s of Dr Kadaba Vedanta Srinath, and Lalitha Srinath; *b* 5 May 1943; *Educ* Univ of Bangaldore India (MB BS); *m* 28 June 1972, Pratibha, da of Mandyam Dhati Narayan; 2 s (Naveen Srinath, Chetan Srinath), 1 da (Archana Srinath); *Career* conslt histopathologist/cytopathologist Dept of Pathology Victoria Hosp Blackpool 1977-, post grad clinical tutor and undergrad tutor Univ of Manchester 1982-; memb Int Acad of Pathologists; memb: Manchester Med Soc, Assoc of Clinical Pathologists; FRCPath 1988; *Recreations* photography, music appreciation, theatre; *Style*— Dr Kadaba Vasudev; 10 Silverdale Rd, St Annes, Lancs FY8 3RE (☎ 0253 720747), Department of Pathology, Victoria Hospital, Whinney Heys Rd, Blackpool, Lancs FY3 8NR (☎ 0253 300000 ext 3751)

VAUGHAN, Lady Auriel Rosemary Malet; da of 7 Earl of Lisburne (d 1965); *b* 1923; *Style*— The Lady Auriel Vaughan

VAUGHAN, Dr Caroline Lesley; da of Frederick Alan Vaughan (d 1970), and Helen Mary, *née* Brackett (d 1983); *b* 5 Feb 1941; *Educ* Croydon HS, Univ of Manchester (BSc), Chelsea Coll London (PhD); *Career* post doctoral fell: MD Anderson Hosp Houston USA 1965-68, King's Coll London 1968-69; fin analyst and mktg mangr WR Grace Euro Consumer Products Div Paris 1969-74, commerical planner Tube Investmts (Domestic Appliances Div and Head Office) 1974-78, divnl exec Nat Enterprise Bd 1978-80; dir of business devpt Celltech Ltd 1980-84, chief exec Newmarket Venture Capital Plc 1984-; *Recreations* theatre, opera, travel; *Style*— Dr Caroline Vaughan; 14-20 Chiswell St, London EC1Y 4TY (☎ 071 638 2521, fax 071 638 8409)

VAUGHAN, David Bertram; s of Leonard Lionel Vaughan (d 1980), and Elizabeth Vaughan, *née* Gibbins; *b* 21 July 1936; *Educ* Wilson GS; *m* 3 Sept 1960, Pamela Druscilla, da of Charles James Brewood; 2 da (Catherine b 1968, Margaret b 1970); *Career* CA; gen ptnr Peat Marwick McLintock 1980- (ptnr 1972-); chm Young Concert Artists Trust, dep chm The Welton Foundation; govr: Nat Heart and Chest SHA, The Cardiothoracic Inst; FCA; *Recreations* golf, music, reading; *Clubs* Athenaeum, MCC, West Hill Golf; *Style*— David Vaughan, Esq; 1 Puddle Dock, Blackfriars, London EC4V 3PO (☎ 071 236 8000, fax 071 248 6552, telex 8811541 PMM Lon G)

VAUGHAN, Prof David John; s of Samuel John Vaughan (d 1982), of Newport, Gwent, and Esther Ruby, *née* Edwards (d 1984); *b* 10 April 1946; *Educ* Newport HS, UCL (BSc), Imperial Coll London (MSc), University Coll Oxford (D Phil, DSc); *m* 31 Dec Heather Elizabeth, da of Alan Marat Ross (d 1979), of Christchurch, Hants; 1 s (Emlyn James b 1979); *Career* res assoc Dept Earth and Planetary Sci Mass Inst of Technol Cambridge USA 1971-74, reader mineralogy Aston Univ 1979-88 (lectr geological scis 1974-79), visiting prof Virginia Poly Inst and State Univ USA 1980, prof mineralogy Univ of Manchester 1988-; pres Mineralogical Soc (GB & Ireland) 1988-89; FIMM 1984, fell Min Soc of America; *Books* Mineral Chemistry of Metal Sulfides (with J Craig, 1978), Ore Microscopy and Ore Petrography (with J Craig, 1981), Resources of The Earth (with J Craig and B Skinner, 1988); *Recreations* painting, walking; *Style*— Prof David Vaughan; Dept of Geology, Univ of Manchester, Manchester M13 9PL (☎ 061 275 3935)

VAUGHAN, Viscount; David John Francis Malet Vaughan; s and h of 8 Earl of Lisburne; *b* 15 June 1945; *Educ* Ampleforth; *m* 1973, Jennifer Jane (an artist), da of late James Desiré John William Fraser Campbell, of Glengarry, Inverness-shire; 1 s (Hon Digby b 3 Jan 1973 but since b before f's marriage legitimated for all purposes except succession to f's and gf's titles), 1 da (Hon Lucy b 2 Aug 1971); *Heir* bro, Hon Michael Vaughan; *Career* artist; *Style*— Viscount Vaughan

VAUGHAN, Sir (George) Edgar; KBE (1963, CBE 1956, OBE 1937); s of William John Vaughan (d 1919), of Cardiff, and Emma Kate Caudle (d 1966); *b* 24 Feb 1907; *Educ* Cheltenham GS, Jesus Coll Oxford; *m* 1, 1933, (Elsie) Winifred (d 1982), da of late Louis Deubert; 1 s (John), 2 da (Doreen, Pauline); m 2, 12 Nov 1987, Mrs Caroleen Mary Sayers, da of late Frank Selley; *Career* former memb Dip Serv; joined Consular Serv 1930, serving at Hamburg, La Paz, Barcelona, Buenos Aires; chargé d'affaires Monrovia 1945-46, consul Seattle 1946-49; consul-gen: Lourenço Marques 1949-53, Amsterdam 1953-56, Buenos Aires 1956-60 (where also minister); ambass and consul-gen Panama 1960-63, ambass Colombia 1964-66; FRHistS; Dean Arts and Science Saskatchewan Univ 1969-73 (prof history 1967-74, lectr 1966-67); First Class Venezuelan Order of Andrés Bello 1990; *Books* author of articles in learned journals mostly concerning British relations with Latin America, Joseph Lancaster en Caracas 1824-1827 y sus relaciones con el Libertador Simón Bolívar (2 vols, Caracas 1987 and 1989); *Clubs* Travellers', RAC; *Style*— Sir Edgar Vaughan, KBE; 9 The Glade, Sandy Lane, Cheam, Surrey SM2 7NZ

VAUGHAN, Dr Elizabeth; da of William Jones (d 1974), and Mary Ellen Morris (d 1987); *b* 12 March 1937; *Educ* Llanfylin GS, RAM London; *m* 1, June 1968, Raymond Peter Brown, s of Stanley Kitchener Brown (d 1980); 1 s (Mark b 21 Oct 1970), 1 da (Sarah b 5 Aug 1974); *Career* Royal Opera House princ soprano roles: Butterfly, Traviata, Leonora, Gilda, Abigaille, Elettra, Donna Elvira, Teresa, Liu, Musetta, Alice; ENO guest artist: Aida, Butterfly, Fidelio; Scottish Opera, WNO and Opera North: Lady Macbeth, Abigaille, Butterfly, Traviata; performed worldwide incl in: Paris Opera, Metropolitan NY, Florence, Vienna, Japan, S America, Canada, Aust; numerous TV and radio performances; prof: Welsh Coll of Music, Guildhall Sch of Music and Drama; Hon DMus Univ of Wales; FRAM (liceniate and assoc); *Recreations* needlepoint, antiques fairs; *Style*— Dr Elizabeth Vaughan

VAUGHAN, Frankie; OBE (1965); *m* 1951, Stella; 2 s (David, Andrew), 1 da (Susan); *Career* singer, actor; turned professional 1951; record hits incl: Green Door, Garden of Eden (first Br chart-topper 1957), Kisses Sweeter than Wine, The Heart of a Man, Tower of Strength (Br No1 1961), Loop de Loop, Made of Fire, There Must be a Way; theatre concert and cabaret engagements all over the world; venues incl: London Palladium, London's Talk of the Town, Rainbow Grill NY, Dunes Hotel LA; film appearances incl: These Dangerous Years, The Heart of a Man, Wonderful Things, The Lady Is a Square, Let's Make Love (with Marilyn Monroe), The Right Approach and It's All Over Town; portrayed Julian Marsh in 42nd Street (West End); tour of GB with the Syd Lawrence Orchestra 1991; patron Nat Boys' Clubs; Past King Rat of the Grand Order of Water Rats 1968; Freeman City of London 1983, Liveryman Worshipful Co of Carmen 1988; hon fell Liverpool Poly 1988; *Style*— Frankie Vaughan, Esq, OBE; Peter Charlesworth Ltd, 2nd Floor, 68 Old Brompton Road, London SW7 3LQ (☎ 071 581 2478, fax 071 589 2922)

VAUGHAN, Sir Gerard Folliott; MP (C) Reading E 1983-; s of Leonard A Vaughan, DSO, DFC, by his w Joan, *née* Folliott; *b* 11 June 1923; *Educ* privately, Univ of London, Guy's Hospital (MB BS), London (DPM); *m* 1955, Joyce Thurle, *née* Laver; 1 s, 1 da; *Career* med conslt emeritus Guy's Hosp; lectr and author; Party candidate (C) Poplar 1955; alderman GLC 1966-72 (LCC 1955-64); MP (C): Reading 1970-74, Reading S 1974-83; PPS to NI Sec 1974, oppn whip 1974, oppn spokesman on Health 1975-79; min of state: for health DHSS 1979-82, for trade with responsibility for Consumer Affrs 1982-1983; Hon FFAS; Liveryman Worshipful Co of Barbers; FRCP, FRCPsych; kt 1984; *Clubs* Carlton, White's; *Style*— Sir Gerard Vaughan, MP; House of Commons, London SW1

VAUGHAN, Hugh Garraway; s of Lt-Col P H Vaughan, of 1 Asplands, Woburn Sands, Bucks, and Dora Mary, *née* Garraway; *b* 23 June 1943; *Educ* Highgate Sch London; *m* 23 March 1968, Diana, da of Frank William Matthews, of Oaklands,

Woburn Sands, Bucks; 1 s (Nicholas James b 3 Jan 1972), 1 da (Claire Louise b 31 Jan 1974); *Career* dir M & J Engineers Ltd (assoc co Abbey plc) 1969-; NRHP, FBIM; *Recreations* swimming, archaeology, boats; *Style*— Hugh Vaughan, Esq; Meadow Ct, Tyrells End, Eversholt, Beds (☎ 0525 28 513); Cashel House, Cadwell Lane, Hitchin, Herts (☎ 0462 452861)

VAUGHAN, Dame Janet Maria; DBE (1957, OBE 1944); da of William Wyamar Vaughan, MVO (sometime headmaster of Rugby and Wellington), and his 1 w, Margaret, *née* Symonds; *b* 18 Oct 1899; *Educ* North Foreland Lodge, Somerville Coll Oxford, UCH; *m* 1930, David Gourlay (d 1963); 2 da; *Career* formerly asst clinical pathologist UCH and Br Post-Grad Med Sch, MO i/c NW London Blood Supply Depot for MRC; princ Somerville Coll Oxford 1945-67 (hon fell), chm Oxford Regnl Hosp Bd 1950-51; hon fell Watson Coll Oxford; Hon DCL: Oxford, London, Bristol; Hon DSc: Wales, Leeds; Hon FRSM, DM, FRCP, FRS; *Books* numerous books and papers on scientific literature; *Style*— Dame Janet Vaughan, DBE, FRS; 5 Fairlawn Flats, First Turn, Wolvercote, Oxford (☎ 0865 514 069)

VAUGHAN, Hon John Edward Malet; s of 8 Earl of Lisburne, and Shelagh Mary, Countess of Lisburne; *b* 3 Oct 1952; *Educ* Ampleforth, RAC Cirencester; *m* 1, 1977 (m dis 1983), Catherine Euphan, da of J P Waterer, of Norton Canon, Hereford; m 2, 29 Nov 1989, Mrs Sandra C J Cooper, da of B H Thomson, of Kemback House, Cupar, Fife; 1 s (Henry John Augustus b 22 Aug 1990); *Career* land agent, agricultural publishing, journalist; dir: South Wales Cable Communications Ltd 1989-, Hygrade Resources Ltd 1990-, chm Newport Cablevision Co (1990); *Clubs* Boodle's; *Style*— The Hon John Vaughan; 19 Bowerdean St, London SW6 3TN (☎ 071 731 3052)

VAUGHAN, Hon Mrs (Mary Patricia); *née* Monck; raised to rank of Viscount's da 1928; da of Capt the Hon Charles Henry Stanley Monck (ka 1918), and Mary Florence, *née* Portal (d 1919); sis of 6 Viscount Monck, OBE (d 1982); *b* 20 June 1911; *Educ* Belstead Southover; *m* 28 Nov 1935, Brig (Charles) Hilary Pritchard, DSO, JP, DL (d 1976, who assumed by deed poll of 1956 the surname Vaughan in lieu of his patronymic), s of Col Charles Hamerton Pritchard (d 1912), late Indian Political Service; 4 da (Susan (Mrs Muirhead) b 1936, Molly (Mrs Davies) b 1941, Patricia (Mrs Engel) b (twin) 1941, Jane (Mrs Allen) b 1945); *Recreations* gardening; *Style*— The Hon Mrs Vaughan; The Old Rectory, Pen Selwood, Wincanton, Somerset (☎ 0747 840 836)

VAUGHAN, Hon Michael John Wilmot Malet; 2 s of 8 Earl of Lisburne; *b* 1948; *Educ* Ampleforth, New Coll Oxford; *m* 1978, Lucinda Mary Louisa, da of the Hon Sir John Francis Harcourt Baring (himself er s & h of 6 Baron Ashburton); *Career* chm Vaughan Ltd; *Style*— The Hon Michael Vaughan; 44 Pembroke Square, London W8

VAUGHAN, Oliver John; s of Maj Joseph Herbert Vaughan (d 1972), and Mary Lavender, *née* Holroyd Smith (d 1989); *b* 28 July 1946; *Educ* Dominican Schs of Llanarth & Laxton, Univ of Neuchatel Switzerland; *m* 16 June 1984, Diana Frances Elizabeth (Boo), da of Cdr Philip Richard Martineau, RN, of Moses Hill Farm, Marley Heights, Haslemere, Surrey; 2 s (Jamie Joseph b 12 July 1986, Jeremy Philip b 22 Oct 1988), 1 fost da (Joanna Eu b 2 Jan 1970); *Career* co fndr Juliana's 1966, subsequently opened offices London Hong Kong Singapore NY, buiness became plc 1983, sold to Wembley plc 1989; currently dir Wembley plc; *Recreations* sailing, computer programming, skiing, shooting, fishing; *Clubs* Brooks's, Royal Thames; *Style*— Oliver Vaughan, Esq; 20 Phillimore Gardens, London W8 7QE; Glen Wye, Courtfield, Ross on Wye, Herefordshire

VAUGHAN, Paul William; s of Albert George Vaughan (d 1987), and Ada Rose, *née* Stocks; *b* 24 Oct 1925; *Educ* Raynes Park Sch, Wadham Coll Oxford; *m* 1, 11 Aug 1951 (m dis 1988), Barbara, da of Arthur Glyn Prys-Jones, OBE (d 1988); 2 s (Timothy Owain b 1955, Matthew David b 1964), 2 da (Katherine Amanda b 1953, Lucy Elizabeth b 1966); m 2, 12 July 1988, Phillipa Jane, *née* Burston; 2 s (Benedict William b 1985, Thomas Edward b 1988); *Career* asst export mangr Menley & James 1951-56, chief press offr BMA 1960-64 (asst PR offr 1956-60), freelance journalist and broadcaster 1964-, dep ed World Med 1970-73; presenter: Sci and Indust, Sci in Action, Discovery (BBC World Serv), New Worlds (Radio 4), Kaleidoscope (Radio 4 1973-), Record Review (Radio 3 1981-88); contrib incl: Today, Woman's Hour, Home This Afternoon (Radio 4); princ narrator Horizon (BBC 2 1970-90); journalist contrib incl: Spectator, Observer, Sunday Times, Truth, Family Doctor, Medical Tribune (NY), Scope Weekly (NY), Medical News, Medical Tribune (London); chm med Journalists Assoc 1968-72 (life memb); memb: NUJ, Equity; *Books* Doctors Commons, A Short History of the British Medical Association (1959), Family Planning - The FPA book of Birth Control (1969), The Pill on Trial (1969); *Recreations* playing the clarinet; *Clubs* BBC, Royal Over-Seas League; *Style*— Paul Vaughan, Esq, 60 King's Rd, Wimbledon, London SW19 8QW (☎ 081 540 5979)

VAUGHAN, Col Peter David Wyamar; MBE (1971), TD (1964), DL (Tyne and Wear 1990); s of David Wyamar Vaughan, CBE, JP (d 1984), of The Old Rectory, Wherwell, Andover, Hampshire, and Norah Agnes, *née* Burn (d 1963); *b* 27 May 1931; *Educ* Rugby; *m* 1, Sept 1956 (m dis 1976), Elizabeth Dobree, *née* Burn; 1 s (David John Wyamar b Nov 1957), 1 da (Laura Katherine b 1960);m 2, 23 May 1978, (Signe) Monica Karin, da of Thor Janzon, of Helsinki, Finland; 1 s (Henry Arthur Peter b 1981); *Career* Nat Serv: Welsh Bde Trg Centre 1949-50, Eaton Hall OTS 1950, 2 Lt 1 Bn Royal Welch Fusiliers 1950-51; TA: Maj (formerly: 2 Lt, Lt, Capt) 4/5 Bn Royal Northumberland Fusiliers 1951-66, 4/5 16 Bn Royal Northumberland Fusiliers 1967-70 (Co Lt-Col 1970), OC 103 Field Sqdn (1 Newcastle) RE (V) 1971-74, Col Dep Cdr NE Dist 1974-76; Hon Col 72 Engr Regt RE (V) 1986-90; Burn Fireclay Co Ltd: joined 1952, works mangr 1955, dir 1958, md 1978, chm and md 1980-; memb Nat Assoc Boys' Clubs; memb Inst Refractory Engrs; *Recreations* walking, bird-watching, gardening, shooting; *Style*— Col Peter Vaughan, MBE, TD, DL; Heatherlea, Tranwell Woods, Morpeth, Northumberland (☎ 0670 512225); The Burn Fireclay Co Ltd, Stobswood, Morpeth, Northumberland (☎ 0670 790234, fax 0670 790745)

VAUGHAN, Dr Roger; s of Benjamin Frederick Vaughan, of Longframmlington, Northumberland, and Marjorie, *née* Wallace; *b* 14 June 1944; *Educ* Manchester GS, Univ of Newcastle Upon Tyne (BSc, PhD); *m* 1; 3 s (Adam John b 1973, Benjamin Nicholas Gray b 1974, Thomas Peter b 1976), 2 da (Ellen Kate b 1979, Anna Cecila b 1980); m 2, Valerie; 2 step s (James Maxwell Phillpott b 1973, Jonathan Peter Phillpott b 1975); *Career* student apprentice Vickers Group 1962, shipbuilding devpt engr Swan Hunter Shipbuilders Ltd 1970-71, md A & P Appledore Ltd (joined 1971), dir Performance Improvement and Productivity Br Shipbuilders 1981-86, jt chief exec Swan Hunter Ltd, chm and chief exec Swan Hunter Shipbuilders Ltd; memb NE Coast Inst of Engrs and Shipbuilders 1963; Shipbuilding Gold medal 1969; FRINA (memb 1963), FEng 1990; *Recreations* music, theatre, ballet, opera, sailing, walking, reading; *Style*— Dr Roger Vaughan; Swan Hunter Ltd, Wallsend Shipyard, Newcastle Upon Tyne NE28 6EQ (☎ 091 295 0295, fax 091 262 0374)

VAUGHAN DAVIES, Geoffrey; s of Hubert Vaughan Davies (d 1963), of Colwyn Bay, N Wales, and Elsie Fielding, *née* Turner (d 1931); *b* 21 July 1928; *Educ* Bishop Vesey's GS, Carlisle GS, Fitzwilliam House Cambridge (MA); *m* 11 Aug 1956, Esther Lockie Menzies, da of Rev Andrew Henderson Anderson (d 1955); 1 s (Andrew b 1966), 2 da (Angela b 1960, Elizabeth b 1962); *Career* RN 1947-49, HMS Wizard 1948-49; called to the Bar Inner Temple 1953, practice Northern circuit 1953-70, dep asst registrar Criminal Appeal Office 1970-74, asst dir Legal Div Office of Fair Trading 1974-88, legal advsr in Consumer Affrs Div DTI 1988-90; elder St Pauls' Utd Reform Church S Croydon 1970-, chm Unified Appeal Ctee Utd Reformed Church 1972-79; Lib Party candidate Withington div of Manchester 1955, 1959, 1964 and 1966; *Recreations* chess, croquet, walking; *Style*— Geoffrey Vaughan Davies, Esq; Ardmore, 13 Norfolk Ave, Sanderstead, South Croydon, Surrey CR2 8BT (☎ 081 657 1449)

VAUGHN, James Hurd; *Educ* Cranbrook Sch, Cornell Univ; *Career* Ensign Supply Corps US Navy 1944-66; pres Vaughn & Blake Inc (insurance brokers) San Francisco 1954-70; Fred S James & Co Inc NY: joined 1970, dir 1973-81, chm 1975-80; dir: Portals Ltd NA 1981-85, Kleinwort Benson, NA NY 1982-85, BNB Resources plc 1983-90, JF Johnson Bahamas 1986-; chm Hogg Group plc 1987- (dir 1983-); name at Lloyds 1973-; tstee Childrens Aid Soc NY 1985-; *Clubs* The Brook and River (New York), City, Queens', Brooks'; *Style*— James Vaughn, Esq; BNB Resources plc, 30 Farringdon Street, London EC4A 4EA

VAUX, John Cuthbert; s of Col Cuthbert Vaux, MC (d 1960), of Moulton Manor, Richmond, N Yorks, and Brenda Mary, *née* Palmer (d 1955); *b* 21 Sept 1933; *Educ* Sandroyd Sch Salisbury, Eton, RMA Sandhurst; *m* 25 Jan 1964, Sara Penelope, da of Gerald Richard Powlett Wilson, JP (d 1986), of Cliffe Hall, Piercebridge, Co Durham; 2 s (Andrew b 1965, Hugo b 1966), 1 da (Camilla b 1973); *Career* 12 Royal Lancers 1954-60, ADC to the Govr of Cyprus 1959-60, Northumberland Hussars Yeo 1962-67; T Pease wine merchants 1961-80, bursar Aysgarth Sch 1980-; Master of Beagles: Eton 1951-52, Sandhurst 1953-54; jt Master of Bedale Hunt 1961-66 and 1969-72; *Recreations* country sports; *Style*— Capt John Vaux; Moulton Manor, Richmond, N Yorks; Aysgarth School, Bedale, N Yorks (☎ 0677 50240)

VAUX, Maj-Gen Nicholas Francis; CB (1989), DSO (1982); s of Harry Vaux, and Penelope Vaux; *b* 15 April 1936; *Educ* Stonyhurst; *m* 1966, Zoya, da of Gen Sir Peter Hellings, KCB, DSC, MC; 1 s (Piers b 1973), 2 da (Zoya b 1967, Tara b 1969); *Career* cmmnd RM 1954, Suez 1956, Far East 1958-61, frigate W Indies 1962-64, Staff Coll Camberley 1969, MOD (Army) 1975-77, 2IC 42 Commando RM 1977-79, Lt Col special advsr US Marine Corps Educn Centre Quantico Virginia 1979-81, CO 42 Commando RM (Operation Corporate) 1981-83, Col 1983, COS to Maj Gen Trg Reserve and Special Forces 1983-85, RCDS 1985, COS Maj-Gen Commando Forces 1986, Maj Gen RM Commando Forces 1987-90; *Books* March to the South Atlantic (1986); *Recreations* skiing, field sports; *Clubs* Farmers; *Style*— Maj-Gen Nicholas Vaux, CB, DSO; c/o Nat West Bank, 14 Old Town St, Plymouth PL1 1DG

VAUX OF HARROWDEN, 10 Baron (E 1523); John Hugh Philip Gilbey; s of William Gordon Gilbey (d 1965), and Grace Mary Eleanor, Baroness Vaux of Harrowden (d 1958); suc bro, 9 Baron, 1977; *b* 4 Aug 1915; *Educ* Ampleforth, Ch Ch Oxford; *m* 5 July 1939, his 1 cous Maureen Pamela, eld da of late Hugh Gilbey, of Shellwood Bend, Leigh, Reigate, Surrey; 3 s, 1 da; *Heir* s, Hon Anthony William Gilbey; *Career* Maj, Duke of Wellington's Regt, served War of 1939-45; sits as Conservative in House of Lords; *Style*— The Rt Hon the Lord Vaux of Harrowden; Cholmondeley Cottage, 2 Cholmondeley Walk, Richmond, Surrey

VAVASOUR, Sir Geoffrey William; 5 Bt (UK 1828), DSC (1943); s of Capt Sir Leonard Pius Vavasour, 4 Bt (d 1961, himself ggs of Hon Sir Edward Vavasour, 1 Bt, né Stourton and 2 surviving s of 17 Baron Stourton, but who changed his name to Vavasour on inheriting the estates of his mother's 1 cous, Sir Thomas Vavasour, 7 & last Bt of the 1628 cr; the 1 Bt of this previous cr was Knight Marshal of the King's Household and ggs through his mother of the 1 Earl of Rutland, while his w Ursula was one of the Giffards of Chillington); *b* 5 Sept 1914; *Educ* RNC Dartmouth; *m* 1, 1940 (m dis 1947), Joan Millicent Kirkland, da of Arthur John Robb; 2 da; m 2, 1971, (m dis 1980), (Marcia) Christine, da of Marshall Shaw Lodge, of Batley, Yorks; *Heir* kinsman, Eric Michel Joseph Marmaduke Vavasour b 1953; *Career* RN (ret) dir W M Still & Sons; *Clubs* All England Lawn Tennis; *Style*— Sir Geoffrey Vavasour, Bt, DSC; 8 Bede House, Manor Fields, Putney, SW15 (☎ 081 788 0707)

VAZ, (Nigel) Keith Anthony Standish; MP (Lab) Leicester East 1987; s of late Tony Vaz, and Merlyn Verona Rosemary, *née* Pereira; *b* 26 Nov 1956; *Educ* Latymer Upper Sch, Gonville & Caius Coll Cambridge (BA, MA); *Career* slr Richmond upon Thames Cncl 1982, sr slr London Borough of Islington 1982-85, slr Highfields & Belgrave Law Centre Leicester 1985-87; called to the Bar 1990; contested Euro elections: Richmond & Barnes 1983, Surrey West 1984; memb Home Affrs Select Ctee House of Commons 1987-; memb Standing Ctees: Immigration Bill 1987-88, Legal Aid Bill 1988, Children Bill 1989, Football Spectators Bill 1989, NHS and Community Care Bill 1989-90, Cts and Legal Servs 1990-, Armed Forces Bill 1991; chm Lab Party Race Action Gp; chair: Parly Nupe Gp, All Party Parly Footwear and Leather Indust Gp; sec: Legal Servs Campaign, Indo-Br Parly Gp, Lab Educn Gp, Parly Lab Party Wool and Textiles Gp; pres: Leicester and S Leicestershire RSPCA 1988-, Hillcroft Football Club 1988-, Thurnby Lodge Boys Club 1987-; govr: Hamilton Community Coll Leicester 1987-, St Patrick's Sch Leicester 1986-; columnist: Tribune, Catholic Herald; memb Nat Advsy Bd Crime Concern; memb: NUPE, Lab Party; MCFI 1988; *Style*— Keith Vaz, Esq, MP; 144 Uppingham Rd, Leicester (☎ 0533 768834, pager 0459109501); House of Commons, London SW1A 0AA

VEALE, Sir Alan John Ralph; s of Leslie Henry Veale (d 1971); *b* 2 Feb 1920; *Educ* Exeter Sch, Manchester Coll of Technol; *m* 1946, Muriel, da of John William Edwards; 2 children; *Career* CEng; dir and gen mangr AEI Motor & Control Group 1966-68; md: GEC Diesels Ltd 1968-70, GEC Power Engineering Ltd 1970-85; dir GEC 1973-85; chm: Rossmore Warwick Ltd 1986-89, RFS Industries Ltd 1987-, Exeter Enterprise Ltd 1989-; pres Inst of Prodn Engrs 1985-86; kt 1984; *Recreations* sailing, walking; *Style*— Sir Alan Veale; 41 Northumberland Rd, Leamington Spa, Warwickshire CV32 6HF (☎ 0926 424349)

VEARNCOMBE, Roderick Andrew George; s of Maj Colin Alexander Vearncombe, of 3 Coxwell Court, Coxwell St, Cirencester, Glos, and Theresa Mary, *née* Bendixson; *b* 9 April 1959; *Educ* Monkton Combe Sch, UCL (BSc, Dip Arch); *Career* architect and designer; sole ptnr Roderick A G Vearncombe, chm Hogarth Trading Co; Memb RIBA; *Recreations* tennis, hockey, theatre, film, opera; *Style*— Roderick Vearncombe, Esq; 18a Walberswick St, London SW8 (☎ 071 582 8524)

VEASEY, Dr Duncan Andrew; s of Frank Veasey, of 31 Arundel Gdns, Westcliff on Sea, Essex SS0 OBL, and (Joyce) Thelma, *née* Robertshaw; *b* 8 April 1953; *Educ* Westcliff HS, St Barts Hosp (BSc, MB BS, LMSSA); *m* 16 July 1977, Alison, da of Ian Gillespie, of The Wilderness, St Swithins Rd, Sherborne, Dorset; 3 s (Max b 1984, Julius b 1985, Robert b 1987), 2 da (Sarah b 1979, Amy b 1981); *Career* RN 1975-86, ret Surgn Lt Cdr; sr specialist psychiatry HMS Drake Devonport 1984-86, conslt psychiatrist Ticehurst House 1986-87, conslt psychogeriatrician E Dorset 1987-89, med dir Huntercombe Manor (private psychiatric hosp) 1989-91, civilian conslt psychiatrist to the Army 1991-; tstee and dir Poole Dementia Care; Freeman City of London 1978, Liveryman Worshipful Soc of Apothecaries 1980; DPM 1982, MRCPsych 1983, FRSM; memb: BMA, HCSA; *Recreations* music, cartophilly, naval photographs; *Style*— Dr Duncan Veasey; Officers Mess, Tedworth House, Tedworth, Hants SP9 7QF

VEATS, John Arthur; s of Arthur Ernest Veats (f 1987), of Woking, Surrey, and Grace Alice, *née* Brooks; *b* 10 Dec 1929; *Educ* Latymer Sch; *m* 1955, Elizabeth Anne, da of Norman Alexander Stemp; 1 s (James b 26 Aug 1961), 3 da (Elizabeth b 13 Jan 1963, Sophie b 24 Jan 1966, Victoria b 23 Oct 1969); *Career* rowing administrator; oarsman: Lensbury Rowing Club 1950-58 (capt and chm), memb Leander Club, rowed Henley Royal Regatta 1951-58; Amateur Rowing Assoc: hon treas 1965-80, chm 1980-89, exec vice pres 1989-; hon treas World Rowing Championships 1975 (vice chm 1986); memb: Mgmnt Ctee Henley 1987- (steward 1982-), Ctee BOA 1985-90, Exec Ctee CCPR 1989- (vice chm Water Recreation Div 1989-); Shell International Petroleum until 1984; MInstD 1985; Desborough medal 1955, Amateur Rowing Assoc Medal of Honour 1986; *Style*— John Veats, Esq; Thorns Brook, Guildford Rd, Cranleigh, Surrey GU6 8PG (☎ 0483 274939)

VEEDER, Van Vechten (Johnny); QC (1986); s of John Van Vechten Veeder (d 1976), and Helen, *née* Townley; *b* 14 Dec 1948; *Educ* Neuilly Paris, Clifton, Jesus Coll Cambridge (MA); *Books* The ICCA National Report on England (with Sir John Steyn, 1988); *Recreations* sailing, reading, travelling; *Clubs* Aldeburgh Yacht, Orford Sailing, Little Ship; *Style*— Johnny Veeder, Esq, QC; 4 Essex Court, Temple, London EC4Y 9AJ (☎ 071 583 9191, fax 071 583 2422, telex COMCAS G)

VELATE, Anthony Spencer; s of Louis Anthony Velate (d 1942), of Altrincham, Cheshire, and Doris Emily, of London (d 1983); *b* 18 Dec 1925; *Educ* Bradbury Central Sch, Birkbeck Coll London (BSc); *m* 29 March 1952, (Gwendoline) Mary, da of Philip David Scott (d 1967), of E Finchley; 1 s (Simon J A b 27 Feb 1956), 2 da (Sara J b 9 May 1960, Rebecca H b 10 Oct 1961); *Career* leading Aircraft Radar Fitter (A) RAFVR 1944-48 (serv in SEAC India 1945-48); experimental staff IMA Ltd 1942-44, devpt engr electro med Electronic and X Ray Applications Ltd 1948-57, chief technician electro-physiology Nat Hosp London 1957-63, res fell MRC St Mary's Hosp Med Sch 1964-67, system conslt patient monitoring TEM Instruments Ltd 1967-71, sales and mktg mangr TEM Engrg Ltd 1971-81, owner Mktg Technol Consultancy 1982-83, membership and qualification mangr IERE 1983-88, sr trg admin IEE 1988-90, conslt Engrg Trg IEE 1991-; chm UK Liaison Ctee for Sci Allied to Med & Biology 1972-74, fndr memb SDP (vice chm Horsham Area 1982-84); Horsham Soc: exec ctee 1973-79, chm 1975-77; Thakeham PC 1983-88 (chm Emergency Planning Ctee 1984-88); CEng 1964, FIEE 1987, CPhys 1986, MIERE 1964, MInst P 1964, MBES 1960; *Recreations* photography, travel, genealogy; *Style*— Anthony Velate, Esq; Goffsland House, Coolham Rd, West Chiltington, Pulborough, West Sussex RH20 2LT (☎ 0798 813120)

VELISSAROPOULOS, Hon Mrs (Penelope Jane); *née* Allsopp; da of 4 Baron Hindlip (d 1966); *b* 1940; *m* 1965, Theodore D Velissaropoulos; *Style*— The Hon Mrs Velissaropoulos; Taxilis 75, Athens 157 71, Greece

VELJANOVSKI, Dr Cento; s of Gavril Veljanovski, of Yugoslavia, and Margaret, *née* Wagenaar; *b* 19 Feb 1953; *Educ* Monash Univ (BEc, MEc), Univ of oxford (DPhil); *m* 1990, Annabel, da of Col William Fazakerley, of Sherborne, Dorset; *Career* jr res fell Wolfson Coll Oxford 1978-84, visiting prof Univ of Toronto 1980-81, lectr YCL 1984-87, res and ed dir Inst of Econ Affrs 1987-; dir Lexecon Ltd 1990-; Royal Econs Soc, Soc of Business Economists, IOD; *Books* The New Law and Economics (1982), Choice by Cable (1983), Selling the State - Privatisation in Britain (1987), Privatisation and Competition - A Market Prospectus (1989), Freedom in Broadcasting (1989), The Media in Britain Today (1990); *Recreations* rowing, art, television, walking; *Clubs* United Oxford and Cambridge Univ, Chelsea Arts; *Style*— Dr Cento Veljanovski; Institute of Economic Affairs, 2 Lord North St, Westminster, London SW1 (☎ 071 799 3745)

VELLACOTT, David Norman Strain; s of James Millner Vellacott (d 1983), and Alice Irene, *née* Strain; *b* 23 Oct 1930; *Educ* Rugby, St John Coll Cambridge (MA); *m* 17 Sept 1955, Patricia Le Souef, da of Dr Robert Baxendale Coleman (d 1963), of Bromley, Kent; 2 s (Iain b 1960, Nicholas b 1968), 1 da (Jacqueline b 1956); *Career* land agent to Sir Francis and Lady Whitmore Orsett Estate Essex 1954-61, bursar Winchester Coll 1982-(estates bursar 1961-82), chm Ind Schs Bursars Assoc; govr Pilgrims Sch Winchester; FRICS; *Recreations* family, photography, golf; *Style*— David Vellacott, Esq; Hideaway, West Street, Alresford, Hants SO24 9AT (☎ 0962 733824); Winchester Coll, Winchester, Hampshire SO23 9NA (☎ 0962 864242)

VELLACOTT, Elisabeth; da of Humphrey Vellacott (d 1926), and Jessie, *née* Evans (d 1961); *b* 28 Jan 1905; *Educ* Louth Girls GS Lincolnshire, Willesden Sch of Art, RCA (Dip); *Career* textile designer and printer 1929-, designs for theatre and opera prodns by Univ of Cambridge Musical Soc, full time painter 1945-; numerous drawings, main subjects landscape, flowers, figures in relation to Landscape (inside and outside), figurative studies for paintings; fndr and memb Cambridge Soc of Painters and Sculptors 1952-; *awards* Artists Gen Benevolent Soc award 1987-; *Style*— Ms Elisabeth Vellacott; Mrs Madeline Ponsonby, The New Art Centre, 41 Sloane St, London SW1 (☎ 071 235 5844)

VELLACOTT, Keith David; s of Hugh Douglas Sempill Vallacott (d 1987), of Tavistock, and Lorraine Freda Vellacott; *b* 25 Feb 1948; *Educ* Kelly Coll, The London Hosp Med Coll; *m* 17 March 1973, Jinette, da of Godfrey Herbert Gibbs, of Teignmouth; 2 s (Darren Adrian b 1975, d 1986, Guy Neil b 1977), 1 da (Adele Fiona b 1980); *Career* res fell Univ of Nottingham 1977-81, conslt gen surgn Bristol Royal Infirmary 1986- (surgical sr registrar 1981-86); memb: Br Soc of Gastroenterology, Assoc of Surgns of England I; FRCS 1976; *Style*— Keith Vellacott, Esq; Glasllwch House, 4 Glasllwch Crescent, Gwent NP9 3SE (☎ 0633 252303); Royal Gwent Hospital, Cardiff Rd, Gwent NP2 2UB

VENABLES, (Harold) David Spenser; s of Maj Cedric Venables TD, of Oatlands, Warborough, Oxford (d 1976), and Gladys, *née* Hall (d 1973); *b* 14 Oct 1932; *Educ* Denstone Coll; *m* 18 July 1964, Teresa Grace, da of James Cornelius Watts, Hove, Sussex (d 1960); 1 s (Julian b 1967), 1 da (Louise b 1965); *Career* pilot offr RAF 1957-58 central reconnaissance estab; admitted slr 1956; entered official slr office 1960; memb Lord Chllrs Ctee on Age of Majority 1965-67, asst official slr 1977-80; official slr 1980-; *Books* A guide to the Law Affecting Mental Patients (1975), Contributor Halsbury's Laws of England (4 edn), The Racing Fifteen-Hundreds: A History of Voiturette Racing 1931-40 (1984); *Recreations* vintage motor cars, military and motoring history; *Style*— David Venables, Esq; 81 Chancery Lane, London WC2A 1DD (☎ 071 911 7116, fax 071 911 7105)

VENABLES, Robert; QC (1990); s of Walter Edwin Venables, MM, of 30 Boswell Rd, Wath upon Dearne, Rotherham, and Mildred Daisy Robson, *née* Taylor; *b* 1 Oct 1947; *Educ* Wath upon Dearne Co GS, Merton Coll Oxford (MA), LSE (LLM); *Career* lectr: Merton Coll Oxford 1972-75, UCL 1973-75; Univ of Oxford 1975-80: official fell and tutor in jurisprudence St Edmund Hall, CUF lectr; called to the Bar Middle Temple 1973, in practice 1976-; FTII 1983; *Books* Inheritance Tax Planning (1988), Non-Resident Trusts (1990), Preserving the Family Farm (1989), Tax Planning and Fundraising for Charities (1989), Lifetime Giving (1989), Tax Planning Through Trusts (1990), National Insurance Contribution Planning (1990), The Company Car (1990), Holdover Relief (1990), Capital Gains Tax Planning for Non UK Residents (1991); *Recreations* music making; *Clubs* Travellers; *Style*— Robert Venables, Esq, QC; 61 Harrington Gardens, London SW7; Chambers, 24 Old Buildings, Lincoln's Inn, London WC2A 3UJ (☎ 071 242 2744, fax 071 831 8095)

VENABLES, Robert Michael Cochrane; s of Cdr Gilbert Henry Venables, DSO, OBE, RN (d 1986), and Muriel Joan, *née* Haes (d 1990); *b* 8 Feb 1939; *Educ* Portsmouth GS; *m* 13 May 1972, Hazel Lesley, da of Wilfred Keith Gowing (d 1990); 2 s (Gilbert b 1974, John b 1977), 2 da (Caroline b 1973, Sarah b 1987); *Career* admitted slr 1962, in private practice London, Petersfield and Portsmouth 1962-70; Treasy Slrs Dept: legal asst 1970-73, sr legal asst 1973-80, asst treasy slr 1980-89; charity commr 1989-; memb: Int Nuclear Law Assoc 1976- (memb Bd 1981-83), Law Soc, City of Westminster Law Soc; *Recreations* opera, collecting domestic anachronisms; *Style*— Robert Venables, Esq; St Albans House, 57-60 Haymarket, London SW1 (☎ 071 210 4419)

VENABLES-LLEWELYN, Sir John Michael Dillwyn-; 4 Bt (UK 1890) of Penllergaer, Llangyfelach and Ynis-y-gerwn, Cadoxton juxta Neath, of Glamorganshire; s of Brig Sir (Charles) Michael Dillwyn-Venables-Llewelyn, 3 Bt, MVO (d 1976); *b* 12 Aug 1938; *Educ* Eton, Magdalene Coll Cambridge; *m* 1, 1963 (m dis 1972), Nina, da of late J S Hallan; 2 da; m 2, 1975, Nina Gay Richardson Oliver; *Career* farmer; *Style*— Sir John Venables-Llewelyn, Bt; Talwen Uchaf Farm, Garthbrengy, Brecon, Powys LD3 9TE; Llysdinam, Newbridge-on-Wye, Llandrindod Wells, Powys (☎ 059 789 351)

VENESS, George Thomas Lionel; s of Robert Veness (d 1962), and Florence Frances, *née* Randall (d 1984); *b* 23 Aug 1936; *Educ* Cuckoo Sch Hanwell; *m* 4 July 1959 (sep), Kathleen, da of late Alfred Powell; 2 da (Jacqueline Susan b 4 Nov 1960, Sharon Nicole b 28 Sept 1962); *Career* Nat Serv RAF 1954-56; md Wilven Finishing Ltd 1972-; *Recreations* art; *Style*— George Veness, Esq; Wilven Finishing Ltd, O'r Diwedd, Penparc, Trefin, nr Haverfordwest, Dyfed, W Wales SA62 5AG (☎ 0348 837 926)

VENGLOS, Jozef; s of Alojz Venglos (d 1982), of Ruzombreok, Czechoslovakia, and Maria, *née* Backorova; *b* 18 Feb 1936; *Educ* Ruzomberok HS, Ruzomberok Technol Sch, Univ of Comenius Bratislava (PhD); *m* 1960, Eva, da of Jozef Matula; 2 c (Jozef b 19 Nov 1961, Juraj b 18 Feb 1965); *Career* professional football manager; player: Ruzomberok 1953-55, Slovan Bratislava 1955-66, represented Czechoslovakia 33 times (full, B, Olympic team); clubs as mangr: FC Sydney Prague 1967-69, VSS Kosice 1969-71, Slovan Bratislava 1973-76, Sporting Club of Lisbon 1983-84, Kuala Lumpur state team 1985-87, Aston Villa 1990-; nat teams as mangr and coach: Aust 1967-69, Czechoslovakia under 23 1970-72, Czechoslovakia 1978-82 and 1988-90 (coach 1973-78), Malaysia 1986-87; coach Europe eleven v Rest of the World (NY) and Italy (Rome) 1981-82; honours as player Slovan Bratislava: Championship 1955, Cup 1961; honours as mangr incl: FC Sydney Prugue Cup and League winners, Slovan Bratislava twice League winners and twice cup winners, Czechoslovakia Euro Championship winners 1976 and third place 1980; FIFA: tech advsr 1976-, presenter numerous lectures and study groups worldwide; Olympic solidarity courses: Uruguay 1982, Costa Rica 1982, Singapore 1983, UAE 1990; assoc prof Faculty of Physical Educn Univ of Comenius Czechoslovakia 1987; former nordic skiing jr champion Czechoslovakia; *Recreations* literature, dramatic plays; *Style*— Dr Jozef Venglos; Aston Villa FC, Villa Park, Birmingham B6 6HE (☎ 021 327 6604, fax 021 322 2107)

VENKAT-RAMAN, Dr Gopalakrishnan; s of Ramachandran Gopalakrishnan, of Madras, and Sakuntala, *née* Sankaran; *b* 11 Sept 1951; *Educ* Poona India (MB BS), Delhi India (MD); *m* 22 April 1979, Kumkum, da of Harbans Lal Vaid (d 1979), of Delhi; 2 da (Lavanya b 1986, Shalini b 1990); *Career* sr res in med Safdarjang Hosp New Delhi 1977-79 (jr res 1974-77), sr house offr in med Sunderland Hosps 1979-80, med registrar Sunderland Royal Infirmary 1980-81, lectr in med St Mary's Hosp Portsmouth 1982-85 (renal registrar 1981-82), conslt and sr lectr in nephrology Wessex Regnl Renal Unit St Mary's Hosp 1985-; memb: Renal Assoc, Med Res Soc, Br Hypertension Soc, Int Soc of Nephrology, Euro Dialysis and Transplant Assoc; numerous scientific pubns in jls; MNAMS (India) 1978, MRCP 1980; *Books* A Handbook on Parenteral Nutrition; *Recreations* travelling, photography, swimming, contract bridge; *Style*— Dr Gopalakrishnan Venkat-Raman; 80 Hill Road, Portchester, Fareham, Hants PO16 8JY; Renal Unit, St Mary's Hospital, Milton Rd, Portsmouth, Hants PO3 6AD

VENNING, Martin John Wentworth; s of Maj Peter Wentworth Venning, of Surrey, and Vera Venning, *née* Heley (d 1956); *b* 30 June 1942; *Educ* Cranleigh Sch Surrey; *m* 1, 5 May 1973, Barbara Lesley; 2 da (Zoe b 1974, Nicola b 1976); m 2, 4 Dec 1982, Marian Kay, da of Ronald Rupert Arthur, of Surrey; *Career* CA; managing ptnr Sheffield Office Finnie & Co; hon treas: High Peak Cons Assoc 1986-90, Sheffield & Dist Soc of CAs 1984-87, W Yorks Soc of CAs 1981-83; hon sec Sheffield & Dist Soc of CAs 1989-, business govr Dore Infant Sch 1990-, chm Hope Valley Tourist Assoc; Insolvency Practitioners Licence; *Recreations* hockey (Yorkshire Co 1972-73), squash, tennis; *Clubs* Purley Hockey, Farsley Hockey, Bamford Tennis; *Style*— Martin J W Venning, Esq; The Old Vicarage, Church Bank, Hathersage, Sheffield S30 1AB (☎ 04 33 51099); Nimrod House, 42 Kingfield Road, Sheffield S11 9AT (☎ 0742 556591)

VENNING, Philip Duncombe Riley; s of Roger Riley Venning, MBE (d 1953), and Rosemary Stella Cenzi, *née* Mann; *b* 24 March 1947; *Educ* Sherborne, Principia Coll Illinois USA, Trinity Hall Cambridge (MA); *m* 4 April 1987, Elizabeth Frances Ann, da of Michael Anthony Robelou Powers, of Grove Terr Mews Highgate London; *Career* journalist Times Educnl Supplement 1970-81 (asst ed 1978), freelance writer 1981-84; sec: Soc for the Protection of Ancient Buildings 1984-, William Morris Craft Fellowship Ctee 1986-; memb: Cncl for Occupational Standards and Qualifications in Environmental Conservation 1988-, Conf on Trg in Architectural Conservation; FSA 1989, FRSA 1990; *Recreations* archaeology, book collecting; *Style*— Philip Venning, Esq, FSA; 17 Highgate High St, London N6 5JT (☎ 081 341 0925); 37 Spital Sq, London E1 6DY (☎ 071 377 1644)

VENNING, Virginia Margaret; da of John Venning, MC (d 1964), of Kendals Hall, nr Radlett, Herts, and Marjorie Beatrice, *née* Close-Brooks; *b* 25 Jan 1913; *Educ* private, Regent St Poly (Sculpture Sch), RA Schs; *m* 11 July 1939, Capt E D T Churcher, CBE, RN (d 1969); *Career* 2 Offr WRNS; sculptor and painter; exhibited: RA, RWA, annually at own studio and locally; cmmnd work (incl sculpture portraits) on and in churches other buildings and gardens in London, Somerset, Dorset, and N Africa; memb SWA; *Recreations* travelling, bridge; *Clubs* (assoc) Army and Navy; *Style*— Miss Virginia Venning; 22 Bimport, Shaftesbury, Dorset SP7 8AZ

VENTHAM, Michael John; s of Percy Ventham, of Rettendon Common, nr Chelmsford, Essex, and Grace Winifred, *née* Rogers; *b* 13 June 1951; *Educ* Wimbledon County Sch for Boys; *m* 14 Sept 1974, Janis, da of Cleaveland Philip Johnson, of Hockley, Essex; 2 s (Mark b 18 June 1975, Graham b 6 June 1977), 1 da (Victoria b 28 Feb 1984); *Career* CA; sr ptnr M J Ventham 1974-; dir: Focusmeer Ltd 1975-, Cotti's House Ltd 1975-, M J Ventham & Co Ltd 1986, Ventham Employment Ltd 1986-, M J Ventham & Co (Computer Services) Ltd 1986-, M J Ventham & Co (Tstees) 1986-, Balance control plc 1987-, Somerly Publications 1987-, M J Ventham & Co (Management Consits) Ltd 1986-; govr Greensward Sch Hockley Essex; FCA 1978 (ACA 1973), FBIM 1986, FIOD 1987; *Recreations* watching and playing football, cricket, reading, travel; *Style*— Michael J Ventham, Esq; Warren House, 10-20 Main Rd, Hockley, Essex SS5 4RY (☎ 0702 206333, fax 0702 207488, car ☎ 0836 252760, telex 946240)

VENTON, Peter Charles; OBE (1989); s of Terence Basil Venton, and Joan Jessica, *née* Smith; *b* 22 Dec 1942; *Educ* Hardye's Sch Dorchester, Univ of London (BSc); *m* 23 Sept 1967, Susan Marilyn, da of Harry James (d 1988); 1 s (Darren James b 20 April 1972), 1 da (Michelle Louise b 20 May 1970); *Career* sr scientist UKAEA Harwell 1962-66; Plessey: devpt engr 1966-70, engr 1970-75, project mangr 1970-75; project dir and gen mangr Plessey defence systems 1982-85 (tech dir 1979-82), md Plessey Radar (now Siemens Plessey Radar) 1985-, dir Siemens Plessey Electronic Systems; memb Cncl Soc of Br Aerospace Cos; MIEE; *Recreations* sailing, golf, squash; *Clubs* Royal Ocean Racing; *Style—* Peter Venton, Esq, OBE; Oakcroft Rd, Chessington, Surrey KT9 1QZ (☎ 081 397 6135, fax 071 381 6196, telex 929755)

VENTRY, 8 Baron (I 1800) Sir Andrew Wesley Daubeny de Moleyns; 8 Bt (1797); assumed by deed poll 1966 the surname of Daubeny de Moleyns; s (by 2nd w) of Hon Francis Alexander Innys Eveleigh-Ross-de-Moleyns (d 1964), s of 6 Baron Ventry, and his 2 w Joan (now Mrs Nigel Springett), eldest da of Harold Wesley, of Surrey; suc uncle, 7 Baron, 1987; *b* 28 May 1943; *Educ* Aldenham; *m* 1, 20 Feb 1963 (m dis 1979), Nelly Edouard Renée, da of Abel Chaumillon, of Loma de los Riseos, Villa Angel, Torremolinos, Malaga, Spain; 1 s, 2 da (Hon Elizabeth-Ann b 1964, Hon Brigitte b 1967); m 2, 1983, Jill Rosemary, da of Cecil Walter Oram; 1 da (Hon Lisa b 1985); *Heir* s, Hon Francis Wesley Daubeny de Moleyns b 1 May 1965, ed Gordonstoun; *Style—* The Rt Hon the Lord Ventry; Hill of Errol House, Errol, Perthshire

VENUGOPAL, Dr Sriramashetty; s of Satyanarayan Sriramashetty (d 1962), and Manikyamma, *née* Akkenapalli; *b* 14 May 1933; *Educ* Osmania Med Coll Hyderabad India (BSc, MB BS), Madras Univ (DMRD); *m* 22 May 1960, Subhadra (Meena), da of Raja Bahadur Sita Ramachander Rao (d 1949); 1 s (Arun b 1964), 1 da (Anu b 1962); *Career* med posts Osmania Hosp, state med servs Hyderabad Singareni Collieries 1959-65, registrar in radiology Selly Oak Hosp Birmingham 1965-66, registrar in radiology Selly Oak Hosp Birmingham 1965-66, registrar in chest med Springfield Hosp Grimsby 1966-67, princ in general practice Aston Birmingham 1967-, hosp practitioner in psychiatry All Saints Hosp Birmingham 1972-, contrib jls on medico-political subjects; fndr memb and chm Link House Cncl 1975-, memb Local Review Ctee for Winston Prison 1981-83, fndr memb Osmania Grad Med Assoc in UK 1984-; memb: W Birmingham Health Authy 1984, Working Gp DHSS 1984- (Local Med Ctee 1975, Dist Med Ctee 1978-), GMC 1984-, Birmingham Community Liaison Advsy Ctee 1985; vice chm: Hyderabad Charitable Tst 1985, Birmingham div BMA 1986-87 (chm 1985-86); nat chm Overseas Drs Assoc 1987- (fndr memb 1975-81, dep treas 1975-81, nat vice chm 1981-87, info and advsy serv 1981), memb and former pres Aston branch Rotary Club; FRSM 1986, FRIPHH 1988, FFCH 1989, MRCGP 1990; *Recreations* medical politics, music, gardening; *Clubs* Aston Rotary; *Style—* Dr Sriramashetty Venugopal; 24 Melville Road, Edgbaston, Birmingham B16 9JT (☎ 021 454 1725); Aston Health Centre, 175 Trinity Rd, Aston, Birmingham B6 6JA (☎ 021 328 3597, car 0831 381 548)

VENUS, Rev John Charles; s of Ernest De Lacey Venus, of St Annes, Binstead, Isle of Wight (d 1971), and Mary Jessie Venus (d 1938); *b* 27 July 1929; *Educ* Newport County GS, Kings Coll London (AKC); *Career* curate Havant Hants 1954-59, chaplain/housemaster St George's GS Cape Town 1960-65; chaplain: RN 1966-70 and 1979-83, Glenalmond Coll 1970-78; rector of Abinger with Coldharbour 1983-; *Recreations* walking, theatre, painting; *Style—* The Rev John Venus; The Rectory, Abinger Common, Dorking, Surrey RH5 6HZ (☎ 0306 730746)

VERCO, Sir Walter John George; KCVO (1981, CVO 1970, MVO 1952); s of John Walter Verco; *b* 18 Jan 1907; *m* 1929, Ada Rose (d 1989), da of Bertram Leonard Bennett, of Lymington, Hants; 1 s, 1 da; *Career* served WWII RAFVR; sec to Garter King of Arms 1949-60, sec Order of Garter 1974-88, sec to Earl Marshal 1961-; Rouge Croix Pursuivant 1954-60, Chester Herald 1960-71, Norroy and Ulster King of Arms 1971-80, Surrey Herald of Arms Extraordinary 1980-; hon genealogist: Order of the British Empire 1959-, Royal Victorian Order 1968-88; inspr: RAF Badges 1970-, RAAF Badges 1971-; advsr on Naval Heraldry 1970-; tstee Coll of Arms Tst; OStJ; *Recreations* travel; *Style—* Sir Walter Verco, KCVO, Surrey Herald of Arms Extraordinary; College of Arms, Queen Victoria St, London EC4 (☎ 071 248 6185); 8 Park Court, Linkfield Lane, Redhill, Surrey RH1 1JG (☎ 0737 71794)

VERCOE, David James; s of Henry Frank Vercoe, of Kegworth, nr Derby, and Lillian Joy, *née* Surrage, of Kegworth; *b* 15 Sept 1949; *Educ* Loughborough GS, Univ of Manchester (BA); *m* 26 April 1976 (m dis), Elizabeth Anne, *née* Latta; *Career* Radio Two Music Dept: ed progs 1988-90, managing ed 1990-91, head of dept 1991-; *Recreations* sailing, skiing; *Style—* David Vercoe, Esq; BBC Radio Two, Broadcasting House, London W1 (☎ 071 927 4539, telex 265781 BBC HQG, fax 071 436 5247)

VERDEN-ANDERSON, (Eric) David Herdman; s of Eric William Verden-Anderson, NP (d 1982), and Dorothy Paton Herdman Verden-Anderson, OBE, JP; *b* 3 Jan 1936; *Educ* Cargilfield Sch Edinburgh, Rugby; *m* 19 Sept 1962, Valery Elizabeth Kennedy, da of David Jamieson, of Newtyle, Coupar Angus; 2 s (Gavin b 17 Dec 1964, Jamie b 4 Dec 1970), 1 da (Sally b 27 May 1966); *Career* Nat Serv RAF 1954-56; chm and md Smith Anderson & Co Ltd Fettykil Mills Leslie Fife 1989- (joined 1956), chm Eagle Envelopes Ltd Bathgate, fndr memb Br Retail Bag Manufacturers Assoc (twice chm); *Recreations* golf, skiing, squash, curling, photography, ecology; *Clubs* R & A (St Andrews), Blairgowrie Golf, Scot Ski, SCGB, DHO; *Style—* David Verden-Anderson, Esq; Smith, Anderson & Co Ltd, Fettykil Mills, Leslie, Glenrothes, Fife KY6 3AQ (☎ 0592 741521, fax 0592743888, telex 72243)

VERDIN, Anthony; s of Jack Arthur Verdin, and Doris Hilda; *b* 16 Nov 1932; *Educ* Christ's Hosp, Merton Coll Oxford (MA, MSc); *m* 1, 1958, Greta; 1 s (John b 1965), 2 da (Julia b 1962, Annemarie b 1963); m 2, 1986, Araminta, da of Michael Henry Carlile Morris; 1 s (Arthur b 1987), 1 da (Aurelia b 1986); *Career* managing ptnr Cherwell Boathouse 1968-; dir: Chelart Ltd 1978-, Chelsea Arts Club Ltd 1987-, Morris & Verdin Ltd 1981-; md Analysis Automation Ltd 1971-90; chm: first Sch on Process Analytical Instrumentation Warwick Univ 1972, cncl of Gas Detection Equipment Manufacturers 1987-90; toured USA and W Indies with Golden Oldies and Miami Rugby Club 1977; Freeman City of London 1989; CEng; *Publications* books incl: Gas Analysis Instrumentation (1973), and numerous articles and lectures on instrumentation techniques and air pollution; *Recreations* family, rugby football, tennis (lawn and real), cricket, music, reading, wine tasting; *Clubs* Chelsea Arts, Henley RFC; *Style—* Anthony Verdin, Esq; Dry Leys, Frilford, Abingdon, Oxon OX13 5HB (☎ 0865 391800)

VERDIN, Peter Anthony; s of Norman Verdin of Northwich, Cheshire (d 1985), and Mary Winifred, *née* McCormack; *b* 4 March 1934; *Educ* Ushaw Coll Durham, Univ of Durham (LLB); *m* 16 Jan 1965, Patricia Marie, da of Joseph Patrick Burke, of Paington, Devon; 2 s (Christopher b 1966, Michael b 1971), 2 da (Catherine b 1968, Caroline b 1972); *Career* admitted slr 1957; ptnr Healds (Wigan); pres Wigan Law Soc 1988-89, chm: Remuneration Ctee 1980-84, Contingency Planning Working Party 1984-87, industl tribunals (pt/t); memb Law Soc (memb Cncl 1974-); *Recreations* golf, opera; *Clubs* RAC, Lymm Golf; *Style—* Peter A Verdin, Esq; 15 Mill Bank, Lymm, Cheshire, WA13 9DG (☎ 092 575 3433); Moot Hall Chambers, 8 Wallgate, Wigan, WN1 1JE (☎ 0942 41511, fax 0942 826 639)

VERDIN, Maj Philip George; MC (1943), DL (1979); s of Lt-Col R N H Verdin, DL, of Garnstone Castle, Weobley, Hereford, (d 1956) and Alison Macfie, *née* Barbour; *b* 27 May 1917; *Educ* Harrow, RMC Sandhurst; *m* 4 Jul 1961, Juliet, da of John Fitzadam Ormiston of Misesden, Glos; 2 s (Richard b 1962, Michael b 1965); *Career* cmmnd 4/7 Royal Dragon Guards 1937, wounded at Dunkirk, instr RMC 1941-42, wounded in accident 1942, returned to regt 1943, took part in D Day (despatches 1945), invalided from army 1950; farmer and landowner; High Sheriff of Herefordshire 1966, chm Hereford Race Course, tax cmmr, pres Royal Br Legion; *Recreations* shooting, fishing; *Clubs* Cavalry, Guards; *Style—* Maj Philip G Verdin, MC, DL; The Buttas, Canon Pyon, Herefordshire (☎ 0432 71231)

VERDON-SMITH, Sir (William) Reginald; DL (Avon 1974); s of Sir William George Verdon-Smith, CBE (d 1957), and Florence Diana, *née* Anders (d 1928); *b* 5 Nov 1912; *Educ* Repton, BNC Oxford (MA, BCL); *m* 1946, Jane Margaret, da of Victor William Hobbs (ka 1918); 1 s, 1 da, 2 step da; *Career* barr; dir Br Aeroplane Co Ltd 1942-66, pres SBAC 1946-48; dir: Br Aircraft Corpn 1960-72 (chm 1955-66), Bristol Siddeley Ltd 1960-66; dep chm Rolls Royce Ltd 1966-68, chm Br Aircraft Hldgs 1969-72, dir Babcock & Wilcox Ltd 1950-70 (dep chm 1960-70), dep chm Lloyds Bank Ltd 1952-83; chm: Lloyds Bank Int Ltd 1973-79, Lloyds Bristol Regnl Bd 1977-83; ptnr George White Evans Tribe & Co Stockbrokers 1952-80; Master: Worshipful Co of Coachmakers 1960-61, Soc of Merchant Venturers of Bristol 1968-69; pro chllr Univ of Bristol 1970-86 (chm of Cncl 1949-56), vice lord-lt for Avon 1980-88; Hon Fell Brasenose Coll Oxford, Hon LLD, and Hon Fell Bristol, Hon DSc Cranfield; kt 1953; *Recreations* sailing, golf; *Clubs* Royal Yacht Squadron, Royal Cruising, Royal Lymington Yacht, Oxford and Cambridge; *Style—* Sir Reginald Verdon-Smith, DL; 3 Spring Leigh, Church Road, Leigh Woods, Bristol BS8 3PG

VERE HODGE, Rev Prebendary Francis; MC (1943); s of Rev Roger Cuthbert Vere Hodge (d 1975), of Somerset, and Juliette Bornèque, *née* Peter (d 1975); *b* 31 Oct 1919; *Educ* Sherborne, Worcester Coll Oxford (MA); *m* 10 Oct 1942, Eleanor Mary, da of Arthur Bentley Connor (d 1960), of Somerset; 2 s (Anthony b 1943, David b 1945), 1 da (Felicity b 1949); *Career* joined Oxford Univ OTC (RA) 1938, 458 Ind Lt Bty RA, 1 Airborne Div 1941-43, No 1 COBU 1943-45, T/Capt 1943, Sicily (attached 2 Para Bn), Italy (attached 1 Para Bde), France (attached 7 Para Bn); Cuddesdon Theol Coll 1946-48; ordained: deacon 1948, priest 1949; curate of Battle 1948-54, rector of Iping and Linch 1954-58; vicar: Kingswood 1958-65, Moorlinch 1965-79; rector: Greinton 1968-79, Lydeard St Lawrence 1979-84; prebendary St Decuman's Wells Cathedral 1979-, chm Glastonbury Abbey Tstees 1986-; *Books* A Handbook for the Newly Ordained and Other Clergy (1986), Glastonbury Gleanings (1991); *Recreations* birdwatching; *Style—* The Rev Prebendary Francis Vere Hodge, MC; Rose Cottage, Ham St, Baltonsborough, Glastonbury, Somerset BA6 8PN (☎ 0458 50032)

VERE-LAURIE, Lt-Col George Edward; o s of Lt-Col George Halliburton Foster Peel Vere-Laurie, JP, DL (d 1981), of Carlton Hall, Notts, and (Caroline) Judith, *née* Francklin (d 1987); Carlton Hall was purchased in 1832 by John Vere (d 1881), descended in an illegitimate line from the de Vere Earls of Oxford, and passed on his death to his niece Clementina Isabella Margaret, Mrs Craig, whose eldest da (by her 1 m to Hon Sydney William Foster-Skeffington (3 s of 10 Viscount Massereene and 3 Viscount Ferrard) Florence Clementina Vere m 1, Lt- Col George Brenton Laurie (ka 1915) and assumed the additional surname of Vere for herself and issue (*see* Burke's Landed Gentry, 18 edn, Vol III, 1972); *b* 3 Sept 1935; *Educ* Eton, RMA Sandhurst, London Univ (BSc); *Career* cmmd 9 Lancers 1955, cmd 9/12 Royal Lancers (PWO) 1974-77; md Trackpower Transmissions Ltd 1979-; Lord of the Manors of Carlton-on-Trent and Willoughby-in-Norwell Notts; Freeman City of London, Master Worshipful Co of Saddlers 1989-90; FBIM 1981; *Recreations* horses, fox hunting, country life; *Style—* Lt-Col George Vere-Laurie; Carlton Hall, Carlton-on-Trent, Newark, Notts (☎ 0636 821421)

VERE NICOLL, Charles Fiennes; s of Maj Raymond Guy Vere Nicoll, MC (d 1981), of Mont Plaisant House, Catel, Guernsey, CI, and Shirley Eugenie Mary, *née* Allen; *b* 2 April 1955; *Educ* Eton; *m* 17 Jan 1985 (m dis 1983), Amanda Mary Howell Crichton-Stuart, da of Michael Pollock Howell Williams, of Orchards, Fordingbridge, Hants; 1 step s (Frederick James b 1981), 1 step da (Katherine Rose b 1979); *Career* admitted slr 1979; co dir Tellydisc Ltd 1980-83; chief exec offr: Telegroup Holdings 1981-83, Ventech Ltd 1983-, Ventech Healthcare Corpn Inc 1986-; *Recreations* shooting; *Clubs* Turf; *Style—* Charles Vere Nicoll, Esq; Drift House, Ashampstead, Berkshire; 11 Old Queen St, London SW1

VEREKER, Hon Foley Robert Standish Prendergast; s and h of 8 Viscount Gort; *b* 24 Oct 1951; *Educ* Harrow; *m* 1979 (m dis 1987), Julie Denise, only da of D W Jones; *Career* Photographer; *Style—* The Hon Foley Vereker

VEREKER, John Michael Medlicott; s of Cdr Charles William Medlicott Vereker, and Marjorie Hughes, *née* Whatley (d 1984); *b* 9 Aug 1944; *Educ* Marlborough, Univ of Keele (BA); *m* 7 Nov 1971, Judith, da of Hobart Rowen, of Washington, DC; 1 s (Andrew b 1975), 1 da (Jennifer b 1973); *Career* asst princ: ODM 1967-69, World Bank Washington 1970-72; princ ODM 1972, private sec to successive Mins at ODM; asst sec 1978, PMs Off 1980-83; under sec 1983- and princ fin offr FCO ODA 1986-88, dep sec (teachers) DES 1988, dep sec (further and higher educn sci) DES 1988-; *Style—* John Vereker, Esq; c/o Dept of Education and Science, Elizabeth House, York Rd, London SE7 7PH (☎ 071 934 9000)

VEREKER, (Charles) John Prendergast; JP (1966); s of Capt M C P Vereker, MC (d 1963), of Byfield, Northants, and Winifred Joan, *née* Twisleton-Wykeham; *b* 28 Dec 1935; *Educ* Kelly Coll Tavistock, Lanchester Coll Coventry; *m* 19 Dec 1975, Jennifer Lesley, da of Frank Ellaby, of Cuddington, Cheshire; 2 s (Richard b 1978, Charles b 1982), 1 da (Elizabeth b 1976); *Career* Lt RA (TA) 1954-62, RA 1958-60, ret 2 Lt; former personnel mangr engrg indust, specialist mgmnt conslt 1981-; former memb Industl Tbnls Panel, memb Warwicks CC 1961- (chm 1982-84), Cons Parly candidate Cannock constituency 1964 and 1979, ldr Controlling Cons Gp 1984-, chm Manpower Sub-Ctee ACC 1989; MIPM, MBIM; *Recreations* rose growing; *Style—* John Vereker, Esq, JP, Lynn Hse, Birdingbury, Rugby, Warwicks CV23 8EN (☎ 0926 632930)

VEREKER, Hon Nicholas Leopold Prendergast; s of 8 Viscount Gort; *b* 1954; *Educ* Harrow; *m* 1985, Nicola F, yst da of Michael W Pitt, of Lias Cottage, Compton Dundon, Somerton, Som; *Style—* The Hon Nicholas Vereker

VEREKER, Peter William Medlicott; s of Cdr C W M Vereker, of Wylye, Wilts, and Marjorie Hughes, *née* Whatley (d 1984); *b* 13 Oct 1939; *Educ* Marlborough, Trinity Coll Cambridge (MA), Harvard Univ (Henry fellow); *m* 7 April 1967, Susan Elisabeth, da of Maj-Gen A J Dyball, CBE, MC, TD (d 1985); 3 s (Connel b 1971, Toby b 1973, Rory b 1981); *Career* Dip Serv: head of Chancery Athens 1975-78, RCDS 1982, cnsllr and consul-gen HM Embassy Bangkok 1983-86 (chargé d'affaires 1984 and 1986), dep perm rep UK Mission Geneva 1987-; *Recreations* tennis, sailing, skiing, poetry; *Clubs* Royal Bangkok Sports, New Sporting (Geneva); *Style—* Peter W M Vereker, Esq; c/o FCO, King Charles St, London SW1A 2AH; UK Mission at Geneva (☎ 34 38 00)

VEREKER, Rupert David Peregrine Medlicott; s of John Stanley Herbert Medlicott Vereker, and Valerie Ann Virginia, *née* Threlfall; *b* 31 July 1957; *Educ* Radley, Univ of Bradford (BA); *m* 9 Aug 1986, Philippa Janet, da of Geoffrey Stocks; 1 s (Frederick

James Herbert Medlicott b 30 June 1990); *Career* Benton & Bowles (now DMB & B) 1980-85 (graduate trainee, account mangr), Doyle Dane Bernbach 1985-87 (account mangr, dir), md Barnes Vereker Allen 1987-; *Style*— Rupert Vereker, Esq; Barnes Vereker Allen, 3 Lloyds Wharf, Mill Street, London SE1 2BA (☎ 071 231 3100, fax 071 231 6868)

VEREKER, Hon Mrs Charles; Yvonne Frances; da of late Maj Geoffrey Arthur Barnett, MBE; *m* 1938, Hon Charles Standish Vereker (d 1941), s of Field Marshal 6 Viscount Gort, VC, GCB, CBE, DSO, MVO, MC (d 1946); *Style*— The Hon Mrs Charles Vereker; Serge Hill, Abbots Langley, Herts

VEREKER-MARSHALL, Hon Mrs (Elizabeth Jane); da of 8 Viscount Gort; *b* 1948; *Educ* Hillcourt Dublin; *m* 1988, Michael L Marshall, s of late A E Marshall, of Baldrine, Isle of Man; 1 s (Jason Colin Vereker b 22 Nov 1974), 1 da (Sarah Jayne Vereker b 9 Jan 1976); *Career* conslt to James Adams (Dublin) Auctioneers in Republic of Ireland; *Style*— The Hon Mrs Vereker-Marshall; The Coach House, Emo Park, Emo, Co Laois, Republic of Ireland; Green Hurst, Grove Mount, Ramsey, Isle of Man

VEREY, Michael John; TD (1945); s of Henry Edward Verey, DSO (d 1968), of Bridge House, Twyford, Berks, and Lucy Alice, *née* Longstaffe (d 1968); *b* 12 Oct 1912; *Educ* Eton, Trinity Coll Cambridge (MA); *m* 26 March 1947, Sylvia Mary, da of Lt-Col Denis Wilson, MC (k 1916); 2 s (Geoffrey b 1949, David b 1950), 1 da (Angela b 1948); *Career* joined Warwicks Yeo 1936; served: ME, Iraq, Syria and Persia Campaigns 1941, El Alamein 1942, Italy 1943; Lt-Col 1945; dir: Helbert Wagg & Co Ltd 1948-77 (joined 1934), Australian Mercantile Land & Finance Co 1950-70; dep chm Commercial Union Assurance Co 1951-82, vice chm The Boots Co 1962-83; chm: Broadstone Investment Trust 1962-83, Brixton Estate Co 1971-83, Schroders Ltd 1973-77; Investment International SA 1968-90, British Petroleum Co 1974-82; memb Covent Garden Mkt Authy 1961-66, chm Charities Official Investmt Fund Accepting Houses Ctee 1974-77, vice pres Br Bankers' Fedn 1974-77; High Sheriff of Berks 1968; *Recreations* gardening, travel; *Clubs* Boodles; *Style*— Michael Verey, Esq, TD; The Lodge, Little Bowden, Pangbourne, Berkshire (☎ 073484 2210); 120 Cheapside, London EC2 (☎ 071 382 6000)

VEREY, Rosemary Isabel Baird; da of Lt-Col Prescott Sandilands, DSO (d 1956), of London, and Gladys Baird, *née* Murton (d 1964); *b* 21 Dec 1918; *Educ* Eversley Sch Folkestone, UCL; *m* 21 Oct 1939, David Cecil Wynter Verey (d 1984), s of Rev Cecil Henry Verey (d 1958), of Barnsley, Glos; 2 s (Charles b 1940, Christopher b 1942), 2 da (Veronica (Mrs Ford) b 1946, Davina (Mrs Wynne-Jones) b 1949); *Career* jt creator Barnsley House Garden Glos, winner of Christies and HHA Garden of the Year Award 1988; lectr on gardening subjects in: America, Aust, Eng; garden designer, author; memb: Ctee The Tradescant Tst St Mary at Lambeth, Gardening History Soc; *Books* The Englishwomans Garden (1980), The Scented Garden (1981), The Englishmans Garden (1982), The American Womans Garden (1983), Classic Garden Design (1984), The New Englishwomans Garden (1987), The Garden in Winter (1988), The Flower Arrangers Garden (1989), The American Mans Garden (1990), Good Planting (1990); *Style*— Mrs Rosemary Verey; The Close, Barnsley, Cirencester, Gloucestershire GL7 5EE (☎ 0285 74 281, fax 0285 74 628)

VERITY, Anthony Courtenay Froude; s of Arthur Verity (d 1962), of Bristol, and Alice Kathleen, *née* Froude (d 1980); *b* 25 Feb 1939; *Educ* Queen Elizabeth's Hosp Bristol, Pembroke Coll Cambridge; *m* 3 Nov 1962, Patricia Ann, da of Walter Siddall, of Northampton; 1 s (James Adam b 1965), 1 da (Alice Lucy b 1968); *Career* metal broker Henry Gardner & Son 1961-62; asst master: Dulwich Coll 1962-65, Manchester GS 1965-69; head of classics Bristol GS 1969-76, headmaster Leeds GS 1976-86, master Dulwich Coll 1986-; memb Admty Interview Bd; FRSA; *Books* Latin as Literature (1969); *Recreations* mountaineering, squash, cricket, theatre and opera-going; *Clubs* Oxford and Cambridge, East India, Academy; *Style*— Anthony Verity, Esq; Elm Lawn, Dulwich Common, London SE21 7EW; 4 Blencathra View, Threlkeld, nr Keswick, Cumbria CA12 4TY; Dulwich College, London SE21 7LD (☎ 081 693 3601)

VERITY, Dr Christopher Michael; s of Rev Harry William Verity (d 1988), of Cambridge, and Gladys, *née* Banks; *b* 18 Feb 1946; *Educ* Merchant Taylors' Sch Crosby, Leeds GS, Keble Coll Oxford (MA, BM BCh), St Thomas' Hosp Med Sch; *m* 5 May 1984, Dorothy Bowes (Kelly), da of Clifford Claud Jupp, of Br Columbia; *Career* MO Save The Children Fund Phnom Penh Cambodia 1974-75, med registrar St Thomas' Hosp 1974-75, house physician Hosp For Sick Children Gt Ormond St 1977, fell Dept of Paediatric Neurology Univ of Br Columbia Canada 1980-81, lectr Dept of Child Health Bristol Royal Hosp For Sick Children 1982-85, conslt paediatric neurologist Addenbrooke's Hosp Cambridge 1985-, assoc lectr Univ of Cambridge Med Sch 1985-; author papers on: the Polle syndrome, follow up after cerebral hemispherectomy, hereditary sensory neuropathies, febrile convulsions in a nat cohort; memb: Br Paediatric Neurology Assoc, Paediatric Res Soc; FRCP 1990; *Recreations* windsurfing, skiing, tennis, painting; *Style*— Dr Christopher Michael; Addenbrooke's Hosp, Dept of Paediatrics, Hills Rd, Cambridge CB2 2QQ (☎ 0223 216662)

VERMA, Dr Shankar Narayan; s of Prabhash Chandra Ghosh (d 1989), of India, and Ambuj Basini, *née* Dutt; *b* 8 Jan 1939; *Educ* Uninv of Patna India (BSc, MB BS); *m* 2 July 1965, Alaka Nanda, da of Dr Sunil Kumar Dutta (d 1975), of Calcutta; 1 s (Amit b 1973), 1 da (Anuradha b 1967); *Career* med registrar S Liverpool HMC 1969-71, asst prof pharmacology Patna Med Coll 1973-75 (1962-66), conslt physician Holy Family Hosp Patna 1973-78, conslt physician in geriatric med Wolverhampton 1982-, registrar and lectr in geriatric med Northern Gen Hosp and Univ of Sheffield 1980-82, memb nat exec ODA 1987-, chm Wolverhampton div: BMA 1988-89, ODA 1983-85; hon fell Indian Coll of GPs; memb Geriatric Soc; *Recreations* hill walking, chrities, photography; *Clubs* Rotary (Wedensfield); *Style*— Dr Shankar Verma; 67 Yew Tree Lane, Tettenhall, Wolverhampton, West Midlands WV6 8UQ (☎ 0902 732255); New Cross hospital, Wolverhampton WV10 0QP (☎ 0902 759385)

VERMES, Prof Geza; s of Ernö Vermes (d 1944), and Terezia, *née* Riesz (d 1944); *b* 22 June 1924; *Educ* Gymnasium of Gyula Hungary, Budapest Univ, Louvain Univ, Coll St Albert of Louvain; *m* 12 May 1958, (Noreen) Pamela, da of Dr Edward Ernest Hobson (Capt RAMC); *Career* lectr (later sr lectr) in biblical studies Univ of Newcastle 1957-65; Wolfson Coll Oxford: prof of Jewish Studies 1989- (reader 1965-89), professorial fell 1965-; govr Oxford Centre for Hebrew Studies 1972-, chm Oxford Cncl of Christians and Jews 1980-86; FBA 1985; *Books* Discovery in the Judean Desert (1956), Scripture and Tradition in Judaism (1961), Jesus the Jew (1973), Post-Biblical Jewish Studies (1975), Jesus and the World of Judaism (1983), History of the Jewish People in the Age of Jesus by E Schüerer (jt reviser, 1973-87), The Dead Sea Scrolls in English (1987); *Recreations* watching wildlife; *Style*— Prof Geza Vermes; West Wood Cottage, Foxcombe Lane, Boars Hill, Oxford OX1 5DH (☎ 0865 735 384); Oriental Institute, Pusey Lane, Oxford OX1 2LE (☎ 0865 278 200/278 208)

VERMONT, David Neville; s of Leon Vermont (d 1949), and Anne MacDonald, *née* Hardy (d 1972); *b* 13 Feb 1931; *Educ* Mercers Sch, Christ's Coll Univ of Cambridge (BA, MA); *m* 16 March 1957, Ann Marion, da of late Lloyd Wilson; 2 s (Christopher b 1959, Charles b 1961), 1 da (Rachel b 1964); *Career* Cadet Bn HAC 1947-50, Nat Serv 2 Regt RHA 1950-52 (served Germany BAOR, cmmnd 1951), 1 Regt HAC RHA 1952-62 (cmmnd 1956); Sedgwick Group plc 1955-88: dep chm gp reinsurance subsid E W Payne Cos Ltd 1975-87, dir Sumitomo Marine & Fire Insurance Co (Europe) Ltd 1975-90, dir City Fire Insurance Co Ltd and Bimeh Iran Insurance Co (UK) Ltd, London rep Compagnie de Réassurance d'Ile de France (Corifrance), gen rep UK New India Assurance Co Ltd; memb Lloyd's 1969-; chm: Reinsurance Brokers' Assoc 1976-77, Brokers' Reinsurance Ctee 1977-78; chm: Cncl Gresham Coll, Anglo-Norse (London) Fund for Disabled; vice pres Argentine Dio Assoc (chm 1973-88), dir London Handel Society Ltd, govr St Paul's Schs (chm 1981-82); memb: Cncl City Univ, City and Insur Advsy Panel City Univ Business Sch (memb Bd Centre for Insurance and Investmnt Studies); tstee Whitechapel Art Gallery Fndn; Freeman City of London 1952, Master Worshipful Co of Mercers 1981-82; FRSA; *Recreations* walking, opera, chamber music; *Clubs* Garrick, MCC, United Oxford & Cambridge Univs, City Livery, Nikaean; *Style*— David Vermont, Esq; Frodsham, Sawbridgeworth, Herts CM21 9EP (☎ 0279 723 415); 6 Lovat Lane, London EC3R 8DT (☎ 071 929 2414, fax 071 626 2099)

VERNER-JEFFREYS, Robert Gerard; s of Lt Robert David Verner-Jeffreys, RN (ka 1942), and Audrey Marion, *née* Bray; *b* 30 Sept 1937; *Educ* Marlborough, RNC Dartmouth; *m* 12 Sept 1964, Anne, da of Col Samuel Alexander Holwell Kirkby, MC (ka 1943); 1 s (Robert b 1969), 1 da (Annabel b 1966); *Career* insur broker; dir John Broadwood & Sons Ltd 1983-86, Pendlehill Ltd 1986-, C T Bowring Reinsurance Ltd 1987-, Bowring International Insurance Brokers Ltd 1988-; tstee: Broadwood Tst, Fullers Almshouses, Neale's Charity; ACII, ABIBA; *Recreations* genealogy, music; *Style*— Robert G Verner-Jeffreys, Esq; 19 High Park Rd, Farnham, Surrey GU9 7JJ (☎ 0252 721 676); C T Bowring & Co Ltd (☎ 071 357 1008); Bowring Building, London EC3

VERNEY, Lt-Cdr David; DL (Cornwall 1982); 2 s of Sir Ralph Verney, 1 Bt, and bro of Sir John Verney, 2 Bt, MC; *b* 31 May 1918; *Educ* Eton; *m* 1948, Hon Mary Kathleen Boscawen, JP, da of 8 Viscount Falmouth; 1 s, 2 da (including Mrs Peter Bickford-Smith); *Career* WWII served RN (ret); High Sheriff Cornwall 1964; *Recreations* fishing; *Clubs* Naval and Military; *Style*— Lt-Cdr David Verney, DL, RN; Trevella, St Erme, Truro, Cornwall

VERNEY, Hon Mrs (Dorothy Cecily); *née* Tollemache; da of 3 Baron Tollemache (d 1955); *b* 1907; *m* 1942, Air Cdre Reynell Henry Verney, CBE, RAF (d 1974); *Style*— The Hon Mrs Verney; Stone House, Bishop's Hill, Lighthorne, Warwick

VERNEY, Edmund Ralph; s and h of Sir Ralph Verney, 5 Bt; *b* 28 June 1950; *Educ* Harrow, York Univ; *m* 1982, Daphne Fausset-Farquhar, of Lovelocks House, Shefford Woodlands, Hungerford; 1 s (b 1983), 1 da (b 1985); *Career* FRICS; *Clubs* Brooks's; *Style*— Edmund Verney, Esq; Rectory Close, Middle Claydon, Buckingham

VERNEY, Sir John; 2 Bt (UK 1946), of Eaton Square, City of Westminster, MC (1944), TD (1970); s of Lt-Col Sir Ralph Verney, 1 Bt, CB, CIE, CVO (d 1959); Sir Ralph's f, Frederick, was 4 s of Sir Harry Verney, 2 Bt, of Claydon (*see* Sir Ralph Bruce Verney, 5 Bt); *b* 30 Sept 1913; *Educ* Eton, Christ Church Oxford; *m* 1939, Jeanie Lucinda, da of late Maj Herbert Musgrave, DSO, RE; 1 s (and 1 s decd), 5 da; *Heir* s, John Sebastian Verney; *Career* served WWII 1939-45 as Maj RAC; painter, illustrator and author; Légion d'Honneur 1945; *Style*— Sir John Verney, Bt, MC, TD; The White House, Clare, Suffolk (☎ 0787 277 494)

VERNEY, His Hon Judge Lawrence John; TD (1955), DL (Bucks 1967); 5 s of Sir Harry Verney, 4 Bt (d 1974), by his w Lady Rachel Bruce (d 1964), da of 9 Earl of Elgin and Kincardine, KG; *b* 19 July 1924; *Educ* Harrow, Oriel Coll Oxford; *m* 1972, Zoë Auriel, da of Lt-Col P G Goodeve-Docker; *Career* Capt Grenadier Gds 1943-46, Lt-Col Royal Bucks Yeo TA 1947-68, Hon Col Bucks Army Cadet Force 1975-80; called to the Bar Inner Temple 1952; dep chm QS: Bucks 1962-71, Middx 1971; circuit judge 1972-90, recorder of London 1990-; govr Harrow Sch 1972-87; *Style*— His Hon Judge Verney, TD, DL; Central Criminal Court, City of London, London EC4M 7EH

VERNEY, Hon Mrs (Mary Kathleen); *née* Boscawen; JP (Cornwall 1960); da of 8 Viscount Falmouth; *b* 11 June 1926; *Educ* Heathfield Ascot; *m* 1948, Lt-Cdr David Verney, DL, *qv*, yr s of Sir Ralph Verney, 1 Bt; 1 s, 2 da; *Style*— The Hon Mrs Verney, JP; Trevella, St Erme, Truro, Cornwall

VERNEY, Sir Ralph Bruce; 5 Bt (UK 1818), of Claydon House, Buckinghamshire, KBE (1974), JP (Bucks 1954), DL (Bucks); s of Sir Harry Calvert Williams Verney, 4 Bt, DSO (d 1974); *b* 18 Jan 1915; *Educ* Canford, Balliol Coll Oxford (BA); *m* 7 July 1948, Mary, da of late Percy Charles Vestey (3 s of Sir Edmund Vestey, 1 Bt) and 2 cous of the present Lord Vestey; 1 s, 3 da; *Heir* s, Edmund Ralph Verney; *Career* Maj RA Java 1945; Vice Lord-Lt for Bucks 1965-85, High Sheriff 1957, Co cnclr 1952-73, Co alderman 1961-73, chm Nat Ctee for England of Forestry Cmmn 1968-80 (produced plan for Chiltern Hills 1971), pres CLA 1961-63, memb Royal Cmmn on Environmental Pollution 1973-79; tstee: Radcliffe, Ernest Cook and Chequers Tsts; chm Nature Conservancy Cncl 1980-83; Hon Doctorate Univ of Buckingham; Hon FRIBA 1977, hon fell Green Coll Oxford; *Clubs* Cavalry and Guards'; *Style*— Sir Ralph Verney, Bt, KBE, JP, DL; Claydon House, Middle Claydon, Buckingham MK18 2EX (☎ 029 6730 297); Plas Rhoscolyn, Holyhead LL65 2NZ (☎ 0407 860288)

VERNEY, Rt Rev Stephen Edmund; MBE (1945); 2 s of Sir Harry Verney, 4 Bt, DSO, by Lady Rachel Bruce, da of 9 Earl of Elgin and Kincardine; *b* 17 April 1919; *Educ* Harrow, Balliol Coll Oxford; *m* 1, 1947, Priscilla (d 1974), da of George Schwerdt, of Alresford; 1 s, 3 da; m 2, 1981, as her 2 husband, Sandra Bailey, of Llandeilo; 1 s (Harry, decd); *Career* late Lt and Temp Capt Intelligence Corps; canon St George's Chapel Windsor 1970-77, suffragan bishop Repton 1977-85; *Books* Fire in Coventry (1964), People & Cities (1969), Into the New Age (1976), Water into Wine (1985), The Dance of Love (1989); *Recreations* conversation and aloneness, music, gardening, walking; *Clubs* English Speaking Union; *Style*— The Rt Rev Stephen Verney, MBE; The Charity School House, Church Rd, Blewbury, Didcot, Oxon OX11 9PY

VERNON, Anthony John; s of John Bloor Vernon; *b* 21 May 1937; *Educ* Abbotsholme Sch Rocester Derbys; *m* 1962, Beatrice Jane, *née* Murray; 2 s; *Career* chm and md Murray Vernon Ltd; chm: Sandfield Securities Ltd, Fastnet Fish Ltd, Sheppard (International Traders) Ltd, UK Provision Trade Fedn 1987-88; govr Ellesmere Coll Salop, fell Midland Div Woodard Schs; Liveryman Worshipful Co of Farmers, Freeman City of London 1988; *Recreations* shooting, sailing; *Clubs* Royal Ocean Racing; *Style*— Anthony Vernon, Esq; Haslington Hall, Haslington, Crewe, Cheshire (☎ 0270 582662)

VERNON, Dr Clare Christine; da of Stephen Vernon, 12 Willows Ave, Lytham St Annes, Lancashire, and Mary, *née* Dewhirst; *b* 23 Oct 1951; *Educ* Queen Mary Sch Lytham Lancs, Girton Coll Cambridge (MA, MB BChir), Bart's; *m* 17 July 1976 (m dis 1988), George, s of Herbert Evans (d 1984); *Career* registrar radiotherapy: Royal Free Hosp 1979, Middx Hosp 1982; sr registrar radiotherapy Mount Vernon Hosp 1984, conslt radiotherapist Hammersmith Hosp 1986-; memb: BMA 1976, GMC 1976, 1951 Club 1986; FRCR 1984, MPS 1989; *Recreations* sports, music, archaeology; *Clubs* 1951; *Style*— Dr Clare Vernon; 60 St Paul St, Islington, London N1 7DA (☎ 081 359 8493); MRC Hyperthermia Clinic, Cyclotron Unit, Hammersmith Hospital, Du Cane Rd, London W12 0HS (☎ 081 740 3177)

VERNON, Denis Stewart; s of Eric Stewart Vernon (d 1964), and Bessie Ferguson, *née* Alder (d 1988); *b* 11 Feb 1931; *Educ* Rossall, King's Coll Newcastle, London

Business Sch; *m* ; 2 s, 2 da; *Career* Nat Serv 2 Lt RASC 1954-56; slr; sr ptnr in Newcastle firm 1956-78; chm and chief exec Ferguson International Hldgs plc 1968-90; chm: Utd Merchants Ltd 1978-87, Rare Breeds Survival Tst Ltd 1988-90; non-exec dir: Expamet International plc, Metro Radio Group plc, Northern Region Barclays Bank; chm Settle and Carlisle Railway Tst 1989-; *Recreations* sailing, skiing, ornithology, art, conservation; *Clubs* Farmers; *Style*— Denis Vernon, Esq; Eden House, Edenhall, Cumbria CA11 8SX (☎ 0768 881536)

VERNON, (John) Fane; s of Capt John Edward Vernon (d 1951), of Co Cavan, Ireland, and Dolores Arnold (d 1931); *b* 16 Jan 1924; *Educ* Winchester; *m* 1948, Pamela Elizabeth, da of Archibald Evander McIver (d 1962), of Dublin; 1 s (John), 1 da (Katharine); *Career* Nat Serv 1942-46, 820 Naval Air Sqdn, HMS Formidable, HMS Indefatigable, Home Fleet, Med and Pacific, demob Lt (A) RNVR; joined Ash & Lacy plc 1951 (chm 1970-89); chm: Br Dredging plc 1980-, Brooke Tool Engrg (Hldgs) plc 1984-90; dir: Shipton Communications Ltd 1982-86, Hargreaves Gp plc 1984-87, Davenports Brewery (Hldgs) plc 1985-86; *Recreations* golf, bridge; *Style*— Fane Vernon, Esq; 60 Richmond Hill Rd, Edgbaston, Birmingham B15 3RZ (☎ 021 454 2047)

VERNON, Hon Jack Leslie; s and h of 6 Baron Lyveden; *b* 10 Nov 1938; *m* 1961, Lynette June, da of William Herbert Lilley; 1 s, 2 da; *Style*— The Hon Jack Vernon; 17 Carlton St, Te Aroha, New Zealand

VERNON, James Loudon; s of Capt Reginald Thornycroft Vernon, RFC (d 1977); *b* 27 Oct 1940; *Educ* Eton, Trinity Coll Dublin; *m* 1971, Elspeth Mary Stewart, da of Rev Cyril Raby Thomson; 2 s, 2 da; *Career* dir Constantine Hldgs Ltd 1977, underwriting memb Lloyd's 1980, Liveryman Worshipful Co of Skinners 1979; *Recreations* sailing (yachts 'Archon' and 'Minx'), shooting, skiing, music (particulary opera); *Clubs* Royal Yacht Sqdn, RAC, Royal St George; *Style*— James Vernon, Esq; 45 Egerton Crescent, London SW3 2ED (☎ 071 589 0858)

VERNON, James William; s and h of Sir Nigel Vernon, 4 Bt; *b* 2 April 1949; *Educ* Shrewsbury; *m* 1981, Davinia, da of Christopher David Howard, of Ryton Corner, Ryton, Shrewsbury; 1 da (Harriet Lucy Howard b 1985), 1 s (George William Howard b 1987); *Career* chartered accountant; *Style*— James Vernon, Esq; The Hall, Lygan-y-Wern, Pentre Halkyn, Holywell, Clwyd

VERNON, John Humphrey; s of Major Humphrey Bagnall Vernon, MC (d 1979), and Sibyl Mason Vernon, of Beechdale House, Stonecross, Exford, Somerset; *b* 7 Dec 1940; *Educ* Charterhouse, Magdalen Coll Oxford; *m* 1973, Alison Margaret, da of William Warnock Watt (d 1986), of Knowlegate, Sheriffhales, Shifnal, Shropshire; 1 s (Andrew b 1981), 1 da (Nicola b 1978); *Career* div chief exec Newship Gp Ltd 1987-, exec with Babcock Int plc 1974-87; md: Dynamo & Electrical Services Ltd 1977-80, Secundalax Emergency Lighting Ltd 1977-80, Piranha Ignition Ltd 1977-80; dep chm Piranha Ignition Ltd 1980-82; dir Pexit Precision Ltd 1981-82; chief exec: Babcock Gardner Ltd 1982-84, Babcock Gears Ltd 1982-85, Babcock Wire Equipment Ltd 1982-85; *Recreations* fishing, photography; *Style*— John Vernon, Esq; Maybank, 36 Gem Brook Rd, Priorslee, Telford, Shropshire (☎ Telford 0952 615381); Newship Gp Ltd, Clive House, Queens Rd, Weybridge (☎ 0932 858044)

VERNON, 10 Baron (GB 1762); John Lawrance Venables-Vernon; s of 9 Baron Vernon (d 1963); *b* 1 Feb 1923; *Educ* Eton, Magdalen Coll Oxford; *m* 1, 1955 (m dis 1982), Sheila Jean, da of W Marshall Clark, OBE, of Johannesburg, S Africa; 2 da; m 2, 1982, Sally June, da of Robin Stratford, QC, and formerly w of (1) Colin Fyfe-Jamieson and (2) Sir (John) Jeremy Eustace Tennyson d'Eyncourt, 3 Bt; *Heir* kinsman, William Ronald Dennis Vernon-Harcourt, OBE, b 1909; *Career* WWII Capt Scots Gds, took Conservative Whip in Lords to 1981, since when has sat as SDP Peer and then Ind Peer; barr Lincoln's Inn 1949; served: Cabinet Office 1953-57, Colonial Office Kenya 1957-58, Foreign Office 1958-60; JP Derbys 1965-77; chm Population Concern 1985-90; *Style*— The Rt Hon the Lord Vernon; Sudbury House, Sudbury, Derbyshire DE6 5HT (☎ 028 378 208); 10 Ringmer Ave, Fulham, London SW6 (☎ 071 736 5900)

VERNON, Sir Nigel John Douglas; 4 Bt (UK 1914), of Shotwick Park, Co Chester; s of Sir (William) Norman Vernon, 3 Bt (d 1967); *b* 2 May 1924; *Educ* Charterhouse; *m* 29 Nov 1947, Margaret Ellen, da of late Robert Lyle Dobell, of The Mount, Waverton, Chester; 2 s (1 s decd), 1 da; *Heir* s, James William Vernon; *Career* Lt RNVR 1942-45; conslt Hogg Robinson Ltd 1984-; *Recreations* gardening, shooting, golf; *Clubs* Naval, Army and Navy; *Style*— Sir Nigel Vernon, Bt; Top-y-Fron Hall, Kelsterton, nr Flint, Clywd CH6 5TF

VERNON, Richard Evelyn; s of Evelyn Vernon, and Violet Mary Stuart, *née* Foley (d 1974); *b* 7 March 1925; *m* 1955 (m dis 1989), Benedicta Lucia, *née* Hoskyns; 1 s (Thomas b 1958), 1 da (Sarah b 1956); partner, Rosemary Frankau; *Career* actor; theatre incl: Stratton (Mercury) 1949 (first professional prodn), Pack of Lies (Lyric) 1983, Look No Hans (Strand) 1985, Dry Rot (Lyric) 1988, Hidden Laughter (Vaudeville) 1990; TV incl: Upstairs Downstairs 1973, Duchess of Duke Street 1976, Ripping Yarns 1978, Paradise Postponed 1985; radio incl: Hitchikers Guide to the Galaxy, Blandings, The Trial of Lady Chatterly, Encyclopedia of Rock; films incl: Indiscreet 1958, Goldfinger 1964, A Hard Days Night 1964, The Pink Panther Strikes Again 1976, Ghandi 1982, A Month in the Country 1986; *Recreations* sailing; *Style*— Richard Vernon, Esq; Julian Belfrage, 68 St James's St, London SW1 (☎ 071 491 4400)

VERNON, Richard Wallace; s of Herbert Wallace Vernon (d 1974), of Aldeburgh, Suffolk, and Gertrude Mary, *née* Jackson (d 1959); *b* 18 Oct 1927; *Educ* Loretto, Univ of Cambridge (MA); *m* 8 Jan 1955, Pamela Violet, da of Lt-Col Alexander George William Grierson (d 1951), of Walmer, Kent; 2 s (David Grierson b 1956, Simon Richard b 1958), 2 da (Sally Pamela Clare Daniell b 1960, Joanna Caroline Bennett b 1963); *Career* Lt RA 1945-48; dir: R K Harrison J I Jacobs (Insurance) Ltd 1967-82, R K Harrison & Co 1975-82, Harrison Horncastle (Insurance) Ltd 1982-84; conslt Towry Law (International) Ltd 1988- (md 1984-88); Freeman City of London; *Recreations* sailing; *Clubs* Aldeburgh Yacht, Lloyds Yacht, Haven Ports Yacht, Little Ship; *Style*— Richard Vernon, Esq; Scotch Corner, Wildernesse Ave, Sevenoaks, Kent TN15 0EA (☎ 0732 61 567)

VERNON, Hon Robert Howard; s of 6 Baron Lyveden; *b* 1942; *m* 1968, Louise Smith; 1 s (Russell Sydney b 1969); *Style*— The Hon Robert Veronon

VERNON, Dr Stephen Andrew; s of Alan Vernon (d 1979), of Alderley Edge, Cheshire, and Phyllis Mary Vernon; *b* 10 Feb 1955; *Educ* King's Sch Macclesfield, Univ of Bristol Med Sch (MB ChB); *m* 1 Sept 1985, Alison Elizabeth Mary, da of Claude Walton (d 1990), of Mansfield, Notts; 1 da (Olivia Katherine b 2 Dec 1989); *Career* house physician Bristol Royal Infirmary 1978-79, house surgn Frenchay Hosp Bristol 1979, demonstrator and lectr in anatomy Bristol Med Sch 1979-80, sr house offr and registrar in ophthalmology Bristol Eye Hosp 1980-83, sr registrar Oxford Eye Hosp 1983-86, sr lectr and founding head Academic Unit of Ophthalmology Univ of Nottingham and hon conslt ophthalmology Nottingham Health Authy 1986-; author of academic pubns on ophthalmic epidemiology and glaucoma detection; memb: Cncl Ophthalmic Section RSM, UK Eye Study Gp; FRCS 1982, FCOpth 1989; *Books* Ophthalmology (1988); *Recreations* inland waterways, skiing, music and drama; *Style*— Dr Stephen Vernon; The Academic Unit of Ophthalmology, University Hospital, Nottingham NG7 2UH (☎ 0602 421421 ext 43200)

VERNON, Hon Mrs (Victoria); *née* Arthur; da of 3 Baron Glenarthur, OBE, DL, by his 2 w; *b* 20 June 1946; *m* 1976, Hugh (Richard) Vernon, 2 s of Mervyn Vernon, MVO (2 s of Rupert Vernon, DSO, JP, 5 s of Hon Greville Vernon, JP, DL, sometime MP Ayrshire and 4 s of 1 Baron Lyveden), by his w, Lady Violet Baring, yr da of 2 Earl of Cromer; 1 s (Andrew Robert Richard b 21 Aug 1979), 2 da (Catherine Victoria b 13 Oct 1977, Emma Mary b 12 Oct 1983); *Style*— The Hon Mrs Vernon; Pierhill, Annbank, Ayrshire

VERNON, William Michael; s of Sir Wilfred Douglas Vernon (d 1973), of Anningsley Park, Ottershaw, Surrey, and Nancy Elizabeth, *née* Jackson; *b* 17 April 1926; *Educ* Marlborough, Trinity Coll Cambridge (MA); *m* 1, 25 April 1952 (m dis 1977), Rosheen Elizabeth Mary, da of George O'Meara (d 1932), of Johannesburg, S Africa; 1 s (Mark Thornycroft Vernon b 7 March 1958); m 2, 7 Sept 1977, Jane Olivia Colston, da of Denys Kilham-Roberts (d 1975); *Career* Lt RM 1944-46; chm and chief exec Spillers Ltd 1968-80 (joined 1948, dir 1960, jt md 1962), dir EMI Ltd 1973-80, chm Famous Names Ltd 1981-85; pres: Nat Assoc of Br and Irish Millers 1965, Br Food Export Cncl 1977-80; vice chm Millers' Mutual Assoc 1968-80, chm RNLI 1989- (dep chm 1981-89); dir Strong & Fisher (Holdings) plc 1980-91, chm Granville Meat Co Ltd 1981-; CBIM; *Recreations* sailing (ASSEGAI VI), skiing, shooting; *Clubs* Royal Yacht Sqdn, Royal Ocean Racing, Hurlingham; *Style*— Michael Vernon, Esq; Fyfield Manor, Andover, Hants

VERRILL, John Rothwell; s of Dr Peter John Verrill, of London, and Christine Mary, *née* Rothwell; *b* 25 March 1954; *Educ* Univ Coll Sch, UCL (LLB); *m* 6 Sept 1980, Katharine Mary, da of Hugh Schofield Spensley; 2 s (William b 27 Aug 1986, Edward b 27 Jan 1989); *Career* articled clerk Ward Bowie 1978-82, admitted slr 1981; Lawrence Graham (previously Crane & Hawkins): asst slr 1982-86, ptnr Co Commercial Dept 1986-; Licensed Insolvency Practitioner 1990-; Freeman Worshipful Co of Slrs 1988; memb: Law Soc, City of Westminster Law Soc, Int Bar Assoc (UK Oil Lawyers Gp), Insolvency Practitioners Assoc, Insolvency Lawyers Assoc; *Recreations* rowing, sailing; *Clubs* Leander Aldeburgh Yacht; *Style*— John Verrill, Esq; Lawrence Graham, 190 Strand, London WC2R 1JN (☎ 071 379 0000, fax 071 379 6854)

VERRILL, Dr Peter John; s of John Edwin Verrill (d 1985), and Ada, *née* James; *b* 17 June 1930; *Educ* UCL; *m* 23 May 1953, Christine Mary, da of Cecil Rothwell (d 1956); 3 s (John, Richard, Mark), 1 da (Jane (Mrs Dacre)); *Career* short serv cmmn Sqdn Ldr RAF 1954-57, fell anaesthesiology Mayo Clinic USA 1960-61, currently conslt anaesthetist UCH (fell UCL 1987); fell Coll of Anaesthetists; *Recreations* golf, sailing, gardening; *Clubs* Aldeburgh Yacht, Aldeburgh Golf; *Style*— Dr Peter Verrill; 40 Southway, London NW11 6SA (☎ 081 458 5705); UCH, Gower St, London WC1 (☎ 071 383 7395)

VERSEN, Lady Cleone Lucinda; eldest da of 6 Earl of Erne; *b* 27 Aug 1959; *m* 23 June 1989, Richard Frederick Versen; *Style*— The Lady Cleone Versen

VERULAM, 7 Earl of (UK 1815); Sir John Duncan Grimston; 14 Bt (E 1629); also Lord Forrester (S 1633), Baron Dunboyne and Viscount Grimston (I 1719), Baron Verulam (GB 1790), Viscount Grimston (UK 1815); s of 6 Earl of Verulam (d 1973); *b* 21 April 1951; *Educ* Eton, Christ Church Oxford; *m* 1976, Dione Angela, da of Jeremy F E Smith, *qv*, of Balcombe House, Balcombe, Sussex; 3 s (Viscount Grimston b 1978, Hon Hugo Guy Sylvester b 1979, Hon Sam George b 1983), 1 da (Lady Flora Hermione b 1981); *Heir* s, Viscount Grimston; *Career* dir Baring Brothers Co Ltd; *Recreations* country pursuits; *Clubs* Beefsteak, White's, Turf; *Style*— The Rt Hon the Earl of Verulam; Gorhambury, St Albans, Herts AL3 6AH (☎ 0727 55000)

VERULAM, Dowager Countess of; Marjorie Ray; da of late Walter Atholl Duncan; *m* 1938, 6 Earl of Verulam (d 1973); 1 s, 4 da; *Style*— The Rt Hon the Dowager Countess of Verulam; Pré Mill House, Redbourn Rd, St Albans, Herts

VESEY, Sir (Nathaniel) Henry Peniston; CBE (1953); s of Hon Nathaniel Vesey, of Devonshire, Bermuda; *b* 1 June 1901; *Educ* Saltus GS; *m* 1920, Louise, da of Capt J Stubbs; 2 s; *Career* chm: H A & E Smith 1939-, Bank of N T Butterfield & Son 1970-; memb House of Assembly Bermuda 1938-72; kt 1965; *Style*— Sir Henry Vesey, CBE; Windward, Shelly Bay, Bermuda (☎ 3 0186)

VESSEY, Prof Martin Paterson; s of Sydney James Vessey (d 1988), of Mill Hill, London, and Catherine, *née* Thompson; *b* 22 July 1936; *Educ* Univ Coll Sch Hampstead, UCL, Univ Coll Hosp Med Sch (MD, MA Oxon); *m* 21 May 1959, Anne, da of Prof Benjamin Stanley Platt, CMG (d 1969); 2 s (Rupert b 1964, Ben b 1967), 1 da (Alice b 1970); *Career* prof of social and community medicine Univ of Oxford 1974-, fell St Cross Coll Oxford 1974-; memb: Oxford Preservation Tst, Nat Tst, Cncl for the Preservation of Rural England, Ctee on Safety of Medicines, BMA, Soc for Social Medicine; author of 3 books and 300 scientific papers; *Recreations* walking, motoring, singing, conservation; *Style*— Prof Martin Vessey; 8 Warnborough Road, Oxford OX2 6HZ (☎ 0865 52698); Dept of Community Medicine and General Practice, Radcliffe (☎ 0865 511293)

VESTEY, Sir (John) Derek; 2 Bt (UK 1921); s of late John Joseph Vestey (eldest s of Sir Edmund Vestey, 1 Bt, the latter being bro of 1 Baron Vestey); suc gf 1953; *b* 4 June 1914; *Educ* The Leys Sch; *m* 21 June 1938, Phyllis Irene, o da of Harry Brewer, of Banstead; 1 s, 1 da; *Heir* s, Paul Edmund Vestey; *Career* WWII Flt Lt RAFVR 1940-45; *Clubs* MCC, RAC; *Style*— Sir Derek Vestey, Bt

VESTEY, Edmund Hoyle; DL (Essex 1978); only s of Ronald Vestey, DL; *b* 1932; *Educ* Eton; *m* 1960, Anne Moubray, yr da of Gen Sir Geoffry Scoones, KCB, KBE, CSI, DSO, MC; 4 s (Timothy b 1961, James b 1962, George b 1964, Robin b 1968); *Career* served as 2 Lt Queen's Bays 1951; chm: Union International, Blue Star Line, Lamport and Holt Line, Albion Insurance; pres Gen Cncl Br Shipping 1981-82; jt master Puckeridge & Thurlow Foxhounds, pres Essex County Scouts Council 1979-87; High Sheriff Essex 1977-78; Lt City of London Yeomanry; *Clubs* Cavalry, Carlton; *Style*— Edmund Vestey, Esq, DL; Glencanisp Lodge, Lochinver, Sutherland; Sunnyside Farmhouse, Hawick, Roxburghshire; Little Thurlow Hall, nr Haverhill, Suffolk CB9 7LQ

VESTEY, Hon Mark William; s of Capt the Hon William Howarth Vestey (ka 1944), and bro of 3 Baron Vestey; raised to the rank of a Baron's younger son 1955; *b* 16 April 1943; *Educ* Eton; *m* 1975, Rose Amelia, da of Lt-Col Peter Thomas Clifton, DSO; 1 s, 2 da; *Career* 2 Lt Scots Gds; *Style*— The Hon Mark Vestey; 20 Eaton Mews South, SW1 (☎ 071 235 8932); Stowell Park, Northleach, nr Cheltenham, Glos

VESTEY, Paul Edmund; s and h of Sir (John) Derek Vestey, 2 Bt; *b* 15 Feb 1944; *Educ* Radley; *m* 1971, Victoria Anne Scudamore, da of John Salter, of Old Ford House, Tiverton, Devon; 3 da; *Clubs* British Racing Drivers', Farmers', Royal Automobile; *Style*— Paul Vestey Esq; 53 Cheval Place, London SW7 (☎ 071 589 0562); Manor House Farm, Bishops Sutton, Hants

VESTEY, 3 Baron (UK 1922); Sir Samuel George Armstrong Vestey; 3 Bt (UK 1913), DL (Glos 1982); s of Capt the Hon William Howarth Vestey, Scots Gds (ka Italy 1944, only s of 2 Baron Vestey), and Pamela, da of George Nesbitt Armstrong, s of Charles Nesbitt Frederick Armstrong and Dame Nellie Melba, the opera singer; suc gf 1954; *b* 19 March 1941; *Educ* Eton; *m* 1, 1970 (m dis), Kathryn Mary, da of John Eccles, of Moor Park, Herts; 2 da (Hon Saffron b 1971, Hon Flora b 1978); m 2, 1981, Celia Elizabeth, yr da of Maj (Hubert) Guy Knight, MC, of Lockinge Manor,

Wantage, and Hester, sis of Countess (w of 6 Earl) of Clanwilliam; 2 s; *Heir* s, Hon William Guy Vestey b 27 Aug 1983; *Career* Lt Scots Gds; dir Union International plc and associated cos; pres: London Meat Trade and Drovers Benevolent Assoc 1973, Inst of Meat 1978-83, Steeplechase Co Cheltenham; Liveryman Worshipful Co of Butchers; patron of one living; GCStJ, Lord Prior of the Order of St John 1991-; *Clubs* White's, Jockey (Newmarket), Melbourne (Melbourne); *Style*— The Rt Hon the Lord Vestey, DL; Stowell Park, Northleach, Glos

VEVERS, David Michael; s of Maj John Bewlay Vevers, MBE (d 1979), of The Manor Ladywood Rd, Roundhay, Leeds, and Kathleen Mary, *née* Wright; *b* 12 June 1942; *Educ* Felsted; *Career* head of PR Charterhouse Gp plc 1975-83, dep chm IPR City and Fin Gp (treas and PR cncl memb 1989), dir Communications J Rothschild Hldgs plc 1983-85, gp public affrs mangr Prudential Corpn plc 1985-89; dir: Wolff Olins Ltd 1989-, London Philharmonic Orchestra Ltd 1989-; MIPR 1975, MCIM 1970, FRSA 1990; *Recreations* music, bridge, contemporary art; *Clubs* Cavalry and Guards'; *Style*— David Vevers, Esq; 91 Lexham Gdns, London W8 6JN (☎ 071 373 0141); Wolff Olins Ltd, 22 Dukes Rd, London WC1H 9AB (☎ 071 387 0891, fax 071 388 6639)

VEY, Hon Mrs (Catharine Gina Amita); *née* Noble; da of Baron Glenkinglas, PC (Life Peer, d 1984), and Baroness Glenkinglas, *qv*; *b* 1943; *m* 1964, Peter Conrad Hamilton Vey; 1 s; *Style*— The Hon Mrs Vey; Godsfield Manor, Alresford, Hants

VIBRAYE; *see*: de Vibraye

VICE, (Henry) Anthony; s of S J Vice (d 1981), and L I Vice; *b* 24 Dec 1930; *Educ* Hymers Coll Hull, Queen's Coll Oxford (MA); *m* 4 Sept 1954, Elizabeth Joan Spencer, da of Prof J N Wright (d 1982); 1 s (John b 6 Aug 1962), 2 da (Susan b 6 Feb 1961, Philippa b 24 Aug 1965); *Career* Somerset LI 1948-50; dir: N M Rothschild 1972-, Bowthorpe Holdings 1978-, Drummond Group 1986-, Cavaghan & Gray 1988-, chm I J Dewhirst 1988-, Chancer Estates 1990-; *Style*— Anthony Vice, Esq; New Court, St Swithin's Lane, London EC4 (☎ 071 280 5000)

VICK, Sir (Francis) Arthur; OBE (1945); s of Wallace Devenport Vick (d 1952), of Birmingham, and Clara, *née* Taylor (d 1932); *b* 5 June 1911; *Educ* Waverley GS Birmingham, Univ of Birmingham (BSc, PhD); *m* 1943, Elizabeth Dorothy (d 1989), da of Ernest Story; 1 da; *Career* physicist; lectr UCL 1936-44, asst dir scientific res Miny of Supply 1939-44, sr lectr Univ of Manchester 1947-50 (lectr 1944-47), physics prof Univ Coll North Staffs (now Univ of Keele) 1950-59 (vice princ 1950-54), dir AERE Harwell 1960-64, memb for res UKAEA 1964-66, pres and vice chllr Queen's Univ Belfast 1966-76, pro chllr Univ of Warwick 1977- (chm of Cncl 1977-90); memb cncl UGC 1959-66; Hon DSc: Keele, Nat Univ of Ireland, Birmingham; Hon LLD: Dublin, Belfast; Hon DCL Kent; FIEE, FInstP, MRIA; kt 1973; *Recreations* music, gardening, DIY; *Clubs* Athenaeum, Savile; *Style*— Sir Arthur Vick, OBE; Fieldhead Cottage, Fieldhead Lane, Myton Rd, Warwick CV34 6QF (☎ 0926 491822)

VICK, David John; s of John Howard George Vick, of W Drayton, Middx, and Pearl Kathleen, *née* Cast; *b* 15 Dec 1951; *Educ* Latymer Upper Sch, Peterhouse Cambridge (MA); *m* 1, 1 Sept 1973 (m dis 1980), (Anne) Sheena Bowyer; m 2, 15 July 1988, Linda, da of Gordon Hunt, of Northallerton, Yorks; *Career* head devpt Radio Authy 1990- (IBA res offr 1975-77, radio servs offr 1977-81, sr radio offr 1981-87, princ radio devpt offr 1987-90); memb: Amnesty Int, Br Film Inst, Mill Hill Preservation Soc, Radio Acad (chm res ctee); *Books* The Voice of Kenya: Radio in a Developing African Nation (1985), Radio Research: An Annotated Bibliography 1975-88 (1989); *Recreations* travel, cinema, sports; *Clubs* Barnet, Everton; *Style*— David Vick, Esq; Swallowfield, 45 Hammers Lane, Mill Hill, London NW7 4DB (☎ 081 906 2310); Radio Authority, 70 Brompton Rd, London SW3 1EY (☎ 071 581 2888, fax 071 823 9113)

VICK, Dr John Alexander Stewart; s of John Oliver Curtis Vick, of 8 Churchfields House, Guessens Rd, Welwyn Garden City, Herts; and Mary Macfarlane, *née* Stewart (d 1988); *b* 4 April 1937; *Educ* Taunton Sch, The London Hosp Med Coll and Univ of London (MB BS); *m* 14 Sept 1963, Patricia Anne Marie, da of William Vincent Cassidy (d 1963), of 7 Grafton St, Londonderry, NI; 1 s (Peter John William b 1965), 1 da (Emma Mary Louise b 1969); *Career* receiving room offr London Hosp 1960, house surgn and house physician Brighton Gen Hosp 1961, med and pediatric registrar Lister Hosp Hitchin 1962-64 (sr house offr of surgery 1962), med registrar Queen Elizabeth II Hosp Welwyn Garden City 1964-66, ptnr Drs Vick, Tidy, Christie, Ingram, Cooper and Kendell, paediatric hosp practitioner Lister Hosp Stevenage, med offr William Ransom & Son Hitchin, dep coroner Hitchin Dist Herts 1979-; former: divnl surgn Hitchin St John Ambulance Bde, memb Herts Local Med Ctee, memb Herts Family Practitioner Ctee, chm E Herts Div BMA; MRCS, memb BMA, MRCGP, LRCP, DObstRCOG; *Recreations* bridge, croquet, philately, photography; *Style*— Dr John Vick; The Pines, 7 Wymondley Close, Hitchin, Herts SG4 9PW (☎ 0462 432904); The Portmill Surgery, 114 Queen St, Hitchin, Herts SG4 9TH (☎ 0462 434246)

VICK, His Hon Judge (Arnold Oughtred) Russell Vick; QC (1980); yr s of His Honour Judge Sir Godfrey Russell Vick, QC (d 1958), of Seal, and Lady Marjorie Vick, JP, *née* Compston (d 1985); *b* 14 Sept 1933; *Educ* The Leys School, Jesus Coll Cambridge (MA); *m* 5 Sept 1959, Zinnia Mary, da of Thomas Brown Yates (d 1968), of Godalming; 2 s (Philip Godfrey Russell b 1960, Mark Thomas b 1964), 1 da (Tessa Louise b 1963); *Career* Nat Serv RAFVR Flying Offr 1952-54; called to the Bar Inner Temple 1958; practised SE Circuit 1958-82: prosecuting counsel to PO 1964-69, rec 1978-80, dep rec Rochester City QS 1971, rec Crown Ct 1972-82; circuit judge Kent 1982-, princ civil judge Kent 1990-; govr New Beacon Sch; Master Worshipful Co of Curriers' 1976-77; *Books* A Hundred Years of Golf at Wildernesse 1890-1990; *Recreations* golf, cricket, bridge, gardening; *Clubs* MCC, Hawks (Cambridge), Wildernesse Golf (capt 1978), Band of Brothers, Royal Worlington and Newmarket Golf, Bromley Hockey; *Style*— His Honour Judge Russell Vick, QC; The Law Courts, Barker Rd, Maidstone, Kent ME16 8EW (☎ 0622 754966, fax 0622 685428)

VICKERMAN, Prof Keith; s of Jack Vickerman, and Mabel, *née* Dyson; *b* 21 March 1933; *Educ* King James Gs Almondbury, UCL (BSc, PhD, DSc), Exeter Univ; *m* 16 Sept 1961, Moira, da of Wilfrid Dutton, MC; 1 da (Louise Charlotte b 1973); *Career* Royal Soc tropical res fell UCL 1963-68 (Wellcome lectr 1958-63), regius prof of zoology Univ of Glasgow 1984- (head of dept 1979-85, prof 1974-84, reader 1968-74); served on various ctees of WHO, ODA and SERC; fell UCL 1985; FRSE 1970, FRS 1984; *Books* The Protozoa (with FEG Cox, 1967); author numerous articles and res papers in learned jls; *Recreations* sketching, gardening; *Style*— Prof Keith Vickerman; 16 Mirrlees Drive, Glasgow G12 0SH (☎ 041 334 2794); Dept of Zoology, Univ of Glasgow, Glasgow G12 8QQ (☎ 041 339 8855, fax 041 330 5971, telex 777079)

VICKERS, Adrian Michael; s of Hugh Anthony Vickers (d 1970), of Greasby, Cheshire, and Margaret, *née* Rae (d 1989); *b* 24 Sept 1938; *Educ* Beaumont Coll, Merton Coll Oxford (MA); *m* 1977 (m dis), Andrea Tyminski; 2 s (Matthew b 29 Jan 1979, Dominic b 25 May 1983), 1 da (Sophie b 8 Nov 1981); *Career* trainee S H Benson 1962-63, dir Robert Sharp & Partners 1963-76, dep chm Abbott Mead Vickers BBDO 1976-; *Recreations* golf, skiing; *Clubs* Royal Mid-Surrey Golf; *Style*— Adrian Vickers, Esq; Abbott Mead Vickers BBDO Ltd, 191 Old Marylebone Rd, London NW1 5DW (☎ 071 402 4100, fax 071 935 5883)

VICKERS, Angus Douglas; TD; s of Douglas Vickers (d 1937); *b* 15 Feb 1904; *Educ* Eton, Magdalen Coll Oxford; *m* 1937, Phyllis Maud, da of Norton Francis, CMG (d 1939); *Career* serv RA (TA) 2 Lt 1939, Bt-Col 1953 (despatches); underwriter Lloyd's; JP 1946-68, DL 1950-68 Ross and Cromarty; hon Sheriff Substitute: Inverness, Moray, Nairn, Ross and Cromarty 1949-; Feudal Baron of Tulloch, memb Royal Co of Archers (Queen's Body Guard for Scotland); *Recreations* photography; *Clubs* New (Edinburgh); *Style*— Angus Vickers, Esq, TD; Casa Sta Catarina, Parque Da Praia, Luz 8600 Lagos, Algarve, Portugal (☎ 082 789660)

VICKERS, Hugo Ralph; s of Ralph Cecil Vickers, MC, *qv*; *b* 12 Nov 1951; *Educ* Eton, Strasbourg Univ; *Career* author, reviewer, and broadcaster; worked with London Celebrations Ctee for Queen's Silver Jubilee 1977, admin Great Children's Pty 1979; literary executor to the late Sir Charles Johnston and the late Sir Cecil Beaton; *Books* We Want The Queen (1977), Gladys, Duchess of Marlborough (1979, reissue 1987), Debrett's Book of the Royal Wedding (1981), Cocktails and Laughter (ed,1983), Cecil Beaton - the Authorized Biography (1985, reissue 1986), Vivien Leigh (1988, reissue 1990); *Recreations* photography, reading, music, travel; *Style*— Hugo Vickers, Esq; 62 Lexham Gardens, London W8 5JA

VICKERS, Jeffrey; s of Edward Vickers (d 1984), and Rose, *née* Soloman; *b* 3 June 1937; *Educ* Harold Co Sch Stratford; *m* 1 (m dis 1982), Angela Vickers; 1 s (Andrew b 11 Feb 1967), 1 da (Joanne b 1 May 1965); m 2, 22 July 1982, Barbara, da of James Ebury Clair May, DSM, RN (d 1986); *Career* chm: DPM Group of Companies 1959-, Chromacopy 1979- (fndr and ptnr Chromacopy of America 1979-), Magog Industries 1984-, Vecone Development Corporation 1984-, Clairmont Properties plc 1989-; finalist Prince of Wales Award for Industl Innovation and Prodn; memb Fulham Cons Assoc; FInstD 1983; *Recreations* skiing, sailing, swimming, classical music/opera; *Clubs* Hurlingham; *Style*— Jeffrey Vickers, Esq; DPM Design Consultants Ltd, 63 Poland St, London W1V 3DF (☎ 071 439 7786, fax 071 434 1528)

VICKERS, Baroness (Life Peer UK 1974), of Devonport, Co Devon; Joan Helen Vickers; DBE (1964, MBE 1946); da of late Horace Cecil Vickers and Lilian Monro Lambert Grose; *b* 1907; *Educ* St Monica's Coll Burgh Heath Surrey; *Career* served BRCS in SE Asia; memb LCC 1937-45, with Colonial Office 1946-50, chm Anglo-Indonesian Soc 1958-, pres Int Bureau for Suppression of Traffic in Persons, Inst for Qualified Private Secretaries 1969-, Int Friendship League 1972-, Status of Women Ctee, Europe China Ctee, London Centre for Homeless Young Persons 1977-; MP (C) Devonport 1955-74; Freedom City of Plymouth 1982; Netherlands Red Cross Medal 1946, Polish Medal 1972; *Style*— The Rt Hon the Lady Vickers, DBE; The Manor House, East Chisenbury, Pewsey, Wilts

VICKERS, Prof Michael Douglas Allen; s of George Alexander Vickers (d 1973), and Freda Kathleen Vickers; *b* 11 May 1929; *Educ* Abingdon Sch, Guy's Hosp Med Sch; *m* 17 July 1959, Ann Hazel; 2 s (Andrew b 1958 d 1988, Guy b 1963), 1 da (Charlotte b 1960); *Career* Nat Serv RAMC 1948-49; lectr Royal Postgrad Med Sch 1965-68, conslt in amaesthetics and clinical measurement and hon lectr Univ of Birmingham 1968-76, prof of anaesthetics Coll of Med Cardiff 1976-, med and hosp dir King Khalid Hosp Jeddah Saudi Arabia 1984-85; pres Assoc of Anaesthetists of GB and Ireland 1982-84, former memb Cncl RCS; currently: pres Euro Acad of Anaesthesiology, chm Exec Ctee World Fedn of Socs of Anaesthesiology; FFARACS 1979, fell Coll of Anaesthesiology; *Books* Drugs in Anaesthetic Practice (7 edn, 1991), Medicine for Anaesthetists (2 edn, 1988), Principles of Measurement (3 edn, 1991); *Recreations* music conducting; *Clubs* RSM; *Style*— Prof Michael Vickers; 2 Windsor Close, Radyr, Cardiff CF4 8BZ (☎ 0222 843097); Les Treilles Hautes, 24250 Grolejac, France (☎ 53 17 55 00); Dept of Anaesthetics, Univ of Wales College of Medicine, Heath Park, Cardiff CF4 4XN (☎ 0222 743110)

VICKERS, The Rt Rev Michael Edwin; s of William Edwin Vickers (d 1967), and Florence Alice, *née* Parsons (d 1975); *b* 13 Jan 1929; *Educ* St Lawrence Coll, Worcester Coll Oxford (MA), Cranmer Hall Durham (Dip in Theology); *m* 3 Sept 1960, Janet Cynthia, da of Arthur Herbert Croasdale (d 1944), of Rostead, Cark-in-Cartmel, N Lancashire; 3 da (Lorna b 1963, Fiona b 1965, Nicola b 1966); *Career* Military Serv 1947-49, Warrant Offr II RAEC serving with Br Troops in Austria; co sec Hoares (Ceylon) Ltd Colombo 1952-56; refugee admin Br Cncl for Aid to Refugees 1956-57; asst curate Christ Church Bexleyheath 1959-62, sr chaplain Lee Abbey 1962-67, vicar of Newland Hull 1967-81, area dean Central Hull 1972-81, chm York Diocesan House of Clergy 1975-85, canon and prebendary York 1981-88, archdeacon of the East Riding 1981-88, bishop of Colchester 1988-; Int Rugby Union caps for Ceylon 1954-55; *Recreations* fell walking, photography, gardening; *Style*— The Rt Rev Michael E Vickers; 1 Fitzwalter Rd, Lexden, Colchester, Essex CO3 3SS (☎ 0206 576 648)

VICKERS, Paul Andrew; s of John Frederick Vickers, of Chislehurst, Kent, and Daphne Rosemary, *née* Reed; *b* 20 Jan 1960; *Educ* Alleyn's Sch, Univ of Southampton (LLB); *m* 21 May 1988, Eileen Anne, da of John Danial MacDonald; *Career* called to the Bar Inner Temple 1983; legal mangr London Daily News 1986, co lawyer TV-am plc 1987, co sec TV-am plc 1988; *Recreations* food, wine, reading, films; *Style*— Paul Vickers, Esq; TV-am plc, Hawley Cres, London NW1 8EF

VICKERS, Ralph Cecil; MC (1944); s of Horace Cecil Vickers (d 1944), and Lilian, *née* Grose (d 1922); bro of Baroness Vickers, DBE; *b* 14 Nov 1913; *Educ* Uppingham, Trinity Coll Cambridge; *m* 1, 1950 (m dis 1986), Dulcie, da of John Metcalf; 1 s (Hugo, *qv*), 1 da (Imogen); m 2 1987, Khorshid, da of Prince Abdual Hossain Farman Farmaian; *Career* served 2 Lt 1 RHA 1939-40, Capt Royal Devon Yeo Artillery 1942-44, Actg Maj; chm: Acorn Investment Trust; hon fell commoner St Catharine's Coll Cambridge; *Recreations* fishing, shooting; *Clubs* BRDC; *Style*— Ralph Vickers, Esq, MC; 33 Egerton Terrace, London SW3 2BU (☎ 071 589 5975)

VICKERS, Rex Adrian; s of Henry Allen Hamilton Vickers (d 1972), and Gladys May, *née* Hardy (d 1976); *b* 27 July 1934; *Educ* Chingford GS, SW Essex Tech Coll; *m* 23 July 1960, Gillian Elizabeth, da of Leonard Frank Edmonds, of Oxted, Surrey; 4 s (Mark b 1961 d 1975, Andrew b 1963, James b 1965, Nicholas b 1972), 1 da (Lucy b 1976); *Career* Nat Serv RE 1955-57; dir: Mott Hay of Anderson Conslt Engrs 1979- (assoc 1978-79, dir overseas ptnrships 1979-), chm SE Gp Assoc Conslting Engrs 1988, memb Bd of Examiners ICE; pres Chinghoppers Cricket Club; CEng 1962, FICE 1973, FFB 1980, MConsE 1980; *Recreations* cricket, rugby, football, golf, gardening; *Clubs* MCC; *Style*— Rex Vickers, Esq; Neb Corner, Neb Lane, Old Oxted, Surrey RH8 9JN; Mott MacDonald, 22/26 Wellesley Rd, Croydon CR9 2UL (☎ 081 686 5041, fax 081 6814 5706, telex 917 241 MOTTAY G)

VICKERS, Lt-Gen Sir Richard Maurice Hilton; KCB (1982), LVO (1959), OBE (1970, MBE 1964); s of Lt-Gen Wilmot Gordon Hilton Vickers, CB, OBE, DL (d 1987); *b* 21 Aug 1928; *Educ* ISC Haileybury, RMA Sandhurst; *m* 1957, Gaie Bradley, da of Maj-Gen George Philip Bradley Roberts, CB, DSO, MC; 3 da; *Career* Capt Tank Regt 1954, Equerry to HM The Queen 1956-59, Maj 1961, Lt-Col 1967, CO The Blues and Royals 1968-70, Brig 1972, dep dir Army Trg 1975-77, GOC 4 Armd Div 1977-79, Cmdt RMA Sandhurst 1979-82; dir-gen: Army Trg 1982-83, Winston Churchill Meml Tst 1983-; Gentleman Usher to The Queen; *Clubs* Cavalry and Guards'; *Style*— Lt-Gen Sir Richard Vickers, KCB, LVO, OBE; Little Minterne, Dorchester, Dorset

VICKERY, David William; s of William James Vickery (d 1986), of Dulwich, London, and Margaret Edith, *née* Bidwell; *b* 29 April 1948; *Educ* Borough Beaufoy Tech Sch Lambeth, East Ham Coll, High Wycombe Coll of Tech and Art (Dip in Interior Design); *m* 7 Sept 1968, Jean Margaret; 3 s (Benjamin David 15 May 1970, Thomas William b 13 May 1981, Joseph James b 12 Jan 1987), 4 da (Sarah Louise b 28 June 1971, Lucy Hannah b 28 Feb 1976, Holly Claire b 5 Dec 1978, Fay Maryanne b 31 Aug 1983); *Career* jr designer Conran Associates 1973; designer: Dale Keller and Associates 1977, Fitch & Co 1978, Wrenn & Co 1979; assoc dir Conran Associates 1980, assoc Wrenn & Co 1984, dir Bd The Jenkins Group 1988 (design dir 1986); external examiner: BA (Hons) interior design courses at: Birmingham Poly 1988-91, Nottingham Poly 1991-94; *Recreations* play association football for Wandsworth Borough FC in Southern Olympian league; *Style—* David Vickery, Esq; The Jenkins Group, 9 Tufton St, London SW1P 3QB (☎ 071 799 1090)

VICTOR, Ed; s of Jack Victor (d 1987), of Los Angeles, and Lydia Victor; *b* 9 Sept 1939; *Educ* Dartmouth Coll USA (BA), Pembroke Coll Cambridge (MLitt); *m* 1, 1963, Michelene Dinah, da of Avram Samuels (d 1985); 2 s (Adam b 1964, Ivan b 1966); m 2, 1980, Carol Ryan, da of Clifton Boggs, of Diego, California; 1 s (Ryan b 1984); *Career* ed dir: Weidenfeld & Nicolson 1965-67, Jonathan Cape Ltd 1967-70; sr ed Alfred A Knopf Inc NY USA 1971-72, dir John Farquharson Ltd 1973-77; chm and md Ed Victor Ltd 1977-; *Recreations* opera, tennis, travel; *Clubs* Groucho; *Style—* Ed Victor, Esq; 10 Cambridge Gate, Regents Park, London NW1 (☎ 071 224 3030); Ed Victor Ltd, 162 Wardour St, London W1 (☎ 071 734 4795, fax 494 3400, car ☎ 0836 225173)

VIGARS, Robert Lewis; s of late Francis Henry Vigars, and Susan Laurina May, *née* Lewis; *b* 26 May 1923; *Educ* Truro Cathedral Sch, Univ of London (LLB); *m* 1962, Margaret Ann Christine, yr da of late Sir John Walton, KCIE, CB, MC; 2 da; *Career* WWII, RA and RCS 1942-47, attached Indian Army (Capt) 1944-47, Capt Princess Louise's Kensington Regt TA 1951-54; admitted slr 1948; ptnr Simmons & Simmons London 1951-75; Kensington Borough Cncl 1953-59 (memb London and Home Cos Traffic Advsy Ctee 1956-58 and London Roads (Nugent) Ctee 1958-59), LCC and GLC Kensington (formerly S Kensington) 1955-86; GLC: chm and memb Environmental Planning Ctee 1967-71, chm and memb Strategic Planning Ctee 1971-73, chm 1979-80; memb Standing Conf on London and SE Regnl Planning and SE Econ Planning Cncl 1968-75, ldr of opposition ILEA 1974-79, memb Ct Univ of London 1977-82; Hist Bldgs and Monuments Cmmn for England: commissioner 1986-89, memb London Advsry Ctee 1986- (chm 1986-89); *Recreations* mountain walking; *Clubs* Hurlingham; *Style—* Robert Vigars, Esq; 24 Cope Place, Kensington, London W8 6AA

VIGGERS, Peter John; MP (C) Gosport Feb 1974-; s of John Sidney Viggers (d 1969), of Gosport; *b* 13 March 1938; *Educ* Alverstoke Sch, Portsmouth GS, Trinity Hall Cambridge (MA); *m* 1968, Jennifer Mary, da of Dr R B McMillan (d 1975); 2 s, 1 da; *Career* RAF pilot 1956-58, TA 1963-70; co slr Chrysler (UK) Ltd 1968-70; dir: Edward Bates & Sons Ltd 1972-74, Premier Consolidated Oilfields Ltd 1973-86, Sweetheart International Ltd 1982-86; vice chm Cons Energy Ctee 1977-79 (sec 1975-76), PPS to Slr Gen 1979-83, delegate to N Atlantic Assembly 1980-86, PPS to Chief Sec to Treasy 1983-85, Parly under sec of state for NI (indust min) 1986-89; Underwriting memb of Lloyds 1973-; memb Nat Ctee RNLI 1980-90 (vice pres 1990-); *Style—* Peter Viggers, Esq, MP; House of Commons, London SW1

VIGIER; *see*: de Vigier

VIGORS, Lt-Col Richard de Cliffe; DSO (1945); s of Thomas Mercer de Cliffe Vigors (d 1951), of Coln St Denys Manor Fossebridge, Glos, and Marjorie, *née* Walwyn (d 1965); *b* 24 Nov 1914; *Educ* Marlborough, RMC Sandhurst; *m* 29 Nov 1939, Rosa, da of Edward Mansfield Weatherby (d 1957), of Brill House, Bucks; 2 s (Richard (Robin) b 1941, Martin b 1944); *Career* 2 Lt 5 Royal Inniskilling Dragoon Gds 1934, ADC to GOC 1 Armd Div 1938, BEF France 1940; 1 Lothians & Border Yeo: Sqdn Ldr UK 1941, BELF France 1944; 2 i/c then CO 1 Fife & Forfar Yeomanry BELF 1945, armd corps instr Sch of Combined Ops 1946-48; 5 Royal Inniskilling Dragoon Gds: 2 i/c BAOR 1950, Korea 1951, (despatches) 1952, CO 1952 served Korea Canal Zone of Egypt and UK; Cmdt RAC Tactical Sch Lulworth 1955, ret 1958; gen mangr CSE Aviation Ltd Oxford Airport 1963-67; pres Brill & Dist Royal Br Legion, vice pres Aylesbury Vale Branch CPRE; *Recreations* shooting; *Style—* Lt-Col Richard Vigors, DSO; The Stable House, Brill, Buckinghamshire (☎ 0844 237 567)

VILLA, (Charles) Peter Wolferstan; s of Sqdn Ldr John Villa, DFC (d 1983), and Sheila Margaret, *née* Reed; *b* 14 March 1941; *Educ* Berkhamsted Sch Herts; *m* 26 March 1966, Jennifer Edith, da of Leonard Alfred Croker; 1 s (Paul Wolferstan b 11 Feb 1967), 2 da (Sarah b 29 April 1968, Anne b 5 June 1970); *Career* chief internal auditor Mobil African Services Ltd 1965-68, co sec Cyclax Ltd 1968-70, md Br Island Airways Ltd 1976-80, (fin controller 1970-76, chm 1982-90), Air UK Ltd 1980-82, md IBA Group Ltd; FCA 1964; *Recreations* sailing, flying; *Style—* Peter Villa, Esq; IBA Church Road, Lowfield Heath, Crawley, Sussex RH11 OPQ (☎ 0293 546301, fax 0293 525285)

VILLANUEVA BRANDT, Hon Mrs (Henrietta Julia); er da of 2 Baron Inchyra, *qv*; *b* 21 Sept 1964; *m* 15 Oct 1988, Carlos Manuel Villanueva Brandt, son of Manuel Villanueva, of Caracas, Venezuela

VILLAR, Anthony Sidney Rex; s of Arthur Andrew Sidney Villar (d 1966), and Betty Helen Fyfe-Jamieson Villar, MBE, *née* Cohen; *b* 4 Sept 1934; *Educ* Stowe; *m* 21 Oct 1961, Clare, da of Henry William Pearson-Rogers, CBE; 4 da (Sally b 1962, Francesca b 1965, Caroline b 1968, Alexandra b 1975); *Career* RNVR ret 1955; farmer; former pres: Racehorse Owners Assoc, St Moritz Curling Club; *Recreations* shooting, curling, racing; *Clubs* Turf, Naval, Jockey Club Rooms, St Moritz Curling; *Style—* Anthony Villar, Esq; Tostock Old Rectory, Bury St Edmunds, Suffolk IP30 9NU; Little Haugh Farm, Norton, Bury St Edmunds, Suffolk (☎ 0359 30468)

VILLAR, Richard Neville; s of George Roger Villar, DSC, RN, and Diana Mary, *née* Thomas; *b* 24 April 1953; *Educ* Marlborough, St Thomas' Hosp Medical Sch (BSc, MB BS), Univ of Southampton (MS), Coll of Surgns; *m* 4 June 1983, (Barbara) Louise Bell Villar, da of Patrick George Arthur Ross Lobban; 2 s (Ruairidh b 1985, Angus b 1988); *Career* RAMC 1979-84; conslt Addenbrookes Hosp Cambridge 1988- (sr registrar 1985-88); overseas liaison offr Br Orthopaedic Assoc, memb World Orthopaedic Concern; fell Br Orthopaedic Assoc 1989; FRCS; *Recreations* fell running, martial arts; *Style—* Richard Villar, Esq; Evelyn Hospital, Cambridge (☎ 0223 329136, fax 0223 312348); Addenbrooke's Hospital, Cambridge

VILLIERS, Sir Charles English Hyde; MC (1945); s of Algernon Hyde Villiers (ka 1917, 3 s of Rt Hon Sir Francis Hyde Villiers, GCMG, GCVO, CB, sometime ambass to Belgium and 4 s of 4 Earl of Clarendon), and Beatrix Elinor, *née* Paul (d 1978, m 1919, 4 Baron Aldenham and (2) Hunsdon, by whom she was mother of the present (5 and 3) Lord Aldenham and Hunsdon; *b* 14 Aug 1912; *Educ* Eton, New Coll Oxford; *m* 1, 9 June 1938, Pamela Constance (d 1943), da of Maj John Flower; 1 s (Nicholas b 1939) & 1 s decd; m 2, 26 Oct 1946, Marie José de la Barre, da of Comte Henri de la Barre d'Erquelinnes (d 1961, original Austrian Netherlands cr of 1722 by Letters Patent by Emperor Charles VI; title recognised by William I of The Netherlands (subsequently Belgium) 1829, while a Countship in the Kingdom of Belgium was also conferred on the 5 Count by King Leopold I of the Belgians in 1844; the original guarantee of the eighteenth century dignity, François Léonard de la Barre, was Seigneur de Maurage et d'Erquelinnes and was descended from the noble Hugues de la Barre, on whom the post of trésorier-général de guerre was conferred by Letters Patent in 1536), of Jurbise, Belgium; 2 da (Diana, Anne); *Career* SRO Grenadier Gds 1936-46, Dunkirk 1940, wounded 1942, SOE Yugoslavia, Italy and Austria (parachuted to Tito Partisans 1944) Lt Col cmd 6 SFSS (1945); md: Glyn Mills and Co Bankers 1931-46, Helbert Wagg (Schroder Wagg) 1947-67, Indust Reorganisation Corpn 1967-71; memb Inst Int Etudes Bancaires 1959-76 (pres 1964); chm: Guinness Mahon and Co 1971-76, Br Steel Corpn 1976-80, BSC (Industry) Ltd 1976-89; exec dep chm Guinness Peat Gp 1973-76; dir: Bass Charrington, Courtaulds, Sun Life Assurance, Banque Belge, Financor SA, Darling and Co Pty Ltd; advsr Deloitte Haskins & Sells (accountants) 1982-; chm: Theatre Royal Windsor, Small Business Research Tst; former tstee Royal Opera Tst, former memb NEDC; 1973 Review of NI Ind; chm: NI Finance Corpn till 1975, thirteenth Int Small Business Congress 1986; Order of People of Yugoslavia, Grande Officier de l'Ordre de Leopold II of Belgium (1974); kt 1975; *Recreations* gardening; *Clubs* Special Forces; *Style—* Sir Charles Villiers, MC; Blacknest House, Sunninghill, Berks (☎ 0990 22137)

VILLIERS, Charles Nigel; s of Capt Robert Alexander Villiers, CBE, RN (d 1990), and Elizabeth Mary, *née* Friend (d 1985); *b* 25 Jan 1941; *Educ* Winchester, New Coll Oxford (MA); *m* 7 Aug 1970, Sally Priscilla, da of Capt David Henry Magnay, RN (d 1968); 1 s (Christopher b 1976), 1 da (Caroline b 1974); *Career* Arthur Andersen & Co 1963-67, Industrial & Commercial Finance Corporation 1967-72; County Bank (subsid of National Westminster Bank): dir 1974, dep chief exec 1977, chm and chief exec 1984-86; dir National Westminster Bank 1985-88, chm County National Westminster 1986-88, md corp devpt Abbey National plc 1988-, non exec dir Conder Group plc 1989-; FCA 1976 (ACA 1966); *Recreations* opera, skiing, squash, tennis; *Clubs* Hurlingham; *Style—* Charles Villiers, Esq; 8 Sutherland St, London SW1V 4LB; Abbey House, Baker St, London NW1 6XL

VILLIERS, George Edward; TD; s of Algernon Edward Villiers, of 15 Salterns Lane, Hayling Island, Hants, and Annie Augusta Merewether, *née* Massy (d 1979); *b* 23 Aug 1931; *Educ* Wellington Coll, Brasenose Coll Oxford (MA); *m* 25 Aug 1962, (Anne) Virginia, da of Cuthbert Raymond Forster Threlfall, MC (d 1965), formerly of Warstone House, Bewdley, Worcs; 2 s (Edward b 1963, Henry b 1965), 1 da (Theresa b 1968); *Career* Nat Serv 2 Lt RHA 1949-51, TA 1951-65 (Maj Berks and Westminster Dragoon); stockjobber Moir & Shand 1956-64, memb Stock Exchange 1960; stockbroker: assoc Sorrell Lamb & Co 1964-65, ptnr H Evans Gordon & Co 1966-70, ptnr Beardsley Bishop & Co 1970-83; assoc Cawood Smithie 1983-; pres Oxford Univ Athletic Club 1953-54; Freeman City of London 1977, Liveryman Worshipful Co of Fanmakers 1977; AMSIA; *Recreations* golf, bridge; *Clubs* Boodles, Wentworth; *Style—* George Villiers, Esq, TD; 73 Carlton Hill, London NW8 0EN (☎ 071 624 2778); Cawood Smithie & Co, 22 East Parade, Harrogate, N Yorks HG1 5LT (☎ 0423 530 035, fax 0423 507 312)

VILLIERS, Viscount; George Henry Child Villiers; s and h of 9 Earl of Jersey; *b* 29 Aug 1948; *Educ* Eton, Millfield; *m* 1, 1969 (m dis 1973), Verna, da of K A Stott, of St Mary, Jersey; 1 da (Hon Sophia Georgiana b 25 June 1971); m 2, 1974, Sacha Jane Hooper, da of Peter Hooper Valpy, step da of Harold Briginshaw, and former w of K F Lauder; 1 s, 2 da (Hon Helen Katherine Luisa b 21 Oct 1978, Hon Luciana Dorothea Sacha b 23 July 1981); *Heir* s, Hon George Francis William Child Villiers b 5 Feb 1976; *Career* late 2 Lt 11 Hussars and the Royal Hussars; md Rouse Woodstock (Jersey) Ltd; *Style—* Viscount Villiers; Rouse Woodstock (Jersey) Ltd, 4 Broad St, St Helier, Jersey (☎ 0534 75989, telex 4192418)

VILLIERS, Hon (William) Nicholas Somers Laurence Hyde; ERD, JP (Hants); s of late 6 Earl of Clarendon; *b* 1916; *Educ* Eton, New Coll Oxford; *m* 1939, Mary Cecilia Georgina, da of Maj the Hon Edric Weld-Forester, CVO (6 s of 5 Baron Forester); 3 da; *Career* Maj Grenadier Gds (Supplementary Res), served ME N Africa and Italy 1943-47; OStJ (pres N Wilts Branch), memb Lloyd's, dir and sec Anderson Finch Villiers (Agencies) Ltd (ret); *Recreations* all field sports, cricket, golf; *Clubs* White's; *Style—* Maj The Hon Nicholas Villiers, ERD, JP; Firs Farm, Milbourne, Malmesbury, Wilts SN16 9JA

VILLIERS, Lt-Col Timothy Charles (Tim); s of Brig Richard Villiers, DSO (d 1973), and Nancy Villiers, *née* Godwin; *b* 16 March 1943; *Educ* Eton, RMA Sandhurst; *m* 30 Jan 1971, Maureen Gwendolen, da of The Ven Reginald George Henry McCahearty (d 1966); 2 s (Nicholas b 1976, Richard b 1980), 1 da (Louise b 1973); *Career* offr 15/19 The Kings Royal Hussars 1963-87, CO Royal Hong Kong Regt (The Volunteers) 1983-86; *Recreations* field sports, horses, family life; *Style—* Lt-Col T C Villiers; Kyrle Rd, London SW11 6BB (☎ 071 350 2531)

VINALL, Paul Stuart; s of Maj Ronald Stuart Vinall (d 1988), of Hartford, Cheshire, and Nora Margaret, *née* Savage; *b* 15 March 1946; *Educ* The Kings Sch Chester, Univ Coll Hosp London (MB BS); *m* 30 Mar 1974, Hilary Anne, da of Frank Attenborough, of West Bridgford, Nottingham; 2 s (John b 1978, David b 1984), 1 da (Elizabeth b 1980); *Career* med cadet 2 Lt RAMC 1966-70, conslt obstetrician and gynaecologist The Gen Infirmary at Leeds 1980-, private practioner; exec ctee memb Br Assoc of Perinatal Med, expert advsr: The Med Protection Soc, The Med Def Union; FRCOG 1988; *Recreations* DIY, rowing; *Style—* Paul Vinall, Esq; 6 Adel Pasture, Adel, Leeds, W Yorks LS16 8HU (☎ 0532 611612; The Clarendon Wing, General Infirmary at Leeds, Belmont Grove, Leeds LS2 9NS (☎ 0532 432799)

VINCE, Dr Frank Peter; s of Dr Rupert James Vince (d 1987), of Doncaster, and Olive Myra Vince, *née* King (d 1985); *b* 19 June 1937; *Educ* Doncaster GS, Sidney Sussex Coll Cambridge (BA), The London Hosp Med Sch (MB BChir); *m* 7 Jan 1967, Sheila, da of Dr Laurence Cleveland Martin (d 1981), of Cambridge; 1 s (Richard James Martin b 1970), 1 da (Joanna b 1968); *Career* med registrar Addenbrookes Hosp Cambridge 1964-66, lectr and sr registrar The London Hosp Whitechapel 1967-71 (house offr 1962-63), conslt physician Coventry Hosp 1971-, princ med offr Equity and Law Insurance soc 1982-, sr lectr in postgrad med Univ of Warwick 1985-; various pubns in med jls on subjects of diabetes, endocrinology and problems of growth and development; coll tutor and examiner for RCP, pres Coventry branch Br Diabetic Assoc, chm Coventry Friends of the Home Farm Tst, co-opted memb Coventry City Cncl; memb: Coventry Health Authy, Coventry Ed Authy 1981-90, Soc for Endocrinology; FRSM, FRCP 1979; *Recreations* music; *Style—* Dr Frank Vince; 42 Kenilworth Rd, Coventry CV3 6PG (☎ 0203 410347); Walsgrave Hospital, Coventry (☎ 0203 602020)

VINCENT, Helen, Lady; Helen Millicent; da of Field Marshal Sir William Robertson, 1 Bt, GCB, GCMG, GCVO, DSO; sis of 1 Baron Robertson of Oakridge, GCB, GBE, KCMG, KCVO, DSO, MC; *b* 17 Dec 1905; *m* 18 Oct 1938, Sir Lacey Eric Vincent, 2 Bt (d 1963); 1 s (Sir William Vincent, 3 Bt), 1 da; *Style—* Helen, Lady Vincent; 44 Eresby House, Rutland Gate, London SW7 (☎ 071 589 4217)

VINCENT, Rev Dr John James; s of David Vincent (d 1976), and Ethel Beatrice, *née* Gadd; *b* 29 Dec 1929; *Educ* Manchester GS, Richmond Coll London (BD), Drew Univ NJ USA (STM), Univ of Basel (DTheol); *m* 4 Dec 1958, Grace Johnston, da of Rev Wilfred Stafford; 2 s (Christopher b 1961, James b 1966), 1 da (Faith b 1964); *Career* Sgt RAMC 1947-79; min Manchester and Salford Mission 1956-62; supt min: Rochdale Mission 1962-69, Sheffield Inner City Ecumenical Mission 1970-; visiting prof of theol:

Univ of Boston Autumn 1969, NY Theol Seminary Spring 1970; dir Urban Theol Unit Sheffield 1970-, visiting prof of theol Drew Univ NJ 1977; chm NW CND 1957-65; founding memb and leader Ashram Community Tst 1967-, chm Urban Mission Training Assoc of GB 1976-77 and 1984-91, memb Cncl Christian Orgns for Social/Political and Economic Change 1981-89, exec Assoc of Adult Theol Educn 1984-90, memb Studiorum Novi Testamenti Societas 1961, hon lectr Biblical Studies Dept Univ of Sheffield (1990-), co-ordinator British Liberation Theology Project (1990-); *Books* Christ in a Nuclear World (1962), Christ and Methodism (1965), Secular Christ (1968), The Race Race (1970), The Jesus Thing (1973), Alternative Church (1976), Starting All Over Again (1981), OK, Let's be Methodists (1984), Radical Jesus (1986), Britain in the 90's (1989), Discipleship in the 90's (1991); *Recreations* writing, jogging; *Style—* The Rev Dr John Vincent; 239 Abbeyfield Rd, Sheffield, S4 7AW (☎ 0742 436688); Urban Theology Unit, 210 Abbeyfield Rd, Sheffield S4 7AZ (☎ 0742 435342)

VINCENT, Paul Howard; s of Stanley Howard Vincent (d 1975); *b* 9 April 1924; *Educ* Bishops Stortford Coll, St John's Coll Cambridge; *m* 1957, Jean, *née* Ford; 1 s, 2 da; *Career* RAF 1942-47; dir: Vincent Fin Co (Yeovil) Ltd, Binding and Payne Ltd, H and C Services Ltd, CB Morgan (Shaftesbury) Ltd, S M V Commercials (Wells) Ltd, Sugg-Vincent Ltd, Vincents Self-Drive Hire Ltd; *Style—* Paul Vincent, Esq; Watermeadows, Turners Barn Lane, Yeovil, Somerset (☎ 0935 23201)

VINCENT, Paul Stephen; s of Ralph Henry Morley Vincent (d 1984) of New Malden, Surrey, and Gladys, *née* Jones; *b* 8 April 1945; *Educ* Stonleigh West Co Tech Sch; *m* 19 Sept 1970, Lynne Patricia, da of Stanley Lawrence Connors, of New Malden, Surrey; 1 s (Edward b 1986), 3 da (Rebecca b 1977, Victoria b 1979, Helena b 1984 d 1985); *Career* audit mangr Cape & Dagleish, fin dir Metal Bulletin plc (formerly Metal Bulletin Ltd) 1980- (accountant 1972, co sec 1973); *Recreations* DIY; *Style—* Paul Vincent, Esq; Metal Bulletin plc, Park House, Park Terrace, Worcester Park, Surrey KT4 7HY (☎ 081 330 4311, fax 081 337 8943, telex 21383 METBUL G)

VINCENT, Gen Sir Richard Frederick; GBE (1990), KCB (1984), DSO (1972); s of Frederick Vincent and late Frances Elizabeth, *née* Coleshill; *b* 23 Aug 1931; *Educ* Aldenham, RMC of Sci Shrivenham; *m* 1955, Jean Paterson, da of late Kenneth Stewart; 1 s, 1 da (and 1 s decd); *Career* Cmdt RMC of Sci 1980-83, Master Gen of the Ordnance MOD 1983-87; Col Cmdt: REME 1983-87, RA 1983; Hon Col: 100 (Yeo) Field Regt RA (Volunteers) TA, 12 Air Def Regt; chief of the Def Staff 1991- (vice chief 1987-91); pres: Combined Servs Winter Sports Assoc 1983-90, Army Skiing Assoc 1983-87; memb Ct Cranfield Inst of Technol 1981-83; govr Aldenham Sch 1987; Kermit Roosevelt lectr USA 1988; Hon DSc Cranfield 1985; FIMechE 1990; FRAeS 1990; *Recreations* travel, reading, film making, theatre; *Style—* Gen Sir Richard Vincent, GBE, KCB, DSO; Chief of the Defence Staff, MOD Main Building (Room 6177), Whitehall, London SW1A 2HB (☎ 071 218 9000)

VINCENT, Sir William Percy Maxwell; 3 Bt (UK 1936), of Watton, Co Norfolk; s of Sir Lacey Vincent, 2 Bt (d 1963), and Helen, Lady Vincent, *qv*; *b* 1 Feb 1945; *Educ* Eton, New York Inst of Finance; *m* 1976, Christine Margaret, da of Rev Edward Gibson Walton (d 1989), of Petersfield; 3 s; *Heir* s, Edward Mark William Vincent b 6 March 1978; *Career* late 2 Lt Irish Gds, served Malaya; dir Save & Prosper Investment Tst 1980-85, Touche Remnant & Co 1985, md and invest dir Touche Remnant Co 1986, dir Société Genérale Touche Remnant 1989; *Recreations* sailing, skiing; *Clubs* Household Div Yacht, City Yacht; *Style—* Sir William Vincent, Bt; Whistlers, Buriton, Petersfield, Hants (☎ 0730 63532)

VINCENZI, Penny; da of Stanley George Hannaford (d 1985), of New Milton, Hants, and Mary Blanche, *née* Hawkey (d 1987); *b* 10 April 1939; *Educ* Notting Hill and Ealing HS; *m* 27 May 1960, Paul Robert Vincenzi, s of Julius Vincenzi, of Essex; 4 da (Polly b 1963, Sophie b 1965, Emily b 1975, Claudia b 1979); *Career* freelance journalist and author; contrib to : Cosmopolitan, Nova, Honey, Options, Over 21, You Magazine, Daily Mail, The Times, Sunday Mirror, Sunday Times, Mail on Sunday; *Books* The Complete Liar (1979), There's One Born Every Minute (1985), Old Sins (1989); *Recreations* family life, surfing, riding, ballet; *Style—* Mrs Penny Vincenzi

VINCZE, Ernest Anthony; *b* 1942; *Educ* BSc; *Career* dir of photography; started in the field of documentaries winning several awards incl: Flaherty Award, Prix Italia, Golden Gate San Francisco, trento, BAFTA; pt/t tutor of Cinematography RCA and Nat Film Sch, nominated Br Acad Award for Best Cinematography 1984 and 1989; features, serials and made-for-TV movies incl: Business As Usual, Escape From Sobibor, Shangai Surprise, Biggles, Behind Enemy Lines, Hitler's SS, A Woman of Substance, Kennedy, Scrubbers, Cream In My Coffee, Roseland, Winstanley, Tell Me No Lies, The Secret Policeman's Ball, A Very British Coup (Emmy Award 1988); memb Br Soc Cinematographers 1978, ACTT; *Style—* Ernest A Vincze, Esq; 25 Marville Rd, London SW6 7BB (☎ 071 385 3413); Agent: CCA Personal Management, 4 Court Lodge, 48 Sloane Square, London SW1 8AT (☎ 071 730 8857)

VINE, Brian John; s of Frank Alexander Vine, of St Leonard's-on-sea, Sussex, and Edith Ellen, *née* Sharp; *b* 11 July 1932; *Educ* Winton House, St Dunstans Coll London; *m* 18 Sept 1972, Beverley Jacqueline, da of Dr Alan Wardale, of Dunedin, NZ; 1 s (Alexander Charles b 1979); *Career* Nat Serv RAF (2 yrs) Zimbabwe; home reporter News Chronicle 1956-60; Daily Express 1960-84: William Hickey Column 1960-69, Chief of Bureau, New York (This is America columnist) 1969-73, foreign ed 1973-74, asst ed 1974-84; Daily Mail: foreign ed 1985-86, asst ed 1986-87, managing ed 1987-; memb Press Cncl, judge Br Press Award; *Books* Zola; *Recreations* racehorse ownership, game shooting, tennis; *Clubs* Turf, Scribes, University NY; *Style—* Brian Vine, Esq; 14 Lisgar Terrace, London W14 (☎ 071 602 3298); Lower Farm Cottage, Haywards Bottom, nr Hungerford, Berkshire; Northcliffe House, Kensington High St, London W8

VINE, Dennis; s of Harold Edward Vine (d 1966), of Ealing London, and Mary Maud Vine (now Nicholls); *b* 24 April 1937; *Educ* Penyrenglyn Treherbert S Wales, Drayton Manor GS Ealing W London, Regent St Poly; *m* 12 June 1965, Anne, da of HS Hawley; 1 s (Richard Edward b 9 March 1967), 1 da Joanna b 6 March 1969); *Career* surveyor; Ealing Borough Cncl 1954, Westminster City Cncl 1960; Vigers Chartered Surveyors: joined 1962, ptnr responsible for Building Surveying 1969, jt sr ptnr 1983, sr ptnr 1990; RICS: memb 1962-, vice chm Educn and Membership Ctee, memb Gen Cncl and Building Surveyors Divnl Cncl, chm Continuing Professional Devpt Sub Ctee, pres Building Surveyors Div 1987-88; chm: Inst and Coll Confs, Advsy Bd Coll of Estate Mgmnt Dip in Building Conservation; external examiner various polys; Freeman City of London 1987, Liveryman Worshipful Co of London Surveyors 1987; *Recreations* tennis, squash, golf; *Clubs* RAC, Bourne (Farnham, Surrey); *Style—* Dennis Vine, Esq; Vigers, 4 Fredericks Place, Old Jewry, London EC2R 8DA (☎ 071 606 7601, fax 071 606 1772, car 0836 773049)

VINE, Col (Roland) Stephen; s of Joseph Soutter Vine (d 1944), and Margaret Mary Josephine, *née* Moylan (d 1976); *b* 26 Dec 1910; *Educ* Southend-on-Sea Boys' HS, Univ of London and Guys Hosp Med Sch (BSc, MRCS, LRCP); *m* 14 Dec 1935, Flora Betty, da of Charles Strutton Brookes, MBE (d 1960), of Dovercourt, Essex; 3 da (Jill (Mrs De Bretton-Gordon) b 8 Jan 1937, Sallie (Mrs Maclay) b 10 May 1939, Joanna (Mrs Marley) b 19 Aug 1950); *Career* short serv cmmn Lt RAMC 1934, Capt 1935, regular cmmn 1939; served in OC mil hosps in India 1936-39, war serv N Africa 1939-44, OC HDS Dover 1944, ADMS Northern France 1944, CO 174 (Highland) Field Ambulance Europe 1944-45 (wounded and invalided to UK), CO 4 Field Ambulance Salonika 1946-47, RAM Coll Millbank 1947-48, qualified as specialist in pathology 1949; asst dir pathology: Northern Cmd UK 1949-51, Canal Zone Egypt 1951-52, Scottish Cmd 1954; OC David Bruce mil hosp Malta 1952-54, Temp Col OC mil hosp Catterick Camp 1955-60, ret 1960 awarded rank of Hon Col; Inspr under the Cruelty to Animals Act at the HO 1960 (chief inspr 1962-75), ret 1975; fndr fell Coll of Pathologists 1962, memb Cncl Res & Def Soc 1976-79, memb Res Team and conslt Biorex Res Laboratories 1976-81; church warden High Hurstwood Trinity Church E Sussex 1970-80; FZS; *Style—* Col Stephen Vine; Shola, Fielden Road, Crowborough, East Sussex TN6 1TR (☎ 0892 661 381)

VINE-LOTT, Anthony Keith; s of Keith Miles Vine-Lott, of Windbreak House, 28 Higham Lane, Gee Cross, Hyde, Cheshire, and Jessie, *née* Meadowcroft; *b* 24 Oct 1947; *Educ* King Edward VI Macclesfield Cheshire, Sheffield Poly (HND); *m* 1, 13 Dec 1969 (m dis 1980), Barbara Elaine; 1 da (Anne Marie Elizabeth b 4 Jan 1974); m 2, 18 June 1982, Dr Ailsa Vine-Lott, da of Capt Frank Edward Webb, of 25 Meridian Ct, Singleton, Ashford, Kent; *Career* engrg scholarship with Wimpey UK Ltd 1966-70, mktg mangr in UK computer software co's 1970-76, md Surlodge Ltd 1976-78, field servs mangr Honeywell UK Ltd (taken over by Gen Electric USA) 1978-81, mktg servs dir WANG UK Ltd 1981-86, chm The Cleaver Co, md Barclays Stockbrokers Ltd 1988-; Lord of the Manor of Beckett; FCIM 1990; *Recreations* yachting, swimming, travel; *Clubs* The Naval; *Style—* Anthony Vine-Lott, Esq; 63 Chiswick High Rd, Chiswick, London W4 2LT (☎ 081 994 1742); Barclays Stockbrokers Ltd, 21 St Thomas' Street, London SE1 (☎ 071 403 4833, fax 071 407 2745)

VINELOTT, Hon Mr Justice; Hon Sir John Evelyn Vinelott; QC (1968); s of Frederick George Vine-Lott (d 1984), and Vera Lilian Mockford (d 1957); *b* 15 Oct 1923; *Educ* Queen Elizabeth's GS Faversham, Queens' Coll Cambridge (MA); *m* 1956, Sally Elizabeth, da of His Hon Sir Walker Kelly Carter (decd), *qv*; 2 s, 1 da; *Career* served WW II Sub-Lt RNVR; barr Gray's Inn 1953, High Court judge (Chancery Div) 1978-; chm Insolvency Rules Advsy Ctee 1984-; kt 1978; *Clubs* Garrick; *Style—* The Hon Mr Justice Vinelott; 22 Portland Rd, London W11 (☎ 071 727 4778)

VINEN, Prof William Frank; s of Gilbert Vinen (d 1945), and Olive Maud, *née* Roach (d 1971); *b* 15 Feb 1930; *Educ* Watford GS, Clare Coll Cambridge (MA, PhD); *m* 16 Sept 1960, Susan Mary Audrey, da of Lt-Col Reginald Arthur Master (d 1954); 1 s (Richard Charles b 1963), 1 da (Catherine Susanna b 1965); *Career* RAF 1948-49; demonstrator Dept of Physics and fell Pembroke Coll Cambridge 1958-62 (res fell Clare Coll 1955-58), visiting prof Univ of Illinois 1964, Poynting prof of physics Univ of Birmingham 1974- (prof of physics 1962-74); memb: bds and ctees SERC, Visiting Ctee Open Univ, Cncl Royal Soc 1976-77, Governing Body Coventry Poly 1984-89, Cncl Inst of Physics 1980; hon fell Coventry Poly 1989; FRS 1973, FInstP 1980; *Recreations* good food; *Style—* Prof William Vinen, FRS; 52 Middle Park Road, Birmingham B29 4BJ (☎ 021 475 1328); School of Physics and Space Research, University of Birmingham, Birmingham B15 2TT (☎ 021 414 4667, fax 021 414 6709)

VINER, Gordon; s of Joseph Viner (d 1982), of Liverpool, and Muriel, *née* Sharp; *b* 14 Nov 1940; *Educ* Kings Sch Chester; *m* 9 Oct 1966, Helen Frances, da of Philip Waters and Beatrice, *née* Cohen, of London; 3 s (Andrew b 1970, Paul b 1970, Richard b 1974), 1 da (Michelle b 1972); *Career* CA; trainee CA Chester 1957-63, H & J Supplies Ltd Chester 1963, ptnr Lerman Quaile Birkenhead 1966-; former chm: Chester and N Wales CAs Students Assoc, Merseyside branch Inst of Taxation 1984-87; chm Chester Jewish Community, memb MENSA; FCA 1963, ATII 1965; *Recreations* golf, tennis, bridge, ball games; *Clubs* Upton-by-Chester Golf, Chester Tennis; *Style—* Gordon Viner, Esq; 5 Nield Court, Upton-By-Chester, Cheshire CH2 1DN (☎ 0244 383 745); Lerman Quaile, 17 Brandon St, Birkenhead, Merseyside L41 5HN (☎ 051 647 7171, fax 051 666 2585)

VINER, Ruben; OBE; s of Adolf Viner (d 1953); *b* 21 Aug 1907; *Educ* King Edward VII Sheffield; *m* 1932, Elaine Rhoda, *née* Aubrey; 2 children; *Career* pres Viners Ltd; underwriting memb of Lloyd's; pres and treas Sheffield C of C 1965, pres Sheffield Cutlery Manufacturers' Assoc 1958-61, Guardian of the Assay; chm: Talbot Tsts, Kelham Is Industl Museum Tst; Freeman Worshipful Co of Cutlers, Liveryman Worshipful Co of Clockmakers; *Recreations* gardening, walking; *Style—* Ruben Viner Esq, OBE; 4 Ivy Park Ct, Ivy Park Rd, Sheffield S10 3LA (☎ 0742 306036)

VINES, HE Eric Victor; CMG (1984), OBE (1981); s of late Henry E Vines; *b* 28 May 1929; *Educ* St Dunstan's Coll London, St Catharine's Coll Cambridge (MA); *m* 1953, Ellen-Grethe Ella Küppers; 1 s; *Career* Nat Serv Army 1947-49; Cwlth Rels Offr 1952: Colombo 1954-55, 1 sec Singapore 1958-61, Canberra 1961-65; Dip Serv Admin Office 1965-68, 1 sec info Mexico City 1968-70, cnsllr exec sec-gen SEATO conf London 1971, head Cultural Exchange Dept FCO 1971-74; cnsllr (commercial) Tel Aviv 1974-77, Stockholm 1977-80; consul-gen Barcelona 1980-83, ambass: Maputo 1984-85, Montevideo 1986-89; *Style—* HE Mr Eric Vines, CMG, OBE; British Embassy, Montevideo, Uruguay; c/o Foreign & Commonwealth Office, King Charles St, London SW1A 2AH

VINEY, Hon Mrs (Anne Margaret); *née* Morton; JP; da of Baron Morton of Henryton, PC, MC (Life Peer, d 1973); *b* 14 June 1926; *Educ* Priorsfield; *m* 1947, Peter Andrew Hopwood Viney, DFC; 1 s, 2 da; *Career* barr Lincoln's Inn 1979; former cllr Kensington & Chelsea Borough Cncl 1960-62; publicity worker with Int Wool Secretariat 1945-47; chm Consumer Protection Advsy Ctee 1973-, jt co-chm Hackney Juvenile Court, chm Inner London Juvenile Court panel 1970 (appointed to panel 1961) (ret 1987); co-fndr (sec 1962-69) London Adventure Playground Assoc 1962; *Style—* The Hon Mrs Viney, JP; Worth House, Worth Matravers, Dorset (☎ 092 943 248)

VINK; *see*: de Vink

VINNICOMBE, John; s of Francis William Vinnicombe (d 1964), of St Saviour, Jersey, CI, and Marjorie Florence, nee Shuff (d 1972); *b* 17 Jan 1930; *Educ* Godalming GS, St Johns Coll Cambridge (MA), St Thomas's Hosp Med Sch (MB MChir); *m* 12 July 1958, Diana Mary, da of Maj-Gen Dennis Charles Tarrant Swan, CB, CBE, of Lordington, Chichester; 3 da (Sarah b 1959, Amanda b 1961, Jane b 1964); *Career* Nat Serv Capt RAEC 1948-49; conslt urological surgn: Portsmouth Dist Hosp 1966, King Edward VII Hosp Midhurst 1970; Br Assoc of Urological Surgns: memb Cncl 1976-79 and 1985-88, hon sec 1981-84, hon treas 1985-86; former pres Portsmouth Div BMA 1981-82; Freeman City of London, Liveryman Worshipful Co of Apothecaries 1972; FRCS, FRSM (pres Urology section 1987-88); *Recreations* travel, sailing, skiing; *Style—* John Vinnicombe, Esq; Hindon House, Emsworth, Hants, (☎ 0243 37 2528); Department of Urology, Saint Mary's Hospital, Portsmouth, Hants, PO3 6AD (☎ 0705 822 331 Extn 2302)

VINSON, Baron (Life Peer UK 1985), of Roddam Dene, Co Northumberland; Nigel Vinson; LVO (1979), DL (1990); s of Ronald Vinson (d 1976), of Nettlestead Place, Wateringbury, Kent, and his 2 w, Bettina Myra Olivia (d 1966), da of Dr Gerald Southwell-Sanders; *b* 27 Jan 1931; *Educ* RNC Pangbourne; *m* 10 June 1972, Yvonne Ann, da of Dr John Olaf Collin, of Forest Row, Sussex; 3 da (Hon Bettina Claire b 1974, Hon Rowena Ann b 1977, Hon Antonia Charlotte b 1979); *Career* Lt Queen's Royal Regt 1949-51; donor Martin Mere Wildfowl Tst; fndr Plastic Coatings Ltd (chm 1952-72); dir: Sugar Bd 1968-75, British Airports Authority 1973-80, Centre for Policy

Studies 1974-80; dep chm: Electra Investment Trust 1975- (dep dir 1990), Barclay's Bank UK 1982-88; memb Cncl King George V Jubilee Tst 1974-78, hon dir Queen's Silver Jubilee Tst 1974-78: dep chm CBI Smaller Firms Cncl 1979-84, chm: Cncl for Small Industries in Rural Areas 1980-82, Newcastle Technol Centre 1985-88, Rural Devpt Cmmn 1980-90, Tstees Inst of Econ Affrs 1987; pres Industrial Participation Assoc 1979-90 (chm 1971-78); FBIM, FRSA; *Books* Personal and Portable Pensions for All (1985); *Recreations* horses, objets d'art, crafts, farming; *Clubs* Boodle's; *Style—* The Rt Hon Lord Vinson, LVO; 34 Kynance Mews, London SW7 4QR (☎ 071 937 4183)

VINTON, Anna-Maria; da of Charles Dugan-Chapman, and Mary Elizabeth Chapman; *b* 17 Nov 1947; *Educ* Chatelard Sch Les Avants Switzerland, Guildhall Sch of Music and Drama; *m* 1, 1970 (m dis 1982), Anthony Greatrex Hawser; m 2, Alfred Merton Vinton; 1 s (George Oliver b 21 Oct 1987), 1 da (Isabel Anusha b 3 Dec 1985); *Career* theatre agent: Cochrane Theatrical Agency 1967-68, Norma Skemp Agency 1969-70; ran private property co 1970-72; fndr and mangr: The Reject Linenshop Beauchamp Place London SW1 1972, The Reject Shops plc 1973 (currently jt chm); dir: Kiki McDonough Ltd, Marie Curie Ltd (memb Advsy Gp); memb: Devpt Ctee Eng Shakespeare Co, Northamptonshire Ctee Wishing Well Appeal 1987-88; *Recreations* skiing, riding, gardening, theatre, reading; *Style—* Mrs Anna-Maria Vinton; Stoke Albany House, nr Market Harborough, Leics; 37 Thurloe Square, London SW7; The Reject Shop plc, RMC House, Townmead Rd, London SW6 (☎ 071 736 7474)

VIRANI, Nazmudin Gulamhusein; s of Gulamhusein Virani, and Fatimah Virani; *b* 2 March 1948; *Educ* Aga Khan Sch Kampala Uganda; *m* 18 July 1990, Yasmin Abdul Rasul Ismail; 2 s, 1 da; *Career* left Uganda for UK 1972, fndr of Virani Group of Cos 1972; chm and chief exec Control Securities plc; tstee: Princes' Youth Business Tst, Home Farm Tst for Mentally Disabled; Freeman City of London; Hon LLD Univ of Warwick; *Recreations* cricket, travel, philanthrophy; *Style—* Nazmudin Virani, Esq; 47-51 Gillingham St, London SW1V 1PS (☎ 071 828 6405)

VIRDI, Prof Kuldeep Singh; s of Gurdial Singh Virdi, of Faridabad, India, and Sital Kaur, *née* Hoogan; *b* 19 May 1944; *Educ* Univ of Agra (BSc), IIT Bombay (BTech), Univ of Roorkee (ME), Univ of London (PhD, DiC); *m* 24 March 1975, Anne Margaret, da of Raymond Robert Pope, of Sydney, Aust; 1 da (Nina, b 1979); *Career* res fell and scientist Structural Engrg Res Centre Roorkee India 1965, asst engr Engrs India Ltd New Delhi Indai 1970, Constrado res fell dept of civil enginr Imperial Coll London 1973 (res asst 1970), lectr in structural engrg dept of civil engrg Univ of Melbourne Aust 1976, prof of struct engrg and dep dean Sch of engrg City Univ London 1988- (lectr engrg 1979, reader 1983, head of dept 1986-), external examiner Poly of Central London 1989-; FICE 1982, FISTruct E 1982; *Recreations* theatre, music, badminton, travel; *Style—* Prof Kuldeep Virdi; Dept of Civil Engineering, City University, London EC1V OHB (☎ 071 253 4399, fax 071 250 0837)

VIRGILS, Katherine Ruth; da of Russell Virgils, of San Marcos, Texas, and Shirley, *née* Koppen; *b* 28 Aug 1954; *Educ* Brighton Art Coll, Ravensbourne Art Coll (BA), RCA (MA); *m* 1990, Peter Raymond Camp, s of Maurice Raymond Camp; 1 s (Louis Elliot Virgils b 4 July 1990); *Career* artist; major solo exhibitions: Head Faces Elevations (Camden Arts Centre) 1983, Spirit Syntax Structure (Thumb Gallery London) 1986, Moguls Myths Minatures (Thumb Gallery London) 1988, Ruth Segel Gallery NY 1988, Tales of Tigers and Temples (Thumb Gallery London) 1989; gp exhibitions: Victoria and Albert Museum 1981, Hayward Annual London 1982, LA Int Art Fair 1987-90; important works in the collections: Contemporary Art Soc, Sainsbury Collection, Crafts Cncl Collection, Merrill Lynch, Calvin Klein, Glaxo Export HQ, IBM, BR, Volvo HQ, Herbert Smith, Lloyd Bank HQ (Crannons Marsh Bristol), Prudential Insurance Co, Harlech TV, Honeywell, Sir Terence Conran, Mitsui, Burton, Woolwich Building Soc HQ, Fitch & Co; *Awards*: Crafts Cncl grant 1982, Oxford Arts Cncl award 1984, Sainsbury prize (Chelsea Fair) 1985; memb: Royal Coll Soc 1982, Crafts Cncl 1983, Ranthamhore Soc 1989; *Recreations* travel in India, exploring Indian forts and wildlife; *Style—* Ms Katherine Virgils; 43 Cambridge Gardens, Notting Hill Gate, London (☎ 081 968 4938)

VISSER, John Bancroft; s of Gilbert Frederick Visser (d 1964), of London, and Ethel Frances Elizabeth, *née* Smith; *b* 29 Jan 1928; *Educ* Mill Hill Sch London, New Coll Oxford (BA, MA); *m* 3 Sept 1955, (Astrid) Margareta, da of Sven Ragnar Olson (d 1976), of London, Cdr of Royal (Swedish) Vasa Order; 2 s (Andrew b 1961, Michael b 1964), 1 da (Helen b 1962); *Career* Nat Serv 1946-48, 2 Lt RA; Civil Serv: entered 1951, princ Miny of Supply 1956 (asst princ 1951), Miny of Aviation 1959, Admin Staff Coll Henley 1965, asst sec 1965, Miny of Technol 1967, RCDS 1970, Civil Serv Dept 1971, procurement exec MOD 1971, sec of Nat Def Industs Cncl 1971-74, under sec 1974, dir admin SERC (formerly SRC) 1974-88, ret 1988; chm Mgmnt Ctee Cirencester CAB, sec Churn Valley Decorative and Fine Arts Soc, ordinary memb Cirencester Civic Soc; *Recreations* classical music, antique furniture and longcase clocks, gardening; *Clubs* Old Millhillians; *Style—* John Visser, Esq; Rosslyn, 3 Berkeley Road, Cirencester, Glos GL7 1TY (☎ 0285 652626)

VITA-FINZI, Prof Claudio; s of Paolo Vita-Finzi (d 1986), of Rome, and Nadia, *née* Touchmalova (d 1952); *b* 21 Nov 1936; *Educ* Univ of Cambridge (BA, MA, PhD, DSc); *m* 1 May 1969, Penelope Jean, da of Robert Lawrence Angus (d 1949), of Prestwick; 1 s (Leo b 1970); *Career* res fell St John's Coll Cambridge 1961-64, prof UCL 1987- (lectr 1964-74, reader 1974-87); *Books* The Mediterranean Valleys (1969), Recent Earth History (1973), Archaeological Sites (1978), Recent Earth Movements (1986); *Recreations* music; *Style—* Prof Claudio Vita-Finzi; 22 South Hill Park, London NW3 2SB (☎ 071 794 4415); Univ Coll, Dept of Geological Sciences, Gower St, London WC1E 6BT (☎ 071 387 7050, fax 071 387 8057, telex 296273 UCLENG G)

VITEZ, Charles Oscar; s of Samuel Thomas Vitez (d 1972), and Suzanne Vitez; *b* 24 Oct 1948; *Educ* Westminster City Sch; *Career* CA 1972, ptnr KPMG Peat Marwick McLintock 1987- (joined as taxation specialist 1973); currently tax ed International Fund Forum and Micropal International Fund Guide; *Books* Taxation of UK Life Assurance Business (1986); *Style—* Charles Vitez, Esq; KPMG Peat Marwick McLintock, 1 Puddle Dock, Blackfriars, London EC4V 3PD (☎ 071 236 8000, fax 071 248 6552)

VIVIAN, 5 Baron (UK 1841); Sir Anthony Crespigny Claud Vivian; 5 Bt (UK 1828); s of 4 Baron Vivian, DSO (d 1940); *b* 4 March 1906; *Educ* Eton; *m* 1930, Victoria (d 1985), da of late Capt Henry Gerard Laurence Oliphant, DSO, MVO, RN; 2 s, 1 da; *Heir* s, Brig the Hon Nicholas Crespigny Laurence Vivian; *Career* WWII 1939-40: RA, Special Constabulary, War correspondent; *Style—* The Rt Hon the Lord Vivian; 154 Coleherne Court, London SW5 (☎ 071 373 1050)

VIVIAN, Rev (Thomas) Keith; s of William Vivian (d 1945), of Cornwall, and Gladys Irene, *née* Thomas (d 1979); *b* 19 Feb 1927; *Educ* Truro Sch, St John's Coll Cambridge (MA); *m* 2 Aug 1952, Audrey Campbell, da of Norman Cowan, of Newcastle upon Tyne; 1 s (Jonathan Mark b 1954), 1 da (Jenefer Clare b 1956); *Career* schoolmaster: Christ's Hosp Horsham 1949-54, Rugby Sch 1954-62; headmaster Lucton Sch Leominster 1962-84; ordained: deacon 1980, priest 1981; priest i/c Chew Stoke, Norton Malreward and Nempnett Thrubwell 1985, Rector 1988-; noted Univ and Co Rugby Football player 1945-57; *Recreations* fishing, golf watching sport, walking; *Clubs* Hawkes (Cambridge), Rotary, Burnham & Berrow Golf; *Style—* The Rev Keith Vivian; The Rectory, Chew Stoke, Bristol BS18 8TV (☎ 0272 332554)

VIVIAN, Hon Mrs Douglas; Mary Alice; da of late Francis John Gordon Borthwick; *m* 1943, Lt-Cdr the Hon Douglas David Edward Vivian, DSC, RN (d 1973, yr s of 4 Baron Vivian); 5 da; *Style—* The Hon Mrs Douglas Vivian; Monastery Garden, Edington, Westbury, Wilts

VIVIAN, Brig the Hon Nicholas Crespigny Laurence; s and h of 5 Baron Vivian; *b* 11 Dec 1935; *Educ* Eton, Madrid Univ; *m* 1, 1960 (m dis 1972), Catherine Joyce, da of James Kenneth Hope, CBE, DL; 1 s, 1 da; m 2, 1972, Carol, da of F Alan Martineau, MBE, JP, of Valley End House, Chobham, Surrey; 2 da; *Career* 16/5 The Queen's Royal Lancers, ret 1990; *Clubs* White's, Cavalry and Guards'; *Style—* Brig the Hon Nicholas Vivian

VIVIAN, Hon Richard Anthony Hussey; s and h of 4 Baron Swansea; *b* 24 Jan 1957; *Educ* Eton, Univ of Durham (BA); *Career* journalist; *Clubs* North London Rifle; *Style—* The Hon Richard Vivian; Flat 3, 37 Dafforne Rd, London SW17 8TY (☎ 081 682 0603)

VIVIAN, Hon Victor Anthony Ralph Brabazon; yr s of 5 Baron Vivian and Victoria Ruth Mary Rosamund, *née* Oliphant (d 1985); *b* 26 March 1940; *Educ* Ludgrove, Nautical Coll Pangbourne, Southampton Univ; *m* 1966, Inger Johanne, da of Advokat Per Gulliksen (d 1981), of Sandejord, Norway; 1 s (Thomas b 1971), 1 da (Arabella b 1973); *Career* Br Merchant Navy 1957-61; overseas managerial contracts 1977-87, French Property Conslts 1989-; *Recreations* sports, shooting; *Clubs* Royal Overseas League; *Style—* The Hon V R B Vivian; Prades, St Martin de Boubaux, 48160 Le Collet de Deze, France (☎ 66455613)

VLASSOPULOS, Antony John; s of John Nicholas Vlassopulos (d 1968), and Edith Alice Vlassopulos (d 1982), *née* Stammers; *b* 13 Nov 1931; *Educ* St George's Weybridge, King's Coll London; *m* 1, 24 Sept 1955, Hon Janet Allanson-Winn, da of Lord Headley, of Sussex; 2 s (Christopher John Antony b 6 Nov 1958, Mark Charles Antony b 27 Nov 1959); m 2, 22 Nov 1969, Sue, da of Frederick Edwards, of USA; 2 s (Jonathan Antony Lee b 5 July 1974, Alexander Frederick Antony b 21 Feb 1981); *Career* called to the Bar Lincoln's Inn 1952; dir: Vlassopulo Bros Ltd 1957-68, dir Howard Tenens Ltd 1963-69; chm and md NEY Shipping 1969-90; (cncllr (cons) Hersham-Walton on Thames 1957-60); returned to the criminal bar 1983; memb Lloyds (underwriter) 1986-; FICS 1958; *Books* Bertie the Bus (with Ingrid Pitt, 1981); *Recreations* motor racing; *Clubs* Ferrari Owners, Porsche Owners; *Style—* Antony Vlassopulos, Esq; The Wishing Well House, Old Avenue, St George's Hill, Weybridge, Surrey KT13 0QB (☎ 0932 842767, 0932 849224); 5 Verulam Buildings, Gray's Inn, London WC1R 5LP (☎ 071 242 1044, fax 071 831 3082, mobile tel 0831 257676, 0831 321943)

VOADEN, Alistair Harold Conway; s of Richard Philip Ball Voaden (d 1957), and Marjorie, *née* Cowlishaw (d 1966); *b* 28 July 1937; *Educ* Perse Sch Cambridge, Coll of Estate Management; *m* 18 Dec 1961, Rosemary Anne, da of Arnold John Wilson (d 1972); 1 s (Jeremy Richard b 1963), 2 da (Katharine Rosemary b 1965, Tania Juliette b 1967); *Career* Nat Serv 3 RHA, Lt 94 Locating Regt RA 1959-61; chartered surveyor; ptnr Grimley & Son 1964 (asst 1961), chm Trident Housing Soc 1965-69, dir Maybrook Properties plc 1970-87, chm Howle Chapman Raymer Ltd 1980-89, chm STS 1980-81, chm Surveyors Holdings Ltd 1986-89 (dir 1980-89), jt sr ptnr Grimley JR Eve 1990 (jt managing ptnr 1988, chm Estates and Finance Ctee 1990-); RICS W Midlands Branch: chm 1968-69 and 1975-76, treas 1970-74; chm RICS/ISVA Code of Measuring Practice Working Party 1978-82; RICS Annual Conf chm York 1984; tstee Hampstead Wells and Campden Tst (chm Estates and Fin Ctee 1990-), chm RICS Regnl Policy Working Party 1986-87; FRICS 1959, FAI 1958; *Recreations* skiing, sailing, gardening, opera; *Clubs* St Stephens Constitutional, Anglo Belgian, RICS Arbrix, 1913 and 1970 (past chm); *Style—* Alistair Voaden, Esq; Norman Chapel, Broad Campden, Gloucestershire GL55 6UR (☎ 0386 840343); Grimley J R Eve Chartered Surveyors, 10 Stratton St, London W1X 5FD (☎ 071 895 1515, fax 071 409 3533, telex 269155)

VOAK, Jonathan Russell Saunders; s of Capt Allan Frederick Voak, of Bel-Air, St Brelade, Jersey, and Annette Mary, *née* Langlois; *b* 25 Oct 1960; *Educ* Victoria Coll Jersey, Leicester Poly (BA); *m* Christina Jane, *née* Pounder; *Career* curatorial asst to dir of V & A (Sir Roy Strong) 1984-87 (museum asst Metalwork Dept 1983-84), curator Aspley House Wellington Museum 1987-; ed V&A Museum Report of the Bd of Tstees 1983-86 and 1986-1989, co ed: (with Sir Hugh Casson) V & A Album Gold Edition 1987, John Le Capelain Exhibition catalogue Jersey 1988; contrib Wellington in Spain exhibition catalogue Madrid 1988, author of numerous articles; memb: Museums Assoc, La Société Jersiase; cncl memb Jersey Soc in London, tstee Chantry Tst; *Recreations* microlight flying, painting; *Style—* Jonathan Voak, Esq; Apsley House, Wellington Museum, 149 Piccadilly, London W1V 9FA (☎ 071 499 5676, fax 071 493 6576)

VOBDAY, Sir Gordon Ivan; s of Alexander Thomas Hobday (d 1971), and Frances Cassandra, *née* Meads; *b* 1 Feb 1916; *Educ* Long Eaton GS, Univ Coll Nottingham (BSc, PhD, LLD); *m* 1940, Margaret Jean Joule; 1 da; *Career* chm: Boots Co Ltd 1972-82, Central Independent TV (covers E and W Midlands franchise area) 1981-85; dir Lloyds Bank 1981-86 (also chm N and E Regnl Bd); Lord-Lt Notts 1983-91, DL 1981-83; chllr Univ of Nottingham 1979- (pres Cncl 1973-82); FRSC; kt 1979; *Style—* Sir Gordon Hobday; c/o Lloyds Bank, St James's St, Nottingham NG1 6FD (☎ 0602 42501)

VOCKINS, Rev Michael David; s of Arthur Donald Vockins, of Thatcham, Newbury, Berkshire, and Evelyn Margaret, *née* Mackay-Ellis; *b* 3 July 1944; *Educ* St Bartholemew's GS Newbury, Oxford Poly, Univ Coll of Wales (BSc), Gloucester Sch for Ministry; *m* 17 Dec 1966, Eileen Grace, da of Walter James Hayward; 2 da (Helen b 23 June 1970, Morag b 1 Jan 1973); *Career* sec Worcestershire County Cricket Club 1971-; mangr: Eng Counties XI Tour to Zimbabwe 1985, Eng Young Cricketers Tour to Aust 1990, Eng Under 19 XI Tour to NZ 1991; principally responsible for devising and promoting game of indoor cricket 1970-71; chm Test and County Cricket Bd Second XI Ctee; memb TCCB Ctees (Cricket, Registration and Discipline); ordained Hereford Cathedral 1988, hon curate of Cradley, Mathon and Storridge Hereford 1988-; *Books* Indoor Cricket, Worcestershire County Cricket Club: An Illustrated History, Barclays World of Cricket (contrib); *Style—* Rev Michael Vockins; Birchwood Lodge, Birchwood, Storridge, Worcs WR13 5EZ (☎ 0886 884366); Worcestershire County Cricket Club, County Ground, New Road, Worcester WRZ 4QQ (☎ 0905 748474, fax 0905 748005)

VOGT, (Susan) Harriet; da of Richard Vogt, of Washington DC, and Joan *née* Davis; *b* 31 July 1952; *Educ* Sidwell Friends Sch Washington DC, Westonbirt Sch, Sussex Univ (BAPsych); common law husband, Philip Gallagher, s of Patrick Gallagher, DFC; *Career* dir of planning Ayer Advertising 1985-, (dir 1984-); *Recreations* consuming books, films, Italian food culture, swimming; *Clubs* YMCA; *Style—* Ms Harriet Vogt; 2 Dunollie Place, London NW5; Ayer Barker, Metropolis House, 22 Percy St, London WIP 9FF (☎ 071 528 8888, fax 071 636 1119, telex 883588)

VOGT, John Julian Charles; s of Charles Vogt, and Evelyn Maude, *née* Smythe; *b* 2 April 1942; *Educ* St Paul's Sch London, The Coll of Law London; *m* 18 April 1970,

Patricia, da of Jack McConnell, of 429 Banbury Road, Oxford; 1 s (Simon), 1 da (Caroline); *Career* slr Parker Chamberlain (private country practice) Wantage Oxon; memb Law Soc, memb Br Legal Assoc; *Recreations* skiing, bridge; *Style*— John Vogt, Esq; 429 Banbury Road, Oxford (☎ 0865 515197); Parker Chamberlain, 9 Victoria Gallery, Wantage, Oxon (☎ 02357 65651, fax 02357 7921)

VOGT, Paul Johan; s of Johan Vogt, and Audrey, *née* Mather; *b* 6 Dec 1938; *Educ* Rugby; *m* 25 Aug 1962, Winifred Ruth, da of Wing Cdr J E Tyrrell; 2 da (Claire b 1965, Charlotte b 1969); *Career* Cheshire Regt 1958-60; chm Vogt and Maguire Ltd 1974, Baltic Exchange Ltd 1989, FICS 1984; *Recreations* bridge, football; *Style*— Paul Vogt, Esq; 24-28 St Mary Ave, London EC3 (☎ 071 283 7222, telex 885101, fax 071 626 0384)

VOICE, Dr Eric Handley; s of Sidney Clayton Voice (d 1936), of Hampstead, London, and Christiana, *née* Brader (d 1970); *b* 2 June 1924; *Educ* Bethany Goudhurst Kent, Univ of Nottingham (BSc), Univ of Bath (PhD); *m* 1 July 1950, Joan, da of Arthur John Lane (d 1965), of Collingham, Notts; 2 s (Michael Iain b 1957, Christopher David b 1961), 1 da (Catherine Hazel b 1959); *Career* distinguished work in penicillin and modern antibiotics 1946-56, res into nuclear reactor R & D for electricity generation and environmental problems 1957-84; currently lectr and broadcaster on: population problems, world energy needs, space travel, environmental matters, author of numerous scientific papers; memb int, Parly and UN Ctees on furtherance of Sci; involved orgns for furtherance of arts and protection of environment, fndr 3 conservation socs; FBIS 1948, FRSC 1970, CChem, FInstP 1989, CPhys; *Recreations* growing camellias, dining with friends; *Style*— Dr Eric Voice; Miller Place, Thurso, Caithness, Scotland KW14 7UH (☎ 0847 64350)

VOKINS, Trevor William Derek; s of William Howard Gilburd Vokins (d 1984), and Gladys Florence Vokins; *b* 14 May 1935; *Educ* Eastbourne Coll; *m* 2 June 1962, Gillian Christine, da of Hugh A Kinney; 3 da (Susan b 1964, Amanda b 1966, Kathryn b 1968); *Career* dir: Anston Hldgs plc 1972-78, Vokins Ltd 1972-, Citizens Regency Building Soc 1973-85, Regency Building Soc 1987; memb Inst Chartered Accountants in England and Wales; FCA; *Recreations* travel, gardening; *Clubs* Brighton and Hove Soiree Rotary; *Style*— Trevor Vokins, Esq; 323 Dyke Road, Hove, E Sussex BN3 6PE (☎ 0273 556317); Vokins Ltd, North Street, Brighton BN1 1FD

VOLCKER, Paul A; *b* 5 Sept 1927; *Educ* Princeton (BA), Harvard Grad Sch of Pub Admin (MA), LSE; *m* Barbara; 1 s, 1 da; *Career* Federal Government: two tours of duty as US Treasury Official, under sec Monetary Affairs 1969-74, pres Federal Reserve Bank of New York 1974-79, chm Bd of Govrs Federal Reserve System 1979-87 (appointed by Pres Carter, reappointed by Pres Reagan); currently non-exec dir: Imperial Chemical Industries plc, Nestle SA, Prudential Insurance USA, MBIA Corp USA, American Stock Exchange; currently chm James D Wolfensohn Incorporated; Frederick H Schultz prof of Int Econ Policy Princeton Univ; chm: Advsy Bd Centre for Strategic and Int Studies, Cmmn on Publc Service 1987-89; various positions with: Mayo Fndn, Trilateral Cmmn, Cncl on Foreign Relations, Aspen Inst, Japan Soc, American Cncl on Germany, Arthritis Fndn, American Diabetes Assoc; Alma Maters: Princeton, Harvard; *Style*— Paul A Volcker, Esq; James D Wolfensohn Inc, 599 Lexington Ave, New York 10022 (☎ 212 909 8173, fax 212 909 5158)

VOLES, Dr Roger; s of Bertram Richard Edward Voles (d 1978), and Winifred Mabel, *née* Barnes (d 1988); *b* 20 July 1930; *Educ* Archbishop Tenison's Sch, London Univ (BSc, MTech, DTech); *m* 24 Sept 1966, Vida Margaret Murray, da of Alec Riley (d 1973); *Career* chief scientist Thorn EMI Electronics 1974-89, technical dir 1989-; contributed 28 papers to jls of IEE and IEEE; granted 81 patents; organised 6 int confs; past chm AGARD Avionics Panel; chm EEA Res Advsy Ctee; vice-chm IEE Electronics Divnl Bd; Freeman Worshipful Co of Engrs 1984; FIEE 1971, FInstP 1971, FEng 1983, FIMA 1989; *Recreations* mountain walking, genealogy, travel; *Style*— Dr Roger Voles; Thorn EMI Electronics, 1 Forest Rd, Feltham, Middx TW13 7HE (☎ 081 751 6464, ext 330)

VON BRENTANO (DI TREMEZZO), (Georg) Michael Robert; s of Bernard von Brentano (d 1964), of Wiesbaden, and Margot, *née* Gerlach; *b* 6 Aug 1933; *m* 26 Feb 1966, Elke, da of Walter Hassel (d 1978), of Frankfurt; 1 da (Meline b 15 Aug 1969); *Career* sr vice pres: Berliner Handels - Gesellschaft Frankfurt until 1964, Deutsche Bank AG Frankfurt 1974-85; md Deutsche Bank Capital Mkts Ltd London 1985-; *Recreations* collecting first editions, golf; *Clubs* IOD, Royal Mid-Surrey Golf, Frankfurter Gesellschaft fuer Handel Industrie und Wissenschaft; *Style*— Michael von Brentano, Esq; Deutsche Bank Capital Mkts Ltd, 150 Leadenhall Street, London EC3V 4RJ (☎ 071 971 7104)

VON HAYEK, Prof Friedrich August; CH (1984); came to Britain 1931, naturalised 1938; *b* Vienna; *Career* Tooke prof of econs London Univ 1931-50, prof of econ sci and statistics Univ of Chicago 1950-62, prof of econs Univ of Freiburg 1962-69, Hon DLitt Univ of Dallas 1975, Hon Doctorate in social scis, Marroquin Univ Guatemala 1977, Santa Maria Univ Valparaiso 1977, Univ of Buenos Aires 1977, Univ of Gessen 1982; Nobel Prize in Econ Science (jtly) 1974; Austrian Distinction for Sci and Art 1975; memb Orders pour le Mérite fur Wissenschaften und Künste Fed Rep of Germany 1977; hon fell: LSE, Austrian Acad of Sci, American Econ Assoc; *Publications* Prices and Production (1931), Monetary Theory and the Trade Cycle (1933, German ed 1929), Monetary Nationalism and International Stability (1937), Profits, Interest and Investment (1939), The Pure Theory of Capital (1941), The Road to Serfdom (1944), Individualism and Economic Order (1948), John Stuart Mill and Harriet Taylor (1950), The Counter-revolution of Science (1952), The Sensory Order (1952), The Political ideal of the Rule of Law (1955), The Constitution of Liberty (1960), Studies in Philosophy, Politics and Economics and the History of Ideas (1978), Beitrage zur Geldtheorie (ed 1933), Collectivist Econ Planning (1935), Capitalism and the Historians (1954); the works of: HH Gossen (1927), F Wieser (1929), C Menger (1933-36), H Thornton (1939); articles in Economic Journal, Economica, and other English and foreign jls; *Clubs* Reform; *Style*— Prof Friedrich von Hayek, CH; c/o Central Chancery of the Order of Knighthood, St James's Palace, London SW1

VON HOYNINGEN-HUENE, Baroness Nancy; *née* Oakes; da of Sir Harry Oakes, 1 Bt; *b* 17 May 1925; *m* 1, 1942 (m annulled 1949), Marie-Alfred Fouquerreaux de Marigny, of Mauritius; m 2, 1952 (m dis 1961), Baron Ernst von Hoyningen-Huene, 2 s of Baron Hermann von Hoyningen-Huene, of Munich; 1 s (Baron Alexander George Lyssardt b 17 Feb 1955); m 3, 1962 (m dis), Patrick Tritton, *qv*; resumed surname of 2 husb; *Style*— Baroness Nancy von Hoyningen-Huene; PO Box N1002, 28 Queen St, Nassau, Bahamas; Marsella 44, Mexico 6, DF Mexico

VON JOEL, Michael David Atkinson (Mike); s of Henry (Todd) von Joel (d 1952), and Annie Doreen, *née* Jones, who m in 1952, George Sawden Atkinson; *b* 13 June 1952; *Educ* GS Yorkshire, Art Sch Winchester Hants; *m* 1, Mandy Stewart; 1 da (Mercedes Kristal b 1980); m 2, 1982 (m dis 1988), Chrissie Shrimpton; 1 s (Todd b 1983), 1 da (Hope b 1985); *Career* fndr ed The New Style Magazine 1976, md AGP Newspapers 1980, ed Art Line Magazine 1982-90, fndr ed Art Issues newspaper 1990, ed Artbooknews Newspaper 1990; chief exec PSi (int management agency for artists) 1991; formerly: curator Line Art Gallery London, chief exec Ziggurat Books; memb Inst of Journalists 1978, NUJ 1981, NGA 1982; *Books* Armageddon - An Eternity (1978), Pirate Radio-Then and Now (1984), Jazz Guitarists (jtly, 1984); *Recreations* sleeping; *Clubs* Chelsea Arts, Groucho, Mortons; *Style*— Mike von Joel, Esq; PSi, 11 Phoenix House, Phoenix St, London WC2 (☎ 071 497 3545, fax 071 379 5846)

VON MALLINCKRODT, Georg Wilhelm Gustav; s of Arnold Wilhelm von Mallinckrodt (d 1982), of 8110 Riegsee, nr Murnau, W Germany, and Valentine, *née* von Joest; *b* 19 Aug 1930; *Educ* Schule Schloss Salem, Hamburg Business Sch; *m* 31 July 1958, Charmaine Brenda, da of Helmut Schroder (d 1967), of Dunlossit, Isle of Islay; 2 s (Philip b 1962, Edward b 1965), 2 da (Claire b 1960, Sophie b 1967); *Career* joined J Henry Schroder Banking Corporation NY 1954, exec chm Schroders plc London 1984-, chm and chief exec Schroders Inc NY 1983-, chm J Henry Schroder Bank A G (Zurich) 1984-, chm and pres Schroder International Ltd 1984-; dir: Schroder Australia Holdings Ltd Sydney 1984-, Wertheim Schroder & Co Inc NY 1986-, J Henry Schroder Wagg & Co Ltd London 1967-, Singapore International Merchant Bankers Ltd 1988-, European Arts Foundation Ltd 1986-, Euris Paris 1987-, Siemens plc 1989-; vice pres German Chamber of Indust and Commerce in UK 1974-, pres German YMCA in London 1971-, memb Br N American Ctee 1988-; CBIM 1986, FRSA 1986; Cross of Order of Merit German Federal Republic 1986 (Officer's Cross 1990); *Recreations* shooting, skiing, gardening, classical music, reading; *Clubs* River (NY); *Style*— George W G von Mallinckrodt, Esq; Schroders plc, 120 Cheapside, London EC2V 6DS (☎ 071 382 6000, fax 071 382 6878, telex 885029)

VON PREUSSEN, Princess Nicholas; Hon Victoria; *née* Mancroft; da of 2 Baron Mancroft, KBE, TD; *b* 1952; *m* 1980, HRH Prince (Frederick) Nicholas von Preussen; 1 s (Frederick Nicholas Stormont b 11 June 1990), 3 da (Beatrice Victoria b 10 Feb 1981, Florence Jessica b 28 July 1983, Augusta Lily b 15 Dec 1986); *Style*— Princess Nicholas von Preussen; Maperton House, Wincanton, Somerset BA9 8EJ

VON SAXE WILSON, Tatiana Alexandra; da of Enrique Sigismundo Von Saxe Tourowitz (d 1979), and Consuelo Trinidad, *née* Yépez; *b* 27 April 1944; *Educ* Lima Peru (Business Admin); *m* 1, 8 June 1968, late Eric A Dilley; m 2, David L Wilson; *Career* sr ptnr Von Saxe Assocs 1970, chm Mainline Corpn 1980, md Mainline Restaurants Ltd 1980; Order of Merit for Distinguished Servs Peru 1980; *Recreations* tennis; *Clubs* St James's, IOD; *Style*— Tatiana von Saxe Wilson; 4 Delancey Passage, London NW1 7NN (☎ 071 387 3544, fax 071 383 5314)

VON SCHRAMEK, Sir Eric Emil; s of Emil von Schramek (d 1947), and Annie von Schramek (d 1981); *b* 4 April 1921; *Educ* Stefans Gymnasium Prague, Tech Univ Prague (Dip Ing Arch); *m* 1948, Edith, da of Dipl Ing W Popper; 1 s (Charles), 2 da (Annette, Therese); *Career* town planner Bavaria 1946-48; sr supervising architect Dept of Works and Housing, Darwin, NT 1948-51; Evans, Bruer & Ptnrs (now von Schramek and Dawes) 1951-, work includes Nat Mutual Centre, State Govt Insur Building, Wales Ho, TAA Building; numerous churches throughout Australia and New Guinea; nat pres Building Sci Forum of Australia 1970-72; pres RAIA 1974-76; former nat dep chm Austcare; former cncllr Cncl of Professions; former chm Lutheran Church of Australia; life fellow RAIA; FRIBA, FIArbA, Affiliate RAPI; kt 1982; *Publications* contributions and articles in architectural pubns; *Style*— Sir Eric von Schramek; 4 Burlington St, Walkerville, S Australia 5081

VON SIMSON, HSH Princess Marie-Anne of Salm-Reiffersheidt, Krautheim und Dyck; Mrs Marie-Anne Helena Emmanuela (Mrs von Simson); da of HSH 6 Prince (Franz Joseph), zu Salm-Reiffersheidt, Krautheim und Dyck; *m* 1, 1964, as his 2 w, Col Hon Alexander Campbell Geddes, OBE, MC, TD, (d 1972, s of 1 Baron Geddes); 1 s (Stephen George b 1969), 1 da (Camilla Johanna Isabel b 1966); m 2, 1978, Prof Dr Otto Georg von Simson, of Berlin; *Style*— HSH Princess Marie-Anne zu Salm-Reif; 55 Chelsea Square, London SW3 6ZH; Max EYTH Strasse 26, 1 Berlin - Dahlem 33, Germany

VON WESTENHOLZ, Lady Mary (Marianella Anne); *née* Kerr; eldest da of 12 Marquess of Lothian, by his w Antonella Newland; *b* 20 March 1944; *Educ* Open Univ (BA); *m* 1970, Charles von Westenholz; 3 s; *Recreations* skiing, tennis, guitar playing, knitting; *Style*— The Lady Mary von Westenholz; Little Blakesware, Widford, Ware, Herts

VOOS, John; s of Kurt Alias Voos, and Amy Jean, *née* Webb; *b* 6 May 1956; *Educ* Netteswell Comp Sch Harlow Essex, Harrow Coll of Technol and Art London; *m* (m dis), Carmen Sik Heng, *née* Lim; *partner* Belinda Alison May; 1 s (James Reith Voos b 26 March 1988), 1 da (Jasmine Emma Voos b 19 Nov 1983); *Career* photographer Fleet St News Agency 1980-82, freelance photographer The Times 1982-86, staff photographer The Independent 1986-; included in World Press Photo Competition Book 1989; *Recreations* sub-aqua diving, backgammon, swimming, walking, jogging; *Style*— John Voos, Esq; The Independent, Newspaper Publishing plc, 40 City Rd, London EC1 (☎ 071 253 1222, car 0836 286526)

VOS, Geoffrey Charles; s of Bernard Vos (d 1974), of London, and Pamela Celeste Rose, *née* Heilbuth; *b* 22 April 1955; *Educ* UCS, Gonville and Caius Coll Cambridge (MA); *m* 31 Mar 1984, Vivien Mary, da of Albert Edward Dowdeswell (d 1982), of Birmingham; 1 da (Charlotte b 1985), 1 step s (Carl b 1973), 2 step da (Maria b 1965, Louise b 1965); *Career* called to the Bar Inner Temple 1977, in practice Chambers of DR Stanford 1979-; Memb Ctee Chancery Bar Assoc, subscriber Senate of the Inns of Ct; memb: Inner Temple, Lincoln's Inn; *Recreations* sheep farming, wine, photography; *Clubs* United Oxford and Cambridge, Worcs GC; *Style*— Geoffrey Vos, Esq; 46 Fordington Rd, Highgate, London N6 4TJ (☎ 081 444 9547); Woodlands, Crumpton Hill, Storridge, Nr Malvern, Worcs (☎ 0886 32556); 3 Stone Buildings, Lincoln's Inn, London WC2A 3XL (☎ 071 242 4937, fax 071 405 3896)

VOSS, Prof Christopher Arnold; s of Dr H J Voss, of Cottingham, Northants, and Matthew, *née* Arnold (d 1989); *b* 23 Dec 1942; *Educ* Bedford Sch, Imperial Coll London (BSc), London Business Sch (MSc, PhD); *m* 14 Dec 1977, Carolyn Jill, da of Sir Richard Kingsland, DFC, of Canberra, Aust; 1 s (Barnaby b 1981), 1 da (Georgina b 1978); *Career* mangr Stuarts & Lloyds Ltd 1960-67, conslt Harbridge House Europe 1970-75, visiting prof Univ of Western Ontario 1975-77, lectr London Business Sch 1977-84, Alan Edward Higgs prof of mfrg strategy and policy Univ of Warwick 1984-90, prof of operations mgmnt London Business Sch 1990-; chm UK Operators Mgmnt Assoc, memb ctee Br Acad of Mgmnt; MBICS 1971, FRSA (1989); *Books* Operation Management in Service Industries and the Public Sector (1985), Just-In-Time Management (1988); *Recreations* skiing, violin, book collecting; *Style*— Prof Christopher Voss; London Business School, Sussex Place, Regents Park, London NW1 4SA (☎ 071 262 5050)

VOSS, Lady Diana France; da of 5 Earl of Listowel, GCMG, PC; *b* 7 Dec 1965; *m* 7 April 1990, Tim J Voss, yst s of D J Voss, of Adelaide, Australia; *Style*— The Lady Diana Voss

VOWLES, Paul Foster; s of Ernest Foster Vowles (d 1929), of Bristol, and Georgina May, *née* Lawrence (d 1983), of Bristol; *b* 12 June 1919; *Educ* Bristol GS, CCC Oxford (MA); *m* 8 Jan 1948, Valerie Eleanor, da of Ralph Theodore Hickman (d 1967); 1 s (John b 1949), 2 da (Penelope b 1952, Deborah b 1955); *Career* Army 1939-46; cmmnd Gloucs Regt 1940, KAR 1942 (despatches), Maj; asst sec: Univ of Birmingham Appts Bd 1947, Inter-Univ Cncl for Higher Educn Overseas 1948-51, registrar Makerere Univ Coll East Africa 1951-63; Univ of London: sr asst to princ 1964-68, external registrar 1968-73, academic registrar 1973-82; vice-chm Cncl Westfield Coll Univ of London 1986-89; fell Queen Mary and Westfield College 1991; *Clubs*

Athenaeum; *Style*— Paul Vowles, Esq; 13 Dale Close, Oxford OX1 1TU (☎ 0865 244042)

VULLIAMY, Patrick David; s of Maj Gen Colwyn Henry Hughes Vulliamy, CB, DSO (d 1972), of Fleet, Hants, and Veronica Mary, *née* Ellis, (d 1978); *b* 25 May 1927; *Educ* Bedford Sch, Peterhouse Cambridge (BA, MA); *m* July 1954, Pamela Elsie, da of Frederick Cottier (d 1974), of Lausanne, Switzerland; 1 s (Christopher Patrick Colwyn b 19 Oct 1956), 1 da (Dominique Fiona b 1 Oct 1958); *Career* Lt Royal Signals 1947 (served 1945-49); mgmnt trainee Purchase Dept Ford Motor Co 1952-54, ptnr Scott Wilson Kirkpatrick Partners Consulting Engineers 1968- (joined 1956); FICE, FASCE; *Recreations* golf, skiing, bridge; *Clubs* NZ Golf, United Oxford and Cambridge Univ; *Style*— Patrick Vulliamy, Esq; The Stables, Coldharbour, Kingsley, nr Bordon, Hants GU35 9LP (☎ 0420 473008); Scott House, Basing View, Basingstoke, Hants (☎ 0256 461161)

VYVYAN, (Ralph) Ferrers Alexander; s and h of Sir John Vyvyan, 12 Bt; *b* 21 Aug 1960; *Educ* Charterhouse, Sandhurst; *Career* short term cmmn Light Infantry; estate mgmnt in conjunction with Sir John Vyvyan Bt; *Recreations* dinghy sailing; *Style*— Ralph Vyvyan, Esq; Trelowarreb, Mawgan, Helston, Cornwall TR12 6AF (☎ 0326 22 224)

VYVYAN, Sir John Stanley; 12 Bt (E 1645); s of late Maj-Gen Ralph Ernest Vyvyan, CBE, MC (himself only s of late Capt Herbert Reginald Vyvyan, OBE, who was in turn 2 s of Rev Herbert Francis Vyvyan, while the Rev Herbert was 3 s of Rev Vyell Francis Vyvyan, the latter being 2 s of Sir Vell Vyvyan, 7 Bt); suc cous Sir Richard Philip Vyvyan, 11 Bt, 1978; *b* 20 Jan 1916; *Educ* Charterhouse, London Sch of Oriental Studies; *m* 1, 1940 (m dis 1946), Joyce Lilia, da of late Frederick Marsh, of Kailan Mining Admin, Peking; 1 da (decd); m 2, 1948 (m dis 1958), Marie, da of late Dr O'Shea, of Hamilton, Ontario; m 3, 1958, Jonet Noel, da of Lt-Col Alexander Hubert Barclay, DSO, MC; 1 s, 1 da; *Heir* s, Ralph Ferrers Alexander Vyvyan; *Career* served 1939-45 War as Maj Royal Signals, in India and Arakan; *Clubs* Army and Navy, Royal Cornwall Yacht (Falmouth); *Style*— Sir John Vyvyan, Bt; Trelowarren Mill, Mawgan, Helston, Cornwall (☎ 0326 22 505)

W

WACE, Michael Gordon; s of Capt Eustace Harold Wace, RN (d 1951) of Liss, Hants, and Marjorie Agnes Wace; *b* 27 Nov 1929; *Educ* Marlborough; *m* May 1952 (m dis 1978), Beryl; 3 da (Josephine, Sara, Jacqueline); *Career* ed: Univ of London Press 1955-62, Rupert Hart Davis Ltd 1962-6, Macmillan and Co Ltd 1966-72; ed dir Macmillan Educn Ltd 1972-79; publishing dir: Macmillan Children's Books 1979-90, Pan Macmillan Children's Books 1990-; *Style*— Michael Wace, Esq; 48 Sussex Square, Brighton BN2 1GE; Pan Macmillan Children's Books, 18-21 Cavaye Place, London SW10 9PG (☎ 01 373 6070)

WADDELL, Sir Alexander Nicol Anton; KCMG (1959, CMG (1955), DSC (1944); s of Rev Alexander Waddell; *b* 8 Nov 1913; *Educ* Fettes, Univ of Edinburgh, Gonville and Caius Coll Cambridge; *m* 1949, Jean Margot Lesbia, da of W Masters; *Career* WWII Serv; Lt RANVR 1942-44 (coastwatcher), Lt-Col (gen list) Br Mil Admin 1945-47; dist offr Br Solomon Islands 1938, DC 1945, princ asst sec N Borneo 1947-52, colonial sec Gambia 1952-56, dep gov Sierra Leone 1958-60 (colonial sec 1956-58), govr and C-in-C Sarawak 1960-63, UK cmmr Br Phosphate Commn 1965-78, memb Panel Ind Insprs Dept Environment 1979-85; *Recreations* golf, hill walking; *Clubs* East India and Sports; *Style*— Sir Alexander Waddell, KCMG, DSC; Pilgrim Cottage, Ashton Keynes, Wilts

WADDELL, Heather; da of Robert Waddell (d 1980), of Glasgow, and Maureen, *née* Buchanan; *b* 11 July 1950; *Educ* Westbourne Sch Glasgow, St Leonard's Sch St Andrews, St Andrews Univ (MA), Byam Shaw Sch of Art London (Dip FA, Leverhulme bursary); *Career* publisher, art critic and photographer; lectr in Eng and gen studies Paddington Coll London 1977, awarded Gulbenkian scholarship to set up and research the Int Artists' Exchange Prog in Aust and NZ 1979, int admin Acme Gallery Covent Garden London 1980, fndr and md Art Guide Publications 1980-87 (publisher Art Guide Publications Imprint 1987-90), set up New Scottish Prints Exhibition as part of Britain salutes NY (toured USA 1983) 1983, conslt Int Contemporary Art Fair London 1984-89, organised Henry Goetz Exhibition London and wrote catalogue 1986; freelance journalist for various pubns incl: The Evening Standard 1974, TES 1978-80, The Glasgow Herald (London art critic) 1980-84, Artnews USA 1986, Blue Guide to Spain 1988, Vie des Arts (London corr) 1979-89, The Independent 1989, Time Out London Guide and New York Guide 1989, The European (arts events ed) 1990, The Artists' Directory; photographer for several pubns incl: two Blue Guides; Int Assoc of Art Critics: memb 1980-, memb Exec Ctee 1982-, treas 1985-86, PR offr 1990-; memb: Exec Ctee Int Assoc of Artists 1978-84, Soc of Young Publishers 1980-86, Ind Publishers' Guild 1980-89, Publishers' Assoc 1983-87 (Map and Guide Book Ctee an Book Publishers Ctee); *Recreations* travel, people, swimming, enjoying life; *Style*— Ms Heather Waddell; 27 Holland Park Avenue, London W11 3RW

WADDELL, Sir James Henderson; CB (1960); s of Donald M Waddell and J C Fleming; *b* 5 Oct 1914; *Educ* George Heriot's Sch, Univ of Edinburgh (MA); *m* 1940, Dorothy Abbie, da of Horace Wright; 1 s, 1 da; *Career* Civil Serv 1936-75: under sec Cabinet Office 1961-63, dep sec Miny for Housing and Local Govt 1963-66, dep under sec Home Office 1966-75; dep chm Police Complaints Bd 1977-81; kt 1974; *Style*— Sir James Waddell, CB; Long Meadow, East Lavant, Chichester, W Sussex (☎ 0243 527 129)

WADDELL, Robert Steele (Robin); s of Col Herbert Waddell, CBE, HLI (d 1988), of 14A Ledcameroch Road, Bearsden, Glasgow, and Jean Cameron, *née* Wallace; *b* 3 Aug 1931; *Educ* Glasgow Acad, St Mary's Melrose, Fettes, Univ of Cambridge; *m* 8 July 1960, Margaret Eileen Monro, da of Dr John Sturrock; 4 da (Elizabeth-Anne (Mrs Wilson) b 1961, Nicola (Dr Markland) b 1963, Alexandra b 1966, Victoria b 1967); *Career* Nat Serv 41 Field Regt RA, Egypt; with Thomson McLintock Glasgow 1955-59, Speirs and Jeffrey Ltd 1960- (sr ptnr 1979, chm 1986-); sec Scottish Wayfarers Over 50's 1982-; *Recreations* golf; *Clubs* Elie Golf, Prestwick Golf, Glasgow Golf, Muirfield, R and A; *Style*— Robin Waddell, Esq; Fairmount, 17 Ledcameroch Road, Bearsden, Glasgow G61 4AB (☎ 041 942 0455); Speirs & Jeffrey Ltd, 36 Renfield Street, Glasgow G2 1NA (☎ 041 248 4311, fax 041 221 4764, telex 777902)

WADDELL, Rear Adm William Angus; CB (1981), OBE (1966); s of late James Whitefield Waddell, and late Christina, *née* Maclean; *b* 5 Nov 1924; *Educ* Univ of Glasgow (BSc); *m* 1950, Thelma Evelyn Tomlins; 1 s, 1 da; *Career* Sub Lt RNVR (Special Branch) 1945, Offr i/c RN Polaris Sch 1966-68, Instr Capt Staff of SACLANT (Dir Info Systems Gp) 1969-72, Dean RN Coll Greenwich 1973-75, assoc teacher The City Univ 1973-75, Dir Naval Offr Appts (Instr) 1975-78, ADC to HM The Queen 1976-79, Chief Naval Instr Offr 1978-81, Rear Adm 1979, Flag Offr Admty Interview Bd 1979-81; sec and chief Exec Royal Inst of Public Health and Hygiene 1982-90; FIEE, CEng; *Style*— Rear Adm William Waddell, CB, OBE; c/o National Westminster Bank plc, 1 Lee Rd, Blackheath, London SE3

WADDICOR, (James) Richard; s of William Waddicor (d 1960), of Bolton, and Marian, *née* Cookson; *b* 2 May 1937; *Educ* Uppingham; *m* 1 March 1962, (Margaret) Gillian, da of Rev Richard Greville Norburn, Canon and Rural Dean of Bolton and of Edgbaston (1978); 1 s (James b 1965), 1 da (Frances b 1963); *Career* fin dir Hawker Siddeley Dynamics Engineering Ltd 1972-79, md Water Engineering Ltd 1979- (formerly Hawker Siddeley Water Engineering Ltd); MIWE, FCA 1970; *Recreations* fly fishing, squash; *Style*— Richard Waddicor, Esq; Oaken Hedges, Enborne Rd, Newbury, Berks RG15 0EY (☎ 0635 344 65); Water Engineering Ltd, Aynho Rd, Adderbury, Banbury, Oxon OX17 3NL (☎ 0295 810 581, fax 0295 811 997, telex 83655)

WADDINGTON, Baron (Life Peer UK 1990), of Read in the County of Lancashire; David Charles Waddington; PC (1987), QC (1971); s of late Charles Waddington, JP, of The Old Vicarage, Read, Lancs, and Minnie Hughan Waddington; *b* 2 Aug 1929; *Educ* Sedbergh, Hertford Coll Oxford; *m* 1958, Gillian Rosemary, da of Alan Green, CBE, of The Stables, Sabden, Lancs; 3 s, 2 da; *Career* 2 Lt 12 Royal Lancers 1951-53; called to the Bar Gray's Inn 1951, rec Crown Ct 1972; former dir: J J Broadley Ltd, J and J Roberts Ltd, Wolstenholme Rink Ltd; Parly candidate (Cons): Farnworth 1955, Nelson and Colne 1964, Heywood and Royton 1966; MP (C): Nelson and Colne 1968-74, Clitheroe March 1979-83, Ribble Valley 1983-90; lord cmmmr treasy 1979-81, Parly under sec employment 1981-83, min of state Home Office 1983-87, govt chief whip 1987-89, home sec 1989-90; Lord Privy Seal and Leader of the House of Lords 1990-; *Style*— The Rt Hon Lord Waddington, PC, QC; Whins House, Sabden, nr Blackburn, Lancs (☎ 0282 71070); 9 Denny St, London SE11 (☎ 071 735 5886)

WADDINGTON, Prof David James; s of Eric James Waddington (d 1958), of 43 Caroline House, London, and Marjorie Edith, *née* Harding; *b* 27 May 1932; *Educ* Marlborough, Imperial Coll (BSc, ARCS, DIC, PhD); *m* 17 Aug 1957, Isobel, da of Ernest Hesketh, of Eastbourne; 2 s (Matthew b 1963, Rupert b 1964), 1 da (Jessica b 1970); *Career* head Sci Dept Wellington Coll 1961-64 (teacher 1956-64); York Univ 1965-: prof of chemical educn 1978-, head dept 1983-, pro vice chllr 1985-; pres educn div Royal Soc Chem 1981-83, chm Ctee Teaching Chemistry, Int Union Pure and Applied Chem 1981-85, sec Ctee Teaching Sci Int Cncl Sci Unions 1985-, Nyholm medal Royal Soc Chem 1985; *Books* Modern Organic Chemistry (1985), Kinetics and Mechanism: Case Studies (1977), Chemistry, The Salters' Approach (1989), Teaching Sch Chemistry (ed 1984), Chemistry in Action (ed 1987), Education Industry and Technology (ed 1987); *Recreations* golf; *Style*— Prof David Waddington; Murton Hall, York YO1 3UQ (☎ 0904 489 393); Dept of Chem, Univ of York, Heslington, York YO1 5DD (☎ 0904 432 500/1, fax 0904 433 433, telex 57933 YORKUL)

WADDINGTON, Robert; s of George Waddington (d 1967), of Lytham, Lancs, and Mary Gwendoline, *née* Briggs; *b* 20 Jan 1942; *Educ* Uppingham; *m* 24 Jan 1976, Jennifer Ann, da of late Sir Anthony Banks Jenkinson, 13 Bt (d 1989); 2 s (Thomas Anthony b 10 May 1977, Guy George b 6 Sept 1979); *Career* Peat Marwick Mitchell 1960-64; Hambros Bank Ltd 1971- (dir 1984); FCA; *Recreations* shooting, golf, gardening; *Style*— Robert Waddington, Esq; 41 Tower Hill, London EC3 (☎ 071 480 5000, fax 071 702 9725)

WADDINGTON, Very Rev Robert Murray; s of Percy Nevill Waddington, MBE (d 1971), and Dorothy, *née* Murray (d 1983); *b* 24 Oct 1927; *Educ* Dulwich, Selwyn Coll Cambridge (MA); *Career* asst curate St John's Bethnal Green 1953-55, chaplain Slade Sch Warwick Qld Aust 1955-59, curate St Luke's Cambridge 1959-61; headmaster St Barnabas Sch Ravenshoe N Qld Aust 1961-70, Dept of Education Oxford Univ 1971-72, residentiary canon Carlisle Cathedral 1972-77, gen sec C of E Bd of Educn and Nat Soc for Promoting Religious Educn 1977-84, dean of Manchester 1984-; *Recreations* cinema, cooking, sociology, travel; *Clubs* St James (Manchester); *Style*— The Very Rev the Dean of Manchester; 44 Shrewsbury Rd, Prestwich, Manchester M25 8GQ (☎ 061 773 2959); The Cathedral, Manchester M3 1SX (☎ 061 834 0019)

WADDY, Lady Olivia Sheelin Davina Anne; *née* Taylour; da of 6 Marquess of Headfort, by his 1 w, *see* Hon Mrs Knight; *b* 4 Oct 1963; *m* 19 April 1986, David Charles Henry Waddy, er s of Ian Waddy, of Mirza Downs, Ward Marlborough, New Zealand; *Style*— The Lady Olivia Waddy; c/o The Hon Mrs Knight, Northfield, Kirk Andreas, Isle of Man

WADE, David Anthony; s of Col Harold Wade (d 1945), and Olive, *née* Baldwin (d 1961); *b* 22 Dec 1925; *Educ* Stonyhurst; *m* 1, 1 Dec 1949, Nancy (d 1965), da of Col R Stalker; 4 da (Linda b 9 Oct 1950, Louise b 2 June 1952 d 1953, Judith b 6 Jan 1955, Annabel b 6 June 1957); m 2, 29 April 1968, Amy Kathrine, da of Thomas Culley (d 1982), of Nova Friburgo, Brazil; 2 s (Mark b 13 March 1969, Sebastian b 3 Feb 1970), 1 da (Alexandra b 21 May 1971); *Career* served WWII Queens Regt 1943, cmmnd 2 KEO Gurkha Rifles, served Assam and Burma 1944-47; FO Singapore Burma and Germany 1947-50; called to the Bar Inner Temple 1959; gen mangr: Synthetic Fibres Div Courtaulds Group 1961-65 (joined 1951), Wm Brandts Sons & Co Ltd 1965-66; gp md Alfred Dunhill Ltd 1967-69, md Australasian Assets Ltd 1969-72, chm Camel Investments Ltd 1975-; *Books* Disaster (1987); *Recreations* skiing, sailing; *Clubs* Reform; *Style*— David Wade, Esq; Roman Way, Benenden, Kent TN17 4ES (☎ 0580 240873); 2 Mitre Court Buildings, Temple, London EC4Y 7BZ (☎ 071 353 1353, fax 071 353 8188)

WADE, Derwent Malcolm Mercer; s of Roland Henry Wade, CBE, JP, and Margaret Elizabeth Wade; n of Baron Wade (Life Peer); *b* 26 June 1939; *Educ* Marlborough, Selwyn Coll Cambridge (MA); *m* 1967, Rosemary, da of Eric Cyprian Perry Whiteley, TD (d 1970); 1 s, 1 da; *Career* solicitor 1965, ptnr Booth & Co 1968-; dir: Wade Gp of Cos 1972-80, BNL Hldgs 1979-82, FTL Hldgs 1974-, Kaye & Co (Huddersfield) 1983-; *Recreations* hunting, gardening; *Clubs* Leeds; *Style*— Derwent Wade, Esq; The Barn House, Bulmer, York YO6 7BL (☎ 065 381 212); PO Box 8, Sovereign House, South Parade, Leeds LS1 1HQ (☎ 0532 469655)

WADE, Hon Donald William Mercer; er s of Baron Wade, DL (Life Peer, d 1988); *b* 1 June 1941; *Educ* Silcoates Sch, Trin Hall Cambridge (BA 1963, MA 1967); *Style*— The Hon Donald Wade; 18 Pinewood Grove, London W5

WADE, Baroness; Ellenora Beatrice; da of late Frank Bentham Holdsworth, of Ilkley; *m* 18 June 1932, Baron Wade, DL (Life Peer UK 1964; d 1988); 2 s (Hon Donald William Mercer, Hon Robert Alexander Mercer, *qqv*), 2 da (Hon Mrs Wickham, Hon Mrs Morrish); *Style*— The Rt Hon Lady Wade; Meadowbank, Wath Road, Pateley Bridge, N Yorkshire (☎ 0423 711431)

WADE, Dr John Philip Huddart; s of Dr Edward Geoffrey Wade, of 22 Hill Top Ave, Cheadle Hulme, Cheshire, and Mary Ward Pickering, *née* Huddart; *b* 19 April 1950; *Educ* Cheadle Hulme Sch, Univ of Cambridge (BA), Manchester Med Sch (MB BChir), (MRCP), Univ of Cambridge (MD); *m* 26 April 1976, Charlotte, da of Dr Elozor Leslie Feinmann (d 1985); 1 da (Jessica Alice Feinmann); *Career* registrar St Thomas's Hosp 1978, sr registrar Nat Hosp for Nervous Disease London and St Bartholomew's Hosp 1984-85, res fell Cerebrovascular Disease Univ of Western Ontario 1985-86, currently conslt neurologist Charing Cross Hosp and Wexham Park Hosp Slough; symposium organiser Int Regnl Cerebral Blood Flow Workshop Brac Yugoslavia 1984 and 1986; present res interests incl: role of functional neuroimaging in neurology, early diagnosis of dementia, evaluation of individual patients with severe extracranial occlusive vascular disease; various grants received for res; scientific reviewer of jnls: Brain, Stroke, Journal of Neurology Neurosurgery and Psychiatry; memb Assoc Br Neurologists 1986, fell stroke cncl American Heart Assoc 1988; *Books* papers incl: Pseudohypertrophy of muscles of thenar eminence in x-linked muscular dystrophy (Becker type) (with H G Boddie, 1980), Reactivity of the cerebral circulation in patients with occlusive carotid disease (with M M Brown, R W Ross

Russell and C Bishop, 1986), CBF and vasoreactivity in patients with arteriovenous malformations (with J K Farrar and V C Hachinski, 1987); various invited chapters in books; letters to jnls incl: Acute renal failure due to polymyositis in Br Med Jnl (1978), Thalamic haemorrhages in Wernick-Korsakoff syndrome demonstrated by computed tomography in Annals of Neurology (with S W Roche and R J M Lane, 1988); abstract papers incl: Cerebral blood flow in subjects with high oxygen affinity haemoglobin at Euro Conf of Haemorheology London (with T C Pearson), Impact of contra lateral ICA stenosis on outcome of symptomatic ICA occlusion at Associates of Br Neurologists Glasgow (with v Hachinski and H J M Barnett, 1989); *Recreations* sailing; *Style*— Dr John Wade; 11 Gardnor Rd, Hampstead, London NW3 (☎ 071 431 2900); Department of Neurosciences, Charing Cross Hospital, Fulham Palace Road, London W6 (☎ 071 846 1195, fax 071 741 7808)

WADE, Prof Kenneth; s of Harry Kennington Wade (d 1983), of Sleaford Lincs, and Anna Elizabeth, *née* Cartwright; *b* 13 Oct 1932; *Educ* Carre's GS Sleaford Lincs, Univ of Nottingham (BSc, PhD, DSc); *m* 14 July 1962, Gertrud Rosmarie (Trudy), da of Willy Hetzel (d 1965), of Grenchen, Solothurn, Switzerland; 1 s (Alan b 1963), 2 da (Marianne b 1965, Julia b 1968); *Career* postdoctoral res fel: Univ of Cambridge 1957-59, Cornell Univ 1959-60; lectr in chemistry Derby Coll Technol 1960-61; Univ of Durham: lectr in chemistry 1961-71, sr lectr 1971-77, reader 1977-83, prof 1983-, chm Dept of Chemistry 1986-89; FRSC; FRS 1989; *Books* Organometallic Compounds: The Main Group Elements (with G E Coates, 1967), Principles of Organometallic Chemistry (with G E Coates, M L H Green, and P Powell, 1968), Electron Deficient Compounds (1971), Chemistry of Aluminium, Gallium, Indium and Thallium (with A J BAnister, 1976), Hypercarbon Chemistry (with G A Olah, G K S Prakash, R E Williams, and L D Field, 1987); *Recreations* walking; *Style*— Prof Kenneth Wade, FRS; Chemistry Dept, University of Durham Science Laboratories, South Rd, Durham DH1 3LE (☎ 091 374 3122, fax 091 374 3741, telex 537351 DURLIB G)

WADE, Kirsty Maragaret; da of Francis Joseph McDermott, of Homefield, Llandrindod Wells, Powys, and Christine, *née* Stuart; *b* 6 Aug 1962; *Educ* Llandrindod Wells HS Millfield, Univ of Loughborough (BA); *m* March 1986, Anthony Douglas (Tony) Wade; 1 da (Rachel Jordan b 29 Oct 1989); *Career* athlete; memb Blaydon Harriers Athletic Club, full UK int 1981-; achievements at 800m: English Schs champion 1980, Welsh champion 5 times, Gold medal Cwlth Games 1982 and 1986; Gold medal 1500m, Cwlth Games 1986; UK and Cwlth record holder 800m and 1000m first woman to win both 800m and 1500m at Cwlth Games 1986; jt fndr Sub Two Fitness Centre Rowlands Gill 1985- (with husband); *Recreations* walking Bruno the Great Dane, reading, sleeping; *Style*— Kirsty Wade; Sub Two Fitness Centre, Rowlands Gill, Tyne & Wear (☎ 0207 542044)

WADE, Michael John; s of Peter Wade, and Lorna A M Harris; *b* 22 May 1954; *Educ* Royal Russell, N Staffs Coll; *Career* fndr Holman Wade Ltd 1980, memb Lloyd's 1980, chm Holman Wade Ltd; dir: Horace Clarkson plc, Holman Wade Gp; memb: Cncl and Ctee Lloyd's 1987-92, Baltic Exchange 1987; *Recreations* music, shooting, flying; *Clubs* Turf; *Style*— Michael J Wade, Esq; 6 Vincent Sq, London SW1; 12 Camomile St, London EC3 (☎ 071 929 1239)

WADE, Prof Owen Lyndon; CBE (1983); s of James Owen David Wade, OBE (d 1962), of 25 Park Place, Cardiff, and Kate, *née* Jones (d 1974); *b* 17 May 1921; *Educ* Repton, Emmanuel Coll Cambridge, UCH (MA, MB BCh, MD, MRCP); *m* 6 March 1948, Margaret, da of Reginald John Burton (d 1972), of Ilfracoombe and New Milton; 3 da (Robin Elizabeth b 1949, Josephine b 1951, Mary Sian Mary b 1953); *Career* RMO UCH 1946, clinical asst Pneumokoniosis Res Unit MRC 1948-51, lectr Dept of Med Univ of Birmingham 1951-56, sr lectr and conslt physician Utd Birmingham Hosps 1956-57, Whitla prof of therapeutics Queen's Univ Belfast and conslt physician NI Hosps Authy 1957-71, dep dean Faculty of Med Queen's Univ Belfast 1968-71, prof of therapeutics and clinical pharmacology Birmingham Univ and conslt physician Queen Elizabeth Hosp Birmingham 1971-85, vice princ and pro vice chllr Univ of Birmingham 1984-85 (dean Faculty of Med and Dentistry 1978-84); memb: NI Gen Health Servs Bd 1957-71, Standing Med Advsy Ctee Min of Health and Social Security NI 1968-71 (Chm Sub Ctees on Community Med and Psychogeriatric Care 1969), Jt Formulary Ctee for the Br Nat Formulary 1963-85 (chm 1978-85), Dunlop Ctee on Safety of Drugs Miny of Health London 1963-70 (chm Sub of Adverse Reactions to Drugs 1967-70), Medicines Cmmn DHSS London 1969-77; chm: Ctee of Review of Medicines 1977-83, Clinical Res Bd MRC 1970-74; consIt advsr WHO: med educn 1960, 1963 and 1965, drug monitoring 1964, intensive hosp drug monitoring 1968, drug monitoring 1968, drug consumption in Europe 1969, Drug Utilisation Res Gp 1968-86; vice pres Res Def Soc 1990-, chm of tstees Arthur Thomson Charitable Tst 1984- (tstee 1978-), Hon MD Queen's Univ of Belfast 1989; memb: Physiological Soc, Br Pharmacological Soc, Assoc of Physicians of GB and Ireland, Med Res Soc; FRCP 1962, hon FRCPI 1969; *Books* Adverse Reactions to Drugs (2 edn, 1976), Cardiac Output and Regional Blood Flow (with JM Bishop 1962); contrib: J Physiology, Clinical Science, J Clinical Investigation; *Recreations* sailing, woodturning, reading, grandchildren; *Clubs* Athenaeum; *Style*— Prof Owen Wade, CBE; The Medical School, Univ of Birmingham, Birmingham B15 2TJ (☎ 021 414 4049)

WADE, Hon Robert Alexander Mercer; yr s of Baron Wade, DL (Life Peer, d 1988); *b* 22 May 1943; *Educ* Mill Hill, Trinity Coll Cambridge (BA 1965, LLB 1966, MA 1969); *m* 1, 29 July 1967, Jennifer Jane, da of Leslie Elliott, of Grantley Grange, High Grantley, nr Ripon; 1 s (Michael Richard b 1968), 1 da (Juliet Helen b 1970); m 2, 1978, Elizabeth, da of James Lobban, of Dundee; 1 s (Alistair James Mercer b 1982), 1 da (Katherine Elizabeth b 1985); *Career* admitted a slr 1968; *Style*— The Hon Robert Wade; The Old Rectory, Barwick-in-Elmet, Leeds, W Yorks

WADE, Robert Edward; s of Edward William Wade, of Southend House, Footscray Rd, Eltham, and Rosina Alice, *née* Gill; *b* 29 Dec 1949; *m* 26 April 1975, Monica Jane, da of Alex Rennie, of Gerrard House, Norwich, Norfolk; 1 da (Joanne Lisa b 7 May 1980); *Career* dir: Bisgood Bishop 1984-86, County Bisgood 1986, Citicorp Scrimgeour Vickers 1986-88, Robert Fleming Secs 1988-90, Bexley Developments Ltd; memb Stock Exchange 1975; *Recreations* golf; *Clubs* Royal Blackheath Golf; *Style*— Robert Wade, Esq; Glebe House, Chislehurst Rd, Bickley, Bromley, Kent BR1 2NJ (☎ 081 467 8964); Bexley Developments Ltd, Epworth House, 25 City Rd, London EC1V 1PT (☎ 071 638 0311)

WADE, Roy; s of Kenneth Wade (d 1978), and Bridle Lily, *née* Westwood (d 1986); *b* 6 Oct 1944; *Educ* Queen Elizabeth's GS, Blackburn Lancs, Gloucester Tech Coll; *m* 1 (m dis 1979), Thirza Dorothy; 1 s (Jasper Kenneth b 1975), 1 da (Amber Elizabeth b 1976); m 2, 16 Nov 1979, Pamela Janis, da of Francis Reece, of 12 Bengal Drive, Christchurch NZ; 1 da (Amelia Jane b 1989); *Career* admitted slr 1969; Shawcross & Co: slr 1970-79; called to the Bar Inner Temple 1980; practice on Midland and Oxford circuit; *Recreations* sea fishing, shooting, travel; *Clubs* Garron Valley Sea Angling; *Style*— Roy Wade, Esq; The Croft, Linton, Ross-on-Wye, Herefordshire HR9 7RZ (☎ 0989 82 476), 1 Fountain Court, Steelhouse Lane, Bimringham B4 6DR (☎ 021 2365721, fax 021 2363639)

WADE, Air Chief Marshal Sir Ruthven Lowry; KCB (1974, CB 1970), DFC (1944); *b* 1920; *Educ* Cheltenham, RAF Cranwell; *Career* RAF 1939-78: Staff Offr Air HQ Malta, Cdr RAF Gaydon 1962-65, Air Exec to Dep for Nuclear Affrs SHAPE 1967-68, AOC 1 Gp Strike Command 1968-71, Dep Cdr RAF Germany 1971-72, vice chief Air Staff 1973-76, Air Marshal 1974, Air Chief Marshal 1976, Chief Personnel & Logistics MOD 1976-78; *Style*— Air Chief Marshal Sir Ruthven Wade, KCB, DFC; White Gables, Westlington, Dinton, Aylesbury, Bucks HP17 8UR (☎ 0296 748884)

WADE, (Sarah) Virginia; OBE (1986, MBE 1969); da of Canon Eustace Holland Wade (d 1988), and Joan Barbara, *née* Gowie (d 1989); *b* 10 July 1945; *Educ* Durban Girls HS, Tunbridge Wells GS, Univ of Sussex (BSc); *Career* tennis player; winner: US Open Tennis Championships 1968, Aust Open 1972, Italian 1972, Wimbledon 1977, Seven Grand Slam titles (three singles, four doubles); played in Wightman Cup for GB twenty times, commentator for BBC and American TV; memb Wimbledon Ctee 1982-, vice pres Greater London Fund for the Blind; Hon LLD Univ of Sussex 1985; *Books* Courting Triumph (1978), Ladies of the Court (1986); *Clubs* All England Lawn Tennis, Queen's; *Style*— Miss Virginia Wade, OBE; IMG, Pier House, Strand on the Green, Chiswick, London W4

WADE, Sir (Henry) William Rawson; QC (1968); s of Col Henry Oswald Wade, DSO, TD (d 1941), and Eileen Lucy *née* Rawson-Ackroyd (d 1973); *b* 16 Jan 1918; *Educ* Shrewsbury, Gonville and Caius Coll Cambrige (BA, MA, LLD), Harvard; *m* 1, 1943, Marie (d 1980), da of G E Osland-Hill (d 1958), of Bucks; 2 s (Michael, Edward); m 2, 1982, Marjorie Grace Hope, wid of B C Browne, da of Surgn-Capt H Hope Gill RN (d 1956), of Devon; *Career* called to the Bar Lincoln's Inn, hon bencher 1964; prof of law: Univ of Oxford 1961-76, Univ of Cambridge 1978-82; master Gonville and Caius Coll Cambridge 1976-88; fell Br Acad 1969 (vice pres 1981-83); kt 1985; *Books* numerous books and articles on administrative, constitutional and real property law; *Recreations* climbing, gardening, music; *Clubs* United Oxford and Cambridge Univs, Alpine; *Style*— Sir William Wade, QC; Gonville and Caius Coll, Cambridge CB2 1TA (☎ 0223 332400); 1A Ludlow Lane, Fulbourn, Cambridge CB1 5BL (☎ 0223 881745)

WADE-GERY, Sir Robert Lucian; KCMG (1982), KCVO (1983); o s of late Prof Henry Theodore Wade-Gery, MC, FBA, and Vivian, *née* Whitfield; *b* 22 April 1929; *Educ* Winchester, New Coll Oxford; *m* 16 June 1962, Sarah, da of Adam Denzil Marris, CMG (d 1989); 1 s (William Richard b 1967), 1 da (Laura Katharine b 1965); *Career* entered For Serv 1951; served: London, Bonn, Tel Aviv, Saigon; under sec Central Policy Review Staff 1971-73; min: Madrid 1973-77, Moscow 1977-79; dep sec of the Cabinet 1979-82, high cmmr New Delhi 1982-87; exec dir Barclays de Zoete Wedd Ltd 1987-89; fell All Souls' Oxford 1951-73 and 1987-89; chm Govrs London School of Oriental and African Studies 1990-; *Recreations* walking, sailing, history, travel; *Clubs* Athenaeum; *Style*— Sir Robert Wade-Gery, KCMG, KCVO; 7 Rothwell St, London NW1A 8YH (☎ 071 722 4754); c/o BZW, Ebbgate House, 2 Swan Lane, London EC4R 3TS (☎ 071 956 4849); Church Cottage, Cold Aston, Cheltenham GL54 3BN (☎ 0451 21115)

WADE-GERY, William Alexander (Sandy); o s of William Robertson Wade-Gery, JP (d 1967), of Bushmead Priory, and Margaret Frances, *née* Dymond; descended from Rev Hugh Wade (d 1832), who assumed the additional name and arms of Gery by Royal Licence on his marriage (1792) to Hester, 3 da and co-heiress of William Gery, of Bushmead Priory (*see* Burke's Landed Gentry, 18 edn, vol II, 1969); *b* 28 Feb 1950; *Educ* Bloxham; *Career* farmer and landowner; *Style*— Sandy Wade-Gery, Esq; Bushmead Priory, Bushmead, nr Colmworth, Beds; Bushmead Farm Office, nr Colmworth, Beds MK44 2LH (☎ 0230 62376, car 0860 627290)

WADE OF CHORLTON, Baron (Life Peer UK 1990), of Chester in the County of Cheshire; Sir (William) Oulton Wade; JP; s of Samuel Norman Wade and Joan Ferris, *née* Wild; *b* 24 Dec 1932; *Educ* Birkenhead Sch, Queen's Univ Belfast; *m* 1959, Gillian Margaret Leete; 1 s, 1 da; *Career* farmer and cheesemaker; md of family farming co, chm Marlow Wade mktg conslts; former Cheshire Cnllr, former chm City of Chester Cons Assoc 1973-76, jt hon treas Cons Pty 1982-, chm Cons Bd of Fin; chm English Cheese Export Cncl 1982-84; Liveryman Worshipful Co of Farmers, Freeman City of London; kt 1982; *Clubs* Carlton, Farmers', Chester City, St James's (Manchester); *Style*— The Rt Hon Lord Wade of Chorlton; Chorlton Lodge Farm, Chorlton by Backford, Chester

WADEY, Lady Bridget Ann; *née* Stuart; o da of 8 Earl Castle Stewart, *qv*; *b* 12 Feb 1957; *Educ* MHort (RHS), DMS; *m* 7 April 1990, Robert W Wadey, o s of Thomas Wadey, of Marine Gardens, Brighton; *Style*— The Lady Bridget Wadey

WADSWORTH, Arthur John; s of John Edwin Wadsworth, of Epsom, Surrey, and Vera May, *née* Merrett; *b* 13 June 1939; *Educ* King's Coll Sch Wimbledon; *m* 2 July 1966, Sheila, da of Charles William Blythe, of Tunbridge Wells, Kent; 1 s (Daniel b 9 Nov 1972), 2 da (Faye b 7 Aug 1970, Zoe b 5 April 1975); *Career* asst gen mangr Midland Bank plc 1982-86 (joined 1958, with various depts/ branches in London 1958-67, appts in Leicester Nottingham London 1967-82), co sec Midland Montagu (Hldgs) Ltd 1987-, co sec and exec dir Samuel Montagu & Co Ltd 1987-, dir London Int Fin Futures Exchange Ltd 1982-85; dir Epsom Sports Club Ltd; Freeman City of London 1979; ACIB 1964, MBIM 1974; *Recreations* playing hockey, gardening; *Clubs* RAC, Epsom Hockey; *Style*— Arthur Wadsworth, Esq; Samuel Montagu & Co Ltd, 10 Lower Thames St, London, EC3R 6AE (☎ 071 260 9777)

WADSWORTH, David Grant; s of Fred Wadsworth (d 1960), and Lona, *née* Booth (d 1970); *b* 30 Dec 1944; *Educ* Hipperholme GS Yorks, Oriel Coll Oxford (MA); *m* Kate Sandra; 1 step s (Simon d 1987), 2 step da (Jill, Helen); *Career* teacher Gloucestershire and Blackpool 1966-73, admin posts ed dept Leeds City Cncl 1973-85, dep dir educn Northumberland 1985-89, chief educn offr Bedfordshire 1989-; memb: Yorkshire: CCC and RFU, Univ of Cambridge RUFC, Harlequins RFC, Northampton RFC; memb Soc Educn Offrs; FBIM 1988, FRSA 1989; *Recreations* rugby and cricket (passively), epicurean delights; *Clubs* Royal Over-Seas League; *Style*— David G Wadsworth, Esq; County Hall, Bedford (☎ 0234 263222)

WADSWORTH, David Jeffrey; s of Arthur Jeffrey Wadsworth, and Gweneth Phyllis, *née* Horsman; *b* 11 Dec 1949; *Educ* Reading Sch, New Coll Oxford (MA); *Career* CA; Peat Marwick Mitchell & Co 1971-79, ptnr Kidsons 1981-90, founder David Wadsworth & Co 1990-; non exec dir: Columbia House Nominees Ltd 1985-90, Kidsons Corporate Fin Ltd 1988-90, Penington Ltd 1988-; dir: Green and Grey Ltd 1988-, Morworth Ltd 1988-, Bramley Heritage Ltd 1988-; memb: Investors in Indust Non-Exec Directors Resource, IOD; FCA; *Recreations* collecting first edition Penguin books, golf, walking, music, gardening; *Clubs* Roehampton; *Style*— David Wadsworth, Esq; (☎ 0831 501494)

WADSWORTH, James Patrick; QC (1981); s of Francis Thomas Bernard Wadsworth (d 1940), of Newcastle, and Geraldine Rosa, *née* Brannan (d 1953); *b* 7 Sept 1940; *Educ* Stonyhurst, Univ Coll Oxford (MA); *m* 1963, Judith, da of Morrison Scott, of Newport on Tay; 1 s (Francis b 1967), 1 da (Katherine (Mrs Ousterman) b 1964); *Career* called to the Bar Inner Temple 1963, bencher 1988, rec of the Crown Ct 1980-; *Style*— James Wadsworth, Esq, QC; 4 Paper Buildings, Temple, London EC4Y 7EX (☎ 071 353 3366, fax 071 353 5778)

WADSWORTH, Roger Leonard; s of Leonard Wadsworth (d 1985), and Irene Nellie, *née* Hughes; *b* 2 May 1950; *Educ* Hurstpierpoint, Kingston Poly (BA); *m* 1988, Sandra Anne, da of RA Carney, of Barry County, Missouri; *Career* chm and md Roger Wadsworth & Co (Holdings) Ltd; chm: Wadsworth Electronics Ltd, Leonard

Wadsworth Group Ltd; *Recreations* wildlife management, stalking, shooting; *Clubs* RAC; *Style—* Roger Wadsworth, Esq; Wadsworth Electronics Ltd, Central Avenue, East Molesey, Surrey KT8 0QB; Camusrory Estate, Mallaig, Inverness-shire; Colony Surf, Honolulu, Hawaii, USA

WADSWORTH, Thomas Gordon; s of Samuel Bertram Wadsworth (d 1955), and Elizabeth Jane, *née* Brown (d 1987); *b* 13 Jan 1930; *Educ* Liverpool Coll, Univs of Liverpool and Wales (MChOrth); *Career* conslt orthopaedic surgn St Bartholomew's Hosp and Homerton Hosp London; former examiner in pathology and section chm Primary FRCS England; examiner in surgy with special interest in pathology FRCSEd, lectr in hand surgy Med Coll of St Bartholomew's Hosp; corresponding memb: American Acad of Orthopaedic Surgns, American Soc for Surgery of the Hand; memb American Shoulder and Elbow Surgns, Med Coll of St Bartholomew's Hosp; memb Cncl: Professions Supplementary to Med, Br Soc for Surgery of the Hand; fndr memb Br Elbow and Shoulder Soc; Freeman City of London; FB OrthA, FRCS, FRCSE, FACS, FICS; *Recreations* walking in country, classical music, travel; *Clubs* Reform, City Livery, Savile; *Style—* Thomas Wadsworth, Esq; 35 Shepherd St, Mayfair, London W1Y 7LH (☎ 071 723 5785); Department of Orthopaedic Surgery, St Bartholomew's Hospital, West Smithfield, London EC1A 7BE (☎ 071 601 8888)

WADWELL, David Martin; s of George Wadwell, of 10 Virginia Beeches, Callow Hill, Virginia Water, Surrey, and Marie, *née* Pickering; *b* 12 March 1946; *Educ* Ipswich Sch, Univ of Southampton (BSc), LSE (MSc); *m* 5 June 1971 (m dis 1978), Valerie, da of Peter Arthur Wilks; *Career* CA; Ernst & Whinney 1968-72, ptnr de Zoete & Bevan Stockbrokers 1972-86, dir Barclays de Zoete Wedd 1986-; FCA; *Recreations* sailing, travel; *Style—* David Wadwell, Esq; 7 Hippodrome Mews, Clarendon Cross, Kensington, London W11 4NN (☎ 071 229 0493); Barclays de Zoete Wedd Securities Ltd, Ebbgate House, 2 Swan Lane London EC4R 3TS (☎ 071 623 2323, fax 071 626 1879, telex 888 221)

WADWELL, George Richard; s of George Wadwell, of Virginia Water, Surrey, and Marie, *née* Pickering; *b* 25 Oct 1942; *Educ* Ipswich Sch Suffolk; *m* 28 Nov 1970, Gladys Yolanda, da of Señor Bricenio Amable Ramirez (d 1972), of Guayaquil, Ecuador, South America; 2 da (Ingrid b 1974, Deborah b 1976); *Career* articled clerk and audit sr Touche Ross and Co London and Cape Town 1960-68, gp accountant Surinvest London 1968-69, asst to finance dir NORAM Ltd London NASSAU 1969-70, various financial posts BOAC, BAB Heathrow Airport 1970-81; British Airways Heathrow Airport: mgr asset and gp accounting 1981-86, gp financial accountant 1986-; FCA 1977; *Recreations* radio ham, marathon running, travel; *Style—* Richard Wadwell, Esq; 7 Barkhart Drive, Wokingham, Berks RG11 1TW (☎ 0734 791398); Group Financial Accountant, British Airways plc, PO Box 10, Hounslow, Middlesex (☎ 081 562 0579, fax 081 562 8764)

WADY, Hon Mrs (Emma); da of 5 Baron Redesdale (d 1991); *b* 27 June 1959; *m* 30 Nov 1985, George F Wady, yr son of G Wady, of Frinton-on-Sea, Essex; 1 s (Alexander Bertram b 1 June 1989); *Style—* The Hon Mrs Wady

WAEBER, Hon Mrs (Jill); *née* Taylor; da of Baron Taylor of Gryfe (Life Peer), and Isobel, *née* Wands; *b* 15 Sept 1945; *Educ* Hutcheson's Girls' GS, Glasgow Sch of Art, Jordanhill Coll of Educn; *m* 1, 1969, Dr Thomas Egli; m 2, 1976, Hans René Waeber; 1 s (Alexander b 1979), 2 da (Kirstie b 1977, Jennifer b 1980); *Career* painter; *Style—* The Hon Mrs Waeber; Marchbachstrasse 24, 4108 Witterswil, Switzerland

WAGEMAKERS, Monique Huberdina Yvonne Maria; da of Corneluis Johannes Maria Wagemakers (d 1972), and Francisca Geertruida Maria, *née* Verbeeten; *b* 29 Sept 1951; *Educ* Brabants Conservatorium; *m* 23 Aug 1985, Aart Bouwmeester, s of Max Eric Bouwmeester, of Stuifzand, Nederland; 1 s (Sebastiaan b 8 Dec 1985), 1 da (Laura b 16 May 1988); *Career* asst dir De Nederlandse Opera Amsterdam 1976-; asst to: Götz Friedrich, Harry Kupfer, John Cox, Gian Carlo Menotti, Lotfi Mansouri, David Poutney, Dario Fo, Tito Capobianco, Michael Geliot; revival dir: The Fantasticks, Don Giovanni, La Vie Parisienne, La Fanciulla del West, Fidelio; debut as dir: Madame Butterfly 1983, Don Giovanni 1986, Rigoletto 1987; choreographies for: La Traviata, Don Giovanni, I Due Foscari, Intermezzo, Roselinda, La vie Parisienne, Arabella; Glyndebourne Festival Opera: asst dir and choreographer Intermezzo 1983, assoc dir and choreographer Arabella 1984 and 1985, revival dir Arabella 1989; *Recreations* photography, video; *Style—* Miss Monique Wagemakers; Gaaspstraat 58, 1079 VG Amsterdam (☎ 020 449 465); De Nederlandse Opera, Waterlooplein 22, 1011PG Amsterdam, Nederland (☎ 020 551 8922)

WAGGETT, Ralph Whitell; s of John Waggett, and Mary, *née* Whitell; *b* 30 Nov 1924; *Educ* Richmond Sch Yorkshire; *Career* RAF 1943-47; slr (ret); tstee: The Richmondshire Museum; re-fndr first warden and present clerk of Co of Fellmongers of Richmond Yorks; Liveryman Worshipful Co of Glovers; *Books* Transcript of the Archives (1580-1980) of the Company of Mercers Grocers and Haberdashers of Richmond Yorkshire (1988); *Recreations* walking, painting, the study of local history, antiquarian book collecting; *Style—* Ralph Waggett, Esq; Hill Hse Cottage, Frenchgate, Richmond, N Yorks (☎ 0748 3000)

WAGNER, Sir Anthony Richard; KCB (1978), KCVO (1961, CVO 1953); s of Orlando Wagner (gggs of George Wagner, godson of George I and hatter to George III. George's f Melchior was hatter to George I and George II and was 2 s of Hans Heinrich Wagner, hatter to the court of Coburg. The Wagners are of Silesian origin). Sir Anthony's sis was m to late Rt Hon Sir Melford Stevenson; *b* 6 Sept 1908; *Educ* Eton, Balliol Coll Oxford (MA); *m* 26 Feb 1953, Gillian Mary Millicent, *qv*, eldest da of Maj Henry Graham (d 1970), of Micheldever, Hants; 2 s, 1 da; *Career* serv WWII War Office and Miny of Town and Country Planning; Portcullis Pursuivant 1931-43, Richmond Herald 1943-61, Garter 1961-78, Clarenceux King of Arms 1978-; ed Soc of Antiquaries' Dictionary of British Arms 1940-, sec Order of the Garter 1952-61, registrar Coll of Arms 1953-60, jt register Ct of Chivalry 1954-, genealogist Order of the Bath 1961-72 and Order of St John 1961-75, kt princ Imperial Soc of Kts Bachelor 1962-83, dir Heralds' Museum Tower of London 1978-83; pres Aldeburgh Soc 1970-83; former: memb Cncl Nat Trust, trustee Nat Portrait Gallery; hon fellow: Balliol Coll Oxford 1979, Heraldry Soc of Canada; KStJ; *Publications include* Heralds and Heraldry in the Middle Ages (1939), Historic Heraldry of Britain (1939), Heraldry in England (1946), The Records and Collections of the College of Arms (1952), English Genealogy (1960), English Genealogy (1960), Heralds of England (1967), Pedigree and Progress (1975); A Herald's World (1988); *Style—* Sir Anthony Wagner, KCB, KCVO, Clarenceux King of Arms; 10 Physic Place, Royal Hospital Road, London SW3 4HQ (☎ 071 352 0934); Wyndham Cottage, Aldeburgh, Suffolk (☎ 072 885) 2596); College of Arms, Queen Victoria St, London EC4 (☎ 071 248 4300)

WAGNER, Lady; Gillian Mary Millicent; *née* Graham; OBE (1977); eldest da of Maj Henry Archibald Roger Graham (d 1970), of Old Mill House, Micheldever, Hants, and Hon Margaret Beatrice Lopes (d 1983), 3 da of 1 Baron Roborough; *b* 25 Oct 1927; *Educ* Cheltenham Ladies' Coll, Geneva Univ (Licencés Sciences Morales), LSE (Dip Social Admin), PhD London (1977); *m* 26 Feb 1953, Sir Anthony Richard Wagner, KCB, KCVO, *qv*; 2 s (Roger Henry Melchior b 28 Feb 1957, Mark Anthony b 18 Dec 1958), 1 da (Lucy Elizabeth Millicent (Mrs Page) b 22 Oct 1954); *Career* chm: Review into Residential Care 1985-88, Barnardos 1978-84 (memb Cncl 1984-), Volunteer Centre 1984-89, Thomas Corau Fndn 1990-; pres IAPS 1984-90; chm Felixstowe Coll 1978-87; pres SKILL Nat Bureau for Students with Disabilities; vice chm: Carnegie UK Tst, Leche Tst; Freeman of City of London; Hon Dr of Social Sciences Univ of Bristol 1989, LLD Univ of Liverpool 1990; *Books* Barnardo (1979), Children of the Empire (1982), The Chocolate Conscience (1987); *Recreations* sailing, gardening, travelling; *Clubs* Aldeburgh Yacht; *Style—* Lady Wagner, OBE; 10 Physic Place, Royal Hospital Road, London SW3 4HQ (☎ 071 352 0934) Wyndham Cottage, Crespigny Rd, Aldeburgh, Suffolk

WAGNER, Dr Nicholas Alan Giles; s of Thomas Donald Wagner, of Croydon, Surrey (d 1980), and Valerie Jacqueline Cameron Peers, *née* Kemp; *b* 17 Jan 1945; *Educ* Whitgift Sch, The Med Coll of St Bartholomew's Hosp Univ of London (MB BS); *m* 1, 14 Aug 1971 (m dis 1982), Patsy, da of Fred Doherty-Bullock, of Worcester (d 1982); m 2, 16 April 1987, Linda, da of James Halstead, of Brentford, Middx; 1 s (Alexander John Halstead b 1984); *Career* conslt: psychiatrist W Middx Univ Hosp 1978-88, mental health of the elderly Herefords Health Authy 1988-; hon sr lectr Charing Cross and Westminster Med Sch 1978-88, chm Herefordshire Alzheimer Disease Soc; *Recreations* gardening, gastronomy; *Style—* Dr Nicholas Wagner; Dept of Mental Health of the Elderly, Cantilupe Wing, General Hosp, Hereford HR1 2PA (☎ 0432 355444)

WAGSTAFF, Ven Christopher John Harold; s of Harold Maurice Wagstaff (d 1982), of London, and Kathleen Mary, *née* Bean (d 1979); *b* 25 June 1936; *Educ* Bishop's Stortford Coll, Essex Inst of Agric, St David's Coll Lampeter (BA); *m* 1964, Margaret Louise, da of John Park Alan Macdonald, of Scotland; 2 s (Alasdair b 1966, Robert b 1968), 1 da (Marianne b 1972); *Career* curate All Saints' Queensbury London 1963-68; vicar: St Michael Wembley 1968-72, Coleford with Staunton Gloucester 1972-82; rural dean South Forest 1975-82; archdeacon of Gloucester 1982-; Freeman City of London, Liveryman Worshipful Co of Armourers and Brasiers; *Recreations* gardening, travel; *Style—* The Ven the Archdeacon of Gloucester; Christchurch Vicarage, Montpellier, Gloucester GL1 1LB (☎ 0452 28500)

WAGSTAFF, David St John Rivers; s of John Edward Pretty Wagstaff (d 1973), and Dorothy Margaret, *née* McRobie (d 1980); *b* 22 June 1930; *Educ* Winchester, Trinity Coll Cambridge (MA, LLB); *m* 31 March 1970, Dorothy Elizabeth, da of Robert Carter Starkie (d 1982), of Pool-in-Wharfedale, nr Leeds; 2 da (Susan b 1971, Patricia b 1973); *Career* called to the Bar Lincoln's Inn 1954; NE circuit, rec of the Crown Court 1974; *Recreations* mountaineering; *Clubs* Alpine, Fell and Rock Climbing (Leeds); *Style—* David Wagstaff, Esq; 8 Breary Lane East, Bramhope, Leeds LS16 9BJ; 22 East Parade, Leeds 1 (☎ 0532 452702)

WAGSTAFF, Edward Malise Wynter; s of Col Henry Wynter Wagstaff, and Jean Everil, *née* Mathieson (d 1965); *b* 27 June 1930; *Educ* Wellington Coll, RMA Sandhurst, Pembroke Coll Cambridge (MA), Staff Coll Camberley; *m* 14 Dec 1957, Eva Margot, da of Fred Erik Oscar Hedelius, Kammarratsrad (Justice), Judge of the Swedish Appeal Court; 1 s (James b 1973), 2 da (Kersti b 1959, Anna b 1962); *Career* cmmnd RE 1949; served UK, Germany, Gibraltar 1950-62; seconded to Fed Regular Army Fedn of South Arabia 1963-65; asst Mil Attaché Amman 1967-69 (Major 1962); joined FCO 1969: first sec Embassy Saigon 1973, FCO 1975, Oslo 1976, Copenhagen 1978, FCO 1981, cnsllr 1983; Gen Serv Medal; South Arabia Radfan Bar 1965; Knight first order of Dannebrog 1979 (Denmark); *Recreations* church work, psychotherapy, house repair; *Clubs* Travellers'; *Style—* Edward Wagstaff, Esq; c/o Lloyds Bank plc, 32 Commercial Way, Woking, Surrey GU21 1ER

WAIN, Christopher Nicholas; s of Andrew Arthur Mackenzie-Wain (d 1973), and Diana Margaret, *née* Douglas; *b* 24 Dec 1939; *Educ* Homefield Sch Bournemouth, Ruskin Coll Oxford, Brasenose Coll Oxford (BA); *m* Jan 1971 (m dis 1975), da of J M Perry (d 1971), of Suffield, Canada; *Career* Reg Army 1957-60: jt intelligence bureau, army PR, HQ Middle East landforces; journalist: New Milton Advertiser 1955-57, Salisbury Journal 1960-62, Southern TV 1966-71, ITN 1971-75; aviation and tport corr 1987- (def corr 1975-87); memb: Breakaway Tst, RNLB, Int Inst Strategic Studies; *Recreations* gliding, travel; *Clubs* Reform, Utd Oxford and Cambridge; *Style—* Christopher Wain, Esq; BBC Television News, TV Centre, Wood Lane, London W12 7IJ (☎ 01 743 8000, fax 01 746 0787)

WAIN, John Barrington; CBE (1984); s of Arnold A Wain, and Anne, *née* Turner (d 1963); *b* 14 March 1925; *Educ* The High Sch Newcastle-under-Lyme, St John's Coll Oxford (BA MA); *m* 1, 1947 (m dis 1956), Marianne, da of Julius Urmston; m 2, 1960, Eirian (d 1988), da of T E James; 3 s (William Brunswick b 1960, Ianto Samuel b 1962, Tobias Hamnet b 1966); m 3, 1989, Patricia Ann, da of R Dunn; *Career* Fereday fell St John's Coll Oxford 1946-49, lectr in Eng lit Univ of Reading 1949-55, prof of poetry Univ of Oxford 1973-78, lectr at various univs in Eng, USA, France, Greece, India, Scandinavia; Hon DLitt: Loughborough Univ of Technol 1984, Univ of Keele 1984; *Books* incl: Hurry on Down (1953), The Smaller Sky (1967), A Winter in the Hills (1970), Young Shoulders (Whitbread award, 1982), Where the Rivers Meet (1988), Comedies (1990), Poems 1949-79 (1980), Dear Shadows (1986), Samuel Johnson (James Tait Black prize, William Heinemann award, 1974), Dear Shadows (memoirs, 1987); *Recreations* walking, travelling by train especially in France; *Style—* John Wain, Esq, CBE; 17 Wolvercote Green, Oxford, Oxon

WAIN, Prof (Ralph) Louis; CBE (1968); s of George Wain (d 1941), of Hyde, Cheshire, and Eliza, *née* Hardy (d 1948); *b* 29 May 1911; *Educ* Hyde Co GS Cheshire, Univ of Sheffield (BSc, MSc, PhD), Univ of London (DSc); *m* Joan, da of Thomas Bowker (d 1941), of Denton, Lancs; 1 s(Michael Louis b 1948), 1 da (Rosemary Joan b 1944); *Career* dir Agric Res Cncl Res Unit Wye Coll Univ of London 1953-78 (prof chemistry 1950-78), hon prof chemistry Univ of Kent 1978-; Hon DAgSci Ghent 1963, hon DSc: Kent 1976, Lausanne 1977, Sheffield 1977; FRS 1960; *Recreations* painting, travel; *Style—* Prof Louis Wain, CBE, FRS; Crown Point, Scotton St, Wye, Kent TN25 5BZ (☎ 0233 812 157); University of Kent, Canterbury, Kent (☎ 0227 764000, telex 965 449)

WAIN, Roger Henry Ashley; s of late Ernest Wain, of Caton, Lancs, and late Muriel Maimie Wain; *b* 28 May 1938; *Educ* Lancaster Royal GS, St Peter's Coll Oxford (MA); *m* 1965, Rosalind, da of late John Laycock, of Moorgarth, Lancaster; 1 s, 2 da (twins); *Career* chm: 1981-88: Laurentian Bank Ltd, Laurentian Investmt Mgmnt Ltd, Laurentian Unit Tst Mgmnt, Castlemere Properties Ltd; dep chm 1981-88: Trident Life Ltd, Imperial Life (UK) Ltd, Laurentian Hldg Co and chief exec); dir 1981-88: Imperial Life of Canada, Abercorn Gen Investmts Ltd, Impco Properties (GB) Ltd, Invicta Investmt Co Ltd, Property Investmt and Fin Lt; dir: Chesterfield Properties plc Centaur Communications Ltd, Br Empire Securities & Gen Tst plc; chm: Madison Tst, LIMRA UK advsy ctee 1985; pres Canada/UK C of C 1985-87, hon fell Life Insur Assoc 1985, vice pres Nat Playbus Assoc 1983, dir Fndn for Canadian Studies 1983; *Recreations* hunting, tennis, travel, shooting, skiing; *Clubs* Buck's; *Style—* Roger Wain, Esq; 15 Lansdowne Walk, London W11 3AH (☎ 071 727 4485)

WAINE, David Michael; s of Capt Leslie Arthur Waine (d 1984), and Linda, *née* Pridmore; *b* 12 June 1944; *Educ* Reading Collegiate Sch; *m* 23 April 1966, Elizabeth Ann, da of John Halls (d 1967); 1 da (Nicola Frances b 1969); *Career* sports ed Newbury Weekly News 1960-64; BBC TV and radio reporter: Radio 4 Today prog, World at One, World Serv, TV news and current affrs, South Today, Points West 1964-67; BBC: prog organiser Radio Brighton 1967-70, mangr Radio Bristol 1970-78, regnl TV mangr South West (Plymouth) 1978-83, head network prodn centre Pebble Mill 1983-86, head of Bdcasting Midlands 1986-; pres Birmingham Press Club 1988-91; memb Royal TV Soc; *Recreations* sport, gardening, reading; *Style—* David Waine, Esq; BBC, BBC in the Midlands, Pebble Mill Road, Edgbaston, Birmingham B5 7QQ (☎ 021 414 8888)

WAINE, Peter Edward; s of Dr Theodore Edward Waine, of Bilton, Rugby, Warwickshire, and Mary Florence, *née* Goodson; *b* 27 June 1949; *Educ* Bilton Grange, Worksop Coll, Univ of Bradford (BSc); *m* 21 June 1973, Stefanie Dale (niece of C P Snow, novelist), da of Philip Albert Snow, OBE, of Angmering, Sussex; 1 da (Philippa Wigmore b 21 May 1981); *Career* personnel mangr: GEC 1970-74, Cape Industs 1974-79, Coopers & Lybrand 1979-83; dir: CBI 1983-88, Blue Arrow 1988-90, W R Royle & Sons (non-exec) 1988-; chief exec Hanson Green 1990; non-exec chm: Corecare Ltd 1990, Arkley House Finance Ltd 1990-, Eurochange plc 1990-; chm Welwyn Garden City Soc; memb: Cncl Euro Business Sch, English Speaking Union Current Affairs Ctee, Ctee Br Atlantic; Parly candidate (Cons) Nottingham North 1979, Nat vice chm The Bow Group 1972 (chm Birmingham Gp 1971), dist cncllr Rugby 1973-77; non-exec dir East Herts Dist Health Authy; Freeman: City of London 1978, Worshipful Co of Carmen; FBIM (former memb Cncl); *Publications* Spring Cleaning Britain (1974), Withering Heights (1976), Weekly Columnist under pseudonym for London Newspaper (1984-87); *Recreations* gardening, walking, tennis; *Clubs* MCC, ESU; *Style—* Peter Waine, Esq; West House, Digswell Place, Welwyn Garden City, Herts (☎ 0707 330 714); Blue Arrow plc, 31 Worship St, London E1 (☎ 071 638 7788, fax 071 374 8412)

WAINSCOAT, Dr James Stephen; s of Arnold John Wainscoat, and Mary Hilda, *née* Bateman (d 1989); *b* 7 May 1949; *Educ* Holme Valley GS, Univ of Liverpool (MB ChB), Univ of Birmingham (MSc); *m* 14 Aug 1971, Beverly Susan, da of Walter Hannah (d 1987); 1 s (Luke), 2 da (Emma, Nancy); *Career* conslt haematologist John Radcliffe Hosp Oxford 1985-, clinical lectr Univ of Oxford 1986, hon dir Molecular and Cytogenic Haematology Unit Leukaemia Res Fund Univ of Oxford 1988-; MRCP 1976, MRCPath 1980; *Books* Molecular Diagnosis of Leukaemia and Lymphoma; *Recreations* music, running; *Clubs* Green Coll Oxford Univ; *Style—* Dr James Wainscoat; 38 Bickerton Rd, Headington, Oxford OX3 7LS (☎ 0865 62928); Dept of Haematology, John Radcliffe Hosp, Headington, Oxford (☎ 0865 817366)

WAINWRIGHT, (Harold) Anthony; s of Herbert Wainwright (d 1945), of Prenton, Cheshire, and Louise, *née* Stewart; *b* 30 Dec 1919; *Educ* Birkenhead Sch; *m* 29 March 1947, (Frances) Jean, da of Edgar Warren (d 1950), of Heswall, Wirral; 2 s (Nicholas b 1948, Michael b 1957), 2 da (Sarah b 1950, Louise b 1960); *Career* RA 1940-45, Lt 1941, Capt 1943, Maj 1945, served 28 LAA Regt (RA) with 14 Army in Burma and Assam 1942-45; chm Boodle and Dunthorne Ltd 1984- (md 1945-84), Hon Consul of Thailand 1965-, chm Nat Jewellers Assoc (JIC) 1971-75, Br rep De Beers Euro Diamond Cncl 1972-75; govr Blue Coat Sch 1974-, sec Birkenhead Boys' Club, assoc on ctees of other Boys' Clubs; Freeman: Worshipful Co of Goldsmiths 1966, City of London 1966; *Recreations* golf, game shooting, gardening; *Clubs* Royal Liverpool Golf (Hoylake), Athenaeum (Liverpool); *Style—* Anthony Wainwright, Esq; Boodle & Dunthorne Ltd, Boodles House, Lord St, Liverpool L2 9SQ (☎ 051 227 2525, fax 051 255 1070)

WAINWRIGHT, Dr (Anthony) Christopher; yr s of Robert Everard Wainwright, CMG (d 1990), of Wagoners Cottage, Cann Common, Shaftesbury, Dorset, and Bridget Doris, *née* Alan-Williams; *b* 25 Oct 1943; *Educ* Marlborough, St Thomas's Hosp Univ of London (MB BS); *m* 6 Sept 1968, Ursula, da of Ernest Herbert Jeans (d 1977), 1 s (James b 1972), 1 da (Sophie b 1975); *Career* sr registrar Univ Hosp Wales 1971-72, lectr anaesthesia Univ of Bristol 1972-75, conslt anaesthetist Univ of Southampton Hosps 1975-, hon clinical teacher Univ of Southampton 1975-, currently involved in beef farming; memb: New Forest Advsy Ctee of Nat Tst, Assoc of Anaesthetists, BMA; co fndr Wig and Scalpel Soc, former chm Copythorne Parish Cncl; FFARCS 1971; *Books* chapters in Anaesthesia Review 4 and Co2 Lasers in Otolaryngology; *Recreations* horses, music, medieval architecture; *Style—* Dr Christopher Wainwright; Ashton Cottage, Cadnam Lane, Cadnam, Southampton SO4 2NS (☎ 0703 812642); Shackleton Dept of Anaesthetics, The Gen Hosp, Tremona Rd, Southampton SO9 4XY (☎ 0703 796135)

WAINWRIGHT, Edgar Worthington; s of John Andrew Worthington Wainwright, of Twyford, Winchester, Hants, and Kathleen, *née* Gillibrand; *b* 17 March 1943; *Educ* Westminster; *m* 14 June 1969, Jill Rosamond, da of Capt Anthony Wilmott Adams, MC; 1 s (Timothy John Alexander Worthington b 26 Sept 1978), 2 da (Amanda Jane b 9 Sept 1970, Lucianne Clare b 2 Sept 1972); *Career* chartered shipbroker and freight forwarder; md Wainwright Bros & Co Ltd and assoc cos 1969-; FICS 1972, FIFF 1975; *Recreations* sailing; *Clubs* Baltic Exchange, Royal Southampton Yacht, Bosham Sailing; *Style—* Edgar Wainwright, Esq; Crofton, Cheriton Rd, Winchester, Hants; Wainwright Bros & Co Ltd, Bowling Green House, Orchard Place, Southampton, Hants (☎ 0703 223671, fax 0703 330880, telex 47 620)

WAINWRIGHT, Geoffrey John; MBE; s of Frederick Wainwright, and Dorothy, *née* Worton; *b* 19 Sept 1937; *Educ* Pembroke Docks Sch, Univ of Wales, Univ of London; *m* 23 Dec 1977, Judith; 1 s (Nicholas b 1966), 2 da (Rhiannon b 1961, Sarah b 1963); *Career* prof of environmental archaeology Univ of Baroda India 1961-63, princ inspector of ancient monuments DOE 1980-89 (inspector 1963-80), chief archaeologist English Heritage 1989-; memb Royal Cmmn on Ancient Monuments (Wales), pres Prehistoric Soc 1981-85, dir Soc of Antiquaries 1984-90; MIFA, FSA, FRSA; *Books* Coygan Camp (1967), Stone Age in India (1967), Durrington Walls (1971), Mount Pleasant (1979), Gussage All Saints (1979), The Henge Monuments (1989); *Recreations* rugby, racing, food and drink, walking; *Style—* Geoffrey Wainwright, Esq, MBE, FSA; Fortress House, 23 Saville Row, London W1X 2HE (☎ 071 973 3013)

WAINWRIGHT, John Andrew Worthington; s of Edgar Worthington Wainwright (d 1941), and Alice Maude, *née* La Mude (d 1979); *b* 11 Jan 1918; *Educ* Heath Mount Sch Hampstead, Westminster; *m* 1, 1939 (m dis 1945), Kathleen, *née* Gillibrand; 1 s (Edgar Worthington, 1 da (Angela); m 2, 1948, Betty Margaret, *née* Schluter; 1 s (Robert Edward Worthington); *Career* dir: British Transit Ltd, H Chaplin & Co Ltd, General Transit Services Ltd, Maccabe-Bower Shipping Ltd, Oscar Harris Son & Co Ltd, Packing and Warehousing Ltd, Bussey Freight Service Ltd, Wainwright Bros & Co Ltd, Yacht Shipping Ltd, Wainwright Bros (Travel) Ltd; Liveryman Worshipful Co of Shipwrights; FICS, FInstFF; *Recreations* gardening, reading, travelling, motoring; *Clubs* Royal Southampton Yacht; *Style—* John Wainwright, Esq; Knighton, Twyford, nr Winchester, Hants SO21 1QU; Bowling Green House, 1 Orchard Place, Southampton, Hants SO1 1BR

WAINWRIGHT, Sam; CBE (1982); *b* 2 Oct 1924; *Educ* LSE; *m* Ruth Strom; 3 s, 1 da; *Career* dep City ed Glasgow Herald 1952, md Rea Bros (merchant bankers) until 1977, md Nat Girobank 1977-85, dep chm Bd PO 1981-85, dir BICC plc 1985-90, chm Manders (Hldgs) plc 1986-87; memb MMC 1985-; *Style—* Sam Wainwright, Esq, CBE; 6 Heath Close, London NW11 7DX (☎ 081 455 4448)

WAITE, David Nicholas; s of George Frederick Waite (d 1989), of Leeds, and Constance, *née* Bouskill; *b* 28 March 1943; *Educ* Leeds GS, Magdalen Coll Oxford (exhibitioner, BA); *m* 1, 1967 (m dis 1979), Valerie May Fortune; 1 s (John b 1981); m 2, 1979, Frances Ann, da of Dominic Sarro; 1 s (Nicholas Sarro-Waite b 1981), 1 da (Mary Sarro-Waite b 1982); *Career* sales asst (later asst mangr Ore Purchases) Noranda Sales Corporation London and Toronto 1964-72, dir of trading (later pres NY Brokerage Subsid) Rudolf Wolff & Co Ltd London and NY 1972-78, vice pres i/c Metals Energy and Trade Finance Units Drexel Burnham Lambert Inc NY 1978-90, sr vice pres i/c Commercial Futures Div (and dir UK Subsid) Paine Webber Inc NY and London 1990-; *Books* Commodities and the Third World (contrib 1974), Rudolf Wolff's Guide to the London Metal Exchange (contrib 1976); *Recreations* family, travel, tennis, squash, reading, movies; *Clubs* Copper (New York); *Style—* David Waite, Esq; Paine Webber International Futures Ltd, 1 Finsbury Avenue, London EC2M 2PA (☎ 071 377 0055)

WAITE, Hon Mr Justice; Hon Sir John Douglas Waite; QC (1975); s of Archibald Waite; *b* 3 July 1932; *Educ* Sherborne, CCC Cambridge; *m* 1966, Julia Mary, da of Joseph Tangye; 3 s and 2 step s; *Career* 2 Lt RA 1951-52; barr Gray's Inn 1956, memb Gen Cncl Bar 1968-69, bencher 1981, High Ct Judge 1982-, pres Employment Appeal Tribunal 1983-85; kt 1982; *Style—* The Hon Sir John Waite; Royal Courts of Justice, Strand, London WC2A 2LL (☎ 01 405 7641)

WAITE, (Winston Anthony) John; s of John Clifford Waite (d 1969), of Gawsworth, Cheshire, and Margaret Ada, *née* Van Schuyk-Smith; *b* 26 Feb 1951; *Educ* Wilmslow GS, Univ of Manchester (BA); *m* 13 July 1984, Cate Anne Valerie, da of Stuart-Campbell, of Islington, London; *Career* BBC: graduate trainee 1973-76, radio presenter 1976-; progs incl: Face the Facts, You and Yours; *Recreations* music, reading, wine; *Style—* John Waite, Esq; 24 Augustus Close, Brentford Dock, Middx TW8 8QE (☎ 081 568 1556); BBC, Broadcasting House, London W1 (☎ 071 580 4468)

WAITE, Jonathan Gilbert Stokes; s of Capt Henry David Stokes Waite, of 8 Priory Close, Aldwick Bay, West Sussex, and Joan Winifred, *née* Paull; *b* 15 Feb 1956; *Educ* Scaitcliffe Sch Surrey, Sherborne, Trinity Coll Cambridge (MA); *Career* called to the Bar Inner Temple 1978, practised in common Law SE Circuit 1978-; hon sec Bar Golfing Soc; *Recreations* golf, skiing, the turf; *Clubs* Woking GC; *Style—* Jonathan Waite, Esq; 1 Paper Buildings, Temple, London EC4Y 7EP (☎ 071 583 7355, fax 071 353 2144)

WAITES, Prof William Michael; s of Lt-Col William Harland Waites (d 1986), and Kathleen, *née* Inglett (d 1985); *b* 18 July 1939; *Educ* Harwich GS, Univ of Durham (BSc), Univ of Sheffield (PhD); *m* 13 Aug 1966, Janet Ashworth; 2 s (Michael b 24 Feb 1968, Richard b 15 Oct 1969); *Career* postdoctorates: Nat Inst For Med Res London 1965-66, Univ of Oxford 1966-69; ARFC Inst of Food res: PSO 1969-85, dep head microbiology 1981-85; vice dean of faculty and head of dept, prof of food microbiology 1985-; convenor microbiology sub-gp food safety Applied Nutrition Res Consultative Ctee 1988-89, chm food safety Advsy Centre 1989-; FIFST 1985, FRSA 1989; *Recreations* walking, squash; *Style—* Prof William Waites; Dept of Applied Biochemistry and Food Science, Faculty of Agricultural and Food Sciences, Nottingham University, Sutton Bonington, Loughbourough, Leics LE12 5RD (☎ 0602 484848, fax 0509 673917)

WAKE, Lady Doune Mabell; *née* Ogilvy; da of 13 Earl of Airlie, DL; *b* 13 Aug 1953; *m* 1977, Hereward Charles Wake, s and h of Sir Hereward Wake, 14 Bt; 1 s; *Style—* The Lady Doune Wake; The Stables, Courteenhall, Northants

WAKE, Sir Hereward; 14 Bt (E 1621), of Clevedon, Somerset, MC (1942), DL (Northants 1955); s of Maj-Gen Sir Hereward Wake, 13 Bt, CB, CMG, DSO, JP, DL (d 1963, himself tenth in descent from the 1 Bt; the latter was in turn fifteenth in descent from Hugh Wac or Wake, feudal Baron by tenure of Bourne and Deeping *temp* King Stephen; this family's descent from Hereward the Wake, albeit in the female line, seems probable although not proven); *b* 7 Oct 1916; *Educ* Eton, RMC; *m* 1952, Julia Rosemary, JP, da of Capt Geoffrey W M Lees, of Falcutt House, nr Brackley, Northants; 1 s, 3 da; *Heir* s, Hereward Charles, b 22 Nov 1952; *Career* served 1937-46 with 1, 2, 7 and 9 Bns 60 Rifles (Burma Egypt, N Africa, NW Europe and Greece), Maj, ret 1947; High Sheriff Northants 1955; *Style—* Sir Hereward Wake, Bt, MC, DL; Courteenhall, Northampton (☎ 0604 204)

WAKE-WALKER, Lady Anne; *née* Spencer; only da of 7 Earl Spencer, TD (d 1975), and Lady Cynthia, *née* Hamilton, DCVO, OBE (d 1972), da of 3 Duke of Abercorn; aunt of HRH The Princess of Wales; *b* 4 Aug 1920; *m* 1944, Capt Christopher Wake-Walker, DL, RN, *qv*; 3 s, 2 da; *Career* served WWII, Third Offr WRNS; *Style—* The Lady Anne Wake-Walker; East Bergholt Lodge, Suffolk (via Colchester) CO7 6QU (☎ 0206 298278)

WAKE-WALKER, Capt Christopher Baldwin Hughes; DL (Suffolk 1983); assumed additional surname of Hughes; s of Adm Sir (William) Frederic Wake-Walker, KCB, CBE (d 1945), Third Sea Lord and Controller of the Navy 1943-45, and Muriel Elsie (d 1963), only da of Sir Collingwood Hughes, 10 Bt; *b* 16 May 1920; *Educ* RNC Dartmouth; *m* 1944, Lady Anne, *qv*, da of 7 Earl Spencer (d 1975); 3 s, 2 da; *Career* served RN, WW II, Cdr RNC Greenwich 1959-61, Naval Attaché Paris 1962-64, Capt Dartmouth Training Sqdn 1964-66, Dir Naval Signals 1966-68, ret 1968; High Sheriff Suffolk 1985; *Recreations* gardening; *Clubs* Army and Navy; *Style—* Capt Christopher Wake-Walker, DL, RN; East Bergholt Lodge, Suffolk (via Colchester) CO7 6QU (☎ 0206 298278)

WAKE-WALKER, David Christopher; s of Capt Christopher Baldwin Hughes Wake-Walker, RN, and Lady Anne, da of 7 Earl Spencer; 1 cous to HRH The Princess of Wales; *b* 11 March 1947; *Educ* Winchester, Univ of St Andrews; *m* 1979, Jennifer Rosemary, only da of Capt Patrick Vaulkhard, of 4 The Terrace, Snape, Saxmundham, Suffolk; 2 s (Frederic b 1981, Nicholas b 1985); *Career* dir Kleinwort Benson Limited 1981, md Kleinwort Benson (Hong Kong) Limited 1983-86, dir Kleinwort Benson Group plc 1990; *Clubs* Wanderers, Aldeburgh Yacht, Hong Kong, Shek O Country, Hurlingham; *Style—* David Wake-Walker Esq; 82 Royal Hill, London SE10 8RT, (☎ 081 691 4666); 20 Fenchurch St London EC3P 3DB, (☎ 071 623 8000)

WAKEFIELD, 10 Bishop of 1985-; Rt Rev David Michael Hope; patron of 74 livings and the archdeaconries and canonries in his cathedral; s of Jack Hope, by his w Florence; *b* 14 April 1940; *Educ* Queen Elizabeth GS, Wakefield, Univ of Nottingham (BA), Linacre House Oxford (DPHIL), St Stephen's House Oxford; *Career* asst curate St John Ivebrook Liverpool 1965-70, chaplain Bucharest 1967-68, vicar St Andrew Warrington 1970-74, princ St Stephen's House Oxford 1974-82; Vicar of All Saints' Margaret St London 1982-85; *Recreations* theatre, walking, travel; *Style—* The Rt Rev the Bishop of Wakefield; Bishop's Lodge, Woodthorpe Lane, Wakefield, W Yorks (☎ 0924 255349)

WAKEFIELD, Derek John; CB (1982); s of Archibald John Thomas Wakefield (d 1971), and Evelyn Bessie, *née* Goddard (d 1971); *b* 21 Jan 1922; *Educ* The Cwlth Sch; *m* 1951, Audrey Ellen, da of Johnathan Smith (d 1961); 1 da (Isobel); *Career* Lt Royal Pioneer Corps 1942-47, served in N Africa, Italy and ME; Air Miny 1939-42 and 1947-52, GCHQ 1952-82 (under sec 1978-82); govr Barnwood House Tst Gloucester 1973-89, memb Airship Assoc; *Recreations* airships; *Clubs* Naval and Military; *Style—* Derek Wakefield, Esq, CB; Dunhurst, Bay Lane, Gillingham, Dorset SP8 4ER (☎ 0747 822932)

WAKEFIELD, Gerald Hugo Cropper (Hady); yr s of Sir Edward Birkbeck

Wakefield, 1 Bt, CIE (d 1969), and (Constance) Lalage, *née* Thompson; *b* 15 Sept 1938; *Educ* Eton, Trinity Coll Cambridge (MA); *m* 4 Dec 1971, Victoria Rose, da of Maj Cecil Henry Feilden; 1 s (Edward Cecil b 7 March 1973); *Career* Nat Serv Lt 12 Royal Lancers 1957; memb Lloyd's; joined Joseph W Hobbs & Co 1961, Anderson Finch Villiers (Insur) Ltd 1963, C T Bowring & Co 1968 (dir 1983-); dir CTB (Insur) Ltd 1972; chm CTB Reinsurance Ltd 1988-, dep chm Guy Carpenter & Co Inc NY; *Recreations* skiing, shooting, fishing; *Clubs* White's; *Style—* Hady Wakefield, Esq; Bramdean House, Alresford, Hants; C T Bowring Reinsurance Ltd, Bowring Building, Tower Place, London EC3 (☎ 071 357 2400; fax 071 929 2705; telex 882 191)

WAKEFIELD, Sir (Edward) Humphry Tyrrell; 2 Bt (UK 1962), of Kendal, Co Westmorland; s of Sir Edward Birkbeck Wakefield, 1 Bt, CIE (d 1969, himself yr bro of 1 Baron Wakefield of Kendal); *b* 11 July 1936; *Educ* Gordonstoun, Trinity Coll Cambridge (MA); *m* 1, 1960 (m dis 1964), Priscilla, da of (Oliver) Robin Bagot; m 2, 1966 (m dis 1971), Hon Elizabeth Sophia Sidney, da of 1 Viscount De L'Isle, VC, KG, GCMG, GCVO, PC; 1 s; m 3, 1974, Hon Katherine Mary Alice Baring, da of 1 Baron Howick of Glendale, KG, GCMG, KCVO (d 1973); 1 s (and 1 s decd), 1 da; *Heir* s, Lieut Maximilian Edward Vereker Wakefield, Royal Hussars (PWO), b 1967; *Career* Capt 10 Royal Hussars; fndr Stately Homes Collection, exec vice-pres Mallett America Ltd 1970-75, former dir Mallett & Son (Antiques) Ltd; chm: Tyrrell & Moore Ltd, Sir Humphry Wakefield & Ptnrs Ltd; dir: Spoleto Festival, Tree of Life Fndn (a UK charity); memb Standing Cncl Baronetage; Pierrepont Morgan Library USA; awarded Freedom of City of Kansas; hon citizen Cities of Houston and New Orleans; Hon Col Louisiana; *Articles* on antique furniture and architecture; *Clubs* Harlequins, Cavalry and Guards', Turf; *Style—* Sir Humphry Wakefield, Bt; Chillingham Castle, Alnwick, Northumberland; c/o Barclays Bank, St James's St, Derby

WAKEFIELD, Hon Lady; Hon Katherine Mary Alice; *née* Baring; da of 1 Baron Howick of Glendale, KG, GCMG, KCVO (d 1973); *b* 1936; *m* 1974, as his 3 wife, Sir (Edward) Humphry Tyrrell Wakefield, 2 Bt; *Style—* The Hon Lady Wakefield

WAKEFIELD, Dowager Lady; (Constance) Lalage; da of Sir John Perronet Thompson, KCSI, KCIE; *b* 2 Oct 1906; *m* 1929, Sir Edward Wakefield, 1 Bt, CIE (d 1969); 2 s (Sir Edward Humphry Tyrrell Wakefield, 2 Bt, *qv*, Hady b 15 Sept 1938), 2 da (Frances Imogen b 4 Dec 1930 (k in Quetta earthquake 1935), Xanthe b 6 Nov 1932 (d Dec 1962)); *Style—* Dowager Lady Wakefield; 13 St Mary Abbot's Terrace, London W14 8NX (☎ 071 602 3042)

WAKEFIELD, Sir Peter George Arthur; KBE (1977), CMG (1973); s of John Bunting Wakefield; *b* 13 May 1922; *Educ* Cranleigh Sch, Corpus Christi Coll Oxford; *m* 1951, Felicity Maurice-Jones; 4 s, 1 da; *Career* RA 1942-47, Mil Govt Eritrea 1946-47; Hulton Press 1947-49; joined Dip Serv 1949; ME Staff Coll for Arab Studies, 2 sec Amman; 1 sec: Nicosia, Cairo; Admin Staff Coll Henley; 1 sec, commercial: Vienna, Tokyo; consul gen and cnsllr Benghazi 1966-69; Tokyo: econ and commercial cnsllr 1970-72, min 1973; seconded BOTB as Japanese mkt special advsr 1973-75; ambass: Lebanon 1975-78, Belgium 1979-82, ret; dir Nat Art Collections Fund 1982-; chm Richmond Theatre, govr Euro Cultural Fndn; *Clubs* Travellers'; *Style—* Sir Peter Wakefield, KBE, CMG; Lincoln House, Montpelier Row, Twickenham, Middx TW1 2NQ (☎ 081 892 6390); La Molineta, Frigiliana, Provincia de Malaga, Spain; National Art Collections Fund, 20 John Islip St, London SW1P 2LL (☎ 071 821 0404)

WAKEFORD, Air Marshal Sir Richard Gordon; KCB (1976), LVO (1961), OBE (1958), AFC (1952); s of Charles Edward Augustus Wakeford; *b* 20 April 1922; *Educ* Kelly Coll; *m* 1948, Anne Butler; 2 s, 1 da (and 1 da decd); *Career* served RAF 1941-78, Cdr The Queen's Flight 1958-61, Air Offr Scotland and NI 1970-72, dir Service Intelligence MOD 1972-73, ANZUK Force cdr Singapore 1974-75, dep chief Def Staff MOD (Intelligence) 1975-78; dir RAF Benevolent Fund Scotland 1978-89, vice chm (air) Lowland TA & VRA 1980-87; tstee McRoberts Tsts, (chm 1982-); dir: Thistle Fndn, Cromar Nominees; cmmr Queen Victoria Sch Dunblane 1980-90; OStJ 1981; CStJ 1986; *Style—* Air Marshal Sir Richard Wakeford, KCB LVO, OBE, AFC; Earlston House, Forgandenny, Perth (☎ 073 881 2392)

WAKEHAM, Bryan Redvers James; s of Stanley Redvers Wakeham (d 1971), and Alice Rose, *née* Taylor (d 1979); *b* 9 April 1929; *Educ* Essex Co Sch Leyton; *m* 11 Sept 1954, Patricia Claire, da of Arthur St Clair-Marston (d 1959); 1 da (Hilary Clair (Mrs Rhodri Huw Williams) b 14 Dec 1960); *Career* Nat Serv LG 1947-49; Thomas Stephens & Sons (Lloyd's broker) 1943-: dir 1961 (co merged into Baindawes 1969), md 1971, resigned 1979; dir Leslie & Godwin Marine, Richard Wood Int Ltd Tampa Florida, Wake Forest Univ Winston Salem N Carolina; Freeman City of London 1981, Liveryman Worshipful Co of Poulters 1981; *Recreations* swimming, gardening, cricket; *Clubs* City of London, MCC; *Style—* Bryan Wakeham, Esq; Windrush, High Trees Rd, Reigate, Surrey, RH2 7EJ (☎ 07372 44696); Leslie & Godwin Ltd, 6 Braham St, London E1 8ED (☎ 071 480 7200, fax 071 480 7450, telex 8950221)

WAKEHAM, Rt Hon John; PC (1983), JP (Inner London 1972), MP (Cons Colchester South and Maldon 1983-); s of Maj Walter John Wakeham (d 1965), of Godalming; *b* 22 June 1932; *Educ* Charterhouse; *m* 1, 1965, Anne Roberta Bailey (d 1984, in IRA bomb blast at Brighton), 2 s; m 2, 1985, Alison Bridget, MBE, da of Ven Edwin J G Ward, of Dorset, 1 s; *Career* CA: memb of Lloyd's, contested (C): Coventry East 1966, Putney Wandsworth 1970; former sec Cons Small Businesses Ctee, govt whip 1979, Ld Cmmr of the Treasy 1981, under sec of state Indust 1981-82, min state Treasy 1982-83, parly sec to the Treasy and Chief Whip 1983-87, Lord Privy Seal 1987-88, Ldr of House of Commons 1987-July 1989, Lord Pres of the Cncl 1988-July 1989, Sec of State for Energy July 1989-; *Recreations* sailing (ketch 'Tias Dancer'), farming, reading; *Clubs* Royal Yacht Squadron, Banks, Carlton, St Stephen's; *Style—* The Rt Hon John Wakeham, JP, MP; House of Commons, London SW1A 0AA

WAKEHAM, Prof William Arnot; s of Stanley William Wakeham (d 1969), of Bristol, and Winifred Gladys, *née* Crocker (d 1946); *b* 25 Sept 1944; *Educ* Bristol Cathedral Sch, Univ of Exeter (BSc, PhD, DSc); *m* 1, 1969 (m dis 1978), Christina Marjorie, da of Kenneth Stone, of Weymouth, Dorset; 1 s (Leigh b 1974); m 2, 23 Dec 1978, Sylvia Frances Tolley; 2 s (Russell Jon b 1983, Nicholas Ashley b 1986); *Career* res assoc Brown Univ Providence USA 1969-71; Imperial Coll London: lectr dept of chemical engrg 1971-79, reader in chemical physics of fluids 1979-85, prof of chemical physics 1985-, head of dept of chemical engrg 1988-; companion memb IChemE, FInstP; *Books* Intermolecular Forces: Their Origin and Determination (1981), The Forces Between Molecules (1986), The Transport Properties of Fluids (1989), International Thermodynamic Tables of the Fluid State: Vol 10 - Ethylene (1989); *Recreations* waterskiing; *Style—* Prof William Wakeham; Department of Chemical Engineering & Chemical Technology, Imperial College of Science, Technology & Medicine, London SW7 2BY (☎ 01 229 8300, fax 01 584 1170, telex 929484 IMPCOL G)

WAKEHURST, 3 Baron (UK 1934); (John) Christopher Loder; s of 2 Baron Wakehurst, KG, KCMG (d 1970), and Margaret, Lady Wakehurst, DBE; *b* 23 Sept 1925; *Educ* Eton, King's Sch Sydney, Trinity Coll Cambridge (MA, LLB); *m* 1, 27 Oct 1956, Ingeborg (d 1977), da of Walther Krumbholz-Hess; 1 s, 1 da; m 2, 10 Sept 1983, (Francine) Brigid, da of William Noble, of Cirencester, Glos; *Heir* s, Hon Timothy Loder; *Career* serv WWII RANVR and RNVR; called to the Bar 1950; chm: Anglo & Overseas Trust plc, The Overseas Investmt Trust plc; dep chm London and Manchester Group plc; CStJ; *Clubs* City of London, Chelsea Arts; *Style—* The Rt Hon the Lord Wakehurst; 26 Wakehurst Road, London SW11 6BY (☎ 071 223 9410); c/o London and Manchester Group plc, Eldon House, Eldon Street, London EC2M 7LB (☎ 071 247 2000; fax , 071 247 2859)

WAKELEY, Sir John Cecil Nicholson; 2 Bt (UK 1952), of Liss, Co Southampton; s of Sir Cecil Pembrey Grey Wakeley, 1 Bt, KBE, CB, FRCS (d 1979), and Dr Elizabeth Muriel Wakeley, *née* Nicholson-Smith (d 1985); *b* 27 Aug 1926; *Educ* Canford, London Univ (MB BS); *m* 10 April 1954, June, o da of Donald Frank Leney; 2 s, 1 da; *Heir* s, Nicholas Jeremy Wakeley b 17 Oct 1957; *Career* former: chief inspr City of London Special Constabulary, sr consulting surgn W Cheshire Gp of Hosps; former memb: Liverpool Regional Hosp Bd, Mersey Regnl Health Authy, Cncl Royal Coll of Surgns of Eng; former conslt advsr (civilian) to RAF; FRCS, FACS; CStJ 1957; *Recreations* photography, music; *Style—* Sir John Wakeley, Bt; Mickle Lodge, Mickle Trafford, Chester CH2 4EB (☎ 0244 300316)

WAKELEY, Dr Richard Michael; s of Sir Cecil Wakeley, 1 Bt, KBE. CB, FRS (d 1979), and Dr Elizabeth Muriel Wakeley, *née* Nicholson-Smith (d 1985); *b* 21 Jan 1933; *Educ* Winchester, King's Coll London (MB BS); *Career* house surgn King's Coll Hosp 1958; actor 1960-66; literary agent 1968-; Freeman City of London 1956; memb: City Co of Barber Surgns, Worshipful Soc of Apothecaries; *Recreations* music, tennis; *Style—* Dr Richard Wakeley; 1 Wordsworth Mansions, Queens Club Gardens, London W14 9TE (☎ 071 385 0908); Coves Cottage, St Peters, Broadstairs, Kent CT10 2TH; Peters Fraser & Dunlop, 5th Floor, The Chambers, Chelsea Harbour, Lots Rd, London SW10 0XF (☎ 071 376 7676, fax 071 352 7356)

WAKELEY, Robin Anthony Wade; GSM (1955); s of Leslie Stuart Pembrey Wakeley (d 1961), of Welwyn Garden City, Herts, and Mary Louise Lloyd, *née* Wade; *b* 1 March 1937; *Educ* Hitchin GS for Boys', King's Coll London, King's Coll Hosp (BDS, Prosthetics prize); *m* 1, 1964 (m dis 1980), Pamela Margaret, da of Trevor James; 1 s (Roderick Stuart James b 15 Oct 1965), 2 da (Annabel Jane b 29 June 1967, Sophie Louise Wade b 1 Nov 1971); m 2, 1987, Carolyn, da of Frank Dakin; *Career* Nat Serv; res house surgn King's Coll Hosp 1964, pt/t lectr Guy's Hosp 1967-71 (pt/t registrar 1965-67), in private practice Harley Street 1971- (pt/t private practice 1965-71); Freeman City of London, memb Worshipful Soc of Apothecaries 1976; *Recreations* golf, walking, collecting antiques; *Clubs* Reform; *Style—* Robin Wakeley, Esq; 106 Harley St, London W1N 1AF (☎ 071 935 1196, fax 071 486 9240)

WAKELEY, Timothy Grey; s of William Grey Pembury Wakeley, Fitzalan Court, Rustington, Sussex, and Daisy Lillian, *née* Poole; *b* 13 Dec 1943; *Educ* Carshalton Coll; *m* 29 April 1967, Anne Caroline Duyland, da of Adm Sir John Fitzroy Duyland Bush, GCB; 2 s (Oliver Grey b 20 Aug 1969, Adam Grey b 2 Oct 1978), 2 da (Fenella Duyland b 8 April 1971, Melissa Emily (twin) b 2 Oct 1978); *Career* ptnr W Greenwell & Co 1972-86 (trainee 1961), md Greenwell Montagu Stockbrokers 1986-; assoc memb Soc of Investmt Analysts, memb Stock Exchange; *Recreations* tennis, skiing, vintage cars; *Clubs* City of London; *Style—* Timothy Wakeley, Esq; Little Green, Thursley, nr Godalming, Surrey GU8 6QE (☎ 0252 702320); 14 Arnold Mansions, Queen's Club Gardens, London W14 9RD (☎ 071 381 4948); Greenwell Montagu Stockbrokers, 114 Old Broad St, London WC2P 2HY (☎ 071 588 8817, fax 071 588 1673)

WAKELING, Rt Rev (John) Denis; MC (1945); s of Rev John Lucas Wakeling (d 1939), and Mary Louisa, *née* Glover (d 1923); *b* 12 Dec 1918; *Educ* Dean Close Sch Cheltenham, St Catharine's Coll Cambridge (MA), Ridley Hall Cambridge; *m* 4 April 1941, Josephine Margaret, da of Benjamin Charles Broomhall (d 1961); 3 s (Antony James b 1943, (John) Gerald b and d 1949, (John) Jeremy b 1954); *Career* Actg Maj Royal Marines 1939-45; clerk in Holy Orders; ordained: deacon 1947, priest 1948; asst curate Barwell Leics 1947-50; chaplain Clare Coll Cambridge and Cambridge Pastorate 1950-52, vicar Emmanuel Plymouth 1952-59, preb Exeter Cathedral 1957 and preb emeritus 1959, vicar Barking Essex 1959-65, archdeacon of West Ham 1965-70, bishop of Southwell 1970-85, entered House of Lords 1974; Hon DD Univ of Nottingham 1985; *Recreations* walking, camping, gardening, hockey, cricket, classical music; *Clubs* Hawk's (Cambridge); *Style—* The Rt Rev Denis Wakeling, MC; The Maples, The Avenue, Porton, Salisbury, Wilts SP4 0NT

WAKELY, Dr Peter George; s of George James Louis Wakely (d 1963), and Winifred Grace Florence, *née* Osborne (d 1961); *b* 15 Feb 1925; *m* 3 April 1954, Constance Mary (Babs), da of Samuel Jeffcote (d 1969); 2 s (Timothy b 1958, Nicholas b 1960); *Career* mathematician and engr previously at: GEC, English Electric Co, Queen's Univ Belfast, Univ of Southampton; hon prof of engrg sci Univ of Warwick 1968-77, chm and md Assoc Engrg Devpts Ltd 1971-80, engrg conslt 1980-; churchwarden St Michael and All Angels Cosby 1965-89, pres Inst of Mathematics and its Applications 1969 (1968), chm CSTI 1969, chm Jt Affrs Ctee CEI and CSTI 1970-71, govr Coventry Poly 1970-73, assessor on Cncl SERC 1977-88, memb Ctee of Inquiry into the Teaching of Mathematics in Schools (The Cockcroft Ctee) 1978-81; former chm: jt SERC and Dept of Indust Advsy Panel on Computer aided Engrg, SERC Cooperative Res Grants Panel, steering gp for the Nat Physical Laboratory numerical analysis and computing div; former memb numerous engrg, scientific and industl ctees; FIMA 1964; *Recreations* social history, sailing; *Style—* Dr Peter Wakely

WAKEMAN, Sir Edward Offley Bertram; 6 Bt (UK 1828), of Perdiswell Hall, Worcestershire; s of Capt Sir Offley Wakeman, 4 Bt, CBE (d 1975), and his 2 w, Josceline Etheldreda, *née* Mitford; suc his half-bro Sir (Offley) David Wakeman, 5 Bt 1991; *b* 31 July 1934; *Heir* none; *Style—* Sir Edward Wakeman, Bt

WAKERLEY, (John) Charles; OBE (1974); s of Charles William Wakerley (d 1978), of Welton, nr Lincoln, and Gladys MacLennon, *née* Skelton (d 1986); brother of Richard Wakerley, *qv*; *b* 18 Jan 1936; *Educ* Lincoln Sch, Univ of Nottingham (LLB); *m* 1, 1958 (m dis 1987), Peggy, da of late George Hayward of Lincoln; m 2, 1987, Diana Louise Seton Adams, da of Fenmore Roger Seton of New Haven, Conn, USA (pres Rehabilitation Int); 2 step s (Christopher Adams b 1969, James Adams b 1971); *Career* cmmnd Army Legal Servs 1960 (asst dir Army Legal Serv HQ NI 1972-74, ret as Lt-Col 1974); called to the Bar Gray's Inn 1960; currently dir and sr counsel SmithKline Beecham (joined 1974); admitted NY Bar 1982; *Recreations* gardening, American civil war; *Clubs* IOD; *Style—* Charles Wakerley, Esq, OBE; SmithKline Beecham plc, SB House, Great West Road, Brentford, Middlesex, TW8 9BD (☎ 081 560 5151, fax 081 975 4244)

WAKERLEY, Richard MacLennon; QC (1982); s of Charles William Wakerley (d 1978), and Gladys MacLennon, *née* Skelton (d 1986), of Lincoln; brother of Charles Wakerley, *qv*; *b* 7 June 1942; *Educ* De Aston Sch Market Rasen, Emmanuel Coll Cambridge (MA); *m* 1966, Marian Heather, da of Stanley William Dawson, of Lincoln; 2 s (Paul b 1968, Simon b 1971), 2 da (Helen b 1966, Emma b 1973); *Career* called to the Bar Gray's Inn 1965; rec Crown Ct 1982-, dep ldr Midland and Oxford Circuit 1989-; *Recreations* bridge, gardening, theatre; *Style—* Richard Wakerley, Esq, QC; Croft House, Grendon, Atherstone, Warwickshire (☎ 0827 712 329); 4 Fountain Ct, Steelhouse Lane, Birmingham (☎ 021 236 3476); 2 Dr Johnson's Buildings, Temple, London (☎ 071 353 4197)

WAKLEY, His Hon Judge Bertram Joseph; MBE (1945); s of Maj Bertram Joseph Wakley (d 1917), and Hon Dorothy Henrietta, *née* Hamilton (d 1951); *b* 7 July 1917;

Educ Wellington, Ch Ch Oxford (MA); *m* 30 July 1953, Alice Margaret, da of Archibald McErvel Lorimer (d 1939), of Linden, 39 Osborne Park, Belfast, NI; *Career* Maj S Lancashire Regt; serv: N Africa, Italy and Greece 1939-46 (despatches); called to the Bar Gray's Inn 1948; circuit judge 1973-; Diocesan Reader Southwark 1977; *Books* History of the Wimbledon Cricket Club (1954), Bradman the Great (1959), Classic Centuries (1964); *Recreations* golf, cricket; *Clubs* Carlton, Roehampton, MCC; *Style—* His Hon Judge Bertram Wakley, MBE

WALCOT, Prof Peter; s of Cedric Ernest William Walcot (d 1956), of London, and Harriet, *née* Reed (d 1988); *b* 10 May 1931; *Educ* Wilson's GS London, UCL (BA, PhD), Univ of Yale (MA); *m* 28 Jan 1956, Jean Margaret Ellen; 2 s (Timothy, Christopher), 1 da (Alison); *Career* Nat Serv Flying Offr RAF 1955-57; visiting prof UCLA 1982, visiting lectr Univ of Florida 1983; prof: Univ Coll Cardiff 1974-88 (asst lectr 1951-59, lectr 1959-66, sr lectr 1966-74), Univ of Wales Coll of Cardiff 1988-; Webster Meml lectr Stamford Univ 1991; ed Greece and Rome 1970-; moderator in classics Univ of London Schools Examination Bd 1974-; memb: Soc For Promotion of Hellenic Studies 1948, Classical Assoc 1957; *Books* Hesiod and the Near East (1966), Greek Peasants Ancient and Modern (1970), Great Drama in its Theatrical and Social Context (1976), Envy and the Greeks (1978); *Recreations* walking; *Style—* Prof Peter Walcot; 28 Rowan Way, Lisvane, Cardiff CF4 5TD (☎ 0222 756653); Sch of History and Archaeology, University of Wales College of Cardiff, PO Box 909, Cardiff CF1 3XU (☎ 0222 874259)

WALD, Prof Nicholas John; s of Adolf Max Wald of London, and Frieda Shastow (d 1986); *b* 31 May 1944; *Educ* Owen's Sch, UCH (MB BS), Univ of London (DSc); *m* 2 Jan 1966, Nancy Evelyn, *née* Miller, 3 s (David b 1968, Richard b 1971, Jonathan b 1977), 1 da (Karen b 1966); *Career* MRC Epidemiology and Med Care Unit 1971- (memb sci staff), ICRF Cancer Epidemiology and Clinical Trials Unit Oxford 1972-83, prof and head of Dept of Environmental and Preventive Med Bart's Hosp 1983-; memb Ctee: MRC, DHSS, RCP, NE Thames RHA Cancer Advisory Gp, Oxford RHA, Action on Smoking and Health; FFCM 1982, FRCP 1986; *Books* Alpha-Fetoprotein Screening-The Current Issues (with JE Haddow, 1981), Antenatal and Neonatal Screening (ed, 1984), Interpretation of Negative Epidemiological Evidence for Carcinogenicity (ed with R Doll, 1985), UK Smoking Statistics (jt ed, 1988), Nicotine Smoking and the Low Tar Programme (ed with P Froggatt, 1989), Smoking and Hormone Related Disorders (ed with J Baron, 1990); *Recreations* skiing, boating, economics; *Clubs* Anthenaeum; *Style—* Prof Nicholas Wald; 22 Staverton Rd, Oxford OX2 6XJ (☎ 0865 52338); 9 Park Cres Mews East, London W1N 5HB (☎ 071 636 2721); Dept of Environmental and Preventive Medicine, The Medical College of St Bartholomew's Hospital, Charterhouse Square, London EC1M 6BQ (☎ 071 982 6121, fax 071 251 8724)

WALDEGRAVE, 12 Earl (GB 1729); Sir Geoffrey Noel Waldegrave; 16 Bt (E 1643), of Hever Castle, Co Kent; KG (1971), GCVO (1976), TD, DL (Somerset 1951); also Baron Waldegrave (E 1686) and Viscount Chewton (GB 1729); s of 11 Earl Waldegrave (d 1936; descended from Sir Richard Walgrave, Speaker of the House of Commons *temp* Richard II), and Anne, da of Rev William Pollexfen Bastard, of Buckland Court, Ashburton, and Kitley, Yealmpton, Devon; *b* 21 Nov 1905; *Educ* Winchester, Trinity Coll Cambridge (BA); *m* 1930, Mary, da of Lt-Col Arthur Grenfell, DSO; 2 s, 5 da; *Heir* s, Viscount Chewton; *Career* served WWII 1939-45, Maj RA (TA); memb Prince's Cncl Duchy of Cornwall 1951-58 and 1965-76; Lord Warden of the Stannaries 1965-76; Vice-Lt Somerset 1955-60; jt Parly sec Miny Ag and Fish 1958-62; chm Forestry Cmmn 1963-65; Offr Legion of Merit (US); *Clubs* Travellers'; *Style—* The Rt Hon Earl Waldegrave, KG, GCVO, TD, DL; Chewton House, Chewton Mendip, Bath BA3 4LQ

WALDEGRAVE, Rt Hon William Arthur; PC (1990), MP (C) Bristol W 1979-; 2 s of 12 Earl Waldegrave (whose ancestor, 1 Baron Waldegrave, m Henrietta FitzJames, child of Arabella Churchill by James II); through the 4 Earl Waldegrave's marriage with his cous Lady Elizabeth Waldegrave, William is direct descendant of Great Britain's First PM, Sir Robert Walpole; William's ancestor the 2 Earl Waldegrave (f of Lady Elizabeth) was also briefly PM (in 'the two days ministry' of 1746), and Mary Hermione Grenfell; *b* 15 Aug 1946; *Educ* Eton, CCC Oxford, Harvard Univ; *m* 1977, Caroline (MA), da of Maj Richard Burrows, of 2A Royal Chase, Tunbridge Wells, Kent; 1 s (James b 1984), 3 da (Katharine b 1980, Elizabeth b 1983, Harriet b 1988); *Career* fell All Souls' Oxford 1971-78, 1979-; CPRS 1971-73, political staff 10 Downing St 1973-74, head of Rt Hon Edward Heath's (oppn ldr) Political Office 1974-75; GEC Ltd 1975-81, memb IBA Advsy Cncl 1980-; jt vice chm Fin Ctee to Sept 1981, under sec state DES (for Higher Educn) 1981-83, chm Ctee for Local Authy Higher Educn 1982-83, under sec state DOE 1983-85; min of state DOE 1985; sec of state for Health 1990-; *Books* The Binding of Leviathan - Conservatism and the Future (1977); *pamphlet*: Changing Gear: What the Government Should Do Next (co-author, 1981); *Clubs* Beefsteak, Pratt's; *Style—* The Rt Hon William Waldegrave, MP; c/o House of Commons, Westminster, London SW1A 0AA

WALDEN, George Gordon Harvey; CMG (1981), MP (Cons Buckingham 1983-); s of G G Walden; *b* 15 Sept 1939; *Educ* Latymer Upper Sch, Jesus Coll Cambridge, Univ of Moscow, Univ of Hong Kong (reading Chinese); *m* 1970, Sarah Nicolette Hunt; 2 s, 1 da; *Career* FO 1962-65, second sec Peking 1967-70, first sec Soviet Desk FCO 1970-73, École Nationale d'Administration Paris 1973-74, first sec Paris 1974-78, princ private sec to: Rt Hon David Owen (1978-79), Rt Hon Lord Carrington 1979-81, fell Harvard Univ 1981-82, head of planning staff FCO 1982-83, ret 1983; PPS to Sec of State for Educn and Sci 1984-85, Parly under sec of state, DES 1985-; columnist for Daily Telegraph; *Books* Ethics and Foreign Policy; *Style—* George Walden, Esq, CMG, MP; House of Commons, London SW1A 0AA (☎ 071 219 6346)

WALDEN, Herbert Richard Charles; CBE (1986); s of Reginald George Walden (d 1954), and late Matilda Ethel, *née* Baker; *b* 6 Oct 1926; *Educ* Westgate Sch Warwick; *m* 1950, Margaret, da of Percy Harold Walker (d 1957); 2 da (Ann, Judith); *Career* serv WWII 1944-47, Royal Warwicks Regt, Royal Leicestershire, serv UK and Gold Coast; dir and gen mangr: Warwicks Building Society 1962-67, Rugby and Warwick Building Soc 1967-74; Heart of England Building Soc 1974-86; chm S Warwickshire HMC 1964-72, fndr pres Warwick Rotary Club 1965, chm The Bldg Socs Assoc 1983-85 (memb Cncl 1974-86), memb Bd Housing Corp 1985-88, govr Warwicks Schs Fndn 1962-90 (chm 1986-90), vice pres Warwicks Scout Cncl (former co tres), cmmnr of taxes, tstee various Warwick charities; pt/t cmmr Bldg Socs Cmmn 1986-; *Recreations* watching cricket and soccer; *Clubs* Naval and Military; *Style—* Herbert Walden, Esq, CBE; Fieldgate House, 24 Hill Wootton Rd, Leek Wootton, Warwick CV35 7QL (☎ 0926 54291)

WALDER WESIERSKA, Ruth Christabel; *née* Walder; OBE (1956); da of Rev Ernest Walder (former rector of Bincombe with Broadwey, d 1951), and Jane, *née* Bull (d 1920); *b* 15 Jan 1906; *Educ* Cheltenham Ladies' Coll; *m* 6 Jan 1955, Maj Gen Jerzy Wesierski (decd), s of Vincent Wesierski; *Career* served WWII Admty 1940-41, air raid warden Chelsea 1941-45; gen organizer Nat Fedn of Womens Insts 1934-40, FO 1942-44, UN Relief and Rehabilitation Admin 1944-47, sec UN Appeal for Children (UK) 1948, nat gen sec YWCA (UK) 1949-67; vice pres Dorset Co Decorative and Fine Arts Soc; memb: RIIA, FAMS, Prayer Book Soc, Nat Tst, RSPB; Polish Gold Cross of Merit 1969; *Recreations* reading, writing, lecturing, gardening; *Clubs* Naval and Military, Royal Dorset Yacht; *Style—* Mrs Ruth Walder Wesierska; Westhope, Langton Herring, nr Weymouth, Dorset DT3 4HZ (☎ 0305 871 233)

WALDMANN, Dr Carl; s of Leon Waldmann (d 1970), and Rewa, *née* Schafer; *b* 25 March 1951; *Educ* Forest Sch Snaresbrook, Sidney Sussex Coll Cambridge (BA), London Hosp (MA, MB BChir), DA; *m* 27 July 1980, Judith; 1 da (Anna b 1981); *Career* Flt-Lt Unit MO RAF Brize Norton 1977-78, Sqdn Ldr 1981-82, sr specialist anaesthetics RAF Ely 1980-82 (specialist 1978-80); sr registrar intensive care Whipps Cross Hosp 1982-83; sr registrar anaesthetics: London Hosp 1984-85 (houseman 1975-76, sr house offr anaethetics 1976-77, lectr anaesthetics 1983-84), Gt Ormond St Hosp 1985-86; conslt anaesthetics and intensive care Reading Hosp 1986-; FFARCS 1980; *Books* Pocket Consultant Intensive Care (1985), Respiration: The Breath of Life (1985), Hazards and Complications of Anaesthesia (1987); *Recreations* fencing, squash, skiing, water-skiing; *Clubs* Kirtons Farm Country (Reading); *Style—* Dr Carl Waldmann, 1 Mohawk Way, Woodley, Reading, Berks (☎ 0734 699418); Intensive Therapy Unit, Royal Berks Hosp, Reading, Berks (☎ 0734 877256); The Tennyson, Sussex Lane, Spencers Wood, Reading RG7 1AT (☎ 0734 884460); Intensive Therapy Unit, Royal Berks Hosp, Reading, Berks (☎ 0734 877256)

WALDRON, Lady Olivia Elsie June; *née* Taylour; da of 5 Marquess of Headfort, TD (d 1960), and Elsie Faith (formerly w of Sir Rupert Clarke, Bt); *b* 20 June 1929; *Educ* St Catherine's Melbourne Australia, St Mary's Convent Ascot; *m* 1955, Victor Echevarri Waldron, s of Ernest Victor Echevarri; 2 da; *Career* dir The Hunger Project Ltd (UK) 1980-84, tstee The Hunger Project Tst 1984-89, chm Waldron Properties Ltd, memb exec cncl UK chapter Soc for Int Devpt, chm advsy cncl The Hunger Project 1989-; *Style—* The Lady Olivia Waldron; Idleigh Cottage, nr Meopham, Kent (☎ 0474 872363)

WALDRON, Victor Echevarri; s of Ernest Echevarri; adopted additional surname of Waldron 1947; *Educ* West Ham Coll, Kings Coll London; *m* 1, 1947, Gladys Leila (d 1952), o da of Col Sir William Waldron; 1 s, 1 da; m 2, 1955, Lady Olivia Elsie June, o da of 5 Marquess of Headfort (d 1960); 2 da; *Career* serv RN 1940-45, Lt RNVR; memb Cons Central Office 1946-53, Parly candidate 1951, fin advsr to Constituencies 1954; former: exec memb Nat Fedn of Property Owners, hon treas Property Cncl; chm: Waldron Group of Cos, Roundwood Development Ltd; memb: Dip & Cwlth Writers Assoc, Foreign Press Assoc, Journalists Devpt Gp of CWDE; awarded Fairfield Int Writer's prize, London Correspondent the Hunger Project Newspaper, ed Aware Digest 1988; pres World Runners UK; memb: AAA, Sports Aid Fndn; Liveryman and Freeman City of London; FRGS; *Clubs* Naval and Military, United and Cecil, Royal Corinthian Yacht, Overseas Press (NY); *Style—* Victor Waldron, Esq; Roundwood Developments Ltd, 81 Cromwell Road, London SW7 5BS; Idleigh Cottage, Meopham, Kent; 362 President St, New York (☎ NY 112 321)

WALDUCK, (Hugh) Richard; JP (Middx 1974); s of Hugh Stanley Walduck (d 1975), of Long Meadow, Hatfield, Herts, and Enid Rosalind (Wendy) Walduck; *b* 21 Nov 1941; *Educ* Harrow, Univ of Cambridge (MA); *m* 1, 1969 (m dis 1979), Meintje Marianne, *née* Stibbe; 2 s (Alexander b 1971, Nicholas b 1972), 2 step s (Richard b 1966, Simon b 1968), 1 step da (Nicola b 1971); m 2, 27 Aug 1980, Susan Marion, da of Frank Sherwood; *Career* dir and sec Imperial London Hotels Ltd 1964-; Liveryman Worshipful Co of Basketmakers 1968; county pres St John Ambulance Hertfordshire 1990; *Recreations* history, skiing, beekeeping; *Style—* Richard Walduck, Esq, JP; Lower Woodside, Hatfield, Herts AL9 6DJ; c/o Directors Off, Imperial Hotel, Russell Sq, London WC1B 5BB (☎ 071 837 3655, fax 071 837 4653, telex 263951 RUSIMP LDN)

WALERAN, Baroness; Valentine; da of Eric Oswald Anderson, CBE; *m* 1954, as his 3 w, 2 and last Baron Waleran (d 1966); *Style—* The Rt Hon Lady Waleran; 42a Cathcart Rd, London SW10 9NN

WALES, Anthony Edward; s of Albert Edward Wales, of Collingham, Nottinghamshire, and Kathleen May, *née* Rosenthal; *b* 20 Dec 1955; *Educ* Stamford Sch Lincs, Worcester Coll Oxford (MA); *m* 1 Sept 1984, Lynda, da of Leonard Page (d 1987), of Swansea, W Glamorgan; 2 s (Edward b 1987, Thomas b 1989); *Career* slr; ptnr Turner Kenneth Brown 1986- (joined 1979); memb: Law Soc 1981, Law Soc Hong Kong 1986; *Recreations* fly fishing, skiing, travelling; *Clubs* Ladies Recreation (Hong Kong); *Style—* Anthony Wales, Esq; Turner Kenneth Brown, 100 Fetter Lane, London EC4A 1DD (☎ 071 242 6006, fax 071 242 3003); 19th Floor Worldwide House, Central, Hong Kong (☎ 8105081, fax 8101295)

WALES, Hon Mrs ((Susan) Clare); *née* Richardson; da of Baron Richardson, LVO; *b* 25 March 1940; *m* 1970, Robert Wales; 1 s; *Style—* The Hon Mrs Wales; 2 Thorne St, London SW13

WALES, Daphne Beatrice; da of Frederick James Wales, and Lilian Frederica, *née* Whitnall; *b* 6 Dec 1917; *Career* princ Bank of England (ret); C of E Gen Synod 1975-90, memb Panel of Chm 1983, chm Bd for Mission and Unity 1983-88; chm St Albans Diocese House of Laity 1979-85; vice chm: S America Missionary Soc, Highway Tst; memb: St Albans Diocese Synod Bd for Mission and Unity, Bishops Cncl, Governing Body Partnership for World Mission, Cncl Oak Hill Theological Coll; *Style—* Miss Daphne Wales; 41 Park Road, Watford, Herts WD1 3QW

WALES, Archbishop of 1987-; Most Rev George Noakes; s of David John Noakes (d 1948), of Bwlchllan, Lampeter, Dyfed, and Elizabeth Mary Noakes (d 1987); *b* 13 Sept 1924; *Educ* Tregaron Co Sch, Univ Coll of Wales Abeystwyth (BA), Wycliffe Hall Oxford; *m* 23 April 1957, Jean Margaretta, da of Samuel Richard Davies (d 1933); *Career* ordained: deacon 1950, priest 1952; curate of Lampeter 1950-56; vicar: Eglwyswrw with Meline 1956-59, Tregaron 1959-67, Eglwys Dewi Sant Cardiff 1967-76; rector Aberystwyth 1976-80, canon St Davids Cath 1977-79, archdeacon of Cardigan 1979-82, vicar Llanychearn with Llanddeiniol 1980-82, bishop of St Davids 1982-; Hon DD Univ of Wales 1990; *Recreations* angling; *Style—* The Most Rev the Archbishop of Wales; Llys Esgob, Abergwili, Carmarthen, Dyfed SA31 2JG (☎ 0267 236 597)

WALES, Gregory John; s of A J Wales, of Guildford, Surrey, and B Wales, *née* Read; *b* 17 May 1949; *Educ* Guildford RGS; *m* 29 July 1972, Jennifer Hilary, da of E Brown, of St Albans; 2 s (Nicholas b 1978, Andrew b 1981); *Career* qualified accountant 1974, sr lectr City 1976-79, mgmnt conslt 1976-80, mangr Arthur Andersen & Co 1980-82, ptnr Coombes Wales Quinnell 1982-; Freeman City of London; FCA; *Recreations* cricket, squash, real tennis; *Clubs* MCC; *Style—* Gregory Wales, Esq; 31 Selwyn Ave, Richmond, Surrey TW9 2HB (☎ 081 940 4398); Coombes Wales Quinnell, 100 Baker St, London W1M 1LA (☎ 071 487 7376)

WALES, Roland John; s of William Frederick Wales (d 1979), of West End, nr Eastleigh, Hants, and Margaret Louise, *née* Landeryou (d 1982); *b* 15 April 1932; *Educ* Brockley Cross, SE London Tech Coll, Borough Poly (NC); *m* 1, 22 March 1958 (m dis 1981), Audrey Mary, da of Walter Mepsted, of Carshalton, Surrey; m 2, 7 April 1984, Gillian Yvonne, da of Terence Addy, of Upper Tysoe, Warwicks; 2 da (Jeannette Deborah (Mrs Scola), Joanne Dorothy (Mrs Stewart)); *Career* Nat Serv RAF (air radar fitter and jr technician) 1953-55; electro-optic systems devpt Hilger & Watts 1955-57, missile testing AV Roe Ltd 1957-59; Beckman Instruments: tech serv 1959-61, UK sales mangr 1962-64, UK mktg mangr 1965-67, int mktg mangr 1968-72; biochemical product gp mangr Rank Hilger 1972-74, Euro devpts OCLI 1974-80, gen mangr Astron Devpts 1980-84, md Ferranti Astron Ltd 1984-88, dir Tayside Optical Technology; memb Nanotechnology Strategy Ctee DTI; MInstM; *Recreations* skiing, sailing, gliding; *Style*— Roland Wales, Esq; 5 Burham Rd, Hughenden Valley, Bucks (☎ 024 024 2633)

WALEY, His Hon Judge (Andrew) Felix; VRD (1962, clasp 1972), QC (1973); s of Guy Felix Waley (d 1959), of Askerswell, Dorset, and Anne Elizabeth, *née* Dickson (d 1959); *b* 14 April 1926; *Educ* Charterhouse, Worcester Coll Oxford (MA); *m* 3 Sept 1955, Petica Mary, da of Sir Philip Humphrey Vivien Rose, 3 Bt (d 1980); 1 s (Simon b 9 Sept 1964), 4 da (Sarah b 17 Feb 1958, Jane b 27 Feb 1959, Juliet b 10 Feb 1960, Victoria b 21 Jan 1961, d 1962); *Career* RN 1944-48, pilot offr RAFVR 1948-51, RNVR and RNR 1951-72 (promoted to Cdr RNR 1965); called to the Bar Middle Temple 1953; rec Crown Ct 1974-81, bencher Middle Temple 1981, circuit judge 1982, resident judge Co of Kent 1985, Judge Advocate of the Fleet 1986; cllr Paddington Borough Cncl 1956-59, parly candidate (C) Dagenham 1959, chm London Flotilla 1980-86; *Recreations* gardens, boats, birds; *Clubs* Garrick, Naval, RNSA; *Style*— His Hon Judge Waley, VRD, QC; The Law Courts, Barker Rd, Maidstone, Kent ME16 8EQ (☎ 0622 754966)

WALEY-COHEN, Sir Bernard Nathaniel; 1 Bt (UK 1961), of Honeymead, Co Somerset; s of late Sir Robert Waley Cohen, KBE (d 1952, first md of Shell Co and WWI petroleum advsr to WO; chm of Palestine Corpn; 1 cous of Sir Herbert Cohen, 2 and last Bt, OBE); assumed by deed poll 1950 his f's final forename as an additional surname; 2 cous of late Baron Cohen (Life Peer d 1973); *b* 29 May 1914; *Educ* HMS Britannia (RNC Dartmouth), Clifton, Magdalene Coll Cambridge; *m* 1943, Hon Joyce Nathan (*see* Hon Lady Waley-Cohen); 2 s (Stephen b 1946 m Pamela Doniger, Robert b 1948 m 1975 Hon Felicity Samuel, da of 3 Visc Bearsted), 2 da (Rosalind b 1945 m 1966 Philip Burdon of NZ; Eleanor b 1952 m 1977 Keith Gallant of Connecticut, USA); *Heir* s, Stephen Harry Waley-Cohen; *Career* serv WWII: River Emergency Serv, Home Gd, princ Miny Fuel and Power 1940-47; underwriting memb Lloyd's 1939, chm Palestine Corpn 1952-54 (vice-chm 1947-52), Exmoor farmer 1952-, chm Simo Properties Ltd 1955-70, dep chm Burston Gp 1971-75(dir: Messrs N Burston & Co Ltd 1962-68, Burston & Texas Commerce Bank Ltd 1968-75); dir: O & M Kleeman Ltd 1957-65, Kleeman Industl Hldgs Ltd 1965-84, Mathews Wrightson Pulbrook Ltd 1971-84; one of HM Lts for City of London 1949-, Sheriff 1955-56, Lord Mayor of London 1960-61; govr Nat Corpn for Care of Old People 1965-72; pres Jewish Museum 1964-84; vice-pres: Trades Advsy Cncl 1963- (pres 1981), Anglo-Jewish Assoc 1962-, Jewish Ctee for HM Forces 1980- (memb 1947-), Fndn Ctee Cambridge Soc 1980- (memb 1975-); chm: Investmts Ctee London U 1966-78, Public Works Loan Bd 1972-79, governing body UCL 1971-80 (memb 1953-80); hon tres Jewish Bd of Guardians 1948-53; tstee College of Arms 1970-; memb: exec ctee Jewish Memorial Cncl 1947-, Senate London Univ 1962-78 and of Ct 1966-78, Girton Coll investmts ctee 1971-78; Liveryman Worshipful Co of Clothworkers'1936- (Master 1975), hon Liveryman Worshipful Co of Farmers' 1961-, hon fell UCL 1963, Hon LLD London Univ 1961, associate KStJ 1961; kt 1957; *Recreations* hunting, racing, shooting, rugger; *Clubs* Boodle's, Pratt's, City Livery, MCC, Pitt, Harlequins RFC; *Style*— Sir Bernard Waley-Cohen, Bt; Honeymead, Simonsbath, Minehead, Somerset TA24 7JX (☎ 064 383 242)

WALEY-COHEN, Hon Mrs (Felicity Ann); *née* Samuel; da of 3 Viscount Bearsted, TD, DL, and his 1 w, (Elizabeth) Heather, da of G Firmston-Williams, now Mrs R H Grierson; *b* 3 April 1948; *m* 1975, Robert Waley-Cohen, 2 s of Sir Bernard Waley-Cohen, 1 Bt, *qv*; 3 s (Marcus b 1977, Sam b 1982, Thomas b 1984), 1 da (Jessica 1979); *Career* Felicity Samuel Gallery 1972-81; chm Patrons of New Art Tate Gallery 1982-87; tstee Tate Fndn 1986, Serpentine Gallery 1987-; memb Exec Ctee NACF 1988-; *Style*— The Hon Mrs R Waley-Cohen; Upton Viva, Banbury, Oxon

WALEY-COHEN, Hon Lady; Joyce Constance Ina; *née* Nathan; JP (Somerset 1959) supplemental list 1987; only da of 1 Baron Nathan, TD, PC (d 1963); *b* 20 Jan 1920; *Educ* St Felix Sch, Girton Coll Cambridge (MA); *m* 1943, Sir Bernard Nathaniel Waley-Cohen, 1 Bt, *qv*; 2 s, 2 da; *Career* JP Middx 1949-59; memb Bd of Govrs Westminster Hosp Gp 1952-68; chm: Westminster Children's Hosp 1952-68, Gordon Hosp 1961-68, Governing Body St Felix Sch 1970-83 (memb 1945-83), Governing Bodies of Girls Schs Assoc 1974-79 (memb 1963-), Independent Schs Jt Ctee 1977-80; govr: Taunton Sch 1978-90, Wellington Coll 1979-90; pres Ind Schs Info Serv Cncl 1981-86 (memb 1972-86) and memb Mgmnt Ctee; *Style*— The Hon Lady Waley-Cohen, JP; Honeymead, Simonsbath, Minehead, Somerset TA24 7JX (☎ 064 383 242)

WALEY-COHEN, Robert Bernard; 2 s of Sir Bernard Waley-Cohen, 1 Bt, and Hon Joyce Nathan, da of 1 Baron Nathan; *b* 10 Nov 1948; *Educ* Eton; *m* 1975, Hon Felicity Anne, da of 3 Viscount Bearsted, TD; 3 s (Marcus Richard b 1977, Sam Bernard b 1982, Thomas Andrew b 1984), 1 da (Jessica Suzanna b 1979); *Career* exec Christie's 1969-81 (gen mangr USA 1970-73); dir Samuel Properties 1977-86; chm and chief exec offr Alliance Imaging Inc 1983-88, chief exec Alliance Medical Ltd 1989- (dir 1988-); *Recreations* the arts, conservation, racing (racehorses include: Sun Lion, Rustle, The Dragon Master, Won't Be Gone Long); *Clubs* Jockey; *Style*— Robert Waley-Cohen, Esq; 18 Gilston Rd, London SW10

WALEY-COHEN, Stephen Harry; s and h of Sir Bernard Waley-Cohen, 1 Bt, and Hon Lady Waley-Cohen, *qqv*; *b* 22 June 1946; *Educ* Eton, Magdalene Coll Cambridge; *m* 1, 1972 (m dis 1986), Pamela Elizabeth, da of J E Doniger, of Knutsford, Cheshire; 2 s (Lionel Robert b 7 Aug 1974, Jack David b 7 Sept 1979), 1 da (Harriet Ann b 20 June 1976); m 2, 1986, Josephine, da of Duncan Spencer, of New York; 2 da (Tamsin Alice b 4 April 1986, Freya Charlotte b 20 Feb 1989); *Career* fin journalist Daily Mail 1968-73, ed Money Mail Handbook 1972-74, dir and publisher Euromoney Pubns Ltd 1969-83, chief exec Maybox Gp plc (theatre and cinema owners and managers) 1984-89; dir Publishing Hldgs plc 1986-88, Willis Faber & Dumes (Agencies) Ltd 1988-, dir St Martin's Theatre Ltd 1989-, md Victoria Palace 1989-, dir Thorndike Hldgs plc 1989-, Stewart Wrightson Member Agency Ltd 1987-; govr Wellesley House Sch; memb Fin Ctee Univ Coll London 1984, memb Cncl Jewish Colonisation Assoc 1984-; *Style*— Stephen Waley-Cohen, Esq; 1 Wallingford Ave, London W10

WALFORD, Hon Mrs (Angela Mary); *née* Bellew; only da of 7 Baron Bellew; *b* 11 April 1944; *m* 1964, Capt Simon Hugh Walford, 17/21 Lancers, s of Lt-Col Hugh Walford (of a family which has been traced to one Sir Hugo de Walford, who held, as a knight's fee, the lordship of Walford, Herefordshire, 1109); 2 da (Jeanie Anne b 1966, Caroline Sarah b 1968); *Style*— The Hon Mrs Walford; Summerstown House, Trim, Co Meath, Eire (☎ 046 31245)

WALFORD, Christopher Rupert; s of John Rupert Charles Walford, MBE, and Gladys Irene Walford, *née* Sperrin; *b* 15 Oct 1935; *Educ* Charterhouse, Oriel Coll Oxford (MA); *m* 1967, Anne Elizabeth, *née* Viggars; 2 s (Rupert, Lawrence) and 1 s decd; *Career* Nat Serv cmmnd RA 1954-56, HAC 1957-72, ret on Warrant Offr; ptnr Allen & Overy 1970- (joined 1959); cncllr Borough of Kensington 1962-65; Borough of Kensington and Chelsea: cncllr 1964-82, dep Mayor 1974-75, Mayor 1979-80; alderman Ward of Farringdon Within 1982-, govr Bridewell Royal Hosp 1984-, memb Cncl CGLI 1984, tstee St Paul's Cathedral Choir Sch Fndn 1985-; IOD 1986- (memb Cncl, memb Policy and Exec Ctee, memb Company Affairs Ctee), memb Ct of Assts and Fin Ctee Corp Sons of the Clergy 1989-, Sheriff City of London 1990-91; Freeman City of London 1964; Liveryman: Worshipful Co of Makers of Playing Card 1978 (Master 1987-88), Worshipful Co of Slrs of City of London 1983 (memb Ct of Assts 1984, jr steward 1990); memb Guild of Freeman; FRSA; *Recreations* listening to music, opera, kitchen bridge, watching rugby and cricket, hill walking; *Clubs* MCC, City Livery, United Wards, Farringdon Ward (patron), Berkhamsted Golf, Craigendarroch Country; *Style*— Christopher Walford, Esq, TEM; Allen & Overy, 9 Cheapside, London EC2V 6AD (☎ 071 248 9898)

WALFORD, Dr Diana Marion; da of Lt-Col Joseph Norton, of Birmingham, and Thelma, *née* Norton; *b* 26 Feb 1944; *Educ* Calder HS for Girls Liverpool, Univ of Liverpool (George Holt scholarship, BSc, MB ChB, MD, George Holt medal, J Hill Abram prize), Univ of London (MSc, N and S Devi prize); *m* 9 Dec 1970, Arthur David Walford, s of Wing Cdr Adolph A Walford, of Bushey Heath, Herts; 1 s (Alexander b 5 May 1982), 1 da (Sally b 8 Aug 1972); *Career* house surgn Liverpool Royal Infirmary March-Aug 1969 (house physician 1968-69); sr registrar rotation 1972-75: St Mary's Hosp (sr house offr 1969-70), Northwick Park Hosp (sr house offr 1970-71), N London Blood Transfusion Centre MRC res fell and hon sr registrar Clinical Res Centre Northwick Park Hosp 1975-76, hon conslt haematologist Central Middx Hosp 1977-87; Dept of Health: sr med offr Medicines Div 1976-79, princ med offr Sci Servs Equipment Building Div 1979-83, sr princ med offr and under sec Med Manpower and Educn Div 1983-86, Sabbatical London Sch of Hygiene and Tropical Med 1986-87, sr princ med offr and under sec Int Health Microbiology of Food and Water and Communicable Disease Div 1987-89, dep chief med offr and med dir NHS Mgmnt Exec 1989-; contrib to various medical books and jls; FRCPath 1986 (MRCPath 1974), FRCP 1990 (MRCP 1972), MFPHM 1989; *Style*— Dr Diana Walford; Department of Health, Richmond House, 79 Whitehall, London SW1A 2NS (☎ 071 210 5593)

WALFORD, John Howard; s of Henry Howard Walford (d 1928), and Marjorie Josephine, *née* Solomon (d 1983); *b* 16 May 1927; *Educ* Cheltenham, Gonville and Caius Coll Cambridge (MA); *m* 6 Aug 1953, Peggy Ann, da of Cdr Richard Frederick Jessel, DSO, OBE, DSC, RN (ret) (d 1988); 2 s (Charles b 1955, Richard b 1960), 2 da (Veronica b 1957, Rosemary b 1964); *Career* admitted slr 1950; conslt Bischoff & Co 1988-91 (sr ptnr 1979-88); memb Cncl Law Soc 1961-69; govr: Coll of Law 1967-88, St John's Hosp for Diseases of the Skin 1967-82; pres Slrs Disciplinary Tribunal 1979-88; chm: Skin Disease Res Fund Appeal Ctee, Bd of Mgmnt Petworth Cottage Nursing and Convalescent Home 1988-, memb: Arbitration Panel The Securities Assoc Consumer Arbitration Scheme 1988-; Master City of London Solicitors Co 1981; Cdr Order of Bernardo O'Higgins (Chile) 1972; *Recreations* being in the country, fly-fishing, travelling abroad; *Clubs* Garrick, City Law, Leconsfield Fly-fishing; *Style*— John Walford, Esq; Pheasant Court, Northchapel, Petworth, West Sussex (☎ 042 878 550); office: Epworth House, 25 City Rd, London EC1 (☎ 071 628 4222, fax 071 638 3345, telex 885062)

WALFORD, John Thomas; OBE (1985), DL (1988); s of Frederick Thomas Walford (d 1973), of London, and Rose Elizabeth, *née* Froud (d 1964); *b* 1 Feb 1933; *Educ* Richmond and East Sheen County GS; *m* 1955 (m dis 1970), June Muriel Harding; 2 s (Martin b 1958, David b 1961), 1 da (Susan Ann b 1964); *Career* Nat Serv RAF 1951-53; CC Wakefield & Co Ltd 1953-55 (1949-51), Stanley Eades & Co 1955-60, MooCow Milk Bars Ltd 1960-64, gen sec of the Multiple Sclerosis Soc 1977- (vol 1954-64, dep gen sec 1965-77); memb RSM; *Recreations* collecting victorian fairings; *Style*— John Walford, Esq, OBE, DL; 109B Holland Rd, London W14 8AS (☎ 071 6036903), Church House, Talley, Llandeilo, Dyfed SA19 7AX (☎ 0558 685744), The Multiple Sclerosis Society of GB & NI, 25 Effie Rd, London SW6 1EE (☎ 071 736 6267, fax 071 7369861)

WALKER; *see*: Forestier-Walker

WALKER, Alexander Alfred; s of Alfred Walker (d 1979), of Protadown, NI, and Ethel, *née* Andrews (d 1974); *b* 22 March 1930; *Educ* Portadown GS, The Queen's Univ Belfast (BA), College d'Europe, Bruges (Diplome), Univ of Michigan USA; *Career* postgrad fell and lectr in political science Univ of Michigan 1952-54, features ed Birmingham Gazette 1954-56, leader writer and film critic The Birmingham Post 1956-59, film critic London Evening Standard 1960- (columnist 1989-), columnist Vogue magazine 1974-86; winner of annual British Press Awards Critic of the Year 1970 and 74 (commended 1985); memb Br Screen Advsy Cncl 1977 (formerly Wilson Interim Action Ctee on the Film Indust), govr The Br Film Inst 1988-, Chevalier de L'Ordre des Arts et des Lettres 1981; *Books* The Celluliod Sacrifice: Aspects of Sex in the Movies (1966), Hollywood, England: The British Film Industry in the Sixties (1974), The Shattered Silents: How The Talkies Came to Stay (1978), Garbo (1980), Peter Sellers: The Authorized Biography (1981), Joan Crawford (1983), Dietrich (1984), National Heroes: British Cinema in the Seventies and Eighties (1985), Elizabeth: The Life of Elizabeth Taylor (1990); author TV series Moviemen, co-producer TV progs on history of Hollywood, Garbo and Chaplin; *Recreations* skiing; *Style*— Alexander Walker, Esq; 1 Marlborough, 38-40 Maida Vale, London W9 1RW (☎ 071 289 0985)

WALKER, Sir Allan Grierson; QC (Scot); s of Joseph Walker; *b* 1 May 1907; *Educ* Whitgift Sch, Univ of Edinburgh; *m* 1935, Audrey, da of Dr T Glover; 1 s; *Career* Scottish Bar 1931-39; Sheriff substitute at: Selkirk and Peebles 1942-45, Dumbarton 1945-50, Glasgow 1950-63; Sheriff princ Lanarks 1963-74; memb Law Reform Ctee for Scotland 1964-70, chm Sheriff Ct Rules Cncl 1972-74; Hon LLD Univ of Glasgow 1967; kt 1968; *Style*— Sir Allan Walker, QC; 24 Moffat Rd, Dumfries (☎ 0387 53583)

WALKER, Prof Andrew Charles; s of Maurice Frederick Walker, of Saffron Walden, Essex, and Margaret Florence, *née* Rust; *b* 24 June 1948; *Educ* Kingsbury County GS, Univ of Essex (BA, MSc, PhD); *m* 2 April 1972, Margaret Elizabeth, da of Arthur Mortimer, of Heckmondwike, Yorks; 1 s (Edmund b 1978), 1 da (Abigail (twin) b 1978); *Career* Nat Res Cncl of Canada postdoctoral fell Ottawa Canada, Sci Res Cncl fell Dept of Physics Univ of Essex 1974-75 (sr res studentship 1969-72), sr scientific offr UK AEA Culham Laboratory 1975-83; Heriot Watt Univ: prof of physics, OCLI Chair of Modern Optics 1988- (lectr 1983-85, reader in physics; memb Ctee: Quantum Electronics Gp Inst of Physics 1979-82 (hon sec 1982-85), Scottish Branch Inst of Physics 1985-88; FInstP 1987; *Recreations* music (piano, guitar), skiing, sailing; *Style*— Prof Andrew Walker; Dept of Physics, Heriot Watt Univ, Riccarton, Edinburgh EH14 4AS (☎ 031 451 3036, fax 031 451 3136)

WALKER, Andrew David; s of Alexander MacPherson Walker, of Norfolk, and Viola Maisie, *née* Pearce; *b* 18 April 1948; *Educ* Norwich Sch, Univ of Bristol (LLB), Univ of Warwick (LLM); *m* 4 Sept 1976, Christine Joan, da of Clifford Horace Hall, of Bedford; 1 s (Alexander Henry b 1982), 1 da (Helen Victoria b 1985); *Career* lectr Univ of Aston 1974-81; slr 1974, private practise Russell & Hallmark 1981-; memb Malvern Hills Dist Cncl, chm Social Security Appeal Tbnl; memb Law Soc 1981; *Books* Law of Industrial Pollution Control (1979); *Recreations* antique collecting, book collecting, cookery; *Style*— Andrew Walker, Esq; 31 Hornyold Rd, Malvern, Hereford & Worcester (☎ 0684 566 991); 4 & 5 Sansome Place, Worcester WR1 1UQ (☎ 0905 726 600, fax 0905 611 093)

WALKER, Hon Mrs (Anna Elizabeth Blackstock); *née* Butterworth; er da of Baron

Butterworth, CBE (Life Peer), *qv*; *b* 1951; *Educ* Benenden, Lady Margaret Hall Oxford; *m* 1983, Timothy Edward Hanson Walker; *Style—* The Hon Mrs Walker; 24 Old Park Ave, London SW12 8RH

WALKER, Anthony; *b* 21 Sept 1937; *Educ* Central Fndn GS London; *Career* ptnr Nicholson Graham & Jones; memb Law Soc; *Recreations* gardening, tennis; *Clubs* Reform; *Style—* Anthony Walker, Esq; Nicholson Graham & Jones, 25 Moorgate, London EC2 (☎ 071 628 9151)

WALKER, Lt-Gen Sir Antony Kenneth Frederick; KCB (1987); s of Kenneth Frederick Andrews Walker (d 1966), and Iris Mary Walker (d 1983); *b* 16 May 1934; *Educ* Merchant Taylors', RMA Sandhurst; *m* 1, 1961 (m dis 1983), Diana Merran Steward; 1 s, 1 da; m 2, 1985, Susan Carol, da of Derrick Stuart Holmes, of Bournemouth; *Career* cmmnd RTR 1954; serv: BAOR, Libya, Ghana, NI (despatches), Hong Kong, UN Force in Cyprus; CO 1 RTR 1974-76, Dep Cdr 4 Armd Div 1978-80, Maj-Gen 1982, GOC 3 Armd Div 1982-84, Col Cmdt RTR 1983-; COS HQ UKLF 1985-87, Dep CDS (Commitments) 1987-; *Recreations* bird-watching, music, theatre, country sports, practical study of wine; *Style—* Lt-Gen Sir Antony Walker, KCB; c/o National Westminster Bank, 151 The Parade, Watford, Herts

WALKER, Archibald George Orr; s of George Edward Orr Walker, MBE, TD, QC (d 1973), of Newark Castle, Ayr, and Margaret Sybil, *née* Orr; *b* 14 Feb 1937; *Educ* Eton; *m* 11 Feb 1967, Fiona Mary Elizabeth, da of Alison Lyle Barr, MC (d 1970), of Brannochlie, Bridge of Weir; 1 s (James b 1968), 1 da (Rosamund b 1970); *Career* Nat Serv 2 Lt Coldstream Gds 1955-57; apprentice CA McClelland Moores Glasgow 1957-62, qualified CA 1962, dep chm Singer and Friedlander Ltd 1983-90 (joined 1968, dir 1973); non exec dir: Clyde Petroleum plc 1973-88, Scot Nat Tst plc 1984; exec dir Singer and Friedlander Gp plc 1987-90, non exec dir Singer and Friedlander Gp plc 1991-, memb Irvine Devpt Corp 1987; memb Queen's Body Gd for Scotland (The Royal Co of Archers) 1968; *Recreations* golf, tennis, stalking, shooting, skiing; *Clubs* Western (Glasgow), Prestwick Golf, The Hon Co of Edinburgh Golfers, Machrihanish Golf, Royal & Ancient Golf St Andrews; *Style—* Archibald Walker, Esq; Newark Castle, Ayr KA7 4ED (☎ 0292 41587)

WALKER, Sir Baldwin Patrick; 4 Bt (UK 1856), of Oakley House, Suffolk; also hereditary Pasha of the Ottoman Empire; s of late Cdr Baldwin Charles Walker, himself s of Sir Francis Walker, 3 Bt (d 1928, in his turn 2 surviving s of Adm Sir Baldwin Wake Walker, 1 Bt, KCB, who was Comptroller of the (Royal) Navy and sometime Adm in the Turkish service, whereby he was cr a Pasha); *b* 10 Sept 1924; *Educ* Gordonstoun; *m* 1, 1948 (m dis 1954), Joy Yvonne, da of Sir Arrol Moir, 2 Bt (d 1957); m 2, 1954, Sandra Stewart; m 3, 1966, Rosemary Ann, da of late Henry Hollingdrake; 1 s, 1 da; m 4, 1980, Vanessa Joyce, da of Dr Alan Clay; *Heir* s, Christopher Robert Baldwin, b 25 Oct 1969; *Career* formerly London regional mangr Planned Music Ltd, Planned Equipment Ltd, Planned Communications Ltd; *Style—* Sir Baldwin Walker, Bt

WALKER, Barry Matthew; *Career* ptnr Ashurst Morris Crisp; *Style—* Barry Walker, Esq; Broadwalk House, 5 Appold St, London EC2A 2HA (☎ 071 638 1111, fax 071 972 7990)

WALKER, Brian Wilson; s of Arthur Harrison Walker (d 1960), and Eleanor Charlotte Mary, *née* Wilson; *b* 31 Oct 1930; *Educ* Heversham Sch Westmorland 1940-50, Leicester Coll of Technol, Manchester Univ, Oxford Univ (MA); *m* 5 April 1954, Nancy Margaret, da of Samuel Henry Gawith (d 1967); 1 s (Peter b 1955), 5 da (Clare b 1957, Dorcas b 1958, Grainne b 1964, Siobhan b 1967, Sarah b 1968); *Career* pres Int Inst for Environment and Devpt 1985-89, dir Earthwatch Europe 1990-; dir Independent Cmmn on Int Humanitarian Issues 1983-85; dir gen Oxfam 1974-83; gen mangr Bridge Port Brass Ltd 1961-74; fndr chm New Ulster Movement 1969; chm: Band Aid, Live Aid 1985-, SOS Sahel 1989-; *Recreations* gardening, walking, reading; *Style—* Brian Walker, Esq; 14 Upland Park Rd, Oxford OX2 7RU (☎ 0865 515473); Earthwatch Europe, Belsyre Court, 57 Woodstock Rd, Oxford OX2 6HU (☎ 0865 311 600)

WALKER, Catherine Marguerite Marie-Therese; d of Remy Baheux and Agnes Lefebvre; *Educ* Univs of Lille and Aix-en-Provence; *m* 1969, John David Walker (decd), 2 da (Naomi Carolyn b 1971, Marianne Emily b 1972); *Career* dir Film Dept French Inst London 1970, memb Lecture Dept French Embassy 1971, dir and proprietor The Chelsea Design Co Ltd 1977-; winner Designer of the Year for Couture 1990-91; *Style—* Mrs Catherine Walker; The Chelsea Design Co Ltd, 65 Sydney St, Chelsea, London SW3 6PX (☎ 071 352 4626)

WALKER, (Alfred) Cecil; JP (1966), MP (UU) Belfast N 1983-; s of Alfred George Walker, and Margaret Lucinda Walker (d 1983); *b* 17 Dec 1924; *Educ* Methodist Coll Belfast; *m* 1953, Ann May Joan; 2 s; *Career* contested (UU): NI Assembly 1973, Belfast N 1979; sales mngr; *Recreations* sailing (yacht 'Nekita'); *Clubs* Down Cruising; *Style—* A Cecil Walker, Esq, JP, MP; 1 Wynnland Rd, Newtownabbey, Belfast BT36 6RZ, NI (☎ 0232 833 463)

WALKER, Chris Ian; s of Peter Earnest Walker, of Hatfield Peveral, Essex, and Kathleen Mary, *née* Partridge; *b* 11 June 1967; *Educ* Manningtree Sch, Colchester Tech Coll; *Career* professional squash player 1986-; represented England at under 12, 14, 16 and 19 level, finalist Br Under 23 Closed 1988, Semi-finalist Austrian Open 1989, winner Jamaican Open 1989, represented England Euro Championships 1989; winner: Tenerife Open 1990 Euro Closed 1990; memb Int Squash Professionals Assoc; *Recreations* golf, all sports, music; *Clubs* Lexden Squash, Ardleigh Hall Squash; *Style—* Chris Walker, Esq; Apartment 4, Claudius Court, St Peter's St, Colchester, Essex CO1 1EQ (☎ 0206 563175)

WALKER, Sir Colin John Shedlock; OBE (1981); s of Arthur John Walker (d 1982), of The Rookery, Hacheston, Woodbridge, Suffolk, and Olave Gertrude, *née* Mann (d 1982); *b* 7 Oct 1934; *Educ* St Edwards Sch Oxford, Royal Agric Coll Cirencester; *m* 26 Sept 1963, Wendy Elizabeth, da of John Hicks Ellis, of Long Stratton, Norfolk; 2 s; *Career* landowner, farmer, businessman; memb: Suffolk CC 1976-80, Central Blood Laboratories Authy 1985-; chm: East Suffolk Health Authy 1986-87, East Anglian RHA 1987- (memb 1983-86), Harwich Harbour Bd 1987-; govr Orwell Park Sch; FRSA, kt 1991; *Recreations* shooting; *Clubs* Royal Over-Seas League; *Style—* Sir Colin Walker, OBE; Blomvyle Hall, Hacheston, Woodbridge, Suffolk IPI3 ODY (☎ 0728 746756), Quel Balcon, La Herradura, Granada, Spain (☎ 58 82 72 62); East Anglian Regional Health Authority, Union Lane, Chesterton, Cambridge (☎ 0223 375375, fax 0223 533209)

WALKER, Prof David Alan; s of Cyril Walker (d 1990), of 33 Hayman Way, Falmouth, and Dorothy, *née* Dobson; *b* 18 Aug 1928; *Educ* South Shields HS, Univ of Durham (BSc, PhD, DSc); *m* 7 July 1956, Shirley Wynne, da of William Chambers Mason (d 1980); 1 s (Rick b 1960), 1 da (Marney b 1957); *Career* RNAS 1946-48; ICI post-doctoral res fell 1956-58, reader in botany QMC London 1963-65 (lectr 1958-63, Charles F Kettering Res Fellowship 1962), reader in enymology Imperial Coll London 1965-70; Univ of Sheffield: prof of biology 1970-84, dir of Res Inst for Photosynthesis 1984-88, prof of photosynthesis Robert Hill Inst 1988-; sr Von Humboldt fell 1991; corr memb American Soc of Plant Physiologists; memb Exec Cncl Save British Science sr von Humbolt fell 1991, FIBiol 1971, FRS 1979; *Books* Energy, Plants and Man (1979), C3 C4 Mechanisms and Cellular and Enviromental Regulation of Photosynthesis (1983), The Use of the Oxygen Electrode and Fluorescence Probes in Simple Measurements of Photosynthesis (1987); *Recreations* singing the Sheffield carols, walking, eating and drinking in good company; *Style—* Prof David Walker; Robert Hill Institute, The University, Sheffield S10 2TN (☎ 0742 768555 ext 6401, fax 0742 682521)

WALKER, Sir David Alan; s of Harold Walker, and Marian Walker; *b* 31 Dec 1939; *Educ* Chesterfield Sch, Queens' Coll Cambridge (MA); *m* 20 April 1963, Isobel, *née* Cooper; 1 s (Jonathan b 29 Jan 1968), 2 da (Elspeth b 4 June 1966, Penelope b 12 April 1970); *Career* HM Treasy: joined 1961, private sec to Jt Perm Sec 1964-66, seconded Staff IMF Washington 1970-73, asst sec 1973-77; Bank of England: chief advsr then chief Econ Intelligence Dept, asst dir 1980, exec dir fin and indust 1982-88; chm Johnson Matthey Bankers Ltd (later Minories Finance Ltd) 1985-88, chm financial markets gp LSE 1987-, pt/t memb Bd CEGB 1987-89, nominated memb Cncl Lloyd's 1988- (chm securities and investmts bd); non exec dir: Bank of England, National Power 1990; chm Exec Ctee Int Securities Cmmns; hon fell Queens' Coll Cambridge; kt 1991; *Recreations* music, long-distance walking; *Clubs* Reform; *Style—* Sir David Walker; Securities and Investments Board, Gavrelle House, 2-14 Bunhill Row, London, EC1Y 8RA (☎ 071 638 1240)

WALKER, David Eaton; s of George Eaton Walker (d 1954), and Ida Christine, *née* Barraclough (d 1979); *b* 16 May 1927; *Educ* Grange GS Bradford, Univ of London (LLB); *m* 10 Sept 1966, Ann Patricia, *née* Haggas; 2 s (Jeremy David Eaton b 6 May 1968, Robert James Eaton b 12 Feb 1971), 1 da (Rosalind Ann b 30 Oct 1973); *Career* articled clerk G T Holden 1946-49, qualified chartered accountant 1949, ptnr Williamson Butterfield & Roberts 1957-65 (joined 1949), ptnr Thornton Baker (following merger) 1965-73, Grant Thornton (following merger): chm Fin Ctee 1973, memb Policy Bd 1973, memb Exec 1975-84, sr ptnr Bradford 1977-; FCA 1954 (ACA 1949); *Recreations* reading, walking; *Clubs* Carlton; *Style—* David Walker, Esq; Grant Thornton, Eldon Lodge, Eldon Place, Bradford BD1 3AP (☎ 0274 734341, fax 0274 390191)

WALKER, (Louis) David; MBE, TD; s of Louis Charles Walker, MBE (d 1981), and Margaret Ann, *née* Phillips (d 1988); *b* 4 July 1932; *Educ* Chipping Sodbury GS, Merchant Ventures Coll, Univ of Bristol; *m* 29 Feb 1964, Moira, da of Lt-Col James Coombe, RFC (d 1974), 1 da (Sarah b 3 Jan 1965); *Career* Nat Serv 2 Lt RA 1953, Lt (later Capt) Royal Aust Artillery (CMF) 1956, Lt RA (TA) 1959, Capt 4 Bn Wiltshire Regt 1963-67; Union Int Group Aust 1955-58 (London 1958-62), Marsh Harris Group Calne 1962-65, G Brazil & Co Ltd 1965-68, Unilever Group London 1968-71, dir Robert Wilson & Sons (1849) Ltd Scot 1971-78, md McKey Food Service Ltd 1978-90 (chm 1990-), chm McKey Holdings (Europe) Ltd 1990-; watch offr Sail Trg Assoc, memb Cncl BMMA 1981-, chm McDonald's Euro Meat Prods Quality Control Ctee, underwriter Lloyd's 1990-; Freeman and Liveryman: Worshipful Co of Tallow Chandlers 1963-, Worshipful Co of Butchers 1985; memb Royal Inst of Meat 1959, MRSH 1959, FRSH 1985; *Recreations* sailing, game shooting, military history; *Clubs* RTYC, RSYC, RAYC; *Style—* L David Walker, Esq, MBE, TD; Ivy Cottage, Aynho, Banbury, Oxfordshire (☎ 0869 810678); McKey Holdings (Europe) Ltd, Northfield Drive, Northfield, Milton Keynes MK15 ODF (☎ 0908 665431, fax 0908 674621, telex 826218, car 0836 290111/0860 890037)

WALKER, Prof David Maxwell; CBE (1986), QC (Scot 1958); s of James Mitchell Walker (d 1934), of Woodbank, Bishopbriggs, Glasgow, and Mary Paton Colquhoun, *née* Irvine (d 1971); *b* 9 April 1920; *Educ* Glasgow HS, Univ of Glasgow (MA, LLB, LLD), Univ of Edinburgh (PhD, LLD), Univ of London (LLB, LLD); *m* 1 Sept 1954, Margaret Walker, OBE, da of Robert Knox (d 1970), of Haystone, Brookfield, Renfrewshire; *Career* WWII: NCO Cameronians (Scottish Rifles) 1939, 2 Lt HLI 1940, transferred to RIASC 1941, served India 1941-42, N Africa 1942-43, 8 Indian Div Italy 1943-46 (Bde Supply and Tport Offr HQ 21 Indian Inf Brig); advocate Scottish Bar 1948, in practice Scottish Bar 1948-53, called to the Bar Middle Temple 1957; regius prof of law Univ of Glasgow 1958-90 (prof of jurisprudence 1954-58, dean Faculty of Law 1956-59, sr res fell 1990-); dir Scottish Univs' Law Inst 1974-80, convenor Sch of Law 1984-88; chm: HS of Glasgow Educn Tst, Hamlyn Tst; hon pres Friends of Glasgow Univ Library; hon LLD Univ of Edinburgh 1974; memb Faculty of Advocates 1948, Middle Temple 1957; FBA 1976, FRSE 1980; *Books* Law of Damages in Scotland (1955), The Scottish Legal System (1959, 5 edn 1981), Law of Delict in Scotland (1966, 2 edn 1981), Principles of Scottish Private Law (2 vols 1970, 4 edn 4 vols 1988-89), Law of Prescription and Limitation in Scotland (1973, 4 edn 1990), Law of Civil Remedies in Scotland (1974), Law of Contracts and Related Obligations in Scotland (1979, 2 edn 1985), The Oxford Companion to Law (1980), Stair's Institutions of the Law of Scotland (ed 1981), Stair Tercentenary Studies (ed 1981), The Scottish Jurists (1985), A Legal History of Scotland (vol 1, 1988, vol 2 1990); author of numerous papers in legal journals; *Recreations* book-collecting, Scottish history; *Clubs* Royal Scottish Automobile; *Style—* Prof David M Walker, CBE, QC, FRSE; 1 Beaumont Gate, Glasgow G12 9EE (☎ 041 339 2802); Department of Private Law, University of Glasgow, Glasgow, Scotland G12 8QQ (☎ 041 339 8855 ext 4556, telex 777070 UNIGLA)

WALKER, (Thomas) Dickson; MBE (1945); s of Tom Brunton Walker (d 1964), and Letitia Flora McDonald, *née* Dickson (d 1964); *b* 23 Sept 1912; *Educ* Mill Hill Sch; *m* 24 June 1939, Joan Mary, da of Herbert Joseph Hawes (d 1966); 1 s (Humphrey 1943), 2 da (Elizabeth b 1941, Janet b 1949); *Career* WW11 RASC 1939-46, enlisted as cadet 1939, cmmnd 1940, 2 Lt Tport UK 1940-42; Capt (1942): Tport N Africa 1942-43 (despatches); Tport Italy 1943-46 (despatches), Maj 1945, released 1946; temporarily recalled Z Reserve Trg; CA; sr ptnr Josolyne Layton-Bennett & Co (formerly Layton Bennett Billingham & Co) 1971-78 (ptnr 1949-71); non-exec dir of various pub cos, latest appts incl: Scapa Group plc 1962-88, William Nash plc 1977-; chm and non-exec dir Sheldon Jones plc 1975-88; sec (later chm) Alford House Youth Club Lambeth 1934-; govr and treas Mill Hill Sch 1953-88, pres Old Millhillians Club 1969-70, memb Ctee Buttle Tst for Children, elder United Reformed Church; FCA 1954, FRSA 1977; *Recreations* gardening, natural history (particularly wildflowers), studying art; *Clubs* East India; *Style—* Dickson Walker, Esq, MBE

WALKER, Douglas Macdonald; s of James Walker (d 1963), of Edinburgh, and Mary Alice, *née* Barton (d 1974); *b* 4 Feb 1928; *Educ* George Heriot's Sch Edinburgh, Edinburgh & East of Scotland Coll of Agric (NDA); *m* 18 Aug 1951, Helen Grant, da of Andrew Bell (d 1979), of Edinburgh; 2 s (Ian b 1956, Duncan b 1958), 1 da (Morag b 1953); *Career* lectr in farm machinery Lancashire Farm Inst 1948-50, lectr in agric engrg Shuttleworth Coll 1950-53, asst export sales mangr David Brown Tractors Ltd 1953-64, md John Deere Ltd 1965-; hon fell Shuttleworth Coll; former pres Agric Engrs Assoc; pres Inst of Agric Engrs, tstee Douglas Bomford Meml Tst 1986, pres Motor Industries Benevolent fund 1988, vice pres Inst of the Motor Industry 1989; Freeman City of London 1974, Liveryman Worshipful Co of Farmers 1975; FIAgrE, FBIM, FIMI, MCIM; *Recreations* walking, travel, photography, collecting wine labels; *Clubs* Farmers; *Style—* Douglas M Walker, Esq; Pentland House, 25 Hallfields, Edwalton, Nottingham NG12 4AA (☎ 0602 233239); John Deere Ltd, Langar, Nottingham NG13 9HT (☎ 0949 60491, fax 0949 60490, telex 37373)

WALKER, Duncan Roy; s of John Hamilton Walker (d 1978), of Uddingston,

Lanarkshire, Scotland, and Sarah Carmichael, *née* Leitch; *b* 1 May 1942; *Educ* Bellshill Acad, Univ of Glasgow; *m* 12 June 1969, Mary Frances, da of Ambrose McNulty (d 1986), of Glasgow; 3 s (Jonathan Johar b 1972, Evan Alexander b 1974, Duncan Robert b 1982), 1 da (Katherine Anne b 1975); *Career* cardiothoracic surgn: Killingbeck Hosp, Gen Infirmary Leeds, St James Univ Hosp 1978-; tstee Children's Heart Surgery Fund; fell RCS; *Recreations* reading, bee keeping, gardening; *Style—* Duncan Walker, Esq; 15 North Grange Mount, Headingley, Leeds LS6 2BY (☎ 0532 783130); Lilypond Cottage, Quinish Estate, Dervaig, Mull; The Killingbeck Hosp York Rd, Leeds LS14 6UQ (☎ 0532 648164)

WALKER, Edward Rognvald Lindsay; s of James Alexander Walker, CBE (d 1967), of Edinburgh, and Edith Marion, *née* Liddle; *b* 30 Jan 1931; *Educ* Edinburgh Acad; *m* 18 April 1956, Lillias McGregor, da of Gregor Eadie, of Edinburgh; 2 s (Douglas b 1958, David b 1964), 1 da (Fiona (Mrs Drew) b 1960); *Career* Nat Serv cmmnd Pilot Offr 1954-56; ptnr: Howden & Molleson CA 1957-64, Scott-Moncrieff Thomson & Shiells 1964-; auditor: St Andrews Tst plc 1964-, Scottish Equitable Life Assur Soc 1967-, Inst of CAs of Scotland 1980-85; dir: Melville Securities Ltd 1971-, Scott-Moncrieff Life & Pensions Ltd 1988-; chm: Pentland Cons Assoc 1969-72, Local Govt Auditors (Scotland) Assoc 1977-79; MICAS; *Recreations* golf, music, photography, reading; *Clubs* New (Edinburgh), The Hon Co of Edinburgh Golfers, Bruntsfield Links Golfing Soc; *Style—* E R L Lindsay, Esq; 9 Woodhall Rd, Edinburgh EH13 0DQ (☎ 031 441 3283); Scott-Moncrieff Thomson & Shiells, 17 Melville St, Edinburgh EH3 7PH (☎ 031 226 6281, fax 031 225 9829, telex 727 186)

WALKER, Geoffrey Hurst; s of Raymond Bennet Walker, of Perth, Scotland, and Joan Edith Agnes, *née* Michie; *b* 7 Feb 1956; *Educ* Bell Baxter HS Cupar Fife, Univ of Edinburgh (BCom); *Career* audit mangr Arthur Young 1978-87; fin dir: Serif Cowells plc 1987-89, DPS Typecraft Ltd 1990-; CA 1981; *Recreations* sailing, badminton, philately; *Style—* Geoffrey Walker, Esq; 2 Ransome Close, Sproughton, Ipswich, Suffolk IP8 3DG (☎ 0473 419 76); Acorn House, Great Oaks, Basildon, Essex SS14 1AH (☎ 0268 523471, fax 0268 281090)

WALKER, George Alfred; s of William James Walker, and Ellen, *née* Page; *b* 14 April 1929; *m* 1957, Jean Maureen, *née* Hatton; 1 s (Jason), 2 da (Sarah (Marchioness of Milford Haven), Romla); *Career* chief exec The Brent Walker Group PLC (leisure gp) 1981-; *Recreations* skiing, climbing, sailing; *Clubs* RAC; *Style—* George Walker, Esq; c/o Brent Walker Group PLC, Brent Walker House, 19 Rupert St, London W1V 7FS (☎ 071 465 0111)

WALKER, Sir Gervas George; JP (Bristol 1969), DL (Avon 1982); s of Harry Walker; *b* 12 Sept 1920; *Educ* Monmouth Sch; *m* 1944, Eileen, *née* Maxwell; 2 s; *Career* formerly: chm Bristol Avon River Authy, memb SW Regnl Planning Cncl, ldr and oppn ldr Bristol City Cncl, chm and ldr Avon CC 1973-81, chm Bristol Cons Assoc 1975-79 and Assoc of CCs 1979-81 (vice chm 1978-79); kt 1979; *Style—* Sir Gervas Walker, JP, DL; Bulverton Well Farm, Sidmouth, Devon EX10 9DW (☎ 0395 516902); The Lodge, Cobblestone Mews, Clifton Park, Bristol BS8 3DQ (☎ 0272 737063)

WALKER, (Victor) Gordon; DL (Co of IOW 1987); s of Edgar Frederick Walker (d 1959), of Mitcham, Melbourne, Victoria, Australia, and Myra Gaskell, *née* Jones (d 1973); *b* 27 Jan 1919; *Educ* Wesley Coll Melbourne, Queen's Coll Univ of Melbourne (MB BS); *m* 1 Sept 1948, Judith Mary, da of Arnold Augustus Phillips (d 1961), of Melbourne, Australia; 2 s (Nicholas b 1949, Jeremy b 1955), 2 da (Philippa b 1951, Belinda b 1956); *Career* Flt Lt RAAF; serv: Australia, France, and UK 1942-47; conslt surgn: IOW Gp of Hosps 1954-86, Home Office 1959-86; memb Ct of Examiners RCS (Eng) 1970-76; High Sheriff Co of IOW 1985-86; FRCS (Eng); *Recreations* sailing; *Clubs* Royal Yacht Sqdn, Melbourne Cricket, Army and Navy; *Style—* Gordon Walker, Esq, DL; Stonelands, Binstead, IOW PO33 3NJ (☎ 0983 63980)

WALKER, Graham Edwards; s of Eric Walker, of North Wales, and Mary, *née* Edwards; *b* 6 July 1939; *Educ* Wallasey GS; *m* Annabel; 2 s (Max b 1 Aug 1966, Jago b 20 Aug 1972), 1 da (Abbey b 15 Feb 1964); *Career* yachtsman; memb Br Admiral Cup team 1983, 1985, 1987, 1989, (capt 1983 and 1987), capt Br Southern Cross team 1983, world 3/4 ton champion 1986, chm Br Americas Cup challenge 1986-87; only Br yachtsman to appear in four consecutive Admiral's Cups; dir: Argyll Group 1983-89, Broad Street Group 1989-90, currently private investor; *Recreations* yachting, shooting, vintage cars; *Style—* Graham Walker, Esq

WALKER, Graham Peter; s of John Henry Walker, of Gidea Park, Essex, and Edna May, *née* Best; *b* 17 June 1948; *Educ* Royal Liberty Sch Gidea Park Essex, The London Film Sch (Dip); *m* 23 April 1977, Josephine Mary, da of Hywel Williams (d 1988), of Birmingham; 1 step s (Simon b 22 May 1988); *Career* BBC film ed 1976-84; progs inc: Play for Today, Bergerac, Miss Marple, Great River Journeys; BBC supervising film ed 1984-86; progs inc: Bergerac, Miss Marple, Hard Travelling; freelance feature film ed 1986-; work inc The Fourth Protocol, The Josephine Baker Story, The Last of the Finest (aka Blue Heat); steward Assoc of Cinematograph and TV Technicians 1982-86; memb Guild of Br Film Eds 1987; *Recreations* cinema and travel; *Style—* Graham Walker, Esq; 64 Chiltern View Rd, Uxbridge, Middx UB8 2PF (☎ 0895 30589)

WALKER, Rt Hon Harold; PC (1979), MP (Doncaster Central 1983 and 1987); s of Harold Walker, and Phyllis Walker; *b* 12 July 1927; *Educ* Manchester Coll of Technol; *m* 1, 1956, Barbara (decd), da of Cecil Hague; 1 da; m 2, 1984, Mary Griffin; *Career* Fleet Air Arm 1946-48; MP (Lab) Doncaster 1964-1983, asst govt whip 1967, Parly under sec of state employment and productivity 1968-70, oppn front bench spokesman industl rels 1970-74, Parly under sec of state employment 1974-76, min of state 1976-79, oppn spokesman 1979-1983; chm Ways and Means Ctee (dep speaker 1983-); chm: Chairmen's Panel, Standing Orders Ctee, Ct of Referees; *Style—* The Rt Hon Harold Walker, MP; House of Commons, London SW1A 0AA

WALKER, Maj Sir Hugh Ronald; 4 Bt (UK 1906), of Pembroke House, City of Dublin; s of Maj Sir Cecil Edward Walker, 3 Bt, DSO, MC (d 1964), and Violet, *née* McMaster; *b* 13 Dec 1925; *Educ* Wellington; *m* 1971, Norna, da of Lt Cdr R D Baird; 2 s (Robert Cecil, Roy Edward b 10 Aug 1977); *Heir* s, Robert Cecil Walker, b 26 Sept 1974; *Career* Maj RA, ret; memb Assoc of Supervisory and Exec Engrs; *Style—* Maj Sir Hugh Walker, Bt; Ballinamona Stud Hospital, Killmallock, Co Limerick, Republic of Ireland; c/o Lloyds Bank Ltd, Somerton, Somerset

WALKER, Ian Hugh; s of John Walker, and Joan, *née* Crowther; *b* 3 Jan 1950; *Educ* Huntley's Tunbridge Wells; *m* 15 July 1975, Lorraine, da of George Armstrong; 2 s (Matthew James Hugh b 1979, Robert George b 1982); *Career* estate agent; ptnr Page & Wells Maidstone, dir Page & Wells Fin Servs Ltd; chm Bearsted Round Table 1989-; FNAEA; *Recreations* golf, squash, running, skiing; *Clubs* Tudor Park, Mote Squash, Bearsted; *Style—* Ian Walker, Esq; 132 Ashford Road, Bearsted, Maidstone, Kent (☎ 0622 39574)

WALKER, Dr Isobel Deda; da of Dr Thomas Alfred Christie, of Auchterarder, Perthshire, Scotland, and Edith Anderson, *née* Young; *b* 4 Oct 1944; *Educ* Jordanhill Coll Sch Glasgow, Univ of Glasgow (MB, ChB, MD); *m* 13 April 1966, Dr Colin Alexander Walker; 2 s (Jason b 1969, Lewis b 1975), 3 da (Nicola b 1972, Emily b 1979, Abigail b 1982); *Career* conslt haematologist Gtr Glasgow Health Bd 1978-, hon clinical lectr Univ of Glasgow 1978-; sec Steering Ctee Nat External Quality Assur Scheme for Blood Coagulation Testing; memb: Nat Panel of Specialists, Haemostasis and Thrombosis Task Force Br Soc Haematology; FRCPath 1984, FRCPEd 1985; *Recreations* French language, needlework; *Style—* Dr Isobel Walker; Dept of Haematology, Glasgow Royal Infirmary, Castle St, Glasgow G4 0SF (☎ 041 552 5692)

WALKER, Rev Dr James Bernard; s of Rev Dr Robert Bernard William Walker, of Edinburgh, and Grace Brownlee, *née* Torrance; *b* 7 May 1946; *Educ* Hamilton Acad Lanarkshire, Univ of Edinburgh (MA, BD), Merton Coll Oxford (D Phil); *m* 18 Aug 1972, Sheila Mary, da of Alexander Ballantyne Easton (d 1948), of Ilford, London; 3 s (Colin Alexander b 1975, Alastair Robert b 1975, Peter Donald b 1978); *Career* ordained Church of Scotland 1975, assoc min Mid Craigie Parish Church (with Wallacetown) Dundee 1975-78, min Old and St Paul's Parish Church Galashiels 1978-87, princ Queen's Theol Coll Birmingham 1987-; *Books* Israel - Covenant and Land (1986); *Recreations* hill walking, squash, swimming; *Style—* The Rev Dr James Walker; The Queen's College, Somerset Rd, Edgbaston, Birmingham B15 2QH (☎ 021 454 1527)

WALKER, Dr James Johnston; s of Sqdn Ldr James Walker, CBE, of 31 Ravenscraig Gdns, Dundee, and Catherine Clark, *née* Johnston; *b* 17 March 1952; *Educ* Dundee HS, Univ of Glasgow; *m* 15 July 1976, Ann Mary, da of Lt-Col Hugh McCulloch Young, of 32 Learmouth St, Falkirk; 2 da (Kate b 5 March 1980, Susan b 3 Aug 1983); *Career* Halt fell in med 1978-79, res fell in obstetrics 1983-84, lectr in obstetrics 1984-86, sr lectr in obstetrics 1987-; memb Royal Coll of Obstetrics, ctee memb Glasgow Obstetrical Soc; MRCOG 1981, MRCP 1981; *Recreations* swimming, music, travel; *Style—* Dr James Walker; 15 Woodburn Rd, Newlands, Glasgow, Scotland (☎ 041 637 0011); University Department of Obstetrics, Royal Maternity Hospital, Rotten Row, Glasgow (☎ 041 552 3400, fax 041 553 1367)

WALKER, His Hon Judge John David; DL (Humberside); s of late Lawrence Cecil Walker, and late Jessie Walker; *b* 13 March 1924; *Educ* Oundle, Univ of Cambridge (MA); *m* 1954, Elizabeth Mary Emma, da of late Victor William Owbridge, of Yorks; 1 s (Nicholas b 1958), 2 da (Belinda b 1955, Emma b 1962); *Career* served WWII Capt Frontier Force Rifles IA 1942-47; called to the Bar Middle Temple 1951, rec 1972; Circuit judge 1972-; pres Mental Health Review Tbnls; *Recreations* shooting, fishing; *Clubs* Lansdowne; *Style—* His Hon Judge John Walker, DL; Arden House, North Bar Without, Beverley, North Humberside

WALKER, Prof John Hilton; s of Lt-Col Arthur Walker (d 1966), of Allendale, Northumberland, and Effie Lilian, *née* Cheetham (d 1979); *b* 28 April 1928; *Educ* Samuel King's Sch Alston Cumberland, Kings Coll Univ of Durham (MB BS, MD), Univ of Newcastle upon Tyne (DPH, MFCM, MRCGP); *m* 9 March 1957, (Margaret) June, da of Capt William Reay Simpson (d 1980), of Allendale, Northumberland; 3 da (Gillian Amanda b 1958, Shona Ruth b 1960, Penelope Kate b 1964); *Career* RNR 1947-49; Luccock res fell Univ of Durham 1957-59, lectr in gen practice Univ of Edinburgh 1959-63; Univ of Newcastle: lectr in public health 1964-68, sr lectr and head of Dept Family and Community Med 1968-76, prof and head of dept 1976-88, emeritus prof; chm Assoc of Univ Teachers of Gen Practice, chief examiner and chm membership div RCGP 1972-83; FRCGP, FFCM 1977; *Recreations* gardening,skiing, motoring, building; *Style—* Prof John Walker; Low Luddick House, Woolsington, Newcastle NE13 8DE, (☎ 2860551)

WALKER, John James; s of Patrick Walker, of Flat 1, Glebe Cottage, Grove Lane, Weston-Super-Mare, Avon, and Claudine, *née* Brown; *b* 26 July 1949; *Educ* Sidcot Sch Winscombe Somerset, Bournemouth Coll of Art (Dip in Design); *Career* freelance film ed 1970-80, dir Bumper Films Ltd 1980-88; prodn of Stop-Frame Puppet; Animation Films: Rocky Hollow, Fireman Sam, Joshua Jones; *Recreations* skiing, squash, wine, travel; *Style—* John Walker, Esq; Bumper Films Ltd, Unit 15, Bridgwater Court, Oldmixon Crescent, Weston-super-Mare, Avon B524 9AY (☎ 0934 418961, fax 0934 624494)

WALKER, Dr John Malcolm; s of Norman Walker (d 1988), of Poole, Dorset, and Jessie Margarita, *née* Bertram; *b* 18 Dec 1950; *Educ* Queen Elizabeth's GS Wimborne Dorset, Univ of Birmingham (BSc, MB, ChB, MD); *m* 28 Aug 1982, Judith May, da of Mervyn Sherwood Brown, of Harrow, London; 1 da (Rachel Emily b 3 March 1988); *Career* conslt; St Thomas's Hospital London 1979-81, Charing Cross and Brompton Hospitals London 1981-84, John Radcliffe Hospital Oxford 1984-87, University College Hospital London 1987-; MRCP, memb British Cardiac Soc; *Style—* Dr Macolm Walker; 2 Westwood Rd, Barnes, London SW13 0LA (☎ 081 876 2935); 48 Heathfield Rd, West Moors, nr Wimborne, Dorset; Dept of Cardiology, Univ Coll Hosp, Gower St, London (☎ 071 387 9709, fax 071 388 5095)

WALKER, Brig (Edward) John Worley; OBE (1987); s of Air Cdre SG Walker, CB, OBE (d 1975) of Bradford-on-Avon, Wilts, and Laura Mabel Mary, *née* Gorton; *b* 5 Dec 1941; *Educ* Dulwich, RMA Sandhurst; *m* 12 June 1965, Susan Vera Anthea, da of Air Vice-Marshal Sir Thomas Shirley, KBE, CB (d 1983), of Wellingore, Lincolnshire; 3 da (Joanna b 1 April, 1967, Tamsin b 28 Oct 1968, Rebecca b 10 March 1972); *Career* cmmnd The Duke of Wellington's Regt 1962; regtl duty 1962-67: UK, Br Honduras, BAOR; ADC to Dep Supreme Allied Cdr Euro 1967-69, signals offr Duke of Wellington's Regt 1969-71, instr Sch of Infantry 1971-73, planning staff HQ NI 1973-75, Staff Coll Toronto 1975-76, Co Cdr Duke of Wellington's Regt BAOR and NI 1976-80, 2 i/c Duke of Wellington's Regt 1981, Lt-Col MOD ASD2 1981-84, CO Duke of Wellington's Regt 1984-87, Chief of Staff HQ dir of Infantry 1987-90, and 49 inf Bde 1990-; dir Br Olympic Nordic Ski Team: Sarajevo 1984, Calgary 1988; memb: Exec Ctee Army Rugby Union 1988, Bd Br Ski Fedn 1990-; chm Combined Servs Nordic and Biathlon; FBIM 1988, memb Br Olympic Assoc; *Recreations* squash, cross country skiing, rugby football; *Clubs* Army & Navy, St James'; *Style—* Brig John Walker, OBE; c/o Royal Bank of Scotland, Victoria Rd, Farnborough, Hants GU14 7NR (☎ 0252 544355, telex QUAESTOR HANTS, fax 0252 540587)

WALKER, Jonathan Gervas; s of Sir Gervas Walker, JP, DL, of Bulverton Well Farm, Sidmouth, Devon, and Lady Jessie Eileen, *née* Maxwell; *b* 26 June 1953; *Educ* Clifton; *m* 25 Feb 1984, Gillian, da of Dr Colin Dodds Drew, of Weston-super-Mare, Avon; 2 s (Edward b 20 May 1986, Giles b 8 March 1989); *Career* accountant Grant Thornton 1973-80, dir Terrett Taylor Ltd 1987-; *Recreations* tennis, shooting; *Clubs* Clifton (Bristol); *Style—* Jonathan Walker, Esq; Old Manor Cottage, Bulverton, Sidmouth, Devon (☎ 0395 514114); Ottery Moor, Honiton, Devon (☎ 0404 41117)

WALKER, Julian Fortay; CMG (1982), MBE (1960); s of Kenneth MacFarlane Walker (d 1963), of Woodcutters, Little London, Ambersham Common, nr Midhurst, W Sussex, and Eileen Marjorie Walker, later Mrs Dahlberg (d 1983); *b* 7 May 1929; *Educ* Harvey Sch NY, Stowe Bryanston, Univ of Cambridge (MA); *m* Aug 1983, Virginia Anne (Mrs Austin), da of Michael Stevens, of Lechdlade, Glos; 3 step da (Rachel b 17 Feb 1969, Kathryn b 6 Oct 1970, Elizabeth b 21 Oct 1972); *Career* Nat Serv RN 1947-49; Cambridge 1949-52, Univ of London Sch of African and Oriental Studies 1952; Foreign Serv: MECAS 1953, asst political agent Trucial States 1953-55, 3 then 2 sec Bahrain 1955-57, FCO and frontier settlement Oman 1957-60, 2 then 1 sec Oslo 1960-63, news dept spokesman FCO 1963-67, 1 sec Baghdad 1967, 1 sec Rabat Morocco 1967-69, FCO 1969-71, political agent Dubai Trucial States 1971, consul gen and cnsllr HM Embassy Dubai United Arab Emirates 1971-72, sabbatical leave Univ of Cambridge 1972-73, political advsr and head of chancery Br Mil Govt

Berlin 1973-76, NI office Stormont Castle 1976-77, dir MECAS 1977-78, ambass to Arab Repub Yemen and Repub of Jibuti 1979-84, ambass to Qatar 1984-87; HM Dip Serv: special advsr (Syria), Res Dept FCO 1987-; order of Isthqaq 1 Class (Qatar, 1985); *Recreations* sailing and sailboarding, music, gardening, tennis; *Clubs* RAC; *Style—* Julian Walker, Esq, CMG, MBE; 23 Woodlands Grove, Isleworth, Middx TW7 6NS (☎ 560 8795); Research and Analysis Dept, Foreign and Commonwealth Office, Whitehall, London SW1A 2AH (☎ 071 210 6214)

WALKER, Kenneth Lane; s of Herbert Arthur Walker (d 1961), and Verona Sophie, *née* Thomas; *b* 26 Feb 1936; *Educ* Moseley GS, Univ Coll Oxford; *m* 1964, Isabella Mary, da of John Moffat (d 1966); *Career* CA, dir of Mono Containers Ltd 1967-77, vice chm Mono Containers International Ltd 1975-77 (dir 1971-77), md Mono Containers, GmbH FDR and (Holdings) AG Switzerland 1975-77; vice chm: Pontneau Mono & Cie SA France 1970-77, Monoplast SA Spain 1972-77, Thurbaform Ltd 1975-77; dir: Kode International Ltd, Kode Investments Ltd, Kode Europe SA Belgium 1977-85; mgmnt conslt 1985-; chm: Wilts Centre IOD 1983-89, West of England branch IOD 1989-; *Recreations* gliding, reading, philately; *Clubs* City Livery; *Style—* Kenneth Walker, Esq; Whitley Grange, Whitley, nr Melksham, Wilts (☎ 0225 702242)

WALKER, (David) Lindsay; s of Rev David Sloan Walker, of Perthshire, and Mary Allan, *née* Ogilvie (d 1987); *b* 11 Sept 1940; *Educ* Stranraer HS, Alloa Acad; *m* 1963, Margaret Anne, da of Capt James Simpson Binnie, of Argyll; 1 s (David b 1969), 1 da (Valerie b 1966); *Career* corporate devpt dir Clydesdale Bank plc; dir: Banff & Buchan Nurseries Ltd 1982, Rhu Marina Ltd 1983, Freeport Scotland Ltd 1984, Clydesdale Bank Equity Ltd 1985, Clydesdale Bank Industl Investmts Ltd 1985, The Buy-Out Syndicate Ltd 1986; memb: Trade Devpt Ctee, Scottish Cncl Devpt and Indust, Rhu and Shandon Community Cncl; Churchill fell 1970; ACIB, FIBScot; *Recreations* sailing; *Style—* Lindsay Walker, Esq; Alt-na-Coille, Shandon, Helensburgh, Dunbartonshire G84 8NP (☎ 0436 820 264); Clydesdale Bank plc, 30 St Vincent Place, Glasgow G1 2HL (☎ 041 248 7070 ext 2581, fax 0436 820 264, telex 77135)

WALKER, Malcolm Conrad; s of Willie Walker (d 1960), and Ethel Mary, *née* Ellam (d 1987); *b* 11 Feb 1946; *Educ* Mirfield GS; *m* 4 Oct 1969, (Nest) Rhianydd, da of Benjamin Jones (d 1976); 3 c; *Career* trainee mangr F W Woolworth & Co 1964-71, Iceland Frozen Foods plc 1970- (jt fndr, chm, chief exec); *Recreations* stalking, skiing, family, home; *Style—* Malcolm Walker, Esq; Iceland Frozen Foods Plc, Second Ave, Deeside Industrial Park, Deeside, Clwyd (☎ 0244 830100, fax 0244 814531, telex 61321)

WALKER, Marjorie G; da of Girsh L Myers, of Miami Beach, Florida, and Miriam, *née* Goldstien, of Philadelphia; *b* 22 Dec 1938; *Educ* Temple Univ (BS), Univ of Miami (MSc, PhD); *m* (m dis); 1 s (Michael b 9 Aug 1967); *Career* writer; lectr Open Univ 1982-87; ed Newsletter New Art at Tate Gallery 1989- (patron 1985-); *books* A Parents' Guide to Child Development - Birth to Adolescence (with Dr Richard Lansdown, 1991); *Clubs* Contemporary Art Soc, Nat Art Collectors Fund; *Style—* Ms Marjorie Walker; 7 Conway Street, London W1P 5HD (☎ 071 637 8804); Cartis Brown (Literary Agent) (☎ 071 631 0503)

WALKER, Michael; s of Wilfred Arthur Walker, of Sudbury, Suffolk, and Molly, *née* Castle; *b* 1 Nov 1948; *Educ* Thomas Lethaby Sch London; *m* 6 June 1970, Jacqueline Margaret, da of John Alexander Bowen, of Witham, Essex; 1 s (Christopher Andrew James b 1984), 2 da (Sarah Jane b 1973, Lucy Anne b 1975); *Career* banker; dir: Clive Discount Co Ltd 1985, Clive Discount Holdings Ltd 1988, Clivwell Securities Ltd 1988; *Recreations* various sports, photography; *Style—* Michael Walker, Esq; 9 Augustus Way, Lodge Park, Witham, Essex CM8 1HH (☎ 0376 513 911); Clive Discount Co Ltd, 9 Devonshire Square, London EC2M 4HP (☎ 071 548 4294, fax 071 548 5306, telex 8958901)

WALKER, Sir (Charles) Michael; GCMG (1976, KCMG 1963, CMG 1960); s of Col Charles William Garne Walker, CMG, DSO (d 1974), and Dorothy Frances (d 1965), da of F Hughes-Gibb, JP, of Manor House, Tarrant Gunville, Dorset; *b* 22 Nov 1916; *Educ* Charterhouse, New Coll Oxford; *m* 1945, Enid Dorothy, da of William Alexander McAdam, CMG (d 1961); 1 s, 1 da; *Career* served WWII RA (attained rank of Lt-Col); clerk House of Lords 1939, served Dominions Office 1947, 1 sec UK Embassy Washington DC 1949-51, High Cmmn New Delhi and Calcutta 1952-55, CRO 1955-58, IDC 1958, asst under sec CRO 1959-62, high cmmr Ceylon 1962-65 and concurrently ambass Maldives 1965, high cmmr Malaysia 1966-71, perm sec Overseas Devpt Admin 1971-73, high cmmr India 1974-76; chm: Cwlth Scholarship Cmmn UK 1977-87, Festival of India Tst 1980-83; *Style—* Sir Michael Walker, GCMG; Herongate House, West Chiltington Common, Pulborough, W Sussex (☎ 079 881 3473)

WALKER, Michael Gervas; s of Sir Gervas Walker, JP, DL, and Lady Eileen Walker, *née* Maxwell; *b* 4 Oct 1949; *Educ* Avonhurst Sch; *m* 14 Aug 1976, Jane Elizabeth, da of George Martin Heslop (d 1979), of Cheltenham; 1 s (Martin Gervas b 3 June 1979), 1 da (Anna Elizabeth b 28 Oct 1977); *Career* dir Terrett Taylor Ltd 1978-; *Recreations* fly fishing, gardening; *Style—* Michael Walker, Esq; Meadow Lea, Boughmore Rd, Sidmouth, Devon (☎ 0395 515105); Ottery Moor, Honiton, Devon (☎ 0404 41117)

WALKER, Michael Giles Neish; CBE (1985); s of Sir William Giles Newsom Walker (d 1989), of Pitlair, Cupar, Fife, and Mildred Brenda, *née* Nairn (d 1983); *b* 28 Aug 1933; *Educ* Shrewsbury, St John's Coll Cambridge (MA); *m* 27 Jan 1960, Margaret Ruby, da of Lt-Col John D Hills, MC (d 1975), of Chirk, North Wales; 2 s (Simon Giles David b 1961, Geordie Michael b 1966), 1 da (Nicola Margaret b 1965); *Career* chm Sidlow Group plc 1988- (joined 1957, chief exec 1976-88); non-exec dir: Scottish Hydro-Electric plc 1982-, Dundee & London Investment Trust plc 1982-, First Charlotte Assets Trust plc 1990-; *Clubs* Cavalry & Guards, Royal & Ancient Golf, Hon Co of Edinburgh Golfers; *Style—* Michael Walker, Esq, CBE; Sidlaw Group plc, Nethergate Centre, Dundee DD1 4BR (☎ 0382 23161, fax 0382 201573, telex 76648)

WALKER, Miles Rawstron; CBE (1991); s of George Denis Walker (d 1970), and Alice, *née* Whittaker; *b* 13 Nov 1940; *Educ* Castle Rushen HS, Shropshire Coll of Agric; *m* 11 Oct 1966, Mary Lilian, da of Thomas Edward Cowell (d 1988); 1 s (Mark), 1 da (Claire); *Career* co dir gen farming and retail dairy trade; memb: House of Keys Rushen Isle of Man 1976-, Bd of Agric 1976-81, Bd of Local Govt 1976-81; chm Broadcasting Cmmn 1979-81; Local Govt Bd: chm 1981-86, memb Exec Cncl 1981-, memb Assessment Bd 1983-86; vice chm IOM PO 1984-86, chief min IOM Govt 1986-; *Style—* The Hon Miles R Walker, CBE; Magher Feailley, Main Road, Colby, Isle of Man (☎ 0624 833728); Office of The Chief Minister, Central Government Offices, Douglas, Isle of Man (☎ 0624 26262, fax 0624 663493)

WALKER, Prof Nigel David; CBE; s of David Boughton Walker (d 1968), and Violet, *née* Johnson (d 1977); *b* 6 Aug 1917; *Educ* Tientsin GS, Edinburgh Acad, ChCh Oxford (Hon scholar); *m* 1939, Sheila Margaret, da of J G Johnston (d 1938); 1 da (Valerie Joan (Mrs O'Farrell) b 1942); *Career* Scottish Office 1939, Cameron Highlanders and Lovat's Scouts Br Army 1940-46 (wounded Appenines), demobbed as Staff Capt Allied Force HQ Italy; princ then asst sec Scottish Office (private sec to Earl of Home when Minister of State) 1946-61, reader in criminology Oxford 1961-73, professorial fell Nuffield Coll Oxford 1961-73; visiting prof: Berkeley California 1965, Yale 1973; dir Cambridge Inst of Criminology 1973-81, professorial fell Kings Coll Cambridge 1973-84, prof of criminology Cambridge 1973-84, visiting prof: Stockholm 1975, Cape Town 1984; chm Home Secs Advsy Cncl on Probation and Aftercare 1970-73, pres Nat Assoc of Probation Offrs 1980-83; Hon DLitt Oxford 1970; Hon LLD: Leicester 1973, Edinburgh 1983; Hon FRCPsych 1987; *Books* Short History of Psychotherapy (1957), Morale in the Civil Service (1961), Crime and Punishment in Britain (1965), Sentencing in a Rational Society (1969), Crime and Insanity in England (2 vols, 1968, 1973), Crimes, Courts and Figures (1971), Behaviour and Misbehaviour (1975), Punishment, Danger and Stigma (1980) Sentencing Theory Law and Practice (1986), Public Attitudes to Sentencing (1987), Crime and Crimonology (1988), Why Punish? (1991); *Recreations* chess, hill climbing; *Clubs* RSM; *Style—* Prof Nigel Walker, CBE; 14A Chaucer Rd, Cambridge, CB2 2EB (☎ 0223 352280); Institute of Criminology, 7 West Rd, Cambridge CB3 9DT

WALKER, Paul Christopher; s of Lt-Col Edward Cummings Walker (d 1953), and Frances Cicely, *née* Bryan; *b* 27 Aug 1950; *Educ* Charterhouse, St John's Coll Oxford (MA); *m* 5 April 1979, (Pamela) Sandra, da of Douglas Hunt; 2 da (Sophie b 1985, Eliza b 1989); *Career* admin trainee HO 1972-74, articled clerk and asst slr Allen & Overy 1974-79, exec then mangr Corp Fin Dept Hill Samuel Co Ltd 1979-84, asst dir Corp Fin Dept J Henry Schroder Wagg & Co Ltd 1985-86, ptnr Corp Fin Dept Lawerence Graham slrs 1986-; Freeman Worshipful Co of Slrs; memb Law Soc; *Books* The City Institutions - A Guide to Their Financial Services (1984); *Style—* Paul Walker, Esq; Lawrence Graham, 190 Strand, London WC2R 1JN (☎ 071 379 0000, fax 071 379 6854, telex 22673)

WALKER, Dr Paul Crawford; JP (Essex Cmmn for the Peace 1980-85); s of Dr Joseph Viccars Walker (d 1986), of Northants, and Mary Tilley, *née* Crawford (d 1984); *b* 9 Dec 1940; *Educ* Queen Elizabeth GS Darlington, Downing Coll Cambridge (BA, MB BChir); *m* 1962, Barbara Georgina, da of Albert Edward Bliss, of Cambridgeshire; 3 da (Kate, Victoria, Caroline); *Career* Capt RAMC(V) 1975-78; area med offr Wakefield Area Health Authority 1976-77, regnl med offr NE Thames RHA 1977-85, gen mangr Frenchay Health Authority 1985-88, hon conslt in community med Bristol and Weston Health Authy 1988-89, dir pub health Norwich Health Authy 1989-, dir Centre for Health Policy Res Univ of E Anglia 1990-, chm CAER Consortium 1985-89; memb: NHS Computer Policy Ctee 1984-85, Advsy Ctee on Misuse of Drugs 1984-87, exec ctee Gtr London Alcohol Advsy Service 1978-85, mgmnt ctee Kings Fund Centre 1980-84; Avon Cmmn for the Peace 1985-89; vice chm professional advisory gp NHSTA, 1987-88; hon sr lectr London Sch of Hygiene and Tropical Medicine 1983-85, visiting prof QMC London 1985-, hon sr lectr Univ of E Anglia 1990-; *Recreations* railway history, anthropology; *Style—* Dr Paul Walker, JP; Chagford, 8 Church Avenue, Stoke Bishop, Bristol BS9 1LD (☎ 0272 687378); District Headquarters, St Andrews Hospital (North Side), Yarmouth Road, Norwich NR7 0SS (☎ 0603 300600)

WALKER, Peter Carl; *b* 1 June 1948; *Educ* Open Univ (BA), Harrow Sch of Photography (Dip in scientific and tech photography); *m* 1 s, 3 da; *Career* area supervisor Sales Dept K Shoes Kendal Cumbria, photographic specialist Hunting Surveys Borehamwood; Ilford Ltd 1972-: technical author, technical ed, currently technical publications mangr; landscape photographer (own business); fell: Br Inst of Professional Photography, Master Photographers Assoc, Inst of Scientific and Technical Communicators; FBIPP; *Recreations* fell walking, running, playing the piano, classical music; *Style—* Peter Walker, Esq; 6 Sunny Lea Mews, Victoria Road, Wilmslow, Cheshire SK9 5HN Ilford Limited, Mobberley, Cheshire

WALKER, Rt Hon Peter Edward; MBE (1960), PC (1970), MP (C) Worcester 1961-; s of Sydney Walker, and Rose Walker; *b* 25 March 1932; *Educ* Latymer Upper Sch; *m* 1969, Tessa, da of G Pout; 3 s, 2 da; *Career* contested (C) Dartford 1955 and 1959, memb NEC Cons Pty 1956, nat chm Young Cons 1958-60, PPS to Ldr House of Commons 1963-64; oppn spokesman: fin and econ 1964-66, tport 1966-68, local govt, housing and land 1968-70; min housing and local govt DOE June-Oct 1970; sec state: environment 1970-72, trade and indust 1972-74; oppn spokesman: trade and indust and consumer affrs Feb-June 1974, def 1974-75; MAFF 1979-83, sec state for energy June 1983-87, sec for Wales 1988-90; currently non-exec dir: British Gas plc, Worcester Group plc, Tate & Lyle plc, Smith New Court plc, DC Gardner Group plc, Dalgety plc; *Style—* The Rt Hon Peter Walker, MBE, MP; Abbots Morton Manor, Gooms Hill, Abbots Morton, Worcestershire

WALKER, Peter Frank; s of Wilfrid Herbert Hornsey Walker (d 1965), and Mildred Sheila, *née* Caddell (d 1984); *b* 27 June 1937; *Educ* Oundle, King's Coll London (BSc); *m* 27 March 1965, Susan Margaret, da of Geoffrey Hugh Sharp, of Leicester; 1 s (Richard b 1972), 2 da (Fiona b 1967, Julia b 1969); *Career* Nat Serv 2 Lt RE 1955-57; CChem; chm Usher-Walker plc 1985- (md 1974-); pres Soc of Br Printing Ink Mfrs 1985-86 (memb Cncl 1973-76, 1979-82 and 1983-87, and 1989-); MRIC, MIOP; *Recreations* racing, antiques, bridge; *Clubs* RAC; *Style—* Peter Walker, Esq; Usher-Walker plc, Chancery House, Chancery Lane, London WC2A 1SA (☎ 071 405 3642, fax 071 831 9921, telex 261293)

WALKER, Rt Rev Peter Knight; s of late George Walker, and Eva Muriel, *née* Knight; *b* 6 Dec 1919; *Educ* Leeds GS, Queen's Coll Oxford; *m* 1973, Mary Jean Walker, JP, yr da of late Lt-Col J A Ferguson, OBE; *Career* RN 1940-45, Lt RNVR; asst master: King's Sch Peterborough 1947-50, Merchant Taylors' Sch 1950-56; ordained 1954, curate Hemel Hempstead 1956-58, fellow, dean of chapel and asst tutor Corpus Christi Coll Cambridge 1958-62, princ Westcott House Cambridge 1962-72, hon canon Ely Cathedral 1966-72, bishop of Dorchester (suffragan for Diocese of Oxford) 1972, canon Christ Church Oxford 1972-77, bishop of Ely 1977-89; chm Hospital Chaplaincies Cncl 1982-86; Hon Fell: CCC Cambridge, Queen's Coll Oxford, St John's Coll Cambridge, St Edmund's Coll Cambridge; Hon DD Univ of Cambridge 1977; *Books* The Anglican Church Today: Rediscovering The Middle Way (1988); *Clubs* Cambridge County; *Style—* The Rt Rev Peter Walker, DD; Anchorage House, The Lanes, Bampton, Oxon OX8 2LA (☎ 0993 850943)

WALKER, Peter Michael; s of Oliver Walker (d 1965), of S Africa, and Freda Miller; *b* 17 Feb 1936; *Educ* Highlands North HS, Johannesburg S Africa; *m* 2, 1979, Susan, da of Harold Davies (d 1969); 1 s (Daniel), (1 s Justin, 1 da Sarah by previous marriage); *Career* former Glamorgan and England cricketer (3 caps v S Africa 1960), former chm Cricketers Assoc, sports columnist for variety of papers and periodicals including The Times, Sunday Telegraph and Mail on Sunday, BBC 2, Refuge Assurance Sunday League, presenter, numerous radio programmes on news, current affairs, sport; md Merlin Film & Video Co Ltd; *Books* Winning Cricket, Cricket Conversations, The All Rounder; *Recreations* golf, music; *Style—* Peter Walker, Esq; 14 Chargot Rd, Llandaff, Cardiff (☎ 0222 563959); Merlin Film & Video Co Ltd, Merlin House, 1 Pontcanna Place, Pontcanna, Cardiff CF5 1JY (☎ 0222 223456)

WALKER, Raymond Augustus; QC; s of Air Chief Marshal Sir Augustus Walker, GCB, CBE, DSO, DFC, AFC, (d 1986), and Dorothy Brenda *née* Brewis; *b* 26 Aug 1943; *Educ* Radley, Univ of Cambridge (BA); *m* 2 Sept 1976, June Rose, da of Thomas Wisby; 1 s (James b 19 June 1979); *Career* called to the Bar Middle Temple 1966; *Recreations* golf, tennis, skiing, sailing, opera; *Clubs* Garrick, Royal West Norfolk Golf, Huntercombe Golf; *Style—* Raymond Walker, Esq, QC; 1 Harcourt Buildings, Temple EC4 (☎ 071 353 0375)

WALKER, Raymond James (Ray); OBE (1990); s of Cyril James Walker (d 1984), and Louie, *née* Hopes (d 1964); *b* 13 April 1943; *Educ* Univ of Lancaster (BA); *m* 29

March 1968, Mary Eastwood, da of George Whittaker (d 1956); 1 da (Claire Louise b 1969); *Career* formerly md of specialised int servs co in textile indust and export dir of key div with leading branded product; currently chief exec Simpler Trade Procedures Bd for HM Govt; UN/EDIFACT rapporteur (UN Economic Cmmn for Europe's New Int Standard for Electronic Data Interchange) co-chair 1987, Western Euro rapporteur, vice-chm Western Euro Bd; special award American Standards Community (ANSI X.12) for outstanding contrib to int data exchange 1986, Man of the Year award International Data Exchange Assoc 1988; *Recreations* collecting wine labels, maps, jazz (at Ronnie Scott's); *Clubs* RAC, Royal Over-Seas League; *Style*— Ray Walker, Esq, OBE; Venture House, 29 Glasshouse St, London W1R 5RG (☎ 071 287 3525, fax 071 287 5751)

WALKER, His Hon Judge Richard; s of Edwin Roland Walker (d 1980), of Epsom, and Barbara Joan, *née* Swann (d 1985); *b* 9 March 1942; *Educ* Epsom Coll, Worcester Coll Oxford (MA); *m* 29 March 1969, Angela Joan, da of John Robert Hodgkinson, of Minehead; 2 da (Rosemary b 1972, Sarah b 1974); *Career* called to the Bar Inner Temple 1966; asst cmmr: Parly Boundary Cmmn 1978-89, Local Govt Boundary Cmmn 1982-89; rec 1989, circuit judge 1989; chm Pathfinders (Anglican Youth Movement) 1978-84, vice chm Church Pastoral-Aid Soc 1978-85; *Books* Carter-Ruck on Libel and Slander (jt ed 3 edn, 1985); *Style*— His Hon Judge Richard Walker; c/o 1 Brick Court, Temple, London, EC4Y 9BY, (☎ 071 353 8845, fax 071 583 9144)

WALKER, Richard John Boileau; s of Kenneth Ralph Walker, and Caroline Jean, *née* Livingstone-Learmonth; *b* 4 June 1916; *Educ* Harrow, Univ of Cambridge, Courtauld Inst; *m* 26 Oct 1946, Margaret Ann Firebrace, da of Brig Roy Firebrace, CBE; 1 s (Nicholas b 3 Oct 1947), 2 da (Susan (Mrs McAlpine) b 8 Oct 1949, Frances (Mrs Goudge) b 23 July 1954); *Career* Lt RNVR 1939-45; asst keeper Tate Gallery 1946-49, govt picture advsr 1949-76, curator Palace of Westminster 1950-76; cataloguer: Nat Portrait Gallery 1976-85, Royal Collection 1985-90, Nat Tst 1990-; tstee: Nat Maritime Museum 1977-84, Army Museums Ogilby Tst 1979-90, Pennington-Mellor Tst 1988-; FSA 1967; *Books* Old Westminster Bridge (1979), Regency Portraits (1985); *Clubs* Athenaeum, United Oxford and Cambridge Univ; *Style*— Richard Walker, Esq; 31 Cadogan Place, London SW1X 9RX

WALKER, Robert; QC (1982); s of Ronald Robert Anthony Walker, of The Retreat, Broadway, Worcs, and Mary Helen, *née* Welsh; *b* 17 March 1938; *Educ* Downside, Trinity Coll Cambridge (BA); *m* 11 Sept 1962, Suzanne Diana, *née* Leggi; 1 s (Robert Thomas b 1963), 3 da (Penelope Mary b 1966, Julian Diana b 1968, Henrietta Solveig b 1972); *Career* 2 Lt Nat Serv RA 1959-61; barr in practice at Chancery Bar 1961-; bencher Lincoln's Inn 1990; *Style*— Robert Walker, Esq, QC; Freeman's Farm, Thaxted, Essex CM6 3PY (☎ 0371 830577); Queen Elizabeth Building, Temple, London EC4Y 9BS (☎ 071 936 3131, fax 071 353 1937, telex 8951414)

WALKER, Robert Ernest; s of William Barrett Walker (d 1989), of Northampton, and Ena Victoria, *née* Mumby (d 1973); *b* 18 March 1946; *Educ* Northampton GS, Royal Sch of Church Music, Jesus Coll Cambridge (MA); *m* 17 Feb 1973 (m dis 1981), Victoria Catherine, da of James Hartung (d 1988), of Grimsby; *Career* organist and master of the choristers Grimsby Parish Church 1968-73, lectr in history and composition London Coll of Music 1983-; composer; works incl: Variations on a theme of Elgar, Chamber Symphony, Symphony No 1, Charms and Exultations of Trumpets, String Quartet, Piano Quintet, Passacaglia For Two Pianos, Requiem, Canticle of the Rose, Missa Brevis, Serenade, The Sun Used to Shine, The Sun on the Celandines, My Dog has Fleas (capriccio for Scratch Orchestra); fndr and artistic dir Petworth Festival; memb Assoc of Professional Composers 1984; *Recreations* reading, gardening, watching television soap operas; *Style*— Robert Walker, Esq; Brinkwells, Fittleworth, Pulborough, W Sussex (☎ 079882 607)

WALKER, Robin Charles; s of Charles Walker (d 1961), of London, and Annie, *née* Vine; *b* 11 July 1932; *Educ* Cardinal Vaughan, Shoreditch Coll, Cardiff Coll of Physical Educn; *m* 16 Aug 1958, Margaret Elizabeth, 2 s (Jeffrey Charles b 1960, Andrew Robin b 1970), (1 da Suzanne Elisabeth b 1972); *Career* Nat Serv RAF 1950-52; teacher Hillbrooke Sch Tooting 1955-56, head of Dept Tylers Croft Sch 1956-61, sr lectr Physical Educn Dept Regent St Poly (now Poly of Central London) 1961-88 (head of Dept 1972-88); sport conslt 1988-; trampolinist 1958-, organiser and mangr first Br team to compete abroad (v W Germany) 1961; Br Trampoline Fedn: fndr and sec 1964, sr coach 1970-, tech dir 1980-, chief exec 1990-; judge World and Euro Championships 1965-82, fndr memb FIT (pres Safety Ctee); rep Middx Basketball 1964, nat grade coach Amateur Basketball Assoc 1964; *Books* Trampolining: Beginner to Competition (1983), Trampolining for Coaches and Performers (1988); *Recreations* music, ornithology, sports psychology, performing arts; *Style*— Robin Walker, Esq; Hamilton, Vine Grove, Uxbridge, Middlesex UB10 9LW (☎ 0895 52114)

WALKER, Robin Charles Andrew; *b* 3 Aug 1944; *Educ* Harrow, McGill Univ Montreal; *m* 30 Aug 1975, Selina Margaret, Riall (see Debrett's Peerage, Walker, Bt (cr 1868), colls); 2 da; *Career* Hill Samuel & Co Ltd London 1967-71, Banque Worms & Cie Paris 1971-74, in private indust 1974-82, dir ANZ McCaughan Merchant Bank Ltd; *Clubs* MCC; *Style*— Robin Walker, Esq; 30 Maida Ave, London W2 1ST; ANZ McCaughan, Merchant Bank Ltd, 3 Cathedral St, London SE1 9AN (☎ 071 378 2300)

WALKER, Rodney Myerscough; JP; s of Norman Walker (d 1943), of Wakefield, and Lucy, *née* Kitchen (d 1987); *b* 10 April 1943; *Educ* Thornes House GS Wakefield; *m* 16 March 1974, Anne Margaret, da of Walter Aspinall (d 1972), of Leeds; 2 s (Alexander b 1976, Timothy b 1977); *Career* currently: maj and controlling shareholder Myerscough Holdings Ltd, chm W Yorks Broadcasting Plc (Radio Aire), dir Red Rose Radio Plc, non-exec dir Bain Clarkson (Northern) Ltd, business advsr to Lord St Oswald of Nostell Priory, chm Yorkshire Life Magazine, memb Investors in Indust Assoc Dirs Resource; dep chm and govr Sports Aid Fndn Yorkshire and Humberside, dir The Rugby Football League, former chm and pres Wakefield Round Table; former chm Wakefield Ctee of the Kirklees; chm: Wakefield Met Festival and Wakefield Metro Arts, Wakefield Theatre Tst, Wakefield Trinity RLFC Bradford (NHS) Hosps Tst; tstee: St Oswald Charitable Tst, The Rowland St Oswald (1984) Charitable Tst, The Clarke Hall Farm Tst Ltd; FRSA; *Recreations* golf, charity work; *Clubs* Landsdowne; *Style*— Rodney Walker, Esq; Walker House, Bond St, Wakefield, West Yorkshire WF1 2QP (☎ 0924 379 443, fax 0924 299 289, car tel 0836 222 814)

WALKER, Prof Roger Michael; s of Jack Walker (d 1986), of Huddersfield, and Lily, *née* Pennock; *b* 25 July 1938; *Educ* Huddersfield Coll Sch, Univ of Manchester (BA), Birkbeck Coll London (PhD); *m* 10 Sept 1960 (m dis 1980), Patricia Mary, da of Maximilian Edmund Eccles (d 1960), of Huddersfield; 1 s (Julian b 1961), 1 da (Sara b 1962); *Career* asst lectr in spanish Univ of Bristol 1961-63, vice master Birkbeck Coll London 1988- (lectr 1963-72, reader 1972-80, prof 1980-), ed Modern Language Review 1985-; memb Ctee Modern Humanities Res Assoc, pres London Medieval Soc, chm Br branch Société Rencesvals; FSA 1983; *Books* Estoria de Santa Maria Egipiaca (1972), Tradition and Technique in 'El Libro del Cavallero Zifar' (1974), Camões e o Pensamento Filosófico do Seu Tempo (1979), El Cavallero Plácidas (1982); *Recreations* heraldry, cricket, beer; *Clubs* Wig and Pen; *Style*— Prof Roger Walker, FSA; 130 Clare Court, Judd St, London WC1H 9QR (☎ 071 833 4945); Birkbeck College, University of London, Malet Street, London WC1E 7HX (☎ 071 580 6622 ext 6143)

WALKER, Sarah Elizabeth Royle (Mrs R G Allum); da of Alan Royle Walker, and Elizabeth Brownrigg; *Educ* Pate's GS for Girls Cheltenham, RCM; *m* 1972, Graham Allum; *Career* mezzo-soprano; maj appearances in Br, America, Aust, NZ, Europe; operatic débuts incl: Coronation of Poppea (Kent Opera 1969, San Francisco Opera 1981), La Calisto (Glyndebourne 1970), Les Troyens (Scottish Opera 1972, Wienstaatsoper 1980), princ mezzo-soprano ENO 1972-77, Die Meistersinger (Chicago Lyric Opera 1977), Werther (Covent Gdn 1979), Giulio Caesare (Le Grand Théâtre Genève 1983), Capriccio (Brussels 1983), Teseo (Sienna 1985), Samson (NY Metro Opera 1986); Numerous Records and video recordings incl title role in Britten's Gloriana; pres Cheltenham Bach Chior 1986-; ARCM, FRCM 1987, LRAM; Hon GSM 1988; *Recreations* interior design, encouraging husband with gardening; *Style*— Ms Sarah Walker; c/o Lies Askonas, 186 Drury Lane, London WC2B 5RY (☎ 071 405 1808)

WALKER, (Richard) Sebastian Maynard; *b* 11 Dec 1942; *Educ* Rugby, New Coll Oxford (BA); *Career* dir: Jonathan Cape Chatto & Windus 1977-79 (joined 1970), Marshall Cavendish Ltd 1975-77; fndr and chm Walker Books 1978; sponsorship activities by Walker Books: annual support of Glyndebourne Touring Opera, Music in Country Churches, The Arvon Writing Fndn; *Recreations* twentieth century British art, piano; *Style*— Sebastian Walker, Esq; Walker Books Ltd, 87 Vauxhall Walk, London SE11 5HJ (☎ 071 793 0909, fax 071 587 1123, telex 8955572)

WALKER, Simon; s of Gerald Bengamin Walker, ISO, and Doreen Elsie, *née* Walker; *b* 14 April 1956; *Educ* Abingdon Sch, Downing Coll Cambridge (BA); *Career* admitted slr 1981; articled clerk and asst slr Allen & Overy 1979-86, asst slr and currently ptnr Needham & James 1986-; memb Law Soc; *Style*— Simon Walker, Esq; Needham & James, Swan House, 37-39 High Hulborn, London WC1 6AA (☎ 071 430 1661, fax 071 430 0380)

WALKER, Simon Jeremy; s of Alan William Walker, of Oxfordshire, and Shirley Ann Lillian, *née* Fremel; *b* 2 April 1967; *Educ* Abingdon Sch, Trent Poly (BA); *m* 11 Aug 1990, Frances Mary, da of William Godfrey Townsend; *Career* photographer; freelance for various Br newspapers and magazines 1988-89, The Independent 1989, corp and advtg work Sunday Telegraph 1990 (joined 1989), Sunday Express 1990-; David Hodge/Observer Young Photojournalist of the Year 1987, Nikon Press Photographer of the Month July 1989, runner-up Most Promising Newcomer Category Br Press Photographer of the Year awards 1990 (commended 1989); memb NUJ; *Recreations* classic cars, travel; *Style*— Simon Walker, Esq; 61 Chardmore Road, Stoke Newington, London N16 6JA (☎ 081 806 0714); Sunday Express, Ludgate House, 245 Blackfriars Rd, London SE1 (☎ 071 922 7343, car 0831 451212)

WALKER, Dame Susan Armour; DBE (1972, CBE 1963); *Educ* Dunbar GS; *Career* chief agent Cons Central Office Yorkshire 1950-56, dep chief orgn offr Cons Central Office 1956-64, dep chm Cons Pty Orgn 1964-68, ret 1968; vice chm WRVS 1969-75; *Style*— Dame Susan Walker, DBE; The Glebe House, Hownam, Kelso, Roxburghshire (☎ 057 34 277)

WALKER, The Ven The Archdeacon of Nottingham Thomas Overington; s of Ernest Thomas Walker (d 1980), and Ethel, *née* Fogden; *b* 7 Dec 1933; *Educ* Dorking County GS, Keble Coll Oxford (MA), Oak Hill Coll (Homiletics prize); *m* 6 July 1957, Molly Anne, da of late Capt Robert Gilmour; 1 s (Timothy Mark b 1969), 2 da (Charis Louise (Mrs Wilson) b 1960, Rachel Joy (Mrs Hopkinson) b 1962); *Books* Renew us by your Spirit (1982), From Here to Heavan (1987), Small Streams, Big Rivers (1991); *Recreations* reading, music, sport, dry stone walling; *Style*— The Ven the Archdeacon of Nottingham; Dunham House, Westgate, Southwell, Notts NG25 0JL (☎ 0636 814490, fax 0636 815084)

WALKER, Tim Philip Buchanan; s of W L B Walker, and Claudine Ella, *née* Mauby; *b* 23 June 1963; *Educ* Millfield; *Career* journalist; regnl newspapers 1983-87, The Observer (London) 1987-90, The European (London) 1990-; freelance presenter LBC London 1989-; Young Journalist of the Year Br Press awards 1987; *Recreations* skiing; *Style*— Tim Walker, Esq; 79 Abingdon Rd, London W8 6XB; The European, Orbit House, 5 New Fetter Lane, London EC4A 1AP (☎ 071 822 3932)

WALKER, Victor Stewart Heron; s and h of Sir James Walker, 5 Bt, by his 1 w Angela; *b* 8 Oct 1942; *Educ* Eton; *m* 1, 1969 (m dis 1982), Caroline Louisa, yst da of late Lt-Col Frederick Edwin Barton Wignall; 2 s, 1 da; m 2, 1982, Svea Borg, only da of late Capt Ernest Hugo Gothard Knutson Borg and Mary Hilary Borg; *Career* late 2 Lt Gren Gds & Lt Royal Wilts Yeo & Royal Yeo; *Clubs* Royal Yacht Sqdn; *Style*— Victor Walker Esq; Villa Josephine, Madliena, Malta

WALKER, Walter Basil Scarlett (Bobby); s of Col James Scarlett Walker, TA (d 1952), of Southport, and Hilda, *née* Sykes (d 1973); *b* 19 Dec 1915; *Educ* Rugby, Clare Coll Cambridge; *m* 10 April 1946, Teresa Mary Louise (Terry), *née* John; 1 s (Peter b 1947 d 1964), 1 da (Sara b 1953); *Career* served RN 1940-46: Sub Lt (S) RNVR HMS Clavermouse Edinburgh 1940, HMS Kenya 1940-42 (Home Fleet), Operation "TORCH" (Algiers Landing) Staff of Adm 1942, asst sec to Adm Gibraltar 1943-45 (Lt Cdr 1945), Staff of Adm Cdr Expeditionary Force Paris and Minden (later C-in-C Germany); CA; ptnr Peat Marwick Mitchell & Co 1956-82 (joined 1937-39 and returned 1946); pt/t dir UK Atomic Energy Authy 1972-81, govr Royal Ballet Covent Gdn 1980-90; chm local Gdn Soc; FCA 1940; *Recreations* gardening, golf; *Style*— Bobby Walker, Esq; 11 Sloane Ave, London SW3 3JD (☎ 071 589 4133); Coles Privett, Nr Alton, Hants GU34 3PH (☎ 073 088 223)

WALKER, Gen Sir Walter Colyear; KCB (1968, CB 1964), CBE (1959, OBE 1949), DSO (1946) and Bars (1953, 1965); s of Arthur Colyear Walker; *b* 11 Nov 1912; *Educ* Blundell's, RMC Sandhurst; *m* 1938, Beryl Catherine (d 1990), da of E N W Johnston; 2 s (Anthony, Nigel), 1 da (Venetia); *Career* served Bde of Gurkhas: Waziristan 1939-41 (despatches twice), Burma 1942 and 1944-46 (despatches), Malaya 1949-59 (Brevet Lt-Col, despatches twice), Atomic Trials Maralinga S Australia 1956, Maj-Gen 1961, dir of ops Borneo 1962-65, Col 7 Duke of Edinburgh's Own Gurkha Rifles 1964-75, dep chief of staff Allied Forces Central Europe 1965-67, Lt-Gen 1967, GOC-in-C Northern Cmd 1967-69, Gen 1969, C-in-C Allied Forces Northern Europe 1969-72; Paduka Stia Negara Brunei 1 class 1964, hon Panglima Mangku Negara Malaysia 1965; *Books* The Bear at the Back Door (1978), The Next Domino (1980); *Recreations* normal; *Clubs* Army & Navy; *Style*— General Sir Walter Walker, KCB, CBE, DSO; Haydon Farmhouse, Sherborne, Dorset DT9 5JB

WALKER, William Connoll (Bill); MP (C) Tayside North 1983-; s of Charles and Willamina Walker; *b* 20 Feb 1929; *Educ* Dundee: Logie and Blackness Schs, Trades Coll, Coll of Arts; Coll of Distributive Trades London; *m* 1956, Mavis Lambert, 3 da; *Career* Sqdn-Ldr RAFVR; Parly candidate (C) Dundee East Oct 1974, gained Perth and E Perthshire from SNP 1979-1983; memb: Select Ctee on Scottish Affrs 1979-, Select Ctee on Parly Cmmn for Admin 1979-; jt sec Aviation Ctee, jt vice chm Cons Backbench Euro Affrs Ctee 1982-; sec Scottish Cons Ctee 1991-; pres: Cons for Euro Reform, Walker Associates, Stagecoach International Ltd, Stagecoach Malawi Ltd; *Clubs* RAF; *Style*— Bill Walker Esq, MP; Candletrees, Golf Course Road, Rosemount, Blairgowrie, Perthshire (☎ 0250 2660)

WALKER, Prof William Farquhar; s of James Walker (d 1939), of Jarmans Hotel, Forfar, Angus, Scotland, and Margaret, *née* Stewart (d 1966); *b* 26 May 1925; *Educ* Forfar Acad, Univ of St Andrews (MB ChM, DSc); *m* Bettie, da of Charles Stanley (d

1965); 2 s (William Stanley b 7 May 1953, Christopher John b 26 Feb 1959), 1 da (Fiona Mary b 22 March 1960); *Career* Nat Serv Sqdn Ldr MO RAF 1949-51; res fell Harvard Med Sch 1956-57, sr lectr in surgery Univ of St Andrews 1956-65, conslt surgn Ninewells Hosp Dundee 1965- (personal chair in surgery 1986), ret 1990; former: pres Assoc of Surgns of GB and Ireland 1983-84; pres Vascular Surgns of GB and Ireland 1988-89, chm Tenovus Tayside; FRSE, FRCS, FRCS(Ed); *Books* Fluid and Electrolyte Therapy (1970), Metabolic Basis of Surgical Care (1971), Intensive Care (1975), Atlas of General Surgery (1976), Atlas of Minor Surgery (1985); *Recreations* golf, fishing, gardening; *Clubs* New (Edinburgh), Royal & Ancient Golf; *Style*— Prof William F Walker; 438 Blackness Rd, Dundee DD2 1TQ (☎ 0382 68179)

WALKER, Hon Mrs (Yvonne Marie); *née* Wall; da of Baron Wall, OBE (Life Peer d 1980); *b* 1942; *m* 1970, Hugh Walker; *Style*— The Hon Mrs Walker; Fieldfare, Seven Hills Close, Walton-on-Thames, Surrey

WALKER-ARNOTT, Edward Ian; s of Charles Douglas Walker-Arnott (d 1980), of Woodford, Essex, and Kathleen Margaret, *née* Brittain; *b* 18 Sept 1939; *Educ* Haileybury, Univ of London (LLB), UCL (LLM); *m* 11 Sept 1971, (Phyllis) Jane, da of Lt-Col J M Ricketts, MC (d 1987), of Weston, Honiton, Devon; 1 s (William b 9 Nov 1981), 2 da (Emily b 7 April 1974, Hannah b 9 July 1979); *Career* admitted slr 1963; ptnr Herbert Smith 1968, dir Sturge Hldgs plc; memb: Cork Ctee on Review of Insolvency Law 1977-82, Insolvency Practitioners Tbnl; cncl memb: Lloyds 1983-88 (hon memb 1988), Haileybury Coll (treas 1977-88), Benenden Sch; Freeman Worshipful Co of Slrs, Asst of Ct Worshipful Co of Loriners; memb Law Soc; *Recreations* cricket, tennis, gardening; *Clubs* City of London; *Style*— Edward Walker-Arnott, Esq; Manuden Hall, Manuden, nr Bishops Stortford, Herts CM23 1 DY; Herbert Smith, Exchange House, Primrose St, London EC2 (☎ 071 374 8000)

WALKER-ARNOTT, (Brian) Richard; s of (Charles) Douglas Walker-Arnott (d 1980), and Kathleen Margaret, *née* Brittain; *b* 8 Sept 1937; *Educ* Haileybury (scholar), Trinity Hall Cambridge (exhibitioner, MA); *m* 23 Jan 1988, Deborah Clare, da of John Ounsted; 1 s (Charles Laurence b 12 Oct 1989); *Career* PR Dept Procter & Gamble Limited (Newcastle upon Tyne) 1960-68, Charles Barker 1968-73, FJ Lyons 1974-76; dir Charles Barker 1976-; Cncllr Royal Borough of Kensington and Chelsea 1974- (former chm various ctees and chief whip Majority Pty, dep ldr Majority Pty 1991), chm Kensington Cons Assoc 1980-83; Master Worshipful Co of Loriners 1990; MIPR 1968, DipCam 1978; *Recreations* mountain walking; *Clubs* City Livery, Tyne Rowing; *Style*— Richard Walker-Arnott, Esq; 27 Finstock Rd, London W10 6LU (☎ 081 968 4448); Charles Barker, 30 Farringdon Street, London EC4A 4EA (☎ 071 634 1317)

WALKER-OKEOVER, Elizabeth, Lady; (Dorothy) Elizabeth; yr da of Josceline Reginald Heber-Percy, DL (gs of Algernon Heber- Percy, n of 5 Duke of Northumberland), and his w, Katharine, da of Lord Algernon Percy, s of 6 Duke of Northumberland; *b* 23 June 1913; *m* 1938, Lt-Col Sir Ian Walker-Okeover, 3 Bt, DSO & bar, TD, JP (d 1982), sometime Ld-Lt Derbyshire; 1 s (Sir Peter W-O, 4 Bt, *qv*), 2 da (Mrs Timothy Clowes, Jane W-O); *Style*— Elizabeth, Lady Walker-Okeover; Park Cottage, Osmaston, Ashbourne, Derbys

WALKER-OKEOVER, Sir Peter Ralph Leopold; 4 Bt (UK 1886), of Gateacre Grange, Co Lancaster, and Osmaston Manor, Co Derby; s of Sir Ian Peter Andrew Monro Walker-Okeover, 3 Bt, DSO, TD (d 1982); *b* 22 July 1947, (King Leopold III of the Belgians stood sponsor); *Educ* Eton, RMA Sandhurst; *m* 1972, Catherine Mary Maule, da of Col George Patrick Maule Ramsay (s of Archibald Ramsay by his w Hon Ismay Preston, formerly w of Lord Ninian Crichton-Stuart (2 s of 3 Marquess of Bute) and da of 14 Viscount Gormanston; Archibald was great nephew of 12 Earl of Dalhousie); 2 s (Andrew b 1978, Ralph b 1982), 1 da (Georgina b 1976); *Heir* s, Andrew Peter Monro Walker-Okeover, b 1978; *Career* Capt Blues and Royals; *Style*— Captain Sir Peter Walker-Okeover, Bt; Okeover Hall, Ashbourne, Derbyshire; House of Glenmuick, Ballater, Aberdeenshire, Scotland

WALKER-SMITH, Prof John Angus; s of Dr Angus Buchanan Walker-Smith (d 1975), of Sydney, Australia, and Alexandra Buckingham, *née* Trindall (d 1970); *b* 1 Dec 1936; *Educ* Sydney C of E GS, Univ of Sydney (MB BS, MD); *m* 29 Aug 1969, Elizabeth Cantley, da of George Blaikie, of Edinburgh; 1 s (James b 15 July 1978), 2 da (Louise b 13 Aug 1970, Laura b 17 March 1975); *Career* house physician: Hammersmith Hosp 1963, Brompton Hosp 1963; res fell: Gastroenterology Royal Prince Alfred Hosp Sydney 1964-66 (res med offr 1960-61), Kinderklinik Zurich Switzerland 1968; student supervisor and hon assoc physician Royal Alexandra Hosp for Children 1969-72 (professorial registrar 1967, res med offr 1962), conslt paediatrician St Bartholomew's Hosp 1973 - (prof paediatric gastroenterology 1985); memb: All Saints Parish Church Woodford Green, Wanstead and Woodford Cons Assoc; Freeman City of London, Liveryman Worshipful Soc Apothecaries; FRACP, FRCP (London and Edinburgh); memb: BMA, Br Paediatric Assoc, Br Soc Gastroenterology; *Books* Diseases of small intestine in childhood (3 edns 1975, 1979, 1988), Practical Paediatric Gastroenterology (with J R Hamilton and W A Walker 1983); *Recreations* swimming, photography, philately; *Style*— Prof John Walker-Smith; 16 Monkham's Drive, Woodford Green, Essex IG8 0LQ (☎ 081 505 7756); Acad Dept of Paediatric Gastroenterology, St Bartholomew's Hosp, London EC1A (☎ 071 601 8888)

WALKER-SMITH, Hon (John) Jonah; s (and h to btcy), of Baron Broxbourne (Life Peer); *b* 6 Sept 1939; *Educ* Westminster, Ch Ch Oxford; *m* 1974, Aileen Marie, o da of late Joseph Smith; 1 s (Daniel b 1980), 1 da (Lucinda b 1977); *Career* barrister; *Style*— The Hon Jonah Walker-Smith; 11 Doughty St, London WC1

WALKINSHAW, Nicholas John Coode; s of David Walkinshaw (d 1966), of Isle of Wight, and Barbara Betty Coode, *née* Coode-Adams; *b* 30 July 1940; *Educ* Marlborough, St John's Coll Cambridge (MA); *m* 1, 14 Sept 1963 (m dis), Sibyl Mary, da of William S Hutton, of Cambridgeshire; 2 s (Christopher b 1965, Anthony b 1967); m 2, 28 May 1977, Barbara Hazel, da of Bertie Ward, of Doncaster; *Career* md Vandenbergh Walkinshaw Ltd Windsor 1972-76, chm Walkinshaw Holdings Ltd Kingsclere Newbury 1976-87, md Walkinshaw Handling Ltd 1987-89, chm Walkinshaw Technologies Ltd 1990-; Freeman: City of London, Worshipful Co of Merchant Taylors; *Recreations* riding/horse trials, sailing; *Clubs* Leander, Henley Royal Regatta; *Style*— Nicholas J C Walkinshaw, Esq; Keepers, Sydmonton, Newbury, Berks (☎ 0635 268216, fax 0635 268780); c/o Lloyds Bank, Thames St, Windsor

WALKLING, (Anthony) Kim; s of William Charles Walkling (d 1989), and Vida Karina, *née* Beare; *b* 27 Sept 1957; *Educ* Sutton HS Plymouth, UCL (LLB); *m* 20 Sept 1986, (Margaret Caroline) Deirdre, *née* Moore, da of Samuel James Moore, of Purley, Surrey; *Career* articled clerk Slaughter and May 1980-82, asst slr Watson Farley & Williams 1982-87, ptnr S J Berwin & Co 1987-; memb law Soc 1982, Holborn Law Soc 1988; *Recreations* photography, music; *Style*— Kim Walkling, Esq; 236 Grays Inn Rd, London WC1X 8HB (☎ 071 278 0444, fax 071 833 2860, telex 8814928 WINLAW G)

WALL, (Dame) (Alice) Anne; DCVO (1981, CVO 1972, MVO 1964); da of Adm Sir Geoffrey Alan Brooke Hawkins, KBE, CB, MVO, DSC (d 1980), by his w Lady Margaret Ida, *née* Montagu-Douglas-Scott (d 1976), eldest da of 7 Duke of Buccleuch; *b* 31 March 1928; *Educ* Miss Faunce's PNEU Sch, Portsmouth Tech Coll; *m* 1975, Cdr Michael Edward St Quintin Wall, RN, s of Capt Bernard St Quintin Wall, Grenadier Gds (d 1976); *Career* asst press sec to HM The Queen 1958-81, extra woman of the bedchamber to HM The Queen 1981-; *Style*— Mrs Michael Wall, DCVO; Ivy House, Lambourn, Berks RG16 7PB (☎ 0488 72348); 6 Chester Way, Kennington, London SE11 4UT (☎ 071 582 0692)

WALL, Brian Owen; s of Maurice Stanley Wall (d 1983), of Newport, Gwent, and Ruby, *née* Holmes; *b* 17 June 1933; *Educ* Newport HS Monmouthshire, Imperial Coll London (BSc, ACGI), RNC Greenwich; *m* 4 Aug 1960, Patricia Thora, da of Percival Spencer Hughes (d 1965), of Langstone, Monmouthshire; 1 s (Andrew b 1969); *Career* with MOD Bath: ship vulnerability 1958-61, submarine design 1961-66; head of propeller design Admty Experiment Works Haslar 1966-71, Staff of C in C Fleet Portsmouth 1971-73, Submarine Support and Modernisation Gp 1973-77, RCDS 1977; MOD Bath: Ship Prodn Div 1978-79, project dir New SSBN Design 1979-84, dir cost estimating and analysis 1985, chief naval architect 1985-90; memb RCNC; CEng 1969, FRINA 1986; *Recreations* photography, golf, music, walking; *Style*— Brian Wall, Esq; Wychwood, 39 High Bannerdown, Batheaston, Bath, Avon BA1 7JZ (☎ 0225 858 694)

WALL, David Richard; CBE (1985); s of Charles Wall, and Dorothy Irene, *née* Barden; *b* 15 March 1946; *Educ* Haliford House Shepperton, Royal Ballet Sch White Lodge Richmond, Royal Ballet Sch Upper Sch; *m* 1 Aug 1967, Alfreda, da of Edward Thorogood (d 1966); 1 s (Daniel b 12 Dec 1974), 1 da (Annaliese b 15 Oct 1971); *Career* Royal Ballet 1963-: soloist 1964, princ dancer 1966-84; danced all major classical roles incl: Rakes Progress 1965, Swan Lake (with Margot Fonteyn) 1966, Giselle (Peter Wright prodn) 1968, Walk to the Paradise Garden 1972, Manon 1974, Dancers at a Gathering 1974, Romeo and Juliet 1975, La Bayadére 1975, Rituals 1975, Mayerling 1977; dir and gen sec Royal Acad of Dancing 1985-91; *Style*— David Wall, Esq, CBE; 34 Croham Manor Rd, South Croydon, Surrey; c/o Royal Academy of Dancing, 48 Vicarage Crescent, London SW11 3LT (☎ 071 223 0091, fax 071 924 3129, telex 8952105 RADANC G)

WALL, Edward Alfred (Ted); ERD (1967); s of Alfred Ernest Wall (d 1944), of Rotherham Yorks, and Katherine Hannah Walker (d 1952); *b* 11 July 1925; *Educ* Spurley Hey Sch Rotherham, Harvard Bus Sch Vevey Switzerland (sr mgmnt programme); *m* 21 Dec 1946, Phyllis Doreen Jean, da of Reginald Harry Pearce (d 1957), of Monmouth; 1 s (Adrian b 1955), 1 da (Vanessa b 1951); *Career* served S Staffs Regt 1943-45, Worcs Regt 1945-47, cmmnd RASC 1947, invalided out 1949; Capt AER 1954-67; articled R A Williams & Co 1949-54, chief accountant Wincanton Tport 1954-68, fin accountant Kuwait Nat Petroleum Co Kuwait 1968; Unigate Ltd: conslt 1969, md Wincanton Tport and dep chm Tport Eng Div 1970-78; NFC: joined 1978, chm NFC Int Hldgs Ltd 1987- (md 1984-87), appointed Main Bd 1985-; past chm Road Haulage Assoc: Milk Carriers Gp, Dairy Trade Fedn Carriers Gp; *Recreations* fishing, swimming, music, reading, travel; *Clubs* Naval and Military; *Style*— Ted Wall, Esq, ERD; Cherry Trees, The Hocket, Northfield End, Henley-on-Thames, Oxon RG9 2JJ (☎ 0491 573 673); NFC plc, The Merton Centre, St Peters St, Bedford MK40 2UB (☎ 0234 272222, fax 0234 270 900, car 0860 530 732, telex 826803)

WALL, Baroness; Gladys Evelyn; da of William Wright and Martha Naomi Cox; *m* 1939, Baron Wall, OBE (Life Peer, d 1980); 2 s, 1 da; *Style*— The Rt Hon the Lady Wall; 93 Church Road, Wimbledon Village, London SW19

WALL, Hon Martin John; er twin s of Baron Wall, OBE (Life Peer, d 1980); *b* 1948; *Style*— The Hon Martin Wall

WALL, Nicholas Peter Rathbone; QC (1988); s of Frederick Stanley Wall (d 1978), of London, and Margaret Helen, *née* Woods; *b* 14 March 1945; *Educ* Dulwich, Trinity Coll Cambridge (Scholar, MA); *m* 31 August 1973, Margaret Diana Wall, JP, da of Norman Sydee, of London; 4 c (Imogen b 1975, Emma b 1977, Rosalind b 1980, Simon b 1983); *Career* called to the Bar Gray's Inn July 1969, rec 1990; *Books* contrib to Rayden and Jackson on Divorce (supplements to 15 edn, 1988); *Recreations* collecting and binding books, attempting to grow vegetables, opera, walking; *Clubs* Athenaeum; *Style*— Nicholas Wall, Esq, QC; 1 Mitre Court Buildings, Temple, London EC4Y 7BS (☎ 071 353 0434, fax 071 353 3988)

WALL, Prof Patrick David; s of Capt Thomas Wall, MC (d 1976), and Ruth, *née* Cresswell (d 1978); *b* 5 April 1925; *Educ* St Pauls, ChCh Oxford (BM, BCH, DM); *Career* instr physiology Yale 1948-50, asst prof anatomy Univ of Chicago 1950-53, instr physiology Harvard 1953-55, assoc prof and prof of biology MIT 1955-67, prof of anatomy UCL 1967- ; visiting prof Hebrew Univ Jerusalem 1972-; Hon MD Siena 1987; FRCP 1984, FRS 1989; *Books* Challenge of Pain (with R Melzack, 2 ed 1988), Textbook of Pain (2 ed 1989); *Style*— Prof Patrick Wall; 141 Grays Inn Rd, London WC1X 8UB (☎ 071 833 0451)

WALL, Maj Sir Patrick Henry Bligh; MC (1945), VRD (1957); s of Henry Benedict Wall; *b* 14 Oct 1916; *Educ* Downside; *m* 1953, Sheila Elizabeth Putnam (d 1983); 1 da; *Career* served with RM 1935-50, Maj 1944; RN Staff Coll 1946, Jt Services Staff Coll 1947; memb Westminster City Cncl 1953-63; MP (C): Haltemprice 1954-55, E Yorkshire 1955-83, Beverley 1983-87; PPS to: Min AFF 1955-57, Chllr of the Exchequer 1958-59; delegate to UN Gen Assembly 1962, vice chm Cons Pty Def Ctee 1965-77, Select Ctee Def 1979-84; chm: Br SA Parly Gp 1970-87, Monday Club 1977-79, Br Taiwan Parly Gp 1979-87, Br Portugese Parly Gp 1979-87; pres North Atlantic Assembly 1983-85 (chm Mil Ctee 1977-79, vice pres 1980-82); Freeman of Beverley 1988; fell Inst of Journalists 1988; US Legion of Merit 1944, Kt SMO Malta; kt 1981, Brilliant Star of Taiwan 1987; *Books* Soviet Maritime Thrust, Indian Ocean and the Threat to the West, Southern Ocean and the Security of the Free World; *Recreations* model ships & aircraft; *Clubs* Royal Yacht Squadron; *Style*— Maj Sir Patrick Wall, MC, VRD, RM (ret); Brantinghamthorp, Brantingham, nr Brough, North Humberside HU15 1QG (☎ 0482 667248); 8 Westminster Gdns, Marsham St, London SW1P 4JA (☎ 071 828 1803)

WALL, Peter Mason; s of Kenneth Mason Wall, of 19 Yateley Rd, Edgbaston, Birmingham, and Margaret, *née* Marsh; *b* 13 Jan 1947; *Educ* Uppingham, Univ of Bristol (BA); *m* 29 March 1975, Jennifer Mary, da of Frank James Evans (d 1983), of Harborne, Birmingham; 1 s (Nicholas James Mason b 14 Feb 1979), 1 da (Sarah Elizabeth b 29 Sept 1976); *Career* admitted slr 1972: managing ptnr Wragge & Co 1976-; cmmr of Taxes 1980-89, memb Cncl Edgaston C of E Coll for Girls; memb Law Soc 1969; *Recreations* golf; *Clubs* Edgbaston Golf (memb Ctee); *Style*— Peter Wall, Esq; Wragge & Co, Bank House, 8 Cherry St, Birmingham B2 5JY (☎ 021 632 4131, fax 021 643 2417, telex 338728 WRAGGE G)

WALL, Maj-Gen Robert Percival Walter; CB (1978); s of Frank Ernest Wall, of Goodmayes, Essex (d 1981), and Ethel Elizabeth, *née* Collins (d 1980); *b* 23 Aug 1927; *Educ* Army & Jt Servs Staff Coll and Royal Coll of Defence Studies; *m* 1, 1953 (m dis 1985), Patricia Kathleen O'Brien; 2 s (Malcolm b 1956, Patrick b 1958), 1 da (Clare b 1961); m 2, 7 Feb 1986, Jennifer Hilary Anning; *Career* RM 1945; served Middle East, Far East, dir staff Jt Servs Staff Coll 1969-71, various MOD appointments, Maj-Gen RM Chief of Staff 1976-79; dir (Land) Decade Educn Cncl 1980-91; mgmnt conslt 1983-; chm: Essex Family Practitioner Ctee 1985, Essex Family Health Servs Authy 1990-; memb North East Thames Regional Health Authy 1990-; Freeman City of London 1978, Craft Owning Freeman Co of Watermen and Lightermen 1979; FBIM 1980; FRSA, JP City of London 1982; *Recreations* reading, walking, cricket, rugby; *Clubs* Army and Navy, MCC; *Style*— Maj-Gen Robert Wall; c/o Barclays Bank, 116

Goodmayes Road, Goodmayes, Ilford, Essex

WALL, Sir Robert William; OBE (1980); s of William George Wall, of Sellack (d 1980), and Gladys Perina, *née* Powell (d 1958); *b* 27 Sept 1929; *Educ* Monmouth, Bristol Coll of Technol; *m* 24 Feb 1968, Jean, da of Harry Clifford Ashworth; 1 s (Matthew b 1970, d 1986), 1 da (Gabrielle b 1971); *Career* cmmnd RAF 1955-58, OC Mountain Rescue Team RAF Valley 1956-58; engr 1958-88: Bristol Aeroplane Co, Br Aerospace plc; memb pro chllr Univ of Bristol; Univ of Bristol, SS Great Britain Project; govr Bristol Old Vic Theatre Tst, pres Bristol Soc of Model and Experimental Engrs, memb The Audit Cmmn; ldr: Cons Gp, Bristol City Cncl; chm: Tport Users Consultative Ctee for W Eng, Western Provincial Area Nat Union of Cons and Unionist Assocs; Freeman: City of London 1986, Worshipful Co of Watermen and Lightermen; Hon MA Univ of Bristol 1982; MBIM 1980, AMRAeS 1985; kt 1987; *Books* Bristol Channel Paddle Steamers (1973), Ocean Liners (1979), Airliners (1981), Bristol-Maritime City (1981), The Story of HMS Bristol (1986); *Recreations* hill walking, collecting postcards; *Clubs* Royal Over-Seas League, Clifton, Bristol Savages; *Style*— Sir Robert Wall, OBE; 1 Ormerod Rd, Stoke Bishop, Bristol BS9 1BA; Lower Deems, Branscombe, Devon (☎ 0272 682 910); The Council House, College Green, Bristol BS1 5TR (☎ 0272 266 031, fax 0272 294 512, telex 449819 CITBRI)

WALL, Hon Robin John; yr twin s of Baron Wall, OBE (Life Peer, d 1980); *b* 1948; *Style*— The Hon Robin Wall

WALL, (John) Stephen; CMG, LVO (1983); s of John Derwent Wall (d 1984), of Pulborough, W Sussex, and Maria Letitia, *née* Whitmarsh (d 1978); *b* 10 Jan 1947; *Educ* Douai Sch, Selwyn Coll Cambridge (BA); *m* 11 Oct 1975, Catharine Jane, da of Norman Reddaway, CBE, of London; 1 s (Matthew b 1979); *Career* joined Her Majesty's Diplomatic Serv 1968; third sec Addis Ababa 1969-72, private sec to Ambass Paris 1972-74, press offr FCO and 10 Downing St 1974-77, asst private sec to Foreign Sec 1977-79, first sec Embassy Washington 1979-83, asst (later head) FCO Euro Community Dept 1983-88, private sec to Foreign Sec 1988-90; *Recreations* reading, walking, photography; *Style*— Stephen Wall, Esq, CMG, LVO; Foreign and Commonwealth Office, King Charles St, London SW1 2AH (☎ 071 270 3100)

WALL, Prof (Charles) Terence Clegg; s of Charles Wall (d 1976), of Woodfield, Dursley, and Ruth, *née* Clegg; *b* 14 Dec 1936; *Educ* Marlborough, Trinity Coll Cambridge (BA, PhD); *m* 22 Aug 1959, Alexandra Joy, da of Prof Leslie Spencer Hearnshaw, of West Kirby; 2 s (Nicholas b 1962, Alexander b 1967), 2 da (Catherine b 1963, Lucy b 1965); *Career* fell Trinity Coll Cambridge, 1959-64, Harkness fell 1960-61, univ reader and fell St Catherines Coll Oxford 1964-65, prof of pure mathematics Univ of Liverpool 1965-, Royal Soc Leverhulme visiting prof Mexico 1967, sr fell SERC 1983-88; treas: Wirral area SDP 1985-88, West Wirral SLD 1988-; fell Cambridge Philosophical Soc 1958-, memb American Mathematical Soc 1961-, pres London Mathematical Soc 1978-80 (memb 1961-, memb cncl 1973-80); Cncl Royal Soc 1973-80 (FRS 1969-), foreign memb Royal Danish Acad 1990-; *Books* Surgery on Compact Manifolds (1970), A Geometric Introduction to Topology (1970); *Recreations* gardening, home winemaking; *Style*— Professor Charles Wall; 5 Kirby Park, West Kirby, Wirral, Merseyside L48 2HA (☎ 051 625 5063); Dept of Pure Mathematics, Univ of Liverpool, PO Box 147, Liverpool L69 3BX (☎ 051 794 4062, fax 051 708 6502, telex 627095)

WALL MORRIS, George Malcolm; s of Richard Wall Morris, of Fuengirola, Spain, and Doris Wall Morris; *b* 16 Sept 1937; *Educ* Radley; *m* 6 Dec 1969, Katherine Mary Lucy, da of Gen Sir Malcolm Cartwright-Taylor, KCB (d 1969); 2 s (Malcolm b 1971, Andrew b 1974); *Career* short service cmmn, 10 Royal Hussars Lt; direct mktg conslt; *Recreations* gourmet, gardening, wine; *Style*— George Wall Morris, Esq; Harlyn House, Manor Rd, Stratford-upon-Avon, Warks CV37 7EA (☎ 0789 292524, car 0860 541316); Tudor Marketing Services (☎ 0789 295568)

WALLACE, (Andrew) Alasdair Cullen; s of James Cullen Wallace (d 1986), of Aberdeen, and Kate Christie Martin, *née* Venters (d 1982); *b* 18 Dec 1928; *Educ* Lanark GS, Univ of Glasgow (BSc); *m* 18 Sept 1954, Norah Gwendoline, da of Thomas Crouther Gordon, DFC, 1 s (Telford Gordon Cullen b 24 Spet 1962); *Career* engr Sir Win Arrol Glasgow 1954-58 (student/graduate apprenticeship 1949-54), mangr Structural Div Blackburn Aircraft 1958-60, ptnr Crouch & Hogg 1971-90 (engr 1960-66, assoc 1966-71), conslt Crouch Hogg & Waterman 1990-; main concern has been design documentation and supervision of construction of steel structures especially bridges; chm: Jt Bldg Gp of Scotland 1970-71, Scottish Branch I Struct E 1973-74; memb: Struct Engrg Bd ICE 1981-84, Wolfson Bridge Res Unit Dundee Univ 1990-; govr Kiel Sch Dumbarton; Miller Prize ICE, Sir Arnold Walter Medal IStructE 1969, Scottish Branch Prize I Struct E (twice); Br Construction Steel Awards for: White Cart Viaduct 1969, Bonar Bridge 1974, Garden Festival Bridge 1989; received: Saltire Design Award (for Garden Festival Bridge), Regeneration of Scotland Award, Br Construction Industry Award; commendation for Glasgow's 1990 Eurodrome Competition IStructE, Euro Architectural Heritage Award for Custom House Quay Glasgow 1970, Lincoln Arc Int Welding Award for Bells Bridge 1990; FEng, FICE, FIStructE, Fell Welding Inst; *Recreations* modelling, photography, art, walking, gardening, history of bridges; *Style*— Alasdair Wallace, Esq; 25 Loch Drive, Helensburgh, Dunbarton (☎ 0436 74134); Crouch Hogg Waterman, The Octagon, 35 Baird St, Glasgow G4 0EE (☎ 041 552 2000, fax 041 552 2525)

WALLACE, Alistair James Wishart Falconer; s of Alexander Lewis Paget Falconer Wallace, TD (d 1975), of Strathdon, Aberdeenshire, and Lois, *née* Wishart-Thomson (d 1940); *b* 17 Aug 1935; *Educ* Eton, Gordonstoun; *m* 1, (m dis 1965), Eileen Mary, *née* Macnaughton; 1 s (James Alexander Falconer b 22 June 1960), 2 da (Caroline Jane b 9 Sept 1958, Emma Mary b 26 Aug 1962); m 2, 10 Feb 1966, Alice Julia, da of Charles John Addison Doughty, QC (d 1973), of London; 1 s (Adam William Doughty Falconer b 29 Aug 1969), 1 da (Arabella Lois b 11 June 1971); *Career* Nat Serv The Lifeguards 1954-56, TA Inns of Ct and City Yeomanry 1957-67, ret Lt TARO; dir Maynard Reeve and Wallace Ltd (Lloyd's Brokers) 1964, dir Edinburgh Gen Insur Servs 1972-83, chm Maynard Wallace and Coffrey (Lloyd's underwriting agents) 1975, chm Andrew Booth Gp 1975-83, dir Laurence Philips Agencies 1986, chm Aragon Agencies 1988 (dir 1983-), chm Alpwood Hldgs 1988 (dir 1984-); former jt chm Dockland Settlements (resigned 1981); Liveryman Worshipful Co of Gunmakers; *Recreations* shooting, fishing, golf; *Clubs* White's, Turf, Pratts, City of London; *Style*— Alistair Wallace, Esq; Manor Farm House, Damerham, Fordingbridge, Hants SP6 3HN (☎ 0725 3229); 11 Aylesford St, London SW1V 3RY (☎ 071 821 8393); Aragon Agencies Ltd, 100 Fenchurch St, London EC3M 5JB (☎ 071 265 1711, fax 071 702 4760)

WALLACE, Constance Armine Louise; da of Maj Graeme Roper Wallace, of North Tregeare Farmhouse, Tresmeer, Launceston, Cornwall, and Katherine Jane Armine, *née* Wodehouse; *b* 27 Sept 1960; *Educ* West Wing Sch Kyneton House Thornbury, Monmouth Sch for Girls, Cambridge Univ; *Career* slr: Bond Pearce Plymouth 1984-88, Simpson Curtis Leeds 1989-; memb Jr C of C; memb Law Soc 1986; *Recreations* haute cuisine, art; *Style*— Miss Constance Wallace; North Tregeare Farmhouse, Tresmeer, Launceston, Cornwall (☎ 0566 81319); Simpson Curtis, 41 Park Sq, Leeds (☎ 0532 433433, fax 0532 445598, telex 55376)

WALLACE, Prof David Alexander Ross; *b* 24 Nov 1933; *Educ* Univ of St Andrews (BSc), Univ of Manchester (PhD); *m* 12 July 1958, Elizabeth Anne, *née* Law (d 1963), 1 da (Elizabeth (Mrs Morrison) b 3 July 1961); *Career* instr Princeton Univ 1958-59, Benjamin Peirce Instr Harvard 1959-60, lectr Univ of Glasgow 1961-65, sr lectr Univ of Aberdeen 1965-73; prof mathematics: Univ of Stirling 1973-86, Univ of Strathclyde 1986-; FRSE 1978, FRSA 1984; *Books* Groups (1974); *Recreations* tennis, badminton, swimming, cultural interests; *Style*— Prof D A R Wallace; 16 Drymen Rd, Bearsden, Glasgow G61 2RB (☎ 041 942 0369); Department of Mathematics, University of Strathclyde, Glasgow G1 1XH (☎ 041 552 4400, fax 041 552 0775, telex 77472)

WALLACE, David Clouston; s of Thomas Clouston Wallace (d 1988), and Pauline Hermina Bradfield, *née* Stevens (d 1981); *b* 3 Feb 1940; *Educ* Harrow; *m* 12 Sept 1969, Ann, da of Sidney Drinkall; 1 s (Mark Clouston b 1971), 1 da (Fiona Harriet b 1970); *Career* md: Euro Slate Co 1965-73, Burlington Slate Ltd 1973-; vice chm Westmoreland and Lonsdale Cons and Unionist Assoc; fell Inst of Roofing; *Recreations* shooting; *Clubs* Sloane; *Style*— David Wallace, Esq; Head House, Newton in Cartmel, Grange over Sands, Cumbria LA11 6JG; Holodyke, Dounby, Orkney; Burlington Slate Ltd, Cavendish House, Kirkby in Furness, Cumbria LA17 7UN (☎ 0229 89661, fax 0229 89466, telex 65157 BURCON G)

WALLACE, (James) Fleming; QC (1985); s of James Fleming Baird Wallace (d 1957), and Margaret Braidwood, *née* Gray; *b* 19 March 1931; *Educ* The Edinburgh Acad, Univ of Edinburgh (MA, LLB); *m* 1, 15 Sept 1964, Valerie Mary (d 1986), da of Leslie Lawrence (d 1957), of Wilts; 2 da (Jennifer b 1966, Gillian b 1969); m 2, 16 Aug 1990, Linda Ann, da of Robert Grant (d 1982); *Career* Nat Serv RA 2 Lt 1954-56, TA RA Lt 1956-60; advocate Scots Bar 1957-60, Scottish Parly draftsman and legal sec to the Lord Advocate London 1960-79, counsel Scottish Law Cmmn Edinburgh 1979-; memb Faculty of Advocates 1957; *Books* Stair Memorial Encyclopaedia of the Laws of Scotland (contrib, 1988); *Recreations* choral singing, hill walking, golf, badminton; *Clubs* Royal Mid Surrey Golf; *Style*— Fleming Wallace, Esq, QC; The Scottish Law Cmmn, 140 Causewayside, Edinburgh (☎ 031 668 2131)

WALLACE, Prof Frank Julius; s of Max Wallach, and Melly, *née* Hollaender; *Educ* Dean Close Sch Cheltenham, Univ of Birmingham (BSc, MSc, PhD, DSc); *m* 8 June 1946, Ruth Betty Ida, da of George Emil Aronstein (d 1942); 2 s (Paul George b 1952, Mark Jonathan b 1967), 1 da (Catherine Melly b 1948); *Career* lectr Univ of Birmingham 1951-56, chief res engr ABE Ltd 1956-60, prof of thermodynamics of fluid mechanics (former reader) Queen's Univ Belfast 1960-66, prof of mechanical engrg Univ of Bath 1966-89, conslt 1989-; author of 72 published papers; memb Power Div Inst Mechanical Engrs 1985-; FIMechE 1972; elected fell: American Soc of Automotive Engrs 1980, Fellowship of Engrg 1984; *Books* Engineering Thermodynamics (1964); *Recreations* tennis, languages; *Style*— Prof Frank Wallace; Cedarwood Cottage, 22 Sion Rd, Bath, Avon BA1 5SG (☎ 0225 314033); School of Mechanical Engineering, Univ of Bath, Bath BA2 7AY (☎ 0225 826399)

WALLACE, Ian Bryce; OBE (1983); s of Sir John Wallace (d 1949), of London, and Mary McAdam Bryce Temple; *b* 10 July 1919; *Educ* Charterhouse, Trinity Hall Cambridge (MA); *m* 1948, Patricia Gordon, da of Michael Gordon Black, OBE (d 1946), of Scotland; 1 s (John), 1 da (Rosemary); *Career* singer, actor, writer & broadcaster; *Books* Promise Me You'll Sing Mud (1975), Nothing Quite Like It (1982), Reflections on Scotland (1988); *Recreations* walking, reading, photography and watching sport; *Clubs* Garrick, MCC; *Style*— Ian Wallace, Esq, OBE; c/o Fraser & Dunlop Ltd, 5th Floor, The Chambers, Chelsea Harbour, Lots Rd, London SW10 0XF (☎ 071 352 4446)

WALLACE, Sir Ian James; CBE (1971, OBE (Mil) 1942); s of John Madder Wallace, CBE; *b* 25 Feb 1916; *Educ* Uppingham, Jesus Coll Cambridge; *m* 1942, Catherine Frost Mitchell; 1 s, 1 da; *Career* WWII Cdr (A) RNVR Fleet Air Arm; dir: Massey Ferguson Hldgs 1952-72, Coventry Motor and Sundries Ltd 1986-; chm SNR (Bearings) UK Ltd 1978-85, commercial conslt TRW Valves; Lloyd's underwriter; chm CBI Midland Regnl Cncl 1967-69; vice pres: W Midlands Cons Cncl (chm 1967-70, pres 1972-74), S Worcestershire Cons Assoc 1990-; Coventry C of C 1972-74, pres Fedn of Coventry Cons Assoc 1987- (chm 1968-87); former memb W Midlands Econ Planning Cncl and Severn-Trent Water Authy; pres: Birmingham and Midlands Inst, Hereford and Worcestershire Rifle Assoc; kt 1982; *Recreations* rifle shooting, antiquarian horology; *Clubs* Carlton, Naval and Military, North London Rifle, Drapers Coventry; *Style*— Sir Ian Wallace, CBE; Little House, 156 High St, Broadway, Worcs WR12 7AJ (☎ 0386 852414)

WALLACE, Ian Norman Duncan; QC (1973); s of Duncan Gardner Wallace (d 1939, HBM Crown Advocate in Egypt), of Alexandria, Egypt, and Eileen Agnes Wilkin, of Smyrna, Turkey; *b* 21 April 1922; *Educ* Loretto, Oriel Coll Oxford (MA); *m* 25 March 1961 (m dis 1965), Valerie Mary, da of Rudolf Karl Walter Hollmann of Beckenham, Kent; *Career* Ordinary Seaman RN 1940-41, Lt RNVR 1941-46; called to the Bar Middle Temple 1948, visiting scholar Univ of California at Berkeley 1977, visiting prof King's Coll London 1987, practicing barr and arbitrator specialising in Construction Law; author: Hudson on Building and Civil Engineering Contracts (1959, 1965, 1970 and 1979 edns), Building and Civil Engineering Standard Forms (1969), Further Building Standard Forms (1973), ICE Conditions (1978), The International Civil Engineering Contract (1980), Construction Contracts: Principles and Policies (1986); contrib: Law Quarterly Review; Construction Law Journal, International Construction Law Review, memb Editorial Bd Construction Law Journal; *Recreations* tennis, shooting; *Clubs* Lansdowne, Hurlingham; *Style*— Ian N D Wallace, Esq, QC; 53 Holland Park, London W11 3RS (☎ 071 727 7640); 1 Atkin Building, Gray's Inn, London WC1R 5BQ (☎ 071 404 0102, fax 071 405 7456, telex 298 623 HUDSON G)

WALLACE, James Robert; MP (Lib) Orkney and Shetland 1983-(Soc & Lib Dem 1988-); s of John Fergus Thomson Wallace, of Ingledene, Annan, Dumfriesshire, and Grace Hannah, *née* Maxwell; *b* 25 Aug 1954; *Educ* Annan Acad, Downing Coll Cambridge (MA), Edinburgh Univ (LLB); *m* 9 July 1983, Rosemary Janet, da of William Grant Paton Fraser, OBE, TD, of Barloch, Mugdock Rd, Milngavie, Glasgow; 2 da (Helen b 1985, Clare b 1987); *Career* memb Scottish Lib Pty Nat Exec 1976-85 (vice chm 1982-85); contested (Lib): Dumfries 1979, S Scotland Euro elections June 1979; admitted to Faculty of Advocates 1979, Lib parly spokesman on defence and dep whip 1985-87; Alliance election spokesman on tport 1987; dep whip 1985-87, elected chief whip and reappointed defence spokesman Oct 1987, elected chief whip Social & Lib Democrats 1988, appointed employment and fisheries spokesman 1988; Elder of Church of Scotland; *Recreations* music, golf, travel; *Clubs* Scottish Liberal; *Style*— James Wallace, Esq, MP; Northwood House, Tankerness, Orkney KW17 2QS (☎ 0856 86 383); House of Commons, London SW1A OAA (☎ 071 219 6254, fax 071 219 5713)

WALLACE, Hon Jim Anthony Hill; s of Baroness Dudley and late Guy Wallace and h to Barony; *b* 9 Nov 1930; *Educ* Lancing; *m* 16 June 1962, Nicola Jane, da of Lt-Col Philip William Edward Leslie Dunsterville, of Hitcham, Suffolk; 2 s (Jeremy William b 12 Sept 1964, Nicholas John Hill b 31 Jan 1967); *Style*— The Hon Jim Wallace; Little Grange, Napleton, Kempsey, Worcs

WALLACE, John Williamson; s of Christopher Kidd Wallace, of Glenrothes, Fife, and Ann Drummond, *née* Allan; *b* 14 April 1949; *Educ* Buckhaven HS, King's Coll Cambridge (MA); *m* 3 July 1971, Elizabeth Jane, da of Prof Ronald Max Hartwell, of Oxford; 2 s (Cosmo b 1979, Esme b 1982); *Career* asst princ trumpet LSO 1974-76, princ trumpet Philharmonia 1976-, performed obligato trumpet at Royal Wedding 1981, performed first performance of Sir Peter Maxwell Davies trumpet concerto Hiroshima 1988; hon memb RCM 1982, FRAM, memb Royal Soc of Musicians; *Books* First Book of Trumpet Solos (1985), Second Book of Trumpet Solos (1985); *Recreations* playing the trumpet; *Style—* John Wallace, Esq; 16 Woodstock Rd, Croydon, Surrey CR0 1JR (☎ 081 688 1170); Seven Muses, 5 Milton Ave, Highgate N6 (☎ 081 348 7256, telex 918774)

WALLACE, Julie T; da of Andrew Keir, and Julia, *née* Wallace; *Educ* Ysgol Y Drenywydd, Twickenham Sixth Form Coll, LAMDA; *Career* actress; theatre work incl: Billy the Kid and Barrel of Laughs (Upstream Theatre Club), The House of Usher (Theatre West), Beauty and the Beast (Bristol), The Worlds (Royal Court), The Cherry Orchard (Dundee); TV incl: The Life and Loves of a She Devil (BBC TV, best actress nomination BAFTA), Stolen (LWT), Morning Sarge (BBC); films incl: The Living Daylights, The Threepenny Opera, Hawks, The Lunatic; *Recreations* going to the cinema, watching TV (esp Barry Norman!); *Style—* Ms Julie Wallace; c/o Annette Stone Associates, 9 Newburgh St, London W1V 1LH (☎ 071 734 0626, fax 071 434 2014)

WALLACE, Hon Mrs (Karis Valerie Violet); *née* Mond; o da of 2 Baron Melchett (d 1949), and Gwen, *née* Wilson; *b* 26 July 1927; *m* 1, 15 Dec 1949 (m dis 1956), John Hackman Sumner, yst s of late Thomas Hackman Sumner, of Redruth, Cornwall; 1 s (Justin b 1953); m 2, 1956, Brian Albert Wallace (d 1986), o s of Peter Daniel Wallace, of Melbourne, Australia; 2 da (Jessica b 1957, Arabella b 1959); *Career* theatre director; *Style—* The Hon Mrs Wallace; Greenways, Lambourn, Berks

WALLACE, Keith; s of William Wallace, CMG, and Sheila Agnes, *née* Hopper; *b* 5 June 1945; *Educ* Mill Hill Sch; *m* 17 March 1973, Christine, da of Alan Beautement (d 1979); 3 s (Jasper b 1975, William b 1977, Dougal b 1983); *Career* admitted slr 1971; ptnr Bird & Bird 1972-84, clerk Richard Cloudesley's Charity 1976-, ed Pension Lawyer 1984-, ptnr Richards Butler 1985-, chm Maldon Unit Tst managers Ltd 1987-; vice pres Holborn Law Soc 1983-4; Freeman: Worshipful Co of Slrs 1985, City of London 1987, memb Ctee Assoc Pension Lawyers, 1984-89; *Style—* Keith Wallace, Esq; Beaufort House, 15 St Botolph St, EC3A 7EE (☎ 071 247 6555, fax 071 247 5091)

WALLACE, (John) Malcolm Agnew; JP (Wigtownshire), DL (1971); s of Maj John Alexander Agnew Wallace, MC (d 1956); *b* 30 Jan 1928; *Educ* Brooks Sch Andover Mass USA, Harrow; *m* 1955, Louise Arden, *née* Haworth-Booth; 1 s, 2 da; *Career* farmer; *Style—* Malcolm Wallace, Esq, JP, DL; Lochryan, Stranraer, Wigtownshire

WALLACE, Maj Malcolm Charles Robarts; s of Lionel John Wallace, MBE, of Beavers, Rowledge, Farnham, Surrey, and Maureen Winefride, *née* Robarts; *b* 12 June 1947; *Educ* Blackrock Coll, Country Dublin; *m* 15 March 1974, Caroline Anne Doyne, da of Maj Philip Edward Churton Vigors Doyne Ditmas (d 1980); 1 s (Harry b 8 April 1980), 1 da (Philippa b 7 Oct 1981); *Career* Cmmnd RA 1967, served Far East and with RHA in BAOR, mounted duty with King's Troop RHA 1970-74 and post CO 1982-85, Troop RHA 1982-85 (mounted duty 1970-74), ret 1985; chef d'equipe (team mangr) int and Olympic three day event team 1979-84, team mangr equestrian teams Seoul Olympics 1988, steward: Sandown Park, Warwick and Lingfield Park; dir gen Br Equestrian Fedn 1985; Freeman: City of London 1984, Worshipful Co of Saddlers; *Books* The King Troop, Royal Horse Artillery (1984); *Recreations* national hunt racing, equestrian sports, field sports; *Clubs* Cavalry and Guards'; *Style—* Maj Malcolm Wallace; Furreux Pelham Hall, nr Buntingford, Hertfordshire SG9 0LB (☎ 0279 777840, fax 0279 777011); British Equestrian Fedn, British Equestrian Centre, Kenilworth, Warwickshire CV8 2LR (☎ 0203 696697, fax 0203 696685, telex 311152, car 0860 371295)

WALLACE, Hon Michael George; o s of Baron Wallace of Coslany (Life Peer); *b* 1944; *m* 1974, Susan, da of Henry William Price, of Orpington, Kent; issue; *Recreations* gardening, amateur radio; *Style—* The Hon Michael Wallace; 17 Leamington Ave, Orpington, Kent

WALLACE, Nicholas Patrick (Nicky); s of James Wallace, of 54 South Main Street, Wexford, Ireland, and Brigid Ita, *née* Lambert; *b* 12 Sept 1952; *Educ* De La Salle Coll Waterford, Jacob Kramer Coll Leeds (Dip Fashion and Design); *m* 2 Sept 1978 (m dis 1988), Carmel Marie Therese, da of Desmond Corish; 1 s (Karl Nicholas b 28 Feb 1981), 1 da (Lauren Catherine b 19 Jan 1985); *Career* int fashion designer (supplies top mkts worldwide), designer wardrobes for TVs Miami Vice, produced own name designer collections for 5 yrs; *Recreations* diving, windsurfing, reading, art; *Style—* Nicky Wallace, Esq; 6 Islington Terrace, Sandy Cove, Co Dublin, Ireland; Nicky Wallace International Trading Ltd, 2c Rockview Terrace, Montenotte, Cork, Ireland (☎ 021 506 930)

WALLACE, Richard Alexander; s of Lawrence Mervyn Wallace, and Norah Wallace; *b* 24 Nov 1946; *Educ* Clifton, King's Coll Cambridge (MA); *m* 1970, Teresa Caroline Harington Smith; 4 c (1 decd); *Career* asst master Woking Co GS for Boys 1967, Miny of Social Security 1968, princ DHSS 1972, asst sec 1981, under sec and head Tport Planning Water and Environment Gp Welsh Office 1988-90 (joined 1986), princ fin offr Welsh Office 1990-; *Style—* R A Wallace, Esq; Welsh Office, Cathays Park, Cardiff CF1 3NQ

WALLACE, Hon Robin Guy Hill; 2 s of Baroness Dudley and her 1 husband, Guy Raymond Hill Wallace (d 1967); *b* 1936; *Educ* Malvern; *m* 1959, Jill Alexandra, da of late Herbert Williams; 2 s (Simon Alexander Hill b 1962, Andrew George Hill b 1964); *Style—* The Hon Robin Wallace; Pond House, Ham Hill, Powick, Worcs WR2 4RD (☎ 0905 830445)

WALLACE, Robin John; s of Patrick John Wallace, and (Lauretta Elizabeth) Anne, *née* Peters; *b* 28 March 1964; *Educ* Thornden Sch Chandlers Ford, Barton Peveril Coll Eastliegh; *Career* skier; Euro ski ballet champion 1984, second place Euro Freestyle Skiing Championships 1987, ninth place in freestyle Calgary Winter Olympics 1988; Br Freestyle Skiing Champion 1989, currently Britian's top professional skier and dir RWI Sports Promotions, winner eight nat titles; pres Br Acrobatic Sports Club; *Recreations* trampolining, windsurfing, computers, chess, golf, stock market; *Style—* Robin Wallace, Esq; 3 Forest Road, Chandler's Ford, Hampshire SO5 1NA (☎ 0703 265214)

WALLACE, (George) Roger; *b* 20 April 1946; *m* 28 June 1969, Susan (Sue); 1 s (Mark b 25 July 1975), 1 da (Helen (twin) b 25 July 1975); *Career* Coalite Group Ltd (formerly Coalite Group plc): gp accountant 1976-80, gp fin controller 1980-82, fin dir 1982-; dir CTC Fisheries Ltd 1986-, chief fin offr Anglo United plc 1990- (fin dir 1990); MCIMA; *Style—* Roger Wallace, Esq; Anglo United plc, Newgate House, Broombank Rd, Chesterfield, Derbys S41 9QJ (☎ 0246 454583, fax 0246 453787)

WALLACE, (Wellesley) Theodore Octavius; s of Dr Caleb Paul Wallace (d 1981), and Dr Lucy Elizabeth Rainsford, *née* Pigott (d 1968); *b* 10 April 1938; *Educ* Charterhouse, Christ Church Oxford (MA); *m* 1 (m dis), Mollie Udale-Smith; m 2, 23 Jan 1988, Maria Amelia, o da of Sir Ian George Abercromby, 10 Bt; 1 s (James Abercromby Octavius b 18 Jan 1989); *Career* 2 Lt RA 1958, Lt Surrey Yeomanry TA 1959; called to the Bar Inner Temple 1963; memb Lloyd's; Inner London Sch govr 1966-86, chm Chelsea Cons Assoc 1981-84, pt/t chm Value Added Tax Tribunals 1989; Cons candidate: Pontypool Feb 1974, South Battersea Oct 1974 and May 1979; *Books* The Case Against Wealth Tax (1968); *Publications*: The Case Against Wealth Tax (1968), A History of Hans Town Chelsea (1986); *Recreations* tennis, racing, skiing; *Clubs* Carlton; *Style—* Theodore Wallace, Esq; Whitecroft, West Clandon, Surrey GU4 7TD (☎ 0483 222574); 46 Belleville Rd, London SW11 4QT (☎ 071 228 7740); 17 Old Buildings, Lincoln's Inn, London WC2A 3UP (☎ 071 405 9653, fax 071 405 5032)

WALLACE, Vivien Rosemary Lumsdaine; da of late Capt James Edward Lumsdaine Wallace, and late Gwynne Wallace, *née* Jones; *b* 11 Feb 1944; *Educ* St Martin's Sch Solihull, Emma Willard Troy New York (on English speaking Union Scholarship), Arts Cncl of GB bursary to study theatre admin; *m* 1, 2 Sept 1964, Anthony Thomas Etridge; m 2, Terence Francis Frank Coleman; 1 s (Jack b 1984), 1 da (Eliza b 1983); *Career* press offr London Festival Ballet 1969-71, first ever press offr Royal Ballet Covent Garden 1972-74, chief press offr National Theatre 1975-77; Granada TV Int 1979-: head of sales 1981, dir of sales 1983, chief exec 1987; dir: Granada TV 1987-, Nat Assoc of TV Production Executives USA 1988-, TBA Films and Television Hamburg 1989-; *Style—* Miss Vivien Wallace; Granada Television International, 36 Golden Square, London W1R 4AH (☎ 071 734 8080, fax 071 494 6280, telex 27937)

WALLACE, Walter Wilkinson; CVO (1977), CBE (1974, OBE 1964), DSC (1944); s of Walter Wilkinson Wallace (d 1960), and Helen Morgan, *née* Douglas; *b* 23 Sept 1923; *Educ* George Heriot's Sch Edinburgh; *m* 11 June 1955, Susan Blanche, da of Brig F W B Parry, CBE (d 1989); 1 s (Andrew Douglas b 1960), 1 da (Susan Emma b 1956); *Career* Capt RM 1942-46; Dip Serv; dist commr then prov commr then devpt sec Sierra Leone 1948-64, estab sec Bahamas 1964-67, sec to the Cabinet Bermuda 1968-73, govr Br Virgin Is 1974-78, FCO 1980-; constitutional cmmr: St Helena 1987, Cayman Is 1991; *Clubs* Army & Navy; *Style—* Walter Wallace, Esq, CVO, CBE, DSC; Becketts, Itchenor, West Sussex PO20 7DE (☎ 0243 512438); Foreign & Commonwealth Office, King Charles St, London SW1 (☎ 071 270 3544)

WALLACE, Prof (William Angus); s of Dr William Bethune Wallace (d 1981), of Dundee, Scotland, and Dr Frances Barret, *née* Early; *b* 31 Oct 1948; *Educ* Dundee HS, Univ of St Andrews (MB ChB); *m* 2 Jan 1971, Jacqueline Vera Studley, da of Dr George William Eglinton, of East Finchley, London; 2 s (Malcolm b 1975, Andrew b 1979), 1 da (Suzanne b 1973); *Career* jr house offr Dundee Royal Infirmary and Maryfield Hosp 1972-73, demonstrator in anatomy Univ of Nottingham 1973-74; sr house off Nottingham 1974-75, Derby 1975; basic surgical trg registrar Newcastle and Gateshead Hosps 1975-77, orthopaedic registrar Nottingham Hosps 1978-81, res fell MRC 1979, lectr in orthopaedic surgery Univ of Nottingham 1981-84, visiting res fell Toronto W Hosp Canada 1983, sr lectr in orthopaedic surgery Univ of Manchester 1984-85, med dir North Western Orthotic Unit and med advsr Dept of Orthopaedic Mechanics Univ of Salford 1984-85, prof of orthopaedic and accident surgery Univ of Nottingham 1985-; memb Cncl Royal Coll of Surgns of Edinburgh, Br Orthopaedic Assoc rep to the IMechE, sec Assoc of Profs of Orthopaedic Surgery, chm Mgmnt Ctee Nottingham Resource Centre for the Disabled, treas Br Elbow and Shoulder Soc; awarded Sir Walter Mercer Gold medal by RCSEd 1985; FRCSEd 1977, FRCSEd (orthopaedic) 1985, memb RSM; *Recreations* jogging, woodwork; *Style—* Prof Angus Wallace; University Hospital, Queen's Medical Centre, Nottingham NG7 2UH (☎ 0602 709407, fax 0602 423656)

WALLACE, Dr William John Lawrence; s of William Edward Wallace, and Mary Agnes, *née* Tricks; *b* 12 March 1941; *Educ* Westminster Abbey Sch, St Edwards Sch Oxford, King's Coll Cambridge (BA), Cornell Univ USA (PhD); *m* 25 Aug 1968, Helen Sarah, da of Edward Rushworth (d 1975); 1 s (Edward b 1981), 1 da (Harriet b 1977); *Career* lectr in govt Univ of Manchester 1966-67, dir of Studies Royal Inst of Int Affrs 1978-90, Hallstein Fell St Antony's Coll Oxford 1990-; memb various Liberal Pty and SDP Liberal Alliance Nat Ctees 1973-87; Parly candidate Liberal Pty: Huddersfield West 1970, Manchester Moss Side 1974, Shipley 1983 and 1987; *Books* The Transformation of Western Europe (1990), The Foreign Policy Process of Britain (1976), Policy Making in the European Community (1983); *Style—* Dr William Wallace; St Antony's College, Oxford (☎ 0865 59651, fax 0865 310518)

WALLACE, Hon William John Sutton; s of Baroness Dudley, and late Guy Wallace; *b* 1938; *Educ* Malvern; *m* 1962, Jean Carol Ann, *née* Shipton; 2 s (Guy Edward John Sutton b 18 Dec 1963, Piers William Somery b 25 April 1965); *Style—* The Hon William Wallace; Beechmount House, Hallow, Worcs (☎ 0905 640413)

WALLACE OF CAMPSIE, Baron (Life Peer UK 1974), of Newlands, Co of City of Glasgow; George Wallace; JP (1968), DL (Glasgow 1971); s of John Wallace and Mary Pollock; *b* 13 Feb 1915; *Educ* Queen's Park Secondary Sch, Univ of Glasgow; *m* 1977, Irene Alice Langdon, er da of Ernest Phipps, of Glasgow; *Career* pres Wallace Cameron Hldgs 1977-; slr Supreme Cts 1950-, Hon Sheriff Hamilton 1971-; memb: Law Soc Scotland, Royal Faculty of Procurators, Int Bar Assoc, Bd of Smith and Nephew plc 1972-77, South of Scotland Electricity Bd 1966-69; chm East Kilbride Devpt Corp 1969-75, fndr memb Scottish Devpt Agency 1976-78, vice pres Scottish Assoc of Youth Clubs, pres East Kilbride Business Centre; chm: Community Indust Support Gp Scotland, Advsy Bd Salvation Army Strathcylde; active with many other gps and assocs; FRSA, FCIM, FBIM, FSA (Scot); KStJ; *Style—* The Lord Wallace of Campsie, JP, DL; 14 Fernleigh Rd, Newlands, Glasgow (☎ 041 637 3337)

WALLACE OF COSLANY, Baron (Life Peer UK 1974), of Coslany, City of Norwich; George Douglas Wallace; s of George Wallace, of Cheltenham, Glos; *b* 18 April 1906; *Educ* Central Sch Cheltenham; *m* 1932, Vera, da of William Joseph Randall, of Guildford, Surrey; 1 s (Hon Michael George b 1944), 1 da (Hon Elizabeth Anne b 1933); *Career* sits as Lab Peer in House of Lords; MP (Lab): Chislehurst 1945-50, Norwich N 1964-74; Govt whip 1947-50, lord in waiting 1977-79, oppn whip 1979-84, oppn spokesman (Lords) on Health 1983-84; memb: Chislehurst and Sidcup UDC 1937-46, Kent CC 1948-53; pres: Radio Soc GB 1977, London Soc of Recreational Gardeners, League of Friends Queen Mary's Hosp Sidcup; *Recreations* gardening, amateur radio; *Style—* The Rt Hon the Lord Wallace of Coslany; 44 Shuttle Close, Sidcup, Kent (☎ 081 300 3634)

WALLACE-TURNER, Robert John Aufrère Carr; s of Alfred Wallace Wallace-Turner (d 1968); *b* 22 July 1931; *Educ* Eton, Trinity Coll Oxford (MA); *m* 1966, Sabine, *née* de Falguerolles; 3 da; *Career* Lt Gren Gds; currently with Broadgate Asset Management Ltd; FCA; *Recreations* France, music, the visual arts; *Clubs* City of London, MCC, First Guards; *Style—* Robert Wallace-Turner, Esq; 39 Marryat Rd, London SW19 5BE (☎ 081 946 6418); Cayenne Par St Germain-des-Prés, Tarn, France; Broadgate Asset Management Ltd, 4 Broadgate, London EC2M 7LE (☎ 071 374 7642)

WALLDEN, Richard James; s of Frederick Edward Wallden, of Frinton on Sea, Essex, and Olive Maud, *née* Jones; *b* 7 Oct 1946; *Educ* Bancroft's Sch Woodford Green Essex; *m* 9 Oct 1971, Sally Barbara, da of Herbert James Ford, of Woodford Green, Essex; 4 s (James b 1975, Toby b 1977, Luke b 1980, Benjamin b 1981); *Career* Barclays Bank plc: mangr 1977-85, dir London NW Region 1985-89, dir Personnel Dept 1989-90; risk management dir UK Domestic Bank 1990-; memb Fyfield PCC 1974-; ACIB; *Recreations* rugby football; *Clubs* Bancroft RFC; *Style—* Richard Wallden, Esq; PO Box 256, Fleetway House, 25 Farringdon St, London EC4A 4LP (☎ 071 489 1995, fax 071 489 1995 ext 450)

WALLEN, David Richard; s of Maurice Wray Wallen (d 1983), and Joan Nicholls; *b* 13 Feb 1951; *Educ* Bolton Sch, Univ of Bradford (BSc); *m* 1976, Kathy Hough; 2 da

(Rebecca b 1983, Camille b 1987); *Career* reporter: Bedfordshire Co Press 1974, Northern Echo 1975-77, Press Association 1977-83 (def corr 1983-86); def and dip corr London Daily News 1986, Euro corr South China Horning Post HK 1987, London ed and dip ed The Scotsman 1990- (dip corr 1988-90); memb: Newspaper Conf 1990, Dip & Cwlth Writers Assoc 1988; *Books* The Chronicle of the 20th Century (contrib, 1989); *Recreations* sailing, motor cruising, skiing, walking, swimming, good music, good food; *Clubs* Bray Cruiser; *Style—* David Wallen, Esq; The Scotsman Publications Ltd, Pemberton House, East Harding St, London EC4A 3AS (☎ 071 353 9051)

WALLER, (Trevor) Alfred Morfey; s of Canon Trevor Waller, of Waldringfield, nr Woodbridge, Suffolk, and Nora Mary, *née* Morfey (d 1973); *b* 23 Sept 1937; *Educ* Ipswich Sch, Selwyn Coll Cambridge (MA); *m* 20 May 1966, (Katherine) Jane, da of Sir Steward Crawford, GCMG, of Henley-On-Thames, Oxon; 2 s (Charles, Edward); *Career* Lt attachment Br Gurkhas Nepal, 1 Bn Suffolk Regt Cyprus 1957-59; md Evans-Methuen SA 1967-70, books offr Br Cncl India 1970-72, publisher Prentice-Hall International 1972-75, ed dir Pitman Publishing Ltd 1976-85; md: Mary Glasgow Group 1985-88, Alfred Waller Ltd 1989-; chm Atlantic Europe Publishing Co Ltd 1989-; former memb Bd Univ Coll and Professional Cncl Publishers Assoc, chm Further Educn Ctee Publishers Assoc; *Recreations* tennis, sailing, ornithology, entomology; *Clubs* Holland Park Lawn Tennis; *Style—* Alfred Waller, Esq; Orchards, Fawley, Nr Henley-On-Thames, Oxon (☎ 049 163 694)

WALLER, Hon Lady (Elizabeth Margery); JP (Petersfield); da of 1 Baron Hacking, OBE, PC (d 1950); aunt of 3 Baron *qv*; *b* 1916; *m* 1936, Rt Hon Sir George Waller, *qv*; 2 s, 1 da; *Style—* The Hon Lady Waller, JP; Hatchway, Hatch Lane, Kingsley Green, Haslemere, Surrey GU27 3LJ (☎ 0428 644629)

WALLER, Gary Peter Anthony; MP (C) Keighley 1983-; s of John Waller (d 1965), and Elizabeth Waller; *b* 24 June 1945; *Educ* Rugby, Univ of Lancaster; *Career* contested (C) Rother Valley Feb and Oct 1974, MP (C) Brighouse and Spenborough 1979-83; memb House of Commons Select Ctee on Tport 1979-82, PPS to David Howell as sec state Tport 1982-83; chm All Party Wool Textile Gp 1984-89; *Style—* Gary Waller, Esq, MP; House of Commons, London SW1A 0AA (☎ 071 219 4010)

WALLER, Rt Hon Sir George Stanley Waller; OBE (1945), QC (1954), PC (1976); s of James Stanley Waller; *b* 3 Aug 1911; *Educ* Oundle, Queens' Coll Cambridge; *m* 1936, Hon Elizabeth Margery, *qv*, da of 1 Baron Hacking; 2 s, 1 da; *Career* RAFO 1931-36; served WWII: RAFVR, 502 Sqdn 1940-41, Wing Cdr 1943 (despatches); called to the Bar Gray's Inn 1934; rec: Doncaster 1953-54, Sunderland 1954-55, Bradford 1955-57, Sheffield 1957-61, Leeds 1961-65; slr gen Durham 1957-61, attorney gen Co Palatine Durham 1961-65, judge High Court Queen's Bench 1965-76, presiding judge NE Circuit 1973-76, Lord Justice of Appeal 1976-84, ret; former memb: Gen Cncl Bar, Parole Bd, Criminal Law Revision Ctee 1977-85; chm Policy Advsy Ctee Sexual Offences 1977-85; kt 1965; *Style—* The Rt Hon Sir George Waller, OBE, QC; Hatchway, Hatch Lane, Kingsley Green, Haslemere, Surrey GU27 3LJ (☎ 0428 644629)

WALLER, Jane Ashton; da of Charles Ashton Waller, of Bucks, and Barbara Mary *née* Batt; *b* 19 May 1944; *Educ* Ladymede Sch Little Kimble, Croham Hurst Sch Croydon, Hornsey Art Sch (BA), RCA (MA); *m* 11 June 1983, Michael Hugh Vaughan-Rees, s of Lyle Vaughan-Rees (d 1962); *Career* since 1982: exhibited in London and many other parts of the country also in Kuwait, collections in LA, Chicago and Miami; work is sold at Bonhams and Sothebys; author of articles in Ceramic Review; started successful one woman campaign to save the Oxo tower on the South bank; involved in Coin St Orgn; *Books* A Stitch in time (1972), Some Things for the Children (1974), A Mans Book (1977), The Thirties Family Knitting Book (1981), Below the Green Pond (1982), The Mans Knitting Book (1984), Women in Wartime (jt 1987), Women in Uniform (jt 1989), Handbuilt Ceramics (1990), Blitz (jtly 1990), The 1940's Knitting Book (1991); *Recreations* reading, gardening, knitting, writing, conservation, cooking, ceramics, walking in the country, collection of fashion magazines and knitting leaflets 1920-60; *Style—* Ms Jane Waller

WALLER, Sir John Stainier Waller; 7 Bt (UK 1815), of Braywick Lodge, Berkshire; s of late Capt Stanier Edmund William Waller, gs of the late Rev Ernest Adolphus Waller, 2 s of 1 Bt; *b* 1917; *Educ* Weymouth Coll, Worcester Coll Oxford; *Career* serv RASC Middle E 1940-46, Capt 1942; features ed and Min of State Cairo 1943-45, chief press offr Br Embassy Baghdad 1945, editorial offr MIME Cairo 1945-46; information offr London Press Serv, Central Off of Information 1954-59; author, poet, journalist, co dir; *Style—* Sir John Waller, Bt; 21 Lyndhurst Road, Hove, East Sussex BN3 6FA

WALLER, Jonathan Neil; s of Douglas Victor Waller, of Fareham, Hampshire, and Kristine Daphne Desmond Rieley (d 1982); *b* 16 April 1956; *Educ* Cherry Orchard HS Northampton, Northampton GS, Nene Coll Northampton, Coventry (Lanchester) Poly, Chelsea Sch of Art (BA, MA); *Career* artist; painting fellowship S Glamorgan Inst of Higher Educn Cardiff 1985-86, full time artist London 1987-; solo exhibitions: Paton Gallery London 1986 and 1988, Flowers East London 1990; gp exhibitions: New Contemporaries (ICA, London) 1984, Midland View 3 (Nottingham and tour) 1984, Four New Painters (Paton Gallery, London) 1986, Royal Over-Seas League London 1986, London Glasgow New York (Metropolitan Museum, New York) 1988, The New British Painting (Cinnatti USA and tour) 1988, Pacesetters (City Art Gallery, Peterborough) 1988, The Thatcher Years: An Artistic Retrospective (Flowers East, London) 1989, Confrontation: Three British Artists (Joy Emery Gallery Detroit USA) 1989, Angela Flowers Gallery 1990 Barbican London 1989, Flowers at Moos (Gallery Moos NY) 1990, This Sporting Life (Flowers East, London) 1990; work in the collections of: Metropolitan Museum NY, Contemporary Art Soc, Unilever plc, Dept of the Environment, Bankers Trust; grants incl: Welsh Arts Cncl 1986, British Cncl 1990; awards: first prize Midland View 3 1984, Mark Rothko Meml Tst travelling scholarship to USA 1988; *Style—* Jonathan Waller, Esq; Studio 51, Acme Studios, 105-107 Carpenters Rd, Stratford, London E15 (☎ 081 519 5240); c/o Matthew Flowers, Flowers East, 199-205 Richmond Road, Hackney, London E8 3NJ (☎ 081 985 3333, fax 081 985 0067)

WALLER, Hon Mrs (Margery Edith); *née* Sugden; da of late Hon Henry Frank Sugden, bro of 2 Baron St Leonards, ggda of 1 Baron St Leonards; raised to the rank of a Baron's da 1912; *b* 1885; *m* 1918, Maj Robert Jocelyn Rowan Waller, DSO (d 1968); 2 da; *Style—* The Hon Mrs Waller; Ickford House, Little Ickford, nr Aylesbury, Bucks

WALLER, The Hon Mr Justice; Sir (George) Mark; s of The Rt Hon Sir George Stanley Waller, OBE (ret Lord Justice of Appeal 1985), of Haslemere, Surrey, and Elizabeth Margery Waller; *b* 13 Oct 1940; *Educ* Oundle, Univ of Durham (LLB); *m* 1967, Rachel Elizabeth, da of His Hon Judge Beaumont, MBE, of Boroughbridge, N Yorks; 3 s (Charles b 1968, Richard b 1969, Philip b 1973); *Career* called to the Bar Gray's Inn 1964, QC 1979, rec 1986, judge of High Ct of Justice Queen's Bench Div 1989-; kt 1989; *Recreations* tennis, golf; *Clubs* Garrick, MCC; *Style—* The Hon Mr Justice Waller; Royal Courts of Justice, Strand, London

WALLER, Michael Garnet; s of Richard Garnet Waller (d 1984), and Joan May Kendrew; *b* 22 Aug 1939; *Educ* Uppingham; *m* 1967, Susan, da of Peter Mercer (d 1979); 2 da (Annabel May b 14 June 1970, Caroline Zoe); *Career* chartered accountant; joined Price Waterhouse 1958; FCA (ACA 1964); *Recreations* shooting, skiing, golf, tennis; *Style—* Michael Waller, Esq; Price Waterhouse, Southwark Towers, 32 London Bridge St, London SE1 9SY (☎ 071 939 2151)

WALLER, Maj Patrick John Ronald; MBE (1959), JP (Herefordshire 1972), DL (Gwent 1983); s of Brig Robert Peel Waller, DSO, MC (d 1978), formerly of Wyastone Leys, Monmouth, and Olave Harriet (d 1966), da of Henry Edward William Fock, 5 Baron de Robeck; *b* 24 Nov 1923; *Educ* St Aubyn's Rottingdean, Wellington; *m* 14 May 1952, Mary Joyce, da of Lt-Col Laton Frewen, DSO (d 1977), of Round Oak Cottage, Bridstow, Herefordshire; 1 s (Richard Patrick b 7 March 1958), 1 da (Olivia Louise (Mrs Stirling) b 14 Nov 1954); *Career* enlisted TA engagement 1941; cmmnd 12 Royal Lancers 1943, served N Africa, Italy and Palestine, Staff Coll 1952, Special Mil Intelligence Staff (Malaya) 1957-59, ret 1968; dir A R Mountain & Son (Lloyd's agents) 1983; past pres Gwent Branch CLA (chm Welsh Ctee 1985-90); memb Herefordshire CC 1970-74, parish cncllr 1970-83, govr Haberdashers' Monmouth Schs 1971- (chm Boys' Sch 1979-89), chm of Mangrs Whitchurch VA Sch; memb Agric Land Tbnl (Wales) 1977-; High Sheriff of Gwent 1978; Freeman City of London 1982, Liveryman Worshipful Co of Haberdashers 1982; *Recreations* country sports; *Clubs* Cavalry and Guards'; *Style—* Maj Patrick Waller, MBE, JP, DL; Hadnock Court, Monmouth, Gwent NP5 3NJ (☎ 0600 2768)

WALLER, Sir Robert William; 9 Bt (I 1780), of Newport, Tipperary; s of 8 Bt (d 1958); *b* 16 June 1934; *Educ* Newark Coll of Engineering, Farleigh Dickinson Univ; *m* 1960 (m dis 1975), Carol Anne, da of John Edward Hines, of Hampton, New Hampshire, and Lynn, Mass, USA; 3 s (1 decd), 2 da; *Heir* s, John Michael Waller b 14 May 1962; *Career* engineer General Electric Co; *Style—* Sir Robert Waller, Bt; 5 Lookout Ter, Lynnfield, Mass 01940, USA

WALLEY, Joan Lorraine; MP (Lab) Stoke-on-Trust North 1987-; da of Arthur Simeon Walley (d 1968), and Mary Emma, *née* Pass; *b* 23 Jan 1949; *Educ* Biddulph GS, Univ of Hull (BA), Univ Coll of Swansea (Dip); *m* 2 Aug 1980, Jan Ostrowski, s of Adam Ostrowski; 2 s (Daniel b 1981, Tom b 1983); *Career* Lambeth cncllr 1982-86; *Style—* Joan Walley, MP; House of Commons, London SW1A 0AA

WALLEY, Sir John; KBE (1965), CB (1950); s of R M Walley; *b* 3 April 1906; *Educ* Hereford HS, Hereford Cathedral Sch, Merton Coll Oxford; *m* 1934, Elisabeth Pinhorn; 2 s, 2 da; *Career* postmaster Merton Coll Oxford 1924-28; asst princ Miny of Labour 1929, sec Cabinet Ctee on Unemployment 1932, princ 1934, asst sec Miny of Nat Serv 1941, promoted under-sec to take charge of legislation and other preparations for Beveridge Nat Insur Scheme in New Miny of Nat Insur 1945, dep sec 1958-66; chm Dental Benefit Cncl 1945-48; chm Hampstead Centre Nat Tst 1969-79 (pres 1980-); *Books* Social Security - Another British Failure? (1972); *Style—* Sir John Walley, KBE, CB; 46 Rotherwick Rd, London NW11 (☎ 081 455 6528)

WALLIKER, Christopher John; RD (1971); s of Richard Harold Walliker, of Wimbledon, and Phyllis Muriel Frances Vincent, *née* Williams (d 1981); *b* 26 April 1936; *Educ* Oundle; *m* 26 Sept 1962, Susan May, da of Eric Windsor Berry (d 1963); 1 s (Michael John Delane b 5 Sept 1964), 1 da (Emma May Delane b 1 May 1967); *Career* Nat Serv RN 1955-56, Sub Lt RNVR, Lt Cdr RNR 1957-72; chief accountant Eucryl Group Ltd 1965-69, divnl fin dir Delta Group 1969-76 (manpower dir 1976-83, main Bd dir 1977-), chm Benjamin Priest Gp plc 1984-91 (vice-chm 1983); chm Cncl CBI W Mids 1980-82 (memb 1976-83), vice pres Mgmnt Bd Engrg Employers W Mids Assoc 1988- (memb 1976-, hon treas 1981-87), chm Central Birmingham Dist Health Authy 1983-; Freeman City of London, memb Worshipful Co of Chartered Accountants; *Recreations* golf, bridge; *Clubs* Naval; *Style—* Christopher Walliker, Esq; Apple Tree Thatch, Chideock, Dorset; P O Box 38, Cradley Heath, Warley, W Mids B64 6JW (☎ 0384 66501, fax 0384 64598)

WALLINGER, John David Arnold; s of Sir Geoffrey Arnold Wallinger, GBE, KCMG (d 1979), and Diana Peel, *née* Nelson (d 1986); *b* 1 May 1940; *Educ* Winchester, Clare Coll Cambridge (BA); *m* 16 Feb 1966, Rosamund Elizabeth, da of Jack Philip Albert Gavin Clifford-Wolff, MBE; 2 da (Rosamund b 1944, Antoinette b 1946); *Career* ptnr: Panmure Gordon & Co 1972-75, Rowe & Pitman 1975-86; dir S G Warburg Securities 1986-; SIA; *Recreations* tennis, skiing, fishing, shooting, racing; *Style—* John Wallinger, Esq; S G Warburg Securities, 1 Finsbury Ave, London, EC2M 2PA (☎ 071 606 1066, fax 071 382 4800, car 0836 232 530, telex 937011)

WALLINGTON, Jeremy Francis; s of Ernest Francis Wallington (d 1962), and Nellie, *née* Howe (d 1953); *b* 7 July 1935; *Educ* Royal GS High Wycombe; *m* 22 Oct 1955, Margaret Ivy, da of Clifford Samuel Willment (d 1988); 3 s (Rupert Francis b 1958, Jake Samuel b 1962, Benjamin Geoffrey b 1965), 1 da (Abigail Margaret b 1959); *Career* asst ed: Sunday Times 1964-65 (co-fndr Insight 1963), Daily Mail 1965-66; ed World in Action 1968- 70 (fndr Investigation Unit 1967), head of documentaries Granada TV 1970-77, dir of programmes Southern TV 1977-81, fndr Southern Pictures 1978, fndr and chief exec Limehouse Studios 1982-86, chm Wallington, Irving, Jackson, Ltd 1990-; *Recreations* Spain, dutch barges; *Clubs* BAFTA and TV; *Style—* Jeremy Wallington, Esq; 6B Newell Street, Limehouse, London E14 7HR (☎ 071 987 8484); M V Josephine, Millharbour, West India Docks, London E14 9XP (☎ 071 537 2113, fax 071 537 2118)

WALLIS, Bill; s of Albert Levi Wallis (d 1967), of Farnham, Surrey, and Edith Annie Robinson (d 1985); *b* 20 Nov 1936; *Educ* Farnham GS, St John's Coll Cambridge; *m* 1, 3 Feb 1960 (m dis 1979), Jean, da of Cdr R L Spalding, RN (decd), of 10 Brambleton Ave, Farnham, Surrey; 2 c (Kathryn b 1960, Dickon b 1970); m 2, 21 Aug 1979, Jean Karen, da of A S H Mills, of Stonerdale, Steep, Hants; 2 c (Rose b 1982, Albert b 1984); *Career* comic and dramatic actor; professional debut Stratford on Avon Royal Shakespeare Theatre for two seasons (with Sir Peter Hall); W End appearances incl: Beyond the Fringe, Mrs Wilson's Diary (as Harold Wilson); numerous TV appearances; in repertory nationwide incl at: Newcastle, Leicester, Young Vic, Nat Theatre, Old Vic; established radio actor incl twenty years of BBC Radio 4 Week Ending; *Recreations* heavy reading and light drinking; *Style—* Bill Wallis, Esq

WALLIS, David Anthony; s of George Arthur Wallis (d 1950), and Marjorie Jane, *née* Faulkner (d 1940); *b* 24 Nov 1932; *Educ* Victoria Sch Watford, Goldsmiths' Coll New Cross (City and Guilds); *m* 11 Aug 1956, Edna, da of Thomas Harold Harrison (d 1977), of Croydon; *Career* Nat Serv RAF 1950-52, instrument specialist; apprentice instrument maker Charles Baker and Sons Ltd Holborn, salesman of wholesale optical prods CS Pyser Ltd of Holborn 1952-56; partnership with Pyser family formed Survey and General Instrument Co Ltd (md 1956-86), chm of Bd Pyser (Holdings) plc 1986; memb Cncl Drawing Office Material Mfrs and Dealers Assoc, former pres Photogrammetric Soc, memb UK Nat Ctee Photogrammetry and Remote Sensing; judge for Kent Exporters of the Year contest 1990-91; Freeman: City of London 1977, Worshipful Co of Scientific Instrument Makers 1977 (memb of Ct); FRGS 1981, FCIM 1986, ARICS 1988; *Recreations* golf, sea fishing; *Clubs* Shortlands Golf, City Livery, United Wards; *Style—* David A Wallis, Esq; Pyser (Holdings) plc, Fircroft Way, Edenbridge, Kent TN8 6HA (☎ 0732 864111, fax 0732 865544, car 0860 391113, telex 95527 OPTSLS G)

WALLIS, Prof David Ian; s of Leonard Stephen Wallis (d 1974), Stevenage, Herts, and Kathleen Muriel, *née* Culpin; *b* 12 March 1934; *Educ* Alleynes GS Stevenage, Downing Coll Cambridge (MA, PhD); *m* 30 April 1960, Mary Elizabeth, da of John

Cecil Ford (d 1985), of Soham, Cambs; 2 s ((David) Stephen b 1965, Dominic John b 1966), 1 da (Naomi Natasha b 1963); *Career* NATO Res Fell Univ of Pennysylvania 1959-61, sr res fell in physiology Aberdeen 1961-67; Univ of Wales Coll Cardiff: lectr in physiology 1967-71, sr lectr 1971-76, reader 1976-83, personal chair and prof 1983, head of dept 1987-, established chair and prof of physiology 1989; memb Ed Bd British Journal of Pharmacology 1981-88; memb: Physiological Soc, Br Pharmacological Soc, Brain Res Assoc; *Books* Cardiovascular Pharmacology of 5HT: Prospective Therapeutic Applications; *Recreations* painting, music; *Style—* Prof David Wallis; Dept of Physiology, University of Wales, College of Cardiff, PO Box 902, Cardiff CF1 1SS (☎ 0222 874801, telex 498635, fax 0222 371921)

WALLIS, Hon Mrs (Juliet); er da of 2 Baron Sinclair of Cleeve, OBE (d 1985); *b* 16 Oct 1951; *m* 1983, Philip Wallis, only s of A P Wallis, of Beaumont, Clacton, Essex; *Style—* The Hon Mrs Wallis

WALLIS, Prof Kenneth Frank; s of Leslie Wallis (d 1982), of Wath-on-Dearne, Yorks, and Vera Daisy, *née* Stone; *b* 26 March 1938; *Educ* Wath-on-Dearne GS, Univ of Manchester (BSc, MScTech), Stanford Univ (PhD); *m* 26 July 1963, Margaret Sheila, da of William Harold Campbell, of Churchill, Somerset; *Career* lectr and reader LSE 1966-77, professor of econometrics Univ of Warwick 1977-, dir ESRC Macroeconomic Modelling Bureau 1983-; exec memb NUS 1961-63; cncl memb: RSS 1972-76, Royal Econ Soc 1989-; chm HM Treasy Acad Panel 1987- (memb 1980-); *Books* Introductory Econometrics (1972, 1981), Topics in Applied Econometrics (1973, 1979), Models of the UK Economy 1-4 (1984-87); *Recreations* travel, music, gardening, swimming; *Style—* Prof Kenneth Wallis; Department of Economics, University of Warwick, Coventry CV4 7AL (☎ 0203 523468, telex 31406 COVLIB G, fax 0203 523032)

WALLIS, Wing Cdr Kenneth Horatio; s of Horace Samuel Wallis (d 1963), of 45A Cambridge Rd, Ely, Cambs, and Emily May, *née* Barker (d 1947); *b* 26 April 1916; *Educ* King's Sch Ely Cambs; *m* 29 April 1942, Peggy Mary, da of Maj Alan Walter Stapley (d 1968), of Surrenden, Surrenden Rd, Brighton, Sussex; 1 s (Jake b 8 Oct 1945), 2 da (Vicky b 29 July 1943, Diz b 15 Jan 1949); *Career* RAFVR AC2 1939, LAC and PO Sch of Army Cooperation 1940, PO operational pilot 268 (Lysanders) and 103 Sqdns (Wellington bombers) 1941, Flt Lt 1942-53 (operational pilot 37 Sqdn Italy 1944, permanent cmmn RAF 1945, MAP 1945, OC Armament at first Canberra Unit 1950), Sqdn Ldr 1953-58 (Air Min 1953, flying and tech exchange post Strategic Air Command HQ 1956), Wing Cdr 1958-64 (weapons offr HQ Fighter Cmd RAF 1958, OC tactical weapons gp Aeroplane and Armament Experimental estab Boscombe Down 1961, ret 1964); first pure Wallis design autogyro built and flown 1961, specialist in autogyro design construction and operation since retirement 1964; all 18 official World Records for autogyro speed range and altitude held by Wallis autogyros, further 6 Records estab by Wallis; mil experimental and film roles (You Only Live Twice, The Martian Chronicles); former dir Weslake Devpts Ltd Rye Sussex (internal combustion engine res co), memb Lloyds 1966-; pres: RAFA Wymondham branch, Norfolk and Suffolk Aviation Museum; vice pres Nat Capital Punishment Campaign; hon fell Manchester Poly 1980; CEng, FRAeS, FRSA; *Recreations* target shooting, hydroplane racing; *Clubs* Royal Air Force, Pathfind Association; *Style—* Wing Cdr Kenneth H Wallis; Reymerston Hall, Norfolk NR9 4QY (☎ 0362 850418)

WALLIS, Pamela June; da of Henry Charles Wallis (d 1954), and Annie, *née* Duffield (d 1976); *b* 27 May 1932; *Educ* St Bernard's Convent Slough Berks, AA London (AADip); *Career* chartered architect in private practice; memb AA 1957, ARIBA 1959; *Recreations* architecture, china painting, gardening, walking, water colours; *Style—* Miss Pamela Wallis; 69 Harvest Bank Rd, West Wickham, Kent BR4 9DP (☎ 081 462 4801)

WALLIS, Victor Harry; s of Harry Stewart Wallis, MBE (d 1966), and Ada Elizabeth, *née* Jarratt (d 1978); *b* 21 Dec 1922; *Educ* Wilson's GS, SOAS; *m* 1 March 1948, (Margaret) Teresa, da of Samuel Meadowcroft (d 1964); 1 s (Stewart Scott b 1949), 3 da (Nicola b 1950, Amanda b 1954, Debra Jane b 1957); *Career* enlisted Royal Scots 1941, Maj (attached Indian Army) 1942-47, Maj RARO 1947-49, TA (Intelligence Corps) 1949-54, TARO (Intelligence Corps) 1954-77; Home Office: Immigration Serv 1947-52, regnl offr 1952-58, Policy and Trg Divs 1958-67, chief trg offr 1967-68, princ estabs 1968-72, asst sec estabs 1972-80, under sec of state Fire and Police Dept 1980-82; assoc BIET 1939; *Books* many HMSO publications on home defence matters 1958-56; *Recreations* philately, military history, painting; *Clubs* Civil Service, St Stephen's Constitutional, British Legion, Old Wilsonians; *Style—* Victor Wallis, Esq; 26 Lumley Rd, Horley, Surrey RH6 7JL (☎ 0293 771925)

WALLIS-KING, Maj-Gen Colin Sainthill; CBE (1975, OBE 1971); s of Lt-Col Frank King, DSO, OBE (d 1934), of Hill House, Northrepps, nr Cromer, Norfolk, and Colline Ammabel, *née* St Hill (d 1985); *b* 13 Sept 1926; *Educ* Stowe; *m* 10 Nov 1962, Lisabeth, da of Swan P Swanstroøm (d 1970), of Oslo, Norway; 2 da (Kathrine, Marianne); *Career* HG 1942-44, enlisted Coldstream Gds 1944 (cmmnd 1945), liaison offr Fleet Air Arm 1954-56, Army Staff Coll 1960-61, Regtl Adj Coldstream Gds 1961-63, seconded to Parachute Regt 1963, ACOS G4 Comland Norway 1965-68, 2 i/c 1 Bn Coldstream Gds 1968-69, Cdr 2 Bn Coldstream Gds 1969-72, Dep Cdr 8 Inf Bde 1972, Col GS Combat Devpt MOD 1972-73, Cdr 3 Inf Bde 1973-75, Brig Intelligence MOD 1975-77, dir Serv Intelligence 1977-80, ret 1980; dir Kongsberg Ltd 1982-87, UK rep Norsk Forsvarsteknologi 1987-; churchwarden Stubbings Parish Church; *Recreations* equitation, fishing, sailing, music, cross-country skiing; *Clubs* Cavalry & Guards; *Style—* Maj-Gen C S Wallis-King, CBE; c/o Royal Bank of Scotland, 21 Gosvenor Gardens, London SW1W 0BW

WALLOP, Hon Nicholas Valoynes Bermingham; s of 9 Earl of Portsmouth (d 1984); *b* 1946; *Educ* Stowe; *m* 1969, Lavinia, da of David Karmel, CBE, QC; 1 s (Henry b 1974), 1 da (Victoria b 1972); *Career* art dealer; *Clubs* Boodles; *Style—* The Hon Nicholas Wallop; 15 Tregunter Rd, London SW10; 90 Jermyn St, London SW1Y 6JD (☎ 071 930 4221)

WALLROCK, John; s of Samuel Wallrock (d 1955), and Marie Kate Wallrock (d 1943); *b* 14 Nov 1922; *Educ* Bradfield; *m* 1967, Audrey Louise, *née* Ariow; 1 s (Giles), 2 da (Marina, Camilla); *Career* Lt RNR 1943, master mariner 1948; chm: J H Minet & Co Ltd 1972-79 (dir 1955-72), Minet Hldgs Ltd 1972-82, Conocean Int Consltts Gp Hong Kong 1984-; dir Tugu Insurance Co Hong Kong 1976-84; memb: Lloyd's Underwriting 1950-84, Cncl of Mgmnt White Ensign Assoc 1974-83; memb: Hon Co Master Mariners, Nautical Inst (MNI) 1970-; Freeman City of London 1965; *Recreations* yachting, painting; *Clubs* Royal London Yacht, Royal South Yacht, East India; *Style—* John Wallrock, Esq; Conocean Int Consltts Gp, Suite 804A, Admiralty Centre (Tower I), 18 Harcourt Rd, Hong Kong

WALLROCK, Raphael John; s of William Wallrock (d 1960), of Westcliff-on-Sea, Essex, and Julia, *née* Joseph (d 1981); ggf Austrian Count Von Tempel Wollrauch; *b* 28 Aug 1920; *Educ* Westcliff HS Essex; *m* 28 Jan 1948, Renée, da of Paul Green (d 1961); 1 da (Louise b 1949), 1 s (David b 1954); *Career* RAF 1939-45; chm Magnolia Group (Mouldings) plc 1966-90; Grantee of the Royal Warrant; FBIM 1973; *Style—* Raphael Wallrock, Esq; Magnolia Group plc, 853B London Road, Westcliff-on-Sea, Essex (☎ 0702 471118, telex 99320, fax 0702 470598)

WALLS, (William) Alan; s of Harold Walls, of 45 Whitehouse Drive, Sedgefield, Cleveland, and Marjorie, *née* Orton; *b* 18 Sept 1956; *Educ* Trinity Hall Cambridge (MA); *m* 29 July 1978, Julie, da of John Brown; 2 s (Thomas William b 4 Sept 1985, Adam Edward b 11 Feb 1991), 1 da (Rachel Hannah Louise b 8 June 1987); *Career* slr; Linklaters & Paines: articled 1979-81, slr 1981-87, ptnr 1987-, licensed insolvency practioner 1990-; memb: Int Bar Assoc, London Slrs Litigation Assoc, Assoc Européenne des Practiceans de Procedures Collectives; memb City of London Slrs Co 1987; memb Law Soc; *Recreations* walking, sailing; *Style—* Alan Walls, Esq; Mitre House, 160 Aldersgate St, London EC1A 4LP (☎ 071 606 7080, fax 071 600 2885, telex 884349/888167)

WALLS, Geoffrey Nowell; s of Andrew Nowell Walls, of Canberra, Aust, and Hilda Margaret, *née* Thompson; *b* 17 Feb 1945; *Educ* Trinity GS Melbourne Aust, Univ of Melbourne Aust (BComm); *m* 8 Aug 1975, Vanessa, da of Capt Alan John Bodger, DFC, of Boston, USA; 1 s (Robert Walls b 20 Jan 1968), 3 da (Tanya b 12 Nov 1969, Jennie b 18 Jan 1977, Sacha b 21 March 1978); *Career* 2 Lt RAAOC 1966-69, active serv S Vietman 1967-68; Aust Dip Serv: asst trade cmmr (Bahrain, Cairo, Singapore, Jakarta, Mecas) 1970-75, trade cmmr Manila 1975-76, asst dir ME section Dept of Trade and Resources Canberra 1976-78, trade cmmr Baghdad 1978-79, regnl dir Adelaide Cwlth Depts of Trade and Indust and Commerce 1980-83; gen mangr central region ATCO Industs Aust 1983-86, agent gen State of S Aust London 1986-; *Recreations* gardening, golf, reading, tennis; *Clubs* RAC, East India; *Style—* Geoffrey Walls, Esq; 53 Chiddingstone St, London SW6 3TQ (☎ 071 371 5988); South Australia House, 50 Strand, London WC2N 5LW (☎ 071 930 7471, fax 01 930 1660, car 0836 588056)

WALLS, Stephen Roderick; s of Ronald William Walls (d 1982); *b* 8 Aug 1947; *Educ* Morecombe GS; *m* 1971, Lynette Janice; 1 s (Roderick William b 28 Jan 1976); *Career* articled clerk Tyson Westall & Co 1963-69, audit sr Deloitte & Co 1969-71, fin planning exec Lindustries Ltd 1971-74, gp fin exec Vernons Ltd 1974-75; Chesebrough Ponds Inc: area fin dir Africa 1975-77, fin dir UK 1977-80, fin dir Europe 1980-81, vice pres fin US and Worldwide 1981-87; fin dir, md and chief exec designate Plessey Co plc 1987-89, chm and chief exec Wiggins Teape Appleton plc 1989-; FCA; *Recreations* running, squash, music; *Clubs* RAC; *Style—* Stephen Walls, Esq; Wiggins Teape Appleton plc, Gateway House, Basingstoke, Hants RG21 2EE (☎ 0256 842020, fax 0256 840068, telex 858031)

WALLWORK, Geoffrey James; s of James Albert Wallwork (d 1986), and Winifred Mary, *née* Dyke; *b* 14 March 1941; *Educ* Boteler GS Warrington, Manchester GS; *m* 5 Aug 1967, Sheila Margaret, da of late Frank Oakley; 1 s (Andrew James b 30 July 1969), 2 da (Rachel Anne b 27 Nov 1971, Susan Catherine b 5 Jan 1978); *Career* CA; articled clerk Walton Watts and Co Manchester 1959, ptnr Thornton Baker & Co (became Grant Thornton) 1976-; Manchester Soc of Chartered Accountants: treas 1986-89, dep pres 1989-90, pres 1990-91; FCA (ACA 1965); *Recreations* DIY, gardening, travel; *Style—* Geoffrey Wallwork, Esq; Grant Thornton, Heron House, Albert Square, Manchester M2 5HD (☎ 061 834 5414, fax 061 832 6042, car 0831 578423)

WALLWORK, John; s of Thomas Wallwork, and Vera, *née* Reid; *b* 8 July 1946; *Educ* Accrington GS, Univ of Edinburgh (BSc, MB CHB), Univ of Cambridge (MA); *m* 1973, Elizabeth (Ann), da of John Selwyn Medley (d 1988), of New Plymouth, NZ; 1 s (Nicolas b 25 March 1982), 2 da (Sarah b 18 April 1977, Alice b 9 May 1989); *Career* surgical registrar Royal Infirmary Edinburgh 1975-76; sr registrar: Royal Infirmary Glasgow 1978-79, Bart's 1979-81, Adelaide Hosp S Aust 1977-78; chief res in cardiovascular and cardiac transplant surgery Stanford Univ 1980-81, currently Papworth Hosp Cambs; memb: Regnl Cardiac and Cardiothoracic Advsy Gp, Regnl Specialities Advsy Ctee, DHSS Multi-Organ Allocation Gp, Br Transplant Soc, Cardiac Soc, Int Soc for Cardiac Transplantation, Scot Thoracic Soc, Soc of Thoracic and Cardiovascular Surgns of GB and Ireland, Euro Assoc for Cardio-Thoracic Surgery, Cardiac Res Club, Transplant Soc, Euro Soc for Organ Transplantation, Paediatric Intensive Care Soc; pres: Euro Heart Transplant Soc; Lister Professorship (RCSEd) 1985-86; FRCSEd; *Books* Heart Disease: What it is and How it is Treated (1987), Heart and Heart-Lung Transplantation (1989); *Clubs* Caledonian; *Style—* John Wallwork, Esq; Papworth Hospital, Papworth Everards, Cambs CB3 8RE (☎ 0480 830541, fax 0480 831114)

WALMSLEY, Dr Katharine Mary; da of David Robert Walmsley, of Ickleford, Hitchin, Herts, and Muriel Jean, *née* McKelvie; *b* 5 May 1948; *Educ* Hitchin Girl's GS, Univ of Bristol (MB ChB); *m* 23 Sept 1972 (m dis 1990), Dr (John) Roy Davies; 2 da (Claire b 1980, Angharad b 1984); *Career* conslt radiologist: UCH 1979-, Royal Free Hosp 1979-, King Edward VII's Hosp 1985-; FRCR 1977; *Recreations* my family; *Style—* Dr Katharine Walmsley; Flat 6, Harmont House, 20 Harley St, London W1N 1AL (☎ 071 580 1442)

WALMSLEY, Kevin James Thomas; s of James Walmsley, and Evelyn Grace, *née* Bunnett; *b* 20 Aug 1959; *Educ* Runshaw Coll Lancs, Univ of Liverpool (BA Hons); *m* 30 June 1990, Dr Sara Rosalind, da of Raymond Percy Luck, JP (d 1982); *Career* King & Co CAs; cncllr Dartford Borough Cncl (Gundulf Ward) 1983-; memb Ctees: Policy, Planning, Contracts, Resources, Dartforce, Housing, Performance, Mgmnt, Fin and Personnel (chm); Dartford Cons Assoc: treas 1986-87, dep chm 1987-89, chm 1989-; prospective Cons Party Parly Candidate Woolwich Constituency 1989-; memb Cons Party 1974-; *Recreations* travel, walking, current affairs, reading, photography, gardening; *Style—* Kevin Walmsley, Esq; Dartford Conservative Assoc, 17 Highfield Rd, Dartford, Kent DA1 2JS (☎ 0322 220704); Dartford Borough Council, Civic Centre, Home Gardens, Dartford, Kent DA1 1DR; King & Co Chartered Accountants, 12 Fife Rd, Kingston Upon Thames, Surrey KT1 1SZ (☎ 081 546 7562, fax 081 541 1387)

WALMSLEY, Peter James; MBE (1975); s of George Stanley Walmsley (d 1985), of Cringle, Whyteleafe, Surrey, and Elizabeth, *née* Martin (d 1977); *b* 29 April 1929; *Educ* Caterham Sch, Royal Sch of Mines, Imperial Coll London (BSc, ARSM); *m* 1, 1958 (m dis 1967), Jane Mary, *née* Budgen; 1 s, 1 da; m 2, 1970, Edna, *née* Gallagher; 2 step s; *Career* geologist: Iraq Petroleum Co 1951-59, BP Trinidad 1959-65, BP London 1965-72; exploration mangr BP Aberdeen 1972-78, dep chief geologist BP London 1978-79, regnl exploration mangr BP London 1979-81; dir petroleum engrg div Dept of Energy 1981-87 (dir gen 1987); chm Petroleum Exploration Soc of GB 1971-72; ret 1990; *Style—* Peter Walmsley, Esq, MBE; Elm Tree Cottage, 10 Great Austins, Farnham, Surrey GU9 8JG (☎ 0252 715622)

WALMSLEY, Dr Thomas; s of Prof Robert Walmsley, of St Andrews, and Isabel, *née* Mathieson; *b* 15 Aug 1946; *Educ* Fettes, Univ of Dundee (MB ChB), Univ of Edinburgh (DPM); *m* 1, 1973 (m dis 1981), (Felicity) Jane, da of Dr E G Walsh, of Edinburgh; 1 da (Anna b 24 May 1976); m 2, 1981, Linda Ann, da of G D Hardwick, of Arbroath, Scotland; 2 s (William George b 27 March 1987, Christpher Robert (Kit) b 31 March 1990); *Career* lectr in psychiatry Univ of Edinburgh 1975-77, conslt psychiatrist Royal Edinburgh Hosp 1977-81 (hon sr lectr 1977-81), conslt psychiatrist Southampton and SW Hants Health Authy 1981-, psychiatric tutor Knowle Hosp 1983-; MRCPsych 1974; *Recreations* reading, railways, maps; *Style—* Dr Thomas Walmsley; Beachcombers, Beeches Hill, Bishops Waltham, Hants SO3 1FF; Knowle Hosp, Fareham, Hants PO17 5NA (☎ 0329 832271)

WALPOLE, Dowager Baroness; Nancy Louisa; *née* Jones; OBE, JP (Norfolk 1941); yst da of late Frank Harding Jones, of 21 Abingdon Court, London W8; *m* 14 July 1937, 9 Baron Walpole (d 1989); 1 s (10 Baron), 1 da (Hon Mrs Phillida Hurn) and 1 s and 1 da decd; *Career* pres Norfolk Red Cross for 25 yrs, now patron; *Style*— The Rt Hon Nancy, Lady Walpole, OBE, JP; Wolterton Hall, Norwich, Norfolk NR11 7LY (☎ 0263 761210, 0263 77274)

WALPOLE, 10 Baron (GB 1723); Robert Horatio Walpole; JP (Norfolk); also 8 Baron Walpole of Wolterton (GB 1756); patron of 6 livings; s of 9 Baron Walpole, TD (d 1989); *b* 8 Dec 1938; *Educ* Eton, King's Coll Cambridge (BA, MA, Dip Agric); *m* 1, 30 June 1962 (m dis 1979), (Sybil) Judith, yr da of late Theodore Thomas Schofield, of Harpenden, Herts; 2 s (Hon Jonathan Robert Hugh b Nov 16 1967, Hon Benedict Thomas Orford b 1 June 1969), 2 da (Hon Alice Louise b 1 Sept 1963, Hon Emma Judith b 10 Oct 1964); m 2, 1980, Laurel Celia, o da of Sidney Tom Ball, of Swindon, Wilts; 2 s (Hon Roger Horatio Calibut b 1980, Hon Henry William b 1982), 1 da (Hon Grace Mary b 1986); *Heir* s, Hon Jonathan Robert Hugh Walpole; *Style*— The Rt Hon the Lord Walpole, JP; Mannington Hall, Norwich, Norfolk NR11 7BB

WALSER, Ven David; s of Rev William Walser (d 1952, formerly vicar of Imber, Wilts), and Eleanor Marguerite Davida, *née* Corelli (d 1923); *b* 12 March 1923; *Educ* Clayesmore Sch, St Edmund Hall Oxford (MA, Dip Theol), St Stephen's House Oxford; *m* 15 Nov 1975, Elizabeth Enid, da of James Francis Shillito, of Old Forge, Staple Cross, Robertsbridge, Sussex; *Career* RA, Capt Royal Indian Artillery served UK, India, Burma, French Indo-China, Malaya 1942-46; ordained: deacon 1950, priest 1951; curate St Gregory's Horfield, vice princ St Stephen's House 1954-60, chaplain the King's Sch Ely and minor canon of Ely Cathedral 1961-71, vicar of Linton Cambs 1971-81, rector Bartlow Cambs 1973-81, rural dean of Linton 1976-81, rector of St Botolph's Cambridge 1981-89, archdeacon of Ely 1981-; hon canon Ely Cathedral 1981-, priest i/c St Clements Cambridge 1985-89; *Recreations* hill walking, caravanning, music, hymn-writing; *Style*— The Ven the Archdeacon of Ely; St Botolph's Rectory, Summerfield, Cambridge CB3 9HE (☎ 0223 350684)

WALSH, Andrew Geoffrey; s of Dr Geoffrey Parkin Walsh, of Blackburn, Lancs, and Dorothy, *née* Baldwin; *b* 26 July 1954; *Educ* Westholme Sch Blackburn, Queen Elizabeth GS Blackburn, Magdalen Coll Oxford (MA), Trinity Hall Cambridge (LLB); *m* 1, (m dis); m 2, Sept 1989, Emma Belmonte; *Career* articled clerk Payne Hicks Beach 1977-79, asst slr Norton Rose Botterell and Roche 1979-83, ptnr McKenna and Co Slrs 1986- (asst slr 1983-86); memb City of London Slrs Co; *Books* Global Mergers and Acquisitions (chapter, 1988), The Companies Bill (1989); *Recreations* soccer, squash, cycling, visiting historic churches and buildings, theatre; *Clubs* Cannons; *Style*— Andrew Walsh, Esq; Mitre House, 160 Aldesgate St, London EC1A 4DD (☎ 071 606 9000, fax 071 606 9100, telex 27251)

WALSH, Arthur Stephen; CBE; s of Wilfrid Walsh (d 1977), and Doris, *née* Gregory; *b* 16 Aug 1926; *Educ* Midsomer Norton GS Somerset, Selwyn Coll Cambridge (MA); *m* 1 (m dis 1983), Gwendoline Mary; 1 s (Gordon Thomas b 1962), 1 da (Catherine Mary b 1964); m 2, Feb 1984, Judith Marth, da of Paul Balmer (d 1983), of Johannesburg, SA; *Career* md: Marconi Space and Defence Systems 1969-82, The Marconi Group 1982-85; dir GEC 1983 (various sr posts 1952-69), chm STC plc 1989- (chief exec 1985-), chm Unitel; Hon DSc Univ of Ulster 1988; FEng 1980, FIEE; *Recreations* sailing and skiing; *Clubs* Little Ship; *Style*— Arthur Walsh, Esq, CBE; STC plc, 16 Portland Place, London W1N 3AA (☎ 071 323 1000, fax 071 323 1000 ext 247)

WALSH, Brian; s of Lt-Col Percy Walsh (d 1978), of Leeds, and Sheila, *née* Frais (d 1988); *b* 17 June 1935; *Educ* Leeds GS, Gonville and Caius Coll Cambridge (BA, LLB, pres of the Union); *m* 19 August 1964, Susan Margaret, da of Eli Kay Frieze (d 1985), of H Leeds; 2 da (Belinda Dayane b 8 June 1967, Alyson Gay b 28 May 1969); *Career* served as Pilot Offr RAF 1954-56; called to the Bar Middle Temple 1961, Blackstone entrance scholar, Harmsworth law scholar, bencher 1988; joined N Eastern Circuit 1961, recorder of the Crown Court 1972, ldr N Eastern Circuit 1990-; govr: Leeds GS 1977, Leeds Girls' HS 1978, chm Yorkshire CCC 1986- (memb Ctee 1984-); *Recreations* golf, cricket, music; *Clubs* National Liberal; *Style*— Brian Walsh, Esq; Park Court Chambers, 40 Park Cross St, Leeds LS1 2QH (☎ 0532 433277, fax 0532 421285, telex 666135)

WALSH, Colin Stephen; *b* 26 Jan 1955; *Educ* Portsmouth GS, Ch Ch Oxford (MA); *Career* asst organist Salisbury Cathedral 1978-85, organist and master of the music St Albans Cathedral 1985-88, organist and master of the Choristers Lincoln Cathedral 1988-; conductor Lincoln Choral Soc; has given many organ recitals in UK and overseas: French organ music from Salisbury 1985, French organ music from St Albans 1987, Great European Organ Series Lincoln Cathedral 1989; ARCM 1972, FRCO 1977; *Recreations* walking, dining out, travel; *Style*— Colin Walsh, Esq; 12 Minster Yard, Lincoln LN2 1PJ (☎ 0522 532877)

WALSH, (Bernard) David James; TD (1956); s of Maj Bernard John Merlin Walsh (d 1928), of Stourbank, Nayland, Suffolk, and Violet Jennie, *née* Pearson (d 1973); *b* 12 July 1923; *Educ* Eton, Trinity Hall Cambridge; *m* 28 Aug 1954, (Gladys) Angela Margot, da of Maj Henry Berry Lees, MC (d 1967), of Stour House, Nayland, Suffolk; 3 da (Sarah (Mrs Blake) b 1955, Jenny (Mrs Pickford) b 1957, Charlotte (Mrs Johnston) b 1960); *Career* WWII RA 1943, cmmnd 1944, serv Field and Medium Regts in UK 1944-45, instr Army Signal Sch India 1945 (cmd Artillery & Engrg Wing 1946-47), 304 Essex Yeo RHA Field Regt RA (UK) 1948-57, ret Maj 1957; called to the Bar Inner Temple 1952; private practice and SE Circuit 1954-62 and 1974-81, Govt Legal Serv (MPNI) 1962-63, asst registrar Criminal Appeals 1969-74 (dep asst registrar 1963-69), standing counsel for DHSS 1979-81, chm Social Security Appeal Tbnls 1983-; author of various articles in Railway Magazine and other periodicals; pres: Stour Valley Railway Preservation Soc 1990-, Gt Eastern Railway Soc 1973-; chm Consultative Panel for the Preservation of Br Tport Relics 1977-82 (hon sec and treas 1958-61), hon sec Essex Yeo Assoc 1981-, pres Railway Club 1982- (hon sec 1951-68, vice pres 1968-82); *Books* The Stour Valley Railway (1971); *Recreations* study of railway operating and history, photography; *Clubs* Carlton, Railway; *Style*— B D J Walsh, Esq, TD; The Old Rectory, Burgate, Diss, Norfolk IP22 1QD

WALSH, Dennis Maxton; OBE, JP; s of Walter Walsh (d 1947), of Bradford, W Yorks, and Edith, *née* Gorrod (d 1955); *b* 28 Dec 1925; *Educ* Hanson HS; *m* (m dis); 1 da (Moira Kay); *Career* travel agent; chm: Briggs and Hill (Insur Conslts) Ltd, Training for Bradford Ltd; princ Briggs and Hill World Travel Serv; former pres Bradford C of C, former pres Nat Assoc of Ind Travel Agents, former pres and chm ABTA, chm Bradford Magistrates 1985; FTS; *Recreations* foreign travel, walking; *Style*— Dennis Walsh, Esq, OBE, JP; Wellfield Cottage, Lane Side, West Scholes, Queensbury, W Yorks BD13 1NE; Briggs and Hill, 20 Rawson Place, Bradford, W Yorks BD1 3QN (☎ 0274 724167)

WALSH, Hon Jane Emily Mary; da of 5 Baron Ormathwaite, MVO (d 1944); *b* 1910; *Career* lady-in-waiting to HRH Princess Alice Duchess of Gloucester 1969-75; *Style*— The Hon Jane Walsh; 13 Mount St, London W1

WALSH, Dr John; *b* 9 Dec 1937; *Educ* Phillip Exeter Acad New Hampshire, Yale (Ranking schoalr, BA), Univ of Columbia (faculty scholar, President's fell, Frederick J E Woodbridge hon fell, Fulbright graduate fell, MA, PhD), Univ of Leyden The Netherlands; *m* 1962, Virginia Alys, *née* Galston; 3 c; *Career* US Naval Reserve 1957-63 (active duty Petty Offr 3 Class on USS Fiske 1957-59); lectr and res asst The Frick Collection 1966-68; Met Museum of Art: assoc for higher educn 1968-71, assoc curator Dept of Europe Paintings 1970-72 (curator 1972-74, vice chm 1974-75); Columbia Univ: lectr in art history 1969-70, adjunct assoc prof of art history 1970-72, adjunct prof 1972-75; prof of art history Barnard Coll and Columbia Univ 1975-77, Mrs Russell W Baker Curator of Paintings Museum of Fine Arts Boston 1977-83, visiting prof of Fine Arts Harvard Univ 1979, dir J Paul Getty Museum 1983-; memb Editorial Bd: Metropolitan Museum Journal 1970-75, Art Bulletin 1987-; memb: Museum Panel New York State Cncl on Fine Arts 1974-77, Governing Bd Yale Univ Art Gallery 1975-, Tstee Ctee on Educn Museum of Modern Art 1976-, Cmmr's Panel on Art Internal Revenue Service 1979-81, Indemnity Panel Nat Endowment for the Arts 1981-84; memb Advsy Bd: Int Fndn for Art Res 1975-, Gazette des Beaux-Arts 1980-; dir: The Museums Collaborative NY 1976-77, Arts International Inc 1979-87; dir and memb Exec Ctee Coll Art Assoc of America 1979-81; memb Visiting Ctee: Sherman Fairchild Paintings Conservation Center Met Museum of Art 1980-, Harvard Univ Art Museums 1981-; pres Assoc of Art Museum Dirs 1989-90 (memb 1983-); memb: American Antiquarian Soc 1984-, Bd of Fellows Claremont Graduate School 1989-; author of numerous catalogues and articles in art jls; *Style*— John Walsh, Esq; J Paul Getty Museum, PO Box 2112, Santa Monica, Calif 90406 USA FOREIGN

WALSH, John Henry Martin; s of Martin Walsh (d 1986), of Galway, Eire, and Anne, *née* Durkin; *b* 24 Oct 1953; *Educ* Wimbledon Coll, Exeter Coll Oxford (BA), Univ Coll Dublin (MA); partner Carolyn Hart; 1 da (Sophie Matilda Hart-Walsh b 11 Aug 1987); *Career* journalist 1978-; Advtg Dept The Tablet, Gollancz publishers 1977-78, assoc ed The Director Magazine 1978-82; freelance feature writer and reviewer for various newspapers and magazines incl: The Times, The Independent, Time Out, Tatler, London Portrait, Executive Travel, Books and Bookmen; lit ed then features and lit ed Evening Standard 1986-88, lit ed and feature writer The Sunday Times 1988-; *Books* Growing Up Catholic (1989); *Recreations* drinking, talking, planning impractical journeys to impossible destinations; *Clubs* Groucho's; *Style*— John Walsh, Esq; Books Dept, Sunday Times, 1 Pennington St, London E1 (☎ 071 782 5770)

WALSH, Dr John James; s of Thomas Walsh (d 1927), of Beaufort, Monmouthshire, and Margaret, *née* O'Sullivan (d 1972); *b* 4 July 1917; *Educ* Mungret Coll Limerick, Univ Coll Cork (MB BCh, BAO, MD); *m* 23 Feb 1946, Joan Mary, da of Henry Teasdale Birks (d 1950), of Four Oaks, Ashley Park Rd, Walton on Thames, Surrey; 3 s (James, Jeremy, John), 1 da (Jacqueline); *Career* hon conslt to med centre for paraplegia (Ireland) 1961, dir Nat Spinal Injuries Centre Stoke Mandeville Bucks 1966-77, conslt to Paraplegic Unit Paddocks Private Hosp Princes Risborough Bucks 1972-; memb Spinal Injuries Assoc; memb RSM, MRCP 1968, FRCS 1969; *Books* Paraplegia (1964); *Recreations* fishing, reading; *Style*— Dr John Walsh; Alena, Bridge St, Great Kimble, Aylesbury, Burks HP17 9TN (☎ 08444 3347); Paddocks Private Hospital, Aylesbury Rd, Princes Risborough, Bucks HP 17 OJS (☎ 08444 6951, fax 08444 4521, telex 837145 PAD HOS G)

WALSH, Jonathan George Michael; s of Charles Arthur Walsh (d 1978), of Surrey, and Joan Violet Braidwood, *née* Allen (d 1969); *b* 21 April 1944; *Educ* Eton, Sorbonne Univ; *m* 24 Feb 1968, Angela Mary, da of Rear-Adm Sir Anthony Cecil Capel Miers, VC, KBE, CB, DSO (d 1985); 4 s (David b 1969, William b 1971, James b 1974, Harry b 1981); *Career* admitted slr 1969, ptnr Joynson-Hicks London; Freeman City of London 1982, Liveryman Worshipful Co of Tin Plate Workers 1982; memb Law Soc 1969; *Recreations* real tennis, lawn tennis, shooting; *Clubs* Boodle's, Queen's, Hurlingham, MCC; *Style*— Jonathan Walsh, Esq; Quarley Down House, Cholderton, nr Salisbury, Wilts SP4 ODZ and 2 Wymond St, London SW15 1DY (☎ 081 788 9907); Taylor Joynson Garrett, 10 Maltravers St, London WC2 (☎ 071 836 8456, fax 071 379 7196, telex 268014 JHICKS G)

WALSH, Michael Jeffrey; s of Kenneth Francis Walsh, of Alford, Lincs, and Edith, *née* Hudson; *b* 1 Oct 1949; *Educ* Hulme GS Oldham, Univ of Durham; *m* Sally, da of Rev Ronald Forbes Shaw; 1 s, 1 da; *Career* advertising exec; Young & Rubicam: graduate trainee 1972, account exec 1972-74, account mangr 1974-78, account dir 1978-80, dir Bd 1980-81, new business dir 1981-82, mgmnt supervisor 1982, memb Exec Ctee 1982; Ogilvy & Mather: dir Bd and mgmnt supervisor 1983-84, head of account mgmnt 1984-85, dir of client service 1985-86, dep md 1986, md 1986-89, elected to Worldwide Bd 1989, chm 1989-90, UK Gp chm 1990-; Chm Alkrington Young Conservatives 1966-67, memb Constituency Parliamentary Selection Ctee 1966-67, Shadow Chancellor Youth Parliament 1967; MInstD, memb Mktg Group Club of GB; *Recreations* collecting Victorian & Edwardian children's books, antiques, tennis, sailing, golf; *Clubs* RSPB, RAC, Hunstanton Golf, Marks, Annabel's, Lawn Tennis Assoc; *Style*— Michael Walsh, Esq; Ogilvy & Mather, Brettenham House, Lancaster Place, London WC2E 7EZ (☎ 071 836 2466)

WALSH, Moya Christine; da of John Patrick Gray-Walsh (d 1986), and Margaret Mary, *née* Vickers; *b* 31 Oct 1954; *Educ* Notre Dame Convent Cobham Surrey, Oxford Poly (BA); *m* 10 May 1986, Mark William Harcourt Cuthbert, s of Nicholas Harcourt Cuthbert; *Career* pub relations conslt 1987-, memb Amnesty Int; *Recreations* tennis, travel, gardening; *Clubs* Dorking Tennis and Squash; *Style*— Ms Moya Walsh

WALSH, Dr Nigel Dennis; s of Arthur Edward Walsh, MBE (d 1974), and Lilian Freda, *née* Schmidt; *b* 17 Oct 1928; *Educ* Epsom, St Georges Hosp Med Sch London; *m* 29 Sept 1956, Walburga Ann, da of George Haywood (d 1941); 1 s (Philip b 1965), 3 da (Victoria b 1957, Rosamund b 1961, Elizabeth b 1962); *Career* Maj RAMC 1952-54, served E Africa; conslt in pharmaceutical med; med dir: Parke Davis and Co UK 1971-79, Warner Lambert International 1981-87; hon med offr Dorrigo Hosp NSW Aust 1966-69; RSM; *Style*— Dr Nigel D Walsh; Steppes, Mill House, Bodenham Moor, Hereford HR1 3HS (☎ 056884 404)

WALSH, Lt-Col Noel Perrings; s of John Walsh (d 1937), of Emsworth, Hants, and Nancy, *née* Perrings (d 1953); *b* 25 Dec 1919; *Educ* Purbrook Park GS, Open Univ (BA), currently at Univ of Birmingham; *m* 1, 9 July 1945, Olive Mary (d 1987), da of Thomas Walsh (d 1921), of Waterford, Eire; 3 s (John b 1947, Richard b 1950, Colin b 1960), 1 da (Mary b 1954); m 2, 27 June 1988, Mary Ruth, da of Rev Reginald David Morgan Hughes (d 1956); *Career* WWII 2 Lt RA Aug 1940-42, Capt RA 1942 (India, Arakan, Burma); Capt 33 Airborne Regt RA BAOR 1949, Staff Coll 1950, Maj DAQMG 52 (Lowland Div 1951-53), 53 LAA Regt RA BAOR 1953-55, GSO 2 RA HQ BAOR 1955-57, 58 Medium Regt RA 1951-61, GSO2 PR WO 1961-64, Lt Col GSO1 PR MOD 1964-66; Civil Serv: princ MPBW 1966-69, sr princ dir Far East 1969-71, regnl dir Midlands 1971-76, under sec dir of home regnl serv DOE 1976-80; vice chm: SSAFA W Midlands (Central) Branch 1990-, Midland Study Centre for Building Team 1982-90; chm: West Midland Regn CIOB 1988-90; govr Henry Thornton Sch Clapham 1977-80, Westminster Diocese Handicapped Childrens Soc 1966-69; FCIOB 1973, FBIM 1980, FRSA 1986; *Recreations* economic history, gardening, railway modelling; *Clubs* Naval and Military, Edgbaston Priory (Birmingham); *Style*— Lt-Col Noel Walsh; 25 Oakfield Rd, Selly Park, Birmingham B29 7HH (☎ 021 472 2031)

WALSH, (Mary) Noelle (Mrs Heslam); da of Thomas Walsh, and Mary Kate, *née* Ferguson; *b* 26 Dec 1954; *Educ* Univ of East Anglia (BA); *m* 15 Oct 1988, David Howard Heslam, s of Capt James William Heslam; 1 da (Ciara b 15 Aug 1989); *Career*

news ed Cosmopolitan Magazine 1979-85, ed Good Housekeeping Magazine 1987-(dep ed, 1985-1987), memb 300 Gp; *Books* Hot Lips, The Ultimate Kiss and Tell Guide (1985), Ragtime to Wartime: The Best of Good Housekeeping 1922-1939 (1986), The Home Front: The Best of Good Housekeeping 1939-1945 (1987), Good Housekeeping: The Christmas Book (1988), Food Glorious Food: Eating and Drinking with Good Housekeeping 1922-42 (1990), Things My Mother Should Have Told Me: The Best of Good Housekeeping 1922-40 (1991); *Recreations* gardening, bargain hunting, antiques, sailing; *Clubs* Network; *Style*— Miss Noelle Walsh; 72 Broadwick St, London W1V 2BP (☎ 071 439 5247, telex 071 263 879, fax 071 439 5591)

WALSH, Paul Anthony Matthew; s of Samual Dominic Egnatius Walsh, of Bexley, Kent, and June Mary, *née* Dean; *b* 1 Oct 1962; *Educ* St Thomas A Becket Secdy Sch, Woolwich Poly; *m* 29 June 1990, Beverley Marie, da of Ronald Clifford Nickolos; *Career* professional footballer; debut: Charlton Athletic FC 1980 (97 League and 13 Cup appearances), Luton FC 1982 (80 League and 4 Cup appearances, 29 goals scored), Liverpool FC 1984 (77 League and 34 Cup appearances, 37 goals scored, League Champions 1985/86, European Cup runners up 1984/85, Littlewood Cup runners up 1986/87), Tottenham Hotspur FC 1988 (89 League and 14 Cup appearances, 16 goals scored); rep: Eng Youth (10 caps), Eng U21 (7 caps), Eng (5 caps); Professional Footballers Assoc: Young Player of the Year 1982-83, All Star Team 1982-83; *Style*— Paul Walsh, Esq; Tottenham Hotspur FC, 748 High Rd, Tottenham, London N17 OAP

WALSH, Peter Anthony Joseph; s of Michael Walsh, of Yorkshire, and Eileen, *née* Duffy; *b* 24 May 1956; *Educ* Ushaw Coll Durham, London Univ (LLB); *Career* barr 1978; memb: MENCAP, Action Aid; *Recreations* skiing, music, tennis, swimming, cycling; *Clubs* Little Ship, Naval; *Style*— Peter Walsh, Esq; Queen Elizabeth Building, Temple, London, EC4, (☎ 071 353 7181)

WALSH, Peter Banbury; s of Raymond Nevile Walsh (d 1950), and Kathleen Mary, *née* Banbury (d 1973); *b* 18 June 1936; *Educ* Cranleigh, New Coll Oxford (BA); *Career* ptnr Coopers & Lybrand Deloitte CAs 1970-; FCA; *Style*— Peter Walsh, Esq; 28 Shawfield St, London SW3 4BD (☎ 071 351 4290); Coopers & Lybrand Deloitte, Plumtree Ct, London EC4A 4HT (☎ 071 822 4602, fax 071 822 4652)

WALSH, Prof (Patrick Gerard) Peter; s of Peter Walsh (d 1985), and Joanna, *née* Fitzpatrick (d 1975); *b* 16 Aug 1923; *Educ* Preston Catholic Coll, Univ of Liverpool (BA, MA); *m* 18 July 1953, Eileen Benson, da of William Friel Quin (d 1979); 4 s (Anthony b 1954, Stephen b 1960, John b 1964, David b 1967), 1 da (Patricia b 1957); *Career* Intelligence Corps 1944-46; lectr in ancient classics Univ Coll Dublin 1952-59, lectr, reader and prof Dept of Humanity Univ of Edinburgh 1959-72, prof of humanity Univ of Glasgow 1972- (dean Faculty of Arts 1985-88); visiting prof Toronto 1966, Yale 1970, Univ of N Carolina 1978, Georgetown 1989; FRSE 1982; *Books* Livy, His Historical Aims and Methods (1961), Letters, Poems of Paulinus of Nola (1966), The Roman Novel (1970), Thirty Poems from the Carmina Burana (1974), Andreas Capellanus On Love (1982), Tragedies of George Buchanan (1982); edns of Livy: XXI (1973), XXVI to XXVII (1982), XXVII to XXX (1986); edn of William of Newburgh 1 (with M J Kennedy, 1988); *Recreations* tennis, travel; *Style*— Prof Peter Walsh; 17 Broom Rd, Glasgow G43 2TP (☎ 041 637 4977); Dept of Classics, Univ of Glasgow, Glasgow G12 8QQ (☎ 041 339 8855 ext 4383)

WALSH, Hon Mrs (Sarah Louise); *née* Wedderburn; da of Baron Wedderburn of Charlton by his 1 w, Nina, da of Dr Myer Salaman; *b* 1954; *m* 1975, Michael Walsh; *Style*— The Hon Mrs Walsh; 76 Cromwell Avenue, London N6

WALSH SPILLER, John Anthony; MBE (1979); s of Clive Henry Spiller, of The Warren, Northam, Devonshire, and Sarah, *née* Walsh (d 1988); *b* 29 Dec 1942; *Educ* Bideford Sch, N Devon Tech Coll, Bideford Art Coll; *m* 1 Sept 1972, Angela, da of Surtees Gleghorn (d 1971); 1 s (Ben b 23 Feb 1976), 1 da (Sarah b 16 July 1974); *Career* chm Devon Young Liberals 1960-62, asst agent to Mark (Lord) Bonham-Carter Torrington Parly Constituency 1962-64, constituency agent Cornwall N Parly Constituency to John W Pardoe, MP 1965-71; N regnl organiser and election agent: (Rochdale By-Election) to Cyril Smith, MP (Berwick-upon-Tweed By-Election) to Alan Beith, MP 1972-; nat agent Lib Central Assoc 1973-78, advsr to J Nkome African Peoples Union Zimbabwe (Independence Elections) 1979-80, marginal seats advsr (UK) Lib Pty 1981-82, sec gen Lib Pty 1983-86, liaison offr for Devonshire PHAB 1991; nat pres Assoc of Lib Agents and Organisers 1983-84; memb: Bd Mgmnt Gladstone Benevolent Fund 1980-91, Amnesty Int, Shelter, Nat Assoc of CABs (Devon), PHAB (UK), RNLI (S West); *Recreations* travel, growing roses, watching amateur boxing, music (folk); *Style*— John Walsh Spiller, Esq, MBE; 5 Royston Rd, Bideford, Devonshire EX39 3AN (☎ 0237 477173); Keogh, Moycullen, County Galway, Eire; 38 Belvedere Rd, Taunton, Somerset TA1 1HD (☎ 0823 251004)

WALSHAM, Rear Adm Sir John Scarlett Warren; 4 Bt (UK 1831), of Knill Court, Herefordshire, CB (1963), OBE (1944); s of Sir John Walsham, 3 Bt (d 1940), by his w Bessie (gda of Sir John Warren, 4 Bt); *b* 29 Nov 1910; *Educ* Rugby; *m* 1936, Sheila Christina, da of late Cdr Bertrand Bannerman, DSO, RN, and herself 2 cous of Sir David Bannerman, 13 Bt; 1 s, 2 da; *Heir* s, Timothy John Walsham b 26 April 1939; *Career* Lt RN 1933, Cdr 1944, Capt 1953, chief engr Singapore Dockyard 1956, CO RNEC Plymouth, Adm Supt HM Dockyard Portsmouth, Rear Adm 1961, ret 1965; *Style*— Rear Adm Sir John Walsham, Bt, CB, OBE; Priory Cottage, Middle Coombe, Shaftesbury, Dorset

WALSINGHAM, 9 Baron (GB 1780); John de Grey; MC (1951); patron of 3 livings; s of 8 Baron Walsingham, DSO, OBE, JP, DL (d 1965, half-n of 6 Baron, FRS considered by some the best game shot of his generation; *b* 21 Feb 1925; *Educ* Wellington, Aberdeen Univ, Magdalen Coll Oxford (MA), Royal Mil Coll of Sci; *m* 30 July 1963, Wendy, er da of Edward Sidney Hoare; 1 s, 2 da (Hon Sarah b 1964, Hon Elizabeth b 1966); *Heir* s, Hon Robert de Grey, b 21 June 1969; *Career* Lt-Col RA; co dir; landowner and farmer; hon life memb Mark Twain Soc (for contributions to peace); FInstD; *Recreations* etymology; *Clubs* Army and Navy, Special Forces, Farmers, Norfolk; *Style*— The Rt Hon the Lord Walsingham, MC; Merton Hall, nr Watton, Thetford, Norfolk IP25 6QJ (☎ 0953 881226, office 0953 883370, fax 0953 881431)

WALSTON, Baron (Life Peer UK 1961), of Newton, Co Cambridge; Henry David Leonard George Walston; CVO (1976), JP (Cambridge 1944); s of Sir Charles Walston (formerly Waldstein) (d 1927), and Florence, da of David L Einstein, of New York; *b* 16 June 1912; *Educ* Eton, King's Coll Cambridge (MA); *m* 1, 1935, Catherine Macdonald (d 1978), da of David H Crompton, of Rye, New York, USA; 3 s (Hon Oliver b 1941, Hon William b 1942, Hon James Patrick Francis b 1949), 2 da (Hon Anne Sheridan (Hon Mrs Brewin) b 1937, Hon Susan b (twin) 1942) (and 1 s decd); m 2, 1979, Elizabeth Rosemary, da of late John Bissett-Robinson and formerly w of Nicholas Paul Scott, MP; *Career* sits as SDP peer House of Lords (formerly Lab 1961-1981), chief whip SDP Peers 1988-89; contested: (Lib) Hunts 1945, (Lab) Cambs 1951, 1955, Gainsborough 1957, 1959; farmer, agriculturist; res fell Bacteriology Harvard USA 1934-35, dir of Agric Br Zone of Germany 1946-47, agric advsr on Germany to FO 1947-48; cnsllr Duchy of Lancaster 1948-54; Parly under sec: FO 1964-67, BOT 1967; sometime special ambass, cmmr Crown Estates 1968-75, chm Inst of Race Relations 1968-71, memb UK delgn to Cncl of Europe and WEU 1970-75, nominated memb Euro Parl 1975-77, dep chm Cwlth Devpt Corpn 1980-83 (memb 1975-83), dir Bayer UK Ltd; chm: East Anglia Econ Planning Cncl 1969-79, GB/East Europe Centre 1972-86; vice pres Royal Cwlth Soc 1970-; Hon DCL East Anglia; *Publications incl*: From Forces to Farming (1944), Land Nationalisation, for and against, (1958), The Farm Gate to Europe (1970), Dealing With Hunger (1976); *Recreations* shooting, sailing; *Clubs* Brooks's, MCC, House of Lords Yacht; *Style*— The Rt Hon the Lord Walston, CVO, JP; Selwood Manor, Frome, Somerset

WALSTON, Hon James Patrick Francis; 3 surviving s of Baron Walston, CVO, JP; *b* 18 July 1949; *Educ* Ampleforth, Eton, Jesus Coll Cambridge, Univ of Rome,Univ of Cambridge (PhD); *Books* The Mafia and Clientelism (1988); *Style*— The Hon James Walston; Via Serpenti 29, Rome, Italy

WALSTON, Hon Oliver; eldest s of Baron Walston, CVO, JP (Life Peer); *b* 1941; *Educ* Eton, King's Coll Cambridge; *m* 1, 1966 (m dis), Leslie, da of Milton A Gordon, of New York; m 2, 1969, Anne Dunbar, of Washington DC; issue includes 1 s (David Charles b 30 May 1982); *Style*— The Hon Oliver Walston; Thriplow Farm, Thriplow, Royston, Herts

WALTER, Hon Sir Harold Edward; s of Rev Edward Walter; *b* 17 April 1920; *Educ* Royal Coll Mauritius; *m* 1942, Yvette Nidza, MBE, da of James Toolsy; *Career* MLA Mauritius 1959-, min External Affrs, Tourism and Emigration 1976-; kt 1972; *Style*— Hon Sir Harold Walter; La Rocca, Eau Coulée, Mauritius

WALTER, Harriet Mary; da of Roderick Walter, of Flat 5, 41 Lexham Gdns, London W8, and Xandra Carandini, *née* Lee; *b* 24 Sept 1950; *Educ* Cranborne Chase Sch, LAMDA; *Career* actress; began career Duke's Playhouse Lancaster 1974; nat tours 1975-78 with: 7:84, Joint Stock, Paines Plough; Royal Court Theatre 1980-81 incl: Cloud Nine, The Seagull, Ophelia in Hamlet (with Jonathan Pryce); RSC 1981-83 incl: Nicholas Nickleby, Helena in a Midsummers Night's Dream, Helena in All's Well That Ends Well (with Dame Peggy Ashcroft, dir Trevor Nunn, toured Broadway 1983); The Possessed (dir Yuri Liubimov) Almeida Theatre 1985 (toured Paris, Milan, Bologna), Skinner in The Castle by Howard Barker (RSC 1985, nominated Best Actress Olivier Awards), Portia in The Merchant of Venice (Royal Exchange Manchester, RSC 1987), Imogen in Cymbeline, Viola in Twelfth Night, Dacha in A Question of Geography, Masha in The Three Sisters (winner of Best Actress Laurence Olivier Awards), title role in The Duchess of Malfi; TV incl: The Imitation Game (by Ian McEwan), Harriet Vane in Dorothy L Sayers Mysteries, Frances in The Price, Benefactors (by Michael Frayn), Charity in the Men's Room; films incl: Turtle Diary, Reflections, The Good Father, Louis Malle's Milou en Mai; winner Sony Radio Best Actress 1988; assoc artist RSC 1987; memb: Amnesty Int, CND, Arts for Labour; *Books* contrib: Women and Theatre (1984), Clamorous Voices Shakespeare's Women Today (1988), Players of Shakespeare Vol 3; *Recreations* music, travel, cinema, theatre, flying, photography; *Style*— Miss Harriet Walter; Meg Poole - Richard Stone Partnership, 25 Whitehall, London SW1A 2BS (☎ 071 839 6421)

WALTER, Jeremy Canning; s of Maj Richard Walter, OBE, and Beryl, *née* Pugh; *b* 22 Aug 1948; *Educ* King's Sch Canterbury, Sidney Sussex Coll Cambridge (MA, LLB); *m* 24 Aug 1973 (m dis 1985), Judith Jane, da of Dr Denton Rowlands, of Tamworth, Staffs (d 1987); 2 da (Emma b 1976, Alison b 1979); *Career* Ellis Piers & Young Jackson 1971-73, admitted slr 1973; ptnr Simmons & Simmons 1976- (slr advising in corporate law commodity and fin servs law and ptnr responsible for Central and E Euro activities); memb: Law Soc, Ctee Br Polish Legal Assoc, Br Privatisation Export cncl, Int bar Assoc East-West Forum, American Bar Assoc (Int Law and Practice Section); *Recreations* theatre, cricket, reading; *Clubs* MCC; *Style*— Jeremy Walter, Esq; 14 Dominion St, London EC2 (☎ 071 628 2020, fax 071 588 4129)

WALTER, Michael; s of late Leonard Walter (d 1990), of 4 Griffin Close, Saxon Park, Blacon, Chester CH1 5TX, and Anne, *née* Rue; *b* 6 May 1956; *Educ* The King's Sch, Christ's Coll Cambridge (BA, MA); *m* 27 Nov 1982, Joan Margaret, da of Arthur Colin Hubbard (d 1978), of Paeroa, nr Auckland, NZ; 1 s (Matthew b 1987), 1 da (Helen b 1984); *Career* admitted slr 1981 (England, Wales and Hong Kong); Stephenson Harwood: articled clerk 1979-81, asst slr 1981-86, ptnr 1986-; Freeman: City of London 1987, Worshipful Co of Slrs 1987; memb: Law Soc, Law Soc of Hong Kong; *Books* Moores & Rowlands Orange Tax Guides; *Recreations* sailing, scuba diving, running, reading, music; *Clubs* Royal Hong Kong Yacht,Royal Hong Kong Jockey, Hong Kong FC, London Road Runners; *Style*— Michael Walter, Esq; 4 Melbourne Terrace, Moore Park Rd, London SW6 2JU (☎ 071 736 7367); Le Grenier, 133 Chemin Du Rocher Nay, Le Tour, Chamonix 74400, France (☎ 33 50 54 13 92); Flat B-20, Po Shan Mansions, 10 Po Shan Rd, Hong Kong (852 8581124); One St Paul's Churchyard, London EC4M 8SH (☎ 071 329 4422, fax 071 606 0822, telex 886789 SHSPC G); 1802 Edinburgh Tower, The Landmark, 15 Queen's Rd Central, Hong Kong (☎ 852 8680789, fax 852 8681504, telex 66278 SHL HX)

WALTER, Robert John; s of Richard John Walter, of Warminster, Wilts, and Irene Gladys, *née* Clements; *b* 30 May 1948; *Educ* Warminster, Univ of Aston (BSc); *m* 28 Aug 1970, Sally, da of Donald Middleton (d 1976); 2 s (Charles b 1976, Alexander b 1977), 1 da (Elizabeth b 1974); *Career* investmt banker and farmer; dir: FW Holst (Europe) Ltd 1984-86, TV-UK Ltd 1988-, Willow Films Ltd 1989; vice pres Aubrey G Lanston & Co Inc 1986-, visiting lectr Central London Poly, farmer in W Country; memb Stock Exchange; Parly candidate (C) Bedwellty 1979, chm Foreign Affrs Forum 1985-87, dep chm Cons Gp for Europe 1989- (vice chm 1984-86); chm: Euro Democrat Forum 1979-84, Aston Univ Cons Assoc 1967-69, W Wilts Young Cons 1972-75, govrs Tachbrook Sch 1980-; memb Sir Francis Chichester Meml Appeal Ctee; Freeman City of London 1983, Liveryman Worshipful Co of Needlemakers 1983; AMSIA; *Recreations* sailing, shooting; *Clubs* Carlton; *Style*— Robert Walter, Esq; Aubrey G Lanston & Co Inc, 3 Queen Victoria St, London EC4N 8HR (☎ 071 248 3955, fax 071 236 2781, telex 945771)

WALTER, Lady Sarah Marion; *née* Coke; yst da of 5 Earl of Leicester (d 1976); *b* 23 July 1944; *m* 1970, Maj David Finlayson Wylie Hill Walter; 2 s; *Style*— The Lady Sarah Walter; Westwood, Balthayock, by Perth

WALTERS, Prof Sir Alan Arthur; s of James Arthur Walters, and Claribel, *née* Heywood; *b* 17 June 1926; *Educ* Alderman Newtons Sch Leicester, Univ Coll Leicester (BSc London), Nuffield Coll Oxford (MA); *m* 1975, Margaret Patricia, da of Leonard Wilson, of Leeds, Yorks; 1 da by previous m (Louise); *Career* Cassel prof of econs LSE 1968-76, prof of political economy Johns Hopkins Univ Maryland USA 1976-, personal econ advsr to PM 1981-84; Hon DLitt Leicester 1981, Hon DSocSc Birmingham 1984; kt 1983; *Clubs* Athenaeum, Political Economy; *Style*— Prof Sir Alan Walters; 2820 P Street NW, Washington, DC 20007, USA; American Enterprise Institute, 1150 17th Street NW, Washington DC 20036, USA (☎ 202 862 6407)

WALTERS, Hon Mrs (Alice Elizabeth); yr da of Field Marshal Baron Carver, GCB, CBE, DSO, MC (Life Peer), *qv*; *b* 1954; *m* 1976, Capt Claude Walters, Gren Guards; *Style*— The Hon Mrs Walters; 122 High Street, Bottisham, Cambridge

WALTERS, Beverley Hugh (Bev); s of Hugh Edward Walters (d 1986), and Florence Mary (d 1987); *b* 1 April 1942; *Educ* St John's Coll Johannesburg, Univ of Witwatersrand (BSc), Univ of South Africa (BComm, MBA); *m* 16 Jan 1965, Helen Paris, da of Patrick Llyod Gooderham, of Johannesburg; 1 s (Mark Hugh b 1965), 2 da (Caren b 1967, Cathy b 1972); *Career* regnl mining geologist Gen Mining & Fin Ltd

Johannesburg 1964-69, gen mangr Citicorp Johannesburg 1969-78, vice pres Bank of Montreal (Toronto, London, Australia) 1978-86, md ANZ Merchant Bank (Australia and London) 1986-; SAGS 1965, SATS 1965, IBSA 1970, AAIS 1968; *Recreations* golf; *Clubs* Hindheard Golf, Metropolitan Golf (Melbourne), Australian Golf (Sydney); *Style—* Bev Walters, Esq; 34 Onslow Gdns, South Kensington, London SW7; ANZ Merchant Bank, 65 Holborn Viaduct, London EC1A 2EU (☎ 071 489 0021, fax 071 3248 1103, telex 888981)

WALTERS, David Grenville; TD; s of Claude Grenville Walters (d 1971), of Notts, and Agnes, *née* Dunkerley; *b* 19 Aug 1942; *Educ* Nottingham HS; *m* 4 Sept 1965, Frances Mary, da of Robert James Cumming (d 1979), of Banff; 1 s (Nigel b 1967), 1 da (Lynne b 1970); *Career* cmmnd TA 1973, Regt Offr 101 (FD) Regt RA (V) 1974, 2 i/c 203 (FD) Battery RA (V) 1983, SO (TA) HQ RA 2 Inf Div 1986-, Maj; sr exec Thomson Regional Newspapers 1968-72, chm Grentex Manufacturing Ltd 1972-, Cds underwriter Lloyds 1973-, pres Grenville SA France 1974-78, chm Grenville Marine 1988-; landowner; vice chm Ponteland Cons Assoc, hon treas Hexham Constituency Cons Assoc; memb, Nat Exec Cons Pty, Bd Visitors HM Prisons, Parole Bd Local Review Ctee, Northumberland Assoc Boys' Clubs; MCIM 1970; *Recreations* flying, sailing, rugby, hill walking, wine; *Style—* David Walters, Esq, TD; Lane End House, Main St, Corbridge Northumberland NE45 5LE (☎ 0434 632281)

WALTERS, Sir Dennis Murray; MBE (1960), MP (C) Westbury 1964-; s of Douglas L Walters (d 1964), and Clara, *née* Pomello; *b* 28 Nov 1928; *Educ* Downside, St Catharine's Coll Cambridge (MA); *m* 1, 1955 (m dis 1969), Vanora, da of Sir Archibald McIndoe, CBE (d 1960); 1 s (Nicholas McIndoe b 1957), 1 da (Lorian b 1960); m 2, 1970 (m dis 1979), Hon Celia Mary, da of Baron Duncan Sandys, CH (d 1987); 1 s (Dominic b 1971); m 3, 22 Jan 1981, Bridgett Louise, da of J F Shearer, CBE, of Wimbledon; 1 s (Oliver Charles b 1985), 1 da (Camilla Clare b 1982); *Career* interned in Italy during early part of WWII, joined Resistance Movement for 11 months; dir Cluff Oil Inc; tstee ANAF Foundation, memb Kuwait Investmt Advsy Ctee, conslt to Balfour Beatty Construction Ltd; writer and broadcaster; contested (C) Blyth 1959 and 1960 by-election; fndr memb Bow Group, chm Fedn of Univ Cons and Unionist Assocs 1949-50, PA to Viscount Hailsham, QC (now Lord Hailsham of Saint Marylebone) as chm of Cons Pty 1957-69, jt sec Cons Parly Foreign Affairs Ctee 1965-71, jt vice chm 1974-78; chm Asthma Res Cncl 1968-88; jt chm Cncl of Advancement of Arab-Br Understanding 1970-82, chm Cons ME Cncl 1980-; Order of the Cedar of Lebanon 1969; kt 1988; *Books* Not Always With The Pack (autobiographical memoirs, 1989); *Recreations* reading, tennis; *Clubs* Boodle's; *Style—* Sir Dennis Walters, MBE, MP; Orchardleigh, Corton, Warminster, Wiltshire (☎ 098 55 369); 43 Royal Avenue, London SW3 4QE (☎ 071 730 9431, fax 071 823 5938)

WALTERS, Very Rev (Rhys) Derrick Chamberlain; s of Ivor Chamberlain Walters, and Rosamund Grace, *née* Jackson; *b* 10 March 1932; *Educ* Gowerton Boys' GS, LSE, Ripon Hall Oxford (BSc); *m* 28 Dec 1959, Joan, da of William George Fisher, 2 s (David b 1962, Michael b 1964); *Career* curate of Manselton Swansea 1957-58, anglican chaplain of Univ Coll Swansea and curate of St Mary's 1958-62; vicar of: All Saints Totley 1962-67, St Mary's Boulton by Derby 1967-74; diocesan missioner Diocese of Salisbury 1974-82, vicar of Burcombe 1974-79, non residentiary canon of Salisbury Cath 1978 (canon and treas 1979-82), dean Liverpool 1983-; hon fell Liverpool Poly 1988; *Recreations* escapist, literature, croquet, classical music; *Style—* The Very Rev the Dean of Liverpool; Liverpool Cathedral, St James Mount, Liverpool L1 7AZ (☎ 051 709 6271, fax 051 709 1112)

WALTERS, Sir (Frederick) Donald; s of Percival Donald Walters, and Irene Walters; *b* 5 Oct 1925; *Educ* Howardian HS Cardiff, LSE (LLB); *m* 1950, Adelaide Jean, *née* McQuistin; 1 s; *Career* called to the Bar Inner Temple 1946; practised Wales and Chester circuit 1948-59; memb: Bd Welsh Devpt Agency 1980- (dep chm 1984-), Devpt Bd for Rural Wales 1984-; dir Chartered Tst plc 1959-85; Cncl chm Univ of Wales Coll of Cardiff 1988-; High Sheriff S Glamorgan 1987-88; *Style—* Sir Donald Walters; 120 Cyncoed Rd, Cardiff CF2 6BL

WALTERS, Eric; *b* 3 Aug 1944; *Educ* Bablake Sch Coventry, Selwyn Coll Cambridge (MA); *m* 12 Aug 1967, Katharina; 1 s (Eric Andrew b 28 Sept 1976), 1 da (Katya b 25 May 1973); *Career* res offr British Petroleum Co plc 1965-67, conslt Cape Industries plc 1967-69, sr conslt International Systems Research Ltd 1969-72, divnl mangr Lex Service Group plc 1976-80 (planner 1972-76); Grand Metropolitan plc: md CC Soft Drinks Ltd 1980-82, chm Soft Drinks and Overseas Brewing 1982, chief exec Retailing Div 1984; gp md Dominion International Group plc 1986-87, ptnr Schroder Ventures 1987-; currently dir: Goldsmith Group plc, Glass Glover Group plc, Burlington International Group plc, Kundert International Ltd, UK Shoe Group Ltd; non-exec chm Molynx Holdings plc 1987-; *Recreations* skiing, hiking, jogging; *Clubs* RAC; *Style—* Eric Walters, Esq; 136 Wades Hill, London N21 1EH; Schroder Ventures, 20 Southampton St, London WC2E 7QG (☎ 071 632 1020, fax 071 240 5072); Molynx Holdings plc, Crindau Works, Albany St, Newport, Gwent NP9 5XW (☎ 0633 821000, fax 0633 850893, telex 497062)

WALTERS, Geraint Gwynn; CBE (1958); s of Rev David D Walters (d 1968), of Gaiman, Argentina and Brynsiencyn, Anglesey, and Rachel Gwynn, *née* Williams (d 1955); *b* 6 June 1910; *Educ* Univ Coll Bangor (BA); *m* 1, July 1942, Doreena (d 1959), da of John Owen (d 1955), of Bethesda, N Wales; m 2, 2 July 1968, (Sarah Ann) Ruth, da of Henry Roberts Price (d 1963), of Mathry, Dyfed; *Career* regnl organiser under Rt Hon David Lloyd George 1935-40, dep regnl dir Miny of Info 1940-45, dir Miny of Public Bldgs and Works 1945-72: Wales 1948-53 and 1966-72, Far East 1963-66; parly housing cmmr Borough of Merthyr Tydfil 1972-73; memb Gorsedd of Bards 1961, memb Cole Cmmn on Bdcasting in Wales 1962-63, ldr Overseas Welsh at Royal Nat Eisteddfod 1965, pres Singapore Welsh Soc 1965-66, former pres S Wales Soc of Public Admin, cncl memb UWIST 1968-86 (vice chm 1980-83), memb ct Univ of Wales 1980-86, life memb of ct Univ of Wales Coll Cardiff; *Recreations* reading (talking books for the blind); *Clubs* Cardiff and County, Civil Service (London); *Style—* Geraint Walters, Esq, CBE; 1 The Mount, Cardiff Rd, Llandaff, Cardiff CF5 2AR (☎ 0222 568739)

WALTERS, Geraint Wyn; s of Thomas Eifion Walters, of Glanyrafon, Rhyd-y-fro, Pontardawe, Swansea, W Glamorgan, and Dilys, *née* Deer; *b* 31 Dec 1957; *Educ* Ysgol Gyfun Ystalyfera, Univ Coll of Wales Aberystwyth (LLB), Inns of Court Sch of Law; *m* 26 May 1986, Kathryn Ann Walters, da of John Jenkins; 2 da (Lowri Angharad b 1 May 1987, Catrin Wyn b 1 Jan 1989); *Career* called to the Bar Gray's Inn 1981; hon sec Guild for Promotion of Welsh Music, dir and exec memb Swansea Festival Ltd, memb Gorsedd of Bards of the Isle of Britain, memb Inst Welsh Affrs; *Style—* Geraint Walters, Esq; Ael-y-bryn, Lone Rd, Clydach, Swansea, W Glamorgan SA6 5JB (☎ 0792 843375); Angel Chambers, 94 Walter Rd, Swansea, W Glamorgan SA1 5QA (☎ 0792 464623, fax 0792 648501)

WALTERS, Lt-Col John Henry; s of the late Henry Blanchard Walters, OBE, and the late Grace Walters; *b* 17 May 1909; *Educ* Clifton, Corpus Christi Coll Cambridge (MD, BCh); *m* 7 Aug 1937, Janet Isobel Norah, da of Ernest McIntyre (d 1964); 1 s (Humphrey b 1942), 1 da (Julia (Mrs Duprée) b 1940); *Career* IMS 1937-46 (specialist physician 1942-), MO i/c MRC Nutritional Res Station The Gambia 1948-51, specialist physician and dep SMO Kuwait State Med Serv 1951-54, MO i/c and sec W African Cncl for Med Res Lagos 1952-54; conslt physician: Hosp for Tropical Diseases London, Tropical Diseases Unit Queens Mary's Hosp Roehampton 1955-63; FRCP 1958, FRCPE 1960; *Publications incl:* contribs to Manson's Tropical Diseases (17 edn, 1972), Recent Advances in Tropical Medicine (3 edn, 1961), Fundamentals of Current Medical Treatment (1965), and papers in many learned jls; *Recreations* observing natural history, fishing, gardening; *Clubs* MCC; *Style—* Lt-Col John Walters; Higher Lawn, Chudleigh, S Devon (☎ 0626 853 160)

WALTERS, Rear Adm John William Townshend; CB (1984); s of William Bernard Walters, and Lilian Martha, *née* Hartridge; *b* 23 April 1926; *Educ* John Fisher Sch Purley; *m* 1949, Margaret Sarah Patricia Jeffkins; 2 s, 1 da; *Career* joined RN 1944, Supply Offr HMS Albion 1967-69, sec to Chief of Fleet Support 1969-72, Chief Naval Judge Advocate 1972-75, Capt Naval Drafting 1975-78, dir Naval Admin Planning 1978-80, Asst Chief of Def Staff (Personnel and Logistics) 1981-84, ret RN 1984; called to the Bar Middle Temple 1956; chm Industl Tbnls 1984, dep chm Data Protection Tbnl 1985, memb Royal Naval Sailing Assoc; *Recreations* sailing (yacht 'Lady Macbeth'); *Clubs* Army and Navy; *Style—* Rear Adm John Walters, CB; Good Holding, 5 Hollycombe Close, Liphook, Hants GU30 7HR

WALTERS, Joyce Dora; da of Wilfred John Davies (d 1961), and Florence May, *née* Fisher; *b* 10 Dec 1932; *Educ* St Anne's Coll Oxford (MA); *m* 29 July 1979, Lt-Col Howard Corey Walters IV (d 1983), s of Col Howard Corey Walters III (d 1982), of California; by prev m, 1 s (Nicholas John Warwick Bailey b 18 Sept 1962); *Career* headmistress: St Mary's Calne 1972-85, Clifton HS 1985-; *Recreations* reading, cooking, travel; *Clubs* United Oxford and Cambridge; *Style—* Mrs Joyce Walters; 4 Longwood House, Failand, Bristol (☎ 0272 392092); Clifton High School, College Rd, Bristol (☎ 0272 730201)

WALTERS, Julie; *b* 22 Feb 1950; *Career* comic actress; film work incl: Rita in Educating Rita (Oscar nomination, BAFTA award, Golden Globe award), Buster, Personal Services (BAFTA nominee), Joe Orton's mother in Prick Up Your Ears, Mrs Peacham in The Threepenny Opera, Killing Dad, Steppin' Out; theatre work incl: seasons at Everyman Theatre Liverpool and Bristol Old Vic, Educating Rita (RSC Warehouse and Piccadilly Theatre) Having a Ball (Lyric), Jumpers (Royal Exchange), Fool for Love (NT and Lyric), When I was a Girl I Used to Scream and Shout (Whitehall), Frankie and Johnnie; TV incl: The Birthday Party, Secret Diary of Adrian Mole, Victoria Wood - As Seen on TV (BAFTA nomination), Boys From the Blackstuff (BAFTA nomination), She'll Be Wearing Pink Pyjamas, Say Something Happened (BAFTA nomination), Intensive Care, Talking Heads, GBH; *Style—* Ms Julie Walters

WALTERS, (Thomas) Mervyn Llewellyn; MBE (1966); s of Hon Canon Thomas William Walters (d 1951), of Whitwick Vicarage, Leics, and Emmeline Florence, *née* Cocks (d 1958); *b* 8 April 1910; *Educ* Loughborough GS; *m* 1, 22 Sept 1942, Jean Margaret (d 1972), da of late Roy Wallace Murray, of Lincoln; 2 s ((Thomas) Rhodri Murray b 1944, Malcolm Hywel b 1948), 1 da (Gwyneth Margaret (Mrs Page) b 1945); m 2, 26 March 1976, Eileen Mary, da of late Sholto Douglas, of Kenilworth; *Career* slr 1931, Bird Wilford & Sale 1931-, Notary Public 1938-; pres Loughborough Rotary Club 1974-75, (Paul Harris fell 1990); memb: Bishop's Cncl Leics 1970-88, Gen Synod C of E 1975-85; lay canon Leicester Cathedral 1977-; govr: Warner C of E Sch 1944-, Garendon HS 1955-87; chm Review Ctee Loughborough Charities (under Charities Act 1960); dir Abbeyfield Loughborough Soc 1964-; scout cmmr: dist 1937, asst county 1954, dep county 1963, hon 1977-, Silverwolf 1957; pres Loughborough Scouts 1989-; memb: Nat Cncl Scout Assoc 1967-77, Co Youth Ctee 1954-77; first chm Leics Standing Conf of Youth Orgns 1965; memb Law Soc; *Books* Loughborough 1888-1988 The Birth Of A Borough (jtly); *Recreations* travel, caravanning, history, photography, philately, Welsh affairs; *Style—* Mervyn Walters, Esq, MBE; 34 Sandalwood Rd, Loughborough, Leics (☎ 0509 212 349); 20 Church Gate, Loughborough, Leics (☎ 0509 232 611, fax 0509 239 081, telex 341995428)

WALTERS, Michael Quentin; s of Leslie Walters, and Helen Marie Walters; *b* 14 Oct 1927; *Educ* Merchant Taylors', Worcester Coll Oxford (MA); *m* 1954, Lysbeth Ann Falconer; *Career* admitted slr 1954; chm EIS Group plc 1977-, dir Delta Group plc 1980-, sr ptnr Theodore Goddard Solicitors 1983-89, chm Tilbury Group plc 1989-; *Style—* Michael Walters, Esq; c/o EIS Group plc, 6 Sloane Sq, London SW1W 8EE (☎ 071 730 9187)

WALTERS, Nicholas McIndoe; s of Sir Dennis Walters, MBE, MP, of London, and Vanora, *née* McIndoe; *b* 16 May 1957; *Educ* Downside, Univ of Exeter; *m* 1 Aug 1987, Emma Mary, yr da of David Blamey; *Career* legislative asst to Howard Baker, majority ldr The Senate, Washington DC 1980-81; exec: The Marconi Company 1981-82, Paul Winner Marketing Ltd 1982-83; dir: Good Relations Ltd 1983-88, McAvoy Bayley Ltd 1988-; Parly candidate (cons) Merthyr Tydfil 1987; *Recreations* skiing, tennis, snooker; *Clubs* Annabels, Raffles, Hurlingham Ritz Snooker; *Style—* Nicholas Walters, Esq; 124 Bennerley Road, London SW11 6DY (☎ 071 223 5277); McAvoy Bayley Ltd, 36 Grosvenor Gardens London SW1W OEB (☎ 071 730 4500)

WALTERS, Sir Peter Ingram; s of Stephen Walters (d 1945), and Edna, *née* Redgate; *b* 11 March 1931; *Educ* King Edward's Sch Birmingham, Univ of Birmingham; *m* 1960, Patricia Anne, *née* Tulloch; 2 s, 1 da; *Career* Lt RASC; md BP Co Ltd 1973, dep chm 1980-81, chm 1981-90; vice pres BP North America 1965-67; chm: BP Chemicals 1976-81, BP Chemicals Int 1981; dir Nat Westminster Bank 1981-89; memb Indust Soc Cncl 1975-90; Post Office Bd 1978-79, chm Blue Circle Industries plc 1990, dep chm Thorn EMI plc 1990, dir SmithKline Beecham plc 1989; Gen Ctee Lloyds Register of Shipping 1976-90; pres: Soc of Chem Indust 1978-80, Gen Cncl of Br Shipping 1977-78, memb Inst of Manpower Studies 1980-88 (vice pres 1977-80, pres 1980-86); chm Governing Body London Business Sch 1987- (dep chm 1986, govr 1981-), London Business Sch 1981-; Int Mgmnt Inst Memb Fdn Bd 1983-90 (chm 1985-87); pres Ctee CBI 1982-90; tstee: Nat Maritime Museum 1983-90, E Malling Res Station 1983-; tstee Police Fndn 1985-, manging tstee Inst of Econ Affairs 1986, pres IOD 1986-, Hon DUniv Stirling 1987, Hon DSc Birmingham 1986; Cdr Order of Leopold (Belgium); kt 1984; *Recreations* golf, gardening, sailing; *Style—* Sir Peter Walters; Blue Circle Industries plc, 84 Eccleston Square, London SW1V 1PX (☎ 071 245 8127, fax 071 245 8195)

WALTERS, Sir Roger Talbot; KBE (1971, CBE 1965); s of Alfred Walters, of Sudbury, Suffolk; *b* 31 March 1917; *Educ* Oundle, AA Sch of Architecture (BA), Univ of Liverpool; *m* 1976, Claire Chappell; *Career* served RE WWII; chief architect (devpt) Directorate of Works WO 1959-62, dep dir gen res and devpt Miny Public Bldgs and Works 1962-67 (dir gen prodn 1967-69), architect and controller construction servs GLC 1971-78; Hon FAIA, FRIBA, FIStructE; *Clubs* Reform; *Style—* Sir Roger Walters, KBE; 46 Princess Rd, London NW1 (☎ 071 722 3740)

WALTERS, William Charles; s of William Dyke Walters (d 1977), of Walsall, and Georgina May, *née* Bayford, JP (d 1975); *b* 5 Dec 1921; *Educ* Edward Shelley HS Walsall, Coll of Accountancy; *m* 6 Feb 1944, Margaret Joan, da of George Gavan (d 1977); 1 s (Michael b 1948); *Career* Secretarial Branch RN 1942-46; served: Africa, India, Ceylon, Aust, Philipines, Hong Kong; NCO in Cmd Admin Gp Ldr Ship: frigates on Ceylon and Burma patrols, aircraft carriers Br Pacific Fleet; rescue work (food and medicines); CA, joined Kimberley Morrison Moore & Co (now Moore Stephens) 1951 (ptnr 1965-76, sr ptnr 1976-); chorister Walsall Parish Church 1930-; memb: Royal Sch of Church Music and Incorporated Assoc of Organists (chm Lichfield Branch organists 1972-), Br Legion 1948-, Church Neighbourhood Care 1968-; FICA 1949, ATII 1950; *Recreations* classical music, photography, travel; *Style—* William Walters, Esq; 7 Seckham Rd, Beacon Place, Lichfield, Staffs WS13 7AN (☎ 0543 251068); Moore Stephens, St Philips House, St Philips Place, Birmingham B3 2PP (☎ 021 200 3077, fax 021 200 2454)

WALTHER, Robert Philippe; s of Prof David Philippe Walther (d 1973), and Barbara, *née* Brook; *b* 31 July 1943; *Educ* Charterhouse, Christ Church Oxford (MA); *m* 21 June 1969, Anne, da of Lionel Wigglesworth, of Hill Brow, Woldingham, Surrey; 1 s (Luke b 1978), 1 da (Julie Clare b 1973); *Career* Clerical Medical Investment Group: joined 1965, dep investmt mangr 1972, investmt mangr 1976, asst gen mangr (investments) 1980, dir 1985-; chm Investmt Ctee Assoc of Br Insurers; FIA 1970, ASIA 1969; *Recreations* hockey, golf, bridge, squash, sailing; *Clubs* United Oxford and Cambridge; *Style—* Robert Walther, Esq; Ashwell's Barn, Chesham Lane, Chalfont St Giles, Bucks HP8 4AS (☎ 024 07 5575); Clerical Medical Investment Group, 15 St James's Square, London SW1Y 4LQ (☎ 071 930 5474, fax 071 321 1846, telex 27432 CMG LDN)

WALTON, Alastair Henry; s of Sir Raymond Henry Walton (d 1988), of Wimbledon, London, and Helen Alexandra, *née* Dingwall; *b* 26 Aug 1954; *Educ* Winchester, Balliol Coll Oxford (BA); *m* 28 July 1984, Hon Mary Synolda, *née* Butler, *qv*, da of Lord Dunboyne, *qv*, of Chelsea, London; 3 da (Alexandra Mary b 1985, Christina Frances b 1986, Stephanie Katherine b 1988); *Career* called to the Bar Lincoln's Inn 1977, in practice 1978-; *Recreations* lawn tennis; *Style—* Alastair Walton, Esq; 26 Paradise Walk, Chelsea, London SW3 4JL (☎ 071 376 5304); 7 Stone Bldgs, Lincoln's Inn, London WC2A 3SZ (☎ 071 405 3886, fax 071 242 8502)

WALTON, Anthony Michael; QC (1970); s of Henry Herbert Walton (d 1975), of Dulwich, and Clara Martha, *née* Dobrantz (d 1974); *b* 4 May 1925; *Educ* Dulwich, Hertford Coll Oxford (MA, BCL); *m* 1955, Jean Frederica, da of William Montague Hey (d 1936), of London; 1 s (Martin b 1969); *Career* called to the Bar Middle Temple 1950; bencher 1978; Liveryman Worshipful Co of Gunmakers; *Publications* Patent Law of Europe and the UK (1978), Russell on Arbitration (1982); *Style—* Anthony Walton, Esq, QC; 62 Kingsmead Rd, Tulse Hill, London SW2 3JG (☎ 081 674 9159); Francis Taylor Building, The Temple, London EC4Y 7BY (☎ 071 353 5657)

WALTON, Dr Bryan; s of Henry Walton (d 1985), and Helen, *née* Pincus (d 1989); *b* 29 Aug 1943; *Educ* City of London Sch, London Hosp Med Coll Univ of London (MB BS, FFARCS); *m* 7 July 1968, (Sarah) Ruth, da of Philip Levitan (d 1989); 1 s (Jonathan b 1976), 1 da (Anne b 1973); *Career* conslt anaesthetist London Hosp 1974-, advsr on anaesthesia and intensive care Princess Grace Hosp London 1984-, dir of intensive care London Ind Hosp 1989-; memb: Med Def Union 1966, Assoc of Anaesthetists 1972, Anaesthetic Res Soc 1980, Hunterians 1985, Chelsea Clinical Soc 1989; *Books* chapters: Adverse Reactions to Anaesthetic Drugs (1981), Scientific Foundations of Anaesthesia (1982), Hazards and Complications of Anaesthesia (1987), Medicine in the Practice of Anaesthesia (1989); many pubns on anaesthesia and the liver, and anaesthesia and immunology; *Recreations* classical music; *Style—* Dr Bryan Walton; Woodlands, 152 High Rd, Chigwell, Essex IG7 5BQ (☎ 081 500 6040); Dept of Anaesthetics, The London Hospital, London E1 1BB (☎ 071 377 7793, car 0836 201560)

WALTON, Christopher Henry; s of Frank Pearson Walton (d 1966), of Eastbourne, and Marion Ada Beasley (d 1989); *b* 20 June 1930; *Educ* Stockport GS, Gonville and Caius Coll Cambridge (MA); *m* 25 April 1959, Judith Vivien, da of Ernest Leslie Philp (d 1950), of Alexandria, Egypt; *Career* 2 Lt Lancs Fus 1949-51, Capt Royal Fus TA 1951-59; Cwlth Devpt Corpn 1954-65, initiator and dir Kenya Tea Devpt Authy 1959-65; exec and dir: Kyle Prods Ltd Gp 1965-67, Eastern Produce Ltd Gp 1967-69, div chief Projects Dept Eastern and Western Africa World Bank Washington 1969-87; bursar Wolfson Coll Oxford 1987, pres UN Student Assoc 1954-55, advsr on Overseas Devpt to Rt Hon Edward Heath, Cons Party Candidates List 1966-69, dep chm Cons party Overseas Devpt Ctee 1967-68; *Recreations* ecclesiastical architecture, conservative politics, rowing; *Clubs* Oriental, Leander; *Style—* Christopher Walton, Esq; The Corner House, Foxcombe Lane, Bodras Hill, Oxford OX1 5DH (☎ 0865 735179); Wolfson College, Oxford OX2 6UD (☎ 0865 274100, 0865 83147)

WALTON, David; JP (Glasgow 1981); s of Isidore Aaron Walton, CBE, JP (d 1979), of Glasgow, and Lena, *née* Franklin (d 1984); *b* 4 Aug 1943; *Educ* Glasgow HS, Lycée Jaccard Lausanne Switzerland; *m* 12 Oct 1964, Carole, da of Michael Schuster-Davis (d 1953), of Glasgow; 2 s (Michael b 18 Oct 1965, John Richard b 1 Dec 1967); *Career* stockbroker; chm: The Scottish Metropolitan Property plc 1979-, Stirling Hendry & Co stockbrokers 1987-; chm and fndr tstee The Isodore and David Walton Fndn 1979; Hon LLD Glasgow 1980, Hon FRCPS Glasgow 1980; CStJ 1981; memb Int Stock Exchange 1964; *Recreations* bridge, travel; *Clubs* Western (Glasgow); *Style—* David Walton, Esq, JP; The Scottish Metropolitan Property plc, 100 Queen Street, Glasgow G1 3DL (☎ 041 248 7333); Stirling Henry & Co, 16 Royal Exchange Square, Glasgow G1 3AD (☎ 041 248 6033)

WALTON, Col Dennis; CBE (1967, OBE 1962), MC, TD; s of Harry Walton (d 1966), of Bury, Lancs, and Eva Kathleen Walton (d 1969); *b* 7 Feb 1920; *Educ* Bury GS, Emmanuel Coll Cambridge (MA, Soccer blue); *m* 1949, Barbara Shirley, da of Leonard Bertram Jones, JP (d 1948), a former Mayor of Bury; 2 da; *Career* serv WWII N Africa and Europe; Col RA (TA), Dep Cdr 42 Div 1962-67; md Dalkeith Knitwear Ltd 1963-78, bd memb Coats Patons Knitwear Div 1976-78; memb Cncl Nat Artillery Assoc 1962-; pres Nottingham and Dist Hosiery Mfrs Assoc 1967-69; chm: E Midland Further Educn Cncl Textiles Panel 1973-77, Technician Educn Cncl Ctee 1975-80; sr advsr Small Firms Serv (DE) 1978-89; pres: E Midland Further Educ Cncl 1985-, RA Offrs' Assoc of the North-West 1985-; Bolton Volunteer Artillery Assoc 1985-; FBIM, FInstD, FIBC; *Clubs* Royal Overseas League; *Style—* Col Dennis Walton, CBE, MC, TD; Riber Manor, Matlock, Derbyshire DE4 5JU (☎ 0629 583864)

WALTON, Ernest Ward; TD (1968); s of Herbert Walton, JP (d 1968), of Newcastle upon Tyne, and Eleanor, *née* Ward (d 1986); *b* 10 July 1926; *Educ* Univ of Durham (MB BS, MD); *m* 11 Oct 1952, Greta Elizabeth, da of Leonard Wray (d 1978), of Newcastle upon Tyne; 3 s (David b 1954, Paul b 1955, Hugh b 1961), 1 da (Caroline b 1959); *Career* Nat Serv 1950-52; TA 1952-72, Maj RAMC 1958; lectr in pathology Univ of St Andrews 1957-60, conslt pathologist N Tees Health Dist 1960-, clinical lectr in pathology Univ of Newcastle upon Tyne 1978-; chm Cleveland Med Laboratories 1981-; JP 1978, med advsr Nat Assoc of Funeral Dirs 1986-, pres Stockton Rotary Club 1990-91; FRCPath 1972 (memb 1963); *Recreations* fellwalking, travel, cross country skiing; *Clubs* Nat Lib; *Style—* Ernest Walton, Esq, TD; 32 The Green, Norton, Stockton on Tees, Cleveland TS20 1DX (☎ 0642 554653); Cleveland Medical Laboratories Ltd, Letch Lane, Carlton, Stockton on Tees, Cleveland TS21 1EE (☎ 0642 673737, fax 0642 602609)

WALTON, The Ven Geoffrey Elmer; s of Maj Harold Walton (d 1978), and Edith Margaret Dawson (d 1983); *b* 19 Feb 1934; *Educ* West Bridgford GS, Univ of Durham (BA), Queens Coll Birmingham (Dip Theol); *m* 9 Sept 1961, Edith Mollie, da of John Patrick O'Connor (d 1970); 1 s (Jeremy Mark b 1968); *Career* vicar of Norwell Notts and Dio Youth chaplain 1965-69, recruitment and selection sec Advsy Cncl for the Church's Min London 1969-75, hon canon of Salisbury Cathedral 1981, rural dean of Weymouth 1980-82, archdeacon of Dorset 1982-, incumbent of Witchampton with Long Crichel and Moor Crichel 1982-, Dorset Co Scout Chaplain, chm Dio Bd of Miny; *Recreations* religious drama, conjuring, walking; *Style—* The Ven the Archdeacon of Dorset; The Vicarage, Witchampton, Wimborne, Dorset BH21 5AP (☎ 0258 840422)

WALTON, John Cannell; *b* 26 Jan 1946; *Educ* King Edward VI Sch Norwich, UCL (BSc Econ); *m* Ann-Margaret Walton; 2 da (Juliet, Caroline); *Career* investmt analyst then head of investmt res Hill Samuel & Co 1968-72, acquisitions analyst Sterling Land 1972-74, investmt mangr then dir of investmts Imperial Life Assurance 1975-85, md Laurwood Limited 1985-; investmt dir: British Empire Securities & General Trust plc 1985-, French Property Trust plc 1990-; AMSIA; *Style—* John Walton, Esq; 24 The Avenue, Kew, Richmond, Surrey TW9 2AJ; Laurwood Limited, Lincoln House, 296-302 High Holborn, London WC1V 7JH (☎ 071 404 8687, fax 071 404 8121)

WALTON, Lt-Col John Cusack; DL (1987); s of Col Granville Walton, CMG, OBE, DL, JP (d 1974), and Joan, *née* McCraken (d 1975); *b* 16 April 1928; *Educ* Marlborough; *m* 29 Jan 1971, Elsabe, da of Brig James Whetstone, OBE (d 1956); 1 s (David b 29 Feb 1972), 1 da (Joanna b 7 Nov 1973); *Career* cmmnd Royal Scots Greys 1947: Capt 1949-58, Adj 1955-58, Maj 1960-71, Lt-Col 1971-77, served Aden, Bahrain, Libya, Germany, UK, ret 1977; chm: Regtl Assoc 1984- (tstee), Old Berks Hunt 1984-; Oxon Scout Cncl 1984-, Thames Valley Police Authy 1985-; memb E Wessex TAVR Assoc 1981-, environment spokesman Oxon 1985-90, cncllr 1981-; *Recreations* field sports; *Clubs* Cavalry and Guards'; *Style—* Lt-Col John Walton, DL; Longworth Manor, Abingdon, Oxfordshire (☎ 0865 820223)

WALTON, John Victor; s of Eric Roscoe Walton (d 1961), of 18 Beech Ave, Radlett, Herts, and Ethel Marjorie, *née* Addinsell (d 1983); *b* 5 Dec 1925; *Educ* Aldenham, Ruskin Sch of Drawing Oxford, Slade Sch of Fine Art London, Univ of London (Dip Fine Art); *m* 1950 (m dis 1970), Annette Rolande Francoise D'Exea; 2 s (James Andre b 1950, Roland Dominic b 1966), 1 da (Victoria Ann b 1953); m 2, 1989, Alice Low, *née* Ellsworth; *Career* portrait painter; princ Heatherley Sch of Fine Art 1974-; exhibitions incl: RA, Royal Soc of Portrait Painters, Paris Salon (hon mention), Institut de France, Academie des Beaux Arts; paintings in national instns and private collections in GB & abroad; co sec Thomas Heatherley Educnl Tst 1976-, chm FBA 1990- (govr 1982-), memb Cncl RSPP 1979-81 and 1983-90; *Recreations* painting, cycling, history; *Clubs* Chelsea Arts; *Style—* John Walton, Esq; 30 Park Road, Radlett, Herts; The Heatherley School of Fine Art, Upcerne Road, Chelsea SW10 0SH (☎ 071 351 4190)

WALTON, Leonard Joseph; *b* 30 May 1911; *Educ* Wallasey GS; *m* 10 July 1937, Vera Freda; 1 da (Deryn); *Career* Gunner RA (TA) 1938, cmmnd RA 1940 (Capt 1941, Maj 1942), served BAOR (despatches) 1939-45; TEM; dep chief gen mangr Martins Bank Ltd 1965-69, gen mangr Barclays Bank plc (on merger) 1969-71, dep chm & chief exec Barclays Merchant Bank and dir various Barclays subsids 1971-76, dep chm Riggs AP Bank Ltd 1976; chm: Riggs AP Leasing Ltd 1988-, Riggs AP Servs Ltd 1988-, Regalian Properties plc 1983-90; chm Inst of Laryngology (Univ of London) 1971-76, govr Royal Throat Nose & Ear Hosp 1971-76, hon treas & dep chm Victoria League for Cwlth Friendship 1972-88; FCIB (hon treas 1966-80); *Recreations* fishing, golf; *Clubs* Royal Liverpool Golf, Hoylake Ches, Wyresdale Anglers; *Style—* L J Walton, Esq; 16 Clifton Place, Hyde Park, London W2 2SN (☎ 071 723 0382); Riggs AP Bank Ltd, 21 Great Winchester St, London EC2N 2HH (☎ 071 588 7575)

WALTON, Malcolm Cranston; s of Cranston Graham Walton, of Amwell, Wheathampstead, nr St Albans, Herts, and Pamela Beatrice, *née* Sharpe; *b* 29 Jan 1950; *Educ* Stowe; *m* 6 Nov 1971, Henrietta Elizabeth, da of Lt-Col Henry Leonard Boultbee; 2 s (Richard b 1974, Henry b 1984), 2 da (Lucy b 1977, Anna b 1979); *Career* admitted slr 1974, ptnr Waltons 1975-77; md and fndr Cambridge Tst plc (property investmt and devpt) 1982-; memb Law Soc; *Recreations* fishing, shooting, gardening, tennis; *Clubs* Lansdowne; *Style—* Malcolm Walton, Esq; Crave Hall, Cow Lane, Gt Chesterford, Saffron Walden, Essex CB10 5JH (☎ 0799 30803); Cambridge Tst plc, Pound Hill House, Pound Hill, Cambridge CB3 OAE (☎ 0223 312457, fax 0223 460401, car 0860 224654)

WALTON, Hon Mrs (Mary Synolda); *née* Butler; eldest da of 28 Baron Dunboyne, *qv*; *b* 29 April 1954; *Educ* Benenden, Girton Coll Cambridge (BA, MA); *m* 1984, Alastair Henry Walton, *qv*, o s of late Sir Raymond Henry Walton; 3 da (Alexandra Mary b 1985, Christina Frances b 1986, Stephanie Katharine b 1988); *Career* admitted slr 1980; *Recreations* tennis (Cambridge 1/2 Blue 1974 and 1975), swimming, tower bell ringing; *Style—* The Hon Mrs Walton; 26 Paradise Walk, London SW3 4JL

WALTON, Miles Henry; s of Rae Walton, MC, AFC, TD, of Tynemouth, and Anne Elizabeth, *née* Flisher; *b* 15 July 1955; *Educ* Ratcliffe Coll, Brasenose Coll Oxford (MA); *m* 11 May 1985, Lorraine, da of Jack Nunn (d 1966); 1 s (Jack b 14 Nov 1987), 1 da (Rachel b 25 June 1989); *Career* admitted slr 1980; currently ptnr Wilde Sapte; memb Law Soc, ATII; *Recreations* wine, sailing, saxophone, scuba diving, skiing; *Style—* Miles Walton, Esq; Wilde Sapte, Queensbridge House, Upper Thames St, London EC2 (☎ 071 236 3050, fax 071 236 9624)

WALTON, Col Peter Sinclair; s of Col William Patrick Everard Walton, CBE, of Tenterden, Kent, and Ruby Marcella Bloomfield, *née* Maffett; *b* 3 Jan 1939; *Educ* St Johns Sch Leatherhead; *m* 3 July 1971, Michelle Frances, da of Philip Edward Aldous, OBE, of Cape Province, SA; 1 s (David Sinclair b 1972), 1 da (Victoria Louise b 1978); *Career* HAC 1957, Int Corps 1958, cmmnd RAOC 1961, Lt-Col HQ BAOR 1979, COS Br Mil Advsy and Trg Team Zimbabwe 1983, CO 2 Ordnance Bn 1983, materials mgmnt strategy review team MOD 1987-89 (Col 1985-), Hon Col RAOC TA 1990; tstee and designer RAOC Museum 1976-, Cncl memb Assoc of Independent Museums 1990-; sec: Army Museums Ogilby Tst 1989-, chm Victorian Mil Soc; chm Corps of Drums Soc; memb: RUSI, SAHR; Sultan of Oman's DSM 1975; *Books* Simkin's Soldiers The British Army in 1890 (vol I 1982, vol II 1986); *Recreations* kicking myself for not doing today what I shall think of tomorrow; *Clubs* HAC; *Style—* Col Peter Walton; Army Museums Ogilby Tst, Connaught Barracks, Duke of Connaughts Rd, Aldershot, Hampshire GU11 2LR (☎ 0252 331393)

WALTON, Hon Mrs (Sarah Lucy); *née* Pym; yr da of Baron Pym, PC, MC (Life Peer), *qv*; *b* 18 Dec 1958; *m* 1985, Peter Walton, s of W C Walton; 1 s (James Peter b 1986), 1 da (Victoria Lucy b 1988); *Style—* The Hon Mrs Walton; c/o The Rt Hon Lord Pym, PC, MC, DL, Everton Park, Sandy, Beds SG19 2DE

WALTON, Stuart Michael; s of James Walton, of 11 Evistones Rd, Gateshead, Tyne and Wear, and Blance May, *née* Crawley; *b* 22 Jan 1945; *Educ* Gateshead GS, Univ of Newcastle (MB BS); *m* 6 Dec 1969, Jennifer Lois, da of James Mathewson (d 1942); 2 s (Jonathan James b 29 Oct 1970, Nicholas Paul b 30 Jan 1972), 1 da (Abigail Naomi b 28 Jan 1976); *Career* obstetrician and gynaecologist: registrar Newcastle 1969-74, lectr Univ of Nairobi Kenya 1974-76, sr lectr Wellington Clinical Sch of Med Univ of Otago NZ 1977-80, conslt North Tees Health Dist 1980-; rep: Nat Family Planning Bodies, regnl trg ctees; coll tutor at dist level; church warden Yarm Parish Church; FRCOG 1985; *Recreations* pastel painting, modern art history, wine; *Style—* Stuart Walton, Esq; The Downs, The Spital, Yarm, Cleveland TS15 9EU (☎ 0642 783898); Department of Obstetrics and Gynaecology, North Tees General Hospital, Stockton-on-Tees, Cleveland TS19 8PE (☎ 0642 672122)

WALTON, William Robert; s of Wiliam Redman Walton (d 1970) and Edith Alice, *née* Levit (d 1980); *b* 4 July 1925; *Educ* Loughborough Coll; *m* 1949, Joyce, da of Ernest Edward Baldwin (d 1960); 1 da (Jacqueline); *Career* mechanical engr; dir Hathorn Davey & Co 1971-88, jt md Sulzer Bros (UK) Ltd 1978-88 (dir 1971-88), chm Sulzer (UK) Pumps Ltd 1987-88; past pres Yorkshire & Humberside Employers Assoc; FIMechE, CEng, CBIM; *Recreations* photography, gardening; *Style—* William Walton, Esq; Willow Court, Tripp Garth, Linton, Wetherby, W Yorks; Enterprise Adviser, DTI Yorkshire & Humberside, 25 Queen St, Leeds LS1 2TW (☎ 0532 338 366)

WALTON JONES, Howard; s of Alfred Hayter Walton Jones, of Majorca, and Carmen Mary, *née* Rowlands; ggf A Jones founded A Jones & Sons 1857 London; Co now has 120 shops in England with int reputation for high quality; *b* 18 Feb 1945; *Educ* Monkton Combe Sch Bath; *m* 20 July 1968, Susan Dorothy Ann, da of John Brian Edwards Penn (d 1980); 2 da (Emma b 1972, Katy b 1975); *Career* md A Jones & Sons plc (shoe retailers) 1976-; dir: Church & Co plc (shoe mfrs) 1976-, Babers of Oxford St (shoe retailers) 1976-; *Recreations* tennis; *Clubs* East India; *Style—* Howard Walton Jones, Esq; 18 Maple Road, Eastbourne, E Sussex BN23 6NZ (☎ 0323 30532, fax 0323 38272)

WALTON OF DETCHANT, Baron (Life Peer UK 1989); John Nicholas Walton; TD (1962); s of Herbert Walton; *b* 16 Sept 1922; *Educ* Alderman Wraith GS, King's Coll Med Sch Univ of Durham (MD); *m* 1946, Mary Harrison; 1 s, 2 da; *Career* Col (late RAMC) CO I(N) Gen Hosp (TA) 1963-66, Hon Col 201 (N) Gen Hosp (T and AVR) 1968-73; conslt neurologist Univ of Newcastle Hosps 1958-83, prof neurology Univ of Newcastle 1968-83, chm Muscular Dystrophy Gp GB 1970-, memb Gen Med Cncl 1971- (chm Educn Ctee 1975-82, pres 1982-89), pres BMA 1980-82, ASME 1982-, ABN 1987-8; first vice pres World Fedn Neurologists 1981-89 (pres 1989-); warden Green Coll Oxford 1983-89; pres RSM 1984-86; FRCP; DSc Newcastle; kt 1979; *Clubs* Athenaeum, United Oxford and Cambridge; *Style—* The Rt Hon Lord Walton of Detchant, TD; 13 Norham Gardens, Oxford OX2 6PS (☎ 0865 512492)

WALWYN, Peter Tyndall; s of Lt-Col C T Walwyn, DSO, OBE, MC (d 1959), and Alexandra Adelaide Walwyn (d 1959); *b* 1 July 1933; *Educ* Charterhouse; *m* 5 Jan 1960, Virginia Clementina, da of Auriol S Gaselee (d 1987); 1 s (Edward b 1969), 1 da (Kate b 1972); *Career* racehorse trainer; leading trainer on the Flat 1974-75, leading trainer Ireland 1974-75; major races won incl: The Thousand Guineas 1970, Oaks Stakes 1974, Irish Derby 1971, King George and Queen Elizabeth Stakes, Epsom Derby, Irish Derby, Irish 2000 Guineas; *Recreations* foxhunting, shooting; *Clubs* Turf, Jockey (Club Rooms); *Style—* Peter Walwyn, Esq; Seven Barrows, Lambourn, Berks

WAN, Dr Horatio Ho-Hee; s of Cheuk-ming Wan (d 1988), of Hong Kong, and Shun-Hing, *née* Au (d 1979); *b* 24 June 1935; *Educ* Ling-nan Middle Sch Hong Kong, Univ of Hong Kong (MB BS), Univ of Manchester (MSc); *m* 24 Feb 1960, Octavia Huang long-long, da of Chen-Ying Huang, of Hong Kong; 1 s (Dennis Jit-Yin b 1971), 1 da (Valeria Jit-Wing Wan Ricci b 1961); *Career* MO Nethersole Hosp Hong Kong, sr house offr Aberdeen Teaching Hosps 1972-74, med registrar SE Kent 1974-75, res fell and med registrar Hosp Manchester 1975-77, lectr and sr med registrar Univ Hosp of S Manchester 1977-78, conslt physician in geriatric med Tameside Gen Hosp 1979-; author of articles in various med jls incl: British Jl of Cancer, Postgraduate Medical Jl, Int Jl of Immunopharmacology; pres Manchester Chinatown Lions Club Int 1987-88; MRCP 1975; *Recreations* travel, reading, investment, walking; *Style—* Dr Horatio Wan; Tameside General Hosp, Ashton-under-Lyne, Lancashire OL6 9RW (☎ 061 3308373, 061 2282548), Room 8, 2nd Floor, Apothecary House, 41 Fauklner St, Manchester M1 4EE

WANAMAKER, Samuel (Sam); s of Maurice Wanamaker (d 1983), of Los Angeles, and Molly, *née* Bobele (d 1978); *b* 14 June 1919; *Educ* Tuley HS Chicago, Drake Univ Des Moines Iowa, Godman Theatre Chicago Art Inst (BDA); *m* 26 May 1940, Charlotte, da of Arnold Holland (d 1936), of Chicago; 3 da (Abby b 14 July 1942, Zoe Mora b 13 May 1948, Jessica Lee b 24 January 1954); *Career* WWII serv: NCO Special Servs Div US Army 1944-46 (serv Pacific with invasion forces in capture of Iwo Jima); Globe players Co (Great Lakes Fair) 1936, dir JPI Theatres Chicago 1939-40; acted in and directed Broadway shows incl: Café Crown 1941, Counterattack 1942, This Too Shall Pass (1946), Joan of Lorraine 1947, Goodbye My Fancy 1949, Caesar and Cleopatra 1950, A Far Country 1961, Children from their Games, Case of Libel, Murder Among US 1962-63; acted in and directed over 50 films incl: My Girl Tisa 1947, Christ in Concrete 1949, Taras Bulba 1962, Those Magnificent Men in Their Flying Machines 1964, The Spy Who Came in From The Cold 1965, Death on the Nile 1978, Private Benjamin 1980, Superman IV 1986, Baby Boom 1987; acted in and directed over 200 films and TV shows in UK, USA and Europe incl: Holocaust 1977, The Berrengers 1984, Baby Boom 1988-89, To Cast a Shadow (MGM) 1990, Guilt By Suspicion (Warner Brothers) 1990, A Time to Remember (USA cable 1990); dir ABC TV movie 'Colombo' 1989, The Shell Seekers (MCA/Universal) 1989; prodr opera incl: King Priam, Forza del Destino, Ice Break (all at Covent Garden), War and Peace (Sydney), Aida (San Francisco), Stravinsky, Oedipus Rex (Tanglewood), Tosca (San Diego); artistic dir New Shakespeare Theatre Liverpool 1957-59, played Iago in Othello RSC 1959-60, played title role and directed Macbeth Chicago 1964, prodr seasons Globe Playhouse Tst 1972-74; fndr: The Globe Playhouse Tst, World Centre for Shakespeare Studies 1970-71, Shakespeare Globe Tst, Int Shakespeare Globe Centre, Bear Gardens Museum and Arts Centre 1982; Hon LLD Univ of New Brunswick 1988, Hon Dr Fine Arts Roosevelt Univ 1990; Benjamin Franklin award RSA 1990, Ambassador Fndn award for Excellence 1991; memb BAFTA; *Recreations* jogging, tennis, swimming; *Clubs* RSA, Athenaeum; *Style—* Sam Wanamaker, Esq; International Shakespeare Globe Centre, Bear Gardens, Bankside, Liberty of the Clink, London SE1 9EB (☎ 071 620 0202, US 213 653 6783, UK Fax 01 928 7968)

WANAMAKER, Zoë Mora; da of Sam Wanamaker of Chicago USA, and Charlotte Holland; *b* 13 May 1949; *Educ* King Alfred Sch, Sidcot Sch Somerset, Hornsey Coll of Art, Central Sch of Speech and Drama; *Career* actress; Manchester 69 Co: Midsummers Night Dream 1970, Guys and Dolls 1972; Edinburgh Lyceum Theatre: The Cherry Orchard 1971 (also at the Stables Theatre Club 1970), Dick Whittington 1971-72; Twelfth Night (Leeds Playhouse 1971, Cambridge Theatre Co 1973-74), Caberet (Farnham) 1974; Young Vic 1974 (Tom Thumb, Much Ado About Nothing), Kiss Me Kate (Oxford Playhouse) 1974, The Taming of the Shrew (New Shakespeare Co Round House) 1975, Nottingham Playhouse 1975-76 (A Streetcar Named Desire, Pygmalion, Beggars Opera, Trumpets and Drums); Piccadilly Theatre: Wild Oats 1977, Once in a Lifetime 1979-80 (RSC 1978-79, SWET award 1979); RSC Stratford and London: The Devils Disciple (Aldwych), Ivanov (Aldwych), The Taming of the Shrew 1978-79 (SWET award 1979), A Comedy of Errors 1984-85, Twelfth Night 1984-85, The Time of Your Life 1984-85, Mother Courage 1984-85 (Drama award 1984), Othello (The Other Place) 1989; Loot (Manhattan Theatre Club, Music Box Theatre Broadway) 1986, Made in Bangkok (The Mark Taper Forum LA) 1988; NT: The Importance of Being Earnest 1984-85, Bay at Nice 1986-87 Wrecked Eggs 1986-87, Mrs Klein 1988-89, The Crucible 1990-91 TV incl: Sally For Keeps 1970, The Eagle Has Landed 1972, Between the Wars 1973, The Silver Mask 1973, Lorna and Ted 1973, The Confederacy of Wives 1974, The Village Hall 1975, Dantons Death 1977, Beaux Strategem 1977, The Devils Crown 1978-79, Strike 1981, Baal 1981, All the Worlds A Stage 1982, Richard III 1982, Enemies of the State 1982, Edge of Darkness 1985, Paradise Postponed 1985, Poor Little Rich Girl 1987, Once in a Lifetime 1987, The Dog it was that Died 1988, Ball Trap on the Coté Sauvage 1989, Othello 1989, Prime Suspect 1990, Love Hurts 1991; films: Inside the Third Reich 1982, The Raggedy Rawney 1987; radio: The Golden Bowl, Plenty 1979, Bay at Nice 1987, A February Morning 1990, Carol (book reading) 1990, Such Rotten Luck 1991 (first series 1989); *Recreations* music, art galleries, films, TV, listening to the radio, dancing, seeing friends, reading, junkshops, shopping, the countryside, the garden; *Style—* Ms Zoe Wanamaker; Jeremy Conway, 18-21 Jermyn St, London SW1Y 6HP (☎ 071 287 0077)

WANDRAG, Graham David; s of late Fl Lt Sarel Johannes Wandrag, MBE, of Pretoria, SA, and Florence Belle Adath, *née* Chedzey; *b* 23 Sept 1949; *Educ* Stationers Co Sch; *m* 1 (m dis 1983), Christine Ann, *née* Johnson; 1 da (Olivia Maria b 19 Feb 1981); m 2, 6 Oct 1986, Jenefer Catherine; *Career* ptnr City Deposit Brokers 1974-87, md Tradition UK Ltd 1987-88; dir Tradition UK Ltd 1989-, CEO Tradition Berisford LP New York 1989-; TSA, NASD, fell RSPB, SRA, fell RZS; *Recreations* squash, wildlife conservation, golf; *Clubs* Roehampton; *Style—* Graham Wandrag, Esq; 14 Wadham Rd, Putney, London SW15 2LR (☎ 081 870 8340); 133 Ryder Way, New Providence, New Jersey 07974, USA (☎ 010 1 201 771 0774); Staple Hall, Stone House Ct, 87-90 Houndsditch, London EC3 7AX (☎ 071 283 7971, fax 071 621 1213, car 0836 211 722); 61 Broadway, New York NY 100006 (☎ 010 1 212 797 7200, fax 010 1 212 797 7207, car 010 1 201 913 4154)

WANE, Peter Ingle; s of Richard Soloman Wane, and Hazel, *née* Whitalker; *b* 15 March 1949; *Educ* Harrogate Sch of Art, Stoke-on-Trent Coll of Art and Design, RCA; *Career* graphic designer BBC 1975-; programmes worked on incl: Bread, Arena, Omnibus, An Ocean Apart, Life without George, You Must be the Husband, Playschool, Fast Forward, Sword and Spirit, The Two Ronnies, Antiques Road Show; also various documentary features, music and art childrens programmes; illustrator: The Pilgrims Progress by John Bunyan, various George McDonald Books (incl The Lost Princess, The Princess and the Goblin), various magazine articles; *Clubs* BBC Squash; *Style—* Peter Wane, Esq; 45 Woodheyes Rd, London NW10 (☎ 081 451 4706); BBC Television Centre, Woodlane, Shepherds Bush, London W7 (☎ 081 576 1339, fax 081 743 0377)

WANT, Dennis Victor John; s of Thomas Victor Want, of Walsall, West Midlands, and Nellie Smith; *b* 12 March 1936; *Educ* Joseph Leckie Comp Sch Walsall, Wednesbury Tech Coll (HNC); *m* 21 May 1960, Brenda Rose, da of John Horace Cope; 3 s (Paul Andrew John b 30 May 1962, Robert Michael b 7 Dec 1965, Jonathan Peter b 14 Aug 19700, 1 da (Susan Mary b 5 March 1968); *Career* Brockhouse Transmissions Ltd: chief designer 1965-73, mangr engrg 1973-83, dir engrg and mktg 1983-84; mktg mangr K A W Engineering Ltd 1985, self-employed engrg conslt 1985-86, chief designer NEI Allen Ltd and Allen Gears 1986-; *Recreations* all sporting activities especially badminton and football (former mangr jr football team), DIY, winemaking; *Style—* Dennis Want, Esq; NEI Allen Limited - Allen Gears, Atlas Works, Station Rd, Pershire, Worcs WR10 2BZ (☎ 0386 552211, fax 0386 554491)

WARBURG, (Christina) Clare Barham; da of Dr Alan Barham Carter, *qv*, of The Bracken, St Georges Hill, Weybridge, Surrey, and Mollie Christina, *née* Sanders; *b* 16 Dec 1946; *Educ* St Michaels Sch, Université de Poitiers; *m* 1, 8 June 1968 (m dis 1975), Andrew Oscar Warburg, s of late Brig Thomas Raphael Warburg, CBE of Maidstone Kent; 2 s (Mark b 9 Jan 1971, Daniel b 2 Dec 1972); m 2, 28 Feb 1983 (m dis 1987) Peter Brian Adie; *Career* paper conservator and watercolour restorer; fine art dealer: Kensington Park Galleries 1975-78, freelance 1978-; memb: Kensington Ctee Save The Children Fund; *Recreations* gardening, antiques, photography; *Clubs* Lansdowne; *Style—* Mrs Clare Warburg; 18 Park Place Villas, London W2 15P; Meadow Cottage, Milland Liphook, Hampshire

WARBURTON, Dame Anne (Marion); DCVO (1979, CVO 1965), CMG (1977); da of Capt Eliot Warburton, MC; *b* 8 June 1927; *Educ* Barnard Coll, Columbia Univ, Somerville Coll Oxford; *Career* Marshall Plan Administration London 1949-52, NATO Paris 1952-54, Lazard Bros 1955-57; joined FO 1957, served FO/FCO; UK perm mission: UN NY 1959-62, Bonn 1962-65; head Guidance and Info Policy Dept FCO 1975-76, ambass Denmark 1976-83, ambass and perm UK rep to UN and other int orgns Geneva 1983-85 (former cnsllr UK Mission to UN Geneva 1970-75), pres Lucy Cavendish Coll Cambridge 1985-; cmmr Equal Opportunities Cmmn 1986-87, memb Bd Br Library 1989-; FRSA 1986; *Style—* Dame Anne Warburton, DCVO, CMG; Lucy Cavendish Coll, Lady Margaret Road, Cambridge

WARBURTON, David; s of Harold Warburton, (d 1988), of Shipley Yorks, and Ada, *née* Sinfield (d 1960); *b* 10 Jan 1942; *Educ* St Walburgas Sch Shipley, Cottingley Manor Sch Bingley, Coleg Harlech N Wales; *m* 15 Oct 1966, Carole Ann Susan, da of Frank Tomney (d 1984), of Rickmansworth, and former MP for Hammersmith; 2 da (Sara Anne b 25 Sept 1968, Caroline Susan b 28 July 1970); *Career* GMWU educn offr 1965-67 (regnl offr 1967-73), Nat industl offr GMBATU 1973-90, nat offr Apex 1990-; vice pres Int Fedn Chemical and Energy Workers 1986-, sec UK Chemical Unions Cncl 1978-85, chm TUC Gen Purpose Ctee 1984-; memb: NEDC 1973-86, Cwlth Devpt Corp 1979-87, MOD Industl Cncl 1988-; sec Friends of Palestine 1983-; memb: Yorkshire Soc 1983-, Upper Wharfedale Museum Soc 1978-; *Books* Pharmaceuticals for the People (1973), Drug Industry (1975), UK Chemicals: The Way Forward (1977), Economic Detente (1980), The Case for Voters Tax Credits (1983), Forward Labour (1985), Facts Figures and Damned Statistics (1987); contrib numerous articles to leading jls; *Recreations* hill climbing, music, 1930-40 film memorabilia; *Clubs* Victoria (Westminster); *Style—* David Warburton, Esq; 47 Hill Rise, Chorleywood, Rickmansworth, Herts WD3 2NY (☎ 0923 778726); GMB Thorne House, Ruxley Ridge Claygate, Esher, Surrey (☎ 0372 62081, fax 0372 67164)

WARBURTON, Ernest; s of Arthur Warburton (d 1946), of Irlam, Lancs, and Jane Warburton (d 1942); *b* 10 June 1937; *Educ* Royal Masonic Sch, Wadham Coll Oxford (MA, DPhil); *m* 31 Dec 1960, (Anne) Jennifer, da of Harry Carding (d 1971), of Cadishead, Lancs; 2 s (Matthew b 1964, Jonathan b 1966); *Career* BBC: head of music North of Eng 1970-77, head of music progs Radio 1977-81, ed music Radio Three 1982-85, external servs music organiser 1986-88, managing ed World Serv 1988-90, ed World Serv 1990-; ed The Collected Works of Johann Christian Bach 1984-; author numerous articles on music in jls incl: The New Grove, The Musical Times, The Listener; memb Radio Acad; FRCO 1968; *Recreations* music, travel, architecture, reading, things Halian; *Style—* Ernest Warburton, Esq; 10a Park Ave, St Albans, Herts AL1 4PB (☎ 0727 52589); BBC World Service, PO Box 76, Bush House, London WC2B 4PH (☎ 071 257 2343, fax 071 379 6785, telex 265781)

WARBURTON, Ivor William; s of Dennis Warburton (d 1990), and Edna Margaret, *née* Ridgway; *b* 13 Aug 1946; *Educ* Dulwich, Queen's Coll Cambridge (BA, MA), Univ of Warwick (MSc); *m* 16 Aug 1969 (m dis 1982), Carole-Ann, *née* Ashton; 3 da (Penny b 1970, Hazel b 1970, Catherine b 1975); *Career* British Railways: local prodn mgmnt posts 1968-74, divnl passenger mangr Bristol 1974-78, overseas tourist mangr Bd headquarters 1978-82, chief passenger mangr Eastern region York 1982-84, dir Passenger Mktg Servs Bd headquarters 1984-85, asst gen mangr London Midland

Region Birmingham 1985-87, employee rels mangr Bd headquarters 1987-88, dir of ops Bd headquarters 1988-90, gen mangr London Midland region Birmingham 1990-; dir Transecon 1984-85; memb: ESRC Indust Econ and Environment Res Devpt Gp 1989-, West Midlands Regnl Cncl CBI 1990-; Liveryman Worshipful Co of Marketors 1987; MCIM 1987, FCIT 1989; *Recreations* cooking Chinese style, music, opera, handicapped scouting; *Style*— Ivor Warburton, Esq; 34 St Clair's Road, Croydon CR0 5NE (☎ 081 688 2742); British Rail London Midland Region, Stanier House, 10 Holliday St, Birmingham B1 1TG (☎ 021 644 4200, fax 021 644 4557)

WARBURTON, John Kenneth; CBE (1983); s of Frederick Hammond Warburton (d 1989), of Wolstanton, Newcastle-under-Lyme, and Winifred Eva, *née* Abbotts (d 1990); *b* 7 May 1932; *Educ* Newcastle-under-Lyme HS, Keble Coll Oxford (MA); *m* 25 June 1960, Patricia Naomi Margaret, da of Stewart Frank Glennie Gordon, ISM (d 1962), of Shrewsbury; 1 da (Moira b 1961); *Career* RAOC 1950-52; called to the Bar Gray's Inn 1977; with London C of C 1956-59, dir and chief exec Birmingham Chamber of Indust and Commerce 1978 (joined 1959); memb: Steering Ctee Int Bureau of C of C 1976-, Nat Cncl Assoc of Br C of C 1978-, review body on Doctors and Dentists Remuneration 1982-, E Euro Trade Cncl BOTB 1984- (Euro Trade Ctee and Business Link Gp 1979-87), MSC Task Gp on Employment Trg 1987-88; regnl sec W Midlands Regnl Gp of C of C 1978-, pres Br C of C Execs 1979-81; dir: Business in the Community 1981-91, Nat Garden Festival 1986 Ltd 1983-87, Birmingham Convention and Visitor Bureau 1986-, Black Business in Birmingham 1986-; alternate dir Birmingham Heartlands Ltd 1988-, govr Univ of Birmingham 1982-; chm: Advsy Cncl W Midlands Industl Devpt Assoc 1983-86, Birmingham Chamber Trg Ltd 1987-; dir Nat Exhibition Centre Ltd 1989-; memb Disciplinary Panels FIMBRA 1989, FRSA; *Style*— John Warburton, Esq, CBE; 35 Hampshire Drive, Edgbaston, Birmingham B15 3NY (☎ 021 454 6764); Birmingham Chamber of Industry & Commerce, PO Box 360, 75 Harborne Rd, Birmingham B15 3DH (☎ 021 454 6171, fax 021 455 8670, telex 338024)

WARBURTON, Laurence; s of John Urquhart Warburton, of Esher, Surrey, and Edith Mary, *née* Rhodes; *b* 8 April 1943; *Educ* Kingston GS, Surbiton GS; *m* 1; 1 s (Julian b 1974), 1 da (Sarah b 1972); m 2, 14 Feb 1986, Geraldine; *Career* mktg dir Trident Life 1974-83, nat sales mangr Life Assoc of Scotland 1983-85, md Regency Fin Gp plc 1985-89; *Recreations* skiing, travel, opera; *Style*— Laurence Warburton, Esq; Little Oak, Fee Farm Rd, Claygate, Surrey KT10 0JX (☎ 0372 68 453)

WARBURTON, Richard Maurice; OBE (1987); s of Richard Warburton (d 1954), of 63 Chorley Rd, Standish, nr Wigan, and Phyllis Abbott (d 1972); *b* 14 June 1928; *Educ* Wigan GS, Univ of Birmingham (BA); *m* 13 Feb 1952, Lois May, da of Sydney Green, of 16 Romney Way, Wigan; 2 s (Ian Richard b 1952, Nicholas b 1953); *Career* HM Inspectorate of Factories 1953-79: HM superintending inspr, dir Accident Prevention Advsy Unit 1972-79, chm Jt Standing Ctee Safety in Paper Mills 1976-78; dir gen ROSPA 1979-91; advsr Worshipful Co of Carmen 1980-; *Recreations* golf, hill walking, gardening, reading; *Style*— Richard Warburton, Esq, OBE; Cornaa, Wyfordby Ave, Blackburn BB2 7AR (☎ 0254 56824)

WARD, Dr Adam Anthony; s of Dennis Harold Ward, of Avening, Mark Cross, Crowborough, East Sussex, and Margaret Maud, *née* Record; *b* 15 June 1947; *Educ* Tonbridge, Springhill Sch, King's Coll London, Westminster Med Sch, Univ of London (MB BS), LSHTM (MSc), Hotel Dieu Univ of Paris (DipOrthMed); *Career* ed Broadway Magazine 1970, lectr and hon sr registrar (epidemiology) Westminster Med Sch 1978-79; physician: Dept of Orthopaedic Med Hotel Dieu Paris 1982-83, Royal London Homoeopathic Hosp 1983-; specialist in complementary med; clinician; lectr; broadcaster; memb: Cncl The Faculty of Homoeopathy London, Medical Homoeopathic Res Gp London; *Recreations* walking in Rupert Bear country; *Style*— Dr Adam A Ward; 41 Frankfield Rise, Tunbridge Wells, Kent TN2 5LF (☎ 0892 25799)

WARD, Sir Alan Hylton; s of Stanley Victor Ward (d 1974), and Mary, *née* Whittingham; *b* 15 Feb 1938; *Educ* Christian Bros Coll Pretoria, Univ of Pretoria (BA, LLB), Cambridge Univ (MA, LLB); *m* 1, 22 June 1963 (m dis 1982); 1 s (Mark b 1968), 2 da (Wendy b 1965, Emma b 1966); m 2, Helen Madeleine, da of Keith Gilbert, of Berkswell, Warwicks; 2 da (Amelia b 1984, Katharine (twin) b 1984); *Career* attorney Supreme Ct SA 1959-61, called to the Bar Gray's Inn 1964, QC (1984), Justice of the High Ct assigned to the Family Div 1988; kt 1988; *Recreations* knocking balls about; *Clubs* MCC; *Style*— The Hon Sir Alan Ward; Royal Courts of Justice, Strand, London WC2A 2LL (☎ 071 936 6000)

WARD, Hon Mrs (Alathea Gwendolen Alys Mary); *née* Fitzalan-Howard; da of late 2 Viscount Fitzalan of Derwent and Joyce Elizabeth, now Countess Fitzwilliam, *qv*; *b* 24 Nov 1923; *m* 1953, Hon Edward Frederick Ward (d 1987), s of 2 Earl of Dudley; *Style*— The Hon Mrs Ward; 21b Ave du Temple, Lausanne, Switzerland (☎ 021 652 6986)

WARD, Hon Mrs (Alice Belinda); eldest da of Hon John Dawson Eccles, CBE, and Baroness Eccles of Moulton (Life Peer), *qqv*; *b* 15 Jan 1958; *Educ* Univ of Durham (BSc); *m* 1981, Rev Robert Charles Irwin Ward, s of late John Lawson Ward, of The Old Vicarage, Salehurst, Robertsbridge, Sussex; 2 s (Samuel John b 1982, James Nicholas b 1984), 1 da (Susanna Mary b 1988); *Style*— The Hon Mrs Ward; 1 Hawthorn Villas, The Green, Wallsend-on-Tyne

WARD, Anthony John Hedderley; s of Dudley John Hedderley Ward (d 1980), of Matching Green, Harlow, Essex, and Winifred Marjorie, *née* Bidwell (d 1979); *b* 21 May 1926; *Educ* Bowden House Sch Seaford Sussex, Eton; *Career* joined Coldstream Gds 1944, cmmnd 1945, ret with rank of Capt 1948; chm and md W J Rendell Ltd Hitchin Herts (family firm, joined 1948), chm Hydrophane Ltd Hitchin; former dir: Ward and Ward (Australia) Ltd, Bliss Chemicals and Pharmaceuticals (India) Ltd; pres: N Herts Cons Assoc 1980-85 (former chm 1975-78), The Queens Club 1984-89 (chm 1977-80); Liveryman Worshipful Co of Mercers 1967; *Recreations* real tennis, lawn tennis, golf; *Clubs* All England Lawn Tennis, The Queen's, Royal Worlington Golf; *Style*— Anthony Ward, Esq; Bunyans Cottage, Preston, Hitchin, Herts SG4 7RS (☎ 0462 452 147); Ickleford Manor, Hitchin, Herts SG5 3XE (☎ 0462 432 596, fax 0462 420 423, car 0860 720 528, telex 82311)

WARD, Anthony Stewart; s of Norman Ward (d 1988), of Woodville, Green Lanes, Sutton Coldfield, W Midlands, and Alice, *née* Patterson; *b* 13 Nov 1943; *Educ* Bishop Vesey GS Sutton Coldfield, Univ of London (MBBS); *m* 25 Aug 1979, Susan Mary, da of Rev Donald Moorhouse Lister (d 1966), of Kenwood, Langsett Avenue, Sheffield; 1 da (Sally Elizabeth b 1986); *Career* surgical registrar United Birmingham Teaching Hosps 1968-70, surgical registrar Middx Hosp 1972, lectr in surgery Univ of Sheffield 1972-75, sr registrar in surgery Sheffield Area Health Authy 1975-82, conslt surgn Basingstoke Dist Hosp 1983-; memb: BMA, Vascular Surgical Soc of GB and I 1988; FRCS 1971, MS 1975; *Books* Operative techniques in arterial surgery (1966); *Recreations* interior design; *Style*— Anthony Ward, Esq; Basingstoke District Hospital, Aldermaston Rd, Basingstoke, Hants RG24 9NA (☎ 0256 473202)

WARD, Antony John (Tony); s of Edgar Frank Ward (d 1979), of Northampton, and Kathleen Muriel Ward, MBE, *née* Hobbs; *b* 23 June 1947; *Educ* Northampton Trinity HS, Lanchester Poly Coventry (LLB); *Career* local govt legal serv 1969-78, slr of Supreme Ct 1971, ptnr Coward Chance 1985-87 (joined 1978), ptnr Clifford Chance 1987-; memb Law Soc Planning Law Ctee 1985-; chm: Bar Cncl, RICS, Law Soc Jt Planning Law Conf Ctee 1987-88; memb Cncl Br Polish Legal Assoc; numerous lectures and articles for professional orgns and pubns; Freeman City of London 1980, Liveryman Worshipful Co of Slrs 1983; memb: Law Soc 1980, Int Bar Assoc 1981; *Recreations* tennis, squash; *Style*— Tony Ward, Esq; 111 Willoughby House, Barbican, London EC2Y 8BL (☎ 071 628 8200); Clifford Chance, Blackfriars House, 19 New Bridge St, London EC4V 6BY (☎ 071 353 0211, fax 071 489 0046, telex 887 847 LEGIS G)

WARD, Brian; s of Stanhope Llewellyn Ward (d 1958), of Huddersfield, and Lily, *née* Wilkinson (d 1982); *b* 12 Dec 1924; *Educ* King James GS, Almondbury Huddersfield; *m* 24 March 1951, Joan Ward, da of Arthur George Enoch (d 1963), of Huddersfield; 2 da (Valerie Ann b 1954, Helen Virginia Wells b 1957); *Career* RNVR 1943-46, Sub Lt; CA 1949; sr ptnr Revell Ward W Yorks, ret; business interests: machine tools, builders' merchants, venture capital; memb: Bd of Govrs for Huddersfield Poly, Colne Valley Cons Assoc; FICA 1949; *Recreations* golf, private flying, travel; *Clubs* Woodsome Hall GC Ltd, Yorkshire Aeroplane; *Style*— Brian Ward, Esq; 8 Occupation Rd, Lindley, Huddersfield, W Yorks HD3 3AZ (☎ 0484 421005, fax 0484 421005)

WARD, Cecil; CBE (1989); s of William Ward (d 1975), of 23 Belgravia Ave, Belfast, and Mary Caroline, *née* Gray (d 1969); *b* 26 Oct 1929; *Educ* Belfast Tech HS, Belfast Coll of Technol, Queen's Univ Belfast (MA); *Career* Belfast Corp: clerk 1947-60, ctee clerk 1960-73; Belfast City Cncl: chief clerk 1973-77, asst town clerk 1977-79, town clerk and chief exec 1979-89, ret 1989; memb: Bd Ulster Orch 1980-, Exec Cncl Soc of Local Authy Chief Execs 1980-89 (chm 1990), ARB Cncl NI 1980-85 and 1987-89, NI Ctee of IBA 1983-88, NI Local Govt Staff Cmmn 1983-89, Bd Tstees Ulster Museum 1989-, Senate Queen's Univ Belfast 1990-B; *Recreations* music walking; *Clubs* Malone Golf; *Style*— Cecil Ward, Esq, CBE, JP; 24 Thornhill, Malone, Belfast BT9 6SS Northern Ireland (☎ 0232 668950)

WARD, Christopher John Ferguson; s of Maj Harry Leeming Ferguson Ward, and Barbara Dorothy, *née* Gurney; *b* 26 Dec 1942; *Educ* Magdalen Coll Oxford; *m* 1 (m dis); 2 s (Julian b 1963, Alexander b 1969), 1 da (Samantha b 1967); m 2, Janet Theresa, da of Ronald Kelly; 1 s (Rupert b 1986), 1 da (Sarah b 1984); *Career* admitted slr 1965; managing ptnr Clarks Solicitors 1990-; MP for Swindon 1969-70, former memb Berks CC (ldr 1979-81); chm: Chiltern Nursery Trg Coll (1989-91), Assoc of Nursery Trg Colls 1990; *Clubs* Carlton, United and Cecil (hon sec 1982-87); *Style*— Christopher Ward, Esq; Ramblings, Maidenhead Thicket, Berks SL6 3QE; Gt Western House, Station Rd, Reading RG1 1SX (☎ 0734 585 321)

WARD, Christopher Margrave; s of Dr Gerald Margrave Ward (d 1979), and Pamela Gwyneth, *née* Owen-Williams; *b* 17 June 1941; *Educ* Felsted, London Hosp Medical Sch, Univ of London (BSc, MB BS); *m* 7 July 1971, Wendy Ann, da of Capt Leslie Edward Campion, of 14 Charlwood, Courtwood Lane, Croydon; 1 s (Matthew b 1972), 1 da (Naomi b 1974); *Career* clinical res fell plastic surgery Hosp for Sick Children Toronto Canada 1976-77, sr registrar plastic surgery Postgrad Med Sch Hammersmith Hosp 1977-78, memb Monospecialist Ctee for Plastic Surgery within EEC 1986-1990, conslt plastic surgn; W Middx Hammersmith and Central Middx Hosps 1978-88, Charing Cross and W Middx Univ Hosps 1988-; advsr: Nat Breast Care and Mastectomy Assoc, Nat Disfigurement Guidance Centre; examiner plastic surgery specialists FRCS intercollegiate exam; pres: plastic surgn section RSM 1986-87, W London Cleft Lip and Palate Assoc; Eng int hockey player 1965; FRCS; *Books* Cosmetic Surgery - Facing The Facts (1986); *Recreations* real tennis; *Clubs* Queen's and Hampton court Real Tennis; *Style*— Christopher Ward, Esq; 44 Wensleydale Rd, Hampton, Middlesex TW12 2LT (☎ 081 979 2897); 310 Kew Rd, Kew Gdns, Richmond, Surrey TW9 3DU (☎ 081 948 4990)

WARD, Clive Richard; s of William Herbert Ward (d 1982), and Muriel, *née* Wright; *b* 30 July 1945; *Educ* Sevenoaks Sch, Univ of Cambridge (MA); *m* 9 Sept 1972, Catherine Angela, da of Lt Cdr Godfrey Joseph Hines, of Droxford, Hants; 3 da (Joanna b 1975, Diana b 1977, Emily b 1979); *Career* CA 1971, asst sec take over panel 1975-77, ptnr Ernst and Young 1979-90, head corp fin London 1987, corp devpt dir Shandwick plc 1990; Freeman Worshipful Co of Barbers 1985, Worshipful Co of Tobacco Pipe Makers and Tobacco Blenders 1975; FCA 1979; *Books* Guide to Company Flotation (1989); *Recreations* fishing, music, gardening; *Style*— Clive Ward, Esq; Market Heath House, Brenchley, Tonbridge, Kent TN12 7PA (☎ 089272 2172); Shandwick plc, 61 Grosvenor St, London W1X 9DA (☎ 071 408 2232, fax 071 493 8246)

WARD, David; s of Frank Ward, of Darfield, and Elizabeth, *née* Pattinson (d 1989); *b* 23 Feb 1937; *Educ* Dame Allan's School Newcastle-upon-Tyne, Queen Elizabeth GS Penrith, St Edmund Hall Oxford (BA); *m* 22 July 1978, Antoinette, da of Maj-Gen Desmond Alexander Bruce Clarke; 2 s (Andrew b 1981, Robin b 1982), 1 da (Rachel b 1979); *Career* admitted slr 1962; with Atkinson and North since articles, now sr ptnr; pres The Law Soc 1989-90 (cncl memb 1972); *Recreations* mountaineering, choral singing; *Clubs* Carlisle Mountaineering; *Style*— David Ward, Esq; The Green, Caldbeck, Wigton, Cumbria CA7 8ER (☎ 0698 220), 15 Fisher St, Carlisle, Cumbria CA3 8RW (☎ 0228 25221, fax 0228 515509)

WARD, Dr David Arthur; s of James Arthur Ward, of Warwickshire, and Elizabeth Irene Ward; *b* 4 March 1955; *Educ* Atherstone GS, Univ of Manchester Med Sch (MB ChB); *m* 1 July 1980, (Anne) Bernadette, da of Francis Cyril Minihan (d 1952); 2 s (Nicholas b 13 July 1982, Paul b 22 Feb 1984); *Career* conslt radiologist Doncaster Royal Infirmary 1986-; MRCP 1980, FPCR 1985; *Recreations* golf; *Clubs* Doncaster Golf; *Style*— Dr David Ward; 40 Stoops Road, Bessacarr, Doncaster, South Yorkshire (☎ 0302 536614), Dept of Medical Imaging, Doncaster Royal Infirmary, Armthorpe Rd, Doncaster (☎ 0302 366666)

WARD, David James; s of Lesley Edward Ward; of Egham, Surrey, and Margaret, *née* Cook; *b* 1 May 1946; *Educ* Manor Croft Sch Egham, Brookland Tech Coll, Richmond Coll of Technol; *m* 10 April 1971, Glenora Ann, da of late Robert Gordon Tott; 2 da (Joanna Louise b 1 March 1980, Sarah Michele b 30 July 1982); *Career* freelance photographer 1978-; press photographer, work published in various magazines papers and books, photographer of Royalty, show business people and actors, specialist in portraiture; winner of many merits and awards incl: Press Photographer of the Year, Kodak Photographer of the Year, Panorama Photographer of the Year; assoc BIPP 1980, Master Photographic Assoc 1986, Br Photographers Assoc 1990; *books* Wonderful World Series (1985); *Recreations* jogging, squash, cycling; *Clubs* Roundtable (Egham); *Style*— David Ward, Esq; Latchets, Harpesford Ave, Virginia Water, Surrey GU25 4RE (☎ 0344 843421); The Studio, Latchets, Harpesford Ave, Virginia Water, Surrey GU25 4RE (☎ 0344 843421)

WARD, Denis John; s of George Hartwell Ward (d 1978), of Rainham, Kent, and Enid Joyce, *née* Randall (d 1982); *b* 3 Dec 1923; *Educ* Kings Sch Rochester; *m* 10 Oct 1959, (Mary) Rosina, da of Cdr Harry Marshall (d 1943), of Hartlip, Kent; 1 s (Timothy b 1964 d 1987), 1 da (Claire b 1961); *Career* Br Army 1943-46: bomb disposal SE Eng, W African Frontier Force in Nigeria, served in Burma; chm and md: Ward Holdings plc, Wards Construction (Medway) Ltd; dir: Wards Construction (Industrial) Ltd, Ward Homes (South East) Ltd, Ward Homes (Anglia) Ltd, Ward Bros (Gillingham) Ltd, Wards Construction (London) Ltd; chm White Seal Stairways Ltd; *Recreations* tennis, squash; *Clubs* Gore Court Cricket, Teynham Squash, Tudor Park

Squash; *Style—* Denis Ward, Esq; Ward Holdings plc, 2 Ashtree Lane, Chatham, Kent ME5 7BZ (☎ 0634 55111)

WARD, Dr Dermot Joseph; s of Richard Ward (d 1985), of Dublin, and Margaret, *née* Whitty (d 1962); *b* 7 June 1933; *Educ* St James Secdy Sch Dublin; *m* 3 Aug 1961, Ruth Eva, da of George Nathaniel Stedmond (d 1978), of Dublin; 2 s (Jonathan Dermot b 1965, Simon Richard b 1969); *Career* sr registrar in psychiatry Bath Clinical Area 1965-68, med dir St Lomans Hosp Dublin 1979-86 (conslt psychiatrist 1969-86); conslt psychiatrist: Graylingwell Hosp Chichester 1986-88, St Davids Hosp Carmarthen 1988-; pubns in: Br Med Jl, Irish Med Jl, Br Jl of Psychiatry; memb Inst of Economic Affrs 1983; LRCPI, LRCSI, LM, FRCPI, FRCPsych, DPM, memb BMA 1961, FRSM 1983; *Recreations* writing, literature, theatre, films and travel; *Clubs* Royal Soc of Med; *Style—* Dr Dermot Ward; 4 Jubilee Terrace, Chichester, West Sussex; Llysneddyg, Jobswell Rd, Carmarathen, Dyfed; St Davids Hosp, Camarthen, Dyfed SA31 3HB (☎ 0269 237481)

WARD, Donald Albert; s of Albert Goerge Ward, and Rosie, *née* Smith; *b* 30 March 1920; *Educ* Southend HS, Queen's Coll Univ of Oxford (MA); *m* 1 Sept 1948, Mary Theresa, da of Michael Molloy; 5 s (Michael b 1949, Anthony John b 1951, Adrian b 1953, Julian Patrick b 1956, Gregory Peter b 1958); *Career* IA 1940-45: RIASC served Middle East and Italy (despatches), final appt OC 10 Indian Inf Bde Tport Co; Miny of Food 1946-53, under sec Export Credits Guarantee Dept 1971-74 (joined 1953), sec gen Int Union Credit and Investmt Insurers (Berne Union) 1974-86; *Clubs* Oxford and Cambridge; *Style—* Donald Ward, Esq; Lindisfarne, St Nicholas Hill, Leatherhead, Surrey

WARD, Gen Sir Dudley; GCB (1959, KCB 1957, CB 1945), KBE (1953, CBE 1945), DSO 1944; s of Lionel Howell Ward of Wimborne Dorset; *Educ* Queen Elizabeth's GS Wimborne, RMC Sandhurst; *m* 1, 1933, Beatrice Constance (d 1962), da of late Rev T F Griffith (d 1950); 1 da; m 2, 1963, Joan Elspeth de Pechell, da of late Col D C Scott, CBE; *Career* 0 Lt Dorset Regt 1929, transferred King's Regt, Capt 1937; served WWII: Central Med Theatre (Italy (despatches), Greece), Cdr 4 Div 1944-45; (acting: Lt-Col 1941, Brig 1942, Maj-Gen 1944) COS 1945, 1945, Maj-Gen 1946, cmdt Staff Coll Camberley 1948-51, cdr 1 Corps BAOR 1951, dep CIGS 1953-56, Gen 1957, cdr Northag and C-in-C BAOR 1957-59, C-in-C Near East 1960-62, govr and C-in-C Gibraltar 1962-65, ret 1965; Col King's Regt 1947-57, Col Cmdt REME 1958-63, ADC Gen to HM The Queen 1958-61, memb Security Cmmn to 1982; DL Suffolk 1968-85; KStJ, Order of Suvorov 3 class (USSR) 1944, Cdr Legion Merit (USA) 1946; *Recreations* golf; *Clubs* Army and Navy; *Style—* Gen Sir Dudley Ward, GCB, KBE, DSO; Wynney's Farmhouse, Dennington, Woodbridge, Suffolk (☎ 072 875 663)

WARD, Dudley Arthur Jonathan; s of Charles Thomas Ward (d 1924), of Colchester, and Eva Louisa Ward (d 1944); *b* 12 Sept 1915; *Educ* Felsted; *m* 17 Nov 1939, Laila (d 1989), da of Brox Bergum (d 1942), of Norway; 2 s (Christopher b 1943, Tim b 1945), 1 da (Rita b 1941); *Career* war serv Capt RASC: France, Belgium, Holland, Germany, N Ireland 1939-45; CA; Ward & Co Frinton Walton & Colchester 1946-83, ptnr Bland Fielden Colchester 1983-85, dir Burkill & Co Ltd; FCA, FTII; *Recreations* golf, yoga; *Clubs* Frinton Golf, Cross Creek Country (Ft Myers); *Style—* Dudley A J Ward, Esq; Marconia, 34 Upper Third Ave, Frinton, Essex CO13 9PS (☎ 0255 676605); 12521 Coldstream Dr 508, Fort Myers, Florida, USA (☎ 813 7689510)

WARD, Hon Edward Nicholas; s (by 4 w) of 7 Viscount Bangor, *qv*; *b* 16 Jan 1953; *m* 1985, Rachel Mary, 2 da of Hon Hugh Waldorf Astor, *qv*; 1 da (Anna Roxelana b 1987); *Style—* The Hon Edward Ward; 9 Kildare Terrace, London W2

WARD, Ven Edwin James Greenfield; LVO (1963); s of Canon Frederick Greenfield Ward, MC (d 1963); *b* 26 Oct 1919; *Educ* St John's Leatherhead, Christ's Coll Cambridge; *m* 1946, Grizell Evelyn (d 1985), da of Capt Harry Gurney Buxton (d 1936); 1 s, 2 da; *Career* Lt King's Dragoon Guards 1940-46; ordained 1948, vicar of North Elmham 1950-55; chaplain to: HM The Queen 1955-89 (extra chaplain 1989-), Windsor Great Park 1955-67, archdeacon of Sherborne and rector of W Stafford 1967-84, archdeacon emeritus 1985-; *Recreations* fishing; *Style—* The Ven Edwin Ward, LVO; Manor Cottage, Poxwell, Dorchester, Dorset

WARD, Elizabeth Despard; MBE (1978); da of Denys Ashley Ferion Rynd (d 1965), of Brookhurst Brook, nr Godalming, Surrey, and Joyce, *née* Fleming (d 1987); *b* 11 Oct 1926; *Educ* Cheltenham Ladies Coll; *m* 1, 21 June 1946 (m dis 1952), Capt Michael Aston; 1 da (Susan b 19 May 1947); m 2, 3 May 1952, Nigel Yeoward Peirce Wad, s of Robert Geoffrey Ward (d 1971); 1 s (Timothy Nigel Peirce b 3 Jan 1953, d 1987), 1 da (Rebecca Elizabeth b 8 Feb 1954); *Career* sales dir NYP Ward and Co 1957-66, PRO Bonhams Fine Art Auctioneers 1959-61, JP 1974-83; local rep SAAFA, vol After Prison Care Serv, founder pres Br Kidney Patient Assoc; Hon LLD Univ of Dundee 1990; memb RSM, FInstD; *Books* Timbo, A Struggle for Survival (1986); *Recreations* tennis, walking, bicycling, opera; *Clubs* Arts, Royal Society of Medicine; *Style—* Mrs Elizabeth Ward, MBE; Oakhanger Place Cottage, nr Bordon, Hampshire GU35 9JP (☎ 04203 87757); British Kidney Patient Association, Bordon, Hants (☎ 04203 2021, fax 04203 5831, telex 858281)

WARD, Geoffrey Wesley; OBE (1982), VRD (1960); s of Rev Clarence Oliver Ward (d 1981), and Beatrice Ellen Ward (d 1940); *b* 6 Oct 1923; *Educ* Kingswood Sch Bath; *m* 1950, Patricia, da of Leonard Bowman Beevers (d 1980); 2 s, 1 da; *Career* joined RNVR 1942, Lt Cdr 1958; dir James Neill (Sheffield) Ltd 1966 (md 1972-), dir James Neill Holdings Ltd 1976-, dep chm and marketing dir Neill Tools Gp Ltd 1982-, chm Stubs Welding Ltd 1979-, dir Edward Pryor and Son Ltd 1981-; *Recreations* golf, gardening, caravanning; *Clubs* RNVR; *Style—* Geoffrey Ward, Esq, OBE, VRD; Robin Hill, Water Lane, Eyam, Sheffield S30 1RG; Neill Tool Ltd, Handsworth Rd, Sheffield S13 9BR (☎ 0742 449 911)

WARD, Gerald John; CBE; s of Col Edward John Sutton Ward LVO, MC (d 1990); *b* 31 May 1938; *Educ* Eton, Sandhurst, RAC Cirencester; *m* 1967 (m dis 1983), Rosalind Elizabeth, da of Hon Richard Lygon (d 1972), 2 da; m 2, 1984, Amanda, da of Sir Lacey Vincent, 2 Bt (d 1963); *Career* Capt RHG; industrialist and farmer; chm: UK Solenoid Ltd, Chilton Farms Ltd; vice pres Nat Cncl of YMCAs; Extra Equerry to HRH The Prince of Wales 1987; *Clubs* White's; *Style—* Gerald Ward, Esq, CBE; Chilton Park Farm, Hungerford, Berks (☎ 0488 682329); 179 Cranmer Court, Whiteheads Grove, London SW3 (☎ 071 589 6955)

WARD, Graham Norman Charles; s of Ronald Charles Edward Ward, and Hazel Winnifred, *née* Ellis; *b* 9 May 1952; *Educ* Dulwich, Jesus Coll Oxford (MA, Boxing blue); *m* 1975, Ingrid Imogten Sylvia, da of Hubert Edward Philip Peter Baden-Powell; 2 s (Peter Ronald Norman b 15 June 1978, Andrew Charles Richard b 16 Sept 1980); *Career* Price Waterhouse: articled clerk 1974-77, personal tech asst to chm Account Standards Ctee 1978-79, seconded to HM Treas 1985, ptnr 1986, dir Electricity Services Europe 1990; chm: Young Chartered Accountants Group 1980-81, London Soc of Chartered Accountants 1989-90 (memb Ctee 1983-); membership sec Pensions Res Accountants Gp 1985-90, memb Cncl Soc of Pension Conslts 1988-90; vice pres: Chartered Accountants Students' Soc of London 1987-, Univ of Oxford Amateur Boxing Club 1990-; pres Jesus Coll Assoc 1990-; FCA 1983 (ACA 1977); *Books* The Work of a Pension Scheme Actuary (1987), Pensions: Your Way Through The Maze (1988); *Recreations* boxing, rugby, jazz; *Clubs* Carlton, Vincent's (Oxford); *Style—* Graham Ward, Esq; Price Waterhouse, Southwark Towers, 32 London Bridge St, London SE1 9SY (☎ 071 939 3101, fax 071 403 0733, car 0860 497125)

WARD, Hon Helen Elizabeth; da of 6 Viscount Bangor, OBE, PC (d 1950), of Castle Ward, Downpatrick, NI, and Agnes Elizabeth Hamilton (d 1972), da of Dacre Hamilton; *b* 9 May 1912; *Style—* The Hon Helen Ward; 7 Chelsea Lodge, 58 Tite St, London SW3

WARD, Dr (Richard) Humphry Thomas; s of Brig Dr William Roy Ward, TD, QHS (d 1985), and Alice Anita Marjorie Ward (d 1983); *b* 29 April 1938; *Educ* Shrewsbury, St John's Coll Cambridge (MA, MB, BChir); *m* 31 July 1965, Hilary Patricia, da of Cedric Ivor Tuckett, OBE (d 1975); 2 s ((William) Harvey Charles b 1967, Jeremy Edward Humphry b 1971), 1 da (Charlotte Rosemary Lucy b 1968); *Career* conslt obstetrician and gynaecologist UCH London 1972-; FRCOG, memb RSM; *Recreations* gardening, skiing; *Style—* Dr Humphrey Ward; UCH, Private Consulting Rooms, Grafton Way, London WC1 (☎ 071 387 8323)

WARD, (William) Ian Roy; s of William Gerald Roy Ward (d 1977), of St Leonards-on-Sea, and Ellinor Ward, *née* Ostergaard (d 1964); *b* 17 Sept 1936; *Educ* Bembridge Sch, Thames Nautical Trg Coll HMS Worcester; *m* 21 Nov 1964, Vivienne, da of George Edward Garton Watson (d 1971), of Capetown; 1 s (Duncan b 30 Sept 1969), 2 da (Michele b 4 Sept 1967, Alison b 31 Aug 1975); *Career* Lt RNR until 1965; merchant navy 1954-58, 1962-64, called to the Bar Admiralty Chambers 1962, ptnr (specialising in shipping) Lovell White Durrant 1976-; Freeman Worshipful Co of Solicitors; memb Law Soc 1976-, FCIArb 1972-; *Recreations* sailing, walking; *Style—* Ian Ward, Esq; 67 The Ave, Kew, Richmond, Surrey TW9 2AH (☎ 081 940 0260); Castle Hill, Newport, Dyfed SA43 OQD (☎ 0239 820263); Lovell White Durrant, 65 Holborn Viaduct, London EC1A 2DY (☎ 071 236 0066, telex 887122 LWDG, fax 071 248 4212)

WARD, Ivor William (Bill); OBE (1969); s of Stanley James (d 1943), of Plymouth, and Emily, *née* Smith (d 1944); *b* 19 Jan 1989; *Educ* Hoe GS; *m* 1, 1939, Patricia Aston, *née* Gold (m dis 1967); m 2, 1970, Betty, *née* Wager (m dis 1981); m 3, 22 Dec 1987, Sandra Calkins Hastie, da of Cdr William Calkins, USN, of Pacific Grove, California, USA; 2 s (David Terence, Martin Sean), 1 da (Mary Kathleen); *Career* gunner RA TA 1939, WO1 REME TA 1942-46 (seconded to SAS 1946); BBC: engr's asst 1932, tech asst Alexandra Palace 1936, maintenance engr 1937, returned to Alexandra Palace as studio mangr 1946, light entertainment to prodr 1947 (responsible for How do you View, This is Show Business, and others), sr light entertainment producer 1951; ITV: head of light entertainment ATV 1935, prodn controller ATV 1956, exec controller TV 1963, bd memb ATV (Network) Ltd 1955, dir of progs and exec dir ATV Ltd 1968, memb ITV Network Prog Ctee 1970, chm Network Sports Ctee 1971, memb EBU Sports Working Party 1973, chm EBU Football Ctee 1974, dep md ATV Ltd 1974, head EBU Ops Gp for all euro broadcasters for coverage of FIFA World Football Cup in Argentina 1978 (Summer Olympic Games in Moscow 1980), assisted Thomson Fndn in improving Thailand's TV prodn techniques 1981, memb UNESCO team assisting Ethiopian Govt in media devpt planning 1982, exec prodr Highway 1983; responsible for shows such as Sunday Night at The Palladium and the Royal Variety Shows working with performers such as: Bob Hope, Nat King Cole, Bing Crosby, Sir Harry Secombe, Shirley Bassey, and many others; Guild of TV Producers-Light Entertainment Producer 1959, BAFTA Desmond Davies Award 1976; Liveryman Fletchers' Co; FRSA 1974; *Recreations* golf; *Clubs* Lord Taverners'; *Style—* Bill Ward, Esq, OBE; 28A Talbot Rd, Lyme Regis, Dorset DT7 3BB; Richmond Film and TV, 87 Charlotte St, London WC1 (☎ 071 631 5424, 071 831 0337)

WARD, Joan, Lady; Joan Mary Haden; da of Maj Thames Patrick Laffey, of Auckland NZ; *m* 1944, Sir Joseph Ward, 3 Bt, LLM (d 1970); 3 s (including 4 Bt), 3 da; *Style—* Joan, Lady Ward

WARD, (Christoher) John (William); s of Gp Capt Thomas Maxfield Ward, CBE, DFC (d 1969), and Peggy, *née* Field; *b* 21 June 1942; *Educ* CCC Oxford, Univ of E Anglia (Dip Econ); *m* 1971 (m dis 1988), Diane, *née* Lelliott; *Career* Bank of England 1965-74; gen sec: Bank of England Staff Organisation 1974-80, Assoc First Div of Civil Servants 1980-88; head of devpt Opera North 1988-; chm Swindon Supporters in London 1987-88; *Style—* John Ward, Esq; Opera North, Grand Theatre, 46 New Briggate, Leeds LS1 6NU (☎ 0532 439 999)

WARD, Dr John Dale; s of John Ward, and Lily, *née* Dale; *b* 25 Dec 1935; *Educ* Mount St Mary's Coll Cerbyshire, The London Hosp Med Coll (BSc, MD); *m* 22 Sept 1962, Ann Deirdre, da of Gp Capt Francis Sumerling, OBE (d 1967); 1 s (Timothy Jerome b 1969), 3 da (Clare Caroline b 1963, Susannah Elizabeth b 1965, Helen Louise b 1967); *Career* med trg Guy's Hosp 1954-71, conslt physician in med and diabetes Royal Hallamshire Hosp Sheffield 1971-; visiting lectr: Budapest 1981, Nairobi 1982; contrib: diabetic res papers, many chapters in diabetic manuals; chm patient servs cmmn Br Diabetic Assoc, memb American Diabetes Assoc 1987, hon treas Euro Assoc for the Study of Diabetes; FRCP 1976; *Books* The Foot in Diabetic Manuals (co-ed 1987); *Recreations* golf, music; *Clubs* Sickleholme Golf (Derbyshire); *Style—* Dr John Ward; 68 Dore Rd, Sheffield S17 3NE (☎ 0742 364698); Royal Hallamshire Hosp, Glossop Rd, Sheffield S17 (☎ 0742 76622)

WARD, John Devereux; CBE (1973), MP (C) Poole 1979-; s of Thomas Edward Ward (d 1981), and Evelyn Victoria Ward (d 1986); *b* 8 March 1925; *Educ* Romford County Tech Sch, Univ of St Andrews (BSc Eng); *m* 1955, Jean Miller, da of Andrew Aitken (d 1974); 1 s, 1 da; *Career* RAF 1943-47, chartered civil and structural engr; joined Taylor Woodrow Ltd 1958, md Taylor Woodrow Arcon 1976-78; contested (C) Portsmouth North Oct 1974; fndr memb Cons Cwlth Cncl; memb: Nat Union Exec Cons Pty 1965-78, Cons Pty Central Bd of Fin 1969-78, jt sec Cons Backbench Indust Ctee 1982-83, vice chm Trade and Indust Ctee (C) 1983-84, representative of UK Parliament at Cncl of Europe and Western Euro Union 1983-87, re-appointed 1989, parly private sec to Fin Sec to Treasy 1984-86, parly private sec to Sec of State for Social Security 1987-89; *Style—* John Ward, Esq, CBE, MP; 54 Parkstone Rd, Poole, Dorset (☎ 0202 674771); House of Commons, London SW1A 0AA

WARD, John Streeton; s of Charles Eric Ward, of Stamford, Lincs, and Agnes Anne, *née* Streeton; *b* 28 Sept 1933; *Educ* Stamford Sch; *m* 28 Sept 1957, Dorothy Sheila; 2 s (Graham b 1960, Richard b 1966); *Career* Barclays Bank: joined 1950, local dir Preston 1974-79, sr local dir Newcastle upon Tyne 1983-88 (local dir 1979-83); non-exec dir: Tyne & Wear Enterprise Trust Ltd (ENTRUST) 1981, Northern Investors Company Ltd 1984-, Theatre Royal Trust Ltd 1988-, Northumbrian Water Group plc 1989-; non-exec dir and dep chm Tyne & Wear Development Corp 1987-, regnl dir Barclays Bank plc 1988-; chm: The Newcastle Initiative 1988- (dir 1990-), memb Bd Business in the Community Tyne & Wear & Northumberland (chm 1985-90), dep chm Bd of Govrs Newcastle upon Tyne Poly, vice chm Tyneside Stables Project Ltd St Thomas St Workshops; chm: Barclays Bank plc (Northern Region) Sports and Social Club, Cruddas Park Community Tst Newcastle upon Tyne, British Olympic Appeal NE Region 1984 and 1988; ACIB; *Recreations* golf, theatre going, Newcastle United FC supporter; *Clubs* Northern Couties (Newcastle upon Tyne), Royal and Ancient Golf (St Andrews), Northumberland Golf; *Style—* John Ward, Esq, OBE; Barclays Bank Ltd, Northern Regional Office, Barclays House, 61/73 Grey St, Newcastle upon Tyne NE99 1LG (☎ 091 261 7676, 091 232 0061, 0860 317452)

WARD, John William; s of George Ward, and Margaret, *née* Ellaway; *b* 25 Dec 1940; *Educ* Elliot Secondary Sch Putney; *Career* PR conslt: Medway Shoes Ltd 1977-82, Mary West PR 1982-87; owner and mangr John Ward PR and Promos; active participant in sports fund raising events for charities incl: Cystic Fibrosis, Save the Children, Haemophiliac Soc; *Recreations* marathon running, reading; *Clubs* Gardens Running and Tennis Wimbledon; *Style*— John Ward, Esq; 31 Trentham St, Southfields, London SW18 3DU; John Ward Public Relations and Promotions, 11 Bolt Ct, Fleet St, London EC4A 3DQ (☎ 071 353 7887/071 936 2127, fax 071 583 2800)

WARD, Sir Joseph James Laffey; 4 Bt (UK 1911), of Wellington, New Zealand; s of 3 Bt (d 1970); *b* 11 Nov 1946; *m* 1968, Robyn Allison, da of William Maitland Martin, of Rotorua, NZ; *Heir* bro, Roderic Anthony Ward b 23 April 1948; *Style*— Sir Joseph Ward, Bt

WARD, Keith John; s of Thomas B Ward; *b* 10 Sept 1933; *Educ* St Christopher's Sch Herts; *m* 1960, Susan Jean Robson; 2 s; *Career* builder's merchant and timber merchant, timber importer; md: Graham-Reeves Ltd 1974-81, Ward Associates Commerical Consultants 1982-; devpt dir The Graham Group 1981 (dir 1974), princ and md Brock's Fireplaces Ltd 1984-; pres Soc of Builder's Merchants 1982-84; *Recreations* fishing, shooting, horticulture; *Clubs* MCC; *Style*— Keith Ward, Esq; Brock's Fireplaces Limited, Centurion Works, Union Rd, Kingsbridge, Devon TQ7 1EF

WARD, Prof (John Stephen) Keith; s of John Ward (d 1983), of Hexham, Northumberland, and Evelyn, *née* Simpson; *b* 22 Aug 1938; *Educ* Hexham GS, Univ of Wales (BA), Linacre Coll Oxford (BLitt), Trinity Hall Cambridge (MA); *m* 21 June 1963, Marian, da of Albert Trotman (d 1942), of Ystrad Rhondda, S Wales; 1 s (Alun James b 1968), 1 da (Fiona Caroline b 1966); *Career* lectr in: logic Univ of Glasgow 1964-69, in philosophy Univ of St Andrews 1969-71, in philosophy of religion King's Coll London 1971-76; fell and dean Trinity Hall Cambridge 1976-83, FD Maurice prof of moral and social theology Univ of London 1983-86, prof of history and philosophy of religion King's Coll London 1986-, priest C of E 1972-; chm World Congress of Faiths, memb Cncl Royal Inst of Philosophy; *Books* Kant's View of Ethics (1972), The Concept of God (1974), Rational Theology and the Creativity of God (1982), The Living God (1984), Images of Eternity (1987), Divine Action (1990); *Recreations* music, walking; *Style*— Prof Keith Ward; The Brewery Cottage, Lower Froyle, nr Alton, Hampshire GU34 4LX (☎ 0420 23148); Kings College, Strand, London WC2R 2LS (☎ 071 836 5454, fax 071 836 1799)

WARD, Hon Lalla - (Sarah); *née* Ward; da of 7 Viscount Bangor, *qv*, and his 4 w, Marjorie Alice, *née* Banks; *b* 28 June 1951; *m* 1980 (m dis 1984), Tom Baker, the actor; *Career* actress and illustrator; *Style*— The Hon Lalla Ward; 13 Durham Terrace, London W2

WARD, Hon Mrs ((Elizabeth) Louise); *née* Astor; 2 da of 2 Baron Astor of Hever (d 1984), and Dowager Baroness Astor of Hever, *qv*; *b* 1951; *Educ* St Agnes and St Michael Convent, Madrid Univ, Westminster Hosp London; *m* 1, 1979 (m dis 1981), David John Shelton Herring; m 2, 1985, David Joseph Ward, s of Joseph Ward, of Canterbury, Kent; 1 s (Oliver Gavin Joseph b 1985), 1 da (Victoria Mary Ward b 1987); *Career* registered nurse; *Recreations* riding (master of foxhounds), painting; *Style*— The Hon Mrs David Ward; Chelworth House, Chelwood Gate, Haywards Heath, West Sussex RH17 7JZ (☎ 082 574 615)

WARD, His Hon Judge Malcolm Beverley; s of Edgar Ward (d 1966), and Dora Mary, *née* Dutton (d 1974); *b* 3 May 1931; *Educ* Wolverhampton GS, St John's Coll Cambridge (MA, LLM); *m* 12 July 1958, Muriel Winifred, da of Dr Edwin Daniel Mackay Wallace (d 1973); 2 s (Simon b 1963, Nicholas b 1967), 2 da (Louise b 1965, Amanda b 1970); *Career* called to the Bar 1956, rec 1974, circuit judge 1979-; chm Wolverhampton GS 1981- (govr 1972-); *Recreations* golf, music, (in theory) horticulture; *Style*— His Hon Judge Malcolm Ward; 1 Fountain Court, Birmingham B4 6DR

WARD, Malcolm Stanley; s of Hugh Ward (d 1979), and Rebecca, *née* Rogerson; *b* 24 Sept 1951; *Educ* Gilberd Sch Colchester; *Career* dep ed Gulf News Dubai 1978-79, ed Woodham and Wickford Chronicle Essex 1979-81, dep ed Gulf Times Qatar 1981-84, dir Daily News Birmingham 1986- (ed 1986-); memb: Guild Br Newspaper Eds, Variety Club of GB; tstee Alexandra Theatre Birmingham; *Recreations* writing, travel, soccer, driving, tennis; *Style*— Malcolm Ward, Esq; 3 Rectory Park Ave, Sutton Coldfield, W Midlands B75 7BL (☎ 021 329 2589); Daily News, 78 Franics Rd, Edgbaston, Birmingham B16 8SP (☎ 021 454 8800, fax 021 455 9162, car 0831 124923)

WARD, Lady; Margaret Mary; da of Anthony Davis, of New York; *m* 1, Capt Ralph Risley, USN (decd); m 2, 1965, as his 3 w, Cdr Sir Melvill Ward, 3 and last Bt, DSC, RN (d 1973); *Style*— Lady Ward; Box 276, Southport, Conn, USA

WARD, Hon Mr Justice; Martyn Eric Ward; s of Arthur George Ward, DSM (d 1969), and Dorothy, *née* Perkins (d 1982); *b* 10 Oct 1927; *m* 1, 1957, Rosaleen Iona Soloman; 1 da (Belinda); m 2, 25 March 1966, Rosanna Maria; 2 s (Rufus b 1969, Henry b 1971); *Career* RN 1945-48 (Palestine); barr Lincoln's Inn 1955-72; HM circuit judge 1972-87; judge Supreme Ct Bermuda 1987-; *Recreations* skiing, swimming, tennis, reading; *Style*— The Hon Mr Justice Ward; c/o The Supreme Court, 21 Parliament St, Hamilton HL12, Bermuda

WARD, Maxwell Colin Bernard; s of Maj Bernard Maxwell Ward, LVO, of Rockalls Hall, Polstead, Colchester, Essex, and Margaret Sunniva, *née* Neven-Spence (d 1962); *b* 22 Aug 1949; *Educ* Harrow, St Catharines Coll Cambridge (MA); *m* 17 April 1982, Sarah, da of Lt Col Peter William Marsham, MBE (d 1970); 2 s (Charles Bernard Maxwell b 27 Feb 1986, Frederick Peter Neven b 15 Feb 1989), 1 da (Laura Sunniva b 2 April 1984); *Career* investment trainee Ballie Gifford & Co 1971-74 (ptnr 1975-), dir Scottish Equitable Life Assur Soc 1988-; main bd memb Scottish Cncl for Spastics 1981-; *Recreations* tennis, squash, bridge, country pursuits; *Clubs* New (Edinburgh); *Style*— Maxwell Ward, Esq; The Old Manse, Crichton, Pathhead, Mid Lothian (☎ 0875 320702); Baillie Gifford & Co, 10 Glenfinlas St, Edinburgh EH3 6YY (☎ 031 225 2581, fax 031 225 2358, telex 72310)

WARD, Michael Jackson; CBE (1980); s of Harry Ward, CBE (d 1988), and Dorothy Julia, *née* Clutterbuck (d 1974); *b* 16 Sept 1931; *Educ* Drayton Manor GS, UCL (BA), Univ of Freiburg Germany, CCC Oxford; *m* 1, Oct 1955, Eileen Patricia, da of John Foster (d 1985); 1 s (Michael b 1962), 1 da (Victoria b 1959); *Career* Nat Serv 2 Lt Royal Signals 1953-55; dist cmmr and asst sec to Govt Gilbert and Ellice Islands HMCOS 1956-61; Br Cncl: Schs Recruitment Dept 1961-64, regnl rep Sarawak 1964-68, dep rep Pakistan 1968-70, dir Appts Servs Dept 1970-72, dir Personnel Dept 1972-75, controller Personnel and Appts Div 1975-77, rep Italy 1977-81, controller Home Div 1981-85, asst dir gen 1985-90, dir Germany 1990-; *Recreations* music, golf; *Clubs* Nat Lib, Gog Magog Golf; *Style*— Michael Ward, Esq, CBE; 1 Knapp Rise, Haslingfield, Cambridge, CB3 7LQ (☎ 0223 871557); The British Council, Hahnenstrasse 6, 5100 Köln 1, Federal Republic of Germany (☎ 0221 20644 0)

WARD, Michael John; s of Stanley William Ward (d 1985), of Romford, and Margaret Annie, *née* Gill (d 1986); *b* 7 April 1931; *Educ* Royal Liberty GS Gidea Park Essex, Univ of Manchester (BA); *m* 1953, Lilian, da of Frederick Lomas, of Hadleigh, Essex; 2 da (Alison, Susan); *Career* Flt Lt RAF 1952-57; MP (Lab) Peterborough 1974-79, ldr London Borough of Havering Cncl 1971-74 (memb 1958-74), sponsored Unfair Contract Terms Act 1977, pps to Sec of State Educn and Science, min for Overseas Devpt, min of state Foreign and Cwlth Office 1976-79, dir of info Inner London Educn Authy 1984-86, public affrs offr Gas Consumers Cncl 1986-88; exec offr to Rt Hon Paddy Ashdown MP 1988-89, asst gen sec Assoc of Chief Offrs of Probation 1989-, parly candidate SDP/Lib All Tonbridge & Malling 1987; MIPR; *Recreations* music, gardens; *Clubs* Reform, National Liberal; *Style*— Michael Ward, Esq; 1A Vanbrugh Terrace, Blackheath, London SE3 7AP

WARD, Hon Peter Alistair; 3 s of 3 Earl of Dudley, MC, TD (d 1969), and his 1 w, Rosemary Millicent Ednam, *née* Leveson-Gower, RRC (who d 1930 prior to 2 Earl's death in 1932), da of 4 Duke of Sutherland, KG; *b* 8 Feb 1926; *Educ* Eton, Univ of British Columbia, ChCh Oxford; *m* 1, 1956 (m dis 1974), Claire Leonora, only da of A E G Baring; 1 s (Alexander b 1961), 2 da (Rachel b 1957, Tracy b 1958); m 2, 1974, Elizabeth Rose, da of Richard V C Westmacott, of Ascona, Switzerland; 2 s (Jeremy b 1975, Benjamin b 1978); *Career* Royal Canadian Air Force 1943-45 and Fleet Air Arm; chm Baggeridge Brick plc; *Clubs* White's, Pratt's, Royal Yacht Squadron; *Style*— The Hon Peter Ward; 7 Elm Park Lane, London SW3 (☎ 071 351 2890); Chipping Norton, Oxon (☎ 060 8658 555)

WARD, Peter Michael John; s of Lt-Col Francis Ward, OBE, MC (d 1950), of 69 Cheyne Ct, Chelsea, London, and Dorothy Aline Augusta, *née* Peile (d 1950); *b* 24 July 1924; *Educ* St Ronan's Sch, Stowe, Clare Coll Cambridge; *m* 16 Sept 1950, Janet Mary, da of Brig I R C G M Bruce, DSO, MBE (d 1956), of The Old Manor House, Letcombe Regis, nr Wantage, Berks; 4 s (Jonathan Francis Bruce b 6 Oct 1954, Robert Richard Craufurd b 29 July 1959, Edmund Giles William b 15 May 1962, Damian Peter Michael b 29 Jan 1966), 4 da (Clare Dorothy b 27 Aug 1951, Catharine Joan b 5 Dec 1952, Magdalen Mary b 6 Dec 1955, Hester Janet Teresa b 30 March 1964); *Career* Nat Serv WWII: Lt 3 (Tank) Bn Scots Guards 1944, Sports Offr Gds Div 1946, Staff Capt A (PS2) Branch HQ 1 Br Corps 1947, demob 1947; Gulf Oil 1947-85: chm Gulf UK Pension Scheme Ctee 1973-85, gen mangr Human Resources 1976-85, dir Eastern Gulf Oil Co Ltd 1976-85; chm and md Thames Valley Wine Co Ltd 1962-71, dir Burgan Oil Co Tstees Ltd 1975-85, dir Kuwait Oil Co Tstees Ltd 1975-85; chm: David Brown Staff Pension Tstee Ltd 1987-90, David Brown Works Pension Tstee Ltd 1987-90, David Brown Pension Tstee Ltd 1990-; p/t ambulance driver Arthritis Care 1986-; *Recreations* sport, theatre, films, music; *Clubs* Oriental; *Style*— Peter Ward, Esq; Waterdell House, Little Green Lane, Croxley Green, Rickmansworth, Herts WD3 3JH (☎ 0923 772 775)

WARD, Dr Peter Roger; s of late Edmund Ward AMIEE, of Moelfre, Anglesey, and Mona MacPhail; *b* 26 Aug 1927; *Educ* Univ of Manchester (MB ChB, DMRD); *m* 7 Dec 1954, Helen Ruth, da of William Ballantyne (d 1956), of Douglas, Lanarkshire; 1 s (Alistair b 1961), 3 da (Fiona (Mrs Cruickshank) b 1958, Frances (Mrs Trainer) b 1959, Kathleen b 1962); *Career* Nat Serv Med branch RAF 1953-55; conslt radiologist Aberdeen Hosps and clinical sr lectr Univ of Aberdeen 1968-; FRCR 1962; *Recreations* mountains; *Clubs* Cairngorm (hon librarian); *Style*— Dr Peter Ward, Esq; X-ray Department, Woodend Hospital, Aberdeen AB9 2YS (☎ 0224 681818 ext 56232)

WARD, Philip; s of Albert Edwin Ward, of Doncaster, and Mildred, *née* Elsey; *Educ* Haberdashers' Aske's Sch Hampstead, Perugia, Coimbra, MECAS (Lebanon); *m* 4 April 1964, Audrey Joan, da of Lawrence Monk, of Newport, Essex; 2 da (Carolyn b 1966, Angela b 1968); *Career* coordinator Library Servs Libya 1963-71, UNESCO expert Library Servs and Documentation Egypt 1973, UNESCO dir of Nat Library Serv Indonesia 1973-74, professional writer 1974-; fndr Private Libraries Assoc 1956-, FRGS, FRSA, ALA; *Books* The Oxford Companion to Spanish Literature 1978, A Dictionary of Common Fallacies (2 vols, 1978-80), A Lifetime's Reading (1982); novels: Forgotten Games (1984); poetry: Lost Songs (1981); plays: Garrity (1970); travel books: Travels in Oman (1986), Finnish Cities (1987), Polish Cities (1988), Bulgaria (1989), Wight Magic (1990); *Recreations* meditative basketball (following the teachings of Hirohide Ogawa) and reading; *Style*— Philip Ward, Esq

WARD, Maj-Gen Sir Philip John Newling; KCVO (1976), CBE (1971, OBE 1967), DL (W Sussex 1981); s of George William Newling Ward (d 1953), of The Old Rectory, Clapham, nr Worthing, and Mary Florence Ward; *b* 10 July 1924; *Educ* Monkton Combe Sch; *m* 1948, Pamela Ann, da of William Horace Edmund Glennie; 2 s, 2 da; *Career* cmd 1 Bn Welsh Gds 1965-67, Cdr LF Gulf 1969-71, GOC London Dist and Maj-Gen Cmd Household Div 1973-76, Cmdt RMA Sandhurst 1976-79 (Adj 1960-62); dir Corporate Affrs (IDV) Int Distillers & Vintners (UK) 1980-89; chm: Hamilton Ingram Ltd 1985-89; memb Southern Regnl Bd Lloyds Bank 1983-90; cmmr of Chichester Cathedral 1980-83; chm: Royal Soldiers' Daughters' Sch until 1983, Queen Alexandra's Hosp Home; govr cmdt Church Lads and Church Girls Bde until 1986; High Sheriff of W Sussex 1985-86, Vice Lord Lt W Sussex 1990; Freeman City of London; *Recreations* gardening; *Clubs* Cavalry and Guards (chm 1987), Buck's; *Style*— Maj-Gen Sir Philip Ward, KCVO, CBE, DL; 15 Tarrant Wharf, Arundel, W Sussex BN18 9NY (☎ 0903 884122)

WARD, Richard; s of Louis Ward, and Rose, *née* Shafer; *b* 14 Jan 1945; *Educ* John Kelly Sch for Boys; *m* 14 Jan 1968, Simone Maureen, da of Samuel Lestor; 1 s (Ellis Andrew b 20 Oct 1972), 1 da (Jannie Laura b 15 Nov 1968); *Career* md G F Dietary Supplies Ltd 1977-85, chm G F Dietary Gp of Cos Ltd 1985-; advsr to: Euro Dietary Cmmn, Health Food Mfrs Assoc, Br Health Food Trade Assoc; memb Harrow Cons Business Club, advsr to Young Enterprise; FInstD 1984, FBIM 1985; memb Ceoliac Soc, Nat Soc of Phenylketonuria; *Recreations* tennis, swimming, opera, sailing; *Clubs* Dyrham Park (Barnett); *Style*— Richard Ward, Esq; G F Dietary Gp of Cos Ltd, 494-496 Honeyport Lane, Stanmore, Middx HA7 1JH (☎ 081 951 5155, fax 081 951 5623, car 0860 413401, 0836 207012, telex 21875 GFS)

WARD, Maj-Gen Robert William; CB (1989), MBE (1972); s of Lt Col William Denby Ward (d 1973), of Fleet, Hants, and Monica Thérese, *née* Collett-White, (d 1985); *b* 17 Oct 1935; *Educ* Rugby, RMA Sandhurst; *m* 16 April 1966, Lavinia Dorothy, da of Col (Alexander James) Henry Cramsie OBE, DL, JP (d 1982), of O'Harabrook, Ballymoney, Co Antrim, N Ireland; 2 s (Thomas b 1968, James b 1973), 1 da (Gemma b 1970); *Career* cmmnd The Queen's Bays (later Queen's Dragoon Gds) 1955; served: Jordan, Libya, Germany, NI, Borneo, 1955-64; student RN Staff Coll 1967, GSO2 Intelligence Bahrain 1968-69, cdr A Squadron, QDG Berlin 1970-72, Nat Def Coll 1972-73, MA to C in C BAOR 1973-75, CO 1 Queen's Dragoon Gds 1975-77, Col GS Army Staff Coll 1977-78, cmd 22 Armoured Bde 1979-82, student Nat Def Coll Canada 1982-83, asst COS Northern Army Gp 1983-86, GOC Western District 1986-89; *Recreations* gardening, outdoor sports, country pursuits, food, wine, travel; *Clubs* Cavalry and Guards, MCC, I Zingari; *Style*— Maj-Gen Robert Ward, CB, MBE; c/o Lloyds Bank plc, Cox's & King's, PO Box 1190, 7 Pall Mall, London SW1Y 5NA

WARD, Prof Roy Charles; s of Charles Henry Ward, of 19 Rosamund Drive, Old Woodstock, Oxford OX7 1YD, and Hilda May, *née* Norris (d 1987); *b* 8 July 1937; *Educ* Reading Sch, Univ of Reading (BA, PhD); *m* 2 April 1966, (Georgina) Kay, da of Percy Frederick Kirby (d 1962); 2 da (Katie b 1970, Sally Ann b 1973); *Career* prof Univ of Maryland USA 1968-69; Univ of Hull: lectr 1960, sr lectr 1972-77, reader 1977-1981, prof 1981-, dean of Sci Faculty 1986-87, pro vice chllr 1987-; memb: Rural Devpt Cmmn, Humberside Business Ctee; memb Inst of Br Geographers; *Books*

Floods (1978), Principles of Hydrology (3 edn, 1989); *Recreations* walking, wine; *Style—* Prof Roy Ward; Sch of Geography and Earth Resources, University of Hull, Hull HU6 7RX (☎ 0482 465215, fax 0482 466340, telex 592592)

WARD, Simon Charles Vivian; s of Maj Vivian Horrocks Ward, of Long Meadow House, Little Cornard, Sudbury, Suffolk, and Leila Penelope, *née* Every; *b* 23 March 1942; *Educ* Shrewsbury, Trinity Coll Cambridge (MA); *m* 18 Sept 1965, Jillian Eileen, da of Thomas Roycroft East (d 1980), of Dublin; 3 da (Victoria Penelope Jane b 1969, Antonia Lisa b 1971, Lucinda Fiona (twin) b 1971); *Career* trainee stockbroker Govett Sons & Co 1963-65; ptnrs asst: Hedderwick Hunt Cox and Co 1965-67, Hedderwick Borthwick and Co 1967-70; ptnr Montagu Loebl Stanley and Co 1972-86; dir: Fleming Montagu Stanley Ltd 1986-89, Fleming Private Asset Management Ltd 1989-; chm Fleming Private Fund Management Ltd 1989 (dir 1975-); memb Int Stock Exchange 1968; *Recreations* skiing, tennis, shooting, gardening, opera, ballet; *Style—* Simon Ward, Esq; The Dower House, Bulmer, Sudbury, Suffolk CO10 7EH (☎ 0787 73257); 107 Andrews House, The Barbican, London EC2 (☎ 071 588 3290); Fleming Private Asset Mgmnt Ltd, 31 Sun St, London EC2M 2QP (☎ 071 377 9242, fax 071 247 3594, telex 885941)

WARD, Simon Roderick; s of Edward John Ward (d 1976), of Grey Barn, Pagham Harbour, W Sussex, and Vera, *née* Braun (d 1985); *b* 4 Aug 1928; *Educ* Clifton, Lincoln Coll Oxford (BA), Cornell Univ NY (MA); *m* 11 Dec 1965, Diana Strafford, da of Col Rowland Marshall Davies (d 1980), of India; 2 da (Clare Lara b 1969, Charlotte Kate b 1972); *Career* 2 Lt 1 Bn Malay Regt 1948-49; Malayan Starr 1949; barr Lincolns Inn 1953-56, slr Slaughter & May 1956-; memb Cncl Charing Cross and Westminster Med Sch; *Style—* Simon R Ward, Esq; 26 Ladbroke Grove, London, W11 3BQ; 35 Basinghall St, London EC2V 5DB (☎ 071 600 1200)

WARD, Sir Terence George; CBE (1961, MBE mil 1945); *b* 16 Jan 1906; *Educ* Edinburgh (DDS, DO); *m* 1931, Elizabeth Wilson (d 1981); 1 s, 1 da; m 2, 1982, Sheila Elizabeth Lawry; *Career* oral surgeon; dean Faculty of Dental Surgery RCS 1965-68; former consulting dental surgeon to: DHSS, RAF, Army, Navy; now conslt emeritus to Navy and Army and hon conslt to RAF and Queen Victoria Hosp East Grinstead; FRCS, FDSRCS, FFDRCSI, FDS Aust, FACD; *Recreations* golf; *Style—* Sir Terence Ward, CBE; 22 Marina Court Ave, Bexhill-on-Sea, E Sussex (☎ 0424 214760)

WARD, Tony; *b* 18 July 1931; *Educ* Loughborough Univ; *m* Gwenda Mary; 1 s (Timothy Matthew); *Career* Southern admin Amateur Athletic Assoc 1965-68, PR conslt offr Amateur Athletic Assoc BAAB 1966-, Recreation Div 3M 1968-79, Setars (UK) Finance 1979-82; *Books* Modern Distance Runners (1968), Athletics For the Seventies (1969), Linford Christie (with Linford Christie, 1989), Athletics: The Golden Decade (1991); *Recreations* theatre, literature; *Style—* Tony Ward, Esq; 7 Garlands Close, Burghfield Common, Berkshire RG7 3JX (☎ 0734 833739); Amateur Athletic Association, Edgbaston House, 3 Duchess Place, Hagley Rd, Birmingham B16 8NM (☎ 0734 833739, fax 0734 834865)

WARD, Walter; s of Alfred Ward, of Edgware, Middx, and Mary, *née* Beck; *b* 22 May 1930; *Educ* Grocers' Co Sch; *m* 1, 21 June 1955, Joan Frances, da of Alfred Cash, of Wembley; 1 da (Lorraine b 1960); m 2, 7 July 1968, Alma, da of Samuel Baars (d 1986); 1 da (Lisa Melanie b 1969); *Career* Corporal RAF 1952-54, Fighter Cmd N Weald Essex, Malta 1953; *Recreations* video filming, painting oils, travel, skiing; *Style—* Walter Ward, Esq; 29 Welbeck Street, London W1M 8DA

WARD, Hon William Maxwell David; s (by 3 m) and h of 7 Viscount Bangor, *qv*; *b* 9 Aug 1948; *Educ* Univ Coll London; *m* 1976, Mrs Sarah Bradford, da of Brig Hilary Anthony Hayes, DSO, OBE; *Style—* The Hon William Ward; 31 Britannia Road, London SW6

WARD-BOOTH, Maj-Gen (John) Antony (Tony); OBE (1969), DL (1987); s of Rev John Vernon Ward Ward-Booth (d 1973); *b* 18 July 1927; *Educ* Worksop Coll; *m* 1952, Margaret Joan, da of Rev Aubrey Hooper, MC; 2 s, 2 da; *Career* joined Army 1945, CO 3 Bn Parachute Regt 1967-69, Cdr 16 Parachute Bde 1970-73, Nat Defence Coll Canada 1973-74, DAG HQ BAOR 1974-75, Maj-Gen 1976, Dir Army Air Corps 1976-79, GOC Western Dist 1979-82, ret; sec Eastern Wessex TAVRA 1982-89; chm Southampton Div SSAFA 1982-, Dep Col R Anglian Regt 1982-86; memb Paracute Regt Cncl 1982; chm Cncl: Clayesmore Sch 1985, govr Enham Village Centre 1982; *Recreations* sports; *Clubs* Army and Navy, MCC; *Style—* Maj-Gen John Ward-Booth, OBE; 22 Winchester Gardens, Andover, Hants SP10 2EH (☎ 0264 54317)

WARD-HOWLETT, Ronald Peter Henry; s of Ronald Desmond Ward-Howlett (d 1972), of Gerrards Cross, Bucks, and Hilda May (d 1970), *née* Stopforth-Rimmer; *b* 5 May 1932; *Educ* Ealing Coll; *Career* served RAF 1950-52; fin investmt controller Arthur Young 1984-, md and chief exec Silkhouse Fin Services Ltd 1987-, dir Berklay Devere (Hldgs) Ltd; life memb Br Herpetological Soc, fndr memb Jersey Wildlife Preservation Soc; FBIM, FInstAA, FZS, fell Linnean Soc; *Recreations* herpetology, numismatics; *Clubs* Royal Overseas, The Victory Services; *Style—* Ronald Ward-Howlett, Esq; 13 Brandon Park Court, Argyle Road, Southport, Lancashire PR9 9LG (☎ 0704 45366); Arthur Young, Silkhouse Court, Tithebarn Street, Liverpool L2 2LE (☎ 051 2368214, telex 629179 AYLI, fax 051 2360258)

WARD-JACKSON, Adrian Alexander; CBE (1991); s of William Alexander Ward-Jackson, of Kensington Court Place, London W8, and Catherine Elizabeth, *née* Trew; *b* 6 June 1950; *Educ* Westminster, Vienna; *Career* Expert Drawings Dept Christie's London 1970-71, dir P&D Colnaghi & Co Ltd 1971-75; chm and dir: Adrian Ward-Jackson Ltd 1975-, Ballet Rambert Ltd 1984-90, Mercury Theatre Tst Ltd 1984-90; dep chm and dir Creative Dance Artists Tst 1985-90, govr Royal Ballet 1985-, tstee Aphrodisias Tst 1985-, memb Ballet Bd Royal Opera House 1985-90, chm and memb Nat Dance House Study Gp (now Action Gp for a Dance House) 1986-, memb Cncl Benesh Inst 1987-90 (tstee Endowment Fund), dir Royal Opera House Tst Ltd 1987-90, tstee Dancers Resettlement Fund 1987-, dep chm Cncl Aids Crisis Tst 1987-, dir Theatre Museum Assoc 1987-, tstee The Silver Tst 1988-, dir Contemporary Art Soc Projects Ltd 1988-, chm Contemporary Art Soc 1990-, dir Soc of Br Theatre Designers Ltd 1989-, memb Cncl Arts Cncl of GB 1989- (chm Dance Panel 1990-), tstee Dancers Pension Fund 1989-, memb Theatre Museum Ctee V&A 1990-, dir American Friends of Covent Garden and Royal Ballet Inc 1990-, memb Steering Gp on Structure of Arts Funding Office of Arts & Libraries 1990-, tstee Margot Fonteyn Scholarship Fund 1990-; *Recreations* performing arts, contemporary art, skiing; *Clubs* Turf; *Style—* Adrian Ward-Jackson, Esq, CBE; 120 Mount St, Mayfair, London W1Y 5HB (☎ 071 493 8768); 37 Great Cumberland Place, London W1H 7LG (☎ 071 262 3558)

WARD-JACKSON, (Audrey) Muriel; *née* Jenkins; da of William James Jenkins (d 1974), of Roehampton, and Alice, *née* Glyde (d 1967); *b* 30 Oct 1914; *Educ* Queenswood Sch Hatfield Herts, Lady Margaret Hall Oxford (BA, MA); *m* 14 March 1946, George Ralph Norman Ward-Jackson (d 1982), s of late Ralph Stapleton Ward-Jackson; *Career* Civil Serv: asst princ 1937, princ 1942, asst sec 1946-55 (served in Miny of Works, Town and Country Planning, HM Treasy, Housing and Local Govt); John Lewis Partnership 1955-74: gen inspr and fin dir, dir 1957-74, dir John Lewis Properties Ltd 1969-74, chm Pensions Trust 1964-74; served on Civil Serv Arbitration Tbnl 1959-64, chm Consumer Ctees (Agric Mktg) 1971-75; govr Br Film Inst 1962-65; memb: Cncl Bedford Coll London Univ 1967-72, Nat Savings Review Ctee 1971-73, Royal Cmmn on Standards of Conduct in Public Life 1974-76; fund-raiser for St Luke's Church Chelsea 1984-(hon treas and memb Ctee Restoration Fund); *Recreations* swimming; *Clubs* Lansdowne; *Style—* Mrs Muriel Ward-Jackson; 195 Cranmer Court, Whiteheads Grove, Chelsea, London SW3 3HG (☎ 071 581 1926)

WARD-JONES, Norman Arthur; CBE (1990), VRD (1959), JP (N Westminster 1966); s of Alfred Thomas Ward-Jones, and Claire Mayall, *née* Lees; *b* 19 Sept 1922; *Educ* Oundle, Brasenose Coll Oxford; *m* Pamela Catherine Ainslie, *née* Glessing; *Career* Capt RM 1941-46; RM Reserve 1948-64, Lt-Col RMR (City of London) 1961-64 (Hon Col 1968-74); admitted slr 1950; sr ptnr Lawrence Messer Co 1981-85, hon slr Magistrates' Assoc 1960-85; chm: East Anglian Real Property Co Ltd 1970-80 (non exec dir 1980-89), Gaming Bd GB 1986 (memb 1984-); *Recreations* wine drinking; *Clubs* East India; *Style—* Norman Ward-Jones, Esq, CBE, VRD, JP; Gaming Board For Great Britain, Berkshire House, 168-173 High Holborn, London WC1V 7AA (☎ 071 240 0821)

WARD THOMPSON, Catharine Joan; da of Peter Michaeljohn Ward, of Waterdell House, Croxley Green, Herts, *qv*, and Janet Mary, *née* Bruce (*see* Debrett's Peerage, Bruce, Bt cr 1628); *b* 5 Dec 1952; *Educ* Holy Cross Convent Chalfont St Peter Bucks, Rickmansworth GS, Univ of Southampton (BSc), Univ of Edinburgh (Dip LA); *m* 30 Dec 1983, Henry Swift Thompson, s of Henry Swift Thompson, of 104 Carrie Drive, Grass Valley, California, 95949, and Hancock Point Maine 04640; 1 s (James b 21 Nov 1987), 1 da (Emma b 27 Sept 1985); *Career* landscape asst Justice and Webb Landscape Architects Vancouver BC Canada 1974-75, landscape architect and sr landscape architect W J Cairns & Ptnrs 1976-81, princ LDS Assocs Landscape Architects and Landscape Scientists 1986-90, head Dept of Landscape Architecture Edinburgh Coll of Art Heriot-Watt Univ 1989- (lectr 1981-88); memb: Amnesty Int (formerly Scottish Co-ordinator for Central America Special Action), Women of Lothian, World Devpt Movement; ALI; *Recreations* dance (ballet, contemporary, tap, Spanish), choreography; *Style—* Mrs Catharine Ward Thompson; 11 Douglas Crescent, Edinburgh EH12 5BB (☎ 031 337 6818); Hancock Point, Maine 04640, USA; Dept of Landscape Architecture, Edinburgh College of Art, Heriot-Watt University, Lauriston Place, Edinburgh EH3 9DF (☎ 031 229 9311, fax 031 229 0089)

WARDALE, Sir Geoffrey Charles; KCB (1979, CB 1974); *b* 29 Nov 1919; *Educ* Altrincham GS, Queens' Coll Cambridge; *m* 1944, Rosemary Octavia Dyer; 1 s, 1 da; *Career* Civil Serv Miny Tport 1942-70: asst sec 1957-66, under sec 1966-70; DOE 1970-80: dep sec 1972-78, 2 perm sec 1978-80; *Style—* Sir Geoffrey Wardale, KCB; 89 Paddock Lane, Lewes, E Sussex (☎ 0273 47368)

WARDE, His Hon John Robins; *b* 25 April 1920; *Educ* Radley, Corpus Christi Coll Oxford (MA); *m* 16 Aug 1941, Edna Holliday (Holly), *née* Gipson; 3 s (Robin b 1944, Simon b 1946, Nicholas b 1952); *Career* WWII served 1940-45 Lt RA, liaison offr with HQRA 53 (W) Div, awarded C-in-C's certificate for oustanding good service in the campaign in NW Europe; admitted slr 1950, ptnr in Waugh & Co Haywards Heath and East Grinstead Sussex 1960-70, registrar Clerkenwell County Ct 1970-77, rec Crown Ct 1972-77, circuit judge SE circuit 1977-90; memb: Devon CC 1946-49, Devon Agric Exec Ctee 1948-53, W Regnl Advsy Cncl of BBC 1950-53; *Recreations* mountaineering, watching cricket, listening to music; *Clubs* MCC, Forty, Law Soc, Assoc of Br Members of the Swiss Alpine, Br Schools Exploring Soc; *Style—* His Hon John Warde; 20 Clifton Terrace, Brighton, Sussex BN1 3HA

WARDE, John St Andrew; o s of Maj John Roberts O'Brien Warde, TD, DL (d 1975), of Squerryes Court, Westerham, Kent, and Millicent Anne Warde, CBE (d 1982), o da of Ralph Montagu Cook, of Roydon Hall, Paddock Wood, Kent; descended from Sir John Warde, Lord Mayor of London 1719, whose s John acquired Squerryes Court (house built 1681), where the family has resided ever since (*see* Burke's Landed Gentry, 18 edn, Volume III, 1972); *b* 8 March 1940; *Educ* Eton, Trinity Coll Cambridge (BA, MA); *m* 16 April 1973, Anthea, da of Anthony Holland, MC; 2 s (Charles b 1974, Henry b 1976), 1 da (Charlotte b 1982); *Career* served with Kent and Co of London Yeo (Sharpshooters) TA 1960-68; farmer and landowner; dir private cos; memb Sevenoaks DC 1976-87 (chm 1980), High Sheriff of Kent 1990-91; past chm: Kent Branch CLA, SE Region Historic Houses Assoc, Home Counties Region Timber Growers UK (and dep chm for England); *Recreations* field sports; *Clubs* Cavalry and Guards'; *Style—* John Warde, Esq; Squerryes Court, Westerham, Kent TN16 1SJ (☎ 0959 63118)

WARDE-ALDAM, Maj William; JP (S Yorks 1972), DL (S Yorks 1979); s of Lt-Col John Ralph Patientius Warde-Aldam, TD (d 1973); *b* 14 June 1925; *Educ* Eton; *m* 1960, Gillian Margaret, da of Malcolm Scott, of Lyons Hall, Great Leighs, Essex; 2 s, 1 da; *Career* served with Coldstream Guards: Germany, Italy, Norway, Malaya, Kenya 1943-64; High Sheriff Hallamshire 1971; *Clubs* Cavalry and Guards', MCC, Pratt's; *Style—* Maj William Warde-Aldam, JP, DL; Frickley Hall, Doncaster DN5 7BU (☎ 0977 642854); Ederline, Ford, Lochgilphead, Argyll PA31 8RJ (☎ 054 681 284)

WARDE-NORBURY, (William George) Antony; DL (S Yorks, 1989); s of Harold George Warde-Norbury, of Hooton Pagnell Hall, nr Doncaster, Yorks, and Mary Betty Warde-Aldam; *b* 13 March 1936; *Educ* Eton, Sandhurst; *m* 15 April 1961, Philippa Marjorie, da of Col Philip Ralph Davies-Cooke, CBE, of Gwysaney Hall, Mold, N Wales; 2 s (Mark b 1962, Alistair b 1966); *Career* Capt Coldstream Gds 1957-64; joined Allied-Lyons 1964, memb Allied Breweries Bd 1979 (jt md 1986-88); dir : Allied-Lyons, Euro Cellars and Britvic Corona 1986-88, Skol Int (also chm), Ind Coope African Investmts, Provident Fin, Selection Res Ltd; *Recreations* shooting, agriculture, golf, music; *Clubs* Cavalry and Guards, RAC; *Style—* Antony Warde-Norbury, Esq; Hooton Pagnell Hall, Doncaster DN5 7BW (☎ 0977 642850, car 0860 31193)

WARDELL, Gareth Lodwig; MP (Lab) Gower 1982-; s of John Thomas and Jenny Ceridwen Wardell; *b* 29 Nov 1944; *Educ* Gwendraeth GS, LSE (BSc, MSc); *m* 1967, Jennifer Dawn Evans; 1 s (Alistair); *Career* college lecturer in Carmarthen; *Recreations* swimming, cross-country running; *Style—* Gareth Wardell, Esq, MP; 67 Elder Grove, Carmarthen, Dyfed SA31 2H

WARDELL, Martin Bernard Peter; s of Bernard John Wardell, of 20 Jacey Rd, Edgbaston, Birmingham, and Audrey Ada, *née* Worrall; *b* 1 April 1951; *Educ* St Philip's GS Edgbaston, Univ of Surrey (BSc), Univ of Aston (MBA); *m* 6 Sept 1975, Julia Sara, da of Geoffrey Norman James Thornley, of 37 Allesley Cl, Sutton Coldfield, West Midlands B74 2NF; 1 s (James Martin Oliver b 28 Oct 1979), 2 da (Sophie Alexandra b 22 Oct 1981, Romilly Julia Helen b 17 Sept 1984); *Career* product mangr Foseco Int Birmingham (developed product range for steel plants) 1973-78, md Foseco Hellas Athens 1978-81, Euro sales mangr Bradley & Foster Ltd Darlaston 1981-83, gen mangr Technal UK Ltd Birmingham 1983-86, md George Wilson Industs Ltd (reintroduced prodn of new gas meters) 1986-; memb Round Table; memb Inst Gas Engrs, CEng; *Style—* Martin Wardell, Esq; 40 Ashdene Close, Sutton Coldfield, West Midlands B73 6HL (☎ 021 355 3990); Valor Flow Control (George Wilson Industries Ltd), 475 Foleshill Rd, Coventry, West Midlands CV6 5AP (☎ 0203 688655, fax 0203 661003, telex 312567, car 0836 272767)

WARDEN-OWEN, Edward; s of Norman Warden-Owen, of Cae Grugog Cottage, Trearddur Bay, Holyhead, Gwynedd, and Gwladys Elinor, *née* Jones; *b* 25 June 1949; *Educ* Holyhead County Secondary Sch, Cardiff Coll of Educn; *m* 18 Aug 1989, Susan

Virginia, da of Thomas Henry Alexander Gill, of The Corner House, The Gardens, Emsworth Rd, Havant, Hants; *Career* teacher of physical educn 1972-74, began career in sailmaking 1974, currently co dir of Bruce Banks Sails Ltd; sporting highlights in yachting; helmsman of Phoenix, memb of 1985 Br Admirals Cup Team and Top Scoring Boat Overall, Skipper of Indulgence V, winner of 3/4 ton cup 1986, navigator of White Crusader in Britains Challenge for America's Cup 1986-87, Silk Cut Helmsman of the year 1987, winner 1987 Congressional Cup, 1988 Nippon Cup skipper of Crusader in 1988 12 metre world championships and winner of Midnight Sun Cup Race, skipper of Indulgence VII, memb British Admirals Cup winning team 1989, runner up One Ton Cup 1989; 470 class yachting representative 1980 Olympic Games; *Recreations* squash, tennis, skiing, golf, horse riding; *Clubs* Royal Ocean Racing, Holyhead Sailing; *Style*— Edward Warden-Owen, Esq; Bruce Banks Sails Ltd, 372 Brook Lane, Sarisbury, Nr Southampton, Hampshire (☎ 0489 582444, fax 0489 589789)

WARDINGTON, 2 Baron (UK 1936); Christopher Henry Beaumont Pease; s of 1 Baron Wardington (d 1950), and Dorothy Charlotte, *née* Forster (d 1983); *b* 22 Jan 1924; *Educ* Eton; *m* 9 Sept 1964, Margaret Audrey, da of John White (d 1962), and former w of Jack Dunfee; 1 adopted s (Christopher William Beaumont b 18 April 1970), 2 adopted da (Lucy Anne b 23 Sept 1966, Helen Elizabeth b 24 Dec 1967); *Heir* bro, Hon William Simon Pease; *Career* served Scots Gds Italy, Capt 1942-47; ptnr Hoare Govett Ltd 1950-86; cmmr Public Works Loan Bd 1964-69; memb: Cncl of Stock Exchange 1963-81, Corp for Bond Holders 1967-; Alderman Broad St Ward London 1960-63, tstee Royal Jubilee Tsts; chm: Athlone Tst, Friends of British Library; *Recreations* books, gardening, golf; *Clubs* RAC, Garrick, Roxburghe, All England Lawn Tennis (Wimbledon); *Style*— The Lord Wardington; 29 Moore St, London SW3 (☎ 071 584 5245); Manor House, Wardington, Banbury, Oxon (☎ 0295 750202)

WARDLAW, Prof Alastair Connell; s of Prof Claude Wilson Wardlaw (d 1985), of Bramhall, Cheshire, and Jessie, *née* Connell (d 1971); *b* 20 Jan 1930; *Educ* Manchester GS, Univ of Manchester (BSc, MSc, PhD, DSc); *m* 1 July 1954, Jacqueline Shirley, da of Reginald Ormsby Jones, of Durrus, Ireland; 1 s (Malcolm b 1963), 2 da (Joanna b 1958, Valerie b 1961); *Career* res fell: W Reserve Univ Cleveland Ohio USA 1953-55, St Marys Hosp Med Sch London 1955-58; res memb Connaught Med Res Laboratories Toronto 1958-66; prof of microbiology: Univ of Toronto 1966-70, Univ of Glasgow 1970-; memb: Marshall Aid Scholarship Cmmn, American Soc for Microbiology 1978; FRSE 1972; *Books* Sourcebook of Experiments for the Teaching of Microbiology, Practical Statistics for Experimental Biologists, Pathogenesis and Immunity in Pertussis; *Recreations* gardening, ceramics, bicycle-camping; *Style*— Prof Alastair Wardlaw, FRSE; 92 Drymen Rd, Bearsden, Glasgow G61 2SY (☎ 041 942 2461); Microbiology Dept, University of Glasgow, Glasgow G12 9QQ (☎ 041 339 8855 ext 4001, fax 041 330 4600)

WARDLAW, Sir Henry; 20 Bt (NS 1631), of Pitreavie, Fifeshire; s of Sir Henry Wardlaw, 19 Bt (d 1954, himself ninth in descent from Sir Henry Wardlaw, 1 Bt, who was Chamberlain to James I's Queen, Anne of Denmark); *b* 30 Aug 1894; *m* 1929, Ellen, da of late John Francis Brady, of Hawthorn, Victoria, Australia; 4 s, 1 da; *Heir* gs, Henry Justin Wardlaw b 10 Aug 1963; *Style*— Sir Henry Wardlaw, Bt; 10120 Florence Rd, Surrey Hills, Victoria, Australia 3127

WARDLE, Anthony Peter; s of Peter John Wardle, of Minehead, Somerset, and Caroline Mina Gertrude, *née* Salter; *b* 9 Aug 1948; *Educ* Hertford GS, Thames Nautical Training Coll, Univ of Southampton Sch of Navigation; *m* 24 June 1972, Susan Margaret, *née* Lewis; 2 da (Jessica Ann b 3 June 1979, Eleanor Katherine b 18 June 1981); *Career* navigating apprenticeship Peninsular & Orient Steam Navigation Co 1966-69, prods mgmnt sales and mktg trg Rossfoods 1972-73, Bd dir BBDO and Promotional Campaigns Ltd 1977-79 (joined 1973), dir and shareholder Merchandising Strategy Ltd 1979-81, co bought out to form Mann Wardle Ltd (jt chm 1981-87); co later became Mann Wardle Group Ltd (acquired by Saatchi & Saatchi plc 1987); chm 1987-: Saatchi & Saatchi/Spa, Saatchi & Saatchi Business Communications, Saatchi & Saatchi Integrated, Equator UK Ltd; memb: BFSS, CLA, The Game Conservancy; *Recreations* shooting, fishing, tennis, food, wine; *Style*— Anthony Wardle, Esq; Norton House, Norton St Philip, Bath, Somerset BA3 6LW (☎ 037 387 239); La Seguinie, Pezuls, 24510 Ste Alvere, Dordogne France (☎ 33 532 34532); Saatchi & Saatchi Integrated, 83-89 Whitfield St, London W1A 1AQ (☎ 071 631 3224, fax 071 436 9522, car 0836 245079)

WARDLE, Charles Frederick; MP (C) Bexhill and Battle 1983-; s of Frederick Maclean Wardle (d 1975), and Constance, *née* Roach; *b* 23 Aug 1939; *Educ* Tonbridge, Lincoln Coll Oxford, Harvard Business Sch; *m* 1964, Lesley Ann, da of Sidney Wells (d 1967); 1 da (Sarah b 1969), and Dorothy, *née* Martin; *Career* chm: Benjamin Priest Group 1977-84, MP Bexhill and Battle 1983, PPS to Sec of State for Social Servs 1984-87; chm One Nation Forum 1989-90, PPS to Sec of State for Scotland 1990-; memb: CBI Cncl 1980-84, Treasy and Civil Serv Ctee 1990-91; *Style*— Charles Wardle, Esq, MP; House of Commons, Westminster, London SW1A 0AA

WARDLE, (John) Irving; s of John Wardle (d 1975), of Bolton, and Nellie, *née* Partington (d 1930); *b* 20 July 1929; *Educ* Bolton Sch, Wadham Coll Oxford (BA), RCM (ARCM); *m* 1, Joan (decd); m 2 (m dis), Fay; 2 s (Benjamin b 1964, Thomas b 1967); m 3, Elizabeth Rosalind; 1 s (Alexander b 1972), 1 da (Judith b 1974); *Career* sub ed Times Educational Supplement 1957-60, dep theatre critic The Observer 1960-63; theatre critic The Times 1963-89, ed Gambit Int Theatre Magazine 1970-72, theatre critic The Independent on Sunday 1990; *Books* The Theatres of George Devine (1978); *Plays*: The Houseboy (Open Space Theatre 1973), Dolls (Soho Poly Theatre 1987); *Recreations* piano playing; *Style*— Irving Wardle, Esq; 51 Richmond Rd, New Barnet, Herts EN5 1SF (☎ 081 440 3671); The Independent on Sunday, 40 City Rd, London ECM 2DB (☎ 071 253 1222)

WARDLE, John Malcolm; s of Hubert Stanley Wardle (d 1988), of Minehead, Somerset, and Annie, *née* Lambert (d 1965); *b* 30 Dec 1928; *Educ* St Edward's Sch Oxford, Birmingham Univ (LLB); *m* 9 Jan 1958, (Nora) Patricia Hilda, JP, da of John Gilbert Saville (d 1982); 1 s (Guy b 1960), 1 da (Jocelyn b 1959), 1 step da (Geraldine b 1955); *Career* Flying Offr RAF 1951-53; slr; ptnr Edge & Ellison (Solicitors) 1956, sr ptnr 1963-90; former chm: Leon Berner Gp, D F Bevan Holdings, Barton Gp, Wm Whittingham Holdings, HB Electronics, Rex Williams Leisure; local dir Barclays Merchant Bank; chm: Metalrax Gp plc, Hampson Industries plc; dep chm Forward Gp plc; dir: Galliford plc, Harding Gp plc; chm Olympic Appeal (W Midlands) 1984 and 1988; tstee Birmingham Hippodrome Theatre Devpt Tst 1981; pres Birmingham and Midland Operatic Soc; memb The Law Soc 1954; author of various newspaper and magazine articles on legal subjects and the duties of a non-exec dir; *Recreations* writing for pleasure, theatre, golf; *Style*— John Wardle, Esq; Norton Grange, Norton Green Lane, Knowle, Solihull, W Midlands B93 8PJ (☎ 0564 772548); Rutland House, 148 Edmund St, Birmingham B3 2JR (☎ 021 200 2001, fax 021 200 1991, telex 336370)

WARDLE, Piers; s Dr of Christopher John Wardle, of Devon, and Mary, *née* Haworth; *b* 20 April 1960; *Educ* Exeter Art Coll, Ruskin Sch of Drawing Oxford; *Career* artist; solo exhibitions: Northcott Theatre Exeter 1979, The Acme Gallery London 1981, Pomeroy Purdy Gallery London 1989 and 1990, Eastbourne Clark Gallery Florida 1990, Bernard Baron Gallery London 1990; group exhibitions: The Museum of Modern Art Oxford 1982, The Crypt London 1987 and 1988, The Summer Show (Pomeroy Purdy Gallery) 1988, New Work By Gallery Artists (Pomeroy Purdy Gallery) 1990; work in the collection of The Courtauld Institute; *media* The Late Show (Chaos Theory and Art) BBC TV 1990; *books* Longinus and Stephaton (with Tim Long, 1990); *Style*— Piers Wardle, Esq; Pomeroy Purdy Gallery, Jacob Street Film Studios, Mill St, London SE1 2BA (☎ 071 237 6062, fax 071 252 0511)

WARDMAN, Arthur Stewart; s of Gp Capt Rex Wardman, OBE, AFC (d 1985), and Edith, *née* Harper; *b* 13 Sept 1941; *Educ* Brighton Coll; *m* 1965 (m dis 1971); 1 s (Iain b 1968), 1 da (Joanne b 1970); *Career* md: Kigass Engineering Ltd 1975-85, Kigass Aero Components Ltd 1975-85, Abex Plastic Products Ltd 1976-, Apco International Ltd 1984-; chm and gp md Kigass Ltd 1985-; dir Premier Springs and Pressings Ltd 1985-; *Recreations* sailing, shooting, skiing, sub-aqua diving; *Clubs* Royal Ocean Racing, Royal Lymington Yacht; *Style*— Arthur Wardman, Esq; Kigass Ltd, Kigass House, Chapel St, Leamington Spa, Warwicks CV31 1EL (☎ 0926 422241, telex 311071, fax 0926 421454)

WARDROPE, James (Jim); s of James Wardrope, of Bathgate, W Lothian, Scotland, and Elizabeth Wilson, *née* Young (d 1989); *b* 14 March 1954; *Educ* Bathgate Acad, Univ of Edinburgh (BSc, MB ChB); *m* 31 March 1978, Diana Jane, da of Bruce Stuart Fothergill, of Sheffield; 1 s (Alistair b 1988), 1 da (Katie b 1986); *Career* registrar and res registrar Leeds Gen Infirmary 1982-85, sr registrar Royal Hallamshire Hosp Sheffield 1985-87, conslt in accident and emergency med Northern Gen Hosp Sheffield 1987-; memb: BAEM Academic Sub Ctee and Disaster Sub Ctee, Nat Hosp Jr Staff Ctee 1982-85, Exec Ctee Sheffield Div BMA 1985-; FRCS (Edin) 1982, FRCS 1982; *Recreations* cycling, running, gardening; *Style*— Jim Wardrope, Esq; Accident and Emergency Department, Northern General Hospital, Herries Rd, Sheffield S5 7AU (☎ 0742 434343)

WARDROPER, Lt-Col Michael John Ferrers; s of Kingsley Ronald Wardroper (d 1970), and Ruth Elizabeth Bunbury (d 1948); *b* 24 July 1935; *Educ* Bedford Sch, Canford; *m* 30 Aug 1969, Angela Yvonne, da of John Kenneth Stanley, of Eastbourne; 2 s (James b 1970, David b 1972); *Career* Lt-Col cmmnd from RMA Sandhurst into 10 Princess Mary's Own Gurkha Rifles 1956, Army Staff Coll 1967-68, Nat Defence Coll 1974-75, cmd 6 Queen Elizabeth's Own Gurkha Rifles 1975-78 (served principally in Far East); gp co-ordinator and dir property devpt LEP Group plc 1985-89, property devpt conslt 1989, Mktg Div Grants Intl 1990-; *Recreations* shooting, gardening, riding; *Style*— Lt-Col Michael Wardroper; Quinces Upper Dicker, Hailsham, East Sussex BN27 3RH (fax 0323442618)

WARE, Jeremy John; s of Col Robert Remington Ware (d 1952), of Collingham, Newark, Notts, and Barbara, *née* Lewellyn; *b* 29 Oct 1932; *Educ* Winchester, Lincoln Coll Oxford (MA); *m* 23 April 1960, Patricia Jane, da of Maj Horace Maylin Vipan Wright; 3 s (Julian b 1963, Henry b 1965, Maylin b 1968); *Career* admitted slr 1958; ptnr Tallents Godfrey & Co; pres: Notts Law Soc 1986-87, Grantham Div Cons Assoc 1986- (chm 1978-86); chm Lincs & E Notts Euro Parly Constituency 1988-; memb Law Soc; *Recreations* shooting, fishing, gardening; *Style*— J J Ware, Esq; Lister Place, Brant Broughton, Lincoln; 3 Middlegate, Newark, Notts (☎ 0636 71881)

WARE, John Desmond; s of Ralph Ernest Ware, MBE (d 1957), of Exeter, and Hilda Marguerite, *née* Croom-Johnson (d 1955); *b* 12 Jan 1920; *Educ* Sherborne; *m* 19 Nov 1966, Constance Wiltshire, da of Sir John Hampden Inskip, KBE (d 1960); 1 s (Nicholas John b 29 Nov 1967); *Career* WWII serv Royal Gloucestershire Hussars (TA) 1937-40, Lt Devonshire Regt 1940-43, Capt Chindits 54 Column 1943-44, Maj Para Regt 1944; WD & HO Wills: mangr Swindon 1949-53, gen factor mangr 1953-59; gen mangr Wills/Clarke Dublin 1959-63; dir: Irish Carton Printers 1959-63, Imperial Tobacco Co 1963-69, WD & HO Wills 1963-69; chm: Imperial Athletic Club, Wills Branches Royal Br Legion; memb Cncl St Monica Home, hon treas Bristol Benevolent Inst, govr Milton Abbey Sch, former pres: Colston Soc; former pres: Anchor Soc, Colston Res Soc, Bristol Hibernian Soc; *Recreations* golf, gardening; *Clubs* Bristol & Clifton; *Style*— John D Ware, Esq; Coach House, 4 Cooks Folly Rd, Bristol BS9 1PL (☎ 0272 681 550)

WARE, Dr Lancelot Lionel; OBE (1987); s of Frederick Richard Ware (d 1940), of Astolat, The Chase, Wallington, Surrey, and Eleanor Gwynne, *née* Emslie (d 1952); *b* 5 June 1915; *Educ* Steyning GS, Royal Coll of Science (BSc, PhD, ARCS, DIC), Lincoln Coll Oxford (MA); *m* 14 June 1980, Joan Francesca Rae; *Career* res worker Nat Inst Med Res 1938-39, lectr in biochemistry St Thomas' Hosp Med Sch 1941-46; called to the Bar Lincoln's Inn 1949, practised 1949-87; Surrey Co Cnclr 1949-55, Alderman London CC 1955-61, memb Cncl of Euro Municipalities 1958-70; vice pres Eurotalent 1988-, Royal Asiatic Soc, Inst of Patentees and Inventors (formerly chm); chm tstees of Shakespearean Authorship Tst, former pres Int Assoc of Inventors Assocs; former chm: Assoc of Voluntary Aided Secdy Schs, Cons Graduate Assoc; former govr: Wye Agric Coll, Coll of St Mark and St John, Imperial Coll, LSE, LSHTM, SOAS, St Olave's and St Saviour's Fndn (warden), St Olave's GS, St Saviour's GS, Weybridge Tech Coll, St Thomas' Hosp; FRIC, FCIArb; Fons et Origo Mensae; *Recreations* field sports, real tennis, rackets, chess (former univ and co player); *Clubs* Athenaeum, Carlton; *Style*— Dr L L Ware, OBE; Homewood, Quarry Rd, Hurtmore, Godalming, Surrey GU7 2RW (☎ 0483 422711); 11 Old Sq, Lincoln's Inn, London WC2A 3TS (☎ 071 2426995)

WARE, Michael John; CB (1985), QC (1988); s of Kenneth George Ware (d 1967), and Phyllis Matilda, *née* Joynes (d 1984); *b* 7 May 1932; *Educ* Cheltenham GS, Trinity Hall Cambridge (BA, LLB); *m* 4 June 1966, Susan Ann, da of Gp Capt C E Maitland, DFC, AFC; 3 da (Victoria b 1967, Johanna b 1970, Katherine b 1974); *Career* called to the Bar Middle Temple 1955; legal dept Bd of Trade (later DTI) 1957-73, legal advsr Office of Fair Trading 1973-77; under-sec (legal) DTI (co inspections and prosecutions) 1977-80; slr Dept of Environment 1980-; *Style*— Michael Ware, Esq, CB, QC; Department of the Environment, 2 Marsham St, London SW1P 3EB (☎ 071 212 4731)

WARE, Peter Morrell; s of late Arthur Coates Ware; *b* 14 Sept 1922; *Educ* Malvern; *m* 1955, Elizabeth Ann, *née* Farrell; 1 s, 2 da; *Career* Warrant Officer 11 UK; md CPC (UK) Ltd 1975-, gen mangr CPC Benelux and Scandinavia 1966-70, chm British Maize Refiners Assoc 1976-77, pres Assoc des Amidonneries de Maïs de la CEE 1978-79; *Recreations* cricket, tennis; *Clubs* MCC; *Style*— Peter Ware, Esq; 1 Fairacres, Roehampton Lane, London SW15 (☎ 081 878 1979)

WAREING, Robert Nelson; MP (Lab) Liverpool, West Derby 1983-; s of Robert Wareing (d 1960), and Florence Patricia, *née* Mallon (d 1964); *b* 20 Aug 1930; *Educ* Ranworth Square Sch, Alsop HS Liverpool, Bolton Coll of Educn, Univ of London (BSc, external degree); *m* 1962, Betty (d 1989), da of Thomas Coward (d 1964); *Career* local govt offr 1946-48, LAC RAF 1948-50, local govt offr 1950-56, coll lectr 1957-83, chm Merseyside Econ Devpt Co Ltd 1981-; contested (Lab): Berwick-upon-Tweed 1970, Liverpool Edge Hill March 1979 (by-election), May 1979; Merseyside Cllr, chief whip Lab gp 1981-83, asst opposition whip 1987-; vice chm Br-Yugoslav Parly Gp; *Recreations* concert-going, soccer, travel; *Clubs* Pirrie Labour, Dovecot Labour (Liverpool); *Style*— Robert Wareing, Esq, MP; House of Commons, London

SW1A 0AA (☎ 071 219 3482)

WARENIUS, Prof Hilmar Meek; s of Tor Adolph Warenius (d 1971), and Ruby Gwendoline, *née* Meek; *b* 12 Jan 1942; *Educ* Penzance GS, Downing Coll Cambridge (MA), Middlesex Hosp (PhD, DMRT); *m* 19 Aug 1972, Rosamund Jean Talbot, da of Leopold Edward Hill (d 1957); 1 s (Christopher b 1976), 2 da (Eleanor b 1979, Fleur b 1985); *Career* sr house offr Royal Marsden Hosp 1970-71, registrar radiotherapy Middlesex Hosp; first asst to Prof Mitchell at Addenbrookes Hosp, MRC clinical res fell Univ of Cambridge, first asst to Mr William Ross Univ of Newcastle and Newcastle Gen Hosp, conslt in radiotherapy and oncology in Newcastle, CRC prof of radiation oncology Univ of Liverpool 1982-90, MRC hon clinical coordinator Fast Neutron Studies 1982-89, currently prof and head Dept Oncology Res Unit Cancer Res Campaign Dept of Med Univ of Liverpool; FRCR, FRCP; *Recreations* swimming, choral society; *Style*— Prof Hilmar Warenius; 14 Delavor Rd, Heswall, Wirral, Merseyside (☎ 051 342 3034); Cancer Research Campaign, Oncology Research Unit, Department of Medicine, The University of Liverpool, PO Box 147, Liverpool L69 3BX (☎ 051 706 2000 Ext 4530, 051 706 4070)

WARHURST, Alan; CBE (1990); s of William Warhurst (d 1965), and Margaret, *née* Holden (d 1953); *b* 6 Feb 1927; *Educ* Canon Slade GS Bolton, Univ of Manchester (BA); *m* 5 Sept 1953, Sheila Lilian, da of John Bradbury (d 1957), of Atherton; 1 s (Nicholas b 1964), 2 da (Alyson b 1958, Frances b 1960); *Career* Nat Serv cmmnd Lancs Fus 1946-48; dir: City Museum Bristol 1960-70, Ulster Museum Belfast 1970-77, Manchester Museum 1977-; pres: Western Fedn of Museums and Galleries 1966-68 and 1979-80, The Museums Assoc 1975-76; chm: Irish Nat Ctee ICOM 1973-75, Gtr Manchester Archaeological Fedn, Hulme Hall Ctee Univ of Manchester; hon sec The Univ Museums Gp 1987, dep chm North West Museum and Art Gallery Serv 1987-, tstee Canon Slade GS; Hon MA Queens Univ Belfast 1983; FSA 1953, FMA 1958; *Recreations* English ceramics, hillwalking; *Style*— Alan Warhurst, Esq, CBE, FSA; Calabar Cottage, Woodville Road, Altrincham, Cheshire WA14 2AL (☎ 061 928 0730); The Manchester Museum, The University, Oxford Rd, Manchester M13 9PL (☎ 061 275 2650)

WARIN, Dr Andrew Peter; s of Dr John Fairbairn Warin, OBE (d 1990), of Tudor Cottage, Iffley, Oxford OX4 4EF, and Dr Kathleen Warin; *b* 16 Jan 1945; *Educ* Radley, Guy's Hosp London Univ (MB BS); *m* 3 Sept 1966 (m dis 1987), Dr Judith M Warin, da of V D H Rutland, of Tregolls Bungalow, 31 The Crescent, Farnborough, Hants; 1 s (Benjamin b 2 Jan 1974), 2 da (Fiona b 11 Nov 1969, Joanna b 10 Nov 1970); *Career* conslt dermatologist and sr lectr St John's Hosp for Diseases of Skin 1976-80, conslt dermatologist Exeter 1980-; articles on psoriasis mycosis fungoides and glucagonoma syndrome; FRSM (memb Ctee), FRCP (memb Ctee), memb Br Assoc Dermatologists (memb Ctee); *Recreations* squash, swimming, windsurfing, running, tennis, skiing, clarinet; *Clubs* Golf and Country; *Style*— Dr Andrew Warin; 14 Barnfield Hill, Exeter, Devon EX1 1SR (☎ 0392 217698); Royal Devon and Exeter Hospital, Barrack Rd, Exeter, Devon (☎ 0392 77833)

WARING, Caroline; da of Peter Waring, of Huntend, Redditch, Hereford and Worcester, and Patricia Margret, *née* Radcliffe; *b* 11 April 1961; *Educ* Harold Cartwright GS for girls, Solihull Coll of Technol, Kingston Poly (BA); *Career* designer; Klaus Wultke & Partners July-Dec 1982, retail and corporate identity for Derek Forsyth Partnership 1983-85, gen graphic design Basten Brewer & Andrews 1985-86 (for BT, BMW, Honeywell Computers); dep gp head Michael Peters & Partners 1986-88 int packaging design (Upim Make-Up Milan, Campbells USA, Fazer Biscuits Finland, Paulig Tea Finland, Warner Lambert, W H Smiths); gp asst creative dir Coley Porter Bell 1988- (Asda Supermarket, Cussons, Crookes Health Care, Eden Vale, Safeway Supermarket, Shell (UK), ICI (UK), Holsten (UK)); *Recreations* skiing, walking; *Style*— Ms Caroline Waring

WARING, Sir (Alfred) Holburt; 3 Bt (UK 1935); s of Sir Alfred Waring, 2 Bt (d 1981), and Winifred, Lady Waring; *b* 2 Aug 1933; *Educ* Rossall; *m* 1958, Ana, da of Valentine Medinilla; 1 s, 2 da; *Heir* s, Michael Holburt Waring, b 3 Jan 1964; *Career* dir: SRM Plastics, Waring Investments, Property Realisation Co Ltd; *Recreations* tennis, golf, squash, swimming; *Clubs* Moor Park Golf; *Style*— Sir Alfred Waring, Bt; 30 Russell Rd, Moor Park, Northwood, Middx

WARING, John; s of Samuel Hugh Waring (d 1940), of Leek, and Mary, *née* Whittington (d 1972); *b* 13 Dec 1927; *Educ* Leek HS, Sacred Heart Coll Droitwich; *m* 1951, Jean Margaret, da of John Norman Hill (d 1968), of Worcs; 1 s (Richard), 2 da (Susan, Claire); *Career* chm John Waring Gp of Cos 1969- (involved in grain shipping, seed and animal feed prodn, intensive pig and cattle farming); *Recreations* shooting, swimming, painting; *Style*— John Waring, Esq; Wellingore Hall, Wellingore, Lincoln LN5 0HX (☎ 0522 810810)

WARING, Stuart James Heaton; s of Walter Heaton Waring (d 1983), and Margaret Helen, *née* Jacobs; *b* 18 Sept 1944; *Educ* Shrewsbury, City Univ London (BSc); *m* 12 Sept 1970, Ann Carol, da of George Henry Vince, of Los Flamencos 6, Guadalmina Alta, San Pedro de Alcantara, Malaga, Spain; 1 s (Daniel b 28 May 1973), 1 da (Zoe b 11 May 1975); *Career* chm: Warings Contractors Ltd 1970-, Heaton Holdings Ltd 1985-, Gatcombe House Properties Ltd 1988-, Sanipor UK Ltd 1989-; govr Portsmouth Poly; Freeman City of London, Liveryman Worshipful Co of Paviors 1968; CEng, FICE; *Recreations* fly-fishing, shooting, tennis, skiing; *Style*— Stuart J H Waring, Esq; Warings Contractors Limited, Gatcombe House, Hilsea, Portsmouth, Hampshire PO2 0TU (☎ 0705 694900)

WARING, Winifred, Lady; Winifred; da of Albert Boston, of Stockton-on-Tees; *m* 1930, Sir Harold Waring, 2 Bt (d 1981); 1 s (Sir Alfred W, 3 Bt), 2 da (Mrs Michael Mark, Mrs John Holderness); *Style*— Winifred, Lady Waring; Pen Moel, Tidenham, Glos

WARLAND, Philip John; s of Ernest Alfred Henry Warland, of Christchurch, and Winifred Mary, *née* Poyntz-Owen; *b* 25 Dec 1945; *Educ* KCS; *m* 19 Sept 1970, Sandra, da of Jack Cross (d 1987); 3 s (David b 1972, Richard b 1973, John b 1978); *Career* head Info Div Bank of England 1985-89, gp personnel resources mangr Standard Chartered Bank 1989-90, dir gen Unit Tst Assoc 1991-; *Recreations* squash, golf, cricket, walking; *Style*— Philip Warland, Esq; Unit Trust Assoc, 65 Kingsway, London WC2B 6TD (☎ 071 831 0898)

WARLOW, Prof Charles Picton; s of Charles Edward Picton Warlow (d 1988), and Nancy Mary McLellan, *née* Hine (d 1987); *b* 9 Sept 1943; *Educ* Univ of Cambridge (BA, MB BChir, MD), St George's Hosp Med Sch London; *m* 4 Sept 1976, Ilona Patricia, da of Max McDowell, of Auckland, NZ; 2 s (Benjamin b 1 Aug 1980, Oliver b 27 Oct 1984), 1 da (Margaret b 25 March 1982); *Career* clinical reader in neurology Univ of Oxford 1977-86, fell Green Coll 1979-86, prof of med neurology Univ of Edinburgh 1987-; memb: Chest Heart and Stroke Assoc, Dept of Tport, Assoc of Br Neurologists, Br Stroke Res Gp, Assoc of Physicians, Euro Neurological Soc, Athero Sclerosis Discussion Gp, American Neurological Assoc, Lab Pty, Woodcraft Folk; FRCP, FRCPE; *Books* Transient Ischaemic Attacks (1982), Dilemmas in the Management of the Neurological Patient (1984), More Dilemmas in the Management of the Neurological Patients (1987), Stroke and Living with Stroke (with Barbara Woodhouse, 1987); *Recreations* sailing, skiing, photography, walking; *Style*— Prof Charles Warlow; Department of Clinical Neurosciences, Western General Hospital, Crewe Rd, Edinburgh EH4 2XU (☎ 031 332 2525, fax 031 332 5150)

WARMAN, Oliver Byrne; *b* 10 June 1932; *Educ* Stowe, Univ of Exeter, Balliol Coll Oxford; *Career* cmmnd Welsh Guards 1953, GSO III Cabinet Office, instr Staff Coll RMCS, ret 1970; artist: first exhibited RA 1980; exhibited: RBA, RWA, RSMA, ROI, NEAC; work in public collections incl: US Embassy, Nat West Bank, Co-op Bank Crown Cmmn; dir: Ship & Boat Builders Fedn 1972, Falmarine 1973, Ashlyns' Wine Shippers 1978, Tulsemead Wine Shippers 1983; chief exec Fedn of Br Artists 1984-; memb Cncl: CBI, Army Ski Assoc; RBA 1984; *Books* Arnhem 1944 (1970), Royal Society of Portrait Painters (1986); contrib to anthologies on wine, painting, military history; *Recreations* painting, France, food, military history, sailing, wine; *Clubs* Cavalry & Guards, Chelsea Arts, Royal Cornwall Yacht; *Style*— Oliver Warman, Esq; 17 Carlton House Terrace, London SW1Y 5BD (☎ 071 930 6844)

WARMINGTON, Anthony Marshall; s of Sir Marshall Warmington, Bt, of Swallowfield Park, Reading, Berkshire, and Eileen Mary, *née* Howes (d 1969); *b* 1 July 1946; *Educ* Charterhouse, Univ of Grenoble; *m* 1973 (m dis 1987), Carolyn Patricia, da of late Micky Simonds; 1 s (Oliver Marshall Simonds b 30 Sept 1974), 1 da (Katherine Louise b 22 Feb 1977); *Career* Lt Queen's Dragoon Gds, served NI Aden Germany 1965-68; Kitcat and Aitken 1968-71, Bisgood Bishop & Co 1971-72, investmt mangr Ionian Bank 1972-74, investmt mangr Kitcat and Aitken 1974-77; dir: Streets Financial PR 1980-87 (joined 1977), fin PR Manning Selvage & Lee 1987-89; dir: Burson-Marsteller 1989-, Burson-Marsteller Financial 1989- (head int investor rels); memb: Investor Relations Soc 1990, MENSA 1990; *Recreations* golf, shooting, theatre, tennis; *Clubs* MCC, Cavalry and Guards; *Style*— Anthony Warmington, Esq; Burson Marsteller, 24-28 Bloomsbury Way, London WC1A 2PX (☎ 071 831 2969, fax 071 430 1052)

WARMINGTON, Sir Marshall George Clitheroe; 3 Bt (UK 1908); s of Sir Marshall Denham Warmington, 2 Bt, JP (d 1935), and his 1 w Alice Daisy, *née* Ing; *b* 26 May 1910; *Educ* Charterhouse; *m* 1, 1933 (m dis 1941), Mollie, da of late Capt Malcolm Alfred Kennard RN; 1 s, 1 da; m 2, 1942, Eileen Mary (d 1969), da of late P J Howes; 2 s; m 3, 1972 (m dis 1977), Sheila (d 1988), da of Stanley Brotherhood, JP, of Thornhaugh Hall, Peterborough, and widow of Adm the Hon Sir Cyril Eustace Douglas-Pennant, KCB, CBE, DSO, DSC (d 1961, s of 5 Baron Penrhyn); *Heir* s, Marshall Denham Malcolm Warmington b 1934; *Career* Lt Cdr RN 1928-54; co sec Securicor 1963-69; *Recreations* fishing, golf; *Clubs* MCC; *Style*— Sir Marshall Warmington, Bt; Swallowfield Park, Reading, Berks (☎ 0734 882210)

WARNE, (Ernest) John David; CB (1982); s of John Warne (d 1954), and Amelia, *née* Hawking (d 1928); *b* 4 Dec 1926; *Educ* Univ of London (BA); *m* 1953, Rena, da of Col Vladimir Vasilievich Alexandrov (d 1937), of Leningrad, USSR; 3 s (Anthony, Steven, Richard); *Career* univ lectr 1951-53; Civil Service: princ 1953-64, asst sec 1964-72, under sec 1972-79, dep sec 1979-82; sec ICAEW 1982-90; *Recreations* reading, collecting prints, theatre, walking; *Clubs* Reform; *Style*— John Warne, Esq, CB; 3 Woodville Rd, Ealing, London W5 (☎ 081 998 0215)

WARNER, Alan Tristram Nicholas; s of Sir Edward Warner, KCMG, OBE, of Blockley, Glouc, and Grizel Margaret, *née* Clerk-Rattray; *b* 18 Oct 1949; *Educ* Rugby, Univ of St Andrews (MA); *m* 7 Jan 1984, Susan Voase, da of Richard Boyle Adderley, MBE, of Pickering, N Yorks; 1 s (Nicholas b 15 April 1985), 1 da (Harriet b 9 Feb 1988); *Career* accountant Touche Ross & Co 1974-78; md Douglas Deakin Young Ltd 1988, Citycall Financial Review 1987-; contrib to fin progs on radio and TV; Liveryman Worshipful Co of Grocers 1980; ACA; *Recreations* family, shooting, skiing; *Clubs* RAC; *Style*— Alan Warner, Esq; 43 Thornhill Rd, London N1 1JS (☎ 071 607 6577); Douglas Deakin Young Ltd, Empire House, 175 Piccadilly, London W1V 9DB (☎ 071 499 1206, fax 071 499 1017)

WARNER, Deborah; da of Roger Harold Metford Warner, of Oxfordshire, and Ruth Ernestine, *née* Hurcombe; *b* 12 May 1959; *Educ* Sidcot Sch Somerset, St Clare's Coll Oxford, Central Sch of Speech and Drama London; *Career* artistic dir Kick Theatre Co 1980-86, res dir RSC 1987-89, assoc dir Royal Nat Theatre Co 1990; *Recreations* travelling; *Style*— Ms Deborah Warner; c/o Jeremy Conway, 18-21 Jermyn St, London SW1Y 6HP (☎ 071 287 0077, fax 071 287 1940)

WARNER, Sir Edward Redston; KCMG (1965, CMG 1955), OBE (1948); s of Sir George Redston Warner, KCVO, CMG (d 1978), and Margery Catherine, *née* Nicol (d 1963); *b* 23 March 1911; *Educ* Oundle, King's Coll Cambridge; *m* 1943, Grizel Margaret, da of Col Paul Robert Clerk Rattray, CBE, JP, DL, RE (d 1937); 3 s (Paul now Ramsay of Bamff, Nigel, Alan), 1 da (Elizabeth (Mrs Berry)); *Career* FO 1935-70: served Athens, dep UK delegate OEEC Paris 1956-59, min Tokyo 1959-62, ambass Cameroon 1963-66, UK rep Econ and Social Cncl UN 1966-67, ambass Tunisia 1968-70, memb Staff Appeals Bd OECD Paris 1971-83; pt/t ed Historical Manuscripts Cmmn 1971-74; *Clubs* Utd Oxford and Cambridge, Royal Cwlth Soc; *Style*— Sir Edward Warner, KCMG, OBE; Old Royal Oak, Blockley, Glos GL56 9EX

WARNER, Francis Robert Le Plastrier; s of Rev Hugh Compton Warner (d 1955), of Epsom, Surrey, and Nancy Le Plastrier, *née* Owen; *b* 21 Oct 1937; *Educ* Christ's Hosp, London Coll of Music, St Catharine's Coll Cambridge (BA, MA), Univ of Oxford (MA); *m* 1, 1958 (m dis 1972), Mary, *née* Hall; 2 da (Georgina b 1962, Lucy b 1967); m 2, 2 July 1983, Penelope Anne, da of John Hugh Davis, of Blagdon, nr Bristol; 1 s (Benedict b 1988), 1 da (Miranda b 1985); *Career* poet and dramatist; Univ of Cambridge: supervisor St Catharine's Coll 1959-63, staff tutor in Eng, memb Bd of Extramural Studies 1963-65; Univ of Oxford Sir Gordon White fell in Eng lit and sr Eng tutor St Peter's Coll 1965-, fell librarian 1966-76, dean of degrees 1984-, vice-master 1987-89, pro sr proctor Univ of Oxford 1989-90 (univ lectr 1965-); Messing Int Award for Distinguished Contribs to Lit 1972; memb Southern Arts Drama Panel Arts Cncl of GB 1976-78 (chm 1978-79 and 1979-80); *poetry:* Perennia (1962), Early Poems (1964), Experimental Sonnets (1965), Madrigals (1967), The Poetry of Francis Warner (USA, 1970), Lucca Quartet (1975), Morning Vespers (1980), Spring Harvest (1981), Epithalamium (1983), Collected Poems 1960-84 (1985); *plays:* Maquettes, a trilogy of one-act plays (1972); Requiem: Pt 1 Lying Figures (1972), Pt 2 Killing Time (1976), Pt 3 Meeting Ends (1974); A Conception of Love (1978), Light Shadows (1980), Moving Reflections (1983), Living Creation (1985), Healing Nature: The Athens of Pericles (1988), Byzantium (1989); *ed:* Eleven Poems by Edmund Blunden (1965), Garland (1968), Studies in the Arts (1968); *Recreations* children, cathedral music, travel; *Clubs* Athenaeum; *Style*— Francis Warner, Esq; St Peter's College, Oxford OX1 2DL (☎ 0865 278 900)

WARNER, Frank Ernest; MBE (1945), TEM (1950); s of Stanley Theodore Warner (d 1953), of Henley-on-Thames, and Ursula Marguerite, *née* Harrison; *b* 7 Jan 1920; *Educ* Reading Sch; *m* 28 Nov 1942, Joan Vera, da of Joseph Cotton (d 1938), of Reading; 1 s (David b 1948), 2 da (Ann b 1944, Jill b 1945); *Career* serv WWII, Maj (1944) RCS UK and Europe, TA 1938-39 and 1947-50; Turquand Youngs & Co 1946-48, co sec and accountant Thresher & Co 1948-50, sr ptnr Urwick Orr & Ptnrs (chm UK and overseas cos) 1950-75; conslt and CA in private practice 1975-89; hon nat treas The Abbeyfield Soc 1977-83; FCA (1948), FIOD (1964-90); *Style*— Frank Warner, Esq, MBE, TEM; 7 Lewes Crescent, Brighton BN2 1FH (☎ 0273 691 093)

WARNER, Sir Fred Archibald; GCVO (1975), KCMG (1972, CMG 1963), MEP (EDG) Somerset 1979-; s of Cdr Frederick Archibald Warner, DSO, RN (ka 1917); *b* 2

May 1918; *Educ* Wixenford Berks, RNC Dartmouth, Magdalen Coll Oxford; *m* 1971, Simone Georgina, formerly w of Basil de Ferranti, MEP (by whom she had 1 da: Alexa Georgina Ziani), and da of Lt-Col Hubert Jocelyn Nangle, DSO (d 1968, tenth in descent from Walter Nangle, 8 s of Sir Thomas Nangle (*floruit temp* Henry VIII), 17 ('Palatine') Baron of Navan, by Sir Thomas's w Elizabeth, eldest da of 3 Viscount Gormanston; This 'Palatine' Barony of Navan was first granted to Jocelyn De Angulo by Hugh de Lacy after Jocelyn accompanied Strongbow to Ireland from Pembrokeshire (in which county the place name Angle, whence De Angulo, is to be found) 1169); 2 s (Valentine b 1972, Orlando b 1974); *Career* Lt Cdr RNVR; served FO (later FCO) 1946-75: ambass Lagos 1965-67, ambass UN 1969-71, ambass Japan 1972-75; dir: Guinness Peat Gp, Loral Int, Job Creation Ltd; chm Nat Tst Wessex Region 1976-78; farmer 1958-82; chm Overseas Ctee CBI; *Clubs* Puffin's, Beefsteak, Turf; *Style—* Sir Fred Warner, GCVO, KCMG, MEP; 4 The Porticos, King's Road SW3 (☎ 071 351 3645); Inkpen House, Newbury, Berks

WARNER, Prof Sir Frederick Edward; s of Frederick Warner; *b* 31 March 1910; *Educ* Bancrofts Sch, UCL; *m* 1, Margaret Anderson McCrea; 2 s, 2 da; m 2, Barbara Reynolds; *Career* chemical engr; Cremer & Warner: joined 1956, sr ptnr 1963-80, now emeritus ptnr; visiting prof: Bartlett Sch of Architecture UCL 1970-73, Imperial Coll London 1970-78, Essex Univ 1983-; chm London Univ Sch of Pharmacy 1971-78, pro chllr Open Univ 1974-79, pres Br Standards Inst 1980-83 (formerly chm Exec Bd and Dep Pres); memb Ct: Cranfield Inst Technol, Essex Univ; fell UCL 1967; DUniv Open Univ, Hon DSc: Aston, Cranfield, Heriot-Watt, Newcastle; Hon DTech Bradford; FRS; kt 1968; *Style—* Prof Sir Frederick Warner, FEng, FRS; Univ of Essex, Wivenhoe Park, Colchester CO4 35Q (☎ 0206 873370); Cellar House, Brightlingsea, Essex CO7 0JR

WARNER, Gerald Chierici; CMG (1984); s of Howard Warner and Elizabeth, *née* Chierici-Kendall; *b* 27 Sept 1931; *Educ* Univ of Oxford (BA); *m* 1956, Mary Wynne Davies; 1 s, 2 da; *Career* 3 sec Peking 1956-58, 2 sec Rangoon 1960-61, 1 sec Warsaw 1964-66 and Geneva 1966-68, cnsllr Kuala Lumpur 1974-76, cnsllr FCO 1976-90; memb Police Complaints Authy 1990-; *Style—* Gerald Warner Esq, CMG; c/o Police Complaints Authority, 10 Great George St, London SW1

WARNER, Sir (Edward Courtenay) Henry; 3 Bt (UK 1910), of Brettenham, Suffolk; s of Col Sir Edward Warner, 2 Bt, DSO, MC (d 1955); *b* 3 Aug 1922; *Educ* Eton, Christ Church Oxford; *m* 1949, Jocelyn Mary, da of Cdr Sir Thomas Lubbock Beevor, 6 Bt, RN (ka 1943); 3 s; *Heir* s, Philip Warner; *Career* served WWII 1939-45 with Scots Gds; chm Law Land Co Ltd 1975-81; *Style—* Sir Henry Warner, Bt; The Grove, Great Baddow, Essex

WARNER, Hon Mr Justice; Hon Sir Jean-Pierre Frank Eugene; s of Frank Cloudesley ffolliott Warner, and Louise Marie Blanche, *née* Gouet; *b* 24 Sept 1924; *Educ* Sainte Croix de Neuilly, Ecole des Roches, Harrow, Trinity Coll Cambridge; *m* 1950, Sylvia Frances, da of Sir Ernest Goodale, CBE, MC; 2 da; *Career* serv WWII Rifle Bde; called to the Bar Lincoln's Inn 1950; jr counsel: Restrictive Trading Agreements Registrar 1961-64, Treasury (Chancery) 1964-72; QC 1972, advocate gen European Communities Ct of Justice 1973-81, vice pres UK Assoc European Law 1975-83 (pres 1983-89), High Ct judge (Chancery) 1981-, judge of Restictive Practices Ct 1982-; master of the walks Lincoln's Inn 1982, keeper of the Black Book 1983, dean of the Chapel 1984 (treas 1985); former chllr Kensington and Chelsea; former dir Warner & Sons; Hon LLD: Exeter 1983, Leicester 1984, Edinburgh 1987; kt 1981; *Style—* The Hon Mr Justice Warner; 32 Abingdon Villas, London W8 6BX (☎ 071 937 7023); Royal Courts of Justice, Strand, London WC2 2LL (☎ 071 936 6769)

WARNER, Capt John Rudyerd; s of Lt-Col Harold Rudyerd Warner, 1/131 UP Regt and Imp Indian Police (d 1964), and Ethel Norah, *née* Elliott (d 1966); *see* Burkes Landed Gentry, 18 edn, vol I, 1965, *sub* Warner formerly of Framlingham; *b* 22 March 1923; *Educ* Pangbourne Sch, Univ of London (BSc); *m* 1, 11 Oct 1958 (m dis 1963), Sheila Lesley, da of Edward Andrew, of Guernsey, CI; m 2, 30 Nov 1974 (m dis 1987), Lesley Ann Collier; 4 da (Madeleine b 26 Sept 1975, Lucy b 27 Nov 1979, Louise b 17 March 1982, Marie b 24 April 1984); *Career* served in IA, Capt RE, co cdr 10 Pathan Engr Bn, India, Burma, France and Germany 1941-46; chm Republic Lands Ltd 1973-; LRSC; *Recreations* tennis, swimming, photography; *Clubs* Naval; *Style—* Capt J R Warner; 131 Wellington Close, Walton-on-Thames, Surrey (☎ 0932 245028); Los Altos, Marbella, Spain

WARNER, Marina Sarah (Mrs John Mathews); da of Col Esmond Pelham Warner, TD (d 1982), of Cambridge, and Emilia, *née* Terzulli; *b* 9 Nov 1946; *Educ* Lady Margaret Hall Oxford (MA); *m* 1, 31 Jan 1972 (m dis 1980), Hon William Hartley Hume Shawcross, s of Baron Shawcross, *qv*; 1 s (Conrad Hartley Pelham b 1977); m 2, 16 Dec 1981, John Piers Dewe Mathews, s of Denys Cosmo Dewe Mathews (d 1986), of London; *Career* writer; Getty scholar Getty Center for the History of Art and the Humanities 1987-88, Tinbergen prof Erasmus Univ Rotterdam 1991; memb: Advsy Bd Royal Mint, Mgmnt Ctee Nat Cncl for One Parent Families; FRSL 1985; *Books* The Dragon Empress (1972), Alone of All Her Sex: the Myth and the Cult of the Virgin Mary (1976), Queen Victoria's Sketchbook (1980), Joan of Arc: the Image of Female Heroism (1981), Monuments and Maidens: the Allegory of the Female Form (1985); fiction: In A Dark Wood (1977), The Skating Party (1983), The Lost Father (1988); children's books: The Impossible Day (1981), The Impossible Night (1981), The Impossible Bath (1982), The Impossible Rocket (1982), The Wobbly Tooth (1984); juvenile: The Crack in the Teacup (1979); contrib: Times Literary Supplement, Independent; *Recreations* travel, gardening, photography, looking at pictures; *Style—* Miss Marina Warner; c/o Peters Fraser & Dunlop, Fifth Floor, The Chambers, Lots Rd, London SW10 (☎ 071 376 7676)

WARNER, Michael John Pelham; s of John Jellicoe Pelham Francis Warner (s of Sir Pelham (Plum) Warner, England Cricket Capt and Pres MCC), and Jean Mary, *née* McWatters; *b* 8 Dec 1943; *Educ* Eton; *m* 27 Feb 1982, Jennifer Jane, da of Nicholas John Inman, of Wendover, Bucks; 3 s (Richard Pelham b 1973, Giles Peter b 1975, James William b 1987); 1 da (Victoria Jean b 1984); *Career* CA; sr ptnr in Warner Marsh; pres Southern Soc of CAs 1983-84; *Recreations* golf, theatre, opera; *Clubs* Stoneham Golf; *Style—* Michael J P Warner, Esq; Quarry Cottage, Quarry Rd, Winchester, Hants (☎ 0962 855799); 11 College Place, Southampton (☎ 0703 638237)

WARNER, Norman Reginald; s of Albert Henry Edwin Warner, and Laura Edith, *née* Bennett; *b* 8 Sept 1940; *Educ* Dulwich, Univ of Calif Berkley (MA, Harkness fell), Nuffield Coll Oxford (Gwilyn Gibbon fell); *m* 1 (m dis 1981), Anne Lesley; 2 s (Andrew Simon b 1967, Joel James Stephen b 1981), 1 da (Justine Emma b 1969); m 2 , Suzanne Elizabeth; *Career* DHSS: various posts concerned with The NHSS 1960-74, principal private sec to Sec of State for Social Services 1974-76, asst sec Supplementary Benefit 1976-79, asst sec Operational Planning 1979-81, regnl controller Wales and SW Region 1981-83, under sec Supplementary Benefit and Housing Benefit 1984-85; dir Social Services Kent County Cncl 1985, memb Kent Family Practitioners' Ctee 1987-90, dir Kent Family Health Service Authy 1990; memb: Assoc of Dirs of Social Services 1985-, RIPA; *Recreations* walking, reading, cinema, theatre; *Style—* Norman Warner, Esq; 8 College Gardens, Dulwich, London SE21 7BE (☎ 081 693 7663); Kent County Council, Springfield, Maidstone, Kent ME14 2LW (☎ 0622 671411 ext 2601)

WARNER, Peter Mark; s of Dr Marcel Mark Warner, of Weybridge, Surrey, and Birthe Johanna Warner; *b* 21 June 1959; *Educ* Woking County GS, Kingston Poly Business Sch (BA); *Career* account exec Tim Arnold and Associates (sales promotion agency) 1981-83, client services dir IMP Ltd 1989- (joined as account exec 1983); *Recreations* gardening, fell walking, motorcycling; *Style—* Peter Warner, Esq; IMP Ltd, 197 Knightsbridge, London SW7 1RP (☎ 071 581 7666, fax 071 589 3903)

WARNER, Philip Arthur William; s of W T Warner (d 1964), of Whitacre, Warks, and M Warner, *née* Rowley (d 1933); *b* 19 May 1914; *Educ* ChCh Oxford, St Catharine's Coll Cambridge (MA); *m* 11 Sept 1946, Patricia Kathleen (d 1971), da of R G Rollinson; 2 s (Richard, John), 1 da (Diana); *Career* Army 1939-46; asst princ HM Treasy 1946, lectr (Spain) Br Cncl 1947, sr lectr RMA Sandhurst 1948-80 (fndr Dept of Communication); reviewer and author military history and biographies incl Auchinleck and Kitchener; *Recreations* fly fishing, tennis, travel, archaeology; *Clubs* Athenaeum, Wig and Pen, Harlequin RFC, Jesters Squash; *Style—* Philip Warner, Esq; The White Cottage, 21 Heatherdale Rd, Camberley, Surrey GU15 2LT (☎ 0276 63623)

WARNER, Philip Courtenay Thomas; s and h of Sir (Edward Courtenay) Henry Warner, 3 Bt, and Jocelyn Mary Beevor; *b* 3 April 1951; *Educ* Eton; *m* 1982, Penelope Anne, yr da of John Lack Elmer (d 1973); 1 s, 2 da; *Career* dir: Lewin & Warner Ltd, Warner Estate Hldgs plc; *Recreations* power-boating, sailing; *Style—* Philip Warner, Esq; 3 Vere St, London W1M 9HQ

WARNER, Simon Metford; s of Roger Harold Metford Warner, of Burford, Oxford, and Ruth Ernestine, *née* Hurcombe; *b* 12 Jan 1951; *Educ* Downs Sch Colwall Herefordshire, Leighton Park Sch Reading, Churchill Coll Cambridge (MA), Univ of Bristol; *m* 1974, Judith, da of Capt W Adams; 1 s (Leo b 1980); *Career* staff photographer Sotheby's 1973-75, freelance photographer 1975-; contrib to many books incl: Best Views of Britain (Geoffrey Young), Wild Britain (Douglas Botting), Bronte Country (ed Glenda Leeming), Pennine Landscapes (with Judith Warner 1984), South Pennines & Bronte Country (with Judith Warner 1984); illustrator of: Pennine Way North 1989, Pennine Way South 1990, These Lonely Mountains 1987, Peddars Way and Norfolk Coast Path 1991, Wolds Way 1982; exhibitions incl: Leeds Playhouse Gallery, Cliffe Castle Art Gallery, Keighley (Bradford Museums) 1988, Grassington Festival, Hebden Bridge Info Centre; *Recreations* cycling, theatre, rearing guinea pigs; *Style—* Simon Warner, Esq; Whitestone Farm, Stanbury, Keighley, W Yorks BD22 0JW (☎ 0535 644644)

WARNFORD-DAVIS, (Karelyn) Mandy; da of John David Warnford-Davis, and Ruth Grace, *née* Clift; *b* 19 June 1954; *Educ* Heathfield Sch Ascot Berks, St Hugh's Coll Oxford (BA); *Career* admitted slr 1979; slr Titmuss Sainer and Webb 1979-82, ptnr Rowe and Maw 1985- (joined 1982); memb Law Soc; *Recreations* opera, theatre, music, travel; *Style—* Miss Mandy Warnford-Davis; Rowe & Maw, 20 Black Friars Lane, London EC4V 6HD (☎ 071 248 4282, fax 071 248 2009, telex 262787 MAWLAW G)

WARNOCK, Hon Felix Geoffrey; er s of Sir Geoffrey James Warnock, and Baroness Warnock (Life Peer), *qqv*; *b* 18 Jan 1952; *Educ* Winchester, Royal Coll of Music (ARCM); *m* 27 Aug 1975, Juliet, da of Arthur Robert Lehwalder, of Seattle, Washington, USA; 1 s (Daniel Arthur Richard b 1985), 2 da (Eleanor Denise b 1982, Polly Patricia b 1986); *Career* bassoonist Acad of St Martin-in-the-Fields 1975-89, principal bassoonist London Classical Players 1978-88, memb Albion Ensemble 1980-, principal bassoonist Acad of Ancient Music 1981-89, prof of bassoon Trinity Coll of Music 1985-90; memb musical Advsy Panel to Arts Cncl of Great Britain 1987-89, gen mangr Orchestra of the Age of Enlightenment 1989-; memb Musicians' Union; *Recreations* cricket, golf; *Style—* The Hon Felix Warnock; 5 Kingsbridge Road, London W10 6PU (☎ 081 969 5738); Age of Enlightenment, 259 New Kings Road, London SW6 4RB (☎ 071 384 2622)

WARNOCK, Sir Geoffrey; s of James Warnock, OBE, MD (d 1953), of Leeds, Yorks, and Kathleen, *née* Hall (d 1976); *b* 16 Aug 1923; *Educ* Winchester, New Coll Oxford (MA); *m* 1949, (Helen) Mary, Baroness Warnock, *qv*, da of Archibald Wilson, of Winchester (d 1924); 2 s (Felix, James), 3 da (Kathleen, Stephana, Grizel); *Career* fell and tutor Brasenose Coll Oxford; hon fell: New Coll Oxford, Magdalen Coll Oxford (fell and tutor in philosophy 1952-71), Hertford Coll Oxford (princ 1971-88); vice chllr Univ of Oxford 1981-85; kt 1986; *Books* Berkeley (1953), English Philosophy since 1900 (1958), Contemporary Moral Philosophy (1967), The Object of Morality (1971), Morality and Language (1983), J L Austin (1989); *Style—* Sir Geoffrey Warnock; Brick House, Axford, Marlborough, Wilts SN8 2EX

WARNOCK, Hon Grizel Maria; da of Sir Geoffrey Warnock, and Baroness Warnock, DBE (Life Peer), *qqv*; *b* 17 July 1961; *Educ* Oxford High Sch, W Surrey Coll of Art & Design, Liverpool Poly; *Career* dir and memb Exec Cncl Breakout Children's Holidays; *Recreations* music; *Style—* The Hon Grizel Warnock

WARNOCK, James; yr s of Sir Geoffrey Warnock, and Baroness Warnock, DBE (Life Peer), *qqv*; *m* 31 March 1986, Fiona Margaret, da of Matthew Stewart Hair, of Stratford-upon-Avon; 1 da; 12 Gambier Terrace, Liverpool 1

WARNOCK, Baroness (Life Peer UK 1985), of Weeke in the City of Winchester; (Helen) Mary Warnock; DBE (1984); da of Archibald Edward Wilson (d 1924), of Winchester, and Ethel Mary (d 1952), eldest da of Sir Felix Otto Schuster, 1 Bt; *b* 14 April 1924; *Educ* St Swithun's Winchester, Lady Margaret Hall Oxford (MA, BPhil); *m* 1949, Sir Geoffrey James Warnock, *qv*; 2 s (Hon Felix Geoffrey b 1952, Hon James Marcus Alexander b 1953), 3 da (Hon Kathleen (Kitty) b 1950, Hon Stephana (Fanny) (Hon Mrs Branson) b 1956, Hon Grizel Maria b 1961); *Career* fell and tutor in philosophy St Hugh's Coll Oxford 1949-66, former headmistress Oxford HS; memb SSRC, chm Ctee of Enquiry into Human Fertilisation, former memb IBA; chm: Advsy Ctee on Animal Experiments, Ctee of Enquiry into Education of Handicapped, memb Royal Cmmn on Environmental Pollution 1979-85; Talbot Res fell LMH to 1976, FCP; mistress Girton Coll Cambridge 1985-; hon degrees: Open Univ, Essex, Melbourne, Bath, Exeter, Manchester, Glasgow, York, Warwick; author of numerous books and journalist (womens magazines and educn jls); *Books* Ethics Since 1900, Existentialism, Imagination, Schools of Thought, What Must We Teach? (with T Devlin), Education: A Way Forward, Memory: A Common Policy for Education; *Recreations* gardening, music; *Style—* The Rt Hon the Lady Warnock, DBE; Girton College, Cambridge; Brick House, Axford, nr Marlborough, Wiltshire SN8 2EX

WARNOCK, Neil; s of William Warnock (d 1974), of Sheffield, and Glady's Mary, *née* Hopkinson (d 1960); *b* 1 Dec 1948; *Educ* Westfield Comp; *m* 19 May 1973, Susan Margaret, da of late Frank Bownes; 1 s (James Andrew Neil b 30 July 1981), 1 da (Natalie Victoria b 20 Feb 1986); *Career* football player/mangr; playing career: Chesterfield 1968-70, Rotherham Utd 1970-72, Hartlepool 1972-73, Scunthorpe Utd 1974, Aldershot 1974-75, Barnsley FC 1975-78, York City 1978-79, Crewe 1979-80; player and mangr: Gainsborough Trinity 1980-81, Burton Albion 1981-85, Scarborough FC (championship) 1986-89, Notts County (promotion to 2nd Division) 1989; four times winner Football League Mangr of the Month awards (twice with Scarborough, twice with Notts County), GM Vauxhall Mangr of the Year 1986-87; memb Br Sch of Chiropody; *Recreations* philately (stamp collecting Queen Elizabeth); *Style—* Neil

Warnock, Esq; Notts County Football Club, Meadow Lane, Nottingham (☎ 0602 861155)

WARRELL, Prof David Alan; s of Alan Theophilus Warrell, ISO, of Steeple Aston, and Mildred Emma, *née* Hunt; *b* 6 Oct 1939; *Educ* Portsmouth GS, ChCh Oxford (MA, DM, BCh, DSc), St Thomas's Hosp Med Sch; *m* 11 Oct 1975, Mary Jean, da of George Prentice, of London; 2 da (Helen b 1981, Clare b 1985); *Career* lectr and conslt physician Royal Postgrad Med Sch London 1974-75, conslt physician Radcliffe Infirmary Oxford 1975-79, fell St Cross Coll Oxford 1977-, hon conslt physician Oxfordshire Health Authy 1979-, fndr dir Welcome-Mahidol Univ of Oxford Tropical Med Prog Bangkok 1979-86, hon clinical dir Alistair Reid Venom Res Unit Liverpool Sch Tropical Med 1983-, prof of tropical med and infectious diseases Univ of Oxford 1987-, hon conslt in malariology to the Army 1989-; chm AIDS Therapeutic Trials Ctee MRC 1987-, memb Expert Advsy Panel on Malaria WHO 1989- (memb Steering Ctee Chemotherapy of Malaria 1986-), tstee Tropical Health and Educn Tst 1988-; FRCP, MRCS, FZS 1967; FRGS 1989-; *Books* Rabies - The Facts (1986), Oxford Textbook of Medicine (1987); *Recreations* music, hill walking, natural history, book collecting; *Style—* Prof David Warrell; Nuffield Dept of Clinical Medicine, University of Oxford, John Radcliffe Hospital, Headington, Oxford OX3 9DU (☎ 0865 60871, fax 0865 750506)

WARREN, Very Rev Alan Christopher; s of Arthur Henry Warren (d 1987), of Durdham Court, Bristol, and Gwendoline Catherine, *née* Hallett; *b* 27 June 1932; *Educ* Dulwich Coll, Corpus Christi Coll Cambridge (MA), Ridley Hall Theol Coll; *m* 24 Aug 1957, Sylvia Mary, da of Charles Edwin Matthews (d 1988), of West Wickham, Kent; 3 da (Susan Rachel b 1958, Catherine Linda b 1960, Helen Judith b 1963); *Career* curate: St Paul's Margate 1957-59, St Andrew's Plymouth 1959-62; chaplain Kelly Coll Tavistock 1962-64, vicar Holy Apostles Leicester 1964-72, diocesan missioner Coventry 1972-78, hon canon Coventry Cathedral 1972-78, proctor in convocation 1977-78 and 1980-85, provost Leicester Cathedral 1978-; memb Cathedral's Statutes Cmmns 1981-, chm Leicester Cncl of Christians and Jews; pres: Leicester Civic Soc, Leicester Cncl of Churches; vice pres Leicester Bach Choir; formerly MCC and minor counties cricketer; *Books* Putting it Across (1975), Dulwich Memories (1990); *organ prelude* Et Incarnatus Est (1979); *Recreations* music, golf, steam trains; *Clubs* Free Foresters, Hunstanton Golf, Leicestershire Golf; *Style—* The Very Rev the Provost of Leicester; Provost's House, St Martin's East, Leicester LE1 5FX (☎ 0533 25295); 9 Queen's Drive, Hunstanton, Norfolk; Cathedral Office, St Martin's East, Leicester (☎ 0533 25294)

WARREN, Dr Alan George; s of George James Warren (d 1964), of Beckenham, Kent, and Edith Elizabeth, *née* Court (d 1982); *b* 15 Aug 1923; *Educ* Co Sch for Boys Beckenham and Penge, Univ of Reading, Royal Vet Coll Univ of London (BSc), Univ of Zurich (Dr Med Vet), RCS; *m* 4 Sept 1948, Elsa, da of Friedrich Franz Uhrig (d 1976), of Bassersdorf, Zurich, Switzerland; 2 s (Louis George b 1960, Jeremy James Alan b 1965), 1 da (Angela Elizabeth b 1951); *Career* Offr Cadet Corps Reading Univ 1941-43, Home Gd 7 BRX 1943-45; asst lectr in animal husbandry Royal Vet Coll 1947-48, lectr in vet surgery and clinical med Gordon Memorial Coll Khartoum (later Univ Coll of Khartoum) 1948-53, vet offr Colonial Vet Serv Nyasaland (later Malawis) 1953-64, inspr under Cruelty to Animals Act 1876 in the Home Office 1965-86, inspr Animals (Sientific Procedures) in Home Office 1987-88; biologist and biomedical advsr 1988-; memb: BVA, BSAVA, Assoc of Anaesthetists 1960, Assoc of Vet Anaesthetists 1964, Laboratory Animal Sci Assoc 1965, Assoc of Faculty of Homoeopathy 1982, Br Assoc of Homoeopathy Vet Surgeons 1982, Int Assoc for Vet Homoepathy 1984; MRCVS, FIBiol; *Books* Cyclopropane Ancesthesia in Animals (1961); *Recreations* travel, walking, photogrphy, cookery, dowsing, countryman; *Style—* Dr Alan Warren

WARREN, Andrew David; s of Walter Warren, of 18 Yarnells Hill, Oxford, and Monica Joyce Warren; *b* 9 May 1944; *Educ* Royal GS High Wycombe, Wadham Coll Oxford (MA); *m* 27 Oct 1973, Joan Mary, da of Arthur Webb; 2 s (Paul b 1978, Ian b 1980), 1 da (Clare b 1976); *Career* Centrefile 1966-69; Deloitte Haskins & Sells 1969-90: ptnr mgmnt consultancy 1975-79, ptnr i/c Computer Servs Div 1979-85, ptnr i/c Mgmnt Consultancy Div 1985-90; exec ptnr i/c Coopers & Lyrand Deloitte 1990-; MBCS 1968, FIMC 1987; *Recreations* flying, sailing, theatre, photography; *Clubs* Le Micro; *Style—* Andrew Warren, Esq; 10 Tring Avenue, Ealing, London W5 3QA (☎ 081 992 0673); Coopers & Lybrand Deloitte, Plumtree Court, London EC4A 4HT (☎ 071 583 5000, fax 071 822 8024, telex 887470)

WARREN, Sir (Harold) Brian Seymour; s of late Harold Warren, and late Marian, *née* Emlyn, of St Ives, Huntingdonshire; *b* 19 Dec 1914; *Educ* Bishop's Stortford Coll, UCL, Univ Coll Hosp; *m* 1, 1942 (m dis 1964), Dame Josephine Barnes; 1 s (Antony), 2 da (Penelope, Amanda); m 2, 1964, (Elizabeth) Anne (d 1983), da of Walter Marsh; 2 s (Marcus, Benedict); *Career* served WWII Regtl MO 1 Bn Grenadier Gds and DADMS Gds Div (despatches); house physician and surgn UCH, pres Chelsea Clinical Soc 1955-56, personal physician to PM 1970-74; memb: Cncl King Edward VII Hosp for Offrs, Governing Body Westminster Hosp 1970-74; former memb: LCC, Westminster City Cncl 1955-64 and 1968-78; fought (C) Brixton Gen Election 1959; Freeman City of London; MRCS, LRCP; kt 1974; *Recreations* travel, gardening, listening to music; *Clubs* Boodle's, Pratt's; *Style—* Sir Brian Warren; 94 Oakley St, London SW3 5NR (☎ 071 351 6462)

WARREN, Lady Carolyn Penelope; *née* Herbert; da of 7 Earl of Carnarvon; *b* 27 Jan 1962; *m* 1985, John F R Warren, s of John Warren, of Harlow, Essex; 1 s (Jakie James b 1986), 1 da (Susanna b 1988); *Career* freelance video producer; *Style—* The Lady Carolyn Warren

WARREN, Sir (Brian) Charles Pennefather; 9 Bt (I 1784), of Warren's Court, Co Cork; s of Sir Thomas Warren, 8 Bt, CBE, DL (d 1961); *b* 23 June 1923; *Educ* Wellington; *m* 1976, Nicola, da of Capt Edward Cazenove, of Great Dalby, Leics, and his w Grania (ggda of Sir John Kennedy, 1 Bt); *Heir* kinsman, Michael Blackley Warren b 1918; *Career* serv with 2 (Armoured) Bn Irish Gds 1941-45; *Style—* Sir Charles Warren, Bt; The Wilderness, Castle Oliver, Kilmallock, Co Limerick, Ireland

WARREN, Dr Graham Barry; s of Charles Graham Thomas Warren, and Joyce Thelma, *née* Roberts; *b* 25 Feb 1948; *Educ* Willesden Co GS, Pembroke Coll Cambridge (BA, MA, PhD); *m* 18 June 1966, Philippa Mary Adeline, da of Alexander Edward Temple-Cole (d 1981), of Shoreham, Kent; 4 da (Joanna b 5 Nov 1966, Eleanor b 20 Aug 1969, Katya b 13 Nov 1979, Alexandra b 7 Dec 1980); *Career* MRC jr res fell Nat Inst for Med Res London 1972-74, res fell Gonville and Caius Coll Cambridge and Stothert res fell of the Royal Soc Biochemistry Dept Univ of Cambridge 1975-77, sr scientist Euro Molecular Biology Lab Heidelberg W Germany (formerly gp ldr) 1977-85, prof and head of Dept of Biochemistry Univ of Dundee 1985-88, princ scientist Imperial Cancer Res Fund 1988-; memb Euro Molecular Biology Orgn; *Style—* Dr Graham Warren; 17 Grosvenor Rd, London N10 2DR (☎ 081 444 5808); Imperial Cancer Research Fund, P O Box 123, Lincoln's Inn Fields, London WC2A 3PX (☎ 071 269 3561)

WARREN, John Cecil Turnbull; s of Cecil George Warren (d 1971), and Jessie Eileen, *née* Parker; *b* 25 April 1931; *Educ* Collyers Sch Horsham, Univ of Durham (BArch), Univ of Newcastle (MLitt); *m* 11 Sept 1957, Judith Boulton, da of Ernest Kershaw (d 1985); 1 s (Philip Heath b 1963), 1 da (Rebecca Jane b 1966); *Career* Pilot Offr RAF 1957; architect and town planner, fndr and sr ptnr Architectural and Planning Partnership; author; exhibitor RA Summer Exhibitions; fndr tstee: Weald and Downland Open Air Museum Singleton Chichester, Chalkpits Museum Amberley; ARIBA 1959, FRTPI 1961, FRAS 1970, FSA 1981; *Books* Greek Mathematics and the Architects to Justinian I (1980), Traditional Houses in Baghdad (1982), Conservation in Baghdad (1983), The History of Architecture by Sir Bannister Fletcher (contrib, 18 and 19 edns), The World's Great Architecture (ed Nuttgens), Architecture of the Islamic World (ed Michell), Edwardian Architecture (ed Service), Conservation and Rehabilitation of Buildings (ed Markus), Cambridge Illustrated Encyclopedia Modern Architecture; contrib to Architectural Review, Art and Archaeology Res Papers, Architectural Design, Industrial Archaeology; *Recreations* painting, writing, travelling and forestry; *Clubs* Oriental; *Style—* John Warren, Esq, FSA; Parsons Farm, Coltstaple Lane, Horsham, W Sussex RH13 7BB (☎ 0403 730022); The Architectural and Planning Partnership, APP House, 100 Station Rd, Horsham, W Sussex RH13 5EU (☎ 0403 210 612, fax 0403 210617, telex 877058 APP HG)

WARREN, Kenneth Robin; MP (C) Hastings and Rye 1983-; s of Edward Charles Warren (d 1987), of St Leonards on Sea, East Sussex; *b* 15 Aug 1926; *Educ* Midsomer Norton, Aldenham, De Havilland Aeronautical Tech Sch, Univ of London; *m* 1962, Elizabeth Anne, da of Russell Chamberlain; *Career* aero and electronics engr; De Havilland Aircraft 1947-51, BOAC 1951-57, Smith Industries Ltd 1957-60, Elliott Automation Ltd 1960-69; chm Warren Woodfield Assocs; dir: Datapoint (UK) Ltd, Loral International; memb Paddington Borough Cncl 19653-65, contested (C) St Pancras North 1964, MP (C) Hastings 1970-1983; chm: Parly Ctee on Offshore Technol 1974-75, Cons Parly Aviation Ctee 1974-76, Western European Univ Sci, Technol and Aerospace Ctee 1977-80; memb Select Ctee on Sci and Technol, PPS to Rt Hon Sir Keith Joseph, Bt, MP, Sec of State for Industry 1979-81 (Educn and Sci 1981-83); chm: Select Ctee on Trade & Indust 1983-, Br-Soviet Parly Gp 1986-; Freeman City of London; Liveryman: Worshipful Co of Coachmakers and Harness Makers, Worshipful Co Air Pilots and Navigators; CEng, FRAeS, FCIT FRSA; *Clubs* Special Forces; *Style—* Kenneth Warren, Esq, MP; Woodfield House, Goudhurst, Kent

WARREN, Prof (Wilfred) Lewis; s of William Arnold Warren (d 1986), and Frances Jessie, *née* Mason (d 1983); *b* 24 Aug 1929; *Educ* The High Sch Newcastle-under-Lyme, Exeter Coll Oxford (MA, DPhil); *m* 7 Sept 1960, Anne Josephine Smyth; 1 s (Nicholas b 1963), 2 da (Rebecca b 1961, Rachael b 1968); *Career* Queen's Univ Belfast: lectr in modern history 1955, warden Alanbrooke Hall 1963-70, prof of modern history 1973-, dean of theology 1975-78, dir Sch of Modern History 1988-; Wolfson Literary prize for history 1973; memb: Arts Cncl NI 1975-79 and 1984-89, Arts Sub-Ctee UGC 1984-89, Cncl RHS 1974-78; FRHistS 1965, FRSL 1974, MRIA 1976; *Books* King John (1961), 1066: The Year of the Three Kings (1966), Henry II (1973), The Governance of Norman and Angevin England 1086-1272 (1987); *Style—* Prof Lewis Warren; 23 Garvey Manor, Lisburn, County Antrim, Northern Ireland BT27 4DQ (☎ 0846 661661); Department of Modern History, The Queen's University, Belfast BT7 1NN (☎ 0232 245133)

WARREN, Margaret Patricia; da of Basil Louis Watkins (d 1983), of Kirby Muxloe, Leics, and Muriel, *née* Wheeldon; *b* 1 Aug 1945; *Educ* Ravenhurst Rd Primary Sch, Nativity Convent Leics, Anstey Martin HS, Loughborough Coll; *m* 31 Aug 1968, Michael Peter Warren, s of Montague Warren (d 1980), of Kirby Muxloe, Leics; 1 s (Matthew Charles b 7 March 1973), 1 da (Rebecca Louise b 25 March 1971); *Career* sec family business 1965-68; dir: S W Wilkinson & Co Ltd 1980-, Warren Beale Ltd 1980-; past memb WRVS and tres local branch Red Cross; *Recreations* swimming, cooking; *Style—* Mrs M P Warren; 78 Oakcroft Ave, Kirby Muxloe, Leics (☎ 0533 392655); S W Wilkinson & Co Ltd, 374 Western Rd, Leics (☎ 0533 546525)

WARREN, Maurice Eric; s of Frederick Leonard Warren, and Winifred Warren (d 1936); *b* 21 June 1933; *Educ* St Brendans Coll Bristol; *m* 21 Aug 1954, Molly, da of Herbert Slater, of Bristol; 1 s (Stephen), 1 da (Sally (Mrs Wilkinson)); *Career* RAF 1951-53; md: Dalgety Agriculture Ltd 1976-81, Dalgety UK Ltd 1981-87; chief exec Dalgety plc 1989- (md 1987-89); FCCA; *Recreations* golf; *Clubs* RAC, Lansdowne; *Style—* Maurice Warren, Esq; Dalgety plc, 100 George St, London W1H 5RH (☎ 071 486 0200, fax 071 493 0892, telex 23874)

WARREN, Prof Michael Donald; s of Charles Warren (d 1966), of Brook Vale, Rattlesden, Bury St Edmunds, Suffolk, and Dorothy Gladys Thornton, *née* Reeks (d 1979); *b* 19 Dec 1923; *Educ* Bedford Sch, Guy's Hosp Med Sch (MB BS), LSHTM (MD, DPH, DIH); *m* 8 March 1946, Joan Lavina, da of Robert Horace Peacock (d 1955), of Green Acre, New Farm Drive, Abridge, Romford, Essex; 1 s (David b 1947), 2 da (Dorothy b 1948, Penelope b 1958); *Career* RAF Med Branch 1947-51, Sqdn Ldr 1948-51; dep med offr of health Hampstead 1952-54, asst princ med offr London CC 1954-58, sr lectr in social and preventive med Royal Free Sch of Med and LSHTM 1958-64, hon conslt in social and rehabilitation med Royal Free Hosp 1958-64, reader in pub health Univ of London 1964-71, prof of social med and dir Health Servs Res Unit Univ of Kent Canterbury 1971-83 (emeritus prof of social med 1984), academic registrar Faculty of Community Med RCP 1971-77; memb: Cncl for Postgrad Med Educn 1972-76, Regnl Res Ctee SE Thames Regnl Health Authy 1974-83, Exec Cncl Kent Postgrad Med Centre Canterbury 1974-88; chm Soc for Social Med 1982-83, FFCM 1972, FRCP 1975; *Books* Public Health and Social Services (3 edn, 1965), Physically Disabled People Living at Home (1978), Recalling the Medical Officer of Health (1987); *Recreations* reading, genealogy, light gardening; *Clubs* RSM, Kent CCC; *Style—* Prof Michael Warren; 2 Bridge Down, Bridge, Canterbury, Kent CT4 5AZ (☎ 0227 830 233)

WARREN, Ven Norman Leonard; s of Arthur Henry Warren (d 1987), and Gwendoline Catharine, Hallett; *b* 19 July 1934; *Educ* Dulwich, CCC Cambridge (MA), Ridley Hall Cambridge; *m* 15 April 1961, Yvonne; 3 s (Andrew Mark b 1962, Philip James b 1965, David John Chi Hanh b 1970), 2 da (Ruth Elizabeth b 1963, Sarah Rachel b 1968); *Career* RN 1953-55; vicar St Paul's Leamington Spa 1963-77, rector Morden Surrey 1977-89, rural dean Merton 1986-89, archdeacon Rochester 1989-; memb: Gen Synod of the C of E 1989-, Cncl Royal Sch of Church Music; pres Music in Worship Tst; *Books* Journey Into Life (1963), The way Ahead (1965), Directions (1968), Signposts (1974), What's The Point? (1986), A Certain Faith (1988), The Path to Peace (1988); *Recreations* music, walking; *Style—* The Ven the Archdeacon of Rochester; The Archdeaconry, Rochester, Kent ME1 1SX (☎ 0634 842527)

WARREN, Prof Peter Michael; s of Arthur George Warren (d 1946), and Alison Joan, *née* White (d 1942); *b* 23 June 1938; *Educ* Sandbach Sch, Llandovery Coll, UCNW Bangor (BA), Corpus Christi Coll Cambridge (BA, MA, PhD); *m* 18 June 1966, Elizabeth Margaret, da of Percy Halliday, of Beaconsfield, Bucks; 1 s (Damian b 1984), 1 da (Diktynna b 1979); *Career* reader in Aegean archaeology Univ of Birmingham 1976 (lectr 1972-74, sr lectr 1974-76), dean Faculty of Arts Univ of Bristol 1988-90 (prof of ancient history and classical archaeology 1977-), visiting prof Univ of Minnesota 1981, Geddes-Harrower prof of Greek art and archaeology Univ of Aberdeen 1986-87, Félix Neubergh lectr Univ of Göteborg 1986; vice pres Cncl Bristol and Glos Archaeological Soc 1989 (vice chm 1980-81, chm 1981-83); pres: Wotton-under-Edge Historical Soc 1986-90, Bristol Anglo-Hellenic Cultural Soc 1987-; chm

Managing Ctee Br Sch Athens 1979-83 (memb 1973-77, 1978-79, 1986-90), memb Cncl Soc for the Promotion of Hellenic Studies 1978-81; FSA 1973, Hon Fell Archaeological Soc of Athens (1987); *Books* Minoan Stone Vases (1969), Myrtos An Early Bronze Age Settlement in Crete (1972), The Aegean Civilizations (1975 and 1989), Minoan Religion as Ritual Action (1988), Aegean Bronze Age Chronology (with V Hankey, 1989); *Recreations* contemporary Br politics, Med travel, history of Med botany; *Style*— Prof Peter Warren, FSA; Claremont House, Merlin Haven, Wotton-under-Edge, Glos GL12 7BA (☎ 0453 842 290); Dept of Classics and Archaeology, University of Bristol, 11 Woodland Rd, Bristol BS8 1TB (☎ 0272 303 030 ext 3476)

WARREN, Dr Peter Tolman; s of Hugh Alan Warren, OBE, of 35 West Hill, Sanderstead, Surrey, and Florence Christine, *née* Tolman; *b* 20 Dec 1937; *Educ* Whitgift Sch S Croydon, Queens' Coll Cambridge (BA, MA); *m* 9 Sept 1961, Angela Mary, da of Thomas Henry Curtis, of 8 Teresa's Walk, Sanderstead, Surrey; 2 s (Simon b 1965, Timothy b 1970), 1 da (Katherine b 1967); *Career* princ sci offr Br Geological Survey (previously Inst Geological Sci, formerly Geological Survey & Museum) 1962-72 (formerly sci offr), chief sci advsr Cabinet Office Whitehall 1972-76, safety advsr NERC 1976-77, exec sec Royal Soc of London 1985- (dep exec sec 1977-1985); memb Cncl GPDST 1989-, govr Croydon HS for Girls; FGS, FInstGeol; *Books* Geology of the Country around Rhyl and Denbigh (jtly, 1984); *Recreations* gardening, geology; *Clubs* Athenaeum; *Style*— Dr Peter Warren; Flat 1, 6 Carlton House Terrace, London SW1Y 5AG (☎ 071 839 5260); The Royal Society, 6 Carlton Hse Terrace, London SW1Y 5AG (☎ 071 839 5561, fax 071 930 2170, telex 917876)

WARREN, Prof Raymond Henry Charles; s of Arthur Henry Warren (d 1987), and Gwendoline, *née* Hallett; *b* 7 Nov 1928; *Educ* Bancroft's Sch, Corpus Christi Coll Cambridge (MA, DMus); *m* 9 April 1953, Roberta, da of Frederick Smith (d 1985); 3 s (Timothy b 1954, Christopher b 1956, Benedict b 1960), 1 da (Clare b 1965); *Career* prof of music: Queen's Univ Belfast 1967-72 (lectr 1955-67), Univ of Bristol 1972-; princ compositions: The Passion (1962), Symphony No 1 (1965), Symphony No 2 (1969), In the Beginning (Opera 1982), Oratorio Continuing Cities (1989); chm: Bristol Chamber Choir, Incorporated Soc Musicians (Bristol Centre), Nat Assoc Univ Music Staffs; memb: Composers' Guild, ISM; *Recreations* walking; *Style*— Prof Raymond Warren, 9 Cabot Rise, Portishead, Bristol BS20 9NX (☎ 0272 844289); Univ of Bristol, Dept of Music, Bristol BS8 1TH (☎ 0272 303030 fax 0272 732657)

WARREN, Dr Roderic Ellis; s of Ronald Thomas Warren (d 1970), of Tadworth, Surrey, and Mabel Elsie Warren; *b* 24 Oct 1948; *Educ* Whitgift Sch Croydon, Gonville and Caius Coll Cambridge (MA, MB BChir), Westminster Med Sch; *m* 6 Sept 1976, Pamela Rose, da of Frederick John Taft (d 1976), of Canterbury; 1 s (Charles), 2 da (Elizabeth, Eleanor); *Career* conslt microbiologist Addenbrooke's Hosp 1976-, assoc lectr Univ of Cambridge 1977-; memb Editorial Bd Drug and Therapeutic Bulletin and reviews in Medical Microbiology; FRCPath 1989; *Recreations* helping bureaucracy and consumer affairs; *Style*— Dr Roderic Warren; Clinical Microbiology Laboratory, Addenbrooke's Hospital, Hills Road, Cambridge

WARREN, Stanley Anthony Treleaven (Tony); CB (1984); s of Stanley Howard Warren, and Mable Harriet, *née* Ham; *b* 26 Sept 1925; *Educ* King's Coll London; *m* 1950, Sheila Gloria May, *née* Rowe; 2 s, 1 da; *Career* Sub Lt RN 1945-47, Constructor Lt RCNC 1947-51, designer Royal Yacht Brittania 1951-54, frigate modernisations 1954-57, constructor HM Dockyard Malta 1957-60, Admty constructor overseer John Brown and Yarrow 1960-64, Polaris submarine design 1964-67, PNO Cammell Laird 1967-72, project mangr HMS Invincible 1972-76, dep dir of Submarines (Polaris) MOD (PE) 1976-79, dir gen Submarines MOD (PE) 1979-85; CEng, FRINA, FIMechE, RCNC; *Style*— Tony Warren, Esq, CB

WARRENDER, Hon Anthony Michael; s (by 2 m) of 1 Baron Bruntisfield, MC; *b* 17 July 1950; *Educ* Eton, Christ Church Oxford; *m* 1, 1976, Christine, da of Serge Semenenko, of Boston, Mass; m 2, 1983, Mrs Patricia Connors Kelly, da of Philip Connors, of Middleburg, Va; 1 s (Patrick Victor Anthony b 1984); *Career* FCA; pres Warrender Associates Inc 1983-; *Clubs* Turf, White's; *Style*— The Hon Anthony Warrender; Little Cotland Farm, PO Box 1431, Middleburg, Virginia 22117, USA

WARRENDER, Col Hon John Robert; OBE (1963), MC (1943), TD (1967), DL (Somerset 1965); s (by 1 m), and h of 1 Baron Bruntisfield, MC; *b* 7 Feb 1921; *Educ* Eton, RMC Sandhurst; *m* 1, 1948, Ann Moireen (d 1976), 2 da of Lt-Col Sir Walter Fendall Campbell, KCIE; 2 s, 2 da; m 2, 1977, Shirley (d 1981), formerly w of Jonathan J Crawley, and da of Sqdn Ldr Edward Ross, RAF ret; 3 step s; m 3, 1985, Joanna (Jan), formerly w of Colin Hugh Campbell Graham, and da of late David Chancellor, of Pencaitland, E Lothian; 2 step s, 1 step da; *Career* Col RARO, Brig Queen's Body Guard for Scotland (Royal Co of Archers), ret 1985, late Capt 2 Dragoons, Royal Scots Greys, ADC to Govr of Madras 1946-48 and cmdg N Som Yeo and 44 Royal Tank Regt 1957-62; *Clubs* Pratt's, New (Edinburgh); *Style*— Col the Hon John Warrender, OBE, MC, TD, DL; 18 Warriston Crescent, Edinburgh, EH3 5LB

WARRENDER, Hon Robin Hugh; 3 s of 1 Baron Bruntisfield, MC; *b* 24 Dec 1927; *Educ* Eton, Trinity Coll Oxford; *m* 1951, Gillian Elizabeth, da of Leonard Lewis Rossiter and his w Elsie Rose, da of late Sir Bernard Oppenheimer, 1 Bt; 1 s, 2 da; *Career* chm London Wall Holdings plc 1986-; underwriting memb of Lloyd's 1953, Tudor & Co (Insur) Ltd 1958-62, md Fenchurch Insurance Holdings Ltd 1963-69, dep chm A W Bain & Sons Ltd 1970, chm Bain Dawes plc and other gp cos 1973-86; dir: Comindus SA (France) 1980-, Worms & Co 1981-; Varity Corp (Canada) 1982; Varity Holdings Ltd 1982-, Heritable Group Holdings Ltd 1983-, Sociëté Centrale Preservatrice Fonciere Assurances 1986-89, Group Athena 1989-; memb: Cncl of Bath Univ 1979-82, Cncl and Ctee Lloyd's 1983-86 (hon treas Governing Ctee); Royal Choral Soc 1979-; *Clubs* City of London, Portland, White's; *Style*— The Hon Robin Warrender; Widcombe Manor, Church St, Bath (☎ 0225 317116); 69 Whitehall Court, London SW1 (☎ 071 839 3848)

WARRENDER, Hon Simon George; DSC; s of 1 Baron Bruntisfield, MC, and Dorothy Etta Rawson (d 1982); *b* 11 Aug 1922; *Educ* Eton; *m* 1950, Pamela, da of Sir Norman Myer (d 1956), of Toorak, Victoria, Australia; 2 s, 2 da; *Career* Lt RNVR, served WWII (USSR Commemorative medal); co dir; conslt aviation and travel, fndr and chm Australia World Airways; ARAeA, fell Br Interplanetary Soc; *Books* Score of Years Biography (1973); Score of Years Biography (1973); *Recreations* fencing, fishing, flying; *Clubs* Turf; *Style*— The Hon Simon Warrender, DSC; 57 Dixon St, Malvern, Victoria 3143, Australia; PO Box 145, Toorak, Victoria 3142, Australia (☎ 03509 0090)

WARSOP, Rear Adm John Charles; CB (1984); s of John Charles Warsop, of Leicester, and Elsie Mary Warsop; *b* 9 May 1927; *Educ* Eaton Hall RNC, RN Engrg Coll; *m* 1958, Josephine; 2 da; *Career* joined RN 1943, RNC Keyham and Greenwich, sr engr HMS Ark Royal 1959-61, staff engr offr Def Staff Washington 1965-68, MOD 1968-70, marine engr offr HMS Blake 1970-72, Capt 1972, MOD 1972-75, CO HMS Fisgard 1975-78, Dep Dir Systems Design and chief marine engr offr Ship Dept 1979-81, Rear Adm 1981, Port Adm Rosyth 1981-83, Flag Offr and Naval Base Cdr Portsmouth 1983, ret 1986; chm Soc of Friends RN Museum and HMS Victory; hon consltg engr HMS Warrior, FIMechE; *Recreations* sailing (yacht Sintra), rugby, tennis, swimming; *Style*— Rear Adm John Warsop, CB; 1 Garden Terrace, Southsea, Hants

WARWICK, Alban Maurice; JP (1973); s of Frederick Maurice Warwick (d 1964), and Constance Mabel, *née* Brightman; *b* 13 Nov 1933; *Educ* St Albans Sch; *m* 1, 1958 (m dis 1980), Janet Rose; 2 s (Neil b 1963, Bruce b 1964); m 2, 1981, Susan Marilyn, da of Walter Arthur Wells (d 1951); 2 step s (William b 1975, Charles b 1976), 1 step da (Zoe b 1973); *Career* dir: Warwicks Ltd 1957-, Rodney Maurice (St Albans) Ltd 1982; chm St Albans Round Table 1973-74; pres St Albans & Dist C of C 1984-85; govr Heathlands Sch; *Recreations* golf, shooting, gardening, cricket; *Clubs* St Albans Rotary, St Albans and Professional; *Style*— Alban M Warwick, JP; Hill End Farm, Gorhambury, St Albans AL3 6AR (☎ 0727 50351)

WARWICK, Diana; *b* 16 July 1945; *Educ* Univ of London (BA); *m* 1969, Sean Terence Bowes Young; *Career* tech asst NUT 1969-72, asst sec Civil and Public Servs Assoc 1972-83, gen sec Assoc of Univ Teachers 1983-; memb: bd of the Br Cncl 1985-, Employment Appeals Tbnl 1987-, exec bd Industl Soc 1987-, TUC Gen Cncl 1989-; govr Cwlth Inst 1988-, memb Cncl of Fndn for Educn Business Partnerships 1990-; *Style*— Ms Diana Warwick; Assoc of Univ Teachers, United House, 1 Pembridge Road, London W11 3HJ (☎ 071 221 4370)

WARWICK, Edwin Stanley Ransom; s of Sir Norman Richard Combe Warwick, KCVO, OBE (d 1962), and Joyce Huskinson, *née* Ransom; *b* 22 March 1928; *Educ* Marlborough; *m* 26 Jan 1963, Marjorie, da of Eden White (d 1982); 1 s (Hugh b 1966), 1 da (Tessa b 1969); *Career* shipowner; dir: Thos and Jas Harrison Ltd, Liverpool & London P and I Club, Liverpool & London War Risks Club (vice chm 1985-86), Thos Tweddle & Co Ltd 1980-86; *Recreations* music, swimming; *Clubs* Liverpool Racquet; *Style*— Edwin Warwick, Esq; Fieldings, 167 Lache Lane, Chester CH4 7LU (☎ 0244 676983)

WARWICK, John William; s of John Alfred Warwick, of Plumstead, London, and Lillian Rose, *née* Stothard; *b* 10 Feb 1932; *Educ* Stratford GS, Univ of Birmingham (BSc); *m* 28 March 1963, Thea Susan, da of Bernard Leeming, of Perth, Western Aust; 1 s (David b 1964), 1 da (Jennifer b 1969); *Career* RA 1953-55, 44 Regt, 5 Army Gp, Br Army of The Rhine; Exploration Geophysicist: Pakistan 1957-60, Aust 1961-64, Saudi Arabia 1965-66, USA 1966-67, Singapore 1969-73, UK 1973-76; geophysical conslt Texas Instruments Inc (Petroleum Exploration Div) 1976-85, geophysical advsr Sirte Oil Co 1986-; memb: Soc of Exploration Geophysicists 1975, American Assoc of Petroleum Geologists 1975, IOD; *Style*— John Warwick, Esq; 32 Bramley Ave, Coulsdon, Surrey CR32DP (☎ 081 660 1232); Crown House, Chobham Rd, Woking, Surrey (☎ 0483 727118)

WARWICK, Richard Carey; s of Dennis Bliss Winter, of Drury Lane Cottage, Redmarley, Glos, and Margaret Joan, *née* Simpson; *b* 29 April 1945; *Educ* Dean Close Sch Cheltenham, RADA; *Career* actor; appeared with: Nat Theatre at Old Vic, Young Vic Co, Cambridge Theatre Co; West End appearances incl: While the Sun Shines, In Praise of Love, The Real Thing; TV appearances incl: The Vortex, The Last of the Mohicans, A Fine Romance; film appearances incl: Romeo & Juliet, If..., The Bedsitting Room, Nicholas & Alexandra, Sebastiane, The Tempest, The Breaking of Bumbo, White Hunter Heart, Hamlet; *Recreations* running, cycling, swimming, music, reading, dancing; *Clubs* YMCA, CND, Troll, Heaven; *Style*— Richard Warwick, Esq; 36 Digby Mansions, Hammersmith Bridge Rd, London W6 9DF (☎ 081 741 3529)

WARWICK-SMITH, Myles Humphrey (Mike); s of Cdr Reginald Warwick-Smith, RN (d 1944), and Eileen, *née* Maclean (d 1984); *b* 26 Dec 1929; *Educ* Nautical Coll Worcester; *m* 1952, Diana Mary Stella, da of Capt R Calum Freeman (d 1982); 2 s (Robert, Peter), 2 da (Penelope, Fenella); *Career* Capt (Leicesters) TA, served Korea; md: LRC Industrial Holdings Ltd, LRC Overseas Ltd; chm United Photographic Laboratories until 1981; chm and md Elsan Ltd and Horton Hygiene Co 1981-; *Recreations* riding, tennis, travel; *Clubs* IOD; *Style*— Mike Warwick-Smith, Esq; Elsan Group Ltd, Buxted, Sussex TN22 4LW (☎ 0825 813 291, telex 957236)

WASE-ROGERS, Nicholas John; s of Lt-Col John Alistair Wase-Rogers (d 1984), and Margery Lillian, *née* Hall; *b* 19 June 1945; *Educ* Shrewsbury; *m* 28 July 1973, Christine Linda, da of Ernest Williams, of Droitwich, Worcs; 1 s (James b 1974), 1 da (Melissa b 1975); *Career* solicitor, ptnr Charles Russell; *Recreations* golf, tennis, skiing, shooting; *Clubs* Blackwell Golf, Royal and Ancient Golf; *Style*— Nicholas Wase-Rogers, Esq; Oakfield Farmhouse, Cakebole, Chaddesley Corbett, Worcs (☎ 0562 777737); 18 Bennetts Hill, Birmingham (☎ 0793 617444)

WASHINGTON, Lt-Col Timothy John Clulow; s of Peter Washington (d 1984), and Catherine Marguerite Beauchamp Waddell (d 1972); *b* 26 June 1923; *Educ* Shrewsbury, Trinity Coll Cambridge; *m* 10 July 1956, Margaret Helen, da of Maj Edward William Hasell (d 1972), 2 da; *Career* served in Army 1941-78, 27 Lancers 1942-45, 12 Lancers 1945-60, 9/12 Lancers 1960-78; *Recreations* horses, farming; *Clubs* Cavalry and Guards'; *Style*— Lt-Col T J C Washington; Dacre Lodge, Penrith CA11 0HH (☎ 07684 86221)

WASILEWSKI, Mark Alexander; s of Stanislaw Wasilewski (d 1979), and Vera, *née* Hudson; *b* 22 June 1960; *Educ* Culcheth HS, Brasenose Coll Oxford; *Career* investmt analyst NCB Pension Fund, dir Marketable Securities, portfolio mangr UK Equities; *Recreations* most sports, football, cricket, golf, music, cinema/theatre; *Clubs* ICPG FC; *Style*— Mark Wasilewski, Esq; 14 Forsyth House, Tachbrook St, London, SW1V 2LE; Cin Management Ltd, PO Box 10, Hobart House, Grosvenor Place, London, SW1X 7AD (☎ 245 6911)

WASON, (Robert) Graham; s of Cathcart Roland Wason, and Margaret Ogilvie, *née* Lamb; gs of Rear Adm Cathcart Romer Wason, CMG, CIE (d 1941), ggs of Rt Hon Eugene Wason, MP (Liberal MP and Chm Scottish Liberal Party), gggs of P R Wason, MP for Ipswich, Promoter of Reform Bill 1832 and co-fndr of Reform Club; *b* 6 Jan 1951; *Educ* Alleyne's GS Stevenage, Univ of Surrey (BSc); *Career* ptnr Touche Ross Management Consultants Greene Belfield-Smith Div 1983-, hotels ops in E and Africa; *Recreations* tennis, badminton, squash; *Style*— Graham Wason, Esq; Touche Ross Management Consultants, Greene Belfield-Smith, Victoria House, Vernon Place, London WC1B 4DB (☎ 071 242 3959, telex 24292 GBS, fax 071 831 8626)

WASS, Sir Douglas William Gretton; GCB (1980, KCB 1975, CB 1971); s of Arthur William Wass (d 1978), of Hampton, Middx, and Winifred Elsie, *née* Gretton (d 1955); *b* 15 April 1923; *Educ* Nottingham HS, St John's Coll Cambridge (BA, MA); *m* 14 July 1954, Dr Milica, da of Tomislav Pavicic (d 1932), of Belgrade, Yugoslavia; 1 s (Andrew b 1960), 1 da (Alexandra b 1958); *Career* entered HM Treasy 1946; private sec to: Chllr of Exchequer 1959-61, Chief Sec Treasy 1961-62; asst sec Treasy 1962, alternate exec dir IMF and fin cnsllr Br Embassy Washington 1965-67; Treasy: under-sec 1968, dep-sec 1970-73, second perm sec 1973-74, perm sec 1974-83; jt head Home Civil Serv 1981-83; dir: Barclays Bank 1984-87, De La Rue Company plc 1984-, Compagnie du Midi SA 1987-; chm: Equity & Law plc 1986-, Nomura International Ltd 1986-; Reith lectr 1983, Shell Int lectr St Andrews 1985, Harry Street Memorial lectr Univ of Manchester 1987; dep chm Centre for Policy Studies Inst 1980-84; chm: Br Selection Ctee of Harkness Fellowships 1981-84, UN Advsy Gp on Fin Flows to Africa 1987-88; dir African Capacity Building Fndn 1990-; memb Cncl: Overseas Development Inst 1990-, Br Heart Fndn 1990-; govr Centre for Econ Policy Res 1983-90, pres Mkt Res Soc 1987-; memb Cncl Univ of Bath 1985-, govr Ditchley Fndn; hon fell St John's Coll Cambridge; Hon DLitt Univ of Bath 1985; *Books* Government and the Governed (1984); *Recreations* swimming, golf; *Clubs* Reform;

Style— Sir Douglas Wass, GCB; 6 Dora Rd, London SW19 7HH (☎ 081 946 5556); Nomura International Ltd, 1 St Martin's-le-Grand, London EC1A 4NP (☎ 071 236 8811, fax 071 248 5958, telex 883119)

WASS, Francis Harry; s of Frank Wass, of Burton Coggles, Grantham, Lincs (d 1955); *b* 6 Aug 1927; *Educ* King's Sch Grantham, Newark Tech Coll; *m* 1951, Phyllis May; 1 s, 1 da; *Career* chartered engr; asst chief engr Aveling Barford Ltd 1966-75, dir Goodwin Barsby Ltd 1977-82; tech conslt (design and drawing serv); MIMechE; *Recreations* author of tech papers on compaction, hydrostatic transmissions; *Style*— Francis H Wass, Esq; 57 Priory Close, Beeston Regis, Sheringham, Norfolk (☎ 0263 825707)

WASS, Prof John Andrew Hall; s of Samuel Hall Wass (d 1970), and June Mary Vaudine, *née* Blaikie; *b* 14 Aug 1947; *Educ* Rugby, Guy's Hosp Med Sch London (MB BS, MD); *m* 4 April 1970, Valerie Jean, da of Donald Vincent, of Shell House, Hedgerley, Bucks; 1 s (Samuel b 1979), 1 da (Katherine b 1974); *Career* registrar: KCH 1973-74, Guy's Hosp 1974-75; sub-dean of Med Coll and prof of clinical endocrinology St Bartholomew's Hosp 1989- (lectr 1976-81, sr lectr 1982-85, reader 1985-89); articles and chapters on: acromegaly, pituitary tumours, growth hormone, growth factors; vice chm Ctee of Mgmnt Royal Med Benevolent Fund 1990- (memb 1982-), advsr to BACUP 1985-, sec Endocrine Section RSM 1988-, memb American Endocrine Soc, ed Clinical Endocrinology 1991-; Freeman City of London 1983; MRCP 1973, FRCP 1986, FRSM; *Books* Neuroendocrine Perspectives (1987); *Recreations* music, opera, theatre, wine; *Style*— Prof John Wass; Department of Endocrinology, St Bartholomew's Hospital, West Smithfield, London EC1A 7BE (☎ 071 601 8346, fax 071 601 7024)

WASSERMAN, Ian; s of Jacob Wasserman, QC (d 1985), and Rachel Wasserman (d 1963); *b* 4 Sept 1939; *Educ* City of London Sch; *m* 23 Sep 1981, Nicola Viveca, da of Major John Bromley, MVO (d 1979); 3 s (Nicholas, Alexander, Joshua), 2 da (Caron, Tanya); *Career* chm: GM Firth plc, Slug & Lettuce Ltd; *Recreations* fishing, travel, bridge, investment; *Clubs* East India; *Style*— Ian Wasserman, Esq; Cotswold Park, Cirencester, Glos (☎ 0285 83414); 40 Catherine Place, London SW1 (☎ 071 828 7425)

WASTELL, Prof Christopher; s of Edgar Barker Wastell (d 1963), and Doris Emmeline, *née* Pett (d 1965); *b* 13 Oct 1932; *Educ* Drax GS; Guy's Hosp Med Sch (MB BS), Univ of London Med Sch (MS); *m* 2 April 1958, Margaret Anne, da of Joseph Fletcher (d 1976); 1 s (Giles Richard b 1965), 2 da (Jacqueline Anne b 1961, Vivien Clare b 1963); *Career* house physician Joyce Green, house surgn Franborough Kent, sr house offr Bristol Royal Infirmary, house surgn Great Ormond St, registrar Westminster Hosp, lectr Westminster Med Sch 1964-67, C and H J Gaisman res fell Mount Sinai Hosp NY USA 1965-66, sr lectr and hon conslt surgn Westminster Med Sch and Hosp 1968-73 (reader 1973-82), prof and hon conslt surgn Charing Cross and Westminster Med Sch London Univ at Westminster Hosp 1983-, conslt to accident and emergency Westminster Hosp 1971-; FRCS; *Books* Chronic Duodenal Ulcer (1972), Westminster Hospital Symposium on Chronic Duodenal Ulcer (1974), Surgery for Nurses (with Ellis, 1976), Surgery of the Stomach and Duodenum (with Nyhus, 1977 and 1986), Cimetidine, The Westminster Hospital Symposium (1978); *Recreations* sailing, gardening, walking; *Clubs* Wilsonian Sailing, RSM; *Style*— Prof Christopher Wastell; 7 Manor Way, Beckenham, Kent BR3 3LH; 3 North Rd, Kingsdown, Deal, Kent CT14 8AG (☎ 081 650 5882); Surgical Unit, Westminster Hosp, Page St Wing, London SW1P 2AP (☎ 081 746 8000/081 746 8466, fax 081 746 8111)

WASTELL, William; s of Capt Charles Henry Wastell, MN (d 1939), and Elsie Alice Perham; *b* 13 Dec 1939; *Educ* Brentwood Sch, Regent St Poly Sch of Architecture; *m* 26 Nov 1966, Rosamund, da of Harold Geoffrey Haden; 3 da (Kerry b 1969, Miranda b 1970, Cindy b 1972); *Career* md William Wastell Architects Ltd; ARIBA; *Recreations* archery (pres Green Dragon Bowman), bridge, travel; *Style*— William Wastell, Esq; Oak House, Mardley Heights, Welwyn, Herts (☎ 043 871 6808); Troopers Yard, 23 Bancroft, Hitchin Herts (☎ 0462 422440, fax 0462 420403)

WATANABE, Nobuyuki; s of Akio Watanabe, of Fujisawa-City, Japan, and Keiko Gorin (d 1970); *b* 13 Dec 1939; *Educ* Keio Univ (BA Economics); *m* 25 Oct 1970, Mariko, da of Haruichi Eguchi (d 1986); 1 s (Clayton b 17 May 1973), 1 da (Meme b 2 Dec 1971); *Career* md Sony (UK) Ltd 1984-; dir: Sony Broadcast Ltd 1978-86, Sony of Canada Ltd 1974-78; *Recreations* golf, tennis; *Style*— Nobuyuki Watanabe, Esq; Hakoyanagi, Queen's Hill Rise, Ascot, Berkshire SL5 7DP (☎ 0990 26930); Sony (UK) Ltd, South St, Staines, Middlesex TW18 4PF (☎ 0784 467202, fax 0784 467183, telex 925671, car 0836 237584)

WATCH, Cecil; s of Samuel Watch (d 1977), of Manchester, and Emma Watch (d 1988); *b* 5 Dec 1934; *Educ* Manchester GS; *m* 9 Sept 1973, (Valerie) Angela, da of Paul Field (d 1983), of Cheshire; 1 s (Jonathan Franklin b 1977), 2 da (Helen Victoria b 1974, Lisa Ruth b 1976); *Career* ptnr Woolfson Watch & Co Manchester; FCA, ATII; *Recreations* sport; *Style*— Cecil Watch, Esq; Reedham House, 31-33 King St, Manchester M3 2PF (☎ 061 834 2432)

WATCHMAN, David; *b* 18 Jan 1937; *Educ* Bishop Gore Sch; *m* Dorothy; 1 s (Hugh), 1 da (Helen); *Career* account exec Park Advertising Ltd London 1958-63, dir ATA Advertising Group London 1963-73, md Intext Inc Australia 1976-79, chief exec West Sydney Radio Pty Ltd 1979-84; dir: Atkins Bros plc (and subsid cos) 1985-90, Mors Technology SA 1988-, Mors SA 1991-, Mors Technology UK Ltd 1991-; chief exec Royal Acad of Dancing 1991-; JP (Aust); FInstD, MInstM; *Recreations* opera, reading, golf, gardening; *Style*— David Watchman, Esq

WATERFIELD, John Percival; er s of Sir Percival Waterfield, KBE, CB (d 1965), and Doris Mary, *née* Siepmann (d 1988); *b* 5 Oct 1921; *Educ* Dragon Sch Oxford, Charterhouse, ChCh Oxford; *m* 5 Feb 1950, (Margaret) Lee (d 1990), da of late Prof H R Thomas, of Univ of Illinois, USA; 2 s (John, James), 1 da (Polly); *Career* WWII 1940-45, 1 Bn KRRC (Adj) served W Desert, Tunisia, Italy and Austria (despatches); Foreign (later Dip) Serv: entered 1946, third sec Moscow 1947, second sec Tokyo 1950, FO 1952, first sec Santiago 1954, consul (commercial) NY 1957, FO 1960, ambass to Mali Rep 1964-65 (concurrently to Guinea 1965), duties connected with NATO 1966, cnsllr and head of Chancery New Delhi 1966-68, head Western Orgns FCO 1969, md BEAMA 1971-73, princ estabs and fin offr NI Office 1973-79; on secondment to International Military Services Ltd 1979-80; chm and dir various cos 1981-84; *Recreations* fishing, water colour painting, gardening; *Clubs* Boodle's; *Style*— John Waterfield, Esq; 5 North St, Somerton, Somerset TA11 7NY

WATERFORD, Marchioness of; Lady Caroline Olein Geraldine; *née* Wyndham-Quin; da of late 6 Earl of Dunraven and Mount-Earl, CB, CBE, MC; *b* 1936; *m* 1957, 8 Marquess of Waterford; *Style*— The Most Hon the Marchioness of Waterford

WATERFORD, 8 Marquess of (I 1789); Sir John Hubert de la Poer Beresford; 12 Bt (I 1665); also Baron of Le Poer (I 1767), Viscount Tyrone, Baron Beresford (both I 1720), Earl of Tyrone (I 1746), and Baron Tyrone (GB 1786, in which title he sits in House of Lords); s of 7 Marquess of Waterford (d 1934); *b* 14 July 1933; *Educ* Eton; *m* 23 July 1957, Lady Caroline Wyndham-Quin, da of 6 Earl of Dunraven and Mount-Earl; 3 s, 1 da (Lady Alice Rose de la Poer b 31 July 1970); *Heir* s, Earl of Tyrone; *Career* Lt RHG Supp Reserve; *Clubs* White's; *Style*— The Most Hon the Marquess of Waterford; Curraghmore, Portlaw, Co Waterford (☎ 051 87102)

WATERHOUSE, Lady Caroline; *née* Spencer-Churchill; da of 10 Duke of Marlborough (d 1972); *b* 1923; *m* 1946, Maj (Charles) Hugo Waterhouse, *qv*; 2 s, 1 da; *Style*— Lady Caroline Waterhouse; Middleton Hall, Bakewell, Derbys (☎ 0629 636224)

WATERHOUSE, Maj (Charles) Hugo; DL (Derbyshire); s of Capt Rt Hon Charles Waterhouse, MC, JP, DL, and Beryl, *née* Ford; *b* 11 June 1918; *Educ* Eton, Trinity Coll Cambridge; *m* 5 Dec 1946, Lady Caroline Spencer-Churchill, *qv*; 2 s, 1 da; *Career* cmmnd Life Guards, served Europe (despatches, Croix de Guerre) WWII, Maj, ret; High Sheriff of Derbys 1981; *Recreations* shooting; *Clubs* White's; *Style*— Maj Hugo Waterhouse, DL; 57 St George's Drive, London SW1 (☎ 081 834 3950); Middleton Hall, Bakewell, Derbys DE4 1RS (☎ 0629 636224)

WATERHOUSE, Keith Spencer; s of Ernest Waterhouse, and Elsie Edith Waterhouse; *b* 6 Feb 1929; *Educ* Osmondthorpe Cncl Sch Leeds, Leeds Coll of Commerce; *m* 1 (m dis); 1 s, 2 da; m 2, 1984 (m dis); *Career* writer and journalist 1950-; Columnist: Daily Mirror 1970-86, Daily Mail 1986-; contrib to various pubns; plays (with Willis Hall) incl: Billy Liar 1960, Celebration 1961, England Our England (revue, music by Dudley Moore), Squat Betty & the Sponge Room, All Things Bright and Beautiful 1963, Say Who You Are 1965, Childrens Day 1969, Who's Who 1972, Saturday, Sunday, Monday; Filuemena (adaption from Edwards de Filippo) 1973, The Card (musical adaption from novel by Arnold Bennet, music and lyrics Tony Hatch and Jackie Trent) 1973, Worzel Gummidge (music Dennis King), Budgie (musical, lyrics Don Black, music Mort Schuman), Mr & Mrs Nobody (play) 1986, Jeffrey Bernard is Unwell (play) 1989, Bookends 1990; Screenplays (with Willis Hall) incl: Whistle Down the Wind, Billy Liar, A Kind of Loving, Man in the Middle, Pretty Polly, Lock up your Daughters; TV Films incl: There is a Happy Land, The Warmonger, Charlie Muffin (from Brian Freemantle's novel) 1983, This Office Life (from own novel) 1985, The Great Paper Chase (from the book Slip Up by Anthony Delano) 1986; TV Series incl: The Upchat Line, The Upchat Connection, West End Tales, The Happy Apple, Charters and Caldicott, Andy Capp; TV series with Willis Hall: Queenie's Castle, Budgie, The Upper Crusts, Billy Liar, Worzel Gummidge (character created by Barbara Euphan Todd); Awards: Granada Columnist of the Year 1970, IPC Descriptive Writer of the Year 1970, IPC Columnist of the Year 1973, Br Press Columnist of the Year 1978, Granada Special Quarter Century Award 1982, Evening Standard Comedy of the Year 1990 (Jeffrey Bernard is Unwell); *Books* Novels incl: There is a Happy Land (1957), Billy Liar (1959), Jubb (1963), The Bucket Shop (1968), Billy Liar on the Moon (1975), Office Life (1978), Maggie Muggins (1981), In the Mood (1983), Thinks (1984), Our Song (1988), Bimbo (1990); general: The Passing of the Third Floor Buck (anthology of Punch pieces, 1974), Mondays, Thursdays (Daily Mirror columns 1976), Rhubarb, Rhubarb (1979), Daily Mirror Style (1980), Fanny Peculiar (1983), Mrs Pooter's Diary (1983), Waterhouse at Large (1985), The Collected Letters of a Nobody (1986), The Theory and Practice of Lunch (1986), The Theory and Practice of Travel (1988), English Our English (1991); *Clubs* Garrick, Pen, Chelsea Arts, Savile; *Style*— Keith Waterhouse, Esq; 29 Kenway Rd, London SW5 0RP; Agent: London Mgmnt, 235/241 Regent St, London W1; Literary Agent: David Higham Assocs, 5-8 Lower John St, London W1

WATERHOUSE, Norman; s of Norman Waterhouse, and Jean Gardner Hamilton Reid; *b* 13 Oct 1954; *Educ* Salesian Coll Farnborough, Univ of Birmingham Med Sch (MB ChB); *Career* plastic surgn trg: Frenchary Hosp Bristol, Hospital Toadu Bordeaux, South Australian Craniofacial Unit Adelaide, Mount Vernon Hosp Northwood, Tokyo Metropolitan Hosp; conslt in plastic and reconstructive surgery: St Bart's Hosp and The London Hosp Whitechapel 1989-91, Charing Cross Hosp 1991-, St Mary's Hosp Paddington 1991-, Westminster Hosp 1991-; FRCS 1982, FRCS (Ed) 1982, FRCS (plastic surgery) 1988; *Recreations* rock climbing, mountaineering; *Style*— Norman Waterhouse, Esq; 55 Harley St, London W1N 1DD (☎ 071 636 4073, fax 071 436 1645)

WATERHOUSE, Dame Rachel Elizabeth; *née* Franklin; DBE (1990, CBE 1980); da of Percival John Franklin (d 1955), and Ruby Susanna, *née* Knight; *b* 2 Jan 1923; *Educ* King Edward's HS for Girls Birmingham, St Hugh's Coll Oxford (MA), Univ of Birmingham (PhD); *m* 16 Aug 1947, John Alfred Humphrey Waterhouse, s of (Thomas Alfred) Foster Waterhouse, of 60 Hagley Road, Edgbaston, Birmingham; 2 s (Matthew b 21 Sept 1950, Edmund b 4 Feb 1952), 2 da (Deborah (Mrs De Haes) b 11 March 1956, Rebecca (Mrs Morgan) b 20 Oct 1958); *Career* WEA/extra-mural tutor 1944-47; res fell Univ of Birmingham 1948-52; memb: Potato Mktg Bd 1969-81, Price Cmmn 1977-79, Nat Consumer Cncl 1975-86, Duke of Edinburgh's Enquiry into Br Housing 1984-85 and 1990-91; chm Consumers' Assoc 1982-90 (memb Cncl 1966-); memb: Nat Economic Devpt Cncl 1981-, Securities & Investmts Bd 1983-, Cncl of Banking Ombudsman 1986-, Advsy Bd Inst of Food Res 1988-; chm Cncl for Licensed Conveyancers 1986-89, memb Health and Safety Cmmn 1990-, tstee Joseph Rowntree Fndn 1990-; Hon D Litt Loughborough Univ 1980, Hon DSocSci Univ of Birmingham 1990; Hon CGIA 1988; CBIM 1988; *Books* History of the Birmingham and Midland Institute 1854-1954 (1954), A Hundred Years of Engineering Craftsmanship (1957), Children in Hospital, 100 Years Child Care in Birmingham (1962); *Clubs* Cwlth Tst; *Style*— Dame Rachel Waterhouse, DBE; 252 Bristol Rd, Birmingham B5 7SL (☎ 021 472 0427); Consumers' Association, 2 Marylebone Rd, London NW1 4DX (☎ 071 486 5544, fax 071 935 1606, telex 918197, car 0836 734673)

WATERHOUSE, Hon Mr Justice; Hon Sir Ronald Gough Waterhouse; QC (1969); s of Thomas Waterhouse, CBE (d 1961), and Doris Helena Gough; *b* 8 May 1926; *Educ* Holywell GS, St John's Coll Cambridge (MA, LLM); *m* 1960, Sarah Selina, da of Capt Ernest Augustus Ingram (d 1954), of Bletchley Park Stud; 1 s, 2 da; *Career* RAFVR 1944-48; called to the Bar Middle Temple 1952; dep chm: Cheshire QS 1964-71, Flintshire QS 1966-71; Crown Ct rec 1972-77, judge of Employment Appeal Tbnl 1979-88, presiding judge Wales and Chester Circuit 1980-84, High Ct Judge (Queen's Bench Div) 1988- (Family Div 1978-88); chm Local Govt Boundary Cmmn for Wales 1974-78, vice pres Zoological Soc of London 1981-84 (cncl memb 1972-89); Hon LLD Univ of Wales 1986; kt 1978; *Recreations* golf, cricket, music; *Clubs* Garrick, MCC, Cardiff and County; *Style*— The Hon Mr Justice Waterhouse; Royal Courts of Justice, Strand, London WC2A 2LL

WATERLOW, Sir Christopher Rupert; 5 Bt (UK 1873), of London; s of (Peter) Rupert Waterlow (d 1969), of Knightsbridge, London, and Jill Elizabeth, *née* Gourlay (d 1961); gs of Sir Philip Alexander Waterlow, 4 Bt (d 1973), and 3 cous twice removed of Sir Thomas Waterlow, 3 Bt, CBE, of Harrow Weald; *b* 12 Aug 1959; *Educ* Stonyhurst; *m* 6 Sept 1986, Sally-Ann, o da of Maurice Bitten, of Abbey Wood, London; *Career* Met Police civil staff; memb: Stonyhurst Assoc, Civil Service Sports Cncl; *Recreations* music, American football, NFL supporter (UK), shooting; *Style*— Sir Christopher Waterlow, Bt; 58D St John's Park, Blackheath, London SE3 (☎ 081 853 4900); New Scotland Yard, Broadway, London SW1 (☎ 071 230 1212)

WATERLOW, Lady; Diana Suzanne; *née* Skyrme; da of Sir Thomas Skyrme, KCVO, CB, CBE, TD, JP, of Elm Barns, Blockley, Gloucs, and Hon Barbara Suzanne, *née* Lyle, da of 1 Baron Lyle of Westbourne; *b* 21 March 1943; *m* 10 July 1965, Sir (James) Gerard Waterlow, 4 Bt, *qv*; 1 s, 1 da; *Career* actress 1963-68; appointed JP S Westminster 1972, transferred to W Berkshire 1982; memb Bd of

Holloway Prison; dir The Securities Assoc; ptnrship in interior design business W Squared Interiors; *Recreations* tennis, bridge; *Style—* Lady Waterlow; Windmills House, Hurstbourne Tarrant, nr Andover, Hants SP11 0DQ (☎ 026476 547)

WATERLOW, Sir (James) Gerard; 4 Bt (UK 1930), of Harrow Weald, Middlesex; s of Sir Thomas Waterlow, 3 Bt, CBE (d 1982); *b* 3 Sept 1939; *Educ* Marlborough, Trinity Coll Cambridge; *m* 1965, Diana Suzanne, *qv*, yr da of Sir Thomas Skyrme, KCVO, CB, CBE, TD, JP, *qv*; 1 s, 1 da (Amanda b 1968); *Heir* s, Thomas James Waterlow b 20 March 1970; *Style—* Sir Gerard Waterlow, Bt; Windmills House, Hurstbourne Tarrant, nr Andover, Hants SP11 0DQ (☎ 026476 547)

WATERLOW, John William; s of Sir Thomas Gordon Waterlow, 3 Bt, CBE, LLD (d 1982), of Edinburgh, and Helen Elizabeth, *née* Robinson (d 1970); *b* 14 Nov 1945; *Educ* Marlborough; *m* 15 July 1972, Camilla Dudley, da of Wing Cdr Dudley Farmer, AFC, DFC, of Frieth, Oxon; 2 s (Rufus b 1976, Alec b 1980); *Career* sales dir Jarrold & Sons 1981-83, dep chm Burrup Mathieson Sales 1989 (memb 1969-81, assoc dir 1984-85, sales dir 1985); Liveryman Worshipful Co of Stationers and Newspapermakers; *Recreations* tennis, golf, fishing, skiing; *Clubs* MCC, Lansdowne, Den Norske; *Style—* John Waterlow, Esq; 81 Streathbourne Rd, London SW17 8RA (☎ 081 767 1398); St Ives House, Lavington St, London SE1 0NX (☎ 071 928 8844)

WATERMAN, Clive Adrian; s of Harvey Waterman (d 1967), of Hendon, London, and Hannah, *née* Spector; *b* 13 Aug 1949; *Educ* Haberdashers' Aske's Sch Elstree, London Hosp Med Coll (BDS), Royal Dental Hosp of London (MSc); *Career* clinical asst London Hosp 1973-75 (house surgn 1973), registrar Eastman Dental Hosp 1976-77, pt/t clinical asst Guy's Hosp 1977-84, gen and specialist practice 1977-, pt/t lectr King's Coll 1985-; chm GP Section Br Soc of Periodontology; memb: Kingston and Richmond local dental ctee, Rotary Club Barnes; memb Cncl BSP 1990- (memb BDA Scientific Programme Sub-Ctee 1990-, LDC 1988-; *Recreations* cricket, skiing, squash, wine, dining; *Clubs* Riverside, Reform; *Style—* Clive Waterman, Esq; 4 Elm Grove Rd, Barnes, London SW13 0BT (☎ 081 392 2288, office 081 878 8986)

WATERMAN, Fanny; OBE (1971); da of Myer Waterman (d 1984), of Leeds, and Mary, *née* Behrmann (d 1978); *b* 22 March 1920; *Educ* Chapel Allerton HS Leeds, RCM; *m* Dr Geoffrey de Keyser; *Career* concert pianist and teacher of int repute; chm Harvey Leeds Int Pianoforte Competition, jury memb of prestigious piano competitions incl the Tchaikovsky and Rubinstein (vice pres), regular broadcaster tv and radio, author of over twenty books on piano-playing and teaching; FRCM; *Recreations* travel, reading, voluntary work, cooking; *Style—* Miss Fanny Waterman, OBE; Woodgarth, Oakwood Grove, Leeds, W Yorks LS8 2PA (☎ 0532 655 771)

WATERMAN, Howard John; *b* 23 May 1953; *Educ* Univ of Southampton (LLB), Coll of Law; *m* 1 Nov 1981, Sharon; 1 da (Lauren b 1 Sept 1988); *Career* admitted slr 1977; departmental mangr Banking Dept Cameron Markby Hewitt 1987- (ptnr 1984-); memb City of London Slrs Co; memb Law Soc 1977; *Recreations* chess, bridge, sports; *Style—* Howard Waterman, Esq; 20 Beaumont Place, Hadley Highstone, Herts (☎ 081 440 7839); Sceptre Court, 40 Tower Hill, London EC3N 4BB (☎ 071 702 2345)

WATERMAN, Peter Alan (Pete); s of John Edward Waterman, of 94 Burlington Rd, Coventry, and Stella, *née* Lord (d 1978); *b* 15 Jan 1947; *Educ* Frederick Bird Secdy Modern Coventry; *m* 1, 1970, Elizabeth Reynolds; 1 s (Paul Andrew b 1972); m 2, 1980, Julie Reeves; 1 s (Peter Alan b 1982); partner, 1987, Denise Gyngell; 1 da (Toni Tuesday); *Career* record producer; former disc jockey at local pubs and Mecca dancehall, former Arts and Repertoire man for various record cos; formed Loose Ends Productions with Peter Collins working with artists incl Musical Youth and Nick Kershaw until 1983, fndr ptnr Stock Aitken Waterman (with Mike Stock and Matt Aitken) 1984; has won numerous Silver, Gold and Platinum Discs since 1985 for writing and/or producing artists incl: Princess, Hazell Dean, Dead or Alive Bananarama, Mel and Kim, Sinitta, Rick Astley, Kylie Minogue, Brother Beyond, Jason Donovan, Donna Summer, Sonia, Big Fun, Cliff Richard; *awards* BPI Best British Producers 1988; Music Week Top Producers for: Singles (1st) and Albums (3rd) 1987, Singles (1st) and Albums (1st) 1988 and 1989; Ivor Novello Awards (UK): Songwriters of the Year 1987, 1988 and 1989, Writers of Most Performed Works 1987, 1988 and 1989; BMI Awards (USA) Writers of Most Performed Works 1987, 1988 and 1989, Jasrac Awards (Japan) and Cash Awards (Hong Kong) Writers of Most Performed Foreign Works 1989; involved with charity work incl SAW Goes to the Albert (Royal Marsden Hosp) and records: Let it Be (Ferry Aid), The Harder I Try (Young Variety Club of GB), Help (Comic Relief), Lets All Chant, I Haven't Stopped Dancing Yet and Use It Up and Wear It Out (Help a London Child), Ferry 'Cross the Mersey (Mersey Aid), Do They Know It's Christmas? (Ethiopia Famine Appeal), You've Got a Friend (Childline); *Recreations* steam railways, model railways, car collection, Koi Carp farming; *Style—* Pete Waterman, Esq; PWL Records, 4-7 The Vineyard, Sanctuary St, London SE1 1QL (☎ 071 403 0007)

WATERPARK, 7 Baron (I 1729); Sir Frederick Caryll Philip Cavendish; 8 Bt (GB 1755); s of Brig-Gen Frederick Cavendish, bro of 6 Baron and 6 in descent from William Cavendish, natural s of 3 Duke of Devonshire; suc unc 1948; *b* 6 Oct 1926; *Educ* Eton; *m* 17 April 1951, Danièle, da of Roger Guirche, of Paris; 1 s, 2 da; *Heir* s, Hon Roderick Cavendish; *Career* served Gren Gds, Kenya Police Reserve; sales dir CSE Aviation Ltd 1962-; dep chm and md CSE Int 1984; *Clubs* Cavalry and Guards'; *Style—* The Rt Hon Lord Waterpark; 2/74 Elm Park Rd, London SW3 (☎ 071 351 3663); Park House, Bletchingdon, Oxford (☎ (0869) 50238)

WATERS, Alexander James Garland; s of Rev Alexander Waters, MA, BD (d 1924), and Isabella Jane, *née* Garland (d 1956); *b* 24 March 1912; *Educ* Sorbonne, Heidelberg, McGill Univ (BSc Eng); *m* 6 March 1940, Eileen Mary, da of Rev Arthur Edwin Thomas Mcnamara, MA, BD (d 1949), of Westbury-on-Severn, Glos; 1 da (Ann Garland b 1943); *Career* engr; research engr Rolls Royce and Rotal Ltd 1938-43, gen sales mangr Landley Alloys Ltd 1943-45; chm: A J G Waters Ltd 1956-, Realm Engineering Ltd 1960, Realm Control, Systems Ltd 1983, Proclin Int 1972; *Recreations* cricket, golf, rugby, squash; *Clubs* MCC, Berkshire Golf, Royal Aero, London Scottish and Wasps Rugby; *Style—* Alexander J G Waters, Esq; Rolls Farm, Tismans Common, Rudawick, Horsham, W Sussex; 8/28 Milton Ave, Croydon, Surrey C24 2JP (☎ 081 689 5521, telex 945411, fax 081 689 1715)

WATERS, Brian Richard Anthony; s of Montague Waters, QC, of London, and Jessica Freedman; *b* 27 March 1944; *Educ* City of London Sch, St John's Coll Cambridge (MA), (Dip Arch, PCL Dip); *m* 1 Nov 1974, Myriam Leiva, da of Jose Ramon Leiva Alvarez, of Bogota, Colombia; *Career* chartered architect & town planner; memb RIBA, RTPI; pres Cities of London and Westminster Soc of Architects 1980-82, vice pres RIBA 1988 (memb Cncl 1987); chm Nat Architecture Conf London 1991, London Devpt Control Forum 1990-; princ The Boisot Waters Cohen Partnership (design), ptnr Studio Crown Reach, dir Gray Lucas Mgmnt Ltd; Architectural Journalist of the Year commendation 1979, 1982, 1984, 1986; Freeman City of London Co of Chartered Architects; *Books* author of articles and reviews for various architectural pubns; *Recreations* tennis, dressage, pots, Siberian huskies; *Clubs* RAC, Hurlingham; *Style—* Brian R A Waters, Esq; Studio Crown Reach, 149a Grosvenor Road, London SW1V 3JY (☎ 071 828 6555, fax 071 834 9470)

WATERS, Brian Wallace; s of Stanley Wallace Waters, of Harpenden, Herts, and Kathleen, *née* Thake; *b* 24 Nov 1936; *Educ* City of London Sch, Harvard Business Sch; *m* 1 April 1961, Gillian, da of Herbert William Harris (d 1976); 4 s (Andrew b 1963, James b 1965, Richard b 1967, Mark b 1975); *Career* Ernst & Young: ptnr 1968, exec vice chm (Europe) 1979-82, chm (Europe) 1982-85, managing ptnr Ernst & Young Cambridge 1984-, dir of Euro affrs UK 1986-; chm London Soc of Chartered Accountants 1976-77, memb ICAEW 1983-87, memb Exec Ctee Union Européenne des Expert Compatables 1983-87; memb Horserace Betting Levy Appeal Tbnl 1986-; Liveryman: Worshipful Co of Chartered Accountants, Worshipful Co of Drapers; FCA 1960, FCMA 1962; *Recreations* cricket, field sports, racing, real tennis; *Clubs* MCC, Institute of Directors, City Livery, Wig and Pen; *Style—* Brian Waters, Esq; Ernst & Young, Compass House, 80 Newmarket Rd, Cambridge CB5 8DZ (☎ 0223 461200)

WATERS, Lady Caroline Mary Victoria; yr da of 9 Earl of Shannon; *b* 12 Oct 1965; *m* 7 July 1990, Mark Nowell Waters, o s of P N Waters, of Guildford, Surrey; *Style—* The Lady Caroline Waters

WATERS, Charles Frobisher Haselar; s of Frank Haselar Waters, MC, of Grange Cottage, Uckfield, Sussex, and Elizabeth Georgina Napier Waters; *b* 31 May 1947; *Educ* The Nautical Coll Pangbourne; *m* 17 April 1972, (Pamela) Rosemary Gordon, da of George Gordon Dodwell Carter; 1 s (James Gordon Frobisher), 1 da (Katharine Jane); *Career* chartered surveyor; FRICS 1979; *Recreations* shooting, fishing, sailing, golf; *Style—* Charles Waters, Esq; 16 Catherine Place, London SW1 (☎ 071 630 6629); Mellersh & Harding, 43 St James's Place, London SW1 (☎ 071 499 0866, 071 408 1387)

WATERS, David Frobisher; s of Frank Haselar Waters, of Grance Cottage, Uckfield Sussex, and Elizabeth Georgina Napier, *née* Frobisher; *b* 20 Sept 1949; *Educ* The King's Sch Canterbury, Univ of Cape Town (BComm, MIndAd); *m* 1, 12 June 1971 (m dis); 2 s (Marcus Damian Napier b 2 Dec 1973, Fraser Henry Hamilton b 31 March 1976); m 2, 8 Dec 1990, Brigid Mary Dowling; *Career* Harwood Banner (London) 1966-70, PA Thomas & Co (London) 1970-71, Coopers & Lybrand (Cape Town) 1971-73 and 1978-86 (ptnr), sr lectr Univ of Cape Town 1973-78, ptnr Ernst & Young (Jersey) 1986-; ATII (1969), FCA (1970), CA (SA, 1972); *Books* Insolvency and Liquidation - A Creditors Handbook (1976), The Law of Insolvency in South Africa (1979); *Recreations* sport, games and puzzles; *Clubs* Hon Artillery Co, Royal Cape Yacht, Western Province Sports, Victoria (Jersey), Mensa; *Style—* David Waters, Esq; Green Lanes, Pont Au Bre, St Peter, Jersey, Channel Islands (☎ 0534 33700); Ernst & Young, Le Callais Chambers, 54 Bath St, St Helier, Jersey, Channel Islands (☎ 0534 33700)

WATERS, Donald Henry; s of Henry Lethbridge Waters (d 1978), of Edinburgh, and Jean Manson, *née* Baxter (d 1987); *b* 17 Dec 1937; *Educ* George Watson's Coll Edinburgh, Inverness Royal Acad; *m* 5 May 1962, June Leslie, da of Andrew Hutchison (d 1984), of Forres, Moray; 1 s (Andrew Henry Lethbridge b 1969), 2 da (Jennifer Dawn b 1963, Gillian Claire b 1966); *Career* dir: John M Henderson Ltd 1972-75, Glenburnie Properties Ltd 1976-, Blenheim Travel Ltd 1981-90, Moray Firth Radio Ltd 1982-, Independent Television Publications Ltd 1987-90, Cablevision Scotland plc 1987-90; chief exec Grampian TV plc 1987-(dir 1979-); former chm Royal Northern and Univ Club Aberdeen; MICAS; *Recreations* gardening, travel, hillwalking; *Clubs* Royal Northern and Univ Aberdeen; *Style—* Donald Waters, Esq; Balquhidder, 141 North Deeside Rd, Milltimber, Aberdeen AB1 0JS (☎ 0224 867 131); Grampian TV plc, Queens Cross, Aberdeen AB9 2XJ (☎ 0224 646 464)

WATERS, Prof (William) Estlin; s of Dr Edward Thomas Waters (d 1977), and Dr Cicely Waters, *née* Weatherall (d 1985); *b* 6 Nov 1934; *Educ* Cardiff HS, Univ of London (MB BS); *m* 14 March 1964, Judith Isabel, da of David Harold Lloyd (d 1963); 2 s (Robert b 26 April 1966, David b 8 Aug 1967); *Career* Nat Serv Capt RAMC; prof of community med Univ of Southampton 1976 (sr lectr and reader clinical epidemiology and community med 1970-75); sec Exec Ctee Int Epidemiological Assoc 1974-77 (memb Cncl 1971-77 and 1981-84), memb Editorial Ctee Jl of Epidemiology and Community Health, ed Int Jl of Epidemiology 1990; MFCM 1974, FFCM 1976 FFPHM 1989; *Books* Community Medicine (1983 and 1987), Headache, Clinical Epidemiology Series (1986); *Recreations* ornithology, visiting remote islands; *Clubs* British Trust for Ornithology, British Ornithologists Union; *Style—* Prof Estlin Waters; Orchards, Broxmore Park, Sherfield English, Romsey, Hants SO51 6FT (☎ 0794 884254); Academic Dept of Community Medicine, South Block, Southampton General Hospital, Southampton, Hants SO9 4XY (☎ 0703 796531)

WATERS, (Suzanne) Fiona; s of Capt Michael Theodore Waters, of Ambleside, Cumbria, and Sylvia, *née* Tingle; *b* 10 April 1956; *Educ* Felixstowe Ladies Coll; *Career* production co-ordinator and at work on several UK and US theatrical prodns Knightsbridge Theatrical Productions 1976, press offr Royal Court Theatre 1980, head of press network co-ordinator Satellite TV plc 1982, head of press Sky Channel 1984, dir of press and publicity: Sky TV 1988, British Sky Broadcasting 1990; *Recreations* sailing, gardening, writing; *Style—* Ms Fiona Waters; 5 Corringway, London NW11 7ED; British Sky Broadcasting, Business Park, Isleworth, Middx TW7 5QD (☎ 071 782 3000, fax 081 783 3113)

WATERS, Gen Sir (Charles) John; KCB (1988), CBE (1981, OBE 1977); s of Patrick George Waters (d 1952), and Margaret Ronaldson, *née* Clark; *b* 2 Sept 1935; *Educ* Oundle, RMA Sandhurst; *m* 1962, Hilary Doyle, da of Harry Sylvester Nettleton (d 1983); 3 s; *Career* CO 1 Bn Gloucestershire cs Regt 1975-77, Col Gen Staff 1 Armd Div 1977-79, Cmd 3 Inf Bde 1979-81, RCDS 1982, Dep Cmd Land Forces Falklands 1982, Cmd 4 Armd Div 1983-85, Col Gloucestershire Regt 1985-91, Cmdt Staff Coll Camberley 1986-88, GOC and dir of ops NI 1988-90, Col Cmdt Prince of Wales Div, Lt-Gen 1988; Gen 1990, C-in-C UKLF 1990-; *Recreations* sailing, skiing, painting, reading, walking; *Clubs* Army and Navy, SCGB, Eagle Ski, Axe Yacht; *Style—* Gen Sir C J Waters, CBE; c/o National Westminster Bank, 4-6 Broad St, Reading, Berks

WATERS, John Stephen; s of Ronald Neil Waters (d 1976), of Ufford Place, Woodbridge, Suffolk, and Eva Louise, *née* Porter (d 1989); *b* 22 Oct 1934; *Educ* Queen Elizabeth's Sch Barnet, Charing Cross Hosp Med Sch (MS); *m* 10 July 1960, Faith, da of Edward Hindle; 3 da (Lynn b 28 May 1963, Jill b 10 July 1966, Susan b 26 Dec 1967); *Career* med trg Charing Cross Hosp: house surgn, house physician, casualty offr; surgical registrar Charing Cross Hosp 1960-64; Royal Surrey Co Hosp, Prince of Wales Hosp London; sr surgical registrar 1965-71: Norfolk and Norwich Hosp, St George's Hosp, Royal Marsden Hosp; conslt surgn Morriston and Singleton Hosps Swansea 1971-; hon tutor Univ of Wales Coll of Med; elected to Welsh Bd RCS; memb: BMA, RSM, Assoc Surgeons; FRCS; *Recreations* sailing, walking; *Style—* John Waters, Esq; 12 Grange Rd, West Cross, Swansea, West Glamorgan SA3 5ES; St Davids House, 1 Uplands Terrace, Swansea (☎ 0792 472922)

WATERS, Prof Ronald Thomas; s of David John Waters (d 1978), of Caerphilly, and Mary Evelyn Rees (d 1982)); *b* 20 June 1930; *Educ* Caerphilly GS, Univ Coll Of Swansea (BSc, PhD); *m* 2 April 1956, Catherine Margaret, da of Richard Cullen (d 1978), of Swansea; 2 da (Janet b 1957, Deborah b 1961); *Career* res engr: AEI Ltd 1954-61, Univ of Wales 1961-; memb Welsh Jt Educn Ctee; FInst P, FIEE, C Eng; *Books* Gas Discharges and the Electricity Supply Industry (1962), Electrical Breakdown of Gases (1978); *Recreations* golf, gardening, travel; *Clubs* Cardiff Golf;

Style— Prof Ronald Waters; 7 South Rise, Llanishen, Cardiff, South Glamorgan CF4 5RF (☎ 0222 754602); University of Wales, College of Cardiff

WATERSTONE, David George Stuart; CBE (1991); s of Malcolm Stuart Waterstone, MBE (d 1979), and Sylvia Catherine, *née* Sawday (d 1974); *b* 9 Aug 1935; *Educ* Tonbridge, St Catherine's Coll Cambridge (MA); *m* 1 (m dis), Dominique, *née* Viriot; 1 s (Mark), 2 da (Caroline, Isabelle); m 2, 10 April 1988, Sandra Kaye, da of George Edward Willey, of Aust; *Career* PO 601 County of London Sqdn RAF 1953-56, Lt 21 SAS 1956-59; HM Dip Serv 1959-70, sr exec IRC 1970-71, md Commercial BSC 1972-77; exec chm: BSC Chemicals 1977-81, Redpath Dorman Long 1977-81; chief exec: Welsh Devpt Agency 1983-90, energy and Technical Services Group Ltd 1990-; memb Bd BSC 1976-81; CBIM 1975; *Recreations* sailing, walking, furniture making, painting; *Clubs* Reform; *Style*— David Waterstone, Esq, CBE; 1 Prior Park Buildings, Prior Park Rd, Bath BA2 4NP; Energy and Technical Services Group Ltd, 8 Headfort Place, London SW1X 7BH (☎ 071 823 2288, fax 071 245 9963)

WATERSTONE, Timothy John Stuart; s of Malcolm Waterstone (d 1977), of Forge Cottage, Maresfield, Sussex, and Sylvia, *née* Sawday (d 1967); *b* 30 May 1939; *Educ* Tonbridge, St Catharine's Coll Cambridge (MA); *m* 1, Oct 1962 (m dis 1971), Patricia Harcourt-Poole; 2 s (Richard b 1963, Martin b 1965), 1 da (Sylvia b 1969); m 2, Oct 1972 (m dis 1990), Clare Perkins; 1 s (Oliver b 1980), 2 da (Amanda b 1975, Maya b 1977); *Career* Carritt Moran & Co Calcutta 1962-64, Allied Breweries plc 1965-73, W H Smith Group plc 1973-81, fndr and exec chm Waterstone & Co 1982-; chm: The Principals Ltd 1987-, Metronome Radio Ltd 1989-90, Priory Investments Ltd 1990-; dep chm Sinclair-Stevenson Publishers Ltd 1990-, dir Classic - FM Radio Ltd 1990-; tstee International House 1986, memb Ctee Booker Prize 1986, treas Church Action with the Unemployed 1987-89; chm: Princes Youth Business Tst 1989, Shelter 25th Anniversary Appeal 1990-, London Int Festival of Theatre 1990-; dir: The Academy of Ancient Music 1989-, The London Philharmonic Orchestra Ltd 1990-; *Recreations* books, music; *Clubs* Athenaeum; *Style*— Timothy Waterstone, Esq; 37 Ixworth Place, London SW3 3QH (☎ 071 584 4448, fax 071 584 6315)

WATERTON, John Brian; s of Laurence Maude Waterton (d 1976); *b* 10 March 1934; *Educ* Giggleswick Sch Yorks; *m* 1959, Jane Pollack, da of Harry Anthony Pitt Wilkinson (d 1966); 2 s, 2 da; *Career* co dir and gp mktg dir: Dawson Int plc 1978-89, House of Hardy Ltd 1989-; *Recreations* golf; *Clubs* Caledonian; *Style*— John Waterton, Esq; House of Hardy Ltd, Willowburn, Alnwick, Northumberland NE66 2PG

WATES, Michael Edward; s of Sir Ronald Wates (d 1986), and Lady Phyllis Mary Wates, *née* Trace; *b* 19 June 1935; *Educ* Oundle, Emmanuel Coll Cambridge (MA), Harvard Business Sch; *m* 24 June 1959, Caroline Josephine, *née* Connolly; *Career* Nat Serv RM 1953-55; Wates Ltd: joined 1959, dir Wates Construction 1963-, dir Wates Built Homes 1966-, chm 1975-; chm Br Bloodstock Agency plc 1986-; memb Worshipful Co of Innholders 1958, Hon FRIBA; *Style*— Michael Wates, Esq; Manor House, Longton Long, Blandford Forum, Dorset DT11 9HS (☎ 0258 455241); Wates Ltd, 1260 London Rd, Norbury, London SW16 4EG (☎ 081 764 5000)

WATHEN, Julian Philip Gerard; s of Gerard Anstruther Wathen, CIE (d 1958), and Melicent Louis, *née* Buxton (d 1984); bro of Rev Mark W G Wathen, *qv*; *b* 21 May 1923; *Educ* Harrow; *m* 1948, Priscilla Florence, da of Maj-Gen Bevil Thomson Wilson (d 1975); 1 s (Simon), 2 da (Lucy (Mrs Floyer-Acland), Henrietta (Mrs Goodall)); *Career* joined Barclays Bank DCO 1948, served Kenya, Tanganyika, Cyprus, New York, Sudan, Ghana; vice chm Barclays Bank 1979-84 (gen mangr 1966); dir Mercantile & Gen Reinsurance; chm Hall Sch Tst; pres Royal African Soc, vice chm London House for Overseas Graduates; govr: St Paul's Schs, Dauntseys, Abingdon, SOAS; Master Mercers' Co 1984-85; *Clubs* Travellers'; *Style*— Julian Wathen, Esq; Woodcock House, Owlpen, Dursley GL11 5BY (☎ 0453 860214); 1 Montagu Place, Marylebone, London W1H 1RG (☎ 071 935 8569)

WATHEN, Rev Mark William Gerard; TD (1946); s of Gerard Anstruther Wathen, CIE (d 1958), and Melicent Louis, *née* Buxton (d 1984); bro of Julian P G Wathen, *qv*; *b* 18 Sept 1912; *Educ* Gresham's Sch Holt; *m* 1940, Rosemary, da of Charles Hartridge, of Findon Place, W Sussex, and his w Kathleen, er da of Sir Fortescue Flannery, 1 Bt; 2 s (Roderick b 1940, Jonathan b 1951), 2 da (Primula b 1946, Erica b 1949); *Career* dir Barclays Bank (City, Ipswich, Norwich) 1948-72; High Sheriff Norfolk 1968; memb Gen Synod C of E 1970-80, church cmmr 1973-78, ordained deacon and priest 1982, priest i/c St Columba's Church Isle of Skye 1982-; Master Mercers' Co 1963; FRSA; *Recreations* shooting, fishing, writing; *Clubs* Brooks's, MCC; *Style*— The Rev Mark Wathen, TD; Talisker House, Carbost, Isle of Skye IV47 8SF (☎ 047 842 245); Bolwick Hall Farm, Marsham, Norwich (☎ 026 373 3130)

WATHERSTON, (John) Michael; s of John Robert Watherston (d 1983); *b* 30 June 1932; *Educ* Sedbergh; *m* 1960, Lorna Kathryn, da of George Warren (d 1956), of Enniskillen; 1 s, 1 da; *Career* exec dir (now ret) Murray Johnstone Ltd; dir: Murray Johnstone Unit Trust Mgmnt Ltd, MJ Finance Ltd, Murraystone Investment Ltd and other cos; high constable Holyrood; MICAS; *Recreations* golf, shooting, skiing; *Clubs* Honourable Co of Edinburgh Golfers, New (Edinburgh); *Style*— Michael Watherston, Esq; 22 Murrayfield Drive, Edinburgh EH12 6EB (☎ 031 337 2948); Kil Modan, N Connel, Argyll (☎ 063 171)

WATKIN, Dr Bernard Curtis; s of Harold Victor Watkin (d 1989), and Mary Curtis (d 1965); *b* 29 Aug 1931; *Educ* Hymers Coll, Tiffin Sch, Univ of London (MB BS), St Bartholomews' Hosp (DPhysMed); *m* 21 Oct 1967, Jennifer Ann, da of Dr Edward Street; 2 da (Eleanor Curtis b 5 April 1971, Jessica Kate b 5 Feb 1973); *Career* hon clinical asst in rheumatology St Stephen's Hosp London; registrar Arthur Stanley Inst of Rheumatology Middx Hosp London, registrar in physical med St Thomas Hosp London, scientific advsr in orthopaedics ICI Ltd, sports injury conslt to IMG (International Management Group); med offr to BCU at 1972 Olympics; memb: Br Assoc of Manipulative Med, Soc of Orthopaedic Med; *Books* contrib to various books on lumbar disorders; paper on Tempero-Mandibula Joint in Rheumatoid Arthritis (1969); *Style*— Dr Bernard Watkin; 62 Wimpole St, London W1M 7DE (☎ 071 486 8684, fax 071 224 3282)

WATKIN, (Francis) David; s of John Wilfrid Watkin and Beatrice Lynda Dadswell; *b* 23 March 1925; *Career* British Army 1944-47; dir of photography; documentary films incl The England of Elizabeth; feature films incl: The Knack, Help, Marat Sade, The Charge of the Light Brigade, Catch 22, The Devils, The Boyfriend, Jesus of Nazareth, Chariots of Fire, White Nights, Out of Africa, Moonstruck, Memphis Belle, Hamlet; American Academy award 1985, British Academy award 1986; *Recreations* music, reading; *Style*— David Watkin; 6 Sussex Mews, Brighton BN12 1GZ

WATKIN, David John; s of Thomas Charles Watkin, and Vera Mary, *née* Saunders; *b* 7 April 1941; *Educ* Farnham GS, Trinity Hall Cambridge (BA, MA, PhD); *Career* head Dept History of Art Univ of Cambridge 1989- (fell Peterhouse 1970-, lectr history of art 1972-); memb: Historic Bldgs Advsy Ctee, Historic Bldgs and Monuments Cmmn, Exec Ctee Georgian Gp; FSA 1979; *Books* Thomas Hope 1769-1831 and The Neo-Classical Idea (1968), The Life and Work of CR Cockerell RA (1974), Morality and Architecture (1977), English Architecture: A Concise History (1979), The Rise of Architectural History (1980), Neo-Classical and Nineteenth Century Architecture (with Robin Middleton, 1980), Athenian Stuart: Pioneer of the Greek Revival (1982), The English Vision: The Picturesque in Architecture, Landscape and Garden Design (1982), A History of Western Architecture (1986), German Architecture and the Classical Ideal: 1740-1840 (with Tilman Mellinghoff, 1987); *Clubs* Beefsteak, Travellers'; *Style*— David Watkin, Esq, FSA; Peterhouse, Cambridge

WATKIN, Dr Ross Rickard; s of Philip James Watkin, OBE, MC (d 1969), of Pulborough, Sussex, and Phyllis, *née* Rickard (d 1987); *b* 18 Dec 1933; *Educ* Westminster, Guy's Hosp Med Sch Univ of London (MB BS, DObst RCOG); *m* 8 Aug 1967, Jacqueline Ruth, da of William John Hole (d 1976), of Sutton, Surrey; 2 da (Frances Rickard b 1967, Antonia Ruth b 1972); *Career* ship's surgn MN 1959; conslt anaesthetist Guy's Hosp 1967; sec and chm SE Thames Anaesthetic Soc 1986, chm SE Thames Anaesthetic Sub-ctee 1987-; memb: BMA, Assoc of Anaesthetists, Coll of Anaesthetists; FFARCS; *Style*— Dr Ross Watkin; Orchard Cottage, Rectory Rd, Mugswell, Surrey CR3 3SY (☎ 0737 557564); Flat 3, Pickfords Wharf, Clink St, London SE1 9DG; Department of Anaesthesia, Guy's Hospital, London SE1 9RT (☎ 071 955 4051)

WATKIN, Steven Llewellyn; s of John Watkin, of Port Talbot, West Glamorgan, and Sandra, *née* Davies; *b* 15 Sept 1964; *Educ* Cymer Afan Comp Sch, Glan Afan Comp Sch, Swansea Coll of Further Educn, S Glamorgan Inst of Higher Educn (BA); *Career* professional cricketer; Glamorgan CCC 1986: debut v Worcs 1986, awarded county cap 1989, 63 appearances taking 211 wickets; 11 caps Welsh Secdy Schs 1981-84; tours: England A to Kenya/Zimbabwe 1990 and Pakistan/Sri Lanka 1991, Br Colls to W Indies 1987, Glamorgan to W Indies 1989; 2 unoffical B Test matches v Zimbabwe; leading wicket taker with 94 wickets 1989; soccer cap Welsh Boys under 16; *Recreations* carpentry, gardening, watching tv, listening to music, a quiet pint, motor mechanics, all sports; *Style*— Steven Watkin, Esq; Glamorgan CCC, Sophia Gardens, Cardiff (☎ 0222 343478)

WATKIN WILLIAMS, Sir Peter; s of Robert Thesiger Watkin Williams; *b* 8 July 1911; *Educ* Sherborne, Pembroke Coll Cambridge; *m* 1938, Jane Dickinson, *née* Wilkin; 2 da; *Career* served WWII; ptnr Hansons (lawyers) Shanghai 1937-40, resident magistrate Uganda 1946-55; puisne judge: Trinidad & Tobago 1955-58, Sierra Leone 1958-61; plebiscite judge Cameroons 1961; CJ: Basutoland, Bechuanaland and Swaziland (also pres Ct Appeal) 1961-65, high court judge Malawi 1967-69, CJ Malawi 1969-70, ret; kt 1963; *Style*— Sir Peter Watkin Williams; Lower East Horner, Stockland, Honiton, Devon (☎ 040 488 374)

WATKINS, Alan (Rhun); s of David John Watkins (d 1980), of Tycroes, Dyfed, and Violet, *née* Harris (d 1986); *b* 3 April 1933; *Educ* Amman Valley GS Ammanford, Queens' Coll Cambridge (MA, LLM); *m* 1955, Ruth Howard (d 1982); 1 s, 1 da (and 1 da decd); *Career* Flying Offr Educn Branch RAF 1955-57; called to the Bar Lincoln's Inn 1957, res asst Dept of Govt LSE 1958-59, editorial staff Sunday Express 1959-69 (NY corr 1961, crossbencher columnist 1963-64); political corr: Spectator 1964-67, New Statesman 1967-76; political columnist Sunday Mirror 1968-69, dir The Statesman and Nation Publishing Co 1973-76, columnist Evening Standard 1974-75, political columnist Observer 1976-; rugby columnist: Field 1984-86, Independent 1986-; chm Political Advsy Gp Br Youth Cncl 1979-81, memb (Lab) Fulham Borough Cncl; *Books* The Liberal Dilemma (1966), The Making of the Prime Minister (with A Alexander, 1970), Brief Lives (1982), Sportswriter's Eye (1989), A Slight Case of Libel (1990); *Recreations* reading, walking; *Clubs* Beefsteak, Garrick; *Style*— Alan Watkins, Esq; 54 Barnsbury St, London N1 1ER (☎ 071 607 0812); Observer, Chelsea Bridge House, London SW8 (☎ 071 350 3251)

WATKINS, Dr Alan Keith; s of Wilfred Victor Watkins (d 1963), and Dorothy Hilda Watkins; *b* 9 Oct 1938; *Educ* Moseley GS, Univ of Birmingham (BSc, PhD); *m* 1963, Diana Edith Wynne, *née* Hughes; 2 s (David Mark b 31 March 1966, Andrew John b 12 Dec 1970); *Career* mfrg process res Lucas Group Research 1962-69, mfrg and prodn engrg Lucas Batteries Ltd 1969-75; md: Lucas Aerospace Ltd 1982-87 (dir Electrical Div 1975-82), Aerospace Lucas Industries 1987-89; md and chief exec Hawker Siddeley Group plc 1989-; currently dir: Hawker Siddeley Management Ltd, hawker Siddeley Canada Inc; *Recreations* tennis, photography, golf, hot-air ballooning; *Style*— Dr Alan Watkins; Hawker Siddeley Group plc, 18 St James's Square, London SW1Y 4LJ (☎ 071 627 7510, fax 071 627 7767, telex 919011 HAWSID G)

WATKINS, Brian; s of James Edward Watkins (d 1981), of Newport, Gwent, and Gladys Ann, *née* Fletcher (d 1942); *b* 26 July 1933; *Educ* Newport HS, LSE (BSc Econ), Worcester Coll of Oxford; *m* 1, 26 Oct 1957 (m dis 1979), Thelma, da of Thomas Horace Waite (d 1963), of Newport, Gwent; 1 s (Mark b 1958); m 2, 31 Dec 1982, Elisabeth, da of Arfon Jones; 1 da (Caroline b 1985); *Career* RAF 1954-58; HMOCS Sierra Leone 1959-63, local govt 1963-66, admin Tristan da Cunha 1966-69; admitted slr 1970; lectr Univ of Manchester 1969-71; HM Dip Serv: FCO 1971-73, NY 1973-76, NI Office 1976-78, FCO 1978-81, cnsllr and dep govr Bermuda 1981-83, cnsllr (econ) Islamabad 1983-86, consul gen Vancouver 1986, high cmmr to Swaziland 1990; memb Law Soc; *Recreations* reading, dancing, theatre; *Clubs* Royal Bermuda Yacht; *Style*— Brian Watkins, Esq; British High Commission, Private Bag, Mbabane, Swaziland (☎ 268 42581, fax 268 42585)

WATKINS, David John; s of Thomas George Watkins (d 1986), and Alice Elizabeth, *née* Allen (d 1955); *b* 27 Aug 1925; *Educ* S Bristol Central Sch, Merrywood GS, Bristol Tech Coll; *Career* Nat Serv RAF 1945-48; engr in indust 1941-45 and 1948-66; MP (Lab) Consett 1966-83 (memb Lab Pty 1950-); hon treas Cncl Advancement of Arab-British Understanding (memb 1968-, dir 1983-90); memb Amalgamated Engrg Union 1941-; *Books* Labour and Palestine (1975), Industrial Common Ownership (1978), The World and Palestine (1980), The Exceptional Conflict (1984); *Recreations* reading, music, swimming; *Clubs* Royal Cwlth Soc; *Style*— David Watkins, Esq; The Arab-British Centre, 21 Collingham Rd, London SW5 0NU (☎ 071 373 8414, fax 071 370 5956, telex 895 3551 PROMEI G)

WATKINS, Rev Gordon Derek; s of Clifford Henry Watkins (d 1967), of Bristol, and Margaret Caroline, *née* Grimley (d 1974); *b* 16 July 1929; *Educ* St Brendan's Coll Clifton; *m* 3 Jan 1957, Beryl Evelyn Watkins, da of Thomas Henry Whitaker (d 1959), of Sydney, NSW; *Career* Nat Serv RAOC 1947-49; minor canon of Grafton Cathedral NSW 1953-56, vicar of Texas Queensland 1956-61, curate of St Wilfrid's Harrogate 1961-63, vicar of Upton Park 1963-67; rector of: Great and Little Bentley 1967-73, Great Canfield 1973-78; asst sec Chelmsford Diocesan Synod 1973-78, sec Chelmsford Redundant Churches Uses Ctee 1973-78, pastoral sec Diocese of London 1978-84, vicar St Martin-within-Ludgate City of London 1984-89, sec London Diocesan Advsy Ctee 1984-, priest vicar of Westminster Abbey 1984-89, Priest-in-Ordinary HM The Queen 1984-; chaplain: Ward of Farringdon within City of London 1984-89, Knights of the Round Table 1984-89; Freeman City of London 1984; Chaplain: Co of Makers of Playing Cards 1987-88, Co of Pipe Makers and Tobacco Blenders 1985-; *Recreations* reading, television, the country; *Clubs* Athenaeum; *Style*— The Rev Gordon Watkins; 30 Causton St, London SW1P 4AU

WATKINS, Maj-Gen Guy Hansard; CB (1986), OBE (1974); s of Col Alfred Norman Mitchell Watkins (d 1970), of Milford-on-Sea, Hants, and Sylvia Christine, *née* Downing (d 1988); *b* 30 Nov 1933; *Educ* The King's Sch Canterbury; *m* 15 Feb 1958, Sylvia Margaret, da of William Lawrence Grant, of Walton-on-the-Hill, Surrey; 2 s (Michael b 1959, Peter b 1971), 2 da (Anne-Marie b 1961, Carol b 1965); *Career* cmmnd RA 1953, Battery Cdr (BAOR) 1969, Instr Staff Coll 1971, Co 39 Regt RA (BAOR) 1973,

Dep Cmd 1 Armoured Div (BAOR) 1977, Dir Public Relations (Army) 1980, Cmd Artillery Div (BAOR) 1982, Dir Gen Army Manning and Recruiting 1985, ret 1986; chief exec The Royal Hong Kong Jockey Club 1986; *Recreations* riding, golf, fishing; *Clubs* Royal Hong Kong Jockey, Shek-O Country, Army and Navy, Littlehampton Golf; *Style*— Maj-Gen Guy Watkins, CB, OBE; c/o National Westminster Bank, 60 High St, Bognor Regis, West Sussex; The Royal Hong Kong Jockey Club, Sports Rd, Happy Valley, Hong Kong (☎ Hong Kong 8378333, telex 65581 RHKJC HX, fax HK 5766410)

WATKINS, James Arthur; s of William Arthur Watkins, of York, England, and Mary Lilian Chapman; *b* 26 Sept 1945; *Educ* Archbishop Holgate's Sch York, Univ of Leeds (LLB); *m* 4 March 1967 (m dis), Ursula Barbara; 2 da (Philippa Jane Langford b 1975, Victoria Joanne Langford b 1977); *Career* Linklaters & Paines: articled clerk 1967, asst slr 1969, ptnr 1975-; memb Worshipful Co of Solicitors 1976, Freeman City of London 1976; memb: Law Soc 1969, Int Bar Assoc 1978, Union Internationale des Avocats 1980; *Recreations* golf, tennis, reading, music, food and wine; *Clubs* Hurlingham, Annabel's, Hong Kong, Shek-O Country; *Style*— James Watkins, Esq; 37 Montpelier Walk, London SW7 1J (☎ 071 606 7080); 5A, 6A Bowen Rd, Hong Kong (☎ 852 525 2921); 14th Floor, Alexander House, Chater Rd, Hong Kong (☎ 852 525 2921, fax 852 8133/1695, telex 83695 LPHK HX); Barrington House, 59-67 Gresham St, London EC2V 7JA

WATKINS, John; s of Charles Watkins, and Kathleen Myrtle, *née* Cullis (d 1969); *b* 16 Dec 1943; *Educ* Yeovil Sch Somerset; *m* 2 Sept 1967, Diane Mary, da of Cyril Charles Hooper; 2 s (James Charles Cullis b 24 Oct 1969, Alastair John Cullis b 2 Aug 1972), 2 da (Philippa Louise b 11 Sept 1974, Gemma Kate b 7 Sept 1978); *Career* articled clerk Howard Howes & Co 1962-68 (latterly personal asst to sr ptnr); ptnr: Neville Russell 1972-89 (personal asst 1969-72), Ernst & Young 1989-; FCA (ACA 1968), assoc memb Lloyd's of London 1986; *Clubs* Gresham; *Style*— John Watkins, Esq; Ernst & Young, Private Client Services, Lonsdale Chambers, 27 Chancery Lane, London W1 (☎ 071 931 6767)

WATKINS, Prof John William Nevill; DSC; s of William Hugh Watkins (d 1952), and Winifred Ellen, *née* Jeffries (d 1966); *b* 31 July 1924; *Educ* RNC Dartmouth, LSE (BSc), Yale Univ (MA); *m* 4 April 1952, Millicent Joan (Micky) *née* Roe; 1 s (Hugh b 1 March 1953), 3 da (Susan (twin) b 1 March 1953, Kate b 21 June 1956, Julie b 2 Sept 1958); *Career* RN: Midshipman HMS Renown 1941-43, HMS Calpe 1943, Sub Lt HMS Ashanti 1943-44, Lt HMS Tyrian 1944-46; prof LSE 1966- (asst lectr 1950-53, lectr 1953-58, reader 1958-66); pres Br Soc for the Philosophy of Sci 1972-75; memb: Mind Assoc, Royal Inst of Philosophy; *Books* Hobbes's System of Ideas (1965, 2 edn 1973), Freiheit und Entscheidung (1978), Libertá e Decisione (1981), Tre Saggi su Scienza e Metafisica(1983), Science and Scepticism (1984, Italian, Polish and Portugese translations); *Recreations* dinghy sailing; *Clubs* Salcombe Yacht; *Style*— Prof John Watkins, DSC; 11 Erskine Hill, London NW11 6HA (☎ 081 455 8813); LSE, Houghton St, London WC2A 2AE (☎ 071 405 7686, fax 071 242 0392)

WATKINS, Nowell St John; s of Josceline Charles Shaw Watkins (d 1974) and Anne Agnes St John Beddow, *née* Hickman; *b* 20 Aug 1930; *Educ* Haileybury; *m* 27 April 1957, Penelope Mary, da of James Herbert Harris, MC (d 1981), of Mayfield; 1 s (Timothy James b 16 May 1961), 1 da (Amanda Mary St John b 14 Jun 1959); *Career* admitted slr 1954, NP and ptnr in firm variously known as Steward Vulliamy and Watkins & Stewards 1960-86; sr ptnr Watkins Stewart & Ross 1986-; HM Coroner for Ipswich Dist of Suffolk, chm Ipswich Social Security Appeal Tribunal; *Recreations* cricket, racing, the garden; *Clubs* MCC; *Style*— Nowell Watkins, Esq; 8 Lower Brook St, Ipswich Suffolk, IP4 1AP (☎ 0473 226 266, fax 0473 230 052)

WATKINS, Paul Alexander; s of Robert Arthur Watkins (d 1980), and Doris Leah, *née* Starling; *b* 29 April 1949; *Educ* Sir Thomas Rich's GS Gloucester, Univ of Manchester (BA); *m* 1, 1970 (m dis 1980), V Swanson; 2 da (Rebecca Ursula b 13 March 1973, Rachel Louise b 20 Jan 1975); m 2, 2 April 1983, Candy Juliet, da of Maj Edward Michael Ling (d 1988); 1 da (Lucinda Elizabeth b 11 Sept 1985); *Career* mgmnt trainee Marks & Spencers 1970-71, md WM Robb Ltd (Robbs of Gloucester) 1984- (co dir 1971-84); memb RETRA trade orgn; FInstD; *Recreations* squash, golf; *Clubs* Old Patesians Cheltenham, Tewkesbury Park Glos, Lileybrook Golf Glos; *Style*— Paul Watkins, Esq; 13-15 Worcester St, Gloucester GL1 3AJ (☎ 0452 302531, car 0836 382342)

WATKINS, Peter Rodney; s of Frank Arthur Watkins (d 1990), of Seaton, Devon, and Mary Gwyneth, *née* Price; *b* 8 Oct 1931; *Educ* Solihull Sch, Emmanuel Coll Cambridge (MA); *m* 23 Aug 1971, Jillian Ann, da of Henry John Burge (d 1973); 2 da (Anna Mary b 1972, Katharine Ruth b 1975); *Career* Nat Serv flying offr RAF 1954-56; history master E Ham GS 1956-59, sixth form history master and house tutor Brentwood Sch Essex 1959-64, sr history master Bristol GS 1964-69; headmaster: King Edward's Five Ways Sch Birmingham 1969-74, Chichester HS for Boys 1974-79; princ Price's Sixth Form Coll Fareham Hants 1980-84, Sch Curriculum Devpt Ctee chief exec 1988 (dep chief exec 1984-88), Nat Curriculum Cncl dep chief exec 1988-; exec Secondary Heads Assoc 1980-84, chm Christian Educn Movement 1980-87, govr Bedales Sch Hants 1986-88, reader St Peter's Bishops Waltham; *Books* The Sixth Form College in Practice (1982), Modular Approaches to the Secondary Curriculum (1986); *Recreations* fell walking, local history, theology; *Clubs* Royal Cwlth Soc; *Style*— Peter R Watkins, Esq; 43 St Andrewgate, York YO1 2BR

WATKINS, Richard Valentine; *b* 23 Sept 1950; *Educ* Wellington, Loughborough Univ of Technol (BSc); *m* 1978, Charlotte, *née* de Laszlo; 2 s, 1 da; *Career* Phillips & Drew Inc 1972-77, mangr and overseas rep Kleinwort Benson 1977-83, md Phillips & Drew Inc (NY) 1983-86, pres Hoare Govett Inc (NY) 1986-88, chm Burns Fry Hoare Govett Inc (NY) 1988, exec dir J Henry Schroder Wagg & Co Ltd 1988-, also currently chief exec Schroder Securities Ltd and dir of related cos in SE Asia, Japan, Korea, Switzerland; *Recreations* skiing; *Clubs* Turf, Racquet (NY); *Style*— Richard Watkins, Esq

WATKINS, Roger Malcolm; s of Ronald Alan Watkins, of London, and Molly Elsie, *née* Bullen; *b* 15 Jan 1952; *Educ* Latymer Upper Sch, Emmanuel Coll Cambridge (MA), Westminster Med Sch Univ of London (MB MChir); *m* 4 April 1981, Mary Jane, da of Maj John Strelley, MBE, of Hereford; *Career* sr registrar in surgery Westminster Hosp London 1984-87, sr registrar and lectr in surgery Royal Marsden Hosp London 1987-88, conslt surgn Derriford Hosp Plymouth 1988-; memb: RSM, BMA, Br Assoc of Surgical Oncology, Surgical Res Assoc, Assoc of Surgns of GB; FRCS; *Books* Aids to Postgraduate Surgery (1989); *Style*— Roger Watkins, Esq; Bay Tree House, The Crescent, Crapstone Yelverton, Devon PL20 7PS (☎ 0822 852504); Derriford Hospital, Plymouth PL6 8DH (☎ 0752 792108)

WATKINS, Dr Sylivia Madeleine; da of Kenneth Harold Watkins (d 1938), of Manchester, and Irmgard, *née* Herrmann (d 1989); *b* 5 Feb 1938; *Educ* Loreto Coll Manchester, Lady Margaret Hall Oxford, St Bartholomew's Hosp London (MA, DM, BCh); *Career* house offr and sr house offr posts 1962-64, Wissenschaftliche Assistentin in neurology Univ of Heidelberg 1964-65, sr registrar in med Royal Free Hosp London 1965-73, conslt physician in med and oncology Lister Hosp Stevenage 1973-; chm N Herts Hospice Care Assoc, memb N Herts District Health Authy; FRCP 1980; *Recreations* playing the violin, theatre, concerts, opera, fell-walking, travel abroad; *Style*— Dr Sylvia Watkins; Stonlegh, 13 Priory Way, Hitchin, Herts SG4 9BJ; Lister Hospital, Stevenage, Herts (☎ 0438 314333)

WATKINS, Rt Hon Lord Justice; Rt Hon Sir Tasker Watkins; VC (1944), GBE (1990), DL (Glamorgan 1956), PC (1980); s of Bertram and Jane Watkins; *b* 18 Nov 1918; *Educ* Pontypridd GS; *m* 1941, Eirwen Evans; 1 s (decd), 1 da; *Career* WWII Maj Welch Regt; barr Middle Temple 1948, QC 1965, dep chm Carmarthenshire QS 1966-71, dep chm Radnor QS 1962-71; rec: Merthyr Tydfil 1968-70, Swansea 1970-71; high ct judge: Family Div 1971-74, Queen's Bench 1974-80; presiding judge Wales and Chester Circuit 1975-80 (ldr 1970-71), lord justice of Appeal 1980-, sr presiding judge England and Wales 1983-, dep chief justice 1988; chm Judicial Studies Bd 1979-80; chm Wales Region Mental Health Review Tribunal 1960-71; Hon LLD Wales 1979; kt 1971; *Style*— The Rt Hon Lord Justice Watkins, VC, GBE, DL; 5 Pump Court, Middle Temple, London EC4 (☎ 071 353 1993); Fairwater Lodge, Fairwater Rd, Llandaff, Glamorgan

WATKINS, William George; s of W H E Watkins, and A M Brown; *b* 29 Aug 1933; *Educ* King's Sch Canterbury, Univ Coll Oxford (MA); *m* Anne, *née* Roper; 3 s (David b 1966, James b 1971, John b 1971), 1 da (Emma b 1968); *Career* Nat Serv 2 Lt 40 Field Regt RA 1952-54; asst slr Slaughter and May 1960-69 (articled clerk 1957-60); Lovell White Durrant (formerly Durrant Piesse, previously Durrant Cooper and Hambling): joined 1969, ptnr 1970-; Liveryman City of London, memb City of London Solicitors Co; memb: Law Soc, Int Bar Assoc; *Recreations* awalking, industrial archaeology; *Style*— William Watkins, Esq; Bramshott Manor, Church Rd, Bramshott, Liphook, Hants GU30 7SQ; Lovell White Durrant, 65 Holborn Viaduct, London EC1A 2DY (☎ 071 236 0066, fax 071 248 4212)

WATKINS-PITCHFORD, Dr John; CB (1968); s of Wilfred Watkins-Pitchford (d 1952), and Olive Mary, *née* Beynon Nicholl (d 1960); *b* 20 April 1912; *Educ* Shrewsbury, St Thomas's Hosp (MB BS, MD, DPH, DIH, MRCS, LTCP); *m* 14 Aug 1945, (Elizabeth) Patricia, da of Hubert Wright (d 1959), of Guernsey; 1 s (Michael); *Career* Sqdn Ldr RAF 1939-46; chief med offr Miny Social Security, chief med advsr in Social Security Miny of Health; memb: Industl Injuries Advsy Cncl 1975-84, Cncl Chest Heart & Stroke Assoc; Queens Hon Physician 1971; *Recreations* gardening; *Style*— Dr John Watkins-Pitchford, CB; Hill House, Farley Lane, Westerham, Kent TN16 1UD (☎ 0959 64448)

WATKINSON, David Robert; s of late Robert Douglas Watkinson, of St Johns, Woking, Surrey, and Muriel Winifred, *née* Reeves; *b* 6 Oct 1947; *Educ* Woking GS for Boys, Clare Coll Cambridge (MA, LLB); *partner* Suzanne Eve Tarlin; 1 da (Eva Rose b 1 July 1980); *Career* called to the Bar Middle Temple 1972; fndr and memb barrs chambers Wellington St London 1974-88 (committed to working in social welfare areas of law), specialist in housing law; legal cases incl: Pulhofer v L B Hillingdon 1986 AC 484 (homeless persons), AG Securities v Vaughan 1989 2 WLR 689 (Rent Act 77 licence/tenancy distinction); memb: Exec Ctee Family Squatting Advsy Ctee 1972-75, N Islington Law Centre 1974-78, memb and legal advsr to campaign v criminal trespass laws 1974-78, occasional legal advsy Advsy Serv to Squatters 1975-, concerned in Publicity for campaign of limitation of rights of def in W Germany late 1970s, campaigned to extend grant of Legal Aid in particular magistrates ct 1979-80, memb Stop the Criminal Trespass Law Campaign 1983-84, teacher of housing law course Univ of Warwick 1984, observer on behalf of Haldane Soc for Socialist Lawyers and on behalf of Agric Allied Workers Branch Tport and Gen Workers Union at trial of agric day labourers in Spain 1986, lectures on legal aspects of Housing Bill S Bank Poly 1988; reviews and articles on housing 1974- (Legal Action Gp Bulletin, Roof, Law Soc's Gazette, Haldane Soc Bulletin-); memb: Haldane Soc Socialist Lawyers, Legal Action Gp, Admin Law Bar Assoc, Housing Law Practitioners Assoc, Industl Law Soc Nicaragua Solidarity Campaign; *Books* contrib: Law in a Housing Crisis (1975), NCCL Civil Rights Guide (1978), Squatting - The Real Story (1980); Squatting Trespass and Civil Liberties (jtly, 1976); *Recreations* travel, theatre, cinema, ethnic music, history, archaeology, fiction, being with daughter, swimming; *Style*— David Watkinson, Esq; 2 Garden Ct, Temple, London EC4 9BL (☎ 071 353 1633, fax 071 353 4621)

WATKINSON, 1 Viscount (UK 1964); Harold Arthur Watkinson; CH (1962), PC (1955); s of Arthur Watkinson; *b* 25 Jan 1910; *Educ* Queen's Coll Taunton, King's Coll London; *m* 1939, Vera, da of John Langmead; 2 da; *Heir* none; *Career* sits as Cons in House of Lords; MP (C) Woking 1950-64, min Tport and Civil Aviation 1955-59, min Def 1959-62; chm Cadbury Schweppes 1969-74, pres CBI 1976-77; *Books* Blueprint for Industrial Survival, Turning Points, The Mountain, Jewels and Old Shoes; *Recreations* sailing, walking; *Style*— The Rt Hon the Viscount Watkinson, CH, PC; Tyma House, Shore Rd, Bosham, nr Chichester, Sussex

WATKINSON, John Taylor; s of William Forshaw Watkinson (d 1963), of Bristol, and Muriel Beatrice, *née* Taylor (d 1979); *b* 25 Jan 1941; *Educ* Bristol GS, Worcester Coll Oxford (MA); *m* 29 Aug 1969, Jane Elizabeth, da of Ian Gerald Miller, of The Knoll, Stowe Nine Churches, Weedon, Northants; 2 s (Benjamin Harry b 11 March 1974, Harry John b 30 Oct 1975), 2 da (Anna Rose b 25 Dec 1979, Polly Rachel b 20 Sept 1982); *Career* schoolmaster: Repton 1964-66, Rugby 1966-71; barr 1971-86; MP (Lab) W Gloucs 1974-79, PPS Home Office 1976-79, memb Public Accounts Ctee 1976-79, memb cncl Europe and Western European Union 1976-79, rapporteur Legal Affairs Ctee 1978-79; reporter Money Programme BBC 1979-83, dir Interconnect Communications 1984-, slr 1986; *Books* UK Telecommunications Approvals Manual (jtly 1987); *Recreations* rackets, golf, squash; *Clubs* Jesters; *Style*— John Watkinson, Esq; Clanna Lodge, Alvington, Lydney, Glos GL15 6AJ (☎ 0594 530005); Watkinson & Co, Merlin House, Chepstow, Gwent (☎ 0291 627172)

WATKINSON, Leonard James; s of Leonard Watkinson (d 1966); *b* 27 June 1928; *Educ* W Leeds HS, Univ of Leeds (MSc, PhD); *m* 1957, Norma, *née* Schofield; 1 s, 2 da; *Career* tech dir Universal Ink Co Ltd 1960-64, dir of res W H Howson Ltd 1964-70, tech dir Howson-Algraphy Group of Vickers plc 1970-85, dir Wychem Ltd 1980-85; graphic arts conslt 1985-; CChem, FRSC; *Recreations* fell walking, photography, botany, choral music; *Style*— Leonard Watkinson, Esq; 95 Cookridge Lane, Leeds, LS16 7NE (☎ 0532 673853)

WATKINSON, Michael; s of Albert Watkinson, of Bolton, and Marian Watkinson; *b* 1 Aug 1961; *Educ* Rivington and Blacrod HS Horwich; *m* Susan; 1 da (Charlotte b 24 Feb 1989); *Career* professional cricketer; debut Lancashire CCC 1982-, awarded county cap 1987; honours: Benson & Hedges Cup 1984 and 1990, Refuge Assurance League 1989, Nat West Trophy 1990; structural engr; *Style*— Michael Watkinson, Esq; Lancashire CCC, Old Trafford, Manchester M16 OPX (☎ 061 848 7021)

WATKISS, Barbara Anne; *née* Needham; da of Ernest Needham (d 1984), and Gertrude Agnes, *née* Glover; *b* 19 Feb 1934; *Educ* St Albans Girls' GS, Bath Domestic Sci Coll, Univ of Bristol (Dip Teaching); *m* 31 March 1956, Christopher Robin Watkiss, s of Arthur Edwin Watkiss (d 1975), of Middlesborough; 1 s (Michael Christopher b 1957), 2 da (Susan Barbara (Mrs Attew) b 1960, Julia Anne (Mrs Wetton) b 1963); *Career* teacher Herts CC 1955-59; dir and co sec: Watkiss Studios Ltd 1959-, Watkiss Group Aviation Ltd 1971-, Multiplex Techniques Ltd 1972-, Multiplex Medway Ltd 1979-; md and co sec Watkiss Automation Ltd 1972-, ptnr Holme Grove Farm 1983-, md Franshams Ltd 1988-; chm: Competition Stallions International Ltd 1988-, NEBC Ltd 1988-; memb BFPMS; *Recreations* supporting equestrian competition, tennis, skiing; *Style*— Mrs Barbara Watkiss; Holme Grove House, Biggleswade, Beds SG18 9SS (☎ 0767 315 182); Holme Ct, Biggleswade, Beds SG18 9ST (☎ 0767 313 853, fax 0767 317 945, telex 826358)

WATKISS, Ronald Frederick; CBE (1981); s of Bertie Miles Watkiss (d 1943), of 71 Pentre St, Cardiff, and Isabella, *née* Blake (d 1966); *b* 21 May 1920; *Educ* Howard Gardens HS Cardiff; *m* 30 April 1941, Marion, da of Harry Preston (d 1976), of Fishguard Close, Cardiff; 1 s (Derek b 21 Jan 1943 d 1964), 1 da (Carolyn b 12 Oct 1955); *Career* TA, RCS 1938, served 1939-43, combined ops 1943-46, Sgt; md Lloyd and Watkiss Ltd 1950-86; pres: Cardiff Credit Traders Assoc 1953-54 and 1963-64, Heath Community Assoc (Cardiff) 1982- (chm 1970-72); vice chm Cardiff 94 Cwlth Games Ctee 1985-88, memb People and Work Unit 1988; Cardiff City Cncl: cncllr 1960, alderman 1967-74, re-elected cncllr 1973, cncl leader 1976-79 and 1983-87, ldr Cons Party 1974-, dep chm Assoc of Dist Cncls 1990- (vice chm 1989-90) hon fell Univ Coll of Cardiff 1986; Queen's Silver Jubilee Medal 1977; *Recreations* all forms of sport (spectator only now); *Clubs* Victory Services; *Style*— Ronald Watkiss, Esq, CBE; 69 King George V Drive, Heath, Cardiff CF4 4EF (☎ 0222 752 716, fax 0222 747 184)

WATLING, His Hon Judge (David) Brian Watling; QC (1979); s of Vernon Watling and Edith, *née* Ridley; *b* 18 June 1935; *Educ* Charterhouse, King's Coll London; *m* 1964, Noelle Bugden, WRNS; *Career* barr 1957, Crown Ct recorder 1979-81, Circuit judge (SE) 1981-, visiting prof law Univ Coll Buckingham 1980; *Style*— His Hon Judge Watling, QC; Queen Elizabeth Building, Temple, EC4 (☎ 071 353 6453)

WATMORE, Leslie John; s of Arthur Watmore (d 1962), of London, and Edith Alice, *née* Giles (d 1986); *b* 8 May 1929; *Educ* St Olave's GS, Keble Coll Oxford (MA); *m* 19 Dec 1953, Iris Daphne, da of Charles William Enever (d 1981), of London; 2 s (Stephen Charles b 26 Nov 1954, David Anthony b 22 Oct 1960); *Career* admitted slr 1957; ptnr L Bingham and Co 1959-76, sr ptnr L Watmore and Co 1976-; chm Legal Aid Area 1981-84; former capt and chm W Kent GC; Freeman City of London, Liveryman Worshipful Co of Slrs 1966; memb Law Soc; *Recreations* golf, hill walking; *Clubs* RAC, City Livery, Cordwainer Ward, West Kent Golf; *Style*— Leslie Watmore, Esq; Tudor Cottage, 10 Downs Hill, Beckenham, Kent (☎ 081 650 4807); L Watmore and Co, Chancery House, 53/66 Chancery Lane, London WC2A 1QU (☎ 071 430 1512, fax 071 405 7382)

WATNEY, (John) Adrain; s of Maj John Douglas Watney, RA (d 1988), of Dorking, Surrey, and Barbara Ann, *née* Smith; *b* 3 Oct 1943; *Educ* Sherborne; *m* 9 Sept 1967, Angela Winifred, da of Dudley Partridge, of Horsley Surrey (d 1982); 1 s (Christopher b 1981), 3 da (Katherine b 1970, Sarah b 1972, Victoria b 1976); *Career* admitted slr 1968; currently ptnr Mason; Freeman: City of London 1964, Worshipful Co Mercers; memb Law Soc; *Recreations* golf, cricket, rugby, opera; *Clubs* Royal and Ancient Golf St Andrews, MCC, Rye Golf, Waton Heath Golf, Working Golf; *Style*— Adrain Watney, Esq; 11/118 Chancery Lane, London WC2A 1PP (☎ 071 583 9990, fax 071 831 4220, telex 8811117 MASONSG

WATNEY, Lady Katherine Felicity; *née* Courtenay; da of 17 Earl of Devon; *b* 1940; *m* 1966, Antony Stephen Pope Watney (d 1986); 1 s; *Style*— Lady Katherine Watney; 1 Playhatch Cottages, Playhatch, nr Reading RG4 9QX

WATSON *see also*: Inglefield-Watson, Milne-Watson

WATSON, Dr Adam; s of Adam Watson, of 10 Hanover Court, Banchory, Kincardineshire, and Margaret Isabella Spence, *née* Rae; *b* 14 April 1930; *Educ* Turriff Acad, Univ of Aberdeen (BSc, PhD, DSc); *m* 19 March 1955, Jenny Mortimer, *née* Sutherland; 1 s (Adam Christopher b 7 Oct 1963), 1 da (Jenny b 13 July 1958); *Career* demonstrator in biological sciences McGill Univ Montreal 1952-53, teacher of sci Aberdeen Acad 1956-57, sr res fell Univ of Aberdeen 1957-60 (asst lectr Dept of Natural History 1953-56), princ scientific offr Nature Conservancy and offr in charge Mountain and Moorland Res Station 1966-71, sr princ scientific offr Inst of Terrestrial Ecology Banchory 1971-90; Neill prize of RSE 1983-85; CBiol, fell Arctic Inst of N America, FRSE, FIBIOL; *Books* Animal Populations in Relation to their Food Resources (ed, 1970), The Cairngorms (1975), The Cairngorms (with D Nethersole-Thompson, 1981), The Place Names of Upper Deeside (1984); *Recreations* hill walking, mountaineering, cross-country skiing; *Clubs* Scot Mountaineering, Scot Ornithologists; *Style*— Dr Adam Watson, FRSE; Clachnaben, Crathes, Banchory, Kincardineshire AB31 3JE (☎ 033 044 609); c/o Institute of Terrestrial Ecology, Hill of Brathens, Glassel, Banchory, Kincardineshire AB31 4BY (☎ 033 02 3434)

WATSON, Alan Carlos; s of William Carlos Watson (d 1990), and Doris May, *née* Putwain; *b* 26 Oct 1940; *Educ* Willesden Tech Coll (HNC); *m* 12 Sept 1964, Sandra Mary, da of John Bruce Gorner; 1 s (Ashley b 8 April 1966), 1 da (Martine b 11 Dec 1968); *Career* student apprentice Matthew Hall Mechanical Services Ltd, resident engr Dungeness Nuclear Power Station A, conslt mechanical and electrical engr working on town centre devpts and hosps 1965-, joined Building Design Partnership 1972 (projects incl: Esso Messmoran Facilities bldgs, Falklands installations, town centres, commercial bldgs), ptnr BDP 1988- (projects incl: Channel Tunnel UK Terminal Infrastructure Works, Theatre at High Wycombe); expert witness for Select Ctee Channel Tunnel Hybrid Bill; FIWEM; *Recreations* sportsmen; *Style*— Alan Watson, Esq; 17 Silver Close, Harrow, Middlesex HA3 6JT; Building Design Partnership, 16 Gresse St, London W1A 4WD (☎ 071 631 4733, fax 071 631 0393)

WATSON, Alan John; CBE (1985); s of Rev John William Watson (d 1980), of Bognor Regis, and Edna Mary, *née* Peters (d 1985); *b* 3 Feb 1941; *Educ* Kingswood Sch Bath, Jesus Coll Cambridge (MA); *m* 1965, Karen, da of Hartwig Lederer (d 1966), of Frankfurt-on-Main; 2 s (Stephen b 1966, Martin b 1968); *Career* history scholar and res asst to Regius Prof of Modern History Cambridge 1962-64; broadcaster: presenter of The Money Programme BBC 2 and Panorama BBC 1 1964-76, head of radio & TV EEC Cmmn 1976-80, presenter You and 92 BBC1; chief exec Charles Barker City Ltd 1980-83, dep chm Sterling PR Ltd 1985-86; chm: City and Corp Cncl Ltd 1987-, Corp Vision Ltd 1989-; dir Threadneedle Publishing Ltd, pres Lib Pty 1984-85, govr Kingswood Sch 1984-90; memb: UNICEF Exec Bd 1985-, Jesus Coll Cambridge Soc Exec 1987, Royal TV Soc Cncl, Anglo-German Assoc Exec; chm: Bd of Govrs Westminster Coll Oxford 1988-, Richmond Theatre Appeal 1990-; visiting fell Louvarvian Business Sch 1990-; visiting prof Louvain Univ of Belgium 1990-; *Books* Europe at Risk (1974); *Recreations* travel, wines, theatre; *Clubs* Brooks's, RAC, Oxford and Cambridge, Kennel; *Style*— Alan Watson, Esq, CBE; Cholmondeley House, 3 Cholmondeley Walk, Richmond, Surrey; Somerset Lodge, Nunney, Somerset

WATSON, Alexander Stuart; s of William Alexander Stuart Watson of Shanghai (d 1960), and Frances Dorothy, *née* Hawes (d 1963); *b* 16 July 1920; *Educ* Worksop Coll, Notts Coll of Aeronautical Engrg Chelsea; *m* 1949, Jean Patricia, da of Capt Charles Geoffrey Kerswell; 1 s (Roderick), 2 da (Katie, Fiona); *Career* Lt (A) RNVR 1942-46; sales dir: Hawker Siddeley Aviation Ltd 1972-77, Dowty-Rotol Ltd 1962-72; dir: Dowty Exports Ltd, Bolton Paul Aircraft Ltd; pres and chm Hawker Siddeley Aviation Inc; mktg dir (Aircraft) Br Aerospace plc 1977-82, conslt aeronautical engr 1982-; *Recreations* sailing (yacht 'Kit V'); *Clubs* Royal Motor Yacht (Poole); *Style*— Alexander Watson, Esq; Saxon Hill, South Cadbury, Somerset (☎ 0963 40516)

WATSON, Prof (George) Alistair; s of George Arthur Watson (d 1972), and Grace Anne, *née* MacDonald; *b* 30 Sept 1942; *Educ* Breadalbane Acad, Univ of Edinburgh (BSc, MSc), Australian Nat Univ (PhD); *m* 6 April 1971, (Margaret) Hilary, da of Robert Whitton Mackay (d 1971); 1 da (Kirsty b 1989); *Career* prof Univ of Dundee 1988- (lectr 1970-82, sr lectr 1982-84, reader 1984-88); FIMA 1972; *Books* Computational Methods for Matrix Eigenproblems (with A R Gourlay, 1973), Approximation Theory and Numerical Methods (1980); *Recreations* opera, photography, gardening; *Style*— Prof Alistair Watson; 7 Albany Rd, Broughty Ferry, Dundee DD5 1PN, Scotland (☎ 0382 79473); Dept of Mathematics and Computer Science, University of Dundee, Dundee DD1 4HN, Scotland (☎ 0382 23181)

WATSON, Sir (James) Andrew; 5 Bt (UK 1866), of Henrietta Street, Cavendish Sq, St Marylebone, Co Middx; s of Sir Thomas Watson, 4 Bt (d 1941), and Ella, Lady Watson, *qv*; *b* 30 Dec 1937; *Educ* Eton; *m* 1965, Christabel Mary, da of Kenneth Ralph Malcolm Carlisle; 2 s, 1 da; *Heir* s, Roland Victor Watson; *Career* Lt Life Gds; barr; recorder of Crown Court; *Style*— Sir Andrew Watson, Bt; Talton House, Newbold-on-Stour, Stratford-on-Avon, Warwicks

WATSON, Maj-Gen Andrew Linton; CB (1981); s of Col William Linton Watson, OBE (d 1961), of Bridge of Allan, and Dorothy Ellen, *née* Lea (d 1950); *b* 9 April 1927; *Educ* Wellington; *m* 23 Feb 1952, Mary Elizabeth (Ginty), da of Albert S Rigby (d 1965), of Edina, Warren Point, Co Down; 2 s (Alastair Alexander Linton b 15 Feb 1953, Patrick Adrian Richard John b 4 April 1955), 1 da (Shane Elizabeth Annabel b 2 Aug 1960); *Career* cmmnd Black Watch 1946; 1 and 2 Bns served: UK, Germany, Cyprus, Br Guyana, UN Force Cyprus; Staff Coll 1958, Jt Servs Staff Coll 1964, GSO1 HQ 17 Div Malaya Dist 1966-68; cmd 1 Bn Black Watch 1969-71: Malaya, UK, Gibraltar, NI; Royal Coll Def Studies 1974, cdr Br Army Staff and mil attaché Washington DC 1975-77, GOC Eastern Dist 1977-80, chief of staff Allied Forces Northern Europe 1980-82, Col The Black Watch 1981-; chm Inner London Branch Army Benevolent Fund 1983-, Lt govr Royal Hosp Chelsea 1984-; *Recreations* tennis, walking; *Clubs* Army and Navy, Highland Brigade; *Style*— Maj-Gen Andrew Watson, CB; Lieutenant-Governor's House, Royal Hospital, Chelsea, London SW3 4SL (☎ 071 730 0161, fax 071 823 6871)

WATSON, Dr (Nicholas) Andrew; s of Phillip Charles Watson, of 2 Station New Rd, Brundall, Norwich, and Venetia Madeline Le Poer, *née* Wyon; *b* 25 Aug 1952; *Educ* Boston GS, Univ of Nottingham Med Sch (BMedSci, MB BS, Dip Child Health); *m* 18 Nov 1977, Elaine Alma, da of late Jack Attack; 1 s (Edward Phillip b 29 Oct 1984), 1 da (Helen Ruth b 5 Jan 1983); *Career* jr house offr Derby Royal Infirmary and Nottingham City Hosp 1975-76; sr house offr in Depts of: Geriatric Med City Hosp 1976-77, Med City Hosp Feb 1977 - July 1977, Traumatology Queens Med Centre Feb 1978 - July 1978, Paediatrics Queens Med Centre 1978-79; postgrad traineeship in gen practice Nottingham 1977-78 and Feb 1979 - July 1979; princ in gen practice Keyworth 1979-82, specialist in orthopaedic med 1982-; lectr in USA and UK with Soc of Orthopaedic Med 1982-; author of numerous published papers letters and articles on orthopaedic med; chm Soc of Orthopaedic Med 1988 (elected to Cncl 1982); MRCGP 1979, fell Soc of Orthopaedic Med 1982 (memb 1981); *Recreations* music (has played piano, viola, mandolin and crumhorn), plays jazz guitar in a jazz band; *Style*— Dr Andrew Watson; 10 Golf Course Rd, Stanton on the Wolds, Notts NG12 5BH (☎ 06077 3603); 32 Wimpole St, London W1M 7AE (☎ 071 486 2160)

WATSON, Andrew Stewart; s of Leslie Donald Watson, of Malvern, Worcestershire, and Joan Beatrice, *née* Everton; *b* 29 March 1950; *Educ* King's Sch Worcester, St John's Coll Oxford; *m* 11 Dec 1976, Lea Karin, da of Eino Arvid Nordberg (d 1963); *Career* admitted slr 1975; Thomson Snell and Passmore: articled clerk 1973, ptnr 1981, head Litigation Dept 1986; memb: Legal Aid Area Ctee 1986, Local Advsy Ctee Headway Gp, Law Soc; *Recreations* running, reading, music, cooking; *Clubs* Tunbridge Wells Runners (chm); *Style*— Andrew Watson, Esq; 3 Lonsdale Gardens, Tunbridge Wells, Kent TN1 1NX (☎ 0892 510000)

WATSON, Anthony; s of Lt Cdr Andrew Patrick Watson, RNR, and Harriet, *née* Hewardine (d 1981); *b* 1 April 1945; *Educ* Campbell Coll Belfast, Queen's Univ Belfast (BSc); *m* 29 July 1972, Heather Jane, da of Lt Cdr Wilfred Norman Dye, RNR (d 1988); 2 s (Edward b 1975, Tom b 1976), 1 da (Tilly b 1980); *Career* barr Lincoln's Inn; dir: Touche Remnant & Co 1978-85, Touche Remnant Hldgs 1978-85; chief investmt offr Citibank NA 1985; chm: Citifunds Ltd 1985-, Citicare Ltd 1985-; played for London Irish RFC first XV 1967-68; AMSIA 1971; *Clubs* RAC; *Style*— Anthony Watson, Esq

WATSON, Anthony Gerard (Tony); s of George Maurice Watson, JP, of Market Deeping, Lincs, and Anne, *née* McDonnell; *b* 28 May 1955; *Educ* St John Fisher Peterborough, North Staffs Poly (BA); *m* 17 Sept 1982, Susan Ann, da of Malcolm Gutteridge, of Stockton on Tees; 2 s (Samuel John b 3 Sept 1983, Tom b 10 Jan 1985), 2 da (Melissa Jane b 12 Feb 1977, Emily Anne b 7 Feb 1987); *Career* reporter Stamford Mercury 1978-79, news ed Evening Despatch Darlington 1983-84 (reporter 1979-81); Yorkshire Post: reporter 1984-86 dep ed 1988-89, ed 1989-, res World in Action Granada TV 1986-88; awarded Br Press Awards 1986 and 1987, YTV Journalist of the Year 1986; memb Guild of Editors; *Style*— Tony Watson, Esq; The Yorkshire Post, Wellington St, Leeds LS1 1RF (☎ 0532 432701, fax 443430, telex 55245, car 0860 484016)

WATSON, Antony Edward Douglas; QC (1986); s of William Edward Watson, of Hanchurch, Staffs, and Margaret Douglas; *b* 6 March 1945; *Educ* Sedbergh, Sidney Sussex Coll Cambridge (MA); *m* 15 Sept 1972, Gillian Mary, da of Alfred John Bevan-Arthur, of Bramishall, Staffs; 2 da (Edwina b 1978, Willa b 1981); *Career* 2LT Staffs Yeomanry (TA) 1964-67; called to the Bar Inner Temple 1968; specialising in Intellectual Property Law; *Recreations* country pursuits, wine, opera; *Style*— Antony Watson, Esq, QC; 6 Pump Court, Temple, London EC4 (☎ 071 353 8588)

WATSON, Arthur James; s of David Lyall Watson, of Aberdeen, and Nance Harding, *née* Nicol; *b* 24 June 1951; *Educ* Aberdeen GS, Grays Sch of Art Aberdeen (Dip Art); *m* 1, 1972 (m dis 1980), Jennifer Moncrieff Sutherland; m 2, 1981 (m dis 1989), Joyce Winifred Cairns; *Career* sculptor and artist; dir Peacock Printmakers 1974-, visiting lectr Duncan of Jordanstone Coll of Art 1988-; maj works incl: sculptures Sea Sign, Northern Light at Peterhead Power Station Boddam 1986, Across The Sea at the Venice Biennale 1990, A New Light Univ of Aberdeen 1991; recordings incl: Beware of the Aberdonian (1976), The Fighting Scot (1991); ARSA; *Style*— Arthur Watson, Esq; 16 Pilot Square, Aberdeen (☎ 0224 580298); Peacock Printmakers, 21 Castle St, Aberdeen AB1 1AJ (☎ 0224 639539)

WATSON, Lady; Beryl; da of Alfred Norris; *m* 1, Sqdn Ldr Basil Davis, RAF (decd); m 2, 1968 (m dis 1973), Sir Frances Cyril Rose, 4 Bt (d 1979); m 3, 1974, Sir Norman James Watson, 2 Bt (d 1983, when title became extinct); *Style*— Lady Watson; Flat 132, 55 Park Lane, London W1

WATSON, Bruce Dunstan; s of James Harvey Watson, and Edith Mary, *née* Crawford; *b* 1 Aug 1928; *Educ* Toowoomba GS, Univ of Queensland (BSc); *m* 18 Dec 1952, June, da of Harry Woolston Kilgour; 1 s (Timothy), 2 da (Sally, Jenny); *Career* engr Tasmanian Hydroelectricity Cmmn and Townsville Electricity Bd 1950-56, design engr and dep chief engr Copper Refineries Pty Ltd 1956-70; MIM Hldgs Ltd: gp industl rels mangr 1973-75, exec dir coal ops and ht ventures 1977-80, md 1980-81, chief exec offr 1981-83, chm and chief exec offr 1983-; gen mangr Agnew Nickel Mine 1975-77; memb: Business Cncl of Aust, Australasian Inst of Mining and Metallurgy, cncl Aust Mgmnt Coll; FIE, FAIM; kt 1985; *Recreations* golf; *Clubs* Brisbane, Queensland, Lions; *Style—* Sir Bruce Watson; MIM Holdings Limited, 410 Ann St, Brisbane, Queensland 4000, Australia (☎ 010 61 7 833 8000, fax 61 7 832 2426, telex AA40160)

WATSON, Brig Bruce Edmeston; s of Prof Herbert Edmeston Watson (d 1980), and Margaret Kathleen, *née* Rowson (d 1952); *b* 5 April 1918; *Educ* Marlborough, UCL; *m* 1941, Joan Elizabeth, da of William Moore (d 1950); 1 s (Andrew), 2 da (Susan, Gillian); *Career* served RA 1939-73; dep dir Inspectorate of Armaments 1967-70, dir Heavy Weapons Projects 1970-73, dir FN(Eng) Ltd 1973-85; tstee Keston Village Hall 1974-; FBIM 1980 (MBIM 1969); *Recreations* photography, gardening; *Style—* Brig B E Watson; Chestnut Cottage, 12 Longdon Wood, Keston Park, Kent BR2 6EW (☎ 0689 852619)

WATSON, Hon Mrs (Catriona Mary Antonia); yr da of Baron Swann (Life Peer, d 1990), and Teresa Ann, *née* Gleadowe; *b* 15 March 1953; *Educ* St George's Sch for Girls Edinburgh, N of Scotland Coll of Agric; *m* 1976, Robert Noble Watson, s of Robert John Watson; 1 s (Jamie), 1 da (Tessa); *Career* farmer; *Recreations* riding, sailing, skiing, gardening; *Style—* The Hon Mrs Watson; Ballingall Farm, Leslie, Fife (☎ 0592 742963)

WATSON, Christopher John; s of Allan John Watson (d 1965), of Uxbridge, and Dorothy C, *née* Perry; *b* 21 June 1940; *Educ* Leighton Park Sch, Univ of Bristol (BA); *m* 20 July 1963, (Sheila) Mary, da of Andrew Warden Vincent (d 1986), of Hereford; 2 s (Angus b 1969, Peter b 1972), 1 da (Clare b 1967); *Career* King's Coll Univ of London 1962-63, Northumberland CC 1963-65, Univ of Sussex 1966-68, res offr Scottish Devpt Dept 1968-72; Univ of Birmingham Centre for Urban and Regional Studies: res fell 1972-79, lectr 1979-83, sr lectr 1983-, head of dept 1988-, dir int affrs 1987-; memb Ctee Mercian Housing Assoc Ltd; *Books* Housing in Clydeside 1970 (with JB Cullingworth, 1971), Housing Policy and the Housing System (with Alan Murie and Pat Niner, 1975), contrib to various books and jls; *Recreations* music, travel; *Style—* Christopher Watson, Esq; Centre for Urban and Regional Studies, The Univ of Birmingham, Edgbaston, Birmingham B15 2TT (☎ 021 414 5018, fax 021 414 4989, telex 333762 UOBHAM G)

WATSON, David Saxton; s of Alfred Ralph Cecil Watson, of Windlesham, and Marion Joy, *née* Saxton (d 1967); *b* 16 April 1942; *Educ* Stowe, Univ of St Andrews; *m* 1, 29 Sept 1965 (m dis), Victoria Jane, da of Rodney Sykes; 1 s (James Daniel b 29 May 1971), 1 da (Juliet Natasha b 4 March 1968); m 2, 22 Dec 1990, Helen, da of Harry Fogarty; *Career* trainee then CA Safferys 1962-70, ptnr (responsible for training) Safferys Champness 1970-; vice chm City Dist Training Bd ICA; FCA; *Recreations* flying (private pilots licence), golf, skiing; *Clubs* West London Aero, Richmond Golf; *Style—* David Watson, Esq; Saffery Champness, Fairfax House, Fulwood Place, Gray's Inn, London WC1V 6UB (☎ 071 405 2828, fax 071 405 7887, telex 889108 RYSAF G)

WATSON, Prof Douglas Hugh; s of Joun Douglas Drummond Watson (d 1975), of Drymen, and Marion Allison, *née* Smellie; *b* 20 Nov 1931; *Educ* King Edward VII Sheffield, HS of Stirling, Univ of Glasgow, (BSc, PhD); *m* 2 Sept 1959 (m dis 1984), Dolina Munro; 1 s (Donald John b 20 June 1960), 1 da (Shirley Anne b 9 March 1965); *Career* Univ of Glasgow: asst lectr chem 1953-57, ICI fell chem 1957-60, MRC experimental virus unit 1960-64; Univ of Birmingham: sr res fell dept of virology 1964-67, sr lectr 1967-69; Univ of Leeds: prof reader dept of microbiology 1972-, dean of staff 1989-; ed in chief Jl of Gen Virology 1971-75; treas soc for Gen Microbiology 1980-87; FI biol 1972; *Style—* Prof Douglas Watson; Dept of Microbiology Univ of Leeds, Leeds LS2 9JT (☎ 0532 335647)

WATSON, Duncan Amos; CBE (1986); s of Duncan Watson (d 1980), of Sheffield, and Sybil Watson (d 1984); *b* 10 May 1926; *Educ* Worcester Coll for the Blind, St Edmund Hall Oxford (BA); *m* 2 June 1954, Mercia Margaret, da of Gilbert S Casey (d 1963), of Auckland, NZ; *Career* Slrs Dept Treasy 1957-86, ret as princ asst treasy slr; chm Exec Cncl Royal Nat Inst for the Blind 1975-90, pres World Blind Union 1988-, chm Access Ctee for England 1989; *Recreations* reading, listening to music; *Clubs* Reform, MCC; *Style—* Duncan Watson, Esq, CBE; 19 Great Russell Mansions, 60 Great Russell St, London, WC1B 3BE (☎ 071 242 7284)

WATSON, Sir (Noel) Duncan; KCMG (1967, CMG 1960); s of Harry Watson, of Bradford, Yorks; *b* 16 Dec 1915; *Educ* Bradford GS, New Coll Oxford; *m* 1951, Aileen (d 1980), da of Charles Bell, of Dublin; *Career* Colonial Admin Serv: admin offr Cyprus 1938-43, asst colonial sec Trinidad 1943-45; seconded to Colonial Office 1946, princ private sec to Sec State Colonies 1947-50, asst sec Colonial Office 1950-62, under sec Central Africa Office 1963, asst under sec Colonial Office & CRO 1964-67; transfered to HM Diplomatic Serv 1965-; political advsr to C-in-C Far East 1967-70, high cmmr Malta 1970-72, dep under sec FCO 1972-75; ret HM Dip Serv 1975; dep chm Central Cncl of Royal Cwlth Soc 1983-87 (vice pres 1987); *Style—* Sir Duncan Watson, KCMG; Sconce, Steels Lane, Oxshott, Surrey

WATSON, Edward Howsley; CB (1968); s of Ernest Watson (d 1945); *b* 16 June 1910; *Educ* Harrogate GS, Univ of Leeds (LLB); *m* 1951, Alice Mary, *née* Atkinson; 1 s; *Career* WWII Serv RA Maj; joined Miny of Health 1946; slr and legal advsr: Miny of Health 1965-68, Miny of Housing and Local Govt 1965-70; *Style—* Edward Watson, Esq, CB; 10 The Terrace, Hales Place, Canterbury, Kent CT2 7AJ (☎ 0227 450 978)

WATSON, Ella, Lady; Ella Marguerite; da of Sir George Farrar, DSO, 1 and last Bt (d 1915); sis of Viscountess Lowther m of 7 Earl of Lonsdale; *m* 1935, Sir Thomas Watson, 4 Bt (ka 1941); 1 s (5 Bt); *Style—* Ella, Lady Watson; Talton Lodge, Newbold-on-Stour, Stratford-on-Avon, Warwicks

WATSON, Sir Francis John Bagott; KCVO (1973, CVO 1965, MVO 1959); s of Hugh Watson, and Helen Marian, *née* Bagott; *b* 24 Aug 1907; *Educ* Shrewsbury, St John's Coll Cambridge (BA); *m* 1941, Mary Rosalie Gray (d 1969), da of George Strong; 1 adopted s; *Career* dir Wallace Collection 1963-74 (asst keeper and dep dir 1938-63), surveyor Queen's Works of Art 1963-72 (dep 1947-63), advsr Works of Art 1972-, tstee Whitechapel Art Gallery, Slade prof of fine art Oxford 1969-70, Wrightsman prof NY Univ 1970-71, Kress prof Nat Gallery Washington DC 1975-76, visiting lectr Univ of California 1970; FBA, FSA; *Books* Canaletto (1947), Wallace Collection Catalogue of Furniture (1956), Louis XVI Furniture (1959), Gt Family Collections (1965), The Guardi Family of Painters (1966), Tiepolo (1966), The Wrightsman Collection Catalogue (5 Vols 1966-70), Fragonard (1967), Systematic Catalogue of 17th and 18th Century French Furniture Nat Gallery of Washington DC 1989, numerous contribs to learned jls; *Style—* Sir Francis Watson, KCVO, FSA; West Farm House, Corton, Wilts BA12 0SY

WATSON, Rear Adm (John) Garth; CB (1965); el s of Alexander Henry St Croix Watson (d 1963), and Gladys Margaret, *née* Payne; *b* 20 Feb 1914; *Educ* UCS, Northampton Engrg Coll, Univ of London; *m* 1943, Barbara Elizabeth, da of Cecil Hugh Falloon (d 1959), of Moor Park, Middx; 2 s (John, Peter), 1 da (Jane); *Career* served WWII, Br Jt Servs Mission Washington 1945-48, Admty 1948-50, 5 Destroyer Sqdn 1950-53, fleet electrical offr Staff of C in C Home Fleet 1955-57, HM Dockyard Gibraltar 1957-60, asst dir electrical engrg Admty 1960-63, Adm Supt HM Dockyard Rosyth 1963-66, ADC to HM The Queen 1962; md Thomas Telford Ltd 1971-79, chm Inst of Civil Engrs Queens Jubilee Scholarship Tst 1980-85, vice chm Civil Engrs Club 1980-86; Hon DSc City Univ 1984; Freeman City of London 1986, Liveryman Worshipful Co of Engrs 1986; *Books* The Civils (1987), The Smeatonians (1989), contrib to Encyclopaedia Britannica 15 Edn (1974); *Recreations* sailing, gardening; *Clubs* Athenaeum, Royal Thames Yacht, Royal Naval & Royal Albert Yacht; *Style—* Rear Adm Garth Watson, CB; Little Hall Court, Shedfield, nr Southampton, Hants (☎ 0329 833216)

WATSON, (Angus) Gavin; s of late Herbert Edward Watson, of Carlisle, and Marjorie, *née* Reid; *b* 14 April 1944; *Educ* Carlisle GS, Merton Coll Oxford, Peterhouse Cambridge; *m* 29 April 1967 (m dis 1991), Susan Naomi, da of Eric Beal, of Manchester; 2 s (Matthew b 1974, Nicholas b 1980); *Career* DOE: joined 1971, princ 1974, Sec of State's Private Office 1975-78, asst sec 1979, under sec 1986-; chm Environment and Tport Branch Assoc of First Div Civil Servants 1983-85; hon fell Inst of Bldg Control 1987; *Recreations* fell walking, looking at buildings, industrial archaeology; *Style—* Gavin Watson, Esq; Department of the Environment, 2 Marsham St, London SW1 (☎ 071 276 3467)

WATSON, George Menzies; s of William George Watson; *b* 15 July 1941; *Educ* Barnard Castle Sch; *m* 1969, Irene, da of Albert Johnson; 1 s, 1 da; *Career* fin dir and co sec Wailes Dove Bitumastic plc; proprietor C and G Model Railways; FCA; *Recreations* golf, photography, railways; *Style—* George Watson, Esq; Avenue House, High Shincliffe, Co Durham DH1 2PY (☎ 091 384 2143)

WATSON, Gerald Walter; s of Reginald Harold Watson (d 1970), and Gertrude Hilda, *née* Ruffell (d 1979); *b* 13 Dec 1934; *Educ* King Edward VI Norwich Sch, CCC Cambridge (MA); *m* 30 Dec 1961, Janet Rosemary, da of Benjamin Henry Hovey (d 1954); 1 s (Rupert b 1968), 2 da (Candida b 1966, Meriel b 1971); *Career* Pilot Offr RAF 1953-55; W O 1958-64, MOD 1964-69; Civil Serv Dept 1969-73 (and 1975-81), NI office 1973-75, HM Treasy 1981-86; dir: Central Computer and Telecommunications Agency 1978-82, Bank of England 1983, dep chm Bldg Socs Cmmn 1986-88; ptnr Arthur Young 1989, ptnr Ernst & Young 1989-; FBCS 1980; *Recreations* opera, theatre, equestrian sports; *Style—* Gerald Watson, Esq; Ernst & Young, Rolls House, Fetter Lane, London EC4A 1NH

WATSON, Graham Forgie; s of George William Forgie Watson (d 1982), and Margaret Kinlay, *née* Hogg (d 1983); *b* 14 Jan 1958; *Educ* George Heriot's Sch Edinburgh, Univ of Edinburgh (LLB); *m* 3 May 1983, (Elspeth) Margaret, da of Alexander Brewster (d 1983); 1 da (Rebecca b 1989); *Career* CA 1982; KPMG Peat Marwick McLintock 1979-83; Noble Grossart Ltd: exec 1984-86, asst dir 1986-87, dir 1987-; *Recreations* golf, squash, skiing; *Clubs* New, Bruntisfield Links Golf, Golf House Club Elie; *Style—* Graham F Watson, Esq; Noble Grossart Ltd, 48 Queen St, Edinburgh EH2 3NR (☎ 031 226 7011, fax 031 226 6032)

WATSON, Dr (James) Graham; s of C Watson, of Kirkcudbright, and Eudora Watson; *b* 4 Aug 1945; *Educ* George Watson's Coll Edinburgh, Univ of Edinburgh (MD, BSc, DCH); *m* 20 June 1981, (Ann) Jeniffer, da of William Edward Meyers, of Harrow; *Career* MO Zambia Flying Dr Serv 1969, sr lectr paediatrics Royal Free Hosp 1981-83, conslt paediatrician Newcastle upon Tyne 1983-; FRCP, FRCPE; memb: Br Soc of Immunology, Br Paediatric Assoc; *Recreations* Munro bagging; *Style—* Dr Graham Watson; 28 Oaklands, Gosforth, Newcastle upon Tyne; Newcastle Gen Hosp, Dept of Child Health, Westgate Rd, Newcastle upon Tyne (☎ 091 273 8811)

WATSON, Hamish; TD (1966); s of John Thomas Richardson Watson (d 1966), of Edinburgh, and Annie Ewing, *née* Spence (d 1961); *b* 26 June 1923; *Educ* George Watson's Coll, Univ of Edinburgh (MB ChB, MD, MRCPEd, MRCP); *m* 8 Feb 1951, Lesley Leigh Dick, da of Andrew Dick Wood (d 1976), of Edinburgh; 1 s (Michael b 1955 d 1956), 2 da (Penny b 1953, Jillian b 1957); *Career* RAMC: War Emergency Cmmn 1946-48, Garrison MO Northern Dist Nigeria Br W Africa, Regtl MO 1 Bn Nigeria Regt, TA Cmmn 1952, Regtl MO Scottish Horse RAC (TA) 1952-57, sr med specialist 1955-78, Regtl MO Fife and Forfar Yeo/Scottish Horse RAC (TA) 1957-67, RARO 1967-78; conslt physician and cardilogist i/c Dept of Cardiology Dundee Teaching Hosps 1964-85, head of cardiology and sr lectr in Dept of Med Univ of Dundee 1964-85, postgrad dean and dir postgrad med educn Faculty of Med and Dentistry 1970-85; RCPEd: tstee 1973-, memb Cncl 1973-75, convenor Cardiology Ctee 1969-76; memb: Jt Cardiology Ctee RCPS Scotland 1978-82, Specialist Advsy Ctee on Cardiovascular Diseases UK Jt Ctee on Higher Med Trg 1970-74; memb: Scientific Bd of Int Soc of Cardiology 1966-72 (chm Scientific Cncl and Section of Paediatric Cardiology 1966-72), UK Conf of Postgrad Deans 1970-85, Educn Advsy Bd Medico-Pharmaceutical Forum 1978-81, Scottish Cncl for Postgrad Med Educn 1970-85 (memb Eastern Regnl Ctee 1970-85); convenor: Scottish Cncls Working Pty on Trg, Blood Transfusion Serv 1973-74, Partime Trg in Med 1977-85; chm Standing Ctee of Conf of Postgrad Med Deans and Dirs of Postgrad Med Educn of Univs of UK 1975-79; WHO: advsr Working Gp on Congenital Cardiac Malformations in Europe 1963-89, conslt to Cncl for Int Orgns of Med Sciences (CIOMS) 1965-; memb: Central Conslts and Specialists Ctee UK 1959-62 and Scotland 1955-62, Central Med Recruitment Ctee (UK) 1959-62, Medical Staffing Sub-Ctee (UK) 1959-62, Med Estab Ctee (Scotland) 1955-62; chm Hosp Jr Staffs Gp Ctee (UK) 1959-62 and (Scotland) 1955-62, sec and treas Sir James MacKenzie Cardiac Club 1963-; memb: Assoc of Physicians GB and Ireland Br Cardiac Soc, Scot Soc of Physicians; memb Master of Foxhounds Assoc 1985-; FRCPEd 1962, FRCP 1974, fell American Coll of Cardiology 1969; *Books* Paediatric Cardiology (1968), The Clinical Anatomy of the Heart (1978), The New Medicine, Cardiology (1983), Disorders of Rate, Rhythm and Conduction (1984); author of many sci papers on cardiovascular diseases; *Recreations* fox hunting, polo, fishing, gardening; *Clubs* New Edinburgh; *Style—* Dr Hamish Watson, TD; Nethermains of Kinnaird, Inchture, Perthshire PH14 9QX (☎ 0828 86303)

WATSON, Maj-Gen Henry Stuart Ramsay; CBE (1973, MBE 1954); s of Maj Henry Angus Watson, CBE, MVO (d 1952), and Dorothy Bannerman Watson, OBE, *née* Ramsay (d 1968); *b* 9 July 1922; *Educ* Winchester; *m* 1965, Susan, o da of Col William Hall Jackson, CBE, DL, of Barford, nr Warwick; 2 s (Angus b 1967, William b 1969), 1 da (Edwina b 1971); *Career* cmmnd 2 Lt 13/18 Royal Hussars 1942, Lt 1943, Capt 1945, Adj 13/18 H 1945-46 and 1948-50; psc 1951, GSO2 HQ 1 Corps, 1952-53, instr RMA Sandhurst 1955-57, instr Staff Coll Camberley 1960-62, CO 13/18 Royal Hussars 1962-64 Col GS, SHAPE 1965-68, Col Def Policy Staff MOD 1968, IDC 1969, BGS HQ BAOR 1970-73, dir Def Policy MOD 1973-74, sr Army Directing Staff RCDS 1974-76, Col 13/18 Royal Hussars 1979-90; dep dir gen IOD 1985-88 (exec dir 1977-85); *Recreations* golf, gardening, shooting; *Clubs* Cavalry and Guards'; *Style—* Maj-Gen H S R Watson, CBE; c/o National Westminster Bank, 39 High Street, Princes Risborough, Aylesbury, Bucks HP17 0AH

WATSON, James Kenneth; s of James Edward Watson, of Phillips Rd, Birchington, Kent, and Helen Grace, *née* Kilby (d 1959); *b* 16 Jan 1935; *Educ* Watford GS, Stanford Univ California; *m* 26 July 1959, Eileen Fay, da of Sidney C Purkiss, of Amberway, Nancy Downs, Oxhey, Herts; 2 s (Jamie Nicholas b 6 April 1970, Mark Robin (twin) b 6 April 1970), 1 da (Sara Ann b 11 Dec 1968); *Career* CA; dir fin Br Rd Servs 1968-75, dep chm Nat Freight Consortium 1982 - (dir fin 1976-82); Freeman City of London, Liveryman Worshipful Co of Carmen 1980; FCA; *Recreations* cricket, theatre, history; *Clubs* RAC, MCC; *Style—* James Watson, Esq; Inlands, Lower Icknield Way, Bucklands, Bucks HP22 5LR (☎ 0296 630829); NFC plc, The Merton Centre, 45 St Peter's St, Bedford MK40 2UB (☎ 0234 272222, fax 0234 270900, telex 0234

826803, car 0860 417652)

WATSON, Prof James Patrick; s of Hubert Timothy Watson (d 1964), of London, and Grace Emily, *née* Mizen (d 1957); *b* 14 May 1936; *Educ* Roan Sch Greenwich, Trinity Coll Cambridge (BA, MB, MD); *m* 4 April 1962, Christine Mary, da of Rev Norman Tasker Colley (d 1987), of Midsomer Norton; 4 s (Peter b 1963, Andrew b 1964, John b 1970, Robert b 1972); *Career* jr hosp appts 1960-64, trainee psychiatrist Inst of Psychiatry 1964-70, sr lectr and hon conslt psychiatrist St George's Hosp and Med Sch 1970-74, prof of psychiatry Guy's Hosp Med Sch 1974-, The United Med and Dental Schs of Guy's and St Thomas's Hosp 1984-; FRCPsych 1977, FRCP 1978; *Recreations* music (especially Mozart), sport in general; *Clubs* Nat Lib; *Style—* Prof James Watson; Guy's Hosp, London SE1 9RT (☎ 071 955 4247)

WATSON, Jennifer Gordon; da of Edward Gordon Eliott, of Bower's Hill House, Bower's Lane, Burpham, Surrey, and June Elizabeth, *née* Cobb; *b* 31 Aug 1952; *Educ* St Mary's Convent Shaftesbury, Branson's Coll Playford Suffolk, St Mathias Coll of Educn Bristol (Cert Ed), King Alfred's Coll Winchester (BEd); *m* 23 July 1977, Thomas Alexander Watson, *qv*, s of Donald Fletcher Watson, of Australia; 2 s (James Donald b 18 Feb 1981, Alexander Edward b 4 Jan 1987), 1 da (Laura Helen b 15 Jan 1983); *Career* dir and co sec Hallmark Marketing Services Ltd 1986-, co sec Hallmark Euro Communications 1987-; treas and sec Macleod Soc 1983-, chm of Govrs Southdown Sch Compton Winchester 1985-87 (govr 1981-87), govr St Bede's Primary Sch Winchester 1989-; *Recreations* tennis, sailing; *Clubs* Littleton Tennis, Western Sailing; *Style—* Mrs Jennifer Watson; 12 Stoke Rd, Winchester, Hants; Northgate Place, Staple Gardens, Winchester SO23 85R (☎ 0962 863850, fax 0962 841 820)

WATSON, John Gillard; s of Albert Watson (d 1962), of Cheapside, Wakefield, Yorkshire, and Margaret Elizabeth, *née* Gillard (d 1981); *b* 30 April 1919; *Educ* Driffield Sch, Ruskin Coll, St Peter's Coll Oxford (BA, MA); *m* 26 July 1954, Kathleen Mary, da of William Harold Raymond (d 1987), of Essex; 1 s (John Stephen b 1959), 1 da (Margaret Mary b 1957); *Career* RASC (England, France, India, Burma) 1939-46 (Sgt); librarian Oxford Univ Inst of Econ & Statistics 1961-86, memb Nat Exec Ctee Assoc of Univ Teachers 1985-, govr St Aloysuis Sch Oxford 1989-, tstee Oxford Preservation Tst 1989-; *Recreations* watching cricket, mountain walking; *Clubs* United Oxford and Cambridge University, Royal United Servs Inst Oxford Union; *Style—* John Gillard Watson, Esq; 11 Beaumont Buildings, Oxford OX1 2LL (☎ 0865 54583)

WATSON, John Grenville Bernard; s of Norman Victor Watson (d 1969), of Leeds, and Rugby Ernestine, *née* Hawker (d 1962); *b* 21 Feb 1943; *Educ* Bootham Sch York, Coll of Law; *m* 12 June 1965, da of Jack Wood (d 1970), of Sheffield; 1 s (Alexander b 1973), 2 da (Melinda b 1975, Sophie b 1975); *Career* asst slr Hepworth & Chadwick 1967-69, mgmnt trainee John Waddingtons Ltd 1969-73, md Waddingtons Games Ltd 1976-79 (mktg dir 1973-76), dir Main Bd John Waddingtons plc 1979-89; MP (C) Skipton 1979-83, Skipton and Ripon 1983-87; PPS 1981-86; dir Goddard Kay Rogers (Northern) Ltd 1989-; nat chm Young Cons Orgn 1970-72, chm Cons Candidates Assoc 1975-79, pres Br Youth Cncl 1979-83, memb Leeds Devpt Corp 1988-; Freeman City of London, memb Ct Worshipful Co of the Makers of Playing Cards; memb Law Soc; *Books* Home from Home (1973), Changing Gear (contrib, 1982), View From The Terrace (contrib, 1986); *Recreations* walking, photography, travel; *Style—* John Watson, Esq; Bay Horse Corner, Ling Lane, Scarcroft, Leeds LS14 3HY (☎ 0532 892209); Goddard Kay Rogers (Northern) Limited, Park House, 6 Killingbeck Drive, York Rd, Leeds LS14 6UF (☎ 0532 484848, fax 0532 484852, car 0831 488829)

WATSON, John Henry; s of Henry William Watson (d 1963), and Rose Hannah, *née* Abley (d 1982); *b* 25 Jan 1944; *Educ* Wolverhampton GS; *m* 1966, Marigold Anne, da of Rev William Young Milne, Rector of Malvern Wells; 1 s (decd), 3 da; *Career* articled with Worcester Country Practice 1960-66, mgmnt conslt Touche Ross & Co 1968-71, fin dir Pillsbury UK Ltd 1975-85, sr vice-pres Pillsbury Cunnda Ltd 1985; vice-pres Finance Int The Pillsbury Co USA; FCA; *Recreations* music; *Style—* John Watson, Esq; 1678 The Pillsbury Center, Minneapolis, Minnesota 55402, USA

WATSON, Lt-Col Lesslie Kenyon; MBE (1944), TD (1944); s of Maj William Ernest Watson, TD (1950), of Gray's Inn Place, and Edith Mary, *née* Kenyon (d 1958); *b* 8 Sept 1906; *Educ* Bradfield Coll, Pembroke Coll Cambridge (MA); *m* 15 June 1929, Josephine Ida (d 1983), da of Edward Gosset-Tanner (d 1922); 2 s (Niall b 1934, Robin b 1941), 1 da (Diana b 1931); *Career* Lt-Col serv RA W Desert, Italy (POW, 4 escapes); architect; town planner; worked under: Louis de Soissons, Cyril Farey, Sir Guy Dawber, Sir Giles Scott, Sir Edward Maufe; site architect of Bomber Cmd HQ building 1938; own practice 1950, later in ptnrship with H J Coates; Power Stations at Ferrybridge, Thorpe Marsh, Richborough, Rugeley A and B, offices LEB, offices Tyne Tunnel, New Scotswood Bridge; jt fndr High Wycombe Arts Assoc 1947, The Assoc of Private Architects 1959, The Doric Club 1973, first chm West Wycombe Parish Cncl 1987; memb RTPI, FCIArb, FRIBA; *Recreations* hunting, fishing, gardening; *Clubs* The Arts; *Style—* Lt-Col Lesslie K Watson, MBE, TD; Silver Birches, W Wycombe, Bucks HP14 3AH (☎ 0494 27905)

WATSON, Marilyn Jane; da of Edwin John Watson, DFC, of Norfolk, and Mary Irene Love, *née* Willmott; *b* 17 Sept 1952; *Educ* St Mary's Convent Bishop's Stortford, Cambridge Coll of Arts and Technol; 1 s (Luke b 1988); *Career* dir MPR Leedex Group Ltd 1986-89, proprietor Watsons 1989-; MIPR; *Recreations* sailing, riding, swimming; *Style—* Ms Marilyn Watson; 1B Terrace Gardens, Barnes, London SW13 0HD (☎ 081 392 2332, fax 081 392 2347)

WATSON, Mervyn Edward Robert; s of Robert George Watson, of Darlington, Co Durham, and Beryl May, *née* Lord; *b* 23 Aug 1945; *Educ* Queen Elizabeth GS Darlington, Univ of Nottingham (BSc), Univ of Sask Canada (BA); *Career* trainee mangr BSC 1963-68, res metallurgist Hudson Bay Mining and Smelting Co Manitoba Canada 1968-70, actor Coventry Theatre in Educn Co 1972-75, actor and assoc dir Humberside Theate Hull 1975-77, assoc dir Alan Ayckbourn's Theatre in the Round Scarborough; playwright and freelance theatre dir 1979-80; plays incl: Big Deal (stage 9 to 11 year olds) 1975, Reversed Charges (stage and radio) 1978, Hands (with Rosemary Leach TV play)1980, Family Man (with Julie Walters and John Duttine TV play) 1983; sr prodr Granada TV 1980-90: Coronation Street 1982-84, First Among Equals (by Jeffrey Archer) 1985-86, Floodtide (by Roger Marshall) 1987, Wipe Out (by Martin Stone and Ric Maher) 1988, Coronation Street 1989-90; *Recreations* DIY, hill walking, skiing; *Style—* Mervyn Watson, Esq; Granada Television, Quay St, Manchester M60 9EA (☎ 061 832 7211, fax 061 835 1508)

WATSON, Col Michael Colvin; OBE (1966), MC (1944), TD, DL (Wilts 1979-86, Gloucs 1986-); s of Lt-Col Forrester Colvin Watson, OBE, MC (d 1951), and Cecilia, *née* Grimston (descended from 1 Earl of Verulam, d 1960); *b* 30 Sept 1918; *Educ* Stowe, Sandhurst; *m* 18 April 1942, Hon (Joan) Sybil, *née* Berry (d 1988), da of 1 Baron Buckland (d 1928); 1 s (Rupert b 1949), 2 da (Mrs Longsdon b 1946, Mrs Hurrell b 1951); *Career* cmmnd 17/21 Lancers 1938, ret 1947; cmd Royal Wilts Yeo 1961-65 (joined 1954), Col TAVR 1967-73, ADC (TAVR) to HM The Queen 1969-73, Col 17/21 Lancers 1975-83; High Sheriff Gloucestershire 1981, Vice Lord Lt Gloucestershire 1987-89; *Recreations* field sports; *Clubs* Cavalry and Guard's; *Style—* Col M C Watson, OBE, MC, TD, DL; The Dower House, Barnsley, Cirencester, Gloucestershire GL7 5EF (☎ 028 574 508)

WATSON, Michael Goodall (Mike); s of Clarke Carter Watson, and Agnes Hope, *née* Goodall; *b* 1 May 1949; *Educ* Dundee HS, Heriot Watt Univ (BA); *m* 31 Oct 1986, Lorraine Therese, da of William McManus (d 1985); *Career* devpt offr Mid-Derbyshire Workers Educnl Assoc 1974-77, trade union official ASTMS 1977- (divnl offr 1977-87, regnl offr 1987-89); memb Exec Ctee Lab Pty Scot Cncl 1987-90; *Books* Rags to Riches - The Official History of Dundee United Football Club (1985); *Recreations* jogging, watching Dundee Utd FC, reading; *Style—* Mike Watson, Esq; 58 Fox St, Glasgow G1 4AU; House of Commons, London SW1 (☎ 071 219 5804)

WATSON, Dr Michael Leonard; s of Col Edgar Stewart Watson, OBE, of Bridlington and Dorothy, *née* Mansfield; *b* 29 March 1949; *Educ* Merchiston Castle Sch, Univ of Edinburgh (BSc, MB ChB, MD); *m* 27 March 1971, Penelope Ann, da of William H A Bartlett, of Elvanfoot; 1 s (James Stuart Michael b 31 Jan 1979), 1 da (Fiona Jane b 15 Oct 1976); *Career* travelling fell MRC 1981-82, conslt physician Royal Infirmary Edinburgh 1984-; sec Symposium Ctee RCP Edinburgh; FRCP 1986; *Recreations* mountaineering; *Style—* Dr Michael Watson; 42 Dreghorn Loan, Edinburgh EH13 0PE (☎ 031 441 3483); Medical Renal Unit, Lauriston Place, Royal Infirmary, Edinburgh EH3 9YW (☎ 031 229 2477)

WATSON, Maj Hon Miles Ronald Marcus; s and h of 3 Baron Manton; (triplet with Hon Thomas and Hon Victoria); *b* 7 May 1958; *Educ* Eton; *m* 17 Oct 1984, Elizabeth A, eldest da of J R Story, of Westcott, Surrey; 2 s (Thomas b 19 April 1985, Ludovic Waldo Rupert b 31 March 1989); *Career* Maj Life Guards; *Recreations* shooting, skiing, hunting, racing, polo; *Style—* Maj The Hon Miles Watson

WATSON, Prof Peter Anthony; s of Henry Watson (d 1974), and Elsie Watson (d 1988); *b* 28 June 1941; *Educ* Queen Elizabeth GS Darlington, Univ of Durham (BSc, PhD); *m* 19 Feb 1966, Joy Carolyn, da of James William Gartside, of Grimsby, Lincs; 3 da (Vivienne b 1967, Jennifer b 1969, Alison b 1970); *Career* sr scientific offr PO res dept London 1962-70 (scientific offr); Univ of Bradford: lectr 1970, sr lectr 1975, reader 1978, prof of communications engrg 1980; seconded as devpt dir BIT Ltd 1984-86 (Euro Space Agency Netherlands 1977-79); delivered IEE Appleton lecture 1980, awarded Marconi Premium Prize IEE 1987 (1978), JJ Thomson Premium 1989; memb and chm various nat ctees IEE, former RS memb Br Nat Ctee for Radio Sci, memb various ctees Int Union of Radio Sci; MIEE; *Recreations* classical music, squash, walking; *Style—* Prof Peter Watson; Department of Electrical and Electronic Engineering, University of Bradford, Bradford, W Yorks BD7 1DP (☎ 0274 733466, fax 0274 305340, telex 51309 UNIBFD)

WATSON, Peter Frank Patrick; s of Frank Patrick Watson (d 1963), of Birmingham, and Lilian Ethel, *née* Hopwood; *b* 23 April 1943; *Educ* Cheltenham, Univ of Durham (Psychology prize), Univ of London, Univ of Rome; *m* 1 (m dis), Nichola Theodas; m 2 (m dis), Lesley Rowlatt; *Career* intern Tavistock Clinic 1966-68; dep ed New Society 1968-71, Sunday Times 1971-81, The Times 1981-83, The Observer 1985-, currently columnist The Spectator, reg contrib New York Times; author of 4 novels set in the art world; *Books* War on the Mind; the Military Uses and Abuses of Psychology (1973), Twins (1978), The Caravaggio Conspiracy (1982), Wisdom & Strength: the biography of a Renaissance Masterpiece (1990); books translated into 12 languages; Halian Govt scholarship (music) 1964, US Govt bursary 1970, Crime Writers of Britain gold Dagger 1982; memb: PEN 1988, Br Psychological Soc; *Recreations* opera, cricket, fishing; *Clubs* Reform; *Style—* Peter Watson, Esq; The Observer, Chelsea Bridge House, Queenstown Rd, London SW8 4NN (☎ 071 627 0700)

WATSON, Peter Gordon; s of Ralph Watson, and Renee, *née* Smith; *b* 30 April 1930; *Educ* The Leys Sch, UCH London, Queens' Coll Cambridge (MA, MB BChir); *m* 6 Aug 1955, Ann Wollaston, da of John Macintosh; 3 s (Andrew Brailsford b 1957, James Bartholomew Wollaston b 1959, Hamish Charles John b 1963), 2 da (Louisa Harriet b 1961, Elizabeth Emma Hutton b 1965); *Career* Nat Serv 2 Lt RHA 1948-50; sr lectr Inst of Opthalmology London 1962-63; posts held 1965-: sr conslt opthalmic surgn Addenbrooke's Hosp Cambridge, conslt Moorfields Eye Hosp London, assoc lectr faculty of clinical med Univ of Cambridge, sr lectr Inst of Opthalmology Univ of London, ed Eye journal; vice pres Coll of Opthalmologists 1965-, dep hospitaller Order of St John of Jerusalem; Freeman City of London, memb Worshipful Soc of Apothecaries; fell commoner Queen's Coll Cambridge 1985; FRCS 1963, FCOpth 1988; *Books* Metabolic Integrations (1954), The Sclera and Systemic Disorders (1976); *Recreations* tennis, sailing, shooting; *Clubs* RSM; *Style—* Peter Watson, Esq; 17 Adams Rd, Cambridge CB3 9AD (☎ 0223 353789, 0223 62900, fax 0223 460910)

WATSON, Vice Adm Sir Philip Alexander; KBE (1976), LVO (1960); s of Alexander Henry St Croix Watson (d 1963); *b* 7 Oct 1919; *Educ* St Alban's Sch; *m* 1948, Jennifer Beatrice, *née* Tanner; 1 s, 2 da; *Career* joined RNVR 1940, transferred to RN 1945, Rear Adm 1970, Dir-Gen Weapons (Navy) MOD 1970-77, Vice Adm 1974, Chief Naval Engr Offr 1974-76, ret 1976; Adm Pres Midland Naval Offrs Assoc 1979-85; dir: Marconi Int Marine Co Ltd, Marconi Radar Systems Ltd (chm 1977-85), naval conslt GEC Marconi Electronics Ltd 1977-85, conslt to Marconi Gp of Companies 1985-87; memb Cncl IEE 1975-78, 1982-87, 1988-; CEng, FIEE 1963, CBIM 1973; *Clubs* Army and Navy; *Style—* Vice Adm Sir Philip Watson, KBE, LVO; The Hermitage, Bodicote, Banbury, Oxon OX15 4BZ

WATSON, Rt Rev Richard Charles Challinor; s of Col Francis William Watson, CB, MC, DL (d 1966), of the Glebe House, Dinton, Aylesbury, Bucks, and Alice Madelein, *née* Collings Wells (d 1952); *b* 16 Feb 1923; *Educ* Rugby, New Coll Oxford, Westcott House Cambridge; *m* 1955, Anna, da of Rt Rev Christopher Maude Chavasse, OBE, MC (d 1962), Bishop of Rochester; 1 s (David b 1956), 1 da (Rachel b 1959); *Career* served WW II Indian Artillery, Capt RA SE Asia 1942-45; curate Stratford E London 1952-53, tutor and chaplain Wycliffe Hall Oxford 1954-57, chaplain Wadham Coll and Oxford Pastorate 1957-61, vicar of Hornchurch 1962-70; examining chaplain to: Bishop of Rochester 1956-61, Bishop of Chelmsford 1962-70; asst rural dean of Havering 1967-70, rector of Burnley 1970-77, bishop suffragan of Burnley 1970-87; *Recreations* reading, gardening; *Clubs* Lansdowne; *Style—* The Rt Rev Richard Watson; 6 Church Rd, Thame, Oxon OX9 3AJ (☎ 0844 213853)

WATSON, Prof (John) Richard; s of Reginald Joseph Watson, and Alice Mabel, *née* Tennant; *b* 15 June 1934; *Educ* Magdalen Coll Oxford (BA, MA), Univ of Glasgow (PhD); *m* 21 July 1962, Pauline Elizabeth, *née* Roberts; 1 s (David James b 1966), 2 da (Elizabeth Emma b 1968, Rachel Clare b 1971); *Career* 2 Lt RA 1953-55; public orator Univ of Durham 1989- (prof of English 1978-); vice chm Landscape Res Gp; chm Modern Humanities Res Assoc 1990-; *Books* Wordsworth's Vital Soul (1982), Everyman's Book of Victorian Verse (ed, 1982), English Poetry of the Romantic Period 1789-1830 (1985), The Poetry of Gerard Manley Hopkins (1987), Companion to Hymns and Psalms (with K Trickett, 1988); *Recreations* playing the cello, walking, windsurfing; *Style—* Prof Richard Watson; 3 Victoria Terrace, Durham DH1 4RW (☎ 091 384 5716); University of Durham, English Dept, Elvet Riverside, New Elvet, Durham (☎ 091 374 2731)

WATSON, Robert Jeffrey; s of Col RM Watson, DSO (d 1936), and V C M Barlow, *née* Arnold (d 1981); *b* 21 July 1934; *Educ* Institut Montana Switzerland, Millfield, UCL; *m* 16 Oct 1969, Maureen Esme; *Career* called to the Bar Inner Temple 1963; former exec chm UK Cncl for Overseas Students, hon treas Br Olympic Assoc 1980-, vice pres Euro Hockey Fedn; memb Worshipful co of Leathersellers; *Recreations* gardening, shooting, sport, fiction; *Style—* Robert Watson, Esq; 3 Temple Gardens, Temple, London EC4 Y 9AU (☎ 071 583 1155, fax 071 353 5446)

WATSON, Robert John; s of Donald George James Watson, and Nabiha, *née* Bulis; *b* 29 June 1955; *Educ* Sir Walter St John Sch, Oxford Sch of Architecture (BA Dip Arch); *m* 11 Aug 1984, Au, da of Dr Hing Tsung Lam; *Career* ptnr Lam and Watson and Woods Partnership, dir and ptnr First Design Gp, dir Mitrech Ltd; hon consulting architect to London Chinatown Assoc and specialist in traditional Chinese architecture and oriental design; fndr memb Progress Architectural Gp; RIBA; *Recreations* private aviation, vintage transport, speed, futurism; *Style—* Robert Watson, Esq; 23 Rydal Rd, London SW16 (☎ 081 769 5853); Lam, Watson & Woods Architects, 88 Clapham Park Rd, London SW4

WATSON, (Lawrence) Roger; s of Lawrence Watson (d 1983), of Alford, Lincs, and Alberta Gertrude, *née* Baker; *b* 25 Jan 1941; *Educ* Maidenhead GS, Univ of London (BA); *m* 19 Oct 1963, Sheila, da of Victor Orlando Dandridge (d 1976), of Bourne End, Bucks; 1 da (Rachel Helen b 1967), 1 s (Neil Lawrence b 1969); *Career* insur co dir; md Paramount Insurance Co Ltd 1986 (dir 1972), dir Robert A Rushton (Life Pensions) Ltd; *Recreations* sport, reading, walking; *Style—* Roger Watson, Esq; 202 Beech Rd, St Albans, Herts AL3 5AX (☎ 0727 63367); 188-196 St Albans Rd, Watford, Herts (☎ 0923 37111, car ☎ 359485)

WATSON, Ronald Norman Stewart; s of Kenneth Watson, of Yeovil, Somerset, and Dorothy Fraser, *née* Peat; *b* 12 Feb 1942; *Educ* Tauntons' GS Southampton; *m* 2 Dec 1972, Sally Virginia, da of Arthur John Wilson; 2 s (Ben b 1974, Ross b 1979); *Career* mangr data servs Conoco Europe 1969-74, mgmnt conslt Booz Allen & Hamilton 1974-76, fin mangr BNOC 1977-83, fin mangr Britoil 1983-86, gp fin dir Howden Group plc 1987-; FCA 1964; *Recreations* sailing, golf; *Clubs* RNC Yacht; *Style—* Ronald Watson, Esq; Howden Group plc, 195 Scotland St, Glasgow G5 8PJ (☎ 041 429 4747, fax 041 429 4244)

WATSON, (James) Roy; CBE (1991); s of Edwin Watson (d 1981), of Leigh, Lancs, and Sarah, *née* Isaacs (d 1988); *b* 25 Aug 1936; *Educ* Westleigh Sch Leigh Lancs, Leigh Mining and Tech Coll; *m* 8 Feb 1958, Josephine Mary, da of Vincent Foster, of Leigh, Lancs; 1 s (Ian Mark b 1959, d 1983), 2 da (Tessa Marie b 1962, Janet Elizabeth b 1970); *Career* Lancs Co Fire Brigade: joined 1962, divnl commander 1976, dep chief offr 1981, chief fire offr 1983; chm: Fire Servs Nat Benevolent Fund 1989-90, Fire Servs Sports and Athletics Assoc Angling Soc, NW Fire Serv Examinations Bd; fell Inst of Fire Engrs 1983, FBIM 1983; German Fire Servs Assoc medal for int co-operation 1989; *Recreations* golf, music, caravanning; *Style—* Roy Watson, Esq, CBE; 2a Ambleside Drive, Darwen, Lancashire BB3 3BG (☎ 0254 703533); Lancashire County Fire Brigade HQ, Garstang Rd, Fulwood, Preston, Lancs PR2 3LH (☎ 0772 862545, telex LANFIR 67444, fax 0772 865144)

WATSON, Shelia Mary; da of Joseph Herbert Watson, OBE, MC (d 1990), and Evelyn Ada, *née* Patching; *b* 8 March 1931; *Educ* The Warren Worthing, King's Coll, Univ of London, Univ of Bordeaux (BA); *m* 1, 2 Sept 1961 (m dis), Neil Francis Elliot Blackmore, s of late William Blackmore, MD; 2 da (Karen Anne b 30 May 1964, Laura b 10 Sept 1967); m 2, 15 April 1972, David Hugh Arthur Christie-Murray; *Career* dir David Higham Assocs (author's agents) 1955-71, dir and sec Bolt & Watson Ltd 1971-83, md Watson & Little Ltd 1983; *Recreations* reading, walking; *Style—* Ms Sheila Watson; Imber Court Cottage, Orchard Lane, East Molesey, Surrey KT8 0BN; Watson Little, 12 Egbert Street, London NW1 8LT (☎ 071 483 1715, fax 071 379 7731)

WATSON, Simon John; s of John Charles Watson, of 3 Rushmead Drive, Loose, Maidstone, Kent, and Lorna Kathleen, *née* Whitehouse; *b* 13 May 1958; *Educ* Maidstone GS, St Catherine's Coll Oxford (MA); *Career* admitted slr 1983; ptnr Simmons & Simmons 1988- (articled clerk 1981-83, asst slr 1983-88); memb ctee Notting Hill Family Service Unit; memb Law Soc; *Recreations* opera, bridge; *Style—* Simon Watson, Esq; 14 Dominion St, London EC2M 2RJ (☎ 071 628 2020, fax 071 588 4129, telex 888562)

WATSON, Prof Stephen Roger; s of John Cole Watson, MBE (d 1987), of Steyning, Sussex, and Marguerite Freda Rose, *née* Seagrief; *b* 29 Aug 1943; *Educ* Univ Coll Sch Hampstead, Emmanuel Coll Cambridge (BA, MA, PhD); *m* 26 July 1969, Rosemary Victoria, da of Rt Rev Cyril James Tucker, CBE, of Cambridge; 1 s (Oliver b 5 Feb 1972), 1 da (Emily b 18 Feb 1975); *Career* planning asst Shell International Petroleum Co 1970-71, fell Emmanuel Coll Cambridge 1971- (res fell 1968-70); Cambridge Univ: lectr Engrg Dept 1971-86, Peat Marwick prof of mgmnt studies 1986-, dir Judge Inst of Mgmnt Studies 1990-; dir: Cambridge Decision Analysts 1984-, Environmental Resources Ltd 1989-; chm Ctee Cambridge Christian Aid; FSS, AFIMA; *Books* Decision Synthesis (with D M Buede, 1988); *Recreations* overseas development, singing; *Style—* Prof Stephen Watson; 120 Huntingdon Rd, Cambridge CB3 0HL (☎ 0223 625 36); Judge Institute of Management Studies, Mill Lane, Cambridge CB2 1RX (☎ 0223 338170, fax 0223 338076, telex 81239)

WATSON, Steuart Charles; s of Edwin Charles Watson, of 10 Ancrum Gdns, Dundee, and Betty, *née* Cuthbert; *b* 29 June 1952; *Educ* Harris Acad Dundee, Canterbury Sch of Architecture (dip arch); *m* 10 June 1980, Claire-Marie, da of Dr Desmond M Burns (d 1985), of Dundee; *Career* architect, qualified 1977; principal in private practice 1979-80 and 1983-85, conslt architect E African Breweries Ltd 1980-83, ptnr Campbell Watson and Walker Architects and Surveyors 1985-; Br Inst's Prize in Arch awarded by the RA 1975; RIBA; *Recreations* golf; *Style—* Steuart C Watson, Esq; c/o Natwest Bank, 98 High Street, Wimbledon, London SW19 5EJ; Campbell Watson & Walker, 2 Wimpole Street, London W1M 7AA (☎ 071 637 4266, fax 071 409 0165)

WATSON, Lady Susan Diana; *née* Wood; yr da of 2 Earl of Halifax (d 1980); *b* 22 Sept 1938; *m* 10 Oct 1959, Brig Ian Darsie Watson, CBE, TD, s of late Darsie Watson, of Blackeshours, Upper Hartfield, Sussex; 2 s (David Charles Darsie b 1960, Richard Ian b 1962); *Style—* The Lady Susan Watson

WATSON, Thomas Alexander (Tom); s of Donald Fletcher Watson, of Bowral, NSW, Aust, and Helen Mary Spedding, *née* Irvine; *b* 17 Sept 1950; *Educ* Grafton HS NSW, Hunters Hill HS NSW, Univ NSW, Sydney, Aust (BA); *m* 23 July 1977, Jennifer, *qv*, da of Edward Gordon Eliott; 2 s (James Donald b 1981, Alexander Edward b 1987), 1 da (Laura Helen 1983); *Career* md: Hallmark Mktg Servs Ltd 1984-, Hallmark European Communications Ltd 1987-; vice-chm: Macleod Soc, dir Prince's Youth Business Tst Southern Counties 1988-90, cncllr Hampshire CC 1981-85, govr Westgate Sch Winchester 1981-85; memb: Prov Cncl Wessex Area Cons 1990-, Ctee PR Cnslts Assoc 1988; MIPR 1983; *Recreations* yachting, reading, politics; *Clubs* Western Sailing; *Style—* Tom Watson, Esq; Northgate Place, Staple Gardens, Winchester SO23 8SR (☎ 0962 863850, fax 0962 841820)

WATSON, Thomas Paul; JP City of Sheffield, (1966), DL S Yorks (1979); s of Clark Bell Porteous Watson (d 1979), of South Shields Co Durham, and Decima Bruce, *née* Coombes; *b* 20 Nov 1925; *Educ* South Shields HS, Appleby GS Westmorland; *m* 11 June 1949, Sheila Thomas, da of William Arthur Thomas (d 1981), of South Shields; 1 s (Stephen Sean Watson b 1951 d 1966), 1 da (Madeleine Anne Watson b 1953); *Career* ed: Evening Telegraph Blackburn 1960-62, The Star Sheffield 1962-68; md Sheffield Newspapers Ltd 1970-82 (dir 1968-), dir United Newspapers plc 1977-86, dep chm United Provincial Newspapers Ltd 1982-86, dir Radio Hallam 1972-89, former dir Yorkshire Radio Network plc; vice chm Pres Cncl 1986-89 (memb 1981-89), hon fell Sheffield City Poly; *Recreations* bridge, travel, military history; *Clubs* The Naval, Hill Street, Mayfair; *Style—* Thomas Watson, Esq, JP, DL; 10 Ivy Park Court, Ivy Park Rd, Sheffield S10 3LA (☎ 0742 306857)

WATSON, Hon Thomas Philip; 2 s of 3 Baron Manton; (triplet with Hon Miles and Hon Victoria); *b* 7 May 1958; *Educ* Eton, RAC; *m* 19 Dec 1988, Venetia Margaret Cadogan, da of Paul Spicer, *qv*, of Ovington Gardens, London SW3; 1 s (Alexander Paul Rupert b 1989); *Career* Lt QOH TAVR 1981, ret 1981, Lt Yorks Yeo; *Clubs* Mombasa (Kenya); *Style—* The Hon Thomas Watson

WATSON, Hon Victoria Monica; da of 3 Baron Manton; *b* 7 May 1958, (triplet, with Hon Miles and Hon Thomas); *Educ* St Mary's Convent Woldingham; *Career* shiatsu practitioner, aromatherapy, massage, reflexology; *Style—* The Hon Victoria Watson

WATSON-GANDY, Dr Carl Donald Tyndale; s of Lt-Col Campbell Vere Watson-Gandy, OBE, and Edit Laura, *née* Falck; *b* 2 March 1939; *Educ* Eton, Univ of Edinburgh (BSc), Univ of London (MSc PhD, DIC); *m* 22 July 1976, Patricia Marion, da of Alexander Hugh Ramsay (d 1962), of Auckland, NZ; 1 s (Hugh b 1981), 1 da (Vere b 1979); *Career* mining engr N Rhodesia 1961-64, lectr Imperial Coll 1967-88, visiting prof Univ of Copenhagen 1984; dir: IPDM Ltd 1981-85, Burman Assoc Ltd 1984-; sr lectr in logistics RMCS Cranfield 1988-; vice chm W Chiswick Residents Assoc 1982-88, memb Hounslow Community Cncl 1984-88, sec Swindon Chapter FGBMFI 1989; Freeman: City of London 1978, Worshipful Co of Gardeners 1981; FBIM 1980, FILDM 1981; *Books* Distribution Management: Mathematics Modelling and Practical Analysis (co author 1971); *Recreations* gardening; *Style—* Dr Carl Watson-Gandy; Systems Assessment Group, RMCS, Shrivenham, Swindon, Wilts (☎ 0793 782551)

WATSON-SMYTH, (Edward) Michael; DFC (1943); s of George Robert Watson-Smyth (Capt 13 Hussars, d 1968), and Madeleine Mary Pedder (d 1971); perfumiers in Bond St W1 1697-1939 Trading as Smyth & Son; James Smyth was a friend of Handel and his home at Wadhurst Castle remained in the family until 1930; *b* 25 March 1923; *Educ* Sunningdale Sch Berks, Fettes Coll Edinburgh, Univ of Miami USA; *m* 7 Aug 1954 (m dis), Monica Amy Merrick, da of Thomas Alderson Scott (d 1951); 1 s (Miles b 1966), 5 da (Melanie b 1955, Madeleine b 1956, Miranda b 1957, Marianne b 1959, Millicent b 1963); m 2, 2 Dec 1988, Rachael Mary Beeson, *née* Fairclough; *Career* Flt Lt RAFVR; navigator: 150 Sqdn N Africa 1943, (DFC), 161 Sqdn Tempsford 1944-45; chm: Window-Boxes Ltd, Yard Arm Club Ltd, Continuous Laminates Ltd; memb of Lloyds; *Recreations* cricket, music, Times Crossword; *Clubs* MCC, Turf; *Style—* Michael Watson-Smyth, Esq, DFC; North Aston Hall, Oxfordshire; 5 Melina Place, London NW8 9SA

WATSON STEWART, Avril, Lady; Avril Veronica; *née* Gibb; o da of late Andrew Adamson Gibb, of Glasgow; *m* 1980, as his 2 w, Sir James Watson Stewart, 4 Bt (d 1988); *Career* artist, calligrapher, lectr (worldwide); FRSA, Hon FBID, Hon MASC; *Clubs* Royal Scottish Automobile, Royal Gourock Yacht; *Style—* Avril, Lady Watson Stewart; Undercliff Court, Wemyss Bay, Renfrewshire PA18 6AL (☎ 0475 521019)

WATT; *see*: Harvie-Watt

WATT, Col Alexander James; MBE (1942), TD (1948), JP (1972), DL (1988); s of Maj James Watt, MC, DL (d 1975), of West Linton, Peeblesshire, and Emily, *née* Burns (d 1972); *b* 3 May 1915; *Educ* Royal HS Edinburgh, Leys Sch; *m* 15 March 1946, Margaret Laura Evelyn, da of Lt-Col John Gibson Anderson (d 1955), of Edinburgh; 2 s (James b 1947, Ian b 1953), 1 da (Pamela b 1950); *Career* WWII joined London Scottish 1939, cmmnd Black Watch 1940, 51 Highland Div; served: N Africa, Sicily, Normandy, Holland, Germany; demob 1946; Maj 6/7 Bn Black Watch TA (Lt-Col cmdg 1956-60), Hon Col 1/51 Bn Highland Volunteers 1976-80; chm and md McEwens Perth 1982; involved locally with the Order of St John (hospitaller 1983-90), KStJ 1981; FSA (Scotland) 1974; *Recreations* fishing; *Clubs* Royal Golf (Perth), Army and Navy; *Style—* Col Alexander Watt, MBE, TD, JP, DL, FSA; Balcanquhal House, Glenfarg, Perthshire PH2 9QD (☎ 057 73 261)

WATT, Alison; s of James Watt, and Annie (Nancy), *née* Sinclair; *b* 11 Dec 1965; *Educ* Glasgow Sch of Art (BA, postgrad studies, first prize Glasgow Competition, Armour prize for still life painting); *Career* artist; solo exhibitions: One Woman Show (The Scottish Gallery, London) 1990, One Woman Show - Contemporary Art Season (Glasgow Art Gallery and Museum, Kelvingrove) 1990; gp exhibitions: Student Competition (Royal Scottish Acad) 1986, Glasgow Competition (Inn On the Green Glasgow) 1986, British Inst Fund (Royal Acad) 1986, Student Competition (Royal Scottish Acad Edinburgh) 1987, Nat Portrait Competition (Nat Portrait Gallery London) 1987, Spring Show (Blythswood Gallery Glasgow) 1988, Recent Graduates (Compass Gallery Glasgow) 1988, Six Women Artists (Scottish Gallery Edinburgh) 1988, London Opening (Scottish Gallery London) 1989, Royal Scottish Portrait Award (Royal Scottish Acad Edinburgh) 1989; commissions: HRH Queen Elizabeth The Queen Mother (Nat Portrait Gallery London), Glasgow Art Gallery and Museum, Kelvingrove, The Observer, EMI Records, News Scotland Ltd, Mirror Group Newspapers, Collins Publishers, numerous private cmmns; works in collections: Nat Portrait Gallery, Glasgow Art Gallery and Museum, BBC Fleming Collection London, Robert and Susan Kasen - Summer NY; awards: first prize for painting Br Inst Fund (Royal Acad) 1986, winner John Player Portrait award (Nat Portrait Gallery) 1987, Elizabeth Greenshields Fndn award Montreal Canada 1989, special commendation Morrison Scottish Portrait award (Royal Scottish Acad, Edinburgh) 1989; *Style—* Ms Alison Watt; Glasgow

WATT, Arthur Alexander; *b* 22 May 1940; *Educ* George Heriot's Sch Edinburgh, Falkirk HS; *m* 1, 1965 (m dis 1977), Judith Mary, *née* Mangles; 2 s, 1 da; m 2, 1979; *Career* chartered accountant, gp md Aurora Holdings Ltd 1974-, gp fin dir Cooper & Turner Ltd 1971-74, consultant PA Management Consultants Ltd 1968-71; *Recreations* running, climbing, squash; *Clubs* Oriental; *Style—* Arthur Watt Esq; Priory Farmhouse, S Leverton, Notts (☎ 0427 880250)

WATT, Dr Hamish; JP; s of late William Watt, of Birkenburn Keith, and late Caroline, *née* Allan; *b* 27 Dec 1925; *Educ* Keith GS, Univ of St Andrews; *m* 1 s, (Michael), 2 da (Maureen, Lorna); *Career* RAF 1944-47 Aircrew; Cons Candidate Caithness gen election 1966, MP SNP Banffshire 1974-79, Grampian regnl cncllr 1984-; farmer, co dir and writer; chm educn ctee COSLA rep 1986-; hon LLD Univ of Aberdeen 1988; *Clubs* Farmers; *Style—* Dr Hamish Watt, JP

WATT, Hew Matthew Brown; OBE (1973), JP (Essex 1951); s of William Orr Watt (d 1949), of Heath Place, Orsett, Grays, Essex, and Jeanie, *née* Dunlop (d 1951); *b* 16 Sept 1915; *Educ* Palmers GS Grays Essex, Essex Inst of Agric; *m* 9 Oct 1937, Molly Annie, da of William John Payne (d 1972), of Gaypenant, Lodge Lane, Grays, Essex; 1 da (Dr Trudy Watt b Jan 1953); *Career* Lt Army Cadet Corp 1941-45; agric broadcaster and writer 1951-, chm Thurrock Licensing Ctee 1961-85, memb Agric Advsy Ctee BBC 1964-76, agric visits to 22 countries incl China and Soviet Union 1967-86, dep chm Thurrock Bench 1970-85, memb Guild Agric Journalists 1970-, chm Apple & Pear Devpt Cncl 1972-77, memb Nature Conservancy Cncl 1972-82; memb and pres Thurrock Rotary Club 1947-, organiser Orsett Agric Show 1950-71, treas and deacon Orsett Congregational Church 1964-; memb and pres Farmers' Club London

1964-, fndr chm: Thurrock Christian Social Cncl 1965-75, chm Thurrock Marriage Guidance Cncl 1968-75, vice-pres Royal Agric Benevolent Inst; Freeman City of London, Liveryman Worshipful Co of Fruiterers 1977; FRAgS 1985; *Recreations* talking, live theatre; *Style—* Hew Watt, Esq, OBE, JP; Wingfield Cottage, Prince Charles Ave, Orsett, Grays, Essex RM16 3HS

WATT, Iain Alasdair; s of Andrew Watt, of Edinburgh, and Margaret Fawns, *née* Brown (d 1967); *b* 30 March 1945; *Educ* Edinburgh Acad, Hull Univ (BSc); *m* 30 Jun 1971, Lynne Neilson, da of Harold Livingston (d 1984), of Kirkcaldy; 3 s (Nicholas b 1973, Christopher Nial b 1975, Oliver Noel b 1980), 1 da (Gemma Stephanie Margaret b 1985); *Career* with Bank of Scotland 1964-86; dir British Liwen Bank 1986-; dir other cos incl: Crescent Japan Investment Trust, New Tokyo Investment Trust, Euro Assets Trust NV, Continental Assets Trust, EFM Dragon Trust, Edinburgh Fund Managers; memb Cncl Queens Nursing Inst in Scotland; AIB; *Recreations* tennis, golf; *Clubs* Golf House Elie, Bruntsfield Golf, N Berwick Golf, Aberdour Tennis, Dean Tennis; *Style—* I A Watt, Esq; Sycamore Bank, North Queensferry, Fife (☎ 0383 413645); 4 Melville Crescent, Edinburgh (☎ 031 226 4931, fax 031 226 2359, telex 72453)

WATT, Ian Glendinning; s of Edward Glendinning Watt (d 1974), of Eastbourne, and Violet Isabel, *née* Eeley; *b* 6 Dec 1932; *Educ* Eastbourne Coll; *m* 27 Sept 1958, Pauline Ann, da of Bertram Roy Shaw (d 1972), of Fareham; 1 s (Jonathan b 1962), 1 da (Louise b 1963); *Career* CA 1957-; ptnr: KMG Thomson McLintock 1963-1987 (chm 1987), KPMG Peat Marwick McLintock 1987-; jt liquidator Rolls Royce Ltd 1977; DTI inspr: Alexander Howden Group plc 1982, Guinness plc 1986; govr: Eastbourne Coll 1965-, Roedean 1976-88, Brambletye Sch E Grinstead (chm) 1969-; FCA; *Recreations* fishing, cricket, golf; *Clubs* MCC, Caledonian, Royal Ashdown Forest GC; *Style—* Ian Watt, Esq; Rough Acre, Furners Green, Uckfield, Sussex TN22 3RP (☎ 082 574 392); KPMG Peat Marwick McLintock, 1 Puddle Dock, Blackfriars, London EC4V 3PD (☎ 071 236 8000, telex 8811541 PMM LONG)

WATT, Surgn Vice Adm Sir James; KBE (1975); s of Thomas Watt (d 1944), and Sarah Alice, *née* Clarkson; *b* 19 Aug 1914; *Educ* King Edward VI Sch Morpeth, Univ of Durham (MB BS, MS), Univ of Newcastle (MD); *Career* joined RN as Surgn Lt RNVR 1941; served: HMS Emerald Far E, HMS Roxborough N Atlantic 1943, HMS Asbury USA 1944, HMS Arbiter Pacific 1945, Surgn Lt Cdr, demobbed 1946; rejoined RN as surgical registrar RN Hosp Haslar 1948; surgical specialist: NI 1949, HM Hosp Ship Maine (Korean War) 1951, RN Hosp Hong Kong 1954; conslt in surgery: RN Hosp Plymouth 1956 (Surgn Cdr), RN Hosp Haslar 1959, RN Hosp Malta 1961, RN Hosp Haslar 1963, Surgn Capt and 1 jt prof of naval surgery RCS and RN Hosp Haslar 1965, Surgn Rear Adm 1 dean of naval med and med offr i/c New Inst of Naval Med 1969, Surgn Vice Adm and med dir gen of the Navy 1972, ret 1977; visiting fell Univ House Aust Nat Univ Canberra 1986; author of numerous papers on: surgery, burns injury, hyperbaric oxygen therapy, christian ethics, med aspects of the history of sea warfare, voyages of discovery, the slave trade and the founding of Aust; pres: Med Soc of London 1980-81 (tstee 1983-), RSM 1982-84; vice pres: Soc for Nautical Res, Churches Cncl for Health and Healing 1988-; pres Inst of Religion and Med 1989-; chm bd of tstees Naval Christian Fellowship 1968-75, tstee Royal Sailors Rests 1972-81, pres RN Lay Readers Soc 1974-83; Erroll Eldridge Prize 1968, Gilbert Blane Gold Medal 1971; Hon Freeman Worshipful Co of Barbers 1978, hon memb Smeatonian Soc of Civil Engrs 1978; Hon FRCS Edinburgh 1976, Hon DCh Newcastle 1978; FRCS, FRCP, FRSM, FICS, FRGS, FSA, fell Assoc of Surgns of GB & Ireland; Cdr OStJ of Jerusalem 1968; *Books* Starving Sailors (ed, 1981), Talking Health: Conventional and Complementary Approaches (ed, 1988); *Recreations* mountain walking; *Clubs* English Speaking Union; *Style—* Surgeon Vice Adm Sir James Watt, KBE, FSA

WATT, Dr James Affleck Gilroy; s of Walter Gilroy Watt (d 1981), and Elizabeth, *née* Christie; *b* 14 July 1934; *Educ* Lasswade Sr Secdy Sch, Univ of Edinburgh (MB ChB, MD, DPM); *m* 26 March 1960 (m dis 1988), (Camilla) Shirley, da of Joseph Wilson, of Scarborough; 2 s (Ewan b 1961, Neil b 1963), 1 da (Alison b 1966); *Career* Nat Serv RAMC 1960, Short Serv Cmmn RAMC until 1964; Bates Mental Health Res Fell 1966-69, lectr in psychiatry Univ of Dundee 1969-71, conslt psychiatrist Gartnavel Royal Hosp 1971- (res into pink spots in schizophrenia and relationship of paranoid states to schizophrenia); articles in: Nature, Br Jnl of Psychiatry, American Jnl of Psychiatry, Acta Psychiatrica Scandinavica; FRCPE 1975, FRCPsych 1982; *Recreations* skiing, windsurfing; *Style—* Dr James Watt; Gartnavel Royal Hospital, 1055 Gt Western Rd, Glasgow G12

WATT, James Muir; OBE (1968); s of James Watt (d 1944), of Ayr, Scotland and Hove, Sussex, and Mary Hewitt, *née* Muir (d 1971); *b* 13 July 1909; *Educ* Glasgow HS, Univ of Glasgow (MA), Balliol Coll Oxford (MA); *m* 28 June 1940, Merlyn Keigwin Duncombe, da of Capt Frederick Duncombe Mann, of Kent and Somerset; 4 da (Betty b 1943, Barbara b 1946, Horatia b 1957, Julia b 1961); *Career* gunner 97 HAA Regt 1940, non cmmnd ranks to SSM 1940-43; staff appts: Lt, Capt, Maj 1943-45; Maj i/c Statistical Branch Northern Cmd; called to the Bar Inner Temple 1935; asst (later dep) sec Chartered Auctioneers and Estate Agents Inst 1946-70, sec Livestock Auctioneers Market Ctee for Eng and Wales 1970-73, legal advsr and vice pres London Rent Assessment Panel 1973-82; ed Estates Gazette Law Reports 1977-; chm St Margaret's Sch for Girls Hampstead 1952-80; ARICS 1973, hon memb CAAV 1973; *Books* Agricultural Holdings (latest edn 1987), Megarry's Rent Accts (jt ed 11 edn, 1988); *Recreations* reading, walking; *Clubs* Naval and Military; *Style—* James Muir Watt, Esq, OBE; 47 Fort St, Ayr, Scotland, KA7 1DH (☎ 0292 283 102)

WATT, Dr Jean Barbara; da of Capt Douglas Maxwell Watt, MM (d 1967), of Kingsheath, Birmingham, and Barbara Gwenllian Havard, *née* Jones; *b* 15 Dec 1948; *Educ* Howells Sch Llandaff Cardiff, King Edward VI Sch for Girls Kings Heath Birmingham, Univ of Birmingham (MB ChB); *m* 15 July 1978, Gavin Neil McKenzie, s of Roderick Charles McKenzie (d 1969), of Warlingham Surrey; 2 da (Molly b 1980, Charlotte b 1985); *Career* sr house offr Univ Hosp of Wales Cardiff 1973-76, registrar The Hosp for Sick Children Great Ormond Street 1976-79, sr registrar in paediatrics St Mary's Hosp Paddington London 1982-87, conslt paediatrician Royal Shrewsbury Hosp 1987-; MRCP 1975; *Recreations* gardening, reading; *Style—* Dr Jean Watt; Cross Houses Hospital, Cross Houses, nr Shrewsbury, Shropshire SY5 (☎ 0743 75 242)

WATT, Capt Kenneth Rupert; s of Gerald Allingham Watt, of Thornhill, Co Londonderry, NI, and Gladys Kathleen, *née* Macky; *b* 12 Sept 1914; *Educ* Malvern, RMC Sandhurst, Trinity Coll Cambridge, (MA); *m* 1946, Elisabeth, da of Capt Edward Hodgson, of Barnfield, Cowfold, Sussex; *Career* regular soldier 15/19 The King's Royal Hussars, active serv France, invalided 1945; sr ptnr Tattersalls 1951-83 (chief shareholder); landowner, salmon fishery mangr, shoot and bird reserve owner; Lord of the Manor of Boulge (Suffolk); *Recreations* hunting, polo, shooting, fishing, music, opera, wildlife sanctuary (private); *Clubs* White's, Cavalry and Guards'; *Style—* Capt Kenneth Watt; Dingle Estate, Dunwich, Suffolk; Barclays, Cambridge; Tattersalls, Terrace House, New Market, Suffolk

WATT, Hon Mrs (Mary); *née* Mackintosh; da of 1 Viscount Mackintosh of Halifax (d 1964); *b* 1927; *m* 1949, (Charles) Michael Watt; 2 s (Charles b 1950, Henry b 1962), 1 da (Susan b 1953); *Career* JP Norfolk, chm Norwich Juvenile Ct 1978-82; *Recreations* horse racing; *Clubs* Jockey Club Rooms; *Style—* The Hon Mrs Watt; Wychwood House, Hethersett, nr Norwich, Norfolk NR9 3AT

WATT, Dr Robert Mackay; s of Robert Mackay Watt, of Southfield Cottage, Summerfield Rd, Dunbar, Scotland, and Helen Good, *née* Pollock (d 1975); *b* 5 Feb 1941; *Educ* Aberdeen GS, Manchester GS, Univ of Edinburgh (BSc, MB ChB, PhD, Dip Comm Med); *m* 28 June 1969, Christine Wendy, da of James Clifford Gregory (d 1990), of Innisfree, 10 Outgaits Close, Hunmanby, Filey, Yorks; 2 s (Andrew b 1970, Mark b 1972); *Career* fell in community med Univ of Edinburgh Med Sch 1975-77 (lectr in physiology 1970-75), superintending inspr Cruelty to Animals Act 1876 1984-87 (inspr 1977-84), chief inspr Animals (Scientific Procedures) Act 1987-; CBiol, FIBiol 1989; *Recreations* painting, model making, wood carving, aviation; *Style—* Dr Robert Watt; Home Office, Animals (Scientific Procedures) Inspectorate, 50 Queen Anne's Gate, London SW1H 9AT (☎ 071 273 2347)

WATT, Prof William Smith; s of John Watt, and Agnes, *née* Smith; *b* 20 June 1913; *Educ* Univ of Glasgow (MA), Balliol Coll Oxford; *m* 7 July 1944, Dorothea, da of Robert James Codrington Smith; 1 s (Robert b 1951); *Career* lectr in Greek Univ of Glasgow 1937-38, fell and tutor in classics Balliol Coll Oxford 1938-52, civilian offr Admty Naval Intelligence Div 1941-45; Univ of Aberdeen: regius prof of humanity 1952-79, curator of library 1954-59, dean of Faculty of Arts 1963-66, Univ Ct 1966-77, vice princ 1969-72; memb: Scot Cncl for Trg of Teachers 1964-67, Gen Teaching Cncl 1967-71 and 1975-78; chm Governing Body Aberdeen Coll of Educn 1971-75 (vice chm 1964-67, govr 1959-75); convener Scot Univs Cncl on Entrance 1973-77 (memb 1968-77), pres Scot Classical Assoc 1983-88, sr fell Br Acad 1989; *Books* Ciceronis Epistulae (vol 3 1958, vol 2.1 1965, vol 1 1982), George Buchanan's Miscellaneorum Liber (jtly, 1982), Vellei Paterculi Historiae (1988); *Clubs* Aberdeen Business and Professional; *Style—* Prof W S Watt; 38 Woodburn Grdns, Aberdeen AB1 8JA (☎ 0224 314369)

WATTERS, James Andrew Donaldson; s of Andrew James Watters, of Dumfriesshire, and Elsa Donaldson, *née* Broatch; *b* 16 March 1948; *Educ* Kings Coll Sch Wimbledon, Pembroke Coll Oxford (BA); *m* 21 July 1973, Lesley Jane Aves, da of Cyril Joseph Churchman (d 1963); 2 s (Alexander b 4 March 1978, Rupert b 11 June 1980), 1 da (Flora b 16 May 1985); *Career* admitted slr 1972, articled clerk and slr Stephenson Harwood 1970-75, slr Norton Rose Botterell & Roche 1976-79, sr legal advsr Investors in Industry plc 1980-82; ptnr: Goodwille & Co 1982-85, Stephenson Harwood 1985-; Freeman: City of London, Worshipful Co of Slrs; memb Law Soc 1972; *Style—* James Watters, Esq; 59 De Beauvoir Rd, London N1 5AU (☎ 071 254 9221); Stephenson Harwood, 1 St Paul's Churchyard, London EC4M 8SH (☎ 071 329 4422, fax 071 606 0822, telex 886789)

WATTIS, Dr John Philip; s of Philip William Wattis, of 8 West Whinn View, Leeds, and (Elizabeth) Joan, *née* Nickson; *b* 4 Feb 1949; *Educ* St Joseph's Coll Blackpool, Univ of Liverpool Med Sch (MB ChB); *m* 12 July 1969, Florence Elizabeth (Libby), da of David John Roberts (d 1980); 2 s (Mark b 1980, Peter b 1985), 2 da (Sharon b 1982, Ruth b 1988); *Career* house offr The Royal Infirmary Liverpool 1972-73, med supt Amudat Mission Hosp Uganda 1973-75, registrar in psychiatry John Conolly Hosp Birmingham 1975-78, lectr in health care of the elderly Univ of Nottingham 1978-81, sr lectr and conslt in old age psychiatry St James's Univ Hosp Leeds 1986- (conslt 1981-86); public educn offr Section for Psychiatry of Old Age RCPsych (past hon sec), former chm and fndr Leeds Branch Alzheimer's Disease Soc; MRCPsych 1981; *Books* Practical Psychiatry of Old Age (with M Church, 1986), Psychological Assessment of Old People (ed with I Hindmarsh, 1988), Confusion in Old Age (1989); *Recreations* hill walking, photography; *Style—* Dr John Wattis; Dept of Psychiatry, St James's University Hospital, Beckett St, Leeds LS9 7TF (☎ 0532 433144)

WATTLEY, Graham Richard; s of Richard Charles Henry Wattley (d 1961), of Plymouth, and Sylvia Joyce, *née* Orman (d 1962); *b* 12 March 1930; *Educ* Devonport HS Plymouth; *m* 5 Sept 1953, Yvonne (d 1990), da of Harold John Heale (d 1985), of Torquay; s (Jeffery b 1957), 2 da (Lesley b 1954, Gillian b 1956); *Career* Nat Serv pilot offr RAF 1949-50; Miny of Works 1950-71, Dept of Environment 1971-73, dir DVLC grade three 1985 (joined Dept of Transport 1973, asst sec Head of DVLC Computer div 1978-85), ret 1990; memb Ctee Dewi Sant Housing Assoc 1990; *Recreations* walking, cooking, photography; *Style—* Graham Wattley, Esq; Caradoc, 36 The Ridge, Derwen Fawr, Swansea, S Wales SA2 8AG (☎ 0792 290408)

WATTS, Anthony Venning; s of William Andrews Watts (d 1954), and Dorothy, *née* Moody; *b* 30 Dec 1933; *Educ* Hymers Coll Hull, Sch of Architecture Hull Coll of Art (Dip Arch); *m* 28 March 1959, Patricia, da of Wilfred Edgar Blake; 3 s (Jonathan b 14 Nov 1961, Andrew b 2 Feb 1963, Matthew b 16 Jan 1966); *Career* architect; ptnr Fisher Hollingsworth Ptnrship Hull; vice chm Hull Missions to Seamen; memb RIBA 1959; *Books* The Humber (1980); *Recreations* sailing, golf, watercolour painting; *Clubs* Humber Yawl, Hull Golf; *Style—* Anthony Watts, Esq; Greenways, Seven Corners Lane, Beverley, Humberside (☎ 0482 882 269); Fisher Hollingsworth Partnership, Haworth House, Clough Road, Hull (☎ 0428 41 455, fax 0428 45 768)

WATTS, Sir Arthur Desmond; KCMG (1989, CMG 1977), QC (1988); s of Col Arthur Edward Watts (d 1958), and Eileen May, *née* Challons (d 1981); *b* 14 Nov 1931; *Educ* Haileybury, RMA Sandhurst, Downing Coll Cambridge (MA, LLB, Whewell scholar in Int Law); *m* 1957, Iris Ann Collier; 1 s (Christopher), 1 da (Catherine); *Career* called to the Bar Gray's Inn 1957; legal asst FO 1957-59, legal advsr Br Property Cmmn (later Br Embassy) Cairo 1959-62, asst legal advsr FO 1962-67, legal advsr Br Embassy Bonn 1967-69, asst slr Law Offrs Dept 1969-70, legal cnsllr FCO 1970-73, cnsllr (legal advsr) Office of UK Permanent Rep to EEC 1973-77, legal cnsllr FCO 1977-82, dep legal advsr FCO 1982-87 and legal advsr 1987-91; *Books* Legal Effects of War (4 edn with Lord McNair, 1966), Encyclopaedic Dictionary of International; Law (jt ed 1986); contribs to: British Year Book of International Law, International and Comparative Law Quarterly, Egyptian Review of International Law; *Style—* Sir Arthur Watts, KCMG, QC; Foreign and Commonwealth Office, Whitehall, London SW1

WATTS, Prof Cedric Thomas; s of Thomas Henry Watts (d 1964), of Cheltenham, and Mary Adelaide, *née* Cheshire (d 1965); *b* 19 Feb 1937; *Educ* Cheltenham GS, Pembroke Coll Cambridge (BA, MA, PhD); *m* 3 Jan 1963, Judith Edna Mary, da of Charles Edward Hill (d 1974), of Bath; 1 s (William b 1967), 2 da (Linda b 1964 decd 1985), (Sarah b 1972); *Career* Nat Serv RN 1956-58; asst lectr Cambridgeshire Coll of Arts and Technol 1964-65, prof English and American Sch Univ of Sussex 1983- (lectr 1965-79, reader 1979-83); *Books* Conrad's Heart of Darkness: A Critical and Contextual Discussion (1977), Cunninghame Graham: A Critical Biography (jtly, 1979), A Preface to Conrad (1982), RB Cunninghame Graham (1983), The Deceptive Text (1984), A Preface to Keats (1985), William Shakespeare: Measure for Measure (1986), Hamlet (1988), Joseph Conrad: A Literary Life (1989); *Style—* Prof Cedric Watts; University of Sussex, Brighton, East Sussex BN1 9QN (☎ 0273 606755)

WATTS, Christopher Charles Philip; s of Rev Bertram Philip Knight Watts (d 1978), and Ethel Mary, *née* Palmer; unc Sir Henry Lumby of Ormskirk, Lord Lieut of Lancs (d 1989); *b* 21 Jan 1943; *Educ* Liverpool Coll, St John's Leatherhead, Northern Poly London (Dip Arch); *m* 5 Sept 1964, Ann Elizabeth, da of George Richard Harding; 1 da (Melanie-Ann b 1969); *Career* architect to the media industry, television and sound recording; conslt to the Virgin Cos; designer patentee of the Frolic fun boat and others; Liveryman Worshipful Co of Needlemakers; *Recreations* mountain pursuits, huskys, the Arts; *Style*— Christopher Watts, Esq; Tressan House, Chapmans Lane, Deddington, Oxon OX15 0SU (☎ 0869 38883)

WATTS, Christopher Nigel Stuart; s of Maj Ronald Henry Watts (d 1982), of Carlisle, and Eva Maria-Louise, *née* Gliese; *b* 6 March 1954; *Educ* Univ of Aberdeen (MA); *m* 24 Dec 1986, Nicola Clare, da of Wilfred Albert Mason, of Ashby de la Zouche; 1 s (Billy b 1990), 1 da (Poppy Mason-Watts b 1988); *Career* admitted slr 1980; ptnr Whitehead Watts, conslt to Williamson and Soden slrs Birmingham; dir Mason-Watts Fine Art; legal memb: Mental Health Act Cmmn, Mental Health Review Tbnl; memb Law Soc Child Care Panel; memb MIND; *Recreations* music, opera, theatre; *Clubs* Lansdowne; *Style*— Christopher Watts, Esq; 16 Lansdowne Circus, Leamington Spa, Warwicks (☎ 0926 316192); Drystones, Stainton, Cumbria

WATTS, Dr David; s of John Mark Watts (d 1956), of Chapel-en-le-Frith, Derbyshire, and Eva Jane, *née* Waterhouse (d 1973); *b* 14 June 1935; *Educ* New Mills GS, UCL (BSc), Univ of California Berkeley (MSc), McGill Univ Montreal (PhD); *m* 1, 7 Aug 1961 (m dis 1966), Judith Harriet, da of Jack Koota (d 1968), of NY; 1 s (Christopher b 1963); m 2, 18 April 1981, Pamela Anne, da of Charles Lee (d 1983), of Montréal; *Career* dean sch of Geography and Earth resources Univ of Hull 1988- (lectr 1963-67, sr lectr 1973-89, reader 1989-); visiting appts incl: McGill Univ Montreal (1966, 1968), Flinders Univ of S Australia (1980), Univ of Adelaide (1980); fndr ed jl of Biogeography 1974-80, chm Biogeography Res Gp UK 1979-82; memb: Inst of British Geographers 1973- (cncl memb 1977-79), Biogeography Res Gp 1976- (chm 1979-82), Caribbean Studies Assoc 1973- (cncl memb 1988-90), Consumers' Assoc 1987-, memb RSPB 1987-; *Books* incl: Principles of Biogeography (1971), The West Indies; patterns of development, culture and environmental change since 1942 (1979, Spanish language edn 1989), Development and Environment in Korea (1990); *Recreations* theatre, opera, mountain walking, travel, wine; *Style*— Dr David Watts; 21 Hall Walk, Walkington, Beverley, N Humberside HU17 8TF (☎ 0482 861137); Dean, School of Geography & Earth Resources, University of Hull, Hull HU6 7RX (☎ 0482 465421, telex 0482 465274, fax 0482 466340)

WATTS, Edward; s of Edward Samuel Window-Watts (d 1975), of Hornchurch, and Louise, *née* Coffey; *b* 19 March 1940; *Educ* East Ham GS for Boys, South West Essex Tech Coll; *m* 18 June 1960, Iris Josephine, da of Edward John Frost, MBE; 2 s (Mark Edward b 3 March 1963, Paul Jonathan b 27 June 1968); *Career* architect; Cotton Ballard & Blow Architects 1959, E Wookey & Co General Practice Surveyors 1962, chief surveyor Ian Fraser & Assoc (Architects & Town Planners) 1964, team leader Housing Devpt Br GLC 1966, fndr Edward Watts & Co 1976 (now Watts & Partners currently chm); Freeman City of London, memb Worshipful Co of Chartered Surveyors; FRICS 1962; ACIArb 1964, FBIM 1982; *Recreations* sailing - offshore racing and cruising; *Clubs* Royal Ocean Racing, Island Sailing, Royal Lymington Yacht, RAC; *Style*— Edward Watts, Esq; Watts & Partners, 11-12 Haymarket, London SW1Y 4BP (☎ 071 930 6652, fax 071 839 4740)

WATTS, Geoffrey Alan Howard; s of Arthur Josiah Watts (d 1977), and Mary Louise *née* Baber; *b* 26 Aug 1921; *Educ* Wycliffe Coll, Univ of Glasgow (BSc); *m* 28 May 1955, Phyllis Mary, da of James Joseph Harris (d 1977); 2 s (John b 1956, Arthur b 1965), 2 da (Louise b 1958, Rebecca b 1961); *Career* WWII RNVR HMS Hunter (air eng offr) serv India and Malaya 1942-46; chief engr Red & White Services 1947; dir: United Transport Company 1948-82, Watts of Lydney 1949-89, Uganda Transport 1953-63, Kenya Bus Serv 1953-63, African Transport 1954-63, Rhodesia Omnibus Co 1953-63, Bulwark Transport 1963-82, BET 1976-82, Electrical Press 1982-87; numerous current directorships incl: Lloyds Bank plc S Wales 1977-, BET Plant Services 1982-, Eddison Plant Ltd 1982-, Grayston-White & Sparrow 1982-; vice pres Wycliffe Coll 1965-, St John's-on-the-Hill Sch 1965-; FCIT, FInst Nuc Eng, MIME; *Recreations* tennis, golf, sailing, skiing, swimming, flying; *Clubs* Lansdowne, St Pierre, Cardiff Business; *Style*— Geoffrey Watts, Esq; Stroat House, Stroat, Glos NP6 7LR (☎ 0594 52330); Watts of Lydney Group Ltd, High St, Lydney, Glos

WATTS, Gerald Edward; s of Reginald Edward Watts, of West Huntspill, Somerset, and late Gladys May, *née* Hussey; *b* 21 Oct 1934; *Educ* Blundell's, Selwyn Coll Cambridge (MA); *m* 1, 16 Aug 1958 (m dis 1981), Anne, da of Thomas Henry Clarke (d 1965), of Battlefields, Bath; 2 da (Philippa Anne, Susannah Jane); m 2, 21 Dec 1981, Barbara Ann, da of Oliver Rawson (d 1952) of Swindon; *Career* headmaster: Malsis Sch Cross Hills Keighley Yorks 1965-75, Hawtreys Savernake Forest Marlborough 1975-90; athletics for Univ of Cambridge and Western Cos; cricket: MCC, I Zingari, Free Foresters; rugby: Blackheath, Bath, Bedford, Headingley; sec Royal St George's Golf Club Sandwich 1990-; *Recreations* collecting prints, sporting, ephemera, golf; *Clubs* Hawk's, MCC; *Style*— Gerald Watts, Esq; St George's Lodge, Sandwich, Kent

WATTS, John Arthur; MP (C) Slough 1983-; *b* 19 April 1947; *Educ* Bishopshalt GS, Hillingdon, Gonville and Caius Coll Cambridge (MA); *m* 1974, Susan Jennifer, *née* Swan; 1 s, 3 da; *Career* CA 1972; former chm Cambridge Univ Cons Assoc, chm Uxbridge Cons Assoc 1973-76, memb Hillingdon Boro Cncl 1973-86 (former dep ldr and leader of oppn) ldr 1978-84; PPS to: Min Housing and Construction 1984-85, Min of State Treasy 1985; under sec Parly and Law Affairs Inst of CA in Eng and Wales 1981-83; memb: Treasy and CS Select Ctee 1986-; FCA; *Style*— John Watts, Esq, MP; House of Commons, London SW1

WATTS, (William) John Bonsall; s of William John Vickery Watts, JP (d 1972), of The Firs, Newton Abbot, Devon, and Ella Winifred, *née* Bonsall; *Educ* Leighton Park Sch Reading; *m* 1, 1940, Myrae Gertrude; 1 s (William John Christpher b 8 Jan 1949); m 2, 1989, Jean Winifred; 1 step da (Susan St Albans Osman b 28 April 1943); *Career* serv WWII RNVR; dir then pres Watts Blake Bearne & Co plc; chm Teignmouth Harbour Cmmn, memb Newton Abbot UDC, capt and pres Teignmouth Golf Club, memb Trinity House Pilot Cmmn; Br Legion Gold Medal awarded for servs rendered; memb CBI; *Recreations* golf, shooting, conservation, gardening; *Style*— John Watts, Esq; Coombe Hatch, Bishopsteignton, Teighmouth, Devon (☎ 0626 775 228); Watts Blake Bearne & Co plc, Park House, Newton Abbot, Devon (☎ 0626 52 345)

WATTS, Col John Cadman; OBE (1959), MC (1945); *b* 13 April 1913; *Educ* Univ of London (MB BS, LRCP); *m* 21 Feb 1938, Joan Lilian, da of Maj Charles Inwood, OBE, MC (d 1944); 3 s (John Inwood Michael b 1941, Jeremy Christopher b 1945, Richard Charles b 1947); 1 da (Stephanie Carol b 1938); *Career* cmmnd Lt RAMC 1937; surgical specialist: 2/5 CCS Palestine 1938, Western Desert 1939-41, 8 Gen Hosp Alexandria 1941, 9 Gen Hosp Cairo 1942, 2 CCS Syria 1942, 3 CCS WDF 1943; Offr cdr 31 FSU Italy 1943-44, surgical specialist 1944, DADMS 6 Airborne Div 1944-45 (despatches 1944), CO 225 Para FD AMB Malaya, Java 1945-46 (despatches 1946), CO 195 Para FD AMR Palestine 1946-47, surgical specialist BCOF Hosp Japan 1950-57, advsr in surgery Br Troops Austria 1953-55, surgical specialist Cyprus 1955-59, prof of mil surgery RCS England 1960-64; conslt surgn Bedford Gen Hosp 1965-76; cmmr St John Ambulance Bedford 1966-68; BMA: memb Cncl 1969-76, chm Armed Forces Ctee 1977-80, pres E Suffolk Branch 1982-84; OStJ 1968; FRCS Eng 1949; *Books* Surgeon at War (1955); *Recreations* sailing, gardening; *Clubs* Deben Yacht Utd Hosp Sailing; *Style*— Colonel John Watts, OBE, MC; Lowood Lodge, Hasketon, Woodbridge, Suffolk (☎ 047 335 326)

WATTS, John Clifford; s of Clifford Watts (d 1987), and Edith, *née* Fenby (d 1972); *b* 13 June 1933; *Educ* Hull GS, Hull Coll of Technol; *m* 1954, Marion Edith, da of John Holroyd (d 1983), of Hull; 2 s (Christopher, Nicholas); *Career* chm and md Lovell Construction Ltd and subsids, dir Y J Lovell (Hldgs) plc; gp chief exec Witshier plc; *Recreations* flying (holder of private pilot's licence); *Clubs* IOD; *Style*— John Watts, Esq; 11 West Drive, Sonning, nr Reading, Berks (☎ 0734 695789); Manor Court, Harmondsworth, Middx (☎ 081 759 331; fax 081 564 7545)

WATTS, Lesley Mary; *née* Samuel; da of Prof Eric Samuel, CBE, of SA, and Vera Eileen; *b* 19 Sept 1953; *Educ* Cheltenham Ladies Coll, Univ of Cambridge (MA); *m* 1983 (m dis); *Career* dir Kleinwort Benson Ltd; *Recreations* fly fishing, piano, collector of comtemporary art; *Style*— Ms Lesley Watts; Kleinwort Benson Ltd, 20 Fenchurch St, London EC3 (☎ 071 623 8000)

WATTS, Rev Michael; s of Henry Moseley Watts (d 1959), of Gloucester, and Kathleen Evelyn, *née* Powell (d 1981); *b* 18 Jan 1932; *Educ* Sir Thomas Rich's Sch Gloucester, St David's Univ Coll Lampeter (BA), St Catherine's Coll Oxford (BA, MA), St Stephen's House Oxford; *Career* asst curate St Michael Summertown Oxford 1958-60, chaplain and precentor Christ Church Oxford 1960-80, admin asst to Dean of Christ Church 1969-80, gen sec Soc for the Maintenance of the Faith 1983-, rector Sulhamstead Abbots Berks 1980-, warden Burnham Abbey Bucks 1988-, priest vicar Westminster Abbey 1982-87; chaplain to the County High Sheriff Berks 1984; chm Oxford Diocesan Liturgical Ctee 1990-; *Books* Christ Church Oxford (1971), The Life of Christ (1975), Oxford City and University (1974), Pope John Paul II - His Life and Travels (1979); *Recreations* music, church architecture; *Style*— The Rev Michael Watts; The Rectory, Ufton Nervet, Reading RG7 4DH (☎ 0734 832328)

WATTS, Michael George; s of George Watts, OBE, of Selsey, W Sussex, and Barbara Grace, *née* Young; *b* 3 Dec 1934; *Educ* St Edward's Sch, Oxford Sch of Architecture, SW Essex Sch of Art; *m* 1, 13 April 1957 (m dis 1979), (Edith) Sylvia, da of Albert Edward Matthews, MBE (d 1975); 3 s (Simon Michael b 1959, Martin Andrew b 1964, Julian b 1967), 1 da (Alison Barbara b 1962); m 2, 15 Dec 1979, Margaret Jennifer (Meg), da of Alfred Cooper (d 1973); *Career* RE 1956-58; formerly architect public authy housing, EPR Architects Ltd 1985-, bldgs incl offices in central London and Glaxo GP Res Bldgs; paintings exhibited in: London, Home Cos, provinces, RIBA; cartoons and caricatures syndicated nationally under pseudonym Septimus Pike, articles illustrations and cartoons in local and nat pubns; memb: art socs London and Sussex; memb Cons Pty: N Shropshire, London, W Sussex; ARIBA 1965, MFPS 1989; *Recreations* travelling, painting, DIY; *Clubs* Thames Art; *Style*— Michael Watts, Esq; 27 Sutherland St, London SW1V 4JU (☎ 071 630 6004); Trinity Cottage, Edgmond, Shropshire TF10 8LB (☎ 0952 813864); Cavalaire, West Drive, Bracklesham Bay, Chichester, W Sussex PO20 8PH (☎ 0243 670614); EPR Architects Ltd, 27 Douglas St, London SW1P 4PE (☎ 071 834 4411, fax 071 630 9027, telex 917940 ELPACK G)

WATTS, Michael John Colin; s of Colin Ernest Watts of Northwood, Middx, and Jenny Brearly, *née* Eatough; *b* 17 July 1947; *Educ* Rugby, Univ of Cambridge (MA); *m* 23 Sept 1983, Katherine Elizabeth, da of Jim Spivey; *Career* CA 1973; articled clerk Cooper Brothers 1969-73, Morgan Grenfell & Co Limited: joined 1973, seconded Br Trade Devpt Office NY 1976-78, dir Morgan Grenfell Finance Limited 1978-87; dir Brown Shipley & Co Limited 1987-; Freeman City of London 1989, memb Worshipful Co of Pattenmakers 1990; FCA 1978; *Clubs* MCC; *Style*— Michael Watts, Esq; Brown, Shipley & Co Ltd, Founders Court, Lothbury, London EC2 (☎ 071 606 9833, fax 071 606 4825)

WATTS, Reginald John; s of Wilfred John Lionel Watts (d 1963), and Julia Doris Watts; *b* 28 Jan 1931; *Educ* Bishop's Stortford Coll; *m* (Susan) Roscoe, *qv*, da of Charles Roscoe Cushman; 2 children; *Career* chm Burson-Marsteller 1968-85, fndr chm Reginald Watts Assoc 1985-; cncllr: Southend Borough Cncl 1954-63, Westminster City Cncl 1974-82; dep Lord Mayor City of Westminster 1981-82, memb CBI London Regnl Cncl, chm BIM Pub Affrs Ctee 1989, pres Inst PR 1989; hon sr visiting fell City Univ Business Sch; FIPR; *Books* Public Relations for Top Management, Reaching the Consumer, The Businessman's Guide to Marketing, The Corporate Revolution; *Recreations* art, ballet, polo, squash; *Clubs* Carlton; *Style*— Reginald Watts, Esq; Reginald Watts Assoc Ltd, 52 St John Street, London EC1M 4DT (☎ 071 490 4747, fax 071 490 4624)

WATTS, (Susan) Roscoe; da of Charles Roscoe Cushman, of Lamberhurst Quarter, Kent, and Marjorie Cushman; *b* 13 Feb 1937; *Educ* Blackheath HS, Rachel McMillan Teacher Trg Coll (teaching Cert), Inst of Educn Univ of London (MA); *m* 13 July 1960, Reginald John Watts, *qv*; 1 s (Marcus Redmayne b 1962), 1 da (Charlotte Amelia Roscoe b 1964); *Career* lectr child devpt N London Coll, princ St Nicholas Montessori Coll; vice-chair: Teaching Cncl Br Assoc of Early Childhood, NNEB Tutors Assoc, govr Dartford Teachers Trg Coll; *Recreations* collecting builders with few skills, creating gardens; *Clubs* Hurlingham; *Style*— Mrs Roscoe Watts; St Nicholas Montessori College, 23-24 Prince's Gate, London SW7 1PT (☎ 071 225 1277, fax 071 823 7557)

WATTS, Roy; CBE (1978); *b* 17 Aug 1925; *Educ* Doncaster GS, Edinburgh Univ (MA); *m* 1951, Jean Rosaline; 1 s, 2 da; *Career* Army 1943-47, cmmnd Sandhurst; dep chm and chief exec BEA 1972-77 (joined 1955); chm: European Airlines 1982-, Thames Water Authy 1983-, Cabeltime Installations Ltd 1984-89, Armstrong Equipment plc, Water Aid 1984; dep chm: Brymon Airways; jt dep chm BA Bd 1980-83 (memb 1974-83); FCIPEA, FRAeS, FCIT, Hon DBA 1987; *Recreations* cricket, squash; *Style*— Roy Watts, Esq, CBE; Thames Water Plc, 14 Cavendish Place, London W1M 9DJ

WATTS, Thomas (Tom) Rowland; CBE (1978); s of Thomas William Watts (d 1947), of Colchester, and Daisy Maud Watts, *née* Bultitude (d 1949); *b* 1 Jan 1917; *Educ* Gresham's Sch Holt Norfolk; *m* 1955, (Hester) Zoë, da of William Kenrick Armitstead (d 1961), of Colchester; 1 s (Nigel), 2 da (Felicity, Claudia); *Career* TA 1939-41, RM 1941-46, Capt; FCA (memb Cncl 1974-82); ptnr Price Waterhouse until retirement 1982 (joined as an articled clerk 1934); dir Jarrold and Sons Ltd Norwich 1982-87; chm: Accounting Standards Ctee (UK and I) 1978-82, EEC Ctees of Accountancy Profession 1974-79; advsr Dept of Trade on EEC Co Law 1974-82; vice pres D'honneur Gp d'etudes des Experts Comptables de la CEE 1979-87 (vice-pres 1975-79), chm: EEC Liaison Ctee of UK Accountancy Bodies 1985-88, Dental Rates Study Gp 1982-85; gen cmmr for Income Tax 1986-; hon visiting prof City of London Poly 1983-87, Laureate Founding Socs Centenary award 1982; author and editor various professional books and papers; *Recreations* travel, music, opera costume designs; *Style*— Tom Watts Esq, CBE; 13 Fitzwalter Road, Colchester, Essex CO3 3SY; 29 Capstan Square, Isle of Dogs, London E14

WATTS, Victor; s of John Edward Watts (d 1977), and Amy Louise, *née* Putley; *b* 7 Aug 1952; *Educ* Roxeth Manor Sch, Lascelles Sch Harrow; *m* 13 May 1972, Eve, da of Charles Coleman; *Career* photographer; freelance asst with numerous photographic studios 1968-75 (work appeared in Times, Observer, Express, Tatler and Harpers), proprietor of own studio 1976-; memb Assoc of Photographers; *Style*— Victor Watts, Esq; 31 Liddell Rd, West Hampstead, London NW6 2EW (☎ 071 624 8228/9, fax 071 328 2288)

WATTS, His Hon Judge Victor Brian; s of Percy William King Watts, of 77 Harland

Rd, Lee (d 1981), and Doris Milicent *née* Peat (d 1971); *b* 7 Jan 1927; *Educ* Coffe's GS, Univ Coll Oxford (MA, BCL); *m* 31 July 1965, Patricia Eileen, da of Richard Cuthbert Steer, of Ferndown, Dorset (d 1982); 1 s (Martin b 1969), 1 da (Julia b 1967); *Career* Flying Offr Educn Branch RAF 1950-52; called to the Bar Middle Temple 1950; memb Western Circuit; rec Crown Ct 1972-80; circuit judge 1980; *Recreations* the arts, tennis, riding; *Clubs* Hurlingham; *Style—* His Hon Judge Victor Watts; 28 Abinger Rd, Bedford Park, London W4 1EL (☎ 081 994 4435)

WATTS, Vincent Challacombe; s of Geoffrey Hilton Watts (d 1987), and Lillian Florence, *née* Pye (d 1955); *b* 11 Aug 1940; *Educ* Sidcot Sch, Peterhouse Cambridge (MA), Univ of Birmingham (MSc); *m* 17 June 1967, Rachel Mary, da of John Arthur Rosser (d 1986); 1 s (Ben b 1977), 1 da (Hannah b 1981); *Career* CA; ptnr Arthur Andersen Consltg 1976- (joined 1963); projects incl: performance indicators for NHS and govt agencies, memb HM Treasy Fin Mgmnt Unit 1982-85, info technol strategies for NHS, BR and MOD; memb Cncl: ICAEW 1987-89, Operational Res Soc 1974-76; FCA; *Recreations* squash; *Clubs* Utd Oxford and Cambridge Univ; *Style—* Vincent Watts, Esq; Bardon Lodge, 21 Westside, Wimbledon Common, London SW19 4UF Andersen Consulting, 2 Arundel St, London WC2R 2PS (☎ 071 438 3560)

WATTS-RUSSELL, David O'Reilly; s of Cdr Nevill David Watts-Russell (d 1962), and Jean, *née* McNair (d 1974); *see* Burke's Landed Gentry 18 edn vol II, 1969; *b* 21 Jan 1944; *Educ* Gordonstoun; *m* 5 April 1974, Susan; 1 s (Edward David b 1976), 3 da (Miranda Jane b 1980, Emily Susan b 1983, Tabitha Rose b 1986); *Career* dir Greig Middleton & Co Ltd 1986-; memb Ayshire and Arran Health Bd 1987-; *Recreations* music, reading, shooting, fishing, travel; *Clubs* Western (Glasgow), Glasgow Arts; *Style—* David Watts-Russell, Esq; Glenlogan, Sorn, Mauchline, Ayshire KA5 6JP; 70 Wellington St G2 6UD, Glasgow

WAUGH, Auberon Alexander; s of Evelyn Waugh (d 1966), the novelist, by his 2 w Laura (d 1973), yst da of Hon Aubrey Herbert, 2 s of 4 Earl of Carnarvon; *b* 17 Nov 1939; *Educ* Downside, Christ Church Oxford; *m* 1 July 1961, Lady Teresa Onslow, da of 6 Earl of Onslow, KBE, MC, TD (d 1971); 2 s (Alexander b 1963, Nathaniel b 1968), 2 da (Sophia b 1962, Daisy b 1967); *Career* served Royal Horse Guards 1957-58; journalist and novelist; formerly with: Catholic Herald, Mirror Group, Times; former chief fiction reviewer Evening Standard 1973-80; columnist: Private Eye 1970-86, The Spectator 1976- (chief fiction reviewer 1970-73), The Sunday Telegraph 1981-90; chief book reviewer: Daily Mail 1981-86, Independent 1986-90; book reviewer Sunday Telegraph 1990-, Way of the World Daily Telegraph 1990-; former contributor Books and Bookmen; ed Literary Review 1986; stood for N Devon Gen Election as Dog Lovers Party Candidate 1979; Nat Press Critic of the Year Commendations 1976 and 1978; Granada TV What the Papers Say Columnist of the Year 1978-88; *Books* Foxglove Saga (1960), Who are the Violets Now? (1966), Consider the Lilies (1968), A Bed of Flowers (1971), The Last Word: The Trial of Jeremy Thorpe (1980), Four Crowded Years: The Diaries of Auberon Waugh 1972-1976, A Turbulent Decade: 1976-85 (1985), Waugh on Wine (1986); *Recreations* gossip, wine; *Style—* Auberon Waugh Esq; Combe Florey House, Combe Florey, Taunton, Somerset (☎ 0823 432297)

WAUGH, Rev Eric Alexander; s of Hugh Waugh (d 1990), and Marion, *née* McLay (d 1972); *b* 9 May 1933; *Educ* Univ of Glasgow, Univ of Edinburgh (LTh); *m* 26 Aug 1955, Agnes-Jean (Sheena), da of James Renton Saunders (d 1985); 2 s (Euan b 1959, Eric James b 1961); *Career* local govt offr 1948-64, asst minister of High Church Bathgate 1969-70, missionary Kenya Highlands 1970-73, minister of Mowbray Presbyterian Church Cape Town 1973-78, missioner of Presbyterian Church of Southern Africa 1978-85, minster of The City Temple URC London 1986-; *Recreations* hill walking, gardening; *Style—* Rev Eric Waugh; 124 Rotherfield St, Islington, London N1 3DA (☎ 071 359 7961); The City Temple, Holborn Viaduct, London EC1A 2DE (☎ 071 583 5532)

WAUGH, Harry Horsburgh; s of Alexander Adam Waugh (d 1908), and Mary Anne, *née* Jennings (d 1926); *b* 9 June 1904; *Educ* Cranleigh; *m* 1, 1936 (m dis 1960), Diane Eleanor, *née* Spengler; m 2, 4 June 1970, Prudence D'Arcy, da of Lt-Col Joseph Waters, OBE, of Down Cottage, Frant, nr Tunbridge Wells; 1 s (Jamie b 3 Sept 1973), 1 da (Harriet (twin) b 3 Sept 1973); *Career* WWII, Welsh Guards 1940-45, capt and co cdr Wellington Barracks 1944-45; wine merchant; Block Grey and Block 1934-39, John Harvey and Sons Ltd Bristol 1946-66 (dir 1950-66), ret 1966; dir Chateau Latour Pauillac 1965-, hon MW 1989; American Ambassadors award Knights of the Vine 1988, certificate of appreciation Wine Inst of San Francisco 1988, Lifetime Achievement award Soc of Bacchus USA 1990; cncllr and co fndr Wine Guild of UK; fndr and pres Les Compagnons du Beaujolais and Zinfandel Club for the Promotion of Californian Wine; Ordre du Mérite Agricole France 1984, Ordre Nationale du Mérite France 1987; *Books* Bacchus on the Wing (1966), The Changing Face of Wine (1968), Pick of the Bunch (1970), Diary of a Wine Taster (1972), Winetaster's Choice (1973), Harry Waugh's Wine diary: Columes 6-10 (1975-87); *Recreations* shooting, collecting china; *Clubs* Saintsbury, Brooks's, Boodle's, Pratt's; *Style—* Harry Waugh, Esq; 14 Camden Square, London NW1 9UY (☎ 071 485 9287)

WAUGH, Dr Michael Anthony; s of Anthony Lawrence Waugh, of Richmond, Surrey, and Nancy Genevieve, *née* Vernon; *b* 19 Sept 1943; *Educ* St George's Coll Weybridge Surrey, Charing Cross Hos Med Sch Univ of London (MB BS); *Career* consIt physician genito urinary medicine Gen Infirmary Leeds 1975-, pres Med Soc for Study of Venereal Diseases 1989- (hon sec 1981-89), sec gen Int Union Against Venereal Diseases and Treponematoses 1984-, observer venereology dermatovenereology specialists ctee Union Euro Med Specialists 1984-, hon sr lectr Univ of Leeds 1985- (Soc Apothecaries lectr in history of medicine 1984-); corresponding memb Austrian Soc for Dermatology and Venereology 1990; DHMSA 1970, Dip Venereology 1974; Liveryman Worshipful Co Apothecaries 1970; *Books* venereology section of Oxford Companion to Medicine (1986), contrib Sexually Transmitted Diseases (2 edn, 1990), History of Sexually Transmitted Diseases (1990); *Recreations* gardening, browsing in second hand bookshops, travelling; *Style—* Dr Michael Waugh; Wellfield House, 151 Roker Lane, Pudsey, Leeds LS28 9ND (☎ 0532 565 255); Dept of Genito Urinary Medicine, Gen Infirmary Leeds, LS1 3EX (☎ 0532 432 799)

WAUGH, Lady Teresa Lorraine; *née* Onslow; da of 6 Earl of Onslow, KBE, MC, TD (d 1971); sister of 7 Earl of Onslow; *b* 1940; *m* 1961, Auberon Waugh, *qv*; 2 s, 2 da; *Career* translator and novelist; *Books* Painting Water (1984), Waterloo Waterloo (1986), An Intolerable Burden (1988), Song at Twilight (1989); *Style—* The Lady Teresa Waugh; Combe Florey House, Combe Florey, Taunton, Somerset (☎ 0823 432297)

WAVERLEY, 3 Viscount (UK 1952); John Desmond Forbes Anderson; o s of 2 Viscount Waverley (d 1990), and Lorna Myrtle Ann, *née* Ledgerwood; *b* 31 Oct 1949; *Educ* Malvern; *Heir* none; *Style—* The Rt Hon the Viscount Waverley; Chanders, Aldworth, Berks RG8 9RU

WAVERLEY, Viscountess; Lorna Myrtle Ann; *née* Ledgerwood; da of Lt-Col Frederick Hill Ledgerwood, IA, and Mrs Alfred John Home Ross; *m* 13 Nov 1948, 2 Viscount Waverley (d 1990); 1 s (3 Viscount, *qv*), 1 da (Hon Patricia Mairead Janet b 1955) (and 1 da decd)

WAY, John Stanley; s of Stanley George Godwin Way (d 1985), of Weybridge, Surrey, and Margaret Jean, *née* Edwards; *b* 18 Dec 1946; *Educ* St John's Sch Leatherhead; *m* 1 Feb 1975, (Diana) Jayne, da of Maj Thomas Herbert Sills, MBE, TD, DL (d 1988), of Sandy, Beds; 2 s (Robert b 1979, Duncan b 1986); *Career* Coopers & Lybrand 1969-73; Continental Illinois Nat Bank & Tst Chicago: far east regnl auditor 1974-79, Euro/Latin America regnl auditor London 1979-83, int auditor 1983-87; int auditor worldwide Prudential Insur Co of America 1987-; FCA 1969, FHKSA 1977, MBIM 1978, MENSA, IIA 1978; *Recreations* golf, tennis; *Style—* John Way, Esq; Fairfield, Pyrford Woods, Pyrford, Woking, Surrey GU22 8UT; 9 Devonshire Square, London EC2M 4HP (☎ 071 548 5045)

WAY, Patrick Edward; s of John Francis Way, of Solihull, and Margaret Helen Laura, *née* Ewins; *b* 6 Feb 1954; *Educ* Solihull Sch, Univ of Leeds (BA); *m* 10 June 1978, Judith Anne, da of Dr Peter Orchard Williams, of Winchester; 3 s (Oliver Christopher Patrick b 16 Dec 1983, Frederick William Patrick b 6 Feb 1987, Dominic Hugo Patrick b 29 Nov 1988); *Career* admitted slr 1979, asst slr Lawrence Graham 1979-82, tax ptnr Nabarro Nathanson 1985-87 (asst 1982-85), ptnr and head of tax dept Gouldens 1987-; founding ed Trusts and Estates 1985, tax ed The BES Magazine 1986; ctee memb BES Assoc; memb Law Soc; *Books* Death and Taxes (1985), Maximising Opportunities under the BES (1986), The BES and Assured Tenancies - The New Rules (1988), Tolley's Tax Planning (contib, 1991), Share Sales and Earn-Outs (1991), Practical Corporate Tax Planning (ed and contrib, 1991); *Recreations* tennis; *Style—* Patrick Way, Esq; 22 Tudor St, London EC4Y OJJ (☎ 071 583 7777, fax 071 583 3051, telex 21520)

WAY, Sir Richard George Kitchener; KCB (1961, CB 1957), CBE (1952); s of Frederick Way; *b* 15 Sept 1914; *Educ* Poly Secdy Sch London; *m* 1947, Ursula Starr; 1 s, 2 da; *Career* dep sec Miny Supply 1958-59, perm under sec WO 1960-63, perm sec Miny Aviation 1963-66; chm: Lansing Bagnall 1967-69, London Transport 1970-74, Royal Cmmn for Exhibition of 1851 1978-87; princ King's Coll London 1975-80; dir Dobson Pk Industs Ltd 1975-85; treas Cncl London Zoological Soc 1983-84 (memb 1977, vice-pres 1979-82 and 1984-87); Hon DSC Univ of Loughborough; CStJ; *Clubs* Brooks's; *Style—* Sir Richard Way, KCB, CBE; The Old Forge, Shalden, Alton, Hants (☎ 0420 82383)

WAYMOUTH, Peter Gordon; s of Capt Gilbert Ridley Waymouth, RN, CBE (d 1974), and Gwyneth Lilian, *née* Rice (d 1987); *b* 11 Nov 1932; *Educ* Radley, Pembroke Coll Cambridge; *m* 2 June 1956, Jean Myddleton, da of Neil Sutherland Eaton (d 1964); 1 s (Harry b 1962), 2 da (Claire b 1958, Sophie b 1960); *Career* Lt RTR serv Germany 1952-53; chief exec Containerbase Federation Ltd and dir assoc cos 1968-70; mangr: Blue Star Line 1970-73, Union International Ltd and dir subsidiary cos 1973-78; chm Continental N Atlantic Westbound Freight Conf 1978-79, dir and md T S Engineering Ltd 1979-86, dir: Turnbull Scott Holdings plc 1981-86, Acoustat Ltd, Hurry & Ptnrs 1984-86, Perth Corp Holdings Ltd 1988-; md Ailsa Perth Shipbuilders Ltd 1987-; govr Radley Coll 1981-86, memb Bd Marr Coll Groom 1990-; *Recreations* golf, painting, walking, fishing, shooting; *Clubs* Woking, Prestwick Golf; *Style—* Peter G Waymouth, Esq; c/o Ailsa-Perth Shipbuilders, Harbour Rd, Troon, Ayrshire KA10 6DN (☎ 0292 311311, fax 0292 317613, telex 778027 AILSA G)

WAYMOUTH, Lady Victoria Mary Verenia Braganza; *née* Yorke; da of 9 Earl of Hardwicke (d 1974); *b* 22 Feb 1947; *Educ* St Mary's Convent Ascot; *m* 1976, Nigel Norman de Glanville, artist, s of Wing Cdr T G Waymouth, of Bideford; 2 s; *Career* interior designer; *Style—* The Lady Victoria Waymouth; 36 Elms Rd, SW4 (☎ 071 622 2985, office 071 376 5244)

WAYNE, Peter Howard; s of Kurt Wolff (d 1944), of Berlin, and Lilli, *née* Wallerstein; *b* 8 May 1920; *Educ* Friends' Sch Great Ayton, Germany, Switzerland; *m* 19 Oct 1968, Waltraud Charlotte, da of Carl Kirsch (d 1985), of Frankfurt, Germany; 1 s (Alexander Simon Howard b 1970), 1 da (Nicola Martina Suzanne b 1973); *Career* mil serv 1941-46 UK, France, Belgium, Germany; mil govt head interpreter at Minden War Crimes Ct, interpreter and investigator of German financial institutions; CA, ptnr Thomas Theobald & Son 1952-67; fin dir: Engway Properties Ltd 1958, Lynjohn Investments Ltd 1959; *Recreations* skiing, music, historic research; *Clubs* Army Ski Assoc; *Style—* Peter H Wayne, Esq; 11 Kensington Park Gardens, London W11 3HD (☎ 071 727 3476); 81 Cromwell Rd, London SW7 (☎ 071 370 3273)

WAYT, John Lancaster; s of Arthur George Wayt, MBE, of Netherstones, Oxshott Way, Cobham, Surrey, and Leonora Lancaster, *née* Shaw; *b* 8 March 1937; *Educ* Cranleigh, Keble Coll Oxford (MA); *m* 30 Sept 1965, Margaret, da of Henry Morris, of Woodcote Ave, Nuneaton, Warks; 3 s (Anthony b 1967, James b 1970, David b 1970); *Career* admitted slr 1961; sr ptnr Lancasters (Slrs) 1963-; dir: National Counties 1968, Lancaster Scott and Co Ltd, Lancaster Shaw Insur Conslts plc (chm 1972-); St Martins-le-Grand Estates Ltd, Lancasters Business Mgmnt Ltd, Nat Counties Fin Servs Ltd; Counties and Guardian Financial Services Ltd; exec dep chm and chief exec National Counties Bldg Soc 1982-; National Counties Estate Agents Ltd, London dir Guardian Royal Exchange Assur; chm National Counties Pension Scheme; memb Law Soc; FCIFA, FFA, FBIM, ACIArb, ANAEA, FInstD; *Recreations* art appreciation, gardening, reading; *Clubs* RAC; *Style—* John Wayt, Esq; Ebbisham House, Church St, Epsom, Surrey; Waterloo House, High St, Epsom, Surrey KT19 8EL (☎ 0372 724931)

WDOWCZYK, Dariusz Janusz; s of Waclaw Wdowczyk, of Warsaw, Poland, and Hanna, *née* Outkiewicz; *b* 25 Sept 1962; *Educ* Tech Coll Warsaw; *m* Iwona Agniszka; 1 s (Rafel Michal b 5 Aug 1983), 1 da (Aleksandra Paulina b 26 Sept 1988); *Career* professional footballer; Gwardia Warszawa 1983-89, Celtic 1989-; Poland caps: 50 jr, 15 Olympic, 20 under 21, 47 full (capt 10 times); honours: Polish Cup Legia Warszawa 1989, runners up Poland Euro Jr Championships 1980 and 1981; *Recreations* fishing, cars, reading, spending time with my wife and children; *Style—* Dariusz Wdowczyk, Esq; Celtic FC, Celtic Park, Glasgow (☎ 041 556 2611)

WEALE, Prof Albert Peter; s of Albert Cecil Weale (d 1978), of Brighton, and Elizabeth Margaret, *née* Granger (d 1975); *b* 30 May 1950; *Educ* Varndean GS for Boys Brighton, Clare Coll Cambridge (MA, PhD); *m* 17 Sept 1976 (m dis 1985), Jane, *née* Leresche; *Career* Sir James Knott res fell Dept of Politics Univ of Newcastle upon Tyne 1974-76, lectr in politics 1976-85, asst dir Inst for Res in the Social Sciences Univ of York 1982-85, prof of politics UEA 1985; memb ESRC: Res Grants Bd, Soc, Politics Res Devpt Gp 1986-90; memb Advsy Ctee Kings Fund Inst 1986-89; *Books* Lone Mothers, Paid Work and Social Security (1984), Cost and Choice in Health Care (ed, 1989), Equality and Social Policy (1978), Political Theory and Social Policy (1983); *Recreations* walking, piano, company of friends, swimming; *Style—* Prof Albert Weale; School of Economic and Social Studies, University of East Anglia, Norwich NR4 7TJ (☎ 0603 592064, fax 0603 58553, telex 975197)

WEALE, Felix Ernest; s of Dr Frederick Julius Weale, and Mary Weale; *b* 15 Feb 1925; *Educ* Kingston GS, Westminster Med Sch (MB BS, MRCS, LRCP, MS, PhD); *m* Audrey, da of Harold Elliott, of Wiveliscombe; 2 s (Peter b 1957, Adrian b 1963); *Career* Nat Serv, Sqdn Ldr Med Branch, served Egypt and Iraq 1949-51; jr posts in surgery radiotherapy and pathology 1947-55, lectr in physiology RCS 1955-57, res fell in cardiac surgery Guy's Hosp 1958-59, sr lectr and asst dir St Bartholomew's Hosp 1960-69, conslt surgeon with interest in vascular surgery Dartford and Gravesham 1969-90; exec Br Exec Servs Overseas 1990-; memb Vascular Soc of GB 1969-;

FRCS; *Books* The Heart (contrib, 1963), Introduction to Surgical Haemodynamics (1966, in French translation 1967), Irreversible Shock (1959), Arterial Stenosis (1966), Current Operative Surgery (1985), Surgical Management of Vascular Diseases (1991); *Recreations* skiing, painting, music; *Clubs* Peripheral Vascular; *Style*— Felix Weale, Esq; Top Corner, 9 Warren View, Shorne, Kent DA12 3EJ; Joyce Green Hospital, Dartford, Kent DA1 5P1

WEALE, Graham Alexander; s of Prof Robert Alexander Weale, of London, and Margaret Elizabeth, *née* Drury; *b* 26 Aug 1953; *Educ* Highgate Sch, Lincoln Coll Oxford (MA), City Univ (MSc), Cranfield Sch of Mgmnt (MBA); *m* 15 March 1978, Anthea, da of Thomas Crompton (d 1986), of Christchurch; 2 s (Thomas b 1979, James b 1983); *Career* supply co ordinator Esso Petroleum Co 1977-81, mgmnt conslt Touche Ross & Co 1982-84, sr energy conslt DRI Europe (McGraw Hill) 1984-86, mangr WEFA Energy 1987-; conslt to various Euro gas, oil and power cos, arbitrator; memb: Hayes Town Chapel, Reformed Evangelical Church; Freeman City of London 1983, memb Worshipful Co of Tin Plate and Wire Workers; FInst Pet, AIArb; *Books* European Gas Markets After Troll, European Coal Markets - Prospects and Risks, Gasoline in Europe; *Recreations* chamber music, travel; *Style*— Graham Weale, Esq; 39 The Park, Ealing, London W5 5NP (☎ 081 567 9886); WEFA Energy, 62 Margaret St, London W1N 7FJ (☎ 071 631 0757, fax 071 631 0754)

WEALE, Timothy Donald; s of Donald Jones Weale (d 1971), of Basingstoke, Hants, and Freda Jessy, *née* Gardiner; *b* 10 April 1951; *Educ* Magdalen Coll Oxford, Coll of Estate Mgmnt Reading; *m* 12 Oct 1974, Pamela Anne, da of Gerard Gordon Moore (d 1972), of Tadley, Hants; 1 s (Edward b 15 April 1981), 1 da (Alice b 21 April 1983); *Career* Wessex Regt (Rifle Vols, TA) 1979-86; Capt Inns of Ct and City Yeo 1986; ptnr Pearsons (auctioneers, estate agents surveyors) 1984-86; dir Prudential Property Services 1986-89, ptnr Healey and Baker 1989-; FSVA 1978, ARVA 1979; *Recreations* sailing, skiing, vintage cars, gardening, field sports, music, antiques; *Clubs* VSCC, Cavalry annd Guards'; *Style*— Timothy Weale, Esq; Thackham Ct, Hartley Wintney, nr Basingstoke, Hants RG27 8JG (☎ 025 126 3900); 29 St Georges St, Hanover Square, London W1 3BG (☎ 071 629 9292)

WEARE, Dr (Trevor) John; OBE (1990); s of Trevor Leslie Weare, and Edna Margaret, *née* Roberts; *b* 31 Dec 1943; *Educ* Aston Tech Coll, Imperial Coll London (Granville studentship prize in physics); *m* 20 June 1964, Margaret Ann, da of Harry Wright; 2 s (Michael John b 1969, Stuart Martin b 1972); *Career* post-doctoral res fell Dept of Theoretical Physics: McGill Univ Montreal Canada 1968-70, Univ of Oxford 1970-72; Hydraulics Res Station: sr scientific offr 1972-75, princ scientific offr 1975-78, sr princ scientific offr 1978-81, chief scientific offr 1981-82; md Hydraulics Research Ltd Wallingford 1982-; FRSA 1987, FIWEM 1989; *Style*— Dr John Weare, OBE; Hydraulics Research Ltd, Wallingford OX10 8BA (☎ 0491 35381, fax 0491 25430, telex 848552, car 0860 390726)

WEARE, Nigel; s of Allan George Weare, of Egham, Surrey, and Sylvia, *née* Trigg; *b* 19 Sept 1962; *Educ* Strodes GS and Sixth Form Coll, Goldsmith Coll London, Homerton Coll Cambridge; *Career* nat rowing coach; started rowing 1976; clubs: Strodes Coll, Burway, Staines, Molesey, Kingston, Tideway Scullers, Univ of London, Univ of Cambridge, Homerton Coll Cambridge, Société Nautique de la Marne France; World Junior Championships: Bronze medallist cox Junior Men's VIIIs (Moscow) 1979, 4 place cox Junior Men's VIIIs (Hazewinkel)) 1980; (as coach) 8 place Junior Women's Quads (Aiguebelette) 1990; nat rowing coach 1988-; French teacher 1986-88; memb Br Inst of Sports Coaches; *Recreations* badminton, role playing; *Style*— Nigel Weare, Esq; Amateur Rowing Association, 6 Lower Mall, Hammersmith, London W6 9DJ (☎ 081 748 3632, fax 081 741 4658)

WEARING, Hon Mrs (Caroline Ruth); *née* Addison; da of 3 Viscount Addison; *b* 30 July 1942; *m* 1965, John Wearing; 1 s (Patrick b 1969), 1 da (Jacalyn b 1966); *Style*— The Hon Mrs Wearing; 12 Hill St North, Richmond, Nelson, N Z

WEARNE, Prof Stephen Hugh; s of Hugh Wearne (d 1941), and Phyllis Marion, *née* Stevens (d 1966); *b* 29 June 1928; *Educ* Woolwich Poly (BSc), Imperial Coll London (DIC), Univ of Manchester (PhD); *m* 3 Oct 1959, (Elizabeth) Jean, da of Prof W E Morton (d 1984), of Hale, Cheshire; 1 s (Christopher b 1960), 1 da (Susan b 1963); *Career* apprentice 1945-50, design, planning and co-ordination of water power projects in Spain, Scotland and S America 1952-57, construction design and mgmnt of nuclear power projects 1957-64, sr lectr UMIST 1964-73, prof of technol mgmnt Univ of Bradford 1973-84, chm UK Engrg Project Mgmnt Forum 1983-86; CEng, FICE, FIMechE; *Books* Principles of Engineering Organization (1973), Control of Engineering Projects (1989), Civil Engineering Contracts (1989); *Recreations* work, family, music; *Style*— Prof Stephen Wearne; Project Management Group, UMIST, PO Box 88, Manchester MCO 1QD (☎ 061 200 4615, fax 061 200 4646, telex 666094)

WEATHERALL, Prof Sir David John; s of Harry Weatherall (d 1973), and Gwendoline Charlotte Miriam, *née* Tharme (d 1985); *b* 9 March 1933; *Educ* Calday Grange GS, Univ of Liverpool (MB ChB, MD); *m* 20 June 1962, Stella Mayorga Isobel, da of Rev Campo Mayorga, of Bogota, Colombia; 1 s (Mark b 1968); *Career* Nuffield prof of clinical med Univ of Oxford 1974-; hon dir: MRC Molecular Haematology Unit 1980, Inst Molecular Med Univ of Oxford; Hon MD: Univ of Leeds, Univ of Sheffield; Hon DSc: Univ of Manchester, Univ of Edinburgh, Univ of Leicester, Univ of Aberdeen; overseas memb Nat Acad of Sciences USA 1990, vice pres Royal Soc 1990-91 (winner Royal medal 1990), hon fell Imperial Coll, Hon FRCOG, Hon FRACP, Hon FACP, FRCP, FRCPath, FRCPE, FRS; *Books* The Thalassaemia Syndromes (with J B Clegg, 3 edn 1982), Blood and Its Disorders (with R M Hardisty, 2 edn 1982), The Oxford Textbook of Medicine (with J G G Ledingham and D A Warrell, 2 edn 1987), The New Genetics and Clinical Practice (3 edn, 1991); *Recreations* music, oriental food; *Style*— Prof Sir David Weatherall, FRS; 8 Cumnor Rise Rd, Cumnor Hill, Oxford OX2 9HD (☎ 0865 862467); Nuffield Dept of Clinical Medicine, John Radcliffe Hosp, Oxford (☎ 0865 60201, telex 83147 viaor GJRH2, fax 0865 750506)

WEATHERALL, Vice Adm Sir James Lamb (Jim); s of Lt Cdr Alwyne Thomas Hirst Weatherall, RNR (d 1939), and Olive Catherine Joan, *née* Cuthbert (d 1977); *b* 28 Feb 1936; *Educ* Gordonstoun; *m* 12 May 1962, Jean Stewart, *née* Macpherson, da of 1 Baron Drumalbyn, KBE, PC; 2 s (Niall b 1967, Ian b 1976), 3 da (Sarah b 1968, Annie b 1974, Elizabeth b 1976); *Career* cadet BRNC Dartmouth, HMS Triumph 1954, midshipman HMS Albion 1955-56; Sub Lt: HMS Scotsman 1956, HM Yacht Britannia 1958; Lt: HMS Lagos 1959-60, HMS Wizard 1960-61, HMS Houghton 1962-64, HMS Tartar 1964, HMS Eastbourne 1965-66; Lt Cdr Advanced Navigation Course 1966, HMS Soberton 1966-67, HMS London 1968-70; Lt Cdr/Cdr HMS Ulster 1970-72 (i/c); Cdr: MOD 1972-74, HMS Tarter 1975-76 (i/c), Cdr Sea Trg 1976-77, HMS Ark Royal 1978; Capt: Nato Def Coll 1979, MOD-Naval Plans 1979-81, HMS Andromeda (i/c), and 8 Frigate Sqdn 1982-84 (inc Falklands), RN Presentation Team 1984-85, HMS Ark Royal (i/c) 1985-87; ADC HM The Queen 1986-87; Rear Adm Staff of Supreme Allied Cdr Europe 1987-89; Vice Adm Dep Supreme Allied Cdr Atlantic 1989-; pres: Bishop's Waltham Branch Royal Br Legion 1983-, London NE Area Sea Cadet Corps 1973-, Leics Fleet Air Arm Assoc 1984-; Liveryman Worshipful Co of Shipwrights 1985 (asst Ct 1989), Freeman City of London 1985, Younger Br Trinity House 1986; *Recreations* fishing, stamp collecting, hockey; *Clubs* RN of 1765 and 1785; *Style*— Vice Adm Sir James Weatherall; Box C-01, Saclant HQ, Naval Party 1964, BFPO Ships (☎ 010 1 804 440 1567, fax 010 1 804 445 3210)

WEATHERALL, Hon Lady (Jean Stewart); *née* Macpherson; er da of 1 Baron Drumalbyn, KBE, PC (d 1987), and Margaret Phyllis, *née* Runge (d 1979); *b* 1938; *m* 1962, Vice Adm Sir James Lamb Weatherall, KBE, s of Alwyn Thomas Lamb Weatherall, RN (d 1939); 2 s (Niall b 1967, Ian b 1976), 3 da (Sarah b 1968, Annie b 1974, Elizabeth b 1976); *Style*— The Hon Lady Weatherall; Craig House, Bishop's Waltham, Hants SO3 1FS

WEATHERBY, Charles (Edward); s of Edward William Weatherby (d 1967), and Ida Rosemary Weatherby, *née* Stratton (d 1984); *b* 28 Dec 1932; *Educ* Winchester; *m* 2 April 1960, Susan (Alison), da of Sir Francis Ley, Bt, MBE, TD; 2 da (Camilla b 1963, Fiona b 1965); *Career* Nat Serv 1 Bn Coldstream Gds (Lt) 1951-53 (Cyprus and Middle E); dir Weatherbys 1956-; dep sec and dir of Field Servs of the Jockey Club 1977-90; *Recreations* fishing, gardening, travelling; *Clubs* Boodle's; *Style*— Charles Weatherby, Esq; Mixbury Lodge Farm, Brackley, Northants, NN13 5RW; Weatherbys, Sanders Rd, Wellingborough, Northamptonshire NN8 4BX

WEATHERHEAD, Alexander Stewart (Sandy); OBE (1985), TD (1964 and clasp 1973); s of Kenneth Kilpatrick Weatherhead (d 1979), and Katharine, *née* Stewart, of Glasgow; *b* 3 Aug 1931; *Educ* George Watson's Edinburgh, Larchfield Sch Helensburgh, Glasgow Acad, Univ of Glasgow (MA, LLB); *m* 22 Dec 1972, (Harriett) Foye, da of Rev Arthur Organ, of Toronto, Canada; 2 da (Foye b 1974, Alison b 1975); *Career* Nat Serv 2 Lt 1950-52 RA 1950; TA 1952-76; Lt-Col cmdg: 277 (A & SH) Field Regt RA (TA) 1965-67, Lowland Regt RA (T) 1967, Univs of Glasgow and Strathclyde OTC 1971-73; chm TAVR (Lowlands West) 1990- (memb 1967, Col 1974-76), ADC to HM The Queen 1977-81, Hon Col Univs of Glasgow and Strathclyde OTC 1982-; slr 1958, ptnr Tindal Oatts 1960-, hon vice pres Law Soc of Scotland 1983-84 (Cncl memb 1971-84); Temp Sheriff 1985-; memb: Royal Cmmn on Legal Servs in Scotland 1976-80, Law Soc of Scotland 1958-, Royal Faculty of Procurators in Glasgow 1960-; *Recreations* reading, sailing, music, tennis; *Clubs* New (Edinburgh), Royal Western Yacht, Clyde Cruising, Royal Highland Yacht; *Style*— A S Weatherhead, Esq, OBE, TD; 52 Partickhill Rd, Glasgow G11 5AB (☎ 041 334 6277); 48 St Vincent St, Glasgow G2 5HS (☎ fax 041 221 8012, 041 221 7803)

WEATHERILL, Rt Hon (Bruce) Bernard; PC (1980), MP (C) Croydon NE 1964-; s of Bernard Weatherill, of Guildford, by his w Annie Gertrude, *née* Creak; *b* 25 Nov 1920; *Educ* Malvern; *m* 1949, Lyn, da of H Eatwell; 2 s, 1 da (Virginia); *Career* serv WWII 4/7 Royal Dragoon Gds & Indian Army; former md Bernard Weatherill Ltd; former: chm Guildford Cons Assoc, memb Nat Union Cons Party; oppn whip 1967, lord cmmr Treasy 1970-71, vice chamberlain HM Household 1971-72, comptroller 1972-73, treas HM Household and Govt dep chief whip 1973-74, oppn dep chief whip 1974-79, chm Ways and Means Ctee 1979-83; elected speaker House of Commons 1983 and 1987; chm Cwlth Speakers and Presiding Offrs 1986 and 1988, High Bailiff Westminster Abbey 1989; Hon Bencher Lincoln's Inn 1989-; Hon DCL Univ of Kent at Canterbury; *Style*— The Rt Hon Bernard Weatherill, MP; Speaker's House, Westminster, London SW1

WEATHERLEY, Dr Michael (Mike); s of Joseph Weatherley (d 1970), of Colchester, Essex, and Louisa Frances, *née* Fowler; *b* 10 July 1935; *Educ* Dean Close Sch Cheltenham, Haberdashers' Aske's, The City Univ (BSc), Univ of Bristol (PhD); *m* 11 Sept 1959 (m dis 1981), Jean Dawn Howard, da of John Pexton, of Colchester, Essex; 1 s (Julian b 1965), 1 da (Helen b 1961); *Career* Nat Serv RAF 1954-56, writer DJ and announcer Aden Forces Bdcasting Assoc; res and devpt engr GEC Ltd 1957-66, res assoc Univ of Bristol 1966-69, prodr/dir BBC TV 1969-; programmes incl: Open Univ tech courses, Bellamy on Botany (1972), Bellamy's Britain (1974), Bellamy's Europe (1976), Up a Gum Tree (1979), Bellamy's Backyard Safari (1981), Bellamy's New World (1983), Favourite Walks (1985), The Trouble with Sex (1987), Business Matters (1989); *Recreations* walking, travel, opera, theatre; *Style*— Dr Mike Weatherley; 73 Archel Rd, London W14 9QL (☎ 071 381 2427); BBC Television, Villiers House, Haven Green, London W5 (☎ 081 743 8000)

WEATHERSBEE, Robin Charles Henry; s of Oliver Charles Weathersbee (d 1973), of Farnham Royal, Berks, and Eileen Daisy, *née* Anstee; *b* 13 April 1938; *Educ* Aldenham Sch Elstree, Northampton Coll of Advanced Technol; *m* 29 July 1961, Jennifer Margaret, da of Richard Frank Sibley (d 1983), of Yeovil, Somerset; 1 s (Michael), 1 da (Sally); *Career* optometrist; FBCO, DCLP; *Recreations* golf, Rotary, travel, wine; *Style*— Robin Weathersbee, Esq; Parkfield, Farthing Green Lane, Stoke Poges, Bucks SL2 1HA (☎ 0753 643459)

WEAVER, Barrie Keith; s of James Richard Weaver (d 1977), of Sutton, Surrey, and Theresa, *née* Cooper; *b* 10 Dec 1946; *Educ* Wallington Sch Surrey, Central Sch of Art (BA); *Career* designer: Conran Assocs 1971-73, Pentagram Design 1973-76; fndr Roberts Weaver Design 1977; cmmns incl: TI Gp 1978-80, Br Telecom 1982-84, STC 1984-85, Applied Materials USA 1985-87, Nixdorf 1986-88, Plessey 1985-87, Matsushita Japan 1988-89; personally retained by Hitachi Japan and Zebra Japan as design dir 1989, fndr Weaver Associates 1990; winner: of three Br Design awards, Industrie form 1988, Prince Philip award, Designer of the Year 1990; memb: Futures Ctee RSA 1988-, Design Cncl 1989- (awards judge 1984-); FRSA 1984, FCSD 1982; *Recreations* antiques, painting, travel; *Clubs* City (Antwerp); *Style*— Barrie Weaver, Esq; 53 Brookenville Rd, London SW6 7BH (☎ 071 385 7112); Weaver Associates, 2a Westbourne Grove Mews, London W11 2SA (☎ 071 221 4420, fax 071 727 1880)

WEAVER, Edward John Martin; s of Edward Algernon Weaver (d 1964), of Berwyn, Mill Lane, Codsall, nr Wolverhampton, and May Evelyn Edwards (d 1974); *b* 7 Nov 1921; *Educ* Clifton, Gonville and Caius Coll Cambridge, St Thomas's Hosp (MA, MB BChir); *m* 2 Sept 1953, Mary Elaine, da of Charles Spitteler (d 1961), of Shevaroy Hill, S India; 3 s (Peter b 1954, James b 1955, Timothy b 1958); *Career* hon conslt cardiothoracic surgeon to The London Hosp, (former head of dept of cardiothoracic surgery at London Hosp), conslt thoracic surgeon Royal Masonic Hosp, former conslt thoracic surgeon Whipps Cross Hosp and Princess Alexander Hosp Harlow; FRCS, LRCP, MRCS; *Recreations* gardening, do-it-yourself; *Style*— John Weaver, Esq; The Lone Pine, Matching Green, nr Harlow, Essex CM17 0QB (☎ 0279 731295); London Independent Hospital, Stepney Green E1 (☎ 071 791 3422)

WEAVER, (Christopher) Giles Herron; s of Lt-Col J F H Weaver, of Greywalls, Gullane, Lothian, and Ursula Priscilla Marie Gabrielle, *née* Horlick; *b* 4 April 1946; *Educ* Eton, London Business Sch (MSc); *m* 30 July 1974, Rosamund Betty, da of Lionel Mayhew, of Whittlesfield, Higher Burwardsley, Tattenhall; 2 s (Freddy b 1977, Jack b 1986), 2 da (Flora b 1975, Johanna b 1983); *Career* CA; Arthur Young 1966-71, asst to chm: Jessel Securities 1973-75, Berry Wiggins 1975-76; i/c of pension funds Ivory and Sime plc 1976-86, md pensions mgmnt Prudential Portfolio Mangrs 1986-; prop Greywalls Hotel Gullane Lothian 1976-; mangr New Club (Edinburgh); ACA 1970, FCA 1977; *Recreations* skiing, golf, tennis, stalking, bridge; *Clubs* New (Edinburgh), HCEG (Muirfield), Hurlingham, Denham; *Style*— Giles Weaver, Esq; Greywalls, Gullane, Lothian; 48 Thurloe Sq, London SW7 (☎ 0620 843205); PPM, 1 Stephen St, London W1 (☎ 071 548 3153, fax 071 936 8424, car 0860 527076, telex 265082)

WEAVER, Leonard John; CBE (1990); s of Alfred Wallace Weaver and Anne, *née*

Geleyns; *b* 10 June 1936; *Educ* St Mary's Sch, Univ of Surrey; *m* 1963, Penelope Ann, *née* Sturge-Young; 5 s, 1 da; *Career* served Kenya Regt 1955-57; AEI Ltd 1962-64, works mangr PYE-TMC 1964-66; P E Consulting Gp: joined 1966, dir 1975, md 1979-82; chm: Polymark Int plc 1982-, Jones & Shipman 1988-, Manifold Industs Ltd 1982-; memb: BIM Cncl 1978-83, IProdE Cncl 1980- (pres 1990-); pres Inst Mngmt Conslts 1983-84; Freeman City of London, Liveryman Worshipful Co of Engrs; CEng, FIEE, FIProdE, CBIM, FIMC, FRSA; *Recreations* cricket, book-collecting, shooting; *Clubs* Reform, MCC; *Style*— Leonard Weaver, Esq, CBE; Crab Apple Court, Oxshott Rd, Leatherhead, Surrey (☎ 0372 843647); Polymark International plc, Dukes Court, Duke St, Woking, Surrey GU21 5BH (☎ 0483 750476)

WEAVER, Oliver; QC (1985); s of Denis Weaver, and Kathleen Nesville, *née* Lynch; *b* 27 March 1942; *Educ* Friends' Sch Saffron Walden, Trinity Coll Cambridge (MA, LLM, pres Cambridge Union Soc); *m* 3 Oct 1964, Julia Mary, *née* MacClymont; 1 s (James b 1969), 2 da (Lucy b 1967, Mary-Ann 1970); *Career* slr; called to the Bar Middle Temple 1965, Lincoln's Inn 1969; memb: Bar Cncl 1981-84, panel of chm of Authorisation and Disciplinary Tribunals of the Securities Assoc 1988-, Cncl of Law Reporting 1986-; *Recreations* fishing, racing, gun dogs; *Style*— Oliver Weaver, Esq, QC; Kennel Farm, Albury End, Ware, Herts SG11 2HS (☎ 027 974 331); Erskine Chambers, 30 Lincoln's Inn Fields, London WC2A 3PF (☎ 071 242 5532)

WEAVER, Simon John; s of Kenneth John Weaver (d 1973), and Hilda Nora *née* Rooke; *b* 4 March 1946; *Educ* King's Sch Canterbury; *m* 28 Oct 1980, Rosemary Jane, da of Leslie John Fuhr (d 1966), of Beckenham; 2 s (Matthew b 1974, Thomas b 1982), 2 da (Lara b 1987, Samantha (twin) b 1987); *Career* account exec W Nally Sports Promotions Gp 1970-75, dir Barwell Sports Mngmnt 1976-83, fndr and ptnr Simon Weaver Sports 1983- assoc memb Inst of Leisure and Amenity Mgmnt; *Recreations* cricket, squash, gardening, walking, conservation; *Clubs* Band of Brothers, Buccaneers, St Lawrence and Highland Ct CC; *Style*— Simon J Weaver, Esq; Castle House, Clifford, Hay-on-Wye, Hereford HR3 5EP (☎ 04973 484 ext 491)

WEAVER, Sir Tobias Rushton (Toby); CB (1962); s of Sir Lawrence Weaver, KBE (d 1930), of London, and Kathleen Purcell (d 1927); *b* 19 July 1911; *Educ* Clifton, Corpus Christi Coll Cambridge (MA); *m* 1941, Marjorie, da of Rt Hon Sir Charles Trevelyan, 3 Bt, of Wallington Hall, Northumberland; 1 s (Lawrence b 1948), 3 da (Kathleen (Mrs Nicholas Abbott), Caroline (Mrs Michael Baker), Rachel (Mrs Charles Munn)); *Career* former master Eton and Barking, Admty 1941, civil servant DES 1946-73 (dep sec 1962-73); prof of educn: Univ of Southampton 1973, Univ of London, Inst of Educn 1974, Open Univ 1976-78; fell Imperial Coll 1986; *Recreations* playing piano; *Style*— Sir Toby Weaver, CB; 14 Marston Close, London NW6 4EU

WEAVERS, Frank Paton; s of Frank Paton Weavers (d 1969), and Ellen, *née* Billing (d 1969); *b* 30 Jan 1927; *Educ* Holly Lodge GS Smethwick; *m* 22 Sept 1951, Meryl June, da of Victor Robert Dixon (d 1984), of Moseley, Birmingham; 2 s (Malcolm Dixon b 1959, Stewart Paton (twin) b 1959); *Career* Nat Serv RAF, mainly in Malaya 1946-48; Carter & Co CAs 1943-61, investmt banking exec and co sec Birmingham Indust Tst Ltd 1962-68, dir and investmt mangr Britannic Assur plc 1980-90 (investmt mangr 1972-79, joined 1969), ret 1990; FCA; *Recreations* walking, reading, opera; *Style*— F P Weavers, Esq; 8 Beechnut Lane, Solihull B91 2NN (☎ 021 704 1543)

WEBB, Prof Adrian Leonard; s of Leonard Webb, of Melksham, Wilts, and Rosina, *née* Staines; *b* 19 July 1943; *Educ* St Julian's HS Newport Gwent, Birmingham Univ (B Soc Sci), LSE (MSC); *m* 21 July 1965, Caroline Frances, da of Arthur Williams (d 1986), of Cardiff; 2 s (Rhicert b 20 April 1967, Geraint b 17 July 1971); *Career* lectr LSE 1966-74, res dir Personal Soc Servs Cncl 1974-76; Loughborough Univ: prof social policy and admin 1976-, head dept social sci 1981-86, dir Centre Res in Social Policy 1982, dean Sch Human and Environmental Studies 1986-88, pro-vice-chllr 1988-; memb: DHSS Birch Ctee on Manpower Trg in Personal Social Servs 1974-76, DHSS res Liason Gp for Local Authy Social Servs 1975-81, SSRC working gp on central govt 1976-77; academic dir mgmnt trg workshop UN Centre Trg and Res in Social Welfare 1976-79, memb Sociology and Social Admin Ctee SSRC 1976-80, chm Social Admin Assoc 1977-80 (treas 1974-77), nat chm bd govrs Volunteer Centre 1978-84, memb Cncl Tbnls 1985-, chm Ctee Workforce Planning and Trg in Social Servs 1987-88, memb DHSS res liaison gp for mental handicap 1987-, sci advsr Chief Scientist's Departmental Res Ctee DHSS 1987-, academic advsr DHSS advsy gp on respite care for mentally handicapped 1987, memb London Univ standing panel of experts in social admin 1987-, vice-pres Leics Regnl Cncl Guideposts Tst Ltd 1988-; memb: Eng Nat Bd Nursing Midwifery and Health Visiting 1988-, UGC Social Studies Sub-Ctee 1989, advsr social policy and social work Univ Funding Cncl 1989-; memb: Social Policy Assoc, Br Sociological Assoc, Political Studies Assoc; FRSA 1987, memb Royal Cwlth Soc; *Books* numerous articles and books on social policy incl jtly: Change Choice and Conflict in Social Policy (1975), Planning Need and Scarcity: Essays on the Personal Social Services (1986), The Economic Approach to Social Policy (1986), Social Work Social Care and Social Planning (1987), Joint Approaches to Social Policy: Rationality and Practice (1988); *Recreations* walking, painting (water colour), ornithology; *Clubs* Nat Liberal; *Style*— Prof Adrian Webb; Loughborough University, Loughborough, Leicestershire LE11 3TU (☎ 0509 223350, fax 0509 610813, telex 34319)

WEBB, Anthony Allan; s of Robert McGraw Webb (d 1967), of Washington DC, and Ruth, *née* Webb (d 1986); *b* 24 May 1943; *Educ* Univ of Colorado (BA, B Int mgmnt); *m* 10 July 1971, Micheline, da of Alphonse Touchette (d 1983), of Montreal, Canada; 1 s (Christian b 1981), 1 da (Annie b 1978); *Career* Lt US Navy 1965-69; Royal Bank of Canada 1970-, The Royal Bank of Canada (Suisse) 1984-88, chm The Royal Bank of Canada (Suisse) Geneva, Royal Bank of Canada (CI) Guernsey; *Recreations* skiing; *Clubs* Club Baur au Lac (Zurich), Annabel's, Overseas Bankers; *Style*— Anthony Webb, Esq; 4030 Marlowe Ave, Montreal, Canada H4A 3MD; The Royal Bank of Canada, 1 Place Ville Marle, Montreal, Canada H3C 3A9 (☎ 514 874 2447)

WEBB, Anthony Michael Francis; CMG (1963), QC (1961), JP (1966); s of Sir Ambrose Henry Webb, QC (d 1964), and Agnes Ellen, *née* Gunn (d 1969); *b* 27 Dec 1914; *Educ* Ampleforth, Magdalen Coll Oxford (MA); *m* 1948, Diana Mary, da of Capt Graham Farley (d 1942); 1 s (Simon), 1 da (Amanda); *Career* 2 Lt Queen's Bays 1940, SOE ME and Europe 1941-46, Maj; called to the Bar Gray's Inn 1939; Colonial Legal Serv: Malaya 1947-55, Kenya 1955-64 (AG and min for legal affrs); Lord Chllrs Office 1964-78 (dep sec of commns and head of court business); chm Indust Tbnls 1978-87; *Clubs* Special Forces; *Style*— Anthony Webb, Esq, CMG, QC, JP; Yew Tree Cottage, Speldhurst Rd, Langton Green, Tunbridge Wells, Kent TN3 0JH

WEBB, Anthony Ronald; s of Ronald Alfred Webb, of East Sutton, Kent, and Muriel Dorothy, *née* Empleton; *b* 17 July 1947; *Educ* Chislehurst and Sidcup GS, Univ of Bristol (LLB); *m* 29 Sept 1979, Sarah Lynette, da of Denzil Edward Kieft, of Lagos, Portugal; 1 da (Camilla b 1986), 1 s (Guy b 1989); *Career* called to Bar Inner Temple 1970; asst rec 1989; *Recreations* equestrian, travel, gardening; *Clubs* Kent CCC; *Style*— Anthony Webb, Esq; Capel Cross, Grovehurst Lane, Horsmonden, Tonbridge, Kent TN12 8BB (☎ 0892 72 3973); Farrar's Building, Temple, London EC4Y 7BD (☎ 071 583 9241, fax 071 583 0090)

WEBB, Brian James; s of Frederick William Webb (d 1972), of Liverpool, and Esther, *née* Foxall; *b* 15 Jan 1945; *Educ* Brookfield Sch Liverpool, Liverpool Coll of Art, Canterbury Coll of Art (DipAD); *m* 1969, Gail Elizabeth, da of George Henderson Barker; 1 s (James William Robin b 4 Jan 1980), 1 da (Holly Katherine b 4 Feb 1976); *Career* asst graphic designer Michael Tucker Assocs 1967-69, graphic designer Derek Forsyth Partnership 1969-71, designer and dir Trickett & Webb Ltd 1971-; work has been exhibited and published throughout the world; contrib Penrose Annual, Best of British Packaging, Best of British Corporate Identity and other jls; winner of nnmerous awards D & AD, Donside and Nat Calendar Awards for work on clients incl: Thames TV, Midland Bank, Royal Mail; memb: Cncl CSD 1980-87 and 1989- (chm Graphics Gp 1980-85), Exec Ctee D & AD 1987-89; memb juries: D & AD 1975-, Design Bursary RSA 1980-; visiting lectr numerous colls in UK, USA and ASIA, external assessor CNAA UK; memb D & AD 1972, fell CSD 1972, FRSA 1980; *Recreations* walking, working; *Style*— Brian Webb, Esq; Trickett and Webb Ltd, The Factory, 84 Marchmont St, London WC1N 1HE (☎ 071 388 5832, fax 071 387 4287)

WEBB, Douglas Geoffrey Larwood; s of Geoffrey Royce Webb (d 1968), of Gt Shelford, Cambs, and Gwendoline Doris, *née* Larwood; *b* 25 Sept 1932; *Educ* Aldenham, Univ of Cambridge (MA, LLM); *m* 29 March 1972, Janet Elizabeth, da of Claud James Walsingham, of Diss, Norfolk (d 1988); 1 s (Cameron Patrick Walsingham b 1975); *Career* admitted slr 1959; sr ptnr Smart & Webb Cambridge; *Recreations* sailing, fishing; *Style*— Douglas G L Webb, Esq; 11 Cavendish Ave, Cambridge CB1 4UP; 1 St Mary's Passage, Cambridge CB2 3PH (☎ 0223 358227)

WEBB, George Hannam; CMG (1984), OBE (1974); s of late George Ernest Webb, and Mary Hannam, *née* Stephens; *b* 24 Dec 1929; *Educ* Malvern Coll, King's Coll Cambridge (MA); *m* 1956, Josephine Chatterton; 2 s, 2 da; *Career* serv 14/20 King's Hussars 1948-49, Parachute Regt (TA) 1950-53; Colonial Serv Kenya 1953-63 (dist offr Central and North Nyanza, dist cmmr Moyale, secretariat Nairobi); Diplomatic Serv 1963-85 (first sec Bangkok and Accra, cnsllr Tehran and Washington); sr fell City Univ London 1989- (dir of mgmnt devpt 1985-89); memb Cncl Royal Soc for Asian Affairs 1984-, tstee Hakluyt Soc 1986-; memb Cncl Gresham Coll 1988-; dep chm Cncl of Friends of Nat Army Museum 1988-; tstee Encounter 1989-91; Liveryman Worshipful Co of Scriveners 1989; FRSA; *publications* Kipling Journal (ed, 1980-), The Bigger Bang: Growth of a Financial Revolution (1987), Kipling's Japan (ed with Sir Hugh Cortazzi, 1988); *Clubs* Travellers', Beefsteak, Royal Cwlth Soc; *Style*— G H Webb, Esq, CMG, OBE; Weavers, Danes Hill, Woking, Surrey GU22 7HQ

WEBB, Prof Hubert Eustace (Hughie); s of Lt-Col Wilfrid Francis Webb, CIE (d 1973), of Rhodesia, and Katherine Leila, *née* Houssemayne du Boulay (d 1971); *b* 30 May 1927; *Educ* Winchester New coll Oxford (MA, BM, BCh, DM; blues: Squash (Capt), Rackets (Capt), Golf, Cricket), FRCP, FRCPath, DSc (London); *m* 13 Sept 1950, (Monica) Jean, da of Roderick Charles MacPherson (d 1965), of Jersey; 1 s (John b 15 Feb 1952), 1 da (Suzanne b 24 Jan 1955); *Career* RAMC: SSC 1953-57, Lt 1953, Capt 1955; assoc Nat Res Cncl Washington 1957, temp staff memb Rockefeller Foundation USA 1958-60, conslt neurologist and sr lectr in medicine St Thomas' Hosp 1963, prof of neurovirology 1987; played squash, cricket for Hampshire; memb Nightingale Fund Cncl; memb: BMA, Assoc of Br Neurologists; *Publications* contrib to numerous pubns and various books; *Recreations* sports, travelling; *Clubs* MCC, All England Lawn Tennis; *Style*— Prof Hughie Webb; 12 Elm Grove, London SW19 4HE (☎ 081 946 1808); Dept of Neurology, St Thomas' Hospital, London SE1 7EH (☎ 071 928 9292 ext 2062)

WEBB, Iain Andrew; s of Eric Webb, of York, and Oris, *née* Dyson; *b* 30 March 1959; *Educ* Scalby Secdy Sch Scarborough, Joseph Rowntree Secdy Sch York, Rambert Sch of Ballet London, The Royal Ballet Sch London; *m* 30 July 1982, Margaret, da of Ettore Barbieri; 1 s (Jason Alexander b 29 July 1987); *Career* Sadlers Well's Royal Ballet (now The Birmingham Royal Ballet) 1979-89; princ roles: Oberon in Ashton's The Dream, The Young Man in Ashton's The Two Pigeons, Franz in Wright's Coppelia, Colas in Ashton's La Fille mal Gardée, Benno in Wright's Swan Lake, Pas de Quatre in Nureyev's Raymonda Act III, Blue Bird and Pas de Quatre in Wright's Sleeping Beauty, The Poet in Les Sylphides; Balanchine's The Prodigal Son, Van Manen's 5 Tango's, Alain in Ashton's La Fille Mal Gardée, Kay in Bintley's The Snow Queen; created roles in: Bintley's Polonia, Night Moves, Choros The Swan of Tuoneh, Flowers of the Forest; performed Petrushka 1988/89 season; joined The Royal Ballet at Covent Garden 1989; debut as the King of the South in MacMillan's The Prince of the Pagodes, Mercury in Bintley's The Plants, danced in first performances of Balanchines Violin Concerts and Page's Bloodline; *Recreations* history of ballet, collecting ballet memorabilia, music, photography; *Style*— Iain Webb, Esq; The Royal Ballet, Royal Opera House, Covent Garden, London WC2E 9DD

WEBB, Hon Mrs (Janet Diana); *née* Allanson-Winn; da of 7 Baron Headley; *b* 1932; *m* 1, 1955 (m dis 1969), Antony John Vlassopulos; 2 s; m 2, 1975, David Walter Webb; *Style*— The Hon Mrs Webb; Springs, Rookery Drive, Westcott, Surrey

WEBB, Jeremy Richard; s of C R Webb, OBE, MC (d 1976); *b* 25 March 1931; *Educ* Radley, Hertford Coll Oxford; *m* 1956, Clover Margaret, da of Maj J Suckling (d 1981); 3 s; *Career* 2 Lt Royal Sussex Regt; advertising (creative dir): Foote Cone & Beldins 1956-61, Lintas Ltd 1961-65, Wasey Campbell Ewald 1966-71, Ferrero & Co Spa Turin 1971-74, Wasey Campbell Ewald 1974-75, Everetts Ltd 1975-85; dir and creative dept mangr Allen Brady and Marsh 1985-87; dir The Word Process 1987-; *Recreations* bridge, swimming, painting, writing; *Style*— Jeremy Webb, Esq; 79 Cowleigh Rd, Malvern, Worcs WR14 1QL (☎ 0684 574748)

WEBB, (Anthony) John; s of Charles Reginald Webb (d 1972), of Bristol, England, and Gwendoline, *née* Moon; *b* 29 Dec 1929; *Educ* Cotham GS Bristol, Univ of Bristol (MB ChM); *m* 5 March 1955, Audrie Ruth; 2 s (Mark Idris, Jason Crispin), 2 da (Dominique Louise, Charlotte Anne); *Career* Nat Serv RAMC 1955-57 Lt-Capt 5 Field Ambulance; conslt surgn Bristol Royal Infirmary and Royal Hosp for Sick Children Bristol 1967, conslt surgn Bristol Royal Infirmary 1985-, currently sr clinical lectr in surgery Univ of Bristol; memb: Br Soc of Clinical Cytology, Br Assoc Endocrine Surgns, IAC; FRCS 1957, fell Int Acad of Cytology; *Books* Operative Surgery and Management (contrib, 1984); *Recreations* choral singing, gardening; *Clubs* Jenner, Bristol Royal Infirmary; *Style*— John Webb, Esq; 7 Percival Rd, Clifton, Bristol BS8 8EL (☎ 0272 738349)

WEBB, John Harold; s of Donald Percy Webb (d 1945), and Helen, *née* Jackson (d 1968); *b* 25 Feb 1929; *Educ* Kings Sch Macclesfield; *m* 1, 25 April 1956 (m dis 1966), Muriel Joan, *née* Gittins; 2 s (Duncan, Simon), 3 da (Jacqueline, Elizabeth, Sophie); m 2, 23 Oct 1968, Sandra Benita, da of late Benjamin Keeling; *Career* md: Kay Metzeler 1960-67, Tangent Ltd 1960-67, Draka Foam Ltd 1970- 86; chm and chief exec Hyman plc; Freeman Worshipful Co of Furniture Manufacturers 1988, Freeman City of London 1989; BRMA; *Recreations* gardening, shooting; *Style*— John Webb, Esq; Henbury Farm, Henbury, Macclesfield, Cheshire SK11 9PY (☎ 0625 34442); Hyman Plc, Spinners Lane, Poynton, Cheshire SK12 IFF (☎ 0625 879944, fax 0625 879943, telex 668307)

WEBB, Dr Jonathan Mark; *b* 24 Aug 1963; *Educ* Univ of Bristol (MB ChB); *m* 25 June 1988, Amanda Claire, da of Finlaw Norman Michael Biddle; 1 da (Harriet Georgina b 17 Aug 1990); *Career* Rugby Union full-back Bath RFC and England; clubs: Northern FC, Bristol FC (leading scorer 1989-90), Bath RFC 1990-; debut England B 1987; England: debut (R) v Aust World Cup 1987, memb World Cup squad (4 appearances) 1987, tour Aust (2 tests) 1988, 17 int caps; doctor; memb BMA; *Recreations* golf, windsurfing, oboe; *Style—* Dr Jonathan Webb; Bath RFC, Recreation Ground, Bath, Avon (☎ 0225 25192)

WEBB, Prof Joseph Ernest; s of Joseph Webb (d 1975), of Worcester Pk, Surrey, and Constance Inman, *née* Hickox (d 1967); *b* 22 March 1915; *Educ* Rutlish Sch Merton, Birkbeck Coll London (BSc, PhD, DSc); *m* 10 Aug 1940, Gwenlilian Clara, da of Herbert Samuel Coldwell (d 1949), of Stoneleigh, Surrey; 3 s (David John b 1943, Ian b 1945, Peter Joseph b 1954); *Career* res entomologist and parasitologist Cooper Tech Bureau 1940-46, lectr zoology Univ of Aberdeen 1946-48, prof zoology Univ Coll Ibadan Nigeria 1950-60 (sr lectr 1948-50), hon fell Westfield Coll London 1986 (prof zoology 1960-80, vice princ 1976-80), emeritus prof zoology Univ of London 1980-, fell Queen Mary and Westfield Coll 1989; author of various pubns on insect physiology, insecticides, systematics, populations, tropical ecology, marine biology and sedimentology; FZS 1943, MIBiol 1952, FIBiol 1963, FLS 1972; *Books* with J A Wallwork and J H Elgood: Guide to Invertebrate Animals (second edn 1978), Guide to Living Mammals (second edn 1979), Guide to Living Reptiles (1978), Guide to Living Birds (1979), Guide to Living Fishes (1981), Guide to Living Amphibians (1981); *Recreations* art, music, photography, gardening; *Clubs* Athenaeum; *Style—* Prof J E Webb; 43 Hill Top, London NW11 6EA (☎ 081 458 2571)

WEBB, Kaye; MBE (1974); da of Arthur Webb, and Ann, *née* Stevens; *b* 26 Jan 1914; *Educ* Hornsey HS, Ashburton GS; *m* 1, Christopher Brierley; m 2, Gp Capt Keith Hunter, OBE; m 3, Ronald Searle *qv*, 1 s (John b 17 July 1947), 1 da (Kate (twin) b 17 July 1947); *Career* journalist; ed: Picturegoer 1931, Picture Post 1938, Lilliput 1939-47; theatre corr The Leader 1947-49, feature writer News Chronicle 1949-55, ed Elizabethan (children's magazine) 1955-58, theatre critic Nat Review 1957-58, children's ed Puffin Books and publishing dir Penguin Books Ltd 1961-79; conslt Goldcrest Films and Curtis Brown Literary Agency, ed in chief Puffin Books, dir Penguin Books; prodr TV series Tootie Eleanor Farjeon Award for Servs to Children's Lit; *Books* ed: C Fry: Experience of Critics, Penguin Patrick Campbell, The Friday Miracle, The St Trinian's Story, I Like This Poem (1979), All the Day Round (1981), Lilliput Goes to War (1985), I Like This Story (1986) Just Six, Meet My Friends (1991); with Ronald Searle: Looking at London, Paris Sketchbook, Refugees 1960; *Recreations* theatre, antiques, reading and working with children; *Style—* Ms Kaye Webb, MBE; 8 Lampard House, 8 Maida Ave, London W2 1SS (☎ 071 262 4695)

WEBB, Keith Stewart; s of Arthur Saunders Webb, of 52 Princes Avenue, Walsall, and Doris Martha, *née* Cheadle; *b* 19 March 1947; *Educ* Joseph Leckie Sch Walsall, Matthew Boulton Coll Birmingham, Sch of Art and Design Walsall (Dip in PR); *m* 13 Aug 1972, Gillian, da of Anthony Anson; 2 da (Nicola Lucy b 5 Aug 1978, Amy Francesca b 27 Dec 1984); *Career* Lucas Industries: in trg Group Advertising Facility 1964-67, prodn controller 1967-68, press offr Lucas Electrical 1968-69, chief press offr 1969-70, dep gp PR mangr 1970-72; Edson Evers and Associates: joined 1973, assoc ptnr 1974, ptnr 1985; MIPR 1974; *Recreations* swimming, yachting; *Style—* Keith Webb, Esq; Yew Tree House, 366 Birmingham Rd, Walsall, West Midlands WS5 3NX (☎ 0922 21032); Edson Evers & Associates, Priory House, Friars Terrace, Stafford ST17 4QG (☎ 0785 49237/55146, fax 0785 211518)

WEBB, Lawrence Desmond; s of Maj George Lawrence Webb, and Evelyn Annie Alice, *née* Wardale; *b* 18 April 1939; *Educ* Harrow, Neuchatel Switzerland; *Career* slr; dir The Investment Co plc 1965-, fin consIt Tico A G Zürich 1981-; *Recreations* squash, sailing, sailboarding, golf; *Clubs* Carlton, Lansdowne; *Style—* Lawrence Webb, Esq; Barclays Bank plc, 6 Clarence St, Kingston upon Thames, Surrey KT1 1NY

WEBB, Hon Mrs (Marigold Elizabeth Cassandra); *née* Neave; da of Airey Neave, DSO, OBE, MC, TD, MP (assas 1979), and Baroness Airey of Abingdon (Life Peeress), *qv*; *b* 5 May 1944; *Educ* St Mary's Sch Wantage Oxon, Pershore Coll of Horticulture, Architectural Assoc (Dip Garden Conservation); *m* 1968, (William) Richard Broughton, s of late Lt Cdr William Frank Broughton Webb, DSC, RN, of Caulin Court, Droitwich; 1 s (Edward Alexander Broughton b 1974), 1 da (Katharine Angela Mary b 1970); *Career* garden designer; *Recreations* gardening; *Style—* The Hon Mrs Webb; Barbers, Martley, Worcs (☎ 08866 362)

WEBB, Neil John; s of Douggie Webb, of Reading, and Joan, *née* Cook; *b* 30 July 1963; *Educ* Little Heath Co-Educnl Sch Reading; *m* 1 June 1985, Shelley, da of A A Alexander; 2 s (Luke b 12 Sept 1986, Joshua b 23 Feb 1990); *Career* professional footballer; Reading 1980-82: apprentice then professional, 69 appearances, 22 goals; Portsmouth 1982-85: joined for a fee of £83,000, 138 appearances, 38 goals; Nottingham Forest 1985-89: joined for a fee of £250,000, 185 appearances, 56 goals; transferred for a fee of £1,500,000 to Manchester Utd 1989-; England caps: 3 under 21, 20 full (3 goals); honours: League Cup and Simod Cup Nottingham Forest 1989, FA Cup Manchester Utd 1990; *Recreations* golf, walking the dogs, the theatre; *Style—* Neil Webb, Esq; Jonathan Holmes, Park Associates Ltd, 6 George St, Nottingham NG1 3BE (☎ 0602 483206, fax 0602 410087)

WEBB, Patrick John Ryall; s of Kenneth Edmund Ryall Webb, of Tadworth, Surrey, and Marjorie Eveline Ryall, *née* Nuthall; *b* 31 March 1944; *Educ* St Edward's Sch Oxford, Trinity Hall Cambridge; *m* 22 March 1969, Dr Joanna Webb, da of Thomas Gilbert Burton (d 1976), of Hull; 1 s (Edward b 1970), 2 da (Georgina b 1971, Elly b 1975); *Career* articled clerk Ernst and Young 1965-69, mangr Peat Marwick McLintock 1969-81; co sec: Touche Remnant and Co 1981-85, James Capel and Co 1986-, dir James Capel Unit Trust Management Ltd 1989-; chm and govr Bramley Sch, treas Betchworth Cons Assoc; FCA 1970; *Recreations* golf, music, tennis; *Style—* Patrick Webb, Esq; Ravenleigh, Betchworth, Surrey RH3 7DF (☎ 073 784 3327); James Capel and Co, 6 Bevis Marks, London EC3A 7JQ (☎ 071 626 0566, fax 071 283 3192, telex 888866)

WEBB, Dr Pauline Mary; da of Rev Leonard Frederick Webb (d 1973), and Daisy Winifred, *née* Barnes (d 1972); *b* 28 June 1927; *Educ* King's Coll London (BA), Union Theol Seminary NY (STM), Univ of Brussels (DTheol), Univ of Victoria Toronto (DLitt), Univ of Mt St Vincent Halifax (DLitt); *Career* ed Methodist Missionary Soc 1955-66; dir: Lay Training Methodist Church 1966-72, First Conf Estate 1978-; exec offr Methodist Overseas Div 1972-79; organiser Religious Bdcasting Overseas BBC External Services 1979-87; dir Hinksey Centre Westminster Coll Oxford 1987-; *Books* Women of Our Company, Women of Our Time, Salvation Today, Faith and Faithfulness, Candles for Advent, Celebrating Friendship; film scripts: Bright Diadem, New Life in Nigeria, Beauty for Ashes, The Road to Dabou; *Recreations* theatre, travel; *Clubs* BBC; *Style—* Dr Pauline Webb; 14 Paddocks Green, Salmon St, London NW9 8NH (☎ 081 904 9088)

WEBB, Philip Alun; s of Frederick Albert George Webb, of Glamorgan, Wales and Bath, Somerset, and D M Webb, *née* Saunders-Jones; *b* 23 Nov 1955; *Educ* Ferndale Glamorgan, Univ Coll of Wales Aberystwyth, Guildford Law Coll; *Career* chief press offr Pilkington plc St Helens 1989, Cons Central Office Community Affrs Dept 1979-82, sr exec the Public Affrs Dept of Sea Containers (SEACO Inc London) 1985-87, dir public affrs Barry Hook Assoc Ltd (advertising and PR) 1987-89; memb: Monarchist League, regnl rep Monarchist League in the Principality of Wales 1975-77, The Heraldry Soc, The Historic Houses Assoc, The Nat Tst, Soc of Cons Lawyers, Soc of Descendants of the Knights of the Garter, Middle Temple Inn of Court; memb Ctee West Area Manchester and Dist Housing Assoc 1990-; *Recreations* tennis, riding, reading; *Style—* Philip A Webb, Esq; Apartment 11, Parsonage Court, Palatine Rd, Withington, Manchester M20 (☎ 061 434 5903); Pilkington PLC, Prescot Rd, St Helens, WA10 3TT (☎ 0744 692141)

WEBB, Richard; s of Lt-Col Richard Webb (d 1988); *b* 26 July 1943; *Educ* Marlborough; *Career* dir Michael Joseph Ltd London (Publishers) 1970-74; co-fndr and md Webb & Bower (Publishers) Ltd 1975-; *Style—* Richard Webb, Esq; Wixels, Ferry Rd, Topsham, Exeter, Devon; Webb & Bower (Publishers) Ltd, 5 Cathedral Close, Exeter, Devon EX1 1EZ (☎ 0392 435362/210445, fax 0392 211652, telex WEBBOW 42544)

WEBB, Robert Stopford; QC (1988); s of R V B Webb, MC, of Styal, Cheshire, and Isabella Raine, *née* Hinks; *b* 4 Oct 1948; *Educ* Wycliffe Coll, Univ of Exeter (LLB); *m* 1 April 1975, Angela Mary, da of Bernard Bruce Freshwater (d 1978), of Darlington, Co Durham; 2 s (Alfred b 1978, William b 1980); *Career* called to the Bar Inner Temple 1971; chm Air Law Ctee Royal Aeronautical Soc, vice chm Air Law Ctee Int Bar Assoc; memb Int Acad of Trial Lawyers; *Recreations* golf, fly fishing; *Clubs* Royal Wimbledon Golf, Royal Lytham St Anne's Golf, Prestbury Golf; *Style—* Robert Webb, Esq, QC; 1 Harcourt Buildings, Temple, London EC4Y 9DA (☎ 071 353 9371, fax 071 583 1656)

WEBB, Rodney Anson John; s of Ernest Herbert Webb (d 1983), of Norwich, and Irene Maud, *née* Gotts; *b* 24 April 1944; *Educ* Bracondale Sch Norwich; *m* 8 Nov 1969, Angela Delys, da of Frederick Lukies (d 1981), of Salhouse, Norfolk; 3 da (Alison b 1971, Victoria b 1977, Hannah b 1986); *Career* md: Bowater Flexible Packaging 1978, Bowater Cartons 1980, Crest Packaging 1985; memb Ctee Br Carton Assoc 1980-81, pres Flexible Packaging Assoc 1983-84; vice pres: Euro Flexible Packaging Assoc 1984-86, UK spokesman Euro Aluminium Foil Assoc 1988-91, FCA; *Recreations* golf, tennis; *Clubs* Bearsted Golf; *Style—* Rodney Webb, Esq; Spitzbrook House, Collier St, Tonbridge, Kent TN12 9RH (☎ 089 273 241); Crest Packaging Limited, Courteney Rd, Gillingham, Kent ME8 ORX (☎ 0634 34444, fax 0634 362473, telex 96153)

WEBB, Stuart Campbell; s of (late) Campbell Owen Webb, and Joan Phyllis, *née* Lewington; *b* 16 May 1940; *Educ* Michaelhouse Natal SA, Cornell Univ USA (BSc), Johnson Sch of Management USA (MBA); *m* 1964, Jacqueline Dorothy, da of Andrew J Lindsley, of New Jersey, USA; 1 s (Cambell Owen b 10 Jan 1968), 1 da (Alexandra Lindsley b 26 April 1970); *Career* investmt analyst FS Smithers & Co 1965-70, dir Robert Fleming & Co Ltd 1970-77, mangr Saudi International Bank 1977-82, dir Chase International Investments Ltd 1982-85, md Lazard Brothers & Co Ltd 1985-; charted fin analyst USA 1971; *Recreations* walking, mountaineering, music, horology; *Style—* Stuart Webb, Esq; Oakelwood, Bunch Lane, Haslemere, Surrey GU27 1ET (☎ 0428 643166); Lazard Brothers & Co Limited, 21 Moorfields, London EC2P 2HT (☎ 071 588 2721)

WEBB, Tom Peel (Tim); MBE (1946); s of Thomas Webb (d 1918), and May Stafford (d 1962); *b* 11 Feb 1919; *Educ* Glossop GS, Manchester Coll of Technol; *m* 18 May 1945, Nancy Eileen, da of Frederick Denny Farrow, OBE; 3 da (Susan b 1946, Anne b 1948, Charlotte b 1958); *Career* Manchester Regt TA 1938, served NW Europe 1939-40, cmmnd RA 1941, Capt/Adj 20 LAA Regt 1944-45, served NW Europe, Maj DAA & QMG 106 AA Bde 1945-46; md Northide Ltd 1946-53, dir Fergusson Wild & Co Ltd 1953-60, exec dir Rank Relay Services Ltd 1960-61, dir G B Trading Ltd 1969-83; sec G B Project 1972-81 (govr 1983-), memb Ctee Nat Union of Mfrs Manchester 1949-53; parish cncllr W Peckham Kent 1963-69; *Recreations* travel, sketching; *Style—* Tim Webb, Esq, MBE; 16 Riverbank Way, Shirebrook Park, Glossop, Derbyshire SK13 8SN (☎ 04574 69579)

WEBB CARTER, Brig David Brian Wynn; OBE (1981), MC (1967); s of Brig Brian Wolseley Webb Carter, DSO, OBE (d 1982), and (Evelyn) Rosemary, *née* Hood (d 1978); *b* 5 Nov 1940; *Educ* Eton, RMA Sandhurst; *m* 15 Oct 1973, Felicity Elisabeth, da of William Lytton de Burgh Young, DL (d 1980), of The Old Rectory, Drewsteignton, Devon; 1 s (Oliver b 1975), 2 da (Margot b 1977, Camilla b 1983); *Career* cmmnd Irish Gds 1961; served BAOR; Libya, Cyprus, Middle East, Singapore, Hong Kong, Belize and USA; CO 1 Bn Irish Gds 1979-81, MA to QMG 1981-83, DCOS HQ 1 (BR) Corps 1983-84, CBF Belize 1984-87, ACOS HQ BAOR 1988-, psc 1972, odc (US) 1978, RCDS 1987; *Books* The Illicit Drug Trade (1989), Britain and Latin America: a Changing Relationship, The Drugs Problem (1989); *Recreations* skiing, cricket, travel; *Clubs* White's, MCC; *Style—* Brig David Webb Carter, OBE, MC; c/o Guards & Cavalry Section, Lloyds Bank, 6 Pall Mall, London SW1

WEBB-CARTER, Hon Mrs (Anne Celia); *née* Wigram; da of 2 Baron Wigram, MC, JP, DL; *b* 23 April 1945; *m* 1973, Col Evelyn Webb-Carter, OBE, Gren Gds, s of Brig Brian Webb-Carter, DSO, OBE (s of Maj-Gen Sir John Carter, KCMG, of Ixworth Court, Bedford), and Evelyn, *née* Hood, gt niece of 4 Viscount Hood; 1 s, 2 da; *Style—* The Hon Mrs Webb-Carter; c/o Lloyds Bank, 6 Pall Mall, London

WEBB-JENKINS, John Esmond; s of David John Jenkins (d 1955), and Winifred Rose, *née* Webb; *b* 20 May 1939; *Educ* Tonbridge, Univ of Bristol (BSc); *m* 15 Aug 1964, Clare Florence, da of Philip Bond Cockshutt (d 1967); 3 s (Timothy b 3 July 1965, Christian b 11 May 1967, Matthew b 27 Aug 1972), 1 da (Lucy b 27 June 1976); *Career* 2 Lt 54 East Anglia Signals TA 1962-64; shift chemist Br Resin Products Ltd 1960-61, commercial asst ICI plastics div 1961-65, dir Dunbee Combex 1972-73, UK mangr TRC div Solvay Etcie 1973-78, md Stanley Smith & Co 1978-79 tech sales mangr 1965-72), dir IRG plc 1985-, chm and dir Richard Daleman Ltd 1989-; chm Assoc of Calendered UPVC Suppliers; memb Mgmnt Ctee PIFA, BPF Environmental Ctee; govt Worple Rd Sch; Freeman Worshipful Co of Lightmongers; MCIM, MBIM MInst Pkg; *Recreations* golf, jazz, travel, my family; *Style—* John Webb-Jenkins, Esq; Kirkstone, 8 High Pine Close, Weybridge, Surrey KT13 9EA (☎ 0932 847611); The Stanley Smith Group Ltd, Worple Rd, Isleworth, Middx TW7 7AU (☎ 081 568 6831, fax 081 847 5322, telex 897918, car 0836 628806)

WEBBER, Lesley Anne; da of Capt Dennis John Webber, of Felpham, West Sussex, and Constance Acie, *née* Greenaway; *b* 10 April 1956; *Educ* Sydenham HS, Univ of Birmingham (LLB); *m* 17 Sept 1983, Nigel Cleevely Wagland, s of James Leslie William Wagland, DFC, of New Milton, Hants; 1 s (Christopher b 1989); *Career* admitted slr 1980; Freshfields 1980-84; Masons: joined 1984-, ptnr 1985-, currently head planning and landlord and tenant depts; memb Law Soc; *Recreations* skiing, theatre; *Style—* Miss Lesley Webber; Masons, 30 Aylesbury St, London EC1R 0ER (☎ 071 490 4000, fax 071 490 2545)

WEBBER, Terence Frank Lees (Terry); s of late Leslie Clifford Ebb Webber, and late Harriet Marjorie, *née* Lees; *b* 28 July 1934; *Educ* Mill Hill Sch; *m* 1970, Susan Yvonne, *née* Knightley; 2 da (Penelope Jane b 12 April 1972, Elizabeth b 19 Aug 1974); *Career* Nat Serv Royal Army Educn Corps 1957-59; articled Percy Mason & Co 1951-56; Peat Marwick Mitchell & Co: sr asst 1959, sr mangr 1968, ptnr ME 1970, ptnr London 1974; transfd to KPMG Peat Marwick McLintock Bristol 1985-; *Style—* Terry Webber, Esq; Frampton Court, Frampton Cotterell, Bristol BS17 2DW (☎ 0454 777 417); KPMG Peat Marwick McLintock, 15 Pembroke Rd, Bristol BS8 3LG (☎ 0272 732291, fax 0272 732191)

WEBER, David Henry; s of Humphrey Norden Weber, of London, and Queenie, *née*

Temple; *b* 11 Aug 1953; *Educ* Haberdashers' Aske's, Clare Coll Cambridge (MA), Coll of Law London; *m* 14 Aug 1977, Dorothy Broughton, da of Frederick Fairhust; 2 da (Clare Louise b 10 July 1981, Helen Victoria b 29 Aug 1984); *Career* articled clerk Linklaters & Paines London 1976, slr 1978, seconded Fulbright & Jaworski (attorneys) Houston Texas 1980-81, ptnr Linklaters & Paines 1984-; memb: Law Soc, Major Projects Assoc, Int Bar Assoc; memb City of London Solicitors' Co; *Recreations* music, sailing; *Style*— David H Weber, Esq; Linklaters & Paines, 59-67 Gresham Street, London EC2V 7JA (☎ 071 606 7080, fax 071 606 5113, telex 884349/888167)

WEBSTER, Rev Dr Alan Brunskill; KCVO (1988); *b* 1 July 1918; *Educ* Oxford (MA, BD), City Univ (DD Hons); *m* 1951, Margaret; 2 s, 2 da; *Career* curate in Sheffield 1942-46, staff of Westcott House 1946-52, vicar of Barnard Castle 1952-59, warden of Lincoln 1959-70, dean of Norwich 1970-78, dean of St Paul's 1978-87; *Books* Joshua Watson, Broken Bones May Joy; Contrib: Historic Episcopate, Strategist of the Spirit, The Reality of God; *Recreations* writing, gardening, travel; *Style*— The Rev Dr Alan Webster, KCVO; 20 Beech Bank, Norwich NR2 2AL (☎ 0603 55833)

WEBSTER, Alistair Stevenson; s of His Honour Judge Ian Webster, of Rochdale, and Margaret, *née* Sharples; *b* 28 April 1953; *Educ* Hulme GS Oldham, BNC Oxford (BA); *m* 4 June 1977, Barbara Anne, da of Dr Donald Longbottom (d 1961); 2 da (Elizabeth b 1982, Alexandra b 1985); *Career* called to the Bar Middle Temple 1976, hon sec Northern Circuit of the Bar 1988-; *Recreations* skiing, cricket, tennis; *Clubs* Manchester Racquets, Rochdale Racquets, I Volenti CC; *Style*— Alistair Webster, Esq; Ashworth Hall, Ashworth Rd, Rochdale, Lancs OL11 5UP (☎ 0706 30779); Rational House, 64 Bridge St, Manchester M3 3BN (☎ 061 832 5701, fax 061 832 0839)

WEBSTER, Maj-Gen Bryan Courtney; CB (1986), CBE (1981); s of Capt Herbert John Webster (ka 1940), and Mabel, *née* Harrison (d 1970); *b* 2 Feb 1931; *Educ* Haileybury, RMA Sandhurst; *m* 1957, Elizabeth Rowland Waldron, da of Prof Sir David Waldron Smithers; 2 s (Julian, Justin), 1 da (Lucinda); *Career* cmmnd Royal Fusiliers 1951, Airborne Forces 1953-56; served: Germany, Korea, Egypt, Gibraltar, Hong Kong, Malta; directing staff Staff Coll 1969-71; cmd: 1 RRF 1971-73, 8 Inf Bde 1975-77; MID 1977, Chief of Staff SE Dist 1977-78, Indian Nat Def Coll 1979, dir of admin Planning (Army) 1980-82-, dir Army Quartering 1982-86; Dep Col (City of London) RRF 1976-89, chm Army Benevolent Fund Surrey; Freeman City of London 1984; FBIM; *Recreations* field sports, ornithology; *Style*— Maj-Gen Bryan Webster, CB, CBE; Ewshot Lodge, Ewshot, Surrey

WEBSTER, Charles (formerly K F Harrer); *b* 23 Oct 1936; *Career* fell Corpus Christi Coll Oxford 1969-88, reader in history of med Univ of Oxford 1972-88, dir Wellcome Unit for History of Med 1972-88, sr res fell All Souls Coll Oxford 1988-; FBA 1982; *Books* The Great Instauration (1975), From Paracelsus to Newton (1982), Problems of Health Care (1988); *Style*— Charles Webster, Esq; All Souls College, Oxford (☎ 0865 279379, fax 0865 299299)

WEBSTER, David Gordon Comyn; s of Alfred Edward Comyn Webster, of St John's Town of Dalry, Castle Douglas, Scotland, and Meryl Mary, *née* Clutterbuck (d 1970); *b* 11 Feb 1945; *Educ* Glasgow Acad, Univ of Glasgow (LLB); *m* 12 Feb 1972, (Pamela) Gail, da of Dr Dennis Frank Runnicles, of Sevenoaks, Kent; 3 s (Michael Gordon Comyn b 2 Sept 1974, Nicholas Gordon Comyn b 9 Jan 1978, Jonathan Hugo Comyn b 9 Feb 1983); *Career* Lt RNR, ret 1970; slr 1968; corp fin Samuel Montagu & Co 1968-72; fin dir: Oriel Foods Ltd 1973-76, Argyll Gp plc 1977-89 (dep chm 1989-); govr Lockers Park Sch Tst Ltd; *Recreations* military history, gardening, skiing, shooting; *Style*— David Webster, Esq; Rodinghead, Ashridge Park, Berkhamsted, Hertfordshire; Argyll Group plc, 8 Chesterfield Hill, London W1X 7RG (☎ 071 493 0808)

WEBSTER, David John; s of Maj Edgar Webster, and Gladys; *b* 14 Jan 1947; *Educ* All Saints, Emerson Coll Michigan USA; *m* 12 Aug 1973, Julie; 1 s (Piers b 1978); *Career* lectr, artist, fine art dealer, portrait painter in fine art gallery; works: largest historical mural in UK, historical restorations of fine art, signed David John Webster sold worldwide; NSPCC supporter; donated works sold 1987 raised £2,500; *Recreations* photography, shooting, hunting; *Clubs* Historic Wine of GB Sloane Square, Dorset; *Style*— David J Webster, Esq; 26b Abbey St, Crewkerne, Somerset (☎ 0460 74665)

WEBSTER, Derek Adrian; CBE (1979); s of James Tulloch and Isobel Webster; *b* 24 March 1927; *Educ* St Peter's Bournemouth; *m* 1966, Dorothy Frances Johnson; 2 s, 1 da; *Career* RN 1944-48; reporter West Morning News 1943, staff journalist Daily Mail 1949-51, joined Mirror Group 1952, Northern ed Daily Mirror 1964-67, ed Daily Record 1967-72, dep chm Scottish Daily Record and Sunday Mail Ltd 1972-74, (chm and editorial dir 1974-87), dir Mirror Group Newspapers 1974-87; memb Press Cncl 1981-83 (jt vice chm 1982-83), vice chm Age Concern Scotland 1977-83, hon vice pres Newspaper Press Fund; *Recreations* boating, gardening; *Style*— Derek Webster, Esq, CBE; Kessog Bank, 60 Glasgow Rd, Blanefield, Glasgow G63 9BP (☎ 0360 70252)

WEBSTER, His Hon Judge; Ian Stevenson; s of Harvey Webster by his w Annabella, *née* MacBain; *b* 20 March 1925; *Educ* Rochdale GS, Univ of Manchester; *m* 1951, Margaret, *née* Sharples; 2 s; *Career* serv Sub-Lt RNVR in WWII; barr 1948, rec Crown Ct 1972-76 (asst rec Oldham 1970, Salford 1971); chm Manchester Industl Tribunals 1976-; Circuit Judge (Northern) 1981-; *Style*— His Hon Judge Webster; 1 Higher Lodge, Norden, Rochdale OL11 5TR

WEBSTER, Jan; da of William Stuart McCallum (d 1940), of Blantyre, Lanarkshire, and Margaret Henderson (d 1977); *b* 10 Aug 1924; *Educ* Hamilton Acad; *m* 1946, Andrew Webster, OBE, s of William Webster; 1 s (Stephen William b 1951), 1 da (Lyn Margaret b 1950); *Career* journalist: Glasgow Evening News and Scottish Sunday Mail 1942-46, Kemsley Newspapers London 1946-48; freelance journalist and writer of short stories 1948-; *books* incl: Colliers Row (1977), Saturday City (1978), Beggarman's Country (1979), Due South (1982), Muckle Annie (1985), One Little Room (1987), The Rags of Time (1987), A Different Woman (1989), Abercrombie's Aunt and Other Stories (1990), I Only Can Dance With You (1990), Bluebell Blue (1991); *Recreations* teaching creative writing, studying Shakespeare; *Style*— Mrs Jan Webster; c/o Robert Hale Ltd, Clerkenwell House, 45-7 Clerkenwell Green, London EC1R OHT

WEBSTER, Prof John; s of Albert Ashcroft Webster (d 1955), of Kirkby-in-Ashfield, Notts, and Alice, *née* Street (d 1957); *b* 25 May 1925; *Educ* Univ Coll Nottingham (external London BSc), Univ of London (external PhD, DSc); *m* 1 Aug 1950, Mary Elizabeth (Brom), da of Thomas Jireh Bromhead (d 1981), of Clenchwarton, Norfolk; 1 s (Christoher b 1956), 1 da (Sarah b 1959); *Career* lectr in botany Univ of Hull 1946-49, lectr then sr lectr then reader in botany Univ of Sheffield 1950-69, prof of biological scis Univ of Exeter 1986-90 (prof and head of Dept 1969-86, emeritus prof 1990); author of numerous pubns on taxonomy and ecology of fungi; pres Int Mycological Assoc 1983- (vice pres 1977-83), hon memb The Br Mycological Soc 1987- (memb 1946, sec 1953-57, pres 1969), corresponding memb Mycological Soc of America 1987-; FIBiol 1970; *Books* Introduction to Fungi (1980); *Recreations* gardening, walking; *Style*— Prof John Webster; University of Exeter, Hatherly Laboratories, Prince of Wales Road, Exeter EX4 4PS (☎ 0392 263784)

WEBSTER, John Dudley; *b* 13 Nov 1939; *Educ* Merchant Taylors', Univ Coll London (BSc); *m* 1967, Barbara Joan; 1 da (Katherine b 1969); *Career* dir and sec Sun Life Corporation plc, md Sun Life Asset Management Ltd, dir Sapphire Petroleum plc 1981-88; dir: Group Investors plc 1984-86, Save and Prosper Return of Assets Investment Trust plc 1984-; chm Br Insur Assoc Investmt Protection Ctee 1982-84, lay memb Cncl of Stock Exchange 1985-86 and 1988-, ind dir Securities Assoc 1986-90, tstee The Charities Official Investmt Fund 1988-; FIA; *Style*— John Webster, Esq; c/o Sun Life Corporation plc, 107 Cheapside London, EC2V 6DU (☎ 071 606 7788); 10 Merrydown Way, Chislehurst, Kent BR7 5RS

WEBSTER, Prof (Anthony) John Francis; Flt Lt John Terence Webster, DFC (ka 1940), and Lilian Hypatia, Mogg; *b* 24 Aug 1938; *Educ* Wellingborough Sch, St John's Coll Cambridge, (MA, Vet MB), Univ of Glasgow (PhD); *m* 31 Aug 1964 Maureen Anne Sanderson, da of Joseph Blair (d 1959); 1 s (Mark b 1965), 1 da (Joanne b 1967); *Career* assoc prof Univ of Alberta Canada 1966-70, princ vet res offr Rowett Res Inst Aberdeen 1970-77, prof of animal husbandry Univ of Bristol 1977-; memb Farm Animal Welfare Cncl (chm Res and Devpt Gp), sr vice pres Br Soc of Animal Prodn 1990, MRCVS (1963); *Books* Calf Husbandry Health and Welfare (1981), Understanding the Dairy Cow (1987); *Recreations* sailing, music; *Style*— Prof John Webster; Department of Animal Husbandry, University of Bristol School of Veterinary Science, Langford, Bristol BS18 7DU (☎ 0934 852581, fax 0934 853145)

WEBSTER, John Lawrence Harvey; CMG (1963); s of Sydney Webster (d 1970), of Grayshott, Surrey, and Elsie Gwendoline, *née* Harvey (d 1970); *b* 10 March 1913; *Educ* Rugby, Balliol Coll Oxford (MA, DipEd); *m* 1, 9 Jan 1940 (m dis 1959), Elizabeth Angela, da of Dr H Gilbertson (d 1972), of Hitchin, Herts; 2 da (Diana b 17 July 1942, Hilary b 10 May 1949); m 2, Jan 1960, Jessica Lilian, *née* Royston-Smith; *Career* Colonial Admin Serv Kenya: dist offr 1935-46, dist cmmr 1947-48, asst sec 1949-50, sec for devpt 1950-54, admin sec 1954-56, sec to cabinet 1956-58, perm sec for Forest Game and Fisheries 1958-62, perm sec for Info and Bdcasting 1963-; ret HMOCS at Kenya Self Govt; served with Br Cncl 1964-80 in: Thailand, Sri Lanka, Hong Kong, Istanbul, London; *Recreations* swimming, badminton; *Clubs* Nairobi, Royal Cwlth Soc, Leander; *Style*— John Webster, Esq, CMG; Timbercroft, 11 Pevensey Rd, Worthing, Sussex (☎ 0903 48617)

WEBSTER, Vice Adm Sir John Morrison; KCB (1986); s of Frank Martin Webster (d 1986), of Lea House, Lymington, and Kathleen Mary, *née* Morrison (d 1986); *b* 3 Nov 1932; *Educ* Pangbourne Coll; *m* 15 Dec 1962, Valerie Anne, da of Vice Adm Sir Michael Villiers KCB, OBE (d 1990), of Decoy House, Melton, Woodbridge; 1 s (Thomas b 1970), 2 da (Lucilla b 1964, Rozelle b 1966); *Career* joined RN 1951, specialised in navigation 1959; served: UK, Far East, Australia; staff appts at Dartmouth and MOD; cmd: HMS Argonaut 1970-71, HMS Cleopatra 1977-79; Naval Advsr and RNLO Ottawa 1974-76, dir Naval Warfare (MOD) 1980-81, Rear Adm 1982, Flag Offr Sea 1982-84, chief of staff to C-in-C Fleet 1984-86, Vice Adm 1985, Flag Offr Plymouth and Naval Base Cmdr Devonport 1987-; landscape and marine painter, exhibitions in Canada and London (King St Gallery 1981, 1984, Oliver Swann Gallery 1986); govr of Canford Sch; yr bro of Trinity House 1970; *Recreations* painting, sailing; *Clubs* Royal Cruising, Royal Naval Sailing Assoc, Armed Forces Art Soc; *Style*— Vice Adm Sir John Webster, KCB

WEBSTER, John Walter; s of Norman Alan Webster (d 1982), and Francis Kate, *née* Simons; *b* 21 Jan 1936; *Educ* De Aston Sch Market Rasen Lincs, LSE (BSc); *m* 12 Aug 1961, Constance Anne, da of Arthur Cartwright (d 1944), of Sch House, Admaston, Rugeley, Staffs; 1 da (Elizabeth b 1966), 1 s (Graham b 1968); *Career* mangr Price Waterhouse & Co 1961-71, finance dir The Penguin Gp; dir: The Penguin Publishing Co Ltd 1980, Penguin Books Ltd 1976, Penguin Books Australia Ltd 1982, Penguin Books Canada Ltd 1982, Penguin Books (NZ) Ltd 1982, Penguin USA Inc 1986, Penguin India (Private) Ltd 1984, Frederick Warne & Co Ltd 1983; FCA; *Recreations* skiing, travel, reading; *Style*— John Webster, Esq; Woodmans Cottage, Bramley Rd, Silchester, Hants (☎ 0734 700670); School House, Admaston, nr Rugeley, Staffs (☎ 088921 285); Penguin Books Ltd, Bath Rd, Harmondsworth, Middx 1JK (☎ 081 759 2184, fax 081 897 6774)

WEBSTER, Nigel Robert; s of Derek Stanley Webster, of Walsall, and Sheila Margaret Flora, *née* Squire; *b* 14 June 1953; *Educ* Univ of Leeds (BSc, MB ChB, PhD); *m* 2 July 1977, Diana Christina Shirley, da of Brian Robert Galt Hutchinson, of York, 1 s (Oliver James b 1986), 2 da (Lorna Elizabeth b 1984, Lucy Anne b 1987); *Career* memb of scientific staff div of anaesthesia MRC Clinical Res Centre 1986-88, conslt in anaesthesia, dir transplant anaesthesia and co-dir of intensive care St James' Univ Hosp Leeds 1988-; memb: Intensive Care Soc, Soc for Free Radical Res, Elgar Soc; FFARCS; *Books* Research Techniques in Anaesthesia (1988); *Recreations* music, gardening; *Style*— Nigel Webster, Esq; 18 Wetherby Rd, Leeds LS8 2QD; St James's University Hospital, Beckett St, Leeds LS9 7TF (☎ 0532 433144)

WEBSTER, Patrick; s of Francis Glyn Webster, and Ann Webster, *née* Harrington (d 1980); *b* 6 Jan 1928; *Educ* Swansea GS, Rockwell Coll Eire, St Edmund's Coll Ware, Downing Coll Cambridge (BA); *m* 6 Aug 1955, Elizabeth, da of Trevor David Knight (d 1976); 2 s (David b 1956, Patrick 1962), 4 da (Anne b 1957, Elizabeth b 1959, Mary b 1961, Catherine b 1965); *Career* called to Bar Gray's Inn 1950, practised at Bar in Swansea, ISCOED Chambers -1975, rec of the Crown Ct 1972, chm of Indust Tribunals Cardiff Region 1976 (pt/t chm 1965-75); pt/t chm Med Appeals Tribunal 1971-75; *Recreations* music, watching grandchildren, rowing, sailing; *Clubs* Penarth Yacht (Penarth), Beechwood (Swansea); *Style*— Patrick Webster, Esq; 103 Plymouth Rd, Penarth, S Glamorgan CF6 2DE; Caradog House, St Andrews Place, Cardiff CF1 3BE

WEBSTER, Hon Mr Justice; Hon Sir Peter Edlin Webster; QC (1967); s of Herbert Edlin Webster, of Cookham, by his w Florence Helen; *b* 16 Feb 1924; *Educ* Haileybury, Merton Coll Oxford; *m* 1, 1955 (m dis), Susan Elizabeth, da of the late Benjamin William Richards; 1 s, 2 da; m 2, 1968, Avril Carolyn Simpson, da of the late Dr John Ernest McCrae Harrisson; *Career* Nat Serv RNVR 1943-46 and 1950; lectr in law Lincoln Coll Oxford 1950-52, called to the Bar Middle Temple 1952; standing jr counsel to Labour Miny 1964-67; chm: London Common Law Bar Assoc 1975-79, Senate of the Inns of Court and the Bar 1976-77; dir Booker McConnell 1978-79; high ct judge (Queen's Bench) 1980, chm Judicial Studies Bd 1981-83; kt 1980; *Style*— The Hon Mr Justice Webster; Royal Courts of Justice, Strand, London WC2

WEBSTER, Richard Edward; s of William Graham Webster, of Port Tennant, Swansea, and June Elizabeth, *née* Richards; *b* 9 July 1967; *Educ* Cefn Hengoed Secdy; *m* ; 1 da (Kelly Joanne Webster b 11 July 1987); *Career* Rugby Union Flanker Swansea RFC and Wales (2 caps); clubs: bonymaen RFC (capt youth team 1984-85 and 1985-86), Swansea RFC, Barbarians RFC; rep: Wales Youth 1985-86, Wales U21 1987; Wales: debut v Aust 1987, memb World Cup Squad 1987; bricklayer, sales rep Manor Bricks; *Recreations* DIY, horse riding, keep fit; *Style*— Richard Webster, Esq; c/o Swansea RFC, Bryn Rd, Swansea

WEBSTER, Richard Joseph; s of Peter Joseph Webster, of Dulwich,London; *b* 7 July 1953; *Educ* William Penn Dulwich; *m* 1980, Patricia Catherine, da of Gerald Stanley Edwards (former Chief Supt Sussex Police), of East Grinstead; 1 s (James Joseph b April 1985), 1 da (Victoria Catherine b Sept 1983); *Career* Lloyd's insur broker; dir: Howden Cross Ltd 1977-82, Alexander Howden insurance Brokers Ltd 1978-82, Hogg

Robinson & Gardner Mountain (reinsurance and non marine) Ltd 1982-87, Hogg Robinson (London) Ltd 1983-87, Hogg Robinson Ltd 1986-87, Hispano American Reinsurance Brokers Ltd 1984-87, J Besso & Co Ltd 1987-; chm: R J Webster insurance Brokers Ltd 1987-, Besso Int Ltd 1989-; *Recreations* family, riding, swimming, watching rugby; *Clubs* Lloyd's of London; *Style*— Richard Webster, Esq; 23a The Glen, Farnborough Park, Locksbotton, Kent BR6 8LP; 57 Mansell St, London E1 8AN (☎ 071 265 0797, fax 071 480 7725, telex 938046 BESS G)

WEBSTER, Richard Stanley; s of Maurice Stanley Webster, JP (d 1971), of Liverpool, and Dorothea Marie, *née* Thompson; *b* 25 March 1938; *Educ* Sedbergh; *m* 6 June 1964, Sheila Elizabeth, da of Richard Stephenson (d 1975), of North Berwick; 2 da (Karen b 1966, Fiona b 1968); *Career* CA; chm James Webster & Bro Ltd and subsids; dir: Diversion Insurance (Timber) Association Ltd, Age Concern Liverpool, Union Pour Le Commerce Des Bois Tropicaux Dans Le CEE; FCA; *Recreations* gardening, gastronomy; *Style*— Richard Webster, Esq; The White Cottage, 11 Derby Rd, Formby, Merseyside L37 7BN (☎ 07048 73730); James Webster & Bro Ltd, 165 Derby Rd, Bootle, Merseyside L20 8LE

WEBSTER, Prof (John) Roger; OBE (1988); s of Samuel Webster (d 1974), and Jessie, *née* Farbrother (d 1951); *b* 24 June 1926; *Educ* Llangefni Co Sch, Univ Coll of Wales Aberystwyth (MA, PhD); *m* 17 April 1963, Ivy Mary, da of Frederick Garlick (d 1956); 1 s (Matthew b 1964), 1 da (Catrin b 1966); *Career* lectr Trinity Coll Carmarthen 1948, lectr in educn Univ Coll Swansea 1951, dir for Wales Art Cncl of GB 1961; prof of educn: Univ Coll of N Wales Bangor 1966, Univ Coll of Wales Aberystwyth 1978; James ctee on Teacher Trg 1971; memb: Lloyd Ctee on Nat Film Sch 1965-66, Welsh Jt Educn Ctee 1967-, Cncl Open Univ 1969-78, Venables Ctee on Continuing Educn 1974-76, Standing Conf on Studies in Educn 1972-76, CNAA 1976-79, Post Office Users Nat Cncl (chm Wales) 1981-88, Educn Sub Ctee UGC 1988-89; chm: Standing Conf on Studies in Educn 1972-76, Wales Telecommunications Advsrs Ctee 1984-88; govr Cwlth Inst 1985-; *Style*— Prof Roger Webster, OBE; Bron Y Glyn, Rhyd Y Felin, Aberystwyth, Dyfed SY23 4QD; Dept of Educn, Univ Coll of Wales, Old College, King St, Aberystwyth

WEBSTER, Sinclair Aubrey; s of Rae Walter Webster, and Alphonsine Maria Brulez Ryngaert; *b* 19 Nov 1948; *Educ* Worth Sch, Trinity Hall Cambridge (MA, Dip Arch); *m* Stephanie Jane, da of E D John Walter Poeeard; 1 s (Hugh Sinclair b 23 May 1980), 1 da (Isabel Mary b 29 Sept 1982); *Career* Llewelyn-Davies Weeks Forrestier Walker & Bor: joined 1973, project architect Decorating Bldg Hammersmith Hosp London 1973, med planner Hammersmith Hosp Phase 1B 1973, project architect Ras Rumman State of Bahrain and memb team formulating policy and standards for state of Bahrain Miny of Devpt 1974; joined Fitzroy Robinson 1974 (project architect Bank of Credit and Commerce Abu Dhabi 1974-76); Sheppard Robson: joined 1976, assoc ptnr 1980, sr assoc ptnr 1986, ptnr 1988, med planner and architect for Shagamu Accident and Orthopaedic Hosp Nigeria 1976-77; project architect for Sheppard Robson: Trade and Exhibition Centre Ibadan Nigeria 1977, Lewisham Hosp redevelopment London 1980-81, Fountain Square redevelopment Baghdad Iraq 1982, Naish Khana redevelopment masterplan Iraq 1982, PO HQ refurbishment London 1983, River Plate House redevelopment London 1984-85, Kern House redevelopment London 1985, Warnford Ct London 1986, Lloyds Bank Head Office London 1986-87, Nat Gallery Extension London 1986-90, BBC HQ London 1987, Westminster and Chelsea Hosp London 1987- (ptnr 1988-), Euston Centre masterplan 1987-; ptnr: Shelley House London Wall 1988-, Broadwater Lake Business Park Hillingdon 1989-; cncllr Woking Borough Cncl 1990-; solo exhibitions: New Stanley Nairobi 1967, Studio Callebert 1968, Britannique 1969, Edinburgh 1970; jt exhibitions: Churchill Coll 1969, Trinity Hall 1970; pictures in collections: UK, USA, Belgium; RIBA 1975; *Recreations* painting, writing, hillwalking, shooting, wind-surfing, running; *Clubs* Anglo-Belgian; *Style*— Sinclair Webster, Esq; Wych-Elm House, Ashwood Rd, Woking, Surrey GU22 7JW (☎ 0483 722913); Sheppard Robson, 77 Parkway, London NW1 7PU (☎ 071 485 4161, 071 267 3861, fax 0836 576 045)

WEBSTER, Dr Stephen George Philip; s of George Stephen Webster (d 1982), and Winifred Ella, *née* Tice (d 1971); *b* 30 Sept 1940; *Educ* County HS for Boys Ilford Essex, The London Hosp Med Coll (MB BS, MD); *m* 23 July 1960, Susan Jane, da of Maurice Hills, of 2 Apthorpe St, Fulbourn, Cambridgeshire; 3 s (Matthew John b 15 June 1968, Thomas Edward b 9 Jan 1970, Richard George b 14 April 1971); *Career* conslt physician in gen and geriatric med 1973, assoc lectr faculty of Clinical Med Univ of Cambridge 1975, hon public info offr Br Geriatrics soc 1987 (hon sec 1984); memb geriatrics ctee RCP 1989, chm CAMTAD Cambridge, med advsr Counsel and Care of the Elderly; hon MA Univ of Cambridge 1975; FRCP 1988; *Books* Ageing: The Facts (1984), Geriatric Medicine (contrib 1988); *Recreations* reading, skiing; *Style*— Dr Stephen Webster; 1 Water Street, Cambridge CB4 1NZ (☎ 0453 359037), Dept of Geriatric Medicine, Addenbrooke's Hospital, Cambridge (☎ 0223 217599)

WEBSTER, Trevor; s of Samuel Webster (d 1982), and Winifred, *née* Chapman (d 1977); *b* 1 Nov 1937; *Educ* Leeds GS, Univ of Leeds (LLB); *m* (m dis); *Career* customs offr Rhodesia and Nyasaland 1956-57, reporter 1960-64 (Financial World, Investors Review, Stock Exchange Gazette), reporter Daily Express 1966; The Scotsman: dep city ed 1964-66 and 1966-70, city ed 1970-86; dep city ed Daily News 1987, Questor ed Daily Telegraph 1987-88, city ed Daily Express 1989- (dep city ed 1988-89); *Books* Where To Go In Greece (1985), Corfu and the Ionian Isles (1986), Athens and Greek Mainland (1987), Rhodes and the Dodecanese (1988), Crete and the Cyclades (1989), Greek Island Delights (1990); *Recreations* tennis, skiing, travel, wine, theatre, cinema; *Clubs* National Liberal, Hunters, City Golf; *Style*— Trevor Webster, Esq

WEDD, George Morton; CB (1989); s of Albert Edward Wedd (d 1970) of Derbyshire, and Dora Wedd (d 1968); *b* 30 March 1930; *Educ* St John's Coll Cambridge (major open scholar, BA); 1953 (sep 1983), Kate Wedd; 2 s, 1 da; partner Dr Joan Bridgman; *Career* joined Miny of Housing and Local Govt 1951: min's private office 1955; private sec to Dame Evelyn Sharp Btss 1956, princ 1957, asst sec 1966, under sec 1976; regnl dir Depts of Tport and Enviroment 1983-90; ret 1990, now conslt; environmental advsr Community Serv Volunteers; *Recreations* reading, walking, listening to music; *Style*— George Wedd, Esq, CB; The Lodge, Church Hill, High Littleton, Avon BS18 5HG; 1 Horsebrook Cottages, Avonwick, nr Totnes, Devon (☎ 0761 71520)

WEDDERBURN, Hon David Roland; s of Baron Wedderburn of Charlton and his 1 w, Nina, da of Dr Myer Salaman; *b* 1956; *Career* BSc, ACA; *Style*— The Hon David Wedderburn; c/o 29 Woodside Av, Highgate, London N6

WEDDERBURN, Prof Dorothy; da of Frederick C Barnard (d 1953), and Ethel C, *née* Lawrence (d 1969); *b* 18 Sept 1925; *Educ* Walthamstow HS For Girls, Girton Coll Cambridge (MA); *Career* res offr Dept of Applied Economics Univ of Cambridge 1950-65; Imperial Coll of Sci and Technol: lectr in industl sociology 1965-70, reader 1970-77, prof 1977-81, dir Industl Sociology Unit 1973-81, head Dept of Social and Econ Studies 1978-81; princ: Bedford Coll 1981-85, Royal Holloway and Bedford New Coll 1985-90; Sr res fell Imperial Coll of Sci and Technol 1990-; hon pres Fawcett Soc 1986-, pt/t memb Royal Cmmn on the Distribution of Income and Wealth 1974- 78; memb: Cncl Advsy Conciliation and Arbitration Serv 1976-82, SSRC 1976-82; Hon DLitt: Univ of Warwick 1984, Univ of Loughborough 1989; Hon D Univ Brunel Univ 1990; fell Ealing Coll of Higher Educn 1985, hon fell Imperial Coll Univ of London 1986; *Books* White Collar Redundancy (1964), Redundancy and the Railwaymen (1964), The Aged in the Welfare State (with P Townsend, 1965), Workers' Attitudes and Technology (1972); *Recreations* politics, walking, cooking; *Style*— Prof Dorothy Wedderburn; Management School, Imperial College, 52/53 Prince's Gate, Exhibition Road, London SW7 2PG (☎ 071 589 5111)

WEDDERBURN, Hon Lucy Rachel; da of Baron Wedderburn of Charlton and his 1 w, Nina, da of Dr Myer Salaman; *b* 28 June 1960; *Educ* Camden Sch for Girls, Camb Univ (BA), London Hosp Med Coll (MB BS, MRCP); *Career* hospital doctor 1986-; memb: Med Practitioners Union (MSF), Socialist Health Assoc, Women in Medicine; *Recreations* health politics, violin, singing, cycling; *Style*— Dr the Hon Lucy Wedderburn

WEDDERBURN OF CHARLTON, Baron (Life Peer UK 1977), of Highgate, Greater London; Kenneth William Wedderburn; QC (1990); s of Herbert John Wedderburn; *b* 13 April 1927; *Educ* Aske's (Hatcham) GS, Whitgift Sch, Queens' Coll Cambridge (MA, LLB); *m* 1, 1951 (m dis 1962), Nina, da of Dr Myer Salaman; 1 s (Hon David Roland b 1956), 2 da (Hon Sarah Louise b 1954, Hon Lucy Rachel b 1960); m 2, 1962 (m dis 1969), Dorothy Enid, da of Frederick C Barnard and formerly w of William A Cole; m 3, 1969, Frances Ann, da of Basil F Knight; 1 s (Hon Jonathan Michael b 1972); *Career* served RAF 1949-51; sits as Lab peer in House of Lords; barr Middle Temple 1953, former lectr at Clare Coll and Faculty of Law Univ of Cambridge, Cassel Prof Commercial Law LSE 1964-; visiting prof: UCLA Law Sch 1967, Harvard Law Sch 1969-70; chm: London and Provincial Theatre Cncls 1973-, Ind Review Ctee 1976-, ed Modern Law Review 1970-88; fell Br Acad 1981; Hon Dott Giur (Univ of Pavia) 1987; *Publications include* The Worker and the Law (1986), Cases and Materials on Labour Law (1967), Employment Grievances and Disputes Procedures (with P L Davies, 1969), Labour Law and Industrial Relations (with R Lewis and J Clark, 1982), Diritto del Lavoro en Europa (with B Veneziani and S Ghimpu, 1987), Clerk and Lindsell on Torts (jt ed, 1989); *Recreations* Charlton Athletic FC; *Style*— Prof the Rt Hon the Lord Wedderburn of Charlton, QC; 29 Woodside Ave, Highgate, London N6 4SP (☎ 081 444 8472); LSE, Aldwych, London WC2A 2AE (☎ 071 405 7686, telex 24655 BLPES G)

WEDDERBURN-OGILVY, Caryl Eustace; s (by 1 m) of late Donald Wedderburn-Ogilvy; hp of cous, Sir Andrew Ogilvy-Wedderburn, 7 Bt; *b* 10 Dec 1925; *m* 1953, Katharine Mary, da of William Steele, of Dundee; 1 s, 2 da; *Career* ARIBA; *Style*— Caryl Wedderburn-Ogilvy Esq; Pucklepeggies, 21 Sth Glassford St, Milngavie, Strathclyde G62 6AT

WEDDERSPOON, Very Rev Alexander Gillan; s of Rev Robert John Wedderspoon (d 1956), and Amy Beatrice, *née* Woolley (d 1972); *b* 3 April 1931; *Educ* Westminster, Jesus Coll Oxford (MA, BD); *m* 2 Aug 1968, Judith Joyce Wynne, da of Arthur Fitzwalter Wynne Plumptree, CBE (d 1977); 1 s (Alexander Michael Wynne b 1975), 1 da (Caroline Joyce b 1972); *Career* Nat Serv 1949-51, cmmnd RA; curate Kingston Parish Church 1961-63, lectr in religious educn Univ of London 1963-66, educn advsr C of E Schools Cncl 1966-69, priest i/c St Margaret's Westminster 1969-70, canon residentiary Winchester Cathedral 1970-87 (vice dean 1980-87), dean of Guildford 1987-; *Books* Religious Education 1944-84 (1964), The Durham Report on Religious Education (1970), Grow or Die (1981); *Recreations* walking, travel; *Style*— The Very Rev the Dean of Guildford; Cathedral Office, Stag Hill, Guildford GU2 5UP (☎ 0483 65287)

WEDDLE, Stephen Norman; s of Norman Harold Weddle, Sutton Coldfield, W Midlands, and Irene, *née* Furniss; *b* 1 Jan 1950; *Educ* Fairfax High Sch Sutton Coldfield, NE London Poly (BSc), Univ of London, Bedford Coll Univ of London; *m* July 1977 (m dis 1980), Brigid, da of late Edward Couch; *Career* graduate trainee journalist Birmingham Post and Mail 1972-75, reporter BBC Radio Stoke-on-Trent 1975-76, researcher, dir and prodr Pebble Mill at One 1976-, prodr Cool It 1985-90, ed Daytime Live 198790, launched and currently ed Daytime UK 1990; winner RTS Best Original TV Achievement award 1987; *Recreations* supporting Tottenham Hotspur FC, cinema, loud music, reading novels, comedy and politics and eccentric dancing; *Style*— Stephen Weddle, Esq; BBC TV, Daytime Live, Pebble Mill Rd, Birmingham B5 7QQ (☎ 021 414 8189, telex 265781, fax 021 414 8031)

WEDELL, Prof (Eberhard Arthur Otto) George; s of Rev Dr H Wedell (d 1964), of Haslemere and Dusseldorf, and Gertrude, *née* Bonhoeffer (d 1982); *b* 4 April 1927; *Educ* Cranbrook Sch, LSE (BSc); *m* 5 April 1948, Rosemarie, da of Rev Dr Paul Winckler; 3 s (Martin b 1950, Crispin b 1954, Philip b 1956), 1 da (Rebecca b 1957); *Career* princ Miny of Educn 1955-60 (asst princ 1950-55), fndr sec gen Bd for Social Responsibility Gen Assembly of the C of E 1958-60 (secondment from Civil Serv), sec ITA 1961-64 (dep sec 1960-61), prof of adult educn and dir extra-mural studies Univ of Manchester 1964-75, head Community Employment Div Cmmn of the Euro Communities 1973-82, visiting prof of employment policy Manchester Business Sch 1975-83, prof of communications policy Univ of Manchester and dir of the Euro Inst for the Media 1983-; chm: Wyndham Place Tst, Beatrice Hankey Fndn (hon memb 1988-); dir: Royal Exchange Theatre 1968-88, Manchester Arts Centre 1983-; vice pres Greater Manchester Lib Pty; candidate (Lib) Greater Manchester West Euro elections 1979, Greater Manchester Central (Alliance) in Euro elections 1984; pres Friends of the Manchester Coll of Adult Educn, Chev de L'Ordre des arts et des Lettres (France) 1989; Lord of the Manor of Clotton Hoofield; Hon MEd Univ of Manchester 1968; memb Int Inst of Communications 1969, FRTS 1982, FRSA 1972; *Books* The Use of Television in Education (1963), Broadcasting and Public Policy (1968), Teaching at a Distance (with HD Perraton, 1968), Structures of Broadcasting (ed, 1970), Study by Correspondence (with R Glatter, 1971), Correspondence Education in Europe (1971), Teachers and Educational Development in Cyprus (1971), Education and the Development of Malawi (ed, 1973), Broadcasting in the Third World (with E Katz, 1977, Book of the Year NAEB USA 1978), Mass Communications in Western Europe (with G M Luyken and R Leonard, 1985), Making Broadcasting Useful (ed, 1986), Media in Competition (with G M Luyken, 1986); *Recreations* gardening, music, theatre; *Clubs* Athenaeum Fondation Univ (Brussels); *Style*— Prof George Wedell; 18 Cranmer Rd, Manchester M20 OAW (☎ 061 445 5106); 94 Eton Place, London NW3 (☎ 071 722 0299); Vigneau, Lachapelle 47350 Seyches, France (☎ 58 83 88 71); The European Institute for the Media, The University of Manchester M13 9PL (☎ 061 273 2754, fax 273 8788)

WEDGE, Prof Peter Joseph; s of John Wedge (d 1983), and Nellie, *née* Clemson (d 1978); *b* 13 June 1935; *Educ* Queen Mary's Sch Walsall, Univ of Oxford (MA), LSE (certificates in social and pub admin and applied social studies); *m* 26 Aug 1961, Dorothy Charlton, da of John Charlton Grieves; 2 s (John, David), 2 da (Sarah, Catherine); *Career* Nat Serv RAF 1953-55; probation offr Hertfordshire 1961-64, res offr Preston 1964-65, tutor caseworker Univ of Manchester and Family Welfare Assoc 1965-68; Nat Children's Bureau 1968-81: sr res offr, princ res offr, asst dir, dep dir (res); UEA: sr lectr then prof of social work 1981-, dean Sch of Econ and Social Studies 1990-; memb Norfolk probation Ctee, The Princes Tst Young Offenders Gp, Ormiston Tst, Child Tst; memb: SPA 1966, ACPP 1969, BASW 1982; *Books* Preston

Family Welfare Survey (1966), Growing Up Adopted (1972), Born to Fail? (1973), Continuities in Childhood Disadvantage (1982), Children in Adversity (1982), Finding Families for Hard-to-Place Children (1986); *Recreations* singing, walking; *Style—* Prof Peter Wedge; School of Economic & Social Studies, University of East Anglia, Norwich, Norfolk NR4 7TJ (☎ 0603 592099)

WEDGWOOD, Chester Dwight; s of Paul Wedgwood, and Phyllis May (now Mrs King); *b* 25 July 1943; *Educ* Catford Tech Coll; *m* 1, (m dis 1978), Linda Hunt; m 2, 6 Oct 1978, Elizabeth Blanche, da of Edmund Hutchinson (d 1983), of 64 Marlow Rd, High Wycombe, Bucks; 1 s (Simon John b 6 Aug 1980); *Career* The Rank Orgn 1960-64: mgmnt trainee 1960-62, mangr The Pye Record Co 1962-64; mangr The Tan-Sqd Chair Co Ltd 1964-70, sales mangr Godfrey Syrett Ltd 1970-72, md and fndr memb Gordon Russell plc (formerly Giroflex Ltd) 1972-; fndr DIA Gordon Russell Awards; memb Design Cncl with New Designers; memb Worshipful Co of Furniture Makers 1988; FCSD 1988; *Recreations* motor racing, collecting cars, reading, resting; *Style—* Chester Wedgwood, Esq; Gordon Russell plc, 44 Eagle St, London WC1 (☎ 071 831 0031, fax 071 831 9172)

WEDGWOOD, Dennis Leveson; s of Stanley Leveson Wedgwood, of Pawlett, Somerset, and Hilda, *née* Millington (d 1977), of Biddulph, Staffs; *b* 14 Sept 1936; *Educ* Bury GS, Univ of London (BDS, MB BS); *m* 18 June 1966, Jean, da of Arthur Oliver (d 1989), of Minsterley, Shrops; 2 da (Elizabeth b 20 May 1968, Rosalind b 5 April 1970); *Career* Col served Falkland Islands and S Georgia 1960-62, dental practice 1962-64, house surgn and registrar Westminster Hosp 1964-66, sr registrar Univ Coll and Mt Vernon Hosps 1972-75, prof and chm Oral and Maxillo-Facial Surgery Univ of Manitoba Winnipeg Canada 1975-80, conslt Oral and Maxillo-Facial Surgn Shrops HA 1980-; dental post grad tutor Shrops Health Dist, chm Br Study Gp for Titanium Implants; FDSRCS, FRCSEd, FRCD (C), BMA, BAOMFS, HCSA; *Books* approx 20 scientific pubns on oral and maxillo-facial surgery; *Recreations* walking, sailing, restoration of steam vehicles; *Style—* Dennis Wedgwood, Esq; Royal Shrewsbury Hospital, Mytton Oak Rd, Shrewsbury SY3 8BR (☎ 0743 231122 ext 3336)

WEDGWOOD, Hon Mrs (Elfrida Sandra); *née* MacLehose; er da of Baron MacLehose of Beoch; *b* 1949; *m* 1971, Martin Amery Wedgwood; 1 s (Richard Martin b 1975), 1 da (Lois Elfrida Margaret b 1977); *Style—* The Hon Mrs Wedgwood; Collalis, Gartocharn, By Alexandria, Dunbartonshire G83 8SD

WEDGWOOD, Baroness; Jane Weymouth; da of William Poulton, of Kenya; *m* 1949, as his 2 w, 3 Baron Wedgwood (d 1970); 1 s (4 Baron), 2 da (Hon Susan Wedgwood and Hon Mrs Wedgwood Bitove); *Style—* The Rt Hon Lady Wedgwood; Harewood Cottage, Chicksgrove, Tisbury, Wilts

WEDGWOOD, Jill; da of Capt George William Thomas Garrood, AFC (d 1968), of The Sheraton, Kenilworth, Capetown, SA, and Winifed Irene, *née* Jeffery (d 1968); *b* 20 March 1931; *Educ* Malvern Girls Coll; *m* 1, 9 March 1959, James Stirrat (d 1966), s of James Stirrat (d 1914), of 16 Westbourne Gdns, Glasgow; 1 s (Hamish b 1959); m 2, 29 Sept 1972, (Arthur) Anthony Wedgwood, s of Robert Amery Wedgwood, TD, DL (D 1988), of The Mill House, Helensburgh; *Career* chm Scottish Trading Co Ltd 1964-67, dir Goosewing Products 1984-86; dist pres Stirlingshire Red Cross 1967-68, memb Tenovus (Scotland) Strathclyde Ladies Ctee 1986-89; *Recreations* art, swimming, tennis, journalism; *Clubs* The Royal Overseas League; *Style—* Mrs Anthony Wedgwood; Artarman Cottage, Rhu, Dunbartonshire G84 8LQ (☎ 0436 820866)

WEDGWOOD, Dr John; CBE (1987); s of Hon Josiah Wedgwood (d 1968, yr s of 1 Baron Wedgwood and sometime chm of Josiah Wedgwood and Sons and dir of Bank of England 1942-46), of Damson Hill, Stone, Staffs, and Dorothy Mary Wedgwood, OBE, *née* Winser; hp to 1 cous once removed, 4 Baron Wedgwood; *b* 28 Sept 1919; *Educ* Abbotsholme, Trinity Coll Cambridge (MA, MD); *m* 1, 17 July 1943 (m dis 1971), Margaret, da of Alfred Sidell Mason, of Bury St Edmunds; 3 s (Anthony John b 31 Jan 1944 (m 1969 Angela Page), Simon James Josiah b 3 Oct 1949, Nicholas Ralph b 30 June 1951), 2 da (Judith Margaret b 24 Aug 1946 (m 1967 Christopher Tracy), Katherine Sarah b 24 Nov 1955); m 2, 1972, Jo Alice, da of Harold Swann Ripsher (d 1958); *Career* Surgn-Lt RNVR, Europe and Far East 1943-46; conslt Middx Hosp 1968-80, med dir Royal Hosp for Incurables 1980-86, conslt emeritus Middx Hosp 1980-; chm Royal Surgical Aid Soc 1987-; dir Wedgwood plc 1967-87; Liveryman Worshipful Soc of Apothecaries; FRCP; *Recreations* ceramics, history, sailing; *Clubs* Savile, Athenaeum, Liveryman Soc of Apothecaries; *Style—* Dr John Wedgwood, CBE; 109 Ashley Gdns, Thirleby Road, London SW1P 1HJ (☎ 071 828 8319)

WEDGWOOD, Sir (Hugo) Martin; 3 Bt (UK 1942), of Etruria, Co Stafford; s of Sir John Hamilton Wedgwood, 2 Bt, TD (d 1989), and his 1 w, Diana, *née* Hawkshaw (d 1976); 7 in descent from Josiah Wedgwood, the potter; *b* 27 Dec 1933; *Educ* Eton, Trinity Coll Oxford (BA); *m* 20 July 1963, Alexandra Mary Gordon, er da of late Judge Alfred Alexander Gordon Clark, of Berry's Croft, Westhumble, Dorking, Surrey; 1 s (Ralph Nicholas), 2 da (Julia Mary b 1966, Frances Veronica Mary b 1969); *Heir* s, Ralph Nicholas Wedgwood b 10 Dec 1964; *Career* memb Stock Exchange 1973-; ptnr Laurence Prust & Co 1973-84, dir Smith New Court International Ltd 1986-; *Style—* Sir Martin Wedgwood, Bt; Pixham Mill, Pixham Lane, Dorking, Surrey (☎ 0306 889941)

WEDGWOOD, 4 Baron (UK 1942); Piers Anthony Weymouth Wedgwood; s of 3 Baron Wedgwood (d 1970, 5 in descent from Josiah Wedgwood, first MP for the newly enfranchised Stoke-on-Trent 1832-34 and s of Josiah Wedgwood, FRS, who founded the pottery), by his 2 w, Jane Weymouth, *née* Poulton; *b* 20 Sept 1954; *Educ* Marlborough, RMA Sandhurst; *m* 30 May 1985, Mary Regina Margaret Kavanagh, da of late Edward Quinn, of Philadelphia, USA; 1 da (Alexandra Mary Kavanagh b 3 Oct 1987); *Heir* first cous once removed, Dr John Wedgwood, CBE; *Career* late Capt Royal Scots (The Royal Regt); *Style—* The Rt Hon the Lord Wedgwood; 152 Ashley Gardens, London SW1 (☎ 071 834 7817)

WEDGWOOD, Dame (Cicely) Veronica; OM (1969), DBE (1968, CBE 1956); da of Sir Ralph Wedgwood, 1 Bt, sis of Sir John Wedgwood, 2 Bt, and 1 cous twice removed of 4 Baron Wedgwood; *b* 20 July 1910; *Educ* privately, Lady Margaret Hall Oxford; *Career* historian, particularly of sixteenth and seventeenth centuries; former memb: Bd Nat Gallery, Arts Cncl, Advsy Cncl V & A, Inst for Advanced Studies Princeton; hon bencher Middle Temple; hon memb: American Soc Arts & Scis, American Philosophical Soc, American Hist Assoc; *Books* incl: The Thirty Years' War (1938), The King's Peace (1955), The King's War (1958), The Trial of Charles I (1964), The Political Career of Rubens (1975), The Spoils of Time (1984); *Style—* Dame Veronica Wedgwood, OM, DBE; c/o Messrs Collins, 8 Grafton St, London W1 (☎ 071 493 7070)

WEDLAKE, William John; s of William John Wedlake, of South Zeal, Devon, and Patricia Mary, *née* Hunt; *b* 24 April 1956; *Educ* Okehampton GS, Exeter Coll of Educn, Univ of Warwick (BSc); *m* 4 July 1987, Elizabeth Kessick, da of late Brian Kessick Bowes; 2 s (Joshua William b 2 May 1989, James Henry b 29 Aug 1990); *Career* Arthur Andersen (Bristol) 1978-82; Price Waterhouse: USA 1982-84, London 1984-86; Continental Bank (London) 1986-87, fin dir Schroders 1990- (fin controller 1987-90); ACA 1982; *Recreations* horse riding, walking; *Style—* William J Wedlake, Esq; J Henry Schroder Wagg & Co Ltd, 120 Cheapside, London EC2V 6DS (☎ 071 382 6334, fax 071 382 3815)

WEDLEY, Dr John Raymond; s of Raymond Wedley (d 1988), of Wallasey, Cheshire, and Marjorie Elizabeth, *née* Howell; *b* 24 April 1945; *Educ* Oldershaw GS, Univ of Liverpool (MB ChB); *m* 27 July 1968, Susan, da of Thomas Reginald Wakefield, of Fovant, nr Salisbury, Wilts; *Career* sr lectr Guy's Hosp Med Sch and hon conslt on anaesthetics Guy's 1976-81, conslt on anaesthetics and pain relief Guy's 1981-, hon conslt on anaesthetics St Lukes Hosp for the Clergy 1990-; memb Anaesthetics Specialist Sub Ctee SE Thames RHA 1978-79, clinical rep for Guy's Med Academic Staff Ctee BMA 1978-81, Guy's linkman to Assoc of Anaesthetics GB and Ireland 1978-81; memb: Ctee SE Thames Soc of Anaesthetics 1982-85, Cncl Section of Anaesthetics RSM 1987-90; FFARCS 1974, FRSM; *Books* chapters in: Emergency Anaesthesia (1986), Surgery for Anaesthetists (1988), Symptom Control (1989); *Recreations* walking, theatre, music; *Style—* Dr John Wedley; 16 Glamorgan Rd, Hampton Wick, Kingston upon Thames, Surrey KT1 4HP (☎ 081 977 3819); Suite 304, Emblem House, London Bridge Hosp, 27 Tooley St, London SE1 2NP (☎ 071 403 3876)

WEEDON, Prof Basil Charles Leicester; CBE (1974); s of Charles William Weedon (d 1954), and Florence May Weedon (d 1963); *b* 18 July 1923; *Educ* Wandsworth Sch, Imperial Coll of Sci and Technol (PhD, DSc); *m* 21 March 1959, Barbara Mary, da of Leonard Sydney Dawe (d 1963); 1 s (Matthew b 1967), 1 da (Sarah b 1962); *Career* special prof Univ of Nottingham 1988- (vice chllr 1976-88), fell QMC London 1984 (prof organic chemistry 1960-76); scientific ed Pure and Applied Chemistry 1960-75; chm: Food Additives and Contaminants Ctee 1968-83, Cncl Nat Stone Centre 1985-; memb: Sci Bd Sci Res Cncl (chm Enzyme Chemistry and Technol Ctee) 1972-75, Univ Grants Ctee (chm Physical Sciences Sub Ctee) 1974-76, EEC Scientific Ctee for Food 1974-81; FRS 1971; Hon DTech Univ of Brunel 1975, Hon LLD Univ of Nottingham 1988; *Recreations* reading, music, walking; *Style—* Prof Basil Weedon, CBE, FRS; Sheepwash Grange, Heighington Rd, Canwick, Lincoln LN4 2RJ (☎ 0522 522488)

WEEDON, Dudley William; s of Reginald Percy Weedon (d 1965), and Ada Kate Weedon (d 1964); *b* 25 June 1920; *Educ* Northampton Polytech, Univ of London (BSc); *m* 28 July 1951, Monica Rose, da of Emerson Edward Smith, of Colchester (d 1975); 2 s (Michael b 1959, John b 1962), 1 da (Sarah b 1957); *Career* dir Cable & Wireless Ltd 1979-81; chm Energy Communications Ltd 1980-82; dir Hogg-Robinson Space & Telecommunications Ltd; FIEE; *Recreations* sailing; *Style—* Dudley Weedon, Esq

WEEKES, Rt Rev Ambrose Walter Marcus; CB (1970); s of Lt Cdr William Charles Tinnoth Weekes (d 1958); *b* 25 April 1919; *Educ* Rochester Cathedral Choir Sch, Sir Joseph Williamson's Rochester, King's Coll London, AKC 1941, FKC 1970, Scholae Cancellarii Lincoln; *Career* deacon 1942, priest 1943, Chaplain RN 1944-72, chaplain of the Fleet 1969-72; QHC 1969, dean of Gibraltar 1973-78; asst bp of Gibraltar 1978; suffragan bishop of Gibraltar in Europe 1980-86; dean, Pro-Cathedral of the Holy Trinity, Brussels 1980-86; hon asst bishop of Rochester 1986-88; *Recreations* music, yachting; *Clubs* RAC; *Style—* The Rt Rev Ambrose Weekes, CB

WEEKS, Alan Frederick; s of Frederick Charles Weeks, Master Mariner (d 1961), and Ada Frances Taylor (d 1959); *b* 8 Sept 1923; *Educ* Brighton Hove and Sussex GS; *m* 6 Sept 1947, Barbara Jane, da of Harold Burleigh Huckle (d 1936); 2 s (Nigel b 1953 (d 1981), Roderick b 1958), 1 da (Beverly b 1948); *Career* Lt RNR served: HMS Renown, HMS Rother, HMS Helmsdale 1941-46; PRO Brighton Sports Stadium 1946-65, commentator BBC (sports) 1951-90, dir Sports Aid Fndn 1976-83, govr Sports Aid Fndn 1983-, life vice-pres Brighton and Hove Entertainment Mangrs Assoc, life memb Nat Skating Assoc GB; memb Cncl GB Ice Hockey Assoc; *Recreations* swimming, ice sports; *Style—* Alan Weeks, Esq; 102 Wick Hall, Furze Hill, Hove, E Sussex BN3 1NH (☎ 0273 779769)

WEEKS, Clive Anthony; s of Donald Alfred Frederick Weeks, of Ewell, and Beryl Mary, *née* Moreton; *b* 5 Sept 1947; *Educ* Wimbledon Coll; *m* 1970, Teresa Mary, da of Rupert Alan Forrester; 1 s (Nicholas Edward Clive b 1986), 2 da (Clare Elizabeth b 1971, Katherine Frances b 1973); *Career* articled clerk then C A F Rowland & Co 1964-70, fin accountant W S Atkins & Partners 1970-71; ptnr: Rowland & Co 1975-76 (staff and training mangr 1971-75), Rowland Nevill & Co 1976-85, Moores Rowland 1985-; ACA 1969; *Recreations* family, music, books, cricket; *Style—* Clive Weeks, Esq; Moores Rowland, Clifford's Inn, Fetter Lane, London EC4A 1AS (☎ 071 831 2345, fax 071 831 6123)

WEEKS, John; CBE (1986); s of Victor John Weeks (d 1983), and Beatrice Anne, *née* Beasley (d 1975); *b* 5 March 1921; *Educ* Dulwich, Architectural Assoc Sch (Dip); *m* 7 Sept 1955, Barbara Lilian, da of Thomas Harry Nunn (d 1937); 1 s (Timothy b 1959), 1 da (Julia b 1957); *Career* dep dir Nuffield Fndn Div of Arch Studies 1956-60, architect in partnership with Richard Llewelyn-Davies (cr Baron 1963, d 1981) 1960-81, chm Llewelyn-Davies Weeks 1981-86, conslt Llewelyn-Davies Weeks 1986-; sr lectr Univ Coll London 1961-72; works include: Student Housing Imperial Coll of Tropical Agric Trinidad (1960), Northwick Park Hospital Harrow (1961), Univ Childrens Hosps Leuven Belgium (1970), Flinders Medical Centre Adelaide S Aust (1972), redevelopment of St Mary's Hosp Paddington London (1978); exhibitions: This is Tomorrow (London 1956), Cybernetic Serendipity (London 1968); cncl memb Architectural Assoc London 1975-83 (vice pres 1976-78), chm Br Health-Care Export Cncl 1982-84; hon memb China Soc of Architects Beijing 1985; FRIBA 1964, FRSA 1980; *Books* Investigation into the Functions and Design of Hospitals (jtly, 1955), Indeterminate Architecture (1964), Multi-Strategy Buildings (1969), Design for Research-Principles of Laboratory Architecture (1986); *Clubs* Architectural Assoc; *Style—* John Weeks, Esq, CBE; Llewelyn-Davies Weeks, Brook House, Torrington Place, London WC1E 7HN (☎ 071 637 0181)

WEETMAN, Prof Anthony Peter; s of Kenneth Weetman, and Evelyn, *née* Healer; *b* 29 April 1953; *Educ* Univ of Newcastle Med Sch (MB BS, MD); *m* 20 Feb 1982, Sheila Lois, da of John Seymour Thompson, OBE, (d 1985); 1 s (James b 1986), 1 da (Chloe b 1989); *Career* MRC trg fell 1981-83, MRC travelling fell 1984-85, Wellcome sr res fell 1985-89, lectr in med Univ of Cambridge and hon conslt physician Addenbrooke's Hosp 1989- and hon conslt physician Addenbrooke's Hosp 1989-91, prof of med Univ of Sheffield 1991-; MRCP 1979, FRCP 1990, Goulstonian lectr RCP 1991; *Recreations* fell walking; *Style—* Prof Anthony Weetman; 271 Hills Rd, Cambridge CB2 2RP (☎ 0223 212615); Dept of Medicine, University of Sheffield Clinical Sciences Centre, Northern General Hosp, Sheffield S7 5AU (☎ 0742 434343, fax 0742 560458)

WEIDEMANN, Hon Mrs (Hilary Mary); *née* Carron; da of Baron Carron (Life Peer, d 1969); *b* 1933; *m* 1959, John Simon, s of late Sidney Weidemann, of Sussex; 1 s, 1 da; *Style—* The Hon Mrs Weidemann; The Gables, 27 Bromley Rd, SE6 (☎ 081 697 3188)

WEIDENFELD, Baron (Life Peer UK 1976), of Chelsea in Greater London; (Arthur) George Weidenfeld; s of Max and Rosa Weidenfeld; *b* 13 Sept 1919; *Educ* Piaristen Gymnasium Vienna, Vienna Univ, Konsular Akademie; *m* 1, 1952, Jane, da of J Edward Sieff; 1 da (Hon Laura Miriam Elizabeth (Hon Mrs Barnett) b 1953); m 2, 1956 (m dis 1961), Barbara, da of Maj George Skelton and former wife of Cyril Connolly; m 3, 1966 (m dis 1973), Sandra, da of Charles Shipman Payson; *Career* takes SDP whip in House of Lords; chm Weidenfeld & Nicolson 1948- and assoc cos; served during WWII in BBC monitoring serv 1939-42; news commentator with BBC 1942-45, News Chronicle columnist 1945-46, fndr Contact Magazine and Books 1945; spent 1 year as political advsr and chief of cabinet to Pres Weizmann of Israel; vice chm Bd of Govrs Ben Gurion Univ of Negev Beer-Sheva; govr: Univ of Tel Aviv, Weizmann Inst of Sci, Bezalel Acad of Arts Jerusalem; tstee emeritus Aspen Inst Colorado, Wolfson History prize, chm Mitchell prize for History of Art; memb: of South Bank Bd 1986, Bd of English Nat Opera 1988; tstee Nat Portrait Gallery 1988; dir Gt Univ Stores Europe AG 1990; kt 1969; *Recreations* opera, travel; *Clubs* Garrick; *Style*— The Rt Hon Lord Weidenfeld; 9 Chelsea Embankment, London SW3 (☎ 071 351 0042)

WEIGH, Brian; CBE (1982), QPM (1976); s of Edwin Walter Weigh (d 1958), and Ellen, *née* Wignall (d 1969); *b* 22 Sept 1926; *Educ* St Joseph's Coll Blackpool, Queens Univ Belfast; *m* 1952, Audrey, da of Arthur Leonard Barker (d 1968); 1 da (Amanda); *Career* Metropolitan Police 1948-67, dep chief constable Somerset and Bath Constabulary 1969-74 (asst chief constable 1967-69), dep chief constable Avon and Somerset Constabulary 1974-75; chief constable: Gloucestershire Constabulary 1975-79, Avon and Somerset 1979-83; HM inspr of constabulary for SW England and pt of E Anglia 1983-88; memb Royal Life Saving Soc (pres UK Branch, Cwlth vice pres); *Recreations* golf, fell walking, gardening; *Style*— Brian Weigh, Esq, CBE, QPM; c/o Home Office, HM Ch Insp of Constabulary, Queen Anne's Gate London SW1H 9AT

WEIGHILL, Francis James; s of Francis Weighill (d 1943), and Ellen, *née* Parkinson (d 1989); *b* 12 Feb 1939; *Educ* Wrekin Coll, Univ of Liverpool (MB ChB, MChOrth); *m* 12 July 1969, Christine Ann Elizabeth, da of Leslie Daniel Houghton (d 1987); 3 s (Michael Francis b 13 May 1970, Peter James b 3 April 1972, Robert Edward Leslie b 8 Nov 1976); *Career* house offr Liverpool Royal Infirmary 1964-65, surgical registrar Leith Edinburgh 1967-68, sr orthopaedic registrar Liverpool 1973, clinical res fell Hosp for Sick Children Toronto 1974-75, conslt orthopaedic surgn Univ Hosp of Manchester 1977, tutor RCS 1982-88; fell Br Orthopaedic Assoc, FRCSE 1969, FRCS 1969; *Recreations* sailing, painting; *Style*— Francis Weighill, Esq; Lane End, 90 Cherry Lane, Lymm, Cheshire WA13 0PD (☎ 092575 2726); 15 St John Street, Manchester M3 4DG (☎ 061 834 7373)

WEIGHT, Richard James; step s of Henry George Richman, of Selsey Sussex, and Ellan Rebecca, *née* Williams; *b* 17 June 1944; *Educ* Sir Joseph Williamsons Mathemathical Sch Rochester Kent; *m* 23 March 1968, Pamela, da of Leonard James Wilkinson (d 1955), of Gillingham Kent; 1 s (David b 27 June 1973), 1 da (Jennifer b 18 Jan 1977); *Career* Life Gds 1962-65; TA & VR: Lt 2 Bn Wessex Regt (V) 1976, Capt 4 Bn The Royal Regt of Wales (V) 1978, Capt Intelligence Corps (V) 1984; computer mangr The Mettoy Co Swansea, computer services mangr London Regnl Tport, vice-pres Citibank NA, currently dir info technol Security Pacific Hoare Govett (Hldgs); *Recreations* private pilot, sailing; *Style*— Richard Weight, Esq; 5 South Lea, Kingsnorth, Nr Ashford, Kent TN23 3EH (☎ 0233 642137); 4 Broadgate, London EC2M 7LE (☎ 071 374 7309, telex 887887, fax 071 256 8500, car 0836 242729)

WEIGHTMAN, John; s of James Weightman, of Newcastle upon Tyne, and Grace Doreen, *née* Fenton; *b* 6 Sept 1949; *Educ* George Stephenson GS, Univ of London (BSc, external); *m* 1 June 1971, Helena Ruby (d 1986), da of Lt Cdr George Daisley, of Horsham, Sussex; 1 s (Kyle b 17 April 1984); m 2, 7 April 1990, Fiona, da of Henry Grey, of Berwick upon Tweed; *Career* H M Inspr of Taxes Bd of Inland Revenue 1970-75, tax mangr Deloitte and Co 1975-77, co dir Concord Pater Sales 1977-84, tax conslt 1984-, fin conslt New Life Assocs, ptnr Interax Associates; tax conslt to CAB Bureau and NFU, choirmaster Berwick Baptist Church; ATII 1974, LIA 1987; *Recreations* angling, sailing; *Clubs* Co Gentlemans, Berwick Sailing; *Style*— John Weightman, Esq; Twizel Smithy, Cornhill-on-Tweed, Northumberland TD12 4UY (☎ 0289 382573); Interax Associates, Twizel Smithy, Cornhill-on-Tweed, Northumberland TD12 4UY; New Life Associates Ltd, 44 Woodville Drive, Old Portsmouth, Hants PO1 2TG (☎ 0705 829327)

WEIL, Daniel; s of late Dr Alfredo Leopoldo Weil, and Mina, *née* Rosenbaum; *b* 7 Sept 1953; *Educ* Universidad Nacional de Buenos Aires (Arquitecto FAU UMBA), RCA (MA); *Career* industrial designer and lectr; unit master Dip sch Architectural Assoc 1983-86, external examiner MA design Glasgow Sch of Art 1987-90; visiting lectr: RCA, Middx Poly, Kingston Poly, Sch of Architecture Univ of Milan, Bezadel Sch of Art Jerusalem; md Parenthesis Ltd 1982-90, fndr and ptnr Weil and Taylor (design consultancy for maj clients) 1985-; Exhibitions: Memphis Milan 1982, 100 Designers Trienala of Milan 1983, Design since 1945 Philedelphia Museum of Art 1983, Heavy Box Architectural Assoc 1985, Contemporary Landscape (Museum of Modern Art) Kyoto 1985, Bitish Design (Kunst Museum) Vienna 1986, Inspiration Tokyo Paris and Milan 1988, Metropolis (ICA) London 1988, The Plastic Age Victoria & Albert Museum 1990; work in public collections incl The Bag Radio (Museum of Modern Art) NY; memb design subcommittee D&AD Jurer BBC Design Awards 1990; FCSD 1989; *Style*— Daniel Weil, Esq

WEIL, Peter Leo John; s of Robert Weil of Berlin, Germany, and Renate Scheyer; *b* 7 Sept 1951; *Educ* Methodist Coll Belfast, Queens' Coll Cambridge (BA); *Career* researcher Granada TV 1973-77 (Granada Reports, World in Action), prodr BBC TV Current Affairs 1977-84, (Nationwide, Newsnight, Panorama), head of Youth Progs BBC NI 1984-86 (actg dep head of progs 1986), ed Open Air BBC NW 1986-88, exec prodr Wogan 1988-89; head: Topical Features 1989-90, Network TV BBC North 1990; *Recreations* cinema, walking, good food; *Style*— Peter Weil, Esq; New Broadcasting House, Manchester (☎ 061 200 2431)

WEINBAUM, Sandra Joy (Sandy); da of Bernard Rader, of London, and Hilda, *née* Garfinkel; *b* 14 Nov 1950; *Educ* Woodford Co HS, Beth Rivkah Seminary France; *m* 30 Aug 1971, Bernard Weinbaum, s of Rev Harry Weinbaum; 12 c (Chana b 14 June 1972, Etelle b 31 May 1973, Shmaryohu b 25 June 1974, Sora b 30 Aug 1976, Rivka b 12 Jan 1978, Dina b 20 Dec 1979, Yehuda b 8 July 1981, Moishe b 25 Nov 1982, David b 12 July 1984, Rachel b 5 Jan 1986, Levi b 20 March 1988, Chaya Mushka b 26 April 1990); *Career* teacher Lubavitch Fndn Schs 1971-72, worked since then on formulating imaginative and innovative extra-curriculum Jewish learning activities, nat dir Tzivos Hashem (International Jewish Educational Programme) 1983-; int speaker on Jewish Women's issues (USA, Toronto, Belgium, SA, UK); *Books* Woman of Valour (contrib, 1976), The Modern Jewish Woman (contrib, 1976), Return To Roots; *Style*— Mrs Sandy Weinbaum; Tzivos Hashem, 11 Ossulton Way, London N2 ODT (☎ 081 458 6372, fax 081 455 8228)

WEINBERG, Prof Felix Jiri; s of Victor Weinberg (d 1988), and late Nelly, *née* Altschul; *Educ* London Univ (BSc, DIC, PhD, DSc); *m* 26 July 1954, Jill Nesta, da of Jack Alfred Piggott (d 1970); 3 s (John Felix b 27 April 1958, Peter David (twin) b 27 April 1958, Michael Jonathan b 8 Jan 1969); *Career* Dept of Chemical Engrg and Chemical Technol Imperial Coll London: res asst 1951-54, asst lectr 1954-56, lectr 1956-60, sr lectr in combustion 1960-64, reader in combustion 1964-67, prof combustion physics 1967-; visiting prof at various univs and insts across the world, fndr and first chm Combustion Physics Gp Inst of Physics 1974-, chm Br Section Combustion Inst 1975-80, cncl memb Inst of Energy (formerly Inst of Fuel) 1976-79; conslt to numerous bodies incl: BHP, Tioxide UK, Frazer Nash, BP, US Army, Univ of California; Silver Combustion medal The Combustion Inst Pittsburgh 1972, Bernard Lewis Gold medal Univ of Waterloo Canada 1980, Rumford medal of the Royal Soc 1988; prolific contrib to scientific literature and memb editorial bds of various specialist jls; fell Inst of Energy 1960, CEng 1960, FInstP 1960, FRS 1983; *Style*— Prof Felix Weinberg, FRS; Dept of Chemical Engineering and Chemical Technology, Imperial Coll, Prince Consort Rd, London SW7 2BY (☎ 071 589 5111, ext 4360 and 4498, fax 071 584 7596, telex 92984)

WEINBERG, Sir Mark Aubrey; s of Philip Weinberg (d 1933); *b* 9 Aug 1931; *Educ* King Edwards Johannesburg, Witwatersrand Univ, LSE; *m* 1980, Anouska, da of Albert Geissler (d 1980); *Career* md Abbey Life Assurance 1961-70, dep chm Hambro Life Assurance 1971- (now renamed Allied Dunbar Assurance), dir BAT Industs 1985-89; dep chm Securities and Investmts Bd 1986-90; kt 1987; *Recreations* tennis, skiing, bridge; *Clubs* Portland; *Style*— Sir Mark Weinberg; St James's Place Capital, 15 St James's Place, London SW1A 1NW (☎ 071 493 8111)

WEINSTOCK, Baron (Life Peer UK 1980), of Bowden, Co Wilts; Arnold Weinstock; s of Simon and Golda Weinstock; *b* 29 July 1924; *Educ* Albion Road Central Sch N London, LSE (BSc); *m* 1949, Netta, da of Sir Michael Sobell; 1 s (Hon Simon Andrew b 1952), 1 da (Hon Susan Gina (Hon Mrs Lacroix) b 1955); *Career* sits as independent in House of Lords; md GEC 1963-, dir Rolls-Royce Ltd 1971-73, hon master of the bench Gray's Inn 1982-; tstee: Br Museum 1985-, Royal Philharmonic Soc Fndn Fund; hon FRCR; Hon DSc: Univ of Salford 1975, Aston Univ 1976, Univ of Bath 1978, Univ of Reading 1978, Univ of Ulster 1987; Hon LLD: Leeds 1978, Wales 1985; Hon DTech Loughborough 1981; hon fell: LSE, Peterhouse Cambridge; kt 1970; *Recreations* racing, music; *Clubs* Jockey; *Style*— The Rt Hon Lord Weinstock; 7 Grosvenor Sq, London W1 (☎ 071 493 7676)

WEINSTOCK, Hon Simon Andrew; s of Baron Weinstock (Life Peer) (*qv*); *b* 1952; *Educ* Winchester, Magdalen Coll Oxford; *m* 1976, Laura Helen, only da of Maj Hon Sir Francis Michael Legh, KCVO (d 1984); 3 da (Pamela Helen b 1982, Celia Rose b 1985, Laetitia Anne Daphne b 1990); *Style*— The Hon Simon Weinstock

WEIR, Adam Clive; s of William Weir, of Milveton, Taunton, Somerset, and Valerie, *née* Spilsbury; *b* 13 May 1964; *Educ* Prince Rupert Sch Rinteln W Germany, Midhurst GS W Sussex, W Sussex Coll of Art & Design Worthing, Kinsgton Poly (BA Hons); *Career* designer; conslt designer: House Style 1986, Eric Marshall Associates 1986-87, Adrian Stokes Associates 1986-87, Complete Studios 1987; Lighting Design Partnership: joined as designer 1987, project designer 1987-89, team ldr 1989-; exhibitions: Kingston Design (Boilerhouse Gallery) 1986, Machines for Living (Ecology Centre) 1986; MSIAD 1986; *Style*— Adam Weir, Esq; Blandings Castle, Richmond, Slipways, Ducks Walk, Twickenham, Middlesex; Lighting Design Partnership, 47 Theobalds Rd, Holborn, London WC1X 8SP (☎ 071 404 4039, fax 071 404 0357)

WEIR, Rear Adm Alexander Fortune Rose; CB (1981), JP (Bodmin 1985-); s of Cdr Patrick Wylie Rose Weir, RN (d 1971), and Minna Ranken Forrester, *née* Fortune (d 1983); *b* 17 June 1928; *Educ* RNC Dartmouth, RNC Greenwich; *m* 5 Sept 1953, Ann Ross Hamilton, da of Col John Atchison Crawford, RAMC (d 1982); 4 da (Phillipa b 1954, Joanna b 1956, Margaret b 1958, Nicola b 1959); *Career* Cadet 1945-46, Midshipman 1946-47, Actg Sub Lt HMS Zephyr, Portland 1947, Sub Lt professional courses 1947-48, Sub Lt and Lt, HMS Loch Arkaig 1949-51, ADC to Govr of Victoria Aust 1951-53; HMS Mariner 1953-54, Navigating Offr 1954, HMS St Austell Bay WI, Navigating Offr 1955-56, HMS Wave, Fishery Protection Sqdn Home Arctic and Iceland 1956-58, Lt Cdr Advanced Navigation Course, 1958; Staff ND Offr, Flag Offr Sea Trg at Portland Dorset 1958-61, HMS Plymouth, Staff Offr Ops, 4 Frigate Sqdn, Far East Station 1961-62, Cdr 1962, Trng Cdr, BRNC Dartmouth 1962-64, CO HMS Rothesay WI Station 1965-66, Staff of C-in-C Portsmouth, Staff Offr Ops 1966-68, 2 in Cmd and Exec Offr HMS Eagle 1968-69, Capt 1969; jssc 1969-70; pres Far East Cmd Midshipman's Bd 1970, Asst Dir Naval Operational Requirments, MOD(N) 1970-72, Capt (F) 6 Frigate Sqdn (8 ships) and HMS Andromeda FEast Mediterranean & Home Waters 1972-74, NATO Def Coll Rome 1974-75, ACOS Strategic Policy Requirements and Long Range Objectives, SACLANT 1975-77, Capt HMS Bristol 1977-78; Rear Adm 1978; Dep Asst Chief of Staff (Ops) to SACEUR 1978-81; ret RN 1981; joined Capt Colin McMullen and Associates, Marine Consultants 1981 and took over 1983-; FBIM, Assoc Victoria Coll of Music; memb: Nautical Inst, Royal Inst of Navigation; licensed RN lay reader, licensed reader St Kew Parish Diocese of Truro 1984-; JP: Chichester 1982-84, Bodmin 1985-; *Recreations* sailing, shooting, golf; *Clubs* IOD; RYS, RYA, RNSA; *Style*— Rear-Adm Alexander Weir, CB, JP; Tipton, St Kew, Bodmin, Cornwall PL30 3ET (☎ 020 884 289, fax 020 884 675); Captain Colin McMullen and Associates, Yeoman House, Croydon Rd, Penge SE20 7TP (☎ 081 778 6060, telex 946171)

WEIR, The Hon Lord; David Bruce; QC (1971); s of James Douglas Weir (d 1981), of Argyll, and Kathleen Maxwell, *née* Auld (d 1975); *b* 19 Dec 1931; *Educ* The Leys Sch Cambridge, Univ of Glasgow (MA, LLB); *m* 1964, Katharine Lindsay, da of The Hon Lord Cameron; 3 s (Donald b 1965, Robert b 1967, John b 1971); *Career* senator of the Coll of Justice in Scotland, pres Pension Appeals Trbnl (Scotland) 1984, memb Criminal Injuries Compensation Bd 1974-79 and 1984-85; *Recreations* sailing (Tryad), music; *Clubs* New (Edinburgh), Royal Highland Yacht; *Style*— The Hon Lord Weir; Parliament House, High St, Edinburgh (☎ 031 225 2595)

WEIR, David Ian; s of Dr Harold Ross Weir, of Masterton, NZ, and Helen Weir; *b* 2 July 1935; *Educ* Dundee High GS Scotland, Wairarapa Coll Masterton NZ, Univ of NZ (BDS), MGDS RCS, MRCS; *m* 29 Dec 1959, Joan Anne, da of Capt William Patrick Sinclair; 2 s (Ian Kenneth b 7 July 1960, John Sinclair b 16 Sept 1961), 2 da (Temo Fiona (Mrs Donovan) b 27 Aug 1962, Linley Ann b 30 Nov 1964); *Career* gen dental practice Masterton NZ 1959-60, assoc Hammersmith dental practice 1960-61, princ practitioner Associate Dentists in Practice 1961-75, private practice Harley St 1975-; pt/t dental surgn: Marks & Spencers stores Hammersmith & Chiswick 1983-, Bush Boake & Allen Ltd 1986-; course tutor MGDS Group 1988-, pt/t sr lectr Maurice Wohl Centre Kings Coll Med & Dental Schs 1989-90; fndr memb: Harley St Occlusion Gp, Br Endosseous Pin Implant Soc; memb: Br Periodontal Soc, Br Dental Assoc, Soc for Advancement of Anaesthesia in Dentistry, Dental Migraine Soc, Asian Odontological Soc (former memb Ctee), Assoc of Industl Dental Surgns (memb Ctee), Med Protection Soc, Dental Practitioner Assoc; former positions: sec London Branch Br Dental Health Fndn, memb London Chapter Alpha-Omega Soc, treas Acad of Gnathology (superceded by Pankey UK); contrib to numerous learned dental jls; *Recreations* sailing, squash, golf, classical music, highland bagpipe, reading; *Style*— David Weir, Esq; 35 Broomwater, Teddington, Middx TW11 9QJ (☎ 081 977 6133); 141 Harley Street, London W1N 1DJ (☎ 071 935 2592, 071 224 3624)

WEIR, Prof Donald MacKay; s of Dr Henry James Blackwell, of Dunbartonshire, and Gwendoline, *née* MacKay (d 1981); *b* 16 Oct 1928; *Educ* Edinburgh Acad, Univ of Edinburgh (MB ChB, MD); *m* 1, 1956, Dr Sylvia Eva Leiman (m dis 1976); 3 s (Michael b 1957, David b 1959, Philip b 1961); m 2, 6 June 1976, Dr (Cecelia) Caroline Weir, da of Cecil Blackwell (d 1987), of Texas; *Career* res fell Rheumatism Res Unit MRC Taplow 1957-61, personal chair microbiol immunology Univ of Edinburgh 1983- (lectr Bacteriology Dept 1961-67, sr lectr and hon conslt 1967-78, reader 1978-83), hon visiting prof Inst Pasteur Athens Greece 1989-; memb: Br Soc Immunology, Br

Soc Cell Biology; FRCPE; *Books* Handbook of Experimental Immunology (1967 and 1986), Immunology For Undergraduates (1970, 71, 73, 77, 83), Principles of Infection and Immunity in Patient Care (1981), Aids To Immunology (1986), Immunology Student Notes (1988); *Recreations* sailing; *Clubs* Royal Forth YC; *Style*— Prof Donald Weir; 36 Drummond Place, Edinburgh EH3 6PW (☎ 031 556 7646); Univ of Edinburgh Med Sch, Dept of Medical Microbiology, Teviot Place, Edinburgh EH8 9AG (☎ 031 667 1011 ext 3170 fax 031 662 4135 telex 727442)

WEIR, (Malcolm) Donald; s of Malcolm Weir (d 1944), of Craigend, Craigmore, Isle of Bute, and Helen Begg, *née* Saunders (d 1960); *b* 8 Sept 1921; *Educ* Rothesay Acad, Merchiston Castle Sch Edinburgh; *m* 30 June 1950, Angela Christine, da of Alexander Murray (d 1958), of Brora, Sutherland; 2 da (Pauline Helen b 1951, Angela Rosemary b 1955); *Career* WWII OCTU Bangalore India cmmnd Maj Indian Army 1941 served: India, Burma, Malaya RIASC; Maj; mentioned in despatches, demob 1946; Maj TA 1947-50; John Bruce & Co Shipowners Glasgow 1939-65: ptnr 1950-57, dir 1957-65; Westcott & Laurence Line Ltd London 1965-72: dir 1965-69, md 1969-72; md Ellerman City Liners London 1972-; memb Glasgow Jr C of C 1955-65, chm Stewardship Ctee Busbridge Church Godalming 1970-84; Freeman City of London 1980, Liveryman Worshipful Co of Shipwrights 1980; FICS 1947; *Recreations* golf; *Clubs* Caledonian; *Style*— Donald Weir, Esq; The Gables, Munstead, Godalming, Surrey GU8 4AR (☎ 0483 892 554)

WEIR, Dorothy, Viscountess; Dorothy; da of William Yerrington Dear; *m* 1, Edward Hutton (decd); m 2, 1973, as his 2 w, 2nd Viscount Weir, CBE (d 1975); *Style*— The Rt Hon Dorothy, Viscountess Weir; Little Pennbrook, Lake Road, Far Hills, N.J. USA 07931

WEIR, Hon Douglas Nigel; s of 2 Viscount Weir, CBE; *b* 6 Oct 1935; *Educ* Eton, Trinity Cambridge; *m* 1964, Penelope, da of Gp Capt John Whitehead; 3 da; *Style*— The Hon Douglas Weir; Creagdubh Lodge, Newtonmore, Inverness-shire

WEIR, Hon George Anthony; s of 2 Viscount Weir, CBE (d 1975), and Dorothy Isobel Lucy, *née* Crowdy (d 1972); *b* 27 April 1940; *Educ* Winchester, Trinity Coll Cambridge (BA), MIT (SM, PhD); *m* 1962, Hon Jane Caroline, da of The Rt Hon Sir William John St Clair Anstruther-Gray, OC, MC, Baron Kilmany, of Kilmany, Cupar, Fife; 2 s (William b 1971, Edward b 1972), 1 da (Belinda b 1974); *Career* engr, presently md Webtec Indust Technol Ltd 1984; dir The Weir Gp plc since 1972; memb Scottish Devpt Agency 1975-82; *Books* The Attraction of Mobile Investments, Scottish and Irish Experience, Centre for Business Strategy (1986); *Recreations* shooting, fishing, racing, bridge; *Clubs* Jockey, Turf; *Style*— The Hon George Weir; 17 Ainslie Place, Edinburgh EH3 6AU (☎ 031 220 4466)

WEIR, George Wilson (Doddie); s of John Wilson Weir, and Margaret Anne, *née* Houston; *b* 4 July 1970; *Educ* Daniel Stewart's and Melville Coll, E of Scot Coll of Agric; *Career* Rugby Union No 8 and lock forward Melrose RFC and Scotland (1 cap); toured NZ with Scottish Schs 1988; clubs: Melrose RFC 1988- (70 appearances); rep: South of Scot (8 appearances), Scottish Students, Scotland U19, Scot U21, Scot B; Scotland: toured NZ 1990, debute v Argentina 1990; agric student; *Recreations* horse riding (one day eventing), clay pigeon shooting, swimming; *Style*— Doddie Weir, Esq; Cortleferry Farm, Stow, Galashels, Scotland (☎ 05786 216); c/o Melrose RFC, The Greenyards, Melrose, Borders, Scotland (☎ 089 682 2993)

WEIR, Gillian Constance; CBE (1989); da of Cecil Alexander Weir (d 1941), of Martinborough, NZ, and Clarice Mildred Foy, *née* Bignell, (d 1965); *b* 14 Jan 1941; *Educ* Wanganui Girls Coll Wanganui NZ, RCM London; *m* 1, 1967 (m dis 1971), Clive Rowland Webster; m 2, 1972, Lawrence Irving Phelps, s of Herbert Spencer Phelps (d 1979), of Somerville, Mass, USA; *Career* int concert organist 1965-; concerto appearances incl: all leading Br orchs, Boston Symphony Orch, Seattle Symphony Orch, Aust ABC Orchs, Euro orchs; regular performer at all int festivals incl: Edinburgh, Bath, Flanders, Proms, Europhalia, Aldeburgh; performed in major int concert halls and cathedrals incl: Royal Albert, Royal Festival, Sydney Opera House, Palais des Beaux Arts, Lincoln Center, Kennedy Center; frequent nat and int radio and TV appearances (incl own 6 part series The King of Instruments (BBC)), adjudicator int competitions, artist in residence at major univs, lectures and master classes held internationally, recordings made for Virgin Classics, Argo, Chandos, Decca; prizes incl: St Alban's Int Organ Competition 1964, Countess Munster Award 1965, Int Performer of the Year American Guild of Organists NY USA 1981, Musician of the Year Int Music Guide 1982, Turnovsky Fndn Award 1985; Hon DMus Univ of Victoria Wellington NZ 1983; hon memb RAM, hon FRCO 1975, hon fell Royal Canadian Coll of Organists 1983; *Recreations* theatre; *Style*— Miss Gillian Weir, CBE; 78 Robin Way, Tilehurst, Berks RG3 5SW (☎ 0734 414078)

WEIR, Hon Mrs (Grania Rachel); *née* O'Brien; da of 16 Baron Inchiquin (d 1968), and Anne Molyneux, *née* Thesiger (d 1973); *b* 31 May 1928; *m* 1973, Hugh William Lindsay Weir, *qv*, s of Maj Terence John Collison Weir (d 1958); *Career* sec to Rt Hon Sir Arthur Salter, MP 1947-52; social sec to Br Ambass to: Spain 1952, Japan 1954-57, Peru 1958-60; dir Ballinakella Pres; pres (Ennis branch) RNLI, dir Craggaunowen Project and Hunt Museum Co Clare; *Recreations* writing, gardening, sewing, reading; *Style*— The Hon Mrs Weir; Ballinakella Lodge, Whitegate, Co Clare, Republic of Ireland (☎ 0619 27030, fax 0619 27030)

WEIR, Hugh William Lindsay; s of Maj Terence John Collison Weir (d 1958), and Rosamund Suzanne, *née* Gibson; *b* 29 Aug 1934; *Educ* Portora Royal Sch; *m* 1973, Hon Grania Rachel O'Brien, da of 16 Baron Inchiquin (d 1968); *Career* md Weir Machinery Ltd; memb Church of Ireland Representative Body 1980-89; Irish Heritage historian 1980-; pres: Young Environmentalist Fedn, Clare Young Environmentalists; teacher, journalist, author and publisher; FRGS; *Books* Houses of Clare, O'Brien - People and Places, Ireland - A Thousand Kings (1988), Trapa - An Adventure in Spanish and English (1990); Oidhreacht Award 1990 for journalism and environmental promotion; *Recreations* writing, drawing, angling, travel, youth work; *Style*— Hugh Weir, Esq; Ballinakella Lodge, Whitegate, Co Clare, Ireland (☎ 0619 27 030)

WEIR, Hon James Richard Canning; 4 s of 2 Viscount Weir, CBE; *b* 1 May 1949; *Educ* Winchester, Strathclyde Univ; *m* 1977, Haude Chantal Gabrielle, da of Marc Charpentier, of Paris; 2 da; *Career* venture capital; *Recreations* shooting, fishing, golf; *Clubs* Prestwick Golf, Gatineau Fish and Game; *Style*— The Hon James Weir; Vieux Moulin de la Planche, 78790 Courgent, France (☎ 331 30934957)

WEIR, Hon James William Hartland; s and h of 3 Viscount Weir; *b* 6 June 1965; *Career* accountant; *Style*— The Hon James Weir; 27 Albany St, Edinburgh EH1 3QN

WEIR, Hon Mrs (Jane Caroline); *née* Anstruther-Gray; da of Baron Kilmany, MC, PC (Life Peer; d 1985); *b* 1943; *m* 1962, Hon George Anthony Weir, s of 2 Viscount Weir (d 1975); 2 s, 1 da; *Career* farmer; *Style*— The Hon Mrs Weir; Kilmany, Cupar, Fife KY15 4QW (☎ 082 624 753)

WEIR, Kenneth George; s of Thomas Weir, 30 Hospital Road, Annan, Dumfriesshire; *b* 30 Oct 1921; *Educ* Alloa Academy; *m* 1950, Mary Whittingham; 2 c; *Career* past pres: Society of Pension Consultants 1972-74, Pensions Management Institute 1979-80; dep chm Hogg Robinson Europe Ltd and Hogg Robinson (Benefit Consultants) Ltd; fell of the Faculty of Actuaries; *Recreations* bridge, tennis, swimming; *Style*— Kenneth Weir, Esq; Castle Point, ll Harebell Hill, Cobham, Surrey (☎ 0932 4604)

WEIR, Sir Michael Scott; KCMG (1980, CMG 1974); s of Archibald Weir; *b* 28 Jan 1925; *Educ* Dunfermline HS, Balliol Coll Oxford; *m* 1, 1953, Alison Walker; 2 s, 2 da; m 2, 1976, Hilary Reid; 2 s; *Career* WWII RAF; joined FO 1950; served: Trucial States, San Francisco, Washington, Cairo; chllr and head Arabian Dept FO 1966-68, dep political resident Bahrain 1968-71, head of chancery, UK Mission to UN (NYC) 1971-73, asst under sec FCO 1974-79, ambassador Cairo 1979-85, ret 1985; princ dir 21 Century Tst 1990-; pres Egypt Exploration Soc 1988-, chm British Egyptian Soc 1990-; *Style*— Sir Michael Weir, KCMG; 37 Lansdowne Gardens, London SW8

WEIR, Richard Stanton; s of Brig Richard Ambrose Weir, OBE (d 1972), and Dr Margaret Lucretia, *née* Cowan (d 1988); *b* 5 Jan 1933; *Educ* Repton, Christ Church Oxford (MA); *m* 17 June 1962, Helen Eugenie, da of Andrew Guthrie (d 1979); 1 da (Nicola Helen (Mrs Wilkinson) b 1964); *Career* cmmnd 3 Carabiniers (Prince of Wales's Dragoon Guards) 1951; barr Inner Temple 1957; head of Legal Dept Soc of Motor Manufacturers and Traders Ltd 1958-61, exec Br Motor Corpn Ltd 1961-64; dep co sec Rank Orgn Ltd 1964-67, head of admin Rank Leisure Services 1967-69, sec CWS Ltd 1969-74; dir: The Retail Consortium 1975-81, Br Retailer Assoc 1986-; sec gen & chief exec Bldg Socs Assoc 1981-86; memb Consumer Protection Advsy Ctee 1973-76; dir-gen: The Retail Consortium 1986-89, Institutional Fund Managers' Assoc 1989-; *Clubs* United Oxford and Cambridge University; *Style*— Richard Weir, Esq; 2 Lamont Rd, London SW10 0HL (☎ 071 352 4809); Insitutional Fund Managers' Assoc, Park House, 6th Floor, 16 Finsbury Circus, London EC2M 7JP (☎ 071 638 1639, fax 071 920 9186)

WEIR, Sir Roderick Bignell; JP; s of Cecil Alexander Weir (d 1940), of Palmerston, NZ, and Clarice Mildred Foy (d 1965); *b* 14 July 1927; *Educ* Wanganui Boys Coll; *m* 1, 1952, Loys Agnes Wilson (d 1952); 1 da (Lesley Alex (Mrs Donaldson) b 28 March 1953); m 2, 22 March 1986, Anna Jane, da of Richard T Peacock, of Barton Rd, Heretaunga, Wellington; *Career* chm: McKechnie Pacific Ltd, Amuri Corporation Ltd, Sherwood Mercantile Co Ltd; dep chm Rangatira Ltd; dir: Sun Alliance Insurance Ltd, Sun Life Assurance Co Ltd, New Zealand Casing Co Ltd, Bain Clarkson, Crocon Meats Ltd; former dir: McKenzies NZ Ltd, Development Finance Corporation Ltd, James Smith Ltd, Allied Farmers Ltd, Crocon Corperation Ltd, Dalgety NZ Ltd, Newton King Ltd, de Peltichet McLeod Ltd, Gisborne Sheepfarmers Mercantile Co Ltd, Canterbury Farmers Cooperative Assoc Ltd; fin conslt NZ Apple & Dear Marketing Board; memb: Salvation Army Advsy Bd, Cncl Wellington Medical Res Fndn (Inc); patron and memb Bd Massey Coll Univ Agric Res Fndn; chm: Massey Coll Business & Property Tst, NZ National Party Business House Ctee, ASEAN/NZ Business Cncl, Electoral Holdings Inc; memb Fin & Property Ctee NZ Nat Party; tstee: NZ Inst of Economic Res (Inc), Medic Alert, Wanganui Boys Coll; memb: Cncl Wellington Sch of Med, Justice of Peace Assoc; dir Listed Cos Assoc; kt 1984; *Recreations* shooting, boxing, fishing; *Clubs* Wellington Mens (Wellington), Heretaunga Golf (Lower Hutt), Levin (Levin); *Style*— Sir Roderick Weir, JP; 78 Salamanca Rd, Kelburn, Wellington, New Zealand (☎ 04 724 033, fax 04 732 685); The Glove, Main Road North, Waikanae, New Zealand (☎ 058 36373)

WEIR, Dr Ronald John; s of John Bishop Weir (d 1974), and Susan Davies, *née* McCleverty (d 1977); *b* 6 April 1935; *Educ* Jordanhill Coll Sch Glasgow, Univ of Glasgow (MB ChB, MD); *m* 2 June 1961, Janette MacKay, da of Thomas Wilson (d 1971); 3 s (Cameron John b 1966, Clifford Ronald b 1967, Gavin Mackay b 1972), 1 da (Kendra-Lynne Isobel b 1969); *Career* conslt physician and hon clinical lectr Gartnavel Gen Hosp and Western Infirmary Glasgow 1974-; memb: Int Soc of Hypertension, Euro Soc of Hypertension, Br Hypertension Soc, Br Diabetic Assoc, Scot Soc of Physicians, Assoc of Physicians of GB and Ireland, Bd of Examiners Royal Coll of Physicians and Surgns of Glasgow, Counselling Accreditation Ctee Tak Tent Cancer Support Scot, Bd of Educn, Eldership Working Party; convener gp rels Church of Scotland; FRCP Glasgow 1976; *Recreations* hill walking, gardening, reading; *Style*— Dr Ronald Weir; 10 Moorfoot Way, Bearsden, Glasgow G61 4RL (☎ 041 943 1367); Gartnavel General Hospital/Western Infirmary, 1053 Great Western Rd, Glasgow G12 0YN (☎ 041 334 8122)

WEIR, William; s of David Weir (d 1949), of Enfield, Middx, and Agnes Craig, *née* Morton (d 1969); *b* 8 Nov 1909; *Educ* Mill Hill Sch, Clare Coll Cambridge (MA); *m* 1, 26 Oct 1937, Jenny (d 1980), da of Dr James Allan Wilson (d 1944), of Glasgow; 1 s (Allan b 1942), 1 da (Joan b 1944); m 2, 26 May 1982, Christine Margaret (d 1989); *Career* res asst GEC 1931-34, dir Bryce Weir Ltd 1934-72, princ tech offr on radar Royal Aircraft Estab Farnborough 1942-45; former: chm Watford Mfrg Assoc, dir Watford Sheltered Workshop, vol worker CAB; Liveryman Worshipful Co Needlemakers 1974; CPhys, FInstP, FBIM; *Recreations* bridge, golf; *Clubs* Cambridge Soc; *Style*— William Weir, Esq; 3 Caroon Drive, Sarratt, Herts WD3 6DD (☎ 0923 267 036)

WEIR, 3 Viscount (UK 1938); William Kenneth James Weir; also Baron Weir (UK 1918); s of 2 Viscount Weir, CBE (d 1975), of Montgreenan, Kilwinning, Ayrshire, and his 1 w, Lucette Isabel, *née* Crowdy (d 1972); *b* 9 Nov 1933; *Educ* Eton, Trinity Coll Cambridge (BA); *m* 1, 1964 (m dis 1972), Diana Lucy, da of late Peter Lewis MacDougall of Ottawa, Canada; 1 s (Hon James William Hartland), 1 da (Hon Lorna Elizabeth b 17 May 1967); m 2, 6 Nov 1976 (m dis), Mrs Jacqueline Mary Marr, da of late Baron Louis de Chollet, of Fribourg, Switzerland; m 3, 24 Nov 1989, Mrs Marina Sevastopoulo, da of late Marc Sevastopoulo; 1 s (Hon Andrew Alexanda Marc); *Heir* s, Hon James William Hartland Weir b 6 June 1965; *Career* Nat Serv with RN 1955-57; chm: Great Northern Investment Trust Ltd 1975-82, Weir Gp PLC 1983- (vice chm 1981-83, chm and chief exec 1972-81); co-chm RIT and Northern plc 1982-83, vice chm St James' Place Capital plc; dir: British Steel Corporation 1972-76, Br Bank of the Middle East 1977-79 (memb London Advsy Ctee of Hongkong and Shanghai Banking Corp 1980-), BICC plc 1977-, Canadian Pacific Ltd 1989-, L F Rothschild Unterberg Towbin 1983-85; memb: Ct of Bank of England 1972-84, Scottish Econ Cncl 1972-84, Engrg Industries Cncl 1975-80; chm: Engrg Design Res Centre, Patrons of Nat Galleries of Scotland; pres BEAMA 1988-89; FIBF 1984, MIES 1985, FRSA 1987; *Recreations* golf, shooting; *Clubs* White's; *Style*— The Rt Hon the Viscount Weir; Rodinghead, Mauchline, Ayrshire KA5 5TR (☎ 056 384 233); The Weir Group PLC, Cathcart, Glasgow G44 4EX (☎ 041 637 7111, fax 041 637 2221, telex 77161 WPLCRT G)

WEISKRANTZ, Prof Lawrence; s of Benjamin Weiskrantz (d 1935), of Russia and the USA, and Rose, *née* Rifkin; *b* 28 March 1926; *Educ* Swarthmore Coll (BA), Oxford Univ (MSc), Harvard (PhD); *m* 11 Feb 1954, Barbara Edna, da of William Collins (d 1979); 1 s (Conrad b 1963), 1 da (Julia b 1966); *Career* cryptographer USAF 1944-46, served Europe, Africa and Middle East; assoc Inst of Living 1952-55, teaching asst Harvard Univ 1952-53, pt/t lectr Tufts Univ 1952, sr post-doctoral fell US Nat Acad of Sci Oxford Univ (prof of psychology 1967-); Cambridge Univ: res assoc 1956-61, asst dir of res 1961-66, reader in physiological psychology 1966-67; FRS 1980, memb US Nat Acad of Sci 1987; *Recreations* music, walking; *Style*— Prof Lawrence Weiskrantz, FRS; c/o Magdalen Coll, Oxford; Dept of Experimental Psychology, South Parks Rd, Oxford OX1 3UD (☎ 0865 271 356)

WEISMAN, Lorenzo David; s of Eduardo Weisman (d 1988), of Guatemala, and Suzanne, *née* Loeb; *b* 22 April 1945; *Educ* Moses Brown Sch Providence Rhode Island USA, Harvard Coll Cambridge Mass USA (BA), Univ of Columbia NY USA

(MBA); *m* 21 June 1971, Danielle Yvonne Camille Maysonnave; 1 s (Thomas b 3 Oct 1980), 2 da (Melissa b 26 July 1973, Alexia b 27 Oct 1976); *Career* Dillon Read and Co Inc NY: joined 1973, vice pres 1977, md 1981, pres (London) 1984; Memb Societé Francaise des Auteurs; *Clubs* Spee (Harvard), Travellers (Paris), RAC, Hurlingham; *Style—* Lorenzo Weisman, Esq; 24 The Little Boltons, London SW10 (☎ 071 373 8092); Dillon Rd Limited, Devonshire House, Mayfair Place, London W1 (☎ 071 493 1239, telex 8811055)

WEISMAN, Malcolm; s of David Weisman (d 1969), and Jeanie Pearl Weisman (d 1980); *Educ* Parmiter's Sch, Harrogate GS, LSE, St Catherine's Coll Oxford (MA); *m* 1958, Rosalie, da of Dr A A Spiro (d 1963), of St John's Wood; 2 s (Brian b 1959, Daniel b 1963); *Career* jewish chaplain RAF 1956, called to the Bar Middle Temple 1961, chaplain Univ of Oxford 1971, sr chaplain HM Forces 1972, asst cmmr Parly Boundaries 1976, sec gen Allied Air Forces Chiefs of Chaplains Ctee 1980, rec Crown Ct 1980; memb of Cts of Univs of East Anglia, Lancaster, Essex and Warwick; ed Menorah magazine; memb: MOD Advsy Ctee on Mil Chaplaincy, Cabinet of Chief Rabbi of Cwlth; Man of Year Award 1980; religious advsr to small Jewish communities and Hillel cnsllr to New Univs; *Recreations* reading, walking, doing nothing; *Style—* Malcolm Weisman, Esq; 1 Grays Inn Square, London WC1R 5AA (☎ 071 405 8946)

WEISS, Prof Robert Anthony (Robin); s of Hans Weiss, and Stefanie, *née* Löwensohn; *b* 20 Feb 1940; *Educ* UCL (BSc, PhD); *m* 1 Aug 1964, Margaret Rose D'Costa; 2 da (Rachel Mary b 1966, Helen Anne b 1968); *Career* lectr in embroyology UCL 1963-70, Eleanor Roosevelt Int Cancer Res fell Univ of Washington Seattle 1970-71, visiting assoc prof of microbiology Univ of Southern Calif 1971-72, staff scientist Imperial Cancer Res Fund Laboratories 1972-80, dir Inst of Cancer Res 1980-89, head Chester Beatty Laboratories Inst of Cancer Res 1990-; memb: Cancer Res Campaign, UK Co-ordinating Ctee on Cancer Res, AIDS charities; advsr on AIDS and gene therapy to Dept of Health; FRCPath 1985, Hon MRCP 1989; Gustar Stern award in Virology 1973; *Books* RNA Tumor Viruses (1982, 2 edn 1985); Aids and The New Viruses (1990), Aids & The New Viruses (1990); author of various articles on cell biology, virology and genetics; *Recreations* music, natural history; *Style—* Prof Robin Weiss; Chester Beatty Laboratories, Institute of Cancer Research, Fulham Road, London SW3 6JB (☎ 071 352 8133, fax 071 352 3299)

WELANDER, Rev Canon David Charles St Vincent; s of Charles Ernest Sven Welander, of Uppsala, Sweden, and Lousia Georgina, Downes, *née* Panter; *b* 22 Jan 1925; *Educ* Unthank Coll Norwich, Univ of London (BD), Univ of Toronto; *m* 12 July 1952, Nancy O'Rourke, da of Dr George Weldale Stanley, MC (d 1960); 2 s (Richard David Edward b 1955, Christopher Peter Graham b 1959), 3 da (Rosemary Aileen Nancy b 1953, Sarah Jane Mary b 1957, Claire Elizabeth Georgina b 1960); *Career* chaplain and lectr in New Testament studies London Coll of Divinity Univ of London 1950-56; vicar: Iver Bucks 1956-61, Christ Church Cheltenham 1962-74; rural dean Cheltenham 1972-75, memb Gen Synod of C of E 1970-85, sr inspr Theol Coll 1975-82, canon residentiary Gloucester Cath 1975-; memb Cncl: Malvern Girls Coll, King's Sch Gloucester; FSA 1979; *Books* Gloucester Cathedral (with David Verey, 1979), The Stained Glass of Gloucester Cathedral (1985), Gloucester Cathedral: Its History, Art and Architecture (1991); *Recreations* walking, golf, music, European travel; *Clubs* Royal Cwlth Soc; *Style—* The Rev Canon David Welander, FSA; 6 College Green, Gloucester GL1 2LX (☎ 0452 21954)

WELBANK, (John) Michael; s of William Stephenson Welbank (d 1970), of London, and Alice Mary, *née* Robson (d 1973); *b* 2 Aug 1930; *Educ* Highgate Sch, UCL (BA); *m* 25 Aug 1956, Alison Mary, da of Cecil William Hopkins (d 1973), of London; 2 s (Juilian b 1 Feb 1959, William David b 22 Oct 1961), 1 da (Katherine Elizabeth Rose b 29 July 1963); *Career* Nat Serv 2 Lt RA 1948-50; planning offr London CC 1951-59, architect Miny of Educn 1959-62, sr architect Miny of Housing and Local Govt 1962-64, dir Shankland Cox 1964-; chm Cncl Br Conslt Bureau 1985, memb Exec Ctee ICOMOS 1986-, vice pres Royal Town Planning Inst 1989; Freeman City of London 1952, Liveryman Worshipful Co of Chartered Architects 1988; ARIBA 1958, MRTPI 1962; *Recreations* sailing, antiquites; *Clubs* Reform; *Style—* Michael Welbank, Esq; 24 South Hill Park, London NW3 2SB; Shankland Cox, Birmingham Rd, Saltisford, Warwick (☎ 0926 410450)

WELBY, Sir (Richard) Bruno Gregory Welby; 7 Bt (UK 1801), of Denton Manor, Lincolnshire; s of Sir Oliver Welby, 6 Bt, TD (d 1977, s of Lady Maria Hervey, sis of 4 Marquess of Bristol), by his w, Barbara Angela, da of John Gregory, CB, CMG, and gda of Sir Philip Gregory; n of Dowager Lady Saltoun and Viscountess Portal of Hungerford, *qqv*; *b* 11 March 1928; *Educ* Eton, Ch Ch Oxford; *m* 1952, Jane Biddulph, da of the late Ralph Hodder-Williams, MC; 3 s, 1 da; *Heir* s, Charles William Hodder Welby; *Style—* Sir Bruno Welby, Bt; 23 Hanover Gdns, London SE11

WELBY, Charles William Hodder; s and h of Sir (Richard) Bruno Welby, 7 Bt, of Denton by Jane Biddulph; *b* 6 May 1953; *Educ* Eton, RAC; *m* 1978, Suzanna, da of Maj Ian Stuart-Routledge (d 1981), of Harston Hall, Grantham; 2 da (Venetia b 1981, Zinnia b 1985); *Career* 2 Lt 1974 Worcestershire and Sherwood Foresters TAVR; chartered surveyor, conslt Humberts, dep dir Cons Bd of Fin 1987; contested (C) Caerphilly 1983; FRICS; *Style—* Charles Welby, Esq; Stroxton House, Grantham, Lincs (☎ 047 683 232)

WELBY-EVERARD, Maj-Gen Sir Christopher Earle; KBE (1965, OBE 1945), CB (1961), DL (Lincs 1966); s of Edward Everard Earle Welby-Everard (d 1951); *b* 9 Aug 1909; *Educ* Charterhouse, CCC Oxford; *m* 1938, Sybil Juliet Wake, *née* Shorrock; 2 s; *Career* 2 Lt Lincoln Regt 1930, served WWII UK and Normandy, Lt-Col 1944, Brig 1957, Maj-Gen 1959, COS to C-in-C Allied Forces Northern Europe 1959-61, GOC Nigerian Army, ret; High Sheriff Lincs 1974-75; *Style—* Maj-Gen Sir Christopher Welby-Everard, KBE, CB, DL; The Manor House, Sapperton, Sleaford, Lincs NG34 0TB (☎ 047 685 273)

WELCH, Ann Courtenay; OBE (1966, MBE 1953); da of Maj Courtenay Harold Wish Edmonds, OBE (d 1953), and Edith Maud, *née* Austin (d 1945); *b* 20 May 1917; *m* 1, 1939 (m dis 1948), Alfred Graham Douglas, DFC; 2 da (Vivien Redman b 1943, Elizabeth Douglas b 1945); m 2, 21 June 1953, Patrick Palles Lorne Elphinstone Welch, s of Brig Gen Malcolm Hammond Edward Welch, CB, CMG (d 1947); 1 da (Jan b 1955); *Career* pilot A licence 1934, Air Tport Aux ferry pilot 1940-42; gliding instr for 40 years, 20 as nat examiner of instrs, fndr Surrey Gliding Club 1938, mangr Br Gliding Team 1948-68; pres Int Jury for championships in gliding, hang gliding, paragliding and microlight flying 1970-; worldwide ed and prodr annual bulletin Féderation Aéronautique Internationale 1978-90, ed Royal Aero Club Gazette, holder Womens Nat Goal Distance Gliding Record 1961-; pres: Br Hang Gliding Assoc, Br Microlight Assoc; hon pres of 2 cmmns Federation Aeronautique Internationale, hon vice chm Royal Aero Club; FRAeS, FRMetS; gold Air Medal, Lilienthal medal, Bronze Medal, Pelagia Mejewska medal of federation Aeronautique Int; *Books* Silent Flight (1939), Cloud Reading for Pilots (1944), Gliding and Advanced Soaring (1947), Woolacombe Bird (1964), Story of Gliding (1965), Pilots Weather (1973), Accidents Happen (1978), Happy to Fly (1983), Complete Microlight and Soaring Guides (1983, 1986); *Recreations* sailing, painting; *Clubs* Royal Aero, Surrey & Hants Gliding, Bosham Sailing; *Style—* Mrs Ann Welch, OBE; 14 Upper Old Park Lane, Farnham, Surrey GU9 0AS (☎ 0252 715991)

WELCH, Clifford; *b* 1925; *Educ* Christ's Coll Finchley, Delft Tech HS Holland; *Career* former visiting lectr Nat Coll of Rubber & Plastics Technol Univ of London; Temple Press Ltd: asst ed Plastics 1953, ed Plastics 1957, editorial dir European Chemical News, Petroleum Times, Light Metals, Nuclear Engineering and Motor Ship 1958-60; md Heywood-Temple Industrial Publications Ltd and Tothill Press Ltd 1960-66, dep chm Business Publishing Div and chief exec IPC Business Press Overseas Ltd Internation Publishing Corporation Limited 1966-73; Lloyds of London Press Limited: chief exec 1973, advsr to Ctee of Lloyds on Public Affairs, Systems and Communications, advsr to Chief Exec of Lloyds until 1987, currently exec dep chm; dep chm Design Council 1991- (chm Publications Ctee 1988-), dir Periodical Publication Assoc Ltd; chm: Katharine Dormandy Tst Royal Free Hosp London, Minories Art Gallery Colchester, City of London Ctee Guide Dogs for the Blind; memb Bd Mercury Theatre Colchester; Freeman City of London 1957, memb Ct Worshipful Court of Horners (Master 1982); FPRI; *publications* contrib: The Penguin Science Survey, History of the British Plastics Federation; author of various papers to IUPAC and other socs; *Style—* Clifford Welch, Esq; Lloyd's of London Press Ltd, Sheepen Place, Colchester, Essex CO3 3LP (☎ 0206 772380)

WELCH, (James) Colin Ross; s of James William Welch, of Ickleton Abbey, Cambridgeshire, and Irene Margherita, *née* Paton; *b* 23 April 1924; *Educ* Stowe, Peterhouse Cambridge (maj scholar, BA); *m* 1950, Sybil Russell; 1 s, 1 da; *Career* Serv WWII cmmnd Royal Warwickshire Regt 1942, served NW Europe, twice wounded; journalist Glasgow Herald 1948, Colonial Office 1949; Daily Telegraph: leader writer, columnist (Peter Simple, with Michael Wharton), Parly sketch writer 1950-64, dep ed 1964-80, reg columnist 1981-83, ed-in-chief and chief exec magazine 1980-82; columnist and critic The Spectator 1982-, Parly sketch writer Daily Mail 1984-; *awards* Granada Journalist of the Year 1974, Specialist Writer Br Press Awards 1986; Knight's Cross Order of Palonia Restituta 1972; *Publications* Sir Frederick Ponsonby: Recollections of Three Reigns (ed 1951), Nestroy: Liberty Comes to Krähwinkel (trans with Sybil Welch 1954); author numerous articles in: Encounter, Spectator, New Statesmen, American Spectator; contribs to Symposia incl The Future That Doesn't work (1977); *Style—* Colin Welch, Esq; The Daily Mail, Northcliffe House, 2 Derry St, Kensington, London W8 5TT

WELCH, Capt (Neville) David; s of Neville Welch (d 1977), and Doreen Jane, *née* Dodd; *b* 25 May 1940; *Educ* Rugeley GS Staffs, City of London Poly (Dip Sci and Technol Navigation); *m* 1970 (m dis 1975); *Career* RAF 1958-63, Flt Lt gen duties and navigator RNZ AF 1979; navigator various UK and Dutch airline companies, flying instr and pilot examiner 1981-83, ops offr (airport inspr) CAA 1984, Capt Skyguard Ltd 1988 (pilot 1985), Dart-Herald Capt Channel Express Air Servs 1989, author articles in magazines; memb Br Airline Pilots Assoc; *Recreations* travel, light/antique aircraft flying, photography; *Style—* Capt David Welch

WELCH, David Reginald Stuart; s of Reginald Welch, and Margaret Cynthia, *née* Hughes; *b* 14 April 1954; *Educ* Moseley Hall GS, Manchester Poly; *m* 25 Sept 1976, Anne, da of Leslie James Vaux (d 1984); 1 s (Mark b 1986), 2 da (Sarah b 1979, Rachael b 1980); *Career* CA; FCA; *Recreations* Sunday sch teacher, reading, poetry; *Style—* David R S Welch, Esq; 3 Alvington Grove, Hazel Grove, Stockport, Cheshire SK7 5LS (☎ 061 456 9140); 220 Wellington Rd South, Stockport, Cheshire SK2 6RT (☎ 061 480 2480)

WELCH, Ivan Edwin; s of William Edwin Welch, Police Inspector, and Edith May Welch; *b* 14 Nov 1926; *Educ* Lansdowne, Leicester Sch of Arch; *m* 10 May 1951, Eileen, da of Leonard Towers, 1 da (Elaine b 1960); *Career* chartered architect; ptnr Welch, Dood, Wright Ptnrship 1966; ARIBA 1966, FFAS 1984; *Recreations* golf, art; *Style—* Ivan Welch, Esq; Launde House, Harborough Rd, Oadby, Leicester (☎ 0533 714141)

WELCH, Sir John Reader; 2 Bt (UK 1957), of Chard, Co Somerset; s of Sir Cullum Welch, 1 Bt, OBE, MC (d 1980); *b* 26 July 1933; *Educ* Marlborough, Hertford Coll Oxford (MA); *m* 25 Sept 1962, Margaret Kerry, o da of Kenneth Victor Douglass; 1 s, 2 da; *Heir* s, James Douglass Cullum, b 10 Nov 1973; *Career* slr; ptnr: Bell Brodrick & Gray 1961-71, Wedlake Bell 1972-; chm: John Fairfax (UK) Ltd 1977-90, London Homes for the Elderly 1981-90; registrar Archdeaconry of London, memb Court of Common Cncl (City of London) 1975-86 and chm Planning and Communications Ctee 1981-1982; Liveryman and memb of Ct of Assts Haberdashers' Co, Freeman and past Master Parish Clerks' Co; pres (1986-87) and hon slr City Livery Club; chm Walbrook Ward Club 1978-79; CStJ 1981; *Clubs* MCC, Surrey County Cricket; *Style—* Sir John Welch, Bt; 28 Rivermead Court, Ranelagh Gardens, London SW6 3RU; office: 16 Bedford St, Covent Gdn, London WC2E 9HF (☎ 071 379 7266)

WELCH, Melvin Dennis (Mel); s of Robert Charles Welch, of Watford, and Rose Elizabeth, *née* Oakley; *b* 21 Nov 1946; *Educ* Bushey GS, Univ of Sussex (BSc, MSc); *m* 18 Sep 1971, Susan Jane, da of Arthur Jeffcoatt (d 1976), of Coventry; 1 s (Timothy b 1972), 1 da (Josephine b 1974); *Career* sec: Eng Basket Ball Assoc 1970-, Br and Irish Basketball Fedn 1971-, Cwlth Basketball Fedn 1978-; memb: Eligibility Ctee Int Basketball Fedn 1984-, Olympic Review Ctee Sports Cncl 1985-86, Exec Ctee Br Assoc Nat Sports Admin 1985 (fndr memb 1979), Grants Ctee Sports Aid Fndn 1986-, coaching review panel Sports Cncl 1989-; dir: Basketball Publishing Ltd 1986-, Basketball Mktg Ltd 1986-87; tournament referee N Leeds tennis league; fndr memb Br Assoc Nat Sports Admin 1979; *Books* EBBA Yearbook (1971-), Intersport Basketball (1981), Encyclopeadia Britannica Book of Year (contrib, 1985-90); *Recreations* tennis, basketball; *Style—* Mel Welch, Esq; 5 Thorn Lane, Roundhay, Leeds LS8 1NF (☎ 0532 668751), The EBBA, 48 Bradford Rd, Leeds LS8 1NF LS9 6EE

WELCH, Patrick William; s of Edgar Albert Welch (d 1952), and Elsie, *née* Grimmitt (d 1978); *b* 12 Aug 1927; *Educ* King Edward's Birmingham, Univ of London (BA); *m* 29 Sept 1956, Marjorie Eileen, da of Lawrence Handel Rushton (d 1979); 1 s (Timothy b 1961), 3 da (Catherine b 1957, Jennifer b 1959, Susannah b 1964); *Career* md Welconstruct Co 1948-, chm Grimmitt Holdings Ltd 1982-; vice-pres Methodist Conference 1979-80, vice-chm Selly Oak Coll 1981-, pres Storage Equipment Manufacturers Assoc 1984-86; High Sheriff W Midlands 1986-87; *Books* A Man-Sized Cross (1979); *Style—* Patrick Welch, Esq; 43 Wellington Rd, Edgbaston, Birmingham B15 2EP (☎ 021 440 3785); Welconstruct Co Ltd, 127 Hagley Rd, Birmingham B16 8XU (☎ 021 445 9798, fax 021 454 8114, telex 339175 WELCON G)

WELCH, Peter John; s of Cyril Vincent Welch (d 1961), of Sutton Coldfield, and Elsie Lilian Ramsden; *b* 4 Jan 1940; *Educ* St Philip's Sch Edgbaston; *m* 12 June 1962, Margaret Mary, da of John Lavelle Bates, of Birmingham; 4 s (Peter b 1963, Andrew b 1964, Julian b 1966, Ian b 1975), 1 da (Elspeth b 1968); *Career* dir: Unicorn Industries plc 1972-78 and 1980-87 (chm 1980-84), Foseco MINSEP plc 1978-87, Thermal Scientific plc 1987-88, Jeyes Group plc 1987-, Holliday Chemical Holdings plc 1988-, Dunham Bush Ltd 1989-; chm Unitary Tax Campaign (Ltd) 1978-, assoc British Consultants plc 1989, Meconic Ltd 1990-; FCA 1961; *Recreations* bridge, music, reading, private flying; *Style—* Peter Welch, Esq; Frankfield, Spinfield Lane, Marlow, Buckinghamshire SL7 2LB (☎ 0628 485975, car 0836 508766)

WELD, Col Sir Joseph William; OBE (1946), TD (1947, and 2 bars), JP (Dorset 1938), DL (Dorset 1952); yr s of Wilfrid Weld (whose paternal grandmother was Hon

Elizabeth Stourton, da of 17 Baron Stourton). Sir Joseph is fourth in descent from Thomas Weld, of Lulworth Castle, who founded Stonyhurst Coll and whose er bro's 2 wife subsequently married Thomas Fitzherbert and, after being widowed as Mrs Fitzherbert, The Prince of Wales, later George IV; *b* 22 Sept 1909; *Educ* Stonyhurst, Balliol Coll Oxford; *m* 1933, Elizabeth Agnes Mary, da of Edmund Joseph Bellord, of Kensington; 1 s (Wilfrid Joseph b 1934), 6 da (Caroline Agnes Mary b and d 1936, Magdalen Josephine b 1937 d 1989, Elizabeth Jane (Mrs Jaggard) b 1939, Clare Harriet Mary b 1945, Katharine Mary b 1948, Georgina Mary b 1952); *Career* served WW II: Staff Coll Camberley 1941 and 1942-43, GSO 2 GHQ Home Forces, GSO 1 HQ SEAC; cmd 4 Bn Dorset Regt 1947-51 (Hon Col TA, served 1932-41), Col 1951; Lord-Lieut Dorset 1964-84, High Sheriff 1951, co cncllr 1961; chm: Wessex Regnl Hosp Bd 1970-74, Wessex Regnl Health Authy 1974-77, Dorset Police Authy 1959-79; pres: St John Cncl for Dorset 1964-84, Dorset Red Cross 1972-89; lord of the manors of Lulworth, Combe Keynes, Winfrith Newburgh, Sutton Pointz; Privy Chamberlain of Sword and Cape to Pope Pius XII; chm: Dorset CLA 1949-60, S Dorset Cons Assoc 1952-55 (pres 1955-59); kStJ 1967; kt 1937; *Clubs* Royal Dorset Yacht; *Style—* Col Sir Joseph Weld, OBE, TD, JP, DL; Lulworth Manor, East Lulworth, Dorset (☎ 092 941 352)

WELD FORESTER, Anthony Edward; s of Capt Charles Robert Cecil Weld Forester (d 1988), of Laverton Lodge, Broadway, Worcs, and Venetia Dawn, *née* Wills; *b* 24 Oct 1954; *Educ* Harrow, Magdalen Coll Oxford (BA); *m* 20 Oct 1979, Joanna Mary, da of Maj Eric Cyprian Perry Whiteley, TD (d 1973), of The Ship, Walton-on-the-Hill, Tadworth, Surrey; 2 s (Harry b 1981, Alfred b 1983), 2 da (Jocelyn b 1986, Clementine b 1989); *Career* cmmnd Royal Green Jackets 1973; Glasgow Office Sothebys 1980-91; memb Cncl of Reference Nat Prayer Breakfast for Scotland; *Recreations* skiing, tennis; *Clubs* Brooks's, Western, Glasgow; *Style—* Anthony Weld Forester, Esq; Old Manse, Gartmore, By Stirling FK8 3RP (☎ 08772-326); Sothebys Glasgow, 130 Douglas Street, Glasgow G2 4HF (☎ 041 221 4817)

WELD-FORESTER, Hon Kythé Priscilla; da of late 7 Baron Forester; *b* 1941; *Career* farmer; *Style—* The Hon Kythé Weld-Forester; Mvura Chena, P O Box 8, Raffingora, Zimbabwe

WELDON, Anthony Henry David; s of Max Weldon (d 1979), and Regina Charlotte, *née* Gideon; *b* 23 Dec 1945; *Educ* Uppingham; *m* 1970 (m dis 1984), Claire Ellen, *née* Gessler; 2 s (Julian b 1972, Oliver b 1975), 1 da (Alexandra b 1974); m 2, 1984, Manina Anne, *née* Mitchell; *Career* chm Durrington Corporation Ltd 1984; dir: NP Record plc 1989, RA Enterprises Ltd 1989, Royal Acad Tst Ltd; tstee Royal Opera House, chm Advsy Bd Royal Acad of Arts; memb Worshipful Co of Masons; FRCM; *Recreations* sport, opera; *Clubs* MCC, RAC, Royal Tennis, Annabel's, Mark's, Brooks', Hurlingham, Chelsea Arts, The Queens, Cumberland Lawn Tennis, Highgate GC; *Style—* Anthony Weldon, Esq; Flat 2, 83-85 Onslow Gardens, London SW7 3BU (☎ 071 373 6263); Durrington Corporation Ltd, 4/5 Grosvenor Place, London SW1X 7HJ (☎ 01 235 6146)

WELDON, Sir Anthony William; 9 Bt (I 1723), of Dunmore, Co Carlow; s of Sir Thomas Weldon, 8 Bt (d 1979), by his w Marie, Lady Weldon, now Countess Cathcart *qv*; *b* 11 May 1947; *Educ* Sherborne; *m* 1980, Amanda, formerly w of Anthony Wigan, and da of Maj Geoffrey North, MC, by his w, Hon Margaret de Grey (2 da of 8 Baron Walsingham, DSO, OBE, JP, DL); 2 da (Alice Louise b 13 Nov 1981, Oonagh Leone b 6 Oct 1983); *Heir* 2 cous, Kevin Weldon; *Career* late Lt Irish Gds, awarded S Arabian GSM; md BFP Design and Communications; *Recreations* stalking, champagne, cricket; *Clubs* White's, The Stranded Whales; *Style—* Sir Anthony Weldon, Bt

WELDON, Duncan Clark; s of Clarence Weldon, of Southport, and Margaret Mary Weldon; *b* 19 March 1941; *Educ* King George V GS Southport; *m* 1 (m dis 1971), Helen Shapiro; m 2, July 1973, Janet, da of Walter Mahoney (d 1982); 1 da (Lucy Jane b Oct 1977); *Career* theatrical prodr; presented over 140 prodns in London notably: When We Are Married 1970, The Chalk Garden 1971, Waters of the Moon 1978, Man and Superman 1982, School for Scandal 1983, Heartbreak House 1983, A Patriot for Me 1983, The Aspern Papers 1984, Aren't We All 1984, The Way of the World 1984, Sweet Bird of Youth 1985, Waste 1985, Mr and Mrs Nobody 1986, Antony and Cleopatra 1986, The Taming of the Shrew 1986, Long Day's Journey into Night 1986, Breaking the Code 1986, Melon 1987, Kiss Me Kate 1987, A Touch of the Poet 1988, The Admirable Crichton 1988, Richard II 1988, A Walk in the Woods 1988, Orpheus Descending 1988, Richard III 1989, Much Ado About Nothing 1989, The Merchant of Venice 1989, London Assurance 1989, Salome 1990, Bent 1990, An Evening With Peter Ustinov 1990, Wild Duck 1990, Henry IV 1990, Kean 1990, The Homecoming 1991; first Broadway prodn Brief Lives 1974; *Recreations* photography; *Style—* Duncan C Weldon, Esq; Brackenhill, Munstead Park, Godalming, Surrey (☎ 0483 415508); Proscenium Productions Ltd, Wardolf Chambers, 11 Aldwych, London, WC2B 4DA (☎ 071 836 0186)

WELDON, Fay; da of Dr Frank Birkinshaw (d 1947), of N Zealand, and Margaret, *née* Jepson; *b* 22 Sept 1931; *Educ* Christ Church Girls HS (NZ), South Hampstead HS; St Andrews Univ (MA); *m* June 1961, Ron Weldon; 4 s (Nicholas b 1954, Daniel b 1963, Thomas b 1970, Samuel b 1977); *Career* screen writer, novelist, critic, essayist; chm of judges Booker McConnell Prize 1983; *Books* The Fat Woman's Joke (1967), Down Among the Women (1971), Female Friends (1975), Remember Me (1976), Little Sisters (1978), Praxis (1978, Booker prize Nomination), Puffball (1980), Watching Me Watching You (1981), The President's Child (1982), Life and Loves' of a She Devil (1984, televised 1986), Letters to Alice-on First Reading Jane Austen (1984), Polaris and other Stories (1985), Rebecca West (1985), The Shrapnel Academy (1986), Heart of the Country (1987, televised 1987), The Hearts and Lives of Men (1987), The Rules of Life (1987), Leader of the Band (1988), The Cloning of Joanna May (1989), Darcy;s Utopia (1990), Moon Over Minneapolis or Why She Couldn't Stay (1991); childrens books: Wolf the Mechanical Dog (1988), Party Puddle (1989); *Style—* Mrs Fay Weldon; c/o Giles Gordon, Anthony Shiels Associates, 43 Doughty St, WC1N 2LF; c/o Casarotto Co Ltd, National House, 60-66 Wardour St, London W1V 3HP

WELENSKY, Rt Hon Sir Roy - Rowland (Roy); KCMG (1959, CMG, 1946), PC (1960); s of Michael Welensky; *b* 20 Jan 1907,Salisbury, S Rhodesia; *Educ* Salisbury, Rhodesia; *m* 1, 1928, Elizabeth Henderson (d 1969); 1 s, 1 da; m 2, 1972, Valerie Scott; 2 da; *Career* former engine driver; Fedn Rhodesia and Nyasaland: MLC N Rhodesia (now Zambia) 1938, memb Exec Cncl 1940-53, dir Manpower N Rhodesia 1941-46, min Tport Communications and Posts 1953-56, ldr House and dep PM 1955-56, PM and min External Affrs 1956-63; kt 1953; *Style—* The Rt Hon Sir Roy Welensky, KCMG; Shaftesbury House, Milldown Rd, Blandford Forum, Dorset DT11 7DE

WELFARE, Jonathan William; s of Kenneth William Welfare (d 1966), of The Old Doctors House, Stradbroke, Suffolk, and (Dorothy) Patience Athole, *née* Ross; *b* 21 Oct 1944; *Educ* Bradfield Coll Berkshire, Emmanuel Coll Cambridge (MA); *m* 6 Sept 1969, Deborah Louise, da of James D'Arcy Nesbitt, of Neston Cheshire; 1 s (Oliver b 1987), 3 da (Harriet b 1973, Laura b 1975, Amy b 1979); *Career* corp planning mangr Milton Keynes Devpt Corp 1970-74, chief economist and dep chief exec S Yorkshire Met CC 1974-84, dir The Landmark Tst 1984-86; co fndr The Oxford Ventures Gp 1986; dir: Granite TV Ltd 1988-, Oxford Innovation Centres Ltd 1988-; md Venture Link Investors Ltd 1990-; chm: The Oxford Tst, Northmoor Tst; *Books* Sources of EEC Funding for Local Authorities (1977); *Recreations* tennis (real and lawn), cricket, sailing; *Clubs* Hawks; *Style—* Jonathan Welfare, Esq; Rooks Orchard, Little Wittenham, Abingdon, Oxfordshire (☎ 086 730 7765); Venture Link Investors Ltd, Tectonic Place, Holyport Rd, Maidenhead, Berkshire SL6 2YG (☎ 0628 771050, fax 0628 770392)

WELFARE, Mary Katharine; *née* Gordon; er adopted da of 4 Marquess of Aberdeen and Temair (d 1974); *b* 30 May 1946; *m* 1968, Simon Piers Welfare, 2 son of late Kenneth William Welfare, of The Old Doctor's House, Stradbroke, Suffolk; *Books* Witchdust (1980), The Yeti of the Glen (1987), Bandit Bad Witch (1988), Who's Afraid of Swapping Spiders? (1989), Growing Up At Haddo (1989); *Style—* Mrs Simon Welfare; The Den of Keithfield, Tarves, Ellon, Aberdeen AB41 0NU

WELFARE, Simon Piers; s of Kenneth William Welfare (d 1966), of Stadbroke, Suffolk, and Dorothy Patience, *née* Ross; *b* 21 Nov 1946; *Educ* Harrow, Magdalen Coll Oxford; *m* 3 Aug 1968, Mary Katharine, da of Marquess of Aberdeen and Temair, CBE (d 1974), of Haddo House, Aberdeenshire; 1 s (Toby b 29 March 1973), 2 da (Hannah b 30 Sept 1969, Alice b 6 Sept 1971); *Career* broadcaster and writer Yorkshire TV Ltd 1968-81, freelance prodr 1982-, md Granite Film and TV Prodns 1989-; *Books* Arthur C Clarke's Mysterious World (with A C Clarke and J Fairley, 1980), Arthur C Clarke's World of Strange Powers (with A C Clarke and J Fairley, 1984), Great Honeymoon Disasters (1986), Arthur C Clarke's Chronicles of the Strange & Mysterious (with A C Clarke and J Fairley, 1987), Red Empire (with Gwyneth Hughes, 1990); *Recreations* collecting arcane knowledge, flying; *Style—* Simon Welfare, Esq; The Den of Keithfield, Tarves, Ellon, Aberdeenshire AB41 0NU (☎ 06515 510/760)

WELHAM, George; s of George Leslie Welham (d 1986), of London, and Dorothy Emily, *née* Peckem; *b* 9 July 1938; *Educ* Dulwich; *m* 1, Yvonne, *née* Adams; 3 s; m 2, Penelope, *née* Connell; 2 step da; *Career* fin journalist 1960-69; co fndr and first chm Welham-McAdam Public Relations 1969-76, dir Extel PR & Advertising 1976-79, dir and dep md Hill & Knowlton London 1979-84, md Gavin Anderson & Co London 1984-88; chief exec then chm: Burson-Marsteller Financial Ltd 1988-, Burson-Marsteller Ltd (memb Exec Ctee) 1988-; *Style—* George Welham, Esq; 47 Westbourne Terrace, London W2 (☎ 071 724 4949); Burson-Marsteller Ltd, 24-28 Bloomsbury Way, London WC1A 2PX (☎ 071 831 2969, fax 071 430 1052)

WELLDON, Dr Estela Valentina; da of Gilao D'Accurzio (d 1983), and Julia, *née* Barbadillo (d 1957); *b* 3 Nov 1936; *Educ* Universidad de Cuyo Argentina (MD), Menninger Sch of Psychiatry USA, Univ of London; *m* Ronald Michael Charles Welldon (d 1970); 1 s (Daniel Alexis b 2 Feb 1970); partner, Sir John Thomson, GCMG; *Career* psychiatrist Henderson Hosp 1964; Portman Clinic London: conslt psychiatrist 1975-, clinic tutor 1987-; specialist in the application of group analysis to social and sexual deviancy, pioneer in teaching of forensic psychotherapy, fndr in forensic psychotherapy Univ of London; assessor British Journal of Psychiatry, expert on female crime and sexual deviation Panel of Specialists RCPsych, Br corr and memb Editorial Bd Argentinian Journal of Group Psychotherapy; Visitante Distinguido Univ & City of Cuzco Peru 1989; memb: Gp Analytic Soc 1968; Br Assoc of Psychotherapists 1972, Inst for Study and Prevention of Delinquency, American Gp Psychotherapy Assoc, Int Assoc of Gp Psychotherapy, Core Planning Gp of Int Symposium on Family Breakdown 1987-; fndr memb Bd of Dirs Int Acad of Law and Mental Health; memb Soc of Authors; MRCPsych 1973, FRCPysch 1987; *Books* Mother, Madonna, Whore (1988); *Recreations* opera, theatre, walking; *Clubs* Groucho; *Style—* Dr Estela Welldon; 121 Harley St, London W1N 1DH (☎ 071 935 9076)

WELLER, (William) Leslie; s of Frederick Leslie Weller (d 1977), of Horsham, W Sussex, and Blanch Mary, *née* Kemp; *b* 23 April 1935; *Educ* Collyers GS, Cranleigh; *m* 1, 6 June 1959 (m dis), Joyce Elizabeth; 1 s (Adrian Leslie b 21 June 1963); m 2, Brenda Olive Wilson; *Career* Nat Serv, RAF 1957-59; chartered surveyor: Newland Tompkins and Taylor 1951-55, King and Chasemore 1959-78 (1955-57, ptnr 1961-78); md: Sothebys Sussex 1978-91 (dir Sothebys London 1991-); chm: Latern House 1973-78 (mental handicap tst), Chichester Cathedral tst 1979-86 (tstee 1986-); tstee Weald & Downland Museum 1990-, govr W Sussex schs of higher educn, Master Crawley and Horsham foxhounds 1979-; Freeman: Worshipful Co of Ironmongers 1984, City of London 1986; FRICS 1961, FSVA 1976; *Recreations* reading, riding, gardening, foxhunting; *Clubs* Naval & Military and Sussex; *Style—* Leslie Weller, Esq; Court Barton, Sullington, Storrington, West Sussex (☎ 0903 742869); Sothebys, 34 New Bond St, London W1 (☎ 071 493 8080, car 0860 562381)

WELLER, Malcolm Philip Isadore; s of Solomon George Weller (d 1958), and Esther, *née* Black; *b* 29 May 1935; *Educ* Perse Sch, Univ of Cambridge (MA, prize winner), Univ of Newcastle (MB BS, prize winner); *m* 8 May 1966, (Celia) Davina, da of Solomon Reisler (d 1973), of Manchester; 2 s (Ben b 19 Aug 1969, Adrian b 17 Dec 1970); *Career* psychiatrist; pubns incl over 100 chapters papers and editorials on psychiatric subjects; external examiner Univs of Manchester and Singapore, chm CONCERN, vice chm N E Thames Regnl Ctee for Hosp Med Servs, memb Central Ctee BMA; former organiser Newcastle Music Festival, former local cncllr, former chm of govrs Gosforth Middle Sch; FBPsS 1986, FCINP 1987, FRCPsych 1987; *Books* Scientific Basis of Psychiatry (1983), International Perspectives in Schizophrenia (1990); *Recreations* history of art, music; *Clubs* New York Acad of Sciences, RSM; *Style—* Dr Malcolm Weller; 30 Arkwright Rd, Hampstead, London NW3 6BH (☎ 071 749 5804); Friern Hospital, Friern Barnet Rd, London N11 3BP (☎ 081 368 1288, fax 081 361 4434)

WELLER, Dr Maurice George Samuel (Sam); MBE (1969), BEM (1959); s of Walter Gerald Weller, of West Mount, Perrancombe, Perranporth, Cornwall, and Violet May, *née* Knight (d 1985); *Educ* Elmhurst Sch, Univ of London (BSc), Univ of Southampton (MSc), Dartmouth, (PhD); *m* 14 April 1952, Rosina Sybil, da of William Henry Flower (d 1963); 3 s (John Lionel Richard b 1953, Peter David b 1954, Kevin Leslie b 1957), 1 da (Wendy Elizabeth b 1956); *Career* RAF 1949-69: scientific branch 1961, seconded Min Tech Royal Radar Estab Malvern; dir Yonder Towan Field Studies Centre Cornwall 1969-76, conslt computer scientist; memb Cncl and tstee Royal Cornwall Geological Soc; memb: Inst Cornish Studies, Cornwall Archaeological Soc; FISC 1968, fell Inst Tech Communicators; *Books* CORAL in Air Defence (1969), Self Compiling Languages (1966), British Gems & Minerals (1975), Archaeology of West Cornwall (1974), Prehistoric, Inorganic Resource (1986); *Recreations* astronomical telescope construction, computer programming, mineralogy, archaeology; *Style—* Dr Sam Weller, MBE, BEM; Barn Cottage, Boscaswell, West Cornwall (☎ 0736 788286); Marsol, Sta Eulalia del Rio, Ibiza, Baleares, Spain; Levant Laboratories, Pendeen, West Cornwall (☎ 0736 788286)

WELLER, Prof Roy Oliver; s of Leonard Albert Ernest Weller (d 1969), and Myrtle Passie, *née* Vivash (d 1979); *b* 27 May 1938; *Educ* St Olaves and St Saviours GS London, Guy's Med Sch Univ of London (MD, PhD); *m* 27 Dec 1960, Francine Michelle, da of Robert Arthur Cranley; 1 s (Timothy b 1965), 1 da (Adrienne b 1964); *Career* US Public Health Serv post doctoral fell Albert Einstein Coll of Med 1967-68, sr lectr in pathology Guy's Med Sch 1969-72 (lectr 1964-67 and 1968-69), conslt neuropathologist Guy's and Maudsley Hosp 1972, clinical serv dir of pathology Univ of

Southampton Med Sch 1989 (sr lectr and reader in pathology 1973-78, prof of neuropathology 1978, dep dean of med 1980-84); ed Neuropathology and Applied Neuropathology; memb Br Neuropathological Soc, FRCPath 1982; *Books* Pathology of Peripheral Nerves (1977), Clinical Neuropathology (1983), Atlas of Neuropathology (1984), Systemic Pathology: Nervous System Muscle and Eyes (ed 1989); *Style*— Prof Roy Weller; 22 Abbey Hill Rd, Winchester, Hants SO23 7AT (☎ 0962 867465); Dept of Pathology, Level E, South Pathology Block, Southampton General Hospital, Tremona Rd, Southampton SO9 4XY (☎ 0703 796669, fax 0703 705580)

WELLER, Walter; s of Walter Weller (d 1982), and Anna Katharina Weller (d 1990); *b* 30 Nov 1939; *Educ* Gymnasium, HS of Music Vienna; *m* 8 June 1966, Elisabeth Maria, da of Prof Franz Samohyl, of Vienna; 1 s (Andreas b 18 June 1978); *Career* musician and conductor; Vienna Philharmonic Orch 1956-57, fndr Weller Quartet 1957-67, first konzertmeister Vienna Philharmonic 1961, debut as conductor 1966, princ conductor RPO 1980-85, conductor laureate Royal Liverpool Philharmonic Orch (princ conductor and artistic advsr), musical dir Nat Orch of Spain 1990- (princ guest conductor 1987-90); recordings incl: all Prokofiev and Rachmaninov symphonies, Smetana, Shostakovitch Grieg, Bartok, Dukas; operas incl: Fidelio and Der Rosenkavalier (Scottish Opera), Der Fliegende Hollander and Ariadne auf Naxos (ENO), Der Frieischutz (Teatro Comunale Bologna), Der Fliegende Hollander (La Scala); conductor of leading orchestras: Britain, Europe, Scandinavia, America; Honoured Cross for Art and Sci (Austria), Mozart Interpretation prize, Beethoven Gold medal; *Style*— Walter Weller, Esq; c/o Harrison-Parrott Ltd, 12 Penzance Place, London W11 4PA (☎ 071 229 9166, fax 071 221 5042, telex 892791 BIRDS G)

WELLESLEY, Hon Brian Timothy; s (by 2 m) of 4 Earl Cowley; *b* 1938; *Educ* Arizona State Coll, Denver Univ, Colorado and Nevada U (BS); *m* 1, 1961 (m dis 1964), Patricia Tribbey; m 2, 1966, Karen Elizabeth Bradbury, of Reno, Nevada, USA; *Career* chm of intelligence div US Treasury Dept Alaska; *Style*— The Hon Brian Wellesley; PO Box 974, Anchorage, Alaska, 99510 USA

WELLESLEY, Lord John Henry; 3 s of 8 Duke of Wellington; *b* 20 April 1954; *Educ* Eton; *m* 1977, Corinne, da of HE Robert Vaes, Belgian ambass; 1 s (b 6 June 1981), 1 da (b 23 July 1983); *Style*— The Lord John Wellesley; 58, Elm Park Road, London SW3 6AU

WELLESLEY, Julian Valerian; s of Gerald Wellesley, MC, of Highfield Park, Sussex (gn of 1 Earl Cowley, KG, GCB, PC, and ggs of 1 Baron Cowley, bro of 1 Duke of Wellington), by Elizabeth, da of Otho Ball, of Chicago, and formerly w of Quintin Gilbey, the racing correspondent; *b* 9 Aug 1933; *Educ* RNCs Dartmouth & Greenwich; *m* 1965, Elizabeth, da of Cyril Stocken and formerly w of David Hall; 1 s (William Valerian b 1966), 1 da (Kate Elizabeth b 1970), 3 step da; *Career* late Lt RN; md Ayer Barker 1971-78, chm Charles Barker Group 1978-83; dir: Horizon Travel plc 1984-87, Chatsworth Food Ltd 1986-90; chm Eastbourne Health Authy 1990 (memb 1986-90); memb Ctee Assoc of Lloyds Members 1985-; *Recreations* reading, music, family, tennis, watching cricket; *Clubs* Brooks's, Sussex; *Style*— Julian Wellesley, Esq; Tidebrook Manor, Wadhurst, Sussex

WELLESLEY, Lord Richard Gerald; 2 s of 8 Duke of Wellington, KG, LVO, OBE, MC; *b* 20 June 1949; *Educ* Eton, RAC Cirencester; *m* 1973, Joanna, eldest da of John Sumner, of Marston St Lawrence, Oxon; 2 da (Natasha Doone b 1975, Davina Chloe b 1977); *Style*— The Lord Richard Wellesley; Knockdolian, Colmonell, Girvan, Ayrshire

WELLESLEY, Robin Alfred; s of Quintin Gilbey (d 1979), of London; step s of Gerald Wellesley (d 1961), of Withyham, Sussex; *b* 23 July 1928; *Educ* Eton; *m* 1953, Marianne, da of John McDonald, of Chicago; 1 s (Gerald), 2 da (Diana, Laura); *Career* dir: Prestige Group 1965-82, Aust Br C of C 1984-, NZ UK C of C and Indust 1984-; *Recreations* gardening, cricket, travel; *Clubs* Buck's; *Style*— Robin Wellesley, Esq; Shingle Barn, Dwelly Lane, Edenbridge, Kent (☎ 0732 862251); 36 Edge St, London W8 (☎ 071 727 4503); Suite 615, 162-168 Regent St, London W1R 5TB

WELLESLEY, Hon Mrs Henry; Valerie Rose; *née* Pitman; da of late Christian Ernest Pitman, CBE, of Doynton House, Doynton, nr Bath, and Eileen Winifred, *née* Clarke; *m* 1969, as his 4 w, Hon Henry Gerald Valerian Francis Wellesley (d 1981), yr s of 3 Earl Cowley (d 1919); 2 s; *Style*— The Hon Mrs Henry Wellesley; Priestown House, Mulhuddart, Co Dublin, Ireland

WELLING, Mark Ronald; s of Kenneth Ronald Welling, of Derby, and Margaret Dorothy, *née* Hunter; *b* 22 March 1956; *Educ* Derby Sch, Emmanuel Coll Cambridge (MA); *m* 28 March 1987, Vanessa Jane, da of W Richard Barker, of Farnley Tyas, W Yorks; *Career* slr 1981, ptnr Allen and Overy 1987-; cncllr (Lib Dem) Royal Borough of Kingston upon Thames 1986-90; memb City of London Slrs Co 1987-; memb Law Soc 1981-; *Recreations* bassoon, clarinet, and piano playing; *Style*— Mark Welling, Esq; Allen and Overy, 9 Cheapside, London EC2V 6AD (☎ 071 248 9898, fax 071 236 2192, telex 8812801)

WELLINGHAM, Air Cdre (John) Bernard; s of Claude Bernard Wellingham (d 1963), and Annetta, *née* Jagoe (d 1980); *b* 21 June 1925; *Educ* Trinity Sch Croydon, Christs Coll Cambridge (MA), Royal Coll of Military Sci Shrivenham, RAF Staff Coll Bracknell, Jt Servs Staff Coll Latimer; *m* 24 July 1948, Patricia Margaret, da of Wing Cdr Patrick John Murphy (d 1965); 2 s (John b 1949, Charles b 1953); *Career* RAF 1945, cmmnd 1946, communications devpt Royal Aircraft Establishment Farnborough 1946-50, served RAF Shaluffa and Abu Sueir 1951-53, HQ RAF Fighter Cmd 1953-54, sr tech offr RAF Patrington 1954-56, Guided Weapons Devpt Royal Radar Estab Malvern 1957-60, Operational Requirements Staff Air Miny 1961-63, Cmd Telecomms Offr NEAF 1964-67, chief instr RAF Coll Cranwell 1967-68, memb Air Force Bd Ctee on RAF Career Structure 1968-69, asst dir signals MOD 1969-72, controller Def Communications Network 1972-74, Air Offr Wales and Station Cdr RAF St Athan 1974-76, Air Cdre Signals RAF Support Cmd 1976-78; Mid Suffolk DC 1983-: chm Environmental Health Ctee 1986-88, chm Policy and Resources Ctee, vice chm Cncl; chm Wingfield Parish Cncl, vice chm Govrs Stradbroke HS, Churchwarden; CEng, FRAes 1976, FBIM 1976; *Recreations* tennis, shooting, horticulture; *Clubs* RAF; *Style*— Air Cdre Bernard Wellingham; The White House, Wingfield, Diss, Norfolk IP21 5QT

WELLINGS, Sir Jack Alfred; CBE (1970); s of late Edward Josiah Wellings, of Surrey; *b* 16 Aug 1917; *Educ* Selhurst GS, London Poly; *m* 1946, Greta, da of late George Tidey, of Sunderland; 1 s, 2 da; *Career* vice-pres Hawker Siddeley (Canada) Ltd 1952-62, chm and md George Cohen 600 Gp Ltd 1968-, memb Nat Enterprise Bd 1977-79, pt/t memb: NCB 1971-, Br Aerospace 1980-; kt 1975; *Style*— Sir Jack Wellings, CBE; Boundary Meadow, Collum Green Rd, Stoke Poges, Bucks (☎ 395 2978); George Cohen 600 Group Ltd, Wood Lane, London W12 (☎ 081 743 2070)

WELLINGS, Victor Gordon; QC (1973); s of late Gordon Arthur Wellings, and Alice Adelaide Wellings (who later m Charles Arthur Poole, decd); *b* 19 July 1919; *Educ* Reading Sch, Exeter Coll Oxford (MA); *m* 1948, Helen Margaret Jill, da of late Henry Lovell; 3 s; *Career* called to the Bar Gray's Inn 1949, in practice 1949-73; dep High Court judge 1975-, pres Lands Tbnl 1989- (memb 1973-88); *Recreations* golf, fishing; *Clubs* Oxford and Cambridge; *Style*— Victor Wellings, Esq, QC; Cherry Tree Cottage, Whitchurch Hill, Pangbourne, Berks; 48-49 Chancery Lane, London WC2 (☎ 071 936 7169)

WELLINGTON, 8 Duke of (UK 1814); Arthur Valerian Wellesley; KG (1990), LVO (1952), OBE (1957), MC (1941), DL (Hants 1975); also Baron of Mornington (I 1746), Earl of Mornington, Viscount Wellesley (both I 1760), Viscount Wellington of Talavera and of Wellington, Baron Douro (both UK 1809), Conde do Vimeiro (Portugal 1811), Earl of Wellington (UK 1812), Marquess of Wellington (UK 1812), Duque de Ciudad Rodrigo and a Grandee of the 1 Class (Spain 1812), Duque da Vittoria, Marques de Torres Vedras (both Portugal 1812), Marquess of Douro (UK 1814), and Prince of Waterloo (Netherlands 1815); s of 7 Duke of Wellington, KG (d 1972); *b* 2 July 1915; *Educ* Eton, New Coll Oxford; *m* 1944, Diana, da of Maj-Gen Douglas McConnel, CB, CBE, DSO, of Knockdolian, Ayrshire; 4 s, 1 da; *Heir* s, Marquess of Douro; *Career* patron of 4 livings; Brig (ret) RHG, CO 1955-58; Silver Stick in Waiting and Lt-Col cmdg Household Cav 1959-60 & OC 22 Armd Bde 1960-61; cdr RAC BAOR 1962-64; defence attaché Madrid 1964-67; Col-in-Chief The Duke of Wellington's Regt 1974-; Hon Col 2 Bn Wessex Regt TA & VRA; nat vice-pres Royal Br Legion; dir Massey Ferguson Holdings 1967 and Massey Ferguson Ltd 1973-89; vice pres and cncl memb Zoological Soc of London 1973-89; pres and dep pres the Game Conservancy 1976-87; pres: Rare Breeds Survival Tst 1982-86, Cncl for Environmental Conservation 1983-86, Atlantic Salmon Trust 1983-; Queen's Tstee Bd of Royal Armouries 1983-; chm Pitt Club, govr Wellington Coll; tstee: Lawes Agric Tst 1989-, Centre for Agric Strategy Univ of Reading 1988-, World Wildlife Fund (UK) 1985-90; vice pres The Kennel Club 1987-; Cncl memb: RASE, OStJ Hants; Gd Cross Order of Isabel the Catholic (Spain) 1986, Légion d'Honneur (France); *Clubs* Turf, Buck's; *Style*— His Grace the Duke of Wellington, KG, LVO, OBE, MC, DL; Stratfield Saye House, Basingstoke, Hants; Apsley House, Piccadilly, London W1

WELLMAN, Derek Morris; s of Morris Francis Ernest Wellman, of 33 Partis Way, Bath, and Doris Laurena Rose, *née* Chappell; *b* 12 April 1944; *Educ* Crypt GS Gloucester, Selwyn Coll Cambridge (MA); *m* 8 Jan 1972, Evelyn Barbara Hall, da of Thomas Richard Lennox (d 1985); 1 s (Edward b 1972), 1 da (Katherine b 1975); *Career* slr Supreme Ct 1969; registrar Diocese of Lincoln 1978; NP 1978; tstee Lincs Old Church Tst, chm Lincoln area RSCM, amateur musician; memb: Law Soc 1969, Ecclesiastical Law Assoc 1978, Ecclesiastical Law Soc 1987; *Recreations* music, sport; *Style*— Derek M Wellman, Esq; 52 Nettleman Rd, Lincoln (☎ 0522 532619); 28 West Parade, Lincoln (☎ 0522 536161)

WELLMAN, Glenn; s of Edward John Wellman, of Castleshaw, Delph, Yorkshire, and Isabella Jean, *née* Fordyce; *b* 5 Jan 1948; *Educ* Audenshaw GS Lancs, Imp Coll Univ of London (BSc), Manchester Business Sch (MBA); *m* 1973, Barbara Ann Howe; 1 s (Benjamin Alexander b 1977), 1 da (Rachel Lucy b 1978); *Career* asst investmt mangr Esso Petroleum Company 1976 (investmnt analyst 1970), sr vice pres and md Alliance Capital Management 1985 (vice pres 1979); memb Inst of Personnel Management 1970, assoc Soc of Investment Analysts 1973; *publications* author of various papers and articles in learned journals; *Recreations* gardening, history, theatre; *Style*— Glenn Wellman, Esq; 15 College Road, Dulwich Village, London SE21 7BG (☎ 081 693 4478); Alliance Capital Limited, 6th Floor, 155 Bishopsgate, London EC2M 3XS (☎ 071 454 7501, fax 071 454 0421)

WELLS, Alan Peter; s of Ernest William Charles Wells, of Newhaven, and Eunice Mae, *née* Dyke; *b* 2 Oct 1961; *Educ* Tideway Comp Sch Newhaven; *m* 26 Sept 1987, Melanie Elizabeth, da of Barry William Last; 1 s (Luke William Peter b 29 Dec 1990); *Career* professional cricketer; Sussex CCC: debut 1981, awarded county cap 1986, 167 first class appearances, capt v Leics 1990 (won game and scored undefeated century); NCA under 19 tour Canada 1979, Young England v India 1981, unofficial England tour SA 1989-90 (1 Test match, 2 one-day Ints); record partnership for brothers in first class cricket with Colin Wells scoring 303 undefeated v Kent 1987; Sussex player of the year 1989, Sussex leading batsman 1989 and 1990; off-seasons: laboratory asst Artex 1981, insurance salesman 1984-87, proprietor corporate outwork business Newhaven 1988- (brother and father co-directors); *Recreations* country pubs, Indian cuisine, music of Sting, other sports; *Style*— Alan Wells, Esq; Sussex CCC, County Ground, Eaton Road, Hove BN3 3AN (☎ 0273 732161)

WELLS, (William Arthur) Andrew; TD (1984); s of Sir John Wells, *qv*; *b* 14 June 1949; *Educ* Eton, Univ of Birmingham, N London Poly; *m* 19 Oct 1974, Tessa Margaret, da of Lt-Col Jocelyn Eustace Gurney, DSO, MC, DL (d 1973), of Tacolneston Hall, and Sprowston, Norfolk; 2 s (William b 1980, Frederick b 1982), 1 da (Augusta b 1984); *Career* TA: cmmnd 1971, extra lectr Jr Div Staff Coll 1978-79, Maj Royal Green Jackets 1981-90, RARO 1990; publisher 1969-81; co sec Minories Holdings Ltd 1981-; landowner Mereworth Kent; memb: Kent TA Ctee, Kent Cobnuts Assoc, Exec Ctee Friends of Kent Churches; pres N Battersea Cons Assoc 1981-83 pres Tooting Cons Assoc 1991- (div chm 1983-86); Clerk Worshipful Co of Watermen's 1986-; *Recreations* country interests, gardening, architectural history; *Clubs* City Univ; *Style*— Andrew Wells, Esq, TD; Mere House, Mereworth, Maidstone, Kent ME18 5NB; 16 St Mary-at-Hill, London EC3R 8EE

WELLS, Benjamin Weston; TD (1954); s of Sir William Henry Wells (d 1933), of Wimbledon, and Dorothy Kate Wells, JP, *née* Horne (d 1946); *b* 17 Feb 1918; *Educ* Bromsgrove, Univ of London, St Thomas's Hosp (MB MS); *m* 7 May 1945, Jean Lowson, da of Millar Mudie, of Madeley, Shropshire; 1 s (Graham b 1947, d 1959), 2 da (Fiona b 1949, Jane b 1960); *Career* cmmnd RAMC 1942, serv MEF Hosps, Arab Legion 1943-44, surgn CMF 1944-45, Maj RAMC TA 1945-66; conslt surgn 1952-83: St Helier Hosp Carshalton, Nelson Hosp Wimbledon, Wilson Hosp Mitcham; ret from NHS 1983, conslt surgn Parkside Hosp Wimbledon and New Victoria Hosp Kingston 1983-; Freeman City of London 1959-, Liveryman Worshipful Soc of Apothecaries 1953; FRSM 1946, MRCS, LRCP, FRCS, FRCSEd, FRCS (Eng); *Publications* numerous papers on bowel cancer in British Journal of Surgery, The Lancet, British Journal of Oncology; *Recreations* shooting, golf; *Clubs* Roehampton; *Style*— Benjamin Wells, Esq, TD; Oakleigh, 20 Sunnyside, Wimbledon SW19 4SH (☎ 081 946 3191)

WELLS, (Petrie) Bowen; MP (C) Hertford & Stortford 1983-; s of Reginald Laird Wells by his w Agnes, *née* Hunter; *b* 4 Aug 1935; *Educ* St Paul's, Univ of Exeter, Regent St Poly Mgmnt Sch; *m* 1975, Rennie Heyde; 2 s; *Career* RN; schoolmaster, sales trainee Br Aluminium, with Cwlth Devpts Corpn, co sec & industl rels mangr Guyana Timbers and owner mangr Substation Gp Servs; MP (C) Hertford and Stevenage 1979-1983, PPS to Michael Alison as Min State Employment 1982-83; memb: Foreign Affrs Select Ctee, Euro Legislation Select Ctee; chm: Utd Nat Parly Gp, Br Caribbean Gp; govr Inst of Devpt Studies Univ of Sussex, tstee Indust and Parly Tst, memb Bd Outward Bound Wales; govr Centre for Caribbean Studies, Univ of Warwick; chm Soc for Int Dev UK Chapter; memb Cncl: World Devpt Movement, Centre for World Devpt Educn; *Books* Managing Third World Debt; *Style*— Bowen Wells, Esq, MP; House of Commons, London, SW1A 0AA

WELLS, Boyan Stewart; s of Gordon Tebbutt Wells, of 6 Edmund Close, Downend, Bristol, and Vera, *née* Stanisic; *b* 3 June 1956; *Educ* Colston's Sch Bristol, Wadham Coll Oxford (MA, Hockey blue); *m* 11 Aug 1984, Alison Jayne, da of Michael Albert Good, of 45 Henbury Rd, Westbury-on-Trym, Bristol; 2 da (Holly Catharine b 8 May 1987, Elena Rose b 2 Dec 1988); *Career* ptnr Allen & Overy 1987- (joined 1979); Freeman: City of London, Worshipful Co of Slrs 1987; memb: Friends of Dulwich Soc, Law Soc; *Recreations* golf, squash, cinema; *Clubs* Dulwich Golf; *Style*— Boyan Wells, Esq; Allen & Overy, 9 Cheapside, London EC2V 6AD (☎ 071 248 9898, fax 071 236

2192)

WELLS, Sir Charles Maltby; 2 Bt (UK 1944), of Felmersham, Co Bedford, TD; s of Sir (Sydney) Richard Wells, 1 Bt, DL (d 1956), and Mary Dorothy (d 1956), da of Christopher Maltby; *b* 24 July 1908; *Educ* Bedford Sch, Pembroke Coll Cambridge; *m* 1935, Katharine Boulton, da of Frank Boteler Kenrick, of Toronto, Canada; 2 s (Christopher *qv*, Anthony Richard b 2 July 1947); *Heir* s, Christopher Wells; *Career* joined RE (TA) 1933, Capt 1939, served 54 Div 1939-41 and 76 Div 1941-43, Lt-Col 1941, Br Army Staff Washington 1943-45, Acting Col 1945; *Style—* Sir Charles Wells, Bt, TD; Apt 507, 350 Lonsdale Road, Toronto, Canada

WELLS, Christopher Charles; s and h of Sir Charles Wells, 2 Bt, TD; *b* 12 Aug 1936; *Educ* McGill Univ, Toronto Univ; *m* 1960, (m dis 1984), Elizabeth, da of I Griffiths, of Outrement, Quebec; 2 s (Michael b 1966, Geoffrey b 1970), 2 da (Felicity b 1964, Megan b 1969); m 2, 1985, Lynda Anne Cormack, of Toronto, Ontario; 1 s (Andrew b 1983); *Career* md in family practice; *Style—* Christopher Wells, Esq; St Michael's Family Practice, 30 Bond St, Toronto, Ontario M5B 1W8, Canada

WELLS, Dr (John) Christopher Durant; s of Colin Durant Wells, of Cae Coch, Bryn Siencyn, Anglesey, and Barbara Gwynneth, *née* Williams; *b* 5 Oct 1947; *Educ* Manchester GS, Univ of Liverpool (MB, ChB); *m* 14 Aug 1971, Sheila Frances, da of Patrick Joseph Murphy, of Wallasey, Merseyside; 2 da (Amanda b 1973, Sally b 1977); *Career* various hosp appts 1970-82, conslt anaesthetist Mersey RHA 1982-; dir: Centre For Pain Relief and Regnl Neuroscience Unit Walton Hosp Liverpool 1983-, Pain Relief Res Unit Liverpool 1983; hon conslt in pain relief Marie Curie Homes 1984-, hon sr lectr Depts of Annasthesia and Neurological Sciences Univ of Liverpool 1985-; recently completed res projects incl: the use of calcitonin in the treatment of bone pain, the length of action in acupuncture analgesia, the use of naloxone in thalamic (central) pain; current res incl: the use of implanted drug delivery systems, causes of trigeminal neuralgia, new therapies for post-herpetic neuralgia; developed a rehabilitation prog for patients with chronic pain for NHS; numerous presentations at maj nat and int meetings incl: acupuncture analgesia Br Med Acupuncture Soc 1982, morphine in cancer pain Toronto 1984, cancer pain (paper) Pain Symposium Israel 1989; pres: Self Help In Pain, People In Pain; memb Ctee: Intractable Pain Soc of GB and NI, Br chapter Int Assoc for Study of Pain; memb: BMA, Euro Soc of Regnl Anaesthesia; fndr memb and past pres Pain Interest Gp; LRCP 1970, MRCS 1970, LMCC 1973, FFARCS 1978; *Books* numerous pubns on pain incl: Epidural Clonidine (Lancet, 1987), The Clinical Neurology of Old Age (contrib, 1989), Ballieres Clinical Rheumatology (contrib, 1987); *Recreations* curling (for Wales), skiing, horse-riding, music, chess; *Style—* Dr Christopher Wells; 48 Rodney St, Liverpool, Merseyside L9 1AA (☎ 051 7089344)

WELLS, Colin Mark; s of Ernest William Charles Wells, of Newhaven, East Sussex, and Eunice Mae, *née* Dyke; *b* 3 March 1960; *Educ* Tideway Sch Newhaven; *m* 25 Sept 1982, Celia Lilian, da of George James Corbett; 1 da (Jessica Louise b 2 Oct 1987); *Career* professional cricketer Sussex CCC: first class debut 1979, awarded county cap 1982, 248 appearances; Border South Africa 1980-81, Western Province South Africa 1984-85; represented MCC v Championship winners 3 times, 2 one day Ints v Australia and Pakistan 1985; amateur player Newhaven and Brighton & Hove; jt dir lighting assembly and packaging co (with brother and father) 1987-; *Recreations* all sports, keep fit, cooking, wines; *Style—* Colin Wells, Esq; Sussex CCC, Eaton Road, Hove, East Sussex BN3 3AN (☎ 0273 732161)

WELLS, Prof David Arthur; s of Arthur William Wells, of Lancing, West Sussex, and Rosina Elizabeth, *née* Jones (d 1986); *b* 26 April 1941; *Educ* Christ's Hosp Horsham, Gonville and Caius Coll Cambridge (MA, PhD); *Career* lectr in German: Univ of Southampton 1966-69, Bedford Coll London 1969-74; prof of German: The Queen's Univ of Belfast 1974-87, Birkbeck Coll London 1987-; hon sec Modern Humanities Res Assoc 1969-, sec-gen Int Fedn for Modern Languages and Literatures 1981-; FRSA 1985; *Books* The Vorau Moses and Balaam (1970), The Wild Man from the Epic of Gilgamesh to Hartmann von Ave's Iwein (1975), A Complete Concordance to the Vorauer Bücher Moses (1976), The Years Work in Modern Language Studies (jt ed, 1976-); *Recreations* travel; *Style—* Prof David Wells; 128 Belgrave Rd, London SW1V 2BL (☎ 071 834 6558); Dept of German, Birkbeck College, Malet St, London WC1E 7HX (☎ 071 631 6103)

WELLS, David George; s of George Henry Wells, of Welford, Northants, and Marian, *née* Trolley (d 1988); *b* 6 Aug 1941; *Educ* Market Harborough GS, Univ of Reading (BA); *m* 27 Oct 1967, Patricia Ann, da of George Fenwick (d 1983), of Southampton; 2 s (Jonathan b 1968, Colin b 1971); *Career* Hancock Gilbert & Morris 1962-67, Esso Chemical Ltd 1967-69, Gas Cncl 1969-72; Br Gas: chief accountant admin 1973-76, chief investmt accountant (HQ) 1976, dir fin (SE Region) 1976-83, dep chm (W Midlands regn) 1983-88, SE regnl chm (plc) 1988-; dep chm Metrogas Bldg Soc 1979-83 (dir 1978-86); chm South London Trg and Enterprise Cncl 1989-; FCA 1966, CBIM 1990, Companion IGasE 1988; *Recreations* walking, reading, photography, gardening; *Style—* David Wells, Esq; British Gas plc South Eastern, Katharine St, Croydon, Surrey CR9 1JU (☎ 081 688 4466)

WELLS, David John; s of Ralph Weston Wells, (d 1973) of Purley, Berks, and Mary Angela, *née* Crawford g da of 17 Baron Saye & Sele (d 1973); *b* 6 Oct 1935; *Educ* Cheltenham, Royal Agric Coll Cirencester (Dip Estate Mgmnt); *m* 9 July 1960, Patricia Meriel, da of Percy Tyson (d 1962), of Lowick, Cumbria; 2 s (Andrew William b 1963, Alan David b 1966); *Career* Nat Serv Midshipman RNVR 1952-54, Lt (SCC) RNVR 1955-63; estate mgmnt in N Wales; chm N Wales Branch: Central Assoc Agric Valuers 1977-78, RICS 1984-85; lectr in land admin and land use NE Wales Inst Wrexham and conslt in private practice, external tutor Coll of Estate Mgmnt (founded by gf the late Sir William Wells); licensed lay reader Dio of St Asaph; Church of Wales: memb Governing Body 1966-, memb Rep Body 1972-, memb Electors' Coll for Appt of Bishops 1973-; community cncllr; FRICS, MRAC, fell Central Assoc of Agric Valuers; *Recreations* Wrexham FC, philumeny; *Style—* D J Wells, Esq; 46 High Park, Gwernaffield, Mold, Clwyd CH7 5EE; North East Wales Institute, Plas Coch, Mold Rd, Wrexham, Clwyd LL11 2AW (☎ 0978 290666)

WELLS, David Patrick Casey; s of late Frank Wells, and Bridget Theresa, *née* Casey; *b* 24 Nov 1950; *Educ* St Joseph's Coll Blackpool Lancs, QMC London (LLB); *m* 25 Sept 1982, Chenoa Geraldine, da of late William Bailey; *Career* admitted slr 1976; ptnr: Reynolds Porter Chamberlain 1976-81, Titmus Sainer & Web 1988-; memb Law Soc; *Recreations* rugby (Blackheath), squash; *Style—* David Wells, Esq; Titmuss Sainer & Webb, 2 Serjeant's Inn, London EC4 (☎ 071 583 53453, fax 071 353 3683, telex 23823 ADVICE G)

WELLS, Prof George Albert; s of George J Wells (d 1960), and Lilian Maud, *née* Bird (d 1986); *b* 22 May 1926; *Educ* Stationers' Company's Sch, UCL (BA, MA, PhD, BSc); *m* 29 May 1969, Elisabeth, da of Franz Delhey, of Aachen; *Career* Nat Serv in coal mines 1944-45; lectr in German UCL 1949-64 (reader 1964-68), prof of German Birkbeck Coll London 1968-88; emeritus prof Univ of London 1988-, hon assoc Rationalist Press Assoc; *Books* Herder and After (1959), The Plays of Grillparzer (1969), The Jesus of the Early Christians (1971), Goethe and the Development of Science (1978), The Historical Evidence for Jesus (1982), Did Jesus Exist? (1986), The Origin of Language (1987), Religious Postures (1988); Who Was Jesus? A Critique of the New Testament Record (1989); J M Robertson, Liberal, Rationalist and Scholar (ed, 1987), F R H Englefield's Language, Its Origin and Relation to Thought (ed jtly, 1977) and the same author's The Mind at Work and Play (1985), Critique of Pure Vertiage, Essays on Abuses of Language in Literary, Religious and Philosophical Writings (1990); *Recreations* walking; *Style—* Prof George Wells; 35 St Stephens Ave, St Albans, Herts AL3 4AA (☎ 0727 51347)

WELLS, Hon Mrs (Gillian Hermione Christian); *née* Turton; da of Baron Tranmire (Life Peer); *b* 1930; *Educ* Slade School of Art, London; *m* 1960, David Poulett Wells; 2 s (Quinton Robert b 1 Feb 1962, Nicholas Michael b 1966, d 1966), 2 da (Fiona Mary b 8 May 1963, Olivia Rosalind b 21 Jan 1969); *Career* artist; *Recreations* dancing, tennis; *Style—* The Hon Mrs Wells; Hilperton House, Hilperton, Trowbridge, Wilts (☎ 0225 75 3845)

WELLS, Graham Holland; s of Edmund Holland Wells, RD (d 1974), and Pamela Doris, *née* Siddall; *b* 28 May 1959; *Educ* Shrewsbury, Brasenose Coll Oxford (MA); *m* 21 Jan 1984, Dr Susan Margaret, da of James Edgar Riley Tompkin, of 22 Manor Rd, Desford, Leicestershire; *Career* called to the Bar Middle Temple 1982; *Recreations* rowing, skiing, hill walking, water colour and oil painting; *Style—* Graham Wells, Esq; Refuge Assurance House, Derby Square, Liverpool, Merseyside L2 1TS (☎ 051 709 4222, fax 051 708 6311)

WELLS, Lt-Col Herbert James; CBE (1958), MC (1918), JP (Surrey 1952), DL (1962); s of late James J Wells, of NSW, Aust; *b* 27 March 1897; *Educ* Newcastle NSW; *m* 1926, Rose Hamilton (d 1983), da of late H D Brown, of Bournemouth; *Career* AIF and Aust Flying Corps WWI, 55 Surrey Bn Home Gd WWII, Lt-Col 1954; former memb Surrey T & AFA; chm Queen Mary's Hosp Carshalton 1958-60; vice chm Surrey CC 1959-62, chm 1962-65; High Sheriff Surrey 1965; chm Wallington Bench 1961-70, gen cmmr for income tax, Baker Tilley CAs; Freeman City of London; vice chm Carshalton UDC (chm 1950-52 and 1955-56); Hon DUniv Surrey 1975; FCA; *Clubs* RAC; *Style—* Lt-Col Herbert Wells, CBE, MC, JP, DL; 17 Oakhurst Rise, Carshalton Beeches, Surrey SM5 4AG (☎ 081 643 4125); Baker Tilley Chartered Accountants, 2 Bloomsbury St, London WC1B 3ST (☎ 071 413 5100, telex 8952387)

WELLS, John Campbell; s of Rev Eric George Wells (d 1984), and Dorothy Mary, *née* Thompson (d 1960); *b* 17 Nov 1936; *Educ* Eastbourne Coll, St Edmund Hall Oxford (MA); *m* Teresa, da of Sir Christopher Chancellor, of The Old Priory, Ditcheat, Somerset; *Career* 2 Lt Royal Sussex Regt 1955; author: Mrs Wilson's Diary (with Richard Ingrams), The Dear Bill Letters (with Richard Ingrams), Anyone for Denis? (in which he played the lead Whitehall Theatre 1982); various translations include: Danton's Death, The Marriage of Figaro (Nat Theatre), La Vie Parisienne (Scottish Opera), The Magic Flute (City of Birmingham Touring Opera); dir: La Vie Parisienne, Mikado (D'Oyly Carte); memb The Literary Soc; *Recreations* walking, talking; *Style—* John Wells, Esq; 1A Scarsdale Villas, London W8 6PT (☎ 071 937 0534)

WELLS, Prof John Christopher; s of Rev Philip Cuthbert Wells (d 1974), of Walton-on-Trent, and Winifred May, *née* Peaker; *b* 11 March 1939; *Educ* St Johns Sch Leatherhead, Trinity Coll Cambridge (BA), Univ Coll London (MA, PhD); *Career* UCL: asst lectr in phonetics 1962-65, lectr 1965-82, reader 1982-88, prof 1988; pres World Esperanto Assoc, chm London Esperanto Club; *Books* Teach Yourself Concise Esperanto Dictionary (1969), Practical Phonetics (1971), Jamaican Pronunciation in London (1973), Accents of English (1982), Longman Pronunciation Dictionary (1990); *Style—* Prof J C Wells; Dept of Phonetics & Linguistics, University College, Gower St, London WC1E 6BT (☎ 071 380 7175, fax 071 383 4108)

WELLS, Capt John Gerard; CBE (1964), DSC (1940); s of Vice Adm Sir Gerard Aylmer Wells, KBE (d 1943); *b* 22 Sept 1915; *Educ* Summerfields Oxford, RNC Darmouth; *m* 1947, Diana, da of Lt-Gen Sir Edmond Schreiber, KCB, DSO; 2 s; *Career* served RN 1929-64; WWII served Atlantic, Med and Pacific; cmd: HMS Dainty 1959, HMS Excellent 1961, HMS Kent 1963-; ret Capt; gen mangr Aviemore Centre 1964-70, dir Clarkson Holidays 1970-74, conslt Wakeman Trower & Ptnrs 1975-76, gen mangr Gulfspan 1977-78, Mgmnt Business Servs (London) 1980-81, res historian HMS Warrior (1860) 1981-87, chm Warrior Assoc 1985; *Books* Whaley - The Story of HMS Excellent 1830-1980, The Immortal Warrior, Britain's first and last battleship; *Recreations* sailing, skiing, shooting, stalking, golf, naval historical research; *Clubs* Army and Navy, Royal Cruising; *Style—* Capt John Wells, CBE, DSC, RN; High Firs House, Hatch Lane, Liss, Hants (☎ 0730 893343)

WELLS, Sir John Julius; o s of Rev (Arthur) Reginald Kemble Wells (d 1964), and Margaret Evelyn, *née* Hodgson; ggg nephew of John Wells, JP, DL, MP for Maidstone 1820-30; *b* 30 March 1925; *Educ* Eton, CCC Oxford (MA); *m* 31 July 1948, Lucinda Mary Helen Francis, eld da of Francis Ralph Meath Baker, JP, of Hasfield Court, Glos; 2 s ((William Arthur) Andrew *qv*, Oliver Reginald b 5 Nov 1955), 2 da (Julia Jane b 1 Feb 1951, Henrietta Frances b 27 Feb 1952); *Career* served WWII in HM Submarines; contested (C) Smethwick 1955, MP (C) Maidstone 1959-87; chm: Cons Pty Horticultural Ctee 1965-71 and 1973-87, Horticulture Sub Ctee of Agric Select Ctee 1968, Parly Waterways Gp 1974-80; vice chm Cons Agric Ctee 1970; memb Mr Speaker's Panel of Chairmen 1974-87; pres Nat Inst of Fresh Produce 1984-; Master Worshipful Co of Fruiterers 1977, Hon Freeman of Maidstone 1979; Kt Cdr Order of Civil Merit (Spain) 1972, Cdr Order of Lion (Finland) 1984; kt 1984; *Clubs* Army and Navy; *Style—* Sir John Wells; Mere House Barn, Mereworth, Kent ME18; Acheillie Lodge, Rogart, Sutherland

WELLS, Kasan Heybourn; JP (1961); s of Arthur George Wells, JP (d 1971), and Violet Caroline Annie, *née* Heybourn (d 1929); *b* 6 June 1917; *Educ* Brighton Coll, Merton Coll Oxford (MA); *m* 9 Dec 1944, Delicia Mary, da of Edwin Lawrence Mitchell, CB, CBE (d 1960); 2 s (Graham b 1948, Robert b 1953 (decd)), 2 da (Tina b 1945, Fiona b 1956); *Career* served BEF Jan-June 1940, Staff Sgt 8 Army ME, N Africa 1940-44, 21 Army Gp France, Belgium, Germany 1945-46; sr ptnr Brandiston Farms 1950-86; farmer, landowner; memb Norfolk Local Valuation Panel 1979-88, govr Taverham Hall Prep Sch 1967-88; *Recreations* golf, music, contract bridge; *Clubs* Royal W Norfolk Golf (Brancaster), Sheringham Golf, Magistrates Golf (vice pres), Norfolk and Norwich Bridge; *Style—* Kasan Wells, Esq, JP; Church Farm, Brandiston, Norwich, Norfolk NR10 4PJ (☎ 0603 871264)

WELLS, Malcolm Henry Weston; s of Lt Cdr Geoffrey Weston Wells (d 1988), and Inez Brenda, *née* Williams (d 1967); *b* 26 July 1927; *Educ* Eton; *m* 20 Dec 1952, (Helen) Elizabeth Agnes, da of Rt Rev Bishop Maurice Henry Harland (d 1986); 1 s (Nicholas Weston b 1954), 1 da (Caroline Felicity b 1956); *Career* bNVR 1945-48; Peat Marwick Mitchell 1948-58 (articled clerk, latterly asst mangr), SIEBE plc 1958-63 (sec, latterly md); dir: Charterhouse Japhet plc 1963-73 (chm 1973-80), Charterhouse Group 1964-80 (joined 1963), CAA 1974-77; chm: Charterhouse Petroleum plc 1977-82, BWD Securities plc 1987-; dep chm: Carclo Engineering Group plc 1982-, German Securities Investment Trust plc 1985-89; dir Nat Home Loans Holdings plc 1989-; Bank in Liechtenstein Ltd 1981-90 (London rep, currently md); memb Solicitors Disciplinary Tbnl 1975-81; *Recreations* sailing; *Clubs* City of London, Overseas Bankers; *Style—* M H W Wells, Esq; Holmbush House, Findon, Worthing BN1X 0SY (☎ 0903 873630)

WELLS, Michael; s of John Thomas Wells (d 1975), of Cannock, Staffs, and Lily, *née*

Ellis; *b* 7 Aug 1952; *Educ* Pool Hayes Sch Willenhall, Univ of Manchester (BSc, MB ChB, MD); *m* 21 Dec 1974, Jane Cecila, da of John Parker Gill, of Gosforth Cumbria; 1 s (James b 1980), 1 da (Rosemary b 1982); *Career* lectr in pathology Univ of Bristol 1978-79 sr lectr in pathology Univ of Leeds 1988- (lectr 1980-88), hon conslt Leeds Western Health Authy 1983-88, clinical sub dean Leeds West Univ of Leeds Sch of Med 1988-; memb: Assoc of Clinical Pathologists Speciality Ctee on Histopathology, hon sec Br Div of the Int Acad of Pathology, chm Burley-in-Wharfedale Round Table 1989-90; memb Royal Coll of Pathologists 1983; *Recreations* choral singing, gardening; *Style*— Michael Wells, Esq; 8 Rosebank, Burley-In-Wharfedale, Ilkley, W Yorkshire LS 29 7PQ (☎ 0943 862719); Dept of Pathology, Univ of Leeds, Leeds LS2 9JT (☎ 0532 33 3372, fax 0532 33 3404)

WELLS, Wing Cdr Oliver John; DL (Beds 1964); s of Sir Richard Wells, 1 Bt, of Felmersham Grange, nr Bedford (d 1956); *b* 10 March 1922; *Educ* Uppingham, RAF Staff Coll; *m* 1949, Felicity Anne, da of Brig M E Mascall, DSO, OBE (d 1958); 2 s, 1 da; *Career* served RAF 1941-56, High Sheriff of Bedfordshire 1970, chm of brewery co and malting co; *Recreations* flying, sailing; *Clubs* RAF; *Style*— Wing Cdr Oliver Wells DL; Ickwell Grange, nr Biggleswade, Beds (☎ 076 727 274)

WELLS, Prof Peter Bernard; s of Kenneth Edward Bainton Wells (d 1974), and Kathleen Mary Newman Wells (d 1988); *b* 9 Aug 1936; *Educ* Marling Sch Glos, Univ of Hull (BSc, PhD); *m* 28 Dec 1963, Maureen, da of Alfred Stephenson (d 1983); 1 s (Richard Peter Kerwin b 1970), 2 da (Catherine Mary b 1964, Sarah Judith b 1967); *Career* prof of physical chemistry Univ of Hull 1981- (asst lectr in chemistry 1961, lectr, sr lectr, reader in physical chemistry); author of several papers on heterogeneous catalysis; memb certain SERC ctees and currently chm: SERC Initiative on Interfaces and Catalysis, Prog Mgmnt Ctee for the LINK Prog on New Catalysts and Catalytic Processes; fell Royal Soc of Chemistry; *Books* author of over 100 scientific papers on heterogeneous catalysis; *Recreations* music; *Style*— Prof Peter Wells; University of Hull, School of Chemisty, Hull HU6 7RX (☎ 0482 465 660, fax 0482 466 410, telex 592530 UNIHUL G)

WELLS, Dr Peter George; s of Joseph Frederick Wells (d 1973), and Daisy Irene, *née* Sissons (d 1963); *b* 27 April 1925; *Educ* Giggleswick Sch, Univ of Sheffield (MB ChB, Dip Child Health, Dip Obstetrics, Dip Psychological Med); *m* 28 Nov 1970, (Finola) Fidelma; 1 s ((John) Oliver Lancaster b 1972), 1 da (Mary Jane b 1973); *Career* RN 1943-46, Sub Lt RNVR 1945 (midshipman 1944); conslt for adolescent psychiatric servs Mersey and NW RHAs 1970-, assoc lectr Univ of Manchester; memb: Nat Exec Assoc for Psychiatric Study of Adolescence 1978-83, Exec Ctee NW Div RCPsych 1982-86l memb BMA, MRCPsych 1971, FRCPsych 1979, MRANZCP 1981, FRANZCP 1983; *Recreations* sailing, skiing, ornithology, family history, pottering about; *Style*— Dr Peter Wells; Young Peoples Unit, Victoria Rd, Macclesfield SK10 3JS

WELLS, Prof Peter Neil Temple; s of Sydney Parker Temple Wells (d 1976), and Elizabeth Beryl Wells (d 1987); *b* 19 May 1936; *Educ* Clifton Coll Bristol, Univ of Aston (BSc), Univ of Bristol (MSc, Phd, DSc); *m* 15 Oct 1960, Valerie Elizabeth, da of Charles Edward Johnson (d 1982), of Burnham-on-Sea, Somerset; 3 s (Andrew b 1963, Alexander b 1965, Thomas b 1970) 1 da (Lucy b 1966); *Career* res asst United Bristol Hosps 1960-71, prof of med physics Univ of Wales Coll of Med (formerly Welsh Nat Sch of Med) 1978-74, area physicist (teaching) Avon AHA 1975-82, chief physicist Bristol and Weston Health Authy 1982-, hon prof in radio diagnosis Univ of Bristol 1986-, over 200 pubns on med applications of ultrasonics; former pres Br Inst of Radiology, vice pres World Fedn for Ultrasound in Med and Biology; FInstP 1970, FIEE 1978, FEng 1983, FIPSM 1988, Hon FRCR 1987; *Books* Physical Principles of Ultrasonic Diagnosis (1969), Biomedical Ultrasonics (1977); *Style*— Prof Peter Wells; Department of Medical Physics and Bioengineering, Bristol General Hospital, Bristol BS1 6SY (☎ 0272 286274)

WELLS, Prof Stanley William; s of Stanley Cecil Wells, MBE (d 1952), of Hull, and Doris, *née* Atkinson (d 1986); *b* 21 May 1930; *Educ* Kingston HS Hull, UCL (BA), The Shakespeare Inst Univ of Birmingham (PhD); *m* 23 April 1975, Susan Elizabeth, *née* Hill; 3 da (Jessica b 1977, Imogen b and d 1984, Clemency b 1985); *Career* Nat Serv RAF 1951 (invalided out); Shakespeare Inst: fell 1962-77, lectr 1962, sr lectr 1971, reader 1973-77, hon fell 1979-88; conslt in eng Wroxton Coll 1964-80, head of Shakespeare Dept OUP 1978-88, gen ed Oxford Shakespeare 1978-, sr res fell Balliol Coll Oxford 1980-88, prof of Shakespeare studies and dir Shakespeare Inst Univ of Birmingham 1988-; dir Royal Shakespeare Theatre Summer Sch 1971-, pres Shakespeare Club of Stratford-upon-Avon 1972-73; memb: Cncl Exec Royal Shakespeare Theatre 1976- (govr 1974-), Exec Ctee Shakespeare's Birthplace 1976-78 and 1988- (tstee 1975-81, 1984-, dep chm 1990-); guest lectr at Br and overseas univs, Br Acad Annual Shakespeare lectr 1987, govr King Edward VI GS for Boys 1973-77, assoc ed New Penguin Shakespeare 1967-77, ed Shakespeare Survey 1980-; author of contrib to: Shakespeare Survey, Shakespeare Quarterly, Shakespeare Jahrbuch, Theatre Notebook, Stratford-upon-Avon Studies, TLS, and others; Hon DLitt Furman Univ 1976; memb: Soc for Theatre Res 1963-, Cncl Malone Soc 1967-90; *Books* Thomas Nashe, Selected Writings (ed, 1964), A Midsummer Night's Dream (ed 1967), Richard II (ed, 1969), Shakespeare, A Reading Guide (1969 and 1970), Literature and Drama (1970), The Comedy of Errors (ed 1972), Shakespeare (ed 1973, 2 edn 1990), English Drama Excluding Shakespeare (ed 1975), Royal Shakespeare (1977 and 1978), Nineteenth Century Burlesques (compiled in 5 vols, 1977), Shakespeare: An Illustrated Dictionary (1978 and 1985), Shakespeare: The Writer and his Work (1978), Thomas Dekker, The Shoemaker's Holiday (ed, with RL Smallwood 1979), Modernizing Shakespeare's Spelling with three studies in the text of Henry V (with Gary Taylor, 1979), Re-editing Shakespeare for the Modern Reader (1984), Shakespeare's Sonnets (ed 1985), The Complete Oxford Shakespeare (ed, with Gary Taylor *et al*, 1986), The Cambridge Companion to Shakespeare Studies (ed, 1986), William Shakespeare: a textual companion (with Gary Taylor *et al*, 1987), An Oxford Anthology of Shakespeare (1987); *Recreations* music, travel; *Style*— Prof Stanley Wells; Midsummer Cottage, Church Lane, Beckley, Oxford (☎ 086735 252); 38 College St, Stratford-upon-Avon, Warwicks (☎ 0789296 047); The Shakespeare Inst, Stratford upon Avon, Warwicks (☎ 0789 293138)

WELLS, Thomas Leonard; s of Leonard Wells, and Lillian May, *née* Butler; *b* 2 May 1930; *Educ* Univ of Toronto; *m* 24 April 1954, Audrey Alice, da of Arthur C Richardson; 1 s (Andrew Thomas), 2 da (Brenda Elizabeth, Beverley Gail); *Career* advertising mangr: Canadian Hosp Jl 1951-61, Canadian Med Assoc Jl 1961-67; chm: Scarborough Ontario Bd Educn 1961 and 1962, MLA (Progressive C) Scarborough N Ontario 1963-85; min: without portfolio responsible for youth affrs 1966-69, of health 1969-71, of social and family servs 1971-72, of educn 1972-78, of intergovernmental affrs 1978-85; govt house ldr Ontario 1980-85, agent gen for Ontario in UK 1985-; *Recreations* photography, walking, theatre, cinema; *Clubs* RAC, Royal Over-Seas League, Royal Cwlth Soc, Albany and Empire (Toronto), United Wards, City Livery; *Style*— Thomas Wells, Esq; 6-12 Reeves Mews, London WIY 3PB (☎ 071 245 1222); Ontario House 21 Knightsbridge, London SWIX 7LY

WELLS, William Henry Weston; s of Sir Henry Wells, CBE (d 1970), and Rosemary Halliday, *née* Whitchurch (d 1977); *b* 3 May 1940; *Educ* Radley, Magdalene Coll Cambridge (BA); *m* 1 Jan 1966, Penelope Jean, da of Col R B Broadbent (d 1979); 3 s (Rupert d 1969, George b 1971, Henry b 1972); *Career* chm: Land and House Property Group 1977, Frincon Holdings Ltd 1977-87, Chesteron 1983-; dir London Life Assoc 1984-89; memb board of governors: Royal Free Hosp (1968-74), Camden and Islington AHA 1972-82; chm Special Tstees of the Royal Free Hosps 1979-; memb Cncl Royal Free Hosp Sch of Med 1977-; chm Hampstead Health Authy 1982-; hon treas Royal Coll of Nursing 1988-, dir AMP London Bd 1989-; FRICS; *Recreations* family, philately, gardening; *Clubs* Boodle's; *Style*— William Wells, Esq; 54 Brook St, London W1A 2BU (☎ 071 499 0404)

WELLS-PESTELL, Hon Philip Anthony; er s of Baron Wells-Pestell, CBE (Life Peer, d 17 Jan 1991), and Irene Mabel, *née* Wells (d 16 Jan 1991); *b* 31 July 1941; *Educ* City of London Sch, London Univ; *m* 1965, Holly, da of Lorne Hopkins, of Conn, USA; issue; *Style*— The Hon Philip Wells-Pestell; 7 Woodberry Avenue, Winchmore Hill, London N21

WELLWOOD, James McKinney; s of James Wellwood (d 1967), of Belfast, and Violet Armstrong McKinney (d 1978); *b* 18 Dec 1940; *Educ* Fettes, Univ of Cambridge, St Thomas' Hosp Medical Sch London; *m* 1, 8 March 1975, Frances Alexandria Ruth, da of Stephen Howard, of Hertfordshire, England; m 2, 24 July 1982, Anne Margaret, da of Sydney Jones Samuel, of Llanelli, Wales; 1 s (James b 1984), 1 da (Laura b 1988); *Career* conslt surgn Whipps Cross Hosp Leytonstone London 1979, lectr Med Coll of St Bartholomew Smithfield London 1979, clinical tutor Waltham Forest District 1983; hon overseas sec The Br Assoc of Surgical Oncology 1986- (hon sec 1982-86), Br del The European Soc of Surgical Oncology 1986-90; memb: Educn Advsy Ctee, Assoc of Surgns of GB and Ireland 1987-90, Waltham Forest DHA 1983-90; Queen's commendation for Brave Conduct (1971); *Recreations* skiing, shooting, travel; *Clubs* Athenaeum, Royal Soc of Medicine; *Style*— James Wellwood, Esq; 24 Willoughby Rd, Hampstead, London NW3 1SA (☎ 071 794 5708); Whipps Cross Hospital, Leytonstone, London E17 (☎ 081 539 5522); 134 Harley St, London W1N 1AH (☎ 071 487 4212)

WELMAN, Douglas Pole (Pat); CBE (1966); s of late Col Arthur Pole Welman, and late Lady Scott; *b* 22 June 1902; *Educ* Tonbridge, Faraday House Engrg Coll; *m* 1, 1929, Denise, da of Charles Steers Peel; 1 da; m 2, 1946, Betty Majorie, da of late Henry Huth; *Career* electrical and mechanical engr; W Indies 1928-32, Ceylon 1932-35, consulting practice 1932-38, md Forster Yates & Thom Ltd (heavy precision engrs) 1938-50; chm various wartime ctees in Lancs incl ESO and armaments prodn 1942, seconded to Miny of Aircraft Prodn as dir of engr prodn 1942, dep dir gen 1943, control of directorate gen (incl propellor and accessory prodn) 1944; chm NW Gas Bd 1950-64 (pt/t memb 1949), memb Gas Cncl 1950-67, chm Southern Gas Bd 1964-67; chm and md Allspeeds Hldgs Ltd 1967-72; memb Ct of Govrs UMIST of Sci and Technol 1956-64 and 1968-72 (cncl memb 1960-64 and 1968-72); DFM, CStJ 1968 (OStJ 1964); author of articles and papers on company mgmnt; FIMechE, FIEE, FRSA; *Recreations* Royal Thames Yacht; *Style*— D.P. Welman, Esq, CBE; 11 St Michael's Gardens, St Cross, Winchester SO23 9JD (☎ 0962 868091)

WELSBY, John Kay; *b* 26 May 1938; *Educ* Exeter Univ (BA), London Univ (MSc); *Career* BR: dir Prov Services 1981-83, dir Mfrg and Maintenance Policy 1984-86, md Procurement and Special Projects 1986-87; bd memb BR Bd 1987; *Style*— John Welsby, Esq; British Railways Board, Euston House, 24 Eversholt St, London NW1 1DZ (☎ 071 922 6928)

WELSBY, Dr Paul Antony; *b* 18 Aug 1920; *Educ* Alcester GS, Univ of Durham (MA), Lincoln Theol Coll, Univ of Sheffield (PhD); *m* 1948, Cynthia Mary Hosmer; 1 da (Rosamund); *Career* curate: Boxley Kent 1944-47, St Mary-le-Tower Ipswich 1947-52; rector Copdock with Washbrook Suffolk 1952-66, rural dean Samford 1964-66, canon residentiary of Rochester Cathedral 1966-88, dir post-ordination training for diocese of Rochester 1966-88, examining chaplain to Bishop of Rochester 1966-88, canon emeritus Rochester Cathedral 1988-, personal chaplain to Bishop of Rochester 1988-90; memb: Church Assembly 1964-70, Gen Synod 1970-80; chm House of Clergy of Gen Synod, prolocutor of Convocation of Canterbury 1974-80; chaplain to HM The Queen 1980-90; former chm City of Rochester Soc; *Books* A Modern Catechism (1956), Lancelot Andrewes (1958), The Unwanted Archbishop: Life of George Abbot (1962), The Bond of Church and State (1962), Sermons and Society (1970), A History of the Church of England 1945-80 (1984), How the Church of England Works (1985); *Recreations* reading detective fiction, genealogy; *Style*— The Rev Canon Dr Paul Welsby; 20 Knights Ridge, Pembury, Tunbridge Wells, Kent TN2 4HP (☎ 089 282 3053)

WELSH, Andrew Paton; MP (SNP) Angus E 1987-; s of William Welsh (d 1979), and Agnes Paton, *née* Reid (d 1977); *b* 19 April 1944; *Educ* Univ of Glasgow (MA, Dip Ed); *m* 1971, Sheena Margaret, da of Douglas Henry Cannon (d 1972); 1 da (Jane b 1980); *Career* contested Dumbarton Central 1974, Stirling dist cncllr 1974, MP (SNP) Angus S 1974-79, chief whip 1978-79; spokesman on: housing and agric 1974-79, small businesses and self employment 1975-79; sr lectr business studies and public admin Dundee Coll of Commerce and Angus Coll of Further Educn; provost Angus Dist Cncl 1984-87, chief SNP whip 1987; SNP exec vice chm: admin 1979-82, local govt 1983-86; SNP vice pres 1987-; *Recreations* music, horseriding, languages; *Style*— Andrew Welsh, Esq, MP; 22 Monymusk Rd, Arbroath DD11 2DB; House of Commons, London SW1A 0AA

WELSH, Frank Reeson; s of Francis Cox Welsh (d 1974), of Westmorland, and Doris (Reeson) Ibbet; *b* 16 Aug 1931; *Educ* Blaydon GS, Magdalene Coll Cambridge (MA); *m* 1954, Agnes, da of John Embleton Cowley, OBE, of Co Durham; 2 s (Benjamin, John), 2 da (Jane, Sophie); *Career* dir: William Brandts Sons 1965-72, Grindlays Bank 1972-85, The Trireme Trust 1983-; chm: Cox & Kings 1972-77, Jensen Motors, Hadfields, Robey of Lincoln 1967-78, The London Industl Assoc 1984-88; memb: Royal Cmmn on the Nat Health Service, Br Waterways Bd, Gen Advsy Cncl of the IBA, Health Educn Cncl; *Books* The Profit of the State (1982), The Afflicted State (1983), First Blood (1985), Bend'or (with George Ridley, 1985), Uneasy City (1987), Building the Trireme (1988), Companion Guide to the Lake District (1989); *Recreations* sailing (yacht 'Remercie'), building triremes; *Clubs* Savile, Utd Oxford and Cambridge; *Style*— Frank Welsh Esq; Le Logis de Lizant, 86400, France

WELSH, Michael Collins; MP (Lab) Doncaster N 1983-; s of Danny Welsh, and Winnie Welsh; *b* 23 Nov 1926; *Educ* Univ of Sheffield, Ruskin Coll Oxford; *m* 1950, Brenda Nicholson, 2 s; *Career* miner, memb Doncaster Cncl 1962-, MP (Lab) Don Valley 1979-83 and 1987-, sponsored by NUM; *Style*— Michael Welsh, Esq, MP; House of Commons, London SW1A 0AA

WELSH, Michael John; MEP (EDG) Lancs Central 1979-; s of Cdr David Welsh, RN; *b* 22 May 1942; *Educ* Dover Coll, Lincoln Coll Oxford; *m* 1963, Jennifer Pollitt; 1 s, 1 da; *Career* formerly with Levi Strauss & Co Europe (dir mkt devpt 1976), non-exec dir Initial 1982-89; chm Positive Euro Gp; *Books* Labour Market Policy In The European Community - The British Presidency (1987), Collective Security - The European Community and the Preservation of Peace (1988), German Unification - The Challenge of Assimilation (1990), Accountability - The Role of Westminster and the European Institutions (1990); *Clubs* Carlton; *Style*— Michael Welsh, Esq, MEP; Watercrook, 181 Town Lane, Whittle le Woods, Chorley, Lancs (☎ 025 72 76992)

WELSH, Maj-Gen Peter Miles; OBE (1973), MC (1966); s of Brig William Miles Moss O'Donnell Welsh, DSO, MC (d 1965), of Lismore, Sonning, Berks, and Mary Margaret Edith Gertrude Louise, *née* Hearn; *b* 23 Dec 1930; *Educ* Winchester, RMA Sandhurst; *m* 1974, June Patricia, da of Francis MacAdam, of Buenos Aires, Argentina, widow of M E McCausland; 2 step s, 1 step da; *Career* Army Offr; directing staff Staff Coll 1968-71, CO 2 Royal Green Jackets 1971-74, cmd 5 Inf Bde 1974-76, RCDS 1977, BGS HQ BAOR 1978-80, Brig Lt Div 1980-83, pres Regular Cmmns Bd 1983-85; *Recreations* golf, shooting; *Clubs* MCC, I-Zingari, Free Foresters, Berks Golf; *Style—* Maj-Gen Peter Welsh, OBE, MC; c/o Lloyds Bank, Maidenhead, Berks

WELTON, Hon Mrs (Kirstin Elizabeth); *née* Lowther; da of late Lt John Arthur Lowther, MVO, RNVR, gs of 1 Viscount Ullswater; sister of 2 Viscount Ullswater; raised to the rank of a Viscount's da 1951; *b* 1939; *m* 1, 1966, Capt Caledon Alexander, late 7 Queen's Own Hussars; 1 s, 1 da; m 2, 1976, Antony Edward Ord Welton; *Style—* The Hon Mrs Welton; Willowbrook House, Lower Dean, North Leach, Glos

WEMYSS, Rear Adm Martin La Touche; CB (1981); s of Cdr David Edward Gillespie Wemyss, DSO, DSC, RN, of Luthrie Fife (d 1989), and Edith Mary (d 1930); *b* 5 Dec 1927; *Educ* Shrewsbury; *m* 1 (m dis), Ann Hall; 1 s, 1 da; m 2, 1973, Elizabeth Loveday, da of Col Robert Harper Alexander, RAMC, of Kingston Gorse, Sussex (d 1969); 1 s, 1 da; *Career* Cmdg Offr: HMS Sentinel, HMS Alliance, Submarine COs Qualifying Course, HMS Norfolk, 3 Submarine Sqdn; Dir Naval Warfare 1974-76, Flag Offr Second Flotilla 1977-78, Rear Adm 1977, asst chief of Naval Staff (Ops) 1979-81; Clerk Worshipful Co of Brewers 1981; *Recreations* sailing, shooting, gardening; *Clubs* White's, Army & Navy; *Style—* Rear-Adm Martin Wemyss, CB; The Old Post House, Emberton, nr Olney, Bucks MK46 5BX (☎ 0234 713838); Brewers' Hall, Aldermanbury Sq, London EC2 (☎ 071 606 1301)

WEMYSS, Lady Victoria Alexandrina Violet; *née* Cavendish-Bentinck; CVO (1953); da of 6 Duke of Portland, KG, GCVO, TD, PC (d 1943); *b* 1890; *m* 1918, Capt Michael John Wemyss, late Household Cavalry; *Career* appointed an extra woman of the bedchamber to HM Queen Elizabeth, the Queen Mother 1937; *Style—* The Lady Victoria Wemyss, CVO; Wemyss Castle, East Wemyss, Fife

WEMYSS AND MARCH, 12 (and 8) Earl of (S 1633 & 1697); Francis David Charteris; KT (1966), JP (E Lothian); also Lord Wemyss of Elcho (S 1628), Lord Elcho and Methil (S 1633), Viscount Peebles, Lord Douglas of Neidpath, Lyne, and Munard (S 1697), and Baron Wemyss of Wemyss (UK 1821); s of Lord Elcho (ka 1916, s and h of 11 Earl, but predeceased him) and Lady Violet Manners (d 1971), 2 da of 8 Duke of Rutland; suc gf 1937; *b* 19 Jan 1912; *Educ* Eton, Balliol Coll Oxford, Trinity Coll Cambridge; *m* 24 Feb 1940, Mavis Lynete Gordon (d 1988), er da of Edwin Edward Murray, of Cape Province, SA; 1 s, 1 da (and 1 s, 1 da decd); *Heir* s, Lord Neidpath; *Career* Basutoland Admin Serv 1937-44 (war serv with Basuto troops ME 1941-44); landowner; former dir: Standard Life Assur, STV; conslt Wemyss and March Estate Mgmnt Co Ltd; chm Royal Cmmn on Ancient and Hist Monuments and Constructions of Scotland 1949-84, Lord High Cmmr to Gen Assembly of Church of Scotland 1959, 1960 and 1977, pres Nat Bible Soc of Scotland 1962-83, Lord Lt E Lothian 1976-87, pres Nat Tst for Scotland 1967-91, Lord Clerk Register of Scotland and Keeper of the Signet 1974-, Ensign Royal Co of Archers (Queen's Bodyguard for Scotland), hon pres The Thistle Fndn; Hon LLD St Andrews 1953, Hon DUniv Edinburgh 1983; *Clubs* New (Edinburgh); *Style—* The Rt Hon the Earl of Wemyss and March, KT, LLD, JP; Gosford House, Longniddry, East Lothian (☎ 087 57 200/389)

WEMYSS OF WEMYSS, Lady Jean Christian; *née* Bruce; da of late 10 Earl of Elgin and (14 of) Kincardine, KT, CMG, TD, CD, and Hon Dame Katherine Cochrane, DBE, da of late 1 Baron Cochrane of Cults and Lady Gertrude Boyle, OBE, da of 6 Earl of Glasgow; *b* 1923; *m* 1945, Capt David Wemyss of Wemyss, late Royal Corps of Signals; 2 s; *Career* formerly in WAAF; *Style—* The Lady Jean Wemyss of Wemyss; Invermay, Forteviot, Perthshire (☎ 0764 84276)

WEN, Eric Lewis; s of Adam Kung Wen, of California, and Mimi, *née* Seetoo; *b* 18 May 1953; *Educ* Dalton Sch, Columbia Univ (BA), Yale Univ (MPhil), Churchill Coll Cambridge (res award); *m* 3 June 1989, Louise Anne, da of Brian Leon Barder; 1 da (Lily Havala b 5 Nov 1990); *Career* lectr in music: Yale Univ 1977-78, Guildhall Sch of Music and Drama 1978-84, Goldsmith's Coll London 1980-84, Mannes Coll of Music 1984-86; ed The Musical Times 1988-90 (The Strad 1986-89), md Biddulph Recordings and Publishing 1990-; *Books* Schenker Studies (contrib, 1990), Trends in Schenkerian Research (contrib, 1990); *Recreations* chess, cookery, film, magic; *Style—* Eric Wen, Esq; 35 St George St, Hanover Square, London W1R 9FA (☎ 071 491 8621, fax 071 495 1428)

WENNIKE, Helge; *b* 10 Nov 1944; *Educ* Commercial Coll Copenhagen; *m* 17 Feb 1973, Grete Else-Marie; 1 s (Nicolai b 1973), 1 da (Anne-Marie b 1976); *Career* mangr Privatbanken until 1978; md: RB-Banken 1978-80, Finansbank 1980-81, Jyske Bank 1981-84; dep md Scandinavian Bank Group plc 1984-90, SVP Skandinaviska Enskilda Banken 1990-; *Recreations* golf, tennis; *Clubs* RAC; *Style—* Helge Wennike, Esq; 10a Pelhams Walk, Esher, Surrey (☎ 0372 4674 53); 2/6 Cannon St, London EC4M 6XX (☎ 071 588 3494, fax 071 588 0929)

WENSLEY, Dr Richard Thomas; s of Thomas Henry Wensley (d 1984), of Liverpool, and Florence Caroline, *née* Palmer; *b* 15 Oct 1939; *Educ* Merchant Taylors Sch Crosby, Univ of Liverpool (MB ChB); *m* 24 Aug 1963, (Juliet) Patricia, da of James Ahearn (d 1972), of Cork, Ireland; 1 s (Richard James b 1966), 3 da (Carolyn Anne b 1964, Susan Kathrine b 1965, Gillian Elizabeth b 1969); *Career* sr registrar in haematology Bristol Royal Infirmary 1969-74, dir regnl haemophilia centre Manchester Royal Infirmary 1979- (conslt haematologist 1974-); numerous papers published and presented at Int Congress on Haemophilia; memb: Br Soc of Haematology, NW Regnl Advsy Ctee on AIDS; MRCPath 1970, MRCP 1973, FRCPath 1982; *Recreations* playing classical piano music, cooking exotic cuisine; *Style—* Dr Richard Wensley; 15 Cherington Rd, Cheadle, Gtr Manchester SK8 1LN (☎ 061 491 1286); Dept of Haematology, The Manchester Clinic, B Floor, Manchester Royal Infirmary, Oxford Rd, Manchester M13 9WL (☎ 061 276 4812)

WENSLEY, Prof (John) Robin Clifton; s of Maj George Leonard, of Cambridge, and Jeanette Marion, *née* Robbins; *b* 26 Oct 1944; *Educ* Perse Sch Cambridge, Univ of Cambridge (BA), London Business Sch (MSc, PhD); *m* 19 Dec 1970, Susan Patricia, da of Kenneth Royden Horner (d 1975); 1 s (Benjamin Royden b 1978), 2 da (Helen Rebecca b 1973, Ruth Elizabeth b 1975); *Career* brand mangr Ranks Hovis McDougal 1966-69 (former PA), conslt Tube Investments Ltd 1971-73, asst dir of Studies Ashridge Coll 1973-74, sr lectr London Business Sch 1974-85 (former lectr), chm Warwick Business Sch 1989- (prof 1985-), dir BRL Ltd 1987-; memb exec UK Mktg Educn Gp; *Books* Marketing Strategy: Planning, Implementation and Control (1986), Readings in Marketing Strategy (1989), Interface of Marketing and Strategy (1990); *Recreations* badminton, gardening, DIY; *Style—* Prof Robin Wensley; 147 Leam Terrace, Leamington Spa, Warwicks CV31 1DF (☎ 0926 425022); Warwick Business Sch, Univ of Warwick, Coventry CV4 7AL (☎ 0203 523923, fax 0203 523719, telex 317472)

WENT, David; s of Arthur Edward James Went (d 1980), of Dublin, and Phyllis, *née* Howell (d 1980); *b* 25 March 1947; *Educ* High Sch Dublin, Trinity Coll Dublin (BA, LLB); *m* 4 Nov 1972, Mary, da of Jack Milligan (d 1972), of Belfast; 1 s (James b 1976), 1 da (Kate b 1978); *Career* barr King's Inn Dublin; gen mangr Citibank Dublin 1974 (Jeddah 1975), banking dir Ulster Investment Bank Dublin 1976 (chief exec 1982), chief exec Ulster Bank 1988-; FIBI 1978; *Recreations* tennis, reading; *Clubs* Royal Belfast Golf, Royal Monte Yacht, Reform, University; *Style—* David Went, Esq; c/o Ulster Bank, Belfast, NI

WENT, Janice; da of Arthur Edward James Went (d 1980), of Dublin, and Phyllis Nelly, *née* Howell (d 1980); *b* 20 June 1939; *Educ* Univ of Dublin (MB BCh, BAO), Univ of Birmingham (MSc); *Career* conslt chem pathologist Plymouth Health Dist 1971-; FRCPath 1982; *Recreations* hill walking, cross country skiing; *Style—* Janice Went; Dept of Clinical Chemistry, Derriford Hospital, Plymouth PL6 8DH (☎ 0752 792291)

WENT, Ven John Stewart; s of Douglas Norman Went (d 1970), and Barbara Adelaide, *née* Rand; *b* 11 March 1944; *Educ* Colchester Royal GS, Corpus Christi Coll Cambridge; *m* 31 Aug 1968, Rosemary Evelyn Amy, da of late Peter Dunn; 3 s (Simon Charles b 28 June 1970, David James b 12 August 1972, Matthew John b 2 June 1975); *Career* asst curate Emmanuel Northwood Middx 1969-75, vicar Holy Trinity Margate Kent 1975-83, vice princ Wycliffe Hall Theol Coll 1983-89, archdeacon of Surrey 1989-; memb Ecclesiastical Law Soc 1989, chm Guildford Diocese DCMU; *Recreations* music, photography, walking; *Style—* The Ven the Archdeacon of Surrey; Tarawera, 71 Boundstone Rd, Rowledge, Farnham, Surrey GU10 4AT (☎ 025 125 3987)

WENTWORTH, Stephen; s of Ronald Wentworth, OBE (d 1983), of London, and Elizabeth Mary, *née* Collins (d 1967); *b* 23 Aug 1943; *Educ* King's Coll Sch Wimbledon, Merton Coll Oxford (MA, MSc); *m* 9 May 1970, Katharine Laura, da of Rev Arthur John Hopkinson, CIE (d 1953), of, Aislaby, N Yorks; 3 da; *Career* Civil Serv: princ MAFF 1970-78 (asst princ 1967-70), on loan to Civil Serv Selection Bd 1974-75, Personnel Div MAFF 1975-76, on loan to HM Dip Serv as first sec (agric), Office of the UK Perm Rep to the Euro Communities Brussels 1976-78, asst sec head of Beef Div MAFF 1978-80, seconded Cabinet Off 1980-82, head of Milk Div MAFF 1982-85, head of Euro Communities Div 1985-86, promoted grade 3 head of meat gp 1986-89, head of livestock products gp 1989; *Style—* Stephen Wentworth, Esq; Ministry of Agriculture Fisheries and Food, Whitehall Place, London SW1A 2HH

WENTWORTH PING, (William) Hugh; s of Capt Andrew Wentworth Ping (d 1973), of York, and Anne Margaret, *née* Varley (d 1977); *b* 7 June 1924; *Educ* St Peters Sch York, Leeds Coll of Commerce, Sheffield Univ Business Sch, Henley Staff Coll; *m* 7 July 1956, (Joan) Carol, da of Carl Eric Holmstrom (d 1968), of Sheffield; 2 s (Jonathan b 25 Sept 1957, Richard b 3 July 1959); *Career* WWII RNVR 1942-47; served on: HMS Thruster, HMS Lizard, HMS Saunders; ranks: Ordinary Seaman, Able Seaman, Midshipman, Sub-Lt, Lt Staff Offr to C-in-C Mediterranean 1946-47; Lt RNR Humber Div 1947-59; Firth-Vickers Stainless Steels Ltd Sheffield 1948-70: sales rep, asst publicity mangr, sales devpt mangr, special dir (sales); commercial dir PI Castings Ltd 1970-72, commercial mangr British Steel Corporation (forges foundries and engrg) 1973-82, conslt Technical Commercial Intertrade Ltd 1989- (commercial mangr 1983-89); memb Sheffield C of C 1956-70, dist cmmr Scouts 1961-66; chm: Sheffield Croft House Boxing Club 1966-70, Sheffield Sea Cadets 1979-85, Conservation Sheffield Heritage Ltd 1989-, Sheriffs Millenium (1992) Ltd 1989-; rep GB World Bobsleigh Championships 1955; High Sheriff South Yorks 1988-89; Freeman Worshipful Co of Cutlers in Hallamshire (1961); *Recreations* golf, riding, advanced motor cycling, vintage cars, stamps, winter sports; *Clubs* Sickleholme, St Moritz Tobogganing, Shrievalty; *Style—* Hugh Wentworth Ping, Esq; Nicholas Hall, Thornhill, Bamford, Sheffield S30 2BR (☎ 0433 51403, fax 0433 50055); Business Innovation Centre, Innovation Way, Barnsley S75 1JL (☎ 0226 249590, fax 0226 249629, telex 84687 BBIC)

WENTWORTH-STANLEY, (David) Michael; s of Geoffrey David Wentworth-Stanley, and Bridget, *née* Pease; *b* 29 Feb 1952; *Educ* Eton; *m* 7 Oct 1975, Jane, da of Col Tom Hall, OBE; 3 da (Laura b 12 Dec 1978, Emma b 28 May 1981, Harriet b 7 Aug 1985); *Career* CA 1974; Cazenove Inc NY 1981-83, ptnr Cazenove & Co 1982- (joined 1975); ACA 1974, FCA 1979; *Recreations* countryside, gardening, skiing; *Clubs* White's; *Style—* Michael Wentworth-Stanley, Esq; 41 Old Church St, London SW3 5BS (☎ 071 352 3419); 12 Tokenhouse Yard, London EC2R 7AN (☎ 071 588 2828)

WENTZELL, Pamela; *née* Moran; da of Herbert Thomas Moran, of London, and Teresa McDaid, *née* Conway; *b* 3 Feb 1950; *Educ* Pitman's Sch Ealing, Marlborough Coll London; *m* 18 Oct 1969, Christopher John, s of Charles John Wentzell, of Gurnard, IOW; *Career* md JP Communicators Ltd PR Consultancy 1980-; former chm Southampton Publicity Assoc 1985-86; MIPR 1980, FInstD 1989; *Recreations* theatre going, classical music, gardening; *Style—* Mrs Pamela Wentzell; Roke Hollow, Woodington Lane, East Wellow, Hampshire (☎ 0794 517583); Bedford House, 81 Bedford Place, Southampton SO1 2DF (☎ 0703 632738, fax 0703 332283)

WERNICK, Joseph; s of Samuel Wernick (d 1967), and Bertha Wernick (d 1955); *b* 28 Aug 1920; *Educ* Wolverhampton Municipal GS, Wolverhampton & Staffs Tech Coll, Licentiate Inst of Technol; *m* 22 Aug 1942, Eileen, da of Harold Berry (d 1976); 3 s (Andrew b 1945, Julian b 1950, Simon b 1952); *Career* Capt RE BAOR 1945-47; chm and jt md Wernick Gp of Companies, pres Birmingham Progressive Synagogue 1982-85; magistrate Wolverhampton; chm Wolverhampton S Lib Assoc 1970-73 and 1987-; Parly candidate: (Lib) Wolverhampton SW Feb 1974, Oct 1974, 1979, and as (Alliance) Wolverhampton SE 1983; *Recreations* bridge, foreign travel, music, tennis (ex); *Clubs* Tettenhall Bridge, Wolverhampton Lawn Tennis, Squash; *Style—* Joseph Wernick, Esq; 39 Newbridge Cres, Wolverhampton, W Midlands WV6 0LH; S Wernick & Sons Ltd, Lindon Rd, Brownhills, Walsall, W Midlands (☎ 0543 3742)

WERNICK, Lionel Rufus; s of Samuel Wernick (d 1967); *b* 6 Nov 1928; *Educ* Wolverhampton Municipal GS, Univ of London; *m* 1955, Sheila Faye, *née* Lambert; 4 children; *Career* former Lt Royal Signal Corps; chm & md The Wernick Group, Lloyd's underwriter; memb Cncl Nat Prefabricated Bldg Assoc Ltd; chm: Essex Ctee The Royal Jubilee and Prince's Tst, Essex Bd Prince's Youth Business Tst; Liveryman Worshipful Co of Wheelwrights, Freeman City of London; *Recreations* bridge, travel, opera, spectator sports; *Style—* Lionel Wernick, Esq; The Lyches, Greenway, Hutton, Brentwood, Essex (☎ 0277 220535)

WESCHKE, Karl Martin; *b* 7 June 1925; *m* 1, 1948 (m dis 1957), Alison de Vere; 2 s (Benjamin, Lucas), 2 da (Lore, Rachel); m 2, 1963 (m dis 1968), Liese Dennis; *Career* artist and art lectr, came to Britain as POW 1948; one man exhibitions incl: New Vision Centre Gallery London 1958, Woodstock Gallery London 1959, Matthiesen Gallery London 1960, Arnolfi Gallery Bristol 1964 and 1968, Grosvenor Gallery London 1964, Dartington Hall 1968, Bear Lane Gallery Oxford 1971, travelling exhibition 1971-72, Kettle's Yard Cambridge 1980, Moira Kelly Fine Arts London 1981, Redfern Gallery 1984, 1987, 1989; retrospective exhibitions: Whitechapel Art Gallery 1974, Newlyn Art Gallery Penzance 1974, travelling exhibition 1980-81; contrib to numerous major mixed exhibitions of Br art 1959-: UK, USA, Asia, Germany, Austria; works in public collections incl: Arts Cncl of GB, City Art Gallery Bristol, Central Selling Orgn, Contemporary Art Soc London, Cornwall Educn Ctee, Ferens Art Gallery Hull, Govt Art Collection, City Art Gallery Plymouth, Tate Gallery

London, Nat Museum of Wales Cardiff, Baltimore Museum of Art Maryland (Print Collection), Museum of Modern Art NY (Print Collection), Nat Gallery of Victoria Melbourne, Art Gallery of NSW Sydney; awards incl: Arts Cncl of GB Major award 1976, S W Arts Major award 1978, prizewinner John Moores Exhibition 1978, Arts Cncl of GB Purchase award 1980; *Style*— Karl Weschke, Esq; Ruston, Cap Cornwall, St Just, Penzance, Cornwall TR19 7NL; Redfern Gallery Ltd, 20 Cork St, London W1X 2HL

WESKER, Arnold; s of Joseph Wesker (d 1959), and Leah, *née* Perlmutter (d 1976); *b* 24 May 1932; *Educ* Upton House Central Sch Hackney; *m* 1958, Doreen Cecile, da of Edwin Bicker, of Norfolk; 2 s (Daniel, Lindsay Joe), 2 da (Tanya Jo, Elsa Sarah); *Career* Nat Serv RAF 1950-52 (material gathered for later play Chips with Everything); various positions Norfolk 1952-54 incl: seed sorter, farm labourer, kitchen porter; trained pastry cook London and Paris 1954-56, awarded Arts Cncl grant 1958; playwright and dir; chm Br Centre of Int Theatre Inst 1978-83, pres Int Playwrights' Ctee 1981-83; 28 stage plays incl: The Kitchen (1957), Chicken Soup with Barley (1958), Roots (1959), Chips with Everything (1962), The Four Seasons (1965), The Old Ones (1970), The Journalists (1972), The Wedding Feast (1974), One More Ride on the Merry-Go-Round (1978), Caritas (1980), Anne Wobbler (1982), Yarsdale (1983), When God wanted a Son (1986), The Mistress (1988), When God Wanted a Son (1989), Shylock (1989), Shoeshine (1989), Letter To A Daughter (1990); radio, film and tv plays incl: Menace (1971), The Wesker Trilogy (19740, Breakfast (1981), Bluey (1984), Thieves in the Night (4 part adaptation of Arthur Koestler's novel, 1984-85), Caritas (libretto for opera, 1988); stories, essays and other writings incl: Six Sundays in January (1971), Love Letters on Blue Paper (1974), Fatlips (1978), Distinctions (1985), A Mini-biography (1988); plays directed incl: The Four Seasons (Havana, 1968), The Old Ones (Munich, 1973), The Entertainer (1983), Yarsdale (1985 and 1987), The Merry Wives of Windsor (Oslo 1990); Hon DLitt UEA 1989; FRSL; *Style*— Arnold Wesker, Esq; 37 Ashley Rd, London N19 3AG (☎ 071 272 0034); Nat Westminster Bank plc, 298 Seven Sisters Rd, London N4 2AF

WESLEY, (Mary Siepmann); da of Col H M Farmar, CMG, DSO (d 1958), of Yarmouth, IOW, and Violet Dalby (d 1972); *b* 24 June 1912; *Educ* at home by foreign governesses, finishing sch Paris, LSE; *m* 1, 1937 (m dis 1945), Lord Swinfen; 2 s (Roger (now Lord Swinfen), Hon Toby Eady); m 2, 1952, Eric Siepmann, s of Otto Siepmann, of Clifton, Bristol; 1 s (William b 1953); *Career* writer; books incl: Speaking Terms (for children, 1968), The Sixth Seal (for children, 1968), Haphazard House (for children, 1983), Jumping the Queue (1983), The Camomile Lawn (1984), Harnessing Peacocks (1985), The Vacillations of Poppy Carew (1986), Not That Sort of Girl (1987), Second Fiddle (1988), A Sensible Life (1990); *Recreations* reading; *Style*— Mrs Mary Wesley; c/o Tessa Sayle, 11 Jubilee Place, London SH3 3TE (☎ 071 823 3883)

WEST; *see*: Granville-West

WEST; *see*: Alston-Roberts-West

WEST, Brian John; s of Herbert Frank West, and Nellie, *née* Painter; *b* 4 Aug 1935; *Educ* Tiffin Sch Kingston-upon-Thames; *m* 2 April 1960 (m dis 1986), Patricia Ivy, da of Reginald White (d 1985), of Old Windsor, Berks; 2 s (Nicholas Guy b 7 July 1962, Jason Philip b 12 July 1966); m 2, 11 April 1987, Gillian, da of Anthony Bond (d 1984), of Flint, Clwyd; *Career* Sub Lt (O) Fleet Air Arm RN 1956-58; journalist 1952-60: Richmond Herald, Surrey Comet, Western Morning News; ed: Surrey Comet 1964-70 (asst ed 1960-64), Leicester Mercury 1970-74; head of advtg and PR Littlewoods Organisation plc 1974-83, dir AIRC 1983-88, dir and chief exec AIRC/RMB 1988-; govr Communications Advtg and Mktg Fndn 1983-; memb Cncl: Radio Acad 1985-, Advtg Assoc 1987-; *Recreations* walking, gardening, photography, music; *Style*— Brian West, Esq; Assoc of Ind Radio Contractors Ltd, Radio Hse, 46 Westbourne Grove, London W2 5SH (☎ 071 727 2646 fax 071 229 0352 telex 24543)

WEST, Christopher John Rodney; s of Norman (Peter) Hartley West (d 1963), of Rio de Janeiro, Brasil, and Epsom, and Lucy Catherine West, *née* Skey (d 1962); *b* 6 April 1932; *Educ* St George's Coll Buenos Aires Argentina, Haileybury, UCL (BSc); *m* 31 March 1956, Patricia Anne, da of Kenneth Arthur Alexander Neilson (d 1972); 1 da (Helen b 1958), 2 s (Martin b 1960, Ian b 1964); *Career* Nat Serv Sub Lt RNVR; indust career plant mangr in ICI Plastics Div and Br Visqueen Ltd 1955-68, gen mgmnt BOC Gases Div 1968-71, Courteny Mgmnt Selection consultant; chm Assoc for Marriage Enrichment (a registered charity); *Recreations* sailing, walking; *Clubs* Naval; *Style*— Christopher West, Esq; Courtenay, 3 Hanover Sq, London W1R 9OAT (☎ 071 491 4014, fax 071 491 4014 ext 10)

WEST, Prof David Richard Frederick; s of Sydney West (d 1990), and Frederica May, *née* Horsman (d 1986); *b* 7 March 1926; *Educ* Bromley County Sch, Univ Coll Cardiff (BSc), Imperial Coll London (PhD, DIC, DSc); *m* 23 June 1951, Phyllis Edith, da of Robert Wade (d 1956), of Bromley, Kent; 2 s (Peter Robert b 1954, Michael John b 1964), 1 da (Elisabeth Susan b 1957); *Career* scientific offr MOS 1949-50; Imperial Coll: lectr 1950-63, sr lectr 1963-70, reader 1970-86, sr tutor metallurgy and materials 1966-, memb Governing Body 1981-89, prof physical metallurgy 1986; vice pres Inst of Metals (memb Cncl, chm Materials Sci Div); memb Rochester Diocesan Synod, lay chm Bromley Deanery Synod; FIM 1978, CEng 1978; *Books* Ternary Equilibrium Diagrams (1982); *Recreations* music, reading; *Style*— Prof David West

WEST, Denison Hayton; s of George Stephen West (d 1918), of Univ of Birmingham, and Minnie Bullock, *née* Pratt (d 1972); *b* 12 June 1914; *Educ* St Peter's York, St John's Coll Oxford (MA); *m* 11 Nov 1944, Sheila, da of Wilfrid Allport (d 1950); 3 da (Jane b 1947, Phillipa b 1949, Jill b 1951); *Career* WWII Maj 7 Ghurka Rifles IA, NW Frontier and Burma; dir Forestry Grosvenor Estates 1966; FICFor; *Recreations* fishing, golf; *Clubs* Farmers'; *Style*— Denison West, Esq; The Kennels, Belgrave, Chester CH4 9DF (☎ 0244 671555)

WEST, Prof John Clifford; CBE (1977); s of John Herbert West (d 1958), of Hindley, Lancs, and Ada, *née* Ascroft (d 1984); *b* 4 June 1922; *Educ* Hindley and Abram GS, Univ of Manchester (BSc, PhD, DSc); *m* 7 Jan 1946, Winefride Mary, da of Francis Herbert Turner, of Blackpool, Lancs (d 1973); 3 da (Angela b 1946, Julia b 1951, Clare b 1960); *Career* Nat Serv, Electrical Lt Anti-Submarine Warfare Branch RNVR 1943-46; lectr Univ of Manchester 1946-57, prof electrical engrg Queen's Univ Belfast 1958-65, dean of applied sciences Univ of Sussex 1965-78, vice chancellor Univ of Bradford 1979-89, pres IEE 1984-85; chm: Civil Serv Cmmn Special Merit Promotions Panel 1966-72, Crawford Cmmn on Broadcasting Coverage 1973-74, Cncl for Educnl Technol 1980-85, Asian Inst of Business Bradford 1987-89; memb: Int Review Cmmn Univ of Botswana 1989, UGC 1973-78; Hon DSc Univ of Sussex 1988, Hon DUniv Bradford 1989; FIEE 1962, FRPSL 1970, FEng 1983, FInstMC 1984, FRGS 1988; *Books* Servomechanisms (1953), Analytical Techniques for Non-Linear Control Systems (1960); *Recreations* philately; *Clubs* Athenaeum, Cwlth Tst; *Style*— Prof John C West, CBE; 6 Park Crescent, Guiseley, Leeds LS20 8EL (☎ 0943 72605); 11 Windlesham Hall, Windlesham Ave, Brighton BN1 3AH (☎ 0273 726913)

WEST, (Sidney) John; s of Robert Osborne West (d 1964), of Willowhurst, Earith, Huntingdonshire, and Rose Emma, *née* French (d 1964); *b* 4 Oct 1918; *Educ* Kingswood Sch Bath; *m* 27 April 1946, Lorna Marion, da of Harry Cecil Cooper (d 1971), of The Mill House, Unstone, nr Sheffield; 2 s (Stephen John b 1956, Peter James b 1959), 3 da (Jane b 1947, Mary b 1949, Sarah b 1952); *Career* War Serv 1939-46, 104 (Essex Yeo) Regt RHA TA, Br Military Mission Pretoria; RA HAA: TA Service 1948-55, 482 (M) HAA Regt RA (Maj 1954); TA Reserve of Offrs 1957-; Barclays Bank Ltd: joined 1935, mangr Framlingham 1961-64, mangr Colchester 1964-68, local dir Exeter Dist 1968-80; chm Dartington & Co Ltd 1984-90 (dir 1980-); pres Inst of Bankers: local centre Ipswich 1956, local centre Exeter 1972; dir Exeter City AFC Ltd 1978-83, chm Exeter and Dist C of C 1972, FCIB 1962; *Recreations* gardening (memb Nat Gardens Scheme); *Style*— John West, Esq; The Glebe House, Whitestone, nr Exeter, Devon EX4 2LF (☎ 0392 81 200); Dartington & Co Ltd, Rockeagle House, Pynes Hill, Rydan Lane, Exeter EX2 5AZ (☎ 0392 410 599, fax 0392 411 135)

WEST, Kenneth; s of Albert West of Barlby, Selby (d 1978); *b* 1 Sept 1930; *Educ* Archbishop Holgate's GS, Univ Coll Oxford; *m* 1, 1957 (m dis 1982), Doreen Isabel; 3 da; m 2, 1982, Elizabeth Ann Borland; 1 s; *Career* Corpl REME; chemist; dir: South African Nylon Spinners 1976-83, Fiber Industries Inc USA 1977-83, Seahorse Int 1985-, ICI Fibres 1978-83; md Thomas Water 1983-85; chm: Harrogate WEA 1960-67, Granby HS PTA 1973-81; govr: Granby HS 1980-83, RNLI; CChem, FRSC; *Recreations* flying (pilot), sailing (yacht 'Indemood Again'), theatre (producing), violin playing; *Clubs* Yorks Aeroplane, Royal Lymington Yacht; *Style*— Kenneth West, Esq; Stone Ridge, Niton Undercliff, Ventor, IOW PO38 2LY

WEST, Martin Graham; s of Edward Graham West, of Bury, and Dorothy West (d 1987); *b* 7 Nov 1938; *Educ* Bury GS; *m* 1962, Jacqueline, da of Alfred Eric Allen (d 1959); 1 s (Jeremy b 1970), 2 da (Angela b 1965, Janine b 1967); *Career* CA; dir: British Mail Order Corpn Ltd 1973-76, London Scottish Bank plc 1976- (chief exec 1988-); FCA; *Recreations* classic car restoration, bridge; *Clubs* St James's (Manchester); *Style*— Martin Graham West, Esq; The Chaplain's House, West Lane, High Legh, Knutsford, Cheshire WA16 6LR (☎ 092 575 4448); Arndale House, Arndale Centre, Manchester M4 3AQ (☎ 061 834 2861, fax 061 834 2536)

WEST, Rev Michael John; s of William Henry West (d 1985), and Elsie Clara, *née* Wright; *b* 14 March 1933; *Educ* Battersea Poly, Royal Sch of Mines Imperial Coll Univ of London (BSc); *m* 1954, Florence Edith; 4 da (Barbara b 1956, Margaret b 1958, Susan b 1959, Catherine b 1962); *Career* Anglo American Corporation Zambia 1954-60, chm Mining Journal Ltd 1966- (ed 1960-66); ordination course Southwark 1985-88; ordained: deacon 1988, priest 1989; Freeman City of London, memb Worshipful Co of Engineers; ARSM, FIMM (pres 1982), FEng 1989; *Clubs* Reform; *Style*— Rev Michael West; 1 Church Rd, Kenley, Surrey CR8 5DW (☎ 081 668 1548); Mining Journal Ltd, 60 Worship St, London EC2A 2HD (☎ 071 377 2020, fax 071 247 4100)

WEST, Nigel; *b* 8 Nov 1951; *Career* BBC TV 1977-81, Euro ed Intelligence Quarterly; *Books* Spy! (with Richard Deacon), MI5: British Security Service Operation 1909-45, MI6: British Secret Intelligence Service Operation 1909-45, A Matter of Trust: M15 1945-72, GARBO (with Juan Pujol), Molehunt, GCHQ: The Secret Wireless War, Unreliable Witness: Espionage Myths of World War II, The Friends: Britain's Postwar Secret Operations, Games of Intelligence: The Classified Conflict of International Espionage, The Blue List, Culan Bluff; *Style*— Nigel West, Esq; Peters Fraser & Dunlop, The Chambers, Chelsea Harbour, London SW10 (☎ 071 376 7676, fax 071 352 7356)

WEST, Peter; s of Harold William West (d 1975), and Dorcas Ann West (d 1972); *b* 12 Aug 1920; *Educ* Cranbrook Sch; *m* 1946, Pauline Mary, da of Lt Cdr Evan Cuthbert Pike, RNVR (d 1929); 2 s (Simon, Stephen), 1 da (Jacqueline); *Career* radio and tv sports commentator/presenter 1947-; sports journalist, rugby corr The Times 1971-82; *Books* Fight for the Ashes (1953), Fight for the Ashes (1956), Flannelled Fool and Muddied Oaf (autobiography 1986), Clean Sweep (1987), Denis Compton-Cricketing Genius (1989); *Recreations* gardening; *Style*— Peter West, Esq; The Paddock, Duntisbourne Abbotts, Cirencester, Glos (☎ 028 582 380)

WEST, Prof Richard Gilbert; s of Arthur Gilbert Dixon West (d 1949), and Daisy Elizabeth Lovesay, MBE; *b* 31 May 1926; *Educ* King's Sch Canterbury, Clare Coll Cambridge (MA, PhD, ScD); *m* 30 June 1973, Hazel Violet; *Career* Univ of Cambridge: dir Sub Dept Quaternary Res 1966-87, prof botany 1977-; FRS 1968, FGS, FSA, Hon MRIA; *Books* Pleistocene Geology and Biology (second edn 1977), Preglacial Pleistocene of the Norfolk and Suffolk Coasts (1980), Pleistocene Palaeoecology of Central Norfolk (1991); *Style*— Prof Richard West; 3A Woollards Lane, Gt Shelford, Cambridge CB2 5LZ; Department of Botany, University of Cambridge

WEST, Dr Richard James; s of Edward West (d 1982), of Edinburgh, and Doreen, *née* Rutherford; *b* 5 Feb 1944; *Educ* Edinburgh Acad, Univ of Edinburgh (MB ChB); *m* 12 April 1969, Christine, da of Reginald Paul (d 1975); 2 s (Timothy b 1970, Gregory b 1981), 2 da (Sophie b 1971, Madeleine b 1977); *Career* conslt radiologist Queen Elizabeth Hosp Birmingham, hon sr clinical lectr Univ of Birmingham, examiner in surgical neurology RCSE(d) 1986-; author of pubns on biliary and interventional radiology 1978-; memb BMA, FRCR 1973; *Books* Advanced Medicine 23 (contrib, 1987), Philosophical Ethics in Reproductive Medicine (contrib, 1990); *Recreations* singing badly in a choir; *Style*— Dr Richard West; 23 Oxford Rd, Birmingham 13, West Midlands B13 9EH (☎ 021 449 6700); Midland Centre for Neurosurgery, Manor Rd, Warley, West Midlands (☎ 021 558 3232)

WEST, Dr Richard John; s of Cecil John West (d 1987), and Alice, *née* Court; *b* 8 May 1939; *Educ* Tiffin Boys Sch, Middx Hosp Med Sch (MB BS, MD); *m* 15 Dec 1962, Dr Jenny Winn, da of Leslie Gaius Hawkins (d 1976); 1 s (Simon b 1964), 2 da (Sarah b 1967, Sophie b 1972); *Career* lectr Inst of Child Health 1974-75, dean St George's Hosp and Med Sch 1982-87 (sr lectr and conslt paediatrician 1975-); memb: Cncl Br Paediatric Assoc 1974-76, Wandsworth Health Authy 1981-82 and 1990, S W Thames RHA 1982-88; chm Dist Med Ctee Wandsworth and E Merton 1978-80; sch govr: Tiffin Boys Sch 1983-86, Wimbledon HS 1987-; gen sec Inst of Med Ethics 1989- (memb Cncl 1986-); MRCP 1967, FRCP 1979; *Books* The Family Guide to Children's Ailments (1983), Royal Society of Medicine Child Health Guide (1991); *Recreations* reading, travel, collecting pap boats; *Style*— Dr Richard West; 6 Dorset Rd, Merton Park, London SW19 (☎ 081 542 5119); Dept of Child Health, St George's Hosp Med Sch, London SW17 ORE (☎ 081 672 9944)

WEST, Timothy Lancaster; CBE (1984); s of (Harry) Lockwood West (d 1989), actor, and Olive Carleton-Crowe; *b* 20 Oct 1934; *Educ* John Lyon Sch Harrow, Regent St Poly; *m* 1, 1956 (m dis), Jacqueline Boyer; 1 da; m 2, 1963, Prunella Scales; 2 s; *Career* actor; memb RSC 1964-66, Prospect Theatre Co 1966-72, artistic dir Old Vic Co 1980-81; *Style*— Timothy West Esq, CBE; James Sharkey Associates, 15 Golden Square, London W1

WEST, William Todd; s of Alfred William West (d 1963), of Humberside, and Annie Beatrice, *née* Todd (d 1969); *b* 7 Aug 1924; *Educ* Sedbergh, Univ of London (LLB); *m* 7 July 1956, Beryl Josephine, da of William Fletcher Taylor (d 1966), of Scarborough, N Yorks; 1 s (Nicholas William b 1958); *Career* slr, ret; called to the Bar Gray's Inn 1989; elected legal memb of Royal Town Planning Inst 1975; *Books* Drugs Law (1982), The County Court (1983), A Shop Hours Casebook (1984), The Trial of Lord de Clifford (1985, 1990); *Recreations* watching county cricket, exercising a rabbiting terrier, fishing, golf; *Style*— William West, Esq; Lindis, Roundhay Road, Bridlington, North Humberside YO15 3JZ (☎ 0262 673116, 0653 693687)

WEST CUMBERLAND, Archdeacon of; *see*: Hodgson, Ven Thomas Richard Burnham

WEST-KNIGHTS, Laurence James (Laurie); s of Maj Jan James West West-Knights (d 1990), and Amy Winifred, *née* Gott; *b* 30 July 1954; *Educ* Perse Sch, Hampton Sch, Emmanuel Coll Cambridge (MA); *Career* seaman offr London Div RNR 1981-; called to the Bar Gray's Inn 1977, practising barr 1978-; CIArb; *Recreations* sailing, amateur radio, football, keeping fit, darts; *Clubs* Royal Solent Yacht, Bar Yacht, Radio Soc of GB; *Style—* LJ West-Knights, Esq; Clarewood House, 2 Brackley Rd, Chiswick, London W4 2HN (☎ 081 994 0325); 4 Paper Buildings, Temple, London EC4Y 7EX (☎ 071 353 3366, fax 071 353 5778)

WEST-RUSSELL, His Hon Sir David Sturrock; s of Sir Alexander West-Russell (d 1962), and Agnes, *née* Sturrock (d 1930); *b* 17 July 1921; *Educ* Rugby, Pembroke Coll Cambridge (MA), Harmsworth Law Sch; *m* 30 April 1949, Christine, *née* Tyler; 1 s (Christopher), 2 da (Fiona, Sarah); *Career* War Serv 1940-46: cmmnd Queens Own Cameron Highlanders 1941, Parachute Regt 1942, N Africa, Italy, France, Greece, Norway, Palestine (despatches), Maj; mgmnt trainee Guest Keen & Nettlefold 1948-50; called to the Bar Middle Temple 1953, bencher 1986, practising SE Circuit, dep chm Inner London QS 1966-72, circuit judge 1972, sr circuit judge Inner London Crown Ct 1979-82 and Southwark Crown Ct 1983-84; pres Industl Tbnls for England and Wales 1984-91, memb Departmental Ctee on Legal Aid in Criminal Proceedings 1964-65, cmmr NI Emergency Provisions Act 1974-; chm: Lord Chancellor's Advsy Ctee on Appointments of Magistrates for Inner London 1976-87, Home Sec's Advsy Bd on Restricted Patients 1985, pres Inner London Magistrates Assoc 1979-83; memb: Inner London Probation Ctee 1979 (chm 1988), Lord Chancellor's Advsy Ctee on Training of Magistrates 1980-85, Judicial Studies Bd 1980-84 and 1987-90, Parole Bd 1980-82, Parole Review Ctee 1987-88, Criminal Injuries Compensation Bd 1991-; kt 1986; *Recreations* gardening, photography, walking; *Clubs* Garrick; *Style—* His Hon Sir David West-Russell; 24 Hamilton Terrace, St John's Wood, London NW8 (☎ 071 286 3718)

WESTABY, Mark; s of Donald Westaby, of Winterton, S Humberside, and Patricia, *née* Morwood; *b* 26 June 1955; *Educ* Frederic Gough, Brunel Univ (BSc); ptnr, Sarah Frances Elizabeth Cox; *Career* Ove Arup & partners and Res Dept British Gas 1979-81; former PRO: John Drewry Associates, HPS Ltd 1983-84, Countryside Communications (London) 1984-90 (latterly dir, work on Tandem Computers responsible for PR Indust Best Consultancy award 1987); Kinnear Ltd management conslts in communication 1990-; chm Business & Technol Gp PR Consultants Assoc (chm elect 1989-91); *Recreations* all sports, music, reading, travel; *Style—* Mark Westaby, Esq; Kinnear Ltd, 25-28 Old Burlington St, London W1X 1LB (☎ 071 287 9700)

WESTALL, Robert Atkinson; s of Robert Atkinson Westall (d 1985), and Maggie Alexandra, *née* Leggett (d 1985); *b* 7 Oct 1929; *Educ* Tynemouth GS, Univ of Durham (BA), Univ of London (Slade Dip); *m* 29 July 1958 (m dis 1990), Jean, da of Alfred Underhill, of Hampstead, London; 1 s (Robert Christopher b 1960 d 1978); *Career* Nat Serv Royal Signals (Suez Canal Zone) 1954-55; head of art and careers Sir John Deane's Coll Northwich Cheshire 1960-85, antique dealer 1985-87, writer; *Books* The Machine-gunners (1975, Carnegie Medal 1975, Horn Book Award 1976, Preis des Leseraten 1988), The Wind Eye (1976), The Watch House (1977), Devil on the Road (1978), Fathom Five (1979), The Haunting of Chas McGill (1980), Scarecrows (1981, Carnegie Medal 1981, Horn Book Award 1982), The Cats of Seroster (1981), Break of Dark (1982), Futuretrack Five 1983, Preis des Leseraten 1990), The Witness (1984), Urn Burial (1985), Children of the Blitz (1985), Rosalie (1985), Rachel and the Angel (1986), Ghost Abbey (1987), Blitzcat (1988, Smarties Prize 1989), The Call (1988), A Walk on the Wildside (1988), The Creature in the Dark (1988), Ghost Stories (anthology 1988), The Promise (1989), Echoes of War (1989), Antique Dust (1989), Old Man on a Horse (1989), The Kingdom by the Sea (1989), If Cats Could Fly (1990), Storm Search (1990), Yaxleys Cat (1990); PEN (America) 1988; *Recreations* photography, local history, antique clocks, cats; *Style—* Robert Westall, Esq; c/o Laura Cecil, Literary Agent, 17 Alwyne Villas, London N1 2HG (☎ 071 354 1790)

WESTBERG, Capt Niels; s of Sigurd Westberg (d 1951), and Christine Mary, *née* Claxton; *b* 10 Sept 1944; *Educ* St Lawrence Coll; *m* 6 Nov 1976, Jane da of Alexander Waugh; 2 da (Alexandra b 1979, Anneke b 1980); *Career* RN (Capt) 1963-: HMS Wizard, HMS Whirlwind, HMS Defender 1964-69, HM Yacht Britannia 1969-70, CO HMS Sabre 1970-71, HMS Rothesay 1972-74, RAN HMAS Vendetta 1974-76, HMS Jupiter 1977-79, Cdr Fishery Protection Sqdn 1980-82, CO HMS Charydis 1982-84, Directorate Naval Plans MOD 1984-86, CO HMS Brazen 1986-88, Directorate Naval Warfare MOD 1988-90, chief exec Rosyth Single Business, Naval Base Cdr 1991-; *Recreations* horiculture, gemstones; *Style—* Capt Niels Westberg, RN; c/o Naval Secretary, Old Admiralty Building, Whitehall, London SW1

WESTBROOK, Hon Mrs (Mary Joan); *née* Fraser; da of late 1 Baron Strathalmond, CBE; *b* 1922; *m* 1945, Neil Gowanloch Westbrook; 1 s, 1 da; *Style—* The Hon Lady Westbrook; White Gables, Prestbury, Cheshire

WESTBROOK, Michael John David (Mike); OBE (1988); s of Philip Beckford Westbrook (d 1981), of Devon, and Vera Agnes, *née* Butler; *b* 21 March 1936; *Educ* Kelly Coll Tavistock Plymouth Coll of Art (NDD), Hornsey Coll of Art (ATD); *m* 1; 1 s (Anthony Guy b 9 April 19 1964), 1 da (Joanna Maria b 14 June 1966); m 2, 23 Sept 1976, Katherine Jane (Kate), da of Prof Alec Naraway Duckham, CBE (d 1988); *Career* composer, pianist and bandleader; formed first band at Plymouth Art Sch 1958; moved to London 1962 and has since led a succession of gps incl: The Mike Westbrook Brass Band (with Phil Minton) 1973-, The Mike Westbrook Orchestra 1974-, A Little Westbrook Music (with Kate Westbrook and Chris Biscoe) 1982-; has toured extensively in Britain, Europe, Australia, Canada and NY, has written cmmnd works for festivals in GB and Europe; has composed music for theatre, radio, tv and films and has made numerous LPs and recordings incl: Marching Song (1967), Metropolis (1969), Tyger (1971), Citadel/Room 315 (1974), On Dukes Birthday (1984), Big Band Rossini (1987), In A Fix (1988), Off The Abbey Road (1988); tv scores incl Caught on a Train (1983), cinema score Moulin Rouge (1990); concert works with Kate Westbrook incorporating Euro poetry and folk song: The Cortege (1979), London Bridge is Broken Down (1987); music theatre pieces incl: Mama Chicago (1978), Westbrook Rossini (1984), The Ass (1985), Pier Rides (1986), Quichotte (1989); current projects incl: saxophone concerto (for John Harle), Good Friday 1663 (an opera for tv, with Kate Westbrook), Coming Through Slaughter (with Michael Morris, based on novel by Michael Ondaatje); *Recreations* walking in the country, drawing, swimming; *Clubs* John Clare Soc, ICA, The Blake Soc (St James), Ronnie Scotts; *Style—* Mike Westbrook, Esq, OBE; 37 Tredegar Square, London E3 5AE; Laurence Aston, PO Box 354, Reading RG2 7JB (☎ 0734 312580, fax 0734 312582)

WESTBROOK, Sir Neil Gowanloch; CBE (1981); s of Frank Westbrook, and Dorothy; *b* 21 Jan 1917; *Educ* Oundle, Clare Coll Cambridge (MA); *m* 1945, Hon Mary Joan Fraser, da of 1 Baron Strathalmond, CBE; 1 s, 1 da; *Career* WWII Actg Lt Col RE and Gen Staff Offr (despatches); chm and mangr: Trafford Park Estate plc, Port of Manchester Warehouses Ltd; farmer; memb CBI NW Regnl Cncl 1982-88, chm CBI NW Inner Cities Study Gp 1985-88, memb IOD Manchester and Area Branch Ctee 1967-86, dep chm Trafford Ctee Manchester C of C and Indust 1983-86; memb: Trafford Indust Cncl 1975-86, Assoc of Br C of C Ctee on Rates and Local Govt Fin 1975-77, memb Bd of Fin Cons Pty 1984-87, memb: Nat Union Industl and Trade Forum 1982-87, Nat Union Exec Ctee 1975-81, NW Area Fin and Gen Purposes Ctee 1974-87; chm of Manchester Cons Assoc 1974-83 (vice chm 1973-74, hon treas 1964-73), chm Greater Manchester Co-ordinating Ctee 1978-86, memb Manchester City Cncl 1949-72 (dep ldr 1968-69), Lord Mayor City of Manchester 1969-70, chm Greater Manchester South Euro Div 1978-84; Kt 1988; *Recreations* shooting, fishing; *Clubs* Carlton, Manchester Tennis and Racquets; *Style—* Sir Neil Westbrook, CBE; Estate Office, Trafford Park, Manchester M17 1AU (☎ 061 872 5426)

WESTBROOK, Roger; CMG (1990); s of Edward George Westbrook, of Sandy Mount, Bearsted, Kent, and Beatrice Minnie, *née* Marshall; *b* 26 May 1941; *Educ* Dulwich, Hertford Coll Oxford (MA); *Career* HM Dip Serv: FO 1964, asst private sec to the Chllr of the Duchy of Lancaster and Min of State FCO 1965, Yaoundé 1967, Rio de Janeiro 1971, Brasilia 1972, private sec to Min of State FCO 1975, head of chancery Lisbon 1977, dep head News Dept FCO 1980, dep head Falkland Islands Dept FCO 1982, overseas inspectorate FCO 1984, high cmmr Negara Brunei Darussalam 1986; *Clubs* Travellers', Royal Brunei Polo; *Style—* Roger Westbrook, Esq, CMG; British High Commission, Bandar Seri Begawan, Negara Brunei Darussalam

WESTBURY, 5 Baron (UK 1861); David Alan Bethell; MC (1942), DL (N Yorks 1973); s of Capt Hon Richard Bethell (d 1929, s of 3 Baron, whom he predeceased), and Lady Agatha Tollemache, sis of 9 Earl of Dysart; suc bro, 4 Baron, 1961; *b* 16 July 1922; *Educ* Harrow, RMC; *m* 21 Oct 1947, Ursula Mary Rose, CBE (1990), er da of Hon Robert James (3 s of 2 Baron Northbourne), and his 2 w, Lady Serena Lumley, da of 10 Earl of Scarbrough; 2 s, 1 da; *Heir* s, Maj Hon Richard Bethell, MBE; *Career* served WWII with Scots Guards in N Africa & Italy (despatches); sits as Conservative peer in House of Lords; equerry to HRH Duke of Gloucester 1947-49; pres British Wheelchair Sports Fedn; chm Counsel and Care, pres Northern Police Convalescent Home, tstee Berkeley Square Ball, memb Exec Ctee of Int Fedn of Multiple Sclerosis Socs; patron: Action Around Bethlehem Children with Disability, Yorks Assoc of Boys' Clubs; KStJ 1977, Bailiff of Egle, GCStJ 1987; *Clubs* Jockey, Pratt's, Buck's; *Style—* The Rt Hon the Lord Westbury, MC, DL; Barton Cottage, Malton, N Yorks (☎ 0653 692293); 8 Rogers Orchard, Danvers St, London SW3 5AX (☎ 071 352 7911)

WESTBURY, Prof David Rex; s of Harold Joseph Westbury (d 1966), of Rubery, Worcs, and Kathleen, *née* Hedderley; *b* 24 June 1942; *Educ* Bromsgrove Co HS Worcestershire, ChCh Oxford (MA, BSc, BM BCh, DM); *m* 19 Feb 1966, Pauline, da of James Robinson (d 1988), of Darlington, Co Durham; 1 s (Paul b 1969), 1 da (Claire b 1971); *Career* prof Univ of Birmingham 1987- (lectr 1968-74, sr lectr 1974-82, reader 1982-86, exec dean Med Faculty 1984-); memb Physiological Soc 1968; *Recreations* eating, walking, amateur radio communications; *Style—* Prof David Westbury; 120 Bunbury Rd, Northfield, Birmingham B31 2DN (☎ 021 4757404), University of Birmingham, Edgbaston, Birmingham B15 2TT (☎ 021 414 4045, fax 021 414 4036)

WESTCOTT, John Miles; s of Leonard George Westcott (d 1977), of Chipping Campden, Glos, and Marion Blanche, *née* Field; *b* 22 Feb 1929; *Educ* Taunton Sch; *m* 1 Sept 1956, Anne Milne, da of Capt Robert Porter, OBE (d 1956), of Blundellsands, Liverpool; 2 s (Andrew John b 1959, d 1969, Timothy Edmund James b 1963), 1 da (Catherine May b 1961); *Career* Nat Serv 2Lt 13/18 Royal Hussars 1949, Lt North Somerset Yeomanry 1950-52; admitted slr 1956; managing ptnr Veale Wasbrough 1988, legal chm (pt/t) Pensions Appeals Tbnl 1989-; former pres Bristol Law Soc, memb Law Soc Family Law Ctee, fell Int Acad Matrimonial Lawyers; contrib: Family Law, Modern Law Review; vice pres Avon Youth Assoc; chm: Kingswood Schs, Bristol Home-Start; memb Law Soc; *Recreations* village cricket, dry stonewall building; *Clubs* Royal Commonwealth Soc; *Style—* John Westcott, Esq; Old Farm, Southwood, Baltonsborough, Somerset (☎ 0458 50416); Veale Wasbrough, Orchard Court, Orchard Lane, Bristol BS1 5ER (☎ 0272 252020)

WESTCOTT, Richard Henry; s of Charles Westcott (d 1984), of S Molton, Devon, and Ruby Alice, *née* Addicott (d 1979); *b* 5 Nov 1947; *Educ* Barnstaple Boys' GS; *m* 26 Nov 1983, Susan, da of George Frederick Read, of Middlesbrough, Cleveland; 1 s (Charles George Frederick b 20 April 1987), 1 da (Emily Margaret Alice b 29 Aug 1985); *Career* called to the Bar Lincoln's Inn 1978; articled to then sr clerk Moore Bedworth & Co CA's Barnstaple 1964-73, tax mangr Arthur Andersen CA's London 1973-75; dir: Morgan Grenfell & Co Ltd 1983-86 (exec mangr 1975-83), Warburg, Akroyd, Rowe & Pitman, Mullens Securites Ltd 1986-89; md Merrill Lynch International Ltd 1989-; FCA 1970, FTII 1974, ACIB 1979; *Recreations* walking, reading, carpentry, music, golf; *Style—* Richard Westcott, Esq; Ropemaker Place, 25 Ropemaker St, London EC2Y 9LY (☎ 071 628 1000, fax 071 867 2040)

WESTENRA, Hon Mrs (Brigid Mary); da of 6 Baron Rossmore; *b* 23 Sept 1928; *m* 1956 (m dis 1969), Hon Jonathan Howard, s of 3 Baron Strathcona and Mountroyal; 2 da; *Career* reverted to maiden name; *Style—* The Hon Mrs Brigid Westenra

WESTERBY, (Stuart) Marcus; s of Ernest (Tim) Westerby (d 1976), and Pollie Westerby; *b* 1 April 1934; *Educ* Leys Sch Cambridge; *m* 30 July 1959, Josephine (Jo), da of Stanley Clegg (d 1982); 3 da (Sally Anne, Penny Jane, Emma Gail); *Career* Nat Serv RN 1952-53 (Royal Gd at HM Queen Elizabeth's Coronation 1953); dir Moët & Chandon (London) Ltd 1956-; *Recreations* golf, shooting; *Clubs* RAC, Motor Park Golf; *Style—* Marcus Westerby, Esq; Woodcroft, Trout Rise, Loudwater, Rickmansworth, Herts WD3 4JS (☎ 0923 772 773); Moët & Chandon (London) Ltd, 13 Grosvenor Crescent, London SW1X 7EE (☎ 071 235 9411, fax 071 235 6937, telex 296235 MODIR G)

WESTHEAD, John Michael; s of Percy Westhead (d 1961); *b* 13 Nov 1928; *Educ* St John's Coll and St Antony's Coll Oxford; *m* 1958, Portia Joan Peters, da of Capt John Wentworth Rooke, OBE; 2 s; *Career* gp md Bowthorpe Holdings Ltd; *Recreations* squash, music, reading; *Clubs* Oxford & Cambridge, RSA; *Style—* John Westhead, Esq; Hapstead Green Cottage, 63 High St, Ardingly, W Sussex (☎ 0444 892 362); 6 Wetherby Mews, Bolton Gdns, London SW5 (☎ 071 370 3685)

WESTLAKE, Gp Capt George Herbert; DSO (1945), DFC (1943); s of Herbert Westlake (d 1953), and Edith Florence Forder (d 1966); *b* 21 April 1918; *Educ* Shoreham-by-Sea GS, De Havilland Aeronautical Tech Sch Hatfield Herts; *m* 1, 14 Oct 1946, Margaret Lesley, da of John Iddon (d 1956), of Lancs; 1 s (Richard b 1953), 1 da (Jennifer b 1955); m 2, 23 June 1976, Susan Frances Chilton, da of John Kennedy, of Northants; 1 step s (Myles Chilton b 1965), 1 step da (Mimi Lucy Chilton b 1968); *Career* aeronautical student 1936-39, RAF service 1939-69; war serv Battle of Britain, Syria, KI Desert, Cyprus, Central Med, Sicily, Italy; post war serv UK, Germany, USA, NATO (Fontainebleau), Singapore, Hong Kong, Cyprus; aviation and gen mangr in Kuwait 1975-; Air Efficiency Award 1944, despatches 1943; *Recreations* game fishing, reading, TV; *Clubs* RAF, Flyfishers'; *Style—* Gp Capt George H Westlake, DSO, DFC; 17 Main Street, Seaton, nr Uppingham, Leics (☎ 057 287 451); Kuwait Overseas Agencies, PO Box 301, 13004 Safat, Kuwait (☎ 2424477/88)

WESTLAKE, Rev Peter Alan Grant; CMG (1972), MC (1943); s of Alan Robert Cecil Westlake, CSI, CIE (d 1978), and Dorothy Louise, *née* Turner (d 1966); *b* 2 Feb 1919; *Educ* Sherborne, CCC Oxford (MA), Univ of Wales (MSc, BD); *m* 1943, Katherine Gertrude (d 1990), da of Rev Harold Charles Spackman; 2 s; *Career* FRAS; RA in Libya and Tobruk (adj 1 RHA) and Italy (despatches), Capt, 1939-46; entered Foreign Serv 1946, head of Chancery Tel Aviv 1955-57; cnsllr: Washington 1965, Canberra 1967-71; min Br Embassy Toyko 1971-76, UK cmmr gen Int Ocean Expo Okinawa 1975; deacon 1981, priest Church in Wales 1982-; Order of Rising Sun (Japan) 1975; *Recreations* sailing, oceanography; *Clubs* RAYC; *Style—* Rev Peter Westlake, CMG, MC; 53 Church St, Beaumaris, Gwynedd LL58 8AB (☎ 0248 810114)

WESTLEY, Alan; s of Frederick Westley (d 1956), of Wellingborough Rd, Northampton, and Alice Westley (d 1944); *b* 30 April 1912; *Educ* John Clare Sch Northampton; *m* 21 Sept 1939, (Alice) Betsy, da of Arthur Cotton (d 1965), of Heath End, Nuneaton; 2 s (Clive Alan b 1 Feb 1945, Mark Julian b 30 Dec 1949), 1 da (Sally Ann b 12 Aug 1953); *Career* entered motor industry 1926; worked with: Arthur Mulliner coach builder Northampton, Pytchley Autocar Co coach builder Northampton, Salmon & Sons Newport Pagnell coachbuilders, motor panels for Coventry Body Pressings, metalwork for Motor Industry, Sir W G Armstrong Whitworth Aircraft aircraft manufacturers Coventry; jt fndr and jt md Airflow Streamlines Ltd 1941-68, chm and chief exec Airflow Streamlines plc 1968-; *Recreations* golf, boating, gardening, travel; *Clubs* Valletta Yacht (Malta), Northamptonshire Co Golf, Northampton Golf, Northampton Co; *Style—* Alan Westley, Esq; The Knowle, 502 Wellingborough Rd, Abington Park, Northampton NN3 3HX (☎ 0604 406 098); Airflow Streamlines plc, Main Rd, Far Cotton, Northampton NN3 3HX (☎ 0604 762 261, fax 0604 701 405, telex 316319)

WESTMACOTT, Richard Kelso; s of Cdr John Rowe Westmacott, RN (d 1983), and Ruth Pharazyn (d 1971); *b* 20 Feb 1934; *Educ* Eton, Royal Navy; *m* 1965, Karen; 1 s (John b 1969), 1 da (Camilla b 1967); *Career* RN 1952-54; stockbroker; joined Hoare & Co 1955, chm: Hoare Govett Ltd 1975, Security Pacific Hoare Govett (Gp) Ltd 1985, Hoare Govett Corporate Fin Ltd; memb Stock Exchange 1960; *Recreations* sailing, shooting; *Clubs* Whites, Royal Yacht Sqdn; *Style—* R K Westmacott, Esq; Calle Juan de Mena 15, 3 i39, 28014 Madrid, Spain (☎ 1 522 1116, fax 1 532 9716)

WESTMEATH, 13 Earl of (I 1621); William Anthony Nugent; also Baron Delvin (I before 1489, evolved from a feudal Barony, of which the date of origin is uncertain); s of 12 Earl of Westmeath (d 1971); *b* 21 Nov 1928; *Educ* Marlborough, RMA Sandhurst; *m* 31 July 1963, Susanna Margaret, o da of His Hon Judge James Charles Beresford Whyte Leonard, of Sutton Courtenay, Berks; 2 s; *Heir* s, Lord Delvin; *Career* RA 1947-61, ret as Capt; sr master St Andrew's Sch Pangbourne, ret 1988; *Style—* The Rt Hon the Earl of Westmeath; Farthings, Tutts Clump, Reading, Berks (☎ 0734 744426)

WESTMINSTER, Anne, Duchess of; Anne Winifred; da of Brig-Gen Edward Sullivan, CB, CMG, of Glanmire House, Co Cork; *m* 1947, as his 4 w, 2 Duke of Westminster, GCVO, DSO (d 1953); *Style—* Her Grace Anne, Duchess of Westminster; Lochmore, Lairg, Sutherland; Eaton Lodge, Eccleston, Chester

WESTMINSTER, Archbishop (RC) of, 1976-; His Eminence (George) Basil Hume; s of late Sir William Errington Hume, CMG, and late Marie Elizabeth, *née* Tisseyre; *b* 2 March 1923; *Educ* Ampleforth, St Benet's Hall Oxford, Fribourg Univ Switzerland; *Career* ordained priest 1950; Ampleforth Sch: sr modern language master 1952-63, housemaster 1955-63, prof of Dogmatic Theology 1955-63, magister scholarum of the English Benedictine Congregation 1957-63, abbot 1963-76; Cardinal 1976; pres: Cncl of Euro Bishops' Conferences 1979-87, Bishops' Conference England and Wales 1979-; memb Cncl for Secretariat of Int Synod of Bishops 1978-87; Hon Bencher Inner Temple; Hon DD: Cambridge 1979, Newcastle 1979, London 1980, Oxford 1981, York 1982, Kent 1983, Durham 1987, Collegio S Anselmo Rome 1987, Hull 1989; Hon DHL: Manhattan Coll NY USA 1980, Catholic Univ of America 1980, Univ of Keele 1990; *Books* Searching for God (1977), In Praise of Benedict (1981), To Be a Pilgrim (1984), Towards a Civilisation of Love (1988); *Style—* His Eminence the Cardinal Archbishop of Westminster; Archbishop's House, Westminster, London SW1P 1QJ (☎ 071 834 4717)

WESTMINSTER, 6 Duke of (UK 1874); Sir Gerald Cavendish Grosvenor; 15 Bt (E 1622), DL (Cheshire 1982); also Baron Grosvenor (GB 1761), Earl Grosvenor, Viscount Belgrave (both GB 1784), and Marquess of Westminster (UK 1831); s of 5 Duke of Westminster, TD (d 1979), and Hon Viola Lyttelton (*see* Viola, Dowager Duchess of Westminster (d 1987)), da of 9 Viscount Cobham; bro of Countess of Lichfield and Duchess of Roxburghe; *b* 22 Dec 1951; *Educ* Harrow; *m* 1978, Natalia Ayesha, yst da of Lt-Col Harold Pedro Joseph Phillips, and Georgina (da of Sir Harold Wernher, 3 Bt, GCVO, TD, and Lady Zia, CBE, *née* Countess Anastasia Mikhailovna, da of HIH Grand Duke Michael of Russia); sis of Duchess of Abercorn; 1 s (Earl Grosvenor b 29 Jan 1991), 2 da (Lady Tamara Katherine b 20 Dec 1979, Lady Edwina Louise b 4 Nov 1981); *Heir* s, Hugh Richard Louis, Earl Grosvenor b 29 Jan 1991; *Career* joined Queen's Own Yeo 1970, cmmnd 1973, Capt 1979, Maj 1985, SO2 G3 (TA) Western Dist, 2 in cmd of Regt; sits as Cons Peer in House of Lords; landowner; tstee Grosvenor Estate 1971-; pres: Chester City Cons Assoc 1975-, NW Industl Cncl 1979-, freemen of England 1979-, Coal Trade Benevolent Assoc 1980-82, London Tourist Bd 1980-, Spastics Soc 1982-, St John's Ambulance London (Prince of Wales) Dist 1983-; chm Hennel, Frazer & Haws Ltd 1979-87; dir: Sun Alliance Insurance London, Stuart-Devlin Ltd 1979-86, Marcher Sound Ltd, Harland & Wolff Ltd 1983-87; govr: King's Sch 1976-87, Int Students Tst 1978-, Chester Teaching Training Coll 1978-; patron: Br Kidney Patients Assoc 1980-86, Dyslexia Inst, Br Holstein Soc 1981-, Worcs County Cricket Club, Royal Fine Art Cmmn; pro-chancellor Keele Univ 1986-; pres: RNIB 1986-, National Kidney Research Fund 1986-, London Federation Boys' Clubs 1985-, Arthritis Care 1986-, Game Conservancy 1986-, Royal Assoc British Dairy Farmers 1987-90, Industrial Cncl N Wales; patron: British Holstein Soc 1985-, Worcester CCC 1986; The Continuing Professional Devpt Fndn 1983-; tstee Civic Tst 1983-; memb Cons NW Area Exec 1979-; Freeman City: Chester 1975, London 1981, Liveryman Worshipful Co of: Marketors, Goldsmiths, Fishmongers, Armourers and Braziers, Gunmakers, Weavers, Liveryman Guild of Air Pilots and Air Navigators; OStJ 1982; CStJ 1987; FRSA 1987; FID 1985; *Recreations* shooting, fishing, scuba diving; *Clubs* Royal Yacht Sqdn, Brooks's, Cavalry & Guards, MCC; *Style—* His Grace the Duke of Westminster, DL; Eaton Hall, Chester, Cheshire; Eaton Estate Office, Eccleston Chester (☎ 0244 680333)

WESTMORE, Geoffrey David (Geoff); s of Alan Herbert Westmore, of Guildford, Surrey, and Mary Elspeth, *née* Brooking; *b* 28 Sept 1950; *Educ* Royal GS Guildford; *m* 21 July 1979, Paula, *née* Clemett; 1 s (Jonathan Henry Clemett b 1987), 1 da (Kathryn May Clemett b 1983); *Career* Deloitte Haskins & Sells (now Coopers & Lybrand Deloitte): mangr 1975-83, ptnr 1983-; FCA 1972; *Recreations* sport, music, theatre, films; *Style—* Geoff Westmore, Esq; Plumtree Court, London EC4A 4HJ (☎ 071 822 8523, fax 071 822 8500)

WESTMORELAND, (George) Michael; s of George Sawden Westmorland (d 1955), of Leeds, and Gladys, *née* Fowler (d 1954); *b* 16 Nov 1931; *Educ* Leeds Moden Sch, Leeds Coll of Art (NDD), Univ of Leeds (Art Teachers Cert); *m* 1966, Joanne Jennifer, da of Jack Camm; 2 s (Thomas Patrick b 1967, Daniel Joseph b 1976); *Career* freelance artist, full and pt/t teacher and lectr 1953-67 (Leeds Coll of Art, Wakefield Sch of Art, Margaret McMillan Coll Bradford, Northumberland Coll of Educn), freelance photographer and filmmaker 1967- (ran various courses in film and photography Leicester Coll of Educn 1967-76), sr lectr Educnl Technol Centre Leicester Poly 1976-85; exhibitions: one-man show Photographers Gallery London 1979, 12 Images Nat Museum of Photography Bradford 1985, A Panoramic View (travelling one-man show) 1986-88, invited contributor to Tomorrow Exhibition (Royal Festival Hall) 1986 and Panoramania Exhbition (Barbican Centre) 1988, various gp shows UK and abroad, various works in public and private collections and numerous Cmmns for panoramic projects; winner: Kodak Bursary 1980, Richard Farrand Award 1984, (jt RPS/BIPP presentation for tech distinction in applied photography); write-up of works: British Journel of Photography (May 1979), Design Magazine (Dec 1980), Camera Magazine (Jan 1985), SLR Magazine (May 1987); FRPS 1982, FBIPP 1983; *Recreations* badminton, snooker; *Style—* Michael Westmoreland, Esq; 358 Victoria Park Rd, Leicester LE2 1XF (☎ 0533 705828)

WESTMORLAND, 15 Earl of (E 1624); David Anthony Thomas Fane; KCVO (1970); also Baron Burghersh (E 1624); s of 14 Earl of Westmorland (d 1948), and Diana, Countess of Westmorland (d 1983); Lord Westmorland is fourth in descent from 11 Earl, soldier, diplomat, ambass Berlin 1841-51, fndr and pres Royal Academy of Music; *b* 31 March 1924; *Educ* Eton; *m* 1950, Barbara, da of Lt-Col Sir Roland Lewis Findlay, 3 Bt; 2 s, 1 da; *Heir* s, Lord Burghersh; *Career* served RHG, wounded WWII, Capt, ret 1950; Lord in Waiting to HM The Queen 1955-78, Master of the Horse 1978-; chm Sotheby's 1980-82 (dir 1982-); dir Crown Life of Canada; OStJ 1981; *Clubs* White's, Buck's; *Style—* The Rt Hon the Earl of Westmorland, KCVO; Kingsmead, Didmarton, Glos (☎ 045 423 634); 26 Laxford House, Cundy St, London SW1 (☎ 071 730 3389)

WESTOLL, James; DL (Cumbria 1963); s of James Westoll (d 1969); *b* 26 July 1918; *Educ* Eton, Trinity Coll Cambridge (MA); *m* 1946, Sylvia Jane, MBE, da of Lord Justice Luxmoore (d 1944); 2 s, 2 da; *Career* served 1939-46 NW Europe (despatches), Maj Border Regt; farmer; called to the Bar 1952; chm Cumberland CC 1958-74, memb NW Electricity Bd 1959-66, dep chm Cumberland QS 1960-71, High Sherriff 1964, chm Cumbria CC 1973-76; Master Worshipful Co of Clothworkers 1983-84; Hon LLD Univ of Leeds 1984; CStJ 1977, KStJ 1984; *Recreations* gardening, shooting; *Clubs* Boodle's, Farmers'; *Style—* James Westoll, Esq, DL; Dykeside, Longtown, Cumbria (☎ 0228 791235)

WESTON, Adrian Robert; s of Harold Gibbons Weston (d 1987), of Leicester, and Alwyne Gabrielle, *née* Applebee; *b* 7 June 1935; *Educ* Ratcliffe Coll, Queen's Coll Oxford (MA); *m* 28 Sept 1963, Bridget Ann, da of William Henry Smith (d 1964), of Leicester; 1 s (Thomas b 1968), 1 da (Alexandra b 1967); *Career* admitted slr 1961; dir: Atkinson Design Assoc Ltd 1982-, Everards Brewery Ltd 1984-, Pal Int Ltd 1985-, Invicta Plastics Ltd 1989-, Leicestershire Employment Treasury Ltd 1989-; sr ptnr Harvey Ingram Slrs; capt Leics Co Hockey Assoc 1965-66; vice pres: The Hockey Assoc 1979- (chm 1972-78), Leics Co CC; dir Portland House Sch Tst Ltd 1982-, chm of govrs Ratcliffe Coll Leicester 1990-; *Recreations* golf, reading, music; *Clubs* Leicestershire Golf, Br Sportsmens, RAF; *Style—* Adrian R Weston, Esq; Home Farm, Smeeton Westerby, Leicester LE8 0JQ (☎ 0533 792514); Harvey Ingram Solicitors, 20 New Walk, Leicester LE1 6TX (☎ 0533 545454)

WESTON, Anthony Paul Cartade (Tony); s of Robert Jean Marcel Cartade Weston, of Bristol, and Edna Lavinia Jago-Burton (d 1949); *b* 14 May 1936; *Educ* King Edwards Southampton, Fairfield Bristol, The West of England Coll of Art (NDD, ATD, MAH); *m* 28 Dec 1961, Jennifer Anne Blaise, da of Arthur Frederick Gore Bird (d 1971); 1 s (Nicholas b 1964), 1 da (Rebecca b 1965); *Career* painter, sculptor, antiquarian, paintings in many private collections, author; exhibitor at The Royal West of England Acad; *Books* The Late Drawings of Mantegna, Paduan Sculpture, West of England Horology et al; *Recreations* riding to hounds, literary research; *Clubs* The Clifton Yacht; *Style—* Tony Weston, Esq; Eaton House, Clifton Down, Clifton, Bristol BS8 3HT

WESTON, Benjamin Charles; s of Robert H Weston, and Alice E Weston; *b* 19 Aug 1954; *Educ* Miami Univ Ohio (BA), The Johns Hopkins Sch of Advanced Int Studies Washington DC (MA); *m* 29 July 1978, Sara, da of Jack W Sigler; 1 da (Emily b 1985); *Career* asst treas Morgan Guaranty Tst Co 1978-82, mangr Morgan Guaranty Ltd 1982-83, exec dir Bankers Tst Int Ltd 1988- (vice-pres 1983-), md Bankers Tst Co 1986-; *Recreations* golf, classic cars, house renovation; *Style—* Benjamin Weston, Esq; Bankers Trust Int Ltd, Dashwood House, 69 Old Broad St, London EC2P 2EE (☎ 071 382 2566, fax 071 382 2274, telex 888707)

WESTON, Hon Mrs (Berenice Mary); *née* Walker-Smith; da of Baron Broxbourne (Life Peer); *b* 1946; *m* 1967, William Andrew Weston; *Style—* The Hon Mrs Weston; 7 Royal Arcade, Albemarle Street, London W1X 3HD

WESTON, Brian Henry; s of Horace Henry Weston, of Stisted, Essex, and Ethel May, *née* Steel; *b* 29 Nov 1933; *Educ* Cornwall Sch, City of London Coll; *m* 21 July 1956, Sheila Elizabeth, da of Edwin George Howard (d 1971); 2 s (Simon Neil b 1964, David Andrew b 1968), 1 da (Amanda Jane b 1963); *Career* Nat Serv RAF 1952-54; Bank of Nova Scotia 1955-73, gen mangr First Interstate Bank 1973-83, chm and chief exec HFC Bank plc 1983-89; chm: Populuxe Productions Ltd, Voiceline Ltd 1989-; dir Wesham Consultants Ltd 1990; memb Exec Cncl Young Enterprise (chm E Berks Bd); FCIB, FFA, FIOD; *Recreations* gardening, art, reading; *Clubs* Les Ambassadeurs, Wig and Pen, Wellington; *Style—* Brian Weston, Esq; Swan House, St Mary's Square, Bury St Edmunds, Suffolk IP33 2AJ (☎ 0284 706089); Populuxe Productions, The Elephant House, Hawley Crescent, London NW1 8NP (☎ 071 284 2159, fax 071 528 0577)

WESTON, Bryan Henry; s of Henry James Weston (d 1973), and Rose Kate Weston (d 1989); *b* 9 April 1930; *Educ* St George GS Bristol, Bristol Tech Coll, Rutherford Tech Coll, Oxford Tech Coll; *m* 21 July 1956, Heather Grace, da of Henry Gordon West, of Redhill, Avon; 2 s (Richard b 21 Jan 1958, Robert b 21 Dec 1960), 2 da (Rebecca b 13 Sept 1962, Rachel b 21 Sept 1967); *Career* 2 Lt RE 1954-56; apprentice engr SW Electricity Bd 1949, various engrg and commercial posts with SW Electricity Bd 1956-73 (latterly commerical mangr 1973); dep chm Yorks Electricity Bd 1977, chm Manweb plc (formerly MANWEB (Merseyside and N Wales Electricity Bd)) 1985-, dir Chloride Silent Power Ltd; CEng, MIEE, CBIM; *Recreations* gardening, walking, caravanning, DIY; *Style—* Bryan Weston, Esq; Fountainhead Cottage, Brassey Green, nr Tarporley, Cheshire CW6 9UG; Manweb plc, Head Office, Sealand Rd, Chester CH1 4LR (☎ 0244 377 111, fax 0244 390 725)

WESTON, Hon Mrs (Caroline Cecily); *née* Douglas-Scott-Montagu; da of 2 Baron, KCIE, CSI (d 1929); *b* 1925; *m* 1950 (George) Grainger Weston; 3 s, 1 da; *Style—* The Hon Mrs Weston; Santa Clara Ranch, Marion, Texas, USA; 301 Wiltshire, San Antonio, Texas, USA

WESTON, Celia Anne; da of Geoffrey Weston, of London, and Elizabeth, *née* Denny; *b* 13 Feb 1956; *Educ* Clifton HS for Girls, City of Bath Girls' Sch, Poly of North London (BSc); *Career* journalist; reporter The Morning Star 1979-82, asst ed The

Teacher 1982-87, SDP Policy and Press Office 1987, freelance journalist (specialising in educn) 1987-88, labour corr The Guardian 1990- (educn corr 1988-90); fndr memb North Kensington Women's Refuge 1974; memb: North Kensington Law Centre Mgmnt Ctee 1973-75, NUS Women's Ctee 1975-78, London Student Orgn Exec 1974-77, Br Youth Cncl 1977-78; memb Mgmnt Ctee and vice chairwoman Nat Cncl for One Parent Families 1985-, conslt on devpt of training policy 1987-; memb NUJ 1979; *Recreations* gardening, playing bridge; *Style*— Ms Celia Weston; Labour Correspondent, The Guardian, 119 Farringdon Rd, London EC1R 3ER (☎ 071 278 2332 ext 3618)

WESTON, Rear Adm Charles Arthur Winfield; CB (1978); s of Charles Winfield Weston (d 1958), of Barton-on-Sea, Hants; *b* 12 July 1922; *Educ* Merchant Taylors'; *m* 1946, Jeanie Findlay, da of William Dick Brown Miller; 1 s, 1 da; *Career* joined RN as cadet 1940; serv WWII: in home waters, Med, Indian Ocean, Atlantic; sec to 2 Sea Lord 1965-67, Capt 1967, CSO to C-in-C Naval Home Cmd 1969-71, dir Naval Physical Trg and Sport 1972; dir: Def Admin Planning Staff 1973-75, Quartering (RN) 1975-76; ADC to HM The Queen 1976, adm pres RNC Greenwich 1976-78, appeals sec King Edward VII's Hosp for Offrs 1979-87; Freeman Worshipful Co of Shipwrights; *Recreations* cricket, golf, gardening; *Clubs* MCC, Army and Navy; *Style*— Rear Adm C A W Weston, CB; Westacre, Liphook, Hants (☎ 0428 723337)

WESTON, Christopher John; s of Eric Tudor Weston, of Plaxtol, Kent, and Evelyn, *née* Snell; *b* 3 March 1937; *Educ* Lancing; *m* 12 July 1969, Josephine Annabel, da of Dr Moir; 1 da (Annabel b 1973); *Career* RAF 1955-57; chm and chief exec Phillips Son & Neale and assoc cos; dir 1972-: F & C Pacific Investmentt plc 1984-, Headline Book Publishing plc 1986-, F & C Enterprise Trust plc 1987-, F & C Ventures Advisers Ltd 1988-; chm Bradford Peters (Holdings) Ltd 1987-; pres Soc of Fine Art Auctioneers; fell Royal Soc for Encouragement of Arts, Manufactures and Commerce (RSA); vice pres Nat Soc of Non Smokers (QUIT); Freeman of City of London, Liveryman Worshipful Co of Painter Stainers; FIA (Scot), FRSA; *Recreations* theatre, music; *Clubs* Oriental; *Style*— Christopher Weston, Esq; 101 New Bond St, London W1Y 0AS (☎ 071 629 6602, fax 071 629 8876, telex 298855 Blen G)

WESTON, Rev David Wilfrid Valentine; s of The Rev William Valentine Weston (d 1937), and Gertrude Hamilton, *née* Erby (d 1979); *b* 8 Dec 1937; *Educ* St Edmund's Sch Canterbury; *m* 9 June 1984, Helen Strachan, da of James R Macdonald; 2 s (Luke b 1986, Alexander b 1989); *Career* monk of Nashdom Abbey 1960; ordained: deacon 1967, priest 1968; novice master 1969-74, prior of Nashdom 1971-74, abbot 1974-84; vicar of Pilling 1985-89, chaplain to the Bishop of Carlisle 1989; Freedom City of London 1959, memb Worshipful Co of Salters 1959; *Recreations* history; *Style*— The Rev David Weston; The Chaplain's House, Rose Castle, Dalston, Carlisle, Cumbria CA5 7BZ (☎ 069 96 568)

WESTON, Ven Frank Valentine; s of Rev William Valentine Weston, VD (d 1937), and Gertrude Hamilton, *née* Erby (d 1979); *b* 16 Sept 1935; *Educ* Christ's Hosp, Queen's Coll Oxford (BA, MA); *m* 20 April 1963, Penelope Brighid, da of Marmaduke Carver Middleton Athorpe (d 1973), formerly of Dinnington Hall, Yorkshire; 1 s (Simon b 1964), 2 da (Victoria b 1966, Lucy b 1968); *Career* 2 Lt RA 1954-56 (Nat Serv); curate St John Baptist Atherton Lancs 1961-65, chaplain Coll of the Ascension Selly Oak Birmingham 1965-69 (princ 1969-76), princ and Pantonian prof of theology Edinburgh Theological Coll 1976-82, archdeacon of Oxford and canon of Christ Church Oxford 1982-; govr: Tudor Hall Sch Banbury, Christ's Hosp, St Augustine's Upper Sch Oxford; memb Ct of Assts Worshipful Co of Salters (Liveryman 1957, memb of Ct 1984); *Recreations* walking, listening to music; *Style*— The Ven the Archdeacon of Oxford; Archdeacon's Lodging, Christ Church, Oxford OX1 1DP (☎ 0865 276185)

WESTON, (Willard Gordon) Galen; s of W Garfield Weston (d 1978, sometime Cons MP), of Toronto, Canada, and London, by his 1 w, Reta Lila Howard (d 1967); yr bro of Garry *see* Garfield Howard Weston; *for further details see: Debrett's Illustrated Guide to The Canadian Establishment*; *b* 29 Oct 1940; *m* 1966, Hilary Mary Frayne; 2 children; *Career* chm and pres: George Weston Ltd, Wittington Investments Ltd; chm: Brown Thomas Group Ltd (Ireland), Holt Renfrew & Co Ltd, Loblaw Companies Ltd, Weston Foods Ltd, Weston Resources Ltd; vice chm Fortnum & Mason plc (UK); dir: Associated British Foods plc (UK), Canadian Imperial Bank of Commerce, George Weston Holdings Ltd (UK), Ritz - Carlton Hotel Inc (Montreal); chm The Lester B Pearson Coll of the Pacific, dir Utd World Colls (UK); pres: The W Garfield Weston Fndn, The Weston Canada Fndn, The Royal Agric Writer Fair (Toronto); life memb: Art Gallery of Ontario, Royal Ontario Museum; Hon LLD Univ of Western Ontario; Officer of the Order of Canada (OC); *Recreations* polo, tennis; *Clubs* Badminton & Racquet (Toronto), Guards Polo (UK), Lyford Cay (Bahamas), Toronto Club, York (Toronto); *Style*— W Galen Weston, Esq; George Weston Ltd, 22 St Clair Avenue East, Toronto, Canada (☎ 416 922 2500, fax 416 922 4394, telex 06 22781 WESTLOB)

WESTON, Garfield Howard (Garry); s of Willard Garfield Weston (d 1978, sometime Cons MP), of Toronto, Canada and London, by his 1 w, Reta Lila, *née* Howard (d 1967); er bro of Galen Weston, *qv*; *for further details see: Debrett's Illustrated Guide to The Canadian Establishment*; *b* 28 April 1927; *Educ* Sir William Borlase Sch, New Coll Oxford, Harvard; *m* 8 Aug 1959, Mary Ruth, da of Maj-Gen Sir Howard Karl Kippenberger (d 1957); 3 s (Guy, George, Garth), 3 da (Jana, Kate, Sophia); *Career* md: Ryvita Co Ltd UK 1951-54, Weston Biscuit Co Aust 1954-67; chm: Associated Br Foods Ltd UK 1967 (vice chm 1960), Fortnum & Mason plc 1979-, Wittington Investments Ltd UK 1979-; *Style*— Garry Weston Esq; Associated British Foods plc, Weston Centre, Bowater House, 68 Knightsbridge, London SW1X 7LR (☎ 071 589 6363, fax 071 584 8560, telex 263255)

WESTON, (Philip) John; CMG (1985); s of Philip George Weston, of London (d 1969), and Edith Alice Bray, *née* Ansell (d 1976); *b* 13 April 1938; *Educ* Sherborne, Worcester Coll Oxford; *m* 28 Jan 1967, Margaret Sally, da of Robert Hermann Ehlers, of Bridgwater; 2 s (Ben b 1969, Rufus b 1973), 1 da (Gabriel b 1970); *Career* served as 2 Lt with 42 Commando RM 1956-58; entered Dip Serv 1962: FO 1962-63; Treasy Centre for Admin Studies 1964; Chinese languages student Hong Kong 1964-66, Peking 1967-68, FO 1969-71, office of Perm Rep to EEC 1972-74; asst private sec to Sec of State for Foreign and Cwlth Affrs (Rt Hon James Callaghan, Rt Hon Anthony Crosland) 1974-76, head of EEC Presidency Secretariat FCO 1976-77, visiting fell All Souls Coll Oxford 1977-78, cncllr Washington 1978-81, head Def Dept FCO 1981-84, asst under-sec of State FCO 1984-85, min Paris 1985-88, dep sec to the Cabinet 1988-89, dep under sec of state FCO 1989-90; political dir FCO 1990-; *Recreations* fly-fishing, running, chess, poetry; *Clubs* Utd Oxford and Cambridge, Fly Fishers; *Style*— John Weston, Esq, CMG; c/o Foreign and Commonwealth Office, London SW1

WESTON, John Pix; s of Lt John Pix Weston (d 1968), of Stickley, Margaret Road, Harborne, Birmingham, and Margaret Elizabeth, *née* Cox (d 1946); *b* 3 Jan 1920; *Educ* King Edward's Birmingham, Univ of Aston Birmingham (BSc), LSE (BSc), Univ of Georgia USA (Dip); *m* 5 Aug 1948, Ivy, da of Walter Glover, of 21 East Road, Northallerton, Yorks; 3 s (John b 1951, David b 1958, Christopher b 1963); *Career* Nat Serv Sgt RAMC 1939, 203 Mil Liaison Mission SA 1940-44, Allied Mil Liaison HQ (Albania) and GHQ (Southern) Cairo 1944-45, HQ NI Dist 1945-46; City of Birmingham Police Dept 1936-39, City of Birmingham Electricity Supply Dept 1939-48 (released for war service), third dist engr Mids Electricity Bd 1948-50, Switchgear Eng EE Co Ltd 1950-51, second asst area engr (tech) N Western Electricity Bd Kendal 1951-58, sr asst commercial engr Eastern Electricity Bd 1958-60, seconded dep ops mangr Jamaica Public Serv Co 1960-61, princ tech engr and princ commercial engr Mids Electricity Bd 1961-64, asst chief commerce offr S of Scotland Electricity Bd 1964-66, sr econ advsr to Min of Transport 1966-69, sr economist and engr Int Bank for Reconstruction and Devpt Washington 1968-70, sr mangr Michelin Tyre Co 1970-72, dir Post Experience Courses Open Univ 1972-75, dir-gen Royal Soc for the Prevention of Accidents 1974-78, industl devpt offr Argyll and Bute DC 1977-79, health and safety advsr Newcastle Poly and Northants CC 1979, chief admin offr W Bromich Coll of Commerce and Technol 1979-85, conslt engr and economist 1985-; Birmingham Photographic Soc 1979-85: prog sec, competition sec, outings sec, cncl memb; memb cncl Midland Counties Photographic Fedn 1982-85, chm Upper Marlbrook Residents' Assoc 1982-87; memb clubs: Probus, Marbeth 1987-, Tenby 1990-, St Clears (fndr 1989, pres 1990-), Laugharne Cons Assoc 1990- (asst and acting treas); lectr: Allen Tech Inst Kendal 1951-58, Ipswich Civic Coll 1958-60, Halesowen Coll of Further Educn 1961-64, Broomsgrove Coll of Further Educn 1964-64, Univ of Aston in Birmingham 1961-64; SBStJ 1965; author of numerous papers on educn, engrg, tport and safety; CEng 1953, AMIEE 1958, FSS 1957, FREconS 1957, MAPLE 1958, MIEE 1964, FIEE 1966, FBIM 1973; *Recreations* fell walking, swimming, gardening, cine and still photography; *Clubs* Farmers, St John House; *Style*— John Weston, Esq; Brook Mill and Woodside, Brook, Pendine, Dyfed SA33 4NX (☎ 099 427 477)

WESTON, Dame Margaret (Kate); DBE (1979); da of Charles Edward and Margaret Weston; *b* 7 March 1926; *Educ* Stroud HS, Coll of Technology Birmingham (now Univ of Aston); *Career* engrg apprenticeship General Electric Company Ltd; asst keeper Dept of Electrical Engrg and Communications, Science Museum 1955 (dep keeper 1962, keeper of Dept of Museum Servs 1967); dir Sci Museum 1973-86; govr: Imp Coll of Sci & Technol 1974-89, Ditchley Fndn 1985- (memb of Cncl of Mgmnt); pres Assoc of Railway Preservation Socs; vice pres Tport Tst; chm Horniman Museum; tstee: Brooklands Museum Tst Queen's Gate Tst, Hunterian Collection; memb: Museum and Galleries Cmmn, 1851 Cmmn Ct RCA, SE Electricty Bd 1981-90, cncl RSA 1985-90; Hon DSc Univ of Aston 1974, Hon DSc Univ of Salford 1984, Hon DEng Univ of Bradford 1984, Hon DSc Univ of Leeds 1987, DUniv of Open Univ 1987, Loughborough Univ; fell: Imperial Coll London 1975, Newham Coll Cambridge 1986; sr fell RCA 1986, FMA, FINucE, FRSA; Medal of Inst of Engrs and Shipbuilders in Scotland 1988; *Recreations* music, travel, gardening, getting involved in a few things; *Style*— Dame Margaret Weston, DBE; 7 Shawley Way, Epsom, Surrey KT18 5NZ (☎ 0737 355885)

WESTON, Prof Richard Henry; s of Raymond Charles Weston (d 1982), and Winifred May, *née* Hook (1985); *b* 20 March 1944; *Educ* Univ of London (BSc), Univ of Southampton (PhD); *m* 1, 14 Feb 1962 (m dis 1976), Sylvia June, *née* Gregg; 2 s (Keith Richard b 1962, Ian Michael b 1964); m 2, 25 May 1985, Betty, da of Leonard Whitear, of 113 Pevensey Rd, Loughborough; 1 da (Nicola Michelle b 1980); *Career* prof of engrg Loughborough Univ of Technol; supervisor of approximately 40 PhD students, various overseas educnl appts, princ investigator for major UK and Euro res studies in mfrg, retained conslt by numerous UK companies, tech advsr to Sci and Engrg Res Cncl and ICL; author of numerous res pubns on mfrg engrg topics with special interest in the use of computer technol and robotics; memb: Bd of Int Jls, Br and Euro Standards Bodies; FIProdE 1984, FRSA; *Books* incl: Software for Modular Robots (contrib, 1984), Integrating Robots Within Production Systems Encyclopoedia of Systems and Control (contrib, 1988), The Automated Manufacturing Director (ed 1 edn, 1985), Fluid Power 8 (contrib, 1988), Modular Robots Encyclopoedia of Systems and Control (contrib, 1988), Contouring with Pneumatic Servo-Driven Robots (contrib, 1988); *Recreations* golf, bridge, squash, football (Univ colours); *Style*— Prof Richard Weston; 18 Fairway Rd, Shepshed, Leics LE12 9DS (☎ 0509 600063); Department of Manufacturing Engineering, Loughborough University of Technology, Loughborough, Leics (☎ 0509 222907, fax 0509 267725)

WESTON, Richard Miles; s of Maj Eric Cecil Knowles Weston (d 1944), and Joan, *née* Price (d 1975); *b* 31 July 1944; *Educ* Sherborne Sch; *m* 5 May 1975, Ella Patricia, da of Eric Drewett, of Somerset; *Career* slr; *Recreations* hockey, tennis, cricket, horse racing, life; *Style*— Richard M Weston, Esq; Tatt House, Kingston St Mary, Taunton, Somerset TA2 8HY (☎ 0823 45489); The Post House, Church Square, Taunton, Somerset TA1 1SD (☎ 0823 257999)

WESTON SMITH, Ian; s of Albert Alexander Smith (d 1921), of Glasgow, and Jessie Lailey Weston (d 1964); *b* 21 Feb 1918; *Educ* Fettes Coll; *m* 1956, Angela Janet, da of Hugh Lloyd Thomas (d 1938); 2 s (Richard, Dominic); *Career* Capt Scots Gds 1940-47, served Western Desert and Italy; (POW Germany 1943, escaped 1945); md The Morgan Crucible Co plc (chm 1975-82), non exec dir Avon Rubber Co 1980-88; chm: Biomechanics International 1983-87, British United Industrialists 1983-88; memb Cncl Prince of Wales Youth Business Tst; High Sheriff of Oxfordshire; *Recreations* shooting, breeding steeplechasers; *Clubs* Guards, Pratt's; *Style*— Ian Weston Smith, Esq; The Old Rectory, Hinton Waldrist, Faringdon, Oxon SN7 8SA

WESTON SMITH, John Harry; s of Cdr Weston Smith, OBE, RN (1986); *b* 3 Feb 1932; *Educ* Fettes, St John's Coll Cambridge (MA); *m* 1955, Margaret Fraser, da of Prof E A Milne (d 1954); 1 s (Hugh b 1961), 2 da (Miranda b 1956, Lucinda b 1964); *Career* jt gen mangr Abbey National 1968-69 (sec 1961-68), dir British Land Co plc 1973-, and dir of other cos; chm Govrs of St Christopher's Sch Hampstead; *Style*— John Weston Smith, Esq; 10 Eldon Grove, London NW3 (☎ 071 435 5069); Sydenhams Farm Hse, Bisley, Glos (☎ 0453 770047)

WESTPHAL, William Henry (Bob); OBE (1972), DFC (1944); s of William Mathias Westphal (d 1950), of Sydney, Aust, and Madeline May, *née* Pepper (d 1962); *b* 5 Nov 1921; *Educ* North Sydney HS, Univ of Sydney (LLB); *m* 23 July 1945, Daphne Meta Astrid; 3 s (John b 1947, Michael b 1949, David b 1954), 1 da (Pamela b 1951); *Career* WWII RAAF Sqdn Ldr 83 Pathfinder Sqdn Europe; dir Rentokil Group plc 1956-87 (chm 1981-87); FRSA; *Recreations* golf, travel; *Clubs* Pathfinder; *Style*— W H Westphal, Esq, OBE, DFC; The Grove, Penshurst, Kent (☎ 0892 870 504); Penshurst Vineyards, Penshurst, Kent (☎ 0892 870255)

WESTROPP, Anthony Henry (Harry); s of Col Lionel Henry Mountefort Westropp (d 1991), of Berry House, Chilham, Kent, and Muriel Constance Lilian, *née* Jorgensen; *b* 22 Dec 1944; *Educ* Sherborne, King's Coll London; *m* 7 Dec 1977, Zoë Rosaleen, da of (Charles) Douglas Walker, of 58 rue Singer, Paris 16ème; *Career* with Lazard Bros & Co Ltd 1967-72; dir of subsidiaries Trafalgar House Gp 1972-75; md private gp of cos 1975-81; gp md: Bardsey plc 1981-90, The Beckenham Group plc 1990-; non-exec dir Portamn Building Soc 1982-; Freeman Co of Cutlers (Sheffield) 1982; *Recreations* hunting, fishing, skiing; *Clubs* Boodle's, City of London; *Style*— Harry Westropp, Esq; Ludwell Farm, Glympton, Oxon OX7 1A2 (☎ 0993 812726); The Beckenham Group plc, 17 Albermarle St, London W1X 3HA (☎ 071 405 9082, fax 071 242 0810, telex 0836 247636)

WESTROPP, Eric Mountefort; CBE (1982); s of Col Lionel Henry Mountefort Westropp, and Muriel Constance Lilian, *née* Jorgensen; *see* Burkes Irish Family

Records; *b* 30 March 1939; *Educ* Wellington, Camberley Staff Coll; *m* 18 Oct 1963, Jill Mary, da of Rear Adm I G Aylen, of Tracy Mill Barn, Honiton, Devon; 2 s (Richard b 1965, Patrick b 1966), 1 da (Victoria b 1969); *Career* cmmnd 11 Hussars (PAO) 1958, served NI, ME, BAOR, Bde Maj 51 Inf Bde Hong Kong 1972-74, exec Offr to Dep SACEUR at SHAPE in Belgium 1976-78, cmd Royal Hussars (PWO) 1978-80, Brig 33 Armd Bde BAOR 1983-85, ret; joined Control Risks Ltd 1985 (dir 1986), md Control Risks Response Services Ltd 1987-; *Recreations* riding, skiing, photography, reading; *Clubs* Cavalry and Guard's; *Style*— Eric Westropp, Esq, CBE; The White House, Bloxworth, Wareham, Dorset (☎ 092945 356); 83 Victoria St, London SW1 (☎ 071 222 1552)

WESTROPP, George Victor; s of Edward L Westropp (d 1962), of Epsom, Surrey, and Mary Breward, *née* Hughes (d 1973); *b* 2 Nov 1943; *Educ* Bedford Sch; *m* 12 Jan 1972 (m dis 1973), Alexander Jeanne, da of Joseph Steinberg; m 2, 9 May 1977 (m dis 1988), Christine June, da of Alan Ashley, of London; 2 s (Edward b 1980, Kit b 1982); *Career* reporter City Press 1961-63, city reporter Sunday Express 1963, fin journalist Evening Standard 1963-68, Extel (asst city ed 1968-69); dir Shareholder Relations Ltd 1969-73, fin PR exec PPR Int Ltd 1974-76, md Hemingway Public Relations Ltd 1977-79, dir communications UK and Europe Touche Ross & Co 1979- (ptnr 1985-); MIPR; *Books* The Lake Vyrnwy Fishing Book (1979); *Recreations* salmon and trout fishing; *Clubs* London Press (chm 1990), Room 74; *Style*— George Westropp, Esq; 36 Holley Rd, London W3 7TS (☎ 081 743 1752); Touche Ross & Co, Hill House, 1 Little New St, London EC4 3TR (☎ 071 936 3000, fax 071 583 8517, car 0860 299 350)

WESTWELL, Alan Reynolds; s of Stanley Westwell (d 1980), of Liverpool, and Margaret, *née* Reynolds (d 1962); *b* 11 April 1940; *Educ* Old Swan Coll, Liverpool Poly (ACT), Univ of Salford (MSc); *m* 30 Oct 1967, (Elizabeth) Aileen, da of John Birrell (d 1975), of Fife, Scotland; 2 s (Stephen b 1972, Colin (twin) b 1972), 1 da (Julie b 1970); *Career* asst works mangr (previously engrg apprentice and tech asst) Liverpool City Tport Dept 1956-67; chief engr: Southport Corpn Tport Dept 1967-69, Coventry Corpn Tport Dept 1969-72, Glasgow Corpn Tport Dept 1972-74 (dir of public tport 1974-79); dir gen Strathclyde Passenger Tport Exec 1979-86, chm and md Strathclyde Buses Ltd 1986-90; chief exec and md Greater Manchester Buses Ltd 1991-; deacon Congregational Church; FCIT, MIMechE, MIProdE; *Recreations* golf, swimming, tennis, music, reading; *Clubs* Helensburgh Golf; *Style*— Alan Westwell, Esq; 12 Glen Dr, Helensburgh, Dunbartonshire G84 9BJ (☎ 0436 71709); Greater Manchester Buses Ltd, 2 Devonshire St North, Ardwick, Manchester M12 6JS (☎ 061 273 3322, fax 061 274 3428)

WESTWOOD, David John Morris; s of Sydney Westwood (d 1989), of W Midlands, and Florence, *née* Thornycroft (d 1973); *b* 21 June 1931; *Educ* Denstone Coll; *m* 1, 20 June 1956, Valerie Ann Dallison, da of Valentine White (d 1956); 1 s (Mark b 1959), 1 da (Johanna Cole b 1957); m 2, 29 May 1982, Patricia, da of Frederick Higgs (d 1973); *Career* md Utd Spring & Steel Gp plc; magistrate 1974-80; FCA; *Recreations* foxhunting, coursing, golf; *Style*— David J M Westwood, Esq; Wales End Farm, Barton-under-Needwood, Burton-on-Trent, Staffordshire DE13 8JN (☎ 028371 3769); Blews St, Birmingham B6 4EP (☎ 021 333 3494)

WESTWOOD, Hon (William) Gavin; s and h of 2 Baron Westwood, JP; *b* 30 Jan 1944; *Educ* Fettes; *m* 1969, Penelope, da of Charles Shafto, VRD; 2 s; *Career* Co dir; FRSA; *Style*— The Hon Gavin Westwood; Ferndale, Clayton Road, Newcastle upon Tyne, NE2 1TL

WESTWOOD, Hon James Young Shaw; 3 s of 1 Baron Westwood, OBE; *b* 1915; *m* 1941 (m dis 1969), Joan, da of Raymond Potts; 1 s; *Style*— The Hon James Westwood

WESTWOOD, Hon Mrs Douglas (Mary Katherine); da of John Carter; *m* 1939, Hon Douglas Westwood (d 1968); 1 da; *Style*— The Hon Mrs Douglas Westwood; Landover Place, Burlington Place, Eastbourne, E Sussex

WESTWOOD, Hon Nigel Alistair; 2 s of 2 Baron Westwood, JP; *b* 1950; *Educ* Fettes; *m* 1977, Joan Ibison; 2 s; *Career* chartered surveyor; hon Norwegian Consul; FRICS, FRSA; *Clubs* The Northern Counties; *Style*— The Hon Nigel Westwood; 7 Fernville Rd, Gosforth, Newcastle-upon-Tyne NE3 4HT

WESTWOOD, Vivienne; *b* 8 April 1941; *Career* designer; designed with Malcolm McLaren a series of influential avant garde collections showcased at World's End 430 King's Road (formerly named Let it Rock, Too Fast to Live Too Young to Die, Sex, Seditionaries) 1971-82; first person to wear a punk hairstyle; shows: Pirate (Olympia) 1981, Savage (Olympia) 1981, Buffalo (Olympia) 1982, Punkature (Court de Louvre Paris) 1982, Witches (Court de Louvre Paris) 1983, Hypnos (Court de Louvre Paris, Best of Five Tokyo) 1983; solo career (when collaboration with Malcolm McLaren ended) 1984-; Clint Eastwood (Paris) 1985, Mini Crini (Paris, Limelight NY) 1985, Harris Tweed (Olympia) 1987, Pagan I (Olympia) 1988, Time Machine (Olympia) 1988, Civilizade (Olympia) 1989, Voyage to Cythera (Olympia) 1989, Pagan V (Olympia) 1989, Portrait (IOD) 1990, Cut & Slash (Villa de Gamberaia) 1990, Cut Slash & Pull (IOD) 1990; opened shop in Davies St Mayfair 1988; prof of fashion Vienna Acad of Applied Arts; profiled South Bank Show (LWT) 1990; British Designer of the Year 1990; *Style*— Ms Vivienne Westwood; Casnell Ltd, 12 Greenland Street, Camden Town, London NW1 OND

WESTWOOD, 2 Baron (UK 1944); William Westwood; JP (Newcastle 1949); s of 1 Baron Westwood (d 1953), by his 1 w, Margaret; *b* 25 Dec 1907; *Educ* Glasgow; *m* 1937, Marjorie, da of Arthur Bonwick; 2 s; *Heir* s, Hon (William) Gavin Westwood; *Career* former pres Football League, now life memb; hon vice-pres FA; FRSA, FCIS; *Style*— The Rt Hon the Lord Westwood, JP; 55 Moor Court, Westfield, Gosforth, Newcastle-upon-Tyne NE3 4YD

WETHERED, Simon Richard; s of Dr Rodney Richard Wethered, of Nupend House, Stonehouse, Glos, and Sarah Meriel, *née* Long-Price; *b* 1 March 1945; *Educ* Clifton, Worcester Coll Oxford (BA); *m* 9 Sept 1978, Victoria, da of Adm of the Fleet Sir Michael Le Fanu, GCB, DSC (d 1970); 2 s (Edward b 1983, Charles b 1988), 1 da (Anna b 1981); *Career* admitted slr 1970; ptnr: Simmons & Simmons 1974-78, Alsop Wilkinson (formerly Wilkinson Kimbers) 1978-; licenced insolvency practitioner 1987-; memb Holy Innocents Community Centre and PCC, dir Academy Concerts Soc 1984-; memb: FIMBRA 1987-, Law Soc 1970-; visitor HMP Wormwood Scrubs 1984-; *Recreations* wine, music, walking; *Clubs* Hogarth; *Style*— Simon Wethered, Esq; 14 Ashchurch Park Villas, London W12 9SP (☎ 081 743 5440); 6 Dowgate Hill, London EC4R 2SS (☎ 071 248 4141, fax 071 623 8286, telex 885543, car 0860 828 664)

WETHERELL, Gordon Geoffrey; s of Geoffrey Wetherell, of Addis Ababa, Ethiopa, and Georgette Maria, *née* Matkovitch; *b* 11 Nov 1948; *Educ* Bradfield, New Coll Oxford (BA, MA), Univ of Chicago (MA); *m* 11 July 1981, Rosemary Anne, da of Cdr Terence Macrae Myles, RN, ret, of Crieff, Perthshire; 4 da (Christine b 1982, Stephanie b 1985, Emily b 1987, Alexandra b 1989); *Career* third sec FCO and vice consul Br Embassy to Chad 1973-74, third then second sec E Berlin 1974-77; first sec: UK delegation to comprehensive test ban negotiations Geneva 1977-80, New Delhi 1980-83; first sec NATO desk defence dept 1983-85, secondment to HM Treasy 1986-87, asst head Euro communities dept (external) FCO 1987-88, cnllr and dep head of mission Warsaw 1988-; *Recreations* tennis, travel, reading, Manchester Utd FC; *Clubs* Oxford and Cambridge; *Style*— Gordon Wetherell, Esq; British Embassy, Aleja Roz, Warsaw, Poland (☎ 010 48 22 281001, fax 010 48 22 217161)

WETHERELL, John Michael Hugh Paxton; s of Paxton Wetherell, MBE (d 1978), of Whitstable, Kent, and Catherine Wilson, *née* Collins; *b* 24 Oct 1942; *Educ* Ampleforth; *m* 2 May 1964, Elizabeth Ann, da of Harold Thompson (d 1988), of Broadstairs, Kent; 1 s (Joseph b 1979), 5 da (Laura b 1966, Kate b 1968, Beatrice b 1972, Gabrielle b 1974, Jessica b 1978); *Career* Lloyd's underwriter Janson Green/Bolton Ingham Non-Marine Syndicate 1983; dir: Bolton Ingham Agency Ltd 1983-88, Janson Green Management Ltd 1986; memb Lloyd's 1973; *Recreations* reading, music, racing; *Clubs* City University; *Style*— John Wetherell, Esq; Claremont House, Claremont Rd, Tunbridge Wells, Kent (☎ 0892 36481); Lloyds Lime Street, London EC3 (☎ 071 623 5190)

WETZEL, Dave; s of Fred Wetzel (d 1982), and Ivy, *née* Donaldson (d 1981); *b* 9 Oct 1942; *Educ* Spring Grove GS Isleworth, Southall Tech Coll (ONC), Ealing Coll, Henry George Sch of Soc Sci; *m* 14 Feb 1973, Heather Jacqueline, da of Edmond John Allman (d 1976), of Staines; 2 da (Emma b 1968, Chantel b 1974); *Career* apprentice Wilkinson Sword 1959-62, inspector London Transport (conductor, driver) 1962-69, branch mangr Initial Serv 1969-70, pilot roster offr BA 1970-74, political organiser London Co-op 1974-81; sch govr, ed of Civil Aviation News 1978-81, dir London Dial-a-Ride Users' Assoc, convenor Trade Union & Co-op Esperanto Gp, chm Labour Land Campaign; ldr London Borough of Hounslow 1987-(cllr 1964-68 and 1986-), transport chair GLC 1981-86; memb TGWU; *Recreations* politics, swimming, windsurfing, reading; *Clubs* Feltham Lab; *Style*— Dave Wetzel; Civic Centre, Lampton Rd, Hounslow, London, TW3 4DN (☎ 081 682 5025)

WEYMES, John Barnard; OBE (1975); s of William Stanley Weymes (d 1965), of Fawdon, Newcastle-on-Tyne, and Irene Innes, *née* Horn (d 1976); *b* 18 Oct 1927; *Educ* King's Coll Durham Univ; *m* 1, 13 Oct 1951 (m dis 1978), Hazel Madaline, *née* Bellairs; 1 s (James b 1959), 2 da (Barbara (Mrs Doré) b 1952, Jan (Mrs Watson) b 1955); m 2, 15 April 1978, Beverley Pauline, *née* Gliddon; *Career* RAC 1945-48, 8 Royal Tank Regt; HM Dip Serv 1949-81: third sec Panama 1952-56, second sec Bogota 1956-60, vice consul Berlin 1960-63, dep consul Tamsui 1963-65, first sec FCO 1965-68, PM's Office 1968-70, consul Guatemala City 1970-74, FCO 1974-77, consul gen Vancouver 1977-78, ambass Tegucigalpa 1978-81; dir Cayman Islands News Bureau 1981-83, ret 1983; *Recreations* cricket, tennis, chess, reading; *Clubs* MCC; *Style*— John Weymes, Esq, OBE; Nuthatches, Balcombe Green, Sedlescombe, Battle, E Sussex TN33 0QL (☎ 042 487 455)

WEYMOUTH, Viscount; Alexander George Thynn (*sic*, reverted to this spelling); s and h of 6 Marquess of Bath, ED; *b* 6 May 1932; *Educ* Eton, Christ Church Oxford (MA); *m* 1969, Anna, da of Laszlo Gyarmathy, originally of Budapest but latterly of Los Angeles (Anna Gael, the actress, journalist and novelist); 1 s, 1 da (Hon Lenka Abigail b 1969); *Heir* s, Hon Ceawlin Henry Laszlo Thynn b 6 June 1974; *Career* late Lt Life Gds & Royal Wilts Yeo; contested: Westbury (Feb 1974) and Wells (1979) in Wessex Regionalist Pty's interest, Wessex (Euro elections 1979) Wessex Regionalist and European Fed Pty; painter; opened perm exhibition of murals in private apartments of Longleat 1973; dir Longleat Enterprises incl Cheddar Caves; *Books* (as Alexander Thynne before 1976, Thynn thereafter); The Carry Cot (1972), Lord Weymouth's Murals (1974), A Regionalist Manifesto (1975), The King is Dead (1976), Pillars of The Establishment (1980); *Record* I Play the Host (1974, singing own compositions); *Style*— Viscount Weymouth; Longleat, Warminster, Wilts (☎ 098 53 300)

WHADDON, Baron (Life Peer UK 1978), of Whaddon, Co Cambridge; (John) Derek Page; s of John Page and Clare, *née* Maher; *b* 14 Aug 1927; *Educ* St Bede's Coll Manchester, Univ of London (BSc); *m* 1, 1948, Catherine Audrey (d 1979), da of John William Halls; 1 s (Hon John Keir b 1955), 1 da (Hon Eve-Ann (Hon Mrs Prentice) b 1952); m 2, 1981, Angela Rixson, da of Luigi della Bella, of Treviso, Italy; *Career* dir Cambridge Chemicals 1962-89; MP (Lab) King's Lynn 1964-70, joined SDP 1981 (Lib Democrats since 1989); memb Cncl Management COSIRA to 1976-83; chm: Microautomatics Ltd 1981-87, Daltrade 1983-, Skorimpex-Rind 1985-; dir Rindalbourne 1983-90; *Recreations* flying; *Clubs* Reform; *Style*— The Rt Hon Lord Whaddon; Letterbock, Liscarney, Westport, Co Mayo, Republic of Ireland; The Old Vicarage, Whaddon, Royston, Herts (☎ 0223 207209)

WHALE, James; s of David L Whale (d 1979), of The Harrison Arms, Harrison St, London WC1, and Anne Elizabeth, *née* Price; *b* 13 May 1951; *Educ* various schs Surrey (Surrey Jr Archery Champion 1965), Marion Ross Sch of Drama; *m* 10 March 1970, Melinda Jane Maxted; 1 s (Peter), 1 da (Jane); *Career* radio and tv presenter; worked for a demolition co 1967-68, trainee buyer Harrods' 1968-69, worked in repertory theatre 1970-71, fndr DJ Radio Top Shop Oxford Circus 1971-73; presenter: Metro Radio Newcastle 1973-80, Line Up (BBC Radio Derby) 1980-81, Whale Up The Tees (Radio Tees) 1981-82, Friday File (Radio Aire, Leeds) 1982-, Three's Company (Tyne Tees TV) 1981-82; several appearances Midweek (BBC Radio Four) 1985, co-presenter Open Exchange (Channel Four) 1987, The James Whale Radio Show (Yorkshire TV) 1988; *Awards* three Sony awards; nominated for: Best Phone In Show 1976, Smash Hits Personality on Local Radio 1984; winner Smash Hits Local Personality of the Year 1988; *Recreations* eating and enjoying life; *Style*— James Whale, Esq; Time Artistes Ltd, Albert House, Albert St, Chadderton, Oldham, Lancs Ol9 7TS (☎ 061 633 6421, 061 627 5471)

WHALEN, Geoffrey Henry; CBE (1989); s of Henry Charles Whalen (d 1981), and Mabel Elizabeth Whalen (d 1965); *b* 8 Jan 1936; *Educ* East Ham GS, Magdalen Coll Oxford (MA); *m* 1961, Elizabeth Charlotte, da of Dr Eric Ward, of Helperby, Yorks; 2 s (Thomas b 1967, Henry b 1977), 3 da (Catherine b 1963, Anna b 1965, Georgina b.1975); *Career* personnel dir Leyland Cars, British Leyland 1975-78; Peugeot Talbot Motor Co Ltd: asst md 1981-84, md 1984-90, dep chm and md 1990-; dir: Robins and Day Ltd, Talbot Ireland Ltd, Proptal UK Ltd, Motaquip Ltd, Sunbeam-Talbot Ltd; pres Soc of Motor Manufacturers & Traders 1988-90, FIPM, Companion BIM, FIMI; Chevalier de la Legion d'Honneur 1990; *Recreations* cricket, tennis; *Clubs* Utd Oxford and Cambridge; *Style*— Geoffrey Whalen, Esq, CBE; 8 Park Crescent, Abingdon, Oxfordshire; Peugeot Talbot Motor Co Ltd, Aldermoor House, PO Box 227, Aldermoor Lane, Coventry CV3 1LT (☎ 0203 884000, fax 0203 884001)

WHALLEY, Anthony; s of Frederic Edward Whalley (d 1989), and Kathleen, *née* Rowan (d 1956); *b* 5 July 1941; *Educ* Salesian Coll Farnborough, St Joseph's Coll Mark Cross; *m* 8 Oct 1966, Eileen Angela, da of Gp Capt Harold Robert Withers, OBE (d 1986); 2 s (Frederick b 1968, James b 1972), 1 da (Caroline b 1967); *Career* chm Neotech Group Ltd (formerly Aeronautical Radio Serv Ltd) 1978-; non-exec dir: Medusa Communications Ltd, Kemutec Group Ltd, WLS Holdings Ltd, Nord Anglia Education plc, Glopec Holdings Ltd, Foundation Systems Ltd; memb CBI (SE Regnl Cncl 1980-86, Co Ctee 1984-88); ACA 1966, FCA 1976; *Recreations* music, literature; *Clubs* Nat Lib; *Style*— Anthony Whalley, Esq; 27 Clarence Rd, Windsor, Berks; 311 Willoughby House, Barbican, London EC2 (☎ 071 628 0026); Neotech Gp Ltd, Doman Rd, Camberley, Surrey (☎ 0276 685005, fax 0276 61524, telex 858779)

WHALLEY, Guy Ainsworth; s of Philip Guy Rothay Whalley, CBE (d 1950), and Norah Helen, *née* Mawdsley (d 1981), direct descendant of Col Edward Whalley, cousin of Oliver Cromwell and Signatory of The Death Warrant of King Charles I; *b* 26

May 1933; *Educ* Rugby, Gonville and Caius Coll Cambridge (BA, MA); *m* 22 Aug 1959, Sarah, da of Walter William Knight (d 1966); 1 s (Philip Mark b 1961), 1 da (Katherine Jane b 1962); *Career* Nat Serv 2 Lt Royal Fus 1951-53, active serv Korean War 1952-53; slr Supreme Ct 1959, ptnr Freshfields Slrs 1964-, non exec dir Higgs and Hill plc 1972-, dir and memb Ctee of Mgmnt RAM 1982-, govr Beechwood Park Sch 1974-88 (chm 1975-84), co-opted memb Oxford Univ Appts Ctee 1982-; tstee: Rugby Sch War Meml Fund 1980-, Rugby Sch Gen Charitable Tst 1986-; *Recreations* gardening, music, cricket, golf, painting; *Clubs* MCC; *Style*— Guy Whalley, Esq; Woodmans Farm, Chipperfield, Hertfordshire (☎ 093 263795); Whitefriars, 65 Fleet St, London EC4Y 1HS (☎ 071 936 4000, telex 889292, fax 071 832 7001)

WHALLEY, Jeffrey; *b* 20 Nov 1942; *Career* non-exec dir: COIL Holdings Limited 1989-, Combined Optical Industries Limited 1990-, Plastic Integral Optics Limited 1990-, Imico Ltd 1991-; dep chm: Cayson Holdings Limited 1989-, Crossley House Developments Capital Limited 1989-, Crossley House Registrars Limited 1982-, Gartland and Whalley Holdings Limited 1989-, Gartland and Whalley Securities Limited 1989-; non-exec dep chm: FKI plc 1982-, Babcock International Group plc 1989-; *Style*— Jeffrey Whalley, Esq; Gartland & Whalley Securities Ltd, Crossley House, Halifax, West Yorks (☎ 0422 349401, fax 0422 349495)

WHALLEY, John Mayson; s of George Mayson Whalley (d 1968), and Ada Florence, *née* Cairns (d 1989); *b* 14 Sept 1932; *Educ* The Grammar Sch Preston, Univ of Liverpool (BArch, MCD, Sir Charles Reilly Medal), Univ of Pennsylvania (MLA); *m* 21 May 1966, (Elizabeth) Gillian, da of Walter Hide; 1 s (James b 1972), 2 da (Emma b 1968, Tamsin b 1970); *Career* landscape architecture Oskar Stonorov Philadelphia 1960-, architect and landscape architect Grenfell Baines & Hargreaves and Bldg Design Ptnrship Preston 1960-62, assoc Derek Lovejoy & Assocs 1963-64, ptnr Derek Lovejoy & Ptnrs 1968-, fndr and sr ptnr DLP Manchester 1963-; Leverhulme and Italian govt fellowships for study in Scandinavia and Univ of Rome 1957-58, Fulbright scholar 1958, Manchester Soc of Architects Winstanley fellowship 1965; Civic Tst awards: W Burton Power Station 1968, Cheshire Constabulary HQ 1969, Rochdale Canal 1973; first prize int competition: Cergy-Pontoise France 1970, regnl park at La Courneuve Paris 1972; first prizes design competition: Liverpool Garden Festival 1984, Stoke-on-Trent Garden Festival 1986, Glasgow Garden Festival 1988, Urban Park Vitoria-Gaskiz Spain 1990; Civic Tst awards assessor 1970-, former chm RIBA NW Reg 1984-85; former pres: Manchester Soc of Architects 1980-81 (nat pres), Landscape Inst 1985-87; contrib radio and tv programmes, author tech press articles and papers; memb French Order of Architects 1977, FRIBA 1968, FRTPI 1971, FLI 1970, FRSA 1986; *Recreations* jazz, collecting classic cars, salmon fishing, cricket, photography, travel, good food and wine; *Clubs* Lansdowne, Ronnie Scott's, St James' (Manchester); *Style*— John M Whalley, Esq; Dilworth House, Longridge, Nr Preston PR3 3ST (☎ 0772 783262), Derek Lovejoy & Partnership, Arkwright House, Parsonage Gardens, Manchester M3 2LE (☎ 061 8348825, fax 061 8320470, telex 666628)

WHALLEY, Capt Richard Carlton; s of Frederick Seymour Whalley, MC (d 1958), of The Lawn, Marlow, Bucks, and Gwendolen, *née* Collingwood (d 1984); *b* 4 July 1922; *Educ* Shrewsbury, 151 OCTU; *m* 1 Aug 1945, Mary Christian, da of George Bradley (d 1954), of Hilltop Farm, Croxton Kerrial, Grantham, Lincs; 2 s (Jonathon b 1946, Peter b 1948), 2 da (Mary b 1951, Margaret (twin) b 1951); *Career* Regular Army 1940, cmmnd Royal Signals 1942, Indian Assam Burma Adj 2 Div Signals 1942-45 (despatches 1945), Staff Capt War Office 1945-48, GHQ Singapore 1948-51; Vulcan Foundry Ltd locomotive builders 1952-68: asst sec, commercial mangr, gen mangr; mangr Diesel Engine Div English Electric, dir and gen mangr Glacier Metals 1968-70, dep chm and md Millspaugh Group 1971-77, divnl md Sulzer Bros UK, memb Bd Br Shipbuilders 1978-81, chm and md Ewden Assoc 1982-; chm Working Pty NEDO, memb Industl Tbnls 1972-; Freeman Worshipful Co of Cutlers; FInstD; *Recreations* rowing, walking; *Clubs* National Liberal, London Rowing, Sheffield; *Style*— Capt Richard Whalley; Sunnybank Farm, Bolsterstone, Sheffield S30 5ZL (☎ 0742 883116); Ewden Associates Ltd, Ewden House, Bolsterstone, Sheffield S30 S2L (☎ 0742 883116, fax 0742 883116, car 0860 534944)

WHALLEY, Maj-Gen William Leonard; CB (1985); s of William Whalley (d 1951), and Doris Patricia, *née* Hallimond; *b* 19 March 1930; *Educ* Sir William Turner's Sch Coatham, Royal Mill Coll of Sci; *m* 30 July 1955, (Honor) Mary, da of Maj Cyril Golden (d 1985); 1 da (Elisabeth Anne Mary b 7 July 1956); *Recreations* cabinet making, bridge, information technology; *Style*— Maj-Gen William Whalley, CB; Corby City Technology College, Old School, Brooke Rd, Great Oakley, Corby, Northants NN18 8HG (☎ 0536 742572, fax 0536 743794)

WHARNCLIFFE, Dowager Countess of; Aline Margaret Montagu-Stuart-Wortley-Mackenzie; *née* Bruce; o da of Robert Fernie Dunlop Bruce (d 1952), of Dyson Holmes House, Wharncliffe Side, nr Sheffield; *m* 1957, 4 Earl of Wharncliffe (d 1987); 2 da (Lady Joanna Margaret b 1959, d 1981, Lady Rowena Montagu Stuart Wortley-Hunt, *qv*, b 1961; *Style*— The Rt Hon the Dowager Countess of Wharncliffe; Wharncliffe House, Wortley, Sheffield

WHARNCLIFFE, 5 Earl of (UK 1876) Richard Alan Montagu Stuart Wortley; also Baron Wharncliffe (UK 1826) and Viscount Carlton (UK 1876); er s of Alan Ralph Montagu Stuart Wortley (d 1986), and Virginia Ann, *née* Claybaugh; suc his kinsman 4 Earl of Wharncliffe (d 1987); *b* 26 May 1953; *Educ* Wesleyan Univ; *m* 1979, Mary Elizabeth, da of Rev William Reed, of Keene, NH, USA; 3 s (Viscount Carlton, Hon Christopher James b 1983, Hon Otis Alexander b 14 Feb 1991); *Heir* s, Reed Montagu Stuart Wortley, Viscount Carlton, b 5 Feb 1980; *Career* construction foreman; *Style*— The Rt Hon the Earl of Wharncliffe; 270 Main Street, Cumberland Center, Maine, USA

WHARTON, Dr Christopher Frederick Percy; s of John Christopher Wharton, of Banbury, Oxon, and Gertrude Margaret, *née* Dingwall; *b* 19 Feb 1937; *Educ* Shrewsbury, Worcester Coll Oxford (BMS BCh, MA, DM), MRCS, MRCP, LRCP; *m* 10 Aug 1963 (m dis 1980), Andrea Mary Puckle, da of Andrew Gordon Leslie Puckle (d 1988), of Loxwood, W Sussex; 2 da (Antonia Helen Jane b 30 May 1969, (Virginia Phillippa Gertrude) Rose b 29 Oct 1972); m 2, 23 May 1980, Pamela Mary, da of Sqdn Ldr William Henry Deane, of Pretoria, SA; *Career* house offr and registrar in cardiology and gen med Guy's 1963-73, conslt physician in med and cardiology Bromley Dist Hosps 1963-, hon tutor Guy's Med Sch 1979-, teacher Univ of London 1986- (clinical tutor 1974-84), dist tutor RCP; memb Mgmnt Bd Bromley DHA, chm Bromley Hosps Med Exec Ctee; memb Mgmnt Ctee Chipstead Lake Cheshire Home; Freeman City of London 1982, Liveryman Worshipful Co of Gunmakers; FRCP 1980; memb: British Cardiac Soc 1982, BMA; *Books* Cardiological Problems in Practice (1981), Management of Common Disease in Practice Cardiology (with A R Archer, 1986); *Publications* various pubns on echocardiography (1967-72), Myocardial Infarct-Management and Rehabilitation article in Cardiac Update (1987), A Case of Angina-Dual Pathology (1989), Silent Ischaemia-What Implications (1989); *Recreations* shooting, golf, tennis, skiing, Chelsea FC, travel, wine and food; *Clubs* Athenaeum; *Style*— Dr Christopher Wharton; 24-26 High St, Chipstead, nr Sevenoaks, Kent (☎ 0732 452906); The Medical Unit, Farnborough Hospital, Farnborough Common, Orpington, Kent (☎ 0689 853333)

WHARTON, Baroness (E 1544/5); Myrtle Olive Felix (Ziki) Robertson; *née* Arbuthnot; er da of David Arbuthnot (s of Maj John Arbuthnot, MVO, gn of Sir Robert Arbuthnot, 2 Bt), and Baroness Wharton, tenth holder of the title (d 1974); suc as eleventh holder of the title on termination of the abeyance in her favour 1990; *b* 20 Feb 1934; *m* 1958, Henry Macleod Robertson, s of Henry Robertson, of Elgin; 3 s (Hon Myles Christopher David b 1964, Hon Christopher James b 1969, Hon Nicholas Charles b (twin) b 1969), 1 da (Hon Patricia Lesley b 1966); *Heir* s, Hon Myles Christopher David Robertson b 1 Oct 1964; *Style*— The Rt Hon Lady Wharton

WHARTON, (John) Steven; s of Jack Illingworth Wharton (d 1969), and Gladys May Wharton, *née* Cundall; *b* 5 Oct 1943; *Educ* Burton-Stather Primary, Oundle; *m* 26 Oct 1978, Fiona Lisbeth, da of Thomas Windle; 1 s (Joseph William b 1981), 1 da (Angela Claire b 1979); *Career* chm J Wharton (Shipping) Ltd 1986- (md from 1969); chm and md of many assoc cos inc: Trent Lighterage Ltd, JS Wharton (Hldgs) Ltd, J Wharton (Farms) Ltd; *Recreations* hockey (over 100 caps for Lincs), hunting, tennis, golf, squash; *Clubs* Farmers; *Style*— Steven Wharton, Esq; JI Wharton (Shipping) Ltd, Grove Wharf, Gunness, Scunthorpe, South Humberside (☎ 0724 782371, telex 52213, fax 782610)

WHATELY, Nina Abigail; da of Alexander MacArthur Finlayson (d 1923), of Montevideo, Uruguay, and Mari Gwendolen, *née* Jones; *b* 9 Oct 1921; *Educ* St John's Bexhill, Lausanne Switzerland; *m* 19 July 1947, Gerald Arthur Whately, OBE (d 1985), s of Maj Ellis George Whately, MC (d 1966), of 59 Cadogan Square, London; 1 s (Julian Richard b 10 Aug 1949), 1 da (Miranda Nina (Mrs Allhusen) b 19 May 1952); *Career* WWII WRNS 3 offr 1941-45; local ctee memb: Arthritis and Rheumatism Res, Friends of the Elderly; sec Herbert and Peter Blagrave Charitable Tst; vice pres: W Berks Macmillan Cancer Care Appeal, Royal UK Benificent Assoc; *Recreations* gardening, painting, grandchildren; *Style*— Mrs Nina Whately

WHATLEY, Frederick Robert; *b* 26 Jan 1924; *Educ* Univ of Cambridge (ARC scholar, BA, PhD); *Career* res assoc Dept of Plant Nutrition UCLA 1948-50, sr lectr Univ of Sydney 1951-53, Guggenheim fell Univ of Oxford and Nobel Inst Stockholm 1959-60; UCLA: asst plant physiologist Dept of Soils and Plant Nutrition 1953-59 and 1960-62, assoc biochemist Dept of Cell Physiology 1962-64; prof of botany King's Coll London 1964-71, Sherardian prof of botany Univ of Oxford 1971-, visiting res fell Res Sch of Biology ANU 1979, head of Dept of Plant Scis Univ of Oxford 1985-; author of 115 res pubns; FRS 1975; *Books* Light and Plant Life (with J M Whatley); *Style*— Prof Frederick Whatley, FRS; Department of Plant Sciences, University of Oxford, Oxford OX1 3RB (☎ 0865 275000, fax 0865 275144, telex 83147 VIA OR G, attn PLANTOX)

WHATMORE, Andrew; s of Charles Sydney Whatmore, of Palmer's Lodge, Tunbridge Wells, Kent TN3 9AD, and Monica Mabel, *née* Tucker; *b* 18 June 1946; *Educ* The Skinners' Sch Tunbridge Wells, Woolwich Poly, London Univ; *m* 17 Dec 1983, Elizabeth, da of James Stewart Morrison Sim, of 32 McNabb St, Dollar, Clacks; 1 s (Charles Stewart b 1984), 1 da (Kathryn Elizabeth b 1985); *Career* resident engr: (EAEC) Kenya 1980, Roughton and Ptnrs Al Ain UAE 1981; chief engr Taylor Woodrow Int Ghana 1983, agent Christiani & Nielsen S Wales 1987; CEng, MICE; *Style*— Mr Andrew Whatmore; Garth Hall, Abertridwr, Caerphilly, Mid-Glamorgan CF8 2DS (☎ 0222 830261); Geoffrey Osborne Ltd, Stockbridge Rd, Chichester PO19 2LL (☎ 0243 787811)

WHEADON, Richard Anthony; s of Ivor Cecil Newman Wheadon (d 1981), and Margarita Augusta; *b* 31 Aug 1933; *Educ* Cranleigh Sch, Balliol Coll Oxford (MA); *m* 1961, Ann Mary, da of Gp Capt Frederick Charles Richardson, CBE; 3 s; *Career* Sword of Honour RAF 1955, Air Radar Offr 1955-57; asst master Eton Coll 1957-66, Eton Coll CCF 1958-66, dep headmaster and head of Science Dept Dauntsey's Sch 1966-71, contingent cdr Dauntsey's Sch CCF 1969-70; memb Wilts Educn Ctee's Science Advsy Panel; princ Elizabeth Coll Guernsey 1972-88; rowing: pres Balliol Coll Boat Club 1954 and 1955, Bow Oxford Univ 100 Boat Race, Capt and coach RAF eight 1956-57, in Br VIII Euro Championships and Olympic Games 1956, coach Oxford Boat Race 1957, nat coach and Olympic selector 1965-66; *Books* The Principles of Light and Optics (1968); *Recreations* french horn, photography, sailing, singing, swimming; *Style*— Richard Wheadon, Esq; L'Enclos Gallienne, Rue du Court Laurent, Torteval, Guernsey, CI (☎ 0481 64988)

WHEARE, Thomas David; s of Sir Kenneth Clinton Wheare, CMG (d 1979), of Oxford, and Joan, *née* Randell, MA; *b* 11 Oct 1944; *Educ* Dragon Sch, Magdalen Coll Sch Oxford, King's Coll Cambridge (MA), Christ Church Oxford (DipEd); *m* 29 Oct 1977, Rosalind Clare, da of J E Spice, of Winchester; 2 da (Clare b 1980, Frances b 1981); *Career* asst master Eton 1967-76, housemaster Shrewsbury Sch 1976-83, headmaster Bryanston Sch 1983-; *Recreations* music; *Style*— Thomas Wheare, Esq; The Headmaster's Ho, Bryanston Sch, Blandford, Dorset (☎ 0258 452728)

WHEAT, Kenneth James (Ken); s of Arthur James Wheat, of Kenilworth, Warwickshire, and Freda, *née* Glasson; *b* 16 April 1948; *Educ* Castle HS Kenilworth, Royal Agricultural Coll Cirencester (MRAC); *m* 2 Oct 1981, Trudi Elizabeth, da of Percival McDonald, of Stratford upon Avon, Warwick; *Career* sr writer: KMP Manchester 1975-77, Cogent Elliot 1977-82, Ayer Barker 1982-83, Crawford Halls 1984-86; creative dir Brookes and Vernons 1986-; memb South Warwicks Flying Sch; *Recreations* athletics, flying, skiing, gardening, rare breeds; *Clubs* Leamington Cycling and Athletics; *Style*— Ken Wheat, Esq; Brookes & Vernons, 109 Hagley Rd, Edgbaston, Birmingham B16 8LA (☎ 021 455 9481)

WHEATCROFT, Christopher John Wildin; s of Harold Wheatcroft (d 1952), and Doris, *née* Wildin; *b* 7 May 1938; *Educ* Winchester Coll; *m* 30 June 1966, (Thelma Clare) Greer, da of Joseph Allison Corkey; 2 s (James b 14 Aug 1970, Jonathan b 10 July 1980), 1 da (Jessica b 28 Feb 1973); *Career* Nat Serv cmmnd Somerset Light Infantry 1956-58; ptnr Spicer and Pegler 1971 (articled clerk 1958-63), sr ptnr Touche Ross & Co (after merger with Spicer and Pegler 1990); FCA; *Style*— Christopher Wheatcroft, Esq; Touche Ross & Co, Friary Court, 65 Crutched Friars, London EC3N 2NP (☎ 071 480 7766, fax 071 480 6958)

WHEATLEY, Baroness; Agnes Mary; *née* Nichol; da of Samuel Nichol; *m* 1935,Baron Wheatley, PC, QC (Life Peer, d 1988); 4 s, 1 da; *Style*— The Rt Hon Lady Wheatley; Flacon House, 91/16 Morningside Road, Edinburgh EH10 4AY

WHEATLEY, Alan Edward; s of Edward Wheatley, and Margaret Rosina Turner; *b* 23 May 1938; *Educ* Ilford GS; *m* 30 June 1962, Marion Frances, da of John Douglas Wilson (d 1968); 1 da (Susan b 1966), 2 s (Michael b 1968, Jonathan b 1974); *Career* Price Waterhouse 1960- (sr ptnr London Office 1985-), non-exec dir EBS Investments Ltd (Bank of England subsid) 1977-90, non-exec dep chm Cable & Wireless plc 1984-85 (govt dir 1981-84), non-exec memb Bd BSC 1984-; memb Bd Industl Devpt Advsy Bd 1985-; govr Solefield Sch; FCA; *Recreations* golf, tennis, badminton, music, bridge; *Clubs* Wildernesse Golf; *Style*— Alan E Wheatley, Esq; Price Waterhouse, Southwark Towers, 32 London Bridge St, London SE1 (☎ 071 939 3000, fax 071 378 0647, telex 884 657/8)

WHEATLEY, Sir (George) Andrew; CBE (1960); s of Robert Wheatley; *b* 1908; *Educ* Rugby, Exeter Coll Oxford; *m* 1937, Mary Vera Hunt; 3 s, 2 da; *Career* BCL, DL Hants 1967-70, clerk of the Peace & clerk Hants CC 1946-67; memb English Local Govt Boundary Commission 1971-; kt 1967; *Style*— Sir Andrew Wheatley, CBE

WHEATLEY, Rear Adm Anthony; CB (1988); s of Edgar Christian Wheatley, and

Audrey Grace Barton Hall, *née* Phillips; *b* 3 Oct 1933; *Educ* Berkhamsted Sch, RNC Dartmouth, RN Engrg Coll Manadon; *m* 17 Nov 1962, Iona Sheila, da of Major Oliver Peter Haig (d 1987); 1 da (Charlotte b 1 Oct 1963); *Career* RN joined 1950, HMS Ceylon 1958-60, HMS Ganges 1960-61, HMS Cambrian 1962-64, Staff of RNEC Manadon 1964-67, Staff of Cdr Br Navy Staff Washington 1967-69, HMS Diomede 1970-72, Staff of C-in-C Fleet 1972-74, Exec Offr RNEC Manadon 1975-76, MOD Procurement Exec 1977-79, Br naval attaché Brasilia 1979-81, RCDS 1982, HMS Collingwood (in cmd) 1982-85; Flag Offr Portsmouth, Naval Base Cdr and Head of Estab of Fleet Maintenance and Repair Orgn Portsmouth 1985-87; placed on ret list 1988; gen mangr Nat Hosps for Nervous Diseases 1988- 77; *Recreations* cricket (pres RN Cricket Club), golf, music; *Clubs* Army and Navy, Free Foresters; *Style*— Rear Adm Anthony Wheatley, CB; 2 Claridge Court, Munster Rd, Fulham, London SW6 4EY

WHEATLEY, Rev Canon Arthur; s of George Wilson Wheatley (d 1971), of Edinburgh, and Elizabeth, *née* Mackenzie (d 1987); *b* 4 March 1931; *Educ* Alloa Acad, The Episcopal Theol Coll Edinburgh; *m* 1 Aug 1959, (Sheena) Morag, *née* Wilde; 2 s (Christopher b 2 Oct 1961, Kenneth b 3 Nov 1969), 2 da (Paula b 1 Sept 1960, Virginia b 14 June 1964); *Career* ordained: deacon 1970, priest 1970; curate St Salvador Dundee Brechin and St Ninian Dundee 1970-71, priest i/c St Ninian Dundee 1971-76, rector Holy Trinity Elgin with St Margaret's Church Lossiemonth Dio of Moray Ross and Caithness 1976-80, canon St Andrew's Cath 1978-80 (provost 1980-83, canon 1983-); priest i/c: Grantown-on-Spey 1983, Rothiemurchus 1983-; chaplain: HM Prison Porterfield Inverness 1978-, RAF Grantown-on-Spey 1983-; *Recreations* shooting, fishing, bee-keeping; *Style*— Rev Canon Arthur Wheatley; The Rectory, Grant Rd, Grantown-on-Spey PH26 3ER (☎ 0479 2866)

WHEATLEY, Derek Peter Francis; QC (1981); s of Edward Pearse Wheatley (d 1967), of Exeter, and Gladys Eugenie, *née* Williams; *b* 18 Dec 1925; *Educ* The Leys Sch Cambridge, Univ Coll Oxford (MA); *m* 1955, Elisabeth Pamela, da of John Morgan Reynolds Fairlawn (d 1983), of Penarth; 2 s (Simon, Jonathan), 1 da (Claire); *Career* 8 King's Royal Hussars, Lt 1946-48; served BAOR in Germany; called to the Bar 1951, practised until 1974 and 1990-, memb Hon Soc of the Middle Temple, recorder Crown Ct 1971-74, memb Bar Cncl 1975-78, 1980-83 and 1986-90, memb Bar Cncl Law Soc Ctee on Banking Law 1976-, chm Legal Ctee Ctee of London and Scottish Bankers 1984-86, chief legal advsr Lloyds Bank plc 1974-90; vice-pres Bar Assoc for Commerce Finance and Industry; *Recreations* yachting; *Clubs* Bar Yacht; *Style*— Derek Wheatley, Esq, QC; 3 The Wardrobe, Old Palace Yard, Richmond, Surrey (☎ 081 940 6242); 3 Grays Inn Place, Grays Inn, London WC1R 5EA (☎ 071 831 8441, fax 071 831 8479, telex 295119 LEXCOL G)

WHEATLEY, John Edward Clive; MC, JP; s of Edward Pearse Wheatley (d 1968, former alderman and sheriff of Exeter), and Gladwys Eugenie, *née* Williams; *b* 7 March 1921; *Educ* The Leys Sch Cambridge, Exeter Univ; *m* 1945, Rosemarie Joy Malet, da of Victor Samuel Rowbotham of Johannesburg, SA; 3 s (Robin, Adam, Benedict), 1 da (Candida); *Career* Staff Capt N Africa, Italy; Staff Capt RMC Sandhurst; metal merchant; former chm: E Pearse & Co Ltd, Pearse Complex Alloys Ltd, C Philipp & Son Ltd; former chm: South Western Industrial Gases Ltd (SWIG), Exeter Housing Soc Ltd, chm Parks (Exeter) Ltd; pres British Scrap Fedn 1978-79; former chm: E Pearse and Co Ltd, C Phillips & Son (Bristol) Ltd, Bay City Radio; former dir West One Prodns Ltd; memb Police Authority for Devon and Cornwall; *Recreations* travel, photography, collecting old books; *Clubs* Army and Navy; *Style*— John Wheatley, Esq, MC, JP; Bellenden, Wreford's Lane, Exeter (☎ 0392 56087); Parks (Exeter) Ltd, 11/12 West St, Exeter (☎ 0392 32145)

WHEATLEY, Hon John Francis; s of Baron Wheatley (Life Peer, d 1988), and Agnes Mary, da of Samuel Nichol; *b* 9 May 1941; *Educ* Mount St Mary's Coll Derbyshire, Univ of Edinburgh (BL); *m* 1970, Bronwen Catherine, da of Alastair Fraser, of Dollar; 2 s; *Career* called to the Bar Scot 1966, advocate depute 1974-78; Sheriff of Perthshire and Kinross-shire 1980-; *Recreations* gardening, music; *Style*— The Hon John Wheatley; Braefoot Farmhouse, Fossoway, Kinross-shire (☎ 057 74 212); Sheriff Court House, Tay St, Perth (☎ 0738-20546)

WHEATLEY, John Robert Glamis; s of Arthur William Robert Wheatley (d 1971), of Westcliff-on-Sea, Essex, and Marjorie, *née* Leeds; *b* 21 Aug 1930; *Educ* Brentwood Sch, Poly Regent Street; *m* 1964, Pamela Christine, da of Maj Victor George Guest; 2 c (Torquil William Glamis b 10 June 1969, Camilla Victoria Jill b 25 May 1971); *Career* asst: Housing Div GLC 1955-58, Campbell-Jones & Sons Architects 1958-59; Covell Matthews & Partners: gp ldr 1959-63, assoc ptnr 1963-66, ptnr 1966; Covell Matthews Wheatley: fndr dir 1976, chm 1977-84, dir 1984-; dir CMW Group plc 1990-, chm Covell Matthews Partnership 1982-88; Worshipful Co of Chartered Architects: fndr memb 1984, Junior Warden 1988-89, Renter Warden 1989-90, Master 1990-91; RIBA 1959, memb Assoc of Architects Kenya 1970, FRSA 1990; *Recreations* music, cricket, skiing; *Style*— John Wheatley, Esq; Cato Cottage, 24 Esher Green, Esher, Surrey KT10 8AD (☎ 0372 464224); Covell Matthews Wheatley Architects Ltd, 10 Bourdon place, London W1X 9HZ (☎ 071 409 2444)

WHEATLEY, Hon Michael; yst s of Baron Wheatley, PC (Life Peer, d 1988); *b* 1949; *Educ* Mount St Mary's Coll Derbyshire; *m* 1971, Anne, da of Thomas Barry; *Clubs* MCC; *Style*— The Hon Michael Wheatley; Millburn, Old Philpstoun, W Lothian EH49 7RY

WHEATLEY, Hon Patrick; 2 s of Baron Wheatley, PC (Life Peer, d 1988); *b* 1943; *m* 1968, Sheena, da of Douglas Lawrie; *Style*— The Hon Patrick Wheatley; c/o The Rt Hon Lady Wheatley, 3 Greenhill Gardens, Edinburgh EH10 4BN

WHEATLEY, Peter Malcolm Bernard Lewin; s of Malcolm Lewin Wheatley, of Wimbledon, and Lady Eileen, *née* O'Neil (d 1988); *b* 13 July 1938; *Educ* St Joseph's Coll Ipswich, John Fisher Sch Purley; *m* ; 1 s (Rupert Peter Martin Lewin b 1965); *Career* Nat Serv 1956-58 (cmmnd offr 15/19 Kings Royal Hussars 1957); freelance PR offr to theatrical ventures 1965-69, restaurant mangr Gibraltar 1969, opened first restaurant Queen's Hotel Gibraltar 1970, (second Royal Gibraltar Yacht Club 1971, third Strings Gibraltar 1974), weekly broadcasts on cookery Br Forces Bdcasting Serv 1970-; chm Licensed Victuallers' Assoc Gilbraltar 1984-88; MCFA 1980; *Recreations* travel, riding, showjumping; *Clubs* Cavalry; *Style*— Peter Wheatley, Esq; 25 Gibraltar Heights, Church Lane, Gibraltar (☎ 350 78800); Strings Restaurant, 44 Cornwall's Lane Gibraltar (☎ 350 78800)

WHEATLEY, Robert Larke Andrew; s of Sir (George) Andrew Wheatley, CBE, of St Thomas Park, Lymington, and the late Vera, *née* Hunt; *b* 14 Aug 1938; *Educ* Rugby, McGill Univ Montreal; *m* 22 Aug 1964, Elizabeth Marian, da of Leonard Amos Oakden, of Winchelsea, Sussex; 1 s (Andrew b 1966), 1 da (Nicola b 1968); *Career* 2 Lt Rifle Bde, Malaya 1957; co sec R & G Cuthbert Ltd 1970-71, product mangr IBM (UK) Ltd 1986-; CA, ACMA; *Recreations* gardening, singing, school governor; *Style*— Robert Wheatley, Esq; The Pines, Edward Rd, St Cross, Winchester, Hants SO23 9RB

WHEATLEY, Simon Derek John Pearse; s of Derek Peter Francis Wheatley, QC, of 3 The Wardrobe, Old Palace Yard, Richmond, Surrey, and Elizabeth Pamela, *née* Reynolds; *b* 8 Aug 1956; *Educ* Marlborough, Brunel Univ (LLB); *Career* called to the Bar Middle Temple 1979; *Recreations* broadcasting; *Style*— Simon Wheatley, Esq; 22 Cedar Terrace, Richmond, Surrey (☎ 081 948 7815); 1 Harcourt Buildings, Temple, London (☎ 081 353 0375, fax 081 583 5816)

WHEATLEY-HUBBARD, (Evelyn) Raymond; OBE (1990); s of Eric Wyndham Hubbard (d 1946); assumed additional name of Wheatley by deed poll 1949; *b* 22 Feb 1921; *Educ* Eton; *m* 1949, Ann Christobel, OBE, da of late Col Charles Joshua Hirst Wheatley, TD, DL, JP; 1 s, 1 da; *Career* Coldstream Gds 1940-46; chartered surveyor and land agent; *Clubs* Cavalry and Guards'; *Style*— Raymond Wheatley-Hubbard, Esq, OBE; The Dower House, Boyton, Warminster, Wilts (☎ 0985 50214)

WHEATLY, Richard John Norwood; s of Patrick Wheatly (d 1986), of Watford, and Doris Mary, *née* Norwood; *b* 9 Feb 1946; *Educ* Watford GS, St John's Coll Cambridge (MA); *m* 1, 8 July 1968 (m dis 1974), Jane Margaret Phillips, da of Frank Thomas, of Rickmansworth, Herts; 1 da (Sophie Catherine Jane b 26 June 1970); m 2, 9 Feb 1980, Mrs Susan Angela Seider, da of Stuart Masson, of Watford, Herts; *Career* mktg mangr Unilever 1968-72; gp exec: Garland Compton Advertising 1972-73, McCann Erickson Advertising 1973-74; divnl mangr Johnson & Johnson 1974-78, chm Leo Burnett Advertising 1978-; FIPA 1988; *Recreations* riding, shooting; *Clubs* Oxford and Cambridge, Royal Southampton Yacht; *Style*— Richard Wheatly, Esq; Penn House, Penn Common, Bramshaw, Hants (☎ 0794 390 843); Leo Burnett Ltd, 48 St Martin's Lane, London WC2N 4EJ (☎ 071 829 7177, fax 071 829 7026/7, telex 24243)

WHEATON, Rev Canon David Harry; s of Harry Wheaton, MBE (d 1982), and Kathleen Mary, *née* Hyde-Frost (d 1957); *b* 2 June 1930; *Educ* Abingdon, St John's Coll Oxford (MA), London Bible Coll (BD); *m* 23 March 1956, Helen Joy, da of Leonard Forrer (d 1953); 1 s (Mark b 1965), 2 da (Mary b 1964, Joanna b 1967); *Career* tutor Oak Hill Coll 1954-62; rector Ludgershall Bucks 1962-66, vicar of St Paul's Onslow Sq London 1966-71, chaplain Brompton Hosp 1969-71; princ Oak Hill Coll 1971-86, vicar of Christ Church Ware 1986-; Hon Canon of St Albans 1976, rural dean of Hertford 1988-, hon chaplain to HM the Queen 1990-; dir: Church Soc Tst (chm 1981-88), Church Pastoral-Aid Society Tst; *Books* New Bible Dictionary (contrib, 1962), New Bible Commentary (contrib, revised 1970), Evangelical Dictionary of Theology (contrib, 1984), Here We Stand (contrib, 1986), Restoring the Vision (contrib, 1990); *Recreations* walking, DIY; *Style*— The Rev Canon David Wheaton; Christchurch Vicarage, 15 Hanbury Close, Ware, Herts SG12 7BZ (☎ 0920 3165); Dalegarth, Hare Lane, Buckland St Mary, Chard, Somerset (☎ 046 034 377)

WHEELER, Alice, Lady; Alice Webster; *née* Stones; yst da of George Heath Stones, of Rutherglen, Lanarkshire; *m* 7 Jan 1938, Sir Arthur Frederick Pullman Wheeler, 2 Bt (d 16 Dec 1964); *Style*— Alice, Lady Wheeler; E12, Marine Gate, Marine Parade, Brighton 7, Sussex

WHEELER, Sir (Harry) Anthony; OBE (1973); s of Herbert George Wheeler (d 1976), of Stranraer, and Laura Emma, *née* Groom; *b* 7 Nov 1919; *Educ* Stranraer HS, Glasgow Sch of Architecture, Univ of Strathclyde (BArch); *m* 6 Oct 1944, Dorothy Jean, da of David Campbell; 1 da (Pamela Jane b 24 Sept 1953); *Career* WWII RA 1939-46 (demobbed Capt); asst to: city architect Oxford 1948, Sir Herbert Baker & Scott 1949; sr architect Glenrothes New Town 1949-51, sr lectr Dundee Sch of Architecture 1952-58, commenced private practice Fife 1952; princ works incl: Woodside Shopping Centre and St Columba's Parish Church Glenrothes, St Peter's Episcopal Church Kirkcaldy, Hunter Bldg Edinburgh Coll of Art, Students' Union Univ of St Andrews, Leonard Horner Hall and Students' Union Heriot Watt Univ, reconstruction The Giles Pittenweem, redevpt Dysart and Old Buckhaven, town centre renewal Grangemouth; memb: Royal Fine Art Cmmn Scotland 1967-86, Scottish Housing Advsy Ctee 1971-75; tstee Scottish Civic Tst 1970-83; MRTPI 1953, ARSA 1963, RSA 1975 (treas 1978-80, sec 1980-83, pres 1983-90), FRSA 1988, FRIBA (vice-pres 1973-75), pres Royal Incorpn of Architects Scotland 1973-75; Hon RA 1983, Hon RGI 1986; kt 1988; *Recreations* water colour painting, sketching, fishing, gardens, music, drama; *Clubs* Scottish Arts, New (Edinburgh); *Style*— Sir Anthony Wheeler, OBE; Hawthornbank House, Dean Village, Edinburgh EH4 3BH (☎ 031 225 2334); The Steading, Logierait, Ballinluig, Perthshire PH9 0LH (☎ 079 682282); 118 Hanover St, Edinburgh EH2 1DR (☎ 031 226 3338, 031 220 4136)

WHEELER, Arthur William Edge; CBE (1979, OBE 1967); eldest s of Arthur William Wheeler (d 1969), of Dublin, and Rowena; *b* 1 Aug 1930; *Educ* Mountjoy Sch, Trinity Coll Dublin; *m* 1956, Gay; 2 s, 1 da; *Career* called to the Bar Grays Inn 1960; crown counsel Nigeria 1955, acting legal sec Southern Cameroons and memb Exec Cncl and House of Assembly 1958, princ crown counsel Fedn of Nigeria 1961, dir Public Prosecutions N Nigeria 1966, high ct judge N Nigeria 1967, chief judge Kaduna State of Nigeria 1975, cmmr for Revision of the Laws of Northern States of Nigeria 1980; chm Foreign Compensation Cmmn 1983-; *Recreations* tennis, golf, music; *Clubs* Royal Cwlth Soc, Kildare Street and University (Dublin); *Style*— Arthur Wheeler, Esq, CBE; c/o Barclays Bank plc, Bowater House, 68 Knightsbridge, London SW1X 7LW; Foreign Compensation Commission, Alexandra House, Kingsway, London WC2B 6TT

WHEELER, (Selwyn) Charles; s of Wing Cdr Charles C Wheeler, and Winifred, *née* Rees; *b* 26 March 1923; *Educ* Cranbrook Sch; *m* 29 March 1961, DIp Wheeler; 2 da (Shirin, Marina); *Career* WWII served RM 1941-46; BBC: World Serv 1946-48, German serv corr Berlin 1949-53, Euro Serv 1954-56, S Asia corr to India 1958-62, Berlin corr 1962-65, Washington corr 1965-69; chief corr: USA 1969-72, Europe 1972-75, BBC TV news 1975-80; presenter Panorama 1980-82 (prodr 1956-58), corr Newsnight 1982-90, writer and narrator of The Road to War series 1988-89; Royal TV Soc: Journalist of the Year 1988, Int Current Affrs award 1989; *Recreations* gardening, travel; *Style*— Charles Wheeler, Esq; 10a Portland Rd, London W11 (☎ 071 221 4300)

WHEELER, David Michael; s of Antony Wheeler, of London, and Edith Wheeler, LVO, *née* Dawkins; *b* 20 March 1940; *Educ* Eton; *m* 21 Oct 1961, Margita, da of The Hon Andrew Vanneck, MC (d 1965), of Heveningham Hall, Suffolk; 2 s (Andrew b 20 July 1963, James b 28 Oct 1966); *Career* memb Stock Exchange London and Int 1963; ptnr Strauss Turnbull & Co London until 1974; Ermitage Gp: fndr, chm, chief exec 1974; dep chm Harris & Dixon Holdings 1984, non-exec dir Sothebys London 1989; holds numerous other directorships in fin and business enterprises; *Recreations* walking, reading, museum visiting; *Clubs* White's; *Style*— David Wheeler, Esq; Broadlands, La Hougue Bie, Grouville, Jersey, CI (☎ 0534 54216); PO Box 79, St Helier, Jersey, CI (☎ 0534 76007, telex 4192135, fax 0534 79151)

WHEELER, Sir John Daniel; JP (Inner London 1978), DL (Greater London 1989), MP (C) Westminster North 1983-; s of late Frederick Harry Wheeler, and Constance Elsie, *née* Foreman; *b* 1 May 1940; *Educ* County Sch Suffolk, Staff Coll Wakefield; *m* 1967, Laura Margaret Langley; 1 s, 1 da; *Career* former asst prison governor; memb: Home Office Standing Ctee on Crime Prevention 1977-85 (chm Sub-ctee on Mobile Crime 1983-84), Home Office Steering Ctee on Crime Prevention 1985-; chm Residential Burglary Working Gp 1986-87; MP (C) Paddington 1979-83; chm: All-Party Penal Affairs Gp 1986- (vice-chm 1979-86), Home Affairs Select Ctee Sub-ctee on Race Relations and Immigration 1980-87, Home Affairs Select Ctee 1987-, Conservative Greater London Area Members' Ctee 1983-90 (jt sec 1979-83), Policy Gp for London 1988-, British-Pakistan Parly Gp 1988-; vice-chm: Conservative Urban Affairs and New Towns Ctee 1980-83, Conservative Home Affairs Ctee 1987-90 (jt sec 1980-87); kt 1990; *Style*— Sir John Wheeler, JP, DL, MP; House of Commons,

London SW1A OAA (☎ 071 219 4615)

WHEELER, John Frederick; s and h of Sir John Wheeler, 3 Bt, and Gwendolen Alice, da of late Alfred Ernest Oram; *b* 3 May 1933; *Educ* Bedales, London Sch of Printing, The Life Guards; *m* 1963, Barbara Mary, da of Raymond Flint, of Stoneygate, Leicester; 2 s (John Radford b 1965, Andrew Charles b 1969), 1 da (Jane Louise b 1964); *Career* company dir and farmer; *Recreations* sailing, field sports; *Style—* John F Wheeler, Esq; Round Hill, Aldeburgh, Suffolk IP15 5PG (☎ 0728 452748)

WHEELER, Sir John Hieron; 3 Bt (UK 1920), of Woodhouse Eaves, Co Leicester; s of Sir Arthur Wheeler, 1 Bt, DL, JP (d 1943), and Mary, *née* Pullman (d 1938); bro of 2 Bt (d 1964); *b* 22 July 1905; *Educ* Charterhouse; *m* 24 July 1929, Gwendolen Alice, da of late Alfred Ernest Oram, of Walberton, Kirby Muxloe, nr Leicester; 2 s (John Frederick, Benjamin b 1935); *Heir* s, John Frederick Wheeler b 3 May 1933; *Style—* Sir John Wheeler, Bt; 39 Morland Ave, Stoneygate, Leicester

WHEELER, John Michael; s of Sir Charles Wheeler, KBE (d 1976), and Frieda, *née* Close (d 1972); *b* 8 Nov 1931; *Educ* Shrewsbury, Queens' Coll Cambridge (BA), Harvard Business Sch (PMD); *m* 22 Sept 1956, (Jean Ruth) Kirsty, da of John McMyn Gilmour, MC (d 1950); 1 s (Richard b 1960), 2 da (Fiona b 1962, Tanya b 1963); *Career* Nat Serv cmmnd 2 Lt Gren Guards 1950-52; dir: H Clarkson & Co Ltd 1967-90, Elder Austral Chartering Pty Ltd 1973-90, Baltic Freight Futures Exchange 1985-88, Baltic Futures Exchange 1988-90; Jt Master Old Berkeley Beagles, memb Cncl Int Social Serv of GB; Liveryman Worshipful Co of Broderers; *Recreations* beagling, wine tasting, golf; *Clubs* MCC, City Univ, The Tasting; *Style—* John Wheeler, Esq; Great Missenden, Bucks (☎ 024 020 232, fax 024 020 741)

WHEELER, John Vashon Tyrwhitt; s of Wing Cdr Vashon James Wheeler, MC, DFC (ka 1944), of Bitterley Court, Ludlow, Shropshire, and Josephine Hermione, *née* Spencer-Phillips (d 1974); *b* 24 Oct 1931; *Educ* Eton, Trinity Coll Cambridge (BA, MA); *m* 1, 7 Sept 1957, Geraldine (d 1970), da of William Noel Jones (d 1982), of Little Gables, Glasllwch Lane, Newport; 3 s (James Vashon b 1960, Nicholas Charles Tyrwhitt b 1965, Justin Alexander Noel b 1970), 1 da (Susan Verity (Mrs Cummings) b 1958); m 2, 1978, Mrs Caroline Susan Chance, da of Patrick Edward Michael Holmes, MBE; 2 step s (Timothy William Holmes b 1966, Henry Charles Hugh b 1968), 1 step da (Lucy Emma b 1971); *Career* Nat Serv Flying Offr; dir Wolseley-Hughes plc 1970-82 (chief exec agric div); chm and md: Benson Heating Ltd 1982-84, Benson Group plc 1984-90; chm: Richardson (Bitterley) Ltd 1970-; memb Bitterley Parish Cncl; MIMechE 1965, FIAgrE 1978; *Recreations* land management; *Clubs* RAF; *Style—* John Wheeler, Esq; Bitterley Court, Ludlow, Shropshire (☎ 0584 890 265)

WHEELER, Hon Mrs (Katharine Jane); er da of Baron Briggs (Life Peer); *b* 1956; *m* July 1980, David Robert Wheeler, er s of C R Wheeler, of Wimbledon SW19; 1 s (Timothy b 1985), 2 da (Caroline b 1982, Charlotte Rose 1987); *Style—* The Hon Mrs Wheeler; 30 Alexandra Rd, Epsom, Surrey

WHEELER, Air Vice-Marshal Leslie William Frederick; s of George Douglas Wheeler (d 1982), and Susan Wheeler; *b* 4 July 1930; *Educ* Creighton Sch Carlisle; *m* 1960, Joan Elizabeth, da of Harry Newton Carpenter (d 1969); 2 da; *Career* RAF cmmnd 1952, OC 360 Sqdn 1970-72, Station Cdr RAF Finningley 1977-79, Dir-Gen RAF Personal Serv 1983-84; independent inspr Public Inquiries 1984-; chm Appt Bd: Civil Serv Cmmn, MOD; *Recreations* walking, philately; *Clubs* RAF; *Style—* Air Vice-Marshal Leslie Wheeler; c/o Midland Bank plc, Brampton, Cumbria

WHEELER, Prof Michael David; s of David Mortimer Wheeler, and Hilda Lois Stansfield, *née* Eke; *b* 1 Sept 1947; *Educ* St Albans Sch, Magdalene Coll Cambridge (scholar, BA), UCL (Quain student PhD); *m* 1970, Vivienne Rees; 1 s (Joshua b 1973), 2 da (Charlotte b 1975, Emily (twin) b 1975); *Career* Univ of Lancaster: lectr in English 1973-85, sr lectr 1985-90, head of Dept 1984-86, assoc dean of humanities 1989-, prof of Eng lit 1990-; dir: Ruskin Prog (interdisciplinary res gp) 1990-, Ruskin Collection Project 1990-; visiting lectr 1975-: USA, India, Iraq, Poland, Yugoslavia, Switzerland, Norway; Gladstone Fndr's Day lectr 1991; conslt RMP Assocs 1987-; *Publications* The Art of Allusion in Victorian Fiction (1979), English Fiction of the Victorian Period 1830-1890 (1985), Death and the Future Life in Victorian Literature and Theology (1990), Longman Literature in English Series 47 vols (jt gen ed 1980-), Literature and Theology (assoc ed 1987-89); *Recreations* choral singing, croquet; *Style—* Prof Michael Wheeler; 15 Meadowside, Lancaster LA1 3AQ (☎ 0524 60097)

WHEELER, Michael Mortimer; QC (1961), TD (1971); s of Sir (Robert Eric) Mortimer Wheeler, MC, TD (d 1975), and 1 wife, Tessa Verney Wheeler (d 1936); *b* 8 Jan 1915; *Educ* Dragon Sch Oxford, Rugby, Ch Ch Oxford (MA); *m* 30 Oct 1939, Sheila, er da of Stephen Mayou (d 1936); 2 da (Susan Patricia (Mrs Donnellan) b 1940, Caroline Jane (Mrs Pettman) b 1943); *Career* served WWII 1938-46 RA (TA) UK and Italy, Lt-Col 1945; called to the Bar Gray's Inn 1938, joined Lincoln's Inn 1946 (treas 1986), dep High Ct judge 1973-88; *Recreations* golf, watching cricket; *Clubs* Garrick, MCC, Berks Golf; *Style—* Michael Wheeler, Esq, QC, TD; 114 Hallam St, London W1N 5LW (☎ 071 580 7284); Clare Cottage, Maidens Green, Winkfield, nr Windsor, Berks (☎ 0344 883780)

WHEELER, Air Chief Marshal Sir (Henry) Neil George; GCB (1975, KCB 1969, CB 1967), CBE (1957, OBE 1949), DSO (1943), DFC (1941, and bar 1943), AFC 1954; s of Thomas Henry Wheeler (d 1933), of Pretoria, S Africa; *b* 8 July 1917; *Educ* St Helen's Coll Southsea; *m* 1942, Alice Elizabeth, da of William Henry Weightman, CMG (d 1970); 2 s, 1 da; *Career* joined RAF 1935, served in Bomber, Fighter and Coastal Cmds WWII, Gp Capt 1954, ADC to HM The Queen 1957-61, Air Cdre 1961, Air memb Research Policy Staff MOD 1962-63, Air Vice-Marshal 1963, SASO RAF Germany 1963-66, Asst Chief of Defence Staff (Operational Requirements) MOD 1966-67 and Dep Chief 1967, Air Marshal 1967, Cdr Far East Air Force 1969-70, Air memb Supply and Organisation MOD 1970, Air Chief Marshal 1972, controller of Aircraft MOD Procurement Exec 1973-75, ret 1976; dir: Rolls Royce Ltd 1977-82, Flight Refuelling Ltd 1977-85; vice pres Cncl of the Air League; chm Anglo-Ecuadorian Soc 1986-89; Liveryman Guild of Air Pilots and Air Navigators (Master 1986-87); CBIM, FRAeS; *Recreations* flyfishing, painting, gardening; *Clubs* Flyfishers', RAF; *Style—* Air Chief Marshal Sir Neil Wheeler, GCB, CBE, DSO, DFC, AFC; Boundary Hall, Cooksbridge, Lewes, Sussex (☎ 0273 400201)

WHEELER, Dr Patrick Clive Gage; s of Cdr Leonard Gage Wheeler, of Alresford, Hants, and Nancy Dorothea, *née* Cross; *b* 6 Oct 1943; *Educ* Sr Edward's Sch Oxford, Christ Church Oxford (MA, DM, BM BCh), St Thomas Hosp London; *m* 7 June 1975, Diana Lilian, da of Cdr Edward Stanley, of Waldringfield, Suffolk; 3 da (Anna b 1976, Kate b 1978, Gemma b 1981); *Career* med registrar St Thomas Hosp 1971-75, sr med registrar Kings Coll Hosp 1975-80, conslt physician and gastroenterologist SE Kent Health Authy 1980-; author of various articles in scientific pubns; memb Br Soc Gastroentorology; FRCP 1987 (MRCP 1971); *Recreations* fly fishing, music, francophilia; *Style—* Dr Patrick Wheeler; Elham Manor, Elham, Canterbury, Kent CT4 6UL; William Harvey Hospital, Ashford, Kent

WHEELER, Paul; s of Dennis Wheeler, and Joan Margaret, *née* Crawte; *b* 8 Nov 1952; *Educ* Wallingford GS, Coll of Law Guildford; *m* 17 Dec 1977, Sally Anne, da of Arthur (Bob) Robert; 2 s (Lewis b 1983, Nicholas b 1986); *Career* slr 1977; lectr Coll of Law 1977-78, prosecuting slr Thames Valley Police 1978-82, ptnr Hedges & Son Wallingford and Didcot 1985; memb: Law Soc 1985 (Berks, Bucks and Oxon), Oxford Dist Slrs Assoc 1987; *Recreations* hockey; *Clubs* Wallingford Sports and Social, Wallingford Dist Lions; *Style—* Paul Wheeler, Esq; 10 Brookmead Drive, Wallingford, Oxon (☎ 0491 35 252); 144a Broadway, Didcot, Oxon (☎ 0235 812 842, fax 0235 815 696)

WHEELER, Raymond Leslie; s of Edmund Francis Wheeler (d 1969), and Ivy Geraldine, *née* Fryer (d 1979); *b* 25 Oct 1927; *Educ* Newport Co Secdy GS, Univ Coll Southampton (BSc), Imperial Coll London (MSc); *m* 22 March 1950, Jean, da of Colin McInnes (d 1942); 1 s (Douglas b 1956), 2 da (Lesley (Mrs Rathmann) b 1952, Jennifer (Mrs Harrison) b 1954); *Career* chief structural designer Saunders-Roe Div Westland Aircraft Ltd 1965-66 (chief stress 1962-65), tech dir Br Hovercraft Corp Ltd 1972-85 (chief designer 1966-85), business devpt dir Westland Aerospace Ltd 1985-89; dir systems support Westland Aerospace Ltd 1989-; pres IOW Area Bd Young Enterprise, chm of govrs Whippingham Co Primary Sch, chm of govrs IOW Coll of Arts and Technol; FRAeS, FRINA, FRSA; *Books* From Sea to Air - The Heritage of Sam Saunders (with A E Tagg, 1989); *Recreations* hockey, photography, archaeology; *Style—* Raymond Wheeler, Esq; Brovacum, 106 Old Rd, East Cowes, IOW PO32 6AX (☎ 0983 292994); Westland Aerospace Ltd, East Cowes, IOW PO32 6RH (☎ 0983 294101, fax 0983 291006, telex 86761)

WHEELER, (John) Richard; JP (Essex 1963); s of John Wheeler, MBE (d 1982), of 10 Alton Drive, Colchester, and Christine Mary, *née* Everett; *b* 16 May 1932; *Educ* Framlingham Coll Suffolk; *m* 16 June 1956, (Christine) Mary, da of Octavius Blyth (d 1947), of Sunnyside, Yorick Rd, West Mersea, Essex; 1 s (Johnny b 1967), 3 da (Bridget b 1958, Susie b 1959, Sacha b 1962); *Career* Nat Serv cmmnd 2 Lt RASC 1950; md Lay & Wheeler Ltd 1958-(chm 1982-); memb Colchester Borough Cncl 1960-88; Mayor of Colchester 1970 (hon Alderman 1988); Freeman Worshipful Co of Distillers 1976; Chevalier du Merite Agricole (France) 1988; *Recreations* salmon fishing, walking; *Clubs* MCC, Colchester Garrison Officers', West Mersea Yacht; *Style—* Richard Wheeler, Esq, JP; West Mersea Hall, West Mersea, Colchester, Essex CO5 8QD (☎ 0206 382391); Lay & Wheeler Ltd, 6 Culver Street West, Colchester, Essex CO1 1JA (☎ 0206 764446, fax 0206 769552, car 0831 158236)

WHEELER, Timothy Carpenter; s of Andrew Wheeler (d 1950), of Philadelphia, USA, and Molly Wheeler; *b* 20 Sept 1933; *Educ* Beaumont Coll, Law Soc Sch of Law; *m* Nov 1967, Diana Katherine, *née* Hillson; 1 da (Katherine Margaret Elizabeth); *Career* Nat Serv RAC 1957-58; articled to Lewis, Lewis and Gisborne 1951-56, admitted slr 1957; ptnr Clifford-Turner 1964-87 (joined as asst slr 1958), ptnr Clifford Chance 1987-; memb: City of London Slrs' Co (incorporating City of London Law Soc), Law Soc, Int Bar Assoc, Br Property Fedn; chm Sub Ctee on Land Law City of London Law Soc; *Recreations* walking, gardening, travelling; *Style—* Timothy Wheeler, Esq; Clifford Chance, Blackfriars House, 19 New Bridge St, London EC4V 6BY (☎ 071 353 0211, fax 071 489 0046)

WHEELER-BENNETT, Richard Clement; s of Dr Clement Wheeler Wheeler-Bennett (d 1957), and Enid Lucy, *née* Boosey (d 1975); *b* 14 June 1927; *Educ* Radley, ChCh Oxford (MA), Harvard Business Sch; *m* 8 May 1954, Joan Ellen, da of the late Prof Eric Alfred Havelock, of Connecticut, USA; 1 s (Clement b 1965 d 1986), 2 da (Joanna b 1957, Emily b 1960); *Career* RM Lt Commando 1944-48; banker; mangr First National City Bank of New York 1960-66, gen mangr (Europe) Australia and New Zealand Banking Group 1978-80 (exec dir 1967-78), chm Thomas Borthwick & Sons Ltd 1980-85; dir Fleming Technol Tst 1983-, chm Roehampton Club Ltd 1988-; *Recreations* fishing, golf, shooting, viticulture; *Clubs* Brooks's, Pratts, MCC; *Style—* Richard Wheeler-Bennett, Esq; The Mill House, Calstone Wellington, nr Calne, Wilts SN11 8QF (☎ 0249 813241); 94 Rosebank, London SW6 6LJ (☎ 071 385 4970); Roehampton Club Ltd, Roehampton Lane, London SW15 (☎ 081 876 5505)

WHEELER-BOOTH, Michael Addison John; s of Addison James Wheeler, and Mary Angela, *née* Blakeney-Booth; *b* 25 Feb 1934; *Educ* Leighton Park Sch, Magdalen Coll Oxford (MA); *m* 1982, Emily Frances Smith; 1 s (Alfred James b 1990), 2 da (Kate, Charlotte); *Career* reading clerk House of Lords 1983-88, clerk asst of the Parl 1988-90, clerk of the Parliaments 1991-; *Clubs* Brook's; *Style—* M A J Wheeler-Booth, Esq; House of Lords, London SW1

WHEELHOUSE, Alan; s of George William Wheelhouse (d 1990), of Nottingham, and Dorothy Marion, *née* Hickling (d 1974); *b* 4 March 1934; *Educ* Nottingham HS, Emmanuel Coll Cambridge (MA, LLM); *m* 1963, Jennifer Mary, da of Donald Stewart Robinson (d 1974), of Nottingham; 3 da (Heather Jane b 1964, Julie Ann b 1966, Emma Louise b 1969); *Career* slr, sr ptnr Freeth Cartwright, pres Nottinghamshire Law Soc 1985-86; Cambridge Cricket blue 1959, Nottinghamshire Co Cricket 1961 (Ctee 1987-); Capt Notts 50+ Cricket XI 1985-88, XL Club Dist Chm 1985-; pres Gunn & Moore Club Cricket Alliance 1991 (chm 1983-85), pres Old Nottinghamians Soc 1982, pres Old Nottinghamians Cricket Club 1988-89; govr Nottingham HS 1988-; *Recreations* cricket, watching sport, concert and theatre going, eating-out; *Clubs* Old Nottinghamians CC (former captain), XL Club, Notts CCC, Nottinghamshire Football (vice-pres); *Style—* Alan Wheelhouse, Esq; Bracken House, Bracken Hill, Caythorpe, Nottingham NG14 7EF (☎ 0602 663047); Willoughby House, 20 Low Pavement, Nottingham (☎ 0602 506861, fax 0602 585079)

WHEEN, Francis James Baird; s of James Francis Thomeycroft Wheen, and Patricia Winifred, *née* Ward; *b* 22 Jan 1957; *Educ* Capthorne Sch Sussex, Harrow, Royal Holloway Coll London (BA); ptnr Joan Smith, *qv*; *Career* journalist; editorial asst The Guardian 1974-75, staff writer New Statesman 1978-84, news ed New Socialist 1983-84, contirbuting ed Tatler 1985, diarist The Independent 1986-87, contributing ed Sunday Correspondent Magazine 1989-90, diarist Independent on Sunday 1990-, reg contrib to Private Eye 1987-; freelance work for numerous pubns GB and overseas incl: The Times, Guardian, Daily Mirror, Observer, London Evening Standard, Los Angeles Times, The Nation (NY), Literary Reviews; was for several years reg presenter of News-Stand (BBC Radio) and What The Papers Say (Granada TV); *Books* The Sixties (1982), World View 1982 (1982), Television: A History (1985), The Battle For London (1985), Tom Driberg: His Life And Indiscretions (1990); *Clubs* Academy (Soho); *Style—* Francis Wheen, Esq; c/o Peters, Fraser & Dunlop, 5th Floor, The Chambers, Chelsea Harbour, Lots Rd, London SW10 0XF (☎ 071 376 7676, fax 071 352 7356)

WHEEN, Richard Francis; s of Rear Adm Charles Kerr Thorneycroft Wheen, CB (d 1989), and Veryan Rosamond, *née* Acworth; *b* 27 May 1941; *Educ* Harrow, Peterhouse Cambridge (MA); *m* 14 Jan 1983, Anne, da of Patrick Joseph Keegan, of Ireland (d 1980); 5 s (Timothy b 1983, Patrick (twin) b 1983, Jonathan b 1985 (d 1987), Christopher b 1986, Peter b 1988); *Career* slr; ptnr Linklaters & Paines; Lt Cdr RNR, ret 1978; author Bridge Player series of programs for home computers 1983-; *Recreations* bridge, shooting, computer programming, golf; *Clubs* Army and Navy, Worplesdon Golf; *Style—* Richard F Wheen, Esq; The Grange, Rectory Lane, Buckland, Betchworth, Surrey RH3 7BH (☎ 0737 842193); Linklaters & Paines, Barrington House, 59-67 Gresham St, London EC2V 7JA (☎ 071 606 7080)

WHELAN, Dr Michael John; s of William Whelan, ISM (d 1978), of Aldershot, Hants, and Ellen, *née* Pound (d 1972); *b* 2 Nov 1931; *Educ* Farnborough GS, Gonville and Caius Coll Cambridge (BA, MA, PhD); *Career* Univ of Cambridge: demonstrator in physics 1961-65, asst dir of res in physics 1965-66, fell Gonville and Caius Coll 1958-66; reader in physical examination of materials Univ of Oxford 1966-, fell Linacre Coll Oxford 1968-; FRS 1976, FInstP 1976; *Books* co author Electron Microscopy of Thin Crystals; *Recreations* gardening, tinkering, Japanese language; *Style*— Dr Michael Whelan, FRS; 18 Salford Rd, Old Marston, Oxford OX3 0RX (☎ 0865 244556); Dept of Materials, Oxford University, Parks Rd, Oxford OX1 3PH (☎ 0865 273700, fax 0865 273789, telex 83295 NUCLOX G)

WHELAN, Michael Joseph; s of Michael Whelan (d 1972), and Mary T, *née* Hynes; *b* 1 May 1932; *Educ* Castleknock Coll Dublin, Univ Coll Dublin (BA), Columbia Univ NY (MSc); *m* 3 June 1955, Maureen Therese, da of John Ryan (d 1972); 3 s (Gerard b 1959, Brian b 1962, Roger b 1966), 1 da (Ann-Maeve b 1956); *Career* called to the Bar King's Inn Dublin 1953; corporate lawyer Shell Oil: Toronto 1955-59, NY 1959-60; devpt and commercial mangr Aer Lingus NY and Dublin 1960-63, mktg dir Irish Tourist Bd Dublin 1963-71, fndr and chief exec Aran Energy plc Dublin and London 1972-; FInstPet, FInstD; *Recreations* sailing; *Clubs* Royal Irish Yacht, Fitzwilliam, St Stephens Green, Milltown Golf, Royal Irish Automobile (All Dublin); *Style*— Michael J Whelan, Esq; 51 Mount St, Mayfair, London W1; The Cove, Baltimore, Co Cork; Ardoyne House, Ballsbridge, Dublin 4; 37 Maddox St, London W1 (☎ 071 629 2080); Clanwilliam Court, Dublin 2 (☎ 0001 760 696)

WHELAN, Paul William; s of William James Whelan (d 1966), and Carol, *née* O'Leary; *b* 24 Sept 1935; *Educ* Southgate County GS, LSE, Borough Road Training Coll; *m* (m dis); 2 s (Patrick John Paul b 7 July 1971, Alexander James b 15 March 1978), 2 da (Holly Anne b 9 June 1969, Rosalind Elizabeth b 31 Dec 1981); *Career* teacher training 1958-59, teacher and lectr 1959-62; joined Brunning Advertising & Marketing 1963, Thomson Group Marketing 1968, Doyle Dane Bernbach 1970; estab: first co Byfield Mead & Partners (later Byfield Whelan Osborn & Cruttonden) 1971, second co Noble Whelan O'Connell (later AAP-Ketchum) 1978; dir Shandwick 1987, estab third co Paul Whelan & Partners 1990-; various awards for pres and TV advtg at Creative Circle, D & AD, Clios; MIPA, memb Mktg Soc; *Style*— Paul Whelan, Esq; Paul Whelan and Partners, 6 Snow Hill, London EC1A 2AL (☎ 071 236 0369, fax 071 236 0296)

WHELAN, Terence Leonard; s of Thomas James Whelan (d 1939), and Gertrude Beatrice, *née* Chick (d 1968); *b* 5 Dec 1936; *Educ* Oakfield Secdy Sch Anerley London, Beckenham Coll of Art (NDD); *m* 1, 1961 (m dis 1971); 2 s; m 2, 15 Dec 1972, Margaret Elizabeth, da of Brinley John Bowen, of Middx; 1 da; *Career* Nat Serv 14 Field Ambulance RAMC Germany 1956-58; art ed Condé Nast Publishers 1959-68 (worked on Vogue Pattern Book, Vogue South Africa, Br Vogue); Ideal Home magazine: art ed 1968-74, asst ed and art dir 1974-77, ed 1977-; md Satellite Editorial Publications Ltd, writer and broadcaster on home improvements, voted Ed of the Year (Special Interest Section) British Soc Magazine Editors 1988; chm Park HS Parent Teacher Assoc 1990-91; memb Soc Typographic Designers 1972; *Recreations* classical guitar, photography; *Style*— Terence Whelan, Esq; Ideal Home magazine, King's Reach Tower, Stamford St, London SE1 9LS (☎ 071 261 6474)

WHELDON, David Robert; s of Derek Wheldon (d 1962), of Silsoe, and Joan Mary, *née* Neville; *b* 15 Aug 1956; *Educ* Royal Masonic Schs Bushey Hertfordshire, Univ of Kent Canterbury (BA); *m* 10 Sept 1982, Macarena, da of Jaime Ruiz-Larrea Congas (d 1981); 2 s (Daniel b 8 Feb 1986, Alexander b 25 March 1989); *Career* teacher of English 1978-82; Saatchi & Saatchi: account exec 1983, account supervisor 1984, account dir 1985, Bd dir 1986, gp account dir 1987; gp account dir then jt managing ptnr WCRS Mathews MarCantonio 1989, md Lowe Howard-Spink 1989-; *Recreations* cinema, music, reading, tennis, travel, cooking, playing with the children; *Clubs* Savile, Riverside, Mossimans; *Style*— David Wheldon, Esq; Lowe Howard-Spink, Bowater House, Knightsbridge, London SW1X 7LT (☎ 071 584 5033, fax 071 225 2761)

WHELER, Sir Edward Woodford; 14 Bt (E 1660, of City of Westminster, Co London); s and h of Sir Trevor Wood Wheler, 13 Bt (d 1986), and Margaret Idris, *née* Birch (d 1987); *b* 13 June 1920; *Educ* Radley; *m* 2 July 1945, Molly Ashworth, da of late Thomas Lever; 1 s (Trevor), 1 da (Dinah); *Heir* s, Trevor Woodford b 11 April 1946; *Career* Royal Sussex Regt and 15 Punjab Regt Indian Army 1941-47, Capt; Colonial Audit Dept 1948-58; *Style*— Sir Edward Wheler, Bt; 34 St Carantoc Way, Crantock, Newquay, Cornwall (☎ 0637 830965)

WHELER, Margaret, Lady; Margaret Idris; *née* Birch; da of late Sir Ernest Woodford Birch, KCMG; *m* 1915, Sir Trevor Wood Wheler, 13 Bt (d 1986); 1 s (Sir Edward Wheler, 14 Bt), 2 da (Audrey Idris, Diana Edmee); *Style*— Margaret, Lady Wheler; 5A Motcombe Court, Bedford Avenue, Bexhill-on-Sea, Sussex

WHELON, (Charles) Patrick Clavell; s of Charles Eric Whelon (d 1975), and Margaret Ethel Salter (d 1960); *b* 18 Jan 1930; *Educ* Wellington, Pembroke Coll Cambridge (BA); *m* 6 Jan 1968, Prudence Mary, da of Samuel Lesley Potter (d 1966); 1 s (Charles b 1969), 1 da (Emily b 1971); *Career* barr, rec Crown Ct 1978-; Liveryman Worshipful Co of Vintners; *Recreations* gardening, travel, drawing; *Style*— Patrick Whelon, Esq; Russetts, Pyott's Hill, Old Basing, Hants; 2 Harcourt Buildings, Temple, London EC4 (☎ 071 353 2112)

WHELPTON, Robert Anthony (Tony); s of Francis Clair William Whelpton (d 1983), and Alice Beatrice, *née* Cresswell (d 1976); *b* 27 Jan 1933; *Educ* High Pavement Sch Nottingham, Goldsmiths' Coll London (BA, PGCE), Birkbeck Coll London (BA), Univ of Lille (Lè SL); *m* 1, 4 Feb 1956, Kathryn, da of Joseph Evans (d 1984), of Nottingham; 2 da (Fiona b 1957, Rachel b 1959); m 2, 5 Sept 1981, Joan Valerie, *née* Williams; *Career* Nat Serv RAF, Sr Aircraftman 1951-53; schoolmaster 1957-65, sr lectr in French Nottingham Coll of Educn 1965-74, princ lectr in French Trent Poly 1974-82; chief examiner: GCE (N Ireland) 1969-72, GCE (Associated Examining Bd 1973-87, Malawi Cert of Educn 1979, GCSE French Southern Examining Gp); freelance writer, author numerous newspaper and magazine articles and school text-books; *Recreations* squash, choral singing, genealogy; *Style*— Tony Whelpton, Esq; 25 Hartlebury Way, Charlton Kings, Cheltenham, Glos GL52 6YB (☎ 0242 36692)

WHETHERLY, Hon Mrs (Rosemary Gertrude Alexandra); *née* Lever; yr da of 2 Viscount Leverhulme (d 1949), and his 1 w Marion Beatrice, *née* Smith; *b* 23 April 1919; *m* 19 Oct 1938, Lt-Col William Erskine Stobart Whetherly, er s of late Lt-Col William Stobart Whetherly, DSO; 2 s, 1 da; *Style*— The Hon Mrs Whetherly; Hallam, Ogbourne St George, Marlborough, Wilts SN8 1SG (☎ 067 284 212)

WHETHERLY, Lt-Col William Erskine Stobart (Toby); s of Lt-Col W S Whetherly, DSO (d 1956), and Marjorie, *née* Holmes (d 1966); *b* 1 July 1909; *Educ* Harrow, Sandhurst; *m* 19 Oct 1938, Rosemary Gertrude Alexandra, da of 2 Viscount Leverhulme (d 1949), of Thornton Manor, Wirral, Cheshire; 2 s (Dennis b 27 Jan 1940, Robin b 19 Oct 1947), 1 da (Dawn b 12 Feb 1946); *Career* 2 Lt Dragoon Gds 1929, Maj i/c sqdn Western Desert 1940, Lt-Col i/c Mil Mission Yugoslavia 1944, Gen Staff Italy, Lt-Col GSO1 WO 1945, ret 1947; High Sheriff of Wiltshire 1973-74; *Clubs* Boodle's; *Style*— Lt-Col Toby Whetherly; Hallam, Ogbourne St George, Marlborough, Wilts (☎ 067 284 212); Flat 12A, 17 Grosvenor Sq, London W1 (☎ 071 493 9111)

WHETSTONE, Rear Adm Anthony John (Tony); CB (1982); s of Albert Whetstone (d 1949), and Hannah Elizabeth (Anne), *née* Hubbard (d 1963); *b* 12 June 1927; *Educ* King Henry VIII Sch Coventry; *m* 7 April 1951, Elizabeth Stewart (Betty), da of Robert Bruce Georgeson, of Alverstoke, Hants; 3 c (Elizabeth Anne b 1952, Alison Mary b 1954, Robert Anthony Stewart b 1963); *Career* RN: joined 1945, cmmnd Sub-Lt 1947, cmd HMS Sea Scout (submarine) 1955-56, cmd HMA Artful (submarine) 1959-61, Cdr 1963, Ops Offr to Flag Offr Submarines 1963-65, cmd HMS Repulse (Polaris submarine) 1967-69, Capt 1969, asst dir Naval Warfare 1970-72, cmd HMS Juno 1972-73, COS to Flag Offr Submarines 1974-75, cmd HMS Norfolk 1977-78, Flag Offr Sea Trg 1978-80, Rear Adm 1979, Asst Chief of Naval Staff (ops) 1981-83, ret 1983; dir: Gen Cable TV Assoc 1983-86, Nat TV Rental Assoc 1983-87, DESC Ltd 1991-; asst sec Def Press and Bdcasting Ctee 1987-, sec Special Tstees St Georges Hosp 1988-, memb Cncl Offrs Pension Soc, area pres Royal Naval Assoc Kent and Surrey, nat pres Submarine Old Comrades Assoc; chm: Tstees RN Submarine Museum, Civil Serv Drama Fedn; FBIM 1976; *Recreations* fly fishing, hill walking, amateur theatre; *Clubs* Army and Navy, Civil Service; *Style*— Rear Adm Tony Whetstone, CB; 17 Anglesey Road, Alverstoke, Hants PO12 2EG (☎ 0702 680632)

WHETSTONE, Lt Cdr (Norman) Keith; OBE (1983), VRD (1964); s of Albert Whetstone (d 1949), of Coventry, and Hannah Elizabeth, *née* Hubbard (d 1963); *b* 17 June 1930; *Educ* King Henry VIII Sch Coventry; *m* 6 Dec 1952, Monica Joan, da of Allan Clayton, of Leamington Spa; 3 s (William b 1954, Neil b 1956, Alastair b 1959); *Career* RNVR 1949-50 and 1952-53; journalist Coventry Evening Telegraph 1950-52, rugby football corr Western Morning News Plymouth 1953-55, sub-ed The Birmingham Post 1955-58, theatre corr Coventry Evening Telegraph 1958-63; ed: Cambridge Evening News 1963-70, Coventry Evening Telegraph 1970-80; ed dir The Birmingham Post and Mail Ltd 1980-86, ed The Birmingham Evening Mail 1980-85, ed in chief The Birmingham Post and Birmingham Evening Mail Series 1984-86, ret 1986; ed conslt freelance writer; memb: Guild of Br Newspaper Editors 1964 (nat pres 1976-77), Press Cncl 1980-86; *Recreations* rugby football (former Warwickshire sch player), golf, squash, theatre, DIY; *Clubs* Coventry and North Warwickshire CC, Coventry FC (rugby); *Style*— Lt Cdr Keith Whetsone, OBE, VRD; Tudor House, Benton Green Lane, Berkswell, Coventry CV7 7AY (☎ 0676 32323)

WHEWELL, Roger William; s of Alfred Thomas Whewell (d 1969), and Dorothy Annie Whewell (d 1988); *b* 24 Jan 1940; *Educ* Harrison Coll Barbados, Clifton; *m* 9 May 1964, (Edith) Elaine, da of George Turcan Chiene, DSO, TD, MC, of Edinburgh; 2 s (Andrew b 1966, Rupert b 1969), 1 da (Lisa b 1968); *Career* CA; articled clerk Jackson Taylor Abernethy & Co 1958-64; KPMG Peat Marwick: joined 1964, ptnr 1974, gen ptnr 1985, chm insur indust gp; chm indust ctee and memb business law ctee ICEAW, co-chm interprofessional working party accountants/actuaries; inspr under Lloyd's Act 1982 (re-extended Warranty Insur); Liveryman Worshipful Co of Chartered Accountants; FCA 1964; *Recreations* equestrian country pursuits; *Style*— Roger Whewell, Esq; Innerwick, Glenlyon, By Aberfeldy, Perthshire; 10 Lexham House, 45 Lexham Gdns, London W8; KPMG Peat Marwick, 1 Puddle Dock, Blackfriars, London EL4V 3PD (☎ 071 236 8000, fax 071 248 6552, telex 811541 PMMLOW G)

WHICHER, Prof John Templeman; s of Leonard Sydney Whicher, of Piddinghoe, Sussex, and Ethel Adelaid, *née* Orton; *b* 30 July 1945; *Educ* Sherborne, Univ of Cambridge (MA, MB BChir), Westminster Hosp Med Sch, Univ of London (MSc); *m* 1 (m dis 1982), Alba Heather Phyllida Leighton Crawford; 1 s (Hugo b 1975), 1 da (Emma b 1973); m 2, 17 Sept 1982, Jennefer Whitney, da of Dr Arthur Benson Unwin, of London; 2 da (Alexandra b 1986, Charlotte b 1989); *Career* dep dir Protein Reference Unit Westminster Hosp 1975-78, conslt chem pathologist Bristol Royal Infirmary 1978-87, prof of chem pathology Univ of Leeds 1987-; chm Scientific Ctee Assoc of Clinical Biochemists, conslt advsr to Chief MD DHSS; FRCPath; *Books* Immunochemistry in Clinical Laboratory Medicine (jointly, 1978), A Short Textbook of Chemical Pathology (jointly, 1989), The Biochemistry of Inflammation (jointly, 1990); *Recreations* hot air ballooning, speleology, geology; *Clubs* British Balloon and Airship; *Style*— Prof John Whicher; Rush House, Deighton, York YO4 6HG (☎ 090487 237); Department of Chemical Pathology, University of Leeds, Old Medical School, Leeds LS2 9JT (☎ 0532 335673, fax 0532 335672)

WHICHER, Peter George; s of Reginald George Whicher (d 1979), of Chichester, and Suzanne, *née* Dexter (d 1986); *b* 10 March 1929; *Educ* Univ of London (BSc); *m* 3 March 1962, Susan Rosemary (d 1989), da of Dr Stephen Victor Strong, of Windsor; 1 s (Martin b 1964), 1 da (Fiona b 1966); *Career* RAF 1951-53; Miny of Aviation 1953-62, princ expert in telecommunications Eurocontrol Agency Paris 1962-64, govt signal planning staff Cabinet Office 1965-67, asst dir telecommunications R & D and mangr Skynet Satellite Communications Project Miny of Technol 1967-71, supt Communications Div RAF 1971-73, dir air radio MOD(PE) 1973-76, RCDS 1977, dir def sci (electronics) MOD 1978-81, dep dir RAE Farnborough 1981-84, conslt Logica 1985-; CEng 1948, FRAeS, MIEE; *Recreations* sailing, innovative ventures, arts; *Clubs* Royal Ocean Racing; *Style*— Peter Whicher, Esq; Logica, 68 Newman St, London W1A 4SE (☎ 071 637 9111, fax 071 387 3578)

WHICKER, Alan Donald; s of late Charles Henry Whicker, and Anne Jane, *née* Cross; *b* 2 Aug 1925; *Educ* Haberdashers' Aske's; *Career* Capt Devonshire Regt, dir Army Film and Photo Section with 8 Army and US 5 Army, war corr in Korea; foreign corr, novelist, writer, television and radio broadcaster; joined BBC TV 1957, Tonight programme; TV series: Whicker's World 1959-60, Whicker Down Under 1961, Whicker on Top of the World! 1962, Whicker in Sweden, Whicker in the Heart of Texas, Whicker down Mexico Way 1963; The Alan Whicker Report series including The Solitary Billionaire (J Paul Getty); wrote and appeared in own series of monthly documentaries on BBC2 (subsequently repeated on BBC1 under series title Whicker's World) 1965-66; BBC radio programmes and articles for various publications; Sunday newspaper columns; left BBC and joined YTV 1968; various cinema films incl: The Angry Silence 1964; completed 16 documentaries for Yorkshire TV during its first year of operation incl Whicker's New World series, and specials on Gen Stroessner of Paraguay, Count von Rosen and Pres Duvalier of Haiti, Whicker in Europe, Whicker's Walkabout, Broken Hill-Walled City, Gairy's Grenada; documentary series: World of Whicker, Whicker's Orient, Whicker within a Woman's World 1972, Whicker's South Seas, Whicker Way Out West 1973, Whicker's World series on Cities 1974; Whicker's World: Down Under 1976, US 1977, India 1978, Indonesia 1979, California 1980, Peter Sellers Meml programme 1980, Whicker's World aboard the Orient Express 1982, Around Whicker's World in 25 years 1982; returned to BBC TV 1982-83, Whicker's World - the First Million Miles 1982; BBC Radio: chaired Start the Week, Whicker's Wireless World 1983; BBC 1 Whicker's World - a Fast Boat to China 1984; BBC 2: Talk Show Whicker! 1984; BBC1: Whicker's World - Living with Uncle Sam 1985, Whicker's World - Living with Waltzing Matilda 1988, Whicker's World - Hong Kong 1990; various awards incl: Screenwriters' Guild Best Documentary Script 1963, Guild of Television Producers and Directors Personality of the Year 1964, Silver medal RTS 1968, Dumont award Univ of California 1970; Best Interview Programme award: Hollywood Festival of TV 1973, Dimbleby award BAFTA 1978, TV Times Special award 1978; FRSA; *Books* Some Rise By Sin (1949), Away - with Alan Whicker (1963), Within Whicker's World (1982), Whicker's New World (1985), Whicker's World Down Under (1988); *Style*— Alan Whicker, Esq; Le Gallais Chambers, St Helier, Jersey

WHICKER, (Mary) Eileen; da of Patrick Alexander Creighton, of 2 Ivanhoe Place,

Stirling, Scotland, and Agnes, *née* Gavin (d 1980); *b* 29 Oct 1937; *Educ* St Modans HS; *m* 2 June 1962, Paul Jonathan Owen Whicker, s of James Whicker (d 1982); 1 da (Karen Suzanne); *Career* psychotherapist, trainer; fndr Assoc for Neuro Linguistic Programming 1984 (chm 1985-86), memb Family Mediators Assoc; *Recreations* sailing, royal tennis, reading, theatre, sculpture, travelling; *Clubs* Network; *Style—* Mrs Eileen Whicker; 14 Weston Park, Thames Ditton, Surrey KT7 0HQ

WHIDBORNE, Hon Mrs (Elaine Barbara Julia); o da of Lt-Col Hon Rowland Tudor St John, DLI (d 1948, s of 16 Baron St John of Bletso), and Katherine Madge, *née* Lockwood (d 1954); sis of late 20 Baron; raised to the rank of a Baron's da 1977; *b* 19 June 1921; *m* 25 Aug 1939, Lt-Col John Francis Whidborne, RA, o s of John Herbert Whidborne, of Stockleigh English, Devon; 1 s (and 1 s decd), 1 da; *Style—* The Hon Mrs Whidborne; Holly Mount, Pethybridge, Lustleigh, Devon TQ13 9TG (☎ 064 77 267)

WHILEY, Reginald Raymond; JP (1979); s of Harry Hewitt Whiley (d 1957); *b* 7 July 1924; *Educ* Kilburn GS; *Career* memb of Lloyds 1969-; dir CT Bowring (UK) 1974-79, chm Shipton Insurance Services 1976-81; hon treas Snowdon Award Scheme 1979-88, Nat Fund for Research into Crippling Diseases 1979-88; govr: Southlands Coll 1979-89, Luton Indust Coll 1981-90; FCII; *Recreations* walking, watching sport, opera; *Clubs* RAC, MCC; *Style—* Reginald R Whiley, Esq, JP; 2l Francis Rd, Pinner, Middx, HA5 2ST (☎ 081 866 6147)

WHINES, Nicholas Rudwick; s of Rudwick Albert Whines, of Salisbury, and Patricia May, *née* Smith; *Educ* Bishop Wordsworth Sch Salisbury, Fitzwilliam Coll Cambridge (BA); *m* 4 April 1975, Jennifer Elizabeth Susan, da of Archibald Frederick Aldhous; 1 s (Thomas Edward Rudwick b 1979), 1 da (Harriet Frances Dora b 1981); *Career* prodr: BBC Sch Radio 1972-86, BBC Sch TV 1986-88; head of Sch Bdcasting Radio 1988; BAFTA (children's documentary and educn) 1989; *Recreations* gardening, swimming; *Style—* Nicholas Whines, Esq; Broadcasting House, London W1A 1AA (☎ 071 927 5423)

WHIPHAM, Thomas Henry Martin; CBE (1990); s of Harry Rowland Whipham (d 1942), and Anne Hilda Muriel Martin (d 1975); *b* 18 May 1923; *Educ* Malvern; *m* 6 May 1972, Bridget Elizabeth, da of Hugh Roger Greville Montgomery (d 1952); 1 da (Sandra Claire b 24 June 1975); *Career* WWII Army 1941-46, cmmnd Lt RAC Duke of Wellington's Regt 1943 served N Africa, Italy, Middle East; called to the Bar Lincoln's Inn 1949 (ad eundem Middle Temple); pres London Rent Assessment Panel 1986- (a vice pres 1978-86), pres Central London Valuation and Community Charge Tbnl 1987-, hon steward Westminster Abbey 1985-; Parly candidate (Cons) Shoreditch and Finsbury by-election 1958 (also gen election 1959); memb: London Electricity Consultative Cncl 1961-70, Friern Hosp Mgmnt Ctee 1960-73, Marylebone Borough Cncl 1962-65, Westminster City Cncl 1968-86 (chm Ctees on: Road Safety, Highways and Works, Town Planning), Lord Mayor of Westminster 1982-83; Freeman: City of London, Worshipful Co of Goldsmiths; Cdr of Order of Orange Nassau 1982; *Recreations* swimming, walking, opera, theatre, reading, travel, enjoying life; *Clubs* MCC, Carlton, Hurlingham; *Style—* Thomas Whipham, Esq, CBE; 73 Clifton Hill, St John's Wood, London NW8 0JN (☎ 071 624 9837); 37-40 Berners St, London W1 (☎ 071 580 2000)

WHIPP, Dr Elisabeth Clare; da of Dr Brian Whipp (d 1985), and Margery Eileen Whipp (d 1977); *b* 9 Sept 1947; *Educ* St Helen's Sch Northwood, Lady Margaret Hall Oxford; *Career* conslt oncologist Bristol Royal Infirmary 1981-; *Style—* Dr Elisabeth Whipp; Bristol Radiotherapy & Oncology Centre Horfield Rd, Bristol BS8 2B2 (☎ 0272 230000)

WHISHAW, Anthony Popham Law; s of Robert Whishaw, and Joyce, *née* Wheeler; *b* 22 May 1930; *Educ* Tonbridge, Chelsea Sch of Art (Higher Cert), RCA (travelling scholarship, drawing prize); *m* 1957, Jean Gibson; 2 da; *Career* artist; collections incl: Arts Cncl GB, Coventry Art Gallery, Euro Parly Strasbourg, Leicester City Art Gallery, Museo de Bahia Brazil, Nat Gallery Victoria Melbourne, The Tate Gallery; one-man exhibitions incl: Liberia Abril Madrid 1957, Roland Browse & Delbanco 1960,1961,1963,1965 and 1968, Hoya Gallery London 1974, ACME Gallery 1978, from Landscape (Kettle's Yard Cambridge, Ferens Art Gallery Hull, Bede Gallery Jarrow) 1982-84, Work on Paper (Nicola Jacobs Gallery) London 1983, Royal Acad of Arts Diploma Galleries London 1987; gp exhibitions incl: Ashmolean Museum Oxford 1957-72, Br Painting 1952-77 (Royal Acad of Arts London) 1977, Walker Art Gallery Liverpool 1980, Hayward Annual (Hayward Gallery London) 1980 and 1982, Nine Artists (Helsinki, touring) 1983, Three Decades 1953-83 (Royal Acad of Arts London) 1983, 30 London Painters (Royal Acad of Arts London) 1985, Whitechapel Open (Whitechapel Art Gallery London) 1981 and 1987, The Romantic Tradition in Contemporary British Painting (Madrid, Murcia, touring) 1988, 8 Contemporary Br Artsists (Galerie Sapet Valeree France) 1988; prizes: Perth International Biennale 1973, Bayer Int Painting 1973, South East Arts Assoc Painting 1975, GLC Painting 1981, John Moores Minor Painting 1982; scholarships: Spanish Govt 1956, Abbey Minor 1956, Abbey Premier 1982, Lorne 1982-83; Greater London Arts Assoc Grant 1977, Arts Cncl GB Award 1978; RA 1989 (ARA 1980), ARCA; *Style—* Anthony Whishaw, Esq; Acme Studios, 15 Robinson Rd, London E2 (☎ 081 981 2139)

WHISHAW, Sir Charles Percival Law; 2 s of Montague Law Whishaw (d 1946), of London, and Erna Louise, *née* Spies; *b* 29 Oct 1909; *Educ* Charterhouse, Worcester Coll Oxford; *m* 1936, (Margaret) Joan, da of Col Thomas Henry Hawkins, CMG (d 1944), of Formby, Lancs; 1 s, 2 da; *Career* called to the Bar 1932, admitted slr 1938, ptnr Freshfields 1943-74; tstee Calouste Gulbenkian Fndn 1956-81; Comendador of Order of Infante D Henrique Portugal 1982; kt 1969; *Style—* Sir Charles Whishaw; Clare Park, nr Farnham, Surrey GU10 5DT (☎ 0252 851333, 0252 850681)

WHISTLER, Laurence; CBE (1973, OBE 1955); s of Henry Whistler (d 1940), of 69 The Close, Salisbury Cathedral, and Helen, *née* Ward; *b* 21 Jan 1912; *Educ* Stowe, Balliol Coll Oxford (MA); *m* 1, 12 Sep 1939, Jill (d 1944), da of Sir Ralph Furse, KCMG, DSO (d 1963); 1 s (Simon b 1940), 1 da (Caroline b 1944); m 2, 15 Aug 1950 (m dis 1986), Theresa, yr sis Jill Furse; 1 s (Daniel b 1954), 1 da (Frances b 1957); m 3, 24 March 1987, Carol, da of John Groves, CB; *Career* WWII RCS 1940-41, 2 Lt RB 1941, Capt RB 1942-45; glass engraver and author; work on glass incl: engraved church windows and panels Sherborne Abbey Dorset, Guards Chapel London, Salisbury Cathedral, Curry Rivel Somerset; exhibitions: Agnews Bond St 1969, Marble Hill Twickenham 1972, Corning Museum USA 1974, Ashmolean 1976 and 1985; hon fell Balliol Coll Oxford 1974, first pres Guild Glass Engravers 1975-80; FRSL 1955; *Books* on glass incl: The Engraved Glass of Laurence Whistler (1952), Engraved Glass 1952-58 (1959), Pictures on Glass (1972), The Image on The Glass (1975), Scenes And Signs On Glass (1985); poetry incl: The World's Room Collected Poems (1949), To Celebrate Her Living (1967), Enter (1987); prose incl: The English Festivals (1947), The Initials In The Heart, The Story of a Marriage (1975); on his brother: Rex Whistler, His Life and Drawings (1948), The Work of Rex Whistler (with Ronald Fuller, 1969), The Laughter And The Urn (biography, 1985); on architecture incl: Sir John Vanbrugh (biography. 1938), The Imagination of Vanbrugh (1954); *Style—* Laurence Whistler, Esq, CBE; c/o Lloyds Bank, Cox's & King's, 7 Pall Mall, London SW1Y 5YZ

WHITAKER, Alan Arthur; s of Sir (Frederick) Arthur Whitaker, KCB (d 1968, formerly civil engr-in-chief Admiralty 1940-53), of Northwood, Middx, and Florence, *née* Overend (d 1978); *b* 21 March 1925; *Educ* Aldenham, ChCh Oxford (MA); *m* 1957, Beulah, da of Ernest C Hatcher (d 1978), of Northwood, Middx; *Career* dir: Pearson plc 1969-88, Yorkshire TV Holdings plc 1985-89, Osprey Communications plc, Madame Tussaud's Ltd 1978-88, Société Civile du Vignoble de Chateau Latour 1981-89; FCA; *Recreations* gardening; *Style—* Alan Whitaker, Esq; Hartfield, Martinsend Lane, Gt Missenden, Bucks (☎ 024 06 5124)

WHITAKER, Barry Carnaby; s of Maj Kenneth Henry Whitaker (d 1987), of Tilford House, Tilford, Surrey, and Millicent, *née* Carnaby (d 1984); *b* 5 Nov 1940; *Educ* Marlborough; *m* 21 Nov 1968, Jacqueline, da of Sqdn Ldr Harold Rothwell; 2 s (Jason b 7 Feb 1970, Max b 11 Dec 1975); *Career* CA; Peat Marwick Mitchell & Co 1959-64, ptnr Joseph Sebag & Co 1970-79 (joined 1965); ptnr: Carr Sebag & Co 1979-84, Grieveson Grant & Co 1984-86, Kleinwort Griveson & Co 1986-88, C L Alexanders Laing & Cruickshank Gilts Ltd 1987-89, Brown Shipley Stockbroking Limited 1990; chm Tilford Parish Cncl 1990- (memb 1977-), pres Tilford Cons Assoc 1988- (chm 1983-88); ACA 1964, FCA 1974, memb Stock Exchange 1961; *Recreations* country sports, bridge, reading; *Clubs* Boodle's; *Style—* Barry Whitaker, Esq; Tilford House, Tilford, Farnham, Surrey GU10 2BX (☎ 025 125 2962); Founders Court, Lothbury, London EC2R 7AE (☎ 071 726 4059, fax 071 726 2896, car 0836 266763)

WHITAKER, Benjamin Charles George (Ben); 3 s of Maj-Gen Sir John Albert Charles Whitaker, 2 Bt, CB, CBE (d 1957), and Pamela Lucy Mary, *née* Snowden (d 1945); bro of Sir James Whitaker, 3 Bt, *qv*; *b* 15 Sept 1934; *Educ* Eton, New Coll Oxford (BA); *m* 18 Dec 1964, Janet Alison, da of Alan Harrison Stewart, of The Small House, Station Rd, Beeston, Notts; 2 s (Daniel b 1966, Rasaq b 1972), 1 da (Quincy b 1968); *Career* Lt Coldstream Guards; called to the Bar Inner Temple 1959; MP (Lab) Hampstead 1966-70, Parly sec for Overseas Devpt 1969-70, exec dir The Minority Rights Gp 1971-88, UK memb The UN Human Rights Sub Cmmn 1975-88, dir The Gurbenkian Fndn (UK) 1988-; *Books* Parks for People (ed, 1971), The Foundation (1974), The Police in Society (1979), A Bridge of People (1983), The Global Connection (1987); *Recreations* writing; *Style—* Benjamin Whitaker, Esq; 13 Elsworthy Rd, London NW3

WHITAKER, Catherine (Kati); da of Dennis Whitaker, of Totteridge, London, and Florence, *née* Gregory; *b* 11 Dec 1957; *Educ* Queen Elizabeth Girls Sch Barnet, Somerville Coll Oxford (read PPE), Coll of Law Lancaster Gate; *m* 29 May 1989, Andrew Jackson Hughes, s of Brian Jackson Hughes, of Aldershot, Hants; *Career* freelance radio and TV journalist 1973-; presenter Radio 4 prog: Does He Take Sugar 1987-, Sunday 1988-90; *Recreations* music, dance, cinema, travel; *Style—* Ms Kati Whitaker; 1 Stockwell Terrace, London SW9 0QD

WHITAKER, David Brian; OBE (1989); s of Denis Whitaker, of Hexton, Hitchin, Herts, and Phyllis, *née* Clark; *b* 16 Aug 1948; *Educ* Hitchin Boys' GS, Univ of Loughborough (BEd); *m* 18 July 1970, Christine (Chris), da of George Clements (d 1987); 2 s (Kester Mark Clement b 19 Dec 1974, Alexander John Clement b 16 May 1977); *Career* teacher: Hitchin Boys' Sch 1972-76, Sherrardswood Sch 1976-78, Marlborough 1978-85; int hockey player and coach; player: Blueharts 1973-74, Southgate 1974-80, 104 caps England and GB 1973-80; coach England and GB 1980-88, dir of coaching Hockey Assoc 1986-89 (professional coach 1985-86); honours as player: Southgate Euro Club champions 1976, 1977, 1978, played in World Cup 1975 and 1978, Euro Cup 1974 and 1977; honours as coach: Bronze Medal Olympic Games 1984, Silver Medal World Cup 1986, Silver Medal Euro Cup 1987, Gold Medal Olympic Games 1988, Champions Trophy 1981-88; UK coach of the year 1985 and 1988; ptnr and dir The Grass Roots Gp plc 1989-; *Books* Coaching Hockey (1986), Coaching Workshop (1991); *Recreations* DIY, golf, history, leadership and team building; *Style—* David Whitaker, Esq, OBE; Trotters, 24 Hallow Rd, St Johns, Worcester WR2 6BU (☎ 0905 420233)

WHITAKER, David Haddon; s of Edgar Haddon Whitaker, MA, OBE (d 1985), and Molly Marion, *née* Seely; *b* 6 March 1931; *Educ* Marlborough, St John's Coll Cambridge (MA); *m* 1, 1959, late Veronica, *née* Leach; m 2, 1976 (m dis), Audrey, *née* Curl; 2 s (Martin, Rupert), 2 da (Lee, Jane); *Career* Nat Serv Coldstream Gds 1949, 2 Lt Queen's Own Royal West Surrey Regt 1950; chm: Soc of Bookmen 1984-86 (sec 1969-78), Br Standards Inst's Working Pty for Standard Book Numbering 1966-67, ISBN 1968-69, J Whitaker & Sons Ltd 1980 (dir 1966); ed The Bookseller 1976-80, dir Teleordering Ltd 1984; memb Library and Info Servs Cncl of the Office of Arts and Libraries 1984-89 (chm Working Pty Financing the Public Library Service 1988-89); chm: Book Trade Electronic Data Interchange Standards Ctee 1986-90, Advsy Panel of Int Standard Book Numbering Agency Berlin 1989 (dep chm 1986), Min for the Arts Advsy Panel for Public Lending Rights 1988, Working Pty on Library and Book Trade Rels 1988 (memb 1965), Fedn Euro Publishers' Ctee for Standards for the Distribution of Bibliographic Info in Europe 1990, Br Nat Bibliography Res Fund 1991; MBIM 1986, hon vice pres The Library Assoc 1990; *Recreations* walking, reading, tennis; *Clubs* Garrick, Leander, Thames Rowing; *Style—* David Whitaker, Esq; 30 Jenner House, Hunter St, London WC1N 1BL (☎ 071 837 8109); J Whitaker & Sons Ltd, 12 Dyott St, London WC1A 1DF (☎ 071 836 8911, fax 071 836 2909)

WHITAKER, Prof Dorothy Stock; da of Charles William Stock (d 1958), of Chicago, Illinois, and Martha Emily, *née* Utesch (d 1985); *b* 30 March 1925; *Educ* Univ of Chicago (PhB, MA, PhD); *m* 21 Dec 1963, Frederic Philip Galvin, s of Capt Charles Frederick Whitaker (d 1988), of Baildon, W Yorks; 1 s (Weem b 1965); *Career* res assoc dept of educn Univ of Chicago 1952-55, res psychologist VA Res Hosp Chicago 1955-57, assoc prof of psychology Univ of Chicago 1957-64 (former asst prof), lectr dept of psychology Univ of Leeds 1964-73, prof of social work dept of social policy and social work Univ of York 1973-; memb: American Psychological Assoc 1952, American Gp Psychotherapy Assoc 1956, Gp Analytic Soc 1964; *Books* Psychotherapy Through The Group Process (with Morton Lieburuan, 1964), Using Groups to Help People (1985), Research by Social Workers (with J Lesley Archer, 1989); *Recreations* sailing, walking; *Style—* Prof Dorothy Whitaker; Dept of Social Policy and Social Work, University of York, Heslington, York YO1 5DD (☎ 0904 433488, fax 0904 433433, telex 57933 YORKUL)

WHITAKER, James Edward Anthony; s of George Edward Dudley Whitaker, OBE (d 1983), and Mary Evelyn Austin, *née* Haslett (d 1989); *b* 4 Oct 1940; *Educ* Cheltenham; *m* 1965, Iwona, da of late Andrzej Karol Milde, of Poland; 2 s (Edward b 1965, Thomas b 1966), 1 da (Victoria b 1973); *Career* journalist: Daily Mail, Daily Express, The Sun, Daily Star; *Books* Prince Charles, Prince of Wales, Settling Down; *Recreations* racing, shooting, skiing; *Clubs* City Golf; *Style—* James Whitaker, Esq; c/o Mirror Group Newspapers, Holborn Circus London EC1 (☎ 071 353 0246)

WHITAKER, Sir James Herbert Ingham Whitaker; 3 Bt (UK 1936), of Babworth, Nottinghamshire; s of Maj-Gen Sir John Albert Charles Whitaker, 2 Bt, CB, CBE (d 1957), and Pamela Lucy Mary, *née* Snowden (d 1945); bro of Benjamin Charles George Whitaker, *qv*; *b* 27 July 1925; *Educ* Eton; *m* 26 July 1948, Mary Elisabeth Lander, JP (who m 1940, Capt David Urling Clark, MC, d 1942), da of Ernest Johnston (d 1965), of Cockshut, Reigate, Surrey, and sis of Sir Charles Hepburn Johnston, GCMG (d 1986); 1 s, 1 da (Shervie m David W J Price, *qv*); *Heir* s, John James Ingham Whitaker b 23 Oct 1952, *qv*; *Career* 2 Lt Coldstream Gds 1944, served in N W Europe, Egypt and Palestine 1945, ret 1947; dep chm Halifax Building Society 1973-; govr Atlantic Coll; High Sheriff Notts 1969; *Recreations* shooting; *Clubs* Boodle's; *Style—* Sir James Whitaker, Bt; Auchnafree, Dunkeld, Perthshire (☎ 035 05 233); Babworth Hall, Retford, Notts (☎ 0777 703454)

WHITAKER, Maj Jeremy Ingham; s of Maj Leith Ingham Tomkins Whitaker, DL (d 1971), and Myrtle Clare, *née* Van de Weyer; *b* 10 Nov 1934; *Educ* Eton, Sandhurst; *m* 18 April 1974, Philippa, da of Lt-Col HH van Straubenzee, DSO, OBE, of The Old Farm House, Hazeley Bottom, Hoartley Wintney, Basingstoke, Hampshire; 1 s (Benjamin Ingham b 17 April 1979), 2 da (Alexandra Marilyn b 27 June 1975, Camilla Isabelle b 31 May 1980); *Career* cmmnd Coldstream Gds 1954, Capt 1960, ADC to Govr Gen Nigeria 1960-61, UNO forces Congo West Africa Frontier Force GSO3 Nigerian Bde 1961, ADC to High Cmmm Malaysia 1963-65, Maj 1 Bn Coldstream Gds Aden 1965-66; professional architecture photographer 1967-; MCSD 1976; *Recreations* skiing, gardening, carpentry; *Clubs* Pratts; *Style—* Maj Jeremy Whitaker; Land of Nod, Headley, Bordon, Hampshire GU35 8SJ (☎ 0428 713609, 0428 712292)

WHITAKER, John James Ingham (Jack); s and h of Sir James Herbert Ingham Whitaker, 3 Bt; *b* 23 Oct 1952; *Educ* Eton, (BSc); *m* 31 Jan 1981, Elizabeth Jane Ravenscroft, da of L J R Starke, of NZ; 1 s (Harry James Ingham b 1984), 3 da (Lucy Harriet Ravenscroft b 1982, Alix Catherine Hepburn b 1987, Eleanor Mary Harvie b 1989); *Career* FCA, AMIEE; *Style—* Jack Whitaker, Esq; The Cottage, Babworth, Retford, Notts DN22 8EW

WHITAKER, Martin; s of Maj Robert Edmund Whitaker, TD, of Shropshire, and Priscilla Kynaston, *née* Mainwaring; *b* 24 Sept 1938; *Educ* Sherborne, RAC Cirencester; *m* 16 July 1966, Susan Mary Sheila, da of Francis Spenceleigh Walker, of Standlake, Oxon; 1 s (Alexander b 1972), 1 da (Anabel b 1969); *Career* chartered surveyor; dir Lane Fox and Ptnrs Ltd 1987-; FRICS; *Recreations* shooting, hunting; *Style—* Martin Whitaker, Esq; Dovecote House, Driffield, Cirencester, Glos GL7 5PY (☎ 028 585 465); The Mead House, Thomas St, Cirencester, Glos

WHITAKER, Michael; s of Donald Whitaker, and Enid, *née* Lockwood; *b* 17 March 1960; *Educ* Salendine Nook Secdy Modern Sch; *m* 13 Dec 1980, Veronique Dalem's, da of Dino Vastapane; *Career* professional show jumper; Jr Euro Team 1976, winner Jr Championships under 16 and under 21, winner Jr Euro Team Championship 1978; Grand Prix wins: Hickstead 1986, Dortmund 1986, Wembley 1987, Brimingham 1989, Calgary 1989; other wins incl: Hickstead Derby 1980, King George V Gold Cup 1982 and 1989, Euro Team Championships 1985, 1987, 1989, Euro Team Championships 1985, 1987, 1989, nat champion 1984 and 1989; runner-up Euro Championships 1989, Silver medal World Team Championships 1986 (Bronze medal 1990), Silver medal team event Olympics LA 1984; 45 int appearances; world bareback high jump record Dublin 1980; *Recreations* sport, spending time at home; *Style—* Michael Whitaker, Esq; Tunstead Knoll Farm, Kettleshulme, Stockport, Cheshire SK12 7RF (☎ 0663 732687)

WHITAKER, Sheila Hazel; da of Charles Whitaker (d 1975), and Hilda Dixon (d 1987); *b* 1 April 1936; *Educ* Cathays HS for Girls Cardiff, King's Norton GS Birmingham, Univ of Warwick (BA); *Career* chief stills offr Nat Film Archive BFI 1968-74, dir Tyneside Cinema Tyneside Film Festival Newcastle Upon Tyne 1979-84, head programming Nat Film Theatre BFI 1984-90, dir London Film Festival 1987-; *Clubs* Groucho; *Style—* Ms Sheila Whitaker; London Film Festival, South Bank, Waterloo, London SE1 8XT (☎ 071 928 3535)

WHITAKER, Steven Dixon; s of George Dixon Whitaker, of Exeter, and Elsie Whitaker; *b* 28 Jan 1950; *Educ* Burnley GS, Churchill Coll Cambridge (MA); *m* 4 Sept 1976, Jacqueline, da of William Ernest Branter (d 1985); 1 da (Emma Louise); *Career* called to the Bar Middle Temple 1973; chm bd govrs Rosemead Prep Sch London 1987-90; *Recreations* choral singing, music, the arts, for travel; *Style—* Steven Whitaker, Esq; Beulah Cottage, Queen Mary Rd, Upper Norwood, London SE19 3NN (☎ 081 670 0861, fax 081 761 8909); Via Marconi 7, Brucciano Mollazana, Lucca 55020, Italy; 199 Strand, London WC2R 1DR (☎ 071 379 9779, fax 071 379 9481); All Saints Chambers, 9/11 Broad Street, Bristol BS1 2HP (☎ 0272 211966, fax 0272 276493)

WHITAKER, Wolstan John; (formerly Churchward, name changed by deed poll 1954); s of Capt Paul Rycaut de Shordiche Churchward (d 1981), and Claire Isabel, *née* Whitaker who m 2 Richard Rusby Kaye (d 1981); *b* 8 Sept 1935; *Educ* Northaw Sch, Tabley House Sch; *m* 1961, Rosemary, da of Capt Stanley William Culverhouse (d 1973); 2 s (Charles James Stanbury b 1963, Piers Francis John b 1965); *Recreations* hunting, shooting; *Style—* Wolstan Whitaker, Esq; Winsley Hall, Westbury, Shrewsbury, Shropshire SY5 9HB

WHITBOURN, Dr Philip Robin; s of Edwin Arthur Whitbourn (d 1953), of Badgers Mount, Sevenoaks, Kent, and Kathleen, *née* Sykes; *b* 10 March 1932; *Educ* Sevenoaks Sch Kent, UCL (PhD); *m* 10 Jan 1959, Anne Pearce, da of Peter Melrose Marks (d 1938), of Glasgow; 1 s (James b 1963), 1 da (Katherine b 1960); *Career* architect; Sir Edwin Cooper RA and Partners 1955-58, Stewart Hendry and Smith 1958-60, Fitzroy Robinson Partnership 1960-66, Historic Bldgs Div GLC 1966-86, divnl architect London Div English Heritage 1988 (joined 1986); chm Royal Tunbridge Wells Civic Soc 1969-70 1972-73 1978-80 and 1990-91; FRIBA 1968, FRTPI 1983, FSA 1984; *Style—* Dr Philip Whitbourn; Rosaville Lodge, 40 Beulah Rd, Tunbridge Wells, Kent TN1 2NR (☎ 0892 23026)

WHITBREAD, David Anthony Llewellyn; s of Sqdn Ldr Jack Leonard Whitbread, of Hertford, and late Eunice, *née* Llewellyn; *b* 20 July 1936; *Educ* Latymer Upper Sch, Selwyn Coll Cambridge (MA); *m* 3 April 1965, Margaret Lilias, da of Geoffrey Luffingham, of Pietermaritzburg, S Africa; 3 da (Emily Jane b 1966, Harriet Ann b 1969, Rosemary b 1973); *Career* MOD 1960-67, sr asst educn offr Norfolk CC 1967-73, princ asst educn offr Hertfordshire CC 1973-84, under sec for educn Assoc of CCs 1984-; *Style—* David Whitbread, Esq; Association of County Councils, Eaton House, 66A Eaton Square, London SW1W 9BH (☎ 071 235 1200, fax 071 235 8458)

WHITBREAD, David Harry; MBE (1977); s of Harry Whitbread (d 1980), and Maud Emily, *née* Deval; *b* 18 April 1938; *Educ* Leyton County High Sch; *m* 15 Aug 1964, Caroline Elizabeth, da of Maurice Aron, of Devon; 1 s (Richard Piers b 1971), 2 da (Claire b 1966, Amanda b 1967); *Career* Nat Serv 10 Royal Hussars 1956-58; FO 1961; British Embassies 1962-89: Kuwait 1962-63, Baghdad 1964-67, Beirut 1970-76, second sec Jedda 1980-82, first sec Amman 1986-89; *Recreations* wildlife conservation, fishing; *Style—* David Whitbread, Esq, MBE; Foreign & Commonwealth Office, King Charles St, London SW1A 2AH

WHITBREAD, Fatima; MBE (1987); *b* 3 March 1961; *Career* javelin thrower; Cwlth Games: Bronze medallist 1982, Silver medallist 1986; Euro Championships Gold medallist 1986; World Championships: Silver medallist 1983, Gold medallist 1987; Olympic Games: Bronze medallist 1984, Silver medallist 1988; world record holder 1986-; womens rep Br Olympic Assoc; memb Mazda Track Club; *Books* Fatima (autobiography, 1988); *Recreations* theatre; *Style—* Miss Fatima Whitbread, MBE; c/o Amateur Athletic Association, Edgbaston House, off Hagley Rd, Edgbaston, Birmingham B16 8NM (☎ 021 456 4050)

WHITBREAD, Hugh William; s of Col William Henry Whitbread, TD, and Betty Parr, *née* Russell; *b* 11 Feb 1942; *Educ* Eton, Cambridge Univ, Harvard Univ; *m* 1972, Katherine Elizabeth, *née* Hall; 3 c; *Career* brewing industry exec, specialist dir Whitbread & Co, md Thomas Wethereds of Marlow 1976-81; HM Diplomatic Serv 1966-71, second sec Vientiane 1968-70 (third sec 1966-68); *Recreations* fishing, shooting, private flying; *Clubs* Brook's, RAC; *Style—* Hugh Whitbread Esq; The Old Rectory, Dennington, Woodbridge, Suffolk; Kinlochewe Lodge, Achnasheen, Ross-shire

WHITBREAD, Michael William; 2 s of Col William William Whitbread; *b* 25 June 1930; *Educ* Stowe; *m* 1965, Helen Mary, *née* Aikenhead; 1 s, 1 da; *Career* brewery dir, pres Licenced Victualler's Nat Homes 1981-82; ret; *Recreations* shooting, stalking, fishing, rugby; *Style—* Michael Whitbread, Esq; The Grey House, Turkdean, Northleach, Glos (☎ 0457 60389)

WHITBREAD, Samuel Charles; s of Maj Simon Whitbread (d 1985), of Bedford, and Helen Beatrice Margaret, *née* Trefusis; family settled in Bedfordshire at time of Conquest, founded Brewery 1742, 1 Tory and 5 Whig/Liberal MPs; *b* 22 Feb 1937; *Educ* Eton, Trinity Coll Cambridge; *m* 1961, Jane Mary, da of Charles William John Hugh Hayter (d 1985), of Oxfordshire; 3 s (Charles, Henry, William), 1 da (Victoria); *Career* dir: Whitbread & Co plc 1972 (chm 1984), Whitbread Investment Co plc 1977, Brewers' Soc Cncl 1984, Whitbread Share Ownership Tstees Ltd 1984, Whitbread Pension Tstees Ltd 1984, SC Whitbread Farms 1985, Sun Alliance Group 1989; landowner (10800 acres); DL 1974, Lord-Lt for Bedfordshire 1991-; *Recreations* shooting, photography, music, travel; *Clubs* Brooks's; *Style—* Samuel Whitbread, Esq; Southill Park, Biggleswade, Beds SG18 9LL (☎ 0462 813272); Brewery, Chiswell St, London EC1Y 4SD (☎ 071 606 4455, telex 888640)

WHITBREAD, Col William Henry; TD (2 bars); s of Henry William Whitbread (d 1947), of Norton Bavant, Westbury, Wilts, and Mary, *née* Ryramond (d 1925); Landed Gentry Family, Robert Wytbred of Gravenhurst mentioned in the subsidy Rolls 1309 Samuel Whitbread (d 1796) the eminent brewer was MP Bedford 1768-90 and had his seat at Southilll rebuilt by Holland, his s Samuel (d 1815) MP Bedford 1790-1815, m Lady Elizabeth Grey eld da 1 Earl Grey, subsequent Whitbread's have been MPs and m into the Peerage; *b* 22 Nov 1900; *Educ* Eton, Corpus Christi Coll Cambridge (MA); *m* 1, 27 April 1927, Anne Joscelyne (d 1936), da of Samuel Howard Whitbread, CB (d 1944), of Southill Park, Beds; 2 s (Henry Charles b 1928, Michael William b 1930), 1 da (Mary Joscelyne, Lady T Tollemache, (*see* Baronetage) b 1933); m 2, 26 April 1941, Betty Parr, da of Samuel Russell (d 1940), of 18 Grange Road, Eastbourne; 1 s (Hugh William b 1942), 2 da (Isabella Margaret Ruth b 1946, Sarah Maud b 1950); *Career* chm Whitbread Investment Co and Whitbread Int 1944-70 (dir 1927); dir: Barclays Bank, Eagle Star Insurance Co; vice pres Brewers Soc (chm 1952-53), Inst of Brewing (chm research ctee); memb: Hurlingham Polo Ctee 1932-45, Field Sports Ctee 1950; Master Trinity Foot Beagles 1921-23; *Recreations* hunting, stalking, shooting, fishing, sailing; *Clubs* Brook's, Pratt's, Thames Yacht, Royal Yacht Squadron, Jockey; *Style—* Col William Whitbread, TD; Haslehurst, Haslemere, Surrey; Farleaze, nr Malmesbury, Wilts; The Heights of Kinlochewe, Ross-shire

WHITBY, Charles Harley; QC (1970); s of Arthur William Whitby (d 1983), of Acton, Middx, and Florence, *née* Edwards (d 1982); *b* 2 April 1926; *Educ* St Johns Leatherhead, Peterhouse Cambridge (MA); *m* 11 Sept 1981, Eileen May, da of Albert George Scott (d 1978), of Palmers Green, London; *Career* RAFVR 1944-48; called to the Bar Middle Temple 1952, bencher 1977, memb Bar Cncl 1969-71 and 1972-78, rec Crown Court 1972-; Criminal Injuries Compensation Bd 1975-; contrib: Halsbury Laws of Eng, Atkins Encyclopedia of Court Forms; *Recreations* reading, golf, watching soccer, fishing, swimming; *Clubs* Utd Oxford and Cambridge Univ, RAC (steward 1985-), Garrick, Woking Golf; *Style—* Charles Whitby, Esq, QC; 12 Kings Bench Walk, Temple, EC4 (☎ 071 583 0811)

WHITBY, Prof (Lionel) Gordon; s of Sir Lionel Ernest Howard Whitby, CVO, MC, MD (d 1956), of The Master's Lodge, Downing Coll, Cambridge, and Ethel, *née* Murgatroyd; *b* 18 July 1926; *Educ* Eton, King's Coll Cambridge (BA, MA, PhD, MB BChir, MD), Middx Hosp Med Sch London; *m* 29 July 1949, Joan Hunter, da of William Sanderson (d 1969), of 14 Blackford Rd, Edinburgh; 1 s ((Lionel) Michael b 1952), 2 da (Anne Rosemary (Mrs Priestley) b 1950, Pamela Jean (Mrs Molyneaux) b 1954); *Career* fell King's Coll Cambridge 1951-55, jr med appts in London 1956-59, Rockefeller travelling scholarship in med Nat Inst of Health USA 1959-60, univ biochemist Addenbrooke's Hosp Cambridge 1960-63, fell Peterhouse Cambridge 1961-62, prof of clinical chemistry Edinburgh Univ 1963-91 (dean Faculty of Med 1969-72 and 1983-86, vice princ 1979-83); tstee Nat Library of Scotland 1982-, vice pres Royal Soc of Edinburgh 1983-86, memb Br Library Advsy Cncl 1986-91; memb: Dept of Health, Scottish Home and Health Dept, professional advsy ctees 1965-81, Med Laboratory Technicians Bd, Cncl for Professions Supplementary to Med 1978-; memb Worshipful Co of Glovers of London; MRCS, LRCP 1956, FRCPE 1968, FRCP 1972, FRCPath 1972, FIBiol 1988; *Books* Lecture Notes on Clinical Chemistry (with A F Smith and G J Beckett, fourth edn 1988), Principles and Practice of Medical Computing (with W Lutz, 1971); *Recreations* gardening, photography; *Clubs* RSM; *Style—* Prof Gordon Whitby; 51 Dick Place, Edinburgh EH9 2JA (☎ 031 667 4358); Dept of Clinical Chemistry, The Royal Infirmary of Edinburgh, Edinburgh EH3 9YW (☎ 031 229 3182 ext 2477)

WHITCOMBE, Hon Mrs (Rosemary Anne Heather); *née* Colville; da of late 1 Baron Clydesmuir, GCIE, TD, PC; *b* 1927; *m* 1954, Philip Arthur Whitcombe; 1 s, 1 da; *Style—* The Hon Mrs Whitcombe; Green Cross Farm, Churt, Farnham, Surrey

WHITE, Adrian Harold Michael; s of Brig Gilbert William White, MBE (d 1977), and Clodagh Marie, *née* Austin (d 1977); *b* 20 Nov 1945; *Educ* Ampleforth; *m* 25 June 1970, Helen Frances McKay, da of Sir Herbert (Charles Fahie) Cox, QC (d 1973); 1 s (Hugh b 5 March 1978); *Career* CA; audit sr Peat Marwick Mitchell & Co 1964-70; exec: Brown Shipley & Co Ltd 1970-72, Old Broad St Securities Ltd 1972-75, Hill Samuel & Co Ltd 1975-78; sr asst dir Morgan Grenfell & Co Ltd 1978-87, currently fin dir Midland Montagu Asset Management; FCA; *Recreations* rifle shooting; *Clubs* MCC, North London Rifle; *Style—* Adrian White, Esq; 54 Lanercost Rd, London SW2 (☎ 081 674 6831); Midland Montagu Asset Management, 10 Lower Thames St, London EC3R 6AE (☎ 071 260 9922, fax 071 260 9140, telex 8956886)

WHITE, Alan Geoffrey; s of John White, and Rose, *née* Dallin; *b* 8 July 1934; *Educ* Mitcham GS; *m* Melanie (decd); *Career* RAF Photographic 1953-57; freelance photographer 1958-67, CPL Ltd 1967-85 (printer, supervisor, salesman, sales mangr, mktg mangr), set up own co Stilled Movie Limited 1986- (dealing with specialised visual effects photography for film and tv indust); has presented papers at various confs; FBIPP, FRPS, memb Royal TV Soc, MBKS, hon memb Br Film Designers Guild; *Recreations* golf; *Clubs* Hurlingham Luncheon, White Elephant; *Style—* Alan White, Esq; Bramble Cottage, Church St, Hartfield, East Sussex TN7 4AG (☎ 0892 770656); Stilled Movie Ltd, Shepperton Studios, Studios Rd, Shepperton, Middx TW17 OQD (☎ 0932 562611 ext 2010, fax 0932 568989, car 0860 399888)

WHITE, Prof Alan Richard; s of George Albert White (d 1937), and Jean Gabriel, *née* Kingston (d 1957); *b* 9 Oct 1922; *Educ* Midleton Coll and Presentation Coll Cork Ireland, Trinity Coll Dublin (BA), Univ of London (PhD); *m* 1, 12 Aug 1948 (m dis 1978), Eileen Anne, *née* Jarvis; 1 s (Nicholas b 15 Feb 1954), 2 da (Helen b 18 April 1956, Hilary b 11 Jan 1958); m 2, 21 Dec 1979, Enid Elizabeth, *née* Alderson; *Career*

42 Dublin Rifles 1941-45; dep lectr in logic Trinity Coll Dublin 1945-46, pro-vice-chllr Univ of Hull 1976-79 (asst lectr, lectr, sr lectr in philosophy 1946-61, prof 1961-89, dean of arts 1969-71); visiting prof: Univ of Maryland 1967-68 and 1980, Temple Univ 1974, Simon Fraser Univ 1983, Univ of Delaware 1986, Bowling Green State Univ Ohio 1988; special prof Univ of Nottingham 1986-; pres: Mind Assoc 1972 (sec 1960-69), Aristotelian Soc 1979-80; articles in philosophical jls; *Books* G E Moore A Critical Exposition (1958), Attention (1964), The Philosophy of Mind (1967), The Philosophy of Action (ed, 1968), Truth (1970), Modal Thinking (1975), The Nature of Knowledge (1982), Rights (1984), Grounds of Liability (1985), Methods of Metaphysics (1987), The Language of Imagination (1990); *Recreations* dilettantism, odd jobbery; *Style—* Prof Alan R White; 77 Newfield Rd, Sherwood, Notts (☎ 0602 605078)

WHITE, Angela Mary; da of Henry William Orman (d 1973), of London, and Irene Isobel, *née* Searle; *Educ* Bromley HS, City of London Coll (Louis H Keik travelling scholarship); *m* 1962, Roger Lowrey White, JP; *Career* advertising agencies 1960-68, dep advtg mangr Br Tourist Authy 1968-71, advtg and mktg mangr English Tourist Bd 1971-90, media affrs mangr Royal Mail 1990-; memb Worshipful Co of Marketors 1990, Freeman City of London 1990; FCIM 1989 (memb 1974, nat vice chm 1990-91); *Clubs* United and Cecil; *Style—* Mrs Angela M White; Royal Mail, Royal Mail House, 148-166 Old St, London EC1V 9HQ (☎ 071 250 2365, fax 071 250 2366)

WHITE, Bryan Oliver; s of Thomas Frederick White, and Olive May, *née* Turvey (d 1985); *b* 3 Oct 1929; *Educ* Perse Sch Cambridge, Wadham Coll Oxford; *m* 3 Nov 1958, Helen McLeod, da of John R Jenkins, of Argyll; 1 s (James), 2 da (Alison, Emma); *Career* FO 1953-79: Kabul, Vienna, Conakry, Rio de Janeiro, Cabinet Office, Havana; cnsllr Paris 1980-82, head Mexico and Central America dept FCO 1982-84, ambass Honduras and (non-res) El Salvador 1984, consul-gen Lyons 1987-89; *Recreations* languages and literature; *Clubs* Cercle de l'Union (Lyon); *Style—* Bryan White, Esq; 45 Westminster Palace Gdns, London SW1P 1RR (☎ 071 222 0176)

WHITE, Hon Caroline Davina; da of 5 Baron Annaly (d 1990) and his 2 w, Jennifer Margaret, *née* Carey; *b* 8 Feb 1963; *Style—* The Hon Caroline White

WHITE, Dr Christopher John; s of Gabriel Edward Ernest Francis White, CBE (d 1988), of London, and Elizabeth Grace, *née* Ardizzone (d 1958); *b* 19 Sept 1930; *Educ* Downside, Courtauld Inst of Art, Univ of London (BA, PhD), Univ of Oxford (MA); *m* 14 Dec 1957, Rosemary Katharine Alice, da of Gordon Paul Desages (d 1960), of London; 1 s (Sebastian Gabriel b 1965), 2 da (Arabella Elizabeth b 1959, Clarisa Grace b 1961); *Career* asst keeper Dept Prints and Drawings British Museum 1954-65, dir Messrs P and D Colnaghi London 1965-71, curator graphic arts Nat Gallery of Art Washington DC 1971-73, dir studies Paul Mellon Centre for Studies in British Art London 1973-85, assoc dir Yale Centre for British Art New Haven USA 1973-85, dir Ashmolean Museum 1985-, fell Worcester Coll Oxford 1985-; FBA 1989; *Books* Rembrandt and his World (1964), The Flower Drawings of Jan van Huysum (1965), Rubens and his World (1968), Rembrandt as an Etcher (1969), Rembrandt's Etchings: a catalogue raisonne (jtly, 1970), Dürer: the artist and his drawings (1972), English Landscape 1630-1850 (1977), Dutch Paintings in the Collection of H M The Queen (1982), Rembrandt in Eighteenth-century England (ed, 1983), Rembrandt (1984), Peter Paul Rubens: man and artist (1987), Drawing in England from Hilliard to Hogarth (jtly, 1987); *Recreations* music, travel; *Style—* Dr Christopher White; 14 South Villas, London NW1 9BS (☎ 071 485 9148); 39 St Giles, Oxford OX1 3LW (☎ 0865 512289); Shingle House, St Cross, Nr Harleston, Norfolk IP20 0NT (☎ 098 682 264); Ashmolean Museum, Oxford OX1 2PH (☎ 0865 278005, fax 0865 278018)

WHITE, Christopher John Waring; s of Arthur John Stanley White, CMG, OBE, of The Red House, Mere, Wilts, and Joan, *née* Elston-Davies; *b* 21 Nov 1933; *Educ* Marlborough, Clare Coll Cambridge (BA); *m* 11 April 1959, Shirley Diana, da of Sir Kenneth Oswald Peppiatt, KBE, MC (d 1983); 1 da (Annabel b 1961); *Career* Lt Royal Hampshire Regt 1952-54; Joseph Travers & Sons Ltd 1957-60, George Harker & Co Ltd 1960-70; chm F & E Clarke Ltd 1983- (joined 1970), dir The Corn Exchange Co Ltd; memb Chiltern Dist Cncl 1979-83, chm Penn Parish Cncl 1983- (memb 1976-); Freeman Worshipful Co of Makers of Playing Cards 1969-; *Style—* Christopher White, Esq; Ray's Yard, Penn, Bucks (☎ 049 481 3238); 52 Mark Lane, London EC3 (☎ 071 481 8707, fax 071 702 3716, telex 886881)

WHITE, Sir Christopher Robert Meadows White; 3 Bt (UK 1937), of Boulge Hall, Co Suffolk; s of Sir (Eric) Richard Meadows White, 2 Bt (d 1972); *b* 26 Aug 1940; *Educ* Bradfield; *m* 1962 (m dis 1968), Anne Marie Ghislaine, da of late Maj Tom Brown, OBE, MC; m 2, 1968 (m dis 1972), Dinah Mary Sutton; m 3, 1976, Ingrid Carolyn, da of Eric Jowett, of Gt Baddow, Essex; *Heir* none; *Career* formerly schoolmaster; housemaster St Michael's Sch Ingoldisthorpe Norfolk 1963-69; *Style—* Sir Christopher White, Bt; 101 Thunder Lane, Norwich, Norfolk

WHITE, David Harry; DL (Notts 1989); s of Harry White, OBE (d 1975), of Nottingham, and Kathleen, *née* Sadler; *b* 12 Oct 1929; *Educ* Nottingham HS, HMS Conway; *m* 5 April 1971, Valerie Jeanne; *Career* apprentice to Master Shell Tankers Ltd 1946-56, Texaco Ltd 1956-64 (terminal mangr, London area mangr), ops mangr UK Distribution and Construction Gulf Oil Ltd 1964-68, chief exec Samuel Williams Ltd 1968-70; gp md: British Road Services Group 1976-82, Pickford Group of Companies 1982-84; non-exec dir British Rail Property Board 1985-87; National Freight Consortium plc: dep chm and dir 1981-89, gp md Property Gp 1984-85, non-exec dir 1989-90; non-exec chm NFC Trustees Ltd 1985-, non-exec dir YS Lovell (Holdings) plc 1987-, dir Whitehaven Consultants Ltd 1987-; chm: Nottingham Development Enterprise Ltd 1987-, Nottingham Health Authority 1987-; chm Nottingham Poly 1987-, dir Gtr Nottingham Training & Enterprise Cncl, tstee Djanogly City Technol Coll; *Clubs* RAC; *Style—* David White, Esq, DL; Nottingham Health Authority, Forest House, Berkeley Ave, Nottingham NG3 5AF (☎ 0602 691692, fax 0602 627802)

WHITE, David Julian; s of Arthur John Stanley White, CMG, OBE, of Mere, Wilts, and Joan, *née* Davies; *b* 17 July 1942; *Educ* Marlborough; *m* 24 June 1967, Claire Rosemary, da of Rowland Emett, OBE, of Ditchling, Sussex; 3 da (Juliet b 1969, Sarah b 1972, Victoria b 1974); *Career* Union Discount Co of London Ltd plc 1965-79; Cater Allen Holdings plc 1979- (dep chm 1985-); *Recreations* tennis, squash; *Style—* David White, Esq; 20 Birchin Lane, London EC3V 9DJ (☎ 071 623 2070, fax 071 929 1641)

WHITE, Diane, Lady; Diane Eleanor Abdy; da of late Bernard Abdy Collins, CIE, of Deccan House, Aldeburgh; *m* 1939, Sir George Stanley Midelton White, 3 Bt (d 1983); 1 s (Sir George White, 4 Bt, *qv*), 1 da; *Style—* Diane, Lady White; Acton House, Park Street, Iron Acton, nr Bristol

WHITE, Sir Dick Goldsmith; KCMG (1960), KBE (CBE 1950, OBE 1942); s of Percy Hall White; *b* 20 Dec 1906; *Educ* Bishop's Stortford Coll, Ch Ch Oxford, Michigan Univ, California Univ; *m* 1945, Kathleen Somers Bellamy; 2 s; *Career* previously with FCO until 1972; *Style—* Sir Dick White, KCMG, KBE; The Leat, Burpham, Arundel, W Sussex

WHITE, Prof Douglas John; s of Douglas John White, of Flat 43, The Oaks, 71 Berryfields Rd, Sutton Coldfield, W Midlands, and Gladys May, *née* Robins; *b* 31 Oct 1933; *Educ* Handsworth GS Birmingham, Magdalen Coll Oxford (BA, MA), Univ of Birmingham (MSc, PhD, DSc); *m* 29 March 1958, Hazel Margaret, da of Albert Edward Roberts (d 1967); 1 s (David John b 29 March 1963), 1 da (Alison Vanessa b 16 Aug 1967); *Career* Nat Serv RAF air radar fitter 1951-53; Kenward res fell Univ of Birmingham 1960-62, prof and head of Dept of Operational Res Univ of Strathclyde 1968-71 (reader in operational res 1965-68), prof and head of Dept of Decision Theory Univ of Manchester 1971- (sr res fell 1962-64); Univ of Virgina: Mac Wade prof of systems engrg 1987-90, chm Dept of Systems Engrg 1988, mem of Center for Advanced Studies; author of many pubns in maths of operational res and decision theory; former: chm Ed and Res Ctee for Operational Res Soc (former chm of Ctee of Profs in Operational Res, memb USA Soc, memb UK Soc); res assessor for SERC and Nat Sci Fndns of USA and Canada; fell Inst of Mathematics and its Applications; hon MA Univ of Manchester 1974; *Books* Dynamic Programming (1969), Decision Theory (1969), The Role and Effectiveness of Theories of Decision in Practice (with KC Bowen, 1973), Operational Research Techniques (with Donaldson and Lawrie, 1969), Operational Research Techniques (vol 2, with Donaldson, Lawrie, Jardine, McKenzie, McFarlane, 1974), Decision Methodology (1975), Fundamentals of Decision Theory (1976), Finite Dynamic Programming (1978), Recent Developements in Markov Decision Processes (with Thomas and Hartley, 1980), Optimality and Efficiency (1982), Multi Objective Decision Making (with French, Thomas and Hartley, 1983), Operational Research (1985), Introduction to Operational Research (with French, Thomas and Hartley, 1986); *Recreations* walking, gardening, reading, listening to music; *Style—* Prof Douglas White; Bollicello, 24 Springbank, Bollington, Macclesfield, Cheshire SK10 5LQ (☎ 0625 572768); Dept of Decision Theory, Univ of Manchester (☎ 061 275 4921, 061 275 5090)

WHITE, Baroness (Life Peeress UK 1970), of Rhymney, Co Monmouth; Eirene Lloyd White; da of Thomas Jones, CH, LLD (d 1955), of Aberystwyth, and Eirene Theodora, *née* Lloyd (d 1935); *b* 7 Nov 1909; *Educ* St Paul's Girls' Sch, Somerville Coll Oxford; *m* 1948, John Cameron White (d 1968); *Career* former journalist and civil servant; MP (Lab) Flint E 1950-70; min state: Foreign Affrs 1966-67, Welsh Office 1967-70; chm Labour NEC 1968-69, takes 1 whip in Lords, chm Select Ctee EEC and princ dep chm Ctees House of Lords 1979-82, a dep Speaker House of Lords 1979-89; memb Royal Commission on Environmental Pollution 1974-80, pres Montgomeryshire Soc 1981-82; chm cncl UWIST 1984-88, vice pres UCW Cardiff 1989-; hon fell Somerville Coll Oxford; Hon LLD: Univ of Wales 1979, Queen's Univ Belfast 1982, Bath 1983; *Style—* The Rt Hon Lady White; 64 Vandon Court, Petty France, SW1H 9HF (☎ 071 222 5107); House of Lords SW1A 0PW (☎ 071 219 5435)

WHITE, Elizabeth, Lady; Elizabeth Victoria Mary; da of Wilfrid Wrightson, JP (3 s of Sir Thomas Wrightson, 1 Bt, JP, DL, sometime MP Stockton and St Pancras E); *m* 1943, Sir Headley White, 3 Bt (d 1971); 1 s (Sir John Woolmer White, 4 Bt, *qv*), 2 da (Morna b 1944, Isabelle b 1948); *Style—* Elizabeth, Lady White; Salle Park, Reepham, Norfolk

WHITE, Eric Stanley Jeston; s of Frank Cogan Jeston White (d 1979), and Minnie Elizabeth, *née* Young; *b* 27 April 1925; *Educ* Ealing GS for Boys; *m* 30 Sept 1950, Joyce Margaret, da of Ernest Hackett (d 1971); 1 s (David John b 1956), 1 da (Susan Elizabeth b 1959); *Career* radar mechanic and educnl instr 1943-47; Law Accident Insurance Society 1941-64, fndr md and chm Jeston Insurance Brokers 1964-; dir: Heston Insurance Brokers Ltd 1966-, Jeston Securities Ltd 1967-; chm Old Ealonians Assoc 1981-; pres: Insur Inst of Ealing 1982-83, Rotary Club of Southall 1983-84 and 1988-89; ACII 1953, ABIIBA 1969, Chartered Insur Practitioner 1989; *Books* Brentford Facts and Figures 1920-81 (jtly, 1981), First 20 Years of Ealing (jtly, 1987), 100 Years of Brentford (jtly and ed, 1989); *Recreations* Brentford football (prog ed 1959-, press off 1954-); *Style—* Eric White, Esq; Casa Bianca, 79 Tentelow Lane, Norwood Green, Southall UB2 4LN (☎ 081 574 3047); 61 The Broadway, Greenford, Middx UB6 9PW (☎ 081 578 0101, fax 081 575 9020)

WHITE, Hon Mrs (Frances Alice); da (by 1 m) of 3 Baron Fisher; *b* 1951; *m* 1981, Angus J White; 1 s (Thomas, b 1983), 1 da (Sally b 1985); *Style—* The Hon Mrs White; Cooks Farm, Nuthurst, nr Horsham, Sussex

WHITE, His Hon Judge Frank John; s of Frank Byron White (d 1984), of Reading, and Renée Marie Therése, *née* Cachou (d 1972); *b* 12 April 1927; *Educ* Reading Sch, King's Coll London (LLB, LLM); *m* 11 April 1953, Anne Rowlandson, da of Sir Harold Gibson Howitt, GBE, DSO, MC; 2 s (Stephen b 29 Sept 1955, Simon b 27 Aug 1963), 2 da (Teresa b 31 Aug 1958, Louise b 8 Sept 1961); *Career* Sub Lt RNVR 1945-47; called to the Bar Gray's Inn 1951, memb Gen Cncl of The Bar 1969-73, dep chm Berks QS 1970-72, rec Crown Ct 1972-74, circuit judge 1974-, pres Cncl HM Circuit Judges 1990-91; memb: Lord Chllr's Legal Aid Advsy Ctee 1977-83, Judicial Studies Bd 1985-89; *Books* Bench Notes for Assistant Recorders (1988); *Recreations* walking, gardening; *Clubs* Athenaeum, Roehampton; *Style—* His Hon Judge Frank White; 8 Queens Ride, London SW13 0JB

WHITE, Frank Richard; JP (1968); s of Arthur Leslie White (d 1944), and Edna Phylis Jackson, *née* Meade (d 1976); *b* 11 Nov 1939; *Educ* Bolton Tech Coll; *m* 28 Jan 1967, Eileen, da of Frank Crook of 4 Ashdown Drive, Bolton; 2 s (John Richard Alexander b 1 Sept 1968, Christopher Niel b 10 July 1973), 1 da (Elizabeth Caroline b 30 July 1970); *Career* MP (Lab) Bury and Radcliffe 1974-83, parly sec Dept of Indust 1975-76, govt whip 1976-79, oppn spokesman church affrs 1979-83; chm: NW Lab MPs 1979-83, Party Paper Indust Gp 1979-83; memb Select Ctee Employment 1979-83 (presented Home Workers Bill), oppn whip 1980-82, dir trg GMB Trade Union 1988-; memb: Bolton Town Cncl 1963-74 and 1986-, Gtr Manchester CC 1973-75; memb: IMS 1966, IPM 1971; *Recreations* history, walking, caravanning, Richard III supporter; *Clubs* Tonge Cricket, Tonge Lab; *Style—* Frank White, Esq; 4 Ashdown Drive, Firwood Fold, Bolton, Lancs BL2 3AX (☎ 0204 58547); National College, College Rd, Whalley Range, Manchester M16 8BP (☎ 061 861 8788)

WHITE, Air Vice-Marshal George Alan; CB (1984), AFC (1973); s of James Magee White, and Evangeline, *née* Henderson; *b* 11 March 1932; *Educ* Univ of London (LLB); *m* 1955, Mary Esmé, *née* Magowan; 2 da; *Career* pilot 1956, RAF Staff Coll 1964, HQ Middle East Command 1966-67, 11 Sqdn 1968-70, 5 Sqdn 1970-72, Nat Defence Coll 1972-73, dir of ops (air defence and overseas) 1977-78, Air Cdre Plans HQ Strike Cmd 1981-82, dep cdr RAF Germany 1982-; *Style—* Air Vice-Marshal George White, CB, AFC; c/o Williams & Glyn's Bank Ltd, Kirkland House, Whitehall, London SW1A 2EB

WHITE, Sir George Stanley James; 4 Bt (UK 1904), of Cotham House, Bristol; s of Sir George Stanley Midelton White, 3 Bt (d 1983, md Bristol Aeroplane Co, and ggs of Sir George White, 1 Bt, pioneer of Electric Street Traction, fndr first Eng aeroplane factory and responsible for introduction of Bristol Biplanes and Monoplanes), and Diane, Lady White, *qv*; *b* 4 Nov 1948; *Educ* Harrow; *m* 1974 (m dis 1979); 1 da; m 2, Elizabeth, da of Sir William Reginald Verdon-Smith; 1 s (George Philip James), 1 da; *Heir* s, George Philip James b 1987; *Career* conslt horologist; High Sheriff Avon 1989; Keeper of the Collection of the Worshipful Co of Clockmakers; *Books* English Lantern Clocks (1988); *Style—* Sir George White, Bt

WHITE, Maj-Gen Gilbert Anthony; MBE (1944); s of Cecil James Lawrence White (ka 1918), and Muriel, *née* Collins (d 1985); *b* 10 June 1916; *Educ* Christ's Hosp; *m* 22 Sept 1939, Margaret Isabel Duncan (Joy), da of Arthur Wallet (d 1952); 2 da (Susan (Mrs Neil Weir), Caroline); *Career* joined Artists Rifles TA 1936, cmmnd E Surrey

Regt 1938, Adj 1/6 Surreys BEF France 1940, Tunisian Campaign 1943, Staff Coll Camberley 1944, Bde Maj 10 Inf Bde Italy 1944, instructor Staff Coll Haifa 1945, memb UK delgn to Mil Staff Ctee UN NYC 1946-48, regtl duty Egypt and UK 1948-54, mil asst CIGS 1954, regtl duty and instr Latimer 1954-59, cmd 1 Bn E Surrey Regt 1959-61, personal staff to Lord Mountbatten MOD 1961-62, Brig cmd 56 (London) TA Bde 1962-64, Imperial Def Coll 1965, BGS HQ BAOR 1966-69, Maj-Gen JSLO 1969-71; clerk with Lloyd's Brokers 1933-39, memb Lloyd's 1938-; memb Cncl Guide Dogs for the Blind 1972-; *Recreations* indifferent golfer and even worse shot; *Clubs* Army and Navy; *Style—* Maj-Gen Gilbert White, MBE; Speedwell, Tekels Ave, Camberley, Surrey (☎ 0276 23812)

WHITE, Prof Gillian Mary; da of Albert George White (d 1990), of Sale, Cheshire, and Mabel Bathurst (d 1988); *b* 13 Jan 1936; *Educ* Ilford Co HS, King's Coll London (LLB, PhD); *m* 1 April 1978, Colin Arthur Fraser, s of Arthur David Fraser (d 1962); *Career* asst examiner estate duty office Inland Revenue 1954-57; called to the Bar Gray's Inn 1960; ed asst Sweet and Maxwell publishers London 1960-61, res and ed asst to Mr Elihu Lauterpacht Trinity Coll Cambridge 1961-67, res fell in law and dir of studies in law New Hall Cambridge 1964-67, dean of Faculty of Law Univ of Manchester 1988-90 (lectr 1967-71, sr lectr 1971-73, reader 1973-75, prof of int law 1975-, dean 1979-81); contribs jls on int law and EC law; chm exec Manchester Univ Settlement 1974-80, memb Jt Cncl St Peter's House University of Manchester 1972-89, memb PHAB 1968-; hon life fell New Hall Cambridge 1977; memb: Soc of Public Teachers of Law, Br Inst of Int and Comparative Law, American Soc of Int Law, Int Law Assoc, UK Assoc for Euro Law, Univs Assoc for Contemporary Euro Studies, Interights, Liberty, Bar Euro Gp; *Books* Nationalization of Foreign Property (1961), The Use of Experts by International Tribunals (1965), Melland Schill Monographs on International Law (gen ed); *Recreations* travel, classical music, cooking, history of architecture; *Style—* Prof Gillian White; Faculty of Law, Univ of Manchester, Manchester M13 9PL (☎ 061 275 3574, fax 061 273 4407)

WHITE, Graham Stewart; s of Cecil Thomas White, and Kathleen May, *née* Banwell; *b* 24 March 1947; *Educ* Sir John Lawes Sch Harpenden; *m* 29 April 1972, Sylvia Mary, da of John Morris Done; 2 s (Oliver Lewis b 15 Dec 1974, Anthony Joe b 25 Feb 1976); *Career* Scholl: mktg dir 1977-80, md 1980-84; business devpt dir Shering-Plough Consumer Products 1984-87; chief exec Londis (Holdings) Ltd 1987-, non-exec dir Nisa Todays Ltd 1987-; memb Mktg Soc; *Recreations* rugby football; *Style—* Graham White, Esq; Euro Group House, 67-71 High St, Hampton Hill, Middlesex TW12 1LZ (☎ 081 941 0344, fax 081 941 6499, telex 928296)

WHITE, Hugh Collins; s of William Mitchell White, of Maybole, Ayrshire, and Mary Ann Luke, *née* Collins; *b* 21 Oct 1944; *Educ* Kilmarnock Acad, MacIntosh Sch of Arch (Cert in Arch); *m* 23 Aug 1968, Betsy, da of Bernard Lizar Zive (d 1977), of Ayr; 2 da (Kirstine b 1971, Sheona b 1974); *Career* chartered architect in private practice; corp memb RIBA; *Recreations* equestrian driving, photography, restoring horse drawn vehicles; *Style—* Hugh White, Esq; 17 Cargill Rd, Maybole, Strathclyde KA19 8AF (☎ 0655 82188)

WHITE, Vice Admiral Hugo Moresby; CBE; s of Hugh Fortescue Moresby White, CMG (d 1979), and Betty Sophia Pennington, *née* Brandt; *b* 22 Oct 1939; *Educ* Dragon Sch, NC Pangbourne, RNC Dartmouth; *m* 16 April 1966, Josephine Mary Lorimer, da of Dr John Meavious Pedler, of Adelaide, S Aust; 2 s (Jonathan b 26 Feb 1968, Thomas b 8 Jan 1971); *Career* RN; Lt HMS Blackpool 1960-61 Kuwait; on diesel submarines: HMS Tabard 1962-64, HMS Tiptoe 1964, HMS Odin 1964-65; navigation course HMS Dryad 1966, navigator HMS Warspite 1966-68, Lt Cdr HMS Osiris 1968-69, CO HMS Oracle 1970-71, staff BRNC Dartmouth 1971-73 Cdr submarine sea trg HMS Neptune 1973-75, CO HMS Salisbury 1975-77 (Cod War), with Naval Secs Dept MOD 1977-78, Capt Naval Plans MOD 1978-80, CO HMS Avenger and Capt 4 Frigate Sqdn (Falklands) 1980-82, Cdre PSO to CDS MOD 1982-85, CO HMS Bristol and Flag Capt to FOF2 1985-87, Rear Adm Flag Offr Flotilla 3 and Cdr ASW Strike Force 1987-88, Asst Chief of Naval Staff MOD 1988-91; Vice Adm Flag Offr Scotland and NI 1991-; *Recreations* sailing, travelling, reading, gardening; *Clubs* Army and Navy; *Style—* Vice Adm Hugo White, CBE; c/o Naval Secretary, Old Admiralty Building, Whitehall, London SW1A 2BE

WHITE, Ian Jeremy; s of Walter Douglas White, of Melcombe, Lewes Rd, Haywards Heath, Sussex, and Eileen Gordon, *née* Ford; *b* 19 Feb 1943; *Educ* Brighton Coll, Coll of Estate Mgmnt, Univ of London; *m* 14 Sept 1968, Julia Louise, da of Charles Leonard Walker (d 1945), and Helen Maud Walker; 1 s (Jeremy Mark b 27 Feb 1975), 2 da (Samantha Louise b 14 Oct 1970, Justine Ruth b 28 June 1972); *Career* dir Richard Ellis SA 1986 (ptnr UK 1982, joined 1962); Brighton Coll: memb gen cncl, memb fin and gen purposes ctee, memb property ctee, former tstee scholarships funds; ctee memb city branch Guide Dogs for Blind Assoc; Freeman City of London, Liveryman Worshipful Co Innholders and Worshipful Co of Surveyors; FRICS 1968; *Recreations* cricket, tennis; *Clubs* MCC, Free Forester, Roehampton; *Style—* Ian White, Esq; Hyannis, Brook Lane, Haywards Heath, Sussex RH16 1SG (☎ 0444 414836); Richard Ellis, Berkeley Sq House, London W1X 6AN (☎ 071 629 6290, car 0836 225285)

WHITE, Ian Shaw; s of Frank White, of May Hill, Glos, and Joan, *née* Shaw; *b* 30 July 1952; *Educ* Bromsgrove, Churchill Coll Cambridge (MA); *m* 18 Oct 1980, Susan Elizabeth (d 1989), da of Capt Alan Francis Bacon, of Purley, Surrey; 2 s (Duncan b 1985, Gordon b 1988); *Career* ptnr W Greenwell and Co 1984-86; dir: Greenwell Montagu 1986-88 (head of res 1987-88), Kleinwort Benson Securities 1988-; AMSIA; *Recreations* travel, philosophy, family; *Style—* Ian White, Esq; 12 Dove Park, Chorleywood, Herts (☎ 092 78 3051); Kleinwort Benson Securities, 20 Fenchurch St, London EC3P 3DB (☎ 071 623 8000, fax 071 623 5606, telex 922241)

WHITE, James; s of John White (d 1985), of Cleland, Lanarkshire, and Helen, *née* Beattie; *b* 22 Oct 1937; *m* 1961, Mary, da of Alex Jardine (d 1940); 2 da (Jane b 1975, Helen b 1976); *Career* chartered accountant (Scotland); former dir: sales and marketing SKF (UK), Lex Service Gp; chm Bunzl plc 1988- (md 1981-88); dir: Lucas Industries plc 1985-, Redland plc, Beecham plc; chm Ashley Gp plc; *Recreations* golf, gardening, athletics; *Clubs* St Stephen's Constitutional; *Style—* James White, Esq; The Moat House, Annables Lane, Kinsbourne Green, Harpenden, Herts (☎ 0582 64387); Bunzl plc, Stoke House, Stoke Green, Stoke Poges, Slough SL2 4JN (☎ 0753 693, fax 0753 694 694, telex 847503)

WHITE, James; s of James White of Whiteinch, Glasgow; *b* 1922; *Educ* Knightswood Secdy Sch; *m* 1948, Mary Elizabeth, da of Peter Dempsey, of Glasgow; 1 s, 2 da; *Career* joined Lab Pty 1946, sponsored by TGWU, md Glasgow Car Collection Ltd 1959-; memb Cwlth Parly Assoc Delgn: Bangladesh 1973, Nepal 1981; MP (Lab) Glasgow Pollok 1970-87; *Style—* James White Esq, MP; 23 Alder Road, Glasgow

WHITE, Hon Mrs (Jessica Jane Vronwy); *née* Scott-Ellis; da of 9 Baron Howard de Walden and 5 Baron Seaford; co-heiress of Barony of Howard de Walden; *b* 6 Aug 1941; *m* 1966, Adrian Tancred White; 4 s; *Style—* The Hon Mrs White; Farnborough Downs Farm, Wantage, Oxon

WHITE, John; s of John Wesley White (d 1972), and Emily, *née* Brown (d 1981); *b* 21 Dec 1934; *Educ* Brentwood Sch Essex; *m* 28 Aug 1960, Annette Kitty, da of Godfrey William Allnutt (d 1985); 2 s (Jeremy b 1965, Timothy b 1968), 1 da (Philippa b 1963); *Career* CA, sr ptnr Peat Marwick McLintock 1986- (ptnr Middle East 1972-85); memb: PCC, Essex Wildlife Tst; FCA 1958, AMCA 1961; *Recreations* walking, gardening, cricket; *Clubs* Reform; *Style—* John White, Esq; Crownfields, Kelvedon Hatch, Brentwood, Essex; 1 Puddle Dock, Blackfriars, London EC4

WHITE, Rev Canon John Austin; s of Charles White (d 1976), and Alice Emily, *née* Precious (d 1967); *b* 27 June 1942; *Educ* Batley GS Yorks, Univ of Hull (BA), Coll of the Resurrection Mirfield; *Career* asst curate St Aidan's Church Leeds 1966-69, asst chaplain Leeds Univ 1969-73, Chaplain Northern Ordination Course 1973-82, canon St George's Chapel Windsor Castle 1982- (canon precentor 1984-); memb directing staff St George's House Windsor Castle 1982-, convenor Nat Conf on the Care of the Dying, vice-chm govrs Princess Margaret Royal Free Sch Windsor; *Recreations* medieval iconography, cooking, poetry; *Style—* The Rev Canon John White; 8 The Cloisters, Windsor Castle, Windsor SL4 1NJ (☎ 0753 860 409); 2 Queen's Staithe Mews, York

WHITE, John Dudley George; s of John Leslie White (d 1962), of Strathdale, Streatham, London, and Winifred Emily, *née* Bachelor (d 1962); *b* 6 Aug 1937; *Educ* Emanuel Sch London; *m* 20 March 1965, Lorraine Judith Anne, da of Raymond Stanley Ives (d 1981), of Dial House, Chipstead, Surrey; 2 s (Harvey b 1966, Gregory b 1969); *Career* chm and md Electrowares Group of Cos 1979-86; chm: WC Pickering Ltd 1972-87, E & M Construction Ltd 1969-88, Electrical Wholesalers Fedn; cncllr Electrical and Electronic Industs Benevolent Assoc; Freeman City of London 1971, Master Worshipful Co Lightmongers 1981, Liveryman Worshipful Co of Tallow Chandlers 1975; FBIM 1973; *Recreations* yachting (motor yacht 'Idle Hours'); *Clubs* RAC, Royal Thames Yacht, Royal Southern Yacht, City Livery; *Style—* John White, Esq; High Woods, The Glade, Kingswood, Surrey KTZO 6LH (☎ 0737 832052)

WHITE, Prof John Edward Clement Twarowski; CBE 1983; s of Brig A E White, and Suzanne, *née* Twarowska; *b* 4 Oct 1924; *Educ* Ampleforth, Trinity Coll Oxford, Courtauld Inst of Art, Univ of London (BA, PhD); *m* 19 Oct 1950, Xenia, *née* Joannides; *Career* WWII Pilot RAF 1943-47, demobbed as Flt Lt; reader in history of art Courtauld Inst 1958-59 (lectr 1952-58), Alexander White visiting prof Univ of Chicago 1958, Pilkington prof of history of art Univ of Manchester and dir of Whitworth Art Gallery 1959-66, Ferens visiting prof of fine art University of Hull 1961-62, chm Art Advsy Panel NW Museum and Art Gallery Servs 1962-66, prof of history of art and chm Dept of History of Art John Hopkins Univ Baltimore 1966-71, Durning-Lawrence prof of history of art UCL 1971- (vice provost 1984-88, pro provost 1990-); vice pres Comité Int d'Histoire de l'Art 1986-, chm Assoc of Art Historians 1976-80; memb: Bd of Dirs Coll Art Assoc 1970, Advsy Cncl V & A 1973-76, Exec Ctee Assoc of Art Historians 1974-81, Art Panel Arts Cncl 1974-78, Reviewing Ctee on Export of Works of Art 1975-82, Visiting Ctee RCA 1976-86, Armed Forces Pay Review Body 1986-; tstee Whitechapel Art Gallery; Hon MA Manchester 1963; FSA, AAH, CIHA; *Books* Perspective in Ancient Drawing and Painting (1956), The Birth and Rebirth of Pictorial Space (1957, 3 edn 1987), Art and Architecture in Italy 1250-1400 (1966, 2 edn 1987), Duccio: Tuscan Art and the Medieval Workshop (1979), Studies in Renaissance Art (1983), Studies in Late Medieval Italian Art (1984); articles in: Art History, Art Bulletin, Burlington Magazine, Jl of Warburg and Courtauld Insts; *Clubs* Athenaeum; *Style—* Prof John White, CBE, FSA; Department of History of Art, University College, Gower St, London WC1E 6BT (☎ 071 387 9594, fax 071 387 8057)

WHITE, John Jameson; s of Jameson Richard White (d 1989), of Chalkwell, Essex, and Betty Annette, *née* Payne; *b* 6 July 1938; *Educ* Wrekin Coll; *m* 18 April 1964, Carolyn Helen, da of Thomas Lyle Morgan (d 1988); 1 s (Matthew Jameson b 22 March 1968), 2 da (Sarah Michele b 19 Sept 1966, Amanda Clare b 23 May 1970); *Career* Cameron Markby Hewitt (formerly Cameron Kemm & Co): articled clerk 1957-62, admitted as slr 1963, ptnr 1964-; lectr on banking circuit, memb Editorial Bd Journal of Int Fin Law; memb Law Soc 1964; *Books* Legal Issues of Cross-Border Banking (contrib, 1989); *Recreations* hockey, student of port; *Clubs* W Herts; *Style—* John White, Esq; Cameron Markby Hewitt, Sceptre Court, 40 Tower Hill, London EC3N 4BB (☎ 071 702 2345, fax 071 702 2303, mobile 0831 384396)

WHITE, Prof John William; CMG (1981); s of George Alexander John White (d 1977), of New Lambton HTS, Newcastle, and Jean, *née* Mackay; *b* 25 April 1937; *Educ* Newcastle Boys HS NSW, Aust, Sydney Univ (BSc, MSc), Oxford Univ (MA, DPhil); *m* 24 July 1966, Ailsa Barbara, da of Arthur Ambrose Vise, of Southport, Queensland; 1 s (David George Blithe b 1973), 3 da (Sarah Kirsten Jean b 1968, Catherine Naomi b 1970, Rachel Mary b 1974); *Career* ICI fell Lincoln Coll Oxford 1961-63, official fell St Johns Coll Oxford 1963-85, Marlowe Medal Faraday Soc 1968, Tilden lectr Royal Soc of Chem 1976, neutron beam co-ordinator AERE Harwell 1973-75, dir Institut von Laue Langevin Grenoble 1977-80 (dep dir 1975-77), assessor Oxford Univ 1981-82, prof of physical and theoretical chem Aust Nat Univ Canberra 1985-; Argonne fell Univ of Chicago and Argonne Nat Laboratory USA 1985-; prof of physical and theoretical chem Hulme Project for Schs Oxford 1983-85; churchwarden Rhowe Alps Parish 1976-80; memb cncl: Epsom Coll 1980-85, Wycliffe Hall Oxford 1981-85; pres: Royal Aust Chem Inst (Canberra 1987), Aust Soc of Crystallographers 1987; FRS Chem 1981, FRAust Chem Inst 1985, FAust Inst Phys 1986; *Recreations* skiing, squash, family; *Style—* Prof John White, CMG; 2 Spencer St, Turner Act 2601, Australia (☎ 062 486836); Research Sch of Chemistry, Australian Univ, PO Box 4, Acton 2601, ACT, Australia (☎ 062 493578, fax 062 487817)

WHITE, Sir John Woolmer; 4 Bt (UK 1922), of Salle Park, Norfolk; s of Sir Headley Dymoke White, 3 Bt (d 1971); *b* 4 Feb 1947; *Educ* Cheltenham, Royal Agric Coll Cirencester; *m* Joan, da of late T D Borland, of Flemington, W Linton, Peeblesshire; 1 s; *Heir* s, Kyle Dymoke Wilfrid White b 16 March 1988; *Style—* Sir John White, Bt; Salle Park, Reepham, Norfolk

WHITE, Keith Christopher; s of Frank White (d 1963), and Gladys Louise, *née* Moore (d 1960); *b* 14 July 1933; *Educ* Glyn GS Epsom, Univ of London (BSc); *m* 10 Sept 1960, Jennifer Mary (Jenny), da of Thomas Mayhew Lewin (d 1985); 1 s (Paul b 1961), 2 da (Gillian b 1963, Judith b 1968); *Career* consltg engr; ptnr R Travers Morgan & Ptnrs Consltg Engrs 1971, vice chm Travers Morgan Consltg Gp 1990 (dir 1988), memb bd Welsh Health Common Servs Authy 1982-; Freeman: City of London 1966, Worshipful Co of Paviors 1966; FIStructE 1969 (pres 1987-88), FIHT 1974, FICE 1987, FEng 1989; *Recreations* golf, reading, gardening; *Clubs* Naval & Military, RAC, City Livery; *Style—* Keith White, Esq; Longmead, 8 Hillcroft Avenue, Purley, Surrey CR8 3DG (☎ 081 660 9883); Travers Morgan Consulting Group, 136 Long Acre, London WC2E 9AE (☎ 071 836 5474, fax 071 240 9595, car 0836 504026, telex 8812307) 504026)

WHITE, Sir Lynton Stuart; MBE (1943), TD, DL (Hants); s of Sir Dymoke White, 2 Bt, JP, DL (d 1968), *qv*, and Isabelle Stuart, *née* MacGowan (d 1982); *b* 11 Aug 1916; *Educ* Harrow, Trinity Coll Cambridge (MA); *m* 1945, Phyllis, da of Sir Newnham Worley, KBE (d 1976); 4 s (Anthony, Richard, Robert, Philip), 1 da; *Career* TA; 2 Lt RA 1939, served WWII UK 1939-40, Far East 1940-45 (despatches), Hon Lt-Col RA (TA) 1946, TARO 1948-71; memb Hampshire CC 1970 (vice chm 1976, chm 1977-85); kt 1985; *Style—* Sir Lynton White, MBE, TD, DL

WHITE, (Edward) Martin Everatt; s of Frank White (d 1983), of Shrewsbury, and

Norah Kathleen, *née* Everatt (d 1959); *b* 22 Feb 1938; *Educ* Priory Boys GS Shrewsbury, King's Coll Cambridge (MA); *m* 10 May 1969, Jean Catherine, da of James Orr Armour (d 1987), of Manchester; 1 s (Robert b 1978), 1 da (Susannah b 1975); *Career* admitted slr 1962; chief exec: Winchester City Cncl 1974-80, Bucks CC 1980-88, Nat Assoc of Citizens Advice Bureaux 1988-90; chm Curlew Partnership Ltd 1990-; CBIM 1987; *Books* The Role of the Chief Executive in Information Technology (1987); *Recreations* gardening, walking, other outdoor pursuits; *Style—* Martin White, Esq; The Spinney, Sevenacres, Long Crendon, Aylesbury, Bucks HP18 9DU (☎ 0844 208914)

WHITE, Michael John; s of Albert Ernest White (d 1979), and Doris Mary, *née* Harvey; *b* 4 April 1955; *Educ* Langdon Sch, Oxford Univ (MA), Inns of Court Law School; *Career* music critic (The Independent on Sunday), broadcaster and librettist; *Books* The Adjudicator (opera libretto); *Recreations* travel, composition, the Church of England (occasionally); *Style—* Michael John White, Esq; c/o The Independent on Sunday, 40 City Road, London EC1

WHITE, Michael Simon; s of Victor R White, and Doris G White; *b* 16 Jan 1936; *Educ* Lyceum Alpinum Zuoz Switzerland, Pisa Univ, Sorbonne Paris; *m* 1, 1965 (m dis 1973), Sarah Hillsdon; 2 s, 1 da; m 2, 1985, Louise, da of Nigel Moores (d 1977); 1 s (b 1985); *Career* theatre and film producer; asst to Sir Peter Daubeny 1956-61; *stage prodns* (London) incl: Rocky Horror Show, Sleuth, America Hurrah, Oh, Calcutta!, The Connection, Joseph and the Amazing Technicolour Dreamcoat, Loot, The Blood Knot, A Chorus Line, Deathtrap, Annie, Pirates of Penzance, On Your Toes, Metropolis, Bus Stop; films incl: Monty Python and the Holy Grail, Rocky Horror Picture Show, My Dinner with André, Ploughman's Lunch, Moonlighting, Stranger's Kiss, The Comic Strip Presents, The Supergrass, High Season, Eat The Rich, White Mischief, Nuns on the Run; *Books* Empty Seats (1984); *Recreations* art, ski-ing, racing; *Clubs* RAC, Rocks (LA); *Style—* Michael White, Esq; 13 Duke St, St James's, London SW1 (☎ 071 839 3971)

WHITE, Michael William; s of Joseph White, and Mary, *née* Ruth; *b* 11 April 1945; *Educ* North Staffs Poly Beaconside, Stafford (BSc); *m* Mary Doris White, 2 da (Elizabeth Ann b 16 Aug 1973, Catherine Frances b 20 Sept 1976); *Career* sr electrical engr GEC Electrical Projects Ltd 1971-74 (began as student apprentice); IDC Consultants Ltd: sr electrical engr, princ mechanical and electrical engr 1974-78, tech mangr electrical and control engrg 1980-82; ptnr Building Design Partnership 1985- (assoc engr 1983-85); CEng, FIEE, MCIBSE; *Recreations* hill-walking; *Clubs* Long Distance Walkers Assoc; *Style—* Michael White, Esq; Building Design Partnership, Vernon St, Moor Lane, Preston, Lancashire PR1 3PQ (☎ 0772 59383, fax 0772 201378)

WHITE, Dr Norman Arthur; s of Charles Brewster White (d 1969), of Co Durham, and Lilian Sarah, *née* Finch (d 1975), of Great Malvern; *b* 11 April 1922; *Educ* Univ of London, Manchester Inst of Science and Technol, Harvard Business Sch, Univ of Philippines, LSE (BSc, MSc, PhD, AMCT, AMP, DMS); *m* 1, 1944, Joyce Marjorie (d 1982), *née* Rogers; 1 s (Howard Russell b 1945), 1 da (Lorraine Avril b 1949); m 2, 1983, Marjorie Iris, da of William Colenso Rushton (d 1947), of London; *Career* Royal Dutch Shell Gp 1945-72; petroleum res engr Thornton Research Centre 1945-51, tech mangr Shell Co Philippines 1951-55; Shell Int Petroleum: dep mangr Product Devpt Div 1955-61, gen mangr Lubricants Bitumen and LPG Divs 1963-66, dir Mktg Devpt and dep to gp mktg co-ordinator 1966-68; chm and dir Shell Oil and mining cos in UK and Europe 1963-72, chief exec New Enterprises Div 1968-72, plural assignments 1972-; dir and princ exec Norman White Assocs 1972-; dir: Environmental Resources Ltd 1973-87, Henley Centre for Forecasting 1974- (dep chm 1974-87); dir chm Exec Ctee Tanks Oil & Gas Ltd 1974-85, dep chm Strategy Int Ltd 1976-82; chm: KBC Advanced Technologies Ltd 1979-90, American Oil Field Systems plc 1980-85; dep chm Br Canadian Resources Ltd 1980-83; chm: Ocean Thermal Energy Conversion Systems Ltd 1982-, Gearhart Tesel plc 1983-85 (dir 1980-85), Process Automation & Computer Systems Ltd 1984-, Kelt Energy plc 1986-87 (dir 1985-88), Andaman Resources plc 1986-90, Technology Transfer Centre Surrey Ltd 1990-; memb int energy/petroleum delgns to: USSR, China, Rumania, East Germany, Japan, Korea, India, Mexico, Argentine, Brazil 1979-; memb Parly and Scientific Ctee House of Commons 1977-83 and 1987-; chm Br Nat Ctee World Petroleum Congresses (WPC) 1987- (vice chm 1977-87); memb: Cncl IMechE 1980-85 and 1987-, Cncl InstPet (vice pres) 1975-81, Royal Soc Mission to People's Republic of China 1985, UK CAA Ctee of Enquiry on Flight Time Limitations (Bader Ctee) 1972-73; visiting prof Univ of Manchester 1981-90, Henley Mgmnt Coll 1979-, The City Univ of London 1990-; memb Senate Univ of London 1974-87, chm Jt Bd for Engrg Mgmnt (for IMechE, ICE, IEE, IChemE) 1990-; govr: King Edward VI Royal GS Guildford 1976-, Reigate GS 1976-; Freeman City of London 1983; Liveryman: Worshipful Co of Engineers 1984, Worshipful Co of Spectacle Makers 1986; memb Royal Inst of Int Affrs and Royal Inst; Eur Ing, CEng, FInstD, FBIM, FRSA, FIMechE; *Books* Financing the International Petroleum Industry (1979); *Recreations* family, country and coastal walking, wild life, browsing, international affairs, comparative religions, domestic odd-jobbing; *Clubs* Athenaeum, City Livery, Harvard (London), IOD; *Style—* Dr Norman A White; Green Ridges, Downside Road, Guildford, Surrey GU4 8PH (☎ 0483 67523); 9 Park House; 123/125 Harley Street, London W1N 1HE (☎ 071 935 7387, telex 262433, fax 071 935 5573)

WHITE, Adm Sir Peter; GBE (1977, KBE 1976, CBE 1960, MBE 1944); s of William White (d 1936), and Gertrude Frances, *née* Turner (d 1972), of Amersham, Bucks; *b* 25 Jan 1919; *Educ* Dover Coll; *m* 1947, Audrey Eileen, da of Ernest Wallin, of Kingsthorpe, Northampton; 2 s; *Career* served RN 1937-1977, Adm (princ staff offr to CDS 1967-69, dir-gen Fleet Services 1969-71, Port Adm Rosyth 1972-74, chief of fleet support 1974-77); conslt Wilkinson Match Ltd 1978-79; assoc dir: Educn for Industl Soc 1979-88, Business in the Community 1988-; chm cncl Offrs Pension Soc 1982-90, memb Fndn Ctee Gordon Boys' Sch 1980-90; *Recreations* riding, gardening; *Clubs* Army and Navy; *Style—* Admiral Sir Peter White, GBE; c/o Westminster Bank, 26 The Haymarket, London SW1Y 4ER

WHITE, Peter Roland; s of Norman Leonard White, and Gene Elwin, *née* McGrah; *b* 9 July 1945; *Educ* Bournville Boys Tech Sch, Univ of Birminghm (BDS); *m* 1, 23 March 1968 (m dis 1980), Elizabeth Susan, da of Thomas Colin Graty, of Leigh Sinton Worcs; 2 s (Gordon Michael White b 6 Aug 1970, Adam Edward White b 12 Jan 1973), 1 da (Frances Elizabeth Graty b 8 Nov 1968); m 2, 20 Dec 1980, Elisabeth Anne, da of Fred Haworth; *Career* conslt oral surgn; Dudley Rd Hosp Birmingham 1968, Birmingham Dental Hosp 1969-70, Wordsley Hosp Stourbridge 1970-71, Univ of Manchester Dental Sch 1971-73, St Luke's Hosp Bradford 1973-74, Liverpool Dental Hosp and Broad Green Hosp 1974-77; conslt oral surgn NW Regnl Health Authy 1977-; post grad tutor Rochdale and Oldham 1989- (Rochdale 1980-87); memb numerous NHS local ctees; publications in learned jls; memb BDA, FBAOMS 1977 (memb 1971-77), memb Manchester Med Soc 1979 (pres-elect 1989); *Recreations* genealogy, sailing; *Clubs* Elton Sailing; *Style—* Peter White, Esq; 65 Highcroft Way, Syke, Rochdale, Lancs (☎ 0706 353577); 14 St John Street, Manchester (☎ 061 832 7904)

WHITE, Reginald James (Reg); MBE (1977); s of Reginald Bert White (d 1966), of Brightlingsea, and Gladys Amela, *née* Carter; *b* 28 Oct 1935; *Educ* Brightlingsea Secdy Sch; *m* 10 Dec 1955, Marylyn, da of Robert James Osborn; 3 s (Robert Reginald b 23 April 1956, David John b 12 Aug 1961, Mark James b 16 July 1969), 1 da (Sallie Ann b 23 Sept 1963); *Career* yachtsman; began sailing 1949, winner various trophies local yacht clubs (Colne, Wivenhoe, Clacton); winner Little America Cup representing GB: v Australia 1963 and 1965, v USA 1964, 1966, 1968; Gold medal Tornado Catamaran Montreal Olympics 1976; major races won: Hornet World Scotland 1964, B Class world England 1968, C Class Euro England 1969, Tornado nat 1969, 1978, 1981, Tornado Euro Italy 1973, Tornado world Aust 1976 and Germany 1979; apprentice boat builder on leaving sch rising to master shipwright, proprietor Reg White Ltd (catamaran builders); yachtsman of the year award 1966 and 1977; *Books* Catamaran Sailing (with Bob Fisher, 1968); *Recreations* squash, snooker; *Style—* Reg White, Esq, MBE; Colne Yacht Club, Waterside, Brightlingsea, Essex

WHITE, Capt Richard Taylor; DSO (1940, and bars 1941 and 1942); s of Sir Archibald Woolaston White, 4 Bt (d 1954), and hp of bro, 5 Bt; *b* 29 Jan 1908; *Educ* RNC Dartmouth; *m* 1936, Gabrielle Ursula, yr da of Capt Robert Style, JP (n of Sir William Style, 9 Bt); 3 s, 2 da; *Career* WWII RN served Atlantic Med and Far E; Capt RNC Dartmouth 1951-53; *Style—* Capt Richard White, DSO, RN; Tilts House, Boughton Monchelsea, Maidstone, Kent ME17 4JE (☎ 0622 743465)

WHITE, Robin Graham; s of Alan White, of Salisbury, and late Celia White; *b* 21 July 1955; *Educ* Oundle; *m* 8 June 1985, Ann, da of Patrick Ingram, of Clare, Suffolk; 2 da (Sarah Celia b 23 March 1988, Madeline Jane b 25 Jan 1990); *Career* reporter; Northants Evening Telegraph 1973-76, Piccadilly Radio Station Manchester 1977, IRN 1978, ITN 1978- (crime corr 1990-); *Recreations* golf, shooting, reading, music; *Style—* Robin White, Esq; Independent Television News Ltd, ITN House, 200 Gray's Inn Road, London WC1 (☎ 071 833 3000)

WHITE, Roderick Douglas Thirkell; s of Noel Thirkell White (d 1974), and Margaret Douglas, *née* Robertson; *b* 27 March 1939; *Educ* Marlborough, Trinity Coll Oxford (BA); *m* 1964, Stephanie Francis, da of C S Powell; 2 s (Jestyn Noel b 17 Sept 1968, Tristram Benedict b 23 Feb 1971); *Career* advertising exec; J Walter Thompson: graduate trainee Marketing Dept 1962-65, marketing gp head 1965, asst dir 1967; head of unit J Walter Thompson Consultancy Unit 1972-75 (memb staff 1968-75), J Walter Thompson Development Group 1975-77; planning dir: Lansdowne Marketing 1979 (head of planning 1977), Lansdownuro 1981-; President's Gold medal IPA 1967; MIPA 1967, assoc memb MRS 1980; *Books* Consumer Product Development (1973), Advertising: What It Is and How To Do It (1980); *Recreations* walking, windsurfing, cinema, music; *Style—* Roderick White, Esq; Lansdownuro Ltd, Abbey House, 215-229 Baker St, London NW1 6YA (☎ 081 486 7111, fax 081 486 5310)

WHITE, Roger; s of Geoffrey White, of Home Cottage, Didmarton, Badminton, Avon, and Zoe, *née* Bowler; *b* 1 Sept 1950; *Educ* Ifield GS, Christs Coll Cambridge (BA), Wadham Coll Oxford; *Career* Hist Building Div GLC 1979-83, sec Georgian Gp 1984-; pres Oxford Univ Architectural Soc 1975-76, memb Ctee Painswick Rococo Garden 1985-; FSA 1986; *Books* John Vardy (in The Architectural Outsiders, 1985), Georgian Arcadia: Architecture for the Park and Garden (exhibition catalogue, 1987); *Recreations* looking at old buildings; *Style—* Roger White, Esq; The Georgian Group, 37 Spital Square, London E1 6DY (☎ 071 377 1722)

WHITE, Roger John Graham; s of Alfred James White (d 1976), of Kingston Hill, Kingston, and Doris Elizabeth, *née* Robinson (d 1973); *b* 30 April 1940; *Educ* Tiffin Sch; *m* 18 Jun 1966, Elizabeth, da of Tom Lionel Greenwood, of Esher, Surrey; 2 s (Graham b 1968, Andrew b 1970), 1 da (Katherine b 1977); *Career* chartered accountant; ptnr KPMG Peat Marwick McLintock 1974- (sr tax ptnr 1981); memb professional and industry tax ctees; lectr and writer on tax matters; FCA 1962, FTII 1970; *Books* The Trading Company (1978), Purchase of Own Shares (1983); *Recreations* bridge, gardening, books; *Style—* Roger White, Esq; 1 Puddle Dock, Blackfriars, London EC4V 3PD (☎ 071 236 8000, fax 071 248 6552 (Group 3), telex 8811541 PMM LON G)

WHITE, (Wilfred) St John; s of Richard St John White (d 1932), of Wellington Lodge, Bristol, and (Gladys) Lucy, *née* Jones; *b* 28 Nov 1922; *Educ* Merchant Venturers Coll, Univ of Bristol; *m* 22 Aug 1974, Kyoko (d 1978), da of Dr Ray Igarashi (d 1938), of Tokyo, Japan; *Career* res engr Telecommunications Res Estab 1942-46 (devpt of RADAR for RAF); Decca Ltd (later Racal Decca Ltd) 1946-: devpt engr 1946-, dir of up to forty cos within the gp, invented Electronic Position Fixing System (won Queen's Award for Technological Innovation 1969), dir responsible for mktg of Decca Navigational System (international standard), dir Decca Avionics Mktg, involved in devpt North Sea Resources 1963-, currently dir Racal Oil and Gas; dir SENA Ltd and DSKK Ltd of Japan 1965-; memb: Sales and Export Ctee SBAC 1982-89, Cncl Electronic Engrg Assoc 1976-88; MIEE 1947, FInstD 1954, MRIN 1955; memb: Air League 1982, Royal Aeronautical Soc 1986; *Books* Christmas Island Cracker (1987); *Recreations* swimming and squash; *Clubs* The Naval & Military; *Style—* St John White, Esq; Dolphin Square, London SW1 (☎ 071 828 3600); Mukoyama, Nerimaku, Tokyo (☎ 03 3990 2546); Racal-Decca Ltd, New Malden, Surrey (☎ 081 942 2460, fax 081 949 1273, telex 22852)

WHITE, Stephen Frank; s of Judge Frank John White, of Queens Ride, London, and Anne Rowlandson, *née* Howitt, MBE; *b* 29 Sept 1955; *Educ* Eton, Univ of Bristol (BA); *Career* accountant Price Waterhouse and Co 1977-81, Phillips and Drew 1981-83, Hill Samuel Investmt Mgmnt Ltd 1983-85, Foreign and Colonial Mgmnt 1985-, dir F & C Eurotrust plc and F & C Germany Investment Trust plc; Freeman Worshipful Co of Merchant Taylors; ACAG; *Recreations* opera, gardening, walking, swimming; *Style—* Stephen F White, Esq; 86 Archel Road, London, W14 9QP (☎ 071 385 5815); c/o Foreign & Colonial Management Ltd, Exchange House, Primrose St, London EC2A 2NY (☎ 071 628 8000)

WHITE, Stephen John; s of George Edward White, and Doreen Ivy White; *b* 23 July 1948; *Educ* St Olaves GS; *m* 24 April 1971; 2 da (Claire Louise b 1975, Victoria Emily b 1978); *Career* dir WCRS Gp plc, dep chm WCRS-Mathews Marcantonio; MAA, MIPA, MCAM; *Recreations* tennis, swimming, boating, vintage cars; *Clubs* RAC, Vanderbilt; *Style—* Stephen White, Esq; c/o Lloyds Bank, 9 High Street, Bromley, Kent; WCRS Group plc, 41/44 Gt Queen St, London WC2B 5AR

WHITE, Stewart Dale; s of Theo Jeffrey White (d 1979), of Sydney, Aust, and Mary Jean, *née* Stewart; *b* 23 July 1951; *Educ* Newington Coll, St Andrew's Coll Univ of Sydney (BA, LLB), Downing Coll Cambridge (LLM); *m* 20 Sept 1980, Elisabeth Mary Hargreaves, da of Geoffrey John Bolton (d 1968), of Eton Coll; 1 s (Andrew b 1 Aug 1983), 1 da (Victoria b 1 July 1982); *Career* admitted slr: NSW 1976, Eng 1979; sr assoc Allen Allen and Hemsley Sydney 1979-83; ptnr: Blake Dawson Waldron Sydney 1983-88, Denton Hall Burgin Warrens London 1988-; chm: Communications Law Ctee of Int Bar Assoc, Standing Ctee Media and Communications Lawasia, Legal Symposium ITU-COM 1989; memb: Legal Symposium TELECOM 87 and TELECOM 91, NSW Ctee Cambridge Cwlth Tst; memb: Law soc, Int Bar; *Recreations* swimming, tennis, walking, bridge, opera; *Clubs* Australian, Royal Sydney Yacht Squadron, Bosham Sailing, Australian Jockey; *Style—* Stewart White, Esq; 13 Radipole Rd, London SW6 (☎ 071 736 4163); Denton Hall Burgin & Warrens, 5 Chancery Lane, Clifford's Inn, London EC4A 1BU (☎ 071 242 1212, fax 071 404 0087, telex 263567

BURGING, car 0860 593337)

WHITE, Susan Margaret (Sue); da of Arthur Frederick Smith, of Gosport, Hants, and Rose Margaret, *née* Lunt; *b* 7 Dec 1948; *Educ* Brune Park County HS, Polytechnic of South Bank, North East London Polytechnic (BA); *m* 7 Sept 1974, Richard Edward White; 1 s (Christopher Richard Arthur b 11 Sept 1985); *Career* student registered gen nurse 1967-70, student registered mental nurse 1971-72, sec 1973-74, pupil midwife 1974, health visitor 1974-78, nursing offr 1978-80, sr nursing offr 1980-83, dep dist nursing offr 1983-86, dir nursing servs Community Unit 1986-88, unit gen mangr Community Servs Unit 1988-; memb Royal Coll of Nursing 1983-; *Recreations* active member of my church, swimming and cycling, reading; *Style—* Mrs Sue White; The Community Services Unit, Basildon & Thurrock Health Authority, The Old School House, The Drive, South Ockendon Hospital, South Ockendon, Essex (☎ 0708 851901 ext 412)

WHITE, Terence de Vere; s of Frederick S de Vere White, and Ethel, *née* Perry; *b* 29 April 1912; *Educ* St Stephen's Green Sch Dublin, Trinity Coll Dublin (BA, LLB); *m* 1, 1941 (m dis 1982), Mary O'Farrell; 2 s, 1 da; m 2, 1982, Hon Victoria Glendinning, *qv*; *Career* admitted slr 1933, memb Cncl Incorporated Law Soc, ret 1961; author; literary ed Irish Times 1961-77, vice chm Bd of Govrs National Gallery of Ireland; tstee: National Library 1946-79, Chester Beatty Library 1959-80; dir Gate Theatre 1969-81, memb Irish Acad of Letters 1968; Hon RHA 1968, hon prof of literature RHA 1973, FRSL; *Books* The Road of Excess (1945), Kevin O'Higgins (1948), The Story of the Royal Dublin Society (1955), A Fretful Midge (1957), A Leaf from the Yellow Book (1958), An Affair with the Moon (1959), Prenez Garde (1962), The Remainder Man (1963), Lucifer Falling (1965), The Parents of Oscar Wilde (1967), Tara (1967), Leinster (1968), Ireland (1968), The Lambert Mile (1969), The March Hare (1970), Mr Stephen (1971), The Anglo-Irish (1972), The Distance and the Dark (1973), The Radish Memoirs (1974), Big Fleas and Little Fleas (1976), Chimes at Midnight (1977), Tom Moore (1977), My Name is Norval (1978), Birds of Prey (1980), Johnnie Cross (1983), Chat Show (1987); *Clubs* Garrick; *Style—* Terence de Vere White; c/o Allied Irish Banks, 100 Grafton St, Dublin 2, Eire

WHITE, Sir Thomas Astley Wollaston; 5 Bt (UK 1802), of Wallingwells, Nottinghamshire; JP (Wigtownshire 1952); s of Lt-Col Sir Archibald White, 4 Bt, TD (d 1945); *b* 13 May 1904; *Educ* Wellington; *m* 1935, Daphne Margaret, da of Lt-Col Francis Remi Imbert Athill, CMG, OBE, DL (d 1958), of Harbottle Castle, Morpeth, Northumberland; *Heir* bro, Capt Richard Taylor White, DSO, RN, *qv*; *Career* FRICS, Hon Sheriff Substitute Wigtownshire; *Style—* Sir Thomas White, Bt, JP; HA Hill, Torhousemuir, Wigtown, Newton Stewart DG8 9DJ (☎ 09884 2238)

WHITE, Victor Oscar ; s of Arthur Albert White (d 1976), and Gisela Lydia, *née* Wilde; *b* 30 Aug 1936; *Educ* Michael Hall Sch Forest Row, London Univ (LLB); *m* 28 March 1967, Susan Raynor, da of Raynor Leslie Jones, of Praia, Daluz, Portugal; 2 s (Christopher b 1968, Jonathan b 1974), 1 da (Katherine b 1971); *Career* slr; joined ICI Legal Dept 1965, appointed gp slr ICI 1980; memb Law Soc; *Style—* Victor White, Esq; Ballards, Tompsets Bank, Forest Row, Susex; ICI Gp Legal Dept, 9 Millbank, London SW1P 2JF (☎ 071 834 4444, fax 071 834 2042, telex 21324)

WHITE-JONES, John Dale; s of George David White-Jones (d 1979), of Llangollen, N Wales, and Vera, *née* Dale (d 1979); *b* 3 Oct 1934; *Educ* Llandovery Coll; *m* 13 May 1972, Hilary Anne, da of Thomas Richard William Porter; 2 da (Gemma b 23 Sept 1975, Kate b 24 March 1977); *Career* Nat Serv RA 1953-55; prodn dir Thames TV plc 1986-, dir Kingston Training and Educn Cncl 1988; *Style—* John White-Jones, Esq; Thames Television plc, Teddington Studios, Teddington Lock, Teddington, Middx TW11 9NT (☎ 081 977 3252)

WHITE OF HULL, Baron (Life Peer UK 1991), of Hull in the County of Humberside; Sir (Vincent) Gordon Lindsay White; KBE (1979); s of late Charles White and Lily May, *née* Wilson; *b* 11 May 1923; *Educ* De Aston Sch Lincs; *m* 1; 2 da; m 2, 1974 (m dis), Virginia Anne; 1 s; *Career* WWII served SOE; chm Welbecson Ltd 1947-65, dep chm Hanson Tst 1965-73, chm Hanson Industs 1983-, memb Bd British Airways Plc 1989-; memb and chm Int Ctee USA Congressional Award Fndn 1984-; hon fell St Peter's Coll Oxford 1984-; Nat Voluntary Leadership Award Congressional Award 1984; memb: cncl for the Police Rehabilitation Appeal 1985-, bd of dirs Shakespeare Theatre Folger Library Washington 1985-, cncl City Technol Colls Tst 1987-, chm Zoological Soc of London Devpt Tst 1988; Aims of Industry Free Enterprise Award 1985-; Hon DSc(Econ) Univ of Hull 1988; *Clubs* Special Forces, The Brook (NY); *Style—* The Rt Hon Lord White of Hull, KBE; 410 Park Ave, New York, NY 10022, USA (☎ 212 759 8477)

WHITE-THOMSON, Christopher Trefusis; yr s of Maj Walter Norman White-Thomson (3 s of Rt Rev Leonard White-Thomson, sometime Bishop of Ely, by his w Hon Margaret Trefusis, 3 da of 20 Baron Clinton); *b* 22 Feb 1940; *Educ* Harrow, RMA Sandhurst; *m* 1967, Juanita Maria, da of Frederick Arthur Rowlands, of Catania, Sicily; 1 s (Charles b 1969), 1 da (Kate b 1971); *Career* formerly Capt Royal Fusiliers; joined Cater Ryder & Co 1969, chief exec Oppenheimer Fund Management 1982-87; dir Mercantile House Hldgs 1980-87, Parrish plc 1988-90; *Clubs* Army and Navy; *Style—* Christopher White-Thomson, Esq; Parrish plc, 4 London Wall Buildings, London EC2M 5NX (☎ 071 638 1282)

WHITE-THOMSON, Very Rev Ian Hugh; s of Rt Rev Leonard Jauncey White-Thomson, Bishop of Ely (d 1933), and Margaret Adela Hepburn Stuart Forbes Trefusis (d 1939); *b* 18 Dec 1904; *Educ* Harrow, Univ of Oxford; *m* 1954, Wendy Ernesta, da of Gp Capt Frank Hawker Woolliams (d 1980); 2 s (Stephen Jauncey b 1955, John Harvey b 1963), 2 da (Lucy Margaret b 1957, Morwenna Anne b 1958); *Career* ordained 1929, curate of St Marys Ashford 1929-34, rector St Martin with St Paul Canterbury 1934-39, chaplain to Archbishops of Canterbury (Lang, Temple and Fisher) 1939-47, vicar of Folkestone 1947-55; chaplain to: HM King George VI 1947-52, HM The Queen 1952-63; archdeacon of Northumberland 1955-63, dean of Canterbury 1963-76; Freeman City of Canterbury 1976; Hon DCL Univ of Kent at Canterbury 1971; *Recreations* painting; *Style—* The Very Rev Ian White-Thomson; Camphill, Wye, Kent (☎ 0233 812210)

WHITECROSS, Richard Peter; s of John Francis Whitecross (d 1977), and Edna Margaret, *née* Robbins (d 1979); *b* 28 July 1945; *Educ* Univ Coll of Wales Aberystwyth (BA); *m* 14 July 1972, Cristina Elvira, da of German Lange Rosario, of Argentina; 2 s (Mathew b 1977, Thomas b 1980); *Career* regnl dir OUP Consortium Latin America 1970-76, dir Blackwell's Mainstream Book Club 1978-79, mktg conslt Phillips Fine Art Auctioneers 1984-; *Recreations* book collecting; *Style—* Richard P Whitecross, Esq; 35 Linkside Ave, Oxford OX2 8JE; Phillips Auctioneers, 39 Park End Street, Oxford OX1 1JD (☎ 0865 723524)

WHITEFIELD, Robert Henry; s of Henry Whitefield (d 1987), and Lily Josephine, *née* Rolt; *b* 9 Jan 1937; *Educ* Charterhouse; *m* 4 Dec 1965, Diana, da of Lt-Col R C Barrow (d 1968), of Farmington, Glos; 1 s (George b 1983), 3 da (Melanie b 1968, Anna b 1970, Serena b 1984); *Career* Nat Serv 1956-58, 2 Lt RE; dir Jamesons Chocolates plc 1960-90 (md 1972, chm 1987), non-exec dir Magna Specialist Confectioners Ltd, confectionary conslt; *Recreations* sailing, skiing, water colour painting, gardening, photography; *Clubs* Royal Cruising, Royal Ocean Racing, Old Carthusian; *Style—* Robert H Whitefield, Esq; The Old Rectory, Stocking Pelham, Buntingford, Herts SG9 0HU (☎ 0279 777303)

WHITEHALL, Barry John; JP (1987); s of Jack Baxter Whitehall (d 1969), and Norah Louise, *née* Kellond (d 1989); *b* 28 Aug 1936; *Educ* Ampleforth; *m* 1, (m dis 1979), Lavinia Antonia, da of Col R P Baily; 1 s (Richard Andrew b 26 April 1969), 1 da (Sarah Christina b 16 Sept 1972); m 2, 1979, Christine Barbara, da of Ralph Coates; *Career* RAF 1953-57; BBC 1957-: head of bdcasting Br Solomon Islands Protectorate 1968-70, head of overseas admin World Serv 1980-88, gen mangr monitoring World Serv 1988-91, controller of resources World Serv 1991-; *Recreations* tennis, bridge; *Clubs* East India; *Style—* Barry Whitehall, Esq, JP; Anchor House, St Leonards Lane, Wallingford, Oxon OX10 0HA (☎ 0491 35937); BBC World Service, Bush House, Strand, London WC2B 4PH (☎ 071 257 2551)

WHITEHEAD, Hon Mrs (Annabel Alice Hoyer); *née* Millar; LVO (1986); yr da of 1 Baron Inchyra, GCMG, CVO (d 1989); *b* 25 Jan 1943; *m* 1973, Christopher James Bovill Whitehead; 1 s (Robert William Bovill b 1977), 1 da (Christine Daisy Elizabeth b 1975); *Career* lady-in-waiting to HRH The Princess Margaret, Countess of Snowdon 1971-75; extra lady-in-waiting 1975-; *Style—* The Hon Mrs Whitehead, LVO; 5 Vicarage Gdns, London W8

WHITEHEAD, Christopher James Bovill; s of Thomas Bovill Whitehead, of Wiltshire, and Christine Margaret, *née* Dixon; *b* 9 Feb 1939; *Educ* Eton; *m* 1973, Annabel Alice, da of Lord Inchyra, of Perthshire; 1 s (Robert William Bovill b 1977), 1 da (Christina Daisy Elizabeth b 1975); *Career* memb The Stock Exchange London 1962-; *Clubs* White's, City of London, MCC; *Style—* Christopher Whitehead, Esq; 5 Vicarage Gardens, London W8 4HA (☎ 071 229 0766)

WHITEHEAD, Capt David; s of Herbert John Whitehead (d 1984), of Sparsholt, Winchester, Hants, and Doreen Mary, *née* Knight; *b* 10 March 1934; *Educ* Bickley Hall Kent, Wrekin Sch; *m* 24 Oct 1959, Annarosa, da of Lt-Col Leonard Henry Dismore, OBE, TD (d 1956), of Canterbury, Kent; 2 s (Nicholas b 9 Oct 1960, James b 23 Oct 1962), 2 da (Tanya b 9 June 1964, Deborah b 10 Jan 1969); *Career* cadet Britannia RN Coll 1950, cmmnd Sub Lt 1954, OC HMS Droxford 1958-60, Long Communications Course 1961, Lt Cdr Flag Lt to Flag Offr Flotillas (Home) 1962, CO HMS Wakeful 1968, CO HMS Grenville 1969, staff communications offr to Cdr Hong Kong and CO Hong Kong Naval Wireless Station 1970, Cdr sr offr Hong Kong Sqdn and CO HMS Yarnton 1971, OC User Requirements and Trials Section Directorate of Naval Signals 1972, Naval Staff 1974-77, exchange serv with US Naval Staff with responsibility for int interoperability in cmd control and communications (cited for Legion of Merit) 1978-80, Capt Asst Dir Cmd Control and Communications Policy Def Staff 1980, Dir Def Fixed Telecommunications System Def Staff 1982, Dep Chief Naval Signal Offr 1984, ret 1985; dir tech liaison Racal Gp Services Ltd 1985-, dir (UK) Nuits St James Ltd 1988-; FBIM 1978, MNI 1979, memb Lloyds; *Recreations* maritime affairs, photography, travel; *Clubs* Special Forces; *Style—* Capt David Whitehead, RN; 33 Harewood Ave, London NW1 6LE (☎ 071 723 0551); Swanmore Pk, Hants SO3 2QS; Chez Spaud, 24410 St Aulaye, France; Racal Group Services Ltd, Western Rd, Bracknell, Berks RG12 1RG (☎ 0344 483 244 ext 2120, fax 0344 54119, telex 848239)

WHITEHEAD, Dr Denis Sword; s of Henry Whitehead (d 1979), and Alice, *née* Sword (d 1942); *b* 8 May 1927; *Educ* Uppingham, Cambridge Univ (MA, PhD); *m* 21 June 1951, Frances Cabot Paine (Frankie), da of Frank Cabot Paine (d 1952), yacht designer and builder, of Wayland, Mass; 3 s (Henry, Frank, Ian), 1 da (Anne (Mrs Prebensen)); *Career* with Rolls-Royce 1948-54, lectr and reader Cambridge Univ 1957-85; engrg conslt 1985-; fell Jesus Coll Cambridge 1962-; contrib chapter on Aerolasticity in Turbomachines to AGARD Manual; MIMechE, MRAeS, CEng; *Recreations* sailing, golf, fishing; *Clubs* RAC; *Style—* Dr Denis Whitehead; Inwoods, Farleigh Wick, Bradford-on-Avon, Wilts BA15 2PU (☎ 02216 3207)

WHITEHEAD, Frances; da of Frank Whitehead (d 1968), and Alice Archibald, *née* Pemberton (d 1972); *Educ* Queen Mary Sch Lytham, St Hilda's Coll Oxford (BA, MA), Univ of Sheffield (MA); *Career* librarian Lancs Co libraries 1970-71, freelance writer 1973-85, editorial dir Mills & Boon 1987- (editorial 1973, dep ed dir 1985-87); author speaker and bdcaster on aspects of writing and mass market fiction; *Books* And Then He Kissed Her ..., A Guide to Writing Fiction (jtly); *Recreations* Times crossword, sumo wrestling, theatre, travel off the beaten track; *Clubs* Soc of Genealogists; *Style—* Ms Frances Whitehead; c/o Mills & Boon Ltd, Eton House, 18-24 Paradise Rd, Richmond, Surrey (☎ 081 948 0444)

WHITEHEAD, Frank Ernest; s of Ernest Whitehead, (d 1963), of Walmer, and Isabel, *née* Leslie (d 1978); *b* 21 Jan 1930; *Educ* Leyton Co HS, LSE (BSc); *m* 7 Jan 1961, Anne Gillian, da of James Clifford Marston (d 1979), of Silverdale, Lancs; 3 s (David Clifford b 1962, (Edward) Peter b 1964, Michael Frank 1968); *Career* Nat Serv LAC RAF 1948-49; Rio Tinto Co 1952-54, professional offr in Statistics Fedn of Rhodesia and Nyasaland 1955-64, statistician Gen Register Office 1964-68, chief statistician Miny of Social Security (later DHSS) 1968-77, dep dir Office of Population Census and Surveys 1982-89 (head of social survey div 1977-82), author of various articles in statistical jls; memb C of E; vice pres RSS 1988-89 (fell 1966, cncl memb 1987); *Recreations* family history, gardening; *Style—* Frank Whitehead, Esq; Queensmead, Pilgrims Way, Kemsing, Kent TN15 6XA (☎ 0732 61787)

WHITEHEAD, His Honour Judge (Garnet) George Archie; DFC (1944); s of Archibald Payne Whitehead (d 1944), of Wisbech St Mary, Cambs, and Margaret Elizabeth, *née* Watson (d 1919); *b* 22 July 1916; *Educ* Wisbech Sch; *m* 24 Aug 1946, Monica, da of Bertie Watson (d 1976), of York; 2 da ((Margaret) Elizabeth b 1949, (Monica) Jane b 1955); *Career* joined RAF 1939, Flt Lt (pilot) Bomber Cmd and Tport Cmd; admitted slr 1949, rec 1972, circuit judge 1977, ret 1989, dep judge 1989-; memb Boston Borough Cncl 1962-74, Alderman, Mayor of Boston 1969-70; *Recreations* walking, photography; *Style—* His Hon Judge Whitehead, DFC; 15 Burton Close, Boston, Lincs PE21 9QW (☎ 0205 364977)

WHITEHEAD, Ian Kenneth; s of Kenneth Bedford Whitehead, of Wrexham, and Doreen, *née* Tomkins; *b* 23 Feb 1955; *Educ* Grove Park GS Wrexham, UCL (BSc); *m* 17 July 1982, Catherine Ann, da of Geoffrey Large, of Norwich; 2 da (Laura, Hannah); *Career* Price Waterhouse 1976-81; Lloyds Merchant Bank: mangr London 1981-84, vice pres New York 1984-87; dir Bank of Montreal London 1987-88, Prime Minister's Policy Unit 1988-90; chif fin offr Berkeley Govett 1990-, non exec dir North Middlesex Hospital; ACA 1979; *Clubs* tennis, golf, skiing; *Style—* Ian Whitehead, Esq

WHITEHEAD, John Michael Stannage; CBE (1990), JP (1968), DL (1988); s of (Arthur) Stannage Whitehead, JP (d 1946), of Stechford, Elms Rd, Leicester, and Isaline, *née* Baker, JP (d 1974); *b* 19 Dec 1927; *Educ* Uppingham, Leicester Tech Coll (now Leicester Poly); *m* 28 April 1962, Alanda Joy, da of Geoffrey Taylor Bentley (d 1987), of Acorns, Esher Park Ave, Esher, Surrey; 1 s (Michael John Stannage b 1968), 2 da (Penelope Josephine b 1963, Belinda Louise b 1964); *Career* 2 Lt Army Cadet Corps 1945-48, Special Constabulary 1950-68; dir: G Stibbe & Co Ltd 1948-74, J & H Hadden Ltd 1954-63; md Stibbe-Hadden Ltd 1963-74 (chm 1963-72), chm John Whitehead Textiles Ltd 1974-, name Lloyds of London 1979-, chm H Harrison & Co Finishers Ltd 1987-, tax cmmr 1966; chm govrs: Leicester Poly 1974-90 (vice chm 1971-74), Leicester Poly Higher Educn Corp 1988- (pro chllr 1990-); memb various charities; Freeman: City of London, City of Leicester; Liveryman Worshipful Co

Merchant Taylors 1951, Master Worshipful Co of Framework Knitters 1978 (Liveryman 1952); FRSA 1978; *Recreations* watching rugby football, sailing, gardening, reading; *Clubs* Leicestershire; *Style—* John Whitehead, Esq, CBE, JP, DL; The Poplars, Main St, Houghton on the Hill, Leicester LE7 9GD (☎ 0533 412 244); John Whitehead Textiles Ltd, 23 Lancaster St, Leicester LE5 4GD (☎ 0533 762 861, fax 0533 460 215, telex 34376 WP LSTR)

WHITEHEAD, Sir John Stainton; KCMG (1986, CMG 1976), CVO (1978); s of John William Whitehead (d 1946), and Kathleen Mary Whitehead (d 1981); *b* 20 Sept 1932; *Educ* Christ's Hosp Horsham, Hertford Coll Oxford (MA); *m* 1 Feb 1964, (Mary) Carolyn, da of Henry Whitworth Hilton (d 1985); 2 s (Simon b 1966, James b 1973), 2 da (Sarah b 1968, Jessica b 1971); *Career* HM Forces 1950-52; HM Dip Serv: FO 1955-56, 3 sec then 2 sec Tokyo 1956-61, FO 1961-64, 1 sec Washington 1964-67, 1 sec (economic) Tokyo 1968-71, FCO 1971-76, head Personnel Servs Dept 1973-76, cnsllr Bonn 1976-80, minister Tokyo 1980-84, dep under-sec of state (chief clerk) FCO 1984-86, Ambass to Japan 1986-; *Recreations* music, travel, golf, tree-felling, chess; *Clubs* Beefsteak, United Oxford and Cambridge Univ, Liphook Golf; *Style—* Sir John Whitehead, KCMG, CVO; Bracken Edge, High Pitfold, Hindhead, Surrey GU26 6BN; British Embassy, Tokyo, Japan

WHITEHEAD, Linda; da of Thomas Herbert Whitehead, of Darwen, Lancs, and Elvira, *née* Macavei, of Bucharest, Romania; *b* 27 Jan 1954; *Educ* Darwen Secdy Tech Sch; *Career* administrator: Blackburn Rovers FC 1974-78, Women's Football Assoc 1980- (first full time administrator); memb: Exec Ctee Football Family Forum, Ctee CCPR Games and Sports; winner Sunday Times Sports Administrator of the Year 1989; *Style—* Miss Linda Whitehead; 448/450 Hanging Ditch, The Corn Exchange, Manchester M4 3ES (☎ 061 832 5911, fax 061 839 0331)

WHITEHEAD, Hon Mrs (Lucia Edith); *née* Lawson; da of Maj-Gen 4 Baron Burnham, CB, DSO, MC, TD (d 1963); *b* 29 Aug 1922; *m* 1, 1946 (m dis 1953), Hon Roger David Marquis (later 2 Earl of Woolton; d 1969); m 2, 1966, John Whitehead (d 1982); *Career* served WW II 1941-46 as CSM ATS (despatches); *Style—* The Hon Mrs Whitehead; Hallin, 18 Burnham Avenue, Beaconsfield, Bucks

WHITEHEAD, Dr (John Ernest) Michael; s of Dr Charles Ernest Whitehead (d 1939), of London, and Bertha Ivy, *née* Harding (d 1945); *b* 7 Aug 1920; *Educ* Merchant Taylors', Gonville and Caius Coll Cambridge (MA, MB BChir), St Thomas's Hosp Med Sch (Dip Bact); *m* 3 Aug 1946, Elizabeth Bacchus, da of Col George Walker Cochran, DSO, IA (d 1970), of Parkstone, Dorset; 1 s (Stephen Michael b 1947), 1 da (Anne Elizabeth b 1951); *Career* co cdr 7 Bn Cambridgeshire HG 1940-42; lectr in bacteriology St Thomas's Hosp Med Sch London 1948-52, dep dir Public Health Laboratory Sheffield 1953-58, hon lectr in bacteriology Univ of Sheffield 1954-58, dir Public Health Laboratory Coventry 1958-75, hon lectr in bacteriology Univ of Birmingham 1962-75, dir Public Health Laboratory Serv 1981-85 (dep dir 1975-81), conslt advsr in med microbiology DHSS 1981-85, temp advsr WHO 1976-80; specialist advsr to House of Commons Select Ctees on Agric 1988- and Social Servs 1989-90; FRCPath (1974, vice pres 1983-86), chm Assoc of Med Microbiologists 1983-85; *Recreations* skiing, modern languages, house and garden maintenance; *Clubs* Athenaeum; *Style—* Dr Michael Whitehead; Martins, Lee Common, Great Missenden, Bucks HP16 9JP (☎ 0494 837 492)

WHITEHEAD, Philip Henry Rathbone; s and h of Sir Rowland Whitehead, 5 Bt; *b* 13 Oct 1957; *Educ* Eton, Univ of Bristol (Bsc); *m* 1987, Emma Charlotte, da of Capt Alexander Michael Darley Milne Home, RN, of Sydney, Australia; *Career* late Capt Welsh Gds; GSM; *Clubs* Special Forces, Cavalry and Guards, Royal Geographical Soc; *Style—* Philip Whitehead, Esq; 8 Herbert Crescent, London SW1X 0EZ

WHITEHEAD, Dr Philip John; s of Lionel Gilbert Whitehead (d 1974), and Leslie Broadbridge *née* Phillips (d 1985); *b* 13 April 1938; *Educ* Wennington Sch Wetherby, Univ of Bristol (MB ChB); *m* 4 April 1964, Mary Elizabeth, da of Harry Fisher (d 1983); 3 da (Sarah b 1964, Naomi b 1966, Rebecca b 1973); *Career* conslt pathologist W Cumberland Hosp Whitehaven Cumbria 1970-79, conslt haematologist Frenchay Hosp Bristol 1979-; MRCPath 1970, FRCPath 1982; *Recreations* reading, music, walking; *Style—* Dr Philip Whitehead; Dept of Haematology, Frenchay Hospital, Bristol BS16 1LE (☎ 0272 701212)

WHITEHEAD, Phillip; s of Harold Whitehead (d 1961), and Frances May, *née* Kingman (d 1966); *b* 30 May 1937; *Educ* Lady Manners Sch Bakewell, Exeter Coll Oxford (MA); *m* 1967, Christine Hilary, da of Thomas George Usborne, of Surrey; 2 s (Joshua b 1969, Robert b 1971), 1 da (Lucy b 1974); *Career* cmmnd Sherwood Foresters 1956 Lt Oxford 1958-61; writer and TV prodr, BBC producer 1961-67; ed This Week Thames TV 1967-70; MP (Lab) Derby N 1970-83, front bench spokesman Higher Educn 1981-83; chm Fabian Soc 1978-79; presenter Credo LWT 1983-85; columnist The Times 1983-85; dir: Goldcrest Film & TV Holdings 1984-87, Consumers Assoc 1982- (chm 1990-); chm: New Society Ltd 1985, Statesman Nation Publications 1984-90 (chm 1985-90); dir Book Productions (1986) Ltd 1986-; visiting fell in Commuications Goldsmiths Coll Univ of London 1985-; FRSA; *Style—* Phillip Whitehead, Esq; Mill House, Rowsley, Matlock, Derbys DE4 2EB (☎ 0629 732 659); Brook Productions, 103 Wardour St, London W1V 1LM (☎ 071 439 9871)

WHITEHEAD, Roland James; s of (Edwin Francis) Romilly Whitehead, of Hornbeam Cottage, West St, Burghclere, nr Newbury, Berkshire RG15 9LB, and Diana Elizabeth Whitehead; *b* 30 May 1964; *Educ* Eton, Univ of Southampton (BSc), RCA (MDes), Imperial Coll of Sci & Technol & Med (Dip Industl Design Engrg); *Career* industl designer; Julian Everitt Yacht Designs 1982, Kelsall Yacht Design 1983, PA Design 1986, Mortimer Technology 1987-88, Prowess Creative 1988-; winner: PA Design & PA Technol bursary 1985-87, Guardian PC Rewards south and south east regions; nat finalist for software design, designer Br challenge for Little America's cup 1987; chm Prof Gp CSD 1990-, assoc memb RINA; *Recreations* yacht racing, music; *Clubs* British Canoe Union, memb UK Int C Class Catamaran Assoc; *Style—* Roland Whitehead, Esq; 1 Graspan Cottages, 92 Chertsey Rd, Windlesham, Surrey GU20 6HP; Prowess Creative Ltd, Windlesham, Surrey GU20 6BX (☎ 0276 51426, fax 0276 51840)

WHITEHEAD, (Edwin Francis) Romilly; s of James Whitehead, KC (d 1936), of 56 Redington Rd, Hampstead, London, and Elsie Heyden, *née* Wakelam (d 1963); *b* 19 May 1924; *Educ* Westminster, Trinity Coll Cambridge (BA); *m* 17 Dec 1969, Diana Elizabeth, da of Archibald Ernest Bacon (d 1960), of Colesmead, Shorne, nr Gravesend, Kent; 1 s (Roland b 1964), 1 da (Henrietta b 1961); *Career* RA 1943-45 (2 Lt 1944); called to the Bar Gray's Inn 1949; bencher Gray's Inn 1976; *Recreations* sailing, the arts; *Clubs* Garrick; *Style—* Romilly Whitehead, Esq; Hornbeam Cottage, West St, Burghclere, nr Newbury, Berkshire RG15 9LB (☎ 063527 480); 4 Stone Buildings, Lincoln's Inn, London WC2A 3XT (☎ 071 242 5524, fax 071 831 7907, telex 892300)

WHITEHEAD, Sir Rowland John Rathbone; 5 Bt (UK 1889), of Highfield House, Catford Bridge, Kent; ggs of 1 Bt, sometime Lord Mayor of London; s of Maj Sir Philip Henry Rathbone Whitehead, 4 Bt (d 1953); *b* 24 June 1930; *Educ* Radley, Trinity Hall Cambridge (BA); *m* 3 April 1954, Marie-Louise, da of Arnold Christian Gausel, of Stavanger, Norway; 1 s, 1 da; *Heir* s, Philip Henry Rathbone Whitehead, *qv*; *Career* chm: Rowland Hill Benevolent Fund (PO) 1983-, govrs of Appleby Sch Cumbria, chm and fndr The Baronets' Tst 1985-88; chm Exec Ctee of Standing Cncl of the Baronetage 1984-86; tstee The Kelmscot House Tst 1970-; Liveryman Worshipful Co of Fruiterers, Freeman City of London; *Books* Cybernetics: Communication of Control (Handbook of Management Technology); *Recreations* poetry, rural indolence; *Clubs* Arts; *Style—* Sir Rowland Whitehead, Bt; Sutton House, Chiswick Mall, London W4 (☎ 081 994 2710); Walnut Tree Cottage, Fyfield, Lechlade, Glos (☎ 036 785 267)

WHITEHEAD, Prof Thomas Patterson (Tom); CBE (1985); *b* 7 May 1923; *Educ* Salford Royal Tech Coll, Univ of Birmingham (PhD); *m* 20 Sept 1947, Doreen Grace, *née* Whitton; 2 s (Paul b 1948, David b 1952), 1 da (Jill b 1955); *Career* biochemist S Warwicks Hosp Gp 1950-60, conslt biochemist Queen Elizabeth Hosp Birmingham 1968-86, dir Wolfson Res Laboratories 1972-84, Dean of Faculty of Medicine Univ of Birmingham 1984-87, scientific advsr BUPA Health Care; MRCP (Hon), FRCPath, FRSC; *Books* Quality Control in Clinical Chemistry (1976); *Recreations* growing and exhibiting sweet peas; *Clubs* Athenaeum; *Style—* Prof Tom Whitehead, CBE; 70 Northumberland Rd, Leamington Spa, Warwickshire CV32 6HB (☎ 0926 421974); BUPA Medical Research BUPA Medical Centre, 300 Grays Inn Rd, London WC1X 8DU (☎ 071 837 6484)

WHITEHORN, John Roland Malcolm; CMG (1974); s of Alan Drummond Whitehorn (d 1980), and Edith Marcia Whitehorn (d 1981); *b* 19 May 1924; *Educ* Rugby, Trinity Coll Cambridge (BA); *m* 1, 1951 (m dis 1973), Josephine, *née* Plummer; m 2, 1973, Marion, *née* Gutmann; *Career* Flying Offr RAFVR 1943-46, Far East; overseas dir: FBI 1963 (joined 1947), CBI 1965-68; dep dir-gen CBI 1966-78, dir Mitchell Cotts plc 1978-86, conslt dir Lilly Industries Ltd 1978-89; memb: BOTB 1975-78, Gen Advsy Ctee BBC 1976-82, Bd Br Cncl 1968-82; *Clubs* Reform; *Style—* John Whitehorn, Esq, CMG; Casters Brook, Cocking, Midhurst, W Sussex GU29 0HJ

WHITEHORN, Katharine Elizabeth; da of Alan Drummond Whitehorn (d 1980), of Marlborough and London, and Edith Marcia, *née* Gray (d 1982); *Educ* Blunt House, Roedean, Glasgow HS for Girls, Newnham Coll Cambridge (MA); *m* 4 Jan 1958, Gavin Tudor Lyall, s of Joseph Tudor Lyall; 2 s (Bernard b 1964, Jake b 1967); *Career* publisher's reader 1950-53, teacher Finland 1953-54, graduate asst Cornell Univ USA 1954-55, Picture Post 1956-57, Woman's Own 1958, Spectator 1959-61; columnist The Observer 1960- (assoc ed 1980-88); dir: Nationwide Anglia (formerly Nationwide) Bldg Soc 1983-, Nationwide Anglia Estate Agents 1987-90; memb: Latey Ctee on Age of Majority 1965-67, BBC Advsy Gp on Social Effects of Television 1971- 72, Bd Br Airports Authy 1972-77, Cncl RSM 1982-85; rector Univ of St Andrew's 1982-85; Hon LLD St Andrews 1985; memb NUJ; *Books* Cooking in a Bedsitter (1960), Roundabout (1961), Only on Sundays (1966), Whitehorn's Social Survival (1968), Observations (1970), How to Survive in Hospital (1972), How to Survive Children (1975), Sunday Best (1976), How to Survive in the Kitchen (1979), View from a Column (1981), How to Survive your Money Problems (1983); *Recreations* river boat; *Clubs* Royal Soc of Med; *Style—* Ms Katharine Whitehorn; c/o The Observer, Chelsea Bridge House, Queenstown Road, London SW8 4NN (☎ 071 627 0700)

WHITEHOUSE, Brian Paul; s of Rev Sydney Paul Whitehouse (d 1978); *b* 24 May 1933; *Educ* Manchester GS, CCC Oxford; *m* 1958, Jane Margaret da of Lt Cdr John Roberts-West (d 1942); 4 children; *Career* 2 Lt Northamptonshire Regt; dir Hambros Bank 1970-; *Recreations* croquet, bridge, racing; *Style—* Brian Whitehouse, Esq; Hambros Bank, 41 Bishopsgate, EC2

WHITEHOUSE, Prof David John; s of Joseph Whitehouse (d 1989), of 1 Purslet Rd, Wolverhampton, and Alice Gertrude, *née* Roberts (d 1985); *b* 15 Oct 1937; *Educ* Univ of Bristol (BSc), Univ of Leicester (PhD), Univ of Warwick (DSc); *m* 17 July 1965, Ruth Lily Epsley, da of William Pannell; 1 s (Steven Charles b 6 April 1971), 1 da (Anne Frances b 14 Jan 1969); *Career* devpt engr Switchgear Wolverhampton 1958-61, res engr Rank Taylor Hobson Leicester 1961-68, chief engr Rank Precision Industries 1968-78, sr fell SERC Univ of Warwick 1985 (prof of mech engrg 1978, prof of engrg sci, chief scientist 1990, dir of Centre for Micro Engrg and Metrology 1981), sr fell SERC 1986-90; author of 140 tech and scientific papers; memb: BSI, CIRP 1976; FInst, MIEE; *Books* Mean Line of Surface Texture (1965); *Recreations* swimming, music; *Style—* Prof David Whitehouse; 171 Cromwell Lane, Burton Green, Coventry CV4 8AN (☎ 0203 473558); Department of Engineering, University of Warwick, Coventry CV4 7AL (☎ 0203 523154, fax 0203 418922, telex 311904)

WHITEHOUSE, David Rae Beckwith; QC (1990); s of (David) Barry Beckwith Whitehouse, and late Mary, *née* Boffey; *b* 5 Sept 1945; *Educ* Ellesmere Coll Shropshire, The Choate Sch Wallingford Connecticut USA, Trinity Coll Cambridge (MA); *m* 1 Jan 1971, Linda Jane, da of Eric Vickers, CB, of Oakham, Rutland, Leics; 1 s (Benedict Harry Beckwith b 1978); *Career* barr Gray's Inn 1969; asst Recorder 1983; Recorder 1987; *Style—* David Whitehouse, Esq, QC; 3 Raymond Buildings, Gray's Inn, London WC1R 5BH

WHITEHOUSE, Dr David Robert; s of Derick William Whitehouse, of Birmingham, and Anne Valmai, *née* Mallet; *b* 7 Jan 1956; *Educ* Duddeston Manor Sch, Univ of Manchester (BSc, PhD); *m* 3 April 1982, Jillian Dorothy, da of Bernard Carey, of Preston; 1 s (Christopher David b 2 May 1985), 1 da (Lucy Claire b 8 June 1987); *Career* res engr Simon Engrg Ltd 1977-78, res asst Nuffield Radio Astronomy Laboratories Jodrell Bank 1979-82, res fell Space Sci Laboratory UCL 1982-85, weekly space columnist Oracle Teletext 1984-88, conslt ed Space magazine 1987-, space technol conslt, writer, broadcaster 1985-88, sci corr BBC News and Current Affrs; FRAS 1979, fell Br Interplanetary Soc 1983; *Books* New Scientist Special Publication; Man in Space (ed), numerous articles in int press and academic jls; *Recreations* mountaineering, music; *Style—* Dr David Whitehouse; BBC Radio News & Current Affairs, BBC, Broadcasting House, London W1A 1AA (☎ 071 927 4474, fax 071 636 4295)

WHITEHOUSE, Gerard Victor; s of Cyril Whitehouse (d 1961), and Rita Jamieson, *née* Rose; *b* 4 Sept 1955; *Educ* Bishop Vesey's GS Sutton Coldfield, Sheffield Univ (LLB); *m* 9 Sept 1978, Margaret, da of Ronald Winter, of Bainbridge, Sunderland; 3 da (Louise b 1984, Emma b 1986, Amy b 1990); *Career* slr, enrolled 1980; ptnr Blakemores Slrs 1981-; *Style—* Gerard Whitehouse, Esq; Watling House, Orton on the Hill, Leicestershire (☎ 0827 880292); Station Tower, Station Square, Coventry (☎ 0203 525858, fax 0203 228440)

WHITEHOUSE, Prof Graham Hugh; s of Raymond Hugh Whitehouse (d 1955), of Hatch End, Middx, and Joyce Miriam Moreton, *née* Powell; *b* 24 Nov 1939; *Educ* Harrow Co GS, Kings Coll London, Westminster Med Sch (MB BS); *m* 22 March 1969, Jacqueline Meadows, da of Benjamin Alfred Charles (d 1987), of Worcester Park, Surrey; 1 s (Richard b 1973), 1 da (Victoria b 1975); *Career* asst prof of radiology Univ of Rochester NY USA 1975-76, prof of diagnostic radiology Univ of Liverpool 1976- (sr lectr 1972-75); memb Cncl and examiner RCR, memb cncl for Br Inst Radiology, vice pres radiology section RSM; FRCR 1971, FRCP 1983; *Books* Gynaecological Radiology (1981), Techniques in Diagnostic Radiology (co ed, 1 edn 1983, 2 edn 1989), Self Assessment in Diagnostic Radiology (jtly, 1986), Exercises in Diagnostic Imaging (jtly, 1989); *Recreations* oil painting, choir singing, cricket, reading widely; *Style—* Prof Graham Whitehouse; 9 Belmont Rd, West Kirby, Merseyside L48 5EY (☎ 051 625 6933); University Department of Radiodiagnosis, Royal Liverpool Hospital, PO Box 147, Liverpool L69 3BX (☎ 051 706 4160, fax 051 708 6502, telex 627095)

WHITEHOUSE, Mary; CBE (1980); da of James Hutcheson, and Beatrice Ethel, *née* Searanckle; *b* 13 June 1910; *Educ* Chester City GS For Girls, Cheshire Co Training Coll Crewe; *m* 23 March 1940, Ernest Raymond Whitehouse; 3 s (Paul b 4 Jan 1941, Richard b 8 June 1944, Christopher b 30 Dec 1945); *Career* art specialist at Wednesfield Sch Wolverhampton 1932-40, Brewood GS 1943, sr mistress and sr art mistress Madeley Sch Shrops 1960-64; co-fndr Clean Up TV Campaign 1964, hon gen sec Nat Viewer's and Listener's Assoc 1965-80 (pres 1980-); freelance journalist/ broadcaster; *Books* Cleaning Up TV (1966), Who Does She Think She is? (1971), Whatever Happened to Sex? (1977), A Most Dangerous Woman (1982), Mightier than the Sword (1985); *Recreations* reading, walking, gardening; *Style*— Mrs Mary Whitehouse, CBE; Ardleigh, Colchester, Essex C07 7RH (☎ 0206 230 123)

WHITEHOUSE, Prof (Julian) Michael Arthur; s of Arthur Arnold Keer Whitehouse, of Olney, Bucks, and Kathleen Ida Elizabeth, *née* Elliston; *b* 2 June 1940; *Educ* Queens' Coll Cambridge (MA, MB BChir), St Bartholomews Hosp of London (MD); *m* 10 April 1965, Diane France, da of Dr Raymond Maximillien Theodore de Saussure (d 1972), of Geneva, Switzerland; 1 s (Michael Alexander de Saussure b 1966) 2 da (Fiona Geraldine b 1968, Vanessa Caroline b 1972); *Career* sr lectr and acting dir Dept of Med Oncology Bart's 1976; hon conslt physician; visiting prof: Univ of Boston 1981, Christchurch Clinical Sch of Med NZ 1986; former: vice pres Euro Soc of Med Oncology, first chm UICC Clinical Oncology Ctee; currently: prof of med oncology and hon conslt physician Southampton Hosps, dir CRC and Wessex Regnl Med Oncology Unit Southampton; ed Haematological Oncology; govr Canford Sch Dorset; Freeman City of London, Liveryman Worshipful Soc of Apothecaries; FRCP, FRSM; *Books* CNS Complications of Malignant Disease (1979), A Pocket Consultant in Clinical Oncology (1989), Investigation and Management (with Christopher J Williams, 1984-85), Recent Advances in Clinical Oncology (1982 and 1986); *Recreations* skiing, sailing, travelling; *Clubs* Athenaeum; *Style*— Prof Michael Whitehouse; CRC Wessex Regional Medical Oncology Unit, CF99 Southampton General Hospital, Tremona Rd, Southampton SO9 4XY (☎ 0703 796185, fax 0703 783839)

WHITEHOUSE, Patrick Bruce; OBE (1967), JP (1971); s of Cecil Norman Whitehouse (d 1952), and Phylis Mabel, *née* Bucknall (d 1976); *b* 25 Feb 1922; *Educ* Ellesmere Coll, Warwick Sch; *m* 16 Oct 1948, Thelma, da of Capt G H Crosbie (d 1967), of Birmingham; 1 s (Christopher Michael b 1952), 1 da (Margaret Anne b 1956); *Career* WWII RAF Flt Navigator/WT Middle East, Greece, N Africa 1941-46; articled pupil OA Wainwright Chartered Quantity Surveyor 1939-41, presenter BBC Railway Roundabout 1959-63, gp bd dir Holland Hannen & Cubitts Ltd (Int Contractors) 1968-71; chm: B Whitehouse & Sons Ltd, Millbrook House Ltd (Publishers) 1976-; chm Birmingham & District Industl Safety Gp 1963-70, vice chm Licensing Ctee Birmingham Magistrates 1985-91, HM Cmmr Income Tax 1971-87; tstee Birmingham Railway Museum Tst, fndr memb Talyllyn Railway Soc 1950-, assoc Royal Photographic Soc 1954, memb Ctee Birmingham Assoc Youth Clubs, chm Birmingham Assoc Boys Club 1972-74; author over of 43 books on railway subjects; FCIoB; *Recreations* photography, travel, railway history; *Clubs* Birmingham Chamber of Commerce & Industry; *Style*— Patrick B Whitehouse, Esq, OBE, JP; 32 Augustus Road, Edgbaston, Birmingham B15 3PQ; Millbrook House Ltd, 90 Hagley Road, Edgbaston, Birmingham B16 5YH (☎ 021 454 1308)

WHITEHOUSE-JANSEN, N Elly; OBE (1980); da of Jacobus Gerrit Jansen, of Wisch, Holland, and Petronella Suzanna, *née* Vellekoop; *b* 5 Oct 1929; *Educ* Paedologisch Inst Free Univ Amsterdam, Boerhave Kliniek (SRN), Univ of London; *m* 1969, Alan Brian Stewart (George) Whitehouse; 3 da; *Career* fndr and dir Richmond fellowship for Community Mental Health 1959-; fndr Richard fellowship: of America 1968, of Australia 1973, of New Zealand 1977, of Austria 1978, International 1981-90 (incl Barbados, Canada, France, Grenada, Hong Kong, India, Israel, Jamaica, Mexico, Peru, Trinidad & Tobago, Uruguay); dep chm Richmond Fellowship Enquiry 1981-82; consIt: Pan-American Health Organisation 1987-, to Min of Social Affairs Holland 1969-73; advsr to many govts on community care legislations and servs; Templeton award 1985-86; organiser Int Confs on Theraputic Communities 1973, 1975, 1976, 1979,1984, 1988; fell German Marshall Meml Fund 1977-78; *Books* The Therapeutic Community outside The Hospital (ed, 1980), Mental Health and the Community (contrib 1983), Towards a Whole Society (contrib, 1985); *Style*— Mrs N Elly Whitehouse-Jansen, OBE; 8 Addison Road, Kensington, London W14 8DL (☎ 071 603 6373)

WHITELAW, Dr Andrew George Lindsay; s of Dr Robert George Whitelaw, DL, of 64 Garvock Hill, Dunfermline, Scotland, and Cicily Mary, *née* Ballard; *b* 31 Aug 1946; *Educ* George Watson's Coll Edinburgh, King's Coll Cambridge (MA, MB BChir, MD); *m* 7 Sept 1968 (m dis 1990), Sara Jane, da of Capt Jack Sparks (d 1979), of Peaslake, Surrey; 1 s (Benjamin Cameron b 12 May 1972), 2 da (Nicola Jane b 26 Dec 1970, Rebecca Catrin b 18 April 1974); *Career* specialist paediatric training at Gr Ormond St and in Toronto 1972-79, conslt neonatologist and hon sr lectr Royal Postgrad Med Sch Hammersmith Hosp 1981-; chm perinatal servs ctee NW Thames, dep chm res ethics ctee Hammersmith Hosp, memb res ctee Birthright; FRCP 1988; *Books* The Very Immature Infant Under 28 Weeks Gestation (with Cooke, 1988); *Recreations* music, mountains, theatre; *Style*— Dr Andrew Whitelaw; Dept of Paediatrics & Neonatal Medicine, Hammersmith Hospital, Du Cane Rd, London W12 0HS (☎ 081 743 2030, fax 081 740 8281)

WHITELAW, Billie Honor; da of Percival Whitelaw, (d 1942), of Bradford, Yorks, and Frances Mary, *née* Williams (d 1980); *b* 6 June 1932; *Educ* Thornton GS; *m* 1, 1952 (m dis 1965), Peter Vaughan; m 2, Robert Muller; 1 s (Matthew Norreys b 1967); *Career* actress; first appearance aged 11 BBC Northern Region 1943, first West End appearance Hotel Paradiso 1954; later theatre (Joan Littlewood) 1959-60; National Theatre at Old Vic 1963-66 incl: Desdemona to Olivier's Othello, Hobson's Choice, work with Samuel Beckett on Play, seasons at Chichester, Moscow and Berlin; West End: Alphabetical Order 1975, Molly 1976; Tales of Hollywood (Nat Theatre) 1984, Who's Afraid of Virginia Woolf; (Young Vic) 1987; RSC incl: After Haggerty 1971, The Greeks 1979, Passion Play 1981; Royal Court with Samuel Beckett 1971-89 incl: Not I, Happy Days, Footfalls, (written especially for her); opened Samuel Beckett Theatre New York with: Rockaby, Footfalls, Enough (also performed in Los Angeles 1984); films incl: Charlie Bubbles (1968 American Film Critics Award and Br Film Acad Best Supporting Actress), Start The Revolution Without Me, Leo the Last, Gumshoe, Frenzy, The Omen, The Dressmaker, The Krays; over 100 TV appearances incl: No Trains to Lime St, The Fifty Pound Note, Beyond the Horizon, Anna Christie, Wessex Tales, Jamaica Inn, The Picnic; awards incl: TV Actress of the Year 1960, Best TV Actress 1972, Evening Standard Best Actress 1977, Variety Club Best Actress 1977, Best Radio Actress 1987, Br Film Award Evening Standard Best Actress; Hon D Litt Bradford Univ 1981; *Style*— Ms Billie Whitelaw; Rose Cottage, Plum St, Glemsford, nr Sudbury, Suffolk; Duncan Heath Associates (agent), Paramount House, Wardour St, London W1 (☎ 071 439 1471)

WHITELAW, Prof James Hunter (Jim); s of James Whitelaw, and Jean Ross, *née* Scott; *b* 28 Jan 1936; *Educ* Glasgow HS, Univ of Glasgow (BSc, PhD), London Univ (DSc); *m* 10 July 1959, Elizabeth, da of David Dewar Williamson Shields; 3 s (Alan Scott b 1962, David Stuart b 1964, James Douglas b 1968); *Career* res assoc Brown Univ 1961-63, prof Imperial Coll 1974-(lectr 1963-69, reader 1969-74), ed Experiments in Fluids 1982-; Hon DSc Univ of Lisbon 1980; FIMechE; *Books* Principles and Practice of Laser-Doppler Anemometry (with F Durst and A Melling, 1981), Calculation Methods for Engineering Flows (with P Bradshaw and T Cebeci, 1981), Series ed Combustion Treatise also over 300 technical papers; *Recreations* music, garden, travel; *Style*— Prof Jim Whitelaw; 149A Coombe Lane West, Kingston Upon Thames, Surrey KT2 7DH (☎ 081 942 1836); Dept of Mechanical Engineering, Imperial College, L London (☎ 071 225 8966)

WHITELAW, 1 Viscount (UK 1983), of Penrith, Co Cumbria; William Stephen Ian Whitelaw; KT (1990), CH (1974), MC (1944), PC (1967), DL (Cumbria 1974, Cumberland 1967); s of William Alexander Whitelaw (s of William Whitelaw, MP Perth and chm LNER, whose unc, Alexander *m* Dorothy, da of Ralph Disraeli and niece of Benjamin, 1 and last Earl of Beaconsfield) and Helen (da of Maj-Gen Francis Russell, CMG, JP, DL, of a family long domiciled in Scotland, one of whom served under Edward III at the siege of Berwick and saw action at Hallydon Hill in 1333; her mother was Philippa, maternal gda of 6 Viscount Strangford, diplomat and author; 7 Viscount Strangford was George Smythe, supposed model for Disraeli's Coningsby); *b* 28 June 1918; *Educ* Winchester, Trinity Coll Cambridge; *m* 1943, Cecilia Doriel, yr da of Maj Mark Sprot, Royal Scots Greys, of Roxburghshire, and Meliora, herself er da of Sir John Hay, 9 Bt; 4 da; *Career* served Scots Gds WW II; landowner; DL Dunbartonshire 1952-66; MP (C) Penrith and Cumberland Borders 1955-83; PPS to pres BOT 1956 and to chllr of Exchequer 1957-58, asst govt whip 1959-61, lord cmmr of Treasury 1961-62, Parly sec Miny of Labour 1962-64, chief oppn whip 1964-70, lord pres of Cncl and leader of House of Commons 1970-72; sec state: Northern Ireland 1972-73, Employment 1973-74; chm Cons Party 1974-75, dep leader of Oppn and Home Affairs spokesman 1975-79, home secretary 1979-83, lord pres of Cncl and leader of House of Lords 1983-88, ret; *Clubs* White's, Carlton, County (Carlisle), Royal and Ancient Golf of St Andrew's; *Style*— The Rt Hon the Viscount Whitelaw, KT, CH, MC, PC, DL; Ennim, Penrith, Cumbria

WHITELEY; *see*: Huntington-Whiteley

WHITELEY, Lady Angela Mary; *née* North; yr da of Francis George, Lord North (d 1940), er s of 8 Earl of Guilford; sister of 9 Earl; raised to the rank of an Earl's da 1950; *b* 28 May 1931; *m* 18 July 1955, Peter John Henry Whiteley, eldest s of late Brig John Percival Whiteley, OBE, TD, MP, of The Grange, Bletchley, Bucks; 2 s, 1 da; *Style*— The Lady Angela Whiteley; 10 Henning St, London SW11 3DR

WHITELEY, Lady Anne Patricia; *née* Nevill; da of 5 Marquess of Abergavenny, KG, OBE, JP; *b* 25 Oct 1938; *m* 1971, Martin Whiteley (d 1984); 3 da (Camilla Mary b 1972, Davina Marian Beatrice b 1973, Lucinda Jane b 1978); *Style*— The Lady Anne Whiteley; Dalmar House, Culworth, Banbury, Oxon OX17 2BD

WHITELEY, Gen Sir Peter John Frederick; GCB (1979, KCB 1976), OBE (1960), DL (Devon 1987); s of John George Whiteley (d 1958), by his w Irene, *née* Course (d 1964); *b* 13 Dec 1920; *Educ* Bishop's Stortford Coll, Bembridge Sch, Ecole des Roches; *m* 1948, Nancy Vivian, da of William Carter Clayden (d 1943); 2 s, 2 da; *Career* joined RM 1940, Fleet Air Arm 1946-51, Staff Offr Staff Coll Camberley 1960-63, CO 42 Commando Malaysia 1965-66 (despatches), NATO Def Coll 1968, Cdr 3 Commando Bde 1968-70, Maj-Gen Commando Forces 1970-72, COS Allied Forces Northern Europe 1972-75, Cmdt Gen RM 1975-77, C-in-C Allied Forces Northern Europe 1977-79, Lt-Govr and C-in-C Jersey 1979-85; pres Devon St John's Ambulance Bde, trustee Jersey Wildlife Preservation Trust; KStJ 1980; *Recreations* sailing, skiing, music, dogs; *Clubs* Royal Commonwealth Society; *Style*— Gen Sir Peter Whiteley, GCB, OBE, DL; Stoneycross, Yealmpton, Devon PL8 2JZ (☎ 0752 880 462)

WHITELOCKE, Rodger Alexander Frederick; s of Leslie W S Whitelocke (d 1955), of Bulstrode, Jamaica, and Ruth, *née* Hopwood; descendent of Sir James Whitelocke b 1570 (and Family Tree in Plantagenet Roll Exeter Vol) and Bulstrode Whitelocke, Keeper of the Great Seal b 1605 (s Sir James); *b* 28 Feb 1943; *Educ* Taunton Sch, Univ of London, Bart's (MB BS); *m* 28 July 1973, Eleonora Valerie, da of Professor W F Maunder, of Tiverton, Devon; 2 s (Nicholas b 1979, James b 1984), 1 da (Katherine b 1978); *Career* house surgn Bart's 1969-70, research on prostaglandins in ocular inflammation Inst of Ophthalmology 1971-73 (PhD London), sr resident surgical offr Moorfields Eye Hosp 1976, sr registrar Bart's 1977-80; conslt ophthalmic surgn: Bart's, Royal Marsden Hosp London; hon conslt St Lukes Hosp for Clergy, visiting prof of visual scis City Univ London; FRCS; *Recreations* music, antiques, travel, gardening; *Clubs* The Fountain; *Style*— Rodger Whitelocke, Esq; Westwood, Heather Drive, Sunningdale, Berks; 152 Harley Street, London W1N 1HH (☎ 071 935 3834)

WHITEMAN, John; *b* 1954; *Educ* Repton, Univ of Bristol (BA, grad dip architecture), Harvard (Kennedy scholar, MA, PhD); *Career* asst prof Graduate Sch of Design Dept of Urban Design and Planning Harvard Univ 1983-88 (instr 1982-83), William Henry Bishop prof of architecture Yale Univ 1989; dir: Chicago Inst for Architecture and Urban Studies 1987-90, Glasgow Sch of Art 1990-; author of numerous published papers on architectural theory and practice; *books*: Regional Dynamics: Studies in Adjustment theory 1980, Strategies of Architectural Thinking (ed, 1986), Divisible By 2: Documentation of a pavilion on the relation between architecture and politics 1990; memb: AIA (Chicago chapter), American Planning Assoc, Urban Design Inst, Assoc of American Geographers, ARCUK; ARIBA; *Style*— Dr John Whiteman; Glasgow School of Art, Mackintosh Building, 167 Renfrew St, Glasgow G3 6RQ (☎ 041 332 9797, fax 041 332 3502)

WHITEMAN, Prof John Robert; s of Robert Whiteman, and Rita, *née* Neale; *b* 7 Dec 1938; *Educ* Bromsgrove Sch, Univ of St Andrew's (BSc), Worcester Coll Oxford (Dip Ed), Univ of London (PhD); *m* 8 Aug 1964, Caroline Mary, da of Oswald B Leigh (d 1941); 2 s (Angus b 1967, Hamish b 1969); *Career* sr lectr RMCS Shrivenham 1963-67; asst prof: Univ of Wisconsin USA 1967-68, Univ of Texas at Austin USA 1968-70; Brunel Univ 1970-: reader numerical analysis 1970-76 (on leave Richard Merton Gäst prof Univ of Münster FRG 1975-76), prof of numerical analysis and dir Brunel Inst of Computational Mathematics 1976- (head Dept Mathematics and Statistics 1982-90), vice princ 1991-; visiting prof: Univ of Kuwait 1986, Texas A and M Univ USA 1986-, Univ of Stuttgart 1990; memb: SERC Mathematics Ctee 1981-86, SERC Sci Bd 1989-, Amersham Deanery Synod C of E; Freeman City of London 1979, Liveryman Worshipful Co of Glass Sellers 1979; FIMA 1970; *Books* numerous pubns on numerical solution of differential equations (particularly finite element methods) incl: The Mathematics of Finite Elements and Applications vols 1-7 (ed 1973-91), Numerical Methods for Partial Differential Equations (ed journal); *Recreations* walking, swimming, golf, tennis, squash; *Style*— Prof John Whiteman; Institute of Computational Mathematics, Brunel University, Uxbridge, Middlesex UB8 3PH (☎ 0895 74000)

WHITEMAN, Michael Norman; s of Norman Vincent Whiteman (d 1943), and Alma Meads Whiteman; *b* 28 May 1937; *Educ* Whitgift Sch; *m* 21 Nov 1959, Josephine, da of George Henry Hobbs, of Garden Cottage, Great Durnford, Salisbury, Wilts; 1 s (James Michael b 1 April 1966), 1 da (Sarah Jane b 15 April 1963); *Career* RAF 1955-75, gen duties navigator, Sqdn Ldr; Ferranti Computer Systems Ltd 1975-82, mktg dir Mel Philips 1982-83, md Plessey Avionics Ltd 1983-91; dir: Soc Br Aerospace Cos Ltd 1984-90, Identification Projects Ltd 1986-90, Stewart Hughes Ltd 1989-90; chm

Candlestar Plessey BV1 1988-90, Skytrading Hldgs Ltd BV1 1988-90, Skytrading BV 1989-90; taking sabbatical until mid 1991; *Recreations* golf, gardening, reading; *Clubs* Liphook Golf; *Style—* Michael Whiteman, Esq; Plessey Avionics Ltd, Martin Rd, Havant, Hants PO9 5DH (☎ 0705 493218, fax 0705 493140, car 0836 212 306, telex 86227)

WHITEMAN, Prof Peter George; QC (1977); s of David Whiteman (d 1988), and Betsy Bessie, *née* Coster; *b* 8 Aug 1942; *Educ* Warwick Secdy Mod Sch, Leyton HS, LSE (LLB, LLM); *m* 24 Oct 1971, Katherine Ruth, da of Gershon Ellenbogen; 2 da (Victoria Elizabeth b 1975, Caroline Venetia b 1977); *Career* lectr London Univ 1966-70, called to the Bar Lincoln's Inn 1967; visiting prof: Univ of Virginia 1978, Univ of California at Berkeley 1980; memb Faculty of Laws Univ of Florida 1977-, prof of Law Univ of Virginia 1980-; attorney and cnsllr NY State 1982, bencher Lincoln's Inn 1985, recorder Crown Ct 1986-; memb: ctee Unitary Tax Campaign (UK) 1982-, Ed Bd Virginia Jl of Int Law 1982-; pres Dulwich Village Preservation Soc 1987-, memb Advsy Ctee Dulwich Estates Govrs Scheme of Mgmnt 1988-; memb: Bar Council, Consultative Ctee Dulwich Picture Gallery 1990-; *Books* Whiteman on Income Tax (1988), Whiteman on Capital Gains Tax (1988), British Tax Encyclopedia (1965), and author numerous articles in learned jls; *Recreations* tennis, jogging, hill-walking, croquet; *Style—* Prof Peter G Whiteman, QC; Queen Elizabeth Building, The Temple, London EC4Y 9BS (☎ 071 936 3131, fax 071 353 1937, telex 8951414)

WHITEMAN, Rodney David Carter; s of Leonard Archibald Whiteman (d 1955), and Sybil Mary, *née* Morshead (d 1990); *b* 6 Oct 1940; *Educ* St Austell GS Cornwall, Ely Theological Coll; *m* 28 Oct 1969, Christine Anne, da of Edward Thomas James Chelton, of 74 The Haven, Sunnyfield Lane, Up Hatherleigh, Cheltenham, Glos; 1 s (James Rodney Charles b 1975), 1 da (Rebecca Mary De Mornay b 1972); *Career* ordained Birmingham Cathedral: deacon 1964, priest 1965; curate All Saints Kings Heath 1964-70, vicar: St Stephen Rednal 1970-79, St Barnabas Erdington 1974-89; rural dean of Aston 1981-89, Archdeacon of Bodmin 1989-, hon canon of Truro Cathedral 1989- (Birmingham Cathedral 1985-89), priest in charge Cardynham with Helland 1989-; *Style—* The Ven the Archdeacon of Bodmin; The Rectory, Cardynham, Bodmin, Cornwall PL30 4BL (☎ 020 882614)

WHITEMORE, Hugh John; s of Samuel George Whitemore (d 1987), and Kathleen, *née* Fletcher; *b* 16 June 1936; *Educ* Judd Sch Tonbridge, King Edward VI Sch Southampton, RADA; *m* 1, July 1961 (m dis 1976), Jill, *née* Brooke; m 2, May 1976, Sheila, *née* Lemon; 1 s (Tom b 1976); *Career* playwright; stage plays: Stevie 1977, Pack of Lies 1983, Breaking the Code 1986, The Best of Friends 1988; films incl 84 Charing Cross Rd (Royal Film Performance 1987); many TV plays and dramatisations incl contribs to: The Wednesday Play, Armchair Theatre, Play for Today; *Recreations* music, movies, reading; *Style—* Hugh Whitemore, Esq; c/o Judy Daish Assocs, 83 Eastbourne Mews, London W2

WHITEOAK, John Edward Harrison; s of Frank Whiteoak, and Marion Whiteoak (d 1955); *b* 5 July 1947; *Educ* Keighley Secdy Tech, Univ of Sheffield (MA); *m* 1, Margaret Elisabeth, *née* Blakey (d 1980); 1 s (Roger b 1969), 2 da (Juliet b 1971, Olivia b 1973); m 2, 23 Sept 1983, Dr Karen Lynne Wallace, *née* Stevenson; 2 da (Georgia b 1988, Francesca b 1990); *Career* positions 1966-76 with: Skipton UDC, Skipton RDC, Solihull CBC, Cleveland CC 1976-79; fin dir Cheshire CC 1988- (dep co treas 1979-81, co treas 1981-88); fin advsr ACC 1984-; memb: Soc of Co Treas 1981-, Accounting Standards Ctee 1984-87, Tech Ctee CIPFA 1984-87, Exec Ctee SCT 1987; Lord of the Manor of Huntington and Cheaveley; CIPFA; *Recreations* golf, tennis; *Clubs* City Club and Eaton GC; *Style—* John Whiteoak, Esq; Huntington Hall, Huntington, Chester CH3 6EA (☎ 0244 312 901); County Hall, Chester, Cheshire (☎ 0244 602 000)

WHITER, Lt-Col David Stuart; MBE (1968); s of Frank Shirley Stuart Whiter (d 1979), and Ethel Marjorie, *née* Shorland (d 1980); *b* 30 July 1930; *Educ* Radley, RMA Sandhurst; *m* 8 Feb 1958, Marcia, da of Norman Ingrey (d 1977); 1 s (Christopher b 1959), 1 da (Carey b 1965); *Career* personal staff Chief of Def MOD 1970-71 (Germany, Aden, Netherlands), Co 20 Medium Regt RA 1972-73, chief plans and exercises Intelligence HQ Allied Forces Central Europe 1973-75, Cabinet Office 1975-78, serv attaché liaison offr FCO 1978-83, admin dir Br Field Sports Soc 1983; *Recreations* gardening, birdwatching; *Style—* Lt-Col David Whiter, MBE; Shorlands, Birch Grove, Pyrford, Woking, Surrey (☎ 0932 343771); 59 Kennington Road, London (☎ 071 928 4742)

WHITER, John Lindsay Pearce; s of Nugent Whiter (d 1966), and Jean Dorothy, *née* Pearce; *b* 10 May 1950; *Educ* Eastbourne GS; *m* 5 July 1975, Janet Dulcie Sarah, da of Dr Kenneth Oswald Albert Vickery, of Eastbourne; 2 s (Timothy b 1976, William b 1989), 1 da (Nancy b 1979); *Career* articled clerk and audit sr Honey Barrett & Co Eastbourne 1968-72, mangr Brebner Allen & Trapp 1973-74, managing ptnr Neville Russell 1988- (ptnr 1977-88); Freeman City of London, Bishopsgate Ward; FCA 1973; *Recreations* golf, tennis, the arts; *Clubs* The Nat, City of London; *Style—* John Whiter, Esq; Twowayes, 29 Dry Hill Rd, Tonbridge, Kent TN9 1LU (☎ 0732 355088); Neville Russell, 246 Bishopsgate, London EC2M 4PB (☎ 071 377 1000, fax 071 377 8931)

WHITEREAD, Rachel; da of Thomas Whiteread (d 1988), of London, and Pat, *née* Lancaster; *b* 20 April 1963; *Educ* Brighton Poly (BA), Slade Sch of Art UCL (DipHe in sculpture); *Career* artist and sculptor; solo exhibitions incl: Carlile Gallery London (1988), Ghost (Chisenhale Gallery London (1990), Arnolfini Gallery Bristol (1991), Karsten Schubert Ltd London (1991); selected gp exhibitions incl: Whitworth Young Contemporaires Manchester (1987), Riverside Open London (1988), Whitechapel Open London (1989), Deichtorhallen Hamburg (1989-90), British Art Show (touring, 1990), Karsten Schubert Ltd London (1990), Metropolis (Martin-Gropius Bau Berlin (1991); winner of awards: The Elephant Trust 1989, GLA Prodn Grant 1989; involved in teaching on various postgrad and undergrad courses; *Style—* Ms Rachel Whiteread; Karsten Schubert Gallery, 85 Charlotte St, London W1T 1LB (☎ 071 631 0031, fax 071 436 9255)

WHITESIDE, Barbara Ann; da of James Walsh of Kennel Bank, Chelford, Cheshire, and Audrey, *née* Dean; *b* 1 March 1955; *Educ* Manchester HS, Univ of Birmingham (BSoc Sci); *m* ; 1 s (James Nicholas b Aug 1984), 1 da (Emma Jane b Oct 1981); *Career* internal audit asst St Marys W2 1976-77, secretariat mangr Brent Dist 1977-78, hosp admin Willesden Gen Hosp 1978-79, admin Coppetts Wood Hosp 1979-80, ward mangr USA 1980-81, asst admin Royal Free Hosp 1979-80 and 1982-85, various posts Hillingdon Health Authy 1985-87, acting unit gen mangr Mount Vernon Hosp 1987-88, unit gen mangr mental health Riverside 1988-; memb Inst Health Servs Mgmnt 1981; *Recreations* reading, gardening, entertaining; *Style—* Ms Barbara Whiteside; Riverside Mental Health Unit, 50-51 Vincent Square, London SW1 (☎ 081 746 8954)

WHITFELD, Hon Mrs (Deborah Mary); *née* Vaughan-Morgan; da of Baron Reigate, PC, *qv*; *b* 1 Sept 1944; *Educ* West Heath Sevenoaks; *m* 3 May 1966, Michael Whitfeld, s of Lt-Col Ernest Hamilton Whitfeld (d 1973, whose m, Mary, *née* Curzon, was gda of 1 Earl Howe), and Iris E, *née* Scully; 2 s (Nicholas b 1968, Mark b 1971), 1 da (Melanie b 1976); *Style—* The Hon Mrs Whitfeld; Querns, Goring Heath, Oxon RG8 7RH (☎ 0491 680400)

WHITFIELD, Adrian; QC (1983); s of Peter Henry Whitfield (d 1967), and Margaret Mary Whitfield; *b* 10 July 1937; *Educ* Ampleforth, Magdalen Coll Oxford (MA); *m* 1, 1962 (m dis), Lucy Caroline, *née* Beckett; 2 da (Teresa, Emily); m 2, 1971, Niamh, da of Prof Cormac O'Ceallaigh, of Dublin; 1 s (Adam), 1 da (Katharine Anna); *Career* called to the Bar Middle Temple 1964, memb Western Circuit, rec 1981-; *Style—* Adrian Whitfield, Esq, QC; 47 Faroe Rd, London W14 0EL (☎ 071 603 8982); 3 Serjeants' Inn, London EC4Y 1BQ (☎ 071 353 5537)

WHITFIELD, Alan; s of Jonathon Whitfield (d 1982), and Annie, *née* Fothergill Rawe (d 1971); *b* 19 April 1939; *Educ* Consett GS, Sunderland and Newcastle Colls of Advanced Tech (now Poly's); *m* 24 Oct 1964, da of John Thomas Carr (d 1976); 2 s (Simon Mark b 12 Jan 1968, Andrew Jonathon b 16 March 1972); *Career* asst surveyor NCB 1960-62 (jr engr/surveyor 1956-60), various posts rising from engrg asst to team leader Northumberland Co Cncl 1962-70; Civil Serv: maingrade 1970-73, princ prof 1973-76, supt engr 1976-78, on secondment to Establishments as personnel mangr 1978-80, asst sec to dep dir of Midlands Road Construction Unit 1980-83, dir of Tport W Midlands 1983-89, road prog dir DOE and Dept of Tport Eastern Region 1989- (regnl dir 1989); memb Nat Cncl Inst of Highway Engrs (memb Ctee Midland Branch, dep chm Construction Bd); CEng, MICE, FIHT; *Recreations* golf, music; *Clubs* RAC; *Style—* Alan Whitfield, Esq; Department of Transport, Friars House, Warwick Rd, Coventry CU1 2TN (☎ 0203 535102, fax 0203 535330); Department of Transport, 2 Marsham St, London SW1P 3EB (☎ 071 276 4950, fax 071 276 4864, car 0831 476723)

WHITFIELD, Dr Ann; da of Dr Gerald A W Whitfield (d 1971), of Lindfield, Sussex, and Dr Nancy L Jones; *b* 28 July 1935; *Educ* Sherborne, Kings Coll Hosp Univ of London (MB BS, DA); *m* 2 Dec 1961, Robert Evan Kendell, s of Owen Kendell (d 1955), of Enfield, Middx; 2 s (Patrick b 1968, Harry b 1970), 2 da (Katherine b 1965, Judith b 1966); *Career* clinical fell Univ of Vermont Med Sch USA 1969-70; conslt anaesthetist: Lewisham Hosp London 1972-74, Royal Infirmary Edinburgh 1976-; FFARCS 1965, MRCS, LRCP; *Recreations* hill walking, cooking, music; *Style—* Dr Ann Whitfield; 3 West Castle Rd, Edinburgh EH10 5AT (☎ 031 229 4966); Department of Anaesthetics, Royal Infirmary of Edinburgh, Edinburgh (☎ 031 229 2477)

WHITFIELD, Lady Fiona Catherine; *née* Sinclair; da (by 1st m) of late 19 Earl of Caithness; *b* 27 Oct 1941; *m* 10 Jan 1969, Maj Michael Stephen Whitfield; 1 s, 1 da; *Style—* The Lady Fiona Whitfield; Plymtree Farm, PO Box 721, Marondera, Zimbabwe

WHITFIELD, Rev George Joshua Newbold; s of Joshua Newbold Whitfield; *b* 2 June 1909; *Educ* Bede GS Sunderland, King's Coll London, Bishops' Coll Cheshunt; *m* 1937, Audrey Priscilla, *née* Dence; 2 s, 2 da; *Career* headmaster: Tavistock GS 1943-46, Stockport Sch 1946-50, Hampton Sch 1950-68; ordained priest 1963; pres Headmasters' Assoc 1967, gen sec Bd of Educn of Gen Synod of C of E 1968-74, memb of Corp of Church House Westminster 1974-, chm Exeter Diocesan Educn Ctee 1981-88; opened The Whitfield Bldg Hampton Sch 1990; *Books Incl:* God and Man in the Old Testament (1949), Philosophy and Religion (1955); *Recreations* gardening, photography; *Clubs* Athenaeum; *Style—* The Rev George Whitfield; Bede Lodge, 31A Rolle Rd, Exmouth, Devon EX8 2AW (☎ 0395 274 162)

WHITFIELD, Hugh Newbold; s of Rev George Joshua Newbold Whitfield, *qv*, of Exmouth, Devon, and Audrey Priscilla, *née* Dence; *b* 15 June 1944; *Educ* Canford, Gonville and Caius Coll Cambridge (MA, MChir); *m* Penelope Joy, da of William Craig; 2 s (Angus Hugh Newbold b 18 April 1976, Alastair James Newbold b 14 Jan 1981); *Career* cmmnd Royal Army Medical Corps 1967-74; various house jobs Bart's, res fell Inst of Urology 1974-76; Bart's: chief asst Dept of Urology 1976-79, conslt urologist 1979-, clinical dir Dept of Urology and dir Lithotripter Unit 1991-; former memb Nat Youth Orch of GB; memb: BMA 1968, Br Assoc of Urological Surgns 1974; FRSM 1975, FRCS 1972; *Books* Textbooks of Genito-Urinary Vols I and II (ed with W F Hendry, 1985), Urology: Pocket Consultant (1985); *Recreations* music, country pursuits; *Clubs* Athenaeum; *Style—* Hugh Whitfield, Esq; Department of Urology, St Bartholomew's Hospital, West Smithfield, London EC1A 7BE (☎ 071 601 8888); 95 Harley St, London W1N 1DF (☎ 071 935 3095, fax 071 224 3567)

WHITFIELD, John Flett; JP (1971), DL (1982); s of John Herbert Whitfield, of London (d 1955), and Bertha Georgina, *née* Flett (d 1982); *b* 1 June 1922; *Educ* Epsom Coll Surrey; *m* 10 Aug 1946, Rosemary Elisabeth Joan, da of Col Raymond Theobald Hartman (d 1961), of London; 2 da (Christine b 1947, Veronica b 1949); *Career* WWII Capt KRRC 1939-46; HM For Serv served: M East, Roumania, Finland 1946-57; export dir Materials Handling Equipment (GB) Ltd 1957-61, London dir Hunslet (Holdings) Ltd 1961-64, dir Sunningdale Golf Club 1973-77; memb: Berkshire CC 1961-70, Surrey CC 1970-89 (chm 1981-84); chm: Police Ctee Assoc of Co Cncls 1985-88, Surrey Police Authy 1985-89, Windsor Co Bench 1978-80, Cncl Univ of Surrey 1986-88; High Sheriff Surrey 1985-86; Parly candidate (C) Pontefract 1964; *Recreations* golf, foreign languages, bookbinding; *Clubs* R & A, Sunningdale, Rye Golf; *Style—* John F Whitfield, Esq, JP, DL; 4 Holiday House, Priory Rd, Sunningdale, Berks, SL5 9RW (☎ 0990 20997)

WHITFIELD, June; OBE (1985); da of John Herbert Whitfield (d 1955), and Bertha Georgina, *née* Flett (d 1982); *b* 11 Nov 1925; *Educ* Streatham Hill HS, RADA; *m* 1955, Timothy John Aitchison, s of Cdr J G Aitchinson, OBE; 1 da (Suzy b 4 June 1960); *Career* actress; stage debut ASM Pinkstring & Sealing Wax (Duke of York's) 1944; theatre incl: Ace of Clubs (Cambridge Theatre and tour) 1950, From Here and There (Royal Court) 1955, Jack and the Beanstalk (Bath) 1985, An Ideal Husband (Chichester) 1987, Over My Dead Body (Savoy) 1988; tv and radio incl: Take It From Here 1953-60, Hancock 1956, Benny Hill 1961, Dick Emery 1973, subject of This is Your Life 1976, Terry and June (6 series 1980-), The News Huddlines 1984 and 1991, French and Saunders 1988, Cluedo 1990; films: Carry on Nurse 1958, Spy with the Cold Nose 1966, The Magnificent Seven Deadly Sins 1971, Carry on Abroad 1972, Bless This House 1972, Carry on Girls 1973, Romance with a Double Base 1974, Not Now Comrade 1975; recordings: Up Je T'aime, Wonderful Children's Songs 1972; *Style—* Miss June Whitfield, OBE; April Young Ltd, The Clockhouse, 6 St Catherine's Mews, Milner St, London SW3 2PX (☎ 071 584 1274)

WHITFIELD, Dr Michael; s of Arthur Whitfield (d 1990), of Wirral, Merseyside, and Ethel, *née* Woodward (d 1986); *b* 15 June 1940; *Educ* King's Sch Chester, Univ of Leeds (BSc, PhD); *m* 31 July 1961, Jean Ann (d 1984), da of Stanley Beige Rowe (d 1964); 1 s (Benjamin b 1968), 3 da (Katherine b 1962, Clare b 1964, Juliet b 1965); *Career* res scientist CSIRO Fisheries and Oceanography Sidney Australia 1964-69, dir Marine Biological Assoc Plymouth 1987- (sr princ res scientist 1970-87), dep dir Plymouth Marine Laboratory 1988-; dir: Sir Alister Hardy Fndn for Ocean Sci, NMA/MBA Ltd, Gaia Tst; tstee Estuarine and Coastal Sciences Assoc, memb Royal Soc Ctee for Antarctic Res; FRSC; memb: Freshwater Biological Assoc, Scottish Marine Biological Assoc; *Books* Ion-selective Electrodes for the Analysis of Natural Waters (1970), Marine Electro Chemistry (1981); *Recreations* hill walking, photography, watching wildlife, running; *Style—* Dr Michael Whitfield; The Marine Biological Association of the UK, The Laboratory, Citadel Hill, Plymouth PL1 2PB (☎ 0752 669762, fax 0752 226865)

WHITFIELD, Patrick John; s of Albert Victor Whitfield (d 1978), and Rose Anna, *née* Maye (d 1971); *b* 7 Nov 1931; *Educ* Wandsworth Sch, Kings Coll London, St

George's Hosp Med Sch (MB BS, LRCP); *m* 23 July 1955, Doris Eileen, da of Herbert Nelson Humphries (d 1962); 2 da (Roseanne Louise 8 Sept 1968, Natalie Anne b 17 Nov 1975); *Career* jr hosp appts 1958-64, trained at Regnl Plastic Surgery Centre Queen Mary's Univ Hosp; sr registrar: seconded Plastic Surgery Centre Oxford 1966, Queen Mary's Univ Hosp 1967-72 (seconded to Paris, Rome, NY); conslt plastic surgn Westminster Hosp and SW Thames Regnl Health Authy 1972; recognised teacher in plastic surgery Univ of London (Westminster and Charing Cross Hosps), Plastic Surgery Section RSM 1973-81 (hon sec, memb Cncl, vice pres, pres), memb Res Ctee Br Assoc of Plastic Surgns 1974-77, hon sec Br Assoc of Aesthetic Plastic Surgns 1977-83; FRSM 1968, FRCS; memb: Br Assoc of Plastic Surgns 1972, Br Assoc of Aesthetic Plastic Surgns 1978 (fndr); *Books* Operative Surgery (contrib); *Recreations* golf, scuba-diving, tennis, art appreciation; *Clubs* Athenaeum, Royal Wimbledon Golf; *Style*— Patrick Whitfield, Esq; 17 Harley St, London W1N 1DA (☎ 071 580 6283)

WHITFIELD, Paul Martin; s of Christopher Gilbert Whitfield (d 1968), of Chipping Campden, Glos, and Frances Audrey, *née* Chandler; *b* 9 Dec 1942; *Educ* Stowe, Middle Temple; *m* 1, 3 July 1965, Rowan, da of late Norman Fleming, of Broadway, Worcs; 1 s (Benjamin b 1971), 1 da (Lucy b 1968); m 2, 22 Sept 1982, Alison, da of late Dr I A B Cathie, of Barton House, Warwick; 1 s (Orlando b 1987), 1 da (Lily b 1988); *Career* dep chm W & FC Bonham Ltd (auctioneers) 1987-, dir Christie's International and Group of Companies (resigned 1987); govr Stowe Sch 1980, chm Stowe Garden Bldgs Tst 1986; *Recreations* music, literature; *Clubs* Brooks's; *Style*— Paul Whitfield, Esq; Bonhams, Montpelier Street, London SW7 1HH (☎ 071 584 9161, fax 071 589 4072, car 0836 794 341)

WHITFIELD, Prof Roderick; s of Prof John Humphreys Whitfield, and Joan, *née* Herrin; *b* 20 July 1937; *Educ* King Edward's Sch Birmingham, Sch of Oriental and African Studies, St Johns Coll Cambridge (BA, MA), Princeton Univ (MFA, PhD); *m* 1, 11 July 1963 (m dis 1983), Dr Frances Elizabeth, da of Prof Richard Charles Oldfield; 1 s (Aldus b 1970), 2 da (Martha-Ming b 1965, Tanya b 1967); m 2, 25 Aug 1983, Dr Youngsook Pak; *Career* Offr Cadet Jt Serv Sch for Linguists, RAF 1955-57, PO RAFVR 1957, Flying Offr RAFVR; res assoc and lectr Princeton Univ 1964-66, res fell St John's Coll Cambridge 1966-68, asst keeper 1st class Dept of Oriental Antiquities The Br Museum 1968-84, prof of Chinese and East Asian art Univ of London and head of Percival David Fndn of Chinese Art 1984-; memb Cncl Oriental Ceramic Soc, tstee Inst of Buddhist Studies; *Books* In Pursuit of Antiquity (1969), The Art of Central Asia, The Stein Collection at the British Museum (3 vols, 1982-85), Treasures From Korea (ed 1984), Korean Art Treasures (ed 1986), Caves of the Thousand Buddhas (1990), Fascination of the Universe (1991); *Style*— Prof Roderick Whitfield; Percival David Foundation of Chinese Art, 53 Gordon Square, London WC1H OPD (☎ 071 387 3909)

WHITFORD, Hon Mr Justice; Hon Sir John Norman Keates Whitford; s of Harry Whitford; *b* 24 June 1913; *Educ* Univ Coll Sch, Munich Univ, Peterhouse Cambridge; *m* 1946, Rosemary, da of John Barcham Green by his w Emily Paillard; 4 da; *Career* served WW II RAFVR; QC 1965; High Court judge (Chancery) 1970-, barr: Inner Temple 1935, Middle Temple 1946; chm Departmental Ctee Copyright & Design Law 1974-76; kt 1970; *Style*— The Hon Mr Justice Whitford; Royal Courts of Justice, WC2

WHITHEAR, (Edward) Roy; s of William Albert Henry Whithear, of Englefield Green, Surrey, and Marjorie Edna, *née* King; *b* 10 July 1940; *Educ* Isleworth GS, Sherwood Union HS, Ealing Coll of Higher Educn; *m* Ann Whithear, da of William John Mager; 3 c (Samantha Jane b 8 Feb 1970, Peter James b 20 July 1971, Jonathan Paul b 22 June 1976); *Career* British Airways 1958-65 (apprentice, auditor, systems analyst), dep chief accountant The Observer Ltd 1965-67, sr fin and support mgmnt IBM (UK) 1967-77, dir of fin & admin Kingston RBC 1977-78, fin & admin dir Computer Tech Ltd 1978-80, Gestetner Group 1980-85 (fin dir Operating subsids, gp fin controller, gen mangr Mfrg); Midland Bank Group: sr systems mangr and fin controller Int Banking 1985-87, fin dir Greenwell Montagu Stockbrokers and Smith Keen Cutler 1987-; American Field Serv scholarship 1956-57, Best Apprentice of the Year Br Airways 1960-61; FCCA, FBIM, MCIT, MBCS; *Recreations* association football (Watford FC supporter), theatre; *Clubs* Stocks (Birmingham), Theatregoers of GB; *Style*— Roy Whithear, Esq; Greenwell Montagu Stockbrokers, 114 Old Broad St, London EC2P 2HY (☎ 021 632 1169, fax 021 643 1295)

WHITING, Alan; s of Albert Edward Whiting, and Marjorie Irene, *née* Rodgers; *b* 14 Jan 1946; *Educ* Acklam Hall Secdy GS Middlesbrough, UEA (BA), UCL (MSc); *m* 17 Aug 1968, Annette Frances, da of James Kitchener Pocknee; 2 s (Matthew Peter b 27 June 1977, Paul Michael b 11 Nov 1982), 2 da (Alison Jane b 8 March 1976, Claire Louise b 17 Dec 1979); *Career* res assoc and asst lectr UEA 1967-68, cadet economist HM Treasy 1968-69, economic asst Dept of Econ Affrs Miny of Technol 1969-70; economist: Euro Free Trade Assoc Geneva 1970-72, CBI 1972-73; DTI: econ advsr 1974-78, sr econ advsr 1979-83, Industl and Commercial Policy Div 1983-85, under sec economics 2 div 1985-88, Econ Mgmnt and Educn Div 1989, Fin and Resource Mgmnt Div 1989-; *Books* The Trade Effects of EFTA and the EEC (jtly, 1972), The Economics of Industrial Subsidies (ed, 1975); *Recreations* building, gardening, sport, music; *Clubs* Littleton Sailing; *Style*— Alan Whiting, Esq; c/o Department of Trade & Industry, Ashdown House, 123 Victoria St, London SW1E 6RB (☎ 071 215 6869, fax 071 828 3258, telex 8813148 DIHQG)

WHITING, Prof Brian; s of Leslie George Whiting (d 1971), and Evelyn Irene Edith, *née* Goss; *b* 6 Jan 1939; *Educ* Stockport GS, Univ of Glasgow (MB ChB, MD); *m* Marlene Shields, *née* Watson; 2 da (Gillian b 1969, Lanie b 1971); *Career* RNR 1965-73, ret as Surgn Lt Cdr; visiting prof of clinical pharmacology Univ of California San Francisco 1978-79, dir Clinical Pharmacokinetics Laboratory Dept of Materia Medica Stobhill Gen Hosp 1980- (former res and hosp posts), visiting prof of clinical pharmacology Univ of Auckland NZ 1987, currently dean elect Faculty of Med and head of Div of Clinical Pharmacology Dept of Med and Therapeutics Univ of Glasgow (Dept of Materia Medica 1965-77); pubns on: clinical pharmacology, pharmacokinetics, population pharmacokinetics; clinical sec treas Br Pharmacological Soc, memb Assoc of Physicians of GB and I Ctee on Dental and Surgical Materials; FRCP (Glasgow), FFPM; *Books* Lecture Notes on Clinical Pharmacology (3 edn, 1989); *Recreations* music, painting, photography, mountaineering; *Style*— Prof Brian Whiting; 2 Milner Rd, Jordanhill, Glasgow G13 1QL (☎ 041 959 2324); Dept of Medicine and Therapeutics, University of Glasgow, Stobhill General Hospital, Glasgow G21 3UW (☎ 041 558 0111, fax 041 558 5745)

WHITING, Derek Alan; s of William Thomas Whiting (d 1981), of Beckenham, Kent, and Gladys Dudfield Whiting (d 1970); *b* 2 Aug 1931; *Educ* Tonbridge Sch; *m* 1, 5 June 1962, Lady Frances Esmee, *née* Curzon, da of 5 Earl Howe, PC (d 1964); 2 s (Francis b 1965, Alexander b 1967); m 2, 14 Dec 1972, Angela Clare Forbes, da of Sir Archibald Forbes, GBE, (d 1990) of Orchard Ct, Portman Square, London SW1; *Career* commodity trading & broking 1952-; chm: Int Petroleum Exchange 1985-89, London Sugar Futures Mkt 1984-87, AFBD 1984-87, Comfin Trading Ltd 1980-89, Sucden (UK) Ltd 1980-90; played rugby for: Harlequins (former chm and hon sec), Kent; Liveryman Worshipful Co of Skinners; *Recreations* shooting, squash, golf, reading; *Clubs* Swinley Forest, Hurlingham, Harlequins; *Style*— Derek Whiting, Esq; 4 Gertrude St, London SW10 0JN (☎ 071 352 6220); 5 London Bridge St London SE1 9SG (☎ 071 378 6322, fax 071 378 6556, car 0836 237518, telex 883780/89)

WHITING, Rev Peter Graham; CBE (1984); s of Rev Arthur Whiting, of Wimborne, Dorset, and Olive, *née* Stebbings (d 1986); *b* 7 Nov 1930; *Educ* Yeovil GS, Irish Baptist Coll, Dublin (Dip Theol); *m* 9 Jan 1960, Lorena, da of Albert Inns (d 1982), of Northampton; 2 s (Julian b 1962, Toby b 1964), 3 da (Clare b 1960, Sophie b 1967, Anna b 1973); *Career* cmmnd RAChD 1962, Regtl Chaplain 1962-69, Chaplain 1 Bn Parachute Regt 1964-66, Sr Chaplain 20 Armd Bde BAOR and Lippe Garrison BAOR 1969-72, Staff Chaplain HQ BAOR 1972-74, Sr Chaplain 20 Airportable Bde 1974-75, Dep Asst Chaplain Gen W Midland Dist Shrewsbury 1975-78, Sr Chaplain Young Entry Units 1976-78, Asst Chaplain Gen 1 Br Corps BAOR 1978-81, Dep Chaplain Gen to the Forces (Army) 1981-84; ordained Baptist Minister 1956; minister: Kings Heath Northampton 1956-62, Beechen Grove Baptist Church Watford 1985-; Queen's Hon Chaplain 1981-84; memb Cncl of Churches; *Style*— The Rev P G Whiting, CBE; The Manse, 264 Hempstead Rd, Watford, Herts WD1 3LY (☎ 0923 53 197); Beechen Grove Baptist Church, Clarendon Rd, Watford WD1 1JJ (☎ 0923 241 858)

WHITLAM, Michael Richard; s of Richard William Whitlam (d 1971), and Mary Elizabeth, *née* Land (d 1983); *b* 25 March 1947; *Educ* Moseley GS, Tadcaster GS, Coventry Coll of Educn, Univ of Warwick (Cert of Educn), Cranfield Inst of Technol (MPhil); *m* 24 Aug 1968, Anne Jane, da of William McCurley (d 1987); 2 da (Rowena b 1971, Kirsty b 1973); *Career* former teacher Ripon Co GS; asst govr 1969-74: HM Borstal Hollesley Bay, HM Prison Brixton; dir Hammersmith Teenager Project Nat Assoc of Care and Resettlement of Offenders, dir (former dep dir) Save The Children Fund UK Ops 1978-86, chief exec Royal Nat Inst for Deaf 1986-90, DG British Red Cross 1991-, dir City Literature Inst 1990-; chm: Sound Advantage plc 1989-90, Assoc of Chief Execs of Nat Voluntary Organisations; memb: Exec Cncl Howard League 1974-84, Community Alternative Young Offenders Ctee NACRO 1979-82; chm: London Intermediate Treatment Assoc 1979-82, Nat Intermediate Treatment Assoc 1980-83; memb Exec Cncl Nat Children's Bureau 1980-86, chm Assoc of Chief Execs of Nat Voluntary Orgns 1988-89; *Recreations* painting, walking, keeping fit, family activities; *Style*— Michael Whitlam, Esq; 105 Gower St, London WC1E 6AH (☎ 071 387 8033, fax 071 388 2346, car 0860 366457)

WHITLEY, Air Marshal Sir John Rene; KBE (1956, CBE 1945), CB (1946), DSO (1943), AFC and bar (1937, 1956); s of Arthur Noel Joseph Whitley (d 1940); *b* 7 Sept 1905; *Educ* Haileybury; *m* 1, 1932, Barbara Alice Patricia (d 1965), da of F R Liscombe; 3 s (Christopher, David, Piers) and 1 s (Guy d 1978); m 2, 1967, Alison (d 1986), widow of John Howard Russell, and da of Sir Nigel Campbell (d 1948, s of Adela Harriet, 2 da of Lord Charles Pelham Clinton, 2 s of 4 Duke of Newcastle), sometime jt MFH Old Berkeley; *Career* served RAF 1926-62: India 1932-37, Bomber Cmd 1937-45, Singapore 1946, India 1947, Dir Organisation (Estabs) Air Miny 1948-49, IDC 1950, AO Admin 2 TAF Germany 1951-52, AOC 1 Gp Bomber Cmd 1953-56, air memb Personnel 1957-59, Inspr-Gen RAF 1959-62, ret; controller RAF Benevolent Fund 1962-68; *Recreations* sailing (yacht 'Condette'), fishing, skiing; *Clubs* RAF, Royal Lymington Yacht; *Style*— Air Marshal Sir John Whitley, KBE, CB, DSO, AFC; 2 Woodside Close, Woodside Ave, Lymington, Hants SO41 8FH (☎ 0590 676920)

WHITLEY, Lady Mary Ilona Margaret; *née* Cambridge; o da of 2 and last Marquess of Cambridge, GCVO (d 1981; HSH Prince George of Teck until 1917; himself s of 1 Marquess of Cambridge, 2 Duke of Teck (which latter title was discontinued 1917), by the 1 Marquess's w Lady Margaret Evelyn Grosvenor, da of 1 Duke of Westminster. The 1 Marquess was eldest s of HH the 1 Prince and Duke of Teck, GCB, GCVO, and bro of late Queen Mary. The 1 Marquess's mother was HRH Princess Mary Adelaide, da of HRH 1 Duke of Cambridge, KG, GCB, GCMG, GCH, 7 s of George III) and Dorothy Isabel Westenra, *née* Hastings (d 1988); *b* 24 Sept 1924; *m* 1950, Peter Whitley, s of Sir Norman Henry Pownall Whitley, MC, and Florence May, *née* Erskine; 1 s (Charles Francis Peter b 1961), 1 da (Sarah Elizabeth b 1954, m 1982, Timothy J F Felton; 2 da); *Career* bridesmaid to HM The Queen; *Recreations* bird watching, beagling, gardening, sailing; *Clubs* Boodle's; *Style*— The Lady Mary Whitley; Leighland House, Road Water, Watchet, Somerset TA23 ORP (☎ 0984 40996)

WHITLEY, Hon Mrs (Tara Olivia); *née* Chichester-Clark; da of Baron Moyola (Life Peer); *b* 8 July 1962; *Educ* Sherborne Sch for Girls; *m* 1984, Edward Thomas Whitley, s of John Whitley, of Hamsey Lodge, nr Lewes, E Sussex; *Career* conference and public relations; *Clubs* The Hong Kong; *Style*— The Hon Mrs Whitley; The Old Vicarage, Wilmington, Nr Polegate, East Sussex BN26 5SL

WHITLOCK, Ralph; s of Edwin Whitlock (d 1964), of Pitton, Wilts, and Alice, *née* White (d 1958); *b* 7 Feb 1914; *Educ* Bishop Wordsworth's Sch Salisbury; *m* 1 Nov 1939, Hilda, da of Alexander Pearce (d 1963), of Pitton, Wilts; 1 s (Edward Ralph b 1948), 2 da (Wendy Anne (Mrs Beauchamp) b 1940, Rosalie Margaret (Mrs Price) b 1945); *Career* WWII serv Home Gd; writer; farming in Wilts 1968, agric conslt Methodist Missionary Soc 1968-73; journalist/broadcaster; Western Gazette 1932-, farming corr/farming ed The Field 1946-73, script writer & lead part Cowlease Farm (BBC Children's Hour) 1946-62, res panellist Slightly Quizzical (BBC TV programme) 1971-74, written many plays for BBC incl The Odstock Curse; numerous articles for many magazines and nat newspapers incl: The Times and Daily Telegraph, weekly column The Guardian Weekly 1981-; former co chm Wilts Fedn of Young Farmers' Club 1947, vice pres Salisbury Nat History Soc, memb Guild of Agric Journalists; organiser & ldr pioneer ornithological safari to The Gambia 1971-72, tstee and hon warden Bentley Wood Nature Reserve; *Books* numerous books published incl: nat history: The Great Cattle Plague (1959), Bulls through the Ages (1977), Rare Breeds (1980), Bird Watch in an English Village (1982); folklore: In Search of Lost Gods (1979), Here be Dragons (1984); history: The Everyday Life of the Maya (1976), The Warrior Kings of Saxon England (1977), A Victorian Village (1990), The Secret Life (1990); children's books: Cowleaze Farm, Royal Farmers (a major work prepared with special encouragement from HM The Queen), Gentle Giants, The English Farm, The Lost Village; *Recreations* natural history, writing; *Style*— Ralph Whitlock, Esq; The Penchet, Winterslow, Salisbury, Wilts SP5 1PY (☎ 0980 862 949)

WHITMORE, Sir Clive Anthony; GCB (1988, KCB 1983), CVO 1983; s of Charles Arthur Whitmore, by his w Louisa; *b* 18 Jan 1935; *Educ* Sutton GS, Christ's Coll Cambridge; *m* 1961, Jennifer Mary Thorpe; 1 s, 2 da; *Career* private sec to Perm Under Sec of State War Office 1961, asst private sec to Sec of State for War 1962, princ 1964, private sec to Perm Under Sec of State MOD 1969, asst sec 1971, asst under sec of state (Def Staff) MOD 1975, under sec Cabinet Office 1977, princ private sec to PM 1979-82, perm under sec of state MOD 1983-88; perm under sec of state Home Office 1988-; *Recreations* music, gardening; *Style*— Sir Clive Whitmore, GCB, CVO; Home Office, 50 Queen Anne's Gate, London SW1H 9AT

WHITMORE, Ellis, Lady; Ellis Christense; *née* Johnsen; da of Herr Direktor Knud Christian Johnsen (d 1945), of Bergen, Norway, and Thora Heltberg, *née* Lampe (d 1978); *b* 29 Aug 1904; *Educ* U Phils Coll Bergen Norway; *m* 1 Oct 1931, as his 2 w, Sir Francis Henry Douglas Charlton Whitmore, 1 Bt, KCB, CMG, DSO, TD (d 1962); 1 s (Sir John Henry Douglas, 2 Bt, *qv*), 1 da (Anne Catherine (Mrs D J E O'Connell) b

1933); *Career* DStJ; *Recreations* gardening, canvas embroidery; *Style—* Ellis, Lady Whitmore; c/o Barclays Bank, 155 Beehive Lane, Chelmsford, Essex CM29 9SG

WHITMORE, Sir John Henry Douglas; 2 Bt (UK 1954), of Orsett, Co Essex; s of Col Sir Francis Henry Douglas Charlton Whitmore, 1 Bt, KCB, CMG, DSO, TD (d 1962, maternal gs of Sir William Cradock-Hartopp, 3 Bt, while his paternal grandmother was Lady Louisa Douglas, eldest da of 5 Marquess of Queensberry); *b* 16 Oct 1937; *Educ* Eton; *m* 1, 1962, Ella Gunilla (m dis 1969), da of Sven A Hansson, of Danderyd, Sweden; 1 da; m 2, 1977, Diana Elaine, da of Fred A Becchetti, of Calif; 1 s; *Heir* s, Jason Whitmore b 26 Jan 1983; *Career* sports psychologist, also concerned with psychology of int relations; dep dir Centre for Int Peacebuilding, author of books on the mental aspects of sport, life and work; *Recreations* squash, skiing, motor racing; *Clubs* British Racing Drivers; *Style—* Sir John Whitmore, Bt; Southfield, Leigh, nr Tonbridge, Kent TN11 8PJ (☎ 0732 454490)

WHITNEY, John Norton Braithwaite; s of Dr Willis Bevan Whitney, and Dorothy Anne, *née* Robertson; *b* 20 Dec 1930; *Educ* Leighton Park Friends' Sch Reading; *m* 9 June 1956, Roma Elizabeth Duncan (former dancer with London Festival Ballet), da of George Hodgson; 1 s (Alexander b 31 Jan 1961), 1 da (Fiona b 17 Nov 1958); *Career* radio prodr 1951-64; fndr: Ross Radio Prodns Ltd 1951, Autocue Ltd 1955, Radio Antilles 1963; fndr dir Sagitta Prodns 1968-82; dir: Consolidated Prodns (UK) Ltd 1980-82, Satellite TV plc 1982; md: Capital Radio 1973-82, Really Useful Gp plc 1989- (chm 1990-); dir gen IBA 1982-89, memb Friends Provident Life Office 1982-, chm Friends Provident Stewardship Tst 1985-; fndr Recidivists Anonymous Fellowship Tst 1962, co fndr and chm Local Radio Assoc 1964, chm Assoc Ind Radio Contractors 1973-75 and 1980, dir Duke of Yorks Theatre 1979-82, memb Bd Royal Nat Theatre 1982-; RCM: memb Centenary Devpt Fund (formerly Appeal Ctee) 1982-, chm Media and Events Ctee 1982-; memb: Cncl Royal London Aid Soc 1966-90, Cncl Fairbridge Drake Soc (formerly Drake Fellowship) 1981, Films TV and Video Advsy Ctee Br Cncl 1983-89, Indust and Commerce Liaison Ctee Royal Jubilee Tsts 1986- (memb Admin Cncl of Tsts 1981-85), Intermediate Technol Gp 1982-85, Cncl for Charitable Support 1989-, Bd Open Coll 1987-89; chm tstees: Soundaround (nat sound mag for the blind) 1981-, Artsline 1983-; tstee Venture Tst 1982-86, vice chm Festival 1991 (chm Festival Media Ctee 1991-); vice pres: Cwlth Youth Exchange Cncl 1982-85, RNID 1988-; London Marriage Guidance Cncl 1983-90; pres TV and Radio Industs Club 1985-86 (memb Cncl 1979-), govr English Nat Ballet (formerly London Festival Ballet) 1989-, chm Theatre Investmt Fund 1990-, patron MusicSpace Tst 1990, fell RTS (vice pres 1986-89), hon memb BAFTA, hon fell RCM, memb SWET; FRSA; *Recreations* chess, photography, sculpture; *Clubs* Garrick, Whitefriars, Pilgrims; *Style—* John N B Whitney, Esq; 2 Eaton Gate, London SW1W 9BL (☎ 071 259 9356)

WHITNEY, Raymond William; OBE (1968), MP (C) Wycombe (by-election) April 1978-; o s of late George Whitney, of Northampton; *b* 28 Nov 1930; *Educ* Wellingborough Sch, RMA Sandhurst, Univ of London (BA), Hong Kong and Australia Nat Univs; *m* 1956, Sheila Margot Beswick Prince; 2 s; *Career* RA Northants Regt 1951-64, seconded to Aust Army HQ 1960-63, served Trieste, Korea, Hong Kong, Germany; FO 1964-78: served Peking, head of Chancery Buenos Aires 1969-72, dep high cmmr Dacca 1973-76, head Overseas Info Dept FCO 1977-78; PPS to Treasy Mins 1979-80, vice chm Cons Backbench Employment Ctee 1980-83, chm Cons Foreign Affrs Ctee 1981-83, Parly under sec of state FCO 1983-84; Parly under sec of state for: Social Security 1984-85, Health 1985-86; *Style—* Ray Whitney, Esq, OBE, MP; The Dial House, Sunninghill, Berks SL5 0AG (☎ 0344 23164); House of Commons, London SW1A 0AA (☎ 071 219 3457)

WHITROW, Benjamin John; s of Philip Benjamin Whitrow, TD (d 1966), and Mary Isabella, *née* Flounders (d 1984); *b* 17 Feb 1937; *Educ* Dragon Sch Oxford, Tonbridge, RADA; *m* 13 Jan 1972, Catherine Elizabeth, da of Jack Kenneth Cook (d 1986); 1 s (Thomas George b 1976), 1 da (Hannah Mary b 1973); *Career* Nat Serv King's Dragoon Gds 1956-58; actor; debut Liverpool Playhouse 1959; rep work Birmingham, Bristol, Harrogate; joined NT under Sir Laurence Olivier 1967-74; West End appearances incl: Otherwise Engaged (1975), Dirty Linen (1976), Ten Times Table (1978), What the Butler Saw (1979), Passion Play (1982), Noises Off (1983), A Little Hotel on the Side (NT, 1984), Uncle Vanya (1988); films incl: Clockwise, Personal Services, Quadrophenia, On the Black Hill, A Shocking Accident (Oscar for Best Short Film 1982); TV work incl: Ffizz, Chancer, J R Ackerley in We Think the World of You (1980), Ulysses in Troilus and Cressida (BBC), A Litle Bit of Singing and Dancing (Granada), Natural Causes (Yorkshire TV), By George (BBC), The Devil's Disciple (BBC), Bergerac (BBC), Hay Fever (BBC), Harry's Game (Yorkshire TV), Chancer (Central TV); radio work incl: comedy series After Henry, own adaptation Mary Russell Mitford's Letters, own adaptation My Grandfather and Father Dear Father by Dennis Constanduras; *Recreations* golf, reading, bridge; *Clubs* Richmond Golf; *Style—* Benjamin Whitrow, Esq; c/o 91 Regent St, London W1 (☎ 071 439 1456)

WHITSEY, Fred; *b* 18 July 1919; *m* 1947, Patricia Searle; *Career* ed Popular Gardening 1967-82 (asst ed 1948-64, assoc ed 1964-67); gardening corr: Sunday Telegraph 1961-71, Daily Telegraph 1971-; contrib Country Life and The Garden; Gold Veitch Meml Medal 1979, Victoria Medal of Honour 1986; *Books* Sunday Telegraph Gardening Book (1966), Fred Whitsey's Garden Calendar (1985); *Recreations* music, gardening; *Style—* Fred Whitsey; Avens Mead, 20 Oast Rd, Oxted, Surrey RH8 9DU

WHITSON, Harold Alexander; CBE (1968); s of Ralph A Whitson (d 1949), of Carlton, Symington, Lanarks, and Annie Laura Morton Greig (d 1970); *b* 20 Sept 1916; *Educ* Rugby, Cambridge Univ (BA); *m* 1942, Rowena, da of George Stanhope Pitt, of Broadlands, Warlingham, Surrey; 1 s (and 1 s decd), 2 da (and 1 da decd); *Career* former pres Glasgow C of C; former chm: M D W (Holdings) Ltd, Public Construction Co, Irvine New Town Development Corporation, Scottish Mutual Assurance Society; dir Ailsa Investment Trust Ltd; *Recreations* gardening, shooting; *Clubs* East India, New (Edinburgh), RSAC; *Style—* Harold Whitson, Esq, CBE; Edmonston House, Biggar, Lanarks (☎ 0899 20063)

WHITSON, Keith Roderick; s of William Cleghorn Whitson, and Ellen, *née* Wade; *b* 25 March 1943; *Educ* Alleyn's Sch Dulwich; *m* 26 July 1968, Sabine Marita, da of Ulrich Wiechert; 1 s (Mark James b 26 July 1980), 2 da (Claudia Sharon b 31 Aug 1971, Julia Caroline b 2 May 1973); *Career* The Hong Kong and Shanghai Banking Corporation 1961-: mangr Frankfurt 1978-80, mangr Indonesia 1981-84, asst gen mangr fin Hong Kong 1985-87, chief exec offr UK 1987-89; exec dir Marine Midland Banks Inc, chm Carroll McEntee and McGinley Inc; chm Concord Leasing USA; dir Euro-Clear Clearance Systems 1987; *Style—* Keith Whitson, Esq; Marine Midland Banks Inc, One Marine Midland Center, Buffalo, NY 14203 (☎ 010 1 716 841 7381)

WHITSON, Cmdt Thomas Jackson; OBE; s of Thomas Whitson, QPM (d 1974), of Springlea, Aberlady, E Lothian, and Susan, *née* Steele; *b* 5 Sept 1930; *Educ* North Berwick HS, Knox Acad; *m* 5 Sept 1953, Patricia Marion, da of Robert Bugden (d 1968), of Soutra, Fair Oak, Hants; 2 s (Kenneth b 17 June 1956, Kevan b 19 Dec 1958); *Career* RN 1949-51; chief supt Lothian and Borders Police 1976-80, dep chief constable Central Scotland Police 1980-87, cmdt Scottish Police Coll; memb Rotary Club of Polmont; *Recreations* golf, curling, reading; *Style—* Cmdt Thomas Whitson, OBE; Tulliallan Castle, Kincardine, Alloa FK10 4BE (☎ 0259 30333)

WHITTAKER, (George) Anthony; s of George Whittaker (d 1980), by his w Muriel (d 1975); *b* 10 May 1930; *Educ* McGill Univ Montreal (BEng), Inst of Technol Charlottesville Virginia USA (MS); *m* 1964, Elizabeth Anne, da of R E Smyth; 1 s, 2 da; *Career* 2 Lt REME; dir: Smith and Nephew Overseas Ltd 1956-63, Deering Milliken Ltd 1963-68 (and int vice pres), Guinness Peat Group Ltd 1968-82, Robin Marlar Ltd 1983-84; non-exec dir: Spillers Ltd 1979-80, Albert Fisher Group plc 1982-, Norman Reeves plc 1983-86, Edeco Holdings Ltd 1985-89, UK Paper plc 1988-90; md Grosvenor Place Amalgamations Ltd 1982-; chm: Bright Walton Homes plc 1986-, Corroless International Ltd 1987-88 (dir 1984-87); *Recreations* cricket, walking, fishing; *Clubs* MCC, IOD; *Style—* G Anthony Whittaker, Esq; Grosvenor Place Amalgamations Ltd, Flat 8, 28 Ormonde Gate, London SW3 4HA (☎ 071 376 5282)

WHITTAKER, Geoffrey Owen; OBE (1974, MBE 1963); s of Alfred James Whittaker (d 1971), of Nottingham, and Gertrude Austin, *née* Holvey (d 1984); *b* 10 Jan 1932; *Educ* Nottingham HS, Univ of Bristol (BA); *m* 6 April 1959, Annette Faith, da of Percy Thomas Harris (d 1977), of Market Harborough; 1 s (Ian b 1965), 1 da (Fiona b 1962); *Career* HM Overseas Audit Service 1956-67: auditor Tanganyika, princ auditor Windward Is 1960-64, dir of audit Grenada 1964-67; audit advsr Br Honduras 1967-69, colonial treasurer St Helena 1970-75, financial sec and dep govr Montserrat 1975-78, financial sec Br Virgin Is 1978-80, admin offr Hong Kong 1980-87, govr Anguilla 1987-89; *Recreations* music, heraldry, genealogy, country pursuits; *Clubs* Royal Commonwealth; *Style—* Geoffrey Whittaker, Esq, OBE; 2 Hall Lane, Ashley, Northants (☎ 085 883 312)

WHITTAKER, (Thomas) Geoffrey; s of Maj William Whittaker (d 1983), and Nellie May, *née* Crabtree; *b* 2 March 1937; *Educ* Ermysted's Sch Skipton, Lincoln Coll Oxford (MA), London Coll of Violinists; *m* 8 Nov 1960, Florence McKay, da of John Glasgow (d 1943); 2 s (William Robert b 1961, Edward Norman b 1963), 1 da (Katherine Margaret (Mrs Saner) b 1966); *Career* Nat Serv radar tech Cyprus 1955-57; dir and gen mangr Harlander Coats AG Austria 1969, md Laidlaw & Fairgrieve Scotland 1983, dir Invergordon Distillers plc Scotland 1983-; playing memb Edinburgh Symphony Orch; memb: Galashiels Mfrs Corp 1975, Soc of Coopers of Glasgow 1984, Keepers of the Quaich 1988, Br Wool Textiles Export Cncl; former deacon Galashiels Mfrs Assoc, former chm Scottish Wool Spinners Fedn; Liveryman: Worshipful Co of Grocers of Paisley 1962, Glasgow Co of Coopers 1984; Freeman Citizen of Glasgow at Far Hand 1984; *Recreations* music, bridge; *Clubs* Caledonian (Edinburgh); *Style—* Geoffrey Whittaker, Esq; Beechlaw Langside Drive, Peebles, Tweeddale EH45 8RF (☎ 0721 214 52); Invergordon Distillers Ltd, 21 Salamander Place, Leith, Edinburgh (☎ 031 554 4404)

WHITTAKER, Malcolm George; s of Rev George Henry Whittaker, of Ilkley, Yorks, and Katherine Clarissa, *née* Salter; *b* 24 Dec 1937; *Educ* Ermysteds GS Skipton Yorks, Univ of Leeds (MB ChB), Univ of Glasgow, Univ of London; *m* 22 March 1969, Susan Jane, *née* Allan; 1 s (James Benjamin b 17 Aug 1976), 1 da (Helen Rachel b 1 Feb 1971); *Career* lectr in surgery UCH London, currently sr conslt surgn Darlington and Northallerton Health Dists and hon clinical lectr in surgery Univ of Newcastle upon Tyne; vice pres section of surgery RSM, memb Societe Internationale de Chirurgie; FRCS, FRCSEd; *Recreations* walking, reading, skiing; *Clubs* Royal Automobile, Kandahar; *Style—* Malcolm Whittaker, Esq; 12 Southend Ave, Darlington (☎ 0325 484293)

WHITTAKER, Michael William Joseph; s of Harry Whittaker, of Dorchester, and Hylda, *née* Roach; *b* 28 Jan 1941; *Educ* Norman Coll Chester, Miller Acad Thurso, Weymouth and Brunel Tech Coll Bristol; *m* 8 Aug 1972, Brenda Pauline, da of Thomas Marsh (d 1987), of Thurnscoe, Yorks; 2 da (Helena Amanda b 7 March 1963, Lindsay Jane b 30 Dec 1974); *Career* British Aerospace (Dynamics) Ltd: sr design engr, private light aircraft projects, 5 aircraft designed and developed 1973-89, 36 flying MW6 microlight manufactured under licence; winner numerous design awards; CEng, MIMechE, FRAes; *Recreations* playing the 5 string banjo, design and development of light aircraft; *Style—* Michael Whittaker, Esq; Dawlish Cottage, Pincots Lane, Wickwar, Wotton under Edge, Gloucestershire GL12 8NY (☎ 0454 294598); British Aerospace Dynamics Ltd, PO Box 5, Filton, Bristol BS12 7QW (☎ 027236 6320)

WHITTAKER, Nigel; *b* 1948; *Educ* Univ of Cambridge, Yale Law Sch; *Career* barr; in-house lawyer Hoffman La Roche, Gen Cncl Br Sugar, exec dir Kingfisher plc 1983- (joined 1982); chm CBI's Distributive Trades Survey Panel, hon treas Br Retailers Assoc; *Style—* Nigel Whittaker, Esq; Kingfisher plc, North West House, 119 Marylebone Rd, London NW1 5PX (☎ 071 724 7749, fax 071 723 9489)

WHITTAKER, Roger Henry Brough; s of Edward Whittaker, and Valda Viola, *née* Showan; *b* 22 March 1936; *Educ* Prince of Wales Sch Nairobi Kenya, Univ of Cape Town SA, Univ of Wales Bangor (BSc); *m* 15 Aug 1964, Natalie Deirdre, da of Edward (Toby) O'Brien (d 1979); 2 s (Edward Guy b 1974, Alexander Michael b 1978), 3 da (Emily, Claire b 1968, Lauren Marie b 1970, Jessica Jane b 1973); *Career* Nat Serv Kenya Regt in Kenya, TA; singer/songwriter; first recorded hit Steelmen (1962), first continental hit If I were a Richman, Mexican Whistler (1967), first UK hit Durham Town (1969), I Don't Believe In If Anymore (1970), New World in the Morning (1970), What Love Is (1971), Why (1971), Mammy Blue (1971); first USA hit The Last Farewell (1976), over 11 million copies sold worldwide, earning major acclaim throughout Europe, Canada, Australia, N Zealand and the third world; Skye Boat Song (with Des O' Connor) 1986; TV series incl: Whittaker's World of Music (LWT 1971), Hallelujah It's Christmas (Thames 1975), Roger Whittaker Show (Westward 1977) Sing Out (Ulster 1987); tv specials in Denmark, Germany, Canada, USA, Australia; Films inc Roger Whittaker in Kenya (a musical safari) SOS (Stars Orgn for Spastics), Birthright (fund raising aim of Royal Soc of Gynaecologists), Rescue the Rhino, Lords Taverners, Br Acad of Songwriters and Composers; L'Invite d'Honneur (Juan Les Pins, Antibes) 1971, key to the City of Atlanta 1975; hon citizen: Baltimore 1978, Winnipeg 1978, Houston 1983, Lowell Mass 1985; B'Nai B'Rith Humanitarian award 1980, Ambassador of Goodwill (Chatanooga) 1983, Seal of the Cwlth of Mass 1985, Gold badge of Merit Basca 1988; MCPS (pres); *Books* So Far So Good; *Recreations* squash, golf, fishing, photography, backgammon, gardening; *Style—* Roger Whittaker, Esq; Kensington (☎ 071 937 1040)

WHITTALL, (Harold) Astley; CBE (1978); s of Harold Whitall, and Margaret Whittall; *b* 8 Sept 1925; *Educ* Handsworth GS, Tech Coll Birmingham; *m* 1952, Diana Margharita Berner; *Career* former chm Amalgmated Power Engrg; former pres Engrg Employers' Fedn; chm: Ransomes plc, BSG Int plc, Turriff Corp plc; trg bd dir APV holdings plc; dir: Sykes Pickervant Holdings plc, Bain Clarkson Ltd, R Platnauer Ltd; chm BRISCC (Br Iron & Steel Consumers Cncl); CEng, FIMechE, FI ProdE, FIMarE, CBIM; *Recreations* shooting; *Clubs* RAC, IOD; *Style—* Astley Whittall, Esq, CBE

WHITTEMORE, Prof Colin Trengove; s of Hugh Ashcroft Whittemore (d 1983), of Mollington, Chester, and Dorothea, *née* Nance; *b* 16 July 1942; *Educ* Rydal Sch Colwyn Bay, Univ of Newcastle upon Tyne (BSc, PhD, DSc, NDA); *m* 24 Sept 1966, Christine, da of John Leslie Featherstone Fenwick (d 1964), of Corbridge, Northumberland; 1 s (Jonathan b 1974), 3 da (Joanna b 1970, Emma b 1976, Rebecca b 1985); *Career* head of Animal Prodn Advsy And Devpt E of Scotland Coll of Agric 1978-84, head of Animal Sci Div Edinburgh Sch of Agric 1984-90, head of Dept of

Agric Univ of Edinburgh 1989-90 (lectr in agric 1970-78, prof of animal prodn 1984-90); head Univ of Edinburgh Inst of Ecology and Resource Mgmnt 1990- (prof of agric and rural economy 1990-); Sir John Hammond Prize, RASE Gold Medal, Mignini Oscar and David Black award for scientific contribs and res; memb: Community Cncl, BSAP; FIBiol; *Books* Lactation (1980), Pig Production (1980), Pig Science (1987); *Recreations* skiing, horses; *Clubs* Farmers; *Style—* Prof Colin Whittemore; Dept of Agriculture, University of Edinburgh, West Mains Rd, Edinburgh EH9 3JG (☎ 031 667 1041, fax 031 667 2601, telex 727617)

WHITTERIDGE, Sir Gordon Coligny; KCMG (1964, CMG 1956), OBE (1946); s of Walter Whitteridge; *b* 6 Nov 1908; *Educ* Whitgift Sch Croydon, Cambridge Univ; *m* 1, 1938, Margaret Lungley (d 1942); 1 s, 1 da (decd); m 2, 1951, Jane (d 1979), da of Frederick Driscoll, of Mass, USA; 1 s; m 3, 1983, Mrs Jill Stanley, da of Bertram Belcham; *Career* joined Consular Serv 1932, 1 sec Moscow 1948-49, consul-gen Stuttgart 1949-51, cnsllr Bangkok 1951-56, consul-gen: Seattle 1956-60, Istanbul 1960-62; ambass: Burma 1962-65, Afghanistan 1965-68; hon treas Soc Afghan Studies 1972-; *Clubs* Travellers'; *Style—* Sir Gordon Whitteridge, KCMG, OBE

WHITTINGDALE, John Flasby Lawrance; OBE (1990); s of John Whittingdale (d 1974), and Margaret Esmé Scott, *née* Napier; *b* 16 Oct 1959; *Educ* Winchester, UCL (BSc); *m* 1990, Ancilla Campbell Murfitt; *Career* head of political section Cons Res Dept 1982-84, special advsr to Sec of State for Trade and Indust 1984-87, mangr NM Rothschild 1987, political sec to PM 1988-90; *Clubs* Reform; *Style—* John Whittingdale, Esq, OBE; c/o Reform Club, 104 Pall Mall, London SW1

WHITTINGHAM, Michael; s of Francis Sadler Whittingham (d 1972), of London, and Jean Mary, *née* Tarlton (d 1989); *b* 11 June 1954; *Educ* Alleyn's Sch Dulwich, Univ of Leicester (BA, MA), Univ of Loughborough (PGCE); *m* Christine Paterson, da of Alexander McMeekin; *Career* athletics coach; memb Herne Hill Harriers; represented: London Schs, English Schs, Surrey Co, Southern Cos, Br Univs, 25 GB caps (400m hurdles, 800m, 4 x 400m); best performances: semi-final Euro Indoor Championships 1981, fourth Cwlth Games 1982; nat sr event coach 400m 1990- (jr event coach 400m hurdles 1987-88); coach to: Roger Black, Kriss Akabusi; Christine McMeekin, Jacqui Parker, Claire Bleasdale, Colin Anderson, Paul Beaumont, Maria Akara; Coach of the Month PO Counters Oct 1990; lectr Univ of Lyon France 1978-80, teacher 1980-85, dir of sport and physical educn 1985-88, head of leisure servs Waverley Borough Cncl 1988-; Winston Churchill fell 1990; memb:L Inst of Leisure Amenity Mgmnt, Int Athletics Club, Nat Tst; *Recreations* languages, piano, reading, arts, natural history, recreational sport; *Style—* Michael Whittingham, Esq; Rhodens, The Green Sands, Farnham, Surrey GU10 1LL (☎ 02518 2223); BAAB, Edgbaston House, 3 Duchess Place, Hagley Rd, Edgbaston, Birmingham B16 8NM

WHITTINGTON, Prof Geoffrey; s of Bruce Whittington (d 1988), and Dorothy Gwendoline, *née* Gent; *b* 21 Sept 1938; *Educ* Sir Roger Manwood's GS, Dudley GS, LSE, Fitzwilliam Coll Cambridge; *m* 7 Sept 1963, Joyce Enid, da of George Smith (d 1963); 2 s (Alan Geoffrey b 1972, Richard John b 1976); *Career* res posts Dept of Applied Economics Cambridge 1962-72, fell Fitzwilliam Coll Cambridge 1966-72; prof of accountancy and finance: Univ of Edinburgh 1972-75, Univ of Bristol 1975-88; Univ of Bristol: head of Dept of Economics 1981-84, dean Faculty of Social Sciences 1985-87; Price Waterhouse prof of fin accounting Univ of Cambridge 1988-, fell Fitzwilliam Coll Cambridge 1988-; memb: MMC 1987-, Ctees and Working Ptys of ICAEW and Accounting Standards Ctee; fell Centre for Econ Policy Res, academic advsr to Accounting Standards Bd 1990-; ACA 1964, FCA 1974; *Books* Growth Profitability and Valuation (with A Singh, 1968), The Prediction of Profitability (1971), Inflation Accounting (1983), The Debate on Inflation Accounting (with D Tweedie, 1984); *Recreations* music, squash, badminton, walking; *Style—* Prof Geoffrey Whittington; Faculty of Economics and Politics, Austin Robinson Building, Sidgwick Ave, Cambridge CB1 4RT (☎ 0223 335209, fax 0223 335299)

WHITTINGTON, Dr Graeme; s of Walter Whittington (d 1985), and Ethel Elizabeth Garrett (d 1985); *b* 25 July 1931; *Educ* King Edward VI Sch Guildford, Univ of Reading (BA, PhD); *Career* Ernest Ridley scholar Univ of Reading 1956-59, visiting lectr Univ of Natal 1971, chm Dept of Geography and Geology Univ of St Andrews 1987- (lectr 1959-72, sr lectr 1972-80, reader 1980-, chm Dept of Geography 1985-87); FRGS 1963, memb Inst Br Geographers 1963; *Books* Environment and Land Use in Africa (jt ed with M F Thomas, 1969), An Historical Geography of Scotland (jt ed with I D Whyte, 1983); *Recreations* gardening; *Style—* Dr Graeme Whittington; Department of Geography and Geology, The University, St Andrews, Fife (☎ 0334 76161, telex 76213, fax 0334 74674)

WHITTINGTON, Dr Richard Michael; s of Dr Theodore Henry Whittington (d 1982), and Cecily Grace, *née* Woodman (d 1973); *b* 9 Sept 1929; *Educ* St Edwards Sch Oxford, Oriel Coll Oxford (MA); *m* 1954, Dorothy Margaret, da of William Fraser Darroch Gardner (d 1977); 1 s (Richard), 1 da (Alison); *Career* HM Coroner Birmingham and Solihull 1976; dir Parly Advsy Ctee on Tport Safety 1980; univ physician Aston Univ 1985; author of numerous papers related to sudden death in med jls; memb Br Acad of Forensic Sci, FRSM; *Recreations* contract bridge, country walking; *Style—* Dr Richard Whittington; Clanrickarde House, 11 Four Oaks Rd, Sutton Coldfield, W Midlands B74 2XP; Coroners Court, Newton St, Birmingham B4 6NE (☎ 021 236 6646)

WHITTLE, Air Cdre Sir Frank; OM (1986), KBE (1948, CBE 1944), CB (1947); *b* 1 June 1907; *Educ* Leamington Coll, RAF Coll Cranwell, Peterhouse Cambridge (MA); *m* 1, 1930 (m dis 1976), Dorothy Lee; 2 s; m 2, 1976, Hazel Hall; *Career* served RAF 1928-48, former test pilot and involved in devpt of jet engine; former hon tech advsr BOAC and Shell Group; former conslt Bristol Siddeley & Rolls Royce; memb Faculty US Naval Acad Annapolis Maryland 1977-; FRS, FEng, Hon FRAeS, Hon FAeSI, Hon FIMechE, Hon FAIAA, hon fell Peterhouse Cambridge; Hon DSc: Oxford, Manchester, Leicester, Bath, Warwick, Exeter; Hon LLD Edinburgh; Hon ScD Cantab, Hon DTech Trondheim; US Legion of Merit (Cdr) 1946; *Style—* Air Cdre Sir Frank Whittle, OM, KBE, CB; 10327 Wilde Lake Terrace, Columbia, MD 21044, USA

WHITTLE, Prof Peter; s of Percy Whittle (d 1970), and Elsie, *née* Tregurtha; *b* 27 Feb 1927; *Educ* Wellington Boys Coll NZ, Univ of NZ (BSc, MSc), Uppsala Univ Sweden (PhD); *m* 20 May 1951, Kathe Hildegard, da of Viktor Blomquist, of Raisio, Finland; 3 s (Martin b 1952, Miles b 1955, Gregory b 1961), 3 da (Lorna b 1954, Jennifer b 1962, Elsie b 1968); *Career* scientist Uppsala Univ 1951-53, NZ DSIR 1953-59 (ultimately sr princ scientific offr), lectr Univ of Cambridge 1959-61, prof of mathematical statistics Univ of Manchester 1961-67, Churchill prof of mathematics of operational res Univ of Cambridge 1967-; Hon DSc Victoria Univ NZ 1982; memb Royal Soc NZ, FRS 1978; *Books* Hypothesis Testing in Time Series Analysis (1951), Prediction and Regulation (1963), Probability (1970), Optimisation under Constraints (1971) Optimisation over Time (vol 1 1982, vol 2 1983) Systems in Stochastic Equilibrium (1986), Risk-Sensitive Optimal Control (1990); *Recreations* home maintenance; *Style—* Prof Peter Whittle, FRS; 268 Queen Edith's Way, Cambridge CB1 4NL (☎ 0223 245422); Statistical Laboratory, 16 Mill Lane, Cambridge CB2 1SB (☎ 0223 337965, telex 81240 CAMSPL G, fax 0223 337920)

WHITTY, (John) Lawrence; s of Frederick James Whitty (d 1981), and Kathleen May Whitty (d 1967); *b* 15 June 1943; *m* 11 Jan 1969 (m dis 1986), Tanya Margaret, da of Tom Gibson; 2 s (Michael Sean b 1970, Daniel James b 1972); *Career* Hawker Siddeley 1962; Civil Serv 1965-70, Miny of Aviation, UKAEA, Miny of Technol; Economics Dept TUC 1970-73, nat res and political offr GMBATU (formerly Gen and Municipal Workers Union) 1973-85, gen sec Lab Pty 1985-; memb: Lab Pty (Islington, Greenwich, Dulwich, Peckham), Fabian Soc; *Recreations* swimming, walking, theatre; *Style—* Lawrence Whitty, Esq; 64 Coleman Rd, London SE5 7TG; Labour Party, 150 Walworth Rd, London, SE17 (☎ 071 703 0833)

WHITWELL, Michael; s of Donald Edward Whitwell, of Bristol, and Doris Evelyn, *née* Vowles (d 1974); *b* 7 Sept 1934; *Educ* Fairfield GS Bristol; *m* 22 March 1958, Ruby Anne, da of William John Smith (d 1972); 2 s (Ian b 1961, Christopher b 1968), 1 da (Claire b 1963); *Career* financial controller Tyndall GP Ltd 1967, chief exec Jordon Group Ltd 1986 (financial dir), dir The West of England Trust Ltd 1986; FCCA 1958, ATII 1959, FCA 1968; *Recreations* swimming, golf, reading, gardening; *Style—* Michael Whitwell, Esq; 17 Lindsay Road, Horfield, Bristol BS7 9NP (☎ 0272 516071); Jordan Group Limited, 21 St Thomas Street, Bristol BS1 6JS (☎ 0272 230600, fax 0272 230063, telex 4149119)

WHITWORTH, Francis John; s of late Capt Herbert Francis Whitworth, OBE, RNVR, and Helen Marguerite, *née* Tait; *b* 1 May 1925; *Educ* Charterhouse, Pembroke Coll Oxford (Holford scholar, MA); *m* 1956, Auriol Myfanwy Medwyn Hughes; 1 s, 1 da; *Career* War Service Royal Marines 1943-46; called to the Bar Middle Temple 1950, personnel dir Cunard Steamship Co 1965 (joined 1950), md Cunard Line 1968 (gp admin dir 1969), dep dir industl rels Br Shipping Fedn 1972, dep dir gen Cncl of Br Shipping 1980-87, dir Int Shipping Fedn 1980-88, memb Econ and Social Ctee of Euro Communities 1986-, chm Merchant Navy Offrs' Pension Fund Tstees 1987-; chm: Int Ctee of Passenger Lines 1968-71, Atlantic Passenger Steamship Conf 1970-71, Employers' Gp Jt Maritime Cmmn ILO 1980-88, Emplolyers' Gp Int Maritime (Labour) Conf ILO 1986-87, Social Affrs Ctee Comité des Assocs d'Amateurs des Communautes Européennes 1983-88, Nat Sea Trg Schs 1980-87; memb: Nat Maritime Bd 1962-87, Industl Tbnls for Eng and Wales 1978-, Cncl Marine Soc 1988-, Cncl Missions to Seamen 1988-; FBIM 1980 (MBIM 1970); *Recreations* racing, opera, music, cricket; *Clubs* United Oxford & Cambridge Univ; *Style—* F J Whitworth, Esq; The Old School House, Farley Chamberlayne, Romsey, Hampshire SO51 0QR

WHITWORTH, John Vincer; s of Hugh Hope Aston Whitworth, of 47 Orford Gardens, Strawberry Hill, Middlesex, and Elizabeth, *née* Boyes (d 1959); *b* 11 Dec 1945; *Educ* Royal HS Edinburgh, Merton Coll Oxford (MA, BPhil), Univ of Edinburgh; *m* 2 Aug 1975, Doreen Ann, da of Cecil Roberts; 2 da (Eleanor Ruth b 1 Jan 1984, Catherine Rebecca b 20 March 1987); *Career* poet; teacher of: English Colchester English Studies Centre 1970-71, business studies and economics Centre of Economic and Political Studies 1971-82; exec dir until 1982 (co bankrupted); *Volumes* Unhistorical Fragments (1980), Poor Butterflies (1982), Lovely Day for a Wedding (1985), Tennis and Sex and Death (1989), The Faber Book of Blue Verse (ed, 1990); Awards: Alice Hunt Bartlett award of the Poetry Society 1980, South East Arts award 1980, Poor Butterflies (an Observer Book of the Year) 1982, Barbara Campion Memorial prize 1983, prize in National Poetry Competition 1984, Cholmondeley award for poetry 1988; *Recreations* cooking, playing with my daughters, suffering with the England cricket team, supporting Middlesex CCC; *Style—* John Whitworth, Esq; 20 Lovell Rd, Rough Common, Canterbury, Kent CT2 9DG (☎ 0227 462400)

WHITWORTH, Maj-Gen Reginald Henry; CB (1969), CBE (1963); s of Aymer William Whitworth (d 1976), and Alice Lucy Patience, *née* Hervey (d 1973, gda of Lord Arthur Hervey (d 1894), Bishop of Bath and Wells and s of 1 Marquis of Bristol); *b* 27 Aug 1916; *Educ* Eton, Balliol Coll and Queen's Coll Oxford; *m* 1946, June Rachel, da of Col Sir Bartle Mordaunt Edwards, CVO, MC, JP, DL, (d 1977), of Hardingham Hall, Norfolk; 2 s (and 1 decd), 1 da; *Career* Grenadier Gds 1940, GSO3 1944, Bde Maj 24 Gds Bde 1945-46, instr Staff Coll Camberley 1953-55; Cdr: 1 Grenadier Gds 1956-57, Berlin Inf Bde Gp 1961-63, GOC Yorks and Northumberland Dists 1966-68, COS Southern Cmd 1968-70; fell and bursar Exeter Coll Oxford 1970-81; chm: St Mary's Sch Wantage, Army Museums Ogilby Tst; tstee Historic Churches Preservation Tst; USA Bronze Star 1946; *Books* Field Marshal Earl Ligonier, Famous Regiments: The Grenadier Guards; Gunner at Large (1988); *Recreations* riding, fishing, military history; *Clubs* Army and Navy; *Style—* Maj-Gen Reginald Whitworth, CB, CBE; Abbey Farm, Goosey, Oxon (☎ 03677 252)

WHORWELL, Dr Peter James; s of Arthur Victor Whorwell, of Canterbury, and Beryl Elizabeth, *née* Walton; *b* 14 June 1946; *Educ* Dover Coll, Univ of London (BSc, MB BS, MD); *Career* conslt physician and sr lectr in med Univ of Manchester 1981-; numerous pubns on gastrointestinal diseases; memb: Br Soc Gastroenterology, American Gastroenterology Assoc; FRCP 1988; *Style—* Dr Peter Whorwell; 33 Bow Green Rd, Bowdon, Cheshire WA14 3LF (☎ 061 447 3826); Dept of Medicine, Univ Hosp of Manchester, Manchester M20 8LR (☎ 061 447 3826)

WHYBREW, Edward Graham (Ted); s of Ernest Whybrew (d 1968), and Winifred Maud, *née* Castle (d 1968); *b* 25 Sept 1938; *Educ* Hertford GS, Balliol Coll Oxford (BA, soccer and cricket first elevens), Nuffield Coll Oxford (studentship); *m* 9 Sept 1967, Julia Helen, da of Michael Baird (d 1969); 1 s (Adam b 1970), 2 da (Katherine b 1973, Anna b 1975); *Career* econ advsr: NEDO 1963-64, Dept of Econ Affrs 1964-69; Dept of Employment: econ advsr 1969-73, sr advsr 1973-77, asst sec youth and employment policy 1977-81, asst sec industl rels 1981-85, under sec industl rels, pay and equal opportunities 1985-89, under sec Dir of Personnel 1989-; treas Triangle Adventure Playground Assoc 1973-; *Recreations* horseriding, gardening, cricket; *Style—* Ted Whybrew, Esq; Department of Employment, Caxton House, Tothill St, London SW1 (☎ 071 273 5785, fax 071 273 5787)

WHYBROW, Christopher John; s of Herbert William Whybrow, OBE (d 1973), of Colchester, Essex, and Ruby Kathleen, *née* Watson; *b* 7 Aug 1942; *Educ* Colchester Royal GS, King's Coll London (LLB); *m* 1, 11 Sep 1969 (m dis 1976), Marian, da of John Macaulay, of Ramsey, Essex; m 2, 4 April 1979 (m dis 1990), Susan, da of Edward Christie Younge, of Loddiswell, Devon; *Career* called to the Bar Inner Temple 1965; *Recreations* cricket, tennis, country life; *Clubs* Lansdowne; *Style—* Christopher Whybrow, Esq; Spring Farm, Leavenheath, Suffolk; 2 Mitre Court Buildings, Temple, London EC4Y 7BX

WHYHAM, Christopher Russell; s of Whyham Russell Littledale Whyham (d 1966), of 1 Berwick Rd, Blackpool, Lancs, and Dorothy, *née* Birchall; *b* 4 July 1940; *Educ* Arnold Sch Blackpool, Univ of Manchester, Blackpool Tech Coll, Univ of Salford; *m* 1, 22 Aug 1964, Sandra Catherine Irving (d 1970), da of Frederick Irving Harris, of 35 North Park Dr, Blackpool, Lancs; 1 s (Iain b 1967), 1 da (Catherine b 1970); m 2, Jane Lesley, *née* Murdoch (d 1978); m 3, Mary Christine, *née* Abbott; *Career* engrg apprentice Eng Electric Aviation Warton Lancs 1960, engr Wind Tunnel Dept BAC Warton 1962, co dir and chief engr Air Navigation and Trading Co Ltd Blackpool Airport 1966- (engr 1965), ptnr and chief engr C and J Aviation Servs 1977-; CEng, MRAeS 1972, licensed aircraft engr (categories A, B, C and X); *Recreations* photography, speleology, walking, squash, (wild life) gardening, flying; *Style—* Christopher Whyham, Esq; Fairview, Mains Lane, Little Singleton, Lancashire FY6 7LD (☎ 0253 893571); Air Navigation & Trading Co Ltd, Blackpool Airport, Blackpool, Lancs FY4 2QS (☎ 0253 45396, fax 0253 45396)

WHYTE, Derek; s of Edward Henry Whyte, of Cumbernauld, and Sarah Ann, *née* McKinnon; *b* 31 Aug 1968; *Educ* Abronhill HS; *m* 2 March 1966, Wilma, da of John Donnachie; 1 da (Chelsey Marie b 30 Aug 1990); *Career* professional footballer; over 200 appearances Celtic 1986-; Scotland caps: under 15, under 16, under 17, under 18, 12 under 21, 3 full (debut v Belgium 1988); honours: Scot League Championship 1986 and 1988, Scot Cup 1988 and 1989; *Style—* Derek Whyte, Esq; 95 Kerrydale St, Glasgow (☎ 041 554 2611)

WHYTE, Donald; JP (City of Edinburgh); s of late John Whyte, of Almondhill, Kirkliston, and late Catherine Dunachie; *b* 26 March 1926; *Educ* Crookston Sch Musselburgh, Inst of Heraldic and Genealogical Studies Canterbury; *m* 1950, Mary, da of George Laird Burton; 3 da; *Career* conslt genealogist, author, lectr; contrib to numerous academic jls; pres Assoc Scot Genealogists and Record Agents; vice pres: Scot Genealogy Soc, family history socs at Glasgow, Aberdeen and Dundee; granted armorial bearings Lyon Office 1986; Citation of Recognition, Ontario Genealogical Soc 1987; *Books* Kirkliston: a Short Parish History (third edn, 1975), Dictionary of Scottish Emigrants to the USA pre-1855 (1972, reprinted 1981, vol 2 1986), Introducing Genealogical Research (fifth edn 1985), Dictionary of Scottish Emigrants to Canada Before Confederation (1986), Walter MacFarlane: Clan Chief and Antiquary (1988), FSG, fell in Heraldry and Genealogy; *Recreations* motoring, heraldry, black and white photography; *Clubs* Edinburgh Airport Social; *Style—* Donald Whyte, Esq, JP; 4 Carmel Rd, Kirkliston, West Lothian EH29 9DD (☎ 031 333 3245)

WHYTE, John Stuart; CBE (1976); s of William Walter Whyte (d 1951), and Ethel Kate, *née* Budd (d 1983); *b* 20 July 1923; *Educ* The John Lyon Sch Harrow, Northampton Engrg Coll, Univ of London (BSc, MSc); *m* 10 March 1953, (Edna) Joan Mary, da of Frank Stark Budd (d 1942); 1 s (Peter b 1954), 1 da (Anne (Mrs McCulloch) b 1959); *Career* HM Treasy 1965-68; Post Office Telecommunications 1968-79, dep md British Telecom 1979-81; md and engr-in-chief British Telecom 1981-83, chm Plessey Telecommunications International 1983-88, pres Stromberg Carlson Corporation (USA) 1984-85; chm: Astronet Corporation 1984-86, GEC/Plessey Telecommunications International 1988-89; vice pres Royal Inst 1972-74, dep chm Nat Electronics Cncl 1976-, pres Inst of Telecommunications Engrs 1977-83, govr Int Cncl for Computer Communications 1982-91, pres Assoc of Br Membs of Swiss Alpine Club 1988-90; Freeman City London 1979, Liveryman Worshipful Co of Scientific Instrument Makers 1979; CEng 1951, FIEE 1966 (vice pres 1981-84), FEng 1982, CBIM 1982; *Recreations* mountaineering, opera; *Clubs* Alpine; *Style—* John Whyte, Esq, CBE; Wild Hatch, Coleshill Lane, Amersham, Bucks HP7 0NT (☎ 0494 722663)

WIBBERLEY, Prof Gerald Percy; CBE (1972); s of Percy Wibberley (d 1915), of Abergavenny, Gwent, and Ellen Mary, *née* Jackson (d 1962); *b* 15 April 1915; *Educ* King Henry VIII GS Abergavenny, Univ Coll of Wales Aberystwyth (BSc,PhD), Univ of Oxford, Univ of Illinois USA (MSc); *m* 1, 18 Sept 1943, Helen Cecilia (d 1964), da of John Youmans (d 1967), of Newport, Indiana, USA; 1 da (Jane b 1945); m 2, Sept 1972, Peggy, *née* Samways; *Career* E Sussex Agric Exec Ctee 1941, chief res offr Land Use Miny of Agric 1948 (asst 1945), head Econs Dept Wye Coll Univ of London 1954-69, personal chair in rural economy 1963-69, personal chair in countryside planning; conslt to Kent CC on rural planning; cncl memb: Ctee for Small Industs in Rural Areas 1960-86, Nature Conservancy 1972-80; memb Kent Educn Ctee 1982-89, vice chm Wye Parish Cncl 1984-; hon memb Royal Town Planning Inst 1949; Hon DSc Univ of Bradford 1984; memb: Br Agric Econ Soc 1939- (pres 1975), Int Assoc of Agric Econs; Order of Merit Univ of Padua Italy 1982; *Books* Agriculture and Urban Growth (1959), Planning and The Rural Environment (with J Davidson, 1977); *Recreations* choral music; *Clubs* Farmers; *Style—* Prof Gerald Wibberley, CBE; Vicarage Cottage, 7 Upper Bridge St, Wye Nr Ashford, Kent TN25 5AW (☎ 0233 812 377)

WICK, Patricia Joyce; da of Dr Douglas George Pollard, of Bristol, and Dorothea Mary, *née* Hunter; *b* 31 Aug 1953; *Educ* Rose Green HS Bristol, Univ of Birmingham (BA); *m* 28 Sept 1984, Graham David, s of Norman Wick, of Tadworth, Surrey; 1 da (Holly b 19 July 1986); *Career* dir FT Int Ltd Farnham 1986-; *Recreations* art; *Style—* Mrs Patricia Wick; 23 Long Garden Walk, Farnham, Surrey (☎ 0252 737615, fax 0252 737265)

WICKENS, Prof Alan Herbert; OBE (1980); s of Leslie Herbert Wickens (d 1986), of Birmingham, and Sylvia Amelia, *née* Hazelgrove (d 1968); *b* 29 March 1929; *Educ* Ashville Coll Harrogate, Loughborough Univ of Technol (DLC, DSc), Univ of London (BSc); *m* 1, 12 Dec 1953, Eleanor Joyce Waggot (d 1984); 1 da (Valerie Joanne b 1958); m 2, 2 July 1987, Patricia Anne McNeil, da of Willoughby Gervaise Cooper, of Dawlish; *Career* res engr: Sir W G Armstrong Whitworth Aircraft Ltd 1951-55, Canadair Ltd Montreal 1955-59, A R Voe & Co Ltd 1959-62; BR: Res Dept 1962-68, dir of advanced projects 1968-71, dir of res 1971-84, dir of engrg devpt and res 1984; prof of dynamics Dept of Mechanical Engrg Loughborough Univ of Technol 1989- (industl prof 1972-76); writer of various pubns on dynamics of railway vehicles, high speed trains and railway technol; jt winner Macrobert award 1975; pres Int Assoc of Vehicle System Dynamics 1981-86, hon fell Derbyshire Coll of Higher Educn 1984, chm Office of Res and Experimentation Union Internationale de Chemin de Fer Utrecht 1988-90; Hon DTech CNAA 1978, Hon Doctorate Open Univ 1980; MAIAA 1958, MRAeS 1963, FIMechE 1971, FEng 1980; *Recreations* gardening, travel, music; *Style—* Prof Alan Wickens, OBE; Department of Mechanical Engineering, University of Technology, Loughborough LE11 3TU (☎ 0509 223201)

WICKENS, Brett Maynard; s of George Andrew Alfred Wickens (d 1984), of Canada, and Daphne Ellen, *née* Maynard; *b* 15 April 1961; *Educ* Aldershot HS Canada, Ontario Coll of Art, Sheridan Poly (first prize Humber Coll Toronto), London Coll of Printing; *Career* asst art dir Din Disc Records 1981-83, ptnr Peter Saville Associates 1986-90 (designer 1983-86), sr designer Pentagram Design Ltd 1990-; regular contributing author to int design magazines; memb Soc of Graphic Designers (Canada), MCSD; *Style—* Brett Wickens, Esq; Pentagram Design Ltd, 11 Needham Rd, London W11 2RP (☎ 071 229 3477, fax 071 727 9932)

WICKERSON, Sir John Michael; s of Walter Wickerson, of London, and Ruth Ivy Constance Field; *b* 22 Sept 1937; *Educ* Christ's Hosp, Univ of London (LLB); *m* 1963, Shirley Maud, da of Andrew Best (d 1980); 1 s (Andrew b 1968); *Career* admitted slr 1960; pres: London Criminal Cts Slrs Assoc 1981-83, Law Soc England and Wales 1986-87; dir R Mansell Ltd, chm Coydon Community Health Tst; hon memb: American Bar Assoc, Canadian Bar Assoc, NZ Law Soc; *Books* Motorist and the Law; kt 1987; *Recreations* sport, music; *Style—* Sir John Wickerson; 10 High St, Croydon, Surrey (☎ 081 686 3841)

WICKHAM, Rt Rev Dr Edward Ralph; s of Edward Wickham, and Minnie, *née* Wanty; *b* 3 Nov 1911; *Educ* Univ of London (BD), St Stephen's House Oxford; *m* June 1944, (Dorothy) Helen, da of Prof K N Moss; 1 s, 2 da; *Career* ordained 1938, curate Christ Church Newcastle upon Tyne 1938-41, chaplain Royal Ordnance Factory No 5 1941-44, fndr and dir Sheffield Industl Mission 1944-59, bishop of Middleton in the Dio of Manchester 1960-84, asst bishop Dio of Manchester 1984-; Hon DLitt Univ of Salford 1973; FRSA; *Books* Church and People in an Industrial City (1959), Encounter with Modern Society (1964); *Recreations* rock climbing, mountaineering; *Style—* The Rt Rev Dr E R Wickham; 12 Westminster Rd, Eccles, Salford, Manchester M30 9HF (☎ 061 789 3144)

WICKHAM, Hon Mrs (Helen Mary); *née* Wade; er da of Baron Wade, DL (Life Peer, d 1988); *b* 14 April 1933; *m* 28 Sept 1963, Rev Dr Lionel Ralph Wickham, s of Harry Temple Wickham, of Bromley, Kent; children; *Style—* The Hon Mrs Wickham; The Vicarage, West Wratting, Cambridge CB1 5NA

WICKHAM, Henry Lewis; s of Henry Albert Wickham (d 1974), and Alice Emily (d 1967); *b* 30 July 1927; *Educ* St Dunstan's Coll Catford, Pinner County Sch, Hammersmith Sch of Architecture (Dip Arch); *m* 5 Oct 1957, Patricia Rose, da of Thomas Pearce (d 1978), of Boreham, Herts; 1 da (Susan b 1959); *Career* architect: London Tport 1955-58, Sir Robert McAlpine and Sons 1958-64, BR 1964-65, Arndale Property Tst 1965-67, London Borough of Ealing 1967-72; ptnr G M Assocs 1972-79, in own private practice 1979-; memb: Guild of Freemen of the City of London, Planning and Tport Ctee Exeter C of C and Trade; project coordinator RIBA Community Gp E Devon; assoc Faculty of Architects and Surveyors, ARIBA; *Recreations* walking, cycling, photography; *Style—* Henry L Wickham, Esq; 2 Clinton Ave, Exeter, Devon EX4 7BA (☎ 0392 51993)

WICKHAM, (William) Jeffry Alexander; RD (1974); s of Lt Col Edward Thomas, Ruscombe Wickham, MVO (d 1957), and Rachel Marguerite, *née* Alexander (d 1955); *b* 5 Aug 1933; *Educ* Eton, Balliol Coll Oxford (BA, MA), LAMDA; *m* April 1962, Clare Marion, da of A R M Stewart (d 1958), of Fearnan; 2 s (Caspar (Fred) b 1962, Rupert b 1964), 1 da (Saskia b 1967); *Career* Nat Serv RN 1962-64, Russian interpreter 1964; actor; West End appearances incl: Othello Old Vic 1963, Catch My Soul (The Rock Othello) (Prince of Wales) 1970, The Unknown Soldier and his Wife (New London) 1973, The Marrying of Ann Leete (Aldwych) 1975, Donkeys' Years (Globe) 1976, The Family Reunion (Vaudeville) 1979, Anyone for Denis? (Whitehall) 1981, Amadeus (Her Majesty's) 1982, Interpreters (Queen's) 1985, Beyond Reasonable Doubt (Queen's) 1987, Exclusive (Strand) 1989; Nat Theatre 1983-85 and 1986-87: Saint Joan, The Spanish Tragedy, A Little Hotel on the Side, The Magistrate; cncllr Br Actors Equity Assoc (vice pres 1986-91), memb cncl Actors' Benevolent Fund; Liveryman Worshipful Co of Skinners 1956; *Recreations* walking, languages; *Style—* Jeffry Wickham, Esq; c/o Markham & Froggati Ltd, 4 Windmill St, London W1 (☎ 071 636 4412)

WICKHAM, John Ewart Alfred; s of Alfred James Wickham (d 1931), of Chichester, Sussex, and Hilda May, *née* Cummins (d 1977); *b* 10 Dec 1927; *Educ* Chichester GS, Univ of London St Bartholomew's Med Coll (BSc, MB BS, MS); *m* 28 July 1961, (Gwendoline) Ann, da of James Henry Loney (d 1975); 3 da (Susan Jane b 31 May 1962, Caroline Elizabeth b 28 July 1963, (Ann) Clare b 4 July 1966); *Career* Nat Serv RAF 1947-49; sr conslt urological surgn St Barts Hosp London 1966-, surgn St Peters Hosp London 1967-, sr lectr Inst of Urology London 1967-, surgn King Edward VIII Hosp for Offrs London 1973, surgn urologist RAF 1973-; dir: Academic Unit Inst of Urology Univ of London 1979-, London Clinic Lithotripter Unit 1987-, N E Thames Regnl Lithotripter Unit 1987-; pres RSM Urological Section 1984, 1 pres Int Soc of Minimal Invasive Surgery 1989; dir: Rencal Ltd, London Lithotripter Co Ltd, Aquaplastics Ltd; Freeman City of London 1971, Liveryman Worshipful Co of Barber Surgns 1971; Hunterian prof and medal RCS 1970, James Berry prize and medal for contribs to renal surgery 1982, Cutlers prize and medal Assoc Surgns GB for surgical instrument design 1985, St Peters Medal Br Assoc of Urological Surgns 1985; FRCS 1959, FRSM; Fulbright scholar of USA 1964; *Books* Urinary Calculous Disease (1979), Percutaneous Renal Surgery (1983), Intra-Renal Surgery (1984), Lithotripsy II (1987), Urinary Stone Metabolic Basis and Clinical Practice (1989), Minimal Invasive Therapy (ed, 1991); *Recreations* mechanical engineering, tennis; *Clubs* Athenaeum, RAC; *Style—* John Wickham, Esq; Stowe Maries, Balchins Lane, Westcott, Surrey RH4 3LR (☎ 0306 885557); 29 Devonshire Pl, London W1N 1PE (☎ 071 935 2232)

WICKHAM, John Francis; *b* 17 Sept 1934; *Educ* Bedales, S Berks Coll of Further Educn, (ONC), LCC Central Sch of Arts and Crafts (dip in design, NDD); *Career* apprentice engr Chilton Electric Products 1952-55, asst designer Robert Welch Associates 1960-63, estab freelance consultancy 1963-, formed Bell Wickham Associates (with Peter Bell now ret) 1972; RSA bursary (used for travel throughout Europe) 1958; Design Cncl awards: Ilford photographic dryer 1975, LKB Biochrom Ultraspec spectrophotometer 1984, Oxford Medical EEG monitor 1985; Br design award: Nautech Autohelm Seatalk instrument range 1990, Nautech Autohelm Wheel Pilot 1990; FCSD; *Style—* John Wickham, Esq; Pittams Farm, Wappenham, Towcester, Northamptonshire NN12 8SP (☎ 0327 860 236, fax 0327 860 990)

WICKHAM, Julyan Michael; s of Michael Whalley Wickham (painter, designer), and Tatiana, *née* van Langandoc (d 1976); *b* 14 Aug 1942; *Educ* Pinewood Sch Herts/Devon, Holloway Comprehensive, Tulse Hill Comprehensive, Architectural Assoc (AADipl, RIBA); *m* 1969, Tess, da of Prof Aldo Ernest van Eyck, of Loenen a/d Vecht, Holland; 1 s (Rufus b 1971), 1 da (Pola Alexandra b 1969); *Career* architect ARCUK, memb RIBA, princ ptnr Wickham & Assocs (established 1971); *Clubs* RAC, Groucho; *Style—* Julyan M Wickham, Esq; 46 St Mary's Mansions, St Mary's Terrace, London W2; 4-5 Crawford Passage, London EC1R 3DP (☎ 071 833 2631, fax 071 833 4993, car ☎ 0836 612 998)

WICKHAM, His Hon Judge; William Rayley; s of Rayley Esmond Wickham (d 1970), and Mary Joyce, *née* Thom (d 1965); *b* 22 Sept 1926; *Educ* Sedbergh, Brasenose Coll Oxford (MA, BCL); *m* 11 May 1957, Elizabeth Mary, da of John Harrison Thompson (d 1957); 1 s (Christopher b 1961), 2 da (Katharine b 1958, Sarah b 1959); *Career* Army 1944-47 Lt; called to the Bar Inner Temple 1951; chief magistrate Aden 1957 (magistrate 1953), crown counsel Tanganyika 1959, asst to law offrs Tanganyika 1961-63, rec 1972, circuit judge 1975; *Style—* His Honour Judge Wickham; 115 Vyner Rd South, Bidston, Birkenhead, Merseyside (☎ 652 2095); Queen Elizabeth II Law Courts, Liverpool

WICKINS, David Allen; s of James Samuel Wickins (d 1940), and Edith Hannah (d 1973); ggs of Adm Sir Robert Henry Wickins; *b* 15 Feb 1920; *Educ* St George's Coll Weybridge; *m* 1960, Dorothy Covington; 1 s, 5 da; *Career* serv South African Naval Forces, seconded to RN Coastal Forces (Lt) WWII; chm: British Car Auction Gp plc, Attwoods plc, Gp of Lotus Car Cos plc; memb IOD; *Recreations* golf, sailing (yacht 'Stavros II'), horse racing (owner: Return to Power and Indianapolis, winner Schweppes Gold Cup); *Clubs* Royal Thames Yacht, Sunningdale Golf; *Style—* David Wickins, Esq; 16 Rutland Mews South, London SW7 (☎ 071 589 6047); The British Car Auction Gp plc, Expedier House, Portsmouth Rd, Hindhead, Surrey (☎ 042 873 7440, telex 858192)

WICKLOW, Countess of; Eleanor; da of Prof Rudolph Butler, of Dublin; *m* 1959, 8 and last Earl of Wicklow (d 1978); *Career* memb Irish Senate 1948-51; *Style—* The Rt Hon Countess of Wicklow; Sea Grange, Sandycove Ave East, Dun Laoghaire, Co Dublin, Eire

WICKRAMASINGHE, Prof (Nalin) Chandra; s of Percival Herbert Wickramasinghe, of Sri Lanka, and Theresa Elizabeth, *née* Soysa; *b* 20 Jan 1939; *Educ* Royal Coll Colombo, Univ of Ceylon, (BSc), Univ of Cambridge (MA, PhD, ScD); *m* 5 April 1966, (Nelum) Priyadarshini, da of Cecil Eustace Pereira; 1 s (Anil Nissanka b 1970), 2 da (Kamala Chandrika b 1972, Janaki Tara b 1981); *Career* fell Jesus Coll Cambridge 1963-73, prof and head Dept of Applied Mathematics and Astronomy Univ Coll Cardiff

1973-88, dir Inst of Fundamental Studies and advsr Pres of Sri Lanka 1982-84; prof of applied maths and astronomy Univ of Wales 1988-; co-author with Prof Sir Fred Hoyle of a series of books of cosmic theory of life 1978-88; Powell Prize for English Verse Trinity Coll Cambridge 1962, Int Dag Hammarskjöld Gold Medal for Science 1986, Scholarly Achievement Award Inst of Oriental Philosophy Japan 1988; *Books* Interstellar Grains (1967), Light Scattering Functions (1973), Lifecloud (with F Hoyle, 1978), Diseases from Space (1979), Evolution from Space (1981), Space Travellers (1981), Living Comets (1985), From Grains to Bacteria (1984), Archaeopteryx (1986), Cosmic Life Force (1988), The Theory of Cosmic Grains (1991); *Recreations* photography, poetry, history of science; *Clubs* Icosahedron Dining (Cardiff); *Style*— Prof Chandra Wickramasinghe; 24 Llwynypia Rd, Lisvane, Cardiff CF4 5SY (☎ 0222 752 146, fax 0222 753 173); School of Mathematics, University of Wales College of Cardiff, Senghennydd Rd, Cardiff CF2 4AG (☎ 0222 874 811, fax 0222 371 921, telex 498635)

WICKS, Brian Cairns; TD; s of Henry Gillies Wicks (d 1970), of Eastbourne, and Ethel (d 1968); *b* 26 March 1934; *Educ* Sedbergh, Univ of Cambridge (BA); *m* 31 March 1959, Judith Anne, da of Kennedy Harrison (d 1961); 1 s (Robert b 1965), 1 da (Pippa b 1962); *Career* Maj 4/5 Btn Green Howards (TA), A/G AVT 1 W African Field Battery Nigeria 1952-54; div sec ICI plc Paints Div 1975-86, dep dir gen Nat Farmers Union 1986-, pres S Bucks and E Berks C of C and Indust 1981-83, chm Berks Business Gp 1983-87, memb Deregulation Panel of the Enterprise & Deregulation Unit DTI 1989-; Freeman City of London, Liveryman Worshipful Co of Glovers 1988; *Recreations* fishing, shooting, squash, gardening; *Style*— Brian C Wicks, Esq; Gracefield Main Rd, Lacey Green, Aylesbury, Bucks HP17 0QU; Knightsbridge, London SW1 (☎ 071 235 5077)

WICKSTEED, Capt Denis George; RD; s of (George Frederick) Kenneth Wicksteed (d 1949), of Stourton, Warwicks, and Christina Nesta Wicksteed (d 1981); *b* 30 Jan 1919; *Educ* King Edward VI Sch Stratford Upon Avon; *m* 14 March 1942, Beryl Sutton da of Albert Gellion (d 1983), of Port St Mary, Isle of Man; 2 s (Antony Sutton b 1943, Michael John b 1946, d 1978); *Career* Midshipman (later Chief Offr) Elder Dempster Lines 1935-46 (camp ldr NW Africa POW Camp 1942-43), King's Commendation for Brave Conduct 1943, Third Offr (later Chief Offr) Cunard Line 1946-58, Lt RNR 1949; Lt: HMS Contest 1950-51, HMS Crossbow 1953-54; Lt Cdr RNR 1957, ADC to Lord High Com Holyroodhouse 1957, Insp and later Dep Chief Insp RNLI 1958-70; Cdr RNR 1960 RD 1965; Capt RNR 1966; cmdg in Pacific Int Line 1977-83; Freeman City of London 1973, Liveryman Honourable Co of Master Mariners; *Recreations* fishing; *Style*— Capt Denis Wicksteed, RD, RNR; 13 The Shimmings, Guildford, Surrey GU1 2NG (☎ 0483 63827)

WIDDECOMBE, Ann Noreen; MP (C) Maidstone 1987-; da of James Murray Widdecombe, CB, OBE, and Rita Noreen Widdecombe; *b* 4 Oct 1947; *Educ* La Sainte Union Convent Bath, Univ of Birmingham, LMH Oxford (MA); *Career* sr admin London Univ 1975-87; Runymede dist cncllr 1976-78, fndr and vice-chm Women and Families for Def 1983-85; contested gen elections (C) (Burnley 1979, Plymouth Devonport 1983); *Books* Layman's Guide to Defence (1984); *Recreations* riding, reading; *Style*— Miss Ann Widdecombe, MP; 9 Tamar House, Kennington Lane, London SE11 4XA (☎ 071 735 5192); House of Commons (☎ 071 219 5091)

WIDDIS, William Thomas (Bill); s of Capt George Thomas Widdis (d 1979), of Bitterne Park, Southampton, and Maud, *née* Jamieson (d 1979); *b* 19 Dec 1940; *Educ* Duke of York's Royal Mil School Dover; *m* 8 Oct 1966, Anne, da of Leslie Robert Biddlesden, of Reading; 1 s (Robert Thomas b 1 June 1969), 1 da (Patricia Anne b 23 Feb 1971); *Career* offr Customs & Excise 1960-70, official assignee The Stock Exchange 1984-86 (systems mangr 1975-85), systems devpt dir The Int Stock Exchange 1986; *Recreations* golf, squash, bridge; *Clubs* Sonning Golf; *Style*— Bill Widdis, Esq; Woodley Cottage, Loddon Bridge, Woodley, Reading, Berks (☎ 0734 695379); The Int Stock Exchange, London EC2N 1HP (☎ 071 588 2355, fax 071 588 7653, telex 886557)

WIDDOWS, Hon Mrs (Angela Hermione); *née* Marshall; er da of Baron Marshall of Leeds (Life Peer, d 1990); *b* 9 Feb 1944; *Educ* Queen Margaret's Sch Escrick York, Les Ambassadrices Paris, The Cygnets House London, Yorkshire Ladies Cncl of Educn; *m* 1, 1966 (m dis 1979), Myles Spencer Harrison Hartley; 1 s (Robert b 1974), 2 da (Annabelle b 1967, Alexandra b 1972); m 2, 1986, Maj Geoffrey Widdows, yr s of Air Cdre Charles Widdows, *qv*, of Guernsey, CI; *Recreations* field sports, music and church music; *Style*— The Hon Mrs Widdows; The Home Farm, Sand Hutton, York YO4 1JZ

WIDDOWSON, Prof Henry George; s of George Percival Widdowson (d 1986), of East Runton, Norfolk, and Edna May, *née* Garrison (d 1980); *b* 28 May 1935; *Educ* Alderman Newton's Sch Leicester, King's Coll Cambridge (MA), Univ of Edinburgh (PhD); *m* 15 July 1966, Dominique Nicole Helene, da of Jean Dixmier, of Paris; 2 s (Marc Alain b 24 May 1968, Arnold b 18 Oct 1972); *Career* Nat Serv RN 1956; english language offr Br Cncl Sri Lanka and Bangladesh 1962-68, lectr dep of linguistics Univ of Edinburgh 1968-77, prof of educn Inst of Educn Univ of London, chm Advsy Ctee Br Cncl English Teaching, vice chm Bell Educn Tst, fndr ed Applied Linguistics, memb Kingman Ctee on the Teaching of English Language; *Books* Stylistics and the Teaching of Literature (1975), Teaching Language as Communication (1978), Explorations in Applied Linguistics (vol I 1979, vol II 1984), Learning Purpose and Language Use (1983), Language Teaching: A Scheme for Teacher Education (ed, 1987), English in the World (with Randolph Quirk, 1985), Aspects of Language Teaching (1990); *Recreations* reading, walking, travel, poetry; *Style*— Prof Henry Widdowson; Institute of Education, 20 Bedford Way, London (☎ 071 636 1500)

WIDGERY, Baroness; Ann; da of William Kermode, of Peel, IOM; *m* 1948, Baron Widgery, OBE, TD, PC, DL (Life Peer cr 1971, d 1981); *Style*— The Rt Hon Lady Widgery; 56 Jubilee Place, Chelsea SW3 3QT

WIEGOLD, Prof James; s of Walter John Wiegold (d 1967), and Elizabeth, *née* Roberts (d 1960); *b* 15 April 1934; *Educ* Caerphilly Boys' GS, Univ of Manchester (BSc, MSc, PhD), Univ of Wales (DSc); *m* 7 April 1958, (Edna) Christine, da of Lewis Norman Dale (d 1989); 1 s (Richard), 2 da (Helen (Mrs Fish), Alison (Dr Sharrock)); *Career* asst lectr Univ Coll N Staffs 1957-60, lectr UMIST 1960-63, prof Univ Coll Cardiff (now Univ Wales Coll Cardiff following merger with UWIST) 1974- (lectr 1963-67, sr lectr 1967-70, reader 1970-74); memb Mathematical Sciences Sub Ctee UGC 1981-86; FIMA 1979; *Books* The Burnside Problems and Identities in Groups (translated from the Russian of S I Adian, with J C Lennox, 1979), Around Burnside (translated from the Russian of A I Kostiikan, 1990); *Recreations* music (choral singing), walking, language; *Style*— Prof James Wiegold; 131 Heol y Deri, Rhiwbina, Cardiff, Wales CF4 6UH (☎ 0222 620469); School of Mathematics, University of Wales, College of Cardiff, Senghenydd Rd, Cardiff CF2 4AG (☎ 0222 874194, fax 0222 874199, telex 498635)

WIELAND, Barry Raymond; s of Otto Charles Wieland, and Hilda Victoria, *née* Ayling (d 1985); *b* 13 Oct 1922; *Educ* St Josephs Coll Beulah Hill London; *m* 4 May 1957, Mary Evelyn (Meryl) (d 1986), da of late Murdo Macrae; 1 da (Alexandra Mary b 23 Jan 1965); *Career* Nat Serv enlisted Army 1942, RMA Sandhurst, cmmnd BUFFS, serv E Africa Cmd, 3 Bn KAR, 2 Bn N Rhodesia Regt Somali Scouts, appt ADC to Mil Govr of Br Somaliland; joined Schlesinger Orgn S Africa 1952; dir: Odeon Cinema Hldgs Ltd, African Consolidated Investmt Corp Ltd, African Caterers Ltd, African Theatres Ltd, African Amalgamated Advtg Ltd; res dir Schlesinger Orgn London, dir Int Variety & Theatrical Agency, ptnr Collingwood of Conduit St Ltd 1959, joined Chaumet Jewellers 1980; Grand Cncl Monarchist League; Freeman City of London; holder Malaysian Illustrious Order of Kinabalu (Datuk) 1975; *Clubs* Oriental, Hurlingham, Anabells, Marks; *Style*— Datuk Capt Barry Wieland; 83 Hamlet Gdns, London W6 0SX; Chaumet (UK) Ltd, 178 New Bond St, London W1Y 9PD (☎ 071 493 5403/629 0136)

WIELD, (William) Adrian Cunningham; s of Captain Ronald Cunningham Wield, CBE, RN (d 1981), of Coburg, Chudleigh, S Devon, and Mary, *née* MacDonald; *b* 19 Feb 1937; *Educ* Downside; *m* 8 June 1979, Benedicte, da of Poul Preben Schoning (d 1984), of Copenhagen; 1 s (Alexander b 1983), 1 da (Isobel b 1980); *Career* 2 Lt Duke of Cornwall LI 1955-57; stockbroker; ptnr W Mortimer 1967-68, dir EB Savory Milln (later SBC1 Savory Milln) 1985-88 (ptnr 1968-85), dir Albert Sharp & Co 1988-, non-exec dir Buzzacot Investment Management Co 1990-; memb London Stock Exchange 1959-1988; *Books* 1973 The Special Steel Industry (pub privately, 1973); *Recreations* golf, shooting, sailing; *Clubs* Reform; *Style*— Adrian Wield, Esq; Tysoe Manor, Tysoe, Warwicks; Scott House Sekforde St, London EC1 (☎ 029 588 709); c/o Albert Sharp & Co, Davies House, 1 Sun St, London EC2 (☎ 071 638 7275, fax 071 638 7270, telex 336550)

WIELER, Anthony Eric; s of Brig Leslie Frederic Ethelbert Wieler, CB, CBE, JP (d 1965), of Feathercombe, Hambledon, Surrey, and Elisabeth Anne, *née* Parker (d 1984); *b* 12 June 1937; *Educ* Shrewsbury, Trinity Coll Oxford (MA); *Career* Nat Serv 1958-60, 2 Lt 7 Duke of Edinburgh's Own Gurkha Rifles (in 1967 organised the appeal which raised £1.5m for Gurkha Welfare Tsts); joined L Messel & Co, memb London Stock Exchange until 1967, sr investmt mangr Ionian Bank Ltd until 1972; fndr chm: Anthony Wieler & Co Ltd 1972-89, Anthony Wieler Unit Tst Mgmnt 1982; dir: Lorne House Tst IOM 1987, Arbuthnot Fund Mangrs Ltd 1988-89; assoc dir Albert E Sharp & Co 1989; fndr Oxford Univ Modern Pentathlon Assoc 1957 (organised first match against Cambridge), chm Hambledon PC 1965-76, initial subscriber Centre for Policy Studies 1972 (Wider Ownership Sub Ctee), memb Fin Ctee Nat Fund for Res into Crippling Diseases (Action Res), fndr One Million Club for XVI Universiade, memb and tstee numerous other charities particularly in Nepal incl King Mahendra Tst for Nature Conservation in Nepal (UK) and Pestalozzi Childrens Village Tst, vice pres St John (Surrey); hon sec AIIM 1974-88; SBStJ; *Recreations* tennis; *Clubs* Boodle's; *Style*— Anthony Wieler, Esq; Feathercombe, Hambledon, nr Godalming, Surrey GU8 4DP (☎ 0483860 200); Albert E Sharp & Co, Davies House, 1 Sun Street, London EC2A 2EP (☎ 071 638 7275, fax 071 638 7270)

WIGAN, Sir Alan Lewis; 5 Bt (UK 1898), of Clare Lawn, Mortlake, Surrey, and Purland Chase, Ross, Herefordshire; s of Sir Roderick Grey Wigan, 3 Bt (d 1954), and bro of Sir Frederick Adair Wigan, 4 Bt (d 1979); *b* 19 Nov 1913; *Educ* Eton, Magdalen Coll Oxford; *m* 1950, Robina, sis of Countess of Arran (w of 8 Earl), aunt of Duchess of Argyll (w of 12 Duke), and da of Lt-Col Sir Iain Colquhoun of Luss, 7 Bt, KT, DSO; 1 s, 1 da (Rebecca, b 1953, m 1, 1976 (m dis 1977), John Spearman; m 2, 1978 (m dis 1986), James Compton, s of Robin Compton, *qv*; 2 s, 1 da); *Heir* s, Michael Iain, b 3 Oct 1951; m 1984, Frances, da of late Flt Lt Angus Barr Fawcett; *Career* serv WWII KRRC (wounded and POW 1940); former dep chm Charrington & Co (Brewers), Master Brewers Co 1959-60; *Style*— Sir Alan Wigan, Bt; Badingham House, Badingham, Woodbridge, Suffolk (☎ 072 875 664); Moorburn, The Lake, Kircudbright

WIGAN, Christopher; 3 s of Maj Algernon Desmond Wigan, MC, TD, Mary, da of Capt Eric Butler-Henderson, 6 s of 1st Baron Faringdon, and Hon Sophia Massey (da of 5th Baron Clarina); *b* 2 Jan 1947; *Educ* Eton; *m* 1970, Hon Caroline Kinnaird (b 1949), eldest da of 13th Lord Kinnaird; 1 s (George b 1977), 1 da (Leila b 1974); *Career* dir Samuel Montagu & Co Ltd Merchant Bankers; FCA; *Recreations* tennis, cinema, theatre; *Clubs* Brooks's; *Style*— Christopher Wigan, Esq; 14 Zetland House, Marloes Rd, W8 (☎ 071 937 4401)

WIGAN, Michael Christian; s of Maj John Derek Wigan (d 1985), and Anne Geraldine Wigan; *b* 3 Nov 1945; *Educ* Heatherdown, Eton; *m* 14 Oct 1971, Eugenie Mary Felicity, da of Peter Egbert Cadbury, of Armsworth Hill, Old Alresford, Hants; 3 s (Charlie Christian b 1976, James Patrick Cameron b 1978, Rollo Richard b 1980); *Career* chm and dir: Wigan Richardson Int Ltd, Hop Developments Ltd, Fanfire Ltd, Wild Neame Gasgain Ltd, Interhop Ltd, Hopair Ltd; sr ptnr Wigan Richardson and Co; memb Lloyd's; *Clubs* White's; *Style*— Michael Wigan, Esq; Bighton House, nr Alresford, Hants; c/o Wigan Richardson & Co, Church Rd, Paddock Wood, Tonbridge, Kent TN12 6EP (☎ 089283 2235, fax 089283 6008)

WIGART, (Bengt) Sture; s of Bengt Eric Wigart (d 1979), and Elsa Margareta Westberg (d 1983); *b* 11 May 1934; *Educ* Univ of Stockholm, Univ of Munich; *m* 1, 1959, Anne Outram; 3 s; m 2, 1981, Asa; m 3, 1985, Carolyn de Havilland; *Career* chm: McGraw-Hill/Dodge Europe, Bau-Data GmbH Germany, BaumarktData GmbH Austria, MDIS Limited, Wigart Properties Limited; *Recreations* sailing, art; *Clubs* Royal Swedish Yacht, Naval and Military; *Style*— Sture Wigart, Esq; Boarmans, Hilltop Road, Beaulieu, Brockenhurst, Hants SO42 7YT (☎ 0590 612467)

WIGG, Simon Antony; s of William Antony Wigg, of Aylesbury, and Rosemary Evelyn Wigg, *née* Smith-Wright; *b* 15 Oct 1960; *Educ* Woodbridge Sch Suffolk, John Hampden Sch High Wycombe; *Career* speedway racer: Br Grass Track champion 1981, 1982, 1983, 1985, 1989, 90; Br Open Pairs champion 1985, 1986, runner-up of World Pairs Championship 1987, Br Speedway champion 1988, 1989, World Long Track champion in Germany 1990 (Czechoslovakia 1989, Denmark 1985, runner-up in Germany 1987), Cwlth Speedway champion 1989, runner-up of World Speedway Championship in Munich 1989; capt of English team 1986, 1987, 1988, memb English World Cup winning side 1989, winner of several int events and four Br League gold medals 1983, 1985, 1986, 1989; *Recreations* skiing, water sports (all, including jetskiing and windsurfing), squash, motocross, keep-fit; *Style*— Simon Wigg, Esq; ☎ and fax 0296 730004)

WIGGIN, Alfred William Jerry; TD (1970), MP (C) Weston-super-Mare 1969-; s of Col Sir William Wiggin, KCB, DSO and Bar, TD, DL, JP, sometime chm Worcs TA & AF Assoc (gs of Sir Henry Wiggin, 1 Bt, being s of Alfred Wiggin, Sir Henry's 4 s, and Margaret, da of Edward John Nettlefold, whose f was fndr of the firm of Nettlefold & Chamberlain and J S Nettlefold & Sons, the latter eventually becoming part of the Guest Keen & Nettlefold conglomerate); *b* 24 Feb 1937; *Educ* Eton, Trinity Coll Cambridge; *m* 1964 (m dis 1981), Rosemary Janet, da of David Orr; 2 s, 1 da; *Career* 2 Lt Queen's Own Warwicks & Worcs Yeo (TA) 1959, Maj Royal Yeo 1975-78; contested Montgomeryshire (C) 1964 & 1966; pps to: Lord Balniel (MOD then FCO) 1970-74, to Sir Ian Gilmour (MOD) 1971-72; parly sec MAFF 1979-81, parly under sec of state MOD 1981-83, chm Select Ctee on Agric 1987-; *Clubs* Beefsteak, Pratt's, Royal Yacht Squadron; *Style*— Jerry Wiggin Esq, TD, MP; The Court, Axbridge, Somerset BS26 2BN (☎ 0934 732527); House of Commons, London SW1A 0AA (☎ 071 219 4522)

WIGGIN, Maj Charles Rupert John; s and h of Sir John Wiggin, 4 Bt, MC, and his 1 w, Lady Cecilia, *née* Anson, da of 4 Earl of Lichfield; *b* 2 July 1949; *Educ* Eton; *m*

1979, Mrs Mary Burnett-Hitchcock; 1 s (Richard b 1980), 1 da (Cecilia b 1984); *Career* Maj Grenadier Gds; *Style—* Maj Charles Wiggin; 10 Ovington St, London SW3

WIGGIN, Fergus Tredennick Francis; s of Clarence Ethelred Wiggin, MBE (1975); *b* 2 Nov 1930; *Educ* Queen's Coll Taunton, Faraday House Electrical Engrg Coll London; *m* 1952, Jennifer Phillis Louise, *née* Burbidge; 3 c; *Career* chartered engr in field of power utilities; sr engr CEGB 1964-68, mangr GLC 1968-75, dir and generation mangr Slough Industrial Estates Ltd 1975-82, dir and gen mangr utilies servs div Slough Trading Estate Ltd 1982-90, conslt 1991-; *Recreations* sailing, fishing; *Style—* Fergus Wiggin, Esq; 24 Clarefield Drive, Pinkneys Green, Maidenhead, Berks SL6 5DP; Slough Estates plc, 234 Bath Rd, Slough, Berks SL1 4EE (☎ 0753 37171, telex 847604)

WIGGIN, Sir John Henry; 4 Bt (UK 1892), of Metchley Grange, Harborne, Staffs, MC (1946), DL (Warwicks 1985); s of Col Sir Charles Richard Henry Wiggin, 3 Bt, TD, JP, DL (d 1972), and Mabel, da of Sir William Jaffray, 2 Bt; *b* 3 March 1921; *Educ* Eton, Trinity Coll Cambridge; *m* 1, 1947 (m dis 1961), Lady Cecilia Evelyn Anson (d 1963), da of 4 Earl of Lichfield; 2 s; m 2, 1963, Sarah, da of Brig Stewart A Forster; 2 s; *Heir* s, Maj Charles Wiggin, Grenadier Gds; *Career* serv WWII Europe and Middle E (POW); Maj Grenadier Gds Res; JP Berks 1966-72, High Sheriff Warwicks 1976-77; *Style—* Sir John Wiggin, Bt, MC, DL; Honington Hall, Shipston-on-Stour, Warwicks (☎ 0608 61434)

WIGGINS, Brian Seymour; s of Edwin Seymour Wiggins, sr civil servant (d 1976), and Lillian May, *née* Clarke; *b* 30 April 1926; *Educ* Purley and Rhyl GS, Liverpool Univ (BSc); *m* 11 Jan 1958, Margaret, da of Edward Byron (d 1978); 4 da (Janet Elizabeth b 1959, Pamela Margaret b 1960, Moira Frances b 1963, Sandra Joan b 1966); *Career* chm MTM plc 1978-87 (ret 1987); chm Marlborough Biopolymers Ltd 1983-87; md: Seal Sands Chemical Co Ltd 1978-80, N W Oil Co Ltd 1971-73, Tekchem Ltd 1973-76, Magnachem Ltd 1974-78, vice-pres Magna Corp (USA) 1977-78, founder of numerous chemical and other cos in the North of England principally: MTM plc, Seal Sands Chemcal Co Ltd, Fine Organics Ltd, Tekchem Ltd, Marchem Ltd, Marlborough Special Products Ltd, Marlborough Biopolymers Ltd, Marlborough Chemicals Inc (USA), Marlborough Chemicals (Far E) Ltd (Hong Kong); *Recreations* vintage motor cars, sailing; *Clubs* Bentley Drivers, Rolls Royce Enthusiast, IOD; *Style—* Brian S Wiggins, Esq; The Old Hall, Coxwold, York YO6 4AD (☎ 03476 676, fax 03476 677); Flat 11, Roseberry, Charles St, London W1

WIGGINS, Prof David; s of Norman Wiggins, OBE, and Diana, *née* Priestley; *b* 8 March 1933; *Educ* St Paul's, Brasenose Coll Oxford (MA); *Career* asst princ Colonial Office 1957-58, Jane Eliza Procter visiting fell Princeton Univ 1958-59, lectr and fell New Coll Oxford 1960-67 (lectr 1959), prof of philosophy Bedford Coll London 1967-80, fell and praelector in philosophy Univ Coll Oxford 1981-89, prof of philosophy Birkbeck Coll London 1989-; visiting appts: Stanford Univ 1964 and 1965, Harvard Univ 1968 and 1972, All Souls Coll Oxford 1973, Princeton Univ 1980, Univ Coll Oxford 1989-; memb various articles in learned jls; memb Ind Cmmn on Tport 1973-74, memb Central Tport Consultative Ctee 1977-79, chm Tport Users Consultative Ctee for SE 1977-79, memb London Tport and Amenity Assoc, memb Aristotelian Soc; FBA 1978; *Books* Identity and Spatio Temporal Continuity (1967), Truth, Invention and the Meaning of Life (1978), Sameness and Substance (1980), Needs, Values, Truth (1987); *Style—* Prof David Wiggins; Birkbeck College, Malet St, London WC1

WIGGINS, (Anthony) John; s of late Rev Sydney Arthur Wiggins, of Wilts, and Mavis Ellen, *née* Brown; *b* 8 July 1938; *Educ* Highgate, The Hotchkiss Sch USA, Oriel Coll Oxford (MA), Harvard Univ (MPA); *m* 1962, Jennifer Anne, da of John Wilson Walkden, of Northampton; 1 s (Nicholas b 1963), 1 da (Victoria b 1967); *Career* asst princ HM Treasy 1961, prince Dept of Econ Affrs 1966, asst sec HM Treasy 1972, PPS to Chllr of the Exchequer 1980-81, under sec head of Oil Div Dept of Energy 1981-84, memb Bd BNOC 1982-84, under sec Cabinet Office 1985-86, under sec Dept of Educn and Sci 1987-88, dep sec 1988-; *Recreations* mountaineering, skiing, opera; *Clubs* Alpine; *Style—* John Wiggins, Esq; Dept of Education & Science, Elizabeth House, York Road, London SE1 7PH

WIGGINS, Linda Margaret; da of Frederick John Coe, of 58 Park Lane, Snettisham, King's Lynn, Norfolk, and Edna May, *née* Winner; *b* 21 Dec 1949; *Educ* W Norfolk King's Lynn HS for Girls, Univ of Essex (BA); *m* 12 Feb 1972, Derek Ernest Wiggins, s of Frank Wiggins, of 33 Fourth Cross Rd, Twickenham (d 1976); *Career* CA 1975-; ptnr in local firm 1978-84, started own practice Wiggins & Co 1984; *Recreations* riding, embroidery; *Style—* Mrs Linda Wiggins; 5 Granada House, Gabriel's Hill, Maidstone, Kent ME15 6JP (☎ 0622 688 189)

WIGGINTON, Michael John; s of Lt-Col Sydney Isaac Wigginton, OBE (d 1945), and Eunice Olive, *née* Piper; *b* 26 March 1941; *Educ* Nottingham HS, Gonville and Caius Coll Cambridge (MA, Dip Arch); *m* 1, 1969 (m dis), Margaret Steven; 1 s (Alexander b 1974), 1 da (Julia b 1972); m 2, 1988, Jennifer Bennett; *Career* architect and author; with YRM architects and planners 1982-85 (responsible for the design of a series of bldgs incl: an innovatory office bldg in the Netherlands, a maj energy sensitive hosp in Singapore and co-designer The Sultan Qaboos Univ in Oman), organiser Glass in the Environment Conf Crafts Cncl 1986; ptnr Richard Horden Assoc 1987-; architect memb UK/USA Govt sponsored res on energy responsive bldg envelopes; winner (with Richard Horden): The Stag plc Competition London 1987, Epsom Club Stand Competition 1989; FRSA; *Publications* Window Design (1969), Office Buildings (1973), Practice in the Netherlands (1976), Design of Health Buildings in Hot Climates (1976), Glass To-day (1987), Towards the Chromogenic Century (1990), Glass in Architecture (1991); *Recreations* music, reading, tennis; *Style—* Michael Wigginton, Esq; 41 Chiddingstone St, London SW6 3TQ (☎ 071 371 5855); Richard Horden Associates Ltd, 4 Golden Square, London W1 (☎ 071 439 0241)

WIGGLESWORTH, David Cade; s of Air Cdre Cecil George Wigglesworth, CB, AFC (d 1961), and Margaret, *née* Cade Bemrose (d 1963); *b* 25 March 1930; *Educ* Tonbridge, London Coll of Printing; *m* 11 Feb 1956, Anne, da of John Cairns Hubbard, of Esher, Surrey; 2 s (George b 1957, Lloyd b 1959), 2 da (Sally b 1962, Joanna b 1963); *Career* Nat Serv PO, FO RAFVR 1948-50; Bemrose Corp plc: salesman London 1952-55, London sales mangr 1955, gen mangr Bemrose Flexible Packaging Spondon Derbyshire 1965-69, md Bemrose Derby Ops 1969-71, gp chief exec 1971-, started acquisitions in USA, chm Bemrose Yattendon Inc (USA) 1984; chm: CBI Economic Situation Ctee, Bd of Govrs Trent Coll Long Eaton Notts; capt Derbyshire Co Golf Team 1974-75; Freeman City of London, Liveryman Worshipful Co of Stationers; memb Faculty Assoc of Mgmnt Centre Europe (of American Mgmnt Assoc); *Recreations* golf, gardening, skiing, tennis, photography; *Clubs* Carlton, Chevin Golf (Derby), Pine Valley Golf (USA); *Style—* David Wigglesworth, Esq; Manor Quarry, Duffield, Derbyshire, DE6 4BG (☎ 0332 840330); Bemrose Corporation Plc, Wayzoose Drive, Derby DE2 6XP (☎ 0332 294242, fax 0332 290367, car 0831 563405)

WIGGLESWORTH, Prof Jonathan Semple; s of Sir Vincent Brian Wigglesworth, KT, CBE, of 14 Shilling St, Lavenham, Suffolk, and Mabel Katherine, *née* Semple (d 1986); *b* 2 Dec 1932; *Educ* Gordonstoun, Gonville and Caius Cambridge (BA), UCH (BChir, MD); *m* 21 July 1960, (Margaret) Joan, da of Christopher Every Rees (d 1974); 3 da (Sara b 1961, Sian b 1965, Kirsty b 1968); *Career* house physician UCH 1960, house surgn Nat Temperance Hosp 1960-61; Graham scholar in morbid anatomy 1961-62, Beit Memorial fell 1962-64, lectr in morbid anatomy 1964-65; reader in paediatric pathology Dept of Paediatrics Hammersmith Hosp 1980-85 (sr lectr 1965-79), hon conslt in neonatal histopathology NW Thames Region 1983-, prof of perinatal pathology Royal Postgrad Med Sch 1985-; memb: Br Paediatric Assoc, Paediatric Pathology Soc, Neonatal Soc; pres Br Paediatric Pathology Assoc; FRCPath 1977; *Books* Haemorrhage Ischaemia and the Perinatal Brain (with K Pape, 1979), Perinatal Pathology (1984); *Recreations* fly-fishing, gardening; *Clubs* RSM; *Style—* Prof Jonathan Wigglesworth; Wason House, Upper High St, Castle Cary, Somerset BA7 7AT (☎ 0963 50360); 55 Stamford Court, Goldhawk Rd, London W6 0XD (☎ 081 748 6806); Dept of Histopathology, Royal Postgraduate Medical School, Hammersmith Hospital, Du Cane Rd, London W12 0HS (☎ 081 740 3280, fax 081 740 7417)

WIGGLESWORTH, Sir Vincent Brian; CBE (1951); s of Sidney Wigglesworth, MRCS (d 1944), and Margaret Emmeline, *née* Pierce (d 1953); *b* 17 April 1899; *Educ* Repton, Gonville and Caius Coll Cambridge (MA, MD BCh), St Thomas's Hosp; *m* 1928, Mabel Katherine, da of Col Sir David Semple, IMS (d 1936); 3 s, 1 da; *Career* 2 Lt RFA (France) 1917-18; lectr in med entomology London Sch of Hygiene and Tropical Med 1926; reader in entomology: London Univ 1936-44, Cambridge Univ 1945-52; dir ARC Unit of Insect Physiology 1943-67, Quick prof of biology Cambridge 1952-66; FRS, FRCP, FRES; fell Gonville and Caius Coll Cambridge 1945; awarded hon doctorates and membership of various UK and foreign socs, acads and insts; medals gained incl Royal medal (Royal Soc) 1955, Gregor Mendel Gold medal (Czechoslovak Acad of Science) 1967; kt 1964; *Publications include* Insect Hormones (1970), The Principles of Insect Physiology (4 edn, 1972), Insect and the Life of Man (1976), Insect Physiology (4 edn, 1984); *Style—* Sir Vincent Wigglesworth, CBE; 14 Shilling St, Lavenham, Suffolk (☎ 0787 247 293); Gonville and Caius Coll, Cambridge

WIGGLESWORTH, William Robert Brian; s of Sir Vincent Brian Wigglesworth, of Suffolk, and Mabel Katherine, *née* Semple (d 1986); *b* 8 Aug 1937; *Educ* Marlborough, Magdalen Coll Oxford (BA); *m* 1969, Susan Mary, da of Arthur Baker, JP (d 1980), of Suffolk; 1 da (Elizabeth b 1979), 1 s (Benjamin b 1982); *Career* Nat Serv 2 Lt Royal Signals 1956-58; Ranks Hovis McDougall Ltd 1961-70, gen mgmnt and PA to Chief Exec; memb Bd of Trade 1970; asst sec: Dept of Prices and Consumer Protection 1975, dept of Indust 1978; dep dir gen Telecommunications 1984-; *Recreations* fishing, gardening, history; *Style—* William Wigglesworth, Esq; Office of Telecommunications, Export House, 50 Ludgate Hill, London EC4M 7SS (☎ 071 822 1604, fax 071 822 1643, telex 883584)

WIGHT, Robin Alexander Fairbairn; s of William Fairbairn Wight (d 1972), of Alwoodley, Leeds, and Olivia Peterina, *née* Clouston (d 1988); *b* 5 June 1938; *Educ* Dollar Acad, Magdalene Coll Cambridge (MA); *m* 27 July 1963, Sheila Mary Lindsay, da of James Forbes (d 1963), of Edinburgh; 3 s (James William Fairbairn b 1966, Alasdair Robin Forbes b 1968, Douglas Clouston Fullerton b 1973), 1 da (Catriona Mary Susan b 1965); *Career* ptnr Coopers & Lybrand CAs 1971-90, regnl ptnr Coopers & Lybrand Scotland 1977-90, exec chm Coopers & Lybrand Deloitte 1990-; FCA 1976; *Recreations* golf, skiing, hill walking, bridge; *Clubs* Caledonian, RAC; *Style—* Robin Wight, Esq; 22 Regent Terrace, Edinburgh EH7 5BS (☎ 031 556 2100); George House, 126 George St, Edinburgh EH2 4JZ (☎ 031 226 2595, fax 031 226 2692, telex 727803, car 0860 254110)

WIGHTMAN, David Richard; s of John William Wightman, of Leatherhead, Surrey, and Nora, *née* Martin; *b* 3 April 1940; *Educ* KCS Wimbledon; *m* Gillian Primrose, *née* Longley (d 1987); *Career* Kenneth Brown Baker Baker (Turner Kenneth Brown since 1983): articled clerk 1957-62, asst slr 1962-65, ptnr 1965-87, sr ptnr 1987-; ed-in-chief Int Construction Law Review 1983-; Freeman City of London, memb Worshipful Co of Slrs 1983; memb: Law Soc 1962, Int Bar Assoc 1976, IOD 1982, Soc of Construction Law 1986; FRSA 1990; *Recreations* tennis, farming; *Clubs* Traveller's; *Style—* David Wightman, Esq; Turner Kenneth Brown, 100 Fetter Lane, London EC4A 1DD (☎ 071 242 6006, fax 071 242 3003)

WIGHTMAN, Gerald; s of Harold Wightman (d 1978), and Evelyn, *née* Reader (d 1963); *b* 18 Sept 1937; *Educ* Hillhouse; *m* 17 Jan 1959, Mavis, da of William Wilson (d 1988); 1 s (Ian Stewart b 1967); 1 da (Andrea Yvonne (Mrs Peel) b 1965); *Career* fin dir Allied Textile Companies plc and subsid cos, Allintex Co Ltd Hong Kong; FCA; *Recreations* sport, music; *Style—* Gerald Wightman, Esq; Belmont, 110 Knowle Rd, Mirfield, W Yorks WF14 9RJ (☎ 0924 494231); Allied Textile Companies plc, Highburton, Huddersfield, W Yorks (☎ 0484 604301, fax 0484 605740)

WIGHTMAN, John Martin; s of John William Wightman, of Leatherhead, Surrey, and Nora *née* Martin; *b* 27 Jan 1944; *Educ* The Oratory; *m* 17 Oct 1970, Anne Leigh, da of William Laurence Paynter, MBE, of Leatherhead, Surrey; 2 s (Dominic Martin b 20 Dec 1972, Patrick John b 22 March 1983), 5 da (Antonia Leigh b 7 Dec 1971, Georgina Mary b 13 July 1975, Francesca Katherine b 13 May 1978, Gemma Theresa b 25 June 1981, Christiana Bernadette b 11 March 1986); *Career* joined David A Bevan Simpson & Co (now Barclays de Zoete Wedd) 1968: ptnr 1978-, dir de Zoete & Bevan Ltd 1986-, dir Barclays de Zoete Wedd Securities Ltd 1986-; memb: City Liaison Group, Cons Assoc Shamley Green; AMSIA; *Recreations* sports; *Clubs* Gresham, Guildford and Godalming RFC; *Style—* John Wightman, Esq; The Manor House, Shamley Green, Surrey GU5 0UD (☎ 0483 893269); de Zoete & Bevan Ltd, Ebbgate House, 2 Swan Lane, London EC4R 3TS (☎ 071 623 2323)

WIGHTMAN, Nigel David; s of Gerald Wightman (d 1983), of Church Brampton, Northants, and Margaret Audrey, *née* Shorrock; *b* 19 July 1953; *Educ* Bolton Sch, Kent Coll, Dundee HS, Brasenose Coll Oxford (MA), Nuffield Coll Oxford (MPhil); *m* 21 Feb 1987, Christine Dorothy, da of Hubert Alexander Nesbitt, of Bangor, Co Down, NI; 2 s (Patrick Gerald Wisdom b 1987, Hugo William Joseph b 1989); *Career* Samuel Montagu and Co 1976-80, Chemical Bank 1980-84, NM Rothschild and Sons 1984-, md NM Rothschild Asset Management Ltd; *Recreations* seasonal; *Clubs* Wildernesse Golf; *Style—* Nigel Wightman, Esq; Five Arrows House, St Swithins Lane, London EC4N 8NR

WIGHTMAN, Richard Edward John; s of Charles Prest Wightman, of Fairfax Hall, Menston, Ilkley, W Yorks; *b* 21 Aug 1944; *Educ* Uppingham, Univ of Edinburgh (BCom); *m* 15 Oct 1966, Elizabeth Constance, da of James Birnie (d 1960), of Dufftown, Banff, Scotland; 2 s (Charles, Alasdair); *Career* dir: Abtrust Scotland Investment Co plc, Beecrofts Tport Ltd, Leeds-Bradford Airport Ltd, Davenport Engrg Co Ltd, Davenport Hldgs Ltd, Normanton Wood Servs Ltd, RG Fowler Ltd, Tait of Hull Ltd, Wightwood Joinery Ltd; dep leader Bradford Met DC 1988- (memb 1983); *Style—* Richard Wightman, Esq; Fairfax Hall, Menston, Ilkley, West Yorks LS29 6EY; 70 Harris St, Bradford, West Yorks BD1 5JB (☎ 0274 729744, fax 0274 307380, telex 517153)

WIGLEY, Dafydd; MP (Welsh Nationalist Party) Plaid Cymrua Caernarfon Feb 1974-; s of Elfyn Edward Wigley; *b* 1 April 1943; *Educ* Caernarfon GS, Rydal Sch Colwyn Bay, Univ of Manchester; *m* Elinor, da of Emrys Bennett Owen, of Dolgellau; 3 s (2 s decd), 1 da; *Career* industl economist; formerly with: Ford Motor Co, Mars Ltd, Hoover Ltd; chm Alpha Dyffryn Ltd (medical equipment manufacturers), Electoral Reform Nat Ctee; Plaid Cymru: indust and econ affrs spokesman and parly whip, pty pres 1981-84; vice pres Fedn of Industl Devpt Authys, pres Spastics Soc Wales; *Style*— Dafydd Wigley, Esq, MP; 21 Penllyn, Caernarfon; House of Commons, London SW1 (☎ 071 219 5021, constituency office ☎ 0286 2076)

WIGLEY, John Robert; s of Jack Wigley, and Eileen Ellen, *née* Murphy; *b* 22 Dec 1945; *Educ* Latymer Upper Sch, Jesus Coll Cambridge (MA); *m* 12 May 1973, Susan Anne (Sam), da of David Thomas Major (d 1974); 2 s (Robert b 1978, Peter b 1982); *Career* ptnr R Watson & Sons 1973 (joined 1969), dir Combined Actuarial Performance Servs Ltd 1984; FIA 1970; *Recreations* music, sport; *Style*— John Wigley, Esq; Bellapais, 9 Beeches Wood, Kingswood, Surrey (☎ 0737 833664); R Watson & Sons, Watson House, London Rd, Reigate, Surrey RH2 9PQ (☎ 0737 241144, fax 0737 241496, telex 946070)

WIGLEY, (Francis) Spencer; s of Frank Wigley (d 1970), Dep Cmmr of Police of Fiji, and Lorna, *née* Wattley; gf Sir Wilfrid Wigley, chief justice Leeward Islands, WI; *b* 28 Oct 1942; *Educ* Dean Close Sch, Univ of Nottingham (BA); *m* 1969, Caroline, da of Dr George Jarratt; 2 s (Francis b 1972, Edward b 1973); 1 da (Elizabeth b 1979); *Career* admitted slr 1967; sec and head of corp admin The RTZ Corporation plc 1983-; chm Amesbury Sch 1987-, govr Cranleigh Sch 1989-; memb Law Soc; *Recreations* sailing, sporting activities, photography; *Clubs* RAC, Cruising Assoc; *Style*— Spencer Wigley, Esq; 6 St James's Square London SW1Y 4LD (☎ 071 930 2399, telex 24639, fax 071 930 3249)

WIGODER, Baron (Life Peer UK 1974), of Cheetham, in City of Manchester; Basil Thomas Wigoder; QC (1966); s of Philip I Wigoder, LRCPI, LRCSI, of Deansgate, Manchester; *b* 12 Feb 1921; *Educ* Manchester GS, Oriel Coll Oxford (MA); *m* 1948, Yoland, da of Ben Levinson; 3 s (Hon Justin b 1951, Hon Charles Francis b 1960, Hon Giles b 1963), 1 da (Hon Carolyn b (twin) 1963); *Career* serv WWII Lt RA N Africa, Italy, Greece; sits as Lib Democrat in House of Lords; contested (Lib): Bournemouth 1945, Westbury 1959 and 1964; pres Oxford Union 1946, barr 1946, vice pres Lib Pty 1966-, memb Crown Ct Rules Ctee 1971-80, master of bench Gray's Inn 1972 (treas 1989), rec Crown Ct 1972-87; Lib dep whip House of Lords 1976-77, chief whip 1977-86; chm Health Servs Bd 1977-80, memb Cncl on Tbnls 1980-86, chm BUPA and dir BUPA Hosps 1981-; *Recreations* cricket, music; *Clubs* Nat Lib, MCC; *Style*— The Rt Hon the Lord Wigoder, QC; BUPA, Provident House, Essex St, London WC2R 3AX; House of Lords, London SW1 (☎ 071 219 3114)

WIGODER, Hon Charles Francis; 2 s of Baron Wigoder, QC (Life Peer); *b* 1960; *m* 1988, Elizabeth Sophia, o da of Elmar Duke-Cohan, of Totteridge

WIGODER, Hon Giles Joel; s (twin with sis Carolyn) of Baron Wigoder, QC (Life Peer); *b* 17 Aug 1963; *Educ* Mill Hill, Leicester Univ; *Career* retail devpt exec, regnl trg mangr and employee relations offr with Rumbelows Ltd 1984-88, management devpt mangr with Comet Gp plc 1988-90, md Lifestyle Diagnostics plc 1990-; memb Marine Archeological Soc; *Recreations* cricket, golf, bridge, scuba diving; *Style*— The Hon Giles Wigoder; 14c Lanark Mansions, Lanark Road, London W9 1DB (☎ 071 289 9702); Lifestyle Diagnostics plc, 52 Abbey Gardens, St John's Wood, London NW8 9AT (☎ 071 328 8011)

WIGODER, Hon Justin; s of Baron Wigoder, QC; *b* 11 May 1951; *m* 1981, Heather, da of late J H Bugler and Mrs William Storey, and step da of William Storey, of Newark-upon-Trent; *Style*— The Hon Justin Wigoder

WIGRAM, Hon Andrew Francis Clive; MVO (1986); s and h of 2 Baron Wigram, MC, JP, DL; *b* 18 March 1949; *Educ* Winchester, RMA Sandhurst; *m* 1974, Gabrielle, yst da of R Moore, of NZ; 3 s (Harry Richard Clive b 1977, Robert Christopher Clive b 1980, William Michael Clive b 1984), 1 da (Alice Poppy Louise b 1989); *Career* Maj Gren Guards 1969-86; Extra Equerry to HRH The Duke of Edinburgh 1982-86; *Clubs* Leander; *Style*— Maj the Hon Andrew Wigram, MVO; Garden House, Poulton, Cirencester, Glos (☎ 0285 851388)

WIGRAM, Rev Canon Sir Clifford Woolmore; 7 Bt (UK 1805), of Walthamstow, Essex; s of Robert Ainger Wigram (d 1915), and Evelyn Dorothy, *née* Henslowe (d 1960); suc unc, Sir Edgar Thomas Ainger Wigram, 6 Bt (d 1935); *b* 24 Jan 1911; *Educ* Winchester, Trinity Coll Cambridge (MA); *m* 24 Aug 1948, Christobel Joan (d 1983; who m 1, Eric Llewellyn Marriott, CIE d 1945), da of late William Winter Goode, of Curry Rivel, Somerset; 1 step s, 1 step da; *Heir* bro Edward Robert Woolmore Wigram, b 19 July 1913; *Career* ordained 1934, vicar Marston St Lawrence with Warkworth and Thenford, non residentiary canon Peterborough Cathedral 1973, ret 1983, canon emeritus Peterborough Cathedral; *Style*— The Rev Canon Sir Clifford Wigram, Bt; 2 Mold Cottages, Marston St Lawrence, Banbury, Oxon OX17 2DB (☎ 0295 71179)

WIGRAM, 2 Baron (UK 1935); (George) Neville Clive Wigram; MC (1945), JP (Glos 1959), DL (1969); s of 1 Baron Wigram, GCB, GCVO, CSI, PC, Equerry to George V both as Prince of Wales and King (d 1960, himself ggs of Sir Robert Wigram, 1 Bt), and his w Nora, da of Sir Neville Chamberlain; *b* 2 Aug 1915; *Educ* Winchester, Magdalen Coll Oxford; *m* 19 July 1941, Margaret Helen (d 1986), da of Gen Sir Andrew Thorne, KCB, CMG, DSO, and Hon Margaret Douglas-Pennant, 10 da of 2 Baron Penrhyn, JP, DL; 1 s, 2 da; *Heir* s, Hon Andrew Wigram; *Career* late Lt-Col Gren Gds; page of honour to HM 1925-32; mil sec and comptroller to Govr-Gen NZ 1946-49; *Clubs* Cavalry and Guards', MCC; *Style*— The Rt Hon Lord Wigram, MC, JP, DL; Poulton Fields, Cirencester, Glos (☎ 0285 851250)

WIGRAM, Hon Mrs (Sally Ann); *née* Bethell; da of Hon William Gladstone Bethell (3 s of 1 Baron) and sis of 4 Baron Bethell, MEP; *b* 1943; *m* 1965, Anthony Francis Wigram; 1 s, 2 da (twin); *Style*— The Hon Mrs Wigram; 7 Gloucester Sq, London W2 (☎ 071 262 8419)

WIIK, OØystein; s of Kjell Wiik, of Oslo, and Liv, *née* Oulie; *b* 7 July 1956; *Educ* The Norwegian State Coll, The Norwegian Acad of Dramatic Arts; *Career* actor; incl: Jesus in Godspell (National Theatre Bergen) 1978, You Never Can Tell (Oslo New Theatre) 1979, West Side Story (The Norwegian Theatre) 1981, A Chorus Line (Chateau Neuf Oslo) 1983, Cats (The Norwegian Theatre) 1985, Fiddler on the Roof (The Norwegian Theatre) 1987, Jean Michel in La Cage aux Folles (Chateau Neuf) 1987, Jean Valjean in Les Miserables (The Norwegian Theatre 1988, Raimund Theatre Vienna 1989, The Palace Theatre London 1989-90), Sweeny Todd in Sweeny Todd (The Norwegian Theatre) 1991; films: The Frogprince 1984, The Sea Dragon 1990; numerous TV appearances in Scandinavia and Austria; recordings: Godspell, Cats, Diaf, Too Many Mornings (songs by Sondheim); *Style*— OØystein Wiik, Esq; Barry Burnett's Organisation, Grafton House, Golden Square, London W1 (☎ 071 437 7048)

WIJETUNGE, Don B; s of Don Dines Wijetunge (d 1963), of Colombo, Sri Lanka, and Prem, *née* Jayatilake; *b* 24 Jan 1941; *Educ* Royal Coll Colombo Sri Lanka, Univ of Ceylon (MB BS); *m* 20 April 1971, Indra, da of Andrew Amerasinghe, of Kandy, Sri Lanka; 1 s (Aruna b 1973), 1 da (Sonalee b 1974); *Career* conslt surgn Univ Hosp Damman Saudi Arabia 1980-82, dir of emergency serv Abdulla Fouad Univ Hosp Saudi Arabia 1982-84, conslt surgn and head of dept emergency serv St George's Hosp London 1984- (first asst Dept of Surgery 1976-80); memb American Coll of Emergency Physicians; FRCSEd, memb BMA; *Recreations* computer applications in medicine; *Style*— Don Wijetunge, Esq; Accident & Emergency Serv, St George's Hospital, Blackshaw Rd, London SW17 0QT (☎ 081 672 1255)

WILBERFORCE, (William) John Antony; CMG (1981); s of Lt-Col William B Wilberforce, DSO (ka 1943), of Markington Hall, Yorks, and Cecilia, *née* Dormer (d 1974); sr descendant of William Wilberforce, The Emancipator; *b* 3 Jan 1930; *Educ* Ampleforth, ChCh Oxford (MA); *m* 20 Aug 1953, Laura Lyon, da of Howard Sykes (d 1966), of Englewood, NJ, USA; 1 s (William b 1958), 2 da (Anne b 1954, Mary b 1955); *Career* Nat Serv 2 Lt KOYLI Malaya 1948-49; Dip Serv 1953-88: asst under sec RCDS 1979, ldr UK delgn to Madrid CSCE Review Meeting 1980-82, high cmmr Cyprus 1982-88; *Recreations* the turf, travel, gardening; *Clubs* Athenaeum; *Style*— John Wilberforce, Esq, CMG; Markington Hall, via Harrogate, N Yorks (☎ 0765 87356)

WILBERFORCE, Baron (Life Peer UK 1964), of City and Co of Kingston-upon-Hull; Richard Orme Wilberforce; CMG (1965), OBE (1944), PC (1964); s of Samuel Wilberforce, of Lavington House, Petworth, Sussex (d 1954, 4 s of Reginald Wilberforce, JP, DL, by Anna Maria, da of Hon Richard Denman, 3 s of 1 Baron Denman; Reginald was 2 s of the Bishop of Oxford who founded Cuddesdon Theological Coll and was himself 3 s of William Wilberforce, the philanthropist) and Katherine, *née* Sheepshanks (d 1963); the family name derives from a Yorkshire village, Wilberfoss (Wild-Boar-Foss); *b* 11 March 1907; *Educ* Winchester, New Coll Oxford (MA); *m* 10 July 1947, Yvette Marie, da of Roger Lenoan, Judge of the Cour de Cassation, Paris; 1 s (Hon Samuel Herbert b 1951), 1 da (Hon Anne Catherine (Hon Mrs Burn) b 1948); *Career* served WWII Norway, France and Germany as Brig; called to the Bar 1932; QC 1954, High Ct judge (Chancery) 1961-64, Lord of Appeal in Ordinary 1964-82, chm Exec Cncl Int Law Assoc, memb Perm Ct of Arbitration, pres Fédération Internationale du Droit Européen 1978; fell All Souls Oxford 1932-; hon fell: New Coll Oxford 1965, Wolfson Coll Oxford 1990; high steward Univ of Oxford 1967-90, chllr Univ of Hull 1978-; Hon FRCM, Hon CRAeS; hon memb: Scottish Faculty of Advocates, Canadian Bar, American Soc of Int Law and American Law Inst; Hon DCL Oxford 1967; Hon LLD: London 1972, Hull 1973, Bristol 1983; Diplôme d'Honneur Corp des Vignerons de Champagne; Gd Cross St Raymond of Penafort (Spain) 1976, Bronze Star (US) 1944; kt 1961; *Clubs* Athenaeum, Oxford and Cambridge; *Style*— The Rt Hon the Lord Wilberforce, CMG, OBE, PC; c/o House of Lords, London SW1

WILBERFORCE, Hon Samuel Herbert (Sam); s of Baron Wilberforce, CMG, OBE, PC; *b* 15 Dec 1951; *Educ* Eton, New Coll Oxford (MA, PGCE, Dip Ed); *m* 1978, Sarah, da of late Arthur Allen, of Northampton; *Style*— The Hon Sam Wilberforce

WILBRAHAM; *see*: Baker Wilbraham

WILBRAHAM, David Charles; s of Anthony Basil Wilbraham, and Sheila Eleanor, *née* Neville; *b* 16 Aug 1957; *Educ* Radley; *m* 2 Oct 1982, Debra Ann, da of Bryan Windass; 3 da (Annabel b 1984, Jennifer b 1984, Davina b 1988); *Career* dir: Vista Securities Ltd, Prospect Industries PLC; *Recreations* golf, shooting; *Style*— David C Wilbraham, Esq; Rosemount, 9 Sands Lane, Elloughton Brough, N Humberside HU15 1JH (☎ 0482 666942); 2 Parliament St, Hull, N Humberside HU1 2AP (☎ 0482 215850, fax 0482 215882)

WILBRAHAM, Hugh Dudley; s of Ralph Venables Wilbraham (d 1983), of Cheshire, and Katharine Mary, *née* Kershaw (d 1984); *b* 18 Feb 1929; *Educ* Wellington; *m* 27 April 1957, Laura Jane, da of George McCorquodale (d 1979), of Bucks; 3 s (Ian b 1958, Philip b 1960, James b 1964), 1 da (Fiona b 1967); *Career* Nat Serv 1947-49, 2 Lt W Yorks Regt; gen mangr Hyde Park Hotel London 1966-71, dir Russell & McIver (wine merchants); *Recreations* tennis, real tennis; *Clubs* Boodle's, RAC; *Style*— Hugh D Wilbraham, Esq; The Gage, Little Berkhamsted, Hertfords SG13 8LR (☎ 099286 233); Russell & McIver Ltd, The Rectory, St Mary-at-Hill, London E3R 8EE (☎ 071 283 3575)

WILBRAHAM, Peter Norman; s of Frank Kenyon Wilbraham (d 1973), of Manchester, and Marian Flitcroft; *b* 30 Aug 1942; *Educ* Bury GS Lancashire; *m* 1, 31 July 1966 (m dis) Jennifer Mary, da of James Dewhurst, MBE (d 1986), of Deganwy, N Wales; 1 da (Kathryn b 1968); m 2, Ann, da of Jack Swift (d 1989), of Dewsbury, W Yorkshire; 1 s (Michael b 1981), 1 da (Sophie b 1983); m 3, 24 June 1988, Anna Julie, da of William Henry Stephen Hitchens (d 1952), of Bridgwater, Somerset; *Career* admitted slr 1966; ptnr: Last Suddards & Co 1975, Hammond Suddards 1988; cncl memb RTPI 1980-84, ctee memb RTPI Yorkshire 1980-86; memb Law Soc 1966, LMTPI 1973; *Recreations* photography; *Clubs* The Bradford; *Style*— Peter Wilbraham, Esq; 47 Main St, Menston, Ilkley, West Yorkshire LS29 6NB (☎ 0943 870548); Hammond Suddards, Josephs Well, Hanover Walk, Leeds LS3 1AB (☎ 0532 450845, fax 0532 460892, telex 55365, car 0836 728094)

WILBRAHAM, Philip Neville; s of Anthony Basil Wilbraham, of N Humberside, and Sheila Eleanor, *née* Neville; *b* 25 Nov 1958; *Educ* Woodleigh Sch, Radley, Univ of Aston Birmingham (BSc); *m* 1981, Stephanie Jane, da of Ian William McClaren Witty; 2 s (Samuel b 1984, Dominic b 1987), 2 da (Rachel b 1982, Rosemary b 1986); *Career* non-exec dir: Britannia Marine plc, Boston Putford Offshore Safety Ltd, Northumbrian Fine Foods plc; chm and chief exec Prospect Industries plc, chief exec Vista Securities Limited; chm Ptarmigan Holdings plc; *Recreations* shooting, politics; *Clubs* Carlton; *Style*— Philip Wilbraham, Esq; Welton Hill, Kidd Lane, Welton, N Humberside HU15 1PM; Vista Securities Ltd, 2 Parliament St, Hull HU1 2AP (☎ 0482 215850, fax 0482 215882)

WILBY, Prof Charles Bryan; s of Charles Edward Wilby (d 1974), of Leeds, and Olive Eleanor, *née* Whitehead (d 1970); *b* 13 July 1926; *Educ* Leeds Mod Sch, Univ of Leeds (BSc, PhD); *m* 19 Aug 1950, Jean Mavis, da of John William Broughton (d 1987), of Leeds; 3 s (Charles b 1952, Christopher b 1955, Mark b 1962); *Career* engr Yorkshire Hennebique Contracting Co Ltd, dep chief engr Twisteel Reinforcement Ltd Manchester, devpt engr Stuart's Granolithic Ltd, lectr and pt/t conslt Univ of Sheffield; currently: prof Univ of Bradford, conslt J Robinson & Son conslt engrs Bradford; pt/t lectr at colls of technol and further educn: Derby, Hull, Leeds, Stockport; chm Civil Engrg Panel Yorkshire Cncl for Further Educn, memb Cncl and chm Yorkshire Branch IStructE, dep chm Yorkshire Assoc, chm Students Section ICE, memb Panel Intermediate Technol, memb Ct Univ of Sheffield, memb Ct Cncl and Senate Univ of Bradford; FICE, FIStructE, CEng; *Books* 16 books incl: Basic Building Science (1963), Concrete Shell Roofs (1977), Post-tensioned Prestressed Concrete (1981), Structural Concrete (1983); author of over 40 technol papers; *Recreations* various and varying; *Style*— Prof Bryan Wilby; Flat 27, Esplanade Court, Harrogate HG2 0LW (☎ 0423 569061)

WILBY, David Christopher; s of Alan Wilby, of Baildon, Yorks, and June, *née* Uppard; *b* 14 June 1952; *Educ* Roundhay Sch Leeds, Downing Coll Cambridge (MA); *m* 23 July 1976, Susan Christine, da of Eric Arding (d 1977), of Bardsey, nr Wetherby, Yorks; 1 s (Edward b 1985), 3 da (Victoria b 1981, Christina b 1983, Charlotte b 1987); *Career* called to the Bar Inner Temple 1974; memb: NE circuit, Hon Soc of Inner Temple, Harrogate Round Table 1978-; *Recreations* golf, watching assocation and rugby football, being in Tenerife; *Clubs* Pannal Golf, Golf Del Sur (Tenerife), Taverners Headingley, 100 (Leeds) United AFC; *Style*— David Wilby, Esq; Stray Holt, Slingsby Walk, Harrogate, North Yorks (☎ 0423 888 019); San Andres, San Miguel, Tenerife, Canary Island; 5th Floor, St Paul's House, 23 Park Square, Leeds LS1 2NI (☎ 0532 455 866, car 0860 204 121); 2 Harcourt Buildings, Temple, London

WILCOCK, Christopher Camplin; s of Arthur Camplin Wilcock, of 66 Constable Road, Ipswich, Suffolk, and Dorothy Wilcock, *née* Haigh; *b* 13 Sept 1939; *Educ* Berkhamsted Sch, Ipswich Sch, Trinity Hall Cambridge (maj scholar, BA, MA); *m* 5 June 1965, Evelyn Clare; da of Geoffrey Joseph Gollin, of 24 Ottways Lane, Ashtead, Surrey; 2 da (Alice Emily b 1967, Florence Mary b 1969); *Career* HM Dip Serv: Arabian Dept FO 1962-63, third sec HM Embassy Khartoum 1964-66, Econ Rels Dept FO 1966-67, UK del NATO 1968-70, W European Dept 1970-72; Hospital Building Div DHSS 1972-74; Dept of Energy: Petroleum Prodn (subsequently Continental Shelf Policy Div) 1974-78 (promoted to asst sec 1976), Electricity Div 1978-81, seconded to Shell UK 1982-83, Estab and Fin Div 1984-88, (promoted to Grade 4 1986), Electricity Div A 1988- (promoted to Grade 3 1988); Order of the Two Niles, Fifth Class (Republic of the Sudan) 1965; *Recreations* reading, history, cinema; *Style*— Christopher Wilcock, Esq; Department of Energy, 1 Palace St, London SW1E 5HE (☎ 071 238 3734)

WILCOX, His Hon Judge David John Reed; s of Sqdn Ldr Leslie Leonard Kennedy Wilcox (d 1990), and Ada Margaret Reed, *née* Rapson (d 1958); *b* 8 March 1939; *Educ* Wednesbury Boys HS, King's Coll London (LLB); *m* 22 June 1962, Wendy Feay Christine, da of Ernest Cyril Whiteley (d 1974), of Singapore; 1 s (Giles Frederick Reed b 16 Nov 1962), 1 da (Hester Margaret Reed b 2 Jan 1965); *Career* Capt Directorate Army Legal Services 1962-65 (Far East Land Forces Singapore 1963-65); called to Bar Gray's Inn 1962, crown counsel Hong Kong 1965-68, practised Midland & Midland & Oxford Circuits 1968-85 (recorder 1979-85), circuit judge 1985-; chm Nottingham Friendship Housing Assoc 1969-75; *Recreations* gardening, travel; *Style*— His Hon Judge Wilcox

WILCOX, Desmond John; s of John Wallace Wilcox, and Alice May, *née* Whittle; *b* 21 May 1931; *Educ* Cheltenham GS, Christ's Coll London, Outward Bound Sea Sch (sail trg apprentice); *m* 1, 6 Jan 1954, Patsy, da of late Harry Price; 1 s (Adam b 1961), 2 da (Cassandra b 1959, Claire (twin) b 1961); m 2, 2 Dec 1977, Esther, OBE (1991), da of Harry Rantzen; 1 s (Joshua b 1981), 2 da (Emily b 1978, Rebecca b 1980); *Career* Nat Serv Army 1949-51; deckhand Merchant Marine 1948; reporter weekly papers 1949, news agency reporter 1951-52, reporter and foreign corr Daily Mirror (incl New York bureau and UN) 1952-60, reporter This Week ITV 1960-65; joined BBC 1965, co-ed and presenter Man Alive 1965, formed Man Alive Unit 1968, head of gen features BBC TV 1972-80, writer and presenter Americans (TV documentaries) 1979, presenter and chm Where it Matters (ITV discussion series), 1981; prodr and presenter BBC TV series: The Visit 1982 (1984-86), The Marriage (series) 1986; presenter 60 Minutes BBC TV 1983-84; SFTA Award for best factual programme series 1967; Richard Dimbleby Award SFTA for Most Important Personal Contrib in Factual TV 1971; tstee WALK Fund (Walk Again Limb Kinetics); memb Conservation Fndn; dir Wilcox Bulmer prodns (corporate videos, and independent prodn); *Publications* Explorers (jtly, 1975), Americans (jtly, 1978); with Esther Rantzen: Kill the Chocolate Biscuit: or Behind the Screen (1981), Baby Love (1985); *Recreations* riding; *Clubs* Arts, BBC; *Style*— Desmond Wilcox, Esq; East Heath Lodge, 1, East Heath Rd, Hampstead, London NW3 1BN (☎ 071 435 1950)

WILCOX, Lady; Judith Ann; *née* Freeman; *b* 31 Dec 1939; *Educ* St Mary's Convent Wantage; *m* 1986, as his 2 w, Sir Malcolm George Wilcox, CBE (d 1986); *Career* dir Morinie SCI; chm Nat Consumer Cncl; FRSA; *Recreations* fishing, sailing, tennis; *Style*— Lady Wilcox; 9 West Eaton Place, London SW1X 8LT (☎ 071 235 4490)

WILD, (James) Anthony; s of James Wild, of Bolton, and Margaret, *née* Warburton; *b* 11 May 1941; *Educ* Bedstone Sch Shropshire; *m* 1964, Jean Margaret, da of Ashton Dootson, of Bolton; 1 s (Daniel b 1976), 2 da (Sarah b 1968, Suzanne b 1970); *Career* CA, ptnr J Wild & Co 1964-87, conslt 1987-; dir: Associated Credits Ltd 1986-, Dean Property Gp Ltd 1984-, Forshaw Watson Hldgs Ltd 1986-; *Recreations* farming, working; *Style*— Anthony Wild, Esq; Orrell Cote Farm, Edgworth, Bolton, Lancs BL7 0JZ (☎ 0204 852771); Lancaster House, Blackburn St, Radcliffe, Manchester M26 9TS (☎ 061 723 3211, fax 061 723 3911)

WILD, (Charles) Barrie; s of Charles Wild (d 1960), of Skellow, Doncaster, and Dorothy Mary Wild (d 1982); *b* 6 Aug 1934; *Educ* Sir Percy Jackson GS; *m* 22 Aug 1959, Beryl Margaret, da of late Reginald Joseph Lowe, of York; 2 da (Karen Beverley b 1962, Katrina Lorraine b 1964); *Career* ptnr Wild & Co (accountants and auditors); auditor: Milk Mktg Bd 1979-, Thomson McLintock (now Peat Marwick McLintock) 1969-79; FCA; *Recreations* cricket, rugby league, horse racing; *Style*— Barrie Wild, Esq; 34 Dringthorpe Rd, Dringhouses, York YO2 2LG (☎ 0904 707227)

WILD, Dr David; s of Frederick Wild (d 1981), of 213 Manchester Road, Heywood, Lancs, and Lena, *née* Thomson (d 1981); *b* 27 Jan 1930; *Educ* Manchester GS, Univ of Manchester (MB ChB), Univ of Liverpool (DPh); *m* 19 June 1954, Sheila, da of Thomas Wightman (d 1981), of 76 Yew Tree Lane, Manchester 23; 1 s (Tom b 1962), 1 da (Christina b 1960); *Career* Nat Serv Capt RAMC 1954-56; dep co MO W Sussex CC 1963-74 (area MO 1974-81), regnl MO SW Thames RHA 1982-86 (dir professional servs 1986-90); memb Worthing DHA 1990-; FFCM 1980; *Recreations* conversation, reading; *Clubs* Royal Soc of Medicine; *Style*— Dr David Wild; 16 Brandy Hole Lane, Chichester, W Sussex PO19 4RY (☎ 024 352 7125); 13 Surrendale Place, London W9 3QW (☎ 071 289 7257)

WILD, (John) David; s of Herbert Winston Wild (d 1982), and Beatrice Mary, *née* Barraclough (d 1982); *b* 15 Aug 1937; *Educ* Bishop Vesey's GS, Sutton Coldfield; *m* 10 Aug 1962, Janet Rosemary, da of Edwin Clover Askew, of 94 Bonsall Rd, Erdington, W Midlands; 2 c (Jonathan b 1966, Zoe b 1974); *Career* dir various cos; memb Institute of CA in England and Wales; *Recreations* watching rugby union football, opera; *Style*— David Wild, Esq; 210 Birmingham Rd, Wylde Green, Sutton Coldfield, W Midlands BT2 1DD

WILD, John Vernon; CMG (1960), OBE (1955); s of James Wild (d 1964), and Ada Gertrude, *née* Clark (d 1947); *b* 26 April 1915; *Educ* Taunton Sch, Kings Coll Cambridge (MA, Cricket blue); *m* 1, 17 Oct 1942, Margaret Patricia, *née* Rendell (d 1975); 1 s (Paul b 1949, d 1986), 1 da (Judith b 1944); m 2, 30 Dec 1976, Marjorie Mary Lovatt Robertson, da of Francis William Lovatt Smith (d 1975); *Career* Colonial Admin Serv Uganda: asst dist offr 1938, asst chief sec 1950, estab sec 1951, admin sec 1955-60, chm Constitutional Ctee 1959; teacher mathematics Hele's Sch Exeter 1960-71, lectr in maths Exeter Sixth Form and Tech Coll 1971-76; *Books* Early Travellers in Acholi (1950), The Uganda Mutiny (1953), The Story of the Uganda Agreement (1957); *Recreations* cricket, golf, music; *Clubs* Rye Golf; *Style*— J V Wild, Esq, CMG, OBE; Maplestone Farm, Brede, Nr Rye, E Sussex TN31 6EP (☎ 0424 882261)

WILD, Jonathan; s of John William Howard Wild, CO (RAF), of Poole, Dorset, and Madeleine Clifford, *née* Hole; *b* 4 Aug 1951; *Educ* Woking GS for Boys, Univ Coll London (BSc, Dip Arch); *m* 27 April 1979, Jacqueline Ann, da of Roland Oliver Cise, of Walton-on-Thames, Surrey; 1 s (Nicholas James b 1980), 1 da (Anna Loise Julie b 1969); *Career* chartered architect, sole princ Wild Assocs, Wild Alliance and Penwild; RIBA; *Recreations* motor sport, windsurfing; *Style*— Jonathan Wild, Esq; Wild Associates, Rosemount Studios, Pyrford Rd, West Byfleet, Surrey KT14 6LD (☎ 0932 349926/342412)

WILD, Kenneth (Ken); s of Ernest Wild, and Ethel Harriet, *née* Singleton; *b* 25 July 1949; *Educ* Chadderton GS, Univ of York (BA); *m* 6 April 1974, Johanna Regina Elizabeth, da of Karl Heinrich Christian Wolf, of Cheltenham; 1 s (Philip b 1981), 1 da (Victoria b 1978); *Career* CA; Peat Marwick Mitchell & Co 1974-78, under ICEAW 1978-80, tech ptnr Touche Ross & Co 1984- (mangr and sr mangr 1980-84); FCA 1978; memb Cncl ICAEW 1989-90 (and vice chm Business Law Ctee); *Books* An Accountants Digest Guide to Accounting Standards - Accounting for Associated Companies (1982), Company Accounting Requirements, A Practical Guide (jtly, 1985), Manual of Financial Reporting and Accounting (jtly, 1990), The Financial Reporting and Accounting Service (jtly, 1990); *Recreations* reading, gardening; *Style*— Ken Wild, Esq; Touche Ross & Co, 13 Bruton St, London W1X 7AH (☎ 071 480 7766, fax 071 480 6861, telex 884257 ESAND G)

WILD, (Robert Rice) Lewis; s of Robert Edward Wild, and Emma Smith, *née* Hibbert (d 1939); *b* 10 Jan 1920; *Educ* Manchester GS, Univ of Manchester (MRCS, LRCP, capt athletic club), London Sch of Hygiene & Tropical Med (DIH, DTM&H); *m* 31 March 1953, Ann Marie, da of Walter Grieve Miller; 1 s (Ian Grieve b 7 Sept 1955), 2 da (Kilbee Ann b 12 Feb 1957, Penelope Marie b 28 July 1959); *Career* RNVR 1944-46; Derbyshire Royal Infirmary 1943-44 (casualty offr, house surgn), med offr Bahrain Petroleum Co 1948-53, asst chief med offr Caltex Pacific Petroleum Co 1953-58, med offr Demerara Bauxite Co 1960-68, sr med offr Sierra Leone Selection Tst 1968-72, med offr SMTF (Anglo-American) Zaire 1972-76, med advsr VSO 1979-85, private practice 1977-; farmer; asst scout master 1938, rep Lancs (Inter-Cos Athletic Championships) 1939; FRSM, FRSTM&H, memb Soc Occupational Med, Hon Life Memb Med Def Union; *Recreations* most spectator sports, philately; *Style*— Lewis Wild, Esq; 53 Wimpole St, London W1M 7DF (☎ 071 486 2289)

WILD, Prof Raymond (Ray); s of Frank Wild, of Chinley, Derbyshire, and Alice, *née* Large; *b* 24 Dec 1940; *Educ* Glossop GS, Stockport Tech Coll, Salford Coll of Tech, John Dalton Coll, Univ of Bradford (MSc, PhD), Brunel Univ (DSc); *m* 25 Sept 1965, Carol Ann, da of William Mellor, of Birchvale, Derbys; 1 s (Duncan Francis b 19 March 1970), 1 da (Virginia Kate b 10 June 1972); *Career* Industry: apprentice and draughtsman 1957-62, design engr 1962-64, res engr 1964-66, prodn controller 1966-67; Univ of Bradford: res fell 1967-69, lectr 1969-73; Henley Mgmnt Coll: prof 1973-77, princ 1990; Brunel Univ: head of Depts 1977-89, pro vice chllr 1988-89; coll govr; Whitworth fell; FIMechE, FIProdE, CBIM, FRSA, CEng; *Books* Work Organization (1975), Concepts For Operations Management (1977), Mass Production Management (1972), Techniques of Production Management (1971), Management And Production (1972), Production and Operations Management (1978), How To Manage (1982), and 7 others; *Recreations* writing, travel, theatre, sports, DIY; *Style*— Prof Ray Wild; Broomfield, New Rd, Shiplake, Henley-on-Thames, Oxfordshire RG9 3LA (☎ 0734 404102); Henley Management College, Greenlands, Henley on Thames, Oxon RG9 3AU (☎ 0491 571454, fax 0491 571635)

WILD, (John) Robin; JP (Ettrick and Lauderdale 1982-); s of John Edward Brooke Wild (ka 1943), of Whin Brow, Cloughton, Scarborough, Yorks, and Teresa, *née* Ballance; *b* 12 Sept 1941; *Educ* Sedbergh, Univ of Edinburgh (BDS), Univ of Dundee (DPD); *m* 31 July 1965, (Eleanor) Daphne, da of Walter Gifford Kerr (d 1975), of Edinburgh; 1 s (Richard b 1978), 2 da (Alison b 1967, Rosemary b 1977); *Career* princ in gen dental practice Scarborough Yorks 1965-71, dental offr E Lothian CC 1971-74, chief admin dental offr Borders Health Bd 1974-87, regnl dental postgrad advsr SE Regnl Ctee for Postgrad Med Educn 1982-87, dir of studies (dental) Edinburgh Postgrad Bd for Med 1986-87, dep chief dental offr Scottish Home and Health Dept 1987-; vice chm Tweeddale Ettrick & Lauderdale Cons & Unionist Assoc 1982-87, chm Scottish Cncl Br Dental Assoc 1985-87; hon fell Univ of Edinburgh 1984; *Recreations* restoration and driving of vintage cars, music, gardening, photography; *Clubs* Royal Cwlth Soc, RSAC; *Style*— Robin Wild, Esq, JP; Braehead House, St Boswells, Roxburghshire TD6 0AZ (☎ 0835 23203); Nether Craigwell, Calton Rd, Edinburgh EH8 8DR (☎ 031 557 6057); Scottish Home & Health Dept, St Andrew's House, Edinburgh EH1 3DR (☎ 031 244 2305)

WILDASH, Richard James; s of Arthur Ernest Wildash, of London, and Sheila Howard, *née* Smith; *b* 24 Dec 1955; *Educ* St Paul's, Corpus Christi Coll Camb (MA); *m* 29 Aug 1981, (Elizabeth) Jane, da of Peter Edward Walmsley, of Dundee; 1 da (Joanna b 1987); *Career* Dip Serv: FCO 1977, E Berlin 1979, Abidjan 1981, FCO 1984, first sec Br High Cmmn Harare 1988-; *Recreations* music, literature, the country; *Style*— Richard Wildash, Esq; British High Commission, P O Box 4490, Harare, Zimbabwe (☎ 793781); Foreign and Cwlth Office, King Charles St, London SW1A 2AH (☎ 071 270 3000)

WILDBLOOD, (Christopher) Michael Garside; s of Richard Garside Wildblood, of Villars, Switzerland, and Rita Muriel, *née* Jellings; *b* 9 Oct 1945; *Educ* Rugby, Corpus Christi Coll Cambridge (MA, Dip Arch); *m* 30 July 1971, Anne Somerville, da of Alun Roberts, of Radyr, Glamorgan; 1 s (Thomas Garside b 1976), 2 da (Shân Catherine Somerville b 1978, Jane Somerville b 1987); *Career* chartered architect; ptnr and principal Wildblood Macdonald Partnership 1975-; chm: RIBA Leeds Soc of Architects 1985-87, RIBA Yorkshire Region 1985-86; ARIBA; *Recreations* golf, choral singing, water-colour painting; *Clubs* Alwoodley Golf, Old Rugbeian Golfing Soc (Northern Sec); *Style*— Michael Wildblood, Esq; 24 Gledhow Lane, Leeds LS8 1SA; Wildblood Macdonald Partnership, Aubdy Studio, Audby Lane, Wetherby LS22 4FD (☎ 0937 65225)

WILDE, Dr Colin Ernest; s of James Wright Wilde (d 1982), of Poynton, Cheshire, and Maria, *née* Booth; *b* 17 Oct 1937; *Educ* Ashton under Lyne GS, Univ of Birmingham (BSc, PhD); *m* 29 Dec 1962, (Marjorie) Julie, da of James Garth Garner, of Doncaster; 2 da (Colette Elizabeth b 16 Jan 1969, Debbie-Jane b 10 Aug 1970); *Career* conslt clinical chemist Doncaster Royal Infirmary 1974-, hon lectr Univ of Sheffield Med Sch 1976-; memb: Scientific Advsy Ctee 1975-84 (chm), Pathology Advsy Ctee RHA 1978-82, Dept of Health Nat External Quality Assessment Scheme Steering Ctee 1979-, Advsy Ctee for Dangerous Pathogens 1981-87, Health Servs Advsy Ctee HSC 1983-, IFCC Educn Ctee Mexico project 1984-; advsr in clinical chemistry Br Cncl 1984-, hon nat treas Assoc of Clinical Biochemists 1987 (hon nat sec 1981-85), memb Panel of Examiners RCPath; FRSC 1964, FRCPath 1973; *Style*— Dr Colin Wilde; Department of Clinical Chemistry, Royal Infirmary, Doncaster, S Yorks DN2 5LT (☎ 0302 366666 ext 529)

WILDE, Ernest; s of Leonard Wilde (d 1970), of Thornton-Cleveleys, Lancs, and Harriet, *née* Hulmes (d 1988); *b* 22 Jan 1936; *Educ* Ashton-under-Lyne GS, Univ of Leeds (BSc, PhD); *m* 21 Aug 1962, Mary Constance, da of William Ingham (d 1960), of Manchester; *Career* Royal Aircraft Estab Bedford 1960-62, lectr Royal Coll of Advanced Technol 1960-66; Univ of Salford: lectr 1966-68, sr lectr 1968-, dir overseas educnl devpt 1982-, pr vice chllr 1987-; C Eng, MRAeS, FIMA; *Recreations* travel, walking, gardening; *Style*— Ernest Wilde, Esq; 10 Stiles Ave, Marple, Stockport, Cheshire SK6 6LR (☎ 061 427 4608); The University of Salford, Salford M5 4WT (☎ 061 745 5000, fax 061 745 5999)

WILDE, Malcolm James; s of Malcolm John Wilde, and Irene Doris, *née* Rickwood; *b* 9 Oct 1950; *Educ* Bishopshalt Sch; *m* 1 Sept 1973, (Helen) Elaine, da of John Bartley, and Doris Bartley; 1 s (Alastair James Rory b 27 Feb 1987), 2 da (Joanne Caroline b 6 July 1976, Julia Felicity b 10 Feb 1981); *Career* mangr Western American Bank

(Europe) Ltd 1970-75, vice pres Crocker Nat Bank 1975-77; dir: Guinness Mahon Holdings Ltd, Guinness Mahon & Co Ltd 1977-87; md: BCMB Group Ltd, British and Commonwealth Merchant Bank plc; chm British & Commonwealth Merchant Bank (Guernsey) Ltd, dir Prov Bank plc; *Recreations* golf, tennis, music, antique furniture; *Style—* Malcolm Wilde, Esq; Copyhold House, Copyhold Lane, Cuckfield, Sussex; British & Commonwealth Merchant Bank plc, 62 Cannon St, London EC4N 6AE (☎ 071 248 0900, fax 071 248 0906, telex 884040)

WILDE, Dr (Robert) Peter Havelock; s of Jack Kenneth Hilary Wilde, of Lamu, Leigh, Sherborne, Dorset, and Kathleen Elizabeth Wilde, *née* Cockerill; *b* 7 Nov 1950; *Educ* Prince of Wales Sch Nairobi, Univ of Liverpool (BSc), Univ of Oxford (BM BCh); *m* 21 March 1974, Helen Mary, da of David Sutherland, of 43 Breach Ave, Southbourne, W Sussex; 2 da (Clare Elizabeth b 20 Jan 1980, Jane Victoria b 1 July 1982); *Career* conslt cardiac radiologist Bristol Royal Infirmary; has published papers on diagnostic cardiac imaging, interventional cardiac therapy, coronary angioplasty and doppler echocardiography; memb ed bd of British Heart Journal: chm cardiac radiology advsy ctee to the RCR, cncl memb Br Cardiovascular Intervention Soc; MRCP, FRCR; *Books* Doppler Echocardiography (1989); *Recreations* family and friends; *Style—* Dr Peter Wilde; Dept of Radiodiagnosis, Bristol Royal Infirmary, Marlborough St, Bristol BS2 8HW (☎ 0272 282690, fax 0272 283267)

WILDING, Richard William Longworth; CB (1979); s of Longworth Allen Wilding (d 1963), of Oxford, and Elizabeth Olga Fenwick, *née* Stokes (d 1968); *b* 22 April 1929; *Educ* Winchester, New Coll Oxford; *m* 1954, Mary Rosamund, da of Sir Nicolas de Villiers (d 1958), of London; 1 s (James), 2 da (Lucy, Clare); *Career* civil servant (ret); head Office of Arts and Libraries 1984-88; former dep sec: HM Treasy, Civil Serv Dept; *Style—* Richard Wilding Esq, CB; 14 The Lodge, Kensington Park Gardens, London W11 3HA

WILDING, Thomas Henry (Tom); s of Jack Wilding (d 1985), and Ivy, *née* Spicer (d 1963); *b* 29 March 1930; *m* 27 Feb 1954, Ruby Edna, da of Charles William Wix (d 1954); 3 s (Andrew b 1958, Gavin b 1960, Mark b 1961), 1 da (Julia b 1967); *Career* chief chemist St Andrews Paper Mill 1950-57; mill mangr: Bowater Scott Walthamstow 1960-62 (dep 1957), Bowaters 1965 (mill dir 1968); dir: Kemsley Mill 1968-71, Southern Mills 1971, Independent Sea Terminals Ltd, Bowaters UK Paper Co Ltd 1971, Thames Mill 1973, Paper and Bd Div 1973 (and gen mangr); md: Paper and Bd Div 1977, Bowaters UK Paper Co Ltd 1978 (chm and md 1981); exec dir Bowaters Industries plc 1984, chief exec UK Paper plc 1988; memb Bd of Wilding Office Equipment Ltd; pres: CEPAC, Euro Paper Indust Fndn; memb Bd of Clares Equipment Hldgs Ltd; appeals pres Nat Playing Fields Assoc; *Recreations* golf, skiing; *Clubs* Tudor Park Golf and Country; *Style—* Tom Wilding, Esq; Garden Lodge, Boxley, Maidstone, Kent ME14 3CX; UK Paper plc, UK Paper House, Kemsley, Sittingbourne, Kent ME10 2SG (☎ 0795 24488, telex 96102, fax 0795 78038)

WILDISH, Gerald; s of Guy Newcomb Wildish, of Eastbourne, and Joyce Mary, *née* Holland; *b* 15 June 1941; *Educ* Magdalen Coll Sch Oxford, Univ of Manchester (Dip Social Admin, Capt hockey); *m* 9 Oct 1971, Brenda Margaret, da of George Whitehorn; 2 da (Helen Claire b 8 Sept 1972, Jennifer Louise b 26 Feb 1975); *Career* regnl trainee Oxford Regnl Hosp Bd 1960-64, nat trainee Univ of Manchester 1964-66, gen admin asst Darlington Meml Hosp 1966-68, sr admin asst United Newcastle upon Tyne Hosp 1968-70, asst gp sec Fulbourn HMC 1970-72, hosp sec St James' Hosp 1972-75, gen servs mangr Maidstone Health Dist 1978-82 (support servs mangr 1975-78), unit admin Chase Farm Hosp Enfield 1982-86, unit gen mangr Victoria Hosp Blackpool 1986-; assoc Royal Soc Health; *Books* Preserved Locomotives of the World (4 vols, 17 edns, 1968-86), Machin Stamps of the British Isles (1985), Steam In Germany (1970), Narrow Guage Preserved Steam (1969), Rail Researcher (1981, 1985); *Recreations* music, photography, railways, computers; *Style—* Gerald Wildish, Esq; Trees, 2 Worsley Rd, Ansdell, Lytham St Annes, Lancs FY8 4DD (☎ 0253 735107); Blackpool, Wyre and Fylde Health Auth, Victoria Hospital, Whinney Heys Rd, Blackpool FY3 8NR (☎ 0253 300000 ext 4400)

WILDMAN, Hon Mrs (Corinna); da of 2 Baron Cunliffe (d 1963); *b* 18 April 1929; *m* 18 May 1957 (m dis 1965), Frederick Starr Wildman; 1 s; *Books* Hand of Fortune (1985), Play of Hearts (1986), The Unsuitable Chaperone (1988); *Style—* The Hon Mrs Wildman; The Applehouse, RR1 Box 979, Dorset, Vermont 05251, USA

WILDMAN, David Aubrey; s of Ronald Aubrey Wildman, of Luton, Beds, and Bridget Teresa, *née* Cotter; *b* 4 July 1955; *Educ* Denbigh HS, Luton Coll; *m* 11 Oct 1975, Gillian, da of Edward Ambrose Close, of Richmond, N Yorks; 1 s (Philip b 1986); *Career* Chase Manhattan Bank 1973-75, Mobil Oil Co 1975-80, Herald Fin Servs 1980-88, owner of General and Medical Finance 1988-89 (md 1989-); *Recreations* theatre, good food, family; *Style—* David A Wildman, Esq; Forest Thatch, Pilton, Oundle, Peterborough PE8 5SN (☎ 080 15 692)

WILDSMITH, Brian Lawrence; s of Paul Wildsmith, of Yorks, and Annie Elizabeth Oxley (d 1984); *b* 22 Jan 1930; *Educ* De La Salle Coll, Slade Sch of Fine Art UCL (DFA); *m* 1955, Aurélie Janet Craigie, da of Bernard I Thurbide (d 1957); 1 s (Simon), 3 da (Clare, Rebecca, Anna); *Career* freelance artist 1957-, prodn design, illustrations, titles and graphics for first USA-USSR Leningrad film co prodn of the Blue Bird, artist and maker of picture books for young children; Kate Greenaway medal 1962, Soka Gakkai Educnl medal 1988; *Books* ABC (1962), The Lion and the Rat (1963), The North Wind and the Sun (1964), Mother Goose (1964), 123 (1965), The Rich Man and the Shoemaker (1965), The Hare and the Tortoise (1966), Birds (1967), Animals (1967), Fish (1968), The Miller, the Boy, and the Donkey (1969), The Circus (1970), Puzzles (1970), The Owl and the Woodpecker (1971), The Twelve Days of Christmas (1972), The Little Wood Duck (1972), Squirrels (1974), Pythons Party (1974), Blue Bird (1976), The True Cross (1977), What The Moon Saw (1978), Hunter and his Dog (1979), Animal Shapes (1980), Animal Homes (1980), Animal Games (1980), Animal Tricks (1980), Seasons (1980), Professor Noah's Spaceship (1980), Bears Adventure (1981), Cat on the Mat (1982), The Trunk (1982), Pelican (1982), Apple Bird (1983), The Island (1983), All Fall Down (1983), The Nest (1983), Whose Shoes (1984), Toot Toot (1984), Daisy (1984), Give a Dog a Bone (1985), What A Tale (1986), My Dream (1986), Goats Trail (1986), Giddy Up (1987), If I Were You (1987), Carousel (1988), The Christmas Story (1989), The Snow Country Prince (1990); *Recreations* piano, tennis; *Clubs* Reform; *Style—* Brian L Wildsmith, Esq; 11 Castellaras, 06370 Mouans-Sartoux, Alpes-Maritimes, France (☎ 0101 33 93752411)

WILDSMITH-TOWLE, Alan Geoffrey; s of Frederick William Towle (d 1973), of Broadmede, Derby, and Cissie Wildsmith, *née* Steeples; *b* 24 July 1939; *Educ* Sturgess Sch, Joseph Wright Sch of Art, Derby and Dist Coll of Art; *Career* served RAF photographer 1960-63; in family pharmacentical business 1957-60, photographer Rolls-Royce Derby 1964-68, started own photographic business 1968, moved to studio in St Neots Huntingdonshire 1972, moved back to Derbyshire 1976, opened studio at St George's House 1977; reg exhibitions USA; *awards* over 100 awards in photography incl: BIPP Photographer of the Year 1980-81, BIPP Midlands Region trophy (eight times winner since 1976), eight Kodak Gold awards for excellence (winner Pictorial and Commercial Sections), Fuji award in portraiture 1990; FBIPP 1977, memb Professional Photographers of America 1980, FRPS 1990, fell Master Photographers Assoc 1990, FRSA 1990; *Recreations* art, the environment, painting and drawing, agriculture, horseriding, gen quality of life; *Style—* Alan Wildsmith-Towle, Esq; Wildsmith-Towle, St George's House, Bridge St, Belper, Derbyshire DE5 1AZ (☎ 0773 825101)

WILDY, Michael Charles William; s of Cyril William Wildy (d 1980), of Woldingham, Surrey, and Isabel Stewart, *née* Ensell (d 1984); *b* 26 Sept 1926; *Educ* Charterhouse; *m* 3 Dec 1954 (m dis 1987), Rosemary Susan, da of late Christopher Browne; 2 s (Guy b 1955, Hugh b 1957), 1 da (Joanna b 1961); *Career* Nat Serv RN Sub Lt RNVR Northern Europe 1945-48; CA 1951; articles with Deloitte Haskins Sells 1958-51, professional experience London and Australia 1951-54; Booker plc 1954-84: fin dir 1964-84, vice chm 1980-84, chm authors div 1971-77, chm engrg 1973-76, chm food distribution div 1981-82; tstee and invest ctee memb Booker Pension Fund 1985-; non exec dir J W Spear and Sons plc 1985-; memb advsy ctee Causeway Develop Capital Funds 1985-, cncl memb C of E Childrens Soc 1982- (finance ctee memb 1978-, chm 1988-) FCA; *Recreations* golf (past club Capt), tennis, bridge, ornithology; *Clubs* Reform, Roehampton; *Style—* Michael Wildy, Esq; 7 The Layne, Middleton on Sea, nr Bognor Regis, W Sussex PO22 6JJ (☎ 024369 5900)

WILEMAN, John Malcolm Hayes; s of Harry Wileman (d 1967), of Mill House, Bishop Burton, Yorkshire, and Doris Hayes (d 1971); *b* 16 April 1938; *Educ* Rydal Sch North Wales, Westminster Hotel Sch; *m* 1 March 1974, Sandra Beatrice, da of Dennis George Russell Northern, of Brambles, Morecombelake, Dorset; 1 s (James b 1978); *Career* Nat Serv Army Catering Corps 1958-60; hotel gen mangr 1966-; memb Worshipful Co of Innholders 1980; hon memb The Society of Master Chefs; chm and fndr memb The Jersey Etching Gp; hon sec Asthma Soc (Jersey Branch) and Friends of the Asthma Research Cncl; FHCIMA; MCFA; *Recreations* etching, painting, concert-going, writing cookery articles; *Style—* John Wileman, Esq; Le Petit Chêne, La Rue de La Botellerie, St Ouen, Jersey, Channel Islands (☎ 0534 82410); Hotel L'Horizon, Jersey, Channel Islands (☎ 0534 43101)

WILEY, Lady (Jane Lily) Serena; *née* Lumley; da of 11 Earl of Scarbrough, KG, GCSI, GCIE, GCVO, TD, PC (d 1969), and Katharine, *née* McEwen, DCVO; *b* 1935; *m* 1963, Hugh Wiley; 3 s; *Style—* The Lady Serena Wiley; Oak Hill, Palmyra, Virginia, USA (☎ 804 589 3475)

WILEY, (William) Struan Ferguson; s of John Nixon Wiley (d 1968), of Hartlepool, and Muriel Isobel, *née* Ferguson (d 1969); *b* 13 Feb 1938; *Educ* Fettes, Univ of New Hampshire USA; *m* 1, 25 Jan 1964 (m dis 1977), Margaret Louise, da of Ian Graham Forsyth, of Crinan, Scotland; 1 s (Fergus b 1966), 2 da (Sarah b 1964, Anna b 1969); m 2, 21 Dec 1977, Rosemary Anne, da of Sir John Cameron, OBE, of Cowesby, Yorks; *Career* Nat Serv 2 Lt 10 Royal Hussars 1956-58, TA 1958-68, Lt Queens Own Yorks Yeo 1958-68; dir: Chunky Chicks (Nichols) Ltd 1962, Sterling Poultry Prods Ltd 1965, Ross Poultry Ltd 1970, Allied Farm Foods Ltd 1970, Imperial Foods Ltd 1975, Golden Lay Eggs UK Ltd (non-exec); chm and md Ross Poultry and Ross Buxted Nitrovit Ltd 1977; chm: J B Eastwood Ltd 1978, J Lyons Catering Ltd 1981, Normand Ltd 1981, Embassy Hotels Ltd 1983; asst md J Lyons & Co Ltd 1981-90, dir Allied-Lyons plc 1986-90, Normand Motor Gp Ltd (and chief exec) 1990; non-exec dir Wembley Stadium Ltd; chm Br Poultry Breeders and Hatcheries Assoc 1976; memb: Governing Body Houghton Poultry Res Station 1974-82, Grand Cncl Hotel Catering Benevolent Assoc 1983, Leisure Industs Ctee NEDC 1987; winner Poultry Indust Mktg Award 1977; Freeman: City of London 1980, Worshipful Co of Poulters 1981; *Recreations* golf, shooting, collecting old golf clubs; *Clubs* Cavalry and Guards, Woodhall Spa Golf; *Style—* Struan Wiley, Esq; Old Rectory, Withcall, Louth, Lincs LN11 9RL (☎ 050 784 218); Normand Motor Group Ltd, Abbey Road, Park Royal, London NW10 7RY (☎ 081 965 7757)

WILFORD, Sir (Kenneth) Michael; GCMG (1980, KCMG 1976, CMG 1967); s of George McLean Wilford (d 1965), and Dorothy Veronica, *née* Wilson, MBE (d 1945); gs of Sir Thomas Wilford, KCMG, KC, formerly NZ high cmmr in London 1929-33; *b* 31 Jan 1922,Wellington, NZ; *Educ* Wrekin Coll Shropshire, Pembroke Coll Cambridge (MA); *m* 1944, Joan Mary, da of Capt E F B Law, RN (d 1977); 3 da; *Career* RE WWII (despatches); entered Foreign Service 1947, Berlin 1947-49, asst private sec to Sec State Foreign Affrs 1949-52 and 1959-60, Paris 1952-55, Singapore 1955-59, private sec to Lord Privy Seal 1960-62, Rabat 1962-64, consul gen Peking 1964-66, cnsllr Washington 1967-69, asst under sec FCO 1969-73, dep under sec 1973-75, ambass Japan 1975-80; dir Lloyds Bank Inter 1982-87; advsr Baring Int Investment Mgmnt 1982-90; visiting fell All Souls Oxford 1966-67, memb IOD; hon pres Japan Assoc 1981-, chm Royal Soc for Asian Affairs 1984-; *Recreations* golf, gardening; *Style—* Sir Michael Wilford, GCMG; Brook Cottage, Abbotts Ann, Andover, Hants SP11 7DS (☎ 0264 710509)

WILKES, Prof Maurice Vincent; s of Vincent J Wilkes, OBE (d 1971), of Hagley, Worcestershire, and Helen, *née* Malone (d 1968); *b* 26 June 1913; *Educ* King Edward's Sch Stourbridge, St John's Coll Cambridge (BA, MA, PhD); *m* 1947, Bertie Mary (Nina), da of Bertie Twyman (d 1914), of Shanghai, China; 1 s (Anthony b 1950), 2 da (Helen b 1951, Margaret b 1953); *Career* WWII serv: sci offr ADRDE Army Ops Res Gp TRE 1939-42 (sr sci offr 1942-45); computer engr; Univ of Cambridge: univ demonstrator 1937-45, head Computer Laboratory (formerly Mathematical Laboratory) 1945-80, prof computer technol (now emeritus prof) 1965-80, fell St John's Coll 1950-; computer engr Digital Equipment Corp Maynard MA USA 1980-86, memb foreign res strategy Olivetti Res Bd 1986-90 (currently conslt); Hon DSc: Newcastle, Hull, Kent, City, Amsterdam, Munich, Bath; Hon DTech Linköpung Sweden; FRS, FEng, FBCS, FIEE; foreign assoc: US Nat Acad of Sci, US Nat Acad of Engrg; foreign hon memb American Acad of Arts & Scis; *Books* Memoirs of a Computer Pioneer (1985), technical books, papers in sci jls; *Clubs* Athenaeum; *Style—* Prof Maurice Wilkes, FRS; 130 Huntingdon Rd, Cambridge CB3 0HL; Olivetti Research Ltd, 24A Trumpington St, Cambridge CB2 1QA (☎ 0223 343 300)

WILKES, Richard Geoffrey; CBE (1990, OBE (mil) 1969), TD (1958), DL (Leics 1967); s of Geoffrey William Wilkes (d 1963), of Leicestershire, and Kathleen Mary, *née* Quinn (d 1932); *b* 12 June 1928; *Educ* Repton; *m* 1953, Wendy Elaine, da of Rev Clarence Oliver Ward (d 1982), of Hampshire; 1 s (Timothy), 3 da (Judi, Jane, Louise); *Career* cmmr RHA 1947, serv TA Leics 1948-72, cdr Royal Leicestershire Regt (TA) 1965-69, TA Col E Midlands Dist 1969-72, ADC (TAVR) to HM The Queen 1972-77, dep hon Col (TA) Royal Anglian Regt (Leics) 1981-88; chm Leicester Co TAVRA 1981-89, vice chm E Midland TAVRA 1981-89; chartered accountant; ptnr Price Waterhouse London 1969-90; dir Cassidy Davis Holdings Ltd 1989-; pres: ICAEW 1980-81, Int Fedn of Accountants 1987-90, advsr to Lloyds of London on self-regulation 1983-85; cmdt Leics Special Constabulary 1972-79; govr Care for Mentally Handicapped 1972-; FCA 1952; *Recreations* shooting, sailing; *Clubs* Army and Navy; *Style—* Richard Wilkes, Esq, CBE, TD, DL; The Hermitage, Foxton, Leicestershire (☎ 085 884213)

WILKES, Roderick Edward; s of Ernest Lawrence Wilkes (d 1987), of Staffordshire, and Sabra Whitehouse Johnson; *b* 26 Feb 1945; *Educ* Kingshill Sch Secdy Modern for Boys Wednesbury, Wednesbury Coll of Commerce (HND, DipH); *m* 28 March 1970, Marie, da of Harold Page; 1 s (James Edward b 6 June 1972), 1 da (Victoria Louise b 6 May 1974); *Career* Guest Keen & Nettlefolds Ltd 1969-70, commercial conslt GKN Sankey Ltd 1970-73, mktg dir Morlock Industries Ltd 1973-84, gp mktg dir Ellison

Circlips Group 1984-86, md Phoenix Rollformed Sections Ltd 1987- (gen mangr 1986-87); Chartered Inst of Mktg: memb Nat Exec, nat cncllr, Pres award; pres Nat Mktg Educn Bd, fndn govr St Peter's Collegiate Sch Wolverhampton; memb Communication Advtg and Mktg, FCIM, FBIM; *Recreations* theatre, swimming, travel; *Clubs* Wolverhampton CC; *Style—* Roderick Wilkes, Esq

WILKIE, David Andrew; MBE (1974); s of Henry George White Wilkie, of Aberdeen, Scotland, and Jean Angus, *née* McDonald; *b* 8 March 1954; *Educ* Royal Overseas Childrens' Sch Sri Lanka, Daniel Stewarts Coll Edinburgh, Univ of Miami Florida (BA); *partner* Helené Margareta, da of Öllaf Isacson; 1 da (Natasha Louisa b 25 June 1989); *Career* international swimmer; first represented GB 1969, currently competes in masters swimming events worldwide; Cwlth Games: Bronze medal 200m breaststroke 1970, Gold medal 200m breaststroke 1974, Gold medal 200m individual medley 1974, Silver medal 100m breaststroke 1976; Olympic Games: Silver medal 200m breaststroke 1972, Gold medal 200m breaststroke 1976, Silver medal 100m breaststroke 1976; World Championships: Gold medal 200m breaststroke 1973, Bronze medal 200m individual medley 1973, Gold medal 200m breaststroke 1975, Gold medal 100m breaststroke 1975; Euro Championships: Gold medal 200m breaststroke 1974, Gold medal 200m individual medley 1974, Silver medal 400m medley relay 1974; records broken: 5 world, 23 Cwlth, 16 Euro, 30 Br; records held: Euro and Br 200m breaststroke, Scot nat 200m breaststroke 1976-, 3 world in masters events; former ptnr Sports Perception; former tv presenter: Splash (Channel 4), Wings Wheels and Water (Channel 4), Winning With Wilkie (STV), Wilkie on Water (STV), Wilkie in Winter (STV); currently swimming analyst Eurosport, md Healthy Body Products; memb Worldwide Fund for Nature; *Books* Wilkie (autobiography), Winning with Wilkie, Splash, The Handbook of Swimming; *Recreations* scuba diving, travelling; *Style—* David Wilkie, Esq, MBE; Healthy Body Products, PO Box 29, Bracknell, Berks RG12 6RY (☎ 0344 425644, fax 0344 300042)

WILKIE, (Alex) Ian; s of Frederick James Wilkie (d 1976), and Florence Gladys Bell (d 1989); direct descendant of Sir David Wilkie, RA (1785-1841); *b* 1 Sept 1935; *Educ* Lancing, Poole Coll of Tech, Brighton Tech Coll (HNC Metallurgy); *m* 4 May 1963, Pamela May, da of William Frank Ross, of Hove, Sussex; 1 s (Andrew), 2 da (Jill, Philippa); *Career* Military Serv: The Gordon Highlanders; dir: The Assoc of Br Pewter Craftsmen Ltd, md Br Pewter Designs Ltd, Anzon Ltd subsid to Cookson Group plc 1980-84; head of corporate relations worldwide Cookson Group plc; memb: Country Landowners Assoc, Game Conservancy and Br Field Sport Soc; regular contributor of articles on: marketing advertising and corporate affrs; *Recreations* shooting, fishing, golf, gardening, property restoration; *Clubs* East India, Wig and Pen; *Style—* A Ian Wilkie, Esq; The Old Post Office, Hail Weston, Cambs; 416 Horsey Road, London W19; 29 Mona Road, Sheffield; 130 Wood St, London EC2V 6EQ (☎ 071 606 4400, car 0836 634153)

WILKIE, Liam; s of William Douglas Wilkie, of Kirkintilloch, and Kathleen, *née* Gormley (d 1984); *b* 15 Dec 1956; *Educ* St Ninian's HS, Kirkintilloch, Strathclyde Univ (LLB); *m* 25 May 1984, Anne, da of Alexander Barrie, of Blantyre; *Career* slr and notary public, for 8 years; *Recreations* swimming, walking, mountaineering, the arts, theatre; *Clubs* Glasgow Bar Assoc; *Style—* Liam Wilkie, Esq; Kennedy Court, 2 Braidholm Crescent, Giffnock, Glasgow (☎ 041 638 2874); Wilkie & Co, Solicitors, 686 Dumbarton Rd, Glasgow (☎ 041 339 0843/7715)

WILKINS, Christopher Scott; s of R S Wilkins (Ronald (Ronny) Scott), and Nora, *née* Mills; *b* 27 March 1945; *Educ* Emanuel Sch, King Coll Cambridge (MA English); *m* 1, 2 Aug 1966 (m dis 1979); 2 s (Ben b 1969, Toby b 1972); m 2, 4 May 1990, Siân, *née* Pearson; *Career* in advtg; copywriter Saatchi & Saatchi 1975-77, creative dir Young & Rubicam 1977-85, fndr Davis Wilkins Advertising Ltd 1985-; TV plays: The Late Wife (Thames 1975), The Day of the Janitor (LWT 1979); *Publications* Finger (1971); *Recreations* cooking, skiing, music; *Clubs* Annabel's, Mark's, Groucho; *Style—* Christopher Wilkins, Esq; 13 Soho Square, London W1V 5FB (☎ 071 287 3020)

WILKINS, Sir Graham John; s of George Wilkins; *b* 22 Jan 1924; *Educ* Yeovil Sch, Univ Coll Exeter; *m* 1, 1945, late Daphne Haynes; m 2, 1990, Helen Catherine MacGregor; *Career* chm and chief exec: Thorn EMI 1985-88 (dir 1978, chm 1988-89), Beecham Group 1975-84 (exec vice chm 1974); dir: Beecham Inc 1967-86, Beecham AG 1973-74, Courtaulds 1975-85, Hill Samuel 1977-88, Rowntree Mackintosh 1984-88, Eastern Electricity Bd 1989-; memb Doctors and Dentists Rem Review Body 1980-87 (chm 1987-90); pres Advertising Assoc 1983-89, chm ICC UK 1985-89; pres: Assoc of Br Pharm Indust 1969-71, European Fed Pharm Industs Assoc 1978-82; memb: BOTB 1977-80, Cncl Sch of Pharmacy Univ of London 1984-88 (chm 1988-); Hon FRCP 1985; *Style—* Sir Graham Wilkins

WILKINS, Prof Malcolm Barrett; s of Barrett Charles Wilkins (d 1962), of 28 Heath Park Av, Cardiff, and Eleanor Mary, *née* Jenkins; *b* 27 Feb 1933; *Educ* Monkton House Sch Cardiff, King's Coll London (BSc, PhD, DSc); *m* 10 July 1959, (Mary) Patricia, da of Lt-Cdr James Edward Maltby, RNR, RD; 1 s (Nigel Edward Barrett b 7 Aug 1961), 1 da (Fiona Louise Emma Barrett b 14 Jan 1965, d 1980); *Career* lectr in botany King's Coll London 1959-64 (assr lectr 1958-59), prof of biol Univ of E Anglia 1965-67 (lectr 1964-65), prof of plant physiology Univ of Nottingham 1967-70, regius prof of botany Glasgow Univ 1970-; chm: Life Sciences Advsy Ctee Euro Space Agency 1987-89, Laurel Bank Sch Co Ltd Glasgow 1980-87; memb Incorpn of Gardeners City of Glasgow, tstee Royal Botanic Gdns Edinburgh 1990-; hon memb American Soc for Plant Physiology; FRSE, FRSA; *Books* Plantwatching (1988), Advanced Plant Physiology (ed, 1984), The Physiology of Plant Growth and Development (ed, 1969); *Recreations* fishing, sailing, model engrg; *Clubs* Caledonian; *Style—* Prof Malcolm Wilkins, FRSE; 5 Hughenden Drive, Glasgow G12 9XS (☎ 041 334 8079); Botany Dept, Glasgow Univ, Glasgow G12 8QQ (☎ 041 330 4450/041 339 8855, ext 4450, fax 041 330 4447, telex 777070 UNIGLA)

WILKINSON, Rev Canon Alan Bassindale; s of Rev John Thomas Wilkinson (d 1980), of Knighton, Powys, and Marian, *née* Elliott (d 1980); *b* 26 Jan 1931; *Educ* William Hulme's GS Manchester, St Catharine's Coll Cambridge (BA, MA, PhD), Coll of the Resurrection Mirfield; *m* 1, 27 July 1961 (m dis 1975), Eva Leonore, da of Curt Michelson (d 1981), of Lausanne; 2 s (John b 1964, Conrad b 1968), 1 da (Sarah b 1962); m 2, 29 Dec 1975, Fenella Ruth, da of Col Rupert Thurstan Holland, CBE, DSO, MC (d 1959), of Salisbury; *Career* ordained: deacon 1959, priest 1960; asst curate St Augustine's Kilburn 1959-61, chaplain of St Catharine's Coll Cambridge 1961-67, vicar of Barrow Gurney 1967-70, chaplain and lectr of St Matthias' Coll Bristol 1967-70, princ Chichester Theol Coll 1970-74, warden Verulam House St Alban's 1974-75, sr lectr Crewe and Alsager Coll 1975-78, dir of training Ripon Diocese 1978-84, priest i/c Darley Thornthwaite and Thruscross 1984-88, hon priest of Portsmouth Cathedral 1988-; Open Univ tutor 1988-; select preacher: Cambridge 1967, Oxford 1982; memb: Gen Synod Bd of Educn 1982-86; memb: Governing Body Coll of Ripon and York St John 1984-88, Governing Body SPCK 1982-; Hon Canon: of Chichester 1970, of Ripon 1984; *Books* The Church of England and the First World War (1978), Would You Believe It? (1983), Christian Choices (1983), More Ready to Hear (1983), Dissent or Conform? War, Peace and the English Churches 1900-1945 (1986); *Style—* The Rev Canon Alan Wilkinson; Hope Cottage, 27 Great Southsea St, Portsmouth PO5 3BY (☎ 0705 825788)

WILKINSON, Alan Richard; s of Rev Richard Brindle Wilkinson, OBE (d 1966), and Mary, *née* Bretherton (d 1970); *b* 19 July 1923; *Educ* Culford Sch Bury St Edmunds; *m* 9 May 1953, Margaret Ruth, da of Dr Cuthwin Eagleston Donaldson (d 1988); 2 s (Andrew b 1956, Richard b 1962), 1 da (Jane b 1959); *Career* RE: sapper 1942, 2 Lt Trg Unit 1944; Lt 1 Para Sqdn RE 1944-45, Lt First Airborne Div, Burma Engrs Field Co 1946, Capt and Adj Depot Burma Engrgs 1946-47; design engr: Lewis & Duvivier, Coode & Partners (consltg engrs) 1947-54; Coode & Partners (later Coode Blizard): asst res engr Baghdad 1954-57, res engr Mombasa Port Kenya 1957-60, engr London 1960-62, res engr Mailsi Siphon Pakistan 1962-65, res chief engr Indus Basin Barrages Pakistan 1965-68 (ptnr 1969, sr ptnr and md 1985-89); FICE 1964 (MICE 1956), MConsE 1969; *Recreations* wood carving, sculpture, swimming, gardening; *Style—* Alan Wilkinson, Esq; Spinneys, Kippington Rd, Sevenoaks, Kent TN13 2LN

WILKINSON, Prof Andrew Wood; CBE; s of late Andrew Wood Wilkinson, of 134 Greenway Rd, Taunton, Somerset, and Caroline, *née* Robinson (d 1921); *b* 19 April 1914; *Educ* Huish Taunton, Weymouth Coll Dorset, Univ of Edinburgh (MB ChB); *m* 18 Sept 1941, Joan Longair, da of Cdr Guy Descarriéres Sharp, RN, of Edinburgh; 2 s (Peter, Angus), 2 da (Caroline, Jane); *Career* surgical specialist RAMC; Lt, Capt, Maj, Lt-Col; clinical tutor and asst surgn Royal Infirmary Edinburgh, sr lectr surgery Univ of Aberdeen, asst surgn Royal Infirmary Aberdeen, surgn Hosp for Sick Children Aberdeen, prof paediatric surgery Inst of Child Health Univ of London (emeritus prof 1979), asst surgn (later surgn) Hosp for Sick Children Gt Ormond St London 1956-79, ret; Freeman Worshipful Co of Apothecaries; FRCSEd, FRCS (pres 1976-79); *Style—* Prof Andrew Wilkinson, CBE; Auchenbrae, Rockcliffe, Dalbeattie, Kircudbrightshire

WILKINSON, Hon Mrs (Anthea Mary); *née* Hall; yr da of Baron Roberthall, KCMG, CB (Life Peer, d 1988), and his 1 w (Laura) Margaret, *née* Linfoot, now Lady MacDougall; *b* 3 June 1939; *Educ* Oxford HS for Girls, LMH Oxford; *m* 19 March 1966, (David) Max Wilkinson, s of Roger Wilkinson, of York; 1 s, 1 da; *Career* journalist with The Sunday Telegraph; *Recreations* music, being a housewife; *Style—* The Hon Mrs Wilkinson; 112 Hemingford Rd, London N1 1DE; The Sunday Telegraph, 1 Peterborough Court, At South Quay, 181 Marsh Wall, London E14 9SR (☎ 071 538 7421)

WILKINSON, Sheriff (Alexander) Birrell; s of Capt Alexander Wilkinson, MBE (d 1938), of Perth, Scotland, and Isabella Bell, *née* Birrell (d 1977); *b* 2 Feb 1932; *Educ* Perth Acad, Univ of St Andrews (MA), Univ of Edinburgh (LLB); *m* 10 Sept 1965, Wendy Imogen, da of Capt Ernest Albert Barrett, RE (d 1949), of Belfast; 1 s (Alan b 1974), 1 da (Jennifer b 1970); *Career* Nat Serv RAEC 1954-56; faculty of advocates 1959, practice Scottish Bar 1959-69, lectr in scots law Univ of Edinburgh 1965-69, Sheriff of Stirling Dunbarton and Clackmannan at Stirling and Alloa 1969-72, chm Industl Tbnls (Scotland) 1972-86, dean of faculty of law Univ of Dundee 1974-76 and 1986 (prof of private law 1972-86), Sheriff: of Tayside Central and Fife at Falkirk 1986-91, of Glasgow and Strathkelvin 1991-; chm: Scottish Marriage Guidance Cncl 1974-77, Legal Servs Gp Scottish Assoc of CAB 1979-83; memb ed bd Scottish Acad Press, chllr Dioceses of Brechin and of Argyll and The Isles; *Books* Gloag and Henderson's Introduction To The Law of Scotland (jt ed, 1980 and 1987), The Scottish Law of Evidence (1986); *Recreations* collecting books and pictures, reading, travel; *Clubs* New (Edinburgh); *Style—* Sheriff Birrell Wilkinson; 267 Perth Rd, Dundee DD2 1JP (☎ 0382 68939); Court of Glasgow and Strathkelvin, PO Box 23, 1 Carlton Place, Glasgow G5 9DA (☎ 041 429 8888)

WILKINSON, Charles Edmund; s of Dr Oliver Charles Wilkinson (d 1987), of Riverholme, Thames St, Wallingford, Oxon, and Sheila Muriel, *née* McMullan; *b* 6 June 1943; *Educ* Haileybury, ISC, Clare Coll Cambridge; *m* 3 June 1967, Gillian Margaret, da of Thomas Patrick Madden Alexander, of Forest Row, East Grinstead, Sussex; 2 da (Claire b 10 March 1972, Juliet b 13 June 1973); *Career* slr; sr ptnr Blyth Dutton 1980-91 (ptnr 1974-), ptnr Lawrence Graham (following merger) 1991-; memb Worshipful Co of Coachmakers and Coach Harness Makers, Freeman City of London; memb Law Soc; *Clubs* Hurlingham, Roehampton; *Style—* Charles Wilkinson, Esq; 190 The Strand, London WC2R 1JN (☎ 071 379 0000, fax 071 379 6854)

WILKINSON, Brig Charles Edward; CBE (1982, OBE 1977),TD (1964, and Clasp 1976), DL (Derbyshire 1985-); s of Charles Dean Wilkinson, of Woking, Surrey, and Florence, *née* Wakefield; *b* 5 May 1932; *Educ* Repton, Manchester Business Sch; *m* 15 Sep 1956, Joy Maureen, da of Arthur Locke, of Colchester, Essex (d 1946); 1 s (Timothy), 1 da (Sarah); *Career* Nat Serv cmmnd Sherwood Foresters 1951, Mercian Volunteers, Worcester-Foresters, staff 1952-85; Brig TA 1982; dir numerous cos including Leigh Interests plc 1990-; Hon Col 3 Worcester Foresters 1983-; chm E Midlands TAVRA 1985-; vice chm Cncl of TAVRAs 1990-; Liveryman Worshipful Co of Fuellers, Freeman City of London; *Recreations* Territorial Army, flying, photography, spectator sports; *Clubs* Army and Navy, City Livery, Royal Fowey Yacht; *Style—* Brigadier Edward Wilkinson, CBE, TD, DL; Thornbury, Ashford in the Water, Bakewell, Derbyshire DE4 1QH (☎ 0629 812535); Leigh Interests plc, Lindon Rd, Brownhills, Walsall, W Midlands WS8 7BB (☎ 0543 452121, fax 0543 374291, car ☎ 0836 500917)

WILKINSON, Christopher John; s of Maj Edward Anthony Wilkinson, of Welwyn Garden City, Herts, and Norma Doreen, *née* Trevelyan-Beer; *b* 1 July 1945; *Educ* St Albans Sch, Regent Street Poly Sch of Architecture (Dip Arch, RIBA); *m* 3 April 1976, Diana Mary, da of Alan Oakley Edmunds, of Limpsfield Chart, Surrey; 1 s (Dominic b 1980), 1 da (Zoe b 1978); *Career* princ ptnr Chris Wilkinson Architects 1983-; formerly with Richard Rogers and Ptnrs, Michael Hopkins Architects and Foster Assocs; assessor on BSC Colorcoat Award 1986 and 1987; works exhibited at Royal Acad Summer Exhibition 1986, 1987 and 1988; *Books* Supersheds (1991); *Recreations* golf, sketching, travel; *Style—* Christopher J Wilkinson, Esq; 52 Park Hall Rd, West Dulwich, London SE21 (☎ 081 761 7021); Studio 2, 10 Bowling Green Lane, London EC1R 0RD (☎ 071 251 8622, fax 071 251 8419)

WILKINSON, Brig Clive Anthony; CBE (1987); s of George Wilkinson (d 1974), of Cheltenham, and Elsie Annie Wilkinson, *née* Reid; *b* 14 Feb 1935; *Educ* Bishop Cotton Sch Simla India, Wrekin Coll Wellington Shropshire; *m* 4 July 1959, Nadine Elizabeth Wilkinson, da of William Humphreys (d 1979), of Southport; 2 da (Juliette b 1960, Caroline b 1962); *Career* Nat Serv 1953-55, cmmnd Lt RA 1955-67, RMC Camberley 1967; Col: RA 1967-74, military asst to C in C AFCE 1974-77, instr German Armed Forces Staff Coll 1977-79, CO 7 Bn UDR 1979-81, cos strategic planning team NATO HQ 1982-84, asst cos logistics HQ BAOR 1985-86; Brig cdr 107 Ulster Bde 1987-; FBIM 1989; *Recreations* dinghy sailing, golf, walking; *Style—* Brig Clive Wilkinson, CBE; c/o AODO, Mod Stanmore

WILKINSON, Clive Victor; *b* 26 May 1938; *Educ* Four Dwellings Secdy Mod Sch; *m* 7 Oct 1961, (Elizabeth) Ann; 2 da (Sarah Jane (Mrs Lamb), Rachel Elizabeth); *Career* Birmingham City Cncl: memb 1970-84, ldr 1973-76 and 1980-82, ldr oppn 1976-80 and 1982-84; chm: Nostrabell Group Business Consultants, Sandwell Health Authy; memb: Customers Servs Ctee Office Water Servs For Severn Trent Area 1990, Audit Cmmn, Black Country Devpt Corpn; former memb: Rural Devpt Agency, Countryside Cmmn; tstee Bournville Village Tst, chm Civil Housing Assoc; hon Alderman Birmingham City Cncl; *Recreations* squash, basketball, soccer; *Style—* Clive Wilkinson; Sandwell Health Authority, PO Box 1953, District General Hospital, Lyndon, W Bromwich, W Midlands

B71 4NA (☎ 021 553 6151)

WILKINSON, (Thomas) David; s of Thomas Lancelot Wilkinson, of Standdlestones, Stitching Lane, Hilcott, Pewsey, and Ruth Margaret, *née* Hedley; *b* 1 May 1940; *Educ* St John's Sch Leatherhead Surrey; *m* 25 July 1964, Angela Mary, da of Peter Martineau, of 54 St Ann St, Salisbury; 1 s (Edward Rupert b 23 June 1969), 1 da (Camilla b 10 May 1974); *Career* 5 Royal Inniskilling Dragoon Guards 1959-63; mktg dir: Del Monte Int 1972, Bacardi Int 1974-79, gen mangr Fourcroy UK 1982, md Finnish Nat Distiller (Alko) Ltd 1983, Alko Ltd Exports; *Recreations* sailing, skiing; *Clubs* Anglo-Belgian; *Style*— David Wilkinson, Esq; Heath House, Hazeley Lea, Hartley Wintney, Basingstoke, Hants RG27 8ND (☎ 0734 326 298); P O Box 350, Helsinki 10, Finland (☎ 010 358 013311, fax 010 3580 1333225)

WILKINSON, Sir Denys Haigh; s of Charles Wilkinson, and Hilda Wilkinson; *b* 5 Sept 1922; *Educ* Loughborough GS, Jesus Coll Cambridge; *m* 1, 1947 (m dis 1967), Christiane, *née* Clavier; 3 da; m 2, 1967, Helen, *née* Sommers; 2 step da; *Career* dir Int Sch Nuclear Physics Erice Sicily 1974-83, vice chllr Univ of Sussex 1976-87; chm: Br Cncl Scientific Advsy Panel and Ctee 1977-86, Radioactive Waste Mgmnt Advsy Ctee 1978-83; memb: Wilton Park Acad Cncl 1979-83, Cncl Assoc Cwlth Univs 1980-87; pres Inst of Physics 1980-82, foreign memb Royal Swedish Acad of Sciences 1980-, Hon FilDr Uppsala; Hon DSc: Saskatchewan, Utah State, Guelph, Queen's (Kingston), Coll of William and Mary Williamsburg; Hon LLD Univ of Sussex; FRS 1956; kt 1974; *Style*— Sir Denys Wilkinson, FRS; Gayles Orchard, Friston, Eastbourne, E Sussex BN20 0BA (☎ 0323 423333)

WILKINSON, Donald John; s of Frederick Wilkinson, of Wigan Lancs, and Tina, *née* Cameron; *b* 14 Feb 1955; *Educ* Lancaster Royal GS, Keble Coll Oxford (BA, MLitt); *m* 1 Aug 1979, Janet Margaret, da of Stanley Wilkinson; 1 s (Ian b 1984), 1 da (Rachael b 1983); *Career* teacher Manchester GS 1979-84, head of history Oakham Sch 1984-86, head of sixth form Newcastle-under-Lyme Sch 1987-89, headmaster Cheadle Hulme Sch 1990-; *Publications* The Normans in Britain (jtly 1988), various articles on seventeenth century English history; *Recreations* sport, especially cricket and running, walking, theatre, reading modern novels; *Style*— Donald Wilkinson, Esq; Cheadle Hulme School, Claremont Rd, Cheadle Hulme, Cheshire SK8 6EF (☎ 061 485 4142)

WILKINSON, Hon Mrs (Elizabeth Jane Molyneux); *née* Fletcher; da of Baron Fletcher, PC (Life Peer); *b* 1938; *m* 1962, David Blair Wilkinson; 3 s, 1 da; *Style*— The Hon Mrs Wilkinson; Charnwood Lodge, Burton Rd, Repton, Derby DE6 6FN (☎ 0283 702339)

WILKINSON, Prof Sir Geoffrey; s of Henry Wilkinson (d 1978), of Todmorden, Yorks, and Ruth Crowther (d 1971); *b* 14 July 1921; *Educ* Imperial Coll London, in the USA; *m* 1951, Lise Sølver, da of Rektor Prof Svend Aa Schou, of Copenhagen; 2 da; *Career* Sir Edward Frankland prof of inorganic chem Imperial Coll 1956-88; sr res fell Imperial Coll (prof emeritus 1988-), hon fell UMIST 1989; memb: Nat Acad of Sciences (US), Royal Danish Acad of Sciences; hon fell Spanish Sci Res Cncl, centennial foreign fell American Chem Soc; Hon DSc: Edinburgh, Granada, Columbia, Bath, Essex; awarded: Lavoisier medal (French Chemical Soc), jt Nobel prize for Chemistry 1973, Galileo Medal Univ of Pisa; FRS; kt 1976; *Books* Advanced Inorganic Chemistry (jt author, 5 edn 1988); *Style*— Prof Sir Geoffrey Wilkinson; Imperial Coll, London SW7 2AY (☎ 071 589 5111 ext 4504)

WILKINSON, Geoffrey Crichton; CBE (1986), AFC (1957); s of Col William Edward Duncan Wilkinson (d 1980), of 15 High St, Rode, Bath, Avon, and Evelyn Katherine Wilkinson; *b* 7 Nov 1926; *Educ* Bedford Sch, Royal Indian Mil Coll; *m* 6 Dec 1958, Virginia Mary, da of Russell Broom (d 1963), of Rodinghead, Mauchline, Ayrshire; 2 da (Susannah (Mrs Wright) b 1961, Samantha (Mrs Barber) b 1963); *Career* aeronautical engrg trg RN 1948-49 (flying trg 1944-47); pilot RAF 1949-59, seconded UASF Korea 1952-53, Empire Test Pilot Sch 1956, engrg test pilot 1957-59, ret 1959; Turner and Newall 1959-61, dir Mercury Airlines 1961-65, dep chief inspr air accidents Dept of Trade 1981 (inspr 1965, ret as chief inspr accidents 1986); Air medal USA 1953; FRAeS 1970; *Recreations* sailing; *Clubs* RAF, RAF YC; *Style*— Geoffrey Wilkinson, Esq, CBE, AFC; Buckingham House, 50 Hyde St, Winchester, Hants SO23 7DY (☎ 0962 865823)

WILKINSON, Glen Alexander Low; s of Cdr James Henry Wilkinson, of 17 Beech Grove, Alverstoke, Gosport, Hants, and Alexia Menny, *née* Low; *b* 2 Sept 1950; *Educ* Churcher's Coll Petersfield Hants, Univ of Birmingham Univ Med Sch (MB ChB); *m* 26 March 1976, Diana Joy, da of George Norman Purdy, of 57 Newlands Drive, Halesowen; 1 s (Matthew James b 11 Feb 1988), 3 da (Rebecca b 9 Feb 1978, Angela b 9 March 1979, Laura b 19 May 1986); *Career* sr registrar in cardiothoracic surgery W Midlands RHA 1985-88, sr fell (actg instr) in cardiothoracic surgery Univ Hosp Washington Seattle USA 1986-87, currently CCS Sheffield Health Authy and Northern Gen Hosp; FRCS 1978, memb Soc of Cardiothoracic Surgns of GB and I 1986; *Recreations* model railway running and collecting, model boat building, photography; *Style*— Glen Wilkinson, Esq; 31 Meadow Bank Ave, Cherry Tree Hill, Nether Edge, Sheffield S71 1PB (☎ 0742 583197); Northern General Hospital, Herries Rd, Sheffield S5 7AU (☎ 0742 434343, fax 0742 560472)

WILKINSON, Sir Graham; 3 Bt (UK 1941), of Brook, Witley, Co Surrey; s of Sir David Wilkinson, 2 Bt, DSC (d 1972); *b* 18 May 1947; *Educ* Millfield, ChCh Oxford; *m* 1977, Sandra Caroline, da of Dr Richard Rossdale; 2 da (Louise Caroline Sylvia b 1979, Tara Katherine Juliet b 1982); *Heir* none; *Career* dir Orion Royal Bank Ltd 1971-85, md SEIC Services (UK) 1985-89, non-exec dir Galveston-Houston Co USA 1986-89; OStJ; *Clubs* Royal Yacht Sqdn; *Style*— Sir Graham Wilkinson, Bt

WILKINSON, James Arthur; s of James Arthur Wilkinson (d 1972), and Mary Allaby (d 1970); *b* 16 July 1928; *Educ* Westham GS, Chelmsford Poly (HNC); *m* 22 July 1961, Margaret, da of John Welsh (d 1958); *Career* engr Crompton Parkinson 1952-68; fndr dir Indust Control Services plc 1968-; developed wind turbine powered catamaran; FInstD, Safety and Reliability Soc; memb Instrument Soc of America; *Publications* author of numerous articles in learned jls on risks in chem, oil and nuclear installations; *Recreations* sailing, golf; *Clubs* Maldon Little Ship, Burnham Golf; *Style*— James Wilkinson, Esq; Beacon Hill House, St Lawrence, Southminster, Essex CM0 7LP (☎ 0621 87721); Industrial Control Services plc, Hall Road, Madon, Essex

WILKINSON, James Hugh; s of Hugh Davy Wilkinson (d 1972), and Marjorie, *née* Prout (d 1965); *b* 19 Sept 1941; *Educ* Westminster Abbey Choir Sch, Sutton GS, Kings Coll Univ of London (BSc), Churchill Coll Cambridge (CertEd); *m* 11 Nov 1978, Elisabeth Ann, da of John Morse, of Cheltenham; 2 s (Christopher b 1979, Matthew b 1982); *Career* corr: science and health Daily Express 1964-74, sci and aviation BBC Radio 1974-83, sci BBC TV News 1983-; sec Brotherhood of St Edward the Confessor Westminster Abbey 1982-; *Books* Conquest of Cancer (1973), Tobacco (1986), Green or Bust (1990); *Recreations* collecting; *Style*— James Wilkinson, Esq; BBC TV Centre, Wood Lane, London W12 7RJ (☎ 081 576 7487, fax 081 749 9016)

WILKINSON, Jeffrey Vernon; s of Arthur Wilkinson (d 1965), and Winifred May Allison (d 1989); *b* 21 Aug 1930; *Educ* Matthew Humberstone Sch, King's Coll Cambridge (MA), Sorbonne; *m* 1955, Jean Vera, da of George Farrow Nurse (d 1959); 2 da (Julie Katherine b 1962, Elizabeth Jane b 1964); *Career* Joseph Lucas Ltd: joined as graduate apprentice 1954, dir CAV 1963, dir and gen mangr Diesel Equipment CAV 1967, dir 1974, divnl md 1978; dir Simon Engineering 1968, gen mangr Lucas Electrical 1974, jt gp and Lucas Industries plc 1979-84, dir Alan Patricof Assocs 1986, chm and chief exec offr Rotaprint Industries Ltd 1988; chm: Automotive Components Manufacturers 1979-84, Plastics Processing Economic Devpt Ctee 1985-88; memb Cncl and Exec SMMT 1979-84; Liveryman Worshipful Co of Wheelwrights 1971-; FBCS, CBIM; *Recreations* tennis, swimming, water skiing, reading, theatre; *Style*— Jeffrey Wilkinson, Esq; Hillcroft, 15 Mearse Lane, Barnt Green, Birmingham B45 8HG (☎ 021 445 1747)

WILKINSON, Jeremy Squire; s of Philip Squire Wilkinson (d 1979), of Butley Rise, Prestbury, Cheshire, and Mary, *née* Betteridge; *b* 4 June 1936; *Educ* Rugby, Univ of Cambridge (MA, LLM); *m* 29 Sept 1962, Alison Margaret, da of Walter Thomas Isaac, OBE, of Pierce Close, Prestbury, Cheshire; 1 s (Timothy), 1 da (Emma); *Career* Nat Serv 2 Lt RCS 1954; admitted slr 1962, chm: bd of mangrs Cheadle Royal Hosp, Talyllyn Railway Preservation Soc; govr Cheadle Hulme Sch, tstee Narrow Gauge Railway Museum; *Recreations* history of mines, quarries and railways; *Style*— Jeremy Wilkinson, Esq; 3 Old Orchard, Wilmslow, Cheshire SK9 5DH (☎ 0625 524535)

WILKINSON, John Arbuthnot Ducane; MP (C) Ruislip-Northwood 1979-; s of Denys Wilkinson; *b* 23 Sept 1940; *Educ* Eton, RAF Coll Cranwell, Churchill Coll Cambridge; *m* 1, 1969 (m dis 1987), 1 da; m 2, 1987, Cecilia, da of Raoul Cienfuegos; 1 s; *Career* RAF Flying Instructor; MP (C) Bradford W 1970-74 (fought Bradford W Sept and Oct 1974); PPS to: Min of State Indust 1979-80, to John Nott as Sec of State Defence 1981-82; chm Anglo-Asian C Soc 1979-82; PA to chm BAC, sales mangr Klingair Ltd, tutor OU, head Univs Dept C and UCO and ex regular RAF, also SAS (TA); delegate to Cncl of Europe and WEU 1979-90; chm: EMC (Comms) Ltd 1985-, chm C Aviation Ctee 1983-85 and 1990 (chm Space Sub Ctee 1986-90); *Books* The Uncertain Ally - British Defence Policy 1960-90 (with Michael Chichester), British Defence, a Blueprint for Reform; *Recreations* flying; *Clubs* IOD; *Style*— John Wilkinson Esq, MP; House of Commons, London SW1

WILKINSON, John Arthur; *b* 3 March 1925; *Educ* Univ of Wales, Univ of London (BSc, MB MCh); *Career* RAMC 1949-50; sr conslt orthopaedic surgn: Univ Hosp Southampton, Lord Major Treloar Hosp Alton, Guernsey CI; FRCS, FRSM, fell Br Orthopaedic Assoc; *Books* Congenital Displacement of the Hip Joint (1985); *Style*— John Wilkinson, Esq; 3 Oakmount Ave, Highfield, Southampton, Hampshire SO2 1DS; 4 Hulse Rd, Banister Park, Southampton, Hants SO1 2JX (☎ 334897)

WILKINSON, John Francis; s of Col W T Wilkinson, DSO (d 1950), and Evelyn Sybil (d 1975); *b* 2 Oct 1926; *Educ* Wellington, Univ of Edinburgh, Cambridge and London Univ Colonial Course; *m* 11 Aug 1951, Alison Jessie, da of Hugh Wilmott Malcolm (d 1961); 2 (Anthony Hugh b 5 April 1953, Roderick William b 26 Oct 1954), 1 da (Julian Margaret Marion b 24 Sept 1960); *Career* trainee pilot Fleet Air ARM 1945, RN 1945-47; HM Colonial Serv Nigeria: asst dist offr Bida 1949, asst sec Land & Mines Kanduna 1950, private sec to Chief Cmmr N Nigeria 1951; Nigerian Bdcasting Serv: controller N Region 1952, controller Nat Progs Lagos 1956-58; BBC African Service: orgn African Prog 1958, E and Central Africa Prog 1961, asst head 1964, head 1969-79; head of prodn and planning BBC World Service 1976; sec BBC 1977, dir Pub Affrs BBC 1980-85; vice pres The Centre for Int Briefing Farnham Castle 1987- (chm 1977-87), tstee One World Bdcasting Tst 1990- (dir 1986-90), vice pres Royal African Soc 1978-80 (chm Speakers and Publications Ctee 1970-78); memb Cncl Mgmnt Centre for World Devpt Educn 1988-; Hon Master Open Univ 1989; *Recreations* sailing, occasional golf; *Clubs* Commonwealth Trust; *Style*— John Wilkinson, Esq; Compass Cottage, Minchinhampton, nr Stroud, Gloucester GL6 9HD (☎ 045 383 3072, fax 045 383 3617)

WILKINSON, John Parker; JP (Cambridgeshire, 1975); s of Lt-Col William Currington Wilkinson, MC, TD, of Peterborough, and Brenda Mary, *née* Parker (d 1989); *b* 3 July 1939; *Educ* Kings Sch Peterborough, Nottingham Coll of Art and Design (DipTP); *m* 29 June 1963, Barbara Ann, da of John George Metcalf (d 1984), of Peterborough); 1 s (James b 1968), 1 da (Anna b 1966); *Career* asst architect Barlett and Grey Nottingham 1962-65, architect co planning dept Huntingdon 1965-68, ptnr Ruddle Wilkinson Ptnrship Peterborough 1972- (architect and planner Ruddle and Wilkinson 1968-72); dir Norwich and Peterborough Bldg Soc 1980-, pres Peterborough Rotary Club 1981-82, memb Peterborough Civic Soc; ARIBA 1964, MRTPI 1968, FInstD 1986; *Recreations* swimming, photography, walking, geology; *Style*— John Wilkinson, Esq, JP; 84 Lincoln Rd, Peterborough, Cambs PE1 2SW (☎ 0733 314314, fax 0733 52242)

WILKINSON, Rev Keith Howard; s of Kenneth John Wilkinson, of Leicester, and Grace Winifred, *née* Bowler; *b* 25 June 1948; *Educ* Beaumont Leys Coll Leicester, The Gateway GS Leicester, Univ of Hull (BA), Emmanuel Coll Cambridge (MA), Westcott House Cambridge; *m* 27 Aug 1972, Carolyn, da of Lewis John Gilbert (d 1985), of Wokingham; 2 da (Rachel b 1979, Claire b 1979); *Career* head of religious studies Bricknell HS 1970-72, head of faculties (humanities) Kelvin Hall Comprehensive Sch Kingston upon Hull 1972-74; ordained: deacon 1976, priest 1977; asst priest St Jude Westwood Peterborough 1976-79, educn offr to the church Peterborough 1977-79, asst master and chaplain Eton Coll 1979-84, sr chaplain and head of religions studies Malvern Coll 1984-89 (sr tutor 1988-89), headmaster Berkhamsted Sch 1989-; chaplain Oxford Conf on Educn 1987-, memb steering ctee The Bloxham Project 1988-; *Recreations* films, music, drama, ecology, walking, buildings, building; *Clubs* United Ushers; *Style*— The Rev Keith Wilkinson; Wilson House, The School, Castle St, Berkhamsted, Herts HP4 2BE (☎ 0442 864827)

WILKINSON, Dr Mark Lawrence; s of Rev Canon Raymond Stewart Wilkinson, QHC, of Warwick, and Dorothy Elinor, *née* Church; *b* 19 May 1950; *Educ* Birkenhead Sch, The Middx Hosp Med Sch, Univ of London (BSc, MB BS, MD); *m* 4 Jan 1975, Anna Maria, da of Nicola Ugo Dante Cassoni, of Kenton, Harrow; 1 s (Nicholas b 1979), 1 da (Elinor b 1985); *Career* registrar Middx Hosp 1979-81; Liver Unit KCS of Med: res fell 1981-84, lectr 1984-86; sr lectr and conslt physician Guy's Hosp and UMDs at Guy's and St Thomas' Hosps 1986-; memb: Endoscopy Ctee of Br Soc of Gastroenterology, Br Euro and Int Assocs for Study of the Liver; MRCP 1977; *Recreations* books, walking, Italy; *Style*— Dr Mark Wilkinson; Gastroenterology Unit, UMDS Guy's and St Thomas's Hosp, 18th Floor, Guy's Tower, St Thomas' St, London SE1 9RT (☎ 071 955 4564, fax 071 407 4564)

WILKINSON, Prof Paul; s of Walter Ross Wilkinson (d 1985), of Bristol, and Joan Rosemary, *née* Paul; *b* 9 May 1937; *Educ* Lower Sch of John Lyon Harrow, Univ Coll Swansea (MA); *m* 19 March 1960, Susan Sherwyn, da of Charles William John Flook (d 1968), of Newport, Gwent; 2 s (John Paul b 1964, Charles Ross b 1969), 1 da (Rachel Margaret b 1962); *Career* served RAF 1959-65, ret as Flt Lt; asst lectr in politics Univ Coll Cardiff 1966-68 (lectr 1968-75), visiting prof Simon Fraser Univ Canada 1973, sr lectr in politics Univ Coll Cardiff 1975-78, reader in politics Univ of Wales 1978-79, prof int relations Univ of Aberdeen 1979- (head Dept Politics and Int Relations 1985-); chm Res Fndn Study of Terrorism 1986-89, dir Res Inst for Study of Conflict and Terrorism 1989-; conslt BBC London and CBS News NY 1986-, jt ed Terrorism And Political Violence (scholarly jnl) 1988-; hon fell Univ Coll Swansea; memb: RIIA, Br Int Studies Assoc, Political Studies Assoc; *Books* Social Movement (1971), Political Terrorism (1974), Terrorism versus Liberal Democracy (1976),

Terrorism and the Liberal State (1977, revised edn 1986), Terrorism: Theory versus Practice (jtly, 1978), British Perspectives on Terrorism (1981), The New Fascists (revised edn, 1983), Contemporary Research on Terrorism (1987), Lessons of Lockerbie (1989), Terrorist Targets and Tactics (1990); *Recreations* walking, modern painting, poetry; *Clubs* Savile; *Style—* Prof Paul Wilkinson; Dept Int Relations, University of St Andrews, St Andrews, Fife KY16 9AJ (☎ 0334 76161, fax 0334 75851, telex 9312110846 SAG)

WILKINSON, Lt-Col Sir Peter Allix; KCMG (1970, CMG 1960), DSO (1944), OBE (1944); s of Capt Osborn Cecil Wilkinson (ka 1915), by his w Esmé Barbara, da of Sir Alexander Wilson; *b* 15 April 1914; *Educ* Rugby, Corpus Christi Coll Cambridge; *m* 1945, Mary Theresa (d 1984), da of Algernon Hyde Villiers (ka 1917, 3 s of Rt Hon Sir Francis Hyde Villiers, GCMG, GCVO, CB, sometime ambass Brussels, 4 s of 4 Earl of Clarendon) by his w Beatrix (who subsequently m (1919) 4 Baron Aldenham & (2 Baron) Hunsdon, by whom she was mother of 5 Baron Aldenham); 2 da (Virginia b 1947, m 1971, Daniel Worsley; 1 s, 1 da; Alexandra b 1953; 1 s, 2 da); *Career* cmmnd 2 Bn Royal Fusiliers 1935, served WWII (Poland, Fr, Balkans, Central Euro, Italy) Lt-Col, ret 1947; joined Dip Serv 1947; 1 sec: Vienna 1947, Washington 1952; cnsllr Bonn 1955-60, under sec Cabinet Office 1963-64, sr civilian instr IDC 1964-66, ambass Vietnam 1966-67, asst under sec FO 1967-68, dep under sec and chief admin Dip Serv 1968-70, ambass Vienna 1970-71, ret 1972; re-employed as dep sec Cabinet Office 1972-73; Polish Cross of Valour 1940, Czech Order of White Lion 1945, Order of Yugoslav Banner (hon) 1984; *Recreations* reading, trout-fishing; *Clubs* White's, Army and Navy; *Style—* Lt-Col Sir Peter Wilkinson, KCMG, DSO, OBE; 28 High St, Charing, Kent (☎ 023 371 2306)

WILKINSON, Prof Peter Charles; s of Michael Charles Wilkinson (d 1980), and Helen Craig, *née* Wilcox (d 1975); *b* 10 July 1932; *Educ* London Hosp Med Coll (MB BS, MD); *m* 28 nov 1958, Eileen mary, da of Joseph Baron (d 1983); 2 s (Anthony b 1960, James b 1964), 1 da (Catherine b 1962); *Career* lectr London Hosp Med Coll 1960-63; bacteriology and immunology dept Univ of Glasgow: lectr 1964-69, sr lectr 1969-77, reader 1977-82, titular prof 1982-; visiting prof Rockefeller Univ New York 1979, hon conslt immunology Western Infirmary Glasgow 1970-; FRSE 1983, FIBiol 1987; *Books* Dictionary of Immunology (3 edn, 1985), Chemotaxis and Inflammation (2 edn, 1982), approximately 150 sci papers; *Recreations* books; *Style—* Prof Peter Wilkinson, FRSE; Bacteriology & Immunology Dept, University of Glasgow, Western Infirmary, Glasgow G11 6NT (☎ 041 339 8822)

WILKINSON, Sir Philip William; *b* 8 May 1927; *Educ* Leyton County HS; *m* 1951, Eileen Patricia, *née* Malkin; 1 s, 2 da; *Career* dep chm Nat Westminster Bank plc 1987- (dir 1979-, dep gp chief exec 1980, gp chief exec 1983-87), dir: Int Westminster Bank 1982, Handels Bank Nat West Zürich (dep chm), Br Aerospace plc; memb Cncl: Confedn of Br Indust 1983-89, Indust Soc 1982-89; dir Eng Nat Opera; FCIB; kt 1988; *Recreations* golf, watching sport; *Clubs* RAC; *Style—* Sir Philip Wilkinson; National Westminster Bank plc, 41 Lothbury, London EC2P 2BP (☎ 071 726 1000)

WILKINSON, Rev Canon Raymond Stewart; s of Sidney Ewart Wilkinson, and Florence Miriam, *née* Lawrence; *b* 5 June 1919; *Educ* Luton GS, King's Coll London (AKC), Bishop's Coll Cheshunt; *m* 8 Sept 1945, Dorothy Elinor, da of Robert Jacob Church (d 1984); 4 s (Francis John b 1946, Andrew Peter b 1948, Mark Lawrence b 1950, Paul Richard b 1953); *Career* curate of Croxley Green Herts 1943; vicar: St Oswald's Croxley Green 1945-50, Abbots Langley 1950-61; rector of Woodchurch 1961-71, proctor in convocation and memb Church Assembly 1964-71, rector of Solihull 1971-87; Hon Canon of Birmingham 1976; Chaplain to HM The Queen 1982; FRSA; *Books* The More Edifying (1952), Church and Parish of Abbots Langley (1955), My Confirmation Search Book (10 edn 1984), An Adult Confirmation Handbook (6 edn 1985), Gospel Sermons for Alternative Service Book (1983), Pocket Guide for Servers (1986); *Recreations* producing, acting in and conducting Gilbert and Sullivan operas, church architecture, education, gardening; *Clubs* Royal Cwlth, Royal Soc of Arts; *Style—* The Rev Canon Raymond Wilkinson; 42 Coten End, Warwick CV34 4NP (☎ 0926 493 510)

WILKINSON, Richard Denys; s of Denys Cooper Wilkinson (d 1961), of Pill House, Llanmadoc, and Gillian Avice, *née* Nairn (d 1973); *b* 11 May 1946; *Educ* Eton, Trinity Coll Cambridge (MA, MLitt), Ecole Nationale des Langues Orientales Vivantes, Paris, Ecole des Langues Orientales Anciennes Institut Catholique de Paris; *m* 8 Dec 1972, (Maria) Angela, da of Frederick Edward Morris, of London; 2 s (Wilfred b 17 Dec 1983, Samuel b 4 Feb 1986); *Career* Hayter post-doctor in Soviet Studies Sch Slavonic and East Euro Studies Univ of London 1971-72, dip serv 1972, Madrid 1973-77, FCO 1977-79, visiting prof faculty of history Univ of Michigan Ann Arbor 1980, FCO 1980-83, Ankara 1983-85, cnsllr and head of chancery Mexico City 1985-88, info cnsllr Paris 1988-; *Recreations* sightseeing, oriental studies; *Clubs* United Oxford and Cambridge; *Style—* Richard Wilkinson, Esq; Foreign & Commonwealth Office, London SW1A 2AH

WILKINSON, Robert Purdy; OBE (1990); s of Robert Purdy Wilkinson (d 1958), and Lily Ingham (d 1987), *née* Robson; *b* 23 Aug 1933; *Educ* Robert Richardson GS, Univ of Durham (BA, rugby 1 XV); *m* 21 Dec 1957, June, da of late Godfrey Palmer; 2 da (Katharine Jane (Dr Warner) b 28 April 1959, Susanna Jean (Mrs Edge-Partington) b 11 Aug 1961); *Career* Kleinwort Sons & Co 1958-62, Estabrook & Co 1962-64, W I Carr Sons & Co 1964-81; Stock Exchange: ptnr and memb 1966, memb Cncl 1978, chm Firms Accounts Ctee 1980-81, first SE inspr 1981, dir Surveillance Div 1984-90, dir Enforcement The Securities Assoc 1987-90, ret 1991; govr Sevenoaks Sch, advsr Assoc of Swiss Stock Exchanges, memb Fin Mkts Gp London Stock Exchange; *Recreations* walking, skiing, gardening; *Style—* Robert Wilkinson, Esq, OBE; Bessels House, Bessels Green, Sevenoaks, Kent TN13 2PS (☎ 0732 457782)

WILKINSON, Dr Ronald Scotthorn; s of Thomas George Wilkinson (d 1965), of 4 Upper Wimpole St, London, and Mary Eleanor, *née* Dawkins (d 1973); *b* 27 April 1920; *Educ* Humphrey Perkins GS, Shrewsbury, Merton Coll Oxford (MA, BM BCh), Radcliffe Infirmary Oxford; *m* 1, 1947 (m dis), Thelma Elizabeth, da of Clifford Exell, of Chippenham; 2 da (Amanda b 18 Sept 1950, Vanessa b 18 March 1952); m 2, 1972 (m dis), Halina Gostford, da of H Luria, of Warsaw; m 3, Muriel Laycock, da of V Jones, of Abergavenny; *Career* house physician Radcliffe Infirmary 1944, resident med offr Royal Victoria and West Hants Hosp Bournemouth 1945-46, medico legal conslt to various slrs and insurance co's in UK and USA 1947-; writes under pseudonym Ronald Scott Thorn; twelve plays incl: Mountain Air (Comedy, 1948), Taking Things Quietly (Ambassadors, 1950); novels 1952-65: Upstairs and Downstairs, The Full Treatment, Second Opinion, The Twin Serpents (NY Book Club Choice), Experiment with Eros; The Last Scramble (1990), Star Doctor (autobiog, 1984); feature films 1960-62: Upstairs and Downstairs, The Full Treatment; FRSM, memb Soc of Authors; *Recreations* writing poetry; *Style—* Dr Ronald Wilkinson; 50 Hanover Steps, St George's Fields, Albion Street, London W2 2YG (☎ 071 262 0716); 152 Harley St, London W1N 1HH

WILKINSON, Sally Ann; da of Derek George Wilkinson (d 1978), of London, and Kathleen Mary Patricia, *née* O'Callaghan (d 1989); *b* 1 Nov 1953; *Educ* Westonbirt Sch Gloucestershire, Watford Coll of Technol (HND, LAMDA Golf medals in speech and drama); *Career* trainee exec Image Makers Ltd 1973, account exec Crawford Heard Ltd 1974, divnl press offr Thorn Domestic Appliances 1975-78, account exec to creative dir Kingsway Rowland 1978-89, divnl md The Rowland Co 1990-; memb: Inst Mktg 1978, Assoc of Women in PR 1990; *Recreations* theatre, music, writing, art and painting; *Style—* Miss Sally Ann Wilkinson; The Rowland Company, 67-69 Whitfield St, London W1P 5RL

WILKINSON, Samuel William; s of Samuel William Wilkinson (d 1981), of Abbey House, Cirencester, and Louisa, *née* Eggitt (d 1978); *b* 31 Dec 1935; *Educ* Dudley GS, Tettenhall Coll Wolverhampton, Swansea GS, UCL (LLB); *m* 2 Sept 1961, Jane Margaret, da of Henry de Witt West (d 1974), of Porteynon, nr Swansea; 1 s (William b 1962), 2 da (Anna b 1965, Mary b 1968); *Career* admitted slr 1961; with Collins Woods and Vaughan Jones Swansea 1958-62, sr ptnr Davey Son and Jones (Cirencester) 1981- (joined 1962, ptnr 1965); sec and treas N Cerney CC, past chm Cirencester Round Table; memb: Law Soc; *Recreations* cricket, squash, tennis, walking, motor racing; *Clubs* Cirencester Squash (team memb); *Style—* Samuel Wilkinson, Esq; Pennings, North Cerney, Cirencester GL7 7BZ (☎ 028 583 342); 10/12 Dollar Street, Cirencester, Glos GL7 2AL (☎ 0285 654875)

WILKINSON, (George) William; s of Thomas Nutter Wilkinson (d 1985), and Elizabeth, *née* Hurst; *b* 21 Oct 1948; *Educ* Chorlton GS Manchester, Univ of Nottingham (BSc); *m* 27 Dec 1969, Carol Susan, da of Albert James Henry Petre; 3 s (Matthew Jon b 13 Nov 1978, Daniel James b 23 June 1982, Samuel Luke b 26 Aug 1989); *Career* actuarial trainee Sun Alliance 1969, overseas posting as chief actuary Protea Assurance Cape Town 1977-80; Sun Alliance: asst mangr 1980-83, business mangr 1983-88, pensions admin mangr 1988-90, pensions mangr 1990-; sch govr 1988, FIA 1975; *Recreations* family, squash playing and coaching; *Clubs* Horsham Squash; *Style—* William Wilkinson, Esq; Sun Alliance Group, North St, Horsham, West Sussex (☎ 0403 64141 ext 3601)

WILKINSON, Sir William Henry Nairn; s of Denys Cooper Wilkinson (d 1961), and Gillian Avice, *née* Nairn (d 1973); *b* 22 July 1932; *Educ* Eton, Trinity Coll Cambridge; *m* 25 July 1964, Katharine Louise Frederica, da of William Francis Hope Loudon (d 1986); 1 s (Matthew b 1969), 2 da (Sophia b 1971, Alice b 1974); *Career* dir: Kleinwort Benson Ltd 1973-85, TSL Gp plc 1976-88 (chm 1984-88), John Mowlem & Co plc 1977-87; memb: RSPB 1970-76 (hon treas 1971-76 and 1977-83, chm Info Ctee 1980-81, vice pres 1990-), Game Conservancy Cncl 1976-83 (vice-chm 1981-83); chm Nature Conservancy Cncl 1983-91, memb Cncl Winston Churchill Meml Tst 1985-, memb CEGB 1986-89; FRSA; kt 1989; *Recreations* ornithology, opera, music, archaeology; *Clubs* Brooks; *Style—* Sir William Wilkinson; 119 Castelnau, Barnes, London SW13 9EL (☎ 081 748 9964); Northminster House, Peterborough PE1 1UA

WILKINSON, Dr William Lionel; CBE (1986); s of Lionel Wilkinson (d 1978), and Dorothy, *née* Steels; *b* 16 Feb 1931; *Educ* Holgate GS Barnsley, Christ's Coll Cambridge (MA, PhD, ScD); *m* 3 Sept 1955, (Josephine) Anne, da of Charles Dennis Pilgrim (d 1954), of Bedford; 5 s (David William b 6 March 1957, Andrew Charles b 15 Nov 1958, Iain Francis b 5 March 1962, Richard John b 24 March 1965, Stephen James b 6 Feb 1970); *Career* lectr Univ Coll Swansea 1956-59, UKAEA 1959-67, prof of chem engrg Univ of Bradford 1967-79, BNF 1979- (dep chief exec and chm of fuel and engr gp 1986-); Hon DEng Bradford 1989; Freeman Worshipful Co of Salters 1985; FIChemE 1957, FEng 1980; FRS 1990; *Books* Non-Newtonian Fluids (1960); *Recreations* fell walking; *Clubs* Athenaeum; *Style—* Dr William Wilkinson, CBE, FRS; Tree Tops, Legh Rd, Knutsford WA16 8LP (☎ 0565 653 344); BNF plc, Risley, Warrington (☎ 0925 832 000)

WILKS, Capt Antony Hugh Francis; MBE; s of Walter Hugh Wilks (d 1964), of Bushey, Herts, and Frances Mary Bradford, *née* Pratt; *b* 29 Dec 1936; *Educ* Oundle; *m* 4 Sept 1971, Susan Chaloner, *née* Reed; 1 s (Rupert b 1973), 1 da (Lalage b 1976); *Career* serv HM Submarines 1958-67, i/c HMS Belton 1967-69, Staff Coll India 1970, HMS Jupiter 1971-72, BRNC Dartmouth 1973-75, ADC to HE Govr Hong Kong 1976, Naval Staff 1977-78; i/c: Royal Brunei Navy 1979-80, HMS Aurora 1981-82, RNC Greenwich 1983-85; Dep Cdr Naval Base Rosyth Scotland and Queen's Harbourmaster Rosyth and Cromarty 1986-90; chief harbourmaster Firth and Forth 1990-; Yr Brother Trinity House London 1976; Liveryman Worshipful Co of Wheelwrights 1965 (Ct Asst); Perwira Agong Negara Brunei (first class) 1979, Dato Seri Laila Jasa (Brunei Knighthood) 1980; MNI; *Recreations* music, squash; *Clubs* St Moritz Tobogganing, Jesters; *Style—* Capt Antony Wilks, MBE; Easter Fossoway, Carnbo, Kinrosshire; Forth Ports Authority (☎ 031 554 3661)

WILKS, Capt Carey Lovell; s of Richard Lovell Wilks, of Bailing Hill Farm, Warnham, Horsham, W Sussex, and Shelia Gillian Jean, *née* Bowack; *b* 10 May 1960; *Educ* Malvern, Lincoln Coll Oxford (MA); *m* 7 May 1983, Alyson Jane Prior, da of Capt Peter Arnold Prior-Willeard; 2 s (Michael b 17 Sept 1987, Edward b 3 May 1989); *Career* cmmnd RE 1978, Troop Cdr Germany 1982-84, Support Troop Cdr UK 1984-86; engrg trg (electrical and mech) 1986-88, attachment to John Holland Engrg Australia; Adj Germany 1989-; target rifle shooting (Capt Oxford Univ Rifle Club, tour of Kenya 1982, shot for England 1983); MIEAust 1988, AMIEE 1987; *Recreations* target rifle shooting, country sports; *Clubs* Vincents; *Style—* Capt Carey Wilks; c/o Bailing Hill Farm, Warnham, Horsham, Sussex

WILKS, Stanley David (Jim); CB (1979); *b* 1 Aug 1920; *Educ* Polytechnic Sch London; *m* 1947, Dorothy Irene, *née* Adamthwaite; 1 s (Howard John b 1955), 1 da (Penelope Jane b 1958); *Career* RAC 1939-46, served with 48 Bn RTR, 3 Carabiniers (Imphal 1944); Home Office 1946-50, BOT (later DTI) 1950-80: 1 sec Br Embassy Washington 1950-53, GATT non-ferrous metals, ECGD, airports policy; chief exec BOTB 1975-80; dir: Matthew Hall Business Development Ltd 1981-89, Hadson Petroleum International plc 1981-, Hadson Corporation (USA) 1985-, Associated Gas Supplies Ltd 1987-90; regnl dir James Hallam Ltd 1984-, chm Export Network Ltd 1985-89; dep chm: Technol Transfer Group 1986-89 (formerly DG 1981-86), Strategy International Ltd 1990- (conslt dir 1981-90); MIEx 1980; *Recreations* sailing, water skiing; *Clubs* Royal Over-Seas League, Medway Yacht, Lloyds Yacht, Tamesis; *Style—* Jim Wilks, Esq, CB; 6 Foxgrove Avenue, Beckenham, Kent BR3 2BA

WILLACY, Michael James Ormerod; CBE 1989; s of James Willacy (d 1977), of Plymouth, Devon, and Majorie Winifred, *née* Sanders; *b* 7 June 1933; *Educ* Taunton Sch Somerset; *m* 1, 25 Nov 1961, Merle Louise, da of Johannes Schrier, of Denia, Spain; 2 s (Richard b 1962, Peter b 1969), 1 da (Jennifer b 1963); m 2, Victoria Stuart, da of Cecil Stuart John, of Mobberley, Cheshire; 2 s (James b 1985, Michael b 1986, David b 1990), 1 da (Elizabeth b 1988); *Career* dir HM Govt Central Unit on Purchasing 1985-, gen mangr Shell UK Materials Services 1983-85; chm Macclesfield C of C 1981-83; fndr chm Macclesfield Business Ventures 1982-83, gen sec Old Tauntonian Assoc 1978- (pres 1988-89); FInstPS; *Recreations* golf, travel, gardening; *Clubs* Royal Cwlth Soc; *Style—* Michael Willacy, Esq, CBE; Lower Barn, Coarsewell, Ugborough, Ivybridge, Devon PL21 OHP (☎ 054 882 536)

WILLAN, Richard Martin; s of Gp Capt Frank Andrew Willan, CBE, DFC, MA, DL (d 1982), of Teffont, Salisbury, Wilts, and Joan Frances Strathern, *née* Wickham Legg; *b* 22 Nov 1946; *Educ* Eton; *m* 17 April 1971 (m dis 1991), Susan St John, da of Maurice St John Howe, of Dorchester, Dorset; 1 da (Clare Elizabeth b 1976); *Career* short service cmmn Royal Green Jackets 1966-70; dir Christie Tyler plc 1982-; *Recreations* shooting, walking, swimming; *Clubs* Army and Navy, RAC; *Style—* Richard Willan, Esq; 3 Lillian Rd, London SW13 9JG (☎ 081 748 0575); Christie Tyler plc,

Brynmenyn, Bridgend, Mid Glamorgan (☎ 0656 721367)

WILLARD, Barbara Mary; da of Edmund Willard (d 1956), of Richmond, Surrey, and Mabel Theresa, *née* Tebbs (d 1944); *b* 12 March 1909; *Educ* Convent HS for Girls Southampton; *Career* author of novels and childrens fiction for over 50 years incl 8 book sequence of historical novels known as The Mantlemass Chronicle (vol 4 winner of The Guardian award), winner Whitbread Childrens Book award; former memb Bd Conservators of Ashdown Forest; *Books* Sussex (1965), Lewes and Chichester (1970), The Queen of the Pharisees' Children (1984), The Forest: Ashdown in East Sussex (1989); *Recreations* gardening, walking, local history; *Clubs* Soc of Authors; *Style—* Miss Barbara Willard

WILLATS, Stephan; *b* 17 Aug 1943; *Educ* Ealing Sch of Art; *m* Stephanie Willats; *Career* artist; ed and publisher Control magazine 1965-, pt/t lectr 1971-, dir The Centre for Behavioural Art 1972-73, DAAD fell W Germany 1979-80, convenor Art Creating Society Symposium Museum of Modern Art Oxford 1990; solo exhibitions incl: Visual Automatics and Visual Transmitters (Museum of Modern Art, Oxford) 1968, The Artist as an Instigator of Changes in Social Cognition and Behaviour (Gallery House, London) 1973, Coding Structure and Behaviour Parameters (Gallery Banco, Bresco Italy) 1975, Allitudes within Four Relationships (Lisson Gallery, London) 1976, Questions About Ourselves (Lisson Gallery) 1978, Concerning our Present Way of Living (Whitechapel Art Gallery) 1979, Berlin Wall Drawings (Galerie Rudiger Schottle, Munich) 1980, Mens en Omgeving De Beyard Centram voor beeldende Kanst (Breda, Holland) 1981, Meta Filler and Related Works (Tate Gallery) 1982, Inside the Night (Lisson Gallery) 1983, Dopelganger (Lisson Gallery) 1985, City of Concrete (Ikon Gallery, Birmingham) 1986, Concepts and Projects Bookworks (Nigel Greenwood Books, London) 1987, Between Objects and People (Leeds City Art Gallery) 1987, Secret Language (Cornerhouse Gallery, Manchester) 1989, Mosaics (Galerie Kaj Forsblom, Helsinki) 1990; gp exhibitions incl: Kinetic Art (Hayward Gallery) 1970, Art as Thought Process (Serpentine Gallery, London) 1974, Social Criticism and Art Practise (San Francisco Art Inst) 1977, La Parola e le Imagine (Commune di Milano) 1979, Sculpture in the Twentieth Century (Whitechapel Art Gallery, London) 1981, New Art at the Tate Gallery (Tate Gallery) 1983, Eye Level (Van Abbemuseum, Eindhoven) 1986, 100 years of British Art (Leeds City Art Gallery) 1988, The New Urban Landscape (World Fin Centre NY) 1990; works in public collections incl: Art Museum Zurich, The Scottish Nat Gallery of Modern Art Edinburgh, The Tate Gallery London, The Arts Cncl of GB, The V & A Museum, The British Museum, Museum of Contemporary Art Utrecht, Stichting Volkshuisvesting in de Kunst Den Hagg Holland; *Style—* Stephan Willats, Esq; c/o Lisson Gallery, 67 Bell St, London NW1

WILLATT, Sir Hugh; s of Robert John Willatt, OBE, JP, of Nottingham; *b* 25 April 1909; *Educ* Repton, Pembroke Coll Oxford; *m* 1945, Evelyn May, da of Horace Edward Gibbs; *Career* serv RAF WWII; practising slr; sec gen Arts Cncl of GB 1968-75 (former chm Drama Panel), chm Nat Opera Studio, pres Riverside Studios; memb Bd English Stage Co (Royal Court Theatre), tstee Shakespeare's Birthplace Tst, former chm and memb Bd Mercury Trust (Ballet Rambert); former memb Bd: Nat Theatre, Nottingham Playhouse; Hon MA Univ of Nottingham; FRSA; kt 1972; *Style—* Sir Hugh Willatt; 4 St Peter's Wharf, Hammersmith Terrace, London W6 (☎ 081 741 2707)

WILLCOCK, David Charles; s of Clarence Harry Willcock (d 1952), of Horsforth, Leeds, and Lena Gladys, *née* Crabtree (d 1960); *b* 5 Oct 1924; *Educ* Woodhouse Grove Sch Yorks, Univ of Leeds; *m* 8 Oct 1953, Kathleen Mary, da of Capt Alfred Pilley (d 1965), of Calverley, Yorks; 1 s (Charles b 1961), 2 da (Louise b 1963, Frances b 1965); *Career* serv KOYLI 1943-47, Middle E, Italy and E Africa; slr; pres Bradford Law Soc 1974-75, chm Legal Aid Area Ctee 1986-; *Books* St Peters Church Rawdon (1984); *Recreations* walking, theatre, genealogy, local history; *Style—* David Willcock, Esq; Calvi, Carr Close, Rawdon, Leeds (☎ 0532 502297); 2 Tyrell St, Bradford (☎ 0274 721104)

WILLCOCKS, Sir David Valentine; CBE (1971), MC (1944); s of late Theophilus Herbert Willcocks and Dorothy, *née* Harding; *b* 30 Dec 1919; *Educ* Clifton, King's Coll Cambridge (MA, MusB); *m* 1947, Rachel Gordon Blyth, da of late Rev Arthur Cecil Blyth, fell of Selwyn Coll Cambridge; 2 s (1 decd), 2 da; *Career* serv WWII DCLI, Capt NW Europe; organist Salisbury Cathedral 1947-50, master choristers and organist Worcester Cathedral 1950-57, music lectr Cambridge 1957-74, fell and organist King's Coll Cambridge 1957-73 (hon fell 1979), Univ organist 1958-74, musical dir Bach Choir 1960-, gen ed OUP Church Music 1961-; past pres: RCO, ISM, Nat Fedn of Music Socs, Birmingham and Midland Inst; former chm Assoc Bd Royal Schs of Music; former conductor: Philharmonic, Salisbury Music Soc, Worcester Festival Choral Soc, City of Birmingham Choir, Bradford Festival Choral Soc, Univ of Cambridge Music Soc; dir: RCM 1974-84, of music at wedding of HRH The Prince of Wales to Lady Diana Spencer 1981; Hon RAM, Hon GSM, Hon FTCL, Hon MA Bradford; Hon DMus: Exeter, Leicester, Bristol, Westminster Choir Coll, Princeton; Hon DLit Sussex; Hon Dr Sacred Letters Trinity Coll Toronto; FRCM, FRCO, FRNCM, FRSAMD, FRSCM; hon fell Royal Canadian Coll of Organists; kt 1977; *Clubs* Athenaeum, Arts; *Style—* Sir David Willcocks, CBE, MC; 13 Grange Road, Cambridge CB3 9AS (☎ 0223 359559)

WILLCOCKS, Brig Michael Alan; s of Henry Willcocks, and Georgina Bernadette, *née* Lawton (d 1990); *b* 27 July 1944; *Educ* St John's, RMA Sandhurst, Univ of London (BSc); *m* 10 Dec 1966, Jean Paton, da of James Burnside Paton Weir (d 1967); 1 s (Julian b 20 June 1968), 2 da (Jessica b 28 April 1971, Hannah b 26 Feb 1976); *Career* cmmnd RA 1964 (serv Malaya, Borneo, UK, Germany), MOD 1977-79, Staff Coll Directing Staff 1981-82, CO 1 Regt RHA 1983-85, Asst COS Intelligence/Ops HQ UKLF 1988, Comd RA 4 Armd Div 1989-90; RCDS 1991; *Books* Airmobility and the Armoured Experience (1989); *Recreations* books, music, tennis, fishing, sailing; *Style—* Brig Michael Willcocks; Royal College of Defence Studies, Seaford House, 37 Belgrave Square, London SW1X 8NS (☎ 071 235 1091); c/o Barclays Bank plc, 6 High St, Marlborough, Wiltshire SN8 1LP

WILLCOX, John Horace; s of Sir William Henry Willcox, KCIE, CB, CMG, FRCP (d 1941), of 40 Wilbeck St, London W1, and Mildred, *née* Griffin; *b* 1 Feb 1909; *Educ* Oundle, Christ's Coll Cambridge (BA); *m* 19 Jan 1946, Diana Tilden, da of John Sydney Walker, JP (d 1939), of Fellcourt, Coulsdon, Surrey; 3 da (Elisabeth b 1946, Jane b 1950, Joanna b 1953); *Career* WWII serv 1942-46: cmmnd Lt RAOC (served Persia/Iraq Force, Egypt, Italy, Austria), Capt OC Light Aid Detachment REME 104 Regt RHA (Essex Yeo) 1943-45; J & E Hall Ltd Dartford Kent 1930-35; Anglo Ecuadorian Oilfields Ltd 1936-57: asst chief engr 1938-41, chief engr, asst field mangr, local dir; exec engr Regent Oil Co and Esso Petroleum Co 1958-68; CEng, MIMechE 1941; *Recreations* riding, gardening; *Style—* John Willcox, Esq; Blegberry, Shootersway, Berkhamsted, Herts HP4 3NN (☎ 0442 865083)

WILLCOX, Toyah Ann; da of Beric Arnold Willcox, of Birmingham, and Barbara Joy, *née* Rollinson; *b* 18 May 1958; *Educ* Edgbaston C of E Coll, Birmingham Old Rep Theatre Sch; *m* 16 May 1986, Robert Fripp, s of Aurthur Fripp (d 1985), of Wimbourne; *Career* actress and singer songwriter; films incl: Jubilee 1978, The Corn is Green 1978, Quadrophenia 1978, The Tempest 1979, URG The Music War 1979, Battle Ship Redwing 1985, Murder 1985, Midnight Breaks 1987, Little Pig Robertson 1990; theatre incl: Tales from the Vienna Woods (Nat Theatre 1977), American Days (ICA 1978), Sugar and Spice (Royal Court 1979), Trafford Tanzi (Mermaid Theatre 1983), Cabaret (Strand Theatre 1987), Three Men on a Horse (Nat Theatre 1987), A Midsummer Nights Dream (Birmingham Rep 1988), Whale (Nat Theatre 1989-90), Therese Raquin (Nottingham Playhouse 1990), Taming of the Shrew (Cambridge Theatre Co 1990); tv incl: Little Girls Don't 1980, Ebony Tower 1983; albums: Sheep Farming in Barnet 1978, Blue Meaning 1979, Toyah Toyah, 1980, Anthem 1981, Changeling 1982, Warrior Rock 1982, Love is the Law 1983, Minx 1985, Lady or the Tiger 1985, Desire 1987, Pro 1988, Ophelia's Shadow 1991, Kneeling At The Shrine 1991; Singles incl: It's a Mystery, I Wanna be Free, Thunder in the Mountains, Good Morning Universe, Brave New World, World in Action, Echo Beach; vice-pres Nat Assoc of Youth Clubs; patron: Birmingham Rape Crisis Centre, Bournemouth Hosp, Salisbury Festival, Sch for the Performing Arts, hon asst Womens Cncl of GB, Wiltshire Victims Support; *Style—* Ms Toyah Willcox; 63A King's Rd, Chelsea, London SW3 (☎ 071 730 2162)

WILLETT, Allan Robert; s of Robert Willett, and Irene Grace Priscilla, *née* Weigall; *b* 24 Aug 1936; *Educ* Eastbourne Coll 1950-54, Military Serv 1955-57; *m* 13 April 1960, Mary, da of Joseph Hillman; 1 s (Robert), 2 da (Joanna, Katherine); *Career* cmmnd The Buffs Royal East Kent Regt and seconded to 23 Kings African Rifles 1955-57, Kenya Campaign Medal 1956; gp md GD Peters Ltd 1969-71, chm Northampton Machinery Co 1970-74, dep chm Rowen and Boden 1973-74, formed Willett Cos 1974; Willett Int Ltd: chm 1983-, winners Queen's Award for Export Achievement 1989; *Recreations* beagling, walking, military history; *Style—* Allan Willett, Esq; 15 Launceston Place, London W8 (☎ 071 938 3768, fax 071 937 1316, car 0836 253556)

WILLETT, Prof Frank; CBE (1985); s of Thomas Willett (d 1965), of Bolton, Lancs, and Frances, *née* Latham (d 1978); *b* 18 Aug 1925; *Educ* Bolton Municipal Secdy Sch, Univ Coll Oxford (MA); *m* 24 July 1950, (Mary) Constance, da of Charles Hewitt (d 1952), of Bolton Lancs; 1 s (Steven b 1955), 3 da (Margaret Mary b 1952, Pauline b 1958, Jean b 1962); *Career* linguist RAF 1943-44; keeper of ethnology and gen archaeology Manchester Museum 1950-58, govt archaeologist i/c Ife Museum Nigeria 1958-63, Leverhulme res fell 1964, res fell Nuffield Coll Oxford 1964-66, prof of African art and archaeology Northwestern Univ USA 1966-76, visiting fell Clare Hall Cambridge 1970-71, dir Hunterian museum and art gallery Univ of Glasgow 1976-90, hon sr res fell Hunterian museum 1990-; memb Cncl Scot Museums, fndr Univ Museums in Scot, memb Scot Catholic Hertiage Cmmn; fell Royal Anthropological Inst 1949, FRS (Edinburgh) 1979, Hon Fell Bolton Inst of Higher Educn 1990; *Books* Ife In The History of West African Sculpture (1967), African Art: An Introduction (1971), Treasures of Ancient Nigeria (with Ekpo Eyo, 1980); *Recreations* baiting architects, relaxing, walking; *Clubs* Royal Cwlth Soc; *Style—* Prof Frank Willett, CBE, FRS; The Hunterian Museum, The Univ of Glasgow, Glasgow G12 8QQ (☎ 041 339 8855 ext 4384, fax 041 330 4920, telex 777070 UNIGLA)

WILLETT, Peter Stirling; s of Maj Kingsley Willett, MC (d 1946), of South Cadbury House, Yeovil, Somerset, and Agnes Mary, *née* Stirling (d 1972); *b* 19 July 1919; *Educ* Wellington, Univ of Cambridge (MA); *m* 1, 1954 Anne Marjorie, *née* Watkins (d 1965); 2 s (David Henry Stirling b 1955, Stephen Murray b 1958); m 2, 1971, Chloë Lister Beamish; *Career* The Queen's Bays 1941-46 (Middle East, Italy); author, journalist, thoroughbred breeding consultant; dir: Goodwood Racecourse 1977, Nat Stud 1985-; pres Thoroughbred Breeders Assoc 1980-85, chm tstee Br Euro Breeders Fund 1983; FRSA; *Books* An Introduction to the Thoroughbred (1960), The Thoroughbred (1970), The Classic Racehorse (1981), Makers of the Modern Thoroughbred (1986), Tattersalls (1987); *Recreations* tennis, following cricket, reading, bridge; *Clubs* Army and Navy, Jockey; *Style—* Peter Willett, Esq; Paddock House, Rotherwick, Basingstoke, Hants RG27 9BG (☎ 0256 76 2488)

WILLETTS, Bernard Frederick (Bill); s of James Frederick Willetts (d 1965), of Dudley, and Effie, *née* Hurst (d 1962); *b* 24 March 1927; *Educ* Birmingham Central GS, Univ of Birmingham (BSc Eng), Univ of Durham (MSc, PhD); *m* 14 June 1952, Norah Elizabeth, da of William S Law (d 1966); 2 s (David Frederick b 1957, Jonathan William Douglas b 1964); *Career* res asst Univ of Durham 1951-54, section head Vickers Armstrong (Engrs) Ltd 1954-58; Massey-Ferguson (UK) Ltd: chief engr 1959-61, dir engrg 1961-64, dir mfrg 1964-67, dep md 1967-68; The Plessey Co Ltd: gp md 1968-69, dir 1969-78, dep chief exec 1973-78; md Vicker Ltd 1979-80 (asst md and chm Roneo 1978-79), conslt Dubai Aluminium Co 1987- (dep chief exec and gen mangr 1981-87), dep chm and md International Development Corporation 1987-; non-exec dir: Trinity Internationl Hldgs plc 1976-, Massey Ferguson (Hldgs) Ltd 1980-83, Telephone Rentals plc 1981-88, Mel Ltd 1983-86; memb: Advsy Ctee Coll of Technol 1964-68, Cncl Univ of Liverpool, Mgmnt Ctee Engrg Employers Fedn 1973-78, Govt Ctee for Industl Technols; vice pres Inst Prodn Engrs 1979-81; CEng, FIMechE, FIProdE, FIIM, MIEE (RSA), CBIM; *Recreations* gardening, swimming; *Clubs* Lansdowne, Dubai Country; *Style—* Bernard Willetts, Esq; Suna Court, Pearson Rd, Sonning-on-Thames, Berks (☎ 0734 695050); PO Box 9354, Dubai, UAE (☎ 446661, fax 444548)

WILLETTS, David Lindsay; s of John Roland Willetts, and Hilary Sheila Willetts; *b* 9 March 1956; *Educ* King Edward's Sch Birmingham, Ch Ch Oxford (BA); *m* 1986, Hon Sarah Harriet Ann, da of Lord Butterfield; 1 da; *Career* res asst to Nigel Lawson MP 1978; HM Teasury 1978-84: energy policy 1978-79, public expenditure control 1980-81, private sec to Fin Sec 1981-82, monetary policy 1982-84; memb PM's Downing St Policy Unit 1984-86, dir studies Centre for Policy Studies 1987-, conslt dir Cors Res Dept 1987-; memb: Lambeth Southwark and Lewisham FPC 1987-90, Parkside Health Authy 1988-90, Social Security Advsy Ctee 1989-; non-exec dir: Retirement Security Ltd 1988-, Electra Corporate Ventures Ltd 1989-; writer and broadcaster; contributions include: The Times, The Spectator, Any Questions, Question Time; lectr Deutsch-Englische Gesellschaft; FRSA; *Books* The Role of the Prime Minister's Policy Unit (Haldane essay prize RIPA, 1987), Managed Health Care (with Dr Goldsmith, 1988), A Mixed Economy Health Care (with Dr Goldsmith, 1988), Reforming the Health Service (1989), Happy Families? Four Points to a Conservative Family Policy (1991); *Style—* David Willetts, Esq; Centre for Policy Studies, 8 Wilfred St, London SW1E 6PL (☎ 071 828 1176)

WILLETTS, Roger William; s of Leonard Willetts (d 1984), and Doreen May Joyce, *née* Hutchinson; *b* 21 Aug 1946; *Educ* Cavendish Sch Eastbourne Sussex; *m* 24 Oct 1970, Linda, da of Robert Mullins; 1 s (Timothy b 7 Aug 1974), 1 da (Karen b 9 Feb 1977); *Career* Abbey Life Assurance: sales agent 1969, unit mangr 1971, branch mangr 1974, exec dir 1984; head of sales City of Westminster Assurance 1989-; charter pres Woodley and Earley Lions Club; FLIA, FInstSM; *Recreations* squash, golf, tennis (Sussex Co player); *Style—* Roger Willetts, Esq; 16 Alyth Rd, Talbot Woods, Bournemouth, Dorset (☎ 0202 769079); City of Westminster Assurance Co Ltd, 500 Avebury Boulevard, Central Milton Keynes MK9 2NU (☎ 0908 690 888)

WILLIAM-POWLETT, Hon Mrs (Katherine Elizabeth); *née* Keyes; 2 da of Adm of the Fleet 1 Baron Keyes, GCB, KCVO, CMG, DSO (d 1945); *b* 24 Oct 1911; *m* 30 July 1935, Major Peter de Barton Vernon Wallop William-Powlett, MC, yst son of late

Maj Barton Newton Wallop William-Powlett, of Cadhay, Ottery St Mary, Devon; 1 s, 1 da; *Career* artist; *Clubs* Hurlingham; *Style—* The Hon Mrs William-Powlett; 22 St Leonard's Terrace, London SW3

WILLIAMS; *see*: Ffowcs Williams

WILLIAMS, Prof Adrian Charles; s of Geoffrey Francis Williams, OBE, of Aberystwyth, and Maureen, *née* Wade; *b* 15 June 1949; *Educ* Epsom Coll, Univ of Birmingham (MB ChB, MD); *m* 19 April 1980, and Linnea Marie, da of Gerald Olsen, of Colorado, USA; 2 s (Alec b 1984, Henry b 1986), 1 da (Sarah b 1981); *Career* visiting fell Nat Inst Health USA 1976-79, registrar Nat Hosp London 1979-81, conslt neurologist Queen Elizabeth Hosp Birmingham 1981-, Bloomer prof clinical neurology Univ of Birmingham 1988-; memb Assoc Br Neurologists; FRCP 1986; *Recreations* sailing, skiing, gardening; *Style—* Prof Adrian Williams; 53 Weoley Hill, Selly Oak, Birmingham B29 4AB (☎ 021 472 0218); Dept of Neurology, Queen Elizabeth Hospital, Edgbaston, Birmingham B15 2TT (☎ 021 472 1311)

WILLIAMS, Prof Alan; s of Ralph James Williams (d 1942), and Muriel, *née* Williams; *b* 26 June 1935; *Educ* Cyfarthfa GS, Merthyr Tydifl, Univ of Leeds (BSc, PhD); *m* 30 July 1960, Maureen Mary, da of Sydney Bagnall, of Leeds; 3 s (Christopher b 1964, Nicholas b 1967, Simon b 1971); *Career* Livesey prof in fuel and combustion sci and head of Dept of Fuel and Energy Univ of Leeds 1973-, author Combustion of Liquid Fuel Sprays; hon sec Inst of Energy (former pres); FRIC, FInst E, FInstPet, FInstGasE; *Style—* Prof Alan Williams; Department of Fuel and Energy, Leeds University, Leeds LS2 9JT (☎ 0532 332508, fax 0532 440572)

WILLIAMS, Prof Alan Frederick; s of Walter Alan Williams, and Mary Elizabeth *née* Parry; *b* 25 May 1945; *Educ* Melbourne Univ (B Agr Sci), Adelaide Univ (PhD); *m* 23 Dec 1967, Rosalind Margaret, da of Douglas Wright; 1 s (Benjamin b 18 Oct 1970), 1 da (Eliza b 20 July 1973); *Career* Univ of Oxford: demonstrator Dept Biochemistry 1970-72, Dept Biochemistry Immunochemistry Unit MRC 1972-77, dir MRC Cellular Immunology Research Unit 1977-, prof Immunology 1989-, fell BNC 1990-; fell the Royal Soc London 1990-; memb: Biochemistry Soc UK, Br Soc Immunology, Euro Molecular Biology Orgn 1984-; hon memb: American Assoc Immunologists 1989-, Scandinavian Soc for Immunology 1990-; *Recreations* gardening, art; *Style—* Prof Alan Williams; MRC Cellular Immunology Res Unit, Sir William Dunn School of Pathology, University of Oxford, Oxford OX1 3RE (☎ 0865 275595, fax 0865 275501)

WILLIAMS, Prof Alan Harold; s of Sgt Harold George Williams (d 1968), and Glady May Clark (d 1962); *b* 9 June 1927; *Educ* King Edwards Sch Birmingham, King Edwards High Sch Birmingham, Univ of Birmingham (BCom); *m* 7 Nov 1953, June Frances, da of Sgt Edward Alexander Porter; 2 s (Mark Alan b 1956, Paul Robert b 1961), 1 da (Susan Heather b 1959); *Career* RAF 1945-48 corpl; lectr Univ of Exeter 1954-63, visiting lectr MIT 1957-58, visiting fell Princeton 1963-64, sr lectr then reader then prof Univ of York 1964-, dir of economic studies HM Treasury Centre for Admin Studies; former memb: Yorkshire Water Authy, Nat Water Cncl, Royal Cmmn on NHS; Hon DPhil Lund Sweden 1977; memb Royal Economic Soc, CIPFA; *Books* Public Finance and Budgetary Policy (1961), Efficency in the Social Services (with Robert Anderson, 1977), Principles of Practical Cost Benefit Analysis (with Robert Sugden, 1978); *Recreations* music, walking, teasing; *Style—* Prof Alan Williams; Dept of Economics, University of York, York YO1 5DD (☎ 0904 433651, fax 0904 433764)

WILLIAMS, Rt Hon Alan John; PC (1977), MP (Lab) Swansea W 1964-; s of Emlyn Williams (d 1951); *b* 14 Oct 1930; *Educ* Cardiff HS, Cardiff Coll Technol, Univ Coll Oxford; *m* 1957, (Mary) Patricia Rees; 2 s, 1 da; *Career* serv RAF 1956-58; former econ lectr and journalist; memb: Lab Pty 1950-, Fabian Soc and Co-op Pty; contested (Lab) Poole 1959; chm Welsh PLP and pps to PMG 1966-67, Parly under-sec Dept Econ Affrs 1967-69, Parly sec Miny Technol 1969-70, oppn spokesman: Consumer Protection, Small Businesses and Minerals 1970-74; min state: prices and consumer protection 1974-76, indust 1976-79; oppn spokesman: Wales 1979-81, civil service 1981-83, indust 1983-; dep shadow leader of the House 1983-, shadow sec of State for Wales 1987-; *Style—* The Rt Hon Alan Williams, MP; Hill View, Plunch Lane, Limeslade, Swansea (☎ 0792 60475); House of Commons, London SW1

WILLIAMS, Alan Lee; OBE (1973); *b* 29 Nov 1930; *Career* Nat Serv RAF Signals 1951-53; Nat Fire Serv messenger 1944-45, cncllr Greenwich Borough Cncl 1951-53, nat youth offr Lab Pty 1955-62, memb Met Police Special Constabulary, helper UNRA Displaced People's Camp Vienna 1956, memb Cncl of Europe and Parly Assembly W Euro Union 1966-70; MP (Lab): Hornchurch 1966-70, Hornchurch and Havering 1974-79; PPS to Sec of State for: Def 1969-70, NI 1976-79; nat youth offr UNA 1962-66, chm World Assembly of Youth 1960-66, memb Albenarle Youth Ctee and fndr memb Cncl for Euro Nat Youth Ctee 1965-66, def corr Socialist Commentary 1968-76, UK del to 4th Ctee UN Gen Assembly 1969, memb Wilton Park Advsy Ctee 1969-71, treas Euro Movement 1972-79 (dep dir 1970-72), sec Trades Union Ctee for Europe 1970-74 (treas Euro Movement 1974), sec Lab Ctee for Europe and fndr ed Trades Union Ctee for Transatlantic Understanding 1975, memb Cwlth Youth Cncl and jt sec Gaitskell Youth Cmmn 1974-79, actg ldr Parly Delgn to N Atlantic Assembly 1974-79, FO lectr on Br Def Policy and NI (USA and Canada) 1974-79, memb Cncl RUSI 1974-78, memb Tri-Lateral Cmmn 1976-, chm Parly Lab Pty Def Ctee 1976-79, Industl fell Plessey 1978, dir gen ESU 1979-86, memb FO Advsy Ctee on Disarmament and Arms Control and Advsy Ctee PRO 1977-81, chm Br Atlantic Ctee 1980-83 (dir 1972-74), chm NATO Fellowships Ctee (Brussels) 1980-87, fndr memb Ctee for a Community of Democracy; *Style—* Alan Williams, Esq, OBE

WILLIAMS, Alan Peter; s of Ronald Benjamin Williams, of 37 William Allen Lane, Lindfield Sussex, and Marcia Elizabeth, *née* Lister; *b* 27 Oct 1944; *Educ* Merchant Taylors', Univ of Exeter (LLB, capt cricket XI); *m* 21 Sept 1968, Lyn Rosemary, da Reginald Ewart Campling; 1 da (Laura Kate Elizabeth b 3 April 1974); *Career* admitted slr 1969; articled clerk Burton Yeates & Hart 1966-67; Denton Hall & Burgin: articled clerk 1967-68, ptnr 1972, opened Hong Kong office 1976, dept exec Entertainment Dept; memb: Law & Copyright Ctee, Publishers Assoc 1983-, Int Media Law Editorial Bd 1986-, RSA 1990, Richard III Soc; Assoc memb Inner Magic Cirle; memb Law Soc 1969; *Books* contrib to Publishing Agreements (Charles Clark); *Recreations* cricket, music, walking, photography, theatre; *Clubs* RAC, MCC, Groucho; *Style—* A P Williams, Esq; Denton Hall Burgin & Warrens, Five Chancery Lane, Cliffords Inn, London EC4A 1BU (☎ 071 242 1212, fax 071 404 0087)

WILLIAMS, Dr Alan Wynne; MP (Lab) Carmarthen 1987; s of Tom Williams (d 1980), and Mary Hannah Williams, *née* Thomas; *b* 21 Dec 1945; *Educ* Carmarthen GS, Jesus Coll Oxford (BA, DPhil); *m* 1973, Marian, da of Tom Williams, of Gwynedd; *Career* lectr Environmental Science Trinity Coll 1970-87; *Recreations* reading, watching sport; *Style—* Dr Alan Williams, MP; Cwmaber, Alltycnar Road, Carmarthen, Dyfed (☎ 0267 235 825); House of Commons, London (☎ 071 219 4533)

WILLIAMS, Albert; s of William Arthur Williams (d 1953), of Stockport, and Phyllis, *née* Barnes; *b* 12 Feb 1927; *Educ* Houldsworth Sch Reddish, Manchester Sch of Building; *m* 20 March 1954, Edna Ethel, da of Frank Bradley (d 1953), of Manchester; 2 s (Christopher David b 18 June 1955, Edward Paul b 29 March 1961); *Career* operatives sec Nat Jt Cncl for Building Indust 1982, chm Civil Engrg Construction Conciliation Bd 1983, gen sec Union of Construction Allied Trades and Technicians 1984; memb: Gen Cncl TUC 1984, Construction NEDO 1985; pres Euro Fedn of Bldg and Woodworkers 1986, memb Construction Indust Training Bd 1990; chm Tstees Working Class Manchester 1973; *Recreations* swimming, walking; *Style—* Albert Williams, Esq; 177 Abbeville Rd, Clapham Common, South Side, London SW4 9RL (☎ 071 622 2442)

WILLIAMS, Alexander (Alex); s of Henry Williams, of 13 Wat's Dyke Way, Garden Village, Wrexham, Clwyd, and Dorothy, *née* Horne; *b* 30 March 1931; *Educ* Grove Park GS Wrexham, Univ Coll of North Wales Bangor (BSc); *m* 27 April 1957, Beryl Wynne, da of Thomas Charles Williams (d 1979) of Crewe, Cheshire; 1 s (Jonathan Mark b 25 May 1962); *Career* Nat Serv REME 1953-55; Monsanto Chemicals 1955-56, Southern Instruments Ltd Camberley 1956-59, head Div of Mechanical and Optical Metrology Nat Physical Laboratory 1978-81 (with Div of Radiation Sci 1959-78), under sec Res and Technol Policy Div DTI 1981-87, The Govt Chemist 1987-; FInstP; *Books* A Code of Practice for the detailed statement of accuracy (with P J Campion and J E Burns, 1973); *Recreations* walking, travel, bell ringing, opera; *Style—* Alex Williams, Esq; Laboratory of the Government Chemist, Queen's Rd, Teddington, Middlesex TW11 OLY (☎ 081 943 7300, fax 081 943 2767, telex 931 2132476GCG)

WILLIAMS, Prof Allan Peter Owen; s of Thomas Williams, of Cardiff, and Hilda Marie Williams (d 1983); *b* 14 Oct 1935; *Educ* Eastbourne GS, Univ of Manchester (BA), Birkbeck Coll London (MA, PhD); *m* 25 July 1959, Rosella, da of Maj Honorio Jose Muschamp d'Assis Fonseca (d 1984); 1 s (Edmond b 1965), 2 da (Hélène b 1963, Roselyne b 1967); *Career* res exec (later res gp head) Marplan Ltd 1960-63, prof City Univ Business Sch 1988- (lectr 1963-74, sr lectr 1974-83, reader 1983-88), dir Centre for Personnel Res and Enterprise Devpt City Univ 1978-, pro-vice-chllr City Univ 1987-; dir Organsiation Surveys Ltd 1966-69, conslt psychologist Civil Serv Selection Bd 1966-80; hon treas Br Psychological Soc 1971-74 (chm occupational psychology section 1979-80), memb army personnel Res Ctee MRC 1983-, chm personnel psychology panel APRC 1987-; memb exec ctee: Int Assoc of Applied Physics, Br Acad of Mgmnt; FBPsS 1979, MAMED 1974, MAAM 1986, CPsychol 1988; *Books* The Role and Educational needs of Occupational Health Nurses (1982), Using Personnel Research (1983), Changing Culture: New Organisational Approaches (1989); *Recreations* lawn tennis, photography, philately, bibliophile; *Clubs* Barnet Lawn Tennis, Royal Photographic Soc; *Style—* Prof Allan Williams; City University Business Sch, Frobisher Crescent, Barbican Centre, London EC2Y 8HB (☎ 071 920 0111, fax 071 588 2756, telex 263896)

WILLIAMS, Sir Alwyn; s of D D Williams; *b* 8 June 1921; *Educ* Aberdare Boys' GS, Univ Coll of Wales Aberystwyth, US Nat Museum; *m* 1949, Joan Bevan; 1 s, 1 da; *Career* prof of geology Queen's Univ Belfast 1954-74, pro vice chllr 1965-74; Lapworth prof of geology and head of dept Univ of Birmingham 1974-76; Univ of Glasgow: princ and vice chllr 1976-88, hon palaeobiology res fell 1988-; Univ of Wales fell 1947-48, Harkness fell 1948-50; chm Bd of Tstees BM (NH) 1974-79; pres RSE 1985-; FRS, FRSE, MRIA; kt 1983; *Books* Treatises and Monographs in Geology and Palaeontology; *Recreations* music, art; *Style—* Sir Alwyn Williams, FRS, FRSE; Palaeobiology Unit, Department of Geology and Applied Geology, Univ of Glasgow, Glasgow G12 8QQ

WILLIAMS, Dr (Hugh) Amphlett; s of Edwin George Williams (d 1917), of Latimers, Knotty Green, Beaconsfield, Bucks, and Florence Mary, *née* Amphlett (d 1948); *b* 5 June 1906; *Educ* City of London Sch, Univ of London (PhD); *m* 9 Sept 1933, Mary Eileen, da of Arthur Ernest Blackwell (d 1951); *Career* pub analyst: City and Port of London, Greenwich, Kensington, Chelsea, Hackney, Woolwich, Bermondsey 1933-71; gas identification offr 1939-45; contrib various scientific jls on food analysis for harmful substances; Freeman City of London 1927, Liveryman Worshipful Co of Goldsmiths 1944 (Freeman 1927); Fell City and Guilds Inst 1968; FRSC, MChemA, FIFST, FRSH, memb Soc of Public Analysts, Chem Ind; *Recreations* tennis, countryside; *Clubs* Nat Lib, English Speaking Union; *Style—* Dr Amphlett Williams; Wood End, 11 Leazes Ave, Chaldon, nr Caterham, Surrey CR3 5AG (☎ 0883 45 766)

WILLIAMS, Andrew Edward; s of Graham Edward Williams, of Baschurch House, Shrewsbury, and Rosaline Joan Amphlett; *b* 16 Sept 1952; *Educ* Wakeman Sch Shrewsbury, Univ of Warwick (LLB), Univ of Sheffield (MA); *Career* called to the Bar Lincoln's Inn 1975; memb Legal Aid Area Ctee (East London); memb Criminal Bar Assoc; *Style—* Andrew E Williams, Esq; 3 Hare Court, Temple, London EC4Y 7BJ (☎ 071 353 7561, fax 071 353 7741, 0836 271 321)

WILLIAMS, Anthony Ffoulkes; s of Edward Gordon Williams, of Birkenhead, and Sarah Elizabeth, *née* Wearing (d 1972); *b* 7 May 1951; *Educ* Birkenhead Sch, UCL (BSc), Westminister Med Sch (MB BS), St Catherine's Coll Oxford (DPhil); *Career* res fell Dept Paediatrics Univ of Oxford 1981-85 lect in child health Univ of Bristol 1985-87, sr lectr child health and conslt paediatrician St Georges Hosp Med Sch 1987-; memb: Nutrition Soc, British Paediatric Assoc, British Assoc for Perinatal Med; MRCP 1978; *Style—* Dr Anthony Williams; Department of Child Health, St George's Hospital Medical School, Cranmer Terrace, London SW17 0RE (☎ 081 672 9944)

WILLIAMS, Anthony Touzeau; s of Frank Chauncy Williams (d 1971), of Keymer, Sussex, and Yvonne Romaine, *née* Touzeau (d 1967); *b* 14 March 1927; *Educ* Cranleigh Sch, A A Sch of Architecture (Dip Arch); *m* 16 May 1953, Eleanor Brigitte, da of Dr Ernst Jellinek (d 1977), of Harpenden; 3 s (Simon b 1956, Michael b 1959, Peter b 1962); *Career* asst architect: Herts CC 1949-56, Br Standards Inst 1956-58, head Tech Dept RIBA 1958-63; ptnr: Alex Gordon & Ptnrs 1963-66, Anthony Williams & Burles 1966-76; series ed Building Dossiers 1973-, Anthony Williams & Ptnrs 1976-; chm Yarsley Quality Assured Firms 1985-; memb Cncl Bldg Standards Gp of Br Standards Soc, memb BSI Ctee, past chm Modular Soc; FRIBA, FCSD, FRSA; *Books* Signs (1984), Energy Design Guide (1985); *Recreations* historic gardens; *Style—* Anthony Williams, Esq; 43A West Common, Harpenden, Herts AL5 2JW (☎ 0582 460 994)

WILLIAMS, Betty, Lady; Betty Kathleen; da of John Taylor, of Hitchin; *m* 1950, Sir William Williams, 8 Bt, of Tregullow (d 1960); *Style—* Betty, Lady Williams; The Flat, St Brannocks House, Braunton, N Devon

WILLIAMS, Dr Brian Owen; s of William Wood Williams (d 1988), of Kilbarchan, Scotland, and Joan Scott, *née* Adam; *b* 27 Feb 1947; *Educ* Kings Park Sch Glasgow, Univ of Glasgow (MD, MB, CWB); *m* 3 Dec 1970, Martha MacDonald, da of James Carmichael (d 1974), of Glasgow; 2 da (Jennifer b 1976, Linzie b 1978); *Career* maj RAMC 32 Scot Signal Regt TA 1976-83; conslt geriatrician Victoria Infirmary Glasgow 1976-79, sr lectr Univ of Glasgow 1979-82, conslt in admin charge W Glasgow Geriatric Med Serv 1982-, hon clinical lectr Univ of Glasgow 1982-; author of over 100 pubns on health care of the elderly; sec UK Specialist Advsy Ctee in Geriatric Med; memb: BMA, BGS, Scot Soc Physicians; FRCP; *Books* Practical Management of the Elderly (with Sir Ferguson Anderson, 4 edn, 1983, 5 edn, 1988); *Recreations* swimming, writing, hill walking; *Style—* Dr Brian Williams; 15 Thorn Drive, High Burnside, Glasgow G73 4RH (☎ 041 634 4480); Gartnavel General Hospital, 1053 Great Western Rd, Glasgow G12 0YN (☎ 041 334 8122)

WILLIAMS, Bryn Owen; BEM (1990); s of Hugh James Owen Williams (d 1983), and Ivy, *née* Heffer; *b* 20 Aug 1933; *Educ* Southgate County GS, Pitman's Coll, Italia Conti Stage Sch; *m* 6 July 1957, Ann Elizabeth Rheidol, da of David Rheidol Powell (d 1932), adopted da of Stephen Llewellyn Jones (d 1963), of Dulwich; 1 s (Timothy

Dorian b 7 April 1959), 1 da (Tracy-Jane b 11 June 1961); *Career* professional toastmaster 1950; co fndr (with father) Nat Assoc of Toastmasters 1956 (pres 1962 and 1990, life vice pres 1984), chm Toastmaster Training Ltd 1988, officiated at over twelve thousand events in over twenty countries; memb Grand Order Water Rats 1965; Freeman City of London 1980, Liveryman Worshipful Co of Butchers 1985; *Recreations* golf, classical music; *Clubs* Wig & Pen, Muswell Hill Golf, Concert Artists Assoc, City Livery, Variety Club of GB Golf Soc (life memb), Jaguar Drivers (life memb); *Style—* Bryn Williams, Esq, BEM; Tanglewood, 50 The Ridgeway, Enfield, Middx EN2 8QS (☎ 081 366 0012); Bryn Williams Enterprise, 6 Gladstone Hse, High Rd, Wood Green N22 6JS (☎ 081 888 2398)

WILLIAMS, Caroline Ann; da of Maurice Henry Jackson, of Almeria, Spain, and Dorothy, *née* Ludlow; *b* 2 March 1954; *Educ* Convent of the Cross Sch Waterlooville Hants, St Hughs Coll Oxford, Univ of Southampton (LLB); *m* 17 March 1973, Richard David Brooke Williams, s of Gp Capt Richard David Williams, CBE, of Hampshire; 1 s (Richard David b 6 Aug 1987), 1 da (Rowena b 27 June 1982); *Career* admitted slr 1978; ptnr Blake Lapthorn; govr and vice chm Portsmouth Coll Art Design and Further Educn, memb industl advsy bd Portsmouth Poly Business Sch; memb Law Soc 1978; *Recreations* sailing; *Clubs* Eastney Cruising Assoc; *Style—* Mrs Caroline Williams; 4 Grand Parade, Old Portsmouth, Hants; New Court, 1 Barnes Wallis Rd, Segensworth, Fareham PO15 5UA (☎ 0489 579990, fax 0489 579127)

WILLIAMS, Catrin Mary; da of Richard Williams, JP (d 1966), of Y Ddol, Pwllheli, Gwynedd, and Margaret, *née* Jones (d 1986); *b* 19 May 1922; *Educ* Pwllheli GS, Welsh Nat Sch of Med; *Career* conslt ear nose and throat surgn Clwyd Health Authy (North) 1956-86; pres Med Women's Fedn 1973-74, elected jt chm Women's Nat Cmmn 1981-83, chm Meniere's Soc 1990-, chm Wales Cncl for the Deaf 1986-88, memb Cncl Exec Ctee Royal Nat Inst for Deaf, exec memb Wales Cncl for the Disabled; memb: BMA, Med Women's Int Assoc; *Recreations* reading, embroidery; *Style—* Miss Catrin Williams; Gwrych House, Abergele, Clwyd LL22 8EU (☎ 0745 832256)

WILLIAMS, Christopher David Curnow; s of John Curnow Gilbart William, and Marie, *née* Addison; *b* 3 May 1959; *Educ* Repton, Univ of Sheffield (LLB); *m* 3 April 1987, Elaine Joy, da of Gordon Brookes Castleton; 1 s (George Maxwell Curnow b 1989, Charles Henry Brookes b 25 Sept 1990); *Career* called to the Bar Grays Inn 1981; practising barrister; *Recreations* squash, music, theatre, hockey; *Style—* Christopher Williams, Esq; 14 Toft Green, York, N Yorks (☎ 0904 620048); £ 2 Harcourt Buildings, Temple, London EC4Y 9DB (☎ 071 353 1394)

WILLIAMS, Clifford Sydney; s of George Frederick Williams (d 1932), and Florence Maud Gapper Williams Maycock; *b* 30 Dec 1926; *Educ* Highbury County GS London; *m* 1962, Josiane Eugenie, da of Auguste Camille Joseph Peset (d 1972), of Paris; 2 da (Anouk, Tara); *Career* Lt RAOC 1946-48; founded and directed Mime Theatre Co 1950-53, dir of productions Marlow Theatre Canterbury 1956 and Queen's Theatre Hornchurch 1957, assoc dir Royal Shakespeare Co 1963-; has directed for Nat Theatres of UK, Finland, Yugoslavia, Bulgaria, Mexico and Spain, and in France, Denmark, Sweden, W Germany, Japan, Canada and USA; productions in London and New York incl premieres of plays by: Friedrich Dürrenmatt, Eugene Ionesco, David Rudkin, Anthony Shaffer, Alan Bennett, Peter Ustinov, Rolf Hochhuth, Alexander Solzhenitsyn, Ian Ogilvie and Hugh Whitemore; dir Man and Superman (film, 1988); author of plays incl: The Sleeping Princess, The Goose Girl, The Secret Kingdom (with Donald Jonson), Stephen Hero (adaptation of James Joyce with Donald Jonson); fell Trinity Coll of Music 1956, govr Welsh Coll of Music and Drama 1980-89; chm: British Theatre Assoc 1978-89, UK Centre of Int Amateur Theatre Assoc 1980-; *Recreations* motor sport; *Style—* Clifford Williams, Esq; 62 Maltings Place, London SW6 2BY (☎ 071 736 4673)

WILLIAMS, David; s of Trevor Kenneth Stuart Williams (d 1961), and Peri Rene Mavis, *née* Morgan (d 1987); *b* 8 June 1926; *Educ* Cathedral Sch Hereford, St John's Coll Oxford (MA); *m* 18 Aug 1951, Brenda Yvonne, da of Dan Campbell Holmes, OBE (d 1964); 1 s (Jonathan b 1955), 1 da (Linda b 1957); *Career* Sub Lt RNVR 1944-47; dir Gordon and Gotch Advertising 1950-58, chm David Williams and Ketchum 1958-78, dir Ketchum Communications Inc USA 1968-86; govr Pusey House Oxford 1963-; vice chm Royal Cwlth Soc for the Blind 1969-85; cncl memb: Advertising Assoc 1963-78, Advertising Standards Authy 1976-80, Impact Fndn 1985-, Chest Heart and Stroke Assoc 1987-; Freeman City of London 1959, Liveryman Worshipful Co of Stationers and Newspaper Makers 1960; MCAM 1959, FIPA 1962; *Novels*: Unholy Writ (1976), Treasure by Degrees (1977), Treasure up in Smoke (1978), Murder for Treasure (1980), Copper, Gold & Treasure (1982), Treasure Preserved (1983), Advertise for Treasure (1984), Wedding Treasure (1985), Murder in Advent (1985), Treasure in Roubles (1986), Divided Treasure (1987), Treasure in Oxford (1988), Holy Treasure (1989), Prescription for Murder (1990), and numerous short stories; *Recreations* golf, music, looking at churches; *Clubs* Carlton, Wentworth Golf; *Style—* David Williams, Esq; Blandings, Pinewood Rd, Wentworth, Virginia Water, Surrey GU25 4PA (☎ 0344 842055)

WILLIAMS, Adm Sir David; GCB (1977, KCB 1975), DL (Devon 1981); s of A Williams; *b* 22 Oct 1921; *Educ* Yardley Ct Sch Tonbridge, RNC Dartmouth; *m* 1947, Philippa Stevens; 2 s; *Career* joined RN as Cadet 1935, Flag Offr and 2 i/c Far East Fleet 1970-72, dir-gen Naval Manpower and Trg 1972-74, Vice-Adm 1973, Adm 1974, Chief Naval Personnel and Second Sea Lord 1974-77, C-in-C Naval Home Cmd and ADC to HM The Queen 1977-79, Gentleman Usher to HM The Queen 1979-82, Extra Gentleman Usher 1982-, govr and C-in-C Gibraltar 1982-85; memb Cwlth War Graves Cmmn 1980-89 (vice-chm 1986-89); KStJ 1983; *Clubs* Royal Yacht Sqdn, Army and Navy; *Style—* Admiral Sir David Williams, GCB, DL; Brockholt, Strete, Dartmouth, Devon TQ6 0RR

WILLIAMS, Rear Adm David Apthorp; CB (1965), DSC (1942); s of Thomas Pettit Williams (d 1962), of 37 Auckland Rd East, Southsea, Hants, and Vera Frederica Dudley, *née* Apthorp (d 1955); *b* 27 Jan 1911; *Educ* Cheltenham; *m* 27 April 1951, Susan Eastlake (d 1987), da of Wharram Henry Lamplough (d 1945), of Bredon, Foster Rd, Alverstoke, Hants; 1 s (Nigel Lamplough), 2 step da (Sarah Ley (Mrs Bradby) b 1939, Shirley Anne (Mrs Palmes) b 1942); *Career* baval Cadet HMS Erebus (trg ship) 1929-30, Midshipman (E) (later Sub Lt (E)) RN Engrg Coll Keyham 1930-34, Sub Lt (E) (later Lt (E)) HMS Nelson 1934-35, Lt (E) sr engine room watchkeeper HMS Barham 1935-37, Lt (E) Mechanical Trg Estab Chatham (HMS Pembroke) 1937-39; Lt (E) (later Lt Cdr (E)) engr offr HMS Hasty 1939-42: 2 Destroyer Flotilla, Med Fleet, S Atlantic Station, Home Fleet, E Med Fleet (sunk Malta convoy 1942, despatches four times); Lt Cdr (E) sr engr HMS Implacable 1942-45, Home Fleet and 1 Aircraft Carrier Sqdn Br Pacific Fleet (C-in-C's Commendation) Cdr (E) 1945, Cdr (E) HMS Argonaut Br Pacific Fleet and Portsmouth 1945-47, RN Engrg Coll Plymouth (HMS Thunderer) 1947, air engrg course 1947, prodn mangr RN Aircraft Repair Yard Gosport 1947-49, Air Equipment and Naval Photography Dept Admty 1949-52, trg cdr and air engr offr RN Air Station Yeovilton 1952-53, trg cdr and air engr offr RN Air Station St Merryn 1953-55, Capt 1955, First Admty Interview Bd Dartmouth and HMS Sultan 1955-57, cmd tech offr staff of Flag Offr Air (Home) HMS Daedalus 1957-59, Co RN Air Station Abbotsinch HMS Sanderling 1959-61, sr offrs war course RN Coll Greencih March-Aug 1961, cmd engr offr staff of Flag Offr Air (Home) Aug-Oct 1961, chief staff offr (tech) staff of C-in-C Plymouth 1961-62, Rear Adm dir-gen (aircraft) Admty (later dir-gen aircraft (naval) MOD) 1962-65; ret 1965; memb Panel of Interviewers for Professional and Tech Grades and Retired Offrs (Civil Serv Cmmn) 1965-82; chm: Gosport Local Ctee Cancer Res Campaign 1967-, chm Portsmouth Annual Area Meeting Offrs' Pension Soc 1986-; CENG, MIMechE 1947; *Clubs* Army and Navy; *Style—* Rear Adm David Williams, CB, DSC; 3 Ellachie Gdns, Alverstoke, Gosport, Hants PO12 2DS (☎ 0705 583 375)

WILLIAMS, Col David Arden Bruce; s of Brig Edward Stephen Bruce Williams, CBE (d 1977), of Old Rectory, Bramdean, Hants, and Evelyn Agnes, *née* Clay; *b* 6 May 1940; *Educ* Winchester, RMA Sandhurst; *m* 30 Dec 1972, Suzie, da of Dr William Benjamin Ellis Ellis-Jones; 1 s (Jamie b June 1978), 2 da (Katie b Jan 1975, Anna Lisa b July 1976); *Career* cmmnd RB 1960, 3GJ 1962, RGJ 1966, Capt 1966, Maj 1972, Lt-Col 1981, Col 1986; GSO2 2 Div 1975, OCPCD 1977, GSO2 UKLF 1979, CO BGT (UK) 1981, CO IJLB 1983-86, COS HQ EDIST 1986-89, Col ARC 4 (NELC) 1989; *Recreations* game shooting, tennis, golf; *Clubs* RB, RGJ; *Style—* Col David Williams; National Employers Liaison Committee, J Block, Duke of Yorks HQ, Chelsea, London SW3 4SS (☎ 071 218 5736, fax 071 218 5612)

WILLIAMS, His Hon Judge David Barry; QC (1975), TD (1964); s of William Barry Williams (d 1967), of Sully Glam, and Gwyneth Williams, *née* John; *b* 20 Feb 1931; *Educ* Cardiff HS for Boys, Wellington Sch Somerset, Exeter Coll Oxford (MA); *m* 1961, Angela Joy, da of David Thomas Davies of 52 Cyncoed Road, Cardiff; 3 s (Rhodri, Cristyn, Rhidian), 1 da (Catrin); *Career* Nat Serv S Wales Borderers 1949-51, 2 Bn The Monmouthshire Regt (TA) 1951-67 (ret as Maj); barr Gray's Inn 1955, Wales and Chester Circuit 1957-79, rec of Crown Ct 1972-79; asst cmmr Local Govt Boundary Cmmn for Wales 1976-79, cmmr for trial of Local Govt Election Petitions 1978-79; circuit judge 1979-; chm: Glamorgan Wanderers RFC 1974-78, Ctee Cardiff and Country Club 1979-80, Legal Affairs Ctee Welsh Centre for Int Affairs 1979-; UWIST: memb Cncl 1982-88, vice chm Cncl 1983-88, vice pres 1984-88, memb Ct of Govrs; memb Ct of Govrs Univ Coll of Wales Cardiff 1988- (memb Cncl 1988-); Dep Sr Judge (non-resident) Sovereign Base Areas Cyprus 1983-, Liaison Judge W Glamorgan 1983-, pres Mental Health Review Tribunals 1983-; *Recreations* rugby football (administration), mountain walking; *Clubs* Army & Navy, Cardiff and County, Glam Wanderers RFC; *Style—* His Hon Judge David Williams, TD, QC; 52 Cyncoed Rd, Cardiff (☎ 0222 498 189); The Law Courts, St Helen's Rd, Swansea, W Glamorgan

WILLIAMS, David Fredrick; s of Fredrick Williams, of Berkshire and Patricia, *née* Devries; *b* 8 Oct 1958; *Educ* Millfield; *m* 15 Sept 1984, Sarah Jane, da of Eric Bailey; 2 da (Amy Charlotte b 22 Feb 1986, Lucy Rebecca b 24 June 1989); *Career* professional golfer; amateur Herts County 1976-79 (co champion 1979), GB youth team 1979, England youth and full amateur team 1979; turned professional 1979, memb PGA Tour 1980-; winner Rolex International 1980, winner Motorola Classic 1988, finished in top 50 Euro Tour order of merit 1988-90; *Recreations* all sports, fitness training; *Style—* David Williams, Esq; International Sports Management Ltd, Mere Golf and Country Club, Knutsford, Cheshire WA16 6LJ (☎ 0565 830417, fax 0565 830434)

WILLIAMS, Sir David Innes; s of Gwynne Evan Owen Williams (d 1957), and Cecily Mary, *née* Innes; *b* 12 June 1919; *Educ* Sherborne, Trinity Hall Cambridge, Univ Coll Hosp Med Sch (MB BCh, MA, MD, MCh); *m* 19 Sept 1944, Margaret Eileen, da of Victor Harding (d 1956); 2 s (Martin Gwynne b 13 March 1948, Michael Innes b 14 Nov 1949); *Career* Maj RAMC 1945-48 (surgical specialist); surgn St Peter's Hosp London 1950-78, urological surgn The Hosp for Sick Children Gt Ormond St 1952-78; urologist: King Edward VII Hosp for Offrs 1961-72, Royal Masonic Hosp 1962-72; civil conslt urologist to RN 1971-78, dir Br Post Grad Med Fedn Univ of London 1978-86, pro vice chllr Univ of London 1985-87, pres Br Assoc of Urological Surgns 1976-78; vice pres: Int Soc of Urology 1973-74, RCS 1983-85; chm: Cncl for Post Grad Med Educn Eng and Wales 1985-88, Cncl Imperial Cancer Res Fund 1982-91; pres: BMA 1988-89, RSM 1990-; hon fell UCL 1986; FRCS Eng 1944, Hon FACS 1983, Hon FRCSI 1984, hon FDSRCS Eng 1986; kt 1985; *Books* Urology of Childhood (1952), Urology of Childhood (1958), Paediatric Urology (1968, 1982); *Recreations* gardening; *Clubs* RSM; *Style—* Sir David Innes Williams; 66 Murray Rd, Wimbledon Common, London SW19 4PE (☎ 081 879 1042); The Old Rectory, East Knoyle, Salisbury, Wilts; Royal Soc of Medicine, 1 Wimpole St, London W1M 8AE (☎ 071 408 2119)

WILLIAMS, David Lincoln; s of Lewis Bernard Williams (d 1976), of Cardiff, and Eileen Elizabeth, *née* Cadogan (d 1989); *b* 10 Feb 1937; *Educ* Cheltenham; *m* 1959, Gillian Elisabeth, da of Dr William Phillips (d 1977); 1 s (Jonathan), 1 da (Sophie); *Career* chm: Allied Profiles Ltd 1981-, John Williams of Cardiff plc 1983-88 (dir 1969-88), Cox (Penarth) Ltd 1987-, Costa Rica Coffee Co 1988-; chm: Vale of Glamorgan Festival 1978-, Cardiff Broadcasting plc 1979-84, Friends of Welsh Nat Opera 1980-; memb Welsh Arts Cncl 1987- (chm Music Ctee 1988-); *Recreations* opera, sailing; *Clubs* Cardiff & County; *Style—* David Williams, Esq; Rose Revived, Llantrithyd, Cowbridge, S Glam (☎ 0446 781357)

WILLIAMS, Prof David Raymond; s of late Eric Thomas Williams, and Amy Gwendoline Williams; *b* 20 March 1941; *Educ* UCNW Bangor (BSc, PhD), Univ of St Andrews (DSc); *m* 22 Aug 1964, Gillian Kirkpatrick, da of late Adam Murray; 2 da (Caroline Susan b 1 Nov 1970, Kerstin Jane b 20 July 1973); *Career* lectr Univ of St Andrews 1966-77, prof of applied chemistry UCW Cardiff 1977-; chm Br Cncl Sci Advsy Ctee 1986-; CChem, FRSC, FRSA; *Books* The Principles of Bioinorganic Chemistry, The Metals of Life; *Recreations* swimming, cycling, travel, photography; *Style—* Prof David R Williams; School of Chemistry & Applied Chemistry, University of Wales College of Cardiff, PO Box 912, Cardiff CF1 3TB (☎ 0222 874779, fax 0222 874030, telex 497368 G)

WILLIAMS, Dr David Wakelin (Lyn); s of John Thomas Williams (d 1967), of 6 Vicarage Rd, Penygraig, Tonypandy, Glamorgan, and Ethel, *née* Lock (d 1979); *b* 2 Oct 1913; *Educ* Porth GS Rhondda, Univ Coll of S Wales and Monmouthshire (MSc, PhD); *m* 2 July 1948, Margaret Mary, da of Rev Richard Henry Wills (d 1963); 1 s (John Richard b 27 Nov 1953); *Career* demonstrator Zoology Dept Univ Coll Cardiff 1937-38, lectr in zoology, botany, anatomy and physiology Tech Coll Crumlin Mon 1938-39, biochemical work on enzymes and rodent control Indust Estate Treforest 1942-43; Miny of Food (later Dept of Agric and Fisheries Scot); food infestation inspr, sr inspr Scot and NI, PSO 1948, SPSO 1961, DCSO 1963; dir Agric Sci Servs DAFS 1963-73, chm Potato Trials Advsy Ctee 1963-, memb Cncl scot branch Inst of Biology 1966-69, FIBiol 1966, MBIM 1970; *Recreations* writing (including many articles for the scientific layman), hi-fi music, computing, natural history, formerly society and circuit stewart Nicolson Methodist Church Edinburgh; *Style—* Dr Lyn Williams; 8 Hillview Rd, Edinburgh, Scotland EH12 8QN (☎ 031 334 1108)

WILLIAMS, Lt-Col David William Bulkeley; s of Capt RA Williams, MC (d 1932), of Porth Yr Aur, Caernarvon, and Winifred, *née* Baker Brown (d 1979); *b* 22 Jan 1922; *Educ* Dover Coll, Univ of Birmingham (special war course), Jesus Coll Cambridge (Mechanical Sci Tripos), Army Staff Coll Camberley; *m* 11 Jan 1947, Frances Felicity, da of Lt-Col GH Latham (d 1969), of Robin Post, Hailsham, Sussex; 1 s (Kenneth

David Bulkeley b 4 Feb 1950), 2 da (Marion Dilys Bulkeley b 17 March 1948, Christine Frances Bulkeley b 27 July 1951); *Career* WWII cmmnd Maj RE served Gds Arm Div UK and NW Europe, ME, Greece, Egypt, Palestine 1941-46; sr planning engr Thames Conservancy 1972-82; former: MIEE, MInstP; memb: IWEM, Geologists Assoc; *Recreations* gardening, wood working, geology; *Style*— Lt-Col David Williams; Maen Melin, Peasemore, nr Newbury, Berks RG16 0JF (☎ 0635 248 415)

WILLIAMS, Derek Gordon; *b* 22 July 1931; *m* Stephanie Anne, *née* Briggs; 2 c; *Career* CA; chm Charterhall plc 1969-87; FCA; *Clubs* East India; *Style*— Derek Williams, Esq; 9 Paultons Square, London SW3 5AP, (☎ 071 352 0519)

WILLIAMS, Desmond James; OBE (1988); s of Sydney Williams (d 1982), and Eleanor Williams; *b* 7 July 1932; *Educ* Douai Sch, Xaverian Coll, Univ of Manchester (Dip Arch); *m* 1 (m dis 1982), 3 s (Dominic Blair b 1965, Andrew Francis b 1970, Jeremy (twin) b 1970), 1 da (Sarah Frances b 1967); m 2, 30 Dec 1988, Susan Alexandra, da of John Richardson, of Bramber, Salty Lane, Shaldon, Devon TQ14 0AP; *Career* architect; private practice 1964-; consultancy work: World Bank, Asian Devpt Bank; specialises in: educnl and leisure buildings incl New Centre Ampleforth Coll 1988, security design, residential, hotels; univ lectures at univs in Canada, London and Manchester; papers in: Education (1980), Building (1988 & 1989), Architects Journal (1989), Security Magazine (1990); past pres Manchester Soc of Architects 1988, examiner Sch of Architecture Univ of Manchester, chm NW regn RIBA 1989; memb: Civic Tst, Georgian Soc; memb RIBA 1967-; *Recreations* music, opera, walking, painting, travel; *Style*— Desmond Williams, Esq, OBE; Ellis Williams Partnership, Oak House, 2 Gatley Rd, Cheadle, Cheshire SK8 1PG (☎ 061 428 0808, fax 061 428 0812, car 0831 481522)

WILLIAMS, Sir Donald Mark; 10 Bt (UK 1866), of Tregullow, Cornwall; s of Sir Robert Ernest Williams, 9 Bt (d 1976); *b* 7 Nov 1954; *Educ* W Buckland Sch; *Heir* bro, Barton Matthew, b 21 Nov 1956; *Style*— Sir Donald Williams, Bt; Kamsack, Saskatchewan, Canada; Upcott House, Barnstaple, N Devon

WILLIAMS, Douglas; CB (1977), CVO (1966); s of James Eli Williams (d 1977), and Elizabeth, *née* Thomas (d 1943); *b* 14 May 1917; *Educ* Wolverhampton GS, Exeter Coll Oxford (MA); *m* 4 Dec 1947, Marie Agathe, da of Charles Leon Jacquot (d 1959); *Career* WWII Maj RA (despatches 1945); princ Colonial Off 1947, colonial attaché Br Embassy Washington 1956-60, memb and Br Co chm Caribbean Cmmn 1960, asst sec Colonial Office (Head of West Indian Div) 1960-67, Miny of Overseas Devpt 1967, under-sec in charge of multilateral aid 1968, govr Asian Devpt Bank & African Devpt Bank 1968-73 (dep sec 1973-77), ret 1977; memb: Bd of Crown Agents 1978-84, Econ and Social Ctee Euro Community 1978-82, Overseas Devpt Inst Governing Cncl 1979-85; tstee Help the Aged 1984, chm various ctees, memb Exec Ctee David Davies Memorial Inst of Int Relations 1984-; *Books* The Specialised Agencies of the United Nations (1987), contrib to The United Kingdom - The United Nations; *Clubs* United Oxford and Cambridge Univ; *Style*— Douglas Williams, Esq, CB, CVO; 14 Gomshall Rd, Cheam, Sutton, Surrey SM2 7JZ (☎ 081 393 7306)

WILLIAMS, Dr Dudley Howard; s of Lawrence Williams, and Evelyn Williams (d 1982); *b* 25 May 1937; *Educ* Pudsey GS Yorks, Univ of Leeds (BSc, PhD), Univ of Cambridge (MA, ScD); *m* 9 March 1963, Lorna Patricia Phyllis, da of Phillip Anthony Herbert Bedford; 2 s (Mark Howard b 1966, Simon Bedford b 1968); *Career* post doctoral fell and res assoc Stanford Univ USA 1961-64; Univ of Cambridge: fell Churchill Coll 1964-, asst dir of res 1966-74, reader in organic chem 1974-; author of numerous sci pubns and books; FRS 1983; *Books* Spectroscopic Methods in Organic Chemistry (with I Fleming, 4 edn); *Recreations* squash, skiing, piano playing; *Style*— Dr Dudley Williams, FRS; 7 Balsham Rd, Fulbourn, Cambridge CB1 5BZ (☎ 0223 880 592); University Chemical Laboratory, Lensfield Rd, Cambridge CB2 1EW (☎ 0223 336 368)

WILLIAMS, Sir Edgar Trevor; CB (1946), CBE (1944), DSO (1943), DL (Oxon 1964-); s of Rev Joseph Edgar Williams, of Greenbank, Chester; *b* 20 Nov 1912; *Educ* Tettenhall Coll, King Edward's Sch Sheffield, Merton Coll Oxford; *m* 1, 1938, Monica, da of Prof P W Robertson; 1 da; m 2, 1946, Gillian, yr da of Maj-Gen Michael Denman Gambier-Parry, MC (gs of Thomas Gambier-Parry, JP, DL, whose mother was niece of Adm 1 and last Baron Gambier, GCB, the man who failed to destroy the French fleet at the Basque Roads in 1809 but was acquitted at the subsequent court martial owing to political considerations. The general's maternal gf was Hon George Denman, 4 s of 1 Baron Denman) by his w Barbara (paternal gda of Eleanor, herself yst da of Rt Rev George Murray, sometime Bishop of Rochester, by the Bishop's w Lady Sarah Hay, 2 da of 10 Earl of Kinnoull; the Bishop's f was 2 s of 3 Duke of Atholl); 1 s, 1 da; *Career* served WWII 1 King's Dragoon Gds; GSO: N Africa, Italy, Normandy Rhine Army; with UN Secretariat 1946-47; asst lectr Univ of Liverpool 1936, govr St Edward's Sch Oxford 1964-, emeritus fell Balliol Coll Oxford 1980- (fell 1945-80), pro vice chllr Univ of Oxford 1968-80; chm Nuffield Provincial Hosps Tst 1966-88, Radcliffe tstee 1960-; Freeman of Chester; hon fell: Wolfson Coll Oxford, Merton Coll Oxford; UK Observer Rhodesian Elections 1980, sec Rhodes Tst 1951-80, memb Devlin Nyasaland Cmmn 1959; ed DNB 1949-80; FRHistS; kt 1973; *Clubs* Athenaeum, Savile, Vincent's; *Style*— Sir Edgar Williams, CB, CBE, DSO, DL; 94 Lonsdale Rd, Oxford OX2 7ER (☎ 0865 515199)

WILLIAMS, Air Cdre Edward Stanley; CBE (1975, OBE 1968); s of William Stanley Williams (d 1957), of Wallasey, Cheshire, and Ethel, *née* Jones (d 1953); *b* 27 Sept 1924; *Educ* Wallasey Central Sch, Sch of Slavonic and Eastern European Studies London Univ, Univ Coll London, St John's Coll Cambridge (MPhil); *m* 12 July 1947, Maureen, da of William Joseph Donovan (d 1974), of Oxton, Merseyside; 2 da ((Susan) Jane b 3 Feb 1950, Sally (Ann) b 23 June 1955); *Career* joined RAF 1942, WWII training in Canada, served in flying boats 1944, seconded BOAC 1944-48, 18 Sqdn RAF Waterbeach 1949, instr Central Navigation Sch RAF Shawbury 1950-52, Russian language study 1952-54; flying appts 1954-61: MEAF, A & AEE Boscombe Down, 216 Sqdn Tpt Cmd; OC RAF Element Army Intelligence Centre 1961-64, asst air attaché Moscow 1964-67, first RAF def fell 1967-68, Sch of Serv Intelligence 1968-71, chief Target Plans HQ Second ATAF 1971-73, chief intelligence offr Br Forces Near East 1973-75, cmd Jt Air Reconnaissance Intelligence Centre (UK) 1976-77, def and air attaché Moscow 1978-81, ret RAF 1981; conslt Soviet mil affrs MOD 1982-85, Soviet res assoc RUSI 1985-; vice-chm (air) TAVR and RAFVR Assoc (NW Area); *Books* The Soviet Military (1987), Soviet Air Power: Prospects for the Future (1990); *Recreations* walking; *Clubs* RAF; *Style*— Air Cdre E S Williams, CBE; c/o Midland Bank, 2 Liscard Way, Wallasey, Merseyside L44 5TR

WILLIAMS, Edward Thomas; s of Capt Thomas Williams, (d 1960), and Mabel Elvira, *née* Thomas (d 1985); *b* 21 Feb 1927; *Educ* Porth Co Sch, Kingswood Sch Bath, Trinity Hall Cambridge (MA, LLM); *m* 22 March 1955, (Marjorie) Jane Stanley, da of Capt Richard Stanley Evans (d 1949), of Bron-wydd Pontypridd; 1 s (Rhodri Clive b 30 Nov 1957), 2 da (Anne Judith b 10 July 1956, Susan Jane b 18 May 1961); *Career* Nat Serv RN 1945-48; slr 1954; pt/t chm: Nat Insur Local Tbnl 1966, Med Appeals Tbnls for Wales 1985; sec Advsy Ctee on Gen Cmmrs of Income Tax Mid Glamorgan 1986; pres: Pontypridd and Rhondda Dist Law Soc 1968-69, Assoc Law Socs of Wales 1976-77, Bridgend and Dist Law Soc 1977-78; clerk to Gen Cmmrs of Income Tax for Pontypridd 1973-, chm S Wales Autistic Soc, pres Rotary Club of Porthcawl 1987-88, former dir Pontypridd Mkts Fairs and Town Hall Co Ltd (resigned 1988); memb Law Soc 1954; *Recreations* golf; *Clubs* Royal Porthcawl; *Style*— Edward Williams, Esq; 2 Mallard Way, Porthcawl, Mid Glamorgan, CF36 3TS (☎ 0656 784031); 65 Mary Street, Porthcawl, Mid Glamorgan (☎ 0656 78415, fax 5532)

WILLIAMS, Eirian John; s of Rev Prof Cyril G Williams of St David's Coll, Univ of Wales, Lampeter, and Irene Williams; *b* 15 May 1952; *Educ* Carleton Univ Ottawa Canada (BA), Univ Coll of Wales Aberystwyth (LLB); *m* 10 Sept 1978, Glesni, da of Glyn Evans, of Dyfed; 2 s (Iwan Marc b 1982, Dylan Sion b 1985); *Career* admitted Canadian (Alberta) Bar 1978, admitted Br Slrs Roll 1983, ptnr Amphlett Lewis & Evans in assoc with Ungoed Thames & King; *Style*— Eirian Williams, Esq; 4/5 Bridge St, LLandysul, Dyfed (☎ 055936 3244, fax 055936 3733)

WILLIAMS, Elizabeth, Lady; Elizabeth Mary Garneys; JP (Dorset 1959), DL (Dorset 1983); da of William Ralph Garneys Bond, JP (d 1952, whose mother was da of Sir Harry Meysey-Thompson, 1 Bt, also sis of 1 and last Baron Knaresborough and the late Countess of Iddesleigh, w of 2 Earl) of Tyneham, Dorset and Evelyn Isobel Bond, OBE, *née* Blake (d 1954); *b* 1 May 1921; *Educ* Downe House; *m* 1948, as his 2 w, Sir David Williams, 3 Bt (d 1970), s of Sir Philip Williams, 2 Bt (d 1958), of Bridehead, Littlebredy, Dorset; 2 s (Philip 4 Bt, *qv*, Michael b 1955), 1 da (Ruth b 1951, m Michael Widén 1975); *Career* ATS (FANY) 1939-46, cmmnd 1942; High Sheriff Dorset 1979; Territorial Medal; *Recreations* country pursuits; *Style*— Elizabeth, Lady Williams, JP, DL; Stable House, Moigne Combe, Nr Dorchester, Dorset DT2 8JA (☎ 0305 852418)

WILLIAMS, Prof (William) Elwyn; s of Owen Williams (d 1972), of Anglesey, and Maggie, *née* Jones (d 1977); *b* 6 July 1931; *Educ* Holyhead Co Secdy Sch, Univ of Manchester (BSc, MSc, PhD, DSc); *m* 1, Judith (d 1976), da of Evan Davies (d 1932), of Llandovery; 1 s (Richard Aled b 26 Jan 1960); m 2, 6 Sept 1984, Janet Hazel, da of Leonard Knight Adams (d 1989), of Guildford; *Career* lectr then sr lectr in applied mathematics Univ of Liverpool 1957-65, prof of mathematics Univ of Surrey 1965-; FIMA 1966; *Books* Fourier Series and Boundary Vale Problems (1973), Dynamics - van Nostrand (1975), Partial Differential Equations (1982); *Style*— Prof Elwyn Williams; Department of Maths, University of Surrey, Guildford, Surrey GU2 5XH (☎ 0483 571281, fax 0483 300803, telex 859331)

WILLIAMS, Emrys; *b* 18 Jan 1958; *Educ* Slade Sch of Art (Boise Travelling scholar, Robert Ross scholar, BA), Stewart Powell Bowen fellowship 1983; artist in residence: Mostyn Art Gallery Llandudno 1983, South Hill Park Arts Centre and Wilde Theatre Bracknell 1985; awards: minor prize John Moores Liverpool Exhibition 1983, third prize Royal Nat Eisteddfod of Wales 1985, third prize Royal Over-Seas League London (Wardair Travel prize to Canada) 1988, Welsh Arts Cncl award for travel to Normandy 1988; *Career* solo exhibiitons: Andrew Knight Gallery Cardiff 1984, Pastimes Past (Wrexham Arts Centre) 1984, The Welsh Mountain Zoo (South Hill Park Arts Centre, Bracknell) 1985, Off Season - Winter Paintings (Oldham Art Gallery) 1985, Lanchester Poly Gallery Coventry 1986, Benjamin Rhodes Gallery London 1986 and 1989, Wrexham Arts Centre 1990; gp exhibitions incl: Clwyd Ten (Wrexham Arts Centre) 1981, Thorugh Artists Eyes (Mostyn Art Gallery Llandudno) 1982, John Moores Liverpool Exhibiiton XIII 1982-83, Serpentine Summer Show II, (Serpentine London) 1983, Pauline Carter & Emrys Williams (Chapter Gallery) Cardiff 1984, John Moores Liverpool Exhibition XIV 1985, Group 56 (Bratislava Czechoslavakia) 1986, David Hepher and Emrys Williams (Castlefield Gallery) Manchester 1987, Big Paintings (Benjamin Rhodes Gallery) 1988, Ways of Telling (Mostyn Art Gallery, Llandudno) 1989, Group 56 (Glynn Vivian Museum, Swansea), 1990; work in public collections: Contemporary Art Soc of Wales, Arthur Andersen & Co, Glynn Vivian Art Gallery and Museum Swansea, Govt Art Fund, Clwyd County Cncl, Clwyd Fine Art Trust; numerous Works in private collections in Britian and USA; *Style*— Emrys Williams, Esq; Benjamin Rhodes Gallery, 4 New Burlington Place, London W1X 1SB (☎ 071 534 1768/9, fax 071 287 8841)

WILLIAMS, Eric Charles; s of Herbert Reginald (d 1969), of Upper House, Clunbury, Shrops, and May Williams (d 1975); *b* 14 Nov 1921; *Educ* Wellingborough GS; *m* 18 Aug 1947, Margaret Goldsworthy, da of Thomas Peregrine (d 1956), of London; 2 s (Simon Eric b 1969, Philip Charles Peregrine b 1966), 3 da (Susan b 1951, Anne (twin) b 1951, Caroline b 1963); *Career* WWII Capt's sec HMS Agamemnon RNR 1943-44, RNVR 1943-46, paymaster branch HMS Rajah 1944, Capt's Sec HMS Highway 1944, official naval reporter CNI Admty 1944-46; journalist provincial newspapers Northampton 1938-41, Reuters 1946, Sunday Dispatch 1946-47; dir Gainsborough Studios 1948-49, PR Foote Cone & Belding Ltd 1949-56 (Greece 1951-52), PR mangr Notley Advertising Ltd 1957-60, PR dir McCann-Erickson Ltd 1960-62, md PR Plan Ltd 1962-67, fndr and md Eric Williams & Partners Ltd 1967-83, sold co to Daniel J Edelman Ltd and joined their board until ret 1987; chm Esher and Dist Christian Aid Ctee; Freeman City of London 1975, Liveryman Worshipful Co of Fruiterers 1975 (Hon Asst 1986-88); FInstPR 1970, FIOD, memb Int PR Assoc; *Recreations* dry fly fishing, boating, travel, gardening, conversation; *Clubs* Solus; *Style*— Eric Williams, Esq; Fair Acre, 20 Meadway, Esher, Surrey KT10 9HF (☎ 0372 464489)

WILLIAMS, Euryn Ogwen; s of Alun Ogwen Williams (d 1970), and Lil Evans (d 1968); *b* 22 Dec 1942; *Educ* Mold Alun GS, UCNW (BA Dip Educ); *m* 1 Jan 1966, Jenny Lewis, da of John Edward Jones, of Theknap, Barry; 1 s (Rhodri Ogwen b 10 May 1968), 1 da (Sara Lisa Ogwen b 17 March 1971); *Career* prog dir TWW, prodr HTV, dir EOS Independent Production Co, dir BBC Radio, dep chief exec and prog controller S4C, hon lectr Univ of Wales; memb: Welsh Language Bd, ABSA Welsh Ctee; govr Nat Film and TV Sch; *Books* Pelydrau Pell (1973); *Recreations* reading, television viewing, spectator sports; *Style*— Euryn Williams, Esq; S4C, Parc Ty Glas, Llanishen, Cardiff CF4 5GG (☎ 0222 747444, fax 0222 754444, telex 94017032 SIAN G and LINK 7500 1903780)

WILLIAMS, Faynia Roberta; da of Michael Manuel Jeffery (d 1968) of Brighton, Sussex, and Sally Caroline, *née* Stone (d 1968); *b* 10 Nov 1938; *Educ* Brighton and Hove HS, RADA (Dip), Univ of London (BA), Nat Film Sch (short course); *m* 1, 1961, Michael Brandis Williams (d 1968), s of Walter Williams; 2 da (Sabra Mildred b 1964, Teohna Eloise b 1966); m 2, 1975, Richard Arthur Crane, s of Rev Robert Bartlett Crane; 2 s (Leo Michael b 1977, Samuel Richard b 1979); *Career* dir theatre, TV and film; actress: first professional appearance Bridlington Repertory Theatre 1958, Stephen Joseph's Theatre in the Round with Harold Pinter and Alan Ayckbourn 1958-60; contract artist MGM USA 1960-61; first directed The Oz Trial (Oxford Playhouse) 1971; artistic dir: Oxford Free Theatre 1972-74, Oxford Arts Festival 1973, Theatre in the Mill 1974-78, Brighton Theatre 1980-85, Tron Theatre Glasgow 1983-84, Univ of Essex Theatre 1985-89; freelance dir: Royal Court, Fortune, Bush, Young Vic; theatres abroad incl USSR, Poland, Romania, Aust, Sweden and USA; fell in theatre: Univ of Bradford 1974-78, Univ of Lancaster 1978; artist in residence Granada TV and visiting prof Univ of Calif 1984; TV work incl: Signals, C4 arts documentary 1990; Edinburgh Festival Fringe First award: 1974, 1975, 1977, 1979, 1980, 1986, 1987, 1988, 1989; nominated: Best Dir/Designer for Satan's Ball London Critics award 1977, Best Dir Brothers Karamazov 1981; Freedom of the City of London 1959; memb: Equity 1959, Eastern Arts Assoc Drama Panel 1986 (vice chm 1989), Cncl Int Theatre

Inst 1989, Exec Cncl Euro Fedn of Audiovisual Dirs 1990; vice chm Directors Guild of GB 1990- (vice pres 1988-89); *Recreations* bellringing, the sea, travel to lesser-known places; *Style*— Ms Faynia Williams; Timbers, 41 The Cross, Wivenhoe, Essex CO7 9QL (☎ 0206 826769); Directors Guild of Great Britain, Suffolk House, 1-8 Whitfield Place, London W1P 5SF (☎ 071 383 3858, fax 071 383 5173)

WILLIAMS, Sir Francis John Watkin; 8 Bt (GB 1798), of Bodelwyddan, Flintshire, QC (1952); s of Col Lawrence Williams, OBE, JP, DL (d 1958, himself gs of Sir John Williams, 1 Bt, whose gggf was Speaker of the House of Commons); suc bro, Sir Reginald Williams, 7 Bt, MBE, TD (d 1971); *b* 24 Jan 1905; *Educ* Malvern, Trinity Hall Cambridge; *m* 1932, Brenda, JP, da of Sir (Joseph) John Jarvis, 1 Bt (d 1950); 4 da; *Heir* half-bro Lawrence Hugh Williams, b 25 Aug 1929; *Career* served WWII, Wing Cdr RAFVR; called to the Bar Middle Temple 1928; rec of: Birkenhead 1950-58, Chester 1958-71; chm: Anglesey QS 1960-71 (dep chm 1949-60), Flint QS 1961-71 (dep chm 1953-61); dep chm Cheshire QS 1952-71, rec of the Crown Ct 1972-75; chm Med Appeal Tbnl N Wales Area 1954-57; JP Denbighshire 1951-74; High Sheriff: Denbighshire 1957, Anglesey 1963; chllr Diocese of St Asaph 1966-83; Freeman City of Chester 1960; hon memb Wales and Chester Circuit 1987; *Recreations* gardening, golf; *Clubs* United Oxford and Cambridge Univ; *Style*— Sir Francis Williams, Bt, QC; Llys, Middle Lane, Denbigh

WILLIAMS, Francis Owen (Frank); CBE (1987); s of Owen Garbett Williams, Liverpool; *b* 16 April 1942; *Educ* St Joseph's Coll Dumfries; *m* 1974, Virginia Jane, da of Raymond Berry, of Marlow, Bucks; 3 c; *Career* md Williams Grand Prix Engineering Ltd; *Recreations* running; *Clubs* BRDC; *Style*— Frank Williams, Esq, CBE; Boxford House, Boxford, Nr Newbury, Berks; Williams Grand Prix Engineering Ltd, Station Road Industrial Estate, Didcot, Oxon OX11 7NA (☎ 0235 818161, telex 837632)

WILLIAMS, Prof Frederic Ward (Fred); s of Prof Sir Frederic Calland Williams (d 1977), of Spinney End, The Village, Prestbury, Cheshire, and Gladys, *née* Ward; *b* 4 March 1940; *Educ* St John's Coll Cambridge (MA, ScD), Univ of Bristol (PhD); *m* 11 April 1964, Jessie Anne Hope, da of Rev William Wyper Wilson (d 1988), of Weston-Super-Mare, Avon; 2 s (Frederic b 21 Aug 1968, David b 11 Feb 1970); *Career* asst engr Freeman Fox and Ptnrs 1964; lectr in civil engrg: Ahmadu Bello Univ Nigeria 1964-67, Univ of Birmingham 1967-75; prof in civil engrg Univ of Wales Inst of Sci and Technol 1975-88, head of div of structural engrg Univ of Wall Coll Cardiff 1988-; conslt to NASA, Br Aerospace; author of numerous papers in jls; active in local churches; FICE 1984, FIStructE 1985; FRAeS 1990; *Recreations* hill walking, jogging; *Style*— Prof Fred Williams; Brandelhow, 12 Ridgeway, Lisvane, Cardiff CF4 5RS (☎ 0222 761772); Head of Structural Engineering, School of Engineering, University of Wales College of Cardiff, PO Box 917, Cardiff CF2 1XH (☎ 0222 874826, fax 0222 874209, telex 498635)

WILLIAMS, Brig (John) Gage; OBE (1987); s of Col George Torquil Gage Williams, DL, of Menkee, St Mabyn, Cornwall, and Yvonne Marguerite, *née* Ogilvy; *b* 12 March 1946; *Educ* Eton, RMA Sandhurst, Magdalene Coll Cambridge (MA); *m* 4 Jul 1970, Elizabeth Anne Kyffin, da of Stephen Marriott Fox (d 1971), of Burlorne, Weybridge, Surrey; 1 s (James b 1973), 2 da (Rebecca b 1971, Meg b 1978); *Career* cmmnd Somerset and Cornwall Light Inf 1966 (The Light Inf 1967); Platoon Cdr: Ethiopia, Aden, Canada, Norway, Kenya, Germany; GSO 3 ops 19 Airportable Bde England and Cyprus 1974-75, instr tactics Sch of Inf Fort Benning USA 1975-77, Royal Mil Coll Sci 1977, Royal Staff Course Greenwich 1978; Co Cdr: Ireland, Canada, Cyprus (UN) 1978-80; GSO2 Jt Warfare MO1 1980-82, Special Ops Liaison Offr Washington DC 1982-83, Mil Asst GOC NI 1983-84; cmmd 1 Bn Light Inf: Lancs, Falklands, Canada, NI 1985-87; Liaison Col to Sch of Advanced Mil Studies Fort Leavenworth Kansas 1987-88, Col Higher Comd and Staff Course Camberley 1988-90, cmmnd UKMF/1 Inf Bde 1991-92; RUSI; *Recreations* shooting, fishing, stalking, golf, skiing, squash, tennis; *Clubs* Light Infantry, Hawks, Cornish, Beefsteak, St Enodoc GC; *Style*— Brig Gage Williams, OBE; HQ UK MF, Jellalabad Bks, Tidworth SP9 7AB (☎ 0980 46221 ext 2562)

WILLIAMS, Prof Gareth Howel; JP (Brent Petty Sessions Area); s of Morgan John Williams (d 1970), of Harrow, Middx, and Miriam, *née* Jones (d 1979); *b* 17 June 1925; *Educ* Pentre GS, UCL (BSc, PhD, DSc); *m* 2 April 1955, Marie Jessie Thomson, da of William Mitchell (d 1951), of Llanrwst, Gwynedd; 1 s (John b 1956), 1 da (Barbara b 1959); *Career* lectr in chemistry King's Coll London 1950-60 (asst lectr 1947-50), reader in organic chemistry Birkbeck Coll London 1960-67, visiting lectr Univ of Ife Nigeria 1965, prof of chemistry head Chemistry Dept Bedford Coll London 1967-84, Rose Morgan visiting prof Univ of Kansas 1969-70, visiting prof Univ of Auckland NZ 1977, emeritus prof Univ of London 1984-, pt/t prof of chemistry Royal Holloway and Bedford New Coll London 1984-87; memb Magistrates Cts Ctee and dep chm Brent Petty Sessions Area; chm: London Welsh Assoc 1987-90, Harrow Philharmonic Choir 1987-; Freeman City of London 1984, Liveryman Worshipful Co of Fletchers 1984-; memb Hon Soc Cymmrodorion; FRSC 1945-; *Books* Homolytic Aromatic Substitution (1960), Advances in Free Radical Chemistry (ed vol 1-6 1965-80), Organic Chemistry: A Conceptual Approach (1977); *Recreations* music; *Clubs* Athenaeum; *Style*— Prof Gareth Williams, JP; Hillside, 22 Watford Rd, Northwood, Middx HA6 3NT (☎ 09274 25297)

WILLIAMS, Gareth James; s of Rev Daniel James Williams, (d 1967), of Cardiff, and Elizabeth Beatrice May, *née* Walters (d 1974); *b* 22 Dec 1944; *Educ* Cardiff HS, Univ of Exeter; *m* 2 Aug 1969, Ruth Elizabeth, da of Sub Lt Albert Gordon Laugharne (d 1944); 1 s (Geraint b 1975), 2 da (Rhian b 1971, Catherine b 1974); *Career* Marks and Spencer plc: joined 1967, exec responsibilities for buying and distribution systems 1974-86, sr exec 1986-87, Business Devpt Gp NY USA 1987-88, divnl dir for Physical Distribution, Retail Systems and Info Tech; memb: Cons Pty, Chalfont St Giles Parish Church, Friend of Covent Garden; hon vice pres Cardiff HSOB RFC; sport: Cardiff and Cardiff HSOB Rugby Clubs 1964-67, capt Univ of Exeter RFC 1967, played for Br Univs Athletic Union 1967, advsr Br Acad 1985-87, memb UK Cncl of Inst of Logistics and Distribution Mgmnt 1989; *Recreations* sport (esp rugby), music (esp opera), education; *Clubs* Rugby (London), Cardiff HSOBRFC; *Style*— Gareth Williams, Esq; Talgarth House, Hervines Rd, Amersham-on-the-Hill, Bucks HP6 5HS (☎ 0494 432168); Michael House, Baker St, London W1A 1DN (☎ 071 935 4422)

WILLIAMS, Gareth Wyn; QC (1978); s of Albert Thomas Williams (d 1964), and Selina Williams (d 1985); *b* 5 Feb 1941; *Educ* Rhyl GS, Queens' Coll Cambridge (MA, LLM); *m* Aug 1962, Pauline, da of Ernest Clarke (d 1962); 1 s (Daniel b 1969), 2 da (Martha b 1963, Emma b 1966); *Career* barr, recorder Crown Court 1978; ldr Wales and Chester circuit 1987-89; *Style*— Gareth Williams, Esq; Southlake House, Shurlock Row, Berks RG10 0PS; Farrars Building Temple, London EC4Y 7BD (☎ 071 583 9241, fax 071 583 0090)

WILLIAMS, Geoffrey Copeland Meirioty; s of William Meirion Williams (d 1939), of Hastings, and Winifred Marjorie, *née* Brice (d 1987); *b* 31 Aug 1937; *Educ* Eastbourne Coll; *m* 29 May 1965, (Carin) Marianne, da of Col Arne Persson (d 1971), of Stockholm; 1 s (Anthony b 1977), 2 da (Ingela b 1968, Katherine b 1968); *Career* md Ansvar Insurance Co Ltd 1977- (gen mangr 1969-77); other directorships incl: South Down Building Society, UK Temperance Alliance Ltd; chm: Friends of the Towner Gallery Eastbourne, Eastbourne Community Health Servs; FCII 1970; *Recreations* reading, jazz; *Style*— Geoffrey Williams, Esq; Ansvar House, St Leonards Rd, Eastbourne, E Sussex BN21 3UR (☎ 0323 37541, fax 0323 39355)

WILLIAMS, Geoffrey Guy; s of Capt Alfred Guy Williams, OBE (d 1956), and Margaret, *née* Thomas; *b* 12 July 1930; *Educ* Blundell's, Christ's Coll Cambridge (MA, LLM); *Career* slr; ptnr Slaughter & May 1961-66 (joined 1952); J Henry Shroder Wagg & Co Ltd: dir 1966-90, vice chm 1974, dep chm 1977-90; chm Nat Film Fin Corpn 1976-85 (dir 1970); dir: Bass plc 1971-, Shroders plc 1976-90, John Brown plc 1977-85; chm Issuing Houses Assoc 1979-81, loan cmmr Pub Works 1990-, dir Standard Chartered plc 1990-; Freeman City of London; *Clubs* Brooks's; *Style*— Geoffrey Williams, Esq; 18G Eaton Square, London SW1W 9DD (☎ 071 235 5212); 120 Cheapside, London EC2V 6DS (☎ 071 382 6000, fax 071 382 6878, telex 885029)

WILLIAMS, George Mervyn; CBE (1977), MC (1944), DL (Glamorgan 1967); yr s of Owain Lloyd Joseph Williams (d 1930), and Maude Elizabeth, *née* Morgan (d 1941); *b* 30 Oct 1918; *Educ* Radley; *m* 1, 8 March 1941 (m dis 1946), Penelope, da of late Sir Frank Herbert Mitchell, KCVO, CBE; m 2, 19 Aug 1950, Grizel Margaretta Cochrane, da of Maj Walter Peter Stewart, DSO, late Highland LI, of Davo House, Kincardineshire; 1 s (Owain Anthony Mervyn b 8 Jan 1955); *Career* Maj Royal Fusiliers N Africa, Italy, Greece; chm: Christie-Tyler plc 1950-86, S Wales Regnl Bd Lloyds Bank Ltd 1975-87, Williams & Morgan Ltd 1986-; High Sheriff Glamorgan 1966, Vice Lord Lt Mid Glamorgan 1986-, JP 1965-70, DL 1967-86, C St J; *Clubs* Brooks's, RAC, Cardiff and County; *Style*— George Williams, Esq, CBE, MC; Llanharan House, Llanharan, Mid Glamorgan CF7 9NR; Craig y Bwla, Crickhowell, Powys NP8 1SU; Williams & Morgan Ltd, 10 St James Crescent, Swansea SA1 6DZ (☎ 0792 473782, fax 0792 51165)

WILLIAMS, Colonel George Torquil Gage; s of Capt John Gage Williams, 19 Hussars (ka 1943), and Nevil Thorne George; *b* 17 May 1920; *Educ* Cheltenham, RMC Sandhurst; *m* 6 Jan 1945, Yvonne Marguerite, da of Louis William Ogilvy (d 1922), of Calcutta, and St Jean de Luz, France; 2 s (Gage, Peter), 2 da (Louella (Mrs Hanbury-Tenison, *qv*), Rosemary (Mrs Anderson)); *Career* cmmnd Duke of Cornwall's LI 1939, served India, Iraq, M East until 1942, POW in Italy, escaped, served Palestine 1945-47, King's African Rifles 1947-49, 10 Gurkha Rifles 1949-51, Duke of Cornwall's LI BAOR, W Indies, Cmd Regtl Depot 1958-62, Cmd TA Bn 1962-65, Cmdt Hong-Kong Mil Serv Corps 1965-68, ret 1968; DL 1968, clerk to Lieutenancy of Cornwall 1968-90; Hon Col 6 Bn Light Infantry (TA) 1978-88; *Recreations* shooting, fishing; *Style*— Col George T G Williams; Menkee, St Mabyn, Bodmin, Cornwall

WILLIAMS, Gerard; s of Frank Williams, of Manchester, and Margaret Rose, *née* Lockwood; *b* 9 July 1959; *Educ* Manchester HS of Art, Manchester Poly, Brighton Poly; *Career* artist; solo exhibitions: Interim Art 1986 and 1990, Anthony d'Offay Gallery 1989, Galleria Franz Paludetto Turin 1990; group exhibitions incl: Whitechapel Open 1985 1986 1987 1988, Summer Show (Anthony d'Offay Gallery) 1988, That Which Appears is Good, That Which is Good Appears (Tanja Grunert Gallery Cologne) 1988, Home Truths (Castello di Rivara) 1989, Richard Wentworth Grenville Davey Gerard Williams (Sala Uno Rome) 1989, Its a Still Life (Arts Cncl of GB, touring) 1989-91, Leche Vitrines (Le Festival ARS Musica Brussels) 1990, TAC 90 (Sala Parpallo/Diputacion de Valencia, touring) 1990, Realismi (Galleria Giorgio Persano Turin, Ileana Toynta Contemporary Art Centre Athens) 1990, What is a Gallery? (Kettles Yard, Univ of Cambridge), Maureen Paley Interim Art 1990-91; *Style*— Gerard Williams, Esq; c/o Maureen Paley, Interim Art, 20 Dering St, London W1R 9AA (☎ 071 495 4580); c/o Anthony d'Offay, 9/21/23 Dering St, New Bond St, London W1R 9AA (☎ 071 499 4100)

WILLIAMS, Prof Glanmor; CBE (1981); s of Daniel Williams (d 1957), of Dowlais, Glamorganshire, and Ceinwen, *née* Evans (d 1970); *b* 5 May 1920; *Educ* Cyfarthfa Sch Merthyr Tydfil, Univ Coll of Wales Aberystwyth (BA, MA, DLitt); *m* 6 April 1946, (Margaret) Fay, da of late William Harold Davies, of Cardiff; 1 s (Huw b 1 Dec 1953), 1 da (Margaret b 31 March 1952); *Career* Univ Coll of Swansea: asst lectr 1945, sr lectr 1952-57, prof of history 1957-82, vice princ 1975-78; vice pres Univ of Coll of Wales 1986-; chm Royal Cmmn on Ancient Monuments (Wales) 1986-90 (memb 1962-); memb: Historic Bldg Cncl (Wales) 1962-89, Bd of Celtic Studies Univ of Wales 1969-, Ancient Monuments Bd (Wales) 1983-, Ctee Welsh Nat Folk Museum 1986-; chm: Nat Broadcasting Cncl of Wales 1965-71, Br Library Bd 1973-80, Br Library Advsy Cncl 1980-85; govr BBC 1965-71, pres Assoc of Teachers of History of Wales 1983-; FRHistS Soc 1954, FSA 1979, FBA 1986; *Books* The Welsh Church From Conquest to Reformation (1962), Welsh Reformation Essays (1967), Religion Language and Literature in Wales (1979), Wales 1415-1642 (1987), Glamorgan County History Vols I-VI (ed 1971-88); *Recreations* gramophone, walking, cine-photography; *Style*— Prof Glanmor William, CBE, FSA; 11 Grosvenor Rd, Sketty, Swansea SA2 0SP (☎ 792 204 113)

WILLIAMS, Prof Glanville Llewelyn; QC (1968); s of Benjamin Elwey Williams (d 1971), of Bridgend, Glamorgan, and Gwladys Llewelyn (d 1959); *b* 15 Feb 1911; *Educ* Cowbridge GS, UCW Aberyswyth, St John's Coll Cambridge (MA, PhD, LLD); *m* 19 Oct 1939, Lorna Margaret, da of Francis Wilfrid Lawfield (d 1950); 1 s (Rendel b 1941); *Career* called to the Bar Middle Temple 1935; fell St John's Coll Cambridge 1936-42; Univ of London 1945-55: reader in English law, prof of public law, Quain prof of jurisprudence; fell Jesus Coll Cambridge 1955 (hon fell 1978); Univ of Cambridge: reader in English law 1957-66, prof 1966, Rouse Ball prof of English law 1968-78; Carpentier lectr Colombia Univ 1956, Cohen lectr Univ of Jerusalem 1957, first Walter E Meyer visiting res prof NY Univ 1959-60, Charles Inglis Thompson guest prof Univ of Colorado 1965; special conslt for American Law Inst Model Penal Code 1956-58; memb Standing Ctee on Criminal Law Revision (Home Office) 1959-80, memb Law Cmmn working party on codification of criminal law 1967; pres Abortion Law Reform Assoc 1962-; Hon LLD: Univ of Nottingham 1963, Univ of Wales 1974, Univ of Glasgow 1980, Univ of Sussex 1987; Hon DCL Durham 1984; Hon Bencher Middle Temple 1966, FBA 1957, fell Galton Inst, foreign hon memb American Acad of Arts and Scis 1985; *Books* Liability for Animals (1939), Chapters in Impossibility of Performance (1941), The Law Reform (Frustrated Contracts) Act (1944), Learning The Law (1 edn 1945, 11 edn 1982), Crown Proceedings (1948), Joint Obligations (1949), Joint Torts and Contributory Negligence (1950), Speedhand Shorthand (1952, 8 edn 1980), Criminal Law: The General Part (1955, 2 edn 1964), The Proof of Guilt (1955, 3 edn 1963), The Sanctity of Life and the Criminal Law (US edn 1956, UK edn 1958), The Mental Element in Crime (1965), Foundations of the Law of Tort (with B A Hepple, 1976, 2 edn 1984), Textbook of Criminal Law (1978, 2 edn 1983); *Style*— Prof Glanville Williams, QC; Merrion Gate, Gazeley Lane, Cambridge CB2 2HB (☎ 0223 841175)

WILLIAMS, Prof Glynn Anthony; s of Idris Merrion Williams, of Cornwall Drive, Bayston Hill, nr Shrewsbury, and Muriel Elizabeth, *née* Purslow (d 1952); *b* 30 March 1939; *Educ* Wolverhampton GS, Wolverhampton Coll of Art (NDD); *m* 6 July 1963, Heather, da of Cyril Woodhall (d 1952); 2 da (Victoria b 2 Jan 1964, Sophie b 6 July 1967); *Career* regular exhibitor of sculpture 1967- (represented by Bernard Jacobson Gallery London), currently prof of sculpture Royal Coll of Art; has exhibited internationally, represented GB in the third Kotara Takamura Exhibition in Japan, has works in nat and int pub collections such at The Tate and V&A; author of articles on sculpture published in various art magazines and reviewer for the Times Literary Supplement; subject panel memb CNAA; hon fellowship for servs to art and educn from Wolverhampton Poly 1989; *Recreations* collecting tribal art, walking, crossword puzzles, cooking; *Style*— Prof Glynn Williams; Royal College of Art, Kensington Gore, London SW7 2EU (☎ 071 584 5020)

WILLIAMS, Gordon; s of Charles Williams, of Anfield, Liverpool, and Marjorie Gerard, *née* Bradborn (d 1984); *b* 27 June 1945; *Educ* Bishop Vesey's GS Sutton Coldfield, UCH Med Sch (MB BS); *m* 1 (m dis 1989), Susan Mary Gubbins; 2 da (Katherine Louise b 1970, Victoria Mary b 1972); m 2, 20 Sept 1989, Clare, da of (Montgomery) Derek Sanderson (d 1976); *Career* conslt urologist and transplant surgn Hammersmith Hosp and hon sr lectr RPMS 1978-, external examiner Univ of Addis Ababa; visiting surgn: Syria, Burma, Poland; numerous pubns on urology, urological cancer, impotence and diseases of the prostate; chm NW Thames Urologists; memb: Br Assoc Urological Surgns, Int Soc of Urology, Euro Soc of Urology, Euro Transplant Soc; memb Worshipful Soc of Apothecaries 1984, Freeman City of London 1985; Hon MS Univ of London 1988, FRCS; *Recreations* travel, Indian food; *Style*— Gordon Williams, Esq; 12 Derwent Rd, Twickenham TW2 7HQ (☎ 081 740 3218); Dept of Surgery, Hammersmith Hospital and Royal Post Graduate Medical Sch, Ducane Rd, London W12 0HS (☎ 081 740 3218, fax 01 740 3179)

WILLIAMS, (James) Gordon; *b* 13 June 1938; *Educ* Toxleth Tech Inst, Farnborough Tech Coll, Imperial Coll London (BSc, PhD, DSc); *Career* Imperial Coll London: res student 1961-62, asst lectr 1962-64, lectr 1964-70, reader 1970-75, prof 1975-, head Mech Engrg Dept 1990; consultancies: BP Chemicals (UK) 1967-, USI Chemicals (USA) 1977-, Du Pont (US) 1982-, ICI; ed Polymer, hon ed Plastics and Rubber: Processing and Applications, regnl ed International Journal of Fracture 1983-; *books*: Stress Analysis of Polymers (2 edn, 1980), Fracture Mechanics of Polymers 91985); *awards*: Unwin Scholarship 1961, Swinburne Medal-PRI 1986; FPRI 1979, FIMechE 1979, FEng 1982, FCGI 1986; *Style*— Gordon Williams, Esq; Breda, 16 Bois Lane, Chesham Bois, Amersham, Buckinghamshire (☎ 0494 726248)

WILLIAMS, Air Vice-Marshal Graham Charles; AFC (1971, and bar 1975); s of Charles Francis Williams (d 1968), and Molly, *née* Chapman (d 1988); *b* 4 June 1937; *Educ* Marlborough, RAF Coll Cranwell; *m* 3 March 1962, Judy Teresa Ann, da of Reginald Walker (d 1972); 1 s (Mark b 1963), 1 da (Kim b 1966); *Career* Pilot 54 Sqdn Odiham 1958-60, instr 229 OCU Chivenor 1961-63, Flt-Cdr 8 Sqdn Khormaskar 1964-65, Empire Test Pilot's Sch 1966, 'A' Sqdn (fighter test) A and AEE Boscombe Down 1967-70, RAF Staff Coll Bracknell 1971, OC 3 (F) Sqdn Wildenrath 1972-74, jr directing staff RCDS 1975-77, Stn Cdr RAF Bruggen 1978-79, Gp Capt Ops HQ RAF Germany 1980-82, CO Experimental Flying RAF Farnborough 1983, Cmdt A and AEE Boscombe Down 1984-85, DOR (Air) MOD 1986, asst chief of def staff Operational Requirements (Air) 1987-; FRAeS 1984; Harmon Trophy USA 1970; *Recreations* squash, golf; *Clubs* RAF; *Style*— Air Vice-Marshal Graham Williams, AFC; 3 The Ramparts, Knightrider St, Sandwich, Kent CT13 9ER (☎ 0304 613030); 31 Chester Way, London SE11; MOD, Whitehall, London SW1A 2HB (☎ 071 218 7221)

WILLIAMS, Dr (Daniel) Gwyn; s of Rev Daviel James Williams (d 1967), of Cardiff, and Elizabeth Beatrice Mary Walters (d 1974); *b* 7 March 1940; *Educ* Cardiff HS, Univ Coll Cardiff (MB BCh), Welsh Nat Sch of Med (MD); *m* 21 Jan 1967, Angela Mary, da of John Edwin Davies (d 1974), of Petts Wood, Kent; 4 da (Rachel b 1968, Sian b 1970, Hannah b 1972, Leah b 1976); *Career* jr hosp appts at Cardiff Royal Infirmary and The Radcliffe Infirmary Oxford, sr registrar in med Radcliffe Infirmary, res fell and asst lectr Royal Postgrad Medical Sch London, conslt physician and sr lectr in med United Medical and Dental Schs of Guy's and St Thomas's Hosp Univ of London; MRS, The Renal Assoc; FRCP 1978; *Books* The Oxford Textbook of Medicine (contrib, 1987), The Oxford Textbook of Clinical Nephrology (contrib, 1990); *Style*— Dr Gwyn Williams; The Renal Unit, Guy's Hospital, St Thomas's St, London SE1 9RT (☎ 071 955 4306, fax 071 407 6689)

WILLIAMS, Prof (John) Gwynn; s of Rev John Ellis Williams (d 1969), of 26 Stanley Ave, Rhyl, Clwyd, and Annie Maude, *née* Rowlands; *b* 19 June 1924; *Educ* Holywell GS Clwyd, Univ Coll of N Wales Bangor (BA, DipEd, MA); *m* 24 July 1954, Beryl, da of Rev Stafford Henry Morgan Thomas (d 1968); 3 s (William Gwynn b 1965, Gruffudd Rowland b 1969, Thomas Ellis b 1972); *Career* RN 1943-46; staff tutor Dept of Extra Mural Studies Univ of Liverpool 1951-54; Univ of N Wales: asst lectr 1955, prof of Welsh history 1963-83, dean Faculty of Arts 1972-74, vice princ 1974-79; chm Press Bd Univ of Wales 1979- (memb Cncl 1973-85), dir Gregynog Press 1979-; pres: Nat Library of Wales 1986- (vice pres 1984-86), Cambrian Archaeological Assoc 1987-88; vice pres Hon Soc of Cymmrodorion 1988-, hon memb Gorsedd of Bards (White Robe); memb Royal Cmmn on Ancient and Historical Monuments in Wales: 1967, 1977, 1987; *Publications* The University College of North Wales: Foundations (1985), contrib on seventeenth century Wales to learned jnls; *Recreations* travelling, walking; *Style*— Prof J Gwynn Williams; Llywenan, Siliwen, Bangor, Gwynedd LL57 2BS (☎ 0248 353065)

WILLIAMS, Helen Elizabeth Webber; da of Maj Alwyn Thomas, JP, of Llwydcoed, Glamorgan, and Eleanor, *née* Evans; *b* 28 April 1938; *Educ* Redland HS Bristol, Girton Coll Cambridge (scholar, MA, DipEd); *m* 1963 (m dis 1974), Prof Peter Williams; 1 s (Daniel b 1969), 1 da (Lucy b 1968); *Career* asst English mistress: St Paul's Girls' Sch 1962-63, St George's Sch Edinburgh 1963-64; lectr in English and dir of studies Faculty of Arts Univ of Edinburgh 1967-78 (asst lectr Dept of English 1964-67), headmistress Blackheath HS 1978-89, high mistress St Paul's Girls' Sch 1989-; govr: SOAS, City Univ; memb Elizabeth Nuffield Ctee, vice pres W London Ctee for the Protection of Children; *Books* T S Eliot : The Wasteland (1968); *Recreations* music, drama, cookery, gardening; *Style*— Mrs Helen Williams; St Paul's Girls' School, Brook Green, London W6 7BS (☎ 071 603 2288, fax 071 602 9932)

WILLIAMS, Huw Rhys Charles; s of David Charles Williams (d 1984), of Llanelli, Dyfed, and Glenys Margaret, *née* Williams; *b* 4 Jan 1954; *Educ* Llanelli GS, Jesus Coll Oxford (MA); *Career* admitted slr 1978; princ asst slr Mid Glamorgan CC 1984, ptnr and ptnr i/c public law Edwards Geldard Derby (Cardiff and London) 1988 (joined 1987); sec Cardiff and SE Wales branch The Oxford Soc; memb Law Soc 1978; *Recreations* skiing, swimming, architecture and art history; *Clubs* United Oxford and Cambridge Univ; *Style*— Huw Williams, Esq; Edwards Geldard, 16 St Andrew's Crescent, Cardiff CF1 3RD (☎ 0222 238239, fax 0222 237268, telex 497913)

WILLIAMS, Huw Tregelles; *b* 13 March 1949; *Educ* Llanelli Boys GS, Univ Coll of Wales Cardiff (BMus, MA); *Career* music prodr 1973-78, sr prodr 1978-86, head of music 1986-; organ performer on Radio 3 and TV, prodr of several major series for BBC TV, recitalist at inaugural recital St Davids Hall Organ Cardiff; memb: Welsh Arts Cncl, music panel Llangollen In Music Festival; FRCO (Turpin prize 1971); *Clubs* Cardiff and County; *Style*— Huw Tregelles Williams, Esq; Music Department, BBC Broadcasting House, Llandaff, Cardiff CF5 7YQ (☎ 0222 512442, fax 0222 572575)

WILLIAMS, Prof (Edward) Idris; *b* 14 Aug 1930; *Educ* Univ of Manchester (MB ChB, MD); *m* Kathleen; 3 da (Mary (Mrs Campbell), Diana (Mrs Tivey), Sarah (Mrs Craig)); *Career* Capt RAMC 1955-58; principal GP Bolton 1960-79, sr lectr GP Univ of Manchester 1979-85, prof GP Univ of Nottingham 1985-; FRCGP, memb BMA; *Books* Caring for Elderly People in the Community (2 edn, 1989); *Recreations* gardening, fell walking, music; *Style*— Prof Idris Williams; The Medical School, Queens Medical Centre, Nottingham

WILLIAMS, James Sinclair; OBE (1957); s of James Annand Williams, CBE (d 1963), and Jessie Catherine, *née* McPherson (d 1968); *b* 27 April 1910; *Educ* King's Coll Sch Wimbledon, George Watson's Coll Edinburgh, Univ of Edinburgh (B Com); *m* 1 Sept 1945, Audrey Irvine, da of Douglas Irvine Watson, AIC; *Career* dir Coal Utilisation Cncl 1946-60 (sec 1937-45), jt sec Govt Fuel Efficiency Ctee 1940-44, dep dir gen of mktg NCB 1960-64, dir gen Advertising Assoc 1964-75; UK del to International CC Paris, pres Nat Fedn of Publicity Assocs 1974-75, chm Euro Assoc of Advertising Assocs 1967-75; chm History of Advertising Tst 1978-85; memb W Sussex CC 1977-85, chm Arundel constituency Cons Assoc, pres Adwick W Cons Branch; hon memb: Int Advertising Assoc, Communication Advertising and Marketing Educn Fndn; *Recreations* gardening, reading, parties, relaxing; *Clubs* Caledonian, London, Bognor (chm); *Style*— James Williams, Esq, OBE; Sea Cottage, 126 Manor Way, Aldwick Bay, West Sussex PO21 4HN (☎ 0243 262 871)

WILLIAMS, John Albert Norman; s of Albert George Williams, of Harbour View, Ilston Way, Mumbles, Swansea, and Norma May Williams; *b* 14 Jan 1948; *Educ* Oystermouth Secdy Sch Swansea; *m* 14 June 1971, Susan Mary, da of Ronald Francis Davies; 3 da (Emma Jayne b 23 June 1972, Claire Louise b 10 April 1974, Katie Victoria b 23 July 1975); *Career* racehorse jockey; apprentice to Fulke Walwyn 1963-65 then Dr A Jones, first ride Worcester 1965, first winner on flat Kempton 1967, first winner nat hunt Newton Abbott 1969, flat racing only 1984- (mainly nat hunt 1965-84); nat hunt achievements: twice winner Norwegian Grand Nat, winner Grosser Preis der Speilbank Germany 1982, ridden in Grand Nat 4 times, ridden in numerous int races Europe and USA, leading jockey West Country courses; flat racing achievements: winner Stewards Cup Goodwood, winner Ayr Gold Cup, ridden various maj races Scandinavia, rode five winners in a day 1990, best season 62 winners 1990; *Recreations* golf; *Style*— John Williams, Esq; Paddock View, Tolldown Way, Burton, nr Chippenham, Wilts SN14 7PD (☎ 045 421 622)

WILLIAMS, John Arthur; s of Arthur Williams (d 1984), and May Lilian, *née* Read; *b* 2 June 1933; *Educ* Guildford GS UK, Perth W Australia, Charterhouse, Jesus Coll Cambridge; *Career* HM Overseas Civil Serv Kenya 1957-62, asst sec rising to under sec responsible for pubns, dist socs, PR, HQ rebuilding ICAEW 1962-71, Australian Def Dept Canberra 1971-72, dir int affrs ICAEW 1990- (responsible for gen policy and fin EC and int 1972-90); *Recreations* sailing, skiing, tennis, walking, music, stamp collecting; *Clubs* Hurlingham, Bookham Sailing; *Style*— John Williams, Esq; 71 Winchendon Rd, London SW6 5DH (☎ 071 736 3545); The Inst of Chartered Accountants in England & Wales, Moorgate Place, London EC2P 2BJ (☎ 071 628 7060, fax 071 920 0547)

WILLIAMS, Dr John Charles; s of Frank Williams (d 1968), of Princes Risboro, Bucks, and Miriam, *née* Rose (d 1988); *b* 17 July 1938; *Educ* High Wycombe Royal GS, Queen Mary Coll London (BSc, PhD, Univ Year prize); *m* 1968, Susan Winifred, *née* Ellis; 1 s (Matthew Richard b 1976), 1 da (Rachel Joanna b 1972); *Career* engr; researcher, conslt and project leader Philips Res Laboratories 1964-77, mangr MSDS Res Laboratory Marconi Space & Defence Systems Ltd 1980-82 (mangr Advanced Shipborne Terminals 1978-80), dir GEC Marconi Res Centre 1987-88 (dir Marconi Res Centre St Baddow 1982-85, md GEC Research Ltd 1985-87), md Cranfield Industrial Development Ltd 1988-89, sec and chief exec Inst of Electrical Engrs; FIEE, FIE (Aust), FEng, MRI; *Recreations* bridge, jazz; *Style*— Dr John Williams; Institution of Electrical Engineers, Savoy Place, London WC2R OBL (☎ 071 240 1871, fax 071 497 8863, car 0860 298272)

WILLIAMS, John Charles Wallis; s of Peter Alfred Williams, of Menston, West Yorks, and Mary, *née* Bower (d 1990); *b* 12 Dec 1953; *Educ* St Peter's York, Queen's Coll Oxford (MA); *m* 28 June 1980, Wendy Irene, da of Harold Doe, of Whitton, Middx; 2 da (Sarah b 1984, Clare b 1988); *Career* advertising exec: J Walter Thompson Co 1975-86, Valin Pollen Ltd 1986-90 (head res and planning 1988-90); fndr dir Fishburn Hedges Boys Williams Ltd 1991-; *Recreations* cinema, music, good food and wine; *Clubs* RAC; *Style*— John Williams, Esq; 128 Rusthall Ave, London W4 1BS (☎ 081 995 8747); Fishburn Hedges Boys Williams Ltd, 1 Northumberland Ave, Trafalgar Square, London WC2N 5BW (☎ 071 872 5793, fax 071 753 2838)

WILLIAMS, Dr John Edmund; s of John Edgar Williams (d 1971), of Penarth, Glamorgan, and Catherine Letitia, *née* Edmunds (d 1958); *b* 27 Aug 1930; *Educ* Penarth GS, Univ Coll Cardiff (BSc), Welsh Nat Sch of Med (MB BCh, DMRD); *m* Gwen Elizabeth, da of Ewart Price (d 1952), of Bethesda, Caenarvonshire; 1 s (Paul Martyn), 2 da (Ann Catherine, Elizabeth Siân (Mrs West)); *Career* conslt radiologist United Cardiff Hosp 1963-72, asst prof of radiology Univ of Washington Seattle USA 1968-69; St George's Hosp London: dir of radiology and conslt radiologist 1972-, hon sr lectr, chm of radiology; warden RCR 1986-90; Hon FFR RCSI 1988, FRCPE, FRCP, FRCR, FRSM; *Style*— Dr John Williams; Director of Radiology, St George's Hospital, Blackshaw Rd, London SW17 0QT (☎ 081 672 1255)

WILLIAMS, (Edward) John; RD (1967); s of David Charles Williams (d 1981), and Sarah Elizabeth, *née* Jones (d 1981); *b* 3 Feb 1928; *Educ* Towyn Sch Wales, London Hosp Med coll, Univ of London (MS BS, MS); *m* 4 April 1959, Susan Allen, da of Eric Percy Rimer (d 1979); 2 da (Sarah b 1961, Nicola b 1964); *Career* Sqdn MO RNR 1952-54, 8 Destroyer Sqdn HMS Cossack Korea 1952-53, HMS Indefatigable 1953-54; sr lectr and hon conslt surgn St Mary's Hosp London, conslt surgn Windsor Gp of Hosps, vascular conslt in surgery BA 1975; chm Oxford Regnl Surgns 1984-87; memb: RSM, Surgical res Soc, Assoc of Surgns GB & I, Vascular Surgical Soc GB & I (pres 1989); FRCS 1958; *Recreations* fishing, country pursuits, horse breeding, aviculture; *Clubs* RSM; *Style*— John Williams, Esq, RD; Upper Meadow, Hedgerley Lane, Gerrards Cross, Bucks SL9 7NP (☎ 0753 882651)

WILLIAMS, Dr John Garret Pascoe; s of Surgn Cdr Edward Rex Pascoe Williams, OBE, RN (d 1950), and Marion May Gibson, *née* Jarvie; *b* 15 Sept 1932; *Educ* Beaumont Coll, Gonville and Caius Coll Cambridge (MB, BChir MD), St Mary's Hosp Sch London (DPhysMed, MSc, MRCS, LRCP); *m* 20 Sept 1958, Sally Jennifer, da of Ranald Montague Handfield-Jones, MC (d 1972); 2 s (Stephen b 1960, David b 1965), 1 da (Philippa b 1962); *Career* conslt physical med and dir Dept Physical Med and Rehabilition 1965-76, Mount Vernon Hosp, Harefield Hosp; med dir Farnham Park Rehabilitation Centre Farnham Royal 1965-88, conslt rehabilitation med and dir Dept Rehabilitation Med Wexham Park Hosp Slough 1965-, fell (former sec gen) Int Fedn Sports Med 1970-80 (Gold medal 1980), civil conslt rehabilition med RN 1981-; chm Ctee PSM 31 Br Standards Inst, med advsr Squash Rackets Assoc, pres Bourne End Jr Sports Club; Philip Noel Baker res prize UNESCO ICSPE 1974, Winston Churchill travelling fellowship; Liveryman Worshipful Soc of Apothecaries; FRCS 1963, FRCP 1986; *Books* Sports Medicine (contrib and ed 1962, 2 edn, 1976), Medical Aspects of Sport and Physical Fitness (1965), Rowing - A Scientific Approach (contrib and ed with A C Scott, 1967), Atlas on Injury in Sport (1980), Diagnostic Picture Tests in Injury in Sport (1988); *Recreations* naval history, music, model making, real tennis; *Clubs* Queens, Leander (Henley-on-Thames); *Style*— Dr John Williams; Little Paddocks,

Brantridge Lane, Bourne End, Bucks SL8 5BZ (☎ 06285 20834); Wexham Pk Hosp, Rehabilitation Departmt, Slough, Berks SL2 4HL (☎ 02814 2271, 0753 34567, 0836 640384)

WILLIAMS, John Godfrey; s of Godfrey Williams (d 1927), of Chapel Farm, and Clara Ellen, *née* Hughes (d 1974); *b* 15 May 1922; *Educ* King Henry the Eighth GS Abergavenny; *m* 10 Nov 1960, Margaret Jean, da of Richard Morgan David (d 1959); 1 s (Richard John b 1961); *Career* served RN 1941-46; slr 1950, clerk to the Justices of the Hay-on-Wye and Talgarth Divs 1957-66, supt registrar Hay-on-Wye Div 1957-74; pres Herefordshire Breconshire & Radnorshire Incorporated Law Soc 1977; life memb Cambria Archaeological Assoc 1955-; memb: British Dowsers Soc 1963-, Research into Lost Knowledge Organisation 1960-; *Books* The Ancient Stones of Wales (with Chris Barber, 1989); *Recreations* investigating prehistoric standing stones; *Clubs* Abergavenny Conservative, Hay-on-Wye, Hereford Conservative; *Style—* John Williams, Esq; Aurora, 129 Chapel Road, Abergavenny, Gwent (☎ 0873 3141)

WILLIAMS, John Griffith; QC (1985); s of Maj Griffith John Williams, TD, of Hedd-yr-Ynys, Common Lane, Beer, Seaton, Devon, and Alison Rundle, *née* Bennett; *b* 20 Dec 1944; *Educ* Kings Sch Bruton, The Queen's Coll Oxford (MA); *m* 3 April 1971, Mair, o da of Major The Right Hon Sir Tasker Watkins VC, GBE, PC, DL; 2 da (Joanna b 1972, Sarah b 1976); *Career* Lt 4 Bn Royal Welch Fus (TA) Welsh Volunteers (TAVR); barr Grays Inn 1968, practice Wales and Chester Circuit, recorder Crown Ct 1984-; memb Bar Cncl 1990-; *Recreations* golf; *Clubs* Army and Navy, Cardiff and County, Cardiff, Royal Porthcawl Golf; *Style—* John Griffith Williams, Esq, QC; 144 Pencisely Rd, Llandaff, Cardiff CF5 1DR (☎ 0222 562981); Goldsmith Building, Temple, EC4Y 7BL (☎ 071 353 7881, fax 071 353 5319)

WILLIAMS, Rev John Herbert; s of Thomas Williams (d 1932), of Gwent, and Mary Williams, *née* Davies (d 1956); *b* 15 Aug 1919; *Educ* Lewis Sch Pengam, St David's Coll Lampeter (BA), Salisbury Theological Coll; *m* 1948, Joan Elizabeth, da of Archibald Morgan, of Gwent; 1 s (Michael); *Career* clerk in holy orders; chaplain (Prison Dept): Manchester 1951, Holloway 1952, Birmingham 1955, Wormwood Scrubs 1964; regional chaplain SE 1971, dep chaplain gen (Home Office) 1974-83, priest-in-ordinary to HM The Queen 1979-83; former: chaplain of the Queen's Chapel of the Savoy, chaplain of the Royal Victorian Order 1983; chaplain to HM The Queen 1988; *Recreations* music (classical, opera, church), rugby, stamp collecting; *Clubs* City Livery; *Style—* The Rev John Williams; 75 Monks Drive, London W3 0ED (☎ 071 992 5206)

WILLIAMS, John Hugh; s of Vivian Theodore Williams (d 1961), of Walsall, and Louisa Green, *née* Richards (d 1965); *b* 10 June 1932; *Educ* Mill Hill Sch, Univ of Birmingham (BCom); *m* 22 Sept 1962, Jenefer Margaret, da of Ivor Grosvenor Hopkins (d 1967), of Bristol; 2 s (Rupert b 1963, Theodore b 1967); *Career* Capt Royal Scots Greys 1957-67; chm J Emlyn Williams Ltd 1965-; chm Birmingham Boys' and Girls' Union, former pres Birmingham Assoc Nat Fedn of Building Trades Employers; ACA 1957, FCA 1967; *Recreations* rugby football, tennis, country pursuits; *Clubs* Birmingham; *Style—* John Williams, Esq; Bow Hill, Bakers Lane, Knowle, Warwicks B93 8PS (☎ 0564 774743)

WILLIAMS, Rev Canon John James; TD (1961, clasp 1967); s of John Ifor Williams (d 1956), of Bromfield, Shaun Drive, Rhyl, Flints, and Marie Williams (d 1969); *b* 4 May 1920; *Educ* Grove Park Sch Wrexham, Lincoln Coll Oxford (MA); *m* 18 March 1953, Kaye, da of Bertram Law (d 1949), of Westroyd, Penrhyn Bay, Llandudno: 2 s (John b 1956, David b 1959), 1 da (Karen b 1961); *Career* ordained: deacon 1944, priest 1945; chaplain Flint and Denbigh Yeo 1949, 4 Bn KSLI (TA) 1955, sr chaplain HQ 48 W Midlands Div (TA) 1962, chaplain 202 (M) Gen Hosp RAMC (TAVR) 1967, ret 1968; Rhosymedre 1944, Flint 1947, Eglwys Rhos 1950; vicar: Whixhall Salop 1953, Prees Salop 1957, Powyke Worcs 1964, ret 1985; chaplain Powick Psychiatric Hosp 1967-, hon canon Worcester Cath 1977; *Style—* The Rev Canon John Williams, TD; 9 St Nicholas Rd, Peopleton, Pershore, Worcs WR10 2EN (☎ 0905 840032)

WILLIAMS, Prof (Lawrence) John; s of Arthur John Williams, of Cardiff, and Elizabeth Jeanetta, *née* Charlton; *b* 12 June 1927; *Educ* Univ of Wales (BA, MA); *m* 18 Aug 1951, Mair Eluned; 2 s (Stephen Richard b 1955, Roger b 1959), 1 da (Katherine b 1958); *Career* Nat Serv RAF 1948-51; res offr Cabinet Off 1951-52, prof of economics UCW 1987- (formerly lectr, then sr lectr); *Books* incl: The South Wales Coal Industry, 1841-75 (with J H Morris, 1958), Britain Since 1945 (with P Madgwick and D Steeds, 1982), Why Are the British Bad at Manufacturing? (with K Williams and D Thomas, 1983), The Aberystwyth Report on Coal (with K Williams and A Cutler, 1985), Modern South Wales: essays in economic history (ed with C Baber, 1986), 1992: The Struggle for Europe (1989); *Recreations* hill-walking; *Style—* Prof John Williams; 22 Danycoed, Aberystwyth, Dyfed; Dept of Economics, University College Wales, Aberystwyth (☎ 0970 622502)

WILLIAMS, Hon John Melville; QC (1977); s of Baron Francis-Williams (Life Peer, d 1970); *b* 20 June 1931; *Educ* St Christopher Sch Letchworth, St John's Coll Cambridge (BA); *m* 1955, Jean Margaret, da of Harold Lucas, of Huddersfield; 3 s, 1 da; *Career* barrister Inner Temple 1955; bencher Inner Temple 1985, rec 1986; pres Assoc of Personal Injury Lawyers 1990-, vice chm Int Section Assoc of Trial Lawyers of America; *Style—* The Hon John Melville Williams, QC; 15 Old Square, Lincoln's Inn, London WC2A 3UH (☎ 071 831 0801, fax 071 405 1387); Deers Hill, Abinger Hammer, Dorking, Surrey

WILLIAMS, John Michael; JP; s of William Robert John Williams (d 1976), of West Wickham, Kent, and Alice Gladys, *née* Holbrow; *b* 13 Nov 1935; *Educ* Beckenham and Penge GS, Downing Coll Cambridge (MA, LLB); *m* 18 Aug 1962, Patricia May, da of James Francis Logan (d 1960), of Beckenham, Kent; 3 s (Duncan b 1965, Daniel b 1967, Benjamin b 1980), 1 da (Kate b 1963); *Career* slr Supreme Ct of Judicature 1962, NP 1966; hon sec Magistrates Assoc SE London Branch, dir Churchill Theatre Tst Bromley; memb: Cncl Magistrates Assoc, Cncl Cwlth Magistrates and Judges Assoc; memb: Law Soc, Prov Notaries Soc; *Recreations* hockey, cricket, theatre, singing; *Clubs* Langley Park Rotary, Kentish Opera Group; *Style—* John Williams, Esq, JP; Normanhurst, Bishops Walk, Croydon CRO 5BA (☎ 081 656 2445); 73 Station Rd, West Wickham, Kent BR4 0RG (☎ 081 777 6698, fax 081 777 7306)

WILLIAMS, Dr John Peter Rhys; MBE (1977); s of Peter Rhys Jervis Williams, of Bridgend, and Margaret, *née* Rhodes; *b* 2 March 1949; *Educ* Bridgend GS, Millfield and St Marys Hosp Med Sch (MB BS LRCP); *m* 10 May 1973, Priscilla, da of Michael Parkin, of Buxton, Derbys; 1 s (Peter b 1987), 3 da (Lauren b 1977, Anneliese b 1979, Francine b 1981); *Career* conslt orthopaedic surgn Princess of Wales Hosp Bridgend 1986-; Br jr tennis champion 1966, 55 Welsh Int rugby caps 1978-79, memb Br Lions tour NZ 1971 and SA 1974; memb Br Orthopaedic Assoc, FRCSE, MRCS; *Books* JPR Autobiography (1977); *Recreations* all sports especially squash, tennis, rugby; *Clubs* Wig & Pen, Lord's Taverners; *Style—* Dr John Williams, MBE; Llansannor Lodge, Llansannor, Cowbridge, South Glamorgan CF7 7RX (☎ 0446 772590); Princess of Wales Hospital, Bridgend, Mid Glam (☎ 0656 662166); BUPA Hospital, Cardiff (☎ 0222 736011)

WILLIAMS, John Robert; s of Edward S Williams (d 1986), of London, and Frances Madge, *née* Porter; *b* 7 April 1931; *Educ* Enfield GS, Queens' Coll Cambridge (MA); *m* 12 Sept 1959, Teresa, da of Joseph Wareing (d 1956), of Preston, Lancs; 3 da (Catherine b 1960, Joanna b 1962, Helen b 1967); *Career* Ogilvy & Mather: res exec, mktg mangr, res dir, account dir, client servs dir, int mgmnt supervisor 1956-68, appointed to Bd 1968, vice chm 1981; chm: Wimbledon CC 1974-89, The Wimbledon Club (cricket, lawn tennis, hockey clubs, Lakeside squash club); FIPA 1968; *Recreations* cricket, tennis, squash, theatre; *Clubs* MCC, RAC; *Style—* John Williams, Esq; 61 Murray Rd, London SW19 4PF (☎ 081 946 9363)

WILLIAMS, Sir John Robert; KCMG (1982, CMG 1973); s of Sydney James Williams, of Salisbury; *b* 15 Sept 1922; *Educ* Sheen Co Sch, Fitzwilliam Coll Cambridge; *m* 1958, Helga Elizabeth, da of Frederick Konow Lund, of Bergen; 2 s, 2 da; *Career* CRO New Delhi and N Malaya; high cmmr Suva 1970-74, min Lagos and non-resident ambass Benin 1974-79, asst under-sec FCO 1979, high cmmr Nairobi and perm Br rep UN Environment Programme and HABITAT (UN Centre for Human Settlements) 1979-82, ret; chm Cwlth Inst London 1984-87; hon fell Fitzwilliam Coll Cambridge 1983; *Style—* Sir John Williams, KCMG; Eton House, Hanging Langford, Salisbury

WILLIAMS, Juliet Susan Durrant; da of Robert Noel Williams (d 1972), of Gower, W Glamorgan, and Frances Alice, *née* Durrant; *b* 17 April 1943; *Educ* Leeds Girls HS, Cheltenham Ladies' Coll, Bedford Coll London (BSc), Hughes Hall Cambridge (PGCE); *Career* ed MacMillan & Co (publishers) 1966-68, asst ed The Geographical Magazine 1968-73, md Readers Union Gp of Books Clubs 1973-79, chief exec Marshall Cavendish Mail Order 1979-82, md Brann Direct Marketing 1982-88, dir The BIS Gp Ltd 1985-, chief exec Bd Mktg Communications Div BIS 1988-; non exec dir Oxfam Trading; cncl memb: Br Direct Mktg Assoc, Advertising Assoc; full blue lacrosse Univs of London and Cambridge; FRGS 1970, MInstM 1975; *Recreations* labrador retrievers, the countryside, motor sport; *Style—* Ms Juliet Williams; Treeton Cottage, Abbotskerswell, Newton Abbot, Devon TQ12 5PW (☎ 0626 61655); 5 Coach House Mews, The Avenue, Circencester, Glos GL7 1EJ; BIS Marketing Communications, Phoenix Way, Circencester, Glos GL7 1RY (☎ 0285 644 744, fax 0285 654 952, car 0860 535 637, telex 43473)

WILLIAMS, June Mary; da of Arthur Lewis Brett (d 1975), of Sutton Coldfield, and Margaret Elizabeth, *née* Morgan (d 1961); *b* 4 June 1930; *Educ* Sutton Coldfield HS for Girls, Univ of Edinburgh (MA), Univ of Birmingham (LLB); *m* 18 April 1959, David Llewelyn Williams (d 1971), s of Rev David Oliver Williams (d 1979), of Northampton; *Career* admitted slr 1955; sr asst slr Dudley BC 1956-63, dep town clerk Oldbury BC 1963-67, slr with Legal Aid Birmingham and Brighton 1967-68, dep dir Legal Aid 1978-89, sec Legal Aid Bd 1989- (dir Policy and Legal Bd 1989); memb Soroptimist Int GB and Ireland, memb Sussex Law Soc, memb Assoc of Women Slrs; memb Law Soc; *Recreations* reading, music, theatre, walking, talking; *Style—* Mrs June Williams; Legal Aid Head Office, Newspaper House, 8-16 Great New St, London EC4A 3BN (☎ 071 353 7411)

WILLIAMS, Karl; s of Joseph Bernard Williams, and Maria, *née* Cavanna; *b* 29 May 1959; *Educ* De La Salle Sch Cardiff, Saint Illtyd's Coll, LSE (LLB); *Career* called to the Bar Middle Temple 1982; *Clubs* The Beverly Hotel (Cardiff); *Style—* Karl Williams, Esq; 34 Park Place, Cardiff CF1 3TN (☎ 0222 382731, fax 0222 222 542)

WILLIAMS, Hon Mrs (Katharine Lucy); *née* Roskill; da of Baron Roskill, PC, QC, JP, DL (Life Baron); *b* 1953; *Educ* St Mary's School Calne Wilts; *m* 1977, Nicholas Richard Melville Williams; 1 s (George Nicholas Melville b 1981), 1 da (Olivia Katharine Elisabeth b 1978); *Clubs* Hurlingham; *Style—* The Hon Mrs Williams; 37 Perrymead Street, London SW6

WILLIAMS, (John) Kyffin; OBE (1982), DL (Gwynedd 1985); s of Henry Inglis Wynne Williams (d 1942), of Doltrement, Abererch, Pwllheli, Gwynedd, and Essyllt Mary, *née* Williams (d 1964); *b* 9 May 1918; *Educ* Shrewsbury, Slade Sch of Fine Art UCL; *Career* 2 Lt 6 Bn RWF (TA) 1937, invalided 1941; artist; sr art master Highgate Sch London 1944-73; works exhibited: Arts Cncl, Nat Museum of Wales (memb Art Ctee) Nat Library of Wales, Walker Art Gallery Liverpool, Nat Portrait Gallery, Contemporary Art Soc, Glyn Vivian Art Gallery Swansea, Chantrey Bequest, Univ of Wales, Imperial Coll London; Winston Churchill Fellowship 1968; hon fell: Univ Coll of Swansea 1989, Univ Coll N Wales Bangor 1991; Hon MA Univ of Wales 1973; ARA 1970, RA 1974; *Books* Across the Straits (autobiography, 1973), A Wider Sky (autobiography, 1991); *Recreations* countryside sports; *Style—* Kyffin Williams, Esq, OBE, DL; Pwllfanogl, Llanfairpwllgwyngyll, Gwynedd LL61 6PD (☎ 0248 714693)

WILLIAMS, Lawrence Hugh; s of Col Lawrence Williams, OBE, JP, DL, by his 2 w and 1 cous once removed, Elinor, da of Sir William Williams, 4 Bt, JP, DL; hp of half-bro Sir Francis Williams, 8 Bt, QC, JP; *b* 25 Aug 1929; *Educ* RNC Dartmouth; *m* 1952, Sara, da of Prof Sir Harry Platt, 1 Bt, MD, MS, FRCS; 2 da (Emma b 1961, Antonia b 1963); *Career* cmmnd RM 1947; served in: Korea 1951, Cyprus 1955, Near East 1956; Capt 1959, ret 1964; Lt Cdr RNXS 1965-87; farmer; chm Parciau Caravans Ltd 1964-, underwriting memb Lloyd's; High Sheriff Anglesey 1970; *Clubs* Army and Navy; *Style—* Lawrence Williams, Esq; Parciau, Marianglas, Anglesey LL73 8PH

WILLIAMS, (John) Leighton; QC (1986); s of Reginald John Williams, of Skewen, Neath, Glamorgan, and Beatrice Beynon; *b* 15 Aug 1941; *Educ* Neath Boys GS; Kings Coll London, (LLB); Trinity Hall Cambridge (MA); *m* 9 Oct 1969, Sally Elizabeth, of Howard Jones Williams, of Abergavenny, Gwent; 2 s (Nicholas b 1970, Thomas b 1972); *Career* called to the Bar Grays Inn 1964; Rec 1985; QC 1986; *Style—* J Leighton Williams, Esq, QC; Farrar's Building, Temple, London EC4 (☎ 071 583 92141)

WILLIAMS, Sir Leonard; KBE (1981), CB (1975); *b* 19 Sept 1919; *Educ* St Olave's GS, King's Coll London; *m* Anne Taylor Witherley; 3 da; *Career* dir-gen Energy Commission of the European Communities 1976-81, served formerly Inland Revenue, MOD, NATO, Miny Supply, Miny Technology, IDC, Energy Dept; *Style—* Sir Leonard Williams, KBE, CB; 200 rue de la Loi, 1049 Brussels, Belgium

WILLIAMS, Leonard Edmund Henry; CBE (1981), DFC (1944); s of William Edmund Williams (d 1965), and Elizabeth, *née* Restall (d 1969); *b* 6 Dec 1919; *Educ* Acton Co Sch; *m* 23 March 1946, Marie Eirina, da of John Harries-Jones (d 1939); 4 s (Graham b 1949, Martin b 1957, Simon b 1961, Andrew b 1965), 1 da (Jennifer b 1947); *Career* served RAF WWII; Acton Borough Cncl 1939-49, The Gas Cncl 1949-53, fin offr Nationwide Building Society 1954-61 (dep gen mangr 1961-67, chief exec 1967-81, dir 1975, chm 1982-87), dir Y J Lovell (Hldgs) plc 1982-89; chm Nationwide Anglia Building Society 1987-88 (pres 1989-); dep chm Br Utd Provident Assoc Ltd 1988-90 (govr 1982-90); chm Bldg Socs Assoc 1979-81, chm Metropolitan Assoc of Bldg Socs 1972-73 (pres 1989-); Freeman City of London 1974, Liveryman Worshipful Co of Basketmakers 1974; FCA, FCBSI, IPFA, CBIM, FRSA; *Books* Building Society Accounts (1966); *Recreations* golf, reading; *Clubs* RAF, Arts; *Style—* Leonard Williams Esq, CBE, DFC; The Romanys, 11 Albury Rd, Burwood Park, Walton-on-Thames, Surrey KT12 5DY (☎ 0932 242758); Nationwide Anglia Building Society, Chesterfield House, Bloomsbury Way, London WC1V 6PW (☎ 071 242 8822)

WILLIAMS, Hon Mrs (Margaret de Hauteville); *née* Udny-Hamilton; da of 11 Lord Belhaven and Stenton, CIE (d 1950, assumed additional surname of Udny 1934); *b* 1939; *m* 1, 1964 (m dis), Keith Schellenberg; 1 s, 2 da; *m* 2 1983, James Frank Williams; *Style—* The Hon Mrs Williams; Udny Castle, Udny, Aberdeenshire (☎ 0224 2428)

WILLIAMS, Martin John; CVO (1983), OBE (1979); s of John Henry Stroud Williams, of Cricklade, Wilts, and Barbara, *née* Benington; *b* 3 Nov 1941; *Educ* Manchester GS, Corpus Christ Coll Oxford (BA); *m* 6 April 1964, Susan, da of Albert Mervyn (Peter) Dent (d 1984); 2 s (Nicholas b 1966, Peter b 1967); *Career* CRO 1963; Dip Serv: joined 1968, Manila 1966-69, Milan 1970-72, Tehran 1977-80, New Delhi 1982-86, Rome 1986-90; FCO 1990-; *Style—* Martin Williams, Esq

WILLIAMS, Lady Mary Rose; *née* FitzRoy; da of late William Henry Alfred, Viscount Ipswich; sister of 9 Duke of Grafton; co-heiress to Barony of Arlington and Earldom of Arlington; *b* 1918,posthumous; *m* 1945 (m dis), Francis Trelawny Williams, late Lt KRRC; 1 da (Linda Jane Auriol b 1947); *Career* show jumping (memb of Br S J Team for 6 years, first ever lady to jump 2 clear rounds in Nations Cup (Rotterdam) which was in Guinness Book of Records); *Recreations* teaching showjumping, building courses, judging horses and ponies; *Style—* The Lady Mary Rose Williams; The Green, Oddington, Moreton-in-Marsh, Glos (☎ 0451 31008)

WILLIAMS, Sir (William) Maxwell Harries (Max); s of Llwyd and Hilary Williams; *b* 18 Feb 1926; *Educ* Nautical Coll Pangbourne; *m* 1951, Jenifer, da of Rt Hon Edward Leslie Burgin (d 1945); 2 da; *Career* served 178 Assault Fd Regt RA Far East (Capt) 1943-47; admitted slr 1950, memb Cncl Law Soc 1962-85 (pres 1982-83), Royal Cmmn on Legal Servs 1976-79, memb Ctee of Mgmnt of Inst of Advanced Legal Studies 1980-86, Crown Agents for Overseas Govts and Admin 1982-86; lay memb Stock Exchange Cncl 1984-; sr ptnr: Clifford-Turner 1984-87, Clifford Chance 1989- (jt sr ptnr 1987-89); dir: Royal Insurance plc 1985-, 3i plc 1988-; chm Review Bd for Govt Contracts 1986-; hon memb: Canadian Bar Assoc, American Bar Assoc; memb Cncl Wildfowl Trust (hon treas 1974-80); pres City of London Law Soc 1986-87; Master Worshipful Co of Slrs' 1986-87; Hon LLD Univ of Birmingham 1983; kt 1983; *Recreations* fishing, golf, ornithology; *Clubs* Garrick, Flyfishers; *Style—* Sir Max Williams; Clifford Chance, Blackfriars House, 19 New Bridge St, London EC4V 6BY (☎ 071 353 0211, telex 887847)

WILLIAMS, Michael; s of Michael Leonard Williams (d 1987), of Stratford upon Avon, and Elizabeth, *née* Mulligan (d 1982); *b* 9 July 1935; *Educ* St Edward's Coll Liverpool, RADA; *m* 5 Feb 1971, (Judi) Olivia Dench, DBE, BE, da of Dr Reginald Arthur Dench (d 1964), of York; 1 da (Finty b 24 Sept 1972); *Career* Nat Serv RAF 1953-55; Coronation Scholarship winner RADA 1957, Nottingham Playhouse 1959-61, West End debut 1961, assoc memb RSC 1963-77 roles include: Pick (A Midsummer Night's Dream), the herald (Marat/Sade) London & N York, Arthur (Tango), Petruchio (Taming of the Shrew), Troilus (Troilus & Cressida), Orlando (As You Like It), the Fool (King Lear), Charles Courtly (London Assurance), title role (Henry V) Private Meek (Too True to be Good), Autolycus (A Winter's Tale); TV: Elizabeth R, A Raging Calm, My Son, My Son, Love in A Cold Climate, A Fine Romance, Bukovsky, Blunt, Double First, Angel Voices, Can You Hear Me Thinking; films: Dead Cert, Enigma, Educating Rita, Henry V; chm Catholic Stage Guild 1977-88; patron: The Surrey Soc of Cncl for the Protection of Rural England, Cumbria Theatre Tst, Chicken Shed, Imperial Cancer Fund; *Recreations* cricket, gardening; *Clubs* Garrick; *Style—* Michael Williams, Esq; c/o Michael Whitehall Ltd, 125 Gloucester Rd, London SW7 4TE (☎ 071 244 8466)

WILLIAMS, Dr Michael; s of late Benjamin Williams, and Ethel Mary, *née* Marshell (d 1954); *b* 24 June 1935; *Educ* Univ Coll Swansea (BA), Univ of Wales (PhD, DLitt), St Catharine's Coll Cambridge (DipEd), Univ of Oxford (MA); *m* 25 June 1955, Eleanore, da of Leopold Lorenz Lerch (d 1940); 2 da (Catherine Dilys b 1962, Tess Jane b 1965); *Career* demonstrator Dept of Geography Swansea Univ Coll 1957-60, lectr rising to sr lectr Univ of Adelaide SA 1960-78, pt/t lectr in planning SA Inst Technol Aust 1963-70; Univ of Oxford: lectr in geography 1978-, fell Oriel Coll 1978-, lectr in charge St Anne's Coll 1978-, reader in geography 1990-; temp academic appointments: visitor UCL 1973 (visitor and lectr 1966-67), visiting fell Dept of Geography Univ of Wisconsin-Madison USA 1973-74, visiting fell Dept of Geography Flinders Univ SA 1984, visiting prof Ctee on Geographical Studies Univ of Chicago 1989; contrib to many academic jls; Inst of Br Geographers: hon ed Transactions of the Institute 1983-88, chm Pubns Ctee 1983-88, memb Special Pubns Ctee 1983-88 (memb Cncl 1983-88); memb: Ed Advsy Bd RGS 1984, Editorial Ctee Progress in Human Geography 1990-, Int Relations Sub Ctee Cncl Br Geography 1990; FBA 1989; John Lewis Gold medal RGS (SA) 1979, Hidy medal and award Forest and Conservation History Soc USA 1988 (hon fell 1989); travel and res grants: Australian Res Grant Cmmn, Br Acad, RGS; *Books* The Making of the Australian Landscape (1976, Biennial literary prize Adelaide Festival of Arts, 1974), Australian Space, Australian Time: Geographical Perspectives 1788-1914 (jt ed, 1975), The Americans and their Forest: An Historical Perspective (1989), Wetlands: A Theatened Landscape (ed, 1991); *Style—* Dr Michael Williams; Westgates, Vernon Avenue, Harcourt Hill, Oxford OX2 9AU (☎ 0865 243725); School of Geography, Mansfield Rd, Oxford OX1 3TB (☎ 0865 271924)

WILLIAMS, Michael Duncan; s of Harry Duncan Williams, of Oxford, and Irene Pamela, *née* Mackenzie; *b* 31 March 1951; *Educ* Oundle, Trinity Hall Cambridge (MA); *Career* vice pres and UK sr credit offr Bank of America NT and SA 1973-89, dir: SFE Bank Ltd, Banque SFE 1988-89; dep gen credit mangr Nomura Bank Int plc 1989-; hon treas: Amateur Rowing Assoc, London Rowing Club; memb Chartered Inst of Bankers; *Recreations* rowing, golf; *Clubs* Leander; *Style—* Michael Williams, Esq; 113 Deodar Rd, London SW15 2NU (☎ 081 871 4377); Nomura Bank Interantional plc, 1 St Martins-le-Grand, London EC1A 4NP (☎ 071 696 6858, fax 071 626 0851, telex 9413063/4)

WILLIAMS, (John) Michael; s of George Keith Williams (d 1980), and Joan Doreen, *née* Selby (d 1969); *b* 15 Oct 1942; *Educ* Cheltenham Coll, Worcester Coll Oxford (MA); *Career* admitted slr 1967, ptnr Cooper Sons Hartley & Williams; conductor Buxton Musical Soc 1968-, sec Buxton & High Peak Law Soc 1984-, organist St Johns Buxton 1985-, vice chm Buxton Opera House 1978-, memb Cncl Rathbone Soc 1990-; *Recreations* music, cricket; *Style—* Michael Williams, Esq; 143 Lightwood Rd, Buxton (☎ 0298 24185); Cooper Sons Hartley & Williams, 25 Market St, Chapel-en-le-Frith, via Stockport (☎ 0298 81 2138)

WILLIAMS, Michael John; s of Stanley Williams, and Phyllis Mary, *née* Wenn; *b* 23 July 1948; *Educ* William Ellis Sch London, Univ of Liverpool (Oliver Elton prize for English literature, BA); *m* 1971, Carol; 2 da (Stella b 1983, Amy b 1988); *Career* indentured graduate trainee Liverpool Daily Post & Echo 1970-73, features sub ed and news sub ed Birmingham Evening Mail 1973-75, home news sub ed and Stone sub ed The Times 1975-78, asst to editorial dir Thames & Hudson Book Publishers 1978-79; New Society Magazine: diary ed feature writer and educn ed 1979-83, jt asst ed 1983-84, dep ed 1984-86; features ed Today 1986; The Sunday Times: dep news ed 1986-87, news ed 1987-89, asst ed (news) 1989-90, managing ed (news) 1990-; *Books* British Society (1984), Britain Now Quiz (1985), Society Today (1986); *Recreations* travelling in Greece; *Style—* Michael Williams, Esq; 51 Hillfield Rd, West Hampstead, London NW6 1QD (☎ 071 435 7587); The Sunday Times, 1 Pennington St, London E1 9XW (☎ 071 782 5653)

WILLIAMS, Rev Michael Joseph; s of James Williams (d 1972), of West Bromwich, Staffs, and Edith, *née* Unsworth (d 1988); *b* 26 Feb 1942; *Educ* West Bromwich Secondary Tech Sch, West Bromwich Tech Coll (HNC) St John's Coll Durham (BA); *m* 31 July 1971, (Mary) Miranda, da of Lawrence Gordon Bayley, MBE, of Stockport; 1 s (James Matthew b 3 Nov 1978), 1 da (Victoria Louise b 5 March 1976); *Career* team vicar St Philemon Toxteth Liverpool 1975-78 (curate 1970-75), dir of pastoral studies St John's Coll Durham 1978-88, princ The Northern Ordination Course 1989-; *Books* The Power and the Kingdom (1989); *Recreations* woodwork; *Style—* The Rev Michael Williams; 75 Framingham Rd, Brooklands, Sale, Cheshire M33 3RH (☎ 061 962 7513); Northern Ordination Course, Luther King House, Brighton Grove, Manchester M14 5JP (☎ 061 225 6668)

WILLIAMS, Michael Roy; s of Edgar Harold Williams, and Joyce, *née* Smith; *b* 29 March 1947; *Educ* Selhurst GS, Univ of Exeter (BA); *Career* UCMDS trainee Unilever plc/prod mangr Bird's Eye Foods 1969-72, account dir Leo Burnett 1972-78, dir Geers Gross plc 1978-86, md Geers Gross UK 1978-86, dir Charles Barker plc 1986-89, chief exec Ayer Ltd 1986-90, dir Ayer Europe 1986-90, managing ptnr Serendipity Ptnrship Ltd 1990-; *Recreations* films, music, windsurfing, travel, France, SE Asia; *Style—* Michael R Williams, Esq; Serendipity Partnership Ltd, 1 West Garden Place, Kendal St, London W2 2AQ

WILLIAMS, (Garnet) Montague Eveleigh; s of Garnet Montague Williams (d 1939), of Coulsdon, Surrey, and Ellen, *née* Eveleigh (d 1968); *b* 19 Dec 1917; *Educ* Reigate GS, London Polys (BSc); *m* 8 May 1948, Phyllis Olive, da of Capt Thomas Mann (d 1950), of Margate, Kent; 1 s (Oliver b 19 March 1961 d 26 Dec 1973), 1 da (Sara b 5 Nov 1957); *Career* sr sci offr Armament Res & Devpt Estab Miny of Supply 1941-55, sr engr Tech Div PE Consulting Group 1955-59, head of dept City Univ London and Northampton CAT 1959-67 (memb Univ Cncl 1989-), tech dir Ferraris Med Ltd & Associates 1967-86, pt/t conslt chartered engr; life memb Old Reigatian Assoc (chm 1960-61), chm Governing Body City Literary Inst 1988-; memb: Barbican Assoc London, Parly and Sci Ctee 1971-74; chm UK Automation Cncl 1971-74; common cncllr Aldersgate Ward Corp of London 1985-; Freeman City of London 1966; Liveryman: Worshipful Co of Scientific Instrument Makers 1966, Worshipful Co of Engrs 1988, Worshipful Co of Blacksmiths 1990; MIEE 1954, FIProdE 1962, FInstMC 1976, FRSA 1969; *Recreations* reading, theatre, cinema, photography, good living, France; *Clubs* City Livery, Guildhall; *Style—* Montague Williams, Esq; 154 Thomas More House, Barbican, London EC2Y 8BU (☎ 071 638 5339); Milton House, 24 Richmond Rd, Horsham, Sussex

WILLIAMS, Hon Mrs (Ursula) Moyra; *née* Lubbock; da of late Capt the Hon Harold Fox Pitt Lubbock (4 s of 1 Baron Avebury ka 1918); sister of late 3 Baron; raised to the rank of a Baron's da 1931; *b* 1917; *Educ* private, Oxford Univ; *m* 1938 (m dis 1949), Dorian Joseph George Williams, OBE (d 1985), BBC TV equestrian commentator; *Career* clinical psychologist; *Books* Brain Damage of the Mind, Horse Psychology; *Recreations* anything with horses; *Style—* The Hon Mrs Williams; Leyland Farm, Gawcott, Buckingham

WILLIAMS, Nicholas Michael Heathcote; s of Sir Edgar Trevor Williams, CB, CBE, DSO, DL, of 94 Lonsdale Rd, Oxford, and Gillian, *née* Gambier-Parry; *b* 5 Nov 1954; *Educ* Marlborough, St Catharine's Coll Cambridge (Briggs scholar MA); *m* 19 Dec 1987, Corinna Mary, da of David Mitchell, of Oxford; 2 s (Benjamin b 1988, Joshua b 1990); *Career* RMA Sandhurst 1977, 2 Lt Royal Green Jackets 1977, Lt 1977; barr Inner Temple 1976; *Recreations* reading, looking at pictures, walking, cricket; *Clubs* Royal Green Jackets, Friends of Tate Gallery; *Style—* N Heathcote Williams, Esq; 12 King's Bench Walk, Inner Temple, London EC4 (☎ 071 583 0811, fax 071 583 7228)

WILLIAMS, Nigel Christopher Ransome; CMG (1985); s of Cecil Gwynne Ransome Williams, and Corinne Belden, *née* Rudd; *b* 29 April 1937; *Educ* Merchant Taylors', St John's Coll Oxford; *Career* entered Foreign Serv 1961: Tokyo 1961-66, FO 1966-70, first sec UK mission to the UN 1970-73, FO 1973-76, econ cnsllr Tokyo 1976-80, head of UN dept FCO 1980-85, min Bonn 1985-88, hon ambass Copenhagen 1989-; *Style—* Nigel Williams, Esq, CMG; c/o Foreign and Commonwealth Office, 1 King Charles St, London SW1

WILLIAMS, Nigel Phillip; s of Stanley Phillip Williams, of Rainham, Kent and Freda Frances, *née* Stone; *b* 9 May 1956; *Educ* Gillingham GS, LSE (BSc); *Career* W Greenwell & Co 1977-78, assoc memb Grieveson Grant & Co 1978-84, md William Cooke Lott & Kissack Ltd 1984-90, dir Exco Int Non-Agency 1987-90; advsr Czechoslovenska Obchodni Banka 1990-; memb: SBE 1978, SE 1983; *Recreations* sailing, skiing, shooting; *Clubs* Royal London Yatch, Carlton, Gresham; *Style—* Nigel Williams, Esq; Czechoslovenska Obchodni Banka, Na Prikope 14, 115 20 Praha 1, Czechoslovenska (☎ 010 42 02 235 2331)

WILLIAMS, Noel Laurence; s of Walter Parry Williams (d 1959), of School House, Branston, nr Lincoln, and Marion, *née* Ward (d 1971); *b* 4 March 1926; *Educ* City GS Lincoln, Loughborough Univ (Miny of Educn Teacher Cert), Harvard Univ Graduate Sch of Business, Univ of Birmingham; *m* 7 March 1953, Margaret, da of Horace Gray (d 1988), of Penryn, Lincoln Rd, Metheringham, nr Lincoln; 3 da (Alison b 7 Oct 1956, Anne b 9 April 1959, Jacqueline b 3 May 1961); *Career* cmmnd 1 Lt Royal Lincs Regt 1946, Capt transferred to Army Educn Corps 1947; Stanley Tools Ltd: brand and selling mgmnt 1953-62, mktg mangr 1962-70, mktg dir 1970-84; md The Stanley Works Ltd 1984-, ret 1989, currently pt/t conslt as enterprise cnsllr DTI Enterprise Initiative; memb Yorks & Humberside Regnl Cncl of the CBI, past pres Fedn of Br Hand Tool Mfrs; Freeman Worshipful Co of Cutlers Hallamshire York; FInstD; *Recreations* tennis, walking, golf; *Style—* Noel Williams, Esq; 9 Birchitt Close, Bradway, Sheffield S17 4QJ (☎ 0742 364 755); Stanley Tools, Woodside, Sheffield S3 9PD (☎ 0742 768 888, fax 0742 739 038, telex 54150)

WILLIAMS, Prof Norman Stanley; s of Julius Williams, of Harewood, nr Leeds, Yorks, and Mable, *née* Sundle (d 1978); *b* 1 March 1947; *Educ* Roundhay Sch Leeds, Univ of London (MB BS, MS); *m* Linda, da of Reuben Feldman, of London; 1 s (Benjamin b 1983), 1 da (Charlotte b 1979); *Career* res fell UCLA 1980-82, sr lectr in surgery Leeds Gen Infirmary 1982-86 (res fell 1977-78, lectr 1978-80), Fullbright scholar 1980, Moynihan fellowship 1985, prof of surgery of London Hosp 1986- (house surgn and physician 1970-71, surgical registrar 1971-76); author of numerous chapters and papers on gastroenterological disease; memb ed ctee of British Journal of Surgery; memb: Res Cncl, cncl section of loloproctology RSM of Digestive Fndn Cncl, Br Soc of Gastroenterology, Surgical Res Soc 1979, jt bd of MRCS and LRCP, Surgical Res Soc, Int Surgical Gp; FRCS 1975; *Recreations* long distance swimming, theatre, cinema; *Style—* Prof Norman Williams; Surgical Unit, The London Hospital, Whitechapel, London E1 1BB (☎ 071 377 7079)

WILLIAMS, Sir (Michael) Osmond; 2 Bt (UK 1909), of Castell Deudraeth, and Borthwen, Co Merioneth; MC (1944), JP (Gwynedd 1960); s of Capt Osmond Trahairn Deudraeth Williams, DSO (d 1915), by his w Lady Gladys Finch-Hatton (da of 13 Earl of Winchilsea); suc gf, Sir Arthur Osmond Williams, 1 Bt, JP, sometime Lord-Lt and MP Merionethshire, 1927; *b* 22 April 1914; *Educ* Eton, Freiburg Univ; *m* 1947, Benita Mary, da of G Henry Booker (d 1953); 2 da; *Heir* none; *Career* 2 Lt Royal Scots Greys 1933-37 and 1939; Mid East, Italy and NW Europe WW II 1939-45, Capt 1940, Maj 1945; memb Merioneth Pk Planning Ctee 1971-74, govr Rainer Fndn Outdoor Pursuits Centre 1963-75, chm Quarry Tours Ltd 1973-77; Chev Order of Leopold II with Palm, Croix de Guerre with Palm (Belgium) 1940; *Recreations* music, travelling; *Clubs* Travellers'; *Style*— Sir Osmond Williams, Bt, MC; Borthwen, Penrhyndeudraeth, Gwynedd LL48 6EN (☎ 0766 770215)

WILLIAMS, Owen John; s of Owen John Williams (d 1975), of St Clears, and Dilys, *née* Evans; *b* 17 May 1950; *Educ* Ysgol Abermâd Aberystwyth, Harrow, Univ Coll Oxford (MA); *m* 2 March 1984, Mary Elizabeth, da of Lewis William Evans, of Cemmaes, Powys; 1 da (Olivia b 23 Dec 1986); *Career* called to the Bar Middle Temple 1974, memb Wales and Chester Circuit 1975; chm 1975: O J Williams & Son Ltd, O J Williams & Son (Transport) Ltd, O J Williams & Son (merchants) Ltd; dir St Clears Market Co 1975, chm O J Williams & Co (Engineers) Ltd 1981; Cons party candidate Ceredigion & Pembroke N 1987, Euro candidate Mid & West Wales 1989; memb Hon Soc Cymmrordorion, govr United Counties Agric Soc, pres St Clears Sr Citizens' Assoc; MInstD, underwriter Lloyds' 1978, non-exec memb E Dyfed Health Authy 1990-; *Recreations* racing, rugby, country & western music; *Style*— O J Williams, Esq; 4 Brick Court, Temple, London EC4Y 9AD (☎ 071 583 8455, fax 071 706 1951, car 0836 747157); O J Williams & Son Ltd, St Clears, Dyfed SA33 4BN (☎ 0994 230355, fax 0994 230732)

WILLIAMS, Owen Tudor; CBE (1969); s of Sir Evan Owen Williams, KBE (d 1969), and Gladys Clarissa, *née* Tustian (d 1947); *b* 4 Oct 1916; *Educ* Shrewsbury, St Catharines Coll Cambridge (MA); *m* 15 Sept 1943, Rosemary Louisa, da of James Curzon Mander (d 1962); 4 s (Richard Owen b 1945, Robert Tudor Owen b 1948, Hugh Curzon b 1951, Shon Gwyn Owen b 1962); *Career* Sir Owen Williams & Ptnrs (consulting civil and structural engrs): asst engr 1937-42, ptnr 1946-62, managing and sr ptnr 1962-87, conslt 1987-; asst engr chief engrs dept Admty 1942-46; engrg work incl: Luton to Doncaster M1 Motorway, Birmingham link of M1, M5 and M6 Motorways, second peripheral highway of Istanbul Turkey; MConsE, MIAT, FEng, FICE, FIHT, FRSA; *Clubs* Naval and Military; *Style*— Owen Williams, Esq, CBE; 18 Little Gaddesden, Herts HP4 1PA

WILLIAMS, Paul Darren; s of Edgar Williams, of Jamaica, and Nina, *née* Gray; *b* 26 March 1971; *Educ* Anderstaff Infants, De Ferrers HS; *Career* professional footballer; Derby County 1989-, debut v Crystal Palace March 1990, 6 appearances on loan Lincoln City; memb England under 21 squad 1990-91; youth player: St Mary's under 14, Measham under 15, Burton Albion under 16 and reserves; *Recreations* snooker; *Style*— Paul Williams, Esq; Derby County FC, Baseball Ground, Shaftesbury Crescent, Derby DE3 8NB (☎ 0332 40105)

WILLIAMS, Paul Glyn; s of Samuel O Williams (d 1967), of Alnmouth, Northumberland, and Esmée Ingledew, *née* Cail (d 1974); *b* 14 Nov 1922; *Educ* Marlborough, Trinity Hall Cambridge (MA); *m* 1, Sept 1947 (m dis 1964), Barbara Joan, da of late Alan Hardy; 2 da ((Heather) Jane b 1949, Jennifer Ann b 1952); *m* 2, 13 Aug 1964, Gillian Dawtrey, step da of late James Foote, MBE; 1 da (Henrietta Caroline b 1966); *Career* serv RAF Canada and Europe 1942-46; MP (Cons) Sunderland S 1953-57, MP (Ind Cons) 1957-58 (after resignation of Pty whip in protest against UK withdrawal from Suez); MP (Cons) 1958-64; former chm and md of Mount Charlotte Investmts Ltd, chm and dir Backer Electric Co Ltd; conslt PE International plc; chm Monday Club 1964-69; FInstD, FBIM; *Recreations* music, literature, watching rugby; *Clubs* Boodle's, IOD; *Style*— Paul Williams, Esq; 65 Perrymead St, London SW6 3SN (☎ 071 731 0045)

WILLIAMS, Prof (Hilary) Paul; s of John Kenneth Williams, and Margaret Rosalind Williams; *b* 22 June 1943; *Educ* Redruth GS, Univ of Cambridge (MA), Univ of Leicester (PhD); *m* 27 Aug 1971, Eileen, da of Ernest Hewart; 1 s (Alexander Paul b 18 Feb 1975), 2 da (Anna Morwenna b 17 Nov 1972, Eleanor Mary b 20 April 1982); *Career* devpt analyst for IBM 1968-71, lectr Univ of Sussex 1971-76, prof of mgmnt sci Univ of Edinburgh 1976-84, dean of faculty of mathematical studies Univ of Southampton 1987-90 (prof of operational res 1984-); memb: Operational Res Soc, Mathematical Programming Soc, Royal Instn of Cornwall; *Books* Model Building In Mathematical Programming (1978); *Recreations* running, walking; *Style*— Prof Paul Williams; 72 Olivers Battery Rd, Winchester, Hants SO22 4JB (☎ 0962 52575); Faculty of Mathematical Studies, The University, Southampton SO9 5NH (☎ 0703 593794, fax 0703 593939, telex 47661)

WILLIAMS, Dr Paul Randall; s of Fred Williams (d 1986), and Eileen Westbrook, *née* Stafford (d 1964); *b* 21 March 1934; *Educ* Baines' GS, Loughborough Coll (DLC, BSc), Univ of Liverpool (PhD); *m* 7 Sept 1957, Marion Frances, da of Frederick Gee Lewis (d 1981); 1 s (John Lewis b 1959), 1 da (Judith Sarah b 1962); *Career* ICI res fell Univ of Liverpool 1957, res physicist Br Nat Bubble Chamber 1958-62, Rutherford Laboratory SRC 1962-79, head Engrg Div SERC 1981-83 (head of Astronomy Radio and Space Div 1979-81), dir Rutherford Appleton Laboratory 1987- (dep dir 1983-87); govr: Westminster Coll Oxford, Abingdon Coll; lay preacher Methodist Church; FInstP; *Recreations* sailing, walking, skiing, choral singing; *Style*— Dr Paul Williams; 5 Tatham Rd, Abingdon, Oxon OX14 1QB (☎ 0235 524654); Rutherford Appleton Laboratory, Chilton, Didcot, Oxon OX11 0QX (☎ 0235 445533, fax 0235 5147, telex 83159 RUTHLB G)

WILLIAMS, Paul Raymond; s of Raymond Williams (d 1979), and Majorie Joyce, *née* Ashby; *b* 11 Feb 1947; *Educ* King Edward GS Sturbridge W Mid; *m* 12 Oct 1970 (m dis 1985); 1 s (Robert Paul 16 May 1974), 1 da (Joanne 28 Oct 1971); *Career* chief accountant BSG Int Fin Co 1970-73, business mgmnt accountant BSG Int plc 1973-82, gen mangr Bristol Street Motors Long Acre 1982-85 (md: Cheltenham Ltd 1985, Birmingham 1990); memb Birmingham C of C; FCCA 1974, FBIM 1983, FInstD 1988; *Recreations* squash, reading, sports writing; *Style*— Paul Williams, Esq; 12 College Rd, Cheltenham, Glos GL53 7HX; Bristol Street Motors Ltd, 156/182 Bristol St, Birmingham B5 7AY (☎ 021 666 6000, fax 021 666 6340, car 0836 324325)

WILLIAMS, Dr Penry Herbert; s of Douglas Herbert Williams (d 1939), of Cheshunt, Herts, and Dorothea Adelaide Blanche, *née* Murray (d 1982); *b* 25 Feb 1925; *Educ* Marlborough, New Coll Oxford, St Antony's Coll Oxford (MA, DPhil); *m* 10 Sept 1952, June Carey, da of George Carey Hobson (d 1945), of Cape Town; 1 s (Jonathan b 1960), 1 da (Sarah b 1957); *Career* RA 1943-45 (cmmnd 1945), Royal Indian Artillary 1945-47 (Lt 1946); Univ of Manchester: asst lectr 1951-54, lectr 1954-63, sr lectr 1963-64, fell lectr and tutor New Coll Oxford 1964; ed English Historical Review 1982-90; FRS; *Books* The Council in the Marches of Wales (1958), Life in Tudor England (1964), The Tudor Regime (1979); *Recreations* hill walking, opera; *Style*— Dr Penry Williams, FRS; 53 Park Town, Oxford OX2 6SL (☎ 0865 57613); Brook House, Llanigon, via Hereford (☎ 0497 820964); New College, Oxford OX1 3BN (☎ 0865 279546)

WILLIAMS, Peter; CBE (1984); s of late Humphrey Richard Williams; *b* 4 Oct 1916; *Educ* St Paul's; *m* 1940, Nona, da of late William Cook-Davies; 1 da (Lowri); *Career* dep chm Wedgwood plc 1975-84, chm: Staffs Devpt Assoc 1984-; FCA; *Recreations* golf, reading, music; *Style*— Peter Williams, Esq, CBE; Una, Barlaston, Stoke-on-Trent (☎ 078 139 2566)

WILLIAMS, Peter John Frederick; s of Clifford Thomas Williams, of Westwinds, Nash, Newport, Gwent, and Ethel, *née* Holmes; *b* 20 Aug 1935; *Educ* Bassaleg GS, Newport Tech Coll, Newport Coll of Art, Welsh Sch of Architecture Cardiff (Dip Arch); *m* 20 Dec 1958, Gladys Bronwen, da of Albert Colbourne (d 1966), of Chestnut Tree Cottage, Goldcliff, Newport, Gwent; 2 s (Simon Nicholas Alexander b 5 April 1960, Andrew John b 11 Oct 1961); *Career* princ: Stowfield Ltd Newport, OLP/Y & H London, OLP/Peter Williams Ltd London, Shoredene Ltd Newport; dir Detention Corp Ltd London; cnsllr Magor & Mellons RDC 1966-67; memb: Westminster C of C, Br Conslts Bureau, CLAWSA, Inst of Welsh Affairs; Freeman: City of London 1984, Worshipful Co of Chartered Architects; memb ARIBA 1960, FRIBA 1970, fell Faculty of Building 1983; *Recreations* sailing, golf, shooting, fishing; *Clubs* St Pierre Golf & Country, Chepstow, City Livery; *Style*— Peter Williams, Esq; Bali Hai, Whitson, Newport, Gwent; 310 Nelson House, Dolphin Square, London SW1; OLP/Peter Williams Ltd, 96 St George Sq, London SW1V 3RA; OLP/Peter Williams Ltd, 15 Goldtops, Newport, Gwent (☎ 01 821 1488/0633 246325, Fax 01 821 7477/0633 244671, car 0836 713761, telex 21792/ref 693)

WILLIAMS, Peter Keegan; s of William Edward Williams and Lilian *née* Spright; *b* 3 April 1938; *Educ* F Calday Grange GS, Univ de Lille, Pembroke Coll Oxford (MA); *m* 1969, Rosamund Mary de Worms; 2 da; *Career* joined Dip Serv 1962, first sec FCO 1973, first sec, head of Chancery and Consul Rabat 1976 (chargé d'Affaires 1978 and 1979), cnsllr GATT UK Mission Geneva 1979-83, ambass S Yemen 1983-85; head UN Dept FCO 1986-; *Recreations* wine, walking; *Clubs* Travellers', United Oxford and Cambridge Univ; *Style*— HE Mr Peter Williams; British Embassy, 28 Shara Ho Chi Minh, Khormaksar, Aden, South Yemen; c/o Foreign and Commonwealth Office, King Charles St, London SW1

WILLIAMS, Dr Peter Orchard; s of Robert Orchard Williams, CBE (d 1967), and Agnes Annie, *née* Birkinshaw (d 1972); *b* 23 Sept 1925; *Educ* Caterham Sch, Queens Royal Coll Trinidad, St John's Coll Cambridge (MA), St Mary's Hosp Med Sch (MB BChir); *m* 19 Dec 1949, Billie Innes, da of William Williams Brown (d 1985); 2 da (Judith Anne Way b 1953, Sheridan Petrea Ford b 1955); *Career* med appts: St Mary's Hosp, Royal Free Hosp 1950-53, med specialist RAMC 1953-55; MO MRC 1956-60, dir Wellcome Tst 1965- (memb staff 1960-65), hon dir Wellcome Inst for History of Med; chm: Hague Club (Euro Fndns), Assoc Med Res Charities, Fndns Forum, various med ctees; memb Worshipful Soc of Apothecaries 1988; Hon DSc Univ of Birmingham 1989, Hon MD Univ of Nottingham 1990; Mary Kingsley medal Liverpool Sch Tropical Med 1983, hon fellowship London Sch of Hygiene and Tropical Med; FRCP 1970 (memb 1952); *Books* Careers in Medicine (1952); *Recreations* gardening, travel, golf; *Clubs* RSM; *Style*— Dr Peter Williams; Symonds House, Symonds St, Winchester, Hampshire SO23 9JS (☎ 0962 852650); The Wellcome Trust, 1 Park Square West, London NW1 4LJ (☎ 071 486 4902, fax 071 935 0359)

WILLIAMS, Prof Peter Richard; s of Calvert Percy Halliday Williams, of Christchurch, Dorset, and Joan Lillian, *née* Cook; *b* 13 July 1946; *Educ* Bedford Mod Sch, Univ of Oxford, Univ of Saskatchewan, Univ of Reading (BA, MSc, PhD); *m* 2 Dec 1972, Esther May, da of Louis Van Der Veen, of Saskatoon, Saskatchewan, Canada; *Career* res fell: Univ of Birmingham 1975-80, Australian Nat Univ 1980-83; dep dir Inst of Housing 1986-88 (asst dir 1980-86); currently prof Univ of Wales Cardiff; bd memb Tai Cymru (Housing for Wales); memb Inst Br Geographers, assoc memb Inst of Housing; *Books* Urban Political Economy (author and ed, 1982), Social Process and The City (ed, 1983), Conflict and Development (ed, 1984), Gentrification and The City (author/ed, 1986), Class and Space (author/ed, 1987), Home Ownership (co-author, 1990), Safe as Houses (co-author, 1991); *Recreations* walking, sailing; *Style*— Prof Peter Williams; Centre for Housing Management and Development, Department of City and Regional Planning, University of Wales, Cardiff (☎ 0222 874462, fax 0222 874845): PO Box 906, Cardiff CF1 3YN

WILLIAMS, Brig Peter Richard Godber; DL (1989); s of Maj William Washington Williams, TD, FRGS, of Am Bogha, Appin, Argyll, and Katherine Beatrice, *née* Godber; *b* 2 Jan 1936; *Educ* The Leys Sch Cambridge, RMA Sandhurst; *m* 30 Oct 1964, Margaret Ellen Nina, da of Maj-Gen John MacKenzie, Matheson, OBE, TD, of 2 Orchard Brae, Edinburgh; 1 s (Richard b 12 March 1968), 1 da (Charlotte b 18 Dec 1965); *Career* Nat Serv 1954, cmmnd Welsh Gds 1957, 1 Bn Welsh Gds UK/BAOR 1957-61, Gds Parachute Co 1962-63, Staff Captain Cyprus 1964, Co-Cdr Welsh Gds 1964-66, Staff Coll 1967, Bde-Maj 16 Para Bde 1967-70, 2 Ic 1 Bn Welsh Gds BAOR N Ireland 1970-72, Lt-Col 1972, Staff Cdr 1 Bn Welsh Gds UK Cyprus Berlin 1975-77, Col MOD and HQ UKLF 1977- 85, Brig Cdr 54 Inf Bde E Midlands Area 1985-88, ret 1989; bursar St Mary's Sch Cambridge 1989; rugby Army XV 1958; *Books* various articles in mil pubns; *Recreations* tennis, shooting, fishing, music; *Clubs* Army and Navy; *Style*— Brig Peter Williams, DL; Croxton Old Rectory, Eltisley, Huntingdon, Cambs PE19 4SU (☎ 048 087 344)

WILLIAMS, Sir (Robert) Philip Nathaniel; 4 Bt (UK 1915), of Bridehead, Co Dorset; s of Sir David Philip Williams, 3 Bt, DL (d 1970), by his 2 w, Elizabeth, Lady Williams, *qv*; *b* 3 May 1950; *Educ* Marlborough, Univ of St Andrews (MA); *m* 1979, Catherine Margaret Godwin, da of Canon Cosmo Gabriel Rivers Pouncey, of Gannicox, Birlingham, Pershore, Worcs; 1 s (David b 1980), 3 da (Sarah b 1982, Margaret b 1984, Clare b 1987); *Heir* s David Robert Mark Williams b 31 Oct 1980; *Career* landowner (2500 acres); *Clubs* MCC; *Style*— Sir Philip Williams, Bt; Bridehead, Littlebredy, Dorchester, Dorset DT2 9JA (☎ 0308 482232)

WILLIAMS, Prof Rhys Waclyn; s of Rev Morgan John Williams, and Barbara, *née* John; *b* 24 May 1946; *Educ* The Bishop Gore Sch Swansea, Jesus Coll Oxford (MA, DPhil); *m* Kathleen, da of William Henry Gould, of Bournemouth; 2 s (Daniel b 1978, Thomas b 1982); *Career* tutorial res fell Bedford Coll Univ of London 1972-74, lectr in German Univ of Manchester 1974-84, dean of Faculty of Arts Univ Coll of Swansea (prof of German 1984-); currently pres Int Carl Einstein Soc; *Books* Carl Sternheim, A Critical Study (1982); *Style*— Prof Rhys Williams; 48 Derwen Fawr Rd, Shetty, Swansea SA2 8AQ (☎ 0792 290697); Dept of German, University College of Swansea, Singleton Park, Swansea SA2 8PP (☎ 0792 295173)

WILLIAMS, Richard Wayne; s of David Victor Williams (d 1964), and Sarah Irene, *née* Jones; *b* 13 June 1948; *Educ* Ystalyfera GS Swansea, Univ Coll of Wales Aberystwyth (LLB), Univ of London (LLM); *m* 7 Sept 1974, Linda Pauline, da of Cecil Ernest Elvins; 2 s (Rhodri Christopher Wyn b 18 Jan 1982, Robin Owen Wyn b 12 Sept 1985); *Career* admitted slr 1973; ptnr Ince & Co 1978-; speaker at conferences on shipping matters UK and abroad; memb: Baltic Exchange, London Maritime Arbitrators Assoc; memb Law Soc; *Books* Limitation of Liability for Maritime Claims (1986); *Recreations* archaeology, reading, guitar, travel; *Style*— Richard Williams, Esq; Ince & Co, Knollys House, 11 Byward St, London EC3R 5EN (☎ 071 623 2011, fax 071 623 3225, telex 8955043 INCES G)

WILLIAMS, Robert Charles; s of (Charles) Bertram Williams, of Sutton Coldfield, and Marjorie Iris, *née* Jones; *b* 29 Sept 1949; *Educ* Bromsgrove Sch, Worcester Coll Oxford (MA); *m* 4 Aug 1976, Caroline Ursula Easwythe, da of Rev David Allan Pope; 3 s (Henry b 1979, George b 1981, Alfred b 1982); *Career* called to the Bar Inner Temple 1973, managing ed The Weekly Law Reports 1990- (asst ed 1983-90); hon sec PCC All Saints Blackheath London; *Style*— Robert Williams, Esq; 65, Micheldever Rd, London SE12 8LU (☎ 081 318 0410); 1 Crown Office Row, Temple, London EC4Y 7HH

WILLIAMS, Prof Robert Charles Gooding; OBE (1969); s of Robert Williams (d 1941), of Westminster, London, and Alice Grace, *née* Gooding (d 1935); *b* 28 Dec

1907; *Educ* Westminster City, Imperial Coll of Sci and Technol (BSc, DIC, PhD); *m* 16 Dec 1937, Edith Emma (Molly) (d 1974), da of Albert James Morrow (d 1948), of Highgate, London; 1 da (Fiona Molly (Mrs Hunt) b 1940); *Career* chief engr Murphy Radio Ltd 1935-45, exec engr N American Philips Inc NY 1946-47, chief engr Philips Electronics and Assoc Industs 1948-69, dir Guildford and Counties Broadcasting Co Ltd 1970-, chm Professional and Scientific Servs Ltd 1974-, vice-pres and tech conslt County Sound plc 1982-; chm Int Confs on: ferrites 1958, transistors 1959, med electronics 1960, tv 1962, educn 1974; memb cncl IEE 1962-65 (chm: former radio and telecommunications section 1956-57, electronics div 1963-64); dir IEEE USA 1967-68 (fndr chm UK and Repub Ireland section 1961-66), memb Br Electrotechnical Approvals Bd 1967-86, visiting prof of electronics Univ of Surrey 1969-74, pres IEEIE 1969-75 (chm cncl 1966-69); memb ctee: Cncl Royal TV Soc 1958-60 and 1963-65, Res Degrees of CNAA 1964-68, Nat Cncl Educnl Technol 1967-72; chm ctee: Int Electrotechnical Cmmn on Safety of Household Appliances 1967-74 (Data Processing Equipment 1974-84); memb: bd govrs Guildford Coll Technol, bd tstees Yvonne Arnaud Theatre Guildford; Freeman City of London, Liveryman Worshipful Co of Clothworkers 1946; FCGI, hon FIEIE, FIEEE (USA), FInstP, CEng, FIMechE, FIEE; *Books* numerous professional papers incl: Tuning Devices for Broadcast Radio Receivers in Journal of the Institution of Electrical Engineers (1946), Industrial Television in Telecommunications Journal (1953), The Technical Opportunities for Community Television in The Royal Television Society Journal (1965), Electronics in the Classroom in Journal of the Royal Society of Arts (1970); feature articles incl: Engineers Look Ahead - What we many expect in The Times Radio and Television Supplement (1956), Colour - A Progress Report in Contrast Autumn (1961), By Wire: An Electronic Grid in The Guardian (1962); *Clubs* Athenaeum, Pilgrims of GB; *Style*— Prof Robert C G Williams, OBE; Field Plot, The Flower Walk, Guildford, Surrey GU2 5EP (☎ 0483 577 777); Professional and Scientific Servs Ltd, PO Box 7, Guildford, Surrey GU2 5HH

WILLIAMS, Sir Robert Evan Owen; s of Gwynne Williams; *b* 30 June 1916; *Educ* Sherborne, UCL, Univ Coll Hosp (MD); *m* 1944, Margaret Lumsden; 1 s, 2 da; *Career* former memb MRC and pres RCPath; prof bacteriology London Univ 1960-73, dean St Mary's Hosp Medical Sch 1967-73, dir Public Health Laboratory Service 1973-81, chm Genetic Manipulation Advsy Gp and Ctee on Genetic Manipulation (HSE) 1981-86; fellow UCL 1968; Hon FRCPA, Hon MD Uppsala, Hon DSc Bath; FRCP, FRCPath, FFCM; kt 1976; *Recreations* horticulture; *Clubs* Athenaeum; *Style*— Sir Robert Williams; Little Platt, Plush, Dorchester, Dorset (☎ 030 04 320)

WILLIAMS, Prof Robert Hughes; s of Emrys Williams (d 1972), of Rhydsarn, Llanuwchllyn, Bala, Gwynedd, N Wales, and Catherine, *née* Hughes; *b* 22 Dec 1941; *Educ* Bala Boys GS, Univ Coll of N Wales Bangor (BSc, PhD, DSc); *m* 18 March 1967, Gillian Mary, da of Basil Harrison, of 1 Ropley Rd, Christ Church, Hants; 1 s (Alun Hughes b 14 Aug 1972), 1 da (Sian Hughes b 17 Dec 1970); *Career* lectr, reader then prof New Univ of Ulster NI 1968-83, prof physics and head of Dept Univ of Wales Cardiff 1984-; author of several chapters, articles and papers; chm S Wales Branch and Semiconductor Gp of Inst of Physics; Br Vacuum Cncl medal 1988, Max Born medal German Physics Soc 1989; CPhys, FInstP 1976, FRS 1990; *Books* Metal Semiconductor Contacts (1988); *Recreations* walking and fishing; *Style*— Prof Robert Williams, FRS; Dolwerdd, Trerhyngyll, Cowbridge, S Glamorgan, Wales (☎ 04463 3402); Physics Department, University of Wales College of Cardiff, PO Box 913, Cardiff CF1 3TH (☎ 0222 874785, fax 0222 874056)

WILLIAMS, Robert James; s of Capt Thomas Edwin Williams, MBE, of Lutterworth, Leicestershire, and Joan Winifred, *née* Nelson; *b* 20 Sept 1948; *Educ* King Edward VII Sch Sheffield, Univ Coll Oxford (BA); *m* 29 July 1972, Margaret, da of Charles Neville Hillier, of Guernsey; 2 da (Katherine b 6 Aug 1979, Caroline b 24 Aug 1983); *Career* Linklaters & Paines: articled clerk 1971-73, asst slr 1973-81, Hong Kong Office 1978-80, ptnr 1981-; Friend of Dulwich Coll; memb City of London Slrs Co 1980; memb Law Soc 1973; *Recreations* swimming, walking, eating, sleeping; *Style*— Robert Williams, Esq; 84 Alleyn Rd, London SE21 8AH (☎ 081 761 1536); Barrington House, 59/67 Gresham St, London EC2V 7JA (☎ 071 606 7080, fax 071 606 5113, telex 884349)

WILLIAMS, Robert James; s of Wyndham James Williams, and Minnie, *née* Thomas; *b* 12 Nov 1943; *Educ* Newport High Sch, Univ of Sheffield (BA); *m* 21 Oct 1967, Janice, da of Frederick John Evan (d 1981); 1 s (Ian James b 23 Nov 1972); *Career* CA, articled with Cooper Brothers 1966-69, various posts Unilever 1970-77, chief accountant United Gas Industs 1977-79, md Mills and Boon 1985- (joined 1979); *Recreations* sports - particularly tennis (jr Wimbledon); *Style*— Robert Williams, Esq; Mills & Boon Ltd, Eton House, 18-24 Paradise Rd, Richmond, Surrey TW9 1SR (☎ 01 948 0444, fax 040 5899, telex 24420 MILBON G)

WILLIAMS, Robert James Royston; s of Kenneth James Williams, of Hollybrook, Hamnish, nr Leominster, Herefordshire, and Gwendoline Betty, *née* Gravestock; *b* 25 Feb 1953; *Educ* Surbiton GS; *m* 18 Nov 1978, Clare Margaret, da of John Francis Cotton, of Moreton Jeffries, Burley Gate, Herefordshire; 2 da (Hannah b 26 Oct 1984, Emily b 25 April 1986); *Career* racehorse trainer 1981-; trained: Chaumiere winner of John Smiths Magnet Cup York 1985 and 1986, Mister Majestic winner of Tattersalls Middle Park Stakes Gr I Newmarket 1986; *Recreations* skiing, golf, shooting; *Style*— Robert Williams, Esq; Marriott Stables, Hamilton Rd, Newmarket, Suffolk CB8 0NY (☎ 0638 663218, fax 0638 660145, car 0891 493629)

WILLIAMS, Prof Robert Joseph Paton; s of Ernest Ivor Williams (d 1968), and Alice, *née* Roberts (d 1988); *b* 25 Feb 1926; *Educ* Wallasey GS, Merton Coll Oxford (BA, MA, DPhil); *m* 19 July 1952, Jelly Klara, da of Mattheüs Jacobus Christiaan Buchli, of The Netherlands; 2 s (Timothy Ivor b 1955, John Matthew b 1957); *Career* Royal Soc Napier res prof Univ of Oxford 1974- (jr res fell Merton Coll 1951-55, lectr in chemistry 1955-72, tutor in biochemistry Wadham Coll 1956-72, reader in chemistry 1972-74, fell 1956-); Buchman Memorial lectr California Inst of Technol 1972; visiting lectr: Univ of Princeton 1976, Univ of Toronto 1980, Univ of Newfoundland 1983; Walter J Chute lectr Univ of Dalhousie 1984, Katritsky lectr UEA 1986; foreign memb: Lisbon Acad of Sci 1981, Royal Soc of Sci Leige 1981, Royal Swedish Acad of Sci 1984, Nat Acad of Sci Czechoslovakia 1989; memb: Lindemann Tst, Oxford Preservation Tst; delegate Oxford Univ Press; *awards* Tilden lectr and medallist Chem Soc 1970, Keilen medal Biochem Soc 1972, Hughes medal The Royal Soc 1979, Claire Brylants medal Univ of Louvain 1980, Sir Hans Krebs medal Euro Biochem Societies 1985, Linderstrom-Lang medal Univ of Bologna 1987, Heyrovsky medal Int Union of Biochemistry 1988, Sir Frederick Gowland Hopkins medal Biochem Soc 1989; Hon DSc: Univ of Leige Belgium 1980, Univ of Leicester 1985; FRS 1972-; *Books* Inorganic Chemistry (with C G S Phillips 1966), Biomineralization (with S Mann and J Webb, 1989); *Recreations* walking in the country; *Style*— Prof Robert Williams, FRS; 115 Victoria Rd, Oxford OX2 7QG (☎ 0865 58926); Wadham College, Oxford OX1 3QR (☎ 0865 272600, fax 0865 272690)

WILLIAMS, Dr (Andrew) Robin; *b* 10 May 1952; *Educ* King Edward VI GS, NE London Poly (Dip Scientific and Med Photography), Univ of London (MA, PhD); *Career* scientific photographer GEC Marconi Res Laboratories 1972, trainee med photographer Cambridge Med Sch and Addenbrooke's Hosp 1973, med photographer Westminster Med Sch 1974-79, head Med Illustration and Teaching Servs Charing Cross Hosp and Med Sch 1979-84, head Combined Dept of Med Illustration and Teaching Servs of Charing Cross and Westminster Med Schs 1984-; Westminster Hosp; memb Safety Ctee 1976-79, memb Teaching Resources Ctee 1979-84, memb Clinical Support Gp 1980-, memb Computor Assisted Learning Ctee 1980; lective convenor RPS Med Gp 1976-79, memb Med Associateship and Fellowship Bd RPS 1979-, memb Med Ctee Inst of Incorporated Photographers 1979-82, teacher London Sch of Med Photography 1979-, examiner Basic Med Photography Examination (IIP) 1979-85; external supervisor: PCL 1979-, Harrow Coll of Art and Design 1980-84; visiting lectr Trent Poly 1979-81, pt/t lectr in mgmnt studies Univ of London 1980-, dir London Sch of Med Photography 1980-, visiting lectr NE Surrey Coll of Technol 1980-, vice chm RPS Med Gp 1981-84, project dir Charing Cross and Westminster's Interactive TV Network 1981-84, specialist advsr Univ of London Computor Ctee 1983-86; chm: Annacreon Soc 1983-88, Med Ctee BIPP 1983-86, RPS Med Gp 1984-86; treas Assoc of Univ Teachers Local Ctee 1983-86 (memb 1980-83), memb Standing Advsy Ctee Univ of London Purchasing Gp 1984-87, memb Working Pty on Communication Technol Senate and Ct Univ of London 1984-89, memb Bd of Examiners BIPP Higher Med Examinations 1984-, abstracts ed Jl of Audio visual Media in Med 1984-89; memb: Int Contract Gp of Med Illustrators 1985-, Special Cmmn of EEC on Project DELTA 1985-88, special advsr to Select Ctee on Higher Educn 1985-, memb Bd Govrs and dir Biological Photographic Assoc 1986-89; memb: Fellowship Ctee Biological Photographic Assoc 1986, RPS Devpt Ctee 1987-89, Cncl RPS 1988-; conslt Euro Space Agency 1986-89; numerous awards incl: Br Med Jl award 1975, Combined Royal Colls' medal 1977 and 1990, Gold award Biological Photographic Assoc (USA) 1983 and 1989, Chm's award RPS 1988; FRMS 1976, FRPS 1976, FBIPP 1977; *Recreations* travel, music, food, wine and archaeology; *Style*— Dr Andrew Williams; Dept of Medical Illustration, Charing Cross Hospital, Fulham Palace Rd, London W6 8RF; (☎ 081 748 1495)

WILLIAMS, Sir Robin Philip; 2 Bt (UK 1953), of Cilgeraint, Co Caernarvon; s of Sir Herbert Geraint Williams, 1 Bt, sometime MP (Reading and also Croydon S) and Parly sec BOT 1928-29 (d 1954), and Dorothy Frances, *née* Jones (d 1957); *b* 27 May 1928; *Educ* Eton, St John's Coll Cambridge; *m* 19 Feb 1955, Wendy Adele Marguerite, da of late Felix Joseph Alexander, of Hong Kong; 2 s; *Heir* s, Anthony Geraint Williams, b 22 Dec 1958; *Career* Lt RA 1947; called to the Bar Middle Temple 1954; insurance broker 1952- and memb Lloyds 1961-; chm: Bow Group 1954, Anti Common Market League 1969; councillor Borough of Haringay 1968-74; hon sec Campaign for an Independent Britain 1990; *Style*— Sir Robin Williams, Bt; 1 Broadlands Close, Broadlands Rd, Highgate, London N6 4AF

WILLIAMS, Rev Canon (John) Roger; s of Sir Gwilym Tecwyn Williams, CBE (d 1989), and Kathleen Isobel Rishworth, *née* Edwards (d 1989); *b* 6 Oct 1937; *Educ* Denstone Coll, Lichfield Theol Coll; *Career* ordained Lichfield Cathedral; deacon 1963, priest 1964; asst curate: Wem Shropshire 1963-66, St Peter's Collegate Church Wolverhampton 1966-69; rector Pudleston-cum-Whyle with Hatfield and priest i/c Stoke Prior Humber and Docklow Hereford 1969-74, vicar Christ Church Fenton Stoke-on-Trent 1974-81, rector Shipston-on-Stour with Honington and Idlicote 1981-, rural dean Shipston 1983-90, hon canon Coventry Cathedral 1990-; chaplain to High Sheriff of Warwicks 1987-88 and 1991; *Recreations* art, architecture, walking, travel; *Style*— The Rev Canon Roger Williams; The Rectory, 8 Glen Close, Shipston-on-Stour, Warwickshire CV36 4ED (☎ 0608 62661)

WILLIAMS, Dr Roger Stanley; s of Stanley George Williams, and Doris, *née* Dagmar; *b* 28 Aug 1931; *Educ* St Mary's Coll Southampton, London Hosp Med Coll (MB, MD, LRCP, MRCP); *m* 1, 8 Aug 1954 (m dis 1977), Lindsay Mary, *née* Elliott; 2 s (Robert b 8 March 1956, Andrew b 3 Jan 1964), 3 da (Anne b 5 March 1958, Fiona b 24 April 1959, Deborah b 12 July 1961); m 2, 15 Sept 1978, Stephanie Gay, da of Gp Capt Patrick De Laszlo (d 1980); 1 s (Aiden b 16 May 1981), 2 da (Clemency b 28 June 1979, Octavia b 4 Sept 1983); *Career* Capt RAMC 1956-58; jr med specialist Queen Alexandra Hosp Millbank 1956-58, med registrar and tutor Royal Postgraduate Med Sch 1958-59, lectr med Royal Free Hosp 1959-65, conslt physician Royal S Hants and Southampton Gen Hosp 1965-66, dir Liver Res Unit and conslt physician King's Coll Hosp and Med Sch 1966-; memb scientific gp on viral hepatitis WHO Geneva 1972, conslt Liver Res Unit Tst 1974-, memb Advsy Gp on Hepatitis DHSS 1980- (memb Transplant Advsy Panel 1974-83), attended Melrose meml lecture Glasgow 1970, Goulstonian lecture RCP 1970, Searle lecture American Assoc for Study of Liver Disease 1972, Fleming lecture Glasgow Coll of Physicians and Surgns 1975, Sir Arthur Hurst meml lecture Br Soc of Gastroenterology 1975, Skinner lecture Royal Coll of Radiologists 1978; Sir Ernest Finch visiting prof Sheffield 1974, hon conslt in med to Army 1988-; memb: RSM (sec of section 1962-71), Euro Assoc for Study of the Liver (sec and tres 1968-71, pres 1984); pres Br Soc of Gastroenterology 1989-90, UK rep select Ctee of Experts Organ Transplantation 1989-; Freeman City of London, Liveryman Worshipful Co of Apothecaries; MRCS, FRCP, FRCS; *Books* ed: Fifth Symposium on Advanced Medicine (1969), Immunology of the Liver (1971), Artificial Liver Support (1975), Immune Reactions in Liver Diseases (1978), Drug Reactions and the Liver (1981), Variceal Bleeding (1982); author of over 800 scientific papers, review articles and book chapters; *Recreations* tennis, sailing, opera; *Clubs* Saints and Sinners, Royal Yacht Sqdn, Royal Ocean Racing; *Style*— Dr Roger Williams; 8 Eldon Rd, London W8 (☎ 01 937 5301); Reed House, Satchell Lane, Hamble, Hants; Inst of Liver Studies, King's Coll Hosp, Denmark Hill, London SE5 9RS (☎ 071 326 3169, fax 071 326 4789)

WILLIAMS, Ronald William; s of Albert Williams (d 1942), and Katherine Teresa, *née* Chilver (d 1962); *b* 19 Dec 1926; *Educ* City of London Sch, Downing Coll Cambridge (BA, LLB); *Career* RN 1945-48; Iraq Petroleum Co and Philips Electrical Industs 1952-64, sr conslt PA Mgmnt Conslt 1964-69; asst sec: Nat Bd for Prices and Incomes 1969-71; Office of Manpower Econs 1971-73; under sec CSD 1980 (asst sec 1973-80), dir of The Officer of Manpower Econs 1980-86; sr advsr Coopers and Lybrand Deloitte 1986-; *Recreations* books, music; *Style*— Ronald Williams, Esq; 126 Defoe House, Barbican, London EC2Y 8DN (☎ 071 638 5456); C/O Coopers & Lybrand Deloitte, Plumtree Ct, London EC4A 4HT (☎ 071 822 4790, fax 071 822 4652, telex 887470)

WILLIAMS, Roy; CB (1989); s of Eric and Ellen Williams; *b* 31 Dec 1934; *Educ* Univ of Liverpool (BA), Univs of Chicago and Berkeley USA; *m* 1959, Shirley, da of Capt O Warwick; 1 s (Justin b 1966), 1 da (Adela b 1961); *Career* asst princ Miny of Power 1956 (princ 1961), princ private sec Miny of Power 1969, paymaster gen 1969, asst sec DTI 1971, princ private Sec of State for Indust 1974, under sec 1976, dep perm sec DTI 1984-; *Style*— Roy Williams, Esq, CB; Department of Trade and Industry, 123 Victoria St, London SW1

WILLIAMS, Lady; Ruth Margaret; da of Charles Butcher, of Hudson Bay; *m* 1948, Sir Robert Williams, 9 Bt, of Tregullow (d 1976); 3 s (1 decd, 10 Bt, Barton), 1 da (Phyllis); *Style*— Lady Williams; Kamsack, Saskatchewan, Canada; Upcott House, Barnstaple, N Devon

WILLIAMS, Hon Mrs (Sarah Sophia Rhiannon); *née* Rhys; 2 da of 9 Baron Dynevor, *qv*; *b* 1963; *m* 1987, Dyfrug Williams, eldest s of Daniel Thomas Williams, of

Carmarthen; 1 s (Stefan Orlando b 1988); *Style*— The Hon Mrs Williams; c/o The Rt Hon Lord Dynevor, The Walk, Carmarthen Road, Llandeilo, Dyfed

WILLIAMS, Rt Hon Shirley Vivien Teresa Brittain (Mrs Richard Neustadt); PC (1974); da of Prof Sir George Catlin and the writer, Vera Brittain (Mrs Catlin); *b* 27 July 1930; *Educ* Somerville Coll Oxford, Columbia Univ New York; *m* 1, 1955 (m dis 1974), Prof Bernard Williams; 1 da (Rebecca Clare); m 2, 19 Dec 1987, Prof Richard E Neustadt; *Career* contested (Lab): Harwich 1954 and 1955, Southampton Test 1959; MP (Lab) Hitchin 1964-74, Hertford and Stevenage 1974-79; MP SDP Crosby (by-election, converted Cons majority of 19,272 to SDP one of 5,289) 1981-83; PPS to Min Health 1964-66, Parly sec: Miny Lab 1966-67, Min State Educn and Sci 1967-69, Home Office 1969-70; oppn spokesman: Social Serv 1970-71, Home Affrs 1971-73, Prices and Consumer Protection 1973-74 (sec state 1974-76); sec state Educn and Sci and paymaster gen 1976-79, chm Fabian Soc 1980 (gen sec 1960-64), memb Lab NEC 1970-81, co-fndr SDP 1981, pres 1982-88; fell Inst of Politics Harvard Univ 1979-80, OECD examiner 1979-, prof fell Policy Studies Inst 1979-85, memb Sr Advsy Ctee Inst of Politics, Harvard; tstee: Twinhick Century Fund (New York), Learning by Experience Tst; dir Turing Inst, Univ of Strathcylde, prof elective politics Kennedy Sch of Govt Harvard Univ 1988-, acting dir Inst of Politics (1988-); *Style*— The Rt Hon Shirley Williams; SDP, 4 Cowley St, London SW1P 3NB (☎ 071 222 7999)

WILLIAMS, Prof Stanley Thomas; s of Thomas Raymond Williams (d 1959), and Martha Alice Rowlands (d 1973); *b* 8 March 1937; *Educ* Birkenhead Sch, Univ of Liverpool (BSc, PhD, DSc); *m* 26 April 1962, Grace Katharine, da of Capt Cyril Twentyman (d 1973); 1 s (David John b 18 July 1967), 1 da (Anne Margaret b 12 Jan 1966); *Career* post doctoral fell Univ Coll Dublin 1962-64; Univ of Liverpool: lectr 1964-73, sr lectr 1973-78, reader 1978-87, prof 1987-; Workers Educnl Assoc; memb: Br Mycological Soc 1961-, Soc Gen Microbiology 1962-, American Soc Microbiology 1965-; *Books* Soil Organisms (1971), Methods in Soil Microbiology (1972), Biology of Actinomycetes (1983); *Recreations* opera, swimming, gardening, politics; *Style*— Prof Stanley Williams; 10 Brimstage Ave, Bebington, Merseyside L63 5QH (☎ 051 608 5385); Dept Genetics and Microbiology, Liverpool University, PO Box 147, Liverpool L69 3BX (☎ 051 794 5125, fax 051 708 6502, telex 627095 UNILPL G)

WILLIAMS, Steve Charles; s of Charles Williams, of Romford, Essex, and Joyce, *née* Clarke; *b* 12 July 1958; *Educ* St Edwards Sch Chadwell Heath Romford; *m* 20 June 1981, Angie, da of Len Toomer; 1 s (Craig Steven b 25 June 1982), 1 da (Sasha Louise b 7 Feb 1984); *Career* professional footballer; Southampton 1976-84 (278 league appearances, 18 goals), Arsenal 1984-88 (95 league appearances, 4 goals), Luton Town 1988- (over 30 appearances); England: 15 under 21 caps 1977-80, 6 full caps 1983-85; Southampton player of the year 1977, Littlewoods Cup Winner's medal Arsenal v Liverpool 1987 (Loser's medal Southampton v Nottm Forest 1979); proprietor A & S Williams Ltd 1980- (building co); *Recreations* snooker, building, gardening; *Style*— Steve Williams, Esq; Luton Town FC, Kenilworth Stadium, 1 Maple Rd, Luton Town, Luton, Beds LU4 8AW (☎ 0582 411622, fax 0582 405070)

WILLIAMS, Steve Michael; s of Michael Willians, and Margaret Maud, *née* Vickers; *b* 3 Oct 1970; *Educ* Glanafon Comp Sch Port Talbot, Neath Tertiary Coll; *Career* Ruby Union No 8 and flanker Swansea RFC; clubs: Neath Tertiary Coll RFC, Bryncoch RFC, Swansea RFC (debut 1988, 60 appearances); rep: Welsh Students, Welsh Schs U19 (7 caps), Wales U21 (2 caps at No 8, capt), Wales B (debut 1990), Wales Sevens (HK Sevens 1990); Wales: tour Namibia 1990; trainee quantity surveyor; other sports: memb Swansea Harriers, Welsh U20 Shot Putt Champion, capt Wales U15 Basketball team (6 appearances), capt Wales Schs Athletics team; voted Most Promising Welsh Rugby player 1990; *Recreations* music, films; *Style*— Steve Williams, Esq; 109 Maes Ty Canol, Baglan, Port Talbot, West Glamorgan SA12 8UR (☎ 0639 812913); c/o Swansea RFC, The Clubhouse, St Helens, Swansea

WILLIAMS, Susan; da of Evan Peter Williams, of High Wycombe, Bucks, and Lesley Elizabeth, *née* Evenden; *b* 12 Sept 1959; *Educ* Lady Verney GS High Wycombe, UCL (BSc); *Career* md James R Adams and Assocs Ltd 1989 (dir 1984-); MRS (1983), BPS (1989); *Recreations* reading, water and snow skiing, travelling, antiques and restoration; *Style*— Ms Susan Williams; James R Adams & Associates Ltd, 5 Langley St, Covent Garden, London WC2H 9JA (☎ 071 836 5012, fax 071 240 2202)

WILLIAMS, Susan Eva; MBE (1958); da of Robert Henry Williams (d 1963), of Bonvilston House, S Glamorgan, by his w, Dorothy Marie (d 1976); *b* 17 Aug 1915; *Educ* St James's Sch W Malvern; *m* 1950, Charles Crofts Llewellyn Williams (d 1952), s of Charles Williams, of The Heath, Cardiff (d 1912); *Career* Wing Offr WAAF WWII; JP Glamorgan 1961, High Sheriff 1968; DL Glamorgan 1973, HM Lt for S Glamorgan 1981-; Lord Lt S Glamorgan 1985-90; *Recreations* nat hunt racing; *Clubs* RAF; *Style*— Mrs Susan Williams, MBE; Caercady, Welsh St Donat's, Cowbridge, S Glamorgan CF7 7ST (☎ 044 677 2346)

WILLIAMS, Susan Jennifer (Sue) (Mrs Stephen Williams); da of Denis J Cottam, of Broomhill, 19 Thornley Park Road, Grotton nr Oldham, Lancs, and Gerda, *née* Hopfinger; *b* 9 Nov 1948; *Educ* Manchester HS for Girls, King's Coll London (Gulbenkian scholar, BA), Univ of Vienna (Dip in Translating); *m* 1972, Stephen Geoffrey Williams, s of Alfred Earnest Williams; 1 s (Thomas Alexander b 8 Aug 1981); *Career* mktg info offr Thorn Electrical Industries Ltd 1971-73, asst to MD Biba Ltd 1973-75, asst buyer Miss Selfridge Ltd 1975-76; Pret-A-Porter Ltd: asst to MD 1976-87, dir 1980-87, ptnr subsid co 1985-87; estab Sue Williams Gallery 1987 (selected by Crafts Cncl for Galleries Index 1988); AKC 1971; memb: Convocation of Univ of London 1971, ICA 1975; *Recreations* family, contemporary art, twentieth century literature, swimming, yoga, cooking; *Clubs* 2 Brydge's Place; *Style*— Ms Sue Williams; 17 Highbury Hill, London N5 1SU (☎ 071 354 3100); Sue Williams, 320 Portobello Rd, London W10 5RU (☎ 081 960 6123)

WILLIAMS, Prof Thomas Eifion Hopkins; CBE (1980); s of David Garfield Williams (d 1974), of Cwmtwrch, Breconshire, and Annie Mary, *née* Hopkins (d 1949); *b* 14 June 1923; *Educ* Ystradgynlais GS, Univ of Wales (BSc, MSc), Univ of Durham (PhD), Univ of California Berkeley (Post Doctoral); *m* 28 June 1947, (Elizabeth) Lois, da of Evan Rees Davies (d 1979), of Cwmtwrch, Breconshire; 1 s (Huw b 2 Feb 1960), 2 da (Maelor b 5 April 1948, Amanda b 19 May 1955); *Career* res Stressman Sir W G Armstrong Whitworth Aircraft 1945, asst engr Trunk Rds Div Glamorgan CC 1946, asst lectr Univ Coll of Swansea 1947, lectr and reader King's Coll Univ of Durham 1948-63, resident conslt engr RT James & Ptnrs 1952, visiting prof Northwestern Univ Illinois 1957, reader and prof Univ of Newcastle upon Tyne 1963-67, res prof Dept of Civil Engrg and Transportation Univ of Southampton 1983- (prof 1967-83); memb and chm NEDO EDC Civil Engrg 1969-78, chm Dept of Tport Trunk Rd Assessment Standing Advsy Ctee 1980-87, pres Inst of Highway Engrs 1979-80, memb Public Policy Ctee RAC 1981-, memb Cncl Church Schs Co 1982-90, visitor Traffic Engr Div Tport & Rd Res Laboratory 1982-88; specialist advsr: H of C Tport Select Ctee 1989, House of Lords Euro Communities Ctee 1990; CEng, FICE, FIHT, FCIT, FRSA; *Books* ed: Urban Survival & Traffic (1961), Inter-City VTOL: Traffic & Sites (1969), Transportation & Environment (1973), Urban Road Appraisal Report (chm, 1986); *Recreations* music; *Clubs* RAC; *Style*— Prof Thomas Williams, CBE; Willowdale, Woodlea Way, Ampfield, Romsey, Hants SO51 9DA (☎ 0703 253 342); Transportation Research Group, Dept of Civil Engineering, Univ of Southampton S0G 5NH (☎ 0703 595 000, telex 47661)

WILLIAMS, Dr Trevor Illtyd; s of Illtyd Williams (d 1947), of Bristol, and Alma Mathilde, *née* Sohlberg (d 1956); *b* 16 July 1921; *Educ* Clifton Coll, The Queen's Coll Oxford (MA, Bsc, DPhil); *m* 13 Sept 1952, Sylvia Iréne, da of Archibald Armstead (d 1942), of Bromley; 4 s (Darryl, Lloyd, Adam, Benjamin), 1 da (Clare); *Career* ed Endeavour 1954-, Outlook on Agriculture 1982-90, academic relations advsr ICI 1962-74; chm: World List of Scientific Periodicals 1966-88, Soc for the History of Alchemy & Chemistry 1967-84, Ctee for Selection of Low-Priced Books for Overseas 1982-84; FRSC 1947, FRHistS 1977; *Books* The Chemical Industry (1953), A History of Technology (jt ed 8 vols 1954-84), A Biographical Dictionary of Scientists (ed 1968), Industrial Research in the United Kingdom (ed 1980), History of the British Gas Industry (1981), Florey, Penicillin and After (1984), The Triumph of Invention (1987), Robert Robinson, Chemist Extraordinary (1990), Science, Invention and Discovery in the 20th Century (1990); *Recreations* gardening, hill walking; *Clubs* Athenaeum; *Style*— Dr Trevor Williams; 20 Blenheim Drive, Oxford OX2 8DG (☎ 0865 58591); Pen-y-Cwm, Corris Uchaf, Machynlleth, Powys SY20 7HN

WILLIAMS, Walter Gordon Mason; CB (1983); s of Rees John Williams DSO (d 1960), of Cardiff, and Gladys Maud Williams, *née* Hull (d 1967); *b* 10 June 1923; *Educ* Cardiff HS, Coll of Estate Mgmnt; *m* 1950, Gwyneth Joyce, da of Thomas Gwyn Lawrence (d 1941), of Caerphilly; 2 da (Lois, Ann); *Career* chartered surveyor; district valuer: Tower Hamlets 1967-68, Westminster 1968-69; superintending valuer North Midlands 1969-73, asst chief valuer 1973-79, dep chief valuer (under sec) 1979-83, vice pres London Rent Assessment Panel 1984-; *Recreations* reading, music, theatre, rugby union football; *Style*— Walter Williams Esq, CB; 33A Sydenham Hill, London, SE26 6SH (☎ 081 670 8580); Newlands House, 37-40, Berners St, London W1P 4BP (☎ 071 580 2000)

WILLIAMS, Prof William Morgan (Bill); CBE (1985); *b* 2 May 1926; *Educ* Univ of Wales (BA, MA); *Career* Welsh Guards 1944 cmmnd JAT regt Indian Army, served India, Java, Sumatra, Singapore, demobbed 1948; reader in social geography Univ of Keele 1963 (lectr 1952, sr lectr 1960), prof of sociology and anthropology Univ Coll Swansea 1963-, dir Inst of Health Care Studies Swansea; memb: Welsh Econ Cncl 1964-73, Assoc of Social Anthropologists of the Cwlth 1965; chm Glamorgan Health Authy 1974-; hon citizen City of Minneapolis 1987; *Books* The Sociology of an English Village: Gosforth (1956), The Country Craftsman (1958), A West Counry Village: Ashworthy (1963), The Medical Use of Psychotropic Drugs (1973), Occupational Choice (1974); *Recreations* reading, music, looking at paintings; *Style*— Prof Bill Williams, CBE; Dept of Sociology and Anthropology, University College of Swansea, Singleton Park, Swansea, Glam (☎ 0792 295308, fax 0792 295643, telex 48358 UL SWAN G)

WILLIAMS, William Trevor (Bill); s of Percy Trevor Williams (d 1987), of Liverpool, and Edith, *née* Hible; *b* 3 June 1935; *Educ* Liverpool Coll Sch; *m* 1, 23 June 1956, Jane Williams; 2 s (Bruce b 1957, Shaun b 1959), 1 da (Heidi b 1961); m 2, 25 March 1967, Pamela Hilda, da of Albert Victor Saunders (d 1988), of Westminster; 1 da (Justine b 1970); *Career* Nat Serv RAF 1953-55; dir gen mangr RMC Ltd: Wales 1963-73, E Midlands 1973-76, London 1976-78; divnl dir North of England RMC (UK) Ltd 1978-84, md Hall & Co Ltd 1984-; Freeman City of London, Liveryman Worshipful Co of Builders Merchants; *Recreations* fly-fishing, gardening; *Clubs* The Flyfishers London; *Style*— Bill Williams, Esq; Quarry House, Springbottom Lane, White Hill, Bletchingley, Surrey RH1 4QZ (☎ 07374 3876); Hall & Co Ltd, RMC House, Victoria Wharf, Brighton Rd, Redhill, Surrey RH1 6QZ (☎ 0737 772415, fax 0737 760567)

WILLIAMS, Col William Trevor (Bill); s of Francis Harold Williams (d 1951), and Ethel Mabel, *née* Gwyther (d 1964); *b* 16 Oct 1925; *Educ* Whitchurch GS, Univ of Kent (MA); *m* 6 Feb 1951, Elizabeth, da of Brig A H Goldie (d 1967); 2 s (Stephen b 15 May 1952, Richard b 16 Nov 1961), 2 da (Mandy b 11 June 1958, Mary b 13 April 1967); *Career* enlisted Grenadier Gds 1943, cmmnd Black Watch, served with Royal Scots RCT, GS to 1977, served Malaysia, South America, Ethiopia, Libya, Germany and Singapore, ret as full Col; dir SATRA (GB) 1978-79, dir gen EIA 1980-; TECs SATROs, FBIM 1965, FCIS 1979, MCIT 1980; *Recreations* golf, photography; *Clubs* IOD; *Style*— Col Bill Williams; 15 Mill Lane, Lower Harbledown, Canterbury, Kent CT2 8NE (☎ 0227 768170); Engineering Industries Association, 16 Dartmouth St, London SW1H 9BL (☎ 071 222 2367, fax 071 222 2782)

WILLIAMS-BULKELEY, Michael; s of Lt-Col Sir R H D Williams-Bulkeley, Bart, of Plas Meigan, Beaumaris, Anglesey, Gwynedd, and Renée Arundell, *née* Neave; see Debrett's Peerage and Baronetage 1985 Edn; *b* 2 April 1943; *Educ* Eton; *m* 4 May 1968, Ellen-Marie, da of L Falkum-Hansen (d 1972); 2 s (James b 1970, David b 1973); *Career* Lt Welsh Gds, served Aden 1965-66; dir CT Bowring Reinsurance Ltd 1981-89, Bowring Int Insur Brokers Ltd 1988-; md Marsh & McLennan Worldwide 1988-; insur broker; *Recreations* golf, gardening, shooting; *Style*— Michael Williams-Bulkeley, Esq; Pigeon Hill, Lilley Bottom, nr Luton LU2 8NH (☎ 0582 31971; Bowring Int Insur Brokers Ltd, PO Box 145, The Bowring Bldg, Tower Place, London EC3 (☎ 071 283 3100)

WILLIAMS-BULKELEY, Sir Richard Harry David; 13 Bt (E 1661), TD, JP (1934); s of late Maj Richard Gerard Wellesley Williams-Bulkeley, MC, only s of 12 Bt; suc gf, Sir Richard Henry Williams-Bulkeley, 12 Bt, KCB, 1942; *b* 5 Oct 1911; *Educ* Eton; *m* 1938, Renée Arundell, da of Sir Thomas Lewis Hughes Neave, 5 Bt; 2 s; *Heir* s, Capt Richard Thomas Williams-Bulkeley; *Career* serv WWII Maj Royal Welsh Fus; former Lt-Col Cmdt of Caernarvonshire and Anglesey Army Cadet Force; Maj of Beaumars 1949-51-; Lord-Lt of: Anglesey 1947-74, Gwynedd 1974-83; memb Anglesey CC 1946-74 (chm 1956-58); CStJ; *Clubs* Army and Navy, Royal Anglesey, Yacht; *Style*— Sir Richard Williams-Bulkeley, Bt, TD, JP; Plas Meigan, Beaumaris, Gwynedd

WILLIAMS-BULKELEY, Richard Thomas; s and h of Sir Richard Williams-Bulkeley, 13 Bt; *b* 25 May 1939; *Educ* Eton; *m* 1964, Sarah Susan, da of late Rt Hon Lord Justice (Sir Henry Josceline) Phillimore, OBE; 2 s (twin), 1 da; *Career* Capt Welsh Gds 1963; FRICS; *Recreations* astronomy; *Clubs* Army and Navy; *Style*— Richard Williams-Bulkeley, Esq; Red Hill, Beaumaris, Anglesey, Gwynedd

WILLIAMS-ELLIS, Elizabeth Ann; JP (Carnarvonshire 1966, Inner London 1977); da of Gp Capt Evan Christopher Lewis, RAF (d 1960), of Berwick Ct, E Sussex, and Madge Constance, *née* Pilkington; *b* 10 Nov 1935; *Educ* Rosemead Littlehampton; *m* 31 May 1958 (m dis 1975), Roger Clough Williams-Ellis, DL, s of Rupert Greaves William-Ellis, JP, DL, of Glasfryn, Caernarvonshire; 3 s (Jonathan b 1959, Christoper b 1960, Mark b 1961); *Career* Christies 1972-74, Winchester Bowring 1977-80, memb Lloyd's 1978-; memb: Arts Purchasing Ctee Nat Gallery and Museum of Wales 1966-74, Home Office Bail Project 1975-77; memb Ctee N Wales Family Planning Assoc 1963-72, vice-pres Caernarvonshire Red Cross 1964-72, chm Pencaenewydd WI 1963-66, life memb Cambrian Archaelogical Soc 1959, memb Nat Health Exec Ctee Caernarvonshire 1970-73; vice-chm: Warwick Square Residents' Assoc 1981-83, chm Westminster NADFAS 1990; memb: Ctee Westminster Soc 1987-, Hon Soc of Cymroddrian; *Recreations* history, sailing; *Clubs* Berkley; *Style*— Mrs Elizabeth Williams-Ellis, JP; 18 Wilton St, London SW1X 7AX

WILLIAMS-ELLIS, Roger Clough; DL (Caernarfonshire/Gwynedd); s of Rupert

Greaves Williams-Ellis, JP (d 1951), of Glasfryn, Pencaenewydd, Pwllheli, and Cecily Edith Williams-Ellis, MBE, *née* Hambro; *b* 12 April 1923; *Educ* Eton; *m* 1 1958 (m dis 1974), Elizabeth Ann, da of Gp Capt E Christopher Lewis (d 1965), of Berwick Court Farm, Polegate, nr Eastbourne; 3 s (Jonathan b 1959, Christopher b 1960, Mark b 1961); m 2, 1 Aug 1975, Jane Susan, da of Wing-Cdr Ralph Seymour Pearce; *Career* cmmd RE 1944, served India, Capt SORE III 14 Army 1945 (despatches), Maj SORE II ALFSEA 1946, Singapore 1946, demobilised 1947; involved in mgmnt and devpt Glasfryn Estate (primarily forestry); EAHY Prince of Wales Award; High Sheriff Caernarfonshire 1965; *Style—* Roger Williams-Ellis, Esq, DL; Glasfryn, Pencaenewydd, Pwllheli, Gwynedd LL53 6RE (☎ 0766 810 203)

WILLIAMS-FREEMAN, Lady Jean Elisabeth; da of Brig 19 Earl of Caithness (d 1965), by his 1 w, Grizel Margaret (d 1943); *b* 11 Feb 1936; *Educ* Seymour Lodge Sch Crieff, Atholl Crescent Domestic Science Coll; *m* 1961, David Peere Williams-Freeman, s of Cdr Frederick Arthur Peere Williams-Freeman, DSO and bar, RN (d 1939), of Constantia Cape; 1 s, 3 da; *Style—* The Lady Jean Williams-Freeman; Glendean Farm, Nottingham Rd, Natal, S Africa

WILLIAMS OF ELVEL, Baron (Life Peer UK 1985), of Llansantffraed in Elvel, Co Powys; Charles Cuthbert Powell Williams; CBE (1980); s of Dr Norman Powell Williams, DD (d 1943), and Muriel de Lerisson (d 1979), da of Arthur Philip Cazenove; *b* 9 Feb 1933; *Educ* Westminster, Christ Church Oxford (MA), LSE; *m* 1 March 1975, Jane Gillian, da of Maj Gervase Edward Portal (d 1960) and formerly w of Gavin Bramhall Bernard Welby; *Career* British Petroleum Co Ltd 1958-64, Bank of London and Montreal 1964-66, Eurofinance SA, Paris 1966-70, Baring Brothers & Co Ltd 1970-77 (md 1971-77), chm Price Cmmn 1977-79, md Henry Ansbacher & Co Ltd 1980-82, chief Exec Henry Ansbacher Holdings plc, chm Henry Ansbacher & Co Ltd 1982-85; *Clubs* Reform, MCC; *Style—* The Rt Hon the Lord Williams of Elvel, CBE; 48 Thurloe Sq, London SW7 2SX

WILLIAMS-WYNN, Sir (David) Watkin; 11 Bt (E 1688), of Gray's Inn, Co Middx; DL (Clwyd 1969); s of Sir Watkin Williams-Wynn, 10 Bt, CBE, JP (d 1988), and his 1 w, Margaret Jean, *née* McBean; *b* 18 Feb 1940; *Educ* Eton; *m* 1, 1968 (m dis 1981), Harriet, da of Gen Sir Norman Tailyour, KCB, DSO; 2 s (Charles b 1970, Robert b 1977), 2 da (Alexandra 1972, Lucinda (twin) b 1972); m 2, 1983, Victoria Jane Dillon, da of Lt-Col Ian Dudley De Ath, DSO, MBE (d 1960); 2 s (Nicholas Watkin b 1988, Harry Watkin (twin) b 1988); *Heir* s, Charles Williams-Wynn b 1970; *Career* Lt Royal Dragoons 1959, Maj Queen's Own Yeo 1970; memb Agric Lands Tbnl (Wales) 1978; High Sheriff Clwyd 1990; *Style—* Sir Watkin Williams-Wynn, Bt, DL; Plas-yn-Cefn, St Asaph, Clwyd LL17 0EY (☎ 0745 582200)

WILLIAMS-WYNNE, Col John Francis; CBE (1972), DSO (1945), JP (Gwynedd 1974); s of Maj Frederick Williams-Wynn, CB (s of Lady Annora Williams-Wynne, yr da of 2 Earl Manvers (Earldom extinct 1955), and ggs of Sir Watkin Williams-Wynn, 4 Bt, by his 2 w Charlotte, *née* Grenville, aunt of Richard Grenville, 1 Duke of Buckingham); Col Williams-Wynne took the name Williams-Wynne instead of Williams-Wynn in 1940; *b* 7 Feb 1947; *Educ* Oundle, Magdalene Coll Cambridge; *m* 1938, Margaret Gwendolen Hayward, da of Rev George Eliot Roper (*see* Williams-Wynne, Hon Mrs);1 s, 2 da (Merion b 1941, m 1, 1964 Maj Peter Abbot-Davies; 2 s; m 2, HH Sayyid Faher bin Taimour Al-Said; Hon Mrs David Douglas-Home, *qv*); *Career* RA 2 Lt 1929, served WWII India and Burma, Col 1954, Hon Col 7 Cadet Bn Royal Welsh Fus 1964-74; Parly candidate (C) Merioneth 1950; pres: Wales and Monmouth Cons and Unionist Assoc 1948-49, Royal Welsh Agric Soc 1967-68 (chm Cncl 1972-76), Timber Growers' Orgn 1974-76; former chm BBC Wales Agric Advsy Ctee, chm and md Cross Foxes Ltd; chm: Advsy Ctee Miny of Agric Experimental Farm Trawscoed 1955-76, Flying-Farmers Assoc 1974-82 (pres 1982-); memb: Gwynedd River Bd 1957-63, Nat Parks Cmmn 1961-66, Forestry Cmmn 1963-65, Forestry Ctee of GB 1967-76, Prince of Wales's Ctee 1971-76, Airline Users' Ctee CAA 1973-80; pt/t memb Merseyside and N Wales Electricity Bd 1953-65; JP Merioneth 1950, constable of Harlech Castle 1964-, Vice Lord-Lt Gwynedd 1980- (Lt 1974-80); Merioneth: DL 1953, Vice-Lt 1954, Lt 1957-74; CStJ, FRAgS; *Clubs* Pratt's, Army & Navy; *Style—* Col John Williams-Wynne, CBE, DSO, JP; Peniarth, Tywyn, Merioneth, Gwynedd LL36 9UD (☎ 0654 710328)

WILLIAMS-WYNNE, Hon Mrs (Veronica Frances); *née* Buxton; 3 da of Baron Buxton of Alsa by his w Pamela Mary; *b* 24 March 1953; *Educ* St Mary's Convent Ascot; *m* 1975, William Robert Charles, s of Col John Williams-Wynne, CBE, DSO, JP, *qv*; 3 da (Chloë b 1978, Leonora b 1980, Rose b 1983); *Career* farmer; *Style—* The Hon Mrs Williams-Wynne; Talybont, Tywyn, Gwynedd (☎ 0654 710101)

WILLIAMS-WYNNE, William Robert Charles; s of Col John Francis Williams-Wynne, CBE, DSO, and Margaret Gwendolin, *née* Roper, DL; *b* 7 Feb 1947; *Educ* Packwood Haugh, Eton; *m* 18 Oct 1975, Veronica Frances, da of The Lord Buxton of Alsa, MC, of Oldhall Farm, Stiffkey, Norfolk; 3 da (Chloë b 14 Oct 1978, Leonora b 20 Oct 1980, Rose b 17 Feb 1983); *Career* Williams Wynne Farms 1969, qualified FRICS 1972, JP 1984, contested Gen Election as Cons candidate for Montgomery 1974, F and GP RWAyS, memb Cncl RASE, chm WASEC, cmmr Nat Parks 1983, memb Prince of Wales Ctee 1983, Mount Pleasant Bakery 1983, Pizza Bella 1985; FRICS; *Style—* William Williams-Wynne, Esq; Williams Wynne Farms, Tywyn, Gwynedd LL36 9LG (☎ 0654 710101/2, fax 0654 710103, telex 0831 130999/131000)

WILLIAMSON, Alison Jane; s of Thomas Stanley Williamson, of Chelmick Forge, Church Stretton, Shropshire, and Susan Elizabeth, *née* Allen; *b* 3 Nov 1971; *Educ* Church Stretton Sch, Ludlow Coll, Arizona State Univ USA; *Career* archer; memb nat youth squad 1983, memb sr nat squad whilst still a jr, represented GB 1985-; competed at Sr Euro Championships 1988 and 1990 (Jr 1987 and 1989); honours incl: Jr Nat Indoor champion 1986, 1987, 1988, Jr Nat Outdoor champion 1987 and 1989, Bronze medal Jr Euro Championships 1989; broken 27 jr and sr nat records, first Br woman to achieve 1300 FITA Star; *Recreations* reading, swimming, green issues; *Style—* Miss Alison Williamson; Chelmick Forge, Church Stretton, Shropshire SY9 7HA (☎ 0694 722767)

WILLIAMSON, Anthony Evelyn (Tony); CBE (1990); s of Arthur Evelyn Williamson (d 1944), and Lucy; *b* 2 Jan 1932; *Educ* East Lane Secondary Modern Willesden Techn Coll; *m* 17 Sept 1953, Sylvia Elizabeth, da of James Alowler (d 1969); 2 da (Sandra b 1960, Joanne b 1960); *Career* md Hoover plc UK 1986-; vice-chm Queens Park Rangers FC, resigned 1987; Freeman City of London; Liveryman Worshipful Co of the Makers of Playing Cards; cncl memb CBI Wales; memb AMDEA Bd; *Recreations* sport, golf; *Style—* Tony Williamson, Esq, CBE; 7 Crofta, Lisvane, Cardiff CF4 5EW; Hoover plc, Dragonparc, Abercanaid, Merthyr Tydfil, Mid Glamorgan CF48 1PQ

WILLIAMSON, OBE Anthony William (Tony); s of Rev Joseph Williamson (d 1988), of St Paul's, Dock St, London, and Audrey Hollist, *née* Barnes (d 1974); *b* 2 Sept 1933; *Educ* Marlborough, Trinity Coll Oxford, Cuddesdon Theological Coll Oxford; *m* 10 Oct 1959, Barbara Jane, da of Louis Freeman (d 1970), of Gullet Lane, Kirby Muxlue, Leicester; 3 s (Paul Joseph b 19 March 1962, Hugh Anthony b 3 May 1964, Ian Thomas b 17 Jan 1967), 1 da (Ruth Elizabeth b 16 Sept 1960); *Career* Nat Serv 1951-53; fork-lift driver Pressed Steel Co Cowley Oxford (now Austin Rover Cowley Body Plant) 1958-87; ordained: deacon 1960, priest 1961; chm: BBC Radio Oxford Local Radio Cncl 1970-73, TGWU Cowley Body Plant 1971-87; currently diocesan dir of educn (schools) Oxford; Oxfordshire CC: memb 1973-88, jt ldr 1985-87, jt chm of educn 1987-88; Oxford City Cncl: memb 1961-67 and 1970-88, former chm of housing, ldr 1980-83, Lord Mayor 1982-83; *Recreations* squash, tennis, hill walking; *Style—* The Rev Tony Williamson, OBE; 9 The Goggs, Watlington, Oxford OX9 5JX (☎ 049 161 2143); Education Dept (Schools), Oxford Diocese, South End, Forest Hill, Oxford OX9 1EQ (☎ 08677 4340)

WILLIAMSON, (Robert) Brian; CBE; *b* 16 Feb 1945; *Educ* Trinity Coll Dublin (MA); *m* June 1986, Diane Marie Christine de Jacquier de Rosee; *Career* cmmnd HAC 1975-; PA to Rt Hon Maurice Macmillan MP (later Viscount Macmillan) 1967-71, ed Int Currency Review 1971, Parly candidate (C) Sheffield Hillsborough 1974, prospective Parly candidate Truro 1976-77, md Gerrard Nat 1978-; chm: London Int Fin Futures Exchange 1985-88 (dir 1980-), GNI Ltd 1985; memb Cncl Br Invisible Exports Cncl 1985-88; dir: Bank of Ireland Br Hldgs 1986- (memb Ct Bank of Ireland 1990-), Securities and Investmts Bd 1986-; memb Br Invisible Export Cncl Euro Ctee 1988-90; *Clubs* Kildare Univ (Dublin); *Style—* Brian Williamson, Esq, CBE; Gerrard National Hldgs plc, 33 Lombard St, London EC3 (☎ 071 623 9981)

WILLIAMSON, David Francis; CB (1984); s of Samuel Charles Wathen Williamson, of Bath, and late Marie Eileen Williamson; *b* 8 May 1934; *Educ* Tonbridge, Exeter Coll Oxford (MA); *m* 1961, Patricia Margaret, da of Eric Cade Smith, of Broadclyst, Exeter; 2 s; *Career* civil servant; MAFF 1958-65 and 1967-77, seconded to HM Dip Serv for Kennedy Round Trade Negotiations 1965-67, dep dir Gen Agric European Cmmn Brussels 1977-83, dep sec Cabinet Office 1983-87, sec gen Euro Cmmn Brussels 1987-; *Style—* David Williamson, Esq, CB; European Commission, 200 Rue de la Loi, 1049 Brussels, Belgium

WILLIAMSON, David Stewart Whittaker; JP (1972); s of John Watt Williamson (d 1951), and Annie Simpson Williamson, *née* Stewart (d 1989); *b* 18 Jan 1943; *Educ* Hamilton Acad, Univ of Glasgow; *m* 1 March 1969, Joy Delia Francis, da of Walter Elliot Francis Wilson (d 1959); 2 s (Robin b 1970, John b 1979), 2 da (Jill b 1972, Nicola b 1975); *Career* CA in private practice, ptnr McMurdo & Williamson 1967-, pt/t lectr in accountancy Univ of Glasgow 1966-76; memb Local Authy Accounts in Scotland 1986-; cnclr (Con): Burgh of Hamilton 1966-75, Hamilton Dist 1975-84; magistrate 1973-75; *Recreations* tennis, hillwalking, swimming, politics; *Style—* David Williamson, Esq, JP; 3 Alder Ave, Hamilton, Lanarkshire ML3 7LL (☎ 0698 422882); McMurdo and Williamson, Chartered Accountants, 47 Cadzow St, Hamilton ML3 6ED (☎ 0698 284888)

WILLIAMSON, Hazel Eleanor (Mrs Harvey Marshall); QC (1988); da of Geoffrey Briddon, of 26 Highlands Rd, Barton on Sea, Hants, and Nancy Briddon, *née* Nicholson; *b* 14 Jan 1947; *Educ* Wimbledon HS for Girls GPDST, St Hilda's Coll Oxford (BA); *m* 1, 24 June 1969, R Williamson; m 2, 16 Sept 1983, H Marshall, FRICS; 1 s (Quentin Noel John Marshall b 7 June 1973); *Career* called to the Bar Gray's Inn 1972; Atkin scholar of Gray's Inn; *Recreations* gardening, opera, occasional offshore sailing; *Style—* Miss Hazel Williamson, QC; 13 Old Square, Lincoln's Inn, London WC2 (☎ 071 404 4800, fax 071 405 4267, telex 22487)

WILLIAMSON, Ian Gordon; s of Edgar Williamson (d 1939), of Hove, Sussex, and Silvia Beatrice, *née* Pilkington (d 1987); *b* 28 Nov 1931; *Educ* Stowe, Univ of London (LLB); *m* 31 Aug 1974, Hylda Josephine, da of Austin Hugh Percival Carbery (d 1969), of Dublin; 2 da (Sarah Louise b 1976, Charlotte Lucy b 1977); *Career* admitted slr 1957; clerk to Worshipful Cos of: Poulters 1968-87, Farmers 1979-86, Framework Knitters 1978-80 (creating a record of 3 clerkships of livery cos held simultaneously); *Recreations* tennis, squash, walking, fly-fishing, genealogy, music; *Clubs* Naval and Military, Lansdowne, Ski; *Style—* Ian G Williamson, Esq; 47 Newstead Way, Wimbledon, London SW19 5HR (☎ 081 947 4496); 54 Wilbury Rd, Hove, E Sussex (☎ 0273 775725)

WILLIAMSON, John Peter; s of John William Stephen Williamson (d 1979), of Camberwell, and Ellen Gladys, *née* Naulls; *b* 19 Jan 1943; *Educ* Addey and Stanhope GS, Hackney Tech Coll, Thames Poly; *m* 17 Oct 1964, Dorothy Shirley Esther, da of Leonard Frederick Farmer, of Blackheath; 2 s (Earl John Grant b 1975, Craig Stephen b 1980); *Career* engr mangr Production Dept Rolex Watch Co 1960-63; jt md and financial controller Dynamic Reading Inst 1968-69, int instr in speed reading, memory and mind control techniques, fndr exec memb BIM Younger Mangr Assoc 1969-70, gp financial controller, co sec and asst md Hunter-Print Gp plc 1971-74; co comptrollers' sr analyst ITT, STC 1975; UK chm: Investigations and Operational Reviews (mangr 1976-80), ITT Bd (USA); consult CE Health 1985-86; princ J P Williamson Co 1981; dir: Prestige Micro-Systems Ltd 1979-, Guardian Services Ltd 1983-88, Guardian Services plc 1988-; fndr memb I Fin Planning 1987, co fndr Assoc of London Hobby Computer Clubs 1980; Freeman City of London 1986; FCA, FInstSM, MCIM, FInstD, MBIM, MIIM, MInstAM; *Books* author ITT/STC EDP Audit Manual; *Recreations* computers, reading, shooting, martial arts; *Style—* John Williamson, Esq; c/o Guardian Services plc, PO Box 56, London SE9 1PA (☎ 081 850 4195, 081 294 1597)

WILLIAMSON, John Robin; s of Samuel Charles Wathen Williamson, of Waterhouse, Monkton Combe, Bath, Avon, and Marie Eileen, *née* Denney (d 1962); *b* 11 May 1931; *Educ* Tonbridge, St John's Coll Cambridge (MA); *m* 28 June 1958, Rosemarie Dorothea, da of Rev Carl Hugo Stelzner (d 1967), of St Jacobus, Pesterwitz, Germany; 2 da (Catherine Anne b 1959, (Susan) Jane b 1962); *Career* Iraq Petroleum Co 1956-68, Qatar and Abu Dhabi Petroleum Cos 1968-77, BP plc 1977-82 (mangr Forties Oilfield, gen mangr Exploration and Prodn, dir BP Petrol Devpt Ltd), dir and md oil and gas subsid cos Trafalgar House plc 1984-89; FIMechE, FInstPet; *Style—* John Williamson, Esq; The Manor House, Mosterton, Dorset

WILLIAMSON, Marshal of the RAF Sir Keith Alec; GCB (1982, KCB 1979), AFC (1968); s of Percy and Gertrude Williamson; *b* 25 Feb 1928; *Educ* Bancroft's Sch, Market Harborough GS, RAF Coll Cranwell; *m* 1953, Patricia Anne, da of Wing Cdr F M N Watts; 2 s, 2 da; *Career* cmmnd 1950, served RAAF Korea, cmd RAF Gütersloh W Germany 1968-70, RCDS 1971, Dir of Air Staff Plans 1972-75, Cmdt RAF Staff Coll 1975-77, ACOS SHAPE Plans and Policy 1977-78, AOC-in-C: RAF Support Cmd 1978-80, RAF Strike Cmd and C-in-C UK Air Forces 1980-82, Chief of Air Staff 1982-85, Air ADC to HM The Queen 1982-85, Marshal of the RAF 1985; *Style—* Marshal of the RAF Sir Keith Williamson, GCB, AFC; c/o Midland Bank Ltd, 25 Notting Hill Gate, London W11

WILLIAMSON, Malcolm Benjamin Graham Christopher; CBE (1976); s of Rev George Williamson, of Sydney; *b* 1931; *Educ* Barker Coll Hornsby NSW, Sydney Conservatorium; *m* 1960, Dolores Daniel; 1 s, 2 da; *Career* composer; Master of The Queen's Music 1975-, pres Royal Philharmonic Orchestra (London) 1977-82; Hon Degree Open Univ 1983; *Style—* Malcolm Williamson, Esq, CBE; c/o Josef Weinberger Ltd, 10-16 Rathbone St, London W1P 2BJ

WILLIAMSON, (George) Malcolm; s of George Williamson (d 1969), and Margery Williamson; *b* 27 Feb 1939; *Educ* Bolton Sch; *m* 6 Oct 1963, Pamela, da of Arthur Stanley Williams (d 1979); 1 s (Stephen b 1964), 1 da (Lea b 1965); *Career* regnl gen mangr (London) Barclays Bank plc 1983-85, memb PO Bd 1985-89, md Girobank plc 1985-89, gp exec dir Standard Chartered Plc 1989-; fell Inst Bankers, companion Br Inst of Mgmnt; *Recreations* mountaineering, running, chess; *Clubs* Rucksack, Manchester Pedestrian; *Style—* Malcolm Williamson, Esq; Martyr Worthy Place,

Martyr Worthy, Winchester, Hants SO2 1AW (☎ 0962 78235); Standard Chartered Plc, London (☎ 071 280 7038)

WILLIAMSON, Dame (Elsie) Marjorie; DBE (1973); da of Leonard Williamson; *b* 30 July 1913; *Educ* Royal Holloway Coll; *Career* dep vice chllr Univ of London 1970-71 and 1971-72; princ: St Mary's Coll Univ of Durham 1955-62, Royal Holloway Coll 1962-73; lectr in physics Bedford 1945-55; memb Cwlth Scholarship Cmmn 1975-84 fell Bedford Coll London; *Style*— Dame Marjorie Williamson, DBE; Priory Barn, Lower Raydon, Ipswich, Suffolk (☎ 0473 824033)

WILLIAMSON, Prof Mark Herbert; s of Herbert Stansfield Williamson (d 1955), and Winifred Lilian, *née* Kenyon (d 1990); *b* 8 June 1928; *Educ* Groton Sch Mass USA, Rugby, ChCh Oxford (DPhil); *m* 5 April 1958, Charlotte Clara Dallas, da of Hugh Macdonald (d 1958); 1 s (Hugh b 1961), 2 da (Emma b 1963, Sophia b 1965); *Career* Nat Serv 2 Lt Oxfordshire and Buckinghamshire LI 1950-52, Capt 100 APIU TA 1952-57; demonstrator in zoology Univ of Oxford 1952-58, with Scottish Marine Biological Assoc Edinburgh 1958-62, lectr in zoology Univ of Edinburgh 1962-65, prof (fndr and head of Dept) Dept of Biology Univ of York 1965-; memb 1965-: SERC, NERC, UGC, HSE, Royal Soc, York Archaelogical Tst; FIBiol 1966; *Books* Analysis of Biological Populations (1972), Ecological Stability (1974), Island Populations (1981), Biological Invasions (1986); *Recreations* natural history, walking, photography; *Style*— Prof Mark Williamson; Dalby Old Rectory, Terrington, York YO6 4PF (☎ 0347 5244); Department of Biology, University of York, York YO1 5DD (☎ 0904 432806, fax 0904 432860)

WILLIAMSON, Martin; s of Albert Williamson (d 1986), and Jocelyn Marjorie, *née* Roe (d 1968); *b* 30 July 1944; *Educ* Wyggeston GS Leicester, Birmingham Catering Coll, Portsmouth Catering Coll, Cornel Univ NY; *m* 29 Jan 1972, Susan Anne; 1 s (James Andrew Thomas b 8 Jan 1982), 1 da (Victoria b 16 Sept 1974); *Career* trainee mangr Strand Hotels Ltd 1964-65, asst mangr Ireland Caterers Fountain Hotel Cowes 1966, Belmont Hotel & Golf Club Bermuda 1966-67; resident mangr: Queen's Hotel Southsea Hants 1968-70, Bay Roc Hotel Montego Bay Jamaica 1970-72; relief mangr Gooderson Group of Hotels Durban SA 1972-73, gen mangr Bear Hotel Havant Hants 1973-84, hotel proprietor 1984-; fndr memb The Master Innholders 1978, Freeman City of London 1978; FHCIMA; *Style*— Martin Williamson, Esq; Cleeve House, Mill Rd, Goring on Thames, Reading RG8 9DD (☎ 0491 873225); The Miller of Mansfield, High St, Goring on Thames, Reading RG8 9AW (☎ 0491 872829, fax 0491 874200)

WILLIAMSON, Gp Capt Michael Edwin; OBE; s of Ernest Harold Williamson, of Clive, Shropshire, and Hilda Ivy, *née* Hiley; *b* 13 April 1937; *Educ* Solihull Sch, RAF Coll Cranwell; *m* 20 Aug 1960, Helen Margaret Isobel, da of William Tunnicliffe (d 1954), of Farcroft, Lapworth, Warwicks; 2 s (Robin b 17 Nov 1964, James b 31 Jan 1980), 1 da (Sarah (Mrs Manford) b 28 March 1963); *Career* Coastal Command 1959-65, qualified as flying instr 1966; flying instr: Bristol Univ Air Sqdn 1966-68, Flt Cdr RAF Coll Cranwell 1968-70, CO Univ of Birmingham Air Sqdn 1970-73, RAF Staff Coll Bracknell 1973; CO no 1 trg sqdn RAF Sch of Recruit Trg Swinderby 1974-76, air staff offr HQ Univ Air Sqdns RAF Coll Cramwell 1976-77, Defence Naval Mil and Air Attache for Embassy Baghdad Irag 1978-81, CO Admin Wing and Dep station cdr RAF Conningsby 1981-83, Naval and Air Attache for Embassy Muscat Sultanate of Oman 1984-85, Gp Capt orgn HQ RAF Germany and regnl Commandant RAF Germany ATC Sqdns 1986-88; business advsr to RC Manford (Agricultural Contractor) Shropshire 1988-; fund raising chm N and W Shropshire RNIB, memb local deanery synod; *Recreations* squash, tennis, watching sport, photography, cooking, gardening, house maintence, walking, music, travel; *Clubs* RAF; *Style*— Gp Capt Michael Williamson, OBE; Rose Cottage, Morton, nr Oswestry, Shropshire SY10 8AH (☎ 0691 830518)

WILLIAMSON, Neil Morton; s of John Glyn Williamson (d 1987), and Vera May, *née* Morton; *b* 14 May 1943; *Educ* Tonbridge, Worcester Coll Oxford (MA); *Career* Henry Ansbacher & Co Ltd 1965-78 (dir 1972-78), 3i Corporate Finance Ltd 1978- (md 1979-); Liveryman Worshipful Co of Skinners' 1972, Freeman City of London 1970; *Recreations* golf, opera, ballet; *Clubs* East India; *Style*— Neil Williamson, Esq; 3i Corporate Finance Ltd, 91 Waterloo Rd, London SE1 8XP (☎ 071 928 3131, fax 071 928 1875, telex 917844)

WILLIAMSON, Sir Nicholas (Frederick Hedworth); 11 Bt (E 1642), of East Markham, Notts; s of Maj William Hedworth Williamson (ka 1942), and Diana (who m 2, 1 and last Baron Hailes, and d 1980), o da of Brig-Gen Hon Charles Lambton, DSO, 4 s of 2 Earl of Durham; suc unc, Sir Charles Williamson, 10 Bt (d 1946); *b* 26 Oct 1937; *Educ* Eton; *Heir* none; *Career* Nat Serv cmmnd 4/7 Royal Dragoon Gds 1957; farmer; *Style*— Sir Nicholas Williamson, Bt; Abbey Croft, Mortimer, Reading, Berks (☎ 0734 332324)

WILLIAMSON, Nigel; s of Neville Albert Williamson, of Arizona, and Ann Maureen Kitson; *b* 4 July 1954; *Educ* Chislehurst and Sidcup GS, UCL; *m* 1976, Magali Patricia; 2 s (Adam b 1977, Piers b 1978); *Career* ed: Tribune 1984-87, Labour Party News 1987-89, New Socialist 1987-89; diary ed The Times 1990- (political corr and columnist 1989-90); *Books* The SDP (1982), The New Right (1984); *Recreations* cricket, opera, gardening; *Clubs* St James's, Skyliners Cricket; *Style*— Nigel Williamson, Esq; High Beeches, 60 Sutherland Ave, Biggin Hill, Westerham, Kent TN16 3HG (☎ 0959 71127); c/o The Times, 1 Pennington St, London E1 (☎ 071 782 5753)

WILLIAMSON, Paul Eric Dominic; s of Peter Williamson, of London, and Mary Teresa, *née* Meagher; *b* 4 Aug 1954; *Educ* Wimbledon Coll, Univ of East Anglia (BA, MPhil); *m* 11 Aug 1984, Emmeline Mary Clare, da of James Mandley (d 1983), of London; *Career* V & A Museum: asst keeper Dept of Sculpture 1979-89, acting keeper Dept of Sculpture 1989, curator Sculpture Collection 1989-; memb: Wells Cathedral West Front Specialist Ctee 1981-83, wall paintings sub ctee Cncl for the Care of Churches 1987-, Lincoln Cathedral Fabric Cncl 1990-; expert advsr on sculpture Reviewing Ctee on the Export of Works of Art 1989-; Freeman Preston 1972; FSA 1983; *Books* An Introduction to Medieval Ivory Carvings (1982), Catalogue of Romanesque Sculpture in the Victoria and Albert Museum (1983), The Medieval Treasury: The Art of the Middle Ages in the Victoria and Albert Museum (ed 1986), The Thyssen-Bornemisza Collection: Medieval sculpture and works of art (1987), Northern Gothic Sculpture 1200-1450 (1988), Early Medieval Wall Painting and Painted Sculpture in England (ed with S Cather and D Park, 1990); *Recreations* wine, tennis, second-hand bookshops; *Style*— Paul Williamson, Esq, FSA; 53 St Maur Rd, London SW6 4DR (☎ 071 384 1446); Sculpture Collection, Victoria and Albert Museum, South Kensington, London SW7 2RL (☎ 071 938 8399, fax 071 938 8477)

WILLIAMSON, Philip Nigel; s of Leonard James Williamson, and Doris, *née* Chapell; *b* 23 Sept 1948; *Educ* Mill Hill, Newcastle Univ (CBA, BArch); *m* 27 May 1983, Victoria Lois, da of Joseph Samuel Brown, of Clwyd, N Wales; 2 s (Nicholas James b 1984, Christopher Patrick b 1988); *Career* architect; princ PNW Design & Co 1979-; chm and md: PNW Associates Ltd (architects and interior designers) 1985-, PNW Properties Ltd 1985-; memb RIBA; *Recreations* sailing, tennis, winter sports; *Clubs* The Queens, London Riverside Racquet Centre; *Style*— Philip Williamson, Esq; 8 Netherton Rd, St Margarets, Twickenham, Middlesex (☎ 081 892 3076); 6 North Rd, Richmond, Surrey (☎ 081 878 8427)

WILLIAMSON, Robert Algie; s of Thomas Algie Williamson (d 1955), of Glasgow, and Laura Evelyn, *née* Littler; *b* 11 Aug 1931; *Educ* Merchiston Castle Edinburgh, Harvard Business Sch (Advanced Mgmnt Prog); *m* 25 Aug 1956, (Sheila) Patricia Langdon (d 1985), da of Air-Cdre Richard Grice, OBE, DFC (d 1952);2 s (Eric Duncan b 26 June 1958, d 1958, Roy Eric b 26 Oct 1963), 2 da (Susan Kay b 18 Feb 1960, Lois Ann b 31 Aug 1961); *Career* RAF Pilot Offr Flying Trg 1954-56; sec and fin dir John Brown & Co (Clydebank) Ltd 1958-67; fin dir: Upper Clyde Shipbuilders Ltd Glasgow 1967-68, Surface Electronics Ltd Poole, Dorset 1984-; gp fin dir Samuel Osborn & Co Ltd Sheffield 1968-78; dir: Seatic Marine Ltd Dorset 1984-, Forelle Ltd 1987-, Bourne Steel Ltd 1988-; Freeman Worshipful Co of Cutlers of Hallamshire 1972; FBIM; *Recreations* fishing, sailing; *Clubs* RAF; *Style*— Robert Williamson, Esq; Chamberlaynes Farm House, Bere Regis, nr Wareham, Dorset BH20 7LS (☎ 0929 471 357); office: (☎ 0202 674 333, fax 0202 678 028, telex , 41184 SURFEL S)

WILLIAMSON, Robert Glenn Edward; s of John David Putnam Williamson, and Eileen Mary, *née* Stokes; *b* 1 Aug 1930; *Educ* Univ of Toronto, Ontario Coll of Art (BA); *partner*, Juliet Barclay, 4 c (Robert Adrian b 1959, Lisa Maria b 1961, Benedict James b 1966, Tamara Nell b 1968); *Career* gold prospector Artic Quebec Cuba 1946-56, sailed from Canada to Gulf of Mexcio and from Hamburg to Cannes 1950 and 1956, made mosaics for Picasso Cannes 1956-57, mosaic designer and maker London 1958-61, freelance advtg and graphic designer 1961-62, art dir/creative dir Alexander - Butterfield and Ayer 1962-69, fndr Robert Williamson Design International Packaging and Corp Graphics 1970-; as design conslt visited: China 1980 and 1983, Cuban Design Cncl and Instituto Superior de Diseno Industrial Havana Cuba (UN rep) 1986, Brazil 1987, Zimbabwe (UN rep) 1989; dir Spanish Caribbean Arts Network/Semana Cubana 1988-89; memb Inst of Packaging, FSIAD; *Books* The Schooner Driftwood, Mosaics, Projects, Dogrib Dictionary, How to be a Doctor; *Recreations* skiing, sailing, painting, exploring; *Style*— Robert Williamson, Esq; Robert Williamson Design, 95 Great Titchfield St, London W1F 7FP (☎ 071 636 8542, fax 071 323 3155)

WILLIAMSON, Robert Martin Eyre (Robin); s of Maj Henry Martin Williamson, MBE, of Balcombe, Sussex, and Margaret Ruth, *née* Lyons; *b* 27 July 1938; *Educ* Tonbridge Sch, Magdalen Coll Oxford (BA); *m* 24 Jan 1970, Priscilla Anne, da of Stephen Benedict Hatch-Barnwell, CBE (d 1989); 2 s (Jonathan b 1970, Timothy b 1975); *Career* Int Computers Ltd 1963-77, hd professional servs Data Logic Ltd 1977-79, dir mktg servs Aregon Int Ltd 1979-84, dir Mandarin Communications Ltd 1984-89, md Context Ltd 1989-; FBCS 1977; *Books* Penguin Dictionary of Computers (co-ed 1970, 3 edn 1985), Practical Systems Analysis (co-author 1975), Electronic Publishing (1988), Electronic Text Archiving (1989), The Knowledge Warehouse (1989); *Recreations* walking, painting in watercolours; *Style*— Robin Williamson, Esq; Greenaway, London Rd, Balcombe, West Sussex RH17 6HS (☎ 0444 811519); Context Rd, Tranley House, Tranley Mews, London NW3 2QW (☎ 071 267 7055, fax 071 267 2745)

WILLIAMSON, Prof Robin Charles Noel; s of James Charles Frederick Lloyd Williamson (d 1970), of Hove, Sussex, and Helena Frances, *née* Madden (d 1984); *b* 19 Dec 1942; *Educ* Rugby, Univ of Cambridge and Bart's Med Sch (BA, BChir, MA, MB MChir, MD); *m* 21 Oct 1967, Judith Marjorie, da of Douglas John Bull (d 1982), of London; 3 s (Richard b 1968, Edward b 1970, James b 1977); *Career* house surgn Bart's 1968, surgical registrar Royal Berks Hosp Reading 1971-73, sr surgical registrar Bristol Royal Infirmary 1973-75, clinical and res fell surgery Mass Gen Hosp and Harvard Med Sch 1975-76; Univ of Bristol: lectr in surgery 1977, conslt sr lectr in surgery 1977-79, prof of surgery 1979-87; prof and dir of surgery Royal Postgraduate Med Sch and Hammersmith Hosp 1987-; Arris and Gale lectr RCS 1977-78, Moynihan fell Assoc of Surgns of GB and I 1979, Hunterian Prof RCS 1981-82, Res Med Br Soc of Gastroenterology 1982, co sec Br Jl of Surgery Soc 1983-91, pres Pancreatic Soc of GB and I 1984-85, sec gen World Assoc of Hepatopancreatobiliary Surgery 1990- (treas 1986-); Finlayson lectr RCS Glasgow 1985, Sir Gordon Bell lectr RACS (NZ) 1988; Hazlett prize RCS 1970; FRCS 1972; *Books* Colonic Carcinogenesis (jtly, 1982), General Surgical Operations (jtly, 1987), Emergency Abdominal Surgery (jtly, 1990), Surgical Management (jtly, 1991); *Recreations* travel, military uniforms and history; *Clubs* United Oxford and Cambridge; *Style*— Prof Robin Williamson; The Barn, 88 Lower Rd, Gerrards Cross, Bucks SL9 8LB (☎ 0753 889816); Department of Surgery RPMS, Hammersmith Hospital, Ducane Rd, London W12 0NN (☎ 081 740 3210, fax 081 740 3179)

WILLINGHAM, Derrick; *b* 29 Dec 1932; *Educ* Brunts GS, Mansfield Notts, Nottingham Univ (BA); *m* 1956, Nancy Patricia, *née* Webb; 1 s, 1 da; *Career* chm Hayward Tyler Pump Gp 1977-86; pres chartered Inst of Mgmnt Accountants 1982-83 (memb cncl 1975-86, vice-pres 1980-82); sr vice-pres Vulcan Indust Serv 1985-87; pres Sterling Pump Co's 1984-85; chm Br Pump Mfrs Assoc 1984-85 (memb cncl 1977-85); FCMA; *Recreations* golf, tennis, travel; *Clubs* RAC, Woburn Golf and Country, Dunstable Downs Golf; *Style*— Derrick Willingham, Esq; TWIL Limited, PO Box 119, Shepchote Lane, Sheffield S9 1TY (☎ 0742 443388); Lindrick Lodge, Lindrick Road, Woodsetts, Nr Worksop, Notts S818 A7 (☎ 0909 568276)

WILLINK, Alma Marion; JP (City of Manchester 1949), DL (Gtr Manchester 1981); da of Rev Hendrick Chignell, sometime Rector of Northenden, Cheshire; *Educ* Manchester Univ (MA); *m* 1930, Lt-Col Francis Arthur Willink (sometime dep chm Lancashire United Transport Ltd), and 2 s of Henry Willink, JP (1 cousin of Wiliam Willink, f of Sir Henry Urmston Willink, 1 Bt, MC, PC, QC); *Career* chm City of Manchester Bench 1978 and 1979; pres Manchester Luncheon Club 1984-85; *Style*— Mrs Francis Willink, JP, DL; 141 The Green, Worsley, M28 4PA

WILLINK, Sir Charles William; 2 Bt (UK 1957), of Dingle Bank, City of Liverpool; s of Rt Hon Sir Henry Urmston Willink, 1 Bt, MC, QC (d 1973, ggs of Daniel Willink, sometime Dutch Consul in Liverpool), and his 1 w, Cynthia Frances (d 1959), da of Herbert Morley Fletcher, MD, FRCP, of Harley Street; *b* 10 Sept 1929; *Educ* Eton, Trinity Coll Cambridge (MA, PhD); *m* 7 Aug 1954, Elizabeth, er da of Humfrey Andrewes, of North Grove, Highgate; 1 s, 1 da; *Heir* s, Edward Daniel Willink b 18 Feb 1957; *Career* housemaster Eton 1964-77; *Books* Euripides Orestes (ed with commentary, 1986); *Style*— Sir Charles Willink, Bt; 20 North Grove, Highgate, London N6 4SL (☎ 071 340 3996)

WILLINK, William Alfred; s of Derek Edward Willink (d 1985), of Mirefoot, Burneside, Cumbria, and Joan Leslie, *née* Smallwood; *b* 11 July 1931; *Educ* Marlborough, St John's Coll Oxford (BA, MA); *m* 7 April 1956, Hester Anne Dymond, da of Wilfred Edmund Mounsey, of Helsington Lodge, Brigsteer, Cumbria; 1 s (Daniel b 1961), 2 da (Jessica b 1963, Priscilla b 1965); *Career* Barclays Bank: local dir Reading 1962-66, local dir Maidstone 1966-70, sr local dir Maidstone 1970-81, sr local dir Preston 1981-87; chm: Kent Nat Savings Ctee 1973-77, Maidstone Cancer Res Campaign 1978-81; fndr govr Satro Cumbria 1982-87, chm and managing tstee Francis C Scott Charitable Tst (tstee 1983-); *Recreations* fly-fishing, travel, fell walking; *Style*— William Willink, Esq; Dalton House, Burton-in-Kendal, Cumbria LA6 1NH (☎ 0524 781203)

WILLIS, Antony Martin Derek; s of Thomas Martin Willis, of Marton, NZ, and Dawn Marie, *née* Christensen; *b* 29 Nov 1941; *Educ* Wanganui Collegiate Sch Wanganui NZ, Victoria Univ Wellington NZ (LLB); *m* 1, 10 Feb 1962 (m dis), Diane Elizabeth, da of late Frederick Willis Gorton (d 1987), of Feilding, NZ; 3 da (Kirsty Elizabeth b 13 April 1963, Sara Jane b 7 June 1966, Nicola Mary b 6 Nov 1968); m 2, 12 April 1975,

Diana Alice, da of Robert Dermot McMahon Williams, of Lenham, Kent; 1 s (Matthew William Dermot b 22 Aug 1988), 2 da (Charlotte Emily Christensen b 5 Jan 1978, Joanna Catherine Dalrymple b 7 Dec 1981); *Career* slr; ptnr: Perry Wylie Pope & Page NZ 1967-70, Coward Chance London 1973-87 (managing ptnr 1987); Clifford Chance (merged firm of Coward Chance with Clifford Turner): jt managing ptnr 1987-88, sr litigation and arbitration ptnr 1989-; memb: Law Soc, City of London Slrs Co, American Arbitration Assoc, Int Bar Assoc, Wellington Dist Law Soc (NZ); Freeman City of London 1975, Liveryman of Worshipful Co of Slrs; ACIArb; *Recreations* music, gardening; *Clubs* Reform, Hurlingham; *Style—* Antony Willis, Esq; 28 Chipstead St, London SW6 (☎ 071 731 4735); Clifford Chance, Royex House, Aldermanbury Sq, London EC2V 7LO (☎ 071 600 0808, fax 071 726 8561, telex 8959991 COWARD G)

WILLIS, David; s of William Willis (d 1986), of Consett, Co Durham, and Rachael Elizabeth, *née* Cant; *b* 13 Jan 1949; *Educ* Consett GS, Univ of Edinburgh (BArch); *m* 12 July 1970, Patricia Ann, da of Charles Cedric Endley, DSO, of Cape Town, S Africa; 2 s (Robert b 1984, Steven b 1988), 1 da (Jennifer b 1978); *Career* architect; ptnr Lang Willis & Galloway, architect Thirlestane Castle Tst 1987-; dir: The Caledonian Racing Club, Cobbscot New Lanark Restoration 1974- (awards incl: RICS The Times Conservation, Europa Nostra Medal of Honours 1988), Old Coll Univ of Edinburgh 1974-87; RIBA, RIAS; *Recreations* racehorse owner; *Clubs* Caledonian Racing; *Style—* David Willis, Esq; 3 Maryfield Place, Bonnyrigg, Midlothian (☎ 031 663 5487); 38 Dean Park Mews, Edinburgh EH4 1ED (☎ 031 315 2940)

WILLIS, Baron (Life Peer UK 1963), of Chislehurst, Co Kent; Edward Henry Willis (Ted); s of Alfred John Willis, of Tottenham, London, and Maria Harriet Willis; *b* 13 Jan 1918; *Educ* Downhills Central Sch Tottenham; *m* 12 Aug 1944, Audrey Mary, da of Alfred Hale, of Enfield, Middx; 1 s (Hon John Edward b 4 April 1946), 1 da (Hon Sally Ann Hale (Hon Mrs Murray) b 8 Jan 1951); *Career* served WWII Royal Fus; sits as Lab Peer in House of Lords; playwright and writer; dir: World Wide Pictures 1967-, Vitalcall Ltd 1983-, Netherburn Ltd 1989-; pres Authors' Lending and Copyright Soc; life pres Writers Guild of GB; FRTS, FRSA; *Books Incl:* Whatever Happened to Tom Mix? (autobiography 1970), The Churchill Commando (1977), The Naked Sun (1980), Spring at the Winged Horse (1983), The Green Leaves of Summer (1988), A Problem for Mother Christmas (1988), The Bells of Autumn (1990); *Plays incl* Hot Summer Night, New (1957), A Slow Roll of Drums (1964), Mr Polly (1977), Stardust (1983), Battle at Lavender Lodge (1985), Tommy Boy (1988), Intent to Kill (1989), Doctor on the Boil (1989); *Films include* Woman in a Dressing Gown (1958, later also a play), A Long Way to Shiloh (1969), Mrs Harris Goes to Monte Carlo (1986), Spy on Ice (1987), The Valley of the Dream (1987), Mrs Harris Goes to Moscow (1988), Mrs Harris Goes to Majorca (1989); *TV scripts include* Dixon of Dock Green, Crime of Passion, Black Beauty, Valley of Kings, Sergeant Cork, A Home for Animals, Racecourse; *Clubs* Garrick, Wig and Pen; *Style—* The Rt Hon the Lord Willis; 5 Shepherds Green, Chislehurst, Kent

WILLIS, Frank William; s of Prof Frank McIlveen Willis, of South Littleton, Worcs, and Jonette Constance, *née* Van Praag; *b* 6 April 1947; *Educ* Bradford GS, Magdalen Coll Oxford (BA, BPhil); *m* 15 July 1972, Jennifer Carol, da of Cecil Stanley Arnold (d 1964); 2 da (Laura b 1973, Harriet b 1976); *Career* diplomat; third sec FCO 1971, third then second sec HM Embassy Moscow 1972-74, Ecole Nationale D'Administration Paris 1974-75, first sec FCO 1975-79, principal then asst sec DTI 1980-87; controller of advertising IBA 1987-90, dir advtg and Sponsorship ITV Cmmn; memb: Marketing Soc, RTS; *Recreations* reading, cinema, hill walking; *Style—* Frank Willis, Esq; IBA, 70 Brompton Rd, London SW3 1EY (☎ 071 584 7011, fax 071 589 5533, telex 24345)

WILLIS, Maj-Gen John Brooker; CB (1981); William Noel Willis (d 1976), and Elaine (d 1978); *b* 28 July 1926; *Educ* Redhill Tech Coll; *m* 1959, Yda Belinda Jane, da of Lt-Col G C Firbank, MC (d 1947); 2 s (Christopher b 1960, Hugo b 1968), 2 da (Richenda b 1961, Abigail b 1967); *Career* cmmnd 10 Hussars 1947, cmd 1964-67, Brig 1974, Maj-Gen 1977, dir gen Fighting Vehicles and Engrg Equipment 1977-81, def mktg conslt; *Recreations* golf, aviation, amateur dramatics; *Clubs* Army and Navy; *Style—* Maj-Gen John Willis, CB; c/o Lloyds Bank plc, 26 Hammersmith Broadway, London W6 7AH

WILLIS, John Frederic Earle d'Anyers; OBE (1945); s of Rev Canon F E d'Anyers Willis (d 1940), and Agnes Hilda, *née* Postlethwaite (d 1954); (paternal ancestry, *see* Burke's Landed Gentry 18th Edn, vol ii); *b* 14 March 1908; *Educ* Marlborough; *m* 1, 6 Aug 1938 (m dis 1946), Constance Flora Margaret, da of late Frederick Edward Hooper, of Madras, India; 1 s (John b 1940); m 2, 20 July 1946, Joan Mary Granvaile, da of late Lt-Col Charles Loughlin Meyler O'Malley, RFA; 1 s (Peter b 1949), 1 da (Anne b 1952); *Career* serv WWII Lt-Col 1940-45 Paiforce, Iraq, Persia, Egypt, Lebanon; chm Gillanders Arbuthnot & Co Ltd India; dir: Anglo Thai Corp Ltd, AD International Ltd (dep chm), Charrington Gardner & Locket Ltd, Home County Newspapers; chm J Gerrard & Sons Ltd; *Recreations* shooting, bridge; *Clubs* Bourne Farnham Surrey; *Style—* John Willis, OBE; South Court, Crondall, Farnham, Surrey GU10 5QF (☎ 0252 850711)

WILLIS, Prof John Raymond; s of John Vindon George Willis, of Bicester, Oxon, and Loveday Gwendoline, *née* Parkin; *b* 27 March 1940; *Educ* Southall GS, Imperial Coll London (BSc, ARCS, PhD, DIC), Univ of Cambridge (MA); *m* 3 Oct 1964, Juliette Louise, da of Horace Albert Edward Ireland (d 1979); 3 da (Estelle b 1966, Lucy b 1967, Charlotte b 1969); *Career* asst lectr Imperial Coll London 1962-64, res assoc Courant Inst NY 1964-65, asst dir of res Univ of Cambridge 1968-72 (sr asst 1965-67), prof of Applied Mathematics Univ of Bath 1972-, ed in chief Jl of the Mechanics and Physics of Solids 1982-; memb: SRC Mathematics Ctee 1975-78, SERC Mathematics Ctee 1984-87, Int Congress Ctee, Int Union for Theoretical and Applied Mechanics 1982-90); FIMA 1966; *Recreations* music, swimming; *Style—* Prof John Willis; School of Mathematical Sciences, University of Bath, Bath BA2 7AY (☎ 0225 826241, fax 0225 826492)

WILLIS, Rear Adm Kenneth Henry George; CB (1981); s of Henry (d 1976), and Elsie Nellie Willis; *Educ* St Olaves GS, Jesus Coll Cambridge (BA); *m* Sheila Catherine; 3 da (Lois, Laura, Sharon); *Career* Chief of Staff to CIC Naval Home Cmmnd to Sept 1981; dir gen Home Farm Trust Ltd Bristol 1982-88; memb IOD, FRSA; *Recreations* rowing, life-saving, amateur theatricals; *Style—* Rear Adm Kenneth H G Willis, CB; c/o Barclays Bank, 1 Manvers St, Bath, Avon

WILLIS, Robert George Dylan; MBE (1982); s of Edward Woodcock Willis (d 1982), and Anne Margaret, *née* Huntington; *b* 30 May 1949; *Educ* King Edward VI Royal GS Guildford; *m* 1980, Juliet, da of William and Barbara Smail, of Wilts; 1 da (Katie-Anne b 1984); *Career* professional cricketer, broadcaster, and chief exec Nat Sporting Club; capt: Warwickshire 1980-84, England 1982-84; 90 tests for England, record number of wickets for England on retirement (325); chm In Style Promotions Ltd; *Books* co-author of eight cricket books; *Recreations* classical music, wine, real ale; *Clubs* MCC, Corinthian Casuals Football, Nat Sporting, RAC, Middx County Cricket, Surrey County Cricket, Warwickshire County Cricket; *Style—* Robert Willis, Esq, MBE; 22 Fitzwilliam Rd, London SW4 0DN; Café Royal, 68 Regent St, London W1R 6EL (☎ 071 437 0144)

WILLIS, His Hon Judge Stephen Murrell; s of John Henry Willis (d 1936), of Hadleigh, Suffolk, and Eileen Marian, *née* Heard (d 1984); *b* 21 June 1929; *Educ* Christ Church Cathedral Choir Sch Oxford (chorister), Bloxham Sch; *m* 1, 1953 (m dis 1974), Jean Irene, *née* Eve; 1 s (Rev Geoffrey Willis), 3 da (Susanna (Mrs Ravestein-Willis), Barbara (Mrs Tregear), Jill (Mrs Warner)); m 2, 1975, Doris Florence Davies, *née* Redding; 2 step da (Mrs Jill Lockhart, Mrs Janette Davies); *Career* Nat Serv RS 16 Ind Para Bde Gp 1948-50; articles Gotetee and Goldsmith 1950-55, admitted slr 1955; ptnr: Chamberlin Talbot and Bracey 1955-63, Pearless de Rougemont & Co 1964-85; dep circuit judge 1975-80, rec 1980-85, circuit judge 1986-; fndr The Suffolk Singers 1962, fndr and dir The Prodigal Singers 1964-; *Recreations* performing early music, sailing, walking, travel; *Clubs* The Noblemen and Gentlemen's Catch; *Style—* His Hon Judge Willis; Croydon Combined Court Centre, Altyre Rd, Croydon CR9 5AB (☎ 081 681 2533)

WILLIS FLEMING, Hon Mrs (Elizabeth Sarah); *née* James; da of 4 Baron Northbourne; *b* 1933; *m* 1960, Michael Edward Willis Fleming; 1 s, 1 da; *Style—* The Hon Mrs Willis Fleming; Updown Farm, Betteshanger, Deal, Kent CT14 0EF

WILLIS-STOVOLD, Andrew; *see*: Stovold, Andrew (Andy)

WILLISON, Lt-Gen Sir David John; KCB (1973), OBE (1958), MC (1945); s of Brig Arthur Cecil Willison, DSO, MC, of Trentishoe Manor, Parracombe, N Devon, and Hyacinth D'Arcy, er da of Maj Philip Urban Walter Vigors, DSO, of Basingstoke; *b* 25 Dec 1919; *Educ* Wellington, RMA Woolwich; *m* 1941, Betty Vernon (d 1989), da of Air Vice-Marshal Sir Leslie Bates, KBE; 1 s (Robin), 2 da (Celia, Janet); *Career* 2 Lt RE 1939, served NW Europe, Java, Malaya, Egypt, Middle East, Berlin and Aden, CO 38 Engr Regt 1960-63; BGS: Intelligence MOD 1967-70, HQ Northag 1970-71; dir of Serv Intelligence MOD 1971-72, dep chief of Def Staff Intelligence MOD 1972-75, dir gen Intelligence 1975-78, Col Cmdt RE 1973-82, Chief RE 1977-82; conslt: Int Affrs Nat Westminster Bank Gp 1980-84, Affrs Co NatWest Investmnts Mgmnt 1984-; pres SJA Western Area Hants 1987-, chm RE Widows' Soc 1987-; Freeman City of London; *Clubs* Naval and Military, Royal Lymington Yacht; *Style—* Lt-Gen Sir David Willison, KCB, OBE, MC; Long Barton, Lower Pennington Lane, Lymington, Hants (☎ 0590 677194)

WILLISON, Sir John Alexander; OBE (1964), QPM (1970), DL (Worcs 1968); s of John Willison Gow Willison (d 1942), and Mabel (d 1964); *b* 3 Jan 1914; *Educ* Sedbergh; *m* 1947, Jess Morris, da of late John Bruce; *Career* chief constable: Berwick Roxburgh and Selkirk Police 1952-58, Worcs Constabulary 1958-67, W Mercia Constabulary 1967-74; KStJ 1970; kt 1970; *Recreations* country pursuits; *Style—* Sir John Willison, OBE, QPM, DL; Ravenhills Green, Lulsley, Worcs (☎ 0886 21688)

WILLMAN, John Romain; s of John Sydney Willman, and Millicent Charlotte, *née* Thornton; *b* 27 May 1949; *Educ* Bolton Sch Lancs, Jesus Coll Cambridge (MA), Westminster Coll Oxford (CertE); *m* 1 April 1978, Margaret, da of Dr John Shanahan (d 1981), of Maida Vale; 1 s (Michael b 1982), 2 da (Kate b 1984, Claire b 1987); *Career* asst teacher Brentford Sch for Girls Middx 1972-76, fin researcher Consumers' Assoc 1976-79, ed of Taxes and Assessment (jls of Inland Revenue Staff Fedn) 1979-83, pubns mangr Peat Marwick Mitchell & Co 1983-85, gen sec Fabian Soc 1985-89, freelance writer and journalist, ed Consumer Policy Review 1990-; fell Inst for Pub Policy Res; *Books* Make Your Will (1989), Labour's Electoral Challenge (1989), Sorting out Someone's Will (1990), Lloyds Bank Tax Guide (4 edn 1990), Which? Guide to Planning and Conservation (1990), Work for Yourself (1991); *Recreations* skiing, making the Lab Pty think; *Clubs* Wessex Cave, Inst of Contemporary Art; *Style—* John Willman, Esq; 33 Reservoir Rd, London SE4 2NU (☎ 071 639 3845, fax 071 277 7615)

WILLMER, John Franklin; QC (1967); s of Rt Hon Sir Henry Gordon Willmer (d 1983), of London, and Mary Barbara, *née* Hurd; according to the privately printed History of the Wilmer Family (1888), the name in various spellings is found in public records from the 12th century and existed prior to the Norman Conquest; *b* 30 May 1930; *Educ* Winchester, CCC Oxford (MA); *m* 1, 1958 (m dis 1979), Nicola Ann Dickinson; 1 s (Stephen), 3 da (Susan, Jennifer, Katherine); m 2, 1979, Margaret Lilian, da of Chester B Berryman, of Marlborough, Wilts; *Career* Nat Serv 1949-50, 2 Lt TA 1950-57, Capt; called to the Bar Inner Temple 1955, bencher 1975; memb: Panel of Lloyd's arbitrators in Salvage Cases 1967, Panel from which wreck cmmrs apptd 1967-79; gen cmmr Income Tax for Inner Temple 1982, re-appointed a wreck cmmr 1987; *Recreations* walking; *Clubs* United Oxford and Cambridge Univ; *Style—* J F Willmer, Esq, QC; Flat 4, 23 Lymington Rd, London NW6 1HZ (☎ 081 435 9245); 7 King's Bench Walk, Temple, London EC4Y 7DS (☎ 071 583 0404, telex 887491 KBLAW)

WILLMER, John Honour; OBE (1989); s of Richard Newman Willmer (d 1963), of Friars Ct, Clanfield, Oxford, and Mary Elizabeth Willmer (d 1974); *b* 11 Nov 1920; *Educ* Kingswood Sch Bath, Bradford Tech Coll; *m* 8 Feb 1964, Frances Irene, da of Alan Amory Jackson (d 1959); 1 s (Charles b 1970), 2 da (Carol b 1966, d 1985, Mary b 1967, d 1975); *Career* environmentally sensitive farming open to public; former chm: West Oxon Tech Coll 1955-, Oxfordshire NFU 1965-, Westminster Teacher Trg Coll 1965-; Cliff Coll 1975-; NFU (memb Land Drainage Ctee 1974-86), chm Oxfordshire YFC 1959 (memb Mgmnt and Travel Ctee), memb Clanfield Parish Cncl 1970- (former chm), jt divnl treas Methodist Home Mission Div Westminster 1975-90; FRAgS; *Recreations* conservation; *Style—* John Willmer, Esq, OBE; Friars Ct, Clanfield, Oxford OX8 2SU

WILLMORE, Prof (Albert) Peter; s of Albert Mervyn Willmore (d 1957), and Kathleen Helen, *née* O'Rourke (d 1987); *b* 28 April 1930; *Educ* Holloway Sch London, UCL (BSc, PhD); *m* 1, 1962 (m dis 1972), Geraldine Anne; 2 s (Nicholas b 1963, Andrew b 1964); m 2, 6 Aug 1972, Stephanie Ruth, da of Leonard Alden, of Surrey; 1 s (Ben b 1976), 1 da (Lucy b 1973); *Career* res fell, lectr, reader and prof of physics UCL 1957-72; prof of space res Univ of Birmingham 1972-; Fell RAS 1960-, Tsiolkowsky medal USSR 1987; *Recreations* ancient history, music, sailing; *Style—* Prof Peter Willmore; School of Physics and Space Research, University of Birmingham, Edgbaston, Birmingham B15 2TT (☎ 021 414 6452, fax 021 414 6709, telex 338938)

WILLMOT, Derrick Robert; s of Jack Willmot (d 1982), and Olive, *née* Yarnall (d 1986); *b* 29 April 1947; *Educ* Chesterfield Boys GS, UCH London (BDS, DDO); *m* 9 Jan 1971, Patricia Marie, da of Robert Creighton, of San Luis, Menorca, Spain; 2 s (Mark b 1973, Andrew b 1974); *Career* dental house surgn Royal Portsmouth Hosp 1970, gen dental practitioner Ashbourne Derbyshire 1971, sr registrar UCH 1979 (registrar 1977), conslt orthodontist Chesterfield Royal Hosp and Sheffield Dental Hosp 1984-; sec conslt orthodontists gp 1989-; memb Round Table 1972-87: Ashbourne, St Albans, Chesterfield; memb Chesterfield Scarsdale Rotary Club 1988, vice chm govrs Chesterfield Sch; FDS 1978, MOrthRCS 1987; *Style—* Derrick Willmot, Esq; Ashcroft, Matlock Rd, Walton, Chesterfield, Derbyshire S42 7LD (☎ 0246 239847); Chesterfield and North Derbyshire Royal Hospital, Calow, Chesterfield, Derbyshire S44 5BL (☎ 0246 277271)

WILLMOTT, Dennis James; CBE (1988), QFSM (1981); s of James Arthur Willmott (d 1970), and Esther Winifred Maude, *née* Styles (d 1989); *b* 10 July 1932; *Educ* St Albans County GS; *m* 1958, Mary Patricia, da of Walter Ball-Currey (d 1975), of Liverpool; 2 s (Christopher, Andrew); *Career* served Korea 1951-52, Royal Norfolk

Regt 1950-57, Sgt; joined Fire Serv 1957; dep chief fire offr: Isle of Wight Fire Bde 1972-74, Wilstshire 1976; chief staff offr London Fire Bde 1976-81, dep chief fire offr London 1981-83; chief fire offr Merseyside Fire Bde 1983-88; gp contingency mangr Avon Rubber plc 1988; *Recreations* walking; *Clubs* Royal Br Legion; *Style—* Dennis Willmott, Esq, CBE, QFSM; 27 Highlands, Potterne, Devizes (☎ 0380 725672)

WILLMOTT, Maj-Gen Edward George; CB (1990), OBE (1980); s of Thomas Edward Willmott (d 1983), of Alvechurch, Worcs, and Eileen Ruth, *née* Murphy; *b* 18 Feb 1936; *Educ* Redditch Co HS, Gonville and Caius Coll Cambridge (MA); *m* 18 June 1960, Sally Penelope, da of George Philip Banyard (d 1946), of Long Rd, Cambridge; 2 s (Philip b 1961, Christopher b 1964), 1 da (Georgina b 1962); *Career* RMCS Shrivenham and Camberley 1967-68, DAA & QMG 8 Inf Bde 1969-70, OC 8 Field Sqdn RE 1971-73, memb Directing Staff RMCS Shrivenham 1973-75; CO: 23 Engr Regt 1976, 2 Armd Div Engr Regt 1976-78, Col MGO Secretariat MOD (PE) 1979-80, Cdr 30 Engr Bde, RCDS 1983, dep Cmdt RMCS Shrivenham 1984-85, pres (Army) Ordnance Bd MOD 1986-88 (vice pres 1985-86), dir gen Weapons (Army) MOD 1988-90, ret Maj-Gen 1991; chief exec Construction Indust Trg Bd 1991-; pres Inst of Royal Engrs; FICE 1989, CEng 1989; *Recreations* sailing, skiing, walking, gardening; *Clubs* IOD; *Style—* Maj-Gen E G Willmott, CB, OBE; (☎ 071 489 1662)

WILLMOTT, Prof John Charles; CBE (1983); s of Arthur George Willmott (d 1960), of Goodmayes, Essex, and Annie Elizabeth, *née* Darby (d 1964); *b* 1 April 1922; *Educ* Bancroft's Sch Woodford, Imperial Coll London (ARCS, BSc, PhD); *m* 10 May 1952, Sheila Madeleine, da of Stanley Dumbell, OBE (d 1966), of Birkenhead; 2 s (Nigel b 24 Sept 1956, Philip b 13 March 1963), 1 da (Stella b 19 Apr 1954); *Career* serv WWII Lt REME 1942-46; Univ of Liverpool: asst lectr 1948-49, lectr 1949-58, sr lectr 1958-63, reader 1963-64; Univ of Manchester: prof nuclear physics 1964-67, dir physical labs 1967-89 (pro vice chllr 1982-85); memb: Physics Bd SERC 1968-73 and 1976-82 (cncl 1978-82), Physical Scis Sub Ctee UGC 1970-80, NATO Sci for Stability Steering Gp 1981-; FInstP 1968; *Books* Tables of Coefficients for the Analysis of Triple Angular Correlations of Gamma-Rays from Aligned Nuclei (1968), Atomic Physics (1975); *Recreations* walking; *Style—* Prof John Willmott, CBE; 37 Hall Moss Lane, Bramhall, Cheshire SK7 1RB (☎ 061 439 4169); Department Research and Technology Transfer, Vice Chancellors Dept, University of Manchester M13 9PL (☎ 061 275 2017)

WILLMOTT, Peter; s of Benjamin Merriman Willmott (d 1959), and Dorothy Nellie, *née* Waymouth (d 1926); *b* 18 Sept 1923; *Educ* Tollington Sch London, Ruskin Coll Oxford, Univ of London (BSc); *m* 31 July 1948, Phyllis Mary, da of Alec George Noble (d 1966); 2 s (Lewis b 1949, Michael b 1952); *Career* res offr Inst of Community Studies 1960-64, co dir 1964-78, dir Centre for Environmental Studies 1978-80, head central policy unit GLC 1981-83, sr fell Policy Studies Inst 1983-, ed Policy Studies 1988-; Hon Dr Univ of Orleans 1990; memb: Br Sociological Assoc, Social Research Assoc; *Books* Family and Kinship in East London (with Michael Young, 1957), Family and Class in a London Suburb (with Michael Young, 1957), The Evolution of a Community (1963), Adolescent Boys of East London (1966), The Symmetrical Family (with Michael Young, 1973), Inner London: policies for dispersal and balance (with Graeme Shankland and David Jordan, 1977), Inner City Poverty in Paris and London (with Charles Madge, 1981), Unemployment, Poverty and Social Policy: a comparative study in Britain, France and Germany (with Roger Mitton and Phyllis Willmott, 1983), Community in Social Policy (with David Thomas, 1984), Social Networks, Informal Care and Public Policy (1986), Friendship Networks and Social Support (1987), Social Polarisation and Social Housing: the British and French Experience (with Alan Murie, 1988), Community Initiatives: Patterns and Prospects (1989); *Style—* Peter Willmott, Esq; Policy Studies Institute, 100 Park Village East, London NW1 3SR (☎ 071 387 2171, fax 071 388 0914)

WILLNER, Stuart; s of Dr Hugo Willner (d 1946), and Elsa, *née* Gruenbaum (d 1981); *b* 31 Aug 1925; *Educ* Taunton's GS Southampton, Univ Coll Southampton (BSc); *m* 1 Sept 1954, Lesley Anita, da of Alexander Kari (d 1957); 1 s (Andrew b 1960), 1 da (Alexandra b 1958); *Career* buyer United Africa Co (Unilever) 1954-59, sales mangr Viners of Sheffield 1959-62, int mktg mangr Wilkinson Sword 1962-65, md Sheaffer Pen Co 1965-70, owner Seager Promotional Gifts 1970-91; gen cmmr of tax Barnet Div 1985-; Freeman City of London 1981, Liveryman Worshipful Co of Tobacco Pipe Makers and Tobacco Blenders 1981; memb IOD 1967; *Recreations* theatre, music, sport; *Style—* Stuart Willner, Esq; 17 Church Crescent, Whetstone, London N20 OJR (☎ 081 368 2989)

WILLOTT, Robert Graham; s of William Arthur Willott (d 1968), and Vera Joanna, *née* Ashton; *b* 9 March 1942; *Educ* Hitchin GS; *m* 1968, Patricia Ann (d 1981); 2 da (Sian Elizabeth b 1971, Carys Ann b 1973); *Career* Pawley & Malyon Chartered Accountants: articled clerk 1959-65, mangr 1965-68, ptnr 1968-69; Haymarket Publishing Ltd: ed Accountancy Age 1969-72, publisher 1972-75, dir 1975-76; ICAEW: sec Parly and Law Ctee 1976-78, tech dir 1978-81; Touche Ross (formerly Spicer & Pegler, Spicer & Oppenheim): ptnr 1981-, i/c Client Devpt Unit 1981-86, fndr and ptnr i/c West End Practice 1987-, memb Nat Exec 1985-86 and 1988; ICAEW: past memb Parly and Law Ctee, past memb Company Law Sub-Ctee, Sub-Ctee Auditing Practice Ctee; special advsr DTI, chm Initial Working Pty and memb Exec Ctee Design Business Assoc 1985-; FCA (1976, ACA 1965); *Books* Going Public (ed 1971-73), Current Accounting Law and Practice (1976-85), Guide to Price Controls 1977-78 (1977), The Purchase or Redemption by a Company of its Own Shares (Tolley's, jtly 1982), How Advertising Agencies Made Their Profits (1984-90); *Style—* Robert Willott, Esq; Touche Ross & Co, 13 Bruton St, London W1X 7AH (☎ 071 480 7766, fax 071 480 6861)

WILLOUGHBY, Anthony James Tweedale; s of John Lucas Willoughby, OBE (d 1985), of 2 The Grange, Water St, Mere, Wilts, and Hilary Winifred Tweedale Tait; *b* 29 Sept 1944; *Educ* Westminister; *m* 8 Feb 1975, Joanna, da of Capt David Clayhills-Henderson, of Stoneygroves Farm, by Liff, Dundee; 2 s (James b 23 July 1978, Nicholas b 21 Jan 1982), 1 da (Rachel b 9 June 1976); *Career* admitted slr 1970; The Distillers Co Ltd 1970, ptnr Herbert Smith 1977- (joined 1973); govr Westminster Sch 1990-; MITMA 1975; *Recreations* cricket, golf, tennis; *Clubs* The Hurlingham, Royal Wimbledon Golf, Blairgowrie Golf, The Royal Tennis Court; *Style—* Anthony Willoughby, Esq; Herbert Smith, Exchange House, Primrose St, London EC2A 2HS (☎ 071 374 8000, fax 071 496 0043, telex 886633)

WILLOUGHBY, Brig the Hon (Henry Ernest) Christopher; 2 s of 11 Baron Middleton, KG, MC, TD (d 1970); *b* 12 June 1932; *Educ* Eton, RMA Sandhurst; *m* 1, 7 May 1955, Jean Adini, er da of Lt-Col John David Hills, MC (d 1976), of House by the Dyke, Chirk, Clwyd, and Lady Rosemary Ethel, *née* Baring, da of 2 Earl of Cromer, GCB, GCIE, GCVO, PC; 1 s (Guy Nesbit John b 2 June 1960), 2 da ((Angela) Jane (Mrs Critchley-Salmonson) b 5 Feb 1956, Caroline Rosemary b 22 May 1957); m 2, 9 Oct 1990, J Elizabeth, da of Robert Philip Sidney Bache, OBE (d 1984), of Himbleton, Worcestershire; *Career* cmmnd Coldstream Gds 1952; passed Staff Coll 1962; serv BAOR, Cyprus, Kenya, S Arabia, Mauritius, Washington DC, N Ireland and Gibraltar, cmd 2 Bn Coldstream Gds 1974-76; def and mil attaché Turkey 1980-83, presently mangr Anglia Area Corps of Commissionaires; *Recreations* field sports; *Clubs* Army and Navy; *Style—* Brig the Hon Christopher Willoughby; National Westminster Bank plc, 7 Connhill, Bury St Edmunds, Suffolk IP33 1BQ; St Edmunds House, Lower Baxter St, Bury St Edmunds, Suffolk IP33 1ET

WILLOUGHBY, Ven David Albert; s of John Robert Willoughby (d 1982), and Jane May, *née* Lilley; *b* 8 Feb 1931; *Educ* Bradford GS, St John's Coll Univ of Durham (BA, Dip Theol); *m* 1959, Brenda Mary, da of Dennis Watson (d 1953); 2 s (Simon, Andrew); *Career* asst curate: St Peter's Shipley 1957-60, Barnoldswick with Bracewell 1960-62; rector St Chad's New Moston Manchester 1962-72; vicar: Marown IOM 1972-80, St George's with All Saints' Douglas IOM 1980-; rural dean Douglas 1980-82, archdeacon IOM 1982-; memb Gen Synod 1982-; *Recreations* motor cycling, involvement in light entertainment; *Style—* The Ven the Archdeacon of the Isle of Man; St George's with All Saints Vicarage,16 Devonshire Rd, Douglas, Isle of Man (☎ 0624 675430)

WILLOUGHBY, Hon (John) Hugh Francis; s of 12 Baron Middleton, MC, of Birdsall House, Malton, Yorks, and Janet Marshall-Cornwall, Lady Middleton; *b* 13 July 1951; *Educ* Eton; *Career* Capt Coldstream Gds, served Dhofar War 1974-76, with Sultan of Omans Armed Forces, Actg Maj; conslt IPS Gp; Distinguished Service Medal (Oman) 1976; *Recreations* country pursuits, skiing; *Style—* The Hon Hugh Willoughby; c/o Birdsall House, Malton, N Yorks; 4 Westmoreland Terrace, London SW1

WILLOUGHBY, Hon Mrs (Lucy Corinna Agneta); *née* Sidney; da of 1 Viscount De L'Isle, VC, KG, GCMG, GCVO, PC, of Penshurst Place, by his 1 w, Jacqueline, *née* Vereker (d 1962), da of Field Marshal 6 Viscount Gort, VC, GCB, CBE, DSO, MVO, MC; *b* 21 Feb 1953; *m* 1974, Hon Michael Charles James Willoughby, s and h of 12 Baron Middleton; 2 s, 3 da; *Style—* The Hon Mrs Michael Willoughby; North Grimston House, Malton, N Yorks

WILLOUGHBY, Hon Michael Charles James; s and h of 12 Baron Middleton, MC; *b* 14 July 1948; *Educ* Eton; *m* 1974, Hon Lucy Corinna Agneta Sidney, da of 1 Viscount De L'Isle, VC, KG, GCMG, GCVO, PC; 2 s (James William Michael b 1976, Charles Edward Henry b 1986), 3 da (Charlotte Jacqueline Louise b 1978, Emma Coralie Sarah b 1981, Rose Arabella Julia b 1984); *Career* Lt Coldstream Gds and Queen's Own Yeomanry; farmer; *Style—* The Hon Michael Willoughby; North Grimston House, Malton, N Yorks YO17 8AX (☎ 094 46 204)

WILLOUGHBY, Rt Rev Noel Vincent; *see*: Cashel and Ossory, Bishop of

WILLOUGHBY, Prof Peter Geoffrey; JP (Hong Kong 1984); s of George James Willoughby (d 1976), and Enid Alberta, *née* Nye; *b* 17 Feb 1937; *Educ* Merchant Taylors', LSE (LLB, LLM); *m* 20 Jan 1962, Ruth Marlyn, da of Frederick William Brunwin (d 1981); 1 s (Richard Stephen William b 1967), 1 da (Sara Jane Bandele b 1964); *Career* RNVR 1954-59; admitted slr 1962, lectr Gibson & Weldon Law Tutor 1962, barr and slr Nigeria 1962, sr lectr The Nigerian Law Sch 1962-66, princ lectr (formerly lectr and sr lectr) The Coll of Law 1966-73, slr Hong Kong 1973, dir of professional legal educn Univ of Hong Kong 1973 (prof of law 1975-86), ptnr Turner Kenneth Brown (London and Hong Kong) 1986-; Hong Kong: memb Advsy Ctee on Legal Educn 1973-86, chm Ctee of Inquiry into Public Works Dept 1977, chm Ctee on Insur Law Reform 1981-85, chm Law Soc Revenue Law Ctee 1974-87, memb Law Soc Disciplinary Panel 1983-, memb Free Legal Advice Panel 1974-87; memb: Hong Kong Inland Revenue Bd of Review 1977-, Hong Kong Law Reform Cmmn 1980-87, Hong Kong Standing Ctee on Company Law Reform 1983-, Hong Kong Securities Cmmn 1984-89, Hong Kong Air Traffic Licensing Authy 1987-, chm Jt Liaison Ctee on Hong Kong Taxation 1986-; memb city of London Slrs Co 1987-; memb: Law Soc 1962 (VAT Ctee 1988-, Law Soc Revenue Law Ctee 1990-), Law Soc and Bar Cncl Ctee on China 1988-; *Books publications*: Hong Kong Revenue Law (Encyclopaedia in 3 looseleaf vols with sixth monthly updates), various articles and lectures; *Recreations* sailing, sport generally, music, gardening, Siamese cats; *Clubs* RORC, Royal Hong Kong YC, Royal Fowry YC, Lagos YC; *Style—* Prof Peter Willoughby, JP; Turner Kenneth Brown, 100 Fetter Lane, London EC4A 1DD (☎ 01 242 6006); 1901 Des Voeux Rd, Hong Kong (☎ 852 8105081)

WILLOUGHBY, Philip John; JP (City of London 1990); s of George James Willoughby (d 1976), of Cawsand, Cornwall, and Enid Alberta, *née* Nye; *b* 6 Oct 1939; *Educ* Merchant Taylors'; *m* 16 May 1964, Susan Elizabeth, da of John Humphries (d 1971), of Northwood, Middlesex; 1 s (Andrew James b 17 Sept 1965), 1 da (Caroline Louise b 3 March 1969); *Career* RNVR Seaman's Branch 1957-60; articled to predecessor of Clark Whitehill 1957, ptnr 1968; CA 1964; hon treas (formerly chm) Pottery and Glass Trades Benevolent Inst, govr Northwood Coll Sch; memb Old Merchant Taylors' Soc, pres Bishopgate Ward Club 1989-90; Freeman City of London 1971, Master Worshipful Co of Glass Sellers 1986-87 (Liveryman 1971, hon clerk 1976-89); FCA 1968; Offr Order of the Niger 1989; *Recreations* sailing, cricket, rugby, football, music, the family, golf; *Clubs* MCC, City Livery, Moor Park Golf, Castletown Golf (IOM); *Style—* Philip Willoughby, Esq, JP; Penlee, 28 Valley Road, Rickmansworth, Herts WD3 4DS (☎ 0923 775409); Clark Whitehill, 25 New Street Sq, London EC4A 3LN (☎ 071 353 1577, fax 01 583 1720)

WILLOUGHBY, Hon (Thomas Henry) Richard; 3 s of 12 Baron Middleton, MC; *b* 20 Nov 1955; *Educ* Harrow, Univ of Manchester (BSc); *Career* electronics engineer; *Style—* The Hon Richard Willoughby; The Croft, Batts Lane, Steeple, Essex

WILLOUGHBY, Roger James; s of Hugh Lloyd Willoughby (d 1965), and Gerd, *née* Pers-Pleym (d 1989); *b* 30 Sept 1939; *Educ* Shrewsbury, Balliol Col Oxford (BA); *m* 21 March 1970, (Jane Helen) Veronica, da of Francis Alfred Lepper, of St Wenn, Cornwall; *Career* House of Commons: clerk 1962-, dep princ clerk 1975, sec to UK Delgn to Euro Parl 1976, clerk of Home Affrs Ctee 1979, clerk of supply Public Bill Office 1984, clerk of private bills 1988-; *Recreations* literature, cricket, walking, bonfires; *Style—* Roger Willoughby, Esq; House of Commons, London SW1 (☎ 071 219 3269)

WILLOUGHBY, Trevor Willoughby; s of Frederick Thomas Willoughby (d 1964), of Red Stacks, Beverly Rd Kirkella, Nr Hull, Yorkshire, and Vera, *née* Ohlson (d 1982); *b* 9 Dec 1926; *Educ* Hymers Coll Hull, Hull Regnl Coll of Art; *m* 1, Nov 1957 (m dis), Katherine Anne McLaren, da of Mr Fulton (d 1987), of Johannesburg, SA; 2 s (Mark b 1958, Simon b 1959, d 1987); m 2, 12 Aug 1969, Nicola Jane, da of Steven Macoun, of Godalming, Surrey; 2 s (John b 1973, George Henry b 1981); *Career* WWII Merchant Navy Cadet 1943-47; freelance illustrator (magazines and leading advertisers), painter; exhibitions incl: eight one man exhibitions (RA); portraits incl: Lord Birkett, James Fisher, Mrs Basil Ferranti, late princ and vice chllr Edinburgh Univ Sir Hugh Robson; memb Royal Soc Portrait Painters 1967; *Recreations* reading, carpentry; *Clubs* Chelsea Arts; *Style—* Trevor Willoughby, Esq; 4 Offerton Rd, Grafton Square, Clapham Old Town, London SW4 0DH (☎ 071 720 5415)

WILLOUGHBY DE BROKE, 21 Baron (E 1491); (Leopold) David Verney; s of 20 Baron Willoughby de Broke (d 1986, descendend from the 1 Baron, who was so cr by Henry VII after being on the winning side at Battle of Bosworth Field (1485), and was 4 in descent from 4 Baron Willoughby de Eresby); *b* 14 Sept 1938; *Educ* Le Rosey, New Coll Oxford; *m* 1965, his kinswoman Petra, 2 da of Col Sir John Aird, 3 Bt, MVO, MC, and Lady Priscilla Heathcote-Drummond-Willoughby (yr da of 2 Earl of Ancaster); 3 s (Rupert Greville b 1966, John Mark b 1967, Edmund Peyto b 1973); *Heir* s, Rupert Greville b 1966; *Clubs* White's; *Style—* The Rt Hon Lord Willoughby de Broke; Ditchford Farm, Moreton-in-Marsh, Glos

WILLOUGHBY DE ERESBY, Baroness (E 1313) (Nancy) Jane Marie Heathcote-Drummond-Willoughby; da of 3 Earl of Ancaster (d 1983, when Earldom of Ancaster and Barony of Aveland became extinct, and the Baronetcy of Heathcote passed to his kinsman) and Hon (Nancy) Phyllis Louise Astor (d 1975), da of 2 Viscount Astor; succeeded father in Barony of Willoughby de Eresby; *b* 1 Dec 1934; *Career* a train bearer to HM The Queen at the Coronation 1953; *Style*— The Rt Hon the Lady Willoughby de Eresby; Grimsthorpe Castle, Lincs

WILLS, Dr Arthur William; OBE (1990); s of Archibald Wills (d 1950), of Market St, Warwick, and Violet Elizabeth, *née* Davies (d 1971); *b* 19 Sept 1926; *Educ* St John's Sch Coventry, St Nicholas Coll Canterbury, Univ of Durham (BMus, DMus); *m* 14 Nov 1953, Mary Elizabeth, da of John Titterton (d 1955), of Downham Rd, Ely; 1 s (Colin b 1956), 1 da (Rachel b 1958); *Career* dir of music King's Sch Ely 1953-65, composer organist Ely Cathedral 1958-, prof and academic tutor RAM 1964-, examiner Royal Schools of Music 1964-; recitals in: Europe, USA, Australia, Hong Kong; Hon RAM, Hon FLCM, ARSCM; FRCO 1948 (cncl memb 1966); *Books* Organ (Menuhin Music Guide Series 1984); compositions: Symphonic Suite The Fenlands (for brass band and organ), Symphony in A Minor, Piano Sonata "1984", Opera "1984", Sonata (for guitar), Concerto (for guitar and organ), A Music of Fire (overture for brass band and organ), Concerto Lirico (for guitar quartet); song cycles: Love's Torment (for counter tenor and guitar or piano/harpsichord), The Dark Lady (for baritone and piano), When the Spirit Comes (for mezzo and piano), A Woman in Love (for Mezzo and guitar), Three Poems of EE Cummings (for tenor, oboe and piano); Sacrae Symphonrae: Veni Creator Spirit (for double wind quintet), Benedicite, Miss Eliensis, Resurrection (for organ); *Recreations* travel, antiques, reading; *Clubs* RAM; *Style*— Dr Arthur Wills, OBE; 26 New Barns Rd, Ely, Cambs CB7 4PN (☎ 0353 662084)

WILLS, Dr Catherine Mary Hamilton; da of Sir David Wills, of Sandford Park, Sandford St Martin, Oxford, and Eva, *née* MacMorrough Kavanagh; *b* 23 Nov 1950; *Educ* Study Centre V & A London, Courtauld Inst of Art (BA, PhD); *Career* freelance writer; govr: Ditchley Fndn, Rendcomb Coll; tstee: Dulverton Tst, Farmington Tst; *Recreations* music, theatre, riding, skiing, fishing; *Style*— Dr Catherine Wills; 11 Crescent Place, London SW3 2EA (☎ 071 589 6862)

WILLS, Colin Spencer; s of Sir John Spencer Wills, of E Sussex & London, and Elizabeth D A C, *née* Garcke; *b* 25 June 1937; *Educ* Eton, Queens' Coll Cambridge (MA); *Career* dir: Thames Television plc 1970-, Euston Films Co 1971-, English Nat Opera 1975-87, BAFTA 1980-, Wembley Stadium 1975-84, govr English Nat Ballet 1988-, chm Visiting Arts Office of GB and NI 1990-; FCA 1962; *Recreations* music, theatre, walking; *Clubs* Whites; *Style*— Colin S Wills, Esq; 12 Campden Hill Square, London W8 7LB (☎ 071 727 0534); Old Brick Farm, Burwash, E Sussex (☎ 0435 882 234)

WILLS, Sir (Hugh) David Hamilton; CBE (1971), MBE (1946) TD (1964), DL (1967); yr s of Frederick Noel Hamilton Wills (d 1927, himself yr bro of 1 Baron Dulverton) by his w Margery Hamilton, da of Hon Sir Hugh Fraser, sometime High Court Judge Mrs Wills m 1942, as her 2 husb, Wing Cdr Huntly Sinclair, RCAF; *b* 19 June 1917; *Educ* Eton, Magdalen Coll Oxford; *m* 1949, Eva Helen Wills, JP, yst da of Maj Arthur Thomas McMorrough Kavanagh, MC (decd); 1 s, 1 da; *Career* serv WWII Queen's Own Cameron Highlanders (TA); France 1940, Aruba 1940-41, GSO 111 (Ops) GHQ Home Forces 1941-42, GSO 11 (Ops) HQ Southern Command 1943-44; chm of Tstees Rendcomb Coll 1955-84, High Sheriff Oxfordshire 1961, memb Governing Body Atlantic Coll 1963-73 and 1980-; dir: Batsford Estates, Farmington Tst; pres Ditchley Fndn; kt 1980; *Recreations* fishing and sailing; *Clubs* Boodles, Grillions; *Style*— Sir David Wills, CBE, MBE, TD, DL; Sandford Park, Sandford St Martin, Middle Barton, Oxford (☎ 060 883 238)

WILLS, David James Vernon; s and h of Sir John Vernon Wills, 4 Bt, *qv*; *b* 2 Jan 1955; *Career* memb cncl Royal Bath & West and Southern Countries Soc; *Recreations* shooting; *Style*— David Wills, Esq

WILLS, Hon Mrs (Elizabeth Anne); *née* Cecil; da of 2 Baron Rockley and Anne Margaret, er da of late Adm Hon Sir Herbert Meade-Featherstonhaugh, GCVO, CB, DSO; *b* 6 July 1939; *m* 1961, Andrew Wills, late Life Gds, s of Maj John Wills (himself gs of Sir Edward Wills, 1 Bt, KCB), of Allanbay Park, Binfield, Berks by Hon Jean, 2 da of 16 Lord Elphinstone, KT, by Lady Mary Bowes-Lyon, DCVO (da of 14 Earl of Strathmore and sis of HM Queen Elizabeth The Queen Mother); 2 s (Richard b 1962, Alexander b 1967), 1 da (Tessa b 1963); *Style*— The Hon Mrs Wills; Middleton House, Longparish, Andover, Hants (☎ 026 472 206)

WILLS, Frederick Hugh Philip Hamilton; s of Capt Michael Desmond Hamilton Wills, MC (ka 1943), and Mary Margaret Gibbs, *née* Mitford; *b* 31 May 1940; *Educ* Eton, RAC Cirencester; *m* 1969, Priscilla Annabelle, da of Capt Alec David Charles Francis, of Malmesbury, Wilts; 2 s (Michael b 1972, Edward b 1974), 1 da (Clare (twin) b 1974); *Career* II Hussars (PAO) 1959-66; TA Royal Wilts Yeomanry 1967-75; landowner, farmer, forester; hon treas Cirencester and Tewkesbury Cons Assoc 1976-86; *Recreations* fishing, stalking; *Style*— Frederick Wills, Esq; The Old House, Rendcomb, Cirencester, Glos GL7 7EY (☎ 028583 671); Coulin Lodge, Kinlochewe by Achnasheen, Ross-shire, Scotland IV22 2ES (☎ 044584 210)

WILLS, Hon (Robert) Ian Hamilton; yr s of 2 Baron Dulverton, CBE, TD by his 1 w, Judith Betty Dulverton, *née* Leslie Melville (d 1983); *b* 28 June 1948; *Educ* Harrow, Warwick Univ (BA), Royal Agric Coll Cirencester; *m* 1979, Elizabeth Jane, da of Michael Taylor Downes; 1 s (James b 1984), 1 da (Emma b 1982); *Career* farmer; *Recreations* all field sports; *Style*— The Hon Ian Wills; Soundborough Farm, Andoversford, Cheltenham (☎ 0242 820576)

WILLS, Hon Mrs (Jean Constance); *née* Elphinstone; LVO (1983); da of 16 Lord Elphinstone, KT, (d 1955), and Lady Mary Bowes-Lyon, DCVO (d 1961), 2 da of 14 Earl of Strathmore and sis of HM Queen Elizabeth The Queen Mother; *m* 1936, Maj John Lycett Wills, Life Gds (ret), s of Capt Arnold Wills and gs of Sir Edward Wills, 1 Bt, KCB; 1 s (Andrew *see* Hon Mrs Elizabeth Wills), 1 da (Susan (Mrs Charles Bertie)), and 2 da decd; *Career* extra Lady-in-Waiting to HRH The Princess Margaret 1970-; *Style*— The Hon Mrs Wills, LVO; Allanbay Park, Binfield, Berks; 11 Rutland Mews, East London SW7

WILLS, Sir John Spencer; s of Cedric Spencer Wills by his w Cécile; *b* 10 Aug 1904; *Educ* Merchant Taylors' Sch; *m* 1936, Elizabeth Drusilla Garcke; 2 s; *Career* chm British Electric Traction 1966-82 (remains full time exec, md 1946-73, dep chm 1951-66); chm: Birmingham & Dist Investmnt Tst, Electrical & Industl Investmnt Co Wembley Stadium Ltd; former chm Rediffusion TV, Birmingham & Midland Motor Omnibus Co; vice-patron Theatre Royal Windsor Tst, memb UK Cncl European Movement 1966-; FCIT; kt 1969; *Style*— Sir John Spencer Wills; Beech Farm, Battle, E Sussex (☎ 042 46 2950)

WILLS, Sir John Vernon; 4 Bt (UK 1923), of Blagdon, Co Somerset, TD, JP (Somerset 1962); s of Sir George Vernon Proctor Wills, 2 Bt, (d 1931) and bro of 3 Bt (ka 1945); Sir George, 1 Bt, was pres of Imperial Tobacco Co of GB and Ireland of which 2 Bt was a dir; *b* 3 July 1928; *Educ* Eton; *m* 1953, Diana Veronica Cecil (Jane), da of Douglas Ryan Midelton Baker of Winsford, Minehead, Somerset; 4 s (David, Anthony, Rupert, Julian); *Heir* s, David James Vernon, *qv*; *Career* Lt-Col (TA) 1965-67, Bt-Col 1967; Somerset Co: alderman 1970, High Sheriff 1968, DL 1968; Lord-Lt and Custos Rotulorum of Avon 1974-; chm Wessex Water Authority to 1982; dep chm: Bristol Evening Post 1978- (dir 1973-), Bristol Waterworks Co 1983- (chm 1986); chm Bristol & West Building Society 1988- (dir 1969-); memb: Nat Water Cncl 1973-82, Bristol Local Bd Barclays Bank to 1987; pro chllr Univ of Bath 1979-; KStJ 1978; Hon LLD Univ of Bristol 1986; hon Capt RNR 1988, FRICS; *Clubs* Cavalry and Guards'; *Style*— Sir John Wills, Bt, TD, JP; Langford Court, Langford, Bristol BS18 7DA (☎ 0934 862338)

WILLS, Juliet, Lady; Juliet Eve; *née* Graham-Clarke; yr da of late Capt John Eagles Henry Graham-Clarke, JP, of Frocester Manor, Glos; *b* 30 Nov 1920; *m* 29 June 1949, as his 2 w, Sir (Ernest) Edward de Winton Wills, 4 Bt (d 1983; suc by n Sir Seton Wills, Bt, *qv*); *Style*— Juliet, Lady Wills; Mount Prosperous, Hungerford, Berks RG17 0RP; Lochs Lodge, Glen Lyon, Perthshire, PH15 2PU

WILLS, (Thomas) Justin; s of Philip Aubrey Wills, CBE (1978), and Katharine, *née* Fisher; *b* 20 Aug 1946; *Educ* Bryanston Sch, Pembroke Coll Oxford (MA); *m* 1980, Gillian, da of Maj Samuel Francis Maxwell Howe; *Career* dir of Wills Gp plc 1973-; dep chief exec Wills Tp plc 1984- (dir 1983-); current holder of 10 UK Gliding Recorder Inc Distance Record, Br Team memb World Gliding Championships 1985 and 1987; memb HAC; *Recreations* gliding, fishing, kayaking, skiing; *Style*— Justin Wills, Esq; 55 Holland Park Mews, London W11 (☎ 071 727 0375); Wills Gp plc, 25/35 City Rd, London EC1 (☎ 071 606 6331, fax 071 628 4379, telex 883323)

WILLS, Lady Katharine Anne; 5 da of 6 Earl of Clanwilliam (d 1989); *b* 10 Aug 1959; *m* 7 Feb 1987, Christopher Aubrey Hamilton Wills, s of Hon (Victor) Patrick Hamilton Wills, *qv*, and Hon Mrs Henry Douglas-Home; *Style*— Lady Katharine Wills; Litchfield Down, Whitchurch, Hants

WILLS, Dr Lesley Alison Margaret; da of Maj Lancelot Kenneth Wills, RAMC (d 1970), and Margaret Rosa, *née* MacIldowie (d 1985); *b* 4 April 1943; *Educ* North London Collegiate Sch Canons Edgware, UCL, UCH (BSc, MB BS, MSc, LRCP, MRCP); *Career* house physician UCH 1969, house surgn South London Hosp for Women and Children 1970, postgrad student London Sch of Hygiene and Tropical Med London 1970-71; sr house offr in: pathology United Oxford Hosps 1972-73, gen med and haematology Kingston Gen Hosp Hull 1973-74; gen practice trainee Godalming Surrey 1974, sr house offr in gen med Poole Gen Hosp Dorset 1974; registrar in: clinical haematology United Sheffield Hosps 1974-75, chest and gen med King Edward VII Hosp Midhurst 1975-77 (sr house offr 1975); rotating registrar to Aberdeen Teaching Hosps 1977-79, registrar in dermatology Edinburgh Royal Infirmary 1979-81, sr registrar to Wessex RHA 1981-82, conslt in geriatric med to SW RHA at Trinity Hosp Taunton Somerset 1982-; contrib to learned med jls; memb: Nat Tst for Nature Conservation, Scot Wild Lands Gp, Br Geriatrics Soc; memb BMA, MRCS 1969; *Recreations* riding, walking, foreign travel; *Style*— Dr Lesley Wills; Trinity Hospital, Trinity Rd, Taunton, Somerset (☎ 0823 333444)

WILLS, Leslie Charles; s of Charles Leslie Wills (d 1968), and Anne Edwards, *née* Wright; *b* 21 Feb 1940; *Educ* Robert Gdns Coll, Univ of Aberdeen (MB ChB); *m* 19 July 1967, Frances Cumming, da of David Gove (d 1972); 3 da (Veronica b 19 Sept 1969, Jocelyn b 27 April 1972, Melanie b 22 Feb 1974); *Career* conslt ENT surgn Grampian Health Bd, sr lectr in surgery Univ of Aberdeen; author of papers on ENT; memb Cncl Br Assoc of Otolarynologists, vice chm NE Soc for The Deaf, govr Albyn Sch For Girls Aberdeen; memb: RSM, Otolarynologists Soc; *Clubs* Royal Northern Univ (Aberdeen); *Style*— Leslie Wills, Esq; Bogjoran, Pitfodels, Cults, Aberdeen (☎ 0224 868149); Consulting Rooms, 24 Albyn Pl, Aberdeen (☎ 0224 595993)

WILLS, Group Captain (Alan) Marcus; CVO (1988), OBE (1982); s of Alan Oliver Wills, OBE, of Brent Knoll, Somerset, and Rosamond Margaret, *née* Batty; *b* 21 Sept 1943; *Educ* Sherborne, RAF Coll Cranwell; *m* 23 Sept 1967, Victoria Katrina, da of Dr Derek Harold Johnson, of Dartmouth, Devon; 3 s (Matthew b 1971, Adam b 1973, Edward b 1976); *Career* Gp Capt RAF 1966-: 111 Sqdn 1966-68, ADC to AO C in C Air Support Cmd 1968-70, 10 Sqdn 1970-76, RAF Staff Coll 1976-78, CO 10 Sqdn 1978-82, COS secretariat MOD 1982-83, personal SO to CAS 1983-85, station cdr RAF Benson, dep capt Queen's Flight, ADC to HM The Queen 1985-87, int military staff HQ NATO Brussels 1987-90; Liveryman Worshipful Co of Coachmakers 1982; *Recreations* home computers, photography; *Clubs* RAF; *Style*— Gp Capt Marcus Wills, CVO, OBE; c/o Air Force Department, Ministry of Defence

WILLS, Hon (Gilbert) Michael Hamilton; s (by 1 m) and h of 2 Baron Dulverton, CBE, TD, DL; *b* 2 May 1944; *Educ* Gordonstoun; *m* 1980, Rosalind J M, da of J van der Velde; 1 s (b 20 Oct 1983), 1 da; *Style*— The Hon Michael Wills

WILLS, Nicholas Kenneth Spencer; s of Sir John Spencer Wills, of Beech Farm, Battle, Sussex, and Elizabeth Drusilla Alice Clare Garcke; *b* 18 May 1941; *Educ* Rugby, Queens' Coll Cambridge (MA); *m* 1973 (m dis 1983), Hilary Ann Flood; 2 s, 2 da; m 2, 1985, Philippa Trench Casson; 1 da; *Career* chm: Argus Press Holdings plc 1974-83, Electrical Press plc 1974-83, Initial plc 1979-87; md: Birmingham & District Investment Trust plc 1970-, Electrical & Industrial Investment plc 1970-, Nat Electric Construction plc 1971-; BET plc: dir 1975-, md 1982-, chief exec 1985-; dir: American C of C (UK) 1985- (vice pres 1988-), St George Assurance Co Ltd 1974-81, National Mutual Life Assurance Society 1974-85, Colonial Securities Trust Co Ltd 1976-82, Cable Trust Ltd 1976-77, Globe Investment Trust plc 1977-90, Drayton Consolidated Trust plc 1982-, National Westminster Bank plc (City & West End Advsy Bds) 1982-, United World Colleges (International) Ltd 1987-; treas and churchwarden Church of St Bride Fleet St 1978-, asst Worshipful Co of Haberdashers' 1981- (jr warden 1987-89); Boulton and Paul plc 1979-84; chm: BET Building Services Ltd 1984-87, Bradbury Agnew and Co Ltd 1974-83; memb: Cncl CBI 1987- (memb Overseas Ctee 1987-, Public Expenditure Task Force 1988), Cncl Business in the Community 1986-, Advsy Bd Fishman-Davidson Center for the Study of the Service Sector Univ of PA 1988-, Advsy Bd Charterhouse Buy-Out Funds 1990-; Princes' Youth Business Tst 1988-, memb Advsy Cncl 1988-, hon treas 1989-; tstee Int Fedn Youth Orgns 1988-, chm IFKYO Int Tstees 1990-; hon fell Queens' Coll Cambridge 1990; FCA; CBIM, FCT, FRSA; *Recreations* shooting, sailing, trying to farm in the Highlands; *Clubs* White's, RAC, City Livery, Clyde Cruising; *Style*— Nicholas Wills, Esq; BET plc, Stratton House, Stratton St, Piccadilly, London W1X 6AS (☎ 071 629 8886, fax 071 975 6607, telex 299573 Betcl G)

WILLS, Hon (Victor) Patrick Hamilton; DL (Hants); s of late 1 Baron Dulverton, OBE; *b* 1926; *Educ* Eton, Coll of Estate Mgmnt; *m* 1, 1948 (m dis 1962), Felicity Betty, da of late Maj Aubrey Jonsson, Royal Irish Rifles; 2 s, 1 da; m 2, 1963, Jean Felicity Strutt, da of late Hon Francis Erskine (s of 12 Earl of Mar and Kellie) (d 1984); m 3, 1988, Mrs Elizabeth Gilmor Shaw; *Career* Grenadier Gds and Para Regt (ret); tstee Dulverton Tst 1949-81, CC Hants 1965-73; chm: Hants Playing Fields Assoc 1969-79, Trident Tst 1978-80 (vice chm 1972), Int Students Tst 1984 (govr 1965), Atlantic Salmon Conservation Tst (Scot) 1985; fell Chartered Land Agents Soc 1957; *Style*— The Hon Patrick Wills, DL; Litchfield Manor, Whitchurch, Hants

WILLS, Peter Gordon Bethune; TD (1967); s of Lionel Wills (d 1967), of Trieste, Italy, and Sita, *née* Stapleton (d 1982); *b* 25 Oct 1931; *Educ* Malvern, Corpus Christi Coll Cambridge; *m* 1, 1957, Linda Hutton; 2 s, 1 da; m 2, 1982, Faith Hines; *Career* served Royal Inniskilling Fusiliers in NI and Korea 1950-52, London Irish Rifles (TA) 1952-67; memb Stock Exchange 1960, ptnr Sheppards and Chase (Stockbrokers)

1960-85 (joined 1955); memb Cncl of Stock Exchange 1973-86 (dep chm 1979-82); chm: Security Settlements Options Ltd 1979-, Sheppards Moneybrokers Ltd 1985-89; dir: Wills Group plc 1969-87, The Securities Assoc 1986-89, London Clear Ltd 1987-89, BAII Holding Ltd 1986-89; *Style*— Peter Wills, Esq, TD; 54 Frant Rd, Tunbridge Wells, Kent (☎ 0892 26705)

WILLS, Sir (David) Seton; 5 Bt (UK 1904), of Hazelwood, Stoke Bishop, Westbury-on-Trym, Glos, and Clapton-in-Gordano, Somerset; s of Maj George Wills by his first w, Lilah, da of Capt Percy Hare, gs of 2 Earl of Listowel; suc unc, Sir Edward Wills, 4 Bt, (d 1983, *see also* his wid, Juliet, Lady Wills); *b* 29 Dec 1939; *Educ* Eton; *m* 1968, Gillian, twin da of Albert Eastoe; 1 s, 3 da; *Heir* s, James Seton Wills, b 1970; *Career* FRICS; *Style*— Sir Seton Wills, Bt; Eastridge House, Ramsbury, Marlborough, Wilts SN8 2HJ (☎ 0672 20015); Estate office (☎ 0672 20042)

WILLS, Maj (Michael) Thomas Noel Hamilton; s of Capt Michael Desmond Hamilton Wills, MC (d 1943), and Mary Margaret, *née* Mitford; *b* 31 May 1940; *Educ* Eton, Royal Agric Coll Cirencester; *m* 23 Oct 1982, Penelope Ann, da of Ben Howard-Baker, of Glascoed Hall, Llansilin, Oswestry, Shropshire; 1 s (Nicholas James Noel Hamilton b 9 Sept 1983), 1 da (Camilla Jane Hamilton b 27 June 1985); *Career* Coldstream Gds 1959-73; memb: CLA, Timber Growers UK, Royal Forestry Soc; chm: League of Friends Stroud Hosp, Gloucs Scout Assoc, Tstees Rendcomb Coll; jt master Cotswold Hunt; High Sheriff Gloucs 1985; *Recreations* country pursuits; *Clubs* Boodles; *Style*— Maj Thomas Wills; Misarden Park, Stroud, Gloucs (☎ 028 582 309); Coulags, Achnashellach, Ross-shire

WILLS, Timothy James Bethune; s of Peter Gordon Bethune Wills, of Tunbridge Wells, Kent, and Linda Margaret, *née* Hutton; *b* 12 Aug 1958; *Educ* Malvern; *m* 11 Aug 1989, Sara Elizabeth, da of Esmond Malcolm Hoyle, of Wisbech, Cambs; *Career* RA 1976-77, Royal Military Acad Sandhurst 1977; toy salesman Harrods 1977, accountant and bed salesman Oxford 1978-79, monetary advsr to central banks and govt inst Irving Tst 1985- (bank clerk 1980-83, foreign exchange dealer 1983-85, Irving Tst merged with Bank of NY 1989); memb: Economic Res Cncl, Greenpeace, FOREX Assoc, MENSA; *Recreations* golf, squash, travel; *Clubs* Machrihanish Golf, Argyllshire South Bank Squash; *Style*— Timothy Wills, Esq; 25 Union Rd, London SW4 6JQ (☎ 071 622 9989); The Bank of New York, 46 Berkeley St, London W1X 6AA (☎ 071 629 8333, fax 071 322 6034, telex 888851)

WILLS-DYER, (formerley Dyer) Simonne Louise Pierre; da of Edward Linssen, and Josephine, *née* Larvelle; *b* 25 April 1914; *Educ* UCL, Bartlett Sch of Arch; *m* 1, Trenwith Wills (decd); m 2, 11 Dec 1974, Ernest William George Dyer (decd); *Career* WWII staff architect Vickers-Armstrong Weybridge, town planning conslt (later ptnr) with Trenwith Wills; specialist in restoration and bldg of country houses incl: Cliveden, Hinton Ampner, Fonthill, Castle Howard; panel memb Nat Assoc of Almeshouses; *Recreations* golf, travel; *Clubs* Yorkshire, Eurogolf, York GC; *Style*— Mrs Simonne Wills-Dyer

WILLSON, Hon Mrs (Anne Mildred); *née* Curzon; da of 2 Viscount Scarsdale (decd); *b* 1923; *m* 1942 (m dis 1960), Maj Walter James Latimer Willson, DSO, Grenadier Gds, s of Sir Walter Willson; 1 s, 1 da; *Career* ATS 1942-44; *Style*— The Hon Mrs Willson; Hill Farm, Garsdale, Sedbergh, Cumbria

WILLSON, Prof (Francis Michael) Glenn; s of Christopher Glenn Willson (d 1940), and Elsie Katrine, *née* Mattick (d 1924); *b* 29 Sept 1924; *Educ* Carlisle GS, Univ of Manchester (BA), Balliol Coll and Nuffield Coll Oxford (MA, DPhil); *m* 23 June 1945, Jean, da of Malcolm Nicol Carlyle (d 1957); 2 da (Judith b 1946, Rosanne b 1953); *Career* MN 1941-42, RAF 1943-47, PO 1944, Flying Offr 1945, Flt Lt 1946; res offr Royal Inst Pub Admin 1953-60; Univ of Oxford: res fell Nuffield Coll 1955-60, lectr in politics St Edmund Hall 1958-60; Univ Coll of Rhodesia & Nyasaland: prof of govt 1960-64, dean Faculty of Social Studies 1962-64; Univ of California Santa Cruz: prof of govt and politics 1965-74, provost Adlai Stevenson Coll 1967-74, vice chllr coll and student affairs 1973-74, visiting prof 1985-; princ Univ of London 1975-78 (warden Goldsmith's Coll 1974-75); Murdoch Univ W Aust: vice chllr 1978-84, emeritus prof 1985; memb: Royal Inst Pub Admin, Political Studies Assoc of UK; *Books* Administrators in Action (1961), The Organization of British Central Govenment (with D N Chester, 2 edn 1964); *Recreations* reading, listening to music; *Style*— Prof Glenn Willson; 32 Digby Mansions, Hammersmith Bridge Rd, London W6 9DF (☎ 081 741 1247)

WILLSON, John Michael; CMG (1988); s of Richard Willson (d 1972), of New Malden, Surrey, and Kathleen, *née* Aldridge (d 1983); *b* 15 July 1931; *Educ* Wimbledon Coll, University Coll Oxford (MA), Trinity Hall Cambridge; *m* 25 Sept 1954, (Phyllis Marian) Dawn, da of William John Richards (d 1970), of Barcombe, Sussex; 2 s (Simon b 8 July 1955, Richard b 17 May 1957), 2 da (Melanie b 2 April 1960, Amanda b 5 March 1962); *Career* Nat Serv Army 1949-51; HM Overseas Civil Serv Nothern Rhodesia 1955-64, Min Overseas Devpt London 1965-70; FCO 1970-: HM ambassador 1983-87 (Ivory Coast, Niger, Burkina), Br High Cmmn Zambia 1988-; *Recreations* photography, music, gardening; *Clubs* Royal Cwlth Soc; *Style*— John Willson, Esq, CMG; British High Commission, Po Box 50050, Lusaka, Zambia (☎ 010 260 1 216770, telex 41150)

WILLSON, Stanley William; s of late Stephen Willson; *b* 17 May 1927; *Educ* George Dixon GS; *m* 1957, Rachel, *née* Nickerson; 3 children; *Career* dir Guardian Royal Exchange Group (Birmingham) 1960-; chm: Co Developments Ltd 1965-, Cheylesmore Garages Ltd 1968-, Birmingham Citizens Building Soc 1968-77, Kean & Scott Ltd 1971-79, Aston Martin Lagonda Ltd 1972-75, Birmingham Building Soc 1980-82 (dir 1977-80), Birmingham & Bridgwater Building Soc 1984-86 (dir 1982-84), Marston Green Garage Ltd 1985-91, Birmingham Midshires Building Soc 1986-88; dir St Peters Urban Village Tst; hon treas: St Mary's and St Chad's Lapworth 1960-, Birmingham Assoc of Youth Clubs 1962-70 (vice pres 1970-); chm Tapster Valley Preservation Soc 1971-; memb: Warwick RDC 1971-74, Cncl Soc of Motor Manufacturers and Traders 1973-75; pres Birmingham Sporting Club 1979-87; FCA; *Recreations* preservation of wild life and countryside, photography; *Style*— Stanley William Willson, Esq; Lapworth House, Wharf Lane, Lapworth, Warwicks B94 5QH (☎ 0564 782994)

WILLSON, Stephen Phillips; s of Douglas Stephen Willson, and Sheila, *née* Phillips; *b* 27 July 1948; *Educ* Battisborough Sch Plymouth Devon, Coll of Law; *m* 20 Dec 1975, Susan Mary, da of Gavin Miller Hunter (d 1978); 1 s (Guy Edward Phillips b 23 Nov 1983), 2 da (Sophie Anna b 1 Nov 1977, Sabine Lara b 22 Jan 1979); *Career* Burton & Ramsden: articled clerk 1966-71, asst slr 1971-73, ptnr 1973-82; ptnr S J Berwin & Co 1982-; memb Law Soc; *Recreations* squash, tennis, country pursuits; *Style*— Stephen Willson, Esq; S J Berwin & Co, 236 Grays Inn Rd, London WC1X 8HB (☎ 071 278 0444, fax 071 833 2860)

WILMOT, Sir Henry Robert; 9 Bt (GB 1759), of Chaddesden, Derbyshire; s of Capt Sir Robert Arthur Wilmot, 8 Bt (d 1974, sometime equerry to HRH The Duke of Gloucester), of Pitcarlie Farm, Auchtermuchty, Fife, and Juliet Elvira, *née* Tufnell; *b* 10 April 1967; *Educ* Eton; *Heir* bro, Charles Sacheverel Wilmot, b 13 Feb 1969; *Recreations* origami, scimitar maintenance; *Style*— Sir Henry Wilmot, Bt; 12 Saxe-Coburg Place, Edinburgh EH3 5BR

WILMOT, Michael John Assheton Eardley; s and h of Sir John Eardley-Wilmot, 5 Bt, MVO, DSC; *b* 13 Jan 1941; *Educ* Clifton; *m* 1, 1971, Wendy, da of A J Wolstenholme; 2 s, 1 da; m 2, 1987, Diana, da of R Wallis; 1 da; *Career* md Famous Names Hldgs 1974-86, md Beaufort Hotel; *Style*— Michael Wilmot, Esq; Beaufort Hotel, 33 Beaufort Gardens, London SW3 (☎ 071 584 5252, telex 929200)

WILMOT, (Reginald) Thomas Dorrien; s of Col Reginald Cameron Wilmot (d 1944), and Mabel Louise, *née* Dorrien (d 1959); *b* 11 March 1915; *Educ* Tonbridge; *Career* Nat Serv Capt Leics Yeo 1939-44, 8 Army HQ Italy 1944; asst to Sec Alliance Insurance Co 1933-46, chief exec Br Insurance Assoc 1946-71, chm France Fenwick (Lloyd's brokers) 1971-75, dir World Fire Statistics Centre Geneva 1978-; common councilman City of London 1973-, chm Kensington Soc 1980-82, dep Cordwainer Ward 1986-; Master Worshipful Co of Tallow Chandlers 1976, Liveryman Worshipful Co of Insurers 1980, memb Build of Firefighters 1989; *Recreations* gardening; *Clubs* Travellers', Guildhall, City Livery, Better City Architecture; *Style*— Thomas Wilmot, Esq; Five Oaks, Park Rd, Forest Row, Sussex RH18 5BX

WILMOT-SITWELL, Peter Sacheverell; s of Capt Robert Bradshaw Wilmot-Sitwell, RN (d 1946), and Barbara Elizabeth Fisher (d 1991); *b* 28 March 1935; *Educ* Eton, Univ of Oxford (BA); *m* 1960, Clare Veronica, da of Ralph H Cobbold; 2 s, 1 da; *Career* memb Stock Exchange 1960, chm Rowe & Pitman (stockbrokers) 1986-(sr ptnr 1982-86), chm SG Warburg Gp 1990- (jt chm 1986-90); *Recreations* shooting, golf; *Clubs* White's, Swinley Forest Golf, Pratt's; *Style*— Peter Wilmot-Sitwell, Esq; Portman House, Dummer, nr Basingstoke, Hants; S G Warburg Akroyd Rowe & Pitman Mullens Securities Ltd, 1 Finsbury Avenue, London EC2M 2PA (☎ 071 606 1066, telex 937011 8952485)

WILMSHURST, John; s of Alfred William Wilmshurst, and Frances May, *née* Handy; *b* 30 Jan 1926; *Educ* Maidstone GS, Univ Coll Oxford (MA); *m* 31 March 1951, Patricia Edith, da of R John W Hollis, MBE; 1 s (Jonathon b 1968), 3 da (Letitia b 1953, Felicity b 1955, Priscilla b 1960); *Career* Lt RASC 1945-48; patents offr Glaxo Laboratories Ltd 1950-52, gp advertising mangr Reed International Ltd 1952-59, dir Roles & Parker Ltd 1959-67, md Stuart Advertising Ltd 1967-71, chm and chief exec John Wilmshurst Marketing Consultants Ltd 1971-; memb: Gen Cncl Church Missionary Soc 1970-78, Kent Playing Fields Assoc, SE Publicity Club, Ctee Oxford Soc; chm Kent Branch Chartered Inst of Mktg 1972, church warden Farleigh Parish Church 1979-82; Freeman City of London, Liveryman asst Worshipful Co of Carmen; FCIM 1986, FCAM 1982; *Books* The Fundamentals and Practice of Marketing (1978), The Fundamentals of Advertising (1985); *Recreations* birdwatching, horse racing, theatre, music, collecting first editions; *Clubs* City Livery; *Style*— John Wilmshurst, Esq; The Stable Cottage, East Farleigh, Kent (☎ 0622 728241)

WILMSHURST, Michael Joseph; s of Eric Joseph Wilmshurst (d 1975), and Elsie, *née* Skinner; *b* 14 Sept 1934; *Educ* Latymer Upper Sch, Christ's Coll Cambridge (BA); *m* 7 June 1958, Mary Elizabeth, da of Arthur Kemp (d 1989); 1 s (Paul Dominic b 1961), 1 da (Jane Mary b 1963); *Career* RCS 1953-55; HM Dip Serv: joined 1953, asst private sec to Foreign Sec 1960-62, second sec The Hague 1962-65, first sec Bogota 1965-67, first sec Cairo 1970-73, asst head of Energy Dept FCO 1974-75, asst head of Energy and Arms Control and Disarmament Depts 1975-77, cncllr and head Joint Nuclear Unit FCO 1977-78, consul Guatemala City 1978-81, UK perm rep to IAEA, UNIDO and UN Vienna 1982-87; dir External Relations IAEA Vienna 1987-; *Publications* The International Nuclear Non-Proliferation System: Challenges and Choices (contrib, 1984); *Recreations* reading, walking; *Style*— Michael Wilmshurst, Esq; Prinz Eugenstrasse 6/10, 1040 Wien, Austria (☎ 65 78 59); IAEA, Wagramerstrasse 5, PO Box 200, A-1400 Wien, Austria (☎ 2360 1250, fax 234564, telex 1-12645)

WILSHERE, Jonathan Edward Owen; s of H Owen Wilshere, MBE (d 1963), of Kirby Muxloe, Leicestershire, and Margaret Elsie, *née* Hughes, LRAM (d 1981); *b* 24 June 1936; *Educ* Rugby; *m* 27 July 1974, Daphne Vivien Maureen, da of Reuben Racey (d 1977), of Leicester; 2 s (Nicholas Edward Antony b 1978, Andrew Thomas Hugh b 1984); *Career* proprietor: Chamberlain Music & Books 1970-, Leicester Research Services 1968-; lectr Leics CC 1970-; fndr and chm Leics Family History Soc (vice pres and life memb 1987); ACIS 1965, FCII 1961, FRMetS 1984, memb AGRA 1976; *Recreations* historical research, photography, music, cricket statistics, meteorology; *Clubs* Leicestershire CCC (life memb), Leicestershire Tst for Nature Conservation (life memb); *Style*— Jonathan Wilshere, Esq; 134 London Rd, Leicester (☎ 0533 543405)

WILSHIRE, David; MP (Cons) Spelthorne 1987-; *b* 16 Sept 1943; *Educ* Kingswood Sch Bath, Fitzwilliam Coll Cambridge; *m* 1967, Margaret; 1 s (Simon b 1971), 1 da (Sarah b 1969, d 1981); *Career* sr ptnr Western Political Res Servs, co-dir political mgmnt prog Brunel Univ; former ldr Wansdyke DC (Avon); *Style*— David Wilshire, Esq, MP; 55 Cherry Orchard, Staines, Middx (☎ 0784 450822); House of Commons, London SW1A 0AA (☎ 071 219 3534)

WILSKI, Andrew; s of Ingénieur Boguslaw Jaloszynski, of Piotrowek, Warsaw, and Janina Zofia Zalewska; *b* 2 April 1947; *Educ* Reytan GS, Med Acad Warsaw (DM), Univ of London (DPM, MRC Psych); *m* 2 April 1982, Phillippa, da of Patrick Green, of Freshfields, Harpenden, Herts; 3 s (Alexis b 1983, Nicholas b 1984, Piers b 1986), 1 da (Francesca b 1989); *Career* conslt psychiatrist Royal Tunbridge Wells Health Authy, former conslt psychotherapist Univ of Essex, lectr Herts Coll of Art, community psychiatrist Mental Health Centre London, sr registrar Westminster Hosp, memb Assoc of Christian Psychiatrists; *Books* Cultural Resources and Psychiatric Rehabilitation (1985); *Recreations* travel, reading, arts, photography; *Style*— Andrew Wilski, Esq; 4 Berkeley Rd, Mount Sion, Royal Tunbridge Wells, Kent (☎ 0892 27304)

WILSON, Prof Alan Geoffrey; s of Harry Wilson (d 1987), of Darlington, County Durham, and Gladys, *née* Naylor (d 1990); *b* 8 Jan 1939; *Educ* Queen Elizabeth GS Darlington, Corpus Christi Coll Cambridge (BA, MA); *m* 17 April 1987, Sarah Caroline Fildes; *Career* scientific offr Rutherford Laboratory 1961-64, res offr Inst of Econs and Statistics Univ of Oxford 1964-66, mathematical advsr Miny of Tport 1966-68, asst dir Centre for Environmental Studies 1968-70; Univ of Leeds: prof of urban and regnl geography 1970-, chm bd of arts econs and social studies and law 1984-86, pro vice chllr 1989-91, vice chllr 1991-; memb Oxford City Cncl 1964-67, memb and vice chm Kirklees AHA 1979-81, vice chm Dewsbury DHA 1982-86; *Books* Entropy in Urban and Regional Modelling (1970), Catastrophe Theory and Bifuration (1981), Geography and the Environment (1981); *Recreations* fell running; *Style*— Prof Alan Wilson; Vice Chancellor's Lodge, Grosvenor Rd, Leeds LS6 2DZ; Vice Chancellor's Office, University of Leeds, Leeds LS2 9JT (☎ 0532 333000, fax 0532 334122)

WILSON, Alan Herbert; s of Herbert Wilson (d 1968), and Muriel Rahab Penelope, *née* Morley (d 1966); *b* 6 Sept 1918; *Educ* Doncaster GS, Leeds Sch of Architecture (Dip Arch); *m* 6 Oct 1952, Gwendoline, da of William Watt (d 1960); 2 da (Janet Ruth (Mrs Warburton) b 2 Oct 1954, Judith Helen b 13 Oct 1960); *Career* Nat Serv RE 1939-46, chief draughtsman to Chief Engr Aerodromes 1942-44 (despatches 1944), superintending draughtsman to Chief Engr MEF 1944-45 (certificate for outstanding serv 1945), chief instr (Bldg) Army Formation Coll Scot 1945-46; sr ptnr T H Johnson & Son 1968-77 (asst 1948-49, jr ptnr 1949-61, full ptnr 1962-77); sr hon architect Sue Ryder Fndn 1977-89, hon architect Burghley House Preservation Tst 1982-; 2nd prize London Airport Competition 1945, Civic Tst award, Design award for Stone 1981;

chm: Doncaster Round Table 1952, Doncaster Devpt Ctee 1970-74, Potteric Carr Drainage Bd 1968-82, Doncaster Civic Tst 1969-77, Sue Ryder Fndn 1988; sec Collyweston Slaters Tst; Doncaster Borough CC: cncllr 1966-68, alderman 1968-74, ldr of Cncl 1968-70; cncllr S Yorks Co Cncl; ARIBA 1949, FRIBA 1957; *Recreations* gardening, drawing, bridge; *Style*— Alan Wilson, Esq; Ostlers House, 1 Stamford Rd, South Luffenham, Rutland LE15 8NT (☎ 0780 721224); 11 rue de Noisitiers, Llauro, Thuir, France 66300 (☎ 010 3368 394036)

WILSON, Sir Alan Herries; s of H Wilson; *b* 2 July 1906; *Educ* Wallasey GS, Emmanuel Coll Cambridge; *m* 1934, Margaret Monks (d 1961); 2 s; *Career* Univ of Cambridge: fell Emmanuel Coll 1929-33, fell and lectr Trinity Coll, univ lectr in mathematics 1933-45; former chm: Glaxo Gp, Ctee on Coal Derivatives, Ctee on Noise, Nuclear Safety Advsy Ctee, Central Advsy Water Ctee; chm: governing body Nat Inst Agric Engrg 1971-76, govrs Bethlehem Royal and Maudsley Hosps 1973-80; dep chm Courtaulds 1957-62 (joined 1945, md 1954); pt/t memb and dep chm Electricity Cncl 1959; prime warden Worshipful Co of Goldsmiths 1969-70; Hon DSc: Univ of Oxford, Univ of Edinburgh; hon fell Emmanuel Coll 1929-33; FRS, Hon FIChemE, Hon FInstP, Hon FIMA; *Style*— Sir Alan Wilson, FRS; 65 Oakleigh Park South, Whetstone, London N20 9JL (☎ 081 445 3030)

WILSON, Alan James; s of Dr John Stanley Wilson, and Ellen Wilson; *b* 23 March 1948; *Educ* Univ of Brimingham (MB, ChB, MD), Univ of Glasgow (MSc); *m* 30 March 1976, Pauline Logan, da of Paul Weatherley, FRS, of Torphins, Aberdeenshire; 2 da (Margaret b 1978, Grace b 1982); *Career* lectr in surgery King's Coll Hosp 1984-87, conslt surgn Whittington Hosp 1987-; FRCS (G); *Recreations* mountaineering; *Style*— Alan Wilson, Esq; 54 Grasmere Rd, Musewell Hill, London N10 (☎ 081 883 1880); Whittington Hospital, Highgate, London N19 (☎ 071 272 3070)

WILSON, Alastair James Drysdale; QC (1987); s of Alastair Robin Wilson, ERD, of Sudbury, Suffolk, and Mary Damaris, *née* Dawson; *b* 26 May 1946; *Educ* Wellington, Pembroke Coll Cambridge; *Career* barr, memb Middle Temple; *Recreations* gardening, restoring old buildings; *Style*— Alastair Wilson, Esq, QC; Vanbrugh Castle, Maze Hill, Greenwich, London SE10 (☎ 081 853 1964); 3 Pump Court, Temple, London, EC4Y (☎ 071 583 5110, fax 071 583 1130)

WILSON, Alexander Duncan (Alex); s of Duncan Hubert Wilson, of 19 Catherine St, Gatehouse of Fleet, Scotland, and Betty, *née* Shakeshapt; *b* 14 Aug 1946; *Educ* Flineck Sch Pudsey Yorkshire; *m* Sue, da of Joe Hull; 2 s (Michael Barry b 20 April 1972, Benjamin Joseph b 30 May 1977), 1 da (Stephanie Jane b 7 Nov 1980); *Career* articled clerk E Warwick Broadbent & Co chartered accountants 1963-68, accountant Pilkington plc 1968-; FCA (ACA 1969); *Recreations* tennis, golf; *Clubs* Rotary Club of St Asaph, Denbigh Golf; *Style*— Alex Wilson, Esq; Pilkington PLC, Prescot Rd, St Helens, Merseyside WA10 3TT (☎ 0744 692244, fax 0744 612637)

WILSON, Alexander Galbraith (Sandy); s of George Walter Wilson (d 1937), and Caroline Elsie, *née* Humphrey (d 1963); *b* 19 May 1924; *Educ* Harrow, Oriel Coll Oxford (BA); *Career* Private RAOC 1943-46; contrib to Homione Gingold's Slings and Arrows and Laurier Lister's Oranges and Lemons 1948; composed words and music for revues See You Later 1951 and See You Again 1952; wrote book music and lyrics for: The Boy Friend 1954, The Buccaneer 1955, Valmouth 1958, Divorce Me Darling! 1964, His Monkey Wife 1971, The Clapham Wonder 1978, Aladdin 1978; one man show Sandy Wilson Thanks The Ladies 1971; composed music for TV progs The World of Wooster and Danny La Rue's Charley's Aunt; *Books* This is Sylvia (1955), I Could Be Happy (autobiography, 1975), Ivor (1975), The Roaring Twenties (1976); *Recreations* cinema, travel, drawing and painting; *Clubs* Players'; *Style*— Sandy Wilson, Esq; Flat 4, 2 Southwell Gardens, London SW7 4SB (☎ 071 373 6172)

WILSON, Lady Alexandra Patricia Gwendoline; da of 2 Earl Jellicoe, DSO, MC, PC; *b* 1944; *m* 1970, (Edward) Philip Wilson *qv*, s of Peter Wilson, CBE, *qv*; 2 s (Anthony Benedict b 1980, Patrick Peter b 1984); *Style*— The Lady Alexandra Wilson; 24 Highbury Place, London N5

WILSON, (Francis) Amcotts; s of Cdr Alec Thomas Lee Wilson, RN (d 1956), of Garth Hse, Llangammard Wells, Powys, and Margaret Mina Philipina, *née* Hirsch (d 1966); *b* 3 Jan 1922; *Educ* Shrewsbury (Nat Cert Mechanical Engrg); *m* 1 March 1968, Katherine Mary, da of Robert Charles Bruce, MC (d 1952), of 79 Cadogan Sq, London SW1; 1 s (Robert Mathew b 21 March 1970), 1 da (Jane Mary b 22 Jan 1972); *Career* HO rating RN 1941, Sub Lt RNVR served Atlantic, home waters and Med 1942-45; farmer 1950, memb Lloyds 1962; memb: Builth RDC 1960-67, Breconshire CC 1967-74; chm: St John Cncl Brecknock 1980-, Community Cncl 1986-; High Sheriff Powys 1974-75; *Recreations* shooting, fishing; *Clubs* Army & Navy; *Style*— Amcotts Wilson, Esq; Garth Hse, Llangammarch Wells, Powys LN4 4AL

WILSON, Andrew Norman; s of Lt-Col Norman Wilson (d 1985), and Jean Dorothy, *née* Crowder; *b* 27 Oct 1950; *Educ* Rugby, New Coll Oxford (BA, MA); *m* 1971 (m dis 1990), Katherine Dorothea, da of late Prof Austin Ernest Duncan-Jones; 2 da; *Career* literary ed: Spectator 1981-84, Evening Standard 1990-; author; Chancellor's Essay Prize 1971, Ellerton Theological Prize 1975, John Llewellyn Rhys Memorial Prize 1978, Somerset Maugham Prize, Arts Cncl Nat Book Award, Southern Arts Prizes 1981, W H Smith Prize 1983; FRSL 1981; *Books* The Sweets of Pimlico (1977), Unguarded Hours (1978), Kindly Light (1979), The Laird of Abbotsford (1980), The Healing Art (1980), Who Was Oswald Fish? (1981), Wise Virgin (1982), The Life of John Milton (1983), Scandal (1983), Hilaire Belloc (1984), How Can We Know? (1985), Gentlemen in England (1985), Love Unknown (1986), Stray (1987), Penfriends from Porlock (1988), Tolstoy (1988), Incline of Hearts (1988), The Tabitha Stories (1988), C S Lewis (1990), A Bottle in The Smove (1990); *Clubs* Academy; *Style*— Andrew Wilson, Esq; 91 Albert St, London NW1 7LX; The Evening Standard, 2 Derry St, London W8 (☎ 071 938 7600)

WILSON, Sir Angus Frank Johnstone; CBE (1968); s of William Johnstone-Wilson; *b* 11 Aug 1913; *Educ* Westminster, Merton Coll Oxford; *Career* novelist and playwright; prof of English lit Univ of E Anglia 1966-78 (emeritus 1978); memb: Royal Literary Fund 1966, Arts Cncl 1967; pres: Powys Soc 1970-80, Dickens Fellowship 1974-75, Kipling Soc 1981-88, Royal Soc of Lit 1982-88; chm Nat Book League 1971-74; FRSL, CLitt; Hon LittD Liverpool; Hon DLit: Leicester, E Anglia, Sussex, Sorbonne; Chev de l'Ordre des Arts et des Lettres 1972; kt 1980; *Books incl*: The Wrong Set (1949), Such Darling Dodos (1950), Hemlock and After (1952), The Middle Age of Mrs Eliot (1958, winner of James Black Memorial Prize and Prix du Meilleur Roman Etranger), The Old Men at the Zoo (1961), Late Call (1964), As If By Magic (1973); *biographies* Emile Zola (1952), The World of Charles Dickens (1970), The Strange Ride of Rudyard Kipling (1976), Setting the World on Fire (1980); *Style*— Sir Angus Wilson, CBE; Pinford Nursing Home, Hawstead, Bury St Edmonds, Suffolk

WILSON, Sir Anthony; s of Charles Ernest Wilson (d 1930), of Kirkstall, Leeds, and Martha Clarice, *née* Mee (d 1943); *b* 17 Feb 1928; *Educ* Giggleswick Sch; *m* 18 June 1955, (Margaret) Josephine, da of Maj Joseph Henry Hudson, CBE, MC, DL (d 1977), of Hill Top House, Wetherby, Yorkshire; 2 s (Duncan Henry b 1957, Oliver Charles b 1964), 1 da (Victoria Margaret (Mrs Mathews) b 1960); *Career* CA, head Govt Accountancy Serv and accountancy advsr to HM Treasy 1984-88; ptnr Price Waterhouse 1961-84; non-exec dir The Capita Group plc 1989-; memb: UK Review Body on Top Salaries, Mgmnt Bd of SW Arts 1983- (chm 1988-), Cncl ICAEW 1985-88, Accounting Standards Ctee 1984-88, Auditing Practices Ctee 1987-88; chm Jt Disciplinary Scheme of the UK accountancy profession 1990-, pres Chandos Chamber Choir 1986-88, chm Dorset Opera 1988-, dir Opera - 80 1989-; Freeman City of London, memb Ct Worshipful Co of Needlemakers 1988, Liveryman Worshipful Co of CAs; FCA; kt 1988; *Recreations* fishing, golf, gardening, opera, music; *Clubs* Reform; *Style*— Sir Anthony Wilson; The Barn House, 89 Newland, Sherborne, Dorset DT9 3AG (☎ 0935 815674)

WILSON, Anthony (Tony); s of George Albert Wilson, of Birmingham; *b* 4 May 1944; *Educ* Birmingham Coll of Art and Crafts, Central Sch of Art and Design; *m* 1966, Julia, da of William Eric Bint; 2 s (Ford James b 1967, Jabe George b 1970); *Career* painter, printmaker, lectr and arts admin; course dir MA in Printmaking Camberwell Coll of Arts 1990-, arts admin 1986-90 (incl advsr and examiner on BA and other courses in printmaking and fine art at various art schs and colls); selected one person and mixed exhibitions: Birmingham City Art Gallery 1964, Musee d'Art Moderne Paris 1970, British Painting (Hayward Galley London) 1974, 12 British Painters (Kjarvalsstader, Reykjavik Iceland) 1977, Ikon Gallery Birmingham 1981, Ferens Art Gallery Hull 1980, 1982 and 1985, South London Art Gallery London 1984, Royal Acad of Arts 1987-90, Square Gallery London 1986 and 1989, Premio Internazionale Biella Italy 1987, Talbot Fine Art Tetbury Glos 1990, others in GB Europe and USA; awards: Arts Cncl of Great Britain major award, major prize Humberside Nat Print Competition Ferens Art Gallery Hull 1985, West Midlands Arts award 1987, Lincolnshire Humberside Arts award 1988, London Paper Works Competition (Square Gallery) prizewinner 1989; *Style*— Tony Wilson, Esq; 26 Chestnut Rd, Kingston upon Thames, Surrey KT2 5AP (☎ 081 549 3090); Camberwell College of Arts, Peckham Rd, London SE5 8UF (☎ 071 703 0987, fax 071 703 3689)

WILSON, Anthony Joseph (Joe); MEP (Lab) North Wales 1989-; s of Joseph Samuel Wilson (d 1987), of Birkenhead, and Eleanor Annie, *née* Jones (d 1990); *b* 6 July 1937; *Educ* Birkenhead Sch, Loughborough Coll (DLC), Univ of Wales (BEd); *m* 1 Aug 1969 (m dis 1987), June Mary, da of Charlie Sockett (d 1985), of Wolverhampton; 1 s (Joseph Glen b 1964), 2 da (Carla Jane b 1965, Jessica Lee b 1967); *Career* Nat Serv RAPC 1955-57; teacher in Guernsey 1960-66, gen mangr St Marys Bay Kent 1966-69, lectr NE Wales Inst 1969-89; *Recreations* basketball, camping; *Style*— Joe Wilson, Esq, MEP; 79 Ruabon Rd, Wrexham, North Wales LL3 7PU (☎ 0978 352808); Labour Euro Office, 14 Post Office Lane, Denbigh LL13 3UN (☎ 0745 814434, fax 0745 814434); Swydfa Ewropeadd, 58 Stryd Lyyn, Caernarfon LL65 2AF (☎ 0286 78950, fax 0286 78950)

WILSON, Dr Ashley John; s of John Wilson, of 4 Harton House Rd, Harton, South Shields, Tyne & Wear, and Gladys Wilson; *b* 2 Nov 1950; *Educ* South Shields GS, Bedford Coll London (BSc), Univ of York (DPhil); *m* 2 Jan 1976, Sheila, da of James Mather, of 18 Ewart Crescent, South Shields, Tyne & Wear; *Career* mangr Centre for Cell and Tissue Res Univ of York 1980-; ed Protocols in Electron Microscopy 1989-; memb: Br Humanist Assoc, Nat Secular Soc; active memb and sec York Humanist Gp, fell Royal Microsopical Soc; MIBiol 1975, CBiol 1979; *Books* An Atlas of Low Temperature Scanning Electron Microscopy (1984), Foams: Chemistry, Physics and Structure (1989), Resins for Light and Electron Microscopy (1991); *Recreations* wine tasting, architectural history, badminton; *Style*— Dr Ashley J Wilson; 8 Manor Drive South, Acomb, York YO2 5SA (☎ 0904 799753); CCTR, University of York, York YO1 5SA (☎ 0904 432935, fax 0904 432917)

WILSON, Vice Adm Sir Barry Nigel; KCB (1990); s of Rear Adm Guy Austin Moore Wilson, CB (d 1986), and Dorothy, *née* Watson, BEM; *b* 5 June 1936; *Educ* St Edward's Sch Oxford, Britannia RN Coll (Queen's Sword, Queen's Gold medal); *m* 26 Dec 1961, Elizabeth Ann, da of William Hardy (d 1986); 1 s (Robert Guy b 1967), 1 da (Harriet Jane b 1965); *Career* CO: HMS Mohawk 1973-74, HMS Cardiff 1978-80, RCDS 1982, dir Navy Plans 1983-85, flag offr Sea Training 1986-87, ACDS progs 1987-89, dep chief of Defence Staff (Prog and Personnel) 1989-; memb RUSI, chm Cncl Bede House Assoc Bermondsey; *Recreations* campanology, gardening; *Style*— Vice Adm Sir Barry Wilson, KCB; c/o Naval Secretary, Ripley Block, Old Admiralty Building, Whitehall, London SW1A (☎ 071 218 9000)

WILSON, Brian David Henderson; MP (Lab) Cunninghame N 1987-; s of late John Forrest Wilson, and Marion, *née* McIntyre; *b* 13 Dec 1948; *Educ* Dunoon GS, Univ of Dundee (MA), Univ Coll (Dip Journalism Studies); *m* 1981, Joni, *née* Buchanan; 1 da; *Career* publisher and founding ed West Highland Free Press 1972-; front bench spokesman on Scot Affrs 1988-; first winner Nicholas Tomalin Meml award 1975; contrib to: The Guardian, Glasgow Herald; *Books* Celtic: a century with honour (1988); *Style*— Brian Wilson, Esq, MP; 22 Glebe Rd, Beith, Ayrshire (☎ 050 55 4783); Miavaig House, Isle of Lewis (☎ 085 175 357); office: 37 Main St, Kilbirnie, Ayrshire (☎ 0505 682847); House of Commons, London SW1A 0AA (☎ 071 219 4033)

WILSON, Brian John; s of Andrew Wilson (d 1983), and Alice Margaret, *née* Dickel; *b* 17 May 1944; *Educ* Enfield GS; *m* 26 March 1966, Pamela Florence, da of Joseph Thomas Wansell; 2 da (Jane b 1967, Susan b 1971); *Career* CA 1966; articled clerk Charles Comins & Co 1960-66; Ernst & Young 1966-: joined 1966, ptnr 1973-, i/c public sector servs 1983-88, ptnr i/c specialist industs 1988-; FCA; *Recreations* sailing; *Clubs* Stone SC; *Style*— B J Wilson, Esq; Ernst & Young, Becket House, 1 Lambeth Palace Rd, London SE1 7EU (☎ 071 931 3635, fax 071 928 1345)

WILSON, Brian Vincent; s of Reginald Wilson (d 1976), of Dublin, and Josephine, *née* Murphy (d 1980); *b* 10 July 1945; *Educ* Clongowes Wood Coll Co Kildare Ireland, Univ Coll Dublin (BA), Trinity Coll Dublin (MBA); *m* 16 Oct 1968, Frances Mary Carroll, da of Thomas Carroll (d 1978), of Dublin; 1 s (Stephen b 11 Dec 1973), 2 da (Samantha b 24 July 1969, Eugenie b 25 May 1971); *Career* private indust 1968-71, sr exec Industl Credit Co 1971-73, mangr banking (later dir and gen mangr GB) Allied Investment Bank 1974-83, gp gen mangr GB Allied Irish Banks 1983-89, dir and gp gen mangr Ireland AIB Group 1989-; *Recreations* cricket, golf, rugby, tennis, opera; *Clubs* Reform, Wentworth Golf, MCC, Fitzwilliam Lawn Tennis; *Style*— Brian V Wilson, Esq; AIB Group, Bankcentre, Ballsbridge, Dublin 4 (☎ 010 600311, fax 010 684502)

WILSON, Brian William John Gregg; s of Cecil Samuel Wilson (d 1978), and Margaret Dorothea, *née* Gregg; *b* 16 June 1937; *Educ* Sedbergh, Christ's Coll Cambridge (scholar, MA, capt Rugby Fives Club); *m* 29 March 1969, Sara Remington, da of Henry Edward Hollins; 2 da (Anna Jane Illingworth, Emma Margaret); *Career* RIrF NI 1955-57; schoolmaster Radley Sch 1960-65, housemaster King's Sch Canterbury 1965-73, dir of studies Eastbourne Coll 1973-76, headmaster Campbell Coll Belfast 1977-87, project mangr Navan Fort Initiative Gp 1987-89, dep head St Mary's Sch Wantage 1989-; memb: Central Religious Advsy Ctee BBC and ITV 1982-87, NI Sci and Technol Regnl Orgn, Advsy Ctee for Schs/Indust Liaison; chief examiner Latin A Level NI Schs Examination Bd, examiner in charge Ancient History A Level Cambridge Local Examination Syndicate; memb: Jt Assoc of Classics Teachers, Asst Masters and Mistresses Assoc; *Books* Res Publica (with Prof W K Lacey, 1970), Stories from Uerodotus (1973); *Recreations* walking, theatre, theology; *Clubs* Jesters, Royal Belfast Golf; *Style*— Brian Wilson, Esq; St Mary's Sch, Wantage, Oxon

WILSON, Dr Bryan Ronald; *b* 25 June 1926; *Educ* Univ Coll Leicester, LSE (Hutchinson medal for res), Univ of London (BSc, PhD), Univ of Oxford (MA, DLitt);

Career lectr in sociology Univ of Leeds 1955-62 (warden Sadler Hall 1959-62); Cwtlth Fund fell Univ of Calif Berkeley 1957-58; Univ of Oxford: reader in sociology 1962-, fell All Souls Coll 1963-, sub warden All Souls Coll 1988-90; Hon DLitt Soka Univ Japan; *Books* Sects and Society (1961), Religion in Secular Society (1966), Patterns of Sectarianism (ed, 1967), Religions Sects (1970), The Youth Culture and the Universities (1970), Rationality (ed, 1970), Magic and the Millennium (1973), The Noble Savages (1975), Contemporary Transformations of Religion (1976), Religion in Sociological Perspective (1982), Human Values in a Changing World (co-author, 1984), Values (ed, 1988), The Social Dimensions of Sectarianism (1990); *Style*— Dr Bryan Wilson; All Souls College, Oxford OX1 4AL (☎ 0865 279290)

WILSON, Charles Martin; s of Adam Wilson (d 1964), and Ruth Ann Wilson (d 1974); *b* 18 Aug 1935; *Educ* Eastbank Acad Glasgow; *m* 1, 18 Jan 1968 (m dis 1973), Anne Josephine, da of Bernard Robinson; 1 da (Emma Alexandra b 1970); m 2, 2 Oct 1980, Sally Angela O'Sullivan, da of L J Connell; 1 s (Luke Adam b 1981), 1 da (Lily Joan b 1985); *Career* dep night news ed Daily Mail 1963, followed by exec jobs at The Daily Mail including sports ed and dep Northern ed, asst ed London Evening News; ed: Glasgow Evening Times 1976, Glasgow Herald 1981, The Sunday Standard from its launch 1982; exec ed Times 1982, ed Chicago Sunday Times 1984, jt dep ed The Times 1984, ed The Times Nov 1985-90, dir News International 1990- March-Dec 1990, md and ed in chief The Sporting Life 1991-; *Recreations* writing, reading, watching steeplechasing; *Clubs* Reform; *Style*— Charles M Wilson, Esq; Sporting Life, Orbit House, 1 New Fetter Lane, London EC4A 1AR

WILSON, Hon Charles Thomas; s of 3 Baron Nunburnholme (d 1974) by his 1 w, late Lady Mary Alexander Thynne, youngest da of 5 Marquess of Bath; hp of bro, 4 Baron; *b* 27 May 1935; *Educ* Ludgrove, Eton; *m* 1969 (m dis), Linda Kay, only da of Cyril James Stephens, of Woodlands, Challock Lees, Ashford, Kent; 1 s (Stephen), 1 da (Nathalia); *Career* page of honour to HM King George VI 1950-52; memb Stock Exchange 1956-66; co dir; *Clubs* White's; *Style*— The Hon Charles Wilson; c/o Banco Fonseca Y Burnay, Portimao, Portugal

WILSON, Colin; s of James Wilson, of Linden House, Lymington, Hants, and Rita Woodhouse, *née* Tyson (d 1971); *b* 16 May 1931; *Educ* Ulverston GS, Wadham Coll Oxford (BA); *m* 1, 31 Dec 1955 (m dis 1982), Gillian Elizabeth, *née* Walker; 2 s (Andrew Robert b 5 Feb 1959, Iain James b 26 July 1963), 2 da (Katherine Jane b 27 Aug 1957, Elizabeth Rachel b 12 Nov 1961); m 2, 19 Aug 1985, Niyaz Martin, da of Burhan Ataergin (d 1962), of Istanbul, Turkey; 1 s (Nicholas Turnham Martin b 31 Oct 1962); *Career* Nat serv RAF 1949-51; diplomat: third sec Embassy of Peking 1956-59, Far Eastern Dept FCO, Br military govt Berlin, first sec Br Embassy Washington, head of China Res Dept FCO, head of chancery Br Embassy Vientiane, dir special project (redesign of FCO), asst sec Cabinet Office, consul-gen Auckland, commercial counsellor Br Embassy The Hague, dir special project (review of long term communications and tech requirements of the FCO); memb Royal Cwlth Soc; *Recreations* tennis, swimming, walking, theatre, visual arts, antique collecting; *Clubs* Union Sydney, Royal Sydney Golf; *Style*— Colin Wilson, Esq; 9 Balliol House, Putney, London SE15 (☎ 081 789 3747); 1/66 Waiataru Rd, Remuera, Auckland, New Zealand (☎ 010 64 9 523 3243); 25 Gilliver Ave, Vaucluse, Sydney, NSW, Australia (☎ 010 61 337 5859); British Consulate General, 10th Floor, Goldfields House, 1 Alfred St, Sydney, NSW 2000 (☎ 247 7521, telex 20680, fax 233 1826)

WILSON, Colin Christopher; s of late Ninian Jameson Reid-Wilson, of Bournemouth, England, and Margaret Elizabeth, *née* Briscoe (d 1958); *b* 6 Sept 1941; *Educ* St Peter's Sch Bournemouth, Coll of Law; *m* 11 Sept 1965, Priscilla Joan, da of Bruce Osborne (d 1960), of Calcutta, India; 2 s (Simon Christopher b 1971, Daniel James b 1977); *Career* admitted slr 1966, sr ptnr Turners Bournemouth 1985-; hon slr: Wimborne and Dist Community Assoc, St Thomas Garnet Sch; memb Law Soc; *Recreations* sailing, tennis, skiing; *Style*— Colin Wilson, Esq; Chalbury Grange, Chalbury, Wimborne, Dorset (☎ 0258 840465); 1 Poole Rd, Bournemouth, Dorset (☎ 0202 291291, fax 0202 553606, telex 41158 JUMBOS G)

WILSON, Colin Henry; s of Arthur Wilson, and Annetta Wilson; *b* 26 June 1931; *Educ* Leicester Gateway Sch; *m* 1; 1 s (Roderick); m 2, 1973, Pamela Joy, da of John Arthur Stewart (d 1972); 2 s (Damon, Rowan), 1 da (Sally); *Career* writer in residence Hollins (VA) Coll 1966-67; visiting prof: Univ of Washington Seattle 1967, Rutgers Univ New Brunswick NJ 1974; author; *Books incl*: The Outsider (1956), Ritual in the Dark (1960), The Mind Parasites (1966), The Black Room (1970), The Occult (1971), Criminal History of Mankind (1983), The Essential Colin Wilson (1984), The Personality Surgeon (1986), Spiderworld (1987), Encyclopedia of Unsolved Mysteries (with Damon Wilson, 1987), Aleister Crowley: the nature of the beast (1987), The Misfits: a study of sexual outsidus (1988), Beyond the Occult (1988), Written in Blood (1989), Serial Killers (with Donald Seaman, 1990); *Recreations* walking, swimming; *Clubs* Savage; *Style*— Colin Wilson, Esq; Gorran Haven, Cornwall PL26 6NT

WILSON, Sir David; 3 Bt (UK 1920), of Carbeth, Killearn, Co Stirling; s of Sir John Mitchell Harvey Wilson, 2 Bt, KCVO (d 1975), by his w, Mary Elizabeth (d 1979); *b* 30 Oct 1928; *Educ* Deerfield Acad Mass USA, Harrow, Oriel Coll Oxford; *m* 1955, Eva Margareta, da of Tore Lindell, of Malmö, Sweden; 2 s, 1 da; *Heir* s, Thomas David Wilson; *Career* called to the Bar Lincoln's Inn 1953, solicitor 1962, ptnr Simmons & Simmons 1963-; *Recreations* sailing; *Clubs* Arts, Royal Southern Yacht; *Style*— Sir David Wilson, Bt; Tandem House, Queen's Drive, Oxshott, Surrey KT22 0PH (☎ 037 284 2061); Simmons & Simmons, 14 Dominion St, London EC2M 2RJ (☎ 071 628 2020, fax 071 588 4129)

WILSON, Sir David Clive; GCMG (1991, KCMG 1987, CMG 1985); s of Rev William Skinner Wilson and Enid Wilson; *b* 14 Feb 1935; *Educ* Trinity Coll, Glenalmond , Keble Coll Oxford (BA), Univ of Hong Kong, Univ of Columbia (visiting scholar), Univ of London (PhD); *m* 1967, Natasha Helen Mary Alexander; 2 s; *Career* HM Dip Serv: joined SE Asia Dept FO 1958, third sec Vientiane, third then second sec Peking 1963-65, first sec Far Eastern Dept 1965-68; exec ed The China Quarterly Contemporary Inst SOAS Univ of London 1968-74; HM Dip Serv 1974, Cabinet Office 1974-77, political advsr to Govr of Hong Kong 1977-81, head S Euro Dept FCO 1981-84, asst under sec of State responsible for Asia and the Pacific, FCO 1984-87, Govr and C-in-C of Hong Kong 1987-; Hon LLD Univ of Aberdeen 1990; *Recreations* mountaineering, skiing, reading; *Clubs* Athaeneum, Alpine, Hong Kong; *Style*— Sir David Wilson, GCMG

WILSON, David Geoffrey; OBE (1986), DL (Greater Manchester 1985); s of Cyril Wilson (d 1950), and Winifred, *née* Sutton (d 1944); *b* 30 April 1933; *Educ* Leeds GS, Oldham Hulme GS; *m* 10 Aug 1980, Dianne Elizabeth, da of Rupert George Morgan (d 1980); *Career* Nat Serv RAOC 1951-53, TA Manchester Regt 9 Battalion 1958-68, ret Maj; sec Williams Deacons Bank 1965-70, area mangr Williams & Glyn's Bank 1977-81 (sec 1970-72, mangr 1973-76), regnl dir Enterprise Bd NW 1981-85, dir of banking The Br Linen Bank Ltd 1986-; pres: Manchester Chamber of Commerce & Industry 1978-80, Manchester Literary and Philosophical Soc 1981-83; treas Hallé Concerts Soc, hon consul for Iceland, memb of Ct Univ of Manchester; chm: Manchester PO Advsy Ctee, Manchester Telecommunications Advsy Ctee; govr: Withington Girls Sch, Salford Coll of Technol; MA Univ of Manchester 1983; FBIM, FCIB; *Recreations* gardening, music; *Clubs* St James (Manchester), Army and Navy, MCC, Lancashire Cricket; *Style*— David Wilson, Esq, OBE, DL; Winton, 28 Macclesfield Rd, Wilmslow, Cheshire SK9 2AF (☎ 0625 524133); The British Linen Bank Ltd, 19/21 Spring Gardens, Manchester M2 1EB (☎ 061 832 4444, fax 061 832 4270, telex 665931)

WILSON, Sir David Mackenzie; s of Rev Joseph Wilson (d 1988), of Castletown, Isle of Man; *b* 30 Oct 1931; *Educ* Kingswood Sch, St John's Coll Cambridge (MA, LittD), Lund Univ Sweden; *m* 1955, Eva, da of late Dr G Sjögren, of Stockholm; 1 s, 1 da; *Career* asst keeper Br Museum 1954-66 (dir 1977-92); reader in archaeology of Anglo-Saxon period Univ of London 1966-71 (prof of medieval archaeology 1971-76), jt head Dept of Scandinavian Studies UCL 1973-76 (dean of Faculty of Arts 1973-76); govr Museum of London 1976-81, tstee Nat Museums of Scotland 1985-87, memb Ancient Monuments Bd for England 1976-84, former pres Br Archaeological Assoc; hon fell: St John's Coll Cambridge, UCL; FSA, FBA; Order of Polar Star (Sweden, first class) 1977; kt 1984; *books incl*: The Anglo Saxons, Viking Art, Catalogue of Anglo-Saxon Metalwork 700-1100 in the British Museum; pubns on the Vikings, St Ninian's Isle Treasure and the Bayeux Tapestry; *Clubs* Athenaeum; *Style*— Sir David Wilson, FSA; The Lifeboat House, Castletown, Isle of Man

WILSON, David Steel; s of John Mill Wilson (d 1954), and Elizabeth Garth, *née* Steel (d 1987); *b* 21 Jan 1936; *Educ* Bishopbriggs HS, Glasgow Coll of Technol (Dip in Mktg); *m* 24 Aug 1965, Patricia Ann, da of James MacDowall Docherty; 1 s (Byron David Kingsley b 10 Dec 1970), 1 da (Saskia Claire Kingsley b 2 Jan 1973); *Career* Nat Serv RAF 1957-59; Fyfe & McGrouther Ltd: apprentice 1953-57, sales rep 1959-66, sales mangr 1966-67; area sales mangr James Neill & Co Ltd Sheffield 1967-69, mktg mangr Pneumatic Components (RTZ Group) 1969-70, commis chef and trainee mangr Pheasant Inn Keyston 1970-72, proprietor The Peat Inn Fife 1972-; *Awards* Cellar of the Year UK Wine award Egon Ronay Guide 1985, chef Laureate Br Gastronomic Acad 1986, Michelin star 1986, Restauranteur of the Year Catey award 1989; memb Master Chefs of GB 1983- (chm Exec Ctee 1987-); *Recreations* music, sport, travel; *Style*— David Wilson, Esq; The Peat Inn, Peat Inn, by Cupar, Fife KY15 5LH (☎ 033 484 206, fax 033 484 530)

WILSON, Derek; s of William Lawson Wilson (d 1980), of Blaydon Co Durham, and Bertha, *née* Heppell (d 1982); *b* 21 Sept 1932; *Educ* Blaydon GS, Univ of Durham (BDS), Univ of London (MB BS); *m* 25 Oct 1958, da of Walter Parkinson (d 1978), of Blaydon, Co Durham; 1 s (David John Sinclair b 1966), 1 da (Kathryn Jane b 1963); *Career* surgn Lt RN 1958-61; conslt oral and maxillo facial surgn Charing Cross Hosp 1972-, hon conslt St Thomas Hosp 1972-, Cambridge Mil Hosp Aldershot 1976-, dean of admissions and chm Selection Ctee Charing Cross and Westminster Med Sch 1976-; memb: BMA, Euro Acad of Facial Surgery; FDS RCS 1970, fell BAOMS; *Recreations* golf, tennis, bridge; *Clubs* Walton Heath Golf; *Style*— Derek Wilson, Esq; Sumners, 28 The Street, West Horsley, Leatherhead, Surrey KT24 6AX (☎ 04865 3791); Dept of Oral & Maxillo-Facial Surgery, Charing Cross Hospital, Fulham Palace Rd, London W6 8RF (☎ 081 846 1471)

WILSON, Derek William; s of William George Wilson (d 1987), of Worthing, and Dorothy Amelia, *née* Austin (d 1951); *b* 23 Oct 1933; *Educ* Bancroft's Sch Woodford Green Essex, UCH Med Sch (MB BS); *m* 6 Dec 1958, Evelyn Alice, da of William Charles Stacey (d 1982), of Harrow; 1 s (Ian b 1965), 2 da (Clare b 1967, Philippa b 1969); *Career* Nat Serv Lt and Capt RAMC 1957-59: 3 Div Signal Regt and 26 Fd Regt RA, serv Colchester and Cyprus (GSM); former conslt orthopaedic surgn Royal Free Hosp 1973-89; hon ed memb Cncl Br Orthopaedic Foot Surgery Soc; FRCS; *Books* The Foot (ed with B Helal, 1988), contrib General Surgical Operations (1978); papers incl: Diastrophic Dwarfism (1969), Synovectomy of Elbow (1971 and 1973), Injuries of the Tarsometatarsal Joints (1972), Supracondylar Fractures of Humerus (1977), Hallux Valgus and Bunion (1980); *Style*— Derek Wilson, Esq; 41 Ridge Lea, Hemel Hampstead, Herts HP1 2AZ (☎ 0442 251066)

WILSON, Des; s of Albert H Wilson (d 1989), of Oamuru, NZ, and Ellen, *née* Hoskins; *b* 5 March 1941; *Educ* Waitiki Boys' HS NZ; *m* 1 (m dis 1984); 1 s (Timothy), 1 da (Jacqueline); m 2, 24 May 1985, Jane, da of Maurice Dunmore, of Brighton; *Career* journalist; columnist: The Guardian 1968-71, The Observer 1971-75; ed Social Work Today 1976-79, dep ed The Illustrated London News 1979-81; dir Shelter 1967-71, memb Nat Exec Nat Cncl for Civil Liberties 1971-73, head public affrs RSC 1974-76; chm: CLEAR 1982-90, Friends of the Earth 1983-86, Citizens Action 1984-90, Campaign for Freedom of Info 1984-90; Lib pty: pres 1986-87, memb Fed Exec 1988-89; dir Gen Election Campaign Lib Democrats 1990-; *Books* I know it was the Place's Fault (1970), Des Wilson's Minority Report - a diary of protest (1973), So you want to be a Prime Minister; a personal view of British politics (1979), The Head Scandal (1982), Pressure, the A to Z of Campaigning in Britain (1984), The Environmental Crisis (ed 1984), The Secrets File (ed 1984), The Citizen Action Handbook (1986), Battle for Power - Inside the Alliance General Election Campaign (1987), Costa del Sol (1990); *Clubs* Nat Lib, Groucho's; *Style*— Des Wilson, Esq; 46 Arundel St, Brighton, Sussex (☎ 0273 606915)

WILSON, Sir (Robert) Donald; DL (Cheshire 1987-); s of John Wilson, and Kate Wilson; *b* 6 June 1922; *Educ* Grove Park Sch Wrexham Clwyd; *m* 1946, Elizabeth; *Career* RAF; landowner; tyre industry 1946-60, dir of various farming and property cos 1954-; chm: Electricity Consultative Cncl (NW) 1981-85, Mersey Regnl Health Authy 1982-, Cheshire CLA 1979-81; bd memb NW Electricity Bd (NORWEB) 1981-85;memb Lloyds 1970-; pres Ayreshire Cattle Soc 1966-67; High Sheriff Cheshire 1985-86; kt 1987; *Recreations* fishing, countryside generally; *Clubs* Chester City, Farmers; *Style*— Sir Donald Wilson, DL; The Oldfields, Pulford, Chester

WILSON, (William) Douglas; s of William Howard Wilson (d 1960), of Marlow, Bucks, and Jane Lambert, *née* Cooper; *b* 31 May 1929; *Educ* Harrow, Hertford Coll Oxford (MA); *m* 1, 23 Jan 1959 (m dis 1972), Penelope Catherine, da of Sir Gerard J R d'Erlanger, CBE (d 1961), of London; 1 s ((William) Matthew b 1959), 1 da (Georgina Harriette Mary b 1960); m 2, 1980, Judith Helen, da of Joseph H Porter, of Haddenham, Cambs; 1 d (Daisy Louise b 1982); *Career* assoc ed The Director (IOD) 1954-59; dir: property investmt and dealing cos, retailing and wholesaling cos; Parly candidate (C) Norwood Div Lambeth 1965; *Style*— Douglas Wilson, Esq; Pilton Manor, Oundle, Northants; 6 Eaton Place, London SW1X 8AD (☎ 071 235 8200)

WILSON, Edward; s of Edward William Wilson, of Wingrove House, South Shields, and Thomasina, *née* Moore; *b* 13 July 1947; *Educ* South Shields GS for Boys, Univ of Manchester (BA); *Career* actor Nat Youth Theatre 1965-70, played leading repertory theatres incl a season with the Traverse Theatre Edinburgh; dir of professional prodns in London incl: Romeo and Juliet, Macbeth, Godspell; dir Newbury Community Theatre 1984, artistic dir Fiftieth Anniversary of the Royal Jubilee Tst (staged The Way of Light St Paul's Cathedral) 1984; dir Nat Youth Theatre 1981-: Murder in the Cathedral (London, Edinburgh Festival Moscow Arts Theatre) A Man For All Seasons, The Royal Hunt of the Sun (Jeanetta Cochrane Theatre London), The Taming of the Shrew, Othello, Night Shriek (Shaw), Caucasian Chalk Circle (His Majesty's Aberdeen, Tyne Opera House Newcastle, Bloomsbury Theatre),Marat Sade and Blitz (Playhouse Theatre) Blood Wedding (Bloomsbury Theatre, Teatro Principal Valencia), artistic dir 1987-; dir: Brit Cncl tours 1986 and 1990; TV appearances in When the Boat Comes In and Rockliffe's Babies; memb Bd Northern Stage Company, Actors Equity, Directors Guild of GB; chm Northern Arts Awards; *Recreations* music; *Clubs* Royal

Overseas League; *Style—* Edward Wilson, Esq; National Youth Theatre of Great Britain, 443-445 Holloway Rd, London N7 6LW (☎ 071 281 3863, fax 071 281 8246, car 0860 380 395)

WILSON, Lady; Elizabeth Anne Martin; da of Charles James Nicol Fleming (d 1947), and Katherine, *née* Cunningham; *b* 7 Sept 1911; *Educ* St Leonard's Scotland, Lady Margaret Hall Oxford (MA); *m* 1937, Sir (Archibald) Duncan Wilson, GCMG (d 1983, ambass to Yugoslavia and USSR, and master of Corpus Christi Coll Cambridge), s of Archibald Edward Wilson (d 1924); 1 s decd, 2 da; *Publications* The Modern Russian Dictionary for English Speakers (1982); *Style—* Lady Wilson; Cala Na Ruadh, Port Charlotte, Islay, Argyll PA48 7TS (☎ 049 685 289)

WILSON, Eric; *b* 8 July 1935; *Educ* Horton-Le-Spring GS; *m* 26 Dec 1963, Irene; 1 s (Mark); *Career* Nat Serv RAF 1953-55; Lloyds Bank 1956-57; various mgmnt appts with: Bank of W Africa 1958-65, Martins bank 1965-67, Barclays Bank 1968-80, corp fin dir Barclays Bank 1980-84, chief exec and regnl dir TSB Scot plc 1989- (gen mangr of banking 1984-86, sr gen mangr 1986-87, chief gen mangr 1987, md 1987-89); memb: CBI Scot Cncl, Scot Cncl Devpt and Indust Exec Ctee; FIB (Scotland), FCIB; *Recreations* running, music, reading and travelling; *Clubs* New (Edinburgh); *Style—* Eric Wilson, Esq; 79 Woodfield Park, Colinton, Edinburgh EH13 0RA; TSB Bank Scotland plc, Henry Duncan House, 120 George St, Edinburgh EH2 4TS (☎ 031 225 4555, telex 727512, fax 031 220 0240, car 0836 717100)

WILSON, (William) Frederick; s of Sidney Stuart Wilson (d 1986), of Sunderland, and Audrey, *née* Evans (d 1988); *b* 28 April 1947; *Educ* Bede GS Sunderland, Univ of Durham (BA); *m* 1968, Angela May, da of Andrew Wilkie Campbell, of Berwick Upon Tweed, Northumberland; 1 s (Timothy b 1974), 1 da (Fiona b 1969); *Career* admitted slr 1972; ptnr Dickinson Dees Newcastle Upon Tyne 1975-; memb Law Soc; *Recreations* walking, reading, music, model railways, snooker; *Style—* Frederick Wilson, Esq; Cross House, Westgate Rd, Newcastle Upon Tyne (☎ 091 261 1991, fax 091 261 5855, telex 537129)

WILSON, Hon Geoffrey Hazlitt; yr s of 1 Baron Moran, MC (d 1977), and Dorothy, *née* Dufton, MBE (d 1983); *b* 28 Dec 1929; *Educ* Eton, King's Coll Cambridge (BA); *m* 19 May 1955, (Barbara) Jane, o da of William Edward Hilary Hebblethwaite, of Itchen Stoke, Alresford, Hants; 2 s (Nicholas b 1957, Hugo b 1963), 2 da (Laura b 1966, Jessica b 1967); *Career* 2 Lt RHG 1948-49; joined English Electric 1956, dep comptroller 1965, fin controller (overseas) GEC 1968; Delta plc: fin dir Cables Divn 1969, elected to Main Bd as gp fin dir 1972, jt md 1977, dep chief exec 1980, chief exec 1981-88, chm 1982-; dir: Blue Circle Industries plc, Drayton English & International Trust plc, Johnson Mathey plc, Nat Westminster Bank plc (W Midlands and Wales region), Southern Electric plc, Viczizye Motorcar Ltd; dep pres Engrg Employers Fedn 1986-90 (vice pres 1990-), pres British Electro-technical and Allied Manufacturers' Assocs 1987-88 (counsellor 1988-); hon memb Hundred Gp 1985 (chm 1979-81); memb: Fin Reporting Cncl 1990-, Cncl Inst of Cost and Management Accountants 1972-78, Accounting Standards Ctee 1978-79, Admin Cncl The Royal Jubilee Tsts 1979-88 (hon treas 1980-89), Cncl Winchester Cathedral Tst, Cncl St Mary's Hosp Med Sch 1985-88, Mgmnt Bd Prince's Royal Jubilee Tsts 1988-89; memb Ct of Assistants, Worshipful Co of CAs (jr warden 1986-87, sr warden 1987-88, master 1988-89); FCA 1955, FCMA 1959; *Recreations* family, reading, walking, skiing, vintage cars; *Clubs* Boodle's, RAC; *Style—* The Hon Geoffrey Wilson; Delta plc, 1 Kingsway, London WC2B 6XF (☎ 071 836 3535, telex 27762)

WILSON, Sir Geoffrey Masterman; KCB (1969, CB 1968), CMG (1962); s of Alexander Wilson; *b* 7 April 1910; *Educ* Manchester GS, Oriel Coll Oxford; *m* 1, 1946 (m dis 1979), Julie Strafford Trowbridge; 2 s, 2 da; m 2, 1989, Stephanie Adrienne Stainsby; *Career* vice pres Int Bank Washington DC 1961, perm sec Miny Overseas Dept 1968-70 (dep sec 1966-68), dep sec gen Cwlth Secretariat 1971, chm Race Rels Bd 1971-77, chm Oxfam 1977-83; hon fellow Wolfson Coll Cambridge 1971; *Style—* Sir Geoffrey Wilson, KCB, CMG; 4 Polstead Rd, Oxford

WILSON, Geoffrey Robin (Geoff); s of John Bedford Wilson (d 1987), of Scarborough, N Yorks, and Ena Marjorie, *née* Hall; *b* 10 Oct 1942; *Educ* Scarboorugh HS, Univ of Leeds, Univ of Bristol (BA, Certificate of Drama); *m* 24 April 1971, Valerie Maureen, da of Harold Gray; *Career* BBC TV: joined film unit Midland region 1965, film cameraman 1970, prodn asst Childrens TV (dir Blue Peter) 1970-73, dep head Sch TV 1988- (joined 1973, prodr 1977, chief asst 1983, exec prodr 1985); memb SLD; memb RTS, exec Educational TV Assoc; *Recreations* photography, theatre; *Style—* Geoff Wilson, Esq; St Marys, Gold Hill North, Chalfont St Peter, Bucks (☎ 0753 886642); School Television, BBC White City, London W12 7TS (☎ 081 752 5252)

WILSON, (William) George; OBE (1960); s of William James Wilson (d 1965), and Susannah, *née* Barnfather (d 1967); *b* 19 Feb 1921; *Educ* Blaydon GS; *m* 29 March 1948, Freda, da of David Richard Huddleston (d 1927); 3 s (David b 1951, Richard b 1962, Edward b 1966); *Career* Royal Signals 1940-46; Miny of Health 1939-40, Colonial Office 1947-57, fin sec Mauritius 1957-60, Dept of Technol Co-op 1960-62; Miny of Health: hosp planning and design 1962-1968, DHSS 1970-81, under sec NHS Mgmnt and controller Social Security Mgmnt, ret 1981; admin UK-Kuwait Health Servs Co-op 1981-83, dir and chief exec Paul James & George Wilson Ltd health serv devpt advsrs 1983-89, assoc dir PA Consulting Group 1989-; memb N Tyneside Community Health Cncl 1976-80, librarian Soc of Antiquaries Newcastle Upon Tyne 1977-81; *Recreations* gardening; *Clubs* Royal Cwlth; *Style—* George Wilson, Esq, OBE; Clarghyll Hall, Alston, Cumbria CA9 3NF; PA Consulting Gp, 123 Buckingham Palace Road, London SW1W 9SR

WILSON, Gerald Robertson; s of Charles Robertson Wilson, of Edinburgh, and Margaret, *née* Early; *b* 7 Sept 1939; *Educ* Univ of Edinburgh (MA); *m* 11 May 1963, Margaret Anne, da of John Wight, of Edinburgh (d 1970); 1 s (Christopher b 1968), 1 da (Catherine b 1964); *Career* private sec Civil Serv (Lord Privy Seal) 1972-74, cncllr UK Representation Brussels 1977-82, asst sec Scot Office 1974-77 (and 1982-84), under sec Indust Dept for Scotland 1984-88, sec Scot Educn Dept 1988-; *Recreations* music; *Clubs* Royal Cwlth Soc, New (Edinburgh); *Style—* Gerald Wilson, Esq; Scottish Educn Dept, Scottish Office, New St Andrews House, Edinburgh

WILSON, Dr (Robert) Gordon; s of Robert George Wilson, of Glasgow; *b* 16 April 1938; *Educ* Douglas HS, Univ of Edinburgh (BL), Univ of Dundee (LLD); *m* 1965, Edith Margaret Hassall; 2 da; *Career* MP (SNP) Dundee East Feb 1974-87; SNP: nat sec 1964-71, vice-chm 1972-73, sr vice-chm 1973-74, dep ldr Parly Gp 1974-79, chm 1979-90; rector Univ of Dundee 1983-86; slr; *Style—* Dr Gordon Wilson; 48 Monifieth Rd, Broughty Ferry, Dundee DD5 2RX (☎ 0382 79009)

WILSON, Graeme McDonald; CMG (1975); s of Robert Linton McDonald Wilson (d 1929), and Sophie Hamilton, *née* Milner (d 1953); *b* 9 May 1919; *Educ* Rendcomb Coll, Schloss Schule Salem, Lincoln Coll Oxford (war degree); *m* 6 Nov 1968, Masae (Mayumi), da of Tokichi Yabu, of Fukui, Japan; 3 s (Mark, Jiro, Christopher); *Career* Lt Cdr Fleet Air Arm RNVR 1950-53 (Lt 1939-46), Lt Cdr RCNR 1953-56; private sec to Parly sec Miny of Civil Aviation 1946-49, planning Miny of Civil Aviation 1949-53, dep UK rep Cncl of Int Civil Aviation Orgn 1953-56, int rels Miny of Tport and Civil Aviation 1956-61; asst sec Miny of Aviation 1961-64: interdependence, exports, electronics; cncllr Br Civil Aviation Rep in Far East FCO 1964-81, UN expert on air servs agreements ICAO 1984-; fell Ford Fndn Nat Translation Centre Austin Texas 1968; *Books* Face at the Bottom of the World: Poems by Hagiwara Sakutaro (1969), Three Contemporary Japanese Poets (1972), Natsume Soseki's I Am a Cat (vol 1 1972, vol 2 1979, vol 3 1986), Natsume Soseki's Ten Nights of Dream (1974); *Clubs* Naval, Pen Club of Japan (Tokyo); *Style—* Graeme Wilson, Esq, CMG; 42 Cranford Ave, Exmouth, Devon (☎ 0395 264786)

WILSON, Guy Edward Nairne Sandilands; s of John Sandilands Wilson (d 1963), of 36 Egerton Crescent, London, and Penelope Ann, *née* Fisher-Rowe; *b* 10 April 1948; *Educ* Heatherdown Sch, Eton, Univ of Aix-en-Provence; *m* 20 Oct 1979, (Marianne) Susan, da of James Drummond D'Arcy Clark, of Oxwold House, Barnsley, Glos; 2 s (John b 5 Feb 1984, Hugh b 27 Aug 1986); *Career* CA; Ernst & Young: joined 1967, ptnr 1979-, currently on secondment to HM Treasy; FCA; *Recreations* cricket, golf, tennis, squash, football, gardening; *Clubs* Brooks's, MCC, IZ, Arabs, Royal St George's Golf, Berkshire Golf; *Style—* Guy Wilson, Esq; Ernst & Young, Becket House, 1 Lambeth Palace Rd, London SE1 7EU (☎ 071 928 2000, fax 071 928 0467)

WILSON, Guy Murray; s of Capt Rowland George Wilson (d 1950), of Tolleshunt D'Arcy, Essex, and Mollie, *née* Munson (d 1987); *b* 18 Feb 1950; *Educ* New Coll Oxford (MA), Univ of Manchester (Dip Art Gallery and Museum Studies); *m* 28 Oct 1972, Pamela Ruth, da of Alan Robert McCredie, OBE, of Yorkshire; 2 s (John b 1976, David b 1986), 2 da (Rebecca b 1978, Elizabeth b 1983); *Career* Royal Armouries HM Tower of London: keeper of edged weapons 1978-81, dep master 1981-88, master of the armouries 1988-; memb: Br Cmmn for Mil History, Arms and Armour Socs of GB and Denmark, Advsy Ctee on Hist Wreck Sites; FSA 1984; *Books* Treasures from The Tower of London (jtly, 1982); *Recreations* walking, reading; *Style—* Guy Wilson, Esq; 15 St Fabians Drive, Chelmsford, Essex CM1 2PR (☎ 0245 352349); The Royal Armouries, HM Tower of London, London EC3N 4AB (☎ 071 480 6358, fax 071 481 2922)

WILSON, Guy Neave; s of Stephen Shipley Wilson (d 1989), and Martha Mott, *née* Kelley (d 1989); *b* 4 June 1942; *Educ* Westminster, Trinity Coll Cambridge (BA); *m* 19 Aug 1978, Annabel Alexandra, da of Robert Alexander Crone (d 1950); 1 s (Robert b 1986), 2 da (Lucy b 1980, Eleanor b 1982); *Career* admitted slr 1966; ptnr Allen & Overy 1972- (joined 1964); memb Law Soc; *Recreations* family, walking, skiing, sailing; *Style—* Guy Wilson, Esq; Allen & Overy, 9 Cheapside, London EC2V 6AD (☎ 071 248 9898, fax 071 236 2192, telex 8812801)

WILSON, Harold James Arthur (Jim); s of James Wilson (d 1965), of Houghton Park, Ampthill, Bedfordshire, and Winifred Wilson (d 1956); *b* 16 April 1935; *Educ* Gresham's; *m* Judith Anne Linda, da of George Badman; 2 s (Jonathan Paul b 1959, Christopher James b 1965); *Career* Nat serv RAF 1953-55; Eastern Counties Newspapers 1956-64; Anglia TV 1964-: head of news 1967-74, controller of news 1988, dir news Anglia Broadcasting 1989-; chm Int PR Ctee Rotary Int 1989-90; memb: Br Assoc of Eds, RTS, Radio and TV News Eds Assoc of America; *Recreations* restoring and maintaining Elizabethan farmhouse; *Style—* Jim Wilson, Esq; Anglia Television, Anglia House, Norwich NR1 3JG (☎ 0603 619261, telex 97424, fax 0603 615494, car 0836 641140)

WILSON, Harry; s of Henry Wilson (d 1960), of Welwyn Garden City, and Elsie, *née* Day (d 1987); *b* 18 Aug 1926; *Educ* Handside Sch Welwyn Garden City, Hatfield Poly; *Career* athletics coach; as athlete represented: Herts at every distance from 100m-Marathon, Wales at 10000m and Cross-Country; started coaching sprinters 1959 (success with Ann Jenner Olympics 1960, Janet Simpson Olympics 1968 and 1972), moved to coaching endurance events 1960 (first success with Richard Jones Euro jr record holder for The Mile 4m 2.8s), has since coached 65 GB internationals incl 10 Olympians; best known incl: Steve Ovett (Euro 1500m champion 1978, Olympic 800m champion 1980, Cwlth 5000m champion 1986, world record holder for Mile, 1500m, 2 miles), Kirsty Wade (Cwlth 800m champion 1982, Cwlth 800m and 1500m champion 1986, British record holder 800m), Tony Simmons (Euro Silver medallist 10000m 1974, fourth place Olympics 10000m 1976), Jill Hunter (Cwlth Silver medallist 10000m 1989), Angela Tooby (Silver medallist World Cross Country Championships 1988), Julian Goater (Cwlth 5000m Bronze medallist 1982), Jo White (Euro Jr 800m Bronze medallist 1977), Nicky Morris (Euro Indoor 3000m Silver medallist 1988), Simon Mugglestone (4 consecutive wins in Varsity Cross Country Match); coach to: GB Team for Olympics World and Euro Championships 1978-91, Indian Nat Endurance squad 1988-89, Sri Lanka Endurance Squad currently; lectr and organiser of training courses in numerous countries worldwide; Master Coach award BAAB 1989, awards for services to athletics from Assocs of Spain Zambia and Finland, mktg mangr Engrg Indust Trg Bd 1968-87; *Books* Complete Middle Distance Runner, Running Dialogue, Running My Way; previously industl magazine ed Rank Organisation; *Style—* Harry Wilson, Esq; 8 Uplands, Croxley Green, Rickmansworth, Hertfordshire WD3 4RD (☎ 0923 897486)

WILSON, Prof Herbert Rees; s of Thomas Rees Wilson (d 1971), of Nefyn, N Wales, and Jane, *née* Humphreys (d 1982); *b* 28 Jan 1929; *Educ* Pwllheli GS, Univ Coll of North Wales Bangor (BSc, PhD); *m* 30 Dec 1952, Elizabeth, da of John Thomas Turner (d 1966), of Nefyn, N Wales; 1 s (Neil b 28 June 1957), 2 da (Iola b 14 June 1955, Helen b 5 Sept 1961); *Career* post doctoral res scientist Wheatstone Physics Laboratory Kings Coll London 1952-57, lectr in physics Univ of St Andrews and Queen's Coll Dundee 1957-64, res assoc Harvard Med Sch Boston 1962, sr lectr and reader in physics Univ of Dundee 1964-83, prof of physics Univ of Stirling; memb Br Fulbright Scholars Assoc; FInstP 1975, FRSE 1975, FRSA 1989; *Books* Diffraction of X-Rays by Proteins Nucleic Acids and Viruses (1966); *Recreations* literature, the theatre, travel; *Style—* Prof Herbert Wilson, FRSE; Lower Bryanston, St Margaret's Drive, Dunblane FK15 0DP (☎ 0786 823105); School of Natural Sciences, University of Stirling, Stirling FK9 4LA (☎ 0786 73171 ext 7761, telex 777 557 STUNIV G)

WILSON, Ven (John) Hewitt; CB (1978); s of John Joseph Wilson (d 1959), of Ireland, and Marion Wilson, *née* Green (d 1980); *b* 14 Feb 1924; *Educ* Kilkenny Coll, Mountjoy Sch Dublin, Trinity Coll Dublin (BA, MA); *m* 1951, Gertrude Elsie Joan, da of Rev Robert Edward Weir (d 1957), of Dublin; 3 s (John, Peter, Timothy), 2 da (Kathryn, Sarah); *Career* clergyman; ordained 1947 for St Georges Church Dublin; joined RAF 1950, Staff Chaplain Air Miny 1961-63, Asst Chaplain in Chief Far E Air Force 1966-69, Strike Cmd 1969-73, Chaplain in Chief RAF 1973-80; hon chaplain to HM The Queen 1972-80; *Recreations* tennis, gardening, travel; *Clubs* RAF; *Style—* Ven Hewitt Wilson, CB; Glencree, Philcote St, Deddington, Banbury, Oxford OX15 0TB (☎ 0869 38903)

WILSON, Ian; s of the late John Wilson, of S Shields, Tyne and Wear, and Gladys Irene, *née* Lascelles; *b* 2 March 1944; *Educ* Argyle House Sunderland (private GS for boys), Marine Sch S Shields; *m* 28 Dec 1968, Elizabeth Rebecca, da of George Wilson Brownless, of Westoe, S Shields; 1 s (Nicholas Ian b 9 Feb 1971), 1 da (Rebecca Jane b 11 Sept 1973); *Career* night ed Newcastle Journal 1979-82 (chief sub ed 1975-79), features ed Evening Chronicle Newcastle 1981-; memb: Bd of Govrs Sunderland Church HS for Girls, Newspaper Press Fund; *Style—* Ian Wilson, Esq; 10 Luffness Drive, Cleadon, S Shields NE34 8AJ (☎ 091 4561092); Evening Chronicle, Thomson House, Newcastle (☎ 232 7500, fax 091 2322256)

WILSON, Ian Matthew; CB (1985); s of Matthew Thomson Wilson, OBE, of 114

Morningside Drive, Edinburgh, and Mary Lily *née* Barnett (d 1968); *b* 12 Dec 1926; *Educ* George Watson's Coll, Univ of Edinburgh (MA); *m* 4 July 1953, Anne, da of Thomas Allan Chalmers (d 1962); 3 s (Alan b 1957, David b 1959, Alastair b 1962); *Career* Nat Serv 1948-50, Capt RAEC 1949-50; joined Scot Home Dept 1950, asst under sec of state Scot Office 1974-77, under sec Scot Educn Dept 1977-86, sec of cmmns for Scotland 1987-; *Style—* Ian M Wilson, Esq, CB; 1 Bonaly Drive, Edinburgh EH13 OEJ (☎ 031 441 2541)

WILSON, Lt-Gen Sir (Alexander) James; KBE (1974, CBE 1966, MBE 1948), MC (1945); s of late Maj-Gen Bevil Thomson Wilson, CB, DSO, of Chelsea, and Florence Erica, da of Sir John Starkey, 1 Bt, JP, DL; *b* 13 April 1921; *Educ* Winchester, New Coll Oxford (BA); *m* 3 Oct 1958, Hon Jean Margaret, *qv*, da of 2 Baron Rankeillour (d 1958); 2 s, 1 step s, 2 step da (1 decd); *Career* WWII served Rifle Bde N Africa and Italy (despatches), Adj Indian Mil Acad Dehra Dun 1945-47, priv sec to C-in-C Pakistan 1947-49, psc 1950, Co Cdr 1 Bn Rifle Bde BAOR 1951-52, Bde Maj 11 Armd Div BAOR 1952-54, Kenya (despatches) 1954-55, Lt-Col 1955, Instr Staff Coll Camberley 1955-58, 2 cmd 3 Green Jackets BAOR, GSO1 Sandhurst 1960-62, CO 1 Bn XX Lancs Fus 1962-64, COS UN Force Cyprus 1964-66 (Actg Force Cdr 1965-66), Cdr 147 Inf Bde (TA) 1966-67, dir Army Recruiting MOD 1967-70, GOC NW Dist 1970-72, Vice Adj-Gen 1972-74, GOC SE Dist 1974-77, Dep Col (Lancs) RRF 1973-77, Col Royal Regt Fus 1977-82; Col Cmdt: Queen's Div 1974-77, RAEC 1975-79, Royal Green Jackets 1977-81; Hon Col Univ of Oxford OTC 1978-82; Sunday Times football corr 1957-90; chm Tobacco Advsy Cncl 1977-83 (chief exec 1983-85); memb: Sports Cncl 1973-82, Cncl CBI 1977-85; hon vice pres FA 1976-82, vice chm NABC 1977-90, chm Rusi 1973-76; dir: Standard Commercial Corpn 1983-, Standard Wool 1986-; pres: Notts Assoc of Boys' and Keyston Clubs 1986-, The Broadway Fndn 1989-; chm Crown and Manor Boys' Club Hoxton 1977-; review ed Army Quarterly 1985-; *Recreations* cricket, association football; *Clubs* Travellers, MCC, Nottinghamshire County Cricket; *Style—* Lt-Gen Sir James Wilson, KBE, MC; 151 Rivermead Court, London SW6 3SF (☎ 071 736 7228)

WILSON, Hon James McMoran; er s of 2 Baron Moran; *b* 6 Aug 1952; *Educ* Eton, Trinity Coll Cambridge; *m* 7 June 1980, Hon (Mary) Jane Hepburne-Scott, yst da of 10 Lord Polwarth; *Career* dir Boston Ventures Management; *Clubs* Somerset, Flyfishers; *Style—* The Hon James Wilson; 65 Upland Rd, Brookline, Mass 02146, USA

WILSON, James Noel Chalmers Barclay; s of Alexander Wilson (d 1957), and Isobel Barbara, *née* Fairweather (d 1961); *b* 25 Dec 1919; *Educ* King Henry VIII Sch Coventry, Univ of Birmingham (MB ChB, ChM); *m* 3 Sept 1945, Patricia Norah, da of Harold Norman McCullough (d 1927); 2 s (Michael b 3 Dec 1956, Richard b 24 March 1960), 2 da (Sheila (Mrs Edwards) b 20 Aug 1947, Jane (Mrs Wentworth) b 30 April 1950); *Career* regtl MO RAMC 1943-46, discharged W/S Capt, qualified as parachutist and served 1 Airborne Div; res surgical posts: Birmingham Gen Hosp 1943 and 1947, Coventry and Warwicks Hosp 1948, Robert Jones and Agnes Hunt Orthopaedic Hosp 1949-52; conslt orthopaedic surgn: Cardiff United Hosps and Welsh Regnl Bd 1952-55, Royal Nat Orthopaedic Hosp London and Stanmore 1955-84, Nat Hosp Queen Square 1962-84; surgn i/c accident serv Stanmore 1955-84, hon conslt orthopaedic surgn Garston Med Rehabilitation Centre Watford 1955-84, teacher in orthopaedics Univ of London 1955-84, BOA travelling fell USA 1954; emeritus orthopaedic surgn and conslt: Royal Nat Orthopaedic Hosp, Nat Hosp for Nervous Diseases Queen Square; prof of orthopaedics Addis Ababa Univ 1989; UK chm World Orthopaedic Concern (pres 1979-84), vice chm IMPACT (Initiative Against Avoidable Disablement); MRCS 1943, LRCP 1943, FRCS 1948, Fell Br Orthopaedic Assoc (editorial sec 1972-76), FRSM 1982 (hon memb orthopaedic section 1989); memb: Egyptian Orthopaedic Assoc, Bangladesh Orthopaedic Soc; *Books* Fractures and Joint Injuries (5 and 6 edns); *Recreations* golf, gardening, photography, old cars; *Clubs* RSM; *Style—* J N Wilson, Esq; The Chequers, Waterdell, nr Watford, Herts WD2 7LP (☎ 0923 672364)

WILSON, Sir James William Douglas; 5 Bt (UK 1906), of Airdrie, New Monkland, Co Lanark; s of Sir Thomas Douglas Wilson, 5 Bt, MC (d 1984), and Pamela Aileen, da of Sir Griffin Wyndham Edward Hanmer, 7 Bt; *b* 8 Oct 1960; *Educ* Marlborough, Univ of London; *m* 1985, Julia Margaret Louise, da of Joseph Charles Francis Mutty, of Mulberry Hall, Melbourn, nr Royston, Herts; *Career* farmer; *Style—* Sir James Wilson, Bt; Lillingstone Lovell Manor, Buckingham MK18 5BQ (☎ 028 06 237)

WILSON, Dr Janet Diane; da of Arnold Wilson, of Gomersal, W Yorks, and Sheila May Audrey, *née* Kingdon; *b* 9 Jan 1956; *Educ* Bradford Girl's GS, Univ of Bristol (MB ChB); *m* 8 Oct 1988, Dr Richard John Charles Dunham, s of John Charles Dunham, of Dronfield, Derbyshire; *Career* conslt in genito-urinary med Sheffield and Barnsley 1987- (sr registrar Sheffield 1984-87), hon clinical lectr Univ of Sheffield 1987-; memb: Trent Region Advsy Sub-Ctee on Genito-Urinary Med, Med Soc for Study Venereal Diseases 1985, Br Soc for Colposcopy and Cervical Pathology 1986, Northern Genito-Urinary Physicians Colposcopy Gp 1988; MRCP 1983; *Recreations* skiing, horse riding, gardening; *Clubs* Ski Club of GB; *Style—* Dr Janet Wilson; Watermill Cottage, 18 Mill Farm Drive, Newmillerdam, Wakefield, W Yorks WF2 6QP; Dept of Genito-Urinary Medicine, Royal Hampshire Hospital, Glossop Rd, Sheffield S10 2JF (☎ 0742 700928)

WILSON, Hon Lady (Jean Margaret); *née* Hope; JP (Inner London); 2 da of 2 Baron Rankeillour, GCIE, MC (d 1958, sometime govr of Madras), by his w Grizel (d 1975), da of Brig-Gen Sir Robert Gordon Gilmour, 1 Bt, CB, CVO, DSO; *b* 7 Jan 1923; *m* 1, 1942 (m dis 1955), Capt Anthony Paul, adopted s of F Paul; 1 s (Anthony), 2 da (Sarah (Mrs Tait), Susan d 1986); m 2, 1958, Lt-Gen Sir James Wilson, KBE, MC, *qv*; 2 s (William, Rupert); *Style—* The Hon Lady Wilson, JP; 151 Rivermead Court, Ranelagh Gdns, London SW6 3SF

WILSON, Jeffery Graham; s of Herbert Charles Wilson (d 1983), and Dora Gladys Wilson; *b* 28 Sept 1939; *Educ* Monkton Combe Sch; *m* 8 June 1962, Lise-Francoise, da of Marcel Fritz Robert (d 1977); 3 s (Anthony Charles b 1964, Martin James b 1965, Richard Graham b 1967), 1 da (Sarah Rachel Jane b 1970); *Career* ptnr Wilson & Watford 1964 (joined 1958), memb Stock Exchange 1961, dir Baring Wilson & Watford 1986-90; *Recreations* church and charitable work, golf; *Style—* Jeffery Wilson, Esq; 1 Grove Rd, Northwood, Middx HA6 2AP (☎ 09274 25495)

WILSON, Jeremy Paul; s of Charles Paul Wilson, CVO (d 1972), of Much Hadham, and Margaret, *née* Fraser Cameron; *b* 27 Jan 1932; *Educ* Bryanston, Downing Coll Cambridge, Middx Hosp Med Sch (MA, MB BChir); *m* 1, 24 Feb 1962 (m dis 1986), (Margaret) Clare, da of Rev Gordon Addenbrooke, of Lympstone, Devon; 1 s (James b 1965), 1 da (Harriett b 1967); *Career* conslt surgn Queen Mary's Hosp Sidcup 1974-, hon clinical lectr St Thomas' Hosp London 1975-; memb Advsy Cncl: Paintings in Hospitals 1976-, Dartington Int Summer Sch 1981-; cncl memb Section of Coloproctology RSM 1982-; princ bassoon and vice chm Sidcup Symphony Orchestra; memb: Assoc of Surgns of GB and I, Br Soc Gastroenterology 1974; FRCS 1963, FRSM 1965; *Recreations* playing bassoon, walking, philandering; *Style—* Jeremy Wilson, Esq; 2 Montpelier Row, Blackheath, London SE3 0RL (☎ 081 463 9111); Queen Mary's Hospital, Sidcup, Kent (☎ 081 302 2678)

WILSON, Jocky; s of William Wilson, of Kirkcaldy, Fife, and Margaret Wilson (d 1990); *b* 22 March 1950; *Educ* Waid Acad Anstruther Fife; *m* 3 May 1968, Malvina Narmantowicz; 2 s (John b 3 April 1970, William b 12 March 1971), 1 da (Anne Marie b 15 March 1972); *Career* professional darts player; over 50 appearances for Scotland (first cap 1976), World Professional Champion 1982 and 1989, British Champion 4 times, British Matchplay Champion twice, BBC 2 Bullseye Champion twice, World Pairs Champion; World record holder for 1,000 in 19 darts; British Darts Personality 1982; *Recreations* fishing, golf; *Style—* Jocky Wilson, Esq; c/o Tommy Cos, 27 Berrishill Grove, Red House Farm, Whitley Bay, Tyne & Wear (☎ 091 252 4181, fax 091 237 4472)

WILSON, John; s of George Wilson (d 1987), and Winefred May, *née* Ball (d 1979); *b* 15 Feb 1941; *Educ* Lordsfield Boarding Sch, Ealing Coll; *m* Malgorzata Janina, da of Jerzy Wojciechowski; 1 da (Amy Janina b 18 Aug 1988); *Career* Colour Processing Labs Ltd 1960-61, prodn dir Golderstat Ltd 1961-, memb of Bd Colour Centre Ltd 1973-; chm: John Wilson Ltd 1979-, Colour Centre Ltd 1985; FBIPP; *Recreations* golf; *Style—* John Wilson, Esq; John Wilson Ltd, 16A D'Arblay St, London W1V 3FP (☎ 071 437 1057)

WILSON, John; s of George Wilson (d 1988), and Mable Wilson (d 1989); *b* 20 Dec 1932; *Educ* Audley Cncl Sch Blackburn Lancs; *m* 6 Sept 1958, Margaret, da of Stanley Holmes (d 1965); 3 da (Edwina Jane b 1961, Clare Margaret b 1963, Joanne Sarah b 1966); *Career* Nat Serv RAF 1951-53; various posts incl chief accountant Jackson Steeple Gp 1946-62, conslt Cotton Bd Productivity Centre 1962-65, chief mgmnt accountant (later fin dir) Viyella Int Ltd (later Carrington Viyella plc) 1965-80, dep chief exec KCA Int plc 1981-83, exec chm H Young Holdings plc 1984-; FCMA 1959, FCT 1978; *Recreations* ballet, cricket; *Style—* John Wilson, Esq; Worleys Hill, Wargrave, Berks RG10 8PA (☎ 0491 572 226); H Young Holdings plc, Old Dominion House, 5 Gravel Hill, Henley-on-Thames, Oxon (☎ 0491 578 988, fax 0491 572 360)

WILSON, Sir John Foster; CBE (1965, OBE 1955); s of Rev George Henry Wilson (d 1959); *b* 20 Jan 1919; *Educ* Worcester Coll for the Blind, St Catherine's Coll Oxford; *m* 1944, Chloe Jean, *née* McDermid, OBE; 2 da; *Career* int health administrator; dir Royal Cwlth Soc for the Blind 1950-83, pres Int Agency for the Prevention of Blindness 1975-83 (now hon life pres); sr conslt UN Devpt Programme (IMPACT) 1983-; kt 1975; *Books* various publications on disability and travel; *Clubs* Royal Commonwealth Society; *Style—* Sir John Wilson, CBE; 22 The Cliff, Roedean, Brighton, E Sussex (☎ 0273 607667)

WILSON, Prof John Furness; s of Arthur Oliver Wilson (d 1963), of W Ardsley, Yorks, and Sarah Elizabeth, *née* Furness (d 1955); *b* 9 Feb 1924; *Educ* Morley GS, New Coll Oxford (BA, MA); *m* 12 April 1950, (Florence) Muriel, da of Arthur Edward Gower (d 1949), of Morley, Yorks; 1 s (Christopher b 1952), 1 da (Helen b 1956); *Career* Nat Serv Flt Lt navigator RAF 1943-46; UCW Aberystwyth: lectr 1949-59, sr lectr in law 1959-66, prof 1966-69; dep vice chllr Univ of Southampton 1970-74 (dean faculty of law 1962-68 and 1975-78); visiting prof: Univ of Auckland NZ 1970, Arizona State Univ 1980, Univ of W Aust 1984, Tulane Univ USA 1957-58 and 1987, Queensland Univ Law Schs 1990; chm Wages Cncls 1970-, chm Police Appeals Tbnl, pres Soc of Public Teachers of Law 1989-90 (memb 1950-); *Books* Principles of the Law of Contract (1952), Survey of Legal Education in the United Kingdom (1966), Carriage of Goods by Sea (1988); *Style—* Prof John Wilson; The Red House, Lakewood Close, Chandlers Ford, Hampshire (☎ 0703 252826)

WILSON, Sir John Gardiner; CBE (1972); s of J S Wilson; *b* 13 July 1913; *Educ* Melbourne GS, Clare Coll Cambridge; *m* 1944, Margaret Louise, da of S M De Ravin; 3 da; *Career* Aust Paper Manufacturers Ltd: joined 1947, dep md 1953-59, md 1959-78, chm 1978-; kt 1982; *see Debrett's Handbook of Australia and New Zealand for further details*; *Style—* Sir John Wilson, CBE; 6 Woorigoleen Rd, Toorak, Vic 3142, Australia

WILSON, John Gilmour (Gil); s of John Gilmour Wilson (d 1964), of Torr Hall, Bridge of Weir, Renfrewshire, and Helen Muirhead, *née* Clark; *b* 22 May 1943; *Educ* Loretto, Paisley Coll (HNC); *m* 28 April 1971, Sally Edgar, da of Dr Edgar Rentoul, MBE, JP, of West Manse, Houston, Scotland; 2 s (Edgar b 8 June 1975, Gregory b 18 Aug 1979), 1 da (Nicola b 4 Aug 1981); *Career* chm and md: Carlton Die Castings Ltd 1964-, Tool Manufacturing & Servs (Glasgow) Ltd 1973-; md Vacuseal Ltd 1977-, chm and md Millstream Devpts Ltd 1981-87, dir Ronnoco Engrg 1985-88; dir Paisley TSB 1975-80; *Recreations* fishing, shooting, photography, gardening; *Style—* Gil Wilson, Esq; Rowallan Mill, Kilmaurs, Kilmarnock, Ayrshire KA3 2LJ (☎ 0563 384 92); Carlton Die Casting Ltd, 88 Greenhill Rd, Paisley PA3 1RG (☎ 041 887 8355, fax 041 848 1157)

WILSON, Sir John Martindale; KCB (1974, CB 1960); s of John Wilson (d 1920) of Edinburgh, and Kate Benson Martindale (d 1963); *b* 3 Sept 1915; *Educ* Bradfield, Gonville and Caius Coll Cambridge (MA); *m* 1941, Penelope Beatrice, da of Francis Alfred Bolton, JP, of Moor Court, Oakamoor, Staffs; 1 s, 1 da; *Career* RA India and Burma (despatches) 1940-46, Maj; civil servant 1938-75: under sec Miny of Supply 1954-55 (private sec 1947-50), Cabinet Office 1955-58, dep sec Miny of Aviation 1960-65, dep under sec of state MOD 1965-72, second perm under sec of state MOD 1972-75; chm: Crown Housing Association 1975-78, Civil Service Appeal Bd 1978-81, Civil Service Retirement Fellowship 1978-82 (vice pres 1982-); *Recreations* gardening; *Clubs* Army & Navy; *Style—* Sir John Wilson, KCB; Bourne Close, Bourne Lane, Twyford, Winchester, Hants SO21 1NX (☎ 0962 713488)

WILSON, John Robert; *b* 13 June 1949; *Educ* Univ of Southampton (BA), LSE (MSc); *m* Dec 1971, Lesley; 1 s (James b June 1983), 1 da (Alice b Aug 1989); *Career* sec: Clothing Manufacturers' Federation, Shirt Manufacturers' Federation, Tie Manufacturers' Assoc and the Corsetry Manufacturers' Assoc 1977-81 (joined secretariat 1972); British Clothing Industry Assoc: gen sec 1981-84, dep dir 1984, dir 1985; dir and sec Mens' and Boys' Wear Exhibitions Ltd 1985- (sec 1984-); dir: British Knitting and Clothing Export Cncl 1987-, British Fashion Cncl, Apparel Marketing Services (Export) Ltd, European Designer Collections; dir gen Br Knitting and Clothing Confederation 1991-; chief exec British Apparel Centre 1987-; *Style—* John Wilson, Esq; British Clothing Industry Association Ltd, British Apparel and Textiles Centre, 7 Swallow Place, London W1R 7AA (☎ 071 408 0020, fax 071 493 6276, telex 25149 CECLDN)

WILSON, His Hon Judge John Warley; s of late John Pearson Wilson, of Kenilworth, and Nancy Wade, *née* Harston; *b* 13 April 1936; *Educ* Warwick Sch, St Catharines Coll Cambridge (MA); *m* 2 June 1962, Rosalind Mary, da of Raymond Harry Pulford; *Career* called to the Bar Lincolns Inn 1960, practised Midland and Oxford circuit until 1982, rec 1979-82, circuit judge 1982; *Recreations* gardening, nat hunt racing; *Style—* His Hon Judge John Wilson; Victoria House, Farm St, Harbury, Leamington Spa CV33 9LR (☎ 0926 612572)

WILSON, Julian David Bonhôte; s of Peter Jardine Bonhôte Wilson, OBE (d 1981), and Helen Angela Mann (d 1961); *b* 21 June 1940; *Educ* Harrow; *m* 1, 29 Dec 1970 (m dis 1980), Carolyn Anne, da of Vivian Michael, of Geneva; 1 s (Thomas b 1973); m 2, 22 June 1981, Alison Christian Findlay, da of late Hugh Ramsay, of W Chiltington, Sussex; *Career* racing corr BBC TV 1966-; *Books* Lester Piggott - The Pictorial Biography (1985), 100 Greatest Racehorses (1987); *Recreations* cricket, cresta run; *Clubs* St Moritz Tobogganing; *Style—* Julian Wilson, Esq; 45 Old Church Street, London SW3 (☎ 071 352 4449); BBC TV, Kensington House, Richmond Way, London W14 (☎ 081 895 6491, fax 081 749 3560, car 0836 501754)

WILSON, Kenneth; s of Leslie Wilson (d 1936), of NY, and Theresa Mary, *née* Holmes (d 1973); *b* 3 Jan 1927; *Educ* Bideford GS, Univ of London (LLB); *m* 6 Sept 1958, Jean Margaret, da of Herbert Fletcher, of Maidstone, Kent; 2 s (Peter b 1960, Grenville b 1966), 2 da (Heidi b 1962, Serena b 1969); *Career* War Serv RE 1945-48; Ctee clerk Kent CC 1952-58, clerk of the cncl Hailsham Dist Cncl 1963-73 (dep clerk 1958-63), chief exec Wealden Dist Cncl 1974-85, ret 1985; chm Sussex branch Inst Chartered Secs and Admins 1972-74, pres Rotary Club of Hailsham 1975, tstee Thomas Scanlan Tst (1979-89), govr Hailsham Grovelands CP Sch; memb: Hon Soc Middle Temple, Bar Cncl, ICSA (FCCS); *Recreations* ornithology, philology; *Style—* Kenneth Wilson, Esq; 42 Hawthylands Rd, Hailsham, East Sussex BN27 1EY (☎ 0323 840 966)

WILSON, Kenneth William; s of Stanley Wilson (d 1939), of 15 Queens Rd, Richmond, Yorks, and Evelyn Marie, *née* Gilling (d 1928); *b* 20 Dec 1928; *Educ* St Peter's Sch York, Univ of St Andrews (MB ChB); *m* 24 Jan 1956, Elizabeth, da of James Stewart, of Edinburgh; 2 da (Valerie b 1957 d 1983, Pamela b 1960); *Career* Nat Serv RAF 1947-49, 17 Bn Parachute Regt 9 DLI TA 1965-67; demonstrator in anatomy Univ of St Andrews 1957-59, surgical registrar United Sheffield Hosps 1960-64, sr surgical registrar Royal Victoria Infirmary Newcastle upon Tyne 1964-68, conslt surgn Calderdale Area Health Authy 1968-; surgical tutor RCS 1981-89; former pres: Halifax Assoc for Hydrocaphalus and Spina Bifida, Halifax Div BMA; FRCS; *Recreations* skiing, windsurfing, horse-riding, reading, music; *Style—* Kenneth Wilson, Esq

WILSON, Kevin James; s of Alan James Wilson, and Jane, *née* McCaul; *b* 18 April 1961; *Educ* Blessed George Napier Secdy Sch Banbury; *m* 7 July 1990, Joanne Sue, da of Graham Noble; *Career* professional footballer; played for Derby County (debut 1980, 131 games (41 League and Cup goals)); 110 games with Ipswich Town (49 League and Cup goals), now plays for Chelsea FC (153 games, 53 goals in all League and Cup Competitions); 18 Full International Cups with Northern Ireland (debut v Israel 1987); winner (with Chelsea) Second Div Championship medal 1988-89, Zenith Data Cup medal 1989-90; *Recreations* all sports; *Style—* Kevin Wilson, Esq; Chelsea FC, Stamford Bridge, Fulham Road, London SW6 (☎ 071 385 5545)

WILSON, Lynn Anthony; s of Connolly Thomas Wilson (d 1970), of Northampton, and Frances, *née* Chapman (d 1975); *b* 8 Dec 1939; *Educ* Oakham Sch Rutland; *m* 4 April 1964, Judith Helen, da of late Jack Ronald Mann; 2 s (Nicholas b 30 May 1967, Giles b 27 May 1969); *Career* chm Wilson (Connolly) Holdings plc 1982- (md 1966); nat pres The House Builders Fedn 1981, tstee Oakham Sch, chm Northants CCC; FCIOB, CBIM; *Recreations* cricket, golf, horseracing, shooting; *Style—* Lynn Wilson, Esq; Wilson (Connolly) Holdings plc, Thomas Wilson House, Tenter Rd, Moulton Park, Northampton NN3 1QJ (☎ 0604 790909, fax 0604 492387)

WILSON, Hon Mrs (Margaret Eleanor); *née* Maybray-King; da of Baron Maybray-King, PC (Life Peer); *b* 1926; *m* 1945, Roy Wilson; *Career* JP (Havant), ret; *Style—* The Hon Mrs Wilson; 26 Blenheim Road, Westbury Park, Bristol

WILSON, (William) Mark Dunlop; s of Maj Thomas Dunlop Wilson, of Glasgow, and Paule Juliette, *née* Durand; *b* 23 Jan 1949; *Educ* Univ of Glasgow (BSc), Univ of Illinois (MSc, PhD); *m* 11 Aug 1973, Nancy, da of Donald Lyle Anderson, of PO Box 127, Hoffman, Illinois 62250, USA; 1 s (Clark Andrew Dunlop b 18 March 1979), 1 da (Megan Christine b 3 Dec 1982); *Career* World Bank: young professional projects undertaken in Europe and Middle E 1975-76, agriculturalist S Asia Projects Dept 1976-80, princ project offr Latin American Projects Dept 1988-90 (sr agriculturalist 1980-88); memb: Lions Club, Presbyterian Church, American Soc of Animal Sciences, Cncl for Agricultural Sciences and Technol USA, Br Soc of Animal Sciences; *Recreations* hiking, soccer, tennis; *Clubs* World Wild Life Fund, Audobon Soc; *Style—* Mark Wilson, Esq; World Bank, 1818 H St NW, Washington DC, 20433 USA (☎ 010 1 202 473 9528, fax 010 1 202 334 0039, telex 440098 ITT)

WILSON, (Alan) Martin; QC (1982); s of Joseph Norris Wilson (d 1986), of London, and Kate, *née* Clusky (d 1982); *b* 12 Feb 1940; *Educ* Kilburn GS, Univ of Nottingham (LLB); *m* 1, 1966 (m dis 1975), Pauline Frances Kibart; 2 da (Rebecca b 1968, Anna b 1971); m 2, 20 March 1976, Julia Mary, da of Patrick Maurice George Carter, OBE, of Malvern, Worcs; 1 da (Alexandra b 1980); *Career* called to the Bar Gray's Inn 1963; Rec of the Crown Ct (Midland and Oxford Circuit) 1979; *Recreations* sailing, shooting, literature, travel; *Clubs* Bar Yacht, Sloane; *Style—* Martin Wilson, Esq, QC; 6 King's Bench Walk, Temple, London EC4Y 7DR (☎ 071 353 9901, fax 071 583 2033)

WILSON, Sir (Mathew) Martin; 5 Bt (UK 1874), of Eshton Hall, Co York; s of Sir Mathew Richard Henry Wilson, 4 Bt, CSI, DSO (d 1958), by his w Hon Barbara Lister (da of 4 & last Baron Ribblesdale); bro of Peter, *qv*; *b* 2 July 1906; *Educ* Eton; *Heir* n, Mathew Wilson, MBE, MC, *qv*; *Career* patron of four livings; *Style—* Sir Martin Wilson, Bt; 1 Sandgate Esplanade, Folkestone, Kent

WILSON, Hon Mrs (Mary Jane); *née* Hepburne-Scott; da of 10 Lord Polwarth, TD; *b* 16 Feb 1955; *m* 7 June 1980, Hon James McMoran Wilson, s of 2 Baron Moran, CMG; *Style—* The Hon Mrs Wilson; 65 Upland Road, Brookline, Mass 02146, USA

WILSON, Brig Mathew John Anthony; OBE (Mil 1979), MBE (Mil 1971), MC (1972); s of Anthony Thomas Wilson (d 1982), by his 1 w Margaret, formerly w of Vernon Motion and da of Alfred Holden (decd); hp to unc, Sir Martin Wilson, 5 Bt; *b* 2 Oct 1935; *Educ* Trinity Coll Sch Port Hope Ontario; *m* 1962, Janet Mary, er da of Edward Worsfold Mowll, JP (decd), of Walmer; 1 s (Mathew Edward Amcotts b 1966), 1 da (Victoria Mary b 1968); *Career* Brig King's Own Yorks LI, ret 1983; exec dir Wilderness Fndn (UK) 1983-85; *Clubs* Explorers; *Style—* Brig Mathew Wilson, OBE, MC

WILSON, Michael Gerald; s of John Charles Wilson, of Hove, Sussex, and Dorothy Beatrice, *née* Harmer (d 1985); *b* 6 Dec 1942; *m* 22 Aug 1964, Maureen Brenda, da of Arthur Charles Hiron (d 1982); 1 s (James Michael b 27 Oct 1981), 1 da (Sarah Michelle b 28 March 1973); *Career* admitted slr 1975; ptnr Berwin Leighton 1979-; Freeman: City of London, Worshipful Co of Slrs; memb: Law Soc 1975, Int Bar Assoc 1975, S Western Legal Fndn 1982, Asia Pacific Lawyers Assoc 1985; assoc memb Lloyds of London 1987; *Recreations* tennis, squash, swimming, travel, reading, music; *Clubs* RAC; *Style—* Michael Wilson, Esq; Berwin Leighton, Adelaide House, London Bridge, London EC4R 9HA (☎ 071 623 3144, fax 071 623 4416, telex 886420)

WILSON, Michael John Francis Thomond; s of Sir Michael Thomond Wilson, KB, MBE, of Clytha, South Ascot, Berks (d 1983), and Lady Jessie Babette, *née* Winnington (d 1984); *b* 9 Sept 1934; *Educ* Rugby, Oriel Coll Oxford (MA); *m* 4 May 1968, (Katharine) Mary Rose, da of Lt-Col Robert Macaulay Fanshawe (d 1974), of Church Cottage, Longborough, Moreton-in-Marsh, Glos; 3 s (James b 1970, Andrew b 1972, Richard b 1976); *Career* Nat Serv, Lt RA 1953-55; admitted slr 1961; head of Litigation Dept Stephenson Harwood 1969- (formerly Stephenson Harwood and Tatham, ptnr 1966-); memb City of London Slrs Co; memb Law Soc; *Recreations* horse racing, tennis; *Clubs* Gresham; *Style—* Michael Wilson, Esq; Andridge House, Radnage, High Wycombe, Bucks HP14 4DZ (☎ 0494 482215); Stephenson Harwood, 1 St Paul's Churchyard, London EC4M 8SH (☎ 071 329 4422, fax 071 606 0822, telex 886789 SHSPC G)

WILSON, Michael Stuart; s of Claude Stuart Wilson, of 39 Bury Fields, Guildford, Surrey, and Vivienne Sinclair Dalrymple Morton, *née* Bell; *b* 22 June 1939; *Educ* Marlborough; *m* 26 Dec 1964, Alyson, da of Sidney Arthur Starkey (d 1982), of 4 Warwick New Rd, Leamington Spa; 2 s (Piers b 1967, Neil b 1969); *Career* ptnr Coopers & Lybrand Deloitte 1969-; memb Crafts Cncl 1988-90; FCA 1969, FRSA 1989; *Recreations* goldf, opera, vintage cars; *Clubs* City of London; *Style—* Michael Wilson, Esq; 22 Crescent Grove, London SW4 7AH (☎ 071 622 6360); Faiths Cottage, Church Lane, Sidlesham, Chichester, W Sussex PO20 7RH; Coopers & Lybrand Deloitte 128 Queen Victoria St, London EC4P 4JX (☎ 071 454 4522, fax 071 248 4897, telex 894941)

WILSON, Michael Sumner; s of Cdr Peter Sumner Wilson, AFC, Lower Middlewood, Dorstone, Hereford, and Margaret Kathleen, *née* Letchworth; *b* 5 Dec 1943; *Educ* St Edwards Sch Oxford; *m* 5 June 1975, Mary Dorothy Wordsworth, da of John Alexander Drysdale (d 1986); 1 da (Amanda Wordsworth b 12 March 1976); *Career* Equity & Law 1963-68, Abbey Life 1968-71; Hambro Life/Allied Dunbar 1971-: broker mangr 1971-73, exec dir 1973-76, main bd dir 1976-82, jt dep md 1982-84, jt md 1984-88, gp chief exec 1988; dir BAT Industs 1989-; tstee Mental Health Fndn; memb Lloyds; *Recreations* tennis, racing; *Style—* Michael Wilson, Esq; Warrens Gorse, nr Cirencester, Glos GL7 7JD; Allied Dunbar, Allied Dunbar Centre, Swindon SN1 1EL (☎ 0793 514 514, fax 0793 512 371, telex 449129 Allied G)

WILSON, Michael Thomas; s of Thomas Wilson (d 1967), and Blanche, *née* Dunne; *b* 27 April 1938; *Educ* Rothwell GS, Manchester Univ (BA); *m* 1 Sept 1962, Diana Frances, da of Harold Frank Pettit (d 1968); 1 s (Simon b 1964), 2 da (Victoria b 1966, Emmeline b 1977); *Career* supervisor truck mktg Ford Motor Co 1959-62, dir residential studies Inst of Mktg 1962-64, md Mktg Improvements Ltd 1964-88, chm Mktg Improvements Gp plc 1988-, visiting prof Cranfield Sch of Mgmnt 1989; FInstM 1985, FInstD 1966; *Books* Managing a Sales Force (1970), The Management of Marketing (1980); *Recreations* sport, theatre, cinema, reading; *Style—* Michael Wilson, Esq; Ulster House, 17 Ulster Terrace, Regents Park Outer Circle, London NW1 (☎ 071 487 5811, fax 071 935 4839, telex 299723 MARIMP G)

WILSON, Miles Robert; s of Maurice James Wilson (d 1969), of Colchester, Essex, and Kathleen Isobel Wilson; *b* 28 Sept 1946; *Educ* Chinthurst Sch Tadworth Surrey, Carshalton Coll Surrey; *m* 15 Nov 1985, Sarah, da of Cyril Deakin (d 1976), of Sheffield; *Career* professional broadcaster and radio presenter 1964-78, involved in the tourist indust, set up PR-advtg agency 1983, chm and md Wasp Gp Worthing Sussex 1986-; pres Sussex Coast Business Club 1990-; vice chm Worthing Post Office Advsy Cncl 1988-; exec memb Worthing Coll Tourism Liaison Ctee 1987-; memb Tourism Soc 1983, MInstPR 1985, MBIM 1989; *Books* Fort Newhaven History (co-author 1984); *Recreations* sailing, country pursuits, equestrian, motoring; *Style—* Miles Wilson, Esq; The Old Dairy, 65A Kingsland Rd, Worthing, W Sussex BN14 9ED (☎ 0903 209327, fax 0903 205157, car 0860 571983)

WILSON, Monique (*née* Monica Anne Esteva Wilson); da of Johnny Wilson, of 1120L Mendoza Street, Otis, Paco, Manila, Philippines, and Teresa Esteva Wilson; *b* 4 May 1970; *Educ* Colegio San Agustin The Philippines, Univ of the Philippines; *Career* actress, singer and model; teacher/dir Repertory Theatre Philippines Summer Theatre Workshop 1985-89; *theatre work* numerous roles in repertory Philippines 1982-; musicals: Molly in Annie 1979, Martha in Sound of Music 1980, Ngana in South Pacific 1981, Isabelle in Pirates of Penzance 1983 and 1985, Chava in Fiddler on the Roof 1983, Frederika in A Little Night Music 1984, Pepper in Annie 1984, Philia in A Funny Thing Happened on the Way to the Forum 1984, Maggie in Chorus Line 1985, Shy in Best Little Whore-house in Texas 1985, Mistress in Evita 1986, Joseph and the Amazing Technicolor Dreamcoat 1986, Antonia in Man of La Mancha 1987, Emily in Yanky Panky 1987, widow in Zorba 1987, Sister Mary Leo in Nunsense 1988, Anne in La Cage Aux Folles 1988, Lizzie in Baby 1988, Audrey in Little Shop of Horrors, Kim in Miss Saigon (Theatre Royale) 1989- (to date 230 shows as lead in Miss Saigon); *Style—* Ms Monique Wilson; Cameron Mackintosh, 1 Bedford Square, London WC2 (☎ 071 637 8666); Agent, Richard Grenville (London Management), Regent Street, London (☎ 071 493 1610)

WILSON, Prof Nairn Hutchison Fulton; s of William Fulton Wilson, of Kilmarnock, Ayrshire, and Anne Hutchison, *née* Stratton; *b* 26 April 1950; *Educ* Strathallan Sch, Univ of Edinburgh (BDS), Univ of Manchester (MSc, PhD); *m* 1; 2 da (Kirsty b 1972, Shona b 1976); m 2, 12 April 1982, Margaret Alexandra, *née* Jones; 1 s (Iain b 1984), 1 da (Hannah b 1983); *Career* lectr in restorative dentistry Univ of Edinburgh 1974-75, prof of restorative dentistry Univ of Manchester 1986- (lectr 1975-82, sr lectr 1982-86); ed Jl of Dentistry; fell: American Coll of Dentists, Acad of Dental Materials; memb: Pierre Fauchard Acad, American Acad of Operative Dentistry; FDS(Ed), DRD; *Recreations* various; *Style—* Prof Nairn Wilson; Unit of Conservative Dentistry, Dept of Restorative Dentistry, Univ Dental Hospital of Manchester, Higher Cambridge St, Manchester M15 6FH (☎ 061 275 6660, fax 061 275 6776)

WILSON, Nicholas Allan Roy; QC (1987); s of (Roderick) Peter Garratt Wilson, of Three Chimneys, Fittleworth, Pulborough, W Sussex, and (Dorothy) Anne, *née* Chenevix-Trench; *b* 9 May 1945; *Educ* Bryanston Sch, Worcester Coll Oxford (BA); *m* 14 Dec 1974, Margaret, da of Reginald Frank Higgins (d 1986); 1 s (Matthew b 1977), 1 da (Camilla b 1981); *Career* called to the Bar Inner Temple 1967, Western Circuit, rec Crown Ct 1987; *Style—* Nicholas Wilson, Esq, QC; Queen Elizabeth Building, Temple, London EC4Y 9BS (☎ 071 583 7837, fax 071 353 5422)

WILSON, Nicholas Samuel; s of Dr John Alexander George Wilson, of Sheffield (d 1985), and Grace, *née* Twiselton (d 1974); *b* 27 Sept 1935; *Educ* Repton, Univ of Sheffield (LLB), Harvard Univ (LLM), Univ of California at Berkeley (post grad res); *m* 1, 1961 (m dis 1980), Rosemary Ann Wilson; 2 s (Simon John b 1964, Justin Nicholas b 1966), 1 da (Sophie Rachael b 1973); m 2, 11 Oct 1982, Penelope Mary Elizabeth Moore; *Career* Nat Serv 2 Lt RA 1954-56, capt TA 1956-61; articled with Keeble Hawson Steele Carr & Co Sheffield 1956-61, asst slr Slaughter and May 1961-67 (ptnr 1968-90), advsr National Westminster Bank plc 1990; memb: DTI Advsy Ctee on Company Law 1970-74, Ctee of Inquiry on Indust Democracy 1975-76, City Capital Markets Ctee 1980- (chm 1990); Freeman Worshipful Co of Slrs; memb Law Soc; *Recreations* music, gardening; *Style—* Nicholas Wilson, Esq; Whitnorth, The Street, Shalford, Guildford, Surrey GU4 8BU (☎ 0483 572 644); National Westminster Bank plc, 41 Lothbury, London EC2P 2BP (☎ 071 726 1222, fax 071 726 1174)

WILSON, Nigel Guy; s of Noel Wilson, and Joan Louise, *née* Lovibond; *b* 23 July 1935; *Educ* Univ Coll Sch, CCC Oxford (BA, MA); *Career* lectr Merton Coll Oxford 1957-62, fell and tutor in classics Lincoln Coll 1962-; visiting prof: Univ of Padua 1985, École Normale Supérieure Paris 1986; FBA 1980; *Books* Scribes and Scholars (with L D Reynolds, 2 edn 1974, 3 edn 1991), Scholars of Byzantium (1983), Oxford Classical Text of Sophocles (with Sir Hugh Lloyd-Jones, 1990); *Recreations* tennis (not lawn), squash, bridge; *Style—* Nigel Wilson, Esq; Lincoln College, Oxford, Oxfordshire OX1 3DR

WILSON, Nigel Richard; s of Lt Col Richard Wilson, of Stamford, Lincolnshire, and Jean Dorothy, *née* Jamieson; *b* 18 Feb 1946; *Educ* Radley; *m* 8 July 1971, late Ann, da of John Rowlands, of Canada; 1 s (William Pennington b 1974), 1 da (Rebecca Pennington b 1977); *Career* ptnr McAnally Mongomery 1980-83 (memb Mgmnt Ctee 1982-83), ptnr F Laing of Cruickshank 1983, dir Alexanders Laing & Cruickshank 1987-88, md Laing & Cruickshank Investment Management Services Ltd 1987-88, dir

CS Investment Ltd 1988-; chm Ski Club of GB 1979-82, dir Nat Ski Fedn 1979-82, hon steward All England Lawn Tennis & Croquet Club 1969-, memb Multiple Sclerosis Fin Ctee 1983-; Freeman City of London 1972, Liveryman Worshipful Co of Skinners 1982; *Books* Silk Cut Ski Guide (1974); *Recreations* skiing, golf, tennis, cricket, shooting; *Clubs* Ski Club of GB; *Style*— Nigel Wilson, Esq; Old Manor Farm, Cublinton, Leighton Buzzard, Bedfordshire LU7 0LE (☎ 0296 681279); CS Investments Ltd, 125 High Holborn, London WC1V 6PY (☎ 071 242 1142, fax 071 430 0742)

WILSON, 2 Baron (UK 1946); Patrick Maitland Wilson; s of 1 Baron Wilson, GCB, GBE, DSO, Supreme Allied Mil Cdr Mediterranean 1944 (d 1964); *b* 14 Sept 1915; *Educ* Eton, King's Coll Cambridge; *m* 1945, Storeen Violet, da of Maj Archibald James Douglas Campbell, OBE (d 1936), of Blythswood, and Hon Anna, *née* Massey (4 da of 5 Baron Clarina, by his 2 w Sophia, and half sis of 6 Baron who d 1952, from which date the title has been extinct); *Heir* none; *Style*— The Rt Hon the Lord Wilson; c/o Barclays Bank, Cambridge

WILSON, Paul; s of Thomas William Wilson (d 1947), of Newcastle upon Tyne, and Gladys Rawden, *née* Scaife (d 1989); *b* 2 Aug 1947; *Educ* Newcastle Polytechnic and Univ of London (Dip in Nursing), Newcastle Poly and CNAA (DMS), Henley Management Coll and Brunel Univ (MBA); *Career* registered mental nurse St Nicholas Hosp Newcastle 1965-68, head of nursing in intensive therapy (formerly staff nurse) Royal Victoria Infirmary Newcastle 1970-74 (registered gen nurse 1968-70), mangr of night nursing services West Sector Hosps Northumberland Health Authy 1974-76, staff offr to area nursing offr Merton Sutton and Wandsworth Area Health Authy 1976-77, divnl nursing offr Roehampton Health Dist 1977-82, dir policy and planning Maidstone Health Authy 1985-87 (chief nursing offr 1982-85), gen mangr Mental Health Services Greater Glasgow Health Bd 1987-; *Recreations* squash, photography, oriental art, opera, sport, reading, music; *Style*— Paul Wilson, Esq; Greater Glasgow Health Board, Gartnavel Royal Hospital, Great Western Rd, Glasgow G12 0XH (☎ 041 334 4416, ext 228 (office), 041 339 5534 (private office), fax 041 334 0875)

WILSON, Peter George Kirke; s of Col H W Wilson, OBE, TD (d 1965), of Enton, Surrey, and Lilian Rosemary, *née* Kirke; *b* 22 Oct 1942; *Educ* Winchester; *m* 18 Sept 1965, Susan Mary, da of Capt David Baynes, MC, DSO (d 1958); 2 s (Nigel b 1968, David b 1971), 1 da (Fiona b 1967); *Career* formerly with Deloitte Haskins & Sells, currently md Mgmnt Appts Ltd; FCA 1966; *Recreations* golf, tennis, study of WWII, old Morris cars; *Style*— Peter Wilson, Esq; Dormers, Kiln Way, Grayshott, Hindhead, Surrey; 84 Ashbury Rd, London SW11; Management Appointments Ltd, Finland House, 56 Haymarket, London SW1

WILSON, Peter John Edgar Malyan; s of Herbert Edgar Wilson (d 1989), of Surbiton, Surrey, and Kathleen Phyllis, *née* Humphries (d 1967); *b* 8 April 1933; *Educ* Surbiton Co Secdy Sch, Guy's Hosp Med Sch (MB BS); *m* 21 July 1962, Patience Mary, da of Harold William Wood (d 1980); 2 s (Mark Richard b 1963, James Alexander b 1964), 1 da (Felicity Jane b 1965); *Career* Nat Serv cmmnd RAMC; conslt neurosurgn to W Glam Health Authy 1968-; pres Headway Wales; memb: SBNS, SRHSB, Brain Res Assoc; FRSM, FRCS, FRCSEd; *Recreations* golf, painting, literature, photography; *Style*— Peter Wilson, Esq; 40 West Cross Lane, Swansea, West Glamorgan SA3 5LS (☎ 0792 406209); Dept of Surgical Neurology, Morriston Hospital, Swansea SA6 6NL (☎ 0792 703382)

WILSON, Peter Michael; s of Michael de Lancey Wilson, of Blandford Forum, Dorset, and Mary Elizabeth, *née* Craufurd (d 1972); *b* 9 June 1941; *Educ* Downside, Oriel Coll Oxford (MA); *m* 5 Sept 1964, Lissa, da of Olaf Trab, of Copenhagen; 1 s (Mark b 1974), 1 da (Juliet b 1972); *Career* dep chm Gallaher Ltd 1987, chm Gallaher Tobacco Ltd 1987; *Style*— Peter Wilson, Esq; Gallaher Ltd, Members' Hill, Brooklands Rd, Weybridge, Surrey (☎ 0932 859777)

WILSON, Prof Peter Northcote; CBE (1987); s of L William Charles Montgomery Wilson (d 1980), and Fanny Louise, *née* White (d 1975); *b* 4 April 1928; *Educ* Whitgift Sch, Wye Coll London (BSc, MSc), Univ of Edinburgh, Univ of London (PhD); *m* 9 Sept 1950, (Maud Ethel) Bunny, da of William Ernest Bunn (d 1962); 2 s (David Richard b 1953, John Peter b 1959), 1 da (Rosemary Margaret b 1951); *Career* lectr in agric Makerere Coll Uganda 1951-57, sr lectr in animal prodn Imp Coll of Tropical Agric 1957-61, prof agric Univ of W Indies, dir Trinidad & Tobago Agric Credit Bank 1962-64, sr scientist and head of biometrics Unilever Res 1968-71, chief agric scientist BOCM Silcock 1971-83, prof of agric and rural economy Univ of Edinburgh 1984-90, princ E of Scotland Coll of Agric 1984-90, head Edinburgh Sch of Agric 1984-90; sci dir Edinburgh Centre for Rural Res 1990-, emeritus Prof Univ of Edinburgh 1991; visiting prof Univ of Reading 1975-83; govr Eastern Caribbean Farm Inst 1961-64, chm Frank Parkinson Agric Tst 1972-, pres Br Soc of Animal Prodn 1977-78, memb Medicines Cmmn 1976-79, vice pres Inst of Biology 1977-79, sec-gen Scottish Agric Colls 1986-87, memb Univ Grants Ctee (now Univ Funding Cncl, Agric Sub Ctee) 1987-; CBiol 1963, FIBiol 1963, FRSE 1987; *Books* Agriculture in The Tropics, Improved Feeding of Cattle and Sheep; *Recreations* photography, philately, ornithology, hill walking; *Clubs* Farmers; *Style*— Prof Peter Wilson, CBE; 8 St Thomas Rd, Edinburgh EH9 2LQ (☎ 031 667 3182); Sch of Agric, W Mains Rd, Edinburgh EH9 3JG (☎ 031 667 1041)

WILSON, Peter Stafford; s of Sir Geoffrey Wilson, and Judy Chamberlain, *née* Trowbridge; *b* 12 Jan 1951; *Educ* St Albans Sch Washington DC, Westminster, Exeter Coll Oxford; *m* 1, 1974 (m dis 1979), Elspeth, *née* Walker; m 2, 1980, Patricia Clare, da of RQ Macarthur Stanham, of Camden Park, NSW, Aust; 3 s (Alexander John b 25 Oct 1983, Timothy Quentin b 9 March 1985, Christopher Cowan b 30 April 1987 d 1987), 1 da (Nicola-Anne Neave b 15 Sept 1989); *Career* asst dir Welsh Nat Drama Co 1974-75, co dir Bush Theatre London 1975-76; assoc dir: Horsehoe Theatre Co Basingstoke 1976-79, Lyric Theatre Hammersmith 1980-83; dir Charley's Aunt (Lyric Hammersmith and Aldwych), ind prodr 1983-88 (Edmund Kean with Ben Kingsley, Showpeople with David Kernan, A Betrothal with Ben Kingsley and Geraldine James, The Woman in Black with John Duttine and Charles Kay), chief exec HM Tennent Ltd 1988-90 (Garrison Keillor (Apollo), Jubilee dir Lindsay Anderson, produced and devised, Victor Spinetti's Very Private Diary), ind prodr 1990-; dir: London Int Festival of Theatre, Edinburgh Int Festival Fringe Society Ltd; memb Arts Cncl Touring Bd; *Books* Forty Games for Frivolous People, The After Dinner Olympics; *Recreations* tennis, swimming; *Clubs* Hurlingham; *Style*— Peter Wilson, Esq; PWP Ltd, 11 Goodwin's Court, London WC2N 4LL (☎ 071 379 7909, fax 071 497 8716)

WILSON, (Edward) Philip; s of Peter Wilson, *qv*, and Grace Helen Wilson; *b* 2 Nov 1940; *Educ* Bryanston, Conservatoire de Musique Paris; *m* 1970, Lady Alexandra Jellicoe, *qv*, er da of 2 Earl Jellicoe, PC, DSO, MC; *Career* md Sotheby Publications; *Style*— Philip Wilson, Esq; 24 Highbury Place, London N5; Sotheby Publications, Russell Chambers, Covent Gdn, London WC2E 8AA (☎ 071 379 7886, telex 22158)

WILSON, Ramon (Ray); s of William Henry Wilson (d 1971), of Shirebrook, Derbyshire, and Elizabeth, *née* Mason; *b* 17 Dec 1934; *Educ* Shirebrook Secdy Modern Sch for Boys; *m* 3 Dec 1956, Patricia, da of Edward Walker Lumb; 2 s (Russell b 4 June 1957, Neil b 17 Nov 1959); *Career* former professional footballer; Huddersfield Town 1952-64 (debut 1955), Everton 1964-69, Oldham Athletic 1969-70, asst mangr and coach Bradford City 1970-72; England: debut v Scotland 1960, 63 full caps 1960-68, played in all matches World Cup Chile 1962 and England 1966; honours: FA Cup winners Everton 1966 (runners up 1968), World Cup winners England 1966; ret from football 1972; ptnr Leeches House Funeral Home Outland Huddersfield 1972-; *Books* My Life in Soccer (with James Mossop, 1969); *Recreations* fell walking, wildlife, buying antiques at an affordable level; *Style*— Ray Wilson, Esq

WILSON, Sir Reginald Holmes; s of Alexander Wilson; *b* 1905; *Educ* St Lawrence Ramsgate, Univ of London (BCom); *m* 1, 1930, Rose Marie von Arnim; 1 s, 1 da; m 2, 1938, Sonia Havell; *Career* CA (Scot) 1927; ptnr Whinney Murray & Co 1937-72, princ asst sec Miny Shipping 1941, dir fin Miny War Tport 1941, under sec Miny Tport 1945, memb Royal Cmmn on the Press 1946, vice chm Hemel Hempstead Devpt Corp 1946-56, comptroller Br Tport Cmmn (BTC) 1947, govr LSE 1954-58; chm BTC: Eastern Area Bd 1955-60, London Midland Area Bd 1960-62; memb Ctee of Enquiry into Civil Air Tport 1967-69; chm: Thomas Cook & Son Ltd 1966-75, Transport Holding Co 1967-70 (dep chm 1962-67), Nat Freight Corp 1969-70, Transport Development Group Ltd 1971-75, Bd for Simplication of Int Trade Procedures 1976-79; chm Brompton Hosp Cardiographic Inst 1960-80; chm bd govrs: Hosp for Diseases of the Chest 1960-71, Nat Heart Hosp 1969-71, Nat Heart and Chest Hosps 1971-80; hon treas Int Hosp Fedn; FCIT, FBIM; kt 1951; *Style*— Sir Reginald Wilson; 49 Gloucester Square, London W2

WILSON, Richard; *b* 1953; *Educ* London Coll of Printing, Hornsey Coll of Art (Dip AD), Univ of Reading (MFA); *Career* artist; solo exhibitions incl: 11 pieces (Coracle Press Gallery London) 1976, 12 pieces (Coracle Press Gallery London) 1978, Viaduct (Aspex Gallery Portsmouth) 1983, Sheer Fluke (Matt's Gallery London) 1985, Hopperhead (Cafe Gallery London) 1985, Stoke Stack Lighting (Stoke Garden Festival Cmmn Stoke on Trent) 1986, Halo (Aperto Venice Biennale) 1986, Heatwave (Ikon Gallery Birmingham) 1986, 20:50 (Matt's Gallery London) 1987, Art of Our Time (The Saatchi Collection The Royal Scot Acad Edinburgh) 1987, Hot Live Still (Plymouth Art Centre) 1987, Leading Lights (Brandts Kunsthallen Odense Denmark) 1989, Sea Level (Arnolfini Gallery Bristol) 1989, She Came In Through the Bathroom Window (Matt's Gallery London) 1989, High-Tec (MOMA Oxford) 1989, High Rise (Saô Paulo Bienal Brazil) 1989, All Mod Cons (Edge Biennale Newcastle) 1990, Take Away (Centre of Contemporary Art Warsaw Poland 1990 and Saatchi Gallery 1991); gp exhibitions incl: The London Group (Camden Arts Centre) 1975, Whitechapel Open (Whitechapel Gallery) 1976, Miniatures (Coracle Press Gallery London) 1977, Coracle Press in Amsterdam (Galerie da Costa) 1978, Sculptural Views (Waterloo Gallery London) 1979, Wind Instruments (Coracle Press Gallery London) 1980, Portsmouth/Duisberg Link Exhibition (Lehnbruch Museum) 1980, Romance Science Endeavour (Portsmouth City Art Gallery) 1981, Bookworks (Southill Park Arts Centre Bracknell) 1981, Paper Works (Aspex Gallery Portsmouth) 1982, South Bank Show (Coracle Press Gallery London) 1982, Pagan Echoes (Riverside Studios Gallery London) 1983, Clifftop Sculpture Park (Portland Dorset) 1983, Four Artists (Galerie Hoffman Germany) 1983, British Artists Books (Atlantic Gallery London) 1984, Sculptors Drawings (Ikon Gallery and tour) 1986, The Elements (Bookworks Milton Keynes and tour) 1986, Made to Measure (Kettle's Yard Cambridge) 1988; numerous art pubns, work in various pub and private collections; musician; co-fndr (with Anne Bean and Paul Burwell) and performer Bow Gamelan Ensemble (with Anne Bean and Paul Burwell) 1983-; *awards* Boise travel scholarship 1977, Arts Cncl minor award 1977, Gtr London Arts Project award 1978, 1981, 1989; *Style*— Richard Wilson, Esq; Matt's Gallery, 10 Martello St, London Fields, London E8 3PE (☎ 071 249 3799, 081 521 4913)

WILSON, Richard Thomas James; CB (1991); s of Richard Ridley Wilson (d 1982), and Frieda Bell, *née* Finlay (d 1980); *b* 11 Oct 1942; *Educ* Radley, Clare Coll Cambridge (BA, LLB); *m* 25 March 1972, Caroline Margaret, da of Rt Hon Sir Frank Lee, GCMG, KCB (d 1971); 1 s (Thomas b 10 March 1979), 1 da (Amy b 16 Feb 1981); *Career* called to the Bar Middle Temple 1965, private sec Bd of Trade 1969-71 (asst princ 1966-), princ Cabinet Office, asst sec Dept of Energy 1977 (joined Dept 1974), team leader privatisation of Britoil 1982, promoted to princ estab and fin offr (under sec) 1982, mgmnt and personnel office Cabinet 1986, economic secretariat (dep sec) Cabinet Office 1987-90, dep sec HM Treasy 1990-; *Style*— Richard Wilson, Esq, CB; HM Treasury, Parliament St, London SW1P 3AG

WILSON, Prof Sir Robert; CBE (1978); s of Robert Graham Wilson (d 1966), and Anne, *née* Riddle (d 1985); *b* 16 April 1927; *Educ* South Shields HS, Univ of Durham (BSc), Univ of Edinburgh (PhD); *m* 4 June 1986, Fiona, da of Lt-Col Kenneth Wheeler Nicholson; *Career* sr scientific offr Royal Observatory Edinburgh 1952-57, res fell Dominion Astrophysical Observatory Canada 1957-58, leader Plasma Spectroscopy Gp Harwell 1959-61, head Spectroscopy Divn Culham Lab 1962-68, dir Astrophysics Res Unit (SRC) 1968-72, head Dept of Physics and Astronomy UCL 1987- (Perren prof of astronomy 1972-, dean of sci 1982-85); Herschel Medal RAS 1986, US Presidential award 1988; FInstP 1966, FRS 1975; kt 1989; *Style*— Prof Sir Robert Wilson, CBE, FRS; Department of Physics & Astronomy, University College London, Gower St, London WC1E 6BT (☎ 071 380 7154, fax 071 380 7145, telex 28722 UCPHYS G)

WILSON, Robert Harold; s of Harold Wilson (d 1969), of London, and Emily May Wilson (d 1972); *b* 11 Aug 1930; *Educ* Latymer GS; *m* 1, 4 Dec 1954, Hilda May (d 1986), da of Henry Charles Christopher Stoneman (d 1972); 1 s (Guy Nicholas Robert b 1963), 1 da (Jane Frances b 1955); m 2, 29 April 1988, Jean, da of William Clayton Riley (d 1976); 2 step da (Juliet Contance Robertson b 1972, Jane Margaret Robertson b 1975); *Career* sales dir Speedwork Labels Ltd 1971-73; sales and mktg dir: Harlands of Hull Ltd 1972-76, Harland Group of Companies 1976- (vice chm 1988); pres Fedn Internationale D'Adhesifs et Theomocollants 1987-90 (memb Bd 1982-), memb Bd Article Number Associates (UK) Ltd London 1974-79; Freeman City of London 1980, Liveryman Worshipful Co of Marketors 1980 (Master 1991); FInstM 1980; *Recreations* riding, antiques restoration; *Clubs* Carlton, Farmers'; *Style*— Robert Wilson, Esq; No 6 Newbegin, Beverley HU17 8EG (☎ 0482 881 487, fax 0482 863192, car 0836 615141)

WILSON, Robert Julian (Robin); s of Prof Frank Percy Wilson (d 1963), and Joanna, *née* Perry-Keene (d 1985); *b* 6 July 1933; *Educ* St Edward's Sch Oxford, Trinity Coll Cambridge (Exhibition); *m* 6 April 1957, Caroline Anne, da of John Edward Maher; 2 da (Dr Katharine Joanna b 1959, Dr Olivia Jane b 1964); *Career* lectr Univ of Münster Westphalia 1955-58, asst master St Peter's Sch York 1958-62, head of English Nottingham HS 1962-72, headmaster Trinity Sch of John Whitgift Croydon 1972-; vice chm Academy Policy Ctee HMC; FRSA 1982; *Books* Bertelsmann Sparchkursus Englisch (co-ed, 1959), Shakespeare: The Merchant of Venice (ed, 1971); *Recreations* drama, travel, skiing, golf; *Clubs* E India, Devonshire, Addington GC; *Style*— Robin Wilson, Esq; 22 Beech House Rd, Croydon, Surrey CRO 1JP (☎ 081 686 1915); Trinity School, Shirley Park, Croydon CR9 7AT (☎ 081 656 9541, fax 081 655 0522)

WILSON, Robert Peter; s of Alfred Wilson (d 1951), and Dorothy Eileen, *née* Mathews, MBE; *b* 2 Sept 1943; *Educ* Epsom Coll, Sussex Univ (BA), Harvard Business Sch (AMP); *m* 7 Feb 1975, Shirley Elisabeth, da of George Robson, of Hunmanby, Yorks; 1 s (Andrew), 1 da (Nicola); *Career* asst economist Dunlop Ltd 1966-67, economist Mobil Oil Co Ltd 1968-70; Rio Tinto Zinc Gp 1970-: md Am and s Europe Ltd 1979-82, head of planning and devpt RTZ plc 1982-87, dir RTZ Corp plc 1987-; dir CRA Ltd (Australia) 1990-; *Recreations* theatre, opera, tennis; *Style*—

Robert Wilson, Esq; The RTZ Corporation plc, 6 St James's Square, London SW17 4LD (☎ 071 930 2399, 071 895 9077, fax 071 930 3249, telex 24639)

WILSON, Dr Robert Stanley Edward; s of Stanley William Wilson (d 1988), of Pontesbury, Shropshire, and Grace Rosetta Harriet, *née* Wicks; *b* 30 Nov 1941; *Educ* S W Essex Co Tech Sch, S W Essex Tech Coll, Univ of Bristol (BSc, MB ChB, Silver medallist, RJ Brocklehurst prize, Richard Clarke prize, Barret Roue prize, proxime accesit surgical suple prize and Lady Haberfield Medical prize, MRCP), Univ of Wales (MA); *m* 3 Feb 1968, Jacqueline Mary Ann, da of Clifford Brown; 2 s (Peter Edward b 25 May 1970, Andrew Robert b 1 June 1971), 1 da (Sarah Elizabeth b 21 Oct 1974); *Career* farm labourer Nazeing Essex 1958-59, jr laboratory technician Queen Mary Coll April-Sept 1959, student laboratory technician Connaught Hosp Walthamstow 1959-60, house physician Bristol Gen Hosp 1968-69, sr house offr in clinical pathology Bristol Royal Infirmary 1969-70 (house surgn Feb-Aug 1969), sr house offr in gen med Bristol Gen Hosp 1970-71, registrar in gen med Gordon and Westminster Hosps London 1971-72, registrar and tutor in gen and thoracic med Hammersmith Hosp and RPMS 1973-74, sr med registrar and tutor in gen and thoracic med Bristol Royal Hosp and Frenchay Hosp 1974-76, conslt physician with interest in thoracic med Royal Shrewsbury Hosp 1976-, unit med advsr Shropshire Health Authy 1990- (former unit gen mangr); chm District Medical Audit Ctee 1990; author of numerous medical papers and booklets; chm: Shrewsbury and District Stroke Club 1982, Shropshire Asthma Soc 1987; govr Longden Primary Sch 1982-85, Mary Webb Sch 1986-88; chm Longden Village Hall 1979-90; FRCP 1985, Licentiate Soc of Health Service Mgmnt 1990; *Recreations* golf, stamp collecting, water colours, watching soccer, running a 10 acre small holding; *Style*— Dr Robert Wilson; Lower Wood House, Lower Common, Longden, Shropshire SY5 8HB; Royal Shrewsbury Hospital, Shrewsbury, Shropshire (☎ 0743 231122)

WILSON, Robert William; s of Alfred Wilson (d 1968), of Retford, Notts, and Winifred, *née* Scarborough (d 1964); *b* 18 Sept 1926; *Educ* Retford GS; *m* 24 March 1951, Pamela Marjorie, da of Horace Utley Dixon (d 1962), of Retford; 2 da (Jillian b 1954, Carol b 1956); *Career* Intelligence Corps 1945-48 (latterly in India); admitted slr 1951; cmmr for oaths 1957, HM Coroner for E Berks 1970-, conslt slrs Maidenhead 1989; chm Waltham St Lawrence Parish Cncl 1986; memb Coroners' Soc for England and Wales 1970, Lloyd's Underwriter 1978; memb Law Soc 1960; *Recreations* yachting (yacht 'Josephine'); *Style*— Robert Wilson, Esq; Oak Trees, West End, Waltham St Lawrence, Berks RG10 0NN (☎ 0734 343406, fax 0734 320599)

WILSON, Dr the Hon Robin James; Dr The Hon; elder s of Baron Wilson of Rievaulx, KG, OBE, PC, FRS (Life Peer); *b* 5 Dec 1943; *Educ* University Coll Sch Hampstead, Balliol Coll Oxford (MA), Univ of Pennsylvania (MA, PhD), MIT; *m* 1968, (Margaret Elizabeth) Joy, da of Brian and Sallie Crispin, of Dawlish; 2 da (Jennifer b 1975, Catherine (twin) b 1975); *Career* sr lectr in mathematics: Jesus Coll Oxford 1969-72, Open Univ 1972-79 (sr lectr 1979-, head Dept Pure Mathematics), Keble Coll Oxford (p/t) 1980-; several times visiting prof of mathematics Colorado Coll USA; *Books* Instruction to Graph Theory (1972), Let Newton Be! (jtly, 1988), thirteen other mathematics books, Gilbert and Sullivan: The D'Oyly Carte Years (jtly, 1984), three other music books; *Recreations* music (performing and listening), travel, philately; *Style*— Dr the Hon Robin Wilson; 15 Chalfont Rd, Oxford OX2 6TL

WILSON, Rt Rev Roger Plumpton; KCVO (1974); s of Canon Clifford Plumpton Wilson; *b* 3 Aug 1905; *Educ* Winchester, Keble Coll Oxford; *m* 1935, Mabel Avery; 2 s, 1 da; *Career* former classical master Shrewsbury and St Andrew's Grahamstown; archdeacon of Nottingham 1945-49, bishop of Wakefield 1949-58, bishop of Chichester 1958-74; clerk of the closet to HM The Queen 1963-75; DD Lambeth; *Style*— The Rt Rev Roger Wilson, KCVO; Kingsett, Wrington, Bristol, Avon

WILSON, Air Vice- Marshal Ronald Andrew Fellowes (Sandy); CB (1990), AFC (1978); s of Ronald Denis Wilson (d 1983), of Great Bookham, Surrey, and Gladys Vera; *b* 27 Feb 1941; *Educ* Tonbridge, RAF Coll Cranwell; *m* 1, 4 Aug 1962 (m dis 1979), Patricia Lesley, da of BD Cauthery (d 1986), of Effingham, Surrey; 1 da (Hayley Ann Fellowes b 7 Oct 1972); m 2, 21 May 1979, Mary Christine, da of Stanley Anderson (d 1978), of Darfield, Yorks; *Career* Flying Instr RAF Leeming 1963-65, Pilot 2 Sqdn RAF Gutersloh 1966-67, ADC to C-in-C RAF Germany 1967-68, Flt Cdr 2 Sqdn RAF Gutersloh 1968-70, Sqdn Ldr 1970, Flt Cdr 2 Sqdn RAF Laarbruch 1970-72, RAF Staff Coll Bracknell 1973, SO HQ Strike Cmd 1974-75, Wing Cdr 1975, OC 2 Sqdn 1975-77, SO Air Plans MOD 1977-79, Gp Capt 1980, OC RAF Lossiemouth 1980-82, Air Cdr Falkland Is and OC RAF Stanley 1982, SO Commitments Staff MOD 1983-85, Air Cdre 1985, Dir of Ops (Strike) MOD 1985, Dir Air Offensive MOD 1986-87, Air Vice-Marshal 1987, SASO Strike Cmd and DCSO HQUKAIR 1987-88, AOC 1 Gp 1989-; awarded: Queens Commendation for Valuable Servs in the Air 1973, Arthur Barratt Meml Prize 1973; govr Tonbridge 1984-87, memb Cncl Br Ski Fedn 1986; Freeman City of London 1966, Liveryman Worshipful Co of Skinners 1970 (Extra Memb of Ct 1984-87); FBIM; *Recreations* skiing, golf, painting, furniture restoration, photography; *Clubs* Royal Air Force; *Style*— Air Vice-Marshal RAF Wilson, CB, AFC; c/o Royal Bank of Scotland, Holts Branch, Whitehall, London SW1

WILSON, Ronald George; s of Robert Paterson Wilson (d 1951), of Aberdeen, and Ena Watson Cowie Wilson (d 1965); *b* 20 April 1937; *Educ* Aberdeen GS, Univ of Aberdeen (MB ChB, MD); *m* 6 April 1963, Muriel, da of James Hutcheon (d 1968), of Aberdeen; 1 s (James Robert b 13 Oct 1967), 1 da (Fiona Alys b 18 Nov 1970); *Career* surgn Lt RN with 40 Commando RM 1963-65, with med branch Royal Marine Reserves until 1982; sr house offr in surgery (Aberdeen 1966-68), Bristol Trg Scheme 1968-70, registrar in gen surgery Bristol 1970-71, res in breast cancer Edinburgh Royal Infirmary 1971-73, lectr in surgery Univ of Nottingham 1973-77 (conslt surgn); Breast Screening Prog mangr: Regnl and Nat Organisational Ctees, Nat Computor Devpt Ctee, Nat Ctee for Evaluation; FRCSEd; *Clubs* Moyniham Chirurgical; *Style*— Ronald Wilson, Esq; Priestfield, Burnopfield, Newcastle upon Tyne (☎ 0207 70305); Dept of Surgery and Dir of Breast Screening/Assessment Centre, General Hospital, Newcastle upon Tyne (☎ 091 273 8811 ext 22323, fax 091 272 2641)

WILSON, (Gerald) Roy; s of Fred Wilson (d 1934), of Oldham, Lancs, and Elsie, *née* Morrison (d 1968); *b* 11 Jan 1930; *Educ* Oldham HS; *m* 1, 18 Sept 1965, Doreen Chadderton (d 1990); 1 s (Jonathan b 1973), 1 da (Susan b 1969); m 2, 9 Nov 1990, Patricia, *née* Ive (widowed as Mrs Henderson 1989); *Career* Min of Works HMSO, sr systems designer PO HQ 1965-66, branch mangr Girobank 1966-69 (sr systems designer 1966); National Savings: asst controller IT systems Durham 1972-78 (IT mangr 1969-72), controller (chief exec) Savings Certificate Office Durham 1978-86, dep dir of savings London (under sec rank) 1986-89, conslt 1990-; memb: Rotary Club of Durham, Probus, BIM, Mensa; FBIM 1984; *Recreations* swimming (its organisation and teaching), reading, drawing, photography, watching sport; *Clubs* Civil Service, Dunelm (Durham), Durham City Swimming (life memb), Durham City Cricket; *Style*— Roy Wilson, Esq; 48 Ancroft Garth, High Shincliffe, Durham DH1 2UD

WILSON, Hon Mrs (Sally Anne Marie Gabrielle); da of 5 Baron Vivian; *b* 1930; *m* 1, 1954 (m dis 1962), Robin Lowe; m 2, 1963, Charles William Munro Wilson; 1 s; *Style*— The Hon Mrs Wilson; 150 Cranmer Ct, Whitehead's Grove, London SW3 (☎ 071 589 8864)

WILSON, Hon Mrs (Shirley Cynthia); da of late 2 Baron Cunliffe; *b* 1926; *m* 1959, Alan Desmond Wilson; 1 s (Matthew Crispin b 1961), 1 da (Richenda Catherine b 1963); *Style*— The Hon Mrs Wilson; Ashbrook, Aston Tirrold, Didcot, Oxon OX11 9DL

WILSON, Snoo; s of Leslie Wilson, and Pamela Mary Wilson; *b* 2 Aug 1948; *Educ* Bradfield, East Anglia Univ (BA); *m* 1976, Ann, *née* McFerran; 2 s, 1 da; *Career* writer 1969-, assoc dir Portable Theatre 1970-75, Dramaturge RSC 1975-76, script ed Play for Today 1976, Henfield Fell Univ of E Anglia 1978, US Bicentennial Fell in Playwriting 1981-82, adapted Gounod's La Colombe Buxton Fextival 1983, assoc prof of theatre Univ of California San Diego 1987; filmscript: Shadey 1986; Plays incl: Layby (jtly 1972), Pignight (1972), The Pleasure Principle (1973), Blowjob (1974), Soul of the White Ant (1976), England England (1978), Vampire (1978), The Glad Hand (1978), A Greenish Man (1978), The Number of the Beast (1982), Flaming Bodies (1982), Grass Widow (1983), Loving Reno (1983), Hamlyn (1984), More Light (1987), 80 days (book, musical 1988); novels: Spaceache (1984), Inside Babel (1985); opera: Orpheus in the Underworld (new version 1984); *Recreations* beekeeping, space travel; *Style*— Snoo Wilson, Esq; 41 The Chase, London SW4 0NP

WILSON, Stanley John; CBE (1981); *b* 23 Oct 1921; *m* 1952, Molly Ann; 2 step s; *Career* md Burmah Oil 1975-82 (chief exec 1980-82); chm Burmah SA Ltd 1983-; *Clubs* City of London, City, Rand; *Style*— Stanley Wilson, Esq, CBE; The Jetty, PO Box 751, Plettenberg Bay, Cape Province 6600, Republic of South Africa (☎ Plettenberg Bay 9624)

WILSON, (Catherine) Thelma; da of John Matters (d 1964), of Ashington, Northumberland, and Eleanor Irene, *née* Hudson (d 1979); *b* 9 June 1929; *Educ* St Margaret's HS Gosforth, Central Newcastle HS, King's College Durham Univ (BA); *m* 26 Sept 1953, Noel, s of the late Andrew Wilson, of Ashington, Northumberland; 2 s ((Peter) Lawrence b 16 Jan 1956, Michael David b 5 Aug 1959); *Career* geriatric social worker Wimbledon Guild of Social Welfare 1952-56, lectr several Colls in London 1958-65, princ lectr in social policy NE London Poly 1965-, conslt on preparation for retirement Tate & Lyle Refineries London 1968-, cncl memb for the educn and trg of health visitors 1973-83, short term expert Social Devpt Fund UN 1973, expert assignment Regnl Office for Euro World Health Orgn 1981, UK rep on the Int Ctee Euro Regnl Clearing House for Community Work 1971-78; advsr Nursing and Social Work Serv Soldiers' Sailors & Airmen's Families Assoc 1983-, hon sec Social Admin & Social Work Ctees of the Jt Univ Cncl for Social & Public Admin 1972-79, memb Exam Ctee Local Govt Trg Bd and several related activities 1979-; mangr (Mental Health Act) Goodmayes Hosp 1990-; CEC Erasmus and Tempus awards 1990 and 1991; Freeman City of London 1984, Liveryman Worshipful Co of Chartered Secs and Admins 1984; ACIS 1964, MISW 1964, FCIS 1974; *Books* over 40 pubns including Penal Services for Offenders; comparative studies of England and Poland 1984-85 (1987); *Recreations* reading, travel; *Clubs* Royal Overseas League; *Style*— Mrs Thelma Wilson; Polytechnic of East London, Romford Rd, London E15 4LZ (☎ 081 590 7722 ext 4542/4477)

WILSON, Prof Thomas; OBE (1946); s of John B Wilson (d 1945), and Margaret, *née* Ellison (d 1977); *b* 23 June 1916; *Educ* Methodist Coll Belfast, Queen's Univ Belfast (BA), Univ of London (PhD), Univ of Oxford (MA); *m* 6 July 1943, Dorothy Joan, da of Arthur Parry; 1 s (John), 2 da (Moya, Margaret); *Career* WWII Miny of Econ Warfare 1940-41, Miny of Aircraft Prodn 1941-42, War Cabinet Offices 1942-45; Econ Section Cabinet 1945-46; fell Univ Coll Oxford 1946-58, Adam Smith prof of political econ Univ of Glasgow 1958-82; numerous govt consultancies; hon fell LSE; Hon DUniv Stirling 1981; FBA, FRSE; *Books* Fluctuations in Income and Employment (1942), Oxford Studies in the Price Mechanism (1951), Inflation (1961), Planning and Growth (1964), Essays on Adam Smith (jt ed with A S Skinner, 1975), The Market and the State (jt ed with A S Skinner, 1976), Welfare State (with D J Wilson, 1982), Inflation, Unemployment and the Market (1984), Ulster - Conflict and Consent (1989); *Recreations* hill walking, photography; *Clubs* Athenaeum; *Style*— Prof Thomas Wilson; 1 Chatford House, The Promenade, Clifton Down, Bristol BJ8 3NC (☎ 0272 730741)

WILSON, Thomas Charles; s of Jeremy Charles Wilson, DFC, of Fulmer, Bucks, and June Patricia, *née* Bucknill; *b* 2 June 1946; *Educ* Eton, Aix-en-Provence Univ; *m* 5 Dec 1980, (Elizabeth) Jane, da of Lt-Gen Sir Napier Crookenden KCB, DSO, OBE; 1 s (James b 1984), 1 da (Tobina b 1981), 1 step s (Geoffrey b 1977); *Career* head of corp fin Price Waterhouse 1987- (articled clerk 1965-77, ptnr 1977-); FCA 1974; *Recreations* golf, tennis, fishing, bridge; *Clubs* Hurlingham Denham Golf; *Style*— Thomas Wilson, Esq; Price Waterhouse, Southwark Towers, 32 London Bridge St, London SE1 9SY (☎ 071 407 8989, fax 071 378 0647)

WILSON, Thomas David; s and h of Sir David Wilson, 3 Bt, *qv*; *b* 6 Jan 1959; *Educ* Harrow; *m* 21 July 1984, Valerie, er da of Vivian David Davies Stogdale, of Monks Farm, Shotover, Oxon; 2 s (Fergus b 24 April 1987, Oscar b 10 June 1989); *Recreations* skiing, shooting, fishing, tennis, sailing; *Clubs* Royal Southern Yacht, Mill Reef (Antigua); *Style*— Thomas Wilson, Esq; 80 Broxash Road, London SW11 6AB (☎ 071 228 5282); Cooper Gay & Co Ltd, International House, 26 Creechurch Lane, London EC3A 5EH (☎ 071 480 7322, fax 071 481 4695, telex 885717)

WILSON, Thomas Dunlop; s of William Wilson (d 1977), of Annwill, Grahamston Rd, Barrhead, Glasgow, and Annie, *née* Stewart (d 1986); *b* 5 Feb 1919; *Educ* Allan Glens Sch Glasgow, Univ of Glasgow (BSc); *m* 29 Nov 1946, (Marie) Paule Juliette, da of Mathieu Durand (d 1974), of Souar, Tunisia; 1 s (William Mark Dunlop b 23 Jan 1949), 2 da (Anne-Marie Paule (Mrs Grove) b 3 April 1953, Gillian Francoise b 31 March 1959); *Career* WWII enlisted RE 1941 served UK, cmmnd 1942, 1 Army N Africa 1942-43, Italy and Austria 1943-46 (Maj dep asst dir tport railways GHQ CHF 1945-46); civil engr asst: Paisley 1946-49, Lanarkshire 1949-54; res engr Miny of Devpt Iraq 1954-58, sr civil engr (bridges) Lanarkshire 1958-60, chief project engr M5 Motorway (Worcs) 1960-62, dep co surveyor bridgemaster and engr Cumberland 1962-68, dir NW Road Construction Unit Dept of Tport 1969-72, dep chief engr Dept of Tport 1972-74, ptnr Mott Hay & Anderson (consulting engrs) 1974-79, private consulting practice in civil engrg (arbitrator) 1979-; memb Rotary Club Glasgow, elder Neilston Church of Scotland; memb int ctees on roads and tunnels; CEng, FICE, FIStructE, FAMunE, FCIArb, FIHT, MAConsE; memb French Soc Civil Engrs; *Books* Civil Engineers Reference Book (highways chapter, 1975); *Recreations* hill walking, fishing, shooting, curling; *Clubs* Naval and Military; *Style*— Thomas D Wilson, Esq; Kilmartin, Neilston, Glasgow G78 3EA (☎ 041 881 1346); 114 Main St, Neilston, Glasgow G78 3EA (☎ 041 881 1346)

WILSON, Thomas Skinner; s of Thomas Wilson, of Carmyle, Glasgow, and Anne, *née* Skinner; *b* 24 Aug 1961; *Educ* Bannerman HS, Bell Coll of Technol; *m* 17 July 1981, Marion, da of George Campbell; 1 da (Chloe Slater b 22 Feb 1984); *Career* professional footballer; pt/t Queens Park 1978-82 (43 appearances), St Mirren 1982-89 (240 appearances incl 8 Euro Cup), Dunfermline Athletic 1989- (over 30 appearances); Scotland: 3 under 18 cups 1978, under 21 cup v Switzerland 1983; Scottish Cup Winner's medal 1987 (v Dundee Utd); qualified coach Scottish Football Assoc 1988; mfrg technician apprentice Caterpillar Tractor Co 1978-82; *Recreations* reading, golf; *Style*— Thomas Wilson, Esq; Dunfermline Athletic FC, Halbeath Rd, East End Park, Dunfermline (☎ 0383 724 295)

WILSON, Col Timothy John Michael; s of Lt-Col A C Wilson (d 1975), of Kent and Devon, and Margaret Beverley, *née* Iliffe; *b* 23 March 1932; *Educ* Cranbrook Sch Kent, Canadian Army Staff Coll, Nat Defence Coll, Indian Nat Defence Coll; *m* 23 Sept 1961, Kitty Maxine, da of Maj Seymour Norton-Taylor, of Poole, Dorset; 2 da (Vanessa b 1963, Jennifer b 1965); *Career* 2 Lt and Lt 1950-53, Lt 2 i/c RM Detachment HMS Gambia 1953-55 (memb earthquake relief team Zante Ionian Islands 1953), Troop Subaltern 40 Commando RM 1955-57, served Cyprus, Near East (severely wounded at Port Said Landings 1956, despatches), housemaster RM Sch of Music 1957-59, motor tport course 1959-60, local Capt ADC to C-in-C Near East HQ Near East Cyprus 1960-61, Capt Motor Tport Offr RM Poole 1961-63, staff course Canadian Army Staff Coll 1963-65, Adj 40 Commando RM (subsequently Maj) 1965-68 (served Malaysia 1965-67), Maj GSO 2 (instr) Jr Div Army Staff Coll Warminster 1968-70, Bde Maj UK Commandos GSO 2 Ops and Planning HQ Commando Forces RM 1970-72, staff course Nat Def Coll 1972-73, Lt-Col Royal Marines Rep USMC Devpt and Educn Cmd 1973-75, CO 42 Commando RM 1975-78 (served N Ireland 1976), Col Dir drafting and records RM HMS Centurion 1978-79, staff course Indian Nat Def Coll New Delhi 1979-80, Asst Adj Gen to Cmdt Gen RM MOD London 1980-83, ADC to HM The Queen 1982-83; ptnrship sec Radcliffes & Co Slrs Westminster; working volunteer memb Kent and E Sussex Steam Railway, memb HM Bodyguard of the Hon Corps of Gentlemen of Arms 1984; Hon MSc (def studies) Allahabad 1980; FBIM 1980, MInstAM 1982; *Recreations* beagling, golf, tennis, travel; *Clubs* Army and Navy; *Style*— Col Timothy Wilson

WILSON, Timothy Peter (Tim); s of Maj Philip Grimwade Wilson, MC (d 1968), of Stoke by Nayland, and Muriel, *née* Martin (d 1985); *b* 16 Dec 1929; *Educ* Radley; *Career* accountant; ICI 1957-84, dir and sec Wilsons Corn and Milling Co Ltd 1961-, chief accountant Pensions Tst 1984-87, hon financial admin Pre Retirement Assoc 1988-90; hon treas Thames Rowing Club 1970-84, memb Ctee Putney Amateur Regatta; FCA 1955; *Recreations* rowing, skiing, shooting; *Clubs* Thames Rowing, Tees Rowing, Remenham, Ski of GB; *Style*— Tim Wilson, Esq

WILSON, Dr William; *b* 29 Oct 1928; *Educ* Glasgow HS, Univ of Glasgow (MB ChB); *m* 14 June 1958, Isabel, da of Col David Mackie, MC (d 1966), of Stamford House, Dundonald, Ayrshire; 1 s (David b 1965), 1 da (Anne b 1961); *Career* sr conslt ophthalmologist Glasgow Royal Infirmary 1962-, hon clinical lectr Univ of Glasgow 1962-; conslt: St Vincent Sch for the Blind Glasgow, Kelvin Sch for Partially Sighted Children; examiner: RCSEd and Glasgow 1964-, Coll Ophthalmologists 1988-; pres Scottish Ophthalmological Soc 1982-84; FRCSEd 1958, fell Coll Ophthalmologists 1988; *Recreations* gardening, DIY; *Clubs* Royal Scottish Automobile; *Style*— Dr William Wilson; 34 Calderwood Rd, Newlands, Glasgow G43 2RU; Crossways, Muthill, Perthshire (☎ 041 637 4898); 22 Sandyford Place, Glasgow G3 7NG (☎ 041 221 7571)

WILSON, Hon William Edward Alexander; yr s of 2 Baron Moran, KCMG; *b* 16 Dec 1956; *Educ* Eton, Inns of Court Sch of Law, Univ of London (LLM); *m* 1989, Juliette Elizabeth Charmian, da of Maj Mungo, of Hampshire; *Career* called to the Bar Middle Temple 1978, Dept of the Dir of Public Prosecutions 1980-86, mangr Legal Dept IMRO Ltd 1986-90, legal and compliance offr Century Asset Management 1990-91, environment lawyer 1991-; *Style*— The Hon William Wilson

WILSON, Hon Mrs (Yvette Latham); o da of 1 Baron Baillieu, KBE, CMG (d 1967), and Ruby Florence Evelyn, *née* Clark (d 1962); *b* 30 Sept 1922; *m* 20 July 1946, Robert Ruttan Wilson, s of late Arthur Alling Wilson (ggs of Rev George Wilson, bro of 9 and 10 Barons Berners), of San Francisco, California, USA; 4 da; *Style*— The Hon Mrs Wilson; Durford Knoll, Upper Durford Wood, Petersfield, Hants

WILSON-FISH, Peter; s of Wilfred Fish, of Longton, Preston, Lancs, and Muriel, *née* Wilson; *b* 20 Oct 1933; *Educ* Giggleswick Sch, Univ of London; *m* 1, 20 July 1961 (m dis), Shirley Gertrude, da of Leopold Augustus Henry Rohlehr (d 1961), of New Amsterdam Guiana; 1 da (Jacqueline b 1963); m 2, 18 Oct 1975, Stella Dawn, da of Sidney Charman (d 1982); 2 s (James b 1977, Oliver b 1979); *Career* RE 1956-; in Pharmaceutical Indust 1979; *Recreations* beagling, sailing, thrashing the water, gardening; *Style*— Peter Wilson-Fish, Esq; Hilltop, Colby, Appleby in Westmorland, Cumbria CA16 6BD

WILSON-JOHNSON, David Robert; s of Harry Kenneth Johnson, of Irthlingborough, Northants, and Sylvia Constance, *née* Wilson; *b* 16 Nov 1950; *Educ* Wellingborough Sch, Br Inst of Florence, St Catharine's Coll Cambridge (BA), RAM; *Career* baritone Royal Opera House; performances incl: We Come to the River (debut) 1976, Billy Budd 1982, L'Enfant et les Sortilèges 1983 and 1987, Boris Godunov 1984, Die Zauberflöte 1985, 1986 and 1987, Turandot 1987, Madam Butterfly 1988, Paris Opera debut Die Meistersinger 1989, St Francois d'Assise (title role) 1988 (winner Evening Standard award for Opera); Eight Songs for a Mad King Paris 1979, Last Night of the Proms 1981 and 1986; festival appearances at: Glyndebourne, Edinburgh, Bath, Bergen, Berlin, Geneva, Graz, Holland, Hong Kong, Jerusalem, Orange, Paris, Vienna; recordings incl: Schubert, Winterreise, Schoenberg's Ode to Napoleon, La Traviata, Lucrezia Borgia, Mozart Masses from King's College, Nelson Mass Haydn, Belshazzar's Feast, The Kingdom (Elgar), L'Enfance du Christ (Berlioz); films incl: The Ice Break (Tippett), The Midsummer Marriage (Tippett), The Lighthouse (Maxwell Davies); ARAM 1984, FRAM 1988; *Recreations* swimming, slimming, gardening, growing walnuts at house in Dordogne; *Style*— David Wilson-Johnson, Esq; 28 Englefield Rd, London N1 4ET (☎ 071 254 0941); Lies Askonas Ltd, 186 Drury Lane, London WC23B 5RY (☎ 071 405 1808, fax 071 242 1831, telex 265914 ASKONA G)

WILSON-MACDONALD, Melody; da of Gp Capt Duncan Stuart Wilson-MacDonald, DSO, DFC, RAF, ret, and Rosemary; *Educ* St Georges Sch Montreux Switzerland, Heathfield Sch Ascot Berks, Villa Curonia Florence Italy; *Career* fashion model 1968-78, house model Fortnum & Mason Ltd 1976, Rolls Royce and Bentley Chauffeuse Jack Barclay Ltd 1978-82, interior designer 1986-; actively involved in campaigning against animal abuse in particular factory farming and vivisection; *Recreations* horse riding, swimming, gardening; *Style*— Ms Melody Wilson-MacDonald

WILSON OF HIGH WRAY, Baroness; Valerie Frances Elizabeth; da of William Baron Fletcher, of Cape Town; *m* 1935, Baron Wilson of High Wray, OBE, DSC (d 1980); *Style*— The Rt Hon Lady Wilson of High Wray; Gillingate House, Kendal, Cumbria

WILSON OF LANGSIDE, Baron (Life Peer UK 1969), of Broughton, in Co Edinburgh; Henry Stephen Wilson; PC (1967), QC (Scot 1965); s of James Wilson, of Glasgow, solicitor; *b* 21 March 1916; *Educ* Glasgow HS, Univ of Glasgow (MA, LLB); *m* 1942, Jessie Forrester, da of late William Nisbet Waters, of Paisley; *Career* serv WWII HLI and RAC; barr 1946, slr-gen Scotland 1965-67, lord-advocate 1967-70, Sheriff Princ Glasgow and Strathkelvin 1975-77; contested (Lab): Dumfriesshire 1950 and 1955, Edinburgh W 1951; joined SDP 1981, sits as SDP peer in House of Lords; *Style*— The Rt Hon the Lord Wilson of Langside, PC, QC; Dunallan, Kippen, Stirlingshire (☎ 078 687 210)

WILSON OF RADCLIFFE, Baroness; Freda; *née* Mather; *b* 23 Jan 1930; *m* 1976, as his 2 w, Baron Wilson of Radcliffe (d 1983, former Lab Peer and chief exec offr Co-operative Wholesale Soc); 1 step da; *Style*— The Rt Hon the Lady Wilson of Radcliffe; The Bungalow, 4 Hey House Mews, off Lumb Carr Road, Holcombe, Nr Bury BL8 4NS

WILSON OF RIEVAULX, Baron (Life Peer UK 1983), of Kirklees, Co W Yorks; Sir (James) Harold Wilson; KG (1976), OBE (1945), PC (1947); s of James Herbert Wilson (d 1971, sometime Lib dep election agent to Sir Winston Churchill), of Rievaulx, Biscovey, Par, Cornwall, formerly of Huddersfield and of Manchester, and Ethel Wilson; *b* 11 March 1916; *Educ* Milnsbridge Cncl Sch, Royds Hall Sch Huddersfield, Wirral GS Bebington, Jesus Coll Oxford; *m* 1940, (Gladys) Mary, da of late Rev Daniel Baldwin, of The Manse, Duxford, Cambridge; 2 s (Hon Robin James b 1943, Hon Giles Daniel John b 1948); *Career* lectr in economics New Coll Oxford 1937, fell Univ Coll Oxford 1938, praelector in economics and domestic bursar 1945; MP (Lab): Ormskirk 1945-50, Huyton 1950-83; dir of economics and statistics Miny of Fuel and Power 1943-44, Parly sec Miny of Works 1945-47, sec Overseas Trade 1947, pres BOT 1947-51, chm Exec Ctee Lab Pty 1961-62 (vice chm 1960-61), ldr oppn 1963-64 and 1970-74, PM and First Lord of the Treasy 1964-70 and 1974-76; chllr Univ of Bradford 1966-85, pres RSS 1972-73, chm Ctee to Review Financing of Fin Instns 1976-80; hon pres GB-USSR Assoc 1976-87; pres RSC 1976-86; hon fell Jesus and Univ Colls Oxford 1963; elder bro Trinity House, hon Freeman City of London; Hon DCL Oxford 1965; Hon LLD: Lancaster, Liverpool, Nottingham, Sussex; HonDTech Bradford; DUniv: Essex and Open Univ (which he founded); FRS; *Clubs* Athenaeum; *Style*— The Rt Hon the Lord Wilson of Rievaulx, KG, OBE, PC; House of Lords, London SW1A 0AA

WILSON SMITH, Lt-Col John Logan; OBE (1976); s of William Arthur Wilson Smith, (d 1948), and Dorothea Grace, *née* Lawes (d 1974); *b* 4 July 1927; *Educ* Wellington Coll; *m* 14 April 1961, Ann Winifred Lyon, da of Kenneth Charles Corsar (d 1967), of Cairniehill; 3 da (Susan b 1962, Caroline b 1964, Jane b 1969); *Career* Regular Army offr cmmnd The Royal Scots 1946, served Palestine, Korea, Aden, Cyprus, NI, The Staff Coll (psc) 1961, jssc 1965, ret Lt-Col 1977, regt sec The Royal Scots; dir The Royal Scots Regt Shop Ltd; chm The Royal Scots Assoc, pres SSAFA and FHS Edinburgh and Midlothian; *Recreations* shooting, forestry, horticulture; *Clubs* The Royal Scots; *Style*— Lt-Col John L Wilson Smith, OBE; Cumledge, Duns, Berwickshire TD11 3TB; The Castle, Edinburgh EH1 2YT (☎ 031 336 1761 ext 4265)

WILTON, (James) Andrew Rutley; *Career* asst Keeper: British Art Walker Gallery Liverpool 1965-67, Dept of Prints and Drawings British Museum 1967-76, curator Prints and Drawings Yale Center for British Art New Haven 1976-80, asst keeper Dept of Prints and Drawings British Muesum 1980-84, keeper of British Art Tate Gallery 1989- (curator Turner Collection The Clore Gallery 1985-89); books: Constable's English Landscape Scenery (1976), The Wood Engravings of William Blake (1976), British Watercolours 1750-1850 (1977), Turner in Switzerland (with John Russell, 1977), William Pars: Journey through the Alps (1979), The Life and Work of JMW Turner (1979), Turner Abroad (1982), Turner in his Time (1987); author of numerous exhibition catalogues; FRSA, Hon OWCS; *Recreations* music, cooking, architecture, people; *Style*— Andrew Wilton, Esq; 11 Musgrove Rd, London SE14 5PP (☎ 071 639 6876); Tate Gallery, Millbank, London SW1P 4RG (☎ 071 821 1313, fax 071 931 7512)

WILTON, Sir (Arthur) John; KCMG (1979, CMG 1967), KCVO (1979), MC (1945); s of Walter Wilton (d 1944); *b* 21 Oct 1921; *Educ* Wanstead HS, St John's Coll Oxford; *m* 1950, Maureen Elizabeth Alison, *née* Meaker; 4 s, 1 da; *Career* Royal Ulster Rifles 1942 (despatches), Maj; HM Dip Serv 1947-79: dir MECAS Shemlan 1960-65, dep high cmmr Aden 1966-67, ambass Kuwait 1970-74, under sec FCO 1974-75, ambass Jedda 1976-79; dir London House for Overseas Graduates 1979-86, chm Arab-Br Centre 1981-86, govr Hele's sch 1989-, pres Plymouth Branch English Speaking Union 1991-; FRSA 1982; *Recreations* reading and current affairs, gardening; *Style*— Sir John Wilton, KCMG, KCVO, MC

WILTON, Rosalyn Susan; *née* Trup; da of Samuel Trup, and Celia, *née* Aronson; *b* 25 Jan 1952; *Educ* Copthall Co GS, L'Alliance Francaise Paris, Univ of London (BSc); *m* 11 April 1978, Gerald Parselle Wilton, s of Orville Wilton; 2 da (Georgina b 1979, Emily b 1981); *Career* sterling money broker Butler Till Ltd 1973-79; dir: GNI Ltd 1982-84, Drexel Burnham Lambert Ltd (md institutional financial futures and options) 1984-90, Drexel Burnham Lambert Securities Ltd (md int fixed income) 1989-90; sr vice pres Transaction Products Reuters Europe Middle East and Africa 1990-; dir The London Int Financial Futures Exchange 1985-90; *Style*— Mrs Rosalyn Wilton; Reuters Limited, 85 Fleet St, London EC4P 4AJ (☎ 071 250 1122, 071 955 0011, telex 23222)

WILTON, 7 Earl of (UK 1801); Seymour William Arthur John Egerton; also Viscount Grey de Wilton (UK 1801); s of 6 Earl of Wilton (d 1927, gs of 2 Earl, himself yr bro of 2 Marquess of Westminster and er bro of 1 Baron Ebury); *b* 29 May 1921; *Educ* Eton; *m* 1962, Diana, da of Roy Galway and formerly w of David Naylor-Leyland, MVO, 3 s of Sir Edward Naylor-Leyland, 2 Bt; *Heir* 4 cous, 6 Baron Ebury; *Clubs* White's; *Style*— The Rt Hon the Earl of Wilton; The Old Vicarage, Castle Hedingham, Halstead, Essex CD9 3EZ

WILTSHIRE, Earl of; Christopher John Hilton Paulet; s and h of 18 Marquess of Winchester; *b* 30 July 1969; *Style*— Earl of Wiltshire

WILTSHIRE, James Gordon; s of Arthur Thomas Wiltshire (d 1984), of Oxshott, and Barbara Gordon, *née* Donald; *b* 17 Jan 1928; *Educ* Dean Close Sch Cheltenham, Queens' Coll Cambridge (BA); *m* 19 May 1961, Philippa Katharine, da of Philip Milholland (d 1976), of Wimbledon; 1 s (Philip Gordon b 1965), 2 da (Nicola Viva b 1962, Penelope Ara b 1967); *Career* Lt RE Gold Coast (Ghana) 1947-48; Kennedy & Donkin (consulting engrs): asst engr 1951-57, ptnr 1958-, jt sr ptnr 1975-86, chief exec 1984-86; ptnr Kennedy & Donkin Int Hong Kong 1960-86 (Africa, Malawi 1960-, Africa Uganda 1960-74, Africa Botswana 1960-); gp conslt Kennedy & Donkin Gp Ltd 1987-; dir Kennedy & Donkin Africa Pty Ltd 1987-; memb Smeatonian Soc of Civil Engrs 1977- (hon treas 1981-); serv on cncls of Assoc of Consulting Engrs and of Br Conslts Bureau; Freeman City of London 1989, Liveryman Worshipful Co of Engrs 1990; FEng, FICE, FIEE, FRSA; *Recreations* tennis, golf, sailing, DIY; *Clubs* Royal Wimbledon Golf; *Style*— James Wiltshire, Esq; Willow Bend, Moles Hill, Oxshott, Surrey KT22 0QB; Kennedy & Donkin Group Ltd, Westbrook Mills, Godalming, Surrey GU7 2AZ (☎ 0483 425900, telex 859373 KDHO G, fax 0483 425136)

WILTSHIRE, Kenneth Frank; s of Theo Wiltshire (d 1977), and Constance Maud, *née* Baker (d 1985); *b* 26 March 1929; *Educ* Bournemouth GS, Royal W of England Acad Bristol; *m* Anne Elizabeth Muschamp, da of Arthur William Pickard (d 1946); 2 s (Andrew b 28 Nov 1952, Tim b 22 June 1965); *Career* Lethaby scholar SPAB 1955; restoration of: Longford Castle 1958-, Wilton House 1963-75, Binghams Melcombe 1963-85, Milton Abbey 1966-, Dodington House 1972-77, Romsey Abbey 1974-, Wimborne Minster 1975-, Sherborne Abbey 1976-, Farnham Castle 1976-, Wilbury Park 1977-, Wadham and All Souls Coll Oxford 1978-, Worcester Cathedral 1986-; memb stained glass Ctee Cncl for Care of Churches; vice pres Salisbury Civic Soc, chm design awards ctee Nat Stone Fedn; Freeman City of London, memb Worshipful Co of Masons 1985; FRIBA, FRSA; *Recreations* walking, photography; *Clubs* Nat Liberal; *Style*— Kenneth Wiltshire, Esq; De Vaux House, Salisbury, Wilts (☎ 0722 335306)

WILTSHIRE, Timothy John; s of Raymond Wiltshire (d 1983), of Farmborough, Bath, Avon, and Kathleen Grace Wiltshire; *b* 18 April 1953; *Educ* S Bristol Poly (Dip Engrg), Lackham Coll of Agric; *m* 14 June 1975, Bridget Eileen, da of Rodney Holbrook Acheson-Crow, of Bristol, Avon; 3 s (Benjamin b 1978, Robert b 1980, Jonathon b 1986), 1 da (Eleanor b 1983); *Career* branch mangr Lloyds Abbey Life plc 1973-82, mgmnt fin serv Property Growth Assur Ltd 1982-83, formed financial servs brokerage 1983, chm and md County Mgmnt Conslts Ltd (business and property investmt servs) 1987; ptnr The Prose Partnership (property investmt brokerage) 1989-; memb C of C, govr Royal Bath & West Soc, clerk to Driffield and Harnhill Parish Cncl, community advsr Civil Def Wilts; FLIA 1979, MInstM 1984; *Recreations* shooting, water sports, historic building conservation; *Style—* Timothy Wiltshire, Esq; Driffield Manor, Driffield, Cirencester, Gloucester (☎ 0285 851205); County Management Consultants, Cirencester, Glos GL7 5PY (☎ 0285 851359, cellnet 0860 369392)

WIMBERLEY, Maj Neil Campbell; MBE (1956); s of Maj-Gen Douglas Wimberley, CB, DSO, MC, DL, LLD (d 1983), of Foxhall, Coupar Angus, Perthshire, and Myrtle Livington Campbell; Wimberley - see Burkes Landed Gentry 1 Ed Vol I; *b* 23 Nov 1927; *Educ* Geelong GS Victoria Aust, Army Staff Coll (psc); *m* 10 Aug 1953, Ann, da of Lt-Col Walter Lloyd Stewart-Meiklejohn (d 1963, late Indian Army); 1 s (Michael Campbell b 1954), 1 da (Sarah b 1958); *Career* serv Queen's Own Cameron Highlanders, Malaya, Suez, Korea, Aden, Brunei, Borneo 1945-67; co dir Appleyard Scottish Division Ltd 1975-79, estates mangr Wm Low & Co Plc 1980-; memb Queen's Bodyguard for Scotland, Royal Co of Archers; *Recreations* shooting, fishing, gardening; *Clubs* Army and Navy, Highland Society of London; *Style—* Major Neil Wimberley; The Old Manse, Lundie by Dundee, Angus (☎ 0382 581230); Wm Low & Co Plc, Baird Avenue, Dundee (☎ 0382 814022)

WIMBORNE, 3 Viscount (UK 1918); Sir Ivor Fox-Strangways Guest; 5 Bt (UK 1838); also Baron Wimborne (UK 1880) and Baron Ashby St Ledgers (UK 1910); s of 2 Viscount Wimborne, OBE (d 1967), and Lady Mabel Fox-Strangways, da of 6 Earl of Ilchester; *b* 2 Dec 1939; *Educ* Eton; *m* 1, 1966 (m dis), Victoria (who m subsequently, 1982, Vincent Poklewski-Koziell), da of Col Mervyn Vigors, DSO, MC, by his 2 w Margaret (da of Maj-Gen Sir George Aston, KCB); 1 s; m 2, 1983, Venetia Margaret, er da of Richard Bridges St John Quarry, and former w of Capt Frederick G Barker; 1 da; *Heir* s, Hon Ivor Mervyn Vigors Guest b 19 Sept 1968; *Career* chm Harris & Dixon 1972-76, jt master Pytchley 1968-76, chm Harris & Dixon Holdings Ltd 1977-; *Clubs* Travellers', Cercle Interalliée, Polo; *Style—* The Rt Hon the Viscount Wimborne; c/o Travellers' Club, 25 Champs Elysées, 75008 Paris, France

WIMBORNE, Dowager Viscountess; Lady Mabel Edith; *née* Fox-Strangways; da of 6 Earl of Ilchester, GBE, and Lady Helen Mary Theresa Vane-Tempest-Stewart, da of 6 Marquess of Londonderry; *b* 17 Feb 1918; *m* 1938, 2 Viscount Wimborne; 3 s (3 Viscount, Hon Julian and Hon Charles Guest), 1 da (Hon Mrs Johnson), *qv*; *Style—* The Rt Hon the Dowager Viscountess Wimborne; Magnolia House, Candie, St Peter Port, Guernsey, CI

WIMBUSH, Rt Rev Richard Knyvet; s of Rev Canon James Sedgwick Wimbush (d 1941), and Judith Isabel, *née* Fox (d 1957); *b* 18 March 1909; *Educ* Haileybury, Oriel Coll Oxford (BA, MA), Cuddesdon Theol Coll; *m* 25 Sept 1937, Mary (Mollie) Margaret (d 1989), da of Rev Ezekiel Harry Smith (d 1934), Vicar of Ripponden, Halifax, and Illingworth, Halifax; 3 s (Martin b 1943, Stephen b 1944, John b 1950), 1 da (Judith b 1940); *Career* ordained: deacon 1934, priest 1935; chaplain Cuddesdon Coll 1934-37; asst curate: Pocklington E Yorks 1937-39, St Wilfrid's Harrogate 1939-42; rector Melsonby N Yorks 1942-48, princ Edinburgh Theol Coll (Scottish Episcopal Church) 1948-62, bishop of Argyll and The Isles 1963-77, primus Scottish Episcopal Church 1974-77, incumbent of Etton with Dalton Holme N Humberside 1977-83, asst bishop dio of York 1977-; *Clubs* New (Edinburgh); *Style—* The Rt Rev Richard Wimbush; 5 Tower Place, York YO1 1RZ (☎ 0904 641971)

WINBERG, Max Henry; s of Abraham Winberg (d 1973), and Betty, *née* Singer; *b* 11 Oct 1937; *Educ* Northwold and Mount Pleasant Secdy Modern Sch; *m* 20 Aug 1981, Jean, da of Robert Ruthen (d 1976); 2 da (Lucy b 1981, Emma b 1985); *Career* chm and md: Tacbrook Ltd, Costa Blanca Villas Ltd, Cycloacre Ltd; *Recreations* chess, windsurfing, amateur poker player; *Style—* Max Winberg, Esq; Costa Blanca Villas, 13/17 Newbury St, Wantage, Oxon OX12 8BU (☎ 02357 65305, telex 837071 CBVROK, fax 02357 60256)

WINCH, Prof Donald Norman; s of Sidney Captain Winch, and Iris Mary, *née* Button; *b* 15 April 1935; *Educ* Sutton GS, LSE (scholar, BSc Econ), Princeton Univ (PhD); *m* 5 Aug 1983, Doreen Alice; *Career* visiting lectr Univ of California Berkeley 1959-60, lectr in economics Univ of Edinburgh 1960-63; Univ of Sussex: lectr 1963-66, reader 1966-69, prof in history of economics 1969-; dean Sch of Social Sciences 1968-74, pro vice chllr arts and social studies 1986-89; pubns sec Royal Econ Soc 1971-; FBA 1986, FRHistS 1987; *Books* Classical Political Economy and Colonies (1965), James Mill: Selected Economic Writings (1966), Economics and Policy (with S K Hanson, 1969), The Economic Advisory Council (1976), Adam Smith's Politics (with S Collini and J Burrow, 1978), That Noble Science of Politics (1983), Malthus (1987); *Recreations* gardening; *Style—* Prof Donald Winch; Universtity of Sussex, Falmer, Brighton, E Sussex BN1 9QN (☎ 0273 606755, fax 0273 678466)

WINCH, Hon Mrs (Jean Rosemary Vera); *née* Cary; da of 14 Viscount Falkland, by his 1 w Joan Sylvia, only da of Capt Charles Bonham Southey; *b* 30 Oct 1928; *Educ* Lady Walsingham's Sch; *m* 1950, Henry Herman Montagu Winch, s of Henry Louis Winch (d 1903), and Vera, Lady Newborough (1 w of 5 Baron); *Recreations* country pursuits, flat racing (racehorses: My Solitaire, Sparkling Halo); *Clubs* Turf; *Style—* The Hon Mrs Winch; Castle Barn, Penrhyndeudraeth, Gwynedd (☎ 0766 770313)

WINCH, Richard Anthony Brooke; s of Maj Stanley Brooke Winch, OBE (d 1959), of Swanington Manor, Norwich, and Eleanor Boville, *née* Morris (d 1951); *b* 6 Sept 1921; *Educ* Charterhouse, Trinity Coll Cambridge (MA); *m* 29 Aug 1959, Frances Evelyn Barbara, da of Robert Ives, of Erpingham House, Erpingham, Norfolk; 1 da (Eleanor Charlotte (Mrs Buxton) b 21 March 1963); *Career* High Sheriff of Norfolk 1972; memb Worshipful Co of Farmers; *Recreations* gardens, shooting; *Style—* Richard Winch, Esq; Kettle Hill, Blakeney, Norfolk (☎ 0263 741147)

WINCH, Thomas Beverley Charles; s of Eric William Winch (d 1964), of St Peter Port, Guernsey, CI, and Jessie Kathleen Jeanette, *née* Garrould; *b* 8 April 1930; *Educ* Rugby, St John's Coll Cambridge (BA, MA); *m* 19 Oct 1963, Jane, da of Col Nathaniel Montague Barnardiston (d 1986), of Cirencester, Glos; 1 s (William Montague b 1970), 1 da (Katherine Jane Amicia b 1972); *Career* fine arts valuer; borough cncl Mayor 1977-78; FRSA 1969; *Recreations* historical research and analysis; *Style—* Thomas B C Winch, Esq; Westport Granary, Malmesbury, Wilts (☎ 0666 822119)

WINCHESTER, Archdeacon of; *see*: Clarkson, Ven Alan Geoffrey

WINCHESTER, Bapsy, Marchioness of; Bapsy; *née* Pavry; da of Most Rev Khurshedji Pavry, High Priest of the Parsees in India; *Educ* Columbia Univ New York (MA); *m* 1952, as 3 wife, 16 Marquess of Winchester (d 1962); *Career* memb cncl World Alliance for Int Peace through Religion; Order of Merit of Iran; *Books* Heroines of Ancient Iran (1930); *Style—* The Most Hon Bapsy, Marchioness of Winchester

WINCHESTER, 95 Bishop of (AD 636) 1985-; Rt Rev Colin Clement Walter James; patron of 78 livings, and 29 alternately with other patrons, the Canonries in his Cathedral, and the Archdeaconries of Winchester and Basingstoke; s of late Canon Charles Clement Hancock James, and Gwenyth Mary James; *b* 20 Sept 1926; *Educ* Aldenham, King's Coll Cambridge (MA), Cuddesdon Theological Coll; *m* 1962, Margaret Joan Henshaw; 1 s, 2 da; *Career* asst curate Stepney Parish Church 1952-55, chaplain Stowe Sch 1955-59, BBC Religious Broadcasting Dept 1959-67, vicar St Peter's Bournemouth 1967-73, bishop suffragan of Basingstoke 1973-77, chm Church Information Ctee 1976-79, bishop of Wakefield 1977-85, chm Central Religious Advsy Ctee to BBC and IBA 1979-84, chm C of E Liturgical Cmmn 1986-; *Recreations* theatre, travelling, radio and television; *Style—* The Rt Rev the Bishop of Winchester; Wolvesey, Winchester, Hants SO23 9ND

WINCHESTER, Colin Robert John; s of Stanley Robert John Winchester (d 1968), of Herts, and Daisy Florence Griffiths; *b* 5 Dec 1933; *Educ* Queen Elizabeth's Barnet; *m* 25 March 1961, Jane Hillier, da of Rodney Guy Margetts (d 1961), of Grange Farm, Stratford upon Avon; 2 s (Dominic b 1969, Luke b 1975); *Career* Nat Serv cmmnd RA 1952-54; dir Ogilvy & Mather Ltd 1975-87; *Recreations* golf, squash, skiing; *Clubs* Army and Navy; *Style—* Colin Winchester, Esq; Cranard Broomrigg Rd, Fleet, Hants (☎ 0252 614808)

WINCHESTER, Ian Sinclair; CMG (1982); s of Dr Alexander Hugh Winchester FRCSEd, of Redroofs, 16 Melville Ave, S Croydon, Surrey, and Mary Stewart Duguid (d 1954); *b* 14 March 1931; *Educ* Lewes County GS, Oxford Univ (BA); *m* 9 Nov 1957, Shirley Louise, da of Frederic Milner CMG (d 1957); 3 s (Charles b 1959, Andrew b 1962, Robert b 1967); *Career* HM Dip Serv; dir Communications and Tech Servs 1985-; min Br Embassy Saudi Arabia 1982-83; commercial cnsllr Br Embassy Brussels 1973-76; *Style—* Ian S Winchester, Esq, CMG

WINCHESTER, 18 Marquess of (Premier Marquess of England, cr 1551); Nigel George Paulet; also Baron St John of Basing (E 1539) and Earl of Wiltshire (E 1550); s of George Paulet (1 cous of 17 Marquess, who d 1968; also eighth in descent from 5 Marquess); *b* 23 Dec 1941; *m* 1967, Rosemary, da of Maj Aubrey Hilton, of Harare, Zimbabwe; 2 s (Earl of Wiltshire, Lord Richard b 1971), 1 da (Lady Susan b 1976); *Heir* s, Earl of Wiltshire; *Career* dir Rhodesia Mineral Ventures Ltd, Sani-Dan Servs Ltd, Rhodesia Prospectors Ltd; *Style—* The Most Hon the Marquess of Winchester; Lydford Cottage, 35 Whyteladies Lane, Borrowdale, Salisbury, Zimbabwe

WINCHILSEA AND NOTTINGHAM, 16 and 11 Earl of (E 1628 and 1681); Sir Christopher Denys Stormont Finch Hatton; 17 and 11 Bt (E 1611 and 1660), of Eastwell and Raunston respectively; also Baron Finch (E 1675), Viscount Maidstone (E 1623) and Hereditary Lord of Royal Manor of Wye; s of 15 and 10 Earl of Winchilsea and Nottingham (d 1950), by his 1 w, Countess Gladys Széchényi, 3 da of Count László Széchényi (sometime Hungarian min in London); *b* 17 Nov 1936; *Educ* Eton, Gordonstoun; *m* 1962, Shirley, da of late Bernard Hatfield, of Wylde Green, Sutton Coldfield; 1 s (Viscount Maidstone), 1 da (Lady Alice b 2 May 1970); *Heir* s, Viscount Maidstone; *Style—* The Rt Hon the Earl of Winchilsea and Nottingham; South Cadbury House, nr Yeovil, Somerset

WINCKLES, Kenneth; MBE (1945); s of Frank Winckles (d 1964), and Emily, *née* Hawksby (d 1956); *b* 17 June 1918; *Educ* Harrow Lower Sch, Besançon Univ, LSE; *m* 22 March 1941, Peggy Joan, da of Hubert Joseph Hodges (d 1949); 1 s (Richard b 1946), 1 da (Sally b 1951); *Career* enlisted 1939, cmmnd Hampshire Regt 1940, Adj 5 Bn 1941, GSO2 (Ops) HQ 2 Army 1943, AAG Personnel HQ BAOR 1945, demobbed Lt-Col 1946; co sec Scribbans-Kemp Ltd 1947; Rank Orgn Ltd 1948-67; md Theatre Div 1953, dir and gp asst md 1956, dir Southern TV 1957, chm Vis News Ltd 1957, dir Rank Xerox Ltd 1960; md: Utd Artists Corp Ltd 1967-69, Cunard Line Ltd 1969-70; fin dir Hill Samuel Gp Ltd 1971-80, business conslt 1980; dir: Horse Race Totalisator Bd 1974-76, CAA 1977-80, inter alia Henley Forklift Truck Co Ltd 1975-89, chm Home and Law Mags Ltd; dep chm: ITL Info Tech plc, Merivale Moore plc; FCA, assoc ICAEW 1946; *Books* The Practice of Successful Business Mangagement (1986), Funding Your Business (1988); *Recreations* swimming, gardening; *Clubs* Sunningdale Golf; *Style—* Kenneth Winckles, Esq, MBE; Sunningdale; Seaview, IOW

WINCKWORTH, Archibald Norman; s of William Norman Winckworth (d 1941), of Dunchideock House, Exeter, and Mary Russell Watson (d 1954), f int footballer (assoc) against Scotland and Wales 1892-93; *b* 14 Oct 1917; *Educ* Westminster, Univ of Reading; *Career* Capt RA 1943, Adj 1943-46, serv M East 1941-45; social worker 1946-51, schoolmaster 1952-65; antique dealer 1965-; *Books* My Twenty One Short Stories; *Recreations* gardening, bridge, antique bottle collecting; *Style—* Archibald Winckworth, Esq; Dunchideock House, nr Exeter EX2 9TS (☎ 0392 832429)

WINDEBANK, Dr William John; Serving Bro Ven OStJ 1982, Serv Medal OStJ 1981, Vol Med Serv Medal 1970; s of William Hori Windebank (d 1989), of Keinton Mandeville, Somerton, Somerset, and Kathleen, *née* Saunders; *b* 1 Nov 1939; *Educ* Purbrook Park Co HS Purbrook Hants, Univ of Glasgow Med Sch (BSc, MB ChB); *m* 25 March 1961, Peggy Julia, da of Norman Miles, of 24 Ilex Walk, Hayling Island, Hants; 1 s (Michael b 17 June 1968), 1 da (Jillian b 6 Oct 1966); *Career* sr registrar in gen and thoracic med Glasgow Hosps 1971-73, conslt physician in gen med and thoracic med Derby Hosps 1973-, conslt in charge Respiratory Div Cardiothoracic Measurement Dept Derbyshire Royal Infirmary 1973-, sr lectr anatomy and physiology Derby Sch of Occupational Therapy 1974-, hon clinical teacher Univ of Nottingham Med Sch 1978-, hon lectr in physiological measurement People's Coll Nottingham 1980-, resuscitation trg offr Derby Hosp 1987-; surgn St John Ambulance Bde Derbyshire S area; med offr: Derby Marathon, Darley Moor motorcycle racing club, Locko park horse trials; memb: BMA 1966, Scot thoracic soc 1968, BTS 1976; MRCP 1970, ARTP 1975, FRCP Glasgow 1980; *Recreations* first aid, wine and bread making; *Style—* Dr John Windebank; Derbyshire Royal Infirmary, London Rd, Derby DE1 2QY (☎ 0332 47141)

WINDELER, John Robert; s of Alfred Stewart, and Ethela Marie, *née* Boremuth; *b* 21 March 1943; *Educ* Ohio State Univ USA (BA, MBA); *m* 15 June 1965, Judith Lynn, da of Robert Francis Taylor; 2 s (Stewart, James); *Career* Irving Tst Co NY: vice pres Liability Mgmnt 1973-75, sr vice pres Money Market Div 1975-80, mangr Loan Syndication Devpt 1981, gen mangr London 1981-83, exec vice pres Investmt Banking Gp 1984; md Irving Tst Int Ltd London 1984-, pres Irving Securities Inc NY 1987-; dir: Trans City Hldgs Sydney Aust, Irving Tst Int Singapore, Little Red Sch House Inc; former dir Int Commercial Bank London; memb: Securities Assoc, Assoc Int Bond Dealers; *Recreations* skiing, tennis, running, history; *Clubs* Hurlingham; *Style—* John Windeler, Esq; 18 Margaretta Terrace, London SW3 (☎ 071 352 5183); 10 Mayfair Place, London W1X 5FJ (☎ 071 322 6100, fax 071 322 6074, telex 888479)

WINDER, (Alexander) John Henry; s of Lt-Col Alexander Stuart Monck Winder (d 1969), of Finches, Castlewalk, Wadhurst, Sussex, and Helen Mary, *née* Swayne (d 1985); *b* 23 Oct 1921; *Educ* Shrewsbury, New Coll Oxford (BA, MA); *m* 2 May 1959, Shirlie (Cherry), da of Norman James Lewis (d 1969), of Tunbridge Wells; 2 s (Mark Henry Stuart b 1960, Paul Alexander Lewis b 1962), 2 da (Rachel Emily b 1965, Jane Helen Esther b 1966); *Career* cmmnd RCS 1941, Signal Offr 90 Field Regt RA 1942-45, Capt 1 Corps HQ Germany 1945-46; served: Sicily Landings with 231 Brigade 50 Div 1943, D Day Landings 50 Div 1944; Colonial Engrg Serv N Rhodesia 1949-52; Binnie & Ptnrs Consulting Engrs 1952-66: sr asst resident engr Hong Kong 1953-56, chief resident engr Grafham Water 1957-66; H Lapworth and Ptnrs (resident engr Scammonden Dam) 1966-70, T & C Hawksley Consulting Engrs (chief resident engr Rutland Water) 1970-74, ptnr Watson Hawksley Consulting Engrs 1974-84; author of various papers for Inst of Civil Engrs and Inst of Water and Enviromental Mgmnt; memb Br Section of the Int Ctee on Large Dams, appointed memb of Panel AR under the Reservoirs Act 1969; chm of various research project steering ctees for CIRIA; FICE 1986, FIWEM 1960, MASCE 1980, FBIS; *Recreations* music, walking, tennis, woodworking; *Style—* John Winder, Esq; 10 Mary Vale, Godalming, Surrey, GU7 1SW; c/o Watson Hawksley, Terriers House, Amersham Rd, High Wycombe, Bucks, HP13 5AJ (☎ 0494 26240)

WINDER, John Lindsay; JP; s of Harold Vickers Winder (d 1969), of Barrow in Furness, and Mary Dick, *née* Card; *b* 8 Nov 1935; *Educ* Barrow GS; *Career* CA 1959; vice chm Furness Building Soc 1988- (dir 1973); pres Barrow Scout Mgmnt Ctee, dep chm Barrow with Bootle Magistrates; FCA; *Recreations* fell-walking, gardening, golf; *Style—* John L Winder, Esq, JP; 32 Dane Avenue, Barrow in Furness LA14 4JS (☎ 0229 8217 26); 125 Ramsden Square, Barrow in Furness, Cumbria LA14 1XA (☎ 0229 8203 90)

WINDEYER, Sir Brian Wellingham; s of Richard Windeyer, KC, of Sydney, NSW; *b* 7 Feb 1904; *Educ* Sydney C of E GS, St Andrew's Coll Univ of Sydney (MD); *m* 1, 1928, Joyce, da of Harry Russell; 1 s, 1 da; m 2, 1948, Elspeth, da of H Bowrey; 1 s, 2 da; *Career* prof of radiology Middx Hosp Med Sch 1942-69 (dean 1954-67), vice chllr Univ of London 1969-72; Hon FRACS, Hon FCRA, Hon FACR; Hon DSc: Br Columbia, Wales, Cantab; Hon LLD Univ of Glasgow; FRCP, FRCS, FRCSE, FRSM, FRCR, DMRE; kt 1961; *Style—* Sir Brian Windeyer; 9 Dale Close, St Ebbe's, Oxford OX1 1TU (☎ 0865 242816)

WINDHAM, John Jeremy; er s of Sir Ralph Windham (d 1980), formerly of Waghen Hall, Yorks and later of Tetbury, and Kathleen Mary, *née* FitzHerbert, *qv*; descended from the ancient family of Wyndham of Felbrigg and Crownthorpe (NW of Wymondham) Norfolk and direct descendant of the family of Smith of Hill Hall, Essex; kinsman and hp of Sir Thomas Bowyer-Smyth, 15 Bt; *b* 22 Nov 1948; *Educ* Wellington Coll; *m* 1976, (Rachel) Mary, da of Lt-Col (Walter) George Finney, TD (d 1973); 1 s ((Thomas) Ralph b 1985), 2 da (Katharine Anne b 1981, Emma Georgina b 1983); *Career* Capt Irish Gds and SAS, ret; Br Trans-Americas Expdn (Darien Gap) 1972, Kleinwort Benson Ltd 1978-84, dir Def Systems Ltd 1980-85, Enterprise Oil plc 1984-88, md and fndr Integrated Def Ltd 1988-; *Recreations* shooting, navigation, farming; *Style—* John Windham, Esq; The Hyde, Woolhope, Herefordshire; Integrated Defence Ltd, 81 Broxash Rd, London SW11 6AD (☎ 071 223 9555)

WINDHAM, Lady Kathleen Mary; da of Capt Cecil Henry FitzHerbert, DSC (d 1952), of Latimerstown, Co Wexford, and Ellen Katherine Lowndes (d 1975); *b* 19 Feb 1918; *Educ* Langford Grove Essex; *m* 1946, Sir Ralph Windham (d 1980), s of Maj Ashe Windham, of Waghen Hall, Hull; 2 s (John, *qv*, Andrew), 2 da (Penelope, Belinda); *Career* served WWII WRNS; *Style—* Lady Windham; Hook's Cottage, Kingscote, nr Tetbury, Glos (☎ 0453 860461)

WINDLE-TAYLOR, Paul Carey; s of Dr Edwin Windle-Taylor, CBE (d 1990), and Diana, *née* Grove (d 1987); *b* 25 Nov 1948; *Educ* Mill Hill, Emmanuel Coll Cambridge (MA, MB BChir), St Thomas Hosp London; *m* 10 Sept 1973, Abina, da of Timothy Walsh (d 1984); *Career* conslt otolaryngologist; FRCS, FRSM, Corr Fell American Acad Otolaryngology; *Recreations* fishing, fine wines; *Clubs* Flyfishers', MCC; *Style—* Paul Windle-Taylor, Esq; Higher Pempwell, Stoke Climsland, Cornwall PL17 8LN; Nuffield Hosp, Derriford Rd, Plymouth PL6 8BG (☎ 0752 707277)

WINDLESHAM, 3 Baron (UK 1937); Sir David James George Hennessy; 3 Bt (UK 1927), CVO, PC (1973); s of 2 Baron Windlesham (d 1962), by his 1 w Angela (d 1956), da of Julian Duggan; *b* 28 Jan 1932; *Educ* Ampleforth, Trinity Coll Oxford; *m* 22 May 1965, Prudence Loveday (d 1986), yr da of Lt-Col Rupert Trevor Wallace Glynn, MC; 1 s (Hon James b 1968), 1 da (Hon Victoria b 1966); *Heir* s, Hon James Rupert Hennessy b 9 Nov 1968; *Career* served Grenadier Gds, Lt; sits as Cons peer in House of Lords; min of state: Home Office 1970-72, NI 1972-73; Lord Privy Seal and ldr House of Lords 1973-74; chm: ATV Network 1981 (md 1975-81), Parole Bd 1982-88; dir: The Observer 1981-89, W H Smith Group 1986-; chm: Oxford Preservation Tst 1979-89, Oxford Soc 1985-88; tstee: Br Museum 1981- (chm 1986-), Community Service Volunteers 1981-; memb Museums and Galleries Cmmn 1984-86; hon fell Trinity Coll Oxford 1982, visiting fell All Souls' Coll 1986, princ BNC 1989-; *Books* Communication and Political Power (1966), Politics in Practice (1975), Broadcasting in a Free Society (1980), Responses to Crime (1987), The Windlesham/Rampton Report on Death on the Rock (with Richard Rampton, QC, 1989); *Style—* The Rt Hon the Lord Windlesham, CVO, PC; Brasenose College, Oxford OX1 4AJ

WINDOWS, Anthony Robin (Tony); s of Frederick Ernest Windows (Lt, RNVR, d 1986), of 9 Ridgewood, Knoll Hill, Sneyd Park, Bristol, and Freda Marjorie *née* Bateman; *b* 25 Sept 1942; *Educ* Clifton, Jesus Coll Cambridge (MA); *m* 28 June 1969, Carolyn Mary, da of Eric Spencer, of 3 Norfolk Rd, Portishead, Avon; 2 s (Matthew b 5 Aug 1973, Tom b 12 Jan 1975); *Career* Cambridge Cricket blue 1962-64, Glos CCC 1960-69 (capped 1967), MCC under 25 tour Pakistan 1967/68, best bowling 8-78 W Indies v Glos 1966; Cambridge Rugby Fives Blue 1961-63 (capt 1963); slr 1969, Glos CCC, Bristol Savages; memb Law Soc; *Clubs* MCC, T & RA, Clifton Club Bristol; *Style—* Tony Windows, Esq; Harley Cottage, Clifton Pk, Clifton, Bristol

WINDRAM, Dr Michael David (Mike); s of Gordon Howard Windram, of 103 Manor Lane, Halesowen, W Midlands, and Ethel May, *née* Hudson (d 1977); *b* 21 Sept 1945; *Educ* King Edward's Sch Birmingham, Queens' Coll Cambridge (MA, PhD); *m* 28 March 1970, Joycelyn Mary, da of Leslie Albert Marsh (d 1972); 2 s (Christopher b 20 Dec 1973, Richard b 7 April 1977); *Career* radio astronomer Univ of Cambridge 1966-69, physicist and sr engr Marconi Avionic Systems Ltd 1969-71; Radio Frequency Section IBA: engr 1971-73, sr engr 1973-77, head of section 1978-82; head of Video and Colour section Experimental and Devpt IBA 1982-87, head of Experimental and Devpt Dept IBA 1987-0; exec mangr (Res & Devpt) National Transcommunications Ltd, vice chm Sub Gp V4 EBU, memb Steering Ctee of Working Pty V of EBU; memb IEE 1976, assoc memb Inst of Physics 1969, memb RTS 1984; *Recreations* music, DIY, caravaning; *Style—* Dr Mike Windram; 37 Winslade Rd, Harestock, Winchester, Hants SO22 6LN (☎ 0962 880226); IBA, Crawley Ct, Winchester, Hants SO22 2QA(☎ 0962 822323, fax 0962 822378, telex 477211)

WINDSOR *see also*: Royal Family

WINDSOR, Viscount; Ivor Edward Other Windsor-Clive; s and h of 3 Earl of Plymouth, DL, and Caroline, *née* Rice; *b* 19 Nov 1951; *Educ* Harrow, RAC Cirencester; *m* 1979, Caroline, da of Frederick Nettlefold and Hon Mrs Juliana Roberts (da of 2 Viscount Scarsdale) ; 2 s (Hon Robert, Hon Frederick b 1983); 1 da (Hon India Harriet b 1988); *Heir* s, Hon Robert Other Ivor Windsor-Clive b 25 March 1981; *Career* co-fndr and dir Centre for Study of Modern Art 1973; *Recreations* cricket, football; *Style—* Viscount Windsor; The Stables, Oakly Park, Ludlow, Shropshire (☎ Bromfield 393); 6 Oakley Street, London, SW3

WINDSOR, Col Rodney Francis Maurice; CBE (1972), DL (Aberdeenshire 1989); s of Maurice Windsor, MBE (d 1945), and Elsie, *née* Meredith (d 1959); *b* 22 Feb 1925; *Educ* Tonbridge; *m* 26 April 1951, Deirdre Willa, da of Col Arthur O'Neill Cubitt Chichester, OBE, MC, DL (d 1972), of Co Antrim; 2 s (Anthony b 1955, Nicholas b 1961), 1 da (Patricia b 1953); *Career* served Royal Armoured Corps 1943, The Queens Bays 1944-52, Capt 1949, ADC to High Cmmr and C-in-C Austria 1949-50; N Irish Horse TA 1959-67, Lt-Col cmdg 1964-67, Col TA N Ireland 1967-71, ADC TA to HM The Queen 1970-75; farmer; chm Banff and Buchan Dist Valuation Appeal Ctee 1989- (memb 1982-); *Recreations* shooting, fishing; *Style—* Col Rodney F M Windsor, CBE, DL; Byth House, Newbyth, Turriff, Aberdeenshire (☎ 08883 230)

WINDSOR, Stuart James; s of E J Windsor (d 1965), and Gwendoline Knott (d 1979); *b* 26 May 1946; *Educ* Chace Sch; *m* Oct 1971, Janet Elizabeth Davidson-Lungley; 3 s (Alexander b 3 Nov 1976, Miles b 4 Jan 1985, Freddie b 26 Dec 1989); *Career* photographer; journalist until 1970, Fleet St photographer 1970-73 (Times, Observer, Daily Mail); photographic projects incl: coast to coast trip of America documenting lifestyles, living with Kabre Tribe in N Togo (as part of Nat Geographic anthropological educnl field trip), project in Galapagos Islands, coverage Mount Kotukinabulu Borneo climb 1988; solo exhibition of retrospective work Embankment Gallery 1979; contrib to magazines and books on numerous travel and architectural topics, picture library contains 5000 world wide images; *Recreations* travel, writing, classic cars, photography, cycling, design, architecture, tennis, golf; *Style—* Stuart Windsor, Esq; 1 Salisbury Rd, Wimbledon, London SW19 4EZ (☎ 081 946 9878); Bellevue Studios, 15 Bellevue Rd, Wandsworth Common, London SW17 7EG (☎ 081 672 7440, fax 081 767 5784, mobile 0836 332117)

WINDSOR-CLIVE, Hon Mrs; Hon (Mary) Alice; *née* Jolliffe; da of 4 Baron Hylton (d 1967); *b* 1937; *m* 1, 1959 (m dis 1968), John Paget Chancellor; 1 s, 3 da; m 2, 1968, Hon Richard Windsor-Clive, *qv*; *Style—* The Hon Mrs Windsor-Clive; Combe, Nettlecombe, Taunton, Somerset (☎ 098 44 0212)

WINDSOR-CLIVE, Hon David Justin; 3 s of 3 Earl of Plymouth; *b* 4 Sept 1960; *Educ* Harrow, RAC Cirencester; *m* 18 Sept 1986, Camilla Jane, eld da of John Squire, of Marbella, Spain; 1 s (James b 12 June 1990); *Career* banker; *Recreations* football, tennis, shooting; *Style—* The Hon David Windsor-Clive; 6 Physic Place, London SW3; King and Shaxson Ltd, 52 Cornhill, London EC3 (☎ 071 623 5433)

WINDSOR-CLIVE, Hon Richard Archer Alan; s of 2 Earl of Plymouth, PC (d 1943); *b* 1928; *Educ* Eton, Trinity Coll Cambridge; *m* 1, 1955 (m dis 1968), Joanna Mary, da of Edward Corbet Woodall, OBE; 1 s, 1 da; m 2, 1968, Hon (Mary) Alice Chancellor; 1 da; *Career* chm Bayfine Ltd 1973-85; *Style—* The Hon Richard Windsor-Clive; Combe, Nettlecombe, Taunton, Somerset (☎ 098 44 0212)

WINDSOR-LEWIS, Geoffrey; s of Dr H Windsor-Lewis (d 1982), of Cambridge, and Phyllis Mary, *née* Harris (d 1989); *b* 7 April 1936; *Educ* Leys Sch Cambridge, Trinity Hall Cambridge (BA, MA, Rugby blue); *m* Jacqueline, *née* Harty; 3 s (Steve b 11 Nov 1962, Guy b 2 April 1964, Tom b 5 Sept 1982); *Career* Nat Serv cmmnd 2 Regt RHA 1954-56; former rugby union player: Wales 1960 (v Eng and Scot), Oxfordshire 1961-66 (capt 1962-66), Richmond (capt 1963); hon sec Barbarian Football Club 1966-; chartered surveyor; asst: King & Co 1959-60, Franklin & Jones Oxford 1960-65; Buckell & Ballard 1965-84: mangr branch office Banbury 1965-69, ptnr 1969-78, jt sr ptnr 1978-84; dir Arundell House plc 1985-90, chm Buckingham Assured Properties; govr: Dragon Sch Oxford, Manchester Coll Oxford; capt Chartered Surveyors Golfing Soc 1988; Liveryman Worshipful Co of Chartered Surveyors; FRICS; *Recreations* vegetable gardening, golf, France; *Clubs* British Sportsman's, Frewen Oxford, Lords Taverners; *Style—* Geoffrey Windsor-Lewis, Esq; The Thatched House, Harcourt Hill, Oxford OX2 9AY (☎ 0865 247803)

WINDUST, Jeremy Paul; s of Norman Albert Windust (d 1963), of Glos, and Pamela Rosie, *née* Frampton (d 1969); *b* 6 Jan 1952; *Educ* Marling Sch Stroud, Middx Poly (BA), Brunel Univ; *m* 8 Jan 1972, Elaine Rosemary, da of Lionel Hubert Jordan; 2 s (Alexander b 1973, Benjamin b 1976), 1 da (Kathryn b 1978); *Career* exec offr GCHQ Cheltenham 1975-87; memb ctee to re-establish trade union rights at GCHQ, co-applicant against Govt's union ban at GCHQ in High Ct, Ct of Appeal and House of Lords 1984 and before European Ct of Human Rights Strasbourg 1987; ed Warning Signal 1985-87; proprietor Willow Press (letterpress printing shop); gen sec (chief negotiator) RBA 1988; *Recreations* music; *Style—* Jeremy Windust, Esq; 189 Prestbury Rd, Cheltenham, Glos

WINEARLS, Dr Christopher Good; s of Capt James Robert Winearls, and Sheila, *née* Boardman; *b* 25 Sept 1949; *Educ* Diocesan Coll Rondebosch Capt Town, Univ of Cape Town (MB ChB), Univ of Oxford (DPhil), MRCP; *m* 6 Dec 1975, Beryl Claire, da of Dr Wilmer Edward George Butler, of Cairns, Queensland, Aust; 3 s (James b 1979, Alastair b 1982, Stuart b 1985); *Career* sr lectr in med Royal Postgrad Med Sch London 1986-88, conslt nephrologist Churchill Hosp Oxford 1988-; memb Exec Ctee Renal Assoc of GB; Rhodes Scholar 1972; *Recreations* tennis; *Style—* Dr Christopher Winearls; Renal Unit, Churchill Hosp, Oxford OX3 7LJ (☎ 0865 741841, fax 0865 225773)

WINER, Colin; *b* 23 Feb 1938; *Educ* Clacton County HS, Br Coll of Neuropathy (DO, ND), Lincoln Coll of Indianapolis USA (DC); *m* 27 Aug 1964, Jill Patricia, *née* Osborn; 2 s (Julian Marcel b 25 Oct 1969, Jason Piers b 22 Oct 1971), 1 da (Chantelle Lisa b 20 June 1966); *Career* osteopath, naturopath and chiropractor; lectr in orthopaedics radiology and diagnosis: BCNO 1965-75, Euro Sch of Osteopathy 1968-75; head of Radiology Dept Tyringham Clinic Newport Pagnell Bucks 1969-76; in private practice London, Clacton-on-Sea and Rome Itlay 1965-; pres Br Naturopathic and Osteopathic Assoc 1974-75, 1987-88 and 1991-; memb Cncl Gen Cncl and register of Neuropaths 1988-; MRO, MRN, memb American Chiropractic Assoc; *Style—* Colin Winer, Esq; 31 Weymouth Street, London W1N 3FJ (☎ 071 580 6939); 27 Canarvon Rd, Clacton-on-Sea CO15 6QF (☎ 0255 421 014); Via Giambattista Vico 31, 00196, Rome, Italy (☎ 010 396 361 3640)

WINFIELD, (Elaine Margaret) Maggie; da of Maj Richard Vivian Taylor (d 1980), and Enid Josephine, *née* Fair; *b* 14 Dec 1957; *Educ* Dudley Girls HS, City of Birmingham Poly (BA); *m* 23 July 1977, Stephen Winfield, s of John William Winfield; 1 da (Anna b 1983); *Career* ptnr and dir Myles Communication Group 1985-; fndr memb Soc of E Midlands Businesswomen 1987; *Recreations* running, gardening; *Style—* Mrs Maggie Winfield; The Old Rectory, Rectory Lane, Claypole, Newark, Notts NG23 5BH (☎ 0623 626775); Myles Communication Group, 2 First Ave, Sherwood Rise, Nottingham NG7 6JL (☎ 0602 691692, fax 0602 691221)

WINFIELD, Peter Stevens; s of Harold Stevens Winfield (d 1945), of Chelsea, and Susan, *née* Cooper (d 1973); *b* 24 March 1927; *Educ* Sloane Sch Chelsea, West London Coll of Commerce; *m* 29 June 1955, Mary Gabrielle, da of Patrick John Kenrick (d 1955), of Chelsea; 4 s (John b 28 May 1961, Michael b 18 Jan 1965, Peter Anthony b 18 May 1966, Edward b 4 April 1968), 2 da (Susan (Mrs Wood) b 10 March 1958, Katherine (Mrs Cardona) b 18 Nov 1959); *Career* RA 1944-48, BQMS, India, Egypt and Palestine; joined Healey & Baker 1951 (sr ptnr 1975-88), dir London Auction Mart Ltd 1970 (chm 1980-); memb: Lloyds of London 1978-, property investmt ctee Save and Prosper Gp Ltd 1980-, Horserace Totalisator Bd 1981-; non-exec dir Manders Hldgs plc 1987-, chm Letinvest plc 1987-; govr Guys Hosp 1973-74 (special tstee 1974-); dir: Osprey Management Company Ltd 1989-, Kingston Theatre Tst 1990-; Liveryman: Worshipful Co of Farriers 1967-, Worshipful Co of Feltmakers 1972-87 (Master 1990-91); FRICS 1953; *Recreations* horseracing, cricket, swimming, reading; *Clubs* Buck's, United and Cecil, Mark's, MCC, Turf, RAC; *Style*— Peter Winfield, Esq; 29 St George St, Hanover Square, London W1A 3BG (☎ 071 629 9292, fax 071 355 4299, telex 21800 HEABAK G)

WING, Dr Antony John; s of (Harry) John Tayler Wing (d 1962), of Oxford, and Helen, *née* Foster; *b* 2 May 1933; *Educ* Rugby, Univ of Oxford (MA, BM BCh, DM), St Thomas' Hosp Med Sch; *m* 23 Jan 1960, Rachel Nora, da of Norman Gray, of Eastbourne, Sussex; 3 s (Mark b 1962, Charles b 1964, Michael b 1970), 1 da (Nicola b 1961); *Career* Sqdn Ldr RAF Med Branch 1960-64; registrar St Thomas' Hosp 1964-66, sr registrar Charing Cross Hosp 1967-68, Nuffield res fell Makerere Univ Uganda 1968-69, conslt physician St Thomas' Hosp 1969-, examiner Soc of Apothecaries 1970-, chm of registray Euro Dialysis and Transplant Assoc 1976-85; memb Grants Ctee: Nat Kidney Res Fund 1979-86, Br Kidney Patients Assoc 1985-; chief med offr: Colonial Mutual Assur Soc 1980, United Friendly Assur Soc 1988; memb Governing Body Stowe Sch 1988-, lay reader St Stephen's Church Twickenham, chm Cicely Northcote Tst 1977-83; Liveryman Worshipful Soc of Apothcaries 1973, Freeman City of London 1974; FRSM 1966, FRCP 1976, fell Assurance Med Soc; *Books* The Renal Unit (with M Magowan, 1972), Decision Making in Medicine (with G Scorer, 1979); *Recreations* golf, tennis, skiing; *Clubs* Vincent's; *Style*— Dr Antony Wing; St Thomas' Hospital, London SE1 7EH (☎ 071 928 9292, fax 071 922 8079, telex 27913)

WING, Prof John Kenneth; CBE (1990); *b* 22 Oct 1923; *Educ* Strand Sch, UCL (MB BS, MD, PhD); *Career* RNVR 1942-46, Lt (A); med and specialist trg 1947-56; scientific staff MRC 1957-64; dir MRC Psychiatry Res Unit 1965-89; conslt psychiatrist Bethlem Royal Hosp and Maudslay Hosp 1960-89, prof of social psychiatry Inst of Psychiatry and London Sch of Hygiene 1970-89; memb Bd of Govrs Nat Inst for Social Work 1981-87, tstee Mental Health Fndn 1983-; memb: MRC 1985-89, Departmental Research Ctee Dept of Health 1987-90; emeritus prof Univ of London 1989, dir of res RCP 1989-; Hon MD Univ of Heidelberg 1976; FRCPsych; *Books* Institutionalism and Schizophrenia (1970), Measurement and Classification of Psychiatric Symptoms (1974), Reasoning about Madness (1978); *Style*— Prof J K Wing, CBE; Royal Collage of Psychiatrists, 17 Belgrave Square, London SW1X 8PG (☎ 071 235 2351, 071 703 5411, ext 3509, fax 071 245 1231)

WING, Dr Lorna Gladys; da of Bernard Newbury Tolchard (d 1969), and Gladys Ethel, *née* Whittell (d 1962); *b* 7 Oct 1928; *Educ* Chatham GS, UCH London (MD, MB BS); *m* 15 May 1950, John Kenneth Wing, CBE, s of William Sidney Wing (d 1928); 1 da (Susan b 1956); *Career* scientific staff MRC Social and Community Psychiatry Unit 1964-90, hon conslt psychiatrist Maudsley Hosp London 1972-90, hon sr lectr Inst of Psychiatry London 1974-90; conslt psychiatrist Nat Autistic Soc 1990- (fndr and exec ctee memb); FRCPsych 1980; *Books* Early Childhood Autism (ed, 1976), Autistic Children - A Guide for Parents (1980), Hospital Closure and the Resettlement of Residents (1989); *Recreations* walking, reading, gardening; *Style*— Dr Lorna Wing; National Autistic Society, 276 Willesden Lane, London NW2 5RB (☎ 081 451 1114, fax 081 45186)

WINGATE, Capt Sir Miles Buckley; KCVO (1981); s of Terrence Wingate; *b* 17 May 1923; *Educ* Taunton GS, Prior Park Coll; *m* 1947, Alicia Forbes Philip; 3 da; *Career* with Royal Mail Lines 1939; master mariner; memb Bd Trinity House 1968-88 (dep master 1976-88); *Style*— Captain Sir Miles Wingate, KCVO; Trinity House, Tower Hill, London EC3N 4DH (☎ 071 480 6601)

WINGATE, His Honour Judge; William Granville; QC (1963); s of Col George Wingate, CIE (d 1936); *b* 28 May 1911; *Educ* Brighton Coll, Lincoln Coll Oxford; *m* 1960, Judith Rosemary, da of late Lt-Col J H B Evatt; 1 s, 1 da (twins); *Career* barr Inner Temple 1933, memb Bar Council 1961-65 and 1966-67, dep chm Essex QS 1965-71, a circuit judge (E Sussex) 1967-, memb: County Court Rule Ctee and Lord Chancellor's Legal Aid Advisory Ctee 1971-77, Lord Chllr's Law Reform Ctee 1974-87; chm of govrs of Brighton Coll 1978-87; *Clubs* Bar Yacht, Royal Corinthian Yacht; *Style*— His Honour Granville Wingate, QC; Cox's Mill, Dallington, Heathfield, Sussex (☎ 0435 830 217); 2 Garden Court, Temple, London EC4 (☎ 071 236 4741)

WINGATE-ROUTLEDGE, Robin Charles Marc; s of Lt-Col Stanley Wingate-Routledge, TD (d 1972), and Ilse Anne-Marie, da of Marquard BöDecker; *b* 26 April 1944; *Educ* Int Diplomatic HS, Nikolaus Cosanus Gymnasium Bonn W Germany; *Career* farmer and linguist; breeder of pedigree sheep (Suffolk); *Recreations* music, theatre, art, wild life and conservation, walking, horses; *Clubs* Guards' Polo, Henley Royal Regatta; *Style*— Robin Wingate-Routledge, Esq; New Barn Farm, Sibford Gower, nr Banbury, Oxon OX15 5RY (☎ 029 578 330)

WINGATE-SAUL, Michael Anthony; s of Anthony Sylvester Wingate-Saul, and Brenda Maxwell, *née* Stoddart (d 1987); *b* 8 Feb 1938; *Educ* Rugby, King's Coll Cambridge (MA); *m* 23 Sept 1967, Eleanor Jane, da of Alan Lawrence Brodie (d 1972); 2 da (Polly b 1969, Rebecca b 1971); *Career* Nat Serv 1956-58, 2 Lt 4 Regt RHA Germany; slr, sr ptnr Letcher & Son, NP; govr Bryanston Sch 1982-; *Recreations* music, theatre, amateur dramatics, shooting, tennis, skiing, photography; *Style*— Michael A Wingate-Saul, Esq; Sandle Lodge, Sandleheath, Hampshire SP6 1PF (☎ 0425 652261); 24 Market Place, Ringwood, Hampshire BH24 1BS (☎ 0425 471424, fax 0425 470917)

WINGFIELD, Charles John; s of Lt-Col Charles Ralph Borlase Wingfield (d 1923), of Onslow, Shrewsbury, and Mary Nesta Harriet, *née* Williams (d 1947); *b* 9 May 1917; *Educ* Eton; *m* 14 June 1956, (Cecily) Maxine d'Eyncourt, da of Percy George Meighar-Lovett, OBE (d 1970), of 71 Cadogan Square, London SW1; 1 s (John b 1957), 2 da (Elisabeth b 1959, Helen b 1963); *Career* KSLI Supplementary Res 1938, France and Belgium 1939-40, Somaliland Scouts, KAR E Africa 1941-45; patron of one living Bicton; chm Midland Gliding Club 1947-50, jt master S Shrops Hunt 1954-57; JP Salop 1949, High Sheriff 1953; *Recreations* gliding, fishing, shooting; *Style*— Charles Wingfield, Esq; Onslow, Bicton Heath, Shrewsbury

WINGFIELD, Hon Mrs (Cynthia Meriel); *née* Hill; da of 6 Baron Sandys (d 1961); *b* 1929; *m* 1954, Charles Talbot Rhys Wingfield; 1 s, 3 da; *Style*— The Hon Mrs Wingfield; Barrington Park, Burford, Oxon (☎ Windrush 045 14 302)

WINGFIELD, Hon Guy Claude Patrick; s of 9 Viscount Powerscourt (d 1973), and Sheila, Viscountess Powerscourt, *qv*; bro of 10 Viscount and Hon Lady Langrishe; *b* 5 Oct 1940; *Educ* Millfield; *Style*— The Hon Guy Wingfield

WINGFIELD, Lady Norah Beryl Cayzer; *née* Jellicoe; da of Adm of the Fleet 1 Earl Jellicoe, GCB, OM, GCVO (d 1935); *b* 1910; *m* 1935, Maj Edward William Rhys Wingfield (d 1984), late King's Royal Rifle Corps; 2 s, 2 da; *Style*— The Lady Norah Wingfield; Salterbridge, Cappoquin, Co Waterford

WINGFIELD DIGBY, (Kenelm) Simon Digby; TD (1946), DL (1953); s of Col Frederick James Bosworth Wingfield Digby, DSO (d 1952), and Gwendolen, *née* Hamilton Fletcher (d 1975); Sir Simon Digby and his brothers fought beside Henry Tudor at Bosworth Field, granted Manor of Coleshill which is still in the family; *b* 13 Feb 1910; *Educ* Harrow, Trinity Coll Cambridge (MA); *m* 1936, Kathleen Elizabeth, da of Hon Mr Justice Courtney Kingstone, of Canada; 1 s (John), 1 da (Venetia); *Career* barr; MP (C) West Dorset 1941-74, Cons whip 1948-51, Civil Lord of Admty 1951-57, ldr Br Delgn Cncl Europe Assembly 1972-74; Order of Leopold, Order of the White Lion; landowner (estates at Sherborne, Dorset and Coleshill, Warwickshire); *Recreations* shooting, fishing; *Clubs* Carlton; *Style*— Simon Wingfield Digby, Esq, TD, DL; Sherborne Castle, Sherborne, Dorset (☎ 07476 2650); Coleshill House, Warwickshire; Digby Estate Office, Sherborne, Dorset (☎ 0935 813182)

WINGFIELD DIGBY, Stephen Hatton; s of Archdeacon Basil Wingfield Digby, of Salisbury, and Barbara Hatton Budge (d 1987); *b* 17 Nov 1944; *Educ* Sherborne, Univ of Bristol (BSc, Queen's Univ Belfast (MBA); *m* 1968, Sarah Jane, da of Osborne Lovell, of Dorset; 2 s (William b 1974, Alexander b 1983), 1 da (Claire b 1972); *Career* dir: Bass Sales Ltd 1978-81, Bass Wales & West Ltd 1981-83, The Harp Lager Co 1983-, Barclays Bank plc 1988-, Crown Brewery plc 1989-; chm London Brewers' Cncl 1990- (vice chm 1987); *Recreations* fishing, shooting; *Clubs* MCC; *Style*— Stephen Wingfield Digby, Esq; The Coach House, Gregories Farm Lane, Beaconsfield; The Harp Lager Co, Southway House, Park Royal, London NW1

WINGROVE, David Terence; s of Alfred Wingrove, of Holmer Green, Bucks, and Kathleen Rose Wingrove; *b* 22 Dec 1947; *Educ* John Hampden Sch High Wycombe, Poly of Central London; *Career* chartered surveyor; dir: Howden Mgmnt Servs Ltd 1984-, Alexander Howden Gp Mgmnt Servs Ltd 1986-; mangr int facilities planning Alexander & Alexander Servs Inc 1990-; FRICS; *Recreations* travel, horticulture, walking, photography, reading, seeking-out good food and drink; *Style*— David Wingrove, Esq; 13 Barn View Rd, Coggeshall, Essex C06 1RS; 8 Devonshire Sq, London EC2M 4PL (☎ 071 623 5500, telex 882171, fax 071 621 1511); Alexander & Alexander Servs Inc, Owings Mills, Baltimore, USA (☎ 010 1 301 363 5934)

WINKELMAN, Joseph William; s of George William Winkelman (d 1956), of Keokuk, Iowa, USA, and Cleo Lucretia, *née* Harness (d 1978); *b* 20 Sept 1941; *Educ* Keokuk HS, Univ of the South, Sewanee Tennessee (BA, pres of graduating class), Wharton Sch of Fin Univ of Pennsylvania, Ruskin Sch of Drawing, Univ of Oxford (Cert in Fine Art); *m* 8 Feb 1969, Harriet Lowell, da of Gaspard D'Andelot Belin, of Cambridge, Mass; 2 da (Alice Mary b 21 March 1973, Harriet Lowell b 28 May 1974); *Career* secondary sch master for US Peace Corps Tabora Sch Tanzania 1965-66; occasional tutor: Univ of Oxford Dept for External Studies 1986-88, Ruskin Sch of Drawing 1978-88, Sch of Architecture Oxford Poly 1987-89; artist; working mainly in relief and Intaglio printmaking 1974-91, handmaking own original fine art prints; hon fellowship Printmakers' Cncl 1988; 2 Int Miniature Print Exhibition: Cadaques Spain 1982, Seoul Korea 1982, Royal W of Eng Acad Bristol for painting 1985; chm Oxford Art Soc, pres Royal Soc of Painter-Etchers 1989-; memb Royal Soc of Painter-Etchers 1982 (assoc 1979), RWA 1989; *Recreations* gardening, hill walking, music; *Style*— Joseph Winkelman, Esq; The Hermitage, 69 Old High St, Headington, Oxfordshire OX3 9HT (☎ 0865 62839)

WINKLE, Anthony Webbe; s of Harry Downing Winkle (d 1974), of Edinburgh, and Gladys, *née* Hughes (d 1977); *b* 28 Dec 1931; *Educ* Newcastle HS, George Watsons Coll, Heriot-Watt Univ; *m* 1959, Patricia Emily Mary, da of George Alfred Parker (d 1984), of Edinburgh; 2 s (Philip b 1964, Paul b 1966); *Career* Nat Serv RAF pilot, Flying Offr 1956-58; project mangr; dir Gibson & Simpson Project Management Ltd Edinburgh; farmer; *Clubs* New (Edinburgh); *Style*— Anthony W Winkle, Esq; Whitmuir Lamancha, West Linton, Peeblesshire EH46 7BB (☎ (0968) 60431); Gibson & Simpson, Project Management, Hailes House, Hailes Ave, Lanark Rd, Edinburgh EH13 OLZ (☎ 031 441 5363, fax 031 441 5348)

WINKLER, Audrey; JP (1977); *b* 8 March 1935; *Educ* Ossett GS; *m* 30 March 1955, Andrew Winkler; 2 s (Alex b 10 March 1958, Michael (twin) b 10 March 1958), 1 da (Kay b 12 June 1963); *Career* dir Profitex Ltd 1987, ed Pretty Big 1990; dep chm Mid-Derbys Area Bd of Young Enterprise, dir Derby Arts Festival 1985-88; memb: Wirksworth and Dist Chamber of Trade and Commerce (pres 1984-86), Derbys Chamber of Commerce and Indust 1987; *Style*— Mrs Audrey Winkler, JP; Pretty Big, The Dale, Wirksworth, Derby DE4 4EJ (☎ 062 982 4949, fax 062 982 4773)

WINKLEY, Dr Linda Mary; da of Reginald Bertram Holland (d 1984), and Vera Mary, *née* Mills; *b* 1 June 1942; *Educ* King Edward's HS for Girls Edgbaston Birmingham, Univ of Birmingham (MB ChB, DPM, DCH, DRCOG); *m* 22 July 1967, David Ross Winkley, s of Donald Winkley, of Sutton Coldfield, Birmingham; 1 s (Joseph b 15 June 1973), 1 da (Katherine b 23 June 1971); *Career* in gen practice 1967-70, trained in adult psychiatry Warnford Hosp Oxford 1970-72, sr registrar Midland Trg Scheme in Child Psychiatry 1973-75, conslt child psychiatrist Selly Oak Hosp Birmingham 1976-, regnl speciality clinical tutor in child psychiatry 1989- (developed child psychiatry servs in Midlands and set up course for psychotherapeutic work with children 1980); memb: Client Gp Planning Team for Children's Mental Health Promotion Sub-Ctee W Midlands, Div of Child Health and Paediatrics Selly Oak Hosp 1988; fndr memb and treas W Midlands Inst of Psychotherapy; memb: ACPP 1973, APP 1985; MACP 1986, FRCPsych 1989; *Recreations* theatre, music, squash; *Style*— Dr Linda Winkley; Oaklands, Selly Oak Hospital, Raddlebarn Rd, Selly Oak, Birmingham B29 6JD (☎ 021 471 5280)

WINKS, David John Ffoulkes; s of Capt Geoffrey Ffoulkes Winks, TD (d 1976), and Marjorie Mary, *née* Hoggarth; *b* 16 Oct 1938; *Educ* Wycliffe Coll Glos; *m* Diane Pamela; 1 s (Peter John b 1966), 1 da (Sian Mary b 1969); *Career* ptnr Peat Marwick McLintock 1968-, chm Milton Keynes Business Venture 1983-; pres Beds Bucks & Herts Soc of CAs 1987-88; FCA, ATII; *Recreations* golf; *Clubs* Royal Porthcawl Golf, Woburn Golf and Country, Br Sportsmans; *Style*— David Winks, Esq; Manor Lodge, Milton Bryan, Milton Keynes MK17 9HS (☎ 0525 210015); Norfolk House, 499 Silbury Boulevard, Milton Keynes MK9 2HA (☎ 0908 661881)

WINKWORTH, Peter Leslie; s of Francis William Henry Winkworth (d 1975), and Ruth Margaret Llewllin, *née* Notley; *b* 9 Aug 1948; *Educ* Tonbridge; *m* 16 June 1973, Tessa Anne, da of Sir Alexander Warren Page; 1 s (Piers b 1976), 2 da (Victoria b 1975, Jessica b 1978); *Career* merchant banker and CA; dir: Close Brothers Gp plc 1984-, Close Brothers Ltd 1977-, Safeguard Investmts Ltd 1984-, Arkstar Ltd 1984-88, Clifford Brown Gp plc 1987-, Jackson-Stops & Staff Ltd 1990-; *Recreations* tennis, horse riding, horse breeding, national hunt racing; *Clubs* St George's Hill Lawn Tennis; *Style*— Peter Winkworth, Esq; Merton Place, Dunsford, Surrey; Close Brothers Ltd, 36 Great St Helens, London EC3A 6AP (☎ 071 283 2241, telex 88142744, fax 071 6239699)

WINN, Hon Charles Rowland Andrew; s and h of 5 Baron St Oswald, *qv*; *b* 22 July 1959; *m* 1985, Louise Alexandra, da of Stewart Mackenzie Scott; 1 s (Rowland Charles Sebastian Henry b 1986); *Career* landowner; *Style*— The Hon Charles Winn

WINN, Geoffrey Frank; s of Capt Frank Winn (d 1987), of Scarborough, and Hettie , *née* Croft (d 1983); *b* 13 Dec 1938; *Educ* Scarborough HS, Univ of Leeds (BComm); *m* 9 July 1966, Jennifer Lynne, JP, da of Jack Winter, DFC, of Scarborough; 2 da (Deborah b 1967, Susie b 1970); *Career* CA; Winn & Co (Scarborough and branch offices) 1962-; dir Scarborough Bldg Soc 1984-; Lloyds External name 1985-; chm Scarborough Flower Fund Homes 1986- (memb 1970-); pres: Rotary Club of Scarborough Cavaliers 1985-86 (memb 1978), Humberside & Dist Soc of CAs 1991-92; tstee Scarborough CC; FCA 1962; *Recreations* golf, skiing, badminton; *Clubs* CLA; *Style*— Geoffrey Winn, Esq; Barmoor House, Scalby, Scarborough, N Yorks YO13 OPG, (☎ 0723 362 414); 62/63 Westborough, Scarborough, N Yorks YO11 1TS, (☎ 0723 364341, car 0836 768902)

WINN, Mrs Winifred; DL (Lancs 1980); da of William Minikin Bradley, and Isabella

Hay Donaldson, *née* Ettershank; *Educ* St Mary's Convent Sch Folkestone; *m* 26 Sept 1946, Frank Winn, s of John Winn (d 1959); *Career* memb Preston RDC 1962-74, Chm Penwortham and Dist RNLI 1962-74; memb: Lancs CC 1967-89 (chm Fire Serv and Public Protection Ctee 1973-81, rep ACC 1976-89), Lancs Police Authy 1969-81; rep ACC on Nat Jt Cncl for Fire Brigades 1976-89, dep pres Lancs Br BRCS 1980-; memb Bd Govrs Royal Cross Sch for Deaf 1967-; chm Lancs br Sea Cadet Assoc 1989-; govr: Penwortham Girls' HS 1967- (chm 1974-81), Moor Hey Special Sch 1968-; tstee Mary Cross Tst for Deaf 1990-; *Recreations* travel, gardening, music, writing and reading; *Clubs* Royal Over-Seas League, St James's; *Style*— Mrs Winifred Winn, DL; Oaklea, Kingsway, Penwortham, Preston (☎ 0772 743239)

WINNER, Michael Robert; s of George Joseph Winner (d 1972), and Helen, *née* Zlota (d 1984); *b* 30 Oct 1935; *Educ* St Christopher Sch Letchworth Herts, Downing Coll Cambridge (MA); *Career* chm: Scimitar Films Ltd, Michael Winner Ltd, Motion Picture & Theatrical Investments Ltd 1957-; memb Cncl and chief censorship offr Dirs Guild of GB 1983-, fndr and chm Police Meml Tst 1984-; dir: Play It Cool 1962, West Eleven 1963, The Mechanic 1972; dir and writer The Cool Mikado 1962; prodr and dir: The System 1963, I'll Never Forget What's 'is name 1967, The Games 1969, Lawman 1970, The Nightcomers 1971, Chato's Land 1971, Scorpio 1972, The Stone Killer 1973, Death Wish 1974, Won Ton Ton The Dog That Saved Hollywood 1975, Firepower 1978, Scream for Help 1984, Death Wish Three 1985; prodr dir and writer: You Must be Joking 1965, The Jokers 1966, Hannibal Brooks 1968, The Sentinel 1976, The Big Sleep 1977, Death Wish Two 1981, The Wicked Lady 1982, Appointment with Death 1987, A Chorus of Disapproval 1988, Bullseye! 1989; theatre prodns: The Tempest 1974, A Day in Hollywood A Night in the Ukraine 1978; *Recreations* being difficult; *Style*— Michael Winner, Esq; 6-8 Sackville St, London W1X 1DD (☎ 071 734 8385)

WINNER, Paul; JP (North Westminster Bench) 1972; s of Emmanuel Winner (d 1967), of Oakwood Ct, London, and Bessie, *née* Taylor (d 1983); *Educ* St Lawrence Coll Ramsgate, Westminster City Sch, La Sorbonne Paris, St John's Coll Oxford; *m* Mary, da of Frank Oppenheimer; 1 s (Daniel b 3 May 1968), 1 da (Sanya b 21 March 1966); *Career* sec World Univ Serv 1953-56, exec Gilbert McAllister & Ptnrs 1959-62, asst dir World Parliament Assoc 1959-63, exec dir Lonsdale Information 1963-67, fndr Paul Winner Marketing Communications 1967-84, dir Good Relations plc 1984-85; fndr: Paul Winner Consultants Ltd 1986, Arts Management Group 1987, Music for the World Fndn 1990; mktg advsr CBI 1985; Parly candidate: (Lib) Spelthorne 1974 and 1979, (Alliance) Windsor and Maidenhead 1983, co-ordinator Alliance gen election fund raising campaign 1987, memb Domestic Panel 1980-, memb Exec Cncl of Christians and Jews (chm 1992 50th Anniversairy Ctee); Freeman City of London 1981, Liveryman Worshipful Co of Marketers; MCIM, MInstD; *Books* Effective PR Management (1987), Da Cuneo Tutto; *Recreations* painting, sketching, tennis, travel, poetry, walking; *Clubs* Reform, Arts, Savile, Hurlingham, Roehampton, Hon Soc of the Knights of the Round Table, Rotary London (chm Speakers Ctee); *Style*— Paul Winner, Esq, JP; Paul Winner Consultants Limited, 141 Sloane St, London SW1X 9AY (☎ 071 730 8525, fax 071 730 7133)

WINNICK, David Julian; MP (Lab) Walsall North 1979-; *b* 26 June 1933; *Educ* LSE; *Career* memb: Willesden Cncl 1959-64, Brent Cncl 1964-66; contested (Lab) Harwich 1964, MP (Lab) Croydon South 1966-70, contested Croydon Central Oct 1974 and Walsall Nov 1976 (regained Walsall North for Lab 1979); memb Select Ctees on: Race Relations and Immigration 1969-70, Environment 1980-83, Procedure 1989-; vice-pres APEX; *Style*— David Winnick Esq, MP; House of Commons, London SW1

WINNIFRITH, Charles Boniface; s of Sir (Alfred) John Digby Winnifrith, KCB, *qv*, and Lesbia Margaret, *née* Cochrane (d 1981); *b* 12 May 1936; *Educ* Tonbridge, ChCh Oxford (MA); *m* 21 April 1962, Josephine Joy Winnifrith, MBE, da of Roger Spencer Poile (d 1974), of Kingston, Kent; 1 s (John b 1964), 2 da (Charlotte b 1966, Laura b 1968); *Career* Nat Serv 2 Lt RAEC 1958-68; Dept of the Clerk of House of Commons 1960-, second clerk of Select Ctees 1983-87, clerk of Select Ctees 1987-89, princ clerk of Table Office 1989-; memb Gen Synod of the C of E 1970-90, chm House of Laity Canterbury Diocesan Synod 1979-; govr Ashford Sch Kent 1973; *Recreations* cricket, American soap opera; *Clubs* MCC; *Style*— Charles Winnifrith, Esq; Cliffe Cottage, St Margaret's at Cliffe, Kent CT15 6BJ (☎ 0304 853280); House of Commons, London SW1 (☎ 071 219 3312)

WINNIFRITH, Sir (Alfred) John Digby; KCB (1959, CB 1950); s of Rev Bertram Thomas Winnifrith, Rector of Ightham, Kent; *b* 16 Oct 1908; *Educ* Westminster, ChCh Oxford; *m* 1935, Lesbia Margaret (d 1981), eldest da of Sir Arthur Cochrane, KCVO, sometime Clarenceux King of Arms; 2 s, 1 da; *Career* civil servant 1932-67: BOT to 1934, transferred to Treasy 1934, asst sec War Cabinet and civil sec Combined Ops HQ 1942-44, 3 sec Treasy 1951-59, perm sec MAFF 1959-67; tstee Nat History Section Br Museum 1967-72, dir gen Nat Tst 1968-70 (chm Regnl Ctee for Kent and E Sussex 1971-78), memb Cwlth War Graves Cmmn 1969-83; *Style*— Sir John Winnifrith, KCB; Hallhouse Farm, Appledore, Ashford, Kent (☎ 023 383 264)

WINNIFRITH, Thomas John; s of Sir John Winnifreth, KCB, of Hall House Farm, Appledore, Kent, and Lesbia Margaret, *née* Cochrane (d 1981); *b* 5 April 1938; *Educ* Tonbridge, ChCh Oxford (BA, MA), CCC Oxford (MPhil), Univ of Liverpool (PhD); *m* 1, 3 July 1967, Joanna Victoria Lee (d 1976); da of John Booker (d 1986); 1 s (Thomas John Zacchaeus b 1968), 2 da (Tabitha Jessie Ann b 1969, Naomi Miranda Alice b 1971); m 2, 19 March 1988, Helen Mary, da of Sir George Peregrine Young, CMG (d 1960); *Career* asst master Eton Coll 1961-66, EK Chambers student Corpus Christi Oxford 1966-68, William Noble fell Univ of Liverpool 1968-70, sr lectr Univ of Warwick 1977-89 (lectr 1970-77); *Books* The Brontës and their Background (1973), The Brontës (1977), Brontë Facts and Problems (jtly, 1983), Nineteen Eighty-Four and All's Well (jtly, 1984), The Vlachs (1987), A New Life of Charlotte Brontë (1988), Charlotte and Emily Brontë (jtly, 1989); *Style*— Thomas Winnifrith, Esq; 10 Grove Street, Leamington Spa, Warwickshire CV32 5AJ (☎ 0926 883543); Department of English, University of Warwick, Coventry CV4 7AL (☎ 0327 523523)

WINNING, Most Rev Thomas Joseph; *see*: Glasgow, Archbishop of

WINNINGTON, Anthony Edward; s of Col Thomas Foley Churchill Winnington, MBE, of 182 Rivermeade Ct, Hurlingham, London, and Lady Betty, *née* Anson, da of 4 Earl of Lichfield; *b* 13 May 1948; *Educ* Eton, Univ of Grenoble; *m* 5 Dec 1978, Karyn Kathryn Kettles, da of Joanne Dayton, of Palm Beach, Florida, USA; 1 s (Edward b 1987), 2 da (Victoria b 1981, Sophia b 1985); *Career* dir (equity sales) Hoare Govett Securities Ltd 1984- (joined 1969); memb Stock Exchange 1984; *Recreations* music; *Clubs* Boodles, Hurlingham; *Style*— Anthony Winnington, Esq; 20 Baskerville Rd, London SW18 3RW (☎ 081 870 8466); Hoare Govett, 4 Broadgate, London EC2M 7CE (☎ 071 374 1116)

WINNINGTON, Lady Betty (Marjorie); *née* Anson; da of 4 Earl of Lichfield (d 1960); *b* 12 March 1917; *m* 20 May 1944, Col Thomas Foley Churchill Winnington, MBE, yr bro of Sir Francis Winnington, 6 Bt; 2 s, 2 da; *Style*— The Lady Betty Winnington; 182 Rivermead Court, Ranelagh Gardens, London SW6 3SG

WINNINGTON, Sir Francis Salwey William; 6 Bt (GB 1755), of Stanford Court, Worcestershire; s of Francis Salwey Winnington (d 1913), and gs of Sir Francis Winnington, 5 Bt, JP, DL (d 1931); *b* 24 June 1907; *Educ* Eton; *m* 1944, Anne Beryl Jane, da of late Capt Lawrence Drury-Lowe, Scots Gds; 1 da; *Heir* bro, Col Thomas Foley Churchill Winnington, MBE b 16 Aug 1910; *Career* Lt Welsh Gds 1928-32; re-employed 1939 (despatches); patron of three livings; landed proprietor (4,700 acres); *Clubs* Cavalry and Guards'; *Style*— Sir Francis Winnington, Bt; Brockhill Court, Shelsley Beauchamp, Worcs

WINNINGTON, Col Thomas Foley Churchill; MBE (1948); s of Francis Winnington (d 1913), and Blanche Emma, *née* Casberd-Boteler, (d 1968); hp to bro, Sir Francis Winnington, 6 Bt; *b* 16 Aug 1910; *Educ* Eton, Balliol Coll Oxford (BA); *m* 20 May 1944, Lady Betty Anson, da of 4 Earl of Lichfield (d 1960); 2 s (Anthony b 1948 (m 1978 Karyn Kettles), Henry b 1961), 2 da (Sarah (Viscountess Campden) b 1951, Emma (Mrs Christopher Milne) b 1956); *Career* joined Grenadier Gds 1933: served WWIIA Dunkirk and NW Europe (despatches) cmd 3 Bn Malaya (despatches) 1948, Col cmdg 1952-55; pres WO Selection Bd 1955, ret 1957; Reed Int 1958-75; appeals advsr Help The Aged 1976-; *Clubs* Pratt's, Hurlingham; *Style*— Col Thomas Winnington, MBE; 182 Rivermead Ct, Ranelagh Gdns, London SW6 3SG (☎ 071 731 0697); Help The Aged, St James Walk, London EC1R 0BE (☎ 071 253 0253)

WINNINGTON-INGRAM, (Edward) John; s of Rev Preb Edward F Winnington-Ingram (d 1963), and Gladys, *née* Armstrong; gn of Rt Rev Arthur Foley Winnington-Ingram, PC, KCVO, Bishop of London 1901-39; *b* 20 April 1926; *Educ* Shrewsbury, Keble Coll Oxford (BA); *m* 1, 1953 (m dis 1966), Shirley Yvoire, da of Gerald Lamotte; 2 s (Nicholas b 1957, Gerald b 1960); m 2, Elizabeth Linda, da of Geoffrey Milling (d 1983); *Career* serv WWII RN 1944-47 (Sub Lt RNVR); joined Assoc Newspapers 1949, circulation mangr Daily Mail 1960, gen mangr Manchester 1965-70, dir assoc Newspapers 1971, md The Mail on Sunday 1982, md Mail Newspapers plc 1986-89, dir Assoc Newspapers Hldgs 1986-89; non-exec dir NAAFI 1987-; *Recreations* tennis, shooting, music, beagling, gardening; *Clubs* Buck's; *Style*— John Winnington-Ingram, Esq; Old Manor Farm, Cottisford, Brackley, Northants NN13 5SW (☎ 028 04 367)

WINROW, Frank Reginald; s of Reginald Winrow, of Southport, and Phylis, *née* Greenhalgh; *b* 8 March 1937; *Educ* King George V GS Southport; *m* 1958, Dorothy Rosalie Moffat, da of Stuart Moffat Walker (d 1983), of Southport; 2 s (Andrew, Michael); *Career* SAC RAF 1955-57, HM inspr of taxes, pres Inland Revenue Staff Fedn; memb: Arts, Entertainment and Sports Advsy Ctee of TUC, Gen Cncl of NW Regional TUC, Cncl of Civil Serv Unions, Exec Ctee Lancs Assoc of Boys Clubs, Lab Pty; former referee Assoc Football; *Recreations* trade union and labour movement, assoc football, gardening, reading, photography; *Style*— Frank Winrow, Esq; 8 Everard Rd, Southport, Merseyside PR8 6NA (☎ 0704 32930); Inland Revenue Staff Federation, 231 Vauxhall Bridge Rd, London SW1V 1EH

WINSER, Nigel de Northop; s of Robert Stephen Winser, of Kintbury, Berks, and Anne, *née* Carrick; *b* 4 July 1952; *Educ* Bradfield Coll, Poly of Central London; *m* 17 July 1982, Shane, da of Arthur James Wesley-Smith, of Sheffield; 1 s (Philip b 1984), 1 da (Kate b 1987); *Career* RGS: field dir Mulu Sarawak expedition 1976, expedition offr 1978 (expeditions carried out in Karakoram Pakistan, Kora Kenya, Wahiba Oman, Kimberley Aust), asst dir and head of exploration 1988; exploration fell commoner Corpus Christi Coll Cambridge 1990; patrons Gold medal for leadership of Wahiba Sands project, Mrs Patrick Ness award for expdn leadership 1977; *Books* Sea of Sands and Mists (1989), contributing ed History of World Exploration (1991); monthly Frontiers column Geographical Magazine 1987; *Recreations* fly fishing on the Kennet, Wylie and Nadder; *Clubs* Geographical, Travellers; *Style*— Nigel Winser, Esq; 22 Swanage Rd, London SW18 2DY (☎ 081 874 0824); Royal Geographical Society, 1 Kensington Gore, London SW7 2AR (☎ 071 589 5466, fax 071 581 9918)

WINSHIP, James Gunn; s of James Gunn Winship (d 1965), of Shearwater, Bishopstone, nr Salisbury, Wilts, and Gladys Winefred, *née* Pine-Coffin; *b* 29 Jan 1950; *Educ* Redrice Public Sch Andover; *m* 6 April 1974, Sarah Jane, da of James Henry Manners, of Hill View, Sevenhampton, Highworth, Wilts; 1 s (Christian b 21 Oct 1981), 1 da (Charlotte); *Career* reporter Southern Evening Echo Southampton 1970-73, industl correspondent United Newspapers London 1973-75, sub ed Aldershot News Series 1975-76, account exec Infoplan PR 1976-78, account mangr Bolton Dickinson Assocs 1978-80; fndr and chm: Shearwater PR 1980-, Stephen Gray Assocs 1986-, Kestrel Publishing 1986-; memb Southern Region Cncl of CBI; *Style*— James Winship, Esq; Manor Farmhouse, Manor Lane, West Hendred, Oxfordshire (☎ 0235 833 396); Shearwater Public Relations Ltd, 29 Market Place, Wantage, Oxfordshire OX12 8BG (☎ 02357 66339, fax 02357 69044)

WINSKELL, Cyril; MBE (1982); s of Robert Winskell (d 1963), of South Shields, and Margaret Wiley (d 1970); *b* 29 Aug 1932; *Educ* South Shields HS, Rutherford GS, King's Coll Newcastle upon Tyne, Univ of Durham (certificate in architecture); *m* 24 Sept 1960, Patricia, da of Leonard George Dolby (d 1967), of North Shields; 4 s (Cy b 1961, Scott b 1962, Dane b 1968, Mark b 1968), 1 da (Patricia b 1965); *Career* Nat Serv, Sapper Christmas Island 1956-57; visiting critic and occasional lectr at various schs of architecture 1972-, one man show Gallery Colbert Durham City 1977, chm Northern Region RIBA 1980-82, chm Northumbria Branch RIBA 1984-86, convenor "Newcastle Cityscape" 1984-; external examiner Sch of Architecture Queen's Univ Belfast 1987-88; architect for the restoration of: St Thomas's Neighbourhood, Newcastle upon Tyne 1978-81, Canning Area, Liverpool 1984-87; founded Winskell Chartered Architects Urban Consultants 1982, memb Historic Areas Advsy Ctee English Heritage 1987-88, pres Northern Architectural Assoc 1990-; ARIBA 1956, FRIBA 1971; *Recreations* painting, travel; *Style*— Cyril Winskell, Esq, MBE; 7 Collingwood St, Newcastle upon Tyne NE1 1JE (☎ 091 261 4436)

WINSKILL, Air Cdre Sir (Archibald) Little; KCVO (1980, CVO 1973), CBE (1960), DFC (and Bar), AE; s of James Winskill, of Penrith; *b* 24 Jan 1917; *Educ* Penrith and Carlisle GS; *m* 1947, Christiane Amélie Pauline, da of M Bailleux, of Calais; 1 s (decd), 1 da; *Career* served WWII: Fighter Pilot Battle of Britain 1941, French Resistance, N Africa 1942-43; Air Cdre 1963, air attaché Paris 1964-67, dir PR (Air) MOD 1967-68, Capt of HM The Queen's Flight 1968-82, extra equerry to HM The Queen 1968-; ret RAF 1982; *Clubs* RAF; *Style*— Air Cdre Sir Archie Winskill, KCVO, CBE, DFC, AE; Anchors, Coastal Rd, West Kingston, East Preston, W Sussex BN16 1SN (☎ 0903 775439)

WINSTANLEY, Alan Kenneth; s of (Albert) Kenneth Winstanley (d 1973), and Doreen, *née* Dunscombe, of Mansfield, Notts; *b* 2 Nov 1952; *Educ* St Clement Danes GS for Boys London; *m* 5 Oct 1975, Christine Susan Anne, da of Raymond Henry Osborne; 1 s (James Alan Kenneth b 7 Jan 1983), 1 da (Eve Alexis b 24 Oct 1978); *Career* record prodr; recording engr (work incl Amii Stewart's Knock on Wood, early Stranglers' records) 1970-79, freelance prodr Stranglers LP The Raven 1979, prodr (in partnership with Clive Langer) 1979-; jt fndr: West Side Studios London 1984, residential studio Henley 1987; artists produced incl: Madness 1981-85, Teardrop Explodes 1981, Dexys Midnight Runners 1982, Elvis Costello 1983-84, Marilyn 1983, Lloyd Cole and the Commotions 1985, David Bowie, Sade, Style Council, Ray Davies, Gil Evans (for Absolute Beginners) 1985, Bowie and Jagger (Dancing in the Street) 1985, China Crisis 1986, Hothouse Flowers 1987-90, The Adventures 1989, Morrissey 1989-91, They Might Be Giants 1989; Platinum albums: One Step Beyond (Madness) 1980, Absolutely (Madness) 1981, Complete Madness 1982, Too-Rye Ay (Dexys

Midnight Runners) 1982; Gold albums: The Raven (The Stranglers) 1980, Dance Craze 1981, 7 (Madness) 1981, Kilimanjaro (Teardrop Explodes) 1982, The Rise and Fall (Madness) 1983, Punch the Clock (Elvis Costello) 1983, Easy Pieces (Lloyd Cole) 1985, People (Hot House Flowers) 1988, Home (Hot House Flowers) 1990; Silver albums: Goodbye Cruel World (Elvis Costello) 1984, Mad Not Mad (Madness) 1985; Platnum single: Come On Eileen (Dexys Midnight Runners) 1982; Gold singles: Madness (Baggy Trousers 1980, Embarrassment 1981, It Must Be Love 1981, Our House 1982), Dancing in the Street (Bowie & Jagger) 1985; Silver singles: Madness (One Step Beyond 1980, My Girl 1980, Work Rest and Play EP 1981, Return of the Los Palmas 7 1981, Shut Up 1981, Grey Day 1981, Driving in my Car 1982, Wings of a Dove 1983), Reward (Teardrop Explodes) 1981, Swords of a Thousand Men (Tenpole Tudor) 1981, Calling Your Name (Marilyn) 1983; *awards* Top Producer (singles) Music Week award 1982, nominee Best British Producer BPI awards 1982 and 1983; *Recreations* tennis, golf, skiing, cycling, travelling; *Style—* Alan Winstanley, Esq; West Side Studios, Olaf Centre, 10 Olaf St, London W11 4BE (☎ 071 221 9494, fax 071 727 0008)

WINSTANLEY, John; MC (1944), TD (1951); s of Capt Bernard Joseph Winstanley (d 1919), and Grace Frances, *née* Taunton (d 1970); *b* 11 May 1919; *Educ* Wellington, Univ of London (MB BS), St Thomas' Hosp Med Sch; *m* 10 Jan 1959, Jane Mary, da of Geoffrey Ryan Frost; 1 s (Richard b 28 May 1964), 2 da (Emma b 1 April 1960, Sophie b 27 April 1962); *Career* cmmnd 4 Bn Queens Own Royal W Kent Regt (TA) 1937, serv BEF (despatches) 1940, 8 Army MB ME Forces 1942, India and Burma 1943-45, ret hon Maj 1945; hon civilian conslt ophthalmic surgn Army 1963-84; hon conslt: ophthalmologist Royal Hosp Chelsea 1963-86, ophthalmic surgn St Thomas' Hosp 1984- (conslt ophthalmic surgn 1960-84); memb Cncl Med Protection Soc 1979-; Exec Ctee memb Ex-Servs Mental Welfare Soc 1980, vice pres Iris Fund 1984; Liveryman Worshipful Soc of Apothecaries; FRCS, FCOphth; *Recreations* field sports, history; *Clubs* Fly-Fishers, Army and Navy; *Style—* John Winstanley, Esq, MC, TD; 10 Pembroke Villas, The Green, Richmond, Surrey TW9 1QF (☎ 081 940 6247)

WINSTANLEY, Baron (Life Peer UK 1975), of Urmston in Greater Manchester; Michael Platt Winstanley; eldest s of Dr Sydney A Winstanley; *b* 27 Aug 1918; *Educ* Manchester GS, Manchester Univ; *m* 1, 1945 (m dis 1952), Nancy Penney; 1 s (Hon Nicholas Clayton Platt b 1945); m 2, 1955, Joyce Mary, da of late Arthur Woodhouse; 1 s (Hon Stephen Woodhouse b 1957), 1 da (Hon Diana Christine b 1960); *Career* sits as Lib in House of Lords; MP (Lib) Cheadle 1966-70, Hazel Grove Feb-Oct 1974; chm Lib Pty Health Ctee 1965-66, Lib Spokesman Health, PO and Broadcasting; memb Water Space Amenity Commission 1980-; GP Urmston Manchester 1948-66; broadcaster; MRCS, LRCP; *Style—* The Rt Hon Lord Winstanley; Hare Hall, Dunnerdale, Broughton-in-Furness, Cumbria

WINSTON, Clive Noel; s of George Winston (d 1947), of London, and Alida Celia Winston (d 1964); *b* 20 April 1925; *Educ* Highgate Sch, Trinity Hall Cambridge (BA); *m* 2 April 1952, Beatrice Jeanette, da of Mark Lawton; 2 da (Celia Penelope b 16 Jan 1953, Clair Wendy b 26 Jan 1957); *Career* Capt (emergency cmmn) Royal Berks attached 15 Punjab Regt 1945-47; dep slr Met Police 1982-85, asst dir Fedn Against Copyright Theft 1985-88; union chm Lib and Progressive Synagogues 1981-85; *Recreations* golf, gardening; *Clubs* Bush Hill Park GC; *Style—* Clive Winston, Esq; 2 Bournwell Close, Cockfosters, Herts EN4 0JX (☎ 081 449 5693)

WINSTON, Malcolm John; s of John Winston (d 1982), of Bexhill, and Sarah, *née* Bates; *b* 8 Nov 1930; *Educ* Stationers' Co Sch; *m* 16 June 1962, Cynthia Mary Boorne, da of Hugh Napier Goodchild (d 1981), of Norwich; 1 s (Mark Jonathan Napier b 1964), 1 da (Sarah Catherine Louise b 1967); *Career* Bank of England 1950-75, seconded Central TSB 1973, sr asst gen mangr Central TSB 1981 (asst gen mangr 1975), joined TSB England & Wales upon merger with Central TSB 1986; pres Assoc of Int Savings Banks in London 1985 (founder 1980, chm 1983-84), chm Lombard Assoc 1989-; Freeman City of London 1952, Liveryman Worshipful Co of Makers of Playing Cards 1979; fell Assoc of Corporate Treasurers 1979; ISBI medal of Honour ISBI World Congress (Rome) 1990; *Recreations* beagling, tennis; *Clubs* Over-seas Bankers'; *Style—* Malcolm Winston, Esq; Maze Pond, Wadhurst, East Sussex (☎ 0892 882 074); St Mary's Court, 100 Lower Thomas St, London EC3R 6AQ (☎ 071 623 6000, telex 881 1829)

WINSTON, Prof Robert Maurice Lipson; s of Lawrence Winston (d 1949), of London, and Ruth, *née* Lipson; *b* 15 July 1940; *Educ* St Paul's, Univ of London (MB BS); *m* 8 March 1973, Lira Helen, da of Simon Joseph Feigenbaum (d 1971), of London; 2 s (Joel, Benjamin), 1 da (Tanya); *Career* sr res accoucher The London Hosp 1965, sr lectr Inst of Obstetrics and Gynaecology 1975-81, visiting res prof Catholic Univ of Leuven Belgium 1976-77, conslt obstetrician and gynaecologist Hammersmith Hosp 1978- (sr res fell 1975-78), presenter of Your Life in Their Hands BBC TV 1979-87, prof of gynaecology Univ of Texas San Antonio 1980-81, reader in fertility studies Royal Postgrad Med Sch 1981-86, prof of fertility studies Univ of London 1986-; author of over 100 scientific papers on reproduction; chm Br Fertility Soc 1990- (fndr memb); pres: Int Fallopius Soc 1987-88, Progress All Party Parliamentary Gp for Res In Reproduction 1988-; FRCOG; *Books* Reversibility of Sterilization (1978), Tubal Infertility (1981), Infertility A Synpathetic Approach (1986), What We Know About Infertility (1987), Getting Pregnant (1989); *Recreations* theatre, music, skiing, wine, broadcasting; *Clubs* RSM; *Style—* Prof Robert Winston; 11 Denham Drive, London NW11 6RE (☎ 081 455 7475); Royal Postgraduate Medical Sch, Hammersmith Hospital, Ducane Rd, London W12 0HS (☎ 081 749 5579, fax 081 740 3169, car 0836 639339)

WINTELER, John Fridolin; s of Fridolin Henry Winteler, formerly of Nairobi Kenya (d 1966), and Margaret Mary, *née* Bairstow; *b* 21 Aug 1946; *Educ* Duke of York Sch Nairobi, Pembroke Coll Cambridge (MA); *m* 10 July 1971, Candida Mary Valerie, da of Jack Donald Theodore Pickering, of Woking; 2 s (James b 1974, David b 1976), 2 da (Anne b 1979, Alison b 1983); *Career* called to the Bar Inner Temple 1969; practised NE circuit 1970-; *Recreations* preaching, walking, gardening; *Style—* John Winteler, Esq; Barristers', Chambers, 6 Park Square East, Leeds, W Yorks LS1 2LW (☎ 0532 459763, fax 0532 424395)

WINTER, The Rev David Brian; s of Walter George Winter (d 1952), of London, and Winifred Ella, *née* Oughton (d 1972); *b* 19 Nov 1929; *Educ* Machynlleth Co Powys, Trinity GS London, Kings Coll London (BA), Inst of Educn London (PGCE), Oak Hill Theological Coll; *m* 15 April 1961, Christine Ellen, da of Bernard Martin, of Hitcham, Suffolk; 2 s (Philip b 1963, Adrian b 1969), 1 da (Rebecca b 1964); *Career* Nat Serv RAF 1948-50; sch teacher 1955-59, ed Crusade 1959-70, freelance writer and broadcaster 1970-71, prodr BBC Radio 1971-, head of religious progs BBC Radio 1982-87, head of religious bdcasting BBC 1987-89; priest i/c of Ducklington Oxfordshire and bishop's offr for evangelism 1989-; memb Radio Acad 1985-; *Books incl* Truth in the Son (1985), Battered Bride? (1988); *Recreations* watching cricket; *Style—* The Rev David Winter; The Rectory, 6 Standlake Rd, Ducklington, Oxon OX8 7XG (☎ 0993 776625)

WINTER, Frederick Thomas; CBE (1963); s of Frederick Neville Winter (d 1965), of Newmarket, and Anne Flanagan (d 1987); *b* 20 Sept 1926; *Educ* Ewell Castle; *m* 1956, Diana Ruth, da of Col T R Pearson (d 1945), of Derby; 3 da (Joanna b 1957, Denise (twin) b 1957, Philippa b 1958); *Career* racehorse jockey and trainer, national hunt jockey 1947-64, champion jockey 4 times; won: Grand Nat (twice), Gold Cup (twice), Champion Hurdle (3 times); trainer 1964-88, champion trainer 8 times; won: Grand Nat (twice), Cheltenham Gold Cup, Champion Hurdle (3 times); ret 1988; *Recreations* golf, gardening; *Style—* Frederick Winter, Esq, CBE; Montague House, Eastbury, Newbury, Berks RG16 7JN (☎ 0488 71438)

WINTER, Prof Gerald Bernard; s of Morris Winter (d 1974), and Edith Winter (d 1984); *b* 24 Nov 1928; *Educ* Coopers' Co Sch, London Hosp Med Coll Univ of London (BDS, MB BS, DCH); *m* 24 April 1960, (Brigitte) Eva, da of Dr Hans Heinemann Fleischhacker (d 1965), of London; 1 s (Simon Michael b 1961), 1 da (Caroline Rosalind b 1965); *Career* Nat Serv RADC 1948-49; dental house surgn 1955, house surgn and house physician 1958, lectr Royal Dental Hosp 1959-62; Inst of Dental Surgery Eastman Dental Hosp London: conslt dental surgn 1962-66, prof of children's dentistry 1966-, dean and dir of studies 1983-; pres Br Paedodontic Soc 1970-71 (hon sec 1961-64), hon sec Int Assoc of Dentistry for Children 1971-79, pres Br Soc of Dentistry for the Handicapped 1976-77; FDSRCS, FFDRCSI; *Style—* Prof Gerald Winter; Inst of Dental Surgery, Eastman Dental Hospital, 256 Gray's Inn Rd, London WC1X 8LD

WINTER, John Anthony; MBE (1984); s of Frank Oliver Winter (d 1989), of Norwich, and Sybil Mary, *née* Rudd (d 1976); *b* 16 May 1930; *Educ* Bishops Stortford Coll, Architectural Assoc Sch of Architecture (AA Dip), Yale (MArch); *m* May 1956, Valerie Ursula, *née* Denison; 2 s (Timothy b 1960, Henry b 1963), 1 da (Martha b 1966); *Career* architect; princ John Winter & Assocs; works incl: Morley Coll Lambeth, Housing Lucas Place Milton Keynes, 83 Mansell St E1 (Offices) etc; frequent contrib to architectural jls and videos; memb: Royal Fine Art Cmmn 1986-, Cncl of Architectural Assoc 1989-; FRSA 1988; *Books* Modern Buildings (1969), Industrial Buildings (1971); *Style—* John Winter, Esq, MBE; 81 Swains Lane, London N6 (☎ 081 340 9864); 80 Lamble St, London NW5 4AB (☎ 071 267 7567)

WINTER, Col John Quentin; LVO 1985 (MVO 1982); s of Lt Cdr The Rev Henry Winter, RN (d 1977), and Lawrell, *née* Quentin; *b* 28 Jan 1943; *Educ* The Judd Sch Tonbridge, RMA Sandhurst; *m* 7 Jan 1967, Susan Elizabeth Jane, da of Arthur John Mortimer (d 1982), of London; 2 s (Guy b 1972, James b 1975); *Career* cmmnd Parachute Regt 1963, served world wide, CO 10th Battalion Parachute Regt 1982-84; cdr Cwlth Military Advsy Team Ghana 1987-89, Military Sec HQ UK Land Forces 1989-, Equerry to HRH The Prince of Wales 1980-82, Extra Equerry to HRH The Prince of Wales 1989-; Freeman City of London 1985; *Recreations* most outdoor pursuits; *Clubs* Army and Navy; *Style—* Col John Winter, LVO; c/o The Royal Bank Of Scotland, Holts Farnborough Branch, Victoria Rd, Farnborough, Hants GU14 7NR

WINTER, Richard Thomas; s of Thomas Alfred Baldwin Winter, of Warwickshire, and Ruth Ethel, *née* Newbury; *b* 6 March 1949; *Educ* Warwick Sch, Univ of Birmingham (LLB); *m* Dorothy Sally Cooper, da of Peter Hancock Filer; 1 da (Hannah Louise b 2 Sept 1990); *Career* articled clerk and asst slr Evershed & Tomkinson 1971-75, slr Fisons plc 1975-78, ptnr Evershed Wells & Hind 1981-90 (joined 1978), managing ptnr London office Eversheds Solicitors 1991- (joined 1990); memb Law Soc; *Recreations* sailing, skiing; *Clubs* Roehampton; *Style—* Richard Winter, Esq; Eversheds, 1 Gunpowder Square, Printer St, London EC4 1DE (☎ 071 936 2553, fax 071 936 2590)

WINTER, Roy William; s of Jared William Winter (d 1967), of Osbourne Court, Cowes, Isle of Wight, and Florence, *née* Heron (d 1978); *b* 25 Nov 1931; *Educ* Solihull Sch, Univ of Durham (DipLD), Birmingham Coll of Arts and Crafts (DipArch); *m* 28 Dec 1957, Diane Maureen Winter, da of John Thomas Williams (d 1973), of 96 Glenavon Rd, Maypole, Birmingham; 2 da (Sally Lydia, Lucy); *Career* sergeant RE 1957-59; architect James A Roberts Birmingham 1959-66, chief landscape architect Redditch Devpt Corpn 1966-83, sr lectr Birmingham Poly 1984-; former chm Midland Landscape Assoc, memb of the landscape advsy ctee Dept of Tport; memb RIBA 1960, Ali 1967; *Recreations* cycling, swimming, sailing; *Clubs* Island Sailing; *Style—* Roy Winter, Esq; Brickley Farmhouse, Hanbury, Bromsgrove, Worcs B60 4HT (☎ 052 784 256); 10 Castle Rd, Cowes, Isle of Wight; Inkberrow Studio, Village Green, Inkberrow, Worcs (☎ 0386 792119)

WINTER, William Geoffrey; s of Henry Edgar Winter, OBE, and Josephine, *née* Sims; *b* 2 July 1933; *Educ* Eton, Magdalen Coll Oxford, Heidelberg Univ; *m* 23 Nov 1986, Elizabeth, da of Trevor Edmondson (d 1966); 2 s (Thomas b 1977, Alexander b 1981); *Career* cmmnd 10 Royal Hussars (PWO); dir G & G Kynoch plc 1966-; *Recreations* golf, tennis; *Clubs* Royal St George's, Royal Wimbledon, IOD, Hurlingham; *Style—* William Winter, Esq; 4 Dewhurst Rd, London W14 0ET (☎ 071 602 0106)

WINTERBONE, Prof Desmond Edward; s of Edward Frederick Winterbone (d 1986), of Tenby Dyfed, and Phoebe Hilda, *née* Lane (d 1986); *b* 15 Jan 1943; *Educ* Tenby GS, Rugby Coll of Engrg Technol (CNAA BSc, English Electric Student Apprentice prize), Univ of Bath (PhD); Univ of Manchester (DSc); *m* 24 Sept 1965, Veronica Mary, da of Thomas Frank Cope; 1 s (Edward Joseph b 24 April 1974), 1 da (Anne Caroline b 28 Oct 1971); *Career* student apprentice English Electric Co Ltd Rugby 1960-65 (design engr Diesel Engine Div 1965-67), res fell Univ of Bath 1967-70; UMIST: lectr Dept of Mechanical Engrg 1970-78, sr lectr 1978-80, prof of mechanical engrg 1980-, head Dep of Mechanical Engrg 1981-83, vice princ for external affairs 1986-88, dep princ 1987-88, head Thermodynamics and Fluid Mechanics Div 1990-, head Dept of Mechanical Engrg 1991-; *Awards* chair professorship Nanjing Aeronautical Inst 1985, Mombusho fellowship Univ of Tokyo 1989; doctorate hc Univ of Gen 1991; FIMechE, MSAE (US), FEng 1989; *Publications* The Thermodynamics and Gas Dynamics of Internal Combustion Engines Vols I and II (jt ed, 1982 and 1986), Internal Combustion Engineering: Science and Technology (contrib, 1990); *Recreations* running, cycling (time trials), windsurfing, travel; *Style—* Prof Desmond Winterbone; UMIST, Department of Mechanical Engineering, PO Box 88, Manchester M60 1QD (☎ 061 200 3710, fax 061 200 3723)

WINTERBORN, Dr Michael Hugh; s of Lt-Col Thomas Hugh Winterborn, CBE (d 1985), of Groombridge, Kent, and Helene, *née* Beichmann; *b* 3 June 1939; *Educ* Stonyhurst, St Mary's Hosp (MB BS); *m* 25 Feb 1967 (m dis 1988), Penelope Anne, da of Stephen Fraser Stephenson, of Solihull, W Midlands; 2 s (Simon b 26 June 1969, James b 2 Dec 1970); *Career* jr doctor: St Mary's W2 1963-64, St Albans 1964, W Middx 1965; chest sr house offr St Mary's Hosp Harrow Rd 1965, sr house offr in nephrology Inst of Urology 1966, paediatric registrar Queen Elizabeth Hosp Hackney 1968-70 (res registrar 1967), paediatric sr registrar Birmingham 1970-73, fell in paediatric nephrology Albert Einstein Coll of Med NY 1973-75, conslt paediatrician and nephrologist E Birmingham and Children's Hosps 1975-, dir W Midlands Regnl Children's Dialysis Unit 1979-; sec gen Euro Soc for Paediatric Nephrology; memb: Birmingham Med Res Expeditionary Soc, NEC Lions Club 1977-86; Liveryman Worshipful Co of Wax Chandlers 1964; FRCP 1979 (MRCP 1966); *Recreations* mountaineering, rock climbing, skiing, squash, water colour painting, poetry, Portuguese; *Style—* Dr Michael Winterborn; 180 Quinton Rd, Harborne, W Midlands B17 0RP (☎ 021 427 9101); Regional children's Dialysis Unit, E Birmingham Hospital, Bordesley Green East, Birmingham B9 5ST (☎ 021 766 6611, fax 021 773 6736)

WINTERBOTHAM, Hon Mrs (Emmeline Veronica Louise); *née* Vanden-Bempde-Johnstone; er da of 5 Baron Derwent, *qv*; *b* 3 Nov 1958; *Educ* St Paul's Girls' Sch, UCL (BA); *m* 1982, James John Winterbotham, s of Richard William Consett Winterbotham, of The Hall, Wittersham, Tenterden, Kent; 2 s (Alexander William Harcourt b 1988, Frederick Charles Leo b 1990), 1 da (Héloise Sophie Laura b (twin) 1990); *Career* md The John Harris Design Partnership London; cncl memb The Franco-British Soc 1985-88, skinner of London, memb The Bach Choir; *Style*— The Hon Mrs Winterbotham; 48 Oakley Rd, London N1

WINTERBOTTOM, Hon Caroline Margaret Alyson; only da of Baron Winterbottom (Life Peer), and his 2 w, Ira Munk; *b* 9 Dec 1950; *Educ* Wispers Sch, Oxford Poly (Dip); *Career* publishing; sales admin for Europe and the Middle E; *Recreations* creative writing; *Style*— The Hon Caroline Winterbottom; c/o The Rt Hon Lord Winterbottom, Lower Farm, Fosbury, Marlborough, Wilts SN8 3NJ (☎ 026489 269)

WINTERBOTTOM, David Stuart; s of Samuel Winterbottom (d 1986), and Gladys Winterbottom; *b* 25 Nov 1936; *Educ* Roudhay Sch Leeds; *m* 24 June 1961, Gillian Margaret; 1 s (Richard David Charles b 19 June 1966), 1 da (Fiona Louise b 14 Feb 1964); *Career* articled clerk Alexander Sagar & Co Leeds Chartered Accountants, sr auditor Price Waterhouse & Co Leeds, fin dir Chester Barrie Ltd, md Arbuthnot Latham & Co Ltd Industl Div, gp chief exec Evode Group plc, non-exec dir Electrocomponents PLC; cncl memb Br Adhesives & Sealants Assoc; FCA, FCT; *Recreations* golf, gardening; *Clubs* E India, Devonshire, Sports and Public Schs, Trentham Golf (Stoke-on-Trent), Br Pottery Mfrs Assoc; *Style*— David S Winterbottom, Esq; Walnut Tree Farm, Cowley, Gnosall, Stafford ST20 0BE (☎ 0785 822438); Evode Group plc, Commom Rd, Stafford ST16 3EH (☎ 0785 57755, fax 0785 214403, telex 36161)

WINTERBOTTOM, Derek Edward; JP (1967); s of Edward Marshall Winterbottom (d 1984), and Mabel Winterbottom, (1960); *b* 29 Sept 1923; *Educ* Archbishop Holgates GS York; *m* 4 June 1949, Daphne Floris, da of Frank Brown (d 1968); 2 s (David Roy, Michael John), 1 da (Alison Frances); *Career* CA 1949, conslt Barron & Barron York 1986 (ptnr 1953-); dep chm York Bench, sec Yorks Bldgs Preservation Tst Ltd; tres: York Georgian Soc, Fairfax House York; FCA; *Recreations* golf, skiing; *Style*— Derek E Winterbottom, Esq, JP; Skelton Croft, Skelton, York (☎ 0904 470 321); Barron & Barron, Bathurst House, Micklegate, York, YO1 2HN (☎ 0904 628 551)

WINTERBOTTOM, Hon Dudley Walter Gordon; 2 s of Baron Winterbottom (Life Peer), and his 2 w, Ira Munk; *b* 25 June 1946; *Educ* Charterhouse, Univ of Kent at Canterbury, Wolfson Coll Oxford; *m* 1, 1978 (m dis 1991), Mirjana; 1 s (Thomas b 1989), 1 da (Olga b 1987); m 2, Lauren, *née* Sproule; *Career* co dir; sec Chelsea Arts Club; *Recreations* children; *Style*— The Hon Dudley Winterbottom; 27 Coleherne Court, London SW5 0DL (☎ 071 835 1117)

WINTERBOTTOM, Hon Graham Anthony; 3 s of Baron Winterbottom (Life Peer), and his 2 w, Ira Munk; *b* 23 June 1948; *Educ* Charterhouse, RNC; *m* 1984, Caroline Joy, o da of Guy Bodgard Webster, of Cranbrook, Toddington, Beds; *Style*— The Hon Graham Winterbottom; 140 Bishops Road, London SW6

WINTERBOTTOM, Baron (Life Peer UK 1965), of Clopton, Co Northampton; Ian Winterbottom; s of George Harold Winterbottom, JP (d 1934, High Sheriff Northants 1908, lord of the manor and patron of livings of Horton, Hackleton and Piddington), and his 2 w, Georgina, da of Rev Ian McLeod, of Skye; *b* 6 April 1913; *Educ* Charterhouse, Clare Coll Cambridge; *m* 1, 1939 (m dis 1944), Rosemary Mills; 1 s (Hon John b 30 Sept 1940); m 2, 1944, Ira (Irene Eva), da of Dr Walter Munk, of Mount Carmel, Haifa; 2 s Hon Dudley Walter Gordon b 26 June 1946, Hon Graham Anthony b 23 June 1948), 1 da (Hon Caroline Margaret Alyson b 9 Dec 1950); *Career* serv RHG 1944-46, NW Europe, Capt 1945; sits as SDP peer in House of Lords; private asst to regnl cmmr Hamburg (Sir Vaughan Berry) 1946-49, private sec to min Civil Aviation 1949, MP (Lab) Nottingham Centl 1950-55, parly under-sec MOD (RN) 1966-67, parly sec Min of Public Bldg and Works 1967-68, parly under-sec (RAF) MOD 1968-70, oppn spokesman: Def 1970-74, Trade and Indust 1976-78; lord-in-waiting to HM The Queen 1974-78 (govt whip), resigned 1978; fndr memb SDP 1981; memb: House of Lords All Pty Def Study Gp, Parly and Scientific Ctee, Cwlth Parly Assoc; chm: Venesta Int 1972-74, Centurion Housing Assoc 1980-, Collins Aircraft Co 1980-, Dynavest Ltd 1982-, Anglo Global Ltd 1983-; conslt C Z Scientific Instruments Ltd 1980-; *Recreations* music, ornithology; *Clubs* Athenaeum; *Style*— The Rt Hon the Lord Winterbottom; Lower Farm, Fosbury, Marlborough, Wilts SN8 3NJ (☎ (026489) 269)

WINTERBOTTOM, Hon John; el s of Baron Winterbottom (Life Peer) and his 1 w, Rosemary Mills; *b* 30 Sept 1940; *Educ* Charterhouse, Clare Coll Cambridge; *m* Sheila Marie Evershed; 1 s; *Style*— The Hon John Winterbottom; 20 Pantile Rd, Oatlands Village, Weybridge, Surrey KT13 9PY (☎ 0932 840393)

WINTERBOTTOM, Dr Michael; s of Allan Winterbottom (d 1982), of East Budleigh, Devon, and Kathleen Mary Winterbottom (d 1990); *b* 22 Sept 1934; *Educ* Dulwich, Pembroke Coll Oxford (BA, MA, D Phil); *m* 1, 31 Aug 1963 (m dis 1983), Helen, da of Harry Spencer (d 1977), of Willenhall, Staffs; m 2, Nicolette Janet Streatfeild Bergel, da of Henry Shorland Gervis (d 1968), of Sherborne; 2 s (Peter, Jonathan); *Career* lectr in Latin and Greek UCL 1962-67, fell and tutor in classics Worcester Coll Oxford 1967- (reader in classical languages 1990-); Dr hc Besanfon 1985; *Books* Quintilian (ed 1970), Ancient Literary Criticism (with DA Russell, 1972), Three Lives of English Saints (1972), The Elder Seneca (ed and translated, 1974), Tacitus, Opera Minora (ed with R M Ogilvie, 1975), Gildas (ed and translated 1978), Roman Declamation (1980), The Minor Declamations Ascribed to Quintilian (ed with commentary, 1984), Sopatros the Rhetor (with D C Innes 1988); *Recreations* hill walking, travel; *Style*— Dr Michael Winterbottom; 172 Walton St, Oxford, OX1 2HD (☎ 0865 515727); Worcester College, Oxford OX1 2HB (☎ 0865 278300)

WINTERBOTTOM, Sir Walter; CBE (1972, OBE 1963); s of James Winterbottom; *b* 31 March 1913; *Educ* Chester Coll of Educn, Carnegie Coll of Physical Educn; *m* 1942, Ann Richards; 1 s, 2 da; *Career* dir of coaching and mangr England Team FA 1946-62; gen sec Central Cncl Physical Educn 1963-72, dir Sports Cncl 1965-78; kt 1978; *Style*— Sir Walter Winterbottom, CBE; 15 Orchard Gdns, Cranleigh, Surrey (☎ 0483 271593)

WINTERFLOOD, Brian Martin; s of Thomas George Winterflood (d 1978), of Slough, Bucks, and Doris Maud, *née* Waddington; *Educ* Frays Coll Uxbridge Middx; *m* 10 Oct 1966, Doreen Stella, da of Albert Frederick McCartney, of London; 2 s (Guy b 2 April 1970, Mark b 8 March 1973), 1 da (Sarah b 9 July 1974); *Career* Nat Serv 1955-57; Greener Dreyfus & Co 1953-57; Bisgood Bishop & Co: joined 1957, ptnr 1967, dir 1971 (Co inc), md 1981 (Co taken over by Co NatWest Investmt Bank 1986), md market making 1986, exec dir Co NatWest Securities 1986-88, fndr and md Winterflood Securities 1988, exec dir Union Discount Co of London plc 1991-; memb Stock Exchange 1966; vice-pres REMEDI (Rehabilitation and Med Res Tst), jt chm USM initiative for The Prince's Youth Business Tst; *Recreations* family, work, travel; *Clubs* IOD; *Style*— Brian Winterflood, Esq; 5 Church Hill, Wimbledon, London SW19 7BN (☎ 081 946 4052); Winterflood Securities Ltd, Knollys House, 47 Mark Lane, London EC3R 7QH (☎ 071 621 0004, fax 071 623 9482)

WINTERS, Prof Leonard Alan; s of Geoffrey Walter Horace Winters, of Ipswich, and Christine Agnes, *née* Ive; *b* 8 April 1950; *Educ* Chingford Co HS, Univ of Bristol (BSc), Univ of Cambridge (MA, PhD); *m* 3 Aug 1971, Margaret Elizabeth (Meg), da of Leonard Clayden John Griffin, of Oxford; 2 da (Victoria b 1972, Catherine b 1973); *Career* jr res offr and res offr Dept of Applied Econs Univ of Cambridge 1971-80, lectr in econs Univ of Bristol 1980-86, economist The World Bank 1983-85, prof of econs Univ of Wales Bangor 1986-90, Univ of Birmingham 1990-; former chm English Folk Dance and Song Soc, co-dir res prog Centre for Econ Policy Res, vice pres Br Assoc for the Advancement of Sci section F; *Books* An Econometric Model of The Export Sector: The Determinants of British Exports and Their Prices 1954- (1981), International Economics (1985), Europes Domestic Market (1988); *Recreations* folk music, walking; *Style*— Prof Alan L Winters; Dept of Economics, University of Birmingham, Birmingham B15 2TT, (☎ 021 414 6641)

WINTERSGILL, Matthew William; s of Harold Heap Wintersgill (d 1973), of Bedford, and Patricia, *née* Gregory; *b* 12 July 1949; *Educ* Stratton Sch Beds, Canterbury Sch of Architecture; *m* 16 Sept 1978, Sara Neill, da of Gerald Bradley (d 1970), of London; *Career* architect; Powell and Moya 1973-78 (incl: Cripps Bldg project for Queen's Coll Cambridge, Sch for Advanced Architectural Studies Bristol, Nat West Bank Devpt Shaftesbury Ave London), Thompstone Harris Design Assocs 1978-80, ptnr Thompston Wintersgill Faulkner 1980-; work projects for: Bowater Corp, BP Oil Int, The Sci Museum, Reuters, Prudential Assurance Co, IVECO Ford Truck Ltd, The PO, Nat West Bank, Rank Leisure, Nationwide Anglia Building Society, Prudential Portfolio Managers Ltd; memb W End Soc of Architects; registered memb ARCUK 1974, memb RIBA 1975; *Recreations* drawing, swimming, travel, walking; *Style*— Matthew Wintersgill, Esq; Thompstone Wintersgill Faulkner, 7-11 Lexington St, London W1R 4BU (☎ 071 734 8671, fax 071 434 1801, telex 21879 TWF)

WINTERSGILL, Dr William; s of Fred Wintersgill (d 1982), of School House, Darton, Barnsley, and Mary, Torkington (d 1982); *b* 20 Dec 1922; *Educ* Barnsley Holgate GS, Leeds Univ Med Sch (MB ChB); *m* 29 March 1952, Iris May, da of William Henry Holland (d 1971), of Swedish Bungalow, Rawcliffe, Goole, Yorks; 3 da (Anne b 1953, Jane b 1956, Billie b 1964); *Career* 2 Lt Yorks and Lancs Regt 1944-46; princ in gen practice Smith 1950-66, regnl med offr Miny of Health DHSS 1967-70; DHSS HQ: sr med offr 1970-72, princ med offr 1972-76, sr princ med offr 1976-83; York Health Authy: specialist community med 1983-87, med policy advsr 1987-88; memb York Med Soc, vice chm Age Concern York, fndr chm Br Assoc of Community Physicains; FFCM 1983, MRCGP 1976; *Recreations* gardening, bridge, old buildings, opera, antiques; *Style*— Dr William Wintersgill; Chandlers Cottage, Flawith, Alne, York (☎ 034 73 310)

WINTERSON, Jeanette; *b* 27 Aug 1959; *Educ* Accrington Girls' HS, St Catherine's Coll Oxford (BA); *Career* author; *Books* Oranges Are Not the Only Fruit (1985, BBC TV adaptation 1990), The Passion (1987), Sexing The Cherry (1989); winner: Whitbread First Novel award 1985, John Llewelyn Rhys prize 1987, Commonwealth Writers' award 1988, E M Forster award (American Acad of Arts and Letters) 1989, Golden Gate San Francisco Int Film Festival 1990, Best Drama Euro TV Festival 1990, FIPA D'Argent Cannes 1991; *Recreations* I try to live my life in one piece, so work is recreation and recreations are also work; *Style*— Ms Jeanette Winterson; Peters Frazer and Dunlop Ltd, The Chambers, Chelsea Harbour, Lots Road, London SW10 0XF (☎ 071 376 7676)

WINTERTON, (Jane) Ann; MP (C) Congleton 1983-; da of Joseph Robert and Ellen Jane Hodgson, of Sutton Coldfield; *b* 6 March 1941; *Educ* Erdington GS for Girls; *m* 1960, Nicholas Raymond Winterton ((C) MP, Macclesfield), *qv*, s of Norman H Winterton (d 1971), of Lysways House, Longdon Green, Staffs; 2 s, 1 da; *Career* memb Agric Select Ctee 1987-, jt master S Staffs Hunt 1959-64, memb W Midlands Cons Women's Advsy Ctee 1969-71; *Style*— Mrs Nicholas Winterton, MP; Whitehall Farm, Mow Lane, Newbold Astbury, Congleton, Cheshire

WINTERTON, Nicholas Raymond; MP (C) Macclesfield 1971-; s of Norman H Winterton (d 1971), of Lysways House, Longdon Green, Staffs; *b* 31 March 1938; *Educ* Rugby; *m* 1960, Jane Ann, *qv*, da of J R Hodgson of Sutton Coldfield; 2 s, 1 da; *Career* Nat Serv 2 Lt 14/20 King's Hussars 1957-59; sales and gen mangr Stevens and Hodgson Ltd 1960-80; CC Warwickshire 1967-1972 (dep chm County Educn Ctee 1970-72, chm Co Youth Serv Sub Ctee 1969-72); contested (C) Newcastle-under-Lyme 1969 (by-election) and 1970; Parly advsr to: Emerson International Ltd, Baird Textile Hldgs Ltd, Construction Plant Hire Assoc, Paper and Bd Indust Fedn Br Paper Machinery Makers Assoc; non exec dir Bridgewater Paper co Ltd; chm Br-Namibian Parly Gp; jt vice chm: Anglo-Danish and Anglo-Swedish Parly Groups; sec Anglo-Austrian Parly Gp; treas: Br Bahamas Parly Gp, Br-Taiwan Parly Gp; vice chm: Br-SA Parly Gp 1979-90, UK Falkland Islands Gp; memb Select Ctees: Social Servs 1979-90, Standing Orders 1981-, Health 1991-; memb House of Commons Chairman's Panel; memb Exec Ctee Anglo-Austrian Soc; Freeman City of London, Liveryman Worshipful Co of Weavers; *Style*— Nicholas Winterton, Esq, MP; Whitehall Farm, Mow Lane, Newbold Astbury, Congleton, Cheshire

WINTERTON, 7 Earl (I 1766); Robert Chad Turnour; also Baron Winterton (I 1761) and Viscount Turnour (I 1766); s of Cecil Turnour (gs of Rev Hon Augustus Turnour, 3 s of 2 Earl Winterton); suc 3 cous once removed, 6 Earl, 1962, but has not yet established right to his Peerages; *b* 13 Sept 1915; *Educ* Nutana Coll; *m* 1, 1941, Kathleen Ella (d 1969), da of D B Whyte, of Saskatoon, Saskatchewan, Canada; m 2, 1971, Marion, da of Arthur Phillips; *Heir* nephew, (Donald) David Turnour, *qv*; *Career* Flt Sgt RCAF, serv WWII and Sardinia 1957-58; *Style*— The Rt Hon Earl Winterton; 1326 55th St, Delta, British Columbia, Canada

WINTOUR, Charles Vere; CBE (1980, MBE (Mil) 1945); s of Maj-Gen F G Wintour, CB, CBE (d 1948), of Broadstone, and Alice Jane Blanche, *née* Foster (d 1977); *b* 18 May 1917; *Educ* Oundle, Peterhouse Cambridge (BA, MA); *m* 1, 1940 (m dis 1979), Eleanor Trego, er da of Prof RJ Baker; 3 s (Gerald Jackson b 1940 (decd), James Charles b 1948, Patrick Walter b 1956), 2 da (Anna, Hilary Nora); m 2, 9 Nov 1979, Audrey Cecilia, da of Frederick George Smith, former w of WA Slaughter; *Career* Royal Norfolk Regt 1940, GSO 2 COSSAC 1944, GSO 2 SHAEF 1945 (despatches); joined Evening Standard 1946 (political ed 1952, dep ed 1959-76 and 1978-80), asst ed Sunday Express 1952-54, managing ed Daily Express 1957-59; ed: Sunday Express Magazine 1981-82, UK Press Gazette 1985-86; dir: Evening Standard Co Ltd 1959-82, Express (formerly Beaverbrook Newspapers Ltd 1964-82, TV-am (News) Ltd 1982-84, Wintour Pubns 1984-85; ombudsman Sunday Times 1990; memb Press Cncl 1978-79; Croix de Guerre: France 1945, Belgium 1945; Bronze Star (US) 1945; *Books* Pressures on the Press (1972), Rise and Fall of Fleet Street (1989); *Recreations* theatre going; *Clubs* Garrick; *Style*— Charles Wintour, Esq, CBE; 60 East Hatch, Tisbury, Wilts SP3 6PH

WINWOOD, Dr Robert Sidney; s of Robert Winwood, of Poole, Dorset, and Mary Theodore, *née* Watson; *b* 31 Dec 1932; *Educ* Univ of London (MB BS); *m* 28 Aug 1954, June Margaret, da of Leslie Frank Sansom, of Broadstone, Dorset; 3 s (Robert Julian b 3 June 1958, Paul John b 9 Aug 1971, Andrew Leslie b 15 June 1969); *Career* Capt and jr med specialist RAMC 1958-62; conslt physician and cardiologist; memb:

Ramblers' Assoc, Nat Tst, CPRE, English Heritage, BMA 1957, Hunterian Soc 1964; FRCP; *Books* Essentials of Clinical Diagnosis in Cardiology (1981), current textbooks of Anatomy and Physiology, Materia Medica and Medicine for Nurses, chapters in other med textbooks; *Recreations* music, photography, running, hill walking; *Clubs* Barbican Health and Fitness Centre; *Style*— Dr Robert Winwood; St Bart's Hospital, London EC1A 7BE; Holly House Hospital, Buckhurst Hill, Essex (☎ 081 505 3311); Roding Hospital, Ilford, Essex (☎ 081 551 1100)

WISBECH, Archdeacon of; *see*: Fleming, Ven David

WISDOM, Dr Anthony Rodwell; s of Col George E C Wisdom, CMG (d 1958), of Edenbridge, Kent, and Dorothea, *née* Rodwell (d 1978); *b* 30 Sept 1930; *Educ* Epsom Coll, London Hosp Med Coll, Univ of London; *m* 1, 25 Feb 1956 (m dis 1966), Charlotte Hartstein; 3 s (Oliver b 1958, Michael b 1960, Julian b1961), 1 da (Lucy b 1956); m 2, 14 Aug 1974, Vaneska, da of Col R Fleury of Rio de Janeiro, Brazil; *Career* Nat Serv RN med branch 1955-57; jr dr 1954-64, conslt physician 1964-; MSSVD, fell Hunterian Soc; *Books* Atlas of Sexually Transmitted Diseases (1 edn 1973, 2 edn 1989); *Recreations* rowing, travelling, food especially foreign; *Clubs* Leander, Tideway Scullers, London Rowing; *Style*— Dr Anthony Wisdom; 24 St Albans Rd, London NW5 (☎ 071 482 2442); Newham Gen Hosp, London E13 (☎ 071 476 1400); Oldchurch Hospital, Romford, Essex (☎ 0708 746090)

WISDOM, Julia Mary; da of Dennis Wisdom (d 1985), and Rosemary Jean, *née* Cutler; *b* 24 Sept 1958; *Educ* Cranbourne Chase, Bryanston, King's Coll London (BA); *m* 15 Sept 1984, John Andrew Paul (Clint) Twist, s of Clinton Twist, of Westerkirk, Dumfriesshire; *Career* commissioning ed of crime fiction Victor Gollancz Ltd; memb CWA 1987; *Recreations* music, travel, reading; *Style*— Ms Julia Wisdom; Victor Gollancz Ltd, 14 Henrietta St, London WC2 (☎ 071 836 2003)

WISE, Gp Capt Adam Nugent; LVO (1983), MBE (1976); s of Lt-Col (Alfred) Roy Wise, MBE, TD (d 1974), and Cassandra Noel Wise (d 1982); *b* 1 Aug 1943; *Educ* Repton, RAF Coll Cranwell, Univ of London (BA); *m* 1983, Jill Amabel, da of (Cyril) Geoffrey Marmaduke Alington, of Lincs (d 1987); *Career* cmmnd 1965 RAF; served ME, Far East, Germany; ADC to Cdr FEAF 1970-71, exchange pilot Federal German Air Force 1972-75; Equerry to HM The Queen 1980-83, OC Univ of London Air Sqdn 1983-86, private sec to TRH The Duke and Duchess of York and The Prince Edward 1983-87; HQ Univ Air Sqdn Cranwell 1988-; *Recreations* sailing, riding; *Clubs* RAF, Royal Ocean Racing; *Style*— Gp Capt Adam Wise, LVO, MBE; c/o C Hoare & Co, 32 Lowndes St, London SW1

WISE, Hon Christopher John Clayton; s and h of 2 Baron Wise; *b* 19 March 1949; *Educ* Norwich Sch, Southampton Univ; *Style*— The Hon Christopher Wise

WISE, Prof Douglass; OBE (1981); s of Horace Watson Wise, BEM (d 1964), of Whitby, Yorks, and Doris Wise; *b* 6 Nov 1927; *Educ* King's Coll Newcastle, Univ of Durham (BArch, Dip TP); *m* 6 March 1959 (m dis 1984), Yvonne Jeannine, da of Emile Czeiler (d 1958), of Newcastle upon Tyne; 1 s ((Matthew) Gregory b 15 May 1966), 1 da (Clare Alexandra b 19 Nov 1964); *Career* Lt RE Mil Survey 1953-55; architect; prof of architecture Univ of Newcastle 1968-75, dir Inst of Advanced Architectural Studies Univ of York 1975; fndr Douglass Wise & Ptnrs Architects Newcastle upon Tyne 1959-; vice chm N Housing Gp 1973-75, govr Bldg Centre Tst 1976-, tstee Interbuild Gp 1986-; FRIBA (cncl memb 1979-81); *Recreations* painting, natural history; *Style*— Prof Douglass Wise, OBE; Flat No 3, Kings Manor, York YO1 2EW (☎ 0904 433987); Institute of Advanced Architectural Studies, University of York, Kings Manor, York YO1 2EP (☎ 0904 433989)

WISE, Ernie; *see*: Wiseman, Ernest

WISE, Hillier Bernard Alexander; s of Emanuel Wise (d 1979), and Minnie, *née* Berg (d 1983); *b* 9 Aug 1928; *Educ* Kilburn GS, Bartlett Sch of Architecture UCL, Birbeck Coll London (BA), Westminster Coll Oxford (PGCE), St Catherine's Coll Oxford (MLitt); *Career* various teaching posts in primary, secdy and further educn; admin offr AEB 1962, pt/t extra-mural tutor in history of art Univ of London 1964-, former special lectr Wallace Collection London, summer sch tutor Open Univ, guest lectr Swans Hellenic Art Treasures Tours, sr lectr Willesden Coll of Technol 1975-, convocation senator in arts Univ of London, vice pres Univ of London Graduates Soc; memb: Nat Art Collections Fund, Friend of Tate Gallery and Royal Acad of Arts, Soc of Architectural Historians of GB, Assoc of Art Historians, History of Educn Soc, Oxford Univ Boat Club Tst; Freeman City of London 1971, Liveryman Worshipful Co of Painter-Stainers 1971; inter RIBA 1950, assoc London Coll of Music 1950; *Recreations* music (piano, organ, opera, ballet, concerts), travel, looking at architecture; *Clubs* United Oxford and Cambridge Univ; *Style*— Hillier Wise, Esq; 8 Dicey Ave, Cricklewood, London NW2 6AT (☎ 081 452 1433); Willesden Coll of Technol, Denzil Rd, London NW10 2XD (☎ 081 452 6509)

WISE, 2 Baron (UK 1951); John Clayton Wise; s of 1 Baron Wise, DL (d 1968); *b* 11 June 1923; *m* 1946, Margaret, da of Frederick Snead; 2 s; *Heir* s, Hon Christopher Wise; *Career* farmer; *Style*— The Rt Hon Lord Wise; Martlets, Blakeney, Norfolk NR25 7NP

WISE, Maj Michael Henry; s of Henry Wise (d 1982), and Edith Mae (d 1990), *née* Parsons; *b* 9 Sept 1927; *Educ* Nautical Coll Pangbourne; *m* 5 Jan 1952, Diane, da of Sydney Cathery; 2 da (Amanda b 1955, Nicola b 1957); *Career* cmmnd 2 Lt Grenadier Gds 1946, Lt 1948, Maj 1961; DAAG HQ Southern Cmd 1969-70, GSO 2 (SO) to UKNMR SHAPE 1971-74, GSO 2 (Home Def) HQ LONDIST 1974-82, ret 1982; treas Household Div Funds 1982, sec and treas Guards Chapel; treas: Guards Magazine, Guards Saddle Club, Guards CC; memb Lloyd's 1987; *Recreations* yachting, fishing, riding; *Clubs* Household Div Yacht; *Style*— Maj Michael Wise; Cornerways, 36 Sea Lane, Middleton-on-Sea, West Sussex PO22 7RT (☎ 0243 582510); Treasurer Household Division Funds, Wellington Barracks, Birdcage Walk, London SW1E 6HQ (☎ 071 414 3253/3459)

WISE, Prof Michael John; CBE (1979), MC (1945); s of Harry Cuthbert Wise (d 1954), of Birmingham, and Sarah Evelyn, *née* Lawton (d 1962); *b* 17 Aug 1918; *Educ* Saltley GS Birmingham, Univ of Birmingham (BA, DipEd, PhD); *m* 4 May 1942, Barbara Mary, da of C L Hodgetts (d 1951), of Wolverhampton; 1 s (John Charles Michael b 6 Sept 1949), 1 da ((Barbara) Janet (Mrs Meyer) b 1 June 1946); *Career* cmmnd RA 1941, serv Middle E 1942-44, Maj 1944, The Northamptonshire Regt 1944-46, serv Italy 1944-46; lectr in geography Univ of Birmingham 1946-51; LSE: lectr in geography 1951-54, Sir Ernest Cassel reader in econ geography 1954-58, prof of geography 1958-83, pro dir 1983-85; Erskine fell Univ of Canterbury NZ 1970; chm: departmental ctee of inquiry into statutory smallholdings Miny of Agric 1964-68, landscape advsy ctee Dept of Tport 1981-90 (memb 1971-90); pres: Inst of Br Geographers 1974, Geographical Assoc 1976-77, Int Geographical Union 1976-80, Royal Geographical Soc 1980-82; memb Social Sci Res Cncl 1976-82, chm of govrs Birkbeck Coll London 1983-89; hon fell LSE 1988, fell Birkbeck Coll London 1990; Fndrs Medal Royal Geographical Soc 1977; Hon DUniv Open Univ 1978, Hon DSc Birmingham 1982, Lauréat d'Honneur Int Geographical Union (1984); FRGS, FRSA, fell Inst Environmental Sci; Alexander Körösi Csoma Medal Hungarian Geographical Soc 1980, Tokyo Geographical Soc Medal 1981, Hon Memb Geographical Socs of Paris, Poland, USSR and Mexico; *Books* Birmingham and its Regional Setting (hon, ed 1950); Consultant: An Atlas of World Resources (1979), The Great Geographical Atlas (1982), Ordnance Survey Atlas of Gr Britain (1982); *Recreations* gardening, music, watching cricket; *Clubs* Athenaeum, Geographical; *Style*— Prof Michael Wise, CBE, MC; 45 Oakleigh Ave, Whetstone, London N20 9JE (☎ 081 445 6057); London Sch of Econs, Houghton St, Aldwych, London WC2A 2AE (☎ 071 405 7686)

WISE, Dr Peter Hermann; s of James Wise, of Adelaide, Aust, and Matilda, *née* Benedikt; *b* 20 April 1937; *Educ* St Peter's Coll Adelaide, Univ of Adelaide (MB BS), Univ of London (PhD); *m* 19 Nov 1964, Carole Margaret, da of Otto Kornitzer (d 1983); 2 s (Nicholas Simon, Daniel Jeremy); *Career* dir of endocrinology Royal Adelaide Hosp Aust 1969-75, assoc prof of med Flinders Univ of S Aust 1976-79, conslt physician Charing Cross Hosp London 1979-; ctee memb: Br Diabetic Assoc, Ethical Res Ctee, RCGP; FRACP 1971, FRCP 1978; *Books* Essential Endocrinology (1983), Knowing About Diabetes (1983), Atlas of Endocrinology (1986); *Recreations* tennis, music; *Style*— Dr Peter Wise; Dept of Endocrinology, Charing Cross Hosp, London W6 8RF (☎ 081 846 1065)

WISE, Very Rev the Dean of Peterborough Randolph George; VRD; s of George Wise (d 1971), and Agnes Lucy Wise (d 1971); *b* 20 Jan 1925; *Educ* St Olave's and St Saviour's GS, The Queen's Coll Oxford; *m* 27 March 1951, Hazel Hebe, da of Ronald Murray Simpson (d 1960); 4 da (Catherine, Ruth, Jane, Nicola); *Career* RNVR 1943-47; asst curate: Lady Margaret Walworth 1951-53, Stocksbridge Sheffield 1953-55; vicar: Lady Margaret Walworth 1955-60, Stockbridge Sheffield 1960-66, industl chaplain 1966-76, rector Notting Hill London 1976-81, dean of Peterborough 1981-; memb Worshipful Co of Plaisterers'; MBIM; *Recreations* music, sculling; *Clubs* Naval; *Style*— The Very Rev the Dean of Peterborough; The Deanery, Peterborough PE1 1XS (☎ 0733 62780)

WISE, Dr Richard; s of James Wise, of Eastbourne, and Joan, *née* Richards; *b* 7 July 1942; *Educ* Burnage HS, Univ of Manchester (MB ChB, MD); *m* 16 Feb 1979, Dr Jane Marion Symonds, da of R C Symonds, of Sedbergh; 1 s (Peter Richard b and d 1989), 1 da (Katherin b July 1972); *Career* conslt and dir W Midlands Antibiotic Res Laboratory Dudley Rd Hosp Birmingham 1974-, reader in clinical microbiology Univ of Birmingham 1985-, author papers and books on antibiotic therapy; FRCPath; *Recreations* viticulture; *Style*— Dr Richard Wise; Dept of Medical Microbiology, Dudley Road Hosp, Birmingham B18 7QH (☎ 021 554 3801)

WISEMAN, Carol Mary; *b* 20 Nov 1942; *Educ* Southport HS, Lady Margaret Hall Oxford (MA); *Career* BBC TV 1965-79: res, dir Schools TV, asst dir Drama; Freelance Film TV drama dir 1979-; prodns incl: Coming Out (play, BBC) 1979, A Question of Guilt (serial, BBC) 1980, Bognor-Deadline (serial, Thames) 1981, Pictures (serial, Central) 1982, Big Deal (series, BBC) 1983-84, Dog Ends (play) 1985, Dear Box Number (play) 1985, A Matter of Will (play) 1985, Cats Eyes (series, TVS) 1986, A Little Princess (BAFTA award for Best Childrens Drama) 1987, Somewhere to Run (Prix Europa) 1988, May Wine (film, Canal Plus), 1989, Finding Sarah (play C4) 1990, Does This Mean We're Married (film, Canal Plus) 1990, Love Hurts (film serial, BBC) 1991; *Style*— Ms Carol Wiseman

WISEMAN, David John; s of James Wiseman (d 1982), and Marjorie, *née* Ward; *b* 25 March 1944; *Educ* Britannia RNC Dartmouth, RNEC Manadon Plymouth (BSc), Univ of Surrey (MSc); *Career* RN 1962-74, Lt 1967-74; asst sec DTI 1980-87 (princ 1974-80), co dir Kingsway Rowland 1987-89, md Rowland Public Affrs 1988-, md The Rowland Co Brussels 1990-; FIEE, CEng, MBIM; *Recreations* travel, gardening, riding, music; *Clubs* Athenaeum; *Style*— David Wiseman, Esq; Cedar Ct, Haslemere, Surrey GU27 2BA; The Rowland Co, 67 Whitfield Street, London W1P 5RL

WISEMAN, Ernest (Ernie Wise); OBE (1976); s of Harry Wiseman, and Connie, *née* Wright; *b* 27 Nov 1925; *Educ* Cncl Sch; *m* 1953, Doreen, da of Henry James William Blyth; *Career* radio, variety, TV and film actor, long running comedy partnership with the late Eric Morecambe; SFTA Awards: 1963, 1971, 1972, 1973; BAFTA award Light Entertainment TV 1973, Silver Heart Variety Club 1964 and 1976, Water Rats 1970, Radio Indust 1971 and 1972, Sun Newspaper 1973; Royal Command Performances: 1955, 1964, 1966, 1968 and 1984; shows incl: Too Close for Comfort (TV Los Angeles 1986), The Mystery of Edwin Drood (Savoy Theatre 1987), Run for your Wife (Criterion Theatre 1988); TV incl: NZ Telethon 1989 and 1990, This is Your Life 1990; *Books* with Eric Morecambe: Eric and Ernie - an autobiography of Morecambe and Wise (1973), Scripts of Morecambe and Wise (1974), Morecambe and Wise Special (1977), There's No Answer to That (1981); *Recreations* boating, tennis, swimming; *Clubs* St James's, White Elephant, Ritz, Casino; *Style*— Ernie Wise, Esq, OBE; Gable End, 22 Dorney Reach Road, Dorney Reach Maidenhead, Berks SL6 0DX

WISEMAN, Sir John William; 11 Bt (E 1628), of Canfield Hall, Essex; s of Sir William Wiseman, 10 Bt, CB, CMG (d 1962), and his 3 w, Joan, Lady Wiseman, *qv*; *b* 16 March 1957; *Educ* Millfield, Hartford Univ Conn USA; *m* 1980, Nancy, da of Casimer Zyla, of New Britain, Conn, USA; 1 da (Elizabeth b 1983); *Heir* fifth cous, Thomas Alan Wiseman b 8 July 1921; *Style*— Sir John Wiseman, Bt; 395 North Rd, Sudbury, Mass 01776, USA

WISEMAN, Kenneth John; s of Stephen Wiseman, of 2 Cranston Park Ave, Upminster, Essex, and Lilian Wiseman; *b* 17 Oct 1945; *Educ* Plaistow GS, NE London Poly (HNC); *m* 2, 13 April 1989, Doreen, da of John Harris (decd); *Career* mktg dir Carless Solvents Ltd 1981, md Carless Refining and Marketing Ltd 1986, chm CRMBV Rotterdam 1986, dir Repsol (UK) Ltd 1990; MBIM, FInstPet, FInstM; *Recreations* gardening, DIY, skiing, tennis, soccer, West Ham Utd FC; *Style*— Kenneth Wiseman, Esq; 72 Castellan Ave, Gidea Park, Essex RM2 6ED (telex 261071, car 0860 388 450)

WISEMAN, Dr Martin Jeremy; s of Leslie Wiseman, of Faversham, Kent, and Sonia Wiseman, *née* Linder; *b* 18 April 1953; *Educ* King's Sch Canterbury, Guy's Hosp Med Sch (MRCP); *m* 5 May 1979, Jane Carol, da of Dennis Bannister, of Bournemouth, Dorset; 1 s (Daniel b 1987), 2 da (Jessica b 1982, Anna b 1985); *Career* res fell Metabolic Unit Guys Hosp 1981-86, head of Nutrition Unit Dept of Health 1986-; author of publications on diabetes nutrition and kidney disease; memb: Br Diabetic Assoc, Nutrition Soc; *Recreations* gastronomy, travel, family, Times crossword; *Style*— Dr Martin Wiseman; Department of Health, London SE1 (☎ 071 972 4019)

WISEMAN, Prof (Timothy) Peter; s of Stephen Wiseman (d 1971), of Manchester, and Winifred Agnes Wiseman; *b* 3 Feb 1940; *Educ* Manchester GS, Balliol Coll Oxford (MA, DPhil); *m* 15 Sept 1962, (Doreen) Anne, da of Harold Williams, of Atherton, Lancs; *Career* reader in Roman history Univ of Leicester 1973-76 (lectr in classics 1963-73), visiting prof of classics Univ of Toronto 1970-71, prof of classics Univ of Exeter 1977-; DLitt Durham 1988; FSA 1977, FBA 1986; *Books* Catullan Questions (1969), New Men in the Roman Senate (1971), Cinna the Poet (1974), Clio's Cosmetics (1979), Catullus and His World (1985), Roman Studies (1987); *Style*— Prof Peter Wiseman; Dept of Classics, The University, Exeter EX4 4QH (☎ 0392 264 201, fax 0392 263 108, telex 42894 EXUNIV G)

WISEMAN, Thomas Alan; s of Thomas Edward Wiseman (d 1959, 5 in descent from Sir Thomas Wiseman, 6 Bt), and Anna Louisa, *née* Allen; hp to fifth cous, Sir John Wiseman, 11 Bt; *b* 8 July 1921; *Educ* Gravesend Co Sch for Boys; *m* 11 Dec 1946, Hildemarie, da of Gustav Domnik, of Allenstein, formerly E Prussia; 1 s (Thomas b 1947), 1 da (Susan b 1949); *Career* Army 1941-46, Staff Quartermaster Sgt RAOC

1946-48; English corr and Eng/German interpreter in Brussels 1949-75, ships agent 1975-86, admin offr Forest Prods Terminal Northfleet Terminal Ltd, ret WEF 1986; *Style*— Thomas Wiseman, Esq; 14 Havisham Rd, Chalk, Gravesend, Kent DA12 4UN (☎ 0474 361575)

WISH, Timothy John; s of Charles Arnold Wish (d 1938), of Sheffield, and Kathleen Mary, *née* Bingley (d 1982); *b* 22 Aug 1933; *Educ* Giggleswick Sch, Univ of Sheffield (BSc); *m* 29 March 1962, Jill Christine, da of Ferguson Bishop; 2 s (Dominic b 1963, James b 1964), 1 da (Emma b 1967); *Career* Nat Serv cmmnd Royal Signals 1955-57, TA 1957-63 (Capt); chm Abrafract Ltd 1978 (joined 1957, works mangr 1960, works dir 1962, md 1978); chm & md Abrafract Holdings Ltd 1988-; UK delegate Fédération Européenne des Fabricants de Produits Abrasifs 1977- (vice pres 1988-), memb Abrasives Industs Assoc (chm tech ctee 1970-78), govr Giggleswick Sch 1986; Freeman Worshipful Co of Cutlers in Hallamshire; *Recreations* golf; *Clubs* Sickleholme Golf (Bamford), Abbeydale Park Sport's; *Style*— T Wish, Esq; Clod Hall Farm, Eastmoor, Chesterfield, S42 7DF (☎ 024 688 2148); Abrafract Holdings Ltd, Beulah Rd, Sheffield S6 2AR (☎ 0742 348971, telex 547202 ABRA G)

WISHART, (Margaret) Ruth (Mrs R McLeod); da of John Wishart (d 1960), and Margaret Smith, *née* Mitchell (d 1989); *b* 27 Aug 1945; *Educ* Eastwood Senior Secdy Sch; *m* 16 Sept 1971, Roderick McLeod, s of Roderick McLeod; *Career* women's ed Scottish Daily Record 1973-78; asst ed: Sunday Mail 1978-82, Sunday Standard 1982-83; freelance journalist and broadcaster 1983-86, sr asst ed The Scotsman 1986-88; columnist and broadcaster 1988-; memb: Standing Cmmn on Scottish Econ, Scottish Ctee Assoc Business Sponsorship of Arts, Scottish Advsy Ctee to Br Cncl; dir: Wildcat Theatre Co, Assembly Theatre, fndr dir MAYFEST; *Recreations* theatre, concerts, galleries, curling; *Style*— Ms R Wishart; Wilson Court, Wilson St, Glasgow, Advocates Close, Edinburgh (☎ 041 552 0367); The Scotsman, North Bridge, Edinburgh (☎ 031 225 2468, fax 031 225 7302, telex 72255)

WISHEART, James Dunwoody; s of Rev James Wisheart (d 1986), of Belfast, and Ena Mary, *née* Dunwoody (d 1986); *b* 2 March 1938; *Educ* Methodist Coll Belfast, Queen's Univ Belfast (BSc, MB, MCh), Univ of Alabama; *m* 11 Sept 1965, Janet Mary, da of Cecil Walter Gibson (d 1973), of Dublin; 2 s (Michael b 1969, Andrew b 1973), 1 da (Linda b 1968); *Career* conslt cardiothoracic surgn Bristol Royal Infirmary and Royal Children's Hosp 1975-; assoc ed Thorax 1984-90; memb Methodist Church; memb: BMA, Br Cardiac Soc, Soc Cardiothoracic Surgns, Euro Assoc Cardiothoracic Surgns; FRCS, FRCSEd (memb bd cardiothoracic surgery 1982-); *Recreations* music, walking, sailing; *Style*— James Wisheart, Esq; Department of Cardiac Surgery, Bristol Royal Infirmary, Bristol BS2 8HW (☎ 0272 28 2821)

WISNER, George John; s of George Phillip Wisner, and Lillian Florence, *née* Butler; *b* 1 June 1949; *Educ* Haverstock Hill Sch, Chelsea Sch of Art; *m* 26 March 1977, Romayne Siobhan, da of Derek Dobson Wood; 2 da (Alice Willow b 29 Dec 1977, Shelley Rose b 11 Feb 1980); *Career* set designer; BBC: apprentice carpenter 1965-70, design asst 1971-74, designer 1974-80, sr TV designer 1980-; productions designed incl: Day in the Death of Joe Egg, The Gambler by Dostoevsky, The Prime of Miss Jean Brodie, The Grand Inquisitor, End Game, Macbeth, Miss Julie, numerous childrens progs; FRSA 1987; *Recreations* cycling, swimming; *Style*— George Wisner, Esq; Barton House, Blakesley, nr Towcester, Northamptonshire NN12 8RE (☎ 0327 860282); BBC Open Univ Production Centre, Room 232 Walton Hall, Milston Keynes, Bucks MK7 6BH (☎ 0908 655580, telex 826485 BBC OUPG)

WISZNIEWSKI, Adrian Ryszard; s of Witold Eugene Wiszniewski, of Renfrew, Glasgow, and Elspeth Mary, *née* Hyland; *b* 31 March 1958; *Educ* Mackintosh Sch of Architecture, Glasgow Sch of Art (BA, postgrad Dip); *m* 11 May 1985, Diane Lennox, da of Ronald Alexander Foley, of Glasgow; 1 s (Max Tristan Charles b 26 June 1987), 1 da (Holly b 21 April 1990); *Career* artist; work in painting, printmaking, ceramics, tapestry, neon, sculpture, writing, film; solo exhibitions in London, Belgium, Australia and Japan; also exhibited in several important int gp exhibitions and surveys throughout the world; Mark Rothko Scholarship 1984; *Books* For Max (1988); *Recreations* gambling; *Style*— Adrian Wiszniewski, Esq; c/o The Nigel Greenwood Gallery, 4 New Burlington St, London W1X 1FE (☎ 071 434 3795, fax 071 287 2396)

WITCHELL, Nicholas N H; s of William Joseph Henshall Witchell, and Barbara Sybil Mary, *née* MacDonald; *b* 23 Sept 1953; *Educ* Epsom Coll, Univ of Leeds (LLB); *Career* joined BBC TV News 1976; reporter NI 1979-81, reporter London 1981-83, Ireland corr 1984, presenter 6 O'Clock News 1984-89, presenter BBC Breakfast News 1989-, assoc prodr News 39 1989; *Books* The Loch Ness Story (1974, 1975, 1982 and 1989); *Style*— Nicholas Witchell, Esq; BBC TV News, BBC TV Centre, London, W12 7RJ (☎ 071 576 7200)

WITHERINGTON, Giles Somerville Gwynne; s of Iltyd Gwynne Witherington (d 1962), and Gage, *née* Spicer (d 1968); *b* 7 June 1919; *Educ* Charterhouse, Univ of Oxford (MA); *m* 1951, Rowena Ann Spencer, da of Lt-Col Hylton S Lynch, MC, TD (d 1976); 1 s, 3 da; *Career* Maj RA, N Africa and Italy 1939-46 (despatches); dep chm Reed Int plc 1976-82 (dir 1963-82), ret; chm Save The Children Fund 1982-87 (cncl memb 1980-); cncl memb Textile Conservation Centre 1984- (chm tstees 1984-); Hon LLD Univ of Birmingham 1983; *Recreations* shooting, gardening, travel; *Clubs* Arts; *Style*— Giles Witherington, Esq; Bishops, Widdington, Saffron Walden, Essex CB11 3SQ (☎ 0799 405 39)

WITHEROW, Air Cdre Marcus Spence; s of Lt-Col T M Witherow (d 1970), of Dumfries, and Florence Eileen, *née* Spence (d 1971); *b* 17 Aug 1936; *Educ* Holt Sch Dumfries; *m* 15 March 1969, Mary Craigie, da of George Henry Paulin (d 1962), of Glasgow and Hampstead; 2 s (Rupert b 1971, Dominic b 1973); *Career* RAF 1956-90; cmmnd RAF Regt 1956 (served Aden, Bahrain, Trucial Oman, Libya and Germany), Sqdn Ldr 1968, cmd 26 Sqdn RAF Regt 1968-70, graduated RAF Staff Coll 1971, Wing Cdr 1974, graduated air warfare course 1976, cmd 3 Wing RAF Regt 1976-78, Gp Capt 1978, ADC to HM The Queen 1980-82, cmd RAF Regtl Depot Cathwick 1980-82, graduated Royal Coll of Def Studies 1983, Air Cdre 1985, dir of Ground Personnel RAF 1985-87, Dir RAF Regt 1987-90, ret as Air Cdre 1990; career conslt 1991-; FBIM 1981; *Recreations* shooting, fishing, photography, natural history, gardening, conservation of nature, reading, current affairs; *Clubs* RAF; *Style*— Air Cdre Marcus Witherow; c/o Holt's, The Royal Bank of Scotland, Kirkland House, Whitehall, London SW1A 2EB

WITHERS, Georgette Lizette (Googie); AO (1980); da of Capt Edgar Clements Withers, CIE, CBE, RN (d 1951), and Lizette Catharina Wilhelmina, *née* Van Wageningen (d 1976); *b* 12 March 1917; *Educ* Fredville Park Nonnington Kent, Sch of the Holy Family London; *m* 1948, John Neil McCallum, CBE (chm & chief exec Fauna Films, Australia, also actor & prodr, as well as sometime pres Australian Film Cncl and theatre manager), s of John Neil McCallum (d 1957), of Brisbane; 1 s (Nicholas), 2 da (Joanna, Amanda); *Career* actress (as Googie Withers) since 1933, starring in 50 films including One of Our Aircraft is Missing, On Approval, It Always Rains on Sunday; plays include Deep Blue Sea, Winter Journey, Hamlet, Much Ado About Nothing, The Cherry Orchard, The Skin Game, Private Lives, The Kingfisher, The Circle, The Importance of Being Earnest, School for Scandal, Time and the Conways, The Chalk Garden; numerous tv plays including Within These Walls, Time After Time, Hotel Dulac, Northanger Abbey; Chichester Festival Theatre: Hay Fever, Ring Round The Moon; UK and Aust Tour The Cocktail Hour, USA Ace award, Best Actress TV Film "Time After Time", BAFTA award best actress 1954; best actress Sun award 1974; *Recreations* travelling, reading, interior decorating; *Clubs* Queens (Sydney); *Style*— Miss Googie Withers, AO; 1740 Pittwater Rd, Bayview, NSW 2104, Australia

WITHERS, Ian Stephen; s of Arnold Frederick Withers, of Edgbaston, Birmingham, and Vera, *née* Ridley; *b* 14 May 1946; *Educ* King Edward VI for Boys, Birmingham, Lancaster Gate Coll of Law, Coll of Commerce Liverpool; *m* 24 Nov 1973, Charlotte Gail, da of Leonard Jennings; 3 s (Nicholas Ian b 31 Oct 1974, Andrew Stephen b 15 Sept 1980, David Arnold b 25 Nov 1983), 1 da (Emily Charlotte b 27 Feb 1979); *Career* articled clerk Redfern & Co 1963-68, asst slr Messrs Lane Clutterbuck & Co 1968-71; O'Dowd & Co: asst slr 1971-72, jr ptnr 1973-75, sr ptnr 1975-85; sr ptnr Glaisyers 1985-90, ptnr Edge & Ellison 1990-; memb Law Soc; *Recreations* eating out, snooker, gardening, family; *Clubs* Birmingham, Harborne; *Style*— Ian Withers, Esq; 88 Fitz Roy Avenue, Harborne, Birmingham, West Midlands B17 8RQ (☎ 021 427 1720); Edge & Ellison, Rutland House, 148 Edmund St, Birmingham B3 2JR (☎ 021 200 2001, fax 021 200 1991)

WITHERS, Michael John; s of Harold Leslie Withers (d 1985), of Dawlish, Devon, and Kathleen Veronica, *née* Chudleigh (d 1988); *b* 15 Jan 1938; *Educ* South-West Essex Tech Sch, City Univ (Dip Tech (Engrg), BSc), Univ of Birmingham (MSc); *m* 1962, Marguerite, *née* Beckett; 1 s (Richard John b 1965), 1 da (Justine Marguerite b 1966); *Career* Radio Indust Cncl apprenticeship Cossor Ltd 1955-60, radar engr Cossor Radar 1960-63, lectr Dept of Electronic and Electrical Engrg Univ of Birmingham 1963-72, visiting prof of telecommunications Tech Inst of Aeronautics Sao Jose dos Campos Brazil 1969-70, hon princ sci offr Royal Signals and Radar Establishment Malvern 1970-72, sr systems engr Br Aerospace Stevenage 1972-77, engrg mangr Andrew Corporation Inc Fife 1977-83, mangr RF Technology Division 1983-87, md and chief exec ERA Technology Ltd 1987-; published over 50 tech papers and patents; FIEE 1983 (MIEE 1966), FEng 1990; *Recreations* photography, video and film production, cabinet-making, gardening; *Style*— Michael Withers, Esq; The Hollies, Arford Rd, Headley, Bordon, Hants GU35 8LJ (☎ 0428 712175); ERA Technology Ltd, Cleve Rd, Leatherhead, Surrey KT22 7SA (☎ 0372 374151)

WITHERS, Roy Joseph; CBE (1983); s of Joseph Withers (d 1973), and Irene Ada, *née* Jones; *b* 18 June 1924; *Educ* Tiffin Sch Kingston-upon-Thames, Trinity Coll Cambridge; *m* 20 Dec 1947, Pauline Mary Gillian, *née* Johnston; 4 s (Christopher, Stephen, Paul, Robert); *Career* sr engr ICI 1948-55, tech dir Humphreys & Glasgow 1955-63, engrg dir Davy Power Gas Corp 1963-70 (md 1970-71), chm exec Davy Powergas 1972-73; Davy Corp: md 1973-83, dep chm 1983-86, vice chm 1986-; non-exec dir Vosper Thornycroft (UK) Ltd 1990- (chm 1985-90), chm Transmark Worldwide 1987- (dep chm 1985-87); memb BOTB 1983-86, chm Overseas Projects Bd 1983-86; FEng 1983, Hon FIChemE; *Recreations* golf, painting; *Clubs* Carlton, Hampstead Golf, Bramshaw Golf; *Style*— Roy Withers Esq, CBE; Davy Corporation plc, 15 Portland Place, London W1A 4DD (☎ 071 637 2821, fax 071 637 0902, telex 22604)

WITHERSPOON, Dr (Edward) William; s of Edward William Witherspoon (d 1982), of Liverpool, and Maude Miranda, *née* Goff (d 1987); *b* 19 Dec 1925; *Educ* King Edward's Sch Birmingham, Univ of Birmingham (MB ChB), Univ of London DTM & H, RCP (Lond), RCS (Eng); *m* 10 June 1954, Jean (d 1988), da of John McKellar (d 1956); *Career* Maj RAMC 2 i/c 3 Field Ambulance, 4 RTR Suez Canal Zone and Cyprus 1953; physician (tropical diseases and clinical pharmacology); asst govt med offr Medico-Legal Dept Sydney 1958-60; med dir: Burroughs Wellcome 1960-71, ABPI Trade Mission Japan 1968, Abbott Labs 1971-77, Warner Lambert/Parke Davis 1977-82; sr med advsr Roussel Labs 1983-, chm BMA pharmaceutical physicians gp ctee 1986-; FFPM, FRSH 1971; author The Pharmaceutical Physician (BMA monograph 1989), Thalidomide - The Aftermath (Pharmaceutical Med 1988); *Recreations* Nat Tst, Nat Tst for Scotland; *Clubs* Royal Soc of Medicine, Royal Cwlth, Sloane; *Style*— Dr William Witherspoon; Brook Cottage, 4 Manor Rd, Oakley, nr Aylesbury, Bucks HP18 9QD; Roussel Laboratories Ltd, Broadwater Park, N Orbital Rd, Denham, Uxbridge, Middlesex UB9 5HP (☎ 0895 834343, fax 0895 834479)

WITHRINGTON, John Kenneth Brookes; s of Ronald Ernest Withrington, of 108 Priests Lane, Brentwood, Essex CM15 8HN, and Eileen Gladys, *née* Green; *b* 23 Feb 1957; *Educ* Coopers Co Sch, Jesus Coll Cambridge (BA), Univ of Leicester (MA), Univ of York; *Career* int div National Westminster Bank 1980-83 (PA to Divnl Fin Controller 1983), pt/time lectr Univ of York 1984-87, hon lectr and admin in office of sec Univ of Lancaster 1987-; sec (local) Assoc of Univ Teachers 1987, branch sec Conf of Univ Admin 1987; Liveryman Worshipful Co of Coopers 1977, Freeman City of London; *Recreations* squash, badminton, study of later Middle-English Arthurian romance; *Style*— John Withrington, Esq; Office of the Secretary, University of Lancaster, University House, Bailrigg, Lancaster (☎ 0524 65201, fax 0524 63806, telex 65111 LANCUL G)

WITNEY, Kenneth Percy; CVO (1976); s of Rev Thomas Charles Witney (d 1952), of Church of S India Theological Coll, Nazareth, Tamil Nadu, India, and Dr Myfanwy Dyfed, *née* Rees (d 1951); *b* 19 March 1916; *Educ* Eltham Coll Mottingham London, Wadham Coll Oxford (BA, MA); *m* 3 April 1947, Joan Agnes, da of Harold Tait, of 76 Simonside Terr, Newcastle-on-Tyne; 1 s (Nicholas b 1949), 1 da (Jane (Mrs Witney-Smith) b 1948); *Career* private sec to Parly Under Sec Miny of Home Security 1942-44 (admin asst 1940-42), asst private sec to Home Sec 1945-47; princ: Home Office 1945-47, Colonial Office (Police Div) 1955-57; asst under-sec of state Home Office 1969-76 (asst sec 1957-69), ret 1976; special advsr Royal Cmmn on Gambling 1976-78; memb: Tonbridge Civic Soc, Romney Marsh Res Tst; chm Kent Fedn of Amenity Socs 1982-84; *Books* The Jutish Forest (1976), The Kingdom of Kent (1982); *Recreations* historical research (dark age and early mediaeval); *Style*— Kenneth Witney, Esq, CVO

WITT, Margaret June; da of Henry Witt (d 1976), of 2 Clarendon Rd, Walthamstow, London; *b* 14 June 1930; *Educ* Walthamstow Co HS for Girls, St Bart's Hosp Med Coll (BSc, MB BS, Treasurer's prize in anatomy, Harvey prize in physiology, Matthew Duncan prize and Gold medal); *Career* St Bart's Hosp: house surgn Gynaecology and Obstetrics Unit 1955, gen surgn 1956, SHO Casualty Dept 1957; lectr in anatomy Anatomy Dept St Bart's Med Coll; surgical registrar: Elizabeth Garrett Anderson Hosp, Peace Meml Hosp; SHO Queen Charlotte's Hosp, two locum appts St Stephen's Hosp Watford, SHO Hosp for Women Soho Square, registrar Dulwich Hosp (branch of King's Coll Hosp), then registrar St Bart's Hosp 1966 (sr registrar 1969), conslt obstetrician and gynaecologist N Middx Hosp 1973, hon conslt St Luke's Hosp for the Clergy, hon conslt gynaecological endocrinology St Bart's Hosp; Freeman City of London 1990; memb: Jarringdon Ward Club, Royal Soc of St George (Parent Body and City Branch), Huntarian Soc 1972, Med Soc of London 1973-; *Recreations* photography, travel; *Style*— Ms Margaret Witt; 95 Harley St, London W1 (☎ 081 935 0588)

WITTICH, John Charles Bird; s of Charles Cyril Wittich (d 1976), and Minnie Amelia Victoria, *née* Daborn; *b* 18 Feb 1929; *Educ* privately (BA); *m* 10 July 1954, June Rose, da of Thomas Frederick Taylor (d 1972); 1 s (Andrew Paul b 1961), 1 da (Margaret Judith b 1957); *Career* SOAS 1951-58, AA 1966-74, Middle East Econ

Digest 1977-78, EPR Partnership 1979-86; freelance writer and lectr 1986-, lectr in adult educn circles, memb Minor Order of Readers of the C of E 1980-; Freeman City of London 1971, memb Ct of Parish Clerks Co 1991, Liveryman Worshipful Co of Woolmen 1977; FRSA 1980; *Books* Off-Beat Walks in London (1969, revised ed 1990), London Curiosities (1973), London Villages (1976, revised ed 1990), London Street Names (1977, revised ed 1990), London's Inns & Taverns (1978), London's Parks & Squares (1981), Catholic London (1988), Churches, Cathedrals & Chapels (1988), Guide to Bayswater (1989), Wesley's London (1991), Regents Park (1991), Unknown London (1991); *Clubs* City Livery, Wig and Pen; *Style—* John Wittich, Esq; 66 Saint Michael's St, London W2 1QR (☎ 071 262 9572)

WITTY, (John) David; CBE (1985); s of Harold Witty (d 1948), of Molescroft, E Yorks, and Olive, *née* Scaife (d 1977); *b* 1 Oct 1924; *Educ* Beverley GS, Balliol Coll Oxford (MA); *m* 1955, Doreen, da of John William Hanlan (d 1952), of Hull; 1 s (Simon); *Career* served RN 1943-46; slr; chief exec Westminster City Cncl 1977-84; hon sec London Boroughs Assoc 1978-84; chm London Enterprise Party Co 1984-85; lawyer memb London Rent Assessment Panel 1984-; dir Great Portland Estates plc 1987-; Order of Infante D Henrique (Portugal) 1978, Order of Right Hand (Nepal) 1980, Order of King Abdul Aziz (Saudi Arabia) 1981, Order of Oman 1982, Order of Orange Nassau 1982; *Recreations* golf, motoring; *Clubs* Royal Mid Surrey Golf; *Style—* David Witty, Esq, CBE; 14 River House, The Terrace, Barnes, London SW13 0NR (☎ 081 876 0038)

WIXLEY, Gordon Robert Alexander; CBE (1979, OBE Mil 1955), TD (1959), DL (1976); s of Walter Henry James (d 1959), and Maud Mary, *née* Neave (d 1971); *b* 22 Nov 1914; *Educ* Lindisfarne Coll; *Career* HAC 1939, RA 1939-46; 290 Field Regt RA (City of London) TA 1947-54, CO 1951-54; Col TA 1955-58; CA; memb Ct of Common Cncl (City of London) 1964- (chief commoner 1985), vice chm Greater London TAVRA 1967-73; chm bd of govrs: Bethlem Royal and Maudsley Hosp 1980-82, City of London Freemen's Sch 1977-78; chm ctee of mgmnt Inst of Psychiatry 1984-87; vice chm Nat Biological Standards Bd 1976-89; ADC (TA) to HM The Queen 1967-73; *Recreations* travel, walking, reading; *Clubs* Bucks, Athenaeum, Army and Navy, City Livery; *Style—* Gordon Wixley, Esq, CBE, TD, DL; 947 Chelsea Cloisters, Sloane Ave London SW3 3EU (☎ 071 589 3109)

WIXON, Capt David George; s of John Charles Wixon (d 1957), and Eneta Mary Saunders, *née* Watts (now Mrs Rushmer); *b* 16 May 1937; *Educ* Aylesbury GS, Britannia RNC, RNEC Manadon Devon (BSc Engrg), RNC Greenwich (AME(N)); *m* 3 April 1961, Rosamond Mary, da of Geoffrey Howard Stevens, of Huel, Yelverton, Devon; 1 s (Rufus b 1965), 2 da (Miranda b 1962, Theresa b 1963); *Career* RN served aboard: HMS Newcastle 1957-58, HMS Aurochs 1963-64, HMS Valiant 1966-69, HMS Courageous 1968-72; sr lectr Dept Nuclear Sci and Tech RNC Greenwich 1972-75 (promoted Cdr 1974), CSST (sub sea trg) 1975-77, Cdr RNEC 1980-83 (promoted Capt 1983), strategic systems exec MOD 1983-86, Job Evaluation judge 1987-90, CO HMS Drake 1990-; MIMechE 1974; *Recreations* rugby football, old cars, Allard card restoration, collecting hollow stemmed wine glasses; *Style—* Capt David Wixon, RN; c/o Naval Secretary, Old Admiralty Building, Whitehall SW1

WODEHOUSE, Rev the Hon Lady (Carol Lylie); *née* Palmer; da of 3 Baron Palmer, OBE; *b* 28 Nov 1951; *Educ* St Mary's Sch Wantage, St Hugh's Coll Oxford, Ripon Coll Cuddesdon; *m* 1973, Lord Wodehouse, *qv*, s and h of 4 Earl of Kimberley; 1 s, 1 da; *Career* teacher; ordained deacon in the Church of England; *Style—* The Rev the Hon Lady Wodehouse; Derry House, North End, Henley-on-Thames, Oxon RG9 6LQ

WODEHOUSE, Hon Edward Abdy; s of 4 Earl of Kimberley (by his 3 w); *b* 1954; *Educ* Eton; *m* 1, 1980 (m dis 1983), Pandora Jeffreys; m 2, 1988, Sarah Katherine, da of Richard Allen, of Ranskill, Retford, Notts; *Career* historic car restoration; *Style—* The Hon Edward Wodehouse; 17 Ada Rd, London SE5 7RW (☎ 071 701 2700)

WODEHOUSE, The Hon Henry Wyndham; s of 4 Earl of Kimberley (by his 3 w); *b* 26 April 1956; *Educ* Millfield; *m* 1979 (m dis 1988), Sarah M, only da of J A Fleming, of Hampton, Middx; 1 s (Thomas Henry John b 1981), 1 da (Clare b 1980); *Recreations* current affairs, golf, fly-fishing, fly-dressing, flying, tennis, photography; *Clubs* Falmouth Shark Angling; *Style—* The Hon Henry Wodehouse

WODEHOUSE, Lord; John Armine Wodehouse; s and h of 4 Earl of Kimberley; *b* 15 Jan 1951; *Educ* Eton, Univ of E Anglia (MSc); *m* 1973, Hon Carol, *qv*, da of 3 Baron Palmer; 1 s, 1 da (Hon Katherine b 1976); *Heir* s, Hon David Simon John Wodehouse b 10 Oct 1978; *Career* systems programmer with Glaxo 1979- (joined as res chemist 1974); chm UK Info Users Gp 1981-83; Fell Br Interplanetary Soc 1984- (Assoc Fell 1981-83); FRSA, MBCS 1988-; *Recreations* photography, computing; *Style—* Lord Wodehouse; Derry House, North End, Henley-on-Thames, Oxon RG9 6LQ; Information Systems, Glaxo Gp Res Ltd, Greenford Rd, Greenford, Middx UB6 0HE (☎ 01 422 3434)

WODEHOUSE, Hon Mrs Edward; Sarah Katherine; da of John Richard Percival Allen, and Susan Dorothea Farquhar; *b* 6 July 1962; *Educ* Wycombe Abbey Sch, Univ of E Anglia (BA); *m* 17 Sept 1988, Hon Edward Wodehouse, s of 4 Earl of Kimberley; *Career* mangr and owner Decibel Designs; *Recreations* tapestries, topiary, tennis; *Style—* The Hon Mrs Edward Wodehouse

WOLF, Martin Harry; s of Edmund Wolf, of London, and Rebecca, *née* Wijnschenk; *b* 16 Aug 1946; *Educ* Univ Coll Sch, Corpus Christi Coll Oxford (open scholar, MA), Nuffield Coll Oxford (MPhil); *m* Aug 1970, Alison Margaret, da of late Herbert Kingsley Potter, of Newbury, Berks; 2 s (Jonathan Thomas b 24 Jan 1975, Benjamin Jacob b 11 Jan 1977), 1 da (Rachel Janet b 11 June 1985); *Career* World Bank: joined Young Professional programme 1971, Office of Vice Pres for East Africa 1972-74, sr economist India Div 1974-77, involved with World Devpt Report 1977-78, sr economist Int Trade and Capital Flows Div 1979-81; dir of studies Trade Policy Res Centre 1981-87, chief economics leader writer and assoc ed Financial Times 1990- (joined 1987); conslt to various orgns, advsr and rapporteur to World Bank's Eminent Persons Gp on World Trade 1990 (winner New Zealand 1990 Commemoration Medal), jt winner Wincott Fndn sr prize for excellence in financial journalism 1990; visiting fell: UCL 1978, Nuffield Coll Oxford 1978-79; memb Nat Consumer Cncl 1987-; memb cncl Royal Economic Soc; *publications* incl: Textile Quotas against Developing Countries (with Donald B Keesing, 1980), India's Exports (1982), Costs of Protecting Jobs in Textiles and Clothing (1984), Global Implications of the European Community's Programme for Completing the Internal Market (1989), Meeting the World Trade Deadline: Path to a Successful Uruguay Round (1990); *Recreations* theatre, reading, skiing; *Clubs* Reform; *Style—* Martin Wolf, Esq; Financial Times, 1 Southwark Bridge, London SE1 9HL (☎ 071 873 3421, fax 071 407 5700)

WOLF, (Colin) Piers; s of Peter Wolf, of Claverdon, nr Stratford upon Avon, and Gladys Mary, *née* Williams; *b* 26 Jan 1943; *Educ* Bedford Sch; *m* 8 April 1972, Jennifer Elisabeth, da of Kingsley Richard Fox, of Surbiton, Surrey; 1 s (Guy Daniel b 1976), 1 da (Jocelyn Ruth b 1975); *Career* admitted slr 1966; ptnr Evershed & Tomkinson 1973- (now Evershed Wells & Hind); memb Law Soc 1972 (memb Standing Ctee on Co Law 1989); *Recreations* music, books, walking, cycling; *Style—* Piers Wolf, Esq; 10 Newhall St, Birmingham B3 3LX (☎ 021 233 2001, fax 021 236 1583, telex 336688 EVSHED G)

WOLFE, Anthony James Garnham; s of Herbert Robert Inglewood Wolfe, VRD (d 1970), and Lesley Winifred, *née* Fox; *b* 30 Aug 1952; *Educ* Haileybury ISC, Univ of Bristol (BSc); *m* 4 Sept 1982, Ommar Aung, da of Lionel Aung Kwa Takwali (d 1956); *Career* CA; London and Hong Kong Offices Peat Marwick Mitchell 1974-81, GT Mgmnt London and Hong Kong Offices 1981-; FCA; *Recreations* rugger, golf, travel, walking; *Clubs* Royal Wimbledon GC, Royal Canoe; *Style—* Anthony Wolfe, Esq; 39 St Winifreds Rd, Teddington, Middx TW11 9JS

WOLFE, John Henry Nicholas; s of Herbert Robert Inglewood Wolfe (1970), amd Lesley Winifred, *née* Fox; *b* 4 June 1947; *Educ* Eastbourne Coll, St Thomas's Hosp Univ of London (MB, BS, MS); *m* 23 June 1973, Jennifer, da of Geoffrey Sutcliffe; 3 s (Robert, Owen, Matthew), 2 da (Tara, Roshean); *Career* res fell Harvard Med Sch Brigham Hosp 1981-82, sr registrar St Thomas's Hosp 1982-84, Hunterian Professor RCS 1983; conslt surgn: St Mary's Hosp Med Sch 1984, Royal Postgrad Med Sch Hammersmith Hosp, Edward VII Hosp for Offrs; memb: Surgical Res Soc, Assoc of Surgns, Vascular Soc of GB and I, Euro Soc of Vascular Surgery, Int Soc of Cardiovascular Surgery; FRCS; *Books* Vascular Surgery (ed 1985, 1989); *Recreations* sailing, cooking for children, walking; *Clubs* RSM; *Style—* John Wolfe, Esq; 66 Harley St, London W1N 1AE (☎ 071 580 5030, fax 071 631 5341)

WOLFE, Richard John Russell; s of Maj John Claude Frank Wolfe, of 14 Kennel Lane, Bookham, Surrey, and Betty Doris, *née* Hopwood; *b* 15 July 1947; *Educ* Ackworth Sch, Ackworth Yorks; *m* 28 Nov 1970 (m dis 1977), Lorraine Louise Hart; 1 da (Pandora b 12 July 1976); *Career* mgmnt trainee NM Rothschild and Son Ltd 1964-68, investmt dealer British and Continental Bank 1968-72, fund mangr Hill Samuel and Co Ltd 1972-75, corporate fin offr NM Rothschild and Sons Ltd 1976-80, vice pres and head of real estate fin UK Security Pacific Nat Bank 1980, md and head of Euro real estate Bankers Trust Co 1990; AIB 1978; *Books* Real Estate Finance (contrib 1988); *Recreations* choir singing, swimming, training, study of ancient civilisations; *Style—* Richard Wolfe, Esq; 52 Claylands Road, London SW8 1PZ (☎ 071 582 1952); Bankers Trust Co, 1 Appold Street, Broadgate, London EC2A 2HE (☎ 071 982 2500, fax 071 982 3391)

WOLFE, William Cuthbertson; s of Maj Thomas Wolfe, TD (d 1957), of Bathgate, and Catherine Jane, *née* Cuthbertson (d 1981); *b* 22 Feb 1924; *Educ* Bathgate Acad, George Watson's Coll Edinburgh; *m* 31 Oct 1953, Maimie, da of late Melville Dinwiddie, CBE, DSO, MC, of Edinburgh; 2 s (David Thomas Melville b 1957, Patrick John Murray b 1963), 2 da (Eileen Margaret b 1955, Sheila Mary b 1960); *Career* RA 1942-47: cmmnd 1944, air observation post pilot 1945-47, NW Europe 1944-45, SE Asia 1945-47, Capt 1946; CA 1952, employed in industry 1952-81, in professional practice 1981-; Scouting 1947-64 (county cmmr for W Lothian 1960-64), memb Cncl Saltire Soc 1990- (hon publications treas 1953-64); SNP: chm 1969-79, pres 1980-82, Parly candidate W Lothian 1962-79; sec Scottish Poetry Library 1986-, treas Scottish CND 1981-84, memb Nat Ctee for Scotland Forestry Cmmn 1974-87; *Books* Scotland Lives (1973), Ten Scarts on Time (1979); *Recreations* supporting causes for a better world; *Style—* William Wolfe; Burnside Forge, Burnside Rd, Bathgate, W Lothian, Scotland EH48 4PU (☎ 0506 54785)

WOLFE MURRAY, James Archibald; s of Lt-Col Malcolm Victor Alexander Wolfe Murray, DL (d 1985; ggs of James Murray, who as a Lord of Session took the title Lord Cringletie; he was gggs of Alexander Murray, 2 Bt, of Blackbarony), and his 1 w, Lady Grizel Mary Boyle (d 1942), eldest da of 8 Earl of Glasgow; *b* 25 April 1936; *Educ* Eton, Worcester Coll Oxford; *m* 1, 8 June 1963 (m dis 1976), Hon (Lady until 1963) Diana Lucy Douglas-Home, da of Lord Home of the Hirsel, KT (14 Earl of Home until 1963); 1 s (Rory James b 1965), 2 da (Fiona Grizel b 1964, Clare Elizabeth b 1969); m 2, 17 July 1978, Amanda Felicity, da of Anthony Frank Street (d 1974); 1 s (Andrew Alexander b 1978); *Career* 2 Lt Black Watch 1954-56; export dir James Buchanan & Co 1969-75, vice chm and md: Macdonald Greenlees Ltd 1975-82, John Haig & Co 1982-87; md White Horse Distillers 1987-, regnl dir United Distillers 1988-; *Recreations* golf, fishing, shooting, cricket; *Clubs* White's, Royal St George's Golf, MCC, Hon Co Edinburgh Golfers; *Style—* James Wolfe Murray, Esq; 13 Howards Lane, London SW15 6NX (☎ 081 788 6369); United Distillers Group, Landmark House, Hammersmith Bridge Road, London W6 9DP (☎ 081 748 8580, fax 081 748 5462, telex 935510)

WOLFE-PARRY, Hon Mrs (Blanche-Neige Juno Palma Odette Denisa); *née* Wynn; da of 5 Baron Newborough (d 1957); *b* 1940; *m* 1963, Philip Wolfe-Parry, LDS, RCS; 1 s; *Style—* The Hon Mrs Wolfe-Parry; 206 Grand Drive, London SW20

WOLFENDALE, Prof Arnold Whittaker; s of Arnold Wolfendale (d 1963), and Doris, *née* Hoyle (d 1983); *b* 25 June 1927; *Educ* Stretford GS, Univ of Manchester (BSc, PhD, DSc); *m* 1952, Audrey, da of Arnold Darby (d 1968); 2 s (twins, Colin and David); *Career* prof of physics Univ of Durham 1965-, chm N Region Manpower Service Cmmn's Job Creation Programme 1975-78; pres Royal Astronomical Soc 1981-83, chm: Cosmic Ray Cmmn of IUPAC 1982-84, SERC'S Astronomy & Planetary Science Bd 1988-; pres Durham Univ Soc of Fells 1988-; Astronomer Royal 1991-; Hon DSc Potchefstroom and Lodz; foreign fell: Nat Acad of Sciences of India 1990, Indian Nat Sci Acad 1991; FRS, FInstP, FRAS; *Recreations* gardening, travel; *Style—* Prof Arnold Wolfendale, FRS; Ansford, Potters Bank, Durham DH1 3RR; Physics Dept, University of Durham (☎ 091 374 2160)

WOLFENDEN, Dr (Ernest) Brian; s of Alfred Ernest Wolfenden, and Winifred Harriet Wolfenden; *b* 20 July 1932; *Educ* Glossop GS, Univ of Manchester (BSc, MSc, PhD); *m* 3 Nov 1956, Marilyn; 2 s (Graham b 7 July 1958, John Robert b 2 April 1961); *Career* geologist Overseas Scientific Civil Serv (Kuching Sarawak) 1956-63, employed by State of Sarawak Malaysia 1963-65; md The Robertson Group plc 1987-, dir Robertson Gould & Co plc; memb: American Assoc of Petroleum Geologists, Inst of Petroleum; *Books* Memoirs on The Geology and Mineral Resources of Sarawak over the Period 1960-65; *Recreations* mountain trekking, gardening, music; *Style—* Dr Brian Wolfenden; The Robertson Group plc, Ty'n-y-Coed, Llanrhos, Gwynedd LL30 1SA (☎ 0492 581811)

WOLFENDEN, Hon Daniel Mark; s of Baron Wolfenden, CBE (d 1985); *b* 1942; *m* 1972, Sally Frankel; *Style—* The Hon Daniel Wolfenden; 44 Mortimer St, London W1

WOLFENDEN, Baroness; Eileen le Messurier Wolfenden; 2 da of A J Spilsbury; *m* 1932, Baron Wolfenden, CBE (d 1985; Life Peer UK 1974); 1 s and 1 s decd, 2 da; *Style—* The Rt Hon the Lady Wolfenden; The White House, Westcott, Dorking, Surrey RH4 3NJ (☎ 0306 885475)

WOLFF *see also*: Clifford Wolff

WOLFF, Prof Heinz Siegfried; s of Oswald Wolff (d 1968), of W Germany, and Margot, *née* Saalfeld; *b* 29 April 1928; *Educ* City of Oxford Sch, UCL (BSc); *m* 21 March 1953, Joan Eleanor Mary, da of Charles Heddon Stephenson, MBE (d 1968); 2 s (Anthony b 1956, Laurence b 1961); *Career* head div of biomedical engrg Nat Inst for Med Res 1962-70 (joined 1954), head div of bioengineering Clinical Res Centre 1970-83, dir Brunel Inst for Bioengineering Brunel Univ 1983-; Action Res Harding Award 1989; chm: Life Sci Working Gp ESA 1976-82, microgravity advsy ctee ESA 1982-, microgravity panel Br Nat Space Centre 1986-87; TV series incl: BBC TV Young Scientist of the Year 1968-81, Royal Inst Christmas Lectures 1975, The Great Egg Race 1978-86, Great Experiments which Changed the World 1985-86; fell UCL 1987;

FIBiol; memb: Physiological Soc, Biological Engrg Soc, Ergonomics Res Soc; FIBiol; *Books* Biological Engineering (1969); *Recreations* working, dignified practical joking; *Style*— Prof Heinz Wolff; Brunel Institue for Bioengineering, Brunel University, Uxbridge, Middlesex UB8 3PH (☎ 0895 71206, fax 0895 74608, telex 261173)

WOLFF, Michael Gordon; s of Sergei Mikhailovich Wolff (d 1979), of London, and Mary, *née* Gordon; *b* 12 Nov 1933; *Educ* Greshams, Architectural Assoc Sch of Architecture; *m* 1, 14 Aug 1976 (m dis 1987), Susan, da of Brig Sydney Kent; 1 da (Rebecca Rose b 27 Oct 1981); m 2, July 1989, Martha Anne *née* Newhouse; *Career* fndr and creative dir Wolff Olins 1965-83, chm Addison Design Conslts Ltd 1987-; pres Design and Art Direction Assoc (D&ADA) 1971, fndr and creative dir of the Consortium 1983-87, pres Chartered Soc of Designers (CSD) 1985-87; dir The Hunger Project (UK) 1978-83 (memb bd of tstees 1983-); FRSA, PPCSD; *Recreations* family life, seeing and walking; *Style*— Michael Wolff, Esq; Addison Design Consultants Ltd, 60 Britton Street, London EC1M 5NA (☎ 071 250 1887)

WOLFFER, Hon Mrs; Hon Naomi Anne; *née* Marks; da of 2 Baron Marks of Broughton; *b* 1952; *m* 1980, Martin Christian Wolffer; 2 da (Joanna Claire b 1982, Georgina Chloe b 1985); *Style*— The Hon Mrs Wolffer

WOLFSON, Sir Brian Gordon; s of Gabriel Wolfson (d 1950), of Liverpool, and Charlotte Eve, *née* Carr (d 1967); *b* 2 Aug 1935; *Educ* Liverpool Coll, Univ of Liverpool; *m* 10 March 1957, Helen, da of Lewis Grodner, of Liverpool; 1 s (David b 28 March 1964), 1 da (Gaye b 5 July 1961); *Career* gp jt md Granada Group 1967-70 (joined 1962); chm: Anglo Nordic Holdings 1976-87, Wembly plc 1986-; chm: Nat Training Task Force, EDC Ctee on Leisure & Tourism, Ashridge MBA Prog; vice pres Br Inst of Mgmnt; memb: Nat Economic Devpt Cncl, Advsy Bd William H Wurster Centre for Int Mgmnt Studies Univ of Pennsylvania, Bd Joseph H Lauder Inst Univ of Pennsylvania; first non-N American pres of Young Presidents' Orgn 1979-80; Dr of Business Admin Liverpool Poly 1989; CBIM, fell Br Inst of Engrs; *Recreations* archaeology, wildlife films; *Style*— Sir Brian Wolfson; Wembley plc, Wembley Stadium, Wembley HA9 0DW (☎ 081 902 8833, fax 081 903 2646)

WOLFSON, Sir Isaac; 1 Bt (UK 1962), of St Marylebone, London; s of Solomon Wolfson, JP (d 1941), of Glasgow, and Nellie, *née* Williamovsky (d 1943); *b* 17 Sept 1897; *Educ* Queen's Park Sch Glasgow; *m* 17 Feb 1926, Edith (d 1981), da of Ralph Specterman; 1 s; *Heir* s, Baron Wolfson, *qv*; *Career* former chm The Great Universal Stores Ltd, now hon pres Wolfson Fndn (created 1955 mainly for advancing health, educn and youth activities in UK and Cwlth); hon pres and hon fell Weizmann Inst of Science Fndn Israel; memb Grand Cncl Cancer Research Campaign; FRS; Hon: FRCP, FRCS; hon fell: St Edmund Hall and LMH Oxford, Jews' Coll; Hon DCL Oxford; Hon LLD: London, Glasgow, Cambridge, Manchester, Strathclyde, Brandeis US, Nottingham; *Style*— Sir Isaac Wolfson, Bt, FRS; c/o The Weizmann Institute of Science, PO Box 26, Rehovot 76100, Israel

WOLFSON, Baron (Life Peer UK 1985), of Marylebone in the City of Westminster; Leonard Gordon Wolfson; s and h of Sir Isaac Wolfson, 1 Bt, *qv*, and Lady Edith Wolfson; *b* 11 Nov 1927; *Educ* King's Sch Worcester; *m* 14 Nov 1949, Ruth, da of Ernest A Sterling; 4 da (Hon Janet b 1952, Hon Laura b 1954, Hon Deborah b 1959, Hon Elizabeth b 1966); *Career* chm and fndr tstee Wolfson Fndn; chm: Great Universal Stores plc, Burberrys Ltd; Hon FRCP 1977; hon fell: St Catherine's Coll Oxford, Wolfson Colls Cambridge and Oxford, UCL, Worcester Coll Oxford; Hon PhD: Tel Aviv 1971, Hebrew Univ 1978; Hon DCL: Oxon 1972, E Anglia 1986; Hon LLD: Strathclyde 1972, Dundee 1979, London 1982, Cambridge 1982; Hon DSc: Hull 1977, Wales 1984; Hon Dr of Hebrew Literature Bar Ilan Univ 1983; Hon DUniv Surrey 1990; patron RCS 1976; hon fell: London Sch of Hygiene and Tropical Med 1985, Queen Mary Coll 1985; memb Ct of Benefactors RSM; FBA 1986; Hon FRCS 1989; kt 1977; *Style*— The Rt Hon the Lord Wolfson; Universal House, 251 Tottenham Court Rd, London W1A 1BZ (☎ 071 580 6441)

WOLFSON, Leslie; s of Aaron Wolfson (d 1964), of Glasgow, and Hannah Frank (d 1956); *b* 12 June 1929; *Educ* The High Sch Glasgow, Univ of Glasgow (BL); *m* 30 Sept 1964, Alma Rosalind, da of Louis Woolfson; 3 da (Monica Natanya b 1966, Georgia b 1967, Jessica Gladys b 1972); *Career* admitted slr; sr ptnr Leslie Wolfson & Co; dir: Heron Equities Ltd, Gander Equities Ltd; govr Tel Aviv Univ; chm: The Tel Aviv Univ Tst (Scotland), Jt Israel Appeal Scotland 1982; memb: Human Rights Ctee Int Bar Assoc (former rep UN Human Rights Cmmn), GB - USSR Assoc; tstee Alma & Leslie Wolfson Charitable Tst; *Recreations* photography, walking, gardening; *Style*— Leslie Wolfson, Esq; Longhill, Whitecraigs, Glasgow G46 6TR; 39 Hill St, Mayfair W1X 7FF; Easdale Island, by Oban, Argyll; 56 Kedoshai Hashoa St, Herzliya Pituach, Israel; 19 Waterloo St, Glasgow G2 6BQ (☎ 041 226 4499, telex 779435, fax 041 221 6070)

WOLFSON, (Geoffrey) Mark; MP (C) Sevenoaks 1979-; s of Capt Vladimir Wolfson, RNVR (d 1954); *b* 7 April 1934; *Educ* Eton, Pembroke Coll Cambridge; *m* 1965, Edna Webb, *née* Hardman; 2 s; *Career* warden Brathay Hall Centre Cumbria 1962-65, head Youth Services Industrial Society 1965-69 (head of personnel 1969), dir Hambros Bank 1973-88 (head of personnel 1969); PPS: to Adam Butler as Min State NI 1983-84, as Min for Def Procurement 1984-85, to Ian Stewart as Min for the Armed Servs 1987-88; *Style*— Mark Wolfson, Esq, MP; House of Commons, London SW1A 0AA

WOLFSON, Baroness; Ruth; *née* Sterling; da of Ernest A Sterling (d 1986), of London, and Fay, *née* Ogus; *Educ* St Albans HS; *m* 14 Nov 1949, Baron Wolfson (Life Peer), *qv*; 5 da (1 decd); *Career* tstee: Wolfson Fndn 1982-, Wolfson Family Charitable Tst, Edith and Isaac Wolfson (Scotland) Tst; memb ctee Prince of Wales Ctee Queen's Silver Jubilee Appeal 1976; Hon Fell St Catherine's Coll Oxford 1988; *Recreations* gardening, photography; *Style*— The Rt Hon Lady Wolfson; Chapter One Bookshop, Pierrepont Arcade, Camden Passage, Islington, London N1 (☎ 071 359 1185)

WOLKIND, Dr Stephen Nathaniel; s of Leonard Wolkind (d 1978), and Nettie, *née* Barbitsky; *b* 5 Aug 1939; *Educ* Christ Coll Finchley, Middlesex Hosp Med Sch, Univ of London (MB BS, MD); *m* 29 Jan 1963, Lilliane Camille Juliette Marcelle, da of Edmond Stanislavs Marie Vin (d 1966); 2 s (Ivan b 14 Oct 1967, Philip b 18 Nov 1969), 1 da (Helen b 14 July 1965); *Career* sr lectr and hon conslt in Child Psychiatry London Hosp 1972-85, conslt in child psychiatry Maudsley Hosp 1985; advsr on child and adolescent psychiatry Dept of Health, psychiatric advsr parents for children adoption agency and the bridge; MRCPsych (memb Ct of Electors) 1971, FRCPsych 1981; *Books* Pregnancy, A Psychological and Social Study (1978), Medical Aspects of Adoption and Foster Care (1979), Child Psychiatry and the Law (1989); *Recreations* walking, wine tasting, cinema; *Style*— Dr Stephen Wolkind; Children's Dept, Maudsley Hosp, Denmark Hill, London (☎ 071 703 6333)

WOLLEY DOD, Anthony Kirk; JP (Cheshire 1965); o s of John Cadogan Wolley Dod, JP (d 1973), of Edge Hall, Malpas, Cheshire, and his 1 w, Hilda Gertrude, *née* Elliott (d 1938); the Dods have been settled at Edge Hall since the time of Henry II (1154-89), but a connected descent can only be traced from Thomas Dod, who lived in the 14th century; The eventual heiress of the family, Frances Lucy Parker, m 1850, Rev Charles Wolley, who assumed the additional surname of Dod 1868, when his wife received the Edge property from her mother; The Wolleys were of equal antiquity in Cheshire and Derbyshire and their heiress, Mary Wolley, m 1822, Rev John Francis Thomas Hurt, who assumed the surname of Wolley in compliance with his father-in-law's will, and was mother of Rev Charles Wolley Dod above named (*see* Burke's Landed Gentry, 18 edn, Vol III, 1972); *b* 21 Dec 1918; *Educ* Rugby; *m* 29 Aug 1960, Ann Keightley, o da of Lt-Col John (Jack) Robertson, MC (d 1944), of Oxton, Birkenhead; *Career* serv in WWII as Flying Offr RAF in England, W Africa and Canada; admitted slr 1947; ptnr Batesons & Co Liverpool 1947-62; farmer at The Dairy House, Edge and Edge Hall, Malpas 1962-; High Sheriff of Cheshire 1977-78; memb: CLA, RASE, NFU, Law Soc 1947; *Recreations* fishing, shooting, forestry; *Clubs* Royal Over-Seas League; *Style*— Anthony Wolley Dod, Esq; Edge Hall, Malpas, Cheshire (☎ 094 885 530)

WOLMAN, Clive Richard; s of Lionel Wolman (d 1969), of Sheffield, and Estell, *née* Davidson; *b* 5 April 1956; *Educ* King Edward VII Sheffield, Carmel Coll Wallingford, St Catherine's Coll Oxford (MA, Philosophy Politics Economics), Poly of Central London (Dip Law), London Business Sch (MBA); *Career* Reading Evening Post reporter 1978-80, Jerusalem Post Israel energy housing and telecoms corr 1980-81; Financial Times: co comments writer 1982-83, personal fin ed 1983-85, securities industry corr (covered Big Bang and City Regulation) 1986-89; city ed (i/c financial, business, personal fin sections) The Mail on Sunday 1989-91; *Recreations* archaeology, cycling; *Style*— Clive Wolman, Esq; 373 Liverpool Rd, London N1 1NL (☎ 071 609 2761); The Mail On Sunday, Temple House, Temple Ave, London EC4Y 0TA (☎ 071 938 6985)

WOLMER, Viscount; William Lewis Palmer; s and h of 4 Earl of Selborne; *b* 1 Sept 1971; *Educ* Eton; *Style*— Viscount Wolmer

WOLPERT, Prof Lewis; CBE (1990); *b* 19 Oct 1929; *Educ* Univ of Witswatersrand SA (BSc), Imperial Coll London (DIC), King's Coll London (PhD); *m* (m dis); 2 s, 2 da; *Career* civil engr 1951-54: SA Cncl for Scientific and Industl Res, Israel Water Planning Dept; career changed to cell biology 1954, reader in zoology Dept of Zoology at King's Coll London 1964, prof of Biology as Applied to Medicine Univ Coll and Middlesex Sch of Medicine 1966-; winner the Scientific Medal of the Zoological Soc 1968; visiting lectr Univ of Warwick, TV presenter for Antenna (BBC2) 1988-89, various interviews and documentaries for Radio 3; Hon MRCP London 1986; FRS 1980; *Books* A Passion for Science (1988); *Recreations* cycling, tennis; *Style*— Prof Lewis Wolpert, CBE; Dept of Anatomy & Developmental Biology, University College and Middlesex School of Medicine, Windeyer Building, Cleveland Street, London W1P 6DB (☎ 071 380 9345, fax 071 380 9346)

WOLRIGE GORDON OF ESSLEMONT, Capt Robert; s of Capt Robert Wolrige Gordon, MC (d 1939), of Esslemont, Ellon, Aberdeenshire, and Joan, *née* Walter (d 1977); *b* 20 Sept 1928; *Educ* Cheam Sch, Eton, RMA Sandhurst; *m* 11 July 1956, Rosemary Jane, da of Vice Adm Sir Conolly Abel Smith, GCVO, CB (d 1986), of Ashiestiel, and The Lady Mary Abel Smith; 1 s (Charles Iain Robert b 19 June 1961), 1 da (Henrietta Anne b 11 April 1959 d 1983); *Career* enlisted Grenadier Guards 1947, RMA Sandhurst 1947-48, 2 Lt 1950, Capt 1953, ret 1959; co cnllr Aberdeen CC 1961-74, regnl cnllr 1978-86 (vice chm Planning Ctee); Grand Master Mason Scotland 1974-79, chm Gordon Constituency Cons Pty 1988-90; *Recreations* shooting, golf, tennis, fishing; *Clubs* New; *Style*— Wolrige Gordon of Esslemont

WOLSELEY, Sir Charles Garnet Richard Mark; 11 Bt (E 1628), of Wolseley, Staffs; s of Capt Stephen Wolseley (ka 1944, s of Sir Edric Wolseley, 10 Bt, JP (d 1954); the Wolseleys of Mt Wolseley, Co Carlow, who produced Sir Garnet, the Victorian general cr Visc Wolseley are a cadet branch) and Pamela, Lady Wolseley, *qv*; *b* 16 June 1944; *Educ* Ampleforth, RAC Cirencester; *m* 1, 1968 (m dis 1984), Anita, da of Hugo Fried, of Epsom; 1 s, 3 da; m 2, 1984, Mrs Imogene E Brown; *Heir* s, Stephen Garnet Hugo Charles b 1980; *Career* ptnr Smiths Gore Chartered Surveyors 1979-87 (conslt 1987-); FRICS; *Recreations* shooting, fishing, water-colour painting; *Clubs* Farmers', Shikar; *Style*— Sir Charles Wolseley, Bt; Wolseley Park, Rugeley, Staffs WS15 2TU (☎ 0889 582346)

WOLSELEY, Sir Garnet; 12 Bt (I 1745), of Mount Wolseley, Co Carlow; s of Richard Bingham Wolseley (d 1938), and kinsman of 11 Bt (d 1950); *b* 27 May 1915; *Educ* Wallasey Central Sch; *m* 1950, Lilian Mary, da of late William Bertram Ellison; *Heir* kinsman, James Douglas Wolseley b 1937; *Career* served 1939-45 with Northants Regt (Madagascar, Sicily, Italy and Germany); *Style*— Sir Garnet Wolseley, Bt; 73 Dorothy St, Brantford, Ontario, Canada

WOLSELEY, Pamela, Lady; Pamela Violette; da of Capt F Barry, of Co Cork and latterly Old Court, Whitchurch, Herefs, and Mrs W N Power; *m* 1942, Capt Stephen Wolseley, RA (ka 1944); 1 s (Sir Charles Wolseley, 11 Bt, *qv*), 1 da; *Career* granted rank of Baronet's wife 1955; *Style*— Pamela, Lady Wolseley; Wolseley Park, Rugeley, Staffs (☎ 088 94 2346)

WOLSTENHOLME, Sir Gordon Ethelbert Ward; OBE (1944); s of Ethelbert Wolstenholme (d 1940), of Sheffield; *b* 28 May 1913; *Educ* Repton, Corpus Christi Coll Cambridge, Middx Hosp Med Sch (MB BChir); *m* 1, Mary Elizabeth, da of Rev Herbert Spackman; 1 s, 2 da; m 2, Dushanka, only da of Arthur Messinger; 2 da; *Career* WWII RAMC 1940-47, serv France, Med, Middle E; dir Ciba Fndn 1949-78; memb: Exec Bd UK Ctee WHO 1961-70 (fndr memb 1954), Cncl Westfield Coll Univ of London 1965-73, Planning Bd Univ Coll Buckingham 1969; chm Nuffield Inst for Comparative Med 1969-70, memb Gen Med Cncl 1973-83, tstee and chm Academic Bd St George's Univ Sch of Med 1978-90, Harveian librarian RCP 1979-89, dir and chief scientific advsr Info Retrieval 1980-88, vice pres Assoc of Special Libraries and Info Bureaux 1979-82, pres Br Soc of History of Med 1983-85, patron Fund for the Replacement of Animals in Med Experiments (FRAME), fndr and first chm Action in Int Med 1988-, tstee and chm Oval and Dental Research Tst 1989-; hon life govr Middx Hosp 1938, hon fell Hunterian Soc (orator 1976), hon FACP, hon FRSM 1982 (hon sec 1964-70, pres library res 1968-70, chm working pty on Soc's future 1972-73, pres 1975-77 and 1978); Hon: LLD Univ of Cambridge 1968, DTech Univ of Brunel 1981, MD Grenada 1983; hon FDSRCS 1991, MRCS, FRCP, FIBiol; kt 1976; *Style*— Sir Gordon Wolstenholme, OBE; 10 Wimpole Mews, London W1M 7TF (☎ 071 486 3884)

WOLTON, Harry; QC (1982); s of Harry William (d 1943), and Dorothy Beatrice, *née* Meaking (d 1982); *b* 1 Jan 1938; *Educ* King Edwards Sch Birmingham, Univ of Birmingham; *m* 3 April 1971, Julie Rosina Josaphine, da of George Edward Mason (d 1985); 3 s (Matthew Harry b 1972, Andrew b 1974, Edward b 1977); *Career* barr 1969; rec Crown Ct 1985; *Style*— Harry Wolton, Esq, QC; Armscote Farm, Armscote, Stratford upon Avon CV37 8DQ (☎ 060 882 234); 10 St Lukes St, SW3 3RS (☎ 071 352 5056); 5 Fountain Ct, Steelhouse Lane, Birmingham B4 6DR (☎ 021 236 5771); Devereux Chambers, Temple WC2R 3JJ (☎ 071 353 7534)

WOLVERSON, Brig (Robert) Christopher; OBE (1982); s of Robert Archibald Wolverson (d 1963), of Cambridge, and Mary Isabel, *née* Barnes; *b* 9 June 1940; *Educ* Bedford Sch, Downing Coll Cambridge (MA); *m* 12 Sept 1973, Deborah Elizabeth, da of Dr James Charles Shee, of Zimbabwe and SA; 2 da (Joscelin b 1978, Thomasina b 1980); *Career* cmmnd Irish Guards 1962, served Germany, UK, Aden, Belize, NI, Zimbabwe, Cyprus, Falkland Is, Bangladesh, Adj Cambridge Univ OTC 1968-70, Staff Coll 1970-72, Bde Maj 4 Guards Armoured Bde 1974-76, DS Staff Coll 1978-80, Mil Asst C-in-C BAOR 1980-81, DS Zimbabwe Staff Coll 1981-82, cmd 1 Bn The Kings

Own Royal Border Regt 1983-85, MOD 1985-89, cmd Br Mil Advsy Team Bangladesh 1990; MBIM 1975; *Clubs* Army and Navy, MCC; *Style*— Brig Christopher Wolverson, OBE

WOLVERSON, Maurice Frank; s of Frank Wolverson (d 1990), of 23 Meryhurst Rd, Wood Green, Wednesbury, W Mids, and (Edith Anne) Nancy, *née* Phillips (d 1973); *b* 7 June 1927; *Educ* Wednesbury Boys HS; *m* 4 June 1949, (Kathleen) Merle, da of Philip Patrick Forrester (d 1986); *Career* conscripted 1946-49, RAOC 1947-49 (demobbed Sgt); ptnr Whitehouse, Wolverson, Armston Cox CAs (formerly Barnfield & Co) 1961-; chm Parklands Housing Soc Ltd 1989- (pt/t treas 1966-82, memb Ctee 1982-, vice chm 1988-89), treas to the tstees of Crumps Almshouses, chm Walsall Family Practitioner Ctee 1983-89 (memb 1973-, vice chm 1975-83); vice chm Walsall Health Authy 1990- (memb 1985-); ACA 1959, FCA 1970; Compagnon de Confrerie St Etienne D'Alsace; *Recreations* wines, music, reading, motoring; *Style*— Maurice Wolverson, Esq; 6 Greenslade Rd, Park Hall, Walsall, W Mids WS5 3QH (☎ 0922 261 33); Six Ways Ct, 24 Birmingham Rd, Walsall, W Mids WS1 2LZ (☎ 0922 721 752)

WOLVERTON, Dowager Baroness; Audrey Margaret; *née* Stubbs; da of late Richard Stubbs, of Haseley Manor, Oxford; *m* 1937, 6 Baron Wolverton, CBE (d 1988); 2 s (7 Baron, Hon Andrew), 2 da (Hon Susan (Hon Mrs Mills), Hon Joanna Caroline b 1955); *Style*— The Rt Hon the Dowager Lady Wolverton; The Dower House, Chute Standen, Andover, Hants

WOLVERTON, 7 Baron (UK 1869); Christopher Richard Glyn; er s of 6 Baron Wolverton, CBE (d 1988), and Dowager Baroness Wolverton, *qv*; *b* 5 Oct 1938; *Educ* Eton; *m* 1, 1961 (m dis 1967), Carolyn Jane, yr da of late Antony Noel Hunter, of 33 Brompton Square, London SW3; 2 da (Hon Sara-Jane b 1963, Hon Amanda Camilla b 1966); m 2, 1975, Mrs Frances Sarah Elisabeth Stuart Black, eldest da of Robert Worboys Skene, of 12 Kensington Gate, London W8; *Heir* bro, Hon Andrew John Glyn, *qv*; *Career* FRICS; *Style*— The Rt Hon the Lord Wolverton

WOMBWELL, Sir George Philip Frederick; 7 Bt (GB 1778), of Wombwell, Yorkshire; s of Maj Sir Philip Wombwell, 6 Bt, MBE (d 1977); *b* 21 May 1949; *Educ* Repton; *m* 1974, Jane, da of Thomas Wrightson, of Ulshaw Grange, Leyburn, N Yorks; 1 s, 1 da; *Heir* s, Stephen Wombwell b 12 May 1977; *Career* farmer; *Style*— Sir George Wombwell, Bt; Newburgh Priory, Coxwold, York YO6 4AS (☎ 034 76 435)

WOMERSLEY, Sir Peter John Walter; 2 Bt (UK 1945), of Grimsby, Co Lincoln; s of late Capt John Walter Womersley (ka 1944), and gs of Rt Hon Sir Walter Womersley, 1 Bt, PC (d 1961); *b* 10 Nov 1941; *Educ* Charterhouse, RMA Sandhurst; *m* 1968, Janet Margaret, da of Alastair Grant; 2 s, 2 da; *Heir* s, John Gavin Grant Womersley b 7 Dec 1971; *Career* serv Regular Army, Offr Cadet at Sandhurst to 1962, 2 Lt King's Own Royal Border Regt 1962, Lt 1964, ret 1968; personnel offr Smith Kline Beecham 1968-72, personnel mangr 1972-; *Books* Collecting Stamps (with Neil Grant 1980); *Recreations* breeding rare poultry; *Style*— Sir Peter Womersley, Bt; Broomfields, Goring Rd, Steyning, W Sussex BN44 3GF

WONNACOTT, John Henry; s of Jack Alfred Wonnacott (d 1974), and Ethel Gwendoline Wonnacott; *b* 15 April 1940; *Educ* Univ Coll Sch, Slade Sch; *m* 10 Aug 1974, Anne Rozaha, da of Tadenz Wesolowski (d 1980); 2 da (Elizabeth Anne b 1978, Emma Zofja b 1982); *Career* artist; selected gp exhibitions: Painting and Perception Univ of Sterling 1971, Br Painting '74 1974, Br Painting '52-77 Royal Acad 1977, Hard Won Image Tate Gallery 1984, Pursuit of the Real Barbican 1990; selected one-man shows: The Minorities of Colchester 1977, Rochdale Art Gallery and Tour 1978, Marlborough Fine Art 1980, 1985 and 1988, Scottish Nat Portrait Gallery 1986; nat public collections: Tate Gallery, Arts Cncl, Edinburgh Scottish Nat Portrait Gallery, Norwich Castle, Rochdale Gallery; *Style*— John Wonnacott, Esq; Thomas Agnew & Sons Ltd, 43 Old Bond Street, London W1X 4BA (☎ 071 629 6176, fax 071 629 4359)

WONTNER, Sir Hugh Walter Kingwell; GBE (1974), CVO (1969, MVO 1950); in Scotland styled Sir Hugh Wontner of Barscobe by authy of Lord Lyon King of Arms; s of Arthur Wontner, of Cherry Cross, Totnes, Devon and 3 Albert Terrace, Regent's Park, London NW1, and Rosecleer Alice Amelia Blanche Kingwell (whose stage name was Rose Pendennis), of Moat Hill House, Totnes; *b* 22 Oct 1908; *Educ* Oundle; *m* 1936, Catherine, da of Lt Thomas William Irvin, Gordon Highlanders (ka 1916), of Peterhead, Aberdeenshire; n of late Sir John Irvin, KBE, JP; 2 s, 1 da; *Career* pres The Savoy Hotel plc 1990-; chm Berkeley and Claridge's Hotels London, Hotel Lancaster Paris, Savoy Theatre; former dir Savoy Hotel (md 1941-79, chm 1948-84), dir other cos, clerk of the Royal Kitchens 1953- (catering advsr 1938-); memb: Lloyds 1937-, London C of C 1927-33; sec Hotels and Restaurants Assoc 1933-38 (dir Savoy 1940); chllr City Univ 1973-74; pres Int Hotels Assoc 1961-64 (memb of honour 1965-); govr Univ Coll Hosp 1945-53; tstee: D'Oyly Carte Opera Tst, Coll of Arms Tst, Southwark Cathedral Devpt Tst, Morden Coll, Temple Bar Tst (chm); chm: Cncl Br Hotels Restaurants and Caterers Assoc 1969-73, Historic Houses Ctee BTA 1966-77; memb: Bd of BTA 1950-69, Historic Bldgs Cncl 1968-73, Br Heritage Ctee 1977-, Barbican Centre Ctee 1979-84, Heritage of London Tst 1980-; Freeman City of London 1934, one of HM Lts and JP City of London 1963-80, Alderman 1963-79, Sheriff 1970-71, chief magistrate 1973-74, Lord Mayor of London 1973-74; Master: Worshipful Co of Feltmakers 1962 and 1974, Worshipful Co of Clockmakers 1975; Liveryman Worshipful Co of Plaisterers and Launderers, Freeman of Seychelles 1974; hon citizen St Emilion 1974, Order of Cisneros Spain 1964, Offr L'Etoile Equatoriale 1970, Ordre de l'Etoile Civique 1972, Médaille de Vermeil City of Paris 1972, Offr du Mérite Agricole 1973, Cdr Nat Order of the Leopard (Zaire) 1974, Kt Cdr Order of the Dannebrog 1974, Order of the Crown of Malaysia 1974, Kt Cdr Royal Swedish Order of the Polar Star 1980; Hon DLitt (1973); kstJ 1973; kt 1972; *Recreations* acting, collecting antiques, genealogy; *Clubs* Garrick, City Livery; *Style*— Sir Hugh Wontner, GBE, CVO; Hedsor Priory, Hedsor, nr Bourne End, Bucks (☎ 062 85 23754); Barscobe, Balmaclellan, by Castle Douglas, Kirkcudbrightshire (☎ 064 42 245); 1 Savoy Hill, London WC2 (☎ 071 836 1533)

WOOD, Alfred Arden; CBE (1988), TD; *b* 8 Sept 1926; *Educ* Ashville Sch, Hertford Coll Oxford, Leeds Sch of Architecture and Town Planning; *Career* offr: Royal Tank Regt 1944-48, Westminster Dragoons TA and Leeds Rifles TA 1948-62; architect 1952-65 (Sweden, Harlow New Town, W Riding County, Leeds, Glasgow), city Planning Offr Norwich 1965-72, County Planner Worcs 1973, Co Architect and Planner W Midlands CC 1973-84; bldgs incl Birmingham Int Airport 1984; head of Historic Areas English Heritage 1985-87; memb: Bd Sheffield Devpt Corp, Historic Areas Advsy Ctee of English Heritage; Civic Tst award 1969, EAHY Outstanding award 1975; memb and chm Grants Ctee UK Exec for Euro Architectural Heritage Year; memb: Historic Bldgs Cncl, Preservation Policy Gp; visiting prof Centre for Conservation Louvain Univ Belgium; advsr: Council of Euro, OECD Paris; *Style*— Alfred Wood, Esq, CBE, TD; The Hall Barn, Dunley nr Stourport, Worcestershire DY13 OTX (☎ 02993 6922)

WOOD, Anthony Hugh Boynton-; Lord of the Manor of Copmanthorpe, nr York (acquired 1568); o s of Frederick Anthony Boynton-Wood (d 1939; s of Capt Albert Charles Wood, JP, 8 QRI Hussars, of Hollin Hall, Ripon), and Gladys Gertrude (d 1986), yr da of Charles Frederick Wray, of Hobberley House, Shadwell (gs of William Wray, of Castle Wray, Co Donegal) (*see* Burke's LG 18 edn, vol III, 1972, Boynton-Wood); ninth in descent from Dame Frances Boynton, da and co-heir of John Barnard, Mayor of Hull, who refused Charles 1 entry to the city, and was great-uncle of Anne Boldero-Barnard, Lady Carrington; ggg nephew of Rev Prof Thomas Robert Malthus, of Haileybury Coll, author of the celebrated 'Essay on Principle of Population'; collateral descendant of Bl Edmund Sykes (martyred 23 March 1587, beatified 22 Nov 1987), through his niece Dame Frances Boynton; *b* 1 May 1917; *Educ* privately, Leeds Univ, Hull Univ; *Career* slr 1947; landowner (manages ancestral 1,000 acre estate in family since 1719 and Hollin Arab Stud); received into Church of Rome at Ampleforth 1987; life memb: The Arab Horse Soc, The British Horse Society, Law Soc, Selden Soc (8 New Sq, Lincoln's Inn), Historic Houses Assoc, Cromwell Assoc, Nat Art-Collections Fund; vice pres Friends of York City Art Gallery; *Recreations* horse trials, riding, gardening, genealogy, heraldry, arts, music, theatre; *Style*— Anthony Boynton-Wood, Esq; Hollin Hall, Ripon, N Yorks (☎ 0765 692466)

WOOD, Anthony Richard; s of Rev Thomas John Wood (d 1973), and Phyllis Margaret, *née* Bold; *b* 13 Feb 1932; *Educ* St Edward's Sch Oxford, Worcester Coll Oxford (BA); *m* 1966 (m dis 1973), Sarah, *née* Drew; 1 s (Nicholas b 1969), 1 da (Lucy b 1971); *Career* Army 1950-52 Lt TA 1952-56; Br Sch of Archaeology in Iraq Nimrud Expedition 1956; joined HM Foreign Serv 1957; serv: Beirut 1957, Bahrain 1958, Paris 1959, Benghazi 1962, Aden 1963, Basra 1966, Tehran 1970, Muscat 1980, cnsllr FCO 1984, ret 1987; *Recreations* walking, singing; *Clubs* Army and Navy, Royal Green Jackets London; *Style*— Anthony R Wood, Esq

WOOD, Prof Bernard Anthony; s of Anthony Frederick Wood, of Burnham-on-Sea, Somerset, and Joan Faith, *née* Slocombe; *b* 17 April 1945; *Educ* King's Sch Gloucester, Middx Hosp Med Sch Univ of London (BSc, MB BS, PhD); *m* 29 March 1982, Alison Margretta, da of Robert Richards, of Studham, Beds; 1 s (Nicholas b 1970), 2 da (Penny b 1972, Hannah b 1986); *Career* SA Courtauld prof Univ of London 1982-85 (lectr 1973-75, sr lectr 1975-87, reader 1978-82), Derby prof of anatomy and head of Dept of Human Anatomy and Cell Biology 1985-; past pres Primate Soc of GB, vice pres Royal Anthropological Inst, past sec Br Assoc of Clinical Anatomists; *Books* Human Evolution (1978), Major Topics in Primate and Human Evolution (1986); *Recreations* gardening, walking; *Style*— Prof Bernard Wood; Huntsman's Cottage, Smiths Lane, Clutton, Cheshire CH3 9EP (☎ 0829 782545); Human Anatomy and Cell Biology, Liverpool University, PO Box 147, Liverpool L69 3BX (☎ 051 794 5494, fax 051 794 5517)

WOOD, Catherine Mary; da of Dr Dennis Frederick James Malins, of Mayfield, Owl Lane, East Lambrook, South Petherton, Somerset, and Kathleen Frances, *née* Carroll; *b* 18 Aug 1958; *Educ* Greenhill CS Sch Tenby Pembrokeshire, Univ of Cardiff (LLB); *m* 18 June 1988, Timothy Peter Wood, s of Peter Wood; *Career* slr; Deacons Hong Kong 1984-87, res ptnr Phillips & Buck London 1987- (slr Cardiff Office 1980-84); memb: City of London Law Soc, Holborn Law Soc; *Recreations* squash, golf; *Clubs* Richard Town Squash; *Style*— Mrs Catherine Wood

WOOD, Charles Anthony; s of Anthony Mewburn Wood, of Chiddingstone, Kent, and Margaret Kathleen, *née* Stordy; *b* 20 Nov 1938; *Educ* Downside, Pembroke Coll Oxford (MA); *m* 10 Oct 1964, Susan Mary, da of Henry Anderson, OBE (d 1975), of Wallingford; 3 s (Robert b 1969, Francis b 1979, Jonathan b 1982), 1 da (Juliette b 1971); *Career* Phillips & Drew 1962-71, L Messel & Co 1971-86, Lehman Brothers Securities 1986-; chm New Islington and Hackney Housing Assoc 1984-; ASIA; *Recreations* houses, gardening; *Style*— Charles Wood, Esq; 14 Compton Terrace, London N1 2UN (☎ 071 226 4056); Lehman Brothers Securities, Shearson Lehman Hutton, One Broadgate, London EC2M 7HA (☎ 071 601 0011)

WOOD, Charles Gerald; s of John Edward Wood; *b* 6 Aug 1932; *Educ* Chesterfield GS, King Charles I Sch Kidderminster, Birmingham Coll of Art; *m* 1954, Valerie Elizabeth Newman; 1 s (John Charles b 1954), 1 da (Katrina b 1959); *Career* dramatist, screenwriter and writer for TV and radio; scenic artist, layout artist and stage mangr 1955-63 (Theatre Workshop, Repertory Theatre, Bristol Old Vic, Co-Operative Wholesale Soc), cartoonist The Stage, The Globe and Mail Toronto; full time writer 1963-; *plays for the theatre 1963-89* Cockade, Dingo, Don't Make Me Laugh, Meals on Wheels, Fill the Stage with Happy Hours, H or Monologues at Front of Burning Cities, Tie Up the Ballcock, Welfare, The Garden, Veterans, The Script, Jingo, Red Star, Has Washington Legs, Across From the Garden of Allah, The Plantagenets, Man Beast and Virtue, Arabia; *works for the cinema 1963-91* The Knack, Help, How I Won the War, The Long Day's Dying, The Charge of the Light Brigade, The Bed Sitting Room, Cuba, Wagner, Red Monarch, Tumbledown; *works for TV 1963-* plays: Not At All, Traitor in a Steel Helmet, Drill Pig, Prisoner and Escort, Drums Along the Avon, Mutzen Ab!, A Bit of a Holiday, A Bit of a Family Feeling, A Bit of Vision, A Bit of an Adventure, Death or Glory Boy, The Emergence of Antony Purdy Esq, Love Lies Bleeding, Do As I Say!; series: Don't Forget to Write, My Family and Other Animals (adaption), The Setting of the Sun; documentaries: Last Summer By the Sea; films: Pucini, Wagner, Tumbledown (Prix Italia RAI prize, Best Single Play BAFTA, Best Single Play RTS, Best Single Play BPG); *work for radio 1962-72* Prisoner and Escort, Cowheel Jelly, Next to Being a Knight; *pubns incl* Cockade, New English Dramatists 8, Dingo, H, Veterans, Man Beast and Virture; *work for TV and film 1991* Eva Trout, Sunday Best, The Black Guard, Shooting the Hero; memb Drama Panel SW ARts 1970-72, conslt Nat Film Devpt Fund 1980-82, memb Cncl BAFTA 1990; FRSL 1984; *Style*— Charles Wood, Esq; c/o William Morris Agency Ltd, 31/32 Soho Square, London W1V 5DG (☎ 071 434 2191)

WOOD, David Bernard; s of Richard Edwin Wood (d 1987), and Audrey Adele Whittle, *née* Fincham; *b* 21 Feb 1944; *Educ* Chichester HS for Boys, Worcester Coll Oxford (BA); *m* 1, 1966 (m dis 1970), Sheila, *née* Ruskin; m 2, Jan 1975, Jacqueline, da of Prof Sydney William Stanbury; 2 da (Katherine b 1976, Rebecca b 1979); *Career* actor, writer, composer, theatre dir and prodr; dir: WSG Productions Ltd 1966-, Verronmead Ltd 1982-, Westwood Theatrical Productions Ltd 1986-; hon pres Friends of Wimbledon Theatre; many plays published by Samuel French; children's books incl The Gingerbread Man (1985), The Operats of Rodent Garden (1984), The Discorats (1985), Playtheatres (1987), Sidney the Monster (1988) Happy Birthday, Mouse (1990); *Recreations* conjuring, collecting old books; *Clubs* Green Room; *Style*— David Wood, Esq; c/o Margaret Ramsay Ltd, 14A Goodwin's Court, St Martin's Lane, London WC2 (☎ 071 240 0691)

WOOD, David Frederick; s of Donald Wood (d 1983), and Deborah, *née* Kaminkovitch; *b* 19 Nov 1934; *Educ* Palmers Endowed Sch Essex; *m* 11 Dec 1960, Carole June, da of Isaac Zietman (ka 1944); 2 s (Ivor b 1966, Roger b 1969); *Career* Nat Serv RAF 1953-55; underwriting memb Lloyds, dir and sec Q Insur Servs plc 1988-; Freeman City of London, memb Guild of Freemen of the City of London 1986, Liveryman Worshipful Co of Arbitrators 1988-; ACII, ACIArb; *Recreations* photography, caravanning; *Style*— David Wood, Esq; 2 Archway Parade, Marsh Rd, Luton, Beds LU3 2RW (☎ 0582 490431, 0582 491045)

WOOD, David John Dargue; s of John Nöel Wood, MC (d 1976), of Sheffield, and Ruth Mary Dargue, *née* Moffitt (d 1987); *b* 17 April 1930; *Educ* King Edward VII Sch Sheffield, Wadham Coll Oxford (MA); *m* 23 March 1957, (Rosemary) Sepha, da of Lt-Col Philip Neill, TD (d 1986), of Whitby; 1 s (Justin b 1959), 1 da (Annabel b 1963); *Career* Flag Offr RAF Airfield Construction Branch Egypt and Libya 1953-54; ptnr

Husband and Co conslt engrs 1967-88 (jt md 1988-90); pres Br section Société des Ingenieurs et Scientifiques de France 1984-85; treas Assoc of Conslting Engrs 1980-81; FEng 1987, FICE 1964, FIWEM 1965, MConsE 1967; *Recreations* sailing; *Clubs* Royal Cruising, Royal Ocean Racing; *Style*— David Wood, Esq; Little Crofton Cottage, Titchfield, Hants PO14 2JE (☎ 0329 47844)

WOOD, Major General Denys Broomfield; CB (1978); s of Maj Percy Neville Wood (d 1952), of Hartfield Sussex, and Meryl, *née* Broomfield (d 1964); *b* 2 Nov 1923; *Educ* Radley, Pembroke Coll Cambridge (BA, MA, Capt of Coll Boat Club and memb Univ of Cambridge Goldie Crew); *m* 12 June 1948, Jennifer Nora, da of Air Cdre William Morton Page, CBE (d 1957), of Wimbledon; 1 s (Andrew Richard b 1950), 2 da (Joanna Margaret b 1954, Bridget Susan b 1956); *Career* War Serv UK and Far East 1944-47, cmmnd REME 1944, staff capt WO 1948; instr RMA Sandhurst 1949, staff coll 1953, DAA & QMG II Inf Bde Gp 1955, OC IO Inf Workshop Malaya 1958, Jt Servs Staff Coll 1960, directing staff Staff Coll 1961, Cmdg REME 3 Div 1963, operational observer Vietnam 1966-67, Col GS Staff Coll 1967, Imp Def Coll 1970, dir admin planning (Army) 1971, dep mil sec 1973, dir Army Quartering 1975-78, Col Cmdt REME 1978-84; exec sec then sec CEI 1978-84; memb Lord Chllrs Panel of Ind Inquiry Inspectors 1984-, gen cmmr of taxes 1985-, lay memb Adjudication Ctee Law Soc 1986-; chartered engr, FIMechE, FRSA; *Style*— Maj-Gen Denys Wood, CB

WOOD, Dudley Ernest; s of Ernest Edward Wood, and Ethel Louise Wood; *b* 18 May 1930; *Educ* Luton GS, St Edmund Hall Oxford (BA); *m* 1955, Mary Christin, *née* Blake; 2 s; *Career* ICI 1954-: Petrochemicals and Plastics Div, overseas mangr 1977-82, sales and mktg mangr 1982-86; played rugby football for: Univ of Oxford, Bedford, Rosslyn Park, Waterloo, Streatham Croydon, E Mids; sec RFU 1986-; hon life memb Squash Racquets Assoc 1984; *Recreations* squash, travel, dog-breeding, ME affrs; *Clubs* E India, Royal Overseas League; *Style*— Dudley Wood, Esq; c/o RFU, Twickenham, Middx TW1 1DZ (☎ 081 892 8161, fax 081 892 9816)

WOOD, Hon Edward Orlando Charles; JP; s of Baron Holderness, PC, DL (Life Peer); *b* 1951; *m* 1977, Joanna H, da of John Pinches and Rosemary Pinches *qv*; 1 da (Leonora Sarah Clare b 1982); *Career* CA; *Style*— The Hon Edward Wood, JP; Flat Top House, Bishop Wilton, Yorks

WOOD, Dr Francis William; s of Harry William Wood (d 1980), and Alfreda Elizabeth Wood (d 1969); *b* 29 Jan 1930; *Educ* Wolverton GS, Univ of London (BSc, PhD); *m* 30 April 1958, Christiane Elizabeth, da of Aloys Marbach (d 1965); 1 s (Robert b 1964), 1 da (Catherine b 1962); *Career* sr scientist Unilever Res 1964-82; conslt chemist, princ Gel Plan Servs; Open Univ tutor; *Recreations* music, sailing; *Style*— Dr Francis Wood; Leslie House, Kenton, Exeter EX6 8JD

WOOD, Sir Frederick Ambrose Stuart; s of Alfred Phillip Wood, of Goole, Yorks, and Patras, Greece, and Charlotte, *née* Barnes; *b* 30 May 1926; *Educ* Felsted Sch, Clare Coll Cambridge; *m* 1947, J R (Su) King; 2 s, 1 da; *Career* serv WWII Sub Lt Fleet Air Arm 1944-47; formerly chm Nat Bus Co 1972-78; chm Croda Int 1960-86 (md 1953), chm NEB 1981, NRDC 1979-81 (memb 1973) and first chm of the Br Tech Gp (after NEB and NRDC merged) 1981-83; Hon LLD Univ of Hull; kt 1977; *Style*— Sir Frederick Wood; Plaster Hill Farm, Churt, Surrey (☎ 0428 712134)

WOOD, Gareth Haydn; s of Haydn William George Wood, and Joyce, *née* Jenkins; *b* 7 June 1950; *Educ* Pontypridd Boys' GS, RAM; *Career* dir RPO (memb 1972-), composer of many pieces for brass bands incl Butlins Youth 1977 and Nat 4 Section 1980; cmmns incl: Overture Suffolk Punch for the RPO, Festivities Overture for the Philharmonic Orch, fanfares for 100 years of the Financial Times, fanfare for 150 years of Cunard, Sinfoniettas 2, 3 and 4 for the Nat Youth Orch of Wales; ARAM; *Style*— Gareth Wood, Esq; 57 Marischal Road, Lewisham, London SE13 5LE (☎ 081 318 3312)

WOOD, Geoffrey Frank; s of Frank Harold Wood, (d 1959), of Rookwood, St Johns Ave, Clevedon, Avon and Elsie May Winifred, *née* Saunders (d 1944); *b* 16 Sept 1917; *Educ* Clifton, Univ of Bristol (LLB); *m* 23 June 1942, Marjorie Sybil (d 1988), da of Phillip George Vowles (d 1949), of 18 Walsingham Rd, Bristol; 1 s (Jonathan b 14 Oct 1947) 1 da (Jennifer (Mrs Warner) b 15 Aug 1944); *Career* serv WWII: Capt RA 1939-45; admitted slr 1945, cmmr for oaths 1946- 82, sr ptnr Sinnott Wood & Co Bristol 1953-82, ret 1982; chm Tickenham Parish Cncl 1975-76, formerly hon sec Old Cliftonian Soc (Bristol branch); memb: Law Soc 1946, Bristol Law Soc 1946-82; *Recreations* photography, gardening; *Style*— Geoffrey Wood, Esq; 18 The Green, Shaldon, Devon TQ14 ODW (☎ 0626 873705)

WOOD, (Francis) Gordon; s of Francis Roberts Wood (d 1953), and Florence Ada, *née* Woodcock (d 1980); *b* 30 Oct 1924; *Educ* Alleyne's GS Stone Staffs; *m* 20 July 1950, Margaret Felicité, da of Albert Edward Parr (d 1944); 2 da (Hilary Christine b 1953, Dereth Margaret b 1956); *Career* RN Air Serv 1943-47; Prudential Assurance Co Ltd: dep chief gen mangr 1981-85, dir 1982-85; dir Prudential Corporation Plc 1984-90; ACII 1949, FIA 1956; *Recreations* golf, walking; *Style*— Gordon Wood, Esq; 6 Matching Lane, Bishops Stortford, Herts CM23 2PP (☎ 0279 652197)

WOOD, Prof Graham Allan; s of William Wales Wood, of Glasgow, and Ann Fleming, *née* Blackwood; *b* 15 Aug 1946; *Educ* Hillhead HS, Univ of Glasgow (BDS), Univ of Dundee (MB ChB); *m* 23 Nov 1970, Lindsay, da of Alfred Balfour; 1 s (Alexander b 1985), 1 da (Nicola b 1975); *Career* gen dental practice 1968-70, house offr and sr house offr Glasgow Dental Hosp 1970-71, registrar in oral and maxillofacial surgery Canniesburn and Victoria Infirmary Hosps 1971-72, dental surgeon Int Grenfell Assoc 1972-73, registrar in oral and maxillofacial surgery Queen Elizabeth Hosp Birmingham 1973-74, sr registrar in oral and maxillofacial surgery N Wales 1979-83 (conslt 1983-), clinical prof in oral and maxillofacial surgery Univ of Texas, post grad tutor in Dentistry; dip in cleft lip and palate surgery Univ of Mexico; memb: BMA, BAOMS, BSi, BrSoc Head and Neck Oncology, Craniofacial Soc of GB, FRCS 1985, FRCS (Ed) 1985, FDSRCPS (Glas) 1973; *Books* Cryosurgery of the Maxillofacial Region Vol II (contrib 1986); *Recreations* golf, squash, sailing, hill walking, skiing (formerly Canadian ski patroller); *Clubs* Rotary (St Asaph), Denbigh Golf Club, Sailing Club (Llyn Aled); *Style*— Prof Graham Wood; Northcote, Mount Road, St Asaph, Clwyd LL17 0DE (☎ 0745 583323); Department of Oral and Maxillofacial Surgery, Glan Clwyd Hospital, Bodelwyddan, Rhyl, Clwyd LL18 5UJ (☎ 0745 583910)

WOOD, Graham Barry; s of Anthony Philip Wood, of Outgate, Cumbria, and Jean Wissett, *née* Snelgrove; *b* 21 June 1959; *Educ* Merchant Taylors' Crosby, Univ of Salford Salford (BSc); *m* 1, 6 Aug 1983 (m dis 1985), Hilene Susan, da of Wilson McCloud Henry, of Thornton, Merseyside; m 2, 2 Sept 1989, Yvonne Alison Owen Ditchfield, da of James Edward Owen, of Heaton Moor, Stockport; *Career* CA, ptnr Hanley & Co Cheshire 1985-; fin dir: Ebony Hldgs Plc, Ebony Devpts Ltd, Ebony Residential Properties Ltd, Stache (UK) Ltd, Brooks Owen Assocs Ltd Hanley & Co Fin Servs Ltd, Hanley & Co Accountants Ltd; ICAEW 1983, ACA 1983; *Recreations* sailing, golf, wine; *Style*— Graham Wood, Esq; Broadway Farm, Luddington Hill, Cotebrook, Tarporley, Cheshire CW6 9DW (☎ 08293 2434); Hanley & Co, The Polygon, Stamford Road, Bowdon, Cheshire (☎ 061 928 7100, fax 061 928 7419, car 0836 588436)

WOOD, Prof Graham Charles; s of Cyril Wood (d 1964) of Farnborough, Kent, and Doris Hilda, *née* Strange (d 1986); *b* 6 Feb 1934; *Educ* Bromley GS Kent, Christ's Coll Cambridge (MA, PhD, ScD); *m* 19 Dec 1959, Freda Nancy, da of Arthur Waithman (d 1973), of Bolton, Lancashire; 1 s (David b 1964), 1 da (Louise b 1963); *Career* Inst of Sci and Technol Univ of Manchester 1961-72 (lectr, sr lectr then reader in corrosion sci), prof of corrosion sci and engrg 1972-, head of Corrosion Protection Centre 1972-82, dean Academic Devpt 1987-89 (vice princ 1982-84); former: pres Inst of Corrosion Sci Technol, chm of Nat Cncl of Corrosion Soc; vice chm Int Corrosion Cncl; FIM 1969, CEng, FEng 1990, FRSC 1969 CChem, FIMF 1972, FICorr 1968; *Recreations* travel, cricket, walking; *Style*— Prof Graham Wood; 8 Amberley Close, Deane, Bolton, Lancashire BL3 4NJ (☎ 0204 63659); Corrosion and Protection Centre, University of Manchester Institute of Science and Technology (UMIST), PO Box 88, Sackville St, Manchester M60 1QD (☎ 061 200 4851, telex 666094, fax 061 200 4865)

WOOD, Prof Hamish Christopher Swan; s of Joseph Wood (d 1958), of Hawick, Roxburghshire, and Robina Leggat, *née* Baptie (d 1959); *b* 8 May 1926; *Educ* Hawick HS, Univ of St Andrews (BSc, PhD); *m* 18 Dec 1951, Jean Dumbreck, da of George Mitchell, of Hawick, Roxburghshire; 1 s (Colin Dumbreck b 16 Dec 1957), 1 da (Sheena Margaret (Mrs Walker) b 22 Feb 1953); *Career* lectr in chemistry Univ of St Andrews 1950-51, res fell Dept of Med Chemistry Aust Nat Univ 1951-53, reader in organic chemistry (also lectr and sr lectr) 1953-69; Univ of Strathclyde: prof of organic chemistry 1969-, dep princ 1982-84, vice princ 1984-86; chm Governing Body Glasgow Polytechnic 1987-); memb Universities Funding Cncl 1989-; FRSE 1968, FRSC 1973; *Style*— Prof Hamish Wood, FRSE; 26 Albert Drive, Bearsden, Glasgow G61 2PG (☎ 041 9424552); Department of Pure and Applied Chemistry, University of Strathclyde, Thomas Graham Building, 295 Cathedral St, Glasgow G1 1XL (☎ 041 5524400, fax 041 5525664, telex UNSLIB G)

WOOD, Sir Henry Peart; CBE (1960); s of Thomas Marshall Wood (d 1968), of Bedlington Northumberland, and Margery Eleanor (d 1941), *née* Peart; *b* 30 Nov 1908; *Educ* Morpeth GS, Univ Of Durham (MSc), Univ of Manchester (MA, MEd); *m* 1937, Isobel Mary, da of William Frederick Stamp (d 1956), of Carbis Bay, Cornwall; 1 s, 2 da; *Career* lectr Univ of Manchester 1937-44, princ Jordanhill Coll of Educn Glasgow 1949-71, visiting prof Univ of Strathclyde 1976-84; Hon LLD: Univ of Glasgow 1972, Univ of Strathclyde 1982; kt 1967; *Style*— Sir Henry Wood, CBE; 15A Hughenden Court, Hughenden Rd, Glasgow G12 9XP (☎ 041 334 3647)

WOOD, Ian Clark; CBE (1982); s of John Wood (d 1986) and Margaret, *née* Clark (d 1981); *b* 21 July 1942; *Educ* Robert Gordon's Coll Aberdeen, Aberdeen Univ (BSc); *m* 1970, Helen, *née* Macrae; 3 s; *Career* chm and md John Wood Gp plc, chm J W Holdings Ltd; awards: Grampian Industrialist of the Year, Young Scottish Businessman of the Year 1979, Scottish Free Enterprise 1985; memb Lloyd's; dir Aberdeen Beyond 2000, chm Grampian Enterprise; memb: Bd Royal Bank of Scot plc, Offshore Indust Advsy Bd, Offshore Indust Export Advsy Gp, Scottish Economic Cncl, Univs Funding Cncl Scottish Sub Ctee, Nat Trg Task force, Carnegie Tst; Hon LLD Aberdeen 1984; FRSA, CBIM; *Recreations* squash, art, family; *Style*— Ian Wood, Esq, CBE; Marchmont, 42 Rubislaw Den South, Aberdeen AB2 6BB (☎ 0224 313625); John Wood Gp plc, John Wood Hse, Greenwell Rd, East Tullos, Aberdeen AB1 4AX (☎ 0224 875464, telex 739977)

WOOD, James Alexander Douglas; s of Lt-Col Alexander Blythe Wood, TD, and Cynthia Mary, *née* Boot; *b* 25 June 1952; *Educ* Haileybury, Univ of Warwick (LLB); *m* 1 s (Nathan b 1988); *Career* called to the Bar Middle Temple 1975; memb: int mission of lawyers to Malaysia 1982, panel of inquiry into visit of Leon Brittan to Univ of Manchester Students Union in March 1985; involved for the defence in many Civil rights incl: The Newham Seven, The Broad Water Farm Trials, The Miners Strike Trials, Birmingham Six Appeal; exec memb NCCL; *Books* The Right of Silence, the Case for Retention (1989); *Recreations* the attainment of socialism and civil liberties; *Style*— James Wood, Esq; 35 Wellington St, London WC2 (☎ 071 836 5917, fax 071 831 1241)

WOOD, Hon Mrs (Joan Mary); *née* Wise; da of 1 Baron Wise, DL; *b* 27 Sept 1912; *m* 1938, John Wood; 3 s (Michael v 1939, David b 1946, Roger b 1947), 1 da (Mary b 1941); *Style*— The Hon Mrs Wood; Ham Farm, Berrow, Burnham-on-Sea, Somerset

WOOD, John; CB (1989); s of Maj Thomas John Wood, IA (d 1962), of Varndean Gardens, Brighton, Sussex, and Rebecca, *née* Grand; *b* 11 Jan 1931; *Educ* King's Coll Sch Wimbledon, Law Soc Sch of Law; *m* 3 April 1958, Jean Iris, da of George Collier (d 1945), of London; 2 s (Simon b 1959, Nicholas b 1961); *Career* slr; dep dir Public Prosecutions 1985; dir Serious Fraud Office 1987, DPP Hong Kong 1990; *Recreations* most sports, theatre, music; *Style*— John Wood, Esq, CB; Director of Public Prosecutions, Hong Kong

WOOD, John Edward; OBE (1977); s of John Wood (d 1965), of Newcastle, Staffs, and Elsie, *née* Rose (d 1985); *b* 23 March 1924; *Educ* Wolstanton Co GS N Staffs, N Staffs Tech Coll (Dip in Mining Engrg), King's Coll Durham (BSc); *m* 9 Sept 1949, Valerie Joy, da of Frederick Heath Grindey; 2 s (Stephen John b 4 Oct 1954, Robert Geoffrey b 13 Dec 1959), 1 da (Helena Judith b 14 Sept 1952); *Career* underground coal miner and trainee mining engr 1940-50, various mgmnt posts rising to colliery mangr N Staffs 1951, mangr several collieries (incl E Midlands 1954) 1951-60; NCB: sr mgmnt posts at gp and area level 1960-71, area dir S Notts, Doncaster N Notts 1972-85; self-employed conslt mining engr 1985-; awards: Futers medal (IMinE) 1975, Lord Edward Cavendish medal (Notts & N Derby Br Inst Mining Engrs) 1985; Freeman City of London 1979, fndr memb Worshipful Co of Engrs; fell Inst of Mining Engrs 1940 (nat pres 1977), CEng 1970, FEng 1980, CBIM, former pres Notts and N Derbyshire Branch Inst Mining Engrs; *Clubs* Freemason, St John; *Style*— John E Wood, Esq, OBE; 6 The Avenue, Mansfield, Nottinghamshire NG18 4PN (☎ 0623 23083)

WOOD, Dr John Edwin; s of John Stanley Wood (d 1974), of Darlington, and Alice Hardy (d 1968); *b* 24 July 1928; *Educ* Darlington GS, Univ of Leeds (BSc, PhD); *m* 13 June 1953 (m dis 1978), Patricia Edith Wilson, da of Alfred Sheppard (d 1956); 2 s (Jonathan (John) b 1954, Andrew b 1956), 2 da (Susan b 1961, Nicola b 1965); *Career* joined RN Sci Serv 1959; Underwater Countermeasures and Weapons Estab 1959-76: head Acoustics Res Div 1968, head Sonar Dept 1972; Admty Surface Weapons Estab: head Weapons Dept 1976, head Communications Cmd and Control Dept 1979; chief scientist (RN) and dir gen res (Army) 1980; Br Aerospace (formerly Sperry Gyroscope) Bracknell 1981 (exec dir Bristol Div 1984-88), dir underwater engrg Br Aerospace (Dynamics) Ltd 1988-90; pres Gp 12 Cncl of Br Archaeology 1984-, chm Undersea Def Technol Conf; *Books* Sun Moon and Standing Stones (second edn, 1980); *Recreations* archaeology and fell walking; *Style*— Dr John Wood; 7 Pennant Hills, Havant, Hants PO9 3JZ (☎ 0705 471 411); British Aerospace (Dynamics) Ltd, PO Box 5, Filton, Bristol BS12 7QW (☎ 0272 366 020, fax 0272 363925)

WOOD, Hon Mr Justice; Hon Sir John Kember Wood; MC (1944); s of John Roskruge Wood; *b* 8 Aug 1922; *Educ* Shrewsbury, Magdalene Coll Cambridge; *m* 1952, Kathleen Lowe; 1 s, 1 da; *Career* serv WWII Rifle Bde; called to the Bar Lincoln's Inn 1949, QC 1969, rec Crown Ct 1975-77, High Ct judge Family Div 1977-; pres of Employment Appeals Tbnl 1988- (judge 1985-88); kt 1977; *Style*— The Hon Mr Justice Wood, MC; Royal Cts of Justice, London WC2A 2LL (☎ 071 936 6000)

WOOD, John Lockhart; JP; s of George Lockhart Wood (d 1959), and Joan Wood, *née* Halsey; *b* 22 Aug 1935; *Educ* Eton, Trinity Coll Cambridge (MA); *m* 26 Oct 1963,

(Rosemary) Sonia Despard, da of Richard Graham Hemsley Hopkins (d 1974); 1 s (Edmund b 1966), 1 da (Kirsty b 1968); *Career* Nat Serv 2 Lt 8 Kings Royal Irish Hussars; McCorquodale plc 1958-86: dir 1964-86, chief exec 1972-86, chm 1986; non-exec dir: Halifax Bldg Soc 1986-, Bibby Line Group Ltd 1987-, Domino Printing Sciences plc 1988-; High Sheriff Hertfordshire 1988-89; *Recreations* gardening, fishing, travel; *Clubs* Cavalry and Guards'; *Style*— John Wood, Esq, JP; The Hoo, Great Gaddesden, Hemel Hempstead, Herts HP2 6HD (☎ 0442 252689)

WOOD, John Lucas; ERD; s of Laurence Hemsley Wood (d 1978), and Lucy, *née* Lucas (d 1972); *b* 29 Sept 1923; *Educ* KCS, Univ of London (BSc); *m* 17 May 1947, (Joyce) Cynthia, da of Frank Victor Gunn (d 1984); 2 s (Michael John Hemsley b 16 Sept 1948, Simon George Victor b 1 Nov 1952); *Career* joined RA 1941, cmmnd W Somerset Yeo Field Artillery 1942, Gds Armd Div 1942-45, qualified as Air OP Pilot; Miny of Agric 1950-56, in private practice as Chartered Surveyor 1956-90; Freeman City of London, Liveryman Worshipful Co of Surveyors; FRICS, FCIArb; *Recreations* golf; *Clubs* Royal Eastbourne Golf; *Style*— John Wood, Esq, ERD; Dolphins, 36 Vicarage Drive, Eastbourne, E Sussex (☎ 0323 34443)

WOOD, John Norris; s of Wilfrid Burton Wood, (d 1943) and Lucy Heald Sutcliffe Boston (d 1977); *b* 29 Nov 1930; *Educ* Bryanston Sch, Goldsmiths' Coll Sch of Art, Anglian Sch of Painting & Design, RCA (Degree with Hons); *m* 12 June 1962, Julie Corsellis Guyatt, da of John Nicholls (d 1968); 1 s (Wilfrid Spencer Conal b 1968), 1 da (Dinah Elizabeth Georgia b 1971); *Career* artist and author; lectr in illustration Goldsmiths' Coll Sch of Art 1956-68, tutor Cambridge Coll of Art 1959-70; fndr scientific, tech, med illustration course at Hornsey Coll of Art 1965; fndr and i/c natural history illustration unit RCA 1971 (sr lectr to present day); regular Exhibits at RA Summer Exhibition; conslt to BBC Life on Earth; provided illustrations for: Time, Life, Knopf, Longmans, BBC Publications, Post Office, Methuen, Penguins, Sunday Times and others; FRCA (1980); *Recreations* conservation, natural history, art, music; *Style*— John N Wood, Esq; The Brook, Dewhurst Lane, Wadhurst, E Sussex TN5 6QE; Royal Coll of Art, Dept Natural History, 1 Darwin Building, Kensington Gore, London SW7

WOOD, John Walter; s of Prof John Walter Wood (d 1958), of New York, and Suzanne J, *née* Cort; *b* 7 July 1941; *Educ* in USA, Trinity Coll Dublin (BA), Univ of Oxford (MA), LSE, Univ of California (MA); *m* Charlotte Mary Baron, da of Robert Ralph Baron Cusack-Jobson of The Old Glebe, Newcastle, Co Dublin, Ireland; 1 s (William Duncan b 12 Feb 1964); *Career* chm: Wood Brigdale Nisbet & Robinson 1969-, Trilateral Communications 1986-; dir: Oxford Analytica Ltd 1982-, Segal Quince Wickstead Ltd; memb: Bd of Advsrs Sch of Int Relations Univ of S California London Prog, Gen Cncl Co-operation Ireland, Cncl Regents Coll, Ctee American Aid Soc; chm Republicans Abroad UK; IISS, RIIA, ISPP, APRA; *Clubs* Buck's, Caledonian, Utd Oxford and Cambridge Univ, Union (NY), Mid-Atlantic, Pilgrims, Monday Luncheon (co-chm); *Style*— John W Wood, Esq; 35 Brompton Square, London SW3; Kent House, Market Place, London W1

WOOD, Kenneth Maynard; s of Frederick Cavendish Wood (d 1928), and Agnes, *née* Maynard (d 1972); *b* 4 Oct 1916; *Educ* Bromley Co Sch; *m* 1, 1944, Laurie Marion (d 1976), da of late Michael McKinlay; 2 s (Michael b 1945, Stuart b 1948), 2 da (Sally b 1949, Gillian b 1955); m 2, 15 Sept 1978, Patricia Rose, da of Herbert William Purser (d 1982); *Career* Cadet MN 1930-34, RAF then transferred for devpt of electronic equipment 1939-46; md Kenwood Gp of Cos 1946-68, chm and md Dawson-Keith Gp of Cos 1972-80, chm Hydrotech Systems Ltd 1984-87, ret; Freeman Worshipful Co of Farriers 1972; Fell Inst Ophthalmology 1967; *Recreations* golf; *Style*— Kenneth Wood, Esq; Dellwood Cottage, Wheatsheaf Enclosure, Liphook, Hants GU30 7EH (☎ 0428 723 108)

WOOD, Leonard George; CBE (1978); s of Leonard George Wood (d 1955), and Miriam *née* Barnes (d 1924); *Educ* Bishopshalt Sch Hillingdon Middx, Univ of London (BCom); *m* 12 Sept 1936, Christine Florence (d 1978), da of William Cooper Reason (d 1935); *Career* Flying Offr RAF 1943-46; exec dir Parent Bd EMI Ltd (now Thorn EMI plc) 1965-80, gp dir records and music EMI Ltd 1966-77, asst md EMI Ltd 1973-77; chm: EMI Records UK Ltd 1966-78 (md 1959-66), EMI Music Publishing Ltd 1972-78; dep chm Phonographic Performance Ltd 1967-80, chm: Cncl of IFPI 1968-73, BPI 1973-80 (hon pres 1980-) Record Merchandisers Ltd 1975-80; vice pres and memb Bd of Int Fedn of Prodrs of Phonograms and Videograms (IFPI) 1967-82 (pres and chm of Bd 1973-76), tstee Br Record Industs Tst 1989-; *Recreations* gardening, music; *Style*— Leonard Wood, Esq, CBE; Lark Rise, 39 Howards Thicket Gerrards Cross, Buckinghamshire SL9 7NT (☎ 0753 884233); BPI Ltd, Roxburghe House, 273-287 Regent St, London W1R 7PB (☎ 071 629 8642)

WOOD, Rt Rev Maurice Arthur Ponsonby; DSC (1944); s of Arthur Wood, and Jane Elspeth Dalzell, *née* Piper; *b* 26 Aug 1916; *Educ* Monkton Combe Sch, Queens' Coll Cambridge (MA), Ridley Hall Cambridge; *m* 1, 1947, Marjorie, *née* Pennell (d 1954); 2 s, 1 da; m 2, 1955, Margaret, da of Rev E Sandford, MC; 2 s, 1 da; *Career* chaplain RN and Royal Marine Commandos 1943-46; rector St Ebbe's Oxford 1947-52, rural dean Islington 1952-61, princ Oak Hill Coll Southgate 1961-71, 69th bishop of Norwich 1971-85 (memb House of Lords 1975-85); hon asst bishop: Diocese of London 1985-, Diocese of Oxford 1988-; chm Order of Christian Unity 1986-, visitor Langley Sch 1975-85, govr Monkton Combe Sch; Chaplain Worshipful Co of Weavers 1986-91; *Books* Like a Mighty Army (1954), Your Suffering (1956), Comfort in Sorrow (1957), Christian Stability (1972), Into the Way of Peace (1982), This is Our Faith (1985); *Clubs* Royal Cwlth Soc; *Style*— The Rt Rev Maurice A P Wood; St Mark's House, Englefield, nr Reading, Berks RG7 5EP (☎ 0734 302227)

WOOD, Nicholas Andrew; s of Charles Stephen Wood, (d 1965), and Celia Patty Wood, *née* Underwood (d 1959); *b* 31 Jan 1943; *Educ* Lewes Co GS, Queen Elizabeth Sch Crediton; *m* 8 July 1972, Mary Kristina, da of Donald Bernard Naulin, of Williamsburg, Virginia; 2 da (Olivia Marian Vicary b 17 Oct 1984, Genevieve Anna Cordelia b 11 Oct 1987); *Career* called to the Bar Inner Temple 1970, asst recorder 1987, bencher of the Inner Temple 1990; Ordnance Survey 1960-61, Meridian Airways Ltd 1961-62, commercial artist, designer, copywriter 1962-67; *Recreations* people, places, art, music, transport; *Style*— Nicholas Wood, Esq; 5 Paper Buildings, Temple, London EC4Y 7HB (☎ 071 583 9275, fax 071 583 1926/2031)

WOOD, (John) Peter; s of Walter Ralph Wood (d 1967), and Henrietta, *née* Martin (d 1944); *b* 27 March 1925; *Educ* Grove Park GS Wrexham, Seale Hayne Agric Coll Newton Abbott, Royal Horticultural Soc Wisley; *m* 1956, Susan Maye, da of Brig Lesley White (d 1971); 1 s (David), 1 da (Victoria); *Career* ed Amateur Gardening 1971-85, conslt ed 1985-89, freelance gardening journalist and broadcaster 1989-; *Recreations* choral singing, sailing, gardening; *Style*— Peter Wood, Esq; 1 Charlton House Court, Charlton Marshall, Blandford Forum, Dorset (☎ 0258 454653)

WOOD, (John) Peter; s of late John Wood, and Louisa, *née* Herrington; *b* 18 June 1933; *Educ* Bradford GS, Univ of Durham (BSc); *m* 28 March 1958, Valerie, da of late William Spencer; 1 s (John b 1965), 1 da (Fiona b 1963); *Career* Nat Serv; J Bibby & Sons plc: md Palethorpes Ltd 1971-76, gen mangr Feeds and Seeds Div 1976-79, md Agricultural Gp 1979-84, chief exec 1984-89; dir Heart of England Building Society 1990-; CBIM; *Clubs* Oriental, Farmers; *Style*— Peter Wood, Esq

WOOD, Philip Barrington; s of James Barrington Wood, of Newcastle, Staffs, and June, *née* Sherratt (d 1983); *b* 20 Feb 1956; *Educ* Wolstanton Co GS Newcastle Staffs, North Staffs Poly; *m* 3 August 1988, Sheila Elizabeth, da of Norman Barton; 1 da (Katie Rebecca b 1 March 1988); *Career* Peat Marwick Mitchell & Co Stoke-on-Trent: articled clerk 1975-79, qualified 1979, (sr, supervisor, tax conslt) 1979-81; ptnr: Archer Britton & Co 1983-86 (mangr 1981-83), Archer Wood 1986-; pres: N Staffs CA Students Assoc 1980-81, Wolverhampton CA Students Assoc 1982-83, N Staffs Soc of CAs 1990-91 (former hon treas, hon sec); FCA 1990 (ACA 1979), ATII 1981-; *Recreations* motor sport, circuit racing, shooting; *Clubs* Rotary (Stoke-on-Trent), BRSCC, Silverstone Racing, Potteries & Newcastle Motor, RS Owners, Jaguar Drivers; *Style*— Philip Wood, Esq; April Cottage, Lower Road, Ashley, nr Market Drayton, Staffordshire TF9 4QJ; Archer Wood, 39/41 Trinity St, Hanley, Stoke on Trent ST1 5LQ (☎ 0782 273273, fax 0782 273588; Archer Wood, Bank House, Granville Square, Stone, Staffs ST15 8AB (☎ 0785 812 414, fax 0785 813822)

WOOD, Prof Philip Henry Nicholls; s of Herbert Wood (d 1969), of Sheffield, and Frances Amelia, *née* Nicholls (d 1961); *b* 23 Oct 1928; *Educ* Churcher's Coll Petersfield, Bart's Med Coll, Univ of London (MB BS); *m* 30 July 1952, Cherry Norma, da of Norman Charlish (d 1928), of Brighton; 4 da (Julia b 1956, Vyvyan b 1958, Eleanor b 1959, Beatrix b 1965); *Career* Nat Serv chief clerk Mil Hosp York RAMC 1947-49; res asst prof of med State Univ of NY at Buffalo USA 1963-65; Univ of Manchester: sr res fell Rheumatism Res Centre 1965-67, dir Arthritis and Rheumatism Cncl Epidemiology Res Unit Med Sch 1968-88 (emeritus dir 1989), hon lectr Dept of Community Med 1968-77, hon reader 1977-83, hon prof 1983-; conslt to WHO 1971-; memb Scientific Ctees Arthritis and Rheumatism Cncl 1971-, hon memb Euro League Against Rheumatism (former ed), scientific advsr to chief scientist DHSS 1977-87, memb ctees various rheumatological and epidemiological learned socs; FFCM 1972, FRCP 1978 (memb 1971), FFPHM 1989; *Books* Salicylates, An International Symposium (ed 1963), Population Studies of the Rheumatic Diseases (ed, 1968), International Classification of Instruments, Disabilities and Handicaps (1980), Oxford Textbooks of Public Health (contrib, 1984); *Recreations* oil and water-colour painting, listening to music, english lit; *Clubs* RSM; *Style*— Prof Philip Wood; Bephillick, Duloe, nr Liskeard, Cornwall PL14 4QA

WOOD, Richard Piers Karslake; s of Professor Ronald Karslake Starr Wood, of Pyrford, Surrey, and Majorie, *née* Schofield; *b* 12 Sept 1952; *Educ* Highgate Sch, Univ of Bristol (BSc); *m* 18 April 1978, Gillian Elisabeth, da of Geoffrey Knowles Ruse 1 s (Michael b 1984), 2 da (Victoria b 1982, Emma b 1989); *Career* Price Waterhouse 1974-79, corp fin Morgan Grenfell & Co Ltd 1979-85, asst dir institutional stockbroking Morgan Grenfell Securities Ltd 1985-87, sr salesman institutional stockbroking Smith New Court plc 1987-90, dir investor rels Streets Communications Limited; ACA 1977; *Recreations* golf, sailing, food and wine; *Clubs* Roehampton; *Style*— Richard Wood, Esq; Streets Communications Limited, 18 Red Lion Court, Fleet St, London EC4A 3HT (☎ 071 353 1090, fax 071 583 0661)

WOOD, Robert Wilson; s of Peter Wilson Wood, of Whitburn, Lothian, and Elizabeth Christie, *née* Campbell; *b* 18 Oct 1948; *Educ* Bathgate Acad, Univ of Strathclyde (BSc, Dip Mgmnt); *m* 6 Aug 1971, Mary Davidson, da of James Stewart Armadale (d 1962), of Lothian; 1 s (Alastair b 5 July 1982), 1 da (Lorna b 16 May 1979); *Career* gen mangr Volvo Trucks GB Ltd 1976-80, sales and serv dir Talbot Motor Co 1980-83, md Motor Div Godfrey Davis Holdings plc 1983-85, chief exec Henlys Ltd 1985-; md Plaxton Group plc 1990-; vice chm Elstree and Borehamwood MENCAP, govr Colnbrook Sch Watford; FBIM 1984, FInstD 1985, FIMI 1986; *Recreations* gardening, family; *Style*— Robert Wood, Esq; Henlys Ltd, 53 Theobald St, Borehamwood, Herts WD6 4RT (☎ 081 953 9953, fax 081 207 6245)

WOOD, Roger Bryan Savage; s of Frank Bryan Wood (d 1984), and Margaret Mary Wilkinson, *née* Done (d 1990); *b* 11 April 1939; *Educ* Bromsgrove Sch; *m* 21 Feb 1970, Dinah, da of Henry Brian Cookson, of Bradford-on-Avon, Wilts; 1 s (Alistair b 17 Feb 1972), 1 da (Philippa b 6 Jan 1974); *Career* CA 1963, Birmingham Industl Tst 1963-67, Neville Industl Securities 1967-70, dir Smith Keen Cutler 1986- (joined 1970, ptnr 1976); sec Birmingham CA's Students Soc 1962; FCA 1973, AMSIA 1980; *Recreations* squash, golf, hockey, watersports, skiing; *Clubs* Edgbaston Priory, Edgbaston Golf, Aberdovey Golf, Harborne Hockey; *Style*— Roger Wood, Esq; Harkaway, 60 Harborne Rd, Edgbaston, Birmingham 15 (☎ 021 454 4913); Smith Keen Cutler Ltd, Exchange Buildings, Stephenson Place, Birmingham B2 4NN (☎ 021 643 9977)

WOOD, Roger Norman Alexander; s of Adrian Theodore Wood, of Bristol, and Doreen Mary, *née* Gordon-Harris; *b* 13 Sept 1947; *Educ* The Leys Sch Cambridge, Univ of Bristol (BSc); *m* 1971, Mary Thomasine Howard, da of Howard Reginald Thomas; 1 s (Alexander b 1973), 2 da (Emily b 1975, Joanna b 1976); *Career* conslt Burmah Castrol plc 1990- (gp fin dir 1987-90); *Clubs* Oriental, West Hill Golf; *Style*— Roger Wood, Esq; High Leybourne, Hascombe, Godalming, Surrey GU8 4AD (☎ 048 632 559); 68 Mount St, London W1Y 5HL (☎ 071 499 9533)

WOOD, Prof Ronald Karslake Starr; s of Percival Thomas Evans Wood (d 1979), of Ferndale, and Florence Dix, *née* Starr (d 1989); *b* 8 April 1919; *Educ* Ferndale GS, Imperial Coll London (BSc, ARCSc, DIC, PhD); *m* 15 Dec 1947, Marjorie, da of Frank Schofield (d 1981), of Alnwick; 1 s (Richard Piers Karkslake b 1952), 1 da (Jessica Laura Anne b 1955); *Career* Imperial Coll London: lectr 1946, reader 1954, prof 1964; hon fell: American Phytopathological Soc, Deutsche Phytomedizinische Gesellschaft; Otto Appel Denkmunze German Fed Repub, first hon memb Int Soc for Plant Pathology, second hon memb Br Soc for Plant Pathology, ed 6 books on plant pathology; memb governing bodies: Imperial Coll, East Malling Res Station, Inst of Horiticultural Res; FRS; *Books* Physiological Plant Pathology (1967); *Recreations* gardening; *Style*— Prof Ronald Wood, FRS; Pryford Woods, Pryford, Surrey GU22 8QL (☎ 09323 43827); Imperial College, London SW7 2BB (☎ 071 589 5111, fax 071 225 1234)

WOOD, Simon Marshall; s of Capt Gordon William Wood (d 1964), and Eileen Mary, *née* Pigott-Smith; *b* 16 Oct 1938; *Educ* Oundle, Univ of Cambridge (MA, MB BChir), Univ of Birmingham (MD); *m* 10 Aug 1968, Gillian Anne, da of Dr Claude Newnham, of Brightwell-cum-Sotwell, Oxford; 4 s (Timothy b 1970, James b 1974, Matthew b 1977, Dominic b 1978); *Career* lectr: Guy's 1968-71, Univ of Rhodesia (now Zimbabwe) 1971-72; Wellcome res fell 1972-74, lectr Univ of Birmingham 1974-76, sr lectr Univ of Exeter 1977; memb: Ctee and sec Blair Bell Res Soc, Section Cncl RSM; FRCOG 1981; *Books* Prescribing in Pregnancy (1981); *Recreations* photography, church music, Islamic history, board sailing; *Style*— Simon Wood, Esq; 3 St Leonards Road, Exeter, Devon (☎ 0392 437435)

WOOD, Simon Richard Browne; s of Lt-Col Browne William Wood, of The Grange, Tadcaster, N Yorks, and Joan Radegunde, *née* Woollcombe; *b* 12 Dec 1947; *Educ* Eton; *m* 17 July 1970, Clare Launa, da of Lord Martin Fitzalan Howard, *qv* (bro 17 Duke of Norfolk), of Brockfield Hall, York; 1 s (Charles b 1973), 2 da (Alethea b 1975, Miranda b 1978); *Career* ptnr Sheppards and Chase 1975-80; dir Cater Allen plc 1981-; *Recreations* shooting, fishing; *Style*— Simon R B Wood, Esq; 17 Ellerby Street, London SW6 6EX (☎ 071 736 2779); 20 Birchin Lane, London EC3V 9DJ (☎ 071 623 2070, fax 071 929 1641, telex 888553)

WOOD, Steve; s of Henry James Wood (d 1989), of Southampton, and Irene Rhoda, *née* Stare; *b* 8 March 1946; *Educ* St Nicholas' New Forest, Southampton Art Coll (NDD); *m* 12 May 1984, Sally Karen Jameson; 2 da (Laura Juliet b 12 March 1987, Natalie Lucy b 21 May 1988); *Career* photographer specializing in portraits of Royal Family 1966-; 3 times runner-up Photographer of the Year; *Style*— Steve Wood, Esq

WOOD, Dr Susan Marion; da of Gerald Colomba Ryan, (d 1986), of Guildford, Surrey, and Marion Audrey, *née* Webb (d 1984); *b* 20 July 1952; *Educ* Tormead Sch Guildford, King's Coll London (BSc), St Bartholomews Hosp London (MB BS), Hammersmith Hosp (MD); *m* 30 Jan 1978, Dr John Roland Wood, s of Roland Wood; *Career* sr med offr Medicines Div DHSS 1983-87; princ med offr: Review of Medicines the Medicines Control Agency Dept of Health 1987, Drug Safety Unit Medicines Control Agency Dept of Health 1987-90, head Pharmacovigilance Unit Medicine Control Agency 1990-; author of pubns on endocrinology and adverse drug effects; UK rep of Safety and Pharmacovigilance Working Parties of Ctee on Proprietary Medicinal Products of EEC Brussels 1985 and 1988, memb Advsy Gp of WHO Collaborate Centre for Adverse Drug Reaction Monitoring 1988-; FRSM, memb Br Pharmacological Soc; *Recreations* travel, oriental cuisine; *Style*— Dr Susan Wood; Medicines Control Agency, Dept of Health, Market Towers, 1 Nine Elms Lane, London SW8 (☎ 071 720 2188 ext 3124, fax 071 498 1954)

WOOD, Lady; Susan Studd; MBE (1990); da of Alfred Barclay Buxton (d 1940), and Edith Mary Crossley, *née* Studd (d 1978); *b* 19 Oct 1918; *Educ* The Manor House Surrey, London House of Citizenship (now Hartwell House Aylesbury, Dip Soc Sci); *m* 6 Nov 1943, Sir (Arthur) Michael Wood, s of Arthur Henry Wood, CB; 2 s (Mark Lionel b 1945, Hugo Charles b 1948), 2 da (Janet Mary b 1946, Katrina Susan b 1951); *Career* WWII nurse Radcliffe Royal Infirmary Oxford; emigrated to Kenya 1947, mangr family farms (Kenya and Tanzania) 1951-75, fndr jewellery designer and md Kazuri Ltd (ceramics) Kenya 1975-; in E Africa helped to found: Red Cross Blood Bank, Flying Doctor Serv, African Med and Res Foundation; memb Capricorn Africa Soc during 1950's; *Books* Kenya - The Tensions of Progress (1955), A Fly in Amber (1964), A Dusty Mirror, This One Thing (published privately); *Recreations* swimming; *Clubs* Sloane; *Style*— Lady Wood, MBE; Mbagathi Ridge, Karen, Nairobi, Kenya; Box 24277, Nairobi, Kenya (☎ 010 254 2 882 362); Kazuri Ltd, Box 24276, Nairobi, Kenya (☎ 010 254 2 882 362, fax 882 501, telex 22992 HOSECS)

WOOD, Dr Timothy Campbell; s of Dr Guy E M Wood (d 1941), of Charterhouse, London EC1, and Margaret Dawson, *née* Campbell (d 1972); *b* 3 Oct 1928; *Educ* Rugby, Hertford Coll Oxford, UCH Med Sch; *m* 4 Aug 1956, (Dorothy) Ann, da of Harold Carpenter (d 1984), of Crakers Mead, Watford; 2 s (Geoffrey Campbell b 1957, Julian James b 1964), 1 da (Alison Elizabeth b 1958); *Career* 2 Lt RA 1955-57; UCH 1956-58: house physician, house surgn, res med offr; GP Watford Herts 1959-88, med offr Merchant Taylors' Sch 1966-88; hon sec W Herts and Watford Med Soc 1970-80, memb Herts Local Med Ctee; Freeman Worshipful Co of Fishmongers; FRCGP 1982; *Recreations* sailing; *Style*— Dr Timothy Wood; 20 Grey's Close, Cavendish, Suffolk CO10 8BT (☎ 0787 281 713)

WOOD, Timothy John Rogerson; MP (C) Stevenage 1983-; *b* 1940; *Educ* King James's GS Knaresborough Yorks, Univ of Manchester; *m* 1969, Elizabeth Mary Spencer; 1 s, 1 da; *Career* former project mangr ICL Ltd, memb Bow Group 1962-; PPS to: Rt Hon John Stanley Min of State for NI 1987-88, Min for Armed Forces 1986-87, Rt Hon Ian Stewart Min of State for NI 1988-89, Rt Hon Peter Brooke Sec of State for NI 1989-90; asst govt whip 1990-; chm Wokingham Cons Assoc 1980-83, vice chm Thames Valley Euro Constituency Cncl 1979-83; memb: Cons Cncl 1968-71, Bracknell Dist Cncl 1975-83 (ldr 1976-78), Bracknell Devpt Corpn. 1977-82; *Books* Bow Gp Pamphlets on educn, computers in Britain, and the Post Office; *Style*— Timothy Wood, Esq, MP; House of Commons, London SW1A 0AA

WOOD, (René) Victor; s of Frederick Wood (d 1973); *b* 4 Oct 1925; *Educ* Jesus Coll Oxford; *m* 1950, Helen Morag, *née* Stewart; *Career* actuary; dir: Sun Life Corporation plc, The Wemyss Devpt Co Ltd; *Style*— Victor Wood, Esq; Little Woodbury, Newchapel, nr Lingfield, Surrey RH7 6HR (☎ 0342 832054)

WOOD, Victoria; da of Stanley Wood, of Bury, Lancs, and Helen, *née* Mape; *b* 19 May 1953; *Educ* Bury GS, Univ of Birmingham (BA, Drama and Theatre Arts); *m* 1980, Geoffrey Durham; 1 da (Grace b 1988); *Career* entertainer and writer; plays: Talent 1978, (TV prodn won 3 Nat Drama Award 1980), Good Fun 1980; TV plays: Talent 1979, Nearly A Happy Ending 1980, Happy Since I Met You 1981; TV series Wood and Walters 1981, Victoria Wood As Seen on TV 1985 (Bdcasting Press Guilds Award, BAFTA Award), 2nd series 1986 (BAFTA Award), special 1987 (BAFTA Award); Audience with Victoria Wood 1988 (BAFTA Award), Victoria Wood 1989; West End Shows: Funny Turns 1982, Lucky Bag 1985, Victora Wood Up West 1990; *Books* Lucky Bag The Victoria Wood Song Book (1985), Up To You Porky The Victoria Wood Sketch Book (1986), Barmy The 2nd Victoria Wood Sketch Book (1987), Mens Sana in Thingummy Doo-Dah (1990); *Style*— Miss Victoria Wood; c/o Richard Stone, 25 Whitehall, London SW1 (☎ 071 839 6421)

WOOD, William Henry Luke (Harry); JP (1990); s of Henry Sydney Wood (d 1965), of Durham, and Mary Sybil Oliver, *née* Luke; *b* 24 Oct 1934; *Educ* Oundle, Emmanuel Coll Cambridge (MA); *m* 31 Aug 1963, Margaret Elaine (Peggy), da of Harold Ashley-Biggs (d 1976), of Sussex; 2 s (Nigel b 12 Jan 1965, Robert b 8 June 1967), 1 da (Emma b 11 Nov 1971); *Career* Nat Serv 36 HAA Regt RA Malta 1953-55, Capt 324 HYAD Regt RA TA Newcastle; CA Winter Robinson Sisson & Benson (now Coopers & Lybrand Deloitte) Newcastle 1958-62, md Wood & Watson Ltd (soft drinks) Durham 1962-, chm Durham Mkts Co; FCA 1973; *Recreations* landscaping, DIY, walking, skiing, tennis; *Clubs* Durham Squash, Derwent Reservoir Sailing; *Style*— Harry Wood, Esq, JP; Wood & Watson Ltd, Gilesgate, Durham DH1 1TR (☎ 091 384 8301)

WOOD, William Jeremy (Jerry); s of Maj Peter Alexander Wood, RA, of Budleigh Salterton, Devon, and Gwendoline Marion, *née* Hebron; *b* 2 June 1947; *Educ* Liverpool Coll, Univ of Manchester (BSc); *m* 17 march 1973, Judienne, da of Anthony Bridgett, of London W8; 1 da (Alexis (Lekki) b 1981); *Career* Euro prod mktg mangr Avon Overseas Ltd 1973-79, conslt PE Consulting Gp 1979-82, Euro strategic mktg dir Schering Plough Corpn 1983-85, bd dir Lowe Bell Fin Ltd 1986-89; *Recreations* squash, skiing, travel; *Style*— Jerry Wood, Esq; Lowe Bell Fin, 1 Red Lion Ct, London EC4A 3EB (☎ 071 353 9203, fax 071 353 7392)

WOOD, William Walker (Willie); s of William Edward Wood (d 1981), of Gifford, and Jennie Aitken, *née* Bisset; *b* 26 April 1938; *Educ* Knox Acad; *m* 12 Aug 1967, Morag Christie, da of John Turnbull (d 1976), of Garvald; 1 s (Colin b 1972), 1 da (Sylvia b 1968); *Career* Nat Serv craftsman REME 1956-59; bowler: Singles Gold medallist: SA Games 1973, Cwlth Games 1982; Singles winner Aust Mazda Tournament 1983; World Championships: Silver and Gold medal team winner 1984, Singles Silver and Triples Silver winner 1988; Singles runner-up Embassy World Indoor Championships 1989, Scottish internationalist for 23 years, Gifford Club champion 13 times; memb: Scottish Bowling (Indoors 1972-, (Outdoors 1966-), E Lothian Team 1956-; *Recreations* bowls; *Clubs* Gifford bowling, E Lothian indoor bowling; *Style*— Willie Wood, Esq; Willie Wood's Garage, 2 Tyne Close, Haddington, E Lothian (☎ 062 082 3579)

WOODALL, Antony Edward; s of Col Edward Corbet Woodall, OBE (d 1972) of The Red House, Clifton, Hampden, Oxon, and Janet Inez, *née* Crawley (d 1964), *see* Crawly-Boevey Bt, 1963 Peerage edition; *b* 18 April 1931; *Educ* Maidwell Hall Northampton, Eton; *m* 23 May 1959, Deirdre Kathleen, da of Sir John Child, 2Bt (d 1972), of Chobham Park House, Surrey; 3 s (James Henry b 1960, Andrew Hugh b 1963, Edward Antony John b 1967); *Career* stockbroker, ptnr Fielding Newson-Smith & Co 1959-83, dir Asset Mangrs plc 1986-; pres Herts Soc for the Blind, memb Cncl of mgmnt Byam Shaw Sch of Art; High Sheriff Co of Herts 1986-87; ct memb: Drapers Co 1983, Corpn of the Sons of The Clegg; *Recreations* golf, gardening; *Clubs* Brooks's, Pratt's, MCC, Royal Norfolk GC, Royal Worlington and Newmarket GC; *Style*— Antony Woodall, Esq; c/o Asset Managers plc, 4 Battle Bridge Lane, London SE1 2QE (☎ 071 378 1850)

WOODALL, Noel; s of Ernest Woodall (d 1966), and Sarah Woodhall, *née* Tromans; *b* 25 Dec 1930; *Educ* Oldbury Tech Coll, Birmingham Commercial Coll; *m* 24 July 1954, Dawn, da of Sydney Brown (d 1968); *Career* fndr memb the Cherished Numbers Dealers Assoc, memb Registration Numbers Club; *Books* Car Numbers Series (1962-88); Club Management Diploma; *Recreations* flying, photography, meeting people; *Clubs* RAF Assoc, Conservative; *Style*— Noel Woodall, Esq; 16 Boston Ave, Bispham, Blackpool FY2 9BZ (☎ 0253 55158); 122 Coronation Street, Blackpool FY1 4QQ (☎ 0253 24951)

WOODARD, Rear Adm Robert Nathaniel; Commodore, RN; s of Francis Alwyne Woodard (d 1974), and Catherine Mary, *née* Hayes; *b* 13 Jan 1939; *Educ* Lancing; *m* 20 July 1963, Rosamund Lucia, da of Lt-Col Denis Lucius Alban Gibbs DSO and Bar (d 1984), and Lady Hilaria Agnes, *née* Edgcumbe; 2 s (Rupert b 1964, Jolyon b 1969), 1 da (Melissa b 1967); *Career* 1958-75 aviator served carriers: Bulwark, Ark Royal, Eagle, Victorious; cmd: 771 and 848 Naval Air Sqdn (Lt-Cdr), HMS Amazon 1978-80 (Cdr), HMS Glasgow 1983-85 (Capt), HMS Osprey 1985-86; Cdre Clyde 1988-90, Flag Offr Royal Yachts 1990-; fell western div Woodard Schs; govr: Kings Taunton Sch, Kings Hall Sch, St Clare's Sch; FBIM 1978; *Recreations* painting, shooting, fishing and village cricket; *Clubs* Royal Cornwall Yacht, Royal Cwlth; *Style*— Rear Adm Robert Woodard, RN; HM Yacht Britannia, BFPO Ships

WOODBERRY, (Graham) George John; adopted; *b* 21 Sept 1938; *Educ* secdy modern sch; *m* 1962, Sheilagh Moira Eblis; 1 s (David b 1969), 2 da (Lynn, Jane); *Career* RN Submarines 1952-65; dir Securicor Int 1981-, vice chm Mint Security (Securicor Gp) 1984- (md 1979-84), md Mint Security (Ulster) Ltd 1984-; *Style*— George Woodberry, Esq; 20 Sydenham Road, Croydon, Surrey (☎ 081 686 0123); Sutton Park House, Carlshalton Rd, Sutton, Surrey (☎ 081 770 7000)

WOODBINE PARISH, Sir David Elmer; CBE (1964); s of Walter Woodbine Parish (d 1952), and Audrey, *née* Makins; *b* 29 June 1911; *Educ* Eton, Lausanne Switzerland; *m* 1939, Mona Blair McGarel, da of Charles McGarel Johnston (d 1918), of Glynn, Co Antrim; 2 da (Vanessa b 1941, Miranda b 1944); *Career* industl conslt; dep chm Marine & General Mutual Life Assur Soc 1976-86; chm: St Thomas's Hosp Med Sch 1970-82, City and Guilds of London Inst 1967-78 (life vice pres 1979), Bovis Ltd 1959-66, Sussex Area Royal Sch Church Music, Florence Nightingale Museum Tst 1981-86; memb Bd of Govrs Clothworkers Fndn 1977-, Master Worshipful Co of Clothworkers 1974-75; memb Ct Russia Co 1937-85, fell Imperial Coll; Hon FCGI, Hon LLD Leeds 1975; CBIM, FRSA; kt 1980; *Recreations* travel, music; *Clubs* Boodle's; *Style*— Sir David Woodbine Parish, CBE; The Glebe Barn, Pulborough, W Sussex RH20 2AF (☎ 07982 2613)

WOODBRIDGE, Anthony Rivers (Tony); s of John Nicholas Woodbridge, of Gerrards Cross, Bucks, and Patricia Madeleine, *née* Rebbeck; *b* 10 Aug 1942; *Educ* Stowe, Trinity Hall Cambridge (MA); *m* 29 Sept 1976, Lynda Anne, da of Charles Henry Nolan, of Stouffville, Ontario, Canada; 1 s (Christian b 30 March 1978); *Career* admitted slr 1967; ptnr Woodbridge & Sons Uxbridge 1969, sr ptnr Turberville Woodbridge Uxbridge 1983; co sec Abbeyfield Uxbridge Soc Ltd 1974-, admin Uxbridge Duty Slr Scheme 1983-, clerk Cmmrs Income Tax 1985-; chm govrs Fulmer Sch Bucks 1988-, memb Hillingdon Health Authy 1990-; memb Law Soc 1967; *Recreations* walking, cycling, touring; *Clubs* Denham Golf; *Style*— Tony Woodbridge, Esq; Cadogan House, 39 North Park, Gerrards Cross, Bucks SL9 8JL (☎ 0753 885 442); 122 High St, Uxbridge, Middx UB8 1JT (☎ 0895 59 871, fax 0895 73 519)

WOODBRIDGE, Robert James; s of Bernard Woodbridge, of Norfolk, and Edith Ellen, *née* Holloway; *b* 2 Dec 1945; *Educ* Ealing GS, Univ of Liverpool (BA); *m* 31 July 1975, Gillian Margaret, da of Harold Morris; 1 s (Daniel b 19 Oct 1976), 1 da (Alice b 27 Oct 1978); *Career* merchant banker; Arthur Andersen & Co 1967-71, credit analyst Chase Manhattan Bank NA 1971-72, vice pres Merrill Lynch International Bank Ltd 1972-77, investor/fin advsr 1977-83, md Houston Financial Services 1983-85, exec vice pres Riggs National Bank of Washington DC 1985-91, md Riggs AP Bank 1989-91; chm Riggs Valmet SA (Geneva) 1989-91, Riggs Bank Europe SA (France) 1990-91; FCA; *Recreations* skiing, golf, tennis, bridge; *Clubs* Ski Club of GB, RAC, Gresham, Vanderbilt Racquet, Overseas Bankers; *Style*— Robert Woodbridge, Esq; 6A Langford Place, London NW8 0LL; Riggs AP Bank Ltd, 21 Great Winchester St, London EC2N 2HH (☎ 071 588 7575)

WOODCOCK, Dr Ashley; s of Arthur Woodcock, of Stoke-on-Trent, and Vera, *née* Jones (d 1973); *b* 13 April 1951; *Educ* Univ of Manchester (BSc, MB ChB, MD); *m* 3 Aug 1974, Fiona Marilyn, da of Raymond Griffiths, of Gwaun-Cae Gurwen, Ammanford, Dyfed; 2 s (Daniel Ashley b 1984, (Benjamin) George b 1986), 1 da (Hannah Vera b 1982); *Career* specialist physician Gen Hosp Bandar-Seri-Begawan Brunei - SE Asia 1977-79; jr dr 1979-86: Brompton Hosp, Nat Heart Hosp, Hammersmith Hosp, St James Hosp; conslt physician Manchester Royal Infirmary 1986-88, conslt physician and dir Regnl Lung Function Laboratory and dir Slumberland Sleep Laboratory 1988-; sec NW Thoracic Soc, public educn offr and memb Cncl and Exec Br Thoracic Soc, Clinical Section chm Euro Soc Respirology; MRCP 1977; *Recreations* jogging, tennis; *Clubs* Hale Tennis; *Style*— Dr Ashley Woodcock; NW Regional Dept Respiratory Physiology, Wythenshawe Hospital, Manchester M23 9LT (☎ 061 998 7070)

WOODCOCK, Christopher Terence; s of Maj Bernard Edward Woodcock, TD, of Norwick, and Patricia Francis Louise, *née* Mason (d 1979); *b* 3 Oct 1946; *Educ* Bredons Coll, Oratory Sch Birmingham; *m* 18 July 1968 (m dis 1986), Nora Patricia, da of Thomas McPartland, of Belfast; 2 s (Simon Edward b 1974, James Thomas b 1975); *Career* National Provincial Bank 1963-72, James Capel & Co 1972-76; md Kirkland Whittaker (Sterling Brokers) Ltd 1983- (joined 1976, dir 1982); *Clubs* RAC; *Style*— Christopher Woodcock, Esq; Quince House, Briston, Melton, Constable, Norfolk

WOODCOCK, (Evan) Clive; s of Percy Woodcock (d 1985), and Lilian Mary, *née* Hanlon; *b* 11 Aug 1938; *Educ* King Edward VI Sch Stafford, Univ of Birmingham (LLB); *m* 7 Sept 1963, Hilary Anne, da of Christopher Allen Pither, (d 1970); 1 s (Andrew b 28 June 1967), 2 da (Susan (Mrs Rush) b 5 Nov 1964, Emma b 24 Aug 1973); *Career* admitted slr 1962; chief asst slr and co prosecuting slr Salop CC 1965-69, chief prosecuting slr Cheshire Police Authy 1969-86, chief crown prosecutor Crown Prosecution Serv Merseyside 1986-; pres Prosecuting Slrs Soc of England and Wales 1980-82 (cncl memb 1970-86); FBIM 1986; *Recreations* fell-walking, photography, music; *Style*— Clive Woodcock, Esq; 7th Floor (South), Royal Liver

Building, Pier Head, Liverpool L3 1HN (☎ 051 236 7575)

WOODCOCK, Graham; OBE (1980); s of Thomas Woodcock (d 1975), of Newfield, Haslingden, Rossendale, Lancs, and Beryl, *née* Duckworth (d 1951); *b* 25 July 1920; *Educ* Uppingham, St John's Coll Cambridge (BA, MA); *Career* Nat Serv WWII: Enlisted RA 1939, active serv Gibraltar and India (seconded to Royal India Artillery) 1939-46, released with hon rank of Capt 1946; admitted slr 1949; ptnr Woodcock & Sons 1949-82 (conslt 1982-), hon legal advsr to RRF 1975-; pres: Haslingden Branch Royal Br Legion, Halingden and Dist Civil Tst, Haslingden and Helmshore Band, Haslingden and Dist Fly Fishing Assoc, Rossendale Fell Rescue Team; fndr chm Higher Mill Textile Museum Helmshore; cncllr Lancs CC 1969-81, chm N Western Area Cons Cncl 1989-, memb Fin Bd Nat Union of Cons and Union Assoc 1985-89 (memb Gen Purposes Ctee 1988- and Exec Ctee 1975-); Guild Burgess of the Borough of Preston in the Co of Lancaster since the Guild Merchant of 1922; memb Law Soc; *Recreations* travel, walking, gardening; *Clubs* Royal Over-Seas League, St Stephen's Constitutional, Cambridge Union Soc; *Style*— Graham Woodcock, Esq, OBE; Heathfield, Haslingden, Rossendale, Lancs BB4 4BW (☎ 0706 214290)

WOODCOCK, HM Chief Inspector of Constabulary Sir John; CBE (1983), QPM (1976); s of Joseph Woodcock (d 1967), and Elizabeth May, *née* Whiteside (d 1982); *b* 14 Jan 1932; *Educ* Preston Tech Coll; *m* 4 April 1953, Kathleen Margaret, da of John Abbott; 2 s (Clive John b 1954, Aidan Edward b 1956), 1 da (Karen Belinda b 1962); *Career* police cadet, Lancs Constabulary 1947-50, Army Special Investigation Branch 1950-52, constable to Chief Inspr Lancs Constabulary 1952-65; supt and chief supt Beds and Luton Constabulary 1965-68, asst chief constable 1968-70; dep chief constable: Gwent 1970-74, Devon & Cornwall 1974-78; chief constable: N Yorks Police 1978-79, S Wales Constabulary 1979-83; HM Inspr of Constabulary 1983-90, HM Chief Inspr of Constabulary 1990-; Intermediate Cmd Course Police Coll 1965, sr Cmd Course 1968, Study Bavarian Police 1977, Euro Discussion Centre 1977; lectr Int Police Course, Sicily and Rome 1978; FBI Nat Exec: Washington 1981, Salt Lake City Utah 1986, Sun Valley Idaho 1988; vice pres study Royal Hong Kong Police 1989; Welsh Assoc of Youth Clubs 1981-87, chm Wales Ctee Royal Jubilee and Prince's Tst 1983-85; memb: Admin Cncl Royal Jubilee Tsts 1981-85, Prince's Tst Ctee for Wales 1981-84, Governing Bd, World Coll of the Atlantic 1980-84; Hon memb Swansea Lions; OStJ 1981; Papal knighthood 1984 (KSG); kt 1989; *Recreations* table tennis, badminton, walking, horticulture; *Clubs* Cardiff Business (vice pres); *Style*— HM Chief Inspector of Constabulary Sir John Woodcock, CBE, QPM; Home Office, 50 Queen Anne's Gate, London SW1H 9AT

WOODCOCK, John Charles; s of Rev Parry John Woodcock (d 1938), and Norah Mabel, *née* Hutchinson; *b* 7 Aug 1926; *Educ* Dragon Sch Oxford, St Edward's Sch Oxford, Trinity Coll Oxford (MA); *Career* Manchester Guardian 1952-54; cricket corr: The Times 1954-87, Country Life 1962-; ed Wisden Cricketers Almanack 1980-86; covered 35 Test Tours 1950- incl: Aust (17 times), S Africa, West Indies, NZ, India, Pakistan; dir The Cricketer, memb Ctee of MCC, pres Cricket Writers Club; *Books* The Ashes (1956), Barclays World of Cricket (with EW Swanton 1980, assoc ed 2 edn, conslt ed 3 edn 1986), Hockey for Oxford versus Cambridge (1946, 1947); Br Press Sportswriter of the Year 1987; *Recreations* golf, country pursuits; *Clubs* Flyfishers, Vincent's (Oxford), MCC; *Style*— John Woodcock, Esq; The Curacy, Longparish, nr Andover, Hants SP11 6PB (☎ 02647 259)

WOODCOCK, Michael (Mike); JP (1971), MP (C) Ellesmere Port and Neston 1983-; s of Herbert Eric Woodcock and Violet Irene Woodcock; *b* 10 April 1943; *Educ* Queen Elizabeth's GS Mansfield; *m* 1969, Carole Ann, da of Victor Arnold Berry; 1 s, 1 da; *Career* co dir; author and co-author; conslt; DLitt 1988; *Books* Unblocking Your Organisation, People at Work, Team Development Manual, Organisation Development through Teambuilding, The Unblocked Boss, 50 Activities for Self Development, Management Development Manual, 50 Activities for Team Development, Clarifying Organisational Values; *Clubs* Farmers; *Style*— Mike Woodcock, Esq, JP, MP; Inkersall Farm, Bilsthorpe, Newark, Notts; House of Commons, London SW1

WOODCOCK, (Keith) Roy; s of Charles Roy William Woodcock, of 24 Grounds Ave, March, Cambs, and Freda Margaret, *née* Smith; *b* 8 Nov 1950; *Educ* March GS; *m* 24 Sept 1977, Christine Ann, da of Ernest Barlow, of Hull; 2 s (Matthew b 9 Nov 1979, Samuel b 15 Aug 1982); *Career* features ed Hull Daily Mail 1986-88, ed Hull Star 1988-89, ed Hull Target series of newspapers 1989-; *Style*— Roy Woodcock, Esq; 30 Southfield Drive, North Ferriby, Humberside HU14 3DX (☎ 0482 631099); Blundell's Corner, Beverley Road, Hull HU3 1XS (☎ 0482 226485, ext 343)

WOODCOCK, Thomas; s of Thomas Woodcock, of Hurst Green, Lancs, and Mary Woodcock; *b* 20 May 1951; *Educ* Eton, Univ of Durham (BA), Darwin Coll Cambridge (LLB); *Career* called to the Bar Inner Temple 1975; Rouge Croix Pursuivant 1978-82, Somerset Herald of Arms 1982-; FSA; *Books* Oxford Guide to Heraldry (with John Martin Robinson, 1988); *Clubs* Travellers'; *Style*— Thomas Woodcock, Esq; College of Arms, Queen Victoria St, London EC4 (☎ 071 236 3634)

WOODD, Charles Basil; s of Rev Canon Frederick Hampden Basil Woodd (d 1986), and Emily Hornby, *née* Foss (d 1981); *b* 8 Oct 1946; *Educ* Canford, Jesus Coll Cambridge (BA), LSE (Dip Social Admin); *m* 27 April 1974, Peggy Joanna, da of Rt Rev John Vernon Taylor, of Oxford; 2 s (Benjamin b 1977, Joseph b 1981), 1 da (Susannah b 1975); *Career* dir Bede House Assoc 1972-80, gen sec Voluntary Action Westminster 1980-86, dir Nat Fedn of Community Orgns 1986-; former: chm Lyndhurst Sch Assoc, sec Southwark Playgrounds Assoc, sec Advice Centre; memb: Social Responsibility Gp, St Barnabas Church Dulwich; tstee Jerusalem Tst, hon treas Nat Coalition for Neighbourhoods, chm Dulwich and Dist Dyslexia Association; Freeman City of London, Liveryman Worshipful Co of Salters 1971; *Recreations* walking, singing, DIY, cycling; *Style*— Charles Woodd, Esq; 36 Talfourd Rd, Peckham, London SE15 5NY (☎ 071 708 0540); National Federation of Community Organisations, 8/9 Upper St, London N1 0PQ (☎ 071 226 0189)

WOODD, Hugh Basil; s of Rev Canon Frederick Hampden Basil Woodd (d 1986), and Emily Hornby, *née* Foss (d 1980); *b* 13 Nov 1940; *Educ* Canford, Univ of Bristol (BA); *m* 21 Oct 1967, Susan Mary (Sue), da of Norman Andrew Armitage, of Four Hedges, Woodlands, nr Wimborne, Dorset; 1 s (Christopher b 24 Nov 1968), 2 da (Rachel b 29 June 1970, Anna b 8 June 1972); *Career* CA; Mann Judd & Co: London 1963-67 and 1969-88, Addis Ababa 1967-69, ptnr 1970; ptnr Touche Ross & Co (upon merger) 1979, ret 1988 to become sole practitioner in Winchester; hon treas: Br Sch of Archaeology in Jerusalem, St Matthews PCC; Freeman City of London 1964, Liveryman Worshipful Co of Salters 1964; ACA 1967; *Recreations* opera, mountain walking, skiing, DIY; *Style*— Hugh Woodd, Esq; Honeywick, 17 Bereweeke Ave, Wincester, Hants SO22 6BH (☎ 0962 852924)

WOODFIELD, Colin Keith; OBE (1982); s of Leonard Norman Woodfield (d 1940), and Norah Elizabeth, *née* Packer (d 1967); *b* 5 April 1936; *Educ* Devonport HS, Birkbeck Coll London (BA); *m* 20 Aug 1960, Lorna, da of Lawrence Brown Sime (d 1968); 2 s (Keith b 1962, Allan b 1965), 1 da (Linda b 1968); *Career* Nat Serv RAF 1954-56; HM Dip Serv: FO 1956-62, info attaché Rio de Janeiro 1962-64, vice-consul and third sec (commercial) Djakarta 1964-65, second sec (info) Madras 1965-68, FCO 1968-71, second sec Berne 1971-74, first sec (admin) Dacca 1974-76, FCO 1976-79, perm sec external affrs Belmopan 1979-81, consul (commercial) Zurich 1982-86, dep head Info Dept FCO 1986-88, dep high cmmr Kaduna 1989-; *Recreations* theatre and concert-going, golf; *Style*— Colin Woodfield, Esq, OBE; 3 Independence Way, Kaduna, Nigeria; 2-4 Lamido Rd, Kaduna, Nigeria

WOODFIELD, Sir Philip John; KCB (1982, CB 1974), CBE 1963); s of Ralph Woodfield; *b* 30 Aug 1923; *Educ* Alleyn's Sch Dulwich, King's Coll London; *m* 1958, Diana, da of Sydney Herington; 3 da; *Career* served WWII RA; civil servant NI and Home Office; dep sec Home Office 1974-81, perm under-sec NI Office 1981-84; *Style*— Sir Philip Woodfield, KCB; c/o Lloyds Bank, 6 Pall Mall, London SW1

WOODFORD, Air Vice-Marshal Anthony Arthur George; s of Arthur George Woodford (d 1989), and May, *née* McRea; *b* 6 Jan 1939; *Educ* Haberdashers' Aske's, Open Univ (BA); *m* 29 Aug 65, Christine Barbara, da of John Tripp (d 1989); 1 s (Adrian b 1970), 2 da (Caroline b 1966, Sarah b 1969); *Career* cmmnd 1959; Pilot with Squadrons 12, 44, 53, 101, until 1978;; directing staff RAF Staff Coll 1972-75, asst air attache Washington DC 1978-81, cmd RAF St Mawgan 1982-83, ADC to HM The Queen 1982-83; RCDS 1984, staff appots HQ RAF Strike Cmd 1985-89, asst chief of staff policy SHAPE 1989-91; *Clubs* RAF; *Style*— Air Vice-Marshal Anthony Woodford; Room B339, Policy Division, Shape BFPO 26 (☎ 065 34 0541)

WOODFORD, Maj-Gen David Milner; CBE (1975); s of Maj Robert Milner Woodford, MC (d 1981), and Marion Rosa (Tessa), *née* Gregory (d 1955); *b* 26 May 1930; *Educ* Prince of Wales Sch Nairobi, Wadham Coll Oxford; *m* 1959 (m dis 1987), Ethel Mary, da of David Stanley Edwardes Jones (d 1963); *Career* CO 3 RRF 1970-72, Col Cyprus 1972-75, Cmd 3 Inf Bde 1976-77, Dep Cdr COS SE Dist 1979-80, ACGS MOD 1981-82, SDS RCDS 1982-83, Cmdt Joint Serv Def Coll 1984-86, ret 1986; memb Lord Chancellor's Panel of Independent Inspectors; *Recreations* literary, historical, golf; *Clubs* Army and Navy, NZ Golf; *Style*— Maj-Gen David Woodford, CBE; c/o Barclays Bank, Fleet, Hants

WOODFORD, Guy James Robert; s of Henry James Thomas William Woodford of Amersham (d 1968), and Winifred, *née* Clarke (d 1987); *b* 30 July 1937; *Educ* Dr Challoners GS Amersham; *m* 1, 29 Sept 1962 (m dis 1987), Carole Anne; 1 s (James b 1969), 1 da (Helen b 1967); m 2, 25 May 1990, Janet, *née* Butterworth; 1 step s (Daren Turner); *Career* RHA 1957-58; mgmnt trainee Unilever 1959-61, sales mangr Imp Food Group 1968-72, fndr chm and md Premium Promotions Ltd Group 1972-; MInstM; *Recreations* bridge, skiing; *Style*— Guy Woodford, Esq; Brinkley Cottage, 62 Gregories Road, Beaconsfield, Bucks HP9 1HQ (☎ 0494 674239), Premium Promotions Ltd, 47 High St, Burnham, Bucks SL1 7JX (☎ 0628 664031, fax 0628 603439, telex 849796)

WOODFORD, Peggy Elizabeth Lainé (Mrs Aylen); da of Ronald Curtis Woodford, OBE (d 1970), of Assam, India, and Ruth Mahy, *née* Lainé (d 1987); *b* 19 Sept 1937; *Educ* Guernsey Ladies' Coll CI, St Anne's Coll Oxford (MA); *m* 1 April 1967, Walter Stafford Aylen, QC, s of Rt Rev Charles Arthur William Aylen (Bishop, d 1972); 3 da (Alison b 1968, Frances b 1970, Imogen b 1974); *Career* writer; Italian govt res scholar Rome 1960-61, script and res asst BBC TV, sr tutor Sixth Form Coll Reading 1964-67; *Books* incl: Abraham's Legacy (1963), Please Don't Go (1972), Backwater War (1975), The Real Thing (1977), Rise of the Raj (1978), See You Tomorrow (1979), You Can't Keep Out the Darkness (1980), The Girl with a Voice (1981), Love Me Love Rome (1984), Misfits (1984), Monster in our Midst (1988), Schubert (2 edn, 1989), Out of the Sun (1990), Mozart (2 edn, 1990); *Style*— Miss Peggy Woodford; c/o Murray Pollinger, Literary Agents, 222 Old Brompton Rd, London SW5 OBZ (☎ 071 373 4711)

WOODFORD, Dr (Frederick) Peter; s of Wilfrid Charles Woodford (d 1931), and Mabel Rose, *née* Scarff (d 1970); *b* 8 Nov 1930; *Educ* The Lewis Sch Glamorgan, Balliol Coll Oxford (BA, MA), Univ of Leeds (PhD); *m* 18 Dec 1964, Susan, da of E A Silberman (d 1969); 1 da (Julia Jacqueline b 21 Nov 1969); *Career* RAF 1956-57 (pilot offr, flying offr); res fell Leiden Univ 1958-62, visiting scientist and lectr Univ of Tennessee Medical Sch and NIH USA 1962-63, guest investigator Rockefeller Univ NY 1963-71, scientific historian Ciba Fndn and scientific assoc Wellcome Trust 1971-74, exec dir Inst for Res into Mental and Multiple Handicap 1974-77, PSO (Clinical Chemistry) DHSS 1977-84, chief scientific offr Dept of Health 1984-; managing exec ed: Jl of Atherosclerosis Res 1960-62, Jl of Lipid Res 1963-69, Proceedings of Nat Acad of Scis USA 1970-71; FRCPath 1984, CChem, FRSC 1990; *Books* Scientific Writing for Graduate Students (1969), Medical Research Systems in Europe (1973), The Ciba Foundation: An Analytic History (1974), Writing Scientific Papers in English (1975), Training Manual for Technicians in Physiological Measurement (1988), Training Manual for Technicians in Medical Physics (1989); *Recreations* playing chamber music (pianist); *Clubs* Athenaeum; *Style*— Dr F Peter Woodford; 1 Akenside Rd, London NW3 5BS (☎ 071 435 2088); Dept of Health, 14 Russell Square, London WC1B 5EP (☎ 071 636 6811 ext 3056, fax 071 436 2194)

WOODGATE, Valerie Ann; da of George Henry Stone of London (missing presumed dead 1942), and Lilian Emily Sculley, *née* Delieu; *b* 3 Oct 1941; *Educ* Waverley Sch London, Open Univ (BA); *m* Frank George Woodgate, s of late Percy Frank Woodgate; *Career* Inland Revenue 1958-64, GLC County Hall 1964-69, Standard Bank Development Co Johannesburg SA 1969, Government Hong Kong 1974-77, guide and Lectr Tate Gallery 1978-, currently ptnr and lectr Gallery Scene and Gallery Scene for Children; freelance lectr to various orgns; lectr NADFAS; *Recreations* chiefly riding; *Style*— Mrs Valerie Woodgate

WOODHAMS, Rev the Hon Sophie Harriet; *née* Liddell; da of Hon Cyril Arthur Liddell (d 1932), and sister of 8 Baron Ravensworth; *b* 6 July 1927; *Educ* King's Coll, Univ of Durham, Cranmer Hall Theological Coll Durham; *m* 1981, Leslie Charles William Woodhams, s of Charles Woodhams, RN (d 1922); *Career* granted title, rank and precedence of a Baron's da 1951; ordained deacon in the C of E 14 March 1987; *Style*— The Rev the Hon Sophie Woodhams; 31 Hanover Close, Shaftgate Ave, Shepton Mallet, Somerset BA4 5YQ (☎ 0749 344124)

WOODHEAD, Col Michael ffolliott; OBE (1969); s of Arnold Hugh Woodhead (d 1980), of Orchard Hse, Clare Mont Park, Esher, and Vivienne Lintorn, *née* Highett (d 1962); *b* 12 May 1923; *Educ* Imperial Serv Coll Windsor, RMC Sandhurst; *m* 15 Jan 1955, Gillian Hazel Woodhead, JP (d 1990), da of Col Hugo Graham de Burgh, OBE, MC (d 1954), of Kildare, Ireland; 3 s (Nicholas ffolliot b 23 Oct 1955, Christopher Michael Anthony b 20 Feb 1957, Timothy Hugh b 28 Dec 1965), 2 da (Jane Caroline (Mrs Matthew) b 20 Feb 1959, Eleanor Mary (The Hon Mrs James Keith) b 25 July 1962); *Career* cmmd 9 Queen's Royal Lancers 1942, serv ME, N Africa, Italy and Palestine, 9/12 Royal Lancers Prince of Wales's 1960, cmmnd Lt-Col 9/12 Lancers 1966-69, Col MOD 1969, Cmdt Royal Mil Sch of Music 1975-78, ret 1978, Col 9/12 Royal Lancers 1986-90; Freeman City of London 1981, Liveryman Worshipful Co of Tallow Chandlers 1981; *Recreations* shooting, gardening; *Style*— Col Michael Woodhead, OBE; The Cedars, Eydon, Daventry, Northamptonshire NN11 6PP (☎ 0327 62091)

WOODHEAD, Rear Adm (Anthony) Peter; s of Leslie Woodhead, and Nancy Woodhead; *b* 30 July 1939; *Educ* Leeds GS, Conway, BRNC Dartmouth; *m* 1964, Carol Woodhead; 1 s (Simon), 1 da (Emma); *Career* RN; Seaman Offr, pilot 1962, aircraft carriers Borneo Campaign; CO HM Ships: Jupiter 1974, Rhyl 1975; NDC 1976, Naval Plans Div MOD 1977, CSO to Flag Offr Third Flotilla 1980, COS to FO cmdg Falklands Task Force 1982, Capt 4 Frigate Sqdn 1983, RCDS 1984, dir Naval Ops 1985, CO HMS Illustrious 1986; Flag Offr: Flotilla Two 1988, Flotilla One 1989; *Recreations* tennis, antique restoration; *Clubs* Royal Navy of 1765 and 1785; *Style—* Rear Adm Peter Woodhead; c/o Naval Secretary, Old Admiralty Building, Whitehall, London SW1A 2BE

WOODHEAD, Robin George; s of Walter Henry Woodhead (d 1976), of Zimbabwe, and Gladys Catherine Woodhead, of Johannesburg, SA; *b* 28 April 1951; *Educ* Mount Pleasant Sch Salisbury Rhodesia, Univ Coll of Rhodesia and Nyasaland (LLB); *m* 28 June 1980, Mary Fitzgerald, da of Fergus Hamilton Allen, CB, *qv*, of Berks; *Career* 1981-86: chm and dir Int Petroleum Exchange of London Ltd, md Premier Mgmnt Ltd, dir E D & F Man Int Ltd, chief exec Nat Investmt Hldgs plc 1986-, chm and chief exec Nat Investmt Gp plc 1986-; treas Contemporary Art Soc, fndr tstee Whitechapel Gallery, memb Ballet Rambert; memb Law Soc 1978; *Recreations* skiing, tennis, riding, contemporary art; *Style—* Robin Woodhead, Esq; National Investment Group plc, Salisbury House, London Wall, London EC2M 5SX (☎ 071 638 7412, fax 081 628 2634)

WOODHEAD-KEITH-DIXON, Rev James Addison; s of James Keith-Dixon (d 1967), of Lorton Hall, Cockermouth, Cumbria, and Margaret Ann, da of James Wright, of Glossop, Derbys; *b* 20 July 1925; *Educ* St Aidan's Coll Birkenhead, Univ of Liverpool; *m* 1, 16 Oct 1951, Mary Constance (d 1977), da of Alfred Tindal Saul (d 1960), of Highcroft, Stanwix, Carlisle (d 1972); 1 s (Andrew James b 14 April 1953); m 2, 1 Aug 1981, Clodagh Anne, da of James Trevor Cather, of Icod, Tenerife; *Career* deacon 1948, priest 1949, curate Upperby Carlisle 1948-50, curate Dalton-in-Furness 1950-52, vicar Blawith-with-Lowick 1952-59, vicar Lorton 1959-50, chaplain of Tenerife 1980-82, team vicar of Falstone, Thorneyburn and Greystead 1982, team rector 1983, lay rector Lorton; Lord of The Manors of Lorton Brigham and Whinfell; *Recreations* shooting, fishing, heraldry and genealogy; *Style—* The Rev James Woodhead-Keith-Dixon; The Rectory, Falstone, Hexham, Northumberland NE48 1AE (☎ 0660 40213)

WOODHOUSE, Ven Andrew Henry; DSC (1945); s of Henry Alfred Woodhouse (d 1961), of Woking, Surrey, and Phyllis, *née* Gemmell (d 1983); *b* 30 Jan 1923; *Educ* Lancing, The Queen's Coll Oxford (MA), Lincoln Theol Coll; *Career* RNVR 1942-46, Lt; curate All Saints Poplar 1950-56, vicar St Martins W Drayton 1956-70, rural dean Hillingdon 1967-70, archdeacon of Ludlow and rector Wistanstow 1970-82, archdeacon of Hereford and canon residentiary Hereford Cathedral 1982-; *Recreations* walking, photography; *Clubs* Naval; *Style—* The Ven the Archdeacon of Hereford, DSC; The Archdeacon's House, The Close, Hereford, Herefordshire HR1 2NG (☎ 0432 272873)

WOODHOUSE, Hon (Georgina) Caroline; da of 4 Baron Terrington; *b* 1 July 1946; *Educ* Downham Sch Essex, Queensgate, Villa d'Assomption Paris; *Career* interior designer; *Recreations* skiing, tennis; *Style—* The Hon Caroline Woodhouse; Flat 7, 171 Sussex Gardens, London W2 (☎ 071 723 2836)

WOODHOUSE, Charles Frederick; s of Wilfrid Meynell Woodhouse (d 1967), of 55 Chester Row, London SW1, and Margaret (Peggy), *née* Kahl; *b* 6 June 1941; *Educ* Marlborough, McGill Univ, Peterhouse Cambridge (BA); *m* 25 Jan 1969, Margaret Joan, da of Tom Cooper, of Hulland Ward, Derbyshire; 1 s (Timothy b 6 Dec 1973), 2 da (Rachel b 11 Nov 1969, Philippa b 1 Nov 1971); *Career* admitted slr, ptnr Farrer & Co 1969-; legal advsr to CCPR 1971-, hon legal advsr Cwlth Games Cncl for Eng 1983-, vice chm Slrs Staff Pension Fund 1987-, dir Peko Exploration (UK) Ltd, legal advsr AAA 1988-, vice chm Land Settlement Assoc Ltd; memb Ctee Surrey CCC, pres Guildford CC; memb Law Soc; *Recreations* cricket, golf; *Clubs* MCC, United Oxford and Cambridge, Worplesdon Golf, Surrey CCC, Free Foresters; *Style—* Charles Woodhouse, Esq; Selborne Lodge, 2 Austen Rd, Guildford, Surrey GU1 3NP (☎ 0483 573676); 66 Lincoln's Inn Fields, London WC2A 3LH (☎ 071 242 2022, telex 24318, fax 071 831 9748)

WOODHOUSE, Christopher Richard James; s of Col the Hon C M Woodhouse, DSO, OBE, of Willow Cottage, Latimer, Chesham, Bucks, and Lady Davina, *née* Lytton; *b* 20 Sept 1946; *Educ* Winchester, Guy's Hosp Med Sch (MB BS); *m* 27 Feb 1975, Anna Margaret, da of the hon Hugo Philipps, of Llanstephan House, Boughrood, Powys; 1 s (Jack b 7 Dec 1978), 1 da (Constance b 1 Jan 1982); *Career* sr lectr Inst of Urology 1981; conslt urologist: Royal Marsden Hosp 1981, St George's Hosp 1985; hon conslt urologist: St Peter's Hosp 1981, Hosp for Sick Children Gt Ormond St 1981; numerous pubns in learned jls; corresponding memb American Urological Assoc 1985; Liveryman Worshipful Soc of Apothecaries; FRSM 1981, FRCS; *Books* Physiological Basis of Medicine-Urology and Nephrology (1987), Long term Paediatric Urology (1991); *Recreations* skiing, stalking; *Clubs* Leander; *Style—* Christopher Woodhouse, Esq; The Institute of Urology, Shaftesbury Hospital, Shaftesbury Ave, London WC2 (☎ 071 240 9115)

WOODHOUSE, Lady Davidema Katharine Cynthia Mary Millicent (Davina); *née* Bulwer-Lytton; da of 2 Earl of Lytton KG, GCSI, GCIE, PC (d 1947); *b* 1909; *m* 1, 1931, 5 Earl of Erne (d 1940); 1 s (*see* 6 Earl), 2 da (*see* Lady Rosanagh Raben-Levetzau and Lady Antonia Beckwith); m 2, 1945, Col the Hon Christopher Montague Woodhouse, DSO, OBE, *qv*; 2 s (Christopher Richard James b 20 Sept 1946, Nicholas Michael John b 27 Feb 1949), 1 da (Emma Davina Mary Johnson-Gilbert b 19 April 1954); *Style—* The Lady Davina Woodhouse; Willow Cottage, Latimer, Bucks (☎ 0494 762627)

WOODHOUSE, James Stephen; s of Rt Rev John Walker Woodhouse (d 1956); *b* 21 May 1933; *Educ* St Edward's Sch Oxford, St Catharine's Coll Cambridge; *m* 1957, Sarah Maud, da of Col Hubert Blount, MC (d 1979); 3 s, 1 da; *Career* asst master Westminster Sch 1957-63, under-master and master of Queen's Scholars 1963-67; headmaster: Rugby Sch 1967-81, Lancing Coll 1981-; *Recreations* sailing, music, hill walking, natural history; *Clubs* East India, Sports and Public Sch; *Style—* James Woodhouse Esq; The Old Farmhouse, Lancing Coll, Sussex

WOODHOUSE, Hon (Christopher) Montague; DSO (1943), OBE (1944); s of 3 Baron Terrington, KBE (d 1961), and hp of bro, 4 Baron Terrington; *b* 11 May 1917; *Educ* Winchester, New Coll Oxford (MA); *m* 28 Aug 1945, Lady Davidema, *qv*, wid of 5 Earl of Erne; 3 stepchildren; *Career* serv WWII organising resistance in occupied Greece; dir-gen Royal Inst of Int Affrs, and dir of studies 1955-59, visiting fell Nuffield Coll Oxford 1956-64; MP (C) Oxford 1959-66 and 1970-74, Parly sec Miny of Aviation 1961-62, jt under-sec of state Home Office 1962-64; dir of educn and trg CBI 1966-70, visiting prof King's Coll London 1978-89, fell Trinity Hall Cambridge 1949, corresponding memb Acad of Athens 1980, hon fellow New Coll Oxford 1982; FRSL 1951; *Books* Karamanlis, the Restorer of Greek Democracy (1982), Something Ventured (autobiography 1982), Gemistos Plethon (1986); *Style—* The Hon Montague Woodhouse, DSO, OBE; Willow Cottage, Latimer, Bucks HP5 1TW (☎ 0494 762627)

WOODHOUSE, The Rt Hon Sir (Arthur) Owen; KBE (1981), DSC (1944), PC (1974); s of A J Woodhouse; *b* 18 July 1916; *Educ* Napier Boys' HS, Auckland Univ; *m* 1940, Margaret Leah Thorp; 4 s, 2 da; *Career* served 1939-45 War RNZNVR, Lt Cdr; asst to Naval Attaché HM Embassy Belgrade 1945; judge: Supreme Ct NZ 1961-86, Ct of Appeal 1974-86; pres Ct of Appeal 1981-86; First pres Law Cmmn 1985-; Hon LLD Victoria Univ of Wellington 1978, Hon LLD York Univ Canada 1981; kt 1974; *Style—* The Rt Hon Sir Owen Woodhouse KBE, DSC, PC; Box 2590, Wellington, NZ

WOODHOUSE, (Bernard) Raymond; s of (Thomas) Bernard Montague Woodhouse (d 1969), of Woodcote Park Ave, Purley, Surrey, and Betty, *née* Harvey (d 1956); *b* 24 Nov 1939; *Educ* Ardingly, St Dunstan's Catford, Nat Coll of Food Tech; *m* 6 Oct 1962, Judith, da of Robert Arnold Roach, of Caterham; 2 s (Richard Thomas Raymond b 5 May 1965, Martyn Bernard Robert b 26 Jan 1970); *Career* chm TSJ Woodhouse Ltd 1973- (joined 1960); life govr RNLI; Freeman City of London 1979, Liveryman Worshipful Co of Butchers 1979; *Recreations* tennis, water skiing, boating, golf; *Clubs* Royal Smithfield; *Style—* Raymond Woodhouse, Esq; T S J Woodhouse Ltd, 72-98 Blundell St, London N7 9TS (☎ 071 609 2200); The Backwater, Upper Ct Rd, Woldingham, Surrey CR3 7BF

WOODHOUSE, Ronald Michael; s of Henry Alfred Woodhouse, of Woking, Surrey (d 1961), and Phyllis, *née* Gemmell (d 1983); *b* 19 Aug 1927; *Educ* Lancing, Queen's Coll Oxford; *m* 15 Oct 1955, Quenilda Mary, da of Rt Rev Neville Gorton, Bishop of Coventry (1942, d 1945); 1 s (Alexander b 1961), 3 da (Harriet b 1956, Isobel b 1958, Anna b 1964); *Career* chm: The Int Paint Co Ltd 1978-84, Br Cellophane Ltd 1979-86, Courtaulds Fibres 1985-86; dep chm Courtaulds plc 1986-; dir Bowater plc 1988-; CBIM 1988; *Clubs* Carlton, Oriental; *Style—* Michael Woodhouse, Esq; Tankards, Wonersh, nr Guildford, Surrey (☎ 0483 892 078); 18 Hanover Square London W1A 2BB (☎ 071 629 9080, telex 28788, fax 071 629 2586)

WOODING, Dr Norman Samuel; s of Samuel Wooding (d 1966), of Street Ashton, and Nellie, *née* White (d 1971); *b* 20 April 1927; *Educ* Lawrence Sheriff Sch Rugby, Univ of London (BSc), Univ of Leeds and Univ of Manchester (PhD); *m* 19 Sept 1949, Dorothy Elizabeth, da of Alfred Smith; 1 s (Richard b 1959), 2 da (Susan b 1956, Lucy b 1968); *Career* dep chm Courtaulds plc 1976-87 (dir 1973-76), non-exec chm Earlys of Witney plc 1978-83 (non-exec dir 1971-78); non-exec dir: British Nuclear Fuels plc 1987-, British Textile Technology Group Ltd 1988-; non-exec dep chm Royal London Mutual Insurance Co Ltd 1987-, non-exec chm Agricultural Genetics Co Ltd 1988-; chm E Euro Trade Cncl, pres Br Soviet C of C; memb: Cncl GB-USSR Assoc, Governing Body GB-E Euro Centre, Cncl Sch of Slavonik and E Euro Studies Univ of London; sr visiting memb St Antony's Coll Oxford; CBIM 1983; *Recreations* gardening, mountain walking, cooking, fast cars; *Clubs* Reform; *Style—* Dr Norman Wooding, CBE; East European Trade Council, Suite 10, Westminster Palace Gardens, Artillery Row, London (☎ 071 222 7622, fax 071 222 5359, telex 291018)

WOODING, Roy; s of Raymond Wooding (d 1957), and Elsie, *née* Lyons; *b* 11 Oct 1953; *Educ* Meyborough Sch; *m* 16 October 1976, Angela, da of George Jones; 1 da (Rachael Emma b 27 Sept 1978); *Career* photographer; MT Walters & Associates Ltd 1970-84 (apprentice then responsible for a large proportion of creative output), fndr ICS Photography 1984-, awarded BIPP Yorkshire Centre Indust/Photographer of the Year on six occasions, BIPP bronze award for nat print exhibition 1990; FBIPP 1982 yst then in indust catagory (assoc BIPP 1976); *Books* contrib photographs to Photography Year Book (1983); *Recreations* Yorkshire league badminton, skiing, tennis, fishing; *Style—* Roy Wooding, Esq; 20 Farmoor Close, Harlington, Doncastor, South Yorkshire DN5 7JP (☎ 0709 896237); ICS Photography, Unit Six Studio, Bentley Moor Lane, Carcroft Common Ind Est, Doncaster DN6 7BD (☎ 0302 330281, FAX 0302 330282)

WOODLEY, Derek George; s of George Edward Woodley (d 1957), of Romford, Essex, and Dorothy Marjorie Gwendoline Roper; *b* 28 March 1931; *Educ* Royal Liberty Sch (Dip Arch); *m* 9 July 1955, Thelma Joan, da of Arthur Legg (d 1971); 2 s (David b 1962, Richard b 1968), 1 da (Jacqueline b 1963); *Career* Capt RE (survey), Cyprus survey and other classified work; chartered architect, sr ptnr Bell & Woodley 1980-; RIBA; *Recreations* cricket, golf; *Style—* Derek Woodley, Esq; Leap House, 45 Ferry Rd, Felixstowe, Suffolk (☎ 0394 284880); Bell & Woodley, 117A Hamilton Rd, Felixstowe, Suffolk (☎ 0394 284550/284289)

WOODLEY, Keith Spencer; s of Charles Spencer Woodley, of Pleshey, Essex, and Hilda Mary, *née* Brown; *b* 23 Oct 1939; *Educ* Stationers Company's Sch; *m* 19 May 1962, Joyce Madeleine, *née* Toon; 1 s (Jonathan b 11 Jan 1972), 2 da (Rachel Jane b 8 March 1962, Helen Elizabeth b 17 July 1966); *Career* articled clerk Deloitte Plender Griffith and Co 1957-62, audit sr and mangr Deloitte & Co 1963-68; Coopers & Lybrand Deloitte (formerly Deloitte Haskins & Sells): ptnr 1969-90, personnel ptnr 1978-82, memb Mgmnt Bd 1985-90; chm Royscot Finance Group 1990-; complaints cmmr: Securities and Investment Bd 1990-, Securities Assoc and Int Stock Exchange 1990-; FIMBRA 1990; FCA 1963 (memb Cncl 1989-); *Recreations* hill-walking, theatre and listening to music; *Clubs* Gresham; *Style—* Keith Woodley, Esq; Monaltrie, Chiltern Road, Chesham Bois, Amersham, Bucks HP6 5PH (☎ 0494 433900); Royscot Finance Group plc, Birchin Court, Birchin Lane, London EC3V 9DJ (☎ 071 623 4356, fax 071 621 1593)

WOODLEY, Ven Ronald John; s of John Owen Woodley (d 1960), and Maggie Woodley, *née* Lord (d 1973); *b* 28 Dec 1925; *Educ* Montagu Rd Sch Edmonton London, Bishops' Coll Cheshunt Herts; *m* 1959, Patricia, da of Thomas Kneeshaw (d 1979); 1 s (John), 2 da (Rachel, Elizabeth); *Career* Sgt BAOR 1944-47; ordained: deacon 1953, priest 1954; curate: St Martin Middlesbrough 1953-58, Whitby 1958-61; curate i/c the Ascension Middlesbrough 1961-66, vicar 1966-71, rector of Stokesley 1971-85, rural dean 1977-84, canon and prebendary of York 1982-, archdeacon of Cleveland 1985-91; *Recreations* walking, gardening, cinema, theatre, wine-making; *Style—* The Ven Ronald Woodley; Brierton House, 52 South Parade, Northallerton DL7 8SL (☎ 0609 778818)

WOODMAN, Prof Anthony John; s of John Woodman (d 1988), of Newcastle upon Tyne, and Alma Clare, *née* Callender (d 1982); *b* 11 April 1945; *Educ* Ushaw Coll Durham, King's Coll Newcastle Univ of Durham (BA), King's Coll Cambridge (PhD); *m* 21 July 1977, Dorothy Joyce, da of Gordon Charles Monk (d 1970), of N Shields; 2 s (David b 1981, John b 1983); *Career* reader in Latin lit Univ of Newcastle upon Tyne 1979-80 (lectr in classics 1968-79); prof of Latin: Univ of Leeds 1980-84, Univ of Durham 1984-; visiting prof Princeton Univ 1989-90; *Books* Quality and Pleasure in Latin Poetry (jtly, 1974), Velleius Paterculus: the Tiberian Narrative (1977), Creative Imitation and Latin Literature (jtly, 1979), Velleius Paterculus: the Caesarian and Augustan Narrative (1983), Poetry and Politics in the Age of Augustus (jtly, 1984), Past Perspectives: Studies in Greek and Roman Historical Writing (jtly, 1986), Rhetoric in Classical Historiography (1988), Tacitus: Annals IV (jtly, 1989); *Style—* Prof A J Woodman; Department of Classics, 38 North Bailey, Durham DH1 3EU (☎ 091 374 2072)

WOODMAN, Roderick Eric; s of Arthur John Woodman (d 1965), of Westbury on Severn, and Sylvia, *née* Cottle (d 1953); *b* 19 Feb 1931; *Educ* Malmesbury GS, Cheltenham Coll of Art; *m* 6 Oct 1951, Marian Nora, da of Robert Gilbert Meadows; 1 s (Michael Phillip b 1956), 1 da (Penelope Jane b 1955); *Career* Nat Serv RE 1952-54; architect ptnr 1960-88: Eric Cole & Partners, Barnard & Partners; specialised in museums, swimming pools, public sector housing, design for the handicapped; involved with conservation areas and general improvement areas incl: Cheltenham, Cirencester, Marlborough, Malmesbury, Chippenham; leader socially orientated schemes for the elderly, and physically and mentally handicapped; rotarian (pres Cirencester Rotary club 1970-71); memb: C of E, Nat Panel of Speakers for change to Metric; FRIBA 1968; *Recreations* reading, walking; *Style—* Roderick Woodman, Esq

WOODROFFE, Peter Mackelcan; s of Kenneth Derry Woodroffe (d 1972), of 8 Westminster Gardens, London, and Raby Alfreda Mackelcan, *née* Ryan; *b* 2 Aug 1927; *Educ* Mill Hill; *m* 15 June 1973, Amanda Aloysia Nicolette, da of Henry Forbes, of Chelsea Lodge, Englefield Green, nr Windsor, Berks; 2 s (Justin Mackelcan b 24 May 1977, Clifford Derry b 10 Dec 1979); *Career* joined Rifle Bde 1945, cmmnd 2 Lt Royal Northumberland Fus 1946 (Lt 1947), ret 1948; admitted slr 1953; sr ptnr Woodroffes 1963- (ptnr 1956-63); underwriting memb of Lloyd's; sec Ct of Govrs Mill Hill Sch, memb (C) Westminster City Cncl 1962-65; hon citizen State of Texas USA 1967, Freeman City of London 1984; memb Law Soc 1953; *Recreations* skiing, golf, tennis; *Clubs* Boodle's, The Berkshire Golf, Rye Golf, Royal Cinque Ports Golf; *Style*— Peter Woodroffe, Esq; 13 Cadogan St, London SW3 2PP (☎ 071 589 9339); Stonewalls, Pett Level, nr Hastings, Sussex TN35 4EH (☎ 042481 3198); Woodroffes, York House, 199 Westminster Bridge Rd, London SE1 7UT (☎ 071 928 6855, fax 071 633 0459)

WOODROOFE, Sir Ernest George; s of Ernest Woodroofe; *b* 6 Jan 1912; *Educ* Cockburn HS, Univ of Leeds (PhD); *m* 1, 1938, Margaret Downes (d 1961); 1 da; m 2, 1962, Enid Arnold; *Career* chm: Unilever 1970-74, Leverhulme Tst 1974-82; memb Br Gas Corp 1973-82; dir: Schroders 1974-89, Burton Gp 1974-83, Guthrie Corp 1974-82; Hon DSc: Cranfield, Liverpool; Hon LLD Leeds, Hon DUniv Surrey, hon fell UMIST, Hon ACT Liverpool; memb Royal Cmmn for 1851 Exhibition 1968-84; FInstP, FIChemE; Cdr Order of Orange Nassau 1972; kt 1973; *Clubs* Athenaeum; *Style*— Sir Ernest Woodroofe; 44 The Street, Puttenham, Guildford, Surrey GU3 1AR (☎ 0483 810977)

WOODROW, Arabella Thomasine; da of Michael Henry Carlile Morris (d 1987), of Basingstoke, Hants, and Margaret Joyce, *née* Flannery (d 1984); *b* 31 March 1954; *Educ* Queen Anne's Sch Caversham Berks, Lady Margaret Hall Oxford (BA, DPhil); *m* 15 Dec 1979, Richard Erskine Woodrow, s of Cyril Erskine Woodrow (d 1960), of Scarborough; *Career* wine merchant; sales rep Harveys of Bristol 1979-84, Wine and Spirit Educn Tst dip 1981, Vinters scholarship from Vinters Co 1983, sales rep Christopher & Co Ltd 1984-85, wine buyer Cooperative Wholesale Soc 1986-; qualified Master of Wine 1986; memb Lancs and NW Wine and Spirit Assoc; memb: Inst of Masters of Wine 1986, Wine Devpt Bd 1986; *Books* Wines Of The Rhone Valley; *Recreations* marathon running, skiing, cookery, wine tasting; *Style*— Mrs Arabella Woodrow; CWS Wines and Spirits, Fairhills Rd, Irlam, Manchester M30 6BD (☎ 061 775 8431, telex 669935 CWSVIN G)

WOODROW, David; CBE (1979); s of Sydney Melson Woodrow (d 1981), of Foston House, Foston, Leics, and Edith Constance, *née* Farmer (d 1936); *b* 16 March 1920; *Educ* Shrewsbury, Trinity Coll Oxford (MA); *m* 1, 1 April 1950 (m dis), Marie-Armande Irène, da of Benjamin Barrios, KBE (d 1928); 2 da (Geraldine b 27 Jan 1951, Joanna b 29 June 1955); m 2, 25 Jan 1983, Mary, da of Rupert Alexander Whitamore (d 1946); *Career* enlisted 1939, cmmnd RA 1940, captured Java 1942 (POW Java and Japan 1942-45), demob 1946; slr private practice partnership 1949-84; chm: Reading & Dist Hosp Mgmnt Ctee 1966-72, Oxford Regnl Hosp Bd 1972-74, Oxford RHA 1974-78, Nat Staff Ctee for Admin and Clinical staff of NHS 1975-79; memb Law Soc; *Recreations* painting and drawing; *Clubs* Leander; *Style*— David Woodrow, Esq, CBE; Dobsons, Brightwell-Cum-Sotwell, Oxfordshire (☎ 0491 36170)

WOODROW, (Charles) James; s of Bernard Joseph Woodrow (d 1956), of 10 The Drive, Hartley, Plymouth, and Winifred Barbara, *née* Tregillus (d 1966); *b* 20 March 1918; *Educ* Plymouth Coll, Loughborough Engrg Coll (now Univ); *m* 1 Feb 1947, Elizabeth Teresa, da of Alfred Churchill Channings Jago (d 1945); 3 da (Josanne b 11 Jan 1948, Rosalind b 19 June 1950, Vanessa b 13 Oct 1953); *Career* WWII Maj REME, i/c port workshop Tobruk (during seige), staff coll Palestine, staff duties 8 Army HQ (mentioned in despatches), control cmmn Germany, demob 1946; chm: Blight & White Ltd Structural Engrs Plymouth 1964-85 (md 1947-80), Sutton Harbour Co 1964-; chm: Plymouth Guild Community Serv 1963-77, Plymouth Mfrs Gp 1982-83, Offshore Energy Plymouth, Area Bd Young Enterprise, Plymouth Barbican Assoc 1957-; memb Regnl Cncl CBI; JP (Plymouth Bench) 1954-88 (chm 1985-88), High Sheriff of Devon 1983-84; FRSA, CEng, FIStructE, MIProdE, MBIM; *Recreations* golf, gardening, walking; *Clubs* 7 Armoured Division Offrs', Royal Western Yacht; *Style*— James Woodrow, Esq; Higher Furlong, Thurlestone, Kingsbridge, Devon TQ7 3NT (☎ 0548 560 206); Sutton Harbour Co, Plymouth PL4 0ES (☎ 0752 664 186)

WOODROW, William Robert (Bill); s of Geoffrey William Woodrow, of Chichester, W Sussex, and Doreen Mary, *née* Fasken; *b* 1 Nov 1948; *Educ* Barton Peveril GS, Winchester Sch of Art, St Martins Sch of Art, Chelsea Sch of Art (Higher Dip Fine Art); *m* 12 Nov 1970, Pauline, da of John Neville Rowley; 1 s (Harry), 1 da (Ellen); *Career* sculptor; individual exhibitions in Europe, Australia, USA and Canada 1972-; work in numerous group exhibitions incl: Br Sculpture in the 20th Century Whitechapel Art Gallery 1981, Biennale of Sydney 1982, Aperto 82 Venice 1982, XII Biennale of Paris 1982, New Art at the Tate Gallery 1983, Transformations Sao Paulo (also Riode Janeiro, Mexico City, Lisbon) 1983, Int Survey of Recent Painting and Sculpture New York 1984, Skulptur im 20 Jahrhundert Basle 1984, ROSC '84 Dublin 1984, Space Invaders toured Canada 1985, The Br Show toured Australia 1985, Carnegie Int Pittsburgh 1985, Entre el objeto y la imagen toured Spain 1986, Painting and Sculpture Today Indianapolis 1986, Br Art of the 1980's Stockholm and Tampere 1987, Documenta 8 Kassel W Germany 1987, Starlit Waters Tate Liverpool 1988, British Now Montreal 1988, GB-USSR Kiev Moscow 1990, Metropolis Berlin 1991; winner Anne Gerber award Seattle Museum of Art USA 1988; work in numerous museum collections inc: Arts Cncl GB, Br Cncl, Imperial War Museum, Kunsthaus Zurich, Malmö Konsthall, Nat Gallery of Canada, Rijksmuseum Kröller-Müller, Tate Gallery; *Style*— W R Woodrow, Esq; c/o Lisson Gallery, 67 Lisson St, London NW1 5DA (☎ 071 724 2739)

WOODRUFF, Prof Alan Waller; CMG (1978), OBE (1989); s of William Henry Woodruff (d 1939), of Sunderland, and Mary Margaret, *née* Thomson (d 1966); *b* 27 June 1916; *Educ* Bede Collegiate Sch Sunderland, Univ of Durham Coll of Med (MB BS, MD); *m* 21 Jan 1946, Mercia Helen, da of Leonard Henry Arnold (d 1949), of Dorking; 2 s (Arnold Henry Waller b 1951, Peter Waller Rolph b 1956), 1 da (Heather Mary Elizabeth b 1949); *Career* WWII Flt Lt (formerly Flying Offr) med branch RAF 1940-42, Sqdn Ldr med specialist 1942-46; conslt in tropical med to Army 1953-81; Wellcome prof of clinical tropical med Univ of London 1952-81 (prof emeritus 1981-), physician Hosp for Tropical Diseases (UCH) London 1952-81 (consulting physician 1981-), prof of med Univ of Juba Southern Sudan 1981-; conslt Br Airways 1959-87; pres: Durham Univ Soc 1964-75, Royal Soc of Tropical Med and Hygiene 1974-76, Med Soc of London 1976-77, History Section RSM London 1977-79; chm Br Burma Soc 1969-80; cncl memb Royal Coll of Physicians 1975-79; memb: Colonial Med Res Ctee 1955-68, Tropical Med Res Bd MRC 1968-72, West African MRC 1955-58, East African MRC 1959-64; hon fell Royal Soc of Painters-Etchers and Engravers 1978; FRCP 1953, FRCP Edin 1961; hon fell: Burma Med Assoc 1966, Brazilian Soc of Tropical Med 1969, Belgian Soc of Tropical Med 1969, Société de pathologie Exotique Paris 1972; *Books* Medicine in the Tropics (with S G Wright, second edn 1984), A Synopsis of Infectious and Tropical Diseases (with S Bell, third edn 1987); *Recreations* sketching and engraving, fishing, tennis; *Clubs* Athenaeum, Queen's, Sunderland, Sudan (Khartoum); *Style*— Prof A W Woodruff, CMG, OBE; 122 Ferndene Rd, London SE24 0BA; Univ of Juba, P O Box 82, Juba, Sudan

WOODRUFF, Hon Mrs (Elizabeth Trilby Charity); da of Baron Taylor (Life Peer); *b* 1943; *Educ* Univ of Sussex; *m* 1, 1971 (m dis 1986), Paul Stephen Masterman; m 2, 1986, Alan George Woodruff; *Career* librarian Br Technol Gp 1981-; *Style*— The Hon Mrs Woodruff; 8 Denman's Close, Lindfield, West Sussex RH16 2JX

WOODRUFF, Hon Mrs (Marie Immaculée Antoinette); *née* Lyon-Dalberg-Acton; da of 2 Baron Acton, KCVO (d 1924); 6 Bt PM of Naples during Napoleonic Wars, his s 7 Bt m heiress of Duke of Dalberg, 8 Cr UK Peer 1869; *b* 1905; *m* 1933, John Douglas Woodruff, CBE (d 1978); *Career* Dame of Honour and Devotion of Sovereign O of Malta; has Cross Pro Ecclesia et Pontifice; *Style*— The Hon Mrs Woodruff; Marcham Priory, Abingdon, Oxon

WOODRUFF, William Charles (Bill); CBE (1985); s of Thomas William Woodruff (d 1943), of Ramsgate, Kent, and Caroline Elizabeth, *née* Windsor (d 1966); *b* 14 Aug 1921; *Educ* St George's Sch Ramsgate; *m* 1, 9 May 1946, Ethel May (d 1981), da of late Frank Miles, of Rochester, Kent; 1 s (Gerald b 1948), 1 da (Pamela b 1951); m 2, 7 April 1987, Olivia Minerva, *née* Barnes; 3 step s (John b 1946, James b 1947, David b 1949); *Career* Flt-Lt navigator/observer 1409 Flight RAF 1941-46, POW 1943-45; Miny of Civil Aviation 1945-: air traffic controller at various airports and London HQ 1946-56, air traffic controller Heathrow 1956-62, sec PATCH long-term ATC Planning Gp 1960-61, dir civil air traffic ops 1967-69 (dep dir 1962-67), controller nat air traffic servs 1977-81 (jt field cdr 1969-74, dep controller 1974-77); aviation assessor airports pub inquiries 1981-84, specialist advsr Parly Select Tport Ctee on air traffic control safety 1988-89; master Guild of Air Traffic Control Offrs 1956 (clerk of Guild 1952-56); FRAeS 1976; *Recreations* reading, gardening, crosswords; *Style*— Bill Woodruff, Esq, CBE; Great Oaks, 36 Court Rd, Ickenham, Uxbridge, Middx UB10 8TF (☎ 0895 639134)

WOODS, (Paul) Anthony John; s of Charles John Woods, of Streatham, London, and Joan Vera *née* Margetts; *b* 14 June 1945; *m* 9 June 1979, Louise Head, da of Jason Richard Head Palmer, of Teddington, Middx; 1 s (Richard b 1982), 1 da (Eleanor b 1980); *Career* admitted slr: England and Wales 1969, NSW Australia 1973; ptnr Norton Rose 1980-; Liveryman The City of London Slrs 1981-; memb Law Soc 1969; *Recreations* theatre, reading, gardening, watching rugby union and cricket; *Clubs* MCC, Tanglin; *Style*— Anthony Woods, Esq; Kempson House, Camomile St, London EC3A 7AN (☎ 071 283 2434, fax 071 588 1181, telex 883652 NOROSE G)

WOODS, Basil Joseph Pontifex; s of Victor Jocelyn Woods (d 1966), and Marie Josephé, *née* Payet (d 1971); *b* 28 Aug 1922; *Educ* Durban Boys' HS Natal SA, Natal Univ (BEcon), Pembroke Coll Cambridge (MA); *m* 1, 1950; 3 da (Mrs Peter Alderton b 1951, Carol Anne b 1953, Mrs Andrew Greenwood b 1956); m 2, 1971, Deborah Mary, da of Robert Charles Thomas (decd); *Career* dir Central Bank of Fedn of Rhodesia and Nyasaland, chm Allied Steel and Wire 1981-85; former dir corporate planning and econ advsr Guest Keen and Nettlefolds plc, dep md GKN plc 1981-84 (ret all GKN appts 1984); chm: European Industrial Services, Ashfield Holdings Ltd; *Recreations* cricket, golf; *Clubs* MCC; *Style*— Basil Woods, Esq; Old Roses, Upton Bishop, Ross-on-Wye, Herefs HR9 7UA; European Industrial Services Ltd, Woden Rd West, Kings Hill, Wednesbury, West Midlands WS10 7TT; Ashfield Holdings Limited, 79-81 Station Road, Sutton-in-Ashfield, Nottingham NG17 5FR

WOODS, His Hon Judge Brian; s of Edward Percival Woods, of Woodmancote, Cheltenham (d 1967), and Beulah Aileen Ruth, *née* Thomas (d 1977); *b* 5 Nov 1928; *Educ* City of Leicester Boys' Sch, Univ of Nottingham (LLB); *m* 23 April 1957, Anne Margaret, da of Frederic James Griffiths, of Parkgate, Wirral (d 1975); 3 da (Rachel b 1962, Helen b 1965, Diana b 1969); *Career* RAF 1947-49; called to the Bar Gray's Inn 1955; memb Midland Circuit, Circuit Judge 1975; dep chm Lincs (Lindsey) Quarter Sessions 1968; Anglican Lay Reader 1970, chllr Diocese of Leicester 1977-79; memb Cncl of Abbots Bromley Sch of St Mary and St Anne 1977-, fell Midland Div Woodard Corp 1978, legal memb Mental Heath Review Tbnls (Trent and Northern Regions) 1983-; *Recreations* music, taking photographs, avoiding complacency; *Style*— His Honour Judge Woods

WOODS, Brian Edwin; s of Norman Eric Woods (d 1972), and Alice Louise, *née* Finch (d 1984); *b* 26 Feb 1940; *Educ* Leeds GS; *m* 10 July 1965 (m dis 1981), Judith Elizabeth, *née* Everitt; 1 da (Jane Louise b 7 Jan 1973); m 2, 2 Oct 1981, Josephine, da of Philip Bradley Canneaux, 1 da (Helen Josephine b 27 Aug 1983); *Career* articled clerk Whitfield & Co Leeds, qualified chartered accountant 1965; Thornton Baker: mangr Birmingham 1970-73, mangr Bedford 1973-75, ptnr 1975, managing ptnr 1983-; dir Bedfordshire Training and Enterprise Cncl 1990-, memb Br Olympic Appeal Ctee for Bedfordshire 1991-92, chm Bedford Branch Haven Childrens Hosp Appeal; FCA 1975 (ACA 1965); *Recreations* photography, music, walking; *Clubs* Rotary (Bedford), Institute of Directors, Bedford Round Table; *Style*— Brian Woods, Esq; Grant Thornton, 49 Mill St, Bedford MK40 3LB (☎ 0234 211521)

WOODS, Christopher Charles Eric (Chris); s of Eric James Sydney Woods, of Boston, Lincs, and Patricia Mary, *née* Dawson; *b* 14 Nov 1959; *Educ* Kirton Secdy Sch; *m* 25 June 1980, Sarah, da of Norman Burden; 1 s (Mark Christopher b 16 June 1981), 1 da (Laura Elizabeth b 23 March 1984); *Career* professional footballer; Nottingham Forest (no league appearances), 63 appearances Queens Park Rangers (league debut 1979), 250 appearances Norwich City, over 200 appearances Glasgow Rangers 1986-; England: 6 under 21 caps, 2 B caps, 20 full caps; League Cup Winner's medal Nottm Forest v Liverpool 1978, Euro Cup medal Nottm Forest v Malmo 1979, Milk Cup Winner's medal Norwich City v Sunderland 1985, Div 2 Championship Norwich City 1986; Glasgow Rangers: Scot League Championships 1987, 1989, 1990, Skol Cup Winner's medal 1986-87, 1987-88, 1988-89, 1990-91 (Loser's medal 1989-90), Scot FA Cup Loser's medal 1988-89; holder Br goalkeeping record for not conceding a goal (1196 minutes 26 Nov 1986 - 31 Jan 1987); proprietor nursing home; *Recreations* golf, snooker, squash; *Style*— Chris Woods, Esq; c/o John Mac, 1st Floor, Keystone, 60 London Rd, St Albans, Herts (☎ 0727 48685); Glasgow Rangers, Ibrox Park, Glasgow (☎ 041 427 8500)

WOODS, Eric Cecil; s of Cecil Vincent Edward Woods, of Rustington, Sussex, and Eileen Sybil, *née* Bays; *b* 2 Oct 1930; *Educ* Highgate Sch, LSE (LLB, LLM); *m* 24 June 1961, (Florence) Mary, da of William Gerald Edington (d 1968); 2 da (Katharine b 1962, Penelope b 1964); *Career* admitted slr 1953, asst slr with Newport and Brighton corps 1953-59, asst slr and ptnr Tucker Hussey and Co London 1959-67, princ slr Legal Dept Midland Bank plc 1971-87 (joined 1967), agent slr Crown Prosecution Serv and private practice for Midland Bank 1987, conslt Stephenson Harwood 1988-89; author of articles in New Law Journal and Journal of Institute of Bankers; chm: Legal Ctee London Cleaning Bankers 1980-82 (memb 1971-87), CBI Co Law Panel 1976-83 (memb 1974-); memb: CBI Ctees and Working Parties, Law Soc Standing Ctee on Co Law 1980-87, Chm's Panel Fin Servs Tbnl 1988; JP Herts 1970-71; Freeman City London 1962, Liveryman of Worshipful Co of Glaziers 1962; *Recreations* history, gardening, music, travel; *Style*— Eric Woods, Esq; The Old Stone House, Stedham, Midhurst, W Sussex GU29 0NG

WOODS, (Hubert) Frank; s of Hubert George Woods (d 1959), of Leeds, and Julia Augusta, *née* Kamlinski (d 1963); *b* 18 Nov 1937; *Educ* St Bees Sch, Univ of Leeds

(BSc), Univ of Oxford (BM BCh, DPhil); *m* 7 Jan 1966, Hilary Sheila, da of Ernest E Cox, of Sheffield; 1 s (Christopher b 21 Oct 1967), 2 da (Katharine b 23 Feb 1971, Rebecca b 5 June 1973); *Career* house offr posts NHS 1965-66, memb external med scientific staff MRC 1972-76, hon conslt physician Sheffield Health Authy 1976-, dean Faculty of Med and Dentistry Univ of Sheffield 1988- (prof of clinical pharmacology and therapeutics 1976-), sr external examiner in med Univ of Oxford 1988- (lectr in med 1967-72), examiner membership exam RCP 1989-, author 115 res papers and 3 books; regnl advsr RCP 1986-89; memb Hunterian Soc 1967, FRCP 1978 (MRCP 1968), FFPM 1989; *Books* Clinical and Biochemical Aspects of Lactic Acidosis (with R D Cohen, 1976); *Style—* Prof Frank Woods; 68 Ivy Park Road, Ranmoor, Sheffield, S Yorks S10 3LD (☎ 0742 301829); Royal Hallamshire Hospital, Glossop Rd, Sheffield, S Yorks (☎ 0742 766222, telex 547216 UGSHEF G, fax 0742 720275)

WOODS, Maj-Gen Henry Gabriel; CB (1979), MBE (1945), DL (N Yorks 1984-); s of G S Woods (d 1961), of Bexhill-on-Sea, Sussex, and Flora, *née* MacNevin (d 1976); *b* 7 May 1924; *Educ* Highgate Sch, Trinity Coll Oxford (MA); *m* 29 April 1953, Imogen Elizabeth Birchenough, da of CES Dodd (d 1975), of Bath; 2 da (Sarah b 1955, Arabella b 1958); *Career* cmmnd 5 Royal Iniskilling Dragoon Gds 1944; served NW Europe (Normandy to Baltic): 1944-45, 1945-51, 1960-62, 1967-69; Adj Korea 1952, served Middle East 1954 and 1964-67, Mil Asst to Vice Chief of Def Staff 1962-64, cmd 5 Royal Inniskilling Dragoon Gds 1965-67, Asst Mil Sec to C-in-C BAOR 1967-69, Cdr RAC Centre 1969-72, Cdr Br Army Staff and Mil Attaché Br Embassy Washington USA 1972-75, GOC NE Dist 1976-80, Army Stall Coll 1956, Jt Servs Staff Coll 1960, RCDS 1972; head Centre for Industl and Educnl Liaison W and N Yorks 1980-87, sec St William's Fndn 1987-, dir Transpennine 1988-; chm: Bradford and W Yorks BIM 1982-84, Yorks Region RSA 1984-, N Yorks Scout Cncl 1984-, 5 Royal Inniskilling Dragoon Gds Assoc 1979-; pres Royal Soc of St George (York and Humberside) 1986-88; memb: York Area Mental Health Appeals Ctee 1984-90, TA and VR Assoc 1982-90, Yorks Agric Soc 1980-, Cncl RSA 1990-; Vice Lord-Lt N Yorks 1986-; memb Merchants of the Staple of England 1982-; Hon DLitt Univ of Bradford 1988; FBIM 1980, FRSA 1981; Order of Leopold Second Class (1966); *Books* Change and Challenge - History of the 5th Iniskilling Dragoon Guards (with Gen Sir Cecil Blacker, 1976); *Recreations* gardening, walking, foot follower (hunting), military history; *Clubs* Cavalry and Guards, Ends of the Earth; *Style—* Maj Gen Henry Woods, CB, MBE, DL; St William's Foundation, 5 College Street, York YO1 2JF (☎ 0904 642744)

WOODS, Humphrey Martin; s of Rev Howard Charles Woods, of Manormead, Tilford Rd, Hindhead, Surrey, and Kathleen Ailsie Clutton, *née* Baker; descendant of the philosopher John Locke; *b* 23 Nov 1937; *Educ* Lancing, Trinity Coll Oxford (BA); *m* 1, 4 May 1963, Dona Leslie; m 2, 25 Jan 1977, Jennifer Mary, da of Brig Edward Hayden Tinker, of 3 Ferguson Ave, Westshore, nr Napier, NZ; 2 da (Eleanor b 1977, Lucy b 1979), 3 s (Mark b 1981, Leo b 1984, Dominic b 1963); *Career* archaeologist with the Historic Bldgs & Monuments Cmmn for England (English Heritage formerly the Directorate of Ancient Monuments & Historic Bldgs of the Dept of the Environment) since 1974; *Publications* Excavations on the Second Site of The Dominican Priory Oxford, in Oxoniensia Vol XLI (1976), The Despoliation of the Abbey of Sts Peter and Paul and St Augustine Between the Years 1542 and 1793, in Historical Essays in Memory of James Hobbs (1980), The Completion of the Abbey Church of St Peter, St Paul and St Augustine, Canterbury, By Abbots Wido and Hugh of Fleury, in British Archaeological Association Conference Transactions (1982), Excavations at Eltham Palace 1975-79, in Transactions of the London and Middlx Archaeological Soc (1982), Excavations on the Site of the Dominican Friary at Guildford in 1974 and 1978, Research Volume Number 9 of the Surrey Archaeological Soc (1984), Excavations at Wenlock Priory 1981-86, Journal Br Archaeological Assoc (1987), St Augustine's Abbey, report on excavations 1960-78, Kent Archaeological Soc Monograph Series Vol IV (1988), Romanesque West Front at The Church of the Holy Trinity Much Wenlock in Transactions of Shropshire Archaeological Soc 1989; *Recreations* walking in the Quantock hills, natural history; *Style—* Humphrey Woods, Esq; 20 Wembdon Hill, Bridgwater, Somerset TA6 7PX (☎ 0278 423 955)

WOODS, Hon Mrs (Isobel Ann); *née* Byron; o child of 11 Baron Byron (d 1983), and Pauline, Baroness Byron, *qv*; *b* 23 May 1932; *Educ* St Mary's Cofe Girls' Sch; *m* 1, 1951, Robert Reford Corr (d 1980); 2 s (John b 1953, Anthony b 1956), 1 da (Helen-Jane b 1961); m 2, 1983, Norman James Woods, s of late James Park Woods, VC; *Style—* The Hon Mrs Woods; 55A Mayfair St, Mount Claremont, W Australia

WOODS, Prof John; s of Charles Thomas Woods (d 1988), of Gorleston, Gt Yarmouth, Norfolk, and Dorothy Eleanor, *née* Poole (d 1978); *b* 2 July 1925; *Educ* Gt Yarmouth GS, QMC London (BSc, PhD); *m* 31 March 1951, Eileen Mabel, da of Frank Heys (d 1965), of Wisbech, Cambs; 2 s (Peter John b 1957, Michael Alan b 1960), 1 da (Carol Ann b 1954); *Career* flying offr Tech Branch (Signals) RAF 1945-48; sr sci staff Gen Res Laboratories Wembley 1950-60, emeritus prof Univ of Durham 1989- (lectr in applied physics 1960-64, sr lectr 1964-66, reader 1966-86, prof 1986-89, dean of sci 1985-88); memb: Br Assoc for Crystal Growth, Soc for Information Display; FInstP 1961, CPhys, FRSA 1985, UK ISES; *Books* The Chemistry of the Semiconductor Industry (contrib 1987), II-VI Compounds (co ed 1982), II-VI Compounds (co ed 1987), Crystal Growth (1989); *Recreations* music, cricket, dogs; *Style—* Prof John Woods; 25 Orchard Drive, Durham DH1 1LA (☎ 091 386 4176); Applied Physics Group, School of Engineering and Applied Science, University of Durham, Science Laboratories, South Rd, Durham DH1 3E (☎ 091 374 2386, fax 091 374 3848, telex 537351 DURLIB G)

WOODS, Dr John David; s of Ronald Ernest Goff Woods (d 1968), and Ethel Marjorie Woods; *b* 26 Oct 1939; *Educ* Imp Coll Univ of London (BSc, PhD, DIC); *m* 7 April 1971, Irina Christine Alix, da of Bernd von Arnim; 1 s (Alexander Jan Roland b 1975), 1 da (Virginia Elizabeth Marina b 1980); *Career* res fell Meteorological Office 1966-72, prof of physical oceanography Univ of Southampton 1972-77, prof of oceanography and dir Institut Fuer Meereskunde Univ of Kiel 1977-86, dir of marine and atmospheric sciences NERC 1986-; contrib papers on oceanography and meteorology to various learned jls; memb: NERC 1979-82, Robert Hooke Inst Univ of Oxford 1986-, Academia Europaea 1988, Meteorological Res Ctee 1976-77 and 1987-; Hon DSc Univ of Liège 1980; ARCS 1961, FRGS 1966, FRMetSoc 1967; *Books* Underwater Science (1971), Underwater Research (1976); *Recreations* underwater swimming, history; *Clubs* Athenaeum; *Style—* Dr John Woods; 30 Feilden Grove, Oxford (☎ 0865 69342); NERC, Polaris House, Swindon (☎ 0793 411637, fax 0793 411545, telex 444293 ENVRE G); Hooke Institute, Clarendon Laboratory, Oxford (☎ 0865 272 093)

WOODS, Prof Leslie Colin; s of Alexander Binny Woodhead (d 1983), of Auckland, NZ, and Gwendoline Isobell, *née* Tew (d 1982); *b* 6 Dec 1922; *Educ* Auckland Univ (BSc, MSc, DSc, BE), Merton Coll Oxford (MA, DPhil, DSc); *m* 1, 21 Aug 1943 (m dis 1977), (Gladys) Elizabeth, da of James Bailey of Ashburton, NZ; 5 da (Coral Anne (Mrs Schofield) b 1944, Jillian Rebecca (Mrs Lloyd) b 1947, Diane Rose b 1949, Elizabeth Gladys b 1950, Patricia Beverley (Mrs Alvarez) b 1950); m 2, 11 Nov 1977 (m dis 1990), Helen Louise, *née* Troughton; m 3, 8 Feb 1990, Jacqueline Suzanne, *née* Griffiths; *Career* pilot 16/17 Fighter Sqdns RNZAF; served 1941-45: Pilot Offr 1942, Flying Offr 1943, Flt-Lt 1944; prof engrg Univ of NSW Sydney 1956-61; Univ of Oxford: fell and tutor in engrg sci Balliol Coll 1961-70 (emeritus fell 1990-), prof of maths 1970-90 (emeritus prof 1990-), chm Maths Inst 1984-89; Hon DSc Auckland Univ 1983; *Books* The Theory of Subsonic Plane Flow (1961), Introduction to Neutron Distribution Theory (1964), The Thermodynamics of Fluid Systems (1975), Principles of Magnetoplasma Dynamics (1987); *Recreations* gardening, clarinet playing; *Style—* Prof Leslie Woods; Mathematical Institute, 24-29 St Giles, Oxford (☎ 0865 270205)

WOODS, Michael John; s of Dr L H Woods, and Margery, *née* Pickard; *Educ* Bradfield; *m* 15 Jan 1966, Carolyn Rosemary, da of William Tadman, of Tracey Hill Cottage, Roborough, nr Winkleigh, N Devon; 1 s (Nicholas John b 13 Aug 1967), 1 da (Jennifer Sarah Rosemary b 29 May 1969); *Career* Nat Serv 1 Bn Royal Fus (serv Suez Crisis) 1955-77; trainee exec Mecca Ltd 1957-63; dir: Silver Blades Ice Rink Ltd 1963-70, Mecca Catering 1968-, Mecca Leisure Ltd 1973-; asst md: Mecca Bingo Social Clubs 1972-80, Mecca Leisure Ltd 1979-85, Mecca Agency International 1983-85; chm: Ison Bros (Newcastle) Ltd 1983-85, Pointer Motor Co 1983-85, Scot Automatic Printing 1983-85; md: Mecca Leisure Speciality Catering Div 1985-, Speciality Catering Div Europe 1989-; vice pres Variety Club of GB (co chm Appeals Ctee), memb Confrérie de la Chaîne des Rôtisseurs; FInstD 1965, FHCIMA 1989; *Recreations* squash, swimming, shooting (Clay and Pheasant), fishing; *Style—* Michael Woods, Esq; Glendale, Farley Gn, Albury, Nr Guildford, Surrey (☎ 048641 2472); Mecca Leisure Ltd, 6 Hanover St, London W1 (☎ 071 491 7341, fax 071 629 4623, car 0860 524022, telex 261448)

WOODS, Rt Rev Robert (Robin) Wilmer; KCMG (1980), KCVO (1971); s of Rt Rev Edward Sydney Woods (d 1953), Bishop of Lichfield, and Clemence Rachel, 2 da of Robert Barclay, JP; *b* 15 Feb 1914; *Educ* Gresham's, Trinity Coll Cambridge; *m* 1942, Henrietta Marion, JP (1966), da of late Kenneth H Wilson, OBE, JP; 2 s, 3 da; *Career* ordained priest 1939; army chaplain 1943-46; Vicar of S Wigston 1946-51; Archdeacon: Singapore 1951-58, Sheffield 1958-62; Dean of Windsor, Chaplain to HM The Queen and Register Most Noble Order of the Garter 1962-71; Bishop of Worcester 1971-81; Prelate Order of St Michael and St George 1971-89; asst bishop Diocese of Gloucester 1982; dir of Christian Aid 1969; *Books* Autobiography (1986); *Clubs* Brooks's; *Style—* The Rt Rev Robin Woods, KCMG, KCVO; Torsend House, Tirley, Glos GL19 4EU

WOODS, Robert Carr; s of Percy Charles Woods (d 1969), of Hookwood, Fittleworth, W Sussex, and Janet Woods, *née* Witney; *b* 25 Nov 1930; *Educ* Rugby, Trinity Hall Camb; *m* 20 Oct 1956, Sonia May, da of Thomas Guichard Savill (d 1984), of 20 Marine Point, Worthing, Sussex; 2 s (Richard b 1958, Nicholas b 1961) 1 da (Sally b 1963); *Career* 2 Lieut RA; 3 RHA Regt, Lieut Bucks Yeo (TA); md Woods and Maslen Ltd, dir Jardine Thompson Graham Ltd; memb of Lloyds 1955 (memb Lloyds Brokers Ctee 1983-86, chm Lloyds Brokers Motor Sub Ctee 1986); gen cmmr of Taxes; *Recreations* bird watching, photography, art, conversation, gardening, cars; *Clubs* City of London; *Style—* Robert Woods, Esq; Jardine House, 6 Crutched Friars, London EC3N 2HT

WOODS, Stephen Mallon; s of Alexander Woods (d 1975), and Annie *née* Donnelly; *b* 15 Jan 1930; *Educ* St Mungo's Acad Glasgow, Glasgow Univ (BSc Pharamacy); *m* 8 Feb 1956, Margaret, da of Samuel Trousdale, of 30 Chalmers Ave, Ayr; 3 s (Mark b 1962, Paul b 1968, Alan b 1973), 3 da (Rhona b 1959, Aileen b 1960, Maureen b 1964); *Career* Ayrshire Pharmaceuticals Ltd 1961-, SM Woods (Pharmacy) Ltd 1971-, Ayrshire Off Services Ltd 1968-, Armstrongs Hawich House 1982-; former chm Drug Accounts Ctee (Scotland), former memb Nat Pharmaceutical Advisory Ctee (Scotland); MPS (chm Gen Cncl 1977-80); *Recreations* golf, bridge; *Clubs* St Cuthbert Golf, Bruce Bridge; *Style—* Stephen Woods, Esq; 15 Wheatfield Rd, Ayr, Scotland; 18 Fullarton St, Ayr (☎ 0292 610032)

WOODS, Hon Mrs (Susan Lesley); eldest da of 2 Baron Gridley; *b* 1950; *m* 1, 1975 (m dis 1982), John Philip Bruce Scott; 1 s (Edward Harry Gridley b 1977), 1 da (Carrie Elizabeth Anne b 1979); m 2, 1983, Andrew Kindebee Woods; *Style—* The Hon Mrs Woods; 7 West Way, Old Greenwich, Connecticut 06870, USA

WOODS, Hon Mrs (Victoria Venetia); da of late 5 Baron Stanley of Alderley, KCMG; *b* 1917; *m* 1942, Lt Cdr James Douglas Woods, Royal Canadian Naval VR; 2 da (Virginia b 1943, Teresa b 1946); *Style—* The Hon Mrs Woods; 31 Boswell Ave, Toronto, Ontario, Canada

WOODSTOCK, Viscount; Timothy Charles Robert Noel Bentinck; o s and h of 11 Earl of Portland, *qv*; *b* 1 June 1953; *Educ* Harrow, Univ of East Anglia (BA); *m* 1979, Judith Ann, da of John Robert Emerson, of 70 Queen Street, Cheadle, Staffs; 2 s (Hon William Jack Henry b 1984, Hon Jasper James Mellowes b 1988); *Heir* s, Hon William Jack Henry Bentinck b 19 May 1984; *Career* actor as Timothy Bentinck; *Style—* Viscount Woodstock; 3 Stock Orchard Crescent, Islington, London N7 9SL

WOODTHORPE, Anthony Edmund; s of Edmund Henry Woodthorpe (d 1974), of Braintree, Essex, and Olivia Constance, *née* Austin (d 1980); *b* 30 July 1935; *Educ* Brighton Coll; *m* 4 Oct 1969, Joan Deborah, da of Maj Sidney Francis Clair (d 1964), of Kingswood; 1 s (Nicholas b 1973), 1 da (Catherine b 1970); *Career* CA; sr ptnr Russell Ohly & Co Hove 1985- (ptnr 1968-85); former memb: Brighton and Hove Jr C of C, Hove Round Table; chm Royal Alexandra Hosp for Sick Children Centenary Fund Brighton, memb Rotary Club Hove (pres 1989-90), former treas Rotary Club Hove Housing Soc Ltd; Freeman City of London 1970; FCA 1964; *Recreations* golf, gardening, walking; *Clubs* Sussex Yacht; *Style—* Anthony Woodthorpe, Esq; Toad Hall, Buckingham Rd, Shoreham-by-Sea, W Sussex BN43 5UD (☎ 0273 461067); 94 Church Rd, Hove, E Sussex BN3 2EF (☎ 0273 778844, fax 0273 25210)

WOODWARD, Antony James Thomas; s of Peter Woodward, of Prestons, Chewton Mendip, Bath, Somerset, and Elizabeth Winsome Howell, *née* Davies; *b* 17 Jan 1963; *Educ* Eton, Selwyn Coll Cambridge (MA); *Career* advertising copywriter; sr writer and bd dir Mavity Gilmore Jaume FCA Ltd 1985-87, sr writer and assoc dir Still Price Court Twivy D'Souza Ltd 1988-89, sr writer Collett Dickenson Pearce and Partners Ltd; *Recreations* mountaineering, microlighting, ornithology, films, photography, reading; *Clubs* Buck's, Shuttlecock, Oxford and Cambridge; *Style—* Antony Woodward, Esq; 95 Ashbury Rd, Battersea, London SW11 5UQ (☎ 071 223 8533); Collett Dickenson Pearce and Partners Ltd, 110 Euston Rd, London NW1 2DQ (☎ 071 388 2424, fax 071 383 0939)

WOODWARD, (John) Charles; s of Eric Jackson Woodward (d 1978), of Belper, Derbyshire, and Maude Woodward, *née* Adams (d 1989); *b* 31 Oct 1935; *Educ* Herbert Strutt GS Belper Derbyshire, Univ of Manchester (BSc); *m* 11 Sept 1962, Kathy, da of Harry Ashton (d 1982), of Hazel Grove, Cheshire; 1 s (Giles b 15 Dec 1967), 2 da (Zoë b 14 Sept 1963, Sarah b 5 Jan 1965); *Career* memb London Stock Exchange 1971-75, ptnr Colegrave & Co 1972-75, investmt mangr Reed International 1975-83, chief exec BA Pensions 1984-; Nat Assoc of Pension Funds: memb Cncl 1982-91, chm Investmt Ctee 1982-84, chm of Cncl 1987-89, vice pres 1989-91; investmt advsr Cleveland CC 1983-86, dir Nat Freight Corporation Tstees Ltd 1986-; ASIA 1964, FIA 1965; *Style—* Charles Woodward, Esq; Whitelocke House, 2-4 Lampton Rd, Hounslow, Middlesex (☎ 081 570 7741)

WOODWARD, Christopher Haldane; s of William Haldane Woodward, of Wirral, Cheshire, and Audrey Woodward; *b* 18 Nov 1946; *Educ* Calday Grange GS, Univ of Birmingham (BSocSc), Manchester Business Sch (MBA); *m* 9 Aug 1969, Frances Maria, da of Richard Alan Beatty, of Edinburgh; 1 s (Matthew b 1974), 2 da (Rosalind b 1976, Charlotte b 1980); *Career* graduate trainee and economist mktg asst GKN 1968-70, mktg mangr GKN Farr Filtration 1970-72, mktg exec Guthrie Corp 1974-75, mktg and devpt exec Tay Textiles 1976-77, gp mktg and planning controller 1978-79; Cape Insulation Ltd 1979-82: mktg mangr, nat sales mangr, sales and mktg dir; mktg dir: Euro Uniroyal Ltd 1982-86, 3i plc 1986-; memb MBA Soc; *Recreations* opera, theatre, music, art; *Clubs* RAC; *Style—* Christopher Woodward, Esq; 91 Waterloo Rd, London SE1 (☎ 071 928 7822, fax 071 928 0058, telex 917844)

WOODWARD, Hon Sir (Albert) Edward; OBE (1969); s of Lt-Gen Sir Eric Winslow Woodward, KCMG, KCVO, CB, CBE, DSO (d 1967); *b* 6 Aug 1928; *Educ* Melbourne C of E GS, Univ of Melbourne (LLM); *m* 1950, Lois, da of Daniel Wrixon Thorpe (d 1976); 1 s, 6 da; *Career* judge: Fed Court of Aust 1977-90, Aust Industl Court and Supreme Court of ACT 1972-90; royal cmmr Aboriginal Land Rights 1973-74, DG of Security 1976-81, head of Royal Cmmn into the Aust Meat Indust 1981-82; chm Cncl: Aust Defence Force Acad 1982-, Camberwell GS 1983-87; chllr Univ of Melbourne 1990-; kt 1982; *see Debrett's Handbook of Australia and New Zealand for further details*; *Style—* The Hon Mr Justice Woodward, OBE; 63 Tivoli Rd, South Yarra, Victoria 3141, Australia

WOODWARD, Adm Sir John Forster (Sandy); KCB (1982); *b* 1 May 1932; *Educ* RNC Dartmouth; *m* 1960, Charlotte Mary, *née* McMurtrie; 1 s, 1 da; *Career* RN 1946, serv HMS: Maidstone, Sheffield, Zodiac; submarine specialist 1954; served HMS: Sanguine, Porpoise; CO HMS Tireless 1961-62; Lt Cdr 1962, CO HMS Grampus 1965, 1 Lt HMS Valiant to 1967; Cdr 1967; CO: qualifying course for COs 1967-69, CO HMS Warspite 1969-71; RCDS 1971-72, Capt 1972, Directorate of Naval Plans MOD 1972-74, Capt SM Sea Trg 1974-76, CO HMS Sheffield 1976-78, dir Naval Plans MOD 1978-81, Rear-Adm 1981, Flag Offr First Flotilla 1981-83, Cmd (from HMS Hermes) S Atlantic Task Gps in Falklands War 1982, Flag Offr Submarines and NATO Cdr Submarines Eastern Atlantic 1983-85, Vice Adm 1984, Dep CDS (Commitments) MOD 1985-87, Adm 1987-89; C in C Naval Home Cmd 1987-89, ret 1989; *Recreations* sailing, golf, bridge, skiing; *Clubs* Royal Yacht Squadron; *Style—* Adm Sir John Woodward, GBE, KCB; c/o Naval Secretary, Old Admiralty Building, Whitehall, London SW1

WOODWARD, Dr Michael Trevor; s of Trevor Woodward, of Weare Giffard Hall, Weare Giffard, N Devon, and Beryl Gladys, *née* Barker; *b* 25 Nov 1957; *Educ* Dartmouth Comprehensive Sch Sandwell, Univ of Aberdeen (MA, PhD); *Career* investmt mangr Ivory and Sime plc Edinburgh 1982-, dir Ivory and Sime Int Ltd 1987-; *Recreations* squash, racketball, golf; *Clubs* Edinburgh Sports; *Style—* Dr Michael Woodward; 11 Castle Terrace, Edinburgh EH1 2DP (☎ 031 229 1229); 1 Charlotte Square, Edinburgh EH2 4DZ (☎ 031 225 1357)

WOODWARD, Sarah Wendy Boston; da of Edward Albert Arthur Woodward, and Venetia Mary, *née* Battine; *b* 3 April 1963; *Educ* Moria House Sch Eastbourne, RADA (Bancroft medal); *Career* actress; RSC: Henry V, Love's Labour's Lost, Hamlet, Richard III, Camille, Red Noses; Birmingham Repertory: Charley's Aunt, The Winter's Tale; other theatre incl: Artist Descending a Staircase (King's Head, Duke of York, Clarence Derwent award), The Rape of Lucrece (Almeida), Romeo and Juliet, Arms And The Man (Regent's Park Open Air Theatre), Angelus From Morning 'Til Midnight (Soho Poly), Build On Sand (Royal Court), Talk of the Devil (Bristol Old Vic), London Assurance (Chichester Theatre, Royal Haymarket), Schism in England (NT); most recent role Anne Danby in Kean (Old Vic, Toronto) 1990-91; *Recreations* all sports, poker, blackjack; *Style—* Miss Sarah Woodward; Duncan Heath Assocs, Paramount Hse, Wardour St, London

WOODWARD, William (Bill) Charles; QC (1985); s of Wilfred Charles Woodward, of Nottingham, and Annie Stewart, *née* Young; *b* 27 May 1940; *Educ* Nottingham HS, St John's Coll Oxford (BA); *m* 1965, Carolyn Edna, da of Francis Doughty Johns, of Kent; 2 s (William b 1968, Fergus b 1974), 1 da (Rebecca b 1966); *Career* called to the Bar Inner Temple 1964; memb Midland and Oxford Circuit, marshall to late Sir Donald Finnemore; head of chambers 1987-, rec 1989; Univ of Nottingham Law Advsy Ctee; fndr memb Nottingham Medico Legal Soc; *Recreations* sporadic cookery, swimming, gardening; *Clubs* Pre-War Austin Seven; *Style—* W C Woodward, Esq, QC; 24 The Ropewalk, Nottingham (☎ 0602 472581)

WOOF, Richard Austin; s of Richard Woof (d 1983), of Launceston, Tasmania, Aust, and Avril Frances Chandler Hopkinson, *née* Clark (d 1984); *b* 14 June 1940; *Educ* Kings Coll Taunton; *m* 17 June 1961, Christine Julia, da of Arthur Seymour Hodgkinson (d 1978), of Devon; 1 s (Julian b 1961), 1 da (Caroline b 1972); *Career* slr; sr ptnr Debenham & Co 1974, commercial property ed The Law Society Gazette 1975-; dir: Caribeach (St Lucia) Ltd 1985-, Cove Hotels (Antigua) Ltd; *Recreations* carriage driving, quarter horse racing; *Style—* Richard A Woof, Esq; Gorebridge House, Loxhill, Nr Godalming, Surrey GU8 4BH; Debenham & Co, 20 Hans Rd, Knightsbridge, London SW3 1RT (☎ 071 581 2471, fax 071 584 1783, telex 8954701)

WOOLDRIDGE, Frank Douglas; s of Frank Wooldridge (d 1956), of London, and Mary Margaret, *née* Douglas (d 1962); *b* 2 March 1916; *Educ* Colfes' Sch London, Coll of Estate Mgmnt; *m* 15 Nov 1941, Elizabeth Julia, da of Engr Capt John Edmund Moloney, CIE (d 1972), of Falmouth, Cornwall; 1 s (John b 1943), 1 da (Anne b 1947); *Career* joined TA 1938, WWII 1939-46, Maj RE served India; princ in private practice joined by s 1968; memb Common Cncl City of London 1988-; Freeman City of London 1965, Liveryman Worshipful Co of Cutlers 1966; FRICS 1949 (ARICS 1939); *Recreations* sailing, appreciation of music; *Clubs* City Livery (asst hon sec), Farringdon Ward (past pres), United Wards (memb Governing Body), Royal Soc of St George (memb Cncl City of London Branch), REYC, Medway Yacht; *Style—* Frank Wooldridge, Esq; 3 Harton Close, Bromley, Kent (☎ 081 290 1466)

WOOLDRIDGE, Ian Edmund; OBE (1991); s of late Edmund James Wooldridge, and late Bertha Wooldridge; *b* 14 Jan 1932; *Educ* Brockenhurst GS; *m* 1, 1957 (m dis 1979), Veronica Ann, *née* Churcher; 3 s (Kevin, Simon, Max); m 2, 1 Dec 1980, Sarah Margaret, da of Leonard Chappell, of Gt Easton, Essex; *Career* RN 1952-54; columnist and chief sportswriter Daily Mail 1972- (cricket corr 1963-71); twice Columnist of the Year and three times Sportswriter of the Year in Br Press, three times Sports Feature Writer of the Year Sports Cncl awards; *Books* Cricket Lovely Cricket (1963), Mary P (with Mary Peters, 1974), MCC, The Autobiography of a Cricketer (with Colin Cowdrey, 1976), The Best of Wooldridge (1978), Travelling Reserve (1982), Sport in the 80's (1989); *Recreations* travel, golf, Beethoven, dry martinis; *Clubs* Scribes; *Style—* Ian Wooldridge, Esq, OBE; 11 Collingham Gdns, London SW5; Daily Mail, Northcliffe House, London W8 (☎ 071 938 6228)

WOOLDRIDGE, Susan Margot; da of John De Lacy Wooldridge DSO, DFC, DFM (d 1958), and Margaretta, *née* Scott; *Educ* Convent of the Holy Child Jesus London, More House London, Central Sch of Speech and Drama London, Ecole Jacques Lecoq Paris; *Career* actress; theatre incl: Map of the Heart, Night Mother, Look Back in Anger, Ubu Roi, Dusa Fish Stas and Vi, The Cherry Orchard, School for Scandal, The Merchant of Venice, Tartuffe, Hayfever; films incl: How to Get Ahead in Advertising, Hope and Glory (BAFTA award for best supporting actress), Loyalties, Butley, The Shout, Dead Man's Folly, Frankenstein, Afraid of the Dark, Twenty-One; tv incl: The Jewel in the Crown (ALVA award for best actress, BAFTA nomination for best actress), The Dark Room, The Devil's Disciple, Time and the Conways, Hay Fever, John MacNab, Ticket to Ride, The Small Assassin, Pastoral Care, The Last Place on Earth, Tickle on the Tum, The Naked Civil Servant, Rep (comedy series), The Racing Game, Changing Step, The Pied Piper, Crimestrike, Broke; *Style—* Miss Susan Wooldridge; Plant and Froggatt Ltd, Julian House, 4 Windmill St, London W1 (☎ 071 636 4412)

WOOLF, Dr Anthony Derek; s of Douglas Langton Woolf, of Woodford, Essex, and Kathorn Beth Woolf, *née* Pearce (d 1980); *b* 12 June 1951; *Educ* Forest Sch, Snaresbrook, London Hosp Med Coll (BSc, MB BS); *m* 4 Dec 1975, Hilary Ann, da of Ronald Ruddock-West (d 1978); 1 s (Richard Thomas b 1981), 1 da (Sarah Louise b 1979); *Career* sr registrar Royal Nat Hosp for Rheumatic Diseases and Bristol Royal Infirmary 1983-87, conslt rheumatologist Royal Cornwall Hosp Truro Cornwall 1987; author of papers on rheumatology, viral arthritis and osteoporosis; memb Editorial Bd Annals of Rheumatic Diseases, memb Cncl and treas Nat Osteoporosis Soc, co-ordinator of Euro Rheumatologists in Trg; Freeman Worshipful Soc of Apothecaries; MRCP 1979; *Books* Osteoporosis - A Clinical Guide (1988), How to Avoid Osteoporosis - A Positive Health Guide (1989); *Style—* Dr Anthony Woolf; Royal Cornwall Hospital, Dept of Rheumatology, Infirmary Hill, Truro TR1 2HZ (☎ 0872 74242)

WOOLF, David; s of Raymond Woolf, of London, and Valerie Belle, *née* Robins (d 1954); *b* 27 Jan 1945; *Educ* Clifton; *m* 19 June 1977, Vivienne Barbara, da of Lt Col David Perk, of Johanesburg; 2 s (James b 1979, John b 1982); *Career* trainee Keyser Ullman 1963-64, accountant Chalmers Imperial 1965-69, PA Corob Hldgs 1969-71, chief exec City Grove plc 1971-; FCA 1969; *Recreations* sailing, tennis, opera; *Clubs* Royal Lymington YC, Vanderbilt; *Style—* David Woolf, Esq; Citygrove plc, 77 South Audley St, London W1 (☎ 071 493 4007, fax 071 409 3515, telex 269918 CITY GG)

WOOLF, Dr Douglas Langton; s of Dr Abraham David Woolf (d 1961), and Celia, *née* Rutkowski (d 1976); *b* 20 Sept 1919; *Educ* St Aubyns Sch, Grocers Co Sch; *m* 1946, Kathorn Beth Pearce, da of Thomas Pearce (d 1948), of Melbourne; 1 s (Anthony b 1951), 1 da (Valerie b 1948); *Career* Mil Serv RAMC (capt) 1947-49; house surgn London Hosp 1945-46, second sr Registrar Dept Physical Medicine-Rheumatology Middx Hosp 1949-53, conslt physician rheumatology Willesden Gen Hosp 1952-84, conslt rheumatologist Waltham Forest Health Authy 1953-84 (hon conslt 1984-); med dir and conslt rheumatologist The Horder Centre for Arthritis 1982-89; memb Attendance Allowance Bd Dept of Health, hon chm Arthritis Care 1982-88 (chm Welfare Ctee and memb Exec Ctee 1954-); vice pres: League of Friends London Hosp 1986, Arthritis Care 1989, Horder Centre 1990; hon memb Br Soc for Rheumatology, hon fell Hunterian Soc (pres 1979-80, Hunterian Orator 1986); FRSM, FMS London; fell: Harveian Soc, Zoological Soc of London; Liveryman Soc of Apothecaries; *Books* guest ed Clinics in Rheumatic Diseases, author of numerous articles on rheumatism and arthritis, hon ed Hunterian Soc Transitions, past ed Rheumatology and Rehabilitation; *Recreations* gardening, antiques; *Style—* Dr Douglas Woolf; 2 The Green, Woodford, Essex (☎ 081 504 8877); 2 Harley St, London W1 (☎ 071 580 1199)

WOOLF, Emile Harold; s of Samuel Woolf (d 1984), of London, and Ethel, *née* Smith (d 1967); *b* 17 Jan 1938; *Educ* Parktown Boys HS Johannesburg S Africa; *m* 1962, Anita, da of Kalman Weitzman; 5 c (Kelly b 1959, Carl b 1962, Alexander b 1964, Matthew b 1966, Gabrielle b 1974); *Career* articled clerk Sinclairs, CA Deloittes 1962-65; dir: Foulks Lynch professional tutors 1965-72, London Sch of Accountancy 1972-75; fndr Emile Woolf & Assocs 1975, ptnr Kingston Smith 1984, currently chm E W Fact plc; ICAEW: memb Members Handbook Ctee, memb Pubns Ctee, chm Practice Insur Requirements Ctee; Auditing Practices Ctee: ICAEW rep, chm True and Fair Sub Ctee; lectr on professional econ and business issues to govts, the profession and indust throughout the world; journalist; reg contrib to : accountancy press, The Guardian, The Times, The Observer; Int Author's award Univ of Hartford Connecticut 1980 (only non-American to win); FCA 1962, FBIM 1972, FCCA 1981; *Publications incl*: Auditing Cassettes and Workbooks 1979-85, Cash Flow Analysis 1984, The Legal Liabilities of Practising Accountants 1985, Auditing 1988, Financial Services Act Compliance Workbook 1988, Understanding Accounting Standards with S V Tanna 1988, Accountants' Liability 1990, Auditing Today 1990; *award* Int Author's award Univ of Hartford Connecticut 1980 (only non-American to win); FCA 1962, FBIM 1972, FCCA 1981; *Recreations* golf, opera; *Style—* Emile Woolf, Esq; Kingston Smith, Chartered Accountants, Devonshire House, 146 Bishopsgate, London EC2M 4JX (☎ 071 377 8888, fax 071 247 7048)

WOOLF, Geoffrey Stephen; s of Edward Woolf, of London, and Ruth, *née* Rosenbaum; *b* 13 Oct 1946; *Educ* Harrow Co GS, Kings Coll London (LLB); *m* 1, 19 March 1972 (m dis 1978), Marcia, da of late Joseph Levy; m 2, 14 Feb 1985, Dr Josephine Kay Likierman, da of Julian Likierman, of London; 2 s (Nicholas b 19 Nov 1986, Simon b 30 July 1988); *Career* articled clerk Stephenson Harwood & Tatham 1968-70, admitted slr 1970, ptnr Stephenson Harwood 1975-; Freeman Worshipful Co of Solicitors 1975; memb Law Soc 1970; *Recreations* opera, theatre; *Style—* Geoffrey Woolf, Esq; Stephenson Harwood, 1 St Paul's Churchyard, London EC4M 8SH (☎ 071 329 4422, fax 071 606 0822)

WOOLF, Rt Hon Lord Justice; Rt Hon Sir Harry Kenneth Woolf; PC (1986); s of late Alexander Woolf, and late Leah, *née* Cussins; *b* 2 May 1933; *Educ* Fettes, UCL (LLB); *m* 1961, Marguerite, da of George Sassoon; 3 s; *Career* Nat Service cmmnd 15/19 Royal Hussars 1954, Capt Army Legal Service 1955; called to the Bar Inner Temple 1954, Crown Ct rec 1972-79, jr counsel Inland Revenue 1973-74, first Treasy jr counsel Common Law 1974-79, High Ct judge (Queen's Bench) 1979-86, presiding judge SE Circuit 1981-84, Lord Justice of Appeal 1986-, memb Senate of Bar and Bench 1981-85; chm Accommodation Ctee 1981-85, chm Lord Chllr's Advsy Ctee on Legal Educn 1987-90, Middx Justice's Advsy Ctee 1987-90, chm Bd of Mgmnt of Inst of Advanced Legal Studies 1986-, pres Law Teachers Assoc 1985-90, Hamlyn Lectures 1989, Inquiry into Prison Disturbances 1990-91, Jt Ctee for Jewish Social Services 1988-, W London Magistrates Assoc 1987-, govr Oxford Centre for Hebrew Studies 1988-, hon memb Pub Soc of Teachers of law 1988-; fell UCL 1981; kt 1979; *Clubs* Garrick; *Style—* The Rt Hon Lord Justice Woolf; Royal Courts of Justice, Strand, London WC2 (☎ 071 936 6000)

WOOLF, Dr Ian Lloyd; s of Dr Sidney Woolf (d 1967), of Newcastle upon Tyne, and Mildred, *née* Wiener (d 1986); *b* 25 Sept 1939; *Educ* Royal GS Newcastle upon Tyne, Univ of Oxford (MA), UCH Med Sch (BM BCh); *m* 7 Sept 1969, Gillian Louise, da of Jonas Bolchover (d 1989), of Manchester; 2 da (Sam b 17 Nov 1975, Joanna b 7 Oct 1973); *Career* res fell Harvard Med Sch USA 1970-71, med registrar UCH 1971-72 (1969-70); lectr in med: Univ of Manchester 1972-74, Kings Coll Hosp Univ of London 1974-76; conslt physician North Middx Hosp London 1977-; med advsr Nat Assoc of Colitis and Crohns Disease; FRCP 1985; *Recreations* reading, tennis; *Style—* Dr Ian Woolf; 75 Cholmeley Crescent, Highgate, London N6 5EX (☎ 081 340 8100); Department of Medicine, North Middlesex Hospital, Sterling Way, London N18 1QX (☎ 081 884 2098)

WOOLF, Sir John; s of late Charles M Woolf, and Vera Woolf; *Educ* Institut Montana Switzerland; *m* 1955, Ann, da of late Victor Saville; 2 s; *Career* WWII, Lt-Col, asst dir Army Kinematography WO 1944-45; film and television prodr; chm: Romulus Films

Ltd, Br & American Film Holdings plc; co fndr and exec dir: Anglia TV Group plc 1958-83, First Leisure Corp plc; tstee and memb Exec Cncl Cinema & TV Benevolent Fund; memb: Cinematograph Films Cncl 1969-79, Bd of Govrs Servs Sound & Vision Corp (formerly Services Kinema Corp) 1974-83; awards incl: Br Film Acad best film of 1958 (Room at the Top), Oscar and Golden Globe best film of 1969 (Oliver!); special awards for contribution to Br Film indust: Cinematograph Exhibitors Assoc 1969, Variety Club of GB 1974; Freeman City of London; FRSA 1975; Bronze Star (USA) 1945; kt 1975; *Films incl* The African Queen, Pandora and The Flying Dutchman, Moulin Rouge, I Am a Camera, Carrington VC, Room At The Top, Beat the Devil, The L-Shaped Room, Life At The Top, Oliver!, Day Of The Jackal, The Odessa File; *TV productions for Anglia TV incl* 10 series of Tales of the Unexpected; *Style—* Sir John Woolf; 214 The Chambers, Chelsea Harbour, London SW10 (☎ 071 376 3791, fax 071 352 7457)

WOOLF, John Moss; CB (1975); s of Alfred Woolf (d 1971), and Maud Woolf (d 1979); *b* 5 June 1918; *Educ* Drayton Manor Sch; *m* 1940, Phyllis Ada Mary (d 1990), da of Thomas Albert Johnson (d 1937); 1 da (Stephanie); *Career* called to the Bar Lincoln's Inn 1948; rep Civil Serv Nat Whitley Cncl (Staff Side) 1953-55, memb Exec Ctee Assoc of First Div Civil Servants 1950-58 and 1961-65 (chm 1955-58 and 1964-65), asst sec HM Customs & Excise 1960, chm Valuation Ctee Customs Co-op Cncl Brussels 1964-65, asst sec Nat Bd for Prices and Incomes 1965 (under-sec 1965), asst under-sec of State Dept of Employment and Productivity 1968-70, advsr on price problems to Govt of Trinidad and Tobago 1969, cmmr HM Customs and Excise 1970 (dep chm bd 1973-78), dir gen Customs and Establishments 1973-78 (dir 1971-73); overseas advsr Central Electricity Generating Bd 1979-82; leader Review Team to examine responsibilities of the Directors of the Nat Museums and Galleries 1978-79, Review of Orgn and Procedures of Chancery Div of High Ct 1979-80; Commandeur d'Honneur Ordre du Bontemps de Médoc et des Graves 1973, hon Borgenerális (Hungary) 1974; *Books* Report on Control of Prices in Trinidad and Tobago (with MM Eccleshall, 1968), Report of the Review Body on the Chancery Divison of the High Court (with Lord Oliver, 1981); *Recreations* gardening, wine, reading; *Clubs* Civil Service; *Style—* J M Woolf Esq, CB; West Lodge, 113 Marsh Lane, Middlesex HA7 4TH (☎ 081 952 1373)

WOOLF, Prof Neville; s of Barnett Woolf (d 1972), of Cape Town SA, and Florence Charlotte, *née* Cohn (d 1973); *b* 17 May 1930; *Educ* Univ of Cape Town SA (MB ChB, MMed Path), Univ of London (PhD); *m* 31 March 1957, Lydia Paulette, da of Harry Joseph Mandelbrote (d 1971), of Cape Town SA; 1 s (Adam b 1964), 1 da (Victoria (Mrs Coren) b 1960); *Career* reader and hon conslt St George's Hosp Med Sch 1968-74 (sr lectr and hon conslt 1965-68), Bland-Sutton prof of histopathology Univ Coll and Middx Sch of Medicine (formerly Middx Hosp Med Sch); former chm Bd of Studies in Pathology Univ of London, memb Pathological Soc; FRCPath; *Books* Cell, Tissue and Disease (1977 and 1986), Pathology of Atherosclerosis (1982); *Recreations* reading, music, cooking; *Style—* Prof Neville Woolf; Dept of Histopathology, University College and Middlesex School of Medicine, The Bland-Sutton Institute, Riding House St, London W1P 7AA (☎ 071 380 9399 9401, fax 071 380 9395)

WOOLF, (John) Nicholas; s of Adrian Jack Woolf, of Hampton, Middlesex, and Lesley Clare, *née* Freeman (d 1980); *b* 7 Sept 1946; *Educ* Hampton Sch, LSE (BSc); *m* 1, 21 Aug 1971, Margaret Anne (d 1988), da of Edward Beal (d 1988); 1 s (Christopher b 1977), 1 da (Elizabeth b 1973); m 2, 28 April 1990, (Catherine) Fiona, da of Dr Richard H Swain (d 1981); *Career* Arthur Andersen & Co 1968 (ptnr 1979); FCA 1971, FTII 1972, memb: Inst of Petroleum 1987; *Recreations* golf, squash, tennis; *Clubs* RAC; *Style—* Nicholas Woolf, Esq; 1 Surrey St, London WC2R 2PS (☎ 071 438 3000, fax 071 831 1133)

WOOLFENDEN, (Kenneth) Alan; s of Frederick John Woolfenden (d 1971), and Mary, *née* Duff; *b* 25 July 1950; *Educ* N Manchester GS for Boys, Univ of Liverpool (MB ChB); *m* 1 April 1972, Susan Irene, da of Alan Eaton, of Manchester; 1 s (Jonathan Frederick b 12 Dec 1980); *Career* conslt urological surgn Royal Liverpool Teaching Hosp 1985-, hon lectr Dept of Surgery Faculty of Med Univ of Liverpool; dir Sr Registrar Trg Mersey Region; memb Cncl: Br Assoc of Urological Surgns, Liverpool Med Inst; memb Exec Cncl Mersey Region for Kidney Res; memb BMA 1973, FRCS 1978; *Clubs* Liverpool Cricket, Neston Cricket; *Style—* Alan Woolfenden, Esq; Riverside, Manorial Rd, Parkgate, South Wirral, Cheshire (☎ 051 336 7229); 48 Rodney St, Liverpool L1 9AA (☎ 051 709 2079)

WOOLFENDEN, Guy Anthony; s of Harold Arthur Woolfenden (d 1986), and Kathleen Norah, *née* (d 1978); *b* 12 July 1937; *Educ* Westminster Abbey Choir Sch, Whitgift Sch, Christ's Coll Cambridge (MA), Guildhall Sch of Music (LGSM); *m* 29 Sept 1962, Jane, da of Leonard George Smerdon Aldrick, of Ewell, Surrey; 3 s (Richard b 1964, Stephen b 1966, James b 1969); *Career* head of music RSC 1963-, artistic dir Cambridge Festival 1985-91; compositions incl: scores for RSC and the Comedie Française, three ballet scores, TV and film music, concert music; has conducted many major Br orchestras; chm Denne Gilkes Meml Fund; vice pres: Beauchamp Sinfonietta, Katharine House Hospice Tst; memb: Nat Campaign for the Arts, MU, PRS, MCPS, Composers' Guild, Assoc of Professional Composers, SPNM; FBSM; *Recreations* photography, table tennis, walking, cricket; *Style—* Guy Woolfenden, Esq; Malvern House, Sibford Ferris, Banbury, Oxfordshire OX15 5RG (☎ 0295 78679); Royal Shakespeare Company, Royal Shakespeare Theatre, Stratford upon Avon, Warwickshire CV37 6BB (☎ 0789 296655); Barbican Theatre, Silk St, London EC2Y 8DS (☎ 071 628 3351)

WOOLFSON, Dr Gerald; s of late Joseph Samuel and Lilian Woolfson; *b* 25 March 1932; *Educ* Milton Sch Buelawayo and Zimbabwe, Capetown Univ (MB); *m* 1, 1955, Sheila Charlaff; 3 s (David b 1955, Adrian b 1965, Alexander b 1978), 1 da (Karen b 1959); m 2, 1980, Lynne Silver; *Career* conslt psychiatrist Hammersmith and St Mary's Hosp Gp; hon sr lectr RPMS; FRSM; *Recreations* chess, doodling; *Style—* Dr Gerald Woolfson; 56 Redington Rd, London NW3 (☎ 071 794 1974); 97 Harley St, London W1 1DF (☎ 071 794 1974)

WOOLFSON, Lynne; da of David Bernard Silver (d 1969), of London, and Fay Butchen (d 1977); *b* 4 July 1946; *Educ* Camden Sch for Girls, Univ of Manchester (BA, ed Manchester Independent, Student Newspaper of the Year1967), Courtland Inst of Art (MA); *m* Dr Gerald Woolfson; 1 s (Alexander b 1978); *Career* TV journalist 1968-78; progs incl: David Frost's progs, World in Action, Russell Harty's progs; art historian, psychotherapist; NUS Mirror Gp student Newspaper of the Year award 1967; patron: Tate Gallery, Camden Arts Centre; memb Guild of Psychotherapists; patron: Tate Gallery, Camden Arts Centre; *Recreations* music, theatre; *Style—* Mrs Lynne Woolfson

WOOLFSON, Prof Michael Mark; s of Maurice Woolfson (d 1956), of 218 Lea View House, Springfield, London E5, and Rose, *née* Solomons; *b* 9 Jan 1927; *Educ* Wellingborough GS, Jesus Coll Oxford (BA, MA), UMIST (PhD, DSc); *m* 19 July 1951, Margaret, da of Dr Mayer Frohlich; 2 s (Mark b 1954, Malcolm b 1957), 1 da (Susan b 1960); *Career* HG 7 Northants Bn 1942-44, Nat Serv cmmnd 2 Lt RE 1947-49; res asst Cavendish Laboratory Cambridge 1952-54, ICI res fell Cambridge 1954-55, reader in physics UMIST 1961-65 (lectr 1953-61), prof of theoretical physics Univ of York 1965-; pres: Yorks Philosophical Soc, York Astronomical Soc; govr York Coll of Arts and Technol; FIP, FRAS, FRS, Br Crystallographic Assoc (pres); *Books* Direct Methods in Crystallography (1961), An Introduction to X-Ray Crystallography (1970), The Origin of the Solar System: The Caphere Theory; *Recreations* gardening, winemaking; *Style—* Prof Michael Woolfson, FRS; 124 Wigton Lane, Leeds, W Yorks LS17 8RZ (☎ 0532 687 890); Department of Physics, University of York, York, N Yorks Y01 5DD (☎ 0904 432230)

WOOLFSON, Rosalind Anne; da of Myer Henry Woolfson (d 1962), of Glasgow, and Miriam, *née* Cohen; *b* 13 Feb 1945; *Educ* Glasgow HS for Girls, Princ/Pessa Colonna Sch Florence, Glasgow Sch of Art; *Career* mgmnt trainee then memb Sales Promotion (PR) Team Marks & Spencer 1963-74; sr account exec: FJ Lyons PR 1974-75, Shandwick PR 1975-78, exec dir Opus Public Relations (a Shandwick co) 1979-85 (joined 1978), Bd dir Shandwick Communications 1985-; memb Network (sr business women's gp); *Recreations* visual arts, travel, literature, music, opera; *Style—* Ms Rosalind Woolfson; Shandwick Communications, 1st Floor, Silvertown House, 87 Vincent Square, London SW1P 2PL (☎ 071 835 1001, fax 071 233 6193)

WOOLHOUSE, Prof John George; CBE (1988); s of George Francis Woolhouse (d 1940), and Doris May, *née* Webber; *b* 17 June 1931; *Educ* Ardingly Coll, BNC Oxford (MA); *m* 12 April 1958, Ruth Carolyn, da of The Rev Thomas Edward Harrison; 2 s (Mark Edward John b 25 April 1959, Hugh Francis b 15 Nov 1961), 1 da (Elinor Clare (twin) b 15 Nov 1961); *Career* Nat Serv 2 Lt RCS 1950-51, Pilot Offr RAFVR 1951-54, R AUX AF aux pilot offr 1954-56; Rolls Royce Ltd: various appts 1954-64, dir personnel and admin (Rolls-Royce and Ass) 1965-68, co educn and training offr 1968-72; asst dir Kingston Poly 1972-78, dir Atkins Planning of WS Atkins Group Conslts 1978-82, under sec MSC and dir Tech and Vocational Educn Initiative 1983-87, prof of educn and dir Centre for Educn and Indust Univ of Warwick 1988; MIPM, FBIM, hon FIIM; *Books* Organisation Development, Gower Handbook of Management (1983); *Recreations* music, walking, boating, fishing; *Clubs* RAF; *Style—* Prof John Woolhouse, CBE; University of Warwick, Coventry CV4 7AL

WOOLLAMS, Christopher John (Chris); s of George James Woollams, and Phyllis Joan, *née* Cox; *b* 4 July 1949; *Educ* Watford Boys GS, St Peter's Coll Univ of Oxford (BA); *m* (m dis); 3 da (Catherine Louise b 1978, Georgina Clair b 1983, Stephanie Louise b 1986); *Career* ahm Spiral Cellars Ltd 1980-, dir Ogilvy and Mather London 1981-84, md Publicis 1984, chm Ted Bates Gp London 1985 (Euro and Worldwide Bd dir 1986), chm Fitness in Home Ltd 1986-, chm and chief exec Woollams Moira Gaskin O'Malley Gp Ltd 1987-; MIPA (1983), FInstD (1986), memb Marketing Soc 1989; *Recreations* flying, squash, hockey, chess, skiing; *Clubs* RAC, IOD, Goodwood Flying, Cheam Sports; *Style—* Chris Woollams, Esq; Flat 10, 51 Drayton Gardens, London SW10 (☎ 071 370 5246); Varazur, Les Issambres, France; Woollams Moira Gaskin O'Malley, Portland House, 12/13 Greek St, London W1V 5LE (☎ 071 494 0770, fax 071 734 6684)

WOOLLARD, Kenneth David; s of Harry Woollard (d 1950), of Clare, Suffolk, and Bush Hill Park, Middx, and Forence Jane, *née* Shore (d 1983); *b* 20 Nov 1930; *Educ* Tottenham Tech Coll; *m* 19 Feb 1955, Edna May, da of Frank Stallwood (d 1976), of London; 2 s (David Gordon b 1960, Peter Kenneth b 1963), 1 da (Karen Ann (twin) b 1963); *Career* Nat Serv RAOC N Africa 1948-50; commercial and mktg career in electrical engrg and telecommunications; regnl mangr major projects UK 1968-74, liaison mangr and conslt UK and overseas offshore and onshore petro-chemical projects (Moss Moran, Morecambe Bay, Esso Fawley, Br Gas N Sea fields) 1974-78, project mangr (Delta Dunmurry) Br Coal and Steel Contracts 1978-87, Dept of Transport Motorway Communications M1, M4, M25, M6 projects; MCIM 1974; *Recreations* sailing, golf; *Style—* Kenneth Woollard, Esq; 6 Langham Close, Marshalswick, St Albans, Herts AL4 9TH

WOOLLETT, Maj-Gen John Castle; CBE (1957, OBE 1955), MC (1945); o s of John Castle Woollett (d 1921), and Lily Bradley Woollett (d 1964); *b* 5 Nov 1915; *Educ* St Benedict's Sch, RMA Woolwich, St John's Coll Cambridge; *m* 1, 1941 (m dis 1957), Joan Eileen, *née* Stranks; 2 s (1 s decd); m 2, 1959, Helen Wendy, *née* Braithwaite; 2 step s; *Career* cmmnd RE 1935, served 1939-45 and Korea, Maj-Gen, chief engr BAOR 1967-70 (ret), Col Cmdt RE 1973-78, princ planning inspr DOE 1975-81; *Recreations* cruising, shooting, sailing (yacht 'Cymbeline'); *Clubs* Army & Navy, Royal Cruising, Royal Engineers Yacht, Royal Ocean Racing, Royal Lymington Yacht, Island Sailing (Cowes); *Style—* Maj-Gen John Woollett, CBE, MC; 42 Rhinefield Close, Brockenhurst, Hants SO42 MSU (☎ 0590 22417)

WOOLLEY, Brian Peter; s of Herbert Woolley, and Edna, *née* Hindley; *b* 28 April 1954; *Educ* Manchester GS St John's Coll, Oxford (MA); *m* 1978, Joy, da of Alan Harbottle; *Career* Citibank NA London 1975-79, Orion Bank Limited 1979-81, exec dir Head of Capital Markets Citicorp Investment Bank Limited 1984-; *Recreations* skiing, opera, gardening; *Style—* Brian Woolley, Esq; Waterside Point, Anhalt Rd, London SW11 (☎ 071 978 4423); Citicorp Investment Bank Ltd, Cottons Centre, Hays Lane, London SE1 (☎ 071 234 2110)

WOOLLEY, Hon David Jeffs; 3 s of Baron Woolley, CBE, DL (Life Peer, d 1986), and his 1 w, Martha Annie, *née* Jeffs (d 1936); bro Hons Peter, Harold Graham *qqv*; *b* 11 Jan 1934; *Educ* Dauntsey's Sch, Seale Hayne Agric Coll; *m* 26 April 1958, Freda Constance, da of late Alfred William Smith Walker, of Barrow-in-Furness; 2 s, 1 da; *Career* Captain, Air Canada; *Style—* The Hon David Woolley; Fernhill Farm, 4222 - 216 Street, RR 14, Langley, British Columbia V3A 7R2

WOOLLEY, David Rorie; QC (1980); s of Albert Walter Woolley, of Wallingford, Oxon, and Ethel Rorie, *née* Linn; *b* 9 June 1939; *Educ* Winchester, Trinity Hall Cambridge (Hons Law); *Career* called to the Bar Middle Temple 1962; rec Crown Ct 1983, inspr DOE Inquiry into Nat Gallery 1984, bencher Middle Temple 1988; *publications* Town Hall and the Property Owner (1965); *Recreations* opera, real tennis, mountaineering; *Clubs* MCC, Oxford and Cambridge; *Style—* David Woolley, Esq, QC; 2 Mitre Court Building, Temple, London EC4Y 7BX (☎ 071 583 1355)

WOOLLEY, Hon Dr (Harold) Ewart; 2 s of Baron Woolley, CBE, DL; *b* 10 July 1929,bro Hons Peter, David Graham, *qqv*; *Educ* Woodhouse Grove Sch Yorks, UBC; *m* 1954, Margaret, da of Alderman Thomas Bennett, JP, of Worcester; 1 s, 2 da; *Career* MD, FRCS; *Style—* The Hon Dr H E Woolley; 1350 Laurier Ave, Vancouver, British Columbia, Canada

WOOLLEY, Hon (William) Graham; s of Baron Woolley, CBE, DL; *b* 27 Oct 1927,bro Hons David, Peter, Harold *qqqv*; *Educ* Wrekin Coll; *m* 1, 1955, Joan (d 1974), da of Ralph Rowlands, of Flint; 2 s, 1 da; m 2, 1984, Shirley Ann, da of Thomas William James, LEGA, mangr Bulolo Papua New Guinea; *Style—* The Hon W Graham Woolley; Hatton Hall, Hatton Heath, Cheshire CH3 9AP

WOOLLEY, Dr Paul Kerrison; s of Robert Charles Woolley (d 1979), and Hilda Kerrison, *née* Barnsley; *b* 9 Nov 1939; *Educ* King Edward VI Sch Birmingham, Univ of York (BA, DPhil); *m* 31 July 1976, Penelope Ann, da of Albert Ewart Baines; 2 s (Nicholas Kerrison b 26 Oct 1977, Robert Ewart b 10 June 1980); *Career* ptnr Murray & Co Birmingham 1965-67 (joined 1959), Esmeé Fairbairn lectr in fin Univ of York 1975-76, specialist advsr House of Lords Ctee on EEC 1971-76, advsr International Monetary Fund Washington DC 1980-83 (economist 1976-78, sr economist 1978-80); dir 1983-87 (Baring Brothers & Co Ltd, Baring Investment Management, Baring International Investment Management, Baring Quantitative Management), fndr and md

GMO Woolley Ltd London 1987-, ptnr Grantham Mayo Van Otterloo & Co Boston USA; author of various articles in academic and fin jls; memb Birmingham Stock Exchange 1964-67; *Recreations* walking, travel; *Clubs* Gresham, Harpenden Lawn Tennis; *Style*— Dr Paul Woolley; 48 Amenbury Lane, Harpenden, Hertfordshire AL5 2DQ (☎ 05827 66186); GMO Woolley Ltd, Winchester House, 77 London Wall, London EC2N 1BE (☎ 071 588 7753, fax 071 638 9047)

WOOLLEY, Hon Peter Jeffs; 4 s of Baron Woolley, CBE, DL; *b* 11 Jan 1934,bro Hons Harold, David Graham, *qqv*; *Educ* Dauntsey's Sch, Trinity Hall Cambridge; *m* 1960, Lois, da of Edward Chanter; 3 da; *Career* CA; *Style*— The Hon Peter Woolley; 2660 Queens Ave, W Vancouver, British Columbia, Canada

WOOLLEY, His Hon Judge Roy Gilbert; s of John Woolley (d 1974), and Edith Mary, *née* Holt (d 1958); *b* 28 Nov 1922; *Educ* Deeside, UCL (LLB); *m* 1953, Doreen, da of Humphrey Morris Farmer (d 1967); 2 s (Christopher, Peter), 2 da (Julie, Carolyn); *Career* served WWII Flying Offr RAF Coastal Cmd 1942-45; called to the Bar Lincoln's Inn, recorder 1975-76, circuit judge 1976-; memb: Gen Synod of Church of England 1990-, Legal Advsy Cmmn of the Church of England 1991-; reader dioceses of: St Asoph Chester, Lichfield 1975-; *Recreations* reading, music, art, antiques; *Style*— His Hon Judge Woolley; Henlle Hall, Gobowen, Oswestry, Shropshire SY10 7AX (☎ 0691 661257)

WOOLLONS, Prof David John; s of Sydney Charles Woollons (d 1958), of Birmingham, and Eileen Annie, *née* Russell; *b* 10 June 1937; *Educ* Solihull Sch, Univ of Bristol (BSc, PhD); *m* 29 Sept 1961, Janice, da of William Hector Evans (d 1975), of Bridgend, Glamorgan; 2 s (Andrew b 1963, Martin b 1968), 1 da (Sian b 1966); *Career* res engr Philips Research Laboratories 1961-67, reader in engrg Univ of Sussex 1972-84 (lectr in engrg 1967-72), prof of engrg Univ of Exeter 1984-; former memb Cncl Inst of Electrical Engrs (memb Control and Automation Divnl Bd and Professional Gp CII); FIEE; *Books* Introduction to Digital Computer Design (1972), Microelectronic Systems (1982); *Recreations* reading, walking, music, car renovation; *Style*— Prof David Woollons; Little Croft, 437 Topsham Rd, Exeter, Devon EX2 7AB (☎ 0392 874270); School of Engineering, University of Exeter, North Park Rd, Exeter EX4 4QF (☎ 0392 263628, fax 0392 217965)

WOOLNOUGH, Lt-Col George Frederick; MC (1943); s of Frederick George Woolnough (d 1934), and Caroline Noel, *née* Isles (d 1982); *b* 7 Dec 1914; *Educ* Bishop Wordsworth's Sch Salisbury, RMC Sandhurst; *Career* cmmnd Wilts Regt 1935; served Palestine 1936-37, BEF France and Belgium 1939-40, Sicily and Italy 1943-44, Germany 1945; cmd 1 Bn Wilts Regt 1958-59 and on amalgamation 1 Bn Duke of Edinburgh's Royal Regt 1959-60; ret 1965; sec Friends of Salisbury Cathedral, area cmmr St John Ambulance; *Style*— Lt-Col George F Woolnough, MC; The Cross, Middle Woodford, Salisbury, Wiltshire (☎ 072 273 304)

WOOLNOUGH, Monique Susan; da of Geoffrey Norman Woolnough, and Louise Isabelle, *née* Beaulieu; *b* 16 Dec 1958; *Educ* Springfield Horsham Sussex, Farlington Sch Strood Park Sussex; *Career* Kingsway Public Relations 1982-85, Lonsdale Wilcox Public Relations 1985-87, account dir The Rowland Co; *Recreations* science fiction novels; *Style*— Miss Monique Woolnough; The Rowland Co, 67-69 Whitfield St, London W1A 4PU (☎ 071 436 4060, fax 071 255 2131, telex 8953033)

WOOLNOUGH, Victor James (Vic); s of Lionel Victor Woolnough, of Basingstoke, Hampshire (d 1989), and Joyce Eileen, *née* Hodder; *b* 1 Nov 1943; *Educ* Queen Mary's GS (Hampshire schs jr 100 yards sprint champion 1957); *m* 21 March 1964, Carla Bettine, da of Albert Ernest Atherton; 1 da (Lisa b 19 Dec 1966); *Career* Lansing Bagnall Ltd (Basingstoke): trainee draughtsman and engrg apprentice 1961-66, detail draughtsman 1966-67, design draughtsman 1966-69; CA Blatchford & Sons Ltd: design draughtsman 1969-73, design engr 1973-87, chief designer 1988-; specialist in the design of artificial limbs (incl Blatchford Endolite System), sole or jt inventor of over a dozen patented mechanisms and devices; FIED 1981 (MIED 1976), I Eng 1981, memb Euro Register of Engineers (Group 2) 1989; *Recreations* small boats and personal computers; *Clubs* Leisure Boat Owners Assoc, The Writing Equipment Soc; *Style*— Vic Woolnough, Esq; Lawrenny, Mary Lane, North Waltham, Hampshire RG25 2BY; Chas A Blatchford & Sons Ltd, Lister Road, Basingstoke, Hampshire RG22 4LU (☎ 0256 465771)

WOOLTON, 3 Earl of (UK 1956); Simon Frederick Marquis; also Baron Woolton (UK 1939), Viscount Woolton (UK 1952), and Viscount Walberton (UK 1956); s of 2 Earl of Woolton (d 1969, s of 1 Earl of Woolton, CH, PC, JP, DL, sometime chm Lewis's Investment Trust and associated cos, min of Food 1940-43, min of Reconstruction and memb War Cabinet 1943-45, lord pres Cncl 1945 and 1951-52, chllr of Duchy of Lancaster 1952-55, chm Cons Pty 1946-55) by his 2 w (Cecily) Josephine, er da of Sir Alastair Penrose Gordon-Cumming 5 Bt (now Countess Lloyd George of Dwyfor *qv*); *b* 24 May 1958; *Educ* Eton, Univ of St Andrews (MA); *m* 30 April 1987, Hon Sophie, o c of 3 Baron Birdwood, *qv*; 1 da (Lady Olivia b 16 April 1990); *Heir* none; *Clubs* Royal and Ancient (St Andrews), New (Edinburgh), White's, Turf, Brooks's; *Style*— The Rt Hon the Earl of Woolton; Glenogil, by Forfar, Angus DD8 3SX (☎ 03565 226)

WOOSNAM, Ian Harold; s of Harold Woosnam, and Joan Woosnam; *b* 2 March 1958; *Educ* St Martins Modern Sch; *m* 12 Nov 1983, Glendryth, da of Terrance Mervyn Pugh; 1 s (Daniel Ian b 5 Feb 1985), 1 da (Rebecca Louise b 16 June 1988); *Career* professional golfer 1976-; tournament victories: News of the World under 23 match-play 1979, Cacharel under 25 Championship 1982, Swiss Open 1982, Silk Cut Masters 1983, Scandinavian Enterprise Open 1984, Zambian Open 1985, Lawrence Batley TPC 1986, 555 Kenya Open 1986, Hong Kong Open 1987, Jersey Open 1987, Cepsa Madrid Open 1987, Bell's Scottish Open 1987 and 1990, Lancome Trophy 1987, Suntory World Match-Play Championship 1987 and 1990, Volvo PGA Championship 1988, Carrolls Irish Open 1988 and 1989, Panasonic Euro Open 1988, Am Express Med Open 1990, Torras Monte Carlo Open 1990, Epson Grand Prix 1990; team events: Ryder Cup 1983, 1985 (winners), 1987 (winners), 1989 (winners), Dunhill Cup 1985, 1986, 1988, 1989, 1990, World Cup 1980, 1982, 1983, 1984, 1985, 1986, 1987 (team and individual winner) 1990; finished top Order of Merit 1987 and 1990 (with a record £574,166), ranked 4 Suntory world rankings 1990; *Recreations* snooker, water skiing; *Style*— Ian Woosnam, Esq

WOOTTON, David Hugh; s of James Wootton, and Muriel Wootton; *b* 21 July 1950; *Educ* Bradford GS, Jesus Coll Cambridge; *m* 23 April 1977, Elizabeth Rosemary, da of Peter Knox; 2 s (James b 1979, Christopher b 1985), 2 da (Alexandra b 1978, Sophie b 1981); *Career* currently ptnr Allen & Overy; memb Law Soc 1975; *Clubs* Leander; *Style*— David Wootton, Esq; Allen & Overy, 9 Cheapside, London EC2V 6AD (☎ 071 248 9898, fax 071 236 2192, telex 8812801)

WOOTTON, Frank A A; *b* 30 July 1914; *Educ* Eastbourne Coll of Art; *m* Virginia Ann; 1 s (Leigh Antony b March 1959), 1 da (Tracy Ann b Feb 1963); *Career* Official war artist RAF 1939-46; artist; exhibitions: Ackermanns Gallery London 1964, Stacy-Marks Gallery Eastbourne 1965, Incurable Collector Gallery NY 1969, Horse Artists of the World Tryon Gallery London 1969, Tryon Gallery London 1974, Smithsonian Inst Nat Air and Space Museum USA 1983-84, EAA Museum Oshkosh Wisconsin; C P Robertson trophy Air Miny 1979, Royal Aero Club Silver medal 1985; companion Royal Aeronautical Soc 1985, Freeman Guild of Air Pilots and Air Navigators 1987, pres Guild of Aviation Artists 1970-88; *Books* How to Draw Aircraft (1940), How to Draw Cars (1949), The Aviation Art of Frank Wootton (1976), At Home in the Sky (1984), The Landscape Paintings of Frank Wootton (1990); *Clubs* RAF; *Style*— Frank Wootton, Esq; Mayflower House, Alfriston, Sussex BN26 5QT (☎ 0323 870 343)

WOOTTON, Robert John; s of William Robert Wootton (d 1987), of Marlow, Bucks, and Linda Rosalie, *née* Gyton; *b* 30 June 1955; *Educ* Oundle, UCL; *Career* trainee media exec: Lintas Ltd 1974-81, Wight Collins Rutherford Scott Ltd 1981-85 (head of TV, assoc media dir), media dir HDM Horner Collis Kirvan Ltd 1985-; MIPA 1986-; *Recreations* active and passive participation in music, cookery, food and wine, mycology; *Clubs* RAC, Fred's; *Style*— Robert Wootton, Esq; HDM Horner Collis & Kirvan Ltd, 11 Great Newport St, London WC2H 7JA (☎ 071 379 0631, fax 071 465 0552)

WOOTTON, Dr (Leslie) Roger; s of Denis Stokes Wootton (d 1965), and Geraldine Amy, *née* Virgo; *b* 29 June 1944; *Educ* Kingston GS, City Univ (BSc, PhD); *m* 15 Sept 1979, Hilary Anne Robinson; 2 s (Marcus Desmond b 21 July 1981, Julian Michael 12 Feb 1986); *Career* Nat Physical Laboratory 1962-71 (joined Aerodynamic Div; projects incl: wind effects on bldgs, vortex induced motion of towers and masts, deep water jetty Humber Estuary at Immingham), W S Atkins consltg engrs 1971-; projects incl: BP Forties platform, Shell Tern devpt; memb Cncl FEng, NE Rowe Medal Royal Aeronautical Soc, Telford Premium ICE; memb: Royal Aeronautical Soc, Wind Engrg Soc, Soc for Underwater Technol, Wind Energy Soc; FICE, FEng; *Books* Dynamics of Marine Structures; *Recreations* being a husband and father, hot air ballooning (as means of escaping from former recreations!); *Clubs* Br Balloon and Airship Club; *Style*— Dr Roger Wootton; W S Atkins, Woodcote Grove, Ashley Rd, Epsom, Surrey KT18 5BW (☎ 0372 726140, fax 0372 740055)

WOOTTON-WOOLLEY, (Charles) Derek; CBE (1971), MM; s of Henry Charles Wootton-Woolley (d 1971), of Hove, and Harriet, *née* Grisdale (d 1960); *b* 22 Jan 1921; *Educ* Haileybury; *m* 25 Aug 1944, Jacqueline Esther, da of Joseph Edmond Cattaui (d 1983), of Alexandria, Egypt; 1 s (Robin b 1949), 2 da (Jennifer b 1946, Valerie b 1949); *Career* TA 1939, 42 RTR 1939-42 served W Desert (MM 1942), Adj 46 RTR 1943-44; served as Temp Maj: N Africa, Sicily, Italy (despatches 1944), Greece; Br American Tobacco Co: China 1947-50, Brazil 1950-61, London 1962-64; chm: Nigerian Tobacco Co 1964-71, Blackman Harvey Ltd 1972-88; ret; Freeman City of London 1972, Liveryman Worshipful Co of Basketmakers 1974; Hon LLD Lagos Univ 1969-; *Recreations* golf; *Style*— Derek Wootton-Woolley, Esq, CBE, MM; Orange Ct Farmhouse, Littleton, Guildford, GU3 1HW (☎ 0483 365 46)

WORAM, Terence Annesley; s of Victor Henry Woram (d 1940), and Helena Mary, *née* Cox; *b* 23 June 1933; *Educ* Christian Brothers Coll Kimberley SA, Univ of Capetown SA (BArch); *m* 14 Oct 1961, Patricia Eileen, da of Frederick Leslie Lawrence; 1 s (Michael Desmond b 27 Aug 1962, d 22 May 1980), 3 da (Catherine Ann b 17 Jan 1964, Frances Mary b 21 May 1965, Joanna Helen b 2 May 1967); *Career* Pallet And Price Salisbury Rhodesia SA 1953-56, Harrison and Abramovitz NY 1956-59, Trehearn Norman Preston and Ptnrs London 1960-64; ptnr: BL Adams Partnership London 1964-69, Green Lloyd and Adams London 1969-79; sr ptnr Terence Woram Associates 1979-; architectural awards: Richmond Soc 1983, Europa Nostra 1986, Aylesbury Soc 1988; rep cricket: combined SA Univs XI 1955, USA All Stars XI v W Indies 1958; memb York House Soc; RIBA; *Recreations* cricket, travel, old Hollywood films; *Clubs* Richmond, Mddx Cricket Union; *Style*— Terence Woram, Esq; 48 Lebanon Park, Twickenham, Middx TW1 3DG (☎ 081 892 2634); 52 Lebanon Park, Twickenham, Middx TW1 3DG (☎ 081 891 6446)

WORCESTER; *see*: Jeffery, Very Rev Robert Martin Colquhoun

WORCESTER, Marquess of; Henry John Fitzroy Somerset; s and h of 11 Duke of Beaufort; *b* 22 May 1952; *Educ* Eton; *m* 13 June 1987, Tracy Louise, the actress, da Hon Peter Ward s of 3 Earl of Dudley; 1 s (Robert, Earl of Glamorgan b 20 Jan 1989); *Heir* s, Earl of Glamorgan; *Style*— Marquess of Worcester; Badminton House, Glos GL9 1DB

WORCESTER, 111 Bishop of 1982-; Rt Rev Philip Harold Ernest Goodrich; patron of sixty-six livings, of seven alternately with others and the Archdeaconries of Dudley and Worcester, and eighteen Hon Canonries. The See was founded by Ethelred of the Mercians in 679; s of Rev Canon Harold Spencer Goodrich and Gertrude Alice Goodrich; *b* 2 Nov 1929; *Educ* Stamford Sch, St John's Coll Cambridge (MA); *m* 1960, Margaret, *née* Bennett; 4 da; *Career* curate Rugby Parish Church 1954-57, chaplain St John's Coll Cambridge 1957-61, rector South Ormsby Gp of Parishes 1961-68, vicar Bromley 1968-73, bishop suffragan Tonbridge 1974-82; *Style*— The Rt Rev the Lord Bishop of Worcester; Bishop's House, Hartlebury Castle, Kidderminster, Worcs DY11 7XX

WORCESTER, Richard Gray; s of George Raleigh Gray Worcester (d 1969), and Doris Lea, *née* Birch (d 1947); *b* 11 March 1917; *m* 7 Jan 1956, Inge; 2 s (Nicholas b 7 Dec 1958, Anthony b 5 Feb 1960), 1 da (Fiona (Mrs Haggie) b 11 Oct 1956); *Career* Nat Serv pilot Tport Aux 1941, Fleet Air Arm RN 1943, Admty Directorate of Air Warfare 1944; Aeroplane and Armament Experimental Estab 1940, aircraft pilot and tech offr TATA 1942, tech ed American Aviation Pubns 1950, fndr Aviation Studies 1951 (specialist titles on mil, civil, space, armaments, nuclear weapons and intelligence affrs); memb Aviation and Space Writers Assoc USA; *Books* Rationalization Measures for British Industry (1955), Roots of British Air Policy (1966); *Style*— Richard Worcester, Esq; Sussex House, Parkside, Wimbledon, London SW19 5NB (☎ 081 946 5082)

WORCESTER, Prof Robert Milton; s of late C M Worcester of Kansas City USA and late Violet Ruth; *b* 21 Dec 1933; *Educ* Univ of Kansas (BSc); *m* 1, 1958 (m dis), Joann (*née* Ransdell); 2 s; m 2, 1982, Margaret Noel, *née* Smallbone; *Career* conslt McKinsey & Co 1962-65; controller Opinion Research Corporation 1965-68, past pres World Assoc for Public Opinion Research; chm and md Market & Opinion Research International (MORI) Ltd 1973-; tstee Worldwide Fund for Nature (UK), vice pres Int Social Sci Cncl, memb UNESCO; visiting prof of journalism City Univ London; conslt: The Times, Sunday Times, Economist; FRSA; *Books* Political Communications (co author 1982), Political Opinion Polling: an International Review (ed 1983), Private Opinions Public Polls (co author 1986), We British (1990), British Public Opinion (1991); *Recreations* choral music (Bart's Hosp Choir), gardening, skiing; *Clubs* Reform; *Style*— Prof Robert Worcester; MORI (Market & Opinion Research International), 32 Old Queen Street, London SW1H 9HP (☎ 071 222 0232, fax 071 222 1653)

WORDIE, Sir John (Stewart); CBE (1975), VRD (1963); s of Sir James Mann Wordie, CBE; *b* 15 Jan 1924; *Educ* Winchester, St John's Cambridge (MA, LLM); *m* 1955, Patricia Kynoch, da of Lt-Col G B Kynoch, CBE, TD, DL; 4 s; *Career* served WW II RNVR, Cdr RNR 1967; called to the bar Inner Temple; chm: Burnham and Pelham Ctee 1966-87, Soulbury Ctee 1966-, Wages Cncls, Nat Jt Cncl for Further Education 1980-; memb: Agric Wages Bd for Eng and Wales 1974-, Central Arbitration Ctee 1976-, Cncl of ACAS 1986-90, Ct Asst Salters' 1971- (and Master 1975); kt 1981; *Recreations* sailing, shooting, tennis; *Clubs* Travellers', RORC, Hawks, Army & Navy, Royal Tennis Ct, Clyde Corinthian Yacht; *Style*— Sir John Wordie, CBE, VRD; Shallows Cottage, Breamore, Fordingbridge, Hants (☎ 0725 22432)

WORDIE, Peter Jeffrey; CBE, TD; s of Sir James Mann Wordie, CBE (d 1962), of

Cambridge, and Gertrude Mary, *née* Henderson; *b* 30 May 1932; *Educ* Winchester, Univ of Cambridge (BA); *m* 27 Feb 1959, Alice Elinor Michele, da of Nicolas de Haller, of St Legier, Vaud, Switzerland; 2 s (Roderick b 1960, Charles b 1969), 3 da (Chantal b 1961, Michaela b 1961, Philippa b 1966); *Career* Nat Serv 1 Argylls 1950-52, TA 8 Argylls 1952-69; dir and vice chm Harrisons (Clyde) Ltd 1959-; memb Ct Univ of Stirling; memb Worshipful Co of Shipwrights 1988; Hon DUniv Stirling 1986; *Books* The Royal Game (1989); *Recreations* fishing, real tennis; *Clubs* Travellers; *Style*— Peter Wordie, Esq, CBE, TD; Harrisons (Clyde) Ltd, 16 Woodside Crescent, Glasgow, Scotland (☎ 041 332 9766)

WORDLEY, Ronald William; s of William Wordley, and Elizabeth Anne, *née* Hackett; *b* 16 June 1928; *Educ* Barnet GS, City of London Coll, RMA Sandhurst; *m* 1953, Pamela Mary Offord; 2 s (and 1 s decd), 1 da; *Career* 2 Lt RA 1948; served: UK, Far East, Europe; liaison offr RM Commando Bde 1951, Capt; air observation post pilot 1953, Army Light Aircraft Sch 1955, seconded Army Air Corps Cadre 1957, ret 1958; Unilever (U Africa Co) 1958-59, Anglia TV Ltd 1959-1967, sales controller Harlech Consortium 1967, sales dir HTV Ltd 1971-78 (md 1978-85, chm and md 1985-87); chm The Buckingham Group (Winslow Press) Ltd, dir BCS Developments Ltd; hon patron Royal Regiment of Wales; fell Inst of Mktg, FRSA; *Recreations* golf, swimming, music, travel, sailing (Tirion II); *Clubs* Bristol and Clifton Golf, RYA, Burnham and Berrow Golf, Clifton (Bristol); *Style*— Ron Wordley Esq; 6 Spring Leigh, Leigh Woods, Bristol BS8 3PG

WORDSWORTH, Antony Christopher Curwen; FIAA; s of Lt Col J G Wordsworth, OBE (John Gordon), of Hereford, and Doreen Blackwood, *née* Butler Henderson; ggggs of William Wordsworth, material ggs of Lords Farringdon and Clarina; *b* 24 April 1940; *Educ* Repton; *m* 3 Nov 1962, Rosamond Anne, da of Maj John David Summers, of Marsh Cottage, Old Romney, Kent; 1 s (Mark b 1965), 2 da (Lucy b 1968, Mary b 1972); *Career* Lt Irish Gds 1958-62; insurance loss adjuster; dir Tyler & Co (Adjusters) Ltd; *Recreations* gardening, DIY, music, dogs, horses; *Style*— Antony Wordsworth, Esq, FIAA; Little Brockholds Farm, Radwinter, Saffron Walden, Essex CB10 2TF (☎ 0799 599 458); 152 Commercial St, London E1 6NU (fax 071 377 6355)

WORKMAN, Hugh John; s of Hugh Workman (d 1966), and Annie Workman (d 1956); *b* 24 May 1925; *Educ* St Mungo's Acad Glasgow, Glasgow Univ (BL); *m* 15 Oct 1956, Audrey Henrietta, da of William Aylmer (d 1962), of Glasgow; *Career* slr; snr ptnr of messrs Sellar & Christie Solicitors Glasgow; dir and sec: Castle View Investmt Co (Stirling) Ltd, Commercial Catering Gp of Cos, Bridge of Allan and London, Commercial Contracting Gp of Cos Ltd London, Borthwick Blending Co Ltd, Glen Talla Blending & Broking Co Ltd, R M Stirling & Co (Contractors) Ltd; sec and tres Glasgow & District Bldg Trades Convalescent Homes Collections Ctee; *Recreations* swimming, walking, music; *Clubs* RSAC and Western Glasgow, Caledonian and Canning London; *Style*— Hugh J Workman, Esq; 11 Lockend Crescent, Bearsden, Glasgow G61 1EA; Messrs Sellar & Christie, Merchants' House, 30 George Square, Glasgow G2 1EG (☎ 041 221 4877, telex 777967 CHACOM G, fax GRP 3 041 204 0206)

WORKMAN, Timothy; s of Jonathan Gordon Russell Workman, and Eileen, *née* Dawson (d 1970); *b* 18 Oct 1943; *Educ* Ruskin GS Croydon; *m* 3 July 1971, Felicity Ann Caroline, da of John Western; 1 s (Jonathan b 1973), 1 da (Nicola b 1975); *Career* probation offr Inner London Probation Serv 1967-69; admitted slr 1969; asst slr then ptnr C R Thomas & Son and Lloyd Howarth & Ptnrs Maidenhead 1969-86, Metropolitan Stipendary Magistrate 1986-; memb Law Soc; *Recreations* skiing; *Clubs* Medico-Legal; *Style*— Timothy Workman, Esq; Orchard House, Fleet Hill, Finchampstead, Berks RG11 4LA (☎ 0734 733 315); Camberwell Green Magistrates Court, London SE5 7UP

WORLEY, (Edward) Michael; JP (1972); *b* 29 March 1936; *Educ* Uppingham, Downing Coll Cambridge; *m* 1966, Ann; 2 s (Andrew, Thomas), 1 da (Rachel); *Career* Steel Co of Wales Ltd (Port Talbot) 1957-62; William King Ltd (West Bromwich): joined 1962, md 1963-, chm 1988-; magistrate 1972-, chm Taxation Ctee Unquoted Companies Gp 1979-, dir Wesleyan Assurance Soc 1980- (vice chm 1987-), memb Birmingham Diocesan Bd of Fin 1980-, chm Birmingham Botanical Gardens & Glasshouses 1981-, memb W Midlands Regnl Health Authy 1982- (vice chm 1990-), memb Cncl Birmingham Chamber of Indust and Commerce 1984-90, memb Bd Black Country Development Corp 1987-, non-exec dir Birmingham Regnl Office Barclays Bank PLC 1987-, pres Nat Assoc of Steel Stockholders 1988-90, govr Sandwell Coll of Further and Higher Educn 1988-, chm Sandwell Trg and Enterprise Cncl 1990-; *Books* co-author: Regional Government (1968), Freedom to Spend (1971), Passing On (1973); *Recreations* gardening, sailing, reading; *Style*— Michael Worley, Esq, JP; William King Ltd, Atlas Centre, Union Rd, West Bromwich, West Midlands B70 9DR (☎ 021 553 2911, fax 021 553 2038)

WORLIDGE, (Edward) John; s of Robert Leonard Worlidge (d 1960), and Kathleen Frances, *née* Bonallack; *b* 31 May 1928; *Educ* Marlborough, St John's Coll Cambridge (MA); *m* 8 Jan 1955, Margaret Elizabeth (Margot), da of John Murray (d 1965); 3 s (David b 1956, Nigel b 1960, Mark b 1963); *Career* 2 Lt RE 1946-48; dir Wiggins Teape Group 1970-89, exec dir BAT Industries plc 1980-89, chm and chief exec Wiggins Teape Group 1984-89; non-exec dir: Rugby Group plc 1987, Thames Water plc 1988; chm CBI Energy Policy Ctee 1989; memb Cncl Marlborough Coll 1988; rowing: Cambridge VIII v Oxford 1951, Cambridge v Harvard & Yale in USA 1951, Lady Margaret Boat Club winning VIII Grand Challenge Cup Henley 1951, Leander VIII Winners Grand Challenge Cup Henley 1952, Great Br VIII Olympics Helsinki 1952; Liveryman Worshipful Co of Ironmongers 1986; CBIM 1982, FRSA 1986; *Recreations* sailing, golf; *Clubs* Hawks, Leander, Royal Yacht Squadron, Liphook Golf; *Style*— John Worlidge, Esq; East Dene, Midhurst Rd, Haslemere, Surrey, GU27 2PT

WORLIDGE, Capt Robert Alan; LVO (1977); s of Robert Leonard Worlidge (d 1960), and Kathleen Frances, *née* Bonallack; *b* 26 Oct 1933,bro John Worlidge *qv*; *Educ* Marlborough Coll, Dartmouth, Royal Naval Engrg Coll; *m* 1, 1961 Pauline Reynolds, da of Stewart Cathie Griffith, CBE, DFC, TD; 2 da (Claire b 1964, Sarah b 1967); m 2, 1979, Agnes Margaret, (Molly) da of Maj-Gen Walter Rutherford Goodman, CB (d 1976), of Woodbridge, Suffolk; *Career* joined RN 1952; HMS Renown 1965-70, HMRY Britannia 1975-77; Capt HMS Sultan 1983-85; John Brown Engineers & Constructors 1986-; *Recreations* golf, cricket, sailing, theatre; *Clubs* Royal Yacht Sqdn, Royal Cinque Ports Golf, NCC; *Style*— Capt Robert Worlidge, LVO, RN; Abbey Rectory, 17 Park Lane, Bath BA1 2XH; 20 Eastbourne Terrace, London 6LE

WORLING, Dr Peter Metcalfe; s of Alexander Davidson Worling (d 1965), of Aberdeen, and Florence, *née* Metcalfe; *b* 16 June 1928; *Educ* New Sch Darjeeling India, Robert Gordon's Coll Aberdeen, Univ of Bradford (PhD); *m* 20 March 1954, Iris Isabella, da of James Peacock McBeath (d 1962), of Dingwall; 1 s (Bruce b 26 Aug 1956 (d 1984), 2 da (Helen (Mrs Hill) b 25 Aug 1958, Fiona b 13 Jan 1962); *Career* home sales mangr Carnegies of Welwyn 1954-56 (export exec 1950-54), sales mangr Bradley & Bliss Ltd 1961-66 (pharmacist 1956-61), md Vestric Ltd Cheshire 1979-88 (mangr Ruislip Branch 1965-66, regnl dir Edinburgh 1966-73, mktg dir Cheshire 197988), chm AAH Pharmaceuticals Ltd Cheshire 1989-; memb Ctee Edinburgh Branch Royal Pharamceutical Soc 1968-73 (chm Reading Branch 1963-64), chm: S Wholesale Druggists Assoc 1970 (memb 1966-73), Nat Assoc of Pharmaceutical Distributors 1983-85, pres Proprietary Articles Trade Assoc 1984-85; FRPharmS 1954; *Recreations* gardening; *Style*— Dr Peter Worling; Riverhurst, 19 Eyebrook Road, Bowdon, Altrincham, Cheshire WA14 3LH (☎ 061 928 3248); 33 Hainburn Park, Edinburgh EH10 7HQ; AAH Pharmaceuticals Ltd, West Lane, Runcorn, Cheshire (☎ 0928 717070, fax 0928 714375, telex 629 859)

WORLOCK, Hon Mrs (Ann); da of Baron Edmund-Davies, PC (Life Peer); *b* 1936; *m* 1959, Frederick Cecil Worlock; *Style*— The Hon Mrs Worlock; Brooklands, Fladbury, Pershore, Worcs

WORMALD, Dame Ethel May; *née* Robinson; DBE (1968); da of late John Robert Robinson, a journalist, of Newcastle on Tyne and late Alice Fulbeck; *b* 19 Nov 1901; *Educ* Whitley Bay HS, Univ of Leeds (BA, DipEd); *m* 1923, Stanley Wormald (decd), s of late Samuel Wormald, of Leeds; 2 s (Derek, Michael Robert); *Career* lectr in further educn; chm Liverpool Educn Ctee 1955-67, pres Assoc of Educn Ctees 1961-62, Lord Mayor Liverpool 1967-68; govr: Liverpool Coll Higher Educn, Burton Manor Residential Coll Further Educn; memb Ct Univ of Liverpool; founder chm Ethel Wormald Coll of Higher Educn; JP Liverpool 1948; DL: Lancs 1970, Merseyside 1974; *Style*— Dame Ethel Wormald, DBE, JP, DL; 17 Rhes James, Bethesda, Gwynedd LL57 3RA (☎ 0248 601800)

WORMELL, Peter Roydon; s of Roydon Wormell (d 1959), of Mackay, Queensland, and Gladys Mary Barrow (d 1987); *b* 28 June 1928; *Educ* Colchester Royal GS; *m* 1, 1951 (m dis), Jean, *née* Holmes; 1 s (Stephen Peter b 1958), 1 da (Carol Elizabeth b 1956); m 2, 26 May 1979, Mary Jo Horkins (authoress Mary Lyons); *Career* landowner, author, broadcaster; ed in chief Farmers Handbook 1976-; chm: Eastern Area Cons Agric Ctee 1968-, Cons Countryside Forum 1978-; memb: Essex CC 1966-77 (chm and ldr 1973-77), Lexden and Winstree RDC 1961-67, Colchester Water Bd 1963-66, Eastern Sports Cncl 1968-71, Eastern Elec Consultative Cncl 1969-73, Ct of Univ of Essex 1968-77; chm: N Essex VSO 1968-76, CUM N Essex, ESU 1971-75, Colchester Colne Round Table 1965 (pres 1970); Liveryman Worshipful Co of Farmers 1975-; Guild of Agric Journalists 1967; chm Journal Ctee Farmers Club 1975-78, Lloyd's 1977; *Books* Anatomy of Agriculture (1978); *Recreations* farming, politics, writing; *Clubs* Farmers, Royal Overseas; *Style*— Peter Wormell, Esq; The Estate Office, Langenhoe Hall, Abberton, Colchester CO5 7NA (☎ 020 6735 265)

WORONIECKA, Princess Marysia Helena Gwenfra Teresa; da of Prince Krysztof Woroniecki, and Julia, *née* Jones; *b* 12 Aug 1956; *Educ* Sacred Heart Sch Hammersmith, Chiswick Polytechnic; *Career* proprietor of Marysia Woroniecka Publicity, one of London's premier fashion PR cos, estab 1978, now handling 25 major fashion designers, shops and manufacturers; *Clubs* Chelsea Arts, Groucho's, Fred's; 44 Finborough Road, London SW10 (☎ 071 352 3144); 1 Chelsea Manor Studios, Flood Street, London SW3 5SR (☎ 071 351 7411, fax 071 352 9541, telex 918259 PANIC G)

WORRALL-THOMPSON, Antony; s of Michael Worrall-Thompson, and Joanna Brenda, *née* Duncan; *b* 1 May 1952; *Educ* Kings Sch Canterbury, Westminster Coll (HMD); *m* 1, 1975, Jill, *née* Thompson; m 2, 1983 (m dis), Melitza Jane Hamilton, da of Hugh Miller; 2 s (Blake Antony Cardew, Sam Michael Hamilton); *Career* chef; food and beverage mangr Coombe Lodge Hotel Essex 1972, head chef and mangr Golden Fleece Restaurant Brentwood 1972; head chef: Ye Olde Logge Brentwood 1974, Adriatico Restaurant Woodland Green 1976, Hedges Restaurant (owned by Elton John) South Woodford 1977, Brinkley's Restaurant Fulham Rd 1978-79 (with 6 month sabbatical to France), Dan's Restaurant Chelsea 1980; Menage a Trois: chef and patron Knightsbridge 1981, opened in Bombay 1983, opened New York 1985, opened in Melbourne 1986, sold 1988 (retains all consultancies); chef and patron Avoirdupois Kings Road 1984, opened Mise-en-Place Limited 1986, purchased KWT Foodshow 1988; chef and patron: One Ninety Queen's Gate 1989-, Bistrot 190 1990-; winner Mouton Rothschild menu competition 1987, Meilleur Ouvrier De Grande Bretagne 1988 (life title); memb: Restaurateurs' Assoc of GB, Académie Culinaire of France; *Books* The Small and Beautiful Cookbook (1984); *Recreations* wine, antiques, art, interior design, gardening, sport, classical music, travel; *Style*— Antony Worrall-Thompson, Esq; One Ninety Queen's Gate and Bistrot, 190 Queen's Gate, London SW7 5EU (☎ 071 581 5666, fax 071 581 8172)

WORSLEY, Albert; s of John Worsley (d 1986), and Ada, *née* Astell; *b* 3 Sept 1935; *Educ* Tech Coll; *m* 5 Sept 1959, Lilian Brenda, da of Albert Cross (d 1988); 1 s (Roger); *Career* Nat Serv Lancs Fus; materials controller Triplex Safety Co Ltd 1969-74, internal audit mangr Pilkington plc 1974-83, fin dir Kitsons Insulation Ltd 1983-; 1983-: Kitson Insulation Contractors Ltd, Kitsons Insulation Products Ltd, Keith Young Insulation Ltd, Hastie Insulation (Ireland) Ltd, chm and dir Kitsons Environmental Servs Ltd; Inst of Internal Auditors: ctee memb NW branch 1980-83 (chm 1981-83), nat cncl memb; FCMA, FIIA; *Recreations* gardening; *Style*— Albert Worsley, Esq; 88 Fairholme Ave, Eccleston Park, Prescot, Merseyside (☎ 051 426 6312); Pilkington Plc, Contracting Division, Prescot Rd, St Helens, Merseyside WA10 3TT (☎ 0744 69 3020, fax 0744 451035, telex 627441 PBSTH G)

WORSLEY, Hon Lady (Caroline Cicely); *née* Dewar; da of 3 Baron Forteviot, MBE; *b* 12 Feb 1934; *m* 1, 1956 (m dis 1966), 3 Duke of Fife, *qv*; 1 s, 1 da; m 2, 1980, Gen Sir Richard Edward Worsley, *qv*; *Style*— The Hon Lady Worsley

WORSLEY, Hon Mrs (Carolyn Mary Wynyard); *née* Hardinge; da of 4 Viscount Hardinge, MBE (d 1979), and Margaret Elizabeth Arnot, *née* Fleming; *b* 5 March 1932; *m* 1954, John Arthington Worsley, s of Col Sir William Worsley, 4 Bt (d 1973), of Hovingham Hall, York, and bro of HRH Duchess of Kent and Sir Marcus Worsley, 5 Bt, JP; 3 s (Henry b 1958, Jonathan b 1960, Dickon b 1966), 2 da (Willa b 1955, Katharine b 1968); *Style*— The Hon Mrs Worsley; RR2, Uxbridge, Ontario LOC IKO, Canada (☎ 416 852 6220)

WORSLEY, Lord; Charles John Pelham; s and h of 7 Earl of Yarborough, JP; *b* 5 Nov 1963; *Educ* Bristol Univ; *m* 26 Jan 1990, Anna-Karin, da of George Zecevic, of 1 Swan Walk, London SW3; 1 s (b 9 Aug 1990); *Style*— Lord Worsley

WORSLEY, Francis Edward (Jock); s of Francis Arthur Worsley, and Mary, *née* Diamond; *b* 15 Feb 1941; *Educ* Stonyhurst, Sorbonne; *m* 12 Sept 1962, Caroline Violet, da of James Hamilton Grey Hatherell (d 1968), of Manor House, Chacombe, Banbury, Oxon; 2 s (Richard, Edward), 2 da (Miranda, Joanna); *Career* CA 1964; chm The Financial Training Co Ltd 1972-; pres ICAEW 1988-, govr Ludgrove Sch; Freeman: City of London, Worshipful Co of CAs (Jr Warden 1990-91); FCA 1964; *Recreations* tennis, wine, cooking; *Clubs* Carlton; *Style*— F E Worsley, Esq; The Financial Training Co Ltd, 151 Freston Road, London W10 6SR (☎ 071 792 9090, fax 071 792 9070)

WORSLEY, John Bertrand; s of Richard Samuel Lancelot Worsley (d 1937), of Broxmead, Cuckfield, Sussex, and Margaret Laura Evelyn (later Mrs Victor Jones); *b* 7 Jan 1929; *Educ* Eton, Trinity Coll Cambridge (MA, LLB); *m* 18 July 1956, Jennifer Jane, da of Brig Sir Andrew Edmund James Clark, 3 Bt, QC, MBE, MC (d 1979); 1 s (James b 1957), 3 da (Harriet (Mrs Mark Vernon) b 1960, Alison b 1963, Victoria b 1966); *Career* Nat Serv 2 Lt RCS 1947-49; called to the Bar Inner Temple 1954; fell Woodard Corporation, chm Incorporated Church Building Society 1987-90 (gen cmmr of taxes 1974-); *Recreations* tennis, shooting, gardening, scuba diving, under water photography; *Style*— John Worsley, Esq; Furlong House, Hurstpierpoint, W Sussex

BN6 9QA (☎ 0273 833320)

WORSLEY, Sir (William) Marcus John; 5 Bt (UK 1838), of Hovingham, Yorks, JP (N Yorks 1957), DL (1978); s of Col Sir William Arthington Worsley, 4 Bt (d 1973, descent from Oliver Cromwell; sis Katharine m HRH the Duke of Kent in 1961), and Joyce Morgan, *née* Brunner; *b* 6 April 1925; *Educ* Eton, New Coll Oxford; *m* 10 Dec 1955, Hon Bridget Assheton, da of 1 Baron Clitheroe, PC; 3 s (William b 1956, Giles b 1961, Peter b 1963), 1 da (Sarah b 1958); *Heir* s, William Ralph Worsley; *Career* served Green Howards, India and W Africa, WWII; MP (C): Keighley 1959-64, Chelsea 1966-74; church cmmr 1970-84, chm Nat Tst Properties Ctee 1980-90, dep chm Nat Tst 1986-, pres Royal Forestry Soc of England Wales and NI 1980-82; High Sheriff N Yorks 1982-83; Lord Lt N Yorks 1987; *Recreations* reading, walking, travel; *Clubs* Boodle's, Yorkshire (York); *Style—* Sir Marcus Worsley, Bt; Hovingham Hall, York YO6 4LU (☎ 0653 628206)

WORSLEY, Michael Dominic; QC (1985); s of Paul Worsley, and Magdalen Teresa, *née* Pestel; *b* 9 Feb 1926; *Educ* Bedford Sch, Inns of Court Sch of Law; *m* 1, Oct 1962, Pamela, *née* Philpot (d 1980); 1 s (Benedict b 28 Sept 1967); m 2, 12 June 1986, Jane, da of late Percival Sharpe; *Career* RN 1944-45; called to the Bar Inner Temple 1955; prosecuting counsel: to the Inland Revenue in London 1968-69, London Sessions 1969-71; jr treas counsel Central Criminal Ct 1971-74 (sr treas counsel 1974-85); *Recreations* music, travelling; *Clubs* Garrick, Lansdowne; *Style—* Michael Worsley, Esq, QC; 6 King's Bench Walk, Temple, London EC4Y 7DR

WORSLEY, Nicholas Jarvis; s of Edgar Taylor Worsley (d 1973), and Vida, *née* McCormick (d 1986); *b* 21 July 1943; *Educ* Clivton, Cambridge (MA,LLB); *m* 4 Nov 1967, Anna Maxine, da of Maxwell George Bekenn, of 55 West St, Stratford upon Avon; 2 da (Sophie Tamaris Worsley b 1970, Jessica Worsley b 1973); *Career* called to Bar Inner Temple 1966, chm Agricultural Tribunal 1980, rec 1984; chm: Worcester Civic Soc 1974-77, City of Worcester Building Preservation Tst 1977-; *Recreations* admiring contemporary British art; *Style—* Nicholas Worsley, Esq

WORSLEY, Paul Frederick; QC (1990); s of Eric Worsley, MBE, GM, and Sheila Mary, *née* Hoskin; *b* 17 Dec 1947; *Educ* Hymers Coll Hull, Mansfield Coll Oxford (MA); *m* 14 Dec 1974, Jennifer Ann Avery, JP, da of late Ernest Avery; 1 s (Nicholas b 1975), 1 da (Charlotte b 1977); *Career* called to the Bar Middle Temple 1970; Astbury Scholar, Recorder of Crown Ct 1987-; *Recreations* Spy prints, Whitby, opera, preaching; *Clubs* Yorkshire (York); *Style—* Paul Worsley, Esq, QC; 40 Park Cross St, Leeds LS1 2QH (☎ 0532 433277)

WORSLEY, Gen Sir Richard Edward; GCB (1981, KCB 1976), OBE (1964); s of H Worsley of Grey Abbey, Co Down; *b* 29 May 1923; *Educ* Radley; *m* 1, 1958, Sarah Mitchell; 1 s, 1 da; m 2, 1980, Caroline, Duchess of Fife (*see* Hon Lady Worsley); *Career* served WWII (Mid East & Italy) & Malayan Emergency in Rifle Bde, Instr RMA Sandhurst and Staff Coll Camberley, CO Royal Dragoons, Cdr 7 Armoured Bde 1965-67, COS Far East Land Force 1969-71; GOC 3 Div 1972-74, Cdr 1st (British) Corps 1976-78; QMG 1979-82 (Vice-QMG 1974-76), ret 1982; joined Pilkington Gp 1982-87, chm Barr and Stroud, Pilkington PE, chief exec Pilkington Electro-Optical Div, chm Western Provident Assoc 1989-; *Clubs* Cavalry & Guards; *Style—* Gen Sir Richard Worsley, GCB, OBE; c/o Barclays Bank, 27 Regent St, London SW1Y 4UB

WORSLEY, William Ralph; s and h of Sir (William) Marcus John Worsley, 5 Bt, of Hovingham, Yorkshire; *b* 12 Sept 1956; *Educ* Harrow, RAC; *m* 26 Sept 1987, Marie-Noelle, yr da of Bernard H Dreesmann, of Mas de la Madone, Miramar, Théole, France; 1 da (Isabella Claire b 24 Oct 1988); *Career* former Lt Queen's Own Yeomanry TAVR; farmer; chartered surveyor; dir Graybourne Properties Ltd, conslt Humberts; ARICS; *Recreations* shooting, skiing; *Clubs* Boodle's, Pratt's; *Style—* William Worsley, Esq; Wool Knoll, Hovingham, York (☎ 065 382 771); 61 Bourne St, London SW1

WORSLEY-TAYLOR, Annette Pamela; da of Sir John Godfrey Worsley-Taylor, 3 Bt (d 1952), and Anne, *née* Paget (now Anne, Lady Jaffray, *qv*); *b* 2 July 1944; *Educ* Downham Sch Hatfield Heath Herts; *Career* fndr London Designer Collections 1975 (dir 1976-); fndr memb British Fashion Cncl 1983 (memb exec 1987-); memb BKCEC Womans Wear Exec; *Recreations* fashion, design, music, people; *Style—* Ms Annette Worsley-Taylor; 3 Ovington Gardens, London SW3 (☎ 071 584 2836); 36 Beauchamp Place, London SW3 1NU (☎ 071 581 2931, fax 071 581 9589)

WORSNOP, Edric Rowland; OBE (1985); s of Rowland Worsnop (d 1977), of 4 Epsom Drive, Ipswich, Suffolk, and Nellie Windsor (d 1985); *b* 6 Sept 1930; *Educ* Ipswich Sch; *m* 27 June 1959, (Joan) Margaret, da of William King Munro, of Greengait, Rattray, Blairgowrie, Perthshire; 3 s (Nigel b 8 March 1962, Andrew b 26 Feb 1964, Robin b 18 April 1967); *Career* Nat Serv RAF 1949-51; FO 1951-54; vice consul: Medan Sumatra 1954-56, MECAS Lebanon 1957-58; second sec Bahrain 1958, political offr Abu Dhabi 1958-59, commercial offr Trucial States Dubai 1959-61, FO 1961-63, vice consul Cairo 1963-65, second and later first sec commercial Nicosia 1966-70, FCO 1970-73, first sec commercial and later first sec economic Tehran 1973-77, Parly clerk FCO 1977-81, dep consul gen Melbourne 1981-86, HM consul gen Casablanca 1987-90; *Recreations* cricket, tennis, golf, music, reading, amateur dramatics; *Clubs* Royal Overseas League; *Style—* Edric Worsnop, Esq, OBE; 15 Leven Terrace, Edinburgh EH3 9LW (☎ 031 229 7108)

WORSTHORNE, Sir Peregrine Gerard; s of Col Alexander Koch de Gooreynd, OBE, formerly Irish Gds (d 1985), who assumed surname of Worsthorne by deed poll in 1923, but reverted to Koch de Gooreynd in 1937; *see also* er bro Simon Towneley from whose estate the Worsthorne name is derived (gd m Manuela, da of Alexandre de Laski by Joaquima, Marquesa de Souza Lisboa da of José Marques Lisboa, sometime Min Plenipotentiary of Emperor of Brazil to Ct of St James), and Priscilla, now Baroness Norman, *qv*; *b* 22 Dec 1923; *Educ* Stowe, Peterhouse Cambridge (BA), Magdalen Coll Oxford; *m* 7 June 1950, Claudie Marie-Hélène (d 1990), da of Victor Edouard Bertrand de Colasse, of Paris, and former w of Geoffrey Baynham; 1 da (Dominique Elizabeth Priscilla b 18 Feb 1952), 1 step s (David); *Career* cmmnd Oxford & Bucks LI 1942, Lt Phantom GHQ Liaison Regt 1944-45; journalist and writer; formerly on editorial staff of: The Glasgow Herald 1946-48, The Times 1948-55, Daily Telegraph 1955-61; assoc ed Sunday Telegraph 1961-86 (ed 1986-); kt 1991; *Books* The Socialist Myth (1972), Peregrinations (1980), By The Right (1987); *Recreations* tennis, reading, walking; *Clubs* Garrick, Beefsteak, Pratt's; *Style—* Sir Peregrine Worsthorne; Westerlies, Wivenhoe, Essex (☎ 020 622 2886); 74A Kensington Church St, London W8; The Sunday Telegraph, Peterborough Court at South Quay, 181 Marsh Wall, London E14 9SR (☎ 071 538 5000, fax 071 538 1330, telex 22874 TELLDN G)

WORTH, Brian Leslie; s of Leslie Worth of Brockenhurst, Hants (d 1988), and Grace Alice *née* Drake (d 1983); *b* 25 Jan 1938; *Educ* Haberdashers Askes Sch; *m* 1 s (Graham 1966), 1 da (Susan 1964); *Career* Nat Serv sr Aircraftsman RAF 1960-62; CA; ptnr Whitehill Marsh Jackson & Co 1964, sr ptnr Fryer Whitehill & Co 1974, mangr ptnr Clark Whitehill Chartered Accountants 1982-86; chm: Clark Whitehill Chartered Accountants 1984-90, Clark Kenneth Leventhal 1988-90, Bd of Res ICAEW 1990-, Folley Bros Ltd 1990-, Annual Survey of Published Accounts 1990; memb Main Ctee London Soc of CAs 1976-85 (chm 1893-84); hon treas Br Cncl of Churches 1973-79; FCA (memb Cncl 1985-), ACIArb; *Books* Planning Your Personal Finances (1973); *Style—* Brian L Worth, Esq; 25 New Street Square, London EC4A 3LN (☎ 071 353 1577, 0453 834914, fax 021 633 3765)

WORTH, Prof Katharine Joyce; da of George Lorimer, and Elizabeth, *née* Jones; *b* 4 Aug 1922; *Educ* Univ of London (MA, PhD); *m* 30 Aug 1947, George, s of Ernest Worth; 2 s (Christopher George b 7 Nov 1952, Charles Robert Edmund b 4 July 1959), 1 da (Elizabeth Lorimer b 5 Nov 1955); *Career* prof of drama and theatre studies Royal Holloway and Bedford New Coll Univ of London (formerly Royal Holloway Coll) 1978-87 (lectr Eng lit 1964-74, reader Eng lit 1974-78), visiting prof King's Coll London 1988-, hon res fell RHBNC 1990-; adaptor and prodr of Beckett's Company performed in Edinburgh 1987, London and New York 1988, co-ed Theatre Notebook, memb ed bd of Yeats Annual and Modern Drama, frequent lectr abroad suported by the Br Cncl and foreign universities; memb: Soc for Theatre Res 1950, Soc of Authors 1988; Friend of the Royal Academy; *Books* Revolutions in Modern English Drama (1973), Beckett the Shape Changer (ed 1975), The Irish Drama of Europe from Yeats to Beckett (1978), Oscar Wilde (1983), Maeterlinck's Plays in Performance (1985), Where There is Nothing (ed 1987), Waiting for Godot and Happy Days (Text and Performance, 1990); *Recreations* theatre-going, walking, travel; *Style—* Prof Katharine Worth; 48 Elmfield Ave, Teddington, Middex TW11 8BT

WORTH, Peter Herman Louis; s of Dr L H Worth (d 1982), and Ruth, *née* Niemeyer (d 1967); *b* 17 Nov 1935; *Educ* Marlborough Coll, Trinity Hall Cambridge (MA, MB BChir), Middlesex Hosp Med Sch; *m* 8 Feb 1969, Judith Katherine Frances, da of Arthur Girling (d 1959), of Langham Essex; 1 s (Hugo b 1970), 1 da (Anna b 1972); *Career* conslt urological surgn: UCH 1976, St Peter's Hosps 1976, Middlesex Hosp 1984, Royal Masonic Hosp 1986; memb: Br Assoc of Urological Surgns, RSM; FRCS 1967; *Books* contrib chapters on urology in several medical text books; *Recreations* classical music, skiing, gardening; *Style—* Peter Worth, Esq; Broad Eaves, Mill Lane, Broxbourne, Herts EN10 7AZ (☎ 0992 462827); 34 Wimpole St, London W1M 7AE (☎ 071 935 3593)

WORTHINGTON, (William) Anthony (Tony); MP (L) Clydebank and Milngavie 1987; s of Malcolm Thomas Henry Worthington (d 1985), and Monica, *née* Wearden; *b* 11 Oct 1941; *Educ* City Sch Lincoln, LSE (BA), Univ of Glasgow (MEd); *m* 26 March 1966, Angela May, da of Cyril Oliver, of The Moat House, Charing, Kent; 1 s (Robert b 1972), 1 da (Jennifer b 1970); *Career* lectr Jordanhill Coll Glasgow 1971-87, regnl cncllr Strathclyde 1974-87 (chm Fin Ctee 1986-87); front bench spokesman: Educn, Employment, Trg and Social Work in Scotland; memb Scottish Community Educn Cncl 1980-87, chm Strathclyde Community Business 1984-87; *Recreations* running, gardening, reading; *Clubs* Clydebank Athletic; *Style—* Tony Worthington, MP; 24 Cleddans Crescent, Hardgate, Clydebank (☎ 0389 73195); House of Commons, London SW1 0AA (☎ 071 219 3507)

WORTHINGTON, (Edgar) Barton; CBE (1962); s of Edgar Worthington (d 1931), and Amy Elizabeth, *née* Beale (d 1946); *b* 13 Jan 1905; *Educ* Rugby, Gonville and Caius Coll Cambridge (MA, PhD); *m* 1, 23 Aug 1930, Stella, da of Menasseh Johnson (d 1950); 3 da (Shelagh b 1932, Grizelda b 1934, Marthe b 1938); m 2, 21 June 1980, Harriett, da of George Alva Stockton (d 1943), of Illinois; *Career* biologist, ecologist, environmental conslt; res expdns to great African Lakes 1927-32, scientist to Lord Hailey's African Survey 1934-37, dir Freshwater Biological Assoc 1937-46, scientific advsr to ME Supply Cncl 1939-45, scientific sec Colonial Res Ctee 1946-, devpt advsr Uganda Govt 1946, seconded to E Africa High Cmmn 1947-51, sec gen Scientific Cncl for Africa 1951-56, dep dir Gen Nature Conservancy (UK) 1956-62, scientific dir Int Biological Prog 1962-72, enviromental conslt to major devpt cos 1973-; author; Knight of Golden Ark (Netherland 1966); *Books* Reports on Fishery Surveys of African Lakes 1928-31, Inland Waters of Africa (with Stella Worthington, 1933), Science in Africa (1937), Life in Lakes and Rivers (with T T Macan, 1951), Science in the Development of Africa (1958), The Ecological Century - a Personal Appraisal (1983); *Recreations* nature conservation, field sports, farming; *Clubs* Athenaeum, Farmer's; *Style—* Barton Worthington, Esq, CBE; Colin Godmans, Furner's Green, nr Uckfield, Sussex (☎ 082 574 322)

WORTHINGTON, Air Vice-Marshal Sir Geoffrey Luis; KBE (1960, CBE 1945), CB (1957); s of the late Cdr H E F Worthington, RN; *b* 26 April 1903; *Educ* HMS Conway, Eastbourne Coll, RAF Coll Cranwell, Open Univ (BA); *m* 1931, Margaret Joan (d 1989), da of the late Maj-Gen A Stevenson, CB, CMG, DSO; 2 s, 1 da; *Career* WWII (despatches, CBE) AOC 40 Gp 1955-58, Air Vice-Marshal 1956, dir gen Equipment Air Min 1958-61; Cdr US Legion of Merit 1955; *Style—* Air Vice-Marshal Sir Geoffrey Worthington, KBE, CB; 30 Brickwall Close, Burnham-on-Crouch, Essex (☎ 0621 782388)

WORTHINGTON, His Hon Judge George Noel; s of George Errol Worthington (d 1976), and Edith Margaret Boys Worthington, *née* Stones (d 1970); *b* 22 June 1923; *Educ* Rossall Sch Lancs; *m* 10 July 1954, Jacqueline Kemble, da of George Lionel Spencer Lightfoot (d 1972), of Carlisle; 2 s (Nicholas b 1968, Jonathan decd), 1 da (Kate b 1962); *Career* WWII 1939-45, serv RAC 1941-46; admitted slr 1949; rec of the Crown Ct 1972, circuit judge 1979-; Liveryman Worshipful Co of Wax Chandlers; *Recreations* gardening; *Style—* His Hon Judge George N Worthington

WORTHINGTON, Nick; s of David Worthington, of Tremadda Farm, Zennor, Cornwall, and Bridgit, *née* Petter; *b* 19 Oct 1962; *Educ* Fitzharry's Comp Abingdon Oxon, Banbury Sch of Art and Design, St Martin's Sch of Art (BA); *Career* advtg copywriter; trainee TBWA London 1984, Symington & Partners London 1984-86, Jenner Keating Becker London 1986-88, Bartle Bogle Megarty London 1988-; winner numerous advtg awards; motor cycle racer, won 13 trophies (Brands Hatch, Snetterton and Lydden); *Recreations* motorcycle racing; *Clubs* Br Motorcycle Racing; *Style—* Nick Worthington, Esq; Bartle Bogle Hegarty, 24-27 Gt Pulteney St, London W1R 3DB (☎ 071 734 1677, fax 071 437 3666)

WORTHINGTON, Philip Michael; s of Col Lancelot Jukes Worthington, TD, JP (d 1975), and 1 w Phyllis Mary, *née* Sadler (d 1981); half-bro Stuart Worthington, *qv*; *b* 24 April 1926; *Educ* Ashby-de-la-Zouch, Univ Coll Nottingham (BSc); *m* 1, 25 June 1955, Gillian Hazel, da of late Sir William Sidney Albert Atkins, CBE, of Chobham Place, Chobham, Surrey; 1 s (Nicholas b 1960), 1 da (Catherine b 1962); m 2, 29 July 1983, Judith Sonia May, da of Henry Peter Robson Hamlin, of Prior Lea, Upper Packington Rd, Asby-de-la-Zouch, Leics; 1 da (Miranda b 1985); *Career* conslt engr and business and project conslt; md WS Atkins and Partners 1971-78 (joined 1946, dir 1965-78), PM Worthington & Associates Ltd 1978-; dir: AJ Worthington (Holdings) plc 1972- (chm 1972-83), Polycast Ltd 1984-; author of papers on engrg and economics; underwriting memb Lloyds 1988-; exec dir Major Projects Assoc 1982-83, assoc fell Templeton Coll Oxford 1982-84; CEng, FICE, CBIM; *Books* The Worthington Families of Medieval England; *Style—* P M Worthington, Esq; The Knoll House, Knossington, Oakham, Leics LE15 8LT (☎ 0664 77315)

WORTHINGTON, Stuart Gibson; s of Col Lancelot Jukes Worthington, TD, JP (d 1975), of Swainsley, nr Leek, Staffs, and Marjorie Brown, *née* Gibson (d 1981); bro Philip Worthington *qv*; *b* 30 Oct 1940; *Educ* Winchester; *m* 2 Dec 1972, Geraldine Judith, da of Lt-Col John James Seth, MBE, of Las Mimomas, Guadalmina Alta, San Pedro de Alcantara, Malaga, Spain; 3 da (Melanie b 1966, Lucinda b 1969, Victoria b 1973); *Career* dir: A J Worthington (Hldgs) plc 1970-84, A J Worthington & Co (Leek)

Ltd 1970-84 (chm 1974-84); dir: Narrow Fabrics Fedn 1969-84 (chm 1973-76), Dine Design Ltd 1990-, Wolsey Lodges Ltd 1991-, Br Man-Made Fibres Fedn 1972-77, Br Textile Confedn 1973-76; princ Blore Assocs 1985-; JP Co Stafford 1976 (resigned 1987); Freeman City of London 1978, Liveryman Worshipful Co of Weavers 1978 (Upper Warden 1990-91); *Recreations* cricket, tennis, crosswords; *Clubs* City Livery; *Style*— Stuart Worthington, Esq; The Old Rectory, Blore, nr Ashbourne, Derbys DE6 2BS (☎ and fax 033529 287); Blore Associates, Blore, nr Ashbourne, Derbys DE6 2BS (☎ and fax 033529 287)

WORTHY, Hon Mrs (Margaret); *née* Bruce; da of 7 Lord Balfour of Burleigh (d 1967); 1 Lord was Ambassador to Tuscany and Lorraine & was er Scots Peer 1607, Title Attained 1716 and reversed by Act of Parliament 1868; *b* 1934; *Educ* St Paul's Girls' Sch; *m* 1967, David Graham Worthy, *qv*; 1 s; *Recreations* horses, mountains, swimming; *Clubs* ROSPA Advanced Drivers Assoc; *Style*— The Hon Mrs Worthy; Keepers Cottage, Hare Warren Hollow, Merrow Downs, Guildford, Surrey GU1 2HJ

WOTHERSPOON, (John Munro) Iain; TD, DL (Lochaber, Inverness, Badenoch and Strathspey 1982), WS (1950); s of Robert Wotherspoon (d 1968), of Inverness, and Jessie MacDonald, *née* Munro (d 1980); *b* 19 July 1924; *Educ* Inverness Royal Acad, Loretto, Trinity Coll Oxford (MA), Univ of Edinburgh (LLB); *m* 30 Aug 1952, Victoria Avril Jean, da of Sir Lawrie Edwards, KBE, DL (d 1968), of Newcastle upon Tyne; 2 s (James b 1955, Jonathan b 1957), 2 da (Ann b 1956, Victoria b 1960); *Career* Lt Royal Signals Europe and Burma 1945-46, TA 1948-78, Lt Col Cmdg 51 (Highland) Div Signals 1963-67, Col Dep Cdr 13 Signals Gp 1970-72, Hon Col 32 Scottish Signal Regt 1972-78, ADC to HM The Queen 1971-76; slr and landowner, sr ptnr Macandrew & Jenkins WS, Inverness; Dep Lt Districts of Lochaber, Inverness, Badenoch and Strathspey 1982-; clerk to the Lieutenancy 1985-; *Recreations* shooting, fishing, stalking; *Clubs* Highland, Inverness and New (Edinburgh); *Style*— Iain Wotherspoon, TD, DL; Maryfield, 62 Midmills Rd, Inverness (☎ 0463 233642); Affaric Lodge, Cannich, by Beauly (☎ 045 65 351); 5 Drummond St, Inverness IV1 1QF (☎ 0463 233001, fax 0463 230743)

WRAGG, Prof Edward Conrad; s of George William Wragg, of 7 Errington Ave, Sheffield, and Maria, *née* Brandstetter; *b* 26 June 1938; *Educ* King Edward VII GS Sheffield, Hatfield Coll, Univ of Durham (BA, DipEd); *m* 29 Dec 1960, Judith, da of Beaumont King (d 1984), of 25 Mortimer Rd, Penistone, nr Sheffield; 1 s (Christopher Beaumont b 1975), 2 da (Josephine b 1966, Caroline Maria b 1967); *Career* master Queen Elizabeth GS Wakefield 1960-64, head of German Wyggeston Boys' Sch 1964-66, lectr in educn Univ of Exeter 1966-73, prof of educn Univ of Nottingham 1973-78, prof of educn and dir of sch educn Univ of Exeter 1978-; memb Devon Educn Ctee, chm Sch Broadcasting Cncl for UK (1981-86), chm Educnl Broadcasting Cncl for UK 1986-87, pres Br Educnl Res Assoc, chm BBC Regnl Advsy Cncl for SW 1989-; chartered fell Coll of Preceptors 1988; DUniv Open Univ 1989; radio/TV presenter: Chalkface (Granada), Crisis in Education (BBC), Education Roadshow (BBC); *Books* Teaching Teaching (1974), Classroom Interaction (1976), Teaching Mixed Ability Groups (1976), A Handbook for School Governors (1980), Class Management and Control (1981), A Review of Research in Teacher Education (1982), Swineshead Revisited (1984), Classroom Teaching Skills (1984), The Domesday Project (1985), Education: An Action Guide for Parents (1986), Teacher Appraisal (1987), Education in the Market Place (1988), The Wragged Edge: Education in Thatcher's Britain (1988), Schools and Parents (1989), Riches from Wragg (1990); *Recreations* football watching, playing and coaching, music, running, cooking; *Style*— Prof Edward Wragg; 14 Doriam Close, Exeter EX4 4RS (☎ 0392 77052); School of Education, Exeter University EX1 2LU (☎ 0392 264877, fax 0392 264736)

WRAGG, John; s of Arthur Wragg, of York, and Ethel, *née* Ransom; *b* 20 Oct 1937; *Educ* York Sch of Art, Royal Coll of Art; *Career* artist; solo exhibitions: Hanover Gallery 1963, 1966 and 1970, Gallerie Alexandre Iolas Paris 1968, York Festival 1969, Bridge Street Gallery Bath 1982, Katherine House Gallery Marlborough 1984, Quinton Green Fine Art 1985; selected gp exhibitions: Lords Gallery 1959, L'Art Vivant 1965 and 1968, Arts Cncl Gallery Belfast 1966, Pittsburg Int 1967, Britische Kuns heute Hamburg 1968, Fndn Maeght 1968, Bath Festival Gallery 1977 and 1984, Artists Market 1978, Biennale di Scultura di Arese (Milan) 1980, King Street Gallery Bristol 1980, Gallerie Bollhagen Worpswede Germany 1981 and 1983, Quinton Green Fine Art 1984, 1985, 1986 and 1987, Abstraction 89 (Cleveland Bridge Gallery) 1989, Sculptors Drawings (Cleveland Bridge Gallery) 1990, Contemporary Br Drawing (Cleveland Bridge Gallery) 1989, The Hunting Art Prizes Exhibition 1991; work in the collection of: Israel Museum Jerusalem, Tate Gallery, Arts Cncl of GB, Arts Cncl of NI, Contemporary Art Soc, Wellington Art Gallery NZ, Chancery Bequest 1981; ARCA 1960, ARA 1983; *Recreations* walking; *Style*— John Wragg, Esq; 4 Lansdowne Terrace, Morris Lane, Devizes, Wilts SN10 1NX (☎ 0380 725819)

WRAGG, Lawrence de Villamil; s of Arthur Donald Wragg (d 1966), of Buxton, Derbys, and Lilia Mary May, *née* Adcock (d 1990); *b* 26 Nov 1943; *Educ* Rendcomb Coll Glos, Univ of Bristol (BA), Sorbonne Paris (Dip), Manchester Business Sch (MBA); *m* 23 July 1971, Aureole Margaret Willoughby, da of Lt-Col Edward Cole Willoughby Fowler (d 1985), of Chislehurst, Kent; 1 s (David b 1979), 2 da (Isabel b 1977, Helen b 1988); *Career* systems analyst National Data Processing Service 1968-69, mgmnt conslt Price Waterhouse Assocs 1969-72, exec dir Chemical Bank International (formerly London Multinational Bank International) 1974-82; dir: Charterhouse Japhet 1982-86, Standard Chartered Merchant Bank 1987-89; dep chm and chief exec Ketton Investments 1990-; chm: Lawrence Wragg Associates Ltd 1989-, Proscyon Partners Ltd 1990-; govrs of Duxford Sch, The Ickleton Soc; vice chm Ickleton PC, chm London Banks Composite Currency Ctee 1980-84, memb Assoc of MBAs 1974-; *Books* Composite Currencies (ed, 1984); *Recreations* music, mountaineering, skiing, gardening, aviation; *Clubs* Overseas Bankers, London Mountaineering (treas); *Style*— Lawrence Wragg, Esq

WRAGG, Hon Mrs (Mary Ann Maud Sigrid); er da of 2 Baron Gretton; *b* 5 Jan 1939; *m* June 1986, Thomas Henry Wragg, o s of late T L Wragg, of Hinckley; *Recreations* breeder and int judge of Arabian Horses; *Style*— The Hon Mrs Wragg; Manor House, Stapleford, Melton Mowbray, Leics LE14 2SF (☎ 057 284 224)

WRAIGHT, Sir John Richard; KBE (1976), CMG (1962); s of Richard George Wraight (d 1964), and Kathleen Elizabeth Mary, *née* Robinson (d 1974); *b* 4 June 1916; *Educ* Selhurst GS, Univ of London; *m* 1947, Marquita, *née* Elliott; *Career* Maj HAC and RHA 1939-45; joined FO 1945, Dip Serv 1947, first sec Athens 1948, Tel Aviv 1950, Washington 1953, asst head econ rel FO 1957, commercial cnsllr Cairo 1959, Brussels and Luxembourg 1962, min and consul gen Milan 1968-73, ambass Switzerland 1973-76, ret; co dir and co conslt 1976-, int conslt to London Stockbrokers Phillips & Drew 1976-88; pres Co Scout Cncl of Gtr London SW 1977-; Cdr of the Order of the Crown (Belgium) 1966, memb RIIA; *Books* The Swiss and the British (1987), A History of the City Swiss Club, London, 1856-1991 (1991); *Recreations* music, gardening, birdwatching; *Style*— Sir John Wraight, KBE, CMG; c/o Lloyds Bank plc, 16 St James's St London SW1A 1EY

WRANGEL, Baroness Alexis; Hon Diana Sylvia; *née* Conolly - Carew; da of 6 Baron Carew; *b* 7 April 1940; *m* 22 May 1985, Baron Alexis Wrangel; *Style*— Baroness Alexis Wrangel; Brownstown Lodge, Navan, Co Meath

WRANGHAM, Peter John; *b* 30 April 1934; *m* 5 Jan 1963, Bridget Ann; 1 da (Fiona); *Career* former dir in Hong Kong: Hang Seng Bank Ltd, Cathay Pacific Airways, Mass Transit Railway Corporation, Windsor Industrial Corporation Limited, Hongkong Electric Company Limited, Hutchinson Whampoa Limited; dir: The Hongkong & Shanghai Banking Corporation Ltd 1987-, The Britain Bank of The Middle East (UK) 1988-, HSBC Holdings UK Ltd 1988-, Hongkong Bank Nominees (UK) Ltd 1988-, HSBC Holdings BV 1989-, James Capel Holdings Ltd UK 1989-, 00 Bishopsgate Ltd 1989-, Hongkong Bank Trustee Holding Ltd 1989-; non-exec chm: International Commercial Bank plc 1988-, James Capel & Co Ltd 1989-, Cubbs Insurance Holdings Ltd 1989-; non-exec dir Midland Bank plc UK 1988-; memb in Hong Kong: Consultative Ctee for Basic Law of Hong Kong Special Admin Region, Trade Devpt Cncl, Cncl of Community Chest; FBIB; *Style*— Peter Wrangham, Esq; The Hongkong and Shanghai Banking Corporation Limited, 99 Bishopsgate, London EC2P 2LA (☎ 071 638 2366, fax 071 588 3318, telex 885945 HSBCLO)

WRATTEN, Donald Peter; s of Frederick George Wratten (d 1936), of Folkestone, Kent, and Majorie, *née* Liverton (d 1979); *b* 3 July 1925; *Educ* Harvey GS Folkestone, LSE (BSc Econ), Open Univ (BA); *m* 6 Sept 1947, Margaret Kathleen, da of Frank Marsh (d 1938), of London; 1 s (Mark b 1955), 1 da (Isobel b 1958); *Career* RAF Meteorological Wing 1943-47; PO: asst princ 1950, private sec to Asst PMG 1955-56, princ POHQ 1956-65, private sec to PMG 1965-66, head of Mktg Div PO Telecom 1966-67, dir E Region PO Telecom 1967-69; chief exec: Nat Girobank 1969-74, Nat Data Processing Serv 1974-75; sr dir personnel Br Telecom 1975-81, mgmnt conslt 1981-85, non exec dir National Companies Building Society 1985-; chm Radlett Soc and Green Belt Assoc, chm Radlett Local History Soc, vice chm Stereoscopic Soc, cncl memb Int Stereoscopic Union, memb then chm Advsy Panel City Univ Business Sch 1974-80; memb: Business Educn Cncl 1975-82, Ct Cranfield Inst of Technol 1975-81; FBIM 1960, LRPS 1984, FRSA 1985; *Books* The Book of Radlett and Aldenham; *Recreations* stereoscopic photography, social history; *Style*— Donald Wratten, Esq; 10 Homefield Rd, Radlett, Herts WD7 8PY (☎ 0923 854 500)

WRAXALL, Sir Charles Frederick Lascelles; 9 Bt (UK 1813), of Wraxall, Somerset; s of Sir Morville Wraxall, 8 Bt (d 1978); *b* 17 Sept 1961; *Educ* Archbishop Tenison's GS Croydon; *m* 1983, Lesley Linda, da of William Albert Allan; 1 s; *Heir* s, William Nathaniel Lascelles b 1987; *Career* assist accountant Morgan Stanley Int 1987-; *Recreations* football, stamps, postcards; *Style*— Sir Charles Wraxall, Bt

WRAXALL, 2 Baron (UK 1928); George Richard Lawley Gibbs; DL (Avon 1974); s of 1 Baron Wraxall, TD, PC (d 1931, s of Antony Gibbs, of the banking family and 2nd cousin of 4 Baron Aldenham), and his 2 w, Hon Ursula Mary Lawley, OBE, ARC (d 1979), el da of 6 and last Baron Wenlock, GCSI, GCIE, KCMG (for whom Queen Mary was Sponsor); *b* 16 May 1928; *Educ* Eton, Sandhurst; *Heir* bro, Hon Sir Eustace Gibbs; KCVO, CMG; *Career* Maj N Somerset and Bristol Yeo, Lt Coldstream Gds; chm N Somerset Cons Assoc 1970-74; govr and chm St Katherine's Comprehensive Sch 1974-81, govr Avon County Scout Assoc 1976-; fell Woodard Corpn and Woodard Schs (Western Div) Ltd 1980-; landowner; *Recreations* shooting; *Clubs* RAC, Cavalry and Guards, Clifton (Bristol); *Style*— The Rt Hon the Lord Wraxall, DL; Tyntesfield, Wraxall, Bristol, Avon BS19 1NU (☎ 0275 46223; Estate Office 462021)

WRAXALL, Lady; Irmgard Wilhelmina Maria; da of Alois Larry Schnidrig, of Pratteln, Switzerland; *m* 1956, Sir Morville Wraxall, 8 Bt (d 1978); 2 s (9 Bt *qv*, Peter *qv*), 1 da (Sylvia b 1951); *Style*— Lady Wraxall

WRAY; *see*: Roberts-Wray

WRAY, Denis Gage; s of Capt Gerald Gage Wray (d 1956), and Mary Alice Elaine, *née* Todd (d 1976); *b* 21 May 1928; *Educ* Rossall Sch, Univ of Edinburgh (MB ChB), Univ of Liverpool (MCh Orth); *m* 23 March 1953, Jean, da of Thomas Henry Simpson (d 1967); 2 s (Peter b 1961, Brian b 1967), 2 da (Sheila b 1955, Carol b 1958); *Career* sr examiner in surgery Br Assoc of Occupational Therapists 1962-82, conslt orthopaedic surgn Stockport Health Authy 1965-89, pt/t conslt orthopaedic surgn in private practice 1968-; memb and sec Orthopaedic Engrg Sub Ctee Br Orthopaedic Assoc 1981-84, memb various ctees of BSI 1983-87, fell: Manchester Med Soc, Br Orthopaedic Assoc; FRCS (Ed); *Books* Journal of Trama (contrib, 1981), Journal of RCS Edinburgh (1982), Journal of Clinical Practice (1983); *Recreations* tennis, squash; *Style*— Denis Wray, Esq; 11 Clifford Rd, Poynton, Cheshire SK12 1HY (☎ 0625872537); 432 Buxton Rd, Stockport SK2 7JQ (☎ 061 483 9333)

WRAY, Prof Gordon Richard; s of Joseph Wray (d 1975), of Farnworth, Bolton, Lancs, and Letitia, *née* Jones (d 1978); *b* 30 Jan 1928; *Educ* pt/t Worsley and Bolton Tech Coll (ONC, HNC), Univ of Manchester (BSc, MSc, PhD), Loughborough Univ of Technol (DSc); *m* 20 Nov 1954, Dr Kathleen Wray, da of Harold Greenwood Senior (d 1984), of Rastrick, Brighouse, Yorks; 1 s (Vaughan Richard b 24 Oct 1959), 1 da (Amanda Diane b 19 July 1961); *Career* engrg apprentice Bolton Lancs 1943-49, Sir Walton Preston scholar Univ of Manchester 1949-52, devpt engr Platt Bros Ltd Manchester 1952-53, lectr in mechanichal engrg Bolton Tech Coll 1953-55, lectr in textile engrg UMIST 1955-66, prof (later head dept of Mechanical Engrg), Loughborough Univ of Technol 1970-88 (reader in mechanical engrg 1966-70); Fellowship of Engrg prof in the principles of engrg design and dir Engrg Design Inst; visiting prof Univ of California (Berkeley) 1977; memb: Dept of Industs Chief Scientist's Requirement Bd 1974-75, Interdisciplinary Bd CEI/CSTI 1978-83 (Brunel lectr Br Assoc Annual Meeting 1980), Ctee on Innovation SEFI Brussels 1980-82, Royal Soc Working Gp on Agric Engrg 1981-82, Applied Mechanics Ctee SERC 1982-85, Fellowship of Engrg Working Pty on Dept of Indust Requirement Bds 1982, Working Pty on Engrg Design SERC 1983, Sectional Ctee 4(i) 1986-, Ctee Engrg Profs Conf 1986-88, Mullard Award Ctee Royal Soc 1986-, Royal Soc/SERC Industl Fellowships Panel 1987-, Royal Soc Technol Activities Ctee 1989; chm Engrg Cncl/ Design Cncl Working Pty on Attaining Competences in Engrg Design (ACED Report) 1989-91; memb Cncl IMechE 1964-67 (chm Manipulation and Mechanichal Handling Machinery Gp 1969-71); IMechE: Viscount Weir Prize 1959, Water Arbitration Prize 1972, James Clayton Prize 1975, 76th Thomas Hawksley Meml lectr 1989; Warner Medal of the Textile Inst 1976, SG Brown Prize of the Royal Soc 1978; Hon MIED 1990; FRS 1986, FEng 1980, FIMechE 1973, FTI 1963, FRSA 1974; Euro Engr (Eur Ing) Paris 1987 (first recipient of title); *Books* Modern Yarn Production from Man-Made Fibres (1960), Modern Developments in Weaving Machinery (1961), An Introduction to the Study of Spinning (third edn 1962), Design or Decline: A National Em ergency? (1990); *Recreations* photography, fell walking, theatre, music, gardening, DIY; *Style*— Eur Ing Prof Gordon Wray, FRS; Director, Engineering Design Institute, Lougborough Univ of Technol, Loughborough, Leics LE11 3TU (☎ 0509 223175, fax 0509 268013, telex 34319)

WREFORD-BROWN, Capt Christopher Louis; DSO (1982); s of Louis Careler Wreford-Brown, of Devon, and Anne, *née* Ridgeway; *Educ* Rugby; *m* 29 March 1969, Jenny, da of John Lawrence Pingent, of Devon; 1 s (Paul b Sept 1972), 2 da (Julia b Feb 1970, Amanda b May 1976); *Career* joined RN 1963, joined submarine service 1969, qualified as navigating offr and princ warfare offr, Lt Cdr Co HMS Opossum 1976, 2 i/c HMS Courageous, staff 2 Submarine Sqdn, Cdr 1980, Nat Def Coll 1981; Co: HMS Dreadnought, HMS Conqueror, HMS Valiant; MOD, Capt 1986, Co HMS

Cornwall 1987, Capt 8 Frigate Sqdn 1988, Royal Coll of Def Studies 1989; Master Britannia Beagles; Freeman City of London 1988; FBIM 1988; *Recreations* hunting, gardening; *Style—* Capt Christopher Wreford-Brown, DSO

WREN, Dr John Josiah; s of Leslie Josiah Wren, of Hertford Heath, and Agnes Eva, *née* Sims; *b* 10 April 1933; *Educ* Hertford GS, Christ's Coll Cambridge (MA, PhD); *m* 13 April 1955, Beryl Wilson (d 1980), da of Geoffrey Alfred Victor Brampton (d 1955), of Sudbury, Suffolk; 2 s (Hugh Josiah b 1959, Colin John b 1962), 1 da (Catherine b 1961); *Career* res fell Calif Inst of Technol 1956-58, J Lyons & Co 1959-69 (various appts incl central res mangr), Grand Metropolitan plc 1969-86 (sr exec and dir of subsid cos), in consultancy 1986-89, gen sec Society of Chemical Industry 1989- (chm Cncl 1987-88); memb: Parly and Scientific Ctee, Civil Serv Final Selection Bd; tstee Catalyst Museum; memb: MAFF Steering Gp on Food Surveillance 1981-90, Food and Drink Indust Ctees, Euro Fedn of Biotechnology; FRSC 1965, CChem, FIFST 1966, MFC, MHCIMA 1984; *Books* Food Quality and Preference (co-ed, 1988), author of various pubns in sci and technol; *Recreations* listening to music, choral singing, walking; *Clubs* Glyndebourne Festival Soc; *Style—* Dr John Wren; SCI, 14-15 Belgrave Square, London SW1X 8PS (☎ 071 235 3681, fax 071 823 1698)

WRENBURY, 3 Baron (UK 1915); John Burton Buckley; s of 2 Baron Wrenbury Bryan Burton Buckley (d 1940), and Helen Baroness Wrenbury (d 1981), *née* Graham; *b* 18 June 1927; *Educ* Eton, King's Coll Cambridge (MA); *m* 1, 1956 (m dis 1961), Carolyn, da of Col Ian Burn-Murdoch, OBE; m 2, 1961, Penelope, da of Edward Dimond Fort, of Wilts; 1 s, 2 da (Hon Elizabeth Margaret (Mrs Andrew Macnaughton) b 1964, Hon Katherine Lucy b 1968); *Heir* s, Hon William Edward Buckley b 19 June 1966; *Career* slr 1952, dep legal advsr Nat Tst 1955-56, ptnr: Freshfields 1956-74, Thomson Snell & Passmore 1974-90; landowner (390 acres); ordained deacon 1990; *Clubs* Oriental; *Style—* The Rev The Rt Hon Lord Wrenbury; Oldcastle, Dallington, Heathfield, Sussex TN21 9JP (☎ 0435 0435 830400)

WREY, Benjamin Harold Bourchier; s of Maj Christopher Bourchier Wrey, TD (d 1976), and Ruth, *née* Bowden; *b* 6 May 1940; *Educ* Blundell's, Clare Coll Cambridge (MA); *m* 19 Feb 1970, (Anne) Christine Aubrey, da of Col Christopher B Stephenson (d 1970); 1 da (Tanya b 20 Jan 1971); *Career* Pensions Advsy Dept Legal & Gen Assur Soc Ltd 1963-66, investmt analyst Hambros Bank Ltd 1966-69, gp investmt dir Henderson Admin Gp plc 1990 (joined 1969, appt to Bd 1971, jt md 1981-82, dep chm 1983); *Recreations* shooting, fishing, photography; *Clubs* Boodle's, City of London, Hurlingham; *Style—* Benjamin Wrey, Esq; Henderson Administration Group plc, 3 Finsbury Ave, London EC2M 2PA (☎ 071 638 5757, fax 071 337 5742, telex 884616)

WREY, Sir (Castel Richard) Bourchier; 14th Bt (E 1628), of Trebitch, Cornwall; s of Edward Castell Wrey (d 1933), and n of Rev Sir Albany Bourchier Sherard Wrey, 13 Bt, JP, sometime rural dean Barnstaple (d 1948). The forename Bourchier has been used, in one position or other, by every Wrey Baronet from, 3 Bt, whose m was Lady Anne Bourchier da and co heir of 4 Earl of Bath on whose d Baronies of Fitzwarin and Daubeny fell into abeyance, 11 Bt, petitioned the House of Lords for the termination of the abeyance in 1914; *b* 27 March 1903; *Educ* Oundle; *m* 15 March 1947, Sybil Mabel Alice, er da of Dr George Lubke, of Durban, S Africa; 2 s; *Heir* s, George Richard Bourchier Wrey; *Career* served 1939-40 in France as 2 Lt RASC; joined RN 1940, Lt RNVR 1942; *Clubs* Natal; *Style—* Sir Bourchier Wrey, Bt; 511 Currie Road, Durban, S Africa

WREY, Lady Caroline Janet; *née* Lindesay-Bethune; only da of 15 Earl of Lindsay (d 1989), by his 1 w, Mary Clare, *née* Douglas-Scott-Montagu (*see* Hon Mrs Horn); *b* 7 July 1957; *Educ* West Heath, Sevenoaks Kent; *m* 1 Aug 1981, George Richard Bourchier Wrey, *qv*, el s of Sir Bourchier Wrey 14 Bt, *qv*; 2 s (Harry b 1984, another b 1991), 1 da (b 1987); *Career* qualified teacher and curtain designer; *Style—* The Lady Caroline Wrey; 60 The Chase, SW4 (☎ 071 622 6625); Hollamoor Farm, Tawstock, Barnstaple, N Devon (☎ 0271 73466)

WREY, George Richard Bourchier; s and h of Sir Bourchier Wrey, 14 Bt, *qv*; *b* 2 Oct 1948; *Educ* Eton; *m* 1 Aug 1981, Lady Caroline Janet Lindesay-Bethune, da of 15 Earl of Lindsay, *qv*; 2 s (Harry b 1984), 1 da (Rachel b 1987); *Career* farmer; *Recreations* shooting; *Clubs* Turf; *Style—* George Wrey Esq; 60 The Chase, London SW4 0NH (☎ 071 622 6625); Hollamoor Farm, Tawstock, Barnstaple, N Devon (☎ 0271 73466)

WRIGGLESWORTH, Sir Ian William; s of Edward Wrigglesworth, of Stockton on Tees; *b* 8 Dec 1939; *Educ* Stockton GS, Stockton Billingham Tech Coll, Coll of St Mark and St John Chelsea; *m* 1968, Patricia Susan, da of Hugh L Truscott; 2 s, 1 da; *Career* PA to Sir Ronald Gould as gen sec NUT 1966-68, head Co-op Pty Res Dept 1968-70, press and pub affrs mangr Nat Giro 1970-74; MP (Lab and Co-op 1974-81, SDP 1981-87) Thornaby, Teesside Feb 1974-83, Stockton South 1983-87; PPS: to Alec Lyon when Min of State Home Office 1974, to Roy Jenkins when Home Sec 1974-76, sec Manifesto Gp within Lab Party 1976-81, vice chm Lab Econ Fin and Taxation Assoc 1976-81, oppn spokesman Civil Service 1979-81, SDP home affrs spokesman Nov 1982-May 1983, SDP econ and industl affrs spokesman 1983-87, Alliance Trade and Indust Spokesman 1987; dep chm John Livingston & Sons Ltd; dir: CIT Research Ltd, Med Div Smiths Industries plc; kt 1991; *Recreations* walking, water sports, music; *Clubs* IOD, Reform; *Style—* Sir Ian Wrigglesworth; 24 Buckingham Gate, London SW1E 6LB (☎ 071 828 8323)

WRIGHT, Adela Lucia Lyndon; da of Maj Frederick Edward Gordon Stanford (d 1958), of Carshalton, Surrey, and Peggy Lucy, *née* Chivers (d 1955); *b* 23 Jan 1924; *Educ* St Michael's Sch, Regent St Poly (Dip Arch); *m* 2 July 1949, George Broughton Wright, s of Joseph William Wright (d 1960), of Carshalton, Surrey; 1 s (Timothy Lyndon b 1951), 2 da (Hilary Teresa b 1954, Antonia Sophie b 1962); *Career* architectural asst: Historic Bldgs Div Miny of Works 1946-48, Architects Div Oxford CC 1948-49, Hulme Chadwick 1949-52; private practice 1952-75, tech advsr Soc for the Protection of Ancient Bldgs 1980; memb Worshipful Co of Gardeners; DipConservation 1980; ARIBA 1947; *Books* Craft Techniques for Traditional Buildings (1990); *Recreations* archaeology, travelling; *Style—* Mrs Adela Wright; The Walled Garden, 118 Kippington Rd, Sevenoaks, Kent TN13 2LN (☎ 0732 451590)

WRIGHT, Master Alan John; s of Rev Henry George Wright, MA (d 1963), and Winifred Annie *née* Watson; *b* 21 April 1925; *Educ* St Olave's and St Saviour's GS Southwark, Keble Coll Oxford (MA); *m* 20 Sept 1952, Alma Beatrice, da of Keith Payne Ridding (d 1961); 2 s (Keith b 1955, Matthew b 1962), 1 da (Fiona b 1958); *Career* RAF serv: India, Burma, China 1943-46; slr Shaen Roscoe and Co 1952-71, legal advsr TUC 1955-71, a Master of the Supreme Ct (Supreme Ct taxing office) 1972-91; Anglican lay reader 1989; *Recreations* Germanic studies, walking, travel, youth work; *Style—* Master Wright; 21 Brockley Park, Forest Hill, London SE23 (☎ 081 690 1929)

WRIGHT, Alfred William Fraser (Tim); s of Wilfred Victor Wright (d 1951), of Edinburgh, and Christina, *née* Fraser (d 1949); *b* 22 Dec 1936; *Educ* George Watsons Coll Edinburgh; *Career* articled clerk then chartered accountant Martin Currie & Co Edinburgh (specialising in investmt mgmnt), asst investmt mangr London and NY Investment Co 1961; Williams de Broe: joined 1967, ptnr 1968, dir 1970-; MICAS 1960; *Recreations* golf, shooting, theatre, opera; *Clubs* New (Edinburgh), Hon Co of Edinburgh Golfers; *Style—* Tim Wright, Esq; Williams de Broe plc, 6 Broadgate, London EC2M 2RP (☎ 071 588 7511, fax 071 588 8860)

WRIGHT, Hon Mrs (Alison Elizabeth); *née* Franks; da of Baron Franks (Life Peer); *b* 1945; *m* 1973, Stanley Harris Wright; *Style—* The Hon Mrs Wright; 6 Holly Place, Holly Walk, Hampstead, London NW3 (☎ 071 435 0237)

WRIGHT, Allan Grant; s of John Johnstone Wright (d 1984), and Mary, *née* Armstrong; *b* 11 Aug 1944; *Educ* Wallace Hall Acad, West of Scot Coll of Agric (SDA); *m* 26 March 1965, Ann Campbell, da of Thomas Savage (d 1944); 1 s (Grant b 1970), 1 da (Shelley b 1967); *Career* reporter The Scottish Farmer 1964-67, dep agric ed The Glasgow Herald 1967-73, agric ed The Press and Journal 1973-79, with BBC 1979-89 (agric ed 1984-89), freelance journalist and PR conslt 1989-; FGAJ 1987, ARAgS 1989; *Style—* Allan Wright, Esq; Halfacre, The Shotts, Thornhill, Dumfriesshire DG3 5JT (☎ 0848 31653, fax 0848 31640)

WRIGHT, (William) Allen; s of William Wright, MBE (d 1972), of Edinburgh, and Agnes Isabel May (d 1980); *b* 22 Feb 1932; *Educ* George Watson's Coll Edinburgh; *m* 9 Feb 1957, Eleanor Brunton, da of George Walker Wallace (d 1949), of Edinburgh; 3 da (Caroline b 1958, Hazel b 1960, Angela b 1962); *Career* Nat Serv RTR 1950-52; drama critic and arts ed The Scotsman 1965- (film critic 1956-65); *Books* J M Barrie: Glamour of Twilight (1976); *Recreations* golf; *Style—* Allen Wright, Esq; The Scotsman, 20 North Bridge, Edinburgh EH1 1YT (☎ 031 225 2468, fax 031 226 7420)

WRIGHT, Andrew Matthew; s of William Robert Taylor Wright, of Baillieston, Glasgow, and Marna, *née* Hood; *b* 21 Dec 1973; *Educ* St Ambrose HS Coatbridge; *Career* professional footballer Heart of Midlothian 1989-; Celtic Boy's Club 1984-88, Tynecastle Boy's Club 1988-89; Scotland: 15 under 15 caps, 20 under 16 caps, 2 under 18 caps; winner Scot Amateur Cup Celtic Boys 1986; *Recreations* swimming, pop music; *Style—* Andrew Wright, Esq; 69 South Scott St, Baillieston, Glasgow G69 7JL (☎ 041 771 6168); Heart of Midlothian FC, Tynecastle Park, Gorgie Rd, Edinburgh EH11 2NL (☎ 031 337 6132)

WRIGHT, Andrew Paul Kilding; s of Harold Maurice Wright (d 1983), and Eileen Mary, *née* Kilding; *b* 11 Feb 1947; *Educ* Queen Mary's GS Walsall, Univ of Liverpool (BArch); *m* 10 Oct 1970, Jean Patricia, da of Alfred John Cross; 1 s (Samuel b 1976), 2 da (Hannah b 1973, Sarah b 1985); *Career* architect; Sir Basil Spence Glover & Ferguson 1973-78, assoc Law & Dunbar Nasmith 1978-81, ptnr Law & Dunbar Nasmith Ptnrship 1981-; Inverness Architectural Assoc: memb Cncl 1981-, vice pres 1985, pres 1986-88; memb: Farm Buildings Assoc 1985-, RIBA Cncl 1988-, Ecclesiastical Surveyors and Architects Assoc 1989-; vice pres Royal Incorporation of Architects in Scotland 1986-88 (memb Cncl 1986-), diocesan architect Dio of Moray Ross and Caithness 1988-; memb RIBA, FRIAS; *Recreations* music, fishing; *Clubs* Highland; *Style—* Andrew P K Wright, Esq; Craiglen, Sanquhar Road, Forres, Moray W36 ODG (☎ 0309 72749); 130 High Street, Forres, Moray (☎ 0309 73221, fax 0309 76397)

WRIGHT, Anthony John; s of Harry Wright (d 1972), and Flora Amelia, *née* Alexander; *b* 16 Feb 1939; *Educ* Merchant Taylors'; *m* 29 June 1968, Jane (d 1989), da of George Hubbard Sumner (d 1962); 1 s (John b 1983), 3 da (Elizabeth b 1969, Katherine b 1971, Sarah b 1976); *Career* Nat Serv Chinese linguist RAF 1958-60; dir JH Little Metals 1960-73, Derby & Co Ltd Philip Bros Ltd 1984-86 (joined 1973), sr vice pres Metallgesellschaft Corpn 1986-; hon ed Old Merchant Taylors' Soc News Sheet; Freeman City of London 1967, Liveryman Merchant Taylors' Co 1972; *Recreations* golf, cricket, reading, watching rugby; *Clubs* Oriental, Pesartes, Moor Park Golf, Old Merchant Taylors' Soc; *Style—* Anthony Wright, Esq; The Orchard, Common Rd, Chorleywood, Herts WD3 5LT (☎ 09278 2937); Metallgesellschaft Corp, 1 Albemarle St, London W1X 3HF (☎ 071 491 1669, fax 071 491 0135, telex 262872)

WRIGHT, Anthony John (Tony); s of Michael David Wright, of Stevenage, Hertfordshire, and Patricia, *née* Bunyan; *Educ* Alleyne's Sch Stevenage; *m* 21 Dec 1986, Rachel Ann, da of Brian Benton; 1 da (Hannah Jean b 3 April 1988); *Career* cricketer; played: Hertfordshire U15 XI 1977, S of England U15 XI 1977; Gloucestershire CCC: debut 1982, 150 matches to date, vice capt 1989, capt 1990-, 1000 runs in a season 3 times, 7000 runs and 120 catches; Port Melbourne CC, 1980-81, 1984-85, 1985-86, 1989-90; *Recreations* golf, horseracing, travel; *Style—* Tony Wright, Esq; 151 Sefton Park Road, St Andrews, Bristol, Avon BS7 9AN (☎ 0272 343494); Gloucestershire CCC, County Ground, Nevil Rd, Bristol, Avon BS7 9EJ (☎ 0272 245216, fax 0272 241193)

WRIGHT, Brig Antony Peter (Tony); MBE (1974); s of Capt Dennis Gordon Wright (ka France 1944), and Vera Rose Jean, *née* Mills; *b* 13 Jan 1939; *Educ* Blundell's RMA Sandhurst; *m* 20 June 1964, Ann Jennifer, da of Harry Thomas Lucas, of Hedges, 80 St Martin's Green, Trimley St Martin, nr Felixtowe, Suffolk; 1 s (Jeremy Gordon b 10 Sept 1968), 2 da (Nicola Louise b 14 May 1970, Sally Victoria b 4 Oct 1974); *Career* cmmnd Sherwood Foresters 1958, RMCS Div II 1970, Staff Coll 1971, cmd 1 WFR 1979-82, Col project mangr Inf Weapons 1986-88, vice pres (Army), Brig Ordnance Bd 1988-89, ret 1989; mktg dir SDE Ltd 1989-91, sec/mangr Ipswich Golf Club 1991-; *Recreations* golf, mountain walking, gardening; *Style—* Brigadier Tony Wright, MBE; Ipswich Golf Club, Purdis Heath, Ipswich IP3 8UQ (☎ 0473 728941)

WRIGHT, Barbara Janet; da of Lt John Sutherland, of Bredhurst, Gillingham, Kent, and Betty Dorothy Gladys, *née* Durrant; *b* 16 March 1955; *Educ* Romford County HS for Girls, Univ of Sheffield (LLB); *m* 23 Oct 1981, Lynton Wright, s of John (Jack) Wright of Stockport, Cheshire; *Career* asst slr Gill Turner and Tucker Maidstone 1979-80 (articled clerk 1977-79); asst slr Cripps Harries Hall and Co: Tunbridge Wells 1980-82, Crowborough 1982-84; Walkers 1984-87 (ptnr from 1986), ptnr Thomson Snell and Passmore Tunbridge Wells 1987-; hon arbitrator: Tunbridge Wells 1987-, Tunbridge Wells Equitable Friendly Soc, 1987-; memb Kent Archaeological Soc; memb Law Soc 1979; *Style—* Mrs Barbara Wright; 3 Lonsdale Gardens, Tunbridge Wells, Kent (☎ 0892 510000, telex 95194 Tsan DPG, fax 0892 549884)

WRIGHT, Bernard Bucknall; s of Clifford Joseph Wright (d 1963), and Catherine Mary, *née* Bucknall (d 1939); *b* 22 Dec 1933; *Educ* West Park GS St Helen's, Univ of Liverpool (LLB); *m* 23 May 1964, Jennifer, da of George Richard Cockram; 5 s (Simon Andrew b 15 Feb 1965, Paul Nicholas b 31 May 1966, Christopher David b 8 Feb 1968, Michael Jonathan b 11 Jan 1970, Nicholas James b 15 June 1980); *Career* Nat Serv educn offr RAF 1957-59; ptnr Cuff Roberts & Co Liverpool 1960- (articled clerk 1954-57); memb Law Soc 1959; Law Soc Liverpool: memb 1959, hon sec 1979-82, pres 1983-; *Recreations* golf, skiing, interest in most sports especially rugby, food and wine; *Clubs* New Brighton Rugby Union (former pres), Heswall Squash, Heswall Golf (former capt), Liverpool Artists; *Style—* Bernard Wright, Esq; Cuff Roberts North Kirk, 25 Castle St, Liverpool L2 4TD (☎ 051 227 4181, fax 051 227 5955)

WRIGHT, Brian Alfred; s of Alexander Wright (d 1947), and Elizabeth, *née* Parfitt (d 1963); *b* 6 Feb 1930; *m* 17 May 1952, Sheila Marion, da of Edward William Wood (d 1965); 2 da (Lesley b 1954, Stephanie b 1957); *Career* actuary; gen mangr Sun Alliance Insur Gp 1981 (dir 1984), gp exec dir Sun Alliance Gp plc 1989, dep chm LAUTRO 1986-89; FIA; *Recreations* golf, gardening, music; *Style—* Brian Wright, Esq; Fairways, Colley Manor Drive, Reigate, Surrey RH2 9JS (☎ 0737 222 046); Sun Alliance Gp plc, 1 Bartholomew Lane, London EC2N 2AB (☎ 071 588 2345, fax 071 638 3728)

WRIGHT, (George) Brian; s of George Wright (d 1945), and Martha, *née* Dundee; *b* 9 April 1939; *Educ* Masonic Boys' Sch Dublin, Trinity Coll Dublin (MA, HDipEd); *m* 6 July 1963, Joyce Avril Frances, da of Rev George Camier (d 1946); 2 s (David b 1964, Simon b 1966); *Career* sch master 1961-67, local govt admin 1967-69; BBC: educn offr 1969-81, chief educn offr 1981-89, currently head of educnl broadcasting servs; memb RTS; *Books* How Britain Earns Its Living (1978); *Recreations* completing crosswords, collecting stamps and good wine; *Clubs* BBC; *Style*— Brian Wright, Esq; 67 Western Rd, Ealing, London W5 5DT (☎ 081 840 3758); BBC, Villiers House, The Broadway, London W5 2PA (☎ 081 991 8053, fax 081 567 9356)

WRIGHT, Cdr Brian Harry; RD; s of Lt Cdr Harry Wright, RNVR (d 1982), and Lilian, *née* James; *b* 15 July 1933; *Educ* King's Coll London (BSc, BCom); *m* 1, 4 Aug 1955 (m dis 1962), Virginia Rose Leslie, da of Col Ion David Leslie Beath, CBE, TD; 2 s (Jeremy b 1956, Peter b 1958); m 2, 12 Dec 1966, Coralie Mary (d 1988), da of Sir Frances Spencer Portal, 5 Bt, DL; 1 s (Alexander b 1968), 1 da (Rowena b 1970); m 3, 9 Nov 1990, Mrs Yvonne Walsh-Taylor, of Andover, Hants; *Career* Nat Serv Sub Lt RNVR 1953-55, eastern area mangr English Electric Co Ltd (mangr Bombay Branch 1959, dep md India 1961), chm and md Zyax plc, chm Hovair Int plc, chm Power Lift Ltd, chm Avia Lift Ltd; Freeman City of London 1969, Liveryman Worshipful Co of Clothworkers 1972; CEng, FIEE, FIMH; *Recreations* sailing, skiing, shooting; *Clubs* Royal Yacht Sqdn, RORC Naval, RNVR Yacht; *Style*— Cdr Brian H Wright, RD, RNR; The Corner House, Ecchinswell, Hampshire RG15 8TT (☎ 0635 298 277); AV2-402 Anzere Valais Switzerland; Hovair Int plc, Ampere Rd, Newbury, Berks (☎ 0635 49525, fax 0635 37949, car 0836 217325, telex 847015 HOVAIR G)

WRIGHT, Christopher Julian; s of Lt Cdr Edward Joseph Wright, of York, and Doreen Lillian, *née* Askew; *b* 1 Jan 1947; *Educ* Ampleforth, Univ of St Andrews (MA); *m* 20 May 1972, Pamela Wendy, da of Geoffrey Denis Adamson (d 1959), of Dorset; 1 da (Alexandra b 1972); *Career* Lt RN; serving: HMS Pembroke, HMS Fishgard, RNAS Yeovilton; slr; snr ptnr Christopher Wright & Co Slrs N Yorks; chm Mgmnt Ctee Richmond CAB; *Recreations* beagling, riding, theatre, racing; *Clubs* English Speaking Union, Law Soc; *Style*— Christopher J Wright, Esq; The Georgian House, Burneston, nr Bedale, N Yorkshire (☎ 0845 567314); 22 Richmond Rd, Catterick Garrison, N Yorkshire (☎ 0748 832431)

WRIGHT, Christopher Norman; s of Walter Reginald Wright, of 3 Butts Lane, Tattersall, Lincs, and Edna May, *née* Corden; *b* 7 Sept 1944; *Educ* King Edward VI GS Louth Lincs, Univ of Manchester (BA), Manchester Business Sch; *m* 15 March 1972, Carolyn Rochelle (Chelle), da of Lloyd B Nelson, of California, USA; 2 s (Timothy b 1973, Thomas b 1974), 1 da (Chloe b 1978); *Career* operator Univ and Coll Booking Agency Manchester 1965-67, formed Ellis Wright Agency (with Terry Ellis) 1967, changed name to Chrysalis and moved into records and music publishing 1968 (became int with offices in London, NYC, Los Angeles, Munich), chm Chrysalis (now Chrysalis plc) 1985-; *Recreations* tennis, bridge, breeding racehorses; *Clubs* Oriental, Turf; *Style*— Christopher Wright, Esq; Chrysalis Group plc, The Chrysalis Building, Bramley Road, London W10 6SP (☎ 071 221 2213)

WRIGHT, Claud William; CB (1969); s of Horace Vipan Wright (d 1945), of E Yorks, and Catherine Margaret, *née* Sales (d 1963); *b* 9 Jan 1917; *Educ* Charterhouse, ChCh Oxford (MA); *m* 1947, Alison Violet, da of John Jeffrey Readman, of Dumfries; 1 s (Crispin), 4 da (Dione, Daphne, Ianthe, Oenone); *Career* WO 1939, Private Essex Regt 1940, 2 Lt KRRC 1940, WO 1942-45, GSO 2; joined MOD 1947, asst under sec (Pol) 1961-66, asst under sec (P Air) 1966-68, dep under sec (Air) 1968-71, dep sec Arts and Libraries Dept of Educn and Sci 1971-76, res fell Wolfson Coll Oxford 1977-83; fil Dr Lc Univ of Uppsala 1979, hon DSc Univ of Hull 1987; Lyell Fund 1947, RH Worth prize 1958, Prestwich medal Geological Soc London 1987, Foulerton award Geologists Assoc 1955, Phillips medal Yorks Geological Soc 1976, Strimple award Galeontological Soc of America 1988; author of numerous papers on geological, palaeontological and archaeological subjects; *Books* Monographs on fossil crabs (with J S H Collins, 1972), ammonites of the middle chalk (with W J Kennedy, 1981), ammonites of the lower chalk (with W J Kennedy, 1984-91), Cretaceous Sea-Urchins (with A B Smith, 1990-); *Recreations* archaeology, botany, palaeontology; *Clubs* Athenaeum; *Style*— C W Wright, Esq, CB; Old Rectory, Seaborough, Beaminster, Dorset DT8 3QY (☎ 0308 68426)

WRIGHT, (Idonea) Daphne; da of Claud William Wright, of Dorset, and Alison Violet, *née* Readman; *b* 19 May 1951; *Educ* St Mary's Wantage; *Career* sec and editorial asst Chatto & Windus 1976-77, ed Hutchinson 1977-83, editorial dir Quartet 1983-84, Bellew Publish 1984-86; *Books* The Distant Kingdom (1987), The Longest Winter (1989), The Parrot Cage (1990), Never Such Innocence (1991); As Natasha Cooper: Festering Lilies (1990), Poison Flowers (1991); winner Tony Godwin Meml Tst award 1980; memb: Crime Writers Assoc 1989, Soc of Authors 1990; *Recreations* reading, entertaining, tennis; *Style*— Ms Daphne Wright; c/o Jennifer Kavanagh, 39 Camden Park Rd, London NW1 9AX (☎ 071 482 3676, fax 071 482 6684)

WRIGHT, David Anthony; s of George Henry Wright, of Hornsea East Yorks, and Theresa, *née* Rooke; *b* 21 March 1949; *Educ* Marist Coll Hull, Sidney Sussex Coll Cambridge (MA, memb cast Oxford and Cambridge Shakespeare Co Tour of USA 1969-70 directed by Jonathan Miller); *m* 1979, Susan Iris Benson, da of William F Benson, of Salford Lancs; 1 s (Daniel), 1 da (Fernanda Maria); *Career* freelance documentary film-maker in TV 1979-; films incl: The Christians, This England, The Pennines: A Writers Notebook, Years of Lightning, N Division, 617: Last Days of a Vulcan Squadron, Village Earth, In the Footsteps of The Incas, Learning How the Maasai See, The Tribe That's Fighting Back, Think Dream Laugh, The World: A Television History, Last Voyage of The Arctic Raider, Abbeystead - The Aftermath, Akong and The Big Shrine Room, Bellamy's Bugle; set up own co 54th Parallel 1988; films: The Heat is On - The Making of Miss Saigon, Under The Sacred Bo Tree, Work in Progress; *Recreations* travel, walking, reading, swimming, chopping logs; *Clubs* The Sloane; *Style*— David Wright, Esq; Wood Hall, Old Ellerby, Hull HU11 5AJ (☎ 0482 811265); 54th Parallel Productions, Wood Hall, Old Ellerby, Hull HU11 5AJ (☎ 0482 811265, fax 0482 815534)

WRIGHT, David Frederick; s of Harry George Durie Wright (d 1989), of St Annes on Sea, Lancs, and Dorothy Emily, *née* Forster (d 1986); *b* 2 Oct 1937; *Educ* Bec Sch London SW17, Christ's Coll Cambridge (MA), Lincoln Coll Oxford; *m* Anne-Marie, da of George MacDonald, OBE, of Edinburgh; 1 s (Andrew b 1967), 1 da (Jennifer b 1970); *Career* dean of Faculty of Divinity Univ of Edinburgh 1988- (lectr in ecclesiastical history 1964-73, sr lectr 1973, memb Univ Ct 1984-87); memb: Cncl of Mgmnt Keston Coll Kent, Cncl of Scot Church History Soc, Bd Nat Bible Soc of Scot; chm Tyndale Fellowship for biblical and theol res, Praesidium Int Congress on Calvin res; memb: Assoc Int d'études Patristiques, N American Patristics Soc, Ecclesiastical History Soc; *Books* Common Places of Martin Bucer (1972), Essays in Evangelical Social Ethics (ed 1978), New Dictionary of Theology (jt ed 1988), Bible in Scottish Life and Literature (ed 1988), Chosen by God: Mary in Evangelical Perspective (ed 1989); *Recreations* walking, gardening; *Style*— David Wright, Esq; 5 Lockharton Gardens, Edinburgh EH14 1AU (☎ 031 443 1001); New College, Mound Place, Edinburgh EH1 2LU (☎ 031 225 8400, fax 031 220 0952, telex 727442 UNIVED G)

WRIGHT, David John; LVO (1990); s of John Frank Wright, of Wolverhampton; *b* 16 June 1944; *Educ* Wolverhampton GS, Peterhouse Cambridge; *m* 3 Feb 1968, Sally Ann Dodkin; 1 s (Nicholas b 1970), 1 da (Laura b 1973); *Career* HM Dip Serv: third sec 1966, third later second sec Tokyo 1966, second later first sec FCO 1972, ENA Paris 1975, first sec Paris 1976, private sec to Sec of Cabinet 1980, cnsllr (econ) Tokyo 1982, head of Personnel Servs Dept FCO 1985, dep private sec to HRH The Prince of Wales 1988-90; ambass Seoul 1990-; *Recreations* running, cooking, military history; *Style*— David J Wright, Esq, LVO; Foreign and Commonwealth Office, King Charles Street, London SW1A 2AH

WRIGHT, David John Murray; s of Gordon Alfred Wright (d 1957), of Johannesburg, SA, and Jean Murray Wright (d 1983); *b* 23 Feb 1920; *Educ* Northampton Sch for the Deaf, Oriel Coll Oxford (MA); *m* 1, 6 Oct 1951, Phillipa (d 1985), da of George Reid (d 1964), of Grassington, NZ; m 2, 13 March 1987, Agnes Mary, *née* Ryan; *Career* Gregory fell in lit Univ of Leeds 1965-67; ed: Nimbus 1955-56, X Magazine 1959-62; author, poet and translator; FRSL 1967; *Books* Poems (1948), Moral Stories (1954), Monologue of a Deaf Man (1958), Roy Campbell (1960), Nerve Ends (1969), Deafness, a Personal Account (1969), A South African Album (1975), A View of the North (1976), To the Gods the Shades, New and Collected Poems (1976), Metrical Observations (1980), Selected Poems (1989), Elegies (1990); translations: Beowulf 1957, The Canterbury Tales (prose version 1964, verse version 1985); *Style*— David Wright, Esq; c/o A D Peters Ltd, 5th Floor, The Chambers, Chelsea Harbour, Lots Rd, London SW10

WRIGHT, Dr David Julian Maurice; s of Herschel Wright (d 1982), and Ann, *née* Hammerman; *b* 12 May 1937; *Educ* Univ of London (MB BS, MD); *m* Rosalind, da of Alfred Kerstein; 3 da (Mandy, Pandy, Candy); *Career* reader in microbiology Charing Cross Hosp and Westminster Med Sch 1982 (conslt 1974), dir Lyme Diagnostic Serv, temp advsr WHO; author of numerous scientific papers on lepresy, syphilis, septic shock and Lyme disease; MRCPath 1982; *Books* Immunology of Sexually Transmitted Diseases (1988); *Recreations* eating, dreaming, televising and if possible all three at once; *Clubs* Willesden Discussion Group; *Style*— Dr David Wright; Microbiology, Charing Cross Hospital, Fulham Palace Rd, London W6 8RF (☎ 081 846 7268, fax 081 846 7261)

WRIGHT, Dr David Stephen; s of Edward Alfred Wright (d 1943), and Winifred May, *née* Oliver; *b* 4 Aug 1935; *Educ* Epsom Coll, Bart's (MB BS, MSc, DPH, DIH); *m* 19 Feb 1966, Caroline Auza, da of George William Black (d 1987), of Leeds; 2 s (Mark b 1967, Adam b 1969), 1 da (Alexandra b 1972); *Career* RN 1960-85 (ret with rank of Surgn Capt, final appt prof of naval occupational med and dir of health); head BP Group Occupational Health Centre 1985-, CMO BP 1989-; BMA: chm Armed Forces Ctee 1985-88, memb Cncl 1985-88; vice-dean Faculty of Occupational Med RCP; Freeman City of London 1982, Liveryman Worshipful Soc of Apothecaries 1982; memb: Soc of Occupational Med, BMA; FFOM, FRCP, FRSM; OStJ 1984; *Recreations* walking, gardening; *Style*— Dr David Wright; BP Group Occupational Health Centre, 10 Occam Rd, Surrey Research Park, Guildford GU2 5YQ (☎ 0483 500200, fax 0483 500 237)

WRIGHT, David William; s of William Richard Douglas Wright of Whitstable, Kent, and Doris Jane, *née* Arnold; *b* 2 May 1942; *Educ* Kent Coll Canterbury, Univ of Edinburgh (MA); *m* 23 Sept 1967, Barbara Rita, da of Gerald Gardiner (d 1973); 1 s (Oliver b 1971), 2 da (Annabel b 1973, Eleanor b 1978); *Career* called to the Bar Lincoln's Inn; posts in various cos 1968-76; co sec: Coates Bros plc 1979-84, First Leisure Corporation plc 1984-; vice pres Royal Tunbridge Wells Civic Soc; Freeman City of London 1983, Liveryman Worshipful Co of Spectaclemakers 1983; FCIS 1977; *Recreations* squash, tennis, theatre; *Style*— David Wright, Esq; Hollin House, Court Rd, Tunbridge Wells, Kent TN4 8EF (☎ 0892 32 943); 7 Soho St, London W1V 5FA (☎ 071 437 9727, fax 071 439 0088)

WRIGHT, Sir Denis Arthur Hepworth; GCMG (1971, KCMG 1961, CMG 1954); s of A E Wright (d 1949), and Margery Hepworth Chapman (d 1973); *b* 23 March 1911; *Educ* Brentwood Sch, St Edmund Hall Oxford; *m* 1939, Iona, da of Granville Craig (d 1941), of Bolney, Sussex; *Career* Diplomatic Serv; served (in commercial and consular capacities): Romania, Turkey, Yugoslavia, USA; asst under sec FO 1955-59, ambass Ethiopia 1959-62, asst under sec FO 1962, ambass Iran 1963-71 (formerly cnsllr 1954-55, chargé d'affaires 1953-54); non-exec dir: Shell Transport and Trading Co, Standard Chartered Bank, Mitchell Cotts Group 1971-81; govr Overseas Serv, Farnham Castle 1971-87; pres: Br Inst of Persian Studies 1978-87, The Iran Soc 1989-; hon fellow: St Edmund Hall 1972, St Antony's Coll Oxford 1976; *Books* Persia (with James Morris and Roger Wood, 1968), The English Amongst the Persians (1977), The Persians Amongst the English (1985); *Clubs* Travellers; *Style*— Sir Denis Wright, GCMG; Duck Bottom, Haddenham, Aylesbury, Bucks HP17 8AL (☎ 0844 291 086)

WRIGHT, Hon Mrs (Doreen Julia); *née* Wingfield; da of 8 Viscount Powerscourt, KP, MVO (d 1947), and Sybil, *née* Pleydell-Bouverie (d 1946); *b* 29 March 1904; *m* 10 Jan 1928, FitzHerbert Wright (d 1975), formerly 15/19 Hussars, s of Henry FitzHerbert Wright, JP, CA, of Yeldersley Hall, Derbys; 1 s, 3 da (of whom Susan Mary m 1, Maj Ronald Ivor Ferguson, and is mother of HRH The Duchess of York *qv*); *Style*— The Hon Mrs Wright; Vern Leaze, Calne, Wiltshire SN11 0JF

WRIGHT, Dorothy Ruth; da of Donald Drinkwater (d 1978), of Knight's Farm, Welland, Malvern, Worc, and Theodora Kathrine Ruth, *née* Boardman (d 1952); *b* 21 Aug 1940; *Educ* Malvern Girls' Sch Malvern Chase; *m* 1, Jan 1961 (m dis 1978), David Dodd, s of Raymond Dodd (d 1977); 1 s (Andrew Peter b 5 May 1966), 1 da (Sarah Jane b 30 July 1963); m 2, 20 July 1978, Colin Richard Marcus Wright; 1 da (Lucy Ruth b 17 Feb 1979); *Career* cadet nurse ENT 1956-58, gen nursing trg 1958-61, shop keeper 1964-67, sales offr supervisor 1969-71, sales rep 1971-74, sales mangr 1975-76; sales dir: own business 1977-86, Crawley Welding Supplies Ltd 1984- (only female sales dir in engrg in country); involved with Crawley Down Community Centre; memb: Student Nurses Assoc, Assoc of Welding Distributors; *Recreations* reading, tennis, darts, travel, history; *Style*— Mrs Dorothy Wright; Crawley Welding Supplies Ltd, 11/12 Royce Road, Fleming Way Industrial Centre, Crawley, W Sussex RH10 2NX (☎ 0292 529761, fax 0292 545081); 23 Tiltwood Drive, Crawley Down, West Sussex RH10 4DP (☎ 0342 715051)

WRIGHT, Edward Arnold; s of John Ernest Wright (d 1976), of Hornsey, and Alice Maud, *née* Arnold (d 1968); *b* 20 Nov 1926; *Educ* Tollington GS Muswell Hill; *Career* 52 RTR 1943-45, KDG 1945-47; 1962-70: sales dir Gothic Press Ltd, md Gothic Display Ltd, md Gothic "Studios" Ltd; chm and md Edward Wright Ltd 1970-; hon treas: Int Cncl for Bird Preservation BR section, Fauna and Flora Preservation Soc; former cncl memb Br Tst Ornithology; Freeman City of London 1980, Liveryman Worshipful Co of Gardeners 1980; *Recreations* squash, gardening, shooting; *Clubs* MCC, City Livery; *Style*— Edward Wright, Esq; Edward Wright Ltd, 5/11 Palfrey Place, London SW8 1PB (☎ 071 735 9535, fax 071 793 0967, mobile 0860 539 806)

WRIGHT, Sir Edward Maitland; s of Maitland Turner Wright (d 1943), and Kate, *née* Owen (d 1954); *b* 13 Feb 1906; *Educ* Jesus Coll and ChCh Oxford, Göttingen Univ (BA, MA, DPhil); *m* 1934, Elizabeth Phyllis (d 1987), da of Harry Percy Harris, JP (d 1952); 1 s (John); *Career* Flt-Lt RAFVR, Princ Sci Offr Air Miny Intelligence 1943-45; prof mathematics Univ of Aberdeen 1936-62, princ and vice chllr 1962-76, res fell 1976-; hon fell Jesus Coll Oxford 1963, Hon DSc Strathclyde; Hon LLD: St Andrews,

Pennsylvania, Aberdeen; Order of Polonia Restituta 1978; FRSE; kt 1977; *Books* Theory of Numbers (with GH Hardy, 1 edn 1938, 5 edn 1979); *Clubs* Caledonian (London); *Style*— Sir Edward Wright, FRSE; 16 Primrosehill Ave, Cults, Aberdeen (☎ 0224 861185)

WRIGHT, Hon Mrs (Emily Ann); *née* Hughes; o da of Baron Cledwyn of Penrhos, CH, PC (Life Peer), *qv*; *b* 1950; *m* 1976, Peter Wright; children; *Style*— The Hon Mrs Wright

WRIGHT, Geoffrey Norman; s of Walter Anthony Wright, MC (d 1939), of W Hartlepool, and Evelyn, *née* Blake (d 1979); *b* 14 April 1925; *Educ* W Hartlepool GS, Univ of Durham; *m* 16 July 1949, Jean, da of Charles Loy Mann (d 1941), of Bath; 3 s (Peter b 1951, Richard b 1954, David b 1957); *Career* groundcrew RAF 1944-47; sr master Bradford on Avon Sch Wilts 1970-76 (joined 1950, head English 1963-70), author; chm: Bradford on Avon Pres Soc 1964-73, Winsley Parish Cncl 1966-71, Dales Centre Nat Tst 1983-85, Herefords Marches Assoc Nat Tst 1988-; *Books* The East Riding (1976), Yorkshire Dales (1977), View of Wessex (1978), Stone Villages of Britain (1985), Roads and Trackways of Yorkshire Dales (1985), The Yorkshire Dales (1986), Road and Trackways of Wessex (1988), The Northumbrian Uplands (1989), The Cotswolds (1991); *Recreations* walking; *Style*— Geoffrey Wright, Esq; 6 Huntington Green, Ashford Carbonel, Ludlow, Shropshire SY8 4DN (☎ 058 474 692)

WRIGHT, Gerald; s of William Arthur Reginald (d 1967), and Olive Annie Neal Wright, of Bexleyheath, Kent; *b* 9 Sept 1935; *Educ* Monmouth, Queens' Coll Cambridge (MA); *m* 1959, Elizabeth Ann, da of Dr William Edward Harris (d 1974), of Llandaff; 3 s (Jeremy, Mathew, William); *Career* Nat Serv 2 Lt Welsh Regt 1954-56; dir Lintas London 1972-73, chm Lintas Scandinavia 1973-74, dep chm and md Lintas London 1974-80, md Thresher and Co Ltd 1980-81, mktg dir (UK) Whitbread & Co 1981-82 (chm Nat Sales Div 1982-83); chm and chief exec Lintas London 1983-89, regnl dir Eastern Europe, Austria, Switzerland and ME Lintas Worldwide 1989-; *Recreations* reading, opera, walking, jogging, rugby, cricket; *Clubs* Reform, Solus; *Style*— Gerald Wright, Esq; 25 Crown Lane, Chislehurst, Kent (☎ 081 467 7918); Lintas Worldwide, 84 Eccleston Square, London SW1; Lintas Worldwide Frankfurt, Zeppellin Allee 77, Frankfurt Am Main, Germany

WRIGHT, Gerald Sheldon; s of Roland Sheldon Malcolm Wright (d 1957), of Liverpool, and Grace, *née* Unwin (d 1961); *b* 24 July 1945; *Educ* Liverpool Coll of Art (City & Guilds Cert); *m* 26 Sept 1970, Anita, da of Newton Pratt; 2 da (Kelly Victoria b 18 Dec 1973, Sophie Rebecca b 12 May 1978); *Career* photographer; apprentice photographer Liverpool, asst photographer Birmingham and London, property asst Alexandra Theatre Birmingham, RAF photographer Brighton, staff photographer Grantham Journal; winner Rothmans Press Photographer of Year award; memb Master Photographers' Assoc; *Recreations* shooting, dog training, climbing, working in wood, theatre; *Style*— Gerald Wright, Esq; 137 Harlaxton Rd, Grantham, Lincs NG31 7AG (☎ 0476 67008)

WRIGHT, Hon Glyn David; s of Baron Wright of Ashton-under-Lyne, CBE (d 1974, Life Peer); bro of Hon Owen Wright *qv*; *b* 22 May 1940; *Educ* Ashton Tech; *m* 1965, May, da of George Frederick Alldridge; 2 da (Lisa, Stephanie); *Career* co dir; *Style*— The Hon Glyn Wright; 12 Brookfield Grove, Ashton-under-Lyne, Lancs OL6 6TL

WRIGHT, Graham; s of Edward George Wright (d 1988), and Doris, *née* Belsham; *b* 28 Dec 1944; *Educ* Archbishop Tenison's GS, Univ of Newcastle upon Tyne (BSc); *m* 29 March 1969, Susan Mary, da of Kenneth Atkinson, of Broxbourne; 1 s (James Kenneth Graham b 7 March 1972), 2 da (Katherine b 29 July 1970, Lucy b 7 Jan 1977); *Career* computer programmer Rolls Royce 1968-71, Int Commodities Clearing House 1971-87 (exec dir 1984-87), dep chief exec Int Petroleum Exchange 1987-; LIMA; *Recreations* golf, bridge; *Clubs* Porters Park; *Style*— Graham Wright, Esq; 8 Falstaff Gardens, St Albans, Herts (☎ 0727 670 88); IPE Ltd, Int House, 1 St Katherine's Way, London E1 9UN (☎ 071 481 0643, fax 071 481 8485, telex 927479)

WRIGHT, Graham John; s of Reginald Steer Wright (d 1973), and Phyllis Eileen, *née* Brooks (d 1987); *b* 18 May 1939; *Educ* St Clement Dane's GS; *m* 8 July 1961, Sandra Judith, da of Wilfred Sidney Chitty; 2 s (Andrew John b 17 Feb 1968, Adam John b 27 May 1971); *Career* actuarial student Law Union and Rock Insurance Co 1956; pensions mangr: Philips Electronics 1972-80 (asst pensions mangr 1963-72), Courtaulds plc 1980-; former tutor Inst of Actuaries, former Speaker Nat Assoc Pension Funds; chm: Purley Bury Tennis Club 1981-, Argonauts Club 1991-; regnl organiser (Surrey) of Occupational Pensions Advsy Serv; FIA 1967, FPMI 1977; *Recreations* tennis, bridge, football (supporter), chess, theatre; *Style*— Graham Wright, Esq; Courtaulds plc, 18 Hanover Square, London W1A 2BB (☎ 071 629 9080, fax 071 629 2586)

WRIGHT, Gregory Arthur; s of Ernest Arthur Wright, and Florence, *née* Swindells; *b* 1 Nov 1946; *Educ* Bournville Tech GS; *m* 21 Nov 1970, Christine, da of late Stanley Allen Tongue, of Northfield, Birmingham; 2 s (Dale b 1974, Adam b 1977), 1 da (Emma b 1982); *Career* CA; Josolyn Layton-Bennett 1969, ptnr Ernst & Whinney Birmingham 1980 (joined 1972), managing ptnr Ernst & Whinney Cardiff 1985 and Edinburgh 1988-89, ptnr Ernst & Young 1989-; FCA 1969; *Recreations* chess, cricket, gardening; *Style*— Gregory Wright, Esq; Little Fosters, 120 Whitehouse Rd, Barnton, Edinburgh EH4 6DH (☎ 031 339 4853); Ernst & Young, 17 Abercromby Place, Edinburgh EH3 6LT (☎ 031 556 8641, fax 031 556 5156, telex 72176 ERNSED)

WRIGHT, Hannah Margaret; da of F J K Cross (d 1950), and Eleanor, *née* Phillimore (d 1949); *b* 25 April 1908; *Educ* Downe House, St Hilda's Coll Oxford (BA); *m* 14 April 1936, Edmund Gordon Wright, s of The Rev Basil Wright; 1 s (Giles b 1945), 1 da (Juliet (Mrs Essen) b 1947); *Career* called to the Bar 1931; first woman memb Bar Cncl 1938; HM Cross; *Style*— Mrs Hannah Wright; The Quay House, Sidlesham, Chichester, W Sussex PO20 7LX (☎ 024 356 258)

WRIGHT, Hugh Raymond; s of Rev Raymond Blayney Wright (d 1980), of Macclesfield, and Alys Mary, *née* Hawksworth (d 1972); *b* 24 Aug 1938; *Educ* Kingswood Sch Bath, The Queen's Coll Oxford (MA); *m* 7 April 1962, Jillian Mary, da of Peter McIldowie Meiklejohn (d 1959), of Bedford; 3 s (Andrew b 1963, William b 1967, James b 1970); *Career* asst master Brentwood Sch 1961-64, head Classics Dept and housemaster Boyne House Cheltenham 1964-79; headmaster: Stockport GS 1979-85, Gresham's Sch Holt 1985-91; chief master King Edward's Sch Birmingham 1991-; chm Community Serv Sub Ctee HMC 1985-90 (chm NW dist 1983); memb: Panel Admty Interview Bd 1982-, ACCM 1987-; lay reader Dio of Chester and Norwich, treas Eastern Div ISIS 1988-90; FRSA 1984, AMMA; *Visual Publications incl* Film Strips on History of Church (1980); *Recreations* walking, ornithology, music, theatre; *Clubs* East India; *Style*— Hugh Wright, Esq

WRIGHT, Col Humphrey Bradshaw Mellor; s of Rev Ernest Hugh Wright (d 1939), and Violet Helen Frances, *née* Mellor (d 1917); *b* 7 March 1907; *Educ* Shrewsbury, RMA Woolwich; *m* 24 May 1935, Sybil Mary (d 1981), da of Maj Hon George Algernon Lascelles (d 1932), of Windleshore, Bembridge, Isle of Wight; *Career* cmmnd 2 Lt RA 1927, served UK 1927-30, Lt 1930, Egypt and Sudan 1930-38, Capt 1936, BEF 1939-40 (POW 1940-45), Staff Coll 1946, WO 1946-48, CO 36 HAA Regt Malta 1949-51, AAG Western Cmd 1951-54, Col AQ Midwest Dist 1954-57, ret 1958; *Recreations* bridge, gardening; *Clubs* Naval and Military, MCC; *Style*— Col Humphrey Wright; Conyers Place, Marnhull, Dorset (☎ 0258 820372)

WRIGHT, Ian James; s of James Wilson Wright (d 1987), of Wishaw, and Dorothy, *née* Ormerod (d 1961); *b* 28 May 1948; *Educ* Liverpool Coll of Art (BA), RCA (MA); *m* 1976, Glenda, da of William Laverick Tindale; 3 s (Stewart James b 1978, Steven William b 1981, James Lewis b 1987); *Career* Kinneir Calvert Tuhill Design Consultants 1973-75; currently design dir The Jenkins Group (joined 1975); *Style*— Ian James Wright, Esq; 61 Warren Rd, Chingford, London E4 6QR (☎ 081 529 8231); The Jenkins Group, 9 Tufton St, Westminster London SW1P 3QB (☎ 071 799 1090, fax 071 222 6751)

WRIGHT, Ian Wheeler; s of Rev Ernest Wright (d 1961), and Emily Elizabeth, *née* Wheeler; *b* 9 March 1934; *Educ* Kingswood Sch Bath, Ch Ch Oxford (MA); *m* 1968, (Janet) Lydia, da of Norman Giles (d 1983); 1 s (Oliver b 1973); *Career* HM Overseas Civil Serv Kenya 1956-59; ed Elliot Lake Standard Ontario Canada 1960; The Guardian: joined 1961, film critic, dep features ed 1964, special corr Sudan Aden 1967, Far East corr, war corr Vietnam 1968-70, foreign ed 1970-76, managing and dep ed 1977-; dir Guardian Newspapers 1984-; *Style*— Ian Wright, Esq; The Guardian, 119 Farringdon Rd, London EC1 (☎ 071 278 2332)

WRIGHT, Hon Mrs (Jane Anne Caroline); *née* Littleton; yr da of 5 Baron Hatherton (d 1969); *b* 10 Sept 1929; *m* 24 Jan 1967, Rev Charles Piachaud Wright (d 1990), s of late Charles Moncrieff Piachaud Wright, of St Andrews, Fife; *Style*— The Hon Mrs Wright; 12 St Swithun St, Winchester, Hants

WRIGHT, Joe Booth; CMG (1979); s of Joe Booth Wright (d 1967), of Notts, and Annie Elizabeth, *née* Stockdale (d 1964); *b* 24 Aug 1920; *Educ* King Edward VI GS Retford, Univ of London (BA); *m* 1, 1945, Pat, *née* Beaumont; 1 s (Christopher), 2 da (Helen, Annie); m 2, 1967, Patricia Maxine, da of Albert Nicholls (d 1965); *Career* serv in Armed Forces 1941-46; HM Dip Serv 1947-79 at Jerusalem, Munich, Basrah, Formosa, Indonesia, Cyprus, Tunisia; HM consul-gen: Hanoi 1971-72, Geneva 1973-75; HM ambass: Ivory Coast, Upper Volta & Niger 1975-78, ret 1979; writer, lectr, translator; memb Inst of Linguists and Translators Guild 1982; FRSA 1987; *Books* Francophone Black Africa Since Independence (1981), Zaire Since Independence (1983), Paris As It Was (1985); *Recreations* cricket, writing, music, cinema; *Clubs* Royal Over-Seas League; *Style*— Joe Wright Esq, CMG; 29 Brittany Rd, St Leonards-on-Sea, E Sussex TN38 0RB (☎ 0424 439563)

WRIGHT, Col John Anthony; MBE (1973); s of Col Thomas Wright, CBE (d 1989), and Joyce Mary, *née* Walker; *b* 10 Oct 1940; *Educ* Wellington, RMA Sandhurst; *m* 4 March 1967, Anstice Gillian, da of Wing Cdr (Charles Percy) Vernon Hervey (ret); 1 s (Peter b 1971), 2 da (Claudia b 1969, Alicia b 1983); *Career* RMAS 1959, 2 Lt RTR 1961, ADC and PS to high cmmr Aden 1964, Adj RHKR(V) 1969, transferred 16/5 Lancers 1970, RN Staff Coll 1973, NDC 1980, CO 16/5 Lancers 1982, DPSO/CDS 1987; chm Pony Club Polo 1989; *Recreations* polo; *Style*— Col John Wright, MBE

WRIGHT, John Derek; s of Leslie Thomas Wright, of Cornwall, and Ceinwen Angharad, *née* Johns (d 1984); *b* 25 June 1937; *Educ* West Bridgford GS; *m* 20 Sept 1958, Maureen Pemberton, da of Albert Edward Butler, of Truro; 2 da (Angela Elizabeth b 10 Aug 1960, Sara Jane b 19 Feb 1966); *Career* regnl dir Contractors Servs Gp 1974-78, md Lomount Construction 1978-83, chm and md Mid Cornwall Plant 1983-89, chm Peterscroft 1989-90; *Recreations* walking, breeding and showing pug dogs; *Clubs* Lighthouse; *Style*— John Wright, Esq; The Coppice, Trebetherick, Wadebridge, Cornwall (☎ 0208 862328)

WRIGHT, John Edward; s of John Nicholas Wright (d 1962), and Ellen Bullen, *née* Mulloy; *b* 23 May 1933; *Educ* Mold GS, Univ of Liverpool (MB ChB, MD); *m* 23 May 1959, Kathleen Teresa, da of John Reid (d 1938); 1 s (John b 1960), 1 da (Elizabeth b 1966); *Career* Nat Serv RAMC 1957-60; conslt ophthalmic surgn St Mary's Hosp London 1969-73; sr lectr in ophthalmology Univ of London 1969-73, consult ophthalmic surgn Moorfields Eye Hosp London 1973- (sr registrar 1964-67), consult ophthalmic surgn Royal ENT Hosp London 1973-; Wendel Hughes Lectr USA 1982, Doyne Lectr Oxford 1987; numerous pubns on orbital disease; past sec of the Ophthalmological Soc, pres Int Orbital Soc, past bd memb Moorfields Eye Hosp; memb: RSM, Coll of Ophthalmologists, American Acad of Ophthalmology; FRCS 1966; *Recreations* golf, fishing; *Clubs* Denham Golf and Piscatorial Soc; *Style*— John Wright, Esq; 44 Wimpole St, London W1M 7DG (☎ 071 580 1251, fax 071 224 3722)

WRIGHT, John Gordon Laurence; s of Rev William Henry Laurence Wright (Chaplain RAF 1939-45), of Edinburgh, and Mary Campbell, *née* Macdonald; *b* 6 June 1944; *Educ* Glenalmond, BNC Oxford (MA); *m* 16 July 1974, (Faith) Alison, da of Dr John Allan Guy (d 1986, Capt RAMC 1939-45), of Kendal; 2 s (Thomas b 1977, Richard b 1981); *Career* Hambros Bank Ltd 1967-71, pres Stewart Ivory and Co Ltd (formerly Stewart Fund Managers Ltd) 1971- (apptd dir 1972); *Recreations* shooting, photography, skiing; *Clubs* New (Edinburgh); *Style*— John Wright, Esq; 34 Greenhill Gardens, Edinburgh EH10 4BP; Stewart Ivory & Co Ltd, 45 Charlotte Sq, Edinburgh EH2 4HW

WRIGHT, John Keith; JP (Dover and E Kent 1983); s of James Henry Wright (d 1965), and Elsie May Willis (d 1984); *b* 30 May 1928; *Educ* Tiffins, King's Coll Cambridge, Yale; *m* 1958, Thérèse Marie Claire, da of René Aubenas (d 1977), of Paris; *Career* OEEC (Paris) 1951-56, UKAEA 1956-61, MOD 1961-66, FCO 1966-71, under sec ODA FCO 1971-84; econ and fin conslt; dir Sadler's Wells (Trading) 1983-; memb Cncl: Queen Elizabeth Coll London 1982-85, King's Coll London 1984-; tstee Thomson Fndn 1986-, memb Bd of Visitors Canterbury Prison 1987-; *Recreations* econ and mil history, music, amateur radio; *Clubs* Athenaeum, Beefsteak; *Style*— John Wright, Esq, JP; Laurie House, Airlie Gardens, London W8 7AW; Bowling Corner, Sandwich, Kent

WRIGHT, Karen Jocelyn Wile; da of Louis David Wile (d 1972), and Grace Carlin Wile; *b* 15 Nov 1950; *Educ* Princeton HS, Brandeis Univ (BA), Univ of Cambridge (MA), London Business Sch Univ of London (MSc); *m* 23 May 1981, Richard Bernard Wright, s of Bernard Gilbert Wright; 2 da (Louisa Karen b 17 April 1985, Rebecca Katherine b 21 Oct 1986); *Career* fndr and proprietor Hobson Gallery Cambridge 1975-84, Bernard Jacobson Gallery Cork St 1985, worked on Victor Willing catalogue Whitechapel Art Gallery 1986; Modern Painters magazine: fndr with Peter Fuller 1987, asst ed 1987-89, managing ed 1989, AICA 1988; *Recreations* tennis, swimming, reading, playing with the children; *Clubs* Groucho; *Style*— Mrs Karen Wright; 10 Barley Mow Passage, London W4 4PH (☎ 081 995 1909)

WRIGHT, Keith Elliot; s of Wilfred Stratten Wright (d 1961), and Dorothea, *née* Elliot (d 1961); *b* 20 Nov 1920; *Educ* Giggleswick Sch Settle, Selwyn Coll Cambridge (BA); *m* 20 Feb 1954, Patricia Ann, da of Raymond Tustin Taylor (d 1985); 1 s (David b 1956), 2 da (Catherine b 1958, Sally b 1959); *Career* WWII offr Duke of Wellington Regt 1939-45; sr ptnr Slaughter & May 1976-84 (slr 1950-, ptnr 1955); memb Cncl and chm Exec Ctee King Edward VII's Hosp for Offrs 1986- (memb 1979-); vice chm London Advsy Bd Salvation Army; memb: Cncl Offr's Assoc, Ctee of Mgmnt Wilts Rural Housing Assoc; memb Law Soc 1950; *Recreations* theatre, walking, gardening; *Style*— Keith Wright, Esq; Kestrels, Oak Lane, Easterton, nr Devizes, Wilts SN10 4PD (☎ 0380 812573); King Edward VII's Hospital for Officers, Beaumont St, London WIN 2AA (☎ 071 486 4411)

WRIGHT, Dr Kenneth Campbell; CMG (1987), OBE (1973); s of James Edwin Wright (d 1981), of Colinton, Edinburgh, and Eva Rebecca, *née* Sayers (d 1964); *b* 31 May 1932; *Educ* George Heriot's Sch, Univ of Edinburgh (MA, PhD), Univ of Paris

(Licence-és-Lettres); *m* 19 April 1958, Diana Yolande, da of Geoffrey Morse Binnie, FRS (d 1989), of Benenden, Kent; 1 s (David b 1963), 2 da (Jacqueline b 1964, Vanessa b 1968); *Career* cadet pilot RAFVR 1950, cmmnd RAFVR 1954, short serv reg commn RAF 1957-60 (Flt Lt 1959); lectr: Lovanium Univ and Institut Politique Congolais 1960-63, Univ of Ghana 1963-65 (sr lectr 1964-65); HM Dip Serv: FO 1965-68, first sec (econ) Bonn 1968-72, FCO 1972-75 (and 1979-82, 1985-89), first sec later cnsllr UK Rep EEC Brussels 1975-79, cnsllr Paris 1982-85; dir: Brit Invisible Exports Cncl 1989- (British Invisibles wef Oct 1990), City Communications Centre 1989; *Recreations* people, places, books; *Clubs* Athenaeum; *Style*— Dr Kenneth Wright, CMG, OBE; British Invisibles, Windsor House, 39 King St, London EC2V 8DQ (☎ 071 600 1198, fax 071 606 4248, telex 941 3342 BIE G)

WRIGHT, Rev Canon Kenyon Edward; s of Charles James Wright (d 1975), and Mary Dunbar, *née* Adamson; *b* 31 Aug 1932; *Educ* Paisly GS, Univ of Glasgow (MA), Cambridge Univ (MA), Univ of Singapore (MTh); *m* 18 Aug 1955, Betty, da of Arthur Robinson (d 1958); 3 da (Lindsey Jane b 1959, Shona May b 1961, Shelagh Ann b 1964); *Career* minister Durgapur United Church Bengal India 1955-59, dir Ecumenical Social and Industl Int India 1961-70, canon residentiary and dir of int ministry Coventry Cath 1970-81, gen sec Scottish Churches Cncl 1981-90, dir elect KAIROS (Scottish Curches Agency for Social and Environmental Studies) 1990-; chm exec Scottish Constitutional Convention, vice pres Christian Peace Conference; *Books* Structures for a Missionary Congregation (1965), Ecology and Christian Responsibility (1974); *Style*— The Rev Canon Kenyon Wright; Scottish Churches House, Dunblane, Perthshire FK15 0AJ (☎ 0786 824712); Scottish Churches Council, Dunblane FK15 0AJ (☎ 0786 823588)

WRIGHT, Leo; s of Harry Robert Wright (d 1990), of Cottingham, East Yorks, and Edna Bede, *née* Nias (d 1971); *b* 9 Aug 1931; *Educ* Beverley GS; *m* 28 Sept 1957 (m dis 1989), Barbara, da of Gordon Billam (d 1983); 2 s (Gordon Robert b 1960, Peter James b 1963), 1 da (Victoria Margaret b 1964); *Career* Nat Serv, Royal Northumberland Fusiliers 1949-51; with City Engraving Co Ltd Hull 1952-64, works mangr Billingham Press 1964-66, dir Doig Bros 1966-67, chm J Billam plc 1974- (dir 1971-); *Recreations* golf, crown green bowls, cricket; *Style*— Leo Wright, Esq; J Billam plc, 75 Milton St, Sheffield S3 7WF (☎ 0742 727374, fax 0742 727376)

WRIGHT, Col Leslie William; TD (1952, clasps 1961 and 1963), DL (Derbyshire 1983); s of Leonard Wright (d 1925), of Glossop, and Gertrude Veronica, *née* Wain (d 1938); *b* 26 June 1920; *Educ* Glossop GS, Univ of Sheffield Inst of Educ; *m* 30 Aug 1941, Kathleen, da of John Howard (d 1964), of Bakewell; 1 da (Christina Mary b 1943); *Career* enlisted 2 (N Midland) Corps Signals TA 1939, 12 Wireless section with Rifle Bde (BEF) def of Calais 1940, 4 Corps Signals, 11 Armd Divnl Signals, cmmnd RCS 1943; 76 Divnl Signals; Central Med Forces 1944-46: II L of C and 8 Army Signals, Battle of Cassino 1944, Chief Signalmaster Naples 1945, memb Allied mission for observing the Greek elections Crete 1946; joined Royal Signals reconstituted TA 1947, Lt-Col cmdg 46 (N Midland) Signal Regt TA 1964-67, Bt-Col 1967; Hon Col: Univ of Sheffield OTC 1977-85, Derbys Cadet Bn Worcs and Sherwood Foresters Regt 1988-; sr lectr in history and def studies (formerly lectr) Sheffield City Poly (formerly Sheffield Coll of Technol), memb Mil Educn Ctee Univ of Sheffield 1970-; vice chm Royal Signals Assoc 1972-84; E Midlands TAVR Assoc 1981-84; pres: Sheffield and Dist branch 1940, Dunkirk Veterans Assoc 1972-, Bakewell and Dist branch Royal Br Legion 1978-; memb: W Derbys DC 1973-83, Peak Park Jt Planning Bd 1973-77; Mayor of Bakewell 1978-79; lectr in principles and Law Br Red Cross Soc 1983; Hon MA Univ of Sheffield 1986; chm Sheffield Def Studies Dining Club 1986-; *Recreations* music, walking, Holy Land; *Style*— Col Leslie Wright, TD, DL; Rock House, Buxton Rd, Bakewell, Derbys DE4 1DA (☎ 0629 812530)

WRIGHT, Malcolm Allan; s of Frederick Thomas Wright (d 1969), and Dorothy Jessie, *née* Crossingham; *b* 25 Jan 1939; *Educ* St Dunstan's Coll, Harvard Business Sch (advanced mgmnt programme); *m* 8 July 1967, Brenda Mary, da of Edward Rupert Nicholson, of Grey Wings, The Warren, Ashtead, Surrey; 2 da (Helen Gail b 1968, Elizabeth Mary b 1971, d 1976); *Career* 2 Lt RR Artillery 25 Field Regt RA 1958-60, 1 Lt (gazetted) on Reserve 1961; fin dir Beck and Pollitzer Engrg Ltd 1961-74; Cape Industs plc 1974-85: md Cape Contracts Ltd 1979-81, gp personnel mangr 1981-85, chm Automotive Div 1983-85; conslt 1985-86, exec dir and chief exec Indust Textiles Div BBA Gp plc, memb Governing Cncl Br Rubber Mfrs Assoc; memb Round Table 1973-79; Freeman City of London 1973, Freeman Worshipful Co of Horners 1973; ACIS 1966, FCIS 1974; *Recreations* golf, gardening, DIY (and occasional cricket), photography; *Clubs* Army and Navy; *Style*— Malcolm Wright, Esq; High Point, 58 The Mount, Fetcham, Surrey KT22 9EA (☎ 0372 376 918); Suites 45-47, The Hop Exchange, 24 Southwark St, London SE1 1TY (☎ 071 407 3461, fax 071 403 7086, car 0860 738 108)

WRIGHT, Malcolm Carter; s of Edward Wright (d 1977); *b* 11 April 1938; *Educ* King's Sch Macclesfield; *m* 1, 1964 (m dis 1980), Susan Helen, *née* Winter; 2 s; m 2, 9 Dec 1989, Margaret Anne, *née* Phillips; *Career* jt md R Bailey & Son plc; chm Surgical Dressings Manufacturers' Assoc 1980-83; memb RYA; *Recreations* yachting (yacht Sunchase); *Clubs* South Caernarvon Yacht, Pwllheli Sailing, Rudyard Lake Sailing; *Style*— Malcolm Wright, Esq; Carters Bottom, Longhurst Lane, Mellor, Stockport, Cheshire SK6 5AH (☎ 061 427 4506); office: Dysart St, Stockport, Cheshire (☎ 061 483 1133, telex 668211)

WRIGHT, Dr Martin; s of Clifford Kent Wright (d 1969), of Sheffield, and Rosalie, *née* Mackenzie (d 1967); *b* 24 April 1930; *Educ* Repton, Jesus Coll Oxford (MA), LSE (PhD); *m* 26 July 1957, Louisa Mary (Lisa), da of John Osborne Nicholls (d 1974), of Yoxall, Staffordshire; 3 s (Edward b 1960, James b 1961, William b 1963), 2 da (Sophie b 1960, Ellie b 1968); *Career* librarian Inst of Criminology Cambridge 1964-71, dir Howard League for Penal Reform 1971-81, information/policy devpt offr Victim Support 1985-; memb Inst for the Study and Treatment of Delinquency; chm Lambeth Mediation Serv; memb: Br Society of Criminology, Forum for Initiatives in Reparation and Mediation; *Books* The Use of Criminology Literature (ed, 1974), Making Good: Prisons, Punishment and Beyond (1982), Mediation and Criminal Justice: Victims, Offenders and Community (jt ed with B Galaway, 1989), Justice for Victims and Offenders: a restorative response to crime (1991); *Recreations* suggesting improvements; *Style*— Dr Martin Wright; 19 Hillside Rd, London SW2 3HL (☎ 081 671 8037); Victim Support, 39 Brixton Rd, London SW9 6DZ (☎ 071 735 9166, fax 071 582 5712)

WRIGHT, Martin Nicholas; s of Bertram Sidney Wright, of Guernsey, and Doris Edna, *née* Baker; *b* 28 Jan 1955; *Educ* Elizabeth Coll Guernsey, Bristol Poly; *m* 29 Aug 1981, Beth Louise, da of Francis Brian Whitehall, of Edinburgh; 2 da (Emily Louise b 1985, Eleanor Charmaine b 1990); *Career* CA; ptnr Horlock & Co 1985, co dir The Charter Group; pt/t teacher Elizabeth Coll Guernsey; FCA (ACA 1980); *Recreations* tennis; *Style*— Martin Wright, Esq; Town Mills, Trinity Square, St Peter Port, Guernsey, CI

WRIGHT, Hon Mr Justice; Hon Sir (John) Michael; s of Prof John George Wright (d 1972), and Elsie Lloyd, *née* Razey (d 1955); *b* 26 Oct 1932; *Educ* The King's Sch Chester, Oriel Coll Oxford (BA, MA); *m* 25 July 1959, Kathleen Esther Gladys, da of Frederick Arthur Meanwell, MM (d 1945); 1 s (Timothy b 1965), 2 da (Elizabeth b 1961, Katharine b 1963); *Career* Nat Serv RA 1951-53, 2 Lt 1952, Lt 1953, TA 1953-56, TARO 1956-; barr Lincoln's Inn 1957, rec Crown Ct 1974-, QC 1974, bencher 1983-, legal assessor RCVS 1984-; ldr SE Circuit 1981-83, chm Bar 1983-84 (vice chm 1982-83); kt 1990; *Style*— The Hon Mr Justice Wright; c/o Royal Courts of Justice, London WC2

WRIGHT, Michael Leslie Beaumont; s of Harold Norman Wright, of Solihull, Warks and Elsie Margaret, *née* Beaumont (d 1971); *b* 18 Oct 1922; *Educ* Wellesbourne Sch Solihull Warks; *m* 1946, Maisie Dawn, da of Dr Adam Turner (d 1926), of Stratford Road, Birmingham; 2 s (Timothy, Andrew), 2 da (Penelope, Susan); *Career* Lt (A) RNVR; chm Newman-Tonks Gp plc and other cos; *Recreations* golf, power boating; *Style*— Michael Wright Esq; Bats Hall, Knowle, Warwickshire (☎ 560 2423); c/o Newman-Tonks Group plc, Hospital St, Birmingham (☎ 021 359 3221)

WRIGHT, Prof Michael Thomas; s of William George Wright (d 1985), and Lily May, *née* Turner; *b* 11 April 1947; *Educ* Sheldon Heath Sch Birmingham, Univ of Aston (BSc, PhD); *m* 29 Aug 1970, Patricia Eunice, da of Stanley Douglas Cox; 1 da (Rebecca Michelle b 19 Sept 1977); *Career* apprentice EPE Co Birmingham 1963-68, res engr Redman Heenan Froude Worcs 1969-76, engrg dir Linear Motors Ltd Loughborough 1976-78, tech dir NEI Peebles Ltd Edinburgh 1978-82, engrg dir GEC Large Machines Rugby 1982-85, Molins PLC 1985-90 (md Tobacco Div then gp md), prof and head Dept of Mechanical Engrg Univ of Aston 1990-; governing dir Scot Engrg Trg Scheme Glasgow 1978-82; IEE Student Paper award 1970, IEEE Petrochemical Indust Author award 1981, IEE Power Div Premium for published work 1983; FIEE 1981, sr memb IEEE (USA) 1981, FEng 1988, FIMechE 1989, FRSA 1989; *Style*— Prof Michael Wright; Department of Mechanical and Production Engineering, Aston University, Aston Triangle, Birmingham B4 7ET (☎ 021 359 3611)

WRIGHT, Miles Francis Melville; s of Montague Francis Melville Wright (d 1968), and Marjorie Isobel, *née* Brook (d 1968); *b* 3 Dec 1943; *Educ* Ampleforth, Ch Ch Oxford (MA); *Career* dir American Int Underwriters (UK) Ltd 1982-84 (asst md 1984-87), md Polwring Underwriting Agency at Lloyds 1988-, Active Underwriter Syndicate 1098 Lloyds 1988-; Freeman: Worshipful Co of Glaziers, Worshipful Co of Insurers; *Recreations* cricket, tennis, shooting, gardening; *Clubs* Naval and Military, MCC, I Zingari, Free Foresters, Old Amplefordians CC; *Style*— Miles Wright, Esq; The Barracks, Cranbrook, Kent TN17 2LG (☎ 0580 712209); 24 Lime Street, London EC3M 7HR; Lloyds, 1 Lime St, London EC3 (☎ 071 623 7100 ext 3634/3675)

WRIGHT, Neville Clarkson; s of Percival Albert Wright, of Petts Wood, Kent (d 1965), and Phyllis Marjorie, *née* Clarkson (d 1984); *b* 21 Feb 1929; *Educ* Aldenham, Queens' Coll Cambridge (MA); *m* 18 April 1959, Jennifer Margaret, da of Geoffrey William Tookey, QC, of Beckenham, Kent (d 1976); 1 s (Andrew b 1962), 2 da (Jane b 1960, Victoria b 1964); *Career* 2 Lt RA; slr in private practice; ptnr Clarkson Wright and Jakes (Orpington); NP; former pres Petts Wood Operatic Soc; memb: The Law Soc, The Prov Notaries Soc; *Clubs* Hawks (Cambridge), West Kent Golf, Bromley Hockey (former pres); *Style*— Neville C Wright, Esq; Vine Cottage, Hollybush Lane, Sevenoaks, Kent TN13 3UJ; Villa San Miguel, Binisafua, Menorca; Clarkson Wright and Jakes, Valiant House, 12 Knoll Rise, Orpington, Kent BR6 0PG (☎ 0689 871621, fax 0689 878537)

WRIGHT, Sir (John) Oliver; GCMG (1981, KCMG 1974, CMG 1964), GCVO (1978), DSC (1944); s of Arthur Wright (d 1963), of Seaford; *b* 6 March 1921; *Educ* Solihull Sch, Christ's Coll Cambridge (MA); *m* 1942, (Lillian) Marjory, da of Hedley Vickers Osborne, of Solihull; 3 s (Nicholas b 1946, John b 1949, Christopher b 1950); *Career* RNVR WWII; joined HM Dip Serv 1945; served: NY, Bucharest, Singapore, Berlin, Pretoria; private sec to: Foreign Sec 1963, PM 1964-66; ambass Denmark 1966-69, seconded to Home Office, UK rep to NI Govt 1969-70, chief clerk 1970-72, dep under sec FCO 1972-75; ambass: FRG 1975-81, ret then recalled from retirement to be ambass to Washington 1982-86; dir: Siemens Ltd 1981-82, Savoy Hotel plc 1987-; pres German Chambers of Indust and Commerce 1989; chm: Br Konigswinter Conf Steering Ctee 1986, Govrs Reigate GS, Anglo-Irish Encounter 1986-91; hon fell and master designate Christ's Coll Cambridge until 1982; dir Bd of Br Cncl 1986- (memb Bd 1981-82); tstee: Br Museum 1986-, Shakespeare Int Globe Centre (vice chm of Int Cncl 1986-); Hon DHL Univ of Nebraska 1983; Grand Cross German Order of Merit 1978, King of Arms, Order of St Michael and St George; *Recreations* theatre, opera; *Clubs* Travellers'; *Style*— Sir Oliver Wright, GCMG, GCVO, DSC; Burstow Hall, Horley, Surrey RH6 9SR (☎ 0293 783494)

WRIGHT, Hon Owen Mortimor; s of Baron Wright of Ashton-under-Lyne, CBE (d 1974) (Life Peer); bro of Hon Glyn Wright, *qv*; *b* 18 Nov 1934; *m* 1960, Barbara, da of Arthur Hudson, of Stalybridge; 1 s, 1 da; *Style*— The Hon Owen Wright; Wingthorne, Slade Rd, Newton, Swansea SA3 4UE

WRIGHT, Sir Patrick Richard Henry; GCMG 1989 (KCMG 1984, CMG 1978); s of Herbert Wright (d 1977), of The Hermitage, Chetwode, Buckingham, and Rachel, *née* Green; *b* 28 June 1931; *Educ* Marlborough, Merton Coll Oxford; *m* 1958, Virginia Anne, step da of Col Samuel John Hannaford (d 1983), of Hove; 2 s (Marcus b 1959, Angus b 1964), 1 da (Olivia b 1963); *Career* Nat Serv Lt RA; entered Foreign Serv 1955; served: Beirut, Washington, Cairo, Bahrain; private sec (overseas affrs) to PM 1974-77; ambass: Luxembourg 1977-79, Syria 1979-81; dep under sec FCO Jan 1982-84, ambass Saudi Arabia 1984-86, perm under sec FCO and head Dip Serv 1986-91; hon fell Merton Coll Oxford 1987; KStJ (1990); *Clubs* Oxford and Cambridge; *Style*— Sir Patrick Wright, GCMG; c/o Barclays Banks plc, 1 Pall Mall East, London SW1 5AX

WRIGHT, Sir Paul Hervé Giraud; KCMG (1975, CMG 1960), OBE (1952); s of Richard Hervé Giraud Wright (sec of White's Club), and Ellen Margaret, da of Lewis Mercier; *b* 12 May 1915; *Educ* Westminster; *m* 1942, Beatrice Frederika Wright, MP Bodmin 1941-45, da of Frank Roland Clough and wid of Flt-Lt John Rankin Rathbone, MP, RAFVR (ka 1940); 1 da; *Career* served WWII, Maj KRRC, HQ 21 Army Gp (despatches); contested (Lib) Bethnal Green 1945; asst dir PR NCB 1946-48, PR dir Festival of Britain 1948-51; joined HM Foreign Serv 1951, Paris and NY 1951-54, FO 1954-56, The Hague 1956-57, head of Info Policy Dept FO 1957-60, Cairo 1960-61, memb UK Delegn to NATO 1961-64, dir gen Br Info Services NY 1964-68, min (info) Washington 1965-68; ambass: Congo (Kinshasa) and Republic of Burundi 1969-71, Lebanon 1971-75, ret; special rep of sec of state for Foreign and Cwlth Affrs 1975-78, hon sec London Celebrations Ctee for Queen's Silver Jubilee 1977; chm: Irvin GB Ltd 1979-88, chm Br American Arts Assoc 1983-88, Br Lebonese Assoc 1987-90; govr Westminster Cathedral Choir Sch 1981-, pres The Elizabethan Club 1988-, memb Trusthouse Forte Cncl 1987-; FRSA; *Books* A Brittle Glory; *Clubs* Garrick; *Style*— Sir Paul Wright, KCMG, OBE; 62 Westminster Gardens, London SW1P 4JG

WRIGHT, Peter Frederick George; s of Frederick Grocott Wright (d 1964), and Eleanor, *née* Luckman (d 1980); *b* 7 Dec 1926; *Educ* British Boys Sch Alexandria Egypt, Military Schs Alex and Cairo, Tech Coll Birmingham; *m* 28 March 1958, Jacqueline Eleanor, da of Arthur Bernard Court (d 1988); 1 s (Paul Jeremy b 1966); *Career* sr Flt Sgt 157 Sqdn ATC Birmingham (Central) 1944-47; sr draughtsman (aircraft): Heliwells Ltd 1955-57, Sir WG Armstrong Whitworth Aircraft Ltd 1957, Whitworth Gloster Aircraft 1960; design engr: Hawker Siddeley Dynamics (weapons div) 1961-66, Lockheed Aircraft Corp Marietta Georgia USA 1967-68; project engr 1968-: BMC, Br Leyland, Austin Rover, Rover; sales mangr Cross and Cockade Int (IWW Aviation Historical Soc); *Books* The Royal Flying Corps in Oxfordshire (1985), The Battle of Britain and Beyond (1990); *Recreations* aviation research and writing; *Clubs* Vintage Sports-Car; *Style*— Peter Wright, Esq; 4 Parklands, Freeland, Oxford OX7 2HX (☎ 0993 881747)

WRIGHT, Peter Michael; s of Dudley Cyril Brazier Wright, of 10 Cadogan Gardens, Finchley, London N3 2HN, and Pamela Deirdre, *née* Peacock; *b* 6 March 1954; *Educ* Highgate Sch London, RCM (Organ exhibitioner, ARCM, LRAM), Emmanuel Coll Cambridge (Organ scholar, MA); *Career* sub organist Guildford Cathedral 1977-89, asst music master Royal GS Guildford 1977-89, organist and dir of music Southwark Cathedral 1989-; conductor: Edington Festival 1984-90, Guildford Chamber Choir 1985-, Surrey Festival Choir 1987; several recordings as organist released; memb: Cncl RCO 1990-, Cathedral Organists' Conference; FRCO; *Recreations* opera, theatre, travel, reading; *Style*— Peter Wright, Esq; 52 Bankside, Southwark, London SE1 9JE (☎ 071 261 1291); Southwark Cathedral, Montague Close, London Bridge, London SE1 9DA (☎ 071 407 3708, fax 071 357 7389)

WRIGHT, Peter Robert; CBE (1985); s of Bernard Wright (d 1981), and Hilda Mary, *née* Foster (d 1973); *b* 25 Nov 1926; *Educ* Bedales, Leighton Park; *m* 1954, Sonya Hana, da of Yoshi Sueyoshi (d 1931); 1 s (Jonathan), 1 da (Poppy); *Career* dancer Ballet Jooss and Sadler's Wells Theatre Ballet 1947-55, ballet master Sadler's Wells Opera Ballet and teacher Royal Ballet Sch 1955-58, ballet master Stuttgart Ballet 1960-63, guest prodr BBC TV 1963-65, freelance choreographer and prodr 1965-69; memb: cncl of mgmnt of Inst of Choreology, cncl Friends of Covent Garden, exec cncl of Royal Acad of Dancing; govr: Royal Ballet Sch, Sadler's Wells Fndn; vice pres Friends of Saddler's Wells Theatre, assoc dir Royal Ballet 1970-76, dir Sadler's Wells Royal Ballet (renamed The Birmingham Royal Ballet) 1976-; noted for prodns of 19C classical ballets, The Sleeping Beauty, Swan Lake, Giselle, The Nutcracker, and Coppelia, for most major cos in Europe and USA, including both Royal Ballet Cos, Dutch and Canadian Nat Ballets, Royal Winnipeg Ballet, The Houston Ballet, Ballet de Rio de Janeiro, Stuttgart Ballet, Bavarian State Opera Ballet; own creations include The Mirror Walkers, The Great Peacock, A Blue Rose, Dance Macabre, Summertide; Standard Award for Most Outstanding Achievement in Ballet 1981; John Newson Award for Greatest Contribution to SWRB 1988; Hon DMus Univ of London 1990, Queen Elizabeth II Coronation Award from Royal Acad of Dancing 1990; *Recreations* ceramics; *Style*— Peter Wright, Esq, CBE; 4 The Old Orchard, Nassington Rd, Hampstead, London NW3 2TR; Royal Opera House, Covent Garden, London WC2E 9DD

WRIGHT, Very Rev Dr Ronald (William Vernon) Selby; CVO (1968), TD (1950), JP (Edinburgh 1963); s of Vernon Oswald Wright (d 1942), of Saxe-Coburg Place, Edinburgh, and Anna Gilberta, *née* Selby; *b* 12 June 1908; *Educ* Edinburgh Acad, Melville Coll, Univ of Edinburgh (MA); *Career* radio padre (HM Forces) 1942-47 and sr chaplain: 52 Lowland Div 1942-43, 10 Indian Div 1944-45; minister Canongate Edinburgh 1937-77, minister emeritus 1977-; chaplain: Edinburgh Castle 1959-91, to HM The Queen 1963-78 and extra chaplain 1978- (and 1961-63); The Queen's Body Guard for Scotland (Royal Co of Archers) 1973-; moderator Church of Scotland 1972-73; extraordinary dir Edinburgh Acad 1973-; FRSE; Hon DD Univ of Edinburgh 1956, CStJ 1976; Hon: Old Lorettonian, Old Fettesian, Old Cargilfield; *Clubs* Athenaeum, New (Edinburgh, hon memb); *Style*— The Very Rev Dr R Selby Wright, CVO, TD, JP, FRSE; The Queen's House, 36 Moray Place, Edinburgh EH3 6BX (☎ 031 226 5566)

WRIGHT, Sir Rowland Sydney; CBE (1970); s of Sydney Wright; *b* 4 Oct 1915; *Educ* High Pavement Sch Nottingham, Univ Coll Nottingham (BSc, London); *m* 1940, Kathleen Hodgkinson; 2 s, 1 da; *Career* joined ICI Ltd 1937 (chm 1975-78, dep chm 1971-75); chm Reorganisation Cmmn for Eggs 1967-68, dep chm AE&CI Ltd 1971-75; dir: Royal Insurance Co 1973-79, Barclays Bank plc 1977-84, Hawker Siddeley Gp 1979-, Shell Tport and Trading Co 1981-86, Blue Circle Industries plc 1983-86 (chm 1978-83); former govr London Graduate Sch of Business Studies, hon pres Inst Manpower Studies 1977- (pres 1971-77); memb: Royal Inst, Ford European Advsy Cncl 1976-83, Court Sussex Univ 1983-; Hon LLD: St Andrews, Belfast, Nottingham; chllr Queen's Univ Belfast 1984-; tstee Westminster Abbey Tst 1984-90, chm Blue Circle Trust 1983-; Hon DSc Belfast 1985; CChem, FRSC, CBIM, FRSA, Hon FIChemE; *Recreations* gardening, music; *Clubs* Athenaeum; *Style*— Sir Rowland Wright, CBE; Merchants, Lower Station Road, Newick, Lewes, East Sussex BN8 4HT

WRIGHT, Samantha; *b* 1 Sept 1965; *Educ* Wreake Valley Coll Leicester, Coll of St Paul's and St Mary's Cheltenham; *Partner*, Ian P Jennings (the England hockey player); *Career* hockey player; debut Leicester Ladies 1979; England: jr debut 1982, sr debut 1983, 3 full caps outdoor, 30 full caps indoor; GB: 9 sr outdoor caps, tour NZ and Aust 1990, memb Olympic training squad 1990-; awards: player of the Year 1989, top indoor 1990-91, top goalscorer indoor 1989-90; teacher Wreake Valley Coll Leicester 1986-87, mktg and mgmnt asst Sci-Sport Ltd Leicester 1989-90, sales rep Monarch Group Reading 1990-; *Recreations* most sports, keeping fit; *Style*— Ms Samantha Wright; 8 Mole Close, Cove, Farnborough, Hants GU14 2NY (☎ 0252 540551)

WRIGHT, Lady Sarah Caroline; *née* Waldegrave; da of 12 Earl Waldegrave; *b* 23 Oct 1931; *m* 1955, Ernest Wright, GM, CPM, *qv*; 2 s; *Style*— The Lady Sarah Wright; Honibere Farmhouse, Burton, Stogursey, Bridgwater TA5 1PZ (☎ 027874 300)

WRIGHT, Stanley Harris; s of John Charles Wright (d 1965); *b* 9 April 1930; *Educ* Bolton Sch, Merton Coll Oxford (MA); *m* 1; 1 s; m 2, 1973, Alison Elizabeth, da of Baron Franks, OM, GCMG, KCB, CBE; 1 s; *Career* Bd of Trade 1952, HM Foreign Serv 1955-57, HM Treasy 1958, first sec (fin) Br Embassy Washington DC 1964-66, HM Treasury 1964-72 (under sec 1970-72), dir Lazard Bros & Co Ltd 1972-81; non exec dir: Wilkinson Match Ltd 1974-81, Law Land Co Ltd 1979-81; chm Inter Commercial Bank 1981-83; dir: Royal Tst Bank 1984-88, Stadium Ltd 1990-; chm Wolstenholme Rink plc 1982-, ptnr Price Waterhouse & Partners 1985-88; *Recreations* various; *Clubs* Reform, MCC; *Style*— S H Wright, Esq; 6 Holly Place, London NW3 (☎ 071 435 0237)

WRIGHT, Stephen Andrew; s of Robert Reuben Wright, of 2 Cheriton Avenue, Bromley, Kent, and Shonach McDonald Fraser; *b* 20 Dec 1967; *Educ* King's Sch Canterbury; *Career* oarsman; King's Sch Canterbury Boat Club 1981-85, Canterbury Pilgrims Boat Club 1986, Nottingham and Union Rowing Club 1987, Notts Co Rowing Assoc 1988-; represented England Home Int Championship 1985, winner Jr Men's Single Sculls; represented GB: under 23 world championships lightweight single sculls 1989, world championships Lightweight Eight 1990 (bronze medallists); records: Br Best Lightweight Coxless Fours 2000m Switzerland 1990, Br Best Lightweight Eights 2000m Tasmania 1990; exec offr HM Land Registry Nottingham 1989-; *Style*— Stephen Wright, Esq; c/o Amateur Rowing Assoc, 6 Lower Mall, Hammersmith, London W6 9DJ

WRIGHT, Stephen Richard (Steve); s of Richard James Wright, of Essex, and June Rosina, *née* Saunders; *b* 26 Aug 1954; *m* 8 June 1985, Cynthia Leigh, da of Lloyd Austin Robinson; 1 s (Thomas Lloyd Stephen b 19 May 1986); *Career* marine insur broker Black Sea and Baltic Co 1972, freelance journalist 1974, promotions exec Warner Brothers Records 1974, record librarian and researcher Kaleidoscope BBC Radio 4 1975, voiceover artiste and singer radio and TV commercials 1976, presenter LBC Radio and Radio Orwell 1976, researcher and prodr Thames Valley Radio 210 1977, writer for Thames TV childrens progs and film reviewer Film Magazine 1978, radio presenter Radio Luxembourg 1979, regular presenter Top of the Pops BBC TV 1981-, developed format for Steve Wright in the Afternoon and invented Mr Angry and various popular charcters BBC Radio 1 1983- (various progs incl film reviews 1980), columnist Chat Magazine (IPC), co dir The Original Radio Co; recorded 5 pop records 1984-89, creator of best selling bd game Steve Wright in the Afternoon; 18 awards for best radio show incl TRIC award and four times Sony award winner, award winning Daily Mirror columnist 1985; *Books* The Book of Confectionary (as Jeff Lewin, 1979), The Steve Wright in the Afternoon Book (1985), It's Another True Story (1989); *Recreations* avid movie goer, world travel, lapsed fisherman; *Clubs* Application Eccentric, Pall Mall; *Style*— Steve Wright, Esq; Steve Wright In The Afternoon, BBC Broadcasting House, London W1A 1AA (☎ 071 580 4468, fax 071 636 2476, car 0836 266266)

WRIGHT, Thomas William John; s of John William Richard Wright (d 1977), of Canterbury, Kent, and Jane Elizabeth, *née* Nash (d 1978); *b* 5 Aug 1928; *Educ* Kent Coll, Simon Langton Sch Canterbury, Wye Coll London (BSc); *m* 4 Jan 1956, Shirley Evelyn, da of Henry Parkinson (d 1943), of Beckenham, Kent; 2 da (Geraldine b 1959, Jane b 1962); *Career* garden estate mgmnt conslt and int lectr; tea plantation mangr Kenya and govt horticultural res offr UK 1953-58, mangr Nursery and Landscape Co Devon 1956-60; lectr Pershore Coll 1962-68, sr lectr in landscape horticulture Wye Coll London 1968-90; visiting prof Univs of Beijing and Shanghai China, main lectr Univ of Kent's Summer Acad on Kent's Historic Gdns; Veitch Memorial Medal (RHS) 1989; tstee: Landscape Design Tst, Kent Gardens Tst, Cobham Hall Heritage Tst, Fortescue Gardens Tst; memb: Gdns Ctee HHA, Gdns Panel Nat Tst, Shows Ctee RHS; ALI 1978, FIHort 1986; *Books* The Gardens of Kent, Sussex and Surrey (No 4 in Batsford Series, 1978), Large Gardens and Parks, Management and Design (1982); *Recreations* travel, natural history, gardening, music; *Style*— Thomas Wright, Esq; Cumberland House, Chilham, Canterbury, Kent (☎ 0227 730 246)

WRIGHT, Col Timothy Blake (Tim); s of Maj Harold Stanley Wright, TD (d 1989), and Gladys Mabel Wright; *b* 18 June 1936; *Educ* Hurstpierpoint Coll; *m* 27 April 1963, Leoné Shirley, da of Clifford Hare Harris (d 1938); *Career* Royal Sussex Regt 1954-57, 5 Battalion The Queen's Regt (volunteer) 1967-69; trainee John Dickinson and Co Ltd 1957, chief inspr Northern Rhodesia Police 1964 (asst inspr 1957, inspr 1960), ret Zambia Police 1966, slr 1970, Capt Army Legal Servs 1970, ADALS Hong Kong 1972-82, DADALS HQ NI 1977-78, Col 1986; memb: Police History Soc, Western Front Assoc, Soc for Army Historical Res; memb Law Soc; *Recreations* model soldiers, gardening, walking; *Style*— Col Tim Wright; Army Legal Aid BAOR, BFPO 39

WRIGHT, Prof Verna; s of Thomas William Wright (d 1934), and Nancy Eleanor, *née* Knight (d 1978); *b* 31 Dec 1928; *Educ* Bedford Sch, Univ of Liverpool (MB ChB 1953, MD 1956); *m* 8 Aug 1952, Esther Margaret, da of John Bruce Brown (d 1962), of Kings Walden, Hertfordshire; 5 s (Stephen b 1953, Paul b 1955, Andrew b 1958, Mark b 1964, James b 1970), 4 da (Susannah b 1956, Miriam b 1959, Deborah b 1962, Philippa b 1968); *Career* res asst Univ of Leeds 1956-58; res fell Div of Applied Physiology Johns Hopkins Hosp Baltimore 1958-59; Univ of Leeds: lectr Dept of Clinical Medicine 1960-64, sr lectr 1964-70, ARC prof of rheumatology 1970-; conslt physician in rheumatology Leeds W Dist and Yorkshire RHA 1970-; former pres: Heberden Soc, Br Assoc for Rheumatology and Rehabilitation, Creation Res Soc; vice-pres Biblical Creation Soc; chm Standing Advsy Ctee for Rheumatology Royal Coll of Physicians, United Beach Mission, Young Life Assoc; chm Standing Ctee on Devpts in Academic Rheumatology Arthritis and Rheumatism Cncl; MRCP 1958, FRCP 1970; *Books* Bone and Joint Disease in the Elderly (1983), Integrated Clinical Science: Musculoskeletal Disease (1984), Personal Peace in a Nuclear Age (1985), Arthritis and Joint Replacement (1987), Introduction to the Biomechanics of Joints and Joint Replacement (1981), Applied Drug Therapy of the Rheumatic Diseases (1982), Diagnostic Picture Tests in Rheumatology (1987); *Recreations* reading; *Style*— Professor Verna Wright; Inglehurst, Park Drive, Harrogate HG2 9AY (☎ 0432 502326); Rheumatology and Rehabilitation Research Unit, Department of Medicine, University of Leeds, 36 Clarendon Road, Leeds LS2 9NZ (☎ 0532 334940, fax 0532 445533, telex 0532 336017)

WRIGHT, Mrs Wendy; *née* Morane-Griffiths; da of Gp Capt Desmond Robert Morane-Griffiths, DFC, and Daphne Eve, *née* Fawke; *b* 9 Aug 1947; *Educ* Kent Coll Pembury, Mme Anita's Villa de L'Assomption Paris, Inchbald Sch of Design (Dip ISGD); *m* 1, 25 Sept 1971, Robert Sullivan Thomas; m 2, 2 June 1978, John Charles Wright,er s of Sir Rowland Sidney Wright, CBE; 1 s (William Rowland Hawksworth b 1984), 1 da (Clemency Sarah b 1980); *Career* garden designer, landscape conslt; lectr The English Gardening Sch, princ The Garden Sch in the North 1989; memb advsy Cncl Inchbald Sch of Design; FSLGD 1987; *Recreations* gardening, horses, bridge; *Style*— Mrs Wendy Wright; Hollybush Place, nr Lanchester, Co Durham

WRIGHTSON, Sir (Charles) Mark Garmondsway; 4 Bt (UK 1900), of Neasham Hall, Co Durham; s of Sir John Wrightson, 3 Bt, TD, DL (d 1983), and Hon Lady Wrightson, *qv*; 1 Bt, chm of Head Wrightson & Co Ltd (bridge builders), and MP (C) for Stockton-on-Tees and E Div of St Pancras; *b* 18 Feb 1951; *Educ* Eton, Queens Coll Cambridge; *m* 1975, Stella, da of late George Dean; 3 s (Barnaby, James, William); *Heir* s, Barnaby Thomas Garmondsway Wrightson b 5 Aug 1979; *Career* dir Hill Samuel Bank Ltd 1984; *Style*— Sir Mark Wrightson, Bt; 39 Westbourne Park Road, London W2 5QE

WRIGHTSON, Hon Lady (Rosemary Monica); *née* Dawson; yr da of 1 and last Viscount Dawson of Penn, GCVO, KCB, KCMG, PC (d 1945); *b* 1913; *m* 30 Nov 1939, Maj Sir John Garmondsway Wrightson, 3 Bt, TD, DL (d 1983), High Sheriff of Co Durham 1959; 1 s (Charles, 4 Bt, *qv*), 3 da (Penelope b 1940, Juliet b 1943, Elizabeth b 1946); *Style*— The Hon Lady Wrightson; Stud Yard House, Neasham, nr Darlington, Co Durham

WRIGLEY, Prof Christopher John; s of Arthur Wrigley, of Shipton Gorge, Dorset, and Eileen Sylvia, *née* Herniman; *b* 18 Aug 1947; *Educ* Kingston GS, UEA (BA), Birkbeck Coll London (PhD); *m* 11 Sept 1987, Margaret, da of Anthony Walsh, of Wigton, Cumbria; *Career* lectr in econ history Queen's Univ Belfast 1971-72; reader in econ history: Loughborough Univ 1984-88 (lectr 1972-78, sr lectr 1978-84); prof of mod Br History Univ of Nottingham 1991- (reader in econ hist 1988-91); chm Loughborough Lab Pty 1977-79 and 1980-85 (treas 1973-77), exec memb Loughborough Trades Cncl 1981-86; Leics cncllr 1981-89 (ldr of Lab Gp 1986-89), Charnwood borough cncllr and dep ldr Lab Gp 1983-87; Parly candidate (Lab): Blaby 1983, Loughborough 1987; memb: Historical Assoc Cncl 1980-, Econ History Soc Cncl 1983-; *Books* David Lloyd George and The British Labour Movement (1976), AJP Taylor A Complete Bibliography (1980), A History of British Industrial Relations Vol 1 1875-1914 (ed, 1982) and Vol 2 1914-1939 (ed, 1986), William Barnes: The Dorset

Poet (1984), Warfare Diplomacy and Politics (ed, 1986), Arthur Henderson (1990), Lloyd George and the Challenge of Labour (1990); *Recreations* swimming, walking; *Style*— Prof Christopher Wrigley; 2 Beacon Drive, Loughborough, Leicestershire LE11 2BD (☎ 0509 217 074); Dept of History, Nottingham University, Nottingham, Notts NG7 2RD (☎ 0602 484 848 ext 2719)

WRIGLEY, Dr Edward Anthony (Tony); s of Edward Ernest Wrigley (d 1953), and Jessie Elizabeth, *née* Holloway (d 1976); *b* 17 Aug 1931; *Educ* King's Sch Macclesfield, Univ of Cambridge (BA, MA, PhD); *m* 2 July 1960, Maria Laura, da of Everhard Dirk Spelberg (d 1968); 1 s (Nicholas b 1963), 3 da (Marieke b 1961, Tamsin b 1966, Rebecca b 1969); *Career* William Volker res fell Univ of Chicago 1953-54, lectr in geography Univ of Cambridge 1958-74; Peterhouse Cambridge: fell 1958-, tutor 1962-64, sr bursar 1964-74; Hinkley visiting prof John Hopkins Univ 1975, Tinbergen visiting prof Erasmus Univ Rotterdam 1979, prof of population studies LSE 1979-88, sr res fell All Souls Coll Oxford 1988-; co dir Cambridge Gp for the History of Population and Social Structure 1974-; memb Inst for Advanced Study Princeton 1970-71, pres Manchester Coll Oxford 1987-, treas Br Acad 1989-; FBA 1980; *Books* Industrial Growth and Population Change (1961), English Historical Demography (ed, 1966), Population and History (1969), Nineteenth Century Society (ed, 1972), Towns in Societies (ed with P Abrams, 1978), Population History of England (ed with R S Schofield, 1981), Works of Thomas Robert Malthus (ed with D Souden, 1987), People, Cities and Wealth (1987), Continuity, Chance and Change (1988); *Recreations* gardening; *Style*— Dr Tony Wrigley; 13 Sedley Taylor Rd, Cambridge CB2 2PW (☎ 0223 247614); All Souls College, Oxford OX1 4AL (☎ 0865 279287)

WRIGLEY, Dr Peter Francis Martyn; s of Fred Wrigley (d 1982), of Hatfield, Herts, and Catherine Margaret, *née* Hogley; *b* 13 May 1939; *Educ* Alleyne's Sch, UCL (BSC, PhD), Magdalen Coll Oxford (BM BCh); *m* 24 Feb 1968; *Career* conslt physician (cancer) and med oncologist St Barts Hosp London 1974-; chm Br Stomach Cancer Gp; memb Cancer Ctees MRC; Maccabean prize and medal Soc of Apothecaries 1961; Freeman City of London, Liveryman Soc of Apothecaries; FRCP 1979; *Recreations* shooting, fishing, canals; *Style*— Dr Peter Wrigley; 134 Harley St, London W1N 1AH (☎ 071 487 3193)

WRIGLEY, Thomas James Borgen; s of Edmund Wrigley (d 1963), of Skipton, and Karen Olga, *née* Borgen (d 1961); *b* 31 Aug 1936; *Educ* Merchant Taylors Sch; *m* 1961, Catherine Ethel, da of Sqdn Ldr Clement James Gittins (d 1969), of Herts; 2 s (Edmund b 1967, Michael b 1970), 1 da (Sarah b 1965); *Career* CA, md: First Nat Finance Corp plc, First Nat Securities Ltd; memb Mgmnt Ctee Finance Houses Assoc; *Recreations* gold, gardening; *Style*— Thomas Wrigley; The Old Malt House, St Peter Street, Marlow, Bucks (☎ 06284 2677); First National House, Harrow, Middx (☎ 081 861 1313; St Alphage House, London EC2 (☎ 071 638 2855)

WRIXON-BECHER, John William Michael; s and h of Sir William Wrixon-Becher, 5 Bt, MC, by his 1 w, later Countess of Glasgow (d 1984); *b* 29 Sept 1950; *Educ* Harrow, Neuchatel Univ Switzerland; *Career* Lloyds broker; *Recreations* shooting, fishing, golf; *Clubs* Whites, MCC; *Style*— John Wrixon-Becher Esq; 113A Alderney St, London SW1

WRIXON-BECHER, Maj Sir William Fane; 5 Bt (UK 1831), MC (1943); s of Sir Eustace William Windham Wrixon-Becher, 4 Bt, of Mallow, Co Cork, Ireland (d 1934), and Hon Constance Gough-Calthorpe (d 1957); *b* 7 Sept 1915; *Educ* Harrow, Magdalene Coll Cambridge (BA); *m* 1, 1946 (m dis 1960), Hon Mrs (Ursula Vanda Maud) Bridgewater (later Countess of Glasgow, d 1984), 2 da of 4 Baron Vivian; 1 s, 1 da; m 2, 1960, Yvonne Margaret, former w of Hon Roger Lloyd-Mostyn (now 5 Baron Mostyn, *qv*), and da of A Stuart Johnson, of Henshall Hall, Congleton, Cheshire (d 1970); 1 s (John); *Heir* s, John Wrixon-Becher; *Career* Temp Maj Rifle Bde (Supp Reserve), served West Desert, Tunisian Campaign 1940-43, (wounded, POW escaped), liaison offr Sidi Rezegh Battle NN 1941, Italian Campaign 1944, ADC to FM Lord Wilson, Supreme and Allied Cdr Mediterranean; Lloyds underwriter 1950; memb: British Boxing Bd of Control 1961-82, Nat Playing Field Assoc 1953-65; pres Wilts Branch NPFA 1950-56; played cricket Sussex 1939, capt Wiltshire 1949-53, sec of I Zingari 1953-; landowner; *Recreations* golf, cricket; *Clubs* White's, Royal Green Jackets, MCC, I Zingari; *Style*— Maj Sir William Wrixon-Becher, Bt, MC; 37 Clabon Mews, London SW1 (☎ 071 589 7780)

WROBEL, Brian John Robert Karen; s of Charles Karen Wrobel, of USA, and Marian, *née* Wiseman; *b* 4 Sept 1949; *Educ* Stowe, Univ of London (LLB, LLM); *Career* called to the Bar Lincoln's Inn 1973, also Gray's Inn and Bars State of California and US Supreme Ct; former memb Ctee of Mgmnt of the Inst of Advanced Legal Studies Univ of London; hon legal advsr to All Party Br Parly Human Rights Gp; participant in human rights fact-finding missions 1975-: Iran (before and after rev), S Korea, S Africa, USA; memb Br Legal Delgn Poland, USSR, China; election observer Zimbabwe 1985; govr Br Inst of Human Rights, chm Readers Int (Publishers), conslt on legal colloquia to GB-USSR Assoc; author of various legal papers, reports and articles; *Style*— Brian Wrobel, Esq; c/o Barclays Bank, 19 Fleet St, London EC4P 4DR

WRONG, Henry Lewellys Barker; CBE (1986); s of Henry Arkel Wrong, and Jean, *née* Barker; *b* 20 April 1930; *Educ* Trinity Coll Univ of Toronto (BA); *m* 18 Dec 1966, Penelope Hamilton, da of Mark Richard Norman, CBE, OBE, of Garden House, Much Hadham, Herts; 2 s (Mark Henry b 1947, Sebastian Murray b 1971), 1 da (Christina Jocelyn b 1970); *Career* admin Met Opera NY 1952-64; dir: programming Nat Arts Centre Ottawa 1964-68, Festival Canada Centennial Prog 1967, Barbican Centre 1970-90, Euro Arts Fndn 1990-; memb advsy ctee: ADAPT, LSO, Heslington Fndn Music and Assoc Arts; tstee Royal Opera House 1989, Liveryman Worshipful Co of Fishmongers 1987; DLitt City Univ 1985; memb RSA 1988 (fell Arts Ctee); Order of Merit France Offr Class 1985, Centennial medal Canada 1967; *Clubs* Marks, Badminton and Racket (Toronto); *Style*— Henry Wrong, Esq, CBE; Yew Tree House, Much Hadham, Herts (☎ 027 984 2106)

WRONG, Prof Oliver Murray; s of Edward Murray Wrong (d 1928), of Toronto, and Rosalind Grace, *née* Smith (d 1984); *b* 7 Feb 1925; *Educ* Upper Canada Coll Toronto, Edinburgh Acad, Magdalen Coll Oxford (BA, MA, DM, MRCP); *m* 9 June 1956, Marilda, da of Angela Musacchio (d 1977), of Aosta, Italy; 3 da (Jessica b 1958, Milchela b 1961, Malinka b 1963, d 1985); *Career* Capt (former Lt) RAMC Singapore and Malaya 1948-50; jr hosp res: Oxford 1947-48, Toronto 1950-52; clinical res Massachusetts Gen Hosp 1952-53, lectr (also res and clinical posts) Manchester UCL and Royal Postgrad Med Sch 1954-69; prof of med and hon conslt physician: Univ of Dundee 1969-72, UCL 1972- (dir dept of med 1972-82); sec Renal Assoc 1960-65, treas Med Res Soc 1969-74; memb: Cncl Int Nephrological Soc 1972-78, Zoological Soc; chm: Nat Teidney Res Fund 1976-80; FRCP 1967, FRCPE 1971, memb RSM; *Books* The Large Intestine Its Role in Mammalian Nutrition and Homeostasis (jtly, 1981); *Recreations* music, walking, gardens, foreign travel; *Style*— Prof Oliver Wrong; Flat 8, 96-100 New Cavendish St, London W1M 7FA (☎ 071 637 4740); Department of Medicine, University College, London WC1E 6JJ (☎ 071 380 9674)

WROTH, Hon Mrs (Mary Octavia); *née* Addington; da of late 6 Viscount Sidmouth; *b* 1927; *m* 1, 1953, David Christopher Leeming; 1 s; m 2, 1959, David Tilling Wroth (d 1986); *Style*— The Hon Mrs Wroth; Santiani, Moscari c/Campanet No.29, Mallorca, Spain

WROTTESLEY, 6 Baron (UK 1838); Sir Clifton Hugh Lancelot de Verdon Wrottesley; 14 Bt (E 1642); s of Hon Richard Wrottesley (d 1970), and Georgina, now Mrs J Seddon-Brown, *qv*; suc gf (5 Baron, sixteenth in descent from Sir Walter Wrottesley, a chamberlain of the Exchequer under Edward IV and himself third in descent from Sir Hugh de Wrottesley, KG (one of the original members of the Order), who fought in the Black Prince's div at Crécy) 1977; *b* 10 Aug 1968; *Educ* Eton; *Heir* half unc, Hon Stephen John b 21 Dec 1955; *Career* patron of three livings; *Style*— The Rt Hon the Lord Wrottesley; c/o Barclays Bank, 8 High Street, Eton, Windsor, Berks, SL4 6AU

WROTTESLEY, Baroness; Mary Ada Van Echten; da of Edgar Dryden Tudhope, of Kenilworth, Cape Province, S Africa; *m* 5 March 1955, as his 3 w, 5 Baron Wrottesley (d 1977); 2 s; *Style*— The Rt Hon the Lady Wrottesley; 18 Sonnehoogte, Thomas Rd, Kenilworth, Cape Province, S Africa

WROTTESLEY, Hon Stephen John; s of 5 Baron Wrottesley (d 1977); half-uncle and h of 6 Baron; *b* 21 Dec 1955; *m* 16 Dec 1982, Mrs Roz Fletcher, *née* Taylor; 1 da (Alexandra b 11 May 1985); *Style*— The Hon Stephen Wrottesley

WU, Kung Chao; s of Wu Kuang Hua (d 1944), of Amoy, China, and Chao Fu Kuan (d 1955); *b* 20 Nov 1922; *Educ* Anglo Chinese Coll Amoy China, LSE; *m* 10 May 1951, Daisy Chan, da of Chan Khay Gwan, of Rangoon (d 1979); 1 s (Ping 1953), 1 da (Ling b 1956); *Career* Bank of China: dep gen mangr London 1978-86, dep gen mangr NY 1981-83, sr dep gen mangr London 1986, advsr London 1989; hon pres Foreign Banks and Securities Houses Assoc London 1990; FCIB 1985; *Recreations* tennis, reading, travel, theatre; *Clubs* Overseas Bankers; *Style*— K C Wu, Esq; 79 Hervey Close, London N3 2HH (☎ 081 346 1827); Bank of China, 8/10 Mansion House Place, London EC4N 8BL (☎ 071 626 8301, fax 071 626 3892)

WULSTAN, Prof David; s of Rev Norman B Jones (d 1948), and (Sarah) Margaret, *née* Simpson (d 1973); *b* 18 Jan 1937; *Educ* Royal Masonic Sch, Coll of Tech Birmingham, Magdalen Coll Oxford (BSc, ARCM, MA, BLitt); *m* 9 Oct 1965, Susan Nelson, da of Frank Nelson Graham (d 1963); 1 s (Philip Richard James b 1969); *Career* fell and lectr Magdalen Coll Oxford 1964-78, visiting prof Univ of California Berkeley USA 1978, statutory lectr Univ Coll Cork 1979-80 (prof of music 1980-83), Gregynog prof of music Univ Coll of Wales 1983-; dir The Clerkes of Oxenford 1964-; numerous recordings and appearances for TV and radio, appearance at festivals, recordings of incidental music for TV and cinema, composer of church music, etc; *Books* Gibbons Church Music (Early English Church Music) Vol 3 (1964) and vol 27 (1979), Anthology of English Church Music (1968), Play of Daniel (1976), Coverdale Chant Book (1978), Sheppard, Complete Works (1979), and many other editions, articles and reviews; *Recreations* tennis, badminton, food and drink, bemoaning the loss of the English language; *Style*— Prof David Wulstan; Ty Isaf, Llanilar, Aberystwyth SY23 4NP (☎ 09747 229); Music Dept, Univ Coll of Wales, Aberystwyth, Dyfed SY23 2AX (☎ 0970 622849)

WURTZEL, David Ira; s of Paul Bernard Wurtzel, of Los Angeles, California, and Shirley Lorraine, *née* Stein; *b* 28 Jan 1949; *Educ* Univ of California Berkeley (BA), QMC London (MA) Fitzwilliam Coll Cambridge (MA); *Career* barr 1976-; arts corr The Diplomat 1989-; novelist; author of articles in Town and Country (NY); memb Laurence Oliver Awards Panel; *Books* Thomas Lyster, A Cambridge Novel (1983); *Recreations* theatre, opera, travelling abroad, taking exercise, architecture, conservation; *Style*— David Wurtzel, Esq; 3 Dr Johnson's Building, Temple, London, ECYY 7BA (☎ 071 353 8778)

WYATT, Arthur Powell; s of Dr Henry George Wyatt (ka 1938), and Edith Maud, *née* Holden (d 1972); *b* 14 Oct 1932; *Educ* Taunton Sch, Eltham Coll, Bart's Med Sch (MB BS); *m* 20 Aug 1955, Margaret Helen, da of Rev W H Cox (d 1988); 4 s (John b 1958, Robert b 1961, David b and d 1964, Andrew b 1966); *Career* lectr in surgery Bart's 1961-63, sr registrar in surgery KCH 1964-67, postgrad res surgn Univ of California San Francisco 1965-66, conslt surgn Greenwich Health Dist 1967-; pres: RSM Surgery Section 1989-90, Eltham Combined Div St Johns Ambulance; memb Ct of Examiners RCS, past pres W Kent Medico Chirurgical Soc; memb: BMA, Vascular Surgery Soc, Br Soc Gastroenterol; fell Assoc of Surgns of GB and I, FRCS, FICS; *Recreations* orchid growing, travel, skiing; *Clubs* Woolwich Rotary, Huntarian Society; *Style*— Arthur Wyatt, Esq; The Cottage, 72 Camden Park Rd, Chislehurst, Kent BR7 5HF (☎ 081 467 9477); The Blackheath AMI Hospital, 40-42 Lee Terrace, Blackheath, London SE3 9UD (☎ 081 318 7722)

WYATT, David Francis; s of Francis Edward Wyatt, of Newent, and Enid, *née* Barrett (d 1981); *b* 3 July 1941; *Educ* Marling Sch Stroud Glos, LSE; *m* 24 April 1976, Rosalind Blair, da of Philip Robert Henwood John (d 1955), of Downside House, Bridge Sollers, Hereford; 2 s (Timothy b 1980, Jeremy b 1982), 1 da (Briony b 1986); *Career* admitted slr and notary public 1968; ptnr Treasure and Whiteman, dir TC Vermeer Ltd (agric machinery); vice pres Notaries Soc 1989 (memb Cncl 1977-), tstee Gloucester Municipal Charities; *Books* Two Hundred Years of True Friendship (1987), Ninety Years without Slumbering (1988) (Histories of Masonic Lodges 218 and 2709, 1988); *Recreations* gardening, golf; *Clubs* Minchinhampton Golf; *Style*— David Wyatt, Esq; 17 St John's Lane, Gloucester GL1 2AZ (☎ 0452 25351, fax 0452 506735)

WYATT, David Joseph; CBE (1977); s of Frederick Wyatt (d 1967), and Selina, *née* Parr (d 1990); *b* 12 Aug 1931; *Educ* Leigh GS Lancashire; *m* 1,1957, Annemarie (d 1978), da of Jakob Angst, of Zurich, Switzerland; 2 s (Simon b 1960, Antony b 1961), 1 da (Caroline b 1967); m 2, 1990, Wendy Baron, da of Dr S B Dimson; *Career* Nat Serv RAF 1950-52; foreign then diplomatic serv: joined 1949, served abroad (Berne 1954-57, Vienna 1961-64, Canberra 1965-69, Ottawa 1971-74, Stockholm 1976-79), under sec on loan to Home Civil Serv 1979-82, ambassador UK Mission to UN 1982, min and dep commandant Br Military Govt Berlin 1983-85, dir Int Div BRCS 1985- (acting dir gen Jan-July 1990); *Style*— David Wyatt, Esq, CBE; c/o British Red Cross Society, 9 Grosvenor Crescent, London SW1X 7EJ (☎ 071 235 5454, fax 071 245 6315)

WYATT, Dr Edward Henry; s of Harry George Wyatt (d 1938), in China, and Edith Maud, *née* Holden (d 1972); *b* 29 Sept 1928; *Educ* Eltham Coll, Taunton Sch, London Hosp Med Coll (MB BS); *m* 1 Aug 1953, Hilda Mary, da of James Thomas Eggleton (d 1939), of Faringdon; 4 s (Christopher b and d 1956, Michael b 1958, Stephen b 1961, Adrian b 1964), 1 da (Valerie b 1962); *Career* house offr: the London Hosp, Hackney Hosp, Forest Gate Hosp 1951-52, MO Baptist Missionary Soc Zaire 1953-65, med registrar Chichester 1965-67, dermatology registrar in United Birmingham Hosps 1967-69, sr registrar dermatology Royal Victoria Infirmary Newcastle 1969-72, conslt dermatologist Hull and Yorks Health Authorities 1972-; memb and pres N England Dermatological Soc, memb Hull Med Soc (past pres), past clinical tutor Hull and E Yorks Postgrad Med Centre; memb: BMA, RSM; FRCPE; *Books* pubns incl papers on clinical dermatology and scanning electron microscopy of hair; *Recreations* preaching, painting, maps, travel; *Style*— Dr Edward Wyatt; 16 St James Road, Melton, N Ferriby, N Humberside HU14 3HZ (☎ 0482 633606); 61 North Bar Within, Beverley, North Humberside HU17 8DG (☎ 0482 860412)

WYATT, Jeremy Gaylord; s of Maj Alan Wyatt, of W Sussex, and Pamela, *née* Jermy; *b* 31 Oct 1943; *Educ* Goring Hall, Salisian Coll; *m* 29 Oct 1968, Jenifer Ann Perry, da of Maj John Moore (d 1958); 1 s (Rupert), 1 da (Charlotte); *Career* RA 1962-67, Capt South Arabian Army 1965-67; PR exec ICI Ltd 1969-73, head PR Fisons Ltd 1973-81, dir of communications John Brown plc 1981-83, Main Bd dir and md Corp Div Good Relations Gp Plc 1983-86, dep md Biss Lancaster Plc 1986-91, dir of communications The Prudential Corporation 1991-; *Books* Marketing for Lawyers (1985); *Recreations* garden design, mil history, sailing; *Style*— Jeremy Wyatt, Esq

WYATT, Hon Mrs (Margaret Agnes); *née* Blades; da (twin) of late 1 Baron Ebbisham, GBE; *b* 1908; *m* 1933, Brig Richard John Penfold Wyatt, MC, TD, DL, JP, late Royal Sussex Regt (TA) (d 1954); 2 s; *Style*— The Hon Mrs Wyatt; Hillbarn Cottage, Findon, nr Worthing, Sussex

WYATT, Robert Laurence (Bob); s of Charles Wyatt (d 1987), and Phyliss Muriel, *née* Wheeler; *b* 20 Jan 1943; *Educ* Portsmouth Northern GS; *m* 15 May 1965, Linda Doreen, da of Alan Patrick Mullin; 2 s (James b 1968, David b 1971); *Career* with Midland Bank plc: joined Portsmouth branch 1959, seconded to Bank of Bermuda 1967, Asst Gen Mangr 1981, Gen Mangr 1984; vice chm/ chief exec Forward Trust Gp Ltd 1987; vice-chm Finance Houses Assoc 1988; AIB 1964; *Recreations* golf, gardening, ballet; *Style*— Bob Wyatt, Esq; 145 City Rd, London EC1V 1JY (☎ 071 251 9090, fax 071 251 0064)

WYATT, (Christopher) Terrel; s of Lionel Harry Wyatt, and Audrey Vere Wyatt; *b* 17 July 1927; *Educ* Kingston GS, Battersea Poly, Imperial College (BSc, DIC); *m* 1 (m dis); 4 s; m 2, 1990, Patricia; *Career* RE 1946-48; Charles Brand & Son Ltd 1948-54, joined Richard Costain Ltd 1955 (dir 1970, gp chief exec 1975-80, dep chm 1979-80), chm Costain Group plc 1980-87, chm and chief exec WS Atkins Ltd 1987; FEng, FICE, FIStructE; *Recreations* sailing; *Style*— Terrel Wyatt, Esq; The White House, St Martin's Avenue, Epson, Surrey KT18 5HS; W S Atkins Ltd, Woodcote Grove, Ashley Rd, Epsom, Surrey KT18 5BW (☎ 03727 26140)

WYATT, (Richard) Wesley; s of James Richard Dinham Wyatt (d 1985), of Croford, Wiveliscombe, Somerset, and Elsie, *née* Reed (d 1977); *b* 16 April 1932; *Educ* Taunton Sch; *m* 1; 1 s (Robert Hugh b 1958), 1 da ((Maria) Jayne b 1959); m 2, 22 April 1989, Olive Louisa, da of Fred Parsons (d 1957); *Career* farmer; dir Rural Devpts of Portugal; chm: Farm Advsy Ctee Liscombe Experimental Husbandry Farm 1983-89, Liscombe Research Ltd 1989-90; memb: R & D Ctee Home Grown Cereals Authy 1986-90, Advsy Sectoral Gp (Ruminants) Priorities Bd 1990-; organist Wiveliscombe Methodist Church 1951-86, chm Wiveliscombe Young Cons 1959-62, vice pres Somerset Young Cons 1962, memb Wiveliscombe Parish Cncl 1970-87, pres Old Tauntonian Assoc 1979, chm Burnham & Berrow GC 1986-88 and 1989-90 (Centenary capt 1990-91); ARAgS; *Recreations* golf, gardening, classical music, rugby, cricket; *Clubs* Burnham & Berrow Golf; *Style*— Wesley Wyatt, Esq; The Nineteenth, Orchard Close, Westford, Wellington, Somerset TA21 0DR (☎ 0823 66 4016)

WYATT, (Alan) Will; s of Basil Wyatt, of Oxford, and Hettie Evelyn, *née* Hooper; *b* 7 Jan 1942; *Educ* Magdalen Coll Sch Oxford, Emmanuel Coll Cambridge (BA); *m* 2 April 1966, Jane Bridgit, da of Beauchamp Bagenal (d 1958), of Kitale, Kenya; 2 da (Hannah b 1967, Rosalind b 1970); *Career* reporter Sheffield Morning Telegraph 1964-65, sub ed BBC Radio News 1965-68; BBC TV: prodr 1968- (programmes include Robinsons Travels, B Traven A Mystery Solved, Late Night Line Up, The Book Programme), head presentation programmes 1977-80, head documentary features 1981-87, head features and documentaries gp 1987-88, asst md Network TV 1988-91, md Network 1991; chm ctee on violence in tv programmes BBC 1983 and 1987, tstee Br Video History Tst, dir Broadcasters Audience Res Bd 1989; *Books* The Man Who Was B Traven (1980); *Recreations* walking, horse racing, theatre; *Style*— Will Wyatt, Esq; 38 Abinger Rd, London W4 1EX; BBC Television, Wood Lane, London W12

WYATT OF WEEFORD, Baron (Life Peer UK 1987), of Weeford, Co Staffs; Sir Woodrow Lyle; s of Robert Harvey Lyle Wyatt (d 1932), and Ethel, *née* Morgan (d 1974); descended from Humphrey Wyatt (d 1610), the ancestor of the Wyatt architects, painters, sculptors and inventors; yr bro of Robert David Lyle, *qv*; *b* 4 July 1918; *Educ* Eastbourne Coll, Worcester Coll Oxford (MA); *m* 1, 1939 (m dis 1944), Susan Cox; m 2, 1948 (m dis 1956), Nora Robbins; m 3, 1957 (m dis 1966), Lady Moorea Hastings (now Black), da of 15 Earl of Huntingdon by his 1 w, Cristina; 1 s (Pericles); m 4, 1966, Verushka, *née* Racz, widow of Baron Dr Lazlo Banszky von Ambroz; 1 da (Petronella); *Career* Maj WWII (despatches); journalist; MP (Lab): Aston 1945-55, Bosworth 1959-70; Parly under sec of state and fin sec War Office 1951; chm Horserace Totalisator Bd 1976-; kt 1983; *Books Incl:* The Jews at Home (1950), Turn Again Westminster (1973), The Exploits of Mr Saucy Squirrel (1976), To the Point (1981), Confessions of an Optimist (1985); *Style*— The Rt Hon the Lord Wyatt of Weeford; 19 Cavendish Ave, London NW8 9JD

WYBREW, John Leonard; s of Leonard Percival Wybrew, of Radlett, Herts, and May Edith Wybrew; *b* 27 Jan 1943; *Educ* Bushey GS, Sir John Cass Coll; *m* 1967, Linda Gillian, da of Wing Cdr John James Frederick Long, of Goddards Lane, Camberley; 1 s, 2 da; *Career* life mangr and actuary Time Assur Soc 1971-72, gen mangr and dir: Windsor Life Assur Co Ltd 1972-76 (md 1976-, chm 1988-), World-Wide Assur Co Ltd 1972-76 (dir 1982-); md Windsor Gp Ltd; chm: Windsor Investmnt Mgmnt 1986-, Windsor Tst Mangrs 1986-, Windsor Home Loans Ltd; memb ctee of mgmnt Family Assurance Soc 1987-; *Recreations* horses, sailing, reading, golf; *Clubs* IOD, Oriental; *Style*— John Wybrew Esq; 15 West Heath Rd, London NW3 7UU (☎ 071 794 1121); Windsor Group Ltd, Windsor House, Telford Centre, Salop TF3 4NB (☎ 0952 292929, telex 849780)

WYFOLD, 3 Baron (UK 1919); Sir Hermon Robert Fleming Hermon-Hodge; 3 Bt (UK 1902); s of 2 Baron Wyfold, DSO, MVO (d 1942), and Dorothy, da of Robert Fleming and aunt of Peter Fleming, the travel writer, and Ian Fleming, the creator of James Bond; *b* 26 June 1915; *Educ* Eton, Le Rosey Switzerland; *Heir* none; *Career* Capt Grenadier Gds (reserve); dir Robert Fleming Holding & other cos; ret; *Recreations* gardening; *Clubs* Carlton, Pratt's, Metropolitan (New York); *Style*— The Rt Hon the Lord Wyfold; c/o Robert Fleming Holdings, 25 Copthall Avenue, London EC2R 7DR (☎ 071 638 5858)

WYKEHAM, Air Marshal Sir Peter; KCB (1965, CB 1961), DSO (1943 and Bar 1944), OBE (1949), DFC (1940 and Bar 1941), AFC (1951); s of Guy Vane Wykeham-Barnes; relinquished surname of Barnes 1955; *b* 13 Sept 1915; *Educ* RAF Halton; *m* 1949, Barbara Elizabeth, da of late John Boynton Priestley, OM, the writer; 2 s, 1 da; *Career* cmmnd RAF 1937; served Fighter Sqdns 73, 257 and 23 WWII; dir Jt Warfare Staff MOD 1962-64, Cdr Far East Air Force 1964-66, Dep Chief Air Staff 1967-69, ret; tech conslt 1969-; FBIM, FRAes; *Style*— Air Marshal Sir Peter Wykeham, KCB, DSO, OBE, DFC, AFC; Green Place, Stockbridge, Hampshire

WYKES-JOYCE, Max Stephen Holmes; s of Frederick Bicknell, MM (d 1965), of Marston Green, Warwicks, and May Elizabeth, *née* Ballard (d 1990); *b* 26 Dec 1924; *Educ* Prince Henry's GS Evesham, LSE, Anglo-French Art Centre London, Goldsmiths Coll Sch of Art London; *m* 30 Oct 1947 (m dis 1967), Liza Margaret, da of Walter Langley-Kemp (d 1972), of Perth, W Aust; 1 da (Sianna b 1949); *Career* WWII, RAF 1943-47; London art critic Int Herald Tribune 1967-87, fine arts corr Antique Dealer and Collectors Guide 1967-, saleroom corr Arts Review 1986-; contrib to: The Collector, Galleries magazine, The Independent and many other newspapers and periodicals; memb Int Assoc of Art Critics; Accademico d'Italia con Medaglia d'Oro 1980; *Books* Triad of Genius - Edith and Osbert Sitwell (1953), 7000 Years of Pottery and Porcelain (1958), Cosmetics and Adornment - Ancient and Contemporary Usage (1961), Les Instants Immobiles - The Work of Bouvier de Cachard (1973), Seven Archangels - The Art of Marian Bohusz-Szyszko (1977), My Heart has Opened unto Every Form - The Art of Basil Alkazzi (1982); *Recreations* fencing, gardening, walking, cat watching; *Style*— Max Wykes-Joyce, Esq; 8 Elm Road, Evesham, Worcestershire WR11 5DL (☎ 0386 40214)

WYLD, David John Charles; s of John Hugh Gilbert Wyld, TD, and Helen Selina, *née* Leslie Melville (d 1946); *b* 11 March 1943; *Educ* Harrow, ChCh Coll Oxford (MA); *m* 1, 19 Dec 1970 (m dis), Sally, da of Ellis Morgan, CMG, of Penhenllan, Cusop, Hay on Waye, Herefordshire; 2 s (Barnaby b 1972, Jonathan b 1973); m 2, 20 June 1987, Caroline Mary, da of Ronald Walter Alexander, CBE, of Moonzie Hill, Barnullo, St Andrews, Fife; 2 da (Charlotte b 1988, Alexandra b 1989); *Career* called to the Bar 1968; admitted slr 1974; practising slr: Linklaters & Paines 1974-79, ptnr Macfarlanes 1981-; chm litigation ctee City of London Law Soc; memb Law Soc 1974; *Recreations* reading, walking, golf; *Clubs* MCC, Berkshire Golf, Liphook Golf; *Style*— David Wyld, Esq; Macfarlanes, 10 Norwich St, London EC4A 1BD (☎ 071 831 9222, fax 071 831 9607, telex 296381 MACFAR G)

WYLDBORE-SMITH, Maj-Gen Sir (Francis) Brian; CB (1964), DSO (1943), OBE (1944); yr s of Rev William Reginald Wyldbore-Smith (d 1943, sometime domestic chaplain to the Marquess of Londonderry and ggs of Sir John Wyldbore Smith, 2 Bt); *b* 10 July 1913; *Educ* Wellington, RMA Woolwich; *m* 1944, Hon Molly Angela Cayzer, *qv*, yr da of 1 Baron Rotherwick; 1 s, 4 da; *Career* GOC 44 Div (TA) and Home Counties dist 1965-68, Maj-Gen ME, Far E, France, Italy, Germany, Col 15/19 Hussars 1970-77, dep constable Dover Castle 1965-68, ret 1968; dir Cons Bd of Fin 1970-; kt 1980; *Recreations* shooting; *Clubs* Buck's, Naval and Military; *Style*— Maj-Gen Sir Brian Wyldbore-Smith, CB, DSO, OBE; Grantham House, Grantham, Lincs (☎ 0476 64705)

WYLDBORE-SMITH, Hon Lady (Molly Angela); *née* Cayzer; yr da of 1 Baron Rotherwick (d 1958); *b* 6 Sept 1917; *m* 1 April 1944, Maj-Gen Sir Brian Wyldbore-Smith, CB, DSO, OBE, *qv*; 1 s, 4 da; *Style*— The Hon Lady Wyldbore-Smith; Grantham House, Grantham, Lincs (☎ 0476 64705)

WYLDBORE-SMITH, Nicolas Hugh; s of Lt Cdr Hugh Deane Wyldbore-Smith, RN (ka 1941), and Rachel Caroline Lucy Orlebar; *b* 23 May 1938; *Educ* Wellington Coll Berks, St James Sch Maryland USA; *m* 1964, Gillian Mary, da of Leslie Boland Carman (d 1968), of Hants; 2 s (Alexander b 1969, James b 1971); *Career* joined Ind Coope Gp 1963; dir: Friary Meux Ltd 1967, Ind Coope Oxford 1971, Benskins 1975; md Design Co 1988-; cmmnd 23 Special Air Serv Regt TA and Leicestershire, Derbyshire Yeomanry; bursar Bruern Abbey Sch 1991; Freeman City of London 1989; FInstD, MCIM, MBII; *Recreations* sailing, shooting, gardening; *Style*— Nicolas Wyldbore-Smith, Esq; The Courtiers, Clifton Hampden, Abingdon, Oxon OX14 3EL (☎ 086 730 7941); 21 Montford Place, Kennington

WYLDBORE-SMITH, William Francis; s of John Henry Wyldbore-Smith (d 1982), of Scaynes Hill, Sussex, and Tighnabruaich, Argyll, and Robina, *née* Ward; *b* 15 Jan 1948; *Educ* Marlborough; *m* 27 Dec 1974, Prisca Faith, da of Rev Peter Nourse, of Leominster, Herefordshire; 1 da (Philippa b 15 April 1977); *Career* admitted slr 1972, ptnr Osborne Clarke of Bristol 1977-85, ptnr Wood & Awdry 1986-; chm: N Wilts Business Assoc 1985-88, N Wilts Enterprise Agency 1986-, Wilts Rural Enterprise Agency 1989-; Under Sheriff of Wilts 1987-; Freeman City of London, Liveryman Worshipful Co of Musicians; memb Law Soc 1972; *Recreations* gardening, shooting, reading; *Clubs* Brooks's; *Style*— W F Wyldbore-Smith, Esq; Wood & Awdry, 3 St Mary Street, Chippenham, Wilts (☎ 0249 444422, fax 0249 443666)

WYLIE, Alastair James Blair; TD (1946); s of Alex Wylie (d 1950), of Turnberry, Ayrshire, and Hilda Gwladys, *née* Paton (d 1973); *b* 21 April 1916; *Educ* Kelvinside Acad Glasgow, Warriston Moffat, Sedbergh; *m* 1 Feb 1951, Jessie Elizabeth Kerr, da of William Walker, JP, of Foreland Island, Islay, Argyll; *Career* cmmnd Argyll and Sutherland Highlanders TA 1935; served RA France 1939-40, Egypt 1941, Italy 1942-45, Lt-Col 1949; Wylie's Ltd Glasgow 1935-: dir 1946, md 1949, chm 1950; dir: James Sword & Son Ltd 1964-83, Hamilton Park Racecourse Co Ltd 1978-; *Recreations* golf, shooting, fishing, racing; *Clubs* Western Glasgow, Royal Scottish Automobile, Ranfurly Castle, Western Gailes; *Style*— Alastair Wylie, Esq, TD; 17 Fotheringay Rd, Glasgow G41 (☎ 041 423 1713); Wylie's Ltd, 370 Pollokshaws Rd, Glasgow G41 (☎ 041 423 6644, telex 778440)

WYLIE, Prof John Cleland Watson; s of George Stewart Wylie (d 1966), of Belfast, and Phyllis Ann, *née* Watson; *b* 6 July 1943; *Educ* Methodist Coll Belfast, Queen's Univ Belfast (LLB, LLD), Harvard (LLM); *m* 22 Sept 1973, Gillian Lindsey, da of Eric Sidney Edward Gardner, of London; 1 s (Nicholas George b 1977), 1 da (Emma Louise b 1979); *Career* lectr in law Queen's Univ Belfast 1965-71, Frank Knox Fell Harvard 1966-67; Univ of Wales Coll of Cardiff: sr lectr 1972-76, reader 1976-79, prof of law 1979-, dean faculty of law 1980-83, dep princ 1990-; ed: N Ireland Legal Quarterly 1970-76; editorial dir: Professional Books Ltd 1981-87, Butterworth (Ireland) 1987-; land law conslt N Ireland Office 1980-90, memb Legal Studies Bd CNAA 1984-87; *Books* Irish Land Law (2 edn, 1986), Irish Conveyancing Law (1978), Land Laws of Trinidad and Tobago (1986), Irish Landlord and Tenant Law (1990); *Recreations* reading, swimming, gardening; *Style*— Prof John Wylie; Cardiff Law School, University of Wales College of Cardiff, PO Box 427, Cardiff CF1 1XD (☎ 0222 874177, fax 0222 874097)

WYLIE, Keith Francis; s of Shaun Wylie, of Cambridge, and Odette Frances, *née* Murray; *b* 29 March 1945; *Educ* Winchester, King's Coll Cambridge; *m* 2 July 1988, Helen Margaret, da of John Francis Cassidy of Stevenage; *Career* computer scientist Applied Res of Cambridge 1970-74, call to the Bar Gray's Inn 1976-; Br Open Croquet Champion 1970 and 1971, memb GB Croquet Test Team 1974 and 1982; *Books* Expert Croquet Tactics (1985); *Recreations* skiing, gardening, wine, opera, croquet; *Style*— Keith Wylie, Esq; 17 Carlton Crescent, Southampton (☎ 0703 639001, fax 0703 339625)

WYLIE, Rt Hon Lord; Norman Russell Wylie; VRD (1961), PC (1970), QC (1964); s of late William Wylie; *b* 26 Oct 1923; *Educ* Paisley GS, St Edmund Hall Oxford, Univ of Glasgow, Univ of Edinburgh; *m* 1963, Gillian, da of late Dr Richard Verney, of Edinburgh; 3 s (Julian b 1964, Russell b 1966, Philip b 1968); *Career* Lt-Cdr RNR, served Fleet Air Arm and Russian and Atlantic Convoys; advocate 1952, standing counsel to Air Miny Scotland 1956-59, crown counsel 1959-64, slr-gen Scotland 1964 (April-Oct), MP (C) Edinburgh Pentlands 1964-74, lord advocate 1970-74, Scottish Lord of Session (senator of the Coll of Justice) 1974-90; hon fell St Edmund Hall 1975-; *Recreations* sailing (yacht 'Niarana'), shooting; *Clubs* New, Royal Highland Yacht, RNSA; *Style*— The Rt Hon Lord Wylie, VRD; 30 Lauder Rd, Edinburgh EH9 (☎ 031 667 8377)

WYLIE, Ronald James; OBE (1984); s of James Baird Wylie (d 1977), of Edinburgh, and Christina, *née* Mathieson (d 1977); *b* 31 Aug 1930; *Educ* Melville Coll, Univ of Edinburgh (CA, JDipMA); *m* 17 Sept 1955, Brenda Margaret, da of George Paterson Wright (d 1952), of Leeds; 2 s (Roderick b 1957, Stuart b 1960); *Career* Tullis Russell Co Ltd: md 1973-81, chief exec 1981-85; exec dir Young Enterprise Scotland 1986-;

Recreations sailing, photography, music; *Clubs* Burntisland Sailing; *Style*— Ronald J Wylie, Esq, OBE; Treetops, 123 Dysart Road, Kirkcaldy KY1 2BB (☎ 0592 51 597)

WYLIE-HARRIS, William Harold; s of Richard Charles Harris (d 1947), of Priory Road, Kilburn, London, and Ellen Mabel, *née* Parsons (d 1957), assumed additional surname of Wylie by Deed Poll 1957; *b* 26 Jan 1898; *Educ* City of London Sch; *m* 26 Jan 1932, (Ada) Margaret, da of George Edwards (d 1964), of 16 Donovan Avenue, Muswell Hill, London; 4 s (Michael b 1933, d 1978, Raymond b 1933, d 1978, Clifton b 1939, Peter b 1942), 3 da (Christine b 1936, Pearl b 1942, Dawn b 1947); *Career* Wylie-Harris & Co (Export) Ltd; chm Gresham Ctee, memb Ct of Common Cncl City of London 1957, DL Farringdon Within 1975; Master Worshipful Co of Plaisterers 1966, Worshipful Co of Loriners 1982; FRSA 1971; *Books* Panorama of the City of London (16 booklets on the topography of City Wards, 1970-75), American Links with the City of London (1977); *Style*— William Wylie-Harris, Esq; 41 Lauderdale Tower, Barbican, London EC2 (☎ 071 628 9097)

WYLLIE, Douglas Stewart; s of (Matthew) Stewart Wyllie, of Edinburgh, and Rowena Margaret Wyllie; *b* 20 May 1963; *Educ* Dulwich, Daniel Stewart's and Melville Coll Edinburgh; *m* 21 June 1985, Jennifer Anne; *Career* Rugby Union fly-half/centre Stewart's Melville FP RFC and Scotland (10 caps); played soccer for England U-13 schoolboys; Clubs: Stewart's Melville FP RFC (over 300 appearances) 1981-, Edinburgh 1982-, Barbarians RFC (5 appearances); capt and memb Scotland U-21, Scotland B (3 caps); Scotland: debut v Australia 1984, Five Nations debut v Wales 1985, tour Romania 1984, tour France and Spain 1986, tour USA and Canada 1985, tour NZ 1987 and 1990, tour Zimbabwe 1988, tour Japan 1989; winner Middx sevens 1982; bank offr Bank of Scotland 1981-88; sales exec: Equity & Law Assurance Co 1988-89, Bukta Sportswear 1989-; *Recreations* all sports; *Style*— Douglas Wyllie, Esq; Scottish Rugby Union, Murrayfield, Edinburgh EH12 5PJ

WYLLIE, Dr George Ralston; s of Andrew Wyllie (d 1965), and Harriet Mills Wyllie (d 1979); *b* 31 Dec 1921; *Educ* Allan Glen's Sch Glasgow, Bellahouston Acad Glasgow; *m* 16 Sept 1944, Daphne Winifred, da of William Herbert Watts, BEM (d 1965); 2 da (Louise b 28 July 1950, Elaine b 7 May 1954); *Career* electrical artificer (petty offr) RN 1942-46, serv HMS Argonaut; Civil Serv: Post Office 1938-42 and 1946-47, Customs & Excise 1948-80; Sculptor, writer and performer; exhibitions: UK, USA, Euro; exhibited and performed 1982-87: Glasgow, Edinburgh, London; Sculpture events: Straw Locomotive Glasgow 1987, Paper Boat Gulbenkein award event 1989; works included and installed in: Glasgow Cathedral, Glasgow Kelvingrove Museum, World HQ GA Insurance Perth, Atrium and UFA- Fabrik Berlin, Getty Fndn Fluxus Archives, Arts Cncl Scotland and GB, Worcester Museum Mass USA; fell Hand Hollow Fndn E Chatham NY 1982-83; *Film* The Why's Man; DLitt Univ of Strathclyde; ARSA; *Books* A Day Down A Goldmine (1982); *Clubs* Royal Gourock YC; *Style*— Dr George Wyllie; 9 McPherson Drive, Gourock, Renfrewshire PA19 1LJ (☎ 0475 32810)

WYMAN, Peter Lewis; s of John Bernard Wyman, MBE, of Sharpthorne, Sussex, and Joan Dorthea, *née* Beighton; *b* 26 Feb 1950; *Educ* Epsom Coll; *m* 16 Sept 1978, Joy Alison, da of Edward George Foster, of Horsted Keynes, Sussex; 1 s (John b 1985), 1 da (Gemma b 1988); *Career* CA, ptnr Coopers & Lybrand Deloitte 1978, chm London Soc of CAs 1987-88; Freeman: Worshipful Co of CA's 1988, City of London 1988; FCA 1973, FBIM 1978; *Recreations* equestrian sports, gardening; *Style*— Peter L Wyman, Esq; Reapyears Corner, Streeters Rough, Chelwood Gate, W Sussex RH17 7LL (☎ 0825 74 243); Coopers and Lybrand Deloitte, Plumtree Court, London EC4A 4HT (☎ 071 822 4777, fax 071 822 8278, car 0860 385900)

WYMER, Michael George Petre; s of Norman George Wymer, of Grassmere Close, Felpham, Sussex (d 1982), and Mary Jean Hamilton, *née* Kinloch; *b* 25 Nov 1936; *Educ* Sherborne; *m* 5 Sept 1964, Patricia Lorraine, da of Tom Bruce Jones, of Redcar, Blairlogie, Stirling, Scotland (d 1984); 1 s (Bruce b 1968), 2 da (Penny b 1966, Joanna b 1971); *Career* served 2 Lt Royal Signals 1955-57; joined Longman's Green 1957, gp sales dir Longman Group Ltd 1973-82 (overseas sales mangr 1967-72); dep chief exec: Longman Holdings Ltd 1983-88, Addison-Wesley-Longman Ltd 1988-89; dep chm Longman Group UK Ltd 1988-89, ops and planning dir Longman Group Ltd 1989-; chm Bd of Govrs Waterside Sch 1990- (govr 1974-83 and 1989-); memb bd Book Devpt Cncl 1979-81; *Recreations* golf, gardening, collecting landscape paintings, watching cricket; *Style*— Michael Wymer, Esq; Old Kiln House, 79 Haymeads Lane, Bishop's Stortford, Herts CM23 5JJ (☎ 0279 654738); Longman Gp Ltd, Longman House, Burnt Mill, Harlow, Essex (☎ 0279 62371, fax 0279 451428)

WYND, Oswald Morris; s of William Oswald Wynd (d 1940), of Edinburgh, and Anna Mary, *née* Morris (d 1963); *b* 4 July 1913; *Educ* American Sch Tokyo Japan, Univ of Edinburgh; *m* Janet Greenlees, da of Thomas Greenlees Muir, MC (d 1967); *Career* Nat Serv Scots Gds, cmmnd Lt Intelligence Corps, 9 Indian Div Malaya, POW Kuala Lumpur, Singapore, Hokkaido Japan from 1942 (despatches 1946); freelance writer 1947-; fourteen suspense novels (pen name Gavin Black), sixteen straight novels incl The Ginger Tree; occasional journalist, reviewer and NY travel writer; memb PEN, memb Soc of Authors; *Recreations* gardening; *Style*— Oswald Wynd, Esq

WYNDHAM, Hon Harry Hugh Patrick; s of late 6 Baron Leconfield and (1) Egremont, and Pamela, *née* Wyndham-Quin, gda of 5 Earl of Dunraven and Mount Earl; bro of present Baron Egremont (and Leconfield); *b* 28 Sept 1957; *Educ* Eton, Ch Ch Oxford (BA); *m* 2 Nov 1985, Susan Fiona McLean, eldest da of Bruce Woodall, of 7 Sheffield Terrace, London W8; 1 s (Alexander Harry John Valentine b 27 Dec 1986); *Career* company dir; *Recreations* football, skiing, motor cars; *Style*— The Hon Harry Wyndham

WYNDHAM, Hon Mark Hugh; OBE, MC; s of late 5 Baron Leconfield, DSO, and Gladys, da of Fitzroy Farquhar, OBE (s of 3 Bt, decd); *b* 1921; *m* 1947 (m dis), Anne, da of Hon Reginald Winn (d 1985; s of 2 Baron St Oswald); 1 s, 2 da (see Lord Charles Spencer-Churchill); m 2; Patricia, da of Esmond Baring (see Baron Asburton); *Career* Capt 12 Royal Lancers, served Middle East and Italy (wounded twice) WWII 1939-45, chm C of E Children's Soc 1967-82, ret; *Style*— The Hon Mark Wyndham, OBE, MC; Newmans Cottage, Froxfield Green, Petersfield, Hants GU32 1DQ (☎ 0730 64333)

WYNDHAM, Hon Ursula Constance; da of 5 Baron Leconfield, DSO (d 1967), and Gladys Mary, *née* Farquhar (d 1971); *b* 20 Sept 1913; *Educ* private; *Books* Astride The Wall, Laughter and the Love of Friends (1989); *Recreations* travel, needlework, reading, gardening; *Style*— The Hon Ursula Wyndham; Honeyway House, Petworth, Sussex (☎ 0798 42291)

WYNDHAM, William Wadham; s of George Colville Wyndham (d 1982), of Orchard Wyndham, Somerset, and Anne Dorothy Hodder, *née* Hodder-Williams; *b* 4 Aug 1940; *Educ* Eton, Wadham Coll Oxford; *Career* barr 1966; Parly Counsel Office 1968-70, legal advsr: Formica Int/ De La Rue 1971-78, Esso/Exxon Chemical 1979-88; co sec and legal advsr AB Electronic Prods Gp plc 1988-89; *Recreations* natural history, forestry, theology; *Clubs* Lansdowne; *Style*— William Wyndham, Esq; Orchard Wyndham, William Taunton, Somerset TA4 4HH (☎ 09 843 2309); AB Electronic Products Group plc, Abercynon, Mid Glamorgan CF45 4SF (☎ 0443 7403 31, fax 443 7416 76)

WYNFORD, 8 Baron (UK 1829); Robert Samuel Best; MBE (Mil 1952), DL (Dorset 1970); s of 7 Baron Wynford (d 1942), and Evelyn (d 1929), da of Maj-Gen Sir Edward Sinclair May, KCB, CMG; *b* 5 Jan 1917; *Educ* Eton, Sandhurst; *m* 1941, Anne, da of Maj-Gen John Minshull-Ford, CB, DSO, MC (d 1948); 1 s, 2 da; *Heir* s, Hon John Best; *Career* Army offr; landowner and farmer, formerly Instructor Jt Serv Staff Coll 1957-60; Croix de Guerre; *Recreations* field sports, walking; *Clubs* Army and Navy; *Style*— The Rt Hon the Lord Wynford, MBE, DL; Wynford House, Wynford Eagle, Dorchester, Dorset DT2 0ER (☎ 0300 20241)

WYNN, Cdr Andrew Guy; LVO (1984); yr s of Lt Cdr Hon Charles Wynn, RN, and Hon Hermione Willoughby, da of 11 Baron Middleton; *b* 26 Nov 1950; *Educ* Eton, Gonville and Caius Coll Cambridge (MA); *m* 1978 (m dis 1987), Susanjane, da of Selwyn Willis Fraser-Smith, CBE, MC, of Crowborough; 1 s (Alexander Charles Guy b 1980); m 2, 1988, Shelagh Jean MacSorley, yr da of Prof I K M Smith, of Welwyn Garden City; *Career* Lt Cdr RN, Equerry to HRH The Duke of Edinburgh 1982-84, Dep Supply Offr HMS Ark Royal 1984-86, Cdr RN, Offr Policy Section 1987-88; Sch Bursar Eton 1988-; *Style*— Cdr Andrew Wynn, LVO; Eton College, Windsor SL4 6DB

WYNN, Hon Mrs (Angela Hermione Ida); *née* Willoughby; da of 11 Baron Middleton, KG, MC, TD (d 1970); *b* 5 May 1924; *m* 1947, Lt Cdr the Hon Charles Henry Romer Wynn, s of 6 Baron Newborough, OBE (d 1965); 2 s (Antony, Andrew); *Style*— The Hon Mrs Wynn; Bunkersland, Withleigh, Tiverton, Devon (☎ 0844 252444)

WYNN, Hon Charles Henry Romer; s of 6 Baron Newborough, OBE (d 1965); *b* 1923; *Educ* Canford School; *m* 1947, Hon Angela Hermione Ida Willoughby, da of 11 Baron Middleton; 2 s; *Career* Lt Cdr RN (ret); *Recreations* fishing; *Style*— Lt Cdr the Hon Charles Wynn, RN; Bunkersland, Withleigh, Tiverton, Devon

WYNN, John Stephen; s of Robert Dennis Wynn, of 98 Ryebank Rd, Firswood, Stretford, and Constance, *née* Johnson; *b* 7 May 1952; *Educ* Chorlton GS, Univ of Manchester (MB ChB, MRCP), Univ of London (DCH); *m* 7 Aug 1974, (Elizabeth) Wendy, da of Philip Randal Desmond Clarendon (d 1985), of Co Down, NI; 1 da (Charlotte b 1988); *Career* conslt obstetrician and gynaecologist Wythenshame Hosp Manchester 1985-; assoc lectr Univ of Manchester; MRCOG 1981; *Recreations* golf, scuba diving, football; *Clubs* Alderley Edge Golf, Hazel Grove Diving; *Style*— John Wynn, Esq; Hillcroft, Chelford Rd, Great Warford, Alderley Edge SK9 7TL (☎ 0625 582553); 41 The Downs, Altrincham, Cheshire WA14 2QG (☎ 061 928 0611)

WYNN, Hon Robert Vaughan; s and h of 7 Baron Newborough, DSC, of Rhug, Corwen, N Wales, by his 1 w, Rosamund, da of late Maj Robert Barbour, of Bolesworth Castle, Tattenhall, Cheshire; *b* 11 Aug 1949; *Educ* Milton Abbey; *m* 1, 1981, Sheila Christine Massey; 1 da (Lucinda); m 2, 16 April 1988, Mrs Susan Hall, da of late Andrew Lloyd, of Malta; *Career* landowner and farmer; dir: Maritime Protection Services (Sierra Leone) Ltd, MaCalister Elliott Resources Ltd; *Recreations* skiing, sailing; *Style*— The Hon Robert Wynn; Peplow Hall, Peplow, Market Drayton, Shropshire; Wynn Electronics Ltd, Wynn House, Halesfield 20, Telford, Shropshire TF7 4QU (☎ 0952 588222; telex : 35740; fax : 0952 583510)

WYNN, Terence; MEP (Lab) Merseyside E 1989-; s of Ernest Wynn (d 1979), and Lily, *née* Hitchen (d 1976); *b* 27 June 1946; *Educ* Leigh Tech Coll, Riversdale Marine Coll, Univ of Salford (MSc); *m* 7 March 1967, Doris, da of Ernest Ogden (d 1971); 1 s (David Mark b 4 March 1968), 1 da (Terry Joanne b 20 Nov 1970); *Career* trg exec MTA 1985-89; councillor Wigan Met Borough Cncl 1979-90; *Recreations* reading, theatre, swimming, music, rugby league; *Style*— Terence Wynn, Esq, MEP; European Office, 105 Corporation St, St Helens, Merseyside WA10 1SX (☎ 0744 451609, fax 0744 29832)

WYNN, Terence Bryan; s of Bernard Wynn (d 1961), of Newcastle upon Tyne, and Elsie, *née* Manges; *b* 20 Nov 1928; *Educ* St Cuthbert's GS Newcastle upon Tyne; *Career* jr reporter Hexham Courant 1945-47; reporter: Blyth News 1947-48, Shields Evening News 1948-50, Sunderland Echo 1950-53, Daily Sketch 1953-58; head of news and current affrs Tyne Tees TV 1958-66, planning ed BBC TV News 1966-67; sr press offr: The Land Cmmn 1967-71, HM Customs and Excise 1971-72; ed: The Universe 1972-77, Lib News Lib Pty Orgn 1977-83, press offr Central Office of Info 1983-85, ed Your Court Lord Chllr's Dept 1985-88, dir More Publicity 1989-, ed Brentwood News 1990-; author Walsingham (a modern mystery play prod at Walsingham and in Westminster Cathedral) 1975; chm and hon vice pres Catholic Writers' Guild 1968; MIPR 1971; *Recreations* reading, writing, talking; *Clubs* Press, Nat Lib; *Style*— Terence Wynn, Esq; Bosco Villa, 30 Queens Rd, South Benfleet, Essex SS7 1JW (☎ 0268 792033)

WYNN PARRY, Dr Christopher Berkeley (Kit); MBE (1954); s of Hon Sir Henry Wynn Parry, KBE (d 1962), of Harpenden, Herts, and Hon Mrs Shelagh Berkeley Wynn Parry (d 1975); *b* 14 Oct 1924; *Educ* Eton, Univ of Oxford (DM, MA); *m* 25 July 1953, Lamorna Cathleen, da of Albert George W Sawyer (d 1970), of Clavering, Essex; 1 s (Simon b 1961), 3 da (Charlotte b 1954, Sarah b 1957, Jane b 1959); *Career* RAF 1948-75, Gp Capt Med Branch, conslt advsr in rheumatology and rehabilitation, dir of rehabilitation Jt Servs Med Rehabitation Units RAF Chessington and RAF Headley Court; dir of rehabilitation Royal Nat Orthopaedic Hosps 1975, hon conslt in applied electrophysiology Nat Hosp for Nervous Diseases Queen Square 1975, civil conslt in rheumatology and rehabilitation RAF 1975, chm Disability Ctee RCP London 1978-88, dir of rehabilitation King Edward VII Hosp Midhurst Sussex; winner William Hyde award for sport and med; author articles on: rehabilitation, rheumatology, orthopaedics, pain, peripheral nerve injuries, resettlement, backpain, organisation of servs; author chapters in 22 books; fndr and first pres Int Rehabilitation Med Assoc, sec Int Fedn Physical Med, past pres physical med section and Kovacs Prizeman RSM, Stanford Cade medallist RAF Med Branch, advsr in rehabilitation to Chief Med Offr 1979-86, member Mac Coll Working Pty into Artifical Limb and Appliance Serv 1986-88, pres Br Soc for Surgery of the Hand; Br Cncl visiting lectr and scholar to: Russia, Hungary, Czechoslovakia; hon pres French Soc for Orthoses of the Upper Limb, co ed International Journal of Rehabilitation Studies, memb Ed Bd Pain Br Soc Surgery of the Hand Injury, past Prime Warden Worshipful Co of Dyers 1984-85 (1981-82); memb: Br Soc for Surgery of the Hand, Br Soc of Rheumatology, Br Soc for Relief of Pain, RSA; FRCP, FRCS; *Books* Rehabilitation of the Hand 4 edn (1982); *Recreations* gardening, music, the arts, walking, wine and food; *Clubs* Savile; *Style*— Dr Kit Wynn Parry, MBE; 51 Nassau Road, Barnes, London SW13 9QJ (☎ 081 748 6288); King Edward VII Hospital, Midhurst, Sussex GU29 OBL (☎ 0730 812341, fax 0730 816333)

WYNN-WILLIAMS, Lady Penelope; da of 1 and last Earl Jowitt, PC (d 1957); *m* 20 Nov 1943, George Wynn-Williams, FRCS, FRCOG; *qv* 2 s, 1 da; *Career* govr two schools Fulham; *Recreations* tennis; *Clubs* Hurlingham; *Style*— The Lady Penelope Wynn-Williams; 39 Hurlingham Court, Ranelagh Gdns, SW6 (☎ 071 736 2139)

WYNNE, David; s of Cdr Charles Edward Wynne, RNR, and Millicent, *née* Beyts; *b* 25 May 1926; *Educ* Stowe, Trinity Coll Cambridge; *m* 1958, Gillian Mary Leslie (d 1990), da of Leslie Grant, of Argentina and Switzerland; 2 s (Edward, Roland), and 2 step children; *Career* served WWII Sub Lt RNVR; sculptor, numerous important public works world wide over the last 36 years; *Recreations* active sports, poetry, travel; *Clubs* Garrick, Leander, Queen's, Cresta Run; *Style*— David Wynne, Esq; 12 Southside, Wimbledon Common, London SW19; (☎ 081 946 1514)

WYNNE, Edward John Carleton; s of Wilfrid Edward Carleton Wynne (d 1973), of

Margate, and Marjorie Frances Sibthorpe (d 1982); *b* 10 Oct 1926; *Educ* Epsom Coll, Trinity Hall Cambridge, Middx Hosp Med Sch, (MA, MChir, MB); *m* 5 Dec 1953, Erica Louise, da of Eric Ferdinando, of Barn House, Upper Basildon, Berks, 1 s (William b 1957), 1 da (Clare b 1954); *Career* conslt surgeon; FRCS; *Recreations* surgery, house work; *Style—* Edward Wynne, Esq; The Mews House, Down Ampney, Cirencester , Glos GL7 5QW (☎ 0285 750400); Princess Margaret Hospital, Swindon (☎ 0793 36231)

WYNNE, Lady Marguerite Mary; *née* Chetwynd-Talbot; yst da of 21 Earl of Shrewsbury (d 1980); *b* 12 June 1950; *m* 1970, Guy William Brisbane; 1 s (Duncan b 1975); *Style—* The Lady Marguerite Wynne; 228 Meadvale Rd, Ealing, London W5 (☎ 081 997 5527)

WYNNE, Thomas Meirion; s of Rev E E Wynne (d 1981), of Flint; *b* 26 April 1934; *Educ* UCW (LLB); *m* 21 June 1958, Elizabeth Gwenda; 2 s (Michael Vaughan b 1960, Gareth Dylan b 1961); *Career* slr; former clerk to Justices of Dolgellau and Barmouth; supt registrar, clerk to Cmmrs of Taxes; former memb Gwynedd Family Practitioner Ctee, former Mental Health Cmmr; FBIM; *Style—* T Meirion Wynne, Esq; Llifor, Friog, Fairbourne, Gwynedd LL38 2RX (☎ 0341 250428); J Charles Hughes & Co, Solicitors, Dolgellau, Gwynedd (☎ 0341 422464)

WYNNE-EDWARDS, Prof Vero Copner; CBE (1973); s of Rev Canon John Rosindale Wynne-Edwards, and Lilian Agnes, *née* Streatfeild; *b* 4 July 1906; *Educ* Leeds GS, Rugby, New Coll Oxford (BA, MA, DSc); *m* 19 Dec 1929, Jeannie Campbell, da of Percy Morris (d 1944), of Exeter; 1 s (Hugh b 1934), 1 da (Janet b 1931); *Career* Lt Cdr (Spec Branch) RCNVR 1942-45; student probationer Marine Biological Assoc Plymouth 1927-29, asst/assoc prof zoology McGill Univ Montreal 1930-46; Univ of Aberdeen: regius prof of nat hist 1946-74, vice princ 1972-74; expeditions to Arctic Canada: Baffin Island 1937, 1950, 1953, Mackenzie River 1943, Yukon 1944; visiting prof Univ of Louisville Kentucky 1959, Br Cncl Cwlth Interchange fell NZ 1962, Leverhulme fell 1978-80; memb: Nature Conservancy 1954-57, Red Deer Cmmn (vice chm) 1959-68, Royal Cmmn on Environmental Pollution 1970-74; pres: Br Ornithologists Union 1965-70, Scot Marine Biological Assoc 1967-73, Section D Br Assoc 1974; chm: Natural Environment Res Cncl 1968-71, Scientific Authy for Animals DoE 1976-77; hon fell Inst of Biology 1980; hon memb: Br Ecological Soc 1977, American Ornithologists Union 1959, Cooper Ornithological Soc (California) 1961, Finnish Societas Scientiarum 1965; Hon DUniv (Stirling) 1974, Hon LLD (Aberdeen) 1976; Godman-Salvin Medal BOU 1977, Neill Prize Royal Soc Edinburgh 1977, Frink Medal Zoological Soc London 1980; FRS (ed 1950, Canada 1940, London 1970); *Books* Animal Dispersion in relation to Social Behaviour (1962), Evolution through Group Selection (1986); *Recreations* hill walking, skiing, gardening, natural history; *Style—* Prof Vero Wynne-Edwards, CBE, FRS; Ravelston, William St, Torphins, Scotland AB3 4JR

WYNNE-JONES, Baroness; Rusheen; da of Neville Preston; *m* 1972, as his 2 w, Baron Wynne-Jones (Life Peer d 1982), sometime Prof Chemistry Newcastle Univ; *Career* chm Friends of Chelsea Gp; *Style—* The Rt Hon the Lady Wynne-Jones; 16 Chelsea Embankment, SW3 (☎ 071 352 8511)

WYNNE-MORGAN, David Wynne; s of Col John Wynne-Morgan, and Marjorie Mary, *née* Wynne; *b* 22 Feb 1931; *Educ* Bryanston; *m* 1 (m dis), Romaine Chevers, *née* Ferguson; m 2 (m dis), Sandra, *née* Paul; 2 s (Nicholas b 1956, Adrian b 1957); m 3, 26 June 1973, Karin Elizabeth, da of Daniel Eugene Stings; 2 s (Jamie b 1975, Harry b 1980); *Career* journalist: Daily Mail 1951-54, Daily Express 1954-57; fndr Partnerplan PR (sold to Extel Gp 1980); chm: Hill and Knowlton 1984-, Mktg Gp GB 1989-; pres and chief exec Hill and Knowlton ME and Africa Regn 1990-; played squash for Wales 1953-56; MIPR; *Books* author of: autiobiography of late Pres Gamal Abdel Nassar (serialised Sunday Times), biography of Pietro Annigoni (serialised Daily Express), I Norman Levy; *Recreations* cricket, tennis, riding, squash; *Clubs* Turf, Lord's Taverners, Annabel's, Bath, Rackets, Queen's; *Style—* David Wynne-Morgan, Esq; Hill and Knowlton, 5/11 Theobalds Rd, London WC1 (☎ 071 405 8755)

WYNNE-WILLIAMS, John Anthony; s of John Gabriel Wynne-Williams, MBE, and Mary Adele Josephine, *née* Corazza; *b* 9 Nov 1949; *Educ* Farleigh House Sch Farleigh Wallop Hants, Stonyhurst Coll Blackburn Lancs; *Career* dir D'Arcy Macmanus and Masius 1970-79; dep chm: Ryman plc 1981-87, Levelmill Ltd 1987-; dir: Holland and Holland Ltd 1989-, Kiki McDonough Ltd 1990-; chm Moyses Stevens Ltd 1989-; dep chm royal Marsden Hosp Cancer Appeal, memb Devpt Bd Ballet Rambert; memb Worshipful Co of Fanmakers; *Recreations* shooting, Cresta Run, backgammon, theatre; *Clubs* Brooks's, Annabel's, Marks, RAC, St Moritz Tobogganing; *Style—* John Wynne-Williams, Esq; 27 St Leonards Terr, London SW3 4QG (☎ 071 730 2189, fax 071 259 9123); Levelmill Ltd, 6 Bruton St, London W1 (☎ 071 493 8171, fax 071 493 0618, car 0831 108 358)

WYVILL, (Marmaduke) Charles Asty; Lord of the Manor of Constable Burton and patron of three livings; s of Marmaduke Frederick Wyvill (d 1953, 7 in descent from D'Arcy Wyvill, yr bro of Sir Marmaduke Wyvill, 5 Bt, unc of 6 Bt and great unc of 7 Bt, since whose death in 1774 the Btcy has been dormant; D'Arcy was himself 11 in descent from Richard Wyvill, one of the 25,000 supporters of Henry VI killed at the rout of Towton 1461), and May Bennet; *b* 30 Aug 1945; *Educ* Stowe, RAC Cirencester; *m* 1972, Margaret Ann, da of Maj Sydney Hardcastle, RA; 3 s (Marmaduke b 1975, Edward b 1977, Frederick b 1983), 1 da (Katherine b 1981); *Career* land agent; patron of the livings of Spennithorne, Fingall and Denton; ARICS; landowner (3000 acres); High Sheriff of North Yorkshire 1986; *Recreations* shooting, fishing; *Clubs* Brooks's; *Style—* Charles Wyvill, Esq; Constable Burton Hall, Leyburn, N Yorks

Y

YAFFÉ, Paul; s of David Yaffe (d 1976), of Manchester, and Dinah Pash; *b* 21 April 1946; *Educ* Delamere Forest Sch, Cheetham Secdy Sch; *m* 21 June 1967, Janis Andrea, da of Eric Brown; 2 s (Mark Daniel b 22 July 1968, Adam James b 23 Oct 1972); *Career* environmental portrait and wedding photographer 1961-; worked in family photographic firm, opened own studio in Southport 1967, numerous exhibitions UK and abroad, lectr on photography and modern promotional methods in photography; fell Royal Soc for the Encouragement of Arts, Manufactures and Commerce 1971, FBIPP 1972, chm Judging Panel BIPP (portraiture, wedding and theatrical photography) 1978 (memb 1974, dep chm 1976), chm Admissions and Qualifications Bd BIPP 1983-87 (dep chm 1980), FRPS 1979, FRSA, fell Master Photographers Assoc 1981, hon PFP of Norwegian Fame Assoc, three times memb Kodak Gold Circle; memb Professional Photographers Assoc of America; *Style—* Paul Yaffé, Esq; Paul Yaffé Ltd, Wayfarers Arcade, Lord St, Southport, Merseyside PR8 1NT (☎ 0704 69990/0704 544004/0831 250217)

YAFFE, Ronnie Malcolm; s of Maurice Yaffe, of Prestwich (d 1963), and Victoria, *née* Hodari (d 1978); *b* 23 Oct 1952; *Educ* Manchester GS; *m* 15 Aug 1978, Marjorie Rachel, da of Frank Lea, Whitefield; 1 s (Adam b 1984), 1 da (Vikki b 1987); *Career* dir Kingsley & Forrester plc 1984-87; md Martin Yaffe Int Ltd 1987-; *Recreations* tennis, golf; *Clubs* Whitefield Golf; *Style—* Ronnie Yaffe, Esq; Martin Yaffe International Ltd, Victoria Lane, off Moorside Rd, Swinton, Manchester (☎ 061 794 5553, car 0836 294458)

YALLOP, Dr (Howard) John; OBE (1974); s of John Bertie Yallop (d 1947), and Edith Mary, *née* Holmes (d 1972); *b* 15 Dec 1918; *Educ* Allhallows Sch, Univ of Oxford (MA, BSc), Univ of Exeter (PhD); *m* 8 Aug 1956, Mary Kathleen, da of Fritz Gerald Beet (d 1959); 1 s (Mark b 1960), 1 da (Rachel b 1962); *Career* HG scientist Miny of Supply 1942-45; scientist: MOD 1945-57, forensic explosive laboratory Home Office 1957-73; forensic sci conslt 1973-82, lay reader C of E 1971, hon curator Allhallows Museum Honiton 1974-; author of many res papers in scientific and historical jls; FRSC 1973; *Books* United Nations Recommendations on the Transport of Dangerous Goods (ed 1977), Explosion Investigation (1980), Protection Against Terrorism (1980), Honiton In Old Picture Postcards (1983), Fire Investigation (1984), The History of the Honiton Lace Industry (1987); *Recreations* research in Devon history; *Clubs* Devon and Exeter Inst; *Style—* Dr John Yallop, OBE; New Inn, Farway, Colyton, Devon EX13 6DG (☎ 040487 397)

YAMADA, Taro; s of Haruo Yamada, and Sayuri, *née* Haraguchi; *b* 19 Nov 1934; *Educ* Asahigaoka HS Nagota Japan, Keio Univ Tokyo; *m* 6 March 1961, Nobuko, da of Matsutaro Gotoh (d 1988); 2 s (Jun b 30 Sept 1965, Tadashi b 21 Feb 1969); *Career* joined Yamaichi Securities Co Ltd 1957, dep gen mangr foreign capital dept Yamaichi Securities Co Ltd 1975; Yamaichi Int: pres (America) 1979, gen mangr foreign capital dept 1983, dir and gen mangr int fin dept 1985, md 1987, chm (Europe) and md i/c Europe and Middle East; Japanese Securities Dealers' Assoc, registered princ Nat Assoc Dealers' Assoc; *Recreations* music; *Clubs* Les Ambassadeurs, Woburn Golf; *Style—* Taro Yamada, Esq; Yamaichi Int (Europe) Ltd, Finsbury Ct, 111-117 Finsbury Pavement, London EC2A 1EQ (☎ 071 638 5599, fax 071 638 2849, telex 887414 YSCLDN G)

YANNOPOULOS, George N; s of Nicolas Yannopoulos (d 1972), and Maria Panagiotakis (d 1975); *b* 23 April 1936; *Educ* Univ of London (MSc), Univ of Reading (PhD); *Career* res fell Memorial Univ St John's Canada 1963-65, lectr and reader in economics Univ of Reading 1966-; Greek rep to UN Gen Assembly 1974-76; advsr: Greek Miny for Foreign Affrs, Nat Bank of Greece, Agric Bank of Greece, Greek Miny for Indust; memb Royal Economic Soc; *Books* Greece and the EEC (1986), Customs Unions and Trade Griffith (1988), European Integration and the Iberian Economies (1989), Shipping Policies for an Open World Economy (1989); *Recreations* reading, listening to music; *Style—* George Yannopoulos, Esq; University of Reading, Whiteknights, PO Box 218, Reading RG6 2AA (☎ 0734 318377, fax 0734 750236, telex 847813 RULIB G)

YAPP, Sir Stanley Graham; s of William Yapp; *m* 1 (m dis); 1 da; m 2 (m dis), Carol; 1 s; m 3, 1983, Christine, da of Ernest Horton, former Lord Mayor of Birmingham; *Career* ldr W Midlands CC 1973-77; vice-chm Local Authorities' Mgmnt Services & Computer Ctee; kt 1975; *Style—* Sir Stanley Yapp; 172 York Road, Hall Green, Birmingham B28 8LW

YARBOROUGH, 7 Earl of (UK 1837); John Edward Pelham; JP (Parts of Lindsey 1965); also Baron Yarborough (GB 1794) and Baron Worsley (UK 1837); s of 6 Earl of Yarborough, DL (d 1966, ggs of 2 Earl, Lord-Lt and Custos Rotulorum of Lincs, who did something to recoup the outlay involved in his father's munificent hospitality as Cdr of the Royal Yacht Sqdn by offering odds of 1,000 to 1 against a 'Yarborough' turning up in a Whist hand, whereas the actual odds are 1,827 to 1; the term 'Yarborough', meaning an honourless hand, is now standard in Bridge), and Hon Pamela Douglas-Pennant, da of 3 Baron Penrhyn; *b* 2 June 1920; *Educ* Eton, Trinity Coll Cambridge; *m* 12 Dec 1957, Florence Ann Petronel, da of John Upton, JP, of Ingmire Hall, Yorks, by his 2 w (Petronel, *née* Fursdon, whose mother was da of Sir William Salusbury-Trelawny, 10 Bt, sometime Capt Roy Cornwall Rangers); 1 s, 3 da; *Heir* s, Lord Worsley; *Career* served WW II France and N W Europe, Maj Gren Gds; High Sheriff Lincs 1964, vice-lord-lieut (formerly vice-lieut) 1964-; contested (C) Grimsby 1955; patron E Midlands British Legion 1974-; pres Royal Forestry Soc of Eng Wales and NI 1987-89; *Clubs* Royal Yacht Sqdn, Cavalry and Guards', Boodle's; *Style—* The Rt Hon The Earl of Yarborough, JP; Brocklesby Park, Habrough, S Humberside (☎ 0469 60242)

YARDE-BULLER, Hon Mrs John; Guendolen; da of late Rev Charles Roots; *m* 1939, Hon John Reginald Henry Yarde-Buller (d 1962); 2 s; *Style—* The Hon Mrs John Yarde-Buller; Le Vallon, Mont Félard, Jersey

YARDE-BULLER, Hon John Francis; s (by 1 m) and h of 4 Baron Churston, VRD; *b* 29 Dec 1934; *Educ* Eton; *m* 1973, Alexandra, da of Anthony Contomichalos; 1 s, 2 da; *Career* late 2 Lt RHG; *Style—* The Hon John Yarde-Buller; Yowlestone House, Puddington, Tiverton, S Devon

YARDLEY, Prof David Charles Miller; s of Geoffrey Miller Yardley (d 1987), and Doris Woodward, *née* Jones (d 1934); *b* 4 June 1929; *Educ* Ellesmere Coll, Univ of Birmingham (LLB, LLD), Lincoln Coll Oxford (DPhil, MA); *m* 30 Aug 1954, Patricia Anne Tempest (Patsy), da of Lt-Col Basil Harry Tempest Olver, MBE (d 1980); 2 s (Adrian b 1956, Alistair b 1962), 2 da (Heather b 1958, Briony b 1960); *Career* Nat Serv Flying Offr Educn Branch RAF 1949-51; called to the Bar Grays Inn 1952; Emeritus fell St Edmund Hall 1974- (fell 1954-74), Barber prof of law Univ of Birmingham 1974-78, head of Dept of Law Politics and Econs Oxford Poly 1978-80, Rank Fndn prof of law Univ of Buckingham 1980-82, chm Cmmn for Local Admin in Eng 1982-; chm: rent assessment ctees, rent tbnls and nat insur local tbnls 1963-82; *Books* Introduction to British Constitutional Law (1960, seventh edn 1990), A Source Book of English Administrative Law (1963, second edn 1970), The Future of the Law (1964), Principles of Administrative Law (1981, second edn 1986), Geldarts Introduction to English Law (ed 1991), Hanbury and Yardley's English Courts of Law (1979), The Protection of Freedom (with I Stevens, 1982); *Recreations* lawn tennis, squash racquets, opera, cats; *Clubs* RAF; *Style—* Prof Yardley; 9 Belbroughton Rd, Oxford OX2 6UZ (☎ 0865 54831); 21 Queen Anne's Gate, London SW1H 9BU (☎ 071 222 5622)

YARKER, Peter Francis; *b* 25 June 1943; *Educ* St Michael's Sch Ingoldisthorpe, Ealing Sch of Hotel Keeping & Catering (Musketeers cup); *m* Rosemary Margaret, *née* Allday; 3 s (James Francis b 1969, Edward Timothy b 1972, William Daniel b 1974); *Career* admin trainee Grosvenor House Park Lane 1965; asst mangr: Dudley Hotel Hove 1966, Grosvenor House Sheffield 1967; mangr Burlington Hotel Eastbourne 1969 (sr asst mangr 1968), gen mangr Beaufort Hotel Bath 1972, dir Myddleton Hotels Ltd 1977, regnl dir Ladbroke Hotels 1980, proprietor Dukes Hotel Bath 1983; winner Master Innholder award 1978; Freeman City of London, Liveryman Worshipful Co of Basketmakers; FHCIMA, memb CIM; *Clubs* Bath & County; *Style—* Peter Yarker, Esq; Dukes Hotel (Bath) Ltd, Dukes Hotel, Gt Pulteney St, Bath BA2 4DN (☎ 0225 463512)

YARMOUTH, Earl of; Henry Jocelyn Seymour (Harry); s and h of 8 Marquess of Hertford; *b* 6 July 1958; *Educ* Harrow, RAC Cirencester; *m* 15 Dec 1990, Beatriz (Bea), da of Jorge Karam, of Copacabana, Rio de Janeiro, Brazil; *Career* farm manager; *Style—* Earl of Yarmouth; The Garden House, Arrow, nr Alcester, Warwickshire B49 5NH (☎ 0789 762513); Ragley Home Farms, Alcester, Warwickshire B49 5LZ (☎ 0789 763131, fax 0789 764791, car 0836 355512)

YARNOLD, Rev Edward John; s of Edward Cabré Yarnold, MM (Sgt Queens Westminster Rifles, d 1972), of Burley-in-Wharfedale, W Yorks, and Agnes, *née* Deakin; *b* 14 Jan 1926; *Educ* St Michael's Coll Leeds, Heythrop Coll, Campion Hall Oxford (MA, DD); *Career* entered Soc of Jesus 1943, ordained 1960; tutor in theology Campion Hall 1964- (Master 1965-72), visiting prof Univ of Notre Dame Indiana 1982-; memb Anglican-RC Int Cmmn 1970-81 and 1982-, pres Catholic Theological Assoc of GB 1986-88; Cross of Order of St Augustine of Canterbury 1981; *Books* The Theology of Original Sin (1971), The Awe-Inspiring Rites of Initiation (1972), The Second Gift (1974), The Study of Liturgy (ed with C Jones and G Wainwright, 1978), They Are in Earnest (1982), Seven Days with the Lord (1984), The Study of Spirituality (ed with C Jones and G Wainwright, 1986), In Search of Unity (1989), Time for God (1991); *Recreations* opera, cricket; *Style—* The Rev Edward Yarnold, SJ; Campion Hall, Oxford OX1 1QS (☎ 0865 726811, 0865 240861)

YARNOLD, Patrick; s of Leonard Francis Yarnold (d 1963), of Hassocks, Sussex, and Gladys Blanche, *née* Merry; *b* 21 March 1937; *Educ* Bancroft's Sch Woodford Green Essex; *m* 14 Jan 1961, Caroline, da of Andrew James Martin (d 1988), of King's Lynn, Norfolk; 2 da (Louise b 2 Feb 1962, Frances b 12 Feb 1964); *Career* Nat Serv 1955-57; joined HM Foreign Serv (now Dip Serv) 1957: FO 1957-60, Addis Ababa 1961-64, Belgrade 1964-66, FO (later FCO) 1966-70; 1 sec and head of chancery Bucharest 1970-73, 1 sec (commercial) Bonn 1973-76, 1 sec FCO 1976-79, cnsllr (econ and commercial) Brussels 1980-83, consul gen Zagreb 1983-85, cnsllr head of chancery and consul gen Belgrade 1985-87, cnsllr FCO 1987-; *Recreations* travel, photography, walking, genealogy, chinese cooking, local history, reading, etc; *Style—* Patrick Yarnold, Esq; c/o FCO, King Charles St, London SW1A 2AH (☎ 071 270 3000)

YARRANTON, Peter George; s of Edward John Yarranton (d 1955), of 8 Mardale Drive, London NW9, and Norah Ellen, *née* Atkins (d 1978); *b* 30 Sept 1924; *Educ* Willesden Tech Coll; *m* 10 April 1947, Mary Avena, da of Sydney Flowitt, MC (d 1957), of Farfield Manor, Granville Rd, Scarborough; 1 s (Ross b 9 Sept 1952), 1 da (Sandy (Mrs Turnbull) b 16 Oct 1950); *Career* RAF 1942-57; WWII Pilot Offr 1944, Flying Offr 1945, served Liberators Burma and SE Asia, Flt Lt 1949; post war served: Canada, USA, Bahamas, Ceylon, Malaya, India, Australia, UK; Shell Mex and BP Ltd: trg 1957-58, ops offr Reading 1958-61, UK industl relations liaison offr 1961-63, i/c industl relations 1963-66, mangr industl relations 1966-69, regnl ops mangr SE Region 1969-75; mangr plant and engrg distribution div Shell UK Oil Ltd 1975-77; gen mangr Lensbury Club 1978-, currently sr vice pres and PR advsr RFU; formerly: pres Middx Co RFU, pres Wasps RFC, chm of selectors for London and Middx; former outside broadcast commentator BBC, presenter on the world's largest TV screen at Twickenham, memb editorial bd Rugby World and Post; England rugby international (5 caps); former capt: Barbarians, London, Middx, Wasps, Br Combined Servs, RAF; former capt RAF Swimming and Water Polo Teams; chm London Regnl Cncl for Sport and Recreation 1983-89, fndr dir London Docklands Arena Tst, fndr dir Golden Globe Charitable Tst; govr: Sports Aid Fndn, London Marathon; chm The Sports Cncl 1989-; Freeman City of London 1977, memb Worshipful Co of Gold and Silver Wyre Drawers 1977 (Ct of Assts 1987); FBIM, FIPM, memb Recreational Mangrs Assoc; *Recreations* all sports; *Clubs* RAF, East India, Devonshire Sports and Public Schs, Rugby Club of London, Cricketers; *Style—* Peter Yarranton, Esq; Broom Point, Broom Water West, Teddington TW11 9QH; Sunnydale Villas, Durlston Rd, Swanage, Dorset; Lensbury Club, Broom Rd, Teddington, Middx (☎ 071 977 8821/071 943 2066, fax 071 943 4283)

YARROW, Sir Eric Grant; 3 Bt (UK 1916), of Homestead, Hindhead, Frensham, Co Surrey; MBE (1946), DL (Renfrewshire 1970); s of Sir Harold Yarrow, 2 Bt, GBE (d 1962), by his 1 w, Eleanor; *b* 23 April 1920; *Educ* Marlborough, Univ of Glasgow; *m* 1, Rosemary Ann (d 1957), da of late H T Young; 1 s (Richard d 1987); m 2, 1959 (m dis 1975), Annette Elizabeth Françoise, da of late A J E Steven; 3 s (Norman b 1960,

Peter (twin) b 1960, David b 1966); m 3, 1982, Caroline Joan Rosa, da of late R F Masters, of Piddinghoe, Sussex, and former w of Philip Botting; *Heir* gs, Ross b 1985; *Career* serv RE Burma 1939-45, Maj 1944; former chm and md Yarrow PLC, chm Clydesdale Bank plc, dir Standard Life Assur Co; pres: Exec Ctee Princess Louise Scottish Hosp at Erskine, Burma Star Assoc; memb Cncl IOD, deacon Incorpn of Hammermen of Glasgow 1961-62, Prime Warden of Worshipful Co of Shipwrights 1970, pres Smeatonian Soc of Civil Engrs 1983, pres Marlburian Club 1984, hon vice pres Cncl of Royal Inst of Naval Architects; FRSE; OStJ; *Style*— Sir Eric Yarrow, Bt, MBE, DL, FRSE; Cloak, Kilmacolm, Renfrewshire PA13 4SD (☎ 050 587 2067); Clydesdale Bank plc, 30 St Vincent Place, Glasgow G1 2HL (☎ 041 248 7070)

YARWOOD, Michael Edward; OBE (1976); s of Wilfred Yarwood, and Bridget Yarwood (d 1983); *b* 14 June 1941; *Educ* Bredbury Secdy Sch Cheshire; *m* 1969 (m dis 1987), Sandra Jean, da of Eric Burville; 2 da (Charlotte b 1970, Clare b 1972); *Career* first TV appearance 1963; BBC TV: Three of a Kind 1967, Look - Mike Yarwood, Mike Yarwood in Persons (series) 1971-82; ATV: Will the Real Mike Yarwood Stand Up? (series) 1968; Thames TV: Mike Yarwood in Persons 1983-87, Mike Yarwood Christmas Show 1984-87, One For The Pot (Nat Tour) 1988; Royal Variety performances 1968, 1972, 1976, 1981, 1987; Variety Club of GB award for BBC TV Personality of The Year 1973, Royal Television Soc award for outstanding creative achievement in front of camera 1978, memb Grand Order of Water Rats; *Books* And This Is Me (1974), Impressions of My Life (1986); *Recreations* golf, tennis; *Clubs* Lord's Taverners; *Style*— Michael Yarwood, Esq, OBE; c/o Billy Marsh, Billy Marsh Assoc, 19 Denmark St, London WC2H 8NA

YASS, Irving; s of Abraham Yass (d 1961), and Fanny, *née* Caplin (d 1980); *b* 20 Dec 1935; *Educ* Harrow Co GS, Balliol Coll Oxford (BA); *m* 14 Aug 1962, Marion Ruth, da of Benjamin Leighton (d 1979); 2 s (David b 1965, Michael b 1966), 1 da (Catherine b 1963); *Career* asst princ Miny of Transport and Civil Aviation 1958, private sec to jt parly sec 1960, princ HM Treasy 1967-70, asst sec DOE 1971, sec Ctee of Inquiry into Local Govt Fin 1974-76; Dept of Transport 1976-: under-sec fin 1982-86, dir London Regnl Office 1987-; *Style*— Irving Yass, Esq; Dept of Transport, 2 Marsham St, London SW1 (☎ 071 276 6089)

YASSUKOVICH, Stanislas Michael; s of Dimitri Yassukovich, and Denise Yassukovich; *b* 5 Feb 1935; *Educ* Deerfield Acad, Harvard; *m* Diana Veronica, da of Ralph Obre Crofton Townsend; 2 s (Michael, Nicholas), 1 da (Tatyana); *Career* US Marine Corps 1957-61; White Weld & Co Zurich 1961 (London 1962, gen ptnr (NY) 1969, md London); md Euro Banking Co Ltd (London) 1973 (dep chm 1983-85), sr advsr Merrill Lynch & Co (NY); dir: Merrill Lynch International Ltd, Merrill Lynch Banque (Suisse) SA; non-exec dir Henderson Administration Group plc; chm: The Securities Assoc, Flextech plc, Merrill Lynch Europe Ltd 1985-89; *Recreations* hunting, shooting, polo; *Clubs* Buck's, Turf, The Brook, Union (USA), Travellers (Paris); *Style*— Stanislas Yassukovich, Esq; Henderson Administration Group plc, 3 Finsbury Ave, London EC2M 2PA (☎ 071 410 4412)

YATES, Ann Elizabeth Alice; da of Thomas Berry (d 1978), and Gwladys May, *née* Thomas; *b* 20 May 1937; *Educ* SE Essex County Tech Sch; *m* 25 March 1961 (m dis 1966), Donald Aubrey Yates; *Career* dir Learoyd Packaging Ltd 1983- (co sec 1976); memb: Gen Purposes Ctee Burnley C of C, Burnley Enterprise Tst; advsr Young Enterprise Ltd; *Recreations* keep fit, aerobics; *Style*— Ms Ann Yates; 26 Harrogate Crescent, Burnley, Lancs BB10 2NX (☎ 0282 26089); Learoyd Packaging Ltd, Heasandford Mill, Queen Victoria Rd, Burnley, Lancs BB10 2EJ (☎ 0282 38016)

YATES, Dr (David) Anthony Hilton; s of Dr H Yates (d 1990), of Sandgate, Kent, and Florence Dora, *née* Fagge (d 1968); *Educ* Greshams's Sch Holt, St Thomas' Hosp London (MB BS, MD); *m* 23 April 1955, Gillian, da of Dr David Cecil Morgan (d 1961); 2 s (Timothy Hilton b 1957, Ian Anthony b 1958), 1 da (Jacqueline Amanda b 1960); *Career* Nat Serv Capt RAMC 1955-57, Hon Brig RAMC, civilian conslt advsr in rheumatology 1980; physician in charge Dept of Rheumatology St Thomas's Hosp London 1966, physician King Edward VII Hosp for Offrs London 1976; FRCP; *Recreations* sailing, skiing; *Clubs* Royal Southern Yacht, RSM; *Style*— Dr Anthony Yates; Flat 2, 26 Devonshire Place, London W1N 1PD (☎ 071 935 8917)

YATES, Prof Bernard; s of John Gordon Yates (d 1972), of York, and Beatrice May, *née* Rawlings; *b* 17 Feb 1929; *Educ* Archbishop Holgate's GS York, Univ of Leeds (BSc, PhD), Univ of Salford (DSc); *m* 10 Sept 1955, Muriel, da of Robert Parvin (d 1954), of Thirsk, N Yorks; *Career* Nat Serv RAF 1947-49; memb: sci staff GEC Res Laboratories Wembley 1955-58, academic staff Bradford Inst of Technol 1958-64; Univ of Salford: reader 1964-80, prof of physics 1980, chm dept of pure and applied physics 1982-, pro-vice chllr 1985-89; FInstP 1964, CEng 1989; *Style*— Prof Bernard Yates; Department of Pure & Applied Physics, University of Salford, Salford M5 4WT (☎ 061 745 5000, fax 061 745 5999, telex 668680 Sulib)

YATES, Douglas Martin; s of Albert Sidney Yates, of West Yelland, N Devon, and Lily Gertrude, *née* Jones; *b* 16 Jan 1943; *Educ* St Clement Danes GS, London Sch of Econs (BSc); *m* 1967, Gillian, da of Edward Gallimore, of Ealing, London; 1 s (Nicholas b 1972), 2 da (Lindsay b 1969, Alexandra b 1979); *Career* chartered accountant; finance dir The Rank Orgn plc 1982-; dir: A Kershaw and Sons plc 1982, Rank Xerox Ltd 1983; *Recreations* tennis, badminton, bridge, music; *Clubs* West Middlesex Lawn Tennis; *Style*— Douglas M Yates, Esq; The Rank Organisation plc, 6 Connaught Place, London W2 2EZ (☎ 071 629 7454)

YATES, Hazel; da of Leonard Brown, of Stamford, Lincs, and Vera, *née* Gray; *b* 15 July 1946; *Educ* Wallsend GS, Somerville Coll Oxford; *m* 16 Sept 1983, Rodney Brooks Yates, s of Henry Bertram Yates, OBE, of Alvechurch, Birmingham; 1 s (Benjamin b 1986); *Career* ptnr WI Carr Sons & Co 1978-81, R Nivison & Co 1982-86; memb Int Stock Exchange (part of initial gp of 6 women membs) 1973; *Recreations* reading, opera; *Style*— Mrs Hazel Yates; The Old Rectory, Marholm, Peterborough PE6 7JA (☎ 0733 269466)

YATES, Ian Humphrey Nelson; s of James Nelson Yates (d 1954), of Carnforth, Lancs, and Martha Wyatt, *née* Nutter (d 1965); *b* 24 Jan 1931; *Educ* Lancaster Royal GS, Canford; *m* 16 June 1956, Daphne June, da of Cyril Henry Hudson (d 1985), of Sanderstead, Surrey; 3 s (David b 1958, Nicholas b 1960, Simon b 1963); *Career* Nat Serv cmmn Lt Royal Scots Greys Germany and ME 1951-53; mgmnt trainee Westminster Press Ltd 1953-58, md Bradford and Dist Newspapers 1969-75 (asst gen mangr 1960, gen mangr 1964), dir Westminster Press Planning Div, chm Tellex Monitors Ltd 1987-90, dir and chief exec Press Assoc Ltd 1989-90 (gen mangr and chief exec 1975); chm: Universal News Services Ltd 1989-90, CRG Communictions Group 1990; pres: Young Newspapermens Assoc 1966, Yorks Newspaper Soc 1968; memb: Newspaper Soc Cncl 1970-75, Cncl Cwlth Press Union 1977-90; pres Alliance of Euro News Agencies 1987-88, chm New Media Ctee of Alliance of Euro News Agencies 1984-90; FRSA 1989; *Recreations* walking, reading, theatre; *Style*— Ian Yates, Esq; Woodbury, 11 Holmwood Close, East Horsley, Surrey (☎ 04865 3873)

YATES, Rt Rev John; *see*: Gloucester, Bishop of

YATES, Matthew Stewart; s of Michael Yates, of Basildon, and Sylvia, *née* Hepton; *b* 4 Feb 1969; *Educ* Mayflower Sch; *Career* athlete; memb Newham & Essex Beagles; England debut 800m 1989, GB debut 1500m 1990, also represented England under 23 and S England 1989; achievements incl: runner up 800m AAA Championships 1989, Bronze medal 800m Cwlth Games 1990, runner up 1500m GB v E Germany 1990, European 800m finalist 1990; Sports Aid Fndn award, Basildon Cncl Sports award; *Recreations* music, art, rugby union, football; *Clubs* Nike International; *Style*— Matthew Yates, Esq; c/o AAA, Edgbaston House, 3 Duchess Place, off Hagley Rd, Edgbaston, Birmingham B16 8NM (☎ 021 456 4050)

YATES, Nicholas; s of Peter Yates, of 4 Downs Bridge Rd, Beckenham, Kent, and Ellen, *née* McDermott; *b* 23 May 1961; *Educ* Langley Park Sch for Boys; *Career* badminton player; singles winner: Dutch and Canadian Open 1981, German Open 1985, bronze and team gold Cwlth Games 1986 (singles silver and doubles silver 1982), winner Japan Open 1988; former Eng no 1, holder of 107 caps; *Recreations* golf, computers; *Clubs* Park Langley Badminton, Sundridge Park Golf; *Style*— Nicholas Yates, Esq

YATES, Peter James; s of Lt-Col Robert Latimer Yates (d 1980), and Constance Leah, *née* Aitken (d 1940); *b* 24 July 1929; *Educ* Charterhouse, RADA; *m* 8 Oct 1960, Virginia Sue, da of Charles Quentin Pope (d 1961); 2 s (Toby Robert Quentin b 1962, Andrew b 1971), 2 da (Victoria Camilla b 1964 d 1965, Miranda Jane b 1965); *Career* film and theatre dir-prodr; credits incl: Cullitt 1968, The Deep 1976, Breaking Away 1978 (Acad Award nominations incl best film and best direction), The Dresser 1983 (Acad Award nominations incl best film and best direction); plays incl: Passing Game 1975, Interpreters 1985; *Clubs* Garrick; *Style*— Peter Yates, Esq; Creative Artists Agency, 9830 Wiltshire Boulevard, Beverly Hills, CA 90212, USA

YATES, Rodney Brooks; s of Henry Bertram Yates, OBE, of Alvechurch, Birmingham, and Emily Barbara, *née* Wenham (d 1984); *b* 7 June 1937; *Educ* Uppingham; *m* 1 (m dis); 2 s (Mark b 1965, Duncan b 1966), 1 da (Camilla b 1970); m 2, 16 Sept 1983, Hazel, da of Leonard Brown, of Stamford, Lincolnshire; 1 s (Benjamin b 1986); *Career* dir: Akroyd & Smithers plc 1976-86, Mercury Group Management 1986-87, Hemsley & Co Securities Ltd 1988-89; md Madoff Securities International Ltd 1987-88, chm Olliff & Partners plc 1987-, dir Bently Capital (Europe) Ltd 1991-; memb Cambs Family Health Serv Authy 1990-; Liveryman Worshipful Co of Tallow Chandlers; FCA, memb Int Stock Exchange; *Recreations* tennis, reading; *Clubs* RAC; *Style*— Rodney Yates, Esq; The Old Rectory, Marholm, Peterborough PE6 7JA (☎ 0733 269466); Olliff & Partners plc, Saddlers House, Gutter Lane, Cheapside, London EC2V 6BR (☎ 071 374 0791)

YATES, Roger Philip; s of Eric Yates, of Warrington, and Joyce Mary, *née* Brown; *b* 4 April 1957; *Educ* Boteler GS Warrington, Worcester Coll Oxford (BA), Univ of Reading; *m* 7 Sept 1985, Kim Patricia, da of Anthony Gerald Gibbons, of Abinger, Surrey; 2 s (Max b 1987, Jeremy b 1989); *Career* joined GT Mgmnt Ltd 1981; dir: GT Management (UK) Ltd 1984, GT Management plc 1986; investmt dir GT Unit Managers Ltd 1988, left GT 1988, dir and chief investment offr Morgan Grenfell Investment Management 1988-; *Recreations* golf, windsurfing, skiing, tennis; *Style*— Roger Yates, Esq; 51 Broxash Road, London SW11 6AD (☎ 071 223 4492); Morgan Grenfell Investment Management, 20 Finsbury Circus, London EC2M INB (☎ 071 256 7500, fax 071 826 0331, telex 920286 MGAM G)

YATES, Prof William Edgar; s of Douglas Yates (d 1955), and Doris, *née* Goode (d 1990); *b* 30 April 1938; *Educ* Fettes, Emmanuel Coll Cambridge (MA, PhD); *m* 6 April 1963, Barbara Anne, da of Wolfgang Fellowes (d 1984); 2 s (Thomas b 1971, Paul b 1974); *Career* 2 Lt RASC 1957-58; lectr in German Univ of Durham 1963-72, prof of German Univ of Exeter 1972- (dep vice chllr 1986-89), Germanic ed Modern Language Review 1981-88; memb: Modern Humanities Res Assoc (memb Ctee 1980-), Eng Goethe Soc (memb Cncl 1984-), Int Nestroy Soc (memb Cncl 1986-); *Books* Grillparzer: A Critical Introduction (1972), Nestroy: Satire and Parody in Viennese Popular Comedy (1972), Humanity in Weimar and Vienna: The Continuity of an Ideal (1973), Tradition in the German Sonnet (1981), Nestroy (ed Stücke 12-14, 1981-82, Stücke 34, 1989), Viennese Popular Theatre (ed with J R P McKenzie, 1985), Grillparzer und die Europäische Tradition (ed with R Pichl and others, 1987); *Recreations* music; *Style*— Prof W E Yates; 7 Clifton Hill, Exeter EX1 2DL; Dept of German, Univ of Exeter, Queen's Building Exeter EX4 4QH (☎ 0392 264337)

YEABSLEY, Lady; Hilda Maude; da of Wilmot C M Willson; *m* 1923, Sir Richard Ernest Yeabsley, CBE (d 1983); 1 da; *Style*— Lady Yeabsley; Ingles Court Hotel, Ingles Rd, Folkestone, Kent CT20 2SN

YEAMAN, Keith Ian Bentley; s of Sir Ian David Yeaman (d 1977), of The Moat House, Uckington, Glos, and Anne Doris, *née* Wood (d 1975); *b* 20 July 1931; *Educ* Cheltenham; *m* 23 Sept 1967, Caroline Clare, da of His Honour Judge Anthony Clare Bulger, of The Dower House, Forthampton, Glos; 2 da ((Katharine) Jemima b 1969, Nicola Clare b 1970); *Career* 2 Lt Gloucestershire Regt, served Kenya, Aden and Persian Gulf 1950-52, Offr TA Inns of Ct Regt and Royal Gloucestershire Hussars (Major); slr 1959; memb Solicitors Disciplinary Tribunal; sec Gloucestershire and Wilts Inc Law Soc 1964-83 (pres 1980-81); dir: Nat Centre for Disabled Youth, slrs Indemnity Fund; *Recreations* gardening, most country sports; *Clubs* East India and Sports; *Style*— Keith Yeaman, Esq; The Dower House, Forthampton, Gloucester (☎ 0684 298498); Flat 5, 65 Onslow Gardens, London SW7; Ellenborough House, Wellington Street, Cheltenham, Glos (☎ 0242 222022)

YEANDLE, Geoffrey Ernest Lascelles; s of Rev Walter Harold Yeandle (d 1952), of Bearsted Vicarage, Maidstone, Kent, and Irene Mary, *née* Snow (d 1972); *b* 12 Oct 1931; *Educ* Maidstone GS; *m* 14 Sept 1957, June Pamela, da of Nathaniel Mendess (d 1957); 2 s (Mark b 1962, Simon b 1966); *Career* Nat Serv 1950-52, cmmnd RA Lt, TA 1952-58, cmmnd Capt Kent Yeo; sales dir Warner Fabrics plc 1972-, chm West End Furnishing Fabrics Assoc 1980-84; vice chm Borden Parish Cncl 1981-; Freeman City of London 1980, Liveryman Worshipful Co of Weavers 1980; MIEK, FBIM, FRSA; *Recreations* shooting, cricket, photography; *Style*— Geoffrey Yeandle, Esq; The Thatched Cottage, Chestnut Wood, Borden, Sittingbourne, Kent (☎ 0795 842343); Warner Fabrics plc, 7-11 Noel St, London W1V 4AL (☎ 071 439 2411)

YEARDLEY, Brian; s of John Henry Yeardley, and Elizabeth Anne, *née* Holmes; *b* 7 May 1948; *Educ* Dinnington Tech Sch; *m* 22 Aug 1975, Sandra, da of John Whitworth Stapleton (d 1968); 1 da (Suzanne Louise b 1976), 1 step s (Dominic Rispin b 1967), 1 step da (Fiona Large b 1965); *Career* chm and md Brian Yeardley Ltd 1975-; dir Leconfield Park Service Station Ltd 1985-, Kiplingcotes Stud Ltd 1987-; chm and md Brian Yeardley Continental Ltd (int haulage co) 1983-; chm Road Haulage Assoc Hull Area 1982-84; *Recreations* snooker, working, golf, walking with dogs and wife; *Clubs* Kirkella Golf, Willerby, Kirkella Gentlemans; *Style*— Brian Yeardley, Esq; Rolling Hills, Goodmanham, Market Weighton, York YO4 3JD; Brian Yeardley Continental Ltd, Strand House, Wakefield Rd, Featherstone WF7 5BP (telex 556213, fax 0977 791856)

YEATES, Hon Mrs (Camilla Patricia Caroline); da of 3 Viscount Rothermere; *b* 28 July 1964; *m* 14 Oct 1989, Andrew R Yeates, yst s of late K P Yeates, of Sydney, NSW, Australia; *Style*— The Hon Mrs Yeates

YEATES, Roger; s of Charles Henry Yeates, of Basingstoke, Hants, and Elsie Victoria May Yeates; *b* 18 Sept 1945; *Educ* Queen Marys GS Basingstoke; *m* 15 Sept 1973 (m dis 1984); 1 s (Robert David b 1971), 1 da (Ellen b 1974); *Career* CA 1967; AMF Legg 1967-71, Alexander Duckham & Co Ltd 1971-73; gp accountant Lansing Linde Ltd 1974-; dir and sec: JE Shay Ltd, Bonser Engrg Ltd, Henley Forklift Gp Ltd,

Lansing Bagnall Ltd, Hawkington Ltd, and numerous other cos; *Recreations* gliding, stock car racing, photography, reading; *Style*— Roger Yeates, Esq; 8 Grainger Close, Basingstoke, Hants RG22 4DY; Linde Hldgs Ltd, Kingsclere Rd, Basingstoke, Hants RG21 2XJ (☎ 0256 473131)

YEATES, W Keith; s of William Ravensbourne Yeates (d 1953), and Winifred Scott (d 1969); *b* 10 March 1920; *Educ* Glasgow Acad, Whitley Bay GS, King's Coll Newcastle, Univ of Durham (MD, MS); *m* 3 April 1946, Jozy McIntyre, da of Paul Fairweather (d 1949); 1 s (Rodney b 1947), 1 da (Deborah b 1949); *Career* house surgn Professorial Unit Royal Victoria Infirmary Newcastle upon Tyne 1942 (gen surgical registrar 1943-44), demonstrator in anatomy Med Sch Newcastle 1944-45, res surgical offr Tynemouth Infirmary 1945-47, asst surgn Dept of Urology Newcastle Gen Hosp 1948-49; sr registrar St Paul's Hosp London 1950, Dept of Urology Newcastle Gen Hosp 1951-52, conslt urologist Newcastle Health Authy 1952-85; hon conslt urologist 1985-; chm: Specialist Advsy Ctee Urology RCS 1984-86, Intercollegiate Bd in Urology RCS 1984-88; conslt advsr in Urology DHSS 1978-84; univ visiting prof: Baghdad 1974 and 1978, California 1976, Texas 1976, Delhi 1977, Cairo 1978, Kuwait 1980; guest prof NY section American Urological Assoc 1977 and 1985; princ guest lectr Urological Soc of Australia 1977; guest lectr: Italian Urological Assoc 1978, Yugoslavian Urological Assoc 1980, Rio de Janiero 1975; British Journal of Urology: ed 1973-78, chm Editorial Ctee 1978-84, hon consulting ed 1985-90; St Peters medal Br Assoc of Urological Surgns 1983; FRCS, FRCSE; memb: Int Soc of Urology 1958 (sr memb 1985-), Euro Assoc of Urology 1974 (sr memb 1985-); hon memb: Br Assoc of Urological Surgns 1985- (pres 1980-82), Urological Soc of Aust 1977-, Canadian Urological Assoc 1981-; *Publications* author of various papers and chapters in text books on urology and andrology; *Style*— W Keith Yeates, Esq; 22 Castleton Grove, Newcastle upon Tyne NE2 2HD (☎ 091 281 4030); 71 King Henry's Rd, London NW3 3QU (☎ 071 586 7633)

YEATES, William Ronald; s of Richard Henry Yeates (d 1972), of Coatbridge, Strathclyde, and Caroline McAra Barclay (d 1983); *b* 24 June 1929; *Educ* Kildonan HS Coatbridge, Cranfield Business Sch; *m* 4 Sept 1955, Jean Valentine, da of Frederick Ernest Boxall (d 1960); 2 s (Douglas b 5 Feb 1957, Colin b 30 Oct 1958); 2 da (Cheryl b 23 Sept 1961, Heather b 18 Nov 1963); *Career* Nat Serv RAF 1947-49; J Sainsbury plc: branch mangr 1964-74, dist mangr 1974-76, area dir 1976-83; md Savacentre Ltd 1982-90; charitable activities: Marwell Zoological Tst, Guide Dogs for the Blind, Cancer Research; MInstD 1983; *Recreations* golf; *Clubs* Ampfield Golf, Bramshaw Golf; *Style*— Ronald Yeates, Esq; Bruma, Southdown Rd, Shawford, Winchester, Hampshire

YEATMAN, Anthony Graham; JP (1972); s of Graham N Yeatman, TD, JP, DL, High Sheriff of Dorset, of Poole, Dorset, and Lilian, *née* Gruning; *b* 13 May 1936; *Educ* Blundell's, RAC Cirencester; *m* 27 May 1961, Wendy Joan, da of Edward Robert West (d 1976); 1 s (Graham Edward b 7 May 1966), 1 da (Belinda Jane b 29 Dec 1963); *Career* md Yeatman Gp of Cos; pres Poole Rotary Club 1973 (memb 1962-); memb: Dorset Magistrates Cts Ctee, Game Conservancy, Soc of Dorset Men, Poole Borough Cncl 1974-76; memb and hon treas IOD Sarum Centre Salisbury; *Recreations* sailing, photography; *Clubs* Naval & Military, Royal Motor Yacht; *Style*— Anthony Yeatman, Esq, JP; Court House, Corfe Mullen, Wimborne, Dorset BH21 3RH (☎ 0258 857 328)

YELLAND, David Ian; s of John Michael Yelland, of Bridlington, East Yorkshire, and Patricia Ann, *née* McIntosh; *b* 14 May 1963; *Educ* Brigg GS Humberside, Lanchester Poly Coventry (BA); *partner* 1988-, Jan Jacques; *Career* graduate trainee journalist Company Sch Hastings Westminster Press 1984-85, jr reporter Bucks Advertiser Gerrards Cross 1985-87, news and industl reporter Northern Echo Darlington 1987-88, journalist North West Times and Sunday Times Manchester 1988, city reporter Thomson Regnl Newspapers London 1989-90, city ed The Sun 1990-; NCTJ professional test 1987; *Recreations* annoying the people in this book; *Style*— David Yelland, Esq; News International, 1 Virginia Street, London E1 9BD (☎ 071 782 5000, fax 071 488 3253)

YELLOLY, Prof Margaret Anne; *b* 7 June 1934; *Educ* Univ of St Andrews (BA), Univ of Liverpool (MA), Univ of Leicester (PhD); *Career* prof of social work and dir of social work educn Univ of Sterling 1986-91, Tavistock Clinic prof of social work Brunel Univ 1991-; memb of the Central Cncl for Educn and Training in Social Work, chm Social Work Educn Ctee of the Jt Univ Cncl; *Books* Behaviour Modification in Social Work (1972), Social Work Theory and Psychoanalysis (1985), Social Work and the Legacy of Freud (1989); *Recreations* classical music, harpsichord; *Style*— Prof Margaret Yelloly; The Tavistock Centre, 20 Belsize Lane, London NW3 5BA (☎ 071 435 7111)

YELLOWLEES, Dr Michael James; s of Dr Walter Walker Yellowlees, MC, of Duiness, Aberfeldy, Perthshire, and Sonia, *née* Doggart; *b* 8 Oct 1959; *Educ* Strathallan Sch Forgandenny Perthshire, Univ of Edinburgh (MA, PhD); *Career* formerly: teacher, civil servant, hockey player; currently studying law at Univ of Edinburgh; former capt GB and Edinburgh Civil Serv Hockey Teams, Scottish international 1981- (capt and vice-capt, 54 caps); *Style*— Dr Michael Yellowlees; 24 Buccleuch Place, Edinburgh EH8 9LN (☎ 031 667 8382)

YELLOWLEES, Dr Walter Walker; MC (1944); s of David Yellowlees (d 1966), of Elderslie, and Mary Ann Wingate, *née* Primrose (d 1978); *b* 13 April 1917; *Educ* Merchiston Castle Sch, Univ of Edinburgh (MB ChB); *m* 16 Sept 1950, Sonia, da of James Hamilton Doggart, MD, of Surrey; 2 s (Robin b 1956, Michael b 1959), 1 da (Jane b 1962); *Career* GP ret; Edinburgh Univ Capt Rugby 1939, cricket 1940, pres Athletic Club 1940, county cricket team Stirling 1947, Perthshire 1947; Capt RAMC 1942-46, 220 Field Ambulance 1st Army N African campaign, 5th Bn Queens Own Cameron Highlanders, Sicily Normandy, NW Europe campaign; SHO Sitling Royal Infirmary 1946 (house surgeon 1942-46), house physician Perth Royal Infirmary 1946-47, house paediatrician Western Gen Hosp Edinburgh 1947-48, GP 1948-81; potter 1981-; fndr memb RCGP (FRCGP 1976), fndr memb McCarrison Soc (pres 1975-86); *Books* Ill Fares the Land (1979, James McKenzie Lecture), Food and Health in the Scottish Highlands (1985); *Recreations* organic gardening, skiing, trout fishing, golf; *Clubs* Edinburgh Univ Staff, Scottish Potters Assoc; *Style*— Dr Walter W Yellowlees, MC; Duiness, Aberfeldy, Perthshire PH15 2ET (☎ 0887 20277); The Haining Pottery, Taybridge Rd, Aberfeldy (☎ 0887 20277)

YEO, Diane Helen; da of Brian Harold Pickard, and Joan Daisy, *née* Packham; *b* 22 July 1945; *Educ* Blackheath HS, Univ of London, Institut Francais de Presse; *m* 30 March 1970, Timothy Stephen Kenneth Yeo, MP, *qv*, s of Dr Kenneth John Yeo; 1 s (Jonathan b 1970), 1 da (Emily b 1972); *Career* BBC Radio prodn 1968-74, dir clearing house scheme Africa Educnl Tst 1974-79, head of fundraising Girl Guides Assoc 1979-82; dir: appeals and public rels YWCA 1982-85, Inst of Charity Fundraising Mangrs 1985-88; conslt Centre for Voluntary Organisation LSE 1988-, charity cmmr 1989-, dir Charity Appts; MICFM 1983, FRSA 1989; *Recreations* photography, music, tennis, swimming; *Style*— Mrs Diane Yeo; The Charity Commission, St Albans House, Haymarket, London SW1Y 4QX (☎ 071 210 3000)

YEO, Jacinta Marina; da of Lt-Col Yeo Kee Meng, of Kuala Lumpar, Malaysia, and Kathleen Callaghan, of Dublin, Ireland; *b* 23 Jan 1962; *Educ* Trinity Coll Dublin (BA, BDentSc); *Career* house surgn Dublin Dental Hosp 1985; assoc in private practice: Dublin 1986-88, Harley Street 1988-89; princ 2 Harley Street 1989-; Irish Dental Bd prizes in: oral medicine, oral surgery, oral pathology periodontics 1984; primary fell Faculty of Dentistry of Ireland 1986, FRSM 1990, memb BDA 1990; *Recreations* tapestry, knitting, watercolour painting, computer literacy; *Style*— Miss Jacinta Yeo; 2 Harley St, London W1N 1AA (☎ 071 323 2057, 0831 420 558)

YEO, Timothy Stephen Kenneth; MP (C) South Suffolk 1983-; s of Dr Kenneth John Yeo (d 1979), and Norah Margaret Yeo; *b* 20 March 1945; *Educ* Charterhouse, Emmanuel Coll Cambridge; *m* 1970, Diane Helen, *qv*, da of Brian Harold Pickard; 1 s (Jonathan b 1970), 1 da (Emily b 1972); *Career* parly candidate (C) Bedwellty 1974; dir Worcester Engrg Co Ltd 1975-86; asst treas Banker's Trust Company; treas Int Voluntary Service 1975-78, dir Spastics Soc 1980-83, chm Charities VAT Reform Gp 1981-88; tstee Tanzania Devpt Tst 1980-; chm Tadworth Ct Tst 1983-91; jt sec: Constructive Back-Bench Fin Ctee 1984-87, Social Services Select Ctee 1985-88; PPS to Rt Hon Douglas Hurd, MP 1988-90, parly under sec Dept of Environment 1990-; *Publications* Public Accountability and Regulation of Charities (1983); *Recreations* skiing; *Clubs* Carlton, Royal St George's; *Style*— Timothy Yeo, Esq, MP; House of Commons, London SW1 (☎ 071 219 3000)

YEOMAN, Maj-Gen Alan; CB (1987); s of George Smith Patterson Yeoman (d 1978), and Wilhelmina Tromans Elwell (d 1944); *b* 17 Nov 1933; *Educ* Dame Allan's Sch Newcastle upon Tyne, RMA Sandhurst; *m* 12 March 1960, Barbara Joan, da of Norman Albert Davies (d 1975); 2 s (Timothy b 1 May 1961, Michael b 1 April 1965), 1 da (Sally b 29 Jan 1963); *Career* cmmnd RCS 1954; served 1954-70: Korea, Malaysia, Singapore, Cyprus, UK, BAOR, Canada; Staff Coll 1963, CO 2 Div Signals Regt BAOR 1970-73; HQ 1 (Br) Corps 1973-74, MOD 1974-77, Col AQ HQLF Cyprus 1978-79, cmd Trg Gp Royal Signal and Catterick Garrison 1979-82, Brig AQ HQ 1 (Br) Corps BAOR 1982-84, cmd Communications BAOR 1984-87, ret 1988; Hon Col 37 (Wessex and Welsh) Signals Regt (V) 1987, Col Cmdt Royal Signals 1987-; dir Army Sport Control Bd; *Recreations* golf, cricket, skiing; *Clubs* Army and Navy, MCC; *Style*— Maj-Gen A Yeoman, CB; c/o Lloyds Bank, Catterick Garrison, North Yorks

YEOMAN, Nigel Robin Edward; s of Robin Edward Ferg Yeoman (d 1985), and Ada Kate, *née* Carpenter (d 1984); *b* 14 Oct 1936; *Educ* Salisbury Cathedral Sch, King Sch Bruton; *m* 15 Oct 1960, Tessa Esme, da of Lt James Edward Hill, RN (ka 1944), of Poole, Dorset; 1 s (Gareth b 1961), 3 da (Joanna b 1962, Elaine b 1966, Suzanne b 1966); *Career* slr, Supreme Court of Judicature; chm Southern Rent Assessment Ctee; *Recreations* yacht racing, rugby, golf, skiing; *Clubs* Bournemouth Sports, Parkstone Yacht, Parkstone Golf; *Style*— Nigel R E Yeoman, Esq; Sea Rigs, 28 Dorset Lake Avenue, Lilliput, Poole, Dorset; 221 The Broadway, Broadstone, Dorset (☎ 0202 692308, fax 0202 601353)

YEOMAN, Capt Paul Stanley Pressick; s of William Gordon Yeoman (d 1978), of Claremont Road, Marlow, Bucks, and Fernande Lidy Susanne Georgette Margurite, *née* Gilles; *b* 30 Dec 1926; *Educ* The Nautical Coll Pangbourne; *m* 20 June 1953, Phyllis Genevieve, da of George Victor Were (d 1972), of Auckland, New Zealand; 3 s (Philip, Mark, Richard), 2 da (Sarah (Mrs Poziades), Clare (Mrs Pritchard)); *Career* cadet RNR 1940-44, jr offr Merchant Navy WWII served Europe and Far East; offr Shaw Savill Line 1946-53; joined Limehouse Paperhouse Mills Gp of Cos 1953 (dir 1960-86), chm Condor Paper Sales Ltd; Freeman: City of London 1973, Worshipful Co of Feltmakers 1973; *Clubs* Marlow RUFC; *Style*— Capt Paul Yeoman; Meadow House, Stoney Ware, Marlow, Bucks SL7 1RN (☎ 06284 4269); Condor Paper Sales Ltd, The Old School House, Station Rd, Bourne End Bucks SL8 5QD (☎ 06285 29747/8, fax 0628 810754)

YEOMANS, Joseph; s of Joseph Yeomans (d 1979), of Grange-over-Sands, and Myra Phyllis, *née* Quigley (d 1963); *b* 19 March 1929; *Educ* Barrow Boys GS, Univ of Nottingham (BA); *m* 7 July 1952, Jacqueline Averil, da of Cyril Arnold (d 1974), of Rhyl; 2 s (John b 1953 d 1988, Paul b 1973), 5 da (Cherry b 1955, Gay b 1956, Christine b 1958, Jacqueline b 1963, Hazel b 1966); *Career* Nat Serv RAF 1947-49; Cyril Arnold & Co CAs Rhyl: joined 1952, ptnr 1955-; memb: Rotary Int 1955-61, Round Table 1953-70 (chm 1962); fell ICEAW 1958; *Style*— Joseph Yeomans, Esq; 14 Clwyd St, Rhyl, Clwyd (☎ 0745 343 476)

YEOMANS, Richard David; s of Richard James Yeomans (d 1964), of Eversley, Basingstoke, Hants, and Elsie Marian, *née* Winson; *b* 15 Feb 1943; *Educ* Hartley Wintney Co Secdy Modern Sch, Hants Coll of Agric, Shuttleworth Coll (NDA); *m* 6 April 1968, Doreen Ann, da of William Herring, of Aldershot; 1 s (Jonathon b 24 Feb 1976), 1 da (Claire b 14 Dec 1972); *Career* with Milk Mktg Bd 1965-71; Unigate plc: area mangr tport 1971-, gen mangr (milk) 1975-, memb Main Bd; md: Wincanton Transport Ltd 1978-, Wincanton Group Ltd 1982; tstee Nat Motor Museum Beaulieu; memb: Bd of Econ Situation CBI 1982, Bd of Groundwork Fndn 1988; Liveryman Worshipful Co of Carmen; FBIM 1982, FCIT 1989; *Recreations* shooting, opera, gardening, photography; *Clubs* RAC; *Style*— David Yeomans, Esq; Newland, 4 Gainsborough, Milborne Port, Sherborne, Dorset, DT9 5BA (☎ 0963 250246); Wincanton Group Ltd, Station Road, Wincanton, Somerset, BA9 9EQ (☎ 0963 33933, fax 0963 32490, telex 46237)

YEOWART, Geoffrey Bernard Brian; s of Brian Albert Yeowart, of Chailey, Sussex, and Vera Ivy, *née* Goring; *b* 28 March 1949; *Educ* Ardingly Coll, Univ of Southampton (LLB), King's Coll London (LLM); *m* 6 Oct 1979, Patricia Eileen, da of Oswald Anthony (d 1984); 2 s (Thomas b 8 June 1983, Matthew b 30 Sept 1986), 1 da (Clare b 7 Nov 1980); *Career* admitted slr 1975 (admitted Hong Kong 1982); ptnr: Durrant Piesse 1985-88, Lovell White Durrant 1988-; memb Law Soc; *Recreations* sailing, swimming, skiing, reading; *Style*— Geoffrey Yeowart, Esq; Lovell White Durrant, 65 Holborn Viaduct, London EC1A 2DY (☎ 071 236 0066, fax 071 248 4212, telex 887122 LWD G)

YERBURGH, Lt-Col John Rochfort; s of Canon Oswald Rochfort Yerburgh (d 1966), and Cicely Joan, *née* Savile (d 1981); *b* 14 Sept 1931; *Educ* Marlborough, RMA Sandhurst, RMCS Shrivenham; *m* 17 Aug 1963, Gillian Elizabeth, da of Derek Plint Clifford, of Hartlip Place, Sittingbourne, Kent; 1 s (Toby b 9 Oct 1965), 1 da (Sophia b 8 Jan 1967); *Career* cmmnd RE 1952, C RE NI 1972-74, ret 1983; High Sheriff of Kent 1988-89; memb for Swale Central Kent CC 1984, vice chm Gillingham Cons Assoc 1987; Freeman City of London 1989; *Recreations* travel, tennis; *Style*— Lt-Col John Yerburgh; Hartlip Place, Sittingbourne, Kent ME9 7TR (☎ 0795 842 583); West Heath, Ashgrove Road, Sevenoaks, Kent (☎ 0732 452 541)

YERBURGH, Capt the Hon Robert Richard Guy; o s and h of 2 Baron Alvingham, CBE, *qv*; *b* 10 Dec 1956; *Educ* Eton; *m* 1981, Vanessa Kelty, yr da of Capt Duncan Kinloch Kirk; 2 s (Robert William Guy b 16 Sept 1983, Edward Alexander Henry b 6 April 1986); *Career* Lt 17/21 Lancers 1978, Capt 1980, attached to Army Air Corps as pilot 1979-83, resigned 1983; *Recreations* shooting, fishing, skiing (jt services instr); *Clubs* Cavalry & Guards; *Style*— Capt the Hon Robert Yerburgh; Valley Farm House, Bix Bottom, Henley-on-Thames, Oxon (☎ 0491 576043)

YHAP, Laetitia Karoline; da of Leslie Neville Yhap (d 1987), and Elizabeth, *née* Kogler; *b* 1 May 1941; *Educ* Fulham Co GS, Camberwell Sch of Arts and Crafts (NDD), Slade School (DFA); *m* 1963 (m dis 1980), Jeffrey Camp; 1 s (Ajax b 1984); *Career* artist in oils; Leverhulme Res Award (travel in Italy) 1962-63; first solo show Norwich Sch of Art 1964, Young Contemporaries FBA galleries and tour 1965, various showings with London Gp 1965-, three solo shows Piccadilly Gallery 1968, 1970 and 1973, solo touring summershow Serpentine Gallery 1975, exhibition of drawings of people Serpentine Gallery London 1975, exhibition John Moores Liverpool, The British Art Show 1979, Art and The Sea ICA and tour 1981, Tolly Cobbold 1983, solo show Air Gallery London 1984, The Hard-Won Image Tate Gallery 1984, solo summer show touring The Business of the Beach Laing Art Gallery Newcastle 1988; memb: London Gp, Hastings Arts; *Recreations* badminton, concert going; *Style—* Ms Laetitia Yhap; Fischer Fine Art, 30 King St, St James's, London SW1Y 6RJ (☎ 071 839 3942, fax 071 930 1062)

YONACE, Dr Adrian Harris; JP (Dorset 1989); s of Dr Jack Yonace (d 1975), of Salford, and Bryna, *née* Fidler; *b* 26 Nov 1943; *Educ* Manchester GS, Univ of Manchester, Univ of Nottingham (BMedSci, BM BS); *m* 9 March 1989, Maureen Wilson, da of Thomas Wilson Ramsay, of Liverpool; *Career* computer systems analyst IBM 1965-67, computer conslt 1967-70; house physician and house surgn Univ Dept Mancheter Royal Infimary 1976-77, lectr in psychiatry Royal Free Hosp Univ of London 1980-83, conslt and hon sr lectr Friern Hosp and Univ of London 1983-89, conslt psychiatrist St Ann's Hosp Poole 1989-, clinical teacher Univ of Southampton, sr examiner MB ChB Finals Univ of London; Silver Dip Eng Bridge Union Teachers Assoc; JP Inner London Juvenile Bench 1985-89; MRCPsych 1983; *Recreations* scrabble, bridge, golf; *Style—* Dr Adrian Yonace, JP; St Ann's Hospital, Haven Rd, Canford Cliffs, Poole, Dorset BH13 7LN (☎ 0202 708881)

YONGE, Dame (Ida) Felicity Ann; DBE (1982); da of Cdr William Humphry Nigel Yonge, RN (d 1973), by his w Kathleen Ida Marion (d 1974); *b* 28 Feb 1921; *Educ* Convent of The Holy Child St Leonards-on-Sea; *Career* WRNS 1940-46, 2 Offr; purser's office P&OSN Co 1947-50; private sec to: chm of Cons Pty 1951-64, ldr of oppn 1964-65, Cons chief whip 1965-70 and 1974-79, ldr of House of Commons 1970-74; special advsr Govt Chief Whip's Office 1979-83; *Style—* Dame Felicity Yonge, DBE; 58 Leopold Rd, Wimbledon, London SW19 7JF (☎ 081 946 3018)

YORK, Maj Christopher; DL (1952); s of Col Edward York, TD, DL (d 1951), of Hutton Wandesley, York, and Violet Helen, *née* Milner; *b* 27 July 1909; *Educ* Eton, RMC Sandhurst; *m* 16 Oct 1934, Pauline Rosemary, da of Lt-Col Sir Lionel Fletcher, KBE (d 1961), of Tanganyika; 1 s (Edward Christopher b 22 Feb 1939), 3 da (Caroline Rosemary (Lady Nuttall m dis 1970) b 28 July 1936, (Lavinia Mary) Louise (Mrs Seymour) b 11 April 1942, Mary Susanna (Mrs Mallaby) b 16 Aug 1947); *Career* joined The Royal Dragoons 1930, supplementary reserve 1934-39, served 1939-45 Maj 1943; landowner & farmer 1951-, chm Hutton Wandesley Farms Co 1966-; MP: (U) Ripon 1939-51, Harrogate 1951-54; hon treas RVC 1948-83, tstee RASE 1979- (memb Cncl 1948, hon treas 1961, pres 1979); QALAS 1936, Hon FRVC 1971; *Recreations* writing; *Clubs* Carlton, Boodle's, Yorkshire (York); *Style—* Maj Christopher York, DL; South Park, Long Marston, York YO5 8LL (☎ 090 483 357)

YORK, 95 Archbishop of (cr 625) 1983-; Most Rev and Rt Hon John Stapylton Habgood; patron of many livings, the Archdeaconries of York, Cleveland and the East Riding, and the Canonries in his Cathedral; the Archbishopric was founded AD 625, and the Province comprises fourteen Sees; s of Arthur Henry Habgood, DSO, MB, BCh, and Vera, da of late Richard Chetwynd-Stapylton, ggggs of 4 Viscount Chetwynd; *b* 23 June 1927; *Educ* Eton, King's Coll Cambridge, Cuddesdon Theol Coll Oxford; *m* 1961, Rosalie Mary Anne, da of Edward Lansdown Boston; 2 s, 2 da; *Career* former demonstrator in pharmacology Cambridge; ordained 1954, rector St John's Jedburgh 1962-67, princ Queen's Coll Birmingham 1967-73, hon canon of Birmingham Cathedral 1971-73, bishop of Durham 1973-83; Privy Cncl 1983; hon fell King's Coll Cambridge 1986; *Books* Religion and Science (1964), A Working Faith (1980), Church and Nation in a Secular Age (1983), Confessions of a Conservative Liberal (1988); *Recreations* DIY, painting; *Clubs* Athenaeum; *Style—* The Most Rev and Rt Hon the Lord Archbishop of York; Bishopthorpe, York YO2 1QE (☎ 0904 707021)

YORK, Michael; s of Joseph Gwynne Johnson, and Florence Edith May Chown; *b* 27 March 1942; *Educ* Hurstpierpoint Coll, Bromley GS, Univ Coll Oxford (BA); *m* 1968, Patricia Frances, da of Richard McCallum; *Career* actor: with Nat Theatre Co; Outcry, Broadway; films: Romeo & Juliet, Cabaret, The Three Musketeers, Conduct Unbecoming, Logans Run, Jesus of Nazareth, For Those I Loved, The Heart of the Day; *Style—* Michael York, Esq; Duncan Heath Associates, Paramount House, 162-170 Wardour St, London W1V 3AT (☎ 071 439 1417)

YORK, Susannah Yolande; da of William Peel Simon Fletcher, and Joan Nita Mary, *née* Bowring; *b* 9 Jan 1942; *Educ* Marr Coll Troon, E Haddon Hall Northants; *m* 2 May 1960 (m dis 1980), Michael Barry Wells; 1 s (Orlando Wells b June 1973), 1 da (Sasha Wells b May 1972); *Career* actress; films: Tunes of Glory, Greengage Summer, Freud, Tom Jones, The Seventh Dawn, Act One Scene Nun, Sands of the Kalahari, Scruggs, Kaleidoscope, A Man for All Seasons, Sebastian, Duffy, Lock up your Daughters, The Killing of Sister George, Images (Best Actress Award at Cannes Film Festival), They Shoot Horses Don't They?, Country Dance, Happy Birthday Wanda June, Conduct Unbecoming, That Lucky Touch, Sky Riders, Eliza Fraser, Zee and Co, Silent Partner, The Shout, Memories, The Awakening, Gold, Jane Eyre, The Maids, Loophole, Superman I and II, Golden Gate Murders, Alice, Christmas Carol, Yellowbeard, Mio My Mio, Bluebeard, A Summer Story, Just ask for Diamond, Melancholia, Barbarblu Barbarblu, Little Women; TV: The Crucible, The Rebel and the Soldier, The First Gentleman, The Richest Man in the World, Fallen Angels, Second Chance, We'll Meet Again, The Other Side of Me, Star Quality, The Two Ronnies, Yellow Beard, A Christmas Carol, Bonnie Jean, Macho, Love Boat - USA, Return Journey, After the War, The Man from the Pru, The Haunting of the New, Devices and Desires, Boon; theatre: Wings of a Dove, A Singular Man, Man and Superman, Private Lives, Hedda Gabblar (London and New York); Appearances (London and Paris): Peter Pan, Cinderella, The Singular Life of Albert Nobbs, Penthesilea, Fatal Attraction, The Women, The Apple Cart, Agnes of God, The Human Voice, Multiple Choice, A Private Treason, Lyric for a Tango, A Glass Menagerie, Streetcar Named Desire; *Books* In Search of Unicorns (2 edns, republished 1985), Larks Castle (1976, republished 1986); *Recreations* gardening, reading, writing, walking, travelling, films and theatre; *Style—* Ms Susannah York; c/o Jeremy Conway, Eagle House, 109 Jermyn St, London SW1Y 6HB (☎ 071 839 2121)

YORK-JOHNSON, Michael; *see*: York, Michael

YORKE, David Harry Robert; s of Harry Reginald Francis Yorke (d 1958), and Marie Christine, *née* Miller Frost; *b* 5 Dec 1931; *Educ* Dean Close Sch Cheltenham, Coll of Estate Mgmnt; *m* 23 April 1955, Patricia Gwynneth, da of Henry Arthur Fowler-Tutt (d 1975); 1 da (Sarah b 1960); *Career* Nat Serv RA 1954-56 (2 Lt 1955); chartered surveyor; Weatherall Green & Smith (UK, France, Germany, USA): ptnr London 1961-84, sr ptnr 1984-89, gp chm 1989-; memb Mgmnt Ctee Schroder Property Fund 1988, memb Bristol Devpt Corp 1989, dir Br Waterways Bd 1989; pres RICS 1988-89; Freeman City of London 1978, Liveryman Worshipful Co of Chartered Surveyors 1979; ARICS 1956, FRICS 1966; *Recreations* narrow-boating, crosswords, swimming, occasional cookery; *Clubs* Bucks; *Style—* David Yorke, Esq; Holford Manor, North Chailey, Sussex (☎ 044 484 277); 2 Chester Cottages, London SW1; 22 Chancery Lane, London WC2 (☎ 071 405 6944)

YORKE, Dwight Eversley; s of Fulton Yorke, of Trinidad & Tobago, and Grace, *née* Joseph; *b* 3 Nov 1971; *Educ* Signal Hill Sr Comp Sch Tobago; *Career* professional footballer; former player Signal Hill Tobago, Aston Villa 1989-; Trinidad & Tobago caps: under 14, under 16, under 19, under 23, over 20 full (scored hat-trick v Sweden); footballer of the year Trinidad & Tobago 1990, Barclays young eagle of the month 1991; *Recreations* all sports, music, dancing; *Style—* Dwight Yorke, Esq; Robert St, Canaan, Tobago (☎ 010 1 809 639 0040); c/o The Cottage, Back Lane, Shustoke, Coleshill, Birmingham B46 2AW (☎ 0675 81203)

YORKE, Richard Michael; QC (1971); s of Gilbert Victor Yorke; *b* 13 July 1930; *Educ* Solihull Sch Warwickshire, Balliol Coll Oxford (MA); *Career* cmmnd 2 Lt RA 1949 (Prize of Honour Best Offr Cadet), Lt Hon Artillery Co 1951, Capt 1953; asst to sec Br Rd Servs 1953-56; called to the Bar Gray's Inn 1956 (Lee Prizeman), bencher 1981; joined Inner Temple 1968, barr Supreme Ct and NSW and High Ct of Aust 1972, QC NSW 1974; conslt Bodington & Yturbe Paris 1973-83; contested (C): Durham 1966, Loughborough Feb and Oct 1974; pres Civil Aviation Review Bd 1972-75; vice chm Senate Law Soc Jt Working Pty on Banking Law 1975-83; memb Special Panel Tport Tbnl 1976-, Panel of Arbitrators Assoc 1984-, vol govr Bart's 1974; rec Crown Ct 1972-83; govr Sadler's Wells Theatre 1986; *Recreations* flying, skiing, sailing, tennis; *Clubs* Royal Ocean Racing, St Stephen's Constitutional, Hurlingham, Island Sailing (Cowes); *Style—* Richard Yorke, Esq, QC; 5 Cliveden Place, London SW1W 8LA; Eden Roc, Rue de Ranson, 1936 Verbier, Switzerland (☎ 026 313 504)

YOUARD, Richard Geoffrey Atkin; s of Lt-Col Geoffrey Youard, MBE (d 1987), of Gwernowddy Old Farmhouse, Llandrinio, Llanymynech, Powys, and Hon Mrs Rosaline Joan, *née* Atkin (d 1973); *b* 27 Jan 1933; *Educ* Bradfield, Magdalen Coll Oxford (BA); *m* 31 Dec 1960, Felicity Ann, da of Kenneth Valentine Freeland Morton, CIE, of Temple End House, 27 Temple End, Great Wilbraham, Cambridge; 1 s (Andrew b 1964), 2 da (Penelope b 1961, Elizabeth b 1966); *Career* Nat Serv 1951-53, cmmnd RA 1952, Lt TA; admitted slr 1959, Slaughter and May 1956-89 (ptnr 1968-89); investmt referee 1989-; chm: Islington Consumers Gp 1965, Nat Fedn of Consumer Gps 1968; memb Home Office Ctee on London Taxicab and Car Hire Trade 1967, inspr DTI 1987, memb governing body Bradfield Coll 1968- (clerk and govr); hon res fell Kings Coll London 1988; memb Law Soc 1968; *Books* various works on banking law and practice incl Butterworths Banking Forms and Precedents (ed 1986); *Recreations* gardening, electronics, beekeeping, map collecting, reading; *Style—* Richard Youard, Esq; 12 Northampton Park, London N1 2PJ; (☎ 071 226 8055); Cwm Mynach Ganol, Bontddu, Dolgellau, Gwynedd; Office of the Investment Referee, 6 Fredericks Place, London EC2R 8BT (☎ 071 796 3065)

YOUDALE, Peter John Michael; s of Reginald John Youdale (d 1966), of Brighton, and Olga, *née* Baume (d 1979); *b* 21 June 1928; *Educ* Brighton Hove & Sussex GS; *m* 1 July 1950, Marie, da of G Hart (d 1939); 1 s (Richard Graham b 24 June 1953), 1 da (Wendy Anne b 3 May 1951); *Career* Nat Serv Grenadier Gds; mgmnt trainee Chubb Group 1950-53, Salesman Dexion Group 1953-56, div mangr British Uralite Group 1956-61, dir int mgmnt trg Eutectic Corp USA 1961-63, dir sales and mktg Eutectic Ltd UK 1963-67, vice pres mktg Mattel Toys California 1967-69, chm and chief exec Pirbic Gp Ltd 1969-; FInstM, FInstD, MBIM; *Books* Setting up an Effective Marketing Operation, Sales Management for Profit; *Recreations* swimming, painting, writing; *Clubs* RAC; *Style—* Peter Youdale, Esq; Birdingbury Hall, Birdingbury, nr Rugby, Warwicks (☎ 0926 633331); The Pirbic Gp Ltd, Tile House, Ridgemount Rd, Sunningdale, Berks (☎ 0990 22291, fax 0990 872996, car 0836 282015)

YOUENS, Ven John Ross; CB (1970), OBE (1959), MC (1946); s of late Canon Fearnley Algernon Cyril Youens, and late Dorothy Mary, *née* Ross; *b* 4 Sept 1914; *Educ* Buxton Coll, Kelham Theol Coll; *m* 1940, Pamela Gordon Lincoln, da of Maj Alfred Lincoln Chandler (d 1948); 1 s (Richard), 2 da (Esme decd, Georgina decd); *Career* Royal Army Chaplain Dept 1940-74, chaplain gen 1966-74, archdeacon emeritus 1974, chaplain to HM The Queen 1969-84; sr treas Corp of the Sons of the Clergy 1982-84, dep chm Keston Coll Centre for the Study of Religion and Communism; *Clubs* Cavalry & Guards; *Style—* The Ven John Youens, CB, OBE, MC; King Edward VII Convalescent Home for Officers, Osborne House, East Cowes, Isle of Wight PO32 6JY

YOUENS, Sir Peter William; CMG (1962), OBE (1960); s of Rev Canon F A C Youens (d 1968), and Dorothy Mary Ross (d 1975); *b* 29 April 1916; *Educ* King Edward VII Sch Sheffield, Wadham Coll Oxford (MA); *m* 1943, Diana Stephanie, da of Edward Hawkins (d 1990); 2 da (Stephanie, Sarah); *Career* dep chief sec Nyasaland 1953-63 (asst sec 1951), sec to PM and Cabinet Malawi 1964-66 and Nyasaland 1963-66; exec dir Lonrho plc 1966-69 and 1981- (non-exec dir 1980-81), ptnr Tyzack and Partners Ltd 1969-81; kt 1965; *Recreations* walking, theatre; *Clubs* East India and Sports, Vincent's (Oxford); *Style—* Sir Peter Youens, CMG, OBE; Lonrho plc, Cheapside House, 138 Cheapside, London EC2V 6BL (☎ 071 606 9898)

YOUNG, Alan Godfrey; s of William Karl Young, of Harrogate, and Friedericke, *née* Kühner (d 1973); *b* 16 June 1936; *Educ* Bradford GS; *m* 29 Jan 1966, Susan Margaret Sadler, da of Frank Sadler Rodber; 2 s (Christopher Edward b 1 Nov 1967, Charles Andrew b 4 April 1969); *Career* Nat Serv RA 1959, 2 Lt 1960; articled clerk Armitage & Norton Bradford 1953-58; Cooper Brothers & Co (now Coopers & Lybrand Deloitte): joined as tax specialist 1962, ptnr 1971, sr tax ptnr Sheffield, head NE Regn Tax Practice; memb Nat Tax Policy Ctee, pres Sheffield & Dist Soc of Chartered Accountants 1982-83; FCA (ACA 1958); *Books* Taxation of Family Businesses (jtly 1988); *Recreations* music (piano playing), squash, wine; *Clubs* Sheffield, Abbeydale Park Squash Racketds, Sickleholme Golf; *Style—* Alan Young, Esq; Coopers & Lybrand Deloitte, 1 East Parade, Sheffield S1 2ET (☎ 0742 729141)

YOUNG, Anthony Elliott; s of Prof Leslie Young, of Esher, Surrey, and Ruth, *née* Elliott; *b* 20 Dec 1943; *Educ* Epsom Coll, St John's Coll Cambridge (MA, MB MChir), St Thomas' Hosp Med Sch; *m* 6 July 1968, Dr Gwyneth Vivien Wright, da of Prof Eldred Walls, of Edinburgh, Scot; 3 s (Adam Elliott b 1974, Oliver Elliott b 1975, Toby Elliott b 1977); *Career* dir surgery St Thomas' Hosp 1988- (conslt surgn 1981-); memb BMA 1968, FRSM 1970, FRCS 1971; *Books* Vascular Malformations (1988); *Recreations* fishing, painting, reading; *Clubs* Savile; *Style—* Anthony Young, Esq; 63 Lee Rd, Blackheath, London SE3 9EN (☎ 081 852 1921); St Thomas' Hospital, London SE1 7EH (☎ 071 928 9292); 38 Devonshire Place, London W1N 1PE (☎ 071 580 3612)

YOUNG, Prof Archie; s of Archibald Young, TD, of Glasgow, and Mary Downie, *née* Fleming; *b* 19 Sept 1946; *Educ* Glasgow HS, Univ of Glasgow (BSc, MB ChB, MD); *m* 24 Dec 1973, Sandra, da of Archibald Clark (d 1969), of Glasgow; 1 s (Archie b 1980), 1 da (Sula b 1979); *Career* clinical lectr Univ of Oxford 1978-85, prof geriatric med Royal Free Hosp London 1988- (conslt physician 1985-88); memb Fitness & Health Advsy Gp; Scottish swimming int 1965-70 (British 1970), Scottish water polo int 1968; memb Incorporation of Tailors Glasgow; FRCPG 1985, FRCP 1989; *Recreations* physical; *Clubs* London Scottish Football; *Style—* Prof Archie Young; Academic Dept of Geriatric Medicine, Royal Free Hosp Sch of Medicine, London NW3 2QG (☎ 071 794 0500 ext 3895)

YOUNG, Bertram Alfred; OBE (1980); s of Bertram William Young, and Dora Elizabeth, *née* Knight; *b* 20 Jan 1912; *Educ* Highgate Sch; *Career* HM Forces 1939-48

(Lancashire Fusiliers, King's African Rifles); Amalgamated Press 1930-35, asst ed Punch 1948-63, drama critic and arts ed Financial Times 1964-77; *Books* Tooth and Claw (1958), Bechuanaland (1966), Cabinet Pudding (1967), The Mirror up to Nature (1982), The Rattigan Version (1986); *Recreations* Surviving; *Clubs* Garrick; *Style*— Bertram Young, Esq, OBE; Clyde House, 1 Station St, Cheltenham, Gloucestershire GL50 3LX (☎ 0242 581485)

YOUNG, Sir Brian Walter Mark; er s of Sir Mark Young, GCMG (d 1974); sometime Govr of: Barbados, Tanganyika and Hong Kong; ggs of Sir George Young, 2 Bt, of Formosa Place; *b* 23 Aug 1922; *Educ* Eton, King's Coll Cambridge; *m* 1947, Fiona Marjorie, only da of Allan Stewart, 16 of Appin; 1 s (Timothy b 1951), 2 da (Joanna b 1949, Deborah b 1953); *Career* serv WWII RNVR; asst master Eton 1947-52, headmaster Charterhouse 1952-64, memb Central Advsy Cncl on Educn 1956-59; dir Nuffield Fndn 1964-70 (managing tstee 1978-90), dir-gen IBA (previously ITA) 1970-82; memb Arts Cncl 1983-88, chm Christian Aid 1983-90; Hon DLitt Heriot-Watt Univ; Hon RNCM 1987; kt 1976; *Style*— Sir Brian Young; Hill End, Woodhill Ave, Gerrards Cross, Bucks (☎ 0753 887793)

YOUNG, Charles Bellamy; s of Harold Buckley Young (d 1988), of Toms River, New Jersey, USA, and Mary Margaretta, *née* Schaefer; *b* 7 Aug 1939; *Educ* Yale Univ (BA), John Hopkins (MA); *m* 31 Aug 1963, Carol Ann, da of Joseph Claude Lombardi (d 1973), Purchase, NY, USA; 2 s (Alexander Bellamy b 1969, Christopher Bellamy b 1973); *Career* Citibank: with NY branch 1965-69, exec vice pres Taiwan First Investmt Tst 1970-72, vice pres NY 1972-73, dir gen France 1974-78, pres Canada 1979-86, county corp offr UK 1986-87; exec dir Olympia & York Canary Wharf Ltd 1987-; *Books* A Nation without Coins (1964); *Recreations* jogging, art, travel; *Clubs* Travellers (Paris), Yale (New York); *Style*— Charles Young, Esq; 9 Wilton Street, London SW1X 7AF (☎ 071 235 7966); 21 Rue Mazarine, Paris 75006, France; Barnes Lane, Purchase, NY 10577; 10 Great George St, London SW1P 3AE (☎ 071 222 8878, fax 071 233 1110)

YOUNG, His Hon Judge; Christopher Godfrey; s of Dr H G Young (d 1949); *b* 9 Sept 1932; *Educ* Bedford Sch, King's Coll London (LLB); *m* 1969, Jeanetta Margaret, *née* Vaughan (d 1984); 1 s; *Career* called to the Bar Gray's Inn 1957, Midland and Oxford Circuit 1959-75, rec 1975-79, circuit judge 1980-; liaison judge with magistrates for Peterborough, Huntingdon and Toseland 1980-87, Leicestershire 1987-; memb Parole Bd 1990-; *Recreations* music, natural history, gardening, foreign travel; *Style*— His Hon Judge Young; Stockshill House, Duddington, Stamford, Lincs

YOUNG, Daniel Greer; s of Gabriel Young, and Julia, *née* McNair; *b* 22 Nov 1932; *Educ* Wishaw HS, Univ of Glasgow; *m* 2 Aug 1957, Agnes Gilchrist (Nan), da of Joseph Donald; 1 s (Kenneth Donald b 1962), 1 da (Rhoda Agnes (Mrs Abel) b 1958); *Career* Nat Serv 1957, special short serv cmmn to Ghana Govt 1959; hon consit paediatric surgn: The Hosp for Sick Children Gt Ormond St London (formerly sr registrar and resident asst surgn), Queen Elizabeth Hosp London; sr lectr in paediatric surgery Inst of Child Health Univ of London, hon conslt paediatric surgn Greater Glasgow Health Bd, reader in paediatric surgery Univ of Glasgow; chm Intercollegiate Bd in Paediatric Surgery, memb Cncl RCPS Glasgow, ex pres Royal Medico-Chirurgical Soc of Glasgow, ed Journal of Paediatric Surgery UK; hon memb: Hungarian Assoc of Paediatric Surgns, South African Assoc of Paediatric Surgns, American Paediatric Surgical Assoc; pres elect Br Assoc of Paediatric Assocs; FRCSEd, FRCS Glasgow; *Books* Baby Surgery (with B F Weller, 1971), Paediatric Surgery (with E Strathdee, 1971), Baby Surgery (with E J Martin, 2 edn, 1979); *Recreations* curling, gardening, fishing; *Style*— Daniel Young, Esq; 49 Sherbrooke Avenue, Glasgow G41 4SE (☎ 041 427 3470); Royal Hospital for Sick Children, Yorkhill, Glasgow G3 8SJ (☎ 041 339 8888)

YOUNG, David Edward Michael; QC (1980); s of George Henry Edward Young, and Audrey, *née* Seymour; *b* 30 Sept 1940; *Educ* Monkton Combe Sch Somerset, Univ of Oxford (MA); *m* 1967, Anne, da of John Henry de Bromhead, of Ireland; 2 da (Yolanda b 1970, Francesca b 1972); *Career* called to the Bar Lincoln's Inn 1966, rec SE Circuit; *Books* Terrell on the Law of Patents (1982, 2 edn 1991), Passing Off (1989); *Recreations* tennis, skiing, country pursuits; *Style*— David Young, Esq, QC; 6 Pump Ct, Temple, London EC4Y 7AR (☎ 071 353 8588)

YOUNG, David Ernest; s of Harold Ernest Young (d 1971), of Sheffield, and Jessie, *née* Turnbull; *b* 8 March 1942; *Educ* King Edward VII Sch Sheffield, Corpus Christi Coll Oxford (BA); *m* 8 Feb 1964, Norma, da of Alwyn Robinson (d 1979); 2 da (Wendy b 1965, Michele b 1968); *Career* asst princ Air Miny 1963; private sec: Chief of Air Staff 1968-70, Min State of Def 1973-75; asst sec Central Policy Review Staff Cabinet Office 1975-77; John Lewis Partnership: joined 1982, md Peter Jones Sloane Square 1984-86, fin dir 1987-; ind memb Steering Bd of Companies House 1988-; memb RIPA 1977; *Recreations* walking, gardening, theatre; *Style*— David Young, Esq; John Lewis Partnership plc, 171 Victoria St, London SW1E 5NN (☎ 071 828 1000, fax 071 828 6609)

YOUNG, Rt Rev David Nigel de Lorentz; *see*: Ripon, Bishop of

YOUNG, David Richard James; TD (1980), JP (1986); s of Wing Cdr Michael James Beaumont Young, DFC, JP (d 1979), and Nina Mary Aline, *née* Seely (d 1980); *b* 23 Oct 1949; *Educ* Worth Abbey Sch; *m* 1971, (m dis 1977), Yvonne, *née* Sytner; m 2, 1979, Katharine Marjorie, *née* Cooper; 2 da (Nina Frances Katherine b 12 July 1981, Harriet Georgina Mary b 26 April 1984); *Career* Lt Col TA; account dir: Rex Stewart Gp 1968-71, Burhart Degenhardt PR 1971-72, PD Design Co 1972-74; chm Oakley Young Associates 1974, dir Rasor Communications (Operating Div of WPP Group plc) 1986; memb Small Firms Cncl CBI 1984-86, FRSA 1989; *Clubs* Cavalry & Guards, St James's; *Style*— David Young, Esq, TD, JP; 1 Holmead Rd, London SW6 7HE; Oakley Young Associates Ltd, Fox House, 46 Oxford St, Leicester LE1 5XW (☎ 0533 558084, fax 0533 54118, mobile 0831 401925)

YOUNG, Lt-Gen Sir David Tod; KBE (1980), CB (1977), DFC (1952); s of William Young (d 1930), by his w Davina Tod, *née* Young (d 1974); *b* 17 May 1926; *Educ* George Watson's Coll Edinburgh; *m* 1, 1950, Joyce Marian Melville (d 1987); 2 s; m 2, 11 June 1988, Mrs Joanna M Oyler, *née* Torin; *Career* cmmnd Royal Scots 1945, Col GS Staff Coll 1969-70, Cdr 12 Mechanised Bde 1970-72, Dep Mil Sec MOD 1972-74, Cdr Land Forces NI 1975-77, Col The Royal Scots 1975-80, Dir Infantry 1977-80, Col Cmdt Scottish Div, GOC Scotland 1980-82; govr Edinburgh Castle 1980-82, ret; chm Cairntech Ltd 1983; HM cmmr Queen Victoria Sch Dunblane 1984, pres Army Cadet Force Assoc Scotland 1984, Col Cmdt Ulster Def Regiment 1986, chm Scottish Ctee Marie Curie Memorial Fndn 1986 (memb 1983), govr St Columba's Hospice 1986, chm St Mary's Cathedral Workshop 1986; *Recreations* golf, shooting; *Clubs* New, Royal Scots (both Edinburgh); *Style*— Lt-Gen Sir David Young, KBE, CB, DFC; c/o Adam & Co plc, 22 Charlotte Sq, Edinburgh EH2 4DF; Cairntech Ltd, 67 Marionville Rd, Edinburgh EH7 6AJ (☎ 031 652 1108, telex 727618-G)

YOUNG, David Tyrrell; s of Tyrrell Francis Young, of 143 Cranmer Court, London, and Patricia Morrison, *née* Spicer; *b* 6 Jan 1938; *Educ* Charterhouse; *m* 11 Sept 1965, Madeline Helen Celia, da of Anthony Burton Capel Philips (d 1983)), of The Heath House, Tean, Stoke-on-Trent; 3 da (Melanie Rosamond b 1969, Annabel Katharine b 1971, Corinna Lucy b 1974); *Career* TA 1 Regt HAC 1955-67, ret Capt 1967; trainee CA Gerard Van De Linde & Son 1955-60, audit mangr James Edwards Dangerfield & Co 1961-65; Spicer & Oppenheim (formerly Spicer & Pegler): audit mangr 1965-68, ptnr 1968-82, managing ptnr 1982-88, sr ptnr and int chm 1988-; cncl memb ICEAW 1979-82; Freeman City of London, Memb Ct Worshipful Co of Fishmongers; FCA; *Recreations* golf, tennis; *Clubs* Royal St Georges Golf, Royal Worlington Golf, City of London; *Style*— David T Young, Esq; Overhall, Ashdon, Saffron Walden, Essex CB10 2JH (☎ 0799 84 556) Friary Court, 65 Crutched Friars, London EC3N 2NP (☎ 071 480 7766, fax 071 480 6958, telex 884257 ESANO G)

YOUNG, David Wright; MP (Lab) Bolton SE 1983-; *Educ* Greenock Acad, Univ of Glasgow, St Paul's Coll Cheltenham; *Career* former: cncllr Coventry Co Borough Cncl, alderman Nuneaton Borough Cncl, Cncllr Nuneaton DC; contested (Lab): S Worcs 1959, Banbury 1966, Bath 1970; chm Coventry E Lab Pty 1964-68, MP (Lab) Bolton E Feb 1974-1983, PPS to Sec of State for Def 1977-79, memb House of Commons Public Accounts Cmmn, offr CPA and IPU Gps House of Commons, memb Select Ctee on Employment; *Style*— David Young, Esq, MP; House of Commons, London SW1

YOUNG, Elizabeth; da of Benn E Glanvill, of Crescent Cottage, Aldeburgh, Suffolk, and (Beatrice) Catherine Benn, *née* Newbald; *b* 21 Dec 1936; *Educ* Winceby House Bexhill Sussex, Pensionat Belri Arosa Switzerland; *m* 16 Feb 1961, Kenneth Charles Stuart Young; 2 da (Kate b 20 Dec 1962, Miranda b 1 Dec 1964 d 1988); *Career* journalist (as Elizabeth Benn) Daily Telegraph 1960-86 (staff and freelance), ed Embroidery Magazine 1980-84, freelance ed and writer books on Embroidery 1988-; chm Embroiderer's Guild Hampton Ct Palace 1985-90; Liveryman Worshipful Co of Stationers and Newspapermakers 1977; *Books* Noah's Ark (jtly, 1989); *Recreations* golf; *Style*— Mrs Kenneth Young; Old Rectory, Buckland, nr Aylesbury, Bucks (☎ 0296 630 461); 3C St John's Wharf, Wapping High St, London E1

YOUNG, Elizabeth Jane; da of Philip John Grattidge, of Wareham, Dorset, and Marion Elizabeth, *née* Dixon; *b* 9 Jan 1957; *Educ* Bedford HS for Girls, Sidney Sussex Coll, Cambridge (BA, MA); *m* 11 April 1981, John Todd Young, *qv*, s of Ian Taylor Young, of Rugby, Warwickshire; *Career* slr; Clifford Chance (formerly Coward Chance): articled clerk 1980-82, admitted 1982, ptnr 1988-; memb Law Soc; *Recreations* mountaineering, windsurfing; *Clubs* Cannons; *Style*— Mrs Elizabeth Young; Clifford Chance, Blackfriars House, New Bridge St, London EC4V 6BY (☎ 071 353 0211)

YOUNG, Hon Emily Tacita; da of 2 Baron Kennet; *b* 13 March 1951; *Educ* various, Chelsea Sch of Arts, St Martins Sch of Art; 1 s (Arthur William Phoenix b 1978); *Career* artist; *Recreations* reading, walking; *Clubs* Chelsea Arts; *Style*— The Hon Emily Young

YOUNG, Eric Alexander Irons; DL (Ayr and Arran 1979); s of George Irons Young (d 1945), of Hall Hill, Howwood, Redfredshire, and May Litster, *née* Ingram (d 1960); *b* 27 Dec 1921; *Educ* Trinity Coll Glenalmond, Jesus Coll Cambridge; *m* 22 Aug 1948, Camilla Campbell, da of Dr Edward Milgrove, of Sydney, Australia (d 1974); 2 s (Mark b 1952, Simon b 1955); *Career* XI Hussars PAO Italy and Europe 1942-45; Maj in the Ayrshire ECO Yeo 1957-58; dir Ingram Bros 1946- (md 1968); chm George Ingram & Assoc Co 1969-; *Recreations* racing, shooting, golf; *Clubs* Royal Scottish Automobile; *Style*— Eric Young, Esq, DL; Hillhouse Lodge, Fenwick, Ayrshire KA3 6BU (☎ 05606 260); George Ingram Ltd, Lawmoor Place, Glasgow G5 0YE

YOUNG, Rev Prof Frances Margaret; da of Alfred Stanley Worrall, CBE, of Birmingham, and Mary Frances, *née* Marshall; *b* 25 Nov 1939; *Educ* Bedford Coll London (BA), Girton Coll Cambridge (MA, PhD); *m* 20 June 1964, Robert Charles, s of Lt Charles William Young (d 1978), of Sherborne, Dorset; 3 s (Arthur Thomas b 1967, Edward Stanley b 1969, William Francis b 1974); *Career* ordained methodist minister 1984; Univ of Birmingham: temporary lectr in theol 1971-73, lectr in New Testament studies 1973-82, sr lectr 1982-86, Edward Cadbury prof of theology 1986-; *Books* Sacrifice and the Death of Christ (1975), Can These Dry Bones Live? (1982), From Nicaea to Chalcedon (1983), Face to Face (1985, revised edn 1990), Focus on God (with Kenneth Wilson, 1986), Meaning and Truth in 2 Corinthians (with David Ford, 1987), The Art of Performance (1990); *Recreations* music, walking, cycling, camping, poetry; *Style*— The Rev Prof Frances Young; 142 Selly Park Rd, Birmingham B29 7LH (☎ 021 472 4841); Dept of Theology, University of Birmingham, PO Box 363, Birmingham B15 2TT (☎ 021 414 5660)

YOUNG, Gavin David; s of Lt Col Gavin David Young (d 1978), and Daphne, *née* Forestier-Walker (d 1981); *b* 24 April 1928; *Educ* Rugby, Trinity Coll Oxford (MA); *Career* Nat Serv Welsh Gds 1946-48, served in Palestine 1947-48; Railli Brothers Iraq 1950-52, Desert Locust Control Tihama and Asir Provinces of Saudi Arabia 1954-56; foreign corr The Observer in Africa Far E and ME 1959-90 (corr in NY 1962-63 and Paris 1967); FRSL 1987, FRSG 1989; *Books* Return to the Marshes (1977), Iraq: Land of Two Rivers (1979), Slow Boats to China (1981), Slow Boats Home (1985), Worlds Apart (1987), Beyond Lion Rock (1988); *Recreations* travel in remote places, reading, walking, music, talking late; *Clubs* Travellers', Cavalry and Guards', Pratt's, Brooks's, Beefsteak, Foreign Correspondents (Hong Kong); *Style*— Gavin Young, Esq; c/o Weil, 49 Earls Court Road, London W8 6EE (☎ 071 937 3538, fax 071 937 3538)

YOUNG, George Bell; CBE (1975); s of George B Young (d 1980), and Jemima, *née* MacKinlay (d 1985); *b* 17 June 1924; *Educ* Queens Park Sch Glasgow; *m* 1, 12 Aug 1946, Margaret (Gretta) Boyd (d 1972); 1 s (Martin George b 1947); m 2, 1979, Joyce Marguerite McAteer; *Career* RNVR telegraphist later Sub-Lt 1942-46; reporter and feature writer Glasgow Herald 1946-48, info offr North of Scotland Hydro-Electric Board 1948-52, chief exec London Scottish Council Development & Industry 1952-68, md East Kilbride Development Corporation 1968-69 (advsr 1990-), fndr George Young Associates 1990-, assoc conslt Coopers & Lybrand Deloitte 1989-, assoc Joyce Young Recruitment 1990-, dir Scotrail; chm: BIM Scotland 1988-, Saints and Sinners Club of Scot 1990-91; memb Merchants House of Glasgow, hon vice pres East Kilbridge Sports Club, fndr East Kilbride & Lanarkshire Branch Order of St John; Freeman Dist of East Kilbride 1990; CStJ 1979, CBIM 1988, FBIM 1989, FRSA 1970; *Recreations* reading, music, writing; *Clubs* Caledonian, RSAC (Glasgow); *Style*— George Young, Esq, CBE; 4 Newlands Place, East Kilbride, Lanarkshire G74 1AE; George Young Associates, 118/120 Olympia House, East Kilbride G74 1LX (☎ 03552 41740, fax 03552 64643)

YOUNG, George Horatio; s and h of Sir George Young, Bt, MP; *b* 11 Oct 1966; *Educ* Windsor CFE, Christ Church Oxford; *Career* CA; *Recreations* cricket, tennis, classical guitar; *Style*— George Young, Esq; Formosa Place, Cookham, Berks; 49 Ealing Village, London W5 2NB

YOUNG, Sir George Samuel Knatchbull; 6 Bt (UK 1813), of Formosa Place, Berks; MP (C) Ealing Acton 1974-; s of Sir George Young, 5 Bt, CMG (d 1960), by his w Elisabeth (herself er da of Sir Hugh Knatchbull-Hugessen, KCMG, who was in turn n of 1 Baron Brabourne); *b* 16 July 1941; *Educ* Eton, Christ Church Oxford; *m* 1964, Aurelia, da of Oscar Nemon, and Mrs Nemon-Stuart, of Boars Hill, Oxford; 2 s, 2 da; *Heir* s, George Horatio Young; *Career* economist NEDO 1966-67, Kobler res fell Univ of Surrey 1967-69, memb Lambeth Borough Cncl 1968-71, econ advsr Post Office Corporation 1969-74, memb GLC (Ealing) 1970-73, oppn whip 1976-79; under sec of state: DHSS 1979-81, DOE 1981-86; comptroller Her Majesty's Household and sr govt whip 1990; Min of State for the Environment 1990-; tstee Guinness Tst 1986-90;

Books Tourism, Blessing or Blight?; *Style—* Sir George Young, Bt, MP; 91 Shakespeare Rd, London W3 (☎ 081 992 2743)

YOUNG, Gerard Francis; CBE (1967), DL (West Riding of Yorkshire 1973); s of Smelter Joseph Young (d 1954), of Richmond Park, Sheffield, and Edith, *née* Aspinall (d 1983); *b* 5 May 1910; *Educ* Ampleforth; *m* 7 Aug 1937, Diana, da of Charles Murray, MD; 2 s (Hugo b 13 Oct 1938, Charles b 29 April 1947), 3 da (Jane b 6 March 1945, Sarah b 8 Dec 1950, Caroline b 8 June 1980); *Career* The Tempered Spring Co Ltd 1930-81 (chm 1954-78); chm 1967-79 Sheffield area Sun Alliance and London Insurance Group (dir 1958), dir Nat Vulcan Engineering Insurance Group 1960-79, chm Radio Hallam Ltd 1973-79 dir Crucible Theatre Trust Ltd 1967-75; memb: Nat Bd for Prices and Incomes 1968-71, Top Salaries Review Body, Armed Forces Pay Review Body 1971-74; tstee: Sheffield Town Tst (town collector 1978-81), JG Graves Charitable Tst (chm 1974-86); Freshgate Tst Fndn (chm 1980-86), govr United Sheffield Hosps 1945-53, memb Cncl Univ of Sheffield 1943-84 (pro chllr 1951-67), gen cmmr of income tax 1947-74; JP Sheffield 1950-74, High Sheriff Hallamshire 1973-74, Lord Lt S Yorks and Custos Rotolorum, 1974-85; KStJ 1976; memb Co of Cutlers in Hallamshire (master 1961-62); Hon LLD Univ of Sheffield 1962; FIMechE; GCSG (Vatican) 1974; *Recreations* gardening, 13 grandchildren; *Clubs* Sheffield; *Style—* Gerard Young, Esq, CBE, DL; Roundfield, 69 Carsick Hill Crescent, Sheffield S10 3LS (☎ 0742 302 834)

YOUNG, Gertrude, Lady; Gertrude Annie; da of John Elliott, of Braunton, N Devon; *m* 1912, Sir Cyril Young, 4 Bt; 3 s (1 - late 5 Bt - decd, also Patrick Young, *qv*), 1 da (Mrs Stanley Claremont); *Style—* Gertrude, Lady Young; Le Copacabana, Jardin des Hesperides, Palm Beach, Cannes, Alpes Maritimes, France; 66 Kensington Mans, Trebovir Rd, SW5

YOUNG, Hon Mrs (Gillian Margaret); *née* Campbell; da of late 2 Baron Colgrain; *b* 1925; *m* 1951, Peter Scott Young (d 1988); 2 s, 2 da; *Style—* The Hon Mrs Young; Orchard House, Broom Lane, Langton Green, Tunbridge Wells TN3 0RA

YOUNG, Gordon John; s of Ernest George Young (d 1973), and Maude Jane *née* Homewood (d 1976); *b* 19 March 1935; *Educ* Tollington Boys GS; *m* 1958 (m dis 1975), Margery Anne Orwin; 2 s (Robert Andrew b 23 June 1960, Stephen John b 25 Feb 1962), 1 da (Judy Elizabeth Anne b 5 Dec 1958); *Career* Nat Serv RAF 1957-59; articled clerk George Hay & Co 1951-50, ptnr Harvey Reen & Co 1964-80 PA to sr ptnr 1959-64), regnl managing ptnr Baker Tilley 1988- (following mergers involving Harvey Reen & Co and Baker Rookie); FCA (ACA 1957), ATII 1962; *Style—* Gordon J Young, Esq; Baker Tilly, 2 Newman Road, Bromley, Kent BR1 1RJ (☎ 081 290 5522, fax 081 460 9156)

YOUNG, (John Andrew) Gordon; s of Harold James Young, of Grantown on Spey, and Agnes Elizabeth, *née* Wilson; *b* 19 March 1945; *Educ* King's Coll Sch Wimbledon; *m* 1, 30 Nov 1968, Jane Pamela (d 1988), da of Ronald Victor Seyd, of W Sussex; 1 s (Angus b 17 Jan 1972), 1 da (Suzanna b 9 May 1969); m 2, 27 Oct 1989, Sylvie Claire, da of George Seassan, of Aix En Provence; 1 da (Margaux b 16 Oct 1990); *Career* Baring Bros & Co Ltd 1970-73; NM Rothschild & Sons Ltd: joined 1973, exec dir 1981-87; exec dir Smith New Court plc 1987; MICAS; *Recreations* golf, travel; *Clubs* Oriental, Sussex Golf, Hong Kong; *Style—* Gordon Young, Esq; 25 Ponsonby Terrace, London SW1P 4PZ (☎ 071 821 5455); Smith New Court plc, Smith New Court House, 20 Farringdon Rd, London EC1M 3NH (☎ 071 772 1000)

YOUNG, Graham Christopher McKenzie; s of Archibald Hamilton Young (d 1964), of Caterham, and Lurline, *née* Chandler; *b* 20 Dec 1935; *Educ* Culford Sch, Trinity Coll Cambridge (MA, LLM); *m* 15 Dec 1962, Pamela Frances, da of Geoffrey Frances Anthony Bisley (d 1989), of Kempsford, Glos; 1 s (Jonathan Graham b 1965), 2 da (Alison b 1964, Caroline b 1968); *Career* admitted slr 1962; ptnr Townsends Swindon 1964-; pres Swindon Lions Club 1970; NSPCC: memb Central Exec Ctee, hon sec Swindon and N Wilts Branch; pres Glos and Wilts Inc Law Soc 1986, memb and co sec Prospect Fndn Swindon; pt/t chm: rent assessment panels, social security appeal tbnls; chm Swindon Alcohol for Enjoyment Forum; Parly candidate (C) Swindon 1974; memb Law Soc; *Books* A Little Law (1991); *Recreations* swimming, DIY; *Style—* Graham Young, Esq; New Milton, Back Lane, Fairford, Glos (☎ 0285 712317); Townsends, 42 Cricklade St, Swindon, Wilts (☎ 0793 535 421, fax 0793 616 294, telex 44712)

YOUNG, Graham Wharton; s of Joseph Norman Young (d 1982) and Gwendoline Mable, *née* Wharton; *b* 28 Oct 1944; *Educ* Barrow GS, for Boys, UCL, Univ Coll Hosp (LDS, RCS, BDS); *Career* opened own practice in Wimpole St 1969 (transferred to Harley St 1971); fndr and dir Rymecare plc 1984-; fndr and chm: Halematch Ltd 1986-, Golden Life SA 1987-; frequent bdcasts and lectures throughout the world and conslt to a number of magazines; obtained Equity membership 1963 (appearances in TV advertisments and plays); LRCS 1967, BDS 1968, FRSM 1986; *Recreations* flying (private pilots licence), skiing; *Clubs* Cowdry Park Polo, Goodwood Flying, Medical Pilots Assoc; *Style—* Graham Young, Esq; 42 Harley St, London W1N 1AB (☎ 071 935 8008)

YOUNG, Hugh Kenneth; s of John Young (d 1974), and Monica, *née* Auckland (d 1936); *b* 6 May 1936; *Educ* Edinburgh Acad; *m* 19 Sept 1962, Marjory Bruce, da of Charles Wilson (d 1987), of Edinburgh; 2 s (Hugh b 1967, Angus b 1970), 1 da (Susan b 1965); *Career* TA 1957-59, Nat Serv 2 Lt Royal Scots 1960, served Libya, TA 1961-69 (Capt 1966), joined HSF 1986; CA; dir Radio Forth Ltd 1974-75, exec dir The British Linen Bank Ltd 1978-84, dir Pentland Oil Exploration Ltd 1980-86, sec and memb Mgmnt Bd Bank of Scotland 1984-, chm Bank of Scotland (Jersey) Ltd 1986-; dir: Bank of Wales (Jersey) 1986-, Edinburgh Sports Club Ltd 1983-87 (chm 1984-87), Scottish Agricultural Securities Corporation plc 1988-; *Recreations* squash, tennis, hill-walking; *Clubs* New (Edinburgh), Edinburgh Sports; *Style—* Hugh K Young, Esq; 30 Braid Hills Rd, Edinburgh EH10 6HY (☎ 031 447 3101); Bank of Scotland, Head Office, PO Box No 5, The Mound, Edinburgh EH1 1YZ (☎ 031 243 5562, switchboard 031 442 7777, telex 72275, fax 031 243 5437)

YOUNG, Air Cdre Ian Matheson; MBE (1967); s of Gp Capt Peter Hutchinson Young (d 1967), of Devon, and Hylda, *née* Matheson; *b* 18 May 1927; *Educ* Blundell's; *m* 31 Dec 1953, Kathleen Scott, da of James William Mathewson, MD (d 1924), of Cambridgeshire; 2 da (Beverley b 1956, Lesley b 1959); *Career* RM 1946-47, RAF 1947-81 (despatches 1960, ret as Air Cdre), provost marshal, dir Security and Chief of RAF Police, served: Aden, Cyprus, Singapore, Germany 1978-81; dir Security Playboy Gp Co and Trident Casinos Ltd 1981-82, md Sprite Security Servs Ltd 1983-84, security conslt 1984-86; Security Eurotunnel: head of 1986-90, conslt 1991-; FBIM, FIPI (princ 1985-87); *Recreations* boating swimming, spectator of sports; *Style—* Air Cdre Ian M Young, MBE; Russets, Ridgeway Rd, Dorking, Surrey RH4 3EY (☎ 0306 888844)

YOUNG, Dr Ian Robert; OBE (1986); s of John Stirling Young (d 1971), and Ruth Muir, *née* Whipple (d 1975); *b* 11 Jan 1932; *Educ* Sedbergh, Univ of Aberdeen (BSc, PhD); *m* 1956, Sylvia Marianne Whewell, da of Frederick George Ralph; 2 s (Graham John b 1958, Neil George b 1960), 1 da (Fiona Marianne b 1966); *Career* Hilger & Watts Ltd 1955-59, Evershed & Vignoles Ltd 1959-67, Evershed Power Optics Ltd 1967-76, EMI Central Res Laboratory 1976-81, sr res fell GEC Hirst Res Centre, vice pres Res Picker International Inc Cleveland Ohio 1981-, visiting prof RPMS Hammersmith Hosp 1983-; Duddell medal Inst of Physics 1983, Gold medal Soc of Magnetic Resonance in Med 1988; FIEE 1967, FEng 1988, hon memb Soc of Magnetic Resonance Imaging 1989, FRS 1989, hon FRCR 1990; *Recreations* ornithology, D.I.Y, walking; *Style—* Dr Ian Young, OBE, FRS; Church Hill Cottage, West Overton, Marlborough, Wiltshire SN8 4ER (☎ 0672 86615); GEC Hirst Research Centre, East Lane, Wembley, Middx HAG 7PP (☎ 081 908 9671)

YOUNG, Baroness (Life Peer UK 1971), of Farnworth, Co Palatine of Lancaster; Janet Mary Young; PC (1981), DL (Oxon 1989); da of John Norman Leonard Baker, and Phyllis, *née* Hancock; *b* 23 Oct 1926; *Educ* Headington Sch Oxford, Prospect Hill Sch New Haven Conn USA, Mount Holyoke Coll USA, St Anne's Coll Oxford (MA); *m* 1950, Dr Geoffrey Tyndale Young (fellow Jesus Coll Oxford); 3 da (Hon Alexandra Janet (Hon Mrs Slater) b 1951, Hon Rosalind Ann (Hon Mrs McIntyre) b 1954, Hon Juliet Marguerite (Hon Mrs Brown) b 1962); *Career* sits as Cons peer in House of Lords; memb Oxford City Cncl 1957-72 (alderman and ldr Cons Gp 1967-72); Baroness-in-Waiting to HM The Queen (first ever Cons woman govt whip in upper chamber) 1972-73, parly under-sec of state DOE 1973-74, vice chm Cons Pty Orgn (with special responsibility for women's orgns) 1975-83 (dep chm 1977-79); min of state DES 1979-81, chllr Duchy of Lancaster 1981-82, Cons ldr House of Lords Sept 1981-83, Lord Privy Seal 1982-83, min of state FCO 1983-87; dir: National Westminster Bank 1987-, Marks and Spencer plc 1987; former dir UK Provident, former memb BR Western Region Advsy Bd, vice pres W India Ctee 1987, chm Independent Schs Jt Cncl 1989; hon fell: Inst of Civil Engrs, St Annes Coll Oxford; tstee Lucy Cavendish Coll Cambridge 1988; Hon DLL Mt Holyoke Coll USA; *Clubs* Univ Women's; *Style—* The Rt Hon the Baroness Young, PC, DL; House of Lords, London SW1A 0PW

YOUNG, Jimmy Leslie Ronald; OBE (1979); s of Frederick George Young (d 1989), and Gertrude Jane *née* Woolford (d 1972); *b* 21 Sept 1923; *Educ* East Dean GS Cinderford Gloucestershire; *m* 1, 1946 (m dis), Wendy Wilkinson; 1 da; m 2, 1950 (m dis), Sally Douglas; *Career* WWII RAF, Sgt (physical trg instructor); broadcaster; first BBC radio bdcast Songs at Piano 1949, pianist/singer/bandleader 1950-51, first theatre appearance Empire Theatre Croydon 1952 (numerous subsequent appearances); BBC Radio series 1953-67 incl: Housewives Choice, The Night is Young, 12 O' Clock Spin, Younger Than Springtime, Saturday Special, Keep Young, Through Till Two; presenter of: Radio Luxembourg programmes 1960-68, Jimmy Young Programme BBC Radio Two 1973- (Radio One 1967-73); tv work incl: Pocket Edition (BBC) 1955, Jimmy Young Asks (BBC) 1972, Whose Baby (ITV) 1973, Jim's World (ITV) 1974, The Jimmy Young Television Programme (ITV) 1984-87, host of first Br Telethon (Thames) 1980; bdcasts live from various countries; records: Too Young 1951, Unchained Melody (number one hit) 1955, The Man from Laramie (number one hit) 1955, Chain Gang 1956, More 1956, Miss You 1963; first Br singer to have two consecutive number one hit records; Radio Personality of the Year Variety Club of GB 1968; HM The Queen's Silver Jubilee medal 1977, Radio Industries Club award for Programme of the Year 1979, Radio Industry's Club award for Programme of the Year 1979, Sony award for Broadcaster of the Year 1985, Daily Mail/BBC Nat Radio award for Best Current Affrs Programme 1988-, Sony Roll of Honour award 1988, TV and Radio Industries Club award for Best Radio Programme of the Year 1989; hon memb Cncl NSPCC; Freeman City of London 1969, memb Worshipful Co of Carmen 1969; *Books* Jimmy Young Cookbooks (1968, 1969, 1970, 1972), JY (autobiography, 1973), Jimmy Young (autobiography, 1982); *Clubs* Wigan Rugby League Social & Working Mens; *Style—* Jimmy Young, Esq, OBE; BBC Broadcasting House, London W1A 1AA (☎ 071 580 4468 ext 7051)

YOUNG, John Adrian Emile; s of John Archibald Campbell Young (d 1979), of Plaxtol, Kent, and Irene Eugenie, *née* Bouvier (d 1976); *b* 28 July 1934; *Educ* Cranbrook Sch Kent, Univ of London (LLB); *m* 20 June 1959, Yvonne Lalage Elizabeth, da of John Digby Hyde Bankes (d 1976), of Twitton House, Otford, Kent; 3 s (Charles b 1961, Paul b 1962, Simon b 1965), 1 da (Anna b 1963); *Career* ptnr Cameron Markby Hewitt Slrs 1965-; nat chm Young Slrs Gp 1965-66, pres Association Internationale des Jeunes Avocats 1968-69, memb Cncl Int Bar Assoc 1983-, choirmaster/organist of local church; Master City of London Slrs Co 1989-90 (Freeman 1967); memb Law Soc 1958 (asst sec 1958-64, memb Cncl 1971-); *Recreations* music, gardening, foreign travel; *Style—* John Young, Esq; Stonewold House, Plaxtol, Kent (☎ 0732 810 289); Cameron Markby Hewitt, Sceptre Court, 40 Tower Hill, London EC3N 4BB (☎ 071 702 2345, fax 071 702 2303, telex 925779)

YOUNG, Sir John Kenyon Roe; 6 Bt (UK 1821), of Bailieborough Castle, Co Cavan; s of Sir John William Roe Young, 5 Bt (d 1981), by his 1 w, Joan Minnie Agnes, *née* Aldous (d 1958); *b* 23 April 1947; *Educ* Hurn Ct Sch Christchurch, Napier Coll; *m* 1977, Frances Elise, only da of W R Thompson; 1 s, 1 da (Tamara Elizabeth Eve b 9 Nov 1986); *Heir* s, Richard Christopher Roe Young, b 14 July 1983; *Career* former hydrographic surveyor; sr buyer; *Recreations* golf; *Style—* Sir John Young, Bt; Bolingey, 159 Chatham Rd, Maidstone, Kent ME14 2ND

YOUNG, John Robert Chester; s of Robert Nisbet Young (d 1956), and Edith Mary Young (d 1981); *b* 6 Sept 1937; *Educ* Bishop Vesey's GS, St Edmund Hall Oxford; *m* 1963, Pauline Joyce, da of George Yates (d 1966); 1 s (and 1 s decd), 1 da; *Career* ptnr Simon & Coates (stockbrokers) 1965-82; memb cncl Stock Exchange 1965-82 (cncl memb 1978-82), dir of policy and planning Stock Exchange 1982-87, chief exec The Securities Assoc 1987-, vice chm exec bd The Int Stock Exchange; *Recreations* rugby football; *Clubs* Harlequin's, Vincent's; *Style—* John Young, Esq; Richmond House, Falkland Grove, Dorking, Surrey; The Stock Exchange, London EC2N 1HP (☎ 071 588 2355)

YOUNG, John Todd; s of Ian Taylor Young, of Rugby, Warwicks, and Flora Leggett, *née* Todd; *b* 14 Jan 1957; *Educ* Manchester GS, Sidney Sussex Coll Cambridge (BA, MA); *m* 11 April 1981, Elizabeth Jane, *qv*, da of Philip John Grattidge, of Wareham, Dorset; *Career* Lovell White Durrant (formerly Lovell, White & King): articled clerk 1979-81, slr 1981-, ptnr 1987-; memb Worshipful Co of Slrs; memb Law Soc; *Recreations* mountaineering, windsurfing; *Clubs* Cannons; *Style—* John Young, Esq; 65 Holborn Viaduct, London EC1A 2DY (☎ 071 236 0066, fax 071 248 4212, telex 887122 LWD)

YOUNG, John William Garne; s of David Richard Young, of Shaftsbury, Dorset, and Pamela Mary *née* Garne; *b* 6 Jan 1945; *Educ* Shaftsbury GS; *m* 1 Jan 1971, (Eleanor) Louise, da of Abryn Walsh Sparks (d 1980), of Swinburne, SA; 3 s (Michael b 1972, David b 1974, Peter b 1980); *Career* dir Wolseley plc 1982-; chm: Parmiter Ltd 1982- (md 1973-87), Kidd Ltd 1980-, McConnel Ltd 1982-, Bypy Ltd 1982-, Dihurst Hldgs Ltd 1986-, Sparex Ltd 1986-, Vapormatic Ltd 1986-; pres Agric Engrs Assoc 1987-88, govr Agric Engrg Res, Silsoe memb Engrg Advsy Gp AFRC; tstee Tisbury Village Hall; CIAgrE; *Recreations* cricket, tennis, water sports; *Style—* John Young, Esq; The Gables, Hindon Lane, Tisbury, Wilts (☎ 0747 870756); c/o P J Parmiter & Sons Ltd, Station Works, Tisbury, Wiltshire (☎ 0747 870 821, fax 0747 871 171, telex 417 197)

YOUNG, (David) Junor; s of David Young (d 1974), and Margaret Mellis; *b* 23 April 1934; *Educ* Robert Gordon's Coll Aberdeen; *m* 6 Nov 1954, Kathleen, da of E Brooks, of Eastbourne; 2 da (Stephanie b 1955, Philippa b 1967), 2 s (Ashley b 1958, Jonathan b 1964); *Career* joined FO 1951, consul Stuttgart 1978-81, first sec Kampala 1981-84, consul-gen Hamburg 1984-86, cnsllr (commercial) British Embassy Bonn

1986-88, British high cmmr Honiara Solomon Islands 1988-90, dep high cmmr Karachi 1991; *Recreations* fishing, shooting; *Clubs* Naval and Military, Commonwealth; *Style*— D J Young, Esq; Pine Cottage, Hintlesham, Suffolk

YOUNG, Dr Kate; da of Rev W P Young (d 1969), and Ann Nielson Cumming (d 1941); *b* 13 June 1938; *Educ* Oxenford Castle Sch Ford Midlothian, LSE (PhD); ptnr Charles Legg; 1 s (Justin Dubon b 1965), 1 step s (Jake Legg b 1970), 1 step da (Jessica Legg 1969); *Career* worked with How (of Edinburgh) and Doubleday (in NY), travelled widely, worked in FAO, Inst of Devpt Studies (Univ of Sussex, promoted study of the impact of devpt on women, set up 18 week course for policy makers and activists on gender relationships and economic devpt and MA course Gender and Devpt) 1975-88, set up Womankind (Worldkind) 1988; *Books* Of Marriage and the Market (1981), Women and Economic Development (1988), Serving Two Masters (1989); *Recreations* gardening, talking with friends over a good meal, walking; *Style*— Dr Kate Young; Womankind (Worldwide), 122 Whitechapel High St, London E1 7PT (☎ 071 247 6931, fax 071 247 3436)

YOUNG, Prof Kenneth George (Ken); s of Henry George Young, Christchurch, Hants, and Olive, *née* Heybeard; *b* 3 Jan 1943; *Educ* Brockenhurst GS, LSE (BSc, MSc, PhD); *m* 11 Sept 1987, Rita Michelle, da of Benjamin Goldberg, of London; *Career* res offr LSE 1966-73, res fell Univ of Kent 1974-77, sr res fell Univ of Bristol 1977-79, sr fell Policy Studies Inst 1979-87, prof and dir Inst Local Govt Studies 1987-89, head Sch of Public Policy Univ of Birmingham 1989-90, prof of politics and head Dept of Political Studies Queen Mary and Westfield Coll London 1990-; FRHistS 1983; *Books* Local Politics and the Rise of Party (1975), Metropolitan London (1982), Managing the Post-Industrial City (1983), New Directions for County Government (1989); *Recreations* reading, travel; *Style*— Prof Ken Young; 22 Woodlands Rd, Moseley, Birmingham B11 4HE (☎ 021 449 8531); Dept of Political Studies, Queen Mary and Westfield College, University of London, Mile End Rd, London E1 4NS (☎ 071 975 5003)

YOUNG, Kenneth Middleton; CBE (1977); s of Cyril William Dix Young, of Cardiff, and Gwladys, *née* Middelton (d 1991); *b* 1 Aug 1931; *Educ* Neath GS, Univ of Wales Aberystwyth (BA), Univ of Manchester (Dip Personnel Mgmnt); *m* 25 Aug 1958, Brenda May, da of John Thomas (d 1951), of Connahs Quay; 1 s (Michael b 1964), 1 da (Pamela b 1961); *Career* cmmnd Pilot Offr and navigator RAF 1952-54; collective agreements mangr Massey-Ferguson (UK) Ltd 1959-64, personnel advsr Aviation Div Smiths Industries Ltd 1964-66, GEC 1966-71 (gp personnel mangr and dir GEC (Management) Ltd); The Post Office: bd memb 1972, vice chm 1986, chm Subscription Services Ltd 1988, chm Girobank plc 1989, dep chm 1990, chm Post Office Counters Ltd 1990; memb: Employment Appeal Tbnl, Liaison Ctee London Business Sch; tstee Post Office Pension Funds; FIPM 1986, CBIM 1990; *Recreations* Wales rugby, Chelsea AFC, photography, theatre; *Style*— Kenneth Young, Esq, CBE; The Post Office, Post Office HQ, 30 St James's Square, London SW1Y 4PY (☎ 071 389 8102)

YOUNG, Sir Leslie Clarence; CBE (1980), DL; s of late Clarence James Young, and Ivy Isabel Young (d 1984); *Educ* LSE (BSc, LLD); *m* 1949, Muriel Howard Pearson; 1 s, 1 da; *Career* formerly with Courtaulds Ltd; chm: NW regnl cncl CBI 1976-78, NW Industl Devpt Bd 1978-81, J Bibby & Sons plc 1979-84, Merseyside Devpt Corpn 1981-84, Br Waterways Bd 1984-87, Natwest Bank 1986-, tstees of Nat Museum and Galleries in Merseyside 1986-, Pioneer Mutual Insur Co Ltd 1986-, SIBEC Devpts Ltd 1988-; non-exec dir Granada TV 1979-83, tstee Civic Tst for NW 1978-83; kt 1984; *Style*— Sir Leslie Young, CBE, DL; Overwood, Vicarage Lane, Burton, S Wirral L64 5TJ

YOUNG, Hon Mrs (Lilian Vida Lechmere); *née* Moncreiff; da of 4 Baron Moncreiff (d 1942); *b* 1912; *m* 1942, David Robert Young; 1 s, 1 da; *Style*— The Hon Mrs Young; Tanworth, Fossoway, Kinross-shire

YOUNG, (Clayton) Mark; s of Arnold Young, and Florence May, *née* Lambert; *b* 7 June 1929; *Educ* Pendower Tech Sch Newcastle-on-Tyne; *m* 1, 1952, Charlotte (d 1978); 2 s (Mark b 14 Aug 1962, Robin b 26 Nov 1964), 2 da (Vanessa b 16 Sept 1957, Ursula b 12 Jan 1960); m 2, 1979, Marie Therese; 1 s (Henry b 16 Sept 1981); *Career* RAF; mining and shipbuilding until 1962, head Res Dept Electrical Trades Union 1962 (nat offr 1963), chm Ford Trade Unions 1965-69, sec Nat Jt Cncl for Civil Air Tport 1964-74 and 1977- (chm 1975-77), gen sec Br Air Line Pilots Assoc 1974, sec Br Airways Trade Union Cncl; *Recreations* ballooning, reading; *Style*— Mark Young, Esq; 44 Sutton Court Rd, Chiswick, London W4 (☎ 081 995 8552); Dovengill, Fell End, nr Kirby Stephen, Cumbria; British Air Line Pilots Assoc, 81 New Rd, Harlington, Hayes, Middx UB3 5BG (☎ 081 759 9331, fax 081 564 7957, telex 265871 MONREF G)

YOUNG, (Peter) Miles; s of Matthew Derek Young (d 1989), and Joyce Doreen, *née* Robson (d 1976); *b* 12 June 1954; *Educ* Bedford Sch Bedford, New Coll Oxford (MA); *Career* advertising; Lintas London 1976-79, Allen Brady & Marsh 1979-83, dir client service Ogilvy & Mather Ltd 1983-90, md Ogilvy & Mather Direct Ltd 1990-; memb Westminster Cncl 1986-; chm: New Technology Ctee 1986-87, Environment Ctee 1987-90; Burdett-Coutts Fndn 1986, govr Harper Tst 1989-, vice chm Conserve 1990; MIPA 1990; *Recreations* gastronomy, walking, Balkan travel; *Clubs* Oxford & Cambridge University; *Style*— Miles Young, Esq; 10 Lesley Court, Strutton Ground, London SW1P 2HZ (☎ 071 222 8871); Ogilvy & Mather Direct, Knightway House, 20 Soho Square, London W1V 6AD (☎ 071 437 9878, fax 071 734 0368)

YOUNG, (Roderic) Neil; JP; s of Frederick Hugh Young, OBE (d 1969), of The Gables, Woodhurst Lane, Oxted, Surrey, and Stella Mary, *née* Robinson; *b* 29 May 1933; *Educ* Eton, Trinity Coll Cambridge (MA); *m* 16 June 1962, Gillian Margaret, da of Col William Alexander Salmon, OBE, of Balcombe Place, Balcombe, W Sussex; 2 s (Peter b 1964, Rupert b 1969), 1 da (Jennifer b 1966); *Career* 2 Lt Queens Own Royal W Kent Regt 1952; dir: Murray Johnstone Ltd 1969-70, Kleinwort Benson Ltd 1972-86, Globe Investment Trust plc 1973-90, Brunner Investment Trust plc 1975-, Merchants Trust plc 1975-85, Kleinwort Grievson Investment Management Ltd 1986-88, Aberdeen Petroleum plc 1988-, Malvern UK Index Trust plc 1990-, London & SE Bd Bradford & Bingley Building Society 1990-; dep chm Assoc of Investmt Tst Cos 1987-89; memb Advsy Ctee Greenwich Hosp, almoner Christ's Hosp, Alderman and JP City of London; Liveryman and memb Ct Worshipful Co of Gunmakers, Liveryman Worshipful Co of CA's; ACA 1959, FCA 1969; *Recreations* shooting, gardening, DIY, golf, tennis; *Style*— Neil Young, Esq, JP; Pembury Hall, Pembury, Kent TN2 4AT (☎ 089 282 2971)

YOUNG, Patrick Chisholm; s of Prof William Henry Young (d 1942), of Villa Collonge, La Conversion, Vaud, Switzerland, and Grace Emily, *née* Chisholm (d 1944); *b* 18 March 1908; *Educ* Baccalauréat-ès-Sciences, Univ of Cambridge (MA), Univ of Oxford (DPhil), Univ of London (post grad Dip Chemical Engrg); Univs of: Strasbourg, Göttingen, Geneva; Middle Temple London; *m* 1 June 1950, Marjorie, da of Frederick Charles Sargent (d 1968), of London; 2 s (Norman Patrick b 1955, Lionel Henry b 1955), 1 da (Janet (Mrs Bills) b 1952); *Career* chief chemist John Heathcoat & Co Ltd 1930-31, plant mangr and devpt offr ICI Plastics Ltd 1934-39, chief engr and tech mangr Jablo Propellers Ltd 1939-41, chief engr and tech advsr ME Stace Ltd and F Bender & Co Ltd 1942-43, works mangr De la Rue Plastics Ltd 1943-45, tech dir De La Rue Plasticos do Brasil SA 1945-46, indust conslt UN Econ Cmmn for Asia and Far E 1948, cnsllr head Central Office OEEC Tech Directorate 1948-51, head of UNESCO Sci Co-operation Office for S Asia 1951-54, md Beecham's Copy Labs (India) Private Ltd 1956-57, divnl gp mangr BSI 1957-70, sec gen CEN (assoc for Euro Standards) 1970-74; involvement in local residents' assocs, participation in socs and instns concerned with Asian, Euro, S American and S African affairs; Freeman City of London 1930-, Liveryman Worshipful Co of Fishmongers 1930-; MRAeS 1940, FIChemE 1941; *Recreations* scientific consideration of biology and human behaviour, genealogy; *Style*— Dr Patrick C Young; 14 Russell Hill, Purley, Surrey CR8 2JA (☎ 081 660 5556)

YOUNG, Richard Aretas Lewry; s of Dr Carmichael Aretas Young (d 1987), and Marie Ethel, *née* Lewry; *b* 17 Jan 1943; *Educ* Haileybury Melbourne Aust, St Catharine's Coll Cambridge (MA, MB BChir), St Mary's Hosp Med Sch London (LRCP, FRCS); *m* 12 July 1972, Lesley Rita, da of Gerald Duckett; 3 s (Simon, Andrew, Peter); *Career* Bernard Sunley res fell RCS 1974-75, surgical registrar Royal Free Hosp 1976-78, sr surgical registrar St Mary's Hosp London 1978-82 consult gen and vascular surgn W Middx Hosp 1982-, teacher Univ of London, hon sr lectr Charing Cross and Westminster Hosps Med Sch; memb BMA, FRSM; *Recreations* golf, sailing; *Clubs* Fulwell Golf, Queen Mary's Sailing; *Style*— Mr Richard Young; 26 Strawberry Hill Rd, Twickenham, Middx TW1 4UP (☎ 081 891 0638); West Middlesex University Hospital, Twickenham Rd, Isleworth, Middx TW7 6AF (☎ 081 565 5768)

YOUNG, Sir Richard Dilworth; s of Philip Young, by his w Constance Maria Lloyd; *b* 9 April 1914; *Educ* Bromsgrove, Univ of Bristol; *m* 1951, Jean Barbara Paterson, *née* Lockwood; 4 s; *Career* Boosey & Hawkes Ltd: dep chm 1978-79, chm 1979-84; dir Tube Investmts Ltd 1958 (md 1961-64), chm Alfred Herbert Ltd 1966-74 (dep chm 1965-66); dir: Rugby Portland Cement Co 1968-88, Cwlth Fin Devpt Corp 1968-83, Ingersoll Engrs Inc (USA) 1966-71; chm Boosey & Hawkes Ltd 1979-84 (dep chm 1978-79); memb: Central Advsy Cncl on Sci and Technol 1967-70, Cncl CBI 1967-74, Cncl Univ of Warwick 1966-89, Cncl SSRC 1973-75, SRC Engrg Bd 1974-76; Hon DSc Univ of Warwick; FIMechE (memb Cncl 1969-76), CBIM; kt 1970; *Clubs* Athenaeum; *Style*— Sir Richard Young; Bearley Manor, Bearley, nr Stratford-on-Avon, Warwicks (☎ 0789 731 220)

YOUNG, Richard Stuart; s of David Young (d 1991), and Hilda, *née* Ellison; *b* 17 Sept 1947; *m* 1, 13 Nov 1975, Riita Sinikka Harju (d 1983); 2 s (Danny Eemil b 27 April 1977, Sammy Richard b 27 April 1979); m 2, 28 June 1985, Susan Manije Walker; 1 da (Hannah Harley b 31 Oct 1987); *Career* photographer 1974-; *Books* By Invitation Only (1981), Paparazzo (1989); *Recreations* riding my Harley Davidson; *Clubs* Guards Polo; *Style*— Richard Young, Esq

YOUNG, Robert; s of Walter Horace Young (d 1963), of Wood Green, London, and Evelyn Joan, *née* Jennings; *b* 27 March 1944; *Educ* The Boys' GS London, Magdalen Coll Oxford (BA); *m* 18 Dec 1965, Patricia Anne, da of Robert Archibald Cowin, of Hest Bank, Lancs; 2 s (Matthew b 1969, Alec b and d 1972), 1 da (Judith b 1974); *Career* dir Rolls-Royce Motors Diesel Div 1977-81, gp commercial dir Vickers plc 1981-83; on secondment from Vickers: memb Central Policy Review Staff Cabinet Office 1983, memb 10 Downing St Policy Unit 1983-84; md Crane Ltd 1985-88, chief exec Plastics Div McKechnie plc 1988-90; dir Beauford plc 1990-; CBI: regnl cncllr W Mids 1980-81, chm Shrops 1981; Monopolies and Mergers Cmmn 1986-; FInstD 1985; *Recreations* music, photography, cats, horse-riding; *Clubs* IOD; *Style*— Robert Young, Esq; 54 Fordhook Ave, Ealing Common, London W5 3LR (☎ 081 992 2228); Beauford plc, Cross Keys House, 9 High Street South, Olney, Bucks MK46 4AA

YOUNG, (John) Robertson (Rob); s of Francis John Young (d 1982), and Marjorie Elizabeth, *née* Imrie; *b* 21 Feb 1945; *Educ* Norwich Sch, Univ of Leicester (BA); *m* 15 July 1967, Catherine Suzanne Françoise, da of Jean Houssait (d 1945); 1 s (Jerome Robertson b 9 Jan 1971), 2 da (Isabelle b 10 April 1969, Juliette Claire b 29 Oct 1978); *Career* joined Diplomatic Service 1967, first sec Cairo 1970, FCO 1972, Paris 1976, FCO 1981, cnsllr Damascus 1984, head of Middle E Dept FCO 1987, min Paris 1991-; *Recreations* sailing, acting, music (playing piano and organ, collecting records); *Clubs* Cruising Assoc; *Style*— Rob Young, Esq; c/o Foreign and Commonwealth Office (Paris), King Charles St, London SW1

YOUNG, Sir Roger William; s of Charles Bowden Young (d 1963), and Dr Ruth Young, *née* Wilson (d 1983); *b* 15 Nov 1923; *Educ* Dragon Sch, Westminster, Christ Church Oxford (MA, STh, LHD); *m* 1950, Caroline Mary, da of Lt-Cdr Charles Perowne Christie, RN (d 1929); 2 s (Patrick, Christopher), 2 da (Elizabeth, Janet); *Career* Sub Lt RNVR (Navigating Offr) 1943-45; res tutor St Catharine's Cumberland Lodge Windsor Gt Park 1949-51, asst master Manchester GS 1951-58, princ George Watson's Coll Edinburgh 1958-85, chm Cheltenham Ladies Cncl 1986-, memb Public Schs Cmmn 1968-70, pres Head Teachers Assoc of Scotland 1972-74; chm Headmasters' Conf 1976, memb GBA Ctee 1986- (dep chm 1987); Scottish nat govr BBC 1979-84; FRSE 1965; kt 1983; *Books* Lines of Thought (1958), Everybody's Business (1968); *Recreations* gardening, hill-climbing, photography, knitting; *Clubs* E India; *Style*— Sir Roger Young; 11 Belgrave Terrace, Bath, Avon BA1 5JR (☎ 0225 336940)

YOUNG, Sir Stephen Stewart Templeton; 3 Bt (UK 1945), of Partick, Co City of Glasgow; s of Sir Alastair Spencer Templeton Young, 2 Bt, DL (d 1963), and (Dorothy Constance) Marcelle (d 1964), widow of Lt John Hollington Grayburn, VC, and da of Lt-Col Charles Ernest Chambers; *b* 24 May 1947; *Educ* Rugby, Trinity Coll Oxford, Edinburgh Univ; *m* 1974, Viola Margaret, da of Prof Patrick Horace Nowell-Smith (whose mother was Cecil, ggda of Most Rev Hon Edward Vernon-Harcourt, sometime archbishop of York and yr bro of 3 Baron Vernon) by his 1 w, Perilla (da of Sir Richard Southwell and who m subsequently, as his 2 w, Baron Roberthall); 2 s (Charles, Alexander David b 6 Feb 1982); *Heir* s, Charles Alastair Stephen Young b 21 July 1979; *Career* advocate; Sheriff of: Glasgow and Strathkelvin March-June 1984, North Strathclyde at Greenock 1984-; *Style*— Sir Stephen Young, Bt; Glen Rowan, Shore Rd, Cove, Dunbartonshire G84 0NU

YOUNG, Susan Caroline; da of David Robert Young, of Alcester, and Pamela Ann, *née* Gee; *b* 7 July 1961; *Educ* Lady Manner Sch Bakewell Derbys, Malvern Hall Warks, Solihull Coll of Technol, Liverpool Poly (BA), Royal Coll of Art Sch of Film and TV (Princess of Wales scholarship, MA, RCA); *Career* film and commercial director; with Barrie Joll Associates until 1987; freelance dir: Practical Pictures 1987-89, Felix Films 1989-91, Initial Film and Television 1991-; clients incl: Arts Channel, United Nations, WEA Records, Young and Rubicam, C4, BBC; filmography: Peyote Hunt 1981, Thin Blue Lines 1982, Trafalgar Square 1983, Tempting Fate 1984, Carnival 1985, The Doomsday Clock 1987, Beleza Tropical 1989; exhibitions incl: Animation (Tate Gallery) 1983, Young Blood (Barbican) 1984, European Illustration Annual 1985, Los Angeles Animation Festival (touring) 1986, Br Design and Art Directors Annual 1990; numerous int film festivals and awards; *Recreations* motorcyclist and fitness enthusiast; *Style*— Ms Susan Young; Initial Film and Television, 10-16 Rathbone St, London W1P 1AH (☎ 071 637 8251, 071 673 5117, fax 071 637 9024)

YOUNG, Hon (William Aldus) Thoby; s and h of 2 Baron Kennet; *b* 24 May 1957; *Educ* Marlborough, Dartington Hall Sch, Sussex Univ; *m* 25 April 1987, Hon Josephine Mary Keyes, 2 da of 2 Baron Keyes; 1 da (Maud Elizabeth Aurora b 8 March 1989); *Career* staff SDP 1980-83; md and chm Offshore Productions Ltd 1984-88; ptnr Ducas

Fish 1988-89; owner The Fresh Fish Co 1989-; *Recreations* playing the trumpet, writing; *Style—* The Hon Thoby Young

YOUNG, Hon Toby Daniel Moorsom; s of Baron Young of Dartington by his 2 w Sasha; *b* 1963; *Educ* Brasenose Coll Oxford, Harvard, Trinity Coll Cambridge; *Career* journalist; *Recreations* swimming, windsurfing; *Clubs* Groucho; *Style—* The Hon Toby Young; 45 Dean St, London W1

YOUNG, William Chalmers (Bill); s of William Henry Young (d 1967), of Reigate, Surrey, and Joan Margaret, *née* McGlashan (d 1978); *b* 8 Oct 1919; *Educ* King's Sch Canterbury, Clare Coll Cambridge (MA); *m* 12 April 1944, Elizabeth Irene, da of Maj Alfred Russel Marshall, DSO, MC; 1 s (Martin), 3 da (Jane, Francesca, Rosemary); *Career* Nat Serv WWII cmmnd RA 1939, Lt Kent Yeo 143 Field Regt, Capt IORA HQ RA 49 Div, Capt OC 60 Field Security Section Intelligence Corps; jt md Smith & Young Ltd (family business) 1947-84 (chm 1980-); chm: Nat Assoc Engravers and Diestampers 1957-58, Envelope Makers and Mfg Stationers Assoc 1963-66; pres: SE Dist London Masterprinters Assoc 1960-61, London Printing Industs Assoc 1973-74; pres Inst of Printing 1976-78 (cncl memb 1969-81); memb Surrey CC educn ctee 1970-74, govr (later vice chm and chm) Camberwell Sch of Arts and Crafts, hon sec (later dir) Surrey Co Playing Fields Assoc 1958-85 (Nat Playing Field Assoc Duke of Edinburgh Award), chm Surrey Play Cncl 1976-79; chm Marshall Tst (C of E charity) 1982-87, pres Old Boys Assoc Kings Sch Canterbury 1970-73, memb Royal Inst of Int Affrs, general cmmr of Income Tax 1973-; Worshipful Co of Stationers and Newspaper Makers: Liveryman 1952, Renter Warden, Chm Livery Ctee 1969-71, Ct Asst 1982-, Under Warden 1989-90 Upper Warden 1990-91; FIOP; *Recreations* hunting beagling, tennis, squash, jogging, music (opera, ballet); *Clubs* Hawks (Cambridge), Cwlth Tst; *Style—* Bill Young, Esq; Rushpond Cottage, School Lane, Winfrith Newburgh, Dorset DT2 8JX (☎ 0305 852 951); 66a Penton Place, London SE17 (☎ 071 708 5858); Smith and Young Ltd, 40 Crimscott St, London SE1 5TP (☎ 071 231 1261, fax 071 262 1512, telex 22403 SAY G)

YOUNG, Sir William Neil; 10 Bt (GB 1769), of North Dean, Buckinghamshire; s of Capt William Elliot Young (ka 1942), and gs of Sir Charles Young, 9 Bt, KCMG, MVO (d 1944); Sir Charles's w was Clara, da of Sir Francis Elliot, GCMG, GCVO (gs of 2 Earl of Minto, also Envoy Extraordinary & Min Plenipotentiary to the King of the Hellenes 1903-17); *b* 22 Jan 1941; *Educ* Wellington, RMA Sandhurst; *m* 1965, Christine Veronica, da of R B Morley, of Buenos Aires; 1 s, 1 da; *Heir* s, William Lawrence Elliot Young, b 26 May 1970; *Career* formerly Capt 16/5 Queen's Royal Lancers; stockbroker with Phillips & Drew; *Style—* Sir William Young, Bt; 41 Blenheim Gdns, Kingston upon Thames, Surrey; 20 Briantspuddle, Dorchester, Dorset

YOUNG-HERRIES; see Herries

YOUNG OF DARTINGTON, Baron (Life Peer UK 1978), of Dartington, Co Devon; Michael Young; s of Gibson Young (musician); *b* 9 Aug 1915; *Educ* Dartington Hall, Univ of London (MA, PhD); *m* 1, 1945, Joan Lawson; 2 s (Hon Christopher Ivan b 1946, Hon David Justin b 1949), 1 da (Hon Emma Dorothy b 1956); m 2, 1960, Sasha, da of Raisley Stewart Moorsom; 1 s (Hon Toby Daniel Moorsom b 1963), 1 da (Hon Sophie Ann b 1961); *Career* sits as Labour peer in House of Lords; called to the Bar Gray's Inn 1939; sec Res Dept Lab Pty 1945-51, dir Inst Community Studies 1953-, fell Churchill Coll Cambridge 1961-66, fndr and chm Social Sci Res Cncl 1965-68, memb NEDC 1975-78; pres: Consumers' Assoc 1965-, Nat Extension Coll 1971-, Advsy Centre for Educn 1976-; chm: Mutual Aid Centre 1977-, Tawney Soc (SDP's think tank) 1982-84, Coll of Health 1983-90, Open Coll of the Arts 1986-91, Open Sch 1988; tstee Dartington Hall 1942-; hon fell LSE 1978; *Books* incl: Family and Kinship in East London (with Peter Willmott, 1957), The Rise of the Meritocracy (1958), Learning Begins at Home (with Patrick McGeeney, 1968), The Symmetrical Family (with Peter Willmott, 1974), The Elmhirsts of Dartington - the creation of an Utopian Community (1982), Social Scientist as Innovator (1984), The Metronomic Society - Natural Rhythms and Human Timetables (1988), Life After Work - The Arrival of the Ageless Society (with Tom Schuller, 1991); *Style—* The Rt Hon the Lord Young of Dartington; 18 Victoria Park Square, London E2 9PF (☎ 081 980 6263)

YOUNG OF GRAFFHAM, Baron (Life Peer UK 1984), of Graffham, Co W Sussex; David Ivor Young; PC (1984); s of late Joseph Young and his w, Rebecca; *b* 27 Feb 1932; *Educ* Christ's Coll Finchley, Univ Coll London (LLB); *m* 1956, Lita Marianne, da of Jonas Shaw; 2 da (of whom Hon Karen Debra b 1957 m 1983, Bernard Anthony Rix, QC, *qv*); *Career* slr 1956; chm Eldonwall Ltd 1961-75, dir Town & City Properties 1972-75, chm: Manufacturers Hanover Property Servs 1974-84, Br Orgn for Rehabilitation by Training (ORT) 1975-80, Admin Ctee World ORT Union 1980-84, Int Cncl of Jewish Social and Welfare Servs 1981-; dir Centre for Policy Studies 1979-82 (memb mgmnt bd 1977-82), industl advsr 1979-80 and special advsr Dept of Indust 1980-81; memb: Eng Industl Estates Corpn 1980-82, Nat Econ Devpt Cncl 1982-; chm Manpower Servs Cmmn 1982-84; min without portfolio 1984-85; sec of state: for Employment 1985-87, for Trade and Indust 1987-July 1989, dep chm Cons Pty 1989-90, dir Salomon Inc 1990-, chm Cable & Wireless plc 1990-; pres: Jewish Care 1990-, World ORT Union 1990-; Hon FRPS 1981; *Clubs* Savile; *Style—* The Rt Hon Lord Young of Graffham; 88 Brook St, London W1

YOUNGER, Hon Alexander James; 2 s of 3 Viscount Younger of Leckie, OBE, TD; *b* 5 May 1933; *Educ* Winchester, Worcester Coll Oxford; *m* 1959, Annabelle Christine, da of late Gerald Furnivall, of Bishop's Waltham, Hants; 2 s (Nicholas Gerald Gilmour b 1963, Rupert Edward Alexander b 1966), 2 da (Amanda Charlotte Frances b 1961, Araminta Lucy b 1967); *Career* late Capt Argyll & Sutherland Highlanders (serv Korea 1952); dir Sir J Causton & Sons 1963-68, md Robert Maclehose & Co 1968-77; dir: Simpson Label Co Ltd (Dalkeith), Stationers Co of Glasgow 1972-77; chm Int Mktg Ctee FINAT 1990-; chm Sch Cncl Balfron 1975-78; dist cmmr Strathblane and Dist Pony Club 1974-78; memb BHS Scottish Ctee 1974-78; *Recreations* golf, music, shooting; *Clubs* Highland Bde; *Style—* The Hon Alexander Younger; Wester Leckie, Kippen, Stirlingshire FK8 3JL

YOUNGER, Anne Rosaleen; JP (Tweeddale); da of Lt-Col John Logan, TD, DL (d 1987), of Wester Craigend, Stirling and Rosaleen Muriel, *née* O'Hara (d 1967); *b* 2 Jan 1939; *Educ* West Heath Sch Sevenoaks Kent, Edinburgh Sch of Mothercraft; *m* 1 Dec 1962, (John) David Bingham, s of Maj O B Younger, MC (d 1989), of The Old Rectory, Etal, Cornhill-on-Tweed, Northumberland; 1 s (Mark Robert b 24 May 1972), 2 da (Sarah Juliet b 29 March 1964, Camilla Jane b 12 Dec 1966); *Career* dir Broughton Brewery Ltd 1979; memb Upper Tweed Community Cncl 1976-86; ARSH 1959; *Recreations* music, country pursuits, family; *Style—* Mrs Anne Younger, JP; Kirkurd House, Blyth Bridge, Peeblesshire EH46 7AH; Broughton Brewery Ltd, Broughton, Peeblesshire ML12 6HQ (☎ 08994 345)

YOUNGER, Capt (John) David Bingham; DL (Borders Region dist of Tweeddale); s of Maj Oswald Bingham Younger, MC (d 1989), of the Old Rectory, Etal, Cornhill-On-Tweed, Northumberland, and Dorothea Elizabeth, *née* Hobbs; *b* 20 May 1939; *Educ* Eton, RMA Sandhurst; *m* 1 Dec 1962, Anne Rosaleen, da of Lt-Col John Logan, TD, DL (d 1987), of Wester Craigend, Stirlingshire; 1 s (Mark Robert b 1972), 2 da (Sarah Juliet b 1964, Camilla Jane b 1966); *Career* Argyll and Sutherland Highlanders cmmnd 1959, Adj 1 Bn Borneo and Singapore 1965-67 (GSM Clasps Borneo and Malaysia), GSO 3 Directorate of Mil Ops MOD 1967-69, ret 1969; memb Queen's Bodyguard for Scotland Royal Co of Archers 1969-; Scottish & Newcastle Breweries Ltd 1969-79: sr exec London 1971-73, sr exec Glasgow 1973-76, sr exec Edinburgh (incl 8 months secondment to GEC Marconi Space and Def Systems) 1976-79; co-fndr and md Broughton Brewery Ltd 1979-; memb Argyll and Sutherland Highlanders Regtl Tst and Ctee; chm: Scottish Borders Tourist Bd, Govrs Belhaven Hill Sch Dunbar; MInstD 1984; *Recreations* country pursuits; *Clubs* MCC; *Style—* Capt David Younger, DL; Kurkurd House, Blyth Bridge, Peeblesshire EH46 7AH (☎ 072152 223); Broughton Brewery Ltd, Broughton, Peeblesshire ML12 6HQ (☎ 08994 345)

YOUNGER, Hon Lady (Elizabeth Kirsteen); da of William Duncan Stewart, JP, of Achara, Duror, Argyll; *m* 1934, Rt Hon Sir Kenneth Younger, KBE, PC, (d 1976, sometime MP (Lab) Grimsby 1945-59 and min state For Affrs 1950-51), 2 s of 2 Viscount Younger of Leckie, DSO, TD, JP, DL; 1 s, 2 da; *Style—* The Hon Lady Younger; Dicker's Farm, Sandy Lane, E Ashling, W Sussex

YOUNGER, Rt Hon George Kenneth Hotson; TD (1964), PC (1979), DL (Stirlingshire 1968), MP (C) Ayr 1964-; s and h of 3 Viscount Younger of Leckie, OBE, TD; *b* 22 Sept 1931; *Educ* Winchester, New Coll Oxford; *m* 7 Aug 1954, Diana Rhona, er da of Capt Gerald Seymour Tuck, DSO, RN (d 1984), of Chichester; 3 s (James b 11 Nov 1955, Charles b 4 Oct 1959, Andrew b 19 Nov 1962), 1 da (Joanna b 16 Jan 1958); *Career* 2 Lt Argyll and Sutherland Highlanders 1950, with 1 Bn BAOR and Korea 1951, 7 Bn (TA) 1952-65; Hon Col 154 (Lowland) Tport Regt RCT TA & VR 1977-85; contested (C) N Lanarks 1959 and stood down from Kinross and W Perths 1963 in favour of Sir Alec Douglas-Home; govr Royal Scottish Acad of Music 1960-70, Scottish Cons whip 1965-67, dir Charrington Vintners Ltd 1966-68, dep chm Cons Pty in Scotland 1967-70 and chm 1974-75, parly under-sec state for Devpt Scottish Off 1970-74, min state Def Jan-March 1974, dir Tennant Caledonian Breweries 1977-79; sec of state for: Scotland May 1979- Jan 1986, Defence Jan 1986-July 1989; delivered Sir Andrew Humphrey Meml lectr on 'The Future of Air Power' 1988; pres Nat Union of Cons Assocs 1987-88; Brig Queen's Body Gd for Scotland (Royal Co of Archers); *Recreations* tennis, sailing; *Clubs* Caledonian (London), Highland Brigade; *Style—* The Hon George Younger, TD, PC, DL; Easter Leckie, Gargunnock, Stirlingshire (☎ 078 686 274)

YOUNGER, Julian William Richard; s and h of Maj-Gen Sir John Younger, 3 Bt, CBE, *qv*; *b* 10 Feb 1950; *Educ* Eton, Grinnell Univ USA; *m* 3 Oct 1981, Deborah Ann Wood; 1 s (Andrew William); *Career* Govt Service; *Books* Who's Who of British Business Travel (annually since 1986, ed); *Style—* Julian Younger, Esq

YOUNGER, Hon Sheriff Robert Edward Gilmour; 3 s of 3 Viscount Younger of Leckie, OBE, TD, DL; bro of Rt Hon George Younger, TD, DL, MP; *b* 25 Sept 1940; *Educ* Winchester, New Coll Oxford, Univ of Edinburgh, Univ of Glasgow; *m* 1972, Helen, da of Eric Hayes (d 1959), and Margaret, sis of Sir John Muir, 3 Bt, TD; 1 s, 1 da; *Career* advocate 1968; Sheriff: Glasgow and Strathkelvin at Glasgow 1979-82, Tayside Central and Fife at Stirling and Falkirk 1982-87, Stirling and Alloa 1987-; *Style—* The Hon Sheriff Robert Younger; Old Leckie, Gargunnock, Stirling (☎ 078 686 213)

YOUNGER, Sir William McEwan; 1 Bt (UK 1964), of Fountainbridge, Co and City of Edinburgh, DSO (1942), DL (Midlothian 1956); s of late William Younger (yr bro of 1 Viscount Younger, and er bro of 1 and last Baron Blanesburgh, GBE, PC), of Ravenswood, Melrose; *b* 6 Sept 1905; *Educ* Winchester, Balliol Coll Oxford; *m* 1, 1936 (m dis 1967), Nora Elizabeth, da of Brig Edward Balfour, CVO, DSO, OBE, MC (d 1955) and Lady Ruth Balfour (eldest da of 2 Earl of Balfour (s of Cons PM 1902-05) by his w Lady Elizabeth Lytton, da of 1 Earl of Lytton), of Balbirnie, Markinch, Fife; 1 da; m 2, 1983, June Peck; *Heir* none; *Career* served WWII RA, Western Desert and Italy (despatches), Lt Col 1944; dir: Br Linen Bank 1955-71, Scottish Television 1964-71; chm: Scottish & Newcastle Breweries 1960-69 (md 1960-67), Second Scottish Investment Trust Co Ltd 1965-75, Highland Tourist (Cairngorm Development) Ltd 1966-78; Cons Pty in Scotland 1971-74; memb Queen's Bodyguard for Scotland (Royal Co of Archers) 1955-; *Recreations* mountaineering, fishery; *Clubs* Carlton, New (Edinburgh), Alpine; *Style—* Sir William Younger, Bt, DSO, DL; 27 Moray Place, Edinburgh, Scotland (☎ 031 225 8173)

YOUNGER OF LECKIE, 3 Viscount (UK 1923); Sir Edward George Younger; 3 Bt (UK 1911), OBE (1940), TD, DL; s of 2 Viscount Younger of Leckie, DSO, TD, JP, DL (d 1946), and Maud (d 1957), er da of Sir John Gilmour, 1 Bt; *b* 21 Nov 1906; *Educ* Winchester, New Coll Oxford (BA); *m* 7 June 1930, Evelyn Margaret, MBE (d 1983), da of late Alexander Logan McClure, KC, sometime Sheriff of Aberdeen, Kincardine and Banff; 3 s, 1 da; *Heir* s, Rt Hon George Younger, TD, DL, MP, *qv*; *Career* Capt A Staff, France 1940, Col Gen Staff, France 1939-40, UK 1940-45, Col Argyll and Sutherland Highlanders (TA); Ld-Lt Stirling and Falkirk 1964-79; *Clubs* New (Edinburgh); *Style—* The Rt Hon the Viscount Younger of Leckie, OBE, TD, DL; Leckie, Gargunnock, Stirling (☎ 078 686 281)

YOUNGMAN, Dr Richard; s of Arthur Henry Youngman (d 1941), of Hillside, Northam, N Devon, and Edith Mary, *née* Taylor (d 1962); *b* 15 Sept 1921; *Educ* Mill Hill, St Bart's Hosp London Univ (MB BS, MRCS, LRCP); *m* 1 Oct 1947 (separated), Nancye Clifford, da of Dudley Clifford Christopherson (d 1962), of Lochinvar, Reigate; 1 s (Paul Dudley b 1952), 1 da (Verna (Mrs Lipinski) b 1949); *Career* RAF Med Branch: Flying Offr 1946, Flt Lt 1947; orthopaedic house surgn St Barts 1945-46, sr house offr Kent & Sussex Hosp 1946, casualty surgn W Middx 1950-52, surgical registrar St Barts Hosp 1952-53, GP 1953-85; chm Med Ctee Iver Cottage Hosp; memb: local med ctee Bucks, Area Health Authy Bucks, Windsor Med Soc 1953 (cncl memb 1979-83); *Clubs* Old Millhillians, Naval; *Style—* Dr Richard Youngman; 64 Bicester Rd, Long Crendon, Bucks (☎ 0844 208 450)

YOUNGREN, Hon Mrs (Catherine Elizabeth); er da of 2 Baron Greenhill, MD, DPH (d 1989); *b* 1948; *Educ* (BA); *m* 1978, Kenneth Youngren; *Career* interior designer and store planner; memb: Interior Designers Inst of British Columbia, Inst of Store Planners (Seattle Washington), Interior Designers of Canada; *Style—* The Hon Mrs Youngren; 4118 Russell Court, North Vancouver, British Columbia, Canada V7G 2C5

YOUNGSON, Prof Alexander John; CBE (1987); s of Dr Alexander Brown (d 1954), and Helen Youngson (d 1945); *b* 28 Sept 1918; *Educ* Aberdeen GS; Univ of Aberdeen (MA, DLitt), Univ of California; *m* 14 Sept 1948, Elizabeth Gisborne, da of Leonard Brown Naylor, CBE (d 1957); 1 s (Graeme b 1952), 1 da (Sheila b 1954); *Career* Lt RNVR serv South Atlantic, Europe 1939-45; lectr Univ of Cambridge 1950-58, prof Univ of Edinburgh 1958-74; dir RSSS Aust Nat Univ 1974-80; chm Royal Fine Art Cmmn for Scot 1983-90; *Books* Possibilities of Economic Progress (1959), The Making of Classical Edinburgh (1966), After the '45 (1973), The Prince and the Pretender (1985), Urban Developement (1990); *Recreations* gardening; *Style—* Prof Alexander Youngson, CBE; Hilltop, Station Rd, Scawby, Brigg, S Humberside DN20 9DW (☎ 0652 55566); RFAC, 9 Atholl Crescent, Edinburgh EH3 8HA (☎ 031 229 1109)

YOUNGSON, George Gray; s of Alexander Keay Youngson, MBE, of Glenrothes, Fife, and Jean Oneil, *née* Kelly; *b* 13 May 1949; *Educ* Buckhaven HS, Univ of Aberdeen (MB ChB, PhD); *m* 17 March 1973, Sandra Jean, *née* Lister; 1 s (Calum

Lister b 1981), 2 da (Kellie Jane b 1973, Louise b 1975); *Career* Univ of Aberdeen: lectr in surgery 1979-82, res fell 1974-76; res in cardiothoracic surgery Univ of W Ontario Canada 1977-79, clinical fell in paediatric surgery Hosp for Sick Children Toronto Ontario Canada 1983, conslt surgn Grampian Health Bd 1985; sec Scot Surgical Paediatric Soc; memb: Br Assoc of Paediatric Surgns, Assoc of Surgns GB and Ireland; FRCS (Edin) 1977; *Recreations* bagpipe music, sport (fishing, tennis, squash, golf); *Style—* George Youngson, Esq; 10 Kennerty Park, Peterculter, Aberdeen AB1 0LE (☎ 0224 734403); Royal Aberdeen Childrens Hosp, Cornhill Rd, Aberdeen (☎ 0224 681818)

YOUNIE, Edward Milne; OBE (1978); s of Rev John Milne Younie (d 1961), of The Manse, Kippen, Stirling, and Mary, *née* Dickie (d 1974); *b* 9 Feb 1926; *Educ* Fettes, Gonville and Caius Coll Cambridge (BA); *m* 1, 26 May 1952, Mary Elizabeth (d 1976), da of Alfred Groves, of Georgetown, Guyana; 2 s (Philip b 1955, Peter b 1957); m 2, 19 June 1979, Mimi Barkeley, da of Col Paul Morris, of Washington DC, USA; *Career* Colonial Serv Tanganyika 1950-61; FCO 1963-: SA 1964-66, Malawi 1966-69, Nigeria 1972-76, Kenya 1977-78, Zimbabwe 1979-81; conslt Trefoil Partnership 1981, chm Kippen Cons Assoc, session clerk; Zimbabwe medal; *Recreations* golf, shooting, music; *Clubs* Brooks's; *Style—* Edward Younie, Esq, OBE; Glebe House, Kippen, Stirling (☎ 078 687 252); Trefoil Parnership Ltd, 50 Pall Mall, London SW1 (☎ 071 839 1030, fax 071 930 1816, telex 918934 DISCOSE G)

YOUNIS, Dr Farouk Mustafa; s of Mustafa Younis, of Amman Jordan, and Wasila Mahmoud Khader; *b* 1 March 1947; *Educ* Markaziyah All HS Baghdad Iraq, Baghdad Univ Med Sch (MB ChB); *m* 13 Sept 1975, Cynthia Karen, da of George Gadsby, of Ilkeston Derbyshire; 1 s (Sami Farouk b 15 Feb 1977); *Career* surgeon; started career in Palestinian refugee camps in Lebanon with Red Crescent Soc Med and Health Prog 1971-72; trg posts UK 1973-: casualty, gen surgery, orthopaedics, thoracic, vascular and urologic surgery; casualty post Chesterfield, gen surgery post Harrogate, Barrow in Furness and Huddersfield, orthopaedics post Cambridge, kidney transplant post Royal Free Hosp London, gen and vascular surgery Chelmsford, conslt surgeon Whittington Hosp 1981-83, private surgical practice 1981-; memb: BMA, RSM, Ind Doctors' Forum; FRCS 1977; *Recreations* tennis, golf, travel, chess; *Clubs* David Lloyd Tennis (Finchley); *Style—* Dr Farouk Younis; 118 Harley St, London W1N (☎ 071 487 4897, fax 071 224 6398)

YOXALL, George Thomas; s of George Thomas Yoxall (d 1983), of Sandbach, Cheshire, and Mary, *née* Bunn; *b* 22 Feb 1949; *Educ* Crewe Co GS, Hertford Coll Oxford (MA); *m* 10 April 1976, Barbara Elizabeth, da of Thomas Donald Gorrie, of Liverpool; 2 s (Matthew b 1980, Richard b 1982); *Career* admin sci offr Sci Res Cncl 1970-72, actuarial student Duncan C Fraser & Ptnrs 1972-73, asst to investmt mangr Nat Farmers Union Mutual Insur Soc 1973-76, UK equity mangr Airways Pension Scheme 1976-82, asst investmt mangr Central Fin Bd Methodist Church 1982-84, sr portfolio mangr Abbey Life N America 1984-86, dir investmts Abbey Life Assur Co 1989-, md Abbey Life Investmts Servs 1989-(dir N America 1986-88); hon sec Poole Hockey Club; AIA 1978; *Recreations* hockey, sailing, railways, civil aviation; *Style—* George Yoxall, Esq; Abbey Life Assurance Co, 80 Holdenhurst Rd, Bournemouth BH8 8AL (☎ 0202 292 373, fax 0202 296 816, telex 41310)

YUGOSLAVIA, HRH Prince Tomislav (Karadjordjević) of; 2 s of King Alexander I of Yugoslavia (reigned from 1921 to 1934, when assassinated at Marseilles) and yr bro of King Peter II; gggs of Queen Victoria through his mother, *née* Princess Marie of Roumania; *b* 19 Jan 1928, Belgrade; *Educ* Oundle, Clare Coll Cambridge (BA); *m* 1, 6 June 1957 (m dis 1982), Her Grand Ducal Highness Margarita Alice Thyra Viktoria Marie Louise Scholastica, only da of HRH The Margrave (Berthold Friedrich Wilhelm Ernst August Heinrich Karl) of Baden (d 1963), and Theodora, 2 da of HRH Prince Andrew of Greece and Denmark and sis of Prince Philip, Duke of Edinburgh; 1 s (HRH Prince Nikola b 15 March 1958, is a lorry driver), 1 da (HRH Princess Katarina b 28 Nov 1959, m 5 Dec 1987, Desmond de Silva, QC, *qv*); m 2, 17 Oct 1982, Linda, da of Holbrook Van Dyke Bonney (d 1988); 2 s (HRH Prince George b 25 May 1984, HRH Prince Michael b 15 Dec 1985); *Career* ptnr in garden centre business; *Style—* HRH Prince Tomislav of Yugoslavia; Orchard Cottage, Redlands Farm, Kirdford, nr Billingshurst, W Sussex (☎ 040 388 263)

YUILL, Dr George Martin; s of Sqdn Ldr George Frew Yuill (d 1981), and Dr Mary Enid Yuill, *née* Barnard (d 1973); *b* 23 Sept 1941; *Educ* Stockport GS, Univ of Manchester (BSc, MB ChB), Cert Aviation Med, Open Univ (BA); *m* 1 June 1968; *Career* conslt neurologist NW RHA 1974; hon assoc lectr Univ of Manchester 1981; MRCP 1968, FRCP 1982; memb: Assoc of British Neurologists, N England Neurological Assoc; *Books* Treatment of Uraemia (1975); *Recreations* sport, flying, maths; *Style—* Dr G M Yuill; 16 St John St, Manchester M34 EA

YUILL, Peter Mortley; s of Cecil Mortley Yuill, and Hilda May, *née* Fothergill; *b* 16 May 1949; *Educ* Oundle, Univ of Birmingham (BSc), Univ of Durham (MSc); *m* 12 April 1980, Margaret Helen, da of James Robinson Booth, of Hartlepool, Cleveland; 1 s (David b 9 April 1981), 2 da (Joanna b 27 Sept 1982, Alexandra b 27 Sept 1984); *Career* civil engr Laings; chm and vice-chm C M Yuill Ltd; dir: C M Yuill Ltd, C M Yuill Investmts, Egglescliffe Prop Ltd, Mowden Park Estate Co Ltd, Owten Fens Props Ltd, Orchard Estate Ltd, Chartstrand Ltd, Yuill Devpts Ltd, Westfield Estates Ltd, C M Yuill Construction Ltd, C M Yuill Hldgs Ltd, Yuill Heritage Homes Ltd, Elco (Stockton) Ltd, Melfort Farms Ltd, Ardenstuir Ltd, J W Hobbs Ltd, Billerford Ltd, Yutec Ltd, Peaklene Ltd, Kingston Wharf Mgmnt Co Ltd, Hollin House Maintainance Co Ltd, George Howe Ltd, Blue Anchor Residents Assoc Ltd; pres Bldg Employers Confedn Northern Co's Region 1988-89; Magistrate, Sch Govr; MICE 1976; *Recreations* squash, golf, snooker, bridge; *Clubs* West Hartlepool Gentlemens, West Hartlepool RFC; *Style—* Peter Yuill, Esq; Magnolias, 8 Pk Ave, Hartlepool, Cleveland TS26 0DZ (☎ 0429 273274); Cecil M Yuill Ltd, Cecil House, Loyalty Rd, Hartlepool, Cleveland TS25 5BD (☎ 0429 266620, fax 0429231359, car 0836 239720)

YULE, (Duncan) Ainslie; s of Edward Campbell Yule (d 1974), of Winchburgh, West Lothian, and Elizabeth Morgan Ainslie; *b* 10 Feb 1941; *Educ* North Berwick HS, Edinburgh Coll of Art (DA); *m* 1, 20 July 1963 (m dis 1982), Patricia Anne, da of John Joseph Carlos; 1 da (Sarah b 27 July 1963); m 2, 9 July 1982, Mary Johnson; *Career* lectr in design Gray's Sch of Art Aberdeen 1966-79, Gregory Fell (sculpture) Univ of Leeds 1974-75, head of sculpture Kingston Poly 1982- (reader 1987-); numerous one man exhibitions and contribs to group exhibitions 1971-; *Clubs* Chelsea Arts; *Style—* Ainslie Yule, Esq; School of Fine Art, Dept of Sculpture, Kingston Polytechnic, Canbury Park Road, Kingston upon Thames (☎ 081 549 0151, fax 081 549 8963)

Z

ZACCOUR, Makram Michel; s of Michel Zaccour (d 1937), former MP and For & Interior Min of Lebanon, and Rose, *née* Gorayeb; *b* 19 Aug 1935; *Educ* Berkeley Coll California Univ (BSc, Phi, BETA, KAPPA); *Career* gen mangr Industrias Textiles Ultratex (Colombia) 1964-66 (sales 1957-64); Merrill Lynch: fin cnslt ME 1967-73, mangr Beirut office 1973, Beirut and Paris 1976, London 1977-83; regnl dir Merrill Lynch Pierce Fenner & Smith Ltd 1983-; Arab Banker Assoc; Phi, BETA, KAPPA Edinburgh Univ; *Clubs* Annabel's Harry's Bar, Mark's, Les Ambassadeurs; *Style—* Makram M Zaccour, Esq; Merrill Lynch, Pierce, Fenner & Smith Ltd, Time Life Building, 153 New Bond St, London, W1Y 0RS (☎ 071 493 7242, fax 071 629 0622, car 0836 280 487, telex 21262 A B MERLEAP London W1)

ZACHARY, Stefan Hedley; s of Jan Bronislaw Zacharkiewicz (d 1987), and Thelma Joyce, *née* Mortimer; *b* 30 June 1948; *Educ* Roundhay Sch Leeds, Leeds Coll of Art (BA); *m* 7 Aug 1971, (Margaret) Patricia, da of Stanley George Wright, of 15 Limmers Mead, Pipers Lane, Great Kingshill, Bucks; 2 s (Alexander Adam, Christopher Jan), 1 da (Halina Patricia); *Career* Royal Yeomanry TA&VR 1972-73, 5 Bn The Queens Regt TA&VR 1973-76, RMA Sandhurst 1975; interior designer Conran Design Gp 1970-71, assoc ptnr Howard Sant Partnership 1971-77, md and dir McColl Gp plc 1977-; vice-pres CSD 1986-89 (chm Inscape Gp 1983-85), memb RIBA Mktg Gp 1987-88, jt hon pres Design Business Assoc 1989- (founding chm 1986-89); Freeman City of London 1988, Liveryman Worshipful Co of Painter Stainers 1989 (Freeman 1988); FCSD 1981, FBID 1979, FRSA 1979, FBIM 1984; *Books* CSD Work's Agreement User's Guide (1983); *Recreations* flying, gliding, shooting, travel, golf, racquet sports, driving, painting and drawing; *Style—* Mr Stefan Zachary; McColl Group International plc, 64 Wigmore St, London W1X 9DJ (☎ 071 935 4788, telex 27392, fax 071 935 0865, car 0836 202419, 0836 544960)

ZAKHAROV, Prof Vasilii; s of Viktor Nikiforovich Zakharov (d 1976), and Varvara Semyenovna, *née* Krzak (d 1962); *Educ* Latymer Upper Sch, Univ of London (BSc, MSc, PhD, DIC, DSc); *m* 1959, Jeanne, da of Horace Hopper (d 1988), of Canterbury; 1 s (Oleg b 1959), 1 da (Anna b 1962); *Career* res in computer systems and applications Birkbeck Coll London 1953-56, res in digital systems Rank Xerox 1956-57, res fell in physics Imperial Coll (RCS) 1957-60, physicist CERN 1960-65, univ reader in experimental physics QMC 1965-66, head Computer Systems and Electronics Div SRC Daresbury Laboratory 1966-78, dir Computer Centre and Prof Computer Systems Univ of London 1978-80, sr assoc CERN Geneva 1980-83 (res assoc 1971-72), prof Univ of Geneva 1984-87, dir info processing Int Orgn for Standards Geneva 1989-; visiting prof of physics: QMC 1968, Westfield Coll London 1974-78; visiting scientist JINR Dubna USSR 1965, conslt AERE Harwell 1965; memb SRC Computer Sci Ctee 1974-77; numerous pubns and contribs to scientific and tech literature; *Books* Digital Systems Logic (1968); *Recreations* rough shooting, amateur radio, collecting Russian miscellania, skiing; *Style—* Prof Vasilii Zakharov; 74rte de Chéne, CH-1208, Geneva, Switzerland; The Firs, Old Castle, Malpas, Cheshire SY14 7NE; ISO, 1 rue de Varembé, CH-1211 Genéve 20, Switzerland (☎ 41 22 734 12 40, telex 41 22 05 iso ch)

ZAMBONI, Richard Frederick Charles; s of Alfred Charles Zamboni (d 1957), and Frances, *née* Hosler (d 1983); descendant of a Swiss (Engiadina) family with lineage traceable to 1465; *b* 28 July 1930; *Educ* Monkton House Sch Cardiff; *m* 2 Jan 1960, Pamela Joan, da of Laurence Brown Marshall; 2 s (Edward b 1962, Rupert b 1967), 1 da (Charlotte b 1964); *Career* CA; Br Egg Mktg Bd 1959-70; chm: Sun Life Investmt Mgmnt Servs Ltd 1985-89, Sun Life Tst Mgmnt Ltd 1985-89; vice chm Sun Life Assur Soc plc 1986-89 (md 1979-89); dep chm Assoc of Br Insurers 1986-88 (chm Life Insur Cncl 1986-88), chm Avon Enterprise Fund plc 1990 (dir 1984); *Recreations* ornithology, gardening, tennis; *Style—* Richard Zamboni, Esq; Long Meadow, Beech Avenue, Effingham, Surrey KT24 5PH (☎ 0372 458211)

ZAMOYSKA, Countess Betka Marya; da of Count Andrzej Zamoyski (yr bro of Count Stefan, whose children are Counts Zdzisz, *chef de famille* in UK, and Adam and Countess Marilena, *qqv*) by Priscilla, 2 da of Sir Hugh Stucley, 4 Bt, JP, DL; *b* 12 March 1948; *Educ* Cranborne Chase, Lady Margaret Hall Oxford; *Career* freelance journalist; *Recreations* reading, theatre, films; *Style—* Countess Betke Zamoyska; 136 Hurlingham Rd, London SW6

ZAMOYSKI, Count Adam Stefan; s of Lt-Col Count Stefan Zamoyski, OBE, VM, LLD, Order of Polonia Restituta (d 1976, fifth in descent from Andreas Zamoyski, cr Count 1778 (confirmed 1780) by Empress Maria Teresa of Austria at the time of the Partitions of Poland) by his w Princess Elizabeth Czartoryska (d 1989); the Princess's gf was Prince Wladyslaw Czartoryski (s of Tsar Alexander I's Foreign Minister Prince Adam, who was also briefly head of Independent Poland 1830), while her grandmother (Wladyslaw's w) was HRH Princess Marguerite d'Orléans (da of HRH The Duc de Nemours, 2 s of Louis Philippe, King of the French); *b* 11 Jan 1949, in New York; *Educ* Downside, Queen's Coll Oxford; *Career* author, books include a biography of Chopin and a History of Poland; Knight of Honour & Devotion Sov Mil Order of Malta 1977, Kt of Justice Constantinian Order of St George (House of Bourbon Sicily) 1978, Order of Polonia Restituta 1982; *Clubs* Pratt's, Polish Hearth; *Style—* Count Adam Zamoyski; 33 Ennismore Gdns, London SW7 (☎ 071 584 9053)

ZAMOYSKI, Tomasz Józef Tadeusz Różyc; s of Tadeusz Kazimierz Juljan Różyc Zamoyski, Kt Cdr Order of Polonia Restituta, Chevalier de la Légion d'Honneur, Cdr de l'Ordre Nat du Mérite (d 1980), of the Poraj clan, the Counts Zamoyski (*qqv*) being of the Jelita clan; Tadeusz's ancestors were involved in defence of Częstochowa during the Swedish invasion of Poland 1655-56), author of Kodeks Honorowy (Code of Honour), published in Warsaw in 1924, and universally acknowledged as the authoritative handbook governing the correct procedure relating to duels in pre-war Poland; *b* 22 May 1935,Warsaw; *Educ* Malvern, Sidney Sussex Coll Cambridge, Johann Wolfgang Goethe Univ Frankfurt, Florence Univ; *m* 1959, Nicole, da of Marcel Tranier (d 1983), of Paris; 1 s (Matthew Tomasz Tadeusz Różyc b 1972), 1 da (Arabella Halina Suzanne Różyc Zamoyska b 1974); *Career* Nat Serv 2 Lt 5 RTR; dir HZI Int Ltd; *Recreations* hunting; *Clubs* Boodle's, Lansdowne; *Style—* Tomasz Zamoyski, Esq; 132 Kensington Park Rd, London W11 (☎ 071 229 8040, office 071 242 6346)

ZAMOYSKI, Count Wojciech Michal; er s of Count Michal Zamoyski (2 s of Count Adam Zamoyski, sometime ADC to Tsar Nicholas II, by his marriage with Countess Maria Potocka; Adam the ADC was youngest bro of Count Stefan, who was the ggf of Count Adam Stefan Zamoyski, *qv*); *b* 12 Sept 1927,Kozlowka Palace; *Educ* Poland, Angola, S Africa; *m* 1955, Isobel Zamoyska, er da of William Forbes-Robertson Mutch; 2 s (Count Paul b 1957, Count Alexander b 1962), 1 da (Countess Anna Isabella Zamoyska b 1960); *Career* formerly official at Rhodesian High Cmmn and Overseas Devpt Admin; *Recreations* Poland, the Third World, travel; *Style—* Count Wojciech Zamoyski; (☎ 071 581 0998)

ZAMOYSKI, Count Zdzisz; s of late Count (Stefan) Zamoyski, *chef de famille* in UK; er bro of Count Adam Zamoyski, *qv*; *Style—* Count Zdzisz Zamoyski; Ashfield House, The Horns, Hawkhurst, Kent

ZAMOYSKI, Count Zygmunty Ignacy Stukely; s of Count Andrzej Zamoyski (s of Count Wladislaw Zamoyski and yr bro of late Count Stefan, f of Counts Zdzisz and Adam and Countess Marelina, *qv*) by Priscilla, 2 da of Sir Hugh Stukeley, 4 Bt, JP, DL; *b* 23 Nov 1937; *Educ* Stowe, Christ Church Oxford, Imede Geneva (MBA); *Style—* Count Zygmunt Zamoyski

ZAMYATIN, HE Leonid Mitrofanovich; s of Mitrofan Zamyatin; *b* 9 March 1922; *Educ* Moscow Aviation Inst and Higher Diplomatic Sch; *m* 1946, Olga Alexeevna; 1 da (Elena); *Career* Miny of Foreign Affairs USSR 1953-: cnsllr on political questions of USSR mission to UN, Soviet dep rep on Preparatory Ctee (later on bd of Govrs), Soviet rep on IAEA 1959-60, dep head of American Countries Dept 1960-62, head of Press Dept; memb Collegium Miny of Foreign Affrs 1962-70, dir gen TASS News Agency 1970-78, chief Dept of Int Info of Centl Ctee 1978-86, ambass to UK 1986-; Lenin Prye 1978, orders and medals of the USSR including the Order of Lenin; *Style—* HE Leonid Zamyatin; 13 Kensington Palace Gardens, London (☎ 071 229 3620)

ZANDER, Prof Michael; s of Dr Walter Zander, of Crohamleigh, S Croydon, and Margaret, *née* Magnus (d 1969); *b* 16 Nov 1932; *Educ* RGS High Wycombe, Jesus Coll Cambridge (BA, LLB), Harvard Law Sch (LLM); *m* 27 Aug 1965, Elizabeth Treeger (Betsy), da of Clarence R Treeger, of NYC; 1 s (Jonathan b 1970), 1 da (Nicola b 1969); *Career* 2 Lt RA; admitted slr 1962, Sydney Morse & Co 1962-63; LSE: asst lectr 1963, lectr 1965, sr lectr 1970, reader 1970, prof 1977, convenor Law Dept 1984-88; frequent broadcasts on radio and TV, legal corr The Guardian 1963-87; *Books* Lawyers and the Public Interest (1968), Legal Services for the Community (1973), The Law-Making Process (1980, 3 edn 1989), The Police and Criminal Evidence Act (1984, 2 edn 1990), A Bill of Rights (3 edn 1985), Cases and Materials on English Legal Systems (5 edn 1988), A Matter of Justice: The Legal System in Ferment (revised edn, 1989); *Recreations* learning the cello; *Style—* Prof Michael Zander; 12 Woodside Ave, London N6 4SS (☎ 081 883 6257); LSE, Houghton St, London WC2 (☎ 071 955 7268, fax 071 242 0392)

ZANKEL, Hon Mrs (Alison Victoria); *née* Poole; da of 1 Baron Poole, CBE, TD, PC; *b* 1936; *m* 1961, Dr Fitz Zankel; 2 s; *Style—* The Hon Mrs Zankel; Staudgasse 75, Vienna

ZAPHIRIOU-ZARIFI, Ari Charles; s of Prof George Aristotle Zaphiriou, of Washington DC, and Frosso, *née* Zarifi; *b* 10 March 1946; *Educ* Stowe, LSE (BSc); *m* 27 Dec 1973, Yana, da of Ulysses Sistovaris (d 1985); 1 s (Stefan b 1975), 1 da (Viki b 1978); *Career* Peat Marwick Mitchell 1967-70, J Henry Schroder Wagg 1970-73, chm and chief exec The Heritable and Gen Investmt Bank Ltd 1988- (dir 1975, md 1979), chief exec Heritable Group plc 1983-, chm Alpha Gamma Gp 1983-; chm Cncl King Alfred Sch; FCA 1970; *Recreations* tennis, swimming, sailing, reading, gardening; *Clubs* The Travellers'; *Style—* Ari Zaphiriou-Zarifi, Esq; 31 Tanza Rd, London NW3 2VA (☎ 071 435 2517); Spence House, Dock Lane, Beaulieu, Hants; 52 Berkeley Square, London W1X 6EH (☎ 071 493 6621, fax 071 629 1958, telex 291184 HERIT G)

ZATOUROFF, Dr Michael Argo; s of Argo Arakel Zatouroff (d 1980), of New York, and Nina, *née* Dragounova (d 1979); *b* 23 Oct 1936; *Educ* Seaford Coll Sussex, Royal London Hosp (MB BS, DCH, FRCP); *m* 13 May 1961, Diana, da of Alan Curtis Heard; 1 s (Justin Alan b 7 Sept 1965), 2 da (Anna Eugenie b 22 July 1963, Catherine Morwenna b 20 April 1968); *Career* house offr Royal London Hosp 1961, sr house offr Royal United Hosp Bath 1962-63; med registrar: UCH Ibadan Nigeria 1963-64, Royal Northern Hosp London 1964-66, conslt physician Kuwait Govt 1966-76; present appts: sr med advsr Marathon Oil Co UK, hon sr lectr in Med Royal Free Hosp London, conslt physician The London Clinic London, lectr in med The London Foot Hosp London, examiner in med (Conjoint Bd of England, Soc of Chiropodists, Med Artists Assoc of GB), memb Editorial Bd Med Int; winner Horder prize in Med 1966; Freeman City of London, Liveryman Worshipful Co of Barber Surgeons; memb: RSM 1965, Med Soc of London 1966, Harvian Soc 1966, Osler Club 1966; *Books* Physical Signs in General Medicine (1976, 2 edn, 1991), Diagnostic Studies in General Medicine (1989), The Foot in Clinical Diagnosis (1991); *Recreations* cross-country cycling, med photography, carriage driving, theatre, eating, reading, dieting; *Clubs* Garrick; *Style—* Dr Michael Zatouroff; 25 Fordington Rd, Highgate, London N6 4TD (☎ 081 883 5118); The London Clinic, 149 Harley St, London W1N 1HF (☎ 071 935 4444, fax 071 486 3782)

ZATZ, Paul Simon Jonah; s of Samuel Zatz (d 1981), and Stella Rachel Morgan, *née* Levy; *b* 21 April 1938; *Educ* King William's Coll, Sidney Sussex Coll Cambridge (MA, LLM); *m* 5 Sept 1965, Patricia Ann, da of Sidney Landau (d 1971); 1 s (Joshua b 1969), 1 da (Rachel b 1967); *Career* admitted slr 1964; ptnr Lawrance Messer & Co 1968-81, co sec Clyde Petroleum plc 1980 (legal and corp dir 1983, fin dir 1989); *Recreations* opera, walking; *Clubs* City Univ; *Style—* Paul Zatz, Esq; Coddington Court, Coddington, Ledbury, Herefordshire HR8 1JL (☎ 0531 86811, fax 0531 86579)

ZEALLEY, Christopher Bennett; s of late Sir Alec Zealley, of Devon, and late Nellie Maude, *née* King; *b* 5 May 1931; *Educ* Sherborne, King's Coll Cambridge (choral scholarship, MA); *m* 23 April 1966, Ann Elizabeth Sandwith; 1 s (Robert Paul b 1969), 1 da (Elizabeth Victoria b 1972); *Career* cmnnd RNVR 1953; ICI 1955-66, IRC 1966-70; dir: Dartington Hall Tst 1970-88, Group Ltd, Grant Instruments Ltd; chm: Pub Interest Res Centre 1972-, Social Audit Ltd 1972-, Consumers Assoc (Which?) 1976-81, Dartington and Co Group plc 1979-; Charity Appointments Ltd 1986-, Dartington Coll of Art 1973, Morwelham Recreation Co Ltd 1978- tstee Charities Aid Fndn

1981-90 and various charitable tsts; *Recreations* music; *Clubs* Naval; *Style*— Christopher Zealley, Esq; Sneydhurst, Broadhempston, Totnes, Devon

ZEEMAN, (Erik) Christopher; s of Christian Zeeman (d 1929), of Aarhus & Yokohama, and Christine, *née* Bushell (d 1968); *b* 4 Feb 1925; *Educ* Christ's Hospital, Christ's Coll Cambridge (BA, MA, PhD); *m* 1, June 1950 (m dis 1959), Elizabeth, da of Evan Jones; 1 da (Nicolette b 1956); m 2, 30 Jan 1960, Rosemary, da of Harold Samuels Gledhill; 3 s (Tristan b 1960, Crispin b 1965, Samuel Christian b 1970), 2 da (Mary Lou b 1961, Francesca b 1967); *Career* Flying Officer RAF 1943-47; fell Gonville & Caius Coll Cambridge 1953-64, Cwlth fell Chicago & Princeton 1954-55, lectr Univ of Cambridge 1955-64, memb Institut des Hautes Etudes Scientifiques Paris 1962-63, fndn prof and dir Mathematics Research Centre Univ of Warwick 1964-88, visiting prof Univ of California Berkeley 1966-67, sr fell SERC 1976-81, prof Royal Inst 1983-, visiting fell CCC Oxford 1985-86, princ Hertford Coll Oxford 1988-, Gresham prof of geometry Gresham Coll London 1988-; visiting prof: Inst for Advanced Study Princeton, Institut des Hautes Etudes Scientifique Paris, Instituto de Matematica Pura e Aplicada Rio de Janeiro, Int Centre for Theoretical Physics Trieste, Univ of Maryland, Florida State Univ, Univ of Pisa; chm Mathematic Ctee SERC 1982-85, pres London Mathematics Soc 1986-88, vice pres Royal Soc 1989-90, fndr chm Scientific Steering Ctee Isaac Newton Inst Cambridge 1990-; Queen's Jubilee medal 1977, Senior Whitehead prize London Mathematical Soc 1982, Faraday medal Royal Soc 1988; Hon DSc: Univ of Hull 1984, Claremont Univ Centre & Graduate Sch 1986, Univ of Leeds 1990, Univ of Durham 1990; Hon DSc & Hon Prof Univ of Warwick 1988, Hon DUniv York 1988, Docteur honoris causa Univ of Strasbourg 1974, hon fell Christ's Coll Cambridge 1989; FRS 1975, memb Brazilian Acad of Sciences 1972; *Books* Catastrophe Theory (1977), Geometry and Perspective (1987), Gyroscopes & Boomerangs (1989); many research papers; *Recreations* family, music, carpentry, walking; *Clubs* United Oxford & Cambridge Univ; *Style*— Prof Christopher Zeeman; Principal's Lodgings, Hertford College, Oxford OX1 3BW (☎ 0865 279408, 0865 279407)

ZEFFERT, Clive Lewis; s of Henry Zeffertt (sic), of Portsmouth, and Ann, *née* Levison; *b* 11 Aug 1938; *Educ* Portsmouth GS, Portsmouth Sch of Architecture (Dip Arch); *m* 21 April 1966, Sherry Lynn, da of Charles Weinstein (d 1966), of Portland, Oregon, USA; 1 s (Simeon b 1977), 1 da (Sara b 1973); *Career* architect; princ Clive Zeffert Assocs 1978; dir Thames Housing Ltd 1981; dir Easefern Ltd 1984; ARIBA; *Recreations* squash, sailing; *Style*— Clive Zeffert, Esq; 32 Crouch Hall Rd, London N8 8HJ (☎ 081 341 3375, (work) 081 340 3963)

ZEHETMAYR, John Walter Lloyd; OBE (1991), VRD (1963); s of Walter Edward Zehetmayr (d 1955), of Twickenham, and Gladys Lindsay, *née* Pembroke (d 1971); *Educ* St Paul's, Keble Coll Oxford (BA); *m* 10 Sept 1945, Isabell (Betty), da of Andrew Neill-Kennedy (d 1950), of Belfast; 2 s (Brian b 1946, Peter b 1951), 1 da (Susan (Mrs Mann) b 1954); *Career* RNVR: Sub Lt Special Branch 1942, Lt 1944 (despatches); Lt Special Branch RNVSR 1946; RNR: Lt (L) 1951, Lt Cdr 1958-66; Forestry Cmmn: silviculturist 1948-56, chief work study offr 1956-64, conservator W Scotland 1964-66, sr offr Wales and conservator S Wales 1966-81; memb: Prince of Wales Ctee 1971-89, Brecon Beacons Nat Park Ctee 1982-91; chm and pres Cardiff Ski Club 1975-82, vice chm Glamorgan Wildlife Tst 1985-88, chm Forestry Safety Cncl 1986-; Fell Inst Chartered Foresters 1955; *Books* Experiments in Tree Planting on Peat (1954), Afforestation of Upland Heaths (1960), The Gwent Small Woods Project 1979-84 (1985), Forestry in Wales (1985); *Recreations* garden, conservation, skiing; *Style*— John Zehetmayr, Esq, OBE, VRD; The Haven, 13 Augusta Road, Penarth, S Glam CF6 2RH (☎ 0222 701694)

ZELLICK, Prof Graham John; s of Reginald Hyman Zellick, of Windsor, Berks, and Beana, *née* Levey; *b* 12 Aug 1948; *Educ* Christ's Coll Finchley, Gonville and Caius Coll Cambridge (MA, PhD), Stanford Univ Sch of Law California (Ford fndn fell); *m* 18 Sept 1975, Prof Jennifer Zellick, da of Michael Temkin, of London; 1 s (Adam b 1977), 1 da (Lara b 1980); *Career* called to the Bar Middle Temple 1967; visiting prof of law Univ of Toronto 1975 and 1978-79; Queen Mary and Westfield Coll (formerly Queen Mary Coll): lectr in laws 1971-78, reader in law 1978-82, prof of public law 1982-88, dean faculty of laws 1984-88, head of dept of law 1984-90, Drapers' prof of law 1988-, sr vice principal and actg principal 1990-91, principal 1991-; Univ of London: dean faculty of laws 1986-88, senator 1985-, dep chm academic cncl 1987-89; visiting scholar St John's Coll Oxford 1989; ed: Euro Human Rights Reports 1978-82, Public Law 1981-86; memb Ed Bds: British Journal of Criminology 1980-90, Public Law 1981-, Howard Journal of Criminal Justice 1984-87, Civil Law Library 1987-; chm: Tel Aviv Univ Tst Lawyer's Gp 1984-1989, Prisoners' Advice and Law Serv 1984-89, Legal Ctee All Party Parly War Crimes Gp 1988-, Ctee of Heads of Univ Law Schs 1988-90; dep chm Justice Ctee on Prisoners' Rights 1981-83, memb: Cncl Howard League for Penal Reform 1973-82, Jellicoe Ctee on Bds of Visitors of Prisons 1973-75, Newham Dist Ethics Ctee 1985-86, West London Synagogue 1990- (chm Educn Ctee 1990-); govr: Central London Poly 1973-77, Pimlico Sch 1973-77, Queen Mary Coll 1983-89, Univ Coll Sch 1983-, N London Poly 1986-, Queen Mary and Westfield Coll 1989-; memb: Data Protection Tbnl 1985-, Lord Chancellor's Advsy Ctee on Legal Aid 1985-1988, Lord Chancellor's Advsy Ctee on Legal Educn 1988-90, Ctee Vice Chancellors and Principals 1990-; JP Inner London 1981-85; *Books* Justice in Prison (with Sir Brian MacKenna, 1983), The Law Commission and Law Reform (ed 1988), Prisons in Halsbury's Laws of England (4 edn, with Louis Blom-Cooper, QC); *Clubs* Reform; *Style*— Prof Graham Zellick; 14 Brookfield Park, London NW5 1ER (☎ 071 485 8219); Queen Mary and Westfield College, London E1 4NS (☎ 071 975 5001, fax 081 981 2848, telex 891750); 34 Mixbury, Oxford (☎ 028 04 848295)

ZEMAN, Zbyněk Anthony Bohuslav; s of Jaroslav Zeman (d 1972), and Růzena Zemanová, *née* Pětníková (d 1980); *b* 18 Oct 1928; *Educ* Prague Univ, Univ of London (BA), Univ of Oxford (DPhil); *m* 1956, Anthea, da of Norman Collins; 2 s (Adam b 1957, Alexander b 1964), 1 da (Sophia b 1966); *Career* res fell St Antony's Coll Oxford 1958-61, memb editorial staff The Economist 1959-62, lectr in modern history Univ of St Andrews 1962-70, head of res Amnesty Int 1970-73, dir East-West SPRL (Brussels) and Euro Co-operation Res Gp 1974-76, prof of central and south east Euro studies dir Comenius Centre Univ of Lancaster 1976-82, res prof in Euro history 1982, professorial fell St Edmund Hall Oxford 1983-; visiting prof Univ of Prague 1990-91; *Books* The Break-up of the Habsburg Empire 1914-18 (1961), Nazi Propaganda, The Merchant of Revolution, A Life of Alexander Helphand, (with W B Scharlau, 1964), Prague Spring (1969), A Diplomatic History of the First World War (co-ed 1971), International Yearbook of East-West Trade (1975), The Masaryks Selling the War: art and propaganda in the First World War (1978), Heckling Hitler: caricatures of the Third Reich (1984), Pursued by a Bear, The Making of Eastern Europe (1989); *Recreations* squash, skiing, cooking; *Style*— Prof Zbyněk Zeman; St Edmund Hall, Oxford

ZERMANSKY, Victor David; s of Isaac Zermansky (d 1987), and Sarah, *née* Cowen; *b* 28 Dec 1931; *Educ* Cowper St Sch, Leeds GS, Univ of Leeds (LLB); *m* 1 June 1958, Anita Ann, da of Victor Levison (d 1973); 2 da (Susan Sadot b 1959, Karin Lobetta b 1962); *Career* Nat Serv Army Legal Aid 1953-55; slr 1953-, sr ptnr Victor D Zermansky & Co 1955-, immigration appeal adjudicator 1970-78, dep circuit judge and asst rec 1976 ; formerly pres: Leeds Jewish Rep Cncl, Leeds Law Soc (current memb), Leeds Zionist Cncl, Leeds Kashrut Cmmn (Beth Din Admin), Leeds Jewish Students Assoc; memb: Law Soc; *Recreations* travel, books; *Style*— Victor Zermansky, Esq; 52 Alwoodley Lane, Leeds 17 (☎ 0535 673523); Victor D. Zermansky & Co, Solicitors 10 Butts Court, Leeds 1 (☎ 0532 459 766, fax 0532 467465)

ZERNY, Richard Guy Frederick; s of Marcus Zerny (d 1984), and Eunice Irene Mary, *née* Diggle (d 1982); *b* 27 June 1944; *Educ* Charterhouse; *m* 11 Sept 1970, Jane Alicia, da of Albert George Steventon (d 1984); 2 s (Charles Marcus Stephen b 1972, Miles Patrick Richard b 1973), 1 da (Clare Louise b 1979); *Career* Zernys Ltd: dir 1969-, md 1979-83, chm 1989-; dir Johnson Group Cleaners Properties plc 1983, md Johnson Group Cleaners plc 1989- (dir 1983), dir Cleaning Tokens Ltd 1986-; chm: Joseph Harris Ltd 1989 (md 1983-89), Bollom Ltd 1989-, Kneels Ltd 1989-, James Hayes & Sons Ltd 1989-, Johnson Bros (Cleaners) Ltd 1989-, JAS Smith & Sons (Cleaners) Ltd 1989-, John Crockatt Ltd 1989-, Hartonclean Ltd 1989-, J Pullar & Sons Ltd 1989-, Johnson Micronclean Ltd 1989-, HF Whitton (Shopfitters) Ltd 1989-; md Johnson Group Management Services Ltd 1989-, dir Apparelmaster Design Ltd 1989-; memb ctee Hull and Dist Lifeboat Branch 1967-83, sec to Hull and Dist Lifeboat Branch 1975-83; Liveryman Worshipful Co of Launderers 1987, Freeman City of London 1986; *Recreations* sailing, golf, squash, bridge; *Clubs* Royal Yorks Yacht; *Style*— Richard G F Zerny, Esq; Clayton House, Liverpool Rd South, Burscough, Lancashire, L40 7TP; Johnson Group Cleaners plc, Mildmay Rd, Bootle, Merseyside L20 5EW (☎ 051 933 6161)

ZERVUDACHI, Nolly Emmanuel; s of Maj Laky Emmanuel, of Daira Draneht, 25 Sh Talaat Harb, BP 1277, Alexandria, Egypt, and Alice, *née* Polymeris (d 1983); *b* 2 Jan 1929; *Educ* Victoria Coll Alexandria, Victoria Coll Cairo, English Sch Heliopolis Cairo, New Coll Oxford, Faculte de Droit Paris; *m* 2 July 1957, Carolyn Elinor, da of Maj John Karney Gorman, MC; 3 s (Laky b 1958, Patrick b 1960, Constantine b 1963), 1 da (Manuela (twin) b 1963); *Career* 2 Lt E Batty RHA RA 1948-49; md: Niarchos Hamburg GmBh 1954-60 (dir 1953-54), Hellenic Shipyards Ltd London 1960-85, special memb gen ctee Lloyd's Register of Shipping 1970-88, dir Hellenic War Risks Assoc 1971-88 (Bermuda 1971-86), md Niarchos (London) Ltd 1972-88 (dir 1958-72), dir UK Mutual Steam Ship Assur Assoc Bermuda Ltd 1972-88; memb cncl Int Tanker Owners Assoc 1972-88, vice chm Inter Tanko 1984-86 (memb exec ctee 1976-86); *Recreations* riding, skiing, sailing; *Style*— Nolly Zervudachi, Esq; 22 Holland Villas Rd, London W14 8DH (☎ 071 603 7133)

ZETLAND, 4 Marquess of (UK 1892); Sir Lawrence Mark Dundas; 7 Bt (GB 1762); also Earl of Ronaldshay (UK 1892), Earl of Zetland (UK 1838), and Baron Dundas (GB 1794); eldest s of 3 Marquess of Zetland, DL (d 1989), and Penelope, Marchioness of Zetland, *qv*; *b* 28 Dec 1937; *Educ* Harrow, Christ's Coll Cambridge; *m* 4 April 1964, Susan Rose, 2 da of Guy Richard Chamberlin, of Shefford House, Great Shefford, Newbury, Berks; 2 s (Earl of Ronaldshay b 5 March 1965, Lord James Edward b 2 May 1967), 2 da (Lady Henrietta Kate b 9 Feb 1970, Lady Victoria Clare b 2 Jan 1973); *Heir* s, Earl of Ronaldshay, *qv*; *Career* late 2 Lt Grenadier Gds; landowner; dir: Redcar Racecourse, Catterick Racecourse, Tocketts Mill Development Co, Escor Toys Ltd, Barony Fishing Co Ltd, Racing Five Ltd, J England Group plc; *Recreations* tennis (lawn and Royal), squash, racing (racehorses: Foggy Buoy, Tatiana, Chance Command); *Clubs* All England Lawn Tennis, Jockey; *Style*— The Most Hon the Marquess of Zetland; Copt Hewick Hall, Ripon, N Yorks HG4 5DE (☎ 0765 3946); 44 Bramerton Street, London SW3

ZETLAND, Penelope, Marchioness of; Penelope; 2 da of Col Ebenezer John Lecky Pike, CBE, MC, DL (d 1965), of Little Glebe, Fontwell, Sussex, and Olive Constance, *née* Snell (d 1962); *b* 19 Feb 1916; *m* 2 Dec 1936, 3 Marquess of Zetland, DL (d 1989); 3 s (4 Marquess, Lord David Dundas, Lord Bruce Dundas, *qqv*), 1 da (Lady Serena Kettlewell, *qv*); *Style*— The Most Hon Penelope, Marchioness of Zetland; Aske, Richmond, Yorkshire; 59 Cadogan Place, London SW1

ZETTER, Paul Isaac; CBE (1981); *b* 9 July 1923; *Educ* City of London; *m* 1954, Helen Lore Morgenster; 1 s (Adam), 1 da (Carolyn); *Career* chm: Zetters Gp plc and assoc Cos; Sports Council (Southern), Sports Aid Fndn; Pres John Carpenter Club 1987-88; *Books* It Could Be Verse; *Recreations* walking; *Clubs* RAC; *Style*— Paul Zetter, Esq, CBE; c/o Zetters Group plc, 86-88 Clerkenwell Rd, London EC1 (☎ 071 251 4971)

ZIEGLER, (Paul) Oliver; s of Maj Colin Louis Ziegler DSO, DL (d 1977), and Dora, *née* Barnwell (d 1941); *b* 9 Dec 1925; *Educ* Eton; *m* 1950, Margaret Sybil, da of Sir Lionel George Archer Cust, CBE (d 1962, s of Sir Lionel Cust, KCVO, and Hon Sybil Lyttelton); 2 s (Adam Charles b 1952, William James Archer b 1956); *Career* slr; sr ptnr Moore & Blatch (Lymington), ret 1990; *Recreations* reading, gardening, theatre; *Style*— Oliver Ziegler, Esq; Hightown Farm, Ringwood, Hants (☎ 0425 474278)

ZIEGLER, Philip Sandeman; s of Maj Colin Louis Ziegler, DSO, DL (d 1977); *b* 24 Dec 1929; *Educ* Eton, New Coll Oxford; *m* 1, 1960, Sarah (decd), da of Sir William Collins (d 1976); 1 s, 1 da; m 2, 1971, Mary Clare, *née* Charrington; 1 s; *Career* HM Dip Serv 1952-67, ed dir William Collins and Sons (joined 1967); chm Soc of Authors 1988-90; commissioned to write official biography of Harold Wilson 1990; *Books* Duchess of Dino (1962), Addington (1965), The Black Death (1968), William IV (1971), Melbourne (1976), Crown and People (1978), Diana Cooper (1981), Mountbatten (1985), The Sixth Great Power: Barings 1762-1929 (1988), King Edward VIII (1990); *Clubs* Brooks's; *Style*— Philip Ziegler, Esq; 22 Cottesmore Gardens, London W8 (☎ 071 937 1903); Picket Orchard, Ringwood, Hants (☎ 042 54 3258)

ZIELENKIEWICZ, Hon Mrs (Catherine); *née* Sinclair; da of 1 Viscount Thurso, KT, CMG, PC (d 1970); *b* 25 Oct 1919; *Educ* Kensington HS, Central Sch of Arts & Crafts London, Academie Ranson Paris, Euston Rd Sch London; *m* 1957, Kazimierz Zielenkiewicz; 1 da (Clementina b 1958); *Career* artist (under name Catherine Sinclair); memb Soc Scottish Women Artists; solo shows in Edinburgh and Paris; exhibited also: London Gp, Royal Scot Acad, Soc of Scot Artists, New English Art Club, Royal Soc of Portrait Painters; *Style*— The Hon Mrs Zielenkiewicz; The Mill House, Isle Brewers, Taunton

ZIENKIEWICZ, Prof Olgierd Cecil; CBE (1989); s of Casimir Rafael Zienkiewicz (d 1958), of 8 Grange Terrace, Edinburgh, and Edith Violet, *née* Penny (d 1974); *b* 18 May 1921; *Educ* Imperial Coll of Sci and Technol London (BSc), Univ of London (PhD, DSc); *m* 17 Sept 1952, Helen Jean, da of Albert Fleming; 2 s (Andrew Olgierd b 17 Sept 1953, John David b 4 May 1955), 1 da (Krystyna Helen (Mrs Beynon) b 3 March 1958); *Career* conslt engr Sir William Halcrow & Partners 1945-49, lectr Univ of Edinburgh 1949-57, prof of structural engrg Northwestern Univ Evanston Illinois USA 1957-61, prof and head of Dept of Civil Engrg Univ of Wales Swansea 1961-88, dir Inst for Numerical Methods in Engrg 1970-88; numerous scientific papers on: solid and fluid mechanics, stress analysis of dams, nuclear reactors, lubrication theory, devpt of the finite element method; fndr and chief ed Int Jl for Numerical Methods in Engrg; memb numerous ed bds of jls incl: Solids & Structures, Earthquake Engrg, Rock Mechanics; memb Cncl ICE 1972-76, chm Ctee of Analysis and Design Int Congress of Large Dams 1973-85, holder visiting res chair of naval sea systems cmd Navl Postgrad Sch Monterey California 1979-80, pres Int Assoc of Computational Mechanics 1986-90;

recipient: James Alfred Ewing medal ICE 1980, Nathan Newmark medal American Soc of Engrs 1980, Worcester Warner Reid medal American Soc of Mechanical Engrs 1980, Carl Friedrich Gauss medal W German Acad of Sci 1987, Queens medal Royal Soc 1990; hon prof Dalian China 1988; Hon DSc: Lisbon 1972, Univ of Ireland 1975, Univ of Brussels 1982, Northwestern Univ USA 1984, Univ of Trondheim Norway 1985, Chalmers Univ of Technol Sweden 1987, Univ of Technol Warsaw 1989, Univ of Technol Krakow Poland 1989; hon fell Univ of Wales Swansea 1989; Hon DLitt Univ of Dundee 1987; fell City and Guilds Inst of London 1979; foreign memb: US Nat Acad of Engrs 1981, Polish Acad of Sci 1985; FRS 1978, FEng 1979; *Books* The Finite Element Method in Structural Mechanics (1967), The Finite Element Method in Engineering Science (1971), The Finite Element Method (1977, 4 edn with R L Taylor, vol I 1989), Finite Elements and Approximations (with K Morgan); *Recreations* sailing, diving; *Clubs* Athenaeum; *Style—* Prof Olgierd Zienkiewicz, CBE, FRS; 29 Somerset Road, Mumbles, Swansea SA3 4PL (☎ 0792 368 776)

ZIERKE, Ulrich; s of Dr Erwin Zierke, of Frankfurt, Germany and Elsbeth Zierke; *b* 24 June 1944; *Educ* GS Germany, J W Goethe Univ Frankfurt (Diplom Kaufmann); *m* 4 April 1975, Kornelia Zierke, da of Robert Saur; *Career* Nat Serv 1965-67, banking apprentice 1963-65; Westdeutsche Landesbank: banker 1972, seconded Libra Bank London and Mexico City 1974-78, various assignments to NY Tokyo and Madrid 1978-90, sr vice pres 1983-, dep chief exec Chartered WestLB Limited 1990-; *Recreations* travelling; *Style—* Ulrich Zierke, Esq; Chartered WestLB Ltd, 33-36 Gracechurch Street, London EC3V 0AX (☎ 071 623 8711, fax 071 626 1610)

ZIFF, (Robert) Paul; s of Max Ziff (d 1954), by his w Annie (d 1953); *b* 20 Dec 1935; *Educ* Giggleswick Sch; *m* 29 April 1987, Lea, da of late Irving Charles Bambage, of Yorks; *Career* chm: Finest Brands International Ltd, Champion Manufacturing Ltd, Aigle-FBI Ltd, Public Eye Enterprises Ltd, Well Worth Watching Productions Ltd, Pentagon Productions & Management Ltd, Whitham & Schofield Ltd; *Recreations* mechanical music; *Clubs* St James's, Annabel's; *Style—* Paul Ziff, Esq; Gallogate House, Weeton, nr Leeds; Finest Brands International Ltd, FBI House, Low Fields Way, Leeds LS12 6HQ (☎ 0532 707007)

ZIGMOND, Jonathan Peter; s of His Hon Judge Joseph Zigmond (d 1980), and Muriel, *née* Lermon; *Educ* Cheadle Hulme Sch, Univ of Reading (BSc); *m* 11 Sept 1976, Sarah Angela Barbara, *née* Roff; 2 s (Andrew Morris b 3 Jan 1981, Robin James b 13 Dec 1982); *Career* articled clerk Hogg Bullimore Chartered Accountants 1972-75, qualified 1975; Coopers & Lybrand Deloitte (formerly Coopers & Lybrand): joined 1976, City practice 1976-82, Leeds 1982-, ptnr 1983-, head of tax practice Leeds; memb Inheritance Tax and Tsts Sub Ctee ICAEW; FCA (ACA 1975), ATII 1975; *Books* Tax Digest: Inheritance Tax on Discretionary and Accumulation Trusts (1987, 2 edn 1988), Inheritance Tax Planning (1987, 2 edn 1988); *Style—* Jonathan Zigmond, Esq; Coopers & Lybrand Deloitte, Albion Court, 5 Albion Place, Leeds LS1 6JP (☎ 0532 431343, fax 0532 342840)

ZILKHA, Selim Khedoury; s of Khedoury A Zilkhe (d 1956), of USA, and Louise, *née* Bashi (d 1985); *b* 7 April 1927; *Educ* English Sch Heliopolis Egypt, Horace Mann NYC, Williams Coll Williamston Mass (BA); *m* 1, 21 Oct 1953 (m dis) 1962, Diane, da of Saleh Bashi (d 1961), of Geneva; 1 s (Michael b 1953), 1 da (Nadia Wellisz b 1955); *Career* US Army Inf 1945; banking apprentice Bank Zilkha Cairo, Hallansche Bank Amsterdam and Hambros Bank London 1946-47, vice pres American Nile Corporation NY 1948-51; banker Amerifin London 1955-60 (Paris 1951-55), fndr Mothercare Ltd and associated Cos 1961-82, dir Habitat Mothercare Group 1982; chm and chief exec: Towner Petroleum Co Houston Texas 1983-85, Zilkha Energy Co Houston Texas 1987-; *Recreations* bridge, tennis, skiing Sunningdale, Travellers (France); *Style—* Selim Zilkha, Esq; 750 Lausanne Road, Los Angeles, Calif 90077, USA; 830 Roaring Fork Rd, Aspen, Colorado 81611 (☎ 213 476 6316, 213 472 6528)

ZIMMER, Dr Robert Mark; s of Norman Zimmer, NY, USA, and Lenore *née* Wasserman; *Educ* Churchill Coll Cambridge, MIT (SB), Columbia Univ NY (MA, MPhil, PhD); *m* 23 July 1983, Joanna Elizabeth Marlow, da of Thomas Gondris, of Ipswich, Suffolk; *Career* lectr: Columbia Univ 1982-85, Brunel Univ 1985-; visiting scholar Dept of Sanskrit and Indian Studies Harvard Univ 1989-; published poetry and articles on mathematics, computer sci, electrical engrg and 18 century Eng Lit; *Recreations* food, books; *Clubs* Young Johnsonians; *Style—* Dr Robert Zimmer; 4 Selwyn Court, Richmond, Surrey TW10 6LR (☎ 081 948 3772); Department Electrical Engineering Brunel University, Uxbridge, Middx, UB8 3PH (☎ 0895 74000 ext 2756, fax 0895 32806, telex 261173 G)

ZINNEMANN, Fred; s of Dr Oskar Zinnemann (d 1941), and Anna (d 1942); *b* 29 April 1907; *Educ* Vienna U Law Sch (BA), Ecole Technique de Cinematographie Paris; *m* 1936, Renée, *née* Bartlett; 1 s (Tim); *Career* film director; *films* The Wave (1934), The Seventh Cross (1942), The Search (1947), Act of Violence (1948), The Men (1949), High Noon (1951), A Member of The Wedding (1952), From Here To Eternity (1953), Oklahoma (1955), The Nun's Story (1958), The Sundowners (1960), Behold A Pale Horse (1963), A Man For All Seasons (1967), The Day Of The Jackal (1973), Julia (1977), Five Days One Summer (1982); 4 motion picture Acad awards (Oscars) for directing: 1951, 1954, 1967 (and for producing); BAFTA awards 1967 and 1978; other prof awards incl: NY Film Critics 1952, 1954, 1959 and 1967, Directors' Guild 1954 and 1967, Moscow Festival 1965, Golden Thistle (Edinburgh) 1965, D W Griffith (LA) 1970, Donatello (Florence) 1978; 2 vice pres Directors' Guild of America 1961-64, co-founder and ex tstee American Film Inst 1967-71, fell BAFTA 1978, fell BFI 1990; US Congressional Life achievement Award 1987, Order of Arts and Letters (Fr) 1982, Gold medal City of Vienna (Austria) 1967; *Recreations* mountaineering, chamber music; *Clubs* Sierra (San Francisco); *Style—* Fred Zinnemann, Esq; 128 Mount St, London W1

ZINS, Stefan; s of Maximilian Zins (d 1966), and Zofia, *née* Kurzman; *b* 5 June 1927; *Educ* Hammersmith Coll of Art and Architecture, UCL (Cert Town Planning); *m* 17 Aug 1959, Harriet Norah, da of Henry Frank Back (d 1968); 1 da (Deborah b 1962); *Career* architect, planning consIt; fndr and dir: Stefan Zins Ltd Associates, PS Mgmnt; i/c numerous building schemes in SE England, for public and private sectors, inc hotels, youth hostels, old peoples' homes etc, also commercial projects; FRIBA; *Recreations* tennis, skiing, swimming, wine tasting; *Clubs* Confrerie des Compagnons Haut Normands du Gouste-Vin; *Style—* Stefan Zins, Esq; 31 Valiant House, London SW11 3LU; 71 Warwick Road, London SW5 (☎ 071 370 3129, fax 071 373 5993)

ZITCER, Hon Mrs (Diane Susan); *née* Morris; da of 2 Baron Morris of Kenwood, and Hon Ruth Joan Gertrude Rahle, *née* Janner; *b* 25 Jan 1960; *Educ* St Paul's Girls' Sch, Central Sch of Drama (dip stage mgmnt); *m* 1981, Cary Haskell Zitcer, er s of Chaim Josek Zitcer; 2 da (Natasha Esther b 1986, Emily Margaret b 1988); *Career* television and radio broadcaster, producer and journalist; memb: NUJ, ACTT; *Recreations* theatre, cinema, water and snow skiing, DIY, interior design, needlework; *Style—* The Hon Mrs Zitcer; c/o 154 Fleet St, London EC4A 2QQ

ZOLLINGER, Fred Edward; s of Alfred Edward Zollinger (d 1957); *b* 6 July 1922; *Educ* Queens' Coll Cambridge; *m* 1953, Flora, da of late Brig-Gen Wallace Wright, VC; *Career* chm: Imperial Continental Gas Association 1974-87, Century Power & Light Ltd 1974-87; dir: Lazard Bros & Co Ltd 1966-87, Pirelli General plc 1971-87, Calor Group Ltd 1974-87; ret 1987; *Recreations* skiing; *Style—* Fred Zollinger, Esq; The House of Barns, Chobham, Woking, Surrey (☎ 0276 858815)

ZOLLNER, Stephen; s of Stephen Zollner (d 1956) and Nina, *née* Dragicevic; *b* 7 May 1946; *Educ* Charterhouse, Pembroke Coll Oxford (MA); *m* July 1982, Alison, da of Gerard Frater; 1 da (Amelia b 1982); *Career* barr Gray's Inn 1969; *Recreations* travel, photography; *Style—* Stephen Zollner, Esq; 23 Fitzjohns Ave, London NW3 5JY (☎ 071 435 9848); 15 Old Sq Lincoln's Inn, London WC2A 3UE (☎ 071 831 0801, fax 071 405 1387)

ZOLLO, Jeffrey Michael; s of Michael Joseph Zollo (d 1981), and Florence Lillian, *née* Green; *b* 4 Jan 1945; *m* 2 July 1976, Sirkka-Liisa, da of Kustaa Malm (d 1974); *Career* freelance journalist; trained with Salisbury Journal and Bournemouth Times; reporter: East London News Agency (nat papers), Stockholm Sweden; foreign corr Helsinki; contrib to: Br, Dutch, American, Spanish, German pubns; currently writing for Br and Finnish magazines; memb: Poole Cons Club, Finnish Spitz Club and Soc; memb: NUJ, Int Press Assoc, Int Fedn of Journalists; *Recreations* reading; *Style—* Jeffrey Zollo, Esq; 39 Tatnam Rd, Poole, Dorset BH15 2DW (☎ 0202 677071, fax 0202 684461)

ZOUCHE, 18 Baron (E 1308); Sir James (Jimmie) Assheton Frankland; 12 Bt (E 1660); s of Hon Sir Thomas Frankland, 11 Bt (d 1944, s of Sir Frederick Frankland, 10 Bt, by his w Baroness Zouche (d 1965), 17 holder of the Peerage and descendant of Eudes La Zouche, yr bro of Sir Roger La Zouche of Ashby after whose family Ashby-de-la-Zouch is named); Lord Zouche is coheir to Baronies of St Maur (abeyant since 1628) and Grey of Codnor; *b* 23 Feb 1943; *Educ* Lycée Jacard Lausanne; *m* 1978, Sally, da of Roderic M Barton, of Brook House, Pulham St Mary, Norfolk; 1 s, 1 da; *Heir* s Hon William Thomas Assheton b 23 July 1984; *Career* Capt 15/19 King's Roy Hussars (ret 1968), ADC to Govr Tasmania 1965-68, Hon ADC to Govr Victoria 1975-; vice pres Multiple Sclerosis Soc Victoria 1973-; co dir; *Recreations* shooting; *Clubs* Cavalry & Guards', Melbourne (Australia); *Style—* The Rt Hon the Lord Zouche; 7 St Vincent's Place, Albert Park, Vic 3206, Australia

ZUCKER, His Hon Judge Kenneth Harry; QC (1981); s of Nathaniel Zucker (d 1989), of London, and Norma Zucker, *née* Mehlberg (d 1937); *b* 4 March 1935; *Educ* Westcliff HS, Exeter Coll Oxford; *m* 1961, Ruth Erica, da of Dr Henry Brudno (d 1967); 1 s (Jonathan), 1 da (Naomi); *Career* called to the Bar Gray's Inn 1959, rec 1982, circuit judge 1989; *Recreations* reading, walking, photography; *Style—* His Hon Judge Zucker, QC

ZUCKERMAN, Arie Jeremy; *b* 30 March 1932; *Educ* Univ of Birmingham (BSc, MSc, DSc), Univ of London (MB BS, MD, Dip Bact, Univ Gold medal, Evans prize, A B Cunning Prize, A B Cunning award); *Career* Flt Lt then Sqdn ldr RAF Med Branch 1959-61; first obstetric house surgn Royal Free Hosp 1957-58, casualty surgn and admissions offr Whittington Hosp London 1958-59 (house physician in gen med Jan - July 1958), Med Branch RAF 1959-62; registrar Public Health Laboratory Serv Central, secondment as hon registrar Dept of Pathology Guy's Hosp Med Sch 1962-63, sr registrar Public Health Laboratory 1963-65; London Sch of Hygiene and Tropical Med: sr lectr Dept of Bacteriology and Immunology 1965-68, reader in virology 1968-72, prof of virology 1972-75, dir Dept of Med Microbiology 1975-88; prof of microbiology Univ of London 1975-, dean of Royal Free Hosp Sch of Med 1989-, WHO: conslt on hepatitis 1970-, memb Expert Advsy Panel on Virus Diseases 1974-, dir Collaborating Centre for Ref and Res on Viral Hepatitis 1974-89, dir Colloborating Centre for Ref and Res on Viral Diseases 1990-; hon conslt virologist: N E Thames Regnl Blood Transfusion Centre 1970-, Charing Cross Hosp 1982-; hon conslt microbiologist Royal Free Hosp 1989-, non-exec dir Royal Free Hampstead NHS Tst 1990-; ed: Journal of Medical Virology 1976-, Journal of Virological Methods 1979-; contrib to numerous learned jls; Stewart prize of the BMA 1981; MRCS, LRCP 1957, DObstRCOG 1958, MRCP 1977, MRCPath 1965, FRCPath 1977, FRCP 1982; *Books* Virus Diseases of the Liver (1970), Hepatitis-associated Antigen and Viruses (1972), Human Viral Hepatitis (2 edn, 1975), Hepatitis Viruses of Man (with C R Howard, 1979), A Decade of Viral Hepatitis (1980), Viral Hepatitis (ed, 1986), Viral Hepatitis and Liver Disease (ed, 1988), Recent Development in Prophylactic Immunization (ed, 1989), Viral Hepatitis (ed, 1990), Principles and Practice of Clinical Virology (2 edn, 1990); *Style—* Prof Arie Zuckerman; Royal Free Hospital School of Medicine, Rowland Hill Street, Hampstead, London NW3 2PF (☎ 071 794 0500)

ZUCKERMAN, Baroness; Lady Joan Alice Violet Rufus; *née* Isaacs; da of 2 Marquess of Reading, GCMG, CBE, TD, PC, QC, and Hon Eva Mond, CBE, JP, da of 1 Baron Melchett; *b* 19 July 1918; *m* 1939, Baron Zuckerman, *qv*; 1 s (Paul, *qv*), 1 da (Stella); *Career* JP: Birmingham 1961, Norfolk 1967; amateur artist exhibiting in Norfolk and London; chm Friends of the Sainsbury Centre for Visual Arts Norwich; *Books* Birmingham Heritage (1979); *Style—* The Rt Hon Lady Zuckerman; The Shooting Box, Burnham Thorpe, King's Lynn, Norfolk PE1 8HW

ZUCKERMAN, Hon Paul Sebastian; s of Baron Zuckerman (Life Peer), and Lady Joan Rufus Isaacs, da of 2 Marquess of Reading; *b* 1945; *Educ* Rugby, Trinity Coll Cambridge (MA), Univ of Reading (PhD); *m* 1972 (m dis 1981), Mrs Janette Hampel, da of R R Mather, of Stoke-by-Clare, Suffolk; *Career* dir S G Warburg & Co Ltd, chm Intermediate Technol Devpt Gp, tstee William Walton Fndn; *Clubs* Brooks's; *Style—* The Hon Paul Zuckerman; The Old Rectory, Grosvenor Rd, London SW1

ZUCKERMAN, Baron (Life Peer UK 1971), of Burnham Thorpe, Co Norfolk; Solly Zuckerman; OM (1968), KCB (1964, CB 1946); s of Moses Zuckerman; *b* 30 May 1904, Cape Town; *Educ* Cape Town Univ; *m* 1939, Lady Joan Alice Violet Rufus Isaacs, da of 2 Marquess of Reading; 1 s (Hon Paul Sebastian b 1945), 1 da (Hon Stella Maria (Hon Mrs Norman) b 1947); *Career* sits as Independent peer in House of Lords; pres: Zoological Soc London 1977-84, Fauna Preservation Soc 1974-81, British Industrial Biological Research Association 1974-; chief scientific advsr: Defence Secretary 1960-66, HM Govt 1964-71; FRS, MRCS, FRCP; kt 1956; *Books* Nuclear Illusion and Reality (1982), From Apes to Warlords (1978), Social Life of Monkeys and Apes (1932,1981), Monkeys, Men and Missiles (1988); *Clubs* Brooks's; *Style—* The Rt Hon Lord Zuckerman, OM, KCB, FRS; University of East Anglia, Norwich, Norfolk, NR4 7TJ

ZUKERMAN, Pinchas; *b* 1948; *Educ* began musical training with father, Israel Conservatory (with Ilona Feher), Acad of Music Tel Aviv, Julliard Sch USA (scholar, studied with Ivan Galamian); *Career* musician; violinist, violist, teacher and conductor; soloist and conductor with many maj orchestras incl: New York Philharmonic, Boston Symphony, Los Angeles Philharmonic, Nat Symphony Orchestra of San Francisco, Montreal, Toronto and Ottawa, Berlin Philharmonic, London Symphony Orchestra, Eng Chamber Orchestra, Israel Philharmonic; former music dir: South Bank Festival, St Paul Chamber Orchestra; performed London premiere of Marc Neikrug's violin concerto with BBC Symphony Orchestra 1989, conducted American staged premiere of opera Where The Wild Things Are; guest conductor Dallas Symphony Orchestra's Int Music Festival 1990-; contemporary repertoire incl works by: Boulez, Knussen, Kraft, Lutoslawski, Neikrug, Takemitsu; toured Australia with Israel Philharmonic and US with Marc Neikrug and the Vermeer Quartet (Chicago) 1989-90; orchestral solo appearances incl: New York Philharmonic, Los Angeles Philharmonic, the Pittsburgh, St Louis, Minnesota and Indianapolis Symphony Orchestra; conducting appearances incl: Montreal, Dallas, Cincinnati and Ottawa Symphony Orchestras; toured UK and Europe with Mark Neikrug 1989-90, conductor and soloist for Frankfurt Radio

Orchestra and Berlin Philharmonic 1989-90, dir and soloist Eng Chamber Orchestra (Edinburgh Festival, London, Italy, Switzerland) 1990, touring US (with Itzhak Perlman) and Europe 1991; discography incl over 75 recordings widely representative of violin and viola repertoires; *awards* first prize Twenty-Fifth Leventritt Int Competition 1967, Achievement award of Int Centre in NY, King Solomon award of America-Israel Cultural Fndn, Medal of Arts 1983; DUniv Brown Univ USA; *Style*— Pinchas Zukerman; c/o Harold Holt Ltd, 31 Sinclair Rd, London W14 ONS (☎ 071 603 4600, fax 071 603 0019, telex 22339)

ZULUETA; *see*: de Zulueta

ZUNZ, Sir Gerhard Jacob (Jack); s of Wilhelm Zunz (d 1959), of Johannesburg, South Africa, and Helene, (d 1973); *b* 25 Dec 1923; *Educ* Athlone HS Johannesburg SA, Univ of The Witwatersrand Johannesburg SA (BSc); *m* 1948, Babs Maisel; 1 s (Leslie Mark b 1956), 2 da (Marion Erica b 1952, Laura Ann b 1955); *Career* served WWII SA Artillery Egypt and Italy 1943-46; asst engr Alpheus Williams & Dowse 1948-50; Ove Arup & Partners: structural and civil engr London 1950-54, co fndr and ptnr SA 1954-61, assoc ptnr and ptnr in all overseas partnerships 1965-77; chm Ove & Arup & Partners 1977-84; Ove Arup Partnership: dir 1977-84, co chm 1984-89, conslt 1989-; *Awards* Oscar Faber Silver medal (with Sir Ove Arup) 1969, Inst Structural Engrs Gold medal 1988, Oscar Faber Bronze medal (with M Manning & C Jofeh) 1990; Industl Commoner Churchill Coll 1967-68; FEng 1983, HonFRIBA 1990, FCGI 1991, FICE, FIStructE; kt 1989; *Recreations* theatre, music, golf; *Style*— Sir Jack Zunz; Ove Arup Partnership, 13 Fitzroy St, London W1P 6BQ (☎ 071 636 1531, fax 071 580 3924)

ZUTSHI, Dr Derek Wyndham Hariram; s of Lambodha Zutshi (d 1964), of Srinagar, Kashmir, and London, and Eileen Dorothy Wyndham Lord (d 1944); *b* 26 April 1930; *Educ* Epsom Coll, Univ of Bristol (MB ChB, MRCP); *m* 11 May 1974, Marguerite Elizabeth, da of Edgar Montague Smith (d 1944), of Lima Peru, and Bournemouth; *Career* rheumatology conslt 1973-; med registrar MRC Rheumatism Res Unit Canadian Red Cross Meml Hosp Taplow 1966-68, sr registrar rheumatology and clinical tutor med The London Hosp 1968-73, med dir Sch of Physiotherapy Prince of Wales Gen Hosp 1973-77; rheumatology conslt Gen Hosps Tottenham (Prince of Wales, St Ann's) 1973-77; sr med offr Medicines and Communicable Disease Divs DHSS 1977-86; examiner: Chartered Soc of Physiotherapy 1974-78, Coll of Occupational Therapists 1980-89; hon treas Federal Cncl of Indian Orgns 1974-; memb: Cncl and hon sec Br Assoc for Rheumatology and Rehabilitation 1974-78, cncl Med Soc of London 1977-80, Cncl Hunterian Soc 1978- (hon treas 1979-); Univ of Bristol (memb Ct 1958, Cncl 1988-, Standing Ctee of Convocation 1981-, chm 1988-); memb: Bd of Tstees The Hindu Centre London 1962- (chm 1984-), Bd of Govrs Tottenham Coll of Further Educn 1974-90 (dep chm 1978-87); Nat Rubella Cncl: memb Advsy Panel 1988-, memb Mgmnt Ctee 1989-; FRSA, FRSM; *Recreations* travel, music, reading; *Clubs* Athenaeum; *Style*— Dr Derek Zutshi; 36 Eton Court, Eton Ave, Hampstead, London NW3 3HJ; 99 Harley St, London W1N 1DF (☎ 071 486 8495)

ZVEGINTZOV, Hon Mrs (Rachel Kathleen); *née* Bailey; da of late Hon Herbert Crawshay Bailey (d 1936), 4 s of 1 Baron Glanusk; sister of 4 Baron; raised to the rank of a Baron's da 1948, and Kathleen Mary, *née* Salt (d 1948); *b* 5 June 1914; *Educ* St Paul's Girls' Sch; *m* 1940, Brig Dimitry Zvegintzov, CBE (d 1984), late Border Regt (ret), s of Col Dimitry Ivanovitch Zvegintzov, CMG, DSO (d 1967), of Parc Gwynne, Glasbury-on-Wye, and Mrs Zvegintzov (*née* Princess Obolensky); 2 s (Ivan Dimitry, Paul David), 1 da (Elizavietta Mary); *Style*— The Hon Mrs Zvegintzov; The Studio, White Lodge, Hill Brow Road, Liss, Hants, GU33 7PS (☎ 0730 893866)

ABBREVIATIONS

A

AA	Automobile Association; Anti-Aircraft; Architectural Association
AAA	Amateur Athletic Association
AAAS	American Association for the Advancement of Science
AACCA	Associate of Association of Certified & Corporate Accountants
AACI	Accredited Appraiser, Canadian Institute
AADipl	Diploma, Architectural Association
A&AEE	Aeroplane and Armament Experimental Association
AAF	Auxiliary Air Force
AAFCE	Allied Air Forces Central Europe
AAG	Assistant Adjutant-General
AAGBI	Associate, Anaesthetists of GB and Ireland
AAI	Association of Chartered Auctioneers' and Estate Agents' Institute
AALPA	Associate of Incorporated Auctioneers & Landed Property Agents
AAM	Association of Assistant Mistresses in Secondary Schools
AAMC	Australian Army Medical Corps
AAPG	American Association of Petroleum Geologists
AA&QMG	Assistant Adjutant & Quarter-Master-General
AASA	Associate of Australian Society of Accountants
AASC	Australian Army Service Corps
AASF	Advanced Air Striking Force
AB	Bachelor of Arts (USA); Able-bodied Seaman
ABA	Associate of British Archaeological Association; Antiquarian Booksellers' Association; Amateur Boxing Association
ABIBA	Associate of the British Institute of Brokers Association
ABIM	Associate of British Institute of Management
ABOD	Advance Base Ordnance Depot
ABPS	Associate of the British Psychological Society
ABSA	Association Business Sponsorship of the Arts
ABTA	Association of British Travel Agents
AC	Companion of the Order of Australia
ACA	Associate of the Institute of Chartered Accountants
Acad	Academy
ACARD	Advisory Council for Applied Research and Development
ACAS	Advisory, Conciliation and Arbitration Service
ACBSI	Associate, Chartered Building Societies Institute
ACC	Association of County Councils
ACCM	Advisory Council for the Church's Ministry
ACCS	Associate of the Corporation of Secretaries
AcDipEd	Academic Diploma in Education
ACDS	Assistant Chief of Defence Staff
ACE	Association of Consulting Engineers
ACF	Army Cadet Force
ACG	Assistant Chaplain General
ACGI	Associate of City & Guilds of London Institute
ACGS	Assistant Chief of General Staff
ACIArb	Associate, Chartered Institute of Arbitrators
ACIB	Associate, Chartered Institute of Bankers
ACII	Associate of Chartered Insurance Institute
ACIS	Associate of Chartered Institute of Secretaries
ACMA	Associate, Institute of Cost and Management Accountants
ACNS	Assistant Chief of Naval Staff
ACommA	Associate, Society of Commercial Accountants
ACORD	Advisory Committee on Research and Development
ACOS	Assistant Chief of Staff
ACOST	Advisory Council on Science and Technology
ACP	Association of Clinical Pathologists
ACPO	Association of Chief of Police Officers
ACRE	Action with Rural Communities in England
ACS	American Chemical Society
ACSEA	Allied Command SE Asia
ACT	Australian Capital Territory; Australian College of Theology; Association of Corporate Treasurers
Actg	Acting
ACTT	Association of Cinematograph, Television and Allied Technicians
ACVO	Assistant Chief Veterinary Officer
ACWA	Associate of Institute of Cost and Works Accountants
AD Corps	Army Dental Corps
ADAS	Agricultural Development and Advisory Service (MAFF)
ADC	Aide-de-Camp
ADC(P)	Personal Aide-de-Camp to HM The Queen
ADGB	Air Defence of Great Britain
ADGMS	Assistant Director-General of Medical Services
Adj	Adjutant
Adj-Gen	Adjutant-General
Adm	Admiral
Admin	Administration; Administrative; Administrator
ADMS	Assistant Director of Medical Services
Admty	Admiralty
ADNI	Assistant Director of Naval Intelligence
ADOS	Assistant Director of Ordnance Service
ADP	Automatic Data Processing
ADPR	Assistant Director Public Relations
ADS&T	Assistant Director of Supplies and Transport
Adv-Gen	Advocate-General
Advsr	Adviser
Advsy	Advisory
ADVS	Assistant Director of Veterinary Services
Advtg	Advertising
A/E	Accident and Emergency
AE	Air Efficiency Award (see AEA)
AEA	Air Efficiency Award; Atomic Energy Authority
AEAF	Allied Expeditionary Air Force
AEC	Army Educational Corps (Now RAEC); Agricultural Executive Committee
AED	Air Efficiency Decoration
AEF	Amalgamated Union of Engineering and Foundry Workers
AEM	Air Efficiency Medal
AER	Army Emergency Reserve
AERE	Atomic Energy Research Establishment
AEU	Amalgamated Engineering Union
AF	Air Force
AFAEP	Association of Fashion Advertising and Editorial Photographers
AFAIM	Associate Fellow of the Australian Institute of Management
AFC	Air Force Cross; Association Football Club
AFCENT	Allied Forces Central Europe
Affrs	Affairs
AFHQ	Allied Force Headquarters
AFI	Associate of the Faculty of Insurance
AFIMA	Associate Fellow, Institute of Mathematics and its applications
AFM	Air Force Medal
AFOM	Associate, Faculty of Occupational Medicine
AFRAeS	Associate Fellow of the Royal Aeronautical Society
AFRC	Agricultural and Food Research Council
AFS	Auxiliary Fire Service
AFV	Armoured Fighting Vehicles
AG	Attorney-General
Agent-Gen	Agent-General
AGI	Artistes Graphiques Internationales
AGRA	Association of Genealogists and Record Agents
Agric	Agriculture, Agricultural
AHA	Area Health Authority
AHQ	Army Head Quarters
AHSM	Associate, Institute of Health Services Management
AIA	American Institute of Architects; Associate, Institute of Actuaries: Association of International Artists
AIAA	Associate of the Institute of Administrative Accountants
AIAC	Associate of the Institute of Company Accountants
AIB	Associate of Institute of Bankers
AIBD	Associate, Institute of British Decorators
AICA	Associate Member Commonwealth Institute of Accountants
AICE	Associate, Institute of Civil Engineers
AIChor	Associate of the Institute of Choreography
AICS	Associate of the Institute of Chartered Shipbuilders
AICTA	Associate, Imperial College of Tropical Medicine
AIEE	Associate of the Institution of Electrical Engineers
AIF	Australian Imperial Forces
AIG	Adjutant-Inspector-General
AIIA	Associate of the Institute of Industrial Administration
AIL	Associate, Institute of Linguists
AIM	Associate of the Institution of Metallurgists
AIMarE	Associate of the Institute of Marine Engineers
AIMSW	Associate, Institute of Medical Social Workers
AINA	Associate of the Institute of Naval Architects
AInstM	Associate Member of the Institute of Marketing
AInstP	Associate of the Institute of Physics
AInstT	Associate, Institute of Taxation
AIP	Association of Independent Producers
AIPM	Associate of the Institute of Personnel Management
AIRC	Association of Independent Radio Contractors
Air Cdre	Air Commodore
AIYL	Association of International Young Lawyers
aka	Also known as
AKC	Associate, King's College London
ALA	Associate, Library Association
ALAS	Associate Member of Chartered Land Agents' Society
ALFSEA	Allied Land Forces South East Asia
ALI	Argyll Light Infantry; Associate, Landscape Institute
ALLC	Association for Literary and Linguistic Computing
Alta	Alberta (Canada)
AM	Member of the Order of Australia; Albert Medal; Master of the Arts (USA); Alpes Maritimes
AMA	Associate, Museum Association; Association of Metropolitan Authorities
Ambass	Ambassador
AMBIM	Associate Member of the British Institute of Management
AMCT	Associate, Manchester College of Technology
AMDEA	Associate of Manufacturers of Domestic and Electrical Appliances
AMEC	Association of Management Education for Clinicians
AMEME	Association of Mining Electrical and Mechanical Engineers
AMF	Australian Military Forces
AMGOT	Allied Military Government Occupied Territory
AMIBE	Associate Member of the Institution of British Engineers
AMICE	Associate Member of the Institution of Civil Engineers
AMIChemE	Associate Member of the Institution of Chemical Engineers
AMIED	Associate Member of the Institution of Engineering Designers
AMIEE	Associate Member of the Institution of Electrical Engineers
AMIMechE	Associate Member of the Institution of Mechanical Engineers

AMIMinE Associate Member of the Institution of Mining Engineers
AMInstNA Associate Member of the Institution of Naval Architects
AMIPE Associate Member of the Institution of Production Engineers
AMIStructE Associate Member, Institute of Structural Engineers
AMP Air Ministry Personnel; (Harvard Business School) Advanced Management Programme
AMPC Auxiliary Military Pioneer Corps
AMRAes Associate Member, Royal Aeronautical Society
AMS Army Medical Service; Assistant Military Secretary
AMSIA Associate Member, Society of Investment Analysts
AMTPI Associate of the Town Planning Institution
ANU Australian National University
AO Air Officer; Officer of the Order of Australia
AOA Air Officer in Charge in Administration
AOC Air Officer Commanding
AOC-in-C Air Officer Commanding-in-Chief
AOD Army Ordnance Department
AOEng Air Officer Engineering
AOER Army Officers' Emergency Reserve
AOM Air Officer Maintenance
APA American Psychiatric Association
APEX Association of Professional, Executive, Clerical and Computer Staffs
APM Assistant Provost Marshal
APP Associate of Psychoanalytic Psychotherapy
Appt Appointment
APRA Association of Political Risks Analysts
APS American Physical Society
AQ Administration and Quartering
AQMG Assistant Quarter-Master General
ARA Associate of the Royal Academy of the Arts
ARAD Associate, Royal Academy of Dancing
ARAeS Associate of the Royal Aeronautical Society
ARAM Associate of the Royal Academy of Music
ARBA Associate of the Royal Society of British Artists
ARBS Associate of the Royal Society of British Sculptors
ARC Agricultural Research Council
ARCA Associate of Royal College of Art
ARCA (Lond) Associate of the Royal Academy of Arts
ARCM Associate of the Royal College of Music
ARCO Associate of the Royal College of Organists
ARCS Associate, Royal College of Science
ARCST Associate, Royal College of Science and Technology
ARCUK Architects' Registration Council of the UK
ARCVS Associate of the Royal College of Veterinary Surgeons
ARE Associate, Royal Society of Painters-Etchers and Engravers
ARELS Association of Recognised English Language Schools
ARIAS Associate, Royal Incorporation of Architects in Scotland
ARIBA Associate of the Royal Institute of British Architects
ARIC Associate of the Royal Institute of Chemistry
ARICS Associate of the Royal Institution of Chartered Surveyors
ARINA Associate of the Royal Institution of Naval Architects
ARMCM Associate, Royal Manchester College of Music
Armd Armoured
ARP Air Raid Precautions
ARPS Associate of the Royal Photographic Society
ARRC Associate of the Royal Red Cross
ARSA Associate of the Royal Scottish Academy
ARSM Associate of the Royal School of Mines
ARTC Associate of the Royal Technical College
ARWS Associate of the Royal Society of Painters in Water Colours
ASA Associate Member of the Society of Actuaries; Australian Society of Accountants; Army Sailing Association
ASAA Associate of the Society of Incorporated Accountants and Auditors
ASC Army Service Corps
ASCAP American Society of Composers, Authors and Publishers
ASD Armament Supply Department
ASEAN Association of South East Asian Nations
ASF Associate of the Institute of Shipping and Forwarding Agents
A&SH Argyll and Sutherland Highlanders
ASIA Associate, Society of Investment Analysts
ASIAD Associate, Society of Industrial Artists and Designers
ASLIB Association of Special Libraries and Information Bureaux
ASME American Society of Mechanical Engineers; Association for Study of Medical Education
ASO Air Staff Officer
assas assassinated
Assoc Association; Associate; Associated
AInstTport Associate of the Institute of Transport
Asst Assistant
Assur Assurance
ASTMS Association of Scientific, Technical and Managerial Staff (now MSF)
ASVO Association of State Veterinary Officers
ATA Air Transport Auxiliary
ATAF Allied Tactical Air Force
ATC Air Training Corps
ATD Art Teachers' Diploma
ATI Associate, Textile Institute
ATII Associate Member, Institute of Taxation
ATO Ammunitions Technical Officer
ATS Auxiliary Territorial Service
AUEW Amalgamated Union of Engineering Workers
Aust Australian, Australia
AUT Association of University Teachers
Authy Authority
Aux Auxiliary
Ave Avenue
AVR Army Volunteer Reserve
AWeldI Associate of the Welding Institute
AWRE Atomic Weapons Research Establishment
AWS Graduate of Air Warfare Course

B

b Born
BA Bachelor of Arts; British Airways
BAAB British Amateur Athletics Board
BAAL British Association for Applied Linguistics
BAAS British Association for the Advancement of Science
BAC British Aircraft Corporation
BADA British Antique Dealers Association
BAFO British Air Forces Occupation
BAFSEA British Air Forces South East Asia
BAFTA British Academy of Film and Television Arts
BAI Baccalarius in Arte Ingeniaria
BAIE British Association of Industrial Editors
BALPA British Airline Pilots Association
BAO Bachelor of Obstetrics
BAOL British Association of Otolaryngologists
BAOMS British Association of Oral and Maxillo-Facial Surgeons
BAOR British Army of the Rhine
BARB Broadcasters' Audience Research Board
BARC British Automobile Racing Club
BArch Bachelor of Architecture
BARR British Association of Rheumatology Rehabilitation (now BSR)
Barr Barrister
Bart's St Bartholomew's Hospital
BAS Bachelor in Agricultural Science
BASc Bachelor of Applied Science
BASCA British Academy of Songwriters, Composers and Authors
Batty Battery
BAUA Business Aviation Users Association
BBA British Banker's Association; Bachelor of Business Administration
BBC British Broadcasting Corporation
BBS Bachelor of Business Studies
BC British Columbia
BCE Bachelor of Civil Engineering
BCh or BChir Bachelor of Surgery
BCL Bachelor in Civil Law
BCOF British Commonwealth Occupation Force in Japan
BCom Bachelor of Commerce
BCS British Computer Society; Bengal Civil Service
BCU British Canoeing Union
BD Bachelor in Divinity
Bd Board
BDA British Dental Association
Bdcast(ing) Broadcast(ing)
Bde Brigade
BDF Barking Dog of Fulham
BDMA British Direct Marketing Association
BDS Bachelor of Dental Surgery
BE Bachelor of Engineering
BEA British European Airways
BEAMA Federation of British Electrotechnical and Allied Manufacturers Association
BEcon Bachelor of Economics
BEd Bachelor of Education
BEE Bachelor of Electrical Engineering
BEF British Expeditionary Force
BEM British Empire Medal
BEng Bachelor of Engineering
BETRO British Export Trade Organisation
BFI British Film Institute
BFME British Forces Middle East
BFPO British Forces Post Office
BFSS British Field Sports Society
BGGS Brigadier-General, General Staff
BGS Brigadier, General Staff
BHRCA British Hotel, Restaurant and Catering Association
BHS British Horse Society
BHy Bachelor of Hygiene
BIBA British Insurance Brokers Association
BICC British Insulated Callender's Cables
BIEE British Institute of Energy Economics
BIM British Institute of Management
BINDT British Institute of Non-destructive Testing
BIPP British Institute of Professional Photography
BIR British Institute of Radiology
BJSM British Joint Service Mission
BL Bachelor of Law; British Leyland
BLA British Army of Liberation
Bldgs Buildings
BLESMA British Limbless Ex-servicemens' Association
BLitt Bachelor of Letters

BM	Bachelor of Medicine (Oxford); Brigade Major
BMA	British Medical Association
BMedSci	Bachelor of Medical Science
BMet	Bachelor of Metallurgy
BMH	British Military Hospital
BMus	Bachelor of Music
Bn	Battalion
BNAF	British North Africa Force
BNC	Brasenose (College)
BNES	British Nuclear Energy Society
BNF	British Nuclear Fuels
BNFL	British Nuclear Fuels Ltd
BNMS	British Nuclear Medicine Society
BNSC	British National Space Centre
BNurs	Bachelor of Nursing
BOA	British Olympic Association
BOAC	British Overseas Airways Corporation
BOT	Board of Trade
BOTB	British Overseas Trade Board
BP	British Petroleum
BPA	British Paediatric Association
BPharm	Bachelor of Pharmacy
BPI	British Phonographic Industry
BPhil	Bachelor of Philosophy
BPIF	British Printing Industries Federation
Br	British
BR	British Railways
BRA	British Rheumatism and Arthiritis Association
BRCS	British Red Cross Society
BRDC	British Racing Drivers' Club
Brig	Brigadier
BRNC	Brittania Royal Naval College
bro	brother
BS	Bachelor of Surgery; Bachelor of Science (US)
BSAC	British Sub Aqua Club
BSACI	British Society for Allergy and Clinical Immunology
BSc	Bachelor of Science
BSC	British Steel Corporation; British Society of Cinematographers
BSI	British Standards Institution; British Society for Immunology
BSR	British Society of Rheumatology
BSS	Bachelor of Social Sciences (USA)
Bt	Baronet
BT	British Telecom
BTA	British Troops in Austria; British Tourist Authority; British Theatre Association
Bt-Col	Brevet-Colonel
Btcy	Baronetcy
BTEC	Business and Technicians Education Council
Btss	Baronetess
BUPA	British United Provident Association
BVA	British Veterinary Association
BVMS	Bachelor of Veterinary Medicine and Surgery
BVSc	Bachelor of Veterinary Science
BWI	British West Indies
BWM	British War Medal
BWS	Member of the British Watercolour Society

C

c	children
ca	circa
CAABU	Council for the Advancement of Arab and British Understanding
C	Conservative
CA	Chartered Accountant; County Alderman
CAA	Civil Aviation Authority
CAB	Citizens Advice Bureau
CACTM	Central Advisory Council of Training for the Ministry
Calif	California
CAMC	Canadian Army Medical Corps
CAMRA	Campaign for Real Ale
Cantab	Of Cambridge University
Capt	Captain
CARE	Cottage and Rural Enterprises
CAS	Chief of Air Staff
CB	Companion of the Order of the Bath
CBA	Council for British Archaeology
CBC	County Borough Council
CBE	Commander of the Order of the British Empire
CBI	Confederation of British Industry
CBIM	Companion, British Institute of Management
CBiol	Chartered Biologist
CBIREE	Companion, British Institute of Radio and Electronic Engineers
CC	County Council: Companion of the Order of Canada; Cricket Club
CCA	County Councils' Association
CCAB	Consultative Committee of Accounting Bodies
CCBE	Consultative Council of European Bars and Law Societies (Commission Consultative des Barreaux de la Communant Européene)
CCC	Corpus Christi College; County Cricket Club
CCF	Combined Cadet Force
CCG(BE)	Control Commission, Germany (British Element)
CChem	Chartered Chemist
CCHMS	Central Committee for Hospital and Medical Services
CCIBS	Companion, Chartered Institute of Building Services
CCnclIr	County Councillor
CCO	Conservative Central Office
CCPR	Central Council of Physical Recreation
CCRE	Commander Corps of Royal Engineers
CCRA	Commander Corps, Royal Artillery
CCRSigs	Commander Corps of Royal Signals
CCS	Casualty Clearing Station
CCSC	Central Consultants and Specialists Committee
CD	Canadian Forces Decoration
CDipAF	Certified Diploma in Accounting and Finance
Cdr	Commander
Cdre	Commodore
CDS	Chief of Defence Staff
CE	Chief Engineer
CEDEP	Centre Européen d'Education Permanente
CEFIC	Counseil Européen des Federations de L'Industrie Chimique
CEGB	Central Electricity Generating Board
CEI	Council of Engineering Institutions
CEng	Chartered Engineer
CERN	Conseil (now Organisation) Européenne pour la Recherche Nucléaire
CertEd	Certificate of Education
CEST	Council for the Exploitation of Science and Technology
CF	Chaplain to the Forces
CFBOA	Companion Fellow, British Orthopaedic Association
CFM	Canadian Forces Medal
CFS	Central Flying School
CGA	Country Gentleman's Association
CGIA	City and Guilds of London Insignia Awards Association
CGLI	City and Guilds of the London Institute
CGS	Chief of the General Staff
CH	Companion of Honour
ChB	Bachelor of Surgery
CHC	Community Health Council
ChCh	Christ Church (Oxford)
Chem	Chemical
Chev	Chevalier
Chllr	Chancellor
Chm	Chairman
ChM	Mastery of Surgery
ChStJ	Chaplain of the Order of St John of Jerusalem
CI	Order of the Crown of India; Channel Islands
CIArb	Chartered Institute of Arbitrators
CIBS	Chartered Institute of Building Services
CIBSE	Chartered Institution of Building Services Engineers
CICeram	Companion, Institute of Ceramics
CICHE	Committee for International Co-operation in Higher Education
CID	Criminal Investigation Department
CIE	Companion of the Order of the Indian Empire
CIEE	Companion, Institution of Electrical Engineers
CIGS	Chief of the Imperial General Staff
CIM	Chartered Institute of Marketing
CIMA	Chartered Institute of Management Accountants
CIMarE	Companion of the Institute of Marine Engineers
CIMechE	Companion of the Institution of Mechanical Engineers
C-in-C	Commander-in-Chief
CIPFA	Chartered Institute of Public Finance and Accountancy
CIPM	Companion, Institute of Personnel Managers
CIRIA	Construction Industry Research and Information Association
CIT	Chartered Institute of Transport
CLA	Country Landowners' Association
CLitt	Companion of the Royal Society of Literature
CLP	Constituency Labour Party
CM	Member of the Order of Canada; Master of Surgery
Cmd	Commanded; command
Cmdg	Commanding
Cmdt	Commandant
CMF	Commonwealth Military Forces; Central Mediterranean Force
CMG	Companion of the Order of St Michael and St George
Cmmn	Commission
cmmnd	Commissioned
Cmmr	Commissioner
CMO	Chief Medical Officer
CMP	Corps of Military Police
CMS	Church Missionary Society
CNAA	Council for National Academic Awards
Cncl	Council
Cncllr	Councillor
CND	Campaign for Nuclear Disarmament
CNRS	Centre Nationale du Recherche Scientifique
Cnsllr	Counsellor
CO	Commanding Officer
Co	Company; County
Co L	Coalition Liberal
COD	Communications and Operations Department (FO)
C of C	Chamber of Commerce
C of E	Church of England
COGS	Chief of General Staff
COHSE	Confederation of Health Service Employees
COI	Central Office of Information
Col	Colonel
Coll	College
COMMET	Council of Mechanical and Metal Trade Associations

Comp Comprehensive
Conf Conference
Confedn Confederation
Conn Connecticut
Cons Conservative
Conslt Consultant
consltg consulting
contrib Contributor, contributed, contribution
Co-op Co-Operative
Corp Corporation, corporate
Corpl Corporal
Corr Correspondent
COS Chief of Staff
COSIRA Council for Smaller Industries in Rural Areas
cous cousin
CPA Commonwealth Parliamentary Association
CPC Conservative Political Centre
CPhys Chartered Physicist
CPM Colonial Police Medal
CPRE Council for the Protection of Rural England
CPRS Central Policy Review Staff
CPS Canadian Pacific Steamships
CPSA Civil and Public Services Association
CPsychol Chartered Psychologist
CPU Commonwealth Press Union
cr created
CRA Commander Royal Artillery
CRAC Careers Research and Advisory Council
CRAeS Companion, Royal Aeronautical Society
CRC Community Relations Commission
CRD Conservative Research Department
CRE Commanding Royal Engineers
CRMP Corps of Royal Military Police
CRO Commonwealth Relations Office
CS Clerk to the Signet
CSA Commonwealth Society of Artists; Chair Schools Association
CSD Chartered Society of Designers
CSERB Computer Systems and Electronics Requirements Board
CSI Companion of the Order of the Star of India; Council for the Securities Industries
CSIR Council for Scientific and Industrial Research
CSIRO Commonwealth Scientific and Industrial Research Organisation
CSO Chief Signal Officer; Chief Staff Officer; Chief Scientific Officer
CStJ Commander of the Order of St John of Jerusalem
CSTI Council of Science and Technology Institutes
CSV Community Service Volunteers
Ct Court
Ctee Committee
CText Chartered Textile Technologist
CUF Common Universities Fund
CUP Cambridge University Press
CVCP Committee of Vice-Chancellors and Principals of the UK
CVO Commander of the Royal Victorian Order
CWA Crime Writers' Association
Cwlth Commonwealth

D

d Died, death
da Daughter
DA Diploma in Anaesthetics; Diploma in Art
DA & QMG Deputy-Adjutant and Quartermaster-General
DAA & QMG Deputy Assistant-Adjutant and Quartermaster-General
DAAG Deputy-Assistant-Adjutant-General
D & AD Designers & Art Directors
DACG Deputy Assistant Chaplain General
DADGMS Deputy Assistant Director General of Medical Services
DADMS Deputy Assistant Director Medical Services
DADR Deputy Assistant Director of Remounts
DAD Deputy-Assistant Director
DADST Deputy Assistant Director of Supplies and Transport
DAG Deputy-Adjutant-General
DAMS Deputy-Assistant Military Secretary
DAPM Deputy Assistant Provost Marshall
DAPS Director of Army Postal Services
DAQMG Deputy-Assistant-Quartermaster-General
DBA Doctor of Business Administration
DBE Dame Commander of the British Empire
DC District Council; Doctor in Chiropractic
DCAS Deputy Chief of Air Staff
DCB Dame Commander Order of the Bath
DCGS Deputy Chief of General Staff
DCH Diploma in Child Health
DCL Doctor of Civil Law
DCLI Duke of Cornwall's Light Infantry
DCM Distinguished Conduct Medal
DCMG Dame Commander Order of St Michael and St George
DCMS Deputy Commissioner Medical Services
DCSO Deputy Chief Scientific Officer
DCVO Dame Commander Royal Victorian Order
DD Doctor in Divinity
DDDS Deputy Director of Dental Services
DDME Deputy Director Mechanical Engineering
DDMS Deputy Director of Medical Services
DDO Diploma in Dental Orthopaedics
DDOS Deputy Director of Ordnance Services
DDPS Deputy Director of Personal Services
DDR Deputy Director of Remounts
DDS Doctor of Dental Surgery; Director of Dental Services
DDS & T Deputy Director Supplies and Transport
DDSD Deputy Director of Staff Duties
DDVS Deputy-Director of Veterinary Services
DDWE & M Deputy Director of Works, Electrical and Mechanical
decd deceased
DEd Doctor of Education
Def Defence
Del Delegate
Delgn Delegation
DEM Diploma in Education Management
DEME Director of Electrical and Mechanical Engineering
DEng Doctor of Engineering
Dep Deputy
Dep-Adv-Gen Deputy-Advocate-General
Dep-Sec Deputy Secretary
Dept Department
DES Department of Education and Science
DèsL Docteur ès Lettres
DesRCA Designer of the Royal College of Art
Devpt Development
DFA Doctor of Fine Arts
DFC Distinguished Flying Cross
DFH Diploma of the Faraday House
DG Director General
DGAMS Director-General of Army Medical Services
DGCStJ Dame Grand Cross of the Order of St John of Jerusalem
DGMS Director-General of Medical Services
DGStJ Dame of Grace of the Order of St John of Jerusalem
DH Doctor of Humanities
DHA District Health Authority
DHMSA Diploma in the History of Medicine (Society of Apothecaries)
DHQ District Headquarters
DHSS Department of Health and Social Security
DHy Doctor of Hygiene
DIC Diploma of the Imperial College
DIH Diploma in Industrial Health
Dio Diocese
Dip Diploma; Diplomatic
DipAD Diploma in Arts and Design
DipAg Diploma in Agriculture
DipArch Diploma in Architecture
DipAvMed Diploma in Aviation Medicine
DipBA Diploma in Business Administration
DipCAM Diploma in Communication, Advertising and Marketing of the CAM Foundation
DipCD Diploma in Civic Design
DipEd Diploma in Education
DipHA Diploma in Hospital Administration
DipHSM Diploma in Health Services Management
DipOR Diploma in Operations Research
DipOrthMed Diploma in Orthopaedic Medicine
DipTP Diploma in Town Planning
Dir Director
dis dissolved (marriage)
Dist District
Div Division
Divnl Divisional
DJAG Deputy Judge Advocate General
DJStJ Dame of Justice of the Order of St John of Jerusalem
DK Most Esteemed Family Order of Brunei
DL Deputy-Lieutenant for the County of
DLC Diploma Loughborough College
DLI Durham Light Infantry
DLitt Doctor of Letters
DLit Doctor of Literature
DLO Diploma in Larynology and Otology
DM Doctor of Medicine
DMD Doctor in Dental Medicine
DME Director of Mechanical Engineering
DMGO Divisional Machine Gun Officer
DMI Director Military Intelligence
DMJ Diploma in Medical Jurisprudence
DMO & I Director Military Operations and Intelligence
DMRD Diploma in Medical Radiological Diagnosis
DMRE Diploma in Medical Radiology and Electrology
DMRT Diploma in Medical Radiotherapy
DMS Director of Medical Services; Diploma in Management Studies
DMSI Director of Management and Support Intelligence
DMT Director of Military Training
DMus Doctor of Music (Oxford)
DNI Director of Naval Intelligence
DNO Director of Naval Ordnance
DO Diploma in Ophthalmology; Divisional Officer; Diploma in Osteopathy

DOAE Defence Operational Analysis Establishment
DObstRCOG Diploma Royal College of Obstetricians and Gynaecologists
DOC District Officer Commanding
DOE Department of Environment
DOI Department of Industry
DOMS Diploma in Ophthalmic Medicine
DOR Director of Operational Requirements
DOS Director of Ordnance Services
DPA Diploma in Public Administration
DPCP Department of Prices and Consumer Protection
DPH Diploma in Public Health
DPhil Doctor of Philosophy
DPL Director of Pioneers and Labour
DPM Diploma in Psychological Medicine
DPMO Deputy Principal Medical Officer
DPR Director of Public Relations
DPS Director of Personal Services
DQMG Deputy Quartermaster-General
DRC Diploma of the Royal College of Science and Technology, Glasgow
DRD Diploma in Restorative Dentistry
DRVO Deputy Regional Veterinary Officer
DS Directing Staff
DS & T Director of Supplies and Transport
DSA Diploma in Social Administration
DSAC Defence Scientific Advisory Committee
DSAO Diplomatic Service Administration Office
DSC Distinguished Service Cross
DSc Doctor of Science
DSCHE Diploma of the Scottish Council for Health Education
DSD Director of Staff Duties
DSIR Department of Scientific and Industrial Research
DSM Distinguished Service Medal (United States of America)
DSO Companion of the Distinguished Service Order
dsp *decessit sine prole* (died without issue)
DSP Docteur en Sciences Politiques (Montreal)
DSS Department of Social Security
DSSC Doctor of Social Science
DStJ Dame of Grace of the Order of St John of Jerusalem
DS & T Director of Supplies and Transport
DTech Doctor of Technology
DTh Doctor of Theology
DTI Dept of Trade and Industry
DTM & H Diploma in Tropical Medicine and Hygiene
DUniv Doctor of the University
DVFS Director, Veterinary Field Services
DVM Doctor of Veterinary Medicine
DVO Divisional Veterinary Officer
DVS Director of Veterinary Services
DVSM Diploma of Veterinary State Medicine

E

E East; Earl; England
EASA Ecclesiastical Architects and Surveyors Association
EBU European Broadcasting Union
EC European Commission
ECGD Export Credit Guarantee Department
Econ Economic
Ed Editor; edited
ED Efficiency Decoration; European Democratic (Group)
EDC Economic Development Committee
EDG European Democratic Group (UK Conservative Group, European Parliament)
edn edition
educnl educational
Educn education
EETPU Electrical, Electronic, Telecommunication and Plumbing Union
EFTA European Free Trade Association
EIU Economist Intelligence Unit
eld eldest
EMBL European Molecular Biology Laboratory
EMBO European Molecular Biology Organisation
EMS Emergency Medical Service
Eng English; England
Engr Engineer
Engrg Engineering
ENO English National Opera
ENSA Entertainments National Services Association
ENT Ear, Nose and Throat
er elder
ERD Emergency Reserve Decoration
ESRC Economic and Social Research Council
ESRO European Space Research Organisation
Estab Established; establishment
ESU English-Speaking Union
Eur Ing European Engineer
Euro European
Exec Executive
Expdn Expedition
Ext Extinct; extension

F

f father
FA Football Association
FAA Fellow of the Australian Academy of Science
FAAAS Fellow, American Academy of Arts & Sciences
FAAP Fellow, American Academy of Paediatrics
FAAV Fellow, Central Association of Agricultural Valuers
FACC Fellow, American College of Cardiology
FACCA Fellow of the Association of Certified and Corporate Accountants
FACD Fellow, American College of Dentristry
FACE Fellow, Australian College of Education
FACOG Fellow, American College of Obstetricians and Gynaecologists
FACP Fellow, American College of Physicians
FACS Fellow, American College of Surgeons
FACVT Fellow, American College of Veterinary Toxicology
FAES Fellow of the Audio Engineering Society
FAI Fellow of the Chartered Auctioneers' and Estate Agents' Institute
FAIA Fellow, American Institute of Architects
FAIM Fellow of the Australian Institute of Management
FAIP Fellow, of the Australian Institute of Physics
FAIRE Fellow of the Australian Institute of Radio Engineers
FALPA Fellow of the Incorporated Auctioneers and Land Property Agents
FAMEME Fellow, Association of Mining, Electrical and Mechanical Engineers
FAMI Fellow of the Australian Marketing Institute
FAMS Fellow of the Ancient Monuments Society
FANY First Aid Nursing Yeomanry
FAO Food and Agricultural Organisation
FAPM Fellow of the Association of Project Managers
FARELF Far East Land Forces
FAS Fellow, Antiquarian Society
FASA Fellow of the Australian Society of Accountants
FASCE Fellow of the American Society of Civil Engineers
FBA Fellow of the British Academy
FBCO Fellow of British College of Opticians
FBCS Fellow, British Computer Society
FBHI Fellow of the British Horological Institute
FBI Federation of British Industries
FBIBA Fellow of the British Insurance Brokers Association
FBIEE Fellow of the British Institute of Energy Economists
FBIM Fellow of the British Institute of Management
FBIPP Fellow of the British Institute of Professional Photographers
FBIS Fellow of the British Interplanetary Society
FBKSTS Fellow, British Kinematograph, Sound and Television Society
FBOA Fellow of the British Optical Association; Fellow, British Orthopaedic Association
FBPsS Fellow, British Psychological Society
FBSI Fellow of the Boot and Shoe Industry
FC Football Club
FCA Fellow of the Institute of Chartered Accountants
FCAI Fellow of the Canadian Aeronautical Institute
FCAM Fellow, Communications Advertising & Marketing Educational Foundation
FCAnaes Fellow, College of Anaesthetists
FCBSI Fellow of the Chartered Building Societies Institute
FCCA Fellow of the Association of Certified and Corporate Accountants
FCCS Fellow of the Corporation of Certified Secretaries
FCDA Fellow of the Company Directors Association of Australia
FCEC Federation of Civil Engineering Contractors
FCFA Fellow of the Cookery and Food Association
FCFI Fellow, Clothing and Footwear Institute
FCGI Fellow, City and Guilds of London Institute
FCIA Fellow, Corporation of Insurance Agents
FCIArb Fellow, Chartered Institute of Arbitrators
FCIB Fellow of the Corporation of Insurance Brokers; Fellow, Chartered Institute of Bankers
FCIBS Fellow, Chartered Institution of Building Services
FCIBSE Fellow, Chartered Institution of Building Service Engineers
FCII Fellow of the Chartered Insurance Institute
FCIM Fellow, Chartered Institute of Marketing
FCIOB Fellow, Chartered Institute of Building
FCIS Fellow of the Chartered Institute of Secretaries
FCIT Fellow of the Chartered Institute of Transport
FCMA Fellow, Institute of Cost and Management Accountants
FCO Foreign and Commonwealth Office
FCOG Fellow of the College of Obstetrics and Gynaecology
FCommA Fellow of the Society of Commercial Accountants
FCOphth Fellow of the College of Ophthalmology
FCP Fellow, College of Preceptors
FCPA Fellow, Australian Society of Certified Practising Accountants
FCPS Fellow of the College of Physicians and Surgeons
FCS Fellow of the Chemical Society
FCSD Fellow, Chartered Society of Designers
FCT Fellow of the Institute of Corporate Treasurers
FCWA Fellow of the Institute of Cost and Works Accountants
FDI Féderation Dentaire Internationale
FDR Federalische Deutsche Republik
FDS Fellow in Dental Surgery
FDSRCS Fellow in Dental Surgery Royal College of Surgeons of England
FEAF Far East Air Force
Fed Federal
Fedn Federation
FEIS Fellow of the Educational Institute of Scotland
Fell Fellow

FEng	Fellow, Fellowship of Engineering
FES	Fellow of the Entomological Society
FFA	Fellow of the Faculty of Actuaries (Scotland)
FFARACS	Fellow, Faculty of Anaesthetists Royal Australasian College of Surgeons
FFARCS	Fellow of the Faculty of Anaesthetists, Royal College of Surgeons
FFARCSI	Fellow, Faculty of Anaesthetists Royal College of Surgeons of Ireland
FFAS	Fellow of the Faculty of Architects and Surveyors
FFB	Fellow of the Faculty of Building
FFCM	Fellow, Faculty of Community Medicine (now FFPHM)
FFDRCSI	Fellow, Faculty of Dentistry, Royal College of Surgeons in Ireland
FFHom	Fellow, Faculty of Homeopathy
FFOM	Fellow, Faculty of Occupational Medicine
FFPHM	Fellow, Faculty of Public Health Medicine
FFPM	Fellow, Faculty of Pharmaceutical Medicine
FFR	Fellow, of the Faculty of Radiologists
FGA	Fellow of the Gemmological Association
FGS	Fellow of the Geological Society
FGSM	Fellow, Guildhall School of Music
FHA	Fellow, Institute of Health Service Administrators
FHCIMA	Fellow of the Hotel Catering and Institutional Management Association
FHKIE	Fellow, Hong Kong Institute of Engineers
FHSM	Fellow, Institute of Health Service Managers
FIA	Fellow, Institute of Actuaries; Fédération Internationale de L'Automobile
FIAAS	Fellow Architect Member of the Incorporated Association of Architects and Surveyors
FIAC	Fellow, Institute of Company Accountants
FIAeS	Fellow of the Institute of Aeronautical Sciences
FIAgrE	Fellow, Institution of Agricultural Engineers
FIAL	Fellow, International Institute of Arts and Letters
FIAM	Fellow, International Academy of Management
FIArb	Fellow of the Institute of Arbitration
FIAS	Fellow, Institute of Aeronautical Sciences (US)
FIB	Fellow of the Institute of Bankers (now FCIB)
FIBC	Fellow, Institute of Business Counsellors
FIBiol	Fellow, Institute of Biology
FIBM	Fellow, Institute of Builders' Merchants
FIBScot	Fellow of the Institute of Bankers in Scotland
FICA	Fellow of the Institute of Chartered Accountants in England and Wales (now FCA)
FICAS	Fellow, Institute of Chartered Accountants in Scotland
FICD	Fellow of the Institute of Civil Defence
FICE	Fellow of the Institution of Civil Engineers
FICeram	Fellow, Institute of Ceramics
FICFor	Fellow, Institute of Chartered Foresters
FIChemE	Fellow of the Institution of Chemical Engineers
FICM	Fellow, Institute of Credit Management
FICMA	Fellow, Institute of Cost and Management Accountants
FICS	Fellow of the Institute of Chartered Shipbrokers
FICSA	Fellow of the Institute of Chartered Secretaries and Administrators
FIDPM	Fellow, Institute of Data Processing Management
FIE(Aust)	Fellow, Institution of Engineers, Australia
FIED	Fellow, Institution of Engineering Design
FIEE	Fellow of the Institution of Electrical Engineers
FIEEE	Fellow, Institution of Electrical and Electronics Engineers (New York)
FIERE	Fellow of the Institution of Electronics and Radio Engineers
FIEx	Fellow, Institute of Export
FIFM	Fellow, Institute of Fisheries Management
FIFor	Fellow, Institute of Forestry
FIFST	Fellow of Food Science and Technology
FIGD	Fellow, Institute of Grocery Distribution
FIGE	Fellow, Institute of Gas Engineers
FIGeol	Fellow, Institute of Geology
FIHE	Fellow, Institute of Health Education
FIHort	Fellow of the Institute of Horticulture
FIHospE	Fellow, Institute of Hospital Engineering
FIHT	Fellow, Institute of Highways and Transportation
FIHVE	Fellow, Institution of Heating and Ventilating Engineers
FIIA	Fellow, Institute of Internal Auditors
FIIM	Fellow, Institute of Industrial Managers
FIInfSc	Fellow, Institute of Information Scientists
FIInst	Fellow of the Imperial Institute
FIL	Fellow of the Institute of Linguists
FILA	Fellow of the Institute of Landscape Architects
FILDM	Fellow, Institute of Logistics and Distribution Management
FilDr	Doctor of Philosophy
FIM	Fellow, Institute of Metals (formerly Institution of Metallurgists)
FIMA	Fellow of the Institute of Mathematics and its Applications
FIMarE	Fellow, Institute of Marine Engineers
FIMBRA	Financial Intermediaries, Managers and Brokers Regulatory Association
FIMC	Fellow, Institute of Management Consultants
FIMechE	Fellow of the Institution of Mechanical Engineers
FIMF	Fellow, Institute of Metal Finishing
FIMFT	Fellow, Institute of Maxillo-Facial Technology
FIMH	Fellow, Institute of Materials Handling; Fellow, Institute of Military History
FIMI	Fellow, Institute of Motor Industry
FIMinE	Fellow, Institute of Mining Engineers
FIMIT	Fellow, Institute of Musical Instrument Technology
FIMLS	Fellow, Institute of Medical and Laboratory Sciences
FIMM	Fellow, Institution of Mining and Metallurgy
FIMT	Fellow of the Institute of the Motor Trade
FIMTA	Fellow of the Institute of Municipal Treasurers & Accountants
Fin	Finance; financial
FInstAA	Fellow of the Institute of Administrative Accountants
FInstAM	Fellow, Institute of Administrative Management
FInstCES	Fellow of the Institution of Civil Engineering Surveyors
FInstCS	Fellow, Institute of Chartered Secretaries
FInstD	Fellow, Institute of Directors
FInstF	Fellow of Institute of Fuel
FinstFF	Fellow, Institute of Freight Forwarders
FInst GasE	Fellow, Institution of Gas Engineers
FInstGeol	Fellow, Institute of Geologists
FInstHE	Fellow, Institution of Highway Engineers
FInstLEx	Fellow, Institute of Legal Executives
FInstM	Fellow, Institute of Marketing (now FCIM)
FInstMC	Fellow, Institute of Measurement and Control
FInstMSM	Fellow of the Institute of Marketing and Sales Management
FInstP	Fellow of the Institute of Physics
FInstPet	Fellow of the Institute of Petroleum
FInstPI	Fellow, Institute Patentees (Incorporated)
FInstPS	Fellow, Institute of Purchasing and Supply
FInstSMM	Fellow, Institute of Sales and Marketing Management
FINucE	Fellow of the Institute of Nuclear Engineers
FIOA	Fellow, Institute of Acoustics
FIOB	Fellow, Institute of Building
FIOP	Fellow of the Institute of Printing
FIOSc	Fellow of the Institute of Optical Science
FIP	Fellow, Australian Institute of Petroleum
FIPA	Fellow of the Institute of Public Administration; Fellow of the Institute of Practitioners in Advertising; Fellow, Insolvency Practitioners' Association
FIPHE	Fellow of the Institution of Public Health Engineers
FIPI	Fellow, Institute of Professional Investigators
FIPlantE	Fellow, Institute of Plant Engineers
FIPM	Fellow, Institute of Personnel Management
FIPR	Fellow of the Institute of Public Relations
FIProdE	Fellow of the Institute of Production Engineers
FIPS	Fellow, Institute of Purchasing and Supply
FIQ	Fellow, Institute of Quarrying
FIQA	Fellow, Institute of Quality Assurance
FIRE	Fellow of the Institution of Radio Engineers
FIRI	Fellow of the Institution of the Rubber Industry
FIS	Fellow, Institute of Stationers
FISA	Fédération Internationale Société d'Aviron
FISE	Fellow of the Institute of Sanitary Engineers
FISTD	Fellow, Imperial Society of Teachers of Dancing
FIStructE	Fellow, Institution of Structural Engineers
FITA	Fellow, International Archery Federation
FITD	Fellow, Institute of Training and Development
FIWEM	Fellow, Institution of Water and Environmental Management
FIWES	Fellow, Institute of Water Engineers and Scientists
FIWSc	Fellow, Institute of Wood Science
FJI	Fellow, Institute of Journalists
FKC	Fellow, King's College London
FLA	Fellow, Library Association
FLAS	Fellow, Land Agents Society
FLCM	Fellow, London College of Music
FLI	Fellow, Landscape Institute
FLIA	Fellow, Life Assurance Association
FLS	Fellow, Linnean Society
Flt	Flight
Flt Lt	Flight Lieutenant
FMA	Fellow of the Museums' Association
FMS	Fellow, Institute of Management Services; Fellow, Institute of Medical Society; Fellow, Manorial Society
FNAEA	Fellow, National Association of Estate Agents
Fndn	Foundation
Fndr	Founder
FNI	Fellow, Nautical Institute
FNIAB	Fellow, National Institute of Agricultural Botany
FO	Foreign Office
FOR	Fellowship of Operational Research
FPA	Family Practitioners' Association
FPC	Family Practitioner Committee
FPCA	Fellow of Practising and Commercial Accountants
FPCS	Fellow, Property Consultants' Society
FPEA	Fellow, Physical Education Association
FPhS(Eng)	Fellow, Philosophical Society of England
FPMI	Fellow, Pensions Management Institute
FPRI	Fellow, Plastics and Rubber Institute
FPS	Fellow of Philological Society of Great Britain
FRACDS	Fellow, Royal Australian College of Dental Surgeons
FRACP	Fellow of the Royal Australasian College of Physicians
FRACR	Fellow, Royal Australian College of Radiologists
FRACS	Fellow of the Royal Australasian College of Surgeons
FRAeS	Fellow, Royal Aeronautical Society
FRAgS	Fellow, Royal Agricultural Societies
FRAI	Fellow of the Royal Anthropological Institute
FRAIC	Fellow, Royal Architectural Institute of Canada
FRAM	Fellow of the Royal Academy of Music
FRAS	Fellow of the Royal Astronomical Society; Fellow, Royal Asiatic Society

FRBS Fellow of the Royal Botanic Society; Fellow of the Royal Society of British Sculptors
FRCAA Fellow of the Royal Cambrian Academy of Art
FRCGP Fellow, Royal College of General Practitioners
FRCM Fellow of the Royal College of Music
FRCN Fellow, Royal College of Nursing
FRCO Fellow of the Royal College of Organists
FRCOG Fellow of the Royal College of Obstetricians and Gynaecologists
FRCP Fellow of the Royal College of Physicians
FRCPA Fellow, Royal College of Pathologists of Australia
FRCPath Fellow, Royal College of Pathologists
FRCPE Fellow of the Royal College of Physicians of Edinburgh
FRCPG Fellow, Royal College of Physicians, Glasgow
FRCPI Fellow, Royal College of Physicians in Ireland
FRCPS Fellow of the Royal College of Physicians and Surgeons (Glasgow)
FRCPsych Fellow, Royal College of Psychiatrists
FRCR Fellow, Royal College of Radiologists
FRCS Fellow of the Royal College of Surgeons; Fellow of the Royal C'wlth Society (formerly Royal Empire Soc)
FRCSEd Fellow, Royal College of Surgeons Edinburgh
FRCSGlas Fellow, Royal College of Surgeons, Glasgow
FRCSI Fellow, Royal College of Surgeons in Ireland
FRCVS Fellow, Royal College of Veterinary Surgeons
FREconS Fellow of the Royal Economic Society
FREntS Fellow of the Royal Entomological Society
FRG Federal Republic of Germany
FRGS Fellow of the Royal Geographical Society
FRHistS Fellow of the Royal Historical Society
FRHS Fellow of the Royal Horticultural Society
FRIA Fellow, Royal Institute of Arbitrators
FRIAS Fellow of the Royal Incorporation of Architects in Scotland
FRIBA Fellow of the Royal Institute of British Architects
FRIC Fellow of the Royal Institute of Chemistry
FRICS Fellow of the Royal Institution of Chartered Surveyors
FRIN Fellow of the Royal Institute of Navigation
FRINA Fellow of the Royal Institution of Naval Architects
FRIPH Fellow of the Royal Institute of Public Health
FRMetS Fellow of the Royal Meteorological Society
FRMIA Fellow of the Retail Management Institute of Australia
FRMS Fellow of the Royal Microscopical Society
FRNCM Fellow, Royal Northern College of Music
FRNS Fellow of the Royal Numismatic Society
FRPharmS Fellow, Royal Pharmaceutical Society
FRPI Fellow, Institute of Rubber and Plastics Industry
FRPS Fellow of the Royal Photographic Society
FRPSL Fellow of the Royal Philatelic Society, London
FRS Fellow of the Royal Society
FRSA Fellow of the Royal Society of Arts
FRSAIre Fellow of the Royal Society of Antiquaries of Ireland
FRSAMD Fellow, Royal Scottish Academy of Music and Drama
FRSC Fellow of the Royal Society of Canada; Fellow, Royal Society of Chemistry
FRSCM Fellow, Royal School of Church Music
FRSE Fellow of the Royal Society of Edinburgh
FRSGS Fellow of the Royal Scottish Geographical Society
FRSH Fellow of the Royal Society of Health
FRSL Fellow of the Royal Society of Literature
FRSM Fellow of the Royal Society of Medicine
FRSNZ Fellow, Royal Society of New Zealand
FRSS Fellow, Royal Statistical Society
FRSTM & H Fellow, Royal Society of Tropical Medicine and Health
FRTPI Fellow, Royal Town Planning Institute
FRTS Fellow, Royal Television Society
FRVA Fellow of the Rating and Valuation Association
FRZS Scot Fellow of the Royal Zoological Society of Scotland
FSA Fellow of the Society of Antiquaries
FSAA Fellow of the Society of Incorporated Accountants and Auditors
FSAE Fellow, Society of Arts Education
FSAS Fellow, Society of Antiquaries of Scotland
FSCA Fellow, Society of Company and Commercial Artists
FSE Fellow of Society of Engineers
FSF Fellow of the Institute of Shipping and Forwarding Agents
FSG Fellow of the Society of Genealogists
FSI Fellow, Royal Institution of Chartered Surveyors *(see also* FRICS)
FSIA Fellow of the Society of Industrial Artists
FSIAD Fellow, Society of Industrial Artists and Designers
FSLAET Fellow, Society of Licensed Aircraft Engineers and Technologists
FSLGD Fellow, Society for Landscape and Garden Designs
FSS Fellow of the Royal Statistical Society
FSScA Fellow of the Society of Science and Art, of London
FSTD Fellow, Society of Typographic Designers
FSUT Fellow, Society for Underwater Technology
FSVA Fellow, Incorporated Society of Valuers and Auctioneers
FTC Flying Training Command
FTCL Fellow of Trinity College of Music, London
FTI Fellow of the Textile Institute
FTII Fellow, Institute of Taxation
FTS Fellow of the Tourism Society
Fus Fusiliers
FVI Fellow, Valuers Institution
FWA Fellow, World Academy of Arts and Sciences
FWeldI Fellow, Welding Institute
FZS Fellow of the Zoological Society

G

g great
Ga Georgia (USA)
GA Geologists' Association
GAA Gaelic Athletic Association
GAMTA General Aviation Manufacturers' Association
GATT General Agreement on Tariffs and Trade
G&MWU General and Municipal Workers' Union
GB Great Britain
GBA Governing Bodies Association
GBE Knight of the Grand Cross of the British Empire
GBSM Graduate, Birmingham and Midland Institute School of Music
GC George Cross; Grand Cross
GCB Knight Grand Cross of the Bath
GCBS General Council of British Shipping
GCH Knight Grand Cross of Hanover
GCHQ Government Communications Headquarters
GCIE Knight/Dame Grand Commander of the Indian Empire
GCMG Knight/Dame Grand Cross of St Michael and St George
GCON Grand Cross, Order of the Niger
GCSE General Certificate in Secondary Education
GCSI Knight Grand Commander of the Star of India
GCStJ Bailiff or Dame Grand Cross of the Order of St John of Jerusalem
GCVO Knight or Dame of the Grand Cross of the Royal Victorian Order
gda granddaughter
GDBA Guide Dogs for the Blind Association
gdns gardens
GDR German Democratic Republic
Gds Guards
Gen General
Ger Germany
gf grandfather
ggda great granddaughter (and so forth)
ggs great grandson (and so forth)
GHQ General Headquarters
GIMechE Graduate Institution of Mechanical Engineers
GLC Greater London Council
GLR Greater London Radio
GM George Medal
gm grandmother
GMB Great Master of the Bath
GMBATU General Municipal Boilermakers and Allied Trade Unions
GMC General Medical Council
GMIE Grand Master of the Indian Empire
GMMG Grand Master of St Michael and St George
GMSI Grand Master of the Star of India
GMWU General Municipal Workers Union
gn great nephew; great niece
GO Grand Officier (de la Légion d'Honneur)
GOC-in-C General Officer Commanding- in-Chief
Govr Governor
Govt Government
GP General Practitioner
Gp Group
Gp Capt Group Captain
GPDST Girls' Public Day School Trust
GPO General Post Office
GRCM Graduate of the Royal College of Music
GRSM Graduate of the Royal Schools of Music
GS General Staff; Grammar School
gs grandson
GSA Girls' School Association
GSM General Service Medal; Guildhall School of Music and Drama
GSO General Staff Officer
Gt Great
Gtr Greater
Guy's Guy's Hospital
GWR Great Western Railway

H

h heir
ha heir apparent
HA Historical Association
HAA Heavy Anti-Aircraft
HAC Honourable Artillery Company
HBM His/Her Britannic Majesty
hc honoris causa
HCF Hon Chaplain to the Forces
HCIMA Hotel, Catering and Institutional Management Association
HCITB Hotel and Catering Industry Training Board
HDip in Ed Honorary Diploma in Education
HE His Excellency
HG Homeguard
HESIN Higher Education Support for Industry in the North
HG Homeguard
HH His/Her Highness
HHA Historic Houses Association
HHD Doctor of Humanities (US)
High Cmmr High Commissioner

HIH His/Her Imperial Highness
HIllH His/Her Illustrious Highness
HIM His/Her Imperial Majesty
Hist Historical
HKIA Member, Hong Kong Institute of Architects
Hldgs Holdings
HLI Highland Light Infantry
HMC Headmasters' Conference; Hospital Management Committee
HMEH His Most Emminent Highness
HMHS Her Majesty's Hospital Ship
HMI Her Majesty's Inspectorate
HMOCS Her Majesty's Overseas Civil Service
HMS Her Majesty's Ship
HMSO Her Majesty's Stationery Office
HNC Higher National Certificate
HND Higher National Diploma
Hon Honourable; Honour (Judges); Honorary
Hons Honours
Hort Horticultural
Hosp Hospital
hp heir presumptive
HRE Holy Roman Empire
HRH His/Her Royal Highness
HRHA Honorary Member, Royal Hibernian Academy
HRI Hon Member of the Royal Institute of Painters in Water Colours
HRSA Hon Member Royal Scottish Academy
HS High School
HSE Health and Safety Executive
HSH His/Her Serene Highness
husb husband
HVCert Health Visitors Certificate

I

I Ireland
IA Indian Army
IAAF International Amateur Athletics Federation
IAB Brazilian Institute of Architects
IACP International Association of Chiefs of Police (USA)
IADR International Association for Dental Research
IAEA International Atomic Energy Agency
IAF Indian Air Force; Indian Auxiliary Force
IAMC Indian Army Medical Corps
IAOC Indian Army Ordnance Corps
IAOMS International Association of Oral and Maxillo-Facial Surgeons
IAP Institute of Analysts and Programmers
IAPS Incorporated Association of Preparatory Schools
IARO Indian Army Reserve of Officers
IAS Indian Administrative Service
IASC Indian Army Service Corps
IATA International Air Transport Association
IATEFL International Association of Teachers of English as a Foreign Language
IBA Independent Broadcasting Authority
IBP Institute of British Photographers
IBPA International Bridge Players Association
IBRC Insurance Brokers' Registration Council
IBRD International Bank for Reconstruction and Devpt (World Bank)
IBRO International Brain Research Organisation
i/c in charge of
ICA Institute of Contemporary Arts
ICE Institute of Civil Engineers; In Car Entertainment
ICAEW Institute of Chartered Accountants of England and Wales
ICF International Canoe Federation
ICFC Industrial and Commercial Finance Corporation
ICI Imperial Chemical Industries
ICL International Computers Ltd
ICOM International Council of Museums
ICS Indian Civil Service
ICSA Institute of Chartered Secretaries and Administrators
ICSID International Council of Societies of Industrial Design
idc has completed a course at, or served for a year on the staff, of The Imperial Defence Coll
IDC Imperial Defence College
IDS Institute of Development Studies
IEE Institution of Electrical Engineers
IEF Indian Expeditionary Force
IERE Institute of Electronic and Radio Engineers
IFC International Finance Corporation
IFLA International Federation of Library Associations
IFPA Industrial Fire Protection Association
IG Instructor in Gunnery
IGasE Institute of Gas Engineers
IIEP International Institute for Educational Planning
IIM Institution of Industrial Managers
IIP Institute of Incorporated Photographers
IISS International Institute of Strategic Studies
ILEA Inner London Education Authority
ILO International Labour Office
ILP Independent Labour Party
IMA International Music Association
IMCB International Management Centre Buckingham
IMRO Investment Management Regulatory Organisation
IMS Indian Medical Service; International Military Services
IMechE Institution of of Mechanical Engineers
IMF International Monetary Fund
Imp Imperial
Inc Incorporated
incl include; including
Ind Independent
Indust Industry
Industl Industrial
Industs Industries
Inf Infantry
Info Information
INSEAD Institut Européen d'Administration des Affaires
Inspr Inspector
Inst Institute
Instn Institution
Instr Instructor
Insur Insurance
Int International
Investmt Investment
IOD Institute of Directors
IOM Isle of Man
IOW Isle of Wight
IPA Institute of Practitioners in Advertising; Insolvency Practitioners Association
IPCS Institution of Professional Civil Servants
IPFA Chartered Institute of Public Finance and Accountancy
IPHE Institution of Public Health Engineers
IPI Institute of Patentees and Inventors
IPM Institute of Personnel Management
IPPA Independent Programme Producers' Association
IProdE Institute of Production Engineers
IPS Indian Political Service
IQA Institute of Quality Assurance
Ir Irish
IRA Irish Republican Army
IRC Industrial Re-organisation Corporation
IRE Indian Corps of Royal Engineers
IRN Independant Radio News
IRRV Institute of Revenues, Rating and Valuation
Is Island(s)
ISBA Incorporated Society of British Advertisers
ISC Indian Staff Corps; Imperial Service College
ISCO Independent Schools Careers Organisation
ISE Indian Service of Engineers
ISI International Statistical Institute
ISID International Society of Interior Design
ISIS Independent Schools Information Service
ISM Imperial Service Medal; Incorporated Society of Musicians (member/associate)
ISO Imperial Service Order
ISOCARP International Society of City and Regional Planning
ISPP International Society of Political Psychology
IStructE Institution of Structural Engineers
IT Information Technology
ITA Independent Television Authority
ITCA Independent Television Companies Association
ITN Independent TV News
ITV Independent Television
IUCN International Union for the Conservation of Nature and Natural Resources
IUPAC International Union of Pure and Applied Chemistry
IUTAM International Union of Theoretical and Applied Mechanics
IY Imperial Yeomanry

J

JAG Judge Advocate General
JCD Doctor of Canon Law (Juris Canonici Doctor)
Jcl Licentiate of Canon Law
JD Doctor of Jurisprudence
JDipMA Joint Diploma in Management Accounting Services
jl/s journal/s
JP Justice of the Peace
jr junior
JSM Johan Seita Mahkota (Malaysia)
jssc Qualified at Joint Services Staff College
Jt Joint
jtly jointly

K

k killed
ka killed in action
KAR King's African Rifles
KASG Knightly Association of St George the Martyr
KBE Knight Commander of the Order of the British Empire
KC King's Counsel
KCB Knight Commander of the Order of the Bath

KCH	King's College Hospital
KCIE	Knight Commander of the Order of the Indian Empire
KCMG	Knight Commander of the Order of St Michael and St George
KCS	King's College School
KCSG	Knight Commander of St Gregory
KCSI	Knight Commander of the Star of India
KCVO	Knight Commander of the Royal Victorian Order
KDG	King's Dragoon Guards
KEH	King Edward's Horse Regiment
KEO	King Edward's Own
KG	Knight of the Order of the Garter
KGStJ	Knight of Grace, Order of St John of Jerusalem *(see also* KSEJ)
KGVO	King George V's Own
KHC	Honorary Chaplain to the King
KHDS	Honorary Dental Surgeon to the King
KHP	Honorary Physician to the King
KHS	Honorary Surgeon to the King
K-i-H	Kaisar-i-Hind
KJStJ	Knight of Justice, Order of St John of Jerusalem
KMN	Kesatria Mangku Negara (Malaysian Decoration)
KORR	King's Own Royal Regiment
KOSB	King's Own Scottish Borderers
KOYLI	King's Own Yorkshire Light Infantry
KP	Knight of the Order of St Patrick
KPFSM	King's Police and Fire Service Medal
KPM	King's Police Medal
KRI	King's Royal Irish
KRRC	King's Royal Rifle Corps
KSG	Knight of St Gregory
KSLI	King's Shropshire Light Infantry
KStJ	Knight of the Order of St John of Jerusalem
KT	Knight of the Order of the Thistle
kt	knighted (Knight Bachelor)

L

L	Labour
LA	Los Angeles
La	Louisiana
LAA	Light Anti-Aircraft
Lab	Labour
LAC	Leading Aircraftsman
LACOTS	Local Authorities Co-ordination of Trading Standards Committee
LACSAB	Local Authorities' Conditions of Service Advisory Board
LAH	Licentiate of Apothecaries Hall, Dublin
LAMDA	London Academy of Music and Dramatic Art
LBC	London Broadcasting Co
LCC	London County Council
LCDS	London Contemporary Dance Studio
LCDT	London Contemporary Dance Theatre
LCJ	Lord Chief Justice
LCP	Licentiate of the College of Preceptors
Ldr	Leader
LDS	Licentiate in Dental Surgery
LDV	Local Defence Volunteers
LEA	Local Education Authority
LEB	London Electricity Board
lectr	lecturer
LesL	Licenciees Lettres
LF	Land Forces
LFAA	Look first, ask afterwards
LG	Life Guards
LGSM	Licentiate, Guildhall School of Music and Drama
LH	Light Horse
LHD	Literarum Humaniorum Doctor
LI	Light Infantry
Lib	Liberal
LIBC	Lloyd's Insurance Brokers' Committee
Lib Dem	Liberal Democrat
Lieut	Lieutenant
LIFFE	London International Financial Futures Exchange
LIOB	Licentiate, Institute of Building
Lit	Literature
LittD	Doctor of Letters (Cambridge & Dublin)
LLA	Lady Literate in Arts
LLB	Bachelor of Laws
LLCM	Licentiate, London College of Music
LLD	Doctor of Laws
LLM	Master of Laws
LM	Licentiate in Midwifery
LMCC	Licentiate of Medical Council of Canada
LMSSA	Licentiate in Medicine and Surgery, Society of Apothecaries
LMTPI	Legal Member of the Town Planning Institute
LNER	London and North East Railway
LPTB	London Passenger Transport Board
LRAM	Licentiate of the Royal Academy of Music
LRCP	Licentiate of the Royal College of Physicians
LRCPE	Licentiate, Royal College of Physicians Edinburgh
LRCSE	Licentiate, Royal College of Surgeons Edinburgh
LRFPS	Licentiate of the Royal Faculty of Physicians and Surgeons (Glasgow)
LRIBA	Licentiate of the Royal Institute of British Architects
LSA	Licentiate of the Society of Apothecaries
LSCA	London Society of Chartered Accountants
LSE	London School of Economics
LSHTM	London School of Hygiene and Tropical Medicine
LSO	London Symphony Orchestra
LTA	Lawn Tennis Association
LTCL	Licentiate, Trinity College of Music, London
Lt-Col	Lieutenant-Colonel
Ltcy	Lieutenancy
Lt-Gen	Lieutenant-General
LTh	Licentiate in Theology
LU	Liberal Unionist
LVO	Lieutenant of the Royal Victorian Order
LWT	London Weekend Television

M

m	married, marriage
m dis	marriage dissolved
MA	Master of Arts; Military Assistant
MAAEM	Member, American Association of Electrodiagnostic Medicine
MAAF	Mediterranean Allied Air Forces
MACE	Member, Association of Conference Executives
MACM	Member, Association of Computing Machines
MACP	Member, Association of Child Psychotherapists
MAFF	Ministry of Agriculture, Fisheries and Food
MAI	Master of Engineering
MAIAA	Member, American Institute of Aeronautics and Astronautics
MAIE	Member, Association of Industrial Editors
Maj	Major
Maj-Gen	Major-General
mangr	manager
Mans	Mansions
MAOT	Member of the Association of Occupational Therapists
MAP	Ministry of Aircraft Production
MArch	Master of Architecture
Marq	Marquess
MASAE	Member, American Society of Agricultural Engineers
MASCE	Member, American Society of Civil Engineers
Mass	Massachusetts (US)
MB	Bachelor of Medicine
MBA	Master of Business Administration
MBAE	Member, British Academy of Experts
MBCS	Member, British Computer Society
MBE	Member of the Order of the British Empire
MBEDA	Member, Bureau of European Designers
MBHI	Member of the British Horological Institute
MBII	Member of the British Institute of Innkeeping
MBIM	Member of the British Institute of Management
MBKS	Member, British Kinematograph Society
MBOU	Member, British Ornithologists' Union
MBSG	Member, British Society of Gastroenterology
MC	Military Cross
MCAM	Member, Institute of Communications, Advertising and Marketing
MCB	Master of Clinical Biochemistry
MCC	Marylebone Cricket Club; Metropolitan County Council
MCD	Master of Civic Design
MCFA	Member of the Cookery and Food Association
MChir	Master in Surgery
MChOrth	Master of Orthopaedic Surgery
MCIA	Member, Chartered Institute of Arbitrators
MCIM	Member, Chartered Institute of Marketing
MCIOB	Member, Chartered Institute of Building
MCIT	Member of the Chartered Institute of Transport
MCom	Master of Commerce
MConsE	Member, Association of Consulting Engineers
MCOphth	Member, College of Ophthalmologists (formerly Faculty of Ophthalmologists, FacOpth, and Ophthalmic Society of UK, OSUK)
MCP	Member of Colonial Parliament
MCPath	Member of the College of Pathologists
MCPS	Member, College of Physicians and Surgeons
MCSD	Member, Chartered Society of Designers
MCSP	Member of the Chartered Society of Physiotherapy
MCT	Member, Association of Corporate Treasurers
MD	Doctor of Medicine
md	managing director
MDC	Metropolitan District Council
MDes	Master of Design
MDS	Master of Dental Surgery
ME	Middle East
MEAF	Middle East Air Force
MEC	Member, Executive Council
MECAS	Middle East Centre for Arab Studies
MECI	Member, Institute of Employment Consultants
MEd	Master of Education
Med	Medical; medicine; Mediterranean
MEF	Mediterranean Expeditionary Force
MEIC	Member of the Engineering Institute of Canada
MELF	Middle East Land Forces
memb	member

Meml Memorial
MENCAP Royal Society for Mentally Handicapped Children and Adults
MEP Member of the European Parliament
Met Metropolitan
MFARCS Member of the Faculty of Anaesthetists, Royal College of Surgeons
MFB Member, Faculty of Building
MFC Mastership in Food Control
MFCM Member, Faculty of Community Medicine
MFH Master of Fox Hounds
MFOM Member, Faculty of Occupational Medicine
mfr/mfrg manufacturer/manufacturing
MGC Machine Gun Corps
MGDS RCS Member in General Dental Surgery, Royal College of Surgeons
MGGS Major-General General Staff
Mgmnt Management
MGO Master General of the Ordnance
Mgr Monsignor
MGRA Major-General Royal Artillery
MH Military Hospital
MHCIMA Member, Hotel Catering and Institutional Management Association
MHK Member of the House of Keys (IOM)
MHR Member of the House of Representatives
MHSM Masters in Health Services Management
MI Military Intelligence
MIAeE Member, Institute of Aeronautical Engineers
MIBE Member of the Institution of British Engineers
MIBG Member, Institute of British Geographers
MIBiol Member, Institute of Biology
MICAS Member of the Institute of Chartered Accountants of Scotland
MICE Member, Institution of Civil Engineers
MICEI Member, Institution of Civil Engineers of Ireland
MICFM Member of the Institute of Charity Fund-Raising Managers
MIChemE Member of the Institution of Chemical Engineers
MICM Member, Institute of Credit Management
MIConsE Member, Institute of Consulting Engineers
MIDPM Member, Institute of Data Processing Management
MIEA Member of the Institution of Engineers, Australia
MIED Member, Institution of Engineering Design
MIEE Member of the Institution of Electrical Engineers
MIEEE Member, Institute of Electrical and Electronics Engineers (NY)
MIEI Member of the Institute of Engineering Inspection
MIERE Member of the Institution of Electronic and Radio Engineers
MIES Member of the Institution of Engineers and Shipbuilders in Scotland
MIEx Member of the Institute of Export
MIFA Member, Institute of Field Archaeologists
MIH Member of the Institute of Housing
MIHort Member, Institute of Horticulture
MIHT Member, Institute of Highways and Transportation
MIInfSc Member, Institute of Information Sciences
MIL Member, Institute of Linguists
Mil Military
MILE Member of the Institution of Locomotive Engineers
MIM Member, Institution of Metallurgists
MIMarE Member of the Institute of Marine Engineers
MIMC Member of the Institute of Management Consultants; Corporate Member of the Institute of Measurement and Control
MIMCE Member of the Institute of Municipal and County Engineers
MIME,MInstME Member of the Institution of Mining Engineers
MIMechE Member of the Institution of Mechanical Engineers
MIMI Member of the Institute of the Motor Industry
MIMM Member of the Institution of Mining & Metallurgy
Min Minister
MIngF Member, Danish Engineers' Association
Miny Ministry
MInstD Member of the Institute of Directors
MInstE Member, Institute of Energy
MInstGasE Member of the Institution of Gas Engineers
MInstHE Member of the Institution of Highway Engineers
MInstMC Member, Institute of Measurement and Control
MInstMet Member of the Institute of Metals
MInstP Member of the Institute of Physics
MInst Pet Member of the Institute of Petroleum
MInstPS Member, Institute of Purchasing and Supply
MInstW Member of the Institution of Welding
MINucE Member of the Institution of Nuclear Engineers
MIOB Member of the Institute of Building
MIPA Member of the Institution of Practitioners in Advertising; Member, Insolvency Practitioners' Association
MIPharmM Member, Institute of Pharmacy Management
MIPHE Member of the Institute of Public Health Engineers
MIPM Member of the Institute of Personnel Management
MIPR Member of the Institute of Public Relations
MIProdE Member of the Institution of Production Engineers
MIQ Member, Institute of Quarrying
MIRE Member of the Institution of Royal Engineers
MIS Member of the Institute of Statisticians
MISA Member, Institute of South African Architects
MISI Member of the Iron and Steel Institute
Miss Mississipi (USA)
MIStructE Member of the Institution of Structural Engineers
MIT Massachusetts Institute of Technology (USA)
MITD Member, Institute of Training and Development
MIWEM Member of the Institution of Water and Environmental Management
MJI Member of the Institute of Journalists
MJInstE Member of the Junior Engineers Institute
Mktg Marketing
MLA Member, Legislative Assembly; Modern Language Association; Master in Landscape Architecture
MLC Member of the Legislative Council
MLitt Master of Literature
MLO Military Liaison Officer
MM Military Medal
MMC Monopolies and Mergers Commission
MMechE Master of Mechanical Engineering
MMet Master of Metallurgy
MMIM Member, Malaysian Institute of Management
MMS Masters in Management Services
MN Merchant Navy
MNECInst Member, North East Coast Institution of Engineers and Shipbuilders
MNI Member, Nautical Institute
MNYAS Member, New York Academy of Sciences
MNZIE Member of the New Zealand Institution of Engineers
Mo Missouri (USA)
MO Medical Officer
MOD Ministry of Defence
MOH Medical Officer of Health
MOI Ministry of Information
MOP Ministry of Power
MOS Ministry of Supply
MP Member of Parliament
MPA Master of Public Administration
MPBW Ministry of Public Building and Works
MPhil Master of Philosophy
MPO Management and Personnel Office
MPRISA Member of the Public Relations Institute of South Africa
MPS Member of the Pharmaceutical Society of Great Britain
MR Master of the Rolls
MRAC Member of the Royal Agricultural College
MRAD Member of the Royal Academy of Dancing
MRAeS Member, Royal Aeronautical Society
MRAS Member of the Royal Asiatic Society
MRC Medical Research Council
MRCGP Member, Royal College of General Practitioners
MRCOG Member of the Royal College of Obstetricians and Gynaecologists
MRCP Member of the Royal College of Physicians
MRCPath Member, Royal College of Pathologists
MRCPI Member, Royal College of Physicians in Ireland
MRCPsych Member, Royal College of Psychiatrists
MRCR Member, Royal College of Radiologists
MRCS Member of the Royal College of Surgeons
MRCVS Member of the Royal College of Veterinary Surgeons
MRI Member, Royal Institution
MRIA Member of the Royal Irish Academy
MRIBA Member of the Royal Institute of British Architects
MRIC Member, Royal Institute of Chemistry
MRICS Member of the Royal Institution of Chartered Surveyors
MRIN Member of the Royal Institute of Navigation
MRINA Member of the Royal Institution of Naval Architects
MRN Member, Register of Naturopaths
MRO Member of the Register of Osteopaths
MRPharmS Member, Royal Pharmaceutical Society
MRS Market Research Society; Medical Research Society
MRSH Member of the Royal Society of Health
MRST Member of the Royal Society of Teachers
MRTPI Member of the Royal Town Planning Institute
MRUSI Member of the Royal United Service Institution
MRVA Member, Rating and Valuation Association
MS Master of Surgery; Manuscript; Master of Science (US)
MSAE Member, Society of Automotive Engineers (US)
MSC Manpower Services Commission
MSc Master of Science
MScD Master of Dental Science
MScL Member, Society of Construction Law
MSE Member of the Society of Engineers
MSF Manufacturing, Science and Finance Union (formerly ASTMS)
MSIA Member of the Society of Industrial Artists
MSIAD Member of the Society of Industrial Artists and Designers
MSM Meritorious Service Medal
MSocSci Master of Social Sciences
MSPI Member, Society of Practitioners of Insolvency
MSST Member of the Society of Surveying Technicians
MTB Motor Torpedo Boat
MTG Member of the Translators' Guild
MTh Master of Theology
MTPI Member, Town Planning Institute
MTTA Machine Tool Trades Association
MusB Bachelor of Music
MusD Doctor of Music (Cambridge and Durham)
MusM Master of Music
MV Motor Vessel
MVO Member, Royal Victorian Order
MVSc Master of Veterinary Science
MW Master of Wine
MWB Metropolitan Water Board
MWeldI Member, Welding Institute
MY Motor Yacht

N

N	Nationalist; North
n	nephew
NAAFI	Navy, Army and Air Force Institutes
NABC	National Association of Boys' Clubs
NAC	National Agriculture Centre
NADFAS	National Association of Decorative and Fine Arts Societies
NAEB	National Association of Educational Broadcasters
NAG	Northern Army Group
NAHT	National Association of Head Teachers
NALGO	National and Local Government Officers' Association
NAMH	National Association for Mental Health
NAO	National Audit Office
NAPM	National Association of Paper Merchants
Nat	National
Nat Lib	National Liberal
NATCS	National Air Traffic Control Services
NATFHE	National Association of Teachers in Further and Higher Education
NATO	North Atlantic Treaty Organisation
NBL	National Book League
NBPI	National Board for Prices and Incomes
NC	Nautical College
NCA	National Cricket Association; National Certificate of Agriculture
NCB	National Coal Board
NCCI	National Committee for Commonwealth Immigrants
NCCL	National Council for Civil Liberties
NCLC	National Council of Labour Colleges
NCO	Non-commissioned officer
NCVO	National Council for Voluntary Organisation
ND	Diploma in Naturopathy
NDA	National Diploma in Agriculture
NDC	National Defence College
NDD	National Diploma in Dairying; National Diploma in Design
NEAC	New English Art Club
NEAF	Near East Air Force
NEC	National Executive Committee
NEDC	National Economic Development Council
NEDO	National Economic Development Office
NERC	Natural Environment Research Council
NFL	National Football League
NFS	National Fire Service
NFU	National Farmers' Union
NFWI	National Federation of Women's Institutes
NGW	Nice Glass of Water
NHS	National Health Service
NI	Northern Ireland
NICS	Northern Ireland Civil Service
NID	Naval Intelligence Department
NIESR	National Institute of Economic and Social Research
NIH	National Institutes of Health (US)
NILP	Northern Ireland Labour Party
NJ	New Jersey (USA)
NLF	National Liberal Federation
NMCU	National Metrological Coordinating Unit Committee
NP	Notary Public
NRA	National Rifle Association
NRDC	National Research Development Corporation
NRPB	National Radiological Protection Board
ns	Graduate of the Royal Naval Staff College, Greenwich
NS	Nova Scotia
NSocIs	Member Societé des Ingenieurs et Scientifiques de France
NSW	New South Wales
NT	National Theatre
NTDA	National Trade Development Association
NUGMW	National Union of General and Municipal Workers
NUI	National University of Ireland
NUJ	National Union of Journalists
NUM	National Union of Mineworkers
NUPE	National Union of Public Employees
NUR	National Union of Railwaymen
NUS	National Union of Students
NUT	National Union of Teachers
NWFP	North West Frontier Province
NY	New York
NYBG	New York Botanical Garden
NYC	New York City
NZ	New Zealand
NZEF	New Zealand Expeditionary Force

O

o	only
O & O	Oriental and Occidental Steamship Co
OA	Officier d'Académie
OB	Order of Barbados
OBE	Officer of the Order of the British Empire
OC	Officer Commanding; Officer of the Order of Canada
OCF	Officiating Chaplain to the Forces
OCS	Officer Cadet School
OCTU	Officer Cadet Training Unit
ODA	Overseas Development Administration
ODI	Overseas Development Institute
ODM	Ministry of Overseas Development
OECD	Organisation for Economic Co-operation and Development
OEEC	Organisation for European Economic Co-operation
OER	Officers' Emergency Reserve
Offr	Officer
OFMCap	Order of Friars Minor Capuchin (Franciscan)
OFS	Orange Free State
OFT	Office of Fair Trading
OIC	Officer in Charge
OJ	Order of Jamaica
OM	Order of Merit
O & M	Organisation and Method
OMC	Oxford Military College
ON	Order of the Nation (Jamaica)
Oppn	Opposition
Ops	Operations
OR	Order of Roraima (Guyana)
Orch	Orchestra
Orgn	Organisation
ORS	Operational Research Society
ORT	Organisation for Rehabilitation by Training
OSB	Order of St Benedict
OSC	Graduate of Overseas Staff College
OSNC	Orient Steam Navigation Company
OSRD	Office of Scientific Research and Development
OStJ	Officer of the Order of St John of Jerusalem
OTC	Officers' Training Corps
OUBC	Oxford University Boat Club
OUDS	Oxford University Dramatic Society
OUP	Oxford University Press

P

pa	per annum
Pa	Pennsylvania (USA)
PA	Personal Assistant
pac	Passed final exam of advanced class Military College of Science
Paiforce	Palestine and Iraq Force
PAO	Prince Albert's Own
Parl	Parliament
Parly	Parliamentary
PBWS	President, British Watercolour Society
PC	Privy Councillor; Peace Commissioner (Ireland)
PCC	Parochial Church Council
PCL	Polytechnic of Central London
PDSA	People's Dispensary for Sick Animals
PDTC	Professional Dancers' Teaching College
PE	Procurement Executive
PEI	Prince Edward Island
PEN	Poets, Playwrights, Editors, Essayists, Novelists Club
PEng	Registered Professional Engineer (Canada)
PEP	Political and Economic Planning
Perm	Permanent
PGA	Professional Golfer's Association
PGCE	Post Graduate Certificate of Education
PHAB	Physically Handicapped and Able Bodied
PhD	Doctor of Philosophy
PhL	Licentiate of Philosophy
PID	Political Intelligence Department
PIRA	Paper Industries Research Association
PLA	Port of London Authority
PLC, plc	Public Limited Company
Plen	Plenipotentiary
PLP	Parliamentary Labour Party
PM	Prime Minister
PMG	Postmaster-General
PMN	Pangilma Mangku Negara (Malaysia)
PMO	Principal Medical Officer
Pmr	Paymaster
PMRAFNS	Princess Mary's Royal Air Force Nursing Service
PNEU	Parents' National Educational Union
PNG	Papua New Guinea
PO	Pilot Officer; Post Office
POD	Personnel Operations Department
POEU	Post Office Engineering Union
Poly	Polytechnic
P & OSNCo	Peninsular and Oriental Steam Navigation Company
post grad	post graduate
POUNC	Post Office Users' National Council
POW	Prisoner of War
PPE	Philosophy, Politics and Economics (Oxford University)
PPRA	Past President of the Royal Academy
PPS	Parliamentary Private Secretary
PR	Public Relations
PRA	President of the Royal Academy
PRCA	Public Relations Consultancy Association
PRE	President of the Royal Society of Painters, Etchers and Engravers
Preb	Prebendary
Prep	Preparatory
Pres	President

prev previously
Princ Principal
PRO Public Relations Officer; Public Records Office
Prodn Production
Prodr Producer
Prods Products
Prof Professor
prog/s programme/s
Prov Provost; Provincial
PRS President of Royal Society
psa Graduate of RAF Staff College
PSA President of the Society of Antiquaries; Property Services Agency
psc Staff College Graduate
PSD Petty Session Division
psm Certificate of the Royal Military School of Music
PSM President of the Society of Miniaturists
PSNC Pacific Steam Navigation Society
PSO Principal Staff Officer
PSPA Professional Sports Photographers' Association
pt part
PT Physical Training
PTE Passenger Transport Executive
ptnr partner
pt/t part time
Pty Proprietary; Party
Pub Public
Pubns Publications
PWD Public Works Department
PWO Prince of Wales's Own

Q

QAIMNS Queen Alexandra's Imperial Military Nursing Service
QALAS Qualified Associate of Land Agents' Society
QARANC Queen Alexandra's Royal Army Nursing Corps
QARNNS Queen Alexandra's Royal Naval Nursing Service
QC Queen's Counsel
QFSM Queen's Fire Service Medal for Distinguished Service
QGM Queens Gallantry Medal
QHC Honorary Chaplain to The Queen
QHDS Honorary Dental Surgeon to The Queen
QHNS Honorary Nursing Sister to The Queen
QHP Honorary Physician to The Queen
QHS Honorary Surgeon to The Queen
Qld Queensland
QMAAC Queen Mary's Army Auxiliary Corps
QMG Quartermaster-General
QO Qualified Officer
QOH Queen's Own Hussars
QPM Queen's Police Medal
qqv Qua Vide (which see-plural)
QRIH Queen's Royal Irish Hussars
QS Quarter Sessions
QSM Queen's Service Medal (NZ)
QSO Queen's Service Order (NZ)
qv Quod Vide (which see)

R

(R) Reserve
R & A Royal and Ancient (St Andrews) Club
R & D Research and Development
R of O Reserve of Officers
RA Royal Artillery; Royal Academician
RAAF Royal Australian Air Force
RAAMC Royal Australian Army Medical Corps
RAC Royal Armoured Corps; Royal Automobile Club; Royal Agricultural College
RACGP Royal Australian College of General Practitioners
RAChD Royal Army Chaplains Department
RACP Royal Australasian College of Physicians
RACS Royal Australasian College of Surgeons
RADA Royal Academy of Dramatic Art
RADC Royal Army Dental Corps
RAE Royal Australian Engineers; Royal Aircraft Establishment
RAEC Royal Army Educational Corps
RAeS Royal Aeronautical Society
RAF Royal Air Force
RAFA Royal Air Force Association
RAFO Reserve of Air Force Officers
RAFRO Royal Air Force Reserve of Officers
RAFVR Royal Air Force Volunteer Reserve
RAI Royal Anthropological Institute
RAIA Royal Australian Institute of Architects
RAIC Royal Architectural Institute of Canada
RAM (member of) Royal Academy of Music
RAMC Royal Army Medical Corps
RAN Royal Australian Navy
RANR Royal Australian Naval Reserve
RANVR Royal Australian Naval Volunteer Reserve
RAOC Royal Army Ordnance Corps
RAPC Royal Army Pay Corps
RARO Regular Army Reserve of Officers
RAS Royal Agricultural Society; Royal Astronomical Society; Royal Asiatic Society
RASC Royal Army Service Corps (now RCT)
RASE Royal Agricultural Society of England
RAuxAF Royal Auxiliary Air Force
RAVC Royal Army Veterinary Corps
RB Rifle Brigade
RBA Royal Society of British Artists
RBC Royal British Colonial Society of Artists
RBK & C Royal Borough of Kensington and Chelsea
RBS Royal Society of British Sculptors
RC Roman Catholic
RCA Royal College of Art
RCAC Royal Canadian Armoured Corps
RCAF Royal Canadian Air Force
RCAMC Royal Canadian Army Medical Corps
RCDS Royal College of Defence Studies
RCGP Royal College of General Practitioners
RCHA Royal Canadian Horse Artillery
RCM Royal College of Music
RCN Royal College of Nursing; Royal Canadian Navy
RCNC Royal Corps of Naval Constructors
RCNR Royal Canadian Naval Reserve
RCNVR Royal Canadian Naval Volunteer Reserve
RCO Royal College of Organists
RCOG Royal College of Obstetricians and Gynaecologists
RCP Royal College of Physicians, London
RCPath Royal College of Pathologists
RCPE(d) Royal College of Physicians, Edinburgh
RCPSGlas Royal College of Physicians and Surgeons, Glasgow
RCPI Royal College of Physicians in Ireland
RCPsych Royal College of Psychiatrists
RCR Royal College of Radiologists
RCS Royal College of Surgeons of England; Royal Corps of Signals; Royal College of Science
RCSE(d) Royal College of Surgeons of Edinburgh
RCSI Royal College of Surgeons in Ireland
RCST Royal College of Science and Technology
RCT Royal Corps of Transport
RCVS Royal College of Veterinary Surgeons
Rd Road
RD Royal Naval Reserve Officers' Decoration
RDA Royal Defence Academy
RDC Rural District Council
RDF Royal Dublin Fusiliers
RDI Royal Designer for Industry (RSA)
RE Royal Engineers; Fellow, Royal Society of Painter-Etchers and Engravers
Rear-Adm Rear-Admiral
Rec Recorder
Reg Regular
Regnl Regional
Regt Regiment
Regtl Regimental
Rels Relations
REME Royal Electrical and Mechanical Engineers
REngDes Registered Engineering Designer
Rep Representative
Repub Republic(an)
RERO Royal Engineers Reserve of Officers
Res Reserve; Research; Resident
RES Royal Empire Soc (Now Royal Commonwealth Soc)
ret retired
Rev Reverend
RFA Royal Field Artillery
RFC Royal Flying Corps; Rugby Football Club
RFU Rugby Football Union
RGA Royal Garrison Artillery
RGI Royal Glasgow Institute of Fine Arts
RGN Registered General Nurse
RGS Royal Geographic Society
RHA Royal Horse Artillery; Royal Hibernian Academy; Regional Health Authority
RHB Regional Hospital Board
RHF Royal Highland Fusiliers
RHG Royal Horse Guards
RHR Royal Highland Regiment
RHS Royal Horticultural Society
RI Royal Institute of Painters in Water Colours; Rhode Island
RIAI Royal Institute of Architects of Ireland
RIAS Royal Incorporation of Architects in Scotland
RIASC Royal Indian Army Service Corps
RIBA Royal Institute of British Architects
RIC Royal Irish Constabulary
RICS Royal Institute of Chartered Surveyors
RIF Royal Irish Fusiliers
RIIA Royal Institute of International Affairs
RIM Royal Indian Marine
RIN Royal Indian Navy

RINA Royal Institute of Naval Architects
RINVR Royal Indian Navy Volunteer Reserve
RIOP Royal Institute of Oil Painters
RIPA Royal Institute of Public Administration
RIPH & H Royal Institute of Public Health and Hygiene
RIrR Royal Irish Rifles
RL Retired List
RLSS Royal Life Saving Society
RM Royal Marines
RMA Royal Military Academy; Royal Marine Artillery
RMC Royal Military College, Sandhurst (now Royal Military Academy)
RMCS Royal Military College of Science
RMFVR Royal Marine Forces Volunteer Reserve
RMLI Royal Marine Light Infantry
RMN Registered Mental Nurse
RMO Resident Medical Officer
RMP Royal Military Police
RMR Royal Marine Reserve
RMS Royal Meterological Society
RN Royal Navy
RNAS Royal Naval Air Service
RNC Royal Nautical College; Royal Naval College
RNCM (Member of) Royal Northern College of Music
RND Royal Naval Division
RNEC Royal Naval Engineering College
RNIB Royal National Institute for the Blind
RNID Royal National Institute for the Deaf
RNLI Royal National Lifeboat Institution
RNR Royal Naval Reserve
RNSA Royal Naval Sailing Association
RNSD Royal Naval Store Depot
RNVR Royal Naval Volunteer Reserve
RNVSR Royal Naval Volunteer Supplementary Reserve
RNZADC Royal New Zealand Army Dental Corps
RNZAF Royal New Zealand Air Force
RNZN Royal New Zealand Navy
RNZNVR Royal New Zealand Naval Volunteer Reserve
ROC Royal Observer Corps
ROI Royal Institute of Painters in Oils
ROSPA Royal Society for the Prevention of Accidents
R of O Reserve of Officers
RP Member of the Royal Society of Portrait Painters
RPC Royal Pioneer Corps
RPMS Royal Postgraduate Medical School
RPO Royal Philharmonic Orchestra
RPS Royal Photographic Society
RR Royal Regiment
RRAF Royal Rhodesian Air Force
RRC Royal Red Cross
RRF Royal Regiment of Fusiliers
RSA Royal Scottish Academician; Royal Society of Arts
RSAA Royal Society for Asian Affairs
RSAC Royal Scottish Automobile Club
RSAMD Royal Scottish Academy of Music and Drama (Diploma of)
RSBA Royal Society of British Artists
RSBS Royal Society of British Sculptors
RSC Royal Shakespeare Co; Royal Society of Canada; Royal Society of Chemistry
RSE Royal Society of Edinburgh
RSF Royal Scots Fusiliers
RSL Royal Society of Literature; Returned Services League of Australia
RSM Royal Society of Medicine; Regimental Sergeant Major
RSMA Royal Society of Marine Artists
RSNC Royal Society for Nature Conservation
RSME Royal School of Military Engineers
RSNC Royal Society for Nature Conservation
RSPB Royal Society for the Protection of Birds
RSPCA Royal Society for the Prevention of Cruelty to Animals
RSPP Royal Society of Portrait Painters
RSRE Royal Signals and Radar Establishment
RSS Royal Statistical Society
RSSPCC Royal Scottish Society for the Prevention of Cruelty to Children
RSW Royal Scottish Water Colours Society
Rt Hon Right Honourable
Rt Rev Right Reverend
RTC Royal Tank Corps
RTE Radio Telefis Eireann
RTO Railway Transport Officer
RTPI Royal Town Planning Institute
RTR Royal Tank Regiment
RTS Royal TV Society
RUC Royal Ulster Constabulary
RUFC Rugby Union Football Club
RUI Royal University of Ireland
RUKBA Royal United Kingdom Beneficent Association
RUR Royal Ulster Regiment
RUSI Royal United Services Institute
RVC Royal Veterinary College
RVO Regional Veterinary Officer
RWA Member, Royal West of England Academy
RWAFF Royal West African Frontier Force
RWAR Royal West African Regiment
RWF Royal Welch Fusiliers
RWS Member, Royal Society of Painters in Water Colours
RYA Royal Yachting Association
RYS Royal Yacht Squadron
RZS Royal Zoological Society

S

s son
S South; Scotland/Scottish (Peerages)
SA South Africa; South Australia; Société Anonyme
SAAF South African Air Force
sac Qualified at Small Arms Technical Long Course
SAC Senior Aircraftsman
SACEUR Supreme Allied Commander Europe
SACLANT Supreme Allied Commander Atlantic
SACSEA Supreme Allied Commander, S E Asia
SADG Societé des Architectes Diplomés par le Gouvernement
Salop (now) Shropshire
SAS Special Air Service
Sask Saskatchewan
SASO Senior Air Staff Officer
SAT Senior Member, Association of Accounting Technicians
SATRO Science & Technology Regional Organisation
SBAC Society of British Aircraft Constructors, now Society of British Aerospace Companies
SBNO Senior British Naval Officer
SBStJ Serving Brother of the Order of St John of Jerusalem
sc Student at the Staff College
ScD Doctor of Science (Cambridge and Dublin)
SCF Senior Chaplain to the Forces
SCGB Ski Club of Great Britain
Sch School
Sci Science
SCI Society of Chemical Engineering
SCL Student in Civil Law
SCM State Certified Midwife
SCONUL Standing Conference of National and University Libraries
Scot Scottish; Scotland
SCUA Scottish Conservative Unionist Association
SDP Social Democratic Party
SDLP Social Democratic and Labour Party
SEAC South East Asia Command
SEATAG South East Asia Trade Advisory Group
Sec Secretary
Secdy Secondary
Sec-Gen Secretary-General
Sen Senator
SEN State Enrolled Nurse
sep separated
SERC Science and Engineering Research Council
SERT Society of Electronic and Radio Technicians
Serv Service
SFInstE Senior Fellow Institute of Energy
SFTA Society of Film and Television Arts
SG Solicitor-General
SGM Sea Gallantry Medal
Sgt Sergeant
SHA Secondary Heads Association
SHAEF Supreme Headquarters, Allied Expeditionary Force
SHAPE Supreme Headquarters, Allied Powers Europe
SHHD Scottish Home and Health Department
SIAD Society of Industrial Artists and Designers
sis sister
SJ Society of Jesus (Jesuits)
SLD Social and Liberal Democrats
SLDP Social, Liberal and Democratic Party
slr solicitor
SM Service Medal of the Order of Canada; Master of Science (USA); Member, Society of Miniaturists
SME School of Military Engineering
SMIEEE Senior Member, Institute of Electrical and Electronic Engineers (NY)
SMMT Society of Motor Manufacturers and Traders
SMN Seri Maharaja Mangku Negara (Malaysia)
SMO Senior Medical Officer; Sovereign Military Order
SMOM Sovereign Military Order of Malta
SNO Senior Naval Officer
SNP Scottish Nationalist Party
SNTS Society for New Testament Studies
SO Scottish Office; Staff Officer
SOAS School of Oriental and African Studies
Soc Society
SOE Special Operations Executive
SOGAT Society of Graphical and Allied Trades
Som Somerset
SOTS Society for Old Testament Studies
Sov Sovereign
sp sine prole (without issue)
SPCK Society for Promoting Christian Knowledge
SPG Society for the Propagation of the Gospel
SPNM Society for the Promotion of New Music
SPSO Senior Personnel Staff Officer
SPTL Society of Public Teaching of Law

Sq Square
Sqdn Squadron
Sqdn Ldr Squadron Leader
sr senior
SR Special Reserve; Southern Railway; Southern Region
SRC Science Research Council
SRDE Signals Research and Development Establishment
SRHE Society for Research in Higher Education
SRN State Registered Nurse
SRO Supplementary Reserve of Officers
SRP State Registered Physiotherapist
SRR State Registered Radiographer
SSA Society of Scottish Artists
SSAFA Soldiers', Sailors', and Airmen's Families' Association
SSC Solicitor, Supreme Court (Scotland); Short Service Commission
SSEES School of Slavonic and East European Studies
SSO Senior Supply Officer
SSRC Social Science Research Council
SSStJ Serving Sister of the Order of St John of Jerusalem
STA Society of Technical Analysts
STC Senior Training Corps
STD Doctor of Sacred Theology
STh Scholar in Theology
STL Licenciate of Sacred Theology
STM Master of Sacred Theology
STSO Senior Technical Staff Officer
Subalt Subaltern
Subs Submarines (RN)
Subsid Subsidiary
Subst Substitute
suc succeeded
Sup Supérieure
Supp Supplementary
Supt Superintendent
Surgn Surgeon
Survg Surviving
SWA Sports Writers' Association
SWB South Wales Borderers
SWET Society of West End Theatres

T

TA Territorial Army
TA & VR Territorial Army and Volunteer Reserve
TA & VRA Territorial Army and Volunteer Reserve Association
TAA Territorial Army Association; Tropical Agriculture Association
TAF Tactical Air Force
T&AFA Territorial and Auxiliary Forces Association
TANS Territorial Army Nursing Service
TARO Territorial Army Reserve of Officers
Tas Tasmania
Tbnl Tribunal
TC Order of Trinity Cross (Trinidad and Tobago)
TCCB Test and County Cricket Board
TD Territorial Officers' Decoration; Teachta Dala (member of the Dail Parliament of Eire)
Tech Technical
Technol Technology; Technological
TEFL Teaching English as a Foreign Language
TEM Territorial Efficiency Medal
Temp Temporary
TES Times Educational Supplement
TF Territorial Force
TGWU Transport and General Workers' Union
Theol Theological
ThM Master of Theology
TLS Times Literary Supplement
TMA Theatre Managers Association
Tport Transport
Trans Translation; translated; translator
TRE Telecommunications Research Establishment
Treasy Treasury
Treas Treasurer
Trg Training
TRH Their Royal Highnesses
Tst Trust
Tstee Trustee
TUC Trades Union Congress
TV Television
TVEI Technical and Vocational Educational Initiative

U

U Unionist
UAE United Arab Emirates
UAR United Arab Republic
UC University College
UCCA Universities Central Council on Admissions
UCH University College Hospital
UCL University College London
UCLA University of California at Los Angeles
UCNS Universities' Council for Non-Academic Staff
UCNW University College of North Wales
UCS University College School
UCW University College of Wales
UDC Urban District Council
UDF Union Defence Force; Ulster Defence Force
UDR Ulster Defence Regiment
UDS United Drapery Stores
UDUP Ulster Democratic Unionist Party
UEA University of East Anglia
UFO Unidentified Flying Object
UGC University Grants Committee
UHS University High School
UK United Kingdom
UKAEA United Kingdom Atomic Energy Authority
UKLF United Kingdom Land Forces
UMDS United Medical and Dental Schools
UMIST University of Manchester Institute of Science and Technology
UN United Nations
UNA United Nations Association
unc uncle
UNCTAD United Nations Commission for Trade and Development
UNDP United Nations Development Programme
UNESCO United Nations Educational, Scientific and Cultural Organisation
UNFAO United Nations Food and Agricultural Organisation
UNICE Union des Industries de la Communauté Européenne
UNICEF United Nations International Children's Emergency Fund
UNIDROIT Institut International pour l'Unification du Droit Privé
Univ University
UNO United Nations Organisation
UNRRA United Nations Relief and Rehabilitation Administration
UP Uttar Pradesh; United Provinces; United Presbyterian
UPNI Unionist Party of Northern Ireland
URCC United Kingdom Central Council for Nurses, Midwives and Health Visitors
URSI Union Radio-Scientifique Internationale
US United States
USA United States of America
USAF United States Air Force
USDAW Union of Shop, Distributive and Allied Workers
USM Unlisted Securities Market
USMC United States Military College
USN United States Navy
USNR United States Naval Reserve
USSR Union of Soviet Socialist Republics
UTC University Training Corps
UU Ulster Unionist
UWIST University of Wales Institute of Science and Technology

V

v versus (against)
V & A Victoria and Albert (Museum)
VA Lady of the Order of Victoria and Albert
Va Virginia
VAD Voluntary Aid Detachment
VAT Value Added Tax
VBF Veterinary Benevolent Fund
VC Victoria Cross
VCAS Vice-Chief of the Air Staff
VCC Vintage Car Club
VD Volunteer Officers' Decoration (now VRD)
VDC Volunteer Defence Corps
Ven Venerable
Very Rev Very Reverend
Vet Veterinary
VHF Very High Frequency
Visc Viscount
VM Victory Medal
VMH Victoria Medal of Honour (Royal Horticultural Society)
VO Veterinary Officer
Vol Volunteer
VRD Volunteer Reserve Officers' Decoration
VSCC Vintage Sports Car Club
VSO Voluntary Service Overseas

W

w wife
W West
WA Western Australia
WAAA Women's Amateur Athletics Association
WAAF Women's Auxiliary Air Force (now WRAF)

WEA Worker's Educational Association
WEU Western European Union
WFN World Fund for Nature, see World Wildlife Fund
WFTU World Federation of Trade Unions
WHO World Health Organisation
WI West Indies
wid widow
WIPO World Intellectual Property Organisation
Wm William
WNO Welsh National Opera
WNSM Welsh National School of Medicine
WO War Office
WRAC Women's Royal Army Corps
WRAF Women's Royal Air Force
WRNR Women's Royal Naval Reserve
WRNS Women's Royal Naval Service
WRVS Women's Royal Voluntary Service (formerly WVS)
WS Writer to the Signet
WVS Women's Voluntary Service
WWI First World War
WWII Second World War
WWF World Wildlife Fund

Y

Yeo Yeomanry
YHA Youth Hostels' Association
YMCA Young Men's Christian Association
yr younger
yst youngest
YWCA Young Women's Christian Association